FRENCH LITERATURE

VOLUME I

HARVARD UNIVERSITY LIBRARY

WIDENER LIBRARY SHELFLIST, 47

FRENCH LITERATURE

VOLUME I

CLASSIFICATION SCHEDULE
CLASSIFIED LISTING BY CALL NUMBER
CHRONOLOGICAL LISTING

Published by the Harvard University Library
Distributed by the Harvard University Press
Cambridge, Massachusetts
1973

SHELFLIST VOLUMES IN PRINT:

5–6. LATIN AMERICA. 1966. 2 VOLS. (LC 67–1722, SBN 674–51247–2)
9–13. AMERICAN HISTORY. 1967. 5 VOLS. (LC 67–30955, SBN 674–02400–1)
14. CHINA, JAPAN AND KOREA. 1968. 494 PP. (LC 68–14151, SBN 674–11850–2)
15. PERIODICAL CLASSES. 1968. 758 PP. (LC 68–14152, SBN 674–66300–4)
16–17. EDUCATION. 1968. 2 VOLS. (LC 68–15925, SBN 674–23800–1)
18. LITERATURE: GENERAL AND COMPARATIVE. 1968. 189 PP. (LC 68–15926, SBN 674–53650–9)
19. SOUTHERN ASIA. 1968. 543 PP. (LC 68–15927, SBN 674–82500–4)
20. CANADIAN HISTORY AND LITERATURE. 1968. 411 PP. (LC 68–22417, SBN 674–09351–8)
21. LATIN AMERICAN LITERATURE. 1969. 498 PP. (LC 68–31060, SBN 674–51251–0)
22. GOVERNMENT. 1969. 263 PP. (LC 68–8886, SBN 674–35786–8)
23–24. ECONOMICS. 1970. 2 VOLS. (LC 69–10587, SBN 674–23125–2)
25. CELTIC LITERATURES. 1970. 192 PP. (LC 69–11162, SBN 674–10480–3)
26–27. AMERICAN LITERATURE. 1970. 2 VOLS. (LC 69–11163, SBN 674–02535–0)
28–31. SLAVIC HISTORY AND LITERATURES. 1971. 4 VOLS. (LC 69–10588, SBN 674–81090–2)
32. GENERAL EUROPEAN AND WORLD HISTORY. 1970. 959 PP. (LC 73–128714, SBN 674–34420–0)
33. REFERENCE COLLECTIONS. 1971. 130 PP. (LC 77– 128715, SBN 674–75201–5)
34. AFRICAN HISTORY AND LITERATURES. 1971. 600 PP. (LC 70–128716, SBN 674–00780–8)
35–38. ENGLISH LITERATURE. 1971. 4 VOLS. (LC 74–128717, SBN 674–25663–8)
39. JUDAICA. 1971. 302 PP. (LC 78–179663, SBN 674–48720–6)
40. FINNISH AND BALTIC HISTORY AND LITERATURES. 1972. 250 PP. (LC 72–75829, SBN 674–30205–2)
41. SPANISH HISTORY AND LITERATURE. 1972. 770 PP. (LC 72–75827, SBN 674–83095–4)
42–43. PHILOSOPHY AND PSYCHOLOGY. 1973. 2 VOLS. (LC 72–83389, SBN 674–66486–8)
44. HUNGARIAN HISTORY AND LITERATURE. *in preparation.* (LC 72–83390, SBN 674–42700–9)
45–46. SOCIOLOGY. 1973. 2 VOLS. (LC 72–83391, SBN 674–81625–0)
47–48. FRENCH LITERATURE. 1973. 2 VOLS. (LC 72–93949, SBN 674–32215–0)

STANDARD BOOK NUMBER: 674–32215–0

LIBRARY OF CONGRESS CATALOGUE CARD NUMBER: 72–93949

PRINTED IN U.S.A.

Preface

As part of its effort to computerize certain of its operations, the Harvard University Library is converting to machine-readable form the shelflist and classification schedules of Widener Library, which houses Harvard's central research collection. After each class or group of related classes is converted, it is published in the *Widener Library Shelflist* series.

Volumes 47–48 of the series list nearly 52,000 titles representing historical and critical works on French literature, anthologies, and individual literary works written in French. Histories and anthologies of global scope appear, but the focus of this collection is on European literature in French. Books relating to the literature of particular French-speaking areas outside of Europe are not included. Reference to the schedules for the classifications presented here (*37530–43899, FL, Mol,* and *Mon*) will provide more detailed information on the scope and arrangement of materials in each class.

This catalogue is arranged in four parts. The classification schedule is the first of these. It serves as an outline of the second part, which presents the entries in shelflist order; that is, in order by call number, as the books are arranged on the shelves. Together these two parts form a classified catalogue and browsing guide to each class. Part three lists the same items (excluding periodicals and other serials) in chronological order by date of publication. In addition to its obvious reference use, this list yields information on the quantity and rate of publication in the field. It can be helpful in determining patterns of collection development and in identifying existing strengths and weaknesses. Access to the collection by author and by title is provided by the alphabetical list which constitutes the fourth part of the catalogue. Computer-generated entries are included for titles of works listed elsewhere by author. (In these added entries the author's name follows the title and is enclosed in parentheses.) This section equips the reader with a subject-oriented subset of the card catalogue — a finding list which offers substantial advantages of conciseness and portability over the catalogue as a whole.

A note of caution is in order. A shelflist has traditionally served as an inventory record of the books in the library and as an indispensable tool for assigning call numbers to books as they are added to the collection. Designed and maintained to fulfill these two functions, the Widener shelflist was never intended to serve the purposes now envisaged for it. The bibliographical standards are not equal to those that prevail in the public card catalogues; shelflist entries are less complete than the public catalogue entries and may contain errors and inconsistencies which have not been eliminated during the conversion process. Cross references and name added entries are not included. Entries for serials rarely reflect changes in title, and serial holding statements give only the year or volume number of the first and last volumes in the library with no indication of gaps. If there is a plus sign after the beginning volume number or date, it can be inferred that the title is being currently received. For a complete record of the holdings of serial titles, the conventional serial records in the Widener Library should be consulted.

The list has other deficiencies. No classification system is perfect, and books are not always classified where the reader would expect to find them. Some books formerly in Widener and subsequently transferred to the Houghton Library or the New England Deposit Library are still to be found in the list; but others had been dropped from the original shelflist and could not be re-inserted.

Special notations indicate the locations of books which are in the shelflist but not in the Widener building. Books transferred to the Houghton Library (for rare books and special collections) are indicated by the letters *Htn.* Books that have been moved to special storage areas are designated by one of the following notations: *NEDL, X Cg,* or a *V* as the first letter of a call number prefix. These books should be requested, by their current numbers, through the Widener Circulation Desk. The letters *RRC* designate books in the Russian Research Center Library. The letter *A* following a call number in the alphabetical or chronological section indicates that the Library holds more than one copy of the book on this number. The classified list, however, includes all copies.

The shelflists of libraries not having classified catalogues have long been used by librarians and readers as implements for systematically surveying holdings in a particular subject. When perusing a shelflist one sees all the titles that have been classified in a given area, and not merely those which happen to be on the shelves and whose spine lettering is legible. In addition, one can take in at a glance the essential bibliographical description of a book — author, title, place and date of publication. However, the potential bibliographical usefulness of the shelflist has been difficult to exploit because it exists in only one copy, which is generally kept in a relatively inaccessible location. In Widener this problem is intensified because the handwritten sheaf shelflist is peculiarly awkward to read and difficult to interpret. Computer technology has made it possible to enlarge the concept of the shelflist and to expand its usefulness and accessibility while improving the techniques of maintaining it.

This shelflist catalogue will be of greatest utility to those using the libraries at Harvard, but in spite of its limitations, it can serve as a general bibliography of the subject and is therefore being made available to other interested libraries and individuals. The computer-based shelflist files are being maintained on a continuing basis so that updated editions of volumes in the series can be published as the need arises.

CHARLES W. HUSBANDS
Systems Librarian

Contents

Statistical Summaries of Classes in this Volume
October 1972

Analysis of Shelflist Entries by Language

Entries in the *37530–43899* Class 45,605

French	35,431	Catalan	2	Yugoslav Languages	14
English	6,992	Rumanian	4	Bulgarian	2
German	1,682	Dutch	100	Hungarian	17
Russian	139	Swedish	26	Turkish	5
Greek	4	Danish	15	Finnish	11
Latin	56	Norwegian	9	Latvian	1
Italian	478	Polish	48	Lithuanian	2
Spanish	240	Ukrainian	4	Other Languages	2
Portuguese	45	Czech & Slovak	43	Uncoded	233

Entries in the *FL* Class 2,178

French	1,558	Italian	60	Norwegian	1
English	352	Spanish	12	Icelandic	1
German	136	Dutch	6	Polish	2
Russian	14	Swedish	11	Hungarian	1
Latin	1	Danish	5	Uncoded	18

Entries in the *Mol* Class 1,710

French	1,296	Italian	38	Polish	3
English	139	Spanish	13	Czech & Slovak	3
German	159	Portuguese	6	Yugoslav Languages	1
Russian	8	Dutch	23	Hungarian	1
Greek	5	Swedish	2	Uncoded	7
Latin	5	Danish	1		

Entries in the *Mon* Class 535

French	326	Latin	1	Swedish	1
English	158	Italian	13	Danish	1
German	25	Spanish	4	Uncoded	2
Russian	1	Dutch	3		

Count of Titles

		Widener	Elsewhere	Total
37530–43899	Monographs	42,989	1,987	44,976
	Serials	143	12	155
	Pamphlets in Tract Volumes	1,624	115	1,739
	Pamphlet Boxes	177	7	184
	Total *37530–43899*	44,933	2,121	47,054
FL	Monographs	1,991	112	2,103
	Serials	47	6	53
	Pamphlets in Tract Volumes	49	8	57
	Pamphlet Boxes	8	0	8
	Total *FL*	2,095	126	2,221
Mol	Monographs	1,567	112	1,679
	Pamphlets in Tract Volumes	188	0	188
	Pamphlet Boxes	10	0	10
	Total *Mol*	1,765	112	1,877
Mon	Monographs	476	42	518
	Serials	1	0	1
	Pamphlets in Tract Volumes	63	3	66
	Pamphlet Boxes	2	0	2
	Total *Mon*	542	45	587
Total Titles		49,335	2,404	51,739

Count of Volumes

		Widener	Elsewhere	Total
37530–43899	Monograph	54,106	2,552	56,658
	Serial	1,028	54	1,082
	Tract	254	36	290
	Total *37530–43899*	55,388	2,642	58,030
FL	Monograph	2,690	169	2,859
	Serial	367	25	392
	Tract	10	4	14
	Total *FL*	3,067	198	3,265
Mol	Monograph	2,225	388	2,613
	Tract	21	0	21
	Total *Mol*	2,246	388	2,634
Mon	Monograph	846	84	930
	Serial	9	0	9
	Tract	13	1	14
	Total *Mon*	868	85	953
Total Volumes		61,569	3,313	64,882

WIDENER LIBRARY SHELFLIST, 47

FRENCH LITERATURE

CLASSIFICATION SCHEDULES

NOTE ON THE CLASSIFICATION

Four classes - one using only numbers (37530-43899) and the FL, Mol, and Mon classes - provide for French literature. The class using only numbers is the principal one. It contains all works on literary history (except for histories of the French drama and theater, which are in the FL class), all anthologies of literature, and all works by and about French authors except as noted below. The FL class contains all histories of the French drama and theater, works relating to literature in special dialects, and all works by and about Jean Jacques Rousseau. The Mol and Mon classes contain all works by and about Molière and Montaigne respectively. (A more detailed account of the FL, Mol, and Mon classes will be found in the special notes for each class.)

The sections of the principal class for individual authors (37591-43899) contain, generally speaking, only books by and about European authors writing in French - primarily, of course, authors who are natives of France, Belgium, and Switzerland. The sections for literary history and anthologies (37530-37588) contain books which deal with European literature in French and also those which deal collectively with French literature written by both European and non-European authors. Books relating to the literature of a particular French-speaking area outside of Europe go in a number of different classes - Afr (Africa), Can (Canadian), AL and SAL (American and Latin American literatures), and IndL and OL (India and Oriental literatures).

The accompanying Outline indicates the main divisions of the principal class for French literature (37530-43899). It should be pointed out that, in the sections for individual authors before 1900, the authors are grouped first by historical period and then by literary form. Within the groups for each form, the authors are arranged in a very rough alphabetical order, but a few major writers are given special treatment outside this arrangement. There is not complete consistency in the form of name chosen for alphabetizing - a pseudonym or the real name, a woman's maiden name or her married name. To add to the confusion, there is sometimes a second alphabetical group for a particular form (cf. 42561-42584 and 42585-42588). Generally speaking, an author is placed with the literary form with which he is usually identified, and all works by and about him are kept together there. However, there are many exceptions, especially with authors of the 19th century - works by an author are then classed in two or more places. In the section for individual authors of the period since 1900 (43500-43899), all authors are arranged in a single alphabet.

The principal class for French literature (37530-43899) is one of the remnants of the old fixed location classification system used in Gore Hall, the predecessor of the Widener Library. In that system, the digits of the base number (before the first period or dot) each had a part in specifying an exact location in the stacks. For example, the first two digits indicated the row of shelving and the fifth digit designated the shelf in a section. Additionally, each shelf was set aside for a particular topic or group of topics, though occasionally gaps were left for future expansion. Therefore, a base number could represent a large set of volumes (which might completely fill one or two shelves), a single topic or author, several topics or authors, or a special topic for a major author. Since the base numbers naturally fell into groups of seven or eight numbers (i.e. the shelves in a section numbered from 1 to 7 or 8), there was usually an attempt to arrange the divisions of the classification to fit into one or more such groups. Very often the first number in a group was used for all folio volumes relating to topics in that group of numbers. The classification schedule was set forth in a way which emphasized such groups of numbers, and the terminology was quite vague.

The system just described was originally used for all of French literature. After 1915, it was adapted to be used for literary history, anthologies, and individual authors before 1900 (in 37530-42588), and the section was added for individual authors after 1900 (43500-43899). Many 20th century authors were reclassified into the new section - but not all (e.g. Charles Maurras and Georges Feydeau).

For the present revision, no changes have been made in the general plan of the class. However, where it seemed feasible, decisions have been set down to show a preferred number if books on a topic have been classified in two places. It has not been possible to reclassify all books to accord with these decisions. Much of the schedule has been rephrased in terminology that will be more familiar to the present-day classifier, and the topics are set forth in a more meaningful hierarchy. Finally, an attempt has been made to list most of the writers prior to 1900 with a precise number or range of numbers assigned to each.

Bartol Brinkler
Classification Specialist
July 1972

OUTLINE

	Literary history
37530	Bibliographies, dictionaries, etc.
37531-37544	General works
37546-37548	Local
	[See also FL 1000-1299]
37551-37558	Special forms
37561-37569	Special periods
37571-37588	Anthologies of literature
	Individual authors, etc.
37591-37598	Before 1300
38511-38518	1300-1499
	1500-1661
	Montaigne. See Mon
38521-38539	Others
	1661-1715
38541-38547	Fiction
38551-38558	Oratory
38561-38568	Philosophy and criticism
38571-38575	Corneille
	Molière. See Mol
38576-38588	Other dramatists
39521-39535	Poetry, humor, etc.
	1715-1799
39536-39551	Voltaire
	Rousseau. See FL 6001-6150
39561-39568	Diderot
39571-39579	Other philosophers
39581-39594	History, criticism, etc.
39595-40525	Fiction
40526-40529	Poetry
40531-40539	Drama
	1800-1849
40541-40548	History
40551-40558	Philosophy
40561-40564	Oratory and criticism
40585-41568	Fiction
41571-41574	Victor Hugo
41576-41578	Lamartine
41581-41588	Drama
41591-41598	Poetry
	1850-1899
42511-42522	History, philosophy, etc.
42523-42538	Criticism
42541-42548	Drama
42551-42559	Poetry
42561-42588	Fiction
43500-43899	1900-

Periodicals. See Philol, PFr, 37571-37588, etc.

General literary history

37530 Bibliographies, dictionaries, etc.

General works

[37531] Folios [Discontinued]
37532 Laharpe's Lycée
37533 Works written in 18th century

Works written in 19th century

37534 Petit de Julleville
37536 Craufurd, Pierrot, Villemain, Nissard
37537 Schnabel, Haas, Baron, Geruzez, Godefroy, Chasles
37538 Roche, Moke, Prat, Saucièr, Demogeot, Grangier
37541 Folios [Discontinued]; Pamphlet volumes

Other general works written since 1800

37542 Multi-volume works
37543 Single volume works

Special periods. See 37561-37569
37544 Special topics
[Include works on special themes and characters in French literature, etc. See also 37558. Prefer to class works relating to a special period with the period in 37561-37569.]

Local
Regions and places of France
[N.B. - Include here works relating to local literature written in standard French. For works about the literature written in special dialects, see FL 1000-1299 and Rom.]

[37546] Folios [Discontinued]
37547 Others
37548 Other countries of Europe
[Include Switzerland, Belgium, Holland, etc.]

Non-European countries. See Afr, Can, OL, SAL, etc.

History of special forms

[Prefer to class works relating to a special period with the period in 37561-37569.]

[37551] Folios [Discontinued]
[37552-37553] Drama [Discontinued. See FL 355-399]
37555 Poetry
[Include works on prosody]
37556.1-.9 Wit and humor, satire
37556.10-.22 Journalism
[Include works about individual journals, memoirs and biographies of journalists.]
37556.23- Fiction
37557 Other prose
[Include the essay as a literary form, oratory, letters, criticism as a literary form, history of translations, etc.]
37558 Miscellany
[Include women authors, history of the French Academy, history of the Jeux floraux, etc. Prefer 37544 for special topics.]

History of special periods

[37561] Folios [Discontinued]
37562 Before 1500
37563 16th century
37564 17th century
37565 18th century

19th century
[Include works relating to the 19th and 20th centuries together.]

37566 General works
37567 Special topics, special forms, etc.

History of special periods (cont.)

20th century

37568 General works
37569 Special topics, special forms, etc.

Anthologies, collections of literature

[37571] Folios [Discontinued]
37572 Chrestomathies and readers
[N.B. - Class here only very general works of this type. Prefer to class below in 37573-37585 whenever possible.]

General collections
[Include works containing both prose and poetry together. See also 37575.]

37573.1-.199 General works

Special periods
Before 1661. See with the period in 37591-38539

37573.200-.299 1661-1715
[See also 38524]
37573.300-.399 1715-1799
[Include 18th century in general]
37573.400-.499 1800-1849
[Include also 19th century in general]
37573.500-.599 1850-1899
[Include 19th and 20th centuries together]
37573.600-.799 1900-

Local. See 37575.101-.399

Collections of poetry
[See also 37575.]

37574.1-.199 General works

Special periods
Before 1661. See with the period in 37591-38539

37574.200-.299 1661-1715
[See also 38524]
37574.300-.399 1715-1799
[Include 18th century in general]
37574.400-.499 1800-1849
[Include also 19th century in general]
37574.500-.599 1850-1899
[Include 19th and 20th centuries together]
37574.600-.799 1900-

Local. See 37575.101-.399
General special collections
[Include works containing both prose and poetry together or separately.]

37575.1-.99 Miscellany

Local

37575.101-.199 Regions and places of France (99 scheme, A-Z by place)
[N.B. - See also FL 1000-1299 and Rom for collections of literature in special dialects.]
37575.200-.399 Other countries of Europe
[Include Switzerland, Belgium, etc.]
Non-European countries. See Afr, Can, OL, SAL, etc.
37575.400- Other special
[Include collections devoted to special themes, etc.]

Collections of prose
[Include here works containing all kinds of prose literature and also works limited to a particular prose form, e.g. fiction. See also 37575.101-.399 and 37577-37585.]

37576.1-.199 General works

Special periods
Before 1661. See with the period in 37591-38539

37576.200-.299 1661-1715
[See also 38524]

Anthologies, collections of literature (cont.)
Collections of prose (cont.)
Special periods (cont.)
37576.300-.399 1715-1799
[Include 18th century in general]
37576.400-.499 1800-1849
[Include also 19th century in general]
37576.500-.599 1850-1899
[Include 19th and 20th centuries together.]
37576.600-.799 1900- (By date, e.g. .660 for 1960)

Local. See 37575.101-.399
37577 Collections of facéties
37578 Collections of wit and humor

Collections of drama
[37581] Folios [Discontinued]
37582 Répertoire Géneral du Théâtre Français
37583.1-.199 General works

Special periods
Before 1661. See with the period in 37591-38539
37583.200-.299 1661-1715
[See also 38524]
37583.300-.399 1715-1799
[Include 18th century in general]
37583.400-.499 1800-1849
[Include also 19th century in general]
37583.500-.599 1850-1899
[Include 19th and 20th centuries together]
37583.600-.799 1900- (By date, e.g. .660 for 1960)
37584 Répertoire du théâtre français, Chefs-d'oeuvres des auteurs comiques, etc.
37585 Local and special
37586 Französische Neudrucke, etc.
37587 Société d'Anciens Textes Français
37588 Almanacs

Individual authors, etc.

Before 1300
Provençal authors, etc. See Rom

Langue d'oc (Southern French)
[37591] Folios [Discontinued]
37592 Anthologies
37593 Known authors and anonymous works
[Include Adam de la Halle, etc.]
37594 Old French dialects
[Prefer FL 1000-1299]

Langue d'oeil (Northern French)
37595 Anthologies; Abelard
37596 Other known authors, etc.
[Include Guillaume de Deguilleville, Philippe de Beaumanoir, Rutebeuf, Chrestien de Troyes, Raoul de Houdenc, Adam (Mystery), St. Alexius Legend, Gautier d'Arras, Thibaut IV of Navarre, Jean Renart, etc.]
37597 Other known authors, etc.
[Include the Roman de la Rose, Robert Wace, Jehan Bodel, Colin Muset, Jean de Condé, Jean de Meun, etc.]
37598 Satirical works
[Include Chastie-musart, etc.]

1300-1499
[38511] Folios [Discontinued]
38512 14th century works
[Include Froissart, LaTour-Landry, Casola, Bozon, Guillaume de Machaut, etc.]
38513 Dramas of the 14th and 15th centuries
[Include mysteries and miracle plays, Pathelin, other farces, etc.]
38514 15th century works
[Include Villon, Charles d'Orléans, Basselin, Deschamps, Christine de Pisan, Alain Chartier, etc.]

Individual authors, etc. (cont.)
1300-1499 (cont.)

Anthologies
38515 Collection des poètes de Champagne
38516 Other anthologies
[Include also anthologies which cover the 15th and 16th centuries together. Some collections of dramas have been classed in 38513.]

1500-1661
[38521] Folios [Discontinued]
38523.1-.13 Clément Marot
38523.14 Jean Marot
38523.15- Malherbe
38524.1-.799 Anthologies
[Include here works covering the 16th and 17th centuries together or singly. For anthologies of 17th century literature which emphasize the age of Louis XIV (1661-1715), see 37573, 37574, 37576, and 37583.]
38524.801-.899 Anonymous plays (99 scheme, A-Z by title)
[38525.1-.6] Selections [Discontinued. See 38524.1-.799]
38525.7-.8 Jodelle
38525.9-.22.49 Ronsard
38525.22.50-.27 Regnier
38525.28-.29 Motin
38525.30-.32 Tahureau
38525.33-.34 Guillaume Bouchet
38525.35-.39 Tristan L'Hermite
38525.45- Rotrou
38526 Other poets and dramatists, 16th century
[N.B. - These are arranged in a rough alphabetic order. Include Autels, Belleau, Jean Bouchet, DuBellay, Desmarets, Desportes, Labé, Lemaire, Marguerite d'Angoulème, Pasquier, Pibrac, Pontus de Tyard, Scève, etc. See also 38523 and 38527-38528.]
38527 Other poets and dramatists, 17th century
[Include Vaquelin, Aubigné, Dolet, Garnier, La Boétie, Magny, etc. See also 38526 and 38528.]
38528.1-.39 Satirical and facetious works in verse
38528.40- Anonymous poems
38529 Satirical and facetious works in prose
Montaigne. See Mon

Rabelais
38531 Folios [Discontinued]
38536 Writings
[N.B. - See also 38537.27-.34]
38537.1-.26 Biography and criticism - General
38537.27-.34 Translations
38537.35- Biography and criticism - Special
38539 Other prose writers
[N.B. - Include anonymous prose works. For satirical and facetious works, see 38529.]

1661-1715
General anthologies. See 37573.200-.299

Fiction
Anthologies. See 37576.200-.299
[38541] Folios [Discontinued]
38542.01-.3 Voiture
38542.4-.12 Balzac, J.L.G. de
[38542.13] Miscellany [Discontinued]
38542.14-.26 Saint-Evremond
38542.27- Blessebois, etc.
38543.1-.2 Rochefort
38543.3-.24 La Rochefoucauld
38543.26 Mme. de Sablé
38543.27 Le Pays
38543.28-.31 La Mothe le Vayer
[38543.32] Lacroix [Discontinued]
38543.33-.34 Méré

	Individual authors, etc. (cont.)
	1661-1715 (cont.)
	Fiction (cont.)
38544.01-.4	La Calprenède
38544.6-.26	Du Verdier, Callière, Ferrand, La Fare, etc.
38544.27	Mme. de La Fayette
38544.28-	Montauban, Ortigne, Prechac, etc.
[38545.1-.9]	Miscellany [Discontinued]
38545.12	Regnerye
38545.18	Saint Maurice
38545.20-.23	Saint Réal
38545.24-.29	Huet
38545.33	L'Heritier de Villandon
38546.1-.21	Madeleine de Scudéry
38546.22-.25	Georges de Scudéry
38546.26-.27	Mme. de Grignan
38546.28-	Mme. de Sévigné
38547.1-.16	Honoré d'Urfé
38547.17-.19	Anne d'Urfé
38547.21-	Anonymous works
	Oratory
	Anthologies. See 37576.200-.299
[38551.1-.18]	Folios [Discontinued]
	Fenelon
38551.19-	Biography and criticism
38552	Complete and selected works
[38553.1-.15]	Selections [Discontinued]
	Telemaque
38553.16-	French editions
38554.1-.3	Translations
38554.4-	Other individual works
[38555]	Portfolios [Discontinued]
[38556]	Criticism [Discontinued. See 38551]
	Bossuet
38557.01-.099	Pamphlet volumes
38557.1	Bibliographies
38557.2-.24	Biography and criticism
38557.25	Complete and selected works
38557.26-	Sermons and other individual works
38558.1-.18	Fléchier
38558.20-.99	Mascaron, etc.
38558.101-.199	Anonymous works (99 scheme, A-Z by title)
	Criticism and philosophy
	Anthologies. See 37576.200-.299
[38561]	Folios [Discontinued]
38562.1-.23	Fontenelle
38562.27-	Bouhours
38563.1-.4	Audin
38563.5-.22	Bayle [N.B. - Works limited to a discussion of his philosophical ideas may go in Phil.]
38563.25-	Pellison, Perrault, etc.
	La Bruyère
38564.1-.39	Writings
38564.40-	Biography and criticism
	Boileau
38565	Complete and selected works
[38566.1-.24]	Selections [Discontinued]
38566.25-	Individual works
38567	Biography and criticism
38568.100-.899	Other critics (800 scheme, A-Z by person)
38568.901-.999	Anonymous works (99 scheme, A-Z by title)
	Drama
	Anthologies. See 37583.200-.299
	Corneille, P.
[38571]	Folios [Discontinued]
	Complete and Selected works
38572	18th and early 19th century editions
38573	Other 19th century editions
38574	Later editions
38575.1-.23	Biography and criticism
38575.24-.89	Individual works
[38575.90-.119]	Criticism [Discontinued. See 38575.1-.23]

	Individual authors, etc. (cont.)
	1661-1715 (cont.)
	Drama (cont.)
	Molière. See Mol
38576	Other dramatists, A-P [Include Barbier, Boursault, Boyer, Brueys, Chevreau, Thomas Corneille, Dancourt, De Visé, Hauteroche, Desjardins (Mme. de Villedieu), La Fosse, Le Noble, Mairet, Montfleury, Palaprat, Pradon, etc. See also 38587-38588.]
	Racine
[38581]	Folios [Discontinued]
	Complete and Selected works
38582	18th and early 19th century editions
38583	Later editions
38585.1-.18	Biography and criticism
38585.19-.54	Individual works
[38585.55-.89]	Criticism [Discontinued. See 38585.1-.18]
	Other dramatists
38587.1-.19	Regnard
38587.21-	Hardy, A.
38588.1-.29	Poisson; Quinault; Dufresny; etc.
38588.31-	Anonymous plays
	Poetry, humor, etc.
	Anthologies. See 37574.200-.299 and 37578
	La Fontaine
[39524]	Folios [Discontinued]
39525	Complete and Selected works
[39526]	Miscellany [Discontinued]
39527.1-.7	Biography and criticism
39527.8-.59	Individual works
[39527.60-.89]	Criticism [Discontinued. See 39527.1-.7]
	Other poets and humorists, etc.
[39531]	Folios [Discontinued]
39532.1-.4	Rousseau, Jean Baptiste
39532.5-.15	Hamilton, A.
39532.16	Chaulieu
39532.17	La Monnoye
39532.18-.20	Loret
39532.24-.26	Lacroix
39532.28-.30	Menage
[39532.32-.33]	Patin [Discontinued. See 39533.32-.34]
39532.34	Perrot
39532.36-.39	Gacon
[39533.2-.4]	Hamilton [Discontinued. See 39532.5-.15]
39533.6-.8	Chapelain
39533.9	Chapelle
39533.10-.12	Miscellany
39533.13	Blainville
39533.15-.16	Segrais
39533.17	Sénecé
39533.18	Cotin
39533.19-.19.10	Chéron
39533.19.11-.20	Cyrano de Bergerac
39533.21	Vitu
39533.22	Sorel
39533.23	Lignières
39533.24	Assouey
39533.25	Pecquet
39533.27	Lauvergne
39533.28	Durand
39533.30	Renoult
39533.32-.34	Patin
39533.35	Sainte Garde
39533.45	Morillon
39534.1-.5	Bussy-Rabutin
39534.6-.7	Benserade
39534.10-.12	Vairasse
39534.15	Drelincourt
39534.19-.22	Furetière
39534.23	Laurent
39534.24-.25	Deshoulières
39534.26-.36	Scarron
39534.37-.40	Brébeuf
39534.43-.45	Gaultier Garguille
39534.46-.59	Miscellany
39534.60-	Anonymous works

Individual authors, etc. (cont.)
1661-1715 (cont.)
Poetry, humor, etc. (cont.)
39535 Satirists and epigrammatists
[Include Le Roy, Naudé, Callières, Sorbiere, etc.]

1715-1799
General anthologies. See 37573.300-.399

Voltaire
[N.B. - See also Phil]
Complete and Selected works
[39536-39542] Folios, etc. [Discontinued]
39543.1-.799 Other editions
[N.B. - Include here complete works and miscellaneous modern selections. See also 39545.23-.34]
39543.800-.999 Bibliographies
39544 Biography and criticism
[Include also Voltaire's memoirs and letters, using .25-.28]
[39545.1-.22] Criticism [Discontinued. See 39544]
39545.23-.34 Collected and Selected plays or tales
39545.35- Individual works
[39551] Miscellaneous complete works [Discontinued]

Rousseau, Jean Jacques. See FL 6001-6150

Diderot
[N.B. - See also Phil]
Complete and selected works
[39561-39563] Folios, etc. [Discontinued]
39564.1-.8 Other editions
39564.9-.23 Individual works
[39564.24-.49] Criticism [Discontinued. See 39566]
39564.60-.69 Letters
[See also 39567-39568]
39566 Biography and criticism
[Include also Diderot's memoirs]
39567-39568 Correspondence with F.M. Grimm
[Include also works about Grimm]

Other philosophers
Anthologies. See 37576.300-.399 or Phil
Condillac
[N.B. - See also Phil]
39571-39572.19 Writings
39572.20- Works about
Alembert
39574.1-.28 Writings
39574.29- Works about
Argens
39576.1-.2 Works about
39576.3-.12 Writings
39576.13-.14 Gondar
39576.15- Miscellany
[Include Henrion, Coyer, Maimieux, Bérenger, Bernard, Benouville, Godard d'Aucour, Brusnoy, etc. See also 39578 or Phil]
Condorcet
[See also Phil]
39577.1-.79 Writings
39577.80- Works about
Du Chatelet
39578.3-.4 Works about
39578.5-.6 Writings
Vauvenargues
39578.7-.8.29 Works about
39578.8.30-.9 Writings
39578.10- Miscellany
[Include Voyer, Eggli, Escherny, Lambert, Saint Martin, etc. See also 39576 or Phil]
39579 Anonymous works (99 scheme, A-Z by title)

History, criticism, etc.
Anthologies. See 37576.300-.399
39581-39582.9 Mably

Individual authors, etc. (cont.)
1715-1799 (cont.)
History, criticism, etc. (cont.)
39582.10-.11 Maury
39582.12-.13 Morellet
39582.15- Arnaud
39583.1-.9 Thomas, A.
39583.11-.17 Servan
39583.18- Trublet
39584.1-.20 La Harpe
39584.30-.39 Saint Foix
39585.1 Chevrier
39585.2 Miscellany
39585.3-.5 Dulaurens
39585.6-.11 Saint Hyacinthe
39585.12-.14 Orbessan
39585.17-.18 Suard
39585.19-.20 Bruhier d'Ablaincourt
39585.21-.22 Caraccioli
39585.23- Miscellany
[Include F. Charpentier, Dreux du Radier, etc. See also 39586.29-]
39586.1-.7 Bachaumont
39586.8-.9 Bondeli
39586.10-.12 Boulanger
39586.14 Miscellany
39586.16-.19 Chamfort
[Use .19.9- for Works about]
39586.20 Constant de Rebeque, San
39586.21 Miscellany
[Include Fréron, Mullot, Parfait, Desfontaines, etc.]
39586.22 Grimod de la Reynière
Rivarol
39586.23-.25 Writings
39586.26-.27 Works about
39586.29- Miscellany
[Include Grosley, etc. See also 39585.23-]
39587 Artigny
Montesquieu
[39591] Folios [Discontinued]
39592 Complete works
39593 Selections
39594.1-.14 Individual works
39594.15 Bibliographies
39594.16-.19 Biography and criticism

Fiction
Anthologies. See 37576.300-.399
Saint Pierre
[39594.20-.39] Folios, etc. [Discontinued]
39595.1-.17 Complete and Selected works
39595.18- Paul et Virginie
39596.1-.19 Other individual works
39596.20- Biography and criticism
Marmontel
39597 Complete and Selected works
39598.1-.36 Individual works
39598.37- Biography and criticism
Le Sage
40511 Folios [Discontinued]; Complete and Selected works
40512 Individual works
40513 Biography and criticism
40515.1-.2 Miscellany
[Include Mme. de Charrière]
40515.3-.6 Épinay
Espinasse
40515.7-.13 Writings
40515.14-.15 Works about
Florian
40515.16-.48 Writings
40515.49- Works about
40516.1-.3 Miscellany
40516.4 Ducray-Dumenil
40516.5-.6 Cazotte
40516.7-.11 Miscellany
40516.12 Gudin
40516.13 Cointreau

Individual authors, etc. (cont.)
1715-1799 (cont.)
Fiction (cont.)

40516.15	Coquelet
40516.16-.17	Miscellany
40516.18-.19	Fromaget
40516.20-.21	Godard d'Aucour
40516.22	Jouin
40516.23-.25.8	Deslandes
40516.25.9-.27	Miscellany
40516.28	Louvet de Couvrai
40516.29-.35	Miscellany
40516.36-.39	Ramsay
40516.40-.46	Miscellany
40516.47-.59	Mercier
40516.60	Sade
40516.61-.63	Kruedener
40516.64-.69	Miscellany
40516.70-.74	Marin
40516.75-	Miscellany
40517.1	Caylus
40517.2-.3	Miscellany
40517.4	Challes
40517.5	Beauharnais
40517.6	Baret
40517.7-.7.49	Aulnoy
40517.7.50-.7.99	Beaurieu
40517.8-.17	Berquin
40517.18	Benseval
40517.19-.21	Miscellany
40517.22-.23.6	Delaunay
40517.23.7-.23.199	Duclos
40517.24	Feutry
40517.25-.28	Gomez
40517.29-.30	La Roche
40517.31	Le Prince de Beaumont
40517.32-.39	Gueullette
40517.40-.42	Miscellany
40517.43	Lambert
40517.44	Choderlos de Laclos
40517.45-.48	Miscellany
40517.49-.51	La Morlière
40517.52-.53	Mouhy
40517.54	La Place
40517.55	Pajon
40517.56-.57	Poujens
40517.58-.60	Miscellany
40517.61-.62	Tiphaigne de la Roche
40517.63-.75	Miscellany
40517.80	Caumont de la Force
40517.86-.88	Bedacier
40517.89-.99	Miscellany
	Prévost
40521	Folios [Discontinued]; Complete and Selected works
40522.1-.9	Individual works
40522.10	Bibliographies
40522.11-	Biography and criticism
40524.1-.2	Tencin
[40524.3-.13]	Marie de La Fayette [Discontinued. See 38544.27]
40524.14	La Fite
40524.15	Fontaines
40524.16-.16.19	Elie de Beaumont
40524.16.20-.17.39	Fiévée
40524.17.40-.20	Miscellany
40524.21-.25	Riccoboni
	Restif de la Bretonne
40524.27-.27.49	Bibliographies
40524.27.50-.27.999	Complete and Selected works
40524.28-.31	Individual works
40524.32	Biography and criticism
40524.33-.99	Miscellany
40525.1-.2	Sénac de Meilham
40525.3-.4	Miscellany
	Tressan
40525.5-.8	Writings
40525.9-.12	Works about

Individual authors, etc. (cont.)
1715-1799 (cont.)
Fiction (cont.)

	Moncrif
40525.15-.17	Writings
40525.18	Works about
40525.20-	Anonymous novels

Poetry

	Anthologies. See 37574.300-.399
40526.1-.3	Blin de Sainmore, Berchoux, etc.
	André Chénier
40526.4-.7	Writings
40526.8	Works about
40526.9-.17	Gresset
40526.18-.21	La Grange-Chancel
40526.22	Malfilâtre
40526.23-.26	Gilbert
40526.27-.28	Miscellany
40526.29-.31	Boufflers
40526.32-.33	Bernis, etc.
40526.34	Dorat
40526.35-.38	Miscellany
40526.39-.40	Monbron
40526.41	Miscellany
40526.42-.44	Louis Racine
40526.45-.46	Miscellany
40526.47	Bourgeois
	Duboccage
40526.48-.50	Writings
40526.51	Works about
40526.52-.57	Le Suire
	Fontanes
40526.58-.59	Writings
40526.60	Works about
40526.61-.66	Miscellany
	Vadé
40526.67-.69	Writings
40526.70	Works about
40526.72-.99	Miscellany
40527.1-.2	L'Attaignant
40527.3-.7	Bernard
[40527.8-.19]	Chénier [Discontinued. See 40526.4-.8]
40527.20	Robbé de Beauveset
40527.21	Miscellany
40527.22-.24	Saint-Lambert
40527.25-.29	Miscellany
40527.30-.99	Anonymous poems
40528	Petites Poètes du XVIIIe Siècle [N.B. - This is a special series. Do not add other publications here.]
40529	Satirists and epigrammatists [Include Bièvre, Bordelon, Marechal, Clement, etc.]

Drama

	Anthologies. See 37583.300-.399
40531.1-.2	Aignan, Amar, etc.
40531.3	Anseaume
40531.4-.5	Armault
40531.6.1-.6.99	Barthès de Marmorières
40531.6.100-.6.199	Beaunoir
40531.7	Bizet
40531.10	Bergasse
40531.14-.16	Miscellany
[40531.20-.30]	Folios [Discontinued]
	Beaumarchais
40532.1-.2	Bibliographies
40532.3	Collected and Selected works
40532.4-.17	Individual works
40532.18-	Biography and criticism
[40534.1-.9]	Anthologies [Discontinued. See 37583.300-.399]
	Belloy
40534.10	Writings
40534.11	Works about
40534.13-.17	Miscellany, B-C [See 40537 for M.J. Chénier]
40534.18-.19.149	Colardeau
40534.19.150-	Carolet

	Individual authors, etc. (cont.)
	1715-1799 (cont.)
	Drama (cont.)
40534.20	Collé
	Collin d'Harleville
40534.21-.23.79	Writings
40534.23.80-.23.249	Works about
40534.23.250-	Collot d'Herbois
	Crébillon, P.J.
40534.24-.29	Writings
40534.30	Works about
	Crébillon, C.P.J.
40534.31-.35	Writings
40534.36	Works about
40534.37-.99	Miscellany, C
40535.1-.3	Miscellany, D
	Destouches
40535.4-.5	Writings
40535.6-.7	Works about
40535.8	Miscellany, D
	Ducis
40535.9-.11	Writings
40535.12-.12.149	Works about
40535.12.150-.13.8	Miscellany, D
40535.13.9	Faur
40535.13.10-.13.99	Falbaire de Quingey
40535.14-.14.19	Fabré d'Eglantine
40535.14.20-.14.99	Fagan
40535.14.500-.15.12	Favart
40535.15.13-.15.999	Miscellany, F
40535.16	Miscellany, G
40535.17-.19.18	Graffigny
40535.19.19-.25.8	Miscellany, G-M
	[See also 40535.36-.99 and 40536.1-.10]
	Marivaux
40535.25.9-.27	Complete and Selected works
40535.28-.30	Individual works
40535.31-.32	Biography and criticism
	La Motte
40535.33-.34	Writings
40535.35	Works about
40535.36-.99	Miscellany, M
	[Include Monvel, etc.]
40536.1-.10	Miscellany, L-O
	[Include Lays, J.B. LeBlanc, La Martelière, Laujon, Legèr, Legouvé, etc. See also 40535]
40536.11-.12	Miscellany, P
	Palissot
40536.13	Works about
40536.14-.17	Writings
40536.18-.19	Miscellany, P-R
40536.20-.20.149	Piron
40536.20.150-.23	Miscellany, P-R
40536.24	Ramond
40536.25-.27	Miscellany, S
	Sedaine
40536.28-.31	Writings
40536.32-.33.8	Works about
40536.33.9-.99	Miscellany, S-Z
40537	Chénier, M.J.
40538	Anonymous dramas
40539	Miscellaneous works
	[Include Jan Potocki, etc.]
	1800-1849
	General anthologies. See 37573.400-.499
	History
	Anthologies. See 37576.400-.499
40541	Roederer
	Ozanam
40542.1-.15	Writings
40542.16-	Works about
	Ségur
40543	Complete works
40544.1-.79	Selections, etc.
40544.80-	Works about
40545	Miscellany, A-Z
	[Include Bazin, Fauriel, etc.]

	Individual authors, etc. (cont.)
	1800-1849 (cont.)
	History (cont.)
	Courier
40546.1-.8	Writings
40546.9-.10	Works about
	Toqueville
40546.11-.24	Writings
40546.25-	Works about
40547	Michelet
	Philosophy, etc.
	[See also Phil]
	Anthologies. See 37576.400-.499 or Phil
40551	Bonald
40552	Miscellany, A-C
	[N.B. - For Cabanis, see Phil]
	Constant de Rebecque
40553.1-.9	Writings
40553.10	Works about
40553.11-.12	Cousin d'Avalon
	Cousin, Victor
[40553.15-.29]	Folios [Discontinued]
40554.1-.15	Writings
40554.16-	Works about
40555	Miscellany, D-Z
	[Include Dutens, Stapfer, Villers, etc. See also 40556.12-.14]
40556.1-.6	Deschamel
40556.7-.11	Droz
40556.12-.14	Miscellany
	[See also 40555]
	Joubert
40556.18-.21	Writings
40556.22-.23	Works about
	Maistre, Joseph de
[40556.24-.26]	Works about [Discontinued]
40556.27-.28	Writings
40556.29-	Works about
40557	Montalembert
	Criticism, etc.
	Anthologies. See 37576.400-.499
[40561]	Folios [Discontinued]
	Lacordaire
40562.1-.12	Writings
40562.13-	Works about
	Ampère
40563.1-.14	Writings
40563.15-.19	Works about
40563.21	Allier
	Ballanche
40563.22-.23	Writings
40563.24-.29	Works about
	Beyle. See 40582-40583
	Boissonade
40563.30-.34	Writings
40563.35-	Works about
	Barante
40564.1-.9	Writings
40564.10-.14	Works about
	Chasles
40564.15-.33	Writings
40564.34	Works about
40564.35	Chauvet
	Cuvillier-Fleury
40565.1-.29	Writings
40565.30-.59	Works about
40565.75	Deplace
	Doudan
40566.1-.5	Writings
40566.6	Works about
40566.7	Miscellany, D
40566.8	Dussault
40566.9	Félitz
40566.10	Fontaney
40566.13	Guizot

	Individual authors, etc. (cont.)
	1800-1849 (cont.)
	Criticism, etc. (cont.)
	Janin
[40566.18-.31]	Folios [Discontinued]
40567.1-.39	Writings
40567.40-	Works about
40571	K-Mi
	[Include Labitte, Magnin, Martin, etc.]
40572.2	Montlaur
40572.5-.9	Muret
	Nisard
40572.20-.34	Writings
40572.35-.39	Works about
40572.45	Ozenne
	Peignot
40573.1-.3	Writings
40573.4	Works about
	Planche
40573.5-.13	Writings
40573.14	Works about
	Pyat
40573.18-.22	Writings
40573.23	Works about
	Rémusat
40573.25-.29	Writings
40573.30	Works about
40573.34	Rigault
40573.45	Salgues
[40574]	Folios [Discontinued]
	Saint Beuve
40575.01-.099	Pamphlet volumes
40575.1	Bibliographies
40575.2-.5	Biography and criticism
40575.6-.9	Correspondence
40575.10-	Collected and Selected works
40576	Individual works
[40577-40578]	Folios, etc. [Discontinued]
[40581]	Folios [Discontinued]
	Stendhal, i.e. H. Beyle
40582.1-.4	Complete works
40582.5-.7	Selected works
40582.8-	Individual works
40583	Biography and criticism
40584.5	Vanderbourg
40584.10	Vinet
	Villemain
40584.13	Works about
40584.15-.20	Writings
	Vitet
40584.21-.30	Writings
40584.31	Works about
40584.35-	Anonymous works
	Fiction
	Anthologies. See 37576.400-.499
	Chateaubriand, F.A.R.
40585.1	Bibliographies
40585.2-.399	Complete works
40585.400-	Selected works
40586	Individual works
	[N.B. - Some criticism dealing with a specific title has been classed here with the editions of the work]
40587.1-.899	Biography and criticism
40587.900-.949	Caud, Lucile (Chateaubriand's sister)
40587.950-.999	Chateaubriand, Celeste B. (his wife)
	Cottin
40588.01-.099	Complete and Selected works
40588.1-.6	Individual works
40588.7-.7.49	Biography and criticism
40588.7.50-.7.999	Miscellany, A-C
	[See also 41522 and 41566]
40588.8	Miscellany, D
	[See also 41522-41540 and 41566]
	Genlis
40588.9-.21	Writings
40588.22	Works about
40588.24-.28	Montolieu
40588.29-.30	Souza, Mme de

	Individual authors, etc. (cont.)
	1800-1849 (cont.)
	Fiction (cont.)
	Maistre, Xavier de
40588.33-.40	Complete and Selected works
40588.41-.69	Individual works
40588.70-	Biography and criticism
[40591]	Folios [Discontinued]
	Staël, Mme de
40592.1	Bibliographies
40592.2-.20	Complete works
40592.21-.39	Corinne
40592.40-.59	Correspondence
[40592.60-.99]	Criticism [Discontinued]
40593.1-.14	Selected works
40593.15-.25	Individual works
40593.26-.899	Criticism
	[N.B. - Include here critical works on Mme de Staël's literary works and ideas. Purely biographical works should go in Fr 1589.]
40593.900-.999	Staël-Holstein, August L.
	Balzac
[40594-40595]	Folios [Discontinued]
40596	Complete and Selected words
40597-40597.099	Pamphlet volumes
40597.1-.9	Biography and criticism
40597.10-	Individual works
[41521]	Folios [Discontinued]
	Barbey d'Aurevilly
41522.1-.2	Writings
41522.3	Works about
	Baudelaire, C.
41522.4-.5	Complete and Selected works
41522.6-.15	Individual works
41522.16-.18	Biography and criticism
41522.19	Beaumont-Vassy
41522.20	Beauvoir
41522.21	Badon
41522.23	Bellin de la Liborlière
41522.24-.25	Belot
	Bernard, Charles de
41522.27-.55	Writings
41522.56	Works about
	Bertrand, Louis
41522.58	Writings
41522.59-.60	Works about
[41522.63]	Bonnellier [Discontinued. See 41566.12-.13]
	Borel d'Hauterive
41522.64-.66	Writings
41522.67	Works about
41522.68	Bouis
41522.69-.70	Miscellany, B-C
	[See also 40588 and 41566]
41522.72	Chevalier, Pierre
41522.75-.78	Cordellier-Delanoue
41522.100	Dondey
41522.150-.155	Drouineau
	Dudevant, Mme. See 41557 (George Sand)
	Dumas père
	Complete works
[41523-41528]	Paris edition in French [Discontinued]
	[N.B. - This is a special edition with each title recorded separately in alphabetical order. Do not add anything here.]
[41529]	Boston and N.Y. editions in English [Discontinued]
41530.1-.299	Other French editions
41530.300-.499	Other English editions
41530.500-	Editions in other languages
41538	Individual works
41539	Biography and criticism
41540.2	Dumesnil, P.
41540.4	Fazy
41540.15	Féré
41540.50	Ferrière
41540.75	Floquet
41540.125	François de Nantes, A.
[41541.1-.4]	Folios [Discontinued]

Individual authors, etc. (cont.)
1800-1849 (cont.)
Fiction (cont.)

41541.5	Girardin, Emile de
	Girardin, Delphine
41541.6-.17	Writings
41541.18-.20.99	Works about
[41541.20.100-]	Folios [Discontinued]
	Gautier
41542.1-.4	Biography and criticism
41542.5	Collected and Selected works
41542.6-.37	Individual works
	Gozlan
41542.38-.79	Writings
41542.80	Works about
41542.81-	Miscellany, G [N.B. - For Mme de Genlis, see 40588.9-.22. See also 41543.25-]
	Gérard de Nerval
41543.1-.5	Complete works
41543.6-.7	Selected works
41543.8-.18	Individual works
41543.19-.22	Biography and criticism
	Guiraud
41543.27-.33	Writings
41543.34	Works about
	Grandville
41543.35-.38	Writings
41543.39	Works about
	Hugo. See 41571-41574
	Karr, Alphonse
41544-41545.79	Writings
41545.80-	Works about
	Pigault-Lebrun
41547.1-.14	Writings
41547.15	Works about
	Privat d'Anglemont
41547.17-.19	Writings
41547.20	Works about
41548.10	Kérardven
41548.25	Kératry
41548.50	Kermel
[41551]	Folios [Discontinued]
	Kock, C.P. de
41552-41553.99	Writings
41553.100-	Works about
41554.3	Labutte
	Lacroix, Jules
41554.4	Works about
41554.5-.11	Writings
	Lacroix, Paul
41554.12-.28	Writings
41554.29	Works about
41554.34	Lacroix, Appoline
41554.35	Lambert de Saumery
41554.36	Lanjiunais, S.J.
41554.37	Lassailly
41554.38	Lebras
41554.39	Lebrun
41554.41	Lourdoueix
41554.45	Manceau
41554.50	Maydieu
41554.54	Mercey
41554.58	Laponneraye
	Mérimée
41555.01-.099	Pamphlet volumes
41555.1	Complete works
41555.2-.19	Selected works, Letters
41555.20-.35	Individual works
41555.36	Bibliographies
41555.37-.54	Biography and criticism
41555.55	Meritens, Mme. H. Allart de
41555.56	Moine
41555.58	Moke
41555.62	Montbrun
	Montgolfier
41555.63-.68	Writings
41555.69	Works about
	Nerval. See 41543.1-.22

Individual authors, etc. (cont.)
1800-1849 (cont.)
Fiction (cont.)

	Nodier
41556.6-.14	Collected and Selected works
41556.15-.33	Individual works
41556.34	Bibliographies
41556.35-	Biography and criticism
	Pigault-Lebrun. See 41547.1-.15
	Privat d'Anglemont. See 41547.17-.20
41557.2	Miscellany, P [See also 41567]
41557.3	Ropartz
	Reybaud, Louis
41557.4-.6	Writings
41557.7	Works about
41557.8-.8.39	Miscellany, R-Sa [See also 41568]
	Sand, George, pseud.
41557.8.40-.8.999	Collected and Selected works [N.B. - 41557.8.50-.8.130 is used for a made-up set of complete works - all published in Paris in the late 19th century; the titles are arranged alphabetically and each has a separate second dot number. Do not add other editions here.]
41557.9	Individual works
41557.10	Biography and criticism [Include Sand's letters and posthumous journal.]
	Sandeau
41557.11-.32	Writings
41557.33	Works about
	Sarrazin
41557.34-.44	Writings
41557.45	Works about
	Soulié
41558.1-.29	Writings
41558.30	Works about
	Souvestre
41558.40-.89	Writings
41558.90	Works about
[41561]	Folios [Discontinued]
	Sue
41562	Complete and Selected works
41563.1-.17	Individual works
41563.18	Biography and criticism
41563.20	Suberwick
41563.23	Thibaudeau
	Toepffer
41563.25-.32	Writings
41563.33	Works about
41563.34	Trognan
41563.35	Vanhove
41563.50	Vidocq
	Vigny
41564.1	Complete works
41564.2	Selected works
41564.3-.31	Individual works
41564.32-.55	Biography and criticism
	Other novelists, A-Z. See 41565-41568
	Anonymous novels. See 41569
[41565]	Folios [Discontinued]
41566.1	Abrantes
41566.2-.5	Arlincourt
41566.6-.7	Arnould
41566.8	Auger
41566.9	Barginet
41566.11	Bazot
41566.12-.13	Bonnellier
41566.14	Bouilly
41566.15	Chabot de Bouin
41566.16-.16.49	Bourgeois
41566.16.50-.16.99	Brucker
41566.17-.18	Buonaparte, L.
41566.19	Cadet
41566.22	Choiseul
41566.24	Corbière
41566.26-.27	Craon

Individual authors, etc. (cont.)
1800-1849 (cont.)
Fiction (cont.)

41566.28 Creuzé du Lesser
41566.30 Daux
41566.31 Defontenay
41566.33 Delafaye-Brehier
41566.36 Delécluze
41566.58 Bonnardot
41567.5 Delrieu
41567.8 Dincourt
Duras
41567.10-.11 Writings
41567.12 Works about
Fouinet
41567.14-.16 Writings
41567.17 Works about
41567.18 Gay, M.F.S.
41567.19 Geoffroy
41567.20 Grandfort
Guizot, Mme de
41567.22-.24 Writings
41567.25 Works about
41567.26 Hilarion
41567.27 Montpezat, Mme de
41567.28 Herbster, Mme de
41567.30 Jauffret
41567.32 Juno
41567.34 Lottin de Laval
41567.37 Lorvergne
41567.40 La Madelaine
41567.42 Manesca
Masson
41567.43-.44 Writings
41567.45 Works about
41567.47-.48 Philipon
41567.50 Ponson du Terrail
41568.1 Rabbé
Reybaud, H.E.F.
41568.6-.7 Writings
41568.8 Works about
41568.9 Saint-Genois
Saintine
41568.10-.12 Writings
41568.13 Works about
41568.14-.14.49 Saunders, M.J.
41568.14.50-.14.99 Say, J.B.
Senancour
41568.15 Works about
41568.16-.19 Writings
Sewrin
41568.20-.21 Writings
41568.22 Works about
41568.24 Thenaisie
Tillier
41568.25-.26.49 Writings
41568.26.50-.26.99 Works about
41568.27 Villiers
41568.28 Viollet-le-Duc
41568.29 Wailly
41568.32 Waldor
41568.70 Yvan
41569 Anonymous novels, etc.

Hugo, Victor
41571.1-.4 Complete works
41571.5 Bibliographies
[41571.6-.49] Folios [Discontinued]
41572 Selected works
41573 Individual works
41574.1-.16 Letters and journals
41574.17- Biography and criticism

Lamartine
41576-41577.11 Complete works
[N.B. - 41576.3-41577.8 are used together for a special edition with a separate dot number for each title. Do not add anything in that range of numbers.]
41577.12 Selected works

Individual authors, etc. (cont.)
1800-1849 (cont.)
Lamartine (cont.)
41577.13- Letters and memoirs
41578.1-.35 Individual works
41578.36- Biography and criticism

Drama
Anthologies. See 37583.400-.499
[41581.1-.28] Folios [Discontinued]
41581.29-.49 Pamphlet volumes
41583.2 Adamoli
41583.3 Antier
41583.4 Ancelot
Andrieux
41583.5 Works about
41583.6 Writings
41583.7 Artois
41583.8-.8.9 Arago
41583.8.20 Arnault, A.
41583.8.25 Arnoult, S.
41583.8.40 Aude
41583.9 Barré
41583.10 Aumer
41583.11 Barthelmy-Hadot; Basté; Bawr; Bazin
41583.12 Bayard; Beffroy de Reigny; Belfort; etc.
41583.13 Blache; etc.
41583.14 Boirie; Bonel; etc.
41583.15 Bonjour; Bouchardy; Bourgeois; etc.
41583.16 Brazier
41583.17 Brifaut
41583.18 Brisebarre; Brunneaux; Caigniez; Chazet; etc.
41583.19 Cuvelier
Delavigne, Casimir
41583.20-.31 Writings
41583.32 Works about
41583.34 Delavigne, G.
41583.45 Désnoyer
41584.2 Debraux
41584.3 Delisle de Sales
41584.4 Delaunay
41584.5 Demoustier
41584.6 Desprey
41584.7 Dieu-la-Foy
41584.8 Goubaux (Denaux)
Doucet
41584.15-.18 Writings
41584.19 Works about
41584.23 Dittmer
41584.26 Drague
41584.27 Druancel; Ducange; Dupetit; etc.
41584.28-.29 Duval, A.
41584.30 Duvert
41584.32 Duveyrier
41584.33 Dumolard
41584.34 Dubois
Etienne, C.G.
41584.35-.36 Works about
41584.37-.39 Writings
41584.40 Eustache
41584.41 Fezet-Mougest; Flareau; etc.
41584.42 Fontan
41584.43 Forneret
41584.44 Fougher
41584.47 Francis
41584.49 Ferrand; Friedalle; etc.
41584.50 Gaillardet; Gain-Montaignac
41584.51 Gardy; Germeau; Gibelin; etc.
41584.52 Gibert
41584.53 Gosse
41584.54 Gouffe
41584.55 Gougibus; Guénard; Grévin; etc.
41584.56 Hapdé; Henrion; etc.
Hoffman, F.B.
41584.57-.58 Writings
41584.59 Works about
41585.2 Imbert de Saint Armand

Individual authors, etc. (cont.)
1800-1849 (cont.)
Drama (cont.)

	Jouy
41585.5-.18	Writings
41585.19	Works about
41585.24	Dulong, J. (M. Jules)
41585.31	La Gleyenhaye
41585.35	Laloue
41585.36	Lamey
41586.1	La Roche; La Rochefoucauld-Liancourt
41586.2	Latour
41586.3	Latouche, H. de; Laurençot; etc.
41586.4	La Ville de Mirmont
	Laya, L.
41586.5-.8	Writings
41586.9	Works about
41586.10	Leblanc; etc.
41586.11	Leclercq
41586.12	Le Feure; Le Hoc; etc.
41586.13-.15	Lemercier, N.L.
41586.16	Le Riche; Leroy; Loaisel; etc.
41586.17	Lombard; Lucas; etc.
41586.18	Luchet; etc.
41586.19	Marie; Marsollier; Martainville; etc.
41586.20-.21	Mazères
41586.22	Mélesville; Merle; etc.
41586.23	Merville; Méry; etc.
41586.24	Maurice
41586.25	Monbion
41586.26	Monperlier; Moreau; Ourliac; etc.
41586.27	Outrepont; Perin; Petit; etc.
	Picard, L. See 41587
41586.28	Pixerécourt; Pourchel; etc.
41586.29	Pyat; Revoil; Saulnier; etc.
	Scribe. See 41587-41588
	Soumet, A.
41586.30-.31	Writings
41586.32	Works about
	Picard, L.B.
41587.5-.18.79	Writings
41587.18.80-.18.99	Works about
41587.19	Pompigny; Ponet; Pradel; etc.
41587.20	Raimond; Ratier; Rousseau, P.J.; etc.
41587.21	Saint-Georges
41587.22	Saint-Hilaire
41587.25	Saint-Just
41587.26	Saint-Maurice; Sadler; etc.
41587.27	Salverte; Sidony; etc.
	Scribe, E.
41587.29-	Complete works
41588.1-.15.8	Selected works; Individual works
41588.15.9-.15.999	Biography and criticism
41588.16-.18	Scribe, A.
41588.19	Arlincourt
41588.20	Barthet
41588.23	Loeve-Weimars
41588.24	Sewrin [See also 41568.20-.22]
41588.25	Gallois
41588.26	Geoffrey, M.
41588.28	Quinet
41588.29	Séjour; Servières; Simonnin; etc.
41588.30	Superville
41588.33	Passard
41588.37	Tardif
41588.38	Theaulon
41588.39	Lambert-Thiboust
41588.40	Trouvé, C.J.
41588.41	Vander-Burch
41588.42	Verez
41588.43	Victor, M.
41588.47	Villemontez
41588.48	Villeterque
	Wafflard
41588.49-.50	Writings
41588.51	Works about
41588.52	Wailly [See also 41568.29]
41588.60-	Anonymous dramas

Individual authors, etc. (cont.)
1800-1849 (cont.)

Poetry

	Anthologies. See 37574.400-.499
[41591]	Folios [Discontinued]
41592.01	Agnant; etc.
41592.1	Alletz; Allo; Arnould; etc.
41592.2	Arvers
	Baudelaire. See 41522
	Béranger, P.J.
41592.3-.10	Works about
41592.11-	Writings
41593.3	Baour-Lormian
41593.5-.8	Barthélemy
41593.9	Boucher de Perthes; Boussot; Brad; etc.
	Brizeux
41593.10-.11	Writings
41593.12	Works about
41593.13	Boulay-Paty; Boyer d'Agen; etc.
41593.14	Brifant; Buchon; etc.
41593.15	Chalette; Chatelain; etc.
41593.16	Chênedollé; Chevigné; Clément, R.; etc.
41593.17	Colet; Coquerel; Daru; etc. [See also 41593.150-]
41593.18	DeFoudras
41593.19	Delasalle; Delaurel; etc.
	Delille, J.
41593.20	Complete and Selected works
41593.21-.26	Individual works
41593.27	Biography and criticism
41593.28	Delonne; Dénoix des Vergnes; etc.
41593.29	Désaugiers; Desbordes-Valmore; Deschamps; etc.
41593.30	Direy; etc.
41593.31	Dierx, L.; etc.
41593.32	Miscellany, Du-Gu [See also 41593.150-]
	Guérin, M. de
41593.33-.36.9	Writings
41593.36.10-.42	Works about
41593.45-.49	Guttinguer
41593.60	Halma
41593.70	Hugo, E.
41593.92	Jouin
41593.125	Jullien
41593.160	Bremond
41593.170	Collet
41593.175	Corday
41593.190	Croiszetière
41593.225	Flamen
41593.240	Forget
[41594]	Miscellany [Discontinued]
	Lamartine. See 41576-41578
41595.1	Lacan
41595.2	Lacenaire
41595.4	Lapointe
41595.5	Le Poitevin
41595.6	Lebrèton
	Lebrun, Pierre
41595.7-.9	Writings
41595.10-.11	Works about
	Le Fevre-Deumier
41595.12-.16	Writings
41595.17	Works about
41595.18	Léon, Louis de
41595.19	Lesseps
41595.20	Luce de Lancival
41595.22	Magalon; Magu; Martin-Maillefer; etc.
41595.23	Massas; Mirecourt; Michaud; etc.
	Millevoye
41595.24-.29	Writings
41595.30	Works about
41595.31	Larrebat; Mercoeur; Mollevant; etc.
	Moreau, Hegesippe
41595.32-.35	Complete and Selected works
41595.36-.49	Individual works
41595.50	Biography and criticism
41595.55	Montlivault
41595.60	Moussard

	Individual authors, etc. (cont.)
	1800-1849 (cont.)
	Poetry (cont.)
41595.70	Manso
	Musset, Alfred de
41596.01-.099	Pamphlet volumes
41596.1-.4	Biography and criticism
41596.5-.8	Complete and Selected works [Include also his "Biographie"]
41596.9	Correspondence
41596.10-.38	Individual works
41596.39-.40	Moyria
41596.41	Norvins
41596.42	Olivier; Ourry; etc.
41596.43	Paillet
41596.44	Pécontal
41596.45	Poncy
41596.46-.48	Parny
41596.49	Parseval; Pellet; Périn; Popelin; etc.
41596.50	Pommier
41596.51	Porchat; Pottier; Raynouard; etc.
41596.52	Reynaud; Richard; etc.
41596.53	Rouget de Lisle
41596.55	Roulland
41596.56-.57	Rouquette
41596.58	Salm-Rufferscheid
41596.59	Ségur, Anatole
41596.60	Servan de Sugny
41596.63	Tastu
41596.64	Treneuil; Tellier; etc.
41596.65	Urbain
41596.66	Veyrat
41596.67-.69	Viennet
	Vigny. See 41564
41596.71	Violeau
41596.80	Weustenraad
41596.100	Yvaren
41596.120	Valori
41597	Anonymous works
41598	Satirical and epigrammatic works
	1850-1899
	History, philosophy, etc.
	Anthologies. See 37576.500-.599, Phil, etc.
[42511]	Folios [Discontinued]
	Adam, Juliette. See 42513.47-.48
42512.3	Albert, P.
42512.4	Amis
42512.5	Aulard
42512.6	Bernard-Derosne
42512.7	Bois
42512.8-.19	Broglie
42512.20-.99	Other A-C
42513.3	Darmesteter
42513.5	Delepierre, O.
42513.7	Denis, F.
42513.10	Despois
42513.16	Diane
42513.22	Didon
42513.23	Dollfus
42513.25	DuLaz
42513.26	Esquiros
42513.27-.30	Favre, Jules
42513.33-.40	Gasparin
42513.42	Guyau
42513.43	Guizot
42513.44	Hauréau
42513.45	Jusserand
42513.46	Kuhn, Emile
	Adam, Juliette (Lamber)
42513.47	Writings
42513.48	Works about
42513.50	Lemoine
42513.60	Laveleye
	Leroy-Beaulieu
42513.73-.89	Writings
42513.90-.95	Works about
42513.99	Littré, E.

	Individual authors, etc. (cont.)
	1850-1899 (cont.)
	History, philosophy, etc. (cont.)
	Laboulaye
42514.3-.4	Works about
42514.5-.24	Writings
42514.25	Lamy
42514.26	Lanfrey
42514.27	Lefébure; Lerne; Lomenie; etc.
42514.28	Maurras, Charles
	Mignet
42514.29-.36	Writings
42514.37	Works about
42514.39	Masson, F.
42515.10	Pelletan, E.
42515.13	Pichot
42515.15	Poulet-Malassis
42515.17	Pirmez
42515.20	Prevost-Paradol
42515.22	Primoli
	Renan
42515.25	Complete and Selected works
	Histoire des origines du Christianisme
42515.27	Complete editions
42515.29	Separate volumes
42515.30	Other individual works
42515.32	Bibliographies
42515.33	Pamphlet volumes
42515.34	Correspondence
	Biography and criticism
42515.35	General works (299 scheme minus 100]
42515.36	Criticism of individual works (299 scheme minus 100, A-Z by author)
42515.37-.38	Special topics
	Quinet, Edgar
42515.39-.44	Biography and criticism
42515.45-.68	Complete works
42515.69-	Individual works
42516.6	Schaeffer
42516.9	Secrétan
42516.16-.17	Sorel
	Veuillot, L.
42521.1-.2	Complete and Selected works
42521.3-.18	Individual works
42521.19-	Biography and criticism
	Vogüé, E.M.
42522.1-.22	Writings
42522.23	Works about
42522.25	Vogüé, C.J.M.
42522.32	Warney
42522.36-.37	Weyer
	Criticism
	Anthologies. See 37576.500-.599, etc.
42524.7	Alaux
42524.8	Babou
42524.9	Baldensperger
42524.10	Bardoux
42524.12	Bonneau; Bonnefou; Bredif; etc.
	Brunetière
42524.13-.18	Writings
42524.19	Works about
42524.20	Büchner
42524.22	Capperon
	Circourt
42524.24-.25	Works about
42524.26-.27	Writings
42524.30-.31	Clement de Ris
42524.34	Contades
42524.38	Desjardins
	Doumic
42524.40	Works about
42524.42	Writings
42524.50	Duret
42524.55	Faguet
42524.58	Foulché-Delbosc
42524.60-.62	Frary
42525.5-.6	Gautier
42525.7	Gazier; Grousset; etc.
42525.8	Hello

Individual authors, etc. (cont.)
1850-1899 (cont.)
Criticism (cont.)

42525.9 Hallays
42525.10 Hugues
42525.22 Jal
42526.3 Lacour
42526.4 Larroumet
42526.5 Lhomme
Lucas, H.
42526.6-.7 Writings
42526.8 Works about
42526.9 Langlois
42526.10 Le Blond
Mauclair, C.
42526.14-.17 Writings
42526.18 Works about
[42527] Miscellany [Discontinued]
[42531-42532] Folios [Discontinued]
42533.1 Marchand
42533.2 Mazade
Merlet, G.
42533.5-.8 Writings
42533.9 Works about
42533.10-.13 Mézières
Montégut
42533.14-.16 Writings
42533.17 Works about
42533.18 Mortier
42533.19 Milsand
42533.20 Mockel
Paris, Gaston
42534.1-.4 Works about
42534.5 Writings
42534.12 Pavie
42534.14 Pons
Pontmartin
42534.15-.35 Writings
42534.36 Works about
42535.3 Romey
42535.5 Savine
42535.11 Rambert
42535.15-.19 Ratisbonne
Saint-Victor
42535.20-.21 Writings
42535.22-.22.49 Works about
42535.22.50-.22.99 Scherer
42535.23 Segur, M. de
42535.24 Silvestre
42535.25 Simon, P.M.
42535.27 Spach
42535.30-.35 Stapfer
42536.4 Taillandier
Taine
42536.8-.24 Writings
42536.25-.43 Works about
42536.45- Troubat
42537.16 Yayssière
42537.20 Weiss
42537.25 Wyzewa

Drama
Anthologies. See 37583.500-.599, etc.
[42541.1-.69] Folios [Discontinued]
42541.71-.99 Pamphlet volumes
42542.1 Abraham; Ajalbert; Alexis; Ancey; Arnault; etc.
Augier
42542.2 Biography and criticism
42542.3 Complete and Selected works
42542.4-.26 Individual works
42542.27 Barbier; Barrière; Bayard; etc.
42542.28 Becque
42542.29 Benière; Bergerat; Bernard; Bernstein; Bisson; Bonnetain; Bornier; etc.
42542.30 Bouchor, M.

Individual authors, etc. (cont.)
1850-1899 (cont.)
Drama (cont.)
Bouilhet
42542.31-.35 Writings
42542.36 Works about
42542.37 Bois
42542.42 Bouché, J.
42542.44 Bourdet
42542.45 Bourgeois
42542.46 Bourget
42542.47 Brieux; Bruno; Burani; Busnach; Cadol; Caillavet; etc.
42542.48 Capus; Carré; etc.
42542.49 Céard
42542.50 Chriecki
42542.52 Clairville
42542.53 Coolus; Copeau; etc.
42542.54 Cottinet; Crémieux; etc.
42542.55 Croisset (Wiener)
Curel
42542.58 Writings
42542.59 Works about
42542.60 Darmont; Dartigues; Decourcelle, A.
42542.61 Decourcelle, P.
42542.62 Delacour
42542.63 Délerot; Demesse; Denayrouze; etc.
42542.64 Déroulède; Descaves; Dieudonne; etc.
42542.65 Donnay; Doucet; etc.
42542.66 Dreyfus; Dugué; etc.
42542.67-.69 Dumanoir
42542.72 Duru
Dumas fils
42543.1 Biography and criticism
42543.2-.11 Complete works
42543.12-.27 Individual works
42543.28 Durantin; Empic; Ennes; Eudel; etc.
42543.29 Erckmann; Eude
42543.30 Fournier, N.
42543.31 Fournier, M.; Fournier, E.
42543.32 Fremy
42543.34 Foussier
42543.36 Fabins
42543.37-.38 Fabre, E.
42543.39 Fallet
42543.40 Faramond; Ferrier; Fauchois
42543.41 Figuies; Feydeau, G.; Flers, P.L.
42543.42 Flers, R.
42543.43 Fonson; Galipaux
42543.44 Gandillot; Ganem; Gassier; etc.
42543.45 Gavault
42543.46 Geffroy
42543.47 Giocosa
42543.48 Giron
42543.49 Glatigny
42543.51 Gohier
42543.53-.55 Gondinet
42543.56 Grenet-Dancourt
42543.57 Goury
42543.60 Grandmougin
42543.61 Guinon; Guillemot
42543.62 Guiard; Guiraud; Haraucourt; Hennique; etc.
42543.63-.67 Hermant
42543.68 Halévy, L.; Hennequin
[See also 42576.40 for novels by Halévy]
42543.69 Hervieu; Hervilly; Humières; Ivry
42543.70 Janvier
42543.71 Jullien
42543.73 Josz
42544.1 Keranbors
42544.2 Kistemaeckers
42544.3 Lafont; Lapommeraye; Laroze; etc.
42544.4 Launay
42544.5-.16 Legouvé, E.
42544.17-.19 Legouvé, G.
42544.20 Lengyel
42544.22-.25 Lavedan
42544.26-.30 Labiche
42544.31 Lapointe; Lecomte; Legendre; etc.
42544.32-.33 Lemaitre, J.

	Individual authors, etc. (cont.)
	1850-1899 (cont.)
	Drama (cont.)
42544.34	Lemercier; Lepelletier; Lomon; Lorde; Louys, P.; etc.
42544.35	Lurine, L.
42544.36	Loyson
42544.40	Lubac
	Maeterlinck
42545.01-.099	Complete and Selected works
42545.1-.3.349	Individual works
42545.3.350-.4	Biography and criticism
42545.5	Manquat; Manuel; Maiziere; etc.
42545.6	Mazel; Maques; Marot; etc.
42545.7-.8	Maquet
42545.9	Martel de Janville
	Meilhac
42545.10-.18	Writings
42545.19	Works about
42545.20	Massonneau; Mazilier; etc.
42545.21	Méry; Méténier; etc.
42545.22-.24	Meurice
42545.26	Mercier; Michaud; etc.
42545.27	Mikhaël, Millanvoye
42545.28-.28.8	Mirbeau
42545.28.9-.28.999	Moinaux (Courteline)
42545.29-.38	Monnier, H.
42545.39-.42	Monselet
42545.43-.44	Moreau; etc.
42545.45	Najac; Népoty; Nigond; etc.
42545.46	Normand
42545.47-.48	Nuitter de Beaumont
42545.50	Nus
42545.55	Olagnier
42545.62-.68	Pailleron
42545.69	Parodi; Pelletier; Petitdidier; Philippe d'Ennery; Pierron; etc.
42545.71	Piestre
42545.75-.77	Picard
42545.78	Plouvier
42545.80	Ply
	Ponsard
42545.82-.83	Writings
42545.84	Works about
42545.85-.88	Porto-Riche
42545.89	Potron
42545.95	Pottecher
42545.100-.101	Prével
42545.105	Prévost
42546.4	Richard
42546.6	Ringal; Rivoire
42546.8	Rodenbach
42546.9	Rosier
	Rostand, Edmond
42546.10-.11	Writings
42546.12	Biography and criticism
42546.13-.15.18	Writings
42546.15.19	Rostand, Maurice
42546.15.20-.15.99	Rothschild; Saint Geniès; Salandri; etc.
	Sardou
42546.16	Complete and Selected works
42546.17-.30	Individual works
42546.31	Biography and criticism
42546.32	Sartène; Second; Sermet; etc.
42546.33-.34	Silvestre
42546.39	Serret
42546.40	Scholl
42546.43	Siraudin
42546.46	Sorbets
42546.47	Sonal
42547.1	Thalasso
42547.2	Thénard
42547.4	Thomas; Thurner; Tourte; etc.
42547.5	Trarieux
42547.6	Trézenik
42547.7-.8	Uchard
42547.10	Vacquerie; Vallette; Vandérem; etc.
42547.11	Vaucaire
42547.12	Veber
42547.13	Verhaeren [Discontinued]; Villemin

	Individual authors, etc. (cont.)
	1850-1899 (cont.)
	Drama (cont.)
	Villiers de l'Isle-Adam
42547.14	Pamphlet volumes; Bibliographies
[42547.15]	Works about [Discontinued]
42547.16-.21	Writings
42547.22	Biography and criticism
42547.23-.25	Weill
	Wolff, P.
42547.28-.48	Writings
42547.49	Works about
[42548.1-.70]	Miscellany [Discontinued]
42548.71-	Anonymous plays
	Poetry
	Anthologies. See 37574.500-.599, etc.
[42551-42552]	Folios [Discontinued]
42553.2-.3	Ackermann
	Autran
42553.5-.9	Complete and Selected works
42553.10-.18	Individual works
42553.19	Biography and criticism
	Amiel
42553.20-.33	Writings
42553.34-.35	Works about
	Angellier
42553.39-.47	Writings
42553.48-.49	Works about
42553.52	Angelés
42553.53	Arnaud
42553.55	Ansaldi
42553.60	Amanieux
42553.62	Amoric
42553.68	Baillet
42553.72	Baldenne
	Banville
42554.1-.10	Writings
42554.11	Works about
42554.12	Barbier, A.
42554.13	Beaufort; Bellot des Minières; Bergerat; etc.
42554.14	Barracand; Bocquet; Boissière; etc.
42554.15	Bonnard; Bouchaud; Botrel; etc.
42554.16	Le Braz, A.; Boutelleau; Breton, J.; etc.
42554.17	Caillaux; Carné; Carrère; Cantacuzène; etc.
42554.18	Cazales (Lahor); Chambrun; Chavanne; Chatillon; Clément, J.B.; etc.
	Coppée, F.
42554.19-.26.24	Writings
42554.26.25-.26.29	Works about
42554.26.33	Circello
42554.26.35	Cremieux
42554.26.80-.26.109	Cros
42554.26.110-	Corbière, T.
42554.27	Dogue
42554.28	Dorchain
42554.29	Debans; Déroulède; DeGuerois; Dujardin; Dupuy; etc.
42554.30	Elskamp
42554.31	Eggis; Eichthal; Errera; etc.
42554.32	Fabie; Fabre des Essarts; Ferrières; etc.
42554.33	Fischer; Fontaines; etc.
42554.34	Fontaubert
42554.35	Floupette; Fertrault; etc.
42554.36	Fontenay, H.
42554.37	Fontenelle; Fret; etc.
42554.38	Le Guyader
42554.39	Gérard
42554.40	Gendry; Gauthiez; etc.
42554.41	Gelu
42554.44-.45	Ghil
42554.46	Gielkens
42554.47	Gnafron
42554.48	Grandmougin
42554.49	Gregh; Guaita; etc.
42554.50	Guérin, C.; Guillemet; etc.
42554.51	Harel, P.
42554.52	Harel, R.

	Individual authors, etc. (cont.)
	1850-1899 (cont.)
	Poetry (cont.)
42554.53	Héré
	Heredia
42554.54	Complete and Selected works
42554.55-.61	Individual works
42554.62-.63	Biography and criticism
42554.64	Herold; Hilbey; etc.
42554.65	Hugues; Ibels; Joncières; etc.
42554.66	Jouy; John Pantaléon; etc.
42554.68	Kahn, G.
42554.70	Kerdaniel
42554.71	Kerhalvé
42554.75	Kerviler
42555.1-.2	Laforgue
42555.3	La Grasserie
42555.4	Laroche
42555.6	Lacaussade
42555.8	Laforest
42555.9	Lalot
42555.11	La Landelle
42555.12	Laluyé; La Morvonnais; etc.
	Laprade
42555.13	Biography and criticism
42555.14	Complete and Selected works
42555.15-.32	Individual works
42555.33	Langel; Laurent; Levey; etc.
	Leconte de Lisle
42555.34-.35	Collected and Selected works
42555.36	Individual works
42555.37	Biography and criticism
42555.38	Lefèvre; Letolle; etc.
42555.39	Lemoyne; Lerberghe; etc.
42555.40	Le Roy, G.; Le Vavasseur; Lonley; etc.
42555.41	Loridan; etc.
42555.42	Lutel; Lys; Magnant; Mahul; etc.
	Mallarmé
42555.43	Writings
42555.44	Works about; Letters
42555.45	Marmier, X.
42555.46-.49.5	Manuel, E.
42555.49.7-.49.99	Marc; Mariéton; Martin; Merrill; etc.
	Monnier, M.
42555.50-.56	Writings
42555.57	Works about
42555.58	Mendès, C.; Merat; etc.
42555.59	Michu; Millet; Mithouard; etc.
42555.60	Montesquiou-Ferenzac; Montoya; etc.
	Moréas
42555.61	Writings
42555.62	Works about
42555.63	Nadaud; Nibor; etc.
42555.64	Nizet
42555.65	Michard
42555.66-.67	Nolhac
42555.68	Olivaint; Paban; Paté; etc.
42555.69	Paul, J.
42555.70	Pollet; Pierron; etc.
42555.72	Pons; Pomairols; etc.
42555.73	Popelin
42556.1-.2	Prarond
42556.4	Quillard
	Reboul
42556.6-.10	Writings
42556.11	Works about
42556.12	Poutgebaud
42556.14	Pradels
42556.15	Prior
	Sully-Prudhomme
42556.16-.17	Biography and criticism
42556.18-.19	Complete and Selected works
42556.20	Individual works
42556.21	Raynaud; Reboux; etc.
42556.22	Richepin
42556.23	Read
42556.24-.27.33	Regnier
42556.27.35-.27.999	Renaud; Retté; Riffard; etc.
42556.28	Rimbaud
42556.29	Rocca de Vergalo; Romberg; Samain; etc.
	Individual authors, etc. (cont.)
	1850-1899 (cont.)
	Poetry (cont.)
42556.30	Schuré
42556.31	Roussel
42556.32	Rollinat
42556.33	Severin
	Sully-Prudhomme. See 42556.16-.20
42556.35	Tellier, J.
42556.36	Potez
42556.37	Pagnerre
42556.38	Sirvey
42557.3-.4	Soulary
42557.5	Tailhade; Thiebault; Turquety; etc.
42557.6	Tiercelin
42557.7	Tisseur
42557.8	Treffier
42557.9	Valade
42557.10	Valabrèque; Vannespennes; Vard; etc.
	Verhaeren
42557.11	Writings
42557.12	Works about
	Verlaine
[42557.14]	Biography and criticism [Discontinued. See 42557.20]
42557.15-.18	Complete and Selected works
42557.19	Individual works
42557.20	Correspondence; Works about
42557.21-.25	Vielé-Griffin
42557.26	Vermersch
42557.27-.29	Vicaire
42557.30	Vibert
[42558.1-.14]	Miscellany [Discontinued]
42558.15	Villemer
42558.30	Rouquette
42558.40-.42	Ronchaud
42558.60	Weil
42558.80	Walzer
42558.100-	Anonymous poems
42559	Satirical and epigrammatic poems; Cabaret songs
	Fiction
	Anthologies. See 37576.500-.599, etc.
[42561.1-.23]	Folios [Discontinued]
	Chandeneux
42561.24-.38	Writings
42561.39	Works about
	About, E.
42562.1-.35	Writings
42562.36	Works about
42562.37	Achard; Achkinasi; etc.
	Adam
42562.38-.38.1	Works about
42562.38.2-.38.14	Writings
42562.38.15-.38.17	Ardel
42562.38.19	Asselines
42562.38.21	Aunet
	Aimard, G.
42562.38.35-.38.51	Writings
42562.38.52	Works about
42562.38.54	Arnold
42562.38.55	Aubert
42562.38.80	Aubier
42562.38.90	Aulnay
42562.38.100	Auschitzky
	Other A. See 42562.55- and 42586
	B. See 42563 and 42586
42562.39	Cauvain
42562.41-.50	Celières
42562.55	Auriol
42562.60	Allais, A.
42562.62	Alméras
42562.65	Aubanel
42563.3	Baudin
42563.5	Beaubourg
42563.8	Bac
42563.13	Barbé; Babut; etc.

Individual authors, etc. (cont.)
1850-1899 (cont.)
Fiction (cont.)

	Barrès, M.
42563.14	Bibliographies, etc.
42563.15-.18.74	Writings
42563.18.75-.18.999	Works about
[42563.19-.20]	Miscellany [Discontinued]
42563.21	Bazin
42563.22	Bassanville; Beaume; Beaumont; Belot; etc.
42563.23	Bérenger; Bernard; Berthet; Bertrand, L.; Bloy, L.; etc.
42563.24	Boisson
42563.26	Blocqueville; Bauer; Boissie; etc.
42563.27	Bosc
42563.28	Biart
42563.30	Blandy
42563.32	Blouet
42563.33	Borden
42563.34	Boissière
[42563.35]	Bourges [Discontinued. See 42563.89]
42563.36	Bordeaux
42563.37	Bourget
42563.38	Bouvier; Bovet; etc.
42563.39	Boylesve; Brown; Buet; Carnoy; Carol; Codet; etc.
	Greville, Henri (Mme. Durand)
42563.40-.64	Writings
42563.65	Works about
42563.66	Cantacuzène; Candeze; etc.
42563.67	Chablas
42563.68	Chabot
42563.70	Chabrillan
42563.71	Challamel
42563.72	Champceix
42563.80	Champsaur
42563.89	Bourges, E.
	Cauvain. See 42562.39
	Celières. See 42562.41-.50
	Chandeneux. See 42561.24-.39
42564.1	Capus
	Champfleury (J. Fleury)
42564.3-.54	Writings
42564.55	Works about
42564.56	Chapuis
	Cherbonnel, A. See 42576.12
	Cherbuliez
42565.1-.47	Writings
42565.48	Works about
42565.50	Chéri, M.
42565.53	Chevalet
	Cladel, L.
42565.54	Works about
42565.55	Writings
	Constant, A.
42565.56-.57	Writings
42565.58	Works about
42565.59	Comminges, M.A.
	Corday, M.
42565.62-.64	Writings
42565.65	Works about
	Favre de Coulevain
42565.70-.75	Writings
42565.76	Works about
42565.100	Courtois
	Craven, P.
42566.3-.13	Writings
42566.14	Works about
42566.15	Danville; Darzens; etc.
	Daudet, A.
42566.16	Biography and criticism
42566.17	Complete and Selected works
42566.18-.999	Individual works
	Daudet, E.
42567.1-.19	Complete and Selected works
42567.20-.48	Individual works
42567.49	Biography and criticism

Individual authors, etc. (cont.)
1850-1899 (cont.)
Fiction (cont.)

	Daudet, L. See 43565.5
	Delattre, L.
42567.100-.118	Writings
42567.119	Works about
42568.1	Derennes
42568.2	Deslys; Deschard; Didier; Double; etc.
	Droz
42568.3-.14	Writings
42568.15	Works about
42568.16	Dinet
	Du Boisgobey
42568.17	Works about
42568.18-.19.20	Writings
	Ducasse, I. (Lautréamont)
42568.19.21	Writings
42568.19.22-.19.999	Works about
42568.20	Dudevant, M.; Dufresne; etc.
	Durand, Mme. A.M.C. See 42563.40-.65
42568.21	Durandal; Duranty; etc.
42568.22	Durny
42568.23	Duval, P.; Eekhoud
	Enault, L.
42568.24-.31	Writings
42568.32	Works about
42568.50	Dollivet
42568.56	Demolder
[42571.1-.21]	Folios [Discontinued]
	Gaboriau, E.
42571.22-.34	Writings
42571.35	Works about
[42571.36-.47]	Miscellany [Discontinued]
	Erckmann, E.
42572.1-.79	Writings
42572.85-.999	Works about
[42573.1-.39]	Writings [Discontinued]
42573.60	Eyma
42574.5	Fabre, A.
	Fabre, F.
42574.14-.36	Writings
42574.37-.39	Works about
	Favre de Coulevain. See 42565.70-.76
42575.3	Fage, E.
	Ferry de Bellemare
42575.5-.12	Writings
42575.13	Works about
42575.21	Feydeau, E.
	Feuillet, O.
42575.23-.24	Complete and Selected works
42575.25-.52	Individual works
42575.53-.53.27	Biography and criticism
42575.53.28	Flammarion
	Flaubert. See 42576.15-.35
42575.53.29	Formont
42575.53.35-.53.99	Fould, W.J.S.
	Goncourt, E. and J.
42575.54	Complete and Selected works
42575.55-.79	Individual works
42575.80-.999	Biography and criticism
	Fleury, J. See 42564.3-.55
42576.3	Flore
	France, A. See 42576.62-.63
42576.4	Gevin-Cassal
42576.5	Gebhart
42576.6	Ginisty
42576.8	Gleizes
42576.9	Godefroy
	Goncourt. See 42575.54-.999
42576.10	Guezenec
42576.11	Guillemot
42576.12	Cherbonnel, A.
42576.13	Garcia, M.
	Other G. See 42576.36-.40
42576.14	Houssaye, A.
	Flaubert
42576.15	Biography and criticism
42576.16-.17	Complete and Selected works
42576.18-.35	Individual works [Use .35 for correspondence]

Individual authors, etc. (cont.)
1850-1899 (cont.)
Fiction (cont.)

42576.36 Fleuriot; Gay; Geffroy; etc.
Goncourt. See 42575.54-.999
42576.37 Gorose; Grave; Grosclaud; etc.
42576.38 Guéroult; Guillemain; Galland; etc.
42576.39-.40.199 Guiches
42576.40.200- Halevy, L.
[N.B. - See also 42543.68]
Houssaye. See 42576.14
Huysmans. See 42576.65
I-K. See 42576.67 and 42587
42576.41 La Bedollière; Le Blanc, M.; etc.
42576.42 Labusquière; Le Barillier; Lermina; etc.
42576.43 Lemonnier, C.
42576.44-.45 Le Roux, H.
42576.46-.46.49 Le Roy; Lesueur; Létang
Viaud, J. (Loti)
[42576.46.50-.46.999] Biography and criticism [Discontinued]
42576.47-.47.24 Complete and Selected works
42576.47.25-.57.74 Individual works
42576.57.75-.57.999 Biography and criticism
42576.58-.59 Foa, E.
42576.60 Fonsegrive; Forbin; etc.
42576.61 Franay; Frémine; Frescaly; etc.
France, A.
42576.62-.63.23 Writings
42576.63.24 Bibliographies
42576.63.25-.63.999 Biography and criticism
42576.64 Giron; Goron; Grin; Gramont; etc.
42576.65-.65.12 Glouvet (Quesnay de Beaurepaire); Harry; etc.
Huysmans
42576.65.13 Works about
42576.65.14-.66.4 Writings
42576.66.5-.66.20 Hericault
42576.67-.67.39 Hervieu, P.
42576.67.46 Jicé
Jourdan. See 42576.78
42576.67.50 Judices de Mirandol
42576.67.100 Karélis
42576.68-.68.19 Lamothe, A.
42576.68.25 La Vaudère
42576.68.40 Le Corbeiller
42576.68.100- Lecomte du Nouÿ
42576.69 Legay
42576.70 Lespinasse; Lescure; etc.
42576.71 Lythe
42576.72 Lombard
42576.73 Lescot; Lucas; Lurine; Luzarche; etc.
42576.74 Macé; Mahon; etc.
42576.76 Margueritte, P.
42576.77 Margueritte, V.
42576.78 Jourdan
42576.79 Geruzez
Maupassant
42577.1 Complete and Selected works
42577.2-.4.30 Individual works
42577.4.31-.4.999 Biography and criticism
42577.5-.11 Malot
42577.12 Marsonnière; Martin; Maygrier; etc.
42577.13 Maynard; Mercier; Montepin; Mouton; etc.
42577.14-.32 Murger, H.
42577.33 Maurel
42577.34 Masson-Forestier; Mattais; etc.
42577.35 Michon; Mirecourt; etc.
42577.36 Monteil
[42577.37] Marmier, X. [Discontinued. See 42555.45]
42577.38 Morin, L.
42577.39 Mossé
42577.40 Muller, E.
42577.41 Meunier, G.
42577.42 Meunier, Mme.
42578.5 Noir
42578.7 Rendade

Individual authors, etc. (cont.)
1850-1899 (cont.)
Fiction (cont.)
Narrey, C.
42578.9 Works about
42578.10-.16 Writings
42578.17 Naurroye; Niboget; Neveux; etc.
42578.18 Quillot; Rabusson; Racot; Rameau; Richebourg; etc.
42578.19 Rod, E.
42578.20-.22 Rosny, J.H.
Noriac, J. (Cairon)
42578.23-.27 Writings
42578.28 Works about
Ohnet, G.
42578.29-.30.38 Writings
42578.30.39 Works about
42578.30.40-.30.99 Péladan, J.
42578.30.150 Pilou
42578.31-.31.19 Pouvillon; Pradels; etc.
Prévost, M.
42578.31.20-.31.69 Writings
42578.31.70-.31.75 Works about
42578.31.76- Psichari; Richet; Puaux; Pierret; Reschal; Radet; Reul; Robida; Samopaloff; etc.
Sarcey, F.
42578.32-.35.14 Writings
42578.35.15-.35.99 Works about
42578.35.100- Sarton, G.
42578.36 Schultz, J.
42578.40 Second, A.
42578.48 Thiaudière
42578.49 Tinan
42578.50 Töpffer, R.
42578.51 Tinayre, M.
42578.52 Tinseau, L.
42578.56 Toretain, P.
42578.58 Uchard, M.
42578.62-.64 Vast, R.
42578.65 Temple, G.
42578.66 Rouslane, V.
[42581.1-.31] Verne [Discontinued. See 42582]
42581.33 Vallès, J.
42581.34 Vaux
42581.35 Vogüé, E.M.
42581.36 Viard, J.
[42581.37-.44] Folios [Discontinued]
Verne, J.
42582.1 Pamphlet volumes
42582.2 Biography and criticism
42582.3-.4 Complete and Selected works
42582.5-.99 Individual works
[42583.1-.15] Individual works [Discontinued]
42583.16 Villars
42583.17-.33 Theuriot, A.
42583.34-.35 Tardieu, J.R.
42583.36-.37 Saint-Germain
42583.50 Véron, P.
Viaud, J. See 42576.47-.57
Zola, E.
42584.1 Complete and Selected works
42584.2 Letters
42584.3-.23 Individual works
42584.24-.25 Biography and criticism
Stahl, P.J. (Hetzel)
42584.26-.31 Writings
42584.32 Works about
42584.37 Simon, J.
42584.47 Ulbach, L.
42584.49 Vallon, G.
42584.50 Vernet
42584.52 Vincent
42584.56 Walsh, J.A.
[42585] Folios [Discontinued]
[42586.2-.3] About, E. [Discontinued. See 42562.1-.36]
42586.4-.6 Achard, A.
42586.7 Aicard
42586.8-.9 Arène, P.
42586.10-.12 Assollant, A.
42586.13 Auriac

Individual authors, etc. (cont.)
1850-1899 (cont.)
Fiction (cont.)

42586.14-.14.8	Audoux
42586.14.9	Badin
42586.14.40	Bascle de Lagrèze
42586.14.55	Baudry, J.
42586.14.75	Baudry, E.
42586.18	Beauvoir
42586.19	Baudoux
42586.20	Bégon
42586.21	Bernard, P.; Blaze de Bury; Bigot; Boissieu; etc.
42586.23	Bounières
42586.24	Boubée; Bravard; etc.
42586.25-.27	Bungener
42586.28	Caro; Casale; etc.
42586.29	Castille; Caragual; Causse; Chabrier; etc.
42586.30	Chazel; Chevalier, E.; Claudin; Coni; etc.
42586.31	Claretié
42586.32-.32.5	Coquelin
42586.32.7-.32.699	Coster, C.
42586.32.710	Cournier
42586.32.910	Dabadie
42586.33	Darien, G.
42586.34	Deltuf
42586.35	Delpit
42586.36	Debrit; Demond; Dewailly; Divat; etc.
42586.37-.38	DuCamp, M.
42586.39	Durantin
42586.40	Dépret; Deschamps; etc.
42586.41	Desjardin
42586.42	Desprez, L.; Eprey; etc.
42586.43	Erckmann, J.
42586.46-.48	Feval
42586.49	Filon, A.
42586.51	Fistié
42586.52	Foley; Fonville; Fortia de Piles (Caillot-Duval); etc.
42586.53	Foudras; Fouillée; etc.
42586.54	Foulon de Vaulx; Fouquier; François; etc.
42586.55	Frappié
	Fromentin, E.
42586.56	Writings
42586.57	Works about
42586.59-.61	Gandon, A.
42586.62	Gauthier, H.; Gauthier-Villars; etc.
	Gobineau, A.
42586.63	Works about
42586.64-.68	Writings
42586.69-.70	Gourdon
42586.71	Grandfort
	Guillaumin, E.
42586.76-.78	Writings
42586.79	Works about
42586.90	Habeneck
42587.1	Heard; Hermant; etc.
	Hetzel. See 42584.26-.32
42587.4	Hudry-Menos
42587.5	Hugo, C.
42587.6	Hugo, F.V.
42587.7	Issaurat
42587.8	Jeannin
42587.9	Jobey
42587.10	Julliot, F.
42587.11	Kock, H.
42587.12	Lapauze
42587.13	Lebrun, C.
42587.14	Lepic, A.
42587.15	Lubomirski
42587.16	Maindron; Maizeroy; Marrast; etc.
42587.19	Martel; Massabuan; Medina; etc.
42587.22	Menard, L.
[42587.23-.25]	Méry, J. [Discontinued. See 41586.23]
42587.26	Meyer, A.
42587.27	Michel, A.; Michel, L.
42587.28	Michelet
42587.30-.33	Molènes, P.
42587.35	Moland
42587.36	Moreau; Morgan; Moselly; etc.

Individual authors, etc. (cont.)
1850-1899 (cont.)
Fiction (cont.)

42587.37	Musset, P.; Mystère; Nefftzer; Nesmy; Noisey; Noussanne; etc.
42587.38	Olivier, U.
42587.39	Olga Cantacuzène-Altieri
42587.40	Paul, V.
42587.41-.42	Pelletan, E.
42587.43	Pène
42587.44-.45	Perret, P.
42587.46	Peyrebrune; Piazzi; etc.
42587.47-.48	Plouvier, E.
42587.49	Poictevin; Pommerol; etc.
42587.50	Pressensé; Quellien, N.; Rambaud; Rattazzi; Rebell, H.; Renard, G.; etc.
42587.51-.52	Renard, J.
42587.53	Regnier, M.S.
42587.55	Rivière, H.; Rivoire, A.; etc.
42587.56	Rochefort, H.; Rostaing; Saillens; etc.
42587.57	Schwob, M.
42587.58	Ségur, S.
42587.59	Sainte-Croix; Soyez; Stapleaux
42587.60	Sternon
42587.61	Summer
42587.63	Torquet; Toudouze; Testard; etc.
42587.64	Uzès, A.; Uzanne; etc.
42587.65	Vaugny; Vachette; etc.
42587.66	Valbezen; Vedel; Vigné; Villain; Verly; etc.
42587.67	Villedeuil
42587.69	Villemessant; Viollet; Wagner; Walras; etc.
42587.70	Weill, A.
42587.71-.74	Witt, H.
42587.84	Zaccone
42588	Anonymous fiction

1900-
Anthologies. See 37573.600-.799, etc.

[43500]	Bizot-Briant collection [Discontinued] [N.B. - Do not add anything on this number. It is used only for the books in the Bizot-Briant library which were purchased as a unit and are being kept together in this way.]
43511-43873	Known authors (363 scheme plus 10, A-Z by person)
43874-43899	Anonymous works (A-Z by title)

NOTE ON THE CLASSIFICATION

The FL class was orginally intended to be the replacement for the old scheme for French literature. Long lists of literary authors were compiled, and a tentative numbering system was devised. The confusion and extra work involved in moving into the new Widener Library combined with staff shortages during World War I made it impracticable to attempt to reclassify the large French literature collection at that time, and the project was never revived. However, three sections of the proposed FL class were activated for varying reasons - history of French drama, literature in French dialects, and Rousseau.

The accompanying outline gives a clear picture of what these sections contain. For the section on French drama, it should be noted that anthologies of French drama and works by or about individual dramatists go in the main French literature class (37500-43900). The section for literature in French dialects provides for histories, anthologies, and works by or about individual authors who write in the special dialects other than Provençal. The section for Rousseau provides for all editions of his writings and for all works about him.

During the present revision, a few minor changes were made to update the section for French drama, and explanatory notes have been added to clarify the scheme. It has not been possible as yet to do the reclassification called for by these changes.

Bartol Brinkler
Classification Specialist
April 1972

OUTLINE

	French drama and stage
355	Reference works
356-361	General history, etc.
362-368	Special topics
370-388	History by periods
390-397	Local history
398	Individual biographies
399	Periodicals
	Literature in French dialects
1000-1099	France proper
1100-1109	Walloon
1200-1259	Franco-Provençal
	Provençal. See Rom
	Jean Jacques Rousseau
6001-6017	Complete and Selected works; Correspondence
6020-6059	Major works
6060-6099	Minor works
6109	Attributed works
6111-6150	Works about Rousseau

French drama and stage
[N.B. - Include here only historical and critical material. Anthologies of French drama and works by or about French dramatists go in the main French literature class.]

	Periodicals. See FL 399
355.1-.699	Reference works [Include bibliographies, indexes, encyclopedias, biographical dictionaries, directories, etc.]
355.700-.999	Exhibition catalogues
356-359	General histories (By date)
	General special
360.01-.099	Pamphlet volumes
360.1-.9	Congresses
360.10-.999	Essays, introductions, etc.
	Biographies of actors, directors, etc.
	Collected
	Biographical dictionaries. See FL 355
361	General works
	19th and 20th centuries. See FL 384
	Individual. See FL 398
	Special topics [N.B. - Works relating to any of these topics which are limited to a specific period should be classed with the particular period in FL 370-389.]
362	Special forms of drama [Include comedy, tragedy, mime, etc.]
363	Special characters and literary types [Include doctors, harlequin, etc. See also FL 367.]
	Special kinds of theatricals
364.1-.24	Court theatricals
	Society theatricals
364.25-.49	General works
364.50-.74	Special topics
364.75-.99	Jesuit theatricals
364.100-.124	School and college theatricals
364.125-.149	Street theater
364.150-.174	Amateur theatricals
365.1-.49	Actors and actresses in relation to the law, the church, etc. [Include also general works on the life of comedians]
365.50-.99	Foreign influences [Include influence of the commedia dell'arte, influence of Shakespeare, etc.]
365.100-.499	Stage setting and scenery
365.500-.699	Costume
366.1-.24	Censorship
366.25-.49	Law
366.50-.74	Employees
366.75-.99	Museums [See also exhibition catalogues in FL 355]
367	Special themes in drama [See also FL 363]
368	Other special topics
	History by periods
	Before ca. 1500 [Include also works covering the period up to 1636]
370	General works
371	Religious drama
372.1-.26	Local (A-Z by place)
373	Stage setting and scenery
374	Other special topics
375	16th century
376	16th and 17th centuries together
377	17th century [See also Mol]
378	17th and 18th centuries together

French drama and stage (cont.)
History by periods (cont.)

18th century
379 General works
380 Revolutionary period
381 18th and 19th centuries together

19th century
382 General works
383 Special periods

19th and 20th centuries together
384 Collected biographies
385 General works (99 scheme, A-Z)

20th century
386.1-.363 General works (363 scheme, A-Z)
Special periods
386.400-.499 1st half, 1900-1945 in general
386.500-.599 1900-1919
386.600-.699 1920-1945
386.700-.799 2nd half, 1945-1999 in general
386.800-.899 1945-1969
386.900-.999 1970-1999

Local history
Paris
390 General works
391 Special periods
[See also FL 372]
393 Special topics
[N.B. - .1-.49 has been used for the "théatres de la foire et des boulevards"]
Individual theaters
Comédie Française
394 General works
395 Special periods
396 Other Paris theaters (99 scheme, A-Z by theater]
397.1-.99 Other French cities, towns, etc. (99 scheme, A-Z by place)
[See also FL 372 for the medieval period]

Other European countries
Belgium
397.100 Periodicals
397.105 Reference works
397.110 General histories
397.111 Special periods
397.112 Special topics
397.114 Brussels
397.115 Other Belgian cities (99 scheme, A-Z by place)
Holland
397.155 Reference works
397.160 General histories
397.161 Special periods
397.162 Special topics
397.165 Individual cities, towns, etc. (99 scheme, A-Z by place)
Switzerland
397.200 Periodicals
397.205 Reference works
397.210 General histories
397.211 Special periods
397.212 Special topics
397.215 Individual cities, towns, etc. (99 scheme, A-Z by place)
Germany
397.255 Reference works
397.260 General histories
397.261 Special periods
397.262 Special topics
397.265 Individual cities, towns, etc. (99 scheme, A-Z by place)

French drama and stage (cont.)
Local history (cont.)
Other European countries (cont.)
Rumania
397.305 Reference works
397.310 General histories
397.311 Special periods
397.312 Special topics
397.315 Individual cities, towns, etc. (99 scheme, A-Z by place)

Biographies of actors, directors, managers, etc.
Collected. See FL 361 and 384
398 Individual (99 scheme, A-Z, by person)
[Include also memoirs, etc.]
399 Periodicals (99 scheme, A-Z by title)
[See also FL 397.100 and 397.200]

Anthologies of French drama. See 37581-37585

Literature in French dialects
[N.B. - This section is only for material pertaining to literature written in these special dialects. Material relating to the standard French literature of a particular locality goes with general French literature.]

[For each, use the special Table for French Dialectal Literatures, unless otherwise indicated.]
1000-1007 General history and anthologies
Dialect of the Île de France. See FL 1050-1059 or with general French literature

Dialects of Normandy
1010-1019 Norman proper
1020-1029 Anglo-Norman, Anglo-French
1030-1039 Dialects of Western France
[Include Bretagne, Manceau, Angevin, etc. But note that works relating to literature in the Breton language go in Celt.]
1040-1049 Dialects of Southwestern France
[Include Poitevin, Angoumoisin, Aunisien, etc.]
1050-1059 Dialects of Central France
[Include Orléanais, Berry, Nivernais, etc.]
1060-1069 Dialects of Southeastern France
[Include Bourbonnais, Morvandeau, Bourguignon, etc. See also the Franco-Provençal dialects in FL 1200-1259 and Provençal in Rom]
1070-1079 Dialects of Northeastern France
[Include Lorrain, Alsace, Meuse, Vosges, etc. See also GerL 1024-1029]
1080-1089 Dialect of Champagne
1090-1099 Dialect of Picardy
1100-1109 Walloon dialect

Franco-Provençal dialects
1200-1207 General history and anthologies
1210-1219 Dauphinois dialect
1220-1229 Lyonnais dialect
1230-1239 Savoisien dialect
1240-1249 Ain dialect
1250-1259 Franche-Comtois dialect

Provençal literature. See Rom

Jean Jacques Rousseau
Complete and Selected works
French editions
6001 Complete works (By date, e.g. .960 for 1960)
6002 Selected works (By date, e.g. .970 for 1970)
6003 Special selections

English editions
6004 Complete works
6005 Selected works

Jean Jacques Rousseau (cont.)
Complete and Selected works (cont.)

German editions
6006 Complete works
6007 Selected works

Italian editions
6008 Complete works
6009 Selected works
6010 Editions in other languages

Correspondence
[See also FL 6077-6082]
6015 French editions
6016 English editions
6017 Editions in other languages

Collected Discours. See FL 6066

Confessions
French editions
6020-6023 Complete (By date, e.g. 6021.80 for 1880, 6022.60 for 1960)
6024 Selections
6026 English editions
6027 Editions in other languages
6029 Criticism
[N.B. - Works written before 1778 go in FL 6127]

Contrat social
French editions
6030-6033 Complete (By date, e.g. 6031.90 for 1890, 6032.70 for 1970)
6034 Selections
6036 English editions
6037 Editions in other languages
6039 Criticism
[N.B. - Works written before 1778 go in FL 6127]

Émile
French editions
6040-6043 Complete (By date, e.g. 6041.70 for 1870, 6042.50 for 1950)
6044 Selections
[See also FL 6048]
6046 English editions
6047 Editions in other languages

Special parts
6048.1-.499 Profession de Foi du Vicaire Savoyard
6048.500-.999 Émile et Sophie
6049 Criticism
[N.B. - Works written before 1778 go in FL 6127]

Nouvelle Héloise
French editions
6050-6053 Complete (By date, e.g. 6051.80 for 1880, 6052.60 for 1960)
6054 Selections
[See also FL 6058]
6056 English editions
6057 Editions in other languages

Special parts
6058.1-.499 Lettres sur le suicide
6059 Criticism
[N.B. - Works written before 1778 go in FL 6127]

Minor works
[For each, use dot numbers as follows:
.1-.49 French editions
.50-.74 Translations
.75-.99 Criticism since 1788
Criticism written before 1778 goes in FL 6127]
6060 Allée de Sylvie

Jean Jacques Rousseau (cont.)
Minor works (cont.)
6061 Allegorie
6062 Botanique
6063 Considérations sur le gouvernement de Pologne
Dernière Réponse à Bordes. See FL 6068
6064 Devin de Village
6065 Dictionnaire de musique

Discours
6066 Collected discours
L'Établissement des Sciences
6067 Editions and modern criticism
Rousseau's replies to contemporary criticism
6068.1-.99 Lettre à Raynal
6068.100-.199 Lettre à Grimm sur la Réfutation par Gautier
6068.200-.299 Observation sur la Réponse du Roi de Pologne
6068.300-.399 Dernière Réponse à Bordes
6068.400-.499 Lettre sur une Nouvelle Réfutation
6069 Quelle est la vertue la plus necessaire aux heros?
6070 Quelle est l'origine de l'inégalité parmi les hommes?
6071 Sur l'economie politique
6072 Sur les richesses
Sur les sciences et les arts. See FL 6067
6073 Dissertation sur la musique moderne
Émile et Sophie. See FL 6048
6074 Essai sur l'origine des langues
6075 Imitation théâtrale
6076 Institutions chimiques

Lettres
[N.B. - Those classed here are "open letters" published by Rousseau during his life. For personal correspondence, see FL 6015-6017.]
6077 Lettre à d'Alembert
6078 Lettre à C. de Baumont
6079 Lettre à Grimm (sur Omphale)
Lettre à Grimm (sur la Réfutation par Gautier). See FL 6068
Lettre à Raynal. See FL 6068
Lettre sur une Nouvelle Réfutation. See FL 6068
6080 Lettres à Malesherbes
6081 Lettres de la Montagne
Lettres sur la botanique. See FL 6062
6082 Lettres sur la musique française
Lettres sur la suicide. See FL 6058
6083 Lévite d'Ephraim
6084 Narcisse
6085 Nouveau Dédale
Observation sur la Réponse du Roi de Pologne. See FL 6068
6086 Oraison funèbre du Duc d'Orléans
6087 Pensées d'un esprit droit
6088 Polysynodie
Profession de foi du Vicaire Savoyard. See FL 6048
6089 Projet concernant de nouveaux signes pour la musique
6090 Projet de paix perpétuelle
6091 Pygmalion
6092 Reine fantasque
6093 Réponse à une memoire: Si le monde est une sphère
6094 Réveries du promeneur solitaire
6095 Rousseau juge de Jean Jacques
6096 Testament
6097 Verger des Charmettes
6109 Attributed works

Works about Rousseau
6111 Societies
6112 Periodicals

Jean Jacques Rousseau (cont.)
Works about Rousseau (cont.)

	Reference works
6113	Bibliographies [Include also exhibition catalogues]
6114	Dictionaries, concordances, etc.
6115	Pamphlet volumes
	Biographical material
6117-6120	General works (By date, e.g. 6119.60 for 1960)
6127-6130	Special topics (By date, e.g. 6129.70 for 1970) [N.B. - All biographical and critical works about Rousseau written before 1788 are classed here by date in 6127.]
	Madame de Warens
6132	Writings
6133	Biography and criticism
6134	Other friends and associates
6135	Monuments; Anniversaries
	Criticism
6137-6140	General works (By date, e.g. 6139.50 for 1950) [N.B. - All critical works about Rousseau written before 1788 go in FL 6127.]
	Criticsm of individual works. See FL 6029, 6039, 6049, 6059, 6060-6109, and 6127
6147-6150	Literary works relating to Rousseau (By date) [Include poems, plays, novels, etc.]

Table for French Dialectal Literatures

[0]	Periodicals. See Philol; also 5-7 below
1	Bibliographies
	Literary history
2	General works
	Special forms
3	Poetry
4	Others
	Anthologies, collections of literature
5	General works
	Special forms
6	Poetry
7	Others
8	Individual authors (363 scheme, A-Z, by writer) [Use regular literature table for second dot numbers]
9	Anonymous works (99 scheme, A-Z, by title)

NOTE ON THE CLASSIFICATION

The Mol class provides for all editions of Molière's writings and for all works about Molière.

The class was constructed to provide for a large Molière collection which had been assembled by Prof. Ferdinand Bôcher of Harvard. The collection was purchased by James Hazen Hyde and given to Harvard in 1903.

The accompanying outline shows the main divisions of the Mol class. It is a simple and straightforward scheme in spite of being quite detailed. The only fact not apparent from the outline is that criticism of the individual plays, etc. goes with the particular work rather than with other books about Molière.

During the present revision, only a few explanatory notes have been added to clarify the scheme.

Bartol Brinkler
Classification Specialist
February 1972

OUTLINE

Molière's writings
6-145 Complete and Selected editions
150-270 Individual plays
305-320 Poems
355-370 Ballets and Fêtes
405-496 Attributed works

Works about Molière
501-570 Periodicals and Reference works
600-626 General critical works
700-775 Biographical works
800-840 Miscellaneous topics
845-886 Literary works relating to Molière
900-925 Collections

Complete and Selected works

French editions
Complete works
[Include complete plays]
[6-9] Folios [Discontinued]
16-20 Other (By date)
36-40 Selected works (By date)
[Include collections containing three or more complete plays]
46-50 Selections (By date)
[Include selected scenes, etc.]

Complete poems. See Mol 305
Complete attributed works. See Mol 405

Translations
[N.B. - Include here also bilingual editions]
60 English
62 German
64 Italian
68 Spanish
Arabic. See OL
Armenian. See OL
75 Catalan
80 Danish
85 Dutch and Flemish
95 Greek
100 Hungarian
105 Latin
110 Norwegian
115 Polish
120 Portuguese
125 Provençal
130 Russian
135 Swedish
Turkish. See OL

Individual plays
[150] Folios [Discontinued]

Les Amants Magnifiques
151 French editions
152 Translations
153 Criticism

L'Amour Médecin
155 French editions
156 Translations
157 Criticism

Amphitryon
161 French editions
162 Translations
163 Criticism

L'Avare
165 French editions
166 Translations
167 Criticism

Le Bourgeois Gentilhomme
171 French editions
172 Translations
173 Criticism

La Comtesse d'Escarbagnas
175 French editions
176 Translations
177 Criticism

La Critique de l'École des Femmes
178 French editions
179 Translations
180 Criticism

Dépit Amoureux
181 French editions
182 Translations
183 Criticism

Individual plays (cont.)

Dom Garcia de Navarre, ou Prince Jaloux
185 French editions
186 Translations
187 Criticism

Dom Juan, ou Le Festin de Pierre
191 French editions
192 Translations
193 Criticism
194 Related works

L'École des Femmes
195 French editions
196 Translations
197 Criticism

La Critique de l'École des Femmes. See Mol 178-180

L'École des Maris
201 French editions
202 Translations
203 Criticism

L'Étourdi, ou Les Contretemps
205 French editions
206 Translations
207 Criticism

Les Fâcheux
208 French editions
209 Translations
210 Criticism

Les Femmes Savantes
211 French editions
212 Translations
213 Criticism

Les Fourberies de Scapin
215 French editions
216 Translations
217 Criticism

George Dandin, ou Le Mari Confondu
218 French editions
219 Translations
220 Criticism

L'Impromptu de Versailles
221 French editions
222 Translations
223 Criticism

Jalousie du Barbouillé
225 French editions
226 Translations
227 Criticism

Le Malade Imaginaire
228 French editions
229 Translations
230 Criticism

Le Mariage Forcé
231 French editions
232 Translations
233 Criticism

Le Médecin Malgré Lui
235 French editions
236 Translations
237 Criticism

Le Médecin Volant
238 French editions
239 Translations
240 Criticism

Individual plays (cont.)

Mélicerte
241 French editions
242 Translations
243 Criticism

Le Misanthrope
245 French editions
246 Translations
247 Criticism

Monsieur de Pourceaugnac
248 French editions
249 Translations
250 Criticism

Plaisirs de l'Isle Enchanté. See Mol 255-257

Les Précieuses Ridicules
251 French editions
252 Translations
253 Criticism

La Princesse d'Elide
255 French editions
256 Translations
257 Criticism

Psyché
258 French editions
259 Translations
260 Criticism

Sganarelle, ou Le Cocu Imaginaire
261 French editions
262 Translations
263 Criticism

Le Sicilien, ou L'Amour Peintre
265 French editions
266 Translations
267 Criticism

Le Tartuffe, ou L'Imposteur
268 French editions
269 Translations
270 Criticism

Poems
305 Collected and Selected editions in French
310 Individual poems in French
315 Translations
320 Criticism

Ballets and Fêtes
355 Collected and Selected editions in French
360 Individual works in French
[N.B. - Ballets and fêtes having the same name as the plays go in Mol 151-270.]
365 Translations
370 Criticism

Attributed works
405 Collected and Selected editions in French
415 Collected and Selected editions in translation

Individual works
Le Docteur Amoureux
438 Editions in French
439 Translations
440 Criticism

Histoire des Révolutions de Naples
445 Editions in French
446 Translations
447 Criticism

Attributed works (cont.)
Individual works (cont.)

Joguenet
451 Editions in French
452 Translations
453 Criticism

Mélisse
464 Editions in French
465 Translations
466 Criticism

L'Oracle du Ballet
471 Editions in French
472 Translations
473 Criticism

Scène d'Arlequin
477 Editions in French
478 Translations
479 Criticism

Secret de ne Payer Jamais
484 Editions in French
485 Translations
486 Criticism

Vers Espanols
491 Editions in French
492 Translations
493 Criticism

Other poems
494 Editions in French
495 Translations
496 Criticism

Works about Molière
501-526 Periodicals (A-Z)
531-556 Societies (A-Z)

Reference works
560 Bibliographies
570 Dictionaries, encyclopedias, etc.

General critical works
[598] Folios [Discontinued]
600 Pamphlet volumes
601-626 Monographs (A-Z)

Special critical topics. See Mol 800-840
Criticism of individual works. See Mol 150-496

Biographical works
[698] Folios [Discontinued]
700 Pamphlet volumes
701-726 General works (A-Z)

Special topics
728 Molière in special localities
730 Special aspects
[Include works on Molière as an actor, as a musician, his love affairs, etc.]
735 Iconography
[See also Mol 925]
740 Habitations
745 Death and Burial
750 Wife of Molière
755 Genealogy and Heraldry
765 Monuments
775 Relics
[Include works on furniture, clothing, etc. belonging to Molière]

Miscellaneous topics
Molière's acting troupe
800 General works
803 Individual actors
805 Molière's theater at Paris

Works about Molière (cont.)
Miscellaneous topics (cont.)
810 French theater in the time of Molière
815 Social conditions in the time of Molière
820 Contemporaries of Molière
825 Molière and the doctors
828 Molière and other professions
840 Molière and folklore

Literary works relating to Molière
845 General collections

Contemporaneous works
850 Poetry
853 Prose
855 Plays

Later works
860 Plays
863 Poetry
865 Prose

Anniversary works
Plays
870 Birth
873 Death
875 Poetry
878 Prose

Works based on Molière's writings
880 Plays
882 Operas
884 Novels
886 Other

Collections
900 Scrapbooks
910 Programs
925 Portraits
[N.B. - Include here collected reproductions of portraits of Molière. Works about the pictorial and other representations of Molière go in Mol 735.]

NOTE ON THE CLASSIFICATION

The Mon class provides for all editions of Montaigne's writings and for all works about Montaigne.

The class was constructed to provide for a large Montaigne collection which had been assembled by Prof. Ferdinand Bôcher of Harvard. The collection was purchased by James Hazen Hyde and given to Harvard in 1903.

The accompanying outline shows the main divisions of the Mon class. It is a simple and straightforward scheme in spite of being quite detailed. The only fact not apparent from the outline is that criticism of Montaigne's individual works other than the Essays goes with the particular work rather than with the other books about Montaigne.

During the present revision, only a few explanatory notes have been added to clarify the scheme.

Bartol Brinkler
Classification Specialist
February 1972

OUTLINE

	Montaigne's writings
5-39	Complete and Selected works; Essays
45-92	Other writings by Montaigne
	Works about Montaigne
100-108	Periodicals and Reference works
110-136	General critical works
140-185	Biographical works
190-198	Miscellaneous topics
200	Literary works relating to Montaigne
210	Anniversary celebrations
215-220	Collections

Complete and Selected works; Essays

	French editions
15-20	Complete works (By date) [Include also complete Essays]
28	Selected works [Include also selections from the Essays and texts of individual essays]
	Translations [N.B. - Include here also bilingual editions]
	English
30	Florio
31	Cotton
32	Other translators
35	German
37	Italian
39	Other languages
	Criticism on the Essays. See Mon 110-136

Other writings by Montaigne

	Journal de Voyage en Italie
45	Complete editions in French
48	Selections in French
	Translations
50	English
52	German
55	Italian
57	Other languages
59	Criticism
	Letters
65	Complete editions in French
68	Selections in French [Include also texts of individual letters]
	Translations
70	English
72	German
75	Italian
77	Other languages
79	Criticism
	Montaigne's translation of Raymond de Sebonde
80	Editions
82	Criticism
	Montaigne's edition of Etienne de la Boetie
85	Editions
88	Criticism
	Attributed works
90	Editions
92	Criticism

Works about Montaigne

100	Periodicals
102	Societies
	Reference works
105	Bibliographies
108	Dictionaries, encyclopedias, etc.
	General critical works [Include critical works relating to the Essays]
110	Pamphlet volumes
111-136	Monographs (A-Z)
	Special critical topics. See Mon 190-198
	Criticism of individual works. See Mon 59, 79, 82, 88, and 92.
	Biographical works
140	Pamphlet volumes
141-166	General works (A-Z)
	Special topics
168	Montaigne in special localities
170	Special aspects [Include works on Montaigne as a public figure, his religious life and ideas, his friends, etc.]
172	Iconography [See also Mon 220]
175	Habitations
178	Family and Heraldry
180	Death and Burial
182	Tomb
185	Monuments
	Miscellaneous topics
190	Montaigne and medicine
192	J.F. Payen as a collector of Montaigne
194	Montaigne and education
198	Other special
200	Literary works relating to Montaigne [Include poems, plays, etc.]
210	Anniversary celebrations
	Collections
215	Scrapbooks
220	Portraits [N.B. - Include here collected reproductions of portraits of Montaigne. Works about the pictorial and other representations of Montaigne go in Mon 172.]

WIDENER LIBRARY SHELFLIST, 47

FRENCH LITERATURE

CLASSIFIED LISTING BY CALL NUMBER

Classified Listing

37530 General literary history - Bibliographies, dictionaries, etc.

37530.4 La Croix du Maine, F.G. Premier vol...bibliothèque du Sieur de la Croix du Maine. Paris, 1584.

Htn 37530.5* Rigoley, J.A. Les bibliothèques françoises de la Croix du Maien. v.1-6. Paris, 1772-73. 3v.

37530.7 Foulet, Lucien. A bibliography of medieval French literature for college libraries. New Haven, 1915.

37530.10 Wolff, Boleslas Maurice. Manuel bibliographique. Catalogue...de la littérature française. St. Petersbourg, 1862.

Htn 37530.10.25* Le Petit, Jules. Bibliographie des principales éditions originales d'ecrivains français. Paris, 1888.

37530.11 Cornu, Sophie. List of French fiction. Boston, 1898.

37530.11.8 Boston Public Library. Works of fiction in the French language. Boston, 1892.

37530.11.10 Beaurepaire-Froment, Paul de. Pour le régionalisme. Paris, 1913.

37530.11.20 Jones, S.P. A list of French prose fiction from 1700 to 1750. N.Y., 1939.

37530.15 Lemcke, Ernst. Additional list of the classics and belles lettres. Supplement. N.Y., n.d.

37530.18 La Chèvre, F. Bibliographie des recueils collectifs de poésies publiés de 1597 à 1700. Paris, 1901-05. 4v.

37530.20 Hague. Bibliotheek. Catalogus der Fransche taal-en-letterkunde. v.1-5. Den Haag, 1918-19. 4v.

37530.25 Asselineau, Charles. Mélanges tirés d'une petite bibliothèque romantique. Paris, 1866.

37530.27 Toinet, R. Essai d'une liste alphabètique des auteurs. Tulle, 1911.

37530.28 Bowerman, S.G. Recent French literature; an annotated list of books recommended for libraries. Chicago, 1916.

Htn 37530.30* Carron, Pierre Siméon. Notice des livres facetieux...Bibliothèque de l'Arsenal. Manuscript. n.p., n.d.

37530.35 Moura, Edouard. Catalogue de beaux livres. Paris, 1923.

37530.40 Lanson, Gustave. Manuel bibliographique de la littérature française moderne. v.1-2. Paris, 1921.

37530.45 Société des Libraires et Éditeurs de la Suisse Romande, Geneva. Catalogue des ouvrages de langue française publiée en Suisse, 1910-1927. n.p., 1929.

37530.50 Strong, Lois. Bibliography of Franco-Spanish literary relations until the XIXth century. N.Y., 1930.

37530.55 Taupin, René. L'interprétation américaine de la poésie française contemporaine. Paris, 1929.

37530.60 Belgium. Ministère des Sciences et des Arts. Les lettres belges d'expression française 1830-1930. Bruxelles, 1930.

37530.64 Escoffier, M. Le mouvement romantique, 1788-1850. Paris, 1934.

Htn 37530.64.5* Escoffier, M. Le mouvement romantique, 1788-1850. Paris, 1934.

37530.65A Thième, Hugo Paul. Guide bibliographique de la littérature française de 1800 à 1906. Paris, 1907.

37530.65B Thième, Hugo Paul. Guide bibliographique de la littérature française de 1800 à 1906. Paris, 1907.

37530.66 Laporte, Antoine. Bibliographie contemporaine. Paris, 1884-90. 7v.

37530.67 Lachèvre, Frédéric. Bibliographie sommaire des keepsakes. v.1-2. Paris, 1929.

37530.68 Lachèvre, Frédéric. Bibliographie sommaire de l'Almanach des Muses (1765-1833). Paris, 1928.

37530.69 Lachèvre, Frédéric. Glanes bibliographiques et littéraires. Paris, 1929. 2v.

37530.69.10 Lachèvre, Frédéric. Nouvelles glanes bibliographiques et littéraires. Paris, 1933.

37530.70A Williams, Ralph C. Bibliography of the seventeenth-century novel in France. N.Y., 1931.

37530.70B Williams, Ralph C. Bibliography of the seventeenth-century novel in France. N.Y., 1931.

37530.71 Peyre, Henri. Bibliographie critique de l'Hellénisme en France de 1843 à 1870. Thèse. New Haven, 1932.

37530.72 Peyre, Henri. Bibliographie critique de l'Hellénisme en France de 1843 à 1870. New Haven, 1932.

37530.74 Hilka, Alfons. Französische Philologie. Göttingen, 1931.

Htn 37530.78* Hatin, Eugène. Bibliographie historique et critique de la presse périodique française. Paris, 1866.

37530.80 Varillon, F. Bibliographie élémentaire de littérature française. Paris, 1935.

37530.85 Princeton University. Library. List of French periodicals of the eighteenth and early nineteenth century. n.p., n.d.

37530.90 Société des lettres et des arts. Association des amis de Sequana. Lectures françaises; catalogue. Paris, 1935.

37530.95 Morize, A. General view of French literature. Ann Arbor, 1940.

37530.97 Popa, N.I. Memoriu de titluri şi lucrari. Iaşi, 1937.

37530.100 Cabeen, David C. A critical bibliography of French literature. Syracuse, 1947-56. 5v.

Htn 37530.105* Talvart, Hector. Bibliographie des auteurs modernes de langue française, 1801-1936. v.2-3,6-10. Paris, 1937. 7v.

37530.110 Fromm, H. Bibliographie deutscher Ubersetzungen. Baden-Baden, 1950-53. 6v.

37530.111 Wenger, I. Zehn Jahre deutsche. Hamburg, 1956.

37530.115 Lanson, Gustave. Manuel bibliographique. v.2-3. Paris, 1909-14. 2v.

37530.116 Lanson, Gustave. Manuel bibliographique. Paris, 1909-14. 5v.

37530.120A Jaffe, A.H. Bibliography of French literature in American magazines in the 18th century. East Lansing, 1951.

37530.120B Jaffe, A.H. Bibliography of French literature in American magazines in the 18th century. East Lansing, 1951.

37530.125 Perceau, L. Bibliographie du roman érotique au XIXe siècle. v.1-2. Paris, 1930.

37530.130 Golden, H.H. Modern French literature and language. Cambridge, Mass., 1953.

37530.135 Clouzat, M. Guide du bibliophile français. Biographie pratique des oeuvres littéraires français. Paris, 1953.

37530.135.5 Clouzat, M. Guide du bibliophile français. Notions générales des bibliophiles pratique. Paris, 1953.

37530.140 Woledge, Brian. Bibliographie des romans et nouvelles en prose française antérieurs. Genève, 1954.

37530.145 Thieme, H.P. Bibliographie de la littérature française de 1800 à 1930. Paris, 1933. 3v.

37530.150 Drevet, M.L. Bibliographie de la littérature française. Genève, 1954-55.

37530.155 Cordie, Carlo. Avviamento allo studio della lingua e della letteratura francese. Milano, 1955.

37530.160 Giraud, Jeanne. Manuel de bibliographie littéraire pour les 16, 17 et 18 siècle français. Paris, 1939-

37530 General literary history - Bibliographies, dictionaries, etc. - cont.

37530.165 National Book League. A thousand years of French books. London, 1948.

37530.170 Langlois, Pierre. Guide bibliographique des études littéraires. Paris, 1958.

37530.170.2 Langlois, Pierre. Guide bibliographique des études littéraires. Paris, 1960.

37530.173 Annuaire mondial des journaux, radios, écrivains et associations culturelles de la langue française hors de France. Paris. 1954.

37530.175 Bibliothèque Nationale, Paris. Répertoire collectif. Paris, 1958.

37530.177 Morize, André. Survey of French periodicals. n.p., 1922.

37530.177.2 Morize, André. Survey of French periodicals of literary interest. Supplement. n.p., 1923.

37530.180 Klein, Hans W. Die Fachbücherei des Neusprachlers. Dortmund, 1960.

37530.185 Paris. Bibliothèque Sainte-Geneviève. Collection Doucet. Première exposition du 21 Juin du 15 Juillet. Paris, 1933.

37530.186 Cioranescu, A. Bibliographie de la littérature française. Paris, 1959.

37530.188 Zambon, Maria R. Bibliographie du roman français en Italie au XVIIIe siècle. Firenze, 1962.

37530.190 France. Archives Nationales. Les sources de l'histoire littéraire aux archives nationales. Paris, 1961.

37530.191 P.E.N. Club. Czechoslovakia. La littérature française en Tchecolovaquie. Prague, 1964.

37530.192 Séguin, J.A.R. French works in English translation. Jersey City, 1965. 8v.

37530.193 Société Littéraire de France. Catalogue de la Société Littéraire de France. Paris, 1916.

37530.194 Société Littéraire de France. Catalogue de la Société Littéraire de France. Paris, 1917.

37530.195F Carteret, Léopold. Manuscrits de Pierre Louys et de divers auteurs contemporains. Paris, 1926.

37530.196 Spaziani, Marcello. Introduzione bibliografica alla lingua e alla letteratura francese. Palermo, 1969.

37530.198 Krauss, Werner. Französische Drucke des 18 Jahrhunderts in den Biliotheken der Deutschen Demokratischen Republik. v.1-2. Berlin, 1970.

37530.200 Littérature classique française. Tournai, 1969-

37530.202 Current research in French studies at universities and university colleges in the United Kingdom. London. 1,1970+

37530.204 Ronge, Peter. Studienbibliographie Französisch; Beiträge zur bibliographischen Erschliessung der französischen Philologie. v.1-2. Frankfurt, 1971.

37531 General literary history - General works - Folios [Discontinued]

37531.2 Histoire litteraire de la France. v.1-38. Paris, 1733-1950. 41v.

37531.2.2 Histoire litteraire de la France. Table générale. Paris, 1875.

37531.3 Laharpe, Jean F de. Lycée, ou Cours de littérature. v.1-16. Paris, 1799-1805. 19v.

37532 General literary history - General works - Laharpe's Lycée

37532.3 Laharpe, Jean F. de. Lycée, ou Cours de littérature. Paris, 1813. 16v.

37532.5 Laharpe, Jean F. de. Lycée, ou Cours de littérature. Paris, 1817. 16v.

37532.7 Laharpe, Jean F. de. Lycée, ou Cours de littérature. Paris, 1827. 18v.

37532.8 Laharpe, Jean F. de. Lycée, ou Cours de littérature. Paris, 1837. 2v.

37533 General literary history - General works - Works written in 18th century

37533.5 Goujet, Claude P. Bibliothèque française, ou Histoire de la littérature. Paris, 1741-56. 18v.

37533.12 Formey, M. La France littéraire, ou Dictionnaire des auteurs français. Berlin, 1757.

37533.15 Sablons, M. (pseud.). Les grands hommes vengés. Amsterdam, 1769. 2v.

37533.17 Sabatier de Castras, A. Les trois siècles de notre littérature. Amsterdam, 1772.

37533.17.10 Sabatier de Castras, A. Les trois siècles de la littérature. 5. éd. La Haye, 1778. 4v.

37533.21 Hébrail, J. La France littéraire. Paris, 1769. 3v.

37533.31 Ersch, J.S. La France littéraire. Hambourg, 1797. 3v.

37533.31.2 Ersch, J.S. La France littéraire. Supplement. Hambourg, 1802. 2v.

37534 General literary history - General works - Works written in 19th century - Petit de Julleville

37534.7 Petit de Julleville, L. Histoire de la langue et de la littérature française. v.1-3,5-8. Paris, 1896. 7v.

37536 General literary history - General works - Works written in 19th century - Craufurd, Pierrot, Villemain, Nissard

37536.3 Craufurd, Quintin. Essais sur la littérature française. Paris, 1815. 3v.

37536.4 Pierrot, Jules. Journal des cours publics. Paris, 1820. 2v.

37536.5 Villemain, A.F. Cours de littérature française. Paris, 1830. 2v.

37536.6 Villemain, A.F. Cours de littérature française. Bruxelles, 1840. 7v.

37536.7 Villemain, A.F. Cours de littérature française. Paris, 1857. 2v.

37536.9 Villemain, A.F. Cours de littérature française. Paris, 1858. 4v.

37536.9.5 Villemain, A.F. Cours de littérature française. Paris, 1861. 2v.

37536.9.10 Villemain, A.F. Cours de littérature française. Paris, 1875. 2v.

37536.10 Villemain, A.F. Cours de littérature française. Paris, 1882. 2v.

37536.12 Nisard, Désiré. Histoire de la littérature française. Paris, 1844-61. 4v.

NEDL 37536.13 Nisard, Désiré. Histoire de la littérature française. v.1-6. Bruxelles, 1846-62. 3v.

37536.14.5 Nisard, Désiré. Histoire de la littérature française. 5e éd. Paris, 1874. 4v.

37536.15 Nisard, Désiré. Histoire de la littérature française. v.2-4. 12. éd. Paris, 1884. 3v.

37537 General literary history - General works - Works written in 19th century - Schnabel, Haas, Baron, Geruzez, Godefroy, Chasles

37537.2 Schnabel, C. Abrégé de l'histoire de la littérature française. Leipzig, 1847.
37537.4 Haas, F. Tableau historique de la littérature française. Darmstadt, 1855.
37537.6 Baron, Auguste. Histoire de la littérature française. Paris, 1842.
37537.7 Geruzez, Eugène. Histoire de la littérature française. Paris, 1861. 2v.
37537.9 Geruzez, Eugène. Essais de littérature française. Paris, n.d. 2v.
37537.12 Godefroy, Frédéric. Histoire de la littérature française. Paris, 1859-76. 9v.
37537.12.5 Godefroy, Frédéric. Histoire de la littérature française. v.5. 2. éd. Paris, 1879-
37537.16 Chasles, Émile. Histoire nationale de la littérature française. Paris, 1870.

37538 General literary history - General works - Works written in 19th century - Roche, Moke, Prat, Saucièr, Demogeot, Grangier

37538.3 Roche, Antonin. Histoire des principaux écrivains français. Paris, 1858-60. 2v.
37538.3.10 Roche, Antonin. Histoire des principaux écrivains français depuis l'origine de la littérature jusqu'a nos jours. 4. éd. Paris, 1868. 2v.
37538.3.12A Roche, Antonin. Histoire des principaux écrivains français. 5. éd. Paris, 1875. 2v.
37538.3.12B Roche, Antonin. Histoire des principaux écrivains français. v.1. 5. éd. Paris, 1875.
37538.6 Moke, Henry G. Histoire de la littérature française. Brussels, n.d. 2v.
37538.9 Prat, Henry. Études littéraires. Moyen Âge. Paris, 1847.
37538.10 Prat, Henry. Études littéraires. XIVe et XVe siècles. Paris, 1853.
37538.11 Prat, Henry. Études littéraires. XVIe siècle. Paris, 1855.
37538.12 Prat, Henry. Études littéraires. XVIIe siècle. Paris, 1856-59. 3v.
37538.14 Prat, Henry. Études littéraires. XVIIIe siècle. Paris, 1860-61. 2v.
37538.15 Prat, Henry. Études littéraires. Époque révolutionaire. Paris, 1868.
37538.23 Saucié, D. Histoire de la littérature française. Tours, 1860.
37538.25 Demogeot, Jacques Claude. Histoire de la littérature française. Paris, 1860.
37538.26 Demogeot, Jacques Claude. Histoire de la littérature française. Paris, 1873.
37538.27 Demogeot, Jacques Claude. Histoire de la littérature française. Paris, 1886.
37538.29 Grangier, Louis. Histoire de la littérature française. Leipzig, 1875.

37541 General literary history - General works - Folios [Discontinued]; Pamphlet volumes

37541.01 Pamphlet vol. French literature. 8 pam.
37541.1 Pamphlet vol. Wells, Benjamin W. 4 pam.
Htn 37541.2PF* Pamphlet box. French literature. Broadside.
37541.3 Diancourt, A. Atlas littéraire de la France. Paris, 1878.
37541.5 Guigniant, J.D. Progrès études classiques et du Moyen Âge. Paris, 1868. 2 pam.
37541.6 Fleury, Jean. Du charactère speciale de la langue française. St. Petersbourg, 1873.
37541.10 Goutier, Léon. La littérature catholique et nationale. Bruges, 1894.
37541.11 Grignard, Jean. Nos gloires littéraires. Bruxelles, 1889.
37541.13 Papillon, Philibert. Bibliothèque des auteurs de Bourgogne. Dijon, 1745.
37541.17 Dessessarts, N.L.N. Les siècles littéraires de la France. Paris, 1800-03. 7v.
37541.17.8 Dessessarts, N.L.N. Nouveau dictionnaire bibliographique portatif. 2. éd. Paris, 1804.
37541.17.18 Chénier, M.J. Fragmens du cours de littérature. Paris, 1818.
37541.21 Odin, A. Genèse des grands hommes. Gens des lettres françaises modernes. Paris, 1895. 2v.
37541.23 Colomb de Batines, Paul. Mélanges...relatifs à l'histoire littéraire. Paris, 1837.
37541.25 Robert, U. Documents inédits concernant l'histoire littéraire de la France. Paris, 1875.
37541.27 Engel, Eduard. Geschichte der Französischen Literatur. Leipzig, 1882.
37541.28 Engel, Eduard. Geschichte der Französischen Literatur. 2. Aufl. Leipzig, 1888.
37541.29 Engel, Eduard. Geschichte der Französischen Literatur. 8. Aufl. Leipzig, 1912.
37541.30 Engel, Eduard. Psychologie der französischen Literatur. Wien, 1884.
37541.32 Bornhak, G. Geschichte der Französischen Literatur. Berlin, 1886.
37541.33 Suchier, H. Geschicihte der Französischen Literatur. Leipzig, 1900.
37541.33.2 Suchier, H. Geschichte der Französischen Literatur. Leipzig, 1913. 2v.
37541.34 Pamphlet vol. French literature. 33 pam.
37541.34.2 Pamphlet vol. French literature. 4 pam.
37541.35 Pamphlet vol. French authors. 38 pam.
37541.36 Pamphlet vol. French authors and literature. 28 pam.

37542 General literary history - General works - Other general works written since 1800 - Multi-volume works

37542.05 Pamphlet box. Clements, Robert John.
37542.2 Ancillon, Charles. Memoires concernant les vies de plusieurs modernes célèbres. Amsterdam, 1709.
37542.3 Noiré, Louis. Résumé de l'histoire de la littérature française. Mayence, 1875.
37542.5 Kreyssig, Friedrich. Geschichte des französischen Nationalliter. Berlin, 1873.
37542.6 Taillefer, Antoine. Tableau historique de l'ésprit et du caractère des littérateurs français. Versailles, 1785. 4v.
37542.8 Maillard, A. Histoire de la littérature française. Dresden, 1874.
37542.9 Martin, Charles. Les classiques et les romantiques. Paris, 1838. 2v.
37542.10 Ventouillac, L.T. The French librarian or literary guide. London, 1829.

37542 General literary history - General works - Other general works written since 1800 - Multi-volume works - cont.

37542.11 Van Laun, Henri. History of French literature. N.Y., 1876-77. 3v.
37542.11.2A Van Laun, Henri. History of French literature. London, 1876-77. 3v.
37542.11.2B Van Laun, Henri. History of French literature. v.2-3. London, 1876-77. 2v.
37542.11.90 Van Laun, Henri. History of French literature. London, 1883.
37542.12 Van Laun, Henri. History of French literature. v.1-3. N.Y., 1885.
37542.13 Shelley, M.W. Godwin (Mrs.). Lives of the most eminent literary and scientific men of France. London, 1838-39. 2v.
37542.13.5 Shelley, M.W. Godwin (Mrs.). Lives of the most eminent French writers. Philadelphia, 1840. 2v.
37542.15 Saintsbury, George. Short history of French literature. Oxford, 1882.
37542.15.2 Saintsbury, George. Short history of French literature. Oxford, 1882.
37542.16A Saintsbury, George. Short history of French literature. Oxford, 1889.
37542.16B Saintsbury, George. Short history of French literature. Oxford, 1889.
37542.16C Saintsbury, George. Short history of French literature. Oxford, 1889.
37542.16.5 Saintsbury, George. A short history of French literature. 4. ed. Oxford, 1892.
37542.17 Saintsbury, George. A short history of French literature. 6th ed. Oxford, 1901.
37542.17.5 Saintsbury, George. A short history of French literature. 5th ed. Oxford, 1897.
37542.17.7 Saintsbury, George. A short history of French literature. 7th ed. Oxford, 1917.
37542.18 Merlet, Gustave. Études littéraires...des classiques français. XVII et XVIII siècles. Paris, 1876.
37542.19 Merlet, Gustave. Études littéraires sur...Racine, Corneille et Molière, Chanson de Roland. Paris, 1882. 2v.
37542.21 Merlet, Gustave. Études littéraires sur Racine, Corneille, Molière, Chanson de Roland. Paris, 1883. 2v.
37542.23A Lintilhac, Gustave. Supplément aux études littéraires de G. Merlet. Paris, 1892.
37542.23B Lintilhac, Gustave. Supplément aux études littéraires de G. Merlet. Paris, 1892.
37542.24 Lintilhac, Gustave. Études littéraires sur les classiques français de G. Merlet. Paris, 1894. 2v.
37542.25 Sandras, Étienne G. Leçons sur l'histoire de la littérature française. Paris, 1887.
37542.26 Chauvin, A. La littérature française par les critiques contemporaines. Paris, 1887-1888. 2v.
37542.27 Henry, A. Les auteurs français. Paris, 1886.
37542.28 Biré, E. Études et portraits. Lyon, n.d.
37542.28.9 Biré, E. Dernières causeries historiques et littéraires. 3. éd. Lyon, 1910.
37542.29 Le Fèvre-Deumier, J. Critique littéraire (1825-1845). Paris, 1896.
37542.30A Frankfurter neuphilologische Beitrage. Frankfurt, 1887.
37542.30B Frankfurter neuphilologische Beitrage. Frankfurt, 1887.
37542.31 Breitinger, H. Aus neuern Litteraturen. Zürich, 1879.
37542.32 Mornet, Daniel. Histoire de la littérature et de la pensée française. Paris, 1924.
37542.32.10 Mornet, Daniel. Déjiny, sou debého pisemn a mýsleni francouzckébo 1870-1927. Praha, 1930.
37542.33 Fournier, E. Les écrivains sur le trône. Paris, 1865.
37542.34 Cournot, A.A. Considérations sur la marche des idées. Paris, 1872. 2v.
NEDL 37542.34 Cournot, A.A. Considérations sur la marche des idées. Paris, 1872. 2v.
37542.34.5 Cournot, A.A. Considérations sur la marche des idées. Paris, 1934. 2v.
37542.34.25 Monselet, Charles. La lorgnette littéraire. Paris, 1857.
37542.35 Monselet, Charles. La lorgnette littéraire dictionnaire de mon temps. Paris, 1870.
37542.35.5 Monselet, Charles. Portraits après décès. Paris, 1866.
37542.37 Cinq cents ans de littérature française. Paris, 1935.
37542.38 Duhamel, Roger. Littérature. Montréal, 1948-
37542.42 Hatzfeld, H. Literature through art. N.Y., 1952.
37542.45 Vier, Jacques. Littérature à l'emporte-pièce. Paris, 1958- 5v.
X Cg 37542.46 Decahors, E. Histoire de la littérature française. Paris, 1949. 2v.
37542.48 Vier, Jacques. Histoire de la littérature française. XVIe - XVIIe siècles. Paris, 1959.
37542.50 Saggi e ricerche di letteratura francese. 1. ed. Milano, 1960. 7v.
37542.52 Kohler, Pierre. Histoire de la littérature française. Lausanne, 1955. 3v.
37542.55 Life and letters in France. London, 1965-70. 3v.
37542.58 Guth, Paul. Histoire de la littérature française. Paris, 1967- 2v.
37542.60 Humanisme actif; mélanges d'art et de littérature offerts à Julien Cain. Paris, 1968. 2v.
37542.62 Cruickshank, John. French literature and its background. London, 1968- 5v.
37542.64 Lemaître, Henri. La littérature française. Paris, 1970-72. 5v.
37542.68 Littérature française. v.1-2,6-8. Paris, 1968- 5v.
37542.70 Lambert, B. L'épreuve littéraire aux concours des grandes écoles scientifiques. Villemomble, 1969. 2v.
37542.72 Chaillet, Jean. Études de grammaire et de style. Paris, 1969. 2v.
37542.74 Abraham, Pierre. Manuel d'histoire littéraire de la France. Paris, 1965- 3v.
37542.76A A literary history of France. v.2-5. London, 1967- 4v.
37542.76B A literary history of France. v.3. London, 1967-
37542.78 Roger, Jacques. Histoire de la littérature française. Paris, 1969-70. 2v.

37543 General literary history - General works - Other general works written since 1800 - Single volume works

37543.2 Montaiglon, Anatole de. Catalogue raisonné de la bibliothèque Elzevirienne, 1853-70. Paris, 1870.
37543.3 Drioux, Claude. Histoire de la littérature française. Paris, n.d.
37543.4 Demogeot, Jacques Claude. Histoire de la littérature française. Paris, 1867.

Classified Listing

37543 **General literary history - General works - Other general works written since 1800 - Single volume works - cont.**

37543.4.5 Leypoldt, Frédérick. Leçons de littérature française classique. N.Y., 1867.
37543.5 Bossange, H. Ma bibliothèque française. Paris, 1855.
37543.6 Bonnefon, D. Écrivains célèbres de la France. Alais, 1871.
37543.8 Marcillac, F. Manuel d'histoire de la littérature française. Lausanne, 1871.
37543.8.4 Marcillac, F. Manuel d'histoire de la littérature française. 5. éd. Genève, 1881.
37543.8.5 Marcillac, F. Manuel d'histoire de la littérature française. Genève, 1886.
37543.8.9 Marcillac, F. Manuel d'histoire de la littérature française. 11. éd. Genève, 1892.
37543.9 Brunet, P.G. La France littéraire au XVe siècle. Paris, 1865.
37543.10 Albert, Paul. Littérature française. Paris, 1872.
37543.10.1A Albert, Paul. Littérature française. 2. éd. Paris, 1875.
37543.10.1B Albert, Paul. Littérature française. 2. éd. Paris, 1875.
37543.10.2 Albert, Paul. La littérature française des origines au XVIe siècle. 8. éd. Paris, 1894.
37543.10.3 Albert, Paul. La littérature française des origines au XVIe siècle. 8. éd. Paris, n.d.
37543.11 Sabatier, A. De l'influence des femmes sur la littérature française. Paris, 1873.
37543.11.5 Bordeaux, Henry. Les pierres du foyer. Paris, 1918.
37543.12 Droz, T. L'ésprit Gaulois dans la littérature française. Zürich, 1885.
37543.13 Noël, Auguste. Histoire de la littérature française. Paris, 1874.
37543.15 Gidel, Charles. Histoire de la littérature française. Paris, 1875.
37543.16 Gidel, Charles. Histoire de la littérature française. Paris, 1877.
37543.17.2 Gidel, Charles. Histoire de la littérature française. Paris, 1878.
37543.17.3 Gidel, Charles. Histoire de la littérature française. Paris, 1878.
37543.18 Deloid, T. Les matinées littéraires. Paris, 1860.
37543.19 Masson, Gustave. Outlines of French literature. London, 1877.
37543.19.5 Masson, Gustave. Introduction to the history of French literature. 3. ed. Edinburgh, 1876.
37543.20 Blaze de Bury, H. Tableaux romantiques de littérature et d'art. Paris, 1878.
37543.20.9A Saintsbury, George. Primer of French literature. Oxford, 1880.
37543.20.9B Saintsbury, George. Primer of French literature. Oxford, 1880.
37543.21 Saintsbury, George. Primer of French literature. Oxford, 1880.
37543.21.1 Saintsbury, George. Primer of French literature. 2. ed. Oxford, 1881.
37543.21.2 Saintsbury, George. Primer of French literature. N.Y., 1881.
37543.21.15 Saintsbury, George. Primer of French literature. 3. ed. Oxford, 1894.
37543.21.30 Saintsbury, George. Primer of French literature. 5. ed. Oxford, 1912.
37543.22.3 Fleury, Jean. Histoire élémentaire de la littérature française. 8. éd. Paris, 1890.
37543.22.4 Fleury, Jean. Histoire élémentaire de la littérature française. 9. éd. Paris, 1894.
37543.22.5 Fleury, Jean. Histoire élémentaire de la littérature française. Paris, 1903.
37543.23 Fleury, Jean. Histoire élémentaire de la littérature française. Paris, 1882.
37543.25 Petit de Julleville, L. Leçons de littérature française. Paris, 1884.
37543.25.5 Petit de Julleville, L. Leçons de littérature française. 9. éd. Paris, 1893.
37543.26 Weiss, J.J. Essais sur l'histoire de la littérature française. Paris, 1865.
37543.27 Collas, Louis. Histoire de la littérature française. Paris, 1885.
37543.28 Deschanel, Émile. Le romantisme des classiques. Paris, 1883.
37543.28.9 Vapereau, L.G. L'année littéraire et dramatique. 1858-1868. Paris, 1860. 11v.
37543.29 Vapereau, L.G. Éléments d'histoire de la littérature française. Paris, 1883. 2v.
37543.30 Vapereau, L.G. Esquise d'histoire de la littérature française. Paris, 1884.
37543.31 Tivier, H. Histoire de la littérature française. Paris, 1884.
37543.32 Parnajon, Félix de. Histoire de la littérature française. Paris, 1883.
37543.33 Doumic, René. Éléments d'histoire littéraire. Paris, 1890.
37543.33.2 Doumic, René. Histoire de la littérature française. Paris, 1891.
37543.34 Gazier, A. Petite histoire de la littérature française. Paris, 1891.
37543.35 Hémon, Félix. Cours de littérature. v.1-25. Paris, 1889-93. 8v.
37543.36 Hémon, Félix. Études littéraires et morales. Paris, 1896.
37543.36.2 Hémon, Félix. Études littéraires et morales. Genève, 1971.
37543.37 Lanson, Gustave. Hommes et livres. Études morales et littéraires. Paris, 1895.
37543.37.10 Lanson, Gustave. Études d'histoire littéraire. Paris, 1929.
37543.38 Lanson, Gustave. Histoire de la littérature française. Paris, 1895.
37543.38.1 Lanson, Gustave. Histoire de la littérature française. 4. éd. Paris, n.d.
37543.38.2 Lanson, Gustave. Histoire de la littérature française. 10. éd. Paris, 1908.
37543.38.3 Lanson, Gustave. Histoire de la littérature française. Paris, 1912.
37543.38.6 Lanson, Gustave. Histoire de la littérature française. 13. éd. Paris, 1916.
37543.38.10F Lanson, Gustave. Histoire illustrée de la littérature française. Paris, 1923. 2v.
37543.38.11F Lanson, Gustave. Histoire illustrée de la littérature française. 2. éd. Paris, 1925-1926. 2v.

37543 **General literary history - General works - Other general works written since 1800 - Single volume works - cont.**

37543.38.13 Lanson, Gustave. Histoire de la littérature française. 19. éd. Paris, 1926?
37543.38.15 Lanson, Gustave. Manuel illustrée d'histoire de la littérature française. 2. éd. Paris, 1930.
37543.38.18 Lanson, Gustave. Manuel d'histoire de la littérature française. 4. éd. Paris, 1932.
37543.38.21A Lanson, Gustave. Manuel d'histoire de la littérature française. 4. éd. Paris, 1935.
37543.38.21B Lanson, Gustave. Manuel d'histoire de la littérature française. 4. éd. Paris, 1935.
37543.38.25 Lanson, Gustave. Manuel illustré d'histoire de la littérature française. Paris, 1953.
37543.38.30 Lanson, Gustave. L'idéal française dans la littérature. Paris, 1927.
37543.38.40 Lanson, Gustave. Histoire de la littérature française. Paris, 1953.
37543.39 Robert, P. Études sur l'histoire de la littérature française. Paris, 1895.
37543.39.9 Junker, Heinrich P. Grundriss des Geschichte der französischen Litteratur. Münster, 1889.
37543.40 Junker, Heinrich P. Grundriss des Geschichte der französischen Litteratur. Münster, 1894.
37543.40.5 Junker, Heinrich P. Grundriss der Geschichte der französischen Literatur. 6. Aufl. Münster, 1909.
37543.41 Doumic, René. Études sur la littérature française. Paris, 1896. 6v.
37543.42 Collignon, Albert. La religion des lettres. Paris, 1896.
37543.42.5 Collignon, Albert. La vie littéraire. Paris, 1895.
37543.43 Fouquet, Férnand. A travers la vie. Paris, 1896.
37543.44 Levallois, Jules. Mémoires d'un critique. Paris, n.d.
Htn 37543.45.5* Dowden, Edward. A history of French literature. N.Y., 1897.
37543.46 Henry, A. Histoire de la littérature française. Paris, 1897.
37543.47.5 Brunetière, Ferdinand. Manuel de l'histoire de la littérature française. Paris, 1899.
37543.47.10 Brunetière, Ferdinand. Manual of the history of French literature. N.Y., 1898.
37543.48 Lanson, Gustav. Dějiny novodobé literatury francouzské. pt. 1-2. Praha, 1900.
37543.49 Tenarg, Paul. Nos bons auteurs. Paris, 1898.
37543.53 Fortier, Alcée. Histoire de la littérature française. N.Y., 1893.
37543.53.5 Fortier, Alcée. Histoire de la littérature française. N.Y., 1913.
37543.55 Legouvé, E. Dernier travail derniers souvenirs. Paris, 1898.
37543.57A Wright, C.H. Conrad. A history of French literature. N.Y., 1912.
37543.57B Wright, C.H. Conrad. A history of French literature. N.Y., 1912.
37543.57C Wright, C.H. Conrad. A history of French literature. N.Y., 1912.
37543.57.5 Wright, C.H. Conrad. A history of French literature. N.Y., 1925.
37543.58 Brunetière, Ferdinand. Histoire de la littérature française classique. Paris, n.d. 4v.
37543.58.2 Brunetière, Ferdinand. Histoire de la littérature française classique. Paris, n.d.
37543.60 Birch-Hirschfeld, A. Geschichte der französischen Literatur. Stuttgart, 1889.
37543.61 Broc, V. de. Paysages poétiques et littéraires. Paris, 1904.
37543.63 Claretie, Léo. Histoire de la littérature française. Paris, 1905. 5v.
37543.63.25 Kastner, Leon Emile. Short history of French literature. N.Y., 1900.
37543.63.27 Kastner, Leon Emile. Short history of French literature. London, 1900.
37543.63.29 Kastner, Leon Emile. Short history of French literature. N.Y., 1901.
37543.64 Kastner, Leon Emile. Short history of French literature. N.Y., 1907.
37543.65 Suran, T. Les ésprits directeurs de la pensée française. Paris, 1903.
37543.66 Dumesnil, G. L'âme et l'évolution de la littérature. Paris, 1903. 2v.
37543.67 Jan, E.F. von. Die Landschaft des französischen Menschen. Weimar, 1935.
37543.68 Mornet, D. Le sentiment de la nature en France. Paris, 1907.
37543.68.15 Mornet, D. Histoire des grandes oeuvres de la littérature française. Paris, 1925.
37543.68.25 Mornet, D. La littérature française enseignée par la dissertation. Paris, 1936.
37543.72 Traccanaglia, G. Contributo allo studio dell'Italianismo in Francia. Lodi, 1907.
37543.73 Mazzoni, Guido. Il teatro della rivoluzione. Bologna, 1894.
37543.74 Hervier, M. Les écrivains français jugés par leurs contemporains. Paris, 1911- 4v.
37543.77 Mercereau, Alex. La littérature et les idées nouvelles. Paris, 1912.
37543.79 Giraud, Victor. Livres et questions d'aujourd'hui. Paris, 1907.
37543.80 Giraud, Victor. Les maîtres de l'heure. 3. éd. Paris, 1912.
37543.80.2 Giraud, Victor. Les maîtres de l'heure. Paris, 1911-
37543.80.5 Giraud, Victor. Les ecrivains et soldats. Paris, 1921.
37543.81 Maury, L. Classiques et romantiques. Paris, 1912.
37543.83 Reckzch, E. Beitrage zur Entwicklungsgeschichte des Frauenideals in der französischenLiteratur am Ausgang der Mittelalter. Greifswald, 1912.
37543.85 Wilmotte, M. Études des critiques sur la tradition littéraire en France. Paris, 1909.
37543.87 Mélanges de philologie et d'histoire littéraire. Paris, 1940.
37543.90A Montégut, E. Mélanges critiques. Paris, 1887.
37543.90B Montégut, E. Mélanges critiques. Paris, 1887.
37543.92 Maillard, F. Le requiem des gens de lettres. Paris, 1901.
37543.95 Gourmont, Rémy de. Promenades littéraires. 6. éd. Paris, 1916.
37543.95.2 Gourmont, Rémy de. Promenades littéraires. Série 2. Paris, 1906.
37543.95.3 Gourmont, Rémy de. Promenades littéraires. Série 3. Paris, 1909.

Classified Listing

37543 General literary history - General works - Other general works written since 1800 - Single volume works - cont.

37543.95.4 Gourmont, Rémy de. Promenades littéraires. Série 4. Paris, 1912.
37543.95.5 Gourmont, Rémy de. Promenades littéraires. Série 5. Paris, 1913.
Htn 37543.96* Gourmont, Rémy de. Promenades littéraires. 6. série. Paris, 1926.
37543.96.5 Gourmont, Rémy de. Promenades littéraires. 7. série. Paris, 1927.
37543.96.10 Gourmont, Rémy de. Promenades littéraires. Paris, 1963. 3v.
37543.98.2A Strachey, Giles Lytton. Landmarks in French literature. N.Y., 1923.
37543.98.2B Strachey, Giles Lytton. Landmarks in French literature. N.Y., 1923.
37543.100 Wells, B.W. Modern French literature. Boston, 1896.
37543.102 Brisson, A. La comédie littéraire. Paris, 1895.
37543.105 Rossel, V. Histoire de la littérature française hors de France. Paris, 1897.
37543.106 Rossel, V. Histoire des relations littéraires entre France et l'Allemagne. Paris, 1897.
37543.109 Brisson, A. Portraits intimes. Paris, 1894. 5v.
37543.110 Sourian, Maurice. Moralistes et poètes. Paris, 1907.
37543.112A Herriot, E. Précis de l'histoire des lettres françaises. 2. éd. Paris, n.d.
37543.112B Herriot, E. Précis de l'histoire des lettres françaises. 2. éd. Paris, n.d.
37543.114 Abry, E. Histoire illustrée de la littérature française. Paris, 1912.
37543.114.2 Abry, E. Histoire illustrée de la littérature française. 2. éd. Paris, 1913.
37543.114.3 Abry, E. Histoire illustrée de la littérature française. 3. éd. Paris, 1916.
37543.114.4A Abry, E. Histoire illustrée de la littérature française. Paris, 1918.
37543.114.4B Abry, E. Histoire illustrée de la littérature française. Paris, 1918.
37543.114.10 Abry, E. Histoire illustrée de la littérature française. 7. éd. Paris, 1922.
37543.114.14 Abry, E. Histoire illustrée de la littérature française. 7. éd. Paris, 1925.
37543.114.15 Abry, E. Histoire illustrée de la littérature française. 7. éd. Paris, 1926.
37543.116 Canat, R. Littérature française par les textes. Paris, n.d.
37543.118 Doumic, René. Histoire de la littérature française. 23. éd. Paris, 1906.
37543.118.5 Doumic, René. Histoire de la littérature française. Paris, 1934.
37543.120A Pellissier, Georges. Précis de l'histoire de la littérature française. Paris, n.d.
37543.120B Pellissier, Georges. Précis de l'histoire de la littérature française. Paris, n.d.
37543.120.5 Pellissier, Georges. Précis de l'histoire de la littérature française. Paris, 1926.
37543.122 Kouta, A.K. The history of French literature. N.Y., 1910.
37543.124 Faguet, E. En lisant les beaux vieux livres. Paris, 1911.
37543.124.2 Faguet, E. En lisant les beaux vieux livres. 2. éd. Paris, 1911.
37543.125 Faguet, E. En lisant les beaux vieux livres. Paris, 1912.
37543.127 Faguet, E. Amours d'hommes de lettres. Paris, 1907.
37543.128 Faguet, E. Petite histoire de la littérature française. Paris, 1913.
37543.129 Faguet, E. A literary history of France. London, 1907.
37543.130 Gillot, Hubert. La querelle des anciens et des modernes. Thèse. Nancy, 1914.
37543.132 Roques, Mario. Précis d'histoire de la littérature française des origines à nos jours. Citta di Castelle, 1914.
37543.132.5A Roques, Mario. Études de littérature française. Lille, 1949.
37543.132.5B Roques, Mario. Études de littérature française. Lille, 1949.
37543.133 Levi, Angelo Raffaello. Histoire de la littérature française depuis les origines jusqu'à nos jours. Venise, 1918.
37543.134 Simek, Otokar. Dějiny literatury francouzské v obrysech. Praha, 1918. 4v.
37543.135 Hudson, W.H. Short history of French literature. London, 1919.
37543.136 Joliet, L. Précis illustré de la littérature française. Paris, 1919.
37543.136.5 Joliet, L. Précis illustré de la littérature française. 3. éd. Paris, 1930.
37543.137.5 Grenier, Abel. Histoire de la littérature française. 5. éd. Paris, 1920.
37543.140.5 Braunschvig, Marcel. Notre littérature étudiée dans les textes. v.2. 2. éd. Paris, 1924.
37543.140.7 Braunschvig, Marcel. Notre littérature étudiée dans les textes. 3. éd., v.1.; 2. éd., v.2. Paris, 1925. 2v.
37543.140.8 Braunschvig, Marcel. Notre littérature étudiée dans les textes. 5. éd. Paris, 1928-29. 2v.
37543.140.12 Braunschvig, Marcel. Notre littérature étudiée dans les textes. Paris, 1946. 2v.
37543.140.15 Braunschvig, Marcel. La littérature française contemporaine. 2. éd. Paris, 1928.
37543.140.17 Braunschvig, Marcel. La littérature française contemporaine. 11. éd. Paris, 1947.
37543.140.20 Braunschvig, Marcel. La littérature française contemporaine étudiée dans les textes. 3. éd. Paris, 1929.
37543.143 Adami, J. Précis de littérature avec de nombreuses citations. Paris, 1921.
37543.143.5 Adami, J. Précis de littérature avec de nombreuses citations. 2. éd. Paris, 1923.
37543.144 Des Granges, C.M. Illustrated history of French literature. Paris, 1921.
37543.144.4 Des Granges, C.M. Histoire illustrée de la littérature française. 2. éd. Paris, 1914.
37543.144.5 Des Granges, C.M. Histoire illustrée de la littérature française. 8. éd. Paris, 1923.
37543.144.10 Des Granges, C.M. Histoire illustrée de la littérature française. 3. éd. Paris, 1933.
37543.144.25 Des Granges, C.M. Histoire de la littérature française des origines à nos jours. 43. éd. Paris, 1948.
37543.144.30.5 Des Granges, C.M. Précis de littérature française. 17. éd. Paris, 1922.

37543 General literary history - General works - Other general works written since 1800 - Single volume works - cont.

37543.145A Morize, André. Problems and methods of literary history. N.Y., 1922.
37543.145B Morize, André. Problems and methods of literary history. N.Y., 1922.
37543.145C Morize, André. Problems and methods of literary history. N.Y., 1922.
37543.146 Allain, Maurice. Histoire générale de littérature française. Paris, 1922.
37543.148A Butler, Kathleen J. A history of French literature. London, 1923. 2v.
37543.148B Butler, Kathleen J. A history of French literature. v.2. London, 1923.
37543.149 Mélanges d'histoire littéraire et de philologie offerts à M. Bernard Bouvier. Genève, 1920.
37543.150 Giraud, Victor. Moralistes français. Paris, 1923.
37543.152F Bedier, Joseph. Histoire de la littérature française illustrée. Paris, 1923. 2v.
37543.154 Badaire, J. Précis de littérature française. Boston, 1926.
37543.157 Haas, Joseph. Kurzgefasste französische Literaturgeschichte von 1549-1900. Halle, 1924-27. 4v.
37543.160A Wright, C.H.C. Background of modern French literature. Boston, 1926.
37543.160B Wright, C.H.C. Background of modern French literature. Boston, 1926.
37543.160C Wright, C.H.C. Background of modern French literature. Boston, 1926.
37543.160D Wright, C.H.C. Background of modern French literature. Boston, 1926.
37543.165A Smith, M. Short history of French literature. N.Y., 1924.
37543.165B Smith, M. Short history of French literature. N.Y., 1924.
37543.167 Rudler, Gustave. Les techniques de la critique et de l'histoire littéraires en littérature française moderne. Oxford, 1923.
37543.170A Strachey, Giles Lytton. Landmarks in French literature. N.Y., 1912.
37543.170B Strachey, Giles Lytton. Landmarks in French literature. N.Y., 1912.
37543.172 Strachey, Giles Lytton. Landmarks in French literature. London, 1912?
37543.175 Sáenz Hayes, Ricardo. Perfiles y caracteres. Buenos Aires, 1927.
37543.178 Nitze, W. Albert. A list of French literature from the earliest times to the great war. N.Y., 1922.
37543.179.5 Nitze, W. Albert. A history of French literature from earliest times to the present. N.Y., 1928.
37543.179.7A Nitze, W. Albert. A history of French literature. 3. ed. N.Y., 1938.
37543.179.7B Nitze, W. Albert. A history of French literature. 3. ed. N.Y., 1938.
37543.187 Pilon, Edmond. Figures françaises et littéraires. Paris, 1921.
37543.190 King, Donald L. L'influence des sciences physiologiques. Thèse. Paris, 1929.
37543.191 Boulenger, J. Le touriste littéraire. 5. éd. Paris, 1928.
37543.192 Gottschalk, Walter. Die humoristische Gestalt in der französischen Literatur. Heidelburg, 1928.
37543.193 Kayer, Hermann. Das Problem der gesellschaftlichen Entwurzelung in der FranzösischenLiteratur. Inaug. Diss. Stuttgart, 1928.
37543.196 Morienval, Jean. De Pathelin à Ubu. Paris, 1929.
37543.198 Preissig, E. Der Völkergedanke. Brunn, 1931.
37543.200 Doutrepont, Georges. Les types populaires de la littérature française. pt. 1. Bruxelles, 1926-27. 2v.
37543.201 Bruyère, Jean. Histoire littéraire des gens de métier en France. Paris, 1932.
37543.203 Calvet, Jean. Histoire de la littérature française. Paris, 1955- 10v.
37543.203.10 Calvet, Jean. Le bestiaire de la littérature française. Paris, 1954.
37543.204 Navarre, Charles. Les grands écrivains étrangers. Paris, 1930.
Htn 37543.206* Ellis, Havelock. From Rousseau to Proust. Boston, 1935.
37543.207 Mornet, D. A short history of French literature. N.Y., 1935.
37543.207.2 Mornet, D. A short history of French literature. N.Y., 1936.
37543.208 Thibaudet, A. Histoire de la littérature française de 1789 à nos jours. Paris, 1936.
37543.208.5 Thibaudet, A. Histoire de la littérature française de 1789 à nos jours. Rio de Janeiro, 1940- 2v.
37543.210 Verriest, Léon. L'évolution de la littérature française. N.Y., 1936.
37543.212 Roustan, M. La littérature française par la dissertation. Paris, 193-. 4v.
37543.214 Sammartino, P. Survey of French literature. N.Y., 1937.
37543.216 Pauphilet, Albert. Le moyen âge. Paris, 1937.
37543.218 Bainville, J. Lectures; préface de Charles Maurras. Paris, 1937.
37543.220 Mélanges de philologie d'histoire et de littérature offerts a Joseph Vianey. Paris, 1934.
37543.225 Guillaume, M.M. Histoire de la littérature française. Lyon, 1938.
37543.228 Krüger, P. Fransk litteraer kritik indtil 1830. København, 1936.
37543.232 Thibaudet, A. Réflexions sur la littérature. 5. éd. Paris, 1938.
37543.232.5 Thibaudet, A. Réflexions sur la critique. 5. éd. Paris, 1939.
37543.232.7 Thibaudet, A. Réflexions sur la littérature. 8. éd. Paris, 1940.
37543.234 Pamphlet box. Françon, Marcel. Collection of reprints from various periodicals.
37543.236 Fay, E.G. A new outline of French literature with reading references. Ithaca, 1939.
37543.238 Smith, H.E. Masters of French literature. N.Y., 1937.
37543.240 Feuillerat, A. Studies by members of the French department of Yale University. New Haven, 1941.
37543.241 Peyre, Henri. Essays in honor of Albert Feuillerat. New Haven, 1943.
37543.242 Peyre, Henri. L'influence des littératures antiques. New Haven, 1941.
37543.243 Rousseaux, André. Le monde classique. Paris, 1943.
37543.243.5 Rousseaux, André. Le monde classique. Paris, 1948.
37543.243.10 Rousseaux, André. Le monde classique. Paris, 1946.

Classified Listing

37543 General literary history - General works - Other general works written since 1800 - Single volume works - cont.

37543.243.15 Rousseaux, André. Le monde classique. 3. série. Paris, 1951.
37543.243.20 Rousseaux, André. Le monde classique. 4. série. Paris, 1956.
37543.245 Schwarz, H.S. An outline history of French literature. N.Y., 1924.
37543.247 Fess, Gilbert Malcolm. The American revolution in creative French literature (1775-1937). Columbia, 1941.
37543.249 Le Bidois, Georges. L'honneur au miroir de nos lettres. Paris, 1921.
37543.251 Saintsbury, George. French literature and its masters. 1. ed. N.Y., 1946.
37543.253 Sauvebois, Gaston. Après le naturalisme. Paris, 1908.
37543.255 Smith, Mabell S.C. The spirit of French letters. N.Y., 1912.
37543.257 Fernandez, R. Itinéraire française. Paris, 1943.
37543.259 Arland, Marcel. Le promeneur. Paris, 1944.
37543.261 Van Tieghem, Philippe. Petite histoire des grandes doctrines littéraire sen France. Paris, 1946.
37543.261.4 Van Tieghem, Philippe. Petite histoire des grandes doctrines littéraires en France. Paris, 1957.
37543.261.16 Van Tieghem, Philippe. Les grandes doctrines littéraires en France. 6. éd. Paris, 1963.
37543.263 Le Maître, Henry. Essai sur le mythe de psyche dans la littérature française. Thèse. Persan, 1939.
37543.263.1 Lemaître, Henri. Essai sur le mythe de Psyché dans la littérature française des origines à 1890. Paris, 194-.
37543.265A Jasinski, René. Histoire de la littérature française. Paris, 1947. 2v.
37543.265B Jasinski, René. Histoire de la littérature française. v.2. Paris, 1947.
37543.265.2 Jasinski, René. Histoire de la littérature française. Paris, 1965-66. 2v.
NEDL 37543.267 Akademiia nauk SSSR. Institut literatury. Istoriia frantsuzskoi literatury. Moskva, 1946.
37543.269 Madaule, Jacques. Reconnaissances. v.3. Paris, 1946.
37543.271 Waite, Vincent. An approach to French literature. London, 1947.
37543.273 Ledésert, R.P.L. Histoire de la littérature française des origines à l'époque contemporaine. London, 1946-47. 2v.
37543.275 Castex, Pierre. Manuel des études littéraires françaises. v.1-6. Paris, 1946-50.
37543.277 Noblot, Jean. Les époques des lettres françaises. Paris, 1947- 2v.
37543.279 André, Paul. Survivants. Neuchâtel, 1939?
37543.281 Raymond, Marcel. Génies de France. Neuchâtel, 1942.
37543.281.5 Raymond, Marcel. Vérité et poésie. Neuchâtel, 1964.
37543.281.80 De Ronsard à Breton, recueil d'éssais, hommages à Marcel Raymond. Paris, 1967.
37543.283 Talagrand, J. Languages. Lausanne, 1947.
37543.285 Jaloux, Édmond. Introduction à l'histoire de la littérature française. v.1-2. Genève, 1946-47.
37543.287 Chazel, Pierre. Figures de proue; de Corneille à Valéry. Neuchâtel, 1948.
37543.289 Studies in French language, literature and history presented to R.L. Graime Ritchie. Cambridge, Eng., 1949.
37543.290 Pons, Roger. L'Yseult a violaine. Paris, 1948.
37543.292 Hartoy, M. d'. De l'inouisme et de quelques autres complexes en littérature. Avignon, 1949.
37543.294 Mauriac, F. Mes grands hommes. Monaco, 1949.
37543.294.5 Mauriac, F. Men I hold great. N.Y., 1951.
37543.294.10 Mauriac, F. Great men. London, 1952.
37543.296 Dieckmann, Heinz. Von Villon bis Eluard. Saarbrücken, 1948.
37543.298A Van Tieghem, Philippe. Histoire de la littérature française. Paris, 1949.
37543.298B Van Tieghem, Philippe. Histoire de la littérature française. Paris, 1949.
37543.300F Littérature française. Paris, 1948-49. 2v.
37543.302 Haedens, K. Une histoire de la littérature française. Paris, 1949.
37543.304 Merquiol, A. La côte d'Azur dans la littérature française. Nice? 1949.
37543.306 Bernardin, N.M. Du XVe au XXe siècle. Paris, 1916.
37543.308 Neubert, Fritz. Geschichte der französischen Literatur. Tübingen, 1949.
37543.308.10 Neubert, Fritz. Studien zur vergleichenden Literaturgeschichte. Berlin, 1952.
37543.308.20 Neubert, Fritz. Französische Literaturprobleme. Berlin, 1962.
37543.310A Hoog, A. Littérature en Silesie. Paris, 1944.
37543.310B Hoog, A. Littérature en Silesie. Paris, 1944.
37543.312 Sage, Pierre. Le bon prêtre dans la littérature française d'Amadis de Gaule au Génie du christianisme. Genève, 1951.
37543.314 The French mind. Studies in honour of Gustave Rudler. Oxford, 1952.
37543.316 Romains, Jules. Saints de notre calendrier. Paris, 1952.
37543.318 Guyer, Foster E. The main stream of French literature. Boston, 1932.
37543.320 Paulhan, J. Les fleurs de tarbes, ou La terreur dans les lettres. 12. éd. Paris, 1950.
37543.322 Nathan, J. La littérature et les écrivains. Paris, 1952?
37543.324 Sofer, Johann. Die Antike in der französischen Geistesgeschichte. Wien, 1951.
37543.326 Glasser, R. Studien zur Geschichte des französischen Zeitbegriffs. München, 1936.
37543.328 Schneider, Pierre. La voix vive. Paris, 1953.
37543.330 Bénac, Henri. Études sur les chefs-d'oeuvre de la littérature française. Paris, 1947-48. 2v.
37543.332 Trnka, J. A propos d'une traduction. Paris, 1953.
37543.333 Widmer, Walter. Fug und Unfug des Übersetzens. Köln, 1959.
37543.335 Tielrooy, J.B. Verkenningen in het land der literatuur. Groningen, 1954.
37543.340 Cazamian, Louis. A history of French literature. Oxford, 1955.
37543.345 Leroy, Jules. Saint-Germain-des Prés. Paris, 1952.
37543.350 Arland, Marcel. La grâce d'écrire. 2. éd. Paris, 1955.
37543.355 Natoli, Glauco. Figure e problemi della cultura francese. Messina, 1956.
37543.360 Kemp, Robert. La vie des livres. Paris, 1955. 2v.
37543.365 Charlier, Gustave. De Montaigne à Verlaine. Bruxelles, 1956.
37543.370 Sauro, Antoine. Études françaises d'esthétique. Napoli, 1949.

37543 General literary history - General works - Other general works written since 1800 - Single volume works - cont.

37543.375 Luzi, Mario. Aspetti della generazione napoleonica. Parma, 1956.
37543.380 Hatzfeld, Helmut. Iniatiation à l'explication de textes français. München, 1957.
37543.385 Bornecque, P.H. La France et sa littérature. Lyon, 1953-57. 2v.
37543.390.4 Albalat, Antoine. Comment il faut lire les auteurs classiques français de Villon à Victor Hugo. 4. éd. Paris, 1920.
37543.395 Lebel, Roland. Le Maroc dans les lettres d'éxpression française. Paris, 1956.
37543.400 Robin, Eugène. Impressions littéraires. Bruxelles, 1957.
37543.405 Henriot, Émile. Neuf siècles de littérature française. Paris, 1958.
37543.410 Waltz, Henriette. Éxplications françaises. Lyon, 1958.
37543.415 Maynial, Édouard. Précis de littérature française. Paris, 1926.
37543.420 Wais, Kurt Karl P. Französische Marksteine von Racine bis Saint-John Peral. Berlin, 1958.
37543.425 Valeri, Diego. Da Racine a Picasso. Firenze, 1956.
37543.426 Valeri, Diego. Précis historique et anthologie de la littérature française. 11. éd. Milano, 1959.
37543.430 Bray, Bernard. L'éxpression de l'inquiétude roman français dans le jeune. Groningen, 1959. 2 pam.
37543.435 Ménard, Jean. De Corneille à Saint-Denys-Garneau. Montréal, 1957.
37543.440 Geyl, Pieter. Franse figuren. Amsterdam, 1959.
37543.445 Yetkin, S.K. Edebî meslekler. Istanbul, 1943.
37543.448 Yetkin, S.K. Edebiyatta akimlar. Istanbul, 1967.
37543.450 Cohn, Robert G. The writer's way in France. Philadelphia, 1960.
37543.455 Morier, Henri. La psychologie des styles. Genève, 1959.
37543.460 Cordie, Carlo. Saggi e studi di letteratura francese. Padova, 1951.
37543.465 The Oxford companion to French literature. Oxford, 1959.
37543.470 Macchia, Giovanni. Il paradiso della ragione. Bari, 1960.
37543.471 Macchia, Giovanni. Storia della letteratura francese. Torino, 1961.
37543.472 Macchia, Giovanni. Il mito di Parigi. Torino, 1965.
37543.475 Hofmiller, Josef. Franzosen. München, 1928.
37543.480 Maranini, L. Visione e personaggio secondo Flaubert. Padova, 1959.
37543.485 Diéguez, M. de. L'écrivain et son langage. Paris, 1960.
37543.490 Pamphlet vol. Franse letterkunde. 2 pam.
37543.495 Macchia, Giovanni. Storia della letteratura francese. Roma, 1960?
37543.500A Ellis, Havelock. From Rousseau to Proust. London, 1936.
37543.500B Ellis, Havelock. From Rousseau to Proust. London, 1936.
37543.505 Haškovec, P.M. Francouzské kapitaly. Praha, 1930.
37543.510 Debidour, V.H. Saveurs des lettres. Paris, 1946.
37543.515 Taha-Hussein, Minis. Présence de l'Islam dans la littérature. La Caire, 1960.
37543.520 Faguet, Émile. Histoire de la littérature française. Paris, 1921. 2v.
37543.523 Université d'Aix-Marseilles. Faculté des lettres, Aix. Hommage au doyen Étienne Gros. Gap, 1959.
37543.525 Fin du Moyen Âge et Renaissance. Anvers, 1961.
37543.530 Van Tieghem, Philippe. Les influences étrangères sur la littérature française. Paris, 1961.
37543.535 Guillemin, Henri. A vrai dire. Paris, 1956.
37543.535.5 Guillemin, Henri. Éclaircissements. Paris, 1961.
37543.535.10 Guillemin, Henri. Pas à pas. Paris, 1969.
37543.538 Nardis, Luigi. Il soniso di Reims. Bologna, 1960.
37543.540 Howard, E. Deutsch-französisches Mosaik. Zürich, 1962.
37543.542 Le Meur, L. Panorama d'histoire de la littérature française. Paris, 1962.
37543.544 Rousset, Jean. Forme et signification. Paris, 1962.
37543.545 Style et littérature. La Haye, 1962.
37543.548 Derche, Roland. Études de textes français. Paris, 1959.
37543.548.2 Derche, Roland. Études de textes français. 2. éd. Paris, 1964. 6v.
37543.550 Mauron, Charles. Des métaphores obsédantes au mythe personnel. Paris, 1963.
37543.550.1 Mauron, Charles. Des métaphores obsédantes au mythe personnel. Paris, 1970.
37543.551 Brockmeier, P. Darstellungen der französischen Literaturgeschichte. Berlin, 1963.
37543.552 Jones, P.M. The assault on French literature. Manchester, Eng., 1963.
37543.553 Studi in onore di Carlo Pellegrini. Torino, 1963.
37543.555 Schneider, Marcel. La littérature fantastique en France. Paris, 1964.
37543.556 Etkind, Efin G. Pisateli Frantsii. Moskva, 1964.
37543.557 Paris. Collège de France. Six conférences. Nogent-le-Rotrou, 1964.
37543.558 Bérard, Léon. Au service de la pensée française. Paris, 1925.
37543.562 Clouard, Henri. Petite histoire de la littérature française des origines à nos jours. Paris, 1965.
37543.563 Clapton, G.J. Currents of thought in French literature. N.Y., 1966.
37543.564 Lanson, Gustave. Essais de méthode. Paris, 1965.
37543.565 Bonnet, Henri. De Malherbe à Sartre. Paris, 1964.
37543.566 Thimann, Ivor Cedric. A short history of French literature. 1. ed. Oxford, 1966.
37543.567 Theisen, Josef. Geschichte der französischen Literatur. Stuttgart, 1964.
37543.568 Tippetts, Marie. Les marines des peintres vues par les littérateurs de Diderot aux Goncour. Paris, 1966.
37543.569 Éthier-Blais, Jean. Signets. v.1-2. Montréal, 1967.
37543.570 Bronne, Carlo. Le promenoir des amis. Bruxelles, 1967.
37543.572 Bénichou, Paul. L'écrivain et ses travaux. Paris, 1967.
37543.580 Dresden, Samuel. La notion de structure. La Haye, 1961.
37543.585 Fowlie, Wallace. Climate of violence; the French literary tradition from Baudelaire to the present. N.Y., 1967.
37543.586 Blin, Georges. Leçon inaugurale faite le...13 janvier 1966. Nogent-le-Rotrou, 1967.
37543.588 Studies in French literature presented to H.W. Lawton by colleagues. Manchester, Eng., 1968.
V37543.589 Polanšćak, Antun. Od povjerenja do sumnje. Zagreb, 1966.
37543.590 Pommier, Jean. Dialogues avec le passé, études et portraits littéraires. Paris, 1967.
37543.592 Le Hir, Yves. Analyses stylistiques. Paris, 1965.
37543.594 Moore, Will G. French achievement in literature. London, 1969.

37543 General literary history - General works - Other general works written since 1800 - Single volume works - cont.

37543.595 Guyot, Charly. De Rousseau à Marcel Proust. Neuchâtel, 1968.
37543.596 Mueller, Armand. De Rabelais à Paul Valery. Paris, 1969.
37543.600 Vestdijk, Simon. Gallische facetten. Den Haag, 1968.
37543.602 Modern miscellany presented to Eugène Vinaver by pupils, colleagues and friends. Manchester, Eng., 1969.
37543.604 Gallica: essays presented to J. Heywood Thomas by collegues, pupils, and friends. Cardiff, 1969.
37543.606 Ponton, Jeanne. La religieuse dans la littérature française. Québec, 1969.
37543.608 Itterbeek, Eugene van. Spreken en zwijgen. Hasselt, 1965.
37543.612 Strömberg, Kjell. Dikt och liv. Fransyska parnassvisiter. Stockholm, 1968.
37543.614 Nurse, Peter H. The art of criticism. Edinburgh, 1969.
37543.615 Bonneau, Georges. Mélanges critiques. Ankara, 1956.
37543.618 Raymond, Marcel. Être et dire. Études. (Recueil). Neuchâtel, 1970.
37543.620 Albouy, Pierre. Mythes et mythologies dans la littérature française. Paris, 1969.
37543.624 Fellows, Otis Edward. Problems and personalities, from Voltaire to La nouvelle critique. Genève, 1970.
37543.626 Caramaschi, Enzo. Études de littérature française. Bari, 1967.
37543.630 Schober, Rita. Von der wirklichen Welt in der Dichtung. 1. Aufl. Berlin, 1970.
37543.632 Losfeld, Georges. Le livre des rencontres, Villon, d'Aubigné, Desportes, Malherbe. Paris, 1969.
37543.634 Tricotel, Édouard. Variétés bibliographiques. Paris, 1863.
37543.636 Strauss, Walter Adolf. Descent and return; the Orphic theme in modern literature. Cambridge, 1971.
37543.638 Osburn, Charles B. The present state of French studies: a collection of research reviews. Metuchen, N.J., 1971.
37543.640 De Jean Lemaire de Belges à Jean Giraudoux. Paris, 1970.

37544 General literary history - Special topics

37544.3 Rathery, Edme J.B. Influence de l'Italie sur les lettres françaises. Paris, 1853.
37544.5.2 Potvin, Charles. De la corruption littéraire en France. 2. éd. Bruxelles, 1873.
37544.7 Lintilhac, Eugène. Précis historique et critique de la littérature française. Paris, 1890. 2v.
37544.7.8 Lintilhac, Eugène. Précis historique et critique de la littérature française. 3. éd. Paris, 18- ?
37544.8 Brunetière, Ferdinand. L'évolution des genres dans l'histoire de la littérature. Paris, 1890.
37544.9 Cohnen, Theodor. Der Rhein in der französischen Literatur. Inaug.-Diss. Bonn, 1926.
37544.10 Süpfle, Theodor. Geschichte des deutschen Kultureinflusses auf Frankreich. v.1-2. Gotha, 1886-90. 3v.
37544.10.5 Dupouy, Auguste. France et Allemagne: littératures comparées. Paris, 1913.
37544.12 Rahstede, Georg. Wanderungen durch und französischen Litteratur. Oppeln, 1891.
37544.15 Keene, H.G. The literature of France. London, 1892.
37544.15.5 Keene, H.G. The literature of France. N.Y., 1892.
37544.22.2 Faguet, Émile. Propos littéraires. 2. séries. Paris, 1904.
37544.22.3 Faguet, Émile. Propos littéraires. 3. séries. Paris, 1905.
37544.22.4 Faguet, Émile. Propos littéraires. 4. séries. Paris, 1907.
37544.22.5 Faguet, Émile. Propos littéraires. 5. séries. Paris, n.d.
37544.23.2 Faguet, Émile. Les dix commandements de la vieillesse. 2. éd. Paris, 191- .
37544.24 Faguet, Émile. Les dix commandements de la vieillesse. 4. éd. Paris, n.d.
37544.25.8 Faguet, Émile. Les dix commandements de l'amitié. 8. éd. Paris, 19- .
37544.30.2 Balzo, Carlo del. L'Italia nella letteratura francese. Torino, 1907.
37544.32 Ravà, Béatrix. Venise dans la littérature française. Paris, 1916.
37544.34 Edwards, Matilda Betham. Literary rambles in France. London, 1907.
37544.36 Dorbee, Prosper. Les lettres française dans leurs contacts avec l'atelier de l'artiste. Paris, 1929.
37544.38 Chassée, Charles. Styles et physiologie. Paris, 1928.
37544.40 Engel, Claire Eliane. La littérature alpestre en France et en Angleterre. Chambéry, 1930.
37544.43 Fransen, J. Iets over vergelijkende literatuurstudie, Perioden en Invaloeden. Groningen, 1936.
37544.45 Jensen, Emeline Maria. The influence of French literature on Europe. Boston, 1919.
37544.46 Samsami, N.D. L'Iran dans la littérature française. Thèse. Paris, 1936.
37544.47 Samsami, N.D. L'Iran dans la littérature française. Paris, 1936.
37544.48 Jourda, P. L'éxotisme dans la littérature française depuis Chateaubriand. Paris, 1938. 2v.
37544.49 Leib, H. Les cas de mésalliances dans le roman et le théâtre. Thèse. Berlin, 1936.
37544.51 Jones, P.M. French introspectives from Montaigne to André Gide. Cambridge, Eng., 1937.
37544.53 Mélanges de littérature d'histoire et de philologie offerts a Paul Laumonier. Paris, 1935.
37544.55 Cabanes, A. Autour de la vie de Bohème. Paris, 1938.
37544.56 Paul Émile, Sister. Le renouveau Marial dans la littérature française. Ottawa, 1936.
37544.58 Giraud, V. Le problème religieux et l'histoire de la littérature française. Paris, 1937.
37544.60 Mello Franco, A.A. de. O indio brasileiro e a revolução francesa. Rio de Janeiro, 1937.
37544.65 Dimier, L. Le nationalisme littéraire et ses mefaits chez les français. Paris, 1935.
37544.67 Brun, Felix. L'alouette; histoire littéraire d'un petit oiseau. Meulan, 1894.
37544.68 Calvet, Jean. L'enfant dans la littérature française. Paris, 1930.
37544.70 Rudwin, M.J. Les écrivains diaboliques de France. Paris, 1937.
37544.71 Milner, Max. Le diable dans la littérature française de Cazotte à Baudelaire, 1772-1861. Paris, 1960. 2v.
37544.73 Knauer, K. Studien zur Geschichte der Farbenbestimmung van den Anfangen vis gegenEnde des 18. Jahrhundert. Genève, 1933.

37544 General literary history - Special topics - cont.

37544.75 Wandruszka von Wanstetten, M.W. Nord und Süd in französischen Geistesleben. Diss. Jena, 1938.
37544.77 Dupouy, Auguste. Géographie des lettres françaises. Paris, 1942.
37544.80 Feigelson, Raph. Écrivains juifs de langue française. Paris, 1960.
37544.82 Lehrmann, C. L'élément juif dans la littérature française. 2. éd. Zürich, 1941.
37544.82.2 Lehrmann, C. L'élément juif dans la littérature française. 2. éd. Paris, 1960- 2v.
37544.85 Picard, Roger. Artifices et mystifications littéraires. Montréal, 1945.
37544.88 Trigon, Jean de. Histoire de la littérature enfantine. Paris, 1950.
37544.90 Hesse-Fine, Evelyne. Études sur la thème de l'inceste dans la littérature française. Berne, 1971.
37544.95 Brunet-Jailly, Jean-Baptiste. Introduction à la practique de l'éxplication de texte. Stockholm, 1971.
37544.100 Dupuy, Aimé. La Tunisie dans les lettres d'éxpression française. Paris, 1956.
37544.105 Dupuy, Aimé. L'Algérie dans les lettres d'éxpression française. Paris, 1956.
37544.110 Vovard, André. Les turqueries dans la littérature française. Toulouse, 1959.
37544.115 Simon, Pierre H. Le domaine héröique des lettres françaises, Xe-XIXe siècle. Paris, 1963.
37544.120 Baroli, Marc. Le train dans la littérature française. Thèse. Paris? 1963.
37544.122 Bourin, André. La France littéraire en zigzag. Bruxelles, 1965.
37544.125 Bissoondoyal, Basdeo. India in French literature. London, 1967.
37544.130 Luchini, Albert Marie. Les chrétiens croient-ils encore au livre? Le livre de religion à la question. Paris, 1967.
37544.135 Marquiset, Jean. Les gens de justice dans la littérature. Paris, 1967.
37544.140 Aubéry, Pierre. Pour une lecture ouvrière de la littérature. Paris, 1970.
37544.141 Ragon, Michel. Histoire de la littérature ouvrière du Moyen Âge à nos jours. Paris, 1953.
37544.145 Newman, Pauline. Hélène de Sparte; la fortune du mythe en France. Paris, 1968.
37544.150 Gachon, Lucien. L'écrivain et le paysan. Moulins, 1970.
37544.155 el Nouty, Hassan. Le Proche-Orient dans la littérature française. Paris, 1958.

37546 General literary history - Local - Regions and places of France - Folios [Discontinued]

37546.2 Rolland, Jules. Histoire littéraire de la Ville d'Albi. Toulouse, 1879.
37546.4 Colletet, Guillaume. Vies des poètes Bordelais. Paris, 1873.
37546.10 Deberre, E. La vie littéraire à Dijon au XVIIIe siècle. Paris, 1902.
37546.14 Jeanroy, Alfred. La poésie académique à Toulouse au XIVe et au XVe siècles. Toulouse, 1914.
37546.20 Hauréau, B. Histoire littéraire du Maine. Paris, 1843-52. 4v.
37546.20.2 Hauréau, B. Histoire littéraire du Maine. Paris, 1870. 10v.
37546.24 Geslain, Théodomir. Littérature contemporaine en Provence. Paris, 1873.
37546.31 Lecouvet, F.F.I. Tournay littéraire. Gand, 1861.
37546.34 Vaschalde, Henry. Histoire des poètes du Vivarais. Paris, 1876.

37547 General literary history - Local - Regions and places of France - Others

37547.1.10 Daire, Louis François. Histoire littéraire de la ville d'Amien. Genève, 1970.
37547.2 Leclerc, Marc. Poètes angevins d'aujourd'hui. Paris, 1922.
37547.2.10 Société archéologique et historique de la Charente, Angoulême. Le trésor des pièces angoumoisines inédites ou rares. Paris, 1863-66. 2v.
37547.3 Gourcuff, O. de. Gens de Bretagne, histoire et littérature, prose et poésie. Paris, 1900.
37547.5 Halgan, Stéphane. Anthologie des poètes breton du XVIIe siècle. Nantes, 1884.
37547.6 Rousse, J. La poésie bretonne au [illegible]e siècle. Paris, 1895.
37547.6.3 Rousse, J. Poésies bretonnes: au pay[illegible] poèmes italiens et bretons. Paris, 1882.
37547.6.5 Chateau-Verdun, Marie de. Legendes bretonnes et autres récits. 2. éd. Lille, 1901.
37547.9 Matern, Erich. Die Bourgogne in den liedern ihrer Dichter. Saalfeld, 1928.
37547.9.10 Bouchard, Marcel. De l'humanisme à l'encyclopédie. Thèse. Paris, 1929.
37547.9.11 Bouchard, Marcel. De l'humanisme à l'encyclopédie. Paris, 1930.
37547.14 Colletet, Guillaume. Vies des poètes gascons. Paris, 1866.
37547.14.1 Colletet, Guillaume. Vies des poètes gascons. Genève, 1970.
37547.14.5 Cuzacq, René. Autour de l'école Gaston-Phébus (1897-1919). Bayonne, 1944.
37547.14.10 Bastit, Gaston. La Gascogne littéraire. Genève, 1970.
37547.14.15 Kirsch, Fritz Peter. Studien zur languedokischen und gaskognischen Literatur der Gegenwart. Wien, 1965.
37547.17 Puymaigre, Théodore de. Poètes et romanciers de la Lorraine. Paris, 1848.
37547.18 Calmon, Jean. Essai de bibliographie du département de lot. pt. 1-4. Cahors, 1934-47. 2v.
37547.18.1 Calmon, Jean. Essai de bibliographie du département de lot. Supplement. pt. 1-3. Cahors, 1960-
37547.20 Nicolas, Michel. Histoire littéraire de Nimes. Nimes, 1854. 3v.
37547.22 Paris, Gaston. La littérature Normande avant annexion. (912-1204). Paris, 1899.
37547.22.10 Baratte, L.H. Poètes normands. Paris, 1846.
37547.22.15 Vaneille, Jean Louis. Les patoisants bas-normands. Saint Lô, 1957-
37547.24 Dreux de Radier, Jean François. Bibliothèque...critique du Poitou. Paris, 1754. 5v.
37547.26 Dreux de Radier, Jean François. Bibliothèque...critique du Poitou. Niort, 1842-49. 3v.

37547 General literary history - Local - Regions and places of France - Others - cont.

37547.28 Pérouse, Gabriel. Causeries sur l'histoire littéraire de la Savoie. Chambery, 1934. 2v.
37547.30 Contades, Gérard de. Bagnoles. (Souvenirs littéraires). Alençon, 1892.
37547.37 Brun, Charles. Littératures provinciales. Paris, 1907.
37547.45 Droux, Georges. La chanson lyonnaise. Lyon, 1907.
37547.45.10 Grosclaude, P. La vie intellectuelle a Lyon dans la deuxième moitié du XVIIIe siècle. Thèse. Paris, 1933.
37547.50 Mandet, F. Histoire poétique et littéraire de l'ancien Velaz. Paris, 1842.
37547.58 Quirielle, Roger de. Bio-bibliographie des écrivains anciens du Bourbonnais. Moulins, 1899.
37547.60 Bouchard, Ernest. Poètes Bourbonnais. Moulins, 1870.
37547.65 Rome, Palozzo Primoli. Hommage à commerce. Roma, 1958.
37547.70 Barrière, P. La vie intellectuelle en Périgord, 1550-1800. Bordeaux, 1936.
37547.75 Trigon, Jean de. Portraits et médaillons morlaisiens Morlaix, France. Brest, 1943.
37547.80 Billy, A. Fontainebleau. Paris, 1949.
37547.85 Susini, Jean. Histoire littéraire des Cévennes. Thèse. Alès, 1949.
37547.90 Semmig, Herman. Kultur- und Litteraturgeschichte der Französischen Schweiz und Savoyens. Zürich, 1882.
37547.95 Goy, Paul. Les poètes patois de la ville de Crest-en-Dauphiné. Crest, 1958.
37547.100 Bordeaux, H. Portrait de la Savoie par ses écrivains. Thonon-les-Bains, 1960.
37547.101 Desayniard, J. L'Auvergne dans les lettres contemporaines. Saint-Félicien, 1943.
37547.103 Lissorgues, Marcellin. Les grands écrivains, écrivains d'Auvergne et du Velay. Aurillac, 1938.
37547.103.5 Larat, Jean. Panorama des lettres en Auvergne. Clermont, 1965.
37547.103.10 Bouvelot, Paule. L'Auvergne à travers la poésie auvergnate contemporaine. Aurillac, 1970?
37547.105 Suffran, Michel. Sur un génération perdue. Bordeaux, 1966.
37547.110 Longeon, Claude. Les écrivains foréziens du XVIe siècle. Saint-Étienne, 1970.

37548 General literary history - Local - Other countries of Europe

37548.01 Pamphlet box. Literary history. Swiss and Belgian. Local.
37548.3 Closset, François. Dictionnaire des littérateurs. Bruxelles, 1946.
37548.5 Senebier, Jean. Histoire littéraire de Genève. Genève, 1786. 3v.
37548.6 Monnier, Marc. Genève et ses poètes. Paris, 1874.
37548.8 Gaullieur, Eusèbe H. Études...littéraires de la Suisse française. Paris, 1856.
NEDL 37548.9 Godet, Philippe. Histoire littéraire de la Suisse Française. Paris, 1890.
37548.10 Godet, Philippe. Histoire littéraire de la Suisse Française. 2. éd. Paris, 1895.
37548.11 Rambert, Eugène. Écrivains nationaux. Geneva, 1874.
37548.13 Rossel, Virgile. Histoire littéraire de la Suisse romande. Geneva, 1891. 2v.
37548.15 Rambert, Eugène. Écrivains de la Suisse romande. Lausanne, 1889.
37548.16 Hasler, A. Les vaudois et le sentiment de la nature à l'époque préromantique et romantique. Thèse. Dijon, 1933.
37548.17 Gribble, Francis. Lake Geneva and its literary landmarks. Westminster, 1901.
37548.18 Gribble, Francis. Lake Geneva and its literary landmarks. Westminster, 1901.
37548.19 Bouvier, J.B. Essai sur l'histoire intellectuelle. (Du romantisme à Genève). Paris, 1930.
37548.20 Littératures de la Suisse. Paris, 1938.
37548.22 Ziégler, Henri de. La Suisse littéraire d'aujourd'hui. Lisboa, 1944.
37548.23 Humbert, Jean. La poésie au pays de Gruyère. Bienne, 1947.
37548.26 Charlier, Gustave. Les lettres françaises de Belgique. Bruxelles, 1938.
37548.26.2 Charlier, Gustave. Les lettres françaises de Belgique. Bruxelles, 1944.
37548.28 Thibaut, F. Marguerite d'Autriche et Jehan Lemaire de Belges. Paris, 1888.
37548.30 Lejeune-Dehousse, Rita. Histoire sommaire de la littérature Wallone. 2. éd. Bruxelles, 1942.
37548.32 Masoin, F. Histoire de la littérature française en Belgique de 1815 à 1830. Bruxelles, 1902.
37548.32.5 Dautrepont, G. Histoire illustrée de la littérature française en Belgique. Bruxelles, 1939.
37548.32.10F Charlier, Gustave. Histoire illustrée des lettres française de Belgique. Bruxelles, 1958.
37548.33 Liebrecht, Henri. Histoire illustrée de la littérature belge de langue française. 2. éd. Bruxelles, 1931.
37548.33.10 Nautet, Francis. Histoire des lettres Belges d'expression française. v.1-2. Bruxelles, 1892?
37548.35 Horrent, D. Écrivains belges d'aujourd'hui. 1. série. Bruxelles, 1904.
37548.36 Wilmotte, M. La culture française en Belgique. Paris, 1912.
37548.37 Gourmont, Remy de. La Belgique littéraire. 4. éd. Paris, 1915.
37548.37.5 Turquet-Milnes, G. Some modern Belgian writers. N.Y., 1917.
37548.38 Bithell, Jethro. Contemporary Belgian literature. London, 1915.
37548.38.6 Lazzeri, Gerolamo. Interpreti dell'anima Belga. Belogna, 1919.
37548.38.7 Berger, Lya. Les femmes poètes de la Belgique. Paris, 1925.
37548.38.9 Ridder, André de. La littérature flamande contemporaine. 1890-1923. Anvers, 1923.
37548.38.10 Hamelius, P. Introduction à la littérature française et flamande de Belgique. Bruxelles, 1921.
37548.38.15 Heumann, A. Le mouvement littéraire belge d'expression française. Paris, 1913.
37548.38.20 Gilles, M. Histoire des lettres françaises de Belgique des origines à nos jours. Bruxelles, 1922.
37548.38.25 Woodbridge, B.M. Le roman belge contemporain. Bruxelles, 1930.
37548.39 Courvoisier, A. Les lettres françaises en Alsace depuis la restauration. Strasbourg, 1877.
37548.39.5 Bever, A. van. Anthologie littéraire de l'Alsace et de la Lorraine. Paris, 1920.

37548 General literary history - Local - Other countries of Europe - cont.

37548.39.10 Bloch, Maurice. Femmes d'Alsace; souvenirs littéraires. Paris, 1896.
37548.52 Pamphlet vol. French literature in Boston. 8 pam.
37548.55 Cohen, Gustave. Écrivains français en Hollande. Thèse. Paris, 1920.
37548.55.2 Cohen, Gustave. Écrivains français en Hollande. Paris, 1920.
37548.65 Lebel, Roland. Histoire de la littérature coloniale en France. Paris, 1931.
37548.132 Matthews, A.J. La Wallonie, 1886-1892. N.Y., 1947.
37548.133.2 Galand, Guy. Les lettres françaises de Wallonie. 2. éd. Charleroi, 1962.
37548.135A Hanlet, C. Les écrivains belges contemporains de langue française. Liège, 1946- 2v.
37548.135B Hanlet, C. Les écrivains belges contemporains de langue française. Liège, 1946- 2v.
37548.137 Gille, Valère. La jeune Belgique au hasard des souvenirs. Bruxelles, 1943.
37548.140 Bibliographie nationale. Bruxelles, 1886-1910. 4v.
37548.145 Seyn, Eugene. Dictionnaire des écrivains belges. Bruges, 1930-31. 2v.
37548.155 Weber-Perret, M. Écrivains romands 1900-1950. Lausanne, 1951.
37548.160 Gilsone, Robert. Les influences Anglo-Saxonnes sur les lettres françaises de Belgique de 1850 à 1880. Bruxelles, 1953.
37548.165 Martinet, E. Portraits d'écrivains romands contemporains. 2. série. Neuchâtel, 1954.
37548.180 Desonay, Fernand. Cinquante ans de littérature Belge. Bruxelles, 1952.
37548.185 Mor, Antonio. Storia delle letterature del Belgio. Milano, 1958.
37548.200 Vanwelkenhuyzen, Gustave. Vocations littéraires. Genève, 1959.
37548.205 Congres national de littérature comparée. Les Flandres dans les mouvements romantique et symboliste. Paris, 1958.
37548.210 Cuzacq, René. L'époque contemporaine. Mont-de-Marsan, 1950.
37548.215 Lebel, Roland. Études de littérature coloniale. Paris, 1928.
37548.220 Société de belles-lettres de Lausanne. Belles lettres de Lausanne. Lausanne, 1960.
37548.221 Guiette, Robert. Écrivains français de Belgique au XIXe siècle. Paris, 1963.
37548.222 Nuffel, Roberto van. Poètes et polémistes: C. Beck. Bruxelles, 1961.
37548.223 Tougas, Gérard. Littérature romande et culture française. Paris, 1963.
37548.224 Mallinson, Vernon. Modern Belgian literature. 1830-1960. London, 1966.
37548.225 Andreev, Leonid G. Sto let bel'giiskoi literatury. Moskva, 1967.
37548.228 Huysmans, Camile. Quatre types: Le Renard et Vlenspiegel. Anvers, 1966.
37548.230 Gsteiger, Manfred. Westwind. Bern, 1968.
37548.232 Congrès national des oeuvres intellectuelles de langue française, 1st,Brussels, 1910. Premier congrès national des oeuvres intellectuelles de langue française. Huy, 1911.
37548.234 Delmelle, Joseph. Panorama littéraire du Luxembourg. Vieux-Virton, 1970.

37551 History of special forms - Folios [Discontinued]

V37551.2 Beauchamps, M. de. Recherches sur les théâtres de France. Paris, 1735.
37551.10 Tougard, A. L'Hellénisme dans les écrivains du Moyen-Age. Paris, 1886.
37551.11 Fremy, E. L'Académie des Derniers Valois. Paris, 1887.
37551.30 Franke. Quelles sont les différences. n.p., n.d.
37551.31 Hecq, Gaëtan. Le lai, le virelai, le rondeau. Bruxelles, 1892.
37551.33 Brisson, J. Les grands journaux de France. Paris, 1862.
37551.35 Kerviler, René. Abel Servien. Le Mans, 1877. 4 pam.
37551.36 Kerviler, René. La Bretagne a l'Academie Française. Paris, 1879.
37551.36.2 Kerviler, René. Bretagne à l'Academie Française. Paris, 1889.
37551.37 Kerviler, René. Guillaume Bautru. Paris, 1876.
37551.38 Kerviler, René. J.F.P. Lefebvre de Caumartin. Vannes, 1876.
37551.39 Kerviler, René. J. Ogier de Gombauld 1570-1666. Paris, 1876.
37551.40 Kerviler, René. Marin le Roy sieur de Gomberville, 1600-1674. Paris, 1876.
37551.41 Kerviler, René. Jean de Silhou. Paris, 1876.
37551.42 Kerviler, René. Jean de Sirmond 1589-1649. Paris, 1876.
37551.43 Kerviler, René. Marin et Pierre Cureau de la chambre. Le Mans, 1877.
37551.50 Franqueville, Charles. Le premier siècle de l'Institut de France 1795-1895. Paris, 1895. 2v.
37551.52 Asse, Eugène. L'Académie Française. Paris, n.d.
37551.58 Titon du Tillet, E. Le Parnasse François. Paris, 1732. 2v.
37551.61 Paris, G. La poésie française au 15 siècle. Paris, 1886.
37551.65 Beaujon, Georges. Contribution à l'histoire de la poésie lyrique française contemporaine. Bâle, 1900.
37551.66 Dubedout, E. Le sentiment chrétien dans la poésie romantique. Paris, 1901.
37551.67 Mendès, Catulle. Rapport...sur le mouvement poétique français de 1867 à 1900. Paris, 1902.
37551.70 Vaganay, H. Bibliographie des sonnets françaises du XIXe siècle. Louvain, 1899.

37555 History of special forms - Poetry

37555.2 Pamphlet box. History of French poetry from 1500.
37555.3 Catalogue de...Viollet le duc. Paris, 1843.
37555.4 Catalogue de...Viollet, chansons, fabliaux. Paris, 1847.
Htn 37555.5* Recueil de l'origine de la langue et poésie française. Paris, 1581.
37555.5.4 Fauchet, C. Recueil de l'origine de la langue et poésie française. Thèse. Paris, 1938.
37555.5.5 Fauchet, C. Recueil de l'origine de la langue et poésie française. Paris, 1938.
37555.5.6 Espèner-Scott, J.G. (Mrs.). Claude Fauchet; sa vie, son oeuvre. Thèse. Paris, 1938.
37555.6 Desfeuilles, Paul. Dictionnaire de rimes. Paris, 1925.

37555 History of special forms - Poetry - cont.

37555.7 Mervesin, Joseph. Histoire de la poésie française. Paris, 1706.
37555.9 Massieu, Guillaume. Histoire de la poésie française. Paris, 1739.
37555.11 Rémond de St. Mard, Toussaint. Réfléxions sur la poésie. Photoreproduction. La Haye, 1734.
37555.11.5 Gailloro, G.H. Poétique française à l'usage des dames. Paris, 1749. 2v.
37555.12 Ritter, Otto. Die Geschichte des französischen Balladenformen. Halle, 1914.
37555.12.10 Papin, M.D. La ballade. Grenoble, 1934.
37555.13 Lespy, V. Notes pour l'histoire de la chanson. Paris, 1861.
37555.13.5 Sévrette, Gaston. Les vieilles chansons des pays de France. Paris, 1922.
37555.14 Malherbe, Jules. Conférence sur la chanson. Caen, 1868.
37555.15 Winegarten, R. French lyric poetry. Manchester, 1954.
37555.16 Veyrières, Louis de. Monographie du sonnet. Paris, 1869. 2v.
37555.17 Gaudin, Paul. Du Rondeau, du Triolet, du Sonnet. Paris, 1870.
37555.18 Jasinski, Max. Histoire du sonnet en France. Douai, 1903.
37555.18.2 Jasinski, Max. Histoire du sonnet en France. Genève, 1970.
37555.18.5 Olmsted, E.W. The sonnet in French literature. Ithaca, 1897.
37555.18.9 Martonne, Alfred de. Le sonnet dans midi de la France. Aix, 1894.
Htn 37555.19* Lemerre, Alphonse. Livre des ballades. Paris, 1876.
37555.20 Schlüter, Joseph. Die Französische Kriegs- und Revanche-Dichtung. Heilbronn, 1878.
37555.20.9 Langfors, Arthur. Les incipit des poèmes français. Paris, 1917.
37555.20.15 Lachèvre, F. Bibliographie des recueils collectifs de poésies du XVI siècle. Paris, 1922.
37555.21 Guy, H. Histoire de la poésie française au XVIe siècle. Paris, 1910. 2v.
37555.22 Besant, Walter. Studies in early French poetry. London, 1868.
37555.22.5 Besant, Walter. Studies in early French poetry. Boston, 1877.
37555.23 Sudre, Léopold. Publii Ovidii Nasonis Metamorphoseon Libros. Paris, 1893.
37555.24 Lefèvre, Frédéric. La jeune poésie française. Paris, 1918.
37555.25 Strobel, Adam W. Französische Volksdichter. Baden, 1846.
37555.27.5 Pfuhl, H. Untersuchungen ueber die Roudeaux und Virelais des XIV und XV Jahrhunderts. Regimonti, 1887.
37555.28 Madeleine, J. Quelques poètes Français des XVIe et XVIIe siècles à Fontainebleau. Fontainebleau, 1900.
37555.29 Neff, T.L. La satire des femmes dans la poésie lyrique française du Moyen Âge. Paris, 1900.
37555.29.9 Schwarzkopf, F. Coulanges, Chanlien und La Fare. Leipzig, 1908.
37555.29.12 Hensel W. Die Vögel in der provenzalischen und nordfranzösischen Lyrik des Mittelalters. Erlangen, 1908.
37555.31 Lenient, Charles. La poésie patriotique en France dans les temps modernes. Paris, 1894. 2v.
37555.31.50 Faguet, Émile. Histoire de la poésie française de la renaissance au romantisme. Paris, 1923-26. 11v.
37555.32 Loise, Ferdinand. Histoire de la poésie...en France. Paris, 1888.
37555.33 Lorel, Charles. Bibliothèque française. Paris, 1664.
37555.34 Géruzez, Eugène. Cours d'éloquence française. Paris, 1836.
37555.35 Aubertin, Charles. L'éloquence politique et parlementaire avant 1789. Paris, 1882.
37555.36 Scudéry, M. de. De la poésie française jusqu'à Henry Quatrième. Paris, 1907.
37555.37 Valbel, H. Les chansonniers et les cabarets artistiques. Paris, n.d.
37555.38 Potez, H. L'élégie en France avant le romantisme. Paris, 1897.
37555.38.5 Schlaeger, G. Studien über das Tagelied. Jena, 1895.
37555.39 Zimmermann, O. Die Totenklage in den altfranzösischen Chansons de Geste. Berlin, 1899.
37555.40 Belloc, Hilaire. Avril: being essays on the poetry of the French renaissance. London, 1904.
37555.40.10 Belloc, Hilaire. Avril, being essays on the poetry of the French renaissance. London, 1945.
37555.41 Thurau, G. Der Refrain in der französischen Chanson. Berlin, 1901.
37555.42 Rosières, Raoul. Recherches sur la poésie contemporaine. Paris, 1896.
37555.43 Vigié-Lecocq, E. La poésie contemporaine, 1884-1896. Paris, 1896.
37555.44 Jouffret, M. De Hugo à Mistral. Leipzig, 1902.
37555.45 Doumic, R. La poésie lyrique en France au dix-neuvième siècle. Montréal, 1898.
37555.47 Visau, T. de. L'attitude du lyrisme contemporain. Paris, 1911.
37555.48A Légouis, Émile. Défense de la poésie française a l'usage des lectures anglaises. Londres, 1912.
37555.48B Légouis, Émile. Defense de la poésie française a l'usage des lectures anglaises. Londres, 1912.
37555.48C Légouis, Émile. Defense de la poésie française a l'usage des lectures anglaises. Londres, 1912.
37555.49 Schaffer, A. Parnassus in France; currents and cross-currents in nineteenth-century French lyric poetry. Austin, 1929.
37555.49.10 Schaffer, A. The genres of Parnassian poetry. Baltimore, Md., 1944.
NEDL 37555.50 Robert, Pierre. Les poètes du XIXe siècle. Période romantique. Paris, 1899.
37555.52 Barat, E. Le style poétique et la révolution romantique. Paris, 1904.
37555.52.5 Clouard, H. La poésie française moderne des romantiques à nos jours. Paris, 1924.
37555.52.12 Raymond, Marcel. De Baudelaire au surréalisme. Paris, 1933.
37555.52.15 Raymond, Marcel. De Baudelaire au surréalisme. Paris, 1947.
37555.52.17 Raymond, Marcel. De Baudelaire au surréalisme. Paris, 1952.
37555.52.20 Raymond, Marcel. From Baudelaire to surrealism. N.Y., 1950.

37555 History of special forms - Poetry - cont.

37555.52.22 Raymond, Marcel. From Baudelaire to surrealism. London, 1970.
37555.53 Gonon, Jean F. Histoire de chanson Stephanoise et Forézienne. St. Étienne, 1906.
NEDL 37555.54 Levrault, L. Le genre pastoral. Paris, 1914.
37555.55 Levrault, L. L'épopée (Évolution du genre). Paris, 1900.
37555.55.10 Levrault, L. La poésie lyrique des origines. Paris, 193-.
37555.56 Davidson, F.J.A. Ueber den Ursprung und die Geschichte der Französischen Ballade. Halle, 1900.
37555.57 Hecq, Gaëtan. La ballade et ses dérivés. Bruxelles, 1891.
37555.60 Théret, Auguste. Littérature du Berry; Poésie XVIe, XVIIe et XVIIIe siècles. Paris, 1899.
37555.61 Bercy, L. de. Montmartre et ses chansons. Paris, 1902.
37555.62 Beaunier, A. La poésie nouvelle. Paris, 1902.
X Cg 37555.65 Bailey, John C. The claims of French poetry. London, 1907.
37555.67 Miomandre, F. Figures d'hier et d'aujourd'hui. Paris, 1911.
37555.68 Moréas, Jean. Réflexions sur quelques poètes. Paris, 1912.
37555.70 Ernest-Charles, J. Théâtre des poètes 1850-1910. Paris, n.d.
37555.72 Séché, A. Les caractères de la poésie contemporaine. Paris, 1913.
37555.73 Bellessort, André. Sur les grands chemins de la poésie classique. Paris, 1914.
37555.74 Brereton, G. An introduction to the French poets. London, 1956.
37555.75 Lowell, Amy. Six French poets, studies in contemporary literature. N.Y., 1915.
37555.76 Rudmose-Brown, T. French literary studies. Dublin, 1917.
37555.77 Fusil, C.A. La poésie scientifique. Thèse. Paris, 1918.
37555.78 Chaix, Marie-Antoinette. La correspondance des arts dans la poésie contemporaine. Paris, 1919.
37555.79 Arreat, Lucien. Nos poètes et la pensée de leur temps. Paris, 1920.
37555.80 Chamard, H. Les origines de la poésie française de la renaissance. Photoreproduction. Paris, 1920.
37555.81 Thibaut de Maisières, Maury. Les poèmes inspirés du début de la genèse a l'époque de la renaissance. Louvain, 1931.
37555.81.10 Berger, Bruno. Vers rapportés. Karlsruhe, 1930.
37555.82 Charbonnier, F. La poésie française et les guerres de religion. Thèse. Paris, 1920.
37555.83 Charbonnier, F. La poésie française et les guerres de religion (1560-1574). Paris, 1919.
37555.83.2 Charbonnier, F. La poésie française et les guerres de religion (1560-1574). Genève, 1970.
37555.85 Noblet, Albert. La poésie lyrique en France des origines à 1914. Londres, 1924.
37555.87 Pardo Bazan, E. El lirismo en la poesia francesca. Madrid, 1922?
37555.89 Ghil, René. La tradition de poésie scientifique. Paris, 1920.
37555.89.10 Ghil, René. Oeuvre. En méthode à l'oeuvre. Thèse. Paris, 1904.
37555.91 Hytier, Jean. Les téchniques modernes du vers français. Paris, 1923.
37555.93 Hytier, Jean. Le plaisir poétique: étude de psychologie. Thèse. Paris, 1923.
37555.95 Liefde, C.L. de. Le Saint-Simonisme dans la poésie française entre 1825 et 1865. Haarlem, 1927.
37555.99 Banville, T. de. Petit traité de poésie française. Paris, 1881.
37555.100 Fobler, A. Vom Französischen Versbau alter und neuer Zeit. Leipzig, 1883.
37555.102 Fort, Paul. Histoire de la poésie française depuis 1850. Paris, 1926.
37555.106 Cameron, Margaret M. L'influence des saisons de Thomson sur la poésie déscriptive en France (1759-1810). Thèse. Paris, 1927.
37555.106.5 Cameron, Margaret M. L'influence des saisons de Thomson sur la poésie déscriptive en France (1759-1810). Paris, 1927.
37555.109 Duhamel, G. Les poètes et la poésie 1912-1914. Paris, 1922.
37555.115 Smith, Nina. L'accord de la science et de la poésie dans la seconde moitié du XIXe siècle. Thèse. Ligugé, 1928.
37555.120 Anzalone, Ernesto. Su la poesia satirica in Francia e in Italia nel secolo XVI. Catania, 1905.
37555.123 Muller, A. La poésie religieuse catholique de Marot à Malherbe. Thèse. Paris, 1950.
37555.123.2 Muller, A. La poésie religieuse catholique de Marot à Malherbe. Paris, 1950.
37555.125 Vittoz, René. Essai sur les conditions de la poésie pure. Paris, 1929.
37555.127 Stewart, Jean. Poetry in France and England. London, 1931.
37555.129 Wann, Harry Vincent. Tradition of the homeric simile in 18th century French poetry. Diss. Terre Haute, Ind., 1931.
37555.131 Fontains, A. Tableau de la poésie française d'aujourd'hui. Paris, 1931.
37555.133 Mönch, Walter. Frankreichs Dichtung von der Renaissance zur Gegenwart im Spiegel geistesgeschichtlicher Probleme. Berlin, 1933.
37555.135 Strauss, L. Uebersetzungen italienischer Dichtwerke in Frankreich zwischen 1789 und 1820. Inaug. Diss. Stuttgart, 1932.
37555.137 Harrison, Ruth. An approach to French poetry. London, 1935.
37555.139 Patterson, W.F. Three centuries of French poetic theory 1328-1630. pt.1-4. Ann Arbor, 1935. 2v.
37555.140 Bejot, Amédée. L'évolution poétique en France. Paris, 1933.
37555.142 Fraenkel, C. Studien zur sozialen Arbeiterlyrik in Frankreich von Beginn des 19. Jahrhundert bis zum Ausbruch des Weltkrieges. Inaug. Diss. Breslau, 1935.
37555.144 Gregh, F. Portrait de la poésie française au XXe siècle. Paris, 1936.
37555.146 Beer, Guillaume (Mme.). La sensibilité dans la poésie française contemporaine, 1885-1912. Paris, 1912.
37555.148 Nanteuil, Jacques. L'inquiétude religieuse et les poètes d'aujourd'hui. Paris, 1925.
37555.149 Carco, Francis. La poésie. Paris, 1919.
37555.150 Charpentier, J. L'évolution de la poésie lyrique. Paris, 1930.
37555.152 Orth, Hildegard. Der Todesgedanke in der französischen Lyrik des 19. Jahrhunderts. Inaug. Diss. Ochsenfurt, 1937.

Classified Listing

37555 **History of special forms - Poetry - cont.**

37555.153 Citoleux, M. La voie royale de la poésie française. Paris, 1935.
37555.155 Cazamian, L. Retour d'un Anglicisant à la poésie française. Oxford, 1938.
37555.156 Hunt, Herbert J. The epic in 19th century France. Oxford, 1941.
37555.157A Noulet, E. Études littéraires. Mexique, 1944.
37555.157B Noulet, E. Études littéraires. Mexique, 1944.
37555.158 Lalou, René. Les étapes de la poésie française. 1. éd. Paris, 1943.
37555.159 Poulaille, Henry. La fleur des chansons d'amour. Paris, 1943.
37555.160 Krieser, Jules. Les ascendances romantiques du surnaturalisme contemporain. Thèse. Paris, 1942.
37555.161 Maria Consolato, mother. Christ in the poetry of Lamartine, Vigny, Hugo and Musset. Bryn Maur, 1947.
37555.165A Lote, Georges. Histoire du vers français. Paris, 1949-51. 2v.
37555.165B Lote, Georges. Histoire du vers français. v.2. Paris, 1949-51.
37555.170 Camagna, E.M. Le epopee francesi. Messina, 1948.
37555.175 Jones, Percy Mansel. The background of modern French poetry. Cambridge, Eng., 1951.
37555.175.1 Jones, Percy Mansell. The background of modern French poetry. Cambridge, 1968.
37555.180 Chisholm, A.R. Towards Hérodiade. Melbourne, 1934.
37555.190A Vivier, Robert. Et la poésie fut langage. Bruxelles, 1954.
37555.190B Vivier, Robert. Et la poésie fut langage. Bruxelles, 1954.
37555.195 Sayce, R.A. The French biblical epic in the seventeenth century. Oxford, 1955.
37555.200 Carter, M.E. The role of the symbol in French romantic poetry. Washington, 1946.
37555.200.10 Glauser, Alfred Charles. Le poème-symbole de Scène à Valéry. Paris, 1967.
37555.201 Lalou, R. Histoire de la poésie française. 7. éd. Paris, 1963.
37555.202 Nadal, Octave. A mésure haute. Paris, 1964.
37555.205 Perticucci Bernardini, Ada. Dal simbolismo all'esistenzialismo. Roma, 1955.
37555.208 Kastner, L.E. History of French versification. Oxford, 1903.
37555.209 Ten Brink, B. Coniectanea in Historiam. Bonnae, 1865.
37555.210 Zschalig, H. Die Verslehren von Fabri, du Pont...Alteren Geschichte der franz Poetik. Leipzig, 1884.
37555.211 Thieme, Hugo P. Essai sur l'histoire du vers français. Paris, 1916.
37555.212 Suberville, Jean. Histoire et théorie de la versification française. 2. éd. Paris, 1946.
37555.212.2 Suberville, Jean. Histoire et théorie de la versification française. Paris, 1956.
37555.216 Souza, Robert de. Du rythme en français. Paris, 1912.
37555.221 Les études poétiques. Paris. 1929+ 8v.
37555.226 Pellissier, Georges. Traité théorique et historique de versification française. 2. éd. Paris, 1936?
37555.228 Verrier, Paul. Le vers français. Paris, 1931-32. 3v.
37555.230 Formont, M. Le vers français. Paris, 1937.
37555.235 Henriot, Émile. De Turold à André Chenier. Lyon, 1944.
37555.240 Henriot, Émile. De Lamartine à Valéry. Lyon, 1946.
37555.245 Le Hir, Yves. Esthétique et structure du vers français. Paris, 1956.
37555.250 Nais, Hélène. Les animaux dans la poésie française de la Renaissance. Paris, 1961.
37555.255 Velikovskii, S.Iz. Poety frantsuzkikh revoliutsii 1789-1898. Moskva, 1963.
37555.257 Danilin, Iu. Iv. Poety Iul'skoi revoliutsii. Moskva, 1935.
37555.300.1 Bonaparte, Louis. Essai sur la versification. v.1-2. Rome, 1825.
37555.300.2 Schnatter, J. Cours de versification française. 2. éd. Berlin, 1877.
37555.300.5 Morier, H. Dictionnaire de poétique et de rhétorique. Paris, 1961.
37555.300.10 Mourgues, M. Traité de la poésie française. Paris, 1724.
37555.300.15 Dresse, Paul. Plaisir au vers; technique et rêve. Paris, 1965.
37555.301 Tobler, A. Vom Französischen Versbau alter und neuer Zeit. Leipzig, 1880.
37555.301.2 Tobler, A. Vom Französischen Versbau alter und neuer Zeit. 3. Aufl. Leipzig, 1894.
37555.301.3 Tobler, A. Vom Französischen Versbau alter und neuer Zeit. 4. Aufl. Leipzig, 1903.
37555.301.5 Tobler, A. Vom Französischen Versbau alter und neuer Zeit. 5. Aufl. Leipzig, 1910.
37555.301.11 Tobler, A. Le vers français ancien et moderne. Paris, 1885.
37555.301.12 Monteverdi, Angelo. L'epopea francese. Roma, 1947.
37555.302.2 Weigand, G. Traité de versification française. Bromberg, 1863.
37555.302.3 Weigand, G. Traité de versification française. Bromberg, 1871.
37555.303 Saran, F. Der Rhythmus der Französischen Verses. Halle, 1904.
37555.304 La Grasserie, R. de la. Des principes scientifiques de la versification française. Paris, 1900.
37555.305.5A Grammont, M. Petit traité de versification française. Paris, 1962.
37555.305.5B Grammont, M. Petit traité de versification française. Paris, 1962.
37555.305.6 Grammont, M. Le vers français ses moyen d'éxpression son harmonie. Paris, 1904.
37555.305.7 Grammont, M. Le vers français ses moyen d'éxpression son harmonie. Paris, 1913.
37555.305.12 Grammont, M. Le vers français; ses moyens d'éxpression son harmonie. 4. éd. Paris, 1937.
37555.306 Souza, R. de. Le rythme poétique. Paris, 1892.
37555.307 Foth, K. Die Französische Metrik. Berlin, 1879.
37555.308 Nebout, P. Gallici Versus metrica ratio facultati. Paris, 1897.
37555.309 Lubarsch, E.O. Französische Verslehre. Berlin, 1879.
37555.310 Gosset, A. Manual of French prosody...use of Engish students. London, 1884.
37555.311 Landry, E. La théorie du rythme et le rythme du français déclamé. Paris, 1911.
37555.312 Sully, R.F.A. Réfléxions sur l'art des vers. Paris, 1892.

37555 **History of special forms - Poetry - cont.**

37555.313 Tisseur, C. Modestes observations sur l'art de versifier. Lyon, 1893.
37555.314 Crouslé, L. Éléments de versification française. Paris, 1891.
Htn 37555.314.25* Sebillet, T. Art poétique français. Lyon, 1556.
37555.315 Sebillet, T. Art poétique françoys. Paris, 1910.
37555.315.2 Sebillet, T. Art poétique françoys. Paris, 1910.
37555.315.5 Lukin, Erich. Du Bellay's Deffence...in ihrem Verhältnis zu Sebillet's Art poetique. Inaug. Diss. Oldenburg, 1913.
37555.315.8 Noo, Hendrik de. Thomas Sebillet. Proefschrift. Utrecht, 1927.
37555.316 Barneville, P. de. Le rythme dans la poésie française. Paris, 1898.
37555.317 Boissière, G. Notions de versification française. Paris, 1893.
37555.318 Le Goffie, C. Nouveau traité de versification française. Paris, 1890.
37555.319 Becq de Fouquières, L. Traité général de versification française. Paris, 1879.
37555.320 Della Rocca de Vergalo, N.A. La poétique nouvelle. 2. éd. Paris, 1880.
37555.321.2 Quicherat, L. Traité de versification française. 2. éd. Paris, 1850.
37555.322 Guillaume, Juleo. Le vers français et les prosodies modernes. Bruxelles, 1898.
37555.323 Gladow, J. Vom französischen Versbau neuerer Zeit. Berlin, 1906.
37555.324 Bock, Moriz. Über Vergleiche...bei einigen altfranzösischen Dichtern. Linz, 1901.
37555.324.3 Bock, Moriz. Vergleich und Gleichnisse. n.p., n.d. 2 pam.
37555.325.3 Bibesco, Alex. La question du vers français. Paris, 1896.
37555.326 Ducondut, J.A. Essai de rhythmique française. Paris, 1856.
37555.327.2 Quitard, Pierre M. Dictionnaire des rimes. 7. éd. Paris, 18- ?
37555.329 Martinon, P. Dictionnaire méthodique...des rimes françaises. 6. éd. Paris, 1915.
37555.332 Suchier, W. Französische Verslehre auf historischer Grundlage. Tübingen, 1952.
37555.332.2 Suchier, W. Französische Verslehre auf historischer Grundlage. 2. Aufl. Tübingen, 1963.
37555.335 Dorchain, Auguste. L'art des vers. Paris, 1919.
37555.338 Spoerri, Theophil. Französische Metrik. München, 1929.
37555.340 Limbosch, R. Le principe et l'évolution du vers français. Bruxelles, 1923-24. 3 pam.
37555.345 Devel, Félix. Le quatrain. Paris, 1871.
37555.350 Olovsson, Halvar. Étude sur les rimes de trois poétes romantiques. Thèse. Lund, 1924.
37555.355 Fabre d'Olivet, A. Un manuscrit inédit de Fabre d'Olivet. Paris, 192-?
37555.365 Derème, Tristan. Guirlande pour deux vers de Gérard de Neroal. Saint-Félicien-en-Vivarais, 1926.
37555.370 Romains, Jules. Petit traité de versification. 9. éd. Paris, 1924.
37555.372 Citron, Pierre. La poésie de Paris dans la littérature française de Rousseau à Baudelaire. Paris, 1961. 2v.
37555.375 Royère, Jean. Le musicisme; Boileau, La Fontaine, Baudelaire. Paris, 1929.
37555.385A Clarke, Charles C. Concerning French verse. New Haven, 1922.
37555.385B Clarke, Charles C. Concerning French verse. New Haven, 1922.
37555.390 Eigeldinger, Marc. Le dynamisme de l'image dans la poésie française. Neuchâtel, 1943.
37555.392 Fournet, Charles. Poètes romantiques. Genève, 1962.
37555.395 Gutmann, René A. Introduction à la lecture des poètes français. Paris, 1946.
37555.398 Verhesen, F. Voies et voix de la poésie française contemporaine. Bruxelles, 1960.
37555.399 Goffin, Robert. Fil d'Ariane pour la poésie. Paris, 1964.
37555.500 Martinon, Philippe. Les Strophes, étude historique et critique. Paris, 1911.
37555.500.2 Martinon, Philippe. Les strophes. Paris, 1912.
37555.500.10 Diéguez, Manuel de. Essai sur l'avenir poétique de Dieu. Paris, 1965.
37555.501 Mornet, Daniel. L'alexandrin français...XVIIIe siècle. Toulouse, 1907.
37555.502.2F Lote, Georges. L'alexandrin d'après la phonétique expérimentale. 2. éd. Paris, 1913. 3v.
37555.504 Martin, Eugène-Louis. Les symétries du français littéraire. Thèse. Paris, 1924.
37555.504.2 Martin, Eugène-Louis. Les symétries du français littéraire. Thèse. Paris, 1924.
37555.510 Hudson, Margaret E. The juxtaposition of accents at the rime in French versification. Thesis. Philadelphia, 1927.
37555.512 Rudrauf, L. Rime et sex. Tartu, 1936.
37555.513 Janik, Dieter. Geschichte der Ode und der "Stances" von Ronsard bis Boileau. Bad Homburg, 1968.
37555.514 Verrier, Paul. L'isochronisme dans le vers français. Paris, 1912.
37555.515 Kahn, Gustave. Le vers libre. 3. éd. Paris, 1912.
37555.517 Morier, Henri. Le rythme du vers libre symboliste. Genève, 1943-44. 3v.
37555.518 Gibson, R.D.D. Modern French poets on poetry. Cambridge, Eng., 1961.
37555.519 Florian Parmentier, Ernest. Essai de codification du vers libre. Paris, 192-?
37555.520 Becker, A. Zur Geschichte der Vers Libres. Halle, 1888.
37555.521 Dondo, M.M. Vers libre, a logical development of France verse. Thesis. Paris, 1922.
37555.523 Isou, Isidore. Introduction à une nouvelle poésie. Paris, 1947.
37555.525 Bougier, Marie. Essai sur la renaissance de la poésie catholique. Thèse. Sète, 1942.
37555.527 Dupouy, A. La poésie de la mer. Paris, 1947.
37555.529 Hatzfeld, H. Die französische Renaissance-Lyrik. München, 1924.
37555.530 Thieme, H.P. The technique of the French Alexandrine. n.p., 1898.
37555.531 Trüger, E. Geschichte der Alexandriners. Leipzig, 1889.
37555.532 Stengel, E. Verwendung, Bau und Auwendung der romanischen Zehn-Silbners. Frankfurt, 1887.
37555.533 Lote, George. L'Alexandrin Français d'après la phonetique expérimental. Paris, 1913.

Classified Listing

37555 History of special forms - Poetry - cont.

37555.535A Gilman, Margaret. The idea of poetry in France. Cambridge, 1958.
37555.535B Gilman, Margaret. The idea of poetry in France. Cambridge, 1958.
37555.536A Balakian, Anna E. Surrealism. N.Y., 1959.
37555.536B Balakian, Anna E. Surrealism. N.Y., 1959.
37555.536.1 Balakian, Anna E. Surrealism. N.Y., 1970.
37555.538 Décaudin, M. La crise des valeurs symbolistes. Toulouse, 1960.
37555.539 Weber, Jean Paul. Genèse de l'oeuvre poétique. Paris, 1960.
37555.540 Jouve, P.J. Apologie du poète. Paris, 1947.
37555.542 Revol, Enrique L. Pensamiento arcaico y poesía moderna. Córdoba, 1960.
37555.545 Parent, Monique. Saint-John Perse et quelques devanciers. Paris, 1960.
37555.547 Krafft, Jacques Gustily. Poésie, corps et âme. Paris, 1961.
37555.550 Chatelain, Henri. Recherches sur le vers français au XVe siècle. Paris, 1908.
37555.553 Pfrommer, Walter. Grundzüge der Strophenentwicklung in der französischen Lyrik vom Baudelaire zu Apollinaire. Tübingen, 1963.
37555.554 Dujardin, Édouard. Les premiers poètes du vers libre. Paris, 1922.
37555.556 Pellissier, Georges. De sexti decimi saeculi in Francia artibus poeticis. Paris, 1882.
37555.558 Wilson, Dudley Butler. Descriptive poetry in France from Blason to Baroque. N.Y., 1967.
37555.560 Fuster, Charles. Les poètes du clocher. Paris, 1889.
37555.565.2 Scollen, Christine M. The birth of the elegy in France, 1500-1550. Genève, 1967.
37555.568 Cave, Terence Christopher. Devotional poetry in France 1570-1613. London, 1969.
37555.570 Shapley, C.S. Studies in French poetry of the fifteenth century. The Hague, 1970.
37555.575 Müller, Oskar. Die Technik des romantischen Verses. Berlin, 1901.
37555.615 Möllman, J. Der Homonyme Reim im Französischen. Münster, 1896.
37555.616 Johannesson, Fritz. Zur Lehre vom französischen Reim. Berlin, 1896. 2v.
37555.617 Wentzel, Julius. Uber den Reim in der neueren französischen Dichtung. Borsdorf, 1907.
37555.645.2 Ackermann, Paul. Traité de l'accent...Versification. 2. éd. Paris, 1843.
37555.647 Musser, Frederic O. Strange clamor; a guide to the critical reading of French poetry. Detroit, 1965.
37555.650 La Grasserie, Raoul de. De la césure. Vannes, 1891.
37555.655 Cellier, Léon. L'épopée romantique. Paris, 1954.
37555.660 Landais, Napoléon. Dictionnaire des rimes françaises. Paris, 1869.
37555.665 Sonet, Jean. Repertoire d'incipit des prières en ancien français. Genève, 1956.
37555.670 Béguin, Albert. Poésie de la présence de chrétien de Troyes à Pierre Emmanuel. Neuchâtel, 1957.
37555.675 Schossig, Alfred. Der Ursprung der Altfranzösischen Lyrik. Halle, 1957.
37555.680 Klemperer, V. Moderne französische Lyrik. Berlin, 1957.
37555.685 Brée, Germaine. French poetry. N.Y., 1959.
37555.690 Huguenin, Daniel. Poésie et monde humain. Saint-Étienne, 1960.
37555.695 Porter, Lambert C. La fatrasie et le fatras. Genève, 1960.
37555.700 Gregh, Fernand. Portrait de la poésie moderne de Rimbaud et Valéry. Paris, 1939.
37555.705 Jelínek, H. Podobizny básníků sladké Francie. Praha, 1946.
37555.710 Sauvage, Marcel. Poésie du temps. Marseille, 1926.
37555.715 Grubbs, H.A. Introduction à la poésie française. Boston, 1962.
37555.716 Chalons, Vincent. Règles de la poésie française. Paris, 1916.
37555.717 Mazaleyrat, J. Pour une étude rythmique du vers français moderne; notes bibliographiques. Paris, 1963.
37555.718 Voss, D. Die Majuskel bie französischen Lyrikern des 19. Jahrhunderts. Bonn, 1963.
37555.719 Clancier, G.E. De Chénier à Baudelaire. Paris, 1963.
37555.720 Bays, Gwendelyn. The Orphic vision. Lincoln, 1964.
37555.721 Gutmann, René A. Introduction à la lecture des poètes français. Paris, 1961.
37555.722 Belaval, Yvon. Poèmes d'aujourd'hui. Paris, 1964.
37555.723 Fukui, Y. Raffinement précieux dans la poésie française du XVIIe siècle. Paris, 1964.
37555.724 Elwert, Wilhelm Theodor. Traité de versification française des origines a nos jours. Paris, 1965.
37555.724.7 Elwert, Wilhelm Theodor. Französische Metrik. 2. Aufl. München, n.d.
37555.725 Mourgues, Odette de. An anthology of French 17th century lyric poetry. London, 1966.
37555.726 Cohen, Jean. Structure du langage poétique. Paris, 1966.
37555.727 Burucoa, Christiane. D'autres horribles travailleurs. Millau, 1966.
37555.728 Finch, Robert. The sixth sense. Toronto, 1966.
37555.730 Gibaudan, René. La lyre mystérieuse: Gérard de Nerval, Aloysius Bertrand, Maurice de Guérin, Theophile Gautier. Paris, 1965.
37555.732 Hercourt, Jean. Éléments d'une poétique. Genève, 1964.
37555.735 Jauss, Hans Robert. Genèse de la poésie allegorique française au Moyen Âge de 1180 à 1240. Heidelberg, 1962.
37555.737 Cattaui, Georges. Orphisme et prophétie chez les poètes français 1850-1950. Paris, 1965.
37555.740 Le vers français au 20e siècle, colloque organisé par le centre de philologie...de l'Université de Strasbourg du 3 mai au 6 mai 1966. Paris, 1967.
37555.742 Braet, Herman. L'accueil fait au symbolisme en Belgique 1885-1900. Bruxelles, 1967.
37555.744 Le mysticisme dans la poésie française contemporaine. Anthologie. Tournai, 1968.
37555.746 Jaccottet, Philippe. L'entretien des muses, chroniques de poésie. Paris, 1968.
37555.748 Denommé, Robert Thomas. Nineteenth-century French romantic poets. Carbondale, 1969.
37555.750 Alyn, Marc. La nouvelle poésie française. Les Hautes Plaines de Mane, 1968.
37555.752 Houston, John Porter. The demonic imagination. Baton Rouge, 1969.

37555 History of special forms - Poetry - cont.

37555.754 Keil, Erika. "Cantique" und "Hymne" in der französischer Lyrik seit der Romantik. Bonn, 1966.
37555.756 Matthews, J.H. Surrealist poetry in France. 1. ed. Syracuse, N.Y., 1969.
37555.758 Beyer, Jürgen. Schwank und Moral. Heidelberg, 1969.
37555.760 Jeanneret, Michel. Poésie et tradition biblique au XVIe siècle recherches stylistiques sur les paraphrases des "Psaumes", de Marot à Malherbe. Paris, 1969.
37555.762 Delley, Gilbert. L'assomption de la nature dans la lyrique française de l'âge baroque. Berne, 1969.
37555.764 Caws, Mary Ann. The poetry of Dada and surrealism. Princeton, 1970.
37555.766 Marissel, André. Poètes vivants; essai. Paris, 1969.
37555.768 Blanchard, André. Trésor de la poésie baroque et precieuse. Paris, 1969.
37555.770 Ireson, J.C. Imagination in French romantic poetry. Hull, 1970.
37555.772 Vipper, Iurii B. Formirovanie klassitsizmo vo frantsusskoi poesii nachala XVII veka. Moskva, 1967.
37555.774 Petrova, Injna I. Spivtsi svobody. Kyïv, 1971.
37555.776 Colletet, Guillaume. Le parnasse français ou L'ecole des muses. Genève, 1970.

37556.1 - .9 History of special forms - Wit and humor, satire

37556.3 Canel, Alfred. Recherches sur les jeux d'esprit. Evreux, 1867. 2v.
37556.4 Rossettini, Olga T. Les influences anciennes et italiennes sur la satire en France au XVIe siècle. Florence, 1958.
37556.4.5 Alter, Jean V. Les origines de la satire antibourgeoise en France. Genève, 1966. 2v.
37556.5 Besant, Walter. The French humorists from the 12th to the 19th century. London, 1873.
37556.6A Besant, Walter. French humorists. Boston, 1874.
37556.6B Besant, Walter. French humorists. Boston, 1874.
37556.7 Bar, Francis. Le genre burlesque en France au XVIIe siècle. Paris, 1960.
37556.8 Sainte-Croix, le roy de (pseud.). L'Alsacien qui rit, boit, chante, et danse. Paris, 1880.
37556.8.12 Bavardages de mesdames mes cousines. Rioz, 1882.
37556.9 Gehring, Christian. Die Entwicklung des politischen Urtzblattes in Deutschland. Inaug. Diss. Leipzig, 1927.

37556.10 - .22 History of special forms - Journalism

37556.10A Funck-Brentano, F. Les nouvellistes. 2. éd. Paris, 1905.
37556.10B Funck-Brentano, F. Les nouvellistes. 2. éd. Paris, 1905.
37556.11 Funck-Brentano, F. Figaro et ses devanciers. Paris, 1909.
37556.11.20 Lacretelle, Jacques de. Face à l'événement, "Le Figaro", 1826-1966. Paris, 1966.
37556.12 Camusat, D.F. Histoire critique des journaux. Amsterdam, 1734.
37556.12.5 Avenel, Henri. Histoire de la presse française depuis 1789 jusqu'à nos jours. Paris, 1900.
37556.12.10 Sirel, Louis. Journalisme et droit. Thèse. Toulouse, 1930.
37556.12.15 Belfort, Roland. Johnny Crapand and his journals. London, 1898.
37556.12.20 Mitton, F. La presse française. Paris, 1943-45. 2v.
37556.12.34 Goedorp, Victor. Figures du temps: Eugène Lautier, G. Lenotri. Paris, 1943.
37556.12.40 Hisard, Claude. Histoire de la spoliation de la presse française. Paris, 1955.
37556.12.45 Vidiasova, L.M. Sovremennaia frantsuzskaia pechat. Moskva, 1963.
37556.12.50 Livois, René de. Histoire de la presse française. Lausanne, 1965. 2v.
37556.12.52 Boegner, Philippe. Presse, argent, liberté. Paris, 1969.
37556.12.55 Histoire générale de la presse française. Paris, 1969- 2v.
37556.13 Texier, E. Biographie des journalistes. Paris, 18- .
37556.13.25 Quéval, Jean. Première page, cinquième collone. 19. éd. Paris, 1945.
37556.13.30 Ester, Carl d'. Die Presse Frankreichs im eigenen Urteil, 1540-1940. Stuttgart, 1942.
37556.13.40 Feron, B. Feu la presse libre? Paris, 1954.
37556.13.50 Gabriel-Robinet, Louis. Journaux et journalistes hier et aujourd'hui. Paris, 1962.
37556.14 Colletet, F. Le journal de Colletet. Paris, 1878.
37556.14.20 Colletet, F. Les journaux pour enfants. Paris, 1954.
37556.15 Hatin, Eugène. Histoire...de la presse en France. Paris, 1859-61. 8v.
37556.15.10A Hunt, Herbert J. Le socialisme et le romantisme, étude de la presse 1830-1848. Oxford, 1935.
37556.15.10B Hunt, Herbert J. Le socialisme et le romantisme, étude de la presse 1830-1848. Oxford, 1935.
37556.15.15 Bellet, Roger. Presse et journalisme sous le Second Empire. Paris, 1967.
37556.15.50 Faucher, Jean André. Le quatrième pouvoir, la presse française de 1830 à 1960. Paris, 1969.
37556.15.100 Trahard, Pierre. Une revue oubliée, La revue poétique du XIXe siècle, 1835. Thèse. Paris, 1924.
37556.15.105 Trahard, Pierre. Une revue oubliée. Paris, 1925.
37556.15.120 Wood, K.L. Criticism of French romantic literature in the Gazette de France 1830-1848. Philadelphia, 1934.
37556.15.200 Paris. École pratique des hautes études. Centre d'études des communications de masse. Deux enquêtes "Flash" sur la presse. Paris, 1960.
37556.15.205 Estier, Claude. La gauche hebdomadaire, 1914-1962. Paris, 1962.
37556.15.210 Morin, Violette. L'écriture de presse. Paris, 1969.
37556.16 King, Helen Maxwell. Les doctrines littéraires de la quotidienne, 1814-30. Durham, N.C., 1920.
37556.16.2 King, Helen Maxwell. Les doctrines littéraires de la quotidienne, 1814-30. Northampton, Mass., 1920.
37556.16.25 Hemfrich, Paul. Le journal littéraire de La Haye, 1713-1737. Berlin, 1915.
37556.16.40 Schmitt, Jakob. Die Literaturpolitik der "Revue des deux mondes" von 1850 bis 1870. Inaug. Diss. Marburg, 1929.
37556.16.43 DuVal, T.E. The subject of realism in the Revue des deux mondes (1831-1863). Philadelphia, 1936.
37556.16.45 DuBled, V. Le salon de la "Revue des deux mondes". Paris, 1930.
37556.16.47 Zdraveva, B.V. Les origines de la revue des deux mondes et les littératures européennes, 1831-1842. Thèse. Sophia, 1930.
37556.16.48 Server, A.W. L'Espagne dans la revue des deux mondes (1829-1848). Thèse. Paris, 1939.

Classified Listing

37556.10 - .22 History of special forms - Journalism - cont.

37556.16.50 Morgan, B. Histoire du journal des Scavane depuis 1665 jusqu'en 1701. Paris, 1929.
37556.16.55 Cocheris, H. Histoire du journal des savants. Paris, 1860.
37556.16.60 Dumas, G. Histoire du journal de Thévaux depuis 1701 jusqu'en 1762. Thèse. Paris, 1936.
37556.16.75 Kanonenberg, H. Die Zeitung "L'avenir" (Paris 1830-1831). Inaug. Diss. Marburg, 1935.
37556.16.100 Fajon, Etienne. En feuilletant L'Humanité. Paris? 1964.
37556.16.150 Barrillon, Raymond. Le cas Paris-soir. Paris, 1959.
37556.17 Hatin, E. Histoire du journal en France. Paris, 1853.
37556.17.5 Iakimovich, T.K. Frantsuzskii realisticheskii ocherk, 1830-1848 gg. Moskva, 1963.
37556.17.10 Estivals, Robert. L'avant-garde; étude historique et sociologique des publications périodiques ayant pour titre l'avangarde. Paris, 1968.
37556.18.12 Petric, D.S. Le groupe littéraire de la Minerve française. 1818-1820. Paris, 1927.
37556.18.25 Shumway, A.E. A study of the Minerva française. (Feb. 1818-Mar. 1920). Diss. Philadelphia, 1934.
37556.18.50 Roncuzzi, Alfredo. La revista esprit ed Emmanuel Mounier. Roma, 1961.
37556.18.75 Chatdain, Abel. Le monde et ses lectures sous la IVe république. Paris, 1962.
37556.19 Maillard, F. Histoire...de la presse Parisienne. Paris, 1859.
37556.19.10 Hinter den Kulissen des französischen Journalismus. Berlin, 1925.
37556.19.50 Awtrey, H. La presse Anglo-Americaine de Paris. Thèse. Paris, 1932.
37556.20 Biré, E. La presse royale de 1830 à 1852, Alfred Nettement sa vie et ses oeuvres. Paris, 1901.
37556.20.30 Delisle de Sales, J.C.I. Essai sur le journalisme depuis 1735 jusqu'à l'an 1800. Paris, 1811. 2 pam.
Htn 37556.20.50* Chateaubriand, François A.R. Du retablissement de la censure par l'ordnance du 24 juin 1827. Paris, 1827.
37556.20.60 Sirven, A. Journaux et journalistes. Paris, 1865-66. 4v.
37556.20.70 Morienval, J. Les créateurs de la grande presse en France. Paris, 1934.
37556.20.90 Schwoebel, Jean. La presse, le pouvoir et l'argent. Paris, 1968.
37556.20.100 Prunières, Bernard. La presse sans politique; étude systématique de la presse lue dans le Calvados. Paris, 1966.
37556.20.150 Blanc-Rouquette, Marie Thérèse. La presse et l'information à Toulouse des origines à 1789. Toulouse, 1967.
37556.20.200 Bennett, Robert L. Les journaux de Caen, 1940-1944. Caen, 1969.
37556.21 Germain, A. Martyrologe de la presse 1789-1861. Paris, 1861.
37556.21.2 Dahl, F. Les débuts de la presse française. Göteborg, 1951.
37556.21.3 Giraudeau, F. La presse périodique de 1789 à 1867. Paris, 1867.
37556.21.5 Söderhjehn, A. Le régime de la presse pendant la révolution française. Helsingforo, 1900-01. 2v.
37556.21.6 Palfrey, T. Le Panorama littéraire de l'Europe. Evanston, 1950.
37556.21.7 Breyne-Dubois, G. de. Ce qu'il y a dans une collection de journaux. Bruxelles, 1881.
37556.21.9 Grages, C.M. des. La presse littéraire sur la restauration, 1815-1830. Paris, 1907.
37556.21.10 Vaudin, J.F. Gazetiers et gazettes; histoire critique. Paris, 1860.
Htn 37556.21.11* Contades, G. L'homme au camélia Lautour-Megeray. Argentan, 1885.
37556.21.12 Perrodil, E. de. Un an de journalisme à Lourdes. Paris, n.d.
37556.21.14 Runge, H. Courtilz de Sandras und die Anfänge des Mercure historique et politique. Inaug. Diss. Halle, 1887.
37556.21.15 Gourmont, P. Les petites revues. Paris, 1900.
37556.21.17 Beuchat, C. La revue contemporaine, 1885-1886. Thèse. Paris, 1930.
37556.21.20 Billy, A. Le monde des journaux, tableau de la presse française contemporaine. Paris, 1924.
37556.21.25 Demaison, A. Les voix de la France. Paris, 1932.
37556.21.30 Delfour, L.C. La presse contre l'église. 2. éd. Paris, 1908.
37556.21.35 Laferrière, E. La censure et la régime correctionnel. Paris, 1868.
37556.21.40 Flotte, G. Révues parisiennes. Marseille, 1860-68. 2v.
37556.21.45 Manevy, Raymond. Histoire de la presse, 1914 à 1939. Paris, 1945.
37556.21.45.5 Manevy, Raymond. L'évolution des formules de présentation de la presse quotidienne. Paris, 1956.
37556.21.45.6 Manevy, Raymond. L'évolution des formules de présentation de la presse quotidienne. Paris, 1956.
37556.21.46 Manevy, Raymond. La presse da la III république. Paris, 1955.
37556.21.48 Manevy, Raymond. La presse française de Renaitdot à Rocheport. Paris, 1958.
37556.21.50 Balch, M. A survey of the Paris daily press. Paris, 1945.
37556.21.55 Seguin, Jean Pierre. L'information en France, à la fin du 15e siècle. Genève, 1961.
37556.21.56 Seguin, Jean-Pierre. L'information en France avant le périodique; 517 canards imprimés entre 1529 et 1631. Paris, 1964.
37556.21.60 Varin d'Ainvelle, Madeleine. La presse en France. Paris, 1965.
37556.21.65 Mottin, Jean. Histoire politique de la presse, 1944-1949. Paris, 1949.
37556.22 Toudouze, G. Albert Wolff. Paris, 1883.
37556.22.3 Joze, V. Les marechieux de la chronique: H. Rochefort, A. Scholl, A. Wolff. Paris, 1888.
37556.22.5 Gärtner, J. Das Journal etranger und seine Bedeutung...in Frankreich. Mainz, 1905.
37556.22.6 Sichel, J. Die Englische Literatur im Journal Etranger. Darmstadt, 1907.
37556.22.10 Lovering, S. L'activité intellectuelle de l'Angleterre d'après l'ancien "Marcure de France", 1672-1778. Thèse. Paris, 1930.
37556.22.25 Levron, J. La presse Creusoise au XIXe siècle. Limoges, 1931.
37556.22.30 Morino, L. La nouvelle revue française dans l'histoire des lettres. 6. éd. Paris, 1939.

37556.10 - .22 History of special forms - Journalism - cont.

37556.22.30.5 Morino, L. La nouvelle revue française dans l'histoire des lettres. Paris, 1939.
37556.22.40 Jones, K. La revue Britannique, son histoire et son action littéraire, 1825-1840. Thèse. Paris, 1939.
37556.22.43 Jones, K. La revue Britannique, son histoire et son action littéraire, 1825-1840. Paris, 1939.
37556.22.50 Lavalley, G. Études sur la presse en Normandie. Paris, 1901-10. 2v.
37556.22.60 Batailler, F. Analyses de presse. Paris, 1963.
37556.22.75 Grenoble. Bibliothèque municipale. La presse Grenobloise, 1788-1888. Grenoble, 1964.
37556.22.80 Godfrin, Jacqueline. Une centrale de presse catholique. Paris, 1965.
37556.22.85 Sullerot, Evelyne. Histoire de la presse feminine en France, des origines à 1848. Paris, 1966.
37556.22.89 Chabrol, Claude. Le récit féminin. The Hague, 1971.
37556.22.90 Pourprix, Bernard. La presse gratuite. Paris, 1971.
37556.22.93 Lachat, François. Le pays d'Ernest Daucourt, 1873-1884. Fribourg, 1969.
37556.22.95 Leclerc, Joseph. Le cinéma, témoin de son temps. Paris, 1970.
37556.22.100 Couperus, Marianne Constance. Un périodique français en Hollande; le glaneur historique, 1731-1733. Proefschrift. The Hague, 1971.

37556.23 - History of special forms - Fiction

37556.23.40 Wilmotte, Maurice. De l'origine du roman en France. Paris, 1923.
37556.23.45 Wilmotte, Maurice. Origines du roman en France. Photoreproduction. Paris, 1942.
37556.23.50 Morillot, Paul. Le roman français durant l'époque classique (1610-1800). London, 1921.
37556.24A Morillot, Paul. Le roman en France depuis 1610 jusqu'à nos jours. Paris, 189-?
37556.24B Morillot, Paul. Le roman en France depuis 1610 jusqu'à nos jours. Paris, 189-?
37556.24.1 Pamphlet box. History of French fiction.
37556.24.5 Langlois, E. Nouvelles françaises inédites du 15e siècle. Paris, 1908.
37556.24.6 Söderhjelm, W. La nouvelle française au XVe siècle. Paris, 1910.
37556.24.7 Toldo, Piétro. Contributo allo studio della novella francese del XVe XVI secolo. Roma, 1895.
37556.24.8 Paris, Gaston. Piétro Toldo. Contributo allo studio della novella francese del XV e XVI secolo. n.p., n.d.
37556.24.10 Topin, Marius. Romanciers contemporains. Paris, 1876.
37556.24.11 Boisdeffre, Pierre de. La cafetière est sur la table. Paris, 1967.
37556.24.12 Boisdeffre, Pierre de. Où va le roman. Paris, 1962.
37556.24.15 Margarido, A. O novo romance. Lisboa, 1962.
37556.25 Le Breton, André. Le roman au dix septième siècle. Photoreproduction. Paris, 1890.
37556.26 Perret, Emile. Le roman. Étude morale. Lausanne, 1892.
37556.26.5 Griswold, W.M. A descriptive list of novels...relating to life in France. Cambridge, 1892.
37556.27 Saintsbury, George. Essays on French novelists. London, 1891.
37556.27.5A Saintsbury, George. A history of the French novel. London, 1917-19. 2v.
37556.27.5B Saintsbury, George. A history of the French novel. London, 1917-19.
37556.27.7 Saintsbury, George. A history of the French novel. N.Y., 1964. 2v.
37556.27.25 Hawkins, R.L. Review of Saintsbury's History of the French novel. N.Y., 1918.
37556.28 Flincksieck, F. Zur Entwicklungsgeschichte der Realismus im französischen Roman des 19 Jahrhunderts. Marburg, 1891.
37556.29 Albalat, A. Le mal d'écrire et le roman contemporain. Paris, n.d.
37556.29.15 Albalat, A. Ouvriers et procédés. Paris, 1896.
37556.30.5 Gilbert, Eugène. Le roman en France pendant le XIXe siècle. Paris, 1909.
37556.31 Pajot, Henri. Le paysan dans la littérature française. Paris, 1896.
37556.31.5 Peters, Rudolf. Der Bauer im Französischen Roman. Inaug. Diss. Strassburg, 1914.
37556.31.9 Dordan, E. Le paysan français d'après les romans du XIXe siècle. Thèse. Toulouse, 1923.
X Cg 37556.32 Maigron, Louis. Le roman historique à l'époque romantique. Paris, 1898.
37556.32.5 Maigron, Louis. Le roman historique à l'époque romantique. Paris, 1912.
37556.33.5 Wells, B.W. A century of French fiction. N.Y., 1912.
37556.34A Le Breton, A. Le roman au dix-huitième siècle. Paris, 1898.
37556.34B Le Breton, A. Le roman au dix-huitième siècle. Paris, 1898.
37556.34.5 Green, F.C. La peinture des moeurs de la bonne société dans le roman français de 1715-1761. Paris, 1924.
37556.34.7 Green, F.C. La peinture des moeurs de la bonne société dans le roman français de 1715-1761. Thèse. Paris, 1924.
37556.35 Levrault, Léon. Le roman (Évolution du genre). Paris, n.d.
37556.35.2 Levrault, Léon. Le roman des origines à nos jours. Paris, 1932?
37556.35.13 Levrault, Léon. La satire. Paris, 1911?
37556.36 Le Breton, A. Le roman français au dix-neuvième siècle. pt. 1. Paris, 1901.
37556.36.2 Le Breton, A. Le roman français au XIXe siècle avant Balzac. Paris, 19- ?
37556.36.3 Schmidt, Bertha. Esquisses littéraires. Karlsruhe, 1903.
37556.36.5 Stephens, Winifred. French novelists of today. London, 1908.
37556.36.9 Biré, Edmond. Romans et romanciers contemporains. Paris, 1908.
37556.36.10 Guérard, Albert L. Five masters of French romance. N.Y., 1916?
37556.36.11 Nettement, Alfred. Études critiques sur le feuilleton, roman. Paris, 1845-46. 2v.
37556.36.13 Bertaut, Jules. Le roman nouveau. Paris, 1920.
X Cg 37556.36.15 Palache, J.G. Four novelists of the old regime. N.Y., 1926.
37556.37 Gerhardt, Max. Der Aberglaube in der Französischen Novelle des 16. Jahrhunderts. Schöneberg, 1906.
37556.38 Flake, O. Der französische Roman und die Novelle. Leipzig, 1912.

Classified Listing

37556.23 - History of special forms - Fiction - cont.

37556.39 Rauchfuss, Arthur. Der französische Hirtenroman am Ende des 18. Jahrhunderts. Leipzig, 1912.
37556.40 Franche, Paul. Le prêtre dans le roman français. Paris, 1902.
X Cg 37556.45 Merlant, J. Le roman personnel. Paris, 1905.
37556.46 Waldberg, M. Der empfindsame Roman in Frankreich. Strassburg, 1906.
37556.50A Reynier, G. Le roman sentimental avant l'Astrée. Paris, 1908.
37556.50B Reynier, G. Le roman sentimental avant l'Astrée. Paris, 1908.
37556.52 Bethleem, L. Romans à lire et romans à proscrire. Cambrai, 1908.
37556.52.7 Bethleem, L. Romans à lire et romans à proscrire. 7. éd. Paris, 1920.
37556.52.10 Bethleem, L. Romans à lire et romans à proscrire. 11. éd. Paris, 1932.
37556.56 Brun, Charles. Le roman social en France au XIXe siècle. Paris, 1910.
37556.58 Jakob, M. Gustave. L'illusion et le désillusion dans le roman réaliste français. Paris, 1911.
37556.58.2 Jakob, M. Gustave. L'illusion et la désillusion dans le roman réaliste français. (1851-1890). Paris, 1912.
37556.61 Clouzet, G. Le roman français. Paris, n.d.
37556.63 Wurzbach, W. von. Geschichte des französischen Romans. Heidelberg, 1912.
37556.66 Reynier, G. Origines du roman réaliste. Photoreproduction. Paris, 1912.
NEDL 37556.68 Bertaut, Jules. Les romanciers du nouveau siècle. Paris, 1912.
37556.70 Martino, P. Le roman réaliste. Paris, 1913.
37556.72 Schomaum, E. Französische Utopisten und ehr Frauenideal. Berlin, 1911.
37556.73 Killen, Alice M. Roman "terrifiant" de Walpole à Anne Radcliffe et son influence sur la littérature française jusqu'en 1840. Paris, 1915.
37556.73.2 Killen, Alice M. Le roman "terrifiant" ou roman "noir". Thèse. Paris, 1915.
37556.73.3 Killen, Alice M. Le roman "terrifiant" ou roman "noir". 2. éd. Paris, 1923.
37556.73.10 Chaplyn, Marjorie. Le roman mauresque en France de Zayde au Dernier Abencérape. Thèse. Nemours, 1928.
37556.74 Hytièr, Jean. Les romans de l'individu constant. Paris, 1928.
37556.75.5 Massis, Henri. En marge de "Jugements". Paris, 1927.
37556.76 Carkes, I. Le roman familial a la fin du XIXe siècle. Thèse. Montpellier, 1929.
37556.77 Levaux, Léopold. Romanciers. Paris, 1929.
37556.78 Duhamel, Georges. Essai sur le roman. Paris, 1925.
37556.79 Mauriac, François. Le roman. Paris, 1928.
37556.80 Lemonnier, L. Populisme. Paris, 1911.
37556.80.10 Lemonnier, L. Edgar Poe et les conteurs français. Paris, 1947.
37556.82 Dupuy, Aimé. Un personnage nouveau du roman français, l'enfant. Thèse. Paris, 1931.
37556.84 Mille, Pierre. Le roman français. 4. éd. Paris, 1930.
37556.84.5 Mille, Pierre. The French novel. 1. ed. Philadelphia, 1930.
37556.86 Refort, Lucien. La caricature littéraire. Paris, 1932.
37556.88 Glaser, Hellmuth. Studien zur Entwicklungsgeschichte des französischen Bauernromans von Rétif de la Bretonne zum Naturalismus. Inaug. Diss. Neirode, 1933.
37556.90 Cailliet, Emile. The themes of magic in nineteenth century French fiction. Paris, 1932.
37556.92 Cumings, E.K. The literary development of the romantic fairy tale in France. Diss. Bryn Mawr, 1934.
37556.94 Fraser E.M. Le renouveau religieux d'après le roman français de 1886 à 1914. Thèse. Paris, 1934.
37556.96 Bertuccioli, A. Les origines du roman maritime français. Livorno, 1931.
37556.98A O'Brien, J. The novel of adolescence in France. N.Y., 1937.
37556.98B O'Brien, J. The novel of adolescence in France. N.Y., 1937.
37556.98C O'Brien, J. The novel of adolescence in France. N.Y., 1937.
37556.98D O'Brien, J. The novel of adolescence in France. N.Y., 1937.
37556.100 Dangelzer, Joan Yvonne. La description du milieu dans le roman français de Balzac à Zola. Thèse. Paris, 1938.
37556.103 Phythian, M.T. La géographie des Alpes françaises dans les romanciers contemporains. Thèse. Grenoble, 1938.
37556.105 Toursch, V. L'enfant français à la fin du XIXe siècle d'après ses principaux romanciers. Thèse. Paris, 1939.
37556.108 Rosier, R. Le couple moderne à travers le roman contemporain. Thèse. Bordeaux, 1937.
37556.110 Friedrich, Hugo. Die Klassiker des französischen Romans. Leipzig, 1939.
37556.111.5 Friedrich, Hugo. Drei Klassiker des französischen Romans. 5. Aufl. Frankfurt, 1966.
37556.112 Lukács, Zsuzsanna. A féltékenység elemzése az ujabb francia regényben. Budapest, 1939.
37556.114 Randall, E.S. The Jewish character in the French novel, 1870-1914. Menasha, 1941.
37556.116 Benedek, A. A francia szellemesség a XVIII században. Budapest, 1936.
37556.118 Deschamp, J.G. The history of French children's books. Paris, 1938.
37556.120 Magendie, M. Le roman français au XVIIe siècle. Paris, 1932.
37556.122 Moore, Margaret. Les doctrines littéraires du constitutionnel (1815-1830) leurs rapports avec la politique. Chicago, Ill., 1945.
37556.125 Prévost, Jean. Problèmes du roman. Lyon, 1943.
37556.127 Haedens, Kléber. Paradoxe sur le roman. Marseille, 1941.
37556.127.5 Haedens, Kléber. Paradoxe sur le roman. Paris, 1964.
37556.129 Giraud, V. La critique littéraire. Paris, 1946.
37556.131 Paraf, Pierre. L'information. Paris, 1946.
37556.133 Dinar, André. A la recherche de romans d'amour. 4. éd. Paris, 1944.
37556.137 Jacoubet, Henri. Varietés de histoire littéraire de methodologie. Paris, 1935.
37556.141 Magny, C.E. Histoire du roman français depuis 1918. Paris, 1950-
37556.143A Turnell, Martin. The novel in France. London, 1950.
37556.143B Turnell, Martin. The novel in France. London, 1950.
37556.143.5 Turnell, Martin. The novel in France. N.Y., 1951.

37556.23 - History of special forms - Fiction - cont.

37556.143.10 Turnell, Martin. The art of French fiction. London, 1959.
37556.143.12 Turnell, Martin. The art of French fiction. Norfolk, 1959.
37556.145 Castex, Pierre. Le conte fantastique en Frnce de Nodier à Maupassant. Paris, 1951.
37556.147 Bridenne, J.J. La littérature française d'imagination scientifique. Paris, 1950.
37556.148 Bacourt, P. de. French of today. N.Y., 1917.
37556.149 Hubert, R.R. The Dreyfus affair and the French novel. Thesis. Cambridge, Mass., 1951.
37556.150A Peyre, Henri. The contemporary French novel. N.Y., 1955.
37556.150B Peyre, Henri. The contemporary French novel. N.Y., 1955.
37556.153 Frédérik, Pierre. Un siècle de chasse aux nouvelles. Paris, 1959.
37556.155 Ferrier, J.M. Forerunners of the French novel. Manchester, 1954.
37556.165A Ullman, Stephen. Style in the French novel. Cambridge, Eng., 1957.
37556.165B Ullman, Stephen. Style in the French novel. Cambridge, Eng., 1957.
37556.166 Ullman, Stephen. Style in the French novel. N.Y., 1964.
37556.170 Ledré, Charles. Histoire de la presse. Paris, 1958.
37556.175 Seguin, Jean Pierre. Nouvelles à sensations canards du XIXe siècle. Paris, 1959.
37556.185 Nattier-Natanson, Evelyn. Les amitiés de la revue blanche et quelques autres. Vincennes, 1959.
37556.190 Roger, Gaston. Maîtres du roman de terroir. Paris, 1959.
37556.195 Roger, Georges. Situation du roman régionaliste français. Paris, 1951.
37556.200 McGhee, D.M. The cult of the conte moral. Menasha, 1960.
37556.205A Ullman, Stephen. The image in modern French novel. Cambridge, Eng., 1960.
37556.205B Ullman, Stephen. The image in modern French novel. Cambridge, Eng., 1960.
37556.210 Zeltner-Neukomm, Gerda. Das Wagnis des französischen Gegenwartromans. Reinbek, 1960.
37556.215 Brombert, Victor. The intellectual hero. Philadelphia, 1961.
37556.230 Uitti, Karl D. The concept of self in the symbolist novel. 's-Gravehhage, 1961.
37556.232 Sauerwein, Jules. Trente aus à la une. Paris, 1962.
37556.238 Evnina, E.M. Sovremennyi frantzsuzkii roman, 1940-1960. Moskva, 1962.
37556.242 May, G.C. Le dilemme du roman au XVIIIe siècle. New Haven, 1963.
37556.243 Vernois, Paul. Le roman rustique de George Sand à Ramuz. Paris, 1962.
37556.245 Xuriguera, Ramón. La idea de l'home en la novella francesa. Barcelona, 1961.
37556.246 Lacher, W. Le réalisme dans le roman contemporain. 2. éd. Genève, 1940.
37556.247 Balashova, T.V. Frantsuzskii roman 60-kh godov. Moskva, 1965.
37556.249 Halimi, André. Tous candidats à l'Élysée. Paris, 1965.
37556.250 Greshoff, C.J. Seven studies in the French novel. Cape Town, 1964.
37556.251 Matthews, J.H. Surrealism and the novel. Ann Arbor, 1966.
37556.255 Desnitskii, Vasilii A. Frantsuzskii realisticheskii roman XIX veka. Leningrad, 1932.
37556.256 Raimond, Michel. Le roman depuis la révolution. Paris, 1967.
37556.258 Bo, Carlo. La crisi del romanzo francese nel'900. Milano, 1967.
37556.260 Coulet, Henri. Le roman jusqu'à la révolution. Paris, 1967. 2v.
37556.262 Deloffre, Frédéric. La nouvelle en France à l'âge classique. Paris, 1968.
37556.263 Sokolov, Valentin S. Pechat' narodnogo fronta i progressinvnaia frantsuzskaia literature. Leningrad, 1967.
37556.266.2 Brooks, Peter Preston. The novel of worldliness: Crebillon, Marivaux, Laclos, Stendhal. Princeton, N.J., 1969.
37556.268 Bo, Carlo. Da Voltaire a Drieu La Rochelle. Milano, 1965.
37556.270 Höhnisch, Erika. Das gefangene Ich. Heidelberg, 1967.
37556.274 Eulenburg, Heilwig. Bewältigung des Leidens im Französischen Roman nach dem zweiten Weltkrieg. München, 1967.
37556.278 Frohock, Wilbur Merrill. Image and theme; studies in modern French fiction. Cambridge, 1969.
37556.280 Stewart, Philip R. Imitation and illusion in the French memoir-novel, 1700-1750. New Haven, 1969.
37556.300 Pollmann, Leo. Der neue Roman in Frankreich und Lateinamérika. Stuttgart, 1968.
37556.300.1 Pollmann, Leo. La "nueva novela" en Francia y en Iberoamérica. Madrid, 1971.
37556.300.5 Pollmann, Leo. Der französische Roman im 20. Jahrhundert. Stuttgart, 1970.
37556.302 Reck, Rima D. Literature and responsibility; the French novelist in the twentieth century. Baton Rouge, 1969.
37556.308 Wilhelm, Kurt. Der nouveau Roman. Berlin, 1969.
37556.310 Sasse, Klaus. Die Entdeckung der courtisan Vertueuse in der französischen Literatur des 18. Jahrhunderts. Hamburg, 1967.
37556.312 Dementev, E.G. Roman velikoi frantsuzskoi reloliutsii. Vladivostok, 1969.
37556.314 Stackelberg, Jürgen. Von Rabelais bis Voltaire. München, 1970.
37556.316 Pashchenko, Vadim Il'ich. Prsty kolonializmu in viiny. Kyiv, 1969.
37556.318 Godenne, René. Histoire de la nouvelle française aux 17e et 18e siècles. Genève, 1970.
37556.320 Vachnadze, Georgii N. Pechat' piatoi respubliki 1958-1968 gg. Moskva, 1968.
37556.330 Belozubov, Leonid. L'Europe savante, 1718-20. Paris, 1968.
37556.340 Mercier, Vivian. The new novel from Queneau to Pinget. 1. ed. N.Y., 1971.
37556.351 Ratner, Moses. Theory and criticism of the novel in France from l'Astree to 1750. N.Y., 1971.
37556.355 Engler, Winfried. Texte zur französischen Romantheorie des 19. Jahrhunderts. Tübingen, 1970.
37556.357 Mylne, Vivienne. The eighteenth-century French novel. Manchester, 1965.
37556.358 Roman et lumière au XVIIe siècle. Paris, 1970.
37556.360.2 Nicoletti, Gianni. Introduzione allo studio del romanzo francese nel Settecento. 2. ed. Bari, 1969.

37556.23 - History of special forms - Fiction - cont.

37556.364 Netzer, Klaus. Der Laser des nouveau Roman. Frankfurt, 1970.

37556.366 Astier, Pierre A.G. La crise du roman français et le nouveau réalisme. Paris, 1969.

37556.368 Positions et oppositions sur le roman contemporain; actes du colloque. Paris, 1971.

37556.370 Tourteau, Jean Jacques. D'Arsène Lupin à San-Antonio; le roman policier français de 1900 à 1970. Paris, 1970.

37557 History of special forms - Other prose

37557.2 Berger de Xivrey. Recherches sur...la littérature française. Paris, 1829.

37557.4A Egger, Émile. L'Hellénisme en France. Paris, 1869. 2v.

37557.4B Egger, Émile. L'Hellénisme en France. v.1-2. Paris, 1869.

37557.6 Franz, Arthur. Das literarische Portrat in Frankreich. Leipzig, 1905.

37557.6.2 Franz, Arthur. Das literarische Portrat in Frankreich Beilage. Leipzig, n.d.

37557.7 Nitsche, Karl. Die Bedeutung derBiographie für die Kulturproblematik des Gegenwärtigen Frankreichs. Berlin, 1931.

NEDL 37557.11 Balzo, C. L'Italia nella letterature francese. Roma, 1905.

37557.12 Bédier, Joseph. Études critiques. Paris, 1903.

37557.13A Brunetière, F. Études critiques sur l'histoire de la littérature française. Série 1-9. Paris, 1889-1932. 9v.

37557.13B Brunetière, F. Études critiques sur l'histoire de la littérature française. Série 1-8. Paris, 1889-1932. 8v.

37557.14 Brunetière, F. Études critiques sur l'histoire de la littérature française. Paris, 1880.

37557.15 Brunetière, F. Nouvelles études critiques sur la littérature française. Paris, 1882.

37557.16 Brunetière, F. Essays in French literature. London, 1898.

37557.17 Monselet, Charles. Curiosités littéraires. Paris, 1890.

37557.18A Littré, E. Études et Glanures. Paris, 1880.

37557.18B Littré, E. Études et Glanures. Paris, 1880.

37557.19 Caro, E. Poètes et romanciers. Paris, 1888.

37557.20A France, Anatole. La vie littéraire. v.1,3-4. Paris, 1889. 3v.

37557.20B France, Anatole. La vie littéraire. Pars, 1889. 4v.

37557.21A Gosse, E. French profiles. N.Y., 1905.

37557.21B Gosse, E. French profiles. N.Y., 1905.

37557.21.10 Gosse, E. French profiles. N.Y., 1914.

37557.22.5 Heiss, Hanns. Studien und einige Beziehungen zur der deutschen und der französischen Literatur. Erlangen, 1907.

37557.23A Harper, G.M. Masters of French literature. N.Y., 1901.

37557.23B Harper, G.M. Masters of French literature. N.Y., 1901.

37557.24 Weigand, Wilhelm. Essays (Voltaire, Rousseau, etc.). München, 1892.

37557.25 Hallard, J.H. Gallica and other essays. London, 1895.

37557.26 Wuscher, Gottlieb. Der Einfluss der englischen Ballad- en Poesie. Trogen, 1891.

37557.28 Larroumet, G. Études de littérature et d'art. Paris, 1893. 3v.

NEDL 37557.28 Larroumet, G. Études de littérature et d'art. v.4. Paris, 1893.

37557.35A Deschamps, G. La vie et les livres. Série 1-5. Paris, 1894. 5v.

37557.35B Deschamps, G. La vie et les livres. Série 2-5. Paris, 1894. 4v.

37557.36 Glaser, E. Le mouvement littéraire. 1905-1912. Paris, n.d. 7v.

37557.38 Levrault, Léon. La fable. Paris, 1919.

37557.38.10 Saillard, G. Essai sur la fable en France au dix-huitième siècle. Toulouse, 1912.

37557.41 Rutten, A. Les grands orateurs belges depuis 1830. Bruxelles, 1954.

37557.42 Rambaud, L. L'éloquence française. Lyon, 1949? 2v.

37557.46 Krafft, J.G. Essai sur l'ésthétique de la prose. Paris, 1952.

37557.48 Charbonnel, J. Roger. Essai sur l'apologetique littéraire du XVII siècle a nos jours. Paris, 1903.

37557.50 Bernard, A. Le sermon au XVIII siècle. Paris, 1901.

37557.51 Étienne, S. Le genre romanesque en France. Paris, 1922.

37557.55 Gotaas, Mary C. Bossuet and Vieira. Washington, 1953.

37557.60 Cherel, Albert. La prose poétique française. 3. éd. Paris, 1940.

37557.70 Lucchini, Pierre. Les polémistes français depuis 1789. Paris, 1962.

37557.75 Roustan, M. La lettre; évolution du genre. Paris, 19- ?

37557.75.5 Duchêne, Roger. Realité vécue et art épistolaire. Paris, 1970.

37557.76 Molho, R. La critique littéraire en France. Paris, 1963.

37557.76.5 Fayolle, Roger. La critique littéraire. Paris, 1964.

37557.76.10 Paulhan, Jean. Petite préface à toute critique. Paris, 1951.

37557.76.15 Allemand, André. Nouvelle critique, nouvelle perspective. Neuchâtel, 1967.

37557.76.20 Fowlie, Wallace. The French critic, 1549-1967. Carbondale, 1968.

37557.76.25 Romani, Bruno. La critica francese. Ravenna, 1968.

37557.76.30A Lawall, Sarah N. Critics of consciousness. Cambridge, 1968.

37557.76.30B Lawall, Sarah N. Critics of consciousness. Cambridge, 1968.

37557.76.35 Picard, Raymond. Nouvelle critique ou nouvelle imposture. Paris, 1965.

37557.76.36 Picard, Raymond. New criticism or new fraud? Pullman, 1969.

37557.76.40 Blin, Georges. La cribleuse de blé, la critique. Paris, 1968.

37557.76.45 Simon, John K. Modern French criticism. Chicago, 1972.

37557.76.50 Moreau, Pierre. La critique littéraire en France. Paris, 1960.

37557.76.55 Mattauch, Hans. Die literarische Kritik der frühen französischenZeitschriften, 1665-1748. 1. Aufl. München, 1968.

37557.76.60 Poulet, Georges. La conscience critique. Paris, 1971.

37557.78 Girard, A. Le journal intime. Paris, 1963.

37557.79 Cary, Edmond. Les grandes traducteurs français. Genève, 1963.

37557 History of special forms - Other prose - cont.

37557.80 La Ferrière-Percy, Hector. Rapport sur les recherches faites à la bibliothèque impériale de Saint-Pétersbourg. Saint Pétersbourg, 1965.

37557.81 Blessing, Marieluise. Der philosophische Dialog als literarische Kurstform von Renan bis Valery. Tübingen, 1965.

37557.82 Leiner, Wolfgang. Der Widmungsbrief in der französischen Literatur (1580-1715). Heidelberg, 1965.

37557.84 Kempf, Roger. Sur le corps romanesque. Paris, 1968.

37557.86 Bollème, Geneviève. Les almanachs populaires aux XVIIe et XVIIIe siècles. Paris, 1969.

37557.90 Howarth, William D. Explications: the technique of French literary appreciation. London, 1971.

37558 History of special forms - Miscellany

37558.1.5 Bibliographie de la France. Guide des prix littéraires. Paris. 1951-1957 3v.

37558.2 Voisenon, Claude Henri de. Anecdotes littéraires. Paris, 1880.

37558.3 Raynal, Thomas G.L. Anecdotes littéraires. La Haye, 1766. 3v.

37558.4 Neré, F. Il maggio delle fate a altri scritti di letteratura francesse. Novara, 1929.

37558.6 Fontaine de Resbecq, Adolphe C.T. Voyages littéraires sur le Quais de Paris. Paris, 1857.

37558.7 Fontaine de Resbecq, Adolphe C.T. Voyages littéraires sur le Quais de Paris. Paris, 1864.

37558.9 Ticknesse, Ann. Sketches of the ladies of France. London, 1780. 3v.

37558.10 Kavanagh, Julia. French women of letters. Leipzig, 1862.

37558.11 Guy, Jules. Les femmes de lettres. Paris, 1878.

37558.12 Jacquinet, P. Les femmes de France. Paris, 1889.

37558.13 Alq, Louise. Anthologie féminine. Paris, 1893.

37558.13.12 Mooij, A.L.A. Caractères principaux. Groningen, 1949.

37558.14 Genlis, Stephanie. De l'influence des femmes sur la littérature française. Paris, 1826. 2v.

37558.14.10 Richardson, Lula. The forerunners of feminism in French literature. Diss. Baltimore, 1929.

37558.14.20 Larnac, Jean. Histoire de la littérature féminine en France. 4. éd. Paris, 1929.

37558.14.30 Gourmont, Jean de. Muses d'aujourd'hui. Paris, 1910.

37558.15 Laurent, Émile. Ruelles, salons, et cabarets. Paris, 1858.

37558.16 Colombey, Émile. Ruelles, salons, et cabarets. Paris, 1892. 2v.

37558.17 Mason, Amelia Gere. The woman of the French salons. N.Y., 1891.

37558.18 Longuemare, P. de. Une famille d'auteurs aux 16e, 17e et 18e siècles. Les Sainte-Marthe. Paris, 1902.

37558.19 Maurras, Charles. Le romantisme féminin. Paris, 1926.

37558.20 Laur, E. Zur Geschichte der französischen Litteratur. Mannheim, 1874.

37558.21 Henry, Stuart. Hours with famous Parisians. Chicago, 1897.

37558.22 Proszwimmer, K. A Francia if júsági irodalom a XVIII szazadban és a XIX század elején. Budapest, 1939.

37558.23 Pamphlet box. French academy.

37558.26 Boissier, G. L'académie française. Paris, 1909.

37558.28 D'Alembert, Jean le Rond. Select eulogies of members of the French academy. London, 1799. 2v.

37558.29 Brunel, Lucien. Les philosophes et l'Académie française. Paris, 1884.

37558.30 Mesnard, Paul. Histoire de l'Académie française. Paris, 1857.

Htn 37558.30.65* Pellison-Fontanier, Paul. The history of the French Academy. London, 1657.

37558.30.75 Pellison-Fontanier, Paul. Histoire de l'Academie française depuis son établissement jusqu'à 1652. Paris, 1729.

37558.31 Pellisson-Fontanier, Paul. Histoire de l'Académie française. Paris, 1858. 2v.

37558.32 Kerviler, René. Les trois cardinaux de Rohan (de l'Académie Française). Nantes, 1881.

37558.33 Kerviler, René. Essai d'une bibliographie raisonnée (de l'Académie française). Paris, 1877.

37558.33.5 Kerviler, René. Bibliographie chronologique. Saint-Nazaire, 1884.

37558.34 Michel, H. Le quarantième fauteuil. Paris, 1898.

37558.35 Houssaye, Arsène. Histoire de 41e fauteuil. Paris, 1864.

37558.35.5 Houssaye, Arsène. Histoire de 41me fauteuil. Paris, 1857.

37558.36 Houssaye, Arsène. Histoire de 41me fauteuil. Paris, 1884.

37558.37 Vedrenne, P. Fauteuils de l'Académie Française. Paris, n.d. 4v.

37558.37.5 Jeanroy-Félix, V. Fauteuils contemporains de l'Académie. Paris, n.d.

37558.38 Tisserand, E. Étude sur la première moitié du XVIIme siècle. Paris, 1870.

37558.39 D., Y. "The forty immortals". N.Y., 1884.

37558.41 Doucet, Camille. A l'institut rapports annuels (1886-1894). Paris, 1896.

37558.42A Vincent, Leon H. The French Academy. Cambridge, 1901.

37558.42B Vincent, Leon H. The French Academy. Cambridge, 1901.

37558.43 Vattier, G. Galerie des Académiciens et 1st et 3d. 2nd Série. Paris, 1864. 3v.

37558.44 Robertson, D.M. The French Academy. N.Y., 1910.

37558.45 Edwards, Edward. Chapters of the biographical history of the French academy. London, 1864.

37558.46 Martin, Jules. Nos Académiciens. Académie Française. Portraits et Biographies. Paris, 1895.

37558.47 Barbat de Bignicourt, Arthur. Les petits mystères de l'Academie Française. Paris, 1844.

Htn 37558.48* Barbey d'Aurevilly, Jules. Les quarante médaillons de l'académie. Paris, 1864.

37558.48.5 Barbey d'Aurevilly, Jules. Les quarante médaillons de l'académie, 1864. Paris, 1966.

37558.48.10 Méry, Joseph. Biographie des quarante de l'Académie française. Paris, 1826.

37558.50 Biré, Edmond. Les poètes lauréats de l'Académie française. Paris, 1864. 2v.

37558.53 Gassier, Émile. Les cinq cents immortels. Paris, 1906.

37558.55 Loliée, Frédéric. L'Académie française devant l'opinion. Paris, 1911.

37558.59A Masson, Frédéric. L'Académie française, 1629-1793. Paris, 1912.

37558.59B Masson, Frédéric. L'Académie française, 1629-1793. Paris, 1912.

37558.60 Masson, Frédéric. L'Académie française 1629-1793. 2. éd. Paris, n.d.

37558 History of special forms - Miscellany - cont.

37558.65 Académie française, Paris. Anthologie de l'Académie française. Paris, 1921. 2v.
37558.66 Peter, René. Vie secrète de l'académie française. Paris, 1934-38. 4v.
37558.67 1635-1935. Trois siècles de l'académie française. Paris, 1935.
37558.67.10 Le rayon annuaire du cercle français de l'université Fordham à New York, 1935. N.Y., 1935?
37558.67.20 Peter, René. L'académie française et le XX siècle. Paris, 1949.
37558.70 Deffoux, L. Chronique de l'académie Goncourt. Paris, 1929.
37558.70.5 Ravon, Georges. L'académie Goncourt en dix couverts. Avignon, 1946.
37558.70.10 Benjamin, René. La galère des Goncourt. Paris, 1948.
37558.72 Alembert, J.L. d'. Histoire des membres de l'Académie française. Paris, 1785-87. 6v.
37558.74 Osborne, Nancy F. The doctor in the French literature of the sixteenth century. N.Y., 1946.
37558.75 Adler, Wolfgang. Hassdichtung in Frankreich. Berlin, 1940.
37558.77 Yates, F.A. The French academies of the sixteenth century. London, 1947.
37558.100 Académie des jeux floraux. Recueil de l'académie des jeux floraux. Toulouse. 1696-1941 99v.
37558.115 Gélis, F. de. Histoire critique des jeux floraux. Toulouse, 1912.
37558.117 Duboul, Axel. Les deux siècles de l'académie des jeux floraux. Toulouse, 1901. 2v.
37558.119 Dawson, John C. Toulouse in the renaissance. pt. 1. N.Y., 1921.
37558.120 Dawson, John C. Toulouse in the renaissance. N.Y., 1923.
37558.125 Praviel, Armand. Histoire anecdotique des jeux floraux. Toulouse, 1923.
37558.127 Ségu, F. L'académie des jeux floraux. Paris, 1935-36. 2v.
37558.130 Anglade, J. Les origines du Gai Savoir. Paris, 1920.
37558.135A Cook, Mercer. Five French Negro authors. Washington, 1943.
37558.135B Cook, Mercer. Five French Negro authors. Washington, 1943.
37558.150 Henriot, Émile. Les livres du second rayon. Paris, 1948.
37558.150.5 Henriot, Émile. Portraits de femmes d'Héloise à Katherine Mansfield. Paris, 1951.
37558.150.10 La Rochefericauld, Edmée. Femmes d'hier et d'aujourd'hui. Paris, 1969.
37558.155 Goldmann, L. Le dieu caché. Paris, 1955.
37558.155.5 Goldmann, L. Le dieu caché. Paris, 1962.
37558.156 Goldmann, L. The hidden God. London, 1964.
37558.180 Bordeaux, Henry. Quarante ans chez les quarante. Paris, 1959.
37558.197 el Nouty, Hassar. Le Proche-Orient dans la littérature française. Paris, 1958.
37558.200 La Force, A. de C. En marge de l'académie. Paris, 1962.
37558.203 Weygand, Maxime. L'année à l'academie. Paris, 1962.
37558.204 Ormesson, Wladimir. Le clergé et l'académie. Paris, 1965.
37558.205 Lévis-Mirepoix, Antoine. Que signifie le parti des ducs à l'Académie? Paris, 1964.
37558.206 Didier, Robert. Isographie de l'académie française. Paris, 1964.
37558.208 Gaxotte, Pierre. L'académie française. Paris, 1965.
37558.210 Garcon, Maurice. Le palais à l'académie. Paris, 1965.
37558.235 Oster, Daniel. Histoire de l'académie française. Paris, 1970.

37561 History of special periods - Folios [Discontinued]

37561.2 Ampère, J.J. Histoire littéraire de la France avant Charlemagne. Paris, 1867-1868. 2v.
37561.2.2 Ampère, J.J. Histoire littéraire de la France sous Charlemagne. v.3. Paris, 1868.
37561.3 Ampère, J.J. Histoire littéraire de la France. Paris, 1839. 3v.
37561.5 Henrion, Mathieu R. Histoire littéraire de la France. Paris, 1827.
37561.8A Ideler, Julius Ludwig. Geschichte der altfranzösischen National-Literatur. Berlin, 1842.
37561.8B Ideler, Julius Ludwig. Geschichte der altfranzösischen National-Literatur. Berlin, 1842.
37561.10 Moland, Louis. Origines littéraires de la France. Paris, 1862.
37561.12A Le Clerc, V. Histoire littéraire de la France au 14th siècle. Paris, 1865. 2v.
37561.12B Le Clerc, V. Histoire littéraire de la France au 14th siècle. Paris, 1865. 2v.
37561.14 Potvin, Charles. Nos premiers siècles littéraires. Brussels, 1870. 2v.
37561.15 Boucherie, A. La langue et la littérature françaises au moyen âge. Paris, 1880.
37561.17 Aubertin, Charles. Histoire de la langue et de la littérature françaises au moyen âge. Paris, 1876-1878.
37561.18 Aubertin, Charles. Histoire de la littérature françaises au moyen âge. Paris, 1883. 2v.
37561.21 Bancel, François Désiré. Histoire des révolutions de l'esprit français. Paris, 1878.
37561.26 Paris, Gaston. Les origines de la poésie lyrique en France au moyen âge. Paris, 1892.
37561.27 Jeanroy, Alfred. Les origines de la poésie lyrique en France au moyen âge. 1. éd. Paris, 1889.
37561.27.1 Jeanroy, Alfred. Les origines de la poésie lyrique en France au moyen âge. Paris, 1889.
37561.27.2 Jeanroy, Alfred. Les origines de la poésie lyrique en France au moyen âge. 2. éd. Paris, 1904.
37561.27.4 Jeanroy, Alfred. Les origines de la poésie lyrique en France au moyen âge. 3e éd. Paris, 1925.
37561.27.5 Jeanroy, Alfred. Les origines de la poésie lyrique en France au moyen âge. 4e éd. Paris, 1965.
37561.28 Études romanes dédiées a G. Paris. Paris, 1891.
37561.29 Legrand d'Aussy, C. Notices sur des Mss. français. Paris, 1799.
37561.31 Darmesteter, Arsène. Cours de littérature française du moyen âge. Paris, 1883.
37561.35 Berblinger, W. Das hotel Rambouillet und seine culturgeschichtliche Bedentung. Berlin, 1875.
37561.36 Lyons. Les trois génies de la chaire Bossuet, Bourdaloue. Nice, 1896.

37562 History of special periods - Before 1500

37562.1 Pamphlet vol. French literary history. Early periods. 14 pam.
37562.1.2F Pamphlet box. French literary history. Early periods.
37562.1.3 Pamphlet box. Early French literary history.
37562.1.4 Pamphlet vol. Becker, H. Die Auffassung de Jungfrau Maria in Altfrän. 13 pam.
37562.2 Masson, Gustave. French literature. London, 1888.
37562.2.9 Hertel, Adolf. Verzauberte Örtlichkeiten und Gegenstände in der altfranzösischen erzählenden Dachtung. Hannover, 1908.
37562.3 La Rue, Gervais de. Essais historiques sur les bardes anglo-normans. Caen, 1834. 3v.
37562.4 Rosny, J. de. Tableau littéraire de la France. Paris, 1809.
37562.5 Benoiston-de-Chateauneuf, Louis François. Essai sur la poésie...au XIIe, XIIIe et XIVe siècles. Paris, 1815.
37562.5.10 Boer, C. de. La Normandie et la renaissance. Groningue, 1912.
37562.6 Galpin, S.L. Cortois and Vilain. New Haven, 1905.
37562.7A Roquefort, Bonaventure. De l'état de la poésie française. Paris, 1821.
37562.7B Roquefort, Bonaventure. De l'état de la poésie française. Paris, 1821.
37562.10 Rocquefort-Flaméricourt, Jean Baptiste B. de. De l'état de la poésie française. Paris, 1815.
37562.11 Paris, Gaston. La poésie du moyen âge. Paris, 1885-1895. 2v.
37562.11.2 Paris, Gaston. La poésie du moyen âge. Paris, 1887.
37562.11.3 Paris, Gaston. La poésie du moyen âge. Paris, 1885.
37562.11.10 Trofimoff, A. Poètes français avant Ronsard. Paris, 1950.
37562.12 Jeanroy, Alfred. De nostratibus medii aevi poetis. Paris, 1889.
37562.12.5 Hecq, G. La poétique française. Paris, 1896.
37562.12.8 Heune, W. Die Casus im Mittelfranzösischen. Greifswald, 1886.
37562.12.11 Binet, H. Le style de la lyrique courtoise en France. Paris, 1891.
37562.12.13 Galino, T. Musique et versification française. Leipzig, 1891.
37562.12.14F Ovidio, F. d'. Studii sulla più antica versificazione francese; memoria. Roma, 1920.
37562.12.15 Ovidio, F. d'. Studii sulla più antica versificazione francese. Milan? 1920.
37562.12.16 Enneccerus, M. Versbau und gesanglicher Vortrag des ältesten Französischen Liedes. Frankfurt, 1901.
37562.12.18 Naetebus, G. Die nicht-lyrischen Strophenformen des altfranzösischen. Leipzig, 1891.
37562.12.20 Melchior, G. Der Achtsilbler in der altfranzösischen Dichtung mit Ausschluss der Lyrik. Leipzig, 1909.
37562.12.22 Orth, F. Ueber Reim und Strophenbau in der altfranzösischen Lyrik. Cassel, 1882.
37562.12.23 Stramwitz, E. Ueber Strophen- und Versenjambement im altfranzösischen. Greifswald, 1886.
37562.12.26 Otten, G. Ueber die Caesur im altfranzösischen. Greifswald, 1884.
37562.12.28 Langlois, Ernest. De artibus rhetoricae rhythmicae. Parisiis, 1890.
37562.12.30 Holborn, G. Wortaccent und Rhythmus. Greifswald, 1905.
37562.13 Weidinger, Anton. Die Schäferlyrik der französischen Vorrenaissance. München, 1892-1893.
37562.13.9A Jones, W.P. The pastourelle. Cambridge, 1931.
37562.13.9B Jones, W.P. The pastourelle. Cambridge, 1931.
37562.13.9C Jones, W.P. The pastourelle. Cambridge, 1931.
37562.14.6 Forkert, F.M. Beiträge zu den Bildern...auf Grund der Miracles de Nostre Dame. Bonn, 1901.
37562.15 Clédat, Léon. La poésie lyrique et satirique en France au moyen âge. Paris, n.d.
37562.16 Tolle, Konrad. Das Betheuern und Beschwöven in Altromanischen Poesie. Erlangen, 1883.
37562.17 Trebe, J. H.H. Les trouvères et leurs exhortations aux croisades. Leipzig, 1886.
37562.18 Lecoy de la Marche, A. Le treizième siècle littéraire et scientifique. Lille, 1887.
37562.18.5 Loubier, Jean. Das Ideal der männlichen Schönheit bei den altfranzösischen XIII Jahrhunderts. Halle, 1890.
37562.19 Formentin, Charles. Essai sur les fabliaux français du XIIe-XIIIe siècles. n.p., n.d.
37562.20 Pilz, Oskar. Beiträge zur Kenntnis der altfranzösischen Fableaux. Stettin, 1889.
37562.20.5 Loth, Johannes. Die Sprichwörter und Sentenzen der altfranzösischen Fabliaux. Greifenberg, 1895-1896.
37562.20.7 Herrmann, F. Schilderung...der gesellschaftliche Verhältnisse Frankreichs in der Fabliauxdichtung des XII und XIII Jahrhunderts. Coburg, 1900.
37562.20.9 Pillet, A. Das Fableau von den trois bossus Ménestrels. Halle, 1901.
37562.20.10 Barth, Bruno. Liebe und Ehe im altfranzösischen Fabel. Berlin, 1910.
37562.21 Bédier, Joseph. Les fabliaux. Paris, 1893.
37562.21.6 Bédier, Joseph. Les fabliaux. 3. éd. Paris, 1911.
37562.21.8 Bédier, Joseph. Les fabliaux. 4. éd. Paris, 1925.
37562.21.10 Recueil de fabliaux. Paris, 1910.
37562.22A Paris, Gaston. La littérature française au moyen âge. Paris, 1888.
37562.22B Paris, Gaston. La littérature française au moyen âge. Paris, 1888.
37562.22.2 Paris, Gaston. La littérature française au moyen âge. 2. éd. Paris, 1890.
37562.22.3 Paris, Gaston. La littérature française au moyen âge. 4. éd. Paris, 1909.
37562.22.4 Paris, Gaston. Mélanges de littérature française du moyen âge. Paris, 1910. 2v.
37562.22.4.1A Paris, Gaston. Mélanges de littérature française du moyen âge. v.1-2. Paris, 1910-1912.
37562.22.4.1B Paris, Gaston. Mélanges de littérature française du moyen âge. v.1-2. Paris, 1910-1912.
37562.22.4.2 Paris, Gaston. La littérature française au moyen âge. 5e éd. Paris, 1914.
37562.22.4.5 Paris, Gaston. La littérature française au moyen âge. 6e éd. Paris, 191-?
37562.22.4.10 Paris, Gaston. Mélanges de littérature française du moyen âge. v. 1-2. Paris, 1912.
37562.22.5 Paris, Gaston. Esquisse historique de la littérature française au moyen âge. Paris, 1907.
37562.22.5.2 Paris, Gaston. Esquisse historique de la littérature française au moyen âge. 2. éd. Paris, 1913.
37562.22.9A Paris, Gaston. Mediaeval French literature. London, 1903.

37562 **History of special periods - Before 1500 - cont.**

37562.22.9B Paris, Gaston. Mediaeval French literature. London, 1903.

37562.22.9C Paris, Gaston. Mediaeval French literature. London, 1903.

37562.24 Sepet, Marius. Les etudes relatives à la littérature française du moyen âge depuis 1867. Paris, 1879.

37562.25 Lecoy de la Marche, A. La chaire française au moyen âge. Paris, 1868.

37562.25.3 Lecoy de la Marche, A. La chaire française au moyen âge. 2. éd. Paris, 1886.

37562.25.4 Bourgain, L. La chaire française au XIIe siècle. Paris, 1879.

37562.25.15 Davy, M.M. Les sermons universitaires parisiens de 1250-1251. Paris, 1931.

37562.26 Garreaud, L. Causeries...sur le moyen âge littéraires de la France. Paris, 1884. 2v.

37562.27 Paris, Gaston. Paulin Paris et la littérature française au moyen âge. Paris, 1882.

37562.30 Strümpell, Gustav. Ersten Bibelübersetzungen der Franzosen. Braunschweig, 1872.

37562.31 Child, T. Christmas mystery in the fifteenth century. n.p., 1888.

37562.32 Pons, S. Les poèmes vaudois et les mystères provençaux du XVe siècle. Pinerolo, 1909.

37562.32.10 Champion, P. Histoire poétique du XVe siècle. Paris, 1923. 2v.

37562.33 Kuttner, Max. Das Naturgefühl der Altfranzösen und sein Einfluss auf ihre Dichtung. Berlin, 1889.

37562.34 Shishmarev, V. Lirika i liriki...istorii frantsii. Paris, 1911.

37562.35 Leibecke, O. Der verabredete Zweikampf in der altfranzösischen Litteratur. Göttingen, 1905.

37562.35.10 Witthoff, Johannes. Motiv des Zweikampfes zwischen Vater und Sohn. Nürnberg, 1921.

37562.36 Laur, Franz. Ueber Krankenbehandlung und Heilkunde in der Litteratur des alten Frankreichs. Arnstadt, 1904.

37562.37 Junge, A. Ueber Gerichtsbeamte...in der Litteratur des alten Frankreich. Göttingen, 1906.

37562.40 Brix, Clemens. Richard I., Herzog von der Normandie der französischen Litteratur. Münster, 1904.

37562.42 Rauschmaier, A. Über den figürlichen Gebrauch der Zahlen in altfranzösischen Litteratur. Erlangen, 1892.

37562.45A Voretzsch, Carl. Einführung in das Studium der altfranzösischen Literatur. Halle, 1905.

37562.45B Voretzsch, Carl. Einführung in das Studium der altfranzösischen Literatur. Halle, 1905.

37562.45.2 Voretzsch, Carl. Einführung in das Studium der altfranzösischen Literatur. Halle, 1913.

37562.45.10 Voretzsch, Carl. Einführung in das Studium der altfranzösischen Literatur. Halle, 1925.

37562.46 Voretzsch, Carl. Altfranzösisches Lesebuch zur Erlänterung der altfranzösischen Literaturgeschichte. Halle, 1921.

37562.46.2 Voretzsch, Carl. Altfranzösisches Lesebuch. 2. Aufl. Halle, 1932.

37562.47 Becker, P.A. Grundriss der altfranzösischen Literatur. Heidelberg, 1907.

37562.50 Doutrepont, G. La littérature française à la cour des ducs de Burgoyne. Paris, 1909.

37562.51 Richter, O. Die französische Litteratur am Hofe der Herzöge von Burgund. Halle, 1882.

37562.57 Guerlich, Robert. Bemerkungen über den Versbau der Anglonormannen. Breslau, 1889.

37562.57.5 Vising, J. Sur la versification Anglo-Normande. Upsala, 1884.

37562.60 Oulmont, Charles. Les débats du Clerc et du chevalier. Paris, 1911.

37562.65 Bardenwerper, K. Die Anwendung fremder Sprachen und Mundarten in den französischen Farcen. Halle, 1911.

37562.68 Mussafia, Adolf. Handschriftliche Studien. Wien, 1862.

37562.69 Reiffenberg, M. de. Histoire litteraire et politique. Bruxelles, 1845.

37562.70 Kühn, Oscar. Ueber Erwähnung und Schilderung von Körperlichen Krankheiten und Körpergebrechen in altfranzösischen Dichtungen. Breslau, 1902.

37562.71 Müller, Martin. Minne und Dienst. Inaug. Diss. Marburg, 1907.

37562.73 Jessel, Marie. Strophenbau und Liedbildung in der altfranzösischen Kunstlyrik des 12. und 13. Jahrhunderts. Greifswald, 1917.

37562.75 Wood, Mary M. The spirit of protest in Old French literature. N.Y., 1917.

37562.77 Gelzer, H. Nature zum Einfluss der Scholastik auf den altfranzösischen Roman. Halle, 1917.

37562.79 Heldt, Elisabeth. Französische Virelais aus dem 15. Jahrhundert. Halle, 1916.

37562.85 Winkler, E. Französische Dichter des Mittelalters. Wien, 1918.

37562.90 Fellinger, F. Das Kind in der altfranzösischen Literatur. Göttingen, 1908.

37562.95 Ahsmann, H.P.J.M. Le culte de la sainte Vierge et la littérature française profane du moyen âge. Utrecht, 1930.

37562.96 Hanm, Gertrud. Das altfranzösische Gedicht zu Mariae Hemmelfahrt...Beziehungen. Inaug. Diss. Würzburg, 1938.

37562.98 Merlino, Camillo P. The French studies of Mario Equicola (1470-1525). Berkeley, Calif., 1929.

37562.100 Beardwood, Jane. Rhymes of Latin and French words in Old French. Thesis. Philadelphia, 1930.

37562.102 Voretzsch, Carl. Introduction to the study of Old French literature. Halle, 1931.

37562.102.5 Voretzsch, Carl. Introduction to the study of Old French literature. N.Y., 1931.

37562.104 Jones, P.J. Prologue and epilogue in Old French lives of saints before 1400. Thesis. Philadelphia, 1933.

37562.106 Schilperoort, G. Le commerçant dans la litérature française du moyen âge (Caractère, Vie, position sociale). Proefschrift. Groningen, 1933.

37562.108 Bruel, Andrée. Romans français du moyen âge; essais. Paris, 1934.

37562.110 Lifschitz-Golden, M. Les juifs dans la littérature française du moyen âge. N.Y., 1935.

37562.120 Dupin, Henri. La courtoisie au moyen âge. Paris, 1931.

37562.130 Tuschen, A. Die Taufe in der altfranzösischen Literatur. Inaug. Diss. Wanne-Eickel, 1936.

37562.140 Don, Blanche H. The varying attitude toward women in French literature of the fifteenth century. N.Y., 1936.

37562.160 Röhl, G. Die idyllisch-ländlichen Motive in der altfranzösischen Literatur. Inaug. Diss. Rostock, 1936.

37562.170 Gambier, H. Les trois grands siècles du moyen âge (XIe-XIIe-XIIIe). Treviso, 1936.

37562 **History of special periods - Before 1500 - cont.**

37562.180A Pagès, A. La poésie française en Catalogne du XIIIe siècle a la fin du XVe. Toulouse, 1936.

37562.180B Pagès, A. La poésie française en Catalogne du XIIIe siècle a la fin du XVe. Toulouse, 1936.

37562.190 Hoffmann, K. Themen der französischen Lyrik im 12. und 13. Jahrhundert. Inaug. Diss. Freiburg, 1936.

37562.195 Wilmotte, M. L'epopée française, origine et élaboration. Paris, 1939.

37562.200 Gröber, G. Geschichte der mittelfranzösischen Literatur. 2e Aufl. Berlin, 1937. 2v.

37562.210 Holmes, U.T. A history of Old French literature from the origins to 1300. N.Y., 1937.

37562.220 Lewels, M. Theologische Streifzüge durch die altfranzösische Literatur. Vechte, 1937.

37562.230A Studies in French language and mediaeval literature. Manchester, 1939.

37562.230B Studies in French language and mediaeval literature. Manchester, 1939.

37562.240 Koch, Marie Pierre. An analysis of the long prayers in Old French literature with special reference to the "Biblical-creed-narrative" prayers. Diss. Washington, 1940.

37562.250 Bossuat, R. Le moyen âge. Paris, 1931.

37562.253 Bossuat, R. La littérature morale au moyen âge. Paris, 1935.

37562.257 Bossuat, R. La poésie lyrique en France au XVe siècle. v.1-3. Paris, 1948.

37562.260 Heft, D. Proverbs and sentences in fifteenth-century French poetry. N.Y., 1942.

37562.265 Nyström, Urban. Poèmes français sur les biens d'un ménage depuis l'Oustillement au villain du XIIIe siècle jusqu'aux Controverses de Gratien du Pont. Thèse. Helsinki, 1940.

37562.270 Études romanes dédiées à Mario Roques, pas ses amis, collegues et élèves de France. Paris, 1946.

37562.272 Merk, J. Die literarische Gestaltung der altfranzösischen Heiligerleben. Affaltern, 1946.

37562.274 Pei, Mario A. French precursors of the Chauson de Roland. N.Y., 1948.

37562.276 Cohen, Gustave. La vie littéraire en France au moyen âge. Paris, 1949.

37562.276.10 Cohen, Gustave. Tableau de la littérature française médiévale. Paris, 1950.

37562.276.15 Cohen, Gustave. Littérature française du moyen âge. Bruxelles, 1951.

37562.278 Ketcham, H. Nature in Old and Middle French poetry. Williamsport, Pa., 1950.

37562.280 Crosland, J.R. The Old French epic. Oxford, 1951.

37562.280.5 Crosland, J.R. Medieval French literature. Oxford, 1956.

37562.282 Weeks, R. A collection of works. n.p., n.d.

37562.284 Ahlström, Axel. Studier i den fornfranska lais-litteraturen. Upsala, 1892.

37562.286 Gennrich, Fredrich. Zwei altfranzösische Lais. Torino, 1942.

37562.288 Zumthor, Paul. Histoire littéraire de la France médiévale. 1. éd. Paris, 1954.

37562.290 Scivoletto, Nino. Spiritualitá medioevale e tradizione scolastica nel secolo XII en Francia. Napoli, 1954.

37562.292 Rickard, Peter. Britain in medieval French literature, 1100-1500. Cambridge, Eng., 1956.

37562.295 Kukenheim, Louis. Guide de la littérature française du moyen âge. Leiden, 1957.

37562.295.2 Kukenheim, Louis. Guide de la littérature française du moyen âge. 2. éd. Leiden, 1959.

37562.297 Frappier, Jean. La poésie lyrique en France au XII et XIII siècle. Paris, 1954.

37562.300 Saulnièr, V.L. La littérature française du moyen âge. 4. éd. Paris, 1957.

37562.300.5 Saulnièr, V.L. La littérature française du moyen âge. 5. éd. Paris, 1962.

37562.300.6 Saulnièr, V.L. La littérature française. 6. éd. Paris, 1964.

37562.303 Rasmussen, Jens. La prose narrative française de XVe siècle. Copenhague, 1958.

37562.305 Nolting-Hauff, Ilse. Die Stellung der Liebeskasuistik im höfischen Roman. Heidelberg, 1959.

37562.306 Schon, Peter. Studien zum Stil der frühen französischen Prosa. Frankfurt, 1960.

37562.310 Tourrier, A. Le courant réaliste dans le roman coutois en France au moyen âge. Paris, 1960.

37562.312 Oxford. University. Studies in medieval French. Oxford, 1961.

37562.313 Pickford, Cedric Edward. Changing attitudes towards medieval French literature. Hull, 1966.

37562.314 Valkhoff, M. Masterpieces of Old French literature. Johannesburg, 1956.

37562.316 Dragonetti, Roger. La technique poétique des trouvères dans la chanson courtoise. Brugge, 1960.

37562.318 Coppin, Joseph L. Amour et mariage dans la littérature française du nord au moyen âge. Paris, 1961.

37562.319 Holmes, Urban. A history of Old French literature, from the origins to 1300. N.Y., 1962.

37562.321 Koehler, Erich. Trobadorlyrik und höfischen Roman. Berlin, 1962.

37562.322 Zumthor, P. Langue et techniques poétiques à l'époque romane. Paris, 1963.

37562.323 LeGentil, P. La littérature française du moyen âge. Paris, 1963.

37562.324 Lechner, G. Zur Zeit und zur Stilistischen. München, 1961?

37562.325 Nelli, René. L'Erotique des troubadours. Toulouse, 1963.

37562.326 Woledge, B. Répertoire des plus anciens textes. Genève, 1964.

37562.327 Dubruck, E. The theme of death in French poetry. The Hague, n.d.

37562.328 Varvaro, Alberto. La narrativa francese alla metà del XII secolo. Napoli, 1964.

37562.330 Poirion, Daniel. Le poète et le prince. Grenoble, 1965.

37562.331 Ferrier, Janet Mackay. French prose writers of the fourteenth and fifteenth centuries. 1st ed. Oxford, 1966.

37562.332 Pollmann, Leo. Die Liebe in der hochmittelalterlichen Literatur Franckreichs. Habilitationsschrift. Frankfurt, 1966.

37562.333 Lyons, Faith. Les éléments descriptifs dans le roman d'aventure au XIIe siècle. Genève, 1965.

37562.334A Payen, Jean C. Le motif du repentir dans la littérature française médiévale. Thèse. Genève, 1967.

Classified Listing

37562 **History of special periods - Before 1500 - cont.**

37562.334B Payen, Jean C. Le motif du repentir dans la littérature française médiévale. Thèse. Genève, 1967.
37562.336 Donovan, Mortimor John. The Breton lay: a guide to varieties. Notre Dame, 1969.
37562.338 Macchia, Giovanni. La letteratura francese dalla crisi del medioevo alla fine del Rinascimento. Roma, 1967.
37562.340 Simone, Franco. Miscellanea di studi e ricerche sul Quattrocento francese. Torono, 1967.
37562.342 Jantzen, Hans-Günther. Untersuchungen zur Entstehung des altfranzösischen Prosaromans. n.p., 1966.
37562.344 Ménard, Philippe. Le rire et la sourire dans le roman courtois en France au moyen âge. Genève, 1969.
37562.346 Heger, Henrik. Die Melancholie bei den französischen Lyriken des Spätmittelalters. Bonn, 1967.
37562.348 Balmas, Enea Henri. L'età del Rinascimento in Francia. Milano, 1969.
37562.350 Moelk, Ulrich. Französische literarästhetik des 12. und 13. Jahrhunderts. Tübingen, 1969.
37562.352 Badel, Pierre Yves. Introduction à la vie littéraire du moyen âge. Paris, 1969.
37562.354A Bayrav, Süheylâ. Symbolisme médiéval: Béroul, Marie, Chrétien. Paris, 1957.
37562.354B Bayrav, Süheylâ. Symbolisme médiéval: Béroul, Marie, Chrétien. Paris, 1957.
37562.356 Klein, Karen Wilk. The partisan voice; a study of the political lyric in France and Germany, 1180-1230. The Hague, 1971.
37562.358 Castellani, Arrigo Ettore. Bédier avait-il raison? Fribourg, 1957.
37562.360 Zumthor, Paul. Essai de poétique médiévale. Paris, 1972.
37562.362 Ryding, William W. Structure in medieval narrative. The Hague, 1971.
37562.364 Owen, Douglas David Roy. The vision of Hell: infernal journeys in medieval French literature. Edinburgh, 1970.
37562.366 Fox, John Howard. The rhetorical tradition in French literature of the later Middle Ages. Exeter, 1969.

37563 **History of special periods - 16th century**

37563.2 Chasles, Philarète. Études sur le seizième siècle. Paris, n.d.
37563.3 Girardin, Saint-Marc. Tableau de la littérature française. Paris, 1862.
37563.3.5 Girardin, Saint-Marc. Tableau de la littérature française. Paris, 1868.
37563.4 Wahlund, Karl. Kronologiskt ordnade geografiska schemata. Uppsala, 1901.
37563.5 Blignières, Auguste de. Essai sur Amyot. Paris, 1851.
37563.6 Sturel, R. Jacques Amyot. Paris, 1908.
37563.7 Cougny, Edouard. François Hotoman-Montesquieu et mad. de Lambert. Vers, 1874-77.
37563.8 Réaume, Eugène. Prosateurs français du XVIe siècle. Paris, 1869.
37563.8.2 Réaume, Eugène. Les prosateurs français du XVIe siècle. 2. éd. Paris, 1869.
37563.9 Revillout, M.C. La prose française avant le XVIIe siècle. Montpellier, 1864.
37563.10 Froment, Théodore. L'éloquence et le barreau. Paris, 1875.
37563.12 Froment, Théodore. Essai sur...l'eloquence judiciare. Paris, 1874.
37563.12.5 Fleury, Claude. Dialogues...sur l'éloquence judiciare (1664). Thèse. Paris, 1925.
37563.13 Feugère, M. Leon. Charactères et portraits littéraires du XVI siècle. Paris, 1859. 2v.
37563.14 Feugère, M. Leon. Les femmes poètes au XVIe siècle. Paris, 1860.
37563.15 Desjardins, Albert. Moralistes français du XVIXe siècle. Paris, 1870.
37563.15.55 Plattard, Jean. La renaissance des lettres en France de Louis XII à Henri IV. 3e éd. Paris, 1938.
37563.16 Dezeimeris, Reinhold. De la renaissance des lettres à Bordeaux. Bordeaux, 1864.
37563.17 Alaux, J.E. La langue et la littérature franc du XVe au XVIIe siècle. Paris, 1884.
37563.17.5 Darmesteter, Arsène. Morceaux choisis des...écrivains du XVIe siècle. Paris, 1876.
37563.17.7 Darmesteter, Arsène. Morceaux choisis des...écrivains du XVIe siècle. 21e éd. Paris, 1934.
37563.17.9 Darmesteter, Arsène. Le seizième siècle en France. v.1-2. 3e éd. Paris, 1887.
37563.18 Darmesteter, Arsène. Le seizième siècle. 5e éd. Paris, 1893.
37563.18.5 Darmesteter, Arsène. Le seizième siècle. 8e éd. Paris, 190-?
37563.20 Faguet, Émile. Seizième siècle; études littéraires. Paris, 1894.
37563.20.7 Faguet, Émile. Seizième siècle; études littéraires. Paris, 19- .
37563.21 Piéri, Marius. Le pétrarquisme au XVIe siècle. Marseille, 1896.
37563.21.2 Piéri, Marius. Le pétrarquisme au XVIe siècle: Petrarque et Ronsard. Genève, 1970.
37563.21.5 Vianey, J. Le pétrarquisme en France au XVIe siècle. Montpellier, 1909.
37563.21.10 Vianey, J. Les prostateure du XVIe siècle. Paris, 1939.
37563.22 Sainte-Beuve, C.A. Tableau...de la poésie française. Paris, 1869.
37563.22.2 Sainte-Beauve, C.A. Tableau historique. Cambridge, 1963.
37563.23 Sainte-Beuve, C.A. Tableau...historique et critique de la poésie française. Paris, 1843.
37563.23.5 Sainte-Beuve, C.A. Tableau historique et critique. Paris, 1843.
37563.23.9 Michaut, G. Quibus rationibus Sainte-Beuve opus suum de 16th seculo. Lutetia Parisiorum, 1903.
37563.23.10 Sainte-Beuve, C.A. Tableau de la poésie française au XVIe siècle. Paris, 1876. 2v.
37563.24A Tilley, Arthur A. Literature of the French renaissance. Cambridge, 1904. 2v.
37563.24B Tilley, Arthur A. Literature of the French renaissance. v.2. Cambridge, 1904.
37563.24.5 Tilley, Arthur A. The literature of the French renaissance. N.Y., 1959. 2v.
37563.24.10 Tilley, Arthur A. Studies in the French renaissance. Cambridge, 1922.
37563.24.15 Redenbacher, F. Die Novellistik der französischen Hoch-Renaissance. Inaug. Diss. München, 1926.

37563 **History of special periods - 16th century - cont.**

37563.26 Picot, Émile. Les français italianisants au XVIe siècle. Paris, 1906. 2v.
37563.27 Sayous, Pierre André. Études littéraires sur...la reformation. Paris, 1854. 2v.
37563.27.48 Moore, W.G. La réforme allemande et la littérature française. Thèse. Strasbourg, 1930.
37563.27.50 Moore, W.G. La réforme allemande et la littérature française. Strasbourg, 1930.
37563.28 Chinard, G. L'exotisme américain dans la littérature française au XVIe siècle. Paris, 1911.
X Cg 37563.28 Chinard, G. L'exotisme américain dans la littérature française au XVIe siècle. Paris, 1911.
37563.29 Revue de la renaissance, organ international des amis du XVIe siècle et de la Pléiade. Paris, 1903.
37563.30 Voigt, J. Das Naturgefühl in der Literatur der französischen Renaissance. Berlin, 1898.
37563.31 Voigt, J. Das Naturgefühl in der Literatur der französischen Renaissance. Berlin, 1897.
37563.32 Mansuy, A. Le monde slave et les classiques français. Paris, 1912.
37563.33A Lenient, Charles. La satire en France au moyen âge. Paris, 1859.
37563.33B Lenient, Charles. La satire en France au moyen âge. Paris, 1859.
37563.33.5 Lenient, Charles. La satire en France au moyen âge. Paris, 1877.
37563.34 Lenient, Charles. La satire en France au XVIe siècle. Paris, 1866.
37563.35 Lenient, Charles. La satire en France au XVIe siècle. v.2. Paris, 1886.
37563.39 Henningsen, W. Das Verhältnis der französischen Plejadendichtung zur älteren französischen Literatur. Kiel, 1914.
37563.40 Lefranc, A. Grands ecrivains français. Paris, 1914.
37563.41 Loviot, Louis. Auteurs et livres anciens, XVIe et XVIIe siècles. Paris, 1917.
37563.42A Morf, H. Geschichte der französischen Literatur im Zeitalter der Renaissance. 2. Aufl. Strassburg, 1914.
37563.42B Morf, H. Geschichte der französischen Literatur im Zeitalter der Renaissance. 2. Aufl. Strassburg, 1914.
37563.43 Saineanu, L. Problèmes littéraires du seizième siècle. Paris, 1927.
37563.45 Plattard, Jean. La renaissance des lettres pour françois. Paris, 1939.
37563.48 Turner, Robert. Didon dans la tragédie de la renaissance italienne et française. Thèse. Paris, 1926.
37563.52 Levengood, S.L. The use of color in the verse of the Pléiade. Diss. Paris, 1927.
37563.54 Strowski, Fortunat. La Pléiade; la doctrine et l'oeuvre poétique. v.1-2. Paris, 1933.
37563.55 Chamard, Henri. La doctrine et l'oeuvre de la Pléiade. Paris, 19- . 2v.
37563.55.12 Chamard, Henri. Histoire de la Pléiade. Paris, 1961-1963. 4v.
37563.55.15 Clements, R.J. Critical theory and practice of the Pléiade. Cambridge, 1942.
37563.55.20 Wittschier, Heinz Willi. Die Lyrik der Pléiade. Frankfurt, 1971.
37563.55.25 Demerson, Guy. La mythologie classique dans l'oeuvre lyrique de la "Pléiade." Genève, 1972.
37563.56 Festugière, Jean. La philosophie de l'amour de Marsile Fecin. Coimbra, 1923.
37563.58 Becker, A. Aus Frankreichs Frührenaissance. München, 1927.
37563.59 Becker, A. Aus Frankreichs Frührenaissance. München, 1927.
37563.60 Humanisme et renaissance. Paris. 1-6,1934-1939 8v.
37563.60.1 Humanisme et renaissance, table 1934-1940. Genève, 1956.
37563.60.2 Bibliothèque d'humanisme et renaissance. Paris. 1,1941+ 28v.
37563.62A Atkinson, G. Les nouveaux horizons de la renaissance française. Paris, 1935.
37563.62B Atkinson, G. Les nouveaux horizons de la renaissance française. Paris, 1935.
37563.64 Haag, H. Der Gestaltwandel der Kupplerin in der französischen Literatur des 16. und 17. Jahrhunderts. Marburg, 1936.
37563.66 Gambier, Henri. Italie et renaissance poétique en France. Padova, 1936.
37563.68 Mönch, Walter. Die italienische Platonrenaissance und ihre Bedeutung für Frankreichs Literatur. Berlin, 1936.
37563.68.5 Mönch, Walter. Frankreichs Literatur im XVI Jahrhundert. Berlin, 1938.
37563.70 Françon, Marcel. Notes sur l'esthétique de la femme au 16e siècle. Cambridge, Mass., 1939.
37563.70.5A Françon, Marcel. Leçons et notes sur la littérature française du XVI siècle. Rochecorbon, 1957.
37563.70.5B Françon, Marcel. Leçons et notes sur la littérature française du XVI siècle. Rochecorbon, 1957.
37563.70.7 Françon, Marcel. Leçons et notes sur la littérature française. 2. éd. Cambridge, Mass., 1959.
37563.70.8A Françon, Marcel. Leçons et notes sur la littérature française au XVIe siècle. 3. éd. Cambridge, Mass., 1965.
37563.70.8B Françon, Marcel. Leçons et notes sur la littérature française au XVIe siècle. 3. éd. Cambridge, Mass., 1965.
37563.70.10 Françon, Marcel. Notes de cours. Cambridge, Mass., 1960.
37563.72 Hulubei, A. L'églogue en France au XVIe siècle. Paris, 1938.
37563.72.2 Hulubei, A. L'eglogue en France au XVIe siècle. Thèse. Paris, 1938.
37563.72.5 Hulubei, A. Repertoire des églogues en France au XVIe siècle. Paris, 1939.
37563.72.6 Hulubei, A. Repertoire des églogues en France au XVIe siècle, époque des valois, 1515-1589. Thèse. Paris, 1939.
37563.74 Schmidt, Albert Marie. La poésie scientifique en France au seizième siècle. Thèse. Paris, 1938?
37563.75 Schmidt, Albert Marie. La poésie scientifique en France au 16e siècle. Paris, 1938.
37563.75.5 Schmidt, Albert Marie. Études sur le XVIe siècle, avec les témoignages de François Mauriac et Marc Boegner. Paris, 1967.
37563.75.10 Schmidt, Albert Marie. La poésie scientifique en France au 16e siècle. Lausanne, 1970.
37563.76 Keating, L.C. Studies on the literary salon in France, 1550-1615. n.p., n.d.
37563.77 Bates, B.W. Literary portraiture in the historical narrative of the French renaissance. N.Y., 1945.

37563 **History of special periods - 16th century - cont.**

37563.78.5 Lebègue, Raymond. La poésie française de 1560 à 1630. v.1-2. Paris, 1951.
37563.79 Baridon, S.F. La Pléiade française. Milano, 1948.
37563.79.5 Castor, G. Pléiade poetics. Cambridge, Eng., 1964.
37563.81 Lebègue, Raymond. La poésie française de 1560 à 1630. v.1-2. Paris, 1947.
37563.83 Mélanges d'histoire littéraire de la renaissance offerts à Henri Chamard. Paris, 1951.
37563.84A Rouillard, Clarence D. The Turk in French history, thought, and literature (1520-1660). Paris, 1941.
37563.84B Rouillard, Clarence D. The Turk in French history, thought, and literature (1520-1660). Paris, 1941.
37563.85 Bailly, A. La vie littéraire sous la renaissance. Paris, 1952.
37563.87 Saulnier, Verdun L. La littérature française de la renaissance. 3. éd. Paris, 1953.
37563.87.2 Saulnier, Verdun L. La littérature française de la renaissance. 4. éd. Paris, 1957.
37563.87.5 Saulnier, Verdun L. La littérature française de la renaissance. 5. éd. Paris, 1959.
37563.87.6 Saulnier, Verdun L. La littérature française de la renaissance. 6e éd. Paris, 1962.
37563.87.7 Saulnier, Verdun L. La littérature française de la renaissance. 7. éd. Paris, 1965.
37563.87.9 Saulnier, Verdun L. La littérature française de la Renaissance. 9e éd. Paris, 1969.
37563.90 Weber, Henri. La création poétique au XVI siècle en France. Paris, 1956. 2v.
37563.92 Weber, Henri. La création poétique au XVI siècle en France. Thèse. Paris, 1956. 2v.
37563.93 Buffum, Imbrie. Studies in the baroque from Montaigne to Rotrau. New Haven, 1957.
37563.95 Merrill, R.V. Platonism in French renaissance poetry. N.Y., 1957.
37563.97 Forster, Elborg H. Die französische Elegie im 16. Jahrhundert. Köln, 1959.
37563.99 Bonnot, Jacques. Humanisme et Pléiade. Paris, 1959.
37563.101 Schenda, R. Die französische Prodigienliteratur in der 2. Hälfte des 16. Jahrhunderts. München, 1961.
37563.102 Brunelli, Giuseppe A. Da Ronsard à Molière. Messina, 1963.
37563.103 Homén, Olaf. Studier i fransk klassicism. v. 1-2. Helsingfors, 1914-1916.
37563.104 Bady, René. L'homme et son institution de Montaigne à Berulle, 1580-1625. Paris, 1964.
37563.104.5 Bady, René. Humanisme chrétien dans les lettres françaises: XVIe-XVIIe siècles. Paris, 1972.
37563.105 Smith, Pauline. The anti-courtier trend in sixteenth century French literature. Geneva, 1966.
37563.107 Stage International d'Études Humanistes. Lumières de la Pléiade. Paris, 1966.
37563.109 Jung, Marc-René. Hercule dans la littérature du XVIe siècle. Genève, 1966.
37563.112 The French renaissance and its heritage: essays presented to Alan M. Boase by colleagues, pupils and friends. London, 1968.
37563.114 Melanges d'histoire littéraire, XVIe-XVIIe siècle. Paris, 1969.
37563.116 Giudici, Enzo. Spiritualismo e carnascialismo. Napoli, 1968.
37563.118 Joukovsky, Françoise. La gloire dans la poésie française et néolatine du 16e siècle. Genève, 1969.
37563.120 Humanism in France at the end of the Middle Ages and in the early renaissance. N.Y., 1970.
37563.122 Ménager, Daniel. Introduction à la vie littéraire du XVIe siècle. Paris, 1968.
37563.124 Simone, Franco. Umanesimo, Rinascimento, Barocco in Francia. Milano, 1968.
37563.126 Macchia, Giovanni. La letteratura francese. Firenze, 1970. 2v.
37563.128 Pineaux, Jacques. La poésie des protestants de langue française. Paris, 1971.

37564 **History of special periods - 17th century**

37564.1 Merlet, Gustave. Études littéraires des classiques français XVII et XVIII siècles. Paris, 1876.
37564.2 Lambert, Claude F. Histoire littéraire du Regne de Louis XIV. Paris, 1751. 3v.
37564.4 Weisser, E. L'Hotel de Rambouillet. Breslau, n.d.
37564.4.50 Fremy, A. Essai sur les variations du style français au dix-septième siècle. Paris, 1843.
37564.5 Venet, A.R. Moralistes des 16me et 17me siècles. Paris, 1859.
37564.6 Venet, A.R. Poètes du siècle de Louis XIV. Paris, 1861.
37564.7 Astié, J.F. Louis XIV and the writers of his age. Boston, 1855.
37564.9 Demogeot, Jacques. Tableau de la littérature française. Paris, 1859.
37564.12 Aubineau, Léon. Notices littéraire sur le XVIIe siècle. Paris, 1859.
Htn 37564.13* Guéret, G. La parnasse reformé. Paris, 1669.
Htn 37564.14* Guéret, G. La guerre des auteurs anciens et modernes. Paris, 1671.
37564.15 Sayous, Pierre André. Histoire de la littérature française. Paris, 1853. 2v.
37564.16 Koerting, H. Geschichte des französischen Romans im XVII Jahrhunderts. Leipzig, 1885. 2v.
37564.17A Koerting, H. Geschichte des französischen Romans im XVII Jahrhunderts. Leipzig, 1891.
37564.17B Koerting, H. Geschichte des französischen Romans im XVII Jahrhunderts. Leipzig, 1891.
37564.18 Follioley, Léopold. Histoire de la littérature françoise. Paris, 1864.
37564.20 Follioley, Léopold. Histoire de la littérature française. 5e éd. Tours, 1885. 3v.
37564.21 Vissac, J.A. De la poésie latine en France. Paris, 1862.
37564.23 Duchesne, Julien. Histoire des poëmes épiques français. Paris, 1870.
37564.25 Beaurepaire, Eugène de Robillard de. Histoire de deux sonnets. n.p., n.d.
37564.26 Roederer, P.L. Mémoire pour servir a l'histoire de la Société Polie en France. Paris, 1835.
37564.26.90 Somaize, Antoine de. Le grand dictionaire des pretieuses. Paris, 1661. 2v.
37564.27A Somaize, Antoine de. Le dictionnaire des precieuses. Paris, 1856. 2v.

37564 **History of special periods - 17th century - cont.**

37564.27B Somaize, Antoine de. Le dictionnaire des precieuses. Paris, 1856. 2v.
37564.28.2 Livet, C.L. Précieux et précieuses. Paris, 1895.
37564.28.7 Vincent, Leon. Hôtel de Rambouillet and The précieuses. Boston, 1900.
37564.28.10 Mongrédien, Georges. Les précieux et les précieuses. Paris, 1939.
37564.28.12 Mongrédien, Georges. Les précieux et les précieuses. Paris, 1963.
37564.28.15A Bray, René. La préciosité et les précieux. Paris, 1948.
37564.28.15B Bray, René. La préciosité et les précieux. Paris, 1948.
37564.29 Fialon, Eugene. Leçons d'histoire littéraires. Paris, 1869.
37564.30 Bourgoin, Auguste. Les maitres de la critique au XVIIeme siècle. Paris, 1889.
37564.32.8 Faguet, Émile. Dix-septième siècle. Paris, 19- .
37564.32.15 Faguet, Émile. Dix-septième siècle. Paris, 191-?
37564.32.20 Faguet, Émile. Dix-septième siècle. Paris, 19- .
37564.32.22 Faguet, Émile. Dix-septième siècle. Paris, 19- .
37564.32.50 Faguet, Émile. Les grands maitres du dix-septième siècle. Paris, 1885.
37564.34 Lotherssen, F. Geschichte der französischen Literatur in XVII Jahrhundert. Vienna, 1877. 2v.
37564.35 Weinberg, Gustav. Das französische Schäferspiel in der 17th Jahrhundert. Frankfurt, 1884.
37564.36 Dupuy, Adrien. Histoire de la littérature française (au XVIIe siècle). Paris, 1892.
37564.37 Janet, Paul. Les passions et les caractères dans la littérature du XVIIe siècle. Paris, 1888.
37564.38 Fournel, Victor. De Malherbe a Bossuet. Paris, 1885.
37564.38.10 Fournel, Victor. La littérature independante et les écrivains oublies. Paris, 1862.
37564.39 Longhaye, R.P.G. Histoire de la littérature française aux dix-septième siècle. Paris, 1895- 4v.
37564.40 Jacquet, A. La vie littéraire dans un ville de Province sous Louis XIV. Paris, 1886.
NEDL 37564.41 Delaporte, P.V. Du merveilleux dans la littérature française sous le règne de Louis XIV. Paris, 1891.
37564.42 Broc, Hervé de. Propos littéraires. Paris, 1898.
37564.43 Lodin de Lalaire, T. De la Mission de Pascal de Bossuet et de Fénélon au 17e siècle. Paris, 1833.
37564.43.5 Chamaillard, E. La poésie et les poètes devant Pascal. Paris, 1904.
X Cg 37564.44 Brun, P. Autour du dix-septième siècle. Grenoble, 1901.
37564.44.25 Albert, Paul. La littérature française au dix-septième siècle. Paris, 1873.
37564.44.27 Albert, Paul. La littérature française au dix-septième siècle. 2e éd. Paris, 1875.
37564.44.34 Albert, Paul. La littérature française au dix-septième siècle. 5e éd. Paris, 1882.
37564.46 Gelin, H. Une famille poitevine d'Ecrivains illustres. Niort, 1905.
37564.48 Jacquinet, P. Des predicateurs du XVIIe siècle avant Bosquet. Paris, 1863.
37564.49 Lezat, A. De la prédication sous Henri IV. Paris, n.d.
37564.50 Desjardins, Paul. La méthode des classiques française Corneille-Poussin-Pascal. Paris, 1904.
37564.52 Martino, Pierre. L'Orient dans la littérature française au XVIIe et au XVIIIe siècle. Paris, 1906.
37564.52.1 Martino, Pierre. L'Orient dans la littérature française au 17e et au 18e siècle. Genève, 1970.
37564.53 Pinot, V. La Chine et la formation de l'esprit philosophique en France 1640-1740. Thèse. Paris, 1932.
37564.55 Tilley, Arthur Augustus. From Montaigne to Molière. London, 1908.
37564.55.2 Tilley, Arthur Augustus. From Montaigne to Molière. 2nd ed. Cambridge, 1923.
37564.58 Toinet, R. Notes pour servir à l'histoire littérature du XVIIe siècle. v.3-4. Tulle, 1899- 2v.
37564.59 Legouvé, Ernest. Dernières pages recueillies, 1898-1903. Evreux, 1904.
37564.60A Wright, Charles H.C. French classicism. Cambridge, 1920.
37564.60B Wright, Charles H.C. French classicism. Cambridge, 1920.
37564.60C Wright, Charles H.C. French classicism. Cambridge, 1920.
37564.61A Stewart, H.F. The classical movement in French literature. Cambridge, Eng., 1923.
37564.61B Stewart, H.F. The classical movement in French literature. Photoreproduction. Cambridge, Eng., 1923.
37564.62 Bailly, A. L'école classique française. Paris, 1921.
37564.63 Chinard, G. L'Amérique et le rêve exotique. Paris, 1913.
X Cg 37564.63 Chinard, G. L'Amérique et le rêve exotique. Paris, 1913.
37564.63.2A Chinard, G. L'Amérique et le rêve exotique. Paris, 1934.
37564.63.2B Chinard, G. L'Amérique et le rêve exotique. Paris, 1934.
37564.65 Fidao-Justiniani, J.E. L'Esprit classique et le preciosité au XVIIe siècle. Paris, 1914.
37564.65.5 Fidao-Justiniani, J.E. Qu'est-ce qu'un classique? Paris, 1929.
37564.65.15 Bray, René. La formation de la doctrine classique en France. Paris, 1927.
37564.66A Merlant, J. De Montaigne a Vauvenargues. Paris, 1914.
37564.66B Merlant, J. De Montaigne a Vauvenargues. Paris, 1914.
37564.68 Lacour, L. Richelieu dramaturge et ses collaborateurs. Paris, 1926.
37564.70A Johnson, A. Lafosse Otway, Saint-Real. Paris, 1901.
37564.70B Johnson, A. Lafosse Otway, Saint-Real. Paris, 1901.
37564.71 Johnson, A. Étude sur...littérature...du XVIIe siècle. Thèse. Paris, 1901.
37564.73 Cauchie, Maurice. Documents pour server à l'histoire littéraire du XVIIe siècle. Paris, 1924.
37564.76 Robiou, Felix. Essai sur l'histoire de la littérature. Paris, 1858.
37564.80 Luschka, W.H. Die Rolle des Fortschrittsgedankens in der Poetik und Literarischen Kritik der Franzosen. Inaug. Diss. München, 1926.
37564.85 Strowski, F.J. La sagesse française: Montaigne, Saint François de Sales, Descartes. Paris, 1925.
37564.87 Morley, Grace Louise (McCann). Le sentiment de la nature en France dans la 1e moitié de 17me siècle. Thèse. Nemours, 1926.
37564.87.5 Morley, Grace Louise (McCann). Le sentiment de la nature en France dans la première moitié du dix-septième siècle. Nemours, 1926.
37564.93A Bray, René. La formation de la doctrine classique en France. Thèse. Dijon, 1926.
37564.93B Bray, René. La formation de la doctrine classique en France. Thèse. Dijon, 1926.

37564 History of special periods - 17th century - cont.

37564.98 Storer, Mary E. Un épisode littéraire de la fin du XVIIe siècle. Paris, 1928.
37564.98.5 Storer, Mary E. Un épisode littéraire de la fin du XVIIIe siècle. Thèse. Paris, 1928.
37564.102 Atkinson, Geoffroy. Les relations de voyages du XVIIIe siècle et l'évolution des idees. Paris, 1924.
37564.102.10 Atkinson, Geoffroy. The extraordinary voyage in French literature before 1700. N.Y., 1920.
37564.102.15A Atkinson, Geoffroy. The extraordinary voyage in French literature from 1700 to 1720. Paris, 1922.
37564.102.15B Atkinson, Geoffroy. The extraordinary voyage in French literature from 1700 to 1720. Paris, 1922.
37564.106 Crump, Phyllis Eirene. Nature in the age of Louis XIV. London, 1928.
37564.109 Wollstein, Rose H. English opinions of French poetry, 1660-1750. N.Y., 1923.
37564.112 Wilson, N.S. The French classic age. London, 1927.
37564.114 Caudwell, H. Introduction to French classicism. London, 1931.
37564.116 Trahard, P. Les maîtres de la sensibilité français au XVIIe siècle (1715-1789). Paris, 1931-1933. 4v.
37564.118 Vial, Francisque. Idées et doctrines littéraires du XVIIe siècle. Paris, 1906.
37564.118.5 Vial, Francisque. Idées et doctrines littéraires du XVIIe siècle. Paris, 1939.
37564.120 Dallas, D.F. Le roman français de 1660 a 1680. Thèse. Paris, 1932.
37564.120.5 Dallas, D.F. Le roman français de 1660 a 1680. Paris, 1932.
37564.122 Karpa, Louise. Themen der französischen Lyrik im 17. Jahrhundert. Inaug. Diss. Homburg-Saar, 1934.
37564.124 Brown, H. Scientific organizations in seventeenth century French (1620-1680). Baltimore, 1934.
37564.126A Marni, A. Allegory in the French heroic poem of the seventeenth century. Princeton, 1936.
37564.126B Marni, A. Allegory in the French heroic poem of the seventeenth century. Princeton, 1936.
37564.128 Ninow, Otto. Die Komposition des französischen idealistischen Romans im 17. Jahrhundert nach seinen Hauptvertretern. Inaug. Diss. Halle, 1935.
37564.131 Irmen, F. Liebe und Freudschaft in der französischen Literatur der 17. Jahrhunderts. Inaug. Diss. Speyer, 1937.
37564.133A Feugère, A. Le mouvement religieux dans la littérature du XVIIe siècle. Paris, 1938.
37564.133B Feugère, A. Le mouvement religieux dans la littérature du XVIIe siècle. Paris, 1938.
37564.135 Ganter, P. Das literarische Porträt in Frankreich im 17. Jahrhundert. Berlin, 1939.
37564.145 Riva Agüero, José de la. Estudios sobre literatura francesca. Lima, 1944.
37564.150 Reynier, Gustave. Le roman réaliste au XVIIe siècle. Paris, 1914.
37564.151 Pizzarusso, A. La poetica del romanzo in Francia, 1660-1685. Rome, 1962.
37564.155 Edelman, Nathan. Attitudes of 17th century France toward the Middle Ages. N.Y., 1946.
37564.160 Reynold, Gonzague. Le XVIIe siècle. Montréal, 1944.
37564.165 Neubert, Fritz. Die französische Klassik und Europa. Stuttgart, 1941.
37564.170A Mongrédien, G. La vie littéraire au XVII siècle. Paris, 1947.
37564.170B Mongrédien, G. La vie littéraire au XVII siècle. Paris, 1947.
37564.175 Mornet, Daniel. Histoire de la littérature française classique. Paris, 1940.
37564.175.5 Mornet, Daniel. Histoire de la littérature française classique, 1660-1700. 2. éd. Paris, 1942.
37564.175.10 Mornet, Daniel. Histoire de la littérature française classique. 3. éd. Paris, 1947.
37564.180 Turnell, Martin. The classical moment. Norfolk, 1946.
37564.187 Saulnier, Verdun L. La littérature française du siècle classique, 1610-1715. 2. éd. Paris, 1947.
37564.187.7 Saulnier, Verdun L. La littérature française du siècle classique. 7. éd. Paris, 1963.
37564.190 Busson, H. La religion des classiques. 1. éd. Paris, 1948.
37564.195 Adam, Antoine. Histoire de la littérature française au XVIII siècle. Paris, 1948-1951. 5v.
37564.200A Borgerhoff, E. The freedom of French classicism. Princeton, 1950.
37564.200B Borgerhoff, E. The freedom of French classicism. Princeton, 1950.
37564.210 Tableau de la littérature française. Paris, 1939.
37564.215 Tortel, Jean. Le préclassicisme français. Paris, 1952.
37564.220 Mourgues, O. de. Metaphysical. Oxford, 1953.
37564.225 Rousset, Jean. La littérature de l'âge baroque en France. Paris, 1953.
37564.225.5 Rousset, Jean. L'intérieur et l'extérieur, essais sur la poésie et sur le théâtre au XVIIe siècle. Paris, 1968.
37564.230 Raymond, Marcel. Baroque et renaissance poétique. Paris, 1955.
37564.235 Bonfantini, Mario. La letteratura francese del XVII secolo. Napoli, 1955.
37564.235.2 Bonfantini, Mario. La letteratura francese del XVII secolo. 2. éd. Napoli, 1964.
37564.240 Lang, Alfred. Gesellschaft und Wirtschaft Frankreichs im Spiegel der klassischen Literatur des 17. Jahrhundert (1660 bis 1715). Bonn, 1959.
37564.245 Haase, Erich. Einführung in die Literatur des Refuge. Berlin, 1959.
37564.250 Moore, W.G. French classical literature. London, 1961.
37564.255 France. Archives. Documents du Minutier central concernant. Paris, 1960.
37564.260 Demorest, Jean J. Studies in seventeenth-century French literature. Ithaca, N.Y., 1962.
37564.261 Krailsheimer, Alban. Studies in self-interest. Oxford, 1962.
37564.262 Mercier, R. L'Afrique Noire dans la littérature française; les premières images, XVIIe-XVIIIe siècles. Dakar, 1962.
37564.263 Bruzzi, Amelia. Studi sul barocco francese. Bologna, 1962.
37564.264 Sassus, Jeannine. The motif of renunciation of love in the seventeenth century French novel. Washington, 1963.
37564.265 Davidson, Hugh McCullough. Audience, words, and art. Columbus, Ohio, 1965.
37564.266 Lathuillère, Roger. La preciosité. Genève, 1966.

37564 History of special periods - 17th century - cont.

37564.267 Macchia, Giovanni. La fine dell' "Etá classica" e la litteratura francese agli. Roma, 1958?
37564.268 Lebois, André. XVIIe siècle; recherches et portraits. Paris, 1966.
37564.269 Oblomievskii, Dmitrii D. Frantsuzskii klassitsizm. Moskva, 1968.
37564.272 Corsaro, Antonio. Astrattismo nella poesia francese del seicento e altri studi. Palermo, 1968.
37564.274 Picard, Raymond. Two centuries of French literature, 1600-1800. London, 1970.
37564.276 Saisselin, Rémy Gilbert. The rule of reason and the ruses of the heart. Cleveland, 1970.
37564.278 Picard, Raymond. Génie de littérature française, 1600-1800. Paris, 1970.
37564.280 Zuber, Roger. Les "Belles infidèles" et la formation du goût classique. Paris, 1968.
37564.282 Mazon, Jeanne (Roche). Autour des contes de fées. Paris, 1968.
37564.284 Tournand, Jean Claude. Introduction à la vie littéraire du XVIIe siècle. Paris, 1970.
37564.286 Valle, Daniela dalla. La frattura. Ravenna, 1970.
37564.288 Nurse, Peter Harold. Classical voices: studies of Corneille, Racine, Molière, Mme de Lafayette. London, 1971.

37565 History of special periods - 18th century

37565.2 Aillaud, P.T. Discours sur cette question: Quels ont été les effets de la décadence des moeurs sur la littérature français? Paris, 1808.
37565.3 Beuchot, A.J.Q. Nouveau nécrologe français. Paris, 1812.
37565.4 Jay, Antoine. Tableau littéraire de la France pendant le XVIII siècle. Paris, 1810.
37565.5 Barante, Amable Guillaume P.B. De la littérature française. 4. éd. Paris, 1824.
37565.6 Barante, Amable Guillaume P.B. De la littérature française pendant le XVIIIe siècle. 5. éd. Paris, 1832.
37565.7 Barante, Amable Guillaume P.B. De la littérature française pendant le dix-huitième siècle. 2. éd. Paris, 1814.
37565.8 Vinet, Alexandre R. Histoire de la littérature française au 18me siècle. Paris, 1853.
37565.9 Vinet, Alexandre R. History of French literature in the 18th century. Edinburgh, 1854.
37565.12 Schnitzler, Johann H. Aperçu sommaire de la littérature française. Strasbourg, 1860.
37565.13 Herrmann, T.A. Resumé de la littérature française au XVIII siècle. Dresden, 1874.
37565.14 Du Bled, Victor. Le prince de ligne et ses contemporains. Paris, 1890.
37565.15 Albert, Paul. Littérature française au XVIII siècle. Paris, 1874.
37565.15.3 Albert, Paul. Littérature française au XVIII siècle. Paris, 1883.
37565.15.6 Albert, Paul. Littérature française au XVIIIe siècle. Paris, 1895.
37565.16 Bonnal, Edmond. Étude sur l'histoire de la littérature pendant de la revolution. Toulouse, 1866.
37565.17 Gidel, Charles. Histoire de la littérature française fin du XVIIe siècle - 1815. Paris, n.d.
37565.18 Jeanroy-Felix, Victor. Nouvelle histoire de la littérature française pendant la revolution. Paris, 1887.
37565.19 Sayous, André. Le dix-huitième siècle à l'etranger. Paris, 1861. 2v.
37565.20 Bersot, Ernest. Études sur le XVIIIe siècle. Études générale. Paris, 1855. 2v.
37565.22 Argonne, Bonaventure d'. Melanges d'histoire et de littérature. Rouen, 1700. 2v.
37565.22.2 Argonne, Bonaventure d'. Melanges d'histoire et de littérature. 2nd ed. Paris, 1700. 2v.
37565.22.5 Argonne, Bonaventure d'. Melanges d'histoire et de littérature. 4th ed. Paris, 1725. 3v.
37565.22.25 Lycée de Paris, club littéraire. Paris, 1784.
37565.23 Barni, Jules. Histoire des idées morales. Paris, 1865. 2v.
37565.24 Barni, Jules. Le moralistes français au 18th siècle. Paris, 1873.
37565.25 Joret, Charles. Des rapports intellectuels et littéraires. Paris, 1884.
37565.29 Desnoiresterres, Gustave. La comédie satirique au XVIIIe siècle. Paris, 1885.
37565.29.2 Desnoiresterres, Gustave. Epicuriens et lettres XVIIe et XVIIIe siècle. Paris, 1879.
37565.30 Duval, Georges. Histoire de la littérature révolutionnaire. Paris, 1879.
37565.30.6 Sargent, George H. The French revolution and Napoleon in literature and caricature. n.p., 1906.
37565.31 Duprat, Pascal. Les encyclopédistes. Paris, 1866.
37565.31.2 Rocafort, J. Les doctrines littéraires de l'encyclopedie. Paris, 1890.
37565.31.5 Ducros, L. Les encyclopédistes. Paris, 1900.
37565.31.6 Dupont-Chatelain, M. Les encyclopédistes et les femmes. Paris, 1911.
37565.31.7 Chaumeix, A.J. La petite encyclopédie. Anvers, 1772. 3 pam.
37565.31.9 Chaudon, Louis M. Anti-dictionnaire philosophique. 4e éd. Paris, 1775. 2v.
37565.31.15 Zeller, Hugo. Die Grammatik in der grossen französischen Enzyklopädie. Inaug. Diss. Weisswasser, 1930.
37565.31.25 Stofflet, D.E. Les "Encyclopédistes" et la Franco-Maçonnerie. Paris, 1938?
37565.32 Caro, E. La fin du dix-huitième siècle. Paris, 1880. 2v.
37565.33 Hennet, Léon. Le régiment de la Calotte. Paris, 1886.
37565.34 Schmidt-Weissenfels, Eduard. Geschichte der französischen Revolutions-Litteratur. Prague, 1859.
37565.35 Merlet, Gustave. Tableau de la littérature française 1800-1815. Paris, 1878. 3v.
37565.35.2 Scherer, Edmond. Etudes sur la littérature au XVIIIe siècle. Paris, 1891.
37565.36 Albert, Maurice. La littérature française sous la révolution. Paris, 1891.
37565.36.4 Albert, Maurice. La littérature française sous la révolution. Paris, 1898.
37565.36.9 Faguet, Émile. Dix-huitième siècle. 4e éd. Paris, 1890.
37565.36.20 Faguet, Émile. Dix-huitième siècle. Paris, 1890.
37565.37 Faguet, Émile. XVIII siècle. Études littéraires. Paris, 1892.

37565 History of special periods - 18th century - cont.

NEDL 37565.37.6 Faguet, Émile. XVIII siècle. Études littéraires. Paris, 1901.

37565.38 Bonhomme, Honoré. Journal et mémoires de Charles Collé (1748-1772). Paris, 1868. 3v.

37565.39 Bertrand, L. La-fin du classicisme. Paris, 1897.

37565.40 Blei, Franz. Die galante Zeit und ihr Ende. Berlin, n.d.

37565.41 Séché, L. Educateurs et moralistes. Paris, 1893.

37565.42 Cushing, Mary G. Pierre le tourneur. [Translator]. N.Y., 1908.

37565.43 Vial, F. Idées et doctrines littéraires du XVIII siècle. Paris, 1909.

37565.43.5 Vial, F. Idées et doctrines littéraires du XVIII siècle. 10e éd. Paris, 1937.

37565.44 Lambert, Claude F. Relation singulière, ou Le courier des Champs Elisées. Cologne, 1771.

37565.45 Candel, Jules. Les prédicateurs français dans la première moitié du XVIIIe siècle. Paris, 1904.

37565.46 Coulanges, A. de. La chaire française au dix-huitième siècle. Paris, 1901.

37565.47 Monselet, Charles. Oubliés et dédaignés. Paris, 1885.

37565.48 Pellisson, M. Les hommes de lettres au XVIIIe siècle. Paris, 1911.

37565.49.3 Mornet, Daniel. Le romantisme en France au XVIII siècle. 3e éd. Paris, 1932.

37565.50 Petermann, B. Streit um Vers und Prosa in der französischen Literatur des XVIII Jahrhundert. Halle, 1913.

37565.51 Van Tieghem, P. L'année littéraire, 1754-1790. Thèse. Paris, 1917.

37565.53 Fournel, Victor. De Jean-Baptiste Rousseau à André Chénier. Études litteraires et morales sur le XVIIIe siècle. Paris, 1886.

37565.55 Estève, E. Études de littérature préromantique. Paris, 1923.

NEDL 37565.60 Hatzfeld, H. Geschichte der französischen Aufklärung. München, 1922.

37565.66 Funck-Brentano, T. Les sophistes français. Paris, 1905.

37565.68.2 Green, Frederick C. French novelists. N.Y., 1930.

37565.68.3A Green, Frederick C. French novelists, manners and ideas, from Renaissance to the revolution. N.Y., 1964.

37565.68.3B Green, Frederick C. French novelists, manners and ideas, from Renaissance to the revolution. N.Y., 1964.

37565.68.5 Green, Frederick C. Eighteenth-century France. N.Y., 1931.

37565.68.6 Green, Frederick C. Eighteenth-century France, six essays. N.Y., 1964.

37565.70A Tilley, Arthur. Decline of the age of Louis XIV. Cambridge, 1929.

37565.70B Tilley, Arthur. Decline of the age of Louis XIV. Cambridge, 1929.

37565.72 Monglond, André. Histoire intérieure du préromantisme français de l'abbé Prevosta Jouvert. Thèse. Grenoble, 1929. 2v.

37565.72.5 Monglond, André. Le préromantisme français. Grenoble, 1930. 2v.

37565.72.10 Monglond, André. Le préromantisme français. Paris, 1965-1966. 2v.

37565.74 Monglond, André. Projets d'une bibliographie methodique. Grenoble, 1929.

37565.76 Francois, A. Les origines lyriques de la phrase moderne. Paris, 1929.

37565.78 Bertaut, Jules. Égéries du XVIIIe siècle. Paris, 1928.

37565.78.5 Bertaut, Jules. La vie littéraire en France au XVIIIe siècle. Paris, 1954.

37565.79 Beck, T.J. Northern antiquities in French learning and literature, 1755-1855. N.Y., 1934-35. 2v.

37565.80 Rohrer, B. Das Erdbeben von Lissabon in der französischen Literatur des achtzehnten Jahrhunderts. Inaug. Diss. Heidelberg, 1933.

37565.82 Werner, Erich. Das Literarische Porträt in Frankreich im 18. Jahrhundert. Inaug. Diss. Leipzig, 1935.

37565.84 Mohrenschildt, D.S. Russia in the intellectual life of eighteenth-century France. N.Y., 1936.

37565.86 Mornet, Daniel. French thought in the eighteenth century. N.Y., 1929.

37565.88 Clayton, Vista. The prose poem in French literature of the eighteenth century. N.Y., 1936.

37565.90 Hastings, H. Man and beast in French thought of the eighteenth century. Baltimore, 1936.

37565.92 Dedieu, J. Les philosophes du XVIIIe siècle. Paris, 1936.

37565.94 Seeber, E.D. Anti-slavery opinion in France during the second half of the eighteenth century. Baltimore, 1937.

37565.94.5 Seeber, E.D. Anti-slavery opinion in France during the second half of the eighteenth century. Baltimore, 1937.

37565.96 Géruzez, Eugéne. Histoire de la littérature française, 1789-1800. 8e éd. Paris, 1884.

37565.97 Géruzez, Eugéne. Histoire de la littérature française. 5. éd. Paris, 1882. 2v.

37565.97.5 Géruzez, Eugéne. Histoire de la littérature française pendant la révolution. 7. éd. Paris, 1881.

37565.98 Wais, Kurt K.T. Das antiphilosophische Weltbild des französischen Sturm und Drang, 1760-1789. Berlin, 1934.

37565.100 Dufrenoy, Marie L. L'Orient romanesque en France, 1704-1789. Montréal, 1946-1947. 2v.

37565.105 Henriot, Émile. Courrier littéraire, XVIIIe siècle. Paris, 1945. 2v.

37565.106 Henriot, Émile. Courrier littéraire, XVIIIe siècle. 9. éd. Paris, 1961. 2v.

37565.110 Bellessort, A. Dix-huitième siècle et romantisme. Paris, 1941.

37565.118A Bénichou, P. Morales du grand siècle. 3. éd. Paris, 1948.

37565.118B Bénichou, P. Morales du grand siècle. 3. éd. Paris, 1948.

37565.120 Schalk, Fritz. Einleitung in die Encyclopädie der französischen Aufklärung. München, 1936.

37565.121 Schalk, Fritz. Studien zur französischen Aufklärung. München, 1964.

37565.124 Poulet, Georges. Études sur le temps humain. Paris, 1952- 4v.

37565.125 Poulet, Georges. Études sur le temps humain. Edinburgh, 1949.

37565.126 Poulet, Georges. Studies in human time. Baltimore, 1956.

37565.126.5 Poulet, Georges. The interior distance. Baltimore, 1959.

37565.135 French thought in the eighteenth century. London, 1953.

37565.140 Klemperer, V. Geschichte der französischen Literatur im 18. Jahrhundert. Berlin, 1954.

37565.145 McGhee, D.M. Fortunes of a tale. Menasha, Wisconsin, 1954.

37565 History of special periods - 18th century - cont.

37565.150 Grundpositionen der französischen Aufklärung. 1. Aufl. Berlin, 1955.

37565.155 Pizzorusso, Arnaldo. Studi sulla letteratura dell'età preromantica in Francia. Pisa, 1956.

37565.158 Pizzorusso, Arnaldo. Teorie letterarie in Francia. Pisa, 1968.

37565.160 Cremonesi, C. Corso di letteratura francese. Milano, 1960.

37565.165 Atkinson, Geoffroy. Le sentiment de la nature et le retour a la vie simple. Geneve, 1960.

37565.165.5 Atkinson, Geoffroy. The sentimental revolution. Seattle, 1965.

37565.165.10 Atkinson, Geoffroy. Prelude to the enlightenment: French literature, 1690-1740. London, 1971.

37565.166 Kraus, Werner. Studien zur deutschen und französischen Aufklärung. Berlin, 1963.

37565.167 Lebois, A. Litterature sous Louis XV. Paris, 1962.

37565.168 Oblomievskii, D.D. Literatura frantsuzskoi revoliutsii. Moskva, 1964.

37565.169A Laufer, Roger. Style rococo. Paris, 1963.

37565.169B Laufer, Roger. Style rococo. Paris, 1963.

37565.170 Saulnier, Verdun L. La litterature française du siècle philosophique. 7e éd. Paris, 1963.

37565.172 Livre et société dans la France du XVIIIe siècle. v.2. Paris, 1965. 2v.

37565.173 Orlando, Francesco. Infanzia, memoria e storia da Rousseau ai romantici. Padova, 1966.

37565.175 Congrès National de Littérature Comparée. Actes. [La France, La Bourgogne et la Suisse au XVIIIe siècle]. Paris, 1960.

37565.178 Pozzo, Gianni M. La storia e il progresso nell'Illuminismo francese. Padova, 1964.

37565.180 Krauss, Werner. Perspektiven und Problems. Zur französische und deutschen Aufklärung und andere Aufsätze. Neuwied, 1965.

37565.182 Juin, Hubert. Les Libertinages de la raison. Paris, 1968.

37565.184 Eighteenth century French studies: literature and the arts. Newcastle upon Tyne, 1969.

37565.186 Etiemble, René. L'Orient philosophique du XVIII siècle. v.1-3. Paris, 1957-59.

37565.188 Launay, Michel. Introduction à la vie littéraire du XVIIIe siècle. Paris, 1969.

37565.190 Vier, Jacques. Histoire de la littérature française, XVIIIe siècle. Paris, 1965- 2v.

37565.192 Ehrard, Jean. L'idée de nature en France à l'aube des lumières. Paris, 1970.

37565.194 Peyre, Henri. Qu'est-ce que le romantisme? Paris, 1971.

37565.196 Beiträge zur französischen Aufklärung und zur spanischen Literatur. Berlin, 1971.

37566 History of special periods - 19th century - General works

37566.2 Chenier, Marie J. Tableau historique de la littérature française. Paris, 1818.

37566.2.5 Chenier, Marie J. Tableau historique de l'etat...de la littérature française. Paris, 1816.

37566.3 Chenier, Marie J. Tableau historique de l'etat...de la littérature française. Paris, 1835.

37566.4 Véricour, L. Raymond. Modern French literature. Edinburgh, 1842.

37566.6 Véricour, L. Raymond. Modern French literature. Boston, 1848.

37566.7A Blaze de Bury, Yetta. French literature of to-day. Boston, 1898.

37566.7B Blaze de Bury, Yetta. French literature of to-day. Boston, 1898.

37566.7.5A Thieme, Hugo P. La littérature française du dix neuvième siècle. Paris, 1897.

37566.7.5B Thieme, Hugo P. La littérature française du dix neuvième siècle. Paris, 1897.

37566.7.9 Thieme, Hugo P. Guide bibliographique de la littérature française de 1800 à 1906. Paris, 1907.

37566.8 Vinet, Alexandre R. Études sur la littérature française au 19me siècle. Paris, 1857. 3v.

37566.9 Schmidt, Julian. Geschichte der französischen Literatur seit der Revolution 1789. Leipzig, 1858. 2v.

37566.10 Schmidt, Julian. Geschichte der französischen Literatur seit Ludwig XVI. 1774. Leipzig, 1873-1874. 2v.

37566.11 Barbey d'Aurevilly, J.A. Les oeuvres et les hommes. Paris, 1860-1878. 7v.

37566.12 Barbey d'Aurevilly, J.A. Les oeuvres et les hommes. Paris, 1891-1898. 6v.

37566.12.15 Barbey d'Aurevilly, J.A. Les philosophes et les écrivains religieux. Paris, 1887.

37566.13 Barbey d'Aurevilly, J.A. Les oeuvres et les hommes. 3rd series. Paris, 1899.

37566.13.8 Barbey d'Aurevilly, J.A. Le XIXe siècle des oeuvres et des hommes. Paris, 1964- 2v.

37566.13.20 Barbey d'Aurevilly, J.A. Philosophes et écrivains. Paris, 1909.

37566.14 Nescis, J.J. La littérature sous les deux empires. Paris, 1874.

37566.15 Michiels, Alfred. Histoire des idées littéraires. Paris, 1863. 2v.

37566.16 Michiels, Alfred. Histoire des idées littéraires. Paris, 1842. 2v.

37566.17 Chaudes-Aigues, J. Les écrivains modernes. Paris, 1841.

37566.18 Bonnefon, D. Les écrivains moderne de la France. Paris, n.d.

37566.18.5 Bonnefon, D. Les écrivains moderne de la France. 7th ed. Paris, n.d.

37566.20 Nettement, A.F. Histoire de la littérature française sous la restauration. Paris, 1858. 2v.

37566.21 Nettement, A.F. Histoire de la littérature française sous le gouvernement de juillet. Paris, 1854. 2v.

37566.22 Jeanroy-Felix, Victor. Nouvelle histoire de la littérature française pendant la restauration. Paris, n.d.

37566.23 Jeanroy-Felix, Victor. Nouvelle histoire de la littérature française sous la monarchie de juillet. Paris, n.d.

37566.25 Menche de Loisne, Charles. Influence de la littérature française 1830. Paris, 1852.

37566.26 Charpentier, P. Une maladie morale, le mal du siècle. Paris, 1880.

37566.27 Albert, Paul. La littérature française au 19th siècle. Paris, 1884. 2v.

37566.27.5 Albert, Paul. La littérature française au 19th siècle. Paris, 1902. 2v.

37566 History of special periods - 19th century - General works - cont.

37566.28 Faguet, Émile. Politiques et moralistes du dix-neuvième siècle. v.3. Paris, 1891.
X Cg 37566.28.5 Faguet, Émile. Politiques et moralistes du dix-neuvième siècle. Paris, 192-.
37566.29.3 Pellissier, G. Le mouvement littéraire au XIXe siècle. 9e éd. Paris, 1912.
37566.29.4 Pellissier, G. Literary movement in France during 19th century. N.Y., 1897.
37566.29.5 Pellissier, G. Essais de littérature contemporaine. Paris, 1893.
37566.30 Huret, Jules. Enquète sur l'évolution littéraire. Paris, 1891.
37566.30.9 Faguet, Émile. Dix-neuvième siècle; études littéraires. Paris, 1887.
37566.30.20 Faguet, Émile. Dix-neuvième siècle; études littéraires. Paris, 1887.
37566.31.10 Faguet, Émile. Dix-neuvième siècle. Paris, 19- .
37566.32 Byvanck, W.G.C. Un hollandais à Paris en 1891. Sensations de literature. Paris, 1892.
37566.33 Brandes, G. L'Ecole romantique en France. Paris, 1902.
NEDL 37566.37 Meunier, G. Le Bilan littéraire du XIXe siècle. Paris, 1898.
37566.38 Perrens, F.T. Histoire sommaire de la littérature française au XIXe siècle. Paris, n.d.
37566.40 Strowski, F. Tableau de la littérature française au XIXe siècle. Paris, 1912.
37566.41A Babbitt, Irving. Masters of modern French criticism. Boston, 1912.
37566.41B Babbitt, Irving. Masters of modern French criticism. Boston, 1912.
37566.41C Babbitt, Irving. Masters of modern French criticism. Boston, 1912.
37566.41.5 Babbitt, Irving. Masters of modern French criticism. Boston, 1912.
37566.42 Babou, Hippolyte. Les sensations d'un juré. Paris, 1875.
37566.43 Pailleron, M.L. (Mme.). François Buloz. Paris, 1919.
37566.43.2 Pailleron, M.L. (Mme.). François Buloz et ses amis: les derniers romantiques. Paris, 1923.
37566.43.5 Pailleron, M.L. (Mme.). François Buloz et ses amis de 1885 a nos jours. Paris, 1924.
37566.43.10 Pailleron, M.L. (Mme.). François Buloz et ses amis;...la vie littéraire sous L. Phillippe. Paris, 1930.
37566.43.15 Pailleron, M.L. (Mme.). François Buloz et ses amis;...la revue des deux mondes et la comédie française. Paris, 1930.
37566.44.5 Le Goffic, Charles. La littérature française aux XIX et XX siècle. Paris, 1919. 2v.
37566.44.15 Le Goffic, Charles. Les romanciers d'aujourd'hui. Paris, 1890.
37566.46 Florian-Parmentier, Ernest. La littérature et l'epoque, histoire de la littérature française. Paris, 1914.
37566.48 Estève, Louis. L'hérédité romantique dans la littérature contemporaine. 2e éd. Paris, 1914.
37566.50 Albalat, Antoine. Souvenirs de la vie littéraire. Paris, 1920.
37566.55 Valois, Georges. D'un siècle à l'autre. 3e éd. Paris, 1922.
37566.55.2 Gressent, A.G. D'un siècle à l'autre. Paris, 1924.
37566.60 Carrere, Jean. Les mauvais maîtres. Paris, 1922.
37566.65 Duquesnel, Félix. Souvenirs littéraires. Paris, 1922.
37566.67A Bacourt, Pierre de. French literature during the last half century. N.Y., 1923.
37566.67B Bacourt, Pierre de. French literature during the last half century. N.Y., 1923.
37566.69 Lalou, René. Histoire de la littérature française contemporaine (1870 à nos jours). Paris, 1923.
37566.69.5A Lalou, René. Histoire de la littérature française contemporaine (1870 à nos jours). Paris, 1924.
37566.69.5B Lalou, René. Histoire de la littérature française contemporaine (1870 à nos jours). Paris, 1924.
37566.70A Lalou, René. Histoire de la littérature française contemporaine (1870 à nos jours). Paris, 1925.
37566.70B Lalou, René. Histoire de la littérature française contemporaine (1870 à nos jours). Paris, 1925.
37566.70.5 Lalou, René. Contemporary French literature. N.Y., 1924.
37566.71 Dix causeries françaises. Paris, 1923.
37566.72A Fäy, Bernard. Panorama de la littérature contemporaine. Paris, 1925.
37566.72B Fäy, Bernard. Panorama de la littérature contemporaine. Paris, 1925.
NEDL 37566.72.2 Fäy, Bernard. Panorama de la littérature contemporaine. 11. éd. Paris, 1925.
37566.72.5 Fäy, Bernard. Panorama de la littérature contemporaine. Paris, 1929.
37566.72.10 Fäy, Bernard. Since Victor Hugo. Boston, 1927.
37566.74 Forst-Battaglia, O. Die französische Literatur der Gegenwart, 1870-1924. Wiesbaden, 1925.
37566.75 Millequant, P. Tableau de la littérature française du romantisme à nos jours. Berlin, 1935.
37566.76A Revue des deux mondes. Le livre du centenaire. Paris, 1929.
37566.76B Revue des deux mondes. Le livre du centenaire. Paris, 1929.
37566.77A Braunschvig, M. La littérature française contemporaine. Paris, 1926.
37566.77B Braunschvig, M. La littérature française contemporaine. Paris, 1926.
37566.80 Gregh, Fernand. La fenêtre ouverte. Paris, 1901.
37566.84 Abraham, P. Avec in texte inédit de Balzac. 4e éd. Paris, 1931.
37566.84.5 Abraham, P. Creatures chez Balzac. Paris, 1931.
37566.86 Deffoux, Léon. Le groupe de Medau; Émile Zola. Paris, 1924.
37566.88 Stock, P.V. Mémorandum d'un éditeur. Paris, 1935.
37566.88.10 Stock, P.V. Mémorandum d'un éditeur. 2e serie. Paris, 1936.
37566.90 Saurat, D. Perspectives. Paris, 1938.
37566.93 Ross, W. Das Bild der römischen Kaiserzeit in der französischen Literatur des 19. Jahrhunderts. Inaug-diss. Bochum, 1938.
37566.95 Lafargue, P. Critiques littéraires. Paris, 1936.
37566.97 Tran Van Tung. L'école de France. Hanoi, 1938.
37566.98 Mornet, Daniel. Histoire de la littérature et de la pensée françaises. Paris, 1924.
37566.99 Mornet, Daniel. Histoire de la littérature et de la pensée françaises contemporaines (1870-1925). 2e éd. Paris, 1928.

37566 History of special periods - 19th century - General works - cont.

37566.99.2 Mornet, Daniel. Histoire de la littérature et de la pensée françaises contemporaines, 1870-1927. Paris, 1927.
37566.101 Guthrie, R. French literature and thought since the revolution. N.Y., 1942.
37566.103 Martino, Pierre. L'époque romantique en France, 1815-1830. Paris, 1945.
37566.105 Grosse, Pierre de. Villegiatures romantiques. Paris, 1944.
37566.106 Henriot, Émile. Courrier littéraire, XIX siècle. Paris, 1954.
37566.107 Henriot, Émile. Courrier littéraire, XIXe siècle. v.1-2. Paris, 1948.
37566.108 Henriot, Émile. Courrier littéraire, XIX siècle. Paris, 1953.
37566.108.5 Henriot, Émile. Courrier littéraire, XIX-XX siècles. Paris, 1955.
37566.109A Beuchat, C. Histoire du naturalisme français. Paris, 1949. 2v.
37566.109B Beuchat, C. Histoire du naturalisme français. Paris, 1949. 2v.
37566.111 Rolland de Renéville, A. Univers de la parole. 5. éd. Paris, 1944.
37566.113 Sauro, A. Il mito del romanticismo francese. Bari, 1953.
37566.115 George, A.J. The development of French romanticism. Syracuse, N.Y., 1955.
37566.117 Lebois, André. Admirable XIX siècle. Paris, 1958.
37566.120 Lacretelle, Jacques de. Les maîtres et les amis. Namur, 1959.
37566.125 Klemperer, Victor. Geschichte der französischen Literatur im 19. und 20. Jahrhunderts. Berlin, 1956- 2v.
37566.130 Perović, St. Iz radionice velikih majstora. Zagreb, 1958.
37566.135 Austin, L.J. Studies in modern French literature presented to P. Mansell Jones by pupils, colleagues and friends. Manchester, 1961.
37566.140 Gourmont, Rémy de. The book of masks. Boston, 1921.
37566.142 Saulnier, Verdun L. La littérature française du siècle romantique. 6. éd. Paris, 1961.
37566.143 Jeune, Simon. De F.T. Graindorge à A.O. Barnabooth. Paris, 1963.
37566.144 Green, Frederick C. French novelists, from the Revolution to Proust. N.Y., 1964.
37566.145 Chevalier, Adrian. Humbles essais. Paris, 1903.
37566.146 Delaporte, Louis. Quelques-uns. 1. série. 5. éd. Paris, 1901.
37566.146.10 Delaporte, Louis. Pastels et figurines. 2. éd. Paris, 1898.
37566.147 Maurevert, Georges. Quelques gentilshommes de lettres. Lyon, 1920.
37566.148 Muhlfeld, Lucien. Le monde oú L'on imprime. Paris, 1897.
37566.149 Poulet, Georges. Trois essais de mythologie romantique. Paris, 1966.
37566.150 Beauchamp, Louis de. Le côté de Vinteuil. Paris, 1966.
37566.155 Pellegrini, Carlo. Letteratura e storia nell'Ottocento francese e altri saggi. Roma, 1967.
37566.158.2 Bonfantini, Mario. Ottocento francese. 2. ed. Torino, 1966.
37566.160 Ley, Francis. Bernardin de Saint-Pierre; Mme de Staël, Chateaubriand, Benjamin Constant et Mme de Krudener. Paris, 1967.
37566.165 Reyes, Salvador. Peregrinajes literarios en Francia. Santiago de Chile, 1968.
37566.166 Voloshin, M.A. Liki tvorchestve. Sankt Peterburg, 1914.
V37566.168 Reizov, Boris G. Frantsuzskii roman XIX veka. Moskva, 1969.
37566.170 Juin, Hubert. Les incertitudes du réel. Bruxelles, 1968.
37566.172 Pia, Pascal. Romanciers, poètes essayistes du XIXe siècle. Paris, 1971.
37566.174 Macchia, Giovanni. I fantasmi dell'opera. Milano, 1971.
37566.176 Vallery-Radot, Vincent Félix. Souvenirs littéraires. Paris, 1877.
37566.178 D'Aló, Oresto À. Algunos hombres, algunas ideas: Amiel, Renán, Becher, Ingenieros. Santa Fe, 1955.
37566.180 Tadié, Jean Yves. Introduction à la vie littéraire du XIXe siècle. Paris, 1970.
37566.182 Portraits du prochain siècle. Paris, 1970.

37567 History of special periods - 19th century - Special topics, special forms, etc.

37567.1 Pamphlet box. Romanticism.
37567.2 Ménégault, A.P.F. Martyrologe littéraire. Paris, 1816.
37567.3 Pérennès, F. Les noviciats littéraires. Paris, 1847.
37567.4 Feletz, Charles Marie de. Jugements historiques et littéraires sur quelques écrivains et...écrits du temps. Paris, 1840.
37567.5 Prarond, Ernest. De quelques écrivains nouveaux. Paris, 1852.
NEDL 37567.7 Gautier, Theophile. Famous French authors. N.Y., 1879.
37567.7.2 Nisard, Desiré. Essais sur l'ecole romantique. Paris, 1891.
37567.7.5 Canat, R. Du sentiment de la solitude morale chez les romantiques. Paris, 1904.
37567.8 Asselineau, Charles. Bibliographie romantique. Paris, 1874.
37567.8.5 Nauroy, C. Bibliographie des plaquettes romantiques. Paris, 1882.
37567.9A James, Henry. French poets and novelists. London, 1878.
37567.9B James, Henry. French poets and novelists. London, 1878.
37567.9.3 James, Henry. French poets and novelists. 2nd ed. London, 1893.
37567.9.5 James, Henry. French poets and novelists. London, 1904.
37567.9.7 James, Henry. French poets and novelists. London, 1908.
37567.9.10 James, Henry. French poets and novelists. London, 1919.
37567.9.15 James, Henry. French poets and novelists. 1st ed. N.Y., 1964.
37567.10 Milliet, Paul. Notes romantiques a propos de Marion Delorme. Paris, 1873.
37567.11 Huber, Victor A. Neuromantische Poesie in Frankreich. Leipzig, 1833.
37567.12 Julien, Bernard. Histoire de la poésie française à l'époque impériale. Paris, 1844. 2v.
37567.14 Honnegger, J.J. Victor Hugo, Lamartine. Zürich, 1858.
37567.15 Bourget, Paul. Essais de psychologie contemporaine. Paris, 1883.
Htn 37567.15* Bourget, Paul. Essais de psychologie contemporaine. Paris, 1883.
37567.15.2 Bourget, Paul. Nouveaux essais de psychologie contemporaine. Paris, 1886.

37567 History of special periods - 19th century - Special topics, special forms, etc. - cont.

37567.15.3 Bourget, Paul. Essais de psychologie contemporaine. 9e éd. Paris, 1893.
37567.15.4 Bourget, Paul. Nouveaux essais de psychologie contemporaine. Paris, 1892.
37567.15.5 Bourget, Paul. Essais de psychologie contemporaine. Paris, 1920. 2v.
X Cg 37567.15.10 Bourget, Paul. Essais de psychologie contemporaine. 9e éd. Paris, 1895.
37567.17 Dugas, L. Les grands timides; J.J. Rousseau, Constant, Chateaubriand. Paris, 1922.
37567.20.5 Brandes, Georg. Die Reaktion in Frankreich. 5e Aufl. Leipzig, 1897.
37567.23 Reymond, W. Corneille, Shakspeare et Goethe. Berlin, 1864.
37567.25 Borcharot, A. Littérature française pendant...1870-1871. Berlin, 1871.
37567.26 Lermina, J. Le mouvement littéraire en France en 1882-1883. Paris, 1884.
37567.27 Desprez, Louis. L'évolution naturaliste. Paris, 1884.
37567.28 Werdet, Edmond. Souvenirs de la vie littéraire. Paris, 1879.
37567.29 Jaubert, Caroline. Souvenirs de la vie littéraire. Paris, n.d.
37567.29.2 Jaubert, Caroline. Souvenirs de Madame Caroline Jaubert; lettres et correspondances. Paris, 1881.
37567.30 Claretie, J. Célébrités contemporaines. Victor Hugo. Paris, 1884.
37567.31 Claretie, J. Célébrités contemporaines. A. Dumas. Paris, 1884.
37567.31.10 Claretie, J. Elisa Mercoeur, Hippolyte de la Morvonnais, George Farcy, Charles Doyalle, Alphonse Rabbe. Paris, 1864.
37567.32A Lemaître, Jules. Les contemporains. 9. éd. Paris, 1887-1899. 8v.
37567.32B Lemaître, Jules. Les contemporains. 9. éd. v.4. Paris, 1887-1899.
37567.32.5 Lemaître, Jules. Les contemporains. 4e serie. 8e éd. Paris, 1889.
37567.32.10 Lemaître, Jules. Les contemporains. Paris, 1897-1903. 7v.
37567.32.15 Lemaître, Jules. Les contemporains. Paris, 18- . 8v.
37567.33 Tellier, Jules. Nos poètes. Paris, 1889.
37567.34 Frommel, Gaston. Esquisses contemporaines. Lausanne, 1891.
37567.35 Doumic, René. Portraits d'écrivains. Paris, 1892.
37567.35.1 Doumic, René. Portraits d'écrivains. Paris, 1902.
37567.35.2 Doumic, René. Écrivains d'aujourd'hui. Paris, 1894.
37567.35.4 Doumic, René. Écrivains d'aujourd'hui. Paris, 1903.
37567.35.5 Doumic, René. Contemporary French novelists. N.Y., 1899.
37567.36.2 Brunetière, Ferdinand. Nouveaux essais sur la littérature contemporaine. Paris, 1895.
37567.36.5 Brunetière, Ferdinand. Essais sur la littérature contemporaine. Paris, 1913.
37567.37 L'année littéraire. Paris. 2-7,1886-1891 3v.
37567.38 Klein, Félix. Le mouvement Néo-Chrétien. Paris, n.d.
37567.38.2 Klein, Félix. Nouvelles tendances en religion et en littérature. Paris, 1893.
37567.39 Tissot, Ernest. Les evolutions de la critique française. Paris, 1890.
37567.40 Audebrand, P. Petits mémoires du XIXe siècle. Paris, 1892.
37567.40.5 Audebrand, P. Derniers jours de La Bohème. Paris, 1905.
37567.40.7 Audebrand, P. Lauriers et cyprès. Paris, 1903.
37567.41 Hennequin, E. Quelques ecrivains français. Photoreproduction. Paris, 1890.
37567.42A Houssaye, Henry. Les hommes et les idées. Paris, 1886.
37567.42B Houssaye, Henry. Les hommes et les idées. Paris, 1886.
37567.43 Sainte-Croix, C. de. Moeurs littéraires. Paris, 1891.
37567.44 Delille, Edward. Some French writers. London, 1893.
37567.45 Brunetière, Ferdinand. L'evolution de la poésie lyrique en France au dix-neuvième siècle. Paris, 1894. 2v.
37567.45.4 Brunetière, Ferdinand. L'evolution de la poésie lyrique en France au dix-neuvième siècle. 2. éd. Paris, 1895.
37567.45.10 Brunetière, Ferdinand. L'evolution de la poésie lyrique en France au dix-neuvième siècle. 10. éd. Paris, 19- . 2v.
37567.46 Monod, Gabriel. Renan, Taine, Michelet. Paris, 1894.
37567.47 Bordeaux, H. La vie et l'art. Ames modernes. Paris, 1895.
37567.47.2 Bordeaux, H. La vie et l'art. Sentiments et idées de ce temps. Paris, 1897.
X Cg 37567.48 Pellissier, G.J.M. Nouveaux essais de littérature contemporaine. Paris, 1895.
37567.48.5 Pellissier, G.J.M. Etudes de littérature contemporaine. 1e et 2e série. Paris, 1898. 2v.
37567.48.10 Pellissier, G.J.M. Le mouvement littéraire contemporain. 2e éd. Paris, 1901.
37567.49 Lazare, B. Figures contemporains. Paris, 1895.
37567.50 Bérenger, H. L'aristocratie intellectuelle. Paris, 1895.
37567.51 Spoelberch de Lovenjoul, Charles. Les lundis d'un chercheur. Paris, 1894.
37567.52 Deschamps, Gaston. La vie et les livres. Paris, 1894. 6v.
37567.53 Doumic, René. Les jeunes. Etudes et portraits. Paris, 1896.
37567.55 Biré, Edmond. Histoire et littérature. Lyon, 1895.
37567.56 Fonsegrive, G.L. Les livres et les idées, 1894-1895. Paris, 1896.
37567.57 Paris, Gaston. Penseurs et poètes. Paris, 1896.
37567.58 Morice, C. La littérature de tout à l'heure. Paris, 1889.
37567.59A Tolstoi, Léon. Zola-Dumas. Guy de Maupassant. Paris, 1896.
37567.59B Tolstoi, Léon. Zola-Dumas. Guy de Maupassant. Paris, 1896.
Htn 37567.60.2* Gourmont, Rémy de. Le livre des masques. 1e éd. Paris, 1896.
37567.60.3 Gourmont, Rémy de. Le livre des masques. v.1: 10. éd.; v.2: 6. éd. Paris, 1917. 2v.
37567.60.10 Gourmont, Rémy de. Le livre des masques. Mercure, 1963.
37567.61 Felgeres, Charles. Essais d'histoire et de littérature. Paris, 1896.
37567.62 Carez, F. Auteurs contemporains. Liége, 1897.
37567.63 Recolin, Charles. L'anarchie littéraire. Paris, 1898.
37567.64 Bérenger, H. La France intellectuelle. Paris, 1899.
37567.65.10 Cario, Louis. L'exotisme. 2e éd. Paris, 1911.

37567 History of special periods - 19th century - Special topics, special forms, etc. - cont.

37567.66.2 Symons, Arthur. The symbolist movement in literature. N.Y., 1908.
37567.66.3 Symons, Arthur. The symbolist movement in literature. N.Y., 1919.
37567.66.4 Symons, Arthur. The symbolist movement in literature. N.Y., 1958.
37567.66.5 Retté, A. Le symbolisme. Anecdotes et souvenirs. Paris, 1903.
37567.66.7 Raynaud, Ernest. La mêlée symboliste, 1870-1910. pts. 1-3. Paris, 1918-22. 3v.
37567.66.8A Raynaud, Ernest. En marge de la mêtée symboliste. 2e éd. Paris, 1936.
37567.66.8B Raynaud, Ernest. En marge de la mêlée symboliste. 2e éd. Paris, 1936.
X Cg 37567.66.9 Poizat, Alfred. Le symbolisme de Baudelaire à Claudel. Paris, 1919.
37567.66.9.2 Poizat, Alfred. Le symbolisme. Paris, 1924.
37567.66.10 Woolley, G. Richard Wagner et le symbolisme français. Paris, 1931.
37567.66.11 Mauclair, Camille. Servitude et grandeur litteraires. Paris, 1922.
37567.66.15 Morrissette, B.A. Les aspects fondamentaux de l'esthétique symboliste. Thèse. Clermont-Ferrand, 1933.
37567.66.20 Rudler, M.G. Parnassiens symbolistes et décadents. Paris, 1938.
37567.66.25 Fiser, Emeric. Le symbole littéraire. Paris, 1941.
37567.67 Thompson, Vance. French portraits. Boston, 1900.
37567.68 Frédérix, G. Trente ans de critique. Paris, 1900. 2v.
37567.69 Segard, A. Les voluptueux et les hommes d'action. Paris, 1900.
37567.70 Bordeaux, H. Les ecrivains et les moeurs (1897-1900). 2e éd. Paris, 1900.
37567.70.2 Bordeaux, H. Les ecrivains et les moeurs, 1900-1902. 2e éd. Paris, n.d.
37567.71 Ernest-Charles, J. La littérature française d'aujourd'hui. Paris, 1902.
37567.71.5 Ernest-Charles, J. Essais critiques. Paris, 1914.
37567.72 Pica, V. Letteratura d'eccezione. Milan, 1898.
37567.73 Kahn, Gustave. Symbolistes et décadents. Paris, 1902.
37567.74 Delfour, L.C. La religion des contemporains. Paris, 1895. 4v.
37567.76 Alméras, H. de. Avant la gloire. Leurs débuts. Paris, 1902.
37567.76.2 Alméras, H. de. Avant la gloire. Leurs débuts. Paris, 1903.
37567.78 Rebell, H. Les inspiratrices de Balzac, Stendhal, Mérimée. Paris, 1902.
37567.79 Nordan, Max. Vus du Dehors. Paris, 1903.
37567.80 Lionnet, J. L'evolution des idées chez quelques-uns de nos contemporains. Paris, 1903.
37567.82 Doumic, René. Hommes et idées du XIXe siècle. Paris, 1903.
37567.83 Spoelberch de Lovenjoul, Charles. Bibliographie et littérature. Paris, 1903.
37567.84 Cim, Albert. Le dîner des gens de lettres. Paris, 1903.
37567.85A Davies, Thomas R. French romanticism and the press: the Globe. Cambridge, 1906.
37567.85B Davies, Thomas R. French romanticism and the press: the Globe. Cambridge, 1906.
37567.86 Casella, G. La nouvelle littérature, 1895-1905. Paris, 1906.
37567.87 Sageret, J. Les grands convertis. Paris, 1906.
37567.88A Lasserre, Pierre. Le romantisme français. Paris, 1907.
37567.88B Lasserre, Pierre. Le romantisme français. Paris, 1907.
37567.88.10 Lasserre, Pierre. Des romantiques à nous. 6e éd. Paris, 1927.
37567.89 Maillard, F. La cité des intellectuels. Paris, 1907.
X Cg 37567.90 Cassagne, Albert. La théorie de l'art pour l'art en France chez les derniers romantiques. Paris, 1906.
37567.90.10A Cassagne, Albert. La théorie de l'art pour l'art en France. Paris, 1959.
37567.90.10B Cassagne, Albert. La théorie de l'art pour l'art en France. Paris, 1959.
NEDL 37567.91 Seillière, E. Le mal romantique. Paris, 1908.
37567.91.5 Seillière, E. Les étapes du mysticisme passionel. Paris, 1919.
37567.91.15 Seillière, E. Sur la psychologie du romantisme-français. Paris, 1933.
37567.92 Lardanchet, H. Les enfants perches du romantisme. Paris, 1905.
37567.93 Asse, Eugène. Les petits romantiques. Paris, 1900.
37567.94 Pavie, A. Médaillons romantiques. Paris, 1909.
37567.95 Ledigne, C. Le Fléan romantique. Photoreproduction. Paris, 1909.
X Cg 37567.96 Maigron, L. Le romantisme et les moeurs. Paris, 1910.
X Cg 37567.96.5 Maigron, L. Le romantisme et la mode. Paris, 1911.
37567.96.8 Rudwin, Max. Romantisme et satanisme. Paris, 1927.
37567.97 Jay, A. La conversion d'un romantique. Paris, 1830.
37567.98 Séché, Alphonse. Au temps du romantisme. Paris, 1909.
37567.99 Finch, M.B. The origins of French romanticism. London, 1920.
37567.100 Bertaut, J. La littérature féminine d'aujourd'hui. Paris, n.d.
37567.101 Nonnenberg-Chun, M. Der französischen Philhell...Jahrhundert. Berlin, 1909.
37567.102 Daudet, A. (Mme.). Souvenirs autour d'un groupe littéraire. Paris, 1910.
37567.103 Retinger, J.H. Le conte fantastique dans le romantisme français. Paris, 1909.
37567.103.25 Tharp, J.B. The fantastic short story in France, 1850-1900. n.p., 1928.
37567.104 Gribble, Francis. The passions of the French romantics. London, 1910.
37567.105 Moréas, J. Esquisses et souvenirs. Paris, 1908.
37567.106 Retinger, J.H. Histoire de la littérature française du romantisme à nos jours. Paris, 1911.
37567.107 Tiercelin, Louis. Bretons de lettres. Paris, 1905.
37567.108 Desmarais, C. Essai sur les classiques et les romantiques. Paris, 1824.
37567.109 Canat, René. La renaissance de la Grèce antique (1820-1850). Paris, 1911.
37567.109.5 Canat, René. La littérature française au XIXe siècle. Paris, 1921. 2v.
37567.110 Le Prévost, M.A. Sur la poésie romantique. Rouen, 1825.
37567.110.9 Les premières armes du symbolisme. Paris, 1889.

37567 History of special periods - 19th century - Special topics, special forms, etc. - cont.

37567.111 Barre, A. Le symbolisme. Paris, 1911.
37567.111.2 Barre, A. Bibliographique poésie symboliste. Paris, 1911.
37567.111.15 Michaud, Guy. La doctrine symboliste. Paris, 1947.
37567.111.20A Lehmann, Andrew G. The symbolist aesthetic in France. Oxford, 1950.
37567.111.20B Lehmann, Andrew G. The symbolist aesthetic in France. Oxford, 1950.
37567.111.22 Lehmann, Andrew G. The symbolist aesthetic in France. 2. ed. Oxford, 1968.
37567.111.25 Lawler, James R. The language of French symbolism. Princeton, 1969.
37567.112 Vincent, Francis. Ames d'aujourd'hui. Paris, 1912.
37567.113 Sprouck, M. Les articles litteraires. Paris, 1889.
37567.114 Küchler, W. Französische Romantik. Heidelberg, 1908.
37567.115 Séché, L. La jeunesse dorée sous Louis-Philippe. Paris, 1910.
37567.116 Bordeaux, H. Vies intimes. 6th ed. Paris, n.d.
37567.118 Pellissier, G. Le réalisme du romantisme. Paris, 1912.
37567.119 Marsau, J. La bataille romantique. Paris, 1912.
37567.119.10A Marsau, J. Autour du romantisme. Toulouse, 1937.
37567.119.10B Marsau, J. Autour du romantisme. Toulouse, 1937.
37567.120 Charlier, G. Le sentiment de la nature chez les romantiques français. Paris, 1912.
37567.121 Derôme, L. Causeries d'un amie des livres. Paris, 1886-1887.
37567.121.2 Derôme, L. Causeries d'un amie des livres. Paris, n.d. 2v.
37567.123 Clouard, H. Les disciplines. Paris, 1913.
37567.124 Muller, J. Les tendances présentes de la littérature française. Paris, 1913.
37567.125 Bersaucourt, A. de. Études et recherches. 2e éd. Paris, 1913.
37567.126 Henriot, Emile. A quoi rêvent les jeunes gens. Paris, 1913.
37567.126.10 Henriot, Emile. Romanesques et romantiques. Paris, 1930.
37567.127 Bisi, A. L'Italie et le romantisme français. Milan, 1914.
37567.128 Giraud, V. Maîtres d'autrefois et d'aujourd'hui. Paris, 1912.
37567.129 Bouvier, E. La bataille realiste. Paris, n.d.
NEDL 37567.130 Maillard, F. Les derniers bohêmes. Paris, 1874.
37567.131 Amicis, Edmondo de. Ritratti letterari. 2a ed. Milano, 1881.
37567.131.5 Amicis, Edmondo de. Ritratti letterari. Milano, 1908.
37567.132 Matthey, Hubert. Essai sur le merveilleux dans la littérature française depuis 1800. Paris, 1915.
37567.133 Du Fresnois, André. Une année de critique. Paris, 1913.
37567.134 Stewart, H.F. The romantic movement in French literature. Cambridge, 1913.
37567.135 Thorold, Algar L. Six masters in disillusion. London, 1909.
37567.136 Bourget, Paul. Pages de critique et de doctrine. Paris, 1912. 2v.
37567.137 Barbey d'Aurevilly, J. Les prophètes du passé. Paris, 1880.
37567.138 Rageot, Gaston. Le succès, auteurs et public. Paris, 1906.
37567.139 Edwards, Matilda. French men, women and books. Chicago, 1911.
37567.140 Ghéon, Henri. Nos directions. Paris, 1911.
37567.141 Dondey, Théophile. Lettre inédite de Philothée O'Neddy. Paris, 1875.
37567.141.10 Dondey, Théophile. Feu et flamme. Paris, 1926.
37567.142 Vial, Francisque. Idées et doctrines littéraires du XIXe siècle. Paris, 1918.
37567.143 Curtius, Ernst Robert. Die literarischen Wegbereiter des neuen Frankreich. Potsdam, 1918.
37567.143.2 Curtius, Ernst Robert. Die literarischen Wegbereiter des neuen Frankreich. 2. Aufl. Potsdam, 1920.
37567.144 Eccles, Francis Yvon. La liquidation du romantisme. Oxford, 1919.
37567.145 Jäger, Karl. Der Empirestil in der schöngeistigen Literatur Frankreichs. Griefswald, 1915.
37567.146 Jullien, Adolphe. Le romantisme et l'éditeur Rendual. Paris, 1897.
37567.147 Viatte, Auguste. Le catholicisme chez les romantiques. Paris, 1922.
37567.147.5 Viatte, Auguste. Les sources occultes du romantisme, illuminisme, théosophie, 1770-1820. Thèse. Paris, 1928. 2v.
37567.147.10 Viatte, Auguste. Les sources occultes du romantisme, illuminisme, théosophie, 1770-1820. Paris, 1928. 2v.
37567.147.12 Viatte, Auguste. Les sources occultes du romantisme. 2e éd. Paris, 1965. 2v.
37567.148 Allais, Gustave. Quelques vues générales sur le romantisme français. Paris, 1897.
37567.150 Pujo, Maurice. Essais de critique générale. Paris, 1898.
37567.151 Pujo, Maurice. Le règne de la grâce. Paris, 1894.
37567.152 Mendes, Catulle. Le mouvement poétique française de 1867-1900. Paris, 1903.
37567.153A Parker, Clifford S. The defense of the child by French novelists. Menasha, 1925.
37567.153B Parker, Clifford S. The defense of the child by French novelists. Menasha, 1925.
37567.155 Monselet, Charles. Petits memoires littéraires. Paris, 1892.
37567.156 Roberto, Diego de. Poeti francesi contemporanei. Milano, 1900.
37567.160 Osmont, Anne. Le mouvement symboliste. Paris, 1917.
37567.165 Ghil, René. Les dates et les oeuvres; symbolisme et poésie scientifique (1883-1922). Paris, 1923.
37567.170 Smith, Maxwell A. L'influence des Lakistes sur les romantiques français. Paris, 1920.
37567.170.2 Smith, Maxwell A. L'influence des Lakistes sur les romantiques français. Thèse. Paris, 1920.
37567.175 Martineau, René. Promenades biographiques, Flaubert, Barbey. Paris, 1920.
37567.180 Deffoux, Léon. Le group de Médan. Paris, 1920.
37567.185 Lasserre, Pierre. Cinquante ans de pensée français. 7e éd. Paris, 1922.
37567.186 Bain, M.I. Les voyageurs français en Écosse, 1770-1830. Thèse. Paris, 1931.
37567.187 Bain, M.I. Les voyageurs français en Écosse, 1770-1830. Paris, 1931.
37567.189 Pichon, Jules E. Promenades littéraires en Tchécoslovaquie. Grenoble, 1938.

37567 History of special periods - 19th century - Special topics, special forms, etc. - cont.

37567.190 Martinenche, E. Histoire de l'influence espagnole sur la littérature française. Paris, 1922.
37567.191 Taha-Hussein, Mu'nis. Le romantisme français et l'Islam. Beirut, 1962.
37567.192 Annuaire des gens de lettres et des dessinateurs 1905. Paris, 1905.
37567.193 Noli, Mlle. Les romantiques français et l'Italie. Thèse. Dijon, 1928.
37567.193.15 Hung Cheng Fu. Un siècle d'influence chinoise sur la littérature française (1815-1930). Thèse. Paris, 1934.
37567.193.30 Lichtenberger, M. Ecrivains français en Égypte contemporaine 1870 à nos jours. Thèse. Paris, 1934.
37567.193.45 Krieg, Wera. Griechenland und der Orient. Inaug. Diss. Würzburg, 1935.
37567.193.50 Malleret, L. L'exotisme indochinois dans la littérature française depuis 1860. Paris, 1934.
37567.193.55 Pujarniscle, E. Philoxène. Paris, 1931.
37567.194 Gille, Philippe. La bataille littéraire, 1875-1894. Paris, 1889-94. 7v.
37567.196 Bersaucourt, A. de. Au temps des parnassiens. Paris, 1921?
37567.196.5 Ditchy, Jay K. Le thème de la mer chez les parnassiens. Paris, 1927.
37567.196.10 Desonay, Fernand. La rêve Hellénique chez les poètes parnassiens. Louvain, 1928.
37567.196.12 Desonay, Fernand. Le rêve Hellénique chez les poètes parnassiens. Paris, 1928.
37567.196.14 Canat, René. L'Hellénisme des romantiques. v.1-2. Paris, 1951-53.
37567.196.15 Therive, A. Le parnasse. Paris, 1929.
37567.196.20 Saurian, M. Histoire du parnasse. Paris, 1929.
37567.196.25 Rosenberg, Z. La persistance du subjectivisme chez les poètes parnassiens. Thèse. Paris, 1939.
37567.197 Fourcassié, Jean. Le romantisme et les Pyrénées. Thèse. Paris, 1940.
37567.198A Maurras, C. Romantisme et révolution. Paris, 1922.
37567.198B Maurras, C. Romantisme et révolution. Paris, 1922.
37567.198.10 Maurras, C. Un débat sur le romantisme. Paris, 1928.
37567.202 Evrard, E. Nos mandarins. Tourcoing, 1920.
37567.204 Beaume, G. Au pays des lettres. Parmi les vivants et les morts. Paris, 1922.
37567.205 Annuaire des lettres, des arts et des théatres du journal "Le Constitutionnel". n.p., n.d.
37567.208A Whitridge, A. Critical ventures in modern French literature. N.Y., 1924.
37567.208B Whitridge, A. Critical ventures in modern French literature. N.Y., 1924.
37567.209 Fisher, M. A group of French critics. Chicago, 1897.
37567.210 Latzarus, M.T. La littérature enfantine en France dans la seconde moitié du XIXe siècle. Thèse. Paris, 1923.
37567.210.5 Latzarus, M.T. La littérature enfantine en France dans la seconde moitié du XIXe siècle. Thèse. Paris, 1924.
37567.211 Mignon, Maurice. Les affinites intellectuelles de l'Italie et de la France. Paris, 1923.
37567.212 Partridge, E. The French romantics' knowledge of English literature (1820-1848). Paris, 1924.
37567.213 Porcelli, Giacomo. Letterature italiano...nella critica francese (1830-1848). Firenze, 1926.
37567.214 Martino, Pierre. Le naturalisme français (1870-1895). Paris, 1923.
37567.215 Deffaux, L.L. Le naturalisme. Paris, 1929.
37567.215.10 Schwesinger, M. Die Literarischen und Buchhändlerischen Erfalge des naturalistischen Romans des 19. Jahrhundert im französischen Publikum. Inaug. Diss. Miltenberg, 1935.
37567.216 Baldensperger, F. Sensibilité musicale et romantisme. Paris, 1925.
37567.218 Trabard, P. Le romantisme; défini par "Le globe". Paris, 1925.
37567.220.13 Martino, Pierre. Parnasse et symbolisme. 9e éd. Paris, 1954.
37567.223 Belis, A. La critique française a la fin du XIXe siècle. Paris, 1926.
37567.226 Strowski, F. Tableau de la littérature française au XIXe siècle et au XXe siècle. Paris, 1924.
37567.226.3 Strowski, F. Tableau de la littérature française au XIXe siècle et au XXe siècle. Paris, 1924.
37567.227 George, Albert J. Short fiction in France, 1800-1850. Syracuse, N.Y., 1964.
37567.233 Thérive, André. Du siècle romantique. Paris, 1927.
37567.234 Grant, Elliott M. French poetry and modern industry, 1830-1870. Cambridge, 1927.
37567.237 Bouteron, Maral. Muses romantiques. Paris, 1926.
37567.240 Lamartine, A. de. Portraits et salons romantiques. Paris, 1927.
37567.246 Pipitone-Federico, G. Il naturalismo contemporaneo in letteratura. Palermo, 1886.
37567.249 Souriau, Maurice. Histoire du romantisme en France. Paris, 1927. 2v.
37567.255 Clerc, Charly. Le génie du paganisme. Paris, 1926.
37567.260 Rosny, J.H. Mémoires de la vie littéraire. Paris, 1927.
37567.270 Tissot, Ernest. Nouvelles princesses de lettres. Paris, 1911.
37567.272 Halflants, Paul. Religion et littérature. 2e éd. Bruxelles, 1912.
37567.273 Halflants, Paul. Religion et littérature. 3e éd. Louvain, 1926.
37567.276 Giraud, Jean. L'école romantique française. Paris, 1927.
37567.279A Faguet, Émile. Politicians and moralists of the nineteenth century. Boston, 1928.
37567.279B Faguet, Émile. Politicians and moralists of the nineteenth century. Boston, 1928.
37567.279.5 Faguet, Émile. Politiques et moralistes du dix-neuvieme siècle. Paris, 191-?
37567.281 Baale-Uittenbosch, A.E.M. Les poétesses dolentes du romantisme. Haarlem, 1928.
Htn 37567.283* Monda, Maurice. Bibliographie des poètes maudits. Paris, 1927. 2v.
37567.287 Fontainas, André. Mes souvenirs du symbolisme. 3e éd. Paris, 1928.
37567.300.5 Bouvier, Émile. Initiation a la littérature d'aujourd'hui. Paris, 1932.
37567.305 Van Roosbroeck, G.L. The legend of the decadents. N.Y., 1927.
37567.310 Jacoubet, Henri. Le genre troubadour et les origines françaises du romantisme. Paris, 1929.
37567.315 Flutre, Fernand. Le romantisme. Paris, 1926.

37567 History of special periods - 19th century - Special topics, special forms, etc. - cont.

37567.319 Paris. Bibliothèque Nationale. Cinquantenaire du symbolisme. Paris, 1936.
37567.320 Paris. Bibliothèque Nationale. Le romantisme. Paris, 1930.
37567.322 Quennell, Peter. Baudelaire and the symbolists. London, 1929.
37567.323 Schinzel, E. Natur und Natursymbolik bei Poe. Inaug. Diss. Düren, 1931.
37567.324 Le romantisme et les lettres par Ferdinand Brunot, Daniel Mornet, Paul Hazard. Paris, 1929.
37567.325 Dijon. Université. Faculté des Lettres. En l'honneur du romantisme. Dijon, 1930.
37567.326 Tronchon, Henri. Romantisme et préromantisme. Paris, 1930.
37567.327 Régnier, Henri de. Faces et profils. Souvenirs sur Villiers de l'Isle-Adam. Paris, 1931.
37567.328 Prévost, Jean L. Les épicuriens français. 2e éd. Paris, 1931.
37567.328.5 Prévost, Jean L. Le prêtre ce héros de roman. 2. éd. Paris, 1953.
37567.329 Carr, P. Days with the French romantics in the Paris of 1830. London, 1932.
37567.329.25 Skerlitch, Jean. L'opinion publique en France d'après la poésie politique et sociale de 1830 à 1848. Diss. Lausanne, 1901.
37567.330 Moreau, P. Le classicisme des romantiques. Paris, 1932.
37567.330.5 Moreau, P. Le classicisme des romantiques. Thèse. Paris, 1932.
37567.331 Bray, René. Chronologie du romantisme (1804-1830). Paris, 1932.
37567.332 Doolittle, Dorothy. The relations between literature and mediaeval studies in France, 1826-1860. Diss. Bryn Mawr, 1933.
37567.333 Evans, R.L. Les romantiques français et la musique. Paris, 1934.
37567.333.5 Evans, R.L. Les romantiques français et la musique. Thèse. Paris, 1934.
37567.334 Eggli, Edmond. Le débat romantique en France, 1813-1830. Paris, 1933.
37567.336 Moraud, Marcel. Le romantisme français en Angleterre de 1814 a 1848. Thèse. Paris, 1933.
37567.336.5 Moraud, Marcel. Le romantisme français en Angleterre de 1814 a 1848. Paris, 1933.
37567.338 Lehrmann, Kuno. Das Humanitätsideal der sozialistischromantischen Epoche Frankreichs. Inaug. Diss. Würzburg, 1932.
37567.339 Schwarz, Adam. Studien zum Fortschritts- und Humanitätsgedanken in der französischen Romantik. Inaug. Diss. Würzburg, 1935.
37567.340 Girard, Henri. Le centenaire du premier cénacle romantique de la "Muse française". Paris, 1926.
37567.341 Orliac, Antoine. La cathédrale symboliste. Paris, 1933-48. 2v.
37567.342 Marie, Aristide. La forêt symboliste; esprits et visages. Paris, 1936.
37567.343 Kahn, Gustave. Silhouettes littéraires. Paris, 1925.
37567.343.10 Kahn, Gustave. Les origines du symbolisme. Paris, 1936.
37567.344A Maurras, Charles M.P. Poètes. Paris, 1924.
37567.344B Maurras, Charles M.P. Poètes. Paris, 1924.
37567.345 Grillet, Claudius. Le diable dans la littérature au XIXe siècle. Paris, 1935.
37567.346 Eckardt, Hans. Die Musikausschauung der französischen Romantik. Kassel, 1935.
37567.347 Plomert, J. Petit glossaire pour servir à l'intelligence des auteurs décadents et symbolistes. Paris, 1888.
37567.348 Venzac, G. De Chateaubriand à Barrès aux pays de leur enfance. Paris, 1936.
37567.350 Weinberg, Bernard. French realism; the critical reaction, 1830-1870. Diss. Chicago, 1937.
37567.350.2 Weinberg, Bernard. French realism; the critical reaction, 1830-1870. N.Y., 1937.
37567.350.5 Weinberg, Bernard. The limits of symbolism. Chicago, 1966.
37567.352 Asztrik, G. Index romain et littérature française à l'époque romantique. Budapest, 1936.
37567.354 Ajalhert, J. Mémoires en Vrac, 1880-1890. Paris, 1938.
37567.356 Schneider, H. Deutsche Art und Sitte im Spiegel französischer...Jahren 1830-1870. Inaug. Diss. Köln, 1928.
37567.358 Iorga, N. Quatre figures françaises en lumière roumaine discours commémoratifs. Bucarest, 1925.
37567.360 Cain, J. Ehanche et premiers éléments d'un musée de la littérature. Paris, 1938.
37567.365 Nettement, A. Le roman contemporain. Paris, 1864.
37567.367 Eloesser, A. Literarische Porträts aus dem modernen Frankreich. Berlin, 1904.
37567.370 Stahl, A. Die Schilderung des Sterbens im französischen Roman des 19. Jahrhunderts. Inaug. Diss. Württemberg, 1938.
37567.375A Giraud, V. De Chateaubriand à Brunetière. Paris, 1938.
37567.375B Giraud, V. De Chateaubriand à Brunetière. Paris, 1938.
37567.378 Beuchat, Charles. De Restif à Flaubert, ou Le naturalisme en Marche. Paris, 1939.
37567.380 Weis, E. Der Elsässer im Französischen Roman des 19. und 20. Jahrhunderts. Inaug. Diss. Tübingen, 1938.
37567.382 Clement, N.H. Romanticism in France. N.Y., 1939.
37567.385 Hazard, P. Quatre études; Baudelaire, romantiques, sur un cycle poétique. N.Y., 1940.
37567.387 Pauly, M.H. Les voyageurs-français en Irlande au temps du romantisme. Thèse. Paris, 1939.
37567.389 Guyette, M.A. The moniteur universel and romanticism, 1813-1830. Thesis. Urbana, Ill., 1940.
37567.390 Mann, Heinrich. Geist und Tat. Berlin, 1931.
37567.390.10 Mann, Heinrich. Geist und Tat. Weimar, 1946.
37567.391.4 Crane, T.F. Le romantisme français, 1824-1848. 4. éd. N.Y., 1894.
37567.392 Jaloux, Edmond. De Pascal à Barrès. 3. éd. Paris, 1927.
37567.393 Souday, Paul. Les romantiques à l'Académie. Paris, 1928.
37567.394 Picard, Roger. Le romantisme social. N.Y., 1944.
37567.395 Charpentier, John. Le symbolisme. Paris, 1927.
37567.396 Verlaine, P. Les poètes maudits. Paris, 1920.
37567.398 Baldensperger, F. La critique et l'histoire en France. N.Y., 1945.
37567.400 Schmidt, Albert M. La littérature symboliste (1870-1900). 1. éd. Paris, 1942.
37567.400.6 Schmidt, Albert M. La littérature symboliste. 6. éd. Paris, 1960.

37567 History of special periods - 19th century - Special topics, special forms, etc. - cont.

37567.405 Johandsen, Svend. Le symbolisme; étude sur le style des symbolistes français. Copenhague, 1945.
37567.409 Dinar, André. La croisade symboliste. Paris, 1943.
37567.411 Martinet, E. Princes de lettres. Genève, 1945.
37567.413 Tuzet, Hélène. Voyageurs français en Sicile au temps du romantisme. Paris, 1945.
37567.415 Tuzet, Hélène. Voyageurs français en Sicile. Thèse. Paris, 1945.
37567.417 Dumont, Francis. Naissance du romantisme contemporain. Paris, 1942.
37567.418 Dumont, Francis. Les petits romantiques français. Ligugé? 1949.
37567.419 Carré, Jean Marie. Les écrivains français et le mirage allemand. Paris, 1947.
37567.420 Michaud, Guy. Message poétique du symbolisme. v.1-2,3. Paris, 1947. 2v.
37567.420.2 Michaud, Guy. Message poétique du symbolisme. Paris, 1947. 3v.
37567.422.7 Meeüs, Adrien des. Les romantismes. 7e éd. Paris, 1948.
37567.424 Charlier, Gustave. Le mouvement romantique en Belgique, 1815-1850. Bruxelles, 1948- 2v.
37567.426 Cassou, Jean. Le quarante-huitard. Paris, 1948.
37567.428 Bertaut, Jules. L'époque romantique. Paris, 1947.
37567.430 Hemmings, F.W.J. The Russian novel in France. London, 1950.
37567.432 Siciliano, Italo. Lirici francesi dell'ottocento. Venezia, 1948.
37567.434 Lugli, V. Jules Renard ed altri amici. Messina, 1948.
37567.436 Jean, Marcel. Genèse de la pensée moderne dans la littérature française. Paris, 1950.
37567.438 Pommier, J. Les écrivains devant la revolution de 1848. 1. éd. Paris, 1948.
37567.440 Cornell, William Kenneth. The symbolist movement. New Haven, 1951.
37567.440.1 Cornell, William Kenneth. The symbolist movement. Hamden, Conn., 1970.
37567.442 Senechal, Christian. La Pologne de 1830 à 1846. Paris, 1937.
37567.444A Evans, David Owen. Social romanticism in France, 1830-1848. Oxford, 1957.
37567.444B Evans, David Owen. Social romanticism in France, 1830-1848. Oxford, 1957.
37567.444.5 Evans, David Owen. Social romanticism in France, 1830-1848. N.Y., 1969.
37567.446 Priddin, Deirdre. The art of the dance in French literature. London, 1952.
37567.448 Lion, F. Der französische Roman in neunzehnten Jahrhundert. Stendhal, 1952.
37567.450 Billy, André. L'époque 1900. Paris, 1951.
37567.452 Gandon, Y. Cent ans de jargon. Paris, 1951.
37567.454 Dale, E.H. La poésie française en Angleterre. Paris, 1954.
37567.456 Sauro, A. La lingua poetica in Francia. Bari, 1954.
37567.460 Valeri, D. Il simbolismo francese da Nerval a de Régnier. Padova, 1954.
37567.465 Clark, Mary Ursula. The cult of enthusiasm in French romanticism. Washington, 1950.
37567.470 Revue des Sciences Humaines. Autour du symbolisme. Lille, 1955.
37567.475 Richard, J.P. Littérature et sensation. Paris, 1954.
37567.480 Marsan, Jules. Bohême romantique. Paris, 1929.
37567.485 Roy, C. La critique littéraire. Québec, 1918.
37567.490 Hamelin, J. Hommes de lettres inculpés. Paris, 1956.
37567.495 Giraud, Raymond. The unheroic hero in the novels of Stendhal. New Brunswick, 1957.
37567.500 Prevost, John C. Le dandysme en France. Genève, 1957.
37567.505 Siciliano, Italo. Romanticismo francese. Venezia, 1955.
37567.505.2 Siciliano, Italo. Il romanticismo francese da Prévost à Sartre. Firenze, 1964.
37567.510 Frey, John A. Motif symbolism in the disciples of Mallarmé. Washington, 1957.
37567.515 Charbonnel, Victor. Les mystiques dans la littérature présente. 1. série. Paris, 1897.
37567.525 Trautner, Erich. Das Bild des Priesters in der französischen Literatur des 19. und 20. Jahrhunderts. München, 1955.
37567.530 Reizov, B.G. Frantsuzskii istoricheskii roman v epokhu romantizma. Leningrad, 1958.
37567.535 Carter, A.E. The idea of decadence in French literature. Toronto, 1958.
37567.537 Richard, Noël. Le mouvement décadent: dandys. Paris, 1968.
37567.540 Lethève, Jacques. Impressionistes et symbolistes devant la presse. Paris, 1959.
37567.545 Pichois, Claude. L'image de la Belgique dans les lettres françaises de 1830. Paris, 1957.
37567.550 Ridge, George R. The hero in French romantic literature. Athens, 1959.
37567.552 Ridge, George R. The hero in French decadent literature. Athens, 1961.
37567.555 Bernard, Suzanne. Le poème en prose de Baudelaire. Paris, 1959.
37567.560 Robichon, Jacques. Le roman des chefs-d'oeuvre. Paris, 1959.
37567.565 Jensen, Christian A.E. L'evolution du romantisme l'année 1826. Genève, 1959.
37567.570 Spatz, I. Die französische Teufelsdarstellung von der Romantik bis zur Gegenwart. München, 1960.
37567.575 Iknayan, M.M. The idea of the novel in France. Genève, 1961.
37567.580 Roche, A.V. Les idées traditionalistes en France de Rivard à Charles Maurras. Urbana, 1937.
37567.585 Shroder, Maurice Z. Icazus. Cambridge, 1961.
37567.590 Bornecyne, J. Henry. Réalisme et naturalisme. Paris, 1961.
37567.595 Marten, Miloš (pseud.). Kniha silných. Praha, 1909.
37567.596 Richard, Noel. A l'aube du symbolisme. Paris, 1961.
37567.598 Ditlevsen, Jytte. Inspirations italiennes dans les oeuvres. Tone, 1962.
37567.600A Levin, Harry. The gates of horn. N.Y., 1963.
37567.600B Levin, Harry. The gates of horn. N.Y., 1963.
37567.600C Levin, Harry. The gates of horn. N.Y., 1963.
37567.600D Levin, Harry. The gates of horn. N.Y., 1963.
37567.601 Rièse, Laure. Les salons littéraires parisiens du Sd. Empire à nos jours. Toulouse, 1962.
37567.603 Hagberg, C.A. Fransk litteratur, 1836. Stockholm, 1963.

37567 History of special periods - 19th century - Special topics, special forms, etc. - cont.

37567.605 Barbagelata, H.D. Les grands romantiques français et le modernisme en Amérique latine. Paris, 1961.
37567.606 Reboul, Pierre. Le mythe anglais dans la littérature française sous la restauration. Lille, 1962.
37567.607 Schmidt, A. La littérature symboliste, 1870-1900. 7. éd. Paris, 1963.
37567.608 Menichelli, G.C. Viaggiatori francesi reali o immaginari. Roma, 1962.
37567.609 Guichard, L. La musique et les lettres en France du temps du Wagnerism. Paris, 1963.
37567.610 Van Tieghem, P. Le romantisme français. 7. éd. Paris, 1963.
37567.611 Brussels. Palais des Beaux-Arts. Le mouvement symboliste. Bruxelles, 1957.
37567.612 Dubois, J. Romanciers français de l'Instantane au XIXe siècle. Bruxelles, 1963.
37567.614 Martino, P. Le naturalisme français, 1870-1895. 6. éd. Paris, 1960.
37567.615 Duhamel, Roger. Aux sources du romantisme français. Ottawa, 1964.
37567.616 Schaub-Koch, E. Contribução para o do fantastico no romance. Lisboa, 1957.
37567.617 Vernois, Paul. La style rustique dans les romans champêtres après George Sand, problèmes de nature et d'emploi. Paris, 1963.
37567.618 Wood, John Sinclair. Sondages, 1830-1848. Toronto, 1965.
37567.619 Evans, David Owen. Le roman social sous la monarchie de juillet. Paris, 1936.
37567.620 Sailland, Maurice Edmond. Souvenirs littéraires et gastronomiques. Paris, 1958.
37567.621 Petitbon, René. Les sources orientales de Jean Lahor. Paris, 1962.
37567.622 Le Blond, Maurice. Essai sur le naturisme. Paris, 1896.
37567.623 Graño, César. Bohemian versus bourgeois. N.Y., 1964.
37567.624 Griffiths, Richard Mathias. The reactionary revolution: the Catholic revival in French literature, 1870-1914. London, 1966.
37567.625 Rebell, Hugues (pseud.). Le culte des idoles. Paris, 1929.
37567.626 Segard, Achille. Itineraire fantaisiste. Paris, 1899.
37567.627 Danilin, Iurii I. Poety Parizhskoi Kommuny. Moskva, 1966.
37567.628 Coeuroy, André. Wagner et l'esprit romantique. Paris, 1965.
37567.629 Moreau, Pierre. Âmes et thèmes romantiques. Paris, 1965.
37567.630 Keller, Luzuis. Piranèse et les romantiques français. Paris, 1966.
37567.635 Lobet, Marcel. Le ceinture de feuillage. Bruxelles, 1966.
37567.640 Raimond, Marcel. La crise du roman, des lendemains du naturalisme aux années vingt. Paris, 1966.
37567.645 Carassus, Émilien. Le snobisme et les lettres françaises de Paul Bourget à Marcel Proust. Thèse. Paris, 1966.
37567.650 Fischer, Alexander. Das Vater-Sohn-Verhältnis in der französischen Literatur des 19. und 20. Jahrhunderts. Diss. München, 1963.
37567.655 Sauro, Antoine. L'opposizione al romanticismo. Bari, 1963.
37567.658 Juden, Brian. Traditions orphiques et tendances mystiques dans le romantisme français (1800-1855). Paris, 1971.
37567.660 Puzikov, Aleksandr I. Portrety frantsuzskikh pisatelei. Moskva, 1967.
37567.665 Descotes, Maurice. La légende de Napoléon et les écrivains français du XIXe siècle. Paris, 1967.
37567.670 Monglond, André. Pélerinages romantiques. Paris, 1968.
37567.675 Ábrangi, Tibor. A francia szinbolizmes lirái formaé. Budapest, 1930.
37567.680 Cailliet, Émile. La tradition littéraire des idéologues. Philadelphia, 1943. 2v.
37567.685 Sagnes, Guy. L'ennui dans la littérature française de Flaubert à Laforgue, 1848-1884. Paris, 1969.
37567.690 Lidsky, Paul. Les écrivains contre la commune. Paris, 1970.
37567.695 La société française, 1815-1914. Paris, 1969.
37567.700 Jourdain, Frantz. Les décorés, ceux qui ne le sont pas. Paris, 1895.
37567.705 Couffignal, Robert. La paraphrase poétique de la "Genèse", de Hugo à Supervielle. Paris, 1970.
37567.710 Debré, Moses. The image of the Jew in French literature from 1800 to 1908. N.Y., 1970.
37567.715 Michaud, Guy. Le romantisme. Paris, 1952.
37567.718 Richard, Jean Pierre. Études sur le romantisme. Paris, 1971.
37567.720 Colloque d'Histoire Littéraire, École Normale Superieure de Saint-Cloud, 1966. Romantisme et politique, 1815-1851. Paris, 1969.
37567.725 Heitmaun, Klaus. Der Immoralismus-Prozess gegen die französische Literatur im 19. Jahrhundert. Bad Homburg, 1970.
37567.730 Chadwick, Charles. Symbolism. London, 1971.
37567.735 Bibescŭ, Marthe Lucie (Lahovary). Le confesseur et les poètes. Paris, 1970.
37567.736 Cutler, Maxine G. Evocations of the eighteenth century in French poetry, 1800-1869. Genève, 1970.
37567.737 Houston, John Porter. Fictional technique in France, 1802-1927. Baton Rouge, 1972.
37567.738 Astier Loutfi, Martine. Littérature et colonialisme; l'expansion coloniale vue dans la littérature romanesque française, 1871-1914. Paris, 1971.
37567.739 Baldick, Robert. Dinner at Magny's. London, 1971.
37567.740 Solinas, Paolo. Notes sur le roman patriotique français de 1870 à 1914. Cagliari, 1970.

37568 History of special periods - 20th century - General works

37568.10 Duclaux, Agnes Mary Frances. Twentieth century French writers. London, 1919.
37568.10.2 Duclaux, Agnes Mary Frances. Twentieth century French writers. N.Y., 1920.
37568.14 Baldensperger, F. L'avant-guerre dans la littérature française. Paris, 1919.
37568.15A Schinz, Albert. French literature of the great war. N.Y., 1920.
37568.15B Schinz, Albert. French literature of the great war. N.Y., 1920.
37568.20 Turquet-Milnes, G. Some modern French writers. N.Y., 1921.
37568.25 Gaultier, Paul. Les maîtres de la pensée française. Paris, 1921.

37568 History of special periods - 20th century - General works - cont.

37568.30 Dupuy, Ernest. Poètes et critiques. Paris, 1913.
37568.35 Strowski, F. La rénaissance littéraire. 4e éd. Paris, 1922.
37568.40A Montfort, Eugène. Vingt-cinq ans de littérature française. Paris, 1922-1926. 2v.
37568.40B Montfort, Eugène. Vingt-cinq ans de littérature française. Paris, 1922-1926. 2v.
37568.43 Pellissier, G. Études de littérature et de morale contemporaines. Paris, 1905.
37568.48 Curtius, Ernst R. Französischer Geist im neuen Europa. Stuttgart, 1925.
37568.48.2 Curtius, Ernst R. Französischer Geist im neuen Europa. Stuttgart, 1925.
37568.52 Palmarocchi, R. Letteratura francese contemporanea. Rome, 1927.
37568.54 Berl, Emmanuel. Mort de la pensée bourgeoise. Paris, 1929.
37568.54.3 Berl, Emmanuel. Mort de la morale bourgeoise. 9e éd. Paris, 1929.
37568.54.4 Berl, Emmanuel. Mort de la morale bourgeoise, 1929. Paris, 1965.
37568.55 Billy, André. La littérature française contemporaine. Paris, 1927.
37568.55.2 Billy, André. La littérature française contemporaine. 2e éd. Paris, 1928.
37568.56 Billy, André. La littérature française contemporaine. 3e éd. Paris, 1929.
37568.57 Billy, André. L'epoque contemporaine. Paris, 1956.
37568.58 Lefèvre, Frédéric. Une heure avec... Série 1. Paris, 1924.
37568.58.3 Lefèvre, Frédéric. Une heure avec... Série 1. 13e éd. Paris, 1924.
37568.58.7 Lefèvre, Frédéric. Une heure avec... Série 2. 16e éd. Paris, 1924.
37568.58.10 Lefèvre, Frédéric. Une heure avec... Série 3. Paris, 1925.
37568.58.12 Lefèvre, Frédéric. Une heure avec... Série 3. 4e éd. Paris, 1925.
37568.58.14 Lefèvre, Frédéric. Une heure avec... Série 4. 6e éd. Paris, 1927.
37568.58.15 Lefèvre, Frédéric. Une heure avec... Série 5. 7e éd. Paris, 1929.
37568.60A Michaud, Régis. Modern thought and literature in France. N.Y., 1934.
37568.60B Michaud, Régis. Modern thought and literature in France. N.Y., 1934.
37568.62A Sénéchal, C. Les grands courants de la littérature française contemporaine. Paris, 1933.
37568.62B Sénéchal, C. Les grands courants de la littérature française contemporaine. Paris, 1933.
37568.64 Friedrich, Hugo. Das antiromantische Denken im modernen Frankreich. München, 1935.
37568.66A Saurat, Denis. Modernes. Paris, 1935.
37568.66B Saurat, Denis. Modernes. Paris, 1935.
37568.66.5A Saurat, Denis. Modern French literature. London, 1946.
37568.66.5B Saurat, Denis. Modern French literature. London, 1946.
37568.67 Gross, René. Les lettres. Paris, 1934.
37568.68 Brasillach, R. Portraits. 4e éd. Paris, 1935.
37568.68.2 Brasillach, R. Portraits. Paris, 1935.
37568.70 Peyre, H. Hommes et oeuvres du XXe siècle. Paris, 1938.
37568.72 Eremburg, I.G. Duhamel, Gide, Malraux, Moraud, Romains, Unamuno. 2e éd. Paris, 1934.
37568.74 Gómez Carrillo, E. La nueva literatura francesa. Madrid, 1927.
37568.76.5A Arland, Marcel. Essais critiques. 6e éd. Paris, 1931.
37568.76.5B Arland, Marcel. Essais critiques. 6e éd. Paris, 1931.
37568.78 Baldensperger, F. La littérature française entre les deux guerres, 1919-1939. Los Angeles, 1941.
37568.80.5 Lalou, René. Histoire de la littérature française contemporaine. v.2. 3e éd. Paris, 1946.
37568.80.10 Lalou, René. Histoire de la littérature française contemporaine. v.1-2. Paris, 1947.
37568.82 Brodin, Pierre. Les écrivains français de l'entre-deux-guerres. Montreal, 1942.
37568.82.10 Brodin, Pierre. Présences contemporaines. Paris, 1954-57. 3v.
37568.84 Fowlie, Wallace. Clowns and angels. N.Y., 1943.
37568.86 Gillouin, René. Esquisses litteraires et morales. 5e éd. Paris, 1926.
37568.88 Fowlie, Wallace. The spirit of France. London, 1944.
37568.88.5 Fowlie, Wallace. A guide to contemporary French literature. N.Y., 1957.
37568.90 Catalogne, G. de. Les compagnons du spirituel: Mauriac - Massis - Ducattillon. Montréal, 1945.
37568.92 Aegerter, E. Au temps de Guillaume Appollinaire. Paris, 1945.
37568.94.10 Benda, Julien. La France byzantine,...essai d'une psychologie originelle du littérature. 12e éd. Paris, 1945.
37568.94.15 Mauriac, Claude. La trahison d'un clerc. Paris, 1945.
37568.94.15.5 Mauriac, Claude. Hommes et idées d'aujourd'hui. Paris, 1953.
37568.96 Rousseaux, André. Portraits littéraires choisis. Genève, 1947.
37568.98 Regards sur l'art contemporain. Bruxelles, 1945.
37568.99 Clouard, Henri. Histoire de la littérature française. Paris, 1947. 2v.
37568.102 Vettard, Camille. Du côté de chez. Albi, 1946.
37568.104 Jamet, Claude. Images mêlées de la littérature et du théâtre. Paris, 1948.
37568.106 Larnac, Jean. La littérature française d'aujourd'hui. Paris, 1948.
37568.108 Marill, René. La révolte des écrivains d'aujourd'hui. Paris, 1949.
37568.108.5 Marill, René. Bilan littéraire du XXe siècle. Paris, 1956.
37568.108.10 Marill, René. Bilan littéraire du XXe siècle. Aubin, 1962.
37568.110 Roy, C. Descriptions critiques. Paris, 1949- 5v.
37568.112 Berger, Marcel. Le style au microscope. Série 2. v.1-2,3,4. Paris, 1949-1952. 3v.
37568.114 Berger, Marcel. Le style au microscope. Série 1. Paris, 1934.
37568.116 Boisdeffre, P. de. Métamorphose de la littérature. Paris, 1951. 2v.
37568.116.5 Boisdeffre, P. de. Métamorphose de la littérature. 5. éd. Paris, 1963. 2v.

Classified Listing

37568 History of special periods - 20th century - General works - cont.

37568.118 Curtius, Ernst R. Französischen Geist im zwanzigsten Jahrhundert. Bern, 1952.
37568.120 Kanters, R. Des écrivains et des hommes. Paris, 1952.
37568.122 Girard, M. Guide illustré de la littérature française moderne. Paris, 1949.
37568.123 Girard, M. Guide illustré de la littérature française moderne, de 1918. Paris, 1962.
37568.124 Nathan, J. Histoire de la littérature comtemporaine. Paris, 1954.
37568.126 Nadeau, M. Littérature présente. Paris, 1952.
37568.128 Greshoff, Jean. Mengelstoffen op het gebied der fransche letterkunde. Maastricht, 1924.
37568.130 Paribatra, M. Le romantisme contemporain. Thèse. Paris, 1954.
37568.132 Maurras, C. Maîtres et témoins de ma vie d'esprit. Paris, 1954.
37568.135 Nanteuil, Jacques. Le fanal exhaussé. Niort, 1955.
37568.138 Garnier, C. L'homme et son personnage. Paris, 1955.
37568.140 Rumilly, Robert. Littérature française moderne. Montréal, 1931.
37568.145 Perroud, R. De Mauriac a gli esistenzialisti. Milano, 1955.
37568.150 Simon, P.H. Histoire de la littérature française du XX siècle. Paris, 1956. 2v.
37568.150.5 Simon, P.H. Diagnostic des lettres françaises contemporaines. Bruxelles, 1966.
37568.155 Declerck, R. Gestalten en gedachten. Antwerpen, 1957.
37568.160 Hatzfeld, H. Trends and styles in twentieth century French literature. Washington, 1957.
37568.160.2 Hatzfeld, H. Trends and styles in twentieth century French literature. Washington, 1966.
37568.165 Boisdeffre, P. de. Une histoire vivante de la littérature d'aujourd'hui. Paris, 1958.
37568.165.2 Boisdeffre, P. de. Une histoire vivante de la littérature d'aujourd'hui. Paris, 1959.
37568.165.3 Boisdeffre, P. de. Une histoire vivante de la littérature d'aujourd'hui. Paris, 1962.
37568.165.5 Boisdeffre, P. de. Une histoire vivante de la littérature. Paris, 1964.
37568.165.7 Boisdeffre, P. de. Une histoire vivante de la littérature d'aujourd'hui. 7. éd. Paris, 1968.
37568.170 Tison-Braun, M. La crise de l'humanisme. Paris, 1958. 2v.
37568.175 Frank, Bernard. Le dernier des mohicans. Paris, 1956.
37568.180 Vigorelli, Giancarlo. Carte francesi. Torino, 1959.
37568.185 Andreev, L.G. Frantsuzskaia literatura, 1917-1956 gg. Moskva, 1959.
37568.190 Balmas, E.H. Aspects et problèmes de la littérature contemporaine. Milano, 1959.
37568.190.2 Balmas, E.H. Aspects et problèmes de la littérature contemporaine. Milano, 1961.
37568.191 Balmas, E.H. Situazioni e profili. Milano, 1960.
37568.195 Curtius, Ernst R. Französischer Geist im zwanzigsten Jahrhundert. 2. Aufl. Bern, 1960.
37568.200 Tfitzer, Leo. Marcel Proust. Torino, 1959.
37568.205 Bémol, Maurice. Essai sur l'orientation des littératures de langue française au XXe siècle. Paris, 1960.
37568.210 Guissard, L. Écrits en notre temps. Paris, 1961.
37568.215 Shkunaeva, I.D. Souremennaia frantzsuzskaia literatura. Moskva, 1961.
37568.216 Thiebaut, M. Entre les lignes. Paris, 1962.
37568.218 Declerck, R. Peidingen doorheen het franse geestesleven. Hasselt, 1962.
37568.219 Bouvier, Émile. Les lettres françaises au XXe siècle. Paris, 1962.
37568.220 Barjon, Louis. De Baudelaire à Mauriac. Tournai, 1962.
37568.222 Maurois, André. De Proust à Camus. Paris, 1962.
37568.222.5A Maurois, André. From Proust to Camus; profiles of modern French writers. 1st ed. Garden City, N.Y., 1966.
37568.222.5B Maurois, André. From Proust to Camus; profiles of modern French writers. 1st ed. Garden City, N.Y., 1966.
37568.223 Nadeau, Maurice. Le roman français depuis la guerre. Paris, 1963.
37568.223.1 Nadeau, Maurice. The French novel since the war. N.Y., 1969.
37568.223.2 Nadeau, Maurice. Le roman français depuis la guerre. Paris, 1970.
37568.224 Bo, Carlo. Saggi e note di una letteratura. Milano, 1963.
37568.225 Roger, Juan. Figuras de la literatura francesa contemporanea. Madrid, 1962.
37568.228 Boisdeffre, P. de. Les écrivains français d'aujourd'hui. Paris, 1963.
37568.228.3 Boisdeffre, P. de. Les écrivains français d'aujourd'hui. 3. éd. Paris, 1967.
37568.228.4 Boisdeffre, Pierre de. Les écrivains français d'aujourd'hui. 4e éd. Paris, 1969.
37568.229 Junod, Roger-Louis. Écrivains français du XXe siècle. Lausanne, 1963.
37568.230 Poulet, Robert. Aveux spontanés. Paris, 1963.
37568.231 Ocvirk, Anton. Razgovori. V Ljubljana, 1933.
37568.232 Barrère, Jean Bertrand. Critique de chambre. Paris, 1964.
37568.233 Nimier, Roger. Journees de lectures. Paris, 1965.
37568.234 Chauveau, Paul. Caractéres. Paris, 1933.
37568.235 Maurois, André. De Gide à Sartre. Paris, 1965.
37568.236 Jeanneau, Augustin. Petit guide de la littérature d'aujourd'hui. Paris, 1966.
37568.237 Lovtsova, Ol'ga V. Literatura frantsii, 1917-1965. Izd. 2. Moskva, 1966.
37568.238 Sénart, Philippe. Chemins critiques, d'Abellio à Sartre. Paris, 1966.
37568.239 Fay, Bernard. Les précieux. Paris, 1966.
37568.240 Moore, Harry Thornton. Twentieth-century French literature. Carbondale, 1966. 2v.
37568.242 Massis, Henri. Au long d'une vie. Paris, 1967.
37568.243 David, Jean. Le procès de l'intelligence dans les lettres françaises au seuil de l'entre-deux-guerres, 1919-1927. Paris, 1966.
37568.250.2 Majault, Joseph. Littérature de notre temps. 2. éd. Tournai, 1967.
37568.255 O'Brien, Justin. The French literary horizon. New Brunswick, 1967.
37568.260 Martin Du Gard, Maurice. Les libéraux, de Renan à Chardonne. Paris, 1967.
37568.262 Perrone-Moises, Leyla. O nôvo romance francês. São Paulo, 1966.
37568.263 Vaksmakher, Moris N. Frantsuzskaie literatura nashikh dnei. Moskva, 1967.

37568 History of special periods - 20th century - General works - cont.

37568.265.2 Greshoff, Jan. Latijnsche lente. 2. Druk. Leiden, 1924.
37568.268 Engler, Winfried. Französische Literatur im 20. Jahrhundert. Bern, 1968.
37568.270 Champigny, Robert. Pour une esthétique de l'essai. Paris, 1967.
37568.272.2 Engler, Winfried. The French novel. N.Y., 1969.
37568.274 Itterbeek, Eugène van. Tekens van leven. Brussel, 1969.
37568.276 Nyssen, Hubert. Les voies de l'écriture. Paris, 1969.
37568.278 Broca, José Brito. Letras francesas. São Paulo, 1969.
37568.280 La littérature in France depuis 1945. Paris, 1970.
37568.282 La Rochefoucauld, Edmée de F. Courts métrages. Paris, 1970.

37569 History of special periods - 20th century - Special topics, special forms, etc.

37569.01 Pamphlet box. French literary history. Twentieth century.
37569.1 Lang, André. Voyage en zigzags dans la république des lettres. Paris, 1922.
37569.1.5 Lang, André. Tiers de siecle. Paris, 1935.
37569.2 Billy, André. La muse aux besicles. Photoreproduction. Paris, 1922.
37569.3 Adam, Paul. La littérature et la guerre. Paris, 1916.
37569.3.10 Duliamel, Georges. Guerre et littérature. Paris, 1920.
37569.4 Varillou, Pierre. Enquête sur les maîtres de la jeune littérature. Paris, 1923.
37569.5 Dubech, L. Les chefs de file de la jeune géneration. Paris, 1925.
37569.10 Calvet, J. Le renouveau catholique dans la littérature contemporaine. Paris, 1927.
37569.15 Schwartz, W.L. The imaginative interpretation of the Far East in modern French literature, 1800-1925. Paris, 1927.
37569.17 Mieille, Paul. Pages de bibliographie pyrénéenne. Paris, 1931.
37569.20 Riviere, Jacques. Études: Baudelaire, Paul Claudel, André Gide. 10e éd. Paris, 1925.
37569.25 Blanche, J.E. Mes modéles. 2. éd. Paris, 1928.
37569.25.5 Blanche, J.E. Mes modéles. Paris, 1928.
37569.26A Maurois, A. Études littéraires. N.Y., 1941-44.
37569.26B Maurois, A. Études littéraires. N.Y., 1941-44.
37569.26.3 Maurois, A. Études littéraires. v.1-2. Paris, 1947.
37569.27 Bonneau, Georges. Le symbolisme dans la poésie française contemporaine. Paris, 1930.
37569.29 Sénéchal, Christian. L'Abbaye de Créteil. Paris, 1930.
37569.29.5 Bidal, M.L. Les écrivains de l'abbaye. Paris, 1938.
37569.30 Ehrhard, J.E. Le roman français depuis Marcel Proust. Paris, 1933?
37569.32 Semiontek, H. D'enfant et la littérature enfantine contemporaine en France. Thèse. Toulouse, 1933.
37569.36 Giraud, V. Les maîtres de l'heure. 4e éd. Paris, 1927?
37569.38 Stansbury, M.H. French novelist of today. Philadelphia, 1935.
37569.40.8 Breton, André. Manifeste du surréalisme. Paris, 1924.
Htn 37569.40.8* Breton, André. Manifeste du surréalisme. Paris, 1924.
Htn 37569.40.10* Breton, André. Second manifeste du surréalisme. Paris, 1930.
37569.40.15 Breton, André. Les manifestes du surréalisme. Paris, 1947.
37569.40.16 Breton, André. Manifestes du surréalisme. Paris, 1962.
37569.40.17 Breton, André. Manifestoes of surrealism. Ann Arbor, 1969.
37569.40.20 Breton, André. What is surrealism? London, 1936.
37569.40.22 Breton, André. L'un dans l'autre. Paris, 1970.
37569.40.30 Levy, Julien. Surrealism. N.Y., 1936.
37569.40.40 Topass, J. La pensée en révolte, essai sur le surrealisme. Photoreproduction. Bruxelles, 1935.
37569.40.45 Gershman, Herbert S. A bibliography of the surrealist revolution in France. Ann Arbor, 1969.
37569.40.46 Gershman, Herbert S. The surrealist revolution in France. Ann Arbor, 1969.
37569.40.50 Read, Herbert. Surrealism. London, 1936.
37569.40.56 Nadeau, M. Histoire du surréalisme. Paris, 1964.
37569.40.57 Nadeau, M. The history of surrealism. N.Y., 1965.
37569.40.60 Mangeat, Guy. Histoire du surréalisme. Bruxelles, 1934.
37569.40.65 Torre, G. de. Qué es el superrealismo. Buenos Aires, 1955.
37569.40.70 Calas, Nicolas. Confound the wise. N.Y., 1942.
37569.40.75 Balakian, Anna E. Literary origins of surrealism. N.Y., 1947.
37569.40.76 Balakian, Anna E. Literary origins of surrealism. N.Y., 1966.
37569.40.77 La surréalisme révolutionnaire. Paris.
37569.40.80 Berger, P.C. Bilanz des Surrealismus. Caburg, 1951.
37569.40.197 Chiare, Joseph. Contemporary French poetry. Manchester, 1952.
37569.40.200 Simon, P.H. L'homme en procès. 3. ed. Neuchâtel, 1951.
37569.40.200.2 Simon, P.H. L'homme en procès: Malraux, Sartre. 6. ed. Paris, 1964.
37569.40.200.5 Simon, P.H. La littérature du péche et de la grace. Paris, 1957.
37569.40.202 Simon, P.H. Témoins de l'homme. Paris, 1967.
37569.40.205 Alquie, F. Philosophie du surrealisme. Paris, 1956.
37569.40.206 Alquie, F. The philosophy of surrealism. Ann Arbor, 1965.
37569.40.210 Carrouges, M. Les machines celibataires. Paris, 1954.
37569.40.215 Bo, Carlo. Bilancio del surrealismo. Padova, 1944.
37569.40.220 Kovač, Bohuslav. Alchýmia zázračného. 1. vyd. Bratislava, 1968.
37569.42 Chaigne, L. Vies et oeuvres d'écrivains. Paris, 1933-38. 4v.
37569.42.5 Chaigne, L. Vie et oeuvres d'écrivains. Paris, 1936.
37569.44 Derieux, Henry. La poesie française contemporaine, 1885-1935. 2. éd. Paris, 1935.
37569.46 Porché, F. Poètes français depuis Uerlaine. Paris, 1929.
37569.47 Richli-Bidal, L. Après le symbolisme. Thèse. Paris, 1938.
37569.48A Bermardini, Ada. Simbolisti e decadenti. Roma, 1935.
37569.48B Bermardini, Ada. Simbolisti e decadenti. Roma, 1935.
37569.50 Bocquet, Léon. Les destinées mauvaises. Amiens, 1923.
37569.50.10 Bocquet, Léon. La commemoration des morts. Amiens, 1925.
37569.52 Gandon, Yves. Mascardes litteraires. Paris, 1930.
37569.53 Gandon, Yves. Imageries critiques. Paris, 1933.
37569.53.10 Gandon, Yves. Le démon du style. Paris, 1938.
37569.54 Lievre, Pierre. Esquisses critiques. 1e Série. Paris, 1921.
37569.54.2 Lievre, Pierre. Esquisses critiques. 2e Série. Paris, 1924.
37569.54.3 Lievre, Pierre. Esquisses critiques. Paris, 1929.
37569.56 Fontainas, André. Dans la lignée de Baudelaire. Paris, 1930.

37569 History of special periods - 20th century - Special topics, special forms, etc. - cont.

37569.58 Cavallucci, G. Quelques maîtres d'aujourd'hui. Naples, 1936.
37569.60 Lemaitre, G. Four French novelists. London, 1938.
37569.62 Crémieux, B. Inventaires. Paris, 1931.
37569.64 Dagher, J.A. L'Orient dans la littérature française d'après guerre 1919-1933. Beyrouth, 1937.
37569.66 Vignaud, J. L'esprit contemporain. Paris, 1938.
37569.68A Germain, A. De Proust à dada. Paris, 1924.
37569.68B Germain, A. De Proust à dada. 3. éd. Paris, 1924.
37569.70 Schildener, E.H. Jüdische Bestrebungen im Spiegel französischer Literatur der Gegenwart. Inaug. Diss. Borna, 1937.
37569.80 Delourme, P. Trente-cinq années de politique religieuse. Paris, 1936.
37569.85 Pierrefeu, Jean de. Les beaux livres de notre temps. Paris, 1938.
37569.87 Rousseaux, A. Ames et visages du XXe siècle. 6e éd. 2. Série. Paris, 1936.
37569.90 Lafourcade, G. Notes sur le roman français contemporain. Buffalo? 1939.
37569.93 Mornet, D. Introduction à l'étude des écrivains français d'aujourd'hui. Paris, 1939.
37569.95 Schinz, A. L'année littéraire mil neuf cent trente-neuf. n.p., 1940.
37569.97F Therive, A. Lettre de Paris. n.p., 1939.
37569.97.5 Therive, A. Galerie de ce temps. Paris, 1931.
37569.97.10 Therive, A. Moralistes de ce temps. Paris, 1948.
37569.105 Manuel de la littérature catholique en France de 1870 à nos jours. Paris, 1939.
37569.110A Lemaitre, G. From cubism to surrealism in French literature. Cambridge, 1941.
37569.110B Lemaitre, G. From cubism to surrealism in French literature. Cambridge, 1941.
37569.115 Lalou, René. Le roman français depuis 1900. Paris, 1941.
37569.115.8 Lalou, René. Le roman français depuis 1900. 8. éd. Paris, 1960.
37569.115.9 Lalou, René. Le roman français depuis 1900. 9. éd. Paris, 1963.
37569.115.10 Lalou, René. Le roman français depuis 1900. 10. éd. Paris, 1966.
37569.118 Manoll, Michel. Introduction à la poésie d'aujourd'hui. n.p., 1945.
37569.120 Cooper, C.B. Women poets of the twentieth century in France. N.Y., 1943.
37569.122 Crastre, Victor. Le drame du surrealisme. Paris, 1963.
37569.123A Fowlie, W. Jacob's night. N.Y., 1947.
37569.123B Fowlie, W. Jacob's night. N.Y., 1947.
37569.125 Brodin, Pierre. Maîtres et temoins de l'entre-deux-guerres. N.Y., 1943.
37569.130 Cohen, Gustave. Ceux que j'ai connus. Montréal, 1946.
37569.135 Stolpe, Sven. Den kristna talangen; transka essayer. Stockholm, 1934.
37569.140 Heppenstall, R. The double image. London, 1947.
37569.145 Brugmans, H. Zoekend frankrijk. Amsterdam, 1947.
37569.150 Peyrade, Jean. Recherche de la joie. Paris, 1946.
37569.155 Morel, Robert. La littérature clandestine 1940-1944. Périgueux, 1945.
37569.160 Farges, Marcel. Poètes des temps présents. Paris, 1946.
37569.165 Annuaire international des lettres et des arts. Carcassonne, 1922.
37569.170 Haseganu, I. La France dans l'oeuvre poétique des écrivains roumains contemporains de langue français. Thèse. Cluj, 1939.
37569.175A Garaudy, Roger. Literature of the graveyard. N.Y., 1948.
37569.175B Garaudy, Roger. Literature of the graveyard. N.Y., 1948.
37569.177 Écrivains dans le siècle; étude sur Georges Bernanos, Paul Claudel, Georges Duhamel and others. Toulouse, 1946?
37569.180 Bendz, E.P. Visages d'écrivains. Paris, 1948.
37569.182 Morrow, Christine. Le roman irréaliste dans les littératures contemporaines de langues française et anglaise. Toulouse, 1941.
37569.184 Fowlie, W. Age of surrealism. N.Y., 1950.
37569.185 Pesis, B.A. Frantsuzskaia progressivnaia literatura v bor'be za mir i demokratiiu. Moskva, 1952.
37569.186 Gmelin, H. Der französische Zyklenroman der Gegenwart. Heidelberg, 1950.
37569.188 Villard, E. La poésie patriotique de l'arrière en France et la guerre de 1914-1918. La Chaux-de-Fonds, 1949.
37569.189 Evnina, E.M. Literatura frantsuzskogo soprotivleniia. Moskva, 1951.
37569.190 Breton, V.M.F. Claudel, Mauriac et Cie. Paris, 1951.
37569.193 Weinert, H. Dichtung aus dem Glauben. Hamburg, 1948.
37569.195 Dumay, R. Mort de la littérature. Paris, 1950.
37569.197 Wilhelm, J. Das Fortleben des Gallikanismus in der französischen Literatur der Gegenwart. München, 1933.
37569.200A Smith, T.M. Transatlantic migration. Durham, 1955.
37569.200B Smith, T.M. Transatlantic migration. Durham, 1955.
37569.203 Benac, Henri. Écrivains français vivants. Alegre, 1956.
37569.205 Prévost, J.L. Le prêtre. 3. éd. Paris, 1952.
37569.207 Rodenbach, André. Condition de la poésie française en Flandre. Tournai, 1956.
37569.210 Hubbard, L.J. The individual and the group in French literature since 1914. Washington, 1955.
37569.215 Guyard, M.F. L'image de la Grande-Bretagne dans le roman français. Paris, 1954.
37569.215.5 Guyard, M.F. La Grande-Bretagne dans le roman français, 1914-1940. Paris, 1954.
37569.220F Guiraud, Pierre. Index du vocabulaire du symbolisme. v.1-3, 5, 7. v.4 lost 1969. Paris, 1953- 5v.
37569.225 Perruchot, H. La haine des masques. Paris, 1955.
37569.230A Brée, Germaine. An age of fiction. New Brunswick, 1957.
37569.230B Brée, Germaine. An age of fiction. New Brunswick, 1957.
37569.230C Brée, Germaine. An age of fiction. New Brunswick, 1957.
37569.230D Brée, Germaine. An age of fiction. New Brunswick, 1957.
37569.230E Brée, Germaine. An age of fiction. New Brunswick, 1957.
37569.232 Brée, Germaine. The French novel from Gide to Camus. N.Y., 1962.
37569.235 Tylden-Wright, David. The image of France. London, 1957.
37569.240 Nahas, Hélène. La femme dans la littérature existentielle. Paris, 1957.
37569.245 Martin du Gard, Maurice. Les mémorables. Paris, 1957- 2v.
37569.250 Callot, Émile. Cinq moments de la sensibilité française contemporaine. Annecy, 1958.
37569.255A Cornell, William Kenneth. The post-symbolist period. New Haven, 1958.

37569 History of special periods - 20th century - Special topics, special forms, etc. - cont.

37569.255B Cornell, William Kenneth. The post-symbolist period. New Haven, 1958.
37569.260 Nourissier, François. Les chiens à fouetter. Paris, 1956.
37569.265 Charensol, G. Comment ils ecrivent. Paris, 1932.
37569.270F Czerefkow, S. Les ecrivains chez eux. Paris, 1925.
37569.275 Germain, André. Les croisés modernes. Paris, 1959.
37569.280 Blanchet, André. La littérature et le spirituel. Paris, 1959- 3v.
37569.285 Starkie, Enid. From Gautier to Eliot. London, 1960.
37569.290 Kamras, Hugo. Om Proust och vågra till. Stockholm, 1956.
37569.295 Bolle, Louis. Les lettres et l'absolu. Genève, 1959.
37569.300 Chapsal, Madeleine. Les écrivains en personne. Paris, 1960.
37569.300.5 Chapsal, Madeleine. Quinze écrivains. Paris, 1963.
37569.305 Colloque internationale des écrivains d'expression française. Le colloque internationale. Paris, 1958.
37569.310A Library of Congress. Gertrude Clarke Whittall Poetry and Literature Fund. French and German letters today. Washington, 1960.
37569.310B Library of Congress. Gertrude Clarke Whittall Poetry and Literature Fund. French and German letters today. Washington, 1960.
37569.315 Sérant, P. Le romantisme fasciste. Paris, 1960.
37569.320 Three studies in modern French literature. New Haven, 1960.
37569.325 Bonneville, G. Prophètes et témoins de l'Europe. Leyde, 1961.
37569.330 Pingaud, B. Écrivains d'aujourd'hui. Paris, 1960.
37569.335 Bazjon, Louis. Mondes d'écrivains, destines d'hommes. Paris, 1960.
37569.340 Truc, Gonzagne. Histoire de la littérature catholique contemporaine. Tournai, 1961.
37569.345 Bùi-Xuân-Bào. Naissance d'un héroïsme nouveau. Paris, 1961.
37569.350 Delbaville, Paul. Poésie et sonorités. Paris, 1961.
37569.355 Cruickshank, John. The novelist as philosopher. London, 1962.
37569.357 Kushner, Eva. Le mythe d'Orphée dans la littérature française contemporaine. Paris, 1961.
37569.358 Lauwick, H. D'Alphonse Allais à Sacha Guitry. Paris, 1963.
37569.359 Krause, Gerd. Tendenzen im französischen Romanschaffen des Zwanzigsten Jahrhunderts. Frankfurt, 1962.
37569.360A Kesteloot, Lilyan. Les écrivains noirs de langue française. Bruxelles, 1963.
37569.360B Kesteloot, Lilyan. Les écrivains noirs de langue française. Bruxelles, 1963.
37569.360.3 Kesteloot, Lilyan. Les écrivains noirs de langue française. 3. éd. Bruxelles, 1967.
37569.362 Tans, Joseph. Romans lisibles et romans illisibles. Groningen, 1963.
37569.363 Trois poètes: Mariel Clarmont. Paris, 1956.
37569.364 Soupault, P. Profils perdus. Paris, 1963.
37569.366 Dreher, S. Bibliographie de la littérature française, 1930-39. Lille, 1948-49.
37569.367 Prémont, Laurent. Le mythe de prométhée dans la littérature française contemporaine. Québec, 1964.
37569.368 Fitch, Brian T. Le sentiment d'étrangeté chez Malraux, Sartre, Camus et S. de Beauvoir. Paris, 1964.
37569.370 Richard, Jean Pierre. Onze études sur la poésie moderne. Paris, 1964.
37569.371 Janvier, Ludovic. Une parole exigeante. Paris, 1964.
37569.373 Wautier, André. La poesie française contemporaine en Wallonie. Charleroi, 1964.
37569.374 Barrère, Jean Bertrand. La cure d'amaigressement du roman. Paris, 1964.
37569.375 Pistorius, Jiri. L'image de l'Allemagne dans le roman français. Paris, 1964.
37569.376 Savage, Catharine. Malraux, Sartre, and Aragon as political novelists. Gainesville, 1964.
37569.377 Monnerot, Jules. La poésie moderne et le sacré. Paris, 1949.
37569.378 Narkir'er, Fedor S. Frantsuzskaia revoliutsionnaia literatura, 1914-1924. Moskva, 1965.
37569.380 Frohock, Wilbur Merrill. Style and temper; studies in French fiction, 1925-1960. Cambridge, 1967.
37569.380.5 Frohock, Wilbur Merrill. Style and temper. Oxford, 1967.
37569.382 Heist, Walter. Genet und Andere; Exkurse über eine faschistische Literatur von Rang. Hamburg, 1965.
37569.384 Eustis, Alvin Allen. Marcel Arland, Benjamin Crémieux. Paris, 1961.
37569.386 Onimus, Jean. La connaissance poétique. Paris, 1966.
37569.388 Ganne, Gilbert. Douze minutes de vérité. Paris, 1966.
37569.390 Zeltner-Neukomm, Gerda. Die eigenmächtige Sprache. Olten, 1965.
37569.392 Le Sage, Laurent. The French new criticism; an introduction and a sampler. University Park, 1967.
37569.393 Mitchell, Bonner. Les manifestes littéraires de la belle époque, 1886-1914. Paris, 1966.
37569.398 Controverses; theatre, roman, cinema. Paris, 1960.
37569.400 Random, Michel. Les puissances du dedans. Paris, 1966.
37569.402 Adereth, Maxwell. Commitment in modern French literature: a brief study of "littérature engagée". London, 1967.
37569.403 Dimić, Ivan. La crise psychologique dans le roman français du 20e siècle. Thèse. Belgrade, 1968.
37569.405 Fontaine, François. La littérature à l'encan. Paris, 1967.
37569.408 Rousselot, Jean. Dictionnaire de la poésie française contemporaine. Paris, 1968.
37569.410 Pabst, Walter. Der moderne französische Roman. Berlin, 1968.
37569.412 Loffler, Paul A. Chronique de la littérature prolétarienne française de 1930 à 1939. Rodez, 1967.
37569.414 Roger, Gaston. La grande alliance. Paris, 1969.
37569.416 Cent écrivains français répondent au "questionnaire Marcel Proust". Paris, 1969.
37569.418 Bloching, Karl Heinz. Die Autoren des literarischen "renouveau catholique" Frankreichs. Bonn, 1966.
37569.420 Halimi, André. Trente-six écrivains...et leurs 4 vérités. Paris, 1969.
37569.422 Marill, René. Le roman d'aujourd'hui, 1960-1970. Paris, 1970.
37569.424 Fassbinder, Klara M. Der Versunkene Garten. Heidelberg, 1968.
37569.426 Cranston, M. Enfance, mon amour. Berkeley, 1966.
37569.428 Isbakh, Aleksandr A. Vo glave kolonny. Moskva, 1970.

37569 History of special periods - 20th century - Special topics, special forms, etc. - cont.

37569.430 Knabenhans, Brigitte. Le thème de la pierre chez Sartre et quelques poètes modernes. Thèse. Zurich, 1969.
37569.432 Random, Michel. Le grand jeu. Paris, 1970. 2v.
37569.434 La Jeunesse, Ernst. Les nuits. Paris, 1896.
37569.436 Goldmann, Lucien. Structure mentales et création culturelle. Paris, 1970.
37569.438 Tauber, Christian. Le thème de l'enfance dans la littérature actuelle. Thèse. Zurich, 1971.
37569.440 Gauger, Rosemarie. Littérature engagée in Frankreich zur Zeit des Zweiten Weltkriegs. Göppingen, 1971.
37569.442 Ricardou, Jean. Pour une théorie du nouveau roman. Paris, 1971.
37569.444 Roudiez, Leon Samuel. French fiction today. New Brunswick, N.J., 1972.
37569.446 Entretiens sur la paralittérature, Cerisy-la-Salle, 1967. Entretiens sur la paralittérature. 1er sept.-10 sept.1967. Paris, 1970.

37571 Anthologies, collections of literature - Folios [Discontinued]

37571.1 Moysant, François. Bibliothèque portative des écrivains françois. 2e éd. Londres, 1803. 3v.
Htn 37571.2* Faucon, Nicolas. Bibliothèque portative. Boston, 1810.
37571.2.3A Faucon, Nicolas. Bibliothèque portative. Boston, 1810.
37571.2.3B Faucon, Nicolas. Bibliothèque portative. Boston, 1810.
37571.3 Noël, François J.M. Leçons françaises de littérature. Paris, 1873.
37571.4 Noël, François J.M. Leçons françaises de littérature. Brussels, 1833-36.
37571.5 Noël, François J.M. Leçon françaises de littérature. 21e éd. Bruxelles, 1836.
37571.6 Lemonnier, A.H. Nouvelles leçons françaises. Paris, 1822. 2v.
37571.9 La lecture en famille. Paris, 1882.
Htn 37571.28* Pagès, Alphonse. Les grands poètes français. Paris, 1874.
37571.29 Pagès, Alphonse. Les grands poètes français. Paris, 1883.
37571.31 Le livre d'or des annales politiques et littéraires. Paris, 1893.
37571.41 Aux pecheurs Bretons. Paris, 1903.
37571.50 Côte, Léon. La flore littéraire du Dauphiné. Grenoble, 1911. 3v.
37571.57 French novels. n.p., n.d. 2v.
37571.60 Les romans populaires. Series 2-7,10,13. Paris, 1849- 3v.
37571.65 Pamphlet vol. Classique populaires. 8 pam.
NEDL 37571.65 Pamphlet vol. Classique populaires.
37571.70 Poëtes français, première anthologie. Paris, 1912.
37571.71 Prosateurs français, deuxième anthologie. Paris, 1912.
37571.75 Revel, Bruno. Introduzione alla letteratura francese. Milano, 1950- 3v.
37571.80 Lagarde, André. Collection, textes et littérature. Paris, 1961- 6v.

37572 Anthologies, collections of literature - Chrestomathies and readers

37572.01 Pamphlet box. Collections of French literature-readers. Miscellaneous pamphlets.
37572.1 Recueil en prose. La Haye, 1714. 2v.
37572.1.5 Pensées. Recueil en prose. Genève, 18- .
37572.2 Kerr, Guillaume. Recueil tire des auteurs français tant en prose qu'en vers. Edinburgh, 1727.
37572.3 Ideler, L. Handbuch der französischen Sprache und Literatur. Berlin, 1804.
37572.4 Noël et La Place. L'abeille française. N.Y., 1811.
37572.5 Recueil des chefs d'oeuvre des plus celebres kauy-esprits françois. Edinbourg, 1798.
37572.5.5 Chef d'oeuvres politiques et littéraires de la fin du 18e siècle. Paris, 1788.
37572.6 Masson, Arthur. Nouveau recueil de pièces. Edinburgh, 1782.
37572.7 Chefs-d'oeuvre d'eloquence et de poèsie française. Paris, 1812.
37572.8 Lycée français. Paris, 1819. 5v.
37572.9 Half-hours with the best French authors. N.Y. 19- ?
37572.11 Soulié, J.B.A. Keepsake français, 1830. Paris, 1830.
37572.13 Bourgoin, A. Récits de nos elèves. Paris, n.d.
37572.14 Petit de Julleville, S. Morceaux choisies des auteurs français. Paris, n.d.
37572.16 Merlet, P.F. Petit tableau littéraire. London, 1833.
37572.21 Ladreyt, Casimir. Chrestomathie de la littérature française. N.Y., 1847.
37572.22 Chapsal, C.P. Leçons de littérature française. N.Y., 1845.
37572.23 Chapsal, C.P. Leçons de littérature française. N.Y., 1857.
37572.24 Masson, Gustave. Class-book of French literature. Edinburgh, 1861.
37572.25 Jacquinet, P. Lettres choisies du dix-septième siècle. Paris, 1890.
37572.25.5 Herriot, Édouard. Lettres choisies du XVII siècle. Paris, 1900.
37572.25.10A Hawkins, Richmond L. Newly discovered French letters of the 17th, 18th, and 19th centuries. Cambridge, 1933.
37572.25.10B Hawkins, Richmond L. Newly discovered French letters of the 17th, 18th, and 19th centuries. Cambridge, 1933.
37572.25.13 Lanson, G. Choix de lettres du XVIIIe siècle. 4. éd. Paris, 1895.
37572.25.14 Lanson, G. Choix de lettres du XVIIIe siècle. 9. éd. Paris, 1914.
37572.26 Labbé, M.J. Choix de lettres du XVIIIe siècle. Paris, 1890.
37572.26.3 Les epistoliers du XVIIIe siècle. Paris, 19- ?
37572.26.5 Lettres diverses. Paris, 1825.
37572.26.20 Angel, P. Lettres inédites sur l'inquiétude moderne. Paris, 1951.
37572.26.30 Maison, André. Anthologie de la correspondance française. Lausanne, 1969. 7v.
37572.27 Oppen, Edward A. French reader. London, 1864.
37572.28 Bernardin, N.M. Morceaux choisis des classiques français. Paris, 1883.
37572.28.2 Bernardin, N.M. Morceaux choisis des classiques français. Paris, 1887.
37572.28.3 Bernardin, N.M. Morceaux choisis des classiques français. Paris, 1891.
37572.29 Louandre, Charles. Histoire de la litterature française. Paris, 1863.
37572.29.5 Louandre, Charles. Histoire de la litterature française. v.1-2. Paris, 1876.

37572 Anthologies, collections of literature - Chrestomathies and readers - cont.

37572.30.2 Saintsbury, George. Specimens of French literature. Oxford, 1892.
37572.31 Marcou, F.L. Morceaux choisis des classiques français prosateurs. Paris, 1885.
37572.31.10 Marcou, F.L. Morceaux choisis des classiques français prosateurs. Paris, 191-?
37572.32 Marcou, F.L. Morceaux choisis des classiques français poètes. 27. éd. Paris, 1885.
37572.32.10 Marcou, F.L. Morceaux choisis des classiques français poètes. Paris, 191-?
37572.33 Roche, Antoine. Les prosateurs français. Paris, 1887.
37572.34 Roche, Antoine. Les prosateurs français. Paris, 1872.
37572.35 French miscellany. n.p., n.d.
37572.35.3 Mélanges sur Charles Nodier, Paillet, Dronineau. Paris, 1806-33.
37572.35.4 Mélanges sur Victor Hugo, De Musset et Charles Nodier. Paris, 1844-1908.
37572.35.9 Nodier, Charles. Le nouveau magasin des enfants. Paris, 1860.
37572.36A Merrill, S. Pastels in prose. N.Y., 1890.
37572.36B Merrill, S. Pastels in prose. N.Y., 1890.
37572.36.2 Merrill, S. Pastels in prose. N.Y., 1890.
37572.36.3 Merrill, S. Pastels in prose. N.Y., 1890.
37572.36.4 Merrill, S. Pastels in prose. N.Y., 1890.
37572.36.5 Pamphlet vol. Molière, Jean B. Le dépit amoureux, comédie. 10 pam.
37572.37 O'connor, B.F. Choix de contes contemporains. N.Y., 1885.
37572.37.9 Journal des débats: Revue hebdomadaire. Supplement. 1914-1931 5v.
37572.38.5 Paris, Gaston. Chrestomathie du moyen âge. Paris, 1897.
37572.38.10 Paris, Gaston. Chrestomathie du moyen âge. 13. éd. Paris, 1921?
37572.38.35 Bossuat, A. Les chroniqueurs français du moyen âge. Paris, 1937-
37572.39 Huguet, E. Portraits et récits extraits des prosateurs du XVIe siècle. Paris, 1897.
37572.39.5 Huguet, E. Portraits et récits extraits des prosateurs du XVIe siècle. Paris, 1909.
37572.40 Bornecque, H. Contes et récits en prose...des XVIIe et VIIIe siècles. Paris, n.d.
37572.42 Pellissier, G. Le XVIIe siècle par les textes. Paris, n.d.
37572.43.3 Pellissier, G. Le XVIIe siècle par les textes. 2. éd. Paris, 1919.
37572.44 Recueil de pièces du regiment de la Calotte. Paris, 1726.
37572.44.2 Regiment de la Calotte. Memoires...à l'histoire de la Calotte. pt.1-4. Amsterdam, 1735. 3v.
37572.45A Rinder, Edith N. The massacre of the innocents and other tales. Chicago, 1895.
37572.45B Rinder, Edith N. The massacre of the innocents and other tales. Chicago, 1895.
37572.46 L'étincelle, souvenirs de littérature. Paris, 18- .
37572.47 Marottes à vendre or Triboulet tabletier. London, 1812.
37572.48A Contes de Figaro. Paris, 1885.
37572.48B Contes de Figaro. Paris, 1885.
37572.49 Almanach du Figaro. Paris. 4,1859
37572.50 Faguet, E. La prose française. Paris, n.d.
37572.51 Faguet, E. Ce que disent les livres. Paris, n.d.
37572.53 Guerlac, Othon. Selections from standard French authors. Boston, 1905.
37572.54 Buffum, D.L. French short stories. N.Y., 1907.
37572.54.5 Buffum, D.L. French short stories. 2. ed. N.Y., 1907.
37572.54.7 Buffum, D.L. French short stories. 2. ed. N.Y., 1927.
37572.54.10 Buffum, D.L. Contes français. N.Y., 1915.
37572.55 Salon bleu d'Arthénice par son ombre. 2. éd. Paris, 1912.
37572.56 Des Granges, C. Pages de littérature française (1800-1920). Paris, 1926.
37572.57 Sirich, E.H. Harper's French anthology, XVII-XVIII-XIX centuries. N.Y., 1923.
37572.58 Plattard, Jean. Anthologie du XVil siècle français. London, 1927.
37572.59 Bush, Stephen H. Sixteenth century French anthology. Boston, 1927.
37572.60 Le conteur suisse; recueil des plus interessantes. v.1-2. Berne, 1853.
37572.65 Petite anthologie des auteurs gais contemporains. Paris, 1918.
37572.70 Schinz, A. Nineteenth century French readings. N.Y., 1939. 2v.
37572.75 Barthélemy, B. Textes choisis pour la lecture et l'explication. Paris, 1958-60. 5v.
37572.80 Nelson, R. Aspects of French literature. N.Y., 1961.

37573.1 - .199 Anthologies, collections of literature - General collections - General works

37573.1 Vinet, Alexander R. Chrestomathie française. Littérature de l'enfance. Bruxelles, 1855.
37573.2 Vinet, Alexander R. Choix de lectures prises dans les auteurs classiques de la littérature française...chrestomathie française. Lausanne, 1840-43. 2v.
37573.2.10 Vinet, Alexander R. Chrestomathie française. Littérature de l'adolescence. v.2. 6. éd. Bale, 1855.
37573.3 Vinet, Alexander R. Chrestomathie française. Littérature de la jeunesse et de l'âge mur. Lausanne, 1871-70. 3v.
NEDL 37573.4 Vinet, Alexander R. Chrestomathie française. Littérature de l'adolescence. v.2. Lausanne, 1860.
37573.7 Staaff, F.N. Lectures choisies de la littérature française. Paris, 1866.
37573.8 Staaff, F.N. La littérature française. Paris, 1875-77. 3v.
37573.8.10 Herrig, L. La France littéraire. 6. éd. Brunsvic, 1862.
37573.9 Herrig, L. La France littéraire. 12. éd. Brunsvic, 1868.
37573.10 Crépet, Eugene. Les poètes français. Paris, 1861-62. 4v.
37573.11A Lucas, St. John. The Oxford book of French verse. N.Y., n.d.
37573.11B Lucas, St. John. The Oxford book of French verse. N.Y., n.d.
37573.11C Lucas, St. John. The Oxford book of French verse. N.Y., n.d.
37573.11.5A Lucas, St. John. The Oxford book of French verse, XIII-XIX centuries. Oxford, 1908.
37573.11.5B Lucas, St. John. The Oxford book of French verse, XIII-XIX centuries. Oxford, 1908.
37573.12 Fuster, Charles. L'année poétique. L'année des poètes. Paris. 1890-1897 8v.

37573.1 - .199 Anthologies, collections of literature - General collections - General works - cont.

NEDL 37573.12 Fu5ter, Charles. L'année poétique. L'année des poètes. Paris. 1899-1909 5v.
37573.13 L'almanach des poètes. Paris. 1898
Htn 37573.15* Société des bibliophiles de Belgique. Recueil de chansons. Bruxelles, 1870-79. 4v.
37573.16 Anthologie des poètes français. Paris, n.d.
37573.17 Anthologie des prosateurs français. Paris, n.d.
37573.18 Ginestier, P. Culture et civilisation françaises. Paris, 1962.
37573.21 Rion, Aldine. Les femmes poètes bretonnes. Nantes, 1892.
NEDL 37573.22 Tiercelin, Louis. Le Parnasse Breton contemporain. Paris, 1889-
X Cg 37573.24 Blocquel, S. Le tresor des bons mots. Paris, 1856.
NEDL 37573.25 Anthologie des poètes français du XIXe siècle. Paris, 1898. 4v.
37573.26 Potter, Henry Austin. Dix contes modernes des meilleurs auteurs du jour. Boston, 1900.
37573.28 Anthologie des poètes français contemporains. Paris, 1958- 5v.
37573.28.5 Walch, Gerard. Antologie des poètes français contemporains, 1866-1914. Paris, 1922-24. 3v.
37573.29 Pellissier, G. Anthologie des poètes du XIXe siècle. Paris, n.d.
37573.30 Walch, Gerard. Anthologie des poètes français contemporains, 1866-1907. Paris, 1906-32. 4v.
37573.31 Pellissier, Jean B. L'abeille poétique du XIIe siècle. Limoges, 1852.
37573.33 Lanson, Gustave. Anthologie des poètes nouveaux. 3. éd. Paris, 1913.
37573.34 Brøndal, Viggo. Franske digte fra Renaissancen til vore dage. København, 1942.
37573.35 Vrignault, P. Anthologie de la chanson française. Paris, n.d.
37573.36 Anthologie des indépendants. Paris, 1920.
37573.36.20 Bournand, F. L'eloquence et la littérature chrétiennes. Lyon, 1892?
37573.37 Ferrières, Gauthier. Anthologie des écrivains français des XVe et XVIe siècles; prose. Paris, 1918.
37573.37.1 Ferrières, Gauthier. Anthologie des écrivains français des XVe et XVIe siècles. Prose. Paris, 1913.
37573.37.2 Ferrières, Gauthier. Anthologie des écrivains français des XVe et XVIe siècles; poésie. Paris, 1918.
37573.37.2.5 Ferrières, Gauthier. Anthologie des écrivains français des XVe et XVIe siècles; poésie. Paris, 1913.
37573.37.3 Ferrières, Gauthier. Anthologie des écrivains français du XVIIe siècle; prose. Paris, 1911.
37573.37.4 Ferrières, Gauthier. Anthologie des écrivains français du XVIIe siècle; poésie. Paris, 1911.
37573.37.5 Ferrières, Gauthier. Anthologie des écrivains français du XVIIIe siècle; prose. Paris, 1910.
37573.37.6 Ferrières, Gauthier. Anthologie des écrivains français du XVIIIe siècle; poésie. Paris, 1911.
37573.37.7 Ferrières, Gauthier. Anthologie des écrivains français du XIXe siècle; prose. v.1-2. Paris, 1919-20.
37573.37.8 Ferrières, Gauthier. Anthologie des écrivains du XIXe siècle; poésie. v.1-2. Paris, 1920.
NEDL 37573.37.9 Ferrières, Gauthier. Anthologie des écrivains français contemporaines; prose. Paris, 1920.
NEDL 37573.37.10 Ferrières, Gauthier. Anthologie des écrivains français contemporaines; poésie. Paris, 1920.
37573.37.12 Ferrières, Gauthier. Anthologie des écrivains français contemporaines. v.1-2. Paris, 1919.
Htn 37573.38* Société de Conférences. Addresses. Monaco.
37573.40 Des Granges, Charles M. Morceaux choisis des auteurs français du moyen âge à nos jours. 23. éd. Paris, 1930.
37573.42 Les amis des cahiers verts. Paris. 1-6,1928-1931 2v.
37573.50 Les grands écrivains de France illustrés. v.1-2. pts.1-6. Paris, 1934-38. 5v.
37573.55 Gifford, G.H. La France à travers les siècles. N.Y., 1939.
37573.60 Montagne. Grenoble, 1941.
37573.70 Daniels, W.M. Poèms et chants de France. Boston, n.d.
37573.72 Varney, J.M.V. Ecrivains français; extraits. N.Y., 1943.
37573.74 Palmer, Ray E. French travellers in England, 1600-1900. London, 1960.

37573.200 - .299 Anthologies, collections of literature - General collections - Special periods - 1661-1715

37573.219 Bremond, Henri. Anthologie des écrivains catholiques. Paris, 1919.
37573.223 Hilka, Alfons. Drei Erzählungen aus dem didaktischen Epos. Halle, 1928.
37573.230 Bibliothèque nationale; collection des meilleurs auteurs anciens et modernes. Paris. 1873
37573.240 Schinz, Albert. Seventeenth century French readings. N.Y., 1931.
37573.250 Peyre, Henri. Seventeenth century French prose and poetry. Boston, 1937.
37573.255 Jan, E. von. Classicisme français. Leipzig, 1951.

37573.300 - .399 Anthologies, collections of literature - General collections - Special periods - 1715-1799

37573.300 Pamphlet vol. French poetry, 1789-1792. 13 pam.
37573.300.5 Pamphlet vol. French poetry, 1793-1798. 20 pam.
37573.300.10 Pamphlet vol. Revolutionary poetry. 15 pam.
37573.300.15 Pamphlet vol. Revolutionary hymns and songs. 47 pam.
37573.310 Chapman, Percy A. An anthology of eighteenth century French literature. Princeton, 1930.
37573.315 Gnostiques de la révolution. Paris, 1946. 2v.
37573.316 Etiemble, René. Romanciers du XVIIIe siècle. Paris, 1960. 2v.
37573.318 Krauss, Werner. Antike und Moderne in der Literaturdiskussion des 18. Jahrhunderts. Selections in French. Berlin, 1966.
37573.320 Almanach litteraire; ou Etrennes d'Apollon. Paris. 1790

37573.400 - .499 Anthologies, collections of literature - General collections - Special periods - 1800-1849

37573.400 Pamphlet vol. French poetry. An IX-X. 17 pam.
37573.400.5 Pamphlet vol. French poetry. An XI-1809. 17 pam.
37573.400.10 Pamphlet vol. French poetry. 1810-1818. 26 pam.
37573.400.15 Pamphlet vol. French poetry. 1820-1827. 16 pam.
37573.400.25 Fleurs de poésie moderne; tirées des oeuvres de A. de Lamartine, V. Hugo, De Béranger, C. De Cavigne. Londres, 1834.
37573.400.30 Le petit moissonneur des théâtres. Paris, 18- .

37573.400 - .499 Anthologies, collections of literature - General collections - Special periods - 1800-1849 - cont.

37573.410 Annales romantiques. v.3. Paris, 1826.
37573.410.5 Annales romantiques. Facsimile. v.1-12, 1823-36. Paris. Genève, 1971. 6v.
37573.415 Duvert, F.A. Ce que femme veut. Poizzy, 18- . 6 pam.
37573.420 Curwen, Harry. French love songs and other poems. N.Y., 1871.
Htn 37573.425* Théâtre de l'hermitage de Catherine II. Paris, 1799. 2v.
Htn 37573.435* Noël, François J.M. Études et leçons françaises de littérature et de morale. v.4. Gand, 1822.
37573.445 Rat, Maurice. Contes et récits du XIXe siècle. Paris, 1939.
Htn 37573.450* Société des gens des lettres de France, Paris. Babel. 1840 3v.
37573.455 Govaert, Marcel. Les lettres françaises. Anvers, 1956.
37573.460 Toesca, Maurice. Le chant romantique, anthologie. Paris, 1967.
37573.465 La psyché; choix de pièces en vers et en prose, 1826-30. Paris. Facsimile. Genève, 1971. 4v.

37573.500 - .599 Anthologies, collections of literature - General collections - Special periods - 1850-1899

37573.510 La syrinx. Aix-en-Provence. 1-12//
37573.515 Le scapin. Ser. 1-2,1885-86// Paris. Facsimile. Genève, 1971.
37573.563 Collection d'auteurs français. Berlin.
37573.580 Ploetz, K. Manuel de litterature française. 6. éd. Berlin, 1880.
37573.587 Nouvelle bibliothèque populaire. Paris.
37573.590 Les heures. Paris.
37573.594 Van Daell, Alphonse Naus. An introduction to French authors. Boston, 1894.
37573.594.5 Leune, Albert. Difficult modern French. Boston, 1894.
Htn 37573.596* Feminies; huit chapitres inédits dévoués à la femme. Paris, 1896.
37573.599 Méras, Baptiste. Cinq histoires. N.Y., 1899.
37573.599.10 Mont, Paul de. Modernités. Almelo, 1899.

37573.600 - .799 Anthologies, collections of literature - General collections - Special periods - 1900-

37573.603 Nouvelles originales. Paris. 1-10 3v.
37573.605 Les cahiers de la pléiade. Paris. 1-12,1946-1951 6v.
37573.613 La pensée française. Paris. 1913-1914
37573.617 Turpin, Georges. Les poètes de la guerre. v.1-2. Paris, 1917.
37573.618 Les Humbles. Anthologie des Humbles. Paris, 1918.
37573.619 Association des écrivains combattants. Anthologie des écrivains morts à la guerre, 1914-1918. Amiens, 1924-26. 5v.
37573.619.10 Association des écrivains combattants. Anthologie des écrivains morts à la guerre,1939-1945. Paris, 1960.
37573.619.25A Poèmes des poilus. Boston, 1917.
37573.619.25B Poèmes des poilus. Boston, 1917.
37573.620 Pévost, Ernest. Le livre épique. Paris, 1920.
37573.621 Almanach de l'etudiant alsacien-lorrain. Strasbourg.
37573.622 Mélanges. Paris, 1922.
37573.624 Vers et prose. Paris. 1928
37573.625 Tondo, M.M. Pathelin, et autres pièces. N.Y., 1924.
37573.631 Wolfenstein, Alfred. Hier Schreit Paris. Berlin, 1931.
37573.632 La poésie d'aujourd'hui; anthologie nouvelle. Paris, 1928.
37573.633A Michaud, Régis. Vingtième siècle. N.Y., 1933.
37573.633B Michaud, Régis. Vingtième siècle. N.Y., 1933.
37573.637 Roosbroeck, Gustave L. van. An anthology of modern French poetry. N.Y., 1927.
37573.638 Chaigne, L. Anthologie de la renaissance catholique. Paris, 1938-39. 2v.
37573.643A Boni, Albert. The modern book of French verse in English translations. N.Y., 1920.
37573.643B Boni, Albert. The modern book of French verse in English translations. N.Y., 1920.
37573.645A Poètes contemporains. Paris, 1938.
37573.645B Poètes contemporains. Paris, 1938.
37573.648 Cairo. Egyptian University. Anthologie de prose française. La Caire, 1930.
37573.650 Mélanges de litterature, philosophie et histoire offerts à M. Louis Arnould. Poitiers, 1934.
37573.652 Cooper, N. A first anthology of French poetry. Oxford, Eng., 1939.
37573.654 David-Sauvageat, A. Morceaux choisis des classiques français. Paris, 1904.
37573.662 Glanes d'Esculape. Nice, 1933.
37573.664 Bovée, A.G. Promenades littéraires et historiques. N.Y., 1941.
37573.667 Wilson, C.I. Modern French prose, 1918-1928. London, 1932.
37573.669 Stewart, Hugh F. The French romanticists. Cambridge, Eng., 1914.
37573.671 Braibant, Marcel. Les paysans d'aujourd'hui. Anthologie d'auteurs contemporaine. 10. éd. Paris, 1940.
37573.671.5 Arland, Marcel. Le paysan français à travers la littérature. 2. éd. Paris, 1941.
37573.673 Les pléiades. Paris, 1946.
37573.674 Osmose; cahier littéraire. Paris.
37573.675 Bady, René. L'âme française à travers la littérature. Lausanne, 1945.
37573.677 Clot, René Jean. L'exil français. Alger, 1944.
37573.679 Demeur, L. Pages choisies des écrivains français de Belgique. Bruxelles, 1936.
37573.680 Le milieu du siècle; collection dirigée par Roger Lannes. Paris. 1,1947 5v.
37573.682 The Oxford book of French verse. Oxford, 1907.
37573.684 Picon, Gaëtan. Panorama de la nouvelle littérature française. Paris, 1949.
37573.684.1 Picon, Gaëtan. Panorama de la nouvelle littérature française. Paris, 1960.
37573.684.5 Picon, Gaëtan. Panorama de la nouvelle littérature française. Paris, 1953.
37573.686 Lecompte, I. Anthology of modern French literature. N.Y., 1932.
37573.687 Almanach littéraire Crès. Paris. 1914-1917
37573.688 Southwell, K. Signposts in French literature. London, 1950.
37573.690 Genève, par Lydia Kerr. Hors-texte de Fanny Gianini. Genève, 1956.
37573.700 Bradley, R.F. Eight centuries of French literature. N.Y., 1951.

37573.600 - .799 Anthologies, collections of literature - General collections - Special periods - 1900- - cont.

37573.702 Anthologie de la poésie française depuis le surréalisme. Paris, 1952.
37573.704 Klemperer, V. Die moderne französische Prosa. 3. Aufl. Leipzig, 1948.
37573.706 Écrits. Paris, 1927.
37573.708 Bagaert, Jean. Les lettres françaises. Paris, 1954-58. 3v.
37573.710 Fortini, Franco. Il movimento surrealista. 1. ed. Milano, 1959.
37573.715 Borchardt, G. New French writing. N.Y., 1961.
37573.718 Vallée, Léon. La sarabande. Paris, 1903. 2v.
37573.720 Dougherty, D.M. Perspectives de la littérature française. N.Y., 1961.
37573.722 Peyre, H. Contemporary French literature. N.Y., 1964.
37573.724 Quatre poèmes de Francis Carco, Philippe Chabaneix, Tristan Dereme et Vincent Muselli. Paris, 1923.
37573.726 Mauro, Walter. La resistenza nella literatura francese dalla 2 guerra mondiale all'Algeria. Roma, 1961.
V37573.730 Journées du livre. Dans le jardin des lettres: parni nos auteurs contemporains. Paris, 1936.
37573.732 Jones, Cyril Meredith. Les lettres en France. N.Y., 1967.
37573.737 Actuels, revue littéraire. Bellegarde. 4,1967+
37573.740 Brée, Germaine. Defeat and beyond; an anthology of French wartime writing, 1940-1945. N.Y., 1970.
37573.742 Écritures; cahiers du cercle interfacultaire de littérature de l'université de Liège. Liège. 1956+
37573.744 Bonheur, Gaston. Qui a cassé le vase de Soissons? Paris, 1965.

37574.1 - .199 Anthologies, collections of literature - Collections of poetry - General works

37574.3 Chasles, Émile. Histoire abrégé de la littérature française. Paris, n.d. 2v.
37574.5 Pamphlet vol. Romantismus. 7 pam.
37574.6A Masson, Gustave. French classics. Oxford, 1867-68. 7v.
37574.6B Masson, Gustave. French classics. v.1-3,5-7. Oxford, 1867-68. 6v.
37574.8 Porte-feuille d'un homme de goute. Amsterdam, 1765. 2v.
37574.9 Le Chansonnier du bon vieux temps. v.1-2. Paris, 1809-10.
37574.10 Brakelmann, J. Les plus anciens chansonniers française. Paris, 1871-91.
37574.11 Les diners du vaudeville. Paris. 1-48 5v.
37574.11.2 Les diners du vaudeville. Paris. 1-6
37574.12 Les petits poètes du XVIIIe siècle. Paris, n.d.
37574.13 La chanson française du XVe au XXe siècle. Paris, 1909.
37574.14 Louandre, Charles. Chefs-d'oeuvres des conteurs français, 1051-1650. Paris, 1874.
37574.14.5 Louandre, Charles. Chefs-d'oeuvres des conteurs français. Paris, 1884.
37574.15 Louandre, Charles. Chefs-d'oeuvres des conteurs français, 17e siècle. Paris, 1874.
37574.16 Louandre, Charles. Chefs-d'oeuvres des conteurs français, 18e siècle. Paris, 1874.
Htn 37574.17* Contes et nouvelles en vers. Paris, 1862. 2v.
37574.18 La récréation et passetemps des tristes. Paris, 1862.
37574.19 Rochè, A. Les poètes français. Recueil de morceaux choisis. Paris, 1869.
37574.20 Batteux, Charles. Chefs-d'oeuvres d'éloquence poetique. Toulouse, 1820.
37574.21 Batteux, Charles. Chefs-d'oeuvres d'éloquence poetique. Paris, 1821.
37574.22 Haupt, Moriz. Französische Volkslieder. Leipzig, 1877.
37574.23 Ventouillac, L.T. French poetry. London, 1831.
37574.24 Coutan, A. (Mme.). Choix de poésies. N.Y., 1850.
37574.24.2 Gouttes de poèsie. Paris, n.d.
37574.25A Both-Hendriksen, Louis. La triade française, A. de Musset, Lamartine, et Victor Hugo. Boston, 1886.
37574.25B Both-Hendriksen, Louis. La triade française, A. de Musset, Lamartine, et Victor Hugo. Boston, 1886.
37574.25.3 Both-Hendriksen, Louis. La triade française, A. de Musset, Lamartine et Victor Hugo. Boston, 1897.
37574.25.4 Bowen, Benjamin Lester. Introduction to modern French lyrics. Boston, 1891.
37574.25.5 Bowen, Benjamin Lester. Introduction to modern French lyrics. Boston, 1897.
37574.26A Masson, Gustave. La lyre française. London, 1867.
37574.26B Masson, Gustave. La lyre française. London, 1867.
37574.26C Masson, Gustave. La lyre française. London, 1867.
37574.26.5 Masson, Gustave. La lyre française. London, 1867.
37574.26.6 Masson, Gustave. La lyre française. London, 1867.
37574.26.8 Masson, Gustave. La lyre française. London, 1881.
37574.26.10A Masson, Gustave. La lyre française. London, 1887.
37574.26.10B Masson, Gustave. La lyre française. London, 1887.
37574.26.12 Masson, Gustave. La lyre française. London, 1892.
37574.26.14 Masson, Gustave. La lyre française. London, 1903.
37574.27 Godefroy, Frédéric. Morceaux choisis des poètes et prosateurs français du IXe au XVIe siècle. Paris, 1883.
37574.28 Godefroy, Frédéric. Morceaux choisis des poètes et prosateurs français du XVIe siècle. Paris, 1875.
37574.28.9 Bever, A. van. Les poètes du terroir du XVe siècle au XXe siècle. Paris, n.d. 4v.
37574.28.12 Bever, A. van. Les poètes du terroir du XVe siècle au XXe siècle. v.1,3-4. Paris, 1918. 3v.
37574.29 Illustrated book of French songs. London, 1855.
37574.29.5 Oxenford, John. Book of French songs. London, n.d.
X Cg 37574.30 Tresor des chansons joyeuses et populaires. Paris, 1861.
37574.31 Joyeux refrains de nos pères. Paris, n.d.
37574.31.5 Gourdon de Genouillac, H. Les refrains de la rue de 1830 à 1870. Paris, 1879.
37574.33.3 Ebener, Gottfried. Album poétique. n.p., n.d.
37574.34 Chansonnier republicain. Paris, 187-.
37574.35 Poésies révolutionnaires. Paris, 1821.
37574.36A Poésies nationale de la révolution française. Paris, 1836.
37574.36B Poésies nationale de la révolution française. Paris, 1836.
37574.36.5 Les republiaines chansons populaires des révolutions. v.1-3. Paris, 1848.
37574.37 Vingtrinier, J. Chants et chansons des soldats de France. Paris, 1902.
37574.38 Pylodet, L. Gouttes de Rosée. French lyric poems. N.Y., 1866?
37574.38.5 Gouttes de Rosée. Petit trésor poétique des jeunes personnes. N.Y., 1866.
37574.39 Pylodet, L. Gouttes de Rosée. N.Y., 1869.
37574.40 Thorley, Wilfrid Charles. Fleurs-de-lys...French poetry. Boston, 1920.

37574.1 - .199 Anthologies, collections of literature - Collections of poetry - General works - cont.

37574.42A Saintsbury, George. French lyrics. London, 1882.
37574.42B Saintsbury, George. French lyrics. London, 1882.
37574.42.2A Saintsbury, George. French lyrics. N.Y., 1883.
37574.42.2B Saintsbury, George. French lyrics. N.Y., 1883.
37574.42.5 Saintsbury, George. French lyrics. London, 1882.
37574.42.10 Saintsbury, George. French lyrics. N.Y., 1889.
37574.43 Lewisohn, Ludwig. The poets of modern France. N.Y., 1918.
37574.44 Robertet, G. Poètes lyriques du XIXe siècle. Paris, 1888. 2v.
37574.45 Merlet, Gustave. Extraits de poètes lyriques du XIXe siècle. Paris, n.d.
37574.46 Henning, G.N. Representative French lyrics of the 19th century. Boston, 1913.
37574.46.5 Henning, G.N. Representative French lyrics of the 19th century. Boston, 1935.
37574.47 Chansonnier de société. Paris, 1812.
37574.49 Pamphlet vol. Portrait de Mme. Geoffrin. French poetry. Amsterdam, 1774-1809. 11 pam.
37574.50 Janon, Camille de. Recueil de poésies à l'usage de la jeunesse américaine. N.Y., 1882.
37574.52 Quitard, Pierre M. Anthologie de l'amour, extraite des poètes français. Paris, 1862.
37574.54 Lewis, Charles B. La lyre d'amour. Anthology of French love poems. London, 1911.
37574.55A Lamartine, Alfred. Love songs of France, from original of De Musset. N.Y., n.d.
37574.55B Lamartine, Alfred. Love songs of France, from original of De Musset. N.Y., n.d.
37574.55.5 Lamartine, Alfred. Love songs of France, from original of De Musset. N.Y., 1896.
37574.57 Zuccaro, L. L'Italie dans la poèsie française contemporaine. Milano, 1894.
37574.65 Payne, John. Flowers of France. 16th century. London, 1907.
Htn 37574.65* Payar, John. Flowers of France. The renaissance period. 16th century. London, 1907.
Htn 37574.66* Payne, John. Flowers of France. The classical period. 17th and 18th century. London, 1915.
37574.66.5 Payne, John. Flowers of France. The classical period. 17th and 18th century. London, 1914.
37574.67 Payne, John. Flowers of France. The romantic period. 19th century. London, 1906. 2v.
Htn 37574.67* Payne, John. Flowers of France. The romantic period. 19th century. London, 1906. 2v.
37574.68 Payne, John. Flowers of France. 19th and 20th centuries. London, 1913. 2v.
Htn 37574.68* Payne, John. Flowers of France. 19th and 20th centuries. London, 1913. 2v.
37574.69 González Martínez, Enrique. Jardines de Francia. México, 1915.
37574.71 Société havraise d'etudes diverses. L'abeille havraise. Havre, 1911.
37574.72 Watrin, Eugène. Echos poétiques de Lorraine. 2. éd. Guénange, 1910.
37574.75 Dorchain, Auguste. Les cent meilleurs poèmes, lyriques, de la langue française. Philadelphia, 19- .
37574.75.3 Dorchain, Auguste. Les cent meilleurs poèmes. 4. éd. Paris, 1906.
37574.75.4 Dorchain, Auguste. Les cent meilleurs poèmes. Paris, 1907.
37574.75.6 Dorchain, Auguste. Les cent meilleurs poèmes. Paris, 1910.
37574.75.8 Dorchain, Auguste. Les cent meilleurs poèmes. Paris, 1927.
37574.75.9 Dorchain, Auguste. Les cent meilleurs poèmes. Philadelphia, 1927.
37574.75.15 Dorchain, Auguste. Chefs-d'oeuvre lyriques de F. de Malherbe et de l'école classique. v.2. Paris, 1909.
37574.77A Ritchie, R.L.G. French verse from Villon to Verlaine. London, 1922.
37574.77B Ritchie, R.L.G. French verse from Villon to Verlaine. London, 1922.
37574.77.10A Ritchie, R.L.G. French verse from Villon to Verlaine. London, 1929.
37574.77.10B Ritchie, R.L.G. French verse from Villon to Verlaine. London, 1929.
37574.79 Mixer, A.H. Manual of French poetry. N.Y., 1874.
37574.80 Anthologie de la nouvelle poésie française. Paris, 1925.
37574.81 Boase, Alan Martin. The poetry of France. v.1,3-4. London, 1964. 3v.
37574.90 The Oxford book of French verse, 13th - 20th centuries. Oxford, 1926.
37574.90.5A The Oxford book of French verse, 13th - 20th centuries chosen by St. John Lucas. 2. ed. Oxford, 1931.
37574.90.5B The Oxford book of French verse, 13th - 20th centuries chosen by St. John Lucas. 2. ed. Oxford, 1931.
37574.90.7 The Oxford book of French verse. 2. ed. Oxford, 1957.
37574.95 Duhamel, Georges. Anthologie de la poésie lyrique...XVe-XIXe. Leipzig, 1923.
37574.95.5 Duhamel, Georges. Anthologie de la poésie lyrique en France. Paris, 1946.
37574.100 Anderson, Frederick. Illustrations of early French literature, 1100-1600. Boston, 1926.
37574.102 Le Goffir, Charles. Les poètes de la mer du moyen age à nos jours. Paris, 1928.
37574.105 Chamberlain, B.H. Huit siècles de poésie française. Paris, 1927.
37574.106 Mazade, F. Anthologie des poètes français des origines à nos jours. Paris, 1927-28. 4v.
37574.108A Sarolea, C. Anthologie des poètes lyriques français. Paris, 1914.
37574.108B Sarolea, C. Anthologie des poètes lyriques français. Paris, 1914.
37574.110 Néel, Henri Charles. French anthology. N.Y., 1929.
37574.112 Arland, M. Anthologie de la poésie française. Paris, 1947.
37574.115 Canfield, Arthur G. French lyrics. N.Y., 1899.
37574.115.3 Canfield, Arthur G. French lyrics. N.Y., 1899.
37574.115.10 Canfield, Arthur G. French poems. N.Y., 1941.
37574.120 Legge, J.G. Chanticleer; a study of the French Muse. London, 1935.
37574.122 Lugli, Vittorio. Da Villon a Valéry; il libro della poesia francese. Messina, 1949.
37574.135 Wais, Kurt. Doppelfassungen Französischer Lyrik von Marot bis Valéry. Halle, 1936.

Classified Listing

37574.1 - .199 Anthologies, collections of literature - Collections of poetry - General works - cont.

37574.140 Steele, Alan J. Three centuries of French verse, 1511-1819. Edinburgh, 1956.
37574.140.2 Steele, Alan J. Three centuries of French verse, 1511-1819. Edinburgh, 1961.
37574.142 Poésies et dessins de Charles d'Orléans à Apollinaire, de Fouguet à Pecasso. Lausanne, 1957.
37574.145 Kastner, L.E. A book of French verse from Marot to Mallarme. Cambridge, Eng., 1936.
37574.150 Vianey, J. Chefs d'oeuvre poétiques du XVIe siècle. 5. éd. Paris, 1938.
37574.155 Talagrand, Jacques. Introduction à la poésie française. Paris, 1939.
37574.160 Lefert de la Morinière, A.C. Bibliothèque poétique. Paris, 1745. 4v.
37574.165 Rabion. Les fleurs de la poésie française. 8. éd. Toura, 1865.
37574.167 Almeida, G. de. Poetas de França. São Paulo, 1936.
37574.167.2 Almeida, G. de. Poetas de França. 2. ed. São Paulo, 1944.
37574.170 Thorley, W.C. The French muse. London, 1944.
37574.175 Thorley, W.C. The French muse. 3. ed. London, 1947.
37574.180 Hartley, Anthony. The Penguin book of French verse. Harmondsworth, 1957. 4v.
37574.185 Graham, Victor. Representative French poetry. Toronto, 1962.
37574.190 Cahiers de Rochefort. Rochefort-sur-Loire. 3-6,1942-1952

37574.200 - .299 Anthologies, collections of literature - Collections of poetry - Special periods - 1661-1715

37574.200 Poésies nouvelles. Paris, 1682.
Htn 37574.205* Rosset, François de. Nouveau recueil des plus beaux vers de temps. Paris, 1609.
37574.212 Aury, Dominique. Poètes précieux et baroques du XVIIe siècle. Angers, 1941.
37574.220 Picard, Raymond. La poésie française de 1640 à 1680. Paris, 1964.

37574.300 - .399 Anthologies, collections of literature - Collections of poetry - Special periods - 1715-1799

37574.300 Lély, Gilbert. Chefs-d'oeuvre des poètes galants du XVIIIe siècle. Paris, 1921.
37574.301 Dufay, Pierre. L'enfer des classiques. Paris, 1936.
37574.302 Adam, Pierre. Étude sur le vocabulaire du chansonnier historique. Thèse. Nancy, 1920.
37574.305 Buisson, J.B. Souvenirs des muses. Paris, 1823.
Htn 37574.310* Roucalli, C. Epigrammi francesi, tradotti i versi italiano. Parma, 1798.
37574.315 Parent, F.N. Recueil d'hymnes philosophiques, civiques, et moraux. Paris, 1798-99.
37574.320 Nouveau recueil de cantiques. n.p., 1797.
37574.325 Lablée, Jacques. Le nouveau parnasse chrétien. 2. éd. Paris, 1808.
37574.330 Rallier, Louis Antoine Esprit. Recueil de chants moraux et patriotiques. Paris, 1798-99.
37574.335 Parent, F.N. Recueil de chants philosophiques, civiques et moraux...fêtes nationales. Paris, 1799.
37574.336 Parent, F.N. Recueil de chants philosophiques, civiques et moraux...fêtes nationales. Paris, 1799.
37574.340 Nougaret, P.B. Hymnes pour toutes les fêtes nationales. Paris, 1796. 2 pam.
37574.345 Recueil d'hymnes, odes, etc., relatifs aux fêtes décadaire. n.p., n.d. 3 pam.
37574.351 Couret de Villeneuve, M. Le trésor du Parnasse. v.1-4. London, 1763-70. 2v.
37574.355 Sauvage, R.N. Poesies latines et française sur la convalescence de Louis XV (1744). Rouen, 1922.
37574.360 Van Roosbroeck, G.L. Unpublished poems by Voltaire. N.Y., 1933.
37574.362 Petits poèmes érotiques du XVIIIe siècle. Paris, 1917.
37574.365 Dumas, André. Anthologie des poètes français du XVIIIe siècle. Paris, 1934.
37574.367.2 Fellows, Otis E. The age of enlightenment. N.Y., 1942.
37574.370 Contes théologiques et autres poésies. Paris, 1800.
37574.380 Allem, M. Anthologie poétique française. Paris, 1919.

37574.400 - .499 Anthologies, collections of literature - Collections of poetry - Special periods - 1800-1849

37574.405 Grant, E.M. French poetry of the nineteenth century. N.Y., 1935.
37574.405.2 Grant, E.M. French poetry of the 19th century. 2. ed. N.Y., 1962.
37574.410 Choix de cantiques a l'usage des églises indépendantes de Jersey et Guernesey. Jersey, 1851.
37574.415 Schwartz, W.L. French romantic poetry. 1. ed. N.Y., 1932.
37574.420 Palfrey, F.R. Petite anthologie. N.Y., 1947.
37574.425 Cassell's anthology of French poetry. London, 1950.
37574.426 Conder, Alan. A treasury of French poetry. N.Y., 1951.
37574.430 Les quatres saisons du Parnasse. Paris. 1-16,1805-1809 16v.

37574.500 - .599 Anthologies, collections of literature - Collections of poetry - Special periods - 1850-1899

V37574.500 Diez Canedo, Enrique. La poesía francesa moderna. Madrid, 1913.
37574.510 Quelques chefs-d'oeuvres de la poésie française. Paris, 1930?
37574.515 Pound, Ezra. A study in French poets. N.Y., 1918.
37574.520 La France a Rome. Lyon, 1870.
37574.525A La poésie symboliste. Paris, 1908.
37574.525B La poésie symboliste. Paris, 1908.
37574.530 Nadaud, G. La chanson depuis Béranger. Paris, 1880.
37574.535 Bastos, V. Anthologie de la poésie française moderne. Buenos Aires, 1945.
37574.540 Bo, Carlo. Anthologia del surrealism. Milano, 1944.
37574.545 Eluard, Paul. Le Meilleur choix de poèmes. Paris, 1947.
37574.545.5 Eluard, Paul. Première anthologie vivante de la poésie du passé. v..1-2. Paris, 1951.
37574.545.10 Eluard, Paul. La poésie du passé. Paris, 1953-54. 3v.
37574.545.12 Eluard, Paul. La poésie du passé. Paris, 1960.
37574.550 LeDantec, Y. La guirlande des muses françaises. Paris, 1948.
37574.555 Gregh, F. Sonnets d'hier et d'aujourd'hui. Paris, 1949.
37574.560 Les poètes de la Commune. Paris, 1951.
37574.565 Hackett, C.A. Anthology of modern French poetry. Oxford, 1952.

37574.500 - .599 Anthologies, collections of literature - Collections of poetry - Special periods - 1850-1899 - cont.

37574.570 Frey, Jules. Les chants de guerre de la France en 1870-71. Paris, 1872.
37574.573 Taylor, A.C. A book of French verse. 5. ed. Carlton 1950.
37574.575 Klee-Palyi, Flora. Anthologie der Französischen Dichtung von Nerval bis zur Gegenwart. Wiesbaden, 1958.
37574.577 Lemaitre, Henri. La poésie depuis Baudelaire. Paris, 1965.

37574.600 - .799 Anthologies, collections of literature - Collections of poetry - Special periods - 1900-

37574.602 La Vaissière, Robert de. Anthologie poétique du XXe siècle. v.1-2. Paris, 1923.
37574.603 Aspel, Alexander. Contemporary French poetry. Ann Arbor, 1965.
37574.605 Walch, G. Poètes d'hier et d'aujourd'hui. Paris, 1921.
37574.606 Florilège poétique. 1,1970+
37574.607 Martin, Dorothy. Sextette. London, 1928.
37574.608 Siecle à mains. London. 1,1963+
37574.610 La petite illustration. Poésies. Paris. 1927-1939
37574.612 Flammes vives, Paris. Anthologie poétique.
37574.618 Séquences; anthologie permanente de poésie française. Paris. 1,1958+ 9v.
37574.625 Walch, G. Anthologie des poètes français contemporains. Paris, 1906. 2v.
37574.628 Oradour, B. d'. Album poétique illustré. 2. éd. Stuttgart, n.d.
37574.632 Le Goffic, Charles. Les poètes de la mer de moyen âge à nos jours. Paris, 1928.
37574.637 Gossez, Alphonse Marius. Les poètes du XXe siècle. Paris, 1929-36. 2v.
37574.642 Lévy, Jules. Les hydropathes. Paris, 1928.
37574.643 Aury, D. Anthologie de la poésie religieuse française. 8. éd. Paris, 1943.
37574.643.25 Aury, D. Poètes d'aujourd'hui. Paris, 1947.
37574.645 Bodkin, Thomas. May it please your lordship. Dublin, 1917.
37574.647 Bever, Adolphe van. Poètes d'aujourd'hui. Paris, 1915-17. 2v.
37574.648 Bever, Adolphe van. Poètes d'aujourd'hui. Paris, 1929. 3v.
37574.650 Petite anthologie poétique du surréalisme. Paris, 1934.
37574.654 Anthologie des poètes de la N.R.F. 8. éd. Paris, 1936.
37574.656 Année poétique. Album de l'Année poétique. Paris, 1935.
37574.658 Shipley, J.T. Modern French poetry. N.Y., 1926.
37574.660 Engwer, T. Choix de poésies françaises. Bielefeld, 1912.
37574.660.5 Engwer, T. Choix de poésies françaises. Ergänzungsband. 8. Aufl. Leipzig, 1913.
37574.662 López-Narváez, C. La voz en el eco. Bogota, 1942.
37574.664 Parisot, Henri. Les poètes voyagent. Paris, 1946.
37574.666 Gaese, William F. French lyrics, in English verse. Madison, 1946.
37574.668.5 Charpentier, John. Fleurs du jardin lyrique. 3. éd. Paris, 1939.
37574.670 Barker, Arthur. Twelve more echoes. Wellington, 1944.
37574.672 Poésie une. Paris. 12,1970+ 4v.
37574.680 Poètes d'aujourd'hui. Paris. 1+ 152v.
37574.685 Giedion-Welcker, C. Poètes à l'Ecart. Bern, 1946.
37574.687 Bray, René. Anthologie de la poésie precieuse de Thibaut de Champagne à Giraudoux. Paris, 1946.
37574.688 Bray, René. Anthologie de la poésie précieuse de Thibaut de Champagne à Giraudoux. Paris, 1957.
37574.689 Seghers, Pierre. Poésie, 39-45. London, 1947.
37574.690 Seghers, Pierre. Le livre d'or de la poésie française. Verviers, 1961.
37574.691 Denux, Roger. Ces roses-ci; sonnets. Isey-les-Monlineaux, 1947.
37574.693 Vaunois, Louis. Les poètes de la vie. Paris, 1945.
37574.694 Cahiers franco-anglais. Genève. 1,1968+
37574.695 Gregh, Fernand. Sonnets du temps jadis. Paris, 1947.
37574.696 Société de Poésie, Paris. Eventail. Paris, 1957.
37574.697 Anthologie des poètes français XIXe siècle. Paris, 1905.
37574.700 Société des poètes français. Anthologie de la Société des poètes français. Paris, 1947.
37574.705 Bournet, S. Anthologie des poètes français du Sud-Est de 1900 à nos jours. Lyon, 1947.
37574.710 Gide, André Paul Guillaume. Anthologie de la poésie française. Paris, 1949.
37574.710.5 Gide, André Paul Guillaume. Anthologie de la poésie française. Paris, 1949.
37574.710.10 Gide, André Paul Guillaume. Anthologie de la poésie française. Paris, 1959.
37574.715 Lalow, René. Les plus beaux poémes français. 2. éd. Paris, 1947.
37574.720 Ramuz, C. Anthologie de la poésie française. Paris, 1943. 2v.
37574.721 Anthologie de poètes français actuels. Grenoble, 1963- 6v.
37574.725 La France nouvelle. Paris, 1945.
37574.730 Lugli, V. Da Villon a Valéry. Messina, 1949.
37574.735 Boase, A.M. The poetry of France from André Chénier to Pierre Emmanuel. London, 1952.
37574.740 Burt, P. Paris et ses poètes. Paris, 1951.
37574.745 Jenkins, T.A. Longer French poems. N.Y., 1904.
37574.755 Anthologie 52. Paris, 1952.
37574.760 Young, C.E. Anthology of French lyric poetry. Chicago, 1925.
37574.765 Bouquet, G. Trésor de la poésie française. Paris, 1950-52. 2v.
37574.770 Clancier, G.E. De Rimbaud au surréalisme. Paris, 1953.
37574.770.5 Clancier, G.E. De Rimbaud au surréalisme. Paris, 1959.
37574.775 Grautoff, Otto. Die lyriche Bewegung im gegenwärtigen Frankreich. Jena, 1911.
37574.780 Fowlie, W. Mid-century French poets. N.Y., 1955.
37574.790 Jones, P.M. Modern French verse. Manchester, Eng., 1954.
37574.795 Aragon, L. Journal d'une poésie nationale. Lyon, 1954.
37574.800 Soupault, P. Les deux cents plus beaux poèmes de la langue française. Paris, 1956.
37574.815 Paris, Jean. Anthologie de la poésie nouvelle. Monaco, 1956.
37574.820 Flores, Angel. An anthology of French poetry from Nerval to Valéry. 1. ed. Garden City, 1958.
37574.825 Roy, Claude. Trésor de la poésie populaire française. Paris, 1954.
37574.830 Bartuschek, H. Der gallische Hahn. Berlin, 1957.
37574.835 Janet, Gaston. Poètes de Paris et de l'Île de France. Paris, 1948.

37574.600 - .799 Anthologies, collections of literature - Collections of poetry - Special periods - 1900- - cont.

37574.835.5 Lacroix de l'Isle, Robert. Poètes de Paris et de l'Île de France. Paris, 1957.
37574.840 Gennes, Renata de. Amours. Paris, 1957.
37574.848 MacIntyre, C.F. French Symbolist poetry. Berkeley, 1958.
37574.850 Chiari, Joseph. The Harrap anthology of French poetry. London, 1958.
37574.852 Le bouquée de Provence. Avignon.
37574.854 Bourgeois, Gaston. Poètes protestants d'aujourd'hui. Paris, 1958. 2v.
37574.856 Académie...Brest. Académie des jeux floraux de Bretagne, Brest. Recueil. 5-12 7v.
37574.858 Ménard, René. Le livre des arbres. Paris, 1956.
37574.860 Fouchet, Max P. De l'amour au voyage. Paris, 1958.
37574.860.5 Fouchet, Max P. La poésie française. Paris, 1964.
37574.865 Flammes vives, Paris. Banquet poétique de printemps. Aurillac, 1958.
37574.870 Bealu, Marcel. Anthologie de la poésie feminine. Paris, 1953.
37574.875 Rousselot, Jean. Les nouveaux poètes français. Paris, 1959.
37574.880 Bever, Adolphe van. Les conteurs libertins du XVIIIe siècle. Paris, 1904.
37574.885 Cordone, Jacques. Les muses chez Thémis. Paris, 1956.
37574.890 L'encyclopédie poétique. Paris. 1,1960+ 6v.
37574.895 Le livre des sonnets. Paris, 1949.
37574.900 Hinderberger, H. Französische Symbolisten. Heidelberg, 1960.
37574.905 Pompidore, G. Anthologie de la poésie française. Paris, 1961.
37574.907 Ekeloef, Gunnar. Hundra år modern fransk dikt. Stockholm, 1960.
37574.909 Sanavio, Piero. Poeti francesi d'Oggi. Roma, 1961.
37574.910 Les Poètes français contre la guerre. Paris, 1957.
37574.911 Moulin, J. La poésie feminine. Paris, 1963. 2v.
37574.912 Valeri, Diego. Lirici francesi. 1. ed. Milano, 1960.
37574.913 Jones, P.M. A book of French verse. London, 1964.
37574.914 Bédouin, Jean Louis. La poésie surréaliste. Paris, 1964.
37574.914.1 Bédouin, Jean Louis. La poésie surréaliste. Paris, 1970.
37574.915 Marks, E. French poetry from Baudelaire to the present. N.Y., 1962.
37574.917 Pornon, Charles. Anthologie (apocryphe) de la poésie française. Paris, 1963.
37574.918 Rousselot, Jean. Poètes français d'aujourd'hui. Paris, 1965.
37574.920 Bernard, Jean Marc. Pages politiques des poètes français. Paris, 1912.
37574.925 Poésie nouvelle. Paris. 1,1960+ 65v.
37574.926 Lisowski, Jerzy. Antologia poezji francuskiej. Warszawa, 1966- 2v.
37574.927 Bédra. Les comédiens poètes. Paris, 1966.
37574.928 Valeri, Diego. Quaderno francese del secolo. Torino, 1965.
37574.930 Matthiews, J. An anthology of French surrealist poetry. London, 1966.
37574.932 Alwyn, William. An anthology of twentieth century French poetry. London, 1969.
37574.934 Chevassus, Paul. Anthologie des jeunes poètes. Lyon, 1969. 2v.
37574.936 La conque. Paris. 1-11,1891-1892//
37574.938 Lippens, Louis. Anthologie de poésie contemporaine, 1962. Bruxelles, 1962.
37574.940 Poèmes de la révolution, mai 1968. Paris, 1969?
37574.942 Richard, Gaston. Anthologie des poètes gadzarts. Paris, 1969?
37574.944 Clodd, Alan. Collected verse translations. London, 1970.
37574.946 Bourgeois, Gaston. Anthologie de l'Académie des poètes classiques. Paris, 1969.
37574.948 Taylor, Simon Watson. French poetry today. London, 1971.
37574.950 L'atrium: grand prix de poésie du pays d'Arles; poèmes primés en 1969. Arles, 1969?

37575.1 - .99 Anthologies, collections of literature - General special collections - Miscellany

37575.2 Nouveaux melanges, philosophiques, historiques, critiques. n.p., 1765-76. 19v.
Htn 37575.4* La Place, Antoine de. Pieces intéressantes. Brussels, 1785-90. 8v.
37575.5 M.P.D.L. Recueil d'épitaphes. Bruxelles, 1782. 3v.
37575.7 Pamphlet vol. Melanges 41. Litterature. 14 pam.
37575.7.2 Pamphlet vol. Melanges 42. Litterature. 8 pam.
Htn 37575.8* Bibliothèque facétieuse. Paris, 1858. 8v.
37575.9 Mesnard, Pierre. De Villon à Rimbaud. Alger, 1945.
Htn 37575.10* Genty, Achille. La Fontaine des amoureux de science. Paris, 1861.
Htn 37575.11* Genty, Achille. L'art poetique de Jean Vauquelin. Paris, 1862.
Htn 37575.12* Genty, Achille. Rimes inédites en patois Percheron. Paris, 1861.
Htn 37575.13* Genty, Achille. Oeuvres poétiques...de Nicolas Ellain. Paris, 1861.
Htn 37575.16* Bibliothèque gothique. v.1-3. n.p. n.d.
Htn 37575.17* Bibliothèque gothique. v.4-6. n.p., n.d.
X Cg 37575.18 Les elegantes. Paris, 1913.
Htn 37575.20* Fournier, Édouard. Variétés historiques et littéraires. Paris, 1855-63. 10v.
37575.22 Fournier, Édouard. Variétés historiques et littéraires. Paris, 1855-63. 10v.
37575.25 Porte-feuille français. Paris. 7-12,1806-1811 2v.
37575.28 Lestrange, R. Les animaux dans la littérature. Gap, 1937.
Htn 37575.30* Collection de poésies, romans, chroniques. v.1-24. n.p., n.d. 5v.
Htn 37575.30.5* Pamphlet vol. Collection de poésies, romans. Paris, 1838-58.

37575.101 - .199 Anthologies, collections of literature - General special collections - Local - Regions and places of France (99 scheme, A-Z by place)

37575.105 Delzangles, Fernand. Biographies et morceaux choisies d'écrivains d'Auvergne. Aurillac, 1933.
37575.105.5 Auvergne et Méditerranée. Millau. 1946-1948//
37575.109 Contes et nouvelles butonnes. Rennes, 1836.
37575.116 Terrebasse, Humbert de. Poésies dauphinoises du XVIIe siècle. Lyon, 1896.
37575.148 Académie...Toulouse. Académie de Toulouse. Haut-Languedoc et Armagnac. Paris, 1958.

37575.101 - .199 Anthologies, collections of literature - General special collections - Local - Regions and places of France (99 scheme, A-Z by place) - cont.

37575.148.5 Académie...Montpellier. Académie de Montpellier. Bas-Languedoc et Roussillon. Paris, 1958.
37575.151.2 Dimoff, Paul. Anthologie des poètes de Lorraine de 1700 à 1950. 2. éd. Nancy, 1965.
37575.151.5 Comité Erckmann-Chatrian. Écrivains lorrains. Verdun, 1964.
37575.160 Drouillet, Jean. Anthologie des poètes nivernais. Moulins, 1945.
37575.161 Féret, Charles Théophile. Anthologie critique des poètes normands de 1900 à 1920. Paris, 1920.
37575.161.5 Vaneille, Jean Louis. Les poètes bas-normands. Saint-Lo, 1934.
37575.161.10 Vaneille, Jean Louis. Les vieux maitres de la littérature bas-normands. Saint-Lo, 194-?

37575.200 - .399 Anthologies, collections of literature - General special collections - Local - Other countries of Europe

37575.205 Dumont-Wilden, Louis. Anthologie des écrivains belges. Paris, 1917.
37575.207 Ridder, André de. Anthologie des écrivains flamands contemporains. Anvers, 1926.
37575.208 Guiette, Robert. Poètes français de Belgique de Verhaeren au surréalisme. Manteau, 1948.
37575.209 Anthologie poétique de l'exposition. Bruxelles, 1958.
37575.210 Poésie française de Belgique. Bruxelles, 1960?
37575.211 Geeraert, Robert L. La nouvelle poésie belge d'expression française. Tournai, 1961.
37575.212 Bodart, Roger. Les poètes du bois de la Cambre. Paris, 1964.
37575.213 Mor, Antonio. Le più belle pagine delle letterature del Belgio. Milano, 1965.
37575.214 Six jeunes poètes...Anthologie. Tournai, 1969.
37575.215 La poésie contemporaine. Bruxelles, 1968.
37575.300 Gérard, Marcel. Anthologie française du Luxembourg. Luxembourg, 1960.
37575.325 Weber-Silvain, L. Anthologie de prosateurs romands de J.J. Rousseau à nos jours. Lucerne, 1917.
37575.327 Boccard, Eugène de. Anthologie des poètes de la Suisse romande. Paris, 1946.
37575.330 Walzer, Pierre O. Anthologie jurassienne. Porrentruy, 1964-65. 2v.
37575.332 Dubacq, Jean. L'école de Rochefort. Paris, 1970.

37575.400 - Anthologies, collections of literature - General special collections - Other special

37575.400 Nouvelles nouvelles, souvenirs de littérature contemporain. Paris, 184-.
37575.405 Nisard, Charles. La Muse pariétaire...ou Les chansons des rues. Paris, 1863.
37575.410 Desbordes-Valmone. Confidences poétiques, dédiées à la jeunesse. Paris, 1850.
37575.415A Leypoldt, F. La littérature française contemporaine. N.Y., 1867.
37575.415B Leypoldt, F. La littérature française contemporaine. N.Y., 1867.
37575.420 Les muses du foyer de l'opéra. Bruxelles, 1883.
37575.440 Junges Frankreich. München, 19- .
37575.450 Genest, Emile. Les belles citations de la littérature française. le série. Paris, 1923.
37575.455 Genest, Emile. Les belles citations de la littérature française suggérées par les mots et les idées. Paris, 1930.
37575.460 LaRoche Folle, Jean de. Morale et maximes d'un simple, un guide dans la vie, sagesse. Guéret, 1970.
37575.525 Contes véridiques de tranchées, 1914-1915. Paris, 1915.
37575.526 Nouveaux contes veridiques des tranchées, 1914-1916. Paris, 1916.
37575.605 Maritain, J. "Les iles". Paris, 1933.
37575.635 Lang, Andrew. Ballads and lyrics of old France. Portland, 1896.
37575.650 Díez-Canedo, E. La poesía francesa del romanticismo al superrealismo. Buenos Aires, 1945.
37575.655 Paulhan, Jean. La patrie se fait tous les jours. Paris, 1947.
37575.660 Roger, G. L'ame de la corse à travers la littérature française. Alger, 1947.
37575.670 Ganzo, R. Cinq poètes assassinés. Paris, 1947.
37575.675 Valette, R. Hippocrate et la muse. Paris, 1949.
37575.685 L'Honneur des poètes. v.1-2. Paris, 1943-44.
37575.690 La Nef. Almanach surréaliste du demi-siècle. Paris, 1950.
37575.695 Bryen, C. Anthologie de la poésie naturelle. Paris, 1949.
37575.700F Galtier-Bossière, Jean. Anthologie de la poésie argotique. Paris, 1952.
37575.705 Gallotti, Jean. Le Paris des poètes et des romanciers. Paris, 1955.
37575.707 Fau, Raymond. Rythmes et chansons pour le Seigneur, 110 chansons. Paris, 1969.
37575.710 Actualité de la poésie. Paris, 1956.
37575.720 Mermod, Française. La Provence. Lausanne, 1956.
37575.725 Pia, Pascal. Bouquet poétique des medecins. Paris, 1933.
37575.735 Hommage des poètes français aux poètes hongrois. Paris, 1957.
37575.740 Cadix, Gaston. En Cevenne. Paris, 1957.
37575.750 Bosquet, Alain. Les vingt meilleures nouvelles françaises. Paris, 1958.
37575.755 Un hommage à la poésie. Nantes, 1946.
37575.765 Gershman, H. Anthology of critical preface to 19th century French novel. Columbia, 1962.
37575.765.5 Gershman, H. Anthologie des prefaces de romans français du XIXe siècle. Paris, 1964.
37575.776 Flouquet, T.L. de. Anthologie de la troisième décade, 1950-60. Dilbeek, 1963.
37575.778A Nola, Jean Paul de. Les poètes de la rue des Sols. Paris, 1963.
37575.778B Nola, Jean Paul de. Les poètes de la rue des Sols. Paris, 1963.
37575.779 Bever, Adolphe van. Contes et conteurs gaillards au XVIIIe siècle. Paris, 1906.
37575.780 Anthologie du XXeme anniversaire du Prix Max Rose de poésie. Bruxelles, 1963.
37575.784 Académie française, Paris. Recueil de plusieurs pièces d'éloquence et de póesie presentées à l'académie française. Paris, 1725.
37575.787 Lemercier d'Erm, Camille. Les ballades d'amour du XIIe siècle à nos jours choix. Paris, 1913.

Classified Listing

37575.400 - Anthologies, collections of literature - General special collections - Other special - cont.

37575.788 Barbier, Joseph. Notre-Dame des poètes. Saint Martin, 1966.
37575.789 Peyrade, Jean. Approche de l'amour. Paris, 1966.
V37575.791 Fischer, Jan O. Manifesty francouzských realisti XIX. a XX. století. Praha, 1950.
37575.792 Weverbergh, Julien. Jij goudgepuute lans. Amsterdam, 1967.
37575.793 Gavronsky, Serge. Poems and texts. N.Y., 1969.
37575.795 Le Brun, Annie. Les mots font l'amour, citations surréalistes. Paris, 1970.

37576.1 - .199 Anthologies, collections of literature - Collections of prose - General works

37576.3 Société des bibliophiles. Mélanges de littérature et d'histoire. Paris, 1850.
37576.4 Société des bibliophiles. Mélanges de littérature et d'histoire. pt.1-2. Paris, 1856-67. 2v.
37576.5 Société des bibliophiles français. Mélanges de littérature et d'histoire. Paris, 1877.
37576.7 Matter, Jacques. Lettres et pièces rares. Paris, 1846.
37576.8 LeClerc de la Herverie, B. Les plus belles lettres d'amour française. Paris, 1947.
37576.14 Continuation des memoires de littérature et d'histoire. Paris, 1730-31. 11v.
37576.15 Fourastié, Françoise. Les écrivains temoins du peuple. Paris, 1964.
37576.16 French belles lettres from 1640 to 1870. Washington, 1901.
37576.16.1 French belles-lettres from 1640 to 1870. N.Y., 1901.
37576.20 Alamanach des petits jeux floraux de Marseille, pour 1884-1885. Marseille, 1884-85.
37576.21 Gorceix, Septime. Le miroir de la France. Paris, 1923.
37576.22 Prior, O.H. Morceaux choisis des penseurs français du XVIe au XIXe siècle. Paris, 1930.
37576.23 Comfort, W.W. Les maîtres de la critique littéraire au XIVe siècle. Boston, 1909.
37576.26 Le rendez-vous. Paris. 1-13 4v.
37576.30 Roman. Anthologie des principaux romans français. Paris. 1,1961+ 6v.
37576.35 Ginisty, Paul. Anthologie du journalisme du XVIIe siècle à nos jours. Paris, 1917.
37576.50 Benjamin, L.S. Great French short stories. N.Y., 1928.

37576.200 - .299 Anthologies, collections of literature - Collections of prose - Special periods - 1661-1715

37576.200 Histoire des ouvrages des Sçravans. Rotterdam. 1-24,1867-1709 24v.
37576.210 Storer, M.E. Contes de fées du grand siècle. N.Y., 1934.
37576.215 Lettres du XVIIe siècle. Paris, 1945.
37576.220 Chapman, P.A. An anthology of seventeenth century French literature. Princeton, 1928.

37576.300 - .399 Anthologies, collections of literature - Collections of prose - Special periods - 1715-1799

37576.305 Bayet, Albert. Les écrivains politiques du XVIIIe siècle. 5. éd. Paris, 1935.
37576.310 Saunier de Beaumont. Lettres philosophiques. Paris, 1733.
37576.320 Saunier de Beaumont. Lettres philosophiques, serieuses. v.1-2. La Haye, 1748.
37576.325 Lettres choisies du XVIIIe siècle. Le Cavie, 1945.
37576.330 Villeneuve-Guibert, Gaston. Le portefeuille de Madame Dupin. Paris, 1884.

37576.400 - .499 Anthologies, collections of literature - Collections of prose - Special periods - 1800-1849

37576.405 Mélanges de politique. Louvain. 1-4,1822-1824 4v.
37576.410 Aird, D.M. The modern novelists of France. London, 1847.
37576.412 Klincksieck, Friedrich. Der Brief in der französischen Literatur des 19. Jahrhunderts; eine Auswahl. Halle, 1912.
37576.415 Comfort, W.W. French romantic prose. N.Y., 1928.

37576.500 - .599 Anthologies, collections of literature - Collections of prose - Special periods - 1850-1899

37576.500A Dow, Louis Henry. Quelques contes des romanciers naturalistes. Boston, 1907.
37576.500B Dow, Louis Henry. Quelques contes des romanciers naturalistes. Boston, 1907.
37576.500C Dow, Louis Henry. Quelques contes des romanciers naturalistes. Boston, 1907.
37576.500.3 Dow, Louis Henry. Quelques contes des romanciers naturalistes. Boston, 1907.
37576.502A Bédé, J.A. Quelques textes naturalistes. N.Y., 1937.
37576.502B Bédé, J.A. Quelques textes naturalistes. N.Y., 1937.
37576.505 Lazare, Jules. Contes et nouvelles des meilleurs auteurs contemporains. Boston, 1906.
Htn 37576.510* Critical notices of French literature. Brighton, 1853.
37576.515 Théatre de la révolution, ou Choix de pièces de théâtre qui ont fair sensation pendant la periode révolutionnaire. Paris, 1877.
Htn 37576.525* Les soirees de médan. Paris, 1880.
37576.527 La serate di Médan. Milano, 1958.
37576.530 Alvarado, H.A. Piedras preciosas. San José, 1903.
37576.535 Cupid's capers, by the chief French artists. Boston, 1897.
37576.537 Terrible tales. Paris, 189-?
37576.539 Pène Du Bois, H. French folly in maxims of philosophy. N.Y., 1894.
Htn 37576.545* Société des trente. Publications. Paris. 1-30,1912-1922 15v.
37576.547 Le nouveau décaméron. 2e, 5e, 9e journée. Paris, 1884-87.
37576.550 Manley, Edward. Eight French stories. Boston, 1920.
37576.555 Dorchain, A. The twelve best short stories in the French language. London, 1915.
37576.557 Rudmose-Brown, T.B. French short stories. Oxford, 1925.
37576.560.5 Bazin, R. The ink-stain (Tache d'encre). Paris, 1905.
37576.560.10A Bernard, Charles de. Gefaut. Paris, 1905.
37576.560.10B Bernard, Charles de. Gerfaut. Paris, 1905.
37576.560.12 Bernard, Charles de. Gerfaut. N.Y., 1910.
37576.560.15A Blanc, T. de S. (Mme.). Jacqueline. Paris, 1905.
37576.560.15B Blanc, T. de S. (Mme.). Jacqueline. Paris, 1905.
37576.560.17 Bourgée, Paul. Cosmopolis. N.Y., 1910.
37576.560.20 Claretie, J. Prince Zilah (Le prince Zilah). Paris, 1905.
37576.560.22 Claretie, J. Prince Zilah. N.Y., 1908.
37576.560.25A Coppée, F. A romance of youth. Paris, 1905.
37576.560.25B Coppée, F. A romance of youth. Paris, 1905.
37576.560.28 Ernst, Paul. Altfranzösische Novellen. Leipzig, 1909. 2v.
37576.560.30A Daudet, A. Fromont and Risler. Paris, 1905.

37576.500 - .599 Anthologies, collections of literature - Collections of prose - Special periods - 1850-1899 - cont.

37576.560.30B Daudet, A. Fromont and Risler. Paris, 1905.
37576.560.31 Droz, Gustave A.G. Monsieur. Paris, 1905.
37576.560.32 Droz, Gustave A.G. Monsieur, madame et bébé. N.Y., 1908.
37576.560.35 France, A. The red lily (le lis rouge). Paris, 1905.
37576.560.40 Malot, H. Conscience (Conscience). Paris, 1905.
37576.560.45A Massa, Philippe de. Zibeline. Paris, 1905.
37576.560.45B Massa, Philippe de. Zibeline. Paris, 1905.
37576.560.50 Musset, A. de. Confession of a child of the century. Paris, 1905.
37576.560.55 Souvestre, E. An "attic" philosopher. Paris, 1905.
37576.560.60 Theuriet, A. A woodland queen (Reine des bois). Paris, 1905.
37576.560.65A Viaud, J. Madame Chrysanthème. Paris, 1905.
37576.560.65B Viaud, J. Madame Chrysanthème. Paris, 1905.
37576.560.70A Vigny, A. Cinq-mars. Paris, 1905. 2v.
37576.560.70B Vigny, A. Cinq-mars. Paris, 1905. 2v.

37576.600 - .799 Anthologies, collections of literature - Collections of prose - Special periods - 1900- (By date, e.g. .660 for 1960)

37576.602 Gossez, Alphonse Marius. Poètes du Nord. Paris, 1902.
37576.610 Les oeuvres libres. Paris. 1+ 206v.
37576.610.5F La misère sociale de la femme d'après les écrivains. Paris, 1910.
37576.615 Anthologie des essayistes français contemporains. Paris, 1929.
37576.621 Macklin, A.E. Twenty nine short stories. London, 1921.
37576.621.3 Macklin, A.E. Twenty nine tales from the French. N.Y., 1922.
37576.621.15 Cario, L. La pensée française. Paris, 1921.
37576.623 Michaud, R. Conteurs français d'aujourd'hui. Boston, 1923.
37576.623.5 Macklin, A.E. Five striking stories. London, 1923.
37576.623.10 The best French short stories of 1923, 1924, 1926, 1927 and the yearbook of the French short stories. Boston, 1923-28. 4v.
37576.623.15 Guyer, F.E. Vingt contes favoris. N.Y., 1942.
37576.625 Picard, Gaston. Nos ecrivains definis par eux-mêmes. Paris, 1925.
37576.626A Anthologie de la nouvelle prise française. Paris, 1926.
37576.626B Anthologie de la nouvelle prise française. Paris, 1926.
37576.629 Pargment, M.S. Trente trois contes et nouvelles. N.Y., 1929.
37576.631 March, H. Types of the French short story. N.Y., 1941.
37576.633 Green, F.C. French stories of the 19th and 20th centuries. London, 1933.
37576.635 Gallaud, J.S. Ten favorite French stories. N.Y., 1935.
37576.636 Mélanges offerts à M. Abel Lefranc par ses élèves et ses amis. Paris, 1936.
37576.636.10 Fage, André. Anthologie des conteurs d'aujourd'hui. Paris, 1936.
37576.637 Calvert, C.V. The French newspaper. London, 1936.
37576.639.5 Speare, M.E. Great French short stories. Cleveland, 1943.
37576.641 Le Figaro, Paris. Suites françaises. N.Y., 1945. 2v.
37576.643A Chroniques interdites. v.1-2. Paris, 1943-44[1945]
37576.643B Chroniques interdites. v.1-2. Paris, 1943-44[1945]
37576.645A Becker, Belle. Bedside book of famous French stories. N.Y., 1945.
37576.645B Becker, Belle. Bedside book of famous French stories. N.Y., 1945.
37576.646 Aldington, Richard. Great French romances. London, 1946.
37576.646.5 Chapelan, Maurice. Anthologie du poème en prose. Paris, 1946.
37576.647 Dix nouvelles par Edmond Teissor. Paris, 1946.
37576.647.5 Saurat, Denis. Angels and beasts. London, 1947.
37576.647.10 Castex, Pierre. Anthologie du conte fantastique français. Paris, 1947.
37576.647.12 Castex, Pierre. Anthologie du conte fantastique français. 2. éd. Paris, 1963.
37576.648 New writing. French stories from New writing. London, 1947.
37576.648.5 Alden, Douglas W. Introduction to French masterpieces. N.Y., 1948.
37576.650 New writing. Modern French stories. N.Y., 1948?
37576.650.5 Goodyear, R.G. Two centuries of French short stories. London, 1950.
37576.651 Arland, M. La prose française. Paris, 1951-
37576.654 Farouche à quatre feuilles. Paris, 1954.
37576.655 Demeur, L. Pages choisies des ecrivains français de Belgique. 2. éd. Bruxelles, 1938.
37576.655.5 Burger, H.C. La France d'hier et d'aujourd'hui. Melbourne, 1955.
37576.655.10 Queneau, R. Anthologie des jeunes auteurs. Paris, 1955.
37576.658 Picard, Gaston. Nouvelles 58. Paris, 1958.
37576.658.5 Widmer, Walter. Meistererzählungen des französischen Rokoko. München, 1958.
37576.659.5 Nouvelle revue française. From the N.R.F. N.Y., 1959.
37576.662 Le Sage, Laurent. The French new novel; an introduction. University Park, 1962.
37576.662.5 Baüer, Gerard. Les moralistes français: La Rochefoucauld. Paris, 1962.
37576.665 Schneider, Marcel. Histoires fantastiques d'aujourd'hui. Paris, 1965.
37576.669 Morton, Miriam. Voices from France; ten stories by French Nobel prize winners. 1. ed. Garden City, N.Y., 1969.
37576.670 Courtine, Robert J. Anthologie de la littérature gastronomique. Paris, 1970.
37576.670.5 Club des intellectuels français. Sélection 1970 de contes et nouvelles. Courbevoie, 1970.
37576.671 Textes. Suivi de la Mort de la littérature. Paris, 1971.

37577 Anthologies, collections of literature - Collections of facéties

Htn 37577.3* Les joyeusetez facecies...et Faceties, rarétiés et cur. Paris, 1829. 16v.
Htn 37577.4* Les quinze joies de mariage. Paris, 1837.
37577.6 Pange, Pauline L.M. de B. Lettres de femmes du XIXe siècle. Monaco, 1947.
37577.10 Larousse, P. Fleurs historiques. Paris, 187-?
37577.12 Martin, P.J. L'esprit de tout le monde. Paris, 1859.
37577.30 Recueil de pieces rares et facetieuses. v.3. Paris, 1873.
37577.35 Dupee, F.W. Great French short novels. N.Y., 1952.
37577.36 Recueil des Plaisants devis recites par les supposts du Seigneur de la Coquille. Lyon, 1857.
37577.37 Tréno, Robert. L'anti-France. Paris, 1962.
X Cg 37577.38 Recueil de bons mots des anciens et des modernes. Paris, 1707.

37577 Anthologies, collections of literature - Collections of facéties - cont.
37577.40 Bienstock, J.W. Le bonheur du jour. Paris, 1926.

37578 Anthologies, collections of literature - Collections of wit and humor
Htn 37578.16* Recueil curieux de contes à rire. Utopie, 1681.
Htn 37578.20* Larchey, Lorédoin. Les joueurs de mots. Paris, 1867.
Htn 37578.22* Facecies et motz subtilz, en françois et italien. Lyon, 1573.
Htn 37578.24* Favoral. Les plaisantes journées. Genève, 1868.
Htn 37578.25* Favoral. Les plaisantes journées. Paris, 1620.
37578.26 Vasconiana, ou Recueil des bons mots. Cologne, 1708.
37578.26.5 Vasconiana, ou Recueil des bons mots. Paris, 1710.
Htn 37578.27* Nouveaux contes à rire. Cologne, 1709.
37578.29.5 Lockman, J. The entertaining instructor. London, 1765.
Htn 37578.30* Contes à rire. Paris, 1781. 3v.
Htn 37578.32* Cousin, Charles Y. Gasconiana. Paris, 1801.
37578.34.5 Capelle, Pierre. Aneries révolutionnaires. Paris, 1815.
Htn 37578.36* Desciseaux, M. Recueil de contes a rire. Paris, n.d.
Htn 37578.37* Desciseaux, M. Recueil de contes a rire. Paris, n.d.
Htn 37578.39* Passard, L. Un million de Calembours. Paris, 1858.
Htn 37578.40* Passard, L. Un million de plaisanteries. Paris, 1859.
Htn 37578.42* Bougy, Alfred de. Un million de rimes gauloises. Paris, 1858.
Htn 37578.43* Album drolatique. Paris, 1879.
37578.44 Fleuret, Fernand. Les satires françaises du XVIe siècle. Paris, 1922. 2v.
37578.45 Fleuret, Fernand. Les satires françaises du XVIIe siècle. Paris, 1923. 2v.
37578.46 Anthologie satyrique. v.1,8. Luxembourg, 1876-78. 2v.
37578.48 Finod, J. de. A thousand flashes of French wit, wisdom. N.Y., 1881.
37578.48.2 Finod, J. de. A thousand flashes of French wit, wisdom. N.Y., 1880.
37578.48.5 Finod, J. de. A thousand flashes of French wit, wisdom. N.Y., 1886.
37578.49 Lutaud, Auguste. Le Parnasse hippocratique. Paris, 1887.
37578.50 Almanach comique. Paris, 1844.
Htn 37578.51* Almanach comique. Paris, 1860-71. 4v.
37578.53 Guégan, Bertrand. Le grand kalendrier et compost des bergiers. Troyes, 1529.
Htn 37578.53.10* Kalendrier des Bergers. Le grand calendier et compost des bergiers. Colophon, 1551.
37578.53.16A Kalendrier des Bergers. Le compost et kalendrier des bergiers. The kalender of shepherdes. v.1-3. London, 1892.
37578.53.16B Kalendrier des Bergers. Le compost et kalendrier des bergiers. The kalender of shepherdes. v.1-3. London, 1892.
37578.53.20 Kalendrier des Bergers. The calendar and compost of shepherds from the original. London, 1930.
Htn 37578.54* Almanach astrologique. Paris, 1850.
37578.56 Almanach prophetique. Paris, 1860.
37578.57 Almanach du Charivari. Paris.
37578.58 Almanach du monde plaisant 1881. Paris, 1881.
37578.61 Almanach amusant. Paris. 1901-1917
37578.62 Almanach des cocottes. Paris. 1901-1902
37578.63 Almanach pour rire. Paris. 1901-1902
37578.64 Almanach du vieux major. Paris. 1911
37578.67 Monselet, Charles. Almanach for 1867. Chaillot, 1867.
37578.70 Treich, Léon. Histoires littéraires. 8. éd. Paris, 1926.
37578.75 L'humour est enfant de Paris. Paris, 1930.
37578.80 Histoires parisiennes. Paris, 1931.
37578.85 Beausacq, M.J. Le livre d'or de la comtesse Diane. Paris, 1889.
37578.87 Marchal, C. Dictionnaire amusant. Paris, 1859.
37578.90 Duliani, Mario. Deux heures de fou rire. Montréal, 1944.
37578.92 Picard, André L. Quelques mots de France. N.Y., 1945.
37578.94 Porchère, Samuel. Musée-dictionnaire d'originalités. 2. éd. Saint-Etienne, 1907.
37578.95 Le livre des singularites. Paris, 1805.

37581 Anthologies, collections of literature - Collections of drama - Folios [Discontinued]
37581 Pamphlet box. French plays.
37581.2 Goizet, M.J. Dictionnaire universel du théâtre en France. Paris, 1867.
37581.2.55 Monmerqué, Louis J.N. Théâtre français au moyen âge. Paris, 1839.
37581.2.57 Monmerqué, Louis J.N. Théâtre français au moyen age. Paris, 1839.
37581.3A Monmerqué, Louis J.N. Théâtre français au moyen age. Paris, 1842.
37581.3B Monmerque, Louis J.N. Théâtre français au moyen age. Paris, 1842.
37581.3.10 Monmerqué, Louis J.N. Théâtre français au moyen age. Paris, 1870.
Htn 37581.6* Tournier, Édouard. Théâtre français avant la Renaissance. Paris, n.d.
Htn 37581.8* Tournier, Édouard. Théâtre français au XVIe et au XVIIe siècle. Paris, n.d.
37581.8.2 Tournier, Édouard. Théâtre français au XVIe et au XVIIe siècle. Paris, n.d.
37581.8.3 Tournier, Édouard. Théâtre français au XVIe et au XVIIe siècle. Paris, 1871.
37581.9 Tournier, Édouard. Théâtre français au XVIe et au XVIIe siècle. Paris, n.d. 2v.
37581.12 Corneille, Pierre. Rodogune. Cologne, 1757-74. 10 pam.
37581.13 Dominique, P. François. Arlequin Hulla. v.1-10,12-13. Paris, 1967-72. 12 pam.
Htn 37581.13* Dominique, P. François. Arlequin Hulla. v.11. Paris, 1767-72.
37581.14 Hauteroche, Noël. Le deuil. Paris, 1762-67. 12 pam.
37581.17 Collot, A.G. Chefs-d'oeuvres dramatiques. N.Y., 1851.
37581.18A Fournel, V. Les contemporains de Molière, recueil de comédies...de 1650 à 1680. Paris, 1863-75. 3v.
37581.18B Fournel, V. Les contemporains de Molière, recueil de comédies...de 1650 à 1680. Paris, 1863-75. 3v.
37581.20 Pamphlet vol. Collected French plays. 10 pam.
37581.21 Pamphlet vol. Collected French plays. 9 pam.
37581.22 Pamphlet vol. Collected French plays. 14 pam.
37581.23 Pamphlet vol. Collected French plays. 16 pam.
37581.26 Pamphlet vol. La France dramatique. 25 pam.
37581.31 Coussemaker, E. de. Drames liturgiques au moyen age. Rennes, 1860.
37581.32 Coussemaker, E. de. Drames liturgiques du moyen age. Paris, 1861.
37581.37 Picard, L.B. Une matinée de Henri IV; comédie. N.Y., 1830-63. 8 pam.

37581 Anthologies, collections of literature - Collections of drama - Folios [Discontinued] - cont.
37581.39 Choix de pièces de théâtres de Paris, 1805-1839. Paris, 1805-39.
37581.39.2 Choix de pièces de théâtres de Paris, 1841-1885. Paris, 1841-1885.
37581.40.3 Magasin théâtral. v.1-31. Paris, 1834-1842. 29v.
37581.40.5 Magasin théâtral. 2. ed. v.7-27. Paris, 1833-1843. 7v.
37581.40.12 Magasin théâtral, 1831-1851. Miscellaneous plays. Paris, 1831-51.
37581.40.14 Magasin théâtral, 1837. Miscellaneous plays. Paris, 1837.
37581.40.16 Magasin théâtral. 2 plays, 1850, 1861. Paris, 1850-61.
37581.40.17 Magasin théâtral. Miscellaneous unbound plays. Paris, n.d.
37581.41 La France dramatique au XIXe siècle, 1834-1839. Paris, 1834-39.
37581.41.2 La France dramatique au XIXe siècle, 1840-1881. Paris, 1840-81.
37581.42 Théâtre contemporain, 1790-1853. Paris, 1790-1853.
37581.43 Théâtre contemporain, 1853-1857. Paris, 1853-57.
37581.44 Théâtre contemporain, 1858-1866. Paris, 1858-66.
37581.50 Le théâtre inédit du XIXe siècle. Paris, 1877.

37582 Anthologies, collections of literature - Collections of drama - Répertoire Géneral du Théâtre Français
37582.1 Répertoire général du théâtre français. v.1-49,51. Paris, 1813. 50v.
37582.2 Répertoire général du théâtre français. Paris, 1818. 67v.
37582.2.25 Théâtre des auteurs du sécond ordre...stéréotype d'Herhan. Paris, 1808-10. 40v.
37582.2.50 Petitot, Claude Bernard. Répertoire du théâtre français. Paris, 1803-04. 23v.
37582.2.53 Répertoire du théâtre français, 3. ordre; ou, Supplement aux deux editions du répertoire publiées en 1803 et on 1807. Paris, 1819-20. 8v.
37582.3 Petitot, Claude Bernard. Répertoire du théâtre français. Tragedies. Paris, 1817-18. 6v.
37582.4 Petitot, Claude Bernard. Répertoire du théâtre français. Drames. v.7. Paris, 1817-18.
37582.5 Petitot, Claude Bernard. Répertoire du théâtre français. v.8-25. Paris, 1817-18. 18v.
37582.6 Suite du répertoire général du théâtre français. v.1-71. Paris, 1822-1823. 69v.
37582.8 Fin du répertoire du théatre français. v.1-45. Paris, 1824. 22v.

37583.1 - .199 Anthologies, collections of literature - Collections of drama - General works
37583.5 Pamphlet vol. French plays. 4 pam.
37583.7 Pamphlet vol. French plays. 6 pam.
37583.12 Auriac, Eugène d'. Théâtre de la foire. Paris, 1878.
37583.13 L'avant-scene. Fémina-théâtre. Paris. 96+ 25v.

37583.200 - .299 Anthologies, collections of literature - Collections of drama - Special periods - 1661-1715
37583.210 Théâtre classique français. Paris, 1964-66. 12v.

37583.300 - .399 Anthologies, collections of literature - Collections of drama - Special periods - 1715-1799
37583.302.1 Brenner, Clarence Dietz. Eighteenth-century French plays. N.Y., 196-?
37583.343 Nouveau recueil choisi et mélé des meilleures pièces du théâtre français et italien. Utrecht, 1743-50. 12v.
37583.383 Baudrais, J. Petite bibliothèque des théâtres. v.2-6. Paris, 1783-84. 5v.
37583.385 Billardon de Sauvigny, L.E. Vashington; ou La liberté du nouveau monde, tragédie en quatré actes. Paris, 1791. 5 pam.
37583.395 Nouvelle bibliothèque dramatique. v.1-7. Jena, 1825-29. 3v.

37583.400 - .499 Anthologies, collections of literature - Collections of drama - Special periods - 1800-1849
37583.400 Francheville, Robert. Mirliton du romantisme. Paris, 1927.
37583.405 Borgerhoff, J.L. Nineteenth century French plays. N.Y., 1931.
37583.410 Comfort, William W. French romantic plays. N.Y., 1933.
37583.420 Pamphlet vol. Gregoire, A. Répertoire dramatique. v.1-41. Bruxelles. 7 pam.

37583.500 - .599 Anthologies, collections of literature - Collections of drama - Special periods - 1850-1899
37583.500 La France dramatique. ser. II, livre 1-4. Leipzig, 1869.
37583.505 Rotrou, Jean de. Chefs-d'oeuvre tragiques de Rotrou. Paris, 18- .
37583.510 Stanton, Stephen Sadler. Camille, and other plays. N.Y., 1957.
37583.561 Buchheim, C.A. Théâtre français. Modern French plays arranged for schools. pt.1. London, 1861.
37583.575F La scène. Paris. 1-2,1877-1882

37583.600 - .799 Anthologies, collections of literature - Collections of drama - Special periods - 1900- (By date, e.g. .660 for 1960)
37583.600 Marnière, Jeanne. Théâtre de madame. Paris, 1906.
37583.600.15 Les cahiers du théâtre chrétien. Paris. 1-31 17v.
37583.600.20 Bravo. Les cahiers de Bravo. Paris. 1930-1933 3v.
37583.615 Clark, Barrett Harper. Four plays of the free theater: the fossils. Cincinnati, 1915.
37583.623 Pellissier, Georges. Anthologie du théâtre français contemporain. 3. éd. Paris, 1923.
37583.625 Setchanove, L.J. Four French comedies. Boston, 1925.
37583.625.5 Setchanove, L.J. Five French comedies. Boston, 1925.
37583.634 Grant, E.M. Chief French plays of the nineteenth century. 1. ed. N.Y., 1934.
37583.640A Harvitt, H.J. Representative plays from the French theatre of today. Boston, 1940.
37583.640B Harvitt, H.J. Representative plays from the French theatre of today. Boston, 1940.
37583.640.5 Schwarz, Henry S. Lever de Rideau. N.Y., 1940. 6 pam.
37583.642 Rhodes, Solomon A. The contemporary French theater. N.Y., 1942.
37583.642.5 Baty, Gaston. Trois p'tits tours et puis s'en vont. Paris, 1942.
37583.645A Pillement, Georges. Anthologie du théâtre français contemporain. Paris, 1945-48. 3v.

37583.600 - .799 Anthologies, collections of literature - Collections of drama - Special periods - 1900- (By date, e.g. .660 for 1960) - cont.

37583.645B Pillement, Georges. Anthologie du théâtre français contemporain. Paris, 1945-48. 3v.
37583.654A Puccioni, O.F. The French theater since 1930. Boston, 1954.
37583.654B Puccioni, O.F. The French theater since 1930. Boston, 1954.
37583.655 Turgeon, F. Quatre pièces moderne en un acte. N.Y., 1955.
37583.657 Le drame romantique. Paris, 1957.
37583.658 Bentley, E.R. Let's get a divorce! and other plays. N.Y., 1958.
37583.658.5 Adamov, Arthur. Théâtre de société. Paris, 1958.
37583.660 Four modern French comedies. N.Y., 1960.
37583.661 Bermel, Albert. The genius of the French theater. N.Y., 1961.
37583.664 Benedikt, M. Modern French theatre: the Avant-garde, Dada, and Surrealism. 1. ed. N.Y., 1964.
37583.670 Pillement, Georges. Le théâtre d'aujourd'hui; de Jean-Paul Sartre à Arrabal. Paris, 1970.

37584 Anthologies, collections of literature - Collections of drama - Répertoire du théâtre français, Chefs-d'oeuvres des auteurs comiques, etc.

37584.1 Répertoire général du théâtre français. v.39. Paris, 1821.
37584.2 Picard, L.B. Répertoire du théâtre français. Paris, 1826. 4v.
37584.5 Théâtre pour rire. Paris, n.d.
Htn 37584.6* Le Sage, Alain René. Le théâtre de La Foire. Paris, 1737. 10v.
37584.8 Chefs-d'oeuvre des auteurs comiques. 1. Paris, 1857.
37584.9 Chefs-d'oeuvre des auteurs comiques. 2. Paris, 1860.
X Cg 37584.10 Chefs-d'oeuvre des auteurs comiques. 3. Paris, 1845.
37584.11 Chefs-d'oeuvre des auteurs comiques. 4. Paris, 1845.
37584.12 Chefs-d'oeuvre des auteurs comiques. 5. Paris, 1846.
37584.13 Chefs-d'oeuvre des auteurs comiques. 6. Paris, 1846.
37584.14 Chefs-d'oeuvre des auteurs comiques. 7. Paris, 1846.
37584.15 Chefs-d'oeuvre des auteurs comiques. 8. Paris, 1860.
37584.19 Desmahis, J.F.E. de C. Chefs-d'oeuvre des auteurs comiques. Paris, 1892.
37584.19.5 Desmahis, J.F.E. de C. Chefs d'oeuvre des auteur comiques. Paris, 1854. 8v.
37584.20A Viollet-Le-Duc, E.L.N. Ancien théâtre français. Paris, 1854-57. 20v.
37584.20B Viollet-Le-Duc, E.L.N. Ancien théâtre français. Paris, 1854-57. 20v.
37584.22 Delepierre, Joseph Octave. Description bibliographique...d'un livre unique. Receuil de 64 pièces dramatique...au XVIe siècle. Bruxelles? 1849.
37584.23 Dumas, Adolphe. El campamento de los cruzados. Habana, 1840.
37584.24 Mistral, Frédéric. Un poète bilingué, Adolph Dumas, 1806-1861. Paris, 1927.
37584.25 Lacroix, Paul. Ballets et Mascarades de Cour de Henri III à Louis XIV. Geneva, 1868. 6v.

37585 Anthologies, collections of literature - Collections of drama - Local and special

37585.2 Archer, William. English analyses of the French plays represented at the Gaiety Theatre, London,...by the Comédie française. London, 1879.
37585.3 Théâtre classique. Paris, 1887.
37585.3.5 Théâtre classique. Paris, n.d.
37585.3.7 Théâtre classique; ouvrage adopté par l'Université de France. Paris, 17- .
37585.3.8 Théâtre classique, contenant Esther, Athalie. Tours, 1832.
37585.3.9 Théâtre classique; contenant Le Cid, Horace. Boston, 1870.
37585.4 Godefroy, Frédéric. Théâtre classique. Paris, 1880.
37585.5 Regnier, A. Théâtre classique. Paris, 1883.
Htn 37585.7* Comédies françaises. Paris, 1670-85.
37585.8 Pixerécourt, G. de. Théâtre choisi. Paris, 1841- 4v.
37585.10 Corneille, T. La mort d'Annibal. Tragedie. Paris, 1673. 9 pam.
37585.10.5 Gherardi, Evaristo. Suplement du théâtre italien. 1. éd. v.2,3. Bruxelles, 1697. 2v.
37585.10.9 Le théâtre italien de Gherardi. Receuil toutes les comédies et scènes françaises. Paris, 1717. 6v.
37585.10.12 Gherardi, Evaristo. Le théâtre italien de Gherardi. v.2,4. Amsterdam, 1721. 2v.
37585.11 Petite bibliothèque des théâtres. Théâtre italien. Paris, 1784- 6v.
37585.11.8 Le nouveau théâtre italien. Paris, 1733. 8v.
37585.11.9 Pièces du nouveau théâtre italien. Paris, 1753. 3v.
37585.11.10 Les parodies du nouveau théâtre italien. Paris, 1738. 4v.
37585.11.12 Les parodies du nouveau théâtre italien. Paris, 1731. 3v.
37585.12 Bibliothèque des théâtres. v.4,5,10,11,12,29,31,35,36,38,39,40. Paris, 1784- 12v.
37585.12.5 Nodier, Charles. Bibliothèque dramatique. v.1-4. Paris, 1825-26. 7v.
37585.13 Comédies françaises. A collection. Paris, 1785-1800. 20v.
37585.15 Saynètes et monologues. Paris, 1881. 8v.
37585.16 Pamphlet vol. Miscellaneous French drama. 8 pam.
37585.17 Pamphlet vol. Scribe et Legouvé. Adriana Lecouvreur. Firenze, 1852. 12 pam.
37585.18 Recueil de pièces de théâtre. Paris, 1826- 8 pam.
37585.19 Recueils de comédies. Paris, 1857-69. 6 pam.
37585.20 Recueils de comédies. Paris, 1857. 6 pam.
37585.21 Théâtre. Paris, 1793-1853. 7 pam.
37585.22 Comédies. Paris, 1771-1809. 5 pam.
37585.23 Essais dramatiques. Moulins, 1858. 3 pam.
37585.24 Pièces de théâtre. Paris, 1777-1808. 13v.
37585.25 Dieulafoy, J. Le théâtre dans l'intimité. Paris, 1900.
37585.27 Armade, F. de. Le théâtre français des origines à nos jours. Paris, n.d.
Htn 37585.30* Recueil des pièces de théâtre relative à la révolution. 1er part. Paris, 1796?
37585.33 Wogue, Jules. La comédie aux XVIIe et XVIIIe siècle. Paris, 1905.
37585.35 Pamphlet vol. Le fils de Babouc a persépolis, ou Le monde nouveau. 9 pam.
37585.35.5 Voisenon, C.H. de G. La coquette fixée; comédie en trois actes et en vers. Copenhague, 1771. 5 pam.

37585 Anthologies, collections of literature - Collections of drama - Local and special - cont.

37585.40 Pillemont, Georges. Anthologie du théâtre français contemporain. Paris, 1945.
37585.45 Le théâtre picard. Abbeville, 1949.

37586 Anthologies, collections of literature - Französische Neudrucke, etc.

37586.2 Sammlung Französisches Neudrucke. v.1-2. Heilbronn, 1881.
37586.3 Sammlung Französisches Neudrucke. v.3-6. Heilbronn, 1883.
37586.4 Sammlung Französisches Neudrucke. v.7-8. Heilbronn, 1888. 2v.
37586.5 Sammlung Französisches Neudrucke. v.9. Heilbronn, 1888.
37586.15 Foote, Samuel. The comic theatre. London, 1762. 5v.
37586.16 Ware, J. Redding. Un soir qu'il neigeat. Opera comique, Oct. 1870. London, 1870?
37586.30 Artigny, Antoine Gachet d'. Nouveaux mémoires d'histoire, et critique et de littérature. Paris, 1749-56. 7v.
37586.34 Fox, J.H. Robert de Blois. Paris? 1948?

37587 Anthologies, collections of literature - Société d'Anciens Textes Français

37587.15 BBulletin de la société des anciens textes français. Paris. 1875-1933 11v.
37587.15.12 Bulletin de la société des anciens textes français. Paris.
37587.30 Société des textes français modernes. Sketch of the purpose of the society. Mâcon, 1905.
37587.32 Société des textes français modernes. Bulletin. Paris.
37587.34 Société des anciens textes français. Compte rendu de la séance tenue à Paris. Paris, 1926.

37588 Anthologies, collections of literature - Almanacs

37588.2 Almanach des muses. Paris. 1765-1833 55v.
37588.4 Almanach de la littérature du théâtre. Paris. 1853-1869 3v.
37588.7 La France littéraire; ou Almanach des beaux arts. Paris, 1754
37588.8 La muse française...Jules Marsan, 1823-24. Paris, 1907-09. 2v.
37588.9 Séché, L. Le cénacle de la muse française, 1823-1827. Paris, 1909.
37588.10 Journal singe, par Fiaud. London, n.d.
37588.12 Annals des lettres françaises. Paris. 1906-1911 6v.
37588.13 Journal chinois. Paris.
37588.15 Eaux-vives de Lutece. Paris.

37591 Individual authors, etc. - Before 1300 - Langue d'oc (Southern French) - Folios.[Discontinued]

37591.15 Aumeric. La passion Sainte Catherine. Paris, 1885.
37591.20 Montille, Léone de. Cronicques de Girart de Roussilou. Paris, 1880.
37591.24.5 Schulze, A. Predigten des St. Bernhard. Tübingen, 1894.
37591.25 Foerster, Wendelin. Li sermon Saint Bernart. Erlangen, 1885.
37591.25.2 Foerster, Wendelin. Li dialoge Gregoire lo Pape. Halle, 1876.
37591.25.4 Pope, Mildred K. Étude sur la langue de Frère Angier. Paris, 1903.
37591.25.5 Wiese, Leo. Die Sprache der Dialoge des Papetes Gregor. Halle, 1900.
37591.29 Link, Theodor. Über du Sprache der Chronique rimée von Philippe Mousket. Erlangen, 1882.
37591.30 Reiffenberg. Chronique rimée de Philippe Mousket. Brussels, 1836. 3v.
37591.30.25 Hasselmann, Fritz. Über die quellen de Chronique rimée von Philippe Mousket. Göttingen, 1916.
37591.31 Perne. Chansons du Châtelain de Coucy. Paris, 1830.
37591.31.9 Davids, S. Strophen- und Versbau der Lieder des Kastellans von Coucy. Hamburg, 1887.
37591.32A Atkinson, Robert. Vie de Seint Auban. London, 1876.
37591.32B Atkinson, Robert. Vie de Seint Auban. London, 1876.
37591.32.2A Suchier, Hermann. Über die M. Paris. Vie de Seïnt Auban. Halle, 1876.
37591.32.2B Suchier, Hermann. Über die M. Paris. Vie de Seïnt Auban. Halle, 1876.
37591.35 Wolf, Ferdinand. Über...Altfranzosische Doctrinen von der Minne. Vienna, 1864.
37591.37 Bédier, J. Le lai de l'ombre. Freiburg, 1890.
37591.37.10A Jean, Renast. Le lai de l'ombre. Edinburgh, 1948.
37591.37.10B Jean, Renast. Le lai de l'ombre. Edinburgh, 1948.
37591.39A Adam de la Halle. Oeuvres complètes (Poésies et musique). Paris, 1872.
37591.39B Adam de la Halle. Oeuvres complètes (Poésies et musique). Paris, 1872.
37591.41 Jeanroy, Alfred. Lais et descorts français du XIIIe siècle. Texte et musique. Paris, 1901.
37591.42F Le chansonnier de l'Arsenal (trouvères du XIIe et XIIIe siècle). Paris, 1909.
37591.46 Huon le Roi de Cambrai. La vie de Saint Quentin. Helsingfors, 1909.

37592 Individual authors, etc. - Before 1300 - Langue d'oc (Southern French) - Anthologies

37592.5 Hofmann, C. Altfranzösische lyrische Gedichte. München, 1868.

37593 Individual authors, etc. - Before 1300 - Langue d'oc (Southern French) - Known authors and anonymous works

37593.54 Peigné-Delacourt, Achille. Analyse du Roman du Hem du trouvère Sarrazin. Arras, 1854.
37593.61A Philippe de Navarre. Les quatres âges de l'homme. Paris, 1888.
37593.61B Philippe de Navarre. Les quatres âges de l'homme. Paris, 1888.
37593.61C Philippe de Navarre. Les quatres âges de l'homme. Paris, 1888.
37593.62 Adam de la Halle. Le jeu de Robin et Marion. n.p., 1896.
37593.62.23A Adam de la Halle. Adam le Bossu. Paris, 1923.
37593.62.23B Adam de la Halle. Adam le Bossu. Paris, 1923.
37593.62.24A Adam de la Halle. Adam le Bossu. 2. éd. Paris, 1923.
37593.62.24B Adam de la Halle. Adam le Bossu. 2. éd. Paris, 1923.
37593.62.40 Adam de la Halle. Le jeu de Robin et Marion. Paris, 1935.
37593.62.42 Adam de la Halle. Rondeaux à trois voix égales. Paris, 1942.
37593.62.80 Mayer, Gilbert. Léxique des oeuvres d'Adam de la Halle. Paris, 1940.
37593.62.85 Cartier, Normand Raymond. Le bossu désenchanté. Étude sur le jeu de la feuillée. Genève, 1971.

37593 Individual authors, etc. - Before 1300 - Langue d'oc (Southern French) - Known authors and anonymous works - cont.

37593.63 Meienriers, Richard. Adam de la Halle's Spiel, "Robin und Marion". München, 1893.
37593.63.5 Jiersot, Julien. Sur le jeu de Robin et Marion d'Adam de la Halle (XIIIe siècle). Paris, 1897.
37593.63.9 Berger, R. Canchoirs und Partures des...Adam de la Halle. Halle, 1899.
37593.63.10 Adam de la Halle. Les partures Adam; les jeux partis. Paris, 1917.
37593.64 Guy, Henry. Essai sur la vie...du trouvère Adam de la Halle. Paris, 1891.
37593.64.2 Guy, Henry. Essai sur la vie et les oeuvres littéraires du trouvère Adam de la Halle. Genève, 1970.
37593.64.5 Guy, Henry. Le trouvère Adam de la Halle. Paris, 1900.
37593.64.9 Guy, Henry. Bibliographie critique du trouvère Adam de la Halle. Toulouse, 1900.
37593.64.10 Bahlsin, L. Adam de la Halle. Marburg, 1884.
37593.64.11 Adam de la Halle. La revue Dunord. n.p., 1896.
37593.64.12A Le Bossi, A. Le jeu de la feuille. Paris, 1911.
37593.64.12B Le Bossi, A. Le jeu de la feuille. Paris, 1911.
37593.64.12.5 Luetgemeier, Gertrud. Beuträge zum Verständnis des "Jeu de la Feuillée" von Adam le Bossu. Thesis. Bonn, 1969.

37594 Individual authors, etc. - Before 1300 - Old French dialects

37594.5 Gauthier, Jules. Un poème franc-comtois inédit du XIIIe siècle. Besancon, 1880.
37594.7 Hippeau, M.C. Sermon du XIIIe siècle. Paris, n.d.
37594.8 Sarrasin, Jean. Lettre à Nicolas Arrode (1249). Paris, 1924.
37594.9 Sarrasin, Jean. Le roman du Hem. Paris, 1938.
37594.10 Wendahl, C.A. Si vers de la mort (Poème artésien anonyme du milieu du XIIIe siècle). Lund, 1887.
37594.11 Hélinandus. Les vers de la mort. Paris, 1905.
37594.12 Hublocher, J.V. Hélinand von Froidmont und sein Verhältnis zu J. von Salisbury. Regensburg, n.d.
37594.12.15 Bernhardt, A. Die altfranzosische Helinandstrophe. Münster, 1912.
37594.13 Jarry, L. Deux chansons normandes. Orléans, 1894.
37594.14 Poème moral. Photoreproduction. Erlangen, 1886.
37594.16 Robert de Ho. Les enseignements. Paris, 1901.
37594.17 Henri d'Andeli. Oeuvres. Rouen, 1880.
37594.18 Henri d'Andeli. La bataille et le mariage des XII arts. Paris, 1838.
37594.18.50 Henri d'Andeli. The battle of the seven arts. Berkeley, 1914.
37594.19 Henri d'Andeli. Le Lai d'Aristote. Rouen, 1901.
37594.19.15 Henri d'Andeli. Le lai d'Aristote. Paris, 1951.
37594.20 Augustin, Friedrich. Sprachliche Untersuchung über die Werke Henri d'Andelis. Inaug. Diss. Marburg, 1885.
37594.23 Hilka, Alfons. Ein bisher unbekanntes Narcissusspiel. Breslau, 1914.
37594.33 Friedivagner, M. Die Vengeance Raguidel. Halle, 1918.
37594.35 Henri d'Arci. Vitas patrum. Washington, 1949[1950]
37594.37 Chaurand, Jacques. Fou, dixième conte de la Vie des Pères. Genève, 1971.
37594.38A Bibliotheca Normannica. Halle. 1-9,1879-1938 9v.
37594.38B Bibliotheca Normannica. Halle. 8
37594.38.3 Bibliotheca Normannica. 2. Aufl. 3,1900
37594.48.5 Hoepffner, E. Les Lais de Marie de France. Paris, 1935.
37594.50 Shapiro, Norman Richard. The comedy of eros. Urbana, 1971.

37595 Individual authors, etc. - Before 1300 - Langue d'oeil (Northern French - Anthologies; Abelard

Htn 37595.1* Nouveau recueil...lettres d'Abailard et d'Héloise. Anvers, 1722.
37595.2 Lettres...d'Héloise et d'Abeilard. Genève, 1777. 2v.
X Cg 37595.2.5 Abailard, P. Lettres et épitres amoureuses d'Héloise et d'Abeilard. Londres, 1780. 2v.
37595.3 Lettres d'Abailard et d'Héloise. Paris, 1839. 2v.
37595.3.5 Pamphlet vol. Abailard and Héloise. French.
37595.3.10 Bonghi, Ruggero. Eloisa: studio. Città di Castello, 1886.
37595.4.8 Charrier, Charlotte. Héloise dans l'histoire et dans la légende. Thèse. Paris, 1933.
37595.4.10 Charrier, Charlotte. Héloise dans l'histoire et dans la légende. Paris, 1933.
37595.5 Abailard, Pierre. Lettres complètes d'Abélard et d'Héloise. Paris, 1885?
37595.5.10 Abailard, Pierre. Lettres d'Abélard et Héloise. 2. éd. Paris, 1875.
37595.7 Neulan, Elizabeth C.P. de. Abailard et Héloise. Paris, 1853.
37595.7.20 Abailard, Pierre. Traduction de la première épitre de Pierre Abélard (l'histoire calamitatum). Thèse. Paris, 1934.
37595.7.25 Abailard, Pierre. The story of Abélard's adversities. Toronto, 1954.
37595.7.30 Abailard, Pierre. The story of my misfortunes. Glencoe, Ill., 1958.
37595.7.35 Abailard, Pierre. Istoriia moikh bedstvii. Moskva, 1959.
37595.8 Sabatini, Francesco. Abelardo ed Eloisa. Roma, 1879.
37595.8.3 Abailard, Pierre. Correspondencia de Abélardo y Eloisa. Madrid, 1810.
37595.8.5 Abailard, Pierre. Lettres amoureuses d'Héloise. Paris, 1888.
37595.9 Berinton, J. History of Abaillard and Héloise. Philadelphia, 1819.
NEDL 37595.9.5 Abailard, Pierre. Love letters. London, 1901.
37595.9.24 Abailard, Pierre. Love letters of Abélard and Héloise. London, 1925.
37595.9.25 Abailard, Pierre. Letters of Abélard and Héloise. London, 1925.
37595.9.75 Abailard, Pierre. Epistolario completo. Palermo, 1934.
37595.9.101 Abailard, Pierre. Die Leidensgeschichte, und der Briefwechsel mit Heloisa. 2. Aufl. Heidelberg, 1954.
37595.9.110 Abailard, Pierre. Historia calamitatum. Paris, 1959.
37595.9.112 Abailard, Pierre. Historia calamitatum. n.p., 1968.
37595.10 Abailard, Pierre. Abaelardi et Héloisae Epistolae. Turici, 1841.
37595.10.5 Schuster, Gustav. Abälard und Heloise. Hamburg, 1860.
37595.10.10 Wight, O.W. Romance of Abélard and Héloise. N.Y., 1853.
37595.10.15 Murray, Albert Victor. Abélard and St. Bernard; a study in 12th century modernism. Manchester, 1967.
37595.11 Michel, Francisque. Lais inédits des XIIe et XIIIe siècles. Paris, 1836.

37595 Individual authors, etc. - Before 1300 - Langue d'oeil (Northern French - Anthologies; Abelard - cont.

37595.11.10 Grimes, Evie M. The lays of Desiré, Graclant, and Mehon. N.Y., 1928.
37595.12 Keller, Von Adelbert. Romvart. Mannheim, 1844.
37595.13 Wackernagel, Wilhelm. Altfranzösische Lieder und Leiche. Basel, 1846.
37595.14 Krensnir, Adolf. Rustebrief's Gedichte. Wolfenbüttel, 1885.
37595.15A Mätzner, Eduard. Altfranzösische Lieder. Berlin, 1853.
37595.15B Mätzner, Eduard. Altfranzösische Lieder. Berlin, 1853.
37595.15C Mätzner, Eduard. Altfranzösische Lieder. Berlin, 1853.
37595.15.5 Hue de Tabarie. L'ordene de chavalerie. Lausanne, 1759.
37595.16 Raynaud, G. Recueil de motets français des XII et XIII siècle. Paris, 1881-84. 3v.
37595.16.5 Stimming, Albert. Die altfranzösische Motette der Bamberger Handschrift. Dresden, 1906.
37595.17 Heyse, Paul. Romanische Inedita auf Italianischen Bibliotheken. Berlin, 1856.
37595.18 Gullberg, Gotthard. Deux lais du XIIIe siècle. Kalmar, 1876.
37595.18.5 Bedier, J. Les chansons de croisade. Paris, 1909.
37595.18.6 Oeding, F. Das altfranzösische Kreuzlied. Braunschweig, 1910.
37595.19 Diez, Friedrich. Altromanische Sprachdenkmale. Bonn, 1846.
37595.20 Jubinal, Achille. Lettre. Paris, 1834-49.
37595.21 Boucherie, Anatole. Fragment d'une anthologie picarde. Photoreproduction. Paris, 1834-72.
37595.22 Génac, Mongeaut. Lettre à...Paul Meyer. Paris, 1867-69.
37595.23 Meyer, Paul. Salut d'amour. Paris, 1867.
37595.23.2 Michel, F. Des XXIII manières de vilains (XIIIe siècle). Paris, 1833.
37595.24 Michel, F. La riote du monde. Paris, 1834.
37595.26A Meyer, Paul. Documents manuscrits de l'ancienne littérature de la France. Paris, 1871.
37595.26B Meyer, Paul. Documents manuscrits de l'ancienne littérature de la France. Paris, 1871.
37595.27 Pannier, L. Les lapidaires français XII-XIV siècles. Paris, 1882.
37595.28 Meyer, Paul. Recueil d'anciens textes bas-latins, provencaux et français. Paris, 1874. 2v.
37595.28.5A Meyer, Paul. Recueil d'anciens textes bas-latins, provencaux et français. Paris, 1877.
37595.28.5B Meyer, Paul. Recueil d'anciens textes bas-latins, provencaux et français. Paris, 1877.
X Cg 37595.29 Scheler, M. Auguste. Trouvères belges du XII au XIV siècle. 1st et 2nd séries. Bruxelles, 1876-79.
37595.30 Bretel, Jean. Les chansons publiées par G. Raynaud. Paris, 1880.
37595.31 Luchier, Herman. Mariengebete. Halle, 1877.
37595.31.2 Luchier, H. Mariengebete. Halle, 1877.
37595.32 Mussafia, A. Handschriftliche Studien. Wien, 1862.
37595.33 Raynaud, Gaston. Bibliographie des chansonniers français des XIIIe et XIXe siècles. Paris, 1884.
37595.33.2A Jeanroy, Alfred. Bibliographie sommaire des chansonniers français du Moyen Age. Paris, 1918.
37595.33.2B Jeanroy, Alfred. Bibliographie sommaire des chansonniers français du Moyen Age. Paris, 1918.
37595.34 Jeanroy, Alfred. Chansons et dits artésiens du XIIIe siècle. Bordeaux, 1898.
37595.34.5 Jeanroy, Alfred. Anthologie des troubadours, XIIe-XIIIe siècles. Paris, 1927.
37595.34.15 Palfrey, T.R. Medieval French literature. N.Y., 1934.
37595.34.20 Pauphilet, A. Poètes et romanciers du Moyen Âge. Paris, 1939.
37595.34.20.5 Pauphilet, A. Poètes et romanciers du Moyen Âge. Paris, 1958.
37595.34.23 Pauphilet, A. Jeux et sapience du Moyen Âge. Paris, 1941.
37595.34.25F Bibliothèque Nationale, Paris. Mss. (Fr. 19152). Le manuscrit 19152 du Fonds français de la bibliothèque nationale. Paris, 1934.
37595.34.30 Bibliothèque nationale, Paris. Mss. (Fr. 19152). Twelve fabliaux. Manchester, 1958.
37595.34.40 Agnes, Saint, Legend. The Old French lives of St. Agnes. Cambridge, 1938.
37595.34.59 Linskill, Joseph. Saint Léger. Thèse. Paris, 1937.
37595.34.60 Linskill, Joseph. Saint Léger. Paris, 1937.
37595.35 Foerster, Wendelin. Altfranzösische Bibliothek. Heilbroun, 1880. 13v.
37595.36A Chrestien de Troyes. Cliges. v.1-2. Halle, 1888.
37595.36B Chrestien de Troyes. Cliges. v.1-2. Halle, 1888.
37595.36.2 Jesus Christ Altprovenzalische Marienklage. v.3-4. Halle, 1890.
37595.36.3 Chrestien de Troyes. Yvain. v.5-6. Halle, 1891.
37595.36.3.5 Chrestien de Troyes. Yvain. Halle, 1891.
37595.36.3.10 Chrestien de Troyes. La chevalier au lion. 4. éd. Paris, 1944.
37595.36.3.15 Chrestien de Troyes. Le chevalier de la charrette. Paris, 1962.
37595.36.3.20 Kelly, Frederick Douglas. Sens and conjointure in the Chevalier de la charrette. The Hague, 1966.
37595.36.4 Gautier D'Arras. Ille und Galeron. v.7-8. Halle, 1891.
37595.36.5 Caravajal, B. de. La bandolera de Flandes. v.9-10. Halle, 1893.
37595.36.6 Sordello de Goito. Vita e poesie, v.11-12. Halle, 1896.
37595.36.7A Chrestien de Troyes. Erec und Ęnide. v.13. Halle, 1896.
37595.36.7B Chrestien de Troyes. Erec und Ęnide. v.13. Halle, 1896.
37595.36.7C Chrestien de Troyes. Erec und Ęnide. v.13. Halle, 1896.
37595.36.7.5 Chrestien de Troyes. Erec und Enide. 3. Aufl. Halle, 1934.
37595.36.7.10 Chrestien de Troyes. Erec et Ęnide. Paris, 1954.
37595.36.7.15 Chrestien de Troyes. Erec et Ęnide. Bologna, 1959.
37595.36.7.20 Chrestien de Troyes. Erec et Enide. Paris, 1965.
37595.36.8 Vincenz, Beauvais. La estoria. v.14. Halle, 1897.
37595.36.9 Charlemagne. Romance. Latin. Gesta Karoli Magni. v.15. Halle, 1898.
37595.36.10 Vega Carpio, Lape Felix de. Los Guzmanes. v.16. Halle, 1899.
37595.36.11 Adam de la Halle. Canchons. v.17. Halle, 1900.
37595.36.12 Perrin d'Angicourt. Lieder. v.18. Halle, 1905.
37595.36.13 Pavla, Saint. La vie Sainte Paule. v.19. Halle, 1908.
37595.36.14A Chrestien de Troyes. Wilhelm von England. v.20. Halle, 1911.
37595.36.14B Chrestien de Troyes. Wilhelm von England. v.20. Halle, 1911.
37595.36.21A Foerster, Wendelin. Kristian von Troyes. Halle, 1914.
37595.36.21B Foerster, Wendelin. Kristian von Troyes. Halle, 1914.

37595 Individual authors, etc. - Before 1300 - Langue d'oeil (Northern French - Anthologies; Abelard - cont.

37595.36.21C Foerster, Wendelin. Kristian von Troyes. Halle, 1914.
37595.36.22 Spanke, Hans. Eine altfranzösische Liedersammlung. Halle, 1925.
37595.36.24 Raynaud, Gaston. Bibliographie des altfranzösischen Liedes. Leiden, 1955.
37595.36.50 Foerster, Wendelin. Romanische Bibliothek. 2. Aufl. v.1,5,6,8,13. Halle, 1901-03. 5v.
37595.36.51 Foerster, Wendelin. Romanische Bibliothek. 3. Aufl. Halle, 1906-28. 3v.
37595.36.52A Foerster, Wendelin. Romanische Bibliothek. 4. Aufl. v.1,5. Halle, 1912. 2v.
37595.36.52B Foerster, Wendelin. Romanische Bibliothek. 4. Aufl. v.5. Halle, 1912.
37595.36.53A Foerster, Wendelin. Romanische Bibliothek. Halle, 1913.
37595.37A Dinaux, Arthur. Les trouvères cambrésiens. v.1-4. Photoreproduction. Paris, 1837-1763. 3v.
37595.37B Dinaux, Arthur. Les trouvères cambrésiens. v.1-4. Paris, 1837-1863. 4v.
37595.40 Dinaux, Arthur. Les trouvères Cambrésiens. 3. éd. Paris, 1837.
37595.42 Paris, Gaston. Récits extraits des poètes et prosateurs du Moyen Âge. Paris, 1896.
37595.42.6 Paris, Gaston. Récits extraits des poètes et prosateurs du Moyen Âge. 6. éd. Paris, 1907.
37595.45 Brandin, L. Inedita der altfranzösischen Liederhandschrift Pb5 bibliothèque nationale 846. Berlin, 1900.
37595.46 Glixelli, Stefan. Les cinq poèmes des trois morts et des trois vifs. Paris, 1914.
37595.47 Gennrich, Friedrich. Rondeaux, Virelais und Ballanden. Dresden, 1921. 2v.
37595.49 Le chansonnier d'Arras. Paris, 1925.
37595.52 Cary, Henry F. The early French poets. N.Y., 1925.
37595.57 Dronart la Vache. Le livres d'amour de Dronart la Vache. Thèse. Paris, 1926.
37595.58 Bossuat, Robert. Drouart la Vache, traducteur d'André le chapelain (1290). Thèse. Paris, 1926.
37595.60 Bastin, Julia. Recueil général des Isopets. Paris, 1929-30. 2v.
37595.62 Streng Renbonen, W.O. Les estampies françaises. Paris, 1930.
37595.64 Abbott, C.C. Early mediaeval French lyrics. London, 1932.
37595.66 Les classiques français du Moyen Âge. Paris, n.d. 5v.
37595.68 Bossaut, R. La poésie lyrique au Moyen Âge. Paris, 1936.
37595.70 Marichal, R. Le théâtre en France au Moyen Âge, 12ème et 13ème siècles. Paris, 1938.
37595.72 Oulmont, Charles. La poésie française du Moyen Âge, XIe-XVe siècles. Paris, 1913.
37595.75 Gossart, A.M. Contes et récits; extraits des prosateurs et poètes du Moyen Âge mis en français moderne. Paris, 1939.
37595.78 Pauphilet, A. Contes du jongleur. Paris, 1932.
37595.80 Groult, Pierre. Anthologie de la littérature française du Moyen Âge. Gembloux, 1942-43. 2v.
37595.81A Cohen, Gustave. Anthologie de la littérature française du Moyen Âge. Paris, 1946.
37595.81B Cohen, Gustave. Anthologie de la littérature française du Moyen Âge. Paris, 1946.
37595.82 Pernond, Régine. La poésie médiévale française. Paris, 1947.
37595.83 Grands poètes français: le Moyen Âge. Lausanne, 1946.
37595.85 Rutebeuf. Onze poèmes concernant la croisade. Paris, 1946.
37595.87 Wagner, R.L. Textes d'étude. Lille, 1949.
37595.87.5 Wagner, R.L. Textes d'étude. Genève, 1961.
37595.89 Sbordone, F. Festi ed appunti per lo studio del medioevo francese. Napoli, 1948-
37595.90 Daix, Pierre. Naissance de la poesie française. Paris, 1958.
37595.91 Schwartzkopff, W. Sagen und Geschichten aus dem Alten Frankreich und England. München, 1925.
37595.93 Mary, André. La fleur de la poésie française depuis les origines jusqu'à la fin du XV siècle. Paris, 1951.
37595.95 Wickelgren, F.L. Some gems of early lyrical poetry. Gloucester, 1939.
37595.97 Viscardi, A. Antologia dei narratori francesi del Medio Eno. Milano, 1960.
37595.97.2 Viscardi, A. Filologia romanza. Milano, 1961.
37595.99 Cluzel, Irénée. Les origines de la poésie. Paris, 1962.
37595.99.2 Cluzel, Irénée Marcel. La poésie lyrique d'oïl. 2. éd. Paris, 1969.
37595.100 Revel, Bruno. Teati bilinqui delle origini. Milano, 1956?
37595.102 Terry, P.A. Lays of courtly love. 1. éd. Garden City, 1963.
37595.104 Boogaard, Nico H.J. Rondeaux et refrains. Paris, 1969.
37595.106 Stimming, Albert. Lebensbericht. Auslieferung, 1967.
37595.108 Guiette, Robert. Fabliaux et contes. Paris, 1960.
37595.110 Pottier, Bernard. Antologia de textos del francés antiquo. Granada, 1959.
37595.110.5 Pottier, Bernard. Textes médiévaux français et romans. Paris, 1964.
37595.112 Chastel, André. Trésors de la poésie médiéval. Paris, 1959.
37595.114 Butler, Isabel. Tales from the old French. Boston, 1910.
37595.116 Finoli, Anna Maria. Artes amandi. Da Maître Elie ad Andrea Cappellano. Milano, 1969.
37595.119 Axton, Richard. Medieval French plays. Oxford, 1971.

37596 Individual authors, etc. - Before 1300 - Langue d'oeil (Northern French - Other known authors, etc.

37596.1 Pamphlet box. Guillaume de Deguilleville.
Htn 37596.2* Guillaume de Deguilleville. Le romant des trois pelerinages. Paris, 1500.
37596.2.3 Guillaume de Deguilleville. Die pilger Fahrt des traumenden Mönchs. Berlin, 1915.
37596.2.3.15 Guillaume de Deguilleville. Die pilger Fahrt des traumenden Mönchs. Bonn, 1925.
37596.2.4 Goetze, F. Untersuchungen über die Pilgerfahrt des träumenden Mönchs. Marburg, 1934.
37596.2.6 Bauer, Fritz. Das personal Pronomen in le Pelerinage de vie humaine de Guileville. Würzburg, 1899.
37596.2.10 Hultman, J.E.E. Guillaume de Deguileville. Upsala, 1902.
37596.2.15 Damave, Helena. Die Sprache der Pilgerfahrt der träumenden Mönchs. Proefschrift. Haarlem, 1964.
37596.3A Beaumanoir, P. de. Oeuvres poétique. Paris, 1884-85. 2v.

37596 Individual authors, etc. - Before 1300 - Langue d'oeil (Northern French - Other known authors, etc. - cont.

37596.3B Beaumanoir, P. de. Oeuvres poétique. Paris, 1884-85. 2v.
37596.3.2 Albert, A.C. Die Sprache Philippes de Beaumanoir in seinen poetischen Werken. Erlangen, 1893.
37596.3.10 Paris, Gaston. Le soir de Beaumanoir. Paris, 1926.
37596.3.15 Philippe de Remi. Roman de la Marekine. Paris, 1840.
37596.4 Klint, A.H. Le miracle de Théophile de Rutebeuf. Upsala, 1869.
37596.4.2 Rutebeuf. Le miracle de Théophile. 2. éd. Paris, 1949.
37596.4.5 Sepet, M. Un drame religieux du Moyen Âge. Paris, 1894.
37596.4.10 Rutebeuf. Le miracle de Théophile. Paris, 1925.
37596.4.15 Rutebeuf. Le miracle de Théophile. Paris, 1934.
37596.5 Tjaden, H.P. Untersuchungen über die Poetik Rutebeufs. Marburg, 1885.
37596.5.10 Dehm, C. Studien zu Rutebeuf. Inaug. Diss. Würzburg, 1935.
37596.6 Jubinal, A. Études sur...Rutebeuf. Paris, 1864.
37596.7 Clédat, Léon. Rutebeuf. Paris, 1891.
37596.7.2 Clédat, Léon. Rutebeuf. 2. éd. Paris, 1909.
37596.7.5 Feger, G. Rutebeufs Kritik an den Zuständen seiner Zeit. Inaug. Diss. Freiburg, 1920.
37596.7.15 Lucas, H. Les poésies personnelles de Rutebeuf. Thèse. Strasbourg, 1938.
37596.7.20 Regalado, Nancy Freeman. Poetic patterns in Rutebeuf; a study in noncourtly poetic modes of the thirteenth century. New Haven, 1970.
37596.8A Jubinal, A. Oeuvres de Rutebeuf. Paris, 1839. 2v.
37596.8B Jubinal, A. Oeuvres de Rutebeuf. Paris, 1839. 2v.
37596.8.3 Jubinal, A. Oeuvres completes de Rutebeuf. Paris, 1874-75. 3v.
37596.8.4 Rutebeuf. Oeuvres completes. v.1-2. Paris, 1957.
37596.8.5 Bida, A. Aucassin et Nicolette. Paris, 1878.
37596.8.10 Rutebeuf. Poèmes concernant l'Université de Paris. Paris, 1952.
37596.8.15 Rutebeuf. Rutebeuf: un tableau synoptique de la vie et des oeuvres de Rutebeuf. Paris, 1966.
37596.8.20 Serper, Arié. Rutebeuf; poète satirique. Paris, 1961.
37596.9 Suchier, H. Aucassin und Nicolite. Paderborn, 1881.
37596.9.75 Chrestien de Troyes. Oeuvres choises. Paris, 1936.
37596.9.80 Fotich, T. The narrative tenses in Chrestien de Troyes. Washington, 1950.
37596.10A Foerster, Wendelin. Christian von Troyes sämtliche Werke. Halle, 1884-1932. 5v.
37596.10B Foerster, Wendelin. Christian von Troyes sämtliche Werke. Halle, 1884-1932. 4v.
37596.10C Foerster, Wendelin. Christian von Troyes sämtliche Werke. v.1,3,4. Halle, 1884-1932. 3v.
37596.10D Foerster, Wendelin. Christian von Troyes sämtliche Werke. v.4. Halle, 1884-1932.
37596.10.2.5 Chrestien de Troyes. Arthurian romances. London, 1913.
37596.10.2.15 Chrestien de Troyes. Arthurian romances. London, 1928.
37596.10.2.20 Chrestien de Troyes. Arthurian romances. N.Y., 1935.
37596.10.2.25 Chrestien de Troyes. Romans. Paris, 1952. 4v.
37596.10.2.30 Chrestien de Troyes. Arthurian romances. London, 1968.
37596.10.4A Chrestien de Troyes. Philomena. Paris, 1909.
37596.10.4B Chrestien de Troyes. Philomena. Paris, 1909.
37596.10.4C Chrestien de Troyes. Philomena. Paris, 1909.
37596.10.4.1 Chrestien de Troyes. Philomena. Concordances et index établis d'après l'édition. Liège, 196-.
37596.10.13 Chrestien de Troyes. Eric und Emile. Halle, 1909.
37596.10.25 Chrestien de Troyes. Cliges. Halle, 1934.
37596.10.30 Chrestien de Troyes. Le manuscrit d'Annonay. Paris, 1934.
37596.10.35 Chrestien de Troyes. Yvain. Der Löwenritter. 3. Aufl. Halle, 1906.
37596.10.80 Pamphlet box. Chrestien de Troyes.
37596.10.85 Fabriek, P. La construction relative dans Chréstien de Troyes. Amsterdam, 1924.
37596.10.90 Euler, H. Recht und Staat in den Romanen des Cretien von Troyes. Inaug. Diss. Marburg, 1906.
37596.10.95 Schulz, Otto. Die Darstellung psychologischer Vorgange in den Romanen des Kristian von Troyes. Inaug. Diss. Breslau, 1903.
37596.10.100 Putz, Rudolf. Chrestiens "Yvain" und Hartmanns "Iwein". Neustrelitz, 1927.
37596.10.105 Lonin, Pierre. Prolégomènes à une édtion d'Yvain. Gap, 1958.
37596.10.110 Cohen, Gustav. Un grand romancier d'amour et d'aventure au XII siècle. Paris, 1931.
37596.10.115 Kramer, Hans-Peter. Erzählerbemerkungen und Erzählerkommentare in Chrestiens und Hartmanns Erec und Iwein. Thesis. Göppingen, 1971.
37596.10.120 Reinhard, J.R. Chréstien de Troyes. Ann Arbor, 1932.
37596.10.130 Königer, H. Die Darstellung der Personen bei Chrétien de Troyes. Inaug. Diss. München, 1936.
37596.10.140 Strassberg, S. Die Entführung und Befreiung der Konigin Ginevra. Inaug. Diss. Berlin, 1937.
37596.10.149 Micha, Alexandre. La tradition manuscrite des romans de Chréstien de Troyes. Thèse. Paris, 1939.
37596.10.150 Micha, Alexandre. La tradition manuscrite des romans de Chréstien de Troyes. Paris, 1939.
37596.10.155A Loomis, R.S. Arthurian tradition and Chréstien de Troyes. N.Y., 1949.
37596.10.155B Loomis, R.S. Arthurian tradition and Chréstien de Troyes. N.Y., 1949.
37596.10.160 Bezzola, Rito R. Le sens de l'aventure et de l'amour. Chréstien de Troyes. Paris, 1947.
37596.10.162 Bezzola, Rito R. Liebe und Abenteuer im hofischen Roman. Hamburg, 1961.
37596.10.170 Ritchie, R.L.G. Chrétien de Troyes and Scotland. Oxford, 1952.
37596.10.175 Guyer, F.E. Chréstien de Troyes. N.Y., 1957.
37596.10.180 Frappier, Jean. Chréstien de Troyes. Paris, 1957.
37596.10.181 Frappier, Jean. Chréstien de Troyes. Paris, 1957.
37596.10.185 Ziltener, Werner. Chréstien und die Aeneis. Graz, 1957.
37596.10.190 Reason, Joseph H. An inquiry into the structural style and originality of Chréstien's Yvain. Washington, 1958.
37596.10.200 Gsteiger, M. Die Landschaftsschilderungen in den Romanen Chrestiens de Troyes. Bern, 1957.
37596.10.205 Jaeger, Hermann. Der Sinnbezirk der Fortbewegung. Erlangen? 1959.
37596.10.210 Colby, Alice M. The portrait in twelfth-century French literature. Genève, 1965.
37596.10.215 Micha, Alexandre. La tradition manuscrite des romans de Chréstien de Troyes. Genève, 1966.

Classified Listing

37596 Individual authors, etc. - Before 1300 - Langue d'oeil (Northern French - Other known authors, etc. - cont.

37596.10.220 Wehrli, Annegret. Semantische Untersuchung der Verben für Begehren, Gewähren, Versprechen, Ubergeben und Verweigern die Chrétien de Troyes. Zürich, 1967.

37596.10.225 Foerster, Wendelin. Wörterbuch zu Kristian von Troyes sämtlichen Werken. 4. Aufl. Tübingen, 1966.

37596.10.230 Holmes, Urban Tigner. Chrétien de Troyes. N.Y., 1970.

37596.10.235 Le Coultre, Jules. De l'ordre des mots dansCrestien de Troyes. Diss. Dresde, 1875.

37596.11A Berneville, G. La vie de Saint Gilles. Paris, 1881.

37596.11B Berneville, G. La vie de Saint Gilles. Paris, 1881.

37596.11.5 Aiol et Mirable und Elie de Saint Gille. Heilbronn, 1876-82.

37596.13A Fath, Fritz. Die Lieder des Castellans von Coucy. Heidelberg, 1883.

37596.13B Fath, Fritz. Die Lieder des Castellans von Coucy. Heidelberg, 1883.

37596.13.3 Coucy, G.C. Le lai de la dame de Fayel. St. Quentin, 1872.

37596.13.5 Coucy, G.C. Chansons attribuées au Chastelain de Couci. Paris, 1964.

37596.14 Meon, D.M. Le roman de Renart. Paris, 1826. 4v.

37596.15 Hofmann, K. Amis et amiles du jourdains de Blaivies. Erlangen, 1882.

37596.16 Étienne, E. La vie Saint Thomas le martir. Paris, 1883.

37596.16.5 Raoul de Houdenc. Sämtliche Werke. Halle, 1897-1909. 2v.

37596.17 Raoul de Houdenc. Le romans des Eles. Brussels, 1868.

37596.17.3 Raoul de Houdenc. Songs d'enfer...La voie de paradis. Photoreproduction. Paris, 1908.

37596.17.5 Livingston, C.H. Li dis Raoul Hosdaing. n.p., 1922.

37596.17.10 Kundert-Forrer, V. Raoul de Houdenc. Bern, 1960.

37596.18 Petit, Louis. Les satires. Paris, 1883.

37596.19 Jean de Tuim. Li hystore de Julius César. Halle, 1881.

37596.19.25 Dedecek, U.L. Étude littéraire de Li hystore de Julius Cesar. Philadelphia, 1925.

37596.20 Charsant, Alphonse. La muse Normande. Rouen, 1853.

37596.20.2 Orpen, Goddard H. Song of Dermont and the Earl. Oxford, 1892.

37596.21.5 Gross, Max. Geffrei Gaimar. Die Komposition seiner Reimchroniek. Erlangen, 1902.

37596.23A Luzarche, Victor. Adam; drame Anglo-Normand. Tours, 1854.

37596.23B Luzarche, Victor. Adam; drame Anglo-Normand. Tours, 1854.

37596.23.5 Grant mal fist Adam. Publié par A. Jubinal. Paris, 1834.

37596.23.6 Suchier, Hermann. Zwei altfranzösische Reimpredigten. Halle, 1949.

37596.23.7A Adam. Reimpredigt. Halle, 1897.

37596.23.7B Adam. Reimpredigt. Halle, 1897.

37596.23.9 Adam (Mystery). Le mystère d'Adam. Manchester, 1918.

37596.23.11 Adam (Mystery). Das altfranzösische Adamsspiel. Photoreproduction. Paris, 1925.

37596.23.15 Adam (Mystery). Le mystère d'Adam. Paris, 1968.

37596.23.20A Adam (Mystery). Le jeu d'Adam et Ève. Paris, 1936.

37596.23.20B Adam (Mystery). Le jeu d'Adam et Ève. Paris, 1936.

37596.23.23 Adam (Mystery). Le mystère d'Adam. Genève, 1963.

37596.23.25 Adam (Mystery). Das altfranzösische Adamsspiel. München, 1968.

37596.23.30 Adam (Mystery). Le jeu d'Adam. Paris, 1971.

37596.24A Hamel, A.G. van. Romans de charité et misère. Paris, 1885. 2v.

37596.24B Hamel, A.G. van. Romans de charité et misère. Paris, 1885. 2v.

37596.24.3 Leendertz, P. Het middelnederlandsche leerdicht rinclus. Amsterdam, 1893.

37596.25 Palustre, Léon. Adam mystère du 12e siècle. Paris, 1877.

37596.25.2 Merguet, V. Anglo-Normannischen religiösen Dramas Adam. Konigsberg, 1892.

37596.25.10A Adam (Mystery). Adam...play of 12th century. Seattle, 1926.

37596.25.10B Adam (Mystery). Adam...play of 12th century. Seattle, 1926.

37596.25.10C Adam (Mystery). Adam...play of 12th century. Seattle, 1926.

37596.25.13 Stone, N. A translation of Chapter XI-XVI of the pseudo-Augustinian sermon against Jews, pagans. Seattle, 1928.

37596.26.5 Stengel, E. La cancun de Saint Alexis. Marburg, 1882.

37596.26.10 Aléxius, Saint. Légend. La vie de Saint Aléxis. Paris, 1885.

X Cg 37596.26.10.5 Aléxius, Saint. Légend. La vie de Saint Aléxis. Paris, 1885.

37596.26.15 Aléxius, Saint. Légend. La vie de Saint Aléxis. Paris, 1872.

37596.26.18 Aléxius, Saint. Légend. The life of Saint Aléxis. N.Y., 1931.

37596.26.20 Aléxius, Saint. Légend. Aléxis. Pariser Glossar. 3692. München, 1868.

37596.26.23 Aléxius, Saint. Légend. Saint Aléxis; étude. Paris, 1934.

37596.26.25 Aléxius, Saint. Légend. La vita di S. Alessio. Firenze, 1936.

37596.26.30 Hahnel, Kurt. Sprachliche Untersuchung zur Alexius-Handschrift "V". Inaug. Diss. Coburg, 1934.

37596.27 Herz, Joseph. De Saint Aléxis. Frankfurt, 1879.

37596.27.2 Braunis, Julius. Über...der altfranzösischen Cancun de St. Alexis. Kiel, 1884.

37596.27.3 Kötting, Georg. Studien über altfranzösische Bearbeitungen der Alexinslegende. Trier, 1890.

37596.27.4 Müller, Paul. Studien über drei dramatisch Bearbeitungen der Alexinslegende. Berlin, 1888.

37596.27.6 Keidel, George C. An old French prose version of La vie de St. Aléxis. Baltimore, 1896.

37596.27.8 Guéry, Charles. Guillaume Aléxis dit le bon moine. Eveux, 1907.

37596.27.9 Aléxius, Saint. Légend. Die altfranzösische Prosareision des Aléxiuslégende. Berlin, 1913.

37596.27.10 Aléxius, Saint. Légend. Sankt Alexius. 2. Aufl. Halle, 1941.

37596.27.12 Rösler, Margarete. Sankt Alexius Altfranzösische Legendendichtung des 11 Jahrhunderts. Halle, 1928.

37596.27.14 Aléxius, Saint. Légend. La vie de Saint Aléxis. Oxford, 1946.

37596.27.15 Aléxius, Saint. Légend. La vie de Saint Aléxis. Paris, 1933.

37596.27.15.2 Aléxius, Saint. Légend. La vie de Saint Aléxis. Genève, 1968.

37596.27.18 Sprissler, Manfred. Das rhythmische Gedicht Pater deus (11 Jht.) und das altfranzösische Aléxiuslied. Münster, 1966.

37596 Individual authors, etc. - Before 1300 - Langue d'oeil (Northern French - Other known authors, etc. - cont.

37596.27.20 Gierden, Karlheinz. Das altfranzösische Alexiuslied. Meisenheim, 1967.

37596.27.25 Aléxius, Saint. Légend. Das Leben des Heiligen Aléxius. München, 1968.

37596.29 Foerster, Wendelin. De Venus la deesse d'amor. Bonn, 1880.

37596.29.5 Cristal und Clarie. Dresden, 1915.

37596.30A Garnier de Pont Sainte Maxence. La vie de Saint Thomas. Paris, 1859.

37596.30B Garnier de Pont Sainte Maxence. La vie de Saint Thomas. Paris, 1859.

37596.30C Garnier de Pont Sainte Maxence. La vie de Saint Thomas. Paris, 1859.

NEDL 37596.30.1 Garnier de Pont Sainte Maxence. La vie de Saint Thomas le martyr. Lund, 1922.

37596.30.2A Meyer, Paul. Fragments d'une vie de Saint Thomas de Canterbury. Paris, 1885.

37596.30.2B Meyer, Paul. Fragments d'une vie de Saint Thomas de Canterbury. Paris, 1885.

37596.30.5 Mebes, A. Über Garnier von Pont Sainte-Maxence. Breslau, 1876.

37596.30.10 Garnier de Pont Sainte Maxence. La vie de Saint Thomas Becket. Paris, 1936.

37596.31 Hucher, Eugène. Le Saint-Graal. Paris, 1875. 3v.

37596.32.75 La résurrection du Sauveur. Strasbourg, 1924.

37596.32.80 La Résurrection du Sauveur. La résurrection du Sauveur. Paris, 1931.

37596.33.8 Robert de Blois. Floris et Liriope. Leipzig, 1891.

37596.34 Colvin, Mary N. Lautliche Untersuchung der Werke Roberts von Blois. Zürich, 1888.

37596.34.5 Berlit, O. Die Sprache des altfranzösischen Dichters Robert von Blois. Halle, 1900.

37596.34.10 Fox, John Howard. Robert de Blois, et narrative;...Son oeuvre didactique. Paris? 1948?

37596.35 Weber, Alfred. Athis und Prophilias. Staefa, 1881.

37596.36 Jubinal, A. La complainte et le jeu. Paris, 1835.

Htn 37596.37* Michelaut, Henri. La clef d'amour. Lyons, 1866.

37596.38A Gautier d'Arras. Oeuvres. Paris, 1890. 2v.

37596.38B Gautier d'Arras. Oeuvres. Paris, 1890. 2v.

37596.38.2 Gautier d'Arras. Ille et Galeron. Paris, 1956.

37596.38.5 Pamphlet box. Gautier d'Arras.

37596.38.9 Stevenson, W.M. Der Einfluss des Gautier d'Arras auf die altfranzösische Kunstepils. Göttingen, 1910.

37596.38.12 Hüppe, W. Der Sprachstil Gautiers von Arras. Inaug. Diss. Bochum, 1937.

37596.38.15 Renzi, Lorenzo. Tradizione cortese e realismo in Gautier d'Arras. Padova, 1964.

37596.38.30 Jehan le teinturier d'Arras. Le mariage des sept arts. Paris, 1923.

37596.39 Bartsch, Karl. Romances et pastourelles françaises. Leipzig, 1870.

Htn 37596.39.5* Abbott, C.C. Nine songs from the 12th century French. Chelsea, 1920.

37596.40 Vietor, W. Die Handschriften der Geste des Loherains. Halle, 1876.

37596.41 Evers, Robert W. Dan Michel's Ayenbite of Inwyt. Erlangen, 1888.

37596.41.5 Lusner, L. La somme des vices et des vertus. Wien, 1905.

37596.41.9 Lorens, Frère. Trattato del Ben Vivere. Firenze, 1848.

37596.41.13 Lorens, Frère. Volgarizzamento dell'esposizione del paternostro fatto da Zucchero Bencivenni. Firenze, 1828.

37596.42 Levisque, Pierre. Poésies du...Thibaut IV. Paris, 1742. 2v.

37596.42.2 Thibaut I, King of Navarre. Chansons. Reins, 1857.

37596.42.5A Thibaut I, King of Navarre. Les chansons de Thibaut de champagne roi de Navarre. Paris, 1925.

37596.42.5B Thibaut I, King of Navarre. Les chansons de Thibaut de champagne roi de Navarre. Paris, 1925.

37596.43 Guillaume le Clerc. Le bestiaire divin. Caen, 1852.

37596.44 Guillaume le Clerc. Le bestiaire. Leipzig, 1890.

37596.44.2A Guillaume le Clerc. Le besant de Dieu. Halle, 1869.

37596.44.2B Guillaume le Clerc. Le besant de Dieu. Halle, 1869.

37596.44.9 Schmidt, Adolf. Guillaume, le clerc de Normandie. Bonn, 1880.

37596.45 Maréchal, Théodore. Sur les chansons de Thibaut. Photoreproduction. Rostock, 1871.

37596.45.3 Davids, Fritz. Über Form und Sprache der Gedichte Thibaults IV. Braunschweig, 1885.

37596.45.25 Guillaume d'Oye. La vie de Saint Thibaut. N.Y., 1929.

37596.45.30 Two old French poems on St. Thibaut. New Haven, 1936.

37596.46A Renaut, Le Trouvère. Le roman de galerent. Montpellier, 1888.

37596.46B Renaut, Le Trouvère. Le roman de galerent. Montpellier, 1888.

37596.47 Weidner, Georg. Der Prosaroman von Joseph von Arimathia. Oppeln, 1881.

37596.48 Reinbrecht, August. Legends von den sieben Schläfern. Göttingen, 1880.

37596.49A Söderhjelm, Werner. De Saint Laurent. Paris, 1888.

37596.49B Söderhjelm, Werner. De Saint Laurent. Paris, 1888.

37596.50 Fournival, Richard de. Le bestiaire d'amour. Paris, 1860.

37596.50.3 Fournival, Richard de. Li bestiaires d'amours di Maistre Richart de Fornival e Li response du bestiaire. Milano, 1957.

37596.50.9 Zarifopol, Paul. Kritischer Text der Lieder Richards de Fournival. Halle, 1904.

37596.51 Guichard de Beaulieu. Le sermon de G. de B. Paris, 1834.

37596.52A Jacques d'Amiens. L'art d'amours. Leipzig, 1868.

37596.52B Jacques d'Amiens. L'art d'amours. Leipzig, 1868.

37596.52.2 Simon, Philipp. Jacques d'Amiens. Berlin, 1895.

37596.52.5 Kühlhorn, G. Das Verhältnis der Art d'amors des Jacques d'Amiens zu Ovido Ars amatoria. Inaug. Diss. Weida, 1908.

37596.53 Guillaume de Ferrières. Chansons et saluts d'amour. Paris, 1856.

37596.54A Paris, Gaston. La vie de Saint Aléxis. Paris, 1872.

37596.54B Paris, Gaston. La vie de Saint Aléxis. Paris, 1872.

37596.54.5 Paris, Gaston. La vie de Saint Aléxis. Paris, 1903.

X Cg 37596.54.9 Paris, Gaston. La vie de Saint Aléxis. Paris, 1911.

37596.54.10 Aléxius, Saint. Légend. La vie de Saint Aléxis. 3. éd. Paris, 1921.

37596.56 Cloetta, Wilhelm. Alfassungszeit und Überlieferung das Poème moral. Erlangen, 1884.

37596.57 Richelet, Charles J. Fragmens de l'éxplication allégorique du cantique des cantiques. Paris, 1826.

37596.59 Kölbing, Eugen. La chanson de Roland. Heilbronn, 1877.

37596.60 Julleville, L. La chanson de Roland. Paris, 1878.

37596 Individual authors, etc. - Before 1300 - Langue d'oeil (Northern French - Other known authors, etc. - cont.

37596.62 Koschwitz, E. Chanson du voyage de Charlemagne à Jérusalem et à Constantinople. Heilbronn, 1876.
37596.63 Koschwitz, E. Karls des grossen Reise nach Jerusalem und Constantin. Heilbronn, 1879.
NEDL 37596.63 Koschwitz, E. Karls des grossen Reise nach Jerusalem und Constantin. Heilbronn, 1883.
37596.64.5 Poem on the assumption. Cambridge, 1924.
37596.64.10 Kjellman, Hilding. La deuxième collection anglo-normande des miracles de la Saint Vierge. Paris, 1922.
37596.64.15 Allen, H.E. Mystical lyrics of Mannuel des Pechiez. N.Y., 1918.
37596.65 Fitz Warine, Fulk. Histoire de fulques Fitz-Warin. Paris, 1840.
37596.65.5 Fitz Warine, Fulk. Fouke Fitz Warin. Paris, 1930.
37596.66 Paris, Gaston. Le lai de l'oiselet. Poème français du XIIIe siècle. Paris, 1884.
37596.67 Faut, Carl. L'image du monde; poème du XIIIe siècle. Upsala, 1886.
37596.67.5 Haase, G. Untersuchung über die Reime in der Image du monde. Halle, 1879.
37596.67.25 Petite philosophie. A critical edition of la Petite Philosophie. Diss. Chicago, 1939.
37596.68 Feilitzen, Hugo. Liver del juise. Photoreproduction. Upsala, 1883.
37596.69 Philippe, de Thaon. Li cumpoz. Strassburg, 1873.
37596.69.2 Mann, M.F. Der Physiologus des Philipp von Thaün und seine Quellen. Halle, 1884.
37596.70 Stengel, F. Codicem manu scriptum Digby 86. Halle, 1871. 2v.
37596.71 Thibaud de Montmorency, seigneur de Marly. Vers sur la mort. Paris, 1835.
37596.71.2 Thibaud de Montmorency, seigneur de Marly. Vers sur la mort. Paris, 19- .
37596.71.10 Marly, T. de M. Les vers de Thibaud de Marly. Thèse. Paris, 1932.
37596.72 Salmon, P. Les demandes faites par le roi Charles VI. Paris, 1833.
37596.73 Eberhardt, Paul. Der Lucidaire Gilleberts. Halle, 1884.
37596.73.5 Schladebach, H. Das Elucidarium des Honorius Augustodunensis. Leipzig, 1884.
Htn 37596.74* Raynaud, Gaston. Un nouveau dit des femmes. Paris, 1886.
37596.75 Ehrismann, Henri. Le sermon des plaies. Strasbourg, 1896.
37596.77 Mondeville, H. de. La chirurgie. Paris, 1897. 2v.
37596.77.5 Mondeville, H. de. Chirurgie de maitre H. de Mondeville. Paris, 1893.
37596.78 Everlien, Hermann. Über Judas Machabee von Gautier de Belle Perche. Halle, 1897.
37596.79 Wagner, Philipp. Gillon le Muisi. Brünn, 1896.
37596.79.7 Schmidt, W. Untersuchung der Reime in den Dichtungen dess Abte Gilles Li Muisis. Inaug. Diss. Leipzig, 1903.
37596.80 Colonna, Egidio. Li livres du gouvernement des rois. N.Y., 1899. 2v.
37596.81 Grebel, Max. Le tornoiment antéchrist par Huon de Mery. Inaug. Diss. Leipzig, 1883.
37596.81.10 Huon de Mery. Das tornoiement de l'antechrist. Reims, 1851.
37596.82 Mann, W. Die Lieder des Dichters Robert de Raius gewannt la Chivre. Halle, 1898.
37596.83 Lindfors, W.E. VII anciens textes français. Lund, 1866.
37596.84A Bible. French. (Old). N.T. Revelation. L'apocalypse en français au XIIIe siècle. Paris, 1901. 2v.
37596.84B Bible. French. (Old). N.T. Revelation. L'apocalypse en français au XIIIe siècle. Paris, 1901.
37596.84.4 Bible. French. (Old). N.T. Revelation. The romaunt version of the Gospel. London, 1848.
37596.84.5 Loh, Hugo. Histoires tirées de l'ancien testament. Münster, 1912.
37596.85A Gace Brulé. Chansons. Paris, 1902.
37596.85B Gace Brulé. Chansons. Paris, 1902.
37596.86 Li Miserere, pikardisches Gedicht aus dem XII. Jahrhundert von Reclus de Mollens. Landshut, 1882.
37596.87 Baudler, A. Guiot von Provins, seine Gönner. Halle, 1902.
37596.88 Baker, Alfred T. Die versifizierte Übersetzung der Französischen Bibel. Cambridge, 1897.
37596.88.3 Burckhardt, A. Über den Lothringer Reimpsalter. Inaug. Diss. Halle, 1890.
37596.89 Kutschera, Oscarus. Le manuscrit des sermons français de Saint Bernard. Halis, 1878.
37596.90 Schauer, Karl. Textkritische Beiträge zu den coutumes du Beauvaisis des Philippe de Beaumanoir. Halle, 1890.
37596.91 Irmer, Eugen. Die altfranzösische Bearbeitung der Formula honestae vitae des Martin von Braga. Halle, 1890.
37596.92 Steuer, Wilhelm. Die altfranzösische Histoire de Joseph; kritischerText. Erlangen, 1902.
37596.92.2 Steuer, Wilhelm. Die altfranzösische Histoire de Joseph; kritischer Text. Erlangen, 1903.
37596.92.6 Sass, Ernst. L'estoire Joseph. Halle, 1906.
37596.92.7 Sass, Ernst. L'estoire Joseph. Dresden, 1906.
37596.93 Werth, Hermann. Über die ältesten französischen Übersetzungen mittelalterlicher Jagd- (Beiz-) Lehrbücher. Inaug. Diss. Göttingen, 1888.
37596.93.5 Werth, Hermann. Altfranzösische Jagdlehrbücher. Halle, 1889.
37596.94 Wiese, Leo. Die Lieder des Blondel de Nesle. Dresden, 1904.
37596.94.1 Lavis, G. Les chansons de Blondel de Nesle. Liège, 1970?
37596.94.2 Blondel de Néele. Oeuvres. Reims, 1862.
37596.95 Lavesne, Douin de. Trubert, altfranzösischer Schelmenroman. Dresden, 1904.
37596.97 Restori, A. La gaite de la Tor. Messina, 1904.
37596.98 Schmidt, A. La vie saint Franchois. Diss. Viersen, 1905.
37596.99 Schmidt, A. La vie saint Franchois. Diss. Leipzig, 1905.
Htn 37596.100* Richelet, Charles J. Du baro mors et vis. Conte du XIIe siècle. Paris, 1832.
37596.101 Craon, Pierre de. Chansons. Caen, 1843.
37596.102 Ravenel, Florence L. La vie seint Edmund le Rei. Philadelphia, 1906.
37596.102.3 Denis Piramus. La vie seint Edmund le Rei. Philadelphia, 1906.
37596.102.5 Haxo, Henry E. Denis Piramus; La vie seint Edmunt. Chicago, 1915.
37596.103 Metcke, Albert. Die Lieder des altfranzösischen Lyrikers Gille le Vinier. Halle, 1906.
37596.103.100 Guillaume Le Vinier. Les poésies de Guillaume Le Vinier. Paris, 1970.

37596 Individual authors, etc. - Before 1300 - Langue d'oeil (Northern French - Other known authors, etc. - cont.

37596.104 Drivernoy, E. Le tournoi de Chauvenoy en 1285. Paris, 1905.
37596.105 McKibben, G.F. The eructavit; an old French poem. Baltimore, 1907.
37596.106 Gastoué, A. Le drame liturgique les vierges sages et folles. Paris, 1906.
37596.106.5 Sponsus. Le Sponsus. 1. éd. Paris, 1951.
37596.106.6 Sponsus. Sponsus; dramma delle vergini prudenti e delle vergini stolte. Milano, 1965.
37596.106.10 Sletsjoe, Leif. Tre middelalderspill. Oslo, 1961.
37596.107 Långfors, Artur. Li regres nostre dame. Paris, 1907.
37596.107.3 Reiche, Paul. Beiträge zu Artur Långfors Ausgabe des Regret Notre Dame. Inaug. Diss. Berlin, 1909.
37596.107.5 Huon le Roi de Cambrai. Huon le Roi de Cambrai. Paris, 1913.
37596.107.7 Huon le Roi de Cambrai. Oeuvres. Paris, 1925.
Htn 37596.108* Hue Archevesque. Les dits de Hue Archevesque. Paris, 1885.
37596.108.2 Hue Archevesque. Les dits de Hue Archevesque. Rouen, 1885.
37596.109 Hård af Segerstad, Kerstin. Quelques commentaires sur la plus ancienne chanson d'états française, Le livre des Manièrs. Uppsala, 1906.
37596.109.5 Hård af Segerstad, Kerstin. Sur les dieux des Sarrasins dans les chansons de geste du XIIe siècle. Uppsala, 1926.
37596.111A Freine, Simund de. Les oeuvres. Paris, 1909.
37596.111B Freine, Simund de. Les oeuvres. Paris, 1909.
37596.112 Jenkins, T.A. Eructairt. Dresden, 1909.
37596.113 Faral, E. Mimes français du XIIIe siècle. Paris, 1910.
37596.114 Aldebrandin de Sienne. Le régime du corps. Paris, 1911.
37596.115 Bible. Anglo-Norman. O.T. Samuel. Li quatre livre des Reis. Dresden, 1911.
37596.116 Courtois d'Arras jeu du XIIIe siècle. Paris, 1911.
37596.117 Roques, M. Le garçon et l'aveugle. Paris, 1911.
37596.117.5 Le Garçon et L'Aveugle. Le garcon et l'aveugle, jeu du XIIIe siècle. 2. éd. Paris, 1921.
37596.118 Guesnon, A. La bataille d'enfer et de paradise. Paris, 1909.
37596.119A Richier. La vie de S. Remi, poème. London, 1912.
37596.119B Richier. La vie de S. Remi, poème. London, 1912.
37596.120 Långfors, Artur. Huon le Roi, Le vair palefroi. Paris, 1912.
37596.120.5 Huon le Roi de Cambrai, 13th cent. Huon le Roi, Le vair palefroi. 2. éd. Paris, 1921.
37596.121 Zipperling, C. Das altfranzösische Fablel du Vilain Mire. Halle, 1912.
37596.122 Gautier de Dargies. Chansons et descorts. Paris, 1912.
37596.123 Guiot de Provins. Les oeuvres de Guiot de Provins. Manchester, 1915.
37596.124 Conon de Béthune. Chansons. Helsingfors, 1891.
37596.124.5A Conon de Béthune. Chansons. Paris, 1921.
37596.124.5B Conon de Béthune. Chansons. Paris, 1921.
37596.125 Bible. O.T. Psalms (French-old). Oxonii, 1860.
37596.126A Meyer, Paul. Le chansonnier français de Saint Germain-des-Près. Tom.1. Paris, 1892.
37596.126B Meyer, Paul. Le chansonnier français de Saint Germain-des-Près. Tom.1. Paris, 1892.
37596.127A Bible. N.T. Gospels Nicodemus. Trois versions rimées de l'evangile Nicodime. Paris, 1885.
37596.127B Bible. N.T. Gospels Nicodemus. Trois versions rimées de l'evangile Nicodime. Paris, 1885.
37596.128 Gutbier, J. Bruchstack einer lateinischen mit französischen Sätzen. Halle, 1908.
37596.130 LeCompte, I.C. The sources of the Anglo-French comentary on the proverbs of Solomon. Collegeville, Pa., 1906.
37596.134.30 Jean Renart. Versions inédites de la chanson de Jean Renaud. Paris, 1882.
37596.135A Jean Renart. Lai de l'ombre. Paris, 1913.
37596.135B Jean Renart. Lai de l'ombre. Paris, 1913.
37596.135.10A Jean Renart. Galeran de Bretagne. Paris, 1925.
37596.135.10B Jean Renart. Galeran de Bretagne. Paris, 1925.
37596.135.12 Dubs, Ingeborg. Galeran de Bretagne. Bern, 1949.
37596.135.15 Renart, Jean. Le roman de l'écoufle. Paris, 1925.
37596.135.30 Bédier, Joseph. La tradition manuscrite du Lai de l'ombre. Paris, 1929.
37596.135.40 Lejeune-Dehousse, R. L'oeuvre de Jean Renart. Liége, 1935.
37596.136.5A Renauld de Beaujeu. Le lai d'Ignaurès ou lai du prisonnier. Paris, 1832.
37596.136.5B Renauld de Beaujeu. Le lai d'Ignaurès ou lai du prisonnier. Paris, 1832.
37596.136.15 Renauld de Beaujeu. Le lai d'Ignaurès ou lai du prisonnier. Bruxelles, 1938.
37596.136.20 Renauld de Beaujeu. Les amours de Frêne et Galeran. Paris, 1920.
37596.136.25 Jean Renart. Les amours de Frêne et Galeran. Paris, 1929.
37596.138 Li romans dou lis. N.Y., 1915.
37596.140 Pamphlet box. Histoire de Guillaume le Marichal.
37596.142 Ilvonen, Eero. Parodies de thèmes pieux dans la poésie française du moyen âge. Thèse. Helsingfors, 1914.
37596.143 Gast, Erich. Die beidenRedaktionen des "Evangile de l'enfence". Greifswald, 1909.
37596.144 Wallheinke, Arndt. Die "Vers de le mort" von Robert le Clerc. Inaug. Diss. Weida, 1911.
37596.145 Monaci, E. Francese antico. Roma, 1902.
37596.146 Schmidt, R. Die Lieder des Andrieu contredit d'Arras. Inaug. Diss. Halle, 1903.
37596.147 Müller, Herbert. Sprachliche Untersuchung der Apokalypse der Kerr-Handschrift. Inaug. Diss. Münster, 1912.
37596.148 Danne, F. Das altfranzösische Ebrulfsleben. Inaug. Diss. Erlangen, 1912.
37596.149 Rose, H. Über die Metrik der Chronik Fantosmès. Bonn, 1880.
37596.150 Spanke, J. Zwei altfranzösische Minnesinger. Inaug. Diss. Leipzig, 1907.
37596.151 Richter, Max. Die Lieder des altfranzösischen Lyrikers Jehan de Nurvile. Halle, 1904.
37596.152 Schmidt, J. Le jugement d'amours. Inaug. Diss. Borna, 1913.
37596.153 Steppuhn, A. Das Fabel vom Prestre comporte und seine Versionen. Inaug. Diss. Königsburg, 1913.
37596.154 Schwan, E. Philippe de Rimi...und seine Werke. Bonn, 1880.
37596.155 Suchier, W. Über das altfranzösische Gedicht von der Zerstörung Jerusalems. Inaug. Diss. Halle, 1899.

Classified Listing

37596 Individual authors, etc. - Before 1300 - Langue d'oeil (Northern French - Other known authors, etc. - cont.

37596.160 L'ordene de chevalerie; an old French poem. Thesis. Chicago, 1918.
37596.160.2 Ordene de chevalerie. L'ordene de chevalerie; an old French poem. Norman, 1919.
37596.166 Le Duc de Danmartin, Herbert. Folque de Candie. Dresden, 1909-36. 3v.
37596.166.2 Le Duc de Danmartin, Herbert. Le roman de Foulque de Candie. Reims, 1860.
37596.168 Raoul de Soissons. Lieder. Herausgegeben von Emil Winkler. Halle, 1914.
37596.169 Carlé, Theodor. Der altfranzösische Dichter Garnier von Pont-Sainte-Maxence und seine Zeit. Münster, 1914.
37596.170 Jodoc, Saint. La vie Saint Joce; eine altfranzösische Heiligenlegende. Greifswald, 1915.
37596.171 Paris. Bibliothèque nationale. Eine altfranzösische Bearbeitung biblischer Stoffe. Halle, 1916.
37596.174 Meyer, Paul. Notice sur le manuscrit de la bibliothèque nationale. Paris, 1895.
37596.175 Aitken, Marion Y.H. Étude sur le Miroir...de Robert de Gretham. Thèse. Paris, 1922.
37596.181A Le siège de Barbastre. Paris, 1926.
37596.181B Le siège de Barbastre. Paris, 1926.
37596.190 Pettersen, Holger. La vie de saint Eustàche. Paris, 1928.
37596.195 Moniot, Jean. Poésies inédites, publiées par Gaston Raynaud. Nogent-le-Rotrou, 1882.
37596.198 Bernart Marti, Robert. Les poésies de Bernart Marti. Paris, 1929.
37596.203 Guiot de Dijon. Les chansons attribuées à Guiot de Dijon et Jocelin. Paris, 1928.
37596.203.5 Guiot de Dijon. Critical edition of poems attributed to Guiot de Dijon and Jocelin de Dijon. Paris, 1928.
37596.204 Göring, Werner. Untersuchung der Sprache des Roman de silence von Heldris de Cornualle. Inaug. Diss. Halle, 1930.
37596.205 Jean de la Chapele de Bois. Le conte Dou Barril. New Haven, 1932.
37596.210 Trois aveugles de compiègne. Cortrebarbe. Paris, 1932.
37596.215 Aimon de Varennes. Florimont. Göttingen, 1932.
37596.220 Des Grantz geanz; an Anglo-Norman poem. Oxford, 1937.
37596.235 Faits Des Romains. Li fet des Romains compilé ensemble de Saluste et de Suetoine et de Lucan. Paris, 1935-38. 2v.
37596.236.10 Flutre, Fernand. Li fait des Romains dans les litteratures française et italienne du XIIIe au XVIe siècle. Thèse. Paris, 1932.
37596.236.15 Flutre, Fernand. Les manuscrits des faits des Romains. Thèse. Paris, 1932.
37596.240 Hugues de Berzy. La "Bible" au seigneur de Berzé. Paris, 1938.
37596.240.5 Hugues de Berzy. La "Bible" au seigneur de Berzé. Thèse. Paris, 1938.
37596.243 Courtois d'Arras. Courtois d'Arras, jeu du XIIIe siècle. Paris, 1922.
37596.245 Nardin, Pierre. Lexique compare des fabliaux Jean Bedel. Paris, 1942.
37596.247 Floriant et Florete. Florian et Florete. Ann Arbor, 1947.
37596.247.2 Floriant et Florete. Floriant and Florete. Edinburgh, 1873.
37596.249 Edward, the Confessor, King of England, Saint. Legend. La vie d'Edouard le confesseur. Uppsala, 1948.
37596.251 Agnès de Navarre. Champagne. Poésies. Paris, 1856.
37596.253 Dialogue de Saint Julien et son disciple. Dialogue de saint Julien et son disciple. Oxford, 1949.
37596.255 Ellebaut. Anticlaudien. Washington, 1944.
37596.260 Smeets, Jean Robert. La chevalerie de Judas Macabé. Assen, 1955.
37596.272 Avalle, d'Arco Silvio. Cultura e lingua francese delle origini nella passion di Clermont-Ferrand. Milano, 1962.
37596.274 Simon de Pouille, chanson de geste. Genève, 1968.
37596.276 Alard de Cambrai. Le livre de philosophie et de moralité d'Alard de Cambrai. Paris, 1970.
37596.278 Ver de Couloigne. Li ver de Couloigne, Du bon ange et du mauves. 1. Aufl. München, 1968.

37597 Individual authors, etc. - Before 1300 - Langue d'oeil (Northern French - Other known authors, etc.

37597.1 Lorris, Guillaume de. Le rommánt de la rose. Paris, 1878.
Htn 37597.2* Lorris, Guillaume de. Le rommant de la rose. Paris, 150-.
Htn 37597.2.5* Lorris, Guillaume de. Cest le romant de la rose. Paris, 1500.
37597.3A Lorris, Guillaume de. Le romant de la rose. Paris, 1814. 4v.
37597.3B Lorris, Guillaume de. Le romant de la rose. Paris, 1814. 4v.
37597.3C Lorris, Guillaume de. Le romant de la rose. Paris, 1814. 4v.
37597.3.5A Lorris, Guillaume de. Le roman de la rose. Paris, 1798-99. 5v.
37597.3.5B Lorris, Guillaume de. Le roman de la rose. v.1-3,5. Paris, 1798-99. 4v.
37597.5A Lorris, Guillaume de. Le roman de la rose. Paris, 1864. 2v.
37597.5B Lorris, Guillaume de. Le roman de la rose. Paris, 1864. 2v.
37597.5C Lorris, Guillaume de. Le roman de la rose. Paris, 1864. 2v.
37597.5D Lorris, Guillaume de. Le roman de la rose. Paris, 1864. 2v.
37597.5E Lorris, Guillaume de. Le roman de la rose. Paris, 1864. 2v.
37597.5.10 Lorris, Guillaume de. Le roman de la rose. Paris, 1928.
37597.5.15 Lorris, Guillaume de. Le roman de la rose. Paris, 1933.
37597.6 Püschell, D. Li romanz de la rose. Berlin, 1872.
37597.6.3 Doinel, Jules. Guy Fabi et Guillaume Rebrachien. Orléans, 1887.
37597.7 Marteau, Pierre. Le roman de la rose. Orléans, 1878. 5v.
37597.8 Lorris, Guillaume de. Die Rose. Gravenhage, 1868.
37597.8.5 Lorris, Guillaume de. De fragmenten van de tweede rose. Zwolle, 1958.
37597.9 Lorris, Guillaume de. Le roman de la rose. Amsterdam, 1735. 3v.
37597.9.7A Lorris, Guillaume de. The romance of the rose. London, 1900. 3v.
37597.9.7B Lorris, Guillaume de. The romance of the rose. London, 1900. 4v.

37597 Individual authors, etc. - Before 1300 - Langue d'oeil (Northern French - Other known authors, etc. - cont.

37597.9.9A Lorris, Guillaume de. Le roman de la rose. Paris, 1914-24. 5v.
37597.9.9B Lorris, Guillaume de. Le roman de la rose. Paris, 1914-24. 5v.
37597.9.9C Lorris, Guillaume de. Le roman de la rose. Paris, 1914-24. 5v.
37597.9.9D Lorris, Guillaume de. Le roman de la rose. v.1,2,5. Paris, 1914-24. 3v.
37597.9.12 Lorris, Guillaume de. Le roman de la rose. Paris, 1928.
37597.9.15F Lorris, Guillaume de. Der Roman von der Rose. Wien, 1921.
37597.9.16 Lorris, Guillaume de. Der Rosenroman. Berlin, 1956.
37597.9.16.5 Lorris, Guillaume de. Der Rosenroman. Tübingen, 1966.
37597.9.17 Lorris, Guillaume de. The romaunt of the rose. London, 1911.
37597.9.18 Lorris, Guillaume de. The romance of the rose. N.Y., 1962.
37597.9.18.5 Lorris, Guillaume de. Roman de la rose. Paris, 1965. 3v.
37597.9.20 Lorris, Guillaume de. Le roman de la rose. 8. éd. Paris, 1949.
37597.9.23 Lorris, Guillaume de. Le roman de la rose. Milano, 1954-57. 2v.
37597.9.25 Lorris, Guillaume de. The romaunt of the rose and Le roman de la rose. Oxford, 1967.
37597.9.30 Lorris, Guillaume de. The romance of the rose. Princeton, 1971.
37597.10 Lorris, Guillaume de. Étude historique et biographique. Photoreproduction. Orléans, 1881.
37597.10.2 Guillon, Félix. Jean Clopinel dit de meung. Le roman de la rose. Photoreproduction. Paris, 1903.
37597.10.5 Pamphlet box. Romance of the rose.
37597.10.7 Bourdillon, F.W. The early editions of the roman de la rose. London, 1906.
37597.10.8 Bourdillon, F.W. A Vérard fragment of the roman de la rose. London, 1913.
37597.10.9 Ettmayer, Karl R. Der Rosenroman. Heidelberg, 1919.
37597.10.11 Högberg, Paul. Une édition rarissime du Roman de la rose. n.p., 1921.
37597.10.15 Fleming, John V. The roman de la rose. Princeton, 1969.
37597.11 Körting, Gustav. Über die Quellen des Roman de rose. Leipzig, 1867.
37597.11.5 Kupka, Paul. Zur Chronologie und Genesis des Roman de la rose. Gardelegen, n.d.
37597.11.6 Lorenz, F.W. Der Stil in Maistre Wace's Roman de Rou. Leipzig, 1885.
37597.11.7 Hormel, H. Untersuchung über die Chronique Ascendante. Inaug. Diss. Marburg, 1880.
37597.11.8 Langlois, E. Les manuscrits du roman de la rose. Lille, 1910.
37597.11.10 Thuasne, Louis. Le roman de la rose. Paris, 1929.
37597.12 Christine de Pizan. Les epistres sur le roman de la rose. Neuburg, 1888.
37597.12.5 Ward, C.F. Epistles on romance of the rose. Chicago, 1911.
37597.12.7 Pluquet, Frédéric. Notice sur la vie et les écrits de Robert Wace. Rouen, 1824.
37597.12.15 Garvey, C. The syntax of the declinable words in the roman de la rose. Washington, 1936.
37597.12.20 Langlois, Ernest. Origines et sources du roman de la rose. Photoreproduction. Paris, 1891.
37597.12.25 Cohen, G. Le roman de la rose. Paris, 1933.
37597.12.30 Paré, Gérard. Les idées et les lettres au XIIIe siècle. Montréal, 1947.
37597.12.35 Müller, Franz Walter. Der Rosenroman und der lateinische Averroismus des 13. Jahrhunderts. Frankfurt, 1947.
37597.14 Stehlich, F. Messire Thibaut, le romanz de la poire. Halle, 1881.
37597.14.2 Abrahams, L. De Roberti Wacii Carmine quod inecribitur Brutus. Hafinae, 1828.
37597.15 Wace, Maistre. Roman de Brutus. Rouen, 1836-38. 4v.
37597.15.2 Wace, Maistre. Le roman de Brut. Rouen, 1836.
37597.15.6 Ulrich, Alfred. Über das Verhältnis von Wace's Roman. Erlangen, 1908.
37597.16.10 Zetsche, A.W. Über den I. Teil der Bearbeitung des "Roman de Brut" des Wace durch Robert Mannyng of Brunne. Inaug. Diss. Reudnitz, 1887.
37597.16.25 Pelan, Margaret. L'influence du Brut de Wace. Paris, 1931.
37597.16.30 Wace, Maistre. La partie arthurienne du Roman de Brut. Paris, 1962.
37597.17 Andersen, Hugo. Maistre Wace's Roman de rou. Heilbronn, 1877-79. 3v.
37597.17.9F Wace, Maistre. The conquest of England from poem of the roman de rou. London, 1860.
37597.17.20 Wace, Maistre. La vie de Sainte Marguerite. Paris, 1932.
37597.18 Bröndsted, P.O. Bidrag til den danske historie. Kjobenhavn, 1817.
37597.19 Kloppe, Gustav A. Recherches sur le dialecte de Guace (Wace). Magdeburg, 1853.
37597.19.9 Schneider, Oskar. Die Verbalformen bei Wace. Halle, 1908.
37597.20 Raynouard, Franc J. Observations sur le roman de rose. Rouen, 1829.
37597.21 Broberg, S. Romanen om rosen. Odense, 1869.
37597.22 Fuhrken, G.E. De David li prophecie. Halle, 1895.
37597.22.5 Hawkins, R.L. The manuscripts of the roman de la rose in the libraries of Harvard and Yale Universities. n.p., 1928.
37597.23 Pamphlet box. French literature, 12th and 13th centuries. Collections. Miscellaneous pamphlet.
37597.24 Wace, Maistre. L'etablisement de la fête de la conception. Caen, 1842.
37597.24.10 Wace, Maistre. The conception Nostre Dame of Wace. Menasha, 1933.
37597.24.15 Keller, H.E. Étude descriptive sur le vocabulaire de Wace. Diss. Berlin, 1953.
37597.26A Wace, Maistre. Saint Nicholas. Bonn, 185-.
37597.26B Wace, Maistre. Saint Nicholas. Bonn, 185-.
37597.26.20 Wace, Maistre. Life of Saint Nicholas. Thesis. Philadelphia, n.d.
37597.26.50 Philpot, J.H. Maistre Wace. London, 1925.
37597.26.60 Bodel, Jehan. Jean Bodel, trouvère artésien du XIIIe siècle. Paris, 1925.
37597.26.62 Bodel, Jehan. Le jeu de Saint Nicolas. Oxford, 1958.
37597.26.63 Bodel, Jehan. Le jeu de Saint Nicolas. Bruxelles, 1962.
37597.26.63.5 Bodel, Jehan. Le jeu de saint Nicolas. 2. éd. Bruxelles, 1965.

37597 Individual authors, etc. - Before 1300 - Langue d'oeil (Northern French - Other known authors, etc. - cont.

37597.26.65 Foulon, Charles. L'oeuvre de Jean Bodel. Rennes, 1958.
37597.26.70 Bodel, Jehan. Les fabliaux de Jean Bodel. Dakar, 1959.
37597.26.75 Ruelle, Pierre. Les congés d'Arras: Jean Bodel. 1. éd. Bruxelles, 1965.
37597.26.80 Langlade, Émile. Jehan Bodel. Paris, 1909.
37597.26.85 Rohnström, Johan Otto. Étude sur Jehan Bodel. Thèse. Uppsala, 1900.
37597.27 Weydig, Otto. Beiträge zur Geschichte des Mirakelspiels. Inaug. Diss. Erfurt, 1910.
37597.28 Amiens, Gerard von. Der Roman von Escanor. Tübingen, 1886.
37597.28.6 Römermann, A. Über das Verhältnis der Handschrift D von Girard d'Amiens'Cheval de fust. Greifswald, 1903.
37597.28.7 Pamphlet box. Amiens, Girard von.
37597.29 Péan Gatineau. Vie de Saint Martin. Tours, 186-.
37597.29.2 Péan Gatineau. Leben und Wunderthaten des Heiligen Martin. Tübingen, 1896.
37597.29.5 Péan Gatineau. Das altfranzösische Martinsleben. Helsingfors, 1899.
37597.29.9 Göderhjehn, T. Die Sprache in dem altfranzösischen Martinsleben des Péan Gatineau aus Tours. Helsingfors, 1906.
37597.30 Der münchener Brutus. Halle, 1877.
37597.31 Seeger, Hermann. Über die Sprache des Guillaume le Clerc de Normandie. Halle, 1888.
37597.32.5 Muset, Colin. Les chansons. Paris, 1912.
37597.32.10 Muset, Colin. Les chansons de Colin Muset. 2. éd. Paris, 1938.
37597.33A Jean de Condé. Gedichte. Stuttgart, 1860.
37597.33B Jean de Condé. Gedichte. Stuttgart, 1860.
37597.33.5 Jean de Condé. La messe des oiseaux et le Dit des jacobins et des fremeneurs. Paris, 1970.
37597.33.9 Krause, A. Bemerkungen zu den Gedichten des Bendouin und des Jean de Condé. Berlin, 1890.
37597.33.40 Pamphlet box. Conde, Jean de.
Htn 37597.34* Meun, Jehan de. Le plaisant jeu du dodechediron de fortune. Lyon, 1581.
37597.34.15 Ralph, D.M. Jean de Meun, the Voltaire of the middle ages. Urbana, 1940.
37597.35 L'urban cortese. Pisa, 1895.
37597.36A Adenès li rois. Li roumans de Cléomodès. Brussels, 1865.
37597.36B Adenès li rois. Li roumans de Cléomodès. Brussels, 1865. 2v.
37597.37 Keidel, George C. Romance and other studies. No.1: Evangile aux femmes; an old French satire on women. Diss. Baltimore, 1895.
37597.38 Keidel, George C. Romance and other studies. No.1: Evangile aux femmes; an old French satire on women. Diss. Baltimore, 1895.
37597.39 Wachter, Hermann. Der Springer unserer lieben Frau. Erlangen, 1899.
37597.42 Roman des romans. Deux poèmes moraux anglo-français. Le roman des romans et le sermon de vers. Paris, 1922.
37597.42.5 Roman des romans. Le roman des romans. Princeton, 1923.
37597.42.9 Gros, Gaston. L'amour dans le roman de la rose. Paris, 1925.
37597.42.20A Gunn, A.M.F. The mirror of love. Lubbock, Texas, 1952.
37597.42.20B Gunn, A.M.F. The mirror of love. Lubbock, Texas, 1952.
37597.43.5 La bataille de Caresme et de Charnage. Paris, 1933.
37597.44 Henry, Albert. L'oeuvre lyrique d'Henri III, duc de Brabant. Brugge, 1948.
37597.45 Guger, F.E. Romance in the making. N.Y., 1954.
37597.46 Paré, G.M. Le roman de la rose et la scolastique courtoise. Paris, 1941.
37597.47 Narcisus; poème du XIIe siècle. Paris, 1964.
37597.50 Avalle, d'Arco Silvio. Alle origini della letteratura francese i giuramenti di Strasburgo e la sequenza di Santa Eulalia. Torino, 1966.
37597.52 Poème du XIIIme siècle en l'honneur de la vierge. Mons, 1936.

37598 Individual authors, etc. - Before 1300 - Langue d'oeil (Northern French - Satirical works

37598.5A Jeanroy, Alfred. Chansons satiriques et bachiques du XIIIe siècle. Paris, 1921.
37598.5B Jeanroy, Alfred. Chansons satiriques et bachiques du XIIIe siècle. Paris, 1921.
37598.10 Livingstone, C.H. Le jongleur Gautier le leu. Cambridge, 1951.
37598.15 Chastie-musart. Il poemetto Chastie-musart della Vaticana. Messina, 1953.
37598.15.5 Chastie-musart. Chastie-musart. Roma, 1970.

38511 Individual authors, etc. - 1300-1499 - Folios [Discontinued]

38511.1 Les Sires de Gavre. Histoire des seigneurs de Gavres. Bruxelles, 1845.
38511.2 René I, d'Anjou, King of Naples. Oeuvres complètes. Angers, 1845. 4v.
38511.3 René I, d'Anjou, King of Naples. Oeuvres choisies. Angers, 1848. 2v.
38511.3.2F René I, d'Anjou, King of Naples. Oeuvres choisies. v.1-2. Paris, 1849.
38511.4 Wailly, Natalis de. Mémoire sur Geffroi de Paris. Paris, 1849.
Htn 38511.5* Moralité des Blasphemateurs de Dieu. Paris, 1831.
Htn 38511.6* Moralité de la Vendition de Joseph. Paris, 1835.
Htn 38511.6.5* Moralité de Mundus, Caro, Demonia. Paris, 1827.
Htn 38511.7* Moralité de Mundus, Caro, Demonia. Paris, 1838.
38511.8 Milet, Jacques. L'istoire de la destruction de Troye la grant. Marburg, 1883.
38511.9 Li romans de Bauduin de Sebourc (XIVe siècle). Valenciennes, 1841. 2v.
38511.10 Le livre des Mestiers. Paris, 1875.
38511.10.5 Le livre des Mestiers. pt.1-6. Brugea, 1931.
38511.10.9 Roy, Emile. Le mystère de la passion en France du XIVe au XVIe siècle. Paris, 1904.
38511.11 Greban, Arnoul. Le mystère de la Passion. Paris, 1878.
Htn 38511.11.1.5* Greban, Arnoul. Le mystère de la nativité de Nostre Saulveur Jhesu Christ. Paris, 1937.
38511.11.2 Sorel, Alexandre. Notice sur Arnoul et Simon Greban. Compiègne, 1875.
38511.11.5 Dannenberger, Otto. Bilder des bürgerlich hauslichen Lebens in Frankreich. Mannheim, 1914.
38511.12 Coke, John. Le débat des hérauts d'armes. Paris, 1877.

38511 Individual authors, etc. - 1300-1499 - Folios [Discontinued] - cont.

38511.12.2 Pyne, H. England and France in the 15th century. "The debate between the heralds of France and England." London, 1870.
38511.13 DuFresne de Beaucourt, G. Les Chartier. Recherches sur Guillaume, Alain et Jean Chartier. Caen, 1869.
38511.14 Deschampes, Eustache. Poésies morales. Paris, 1832.
38511.14.2 Le combat de trente Bretons contre trente Anglois. Paris, 1827.
38511.16A Mystère de Saint Crespin. Paris, 1836.
38511.16B Mystère de Saint Crespin. Paris, 1836.
NEDL 38511.18A Froissart, Jean. Oeuvres. v.2-3. Bruxelles, 1870-72. 2v.
NEDL 38511.18B Froissart, Jean. Oeuvres. v.1. Bruxelles, 1870-72.
38511.18.20 Pamphlet box. Jean Froissart.
38511.19 Paris, Paulin. Nouvelles recherches sur la vie de Froissart. Paris, 1860.
Htn 38511.20* Abel, Charles. Le mystère de Clement. Metz, 1861.
38511.21 Joret, Jean. La jardrin salutaire. Paris, 1841.
Htn 38511.22* Chandos, the herald. Le prince noir. London, 1883.
38511.22.2 Chandos, the herald. Le prince noir. London, 1883.
38511.22.5 Chandos, the herald. Life of the black prince. Oxford, 1910.
38511.22.9 Gollancz, Israel. Some observations on a manuscript of the life and feats of arms of Edward, prince of Wales. London, 1921.
38511.23 Bullrich, G. Über Charles d'Orléans. Berlin, 1893.
38511.23.5 Champion, Pierre. Charles d'Orléans joueur d'echecs. Paris, 1908.
38511.24 Keller, Adelbert von. Miracle de Notre Dame. Tübingen, 1865.
38511.25A Pra, Siboud. Le mystère des trois doms joué à Romans en MDIX. Lyon, 1887.
38511.25B Pra, Siboud. Le mystère des trois doms joué à Romans en MDIX. Lyon, 1887.
38511.26 Chatelain, H. Le mistere de Saint Quentin. St. Quentin, 1907.
38511.26.5 Chatelain, H. Le mistere de Saint Quentin. St. Quentin, 1909.
38511.27 Pathelin. Maistre Pierre Patelin. Paris, 1854.
38511.29 Parmentier, J. Le henno de Reuchlin et la farce de Maistre Pathelin. Paris, 1884.
38511.30 Débat de l'ame et du corps. Basel, 1908.
38511.31 Beauvau, Louis de. Le pas d'armes de la Bergère. 2e éd. Paris, 1835.
38511.33 Ovidius. Phaetonfabel im Ovide moralise. Bern, 1897.
38511.33.5 Philippe de Vitry. Les oeuvres de Philippe de Vitry. Reims, 1850.
38511.34 Engels, Joseph. Études sur l'Ovide moralisé. Groningen, 1945.
38511.35 Oresme, N. Traictie de la première invention des monnoies. Paris, 1864.
38511.41A Le jardin de plaisance. Paris, 1910-25. 2v.
38511.41B Le jardin de plaisance. Paris, 1910-25. 2v.

38512 Individual authors, etc. - 1300-1499 - 14th century works

38512.2 Bertoni, G. Liriche di Oton de Grandson. Genève, 1932.
38512.2.5 Braddy, Haldeen. Chaucer and the French poet Graunson. Baton Rouge, La., 1947.
38512.2.10 Igly, France. Oton de Grandson. Travers, 1969.
38512.3 Auguis, Pierre René. Les poets français...jusqu'à Malherbe. Paris, 1824. 6v.
Htn 38512.5* Le bibliophile Troyen. Troyes, 1851.
38512.6 Costello, Louisa S. Specimens of the early poetry of France. London, 1835.
38512.6.2 Costello, Louisa S. Specimens of the early poetry of France. London, 1835.
38512.7 Scheler, Auguste. Notice et extraits de deux manuscrits français. Bruxelles, 1867.
Htn 38512.8F* Saint-Pierre. Novella e poesie francesi inedite o rarissime del secolo XIV. Firenze, 1888.
38512.9 Meunier, Francis. Essai sur Nicole Oresme. Paris, 1857.
38512.10 Wailly, Natalis de. Notice sur Guillaume Guiart. n.p., n.d.
38512.10.50 Les chroniqueurs français: Villehardouin, Froissart, Joinville, Commines. Paris, 1912.
38512.11A Froissart, Jean. Méliador. Paris, 1895. 3v.
38512.11B Froissart, Jean. Méliador. Paris, 1895. 3v.
38512.11.5 Froissart, Jean. L'espinette amoureuse. Paris, 1963.
38512.12 La Curne de St. Palaye. Memoirs of Froissart. London, 1801.
38512.13A Darmesteter, Mary. Froissart. Paris, 1894.
38512.13B Darmesteter, Mary. Froissart. Paris, 1894.
38512.13.2 Darmesteter, Mary. Froissart. N.Y., 1895.
NEDL 38512.14 Kervyn de Lettenhove. Froissart. Étude littéraire. Brussels, 1857. 2v.
38512.15 Ebering, Emil. Syntaktische Studien zu Froissart. Halle, 1881.
38512.16 Riese, Julius. Recherches sur l'usage syntaxique de Froissart. Halle, 1880.
38512.17 Mann, G. Die Sprache Froissarts auf Grund seiner Gedichte. Halle, 1898.
38512.17.9 Blume, F. Metrik Froissarts. Greifswald, 1889.
38512.17.15 Coulton, G.G. The chronicler of European chivalry. (Froissart). London, 1930.
38512.17.20A Sears, F.S. Froissart, chronicler and poet. London, 1930.
38512.17.20B Sears, F.S. Froissart, chronicler and poet. London, 1930.
38512.17.25 Bekkers, F.H.H.A. Étude sur l'emploi que Froissart fait de la préposition. Amsterdam, 1931.
38512.17.30 Schreijir, Willem. Étude sur la négation dans les chroniques de Froissart. Amsterdam, 1931.
38512.17.35 Senonnes. Jean Froissart, ne vers l'an 1337; mort vers 1410. Paris? 1838?
38512.17.40 Wilmatte, M. Froissart. Bruxelles, 1948.
38512.18A Lescurel, Jehannot de. Chansons, ballades. Paris, 1855.
38512.18B Lescurel, Jehannot de. Chansons, ballades. Paris, 1855.
38512.18C Lescurel, Jehannot de. Chansons, ballades. Paris, 1855.
38512.20 Collin de Plancy, Jacques. Mémoires d'un vilain. Paris, 1820.
38512.22A Chassant, Alphonse. L'advocacie Notre Dame. Paris, 1855.
38512.22B Chassant, Alphonse. L'advocacie Notre Dame. Paris, 1855.
38512.24A Chavannes, Félix. Le mireour du monde. Lausanne, 1845.
38512.24B Chavannes, Félix. Le mireour du monde. Lausanne, 1845.
38512.25A De Queux de St. Hilaire. Livre des cent ballades. Paris, 1868.
38512.25B De Queux de St. Hilaire. Livre des cent ballades. Paris, 1868.

38512 Individual authors, etc. - 1300-1499 - 14th century works - cont.

38512.25.2 De Queux de St. Hilaire. Livre des cent ballades. Paris, 1874.
38512.26A Jean le Seneschal. Les cent ballades. Poème du XIVe siècle. Paris, 1905.
38512.26B Jean le Seneschal. Les cent ballades. Poème du XIVe siècle. Paris, 1905.
38512.26C Jean le Seneschal. Les cent ballades. Poème du XIVe siècle. Paris, 1905.
Htn 38512.27* Tross, Edwin. Cent cinq rondeaux d'amour. Paris, 1863.
Htn 38512.29* Malo, Charles. Livre d'amour. Paris, 1821.
38512.31 Kehrmann, Alexander. Die deutsche Übersetzung der Novellen des Ritters vom Turn. Inaug. Diss. Marburg, 1905.
38512.32 La Tour-Landry, Geoffrey de. Livre. Paris, 1854.
38512.32.10 La Tour-Landry, Geoffrey de. The book of thenseygnementes and techynge. London, 1902.
38512.32.20 La Tour-Landry, Geoffrey de. The book of the knight of La Tour-Landry. London, 1930?
38512.33 Montaiglon, Anatole de. Livre du chevalier de La Tour-Landry. Paris, 1854.
38512.33.5 La Tour-Landry, Geoffrey de. Der Ritter vom Turn von den Exempeln der Gotsforcht vñ Erberkeit. Basel, 1493. Unterschneidheim, 1970.
38512.34 Pamphlet box. Livre du chevalier de La Tour-Landry.
38512.35 Le dit de ménage, pièce en vers du XIVe siècle. Paris, 1835.
38512.36 La guerre de Metz en 1324. Paris, 1875.
38512.37 Casola, Nicola da. Attila, poema franco-italiano per G. Bertoni. Friburgo, 1907.
38512.37.5 Casola, Nicola da. La guerra d'Attila. Modena, 1941. 2v.
38512.38 Casola, Nicola da. Il padiglione foresto. Imola, 1871.
38512.41A Bozon, Nicole. Les contes moralisés. Paris, 1889.
38512.41B Bozon, Nicole. Les contes moralisés. Paris, 1889.
38512.42 Bozon, Nicole. Metaphoro of Brother Bozon. London, 1913.
38512.42.5 Bozon, Nicole. Three saints' lives. N.Y., 1947.
38512.42.10 Bozon, Nicole. Seven more poems. N.Y., 1951.
38512.42.25 Küter, Egon. Die Predigtmarlein (contes moralisés) des Fr. Nicole Bozon. Werl in Westfalen, 1938.
38512.44 Scheler, Auguste. Dits de Watriquet de Couvin. Bruxelles, 1868.
38512.46 Jean d'Arkel. Li ars d'amour. Bruxelles, 1867. 2v.
38512.48 Rühlemann, Otto. Altfranzösischen Lebens Gregor des Grossen. Halle, 1885.
38512.50 Henry VII. Les voeux de l'Epervier. Metz, 1895.
38512.52 Bohnstedt, K.R. Vie Saint Nicholas altfranzösisches Gedicht. Erlangen, 1897.
Htn 38512.56* Bonet, Honoré. L'apparition de Jehan de Meun. Paris, 1845.
38512.57 Bonet, Honoré. L'apparicion maistre Jehan de Meun. Paris, 1926.
38512.57.5 Bonet, Honoré. L'apparicion maistre Jehan de Meun. Thèse. Strasbourg, 1926.
38512.57.10 Bonet, Honoré. The tree of battles. Cambridge, Mass., 1949.
38512.60 Crescini, V. On the Pharsalia of Nicolo da Verona. n.p., n.d.
38512.63 Brush, H.R. La bataille de Trente. Chicago, 1912.
38512.64 De Laigue, R. Le combat des trente et les champions. n.p., 1913.
38512.65 Mettlich, Josef. Die Schachpartie in der Prosabearbeitung der allegorisch-didaktischen Dichtung "Les eschez amoureux." Münster, 1907.
38512.66A Ovidius. Altfranzösische Übersetzung des Remedia amoris. Leipzig, 1871.
38512.66B Ovidius. Altfranzösische Übersetzung des Remedia amoris. Leipzig, 1871.
38512.67 Sieper, Ernst. Les échecs amoureux. Weimar, 1898.
38512.68 Höfler, Hans. Les échecs amoureux. Neustadt, 1905.
38512.69 Jordan, Otto. Jehan du Vingnai und sein Kirchenspiegel. Halle, 1905.
38512.70 Snavely, G.E. Aesopic fables in the Mireoir historial of Jehan de Vignay. Baltimore, 1908.
38512.75 Hoepffner, E. La prise amoureuse. Dresden, 1910.
38512.76 Weingärtner, Paul. Quellenverhältnis und Allegorie in der Prise amoureuse des Jehan Acart de Headin. Inaug. Diss. Würzburg, 1926.
38512.82 Vital de Blois. Le traicté de Getta et d'Amphitrion. Paris, 1872.
38512.85 Jean de Mote. Li regret Guillaume Comte de Haunaut. Louvain, 1882.
38512.88 Karl, Louis. Un moraliste...Jean Dupin. Paris, 1912.
38512.89 Le ménagier de Paris. Le ménagier de Paris. Paris, 1846. 2v.
38512.89.3 Le ménagier de Paris. Le ménagier de Paris. Genève, 1966. 2v.
38512.89.5 Le ménagier de Paris. The goodman of Paris. London, 1928.
38512.89.10 Le ménagier de Paris. The goodman of Paris. N.Y., 1928.
38512.90 L'estoire de Griseldis. (1395). Paris, 1910.
38512.91 Matheolus. Les lamentations. Paris, 1892. 2v.
38512.94 Brasdefer, Jean. Pamphile et Galatie. Thèse. Paris, 1917.
38512.97A Langfors, Arthur. Recueil général des jeux-partis français. v.1-2. Paris, 1926.
38512.97B Langfors, Arthur. Recueil général des jeux-partis français. v.1-2. Paris, 1926.
38512.100 Bible. O.T. Psalms. French (Old French). Le Psautier de Metz. Paris, 1884.
38512.102 Le laie Bible. Le laie Bible, a poem of the fourteenth century. N.Y., 1923.
38512.104 Frank, Grace. Le livre de la passion. Paris, 1930.
38512.109 Fletcher, Frank. Études sur la langue des voeux du Paon. Thèse. Paris, 1924.
Htn 38512.110* Marguerite de Beaujeu. Les heures de Marguerite de Beaujeu. Paris, 1925.
38512.112 Maillart, Jean. Le roman du comte d'Anjou. Paris, 1931.
38512.115A Guillaume de Machaut. Oeuvres. Paris, 1908-11. 3v.
38512.115B Guillaume de Machaut. Oeuvres. Paris, 1908-11. 3v.
38512.115C Guillaume de Machaut. Oeuvres. Paris, 1908-11. 3v.
38512.115.2 Guillaume de Machaut. Oeuvres. Reims, 1849.
38512.115.10A Guillaume de Machaut. Le livre du voir-dit. Paris, 1875.
38512.115.10B Guillaume de Machaut. Le livre du voir-dit. Paris, 1875.
38512.115.14 Guillaume de Machaut. Poésies lyriques. Paris, 1909. 2v.
38512.115.50 Hanf, G. Über Guillaume de Machauts Voir-dit. Halle, 1898.
38512.120 LeMote, J. de. La voie d'enfer et de paradis. Diss. Washington, 1940.

38512.125 Geoffroi de Paris. Six historical poems, written in 1314-1318. Chapel Hill, 1950.
38512.126 Geoffroi de Paris. La chronique métrique attribuée à Geoffroy de Paris. Paris, 1956.
38512.126.2 Geoffroy de Paris. La chronique métrique attribuée à Geoffroy de Paris. Thèse. Strasbourg, 1956.
38512.130 Bell, Dora M. Étude sur le songe du vieil pèlerin de Philippe de Mézières. Genève, 1955.
38512.135 Mézières, Philippe de. Description of the Festum praesentalionis Beatae Mariae. New Haven, 1958.
38512.140 Arnould, Emile Jules F. Étude sur Le livre des saintes medecines du duc Henri de Lancastre. Paris, 1948.
38512.141 Gaston III Phoebus, Count of Foix. Le livre des oraisons de Gaston Phébus. Paris, 1920.
38512.142 Jean le Court, dit Brisebare. Le restor du paon. Genève, 1966.
38512.143 Ribard, Jacques. Un ménestrel du 14e siècle: Jean de Condé. Genève, 1969.
38512.145.2 Orsier, Joseph. Un ambassadeur de Savoie en Angleterre. 2e éd. Paris, 1921.
38512.150 Délivrance du peuple d'Israël. La délivrance du peuple d'Israël. 1. Aufl. München, 1970.

38513 Individual authors, etc. - 1300-1499 - Dramas of the 14th and 15th centuries

38513.01 Pamphlet vol. French literature. (14th and 15th centuries). 6 pam.
Htn 38513.2* Le mistère de la Saincte Hostie. Paris, n.d.
38513.2.9 Roy, Emile. Le jour du jugement. Mystère français sur le grande schisme. Paris, 1902.
38513.3 Pottier, L. La vie et histoire de madame Saint Barbe. Laval, 1902.
38513.3.5 Seefeldt, P. Studien über die...Fassungen...des ältesten Mystère français de Saint Barbe en deux journées. Griefswald, 1908.
38513.3.6 Brandenburg, Max. Die festen Strophengebilde...des Mystère de Saint Barbe. Griefswald, 1907.
38513.4 Fournier, Eugene. Le mystère de Robert le Diable. Paris, n.d.
Htn 38513.5* Miracle de...Robert de Dyable. Rouen, 1836.
38513.5.2A Miracle de...Robert de Dyable. Rouen, 1836.
38513.5.2B Miracle de...Robert de Dyable. Rouen, 1836.
38513.6 Miracle de mon Seigneur Saint Nicolas. n.p., n.d.
38513.6.5 Manz, G. Li jus de Saint Nicholas des A. Jean Bodel. Erlangen, 1904.
38513.7 Mostert, Wilhelm. Das Mystère de Saint Genis. Marburg, 1894.
Htn 38513.8* Le mystère de Griselidis. Paris, 1832.
38513.9 Erler, Otto. Das Mystère de Saint Denis...und seine Quelle. Marburg, 1896.
38513.10 Flamang, Guillaume. La vie et passion de Monseigneur Sainct Didier. Paris, 1855.
38513.11A Jubinal, Achille. Mystères inédits. Paris, 1837. 2v.
38513.11B Jubinal, Achille. Mystères inédits. Paris, 1837. 2v.
38513.12A Rothschild, James de. Le mistère du Viel Testament. Paris, 1878-81. 6v.
38513.12B Rothschild, James de. Le mistère du Viel Testament. Paris, 1878-81. 6v.
38513.13 Robillard de Beaupaire. Les miracles du Mont Saint Michel - Théâtre arranches. Paris, 1862.
38513.14A Miracle de Nostre Dame. Stockholm, 1875.
38513.14B Miracle de Nostre Dame. Stockholm, 1875.
38513.14.3A Mielot, Jean. Miracles de Nostre Dame. Paris, 1876-93. 8v.
38513.14.3B Mielot, Jean. Miracles de Nostre Dame. Paris, 1876-93. 8v.
38513.14.3C Mielot, Jean. Miracles de Nostre Dame. v.2,3,5,7,8. Paris, 1876-93. 5v.
38513.14.3.10 Mielot, Jean. Miracles de Nostre Dame. Strasbourg, 1928.
38513.14.4 Pamphlet box. Notre Dame legends.
38513.14.4.5 Loewinski, Henri. Die Lyrik in den Miracles de Notre Dame. Berlin, 1900.
38513.14.4.15 Penn, Dorothy. The staging of the "Miracles de Nostre Dame par personnages" of M. Cangé. N.Y., 1933.
38513.14.5 Intemann, F. Das Verhältnis des "Nouveau Testament" von Geffroi de Paris zu der "Conception Notre-Dame von Wace". Greifswald, 1907.
38513.14.7 Vingt miracles de Notre Dame. Paris, 1929.
38513.14.9 Schroeder, R. Handschriftenverhältnis und Text der altfranzösischen Achtsilbnerredaktionen der "Heirat Mariae". Greifswald, 1908.
38513.14.11 Heinz, Annemarie. Der Wortschatz des Jean Mielot. Wien, 1964.
38513.15 Pein, E. Untersuchungen über die Verfasser der Passion und der Vengence. Greifswald, 1903.
38513.15.2 Oldörp, Bernhard. Untersuchungen über das Mystère "La vengeance nostre seigneur". Greifswald, 1907.
38513.16 Mystères du Moyen-Age. Mystères liturgiques. Paris, 1892.
38513.18 Quedenfeldt, Gustav. Die Mysterien des heilige Sebastian. Berlin, 1895.
38513.18.10 Le mystère de Saint Sébastien. Genève, 1965.
38513.19 Mystère des actes des apôtres. Paris, 1854.
Htn 38513.19.3* Le triumphant mystère des actes des apôtres. Paris, 1540. 2v.
38513.19.4 Picot, Emile. Notice sur Jehan Chaponneau, docteur de l'église réformée, metteur en scène du Mistère des actes des apostres...1536. Paris, 1879.
38513.19.4.10 Lebegue, Raymond. Le mystère des actes des apôtres. Thèse. Paris, 1929.
38513.19.5 Serrigny, Ernest. La representation d'un mystère de Saint Martin à Seurre en 1496. Dijon, 1888.
38513.19.7 Moreau, Georges. Grande pastorale de Noël. Drame-mystère. Tours, 1884.
38513.19.9 David, Carl. Die drei Mysterien des heiligen Martin von Tours. Frankfurt am Main, 1899.
38513.19.15 Whittredge, R. La nativité et le geu des trois roys. Bryn Mawr, Pa., 1944.
38513.19.20 Gréban, Arnoul. The true mistery of the nativity. London, 1956.
38513.19.25 Gréban, Arnoul. The true mistery of the passion. London, 1962.
38513.19.30 Jehan du Prier. Le mystère du Roy Advenir. Genève, 1970.
38513.20 Pathelin. La farce de Maistre Pierre Pathelin. Paris, 1762.
38513.22 Pathelin. La farce de Maître Pathelin. Paris, 1872.

38513 Individual authors, etc. - 1300-1499 - Dramas of the 14th and 15th centuries - cont.

38513.22.9 Pathelin. La farce de maître Pathelin. Paris, 1909?
38513.22.10 Pathelin. Maistre Pierre Pathelin. Strasbourg, n.d.
38513.22.11 La farce du pâté et de la tarte, tres bonne effort joyeuse à quatre personnages. 10. éd. Paris, 1931.
38513.22.15 Lange, C. Die Farce von Pierre Pathelin. Berlin, 1871.
38513.23 Schaumburg, K. La farce de Pathelin. Paris, 1889.
38513.23.5 Chevaldin, E.E. Les jargons de la farce de Pathelin. Paris, 1903.
38513.23.7 Holbrook, Richard T. Étude sur Pathelin. Baltimore, 1917.
38513.23.10 Schumacher, Joseph. Studien zur Farce Pathelin. Rostock, 1911.
38513.24 Pathelin. Maistre Pierre Pathelin. Nouveau Pathelin...Testament de Pathelin. Paris, 1859.
38513.24.5 Pathelin. Maistre Pierre Pathelin. Paris, 1907.
38513.24.10 Pathelin. Maître Pierre Pathelin. Paris, 1931.
38513.24.15 Pathelin. La farce de Maître Pathelin. Paris, 1937.
38513.25 Pathelin. Maistre Pierre Pathelin Hystorié. Paris, 1904.
38513.25.10 Cons, Louis. L'auteur de la farce de Pathelin. Princeton, N.J., 1926.
Htn 38513.26* Lacroix, Paul. Recueil de farces. Paris, 1859.
38513.26.5 Lacroix, Paul. Recueil de farces. Paris, 1859.
38513.26.10 Lacroix, Paul. Recueil de farces. Paris, 1922?
Htn 38513.30* Leroux de Lincy. Recueil de farces. Paris, 1837. 4v.
38513.32A Picot, Émile. Recueil général des soties. Paris, 1902. 3v.
38513.32B Picot, Émile. Recueil général des soties. Paris, 1902. 3v.
38513.33 Picot, Émile. Nouveau recueil de farces françaises des XVe et XVIe siècles. Paris, 1880.
Htn 38513.33.5* Mabille, E. Choix de farces soties et moralités de XVe et XVIe siècles. Nice, 1872-75. 2v.
38513.33.7 Werner, R. Drei Farcen des 15. Jahrhunderts. Berlin, 1879.
38513.34 Lackner, E. Les 5 moralités publiées dans le IIIe volume de l'ancien théâtre. Bartenstein, 1879.
Htn 38513.36* Nouvelle moralité d'une pauvre fille villageoise. Paris, n.d.
38513.40 Lohmann, N. Untersuchungen über J. Louvets 12 Mysterien. Greifswald, 1900.
38513.45 Kruse, Kurt. J. Michel: Das Mystère de la passion Jesu Crist. Greifswald, 1907.
38513.45.5 Michel, J. Le mystère de la passion. Gembloux, 1959.
38513.47 Frank, Grace. La passion du Palatinus - Mystère du XIVe siècle. Paris, 1922.
38513.48 La passion d'Autun. Paris, 1934.
38513.50 Hinriche, B. Le mystère de Saint Remi. Greifswald, 1907.
38513.53 Briand, François. Quatre histoires...sur quatre évangiles. Paris, 1906.
38513.55 Mystère de Saint Eustache joué en 1504. Gap, 1883.
38513.57 Ostrowski, Otto. Le mystère de Saint Crespin et Crispinien. Greifswald, 1909.
38513.58 Ante, Elizabeth. Sprachliche Untersuchung der Mysterien La passion d'Arnoul Gréban. Inaug. Diss. Darmstadt, 1912.
38513.60 Fourmann, J. Über die Uberlieferung und den Versbau des Mystère. Erlangen, 1911.
38513.61 Tinius, Fritz. Studium über das Mystère de Saint Clement. Griefswald, 1909.
38513.62 Franke, Ernst. Untersuchung über Le mistere. Griefswald, 1909.
38513.65 Becker, Rudolf. Das "La Genesi de Nostre Dame Sainte Marie". Griefswald, 1908.
38513.66 Wimmer, Georg. Prolegomena zu einer kritischen Bearbeitung. Marburg, 1886.
38513.67 Fleischer, M. Christi Leben von der Geschichte von der Samariterin bis zur Passion. Greifswald, n.d. 4 pam.
38513.68 Pfühl, E. Die weitere Fassung der alterfranzösischen Dichtung in achtsilbigen Reimpaaren. Greifswald, n.d. 2 pam.
38513.69 Mons Passion play. Le mystère de la Passion joué à Mons en juillet 1501. Mons, 1957.
38513.70 Cohen, Gustave. Mystères et moralités du manuscrit 617 de Chantilly. Paris, 1920.
38513.70.5 Cohen, Gustave. Mystères et moralités du manuscrit 617 de Chantilly. Thèse. Paris, 1920.
38513.70.10 Cohen, Gustave. Anthologie du drame liturgique en France au Moyen-Âge. Paris, 1955.
38513.72 Droz, Eugenie. Le recueil Trepperel. Paris, 1935. 2v.
38513.73 Schneegans, F.E. Le théâtre édifiant en France aux XIVe et XVe siècles. Paris, 1928.
X Cg 38513.75 Magariños, S. Farsas francesas de la edad media. Madrid, 1945.
38513.80 Cohen, Gustave. Recueil de farces françaises inédites du XVe siècle. Cambridge, Mass., 1949.
38513.85 Jouhan. La farce du pauvre Jouhan. Genève, 1959.
38513.90 Bergerie de l'Agneau de France. Genève, 1961.
38513.92 La farce d'Esopet et du couturier. Paris, 1925.
38513.93 Robert-Busquet, L. Farces du Moyen-Âge. Paris, 1964.
38513.96 Kleine, Félix. Sept comédies du Moyen-Âge. Paris, 1927.

38514 Individual authors, etc. - 1300-1499 - 15th century works

38514.01 Pamphlet box. 15th century literature.
38514.4 Bruyant, Jean. Le livre du Chastel de labour. n.p., 1909.
38514.6 Molinier, H.J. Essai biographique et littéraire sur Octovien de Saint-Gelays. Rodez, 1910.
38514.8 Koenig, Wilhelm. Étude sur...Clotilde de Surville. Halle, 1875.
38514.11 Macé, Antonin. Poésies de Clotilde de Surville. Grenoble, 1870.
Htn 38514.13* Surville, Joseph Étienne. Poésies de Madame de Surville. Paris, 1803.
38514.14 Surville, Joseph Étienne. Poésies de Madame de Surville. Paris, 1804.
38514.14.10 Surville, Joseph Étienne. Poésies inédites de Marguerite Eleonore Clotilde. Paris, 1827.
38514.14.15 Surville, Joseph Étienne. Clotilde von Vallon-Chalys. Berlin, 1837.
Htn 38514.15* Regnier, Jehan. Les fortunes et adversitez. Genève, 1867.
38514.15.2 Regnier, Jehan. Les fortunes et adversitez. Genève, 1867.
Htn 38514.15.10* Regnier, Jehan. Les fortunes et adversitez. Paris, 1923.
38514.15.10.2A Regnier, Jehan. Les fortunes et adversitez. Paris, 1923.
38514.15.10.2B Regnier, Jehan. Les fortunes et adversitez. Paris, 1923.
38514.17 Scholl, Sigmund. Guillaume Tardif und seine französische Übersetzung. Kempten, 1903.
38514.18 Villon, François. Les deux Testaments. Paris, 1866.
38514.18.2 Pamphlet box. François Villon.

38514 Individual authors, etc. - 1300-1499 - 15th century works - cont.

Htn 38514.18.5* Villon, François. Le Petit et le Grant Testament. Paris, 1905.
38514.18.7 Villon, François. Oeuvres le Petit et le Grant Testament, poésies diverses. Paris, 1910.
38514.18.9 Villon, François. Le Jargon du XV siècle. Onze ballades. Paris, 1884.
38514.18.10A Villon, François. Jargon. Boston, 1918.
38514.18.10B Villon, François. Jargon. Boston, 1918.
38514.18.10C Villon, François. Jargon. Boston, 1918.
38514.18.11 Villon, François. Les ballads en jargon du manuscrit de Stockholm. Groningen, 1920.
38514.18.12 Ziwes, Armand. Le jargon de François Villon. Paris, 1954. 2v.
38514.18.13A Ziwes, Armand. Oeuvres. Paris, 1854. 2 pam.
38514.18.13B Ziwes, Armand. Oeuvres. Paris, 1854. 2 pam.
Htn 38514.18.25* Ziwes, Armand. Le Grant Testament et le Petit. Paris, 1924.
38514.18.30 Villon, François. The testaments of François Villon. London, 1947.
38514.18.35 Villon, François. Det stora testamentet. Stockholm, 1958.
38514.18.40 Villon, François. Het goote testament. Utrecht, 1961.
38514.19 Villon, François. Oeuvres. Paris, 1877.
38514.19.25 Villon, François. Oeuvres. Paris, 1832.
38514.20 Prompsault, Jean H.R. Oeuvres de...Villon. Paris, 1835.
38514.20.1 Villon, François. François Villon, un tableau synoptique. Paris, 1958.
38514.20.2A Villon, François. Oeuvres complètes. Paris, 1892.
38514.20.2B Villon, François. Oeuvres complètes. Paris, 1892.
38514.20.3 Villon, François. Oeuvres. 2e éd. Paris, 1914.
38514.20.5 Villon, François. Les oeuvres de François Villon. Paris, 1919.
38514.20.7 Villon, François. Oeuvres. Paris, 1959.
38514.20.8 Villon, François. Oeuvres complètes. Mulhouse, 1949.
38514.20.9A Villon, François. Oeuvres complètes. Paris, n.d.
38514.20.9B Villon, François. Oeuvres complètes. Paris, n.d.
38514.20.10A Villon, François. Oeuvres de Maître François Villon. Strasbourg, n.d.
38514.20.10B Villon, François. Oeuvres de Maître François Villon. Strasbourg, n.d.
38514.20.11A Villon, François. Oeuvres. Paris, 1911.
38514.20.11B Villon, François. Oeuvres. Paris, 1911.
38514.20.11.5 Villon, François. Oeuvres. Paris, 1969. 2v.
38514.20.12A Moland, M.L. Oeuvres complètes de François Villon. Paris, 1879.
38514.20.12B Moland, M.L. Oeuvres complètes de François Villon. Paris, 1879.
38514.20.13 Villon, François. Oeuvres complètes de Villon. Paris, 1879?
38514.20.14 Villon, François. Oeuvres complètes de Villon. Paris, 1927.
38514.20.14.25 Villon, François. Les lais. Paris, 1922.
38514.20.15A Villon, François. Oeuvres. Paris, 1923. 3v.
38514.20.15B Villon, François. Oeuvres. Paris, 1923. 3v.
38514.20.15.10 Villon, François. Oeuvres. Paris, 1934.
38514.20.15.13 Villon, François. Oeuvres. Paris, 1935.
38514.20.15.20 Villon, François. Les deux testaments et les ballades de François Villon. Paris, 1936.
38514.20.15.28 Villon, François. Oeuvres complètes. Grenoble, 1945.
38514.20.15.30A Villon, François. Oeuvres. Paris, 1946.
38514.20.15.30B Villon, François. Oeuvres. Paris, 1946.
38514.20.17 Villon, François. Oeuvres. 3. éd. Paris, 1923.
38514.20.17.10 Villon, François. Oeuvres. Evreux, 1969.
38514.20.18 Jeanroy, A. Deux manuscrits de François Villon. Paris, 1930.
38514.20.19A Villon, François. The poems of François Villon. London, 1913.
38514.20.19B Villon, François. The poems of François Villon. London, 1913.
38514.20.20 Villon, François. Oeuvres. Paris, 1934.
Htn 38514.20.21* Villon, François. Two ballades transcribed from the French of Master François Villon. Rugby, 1933.
38514.20.22 Villon, François. Ballades. London, 1946.
38514.20.25 Villon, François. Le poésie. Torino, 1923.
38514.20.27 Villon, François. Poems. London, 1892.
38514.20.28A Villon, François. Poems. N.Y., 192-.
38514.20.28B Villon, François. Poems. N.Y., 192-.
38514.20.28.5 Villon, François. Poems. Portland, 1905.
38514.20.29 Villon, François. Poems. London, 1950.
38514.20.29.5 Villon, François. Poems. London, 1952.
38514.20.29.10 Villon, François. Seven poems. n.p., 1953.
38514.20.30 Villon, François. Poems. Oxford, 1940.
38514.20.31 Villon, François. Poésies. Paris, 1941.
38514.20.31.3 Villon, François. Poésies. Paris, 1945.
38514.20.32 Villon, François. The retrospect of François Villon. London, 1924.
38514.20.33 Villon, François. The free meals of François Villon and his companions and The monologue of the free archer of Baignollet. Paris, 1941.
38514.20.35A Villon, François. Works. London, 1930.
38514.20.35B Villon, François. Works. London, 1930.
38514.20.40A Villon, François. Book of François Villon. Boston, 1931.
38514.20.40B Villon, François. Book of François Villon. Boston, 1931.
38514.20.45 Villon, François. Oeuvres de François Villon. Paris, 1931.
38514.20.50 Lewis, D.B. Wyndham. François Villon; a documented survey. London, 1928.
38514.20.52 Lewis, D.B. Wyndham. François Villon; a documented survey. N.Y., 1928.
38514.20.53A Lewis, D.B. Wyndham. François Villon. N.Y., 1928.
38514.20.53B Lewis, D.B. Wyndham. François Villon. N.Y., 1928.
38514.20.53C Lewis, D.B. Wyndham. François Villon. N.Y., 1928.
38514.20.54A Lewis, D.B. Wyndham. François Villon. Garden City, 1928.
38514.20.54B Lewis, D.B. Wyndham. François Villon. Garden City, 1928.
38514.20.70 Rice, W.H. The European ancestry of Villon's Satirical testaments. N.Y., 1941.
38514.20.80 Villon, François. Poésies. Ballades. Strasbourg, 1958.
38514.20.85A Villon, François. Complete works. N.Y., 1960.
38514.20.85B Villon, François. Complete works. N.Y., 1960.
38514.20.90 Villon, François. Balladai. London, 1958.
38514.20.100 Villon, François. Verzamelde gedichten. Amsterdam, 1963.
38514.21 Villon, François. Oeuvres complètes. Paris, 1873.
38514.21.1 Campaux, Antoine. François Villon, sa vie et ses oeuvres. Paris, 1859.
38514.21.2 Villon, François. Oeuvres complètes. N.Y., 1876.
38514.21.2.5 Villon, François. The complete works of François Villon. N.Y., 1928. 2v.

38514 **Individual authors, etc. - 1300-1499 - 15th century works - cont.**

38514.21.3 Villon, François. Le jargon Jobelin de Maistre François Villon. Paris, 1892.
38514.21.4 Villon, François. Le Jargon et Jobelin, avec un dictionaire analytique. Paris, 1889.
38514.21.5 Villon, François. Le Jargon de François Villon. Paris, 1895.
38514.21.5.2A Villon, François. Le Jargon de François Villon. Paris, 1909.
38514.21.5.2B Villon, François. Le Jargon de François Villon. Paris, 1909.
38514.21.6A Paris, Gaston. François Villon. Paris, 1901.
38514.21.6B Paris, Gaston. François Villon. Paris, 1901.
38514.21.6.5 Paris, Gaston. François Villon. 3e éd. Paris, 1921.
38514.21.7 Reichel, H. Syntaktische Studien zu Villon. Leipzig, 1891.
38514.21.8 Thuasne, L. Villon et Rabelais. Paris, 1911.
38514.21.9 Le Pileur, L. Les maladies de Vénus dans l'oeuvre de François Villon. Paris, 1910.
38514.21.10 Villioniana. François Villon; drame historique. Paris, 1865.
38514.21.12 Reure. Simple conjecture sur les origines paternelles de François Villon. Paris, 1902.
38514.21.13 Watripon, Antonio. Les génies de la tradition française. François Villon. Paris, 1857.
38514.21.14 Alheim, Pierre d'. La passion de Maître François Villon. Paris, 1900.
38514.21.15 Profillet, A. De la vie et des ouvrage de François Villon. Chalans-sur-Maine, 1856.
38514.21.16 Stacpoole, H. De Vere. François Villon, his life and times. N.Y., 1916.
38514.21.16.5 Stacpoole, H. De Vere. François Villon. N.Y., 1917.
38514.21.17 Cox, Edwin Marion. The ballads of François Villon. London, 1917.
38514.21.20 Thomas, Louis. Les dernières leçons de Marcel Schwob sur François Villon. Paris, 1906.
38514.21.25 Yve-Plessis, R. La psychose de François Villon. Paris, 1925.
38514.22 Nagel, G. François Villon. Berlin, 1877.
38514.22.5 Longnon, Auguste. Étude biographique sur François Villon. Paris, 1877.
38514.23 Vitu, Auguste. Notice sur François Villon. Paris, 1873.
38514.23.3 Bijvanck, W.G.C. Specimen d'un essai sur François Villon. v.1-2. Leyden, 1882.
38514.23.5A Champion, P. François Villon, sa vie et son temps. Paris, 1913. 2v.
38514.23.5B Champion, P. François Villon, sa vie et son temps. Paris, 1913. 2v.
38514.23.10 Bernard, Jean Marc. François Villon, 1431-1463. Paris, 1918.
Htn 38514.23.15* Beebe, Lucius M. François Villon, certain aspects. Cambridge, Mass., 1925.
38514.23.18 Foschini, Antonio. L'avventura di Villon. Milano, 1932.
38514.23.20 Siciliano, Italo. François Villon et les thèmes poétiques de Moyen-Âge. Paris, 1934.
38514.23.25 Desonay, F. Villon. Paris, 1933.
38514.23.31 Marthold, E. de. François Villon. Roma, 193-.
38514.23.35 Charpentier, L. François Villon, le personnage. Paris, 1933.
38514.23.40 Saisset, L. Le Grand Testament de François Villon. Paris, 1937.
38514.23.45 Valéry, Paul. Villon et Verlaine. Maestricht, 1937.
38514.23.50 Cons, Louis. Etat présent des études sur Villon. Paris, 1936.
38514.23.55 Castelnau, J. François Villon. Paris, 1942.
38514.23.60 Maas, P.M. François Villon. Utrecht, 1946.
38514.23.65A Chaney, Edward F. François Villon in his environment. Oxford, 1946.
38514.23.65B Chaney, Edward F. François Villon in his environment. Oxford, 1946.
38514.23.70 Macworth, Cecily. François Villon. London, 1947.
38514.23.75 Schneider, Pierre B. Étude sur la criminalité de François Villon. Lausanne, 1944.
38514.23.77 Lôo, Pierre. Villon; étude psychologique et médico-legale. Paris, 1947.
38514.23.80 Sommer, Ernst. Villon. Berlin, 1949.
38514.23.85 Villon, François. Villon. Fribourg, 1944.
38514.23.90 Burger, André. Lexique de la langue de Villon. Genève, 1957.
38514.23.92 Simons, W.J. Portret van François. Baarn, 1961.
38514.23.94 Brunelli, Giuseppe Antonio. François Villon. Milano, 1961.
38514.23.94.10 Brunelli, Giuseppe Antonio. Saggi critici. Messina, 1967.
38514.23.96 Fox, John H. The poetry of Villon. London, 1962.
38514.23.97 Las Vergnas, Georges. François Villon. Paris, 1963.
38514.23.100 Battaglia, S. François Villon. Napoli, 1963.
38514.23.105 Hansen, Karl Heinz. Holzschnitte zu den Balladen des François Villon. Hannover, 1963.
38514.23.110 Dupont, Claude. Le thème de la solidarité humaine dans l'oeuvre de Villon. Alençon, 1961.
38514.23.115 Kuhn, David. La poétique de François Villon. Paris, 1967.
38514.23.120 Le Gentil, Pierre. Villon. Paris, 1967.
38514.23.125 Anacker, Robert. François Villon. N.Y., 1968.
38514.23.130 Süpek, Otto. Villon kis testamentumának keletkezése. Budapest, 1966.
38514.23.135 Guiraud, Pierre. Le Jargon de Villon, ou le Gai savoir de la Coquille. Paris, 1968.
38514.23.140 Dufournet, Jean. Recherches sur le testament de François Villon. v.1-3. Paris, 1967-
38514.23.141 Guiraud, Pierre. Le testament de Villon. Paris, 1970.
38514.23.145 Deroy, Jean Prosper Theodorus. François Villon. Recherches sur le testament. La Haye, 1967.
38514.23.150 Demarolle, Pierre. L'esprit de Villon, étude de style. Paris, 1968.
38514.23.155 Byvanck, W.G.C. Un poéte inconnu de la Société de François Villon. Paris, 1891.
38514.23.160 Habeck, Fritz. François Villon, oder Die Legende eines Rebellen. Wien, 1969.
38514.23.165 Catani, Nazzareno. La misère et la sensualité de Villon. Crema, 1911.
38514.23.170 Fife, Austin E. The life and poetry of François Villon. Logan, 1969?
38514.24 Guichard, J. Marie. Poésies de Charles d'Orleans. Paris, 1842.
38514.24.5A Charles d'Orleans. Les poésies. Paris, 1843.
38514.24.5B Charles d'Orleans. Les poésies. Paris, 1843.
38514.25 Charles d'Orleans. Poésies complètes. v.1-2. Paris, 1874.

38514 **Individual authors, etc. - 1300-1499 - 15th century works - cont.**

38514.26 Charles d'Orleans. Poésies complètes. Paris, 1896. 2v.
38514.26.10 Charles d'Orleans. Poème, ballades, caroles, chansons, complaintes, rondeaux. Paris, 1909.
38514.26.25A Charles d'Orleans. Poésies. Paris, 1923-24. 2v.
38514.26.25B Charles d'Orleans. Poésies. Paris, 1923-24.
38514.26.40 Charles d'Orleans. Rondeaux choisis. Paris, 1913.
38514.26.50 Charles d'Orleans. Chansons. Blaricum, 193-.
38514.26.60 Charles d'Orleans. Charles d'Orleans. Paris, 1958.
38514.26.80 Fox, John Howard. The lyric poetry of Charles d'Orleans. Oxford, 1969.
38514.27 Beaufils, Constant. Étude sur Charles d'Orleans. Paris, 1861.
38514.27.5 Kuhl, F. Die Allegorie bei Charles d'Orleans. Marburg, 1886.
38514.27.10 Seaton, Ethel. Studies in Villon. Oxford, 1957.
38514.28 Sauerstein, Paul. Charles d'Orleans und die englische Übersetzung seiner Dichtungen. Halle, 1899.
38514.28.10 McLeod, Enid. Charles of Orleans, prince and poet. London, 1969.
X Cg 38514.29 Champion, Pierre. Le manuscrit autographe de Charles d'Orleans. Paris, 1907.
38514.29.5 Cigada, Sergio. L'opera poetica di Charles d'Orleans. Milano, 1960.
38514.30A Cigada, Sergio. Vie de Charles d'Orleans (1394-1465). Milano, 1911.
38514.30B Cigada, Sergio. Vie de Charles d'Orleans (1394-1465). Milano, 1911.
38514.30.10 Goodrich, Norma Lorre. Charles, duke of Orleans. N.Y., 1963.
38514.30.20 Poirion, Daniel. Le lexique de Charles d'Orleans dans les ballades. Genève, 1967.
38514.30.25 Goodrich, Norma Lorre. Charles of Orleans; a study of themes in his French and English poetry. Genève, 1967.
38514.31 Travers, Julien. Olivier Basselin. Caen, 1867.
38514.34 Du Bois, Louis. Vaux-de-vire d'Olivier Basselin. Paris, 1821.
38514.36 Lacroix, Paul. Vaux-de-vire d'Olivier Basselin. Paris, 1858.
38514.36.15 Pamphlet box. Olivier Basselin.
38514.37 Meschinot, Jean. Les lunettes des princes. Nantes, 1891.
Htn 38514.37.10* Meschinot, Jean. Les lunettes des princes. Paris, 1534.
38514.38 Borderie, A. de. Jean Meschinot. Sa vie et ses oeuvres. Paris, 1896.
38514.38.5 Kerdaniel, Edouard L. Un soldat-poète du XVe siècle Jehan Meschinot. Paris, 1916.
38514.39 Gasté, Armand. Étude sur Olivier Basselin. Caen, 1866.
38514.40 Gasté, Armand. Olivier Basselin et le Vau de vire. Paris, 1887.
38514.42 Gasté, Armand. Les Vaux-de-vire de Jean Le Houx. Paris, 1875.
38514.42.5 Le Houx, Jean. The Vaux-de vire. London, 1875.
38514.42.10 Le Houx, Jean. Le livre des chants nouveaux de Vau de vire. Rouen, 1901.
38514.43 Gasté, Armand. Jean Le Houx et le Vau de vire. Paris, 1874.
38514.44A Deschamps, Eustache. Oeuvres complètes. Paris, 1878-80. 11v.
38514.44B Deschamps, Eustache. Oeuvres complètes. Paris, 1878-80. 11v.
38514.44.5 Deschamps, Eustache. Le miroir de marriage. Reims, 1865.
38514.44.9 Sarradin, A. Étude sur Eustache Deschamps. Versailles, 1878.
38514.44.10 Hoepffer, Ernst. Eustache Deschamps. Strassburg, 1903.
38514.44.11 Hoepffer, Ernst. Eustache Deschamps. Strassburg, 1904.
38514.44.12 Fehse, Erich. Sprichwort und Sentenz bei Eustache Deschamps. n.p., 1905.
38514.44.15 Bruins, Jan Gerard. Observation sur la langue d'Eustache Deschamps. Amsterdam, 1925.
38514.44.20 Frise, F. Allegorische und mythologische Gestalten in den Dichtungen Eustache Deschamps'. Inaug. Diss. Bottrop, 1934.
38514.44.25 Dickmann, A. Eustache Deschamps als Schilderer der Sitten seiner Zeit. Inaug. Diss. Bochum, 1935.
38514.45 Guilloche, Bourdelois. La prophécie du Roy Charles VIII. Paris, 1869.
38514.46 Piaget, Arthur. Martin Le Franc. Lausanne, 1888.
Htn 38514.46.5* Le Franc, Martin. L'estrif de fortune et de vertu. Bruxelles, 1928.
38514.46.10 Roth, Oskar. Studien zum Estrif de fortune et vertu des Martin Le Franc. Bern, 1970.
38514.47 Michel, F. Chroniques françaises de Jacques Gondar. Paris, n.d.
38514.48 Brézé, Jacques de. Le livre de la chasse du grand seneschal. Paris, 1858.
38514.49A St. Bernard de Menthon. Le mystère de Saint Bernard de Menthon. Paris, 1888.
38514.49B St. Bernard de Menthon. Le mystère de Saint Bernard de Menthon. Paris, 1888.
38514.50A Paris, Gaston. Chansons du XVe siècle. Paris, 1875.
38514.50B Paris, Gaston. Chansons du XVe siècle. Paris, 1875.
38514.50C Paris, Gaston. Chansons du XVe siècle. Paris, 1875.
38514.50.5 Paris, Gaston. Chansons du XVe siècle. Paris, 1935.
38514.51A Raynaud, G. Rondeaux et autres poésies du XVe siècle. Paris, 1889.
38514.51B Raynaud, G. Rondeaux et autres poésies du XVe siècle. Paris, 1889.
38514.51.50 La Sale, Antoine de. Oeuvres complètes. Liège, 1935- 2v.
38514.51.80 Desonay, F. Antoine de la Sale. Liège, 1940.
38514.52 La Sale, Antoine de. L'histoire...du Jehan de Saintré. Paris, 1843.
38514.52.10 Bronarski, Alphonse. Le petit Jehan de Saintré, une énigme littéraire. Florence, 1922.
38514.53 La Sale, Antoine de. L'histoire...du Jehan de Saintré. Paris, 1830.
38514.53.5 La Sale, Antoine de. L'hystoyre...du Petit Jehan de Saintré. Paris, 1890.
38514.53.9 La Sale, Antoine de. Histoire...du Petit Jehan de Saintré. Paris, 1910.
38514.53.12 Champion, Pierre. Le manuscrit d'auteur du Petit Jehan de Saintré. Paris, 1926.
38514.53.15 La Sale, Antoine de. Le Petit Jehan de Saintré. Paris, 1926.
38514.54 La Sale, Antoine de. History...of Little Jehan de Saintré. London, 1862.

38514 Individual authors, etc. - 1300-1499 - 15th century works - cont.

38514.54.15 La Sale, Antoine de. Little John of Saintré. London, 1931.
38514.54.20 La Sale, Antoine de. Jehan de Saintré. Genève, 1965.
38514.54.50 La Sale, Antoine de. Le paradis de la reine Sibylle. Paris, 1930.
38514.55.9 Les quinze joyes de mariage. Paris, 1880.
38514.55.13 La Sale, Antoine de. The fifteen joys of marriage. London, 1926.
38514.55.15 Les quinze joyes de mariage. Paris, 1929.
38514.55.20 Quinze joyes de mariage. Les quinze joyes de mariage. Paris, 1936.
38514.55.25 Quinze joyes de mariage. Les XV joyes de mariage. Genève, 1963.
38514.56 La Sale, Antoine de. Les quinze joyes de mariage. Paris, 1853.
38514.56.3 La Sale, Antoine de. Les quinze joyes de mariage. Paris, 1857.
38514.56.4 Soderhjelm, W. Les inspirateurs des Quinze joyes de mariage. n.p., 1908-09.
38514.56.5 Henckenkamp, F. Les quinze joyes de mariage. Halle, 1901.
38514.56.7 Dressler, A. Die Chantilly Handschrift der "Quinze joyes de mariage". Greifswald, 1903.
38514.56.8 Fleig, Arthur. Der Treperel-Druck der Quinze joyes de mariage. Greifswald, 1903.
38514.56.9 Cressot, M. Vocabulaire des Quinze joyes de mariage. Thèse. Paris, 1939.
38514.56.10 Une énigme d'histoire littéraire. Paris, 1903.
38514.56.15 Nève, Joseph. Antoine de la Sale, sa vie et ses ouvrages. Paris, 1903.
38514.56.18A Coville, Alfred. Jean Petit. Paris, 1932.
38514.56.18B Coville, Alfred. Jean Petit. Paris, 1932.
38514.56.20 Coville, Alfred. Le petit Jehan de Saintré. Paris, 1937.
38514.56.25 Desonay, F. Nouvelles notes autographes d'Antoine de la Sale. Paris, 1931.
38514.57A Pisan, Christine de. Oeuvres poétiques. Paris, 1886- 3v.
38514.57B Pisan, Christine de. Oeuvres poétiques. Paris, 1886- 3v.
38514.57C Pisan, Christine de. Oeuvres poétiques. Paris, 1886- 3v.
38514.57D Pisan, Christine de. Oeuvres poétiques. Paris, 1886-
38514.57.2 Pisan, Christine de. Le livre du chemin de long estude. Berlin, 1881.
38514.57.3A Pisan, Christine de. Le dit de la rose. Halle, 1891.
38514.57.3B Pisan, Christine de. Le dit de la rose. Halle, 1891.
38514.57.4 Pisan, Christine de. The book of the duke of true lovers. London, 1908.
38514.57.4.5 Pisan, Christine de. The book of the duke of true lovers. N.Y., 1908.
38514.57.5A Laigle, Mathilde. Le livre des trois vertues de Christine de Pisan. Paris, 1912.
38514.57.5B Laigle, Mathilde. Le livre des trois vertues de Christine de Pisan. Paris, 1912.
38514.57.10 Pisan, Christine de. The book of fayttes of armes and of chyvalrye. London, 1932.
38514.57.15 Pisan, Christine de. The epistle of Othea to Hector. Philadelphia, 1942.
38514.57.20 Pisan, Christine de. The livre de la paire of Christine de Pisan. 's-Gravenhage, 1958.
38514.57.25 Pisan, Christine de. Christine de Pisan. Paris, 1962.
38514.57.30 Pisan, Christine de. Ballades, rondeaux, and virelais. Leicester, Eng., 1965.
38514.57.35 Pisan, Christine de. Le livre du corps de policie. Genève, 1967.
38514.57.50 Campbell, P.G.C. L'épêtre d'Othea; étude sur les sources de Christine de Pisan. Thèse. Paris, 1924.
38514.58 Thomassy, Raimond. Essai sur...Christine de Pisan. Paris, 1838.
38514.58.1.5 Vanblanc, V.V.H. de. Christine de Pisan, née en 1363. n.p., 1838?
38514.58.2 Koch, F. Leben und Werke der Christine de Pisan. Goslar, 1885.
38514.58.5 Müller, Ernst. Zur Syntax der Christine de Pisan. Greifswald, 1886.
38514.58.8 Delisle, Léopold. Notice sur les sept psaumes allegorises de Christine de Pisan. Paris, 1896.
38514.58.9 Pinet, Marie-Josèphe. Christine de Pisan, 1364-1430. Paris, 1927.
38514.58.10 Pinet, Marie-Josèphe. Christine de Pisan, 1364-1430. Thèse. Paris, 1927.
38514.58.15 Du Castel, F.P.D. Ma grand-mère, Christine de Pisan. Paris, 1936.
38514.58.20 Coville, Alfred. Sur une ballade de Christine de Pisan. n.p., 1901.
38514.58.25 Boldingh-Goemans, W.L. Christine de Pisan. Rotterdam, 1948.
38514.58.30 Pisan, Christine de. Le livre de la mutacion de fortune. Paris, 1959. 2v.
38514.59 Les evangiles des quenouilles. Paris, 1855.
38514.59.3 Hoochstraten, M.H. van. Die Evangelien van den Spinrocke. 's Gravenhage, 1910.
38514.59.5A The farce of Master Pierre Patelin. Boston, 1905.
38514.59.5B The farce of Master Pierre Patelin. Boston, 1905.
38514.59.5C The farce of Master Pierre Patelin. Boston, 1905.
38514.59.6A Pathelin. Master Pierre Patelin. Boston, 1914.
38514.59.6B Pathelin. Master Pierre Patelin. Boston, 1914.
38514.59.6C Pathelin. Master Pierre Patelin. Boston, 1914.
38514.59.6.5 Pathelin. Master Pierre Patelin. Boston, 1914.
38514.59.7 Pathelin. Maistre Pierre Pathelin. Genève, 1953.
38514.59.12 Pathelin. Maistre Pierre Pathelin, farce du XV siècle. 2e éd. Paris, 1937.
38514.59.15 Pathelin. The farce of the worthy Master Pierre Patelin. N.Y., 1925.
38514.59.20 Pathelin. Mistrz Piotr Pathelin. Warszawa, 1953.
38514.60 Le songe veritable. Paris, 1891.
38514.60.75 La Marche, Olivier de. Le chevalier délibéré. London, 1898.
38514.60.85A La Marche, Olivier de. Le chevalier délibéré. Washington, 1946.
38514.60.85B La Marche, Olivier de. Le chevalier délibéré. Washington, 1946.
38514.60.90 La Marche, Olivier de. Den camp vander doot. Antwerpen, 1948.
38514.60.180 Claneria, C. Le chevalier délibéré. Zaragoza, 1950.
Htn 38514.61* La Marche, Olivier de. El cavallero determmado. Salamanca, 1573.

38514 Individual authors, etc. - 1300-1499 - 15th century works - cont.

Htn 38514.61.20* La Marche, Olivier de. The resolved gentleman. London, 1594.
38514.62 La Marche, Olivier de. Le triumphe des dames. Rostock, 1901.
38514.63.2 Coquillart, Guillaume. Oeuvres. Paris, 1847. 2v.
38514.63.3A Coquillart, Guillaume. Oeuvres. Paris, 1857. 2v.
38514.63.3B Coquillart, Guillaume. Oeuvres. Paris, 1857. 2v.
Htn 38514.64* Oeuvres de...Alain-Chartier. Paris, 1617.
38514.64.6 Chartier, Alain. Le curial. Halle, 1899.
38514.64.8 Chartier, Alain. Le quadriloque invectif. Paris, 1923.
38514.64.8.5 Chartier, Alain. Le quadriloque invectif. Paris, 1944.
38514.64.9 Chartier, Alain. Dialogus familiaris amici et sodalis. Halle, 1901.
38514.64.10 Chartier, Alain. Die französische Version von Alain Chartiers Dialogus familiaris. Rossleben, 1912.
Htn 38514.64.25* Chartier, Alain. Delectable demaundes and pleasant questions. London, 1596.
38514.64.33 Chartier, Alain. La belle dame sans mercy et les poésies lyriques. 2e éd. Lille, 1949.
38514.64.35 Chartier, Alain. Le livre de l'esperance. Brest? 1967.
38514.65 Delaunay, D. Étude sur Alain Chartier. Rennes, 1876.
38514.66 Hannappel, M. Poetik Alain Chartiers. Altenburg, 1881.
38514.67 Gröhler, H. Über Richard Ros' mittenglische Übersetzung des Gedichtes von Alain Chartier, La belle dame sans mercy. Breslau, 1886.
38514.68 Joret-Desclosières, G. Un écrivain national au XVe siècle Alain Chartier. Paris, 1897.
38514.68.2 Joret-Desclosières, G. Un écrivain national au XVe siècle Alain Chartier. Paris, 1899.
38514.68.3 Joret-Desclosières, G. Un écrivain national au XVe siècle Alain Chartier. Thèse. Paris, 1876.
38514.68.5 Pamphlet box. Chartier, Alain.
38514.68.10 Hirschel, Grete. Le livre des quatre dames von Alain Chartier. Inaug. Diss. Wertheim, 1930.
38514.68.15 Hoffman, E.J. Alain Chartier. N.Y., 1942.
38514.68.18 Gerig, John L. On a review. N.Y., 1945.
38514.68.200 Margny, J. de. L'aventurier. Paris, 1938.
38514.69 Oliver, T.E. Jacques Milet's Drama "La destruction de Troye la Grant". Heidelberg, 1899.
38514.69.4 Becker, Karl. Die Mysterien le Siège d'Orléans. Marburg, 1886.
38514.69.5 Tivier, H. Étude sur le Mystère du siège d'Orléans. Paris, 1868.
38514.69.6 Meyer, A. Das Kulturhistorische in Le mystère du Siège d'Orléans. Leipzig, 1906.
38514.69.7 Wunder, Curt. Über Jacques Milet's Destruction de Troye la Grant. Leipzig, 1868.
Htn 38514.69.7.40* Martial de Paris. Aresta amorum. Lugduni, 1538.
Htn 38514.69.7.50* Martial de Paris. Aresta amorum. Lugduni, 1546.
38514.69.15 Martial de Paris. Martines de la Vierge. Genève, 1970.
Htn 38514.70* Martial d'Auvergne. Les arrêts d'amour. Amsterdam, 1731.
38514.70.5 Martial de Paris. Les arrêts d'amour. Paris, 1951.
38514.70.10 Mazzariol, Emma S. Gli arrêts d'amour di Martial d'Auvergne. Venezia, 1964.
38514.70.15 Martial de Paris. Martines de la Vierge. Genève, 1970.
38514.71A Martial de Paris. L'amant rendu cordelier. Paris, 1881.
38514.71B Martial de Paris. L'amant rendu cordelier. Paris, 1881.
38514.71.25 Molinet, J. Les faictz et dictz de Jean Molinet. Paris, 1936-39. 3v.
38514.71.80 Reiffenbery, F.A.F.T. Mémoire sur Jean Molinet. Cambrai, 1835.
38514.71.83 Dupire, Noël. Jean Molinet: la vie - les oeuvres. Thèse. Paris, 1932.
38514.71.85 Dupire, Noël. Jean Molinet: la vie. Paris, 1932.
38514.71.88 Dupire, Noël. Étude critique des manuscrits et éditions des poésies de Jean Molinet. Thèse. Paris, 1932.
38514.71.90 Dupire, Noël. Étude critique des manuscrits et éditions des poésies de Jean Molinet. Paris, 1932.
38514.72A Piaget, A. Oeuvres poétiques de Guillaume Alexis. Paris, 1896. 3v.
38514.72B Piaget, A. Oeuvres poétiques de Guillaume Alexis. Paris, 1896. 3v.
38514.72.15 Holbrook, Richard T. Guillaume Alexis et Pathelin. Berkeley, Calif., 1928.
38514.75 Le prisonnier desconforté. Paris, 1908.
38514.80 Klein, A. Die altfranzösischen Minnefragen. Marburg, 1911.
38514.85 Kerdaniel, Edouard L. de. Un rhetorique, André de la Vigne. Paris, 1919.
38514.90 Bible. Old Testament. Psalms. French (Old). 1872. Les psaumes de David. Paris, 1872.
38514.100 Fabre, Adolphe. Les clercs du palais. Vienne en Dauphiné, 1882.
38514.115 Nesson, Pierre de. Pierre de Nesson et ses oeuvres. Paris, 1925.
38514.120 Baude, Henri. Les vers de maître Henri Baude. Paris, 1856.
38514.125 Baude, Henri. Dictz moraulx pour faire tapisserie. Genève, 1959.
38514.130 Le mors de la pomme. N.Y., 1937.
38514.130.5 Le mors de la pomme. Messina, 1967.
38514.140 Bertrand de Broussillon, A. René d'Orange, poète du Bas-Maine. Laval, 1892.
38514.150 Ferrier, J. L'histoire de Messire Guido. Manchester, Eng., 1949.
38514.155 Ovide moralisé. Ovide moralisé en prose. Amsterdam, 1954.
38514.155.5 Ovide moralisé. Le commentaire de Copenhague. Amsterdam, 1929.
38514.160 Jean de Garencières. Le chevalier poète Jehan de Garencières, 1372-1415. pts.1-2. Paris, 1953.
38514.165 Le Lyon coronné. Genève, 1958.
38514.166F Candille, Marcel. Étude du livre de vie active de l'hotel-Dieu de Paris. Paris, 1964.
38514.170 Le monologue du franc archier de Baignolles. Le franc archier de Baignolles, suivi de deux autres monologues dramatiques. Genève, 1966.
38514.175 Alisandre l'Orfelin. Alixandre l'Orphelin. Manchester, Eng., 1951.
38514.180 Robertet, Jean. Oeuvres. Genève, 1970.

38515 Individual authors, etc. - 1300-1499 - Anthologies - Collection des poètes de Champagne

38515.3 Coquillart, Guillaume. Oeuvres. Paris, 1847. 2v.
38515.4 Tarbé, Prosper. Oeuvres de Guillaume de Machault. Paris, 1849.
38515.5 Oeuvres inédites d'Eustache Deschamps. Paris, 1849. 2v.

38515 Individual authors, etc. - 1300-1499 - Anthologies - Collection des poètes de Champagne - cont.

38515.6 Tarbé, Prosper. Le roman d'Aubrey le Bourgoing. Reims, 1849.
38515.7 Chrestien de Troyes. Roman du chevalier de la charette. Reims, 1849.
38515.8 Tarbé, Prosper. Oeuvres de Philippe de Vitry. Reims, 1850.
38515.9 Tarbé, Prosper. Chansonniers de Champagne aux XIIe et XIIIe siècles. Reims, 1850.
38515.10 Bertrand of Bar-sur-Aube. Roman de Girard de Viane. Reims, 1850.
38515.11 Chansons de Thibault IV. Reims, 1851.
38515.12 Huon de Mery. Tornoiement de l'antichrist. Reims, 1851.
38515.13 Tarbé, Prosper. Poétes de Champagne...proverbes. Reims, 1851.
38515.14 Tarbé, Prosper. Recherches sur...Champagne. Reims, 1851. 2v.
38515.15 Poésies d'Agnès...Dame de Foia. Reims, 1856.
38515.16 Leduc, Herbert. Roman de Foulgue de Candie. Reims, 1860.
38515.16.2 Tarbé, Prosper. Le roman des quatres fils aymon. Reims, 1861.
38515.17 Oeuvres de Blondel de Nésle. Reims, 1862.
38515.18 Romancero de Champagne. Reims, 1863-64. 5v.

38516 Individual authors, etc. - 1300-1499 - Anthologies - Other anthologies

Htn 38516.3*A Montaiglon, Anatole. Recueil de poésies françaises des XVe et XVIe siècles. n.p., 1855-78. 13v.
38516.3B Montaiglon, Anatole. Recueil de poésies françaises des XVe et XVIe siècles. n.p., 1855-78. 9v.
Htn 38516.4* Poésies des XVe et XVIe siècles. Paris, 1830-32.
38516.4.25A Francon, M. Poèmes de transition, XVe et XVIe siècles. Cambridge, 1938.
38516.4.25B Francon, M. Poèmes de transition, XVe et XVIe siècles. Cambridge, 1938.
38516.4.25C Francon, M. Poèmes de transition, XVe et XVIe siècles. Cambridge, 1938.
38516.4.26 Chesney, Kathleen. More poèmes de transition. Oxford, 1965.
38516.4.35 Duviard, Ferdinaud. Antologie des poètes français. Paris, 1947.
38516.5 Joly, A. La vraye histoire de Triboulet et autres poésies des XVe et XVIe siècles. Lyon, 1867.
38516.6 Malmberg, T. Le passe-temps Michault. Upsala, 1877.
38516.8 Wright, Charles H.C. French verse of the XVI century. Boston, 1916.
38516.10 Chastellain, Georges. Oeuvres. Bruxelles, 1863-66. 8v.
38516.10.14 Urwin, K. Georges Chastellain. Thèse. Paris, 1937.
38516.10.15 Urwin, K. Georges Chastellain. Paris, 1937.
38516.10.25 Heilemann, K. Der Wortschatz von Georges Chastellain. Inaug. Diss. Grimma, 1937.
38516.10.30 Hemmer, K. Georges Chastellain (1405-75). Inaug. Diss. Lengerich, 1937.
38516.11 Kervyn de Lettenhove. Le telemaque du XVe siècle. Bruxelles, n.d.
38516.12 Le débat de deux demoyselles. Paris, 1825.
38516.18 Michault, Pierre. La dance aux aveugles et autres poésies du XVe siècle. Lille, 1748.
38516.19 Michault, Pierre. La dance aux aveugles et autres poésies du XVe siècle. Amsterdam, 1749.
38516.20.5 Michault, Pierre. Le doctrinal du temps présent de Pierre Michault (1466). Thèse. Paris, 1931.
38516.20.10 Michault, Pierre. Van den drie boinde danssen. Amsterdam, 1955.
38516.22A Löpelmann, M. Die Liederhandschrift des Cardinals de Rohan. Göttingen, 1923.
38516.22B Löpelmann, M. Die Liederhandschrift des Cardinals de Rohan. Göttingen, 1923.
38516.26 Schwob, Marcel. Le parnasse satyrique du XVe siècle. Paris, 1905.
38516.28 Wallis, N.H. Anonymous French verse. London, 1929.
Htn 38516.31* Recueil de vraye poésie françoise. Genève, 1869.
Htn 38516.36* La fleur de poésie françoyse. Paris, 1864.
38516.40 Cent quarante cinq rondeaux d'amour. Paris, 1875.
38516.45 Martin, C.B.W. A few early French verses done into English. Albany, 1949.
38516.50 Currey, R.N. Formal spring. London, 1950.
38516.52 Méon, Dominique Martin. Blasons. Paris, 1809.

38521 Individual authors, etc. - 1500-1661 - Folios [Discontinued]

38521.6A Durand-Lapie, P. Saint-Amant, son temps...1594-1661. Paris, 1898.
38521.6B Durand-Lapie, P. Saint-Amant, son temps...1594-1661. Paris, 1898.
38521.7 Bible. O.T. Psalms. French. Paraphrases. Le pseautier Huguenot du XVIe siècle. Paris, 1902.
38521.8 Douen, O. Clement Marot et le Psautier Huguenot. Paris, 1878. 2v.
38521.10 Du Bellay, Joachim. Oeuvres complètes. Paris, 1903. 4v.
38521.11 Du Bellay, Joachim. Oeuvres choisies. Paris, 1894.
38521.12 Séché, Léon. Joachim du Bellay et la Bretagne-Angevine. n.p., n.d.
38521.13 Stoetzer, O.G. Étude sur Ronsard et son école. Buetzow, 1874.
38521.14 Lange, Paul. Über Ronsards Franciade. Wurzen, 1887.
38521.15 Rochambeau, Eugène Achille Lacroix de Vimeur. La famille de Ronsard. Paris, 1868.
38521.16 Büscher. La versification de Ronsard. Weimar, 1867.
38521.18 Pellisier, Georges. La vie et les oeuvres de Du Bartas. Paris, 1883.
38521.19.5 Beekman, A. Influence de Du Bartas. Poitiers, 1912.
38521.19.9 Weller, P. Joshuah Sylvesters englische Übersetzungen der religiösen Epen des Du Bartas. Tübingen, 1902.
38521.25.5 Radouant, R. Guillaume du Vair. Paris, 1908.
38521.29 François I. Poésies. Paris, 1847.
38521.30 Lachèvre, Frédéric. Le procès du poète Thèophile de Viau. v.2. Paris, 1909.
38521.30.1 Lachèvre, Frédéric. Le procès du poète Thèophile de Viau. Genève, 1968. 2v.
38521.30.2 Lachèvre, Frédéric. Disciplines et successeurs de Théophile de Viau. Paris, 1911.
38521.30.3 Lachèvre, Frédéric. Une seconde revision des oeuvres du poète Théophile de Viau. Paris, 1911.
38521.30.4 Lachèvre, Frédéric. Les recueils collectifs de poésies. Paris, 1914.

38521 Individual authors, etc. - 1500-1661 - Folios [Discontinued] - cont.

38521.30.4.2 Lachèvre, Frédéric. Supplément. Additions et corrections. Les recueils collectifs de poésies. Supplément. Paris, 1922.
38521.30.5 Le Petit, Claude. Oeuvres libertines. Paris, 1918.
38521.30.6 Blot-l'Église, Claude de Chouvigny. Chansons libertines. Paris, 1919.
38521.30.7 Lachèvre, Frédéric. Mélanges. Paris, 1920.
38521.30.8 Lachèvre, Frédéric. Les oeuvres libertines de Cyrano de Bergerac. Paris, 1921. 2v.
38521.30.9 Dehénault, Jean. Les oeuvres de Jean Dehénault. Paris, 1922.
38521.30.10 Lachèvre, Frédéric. Les successeurs de Cyrano de Bergerac. n.p., 1922.
38521.30.11 Lachèvre, Frédéric. Les derniers libertines. Paris, 1924.
38521.30.15 Lefèvre, Louis R. La vie de Cyrano de Bergerac. Paris, 1927.
38521.31 Garrisson, C. Théophile et Paul de Viau. Paris, 1899.
38521.33 Grente, Georges. Jean Bertant. 1552-1611. Paris, 1903.
38521.34 Pinvert, L. Jacques Grévin. Paris, 1898.
38521.36 Lefranc, Abel. Marguerite de Navarre et le platonisme de la renaissance. Paris, 1897.
38521.37A Lefranc, Abel. Les idées réligieuses de Marguerite de Navarre. Paris, 1898.
38521.37B Lefranc, Abel. Les idées réligieuses de Marguerite de Navarre. Paris, 1898.
38521.39 Sporleder, Carl. Uber Montchrestiens "Escossoise." Marburg, 1892.
38521.50 Chardon, Henri. La vie de Rotrou mieux connue. Paris, 1884.
38521.53 Pamphlet box. Sorel, Charles.
Htn 38521.54* Sorel, Charles. Les berger extravagant. Rouen, 1646.
38521.68.5 Audiguier, Vital d'. Histoire trage-comique de nostre temps. Paris, 1633.
38521.71 Sesportes, Philippe. Le mariage. Texte de 1573, 1583, 1585, 1586. Macon, 1908.

38523.1 - .13 Individual authors, etc. - 1500-1661 - Clément Marot

38523.1 Pamphlet box. Clément Marot.
38523.2 Morley, Henry. Clément Marot, and other studies. London, 1877. 2v.
38523.3 Rose, Hermann. Der Einfluss Villons auf Marot. Glückstadt, 1878.
38523.3.3 Glauning, F. Syntaktische Studien zu Marot. Nördlingen, 1873.
38523.3.5 Lerber, Walther de. L'influence de Clement Marot aut XVIIme et XVIIIme siècles. Lausanne, 1920.
38523.3.9 Mensch, J. Das Tier in der Dichtung Marots. Leipzig, 1906.
38523.3.10 Mensch, J. Das Tier in der Dichtung Marots. Naumburg, 1906.
38523.3.12 Villey, Pierre. Tableau chronologique des publications de Marot. Paris, 1921.
38523.3.15A Villey, Pierre. Marot et Rabelais, avec une table chronologique des oeuvres de Marots. Paris, 1923.
38523.3.15B Villey, Pierre. Marot et Rabelais, avec une table chronologique des oeuvres de Marots. Paris, 1923.
Htn 38523.3.20* Plusieurs traictez du different de Marot, Sagon et La Hueterie. Paris, 1539.
Htn 38523.3.25* Les disciples et amys de Marot. Paris, 1537.
38523.3.27 Duvergie, J. L'hérésie de Clément Marot, 1524-1527. Chartres, 1924.
38523.3.30 Becker, P.A. Clément Marot sein Leben und seine Dichtung. München, 1926.
38523.3.32 Pauphilet, A. Clément Marot. Paris, 1936.
38523.3.35 Plattard, J. Clément Marot, 1518. Paris, 1938.
38523.3.36A Plattard, J. Marot, sa carrière poétique, son oeuvre. Paris, 1938.
38523.3.36B Plattard, J. Marot, sa carrière poétique, son oeuvre. Paris, 1938.
38523.3.40 Dettmer, Gustav. Die Geisteshaltung Clément Marots. Inaug. Diss. Bottrop, 1940.
38523.3.45 Kinch, Charles E. La poésie satirique de Clément Marot. Thèse. Paris, 1940.
38523.3.50 Kinch, Charles E. La poésie satirique de Clément Marot. Paris, 1940.
38523.3.55 Jourda, Pierre. Marot, l'homme et l'oeuvre. Paris, 1950.
38523.3.56 Jourda, Pierre. Marot. 2. éd. Paris, 1967.
38523.3.60 Regius, Karl. Untersuchungen zum Übersetzerstil Clément Marots. Diss. Scwarzenbach, 1951.
38523.3.65 Saulnier, V.L. Les élégies de Clément Marot. Paris, 1952.
38523.3.70 Mayer, C.A. Bibliographie des oeuvres de Clément Marot. v.1-2. Genève, 1954.
38523.3.71 Mayer, C.A. La religion de Marot. Genève, 1960.
38523.3.75 Leblanc, Paulette. La poésie religieuse de Clément Marot. Thèse. Paris, 1955.
38523.3.80 Marot, Clément. Marot et sons temps. Angers, 1941.
38523.3.85 Vianey, Joseph. Les epêtres de Marot. Paris, 1962.
38523.3.90 Patocchi, Pericle. Quando Marot traduceva Petrarca. Lugano, 1953.
38523.3.95 Neuhofer, Peter. Das Adjektiv als Stilelement bei Clément Marot. Wien, 1963.
38523.3.100 Screech, Michael A. Marot évangélique. Genève, 1967.
38523.4 Lacroix, Paul. Oeuvres de Clément Marot. Paris, 1824. 3v.
Htn 38523.5* Marot, Clément. Oeuvres. Paris, 1568.
Htn 38523.5.2* Marot, Clément. Oeuvres. Paris, 1557.
Htn 38523.6* Marot, Clément. Oeuvres. Lyon, 1573. 2v.
Htn 38523.6.3* Marot, Clément. Clément Marot [works]. Lyon, 1579.
Htn 38523.6.5* Marot, Clément. Oeuvres. Rouen, 1596.
38523.6.9 Marot, Clément. Les oeuvres. La Haye, 1702. 2v.
38523.6.12 Marot, Clément. Oeuvres. La Haye, 1731. 6v.
38523.6.30 Marot, Clément. L'adolescence clementine. Paris, 1958.
38523.6.50 Marot, Clément. L'edition originale de la deploration sur le trespas de feu messire Florimond Robertet. Paris, 1938.
38523.7 Héricault, C. Oeuvres de Clément Marot. Paris, 1867.
38523.8 Marot, Clément. Oeuvres. v.1,4,5. Paris, 1911-31. 3v.
38523.9A Marot, Clément. Oeuvres. Paris, 1873. 4v.
38523.9B Marot, Clément. Oeuvres. Paris, 1873. 4v.
38523.9.3A Marot, Clément. Oeuvres complètes. Paris, 1873. 4v.
38523.9.3B Marot, Clément. Oeuvres complètes. Paris, 1873. 4v.
38523.9.15 Marot, Clément. Oeuvres complètes. v.1-4. Paris, 18- ? 2v.
X Cg 38523.10 Marot, Clement. Oeuvres de Clément Marot. v.2. Paris, 1876.

Classified Listing

38523.1 - .13 Individual authors, etc. - 1500-1661 - Clément Marot - cont.
38523.10.15 Marot, Clément. Oeuvres. La Haye, 1731. 4v.
38523.10.25 Marot, Clément. Oeuvres. Paris, 1911.
38523.10.30A Marot, Clément. Oeuvres. London, 1958- 5v.
38523.10.30B Marot, Clément. Oeuvres. v.2. London, 1958-
38523.11 Marot, Clément. Les chansons de Clément Marot. Paris, 1951.
38523.12A Saint-Marc, B. Oeuvres complètes de Clèment Marot. Paris, 1879. 2v.
38523.12B Saint-Marc, B. Oeuvres complètes de Clèment Marot. Paris, 1879. 2v.
38523.12C Saint-Marc, B. Oeuvres complètes de Clèment Marot. Paris, 1879. 2v.
38523.12.3 Marot, Clément. Oeuvres complètes. Paris, 1951?
Htn 38523.12.5* Marot, Clément. L'adolescence Clementine ou Autrement. Bourgogne, 1536? 3 pam.
38523.12.10 Marot, Clément. Dialogue de deux amoureux. Paris, 1945.
38523.12.15 Marot, Clément. Choix de poèmes. Lyon, 1946.
38523.12.30 Marot, Clément. L'enfer. 1. ed. Cambridge, Mass., 1960.
38523.12.40 Marot, Clément. Clément Marot. Paris, 1964.
38523.12.80 Smith, Pauline M. Clément Marot, poet of the French renaissance. London, 1970.
38523.13 Bible. O.T. Psalms. French. Les pseaumes mis en rime françoise. Delf, 1602.
38523.13.5 Bible. O.T. Psalms. French. Psaumes, avec les mélodies. Strasbourg, 191-?
38523.13.10 Bible. O.T. Psalms. French. Les pseaumes mis en rime françoise. Kassel, 1935.
38523.13.15 Bible. O.T. Psalms. French. Paraphrases. Les pseaumes de Clément Marot. Assen, 1969.

38523.14 Individual authors, etc. - 1500-1661 - Jean Marot
Htn 38523.14* Guiffrey, G. Poeme inedit de Jehan Marot. Paris, 1860.
38523.14.5 Theureau, Louis. Étude sur la vie et les oeuvres de Jean Marot. Genève, 1970.

38523.15 - Individual authors, etc. - 1500-1661 - Malherbe
38523.15A Brunot, Ferdinand. Doctrine de Malherbe. Paris, 1891.
38523.15B Brunot, Ferdinand. Doctrine de Malherbe. Paris, 1891.
38523.16 Allais, Gustave. Malherbe et la poésie française. Paris, 1892.
38523.17 Bourrienne, Gustave. Malherbe, Points obscurs de sa vie Normande. Paris, 1895.
38523.18A Broglie, Albert. Malherbe. Paris, 1897.
38523.18B Broglie, Albert. Malherbe. Paris, 1897.
38523.19 Counson, A. Malherbe et ses sources. Liège, 1904.
38523.19.2 Gosse, Edmund W. Malherbe and the classical reaction in the 17th century. Oxford, 1920.
38523.20 Gournay, François A. Malherbe; recherches sur sa vie. Caen, 1852.
38523.21 Chevreau, Urbain. Remarque sur les poésies de Malherbe. Niort, 1909.
38523.21.25 Lair, J. Recherches sur une maison de Paris ou demeura Malherbe. Caen, 1899.
38523.21.30 Celles, J. de. Malherbe; sa vie. Paris, 1937.
38523.22 Lettres inédites de Malherbe. Caen, 1852.
Htn 38523.22.45* Malherbe, François de. Oeuvres. 2. éd. Paris, 1631.
Htn 38523.22.47* Malherbe, François de. Oeuvres. 3. éd. Troyes, 1638.
Htn 38523.22.50* Malherbe, François de. Oeuvres. 3. éd. Paris, 1638.
Htn 38523.22.60* Malherbe, François de. Les oeuvres. Paris, 1642.
Htn 38523.22.65* Malherbe, François de. Oeuvres. Paris, 1659. 2 pam.
Htn 38523.22.80* Malherbe, François de. Poésies avec les observations de M. Menage. Paris, 1666.
38523.22.85 Malherbe, François de. Poésies. Paris, 1757.
Htn 38523.22.90* Malherbe, François de. Les poésies. Paris, 1660.
38523.23 Malherbe, François de. Poésies de Malherbe. Paris, 1776.
38523.23.5 Malherbe, François de. Poésies. Genève, 1777.
38523.24.10 Malherbe, François de. Poésies. Paris, 1817.
38523.25 Malherbe, François de. Poésies de Malherbe. Paris, 1822.
38523.26 Malherbe, François de. Poésies, suivies d'un choix de lettres. Paris, 1828.
38523.27 Malherbe, François de. Oeuvres; oeuvres de J.B. Rousseau. Paris, 1843.
38523.28A Malherbe, François de. Oeuvres de Malherbe. v.1-5 et album. Paris, 1862-69. 6v.
38523.28B Malherbe, François de. Oeuvres de Malherbe. v.2-5 et album. Paris, 1862-69. 5v.
Htn 38523.29* Malherbe, François de. Poésies. 2. éd. Paris, 1689.
38523.30.10 Malherbe, François de. Les poésies de Malherbe. Paris, 1926.
38523.30.15A Malherbe, François de. Poésies. Paris, 1936-37. 2v.
38523.30.15B Malherbe, François de. Poésies. Paris, 1936-37.
38523.30.35 Malherbe, François de. Oeuvres poétiques. Paris, 1874.
38523.30.40 Malherbe, François de. Oeuvres poétiques. Paris, 1968. 2v.
38523.31 Malherbe, François de. Oeuvres poétiques. Paris, 1877.
38523.31.5A Malherbe, François de. Oeuvres poétiques de Malherbe réimprimées sur l'édition de 1630. Paris, 1877.
38523.31.5B Malherbe, François de. Oeuvres poétiques de Malherbe réimprimées sur l'édition de 1630. Paris, 1877.
38523.32 Johannesson, Fritz. Die Bestrebungen Malherbes. Halle, 1881.
38523.33 Fromilhague, R. La vie de Malherbe. Paris, 1954.
38523.33.2 Fromilhague, R. La vie de Malherbe. Thèse. Paris, 1954.
38523.33.5 Fromilhague, R. Malherbe. Paris, 1954.
38523.33.6 Fromilhague, R. Malherbe. Thèse. Paris, 1954.
38523.36 Bibliotèque Nationale, Paris. Malherbe et les poétes de son temps. Paris, 1955.
38523.37 Comité aixois du 4e centenaire de la naissance de Malherbe. Malherbe et la Provence. Aix-en-Provence, 1955.
38523.38 Caen, France. Malherbe et son temps. Caen, 1956.
38523.38.5 Ponge, Francis. Pour un Malherbe. Paris, 1965.
38523.41 Jannini, Pasquale Aniel. Tra momenti della poesia francese al tempo di Malherbe. Milano, 1964.
38523.44 Abraham, Claude Kurt. Enfin Malherbe. Lexington, 1971.

38524.1 - .799 Individual authors, etc. - 1500-1661 - Anthologies
38524.4 Jamyn, Amadis. Oeuvres poetiques. Paris, 1878. 2v.
38524.5 Guy de Tours. Premières oeuvres. Paris, 1878.
38524.6 Guy de Tours. Le paradis d'amour. Paris, 1878.
38524.7 Jean de la Taille. Oeuvres. Paris, 1878. 4v.
Htn 38524.11.25* Baïf, Jean A. de. Euvres en rime. Paris, 1573.
Htn 38524.11.50* Baïf, Jean A. de. Les mimes. Paris, 1581.
38524.12 Baïf, Jean A. de. Les mimes. Paris, 1880. 2v.
38524.13 Hémard, Le Sieur. Les restes de la Guerre d'Estampes. Paris, 1880.

38524.1 - .799 Individual authors, etc. - 1500-1661 - Anthologies - cont.
38524.18 Julyot, Ferry. Les élégies de la belle fille. Paris, 1883.
38524.19 Martin, Nicolas. Les Noelz et Chansons. Paris, 1883.
38524.19.5 Martin, Nichlas. Noelz et Chansons. Annecy, 1942.
38524.20 Faifeu, Pierre. La legende joyeuse. Paris, 1883.
Htn 38524.28* Palinodz. Chantz royaulx. Facsimile. Paris, 1897.
38524.30 Merlet, Gustave. Les grands ecrivains du seizième siècle. Paris, 1881.
38524.31 Baïf, Jean A. de. Oeuvres en rime. Paris, 1881- 5v.
38524.32 Belleau, Renny. Oeuvres poétiques. Paris, 1878. 2v.
38524.33 Dorat, Jean. Oeuvres poétiques. Paris, 1875.
38524.34 Du Bellay, Joachim. Oeuvres Françoises. Paris, 1866. 2v.
38524.35 Jodelle, d'Estienne. Les oeuvres et meslanges poétique. Paris, 1868. 2v.
38524.36 Ronsard, P. de. Oeuvres. Paris, 1887. 6v.
38524.36.2 Marty-Laveaux, C. La Pléiade françoise. Appendice. Paris, 1896. 2v.
38524.36.5 Marty-Laveaux, C. La pléiade françoise. Genève, 1966. 2v.
Htn 38524.42* Le seiour des muses ou La cresme des Bons Vers. Lyon, 1722.
38524.50 Thresor du soñet. XVIe-XVIIe siècles. Macon, 1899-
Htn 38524.53* Alizet, Benoit. La calliope chretienne. Genève, 1593.
38524.56 Villey, P. Les sources d'idées. Textes choisis et commentées. Paris, 1912.
Htn 38524.60* Tragédies. Paris, 1637-47.
Htn 38524.62* Nouveau recueil de plusieurs et diverses pièces galantes de ce temps. n.p., 1665. 2v.
38524.63 Fleuret, F. Les amoureux passe-temps. Paris, 1925.
38524.64 Choix de poésies politiques et satiriques du temps de la Fronde. Strasbourg, 1914.
Htn 38524.65* Corrozet, Gilles. Le Parnasse des poetes françois modernes. Paris, 1571.
Htn 38524.66* Le parnasse des plus excellens poètes de ce temps. Paris, 1607.
X Cg 38524.70 Allem, Maurice (pseud.). Anthologie poétique française XVIe siècle. Paris, 1918. 2v.
38524.72A Cons, Louis. Anthologie littéraire de la renaissance française. N.Y., 1931.
38524.72B Cons, Louis. Anthologie littéraire de la renaissance française. N.Y., 1931.
38524.75 Helbig, H. Fleurs des vieux poètes Liègeois (1550-1650). Liège, 1859.
38524.78 Perceau, Louis. Mathurin Regnier et les satyriques. Paris, 1930.
38524.80 Bordier, H.L. Le chansonnier Huguenot du XVIe siècle. Paris, 1870.
Htn 38524.83* Poésies choisies de Messieurs Corneille. Paris, 1655. 2 pam.
Htn 38524.85* Le théâtre françois. Paris, 1624.
38524.87 Picot, E. Recueil de pièces historiques imprimées dans les provinces françaises au XVIe siècle. Paris, 1913.
38524.90 Cart, A. La poésie française au XVII siècle, 1594-1630. Paris, 1939.
38524.98 Hasselmann, Jules. Les conteurs français du XVIe siécle. Paris, 1945.
38524.100 Dans les jardins de la poésie française. Seizième siècle. Paris, 1945.
38524.105 Driano, Maturin. La Pléiade. Angers, 1946.
38524.110A Weinberg, B. Critical prefaces of the French renaissance. Evanston, Ill., 1950.
38524.110B Weinberg, B. Critical prefaces of the French renaissance. Evanston, Ill., 1950.
38524.110.5 Weinberg, B. French poetry of the renaissance. N.Y., 1954.
38524.115 Grands poètes français. Lausanne, 1947. 2v.
38524.118 Rickard, Peter. La langue française au seizième siècle, étude suivie de textes. Cambridge, 1968.
38524.120 Chesney, K. Fleurs de rhétorique. Oxford, 1950.
38524.122A Porteau, Paul. Contes. Paris, 1948.
38524.122B Porteau, Paul. Contes. Paris, 1948.
38524.125 Antoine, G. Le XVIe siècle. Paris, 1950.
38524.130 Gerard de Neval, G.L. Choix des poésies de Ronsard, Dubellay, Baïf, Belleau. Paris, 1830.
38524.135 Schmidt, A.M. Poètes du XVI siècle. Paris, 1953.
Htn 38524.140* Recueil des plus belles pièces des poètes françois. Paris, 1692.
38524.146 Petroni, Liano. La commedia letteraria francese nella seconda metà de Cinquecento. Bologna, 1964.
38524.147 Jourda, Pierre. Conteurs français du XVIe siècle. Paris, 1965.
38524.148 Stone, Donald. Four renaissance tragedies. Cambridge, 1966.
38524.150 Adam, Antoine. Les libertins au XVIIe siècle. Paris, 1964.
38524.152 Elledge, Scott. The continental model; selected French critical essays of the seventeenth century. Minneapolis, 1960.
38524.154 Alyn, Marc. Poètes du XVIe siècle. Paris, 1962.

38524.801 - .899 Individual authors, etc. - 1500-1661 - Anonymous plays (99 scheme, A-Z by title)
Htn 38524.817* Les delices satyriques. Paris, 1620.
38524.826 Farce nouvelle. Strassbourg, 1924.
38524.827 Trois farces du recueil de Londres. Rennes, 1931.
38524.842 Jesus Maria, sur le martyre des SS. Innocens. n.p., n.d.
Htn 38524.869* Perselide. Paris, 1646.
38524.871.10 John, Hans. Pompee. Inaug. Diss. Nürnberg, 1934.
38524.874 Gill, Austin. Les ramonneurs. Paris, 1957.
Htn 38524.879* Le sage jaloux. Paris, 1648.

38525.1 - .6 Individual authors, etc. - 1500-1661 - Selections [Discontinued]
38525.2 Chotard, Raoul. Les ecrivains français du XVIe siècle. Tours, 1872.
38525.3 Talbot, Eugène. Morceaux choisis...du XVIe siècle. 2e éd. Paris, 1875.
38525.3.3 Talbot, Eugène. Morceaux choisis...du XVIe siècle. Paris, 1874-75.
38525.4 Aynard, J. Les poëtes lyonnais. Paris, 1924.
38525.5 Brachet, Auguste. Morceaux choisis...du XVIe siècle. Paris, 1875.
NEDL 38525.5.3 Brachet, Auguste. Morceaux choisis...du XVIe siècle. 7e éd. Paris, 1894.

Classified Listing

38525.1 - .6 Individual authors, etc. - 1500-1661 - Selections [Discontinued] - cont.

38525.5.9 Ulrich, J. Proben der französischen Novellistik des 16. Jahrhunderts. Leipzig, 1906.
38525.5.15 Anthologie des poètes du seizième siècle. Paris, 1955.
38525.5.25 Bégne, C. Les humanistes français. Paris, 1937.
38525.5.30 Allem, Maurice (pseud.). Anthologie poétique française XVIe siècle. Paris, 1914?
38525.5.35 Raymond, Marcel. La poésie française et la manièrisme, 1546-1610(?) Genève, 1971.
38525.6 Lemercier, A.P. Chefs-d'oeuvre des poètes du XVIe siècle. Paris, 1896.
38525.6.5 Lockert, Lacy. The chief rivals of Corneille and Racine. Nashville, 1956.
38525.6.5.5 Lockert, Lacy. More plays by rivals of Corneille and Racine. Nashville, 1968.
38525.6.10 Allem, Maurice (pseud.). Sonnets du XVIe siècle. Grenoble, 1953.
38525.6.15 Rousset, Jean. Anthologie de al poésie baroque française. v.1-2. Paris, 1961.
38525.6.20 Graham, V.E. Sixteenth-century French poetry. Toronto, 1964.
38525.6.25 Schmidt, Albert M. L'amour noir. Monaco, 1959.
38525.6.30 Krailsheimer, Allan John. Three sixteenth-century conteurs. London, 1966.
38525.6.35 Dubois, Claude Gilbert. La poésie baroque...choix de poèmes. Paris, 1969. 2v.

38525.7 - .8 Individual authors, etc. - 1500-1661 - Jodelle

Htn 38525.7.3* Pamphlet box. Jodelle, d'Estienne.
Htn 38525.7.5* Jodelle, d'Estienne. Les oeuvres et meslanges. Paris, 1583.
NEDL 38525.7.9 Jodelle, d'Estienne. Les amours et autres poésies. Paris, 1907.
38525.7.11 Jodelle, d'Estienne. Oeuvres complètes. Paris, 1965. 2v.
38525.7.15A Jodelle, d'Estienne. Cleopâtre captive; tragédie. Paris, 1925.
38525.7.15B Jodelle, d'Estienne. Cleopâtre captive; tragédie. Paris, 1925.
38525.7.20 Jodelle, d'Estienne. Cleopâtre captive. Philadelphia, 1946.
38525.7.25 Jodelle, d'Estienne. L'Eugene. Milano, 1955.
38525.7.80 Ellis, Lowell Bryce. Estienne Jodelle; Cleopâtre captive, a critical edition. Philadelphia, 1946.
38525.8 Fehse, Hermann. Estienne Jodelle's Lyrik. Oppeln, 1880.
38525.8.5 Herting, A. Der Versbau Étienne Jodelle's. Kiel, 1884.
38525.8.10 Horváth, K.A. Étienne Jodelle. Budapest, 1932.

38525.9 - .22.49 Individual authors, etc. - 1500-1661 - Ronsard

38525.9 Wyndham, George. Ronsard and la Pléiade with selections from poetry. London, 1906.
38525.9.5 Franchet, Henri. Le poète et son oeuvre d'après Ronsard. Thèse. Paris, 1922.
38525.9.10 Gordon, Alexandre L. Ronsard et la rhétorique. Genève, 1970.
38525.10 Rochambeau, Vimeur. La famille de Ronsart. Paris, 1857.
38525.11 Longnon, Henri. Pierre de Ronsard. Paris, 1912.
38525.11.5 Storer, Walter Henry. Virgil and Ronsard. Thesis. Paris, 1923.
38525.11.10 Klengel, Alice. Pierre de Ronsards Hymnendichtung. Inaug. Diss. Leipzig, 1931.
Htn 38525.12* Ronsard, Pierre de. Les oeuvres. v.1-2,3-4,5-6. Paris, 1571. 3v.
Htn 38525.12.2* Ronsard, Pierre de. Les oeuvres. v.1,2,3,4,5-6. Paris, 1572-73. 5v.
Htn 38525.12.9* Ronsard, Pierre de. Les oeuvres. Lyon, 1592. 5v.
Htn 38525.12.12* Ronsard, Pierre de. Les oeuvres. v.1-10. Paris, 1597. 5v.
Htn 38525.12.19* Ronsard, Pierre de. Les oeuvres. Paris, 1610. 5v.
38525.12.20 Ronsard, Pierre de. Oeuvres complètes. Paris, 1914-48. 18v.
38525.12.25 Ronsard, Pierre de. Oeuvres complètes. v.7. Paris, 1957.
38525.12.28 Ronsard, Pierre de. Les oeuvres de Pierre de Ronsard. Text de 1587. Chicago, 1966. 6v.
Htn 38525.13* Ronsard, Pierre de. Les oeuvres. v.1-11. Paris, 1617. 5v.
38525.14A Ronsard, Pierre de. Oeuvres. Paris, 1857. 8v.
38525.14B Ronsard, Pierre de. Oeuvres. Paris, 1857. 8v.
38525.14.2 Vaganay, H. Pierre de Ronsard. Oeuvres poétiques. Lyon, 1905.
38525.14.4 Raymond, Marcel. Bibliographie critique de Ronsard. Paris, 1927.
38525.14.5 Ronsard, Pierre de. Oeuvres complètes. Paris, 1923-25. 7v.
38525.14.9 Ronsard, Pierre de. Oeuvres complètes. Paris, 1914-19. 8v.
38525.14.11 Ronsard, Pierre de. Oeuvres complètes. Paris, 1938. 2v.
38525.14.15 Ronsard, Pierre de. La fleur des poésies. v.1-2,3-4. Paris, 1923. 2v.
38525.14.25 Ronsard, Pierre de. La fleur des musiciens. Paris, 1923.
Htn 38525.14.75* Ronsard, Pierre de. Les quatres premiers livres des odes. Paris, 1555.
Htn 38525.14.80* Ronsard, Pierre de. Les cinquieme [!] des odes augmente. Paris, 1553.
Htn 38525.15* Ronsard, Pierre de. Oeuvres - odes. v.1, 2, 3-5. Strassbourg, n.d. 3v.
Htn 38525.15.75* Ronsard, Pierre de. Les amours de Pierre de Ronsard Vaudomois. Paris, 1553. 2v.
Htn 38525.16* Ronsard, Pierre de. Les odes. n.p., 1553.
38525.16.10 Ronsard, Pierre de. Les odes. Paris, 1952.
Htn 38525.16.50* Ronsard, Pierre de. Recueil des sonnets, odes. Paris, 1617.
38525.17 Ronsard, Pierre de. Choix de poésies. Paris, 1862. 2v.
Htn 38525.17.5* Ronsard, Pierre de. Choix de sonnets. n.p., n.d.
38525.17.10 Ronsard, Pierre de. Pierre de Ronsard et ses musiciens. Paris, 1955.
38525.17.20 Ronsard, Pierre de. Pierre de Ronsard. Paris, 1958.
38525.18 Ronsard, Pierre de. XI sonnets nouvellement recueillis. Texte de 1552 et 1578. n.p., n.d.
38525.18.3A Ronsard, Pierre de. Songs and sonnets of Pierre de Ronsard. Boston, 1903.
38525.18.3B Ronsard, Pierre de. Songs and sonnets of Pierre de Ronsard. Boston, 1903.
38525.18.3.20 Ronsard, Pierre de. Songs and sonnets of Pierre de Ronsard. Boston, 1924.

38525.9 - .22.49 Individual authors, etc. - 1500-1661 - Ronsard - cont.

38525.18.5 Ronsard, Pierre de. Sonnets pour Hélène. Paris, 1921.
38525.18.7 Ronsard, Pierre de. Sonnets pour Hélène. Paris, 1947.
38525.18.8 Ronsard, Pierre de. Sonnets pour Hélène. Genève, 1970.
38525.18.30 Ronsard, Pierre de. Amours de Marie. Paris, 1942.
38525.18.80 Ronsard, Pierre de. Oeuvres choisies. Paris, 1841.
NEDL 38525.19 Ronsard, Pierre de. Oeuvres choisies. Paris, 1890.
38525.19.5A Ronsard, Pierre de. Oeuvres choisies. Paris, 1879.
38525.19.5B Ronsard, Pierre de. Oeuvres choisies. Paris, 1879.
38525.20 Ronsard, Pierre de. Poésies choisies. Paris, 1875.
38525.20.5 Ronsard, Pierre de. Selected poems. Oxford, 1908.
Htn 38525.20.7* Ronsard, Pierre de. Les quatres premiers livres de la Franciade. Paris, 1573.
38525.20.9 Ronsard, Pierre de. Livret de folastries. Paris, 1907.
38525.20.9.2 Ronsard, Pierre de. Livret de folastries à janot parisien. Paris, 1920.
38525.20.10A Ronsard, Pierre de. Lyrics. London? 1946.
38525.20.10B Ronsard, Pierre de. Lyrics. London? 1946.
38525.20.15 Ronsard, Pierre de. Poèmes choisis et commentes par André Barlier. Oxford, 1946.
38525.20.21 Ronsard, Pierre de. Poésies. Paris, 1924.
38525.20.21.2 Ronsard, Pierre de. Poésies choisies. Paris, 1969.
38525.20.22 Ronsard, Pierre de. Poésies. Lausanne, 1949.
38525.20.23 Ronsard, Pierre de. Discours des misères de ce temps à la Royne mere du Roy. Paris, 1924.
38525.20.24 Ronsard, Pierre de. Discours des misères de ce temps. Paris, 1949.
38525.20.25A Ronsard, Pierre de. Ronsard lyrique et amoureux. Paris, 1922.
38525.20.25B Ronsard, Pierre de. Ronsard lyrique et amoureux. Paris, 1922.
38525.20.26 Ronsard, Pierre de. Poésies choisies. Paris, 1924.
38525.20.27 Ronsard, Pierre de. Les amours. Paris, 1926. 3v.
38525.20.28 Ronsard, Pierre de. Les amours. 1. ed. Milano, 1947.
38525.20.28.3 Ronsard, Pierre de. Les amours. v.1-2. Paris, 1954.
38525.20.28.8 Ronsard, Pierre de. Les amours. Paris, 1963.
38525.20.28.10 Ronsard, Pierre de. Les amours. Genève, 1970.
38525.20.29A Ronsard, Pierre de. Les chefs d'oeuvres lyriques. Paris, 1907.
38525.20.29B Ronsard, Pierre de. Les chefs d'oeuvres lyriques. Paris, 1907.
38525.20.40 Ronsard, Pierre de. Sonnets pour Hélène. London, 1934.
38525.20.45 Ronsard, Pierre de. Sonnets d'amour. Mainz, 1948.
38525.20.49 Ronsard, Pierre de. Hymne des daimons. Thèse. Paris, 193-?
38525.20.50A Ronsard, Pierre de. Hymne des daimons. Paris, 1939?
38525.20.50B Ronsard, Pierre de. Hymne des daimons. Paris, 1939?
38525.20.58 Ronsard, Pierre de. Lyrics of Pierre de Ronsard, Vandomois. Edinburg, 1967.
38525.20.60 Ronsard, Pierre de. Le second livre des amours. Genève, 1951.
38525.20.62 Ronsard, Pierre de. Les bacchanales. Genève, 1953.
38525.20.65 Ronsard, Pierre de. La bouquinade et autres gaillardises. Paris, 1921.
38525.20.75 Ronsard, Pierre de. Ronsard. Paris, 1960.
38525.20.250 DeRicci, S. Catalogue d'une collection unique des editions orginales de Ronsard. Paris, 1925.
Htn 38525.20.253* DeRicci, S. Catalogue of a unique collection of early editions of Ronsard. London, 1927.
38525.20.255 Raymond, M. Bibliographie critique de Ronsard en France, 1550-1585. Paris, 1927.
38525.20.260 Laumonier, P. Tableau chronologique des oeuvres de Ronsard. 2e éd. Paris, 1911.
38525.20.283 Ronsard, Pierre de. Amori. Firenze, 1955.
38525.21 Bizos, G. Ronsard. Paris, 1891.
38525.21.2 Rosenbauer, A. Die poetischen Theorien der Plejadi nach Ronsard und Dubellay. Erlangen, 1895.
38525.21.3A Mellerio, Louis. Lexique de Ronsard. Paris, 1895.
38525.21.3B Mellerio, Louis. Lexique de Ronsard. Paris, 1895.
38525.21.5 Perdrizet, Pierre. Ronsard et la réforme. Paris, 1902.
38525.21.5.1 Perdrizet, Pierre. Ronsard et la réforme. Genève, 1970.
38525.21.7 Laumonier, P. Ronsard et sa province; anthologie régionale. Paris, 1924.
38525.21.8 Laumonier, P. La vie de Pierre de Ronsard. Paris, 1910.
38525.21.9.5 Laumonier, P. Ronsard poète lyrique. 2. ed. Paris, 1923.
38525.21.10 Jusserand, J.J. Ronsard. Paris, 1913.
38525.21.15 Charbonnier, F. Pamphlets: Protestants contre Ronsard, 1560-1577. Paris, 1923.
38525.21.20 Ronsard, Pierre de. Pierre de Ronsard. Paris, 1914.
38525.21.25 Buhler, Karl. Ronsard und seine Stellung zur mittelalterlichen französischen Litteratur. Inaug. Diss. Frankfurt, 1917.
38525.21.30A Lebègue, Raymond. Ronsard. Paris, 1950.
38525.21.30B Lebègue, Raymond. Ronsard. Paris, 1950.
38525.21.33 Lebègue, Raymond. Ronsard. 3. éd. Paris, 1961.
38525.21.35 Stone, Donald. Ronsard's sonnet cyles. New Haven, 1966.
38525.21.40 Armstrong, Elizabeth. Ronsard and the Age of Gold. London, 1968.
38525.21.45 Dassonville, Michel. Ronsard. Genève, 1968-
38525.21.50 Terreaux, Louis. Ronsard, correcteur de ses oeuvres. Genève, 1968.
38525.22 Prarond, Ernest. Les poëtes historiens, Ronsard et d'Aubigné. Paris, 1873.
38525.22.2 Gandar, E. Ronsard considéré comme imitateur d'Homère et de Pindare. Metz, 1854.
38525.22.4 Tiersot, J. Ronsard et la musiques de son temps. Paris, 1903.
38525.22.5 Froger, L. Les premières poésies de Ronsard. Mamers, 1892.
38525.22.6 Binet, Claude. Critical edition of the Discours de la vie de Pierre de Ronsard. Philadelphia, 1905.
38525.22.6.5 Binet, Claude. Critical edition of the Discours de la vie de Pierre de Ronsard. Philadelphia, 1905.
38525.22.6.10 Binet, Claude. Discours de la vie de Pierre de Ronsard. Paris, 1944.
38525.22.7 Köhler, F. Die Allitteration bei Ronsard. Erlangen, 1901.
38525.22.8 Dufay, Pierre. Le portrait, le buste et l'épitaphe de Ronsard au musée de Plois. Paris, 1907.
38525.22.9 Pamphlet box. Ronsard, Pierre de.
38525.22.10 Ronsard, Pierre de. Amours de Cassandre. Paris, 1907.
38525.22.11 Ronsard, Pierre de. Amours de Pierre de Ronsard Vandomois. Paris, 1910.
38525.22.12 Ronsard, Pierre de. Amours de Pierre de Ronsard. Paris, 1918. 2v.
38525.22.13 Charlier, Gustave. Un amour de Ronsard: "Austrée". Paris, 1920.
38525.22.15 Nolhac, Pierre de. Ronsard et l'humanisme. Paris, 1921.

38525.9 - .22.49 Individual authors, etc. - 1500-1661 - Ronsard - cont.

38525.22.16 Nolhac, Pierre de. La dernière amour de Ronsard. Paris, 1914.
38525.22.20 Cohen, Gustave. Ronsard; sa vie et son oeuvre. Photoreproduction. Paris, 1924.
38525.22.23 Cohen, Gustave. Ronsard; sa vie et son oeuvre. Paris, 1932.
38525.22.24 Cohen, Gustave. Ronsard; sa vie et son oeuvre. Paris, 1956.
38525.22.25 Martellière, Jean. Pierre de Ronsard gentilhomme vandomois. Paris, 1924.
38525.22.30 Champion, Pierre. Ronsard et son temps. Paris, 1925.
38525.22.34 Schweinitz, M. de. Les épitaphes de Ronsard. Thèse. Paris, 1925.
38525.22.35 Schweinitz, M. de. Les épitaphes de Ronsard. Paris, 1925.
38525.22.40 Ronsard et son temps. Paris, 1925.
38525.22.40.5 Ronsard et son temps. Paris, 1925.
38525.22.42 Photiades, C. Ronsard et son luth. 4e éd. Paris, 1925.
38525.22.45 Sorg, Roger. Cassandre ou Le secret de Ronsard. Paris, 1925.
38525.22.45.10F Champion, Pierre. Contribution à l'histoire de la société polie, Ronsard et Villeroy. Paris, 1925.
38525.22.45.15A Champion, Pierre. Pierre de Ronsard et Amadis Jamyn; leur autographs. Paris, 1924.
38525.22.45.15B Champion, Pierre. Pierre de Ronsard et Amadis Jamyn; leur autographs. Paris, 1924.
38525.22.45.20 Addamiano, Natale. Il rinascimento in Francia. Palermo, 1925.
38525.22.45.25 Rocher, E. Pierre de Ronsard, prince des poètes, 1524-1585. Paris, 1924.
38525.22.45.30 Rayon, E. Ronsard en France et dans la région de Brie-Gatinais. Melun, 1925.
38525.22.45.35A Nolhac, Pierre de. La vie amoureuse de Pierre de Ronsard. Paris, 1926.
38525.22.45.35B Nolhac, Pierre de. La vie amoureuse de Pierre de Ronsard. Paris, 1926.
38525.22.45.40 Raymond, Marcel. L'influence de Ronsard sur la poésie française (1550-1585). Thèse. Paris, 1927.
38525.22.45.41 Raymond, Marcel. L'influence de Ronsard sur la poésie française (1550-1585). Paris, 1927. 2v.
38525.22.45.42 Raymond, Marcel. L'influence de Ronsard sur la poésie française, 1550-1585. Genève, 1965.
38525.22.45.43 Maugain, Gabriel. Ronsard en Italie. Paris, 1926.
38525.22.45.50 Cornelia, W.B. The classical sources of the nature references in Ronsard's poetry. N.Y., 1934.
38525.22.45.55A Wolfe, Humbert. Ronsard and French romantic poetry. Oxford, 1935.
38525.22.45.55B Wolfe, Humbert. Ronsard and French romantic poetry. Oxford, 1935.
38525.22.45.60A Silver, Isidore. The Pindaric odes of Ronsard. Paris, 1937.
38525.22.45.60B Silver, Isidore. The Pindaric odes of Ronsard. Paris, 1937.
38525.22.45.61 Sliver, Isidore. Ronsard and the Hellenic renaissance in France. St. Louis, 1961.
38525.22.45.62 Silver, Isidore. The intellectual evolution of Ronsard. St. Louis, 1969.
38525.22.45.65 Bishop, M. Ronsard, prince and poet. London, 1940.
38525.22.45.70 Frey, Dora E. Le genre elegiaque dans l'oeuvre de Ronsard. Inaug. Diss. Liège, 1939.
38525.22.45.75 Scheffler, W. Essai sur Ronsard et sa réforme litteraire. Dresde, 1873.
38525.22.45.80 Lewis, D.B.W. Ronsard. London, 1944.
38525.22.45.83 Thibault, G. Bibliographie des poésies de Pierre de Ronsard. Paris, 1941.
38525.22.45.84 Vianey, Joseph. Les odes de Ronsard. Paris, 1932.
38525.22.45.85 Vianey, Joseph. Les odes de Ronsard. Paris, 1946.
38525.22.45.90 Desonay, F. Ronsard. Bruxelles, 1952. 3v.
38525.22.45.95 Hallowell, R.E. Ronsard and the conventional Roman elegy. Urbana, 1954.
38525.22.45.100 Berry, André. Ronsard. Paris, 1961.
38525.22.45.105 Wilson, D.B. Ronsard. Manchester, 1961.
38525.22.45.110 Katz, R.A. Ronsard's French critics, 1585-1828. Genève, 1966.
38525.22.45.115 Gendre, André. Ronsard; poète de la conquête amoureuse. Neuchâtel, 1970.
38525.22.45.120 Jones, Kenneth R. Wilson. Pierre de Ronsard. N.Y., 1970.

38525.22.50 - .27 Individual authors, etc. - 1500-1661 - Regnier

Htn 38525.22.50* Régnier, Mathurin. Oeuvres. Genève, 1777. 2v.
38525.22.51 Régnier, Mathurin. Oeuvres. London, 1746. 2v.
38525.22.60 Régnier, Mathurin. Oeuvres complètes. Paris, 1853. 2 pam.
38525.22.62 Régnier, Mathurin. Oeuvres complètes. Paris, 1912?
38525.22.65 Régnier, Mathurin. Oeuvres de Mathurin Régnier. Paris, 1862.
Htn 38525.22.68* Régnier, Mathurin. Satyres. Paris, 1614.
Htn 38525.22.70* Régnier, Mathurin. Les satyres de sieur Régnier. Paris, 1619.
Htn 38525.22.75* Régnier, Mathurin. Les satyres du sieur Régnier. Paris, 1645.
Htn 38525.22.80* Régnier, Mathurin. Les satyres et autres oeuvres. Paris, 1655.
38525.22.82 Régnier, Mathurin. Satyres et autres oeuvres de Régnier. Londres, 1733.
38525.23 Régnier, Mathurin. Oeuvres complètes. Paris, 1874.
38525.23.5 Régnier, Mathurin. Oeuvres complètes. Paris, 1869.
38525.24 Régnier, Mathurin. Oeuvres complètes. Paris, 1875.
38525.25 Régnier, Mathurin. Oeuvres complètes. Paris, 1876.
38525.25.5 Régnier, Mathurin. Oeuvres complètes. Paris, 1876.
38525.26 Régnier, Mathurin. Oeuvres complètes. Paris, 1872.
38525.26.3 Régnier, Mathurin. Oeuvres complètes. Paris, 1873.
38525.26.5 Régnier, Mathurin. Quelques pièces attribuées à Régnier. Paris, 1870?
38525.26.20A Régnier, Mathurin. Oeuvres complètes. Paris, 1930.
38525.26.20B Régnier, Mathurin. Oeuvres complètes. Paris, 1930.
38525.26.25 Régnier, Mathurin. Oeuvres complètes. Paris, 1958.
X Cg 38525.26.26 Régnier, Mathurin. Oeuvres. 9. éd. Londres, 1780. 2v.
38525.27 Cherrier, Henri. Bibliographie de Mathurin Régnier. Paris, 1884.
38525.27.5 Vianey, Joseph. Mathurin Régnier. Paris, 1896.
38525.27.7 Nordström, T. Observations sur la langue...de Mathurin Régnier. Lund, 1870.
38525.27.8 Rothschild, J. de. Essai sur les satires de Mathurin Régnier, 1573-1613. Paris, 1863.
38525.27.15 Reger, K.F. Mathurin Régniers literargeschichtliche Bedeutung. Inaug. Diss. München, 1937.

38525.28 - .29 Individual authors, etc. - 1500-1661 - Motin

38525.28 Motin, Pierre. Oeuvres inédites. Paris, 1882.

38525.30 - .32 Individual authors, etc. - 1500-1661 - Tahureau

38525.30 Blanchemain, Prosper. Poésies de Jacques Tahureau. Paris, 1870. 2v.
Htn 38525.30.5* Tahureau, Jacques. Dialogues. Paris, 1568.
38525.31 Conscience, F. Les dialogues de Jacques Tahureau. Paris, 1870.

38525.33 - .34 Individual authors, etc. - 1500-1661 - Guillaume Bouchet

38525.33 Pamphlet box. Bouchet, Guillaume.
38525.34A Bouchet, Guillaume. Les serees. Paris, 1873. 6v.
38525.34B Bouchet, Guillaume. Les serees. Paris, 1873. 6v.
Htn 38525.34.5* Bouchet, Guillaume. Les serees. Poitiers, 1588.
Htn 38525.34.10* Bouchet, Guillaume. Premier-douzième livres de serées. Paris, 1608.
38525.34.15 Liotard, Charles. Étude sur les serées de Guillaume Bouchet. Nimes, 1875.
38525.34.17 Henke, Karl. Syntaktische Untersuchungen zu Guillaume Bouchets "Serées". Marburg, 1908.

38525.35 - .39 Individual authors, etc. - 1500-1661 - Tristan L'Hermite

38525.35.9 Tristan L'Hermite, F. Le parasite. I. Paris, n.d.
38525.35.10 Tristan L'Hermite, F. La mariane. II. Paris, n.d.
38525.35.11 Tristan L'Hermite, F. La mort de Sénèque. III. Paris, n.d.
38525.35.12 Tristan L'Hermite, F. La folie du sage. IV. Paris, n.d.
38525.35.13 Tristan L'Hermite, F. Panthée. V. Paris, n.d.
38525.35.14 Tristan L'Hermite, F. La mort de Chrispe. VI. Paris, n.d.
38525.35.15 Tristan L'Hermite, F. Osman. VII. Paris, n.d.
38525.35.16 Tristan L'Hermite, F. Amarillis. VIII. Paris, n.d.
38525.35.23 Tristan L'Hermite, F. Tristan L'Hermite; les amours, la lyre. 3e éd. Paris, 1909.
38525.35.30A Tristan L'Hermite, F. Le parasite. Paris, 1934.
38525.35.30B Tristan L'Hermite, F. Le parasite. Paris, 1934.
38525.35.35 Tristan L'Hermite, F. Poésies. Paris, 1962.
Htn 38525.35.50* Tristan L'Hermite, F. Poésies galantes et heroiques. Paris, 1662.
38525.35.55 Tristan L'Hermite, F. Les vers héroiques. Genève, 1967.
Htn 38525.36* Tristan L'Hermite, F. La lyre, l'Orphée. Paris, 1641.
Htn 38525.36.2* Tristan L'Hermite, F. La Mariane. Paris, 1637.
X Cg 38525.36.2.5 Tristan L'Hermite, F. La Mariane, tragédie. Paris, 1917.
Htn 38525.36.2.50* Tristan L'Hermite, F. La mort de Chrispe ou Les maleurs domestiques du grand Constantin. Paris, 1645.
38525.36.3 Tristan L'Hermite, F. La mort de Chrispe. Marian. n.p., n.d.
Htn 38525.36.4* Tristan L'Hermite, F. La mort de Sénèque. Paris, 1645.
38525.36.5 Tristan L'Hermite, F. La mort de Sénèque. Paris, 1919.
Htn 38525.36.6* Tristan L'Hermite, F. Panthée. Paris, 1639.
38525.36.7 Tristan L'Hermite, F. Oeuvres.. Paris, 1909.
38525.36.8 Tristan L'Hermite, F. Les plaintes d'Acante et autres oeuvres. Paris, 1909.
38525.36.9 Tristan L'Hermite, F. Le page disgracié. Paris, 1898.
38525.36.9.1 Tristan L'Hermite, F. Le page disgracié. Paris, 1898. Nendeln, 1972.
38525.36.10 Tristan L'Hermite, F. Les amours de Tristan. Paris, 1638.
38525.36.12 Tristan L'Hermite, F. Les amours et autres poesies. Paris, 1925.
38525.36.25 Tristan L'Hermite, F. La folie du sage. Paris, 1936.
38525.36.30 Tristan L'Hermite, F. Choix de pages. Limoges, 1960.
38525.37.2 Bernardin, Napoléon Maurice. Un precurseur de Racine. Genève, 1967.
38525.38 Carriat, A. Bibliographie des oeuvres de Tristan L'Hermite. Limoges, 1955.
38525.38.10 Carriat, A. Tristan. Limoges, 1955.
38525.38.15 Abraham, Claude Kurt. The strangers. Gainesville, 1966.

38525.45 - Individual authors, etc. - 1500-1661 - Rotrou

38525.45 Rotrou, Jean de. Oeuvres. Paris, 1820. 5v.
X Cg 38525.50 Rotrou, Jean de. Théâtre choisi. Paris, 1882. 2v.
38525.51 Rotrou, Jean de. Théâtre choisi. Paris, 1883.
Htn 38525.55* Rotrou, Jean de. Agesilan de Colchos. Paris, 1637.
Htn 38525.56* Rotrou, Jean de. Amélie. Paris, 1638.
Htn 38525.57* Rotrou, Jean de. Antigone. Paris, 1639.
Htn 38525.58* Rotrou, Jean de. La bague de l'oubly. Paris, 1635.
Htn 38525.59* Rotrou, Jean de. Le Belissaire. Paris, 1644.
Htn 38525.60* Rotrou, Jean de. La belle Alphrède. Paris, 1639.
Htn 38525.61* Rotrou, Jean de. Les captifs; ou, Les esclaves. Paris, 1640.
Htn 38525.62* Rotrou, Jean de. La Celiane. Paris, 1637.
Htn 38525.63* Rotrou, Jean de. La Celimene. Paris, 1637.
Htn 38525.64* Rotrou, Jean de. Clarice; ou, L'amour constant. Paris, 1643.
Htn 38525.65* Rotrou, Jean de. Cosroes. Paris, 1649.
38525.65.10 Rotrou, Jean de. Cosroès. Paris, 1950.
Htn 38525.66* Rotrou, Jean de. Crisante. Paris, 1640.
Htn 38525.67* Rotrou, Jean de. Les deux pucelles. Lyon, 1653.
Htn 38525.68* Rotrou, Jean de. La Diane. Paris, 1635.
Htn 38525.69* Rotrou, Jean de. Dom Bernard de Cabrère. Paris, 1647.
Htn 38525.70* Rotrou, Jean de. La Doristée. Paris, 1635.
Htn 38525.71* Rotrou, Jean de. Le filandre. Paris, 1637.
Htn 38525.72* Rotrou, Jean de. Hercule mourant. Paris, 1636.
Htn 38525.73* Rotrou, Jean de. L'heureuse Constance. Paris, 1636.
Htn 38525.74* Rotrou, Jean de. L'heureux naufrage. Paris, 1638.
Htn 38525.75* Rotrou, Jean de. L'hypocondriaque; ou, le mort amoureux. Paris, 1631.
Htn 38525.76* Rotrou, Jean de. L'innocente infidélité. Paris, 1637.
Htn 38525.77* Rotrou, Jean de. Iphygénie. Paris, 1641.
Htn 38525.78* Rotrou, Jean de. Laure persécutée. Paris, 1639.
Htn 38525.79* Rotrou, Jean de. Les Ménechmes. Paris, 1636.
Htn 38525.80* Rotrou, Jean de. Les occasions perdues. Paris, 1635.
Htn 38525.81* Rotrou, Jean de. La pèlerine amoureuse. Paris, 1637.
Htn 38525.82* Rotrou, Jean de. La soeur. Paris, 1647.
Htn 38525.82.5* Rotrou, Jean de. La soeur généreuse. Paris, 1647.
Htn 38525.83* Rotrou, Jean de. Les sosies. Paris, 1647.
Htn 38525.84* Rotrou, Jean de. Venceslas. Paris, 1648.
38525.84.5 Rotrou, Jean de. Venceslas. Paris, 1802.
38525.84.10 Rotrou, Jean de. Venceslas. Saarbrücken, 1956.
Htn 38525.85* Rotrou, Jean de. Le veritable St.Genest. Paris, 1648.
38525.88A Rotrou, Jean de. Saint Genest and Venceslas. Boston, 1907.
38525.88B Rotrou, Jean de. Saint Genest and Venceslas. Boston, 1907.
38525.90 Buchetmann, F.E. Jean de Rotrou's Antigone und ihre Quellen. Erlangen, 1901.

38525.45 - Individual authors, etc. - 1500-1661 - Rotrou - cont.

	38525.91	Jarry, J. Essai sur les oeuvres dramatiques de Jean Rotrou. Lille, 1868.
	38525.92	Merlet, L.V.C. Notice biographique sur Jean Rotrou. Chartres, 1885.
	38525.93	Person, Léonce. Histoire du Venceslas de Rotrou. Paris, 1882.
	38525.94	Person, Léonce. Histoire du Véritable Saint-Genest de Rotrou. Paris, 1882.
	38525.95	Steffens, Georg. Rotrou-Studien. Oppeln, 1891.
	38525.96	Vianey, Joseph. Deux sources inconnues de Rotrou. Dole, 1891.
	38525.97	Neri, F. La sorte del Rotrou. Torino, 1930.
	38525.98	Fries, Wilhelm. Der Stil der Theaterstücke Rotrous. Inaug. Diss. Würzburg, 1933.
	38525.99	Leiner, W. Étude stylistique et litteraire de Venceslas. Saarbrücken, 1955.
	38525.100	Valle Abad, F. del. Influencia española sobre la literatura francesa. Avila, 1946.
	38525.106	Orlando, Francesco. Rotrou dalla tragicomedia alla tragedia. Torino, 1963.
	38525.107	Baden, Jacqueline van. Rotrou, le héros tragique et la révolte. Paris, 1965.
	38525.108	Nelson, Robert James. Immanence and transcendence; the theater of Jean Rotrou, 1609-1650. Columbus, 1969.
	38525.110	Morel, Jacques. Jean Rotrou, dramaturge de l'ambigüité. Paris, 1968.
	38525.111	Schueler, Gerda. Die Rezeption der spanischen Comedia in Frankreich...Lope de Vega und Jean Rotrou. Köln, 1966.

38526 Individual authors, etc. - 1500-1661 - Other poets and dramatists, 16th century

Htn	38526.01.15*	Ambillon, R. Sidere; pastorelle. Paris, 1609.
	38526.01.20	Arnauld d'Andilly, R. Oeuvres chrestiennes. 9e éd. Paris, 1659. 2 pam.
Htn	38526.01.35*	Arnauld d'Andilly, R. Lettres. Paris, 1645.
	38526.01.45	Arnauld d'Andilly, R. Lettres. Lyon, 1674.
Htn	38526.1*	Auger, Jacques. La mort de Caton. Paris, 1648.
	38526.1.9	Hartmann, Hans. Guillaume des Autels (1529-1581?). Zürich, 1907.
	38526.1.12	Young, Margaret. Guillaume des Autelz. Genève, 1969.
Htn	38526.1.15*	Avity, Pierre de. Les travaux sans travail. Paris, 1602.
Htn	38526.1.20*	Bauter, Charles. La rodomontade, Mort de Roger; tragedies et amours de Catherine. Paris, 1605.
	38526.1.25	Harvitt, Hélène. Eustorg de Beaulieu, a disciple of Marot. Lancaster, 1918.
	38526.1.30	Beaulieu, E. Les divers rapportz. Genève, 1964.
	38526.1.35	Eckhardt, Alex. Reandremy Belleau. Budapest, 1917.
Htn	38526.1.35.15*	Belleau, R. Les oeuvres poétiques. Paris, 1578. 2v.
	38526.1.35.18	Belleau, R. La bergerie. Genève, 1954.
	38526.1.35.20	Delacourcelle, D. Le sentiment de l'art dans la Bergerie de Remy Belleau. Oxford, 1945.
Htn	38526.2*	Beys, Charles. Theatre. Paris, 1636-53.
	38526.2.2	Beys, Charles. Les illustres fous of Charles Beys. Baltimore, 1942.
	38526.2.3A	Bèze, Théodore de. Abraham sacrifiant (1550). Genève, 1874.
	38526.2.3B	Bèze, Théodore de. Abraham sacrifiant (1550). Photoreproduction. Genève, 1874.
	38526.2.3.5	Bèze, Théodore de. Abraham sacrifiant. Genève, 1967.
	38526.2.3.6	Bèze, Théodore de. Abraham sacrifiant. N.Y., 1969.
	38526.2.4	Bèze, Théodore de. Tragédie Françoise du sacrifice d'Abraham. N.Y., 1856.
	38526.2.4.25	Keegstra, Pieter. Abraham sacrifiant de Théodore de Bèze. Proefschrift. Den Haag, 1928.
	38526.2.4.100	Billard, C. Gaston de Foix. N.Y., 1931.
	38526.2.4.125	Dabney, L.E. Claude Billard. Baltimore, 1931.
Htn	38526.2.4.150*	Billaut, Adam. Le ville brequin de Me Adam, menvisier de Nevers. Paris, 1663.
Htn	38526.2.4.200*	Blanchon, Joachim. Les premières oeuvres poétiques. Paris, 1583.
Htn	38526.2.5*	Boisrobert, F. le M. de. Cassandre. Paris, 1654.
Htn	38526.2.7*	Boisrobert, F. le M. de. La folle gageure. Paris, 1653.
Htn	38526.2.9*	Boisrobert, F. le M. de. Palène. Paris, 1640.
Htn	38526.2.11*	Boisrobert, F. le M. de. Le pyrandre. Paris, 1633.
Htn	38526.2.13*	Boisrobert, F. le M. de. Le Parnasse royal. Paris, 1635.
	38526.2.15	Boisrobert, F. le M. de. Epistre en vers. Paris, 1921. 2v.
Htn	38526.2.17*	Boisrobert, F. le M. de. Les epistres en vers et autres oeuvres poétiques. Paris, 1659.
Htn	38526.2.19*	Boisrobert, F. le M. de. La jalouse d'elle-mesme. Paris, 1659.
Htn	38526.2.21*	Boisrobert, F. le M. de. Les apparences trompeuses. Paris, 1656. 5 pam.
	38526.2.30	Tenner, Fritz. François le Metel de Boisrobert als Dramatiker und Nachahmer des spanischen Dramas. Leipzig, 1907.
	38526.2.31	Magne, E. Le plaisant Abbé de Boisrobert. Paris, 1909.
Htn	38526.3*	Borce, M. Les princes victorieux. Lyon, 1627.
Htn	38526.3.5*	Bosquier, F.P. Tragoedie nouvelle. Mons, 1589.
	38526.3.5.140	Bouchet, Jean. Epistres morales et familières du traverseur. N.Y., 1969.
Htn	38526.3.5.150*	Bouchet, Jean. Epistres morales et familières du traverseur. Poictieurs, 1545.
Htn	38526.3.5.155*	Bouchet, Jean. Triumphes de la noble et amoureuse dame. Paris, 1545.
Htn	38526.3.5.165*	Bouchet, Jean. Les angoyses et remedes daniouis. Poictiers, 1536. 2 pam.
	38526.3.5.200	Hamon, Auguste. Un grand rhétoriqueur poitevin. Thèse. Paris, 1901.
	38526.3.5.201	Hamon, Auguste. Un grand rhétoriqueur poitevin; Jean Bouchet, 1476-1557? Genève, 1970.
Htn	38526.3.6*	Bougeant, G.H. La critique de la femme docteur. London, 1731.
Htn	38526.3.6.3*	Bougeant, G.H. Le saint Deniche ou La bauqueroute. La Haye, 1732.
Htn	38526.3.6.8*	Bougeant, G.H. Suite de la femme docteur. La Haye, 1732.
Htn	38526.3.6.10*	Bougeant, G.H. La femme docteur ou la theologie tombée en quenouille. Liege, 1731.
	38526.3.7	Vulliod, A. La femme docteur (Bougeant). Lyon, 1912.
Htn	38526.3.7.50*	Boüillon. Les oeuvres de feu Monsieur de Boüillon. Paris, 1663.
	38526.3.7.100	Bourdigné, C. La légende de Pierre Faifeu. Paris, 1880.
Htn	38526.3.7.150*	Bourneuf, Sieur. L'algouasil burlesque, imité du visions. Paris, 1657.
	38526.4	Béreau, Jacques. Oeuvres poétiques de Jacques Béreau. Paris, 1884.

38526 Individual authors, etc. - 1500-1661 - Other poets and dramatists, 16th century - cont.

	38526.5	Frank, Félix. Les comptes du monde adventureux. Paris, 1878. 2v.
	38526.6	Montaiglon, Anatole de. Huit sonnets de...Du Bellay. Paris, 1849.
Htn	38526.6.2*	Du Bellay, Joachim. Les oeuvres françoises. Paris, 1584.
Htn	38526.6.3*	Du Bellay, Joachim. Oeuvres. Rouen, 1597. 2v.
	38526.6.5	Du Bellay, Joachim. Oeuvres poétiques. Paris, 1908-1931. 7v.
	38526.6.6	Du Bellay, Joachim. Oeuvres poétiques. Paris, 1961.
	38526.6.7	Du Bellay, Joachim. Oeuvres choisies. Paris, 1946.
	38526.6.8	Du Bellay, Joachim. Oeuvres choisies. Paris, 1953.
	38526.6.9	Du Bellay, Joachim. Poésies françaises et latines. Paris, 1918. 2v.
Htn	38526.6.10*	Du Bellay, Joachim. Recueil de poésie. Paris, 1561.
	38526.6.13	Du Bellay, Joachim. La defense et illustration de la langue française. Paris, 1936.
Htn	38526.6.14*	Du Bellay, Joachim. Les regrets et autres oeuvres. Paris, 1559.
	38526.6.15	Du Bellay, Joachim. Les regrets. Paris, 19- .
	38526.6.17	Du Bellay, Joachim. Les regrets. Paris, 1925.
	38526.6.18	Du Bellay, Joachim. Les regrets. Genève, 1943.
	38526.6.18.5	Du Bellay, Joachim. Les regrets. Paris, 1949.
	38526.6.18.10	Du Bellay, Joachim. Les regrets. Paris, 1955.
	38526.6.18.15	Du Bellay, Joachim. Les regrets. Paris, 1958.
	38526.6.19	Du Bellay, Joachim. Les amours de Faustine. Amiens, 1923.
Htn	38526.6.20*	Du Bellay, Joachim. Ample discours au roy. Paris, 1588.
Htn	38526.6.25*	Du Bellay, Joachim. L'olive. Paris, 1554.
Htn	38526.6.30*	Du Bellay, Joachim. Le premier livre des antiquitez de Rome. Paris, 1558.
	38526.6.35	Du Bellay, Joachim. Louange de la France et du roy. Paris, 1560.
Htn	38526.6.40*	Du Bellay, Joachim. Entreprise du roy-daulphin pour le tournoy. Paris, 1559.
	38526.6.45	Du Bellay, Joachim. Les antiquitez de Rome et les regrets. Paris, 1945.
	38526.6.47	Du Bellay, Joachim. Les antiquitez de Rome et les regrets. Genève, 1960.
	38526.6.50	Du Bellay, Joachim. Poems. Oxford, 1961.
	38526.6.55	Du Bellay, Joachim. Les regrets. Genève, 1966.
	38526.6.60	Du Bellay, Joachim. Divers jeux rustiques. Lille, 1947.
	38526.6.61	Du Bellay, Joachim. Divers jeux rustiques. Genève, 1947.
	38526.6.63	Du Bellay, Joachim. Divers jeux rustiques. Paris, 1947.
	38526.6.785	Du Bellay, Joachim. Stesky. Praha, 1964.
	38526.7	Du Bellay, Joachim. Lettres de Joachim Du Bellay. Paris, 1883.
	38526.7.8	Du Bellay, Joachim. Joachim Du Bellay. Paris, 1958.
	38526.7.9	Pamphlet box. Du Bellay, Joachim. Paris, 1874.
	38526.7.10	Addamiano, Natale. Delle opere poetiche francesi di Joachim Du Bellay. Cagliari, 1920.
	38526.7.15	Merrill, R.V. Platonism of Joachim Du Bellay. Chicago, 1925.
	38526.7.25	Vianey, Joseph. Les regrets de Joachim Du Bellay. Paris, 1930.
	38526.7.30	Cameron, Alice. The influence of Ariosto's epic and lyric poetry on Ronsard and his group. A portion of a diss. Baltimore, 1930.
	38526.7.35	Ambrière, F. Joachim Du Bellay. Paris, 1930.
	38526.7.40	François, A. Les sonnets suisses de Joachim Du Bellay. Lausanne, 1946.
	38526.7.45	Saulnier, V.L. Du Bellay. Paris, 1951.
	38526.7.50	Dickinson, G. Du Bellay in Rome. Leiden, 1960.
	38526.7.55	Saba, Guido. La poesia di Joachim Du Bellay. Messina, 1962.
	38526.7.60	Keating, Louis Clark. Joachim Du Bellay. N.Y., 1971.
	38526.8A	Baif, Jean Antoine de. Poésies choisies. Paris, 1874.
	38526.8B	Baif, Jean Antoine de. Poésies choisies. Paris, 1874.
	38526.8.2	Baif, Jean Antoine de. Chansonnettes. Vancouver, 1964.
	38526.8.4	Baif, Jean Antoine de. Les amours de Francine. Genève, 1966. 2v.
	38526.8.5	Baif, Jean Antoine de. Les amours. Paris, 1909.
	38526.8.6	Baif, Jean Antoine de. Le psautier de 1587. Paris, 1963.
	38526.8.7	Lehmann, Johanna. Baifs dichterische Vorstellung von Meer und Wasser. Greifswald, 1917.
	38526.8.9	Nagel, H. Die metrischen Verse Jean Antoine de Baifs. Leipzig, 1878.
	38526.8.10A	Ingraham, E.S. The sources of Les amours de Jean Antoine de Baif. Columbus, 1905.
	38526.8.10B	Ingraham, E.S. The sources of Les amours de Jean Antoine de Baif. Columbus, 1905.
NEDL	38526.8.12	Auge-Chiquet, Mathieu. La vie, les idéees et l'oeuvres de Baif. Paris, 1909.
	38526.8.16	Augé-Chiquet, Mathieu. La vie, les idées et l'oeuvre de Jean Antoin e de Baif. Genève, 1969.
Htn	38526.8.30*	Baro, Balthasar. La clarimonde. Paris, 1643.
Htn	38526.8.75*	Bertaut, Jean. Recueil des oeuvres poétiques de Jean Bertaut. Paris, 1601.
	38526.9	Bertaut, Jean. Les oeuvres poétiques. Paris, 1891.
Htn	38526.9.5*	Bertaut, Jean. Les oeuvres poétiques. Paris, 1633.
	38526.9.10	Bertaut, Jean. Recueil de quelques vers amoureux. Paris, 1970.
	38526.9.20	Contades, G. de. Les prédécesseurs de Bertaut. Alençon, 1897.
Htn	38526.9.22*	Billaut, Adam. Les chevilles de Maître Adam, manuisier de Nevers. Paris, 1644.
Htn	38526.9.23*	Birague, Flaminio de. Premières oeuvres poétiques. Paris, 1585.
	38526.9.25	Venema, Johannes. Über die "Soltane". Inaug. Diss. Marburg, 1888.
	38526.9.50	Bassecourt, Claude de. Trage-comédie pastoralle. Bruxelles, 1931.
	38526.10	Mugnier, F. La vie et les poésies de Jean de Boyssomé. Paris, 1897.
	38526.10.2	Corrozet, Gilles. Le compte du rossignol. Paris, 1924.
	38526.10.5	Boysson, Richard de. Un humaniste toulousain Jéhan de Boysson, 1505-1559. Paris, 1897.
	38526.10.7	Boysson, Jéhan de. Les trois centuries. Toulouse, 1923.
	38526.10.7.2	Boysson, Jéhan de. Les trois centuries. Thèse. Toulouse, 1923.
	38526.10.8.2	Brach, Pierre de. Oeuvres poétiques. Paris, 1861-62. 2v.
	38526.10.8.2.5	Brach, Pierre de. Les amours d'Aymée. Genève, 1971.
	38526.10.8.4	Bruès, Guy de. Dialogues. Baltimore, 1953.
Htn	38526.10.8.5*	Chapoton. Coriolan. Paris, 1638.
	38526.10.8.7	Chapoton. La grande iovrnee des machines. Paris, 1648.
	38526.10.8.10	Chassignet, Jean Baptiste. Le mespris de la vie et consolation contre la mort. Genève, 1967.

38526 Individual authors, etc. - 1500-1661 - Other poets and dramatists, 16th century - cont.

38526.10.8.15 Chassignet, Jean Baptiste. Sonnets franc-comtois, inédits. Paris, 1892.
38526.10.8.16 Chassignet, Jean Baptiste. Le mespris de la vie et consolation contre la mort. Genève, 1953.
38526.10.8.17 Müller, A. Un poète religieux du XVIe siècle. Paris, 1951.
38526.10.8.17.2 Müller, A. Un poète religieux du XVIe siècle. Thèse. Paris, 1951.
38526.10.8.22 Buttet, M.C. de. Oeuvres poétiques. v.1-2. Paris, 1880.
38526.10.8.23 Ortali, Raymond. Un poète de la mort: Jean Baptiste Chassignet. Genève, 1968.
Htn 38526.10.8.25* Cholières, Nicolas de. Les apres disness du Seigneur de Cholières. Paris, 1588.
Htn 38526.10.8.27* Cholières, Nicolas de. La guerre des masles contre les femelles. Paris, 1588.
38526.10.8.28 Roche, Louis P. Claude Chappuys (?-1575). Paris, 1929.
38526.10.8.28.1 Roche, Louis P. Claude Chappuys (?-1575). Genève, 1970.
38526.10.8.28.5 Roche, Louis P. Claude Chappuys (?-1575). Thèse. Poitiers, 1929.
38526.10.8.29 Chappuys, Claude de. Poésies intimes. Genève, 1966.
Htn 38526.10.8.29* Chevalier, Guillaume. Le decez ov fin dv monde. Paris, 1584.
Htn 38526.10.8.30* Chrestien, Nicolas. Les amantes. Rouen, 1613.
Htn 38526.10.8.50* Claveret, Jean. Le ravissement de Proserpine. Paris, 1640.
Htn 38526.10.8.55* Claveret, Jean. Le cuyer. Paris, 1665.
Htn 38526.10.8.65* Coeffeteau, N. Paraphrase de la prose des morts. Nantes, 1606. 3 pam.
Htn 38526.10.8.75* Coignard, G. Oeuvres chrestiennes. Tournon, 1595.
38526.10.9 Collerye, Roger de. Oeuvres. Paris, 1855.
38526.10.9.15 Collerye, Roger de. Roger de Collerye et ses poésies dolentes. Paris, 1942.
Htn 38526.10.10* Colletet, Guillaume. Cyminde. Paris, 1642.
38526.10.10.31 Colletet, Guillaume. Traitté de l'épigramme et Traitté du sonnet. Genève, 1965.
38526.10.10.80 Jannini, Pasquale Aneil. Verso il tempo della ragione. Milano, 1965.
Htn 38526.10.11* Colletet, Guillaume. Les amours de Melisse. Paris, 1625.
Htn 38526.10.11.100* Corrozet, Gilles. Les divers et memorables propos des nobles et illustres hommes. Lyon, 1558.
38526.10.11.150 Corrozet, Gilles. Les blasons domestiques. Paris, 1865.
38526.10.12 Corrozet, Gilles. Le compte du rossignol. Paris, 1924.
38526.10.13 Corrozet, Gilles. Hecatomgraphie. Paris, 1905.
38526.10.14 Champier, S. Le livre de vraye amour. 's-Gravenhage, 1962.
38526.10.15 Collas, Georges. Jean Chapelain, 1595-1674. Paris, 1912.
Htn 38526.10.15.20* Colomby, François. Les plaintes de la captive Caliston. n.p., 1605.
Htn 38526.10.15.30* Colomby, François. Consolation à la royne regente. Paris, 1611.
Htn 38526.10.15.50* Colony, J.D. Enseignemens moraux. Coloniae Allgbrogum, 1619. 3 pam.
38526.10.16 Pamphlet box. Charles Cotin.
38526.10.16.5 Kunckel, C. Leben und Werke Charles Cotin's. Strassburg, 1914.
38526.10.17 Gohin, F. De Lud. Charondae, vita et versibus. Lutetiae Parisiorum, 1902.
Htn 38526.10.17.25* Crenne, Helisenne de. Les angoysses douloureuses qui procedent d'amours. n.p., n.d.
Htn 38526.10.17.65* Cretin, Guillaume D. Les poésies. Paris, 1723.
38526.10.17.75 Cretin, Guillaume D. Oeuvres poétiques. Paris, 1932.
Htn 38526.10.17.200* Deimier, P. de. Illustres avantures. Lyon, 1603.
38526.10.18 Lechèvre, Frédéric. Le prince des libertins du XVIIe siècle: Jacques Vallée Des Barreaux, sa vie et ses poésies, 1599-1673. Paris, 1907.
38526.10.19 Juge, Clement. Nicolas Denisot du mans. Paris, 1907.
Htn 38526.10.75* Desfontaines. Saint Alexis; tragédie. Rouen, 16- ?
Htn 38526.10.100* Desiré, Artus. Les batailles et victoires du Chevalier Celeste côtre le Chevalier Terrestre. Paris, 1564.
Htn 38526.11.5* Desmarets de Saint Sorlin, Jean. Mirame. Paris, 1641.
Htn 38526.11.6* Desmarets de Saint Sorlin, Jean. Roxane. Paris, 1640. 5 pam.
Htn 38526.11.7* Desmarets de Saint Sorlin, Jean. Les visionnaires. Paris, 1637.
38526.11.7.2 Desmarets de Saint Sorlin, Jean. Les visionnaires. Paris, 1963.
Htn 38526.11.8* Desmarets de Saint Sorlin, Jean. Ariana in two parts. 2d ed. London, 1641.
Htn 38526.11.8.5* Desmarets de Saint Sorlin, Jean. Clovis, ou La France chrestienne. Paris, 1657.
38526.11.9 Reibetanz, A. Jean Desmarets de Saint Sorlin, sein Leben. Leipzig, 1910.
38526.11.11 Gebhardt, Rudolf. Jean Desmarets de Saint Sorlin als dramatischer Dichter. Leipzig, 1912.
38526.11.15 Des Masures, Louis. Tragédies saintes. Paris, 1907.
38526.11.19 Pamphlet box. Louis Des Masures.
Htn 38526.11.20* Despinelle. Muses françoises. Paris, 1599.
Htn 38526.12.24* Desportes, Philippe. Les oeuvres. Lyon, 1606.
Htn 38526.12.25* Desportes, Philippe. Les premières oeuvres. Rouen, 1607.
Htn 38526.12.26* Desportes, Philippe. Les oeuvres. Lyon, 1608.
38526.12.33 Desportes, Philippe. Oeuvres. Paris, 1858.
38526.12.35 Desportes, Philippe. Oeuvres. pts.1-2. Strasbourg, 1925.
Htn 38526.12.40* Bible. O.T. Psalms. French. Paraphras. 1603. Les CL. Pseavmes de David, mis en vers françois, par Philippe Desportes. Paris, 1603.
38526.12.45 Desportes, Philippe. Élégies. Genève, 1961.
38526.12.49 Desportes, Philippe. Les imitations de l'Arioste. Thèse. Paris, 1936.
38526.12.50 Desportes, Philippe. Les imitations de l'Arioste. Paris, 1936.
38526.12.55 Desportes, Philippe. Cartels et masquarades. Genève, 1958.
38526.12.60 Desportes, Philippe. Cléonice; dernières amours. Genève, 1962.
Htn 38526.12.75* Desportes, Philippe. Rodomonths infernall, or The divell conquered. London, 1607.
38526.12.76 Desportes, Philippe. Diverses amours et autres oeuvres meslées. Genève, 1963.
38526.12.80 Lavaud, J. Un poète de cour au temps des derniers valois. Philippe Desportes, 1546-1606. Thèse. Paris, 1936.
38526.12.81 Lavaud, J. Un poète de cour. Paris, 1936.
38526.12.85 Cioranescu, A. Les imitations de l'Arioste de Philippe Desportes. Paris, 1936.
38526.13 Mucha, Oscar. Über Stil und Sprache von Philippe Desportes. Hamburg, 1895.

38526 Individual authors, etc. - 1500-1661 - Other poets and dramatists, 16th century - cont.

38526.13.2 Kreutzberg, P. Die Grammatik Malherbe's nach dem "Commentaire sur Desportes". Neisse, 1890.
38526.13.4 Groebedinkel, P. Der Versbau bei Philippe Desportes und François de Malherbe. Altenburg, 1880.
38526.13.60 Desportes, Philippe. Les amours de Diane. v.1-2. Genève, 1959.
38526.13.65 Desportes, Philippe. Les amours d'Hippolyte. Genève, 1960.
Htn 38526.13.200* Descret, L.C. Alizon. 2e éd. Paris, 1664.
38526.13.215A Diller, Georges E. Les dames des Roches. Diss. Paris, 1936.
38526.13.215B Diller, Georges E. Les dames des Roches. Diss. Paris, 1936.
Htn 38526.13.225* Tombeau de feu de...Fremin Douri. Paris, 1528.
Htn 38526.13.250* Du Buys, Guillaume. L'oreille du prince. Paris, 1582.
Htn 38526.13.265* Du Chesne, Joseph. Le grand miroir dv monde. Lyon, 1587.
38526.13.270 Du Hamel, J. d. The earliest French play about America. N.Y., 1931.
38526.13.273 Bergounioux, L.A. Un poète quercynois du XVIe siècle; Guillaume Du Buys, 1520?-1594. Thèse. Paris, 1935.
38526.13.275 Bergounioux, L.A. Guillaume Du Buys, 1520?-1594. Paris, 1936.
Htn 38526.13.300* Durval, J.G. Agarite. Paris, 1636.
38526.13.500 Durand, Estienne. Méditations. Paris, 1906.
Htn 38526.14.20* Du Ryer, Pierre. Thémistocle. Paris, 1648.
Htn 38526.14.25* Du Ryer, Pierre. Anaxandre; tragi-comédie. Paris, 1655.
38526.14.30 Du Ryer, Pierre. Scevole. Texte établi et présenté par Giancarlo Fasano. Bologna, 1966.
38526.14.40 Philipp, K. Pierre Du Ryers Leben und dramatische Werke. Zwickau, 1905.
38526.14.45 Lancaster, H.C. Pierre Du Ryer, dramatist. Washington, 1913.
38526.14.50 Du Val, Pierre. Théâtre mystique de Pierre Du Val. Paris, 1882.
Htn 38526.14.65* Du Verdier, Antoine. Les omonimes; satire des moeurs. Lyon, 1572.
38526.14.75 Reure, Odon Claude. Le bibliographie Antoine Du Verdier. Paris, 1897.
Htn 38526.14.85* Elis, Charles. Paranymph de la cour. Rouen, 1638.
38526.14.100 Esternod, C. d'. L'espadon satyrique. 1e éd. Paris, 1922.
Htn 38526.14.115* Ezanville, R. d'. Invention nouvelle des esperviers. Paris, 1610.
38526.14.125 Pamphlet box. Charles Estienne.
Htn 38526.14.128* Favereau, J.I. France consolée. Paris, 1625.
38526.14.129 Filleul, Nicolas. Les théâtres de Gaillon. Genève, 1971.
38526.14.130A Hawkins, R.L. Maistre Charles Fontaine, parisien. Cambridge, 1916.
38526.14.130B Hawkins, R.L. Maistre Charles Fontaine, parisien. Cambridge, 1916.
38526.14.131.80 Secret, François. L'ésotérisme de Guy Le Fèvre de La Bodevie. Genève, 1969.
Htn 38526.14.140* Gamon, Christophe de. La semaine, ou Création du monde. 2. éd. Niort, 1615.
38526.14.142 Gamon, Christophe de. Excerpte, prélection de Juliette Roche. Paris, 1927.
38526.14.150 Garaby, Antoine. Satires inédites. Rouen, 1888.
Htn 38526.14.175* Garel, Hélye. Le triomphe d'Astrée; [poem]. Bordeaux, 1607.
38526.14.200 Garnier, S. La henriade et la loyssée. 2e éd. Paris, 1770.
Htn 38526.15* Gillet de la Tessonerie. Le desniaise. Paris, 1658.
Htn 38526.15.2* Gillet de la Tessonerie. Policritte. Paris, 1643.
Htn 38526.15.2.5* Gillet de la Tessonerie. La belle Quixaire; tragi-comédie. Paris, 1640.
Htn 38526.15.15* Gilbert, Gabriel. Les amours d'Angélique et de Médor. Paris, 1664.
Htn 38526.15.17* Gilbert, Gabriel. Les amours d'Ovide. Paris, 1663.
Htn 38526.15.19* Gilbert, Gabriel. Arie et Petus. Paris, 1660.
Htn 38526.15.21* Gilbert, Gabriel. Hypolite. Paris, 1647.
Htn 38526.15.23* Gilbert, Gabriel. Marguerite de France. Paris, 1641.
Htn 38526.15.25* Gilbert, Gabriel. Opera pastorale héroique. Paris, 1672.
Htn 38526.15.27* Gilbert, Gabriel. Rodogune. Paris, 1646.
Htn 38526.15.29* Gilbert, Gabriel. Sémiramis. Paris, 1647.
Htn 38526.15.31* Gilbert, Gabriel. Téléphonte. Paris, 1642.
38526.15.81 Pellet, E.J. Gabriel Gilbert, 1620?-1680? Baltimore, 1930.
38526.16.25 Claus, F. Jean Godard, Leben und Werke (1564-1630). Greifswald, 1913.
Htn 38526.16.50* Frenicle, Nicolas. Palemon, fable bocagère, et pastoralle. Paris, 1632.
Htn 38526.16.51* Frenicle, Nicolas. L'entreien des illustres berges. Paris, 1634.
Htn 38526.16.250* Gody, Simplicien. Les honestes poësies de Placidas Philemon Gody [pseud.]. Paris, 1632.
38526.16.265 Godefroy, J.E. La vie de Dom Simplicien Gody. Vienne, 1931.
Htn 38526.16.300* Godard, Jeane. Oeuvres. v.1-2. Lyon, 1594.
Htn 38526.16.350* Godeau, A. Poésies chrestiennes. Paris, 1660.
Htn 38526.17* Gombauld, J.O. de. Les danaides. Paris, 1658.
Htn 38526.17.2* Gombauld, J.O. de. L'amaranthe. Paris, 1631.
Htn 38526.17.3* Gombauld, J.O. de. Epigrammes. Paris, 1657.
Htn 38526.17.4* Gombauld, J.O. de. Endimion. Paris, 1624.
Htn 38526.17.5* Gombauld, J.O. de. Endimion. London, 1639.
38526.17.9 Morel, L. Jean Ogier de Gombauld: sa vie, son oeuvre. Neuchâtel, 1910.
38526.17.12 Grévin, Jacques. Théâtre complet et poésies choises. Paris, 1922.
38526.17.19 Collischonn, G.A.O. Jacques Grévin's Tragödie "Caesar". Inaug. Diss. Marburg, 1885.
38526.17.30 Grévin, Jacques. César. Paris, 1971.
38526.17.100 Brenier de Montmorand, Antoine F.J.H.L. Anne de Graville. Paris, 1917.
38526.17.105 Graville, Anne de. Le beau romant des deux amans Palamon et Arcita et de la belle et saige Emilia. Paris, 1965.
38526.18 Gringore, Pierre. Oeuvres complètes. Paris, 1858. 2v.
38526.18.3 Gringore, Pierre. La vie Monseigneur Saint Louis. Paris, 1877.
38526.18.8 Pamphlet box. Gringore, Pierre.
38526.18.9 Oulmont, Charles. Pierre Gringore. Paris, 1911.
38526.18.10 Oulmont, Charles. Étude sur la langue de Pierre Gringore. Paris, 1911.
38526.18.12 Dittmann, W. Pierre Gringore als Dramatiker. Berlin, 1923.
38526.18.14 Picot, Emile. Pierre Gringore et les comédiens italiens. Paris, 1878.

Classified Listing

38526 Individual authors, etc. - 1500-1661 - Other poets and dramatists, 16th century - cont.

38526.19.5 Groulot, Arsène. Arsène Groulot. Torino, 1952. 2v.

38526.19.25 Surin, Jean Joseph. Poésies spirituelles suivis des contrats spirituels. Paris, 1957.

Htn 38526.20* Gournay, Marie de Jars de. Les advis. Paris, 1634.

38526.20.50 Whittem, Arthur F. Two fable collections. [Les fables morales de Philibert Guide]. Cambridge, 1932.

Htn 38526.20.75* Guyet, Nicolas. Pila palmaria. Aureliae, 1598.

38526.20.80 Le Vert. Le docteur amoureux. Genève, 1960.

38526.21.5 Guymond de la Touche. Iphigénie en Tauride. Paris, n.d.

38526.21.7 Guymond de la Touche. Iphigénie en Tauride. Paris, 1773.

Htn 38526.21.12* Habert, Isaac. Les trois livres des meteors avecques autres oeuvres. Paris, 1585.

38526.21.19 Héroet, A. Oeuvres poétiques. Paris, 1909.

38526.21.29 Arnoux, J. Un précurseur de Ronsard, Antoine Héroët. Digne, 1912.

38526.21.31 Larbaud, V. Notes sur Antoine Héroët et Jean de Lingendes. Paris, 1927.

38526.21.100 Indermuehle, Werner. Essai sur l'oeuvre de Claude Hopil. Thèse. Zürich, 1970.

38526.22 Leykauff, A. François Habert. Leipzig, 1904.

38526.22.01 Habert, François. Le philosophe parfaict, et Le temple de vertu. Thèse. Paris, 1922.

38526.22.2 Leykauff, A. François Habert's Leben und Weltanschauung. Naumberg, 1903.

38526.22.4 Wichert, Hans. François Habert und der christliche Humanismus. Inaug. Diss. Elberfeld, 1929.

Htn 38526.22.5* Jamyn, Amadis. Oeuvres poétiques. v.1-2. Paris, 1579-84.

38526.22.5.80 Hammerschmidt, Wilhelm. Amadis Jamyn; sein Leben und seine Werke. Weimar, 1915.

38526.22.5.85 Graur, Theodosia. Un disciple de Ronsard, Amadis Jamyn. Thèse. Paris, 1929.

38526.22.5.86 Graur, Theodosia. Un disciple de Ronsard, Amadis Jamyn. Paris, 1929.

38526.22.5.90 Cameron, Alice. The influence of Ariosto's epic and lyric poetry on the work of Amadis Jamyn. Baltimore, 1933.

38526.22.6 Baridon, Silvio F. Claude de Kerquefinen. Genève, 1954.

38526.22.8 La Caze. L'inceste suposé, cammane. Paris, 1641. 2 pam.

Htn 38526.22.10* La Croix, C.S. de. L'inconstance punie. Paris, 1641.

38526.22.12 Banachévitch, N. Jean Bastier de La Péruse, 1529-1554. Paris, 1923.

38526.22.12.2 Banachévitch, N. Jean Bastier de La Péruse, 1529-1554. Genève, 1970.

38526.22.13 Jacques, J. Le faut-mourir. v.1-2. Lyon, 1661.

38526.22.14.10 Livingston, C.H. Un disciple de Clément Marot. Paris, 1930.

Htn 38526.22.15* La Pinelière, G. de. Hippolyte. Paris, 1635.

38526.22.17 La Perrière, G. de. Le théâtre des bons engins. Gainesville, Florida, 1964.

Htn 38526.22.20* La Perrière, G. de. Les considerations des quatre mondes. Lyon, 1552.

Htn 38526.22.24* La Primaudaye, Pierre de. Cent quatrains consolatoires. Lyon, 1582.

Htn 38526.22.30* Le Royer de Prade, Jean. La victime d'estat. Paris, 1649.

38526.23 Laur, E. Louize Labé. Strassburg, 1873.

Htn 38526.24* La Mesnadière, H.J. La poétique. Paris, 1640.

38526.24.20 Reese, H.R. La Mesnadière's poétique (1639). Diss. Baltimore, 1937.

38526.25.5 Haacke, M. Un précurseur de Molière [Pierre de Larivey]. Halle, 1906.

38526.25.15 Cox, E.M. Notes, critical and bibliographical. London, 1915.

38526.25.100 Laudun d'Aigaliers, P. de. L'art poétique français. Toulouse, 1909.

Htn 38526.25.140* Laudun d'Aigaliers, P. de. Franciade. Paris, 1604.

38526.25.150 Allais, Gustave. De Franciades epica fabula in posteriore XVImi saeculi parte. Paris, 1891.

38526.26 Tross, Edwin. Oeuvres de Louise Labé. Paris, 1871.

38526.26.5 Labé, Louise Charly. Louise Labé. Paris, 1962.

38526.26.12 Labé, Louise Charly. Oeuvres. Lyon, 1824.

38526.26.30 Labé, Louise Charly. The debate between Folly and Cupid. London, 1925.

38526.26.50 Labé, Louise Charly. Oeuvres complètes. Maestricht, 1928.

38526.26.55 Labé, Louise Charly. Oeuvres de Louize Labé. Lyon, 1862.

38526.26.65 Labé, Louise Charly. De vijfentwintig sonnetten van Louïze Labé. Antwerpen, 1960.

38526.26.70 Labé, Louise Charly. Die vierundzwanzig Sonette der Louïze Labé, Lyoneserin, 1555. Leipzig, 191-.

38526.26.75 Labé, Louise Charly. De sonnetten van Lovize Labé. Maastricht, 1924.

38526.26.76 Labé, Louise Charly. Oeuvres poétiques. Paris, 1961.

38526.26.77 Labé, Louise Charly. Love sonnets. N.Y., 1947.

38526.26.78 Labé, Louise Charly. Die vierundzwanzig Sonette der Louïze Labé. Wiesbaden, 1950.

38526.26.79 Labé, Louise Charly. Das lyrische Gesamtwerk. Wiesbaden, 1957.

38526.26.80 Labé, Louise Charly. Sechs Sonnette. Hamburg, 1933.

38526.26.82 Labé, Louise Charly. Sonnets. Toronto, 1950.

38526.26.83 Labé, Louise Charly. Die Liebesgedichte einer schönen Lyoneser Seilerin namens Louïze Labé. Rudolstadt, 1956.

38526.26.84 Labé, Louise Charly. The twenty-four love sonnets. London, 1950.

38526.26.85 Labé, Louise Charly. Il canzoniere. Parma, 1955.

38526.26.86 Guidici, Enzo. Influssi italiani nel Débat di Louise Labé. Roma, 1953.

38526.26.87 Guidici, Enzo. Louise Labé e l'école lyonnaise. Napoli, 1964.

Htn 38526.26.88* Steeg, Gertrud von. Louise Labé. Baruth, 1940.

38526.26.89 Guidici, Enzo. Amore e follia nell'opera della Belle Cordière. Napoli, 1965.

38526.26.90 Fargue, Léon Paul. Louise Labé. Liège, 1956.

38526.26.92 Harvey, Lawrence Elliot. The aesthetics of the renaissance love sonnet. Geneva, 1962.

38526.26.95 Brabant, Luc van. Louize Labé. Coxyde, Belgique, 1966. 2v.

38526.26.100 Zamaron, Fernand. Louise Labé, dame de franchise. Paris, 1968.

38526.27 Labé, Louise Charly. Oeuvres. Paris, 1887. 2v.

38526.27.03 Larnac, Jean. Louise Labé, la belle cordière de Lyon (1522?-1566). Paris, 1934.

38526.27.05 Koczorowski, S.P. Louise Labé; étude littéraire. Paris, 1925.

38526.27.07 O'Connor, D. Louise Labé, sa vie et son oeuvre. Paris, 1926.

38526 Individual authors, etc. - 1500-1661 - Other poets and dramatists, 16th century - cont.

38526.27.08 Elfert, Anna. Die Dichtung der Louise Labé. Inaug. Diss. Ahlen, 1935.

38526.27.09 O'Connor, D. Louise Labé. Thèse. Abbeville, 1926.

Htn 38526.27.2* Lambert. La magie sans magie. Paris, 1661.

Htn 38526.27.3* Larivey, P. de. Les six premières comédies. Paris, 1579.

Htn 38526.27.4* Larivey, P. de. Les comédies facecievses de Pierre de Larivey. 2e éd. Lyon, 1597.

Htn 38526.27.4.8* Larivey, P. de. Trois comédies des six dernières de Pierre de Larivey chanpenois. Troyes, 1611.

38526.27.4.9 Larivey, P. de. Les esprits. Paris, 1953.

38526.27.5.10 Le Blanc, J. Neotemachie poétiques. Poèmes. Paris, 1610. 2 pam.

38526.27.5.15 Le Gras, J. Le tombeau de...Richard Le Gras. Paris, 1586. 2 pam.

38526.27.5.55 La Taille, Jean de. Jean de La Taille und sein Saül le furieux. Leipzig, 1908.

38526.27.5.55.1 Werner, Andreas. Jean de La Taille und sein Saül le furieux. Naumburg, 1908.

38526.27.5.60 La Taille, Jean de. De l'art de la tragédie. Manchester, 1939.

38526.27.5.65 La Taille, Jean de. Saül le furieux, la famine, ou les gabéonites. Paris, 1968.

38526.27.5.100 Daley, Tatham A. Jean de la Taille, 1533-1608. Thèse. Paris, 1934.

38526.27.5.101 Daley, Tatham A. Jean de la Taillé, 1533-1608. Paris, 1934.

38526.27.5.106 Baguenault de Puchesse, Gustave. Jean et Jacques de La Taille. Genève, 1970.

Htn 38526.27.5.250* La Roque, Siméon G. Les premières oeuvres de sieur de la Roque de Clermont. Rouen, 1596.

Htn 38526.27.5.260* La Roque, Siméon G. Oeuvres. Paris, 1609.

38526.27.5.261 Perkins, Jeanne G. Siméon La Roque, poète de l'absence, 1550-1615. Paris, 1967.

Htn 38526.27.5.270* La Tayssonière, G.C. de. Sourdine royale, sonnant le bouteselle. Paris, 1569.

Htn 38526.27.5.300* Le Fèvre. Hymnes ecclesiastiques. pts.1-2. Paris, 1578-79.

38526.27.5.500 Jolimont, T. de. Notice historique sur la vie et les oeuvres de Jacques Le Lieur. Moulins, 1847.

38526.27.6 Pamphlet box. Le Loyer, Pierre.

Htn 38526.27.7* Le Loyer, Pierre. L'erotopegnie. Paris, 1576.

38526.27.7.5 Le Loyer, Pierre. Pierre Le Loyer's version of the Ars amatoria. Chapel Hill, 1941.

38526.27.8 La Ceppède, Jean de. Les théorèmes sur le sacré mystère de notre rédemption. Genève, 1966.

38526.27.8.5 La Ceppède, Jean de. Essai sur la vie et l'oeuvre de Jean de La Ceppède. Genève, 1953.

38526.27.8.80 Donaldson-Evans, Lance K. Poésie et méditation chez Jean de La Ceppède. Genève, 1969.

38526.27.9 Stecher, J. Oeuvres de Jean Lemaire de Belges. Louvain, 1882. 4v.

Htn 38526.27.12* Lesfargus, B. David. Paris, 1660.

38526.27.13A Lemaire de Belges, Jean. La concorde des deux langages. Paris, 1947.

38526.27.13B Lemaire de Belges, Jean. La concorde des deux langages. Paris, 1947.

38526.27.13.2 Lemaire de Belges, Jean. La concorde des deux langages. Cambridge, 1964.

38526.27.14 Lemaire de Belges, Jean. La plainte du désiré. Paris, 1932.

38526.27.15 Lemaire de Belges, Jean. Les épîtres de l'amant vert. Lille, 1948.

Htn 38526.27.15* Lemaire de Belges, Jean. L'epistre du Roy à Hector de Troye. Paris, 1533.

38526.27.15.7 Lamaire de Belges, Jean. Die Briefe des grünen Liebhaben. München, 1970.

38526.27.16 Lemaire de Belges, Jean. Le temple d'honneur et de vertus. Genève, 1957.

38526.27.17 Lemaire de Belges, Jean. Jean Lemaire de Belges (um 1473 - um 1515). Berlin, 1924.

38526.27.18 Champion, P. Le canonicat pour Jean Lemaire de Belges à Lyon. Lyon, 1926.

Htn 38526.27.25* Le Petit, Claude. L'heure du berger. Revue. Paris, 1662.

38526.27.30 Le Petit, Claude. La chronique scandaleuse, ou Paris ridicule. Paris, 1927.

38526.27.35 Schroeder, F. Claude Le Petit; sein Leben. Wismar, 1913.

38526.27.40 Spaak, Paul. Jean Lemaire de Belges. Paris, 1926.

38526.27.45 Munn, K.M. A contribution to the study of Jean Lemaire de Belges. Diss. N.Y., 1936.

38526.28 Becker, P.A. Jean Lemaire. Der erste humanistische Dichter Frankreichs. Strassburg, 1893.

38526.28.3 Stecher, J. Notice Jean Lemaire de Belges. Bruxelles, 1891.

Htn 38526.28.5* Lestoile, C. de. L'intrigue des filous. Paris, 1682.

38526.28.5.55 Parker, R.A. Claude de l'Estoille, poet and dramatist, 1597-1652. Part of a Diss. Baltimore, 1930.

Htn 38526.28.7* Le Vert. Aricidie, ou Le mariage de Tite. Rouen, 1646.

38526.28.9 Lingendes, J. de. Oeuvres poétiques. Manchester, 1916.

38526.28.10 Lingendes, J. de. Oeuvres poétiques. Paris, 1916.

X Cg 38526.28.15 Contes et nouvelles. v.1-5. Paris, 1827. 3v.

Htn 38526.28.50* Lortique, A. Les poemes divers, ou Il est traicté de guerre. Paris, 1617.

38526.28.60 Lorgnier, Louis. Un homme à la mode. Amiens, 1942.

Htn 38526.28.75* Maillet, M. de. Les poésies de M. de Mailliet. Bourdeaux, 1616.

Htn 38526.28.100* Marbeuf, P. de. Recueil des vers de Pierre de Marbeuf. Rouen, 1897.

38526.28.280 Durel, L.C. L'oeuvre d'Andre Mareschal. Baltimore, 1932.

38526.29 Navarre, M. de. L'Heptaméron. Paris, 1879. 3v.

38526.29.01 Pamphlet box. Margaret de Navarre.

Htn 38526.29.2* Navarre, M. de. L'Heptaméron. Lyon, 1578.

Htn 38526.29.4* Navarre, M. de. Contes et nouvelles. Amsterdam, 1700. 2v.

Htn 38526.29.5* Navarre, M. de. Les nouvelles de Marguerite, reine de Navarre. Berne, 1792. 3v.

38526.30 Navarre, M. de. Heptaméron. Paris, 1879. 2v.

38526.30.2 Navarre, M. de. Heptaméron. Paris, 1879. 3v.

38526.31 Navarre, M. de. Heptaméron. Paris, 1879. 2v.

38526.32A Navarre, M. de. Heptaméron. Paris, 1880. 4v.

38526.32B Navarre, M. de. Heptaméron. Paris, 1880. 4v.

38526.32.2 Navarre, M. de. Heptaméron. Paris, 1880. 3v.

38526.32.4 Marguerite d'Angoulême. L'Heptaméron des nouvelles. Paris, 1884.

38526.32.4.5 Marguerite d'Angoulême. L'Heptaméron. Paris, 1960.

38526.32.4.10 Marguerite d'Angoulême. Tales from the Heptaméron. London, 1970.

38526 Individual authors, etc. - 1500-1661 - Other poets and dramatists, 16th century - cont.

38526.32.6 Marguerite d'Angoulême. L'Heptaméron des nouvelles de la reine de Navarre. Paris, 1945-46. 4v.

Htn 38526.32.7* Marguerite d'Angoulême. Heptaméron, or The history of the fortunate lovers. London, 1654.

38526.32.9 Marguerite d'Angoulême. The Heptaméron of Margaret, queen of Navarre. London, 1855.

38526.32.9.5 Marguerite d'Angoulême. The Heptaméron of Margaret, queen of Navarre. London, 1855.

38526.32.10 Marguerite d'Angoulême. The Heptaméron. London, 1849.

38526.32.11 Marguerite d'Angoulême. The Heptaméron. Philadelphia, 18-

38526.32.12 Marguerite d'Angoulême. The Heptaméron. Philadelphia, 18-

38526.32.13 Marguerite d'Angoulême. The Heptaméron. N.Y., 189-?

38526.32.14 Marguerite d'Angoulême. The Heptaméron. Philadelphia, 189-?

38526.32.17A Marguerite d'Angoulême. The Heptaméron. London, n.d.

38526.32.17B Marguerite d'Angoulême. The Heptaméron. London, n.d.

38526.32.18A Marguerite d'Angoulême. The Heptaméron. London, 18- .

38526.32.18B Marguerite d'Angoulême. The Heptaméron. London, 18- .

38526.32.19 Marguerite d'Angoulême. The Heptaméron. London, 18- .

38526.32.20 Marguerite d'Angoulême. The Heptaméron. London, 1894. 5v.

38526.32.21 Marguerite d'Angoulême. The Heptaméron. Philadelphia, 189-. 2v.

38526.32.22 Marguerite d'Angoulême. The Heptaméron. London, 1903. 2v.

38526.32.25 Marguerite d'Angoulême. The Heptaméron. N.Y., 1925.

38526.32.30 Marguerite d'Angoulême. Petit oeuvre dévot et contemplatif. Frankfurt am Main, 1960.

38526.32.35 Marguerite d'Angoulême. Chansons spirituelles. Paris, 1971.

38526.32.40 Marguerite d'Angoulême. Das Heptaméron. Lübeck, 1939.

38526.32.45 Marguerite d'Angoulême. L'Heptaméron. Paris, 1943.

38526.32.48 Marguerite d'Angoulême. Geptameron. Leningrad, 1967.

38526.32.49 Marguerite d'Angoulême. Heptaméron. Budapest, 1969.

38526.32.50 Pellegrini, C. La prima opera di Margherita di Navarra. Catania, 1920.

38526.32.55 Pellegrini, C. La prima opera di Margherita di Navarra. Catania, 1920.

38526.32.60 Febvre, Lucien. Autour de l'Heptaméron. 2e éd. Paris, 1944.

38526.32.61 Febvre, Lucien. Amour sacré, amour profane, autour de l'"Heptaméron". Paris, 1971.

38526.32.65 Ritter, R. Les solitudes de Marguerite de Navarre. Paris, 1953.

38526.32.70 Marguerite d'Angoulême. Nouvelles. Paris, 1967.

Htn 38526.32.100* Marguerite d'Angoulême. Les Marguerites de la Marguerite. Paris, 1558.

38526.33 Frank, Félix. Les Marguerites de la Marguerite. Paris, 1873. 4v.

38526.33.1 Marguerite d'Angoulême. Marguerites de la Marguerite des princesses. N.Y., 1970. 2v.

38526.33.2 Lefranc, Abel. Les dernières poésies de Marguerite de Navarre. Paris, 1896.

Htn 38526.33.2.5* Marguerite d'Angoulême. La navire. Paris, 1956.

38526.33.3A Marguerite d'Angoulême. The mirror of the sinful soul. London, 1897.

38526.33.3B Marguerite d'Angoulême. The mirror of the sinful soul. London, 1897.

38526.34 Marguerite d'Angoulême. Contes. Londres, 1744. 2v.

38526.34.5 Marguerite d'Angoulême. Contes et nouvelles de Marguerite de Valois. La Haye, 1733. 2v.

38526.34.25 Marguerite d'Angoulême. Comédies. Strasbourg, 1923.

38526.34.30 Marguerite d'Angoulême. La coche. Strasbourg, 1936.

38526.34.31 Marguerite d'Angoulême. La coche. Genève, 1971.

38526.34.35A Marguerite d'Angoulême. Comédie de la nativité de Jesus Christ. Paris, 1939.

38526.34.35B Marguerite d'Angoulême. Comédie de la nativité de Jesus Christ. Paris, 1939.

38526.34.40 Marguerite d'Angoulême. Théâtre profane. Paris, 1946.

38526.34.45 Margarete of Austria. Gedichte Margarethe's von Österreich. Wien, 1954.

38526.34.98 Jourda, Pierre. Marguerite d'Angoulême...1492-1549. Thèse. Paris, 1930. 2v.

38526.34.100 Jourda, Pierre. Marguerite d'Angoulême...1492-1549. Paris, 1930. 2v.

38526.34.101 Jourda, Pierre. Répertoire analytique et chronologique de la correspondance de Marguerite d'Angoulême. Paris, 1930.

38526.34.102 Jourda, Pierre. Répertoire analytique et chronologique de la correspondance de Marguerite d'Angoulême. Paris, 1930.

38526.34.104 Telle, E.V. L'oeuvre de Marguerite d'Angoulême. Thèse. Toulouse, 1937.

38526.34.105A Telle, E.V. L'oeuvre de Marguerite d'Angoulême. Toulouse, 1937.

38526.34.105B Telle, E.V. L'oeuvre de Marguerite d'Angoulême. Toulouse, 1937.

38526.34.110 Molnar, R. A Francia élet a Heptaméronban. Pécs, 1936.

38526.34.115 Pauphilet, A. Marguerite de Navarre. Paris, 1938.

38526.34.120 Vernay, Henri. Les divers sens du mot raison. Heidelberg, 1962.

38526.34.125 Gelernt, Jules. World of many loves: the Heptaméron of Marguerite de Navarre. Chapel Hill, 1966.

38526.34.530A Margarete of Austria. Albums poétiques. Cambridge, 1934.

38526.34.530B Margarete of Austria. Albums poétiques. Cambridge, 1934.

38526.34.530C Margarete of Austria. Albums poétiques. Cambridge, 1934.

38526.34.531 Margarete of Austria. The chanson albums of Marguerite of Austria. Berkeley, 1965.

Htn 38526.35* Maréchal, Antoine. La cour bergère. Paris, 1640.

Htn 38526.35.2* Maréchal, Antoine. La genereuse allemande. Paris, 1631.

Htn 38526.35.4* Maréchal, Antoine. Le mauzolée. Paris, 1642.

Htn 38526.35.6* Maréchal, Antoine. Le railleur. Paris, 1638.

Htn 38526.35.6.5* Maréchal, Antoine. Le railleur. N.Y., 1938.

Htn 38526.35.8* Maréchal, Antoine. Le veritable Capitan Matamore. Paris, 1640.

38526.35.75 Marion, J. Rondeaulx et vers d'amour. Paris, 1873.

38526.35.150 Seider, M.H. Anne de Marquets poétesse religieuse du XVIe siècle. Thèse. Washington, 1931.

Htn 38526.35.250* Massac, R. de. Les fontenes de Pougues. Paris, 1605.

38526.36 Maucroix, F. de. Oeuvres diverses. Paris, 1854. 2v.

38526.36.61 Maucroix, F. de. Lettres. Paris, 1962.

38526.36.62 Maucroix, F. de. Lettres. Grenoble, 1962.

38526.37 Maynard, F. de. Oeuvres poétiques. Paris, 1885. 3v.

Htn 38526.37.4* Maynard, F. de. Oeuvres. Paris, 1646.

38526.37.6 Maynard, F. de. Poésies de François Maynard. Paris, 1927.

38526 Individual authors, etc. - 1500-1661 - Other poets and dramatists, 16th century - cont.

38526.37.9 Drouhet, Charles. Tableau des lettres du poète François Mainard. Paris, 1909.

38526.37.10 Drouhet, Charles. Le poète François Mainard (1583-1646). Paris, 1909.

38526.37.11 Durand-Lapie, Paul. François Maynerd et François Menard. Paris, 1899.

38526.37.100 Werth, Werner. François de Molière. Inaug. Diss. Berlin, 1916.

Htn 38526.37.225* Mondin, Jean. Deploration et vers lamentables sur la mort de Monseigneur le duc de Guyse. Paris, 1589.

Htn 38526.38* Monléon, de. Le Thyeste. Paris, 1637. 3 pam.

Htn 38526.39* Montfleury, A. Jacob. La mort d'Asdrubal. Paris, 1647.

Htn 38526.39.25* Montreux, N. de. Les premières oeuvres poétiques chrestiennes. Paris, 1587.

Htn 38526.39.27* Montreux, N. de. Le premier livre des bergeries de Juelliette. 2e éd. Paris, 1587.

Htn 38526.39.29* Montreux, N. de. Second livre des bergeries de Juelliette. Lyon, 1591. 2v.

Htn 38526.39.35* Montreux, N. de. Les chastes et delectables jardins d'amour. Paris, 1599.

38526.39.45 Daele, Rose M. Nicolas de Montreux (Ollenix du Mont-Sacre . N.Y., 1946.

38526.39.50 Morenne, C. de. Poésies profanes. Caen, 1864.

Htn 38526.39.55* Morenne, C. de. Poèmes divers. Paris, 1605. 3 pam.

38526.42 Montluc, A. de. La comédie des proverbes. Paris, 1665.

38526.42.5 Montluc, A. de. La comédie des proverbes. Paris, 1715.

Htn 38526.42.6* Nancel, P. de. De la soveraineté des roys. Poems. n.p., 1610.

Htn 38526.42.6.25* Nostredame, C. de. Pièces héroiques. Colonuéz, 1608. 2 pam.

Htn 38526.42.7* Nouvelon, N. Hercule furieux; tragédie. Paris, 1639.

38526.42.10 Palissy, B. Recepte veritable. Strasbourg, 1921.

38526.42.10.35 Keeler, M.J. Etude sur la poésie et sur le vocabulaire de Loys Papon. Washington, D.C., 1930.

Htn 38526.42.10.50* Paquelin, G. Apologem. Lyon, 1577.

38526.42.10.70 Parmentier, Jean. Oeuvres poétiques. Paris, 1971.

38526.42.10.75 Posadowsky-Wehner, K. Jean Parmentier, 1494-1529. München, 1937.

38526.42.11 Parthenay, C. Ballets allégoriques en vers 1592-1593. Paris, 1927.

38526.42.12F Pasquier, Étienne. Les oeuvres. Amsterdam, 1723. 2v.

38526.42.12.20 Pasquier, Étienne. Le monophile. Varese, 1957.

38526.42.13 Pamphlet box. Estienne Pasquier.

38526.42.13.10 Pasquier, Étienne. Choix de lettres sur la littérature, la langue et la traduction. Genève, 1956.

38526.42.13.12 Pasquier, Étienne. Lettres historiques pour les années 1556-1594. Genève, 1966.

38526.42.13.15 Pasquier, Étienne. Ecrits politiques. Textes réunis, publiés. Genève, 1966.

Htn 38526.42.14* Pasquier, Étienne. Les lettres d'Estienne Pasquier. Avignon, 1590.

Htn 38526.42.14.3* Pasquier, Étienne. Jeunesse d'Estienne Pasquier. Paris, 1610.

Htn 38526.42.14.5* Pasquier, Étienne. La jeunesse d'Estienne Pasquier et sa suite. Paris, 1610.

38526.42.15 Zilch, Georg. Der Gebrauch des französischen Pronomens in der 2. Hälfte des XVI. Jahrhunderts. Heppenheim, 1891.

38526.42.16 Pamphlet box. Estienne Pasquier.

38526.42.17 Thickett, D. Bibliographie des oeuvres d'Estienne Pasquier. Genève, 1956.

38526.42.20 Moore, M.J. Estienne Pasquier. Thèse. Poitiers, 1934.

38526.42.30 Butler, R. Nationales und universales Denken in Werke Estienne Pasquiers. Basel, 1948.

Htn 38526.42.75* Passerat, Jean. Recueil des oeuvres poétiques de Ian Passerat. Paris, 1606. 2 pam.

38526.43 Peletier, Jacques. Oeuvres poétiques. Paris, 1904.

38526.43.1 Peletier, Jacques. Oeuvres poétiques. Genève, 1970.

38526.43.5 Peletier, Jacques. Oeuvres poétiques. Rochecorbon, 1958. 2v.

38526.43.9 Jugé, C. Jacques Peletier du Mans. Paris, 1907.

38526.43.10 Staub, Hans. Le curieux désir; Scève et Peletier du Mans. Genève, 1967.

38526.43.21 Percheron, Luc. Pyrrhe. Genève, 1970.

Htn 38526.43.30* Perrache, J. Vanité du jeu. Paris, 1587.

38526.44 Perrin, François. Les escoliers. Bruxelles, 1866.

Htn 38526.44.3* Perrot de La Sale, Paul. Gigantomachie. Middleburg, 1593.

Htn 38526.44.5* Perrot de La Sale, Paul. Le contr'empire des sciences. Lyon, 1599.

Htn 38526.44.5.10* Perrot de La Sale, Paul. Tableaus sacrey. Francfort, 1594.

Htn 38526.44.10* Pibrac, Guy du Faur. Les quatrains du seigneur de Pybrac. n.p., 1615.

Htn 38526.44.19* Pibrac, Guy du Faur. Les quatrains. Paris, 1646.

38526.45 Pibrac, Guy du Faur. Quatrains. Paris, 1802.

38526.45.5 Pibrac, Guy du Faur. Quatrains. Paris, 1874.

38526.45.15 Catalogue des ouvrages...de Guy du Faur Signeur de Pibrac. Orléans, 1901.

Htn 38526.45.25* Pibrac, Guy du Faur. Recueil de plusieurs pieces. Paris, 1635.

38526.45.30 Cabos, Alban. Guy du Faur de Pibrac. Thèse. Paris, 1922.

38526.45.30.2 Cabos, Alban. Guy du Faur de Pibrac. Paris, 1922.

38526.45.35 Auacker, Robert d'. Les traductions d'Antoine Stettler. Berne, 1927.

Htn 38526.45.100* Picardet, Anne. Odes spirituelles. Lyon, 1618.

Htn 38526.46* Pichou. Les folies de Cardenio. Paris, 1630.

38526.46.100 Pierre de Laval. Les rimes de Pierre de Laval. Bordeaux, 1937.

Htn 38526.46.175* Poille, Jacques. Oeuvres divisées en onze livres. Paris, 1623.

Htn 38526.46.205* Poirier, Hélie. Les soupirs salutaires. Amsterdam, 1646.

38526.46.305 Gasté, A. Noels et vaudevires de manuscrit de Jehan Porée. Caen, 1883.

38526.46.350 Poupo, Pierre. Poésies diverses tirées de la muse chrestienne. Paris, 1886.

38526.46.360 Hester, Ralph M. A Protestant Baroque poet, Pierre Poupo. The Hague, 1970.

38526.46.400 Passerat, Jean. Les poésies françaises. Genève, 1968. 2v.

Htn 38526.46.500* Quillian, M. Dernière semaine. Rouen, 1597.

Htn 38526.46.550* Prevost, J. Tragédies et autres oeuvres. Poictiers, 1618.

38526.46.1500 Quinault, Philippe. Persée, tragédie. n.p., n.d.

38526.47.5 Racan, Honorat de Bueil. Poésies lyriques profanes. Maestricht, 1928.

38526.47.6 Racan, Honorat de Bueil. Les bergeries et autres poésies lyriques. Paris, 1929.

38526 Individual authors, etc. - 1500-1661 - Other poets and dramatists, 16th century - cont.

	38526.47.7	Racan, Honorat de Bueil. Poésies. Paris, 1930-37. 2v.
	38526.47.8.10	Racan, Honorat de Bueil. Poésies. v.2. Paris, 1937.
	38526.47.9	Arnould, S. Un gentil homme de lettres au XVIIe siècle. Racan. Paris, 1901.
	38526.47.10	Pamphlet box. Honorat Racan.
	38526.47.11	Larbaud, Valery. Notes sur Racan. Maestricht, 1928.
Htn	38526.47.12*	Rampalle, M. La belinde. Lyons, 1630.
Htn	38526.47.13*	Rapin, Nicolas. Les oeuvres latines et françoises. Paris, 1610.
	38526.47.14	Arnould, Louis. Racan. Paris, 1896.
Htn	38526.47.15*	Rayssiguier, N. Tragicomédie pastorale. Paris, 1632.
Htn	38526.47.18*	Regnault. Marie Stvard. Paris, 1639.
Htn	38526.47.18.25*	Remi de Beauvais. La Magdaleine. Tournay, 1617.
Htn	38526.47.19*	Richemont. L'esperance glorieuse. Paris, 1632. 2 pam.
	38526.47.20	Rivaudeau, André de. Les oeuvres poétiques. Paris, 1859.
	38526.47.20.5	Rivaudeau, André de. A man. Tragédie sainte. Genève, 1969.
Htn	38526.47.22*	Roland de Richeville, L. Expicedión de Diane. Paris, 1604.
	38526.47.23	Begemann, H. M. Christian Roses geistliche Schauspiele S. Theophania und Holofern, 1647/8. Berlin, 1913.
	38526.47.23.100	Romieu, Marie de. Oeuvres poétiques. Paris, 1878.
Htn	38526.47.23.200*	Rosset, François de. Les XII beautez de Phyllis. Paris, 1604.
Htn	38526.47.23.250*	Rus, Jean. Description poétique de l'histoire du beau Narcissus. Lyon, 1550.
Htn	38526.47.25*	Saint-Amant, Marc Antoine Gérard. Moyse saove. Leyde, 1654.
	38526.47.26	Saint-Amant, Marc Antoine Gérard. Oeuvres. v.2-3. Paris, 1967- 2v.
	38526.47.29	Gourier, F. Étude des oeuvres poétiques de Saint-Amant. Genève, 1961.
	38526.47.30	Saint-Amant, Marc Antoine Gérard. Oeuvres. Paris, 1907.
	38526.47.31	Saint-Amant, Marc Antoine Gérard. Poésies baroques de Marc Antoine Gérard. Paris, 1968.
	38526.47.32	Saint-Amant, Marc Antoine Gérard. Oeuvres poétiques. Photoreproduction. Paris, 1930.
	38526.47.33	Buls, Johannes. Das Naturgefühl bei Saint-Amant. Rostock, 1913.
	38526.47.33.5	Aubin, R.A. Saint-Amant as "preromantic". n.p., 1935.
	38526.47.33.10	Lagny, Jean. Bibliographie des éditions anciennes des oeuvres. Paris, 1961.
	38526.47.33.15	Lagny, Jean. Le poète Saint-Amant. Paris, 1964.
	38526.47.33.20	Borton, Samuel L. Six modes of sensibility in Saint-Amant. The Hague, 1966.
	38526.47.33.25	Wentzloff-Eggebert, Christian. Forminteresse. 1e Aufl. München, 1970.
	38526.47.35	Ruutz-Rees, Caroline. Charles de Sainte-Marthe. N.Y., 1910.
	38526.47.35.3	Ruutz-Rees, Caroline. Charles de Sainte-Marthe. Paris, 1914.
	38526.47.37	Farmer, A.J. Les oeuvres françaises de Scevole de Sainte Marthe, 1536-1623. Toulouse, 1920.
	38526.47.37.2	Farmer, A.J. Les oeuvres françaises de Scevole de Sainte Marthe, 1536-1623. Thèse. Toulouse, 1920.
Htn	38526.47.39*	Saint-Julien. Le courrier burlesque de la guerre de Paris. Anvers, 1650.
	38526.47.40	Saint-Pavin, Denis Sanguin de. Poésies choisies. Paris, 1912.
	38526.47.45	Molinier, H.J. Mellin de Saint-Gelays (1490-1558). Rodez, 1910.
Htn	38526.47.73*	Saint-Gelais, Mellin de. Oeuvres poétiques. Lyon, 1574.
	38526.47.75	Saint-Gelais, Mellin de. Oeuvres poétiques de Mellin S.Gelais. Paris, 1719.
	38526.47.77	Saint-Gelais, Mellin de. Oeuvres complètes de Melin de Sainct-Gelais. Paris, 1873. 3v.
	38526.47.200	Salel, H. Hugues Salel de Cazals-en-Quercy, 1504-1553. Paris, 1929.
	38526.47.300	Sedege. Le légat de la Vache. Paris, 1868.
Htn	38526.48*	Sarasin, Jean F. Oeuvres. Paris, 1656.
Htn	38526.48.1*	Sarasin, Jean F. Oeuvres. Rouen, 1658.
	38526.48.2	Sarasin, Jean F. Oeuvres de Sarasin. Paris, 1694.
	38526.48.2.25	Sarasin, Jean F. Oeuvres rassemblées. Paris, 1926. 2v.
	38526.48.2.75	Mennung, A.G.H.A. J.F. Sarasin's Leben und Werke. v.1-2. Halle, 1902-04.
	38526.48.3	S., I.M. La mort de Roxane. Paris, 1648.
	38526.48.4	Saint Germain. Le grand Timoléon. Paris, 1648.
Htn	38526.48.5*	Sottie à dix personnages. Lyon, 1523.
	38526.48.6	Saint-Julien. Les courriers de la fronde. Paris, 1857. 2v.
Htn	38526.48.8*	Sainte-Marthe, S. Oeuvres. Paris, 1579. 2 pam.
Htn	38526.48.10*	Sallebray. L'amante ennemie. Paris, 1642.
Htn	38526.48.12*	Sallebray. Le jugement de Paris. Paris, 1639.
Htn	38526.48.14*	Sallebray. La troade. Paris, 1641.
Htn	38526.48.15*	Du Bartas, Guillaume de Salluste. Les oeuvres. n.p., 1582. 2v.
	38526.48.15.5	Du Bartas, Guillaume de Salluste. Oeuvres. Toulouse, 1971-
	38526.48.15.10	Du Bartas, Guillaume de Salluste. Works. Chapel Hill, 1935-38. 3v.
Htn	38526.48.16*	Du Bartas, Guillaume de Salluste. Le sepmaine ou création du monde. Paris, 1583.
Htn	38526.48.16.3*	Du Bartas, Guillaume de Salluste. Le sepmaine ou création du monde. v.1-4. Rouen, 1591.
Htn	38526.48.16.5*	Du Bartas, Guillaume de Salluste. Commentaires et annotations du monde. Paris, 1584.
	38526.48.16.9	Braspart, Michel. Du Bartas, Poète chrétien. Neuchâtel, 1947.
	38526.48.17	Reichenberger, K. Du Bartas und sein Schöpfungsepos. München, 1962.
Htn	38526.48.17*	Du Bartas, Guillaume de Salluste. Commentaires sur la sepmaine de la création du monde. Rouen, 1599.
Htn	38526.48.17.2*	Du Bartas, Guillaume de Salluste. Commentaires sur la second sepmaine. Rouen, 1599.
	38526.48.17.10	Du Bartas, Guillaume de Salluste. Die Schöpfungswerke des Du Bartas. Tübingen, 1963.
Htn	38526.48.18F*	Du Bartas, Guillaume de Salluste. Du Bartas - his works. London, 1633.
Htn	38526.48.18.2F*	Du Bartas, Guillaume de Salluste. Du Bartas - his works. London, 1641.
	38526.48.18.3	Du Bartas, Guillaume de Salluste. Bartas: his devine weekes and works, 1605. Gainesville, Florida, 1965.
Htn	38526.48.18.5*	A learned summarie upon the famous poems of William of Salvst. London, 1637.

38526 Individual authors, etc. - 1500-1661 - Other poets and dramatists, 16th century - cont.

	38526.48.19	Du Bartas, Guillaume de Salluste. Judith. Lipsk, 1841.
	38526.48.20	Ashton, H. Du Bartas en Angleterre. Paris, 1908.
Htn	38526.48.21*	Du Bartas, Guillaume de Salluste. Bartas: his divine weekes and workes. London, n.d.
Htn	38526.48.22*	Du Bartas, Guillaume de Salluste. Bartas: his divine weekes and workes. London, 1605-06.
X Cg	38526.48.24	Du Bartas, Guillaume de Salluste. The divine weeks of Josuah Sylvester. Waukesha, 1908.
Htn	38526.48.26*	Du Bartas, Guillaume de Salluste. Hebdomas a Gabriele Lermaeo latinitate donata. Londini, 1591.
Htn	38526.48.27*	Du Bartas, Guillaume de Salluste. Wilhelms von Saluste, Herren zu Bartas vornemsten Sinn. Leipzig, 1631.
Htn	38526.48.27.10*	Du Bartas, Guillaume de Salluste. Die erste und andere Woche Wilhelms von Saluste. Cöthen, 1640.
	38526.48.28.30	Guore, A.E. The language of Du Bartas. Seattle, 1940.
Htn	38526.48.28.50*	Scalion de Virbluneau. Loyales et pudiques amours. Paris, 1599.
	38526.48.29	Baur, Albert. M. Scève et la renaissance lyonnaise. Paris, 1906.
	38526.48.29.5	Plattard, Jean. La vie et l'oeuvre de Scévole de Sainte-Marthe. Paris, 1924.
	38526.48.29.10	Saulnier, Verdum L. Maurice Scève. Paris, 1948-49. 2v.
	38526.48.29.11	Saulnier, Verdum L. Maurice Scève. v.1-2. Paris, 1948-49.
	38526.48.29.20	Boutang, Pierre. Commentaire sur quarante-neuf dizains de la Délie. Paris, 1953.
	38526.48.30	Scève, Maurice. La saulsaye; eglogue de la vie solitaire. Paris, 1918.
	38526.48.30.5	Scève, Maurice. Saulsaye. Cambridge, Mass., 1959.
	38526.48.31	Scève, Maurice. Délie, object de plus haulte vertu. Paris, 1916.
	38526.48.31.5	Scève, Maurice. Délie, object de plus haulte vertu. Paris, 1961.
	38526.48.31.7	Scève, Maurice. Délie. Cambridge, Eng., 1966.
	38526.48.32	Scève, Maurice. Sixty poems. N.Y., 1949.
	38526.48.33	Scève, Maurice. Poésies de Maurice Scève. Lausanne, 1961.
	38526.48.34	Scève, Maurice. Oeuvres poétiques complètes. Paris, 1927.
	38526.48.34.1	Scève, Maurice. Oeuvres poétiques complètes. Paris, 1971. 2v.
	38526.48.35	Scève, Maurice. Maurice Scève. Paris, 1947.
	38526.48.36	Scève, Maurice. Les hommes de la Renaissance. Paris, 1959.
	38526.48.38	Giudici, Enzo. Le opere minori di Maurice Scève. Parma, 1958.
	38526.48.38.5	Giudici, Enzo. Il rinascimento a Lione e la Délie di Maurice Scève. Napoli, 1962.
	38526.48.38.10	Giudici, Enzo. Maurice Scève. Roma, 1965. 2v.
	38526.48.38.12	Giudici, Enzo. Maurice Scève, bucolico e "Blasonneur". Napoli, 1965.
	38526.48.38.37	Scève, Maurice. Opere poetiche minori. Napoli, 1965.
	38526.48.38.40	Risset, Jacqueline. L'anagramme du désir. Roma, 1971.
	38526.48.39	Schelandre, J. de. Tyr et Sidon ou Les funestes amours de Belcar. Paris, 1908.
	38526.48.45	Aulard, F.A. Les théories dramatiques de Jean de Schelandre. Poitiers, 1883.
	38526.48.75	Sconin, Adrin. L'oeuvre poétique d'Adrien Sconin. Paris, 1933.
	38526.48.140	Ruchon, J. La vie et l'oeuvre de Jean de Sponde. Genève, 1949.
	38526.48.150	Sponde, Jean de. Stances et sonnets de la mort. Paris, 1947.
	38526.48.150.5	Sponde, Jean de. Les amours et la mort. Paris, 1949.
	38526.48.155	Sponde, Jean de. Oeuvre poétique pour le premier fois réunie en un volume. Paris, 1945.
	38526.48.157	Sponde, Jean de. Poésies. Genève, 1949.
	38526.48.160	Sponde, Jean de. Meditation, avec un Essai de poèmes chretiens. Paris, 1954.
	38526.48.170	Sponde, Jean de. Sonnet on love and death. Painesville, 1962.
	38526.48.172	Sponde, Jean de. Poems of love and death. Edinburgh, 1964.
	38526.48.244	Attal, J.P. Maurice Scève. Paris, 1963.
Htn	38526.48.245*	Théophile de Viau. Oeuvres. Avignon, 1633.
	38526.48.250	Falbe, A. Die Dichtung Maurice Scèves. Berlin, 1964.
Htn	38526.48.250*	Théophile de Viau. Les oeuvres de Théophile, en trois parties divisées. Paris, 1636.
	38526.48.257	Théophile de Viau. Les oeuvres de Théophile, en trois parties divisées. Rouen, 1649.
	38526.49	Théophile de Viau. Oeuvres complètes. Paris, 1856. 2v.
	38526.49.2	Théophile de Viau. Oeuvres poétiques. Genève, 1951. 2v.
X Cg	38526.49.3	Théophile de Viau. Oeuvres. Paris, 1907.
	38526.49.4A	Théophile de Viau. Oeuvres poétiques. Paris, 1926.
	38526.49.4B	Théophile de Viau. Oeuvres poétiques. Paris, 1926.
	38526.49.5	Théophile de Viau. La tragédie de Pasiphaë. Paris, 1862.
	38526.49.10	Théophile de Viau. Théophile en prison et autres pamphlets. Paris, 1967.
	38526.49.15	Théophile de Viau. Pyrame et Thisbe. Strasbourg, 1933.
	38526.49.20	Théophile de Viau. La maison de Sylvia. n.p., 1946.
	38526.49.25	Théophile de Viau. Prose. Torino, 1965.
	38526.50	Andrieu, Jules. Théophile de Viau. Paris, 1887.
	38526.51	Schirmacher, K. Théophile de Viau. Sein Leben und seine Werke (1591-1626). Leipzig, 1897.
	38526.51.9	Adam, Antoine. Théophile de Viau et la libre pensée française en 1620. Thèse. Paris, 1935.
	38526.51.10	Adam, Antoine. Théophile de Viau et la libre pensée française en 1620. Paris, 1935.
	38526.51.15	Adam, Antoine. Théophile de Viau et la libre pensée française en 1620. Genève, 1966.
	38526.51.80	Bruzzi, Amelia. Il barocco nella poesia di Théophile de Viau. Bologna, 1965.
	38526.51.85	Müller, Gerhard. Untersuchung des poetischen Stils Théophiles de Viau. München, 1968.
	38526.51.90	Meyer-Minnemann, Klaus. Die Tradition der klassischen Satire in Frankreich. Bad Homburg, 1969.
	38526.52.5	Tyard, Pontus. Le solitaire premier. Lille, 1950.
Htn	38526.52.15*	Tyard, Pontus. Solitaire premier, ou Dialogue de la fureur poétique. Paris, 1575?
	38526.52.18	Tyard, Pontus. Oeuvres poétiques complètes. Paris, 1966.
Htn	38526.52.31*	Tyard, Pontus. Les discours philosophiques. Paris, 1587.
	38526.52.35	Tyard, Pontus. Les erreurs amoureuses. Genève, 1967.
	38526.52.80	Baridon, S.F. Pontus de Tyard. Milano, 1953.
	38526.52.85	Hall, Kathleen. Pontus de Tyard and his Discours philosophiques. London, 1963.
	38526.53	Jeandet, Jean Pierre A. Pontus de Tyard. Paris, 1860.

38526 Individual authors, etc. - 1500-1661 - Other poets and dramatists, 16th century - cont.

Htn	38526.56*	Tabourot, Étienne. Les touches du seigneur des accords. Livre 1-5. Paris, 1585. 2v.
	38526.56.5	Tabourot, Étienne. Les touches du seigneur des accords. Rouen, 1626.
Htn	38526.56.25*	Tabourot, Étienne. Les bigarrvres du seigneur. Paris, 1585. 3 pam.
Htn	38526.57.2*	Tabourot, Étienne. Les bigarrvres. Paris, 1608.
	38526.57.5	Tabourot, Étienne. Les bigarrvres. Rouen, 1648.
	38526.58.10	Choptrayanovitch, G. Étienne Tabourot des accords, 1549-1590. Thèse. Dijon, 1935.
	38526.62.10	Théophile de Viau. Oeuvres choisies. Paris, 1949.
	38526.63	Tausianus, P. Latina interpretatio eximii poematis Gallici à Arnaldo d'Andilly. 2a ed. Paris, 1664.
	38526.64	Boyer, H. Un ménage littéraire en Berry au 16 siècle (Jacques Thiboust et Jeanne de la Font). Bourges, 1859.
Htn	38526.65*	Trellon, C. La muse guerrière. Rouen, 1604.
Htn	38526.66*	Trelon, G. Six chants des vertus. Paris, 1587.
	38526.66.75	Thomas, Jean. Isabelle; tragédie imitée de l'Arioste. Thèse. Paris, 1938.
	38526.66.77	Thomas, Jean. Isabelle; tragédie imitée de l'Arioste. Paris, 1939.
	38526.67	Firnelie, Odet de. Les contens. Paris, 1961.
Htn	38526.68*	Regnier, Mathurin. Les satyres, et autres oeuvres. Leiden, 1652.
Htn	38526.68.5*	Regnier, Mathurin. Satyres. Paris, 1645.
Htn	38526.69.25*	Veins, Aymard de. Clorinde; tragedie. Paris, 1599. 2 pam.
Htn	38526.69.50*	Viel, Marc A. Consolation et reconfort de noble, et illustre dame, Helen d'O. Paris, 1589.
Htn	38526.70*	Vievget. Les adventures de policandre. Paris, 1632.
Htn	38526.70.8*	Viret, Pierre. Satyres chrestienes de la cuisine papale. Genève, 1560.
	38526.70.9	Viret, Pierre. Satyres chrestienes de la cuisine papale. Genève, 1857.
	38526.70.20	Shaw, Helen A. Conrad Badius and the Comedie du Pape Malade. Diss. Philadelphia, 1934.
	38526.70.100	Livingston, C.H. Les cent nouvelles nouvelles de Philippe de Vigneulles. Paris, 1924.
Htn	38526.70.125*	Vitel, Jean de. Premiers exercices poétiques. Paris, 1588.
	38526.70.130	Vitel, Jean de. La prinse du Mont-Saint-Michel de Jan de Vitel. Auranches, 1861.
	38526.70.145	Vivonne, H. de. Les chansons de Callianthe. Paris, 1926.
	38526.70.150	Vivonne, H. de. Poésies de Heliette de Vivonne. Paris, 1932.
Htn	38526.71*	De Vaynes, J.H.L. A Huguenot garland. Hertford, 1890.
Htn	38526.73*	Ponte, Petrus de. Petru de Pote ceci burgensis incomparanda G. Colophon, 1512.
	38526.76	Du Bois-Hus, Gabriel. La nuict des nuicts, Les jour des jours, Le miroir du destin, ou La nativité du Daufin du Ciel. Bologna, 1967.
	38526.76.5	Du Bois-Hus, Gabriel. Le prince illustre. Paris, 1645.
	38526.80	Du Guillet, Pernette. Rymes. Genève, 1968.

38527 Individual authors, etc. - 1500-1661 - Other poets and dramatists, 17th century

	38527.4	Travers, Julien. Essai sur...Jean Vauquelin. Caen, 1872.
	38527.5	Lemercier, Aimé Prosper. Étude sur Jean Vauquelin. Nancy, 1887.
	38527.5.1	Lemercier, Aimé Prosper. Étude littéraire et morale sur les poésies de Jean Vauquelin de la Fresnaye. Genève, 1970.
	38527.8	Travers, Julien. Les diverses poésies de Jean Vauquelin. Caen, 1869-72. 3v.
	38527.9	Vauquelin de la Fresnaye, Jean. L'art poétique. Paris, 1885.
Htn	38527.9.5*	Vauquelin de la Fresnaye, Jean. Foresteries. Caen, 1869.
	38527.9.20	Vauquelin des Yveteaux, N. Les oeuvres poétiques de Vauquelin. Paris, 1854.
	38527.9.25	Mongreclien, Georges. Étude sur la vie et l'oeuvre de Nicolas Vauquelin. Paris, 1921. 2 pam.
	38527.9.26	Rathery, E.J.B. Vauquelin des Yveteaux. Paris, 1854.
	38527.9.30	Contades, Gérard de. Le cabaliste. Argentan, 1889.
	38527.9.33	Vauquelin de la Fresnaye, Jean. Les foresteries. Genève, 1956.
	38527.10	Du Lorens, J. Satire. Genève, 1868.
	38527.10.5	Du Lorens, J. Satires. Paris, 1869.
	38527.11	Blanchemain, Prosper. Premières satires de Du Lorens. Paris, 1881.
	38527.13	Bourgoin, Auguste. Valentin Conrart. Paris, 1883.
	38527.14	Kerviler, René. Valentin Conrart. Paris, 1881.
	38527.14.10	Mabille de Poncheville, A. Valentin Conrart, le père de l'Académie française. Paris, 1935.
	38527.16	Aubigné, Théodore Agrippa d'. Oeuvres complètes. Paris, 1873-77. 6v.
	38527.17	Aubigné, Théodore Agrippa d'. Oeuvres poétiques choisies. Paris, 1905.
	38527.17.20	Aubigné, Théodore Agrippa d'. Prose. Neuchâtel, 1943. 2v.
	38527.17.30	Aubigné, Théodore Agrippa d'. Oeuvres. Paris, 1969.
Htn	38527.17.75*	Aubigné, Théodore Agrippa d'. Les avantures du Baron de Foeneste. Dezert, 1630.
	38527.18	Aubigné, Théodore Agrippa d'. Avantures du Baron de Foeneste. Cologne, 1729. 2v.
	38527.19	Aubigné, Théodore Agrippa d'. Avantures du Baron de Foeneste. Amsterdam, 1731. 2v.
	38527.19.5	Aubigné, Théodore Agrippa d'. Avantures du Baron de Foeneste. Paris, 1855.
	38527.19.10	Aubigné, Théodore Agrippa d'. Sa vie à ses enfants. 4e éd. Photoreproduction. Paris, 1928.
	38527.19.20	Prévost, Jean. Agrippa d'Aubigné: sa vie à ses enfants. 2e éd. Paris, 1928.
	38527.20	Aubigné, Théodore Agrippa d'. Avantures du Baron de Foeneste. v.1-2. Paris, 1895.
	38527.21	Audiat, L. Prosper mérimée et son édition de Foeneste. La Rochelle, 1893.
	38527.22	Aubigné, Théodore Agrippa d'. Le printemps. Lille, 1948.
	38527.22.3	Aubigné, Théodore Agrippa d'. Le printemps. Genève, 1952.
	38527.22.5	Aubigné, Théodore Agrippa d'. Le printemps. Paris, 1960.
	38527.22.30	Salis, Arnold von. Agrippa d'Aubigné. 2e Aufl. Heidelberg, 1885.
	38527.23	Aubigné, Théodore Agrippa d'. L'enfer. Satire. Paris, 1873.
	38527.24	Mazon, A. Notice sur la vie et les oeuvres d'Achille Gamon. Lyon, 1885.

38527 Individual authors, etc. - 1500-1661 - Other poets and dramatists, 17th century - cont.

	38527.25	Kaiser, Hermann. Über die Schöpfungsgedichte des Chr. de Gamon und Agrippa d'Aubigné. Bremen, 1896.
	38527.26	Pamphlet box. Théodore Agrippa d'Aubigné.
	38527.27	Rocheblave, S. La vie d'un hiros Agrippa d'Aubigné. Paris, 1912.
	38527.28A	Aubigné, Théodore Agrippa d'. Les tragiques. Paris, 1872.
	38527.28B	Aubigné, Théodore Agrippa d'. Les tragiques. Paris, 1872.
	38527.28.2	Aubigné, Théodore Agrippa d'. Les tragiques. Paris, 1857.
	38527.28.3	Aubigné, Théodore Agrippa d'. Les tragiques. Paris, 1896.
	38527.28.6A	Aubigné, Théodore Agrippa d'. Les tragiques. Paris, 1932-33. 4v.
	38527.28.6B	Aubigné, Théodore Agrippa d'. Les tragigues. Paris, 1932-33. 2v.
	38527.28.9C	Aubigné, Théodore Agrippa d'. Les tragigues. Paris, 1932-33. 2v.
	38527.28.15	Aubigné, Théodore Agrippa d'. Les tragiques. Paris, 1936.
	38527.28.16	Aubigné, Théodore Agrippa d'. Les tragiques. Lausanne, 1966.
	38527.28.17	Aubigné, Théodore Agrippa d'. Les tragiques. London, 1970.
	38527.29	Réaume, Eugene. Étude sur Agrippa d'Aubigné. Paris, 1883.
	38527.29.5	Galzy, Jeanne. Agrippa d'Aubigné. Paris, 1965.
	38527.29.6	Aubigné, Théodore Agrippa d'. Agrippa d'Aubigné...une étude. Paris, 1966.
	38527.29.9	Trenel, J. L'element biilique dans l'oeuvre poétique d'Aubigné. Paris, 1904.
	38527.29.10	Palmgren, V. Observations sur l'infinitif dans Agrippa d'Aubigné. Stockholm, 1905.
	38527.29.11	Schwerd, Karl. Vergleich, Metapher...in den "Tragiques" des Agrippa d'Aubigné. Leipzig, 1909.
	38527.29.13	Pergameni, H. La satire au XVIe siècle et les tragiques d'Agrippa d'Aubigné. n.p., 1881.
	38527.29.15	Ellerbroek, G.G. Observations sur la langue de l'histoire universelle de Théodore Agrippa d'Aubigné. Enschede, 1925.
	38527.29.18	Bietenbeck, K. Der Dichter Agrippa d'Aubigné als Kritiker seiner Zeit. Inaug. Diss. Borken, 1937.
	38527.29.20	Buffum, Imbrie. Agrippa d'Aubigné's Les tragiques. New Haven, 1951.
	38527.29.25	Sauerwein, H.A. Agrippa d'Aubigné's Les tragiques. Baltimore, 1953.
	38527.30	Postansque, M.A. Théodore Agrippa d'Aubigné. Montpellier, 1854.
	38527.30.3	Feugère, L. Agrippa d'Aubigné. Paris, 1853.
	38527.30.5	Rocheblave, S. Agrippa d'Aubigné. Paris, 1910.
	38527.30.8	Plattard, Jean. Une figure de premier plan dans nos lettres de la renaissance. Photoreproduction. Paris, 1931.
	38527.30.10	Bailbé, Jacques. Agrippa d'Aubigné, poète des "Tragiques". Caen, 1968.
Htn	38527.31*	Montchrétien, Antoine de. Les tragédies. Rouen, 1627.
	38527.31.3A	Montchrétien, Antoine de. Les tragédies. Paris, 1891.
	38527.31.3B	Montchrétien, Antoine de. Les tragédies. Paris, 1891.
X Cg	38527.31.5	Montchrétien, Antoine de. La reine d'Escosse. Paris, 1905.
	38527.31.8.2	Montchrétien, Antoine de. Aman; a critical edition. Thesis. Philadelphia, 1939.
	38527.31.8.5	Montchrétien, Antoine de. Les lacenes; a critical edition. Philadelphia, 1943.
	38527.31.9	Lücken, E. Zur Syntax Montchrétiens. Darmstadt, 1894.
	38527.31.10	Scholl, Sigmund. Die Vergleiche in Montchrétiens Tragödien. Nördlingen, 1894.
	38527.31.11	Willner, Kurt. Montchrétiens Tragödien und die stoische Lebensweisheit. Inaug. Diss. Berlin, 1932.
	38527.31.12	Willner, Kurt. Montchrétiens Tragödien und die stoische Lebensweisheit. Berlin, 1932.
	38527.31.20	Griffiths, Richard. The dramatic technique of Antoine de Montchrétien. Oxford, 1970.
	38527.32	Joly, A. Antoine de Montchrétien. Caen, 1865.
	38527.32.5	Pamphlet box. Montchrétien, Antoine de.
	38527.33	La puce de Mme. Desroches. Paris, 1872.
	38527.33.9	Ceriziers, R. de. L'innocence reconnuë en la personne de s. Geneviève de Brabant. 5e éd. Tournay, 1644.
Htn	38527.33.20*	Ceriziers, R. de. The innocent lady. 2nd ed. London, 1674.
Htn	38527.34*	Ceriziers, R. de. The triumphant lady or The crowned innocence. London, 1880.
	38527.34.5	Ceriziers, R. de. Het leven van de heylige Susanna ofte Genoveva. Antwerpen, n.d.
	38527.35	Christie, R.C. Etienne Dolet. London, 1880.
	38527.35.5	Christie, R.C. Etienne Dolet. London, 1899.
	38527.35.10	Née de La Rochelle. Vie d'Etienne Dolet. Paris, 1779.
Htn	38527.37*	Dolet, Etienne. La manière de bien traduire. Lyon, 1540.
	38527.37.10	Dolet, Etienne. Le second enfer. Paris, 1868.
	38527.37.50	Galtier, Octave. Etienne Dolet. Paris, 1908.
	38527.37.55	Boulmier, J. Etienne Dolet. Paris, 1857.
Htn	38527.38*	Taillandier, Alphonse H. Proces d'Etienne Dolet. Paris, 1836.
	38527.38.5	Chassaigne, Marc. Etienne Dolet. Paris, 1930.
	38527.38.11	Alary, Jacques. L'imprimerie au 16e siècle: Etienne Dolet et ses luttes avec la Sorbonne. Genève, 1970.
Htn	38527.39*	Le second enfer d'Etienne Dolet. Lyon, 1544.
	38527.40	Dupérier, Scipion. Harangue pour le prince de Joinville. Paris, 1956.
	38527.41	Busson, Henri. Charles d'Espinay évêque de Dol, et son oeuvre poétique (1531?-1591). Paris, 1923.
	38527.41.2	Busson, Henri. Dans l'orbe de la pléiade. Charles d'Espinay évêque de Dol. Thèse. Paris, 1922.
Htn	38527.42*	Garnier, Robert. Les tragédies. Paris, 1582.
Htn	38527.42.3*	Garnier, Robert. Tragédies. Tholose, 1588.
Htn	38527.42.3.12*	Garnier, Robert. Tragédies. Lyon, 1597.
	38527.42.3.20	Garnier, Robert. Tragédies. Saumur, 1602.
Htn	38527.42.3.22*	Garnier, Robert. Tragédies. Rouen, 1604.
Htn	38527.42.3.25*	Garnier, Robert. Tragédies. Paris, 1607.
	38527.42.3.30	Garnier, Robert. Les Juifves, tragédie. Paris, 1945.
	38527.42.3.32	Garnier, Robert. Les Juifves. Paris, 1949.
	38527.42.5	Garnier, Robert. Oeuvres complètes. Paris, 1923. 2v.
	38527.42.10	Garnier, Robert. Oeuvres complètes. Paris, 1923. 2v.
	38527.42.20	Garnier, Robert. La troade antigone. Paris, 1952.
	38527.43	Garnier, Robert. Cornelia von Thomas Kyd. München, 1894.
	38527.43.10	Garnier, Robert. Bradamante. Paris, 1949.
	38527.44	Garnier, Robert. Countess of Pembroke's Antoine. Photoreproduction. Weimar, 1897.
	38527.45	Jensen, A. Syntactische Studien zu Robert Garnier. Kiel, 1885.

38527 Individual authors, etc. - 1500-1661 - Other poets and dramatists, 17th century - cont.

38527.45.5 Procop, W. Syntactische Studien zu Robert Garnier. Eichstätt, 1885.
38527.46 Körner, Paul. Der Versbau Robert Garniers. Berlin, 1894.
38527.47 Raeder, Hans. Die Tropen und Figuren bei Robert Garnier. Wandsbeck, 1886.
X Cg 38527.47.5 Mysing, O. Robert Garnier und die antike Tragödie. Leipzig, 1891.
38527.47.9 Rolland, J. La tragédie française au XVIe siècle. "Les juifves". Photoreproduction. Paris, 1911.
38527.47.15 Mouflard, M.M. Robert Garnier, 1545-1590. La Ferté-Bernard, 1961-63. 3v.
38527.48 Bernage, Siméon. Étude sur Robert Garnier. Paris, n.d.
38527.48.1 Bernage, Siméon. Étude sur Robert Garnier. Genève, 1970.
38527.48.5 Chardon, Henri. Robert Garnier; sa vie, ses poésies inédites. Paris, 1905.
38527.49 Schmidt-Wartenberg, H.M. Seneca's influence on Robert Garnier. Darmstadt, 1888.
38527.49.5 Lebèque, R. Robert Garnier, Les juives. v.1-2. Paris, 1946.
38527.49.10 Gras, Maurice. Robert Garnier, son art et sa méthode. Genève, 1965.
38527.49.15 Jandorf, Gillian. Robert Garnier and the themes of political tragedy in the sixteenth century. Thesis. London, 1969.
38527.49.20 Wierenga, Lambertus. La troade de Robert Garnier. Proefschrift. Assen, 1970.
38527.50 Payen, Jean François. Notice sur...La Boëtie. Paris, 1853.
38527.50.10 Schmidt, Hans. Estienne de La Boétie's "Discours de la servitude volontaire". Inaug. Diss. Marburg, 1934.
38527.50.12 Dezeimeris, R. Sur l'objectif réel du discours d'Estienne de La Boétie de la servitude volontaire. Bordeaux, 1907.
38527.51.2 Bonnefon, Paul. Estienne de La Boétie. Genève, 1970.
38527.53 Feugère, Léon. Etienne de La Boëtie. Paris, 1845.
38527.54 Barrère, J. Estienne de La Boëtie contre Nicolas Machiavel. Bordeaux, 1908.
38527.56 Lambin, Denys. Lettres galantes de Denys Lambin, 1552-1554. Paris, 1941.
38527.58A La Boétie, Estienne de. Oeuvres...d'Estienne de La Boëtie. Paris, 1846.
38527.58B La Boétie, Estienne de. Oeuvres...d'Estienne de La Boëtie. Paris, 1846.
38527.58.5 La Boétie, Estienne de. Oeuvres politiques. Paris, 1963.
38527.58.10 La Boétie, Estienne de. Über freiwillige Knechtschaft. Berlin, 1924.
38527.58.11 La Boétie, Estienne de. Discours de la servitude volontaire. Paris, 1963.
38527.59 Bonnefon, Paul. Oeuvres complètes d'Estienne de La Boëtie. Paris, 1892.
38527.60 La Boétie, Estienne de. La servitude volontaire. Paris, 1872.
38527.60.5 La Boétie, Estienne de. Discours de la servitude volontaire. Paris, 1922.
38527.60.6A La Boétie, Estienne de. Anti-dictator. N.Y., 1942.
38527.60.6B La Boétie, Estienne de. Anti-dictator. N.Y., 1942.
38527.60.7 Barrère, Joseph. L'humanisme et la politique. Paris, 1923.
38527.60.8 La Boétie, Estienne de. Rassuzhdenie o dobrovol'nom rabstve. 2. izd. Moskva, 1962.
38527.60.10 Hoffmann-Harnisch, W. In dir selber suche den Sklaven. Bonn, 1961.
38527.60.25 Faure, H. Antoine de Laval et les écrivains bourbonnais. Moulins, 1870.
38527.61 Magny, Olivier de. Les odes d'Olivier de Magny. Paris, 1876. 2v.
38527.61.5 Magny, Olivier de. Dernières poésies. Paris, 1880.
38527.61.7 Magny, Olivier de. Les amours. Paris, 1878.
38527.61.7.5 Magny, Olivier de. Les cent deux sonnets des amours de 1553. Genève, 1970.
38527.61.8 Magny, Olivier de. Les gayetez. Paris, 1871.
38527.61.9 Magny, Olivier de. Les gayetez (Recueil de poésie). Genève, 1968.
38527.61.15 Magny, Olivier de. Le odes amoureuses de 1559. Genève, 1964.
38527.62 Magny, Olivier de. Les souspirs. Paris, 1874.
38527.63 Favre, Jules. Olivier de Magny. Paris, 1885.
38527.65 Mermet, Thomas. La vie de l'homme...et la destruction de Jérusalem. Vienne, 1838.
38527.66 Sanlecque, Louis de. Poésies du Père Sanlecque. v.1-2. n.p., n.d.
38527.67 Vion d'Alibray, Charles. Oeuvres poétiques. Paris, 1906.
38527.68A Becq de Fouquières, L. Oeuvres choisies des poètes français du XVIe siècle. Paris, 1879.
38527.68B Becq de Fouquières, L. Oeuvres choisies des poètes français du XVIe siècle. Paris, 1879.
38527.72 Le dict des jardiniers. Paris? 1895?
38527.76 Le banquet du Boys. Paris, n.d.
38527.77 Le banquet du Boys. Paris, 1875.
38527.85 La mort de Silvandre...Poème, 1660. Paris, 1878.
38527.90 Marcel, P. Jean Martin. Paris, 1927.
38527.100 Graces de la Bugne. Le roman des deduis. Karlshamn, 1951.
38527.105 Constans, Jacques de. Jacques de Constans. Genève, 1962.
38527.110 Gross-Kiefer, Esther. Le dynamisme cosmique chez Le Moyne. Thèse. Zurich, 1968.

38528.1 - .39 Individual authors, etc. - 1500-1661 - Satirical and facetious works in verse

Htn 38528.1.5* Caron, P.S. Collection de différens ouvrages anciens. Paris, 1798-1806. 4v.
Htn 38528.1.6* Recueil de livrets singuliers et rares. Paris, 1829-30.
Htn 38528.1.7* Recueil de livrets singuliers et rares. Paris, 1829-30.
Htn 38528.1.20* Le cabinet satyrique. Rouen, 1634.
38528.1.30 Gringore, Pierre. La sottie du Prince des Sotz. Milano, 1957.
38528.2 Bever, A. van. Les poètes satyriques des XVIe et XVIIe siècles. Paris, 1903.
38528.3 Tanizey de Larroque. Essai sur...Florimond de Raymond. Paris, 1867.
Htn 38528.4* Bouaistuau, Pierre. Histoire de Chelidonius Tigurinus. Paris, 1556.
Htn 38528.4.9* Deslauriers, N. Fantaisies. n.p., 1610?
Htn 38528.4.11* Deslauriers, N. Les nouvelles et plaisantes imaginations de Bruscambile. Bergerac, 1615.
Htn 38528.4.13* Deslauriers, N. Les fantaisies de Bruscambille. Paris, 1615.
Htn 38528.4.15* Deslauriers, N. Les oeuvres de Bruscambille. Rouen, 1626.

38528.1 - .39 Individual authors, etc. - 1500-1661 - Satirical and facetious works in verse - cont.

Htn 38528.4.75* Du Lorens, J. Satyres, divisees en deux livres. Paris, 1624.
38528.5 Estienne, Henri. Conformité du Langagu François avec le Grec. Paris, 1853.
38528.6 Grouchy, Ernest Henri. Étude sur Nicolas de Grouchy. Paris, 1878.
Htn 38528.6.3* Estienne, Henri. A world of wonders. London, 1607.
Htn 38528.6.4* Estienne, Henri. A world of wonders. London, 1607.
Htn 38528.6.5* Estienne, Henri. A world of wonders. Edinburgh, 1608.
Htn 38528.6.8* Estienne, Henri. L'introduction au Traité...ou Traité...à l'Apologie pour Hérodote. Paris, 1566.
38528.6.9 Estienne, Henri. L'introduction au Traité...ou Traité...à l'Apologie pour Hérodote. Hasles, 1607.
38528.6.12 Estienne, Henri. Apologie pour Hérodote. La Haye, 1735. 3v.
38528.7A Estienne, Henri. Apologie pour Hérodote. Paris, 1879. 2v.
38528.7B Estienne, Henri. Apologie pour Hérodote. Paris, 1879. 2v.
38528.8 Estienne, Henri. Deux dialogues du nouveau langage françois, italianizé. Paris, 1883. 2v.
38528.8.2 Estienne, Henri. Deux dialogues du nouveau langage françois, italianizé. Paris, 1885. 2v.
38528.8.8 Dieterle, Hans. Henri Estienne. Strassburg, 1895.
38528.8.9 Clément, S. Henri Estienne et son oeuvre française. Paris, 1899.
38528.8.12 Weber, E. Die Bedeutung der Analogie für die Beschäftigung Henri Estiennes. Marburg, 1939.
Htn 38528.8.19* Satyre Ménippée de la vertu du catholicon d'Espagne. n.p., 1593.
Htn 38528.8.25* Satyre Ménippée de la vertu du catholicon d'Espagne. n.p., 1632.
Htn 38528.9* Satyre Ménippée. Ratisbon, 1664.
Htn 38528.9.5* Satyre Ménippée. Brussels, 1709. 3v.
38528.10 Labitte, Charles. Satyre Ménippée. Ratisbon, 1865.
38528.11 Satyre Ménippée. Paris, 1824. 2v.
38528.12 Satyre Ménippée. Paris, 1877. 2v.
38528.13 Le texte primitif de la satyre Ménippée. Paris, 1878.
38528.13.5A Satyre Ménippée de la vertu du catholicon. Paris, 1882.
38528.13.5B Satyre Ménippée de la vertu du catholicon. Paris, 1882.
38528.13.7 Satyre Ménippée; ou La vertu du catholicon. Paris, 1924.
38528.13.9 Alcripe, Philippe de. La nouvelle fabrique. Paris, 1853.
Htn 38528.14* Auvray, Jean. Le banquet des muses, ou Les divers satires. Rouen, 1636.
38528.14.3 Brantôme, P. de B. de. Vies des dames galantes. Paris, 18- .
38528.14.5 Brantôme, P. de B. de. Vies des dames galantes. Paris, 1848.
38528.14.7 Brantôme, P. de B. de. Oeuvres. Paris, 1857.
38528.14.9 Brantôme, P. de B. de. Vie des dames galantes. Paris, 1883.
38528.14.10 Brantôme, P. de B. de. Recueil d'aulcunes rymes de mes jeunes amours. Paris, 1927.
38528.14.81 Crucy, François. Brantôme. Paris, 1934.
38528.14.83 Stevens, L.C. La langue de Brantôme. Paris, 1939.
38528.14.85 Cottrell, Robert D. Brantôme: the writer as portraitist of his age. Genève, 1970.
Htn 38528.15* Béroalde de Verville. Le cabinet de Minerve. Rouen, 1597.
Htn 38528.16* Béroalde de Verville. Le moyen de parvenir. London, 1786. 3v.
38528.16.5 Béroalde de Verville. Le moyen de parvenir. Paris, 1841.
38528.16.6 Béroalde de Verville. Le moyen de parvenir. Paris, 1868.
38528.16.7 Béroalde de Verville. Le moyen de parvenir. Paris, 1870-72. 2v.
38528.16.7.5 Béroalde de Verville. Contes en vers imités du Moyen de parvenir. Paris, 1874.
38528.16.8.12 Béroalde de Verville. Le moyen de parvenir. Paris, 1879.
Htn 38528.16.8.23* Béroalde de Verville. L'histoire véritable, ou Le voyage des princes fortunez. Paris, 1610.
38528.16.8.25 Béroalde de Verville. L'histoire véritable, ou Le voyage des princes fortunez. Paris, 1896.
38528.16.9 Pamphlet box. Béroalde de Verville.
Htn 38528.16.10* Béroalde de Verville. Le moyen de parvenir. Manuscript. n.p., n.d.
Htn 38528.16.40* Béroalde de Verville. Les souspirs amoureux. Paris, 1583.
Htn 38528.16.45* Béroalde de Verville. L'histoire véritable, ou Le voyage des princes fortunez. Paris, 1610.
38528.16.80 Pallister, Janis. The world view of Béroalde de Verville. Paris, 1971.
38528.17 Passerat, Jean. Le chien courant. Paris, 1864.
38528.17.9 Mojsisovics, E. von. Jean Passerat. Halle, 1907.
Htn 38528.17.30* Philippot, the Savoyard. Recueil nouveau des chansons du Savoyart. Paris, 1661.
Htn 38528.18* Nicolas de Troyes. Le grand parangon. Brussels, 1866.
38528.18.5 Nicolas de Troyes. Le grand parangon des nouvelles nouvelles (choix). Paris, 1970.
38528.19 Mabille, E. Le grand parangon. Paris, 1869.
38528.19.5 Kasprzyh, K. Nicolas de Troyes. Warszawa, 1963.
38528.19.9 Pamphlet box. Nicolas de Troyes.
38528.20 Du Fail, Noël. Oeuvres facetieuses. Paris, 1874. 2v.
Htn 38528.20.3* Du Fail, Noël. Les contes et discours d'Eutrapel. Rennes, 1597.
Htn 38528.20.5* Du Fail, Noël. Les contes et discours d'Eutrapel. Rennes, 1598.
Htn 38528.20.8* Du Fail, Noël. Les contes et discours d'Eutrapel. Rennes, 1603.
38528.20.9 Du Fail, Noël. Propos rustique...contes et discours d'Eutrapel. Paris, 1842.
38528.20.10 Du Fail, Noël. Propos rustiques. Paris, 1921.
38528.20.12 Du Fail, Noël. Contes et discours d'Eutrapel. Paris, 1875. 2v.
38528.20.15 Du Fail, Noël. Les baliverneries d'Eutrapel. Paris, 1970.
38528.21 Defrémery, C. Examen de la nouvelle édition de Noël du Fail. Paris, 1875.
38528.21.9 Du Fail, Noël. Das Leben und die Werke. Borna, 1909.
38528.21.10 Förster, Richard. Die sogenannten facetiösen Werke Noëls du Faill. Halle, 1912.
38528.21.11 Philipot, E. Essai sur le style et la langue de Noël du Fail. Paris, 1914.
38528.21.12 Philipot, E. La vie et l'oeuvre litteraire de Noël du Fail. Paris, 1914.
Htn 38528.22* Lacour, Louis. Oeuvres des Periers. Paris, 1856. 2v.
38528.22.2A Lacour, Louis. Oeuvres des Periers. Paris, 1856. 2v.
38528.22.2B Lacour, Louis. Oeuvres des Periers. Paris, 1856. 2v.
38528.23 Despériers, Bonaventure. Cymbalum mundi. Paris, 1858.

38528.1 - .39 Individual authors, etc. - 1500-1661 - Satirical and facetious works in verse - cont.

	38528.24	Despériers, Bonaventure. Cymbalum mundi. Paris, 1873.
	38528.24.5	Despériers, Bonaventure. Cymbalum mundi. Manchester, 1958.
	38528.24.6	Despériers, Bonaventure. Cymbalum mundi. N.Y., 1965.
	38528.24.10	Needhart, Dorothea. Das Cymbalum mundi des Bonaventure des Periers. Genève, 1959.
Htn	38528.25*	Despériers, Bonaventure. Cymbalum mundi. London, 1723.
	38528.25.3	Despériers, Bonaventure. Cymbalum mundi. Amsterdam, 1732.
	38528.25.10A	Febvre, Lucien. Origène et des Periers ou l'énigme du Cymbalum mundi. Paris, 1942.
	38528.25.10B	Febvre, Lucien. Origène et Periers ou l'énigme du Cymbalum mundi. Paris, 1942.
	38528.25.20	Frank, Félix. Léxique de la langue de Bonaventure des Periers. Paris, 1888.
X Cg	38528.25.20	Frank, Félix. Léxique de la lanque de Bonaventure des Periers. Paris, 1888.
	38528.26	Tabarin. Oeuvres complètes. Paris, 1858. 2v.
	38528.27	Le triumphe de Haulte Folie. Poème du XVIe siècle. Paris, n.d.
	38528.28.9	Brunot, F. De Philiberti Bugnonii vita et eroticis versibus. Lugduni, 1891.
	38528.29	Angot, Robert. Les éxercices de ce temps. Paris, 1924.
	38528.29.10	Angot, Robert. Oeuvres satyriques. Paris, 1929.
Htn	38528.30*	Despériers, Bonaventure. Contes...Cymbalum mundi. Paris, 1872.
Htn	38528.31*	Croque-Lardon, Josselin. La grande et universelle pronostication de Maistre Josselin Croque-Lardon. Paris, 1628.
Htn	38528.32*	Despériers, Bonaventure. Nouvelles recréations. Paris, 1874. 2v.
	38528.32.20A	Despériers, Bonaventure. The mirrour of mirth and pleasant conceits . Columbia, S.C., 1959.
	38528.32.20B	Despériers, Bonaventure. The mirrour of mirth and pleasant conceits. Columbia, S.C., 1959.
	38528.33	Chenevière, A. Bonaventure des Periers. Sa vie, ses poésies. Paris, 1886.
Htn	38528.34*	Ouville, Antoine. L'élite des contes. Rouen, 1599.
	38528.35	Ouville, Antoine. L'élite des contes. Paris, 1876.
Htn	38528.36*	Valcroissant, Pierre de Marmet. Entertainment of the cours. London, 1658.
	38528.37	Beauxoncles, Charles T. de. Oeuvres satyriques. 1. éd. Paris, 1920.
Htn	38528.38*	Demons, Jean. La sextessence diallactique. Paris, 1595.
Htn	38528.38.10*	Saint Julien. L'esclite des bouts rimez de ce temps. pt.1. Paris, 1651.
Htn	38528.38.15*	Sonnet, Thomas. Satyre contre les charlatans. Paris, 1610.
Htn	38528.38.20*	Sonnet, Thomas. Satyre Menippee contre les femmes. Lyon, 1623.
	38528.38.25	Sonnet, Thomas . Oeuvres poétiques. Paris, 1876.
Htn	38528.38.30*	Sonnet, Thomas. Oeuvres satyriques. 2. éd. Paris, 1622.
	38528.38.35	Meylan, Henri. Épitres du coq à l'âne. Genève, 1956.

38528.40 - Individual authors, etc. - 1500-1661 - Anonymous poems

	38528.40	Les Caquets de l'accouchée. Paris, 18- .
Htn	38528.45*	Le danger de mariage. Paris, 1577.
Htn	38528.50*	Le Mathois, ou Marchand meslé propre à tout faire. Paris, 1614.
Htn	38528.55*	Le passe par tout des Ponts-Bretons. n.p., 1624.
Htn	38528.60*	Le normant sourt, aveugle et muet. Paris, 1617.
Htn	38528.65*	Les fleurs des musés françaises. Rouen, 16- ?
Htn	38528.70*	La mode qui court au temps présent avec le supplement. Rouen, 15- ?
Htn	38528.70.5*	La mode qui court au temps present avec le supplement. Paris, 161-?
Htn	38528.75*	Les médecins au XVIIe siècle. Paris, 1869.
Htn	38528.80*	Ode sacrée de l'église française. n.p., 1586.
Htn	38528.90*	La Polymachie des marmitons. Lyon, 1563.
	38528.95	Le petit oeuvre d'amour et gaige d'amytié. François Roussin. Paris, 1941.

38529 Individual authors, etc. - 1500-1661 - Satirical and facetious works in prose

	38529.3	Pithoys, Claude. L'apocalypse de Meliton ou révélation. St. Leger, 1662.
Htn	38529.5*	Goulart, Simon. Histoires admirables et mémorables. Paris, 1603.
Htn	38529.6*	Goulart, Simon. Histoires admirables et memorables. Paris, 1603.
	38529.8	Jones, Léonard Chester. Simon Goulart. Genève, 1917.
	38529.9	La petite bourgeoise poème satirique de l'an 1610. Strasbourg, n.d.
	38529.12	La gazette de 1609. Paris, 1914.
Htn	38529.20*	Barry, René. L'esprit de cour. Bruxelles, 1664.
Htn	38529.25*	Des Rues, F. Les marguerites françoyses. Rouen, 1608?
	38529.35A	Girault, F. The tale of Gargantua and King Arthur. Cambridge, 1932.
	38529.35B	Girault, F. The tale of Gargantua and King Arthur. Cambridge, 1932.
Htn	38529.45*	Langlois. The favourites chronicle. London, 1621.
Htn	38529.50*	Lescale. Alphabet de l'éccellence...des femmes. Paris, 1631.
	38529.60	Mathorez, J. Mathurine et les libelles publiés sous son nom. Paris, 1922.
Htn	38529.75*	Romany, Richard de. Le carabinage et matoiserie soldatesque. Paris, 1616.
Htn	38529.77*	Roulhard, Sibout. La magnifique déxologie du festu. Paris, 1610.
Htn	38529.80*	Vigoureux. La défense des femmes, contre l'alphabet. Paris, 1617.
Htn	38529.95*	Montreux, N. de. Les amours de Cleandre et Dorniphille. Paris, 1598.
	38529.105	Hassell, James W. Sources and analogues of the Nouvelles récréations et joyeux. Chapel Hill, N.C., 1957-69. 2v.
Htn	38529.150*	La grande division arrivée ces derniers iours, entre les femmes et les filles de Montpellier. Paris, 1622.

38531 Individual authors, etc. - 1500-1661 - Rabelais - Folios

	38531.11	Rabelais, F. Works. London, 1892. 2v.
NEDL	38531.12	Rabelais, F. Works. London, 1893. 2v.
Htn	38531.12.9*	Rabelais, F. Oeuvres de...nouvelle. Paris, 1854.
	38531.13A	Rabelais, F. Oeuvres. Paris, 1857.
	38531.13B	Rabelais, F. Oeuvres. Paris, 1857.
	38531.14	Heulhard, Arthur. Une lettre fameuse. Paris, 1902.
	38531.16	Lefranc, A. Les navigations de Pantagruel. Paris, 1905.

38531 Individual authors, etc. - 1500-1661 - Rabelais - Folios - cont.

	38531.17	Birch Hirschfeld, A. Das Fümfte Buch das Pantagruel. Lipsiae, 1900-01.
Htn	38531.18*	Plan, P.P. Les éditions de Rabelais à la faculté de Médecine de Montpellier. Montpellier, 1876.
	38531.19	Gordon, R. F. Rabelais à la faculté de médecine de Montpellier. Montpellier, 1876.

38536 Individual authors, etc. - 1500-1661 - Rabelais - Writings

	38536.1	Rabelais, F. Pantagruel. Paris, 1904.
	38536.1.1	Rabelais, F. Pantagruel. Paris, 1946.
	38536.1.2	Rabelais, F. L'isle sonante. Paris, 1905.
	38536.1.3	Rabelais, F. Le quatre livres de Pantagruel. Paris, 1910.
	38536.1.4	Rabelais, F. Lettres écrites. Paris, 1910.
Htn	38536.1.5*	Rabelais, F. Les épistres...pendant son voyage d'Italie. Paris, 1651.
	38536.1.6	Rabelais, F. Les lettres...écrites pendant son voyage d'Italie. Bruxelles, 1710.
Htn	38536.2.15*	Rabelais, F. Oeuvres. Lyon, 1558.
Htn	38536.2.45*	Rabelais, F. Les oeuvres. Lion, 1596.
Htn	38536.2.50*	Rabelais, F. Les oeuvres. Anvers, 1605.
Htn	38536.2.55*	Rabelais, F. Oeuvres. Lyon, 1608.
Htn	38536.4*	Le Duchat. Oeuvres de Rabelais. Amsterdam, 1741. 3v.
	38536.4.10	Rabelais, F. La Rabelais moderne, ou Les oeuvres de maitre. v1,3-6. Amsterdam, 1752. 6v.
	38536.4.20	Rabelais, F. Oeuvres. Paris, 1797-98. 3v.
	38536.5	Rabelais, F. Oeuvres. Paris, 1820. 3v.
	38536.6	Rabelais, F. Oeuvres. Paris, 1823. 9v.
	38536.7	Rabelais, F. Oeuvres. Paris, 1861.
	38536.7.5A	Rabelais, F. Oeuvres. Paris, 1861.
	38536.7.5B	Rabelais, F. Oeuvres. Paris, 1861.
	38536.8	Rabelais, F. Les songes drolatiques. Genve, 1868.
	38536.10	Rabelais, F. Oeuvres. v.1-2. Paris, 1858.
	38536.12	Montaiglon, Anatole. Les quarte livres de...Rabelais. Paris, 1868-70. 3v.
	38536.15	Marly-Laveaux, Charles. Les oeuvres de...Rabelais. Paris, 1868-73. 6v.
	38536.16	Rabelais, F. Oeuvres. Paris, 1877.
	38536.16.10A	Rabelais, F. François Rabelais. Tout ce-qui éxiste de ses oeuvres. Paris, 188-.
	38536.16.10B	Rabelais, F. François Rabelais. Tout ce-qui éxiste de ses oeuvres. Paris, 188-.
	38536.17	Rabelais, F. Oeuvres. Paris, 1912-31. 5v.
	38536.18	Rabelais, F. Oeuvres. 2. éd. Paris, 1870-73. 2v.
	38536.18.5	Rabelais, F. Oeuvres. 3. éd., v.1; 2. éd., v.2. Paris, 1893. 2v.
	38536.18.15A	Rabelais, F. Oeuvres de Rabelais. Paris, 1920. 2v.
	38536.18.15B	Rabelais, F. Oeuvres de Rabelais. Paris, 1920. 2v.
	38536.18.17	Rabelais, F. Oeuvres complètes de Rabelais. Paris, 1929. 5v.
	38536.18.23	Rabelais, F. Oeuvres. Paris, 1927-1928. 4v.
	38536.18.25	Rabelais, F. Oeuvres complètes. Bruxelles, 1947. 3v.
	38536.18.30.2	Rabelais, F. Oeuvres complètes. Paris, 1955.
	38536.18.35	Rabelais, F. Oeuvres complètes. Paris, 1957. 5v.
	38536.18.36	Rabelais, F. Oeuvres complètes. Paris, 1962. 2v.
	38536.18.40	Rabelais, F. Pantagruel de François Rabelais. Paris, 1959.
	38536.18.41	Rabelais, F. Pantagruel. Genève, 1959.
	38536.18.42	Rabelais, F. Pantagruel. Publié sur le texte définitif. Paris, 1962.
	38536.18.50A	Rabelais, F. Works. London, 18- .
	38536.18.50B	Rabelais, F. Works. London, 18- .
	38536.18.50C	Rabelais, F. Works. London, 18- .
	38536.18.55	Rabelais, F. Works. London, 189-?
	38536.18.56	Rabelais, F. Works. London, 1872?
	38536.18.57	Rabelais, F. Works. London, 19- .
	38536.18.60	Rabelais, F. Rabelais; the fine books and minor writings. v.1. 2. ed. Cambridge, Eng., 1934.
	38536.18.85	Rabelais, F. Hours with Rabelais. London, 1905.
	38536.19A	Rabelais, F. Les cinq livres de F. Rabelais. Paris, 1885. 4v.
	38536.19B	Rabelais, F. Les cinq livres de F. Rabelais. Paris, 1885. 4v.
Htn	38536.19.25*	Rabelais, F. Gargantua. Dijon, 1937.
	38536.20.3	Rabelais, F. Five books of the lives...of Gargantua. Philadelphia, 189-.
	38536.20.5	Rabelais, F. Gargantua and Pantagruel. v.2. London, 1900.
	38536.20.10	Rabelais, F. Five books of the lives...of Gargantua and his son Pantagruel. London, 1904. 3v.
	38536.21	Rabelais, F. Gargantua and Pantagruel. Leipzig, 1832. 3v.
Htn	38536.22*	Rabelais, F. La chronique de Gargantua. 1. éd. Paris, 1868.
	38536.22.5	Rabelais, F. Les grandes et inestimables croniques...Gargantua. n.p., 1532.
Htn	38536.22.10*	Rabelais, F. Les grandes et inestimables croniques...Gargantua. London, 1532.
Htn	38536.22.11*	Champion, Pierre. Deux publications lyonnais de 1532 (Les grandes et inestimables croniques). Paris, 1925.
	38536.22.15	Rabelais, F. Les croniques admirables du puissant Roy Gargantua. Rochecorbon, 1956.
	38536.23	Rabelais, F. La seconde chronique de Gargantua. Paris, 1872.
	38536.23.10	Rabelais, F. Le vroy Gargantua. Paris, 1949.
	38536.24	Rabelais, F. Gargantua et Pantagruel. Paris, n.d.
	38536.24.3	Rabelais, F. Gargantua et Pantagruel. Paris, n.d. 3v.
	38536.24.5	Rabelais, F. Gargantua und Pantagruel. München, 1964. 2v.
	38536.24.6	Rabelais, F. Gargantua. Paris, 1939.
	38536.24.9A	Rabelais, F. Selections from Gargantua. N.Y., 1904.
	38536.24.9B	Rabelais, F. Selections from Gargantua. N.Y., 1904.
	38536.24.9C	Rabelais, F. Selections from Gargantua. N.Y., 1904.
Htn	38536.24.11*	Rabelais, F. Le quart livres des faicts et dictz hëroiques du bon Pantagruel. Lyon, 1552.
	38536.24.15	Rabelais, F. Pantagruel. Paris, 1903.
Htn	38536.24.20*	Plan, Pierre Paul. Une réimpression ignorée du Pantagruel de Dresde. Paris, 1910.
	38536.24.25	Rabelais, F. Rabelais médecin: notes et commentaires. Paris, 1911.
	38536.24.40	Rabelais, F. Le quart livre...Pantagruel. Genève, 1947.
	38536.25A	Besant, Walter. Readings in Rabelais. London, 1883.
	38536.25B	Besant, Walter. Readings in Rabelais. London, 1883.
	38536.25.5	Rabelais, F. Readings selected by W.F. Smith. Cambridge, Eng., 1920.
	38536.25.15	Rabelais, F. L'Abbage de Thélème. Paris, 1934.
	38536.25.16	Rabelais, F. L'Abbaye de Thélème. Genève, 1949.

38536 Individual authors, etc. - 1500-1661 - Rabelais - Writings - cont.

38536.26A Rabelais, F. Five books of Gargantua and his son Pantagruel. N.Y., 1905.
38536.26B Rabelais, F. Five books of Gargantua and his son Pantagruel. N.Y., 1905.
38536.26C Rabelais, F. Five books of Gargantua and his son Pantagruel. N.Y., 1905.
38536.26.4 Rabelais, F. Five books of Gargantua and Pantagruel. N.Y., 1944.
38536.26.5 Rabelais, F. Le disciple de Pantagruel. Paris, 1875.
38536.27 Bertoni, G. Rabelais; espisodi scelti. Modena, 1938-
38536.28.5 Rabelais, F. Pantagruel's prognostication. Oxford, 1947.
38536.29 Rabelais, F. La grande et vraye pronostication nouvelle. Paris, 1947.
38536.30 Schönermark, W. Beitrage zur Geschichte Rabelais' Werken. Breslau, 1861.
38536.31 Rabelais, F. Gargantua. Paris, 1951.
38536.32 Rabelais, F. Pantagruel. Paris, 1952.
38536.33 Rabelais, F. Gargantua. Paris, 1949.
38536.34 Rabelais, F. Rabelais. Paris, 1960.
38536.35 Facsimilé intéqral de l'un des trois éxemplaires conservés. Paris, 1959.
38536.36 Rabelais, F. Pantagruel. Paris, 1959.
38536.36.5 Rabelais, F. Pantagruel. 2. éd. Genève, 1965.
38536.36.6 Rabelais, François. Pantagruel. Paris, 1969.
38536.37 Rabelais, F. Le guart livre. Paris, 1959.
38536.38 Rabelais, F. Sunren Gargantuan hirmuinen elämä. Jyväshylä, 1947.
38536.39 Rabelais, F. Le tiers livre de F. Rabelais. Paris, 1962.
38536.40 Rabelais, F. Le tiers livre. Genève, 1964.
38536.42 Rabelais, F. Gargantua. 1. éd. Genève, 1970.

38537.1 - .26 Individual authors, etc. - 1500-1661 - Rabelais - Biography and criticism - General

38537.1 Revue des études Rabelaisiennes. Paris, 1903. 10v.
38537.1.05 Table de la revue des études Rabelaisienne. n.p., n.d.
38537.1.2 Revue du seizième siècle. 1913-1933 14v.
38537.1.3 Revue du seizième siècle. Table. v.1-19, 1913-1933. Genève, 1959.
38537.1.5 Association des amis de Rabelais et de la Dévinière. Bulletin. Tours. 1-10,1951-1961
38537.1.15 Boulenger, Jacques. Rabelais. Paris, 1925.
38537.1.20 Boulenger, Jacques. Rabelais. Paris, 1942.
38537.2 Martin, Henri. De l'autorité de Rabelais dans la revues present. Paris, 1879.
38537.2.5 Ginguené, P.L. De l'autorité de Rabelais dans la revues present. Utopie, 1791.
38537.3 Mayrargues, A. Rabelais, étude sur le seizième siècle. Paris, 1868.
38537.3.5 Febvre, Lucien. Le problème de l'incroyance au XVIe siècle; la religion de Rabelais. Paris, 1962.
38537.4A Brunet, Jacques C. Recherches sur...Rabelais. Paris, 1852.
38537.4B Brunet, Jacques C. Recherches sur...Rabelais. Paris, 1852.
38537.5 Fleury, Jean. Rebelais et ses oeuvres. Paris, 1877. 2v.
38537.6 Noël, Eugène. Rabelais et son oeuvre. Paris, 1870.
38537.7 Michel, Louis. Essai sur Rabelais. Paris, 1877.
38537.8 Arnstadt, F.A. François Rabelais. Leipzig, 1872.
38537.9 Ligier, Hermann. La politique de Rabelais. Paris, 1880.
38537.10 Réaume, Eugène. Rabelais et Montaine pédagogues. Paris, 1886.
38537.11 Heulhard, Arthur. Rabelais légiste. Paris, 1887.
38537.12 Stapfer, Paul. Rabelais. Paris, 1889.
38537.13 Schwarz, Gottlieb. Rabelais und Fischart. Winterthur, 1885.
38537.13.5 Ellmer, W. Rabelais' Gargantua und Fischarts Geschichtklitterung. Weimar, 1895.
38537.13.9 Frantzen, J.J.A.A. Kritische Bemerkungen zu Fischarts Übersetzung von Rabelais' Gargantua. Inaug. Diss. Strassbourg, 1892.
38537.14A Millet, René. Les grands écrivains français. Rabelais. Paris, 1892.
38537.14B Millet, René. Les grands écrivains français. Rabelais. Paris, 1892.
38537.14.2 Millet, René. Les grands écrivains français. Rabelais. Paris, 1903.
38537.15 Eriches, Ludwig. Les grandes et inestimables chroniques de Gargantua und Rabelais. Strassburg, 1889.
38537.16 Klett, Adolf. Lexikographische Beiträge zur Rabelais Gargantua. Bühl, 1890.
38537.16.5 Pfeffer, G. Beiträge zum Wortschatz des 3. Buches Rabelais. Marburg, 1901.
38537.17 Ernst, Karl. Syntaktische Studien zu Rabelais. Greifswald, 1890.
38537.18 Loiseau, Arthur. Rapports de la langue de Rabelais. Angers, 1867.
X Cg 38537.18.5 Sainéau, L. La langue de Rabelais. Paris, 1922-23. 2v.
38537.18.10 Sainéau, Lazar. L'influence et la réputation de Rabelais. Paris, 1930.
38537.19 Huguet, Edmond. Étude sur la syntax de Rabelais. Paris, 1894.
38537.19.5 Platen, Eugen. Syntaktische Untersuchungen zu Rabelais. Leipzig, 1890.
38537.19.9 Töpel, Carl. Syntaktische Untersuchungen zu Rabelais. Oppeln, 1887.
38537.19.10 Saenger, S. Syntaktische Untersuchungen zu Rabelais. Halle, 1888.
38537.20 Pamphlet box. Rabelais, F.
38537.20.50 Paris. Bibliothèque Nationale. Rabelais; exposition organisée à l'occasion du quatrième centenaire de la publication de Pantagruel. Paris, 1933.
38537.21 Besant, Walter. Rabelais. Edinburgh, 1879.
38537.22.3A Gebhart, Émile. Rabelais. Paris, 1877.
38537.22.3B Gebhart, Émile. Rabelais. Paris, 1877.
38537.23 Vallat, Gustave. Rabelais sa vie, son génie et son oeuvre. Paris, 1899.
38537.24 Mättig, J. Über den Einfluss der heimischen volkstümlichen literatur auf Rabelais. Leipzig, 1900.
38537.25 Thuasne, L. Étude sur Rabelais. Paris, 1904.
38537.25.5A Tilley, Arthur. François Rabelais. Philadelphia, 1907.
38537.25.5B Tilley, Arthur. François Rabelais. Philadelphia, 1907.
38537.25.5C Tilley, Arthur. François Rabelais. Philadelphia, 1907.
38537.25.5D Tilley, Arthur. François Rabelais. Philadelphia, 1907.
38537.25.6 Le Double, A. Rabelais anatomiste et physiologiste. Paris, 1899.

38537.1 - .26 Individual authors, etc. - 1500-1661 - Rabelais - Biography and criticism - General - cont.

38537.25.7 Precicou, A. Rabelais et les Limosins. Limoges, 1906.
38537.25.8 Thuasne, L. Rabelais et Villon. Paris, 1907.
38537.25.9 Stoppoloni, A. Francesco Rabelais. Roma, 1906.
38537.25.10 Albenas, G. d'. Les portraits de Rabelais. Montpellier, 1880.
38537.25.11 Dubouchet, A. François Rabelais à Montpellier 1530-1538. Montpellier, 1887.
38537.25.12 Noël, E. Rabelais. Bruxelles, 1859.
38537.25.13 Loviot, L. Au pays de Rabelais. Paris, 1907.
38537.25.14A Plattard, G. L'invention...dans l'oeuvre de Rabelais. Paris, 1909.
38537.25.14B Plattard, G. L'invention...dans l'oeuvre de Rabelais. Paris, 1909.
38537.25.15 Ravá, B. L'art de Rabelais. Rome, 1910.
38537.25.16 Plattard, Jean. L'oeuvre de Rabelais. Paris, 1910.
38537.25.16.3 Plattard, Jean. L'adolescence de Rabelais en Poitow. Paris, 1923.
38537.25.16.7 Plattard, Jean. Life of François Rabelais. N.Y., 1931.
38537.25.16.11 Plattard, Jean. Guide illustré au pays de Rabelais. Paris, 1931.
38537.25.16.15A Plattard, Jean. La vie et l'oeuvre de Rabelais. Paris, 1939.
38537.25.16.15B Plattard, Jean. La vie et l'oeuvre de Rabelais. Paris, 1939.
38537.25.16.20 Plattard, Jean. François Rabelais. Paris, 1932.
38537.25.17 Talant, L. Rabelais et la réforme. Cahors, 1902.
38537.25.18 Walter, Dott. Rabelais e la circulazione del sangue. Genova, 1894.
38537.25.19 Smith, W.F. Rabelais in his writings. Cambridge, n.d.
38537.25.20 Jacob, P.L. Rabelais, sa vie et ses ouvrages. Paris, 1859.
38537.25.21 Fiume, Cordelia del. De l'influence de quelques auteurs italiens sur...Rabelais. Firenze, 1918.
38537.25.25 Sainéau, Lazar. L'histoire naturelle et les branches connexes dans l'oeuvre de Rabelais. Paris, 1921.
Htn 38537.25.26* Silvestre, Armand. Le nu de Rabelais. Paris, 1892.
38537.25.30 Hatzfield, H. François Rabelais. München, 1923.
38537.25.35 Chappell, A.F. The enigma of Rabelais, an essay in interpretation. Cambridge, 1924.
38537.25.40 Porto, Filippo. Studi Rabelesiani. Catania, 1921.
38537.25.45 Anna, Luigi de. Rabelais e la sua epopea burlesca. Firenze, 1924.
38537.25.50 Nicati, William. Rabelais notre maitre, son oeuvre, sa doctrine, le pantagruelisme. Marseille, 1926.
38537.25.55 Fetzer, Herman. The book of Rabelais. Garden City, 1928.
38537.25.60 Causeret, Charles. Ce qu'il faut connaître de Rabelais. Paris, 1927.
38537.25.62 Clement, N.H. The influence of the Arthurian romances on the five books of Rabelais. Berkeley, 1926.
38537.25.65 Plattard, Jean. Vie de François Rabelais. Paris, 1928.
38537.25.70A Nock, Albert J. Francis Rabelais, the man et his work. N.Y., 1929.
38537.25.70B Nock, Albert J. Francis Rabelais, the man et his work. N.Y., 1929.
38537.25.70C Nock, Albert J. Francis Rabelais, the man et his work. N.Y., 1929.
38537.25.73 Nock, Albert J. A journey into Rabelais's France. N.Y., 1934.
38537.25.74 Nock, Albert J. A journey into Rabelais's France. N.Y., 1934.
38537.25.75 Besant, Walter. Rabelais. Philadelphia, 1879.
38537.25.80 Putnam, Samuel. François Rabelais, man of the Renaissance. N.Y., 1929.
38537.25.85 France, Anatole. Rabelais. Paris, 1929.
38537.25.86A France, Anatole. Rabelais. London, 1929.
38537.25.86B France, Anatole. Rabelais. London, 1929.
38537.25.90 Schmidt, Konrad. Rabelais, als Artz in seinen Roman "Gargantua und Pantagruel". Greifswald, 1926.
Htn 38537.25.95* Holmes, Oliver. To the honorary secretaries of the Rabelais club. Letter, 21 mr. 1880. n.p., 1880.
Htn 38537.25.100* Hugo, Victor. To the members of the Rabelais Club. Letter dated 10 April, 1880. n.p., 1880.
38537.25.110 Watson, Francis. Laughter for Pluto. London, 1933.
38537.25.130 Carvalho, R. de. Rabelais et le rire de la renaissance. Paris, 1932.
38537.25.138 Kummer, G. Das Nachwirken der antiken komischen Dichtung in den Werken von Rabelais. Inaug. Diss. Berlin, 1937.
38537.25.140 Kummer, G. Das Nachwirken der antiken komischen Dichtung in denWerken von Rabelais. Berlin, 1937.
38537.25.145 Lote, Georges. La vie et l'oeuvre de François Rabelais. Aix-en-Provence, 1938.
38537.25.150 Bernier, Jean. Jugement et observations sur la vie de F. Rabelais. Paris, 1699.
38537.25.155 Powys, John C. Rabelais. London, 1948.
38537.25.165 Charpentier, John. Rabelais. Paris, 1946.
38537.25.170 Jourda, P. La Gargantua de Rabelais. Paris, 1948.
38537.25.175 Valot, S. Regardons vivre François Rabelais. Paris, 1948.
38537.25.180 Besant, W. Rabelais. Edinburgh, 1905.
38537.25.185 Willcocks, M.P. The laughing philosopher. London, 1950.
38537.25.190 Association d'humanisme et Renaissance. François Rabelais. Genève, 1953.
38537.25.200 Carpenter, N.C. Rabelais and music. Chapel Hill, 1954.
38537.25.205 Association des amis de Rabelais et de La Devinière. Quatrième centenaire de la mort de Rabelais. Tours, 1953.
38537.25.210 Études rabelaisiennes. Genève, 1956. 9v.
38537.25.215 Lebègue, R. Rabelais. Tübingen, 1952.
38537.25.220 Naudon, Paul. Rabelais. Paris, 1954.
38537.25.225 Saulnier, V.L. Le dessein de Rabelais. Paris, 1957.
38537.25.230 Cohen, Gustave. Rabelais. Paris, 1936?
38537.25.235 Roe, Fredrick Charles. Sir Thomas Urguhart and Rabelais. Oxford, 1957.
38537.25.240 Wickler, Franz Josef. Rabelais und Sterne. Bonn, 1963.
38537.25.245 Michel, Pierre. Continuité de la sagesse française. Paris, 1965.
38537.25.250 Coleman, D.G. Rabelais: a critical study in prose fiction. Cambridge, Eng., 1971.
38537.26 Coutaud, Albert. La pedagogie de Rabelais. Paris, 1899.

38537.27 - .34 Individual authors, etc. - 1500-1661 - Rabelais - Translations

Htn 38537.27* Urchard, Thomas. Works of François Rabelais. London, 1694. 4v.
38537.29.5A Rabelais, F. The works of Rabelais faithfully translated from the French. n.p., 19- .
38537.29.5B Rabelais, F. The works of Rabelais faithfully translated from the French. n.p., 19- .

38537.27 - .34 Individual authors, etc. - 1500-1661 - Rabelais - Translations - cont.

	38537.29.10	Rabelais, F. Works. v.1,3-5. London, 1737. 4v.
	38537.30	Rabelais, F. Works. Dublin, 1738. 4v.
	38537.30.7	Rabelais, F. Works. London, 1849. 2v.
	38537.30.9	Rabelais, F. Works. London, 1854-55. 2v.
	38537.30.15	Rabelais, F. The portable Rabelais. N.Y., 1946.
	38537.31	Rabelais, F. Three good giants. Boston, 1888.
	38537.32.5A	Rabelais, F. The life of Gargantua and the heroic deeds of Pantagruel. 4. éd. London, 1887.
	38537.32.5B	Rabelais, F. The life of Gargantua and the heroic deeds of Pantagruel. 4. éd. London, 1887.
	38537.33A	Rabelais, F. The sequel to Pantagruel. London, 1888.
	38537.33B	Rabelais, F. The sequel to Pantagruel. London, 1888.
	38537.33C	Rabelais, F. The sequel to Pantagruel. London, 1888.
	38537.33.20	Rabelais, F. Rabelais Gargantus und Pantagruel. Leipzig, 1880. 2v.
	38537.33.25	Rabelais, F. The history of Gargantua and Pantagruel. Harmondsworth, Middlesex, 1955.
	38537.34	Rabelais, F. The heroic deeds of Gargantua and Pantagruel. London, 1929. 2v.

38537.35 - Individual authors, etc. - 1500-1661 - Rabelais - Biography and criticism - Special

	38537.35	Stein, H. Un Rabelais apocryphe de 1549. Paris, 1901.
	38537.36	Lenoir, P. Quelques aspects de la pensée de Rabelais. Paris, 1954.
	38537.37	Lefebvre, Henri. Rabelais. Paris, 1955.
	38537.38	Lewis, D.B.W. Doctor Rabelais. N.Y., 1957.
	38537.40	Screech, Michael Andrew. The Rabelaisian marriage. London, 1958.
	38537.42A	Francon, Marcel. Autour de la lettre de Gargantua à son fils. Rachecorbon, 1857.
	38537.42B	Francon, Marcel. Autour de la lettre de Gargantua à son fils. Rachecorbon, 1857.
	38537.42.2A	Francon, Marcel. Autour de la lettre de Gargantua à son fils. Cambridge, 1964.
	38537.42.2B	Francon, Marcel. Autour de la lettre de Gargantua à son fils. Cambridge, 1964.
	38537.44	Rabelais écrivain-médecin. Paris, 1959.
	38537.46F	Heulhard, Arthur. Rabelais. 2. éd. Paris, 189-?
	38537.48	Krailsheimer, Alban J. Rabelais and the Françiscans. Oxford, 1963.
	38537.49	Keller, A.C. The telling of tales in Rabelais. Frankfurt, 1963.
	38537.50	Schrader, Ludwig. Pamarge und Hermes. Bonn, 1958.
	38537.51	Mardi, Enzo. Rabelais e il diritto romano. Milano, 1962.
	38537.52	Artamonov, S.D. Fransua Rable. Moskva, 1964.
	38537.53	Doutenville, H. Rabelais dedans Touraine. Tours, 1963.
	38537.54	Montpellier, France. Musée Fabre. Expositon commémorative du 400me anniversaire de la mort de François Rabelais. Montpellier, 1953.
	38537.55	Bakhtin, Mikhail M. Tvorchestvo Fransua Rable i narodnaia kul'tura sredrevekov'ia i Renessansa. Moskva, 1965.
	38537.55.5	Bakhtin, Mikhail M. Rabelais and his world. Cambridge, Mass., 1968.
	38537.56	Tetel, Marcel. Rabelais. N.Y., 1967.
	38537.59	Glauser, Alfred Charles. Rabelais créateur. Paris, 1966.
	38537.60	Greene, Thomas M. Rabelais; a study in comic courage. Englewood Cliffs, N.J., 1970.
	38537.62	Leonarduzzi, Alessandro. F. Rabelais e la sua prospettiva pedagogica. Trieste, 1966.
	38537.64	Screech, Michael Andrew. Aspects of Rabelais's christian comedy. London, 1968.
	38537.66	Krailsheimer, Alban J. Rabelais. Paris, 1967.
	38537.68	Beaujour, Michel. Le jeu de Rabelais. Paris, 1969.
	38537.70	Brown, Huntington. Rabelais in English literature. N.Y., 1967.
	38537.74	Masters, George Mallary. Rabelaisian dialectic and the platonic-hermetic tradition. Albany, 1969.
	38537.76	Paris, Jean. Rabelais au futur. Paris, 1970.
	38537.78	Lindfors-Nordin, Elsa G. Berne, berner, expressions rabelaisiennes. Stockholm, 1948.
	38537.80	Eldridge, Paul. François Rabelais, the great story teller. South Brunswick, 1971.
	38537.82	Bowen, Barbara C. The age of bluff: paradox and ambiguity in Rabelais and Montaigne. Urbana, 1972.
	38537.84	Laurent, Marcel. Rabelais; le monde paysan et le langage auvergnat. Clemont-Ferrand, 1971.
	38537.86	Weinberg, Florence M. The wine and the will; Rabelais's Bacchic Christianity. Detroit, 1972.

38539 Individual authors, etc. - 1500-1661 - Other prose writers

	38539.01	Pamphlet box. 16th century prose.
Htn	38539.1.50*	Beroaede de Verville, F. Apprehensions spirituelles, poems. Paris, 1584.
Htn	38539.2.5*	Camus, Jean P. Le rabat-joye du triomphe monacal. L'Isle, 1634.
Htn	38539.2.10*	Camus, Jean P. The loving enemie. London, 1650.
Htn	38539.2.15*	Camus, Jean P. Admirable events. London, 1639.
Htn	38539.2.18*	Camus, Jean P. La pieuse Jullie. Paris, 1625.
Htn	38539.2.25*	Camus, Jean P. Nature's paradox or The innocent impostor. London, 1652.
	38539.2.30	Camus, Jean P. Agathonphile, récit de philargayrippe. Genève, 1951.
Htn	38539.2.35*	Camus, Jean P. A true tragical history of two illustrious families...Alcimus and Vannoza. London, 1677.
	38539.2.50	Bayer, Albert. Jean Pierre Camus; sein Leben und seine Romae. Inaug. Diss. Leipzig, 1906.
Htn	38539.2.55*	Godeau, Antoine. Oraison funèbre de Messieur Jean Pierre Camus. Paris, 1653.
	38539.2.57	Hartmann, B. Jean Pierre Camus, Erziehung und Erbauung in seinen Unterhaltungsschriften. Inaug. Diss. München, 1937.
	38539.2.59	Joppin, G. Une querelle autour de l'amour pur, Jean Pierre Camus. Thèse. Paris, 1938.
	38539.2.60	Joppin, G. Une querelle autour de l'amour pur, Jean Pierre Camus. Paris, 1938.
	38539.2.65	Angers, J.E. Du stoicisme chrétien à l'humanisme chrétien. Meaux? 1952.
	38539.2.70	Sufuma, Louis. Les histoires dévotes de Jean Pierre Camus. Paris, 1940.
	38539.2.75	Gastaldi, Vittoria. Jean Pierre Camus, romantière barocco e vescovo di Francia. Catania, 1964.
	38539.2.80	Garreau, Albert. Jean-Pierre Camus. Paris, 1586.
	38539.2.200	Cholières, Nicolas de. Paris, 1879. 2v.
Htn	38539.2.250*	Cholières, Nicolas de. Les neuf matinées. Paris, 1586.
Htn	38539.2.260*	Cholières, Nicolas de. La guerre des masles contre les femelles. Paris, 1588.

38539 Individual authors, etc. - 1500-1661 - Other prose writers - cont.

Htn	38539.2.270*	Cholières, Nicolas de. Les aprèsdisnees. Paris, 1588.
	38539.2.500	Cholières, Nicolas de. Oeuvre. Paris, 1910.
	38539.2.5100	Ciorxenescu, A. Les Romans de la princesse de Conti. Paris, 1936.
Htn	38539.3.10*	Contreras, Jeonimo de. Les etranges avantures. Lyon, 1580.
Htn	38539.3.250*	Des Autels, Guillaume. Mythistoire barragouyne de Fanfreluche et Gandichon. Rouen, 1578.
	38539.3.275	Bichemaier, Karl. Die Preziositöt das senimentalen Romane des Sieur des Escuteaux, Wertheim, 1931.
	38539.3.310	Sullivan, Sister M. St. F. Étienne du Trouchet. Washington, 1931.
	38539.4	Du Vair, Guillaume. Oeuvres. 2. éd. Rouen, 1614. 2v.
	38539.5	Du Vair, Guillaume. Recueil des harangues et traictez. Paris, 1606.
Htn	38539.5.15*	Desfontaines. L'inceste innocent; histoire véritable. Paris, 1644.
	38539.6	Du Vair, Guillaume. Actions et traictez oratoires. Paris, 1911.
	38539.6.5	Du Vair, Guillaume. De la sainte philosophie. Paris, 1945.
	38539.6.10	Du Vair, Guillaume. The moral philosophie of the Stoicks. New Brunswick, N.J., 1951.
	38539.6.20	Radouant, René. Guillaume du Vair. Thèse. Genève, 1970.
Htn	38539.6.25*	Doré, Pierre. La tourtrelle de viduité; enseignant les vefues comment elles doivent vivre en leur estat. Arras, 1605.
Htn	38539.6.50*	Duperier, Antoine. Les amours de Lozie. Lyon, 1619. 2 pam.
	38539.7	Gougny, Édmond. Guillaume Du Vair. Paris, 1857.
	38539.7.5	Du Vair, Guillaume. De l'éloquence françoise. Paris, n.d.
	38539.7.9	Sapey, Charles A. Essai sur la vie et les ouvrages de Guillaume Du Vair. Boston, 1847.
Htn	38539.8*	Guyon, Louis. Les diverses leçons de Loys Guyon, Dolois, sieur de la Nanche. 2. éd. Lyon, 1610-25. 3v.
	38539.8.25	Wadsworth, P.A. The novels of Gomberville; critical study of Palexandre and Cythérée. New Haven, 1942.
Htn	38539.9*	Du Verdier, G.S. Les chevalier hipocondriaque. Paris, 1632.
	38539.9.15	Du Verdier, G.S. Don Clarazce de Gontarnos. Amsterdam, 1697.
Htn	38539.11*	Lannel, Jean de. Le romant satyrique. Paris, 1624.
	38539.11.20	Hardee, A. Maynor. Jean de Lannel and the pre-classical French novel. Diss. Geneva, 1967.
	38539.13	La Serre, Jean Puget de. La Clytie, ou le romant de la cour. Paris, 1640.
Htn	38539.13.5*	La Serre, Jean Puget de. Le brevière des courtisans. Paris, 1630.
	38539.13.81	Ginzl, W. Puget de La Serre. Inaug. Diss. Rostock, 1936.
Htn	38539.15*	Le Roux, C. de. La tourterelle gemissante sur Hierusalem. Paris, 1631.
Htn	38539.16*	Montluc, A. de. Deux de l'incognu. Paris, 1630.
	38539.16.5	Montluc, A. de. La comédie des proverbes; pièce comique. 5. éd. Troyes, 1715.
Htn	38539.18*	Faret, Nicolas. L'honeste homme, ou L'art de plaire à la cour. Paris, 1637.
	38539.18.10	Faret, Nicolas. L'honeste homme, ou L'art de plaire à la cour. Thèse. Photoreproduction. Paris, 1925.
	38539.20	Humbert, H. Les amours d'Ircandre et Sophonie. Paris, 1637.
Htn	38539.21.15*	Intras de Bazas, Jean d'. Le duel de Tithamante; histoire Gascone. Paris, 1609.
Htn	38539.23.5*	Le Vayer de Boutigny, R. The famous romance of Taris and Zelie. London, 1685. 2 pam.
Htn	38539.23.10*	Le Vayer de Boutigny, R. Le grand Selim. Paris, 1645.
Htn	38539.25*	Logeas, H.M. de. Le romant héroique. Paris, 1632.
Htn	38539.27.75*	Maisonneuve, Étienne de. La plaisante et delectable histoire de Gerilon d'Angleterre. 3. éd. Lyon, 1602.
Htn	38539.28*	Maisonneuve, Étienne de. Le premier livre de la plaisante et délectable histoire de Gerlon d'Angleterre. Paris, 1572.
	38539.28.50	Grubbs, H.A. Damien Mitton, 1618-1690. Princeton, 1932.
Htn	38539.29.5*	Pielat, B. Le secrétaire incogne. Amsterdam, 1671. 2 pam.
Htn	38539.29.50*	Ravand, Abraham. Les amours d'Endimion et de la lune. Paris, 1624.
Htn	38539.30*	Renaudot, I. Recueil général des questions traitées. Paris, 1655.
Htn	38539.30.5*	Renaudot, I. Recueil général des questions traitées. Paris, 1655-56. 5v.
	38539.32	Rosset, François de. Les histoires tragiques de nos temps. 2. éd. Lyon, 1708.
Htn	38539.32.5*	Rosset, François de. Theatrum tragicum das ist neue Wahrhaftige traurig claeglich und wunderliche Geschichten. Tübingen, 1634.
Htn	38539.33.15*	Saillans, Gaspar de. Premier livre de Gaspar de Saillans. Lyon, 1569.
	38539.35	Vanel, Charles. Histoire du temps ou Journal. Paris, 1685.
Htn	38539.55*	Villiers, J. de. The gentleman-apothecary. London, 1678.
	38539.60	La prison sans chagrin; histoire comique du temps. Paris, 1669.
Htn	38539.65*	Yver, Jacques. Le printemps. Paris, 1578.
Htn	38539.70*	Yver, Jacques. Le printemps. Lyon, 1589.
Htn	38539.75*	Yver, Jacques. Le printemps. Rouen, 1599.
	38539.80	Belliévre, C. Souvenirs de voyages en Italie et en Orient. Genève, 1956.
	38539.85	L'oeuvres des conteurs français. Paris, 1921.
	38539.90	Adam, Antoine. Romanciers du XVIIIe siècle. Paris, 1958.
	38539.95	Bejart, M. Araspe. Avignon, 1959.
	38539.96	Cartigny, J. de. The wandering knight. Seattle, 1951.
	38539.98	Deloffre, F. Agréables conférences de deux paysans de Saint-Ouen et de Montmorency. Paris, 1961.
	38539.100	Crenne, Hilisenne de. Les Angovysses ou Loureuses qui procédént d'amours (1538). Paris, 1968-
	38539.102.80	Harris, Margaret A. A study of Théodore Valentinen's Amant resucité de la mort d'amour. n.p., n.d.
	38539.104	DuSoucy, François. Histoire asiatique de Cerinthe, de Calianthe et d'Artenice. Paris, 1634.
	38539.106	Millot, Michel. L'école des filles ou La philosophie des dames. Paris, 1969.

38541 Individual authors, etc. - 1661-1715 - Fiction - Folios [Discontinued]

Htn 38541.4* Oeuvres de La Mothe le Vayer. Paris, 1862. 2v.
38541.8 Oeuvres de Monsieur Jean L.G. Balzac. Paris, 1665. 2v.
38541.11 Moralistes français. Paris, 1834.
38541.12 Moralistes français. Paris, 1838.
38541.13 Moralistes français. Paris, 1841.
38541.16 Urbain, Charles. Nicolas Coeffeteau Dominican. Paris, 1893.
Htn 38541.18* Duverdier, Gilbert. Loves...of the Greek Princes. London, 1640.
Htn 38541.19* Duverdier, Gilbert. Loves...of the Greek Princes. London, 1640.
Htn 38541.19.75* La Calprenede, G. de C. Hymen's praeludia, or Love's masterpieces. Pt. 1-12. London, 1654-59. 6v.
Htn 38541.20* La Calprenede, G. de C. Hymen's praeludia, or Love's masterpieces. London, 1668.
Htn 38541.21* La Calprenede, G. de C. Hymen's praeludia, or Cleopatra. London, 1674.
Htn 38541.22* La Calprenede, G. de C. Pharamond, or The history of France. London, 1677.
Htn 38541.22.50* La Calprenede, G. de C. Cassandra, the fam'd romance. London, 1661.
Htn 38541.24F* La Calprenede, G. de C. Cassandra, the fam'd romance. 1. ed. pt. 1-5. London, 1652.
Htn 38541.24.20* La Calprenede, G. de C. La mort des enfans d'Herode, ou Suite a la Marian. Tolose, 1652.
38541.25 Woelffel, Paul. Die Reisebilder in den Romanen la Calprenèdes. Greifswald, 1915.
Htn 38541.27* Scudery, Madeleine de. Almahide. London, 1702.
Htn 38541.28F* Scudery, Madeleine de. Almahide, or The captive queen. London, 1677.

38542.01 - .3 Individual authors, etc. - 1661-1715 - Fiction - Voiture

38542.01 Pamphlet box. Voiture, Vincent.
Htn 38542.01.9* Voiture, Vincent. Les oeuvres. Paris, 1652.
38542.1 Voiture, Vincent. Les oeuvres. Paris, 1856.
38542.2 Voiture, Vincent. Oeuvres. Lettres et poésies. Paris, 1855. 2v.
38542.2.5 Voiture, Vincent. Les lettres (and other works). n.p., n.d.
38542.2.7 Voiture, Vincent. Les lettres de Mr. de Voiture. Paris, 1654.
38542.2.7.5 Voiture, Vincent. Lettres de Monsieur de Voiture: Lettres aux Rambouillet. Paris, 1969.
38542.2.15 Voiture, Vincent. Stances, sonnets, rondeaux et chansons. Paris, 1907.
Htn 38542.2.19* Voiture, Vincent. Works. London, 1705.
Htn 38542.2.30* Voiture, Vincent. Zelinda. London, 1676.
38542.3 Lettres...de Voiture et Balzac. Paris, 1807.
38542.3.5 Magne, Emile. Voiture et les origines de l'hotel de Rambouillet. 1597-1635. Paris, 1911.
38542.3.7 Magne, Emile. Voiture et l'hotel de Rambouillet. Paris, 1930.

38542.4 - .12 Individual authors, etc. - 1661-1715 - Fiction - Balzac, J.L.G. de

Htn 38542.4* Balzac, J.L.G. de. Lettres de feu M. de Balzac à M. Conrart. Paris, 1659.
Htn 38542.4.5* Balzac, J.L.G. de. Lettres de feu Monsieur de Balzac à Monsieur Conrart. Amsterdam, 1664.
Htn 38542.4.9* Balzac, J.L.G. de. Letters. London, 1634.
Htn 38542.4.9.20* Balzac, J.L.G. de. Lettres choisies. Paris, 1647. 2v.
38542.4.10 Balzac, J.L.G. de. Lettres choisies. Amsterdam, 1678.
38542.4.11 Balzac, J.L.G. de. Les lettres diverses. Paris, 1659.
Htn 38542.4.12* Balzac, J.L.G. de. Lettres familières de M. de Balzac à M. Chapelain. Amsterdam, 1661.
Htn 38542.4.15* Balzac, J.L.G. de. Les entretiens. Leide, 1659.
Htn 38542.4.16* Balzac, J.L.G. de. Les entretiens. Paris, 1660.
38542.4.20 Balzac, J.L.G. de. Les premières lettres de Guez de Balzac, 1618-1627. Paris, 1933-34. 2v.
Htn 38542.5* Balzac, J.L.G. de. Oeuvres...du Sieur de Balzac. Leide, 1651.
38542.8 Balzac, J.L.G. de. Oeuvres de Jean Louis de Balzac. Paris, 1822. 2v.
38542.9 Balzac, J.L.G. de. Oeuvres choisies. Paris, 1936.
38542.10 Balzac, J.L.G. de. Oeuvres de Jean Louis de Balzac. Paris, 1854. 2v.
38542.10.5 Balzac, J.L.G. de. Les oeuvres diverses. Paris, 1664.
38542.10.8 Balzac, J.L.G. de. Aristippe. Leide, 1658.
38542.10.9 Balzac, J.L.G. de. Aristippe. Leide, 1658.
38542.11 Balzac, J.L.G. de. Aristippe. Amsterdam, 1664.
38542.12 Vogler, H. Die literargeschichtlichen Kenntnisse und Urteile des J.L.G. de Balzac. Altona, 1906.
38542.12.5 Sabrié, J.B. Les idées religieuse de J.L. Guez de Balzac. Paris, 1913.
38542.12.6 Declareuil, J. Idées politiques de Guez de Balzac. Paris, 1907.
38542.12.9 Guillaumie, Gaston. J.L. Guez de Balzac et la prose française. Paris, 1927.
38542.12.11A Guillaumie, Gaston. J.L. Guez de Balzac et la prose française. Thèse. Paris, 1927.
38542.12.11B Guillaumie, Gaston. J.L. Guez de Balzac et la prose française. Thèse. Paris, 1927.
38542.12.15 Beugnot, Bernard. J.L. Guez de Balzac. Montréal, 1967.
38542.12.16 Beugnot, Bernard. J.L. Guez de Balzac. Supplement. Montréal, 1969.
38542.12.20 Sutcliffe, Frank Edmund. Guez de Balzac et son temps. Paris, 1959.

38542.13 Individual authors, etc. - 1661-1715 - Fiction - Miscellany [Discontinued]

38542.13 Baudoin, I. Diversitez historiques. Paris, 1621.
38542.13.5 Brémond, Sébastien. L'heureux esclave. Paris, 1726.
Htn 38542.13.6* Brémond, Sébastien. The happy slave. London, 1686.
Htn 38542.13.7* Brémond, Sébastien. Haltige ou Les amours. Cologne, 1676.

38542.14 - .26 Individual authors, etc. - 1661-1715 - Fiction - Saint-Evremond

38542.14 Merlet, G. Saint-Evremond, étude historique. Paris, 1870.
38542.14.25 Dubosco de la Roberdière. Love victorious. London, 1684.
38542.15 Broglé, Adolphe. Étude sur Saint Evremond. Rostock, 1873.
38542.16 Daniel, W.M. Saint-Evremond en Angleterre. Versailles, 1907.
38542.16.5 Mollenhauer, Ernst. Saint-Evremond als Kritiker. Greifswald, 1914.

38542.14 - .26 Individual authors, etc. - 1661-1715 - Fiction - Saint-Evremond - cont.

38542.16.6 Mollenhauer, Ernst. Saint-Evremond als Kritiker. Greifswald, 1914.
38542.16.10 Schmidt, A.M. Saint-Evremond ou L'humaniste impur. Paris, 1932.
38542.17 Saint-Evremond, C. de M. de S.D. Oeuvres. Paris, 1740. 10v.
38542.17.2 Saint-Evremond, C. de M. de S.D. Oeuvres. Paris, 1753. 12v.
38542.17.9 Saint-Evremond, C. de M. de S.D. Oeuvres melées. Paris, 1866. 3v.
38542.17.12 Saint-Evremond, C. de M. de S.D. Works. London, 1728. 2v.
38542.19.5 Saint-Evremond, C. de M. de S.D. Recueil de diverses pièces. La Haye, 1669.
Htn 38542.19.6* Saint Evremond, C. de M. de S.D. Miscellaneous essays. London, 1692.
38542.20 Saint-Evremond, C. de M. de S.D. Lettres. Paris, 1967-68.
Htn 38542.21* Saint-Evremond, C. de M. de S.D. Jugement sur Seneque, Plutarque et Petrone. Paris, 1670.
38542.22 Saint-Evremond, C. de M. de S.D. Oeuvres choisies. Paris, n.d.
38542.23 Saint-Evremond, C. de M. de S.D. Oeuvres choisies de Saint Evremont. Paris, 1804.
38542.23.5 Saint-Evremond, C. de M. de S.D. Oeuvres en prose. Paris, 1962. 4v.
38542.24 Saint Evremond, C. de M. de S.D. Oeuvres choisies. Paris, 1881.
38542.24.5 Saint Evremond, C. de M. de S.D. Oeuvres. Paris, 1927. 3v.
38542.25 Saint Evremond, C. de M. de S.D. Les académiciens. Étude par Robert de Bonnières. Paris, 1879.
38542.25.2 Saint Evremond, C. de M. de S.D. Les académiciens. Étude par Robert de Bonnières. Paris, 1879.
38542.25.15 Saint Evremond, C. de M. de S.D. La comédie des académistes. N.Y., 1931.
38542.26 Saint-Evremond, C. de M. de S.D. Schriften und Briefe. München, 1912. 2v.
38542.26.5 Saint Evremond, C. de M. de S.D. Critique littéraire. Paris, 1921.
Htn 38542.26.9* Cotolendi, C. Saint-Evremoniana ou dialogues. Paris, 1700.
38542.26.10 Barnwell, H.T. Les idées morales et critiques de Saint Evremond. Paris, 1957.
38542.26.12 Spalatin, Krsto. Saint Evremond. Thèse. Zagreb, 1934.
38542.26.15 Nardis, Luigi de. Il cortegiano e l'eroe. Firenze, 1964.

38542.27 - Individual authors, etc. - 1661-1715 - Fiction - Blessebois, etc.

Htn 38542.27* Saint Dennis, C.M. de. Works. London, 1700. 3v.
Htn 38542.28* Gaultier, Jacques. Al-man-sir. London, 1672.
38542.29 Blessebois, P.C. Alosie ou Les amours de Madame T.P. Paris, 1876.
38542.29.5 Blessebois, P.C. Oeuvre. Paris, 1921.
38542.29.10 Blessebois, Pierre Corneille. Le Zombi du Grand-Pérou et autres oeuvres érotiques. Paris, 1970.
38542.30 Blessebois, P.C. Pastorale tirée des oeuvres satyriques (1676). Alençon, 1892.
38542.30.25 Lachèvre, Frédéric. La Casanova du XVIIIe siècle: Pierre Corneille Blessebois, normand (1646?-1700?). Paris, 1927.
38542.31 Du Pré, M. Le moine seculaire. Franche, 1675?
38542.33 Passard, F.L. Bibliothèque épistolaire. Paris, n.d.
38542.34 Colin, Claude. Eraste, ou Les amours du grand Alcandre. Paris, 1665.
Htn 38542.35* Cotolendi, C. Arliquiniana, ou Les bons mots. Paris, 1694.
38542.36 Barrin, Jean. Venus dans le cloitre. 1. éd. canadienne. Montréal, 1967.

38543.1 - .2 Individual authors, etc. - 1661-1715 - Fiction - Rochefort

38543.1 Rochefort, J. de. Le passe temps agréable. Rotterdam, 1715.
38543.1.5 Rochefort, J. de. Le passe temps agréable. Rotterdam, 17- .
38543.1.10 Le passe temps agréable. v. 1-2. Rotterdam, 1718.
38543.1.15 Le passe temps agréable, ou Nouveaux choix de Bons-Mots. 2. éd. Rotterdam, 1711.

38543.3 - .24 Individual authors, etc. - 1661-1715 - Fiction - La Rochefoucauld

38543.3A Bourdeaux, J. La Rochefoucauld. 1930. Paris, 1895.
38543.3B Bourdeaux, J. La Rochefoucauld. 1930. Paris, 1895.
38543.3.5 Hémon, Félix. La Rochefoucauld. Paris, 1896.
NEDL 38543.3.9 Graudsaignes D'Hauterise, R. Le pessimisme de La Rochefoucauld. Paris, 1914.
38543.4 Oeuvres de...La Rochefoucauld. Paris, 1825.
38543.5 La Rochefoucauld, François. Oeuvres complètes. Paris, 1883. 2v.
38543.5.10 La Rochefoucauld, François. Oeuvres complètes. Paris, 1964.
38543.6 La Rochefoucauld, François. Oeuvres de La Rochefoucauld. v.1-3 et album. Paris, 1868-74. 4v.
38543.6.5 La Rochefoucauld, François. Maximes et réflexions morales. Paris, 1931.
38543.6.7 La Rochefoucauld, François. Réflexions ou Sentences et maximes morales. Paris, 1932.
Htn 38543.6.9* La Rochefoucauld, François. Réflexions ou Sentences et maximes morales. Paris, 1665.
38543.6.25 La Rochefoucauld, François. Réflexions ou Sentences et maximes morales. Amsterdam, 1712.
Htn 38543.7* La Rochefoucauld, François. Réflexions, sentences et maximes morales. Paris, 1736.
38543.8 La Rochefoucauld, François. Réflexions, sentences et maximes morales. Lausanne, 1760.
38543.9 La Rochefoucauld, François. Maximes et réflexions morales. Calais, 1797.
38543.10 La Rochefoucauld, François. Maximes et réflexions. Paris, 1815.
38543.10.3 La Rochefoucauld, François. Réflexions ou Sentences et maximes morales. Paris, 1822.
38543.10.7 La Rochefoucauld, François. Maximes. Pensées...Montesquieu oeuvres...Vauvenagues. Paris, 1858.
X Cg 38543.10.8 La Rochefoucauld, François. Pensées et maximes. Paris, 1824.
38543.10.9 La Rochefoucauld, François. Maximes et réflexions morales. 2. éd. Paris, 1829.

38543.3 - .24 Individual authors, etc. - 1661-1715 - Fiction - La Rochefoucauld - cont.

38543.10.10 La Rochefoucauld, François. Réfléxions, sentences. Paris, 1867.
38543.10.12 La Rochefoucauld, François. La première rédaction des maximes. Paris, 1927.
38543.10.14 La Rochefoucauld, François. Mémoires. Paris, 1804.
38543.10.15A La Rochefoucauld, François. Mémoires. Paris, 1925.
38543.10.15B La Rochefoucauld, François. Mémoires. Paris, 1925.
38543.10.18 La Rochefoucauld, François. Les maximes. 2. éd. Londres, 1908.
38543.10.19 La Rochefoucauld, François. Maximes. London, 1912.
38543.10.20A La Rochefoucauld, François. Maximes. Paris, 1913.
38543.10.20B La Rochefoucauld, François. Maximes. Paris, 1913.
38543.10.22 La Rochefoucauld, François. Les maximes. Pairs, 1881.
38543.10.25 La Rochefoucauld, François. Maximes et réfléxions morales. Paris, 1873.
38543.10.27 La Rochefoucauld, François. Maximes et réfléxions morales. Paris, 1880.
38543.10.30 La Rochefoucauld, François. Maximes. Paris, 1883.
38543.10.40 La Rochefoucauld, François. Les maximes suivies des réfléxions diverses. Paris, 1935.
38543.10.45 La Rochefoucauld, François. Les maximes. Paris, 1945.
38543.10.50A La Rochefoucauld, François. Maximes, suivies des réfléxions diverses. Paris, 1967.
38543.10.50B La Rochefoucauld, François. Maximes, suivies des réfléxions diverses. Paris, 1967.
38543.10.52 La Rochefoucauld, François. Maximes. Genève, 1971?
38543.11 La Rochefoucauld, François. Réfléxions ou sentences et maximes morales. Paris, 1868.
38543.11.10 La Rochefoucauld, François. Réfléxions. Porrentruy, 1947.
38543.12 La Rochefoucauld, François. Le premier texte de La Rochefoucauld. Paris, 1869.
38543.13 Aimé-Martin, Louis. Examen critique. Paris, 1822.
38543.14 Granges de Surgères, Anatole. Traductions en langues étrangères des réfléxions ou sentences et maximes morales de La Rochefoucauld. Paris, 1883.
38543.15 La Rochefoucauld, François. Oeuvres inédites. Paris, 1863.
Htn 38543.16* La Rochefoucauld, François. Moral maxims and reflections. 2. ed. London, 1706.
38543.16.5 La Rochefoucauld, François. Maxims and moral reflexions. London, 1775.
38543.16.10 La Rochefoucauld, François. Maxims and moral reflexions. London, 1781.
38543.17 La Rochefoucauld, François. Maxims and moral reflexions. Edinburgh, 1783.
38543.18 La Rochefoucauld, François. Maxims and moral reflexions. London, 1788.
38543.19 La Rochefoucauld, François. Maxims and moral reflexions. London, 1795.
38543.19.5 La Rochefoucauld, François. Maxims and moral reflections. Edinburgh, 1796.
38543.19.20 La Rochefoucauld, François. Maxims and moral reflections. N.Y., 1835.
38543.19.25 La Rochefoucauld, François. Moral reflections. N.Y., 1851.
38543.19.30 La Rochefoucauld, François. Reflections, or Sentences and moral maxims. London, 1871.
38543.19.40 La Rochefoucauld, François. Reflections, or sentences and moral maxims. N.Y., 19- .
38543.19.42 La Rochefoucauld, François. Reflections, or sentences and moral maxims. N.Y., 1900.
38543.19.43 La Rochefoucauld, François. Maxims. N.Y., 1900.
38543.19.50 La Rochefoucauld, François. Maxims. London, 1939.
38543.19.52 La Rochefoucauld, François. Maxims. London, 1957.
38543.19.60 La Rochefoucauld, François. Maxims. N.Y., 1959.
38543.19.65 La Rochefoucauld, François. Réfléxions ou Sentences et maximes morales. Genève, 1967.
38543.21 Pamphlet box. La Rochefoucauld.
38543.21.5 Marchand, J. Bibliographie générale raisonée de La Rochefoucauld. Paris, 1948.
38543.22 Brix, Ernst. Die Entwicklungsphasen der Maximen La Rochefoucaulds. Inaug. Diss. Erlangen, 1913.
38543.22.20A Bishop, Morris. The life and adventures of La Rochefoucauld. Ithaca, 1951.
38543.22.20B Bishop, Morris. The life and adventures of La Rochefoucauld. Ithaca, 1951.
38543.22.30 Zeller, Mary F. New aspects of style in the Maxims of La Rochefoucauld. Washington, 1954.
38543.22.40 Bruzzi, Amelia. La formazione delle Maximes di La Rochefoucauld attraverso le edizioni originali. Bologna, 1968.
X Cg 38543.23.15 Grubbs, Henry A. The originality of La Rochefoucauld's Maxims. Diss. Paris, 1929.
38543.23.20 Granges de Surgères, Anatole. Les portraits du duc de La Rochefoucauld. Paris, 1882.
38543.23.25 Bruzzi, Amelia. La Rochefoucauld. Bologna, 1958.
38543.23.30 Bruzzi, Amelia. Dai "Memoires" alle "Maximes" di La Rochefoucauld. Bologna, 1965.
38543.23.35 Bochénski, Aleksander. Nienawiść i miłość La Rochefoucauld. Warszawa, 1926.
38543.23.40 La Rochefoucauld, François. Memuary, maksimy. Leningrad, 1971.
38543.23.45 Razumovskaia, Margarita V. Laroshfuko, autor Maksim. Leningrad, 1971.
X Cg 38543.24.5 Magne, Émile. Le vrai visage de La Rochefoucauld. 3. éd. Paris, 1923.
38543.24.10 Sivasriyananda, W. L'éspecurisme de La Rochefoucauld. Thèse. Paris, 1939.
38543.24.20 Hippeau, Louis. Essai sur la morale de La Rochefoucauld. Paris, 1967.
38543.24.25 Moore, Will Grayburn. La Rochefoucauld, his mind and art. Oxford, 1969.

38543.26 Individual authors, etc. - 1661-1715 - Fiction - Mme. de Sablé

38543.26 Jouanst, D. Maximes de Mme. de Sablé. Paris, 1870.
38543.26.80 Ivanoff, N. La marquise de Sablé et son salon. Thèse. Paris, 1927.

38543.27 Individual authors, etc. - 1661-1715 - Fiction - Le Pays

38543.27 Le Pays, René. Les nouvelles oeuvres. Amsterdam, 1715.
38543.27.15 Le Pays, René. Nouvelles oeuvres suivies du dialogue de l'amour et de la raison. Paris, 1925.
38543.27.17 Le Pays, René. Un précieux pient par lui-mème. Portrait de M. Le Pays. Thèse. Paris, 1925.
Htn 38543.27.35* Le Pays, René. The drudge: or The jealous extravagant. London, 1673.

38543.27 Individual authors, etc. - 1661-1715 - Fiction - Le Pays - cont.

38543.27.50 Igel, Johann. René Le Pays, sein Leben und seine Werke. Inaug. Diss. Nürmberg, 1919.
38543.27.55 Rémy, Gabriel. Un précieux de Province au XVIIe siècle, René Le Pays. Thèse. Paris, 1925.

38543.28 - .31 Individual authors, etc. - 1661-1715 - Fiction - La Mothe le Vayer

38543.28 La Mothe le Vayer, F. de. Soliloques sceptiques. Paris, 1875.
38543.28.2 La Mothe le Vayer, F. de. Oeuvres. Précédé de L'Abrégé de la vie de M. de la Mothe de la Vayer. v.1-7, (Pt.1-2). Dresde, 1756-59. 14v.
Htn 38543.28.5* La Mothe le Vayer, F. de. Opuscules ou petits traictez. Paris, 1644.
Htn 38543.28.7* La Mothe le Vayer, F. de. Soliloques sceptiques. Paris, 1670.
Htn 38543.28.10* La Mothe le Vayer, F. de. Homilies académiques. Paris, 1664.
Htn 38543.28.15* La Mothe le Vayer, F. de. Suite des homiliés académiques. Paris, 1665.
Htn 38543.28.20* La Mothe le Vayer, F. de. Dernières homiliés académiques. Paris, 1666.
Htn 38543.28.30* La Mothe le Vayer, F. de. Quatre dialogues. Francfort, 1604.
Htn 38543.29* La Mothe le Vayer, F. de. Cincq dialogues. Amons, 1671.
38543.29.5 La Mothe le Vayer, F. de. La philosophie de La Mothe le Vayer. Paris, 1783.
38543.29.10 La Mothe le Vayer, F. de. L'ésprit de La Mothe le Vayer. n.p., 1703.
Htn 38543.30* La Mothe le Vayer, F. de. Cincq dialogues. Frankfort, 1716. 2v.
Htn 38543.30.2* La Mothe le Vayer, F. de. Quatres dialogues. Frankfort, 1606.
38543.30.5 La Mothe le Vayer, F. de. Deux dialogues faits à l'imitation des anciens. Paris, 1922.
Htn 38543.30.8* La Mothe le Vayer, F. de. Prose chagrine. Pt.1-3. Paris, 1661.
Htn 38543.30.10* La Mothe le Vayer, F. de. La promenade dialogue entre Tubertus Ocella et Marcus Bibulus. Paris, 1662-64. 4v.
Htn 38543.30.15* La Mothe le Vayer, F. de. Observations diverses sur la composition. Paris, 1668.
Htn 38543.30.20* La Mothe le Vayer, F. de. Problems sceptiques. Paris, 1666.
Htn 38543.30.25* La Mothe le Vayer, F. de. Doubte sceptique. Paris, 1667.
Htn 38543.30.29* La Mothe le Vayer, F. de. Discours pour montrer que les doutes de la philosophie sceptique sont de grand usage. Paris, 1669.
Htn 38543.30.36* La Mothe le Vayer, F. de. Mémorial de quelques conférences. Paris, 1669.
Htn 38543.30.40* La Mothe le Vayer, F. de. Hexaméron rustique. Paris, 1670.
38543.30.42 La Mothe le Vayer, F. de. Hexaméron rustique. 2. éd. Paris, 1875.
38543.31 Étienne, Louis. Essai sur La Mothe le Vayer. Rennes, 1849.
38543.31.8 Wickelgren, F.L. La Mothe le Vayer. Thèse. Paris, 1934.
38543.31.10 Wickelgren, F.L. La Mothe le Vayer. Paris, 1934.
38543.31.25 Kerviler, René. François de la Mothe le Vayer. Paris, 1879.

38543.32 Individual authors, etc. - 1661-1715 - Fiction - Lacroix [Discontinued]

38543.32 Lacroix, L. Quid de instituendo principe senserit Vayerius. Paris, 1890.

38543.33 - .34 Individual authors, etc. - 1661-1715 - Fiction - Méré

38543.33.5 Méré, Antoine G. Oeuvres complètes. Paris, 1930. 3v.
38543.33.15 Méré, Antoine G. Les conversations du Chevalier de Méré avec le maréchal de Clerambault. Paris, 1929.
38543.34 Viguié, Pierre. L'honnête homme au XVIIe siècle le Chevalier de Méré. Paris, 1922.
38543.34.5 Wilhelm, Kurt. Chevalier de Méré und sein Verhaltnis zu Blaise Pascal. Berlin, 1936.

38544.01 - .4 Individual authors, etc. - 1661-1715 - Fiction - La Calprenède

38544.01 Pamphlet box. La Calprenède.
38544.1 Hill, H.W. La Calprenède's romances and restoration drama. Chicago, 1911.
38544.1.5 Lancaster, Henry Carrington. La Calprenède, dramatist. Chicago, 1920?
38544.1.10 Seillière, Ernest. Le romancier du Grand Condé. Paris, 1921.
38544.1.15 Pitou, Spire. La Calprenède's Faramond. Baltimore, 1938.
38544.2 La Calprenède, G. de. Cassandre. Paris, 1642-45. 10v.
38544.3 La Calprenède, G. de. Cléopatre. Paris, 1657-58. 24v.
38544.3.25 La Calprenède, G. de. La Cléopatra. Venetia, 1715.
38544.4 La Calprenède, G. de. Faramond ou L'histoire de France. Paris, 1664. 12v.
Htn 38544.4.15* La Calprenède, G. de. Le comte Dessex; tragédie. Paris, 1651.

38544.6 - .26 Individual authors, etc. - 1661-1715 - Fiction - Du Verdier, Callière, Ferrand, La Fare, etc.

38544.6 Du Verdier, Gilbert. Le roman des romans. n.p., 1626-29. 7v.
38544.8 Sonan. Chrisérionte de Gaule, histoire...trouvée en la Terre Sainte. Lyon, 1620.
38544.12 Caillière, Jacques de. Courtisan prédestiné. Paris, 1728.
38544.13 Callières, François de. Histoire poétique. Amsterdam, 1688.
Htn 38544.14* Brilhac, J.B. de. Agnes de Castro. Amsterdam, 1688.
38544.16 Mailly. Les disgrâces des Amans. La Haye, 1725.
38544.20 Claude, I. Les amours de Madame d'Elbeuf. Amsterdam, 1739.
38544.24 Ferrand, B. Histoire des amours de Cleante et Bélise. Leyde, 1691.
38544.25 Ferrand, Anne B. Lettres au Baron de Breteuil. Paris, 1880.
38544.26 La Fare, C.A. Poésies inédites du marquis de la Fare. Paris, 1924.
38544.26.20 La Fare, C.A. The unpublished poems of the...1644-1712. N.Y., 19- .

Classified Listing

38544.6 - .26 Individual authors, etc. - 1661-1715 - Fiction - Du Verdier, Callière, Ferrand, La Fare, etc. - cont.

38544.26.100 La Rüe, C. Oraisons funèbres. Paris, 1940.

38544.27 Individual authors, etc. - 1661-1715 - Fiction - Mme. de La Fayette

38544.27.5 La Fayette, Marie M. Oeuvres complètes. Paris, 1825. 5v.
38544.27.10 La Fayette, Marie M. Oeuvres de Madame de la Fayette. Paris, 1925-30. 3v.
38544.27.12 La Fayette, Marie M. Me. de la Fayette, par elle même. Paris, 1959.
38544.27.15 La Fayette, Marie M. Romans et nouvelles. Paris, 1967.
38544.27.25 La Fayette, Marie M. La Princesse de Clèves. Paris, 1719. 3 pam.
Htn 38544.27.30* La Fayette, Marie M. La Princesse de Clèves. Paris, 1815. 2v.
38544.27.32 La Fayette, Marie M. La Princesse de Clèves. Paris, 1877.
38544.27.35 La Fayette, Marie M. La Princesse de Clèves. Paris, 1889.
38544.27.40 La Fayette, Marie M. La Princesse de Clèves. Boston, 1896.
38544.27.42 La Fayette, Marie M. La Princesse de Clèves. Boston, 1896.
38544.27.45 La Fayette, Marie M. La Princesse de Clèves. London, 19- .
38544.27.46 La Fayette, Marie M. La Princesse de Clèves. Paris, 1911.
38544.27.47 La Fayette, Marie M. La Princesse de Clèves. Paris, 1934.
Htn 38544.27.50.5* La Fayette, Marie M. The Princess of Cleves. London, 1679.
38544.27.55 La Fayette, Marie M. The Princess of Cleves. Boston, 1891. 2v.
38544.27.60 La Fayette, Marie M. La Princesse de Clèves. Paris, 1946.
38544.27.63 La Fayette, Marie M. La Princesse de Clèves. Genève, 1950.
38544.27.65 La Fayette, Marie M. The Princesse de Cleves. London, 1950.
38544.27.66 La Fayette, Marie M. The Princess of Cleves. N.Y., 1951.
38544.27.70 La Fayette, Marie M. La Princesse de Clèves. Paris, 1957.
38544.27.72 La Fayette, Marie M. La Princesse de Clèves. Paris, 1958.
38544.27.250 La Fayette, Marie M. La Princesse de Monpensier. Paris, 1732.
Htn 38544.27.275* La Fayette, Marie M. The princess of Monpensier. London, 1666.
Htn 38544.27.290* La Fayette, Marie M. The princess of Monpensier. London, 1805.
38544.27.295 La Fayette, Marie M. Histoire de la Princesse de Monpensier. Paris, 1926.
38544.27.300 La Fayette, Marie M. Histoire de Madame Henriette. Paris, 1965.
38544.27.310 La Fayette, Marie M. Vie de la Princesse d'Angleterre. Genève, 1967.
Htn 38544.27.400* La Fayette, Marie M. Zayde: a Spanish history, or romance. 2. ed. London, 1690.
38544.27.450 La Fayette, Marie M. Mémoire de Mme. de La Fayette. Paris, 1890.
38544.27.453 La Fayette, Marie M. Lettres de M.M. Pioche de la Vergne. London, 1924.
38544.27.455 La Fayette, Marie M. Isabelle ou le journal amoureux d'Espagne. Paris, 1961.
38544.27.510 Haussonville, Gabriel. Mme. de La Fayette. Paris, 1891.
38544.27.520 Scheuer, Ernst. Frau von La Fayette. Bonn, 1898.
38544.27.530A Rea, Lilian. The life and times of Marie Madeleine countess of La Fayette. London, 1908.
38544.27.530B Rea, Lilian. The life and times of Marie Madeleine countess of La Fayette. London, 1908.
38544.27.540 Beaunier, André. La jeunesse de Mme. de La Fayette. Paris, 1921.
38544.27.550 Ashton, Harry. Mme. de La Fayette, sa vie et ses oeuvres. Cambridge, Eng., 1922.
38544.27.565 Magne, Emile. Madame de La Fayette en ménage. Paris, 1926.
38544.27.570 Raynal, Marie-Aline. Le talent de Mme. de La Fayette. Thèse. Paris, 1926.
38544.27.575A Dédéyan, Charles. Madame de La Fayette. Paris, 1955.
38544.27.575B Dédéyan, Charles. Madame de La Fayette. Paris, 1955.
38544.27.575.2 Dédéyan, Charles. Madame de La Fayette. 2. éd. Paris, 1965.
38544.27.580 Durry, M.J. Madame de La Fayette. Paris, 1962.
38544.27.585 Styger, Flora. Essai sur l'oeuvre de Mme. de La Fayette. Affoltems, 1944.
38544.27.590 Rémy, Jean-Charles. Madame de La Fayette. L'ésprit et les lettres. Lausanne, 1967.
38544.27.595 Bazin de Bezons, Jean de. Vocabulaire de la Princesse de Clèves. Paris, 1967.
38544.27.595.5 Bazin de Bezons, Jean de. Étude de l'attribution de la Princesse de Clèves par des moyens de statistique du vocabulaire. Paris, 1970.
38544.27.605 Burkart, Rosemarie. Die Kunst des Masses in Mme. de La Fayette's Princesse de Clèves. Bonn, 1968.
38544.27.610 Haig, Stirling. Madame de La Fayette. N.Y., 1970.
38544.27.615 Fabre, Jean. L'art de l'analyse dans la Princesse de Clèves. Paris, 1970.
38544.27.620 Beaunier, André. L'amie de La Rochefoucauld. Paris, 1927.
38544.27.625 Niderst, Alain. "La Princesse de Clèves". Sens, 1970?

38544.28 - Individual authors, etc. - 1661-1715 - Fiction - Montauban, Ortigne, Prechac, etc.

Htn 38544.28* Montauban, Jacques P. de. Zenobie, reyne d'Armenie. v.1-5. Paris, 1653.
38544.28.31 Montauban, Jacques P. de. Les aventures et le mariage de Panurge (1674). Baltimore, 1933.
38544.29 Moisant de Brieux, J. Oeuvres choisies. Caen, 1875.
38544.30 Ortigue, P. de. Les galanteries amoureuses de la cour de grêce. Paris, 1693.
Htn 38544.30.5* Ortigue, P. de. Agiatis, queen of Sparta. London, 1686.
Htn 38544.30.15* Ortigue, P. de. The grand Scipio. London, 1660.
38544.40 Préchac, L.M. de. L'illustre parisienne historique, galante et véritable. v.1-2. Paris, 1679.
38544.42 Préchac, L.M. de. L'illustre génoise. Paris, 1685.
Htn 38544.43* Préchac, L.M. de. The chaste Seraglian. London, 1685.
Htn 38544.44.5* Préchac, L.M. de. The serasquier bassa: an historical novel of the times. London, 1700?
Htn 38544.44.25* Préchac, L.M. de. L'heroïne mousquetaire. Amsterdam, 1692.
Htn 38544.44.35* Préchac, L.M. de. Yolande de Sicile. Paris, 1678.
Htn 38544.44.45* Préchac, L.M. de. The lovely polander. London, 1683.
38544.46.35A Pure, Michel. La prétieuse, ou Le mystère des ruelles. Paris, 1938. 2v.

38544.28 - Individual authors, etc. - 1661-1715 - Fiction - Montauban, Ortigne, Prechac, etc. - cont.

38544.46.35B Pure, Michel. La prétieuse, ou Le mystère des ruelles. Paris, 1938. 2v.
38544.55 Subligny, A.F.P. de. La fausse Clélie. Histoire française galante. Nymegue, 1680.
Htn 38544.56* Subligny, A.F.P. de. The mock Clelia. London, 1678.
38544.60 Grandchamp. Le Télémaque moderne. Cologne, 1701. 2 pam.

38545.12 Individual authors, etc. - 1661-1715 - Fiction - Regnerye

Htn 38545.12* Regnerye. Les constantes...amours de Lintason. Paris, 1601.

38545.18 Individual authors, etc. - 1661-1715 - Fiction - Saint Maurice

38545.18 Saint Maurice, A. de. Les fleurs des nouvelles galantes. Paris, 1668.

38545.20 - .23 Individual authors, etc. - 1661-1715 - Fiction - Saint Réal

38545.20 Saint Réal, César V. de. Oeuvres de l'abbé Saint-Réal. Amsterdam, 1740. 3v.
38545.20.3A Saint Réal, César V. de. Oeuvres. Paris, 1730. 5v.
38545.20.3B Saint Réal, César V. de. Oeuvres. v.3. Paris, 1730.
38545.20.5 Saint Réal, César V. de. Histoire de Dom Carlos. Halle, 1914.
Htn 38545.20.9* Saint Réal, César V. de. Don Carlos. London, 1676.
38545.20.10 Saint Réal, César V. de. Oeuvres choisies. Paris, 1819.
38545.21 Dulong, Gustave. L'abbé de Saint Réal. Paris, 1924. 2 pam.
38545.22A Dulong, Gustave. L'abbé de Saint Réal; étude sur les rapports. Paris, 1921. 2v.
38545.22B Dulong, Gustave. L'abbé de Saint Réal; étude sur les rapports. v.1-2. Paris, 1921.

38545.24 - .29 Individual authors, etc. - 1661-1715 - Fiction - Huet

38545.25 Nisard, Charles. Mémoires de Daniel Huet. Paris, 1853.
38545.26 Barach, Karl Sigmund. Pierre Daniel Huet als Philosoph. Wien, 1862.
38545.28 Aiken, John. Memoirs of...Pierre Daniel Huet. London, 1810. 2v.
Htn 38545.29* Huet, M.P.D. Heutiana, ou Pensées diverses. Paris, 1722.

38545.33 Individual authors, etc. - 1661-1715 - Fiction - L'Heritier de Villandon

38545.33 L'Heritier de Villandon, Marie J. La tour ténébreuse et les jours lumineux. Amsterdam, 1706.
Htn 38545.40* Recueil de quelques pièces. Pt.1-2. Cologne, 1667. 2v.

38546.1 - .21 Individual authors, etc. - 1661-1715 - Fiction - Madeleine de Scudéry

38546.3 Mongrédien, Georges. Madeleine de Scudéry et son salon. Paris, 1946.
38546.4 Rathéry, Edme J.B. Mademoiselle de Scudéry. Paris, 1873.
38546.4.5 Scudéry, Madeleine de. Lettres de Mlle. de Scudéry à M. Godeau. Paris, 1835.
38546.5 Barthélemy, Édouard. Sapho le mage de Sidon. Zenocrate. Paris, 1880.
38546.6 Gasté, A. Madeleine de Scudéry et le dialogue des héros de roman. Rouen, 1902.
38546.6.15 Aragonnès, Claude. Madeleine de Scudéry, reine du Tendre. Paris, 1934.
Htn 38546.7*A Scudéry, Madeleine de. Artamenes, or The grand Cyrus. v.1-10. London, 1690-91. 5v.
Htn 38546.7*B Scudéry, Madeleine de. Artamenes, or The grand Cyrus. Pt.6-7. London, 1690. 2v.
Htn 38546.8* Scudéry, Madeleine de. Nouvelles conversations de morale. La Haye, 1692.
Htn 38546.8.5* Scudéry, Madeleine de. Conversations nouvelles sur divers sujets. La Haye, 1685.
Htn 38546.8.5.5* Scudéry, Madeleine de. Conversations nouvelles sur divers sujets. Amsterdam, 1682.
Htn 38546.8.6* Scudéry, Madeleine de. Conversations nouvelles sur divers sujets. Amsterdam, 1685.
Htn 38546.9* Scudéry, Madeleine de. La morale du monde, ou Conversations. Amsterdam, 1686.
38546.9.9 Scudéry, Madeleine de. La promenade de Versailles. Paris, 1920.
Htn 38546.10* Scudéry, Madeleine de. Clélie, histoire romaine. Paris, 1656-61. 16v.
Htn 38546.10.5* Scudéry, Madeleine de. Clélia; an excellent new romance. v.1-5. London, 1658-60. 2v.
Htn 38546.11* Scudéry, Madeleine de. Célinte; nouvelle. Paris, 1661.
38546.12 Scudéry, Madeleine de. Artemene, ou Le Grand Cyrus. Paris, 1659. 10v.
Htn 38546.14* Scudéry, Madeleine de. Almahide. Paris, 1660-63. 8v.
Htn 38546.19.2* Scudéry, Madeleine de. Ibrahim...romance. pt. 1-4. 1. ed. London, 1652.
38546.19.3 Scudéry, Madeleine de. Ibrahim, or The illustrious Bassa. London, 1674.
38546.19.5 Scudéry, Madeleine de. Ibrahim; ou L'illustre Bassa. Paris, 1723. 4v.
Htn 38546.19.9* Scudéry, Madeleine de. Mathilde. Paris, 1667.
38546.20 Scudéry, Madeleine de. Les conversations sur divers sujets. 4. éd. Amsterdam, 1685.
Htn 38546.21* Scudéry, Madeleine de. Triumphant arch...to the...feminine sexe. London, 1656.
38546.21.14 Scudéry, Madeleine de. Isabelle, Grimaldi, princesse de Monaco; roman. 4. éd. Paris, 1923.
Htn 38546.21.20* Scudéry, Madeleine de. Les femmes illustrées. Paris, 1644-54. 2v.

38546.22 - .25 Individual authors, etc. - 1661-1715 - Fiction - Georges de Scudéry

38546.22.3 Scudéry, Georges de. Alaric, ou Rome vaincue. Bruxelles, 1656.
Htn 38546.22.6* Scudéry, Georges de. Alaric, ou Rome vaincue. Rouen, 1659.
38546.22.9 Scudéry, Georges de. Alaric, ou Rome vaincue. La Haye, 1685.
Htn 38546.22.12* Scudéry, Georges de. L'amour tirannique. Paris, 1639.
Htn 38546.22.15* Scudéry, Georges de. L'amour tirannique. Paris, 1640.
38546.22.15.37 Farinholt, V.C. A critical edition of Georges de Scudéry's L'amour tyrannique. Chicago, 1938.
Htn 38546.22.18* Scudéry, Georges de. Eudoxe. Paris, 1641.

38546.22 - .25 Individual authors, etc. - 1661-1715 - Fiction - Georges de Scudéry - cont.

Htn 38546.22.21* Scudéry, Georges de. Ibrahim. Paris, 1643.
Htn 38546.22.24* Scudéry, Georges de. La mort de Caesar. Paris, 1636.
Htn 38546.22.25* Scudéry, Georges de. La mort de Caesar. Tolose, 1652.
38546.22.26 Scudéry, Georges de. La mort de Caesar. N.Y., 1930.
Htn 38546.22.28* Scudéry, Georges de. Le trompeur puny. Paris, 1634.
Htn 38546.22.31* Scudéry, Georges de. Poésies diverses. Paris, 1649. 2 pam.
Htn 38546.22.35* Scudéry, Georges de. Le prince d'éguise. Paris, 1636.
Htn 38546.22.40* Scudéry, Georges de. L'ombre du grand Armand. Paris, 1643.
38546.22.45 Scudéry, Georges de. Le prince déguise. N.Y., 1929.
Htn 38546.22.61* Scudéry, Georges de. Lettres amoureuses de divers auteurs de ce temps. Paris, 1641.
38546.23 Batereau, A. Georges de Scudéry als Dramatiker. Leipzig, 1902.
38546.23.5 Reumann, R. Georges de Scudéry als Epiker. Coburg, 1911.
38546.23.15 Clerc, Charles. Un matamore des lettres. Paris, 1929.
38546.23.20 Schweitzer, J.W. Georges de Scudéry's Almahide. Baltimore, 1939.
X Cg 38546.24 Perrier, E. Scudéry et sa soeur à Marseille. Valence, 1908.
38546.25 Lettres de Mesdames de Scudéry, de S. de Saliez. Paris, 1806.

38546.26 - .27 Individual authors, etc. - 1661-1715 - Fiction - Mme. de Grignan

38546.27 Janet, Paul. Les lettres de Mme. de Grignan. Paris, 1895.
38546.27.5 Murbach, Janet M. La vrai visage de la comtesse de Grignan. Toulouse, 1939.

38546.28 - Individual authors, etc. - 1661-1715 - Fiction - Mme. de Sévigné

38546.28 Walckenaer, Charles Athanase. Mémoire sur Mme. de Sévigné. Paris, 1842. 4v.
38546.29 Walckenaer, Charles Athanase. Mémoire sur Mme. de Sévigné. Paris, 1852. 5v.
38546.30 Walckenaer, Charles Athanase. Mémoire sur Mme. de Sévigné. Paris, 1852. 5v.
38546.31 Depping, G. Quelques pièces inédites concernant Mme. de Sévigné. Paris, 1882.
38546.32 Babon, H. Les amoreux de Mme. de Sévigné. Paris, 1862.
38546.33 Briere, L. de la. Madame de Sévigné. Paris, 1882.
38546.33.2 Roger, Jules. Madame de Sévigné malade. Paris, 1895.
38546.33.5 Pradel, Genès. Madame de Sévigné en Bourbonnais. Montluçon, 1926.
38546.33.8 Pradel, Genès. Madame de Sévigné en Provence. Montluçon, 1932.
38546.33.9 Pradel, Genès. Madame de Sévigné en Provence. Paris, 1936.
38546.33.10 Lemoine, J. Madame de Sévigné aux Rochers;...1669-1676. Rennes, 1930.
38546.33.15 Gazier, Cécile. Madame de Sévigné. Paris, 1933.
38546.33.20 Schmidt, M. Madame de Sévigné. Inaug. Diss. München, 1938.
38546.33.25 Tilley, A. Madame de Sévigné. Cambridge, Eng., 1936.
38546.33.30 Saint-René Taillandier, M.M.L.C. (Mme.). Madame de Sévigné et sa fille. Paris, 1938.
38546.33.35 Hérard, Madeleine. Madame de Sévigné. Dijon, 1959.
38546.33.40 Callot, A. Pages d'histoire bourguignonne: Madame de Sévigné dans les vignes du seigneur à Saulieu en août 1677. Nuits, 1959.
38546.33.45 Duchêne, Roger. Mme. de Sévigné. Paris, 1968.
38546.33.50 Gérard-Gailly, Émile. Madame de Sévigné. Paris, 1971.
38546.34 Sévigné, Marie de R.C. Recueil des lettres. Paris, 1785. 8v.
38546.34.2 Sévigné, Marie de R.C. Recueil des lettres. v.1-9. Paris, 1786. 7v.
38546.34.25 Sévigné, Marie de R.C. Lettres. Paris, 1849.
38546.35A Sévigné, Marie de R.C. Lettres choisies. Paris, 1865.
38546.35B Sévigné, Marie de R.C. Lettres choisies. Paris, 1865.
38546.36 Sévigné, Marie de R.C. Lettres choisies. Paris, 1862.
38546.36.3 Sévigné, Marie de R.C. Lettres choisies. Paris, 1870.
38546.36.4 Sévigné, Marie de R.C. Lettres choisies. 3e éd. Paris, 1927.
38546.36.7 Sévigné, Marie de R.C. Choix de lettres. v.1-3. Paris, 1877-80.
38546.36.8 Sévigné, Marie de R.C. Lettres choisies de Madame de Sévigné. Lille, 1886.
38546.36.12 Sévigné, Marie de R.C. Lettres choisies. Paris, 1907.
38546.36.15A Sévigné, Marie de R.C. Lettres choisies, suivis d'un choix de lettres. v.1-2. Paris, 1923?
38546.36.15B Sévigné, Marie de R.C. Lettres choisies, suivis d'un choix de lettres. v.1-2. Paris, 1923?
38546.36.16 Sévigné, Marie de R.C. Lettres choisies, suivis d'un choix de lettres. Paris, 1923.
38546.36.20 Sévigné, Marie de R.C. Le premier texte des lettres de Mme. de Sévigné, réimpression de l'édition de 1725. Paris, 1880.
38546.36.25 Sévigné, Marie de R.C. Lettres. Paris, 1953- 3v.
38546.36.30 Sévigné, Marie de R.C. Lettres. v.3. Paris, 1963.
38546.37 Sévigné, Marie de R.C. Lettres. Paris, 1900.
38546.38 Sévigné, Marie de R.C. Letters from the marchioness de Sévigné to her daughter. v.1-10. Dublin, 1768. 5v.
38546.38.5 Sévigné, Marie de R.C. Recueil des lettres...à...sa fille. Rouen, 1784. 10v.
38546.38.10 Sévigné, Marie de R.C. Lettres choisies de Mones. de Sévigné. Paris, 1810.
38546.39 Sévigné, Marie de R.C. Lettres de...avec les notes de tous les commentateurs. Paris, 1853. 6v.
38546.39.5 Sévigné, Marie de R.C. Lettres de...avec les notes de tous les commentateurs. Paris, 185-? 6v.
38546.40 Sévigné, Marie de R.C. Letters from...to her daughter. London, 1760-65. 8v.
38546.41 Sévigné, Marie de R.C. Selected letters. Manchester, 1918.
Htn 38546.41.15* Sévigné, Marie de R.C. Memoranda of memorabilia. Oxford, 1928.
38546.42 Sévigné, Marie de R.C. Letters. London, 1811. 9v.
38546.42.5 Sévigné, Marie de R.C. Letters. N.Y., 1856.
38546.42.15 Sévigné, Marie de R.C. Letters. Boston, 1874.
38546.43 Sévigné, Marie de R.C. Letters. Boston, 1899.
38546.44 Sévigné, Marie de R.C. Lettres. Paris, 1818. 10v.
38546.44.2 Sévigné, Marie de R.C. Lettres. Paris, 1856.

38546.28 - Individual authors, etc. - 1661-1715 - Fiction - Mme. de Sévigné - cont.

38546.45A Sévigné, Marie de R.C. Lettres. v.1-14 and album. Paris, 1862. 15v.
38546.45B Sévigné, Marie de R.C. Lettres. v.1-14 and album. Paris, 1862. 15v.
38546.46 Sévigné, Marie de R.C. Lettres. v.1-8. Paris, 1863. 7v.
38546.47 Sévigné, Marie de R.C. Lettres inédites à Mme. de Grignan. Paris, 1876. 2v.
38546.48 Grignan, Françoise M. Éxtrait de quelques lettres de Mme. la comtesse de Grignan. Troyes, 1854.
38546.49 Grignan, Françoise M. Lettres. Paris, 1880.
38546.49.10 Grignan, Françoise M. Lettres choisies. Paris, 1926.
38546.49.15 Grignan, Françoise M. Madame de Sévigné, her letters and her world. London, 1946.
38546.49.20 Sévigné, Marie de R.C. Letters from Madame la marquise de Sévigné. 1st American ed. N.Y., 1956.
38546.50F Pamphlet box. Sévigné.
38546.51.3 Boissier, G. Mme. de Sévigné. 2. éd. Paris, 1887.
38546.51.5A Boissier, G. Mme. de Sévigné. 3. éd. Paris, 1888.
38546.51.5B Boissier, G. Mme. de Sévigné. 3. éd. Paris, 1888.
38546.51.10 Boissier, G. Mme. de Sévigné. Chicago, 1888.
38546.51.20 Boissier, G. Mme. de Sévigné. 4. éd. Paris, 1896.
38546.52 Boissier, G. Mme. de Sévigné. London, 1887.
38546.52.10 Boissier, G. Mme. de Sévigné. 10. éd. Paris, 1922.
38546.53 Vallery-Radot. Mme. de Sévigné. Paris, 1889.
38546.54 Vallery-Radot. Mme. de Sévigné. Paris, 1888.
38546.55 Aubenas, J.A. Histoire de Mme. de Sévigné. Paris, 1842.
Htn 38546.56.2* Ritchie, Anne Isabella Thackeray. Mme. de Sévigné. Edinburgh, 1881.
38546.56.4 Ritchie, Anne Isabella Thackeray. Mme. de Sévigné. Philadelphia, 1881.
38546.57 Montigny, Maurice. En voyageant avec Mme. de Sévigné. Paris, 1920.
38546.58A Puliga, Henriette C.S. Mme. de Sévigné. London, 1873. 2v.
38546.58B Puliga, Henriette C.S. Mme. de Sévigné. London, 1873. 2v.
38546.59 Dorbec, Prosper. L'hotel carnavale et marquis de Sévigné. Paris, 1916.
38546.60 Hallays, André. Madame de Sévigné. Paris, 1921.
38546.61 Clarie, Henriette. Madame de Sévigné. Paris, 1925.
38546.62 Fitzgerald, C. Dictionary of Madame de Sévigné. London, 1914. 2v.
38546.64 Lemoine, Jean. Madame de Sévigné. Paris, 1926.
38546.66 Sonnié-Moret, P. La marquise de Sévigné. Paris, 1926.
38546.66.10A Aldis, Janet. The queen of letter writers, Marquise de Sévigné. N.Y., 1907.
38546.66.10B Aldis, Janet. The queen of letter writers, Marquise de Sévigné. N.Y., 1907.
Htn 38546.68* Torche, Antoine de. La cassette des bijovx. Paris, 1668.
Htn 38546.70* Tyssot de Patot, Simon. Voyages et avantures de Jacques Massé. Bordeaux, 1710.
38546.74 Kögel, T. Bilder bei Mme. de Sévigné. Inaug. Diss. Würzburg, 1937.
38546.78A Brodin, P. Madame de Sévigné. N.Y., 1938.
38546.78B Brodin, P. Madame de Sévigné. N.Y., 1938.
38546.82 Saint René Taillandier, M.M.L.C. (Mme.). Adieu! Paris, 1947.
38546.85 Bailly, A. Madame de Sévigné. Paris, 1955.
38546.90 Kauffmann, Lida. Die Briefe der Madame de Sévigné. Köln, 1954.
38546.95 Choleau, Jean. Le grand coeur de Madame de Sévigné. Vitré, 1959.
38546.100 Pirat, Yvonne. Madame de Sévigné. Paris, 1959.
38546.105 Chaffanjon, A. La Marquise de Sévigné et sa descendance. Paris, 1962.
38546.106 Allentuch, H.R. Madame de Sévigné. Baltimore, 1963.
38546.107 Saporta, Gaston. La famille de Madame de Sévigné. Paris, 1889.
38546.109 Cordelier, Jean. Madame de Sévigné par elle-même. Paris, 1967.
38546.110 Munk, Gerda. Madame de Sévigné et Madame de Grignan dans la correspondance et dans le critique. Utrecht, 1966.

38547.1 - .16 Individual authors, etc. - 1661-1715 - Fiction - Honoré d'Urfé

38547.1 Reure, O.C. Le vie et les oeuvres de Honoré d'Urfé. Paris, 1910.
38547.1.10 Goudard, M.L. Étude sur les épistres morales d'Honoré d'Urfé. Washington, 1933.
38547.2A Rostand, Edmond. Deux romanciers de Provence. Paris, 1921.
38547.2B Rostand, Edmond. Deux romanciers de Provence. Paris, 1921.
38547.3 Urfé, Honoré d'. Oeuvres poétiques choisies. Paris, 1909.
38547.5 Urfé, Honoré d'. L'Astrée. Paris, n.d. 5v.
38547.6 Urfé, Honoré d'. L'Astrée. Pastorale allégorique. Paris, 1733. 10v.
38547.7 Urfé, Honoré d'. L'Astrée de Honoré d'Urfé. pt. 1, book 1-8,9-12. Strassbourg, 1920?
38547.7.5A Urfé, Honoré d'. L'Astrée. Lyon, 1925-28. 5v.
38547.7.5B Urfé, Honoré d'. L'Astrée. Lyon, 1925-28. 5v.
Htn 38547.7.15* Baro, Balthasar. La conclusion et dernière partie d'Astrée. 3. éd. Paris, 1632.
38547.7.20A Urfé, Honoré d'. Le premier des grands romans français l'Astrée. Paris, 1928.
38547.7.20B Urfé, Honoré d'. Le premier des grands romans français l'Astrée. Paris, 1928.
38547.8 Bonafous, Norbert. Études sur l'Astrée et sur Honoré d'Urfé. Paris, 1846.
38547.9 Banti, Charlotte. L'Amyntas du Tasse et l'Astrée d'Honoré d'Urfé. Milan, 1895.
NEDL 38547.10 Germa, B. L'Astrée d'Honoré d'Urfé. Sa composition. Son influence. Paris, 1904.
38547.11 Urfé, Honoré d'. Un épisode de l'Astrée. Les amours d'Alcedon. Paris, 1920.
38547.12 McMahon, Mary C. (Sister). Aesthetics and art in the Astrée of Honoré d'Urfé. Washington, D.C., 1925.
38547.13 Bochet, Henri. L'Astrée...formation de la littérature. Genève, 1923.
38547.14 Werner, Ernst. Die Dastellung des Empfindungslebens in der "Astrée" des Honoré d'Urfé. Inaug. Diss. Nürmberg, 1920.
38547.15 Magendie, Maurice. Du nouveau sur l'Astrée. Paris, 1927.
38547.15.10 Winkler, Egon. Komposition und Liebestheorieen der "Astrée" des Honoré d'Urfé. Diss. Oblau, 1930.
38547.16 Ehrmann, J. Un paradis désespéré. 1. éd. New Haven, 1963.

38547.17 - .19 Individual authors, etc. - 1661-1715 - Fiction - Anne d'Urfé

38547.18 Badolle, Maurice. Anne d'Urfé, l'homme, le poète. Paris, n.d.

38547.18.3 Badolle, Maurice. Anne d'Urfé, l'homme, le poète. Thèse. Paris, 1927.

38547.21 - Individual authors, etc. - 1661-1715 - Fiction - Anonymous works

38547.21 Anonimiana, ou Mélanges de poésies d'éloquence. Paris, 1700.

38547.25 Le comte de Dunois. Paris, 1671.

Htn 38547.27* Dom Sébastien. Paris, 1680.

38547.28 Les entretiens de Thémiste et de Lisias. Saumur, 1678.

38547.30 Ismaël, prince de Maroc; nouvelle historique. Paris, 1698.

38547.33 Ariane, ou Se voit les aventures de Mélinte. v.1-2. Lyon, 1661.

38547.37 Pluton maltotier. Cologne, 1708.

38547.38 Mémoires de Hollande. Paris, 1856.

Htn 38547.43* Courtilz, G. de. Les conquestes amoureuses du grand Alcandre dans les Pays-Bas. Cologne, 1684.

38547.45 Alluis, Jacques. Le chat d'Espagne. Cologne, 1669.

38547.45.5 Alluis, Jacques. Le accommodement de l'ésprit et du coeur. Paris, 1668.

38547.46 La princesse de Portien. Paris, 1724.

38547.47 Histoire curieuse du fameux Francion. Amsterdam, 1697. 2v.

38551.19 - Individual authors, etc. - 1661-1715 - Oratory - Fenelon - Biography and criticism

38551.19 Maugain, G. Documenti bibliografici e critici...del Fénelon in Italia. Paris, 1910.

38551.19.5 Caron, Augustin P.P. Recherches bibliographiques sur le Télémaque, les oraisons de Bossuet et le Discours sur l'histoire universelle. 2. éd. Paris, 1840.

38551.20 Delphanque, A. Fénelon et la doctrine de l'amour. Lille, 1907.

38551.21 Broglie, Emmanuel de. Fénelon a Cambrai 1699-1715. Paris, 1884.

38551.22.5 Funk-Brentano, F. Fénelon. Paris, 1902.

38551.23 Delmont, T. Fénelon et Bossuet. Paris, 1896.

38551.24 Boulve, L. Der l'Hellénisme chez Fénelon. Paris, 1897.

38551.24.4 Cagnac, Moïse. Fénelon directeur de conscience. Paris, 1901.

38551.24.5 Cagnac, Moïse. Fénelon directeur de conscience. 2. éd. Paris, 1903.

38551.24.15 Cagnac, Moïse. Fénelon. Études critiques. Paris, 1910.

38551.30F Bayle, Pierre. Oeuvres diverses. Haye, 1727-31. 4v.

38551.36.40 Bastier, Paul. Fénelon. Paris, 1903.

38551.37 Bertolino, A. La politica economica di Fénelon e il pensiero politico el economico del suo tiempo. Siena, 1927.

38551.38 Blörklund, J. Fénélon. Göteborg, 1874.

38551.39 Bremond, Henri. Apologie pour Fénelon. Paris, 1910.

38551.40.10 Butler, Charles. The life of Fénelon. Philadelphia, 1811.

38551.40.12 Butler, Charles. The life of Fénelon. Baltimore, 1811.

38551.41A Carcassone, E. Fénelon, l'homme et l'oeuvre. Paris, 1946.

38551.41B Carcassone, E. Fénelon, l'homme et l'oeuvre. Paris, 1946.

X Cg 38551.43.5 Chérel, Albert. Fénelon au XVIIIe siècle en France (1715-1820). Paris, 1917.

38551.43.6 Chérel, Albert. Fénelon au XVIIIe siècle en France. Supplément. Fribourg, 1917.

38551.43.8 Chérel, Albert. Fénelon au XVIIIe siècle en France. 1715-1820. Genève, 1970.

38551.43.10 Chérel, Albert. Fénelon. Paris, 1934.

38551.45 Compigny des Bordes, A. de. Fénelon et le chevalier de Ramsay. Paris, 1929.

38551.47.15 Delplanque, A. Fénelon et la doctrine de l'amour pur d'après sa correspondance avec ses principaux amis. Lille, 1907.

38551.49.50 Douen, O. L'intolerance de Fénelon; étude historique. Paris, 1875.

38551.50.10 Dumolard, Joseph Vincent. Éloge de Fénelon. Cambrai, 18-?

38551.65.20 Griselle, Eugène. Fénelon; études historiques. Paris, 1911.

38551.72A Janet, Paul. Fénelon. Paris, 1892.

38551.72B Janet, Paul. Fénelon. Paris, 1892.

38551.72.5 Janet, Paul. Fénelon, his life and works. Port Washington, 1970.

38551.73 Joppin, G. Fénelon et la mystique du pur amour. Paris, 1938.

38551.73.2 Joppin, G. Fénelon et la mystique de pur amour. Thèse. Paris, 1938.

38551.74 Krause, K.E. Beitrage zur Würdigung Fénelons als praktischer Theologe. Freiburg, 1883.

38551.74.20 Kraus, J. Fénelon. Baden Baden, 1953.

38551.75.10 Lamartine, A. de. Fénelon (1651-1715). Paris, 1853.

38551.76.10A Leroy, Maxime. Fénelon. Paris, 1928.

38551.76.10B Leroy, Maxime. Fénelon. Paris, 1928.

38551.79 Lemaître, Jules. Fénelon. Pairs, 1910.

38551.83.15 Martin, Henri G. Fénelon en Hollande. Amsterdam, 1928.

38551.83.16 Martin, Henri G. Fénelon en Hollande. Amsterdam, 1928.

38551.83.50 May, James L. Fénelon; a study. London, 1938.

38551.88.30 Navatel, Ludovic. Fénelon; la confrérie secrète du pur amour. Paris, 1914.

38551.104.20 Ramsay, A.M. de. The life of François de Salignac de la Motte Fénelon. London, 1723.

38551.110 Sackebant, X. Fénelon et le Seminaire de Cambrai d'après des documents la plupart inédits. Cambrai, 1902.

38551.112 Société historique et archéologique du Périgord, Périgueux. III centenaire de la naissance de Fénelon. Périgueux, 1951.

38551.116 St. Cyres, S.H.N. François de Fénelon. London, 1901.

38551.120 Sanders, E.K. Fénelon. London, 1901.

38551.124.5 Wieser, Max. Deutsche und romanische Religiösitat. Berlin, 1919.

38551.126.10 Wunderlich, F.R. Fenelon, ein Lebensbild. Hamburg, n.d.

38551.128 Zermati, D.J. La place de Fénelon dans l'histoire des doctrines économiques. Thèse. Alger, 1934.

38551.130 Amis des lettres, Paris. Fénelon et son temps. Paris, 1952.

38551.135 Bédoyere, M. de la. The archbishop and the lady. London, 1956.

38551.137 Little, Katherine D. François de Fénelon. N.Y., 1951.

38551.139 The life of Salignac de la Mothe Fénelon. N.Y., 1804.

38551.140 Lombard, Alfred. Fénelon et le retour a l'antique au XVIIIe siècle. Neuchâtel, 1954.

38551.19 - Individual authors, etc. - 1661-1715 - Oratory - Fenelon - Biography and criticism - cont.

38551.145 Goré, Jeanne-Lydie. La notion d'indifférence chez Fénelon et ses sources. 1. éd. Grenoble, 1956.

38551.145.5 Goré, Jeanne-Lydie. L'intinéraire de Fénelon. Grenoble, 1957.

38551.145.10 Goré, Jeanne-Lydie. La notion d'indifférence chez Fénelon et ses sources. Paris, 1956.

38551.150 La Gorce, Agnès de. Le vrai visage de Fénelon. Paris, 1958.

38551.152 Danielou, Madeleine C. Fénelon et le duc de Bourgogne. Paris, 1955.

38551.155 Pizzorusso, Arnaldo. La poetica di Fénelon. 1. ed. Milano, 1959.

38551.160 Dupriez, B. Fénelon et la Bible. Paris, 1961.

38551.161 Spaemann, Robert. Reflexion und Spontaneität. Stuttgart, 1963.

38551.165 Hillenaar, Henk. Fénelon et les jésuites. La Haye, 1967.

38551.170 Zovatto, Pietro. Fénelon e il quietismo. Udine, 1968.

38551.175 Haillant, Marguerite. Fénelon et la prédication. Paris, 1969.

38552 Individual authors, etc. - 1661-1715 - Oratory - Fenelon - Complete and selected works

38552.2 Oeuvres de Fénelon. Paris, 1787-92. 9v.

38552.3 Oeuvres de Fénelon. Toulouse, 1810. 19v.

38552.4 Fénelon, F. de S. de la Mothe. Oeuvres. Paris, 1826. 12v.

38552.7 Fénelon, F. de S. de la Mothe. Oeuvres de Fénelon. Paris, 1866.

38552.7.20 Fénelon, F. de S. de la Mothe. Oeuvres choisies. Paris, 1879-81. 4v.

38552.9 Fénelon, F. de S. de la Mothe. Sermons choisis. Paris, 1718.

38552.10 Fénelon, F. de S. de la Mothe. Sermons choisis. Paris, 1744.

38552.10.10 Fénelon, F. de S. de la Mothe. Sermons choisis. Paris, 1803.

Htn 38552.12* Fénelon, F. de S. de la Mothe. Oeuvres spirituelles. Anvers, 1718. 2v.

38552.12.8 Fénelon, F. de S. de la Mothe. Oeuvres spirituelles. n.p., 1752. 4v.

38552.12.10 Fénelon, F. de S. de la Mothe. Oeuvres spirituelles. Paris, 1954.

38552.15 Fénelon, F. de S. de la Mothe. Werke, religiösen Inhalte. Hamburg, 1823. 3v.

NEDL 38552.16 Fénelon, F. de S. de la Mothe. Fénelon; pages choisies. Paris, n.d.

38553.1 - .15 Individual authors, etc. - 1661-1715 - Oratory - Fenelon - Selections [Discontinued]

38553.10 Cagnac, M. Lettres inédites de Fénelon. Paris, 1910.

38553.11 Fénelon, F. de S. de la Mothe. Lettres de direction. Paris, 1702.

Htn 38553.13* Kendall, John. Extracts from the writings of François Fénelon. Philadelphia, 1804.

Htn 38553.13.2* Kendall, John. Extracts from...Fénelon. Philadelphia, 1804.

Htn 38553.13.5* Fénelon, F. de S. de la Mothe. Pious reflections for every day of the month. Salem, 1804.

Htn 38553.13.15* Fénelon, F. de S. de la Mothe. Pious reflections for every day of the month. Salem, 1811.

38553.13.25 Fénelon, F. de S. de la Mothe. A guide to true peace. 1st Aamerican ed. N.Y., 1816.

38553.14 Selections from the writings of Fénelon. Boston, 1829.

38553.15 Selections from the writings of Fénelon. 2. ed. Boston, 1829.

38553.15.2A Selections from the writings of Fénelon. 6th ed. Boston, 1851.

38553.15.2B Selections from the writings of Fénelon. 6th ed. Boston, 1851.

38553.15.3A Fénelon, F. de S. de la Mothe. Selections from the writings. 3. ed. Boston, 1831.

38553.15.3B Fénelon, F. de S. de la Mothe. Selections from the writings. 3. ed. Boston, 1831.

38553.15.4 Fénelon, F. de S. de la Mothe. Selections from the writings. 4. ed. Boston, 1841.

38553.15.4.10 Fénelon, F. de S. de la Mothe. Selections from the writings. Boston, 1859.

38553.15.4.35 Fénelon, F. de S. de la Mothe. Selections from Fénelon. Boston, 1879.

38553.15.4.37 Fénelon, F. de S. de la Mothe. Selections from Fénelon. Boston, 1879.

38553.15.4.38 Fénelon, F. de S. de la Mothe. Selections. Boston, 1888.

38553.15.4.40A fénelon, F. de S. de la Mothe. Selections from Fénelon. Boston, 1890.

38553.15.4.40B Fénelon, F. de S. de la Mothe. Selections from Fénelon. Boston, 1890.

38553.15.4.45 Fénelon, F. de S. de la Mothe. Selections from Fénelon. Boston, 1892.

38553.15.4.50 Fénelon, F. de S. de la Mothe. Christian perfection. N.Y., 1947.

38553.15.5 Fénelon, F. de S. de la Mothe. Fénelon inédit. Vitry-le-France, 1917.

38553.15.7 Fénelon, F. de S. de la Mothe. La vraie et solide vertu sacerdotale; recueillie. Paris, 1837.

Htn 38553.15.15* Gueudeville, Nicolas. Critique générale des aventures. Cologne, 1701.

38553.16 - Individual authors, etc. - 1661-1715 - Oratory - Fenelon - Telemaque - French editions

Htn 38553.16.5* Fénelon, F. de S. de la Mothe. Les avantures de Télémaque fils d'Ulysse. Bruxelles, 1699. 2v.

Htn 38553.16.10* Fénelon, F. de S. de la Mothe. Les avantures de Télémaque. Paris, 1699.

Htn 38553.16.40* Fénelon, F. de S. de la Mothe. Avantures de Télémaque. La Haye, 1701.

38553.16.45 Fenelon, F. de S. de la Mothe. Avantures de Télémaque. La Haye, 1705-17. 2v.

Htn 38553.16.50* Fénelon, F. de S. de la Mothe. Les avantures de Télémaque. Bruxelles, 1706. 3v.

38553.16.75 Fénelon, F. de S. de la Mothe. Les aventures de Télémaque. Paris, 1735.

38553.16.90 Fénelon, F. de S. de la Mothe. Les aventures de Télémaque, fils d'Ulysse. Genève, 1777. 2v.

38553.16.95 Fénelon, F. de S. de la Mothe. Les aventures de Télémaque, fils d'Ulysse. Ulm, 1783.

38553.16 - Individual authors, etc. - 1661-1715 - Oratory - Fenelon - Telemaque - French editions - cont.

38553.17 Fénelon, F. de S. de la Mothe. Les aventures de Télémaque. London, 1792.
38553.18 Fénelon, F. de S. de la Mothe. Les aventures de Télémaque. Paris, 1804.
38553.18.2 Fénelon, F. de S. de la Mothe. Les aventures de Télémaque. Amsterdam, 1741.
Htn 38553.18.5* Fénelon, F. de S. de la Mothe. Les aventures de Télémaque. Ulm, 1761.
38553.19 Fénelon, F. de S. de la Mothe. Les aventures de Télémaque. Paris, 1763. 2v.
38553.19.2 Fénelon, F. de S. de la Mothe. Les aventures de Télémaque, fils d'Ulysse. Leyde, 1773.
Htn 38553.19.3F* Fénelon, F. de S. de la Mothe. Les aventures de Télémaque. Paris, 1785. 2v.
Htn 38553.19.4* Fénelon, F. de S. de la Mothe. Les aventures de Télémaque. Paris, 1790. 2v.
38553.19.5 Fénelon, F. de S. de la Mothe. Les aventures de Télémaque. Maestricht, 1793. 2v.
38553.20 Fénelon, F. de S. de la Mothe. Les aventures de Télémaque. London, 1796.
38553.21 Fénelon, F. de S. de la Mothe. Les aventures de Télémaque. Paris, 1797.
38553.21.5 Fénelon, F. de S. de la Mothe. Les adventures de Télémaque, fils d'Ulysse. N.Y., 1805.
38553.22 Fénelon, F. de S. de la Mothe. Les adventures de Télémaque. Philadelphia, 1806-07. 2v.
Htn 38553.23* Fénelon, F. de S. de la Mothe. Le Télémaque. N.Y., 1818.
38553.24 Fénelon, F. de S. de la Mothe. Les aventures de Télémaque. Paris, 1818.
38553.24.5 Fénelon, F. de S. de la Mothe. Les aventures de Télémague. Philadelphia, 1821.
38553.24.7 Fénelon, F. de S. de la Mothe. Les aventures de Télémaque. Philadelphia, 1824.
38553.24.15 Fénelon, F. de S. de la Mothe. Aventures de Télémaque. Livre III. Paris, 1830.
38553.24.20 Fénelon, F. de S. de la Mothe. Les aventures de Télémaque. Paris, 1832.
38553.24.22 Fénelon, F. de S. de la Mothe. Les aventures de Télémaque. Philadelphia, 1832.
38553.24.23 Fénelon, F. de S. de la Mothe. Les aventures de Télémaque. Philadelphia, 1833.
38553.25 Fénelon, F. de S. de la Mothe. Les aventures de Télémaque. Paris, 1848.
38553.25.2 Fénelon, F. de S. de la Mothe. Les aventures de Télémaque. Paris, 1824. 2v.
38553.25.5 Fénelon, F. de S. de la Mothe. Les aventures de Télémaque. Paris, 1841.
38553.25.6 Fénelon, F. de S. de la Mothe. Les aventures de Télémaque. Paris, 1842.
38553.25.7 Fénelon, F. de S. de la Mothe. Les aventures de Télémaque. Paris, 1856.
38553.25.9 Fénelon, F. de S. de la Mothe. Les aventures de Télémaque. London, 1750.
38553.26 Fénelon, F. de S. de la Mothe. Les aventures de Télémaque. Philadelphia, 1865.
38553.27A Fénelon, F. de S. de la Mothe. Aventures de Télémaque. Philadelphia, 1834.
38553.27B Fénelon, F. de S. de la Mothe. Aventures de Télémaque. Philadelphia, 1834.
38553.27.4 Fénelon, F. de S. de la Mothe. Aventures de Télémaque. Paris, 1872.
38553.27.5 Fénelon, F. de S. de la Mothe. Aventures de Télémaque. Philadelphia, n.d.
38553.27.6 Fénelon, F. de S. de la Mothe. Aventures de Télémaque. Paris, 1873.
38553.27.10 Fénelon, F. de S. de la Mothe. Aventures de Télémaque. N.Y., 1881.
38553.27.15 Fénelon, F. de S. de la Mothe. Aventures de Télémaque. Paris, 1890.
38553.27.20 Fénelon, F. de S. de la Mothe. Aventures de Télémaque. Paris, 1920. 2v.
38553.27.21 Fénelon, F. de S. de la Mothe. Aventures de Télémaque. Paris, 1920?
38553.27.22 Fénelon, F. de S. de la Mothe. Les aventures de Télémaque. Philadelphia, 18- .
38553.28 Fénelon, F. de S. de la Mothe. Les aventures de Télémaque. Boston, n.d.
38553.29 Fénelon, F. de S. de la Mothe. Telemak. Copenhagen, 1835.
Htn 38553.29.100* Fénelon, F. de S. de la Mothe. Telemace. Rome, 1747. 2v.
38553.30 Fénelon, F. de S. de la Mothe. Le aventure di Telemace. Paris, 1804. 2v.
38553.31A Fénelon, F. de S. de la Mothe. Le aventure di Telemace. London, 1801. 2v.
38553.31B Fénelon, F. de S. de la Mothe. Le aventure di Telemace. London, 1801. 2v.
38553.31.5 Fénelon, F. de S. de la Mothe. Le aventure di Telemace. v.1-2. Livorno, 1828.
38553.32F Fénelon, F. de S. de la Mothe. Télémaque Polyglotte. Paris, 1837.
38553.33 Fénelon, F. de S. de la Mothe. Aventuras de Telemaco. Paris, 1733. 2v.
38553.34 Fénelon, F. de S. de la Mothe. Aventuras de Telemaco. Paris, 1804.
38553.35 Fénelon, F. de S. de la Mothe. Adventures of Telemachus. N.Y., n.d. 2v.
38553.36 Fénelon, F. de S. de la Mothe. Telemachiada. Paris, 1814.
38553.37 Fénelon, F. de S. de la Mothe. Les aventures de Télémaque. Paris, 1723.

38554.1 - .3 Individual authors, etc. - 1661-1715 - Oratory - Fenelon - Telemaque - Translations

Htn 38554.1* Fénelon, F. de S. de la Mothe. Adventures of Telemachus. v.1-2. London, 1715.
38554.1.3 Fénelon, F. de S. de la Mothe. Adventures of Telemachus. Books 1-24. n.p., n.d.
38554.1.4 Fénelon, F. de S. de la Mothe. Adventures of Telemachus. Dublin, 1769.
Htn 38554.1.5* Fénelon, F. de S. de la Mothe. The adventures of Telemachus. London, 1768.
38554.1.9 Fénelon, F. de S. de la Mothe. The adventures of Telemachus. 7th ed. Rouen, 1781.
38554.1.15 Fénelon, F. de S. de la Mothe. Adventures of Telemachus. London, 1792.
38554.1.20 Fénelon, F. de S. de la Mothe. The adventures of Telemachus. London, 1794. 2v.

38554.1 - .3 Individual authors, etc. - 1661-1715 - Oratory - Fenelon - Telemaque - Translations - cont.

38554.2 Fénelon, F. de S. de la Mothe. The adventures of Telemachus. N.Y., 1818.
38554.2.5 Fénelon, F. de S. de la Mothe. Telemachus. London, 1807.
38554.2.7 Fénelon, F. de S. de la Mothe. Adventures of Telemachus. N.Y., 1875.
38554.3 Fénelon, F. de S. de la Mothe. Adventures of Telemachus. v.2. N.Y., 1825.
38554.3.3 Fénelon, F. de S. de la Mothe. Adventures of Telemachus. N.Y., 1847.
38554.3.5 Fénelon, F. de S. de la Mothe. Adventures of Telemachus. n.p., 185-?
38554.3.10 Fénelon, F. de S. de la Mothe. Aventuras de Telémaco. Paris, 1804.
38554.3.14 Fénelon, F. de S. de la Mothe. Die Begebenheiten des Printzen von Ithaca. v.1-3. Berlin, 1738-39.
38554.3.15 Fénelon, F. de S. de la Mothe. Die seltsame Begebenheiten des Telemach. Frankfurt, 1741.

38554.4 - Individual authors, etc. - 1661-1715 - Oratory - Fenelon - Other individual works

38554.4.10 Fénelon, F. de S. de la Mothe. Fables. Cambridge, 18- .
38554.4.15 Fénelon, F. de S. de la Mothe. Fables. Paris, 18- ?
38554.6 Fénelon, F. de S. de la Mothe. Fables. 2. éd. Paris, 1865.
38554.7 Les adieux du Duc de Bourgogne et de l'Abbé de Fénelon. Stockholm, 1733.
38554.8 Fénelon, F. de S. de la Mothe. A dialogue between Dionysius, Damon. Lowell, Mass., 1879?
38554.9 Fénelon, F. de S. de la Mothe. Explication des articles d'Issy. Paris, 1915.
38554.11 Fénelon, F. de S. de la Mothe. Le livre de prières. 2. éd. Paris, 1825.
38554.11.3 Fénelon, F. de S. de la Mothe. Le livre de prières de M. de Fénelon. Besancon, 1828.
38554.13 Griveau, Algar. Étude sur la condamnation du livre des maximes des saints. Paris, 1878. 2v.
38554.19 Fénelon, F. de S. de la Mothe. Dissertation on pure love. 2. ed. London, 1738.
38554.20 Fénelon, F. de. S. de la Mothe. A dissertation on pure love. Dublin, 1739.
Htn 38554.25* Fénelon, F. de S. de la Mothe. Dissertation on pure love. London, 1750.
Htn 38554.107* Fénelon, F. de S. de la Mothe. Abrégé des vies des anciens philosophes. Paris, 1726.
38554.107.40 Fénelon, F. de S. de la Mothe. Abrégé des vies des anciens philosophes. Londres, 1832.
38554.107.100 Fénelon, F. de S. de la Mothe. Lives of the ancient philosophers. v.2. Edinburgh, 1803.
38554.107.105 Fénelon, F. de S. de la Mothe. Lives of the ancient philosophers. London, 1825.
Htn 38554.297* Fénelon, F. de S. de la Mothe. Les commandements de l'honnête homme. Paris, 1776.
38554.299 Ramsay, A.M. Fénelon's conversations with M. de Ramsay on the truth of religion. Photoreproduction. n.p., 1869.
Htn 38554.320* Fénelon, F. de S. de la Mothe. Démonstration de l'existence de Dieu. Paris, 1713.
38554.320.5 Fénelon, F. de S. de la Mothe. Démonstration de l'existence de Dieu. Amsterdam, 1713.
Htn 38554.322* Fénelon, F. de S. de la Mothe. Oeuvres philosophiques; démonstration de l'existence de Dieu. Paris, 1718.
38554.322.20 Fénelon, F. de S. de la Mothe. Oeuvres philosophiques. Demonstration de l'existence de Dieu. Paris, 1739.
38554.322.60 Fénelon, F. de S. de la Mothe. De l'existence et des attributs de Dieu. Paris, 1857.
38554.322.65 Fénelon, F. de S. de la Mothe. De l'existence de Dieu. Paris, 1885.
38554.322.68 Fénelon, F. de S. de la Mothe. Triaté de l'existence de Dieu. Paris, 1866.
38554.322.102 Fénelon, F. de. S. de la Mothe. Demonstration...existence...God. London, 1713.
38554.322.105 Fénelon, F. de S. de la Mothe. A demonstration of the existence and attributes of God. London, 1720.
X Cg 38554.322.225 Fénelon, F. de S. de la Mothe. On the knowledge and love of God. Worcester, 185-.
Htn 38554.324.250* Fénelon, F. de S. de la Mothe. Dialogues des morts. Paris, 1712.
Htn 38554.325* Fénelon, F. de S. de la Mothe. Dialogues des morts anciens et modernes. Paris, 1718. 2v.
38554.325.30 Fénelon, F. de S. de la Mothe. Dialogues des morts anciens et modernes. Paris, 1752. 2v.
38554.325.50 Fénelon, F. de S. de la Mothe. Dialogues des morts anciens et modernes. Paris, 1775.
38554.325.65 Fénelon, F. de S. de la Mothe. Dialogues des morts anciens et modernes. Limoges, 1805.
38554.325.80 Fénelon, F. de S. de la Mothe. Dialogues des morts anciens et modernes. Paris, 1862.
Htn 38554.326* Fénelon, F. de S. de la Mothe. Dialogues sur l'éloquence en général. Paris, 1718.
38554.326.10 Fénelon, F. de S. de la Mothe. Dialogues concerning eloquence in general. London, 1722.
38554.326.50 Fénelon, F. de S. de la Mothe. Dialogues sur l'éloquence en général. Paris, 1764.
38554.326.80 Fénelon, F. de S. de la Mothe. Dialogues sur l'éloquence en général et sur celle de la chaire en particulier. Paris, 1861.
38554.326.100 Fénelon, F. de S. de la Mothe. Dialogues concerning eloquence in general. 1st American ed. Boston, 1810.
38554.326.110 Fénelon, F. de S. de la Mothe. Dialogues on eloquence. Princeton, 1951.
Htn 38554.327* Fénelon, F. de S. de la Mothe. Directions pour la conscience d'un roi. La Haye, 1747.
Htn 38554.327.2* Fénelon, F. de S. de la Mothe. Directions pour la conscience d'un roi. La Haye, 1747.
Htn 38554.327.5* Fénelon, F. de S. de la Mothe. Examen de conscience pour un roi. Londres, 1747.
38554.327.8 Fénelon, F. de S. de la Mothe. Directions pour la conscience d'un roi. La Haye, 1748.
Htn 38554.350* Fénelon, F. de S. de la Mothe. Éducation des filles. Paris, 1687.
38554.350.80 Fénelon, F. de S. de la Mothe. De l'éducation des filles. Paris, 1821.
Htn 38554.350.223* Fénelon, F. de S. de la Mothe. Instructions for the education of a daughter. London, 1707.
38554.350.225 Fénelon, F. de S. de la Mothe. Instructions for the education of daughters. Glasgow, 1750.

Classified Listing

38554.4 - Individual authors, etc. - 1661-1715 - Oratory - Fenelon - Other individual works - cont.

38554.350.245 Fénelon, F. de S. de la Mothe. Treatise on the education of daughters. Boston, 1820.
38554.350.250 Fénelon, F. de S. de la Mothe. Treatise on the education of daughters. Boston, 1821.
38554.350.260 Fénelon, F. de S. de la Mothe. Treatise on the education of daughters. Baltimore, 1852.
38554.350.265 Fénelon, F. de S. de la Mothe. Fénelon on education. Cambridge, Eng., 1966.
38554.350.275 Fénelon, F. de S. de la Mothe. Concerning education. N.Y., 1900.
Htn 38554.378* Fénelon, F. de S. de la Mothe. Explication des maximes des saints sur la vie intérieure. Paris, 1697.
Htn 38554.378.2* Fénelon, F. de S. de la Mothe. Explication des maximes des saints sur la vie intérieure. Paris, 1697.
38554.378.10.2 Fénelon, F. de S. de la Mothe. Explication des principales vérités de la foi catholique. Tours, 1875.
38554.379.5 Fénelon, F. de S. de la Mothe. Instruction pastorale touchant son livre Des maximes des Saints. A'darn, 1698.
Htn 38554.462* Fénelon, F. de S. de la Mothe. Mandement et instruction pastorale de Monseigneur l'Archévêque Duc de Cambrai. Cambrai, 1714.
Htn 38554.462.2* Fénelon, F. de S. de la Mothe. Instruction pastorale de Monseigneur l'Archévêque Duc de Cambrai. Cambrai, 1714.
38554.462.10 Fénelon, F. de S. de la Mothe. Instruction pastorale de Monseigneur l'Archévêque Duc de Cambrai. Cambrai, 1715.
Htn 38554.515* Fénelon, F. de S. de la Mothe. Lettres de Monseigneur l'Archécêque de Cambrai. n.p., 1711.
Htn 38554.516* Fénelon, F. de S. de la Mothe. 1ère-5ème lettre de Monseigneur l'Archévêque Duc de Cambrai à Monseigneur l'Evêque de Meaux. n.p., n.d.
Htn 38554.516.50* Fénelon, F. de S. de la Mothe. Première lettre de Monseigneur l'Archévêque Duc de Cambray. v.1-4. n.p., 1698.
Htn 38554.517* Fénelon, F. de S. de la Mothe. Lettre de Monseigneur l'Archévêque Duc de Cambrai [Fénelon] à Monseigneur l'Evêque de Meaux, sur la charité. n.p., 1698?
38554.518.37 Fénelon, F. de S. de la Mothe. Lettre sur les occupations de l'Académie française. Paris, 1868.
38554.518.40 Fénelon, F. de S. de la Mothe. Lettre sur les occupations de l'Académie Française. Paris, 1888.
38554.518.44 Fénelon, F. de S. de la Mothe. Lettre à l'Académie, avec les versions primitives. Genève, 1970.
38554.518.46 Fénelon, F. de S. de la Mothe. Lettre à l'Académie. 6. éd. Paris, 1914.
38554.518.47 Fénelon, F. de S. de la Mothe. Lettre à l'Académie. Genève, 1970.
Htn 38554.518.50* Fénelon, F. de S. de la Mothe. Lettre de M. de S. Fénelon et duc de Cambrai. Roterdam, 1697.
38554.518.55 Fénelon, F. de S. de la Mothe. Letters from Cambrai written to the Contess de Montberon. Cornwall-on-Hudson, 1949.
38554.518.100 Fénelon, F. de S. de la Mothe. Letters of love and counsel. 1st American ed. N.Y., 1964.
Htn 38554.520* Fénelon, F. de S. de la Mothe. Lettres sur divers sujets concernant la religion et la métaphysique. Paris, 1718.
Htn 38554.520.5* Fénelon, F. de S. de la Mothe. Lettres sur divers sujets concernant la religion et la métaphysique. Paris, 1713.
38554.520.10 Fénelon, F. de S. de la Mothe. Letters upon divers subjects. Glasgow, 1750.
38554.522.5 Fénelon, F. de S. de la Mothe. Spiritual counsels from the letters of Fénelon. 1st-2nd series. London, 1910.
38554.523 Fénelon, F. de S. de la Mothe. Spiritual letters, letters to women. London, 1921.
38554.524A Fénelon, F. de S. de la Mothe. Fénelon et Mme. Guyon. Paris, 1907.
38554.524B Fénelon, F. de S. de la Mothe. Fénelon et Mme. Guyon. Paris, 1907.
38554.526 Fénelon, F. de S. de la Mothe. Spiritual letters: letters to men. London, 1877.
38554.526.10 Fénelon, F. de S. de la Mothe. Spiritual letters: letters to men. N.Y., 1914.
38554.526.20 Fénelon, F. de S. de la Mothe. Spiritual letters. Cornwall-on-Hudson, 1945.
38554.527 Fénelon, F. de S. de la Mothe. Letters to men and women. London, 1957.
38554.528 Fénelon, F. de S. de la Mothe. Letters. London, 1964.
Htn 38554.656* Fénelon, F. de S. de la Mothe. Ordonnance et instruction pastorale de Monseigneur l'Archévêque. Valenciennes, 1704. 2 pam.
Htn 38554.735* Fénelon, F. de S. de la Mothe. Recueil des mandements a l'occasion des jubilés. Paris, 1713.
Htn 38554.737.35* Fénelon, F. de S. de la Mothe. Réponce de Monseignenr l'Archévêque de Cambrai à l'ecrit de Monseigneur l'Evêque de Meaux. Paris, 1698.
38554.737.40 Fénelon, F. de S. de la Mothe. Réponse inédite à Bossuet. Paris, 1901.
Htn 38554.737.45* Fénelon, F. de S. de la Mothe. Réponse de Monseigneur l'Archévêque de Cambrai à la déclaration....Explication des maximes des saints. n.p., 1697.
Htn 38554.738* Fénelon, F. de S. de la Mothe. Responsio illustrissimi ac reverenendissimi archiepiscopi Cameracensis. n.p., n.d.
Htn 38554.738.15* Fénelon, F. de S. de la Mothe. Responsio archiepiscopi. n.p., 169-.
Htn 38554.846* Fénelon, F. de S. de la Mothe. Traité du ministère des pasteurs. Paris, 1688.
Htn 38554.867* Fénelon, F. de S. de la Mothe. Verae oppositiones inter doctrinam Meldensis episcopi et doctrinam archiepiscopi Cameracensis. n.p., 1698.

38556 Individual authors, etc. - 1661-1715 - Oratory - Fenelon - Criticism [Discontinued]

38556.7 Beausset, Le Card. Histoire de Fénelon. Paris, 1850. 4v.
38556.10 Tabaraud, M.M. Lettre à M. de Beausset, pour servir de supplement à son histoire de Fénelon. Paris, 1809.
38556.10.15 Tabaraud, M.M. Second lettre à M. de Beausset, pour servir de supplement à histoire de Fénelon. Supplement. Limoges, 1810.

38557.01 - .099 Individual authors, etc. - 1661-1715 - Oratory - Bossuet - Pamphlet volumes

38557.01 Pamphlet box. French literature. Age of Louis XIV.

38557.1 Individual authors, etc. - 1661-1715 - Oratory - Bossuet - Bibliographies

38557.1 Verlaque, V. Bibliographie raisonnée des oeuvres de Bossuet. Paris, 1908.
38557.1.5 Paris. Bibliothèque Nationale. Département des imprimés. Catalogue des ouvrages de Bossuet. Paris, 1904.
38557.1.15F Porcher, Jean. Catalogue des manuscrits de Bossuet de la collection Henri de Rothschild. Paris, 1932.
38557.1.35 Observations sur le prospectus...de la nouvelle édition des oeuvres de Bossuet. Paris, 1813.

38557.2 - .24 Individual authors, etc. - 1661-1715 - Oratory - Bossuet - Biography and criticism

38557.2 Urbain, Charles. Bossuet. Paris, 1899.
38557.2.5 Jovy, Ernest. Bossuet...et Pierre du Laurens. n.p., 1899.
38557.2.20 Maury. Eloge à l'Allemande. Eleutheropolis, 1773.
38557.2.30 Girault, C.X. Notice historique sur les aïeux de J.B. Bossuet. Dijon, 1808.
38557.2.40 Lambin, G. Les rapports de Bossuet avec l'Angleterre. Paris, 1909.
38557.2.50 Tabaraud, M.M. Lettre à M. de Beausset. Paris, 1809. 2 pam.
38557.2.55 Baudot, Pierre Louis. Lettre à M. C.X. Girault. Dijon, 1808.
38557.3 Tabaraud, M.M. Supplément aux histoires de Bossuet. Paris, 1822.
38557.4 Bausset, L.F. Histoire de J.B. Bossuet. Versailles, 1814. 4v.
38557.4.5 Bausset, L.F. Histoire de J.B. Bossuet. 2. éd. Versailles, 1819. 4v.
38557.4.10 Bausset, L.F. Histoire de Bossuet. Besançon, 1846. 3v.
38557.5 Bossuet. London, 1874.
38557.5.1 Nourrisson, J.F. Essai sur la philosophie de Bossuet. Paris, 1852.
38557.5.3 Delondre, Adrien. Doctrine philosophique de Bossuet. Paris, 1855.
38557.5.6 Bonet, Pierre. Bossuet moraliste. Paris, 1912.
38557.5.9 Dimier, Louis. Bossuet. Paris, 1916.
Htn 38557.5.15* Delarue, Charles. Oraison funèbre de Jacques-Benigne Bossuet. Paris, 1704.
38557.6 Revue Bossuet. Paris. 1-7 4v.
38557.8 Le Dieu, François. Mémoires...sur Bossuet. Paris, 1856-57. 4v.
38557.9 Vaillant, V. Etudes sur les sermons de Bossuet. Paris, 1851.
38557.10 Allou, A. Reconnaissance du tombeau de Bossuet. Meaux, 1854.
38557.11 Floquet, Amable. Mémoires...sur Bossuet. Paris, 1855. 3v.
38557.11.5 Floquet, Amable. Eloge de Bossuet. Paris, 1827.
38557.12 Gazier, Augustin. Bossuet et Lois XIV (1662-1704). Paris, 1914.
38557.13 Floquet, Amable. Bossuet, précepteur du Dauphin. Paris, 1864.
38557.13.5 Denis, J.F. Critique et controverse ou Richard Simon et Bossuet. Caen, 1870.
38557.14 Lapommeraye, H. de. Molière et Bossuet. Paris, 1877.
38557.14.5 Le Bidois, G. De comoedia...quid judicaverit Bossuetius. Paris, 1900.
38557.14.50 Moët, E. Bossuetius et Fenelo. Thesis. Paris, 1859.
38557.14.75 Monty, Léopold. De politica Bossuetii doctrina. Thesis. Paris, 1844.
38557.15 Nourrisson, J.F. La politique de Bossuet. Paris, 1867.
38557.15.5 Reaume, A. Histoire de Jacques Bénigne Bossuet. Paris, 1869. 3v.
NEDL 38557.16 Lebarq, J. Histoire critique de la prédication de Bossuet. Lille, 1888.
38557.17 Lanson, G. Bossuet. Paris, 1891.
NEDL 38557.18 Lanson, G. Bossuet. Paris, 1894.
38557.19 Rébelliau, A. Bossuet. Paris, 1900.
38557.19.10 Rébelliau, A. Bossuet historien du protestantisme. Thèse. Paris, 1891.
38557.19.13 Rébelliau, A. Bossuet historien du protestantisme. 3. éd. Paris, 1909.
38557.20 Freppel, Charles Emile. Bossuet et l'éloquence sacrée au XVIIe siècle. Paris, 1893. 2v.
38557.21 Druon, H. Bossuet à Meaux. Paris, n.d.
38557.21.5 Autour d'une brochure. Sept lettres...Bossuet. Paris, 1908.
38557.22 Delmont, T. Autour de Bossuet. Paris, 1901. 2v.
38557.22.6 Longuemare, E. Bossuet et la société française. Paris, 1910.
38557.22.9 Brunetière, F. Bossuet. Paris, 1913.
38557.22.10 La Broise, R. de. Bossuet et la Bible. Paris, 1891.
38557.22.12 Letellier, Albert. Bossuet. Paris, 1920.
38557.22.15 Sanders, E.K. Jacques Benigne Bossuet. London, 1921.
38557.22.17 Ingold, A.M.P. Bossuet et le Jansénisme. Paris, 1897.
38557.23 Bourseaud, H.M. Histoire et description des MS. set des éditions originales des ouvrages de Bossuet. Paris, 1897.
38557.24 Stapfer, Paul. La grande prédication chrétienne en France. Paris, 1898.
38557.24.10 Jovy, Ernest. Etudes et recherches sur Jacques Benigne Bossuet. Vitry-le-François, 1903.
38557.24.15 Rouvier, Frédèric. Le coeur du Maitre d'après Bossuet. Lille, 1922.
38557.24.20 Bellon, E. Bossuet directeur de conscience. Paris, n.d.
38557.24.23 Hardy, Georges. Le "De civitate Dei" source principale du "Discours sur l'histoire universelle". Paris, 1913.
38557.24.25 Courten, C. de. Bossuet e il suo "Discours sur l'histoire universelle" 1627-1704. Milano, 1927.
38557.24.28 Bertault, Philippe. Bossuet intime. Paris, 1927.
38557.24.32 Villemot, Henri. Bossuet et notre temps. Dijon, 1928.
38557.24.36 Baumann, E. Bossuet. Paris, 1929.
38557.24.37 Baumann, E. Bossuet. 19. éd. Paris, 1929.
38557.24.40 Souday, Paul. Bossuet. Liège, 1929.
38557.24.45 Truc, Gonzague. Bossuet et le classicisme religieux. Paris, 1934.
38557.24.50 Polenghi, M. Benigno Bossuet. Torino, 1935.
38557.24.55 Simpson, W.J.S. A study of Bossuet. London, 1937.
38557.24.60 Virely, A. Bossuet. Macon, 1938.
38557.24.65 Pissère, Robert. Les idées politiques de Bossuet. Thèse. Montpellier, 1943.

38557.2 - .24 Individual authors, etc. - 1661-1715 - Oratory - Bossuet - Biography and criticism - cont.

38557.24.70 Tans, J.A.G. Bossuet en Hollande. Thèse. Maastricht, 1949.
38557.24.71 Tans, J.A.G. Bossuet en Hollande. Thèse. Paris, 1949?
38557.24.75 Hüppi, Beda. Versuch über den Stil Bossuets. Freiburg, 1950.
38557.24.78 Martimort, A.G. Le gallicanisme de Bossuet. Paris, 1953.
38557.24.78.2 Martimort, A.G. Le gallicanisme de Bossuet. Thèse. Paris, 1953.
38557.24.80 La Batut, G. de. Oraison funèbre d'Henriette d'Angleterre par Bossuet. Paris, 1931.
38557.24.85 Calvet, Jean. Bossuet. Paris, 1941.
38557.24.86 Calvet, Jean. Bossuet. Paris, 1968.
38557.24.90 Schmittlein, R. L'aspect politique du différend Bossuet-Fénelon. Bade, 1954.
38557.24.95 Terstegge, G. Providence as Idée-Maîtresse in the works of Bossuet. Washington, 1948.
38557.24.100 Hubert, Jean. Manuscrits de J.B. Bossuet. Melun, 1955.
38557.24.105 Le Dieu, François. Les dernières années de Bossuet. v.1-2. Paris, 1928-29.
38557.24.110 Panov, Ioann I. Bossiuet i ego propovedi. Sankt Peterburg, 1888.
38557.24.115 Gasté, Armand. Bossuet en Normandie. Caen, 1893.
38557.24.120 Truchet, Jacques. La prédication de Bossuet. Paris, 1960. 2v.
38557.24.120.10 Truchet, Jacques. Bossuet panégyriste. Paris, 1962.
38557.24.125 Reynolds, E.E. Bossuet. 1. ed. Garden City, 1963.
38557.24.130 Truchet, Jacques. Bossuet panegyriste. Paris, 1962.
38557.24.140 Gaquère, François. Vers l'unité chrétienne. Paris, 1963.
38557.24.145 Goyet, Thérèse. L'humanisme de Bossuet. v.1-2. Paris, 1965.
38557.24.150 Zovatto, Pietro. La polemica Bossuet-Fénelon. Padova, 1968.
38557.24.152 Gaquère, François. Le dialogue irénique Bossuet-Leibniz. Paris, 1966.
38557.24.154 Gaquère, François. Le Dialogue irénique Bossuet-Paul Ferry à Metz (1652-1669). Paris, 1967.
38557.24.156 Gaquère, François. Les suprêmes appels de Bossuet à l'unité chrétienne, 1668-1691. Paris, 1969.

38557.25 Individual authors, etc. - 1661-1715 - Oratory - Bossuet - Complete and selected works

38557.25 Oeuvres choisies de Bossuet. Nimes, 1784. 10v.
38557.25.23 Bossuet, J.B. Oeuvres. Versailles, 1815-19. 43v.
38557.25.30 Bossuet, J.B. Oeuvres. Paris, 1841. 4v.
38557.25.35 Bossuet, J.B. Oeuvres complètes. Paris, 1867.
38557.25.50 Bossuet, J.B. Oeuvres inédites. Paris, 1862.
38557.25.55 Bossuet, J.B. Oeuvres choisies. v.1-3,5. Paris, 1868. 4v.
38557.25.60 Bremond, H. Bossuet. Paris, 1913. 3v.
38557.25.65 Bossuet, J.B. Oeuvres. Paris, 1961.
38557.25.75 Bossuet, J.B. Oeuvres oratoires. Lille, 1890. 6v.
38557.25.80 Bossuet, J.B. Oeuvres oratoires. Paris, 1926-27. 7v.
38557.25.100 Bossuet, J.B. Oeuvres posthumes. Amsterdam, 1753. 3v.
38557.25.125 Bossuet, J.B. Opuscules. Paris, 1751. 5v.
38557.25.195 Bossuet, J.B. Oraisons funèbres. 3. éd. Paris, 1680. 2 pam.
Htn 38557.25.200* Bossuet, J.B. Recueil des oraisons funèbres. Paris, 1699.

38557.26 - Individual authors, etc. - 1661-1715 - Oratory - Bossuet - Sermons and other individual works

38557.26 Bossuet, J.B. Oraisons funèbres. Paris, 1802.
38557.26.2 Bossuet, J.B. Oraisons funèbres. Paris, 1827.
38557.26.3A Bossuet, J.B. Oraisons funèbres. Paris, 1815.
38557.26.3B Bossuet, J.B. Oraisons funèbres. Paris, 1815.
38557.26.4 Dussault, Jean Joseph. Oraisons funèbres de Bossuet, Fléchier, et autres orateurs. Paris, 1826. 4v.
38557.26.5 Bossuet, J.B. Oraisons funèbres. Paris, 1850.
38557.26.8 Bossuet, J.B. Oraisons funèbres. Paris, 1814.
38557.26.10 Dussault, Jean Joseph. Oraisons funèbres de Bossuet, Fléchier, et autres orateurs. Paris, 1837. 3v.
38557.26.50 Bossuet, J.B. Oraisons funèbres. Paris, 1870.
38557.27A Bossuet, J.B. Oraisons funèbres. Paris, 1883.
38557.27B Bossuet, J.B. Oraisons funèbres. Paris, 1883.
38557.27.10 Bossuet, J.B. Oraisons funèbres. Paris, 1885.
38557.27.15 Bossuet, J.B. Oraisons funèbres. Paris, 1885?
Htn 38557.28* Bossuet, J.B. Oraisons funèbres. Paris, 1886.
38557.29 Bossuet, J.B. Oraisons funèbres. v.1-2. Paris, 1875.
38557.30 Bossuet, J.B. Oraisons funèbres. Paris, 1897.
38557.30.36 Bossuet, J.B. Oraisons funèbres. Argenteuil, 1936.
Htn 38557.31* Bossuet, J.B. Oraisons funèbres du Prince de Condé. Paris, 1899.
Htn 38557.31.2* Bossuet, J.B. Oraisons funèbres, Louis de Bourbon. Paris, 1687.
38557.31.5 Bossuet, J.B. Oraison funèbre de Henriette d'Angleterre. Paris, 1896.
Htn 38557.31.6* Bossuet, J.B. Oraison funèbre de Henriette d'Angleterre. Paris, 1670.
38557.31.8 Bossuet, J.B. Oraison funèbre de Henriette d'Angleterre. Lyon, 1676.
38557.31.9 Bossuet, J.B. Oraison funèbre de Henriette-Marie de France. Paris, 1898.
Htn 38557.31.12* Bossuet, J.B. Oraison funèbre de Marie Terese d'Austriche. Paris, 1683.
Htn 38557.31.13* Bossuet, J.B. A sermon preached at the funeral of Mary Terese of Austria. London, 1684.
38557.31.14 Bossuet, J.B. Oraison funèbre de Henriette Marie de France. Lyon, 1676.
Htn 38557.31.15* Bossuet, J.B. Oraison funèbre de Michel Le Tellier. Paris, 1686.
Htn 38557.31.20* Bossuet, J.B. Oraison funèbre de tres haute et tres puissante Princesse Anne de Gonzague de Clèves. Paris, 1685.
38557.31.25 Bossuet, J.B. Oraisons funèbres. Paris, 1959.
38557.31.30 Bossuet, J.B. Oraisons funèbres. Paris, 19- ?
38557.31.35 Bossuet, J.B. Oraisons funèbres de Bossuet. Paris, 1967.
Htn 38557.32* Bossuet, J.B. Select sermons and funeral orations. Boston, 1803.
38557.32.7 Bossuet, J.B. Choix de sermons. Paris, 1867.
38557.32.9 Bossuet, J.B. Choix de sermons. Paris, 1883.
38557.33 Bossuet, J.B. Choix de sermons. Paris, 1885.
38557.33.5 Bossuet, J.B. Sermons choisis. Paris, 1845.
38557.33.10 Bossuet, J.B. Choix de sermons de la jeunesse de Bossuet. 2. éd. Paris, 1868.
38557.33.11 Gandar, E. Bossuet orateur. 2. éd. Paris, 1868.
38557.34 Bossuet, J.B. Sermons. Paris, 1889.

38557.26 - Individual authors, etc. - 1661-1715 - Oratory - Bossuet - Sermons and other individual works - cont.

Htn 38557.34.5* Bossuet, J.B. Instruction sur les états d'oraison. Paris, 1697.
38557.34.8 Bossuet, J.B. Instruction sur les états d'oraison. 2. éd. Paris, 1697.
38557.34.9 Bossuet, J.B. Instruction sur les états d'oraison. Paris, 1897.
Htn 38557.35* Bossuet, J.B. Lettres spirituelles. Paris, 1746.
38557.35.2 Bossuet, J.B. Letters of spiritual direction. London, 1958.
Htn 38557.35.5* Bossuet, J.B. Lettres et opuscules. Paris, 1748. 2v.
Htn 38557.35.20* Bossuet, J.B. Lettres inédites. Versailles, 1820.
Htn 38557.35.22* Bossuet, J.B. Lettres inédites. Versailles, 1820.
Htn 38557.35.30* Bossuet, J.B. Lettres inédites de Bossuet à Madame de la Maisonfort. Paris, 1829.
38557.36 Bossuet, J.B. Six lettres originales. Paris, 1912.
Htn 38557.36.5* Bossuet, J.B. Lettre de M. l'evesque de Meaux à frère N. moine de l'abbaye de N. Paris, 1692.
Htn 38557.36.10* Bossuet, J.B. Lettre pastorale de monseigneur l'evesque de Meaux. Paris, 1686.
Htn 38557.36.12* Bossuet, J.B. A pastoral letter from the Lord Bishop of Meaux to the new Catholics. London, 1686.
38557.36.27 Bossuet, J.B. Lettres. Paris, 1927.
38557.37 Bossuet, J.B. Correspondance. v.1-9,11-14. Paris, 1909-23. 12v.
38557.39 Bossuet, J.B. Fac-simile du sermon sur le jugement dernier. Paris, 1884.
38557.40.10 Bossuet, J.B. Betrachtungen über die Zeit des Jubiläum. 3. Aufl. Würzburg, 1826.
38557.41 Bossuet, J.B. Premier avertissement aux protestans. Paris, 1689.
Htn 38557.41.5* Bossuet, J.B. Avertissement aux protestans sur les lettres du ministère Jurieu. Paris, 1689-91. 2v.
Htn 38557.41.15* Bossuet, J.B. Histoire des variations des églises protestantes. Paris, 1688. 2v.
Htn 38557.41.17* Bossuet, J.B. Histoire des variations des églises protestantes. 2e éd. Paris, 1689. 4v.
38557.41.19 Bossuet, J.B. Histoire des variations des églises protestantes. 2e éd. Paris, 1691. 4v.
38557.41.22 Bossuet, J.B. Histoire des variations des églises protestantes. Paris, 1740. 4v.
38557.41.23 Bossuet, J.B. Histoire des variations des églises protestantes. Paris, 1772. 5v.
38557.41.25 Bossuet, J.B. Histoire des variations des églises protestantes. Paris, 1821. 3v.
38557.41.30 Bossuet, J.B. History of the variations of the protestant churches. 2nd ed. Dublin, 1836. 2v.
38557.41.31 Bossuet, J.B. History of the variations of the protestant churches. Paris, 1845. 2v.
38557.41.35 Bossuet, J.B. History of the variations of the protestant churches. v.2. N.Y., 187-?
38557.41.38 Bossuet, J.B. Histoire des variations des églises protestantes. n.p., n.d. 2v.
Htn 38557.41.75* Bossuet, J.B. Défense de l'histoire des variations contre la réponse de M. Basnage. Paris, 1691.
38557.41.77 Bossuet, J.B. Défense de l'histoire des variations contre la réponse de M. Basnage. Paris, 1727.
38557.41.80 Bossuet, J.B. Histoire universelle. Paris, 1819.
Htn 38557.43* Bible. Latin. O.T. Selections. Libri Salomonis. Paris, 1693.
Htn 38557.44* Bible. Latin. O.T. Psalms. 1690. Liber psalmorum cum notis Jacobi Benigni Bossueti. Lugduni, 1690.
Htn 38557.44.5* Bible. Latin. O.T. Psalms. Liber psalmorum cum notis Jacobi Benigni Bossueti. Lugduni, 1691.
Htn 38557.44.6* Bible. Latin. O.T. Psalms. Liber psalmorum cum notis Jacobi Benigni Bossueti. Lugduni, 1691.
Htn 38557.44.150* Catholic Church. France. Catechisme du diocese de Meaux. Paris, 1687.
38557.45 Bossuet, J.B. The Catholic's manual. N.Y., 1836.
38557.45.10 Scheiding, O. Bossuets Stellung zur Reformatiobewegung. Hamburg, 1899.
Htn 38557.46.25* Bossuet, J.B. Conference avec M. Claude. Paris, 1682.
Htn 38557.46.28* Bossuet, J.B. Conference avec M. Claude. Paris, 1683.
38557.46.31 Bossuet, J.B. Conference avec M. Claude. 2e éd. Paris, 1687.
38557.46.32 Bossuet, J.B. Conference avec M. Claude. 2e éd. Paris, 1691.
38557.46.45 Bossuet, J.B. Conference avec M. Claude. 3e éd. Paris, 1727.
Htn 38557.47* Bossuet, J.B. L'apocalypse avec une explication. Paris, 1689.
Htn 38557.47.5* Bossuet, J.B. L'apocalypse avec une explication. Paris, 1690.
Htn 38557.47.250* Bossuet, J.B. Defensio declarationis conventus cleri Gallicani an. 1682. Amstelodami, 1745. 2v.
38557.47.260 Bossuet, J.B. Défense de la déclaration de l'assemblé...1682. Amsterdam, 1745. 3v.
38557.47.265 Bossuet, J.B. L'établissement du texte de la defensio declarationis de Bossuet. Paris, 1956.
Htn 38557.48* Bossuet, J.B. Defensio declarationis celeberrimae. Chevalier, 1730. 2v.
Htn 38557.48.2* Bossuet, J.B. Defensio declarationis celeberrimae. v.1-2. Chevalier, 1730.
38557.48.3 Bossuet, J.B. Défense de la tradition et des saints pères. Paris, 1763. 2v.
Htn 38557.48.5* Noailles, L.A. Declaratio ecclesiae principium Ludovici Antonii de Noailles. Paris, 1697.
38557.48.8 Bossuet, J.B. Abrégé du célèbre ouvrage de M. Bossuet. Londres, 1813.
38557.48.9 Bossuet, J.B. Abrégé du célèbre ouvrage de M. Bossuet. Paris, 1814.
Htn 38557.48.10* Bossuet, J.B. Divers écrits, ou Mémoires sur...Explication des maximes des saints. Paris, 1698.
Htn 38557.48.15* Bossuet, J.B. De la connaissance de Dieu et de soi-même. Paris, 1741.
38557.48.35 Bossuet, J.B. De la connaissance de Dieu et de soi-même. Paris, 1761.
38557.48.50 Bossuet, J.B. Traité de la connaissance de Dieu et de soi-même. Paris, 1864.
38557.48.70 Bossuet, J.B. De la connaissance de Dieu et de soi-même. Paris, 1891.
Htn 38557.49* Bossuet, J.B. De nova quaestione tractatus tres. Paris, 1698.
38557.49.15 Bossuet, J.B. Discours sur l'histoire universelle. Paris, 1823. 2v.
Htn 38557.49.25* Bossuet, J.B. Explication de la prophétie d'Isaie sur l'enfantement de la Sainte Vierge. Paris, 1704.

Classified Listing

38557.26 - Individual authors, etc. - 1661-1715 - Oratory - Bossuet - Sermons and other individual works - cont.

Htn 38557.49.28* Bossuet, J.B. Instructions sur la version du Nouveau Testament. Paris, 1702.
Htn 38557.49.30* Bossuet, J.B. Seconde instruction: sur les passages particuliers de la version du Nouveau Testament. Paris, 1703.
Htn 38557.49.35* Bossuet, J.B. Justification des réfléxions sur le Nouveau Testament. Lille, 1710.
38557.49.40 Monod, A. La controverse de Bossuet et de R. Simon au sujet de la "Version de Trévoux". Strasbourg, 1922.
38557.50 Bossuet, J.B. Lettres sur l'éducation du Dauphin. Paris, 1920.
38557.50.30 Bossuet, J.B. Le Bossuet des gens du monde. Paris, 1858.
Htn 38557.50.75* Bossuet, J.B. Élévations à Dieu sur tous les mystères. 1. éd. Paris, 1727. 2v.
Htn 38557.51* Bossuet, J.B. Élévations à Dieu sur tous les mystères de la religion chrétienne. Paris, 1727. 2v.
38557.51.20 Bossuet, J.B. Élévations à Dieu sur tous les mystères de la religion chrétienne. Paris, n.d.
38557.51.25 Bossuet, J.B. Élévations sur les mystères. Paris, 1962.
Htn 38557.51.75* Bossuet, J.B. Explication des prières de la messe. Paris, 1691.
Htn 38557.52* Bossuet, J.B. Exposition de la doctrine de l'église catholique sur les matières de controverse. Paris, 1671.
38557.52.2 Bossuet, J.B. Exposition de la doctrine de l'église catholique sur les matières de controverse. 4. éd. Paris, 1680.
38557.52.2.3 Bossuet, J.B. Exposition de la doctrine de l'église catholique sur les matières de controverse. 5. éd. Paris, 1680.
Htn 38557.52.2.10* Bossuet, J.B. Exposition de la doctrine de l'église catholique sur les matières de controverse. Paris, 1680. 3 pam.
Htn 38557.52.3* Bossuet, J.B. Exposition de la doctrine de l'église catholique sur les matières de controverse. 6. éd. Paris, 1686.
38557.52.4 Bossuet, J.B. Exposition de la doctrine de l'église catholique sur les matières de controverse. 7. éd. Paris, 1686.
38557.52.4.5 Bossuet, J.B. Exposition de la doctrine de l'église catholique sur les matières de controverse. 8. éd. Paris, 1686.
38557.52.4.9 Bossuet, J.B. Exposition de la doctrine de l'église catholique sur les matières de controverse. 9. éd. Paris, 1686.
38557.52.4.12 Bossuet, J.B. Exposition de la doctrine de l'église catholique sur les matières de controverse. 12. éd. Paris, 1686.
38557.52.4.15 Bossuet, J.B. Exposition de la doctrine de l'église catholique sur les matières de controverse. 12. éd. Paris, 1706.
38557.52.4.75 Bossuet, J.B. Exposition de la doctrine de l'église catholique sur les matières de controverse. Paris, 1756.
38557.52.4.81 Bossuet, J.B. Exposition de la doctrine de l'église catholique sur les matières de controverse. Paris, 1750.
Htn 38557.52.5* Bossuet, J.B. Exposition de la doctrine de l'église catholique. Paris, 1769.
38557.52.10 Bossuet, J.B. Exposition de la doctrine de l'église catholique sur les matières de controverse. St. Brieuc, 1801.
Htn 38557.52.24* Bossuet, J.B. An exposition of the doctrine of the Catholic Church in matters of controversie. London, 1686.
Htn 38557.52.25* Bossuet, J.B. Explication de quelques difficultez sur les prières de la messe. Paris, 1689.
38557.52.35 Bossuet, J.B. An exposition of the doctrine of the Catholic Church in matters of controversy. London, 1790.
Htn 38557.53.200* Bossuet, J.B. Maximes et réfléxions sur la comédie. Paris, 1694.
38557.53.200.45 Bossuet, J.B. Maximes et réfléxions sur la comédie. Photoreproduction. Paris, 1881.
38557.53.200.60 Bossuet, J.B. L'église et le théâtre. Paris, 1930.
38557.53.232 Bossuet, J.B. Maximes et réfléxions sur la comédie. Paris, 1728. 3 pam.
Htn 38557.53.250* Bossuet, J.B. Méditations sur l'évangile. Paris, 1731. 4v.
38557.53.260 Bossuet, J.B. Méditations sur l'évangile. Paris, 1937. 2v.
Htn 38557.54* Bossuet, J.B. Méditations sur la rémission des pechez. Paris, 1696.
Htn 38557.54.10* Bossuet, J.B. Mandement...pour la publication de la constitution de nostre saint pere le pape Innocent XII. Paris, 1699.
Htn 38557.54.12* Bossuet, J.B. Mandement...pour la publication de la constitution de nostre saint pere le pape Innocent XII. Paris? 1699?
38557.54.25 Bossuet, J.B. Panegyrics of the Saints, from French of Bossuet and Bourdaloue. London, 1924.
Htn 38557.54.40* Bossuet, J.B. Politique tirée des propres paroles de l'Écriture Sainte. Paris, 1709.
38557.54.40.5 Bossuet, J.B. Politique tirée des propres paroles de l'Écriture Sainte. Genève, 1967.
Htn 38557.54.50* Bossuet, J.B. Propositiones examinandae. Paris? 1700?
Htn 38557.55* Bossuet, J.B. Quakerism a-la-mode. London, 1698.
Htn 38557.55.10* Bossuet, J.B. Remarques sur la réponse de M. l'Archévèque de Cambray. Paris, 1698.
Htn 38557.55.12* Bossuet, J.B. Relation sur le quiétisme. Paris, 1698.
Htn 38557.55.80* Bossuet, J.B. Réponse de M. l'Archévèque de Cambray. Paris? 1698?
38557.55.85 Maximes et réfléxions de Bossuet sur la politique. Paris, 1964.
Htn 38557.56.50* Bossuet, J.B. Instruction pastorale au sujet des calomnies avancées dans le Journal de Trévoux. Paris, 1733.
Htn 38557.56.60* Bossuet, J.B. Instruction pastorale sur les promesses de l'église. Paris, 1700. 2 pam.
38557.56.65 Bossuet, J.B. Instruction pastorale sur les promesses de Jésus-Christ à son église. Paris, 1729. 2 pam.
38557.56.75 Bossuet, J.B. Oeuvres philosophiques de Bossuet. Paris, 1844.
38557.56.80 Bossuet, J.B. Oeuvres philosophiques. Paris, 1863.
38557.57 Bossuet, J.B. Introduction à la philosophie. Paris, 1722.
38557.57.5 Bossuet, J.B. Introduction à la philosophie. Paris, 1722.
Htn 38557.57.6* Bossuet, J.B. Introduction à la philosophie. Paris, 1722.
38557.57.10 Bossuet, J.B. Écrits philosophiques. Paris, 1861.
Htn 38557.58.25* Bossuet, J.B. Prières écclésiastiques à l'usage de Meaux. Paris, 1689.
Htn 38557.59* Bossuet, J.B. Réponse aux prejugez décisifs pour M. l'Archévèque de Cambray. Paris, 1699.

38557.26 - Individual authors, etc. - 1661-1715 - Oratory - Bossuet - Sermons and other individual works - cont.

Htn 38557.59.10* Bossuet, J.B. Réponse au huitième et dernier moyen decassation. Paris? 1690.
Htn 38557.59.150* Bossuet, J.B. Sermon presché à l'ouverture de l'assemblée generale du clergé de France. Paris, 1682.
38557.59.155 Bossuet, J.B. Sermon sur la mort. Paris, 1921.
Htn 38557.59.250* Meaux, France (Diocese). Statuts et ordonnances synodales. Paris, 1691.
38557.60 Bossuet, J.B. Traitez du libre-arbitre et de la concupiscence. Paris, 1731.
38557.60.10 Bossuet, J.B. Traité du libre-arbitre. Tucumán, 1948.
38557.60.100 Bossuet, J.B. Traité de la concupiscence. Paris, 1879.
38557.60.110 Bossuet, J.B. Traité de la concupiscence. Paris, 1930.
38557.64 Bossuet, J.B. Traité de la communion sous les deux espèces. Paris, 1727.
Htn 38557.65* Bossuet, J.B. Traité de l'amour de Dieu. Paris, 1736.
Htn 38557.67* Bossuet, J.B. Traité de la communion sous les deux espèces. Paris, 1682.
38557.67.5* fBossuet, J.B. Traité de la communion sous les deux espèces. 2. éd. Paris, 1686.
Htn 38557.67.5* Bossuet, J.B. Traité de la communion sous les deux espèces. 2. éd. Paris, 1686.
Htn 38557.68* Bossuet, J.B. A treatise of communion under both kinds. London, 1687.
Htn 38557.70* Bossuet, J.B. Témoignage sur la vie et les vertus éminentes de Monsieur Vincent de Paul. Paris, 1892.

38558.1 - .18 Individual authors, etc. - 1661-1715 - Oratory - Fléchier

38558.3 Fabre, Antonin. De la correspondance de Fléchier avec Mme. Des Houlières et sa fille. Paris, 1871.
38558.4 Fabre, Antonin. La jeunesse de Fléchier. Paris, 1882. 2v.
38558.5 Fléchier, Esprit. Oeuvres. Nimes, 1782. 10v.
38558.5.5 Fléchier, Esprit. Oeuvres complètes. Paris, 1856. 2v.
38558.6 Fléchier, Esprit. Recueil des oraisons funèbres. Paris, 1740.
38558.6.5 Fléchier, Esprit. Recueil des oraisons funèbres. Paris, 1749.
38558.7 Fléchier, Esprit. Recueil des oraisons. Paris, 1760.
38558.8 Fléchier, Esprit. Oraisons funèbres. Paris, 1803. 2v.
38558.8.2 Fléchier, Esprit. Oraisons funèbres. Paris, 1811. 2v.
38558.8.5 Fléchier, Esprit. Oraisons funèbres. Paris, 1829.
38558.10 Fléchier, Esprit. Choix d'oraisons funèbres. Paris, 1825.
38558.15 Fléchier, Esprit. Dess Hochwürdigsten in Gott Herzens Spiritus Fleschier. Constanz, 1713.
38558.16 Fléchier, Esprit. Lettres choisies, avec une relation des fanatiques du vivarez et des réfléxions sur les différens caractères des hommes. Paris, 1715. 2v.

38558.20 - .99 Individual authors, etc. - 1661-1715 - Oratory - Mascaron, etc.

38558.20 Mascaron, Jules. Recueil des oraisons funèbres. Paris, 1740.
38558.28 Lehanneur, L. Mascaron. La Rochelle, 1878.
38558.32 Revillout, M.C.J. Un maitre de conférences au milieu du XVIIe siècle. Montpellier, 1881.
38558.35 La Ruë, Charles de. Oraisons funèbres. Paris, 1740.

38561 Individual authors, etc. - 1661-1715 - Criticism and philosophy - Folios [Discontinued]

38561.4F Bayle, Pierre. Oeuvres. La Haye, 1727-31. 4v.
38561.6F Bayle, Pierre. Oeuvres. La Haye, 1727-37. 4v.
38561.9 Bayle, Pierre. Dictionnaire historique et critique. 5e éd. Basle, 1738. 4v.
38561.10A Bayle, Pierre. Dictionnaire historique et critique. Amsterdam, 1740. 4v.
38561.10B Bayle, Pierre. Dictionnaire historique et critique. Amsterdam, 1740. 4v.
Htn 38561.15* Oeuvres de Fontenelle. La Haye, 1728-29. 3v.
38561.22 Chassong, A. Oeuvres complètes de J. de la Bruyère. Paris, 1876. 2v.
38561.25 Fournier, E. La Bruyère. Paris, 1857.
Htn 38561.28* La Bruyère, J. Les caracteres de Théophraste. Paris, 1765.
38561.29 La Bruyère, J. Les caracteres ou les moeurs de ce siècle. Paris, 1845.
38561.30 La Bruyère, J. Les caracteres ou les moeurs de ce siècle. Paris, 1864.
38561.61 Boileau-Despréaux, Nicolas. Satires, commentées par lui-même. Paris, 1906.

38562.1 - .23 Individual authors, etc. - 1661-1715 - Criticism and philosophy - Fontenelle

38562.12 Trublet, N.C.J. Mémoires...de Fontenelle. Amsterdam, 1769.
38562.12.5 Bibliothèque Fontenelle, 1657-1757. Paris, 1957.
38562.14 Fontenelle, B. Le B. de. Oeuvres. Amsterdam, 1764. 12v.
38562.15 Oeuvres de Fontenelle. Paris, 1766. 11v.
38562.16A Oeuvres de Fontenelle. Paris, 1790-92. 8v.
38562.16B Oeuvres de Fontenelle. Paris, 1790-92. 8v.
38562.16.2 Fontenelle, B. Le B. de. Oeuvres. Paris, 1818.
38562.17 Fontenelle, B. Le B. de. Pages choisies des grands écrivains. Paris, 1909.
38562.17.5 Fontenelle, B. Le B. de. Fontenelle. Paris, 1929?
Htn 38562.17.25* Fontenelle, B. Le B. de. Poésies pastorales. London, 1707.
Htn 38562.18* Fontenelle, B. Le B. de. République des philosophes. Geneva, 1788.
38562.18.9A Fontenelle, B. Le B. de. Histoire des Oracles. Paris, 1908.
38562.18.9B Fontenelle, B. Le B. de. Histoire des Oracles. Paris, 1908.
38562.18.9C Fontenelle, B. Le B. de. Histoire des Oracles. Paris, 1908.
38562.18.10 Fontenelle, B. Le B. de. Histoire des Oracles. Paris, 1698.
38562.18.15 Fontenelle, B. Le B. de. L'ésprit de Fontenelle. Paris, 1922.
38562.18.20 Fontenelle, B. Le B. de. Dialogues of the dead. London, 1730.
38562.18.25 Bauchard, Marcel. L'histoire des Oracles de Fontenelle. Paris, 1947.

38562.1 - .23 Individual authors, etc. - 1661-1715 - Criticism and philosophy - Fontenelle - cont.

38562.18.30 Schmidt, Christian. Fontenelles "Nouveaux dialogues des morts" als moralistisches Werk zwischen Preziosität und Aufklärung. Hamburg, 1971.
38562.19 Fontenelle, B. Le B. de. Éloges des académiciens. v.2. Paris, 1766.
38562.20 Bouillier, F. Éloges de Fontenelle. Paris, n.d.
38562.20.15 Fontenelle, B. Le B. de. Choix d'éloges. Paris, 1888.
38562.20.20 Fontenelle, B. Le B. de. Entretiens sur la pluralité des mondes. Oxford, 1955.
38562.20.21 Fontenelle, B. Le B. de. Entretiens sur la pluralité des mondes. Paris, 1970.
Htn 38562.21.3* Fontenelle, B. Le B. de. Lettres galantes de M. le chevalier d'Her***. Paris, 1599.
38562.21.10 Fontenelle, B. Le B. de. Lettres galantes. Paris, 1961.
38562.21.15 Fontenelle, B. Le B. de. Fontenelle und die Aufklärung. München, 1969.
38562.21.25 Fontenelle, B. Le B. de. The achievement of Bernard le Bovier de Fontenelle. N.Y., 1970.
38562.22A Laborde-Milaa, A. Fontenelle. Paris, 1905.
38562.22B Laborde-Milaa, A. Fontenelle. Paris, 1905.
38562.23 Maigron, L. Fontenelle. Paris, 1906.
38562.23.8 Carré, J.R. La philosophie de Fontenelle ou Le sourire de la raison. Thèse. Paris, 1932.
38562.23.10 Carré, J.R. La philosophie de Fontenelle. Paris, 1932.
38562.23.15 Neumüller, Josef. Fontenelles Stil im Lichte des Satzverknüpfung. Inaug. Diss. Murnan, 1933.
38562.23.20 Breinbauer, S.A. Bedingungssätze bei Fontenelle. Inaug. Diss. Würzburg, 1937.
38562.23.25 Gregoire, Franz. Fontenelle. Thèse. Nancy, 1947.
38562.23.30 Counillon, J.F. Fontenelle. Fecamp, 1959.
38562.23.35 Consentini, John W. Fontenelle's art of dialogue. N.Y., 1952.
38562.23.40 Nedeljković, D. Fontenel. Beograd, 1963.
38562.23.45 Pizzorusso, Arnoldo. Il ventaglio e il compasso. Napoli, 1964.
38562.23.50 Lissa, Giuseppe. Cartesianesimo e anticartesianesimo in Fontenelle. Napoli, 1971.

38562.27 - Individual authors, etc. - 1661-1715 - Criticism and philosophy - Bouhours

38562.27 Doncieux, G. Le père Bouhours. Paris, 1886.
38562.30 Bouhours, D. Les entretiens d'Ariste et d'Eugène. Paris, 1691.
38562.31A Bouhours, D. Entretiens d'Ariste et d'Eugène. Paris, 1920.
38562.31B Bouhours, D. Entretiens d'Ariste et d'Eugène. Paris, 1920.
38562.32 Bouhours, D. La manière de bien penser dans les ouvrages d'ésprit. Amsterdam, 1525.
Htn 38562.33* Bouhours, D. La manière de bien penser dans les ouvrages d'ésprit. Paris, 1687.
38562.34 Bouhours, D. Pensées ingénieuses des anciens et des modernes. La Haye, 1721.
38562.35 Bouhours, D. Pensées ingénieuses des anciens et des modernes. Lyon, 1693.
38562.36 Bouhours, D. Pensées ingénieuses des anciens et des modernes. Paris, 1707.

38563.1 - .4 Individual authors, etc. - 1661-1715 - Criticism and philosophy - Audin

38563.4 Audin, Prieur de Termes et de la Fage. Favole Heroiche. Venice, 1690.
38563.4.5 Audin, Prieur de Termes et de la Fage. Fables héroïques. 1. partie. Paris, 1648.

38563.5 - .22 Individual authors, etc. - 1661-1715 - Criticism and philosophy - Bayle

38563.5.5 Bayle, Pierre. Oeuvres diverses. Hildesheim, 1964-68. 4v.
38563.6A Bayle, Pierre. Pensées diverses sur la Cornète. Paris, 1911. 2v.
38563.6B Bayle, Pierre. Pensées diverses sur la Cornète. Paris, 1911. 2v.
38563.6.5 Bayle, Pierre. Verschiedene Gedanken bey Gelegenheit des Cometen, der im Christmonate 1680 erschienen. Hamburg, 1741.
38563.6.20 Bayle, Pierre. Analyse raisonnée de Bayle, ou Abrégé méthodique de ses ouvrages. London, 1755- 8v.
38563.6.31 Bayle, Pierre. Projet et fragments d'un dictionnaire critique. Genève, 1970.
38563.7 Bayle, Pierre. Commentaire philosophique sur ces paroles de Jésus-Christ. n.p., n.d.
38563.7.5 Bayle, Pierre. The great contest of faith and reason. N.Y., 1963.
38563.8 Bayle, Pierre. Lettres choises. Rotterdam, 1714. 3v.
38563.9 Bayle, Pierre. Lettres. Amsterdam, 1729. 3v.
38563.10 Bayle, Pierre. Choix de la correspondance. Copenhague, 1890.
38563.10.25 Bayle, Pierre. Sur les obscénités. Bruxelles, 1879.
38563.11 Lenient, C. Étude sur Bayle. Paris, 1855.
38563.12 Des Maizeaux, Pierre. Das Leben des Weltberühmten Peter Bayle. Hamburg, 1731.
38563.13 Betz, Louis P. Pierre Bayle. Zürich, 1896.
38563.14A Cazes, A. Pierre Bayle. Paris, 1905.
38563.14B Cazes, A. Pierre Bayle. Paris, 1905.
38563.14C Cazes, A. Pierre Bayle. Paris, 1905.
38563.15 Dubois, L. Bayle et la tolérance. Photoreproduction. Paris, 1902.
38563.15.2 Dubois, L. Bayle et la tolérance. Thèse. Paris, 1902.
38563.17A Dévolve, J. Religion, critique et philosophie positive chez Pierre Bayle. Paris, 1906.
38563.17B Dévolve, J. Religion, critique et philosophie positive chez Pierre Bayle. Paris, 1906.
38563.18 Bolin, W. Pierre Bayle, sein Leben und seine Schriften. Stuttgart, 1905.
38563.19 Smith, H.E. The literary criticism of Pierre Bayle. Albany, 1912.
38563.19.5 Jeanmaire, Emile. Essai sur la critique religieuse de Pierre Bayle. Thèse. Strasbourg, 1862.
38563.19.10 Sandberg, Karl C. At the crossroads of faith and reason. Tucson, 1966.
38563.19.15 Deschamps, Arsène. La genèse du scepticisme erudit chez Bayle. Liége, 1878.
38563.20 Robinson, Howard. Bayle the sceptic. N.Y., 1931.
38563.21 Bayle, Pierre. Pierre Bayle. Paris, 1948.

38563.5 - .22 Individual authors, etc. - 1661-1715 - Criticism and philosophy - Bayle - cont.

38563.22.10 Montgomery, F.K. La vie et l'oeuvre du père Buffier. Paris, 1930.
38563.22.25 Serrurier, C. Pierre Bayle en Hollande. Apeldoorn, 1912.
38563.22.30 Courtines, L.P. Bayle's relations with England and the English. N.Y., 1938.
38563.22.35 André, P. La jeunesse de Bayle. Genève, 1953.
38563.22.40 Labrousse, Élisabeth. Inventaire critique de la correspondance de Pierre Bayle. Paris, 1961.
38563.22.41 Labrousse, Élisabeth. Pierre Bayle. La Haye, 1963-64. 2v.
38563.22.42 Labrousse, Élisabeth. Pierre Bayle: Hétérodoxie et rigorisme. La Haye, 1964.
38563.22.50 Talluri, Bruna. Pierre Bayle. Milano, 1963.
38563.22.55 La Monnoye, Bernard de. Histoire de Mr. Bayle et de ses ouvrages. Amsterdam, 1716.
38563.22.60A Cowdrick, Ruth Elizabeth. The early reading of Pierre Bayle. Scottdale, Pa., 1939.
38563.22.60B Cowdrick, Ruth Elizabeth. The early reading of Pierre Bayle. Scottdale, Pa., 1939.

38563.25 - Individual authors, etc. - 1661-1715 - Criticism and philosophy - Pellison, Perrault, etc.

38563.25 Larroque, P.T. de. Les correspondants de Peiresc. Marseille, 1880-91. 5v.
38563.27 Marcou, F.L. Étude sur la vie et les oeuvres de Pellisson. Paris, 1859.
NEDL 38563.28 F.A.M.D. Le Parnasse assiégé. Lyon, 1697.
38563.29 Perrault, C. Mémoires de ma vie. Paris, 1909.
38563.29.10 Perrault, C. Mémoires. Paris, 1878.
Htn 38563.29.15* Perrault, C. Recueil de divers ouvrages en prose et en vers. 2. éd. Paris, 1676.
38563.29.80 Kortum, Hans. Charles Perrault und Nicolas Boileau. Berlin, 1966.
Htn 38563.30* Perrault, C. Paralelle des anciens. Amsterdam, 1693.
38563.30.5 Perrault, C. Parallele des anciens et des modernes en ce qui. München, 1964.
38563.31 Perrault, C. L'oublieux, petite comédie. Paris, 1868.
38563.32 Perrault, C. Histoire de Peau d'Ane; conte de ma mère Laye. Londres, 1902.
38563.32.15 Perrault, C. Les contes des fées de Charles Perrault. Paris, 18- .
38563.33 Hallays, André. Les Perrault. 2. éd. Paris, 1926.
38563.33.2 Hallays, André. Les Perrault. 3. éd. Paris, 1926.
38563.34 Rapin, P. Les oeuvres. Amsterdam, 1709-10. 3v.
Htn 38563.46* Leclerc, Jean. Parrhasiana, ou Pensées diverses. Amsterdam, 1701. 2v.
38563.55 Leclerc, Jean. Parrhasiana; or Thoughts on several subjects. London, 1700.
38563.58 Legauz, Pierre. Caractères véritables ou Recherche de la vérité dans les moeurs des hommes. Paris, 1929.
Htn 38563.65* Valois, D.A. Valeseana, ou Les pensées critiques. Paris, 1694.
38563.65.2 Valois, D.A. Valeseana, ou Les pensées critiques. Paris, 1694.
Htn 38563.66* Valois, D.A. Valeseana, ou Les pensées critiques. Paris, 1695.

38564.1 - .39 Individual authors, etc. - 1661-1715 - Criticism and philosophy - La Bruyère - Writings

38564.6 Fournier, E. Comédie de...Bruyère. Pairs, 1872. 2v.
Htn 38564.7* La Bruyère, J. de. Les caractères de Théophraste. Lyon, 1688.
Htn 38564.8* La Bruyère, J. de. Les caractères de Théophraste. 4. éd. Lyon, 1689.
Htn 38564.9* La Bruyère, J. de. Les caractères de Théophraste. 6. éd. Paris, 1691.
Htn 38564.9.5* La Bruyère, J. de. Les caractères de Théophraste. 7. éd. Paris, 1692.
Htn 38564.10* La Bruyère, J. de. Les caractères de Théophraste. 8. éd. Paris, 1694.
Htn 38564.10.2* La Bruyère, J. de. Les caractères de Théophraste. 8. éd. Paris, 1694.
Htn 38564.12* La Bruyère, J. de. Discours sur Théophraste. n.p., n.d.
38564.13 La Bruyère, J. de. Les caractères de Théophraste. 10. éd. Paris, 1699.
38564.14 La Bruyère, J. de. Les caractères de Théophraste. Lyon, 1804.
38564.17 La Bruyère, J. de. Les caractères de Théophraste. Paris, 1700.
Htn 38564.18* La Bruyère, J. de. Les caractères de Théophraste. Amsterdam, 1739. 2v.
38564.18.75 La Bruyère, J. de. Les caractères de La Bruyère. Paris, 1813.
38564.19 La Bruyère, J. de. Les caractères de Théophraste. Avignon, 1817. 2v.
38564.20 La Bruyère, J. de. Les caractères de La Bruyère suivis des caractères de Théophraste. Paris, 1818. 2v.
38564.21 La Bruyère, J. de. Les caractères de La Bruyère suivis des caractères de Théophraste. Paris, 1819. 2v.
38564.22 La Bruyère, J. de. Les caractères de La Bruyère suivis des caractères de Théophraste. Paris, 1824. 2v.
38564.22.5 La Bruyère, J. de. Les caractères de La Bruyère suivis des caractères de Théophraste. Paris, 1826. 2v.
38564.23 La Bruyère, J. de. Oeuvres. Paris, 1820. 2 pam.
38564.24 La Bruyère, J. de. Oeuvres. Strasbourg, n.d.
38564.24.9 La Bruyère, J. de. Les caractères de La Bruyère. Paris, 1829.
38564.25 La Bruyère, J. de. Caractères. Paris, 1843.
38564.25.6 La Bruyère, J. de. Les caractères. Paris, 1853.
38564.25.8 La Bruyère, J. de. Les caractères. Paris, 1854.
38564.25.10 La Bruyère, J. de. Les caractères de Théophraste. Paris, 1861. 2v.
38564.25.50 La Bruyère, J. de. La Bruyère avec introduction, bibliographique, notes. Paris, 1920.
38564.26 La Bruyère, J. de. Le premier texte de La Bruyère. Paris, 1868.
38564.27 La Bruyère, J. de. Oeuvres. v.1-3 and album. Paris, 1865. 4v.
38564.28 La Bruyère, J. de. Les caractères. Paris, 1871. 2v.
38564.28.2 La Bruyère, J. de. Les caractères des caractères de Théophraste. Paris, 1869.
38564.29 La Bruyère, J. de. Les caractères. Paris, 1874.
38564.30 La Bruyère, J. de. Les caractères. Paris, 1872-73. 2v.

38564.1 - .39 Individual authors, etc. - 1661-1715 - Criticism and philosophy - La Bruyère - Writings - cont.

38564.30.3 La Bruyère, J. de. Les caractères ou Les moeurs...Suivis des caractères de Théophraste. Paris, 1875.
38564.30.5 La Bruyère, J. de. Les caractères. Paris, 1881. 2v.
38564.31 La Bruyère, J. de. Les caractères. Paris, 1883. 2v.
38564.32 La Bruyère, J. de. Les caractères. Paris, 1886.
38564.32.5 La Bruyère, J. de. Les caractères. Paris, 1897.
38564.32.9 La Bruyère, J. de. Les caractères. Paris, 1906.
38564.32.15 La Bruyère, J. de. Les caractères. Paris, 1913.
38564.32.25 La Bruyère, J. de. Les caractères. Paris, 1926.
38564.32.28 La Bruyère, J. de. Les caractères. Paris, 1928. 3v.
38564.32.33 La Bruyère, J. de. Les caractères. v.1-2. Paris, 1952.
38564.32.35 La Bruyère, J. de. Oeuvres complètes. Paris, 1934.
38564.32.36 La Bruyère, J. de. Les caractères ou Les moeurs de ce siècle. Paris, 1963.
38564.32.40 La Bruyère, J. de. Les caractères de Théophraste, traduits du grec avec les caractères ou Les moeurs de ce siècle. Paris, 1964.
38564.32.41 La Bruyère, J. de. Les Caractères de Théophraste. Évreux, 1970.
Htn 38564.33* La Bruyère, J. de. The works. London, 1723. 2v.
Htn 38564.34* La Bruyère, J. de. The characters. London, 1689.
Htn 38564.34.5* La Bruyère, J. de. Characters, or The manners of the age. 5. ed. London, 1709.
38564.35 La Bruyère, J. de. The characters. London, 1885.
38564.35.3 La Bruyère, J. de. The "characters". N.Y., 1885.
38564.35.9 La Bruyère, J. de. Des ouvrages de l'Esprit. Paris, 1882.
38564.35.11 La Bruyère, J. de. Des ouvrages de l'Esprit. Paris, 1887.
Htn 38564.35.15* La Bruyère, J. de. Dialogues posthumus. Paris, 1699.
38564.36.5 La Bruyère, J. de. Extraits des caractères de La Bruyère. Paris, 1921.

38564.40 - Individual authors, etc. - 1661-1715 - Criticism and philosophy - La Bruyère - Biography and criticism

38564.40 Morillot, P. La Bruyère. Paris, 1904.
NEDL 38564.41 Brillon, J.P. Apologie de Monsieur de La Bruyère. Paris, 1701.
38564.43 Lange, Maurice. La Bruyère. Paris, 1909.
38564.45 Rahstede, H.G. Ueber La Bruyère und seine Charaktere. Oppeln, 1886.
38564.47 Speckert, L. De politica et sociali Bruyerii doctrina. Tolosae, 1848.
38564.49 Klaus, Hermann. Jean de la Bruyère. Inaug. Diss. Berlin, 1935.
38564.51 Assollant, Georges. La Bruyère, les caractères. Paris, 1932.
38564.53 Michaut, G. La Bruyère. Paris, 1936.
38564.55 Richard, Pierre. La Bruyère et ses "Caractères". Amiens, 1946.
38564.55.10 Richard, Pierre. La Bruyère et ses caractères; éssai biographique et critique. Paris, 1965.
38564.60 Jasinski, René. Deux accès à La Bruyère. Paris, 1971.
38564.62 Pellisson, Maurice. La Bruyère. Genève, 1970.

38565 Individual authors, etc. - 1661-1715 - Criticism and philosophy - Boileau - Complete and selected works

38565.2 Boileau Despréaux, Nicolas. Oeuvres. Paris, 1713.
Htn 38565.3* Brossette, C. Oeuvres de...Nicolas Boileau. Geneva, 1716. 2v.
Htn 38565.3.10* Boileau Despréaux, Nicolas. Oeuvres de Nicolas Boileau. Amsterdam, 1718. 2v.
38565.5 Boileau Despréaux, Nicolas. Oeuvres. Paris, 1766. 2v.
Htn 38565.6* Saint-Marc, Charles H. Oeuvres de Boileau. Paris, 1772. 5v.
38565.6.9 Boileau Despréaux, Nicolas. Oeuvres. Londres, 1780. 2v.
38565.8 Boileau Despréaux, Nicolas. Oeuvres à l'usage des lycées. Paris, 1810.
38565.8.15 Boileau Despréaux, Nicolas. Oeuvres à l'usage des collèges. Lyon, 1814. 2 pam.
38565.9 Boileau Despréaux, Nicolas. Oeuvres. Paris, 1815. 3v.
38565.10 Saint-Surin, M. de. Oeuvres de Boileau. v.2-4. Paris, 1821. 3v.
38565.10.5 Boileau Despréaux, Nicolas. Oeuvres complètes, contenant ses poésies, ses écrits en prose. Paris, 1821. 3v.
38565.10.8A Boileau Despréaux, Nicolas. Oeuvres. Paris, 1821. 4v.
38565.10.8B Boileau Despréaux, Nicolas. Oeuvres. Paris, 1821. 4v.
38565.13 Viollet-Le-Duc, Emmanuel L.N. Oeuvres de Boileau. Paris, 1823.
38565.14 Boileau Despréaux, Nicolas. Oeuvres. Paris, 1823.
38565.16 Amar, Jean A. Oeuvres de Boileau. Paris, 1824. 4v.
38565.17 Boileau Despréaux, Nicolas. Oeuvres. Paris, 1832. 3v.
38565.18 Amar, M. Oeuvres de Boileau. Paris, 1844.
38565.20 Boileau Despréaux, Nicolas. Oeuvres. Paris, 1853.
38565.20.50 Boileau Despréaux, Nicolas. Oeuvres. Paris, 1869.
38565.21 Fournier, E. Oeuvres complètes de Nicolas Boileau. Paris, 1873.
38565.21.5 Boileau Despréaux, Nicolas. Oeuvres de Boileau. Paris, 1928.
38565.21.6 Boileau Despréaux, Nicolas. Oeuvres. Paris, 1910?
38565.21.10 Boileau Despréaux, Nicolas. Oeuvres de Boileau. Paris, 1928-29. 5v.
38565.21.15 Boileau Despréaux, Nicolas. Boileau. Paris, 1936.
38565.21.20 Boileau Despréaux, Nicolas. Oeuvres complètes. Paris, 1846. 3v.
38565.21.25 Boileau Despréaux, Nicolas. Épitres, Art poétique, Lutrin. Paris, 1939.

38566.1 - .24 Individual authors, etc. - 1661-1715 - Criticism and philosophy - Boileau - Selections [Discontinued]

Htn 38566.2* Boileau Despréaux, Nicolas. Oeuvres diverses. Paris, 1692.
Htn 38566.3* Boileau Despréaux, Nicolas. Oeuvres diverses. Paris, 1675.
38566.3.25 Boileau Despréaux, Nicolas. Oeuvres diverses. v.1-2. Amsterdam, 1702.
38566.4 Boileau Despréaux, Nicolas. Oeuvres. Paris, 1768. 2v.

38566.1 - .24 Individual authors, etc. - 1661-1715 - Criticism and philosophy - Boileau - Selections [Discontinued] - cont.

Htn 38566.4.10* Boileau Despréaux, Nicolas. Oeuvres. Amsterdam, 1772. 5v.
38566.4.15 Boileau Despréaux, Nicolas. Oeuvres complètes. Paris, 1966.
38566.5 Boileau Despréaux, Nicolas. Dialogues. Paris, 1942.
38566.6 Boileau Despréaux, Nicolas. Poésies. Paris, 1781.
38566.6.5 Boileau Despréaux, Nicolas. Oeuvres. Paris, 1788. 3v.
38566.6.9 Boileau Despréaux, Nicolas. Oeuvres. v.1-2. Paris, 1800.
38566.7 Boileau Despréaux, Nicolas. Oeuvres. Paris, 1813. 2v.
38566.8 Boileau Despréaux, Nicolas. Oeuvres. Paris, 1815.
38566.9 Boileau Despréaux, Nicolas. Oeuvres. Paris, 1810.
38566.10 Boileau Despréaux, Nicolas. Oeuvres de Nicolas Boileau Despréaux. La Haye, 1722. 4v.
38566.11 Boileau Despréaux, Nicolas. Oeuvres. Paris, 1814.
38566.15 Boileau Despréaux, Nicolas. Oeuvres. Paris, 1825. 4v.
38566.17 Boileau Despréaux, Nicolas. Oeuvres poétiques. Paris, 1845.
38566.17.3 Boileau Despréaux, Nicolas. Oeuvres poétiques. 3. éd. Paris, 1847.
38566.17.5 Boileau Despréaux, Nicolas. Oeuvres. Paris, 1851.
38566.17.8 Boileau Despréaux, Nicolas. Oeuvres poétiques. Paris, 1857.
38566.17.10 Boileau Despréaux, Nicolas. Oeuvres poétiques. Paris, 1878.
38566.17.12 Boileau Despréaux, Nicolas. Oeuvres poétiques. 12. éd. Paris, 1920.
38566.17.15 Boileau Despréaux, Nicolas. Oeuvres poétiques. Paris, 1889.
38566.17.20 Boileau Despréaux, Nicolas. Oeuvres poétiques. Paris, 189-?
38566.18 Boileau Despréaux, Nicolas. Oeuvres. Paris, 1870-73. 4v.
38566.21 Boileau Despréaux, Nicolas. Oeuvres poétiques. Paris, 1876-92. 2v.
38566.22 Boileau Despréaux, Nicolas. Oeuvres de Boileau. Paris, 1889.
38566.24 Boileau Despréaux, Nicolas. Oeuvres poétiques. 19. éd. Paris, 1899.

38566.25 - Individual authors, etc. - 1661-1715 - Criticism and philosophy - Boileau - Individual works

38566.25 Castres, G.H.F. de. L'art poétique de Boileau. Leipzig, 1856.
38566.26.4 Boileau Despréaux, Nicolas. Art poétique. Paris, 1870?
38566.26.7 Boileau Despréaux, Nicolas. Art poétique...Bibliothèque nationale. Paris, 1901. 2v.
38566.26.9 Boileau Despréaux, Nicolas. L'art poétique. 7. éd. Paris, 1911.
38566.26.14 Boileau Despréaux, Nicolas. L'art poétique. Cambridge, 1919.
Htn 38566.27* Boileau Despréaux, Nicolas. The art of poetry. London, 1683.
38566.28.10 Boileau Despréaux, Nicolas. The art of poetry. Glasgow, 1755.
Htn 38566.29* Boileau Despréaux, Nicolas. Ode pindarique...sur la prise de Namur. London, 1695.
Htn 38566.30* Boileau Despréaux, Nicolas. The Lutrin. London, 1708.
38566.31 Boileau Despréaux, Nicolas. The Lutrin. London, 1714.
38566.32 Boileau Despréaux, Nicolas. Le Lutrin. Poetry. Paris, 1893.
38566.32.2 Boileau Despréaux, Nicolas. Le Lutrin. Paris, 1907.
38566.33 Boileau Despréaux, Nicolas. Le Lutrin. Strasbourg, n.d.
Htn 38566.34* Boileau Despréaux, Nicolas. Le Lutrin. London, 1682.
38566.35 Boileau Despréaux, Nicolas. A estante do coro. Lisboa, 1834.
38566.36A Boileau Despréaux, Nicolas. Les héros de Roman. Dialogue. Boston, 1902.
38566.36B Boileau Despréaux, Nicolas. Les héros de Roman. Dialogue. Boston, 1902.
38566.36.2A Boileau Despréaux, Nicolas. Les héros de Roman. Dialogue. Boston, 19- .
38566.40 Boileau Despréaux, Nicolas. Dissertation sur la Joconde. Paris, 1942.
38566.54.10A Boileau Despréaux, Nicolas. Satires. Paris, 1932.
38566.54.10B Boileau Despréaux, Nicolas. Satires. Paris, 1932.
38566.54.15 Boileau Despréaux, Nicolas. Satires. Paris, 1934.
38566.56 Boileau Despréaux, Nicolas. The satires. Glasgow, 1904.
38566.57 Boileau Despréaux, Nicolas. Les premières satires, I-IX. Lille, 1941.
38566.63 Boileau Despréaux, Nicolas. Épitres. Paris, 1937.
38566.65 Boileau Despréaux, Nicolas. Lettres à Racine et à divers. Paris, 1943.
38566.66 Boileau Despréaux, Nicolas. Lettres à Brossette. Paris, 1942.
Htn 38566.70* The works of Monsieur Boileau. London, 1712. 2v.

38567 Individual authors, etc. - 1661-1715 - Criticism and philosophy - Boileau - Biography and criticism

38567.1 Magne, Émile. Bibliographie générale des oeuvres de Nicolas Boileau Despréaux. Paris, 1929. 2v.
38567.4 Laverdet, Auguste. Correspondence entre Boileau et Brossette. Paris, 1858.
38567.7 Pamphlet box. Boileau.
38567.8 Walter, Ulrich. Boileaus Wirkung auf seine englischen Zeitgenossen. Inaug. Diss. Strassburg, 1911.
Htn 38567.9* Pradon, Jacques. Nouvelles remarques sur tous les ouvrages du sieur D***. La Hague, 1685.
X Cg 38567.10 Deschanel, Émile. Boileau, Charles Perrault. Paris, 1888.
38567.12A Lanson, Gustave. Boileau. Paris, 1892.
38567.12B Lanson, Gustave. Boileau. Paris, 1892.
38567.12.10 Lanson, Gustave. Boileau. 3. éd. Paris, 1906.
38567.12.15 Lanson, Gustave. Boileau. 6. éd. Paris, 1922.
38567.14 Morillot, Paul. Boileau. Paris, 189-.
38567.15 Geissler, A. Die Theorien Boileaus. Leipzig, 1909.
38567.17 Dreyfus-Brisac, E. Un faux classique. Nicolas Boileau. Paris, 1901.
38567.18 Chiarini, M. Nicolas Boileau Despréaux. Imola, 1911.
38567.21 Delaporte, P.V. L'art poétique. Lille, 1888. 3v.
38567.22 Maugain, Gabriel. Boileaux et l'Italie. Paris, 1912.
38567.23 Petersen, Karl. Die Urteile Boileaus über die Dichter seiner Zeit. Kiel, 1906.
38567.25 Clark, A.F. Bruce. Boileau and the French classical critics in England. (1660-1830). Paris, 1925.

Classified Listing

38567 Individual authors, etc. - 1661-1715 - Criticism and philosophy - Boileau - Biography and criticism - cont.

38567.26 Miller, J.R. Boileau en France au dix-huitième siècle. Baltimore, 1942.
38567.27 Englander, D. La Xe satire de Boileau comparée à la VIe de Juvénal. Berlin, 1904.
38567.29 Une parodie curieuse de l'art poétique de Boileau. Rouen, 1879.
38567.30 Stein, Henricus J.A. Boileau en Hollande. Nijmegon, 1929.
38567.31 Noss, Mary T. La sensibilité de Boileau. Thèse. Paris, 1932.
38567.35 Hervier, M. L'art poétique de Boileau. Paris, 1936.
38567.37 Bray, René. Boileau; l'homme et l'oeuvre. Paris, 1942.
38567.39 Dumesnil, René. Boileau. Paris, 1943.
38567.41 Kopal, Josef. Literarni teorie Boileau na. Praha, 1927.
38567.43 Bonfantini, Mario. L'art poétique. Napoli, 1957.
38567.43.10 Bonfantini, Mario. Boileau e la sue idee. Milano, 1965.
38567.45A Brody, Jules. Boileau and Longinus. Genève, 1958.
38567.45B Brody, Jules. Boileau and Longinus. Genève, 1958.
38567.48 Albalat, Antoine. L'art poétique de Boileau. Paris, 1929.
38567.50 Des Maizeaux, Pierre. La vie de monsieur Boileau Despréaux. Amsterdam, 1715.
38567.51 Emard, P. La Sainte-Chapelle du Lutrin. Genève, 1963.
38567.52 Clarac, Pierre. Boileau. Paris, 1964.
38567.54 Bonfantini, Mario. Le idee di Boileau. Torino, 1965.
38567.56 White, Julian Eugene. Nicolas Boileau. N.Y., 1969.
38567.58 Vitanović, Slobodan. Poetika Nikole Boaloa i francuski klasicizm. Beograd, 1971.

38568.100 - .899 Individual authors, etc. - 1661-1715 - Criticism and philosophy - Other critics (800 scheme, A-Z by person)

38568.790 Simon, R. Lettres choisies. Amsterdam, 1730. 4v.
38568.790.2 Simon, R. Lettres choisies de M. Simon. v.1-4. 2. éd. Frankfurt, 1967.
38568.855 McKee, David Rice. Simon Tyssot de Patot and the 17th century background of critical deism. Thesis. Baltimore, 1941.
38568.870 Villiers, P. de. Traité de la satire. Paris, 1695.

38568.901 - .999 Individual authors, etc. - 1661-1715 - Criticism and philosophy - Anonymous works (99 scheme, A-Z by title)

38568.903 L'amour de Madeleine. Paris, 1909?

38571 Individual authors, etc. - 1661-1715 - Drama - Corneille, P. - Folios [Discontinued]

Htn 38571.3* Corneille, Pierre. Le théâtre. Paris, 1664. 2v.
38571.5 Corneille, Pierre. Théâtre. Genève, 1774. 8v.
38571.6F Corneille, Pierre. Oeuvres. Paris, n.d.
38571.6.9 Corneille, Pierre. Oeuvres. Paris, 1869.
38571.7 Corneille, Pierre. Oeuvres. Paris, 1873.
38571.8 Corneille, Pierre. Oeuvres des deux Corneille (Pierre et Thomas). Paris, 1865. 2v.
38571.8.5 Corneille, Pierre. Oeuvres de Pierre et Thomas Corneille. Paris, 1844.
38571.10 Corneille, Pierre. Chefs-d'oeuvre. Paris, 1876.
38571.12 Vignier, Adrien. Anecdotes...sur Pierre Corneille. Rouen, 1846.
38571.14 Adeline, Jules. Un portrait de Pierre Corneille. Paris, 1882.
38571.16 Les fêtes du IIIe centenaire de Pierre Corneille. Rouen, 1909.
38571.21 Ayer, Charles C. Tragic heroines of Pierre Corneille. Strassburg, 1898.
38571.22 Tastevin, Maria. Les héroines de Corneille. Paris, 1924.
38571.22.5 Cretin, Roger. Les imagines dans l'oeuvre de Corneille. Paris, 1927.
38571.22.10 Calvet, J. Polyenete de Corneille. Paris, 1932.
38571.26 Vedel, Valdemar. Fransk Klassik. København, 1927.
38571.26.10 Vedel, Valdemar. Deux classiques Français. Paris, 1935.

38572 Individual authors, etc. - 1661-1715 - Drama - Corneille, P. - Complete and Selected works - 18th and early 19th century editions

38572.6 Corneille, Pierre. Chefs-d'oeuvres. Paris, 1823. 2v.
Htn 38572.7.5* Corneille, Pierre. Le théâtre. Rouen, 1660. 3v.
Htn 38572.7.25* Corneille, Pierre. Théâtre. Tome III-XII. Genève, 1764. 10v.
38572.8 Corneille, Pierre. Théâtre. Paris, 1765. 12v.
38572.9A Corneille, Pierre. Théâtre. n.p., 1797. 12v.
38572.9B Corneille, Pierre. Théâtre. n.p., 1797. 12v.

38573 Individual authors, etc. - 1661-1715 - Drama - Corneille, P. - Complete and Selected works - Other 19th century editions

38573.2 Corneille, Pierre. Oeuvres. v.1-3, 5-12; v.4, lost. Paris, 1801. 11v.
38573.3 Corneille, Pierre. Oeuvres. Paris, 1824. 12v.
38573.4 Corneille, Pierre. Oeuvres. Paris, 1830-31. 12v.
38573.5 Corneille, Pierre. Oeuvres. v.1-12 and album. Paris, 1862-68. 13v.

38574 Individual authors, etc. - 1661-1715 - Drama - Corneille, P. - Complete and Selected works - Later editions

Htn 38574.1* Corneille, Pierre. Le théâtre. Paris, 1664.
38574.2 Corneille, Pierre. Le théâtre. Paris, 1723. 5v.
38574.2.3 Corneille, Pierre. Le théâtre de Pierre Corneille. 9. éd. Amsterdam, 1723. 5v.
38574.2.5 Corneille, Pierre. Théâtre. n.p., 1776. 10v.
38574.3 Corneille, Pierre. Théâtre. Paris, 1853.
38574.3.2 Corneille, Pierre. Théâtre. Paris, 1853. 2v.
38574.4 Corneille, Pierre. Oeuvres complètes. Paris, 1857. 2v.
38574.5 Corneille, Pierre. Théâtre. Texte de 1682. Paris, n.d. 8v.
38574.6 Corneille, Pierre. Théâtre. Paris, 1877-79. 5v.
38574.7A Corneille, Pierre. Théâtre. Paris, n.d.
38574.7B Corneille, Pierre. Théâtre. Paris, n.d.
38574.8 Corneille, Pierre. Théâtre. Paris, n.d. 2v.
38574.8.5 Corneille, Pierre. Oeuvres...théâtre complet. Paris, 18- 3v.
38574.8.15 Corneille, Pierre. Théâtre. Paris, 1934. 2v.
38574.9 Corneille, Pierre. Chefs-d'oeuvre...et de nouvelles remarques par C. Nodier et P. Lepeintre. Paris, 1824-25. 2v.
38574.10 Corneille, Pierre. Chefs-d'oeuvres; suivies des oeuvres...T. Corneille. Paris, 1859.
38574.11 Corneille, Pierre. Chefs-d'oeuvres. Paris, 1807. 3v.
38574.11.5 Corneille, Pierre. Chefs-d'oeuvres. v.1-4. Paris, 1836. 2v.

38574 Individual authors, etc. - 1661-1715 - Drama - Corneille, P. - Complete and Selected works - Later editions - cont.

38574.12.5 Corneille, Pierre. Oeuvres des deux Corneille. Paris, 1889. 2v.
38574.15 Corneille, Pierre. Théâtre. Paris, 1872. 2v.
38574.16 Corneille, Pierre. Théâtre. Paris, 1916. 2v.
38574.16.5 Corneille, Pierre. Writings on the theatre. Oxford, 1965.
NEDL 38574.19 Corneille, Pierre. Théâtre choisi illustré. Paris, 1909.
38574.23 Corneille, Pierre. Théâtre choisi. Paris, 1922.
38574.23.5 Corneille, Pierre. Théâtre choisi. Paris, 1932. 2v.
38574.23.7 Corneille, Pierre. Théâtre choisi. Montreal, 1945. 2v.
38574.23.10 Corneille, Pierre. Corneille inconnu. München, 1933.
38574.24 Pamphlet box. Corneille, Pierre. Drama.
38574.25 Corneille, Pierre. Corneille par lui-même. Paris, 1954.
38574.28 Corneille, Pierre. Moot plays. Nashville, 1959.
38574.30 Corneille, Pierre. Théâtre choisi de Corneille. Paris, 1968.

38575.1 - .23 Individual authors, etc. - 1661-1715 - Drama - Corneille, P. - Biography and criticism

38575.3 Tachereau, Jules. Histoire de...Pierre Corneille. Paris, 1829.
38575.4 Tachereau, Jules. Histoire de...Pierre Corneille. 2e éd. Paris, 1855.
38575.5 Guizot, François. Corneille and his time. N.Y., 1852.
38575.6 Guizot, François. Corneille and his time. Paris, 1858.
38575.9 Desjardins, Ernest. Le grand Corneille. Paris, 1861.
38575.11 Geoffrey, M. La revue des Feuilletons du journal de l'empire. Paris, 1807.
38575.12 Levallois, Jules. Corneille inconnu. Paris, 1876.
38575.12.5 Bouquet, F. Points obscurs..de la vie de Pierre Corneille. Paris, 1888.
38575.13 Lemaitre, Jules. Corneille et la poetique d'Aristote. Paris, 1888.
38575.13.5A Segall, J.B. Corneille and the Spanish drama. N.Y., 1902.
38575.13.5B Segall, J.B. Corneille and the Spanish drama. N.Y., 1902.
38575.13.5C Segall, J.B. Corneille and the Spanish drama. N.Y., 1902.
38575.14 Faguet, Émile. Corneille. Paris, 1888.
38575.14.5 Faguet, Émile. En lisant Corneille. Paris, 1913.
X Cg 38575.15 Liéby, A. Corneille. Études sur le théâtre classique. Paris, 1892.
38575.15.5 LeBrun, Roger. Corneille devant trois siècles. Paris, 1906.
38575.16 Lisle, J.A. Essai sur les théories dramatiques de Corneille. Paris, 1852.
38575.16.3 Duparay, B. Des principes de Corneille sur l'art dramatique. Lyon, 1857.
38575.16.5 Böhm, J. Die dramatischen Theorien Pierre Corneilles. Berlin, 1901.
38575.17 Lodge, Lee Davis. A study in Corneille. Baltimore, 1891.
38575.17.5 Mulert, A. Pierre Corneille auf der englischen Bühne. Erlangen, 1900.
38575.17.6A Canfield, Dorothea F. Corneille and Racine in England. N.Y., 1904.
38575.17.6B Canfield, Dorothea F. Corneille and Racine in England. N.Y., 1904.
38575.17.9 Raab, Rudolf. Pierre Corneille in deutschen Ubersetzungen. Heidelberg, 1910.
38575.18 Trollope, H.M. Corneille and Racine. Edinburgh, 1881.
38575.18.3 Trollope, H.M. Corneille and Racine. Edinburgh, 1898.
38575.18.5 Bonieux, B. Critique des tragedies de Corneille et de Racine par Voltaire. Paris, 1866.
38575.18.7 Aretz, P. Remarques gramaticales et lexicologiques sur la langue de Corneille. Bonn, 1871.
38575.19 Lanson, G. Corneille. Paris, 1898?
38575.19.3 Lanson, G. Corneille. 3. éd. Paris, 1909.
38575.19.5 Huszár, Guil. Pierre Corneille et le théâtre Espagnol. Photoreproduction. Paris, 1903.
38575.20 Jacobi, Philipp. Syntactische Studien über Pierre Corneille. Giessen, 1887.
38575.20.5A Vincent, Leon H. Corneille. Boston, 1901.
38575.20.5B Vincent, Leon H. Corneille. Boston, 1901.
38575.20.7 Vincent, Leon H. Corneille. Boston, 1901.
Htn 38575.22* Picot, Émile. Bibliographie Cornélienne. Paris, 1876.
38575.22.3 Picot, Émile. Bibliographie Cornélienne. Paris, 1876.
Htn 38575.22.5* Verdier, P. Additions à la bibliographie Cornelienne. Rouen, 1908.
38575.22.10 Lemonnier, Leon. Corneille. Paris, 1945.
38575.23 Paris. Bibliothèque Nationale. Objets exposés à le second centenaire à Pierre Corneille. Paris, 1945.
38575.23.5 Le Guiner, Jeanne. Les femmes dans les tragédies de Corneille. Paris, 1920.
38575.23.7 Pamphlet vol. Corneille. Dissertations. 7 pam.
38575.23.9 Lyonnet, Henry. Les "premières" de Pierre Corneille. Paris, 1923.
38575.23.25 Bray, René. La tragédie cornélienne devant la critique classique. Paris, 1927.
38575.23.26 Bray, René. La tragédie cornélienne devant al critique classique. Thèse. Dÿon, 1927.
38575.23.30 Cretin, Roger. Les images dans l'oeuvre de Corneille. Thèse. Caen, 1927.
38575.23.32 Cretin, Roger. Lexique comparé des metaphores dans le théâtre de Corneille et de Racine. Thèse. Caen, 1927.
38575.23.35 Mariolle-Pilté, R. La descendance des Corneille. Paris, 1911.
38575.23.40 Lyonnet, Henry. Le Cid de Corneille. Paris, 1929.
38575.23.42 Lemoine, Jean. La première du Cid, le théâtre, les interprètes d'après des documents inédits. Paris, 1936.
38575.23.45 Hoyer, Luise. Die Anrede in Corneille Dramen. Inaug. Diss. Berlin, 1932.
38575.23.50 Braun, Ernst. Die Stellung des Dichters Pierre Corneille zu den "Remarques" des Grammatikers Vaugelas. Inaug. Diss. Kaiserslautern, 1933.
38575.23.55 Le Corbeiller, A. Pierre Corneille intime. Paris, 1936.
38575.23.60 Doenhardt, Willibaldis S. Lessing und Corneille. n.p., n.d.
38575.23.65 Krauss, Werner. Corneille als politischer Dichter. Marburg, 1936.
38575.23.66 Rivaille, Louis. Les débuts de Pierre Corneille. Thèse. Paris, 1936.
38575.23.67 Rivaille, Louis. Les débuts de Pierre Corneille. Paris, 1936.
38575.23.69A Schlumberger, J. Plaisir à Corneille. 5th éd. Paris, 1936.
38575.23.69B Schlumberger, J. Plaisir à Corneille. 6th éd. Paris, 1936.

Classified Listing

38575.1 - .23 Individual authors, etc. - 1661-1715 - Drama - Corneille, P. - Biography and criticism - cont.

38575.23.72 Brasillach, Robert. Pierre Corneille. Paris, 1938.
38575.23.73 Brasillach, Robert. Corneille. Paris, 1961.
38575.23.75 Al Bassir, Mahdi. Le lyrisme de Corneille. Thèse. Montpellier, 1937.
38575.23.80 Schwartz, W.L. The sentential in the dramas of Corneille. Stanford, 1939.
38575.23.85 Rostand, François. L'imitation de soi chez Corneille. Paris, 1945.
38575.23.90 May, G.C. Tragédie cornélienne, tragédie racionienne. Urbana, 1948.
38575.23.95 Nadel, O. Le sentiment de l'amour dans l'oeuvre de Corneille. Thèse. Paris, 1948.
38575.23.100 Couton, Georges. La vieillesse de Corneille. Thèse. Paris, 1949.
38575.23.100.5 Couton, Georges. La vieillesse de Corneille. Paris, 1949.
38575.23.100.10 Couton, Georges. Corneille et la Fronde. Clermont, 1951.
38575.23.100.15 Doubrovsky, Serge. Corneille et la dialectique du héros. Paris, 1963.
38575.23.102 Schneider, R. Corneilles Ethos in der Ära Ludwigs XIV, 1-10 Tourend. Baden-Baden, 1948.
38575.23.105 Pietsch, Franz. Der Einfluss der Ethik Corneilles auf seine Zeitgenassen. Inaug. Diss. n.p., 1940.
38575.23.106 Descates, Mauriel. Les grands rôles du théâtre. Paris, 1962.
38575.23.108 Herland, Louis. Horace. Paris, 1952.
38575.23.110 Écorcheville, J. Corneille et la musique. Paris, 1906.
38575.23.112 Siciliano, Italo. Corneille. Venezia, 1959.
38575.23.115 Couton, Georges. Réalisme de Corneille. Paris, 1953.
38575.23.117 Couton, Georges. Corneille. Paris, 1958.
38575.23.120 Dort, Bernard. Pierre Corneille, dramaturge. Paris, 1957.
38575.23.123PF Corneille, Pierre. Les autographies de Pierre Corneille. Paris, 1929.
38575.23.125 Zanghi, Rosario. Introduzione a Cinna di Corneille. Torino, 1948.
38575.23.140 Arcine, Roland d'. Corneille, l'homme à travers l'oeuvre. Vienne, 1964.
38575.23.150 Currier, Peter. Corneille: Polyeucte. London, 1965.
38575.23.155 Maurens, Jacques. La tragédie sans tragique. Paris, 1966.
38575.23.157 Besançon, France. Université. Laboratoire d'analyse lexicologique. P. Corneille, "Cinna." Paris, 1971.
38575.23.160 Fogel, Herbert. The criticism of Cornelian tragedy; a study of critical writing from the seventeenth to the twentieth century. 1. ed. N.Y., 1967.

38575.24 - .89 Individual authors, etc. - 1661-1715 - Drama - Corneille, P. - Individual works

38575.24 Pierre Corneille. Münster, 1932.
Htn 38575.24.9* Corneille, Pierre. Agesilas. Paris, 1666.
38575.25 Corneille, Pierre. Le Cid. Horace. Polyeucte. Scènes choisies...par M. Bouchor. Paris, 1899.
38575.26 Corneille, Pierre. Le Cid. Paris, n.d.
Htn 38575.26.5* Corneille, Pierre. Le Cid. London, 1650.
38575.26.8 Corneille, Pierre. Corneille's the Cid. Harrisburg, 1896.
X Cg 38575.26.10 Corneille, Pierre. Le Cid. N.Y., 1894.
38575.26.15 Corneille, Pierre. Corneille's Le Cid. N.Y., 1929.
38575.27 Corneille, Pierre. Le Cid. Horace (chef d'oeuvre). Boston, 1873.
38575.27.2 Corneille, Pierre. Le Cid. 10. éd. Bielefeld, 1874.
38575.27.3 Corneille, Pierre. Le Cid. 8. éd. Paris, 1896.
38575.27.4 Corneille, Pierre. Le Cid. 13. éd. Paris, 1908.
38575.27.5 Corneille, Pierre. Le Cid. London, 1909.
X Cg 38575.27.20 Corneille, Pierre. Le Cid. Lyon, 1945.
38575.28 Lucas, Hippolyte. Documents relatifs à l'historie du Cid. Paris, 1860.
38575.28.5 Gasté, Armand. La querelle du Cid, pièces et pamphlets. Paris, 1898.
38575.28.7 Bernard, G. Le Cid espagne et le Cid français. Lille, 1910.
Htn 38575.28.8* Chapelain, J. Les sentimens de l'Académie français sur la tragi-comédie du Cid. Paris, 1638.
38575.28.9 Collas, Georges. Les sentiments de l'Académie français sur la tragi-comédie du Cid. Paris, 1912.
38575.28.9.5 Académie française, Paris. Les sentiments de l'Académie française sur le Cid. Minneapolis, 1916.
38575.28.10 Reynier, Gustave. Le Cid de Corneille. Paris, 1929.
Htn 38575.28.12* Corneille, Pierre. Le défense du Cid. v.1-2. Rouen, 1879.
38575.28.15 Milon, F.J. Le troisième centenaire du "Cid". Paris, 1937.
V38575.28.20 Brandwajn, Rachmiel. Corneille i jego "Cyd". Warszawa, 1968.
38575.28.25 Besançon, France. Université. Centre d'étude du vocabulaire français. P. Corneille. Le Cid. Paris, 1966.
38575.29.1.5 Corneille, Pierre. Le Cid. 2d éd. N.Y., 1870.
38575.29.2.7 Corneille, Pierre. Le Cid. N.Y., 1889.
38575.29.3 Corneille, Pierre. Le Cid. London, 1891.
38575.29.4 Corneille, Pierre. Le Cid. Tournai, 1899.
38575.29.6 Corneille, Pierre. Le Cid. Strasbourg, n.d.
38575.30 Corneille, Pierre. Le Cid...de Pierre Corneille. Paris, 1810.
38575.30.3 Corneille, Pierre. Le Cid. Paris, 1817.
38575.31.2 Corneille, Pierre. Cinna. Paris, 1882.
38575.31.4 Corneille, Pierre. Polyeucte. London, 1886.
38575.31.4.2 Corneille, Pierre. Polyeucte. London, 1892.
38575.31.5 Corneille, Pierre. Polyeucte. Paris, 1771.
38575.31.6 Corneille, Pierre. Polyeucte. Strasbourg, n.d.
38575.31.8 Corneille, Pierre. Cinna; tragédie. Nouvelle éd. Paris, 1906.
38575.31.9 Corneille, Pierre. Cinna, ou La Clémence d'Auguste; tragédie. Paris, 1862.
38575.31.9.2 Corneille, Pierre. Cinna, ou La Clémence d'Auguste. 2. éd. Paris, 1862.
38575.31.9.30 Corneille, Pierre. Cinna. Paris, 1948.
38575.31.9.35 Corneille, Pierre. Cinna. Paris, 1948.
38575.31.10 Lippold, F. Bemerkungen zu Corneilles Cinna. Zwickan, 1893.
Htn 38575.31.18* Corneille, Pierre. Don Sanche d'Arragon. Comédie hèroique. Paris, 1650.
Htn 38575.31.20* Corneille, Pierre. Don Sanche d'Arragon. Comédie hèroique. Paris, 1655.
38575.31.25 Corneille, Pierre. Don Sanche d'Arragon. Comédie hèroique. Paris, 1896.
38575.31.30 Corneille, Pierre. Don Sanche d'Arragon. Paris, 1969.
38575.31.35 Corneille, Pierre. La galerie du Palais. London, 1920.
38575.32 Corneille, Pierre. Horace. Paris, 1848.
38575.32.4 Corneille, Pierre. Horace. Paris, 18- .
38575.32.5 Corneille, Pierre. Horace. Strasbourg, n.d.

38575.24 - .89 Individual authors, etc. - 1661-1715 - Drama - Corneille, P. - Individual works - cont.

38575.32.9 Corneille, Pierre. Horacio...Original Frances con la traduccion...española. Naveva York, 1855.
38575.33.1 Corneille, Pierre. Horace. Oxford, 1882.
NEDL 38575.33.1 Corneille, Pierre. Horace. Oxford, 1882.
38575.33.2 Corneille, Pierre. Horace. N.Y., 1890.
38575.33.3 Corneille, Pierre. Horace. Paris, 1868.
38575.33.4 Corneille, Pierre. Horace; a tragedy. N.Y., 1885.
38575.33.6 Corneille, Pierre. Horace; tragédie. London, 1874.
NEDL 38575.33.7 Corneille, Pierre. Horace. London, 19- .
38575.33.8 Corneille, Pierre. Horace. 7 éd. Paris, 1907.
38575.33.9 Roosbroeck, Gustave L. van. The genesis of Corneille's Mélite. Vinton, 191-.
38575.33.10 Corneille, Pierre. La veuve. Genéve, 1954.
38575.33.11 Corneille, Pierre. La suite du menteur. Cambridge, 1878.
38575.33.12 Corneille, Pierre. Le menteur. London, 1891.
38575.33.13 Corneille, Pierre. Le menteur. Strasbourg, n.d.
38575.33.20 Corneille, Pierre. Le menteur. London, 1879.
38575.33.25A Corneille, Pierre. Rodogune. Paris, 1945.
38575.33.25B Corneille, Pierre. Rodogune. Paris, 1945.
38575.33.35 Corneille, Pierre. Rodogune. Paris, 1900.
38575.33.40 Corneille, Pierre. Rodogune; tragédie. Paris, 1946.
38575.34 Corneille, Pierre. Le menteur et Rodogune. Paris, 1883.
38575.34.1.5 Corneille, Pierre. Le menteur. Paris, 1910.
38575.34.2 Corneille, Pierre. Nicomède. Paris, 1886.
38575.34.3 Corneille, Pierre. Nicomède. Paris, 1888.
38575.34.4 Corneille, Pierre. Nicomède. Paris, 1890.
38575.34.4.15 Corneille, Pierre. Nicomède. London, 1900.
Htn 38575.34.5* Corneille, Pierre. Nicomède. London, 1671.
38575.34.5.25 Corneille, Pierre. Polyeucte martyr. Paris, 1850.
38575.34.6 Corneille, Pierre. Polyeucte par Felix Hermon. Paris, 1887.
38575.34.6.5 Corneille, Pierre. Polyeucte. London, 1887.
38575.34.7 Corneille, Pierre. Polyeucte. London, 1889.
38575.34.7.5 Corneille, Pierre. Polyeucte. Boston, 1891.
38575.34.7.7 Corneille, Pierre. Polyeucte. Cambridge, 1892.
38575.34.8.9 Corneille, Pierre. Polyeucte. Boston, 1906.
38575.34.8.10 Corneille, Pierre. Polyeucte. Strasbourg, n.d.
38575.34.8.12 Corneille, Pierre. Polyeucte. Bielefeld, 1875.
38575.34.8.14 Corneille, Pierre. Polyeucte. Boston, 1909.
38575.34.9.20 Corneille, Pierre. Polyeucte. N.Y., 1923.
Htn 38575.34.10* Corneille, Pierre. Pompey the great. London, 1664.
38575.34.11 Corneille, Pierre. Pompée. 5e éd. Paris, 189-.
38575.34.12 Corneille, Pierre. Pompejus. Amsterdam, 1737.
38575.34.13 Corneille, Pierre. Pompée. London, 1971.
38575.34.15 Corneille, Pierre. La place royale. Paris, 1962.
38575.34.20 Corneille, Pierre. Le menteur. Paris, 1964.
Htn 38575.34.40* Corneille, Pierre. Pertharite roy des Lombards. Tragédie. Paris, 1656.
38575.34.60 Corneille, Pierre. La mort de solon. Paris, 1949.
38575.35 Corneille, Pierre. Sertorius. Paris, 1881.
38575.35.5 Corneille, Pierre. Sertorius. Genève, 1959.
Htn 38575.36* Corneille, Pierre. Oedipe. Paris, 1659.
38575.37 Corneille, Pierre. L'illusion comique. Strasbourg, 1918?
38575.37.10 Corneille, Pierre. L'illusion comique. Manchester, 1944.
38575.37.15 Corneille, Pierre. L'illusion comique. Paris, 1957.
38575.40 Corneille, Pierre. De dood van Hannibal; treurspel. Amsterdam, 1693.
38575.42 Rivaille, L. Pierre Corneille, correcteur de ses premières. Thèse. Paris, 1935.
Htn 38575.50* Corneille, Pierre. Rodogune. Rouen, 1647.
Htn 38575.55* Corneille, Thomas. Darius, tragédie. Paris, 1659.
38575.70 Corneille, Pierre. Trois discours sur le poème dramatique. Paris, 1963.
38575.75 Corneille, Pierre. Mélite. Lille, 1950.
38575.80 Corneille, Pierre. Clitandre. Lille, 1949.
38575.82 Corneille, Pierre. Seven plays. N.Y., 1969.
38575.85 Corneille, Pierre. The chief plays of Corneille. Princeton, 1952.

38575.90 - .119 Individual authors, etc. - 1661-1715 - Drama - Corneille, P. - Criticism [Discontinued]

38575.90 Leroy, L. Polyeucte et la critique. Abbaye de Pontigny, 1954.
38575.93 Mony, Gabriel. La chanson de Rodrique. Nice, 1957.
38575.94 Neukomm, Gerda. Formwerdung und Formzerfall bei Pierre Corneille. Zürich, 1941.
38575.95 Yarrow, Philip J. Corneille. London, 1963.
38575.96 Sweetser, M.O. Les conceptions dramatiques de Corneille. Genève, 1962.
38575.97 Nelson, R.J. Corneille, his heroes and their worlds. Philadelphia, 1963.
38575.98 Manters, Robert. Corneille critique son temps. Paris, 1964.
38575.99 Wanke, C. Seneca, Lucan, Corneille. Heidelberg, 1964.
38575.101 Langéac, Eyide Louis Edome Joseph de l'Espenasse. Eloge de Corneille. Paris, 1768.
38575.103 Muller, Charles. Essai de statisque lexicale. Paris, 1964.
38575.103.2 Muller, Charles. Étude de statistique lexicale. Thèse. Paris, 1967.
38575.103.2.2 Muller, Charles. Étude statistique lexicale. Thèse. Paris, 1967.
38575.105 Maillet du Boullay, Charles. La maison de pierre Corneille au petit Couronne. Rouen, 1884.
38575.108 Stegmann, André. L'héroisme cornélien; genèse et signification. Thèse. Paris, 1968. 2v.
V38575.109 Bartkus, G. Kornelio teatras. Vilnius, 1967.
38575.110 Voss, Harald. Corneille, oder das Werden einer menschlichen Ordnung. Bonn, 1967?
38575.112 Eder, Klaus. Pierre Corneille und Jean Racine. 1. Aufl. Velber, 1969.
38575.114 Besançon, France. Université. Centre d'étude du vocabulaire français. Pierre Corneille, Polyeucte, Concordances. Paris, 1967.
38575.116 Delû-Bridel, Jacques. La préciosité, conception heroique de la vie. Bologna, 1965.

38576 Individual authors, etc. - 1661-1715 - Drama - Other dramatists, A-P

38576.1 Barbier, Marie Anne. La mort de Cesar. Paris, 1710.
38576.1.50 Barbier, Marie Anne. Théâtre de Mademoiselle Barbier. Paris, 1745.
Htn 38576.2* Baron, M.B. Le théâtre. Paris, 1759. 3v.
Htn 38576.2.3* Baron, M.B. L'homme à bonne fortune. Paris, 1686.
38576.3 Bernard, Catherine. Brutus: tragédie. Paris, 1691.
Htn 38576.3.50* Bernard, Catherine. The female, or Frederick of Sicily. London, 1682.

Classified Listing

38576 Individual authors, etc. - 1661-1715 - Drama - Other dramatists, A-P - cont.

	38576.4	Boursault, Edme. Théâtre. Paris, 1746. 3v.
	38576.4.6	Boursault, Edme. Les apparences trompeuses, ou Ne pas croire ce qu'ou void. Amsterdam, 1718.
	38576.4.7	Boursault, Edme. Les Bavardes. Paris, 1890.
	38576.5	Boursault, Edme. Le medicine volant. Paris, 1884.
	38576.6	Boursault, Edme. Le portrait du peintre. Paris, 1879.
	38576.6.2	Boursault, Edme. Théâtre choisi. Paris, 1883.
	38576.7	Boursault, Edme. Lettres par E. Colombey. Paris, 1891.
	38576.7.5	Boursault, Edme. Lettres à Babet. Paris, 1886.
	38576.7.10	Boursault, Edme. Lettres nouvelles. Paris, 1738. 3v.
	38576.7.30	Hoffmann, A. Edme Boursault nach seinem Leben und in seinen Werken. Metz, 1902.
	38576.7.32	Grawe, Ludwig. Edme Boursault Leben und Werke. Inaug. Diss. Lingen, 1887.
Htn	38576.7.50*	Boyer, Claude. Les amours de Jupiter et de Sémélé. Paris, 1666.
Htn	38576.7.52*	Boyer, Claude. Aristodème. Paris, 1649.
Htn	38576.7.54*	Boyer, Claude. Artaxerce. Paris, 1683.
Htn	38576.7.56*	Boyer, Claude. Clotilde; tragédie. Paris, 1659.
Htn	38576.7.58*	Boyer, Claude. Fédéric; tragicomédie. Paris, 1660.
Htn	38576.7.60*	Boyer, Claude. La feste de Venus. Paris, 1669.
Htn	38576.7.62*	Boyer, Claude. Le fils supposé. Paris, 1672.
Htn	38576.7.64*	Boyer, Claude. Le jeune Marius; tragédie. Paris, 1669.
Htn	38576.7.66*	Boyer, Claude. Judith; tragédie. Paris, 1695.
Htn	38576.7.68*	Boyer, Claude. Lisimène, ou Le jeune bergère. Paris, 1672.
NEDL	38576.7.70	Boyer, Claude. La mort de Démétrius, ou Le rétablissement. Paris, 1661.
Htn	38576.7.72*	Boyer, Claude. Oropaste, ou Le faux Tonaxare. Paris, 1663.
Htn	38576.7.74*	Boyer, Claude. Policrate. Paris, 1670.
Htn	38576.7.76*	Boyer, Claude. La Porcie romaine. Paris, 1646.
Htn	38576.7.78*	Boyer, Claude. Porus; ou La generosité d'Alexandre. Paris, 1648.
Htn	38576.7.80*	Boyer, Claude. La soeur généreuse. Paris, 1647.
Htn	38576.7.82*	Boyer, Claude. Tyridate; tragédie. Paris, 1649.
Htn	38576.7.84*	Boyer, Claude. Ulysse dans l'isle de Circé. Paris, 1650.
	38576.7.95	Goehlert, Ernst. Abbé Claude Boyer. Leipzig, 1915.
	38576.8	Brécourt, G.M. de. L'ombre de Molière. Paris, 1880.
	38576.8.2	Brécourt, G.M. de. La feinte mort de Jodelet. Paris, 1660.
	38576.8.4	Brécourt, G.M. de. Les flateurs trompez...par Mr. B. Caen, 1699.
Htn	38576.10*	Brosse, N. de. Les innocens coupables. Paris, 1645.
Htn	38576.10.2*	Brosse, N. de. Les songes des hommes esveillez. Paris, 1646.
	38576.11	Brueys, D.A. de. L'avocat Pathelin. Paris, n.d.
	38576.11.1	Brueys, D.A. de. L'avocat Pathelin. Paris, 1859.
	38576.11.2	Brueys, D.A. de. L'avocat Pathelin. London, 1892.
	38576.11.3	Brueys, D.A. de. L'avocat Pathelin. N.Y., 1909.
	38576.11.4	Brueys, D.A. de. Les oeuvres de théâtre. Paris, 1735. 3v.
	38576.11.6	Brueys, D.A. de. Choix de pieces de théâtre de Brueys et Palaprat. Londres, 1787.
	38576.11.19	Koch, J. Brueys und Palaprat und ihre dramatischen Werke. Dresden, 1906.
Htn	38576.11.23*	Chevreau, U. La suite et le mariage du Cid. Caen, 1702.
Htn	38576.11.25*	Chevreau, U. Coriolan; tragédie. Paris, 1638.
Htn	38576.11.30*	Chevreau, U. Cheveraenna. Paris, 1697-1700. 2v.
	38576.11.35	Boissière, G. Urbain Chevreau, 1613-1701 Moit, 1909.
	38576.12	Cheffault, F. de. Le martyre de Saint Gervais. Paris, 1670.
	38576.12.20	Campistron, J.G. de. Oeuvres. Paris, 1750. 3v.
	38576.12.21	Hausding, Curt. Jean Galhert de Campistron. Leipzig, 1903.
Htn	38576.12.25*	Champmesle, C.C. Les oeuvres. Paris, 1742. 2v.
Htn	38576.12.27*	Champmesle, C.C. Délie; pastorale. Paris, 1668.
Htn	38576.12.30*	Chappuzeau, Samuel. L'avare duppé; ou L'homme de paille. Paris, 1663.
Htn	38576.12.32*	Chappuzeau, Samuel. Le riche mécontent; ou Le noble imaginaire. Paris, 1662.
	38576.12.39	Meinel, Friedrich. Samuel Chappuzeau. Inaug. Diss. Borna, 1908.
	38576.12.40	Chappuzeau, Samuel. Genève delivrée; comédie. Genève, 1862.
	38576.12.42.2	Corneille, Thomas. Poèmes dramatiques. Paris, 1722. 5v.
	38576.12.42.3	Corneille, Thomas. Poèmes dramatiques. Paris, 1738. 5v.
	38576.12.42.10	Corneille, Thomas. Théâtre complet. Paris, 1881.
	38576.12.42.20	Corneille, Thomas. Chefs-d'oeuvre de Thomas Corneille. Paris, 1800.
	38576.12.42.21	Corneille, Thomas. Chefs-d'oeuvre. Paris, 1823.
	38576.12.42.22	Corneille, Thomas. Chefs-d'oeuvre. v.1-2. Paris, 1836.
	38576.12.42.30	Corneille, Thomas. Antiochus. Paris, 1691.
	38576.12.42.35	Corneille, Thomas. La forza dell'ambizione. Bologna, 1711.
	38576.12.42.40	Corneille, Thomas. Ariane. Paris, 1764.
	38576.12.42.45	Corneille, Thomas. The labyrinth. Dublin, 1795.
	38576.12.42.50	Corneille, Thomas. Le berger extravagant. Genève, 1960.
	38576.12.42.51	Corneille, Thomas. Le berger extravagant. Thèse. Genève, 1960.
	38576.12.42.55	Corneille, Thomas. Timocrate. Genève, 1970.
	38576.12.42.80	Reynier, Gustave. Thomas Corneille, sa vie et son théâtre. Paris, 1892.
	38576.12.42.85	Michaelis, Georg. Die Sogenannten "comédies espagnoles" des Thomas Corneille. Berlin, 1914.
	38576.12.42.90	Collins, David A. Thomas Corneille; protean dramatist. The Hague, 1966.
	38576.12.42.95	Coutil, Léon. IIe Centenaire de Thomas Corneille né à Rouen, le 20 août, 1625. Les Andelys, 1909.
	38576.12.43	Barthelemy, Charles. La comédie de Dancourt, 1685-1714. Paris, 1882.
	38576.12.44	Dancourt, Florent C. Le mari retrouvé; comédie. n.p., n.d.
	38576.12.44.10	Dancourt, Florent C. Le chevalier à la mode. Strassbourg, 1920.
	38576.12.45	Dancourt, Florent C. Les oeuvres de théâtre. Paris, 1760. 12v.
	38576.12.49	Pamphlet box. Dancourt, Florent C.
Htn	38576.12.50*	Desmares. La dragonne; ou Merlin dragon. La Haye, 1696.
Htn	38576.12.52*	Desmares. Roxelane; tragédie-comédie. Paris, 1643.
	38576.13	Donneau de Vizé, Jean. La veuve à la mode. Paris, 1881.
	38576.13.30	Donneau de Vizé, Jean. Trois comédies. Paris, 1940.
Htn	38576.14*	Donneau de Vizé, Jean. Les dames Vangées. Paris, 1695.
	38576.14.81	Mélèse, P. Donneau de Visé, fondateur du Mercure Galant. Paris, 1936.
	38576.14.83	Langheim, O. De Visé. Inaug. Diss. Wolfenbüttel, 1903.
	38576.15	Dumas. Le cocu en herbe et en gerbe. Turin, 1871.
	38576.16	Genest, C.C. Zelonide. Paris, 1682.
	38576.16.9	Pamphlet box. Genest, Charles Claude.
	38576.17	Guerin, N.A.M. Myrtil et Mélicerte. Paris, 1882.
	38576.19	Hauteroche, N. le B. de. Les apparences trompeuses. Paris, 1673.
	38576.19.1	Hauteroche, N. le B. de. Les oeuvres de théâtre. Paris, 1736. 2v.
	38576.19.2	Hauteroche, N. le B. de. Le cocher. Paris, 1685.
	38576.19.3	Hauteroche, N. le B. de. Crispin médecin. Paris, 1680.
	38576.19.3.2	Hauteroche, N. le B. de. Crispin médecin. Paris, 1894.
Htn	38576.19.5*	Hauteroche, N. le B. de. Crispin musicien. Paris, 1674.
	38576.19.7	Hauteroche, N. le B. de. Le deüil. Paris, 1673.
	38576.19.9	Hauteroche, N. le B. de. Les nobles de province. Lyon, 1678.
	38576.21	Arnaud, C. Étude sur la vie et les oeuvres de l'abbé d'Aubignac (Hédelin François). Paris, 1887.
Htn	38576.21.25*	Desjardins, Marie C.H. Le jaloux par force et le bonheur des femmes. Fribourch, 1668.
	38576.21.29	Magne, Émile. Madame de Villedieu. Paris, 1907.
	38576.21.30	Kretschmar, Amo. Madame de Villedieu. Weida, 1907.
	38576.21.31	Chatenet, H.E. Le roman...Mme. de Villedieu (1632-1683). Paris, 1911.
	38576.21.35	Desjardins, Marie C.H. Annales Galantes (Mme. de Villedieu de 1683). La Haye, 1700.
	38576.21.40	Desjardins, Marie C.H. Les désordres de l'amour. Genève, 1970.
Htn	38576.21.45*	Desjardins, Marie C.H. The disorders of love. London, 1677.
	38576.21.50	Desjardins, Marie C.H. Les amours des grands hommes. v.1-2. Amsterdam, 1712.
	38576.22	La Chapelle, Jean de. Oeuvres. Paris, 1683.
	38576.23	La Fosse d'Aubigny, A. de. Manlius Capitolinus. Paris, n.d.
	38576.23.5	La Fosse d'Aubigny, A. de. Manlius Capitolinus. Amsterdam, 1711.
Htn	38576.23.6*	La Fosse d'Aubigny, A. de. Polixene; tragédie. Paris, 1696.
	38576.24	Pamphlet box. La Fosse d'Aubigny, A. de.
Htn	38576.25*	Latuillerie, M. Les oeuvres. Paris, 1684.
	38576.25.5	Latuillerie, M. Théâtre. Amsterdam, 1745.
	38576.25.15	Le Noble, E. Les aventures provinciales. La Haye, 1710.
	38576.25.17	Le Noble, E. Les avantures provinciales, ou, Le voyage de Falaize. Paris, 1697.
Htn	38576.26*	Le Noble, E. Esope. Paris, 1691.
	38576.26.5	Le Noble, E. L'histoire...de la conjuration des Pazzi. v.1-2. Paris, 1698.
	38576.27	Le Noble, E. Le gage touché. Histoires galantes et comiques. Amsterdam, 1724.
	38576.27.5	Le Noble, E. Pure love. London, 1750.
	38576.27.25	Pamphlet box. Magnon, Joannes.
	38576.27.28	Magnon, J. de. Josaphat, tragi-comédie. Paris, 1647.
	38576.27.31	Magnon, J. de. Tite: a tragi-comedy. Diss. Baltimore, 1936.
	38576.27.35	Longepierre, M. de. Medée. Paris? 16- ?
	38576.28.2	Mairet, Jean de. Silva. Bamberg, 1890.
Htn	38576.28.5*	Mairet, Jean de. L'illustre corsaire. Paris, 1640.
Htn	38576.29*	Mairet, Jean de. La Sylvie et autres oeuvres poétiques. Paris, 1631.
Htn	38576.29.3*	Mairet, Jean de. La Sylvie. Paris, 1635.
	38576.29.5	Mairet, Jean de. La Sylvie. Paris, 1905.
	38576.29.6	Mairet, Jean de. La Sylvie. Paris, 1905.
Htn	38576.30*	Mairet, Jean de. La Sophonisbe. Paris, 1635.
Htn	38576.30.5*	Mairet, Jean de. L'Athenais. Paris, 1642.
	38576.32	Bizos, G. Étude sur la vie et les oeuvres de Jean de Mairet. Paris, 1877.
	38576.32.5	Dannheiser, E. Studien zu Jean de Mairet's Leben und Werken. Sudwigshafen, 1888.
	38576.32.9	Pamphlet box. Mairet, Jean de.
	38576.33	Montfleury, Zacherie Jacob. Théâtre de Messieurs de Montfleury. Paris, 1739. 3v.
	38576.34	Montfleury, Zacherie Jacob. Théâtre de Messieurs de Montfleury, père et fils. Paris, 1775. 4v.
Htn	38576.34.2*	Montfleury, Antoine Jacob. L'ambigu comique. Paris, 1673.
Htn	38576.34.4*	Montfleury, Antoine Jacob. L'escole des filles. Paris, 1666.
Htn	38576.34.6*	Montfleury, Antoine Jacob. L'escole des jaloux. Paris, 1668.
Htn	38576.34.8*	Montfleury, Antoine Jacob. La femme juge et partie. Paris, 1669.
Htn	38576.34.10*	Montfleury, Antoine Jacob. La fille capitaine. Paris, 1672.
Htn	38576.34.12*	Montfleury, Antoine Jacob. Le mariage de rien. Paris, 1680.
Htn	38576.34.14*	Montfleury, Antoine Jacob. Trasibule. Paris, 1705.
Htn	38576.34.16*	Montfleury, Antoine Jacob. Trigaudin. Paris, 1674.
	38576.34.20	Montfleury, Antoine Jacob. Les oeuvres de Monsieur Montfleury. Paris, 1705.
	38576.35	Pamphlet box. Montfleury.
	38576.39	Palaprat, Jean. Oeuvres. Paris, 1712. 2v.
	38576.39.80	Franz, Henry. Palaprat; son temps, ses oeuvres. Paris, 1916.
Htn	38576.41*	Perrin, Pierre. Les oeuvres de poesie. Paris, 1661.
	38576.42	Perrin, Pierre. Bacchus et Ariane. n.p., n.d.
Htn	38576.45*	Pradon, J. Le théâtre. Paris, 1695.
Htn	38576.46*	Pradon, J. Oeuvres. Paris, 1688.
Htn	38576.47*	Pradon, J. Phèdre et Hippolyte; tragédie. Paris, 1679.
Htn	38576.47.5*	Pradon, J. Phèdre et Hippolyte. Paris, 1677.
	38576.48	Rosimond, C. la R. Le duel fantasque; ou Les valets. Grenoble, 1668.
	38576.48.50	Bussom, Thomas W. The life and dramatic works of Pradon. Paris, 1922.
	38576.48.52	Bussom, Thomas W. A rival of Racine. Paris, 1922.
Htn	38576.49*	Rosimond, C. la R. Le volontaire. Paris, 1676.
Htn	38576.55*	Les privileges du Cocuage. Vicon, 1725.

38581 Individual authors, etc. - 1661-1715 - Drama - Racine - Folios [Discontinued]

	38581.3	Racine, Jean. Oeuvres. Paris, 1760. 3v.
	38581.7A	Racine, Jean. Oeuvres complètes. Paris, 1825. 7v.
	38581.7B	Racine, Jean. Oeuvres complètes. Paris, 1825. 7v.
	38581.8	Racine, Jean. Oeuvres complètes. Paris, 1825-1826. 5v.
	38581.10	Racine, Jean. Oeuvres. Paris, 1833.
	38581.15	Racine, Jean. Oeuvres. Paris, 1873.
	38581.16	Racine, Jean. Oeuvres. Paris, 1882.

38581 Individual authors, etc. - 1661-1715 - Drama - Racine - Folios [Discontinued] - cont.

Htn 38581.17* Racine, Jean. Athalie. Paris, 1691.
38581.22 Delfour, S.C. La Bible dans Racine. Paris, 1891.

38582 Individual authors, etc. - 1661-1715 - Drama - Racine - Complete and Selected works - 18th and early 19th century editions

Htn 38582.2* Racine, Jean. Oeuvres. Paris, 1697. 2v.
38582.2.5 Racine, Jean. Oeuvres. Paris, 1702. 2v.
38582.2.9 Racine, Jean. Oeuvres. Amsterdam, 1714. 2v.
Htn 38582.3* Racine, Jean. Oeuvres. Paris, 1741. 2v.
38582.3.7 Racine, Jean. Oeuvres. Amsterdam, 1743. 3v.
38582.4 Racine, Jean. Oeuvres. Paris, 1779. 3v.
38582.5 Racine, Jean. Oeuvres. Paris, 1789. 3v.
38582.6 Racine, Jean. Oeuvres. v.1-2,4-5. Paris, 1799. 4v.
Htn 38582.6.10F* Racine, Jean. Oeuvres. The 56 plates only. Paris, 1801-05.
38582.7 Racine, Jean. Oeuvres. Paris, 1807. 5v.
38582.7.5 Racine, Jean. Oeuvres. Paris, 1808. 7v.
38582.8 Racine, Jean. Oeuvres. Paris, 1810. 4v.
38582.9 Racine, Jean. Oeuvres. v.5. Paris, 1810.
38582.10 Racine, Jean. Oeuvres. Paris, 1822. 4v.
38582.10.5A Racine, Jean. Oeuvres. Paris, 1827-1828. 5v.
38582.10.5B Racine, Jean. Oeuvres. Paris, 1827-1828. 5v.
38582.11 Racine, Jean. Oeuvres. Paris, 1829. 5v.
38582.11.2 Racine, Jean. Oeuvres. v.4. Paris, 1830.
38582.11.25 Racine, Jean. Oeuvres dramatiques. London, 1824-34. 3v.
38582.12 Racine, Jean. Oeuvres. v.3-4. Paris, 1835.
38582.12.3 Racine, Jean. Oeuvres. Angers, 1836. 3v.
38582.12.5 Racine, Jean. Oeuvres. v.1-4. Paris, 1837. 2v.
38582.13 Racine, Jean. Oeuvres complètes. Paris, 1856. 2v.
38582.18 Racine, Jean. Théâtre complète. Paris, 1844.
38582.19 Racine, Jean. Théâtre complète. Paris, 1847.
38582.19.15 Racine, Jean. Théâtre complète. Paris, 1855.
38582.19.525 Racine, Jean. Oeuvres choisies. N.Y., 1855.
38582.20 Fasquelle, Louis. Chefs d'oeuvre de Jean Racine. N.Y., 1856.
38582.20.5 Fasquelle, Louis. Chefs d'oeuvre de Jean Racine. N.Y., 1861.
38582.22 Racine, Jean. Ausgewählte Tragödien. Leipzig, 1886.

38583 Individual authors, etc. - 1661-1715 - Drama - Racine - Complete and Selected works - Later editions

38583.3 Mensard, Paul. Oeuvres de Jean Racine. Album et musique. Paris, 1865-73. 10v.
38583.3.2 Racine, Jean. Oeuvres. Paris, 1864.
38583.3.4 Racine, Jean. Oeuvres complètes. 2. éd. Paris, 1822. 6v.
38583.3.5 Racine, Jean. Oeuvres. Paris, 1870.
38583.3.7 Racine, Jean. Oeuvres. Amsterdam, 1744. 2v.
38583.3.15 Racine, Jean. Oeuvres. Paris, 1885. 8v.
38583.3.16 Racine, Jean. Album. Paris, 1873.
38583.3.17 Racine, Jean. Musique des choeurs. Paris, 1873.
38583.3.20 Racine, Jean. Oeuvres complètes. Paris, 1951.
38583.3.22 Racine, Jean. Oeuvres complètes. v.1. Paris, 1956.
38583.4 Racine, Jean. Oeuvres. Paris, n.d. 5v.
38583.4.20 Racine, Jean. Théâtre complet. Paris, 1852.
38583.4.21 Racine, Jean. Théâtre complet. Paris, 1854.
38583.4.23 Racine, Jean. Théâtre complet. Paris, 1857.
38583.4.25 Racine, Jean. Théâtre complet. N.Y., 1861.
38583.4.30A Racine, Jean. Théâtre complet. Paris, 1863.
38583.4.30B Racine, Jean. Théâtre complet. Paris, 1863.
38583.5 Racine, Jean. Théâtre complet. Paris, 1869.
38583.5.5 Racine, Jean. Théâtre complet. Paris, n.d.
NEDL 38583.5.10 Racine, Jean. Théâtre complet. Paris, n.d.
38583.5.12 Racine, Jean. Théâtre complet. Paris, n.d.
38583.6 Albert, Paul. Théâtre de J. Racine. Paris, 1878. 2v.
38583.6.5 Racine, Jean. Théâtre. Paris, 1880. 3v.
38583.6.9 Racine, Jean. Théâtre complet. Paris, 1882. 4v.
38583.6.12 Racine, Jean. Théâtre complet. Paris, 1889.
38583.6.13 Racine, Jean. Théâtre complet. Paris, n.d.
38583.6.14 Racine, Jean. Complete plays. N.Y., 1967. 2v.
38583.6.15 Racine, Jean. Théâtre complet. Illustré. v.1-3. Paris, n.d.
38583.6.20A Racine, Jean. Théâtre. Paris, 1933. 2v.
38583.6.20B Racine,Jean. Théâtre. Paris, 1933.
38583.6.30 Racine, Jean. Théâtre. Paris, 1951-52. 5v.
38583.6.35 Racine, Jean. Théâtre complet. Lausanne, 1962. 2v.
38583.6.40 Racine, Jean. Théâtre complet. Paris, 1967.
38583.7.10 Racine, Jean. Théâtre complet. Paris, 1847.
38583.8 Racine, Jean. Théâtre complet. Paris, n.d.
38583.8.15 Racine, Jean. Théâtre choisi. 8. éd. Paris, 1913.
38583.8.25 Racine, Jean. Théâtre de 1664 à 1667. Paris, 1929.
38583.9 Racine, Jean. Lettres inédites. Paris, 1862.
38583.10 Racine, Jean. Letters from Mons. Racine...to his son. London, 1785.
38583.11 Racine, Jean. Lettres à son fils. Paris, 1922.
38583.11.10 Racine, Jean. Lettres d'Uzès. Uzès, 1929.
38583.11.11 Racine, Jean. Lettres d'Uzès. Uzès, 1963.
38583.11.50 Racine, Jean. Poesies. Paris, 1936.
38583.11.60 Racine, Jean. Intimité de Racine. Le Raincy, 1947.
38583.12.10 Racine, Jean. Dramatic works. v.2. London, 1911.
38583.12.25A Racine, Jean. The best plays of Racine. Princeton, 1936.
38583.12.25B Racine, Jean. The best plays of Racine. Princeton, 1936.
38583.12.26 Racine, Jean. The best plays of Racine. Princeton, 1957.
38583.12.27 Racine, Jean. Five plays. N.Y., 1960.
38583.12.30 Racine, Jean. Racine's mid-career tragedies. Princeton, 1958.
38583.14 Racine, Jean. Oeuvres inconnues. n.p., 1911.
38583.18 Racine, Jean. Poésies religieuses inconnues. Landerman, 1954.
38583.20 Racine, Jean. Fedra, Andromaca, Britanico, Ester. Buenos Aires, 1939. 2v.
38583.21 Racine, Jean. Three plays. Chicago, 1961.
38583.22 Racine, Jean. Abrégé de l'histoire de Port-Royal, suivi de la Thébaide et de Alexandre le Grand. Paris, 1969.

38585.1 - .18 Individual authors, etc. - 1661-1715 - Drama - Racine - Biography and criticism

38585.1 Pamphlet box. Racine.
X Cg 38585.2.3 Bury, Blaize (Mme.). Racine and the French classical drama. London, 1845.
38585.3 Deltour, Felix. Les enemis de Racine. Paris, 1859.
38585.4 Pons, A.J. Les éditions illustrées de Racine. Paris, 1878.

38585.1 - .18 Individual authors, etc. - 1661-1715 - Drama - Racine - Biography and criticism - cont.

38585.5 Séché, Léon. Port-Royal des Champs, petit manuel...suivi de Racine à Port-Royal. Paris, 1899.
38585.5.9 Michaut, G. La Bérénice de Racine. Paris, 1907.
38585.6 Roy, Just Jean Ést. Histoire de Jean Racine. Tours, 1872.
38585.7 Soullie, P. Études sur les tragédies de Racine. Paris, 1878.
38585.7.10 Orgel, Vera. A new view of the plays of Racine. London, 1948.
38585.8 Deschanel, Émile. Racine. Paris, 1884. 2v.
38585.8.2 Deschanel, Émile. Racine. Paris, 1885. 2v.
38585.8.5 Truc, Gonzague. Jean Racine, l'oeuvre, l'artiste, l'homme et le temps. Paris, 1926.
38585.8.7 Dubech, Lucien. Jean Racine politique. Paris, 1926.
38585.8.12 Fubini, Mario. Jean Racine é la critica delle sue tragédie. Torino, 1925.
38585.8.17 Saint-René Taillandier, Madeleine M.L. (Mme.). Racine. Paris, 1927.
38585.8.19 Saint-René Taillandier, Madeleine M.L. (Mme.). Racine. 4e éd. Paris, 1940.
38585.9 Larochefoucauld-Liancourt, Frédéric Gaëtan. Études littéraires et morales de Racine. Paris, 1855.
38585.9.5 Fontanier, Pierre. Études de la langue française sur Racine. Paris, 1818.
38585.9.10 Fontanier, Pierre. Études de la langue française sur Racine. v.1-2. Paris, 1818.
38585.10 Dugit, Ernest. Racine. Paris, 1878.
38585.11 Robert, Pierre. La poètique de France. Paris, 1890.
38585.12 Dupin, Charles. Lettre à mylady Morgan sur Racine et Shakespeare. Paris, 1818.
38585.13 Monceaux, Paul. Racine. Paris, 1892.
38585.14 Larroumet, Gustave. Racine. Paris, 1898.
NEDL 38585.14.5 Lemaitre, J. Jean Racine. 15e éd. Paris, 1908.
38585.14.7 Lemaitre, Jules. Jean Racine. 21e éd. Paris, 1908.
X Cg 38585.14.7 Lemaitre, Jules. Jean Racine. 21e éd. Paris, 1908.
38585.14.7.5 Lemaitre, Jules. Jean Racine. Paris, 1922.
Htn 38585.14.8* Jovy, Ernest. Une contribution indirecte à l'histoire de Racine. Paris, 1928.
38585.14.9 Jovy, Ernest. De Royer-Collard à Racine. Saint-Dizier, 1917.
38585.14.10 Jovy, Ernest. La bibliothèque des Racines; Jean, Jean-Baptiste et L. Racine. Paris, 1933.
38585.14.11 Martinez Ruiz, José. Racine y Molière. Madrid, 1924.
38585.15 Dreyfus-Brisac, E. Plagiats et réminiscences. Paris, n.d.
38585.16 Bidois, Georges le. La vie la tragédie de Racine. Paris, 1901.
38585.16.10 Truc, Gonzague. Le cas Racine. Paris, 1921.
38585.16.24A Duclaux, A. (Mme.). The life of Racine. N.Y., 1925?
38585.16.24B Duclaux, A. (Mme.). The life of Racine. N.Y., 1925?
38585.16.25 Duclaux, A. (Mme.). The life of Racine. London, 1925.
38585.16.26 Duclaux, A. (Mme.). Racine. Paris, 1940.
38585.16.30A Mauriac, François. La vie de Jean Racine. Paris, 1928.
38585.16.30B Mauriac, François. La vie de Jean Racine. Paris, 1928.
38585.16.35 Bentmann, F. Die Geschichte der Racine-Kritik in der französischen Romantik. Wertheim, 1930.
38585.16.35.5 Bentmann, F. Die Geschichte der Racine-Kritik in der französischen Romantik. Wertheim, 1931.
38585.16.40 Brémond, Henri. Racine et Valéry. Paris, 1930.
38585.16.45 Maulnier, Thierry. Racine. Paris, 1935.
38585.16.48 Talagrand, J. Racine. 32e éd. Paris, 1947.
38585.16.49 Maulnier, Thierry. Racine. 49e éd. Paris, 1958.
38585.16.50 Lichtenstein, J. Racine, poète biblique. Paris, 1934.
38585.16.55 Müller, Curt. Die "Phlldra" Racines. Inaug. Diss. Leipzig, 1936.
38585.16.60 Lyonnet, Henry. Les "premières" de Jean Racine. Paris, 1924.
38585.16.65 Geleerd, Sara. Les traductions hollandaises de Racine au XVIIe et au XIIIe siècles. Zutphen, 1936.
38585.16.70 Karl, Ludwig. Jean Racine. Wien, 1937.
38585.16.75 Haley, Marie P. Racine and the Art poètique of Boileau. Baltimore, 1938.
38585.16.80 Clark, Alexander Frederick Bruce. Jean Racine. Cambridge, 1939.
38585.16.80.2 Clark, Alexander Frederick Bruce. Jean Racine. N.Y., 1969.
38585.16.84 Baldensperger, F. La souplesse du monosyllable dans diction de Racine. n.p., 1939.
38585.16.84.10 Baldensperger, F. Racine et la tradition romanesque. Paris, 1939.
38585.16.86 Giraudoux, J. Racine. Cambridge, 1938.
38585.16.90 Savory, D.L. Jean Racine. London, 1940.
38585.16.95 William, E.E. Racine depuis 1885. Baltimore, 1940.
38585.16.100 Houben, H. Der Chor in den Tragödien des Racine. Düsseldorf, 1894.
38585.16.105 Vossler, Karl. Jean Racine. München, 1926
38585.16.106 Vossler, Karl. Jean Racine. N.Y., 1972.
38585.16.110 Segond, Joseph. Psychologie de Jean Racine. Paris, 1940.
38585.16.115 Mersch, Ernest. Racine et nous, 1639-1939. Liége, 1939.
38585.16.120 Becthum le Ducq, M. Défense de Racine. Paris, 1934.
38585.16.125 Moreau, Pierre. Racine, l'homme et l'oeuvre. Paris, 1943.
38585.16.130 Crouzet, Paul. Tout Racine ici, à Port-Royal. Paris, 1940.
38585.16.135 Dimier, Louis. Racine perdu et retrouvé. Paris, 1941.
38585.16.140 Schröder, R.A. Racine und die deutsche Humanität. München, 1932.
38585.16.145A Guéguen, Pierre. Poésie de Racine. Paris, 1946.
38585.16.145B Guéguen, Pierre. Poésie de Racine. Paris, 1946.
38585.16.150 Grimmer, G. Andromaque de Racine. Paris, 1946.
38585.16.155 Freudeman, Erika R. Das Adjektiv und seine Ausdruckswerte im Stils Racine. Berlin, 1941.
38585.16.163 Lion, Fernand. Les rêves de Racine. 6. éd. Paris, 1948.
38585.16.165 May, Georges C. D'Ovide à Racine. Paris, 1949.
38585.16.170 Lacretelle, Pierre de. La vie privée de Racine. Paris, 1949.
38585.16.175 Bailly, A. Racine. Paris, 1949.
38585.16.180 Brereton, G. Jean Racine. London, 1951.
38585.16.185 Siciliano, Italo. Racine. Padova, 1950.
38585.16.190 Orcibal, Jean. La genèse d'Esther et d'Athalie...Racine. Paris, 1950.
38585.16.195 Knight, Roy Clement. Racine et la Grèce. Paris, 1951.
38585.16.195.2 Knight, Roy Clement. Racine et la Grèce. Thèse. Paris, 1950.
38585.16.200 Tielrooy, J.B. Jean Racine. Amsterdam, 1951.
38585.16.205 Vinaver, E. Racine et la poésie tragique. Paris, 1951.
38585.16.206 Vinaver, E. Racine and poetic tragedy. Manchester, 1955.
38585.16.210 Pommier, Jean. Aspects de Racine. Paris, 1954.

38585.1 - .18 Individual authors, etc. - 1661-1715 - Drama - Racine - Biography and criticism - cont.

38585.16.215 Grasclaude, P. Le renoncement de Jean Racine. Paris, 1955.
38585.16.220 Lapp, John C. Aspects of Racinian tragedy. Toronto, 1955.
38585.16.225 Port Royal, France. Musée national des Granges de Port Royal. Racine et Port-Royal. Paris, 1955.
38585.16.230 Wheatley, K.E. Racine and English classicism. Austin, 1956.
38585.16.235 Claudel, Paul. Conversation sur Jean Racine. Paris, 1956.
38585.16.240 Goldmann, Lucien. Jean Racine. Paris, 1956.
38585.16.241 Goldmann, Lucien. Jean Racine. Paris, 1970.
38585.16.245 Dédéyan, Charles. La Phèdre de Racine. Paris, 1956.
38585.16.250 Knight, Roy Clement. Racine, convention and classicism. Swansea, 1952.
38585.16.255 Jasinski, René. Vers le vrai Racine. Paris, 1958. 2v.
38585.16.260 Cahiers raciniens. Paris. 1,1957+ 4v.
38585.16.265 Hubert, J.D. Essai d'exégèse racinienne. Paris, 1956.
38585.16.270 Descotes, Maurice. Les grands rôles du théâtre de Jean Racine. 1. éd. Paris, 1957.
38585.16.275 Mongredien, Georges. Athalée. Paris, 1929.
38585.16.280 Moore, Will G. Racine. London, 1960.
38585.16.285 Weinrich, Harald. Tragische und komische Elemente in Racines Andromaque. Münster, 1958.
38585.16.290 Vinaver, Eugene. L'action poètique dans le théâtre de Racine. Oxford, 1960.
38585.16.295 Tans, J.A.G. Vrijheid en voorbeschibbing bij Racine. Groningen, 1959.
38585.16.300 Butler, Philip. Classicisme et baroque dans l'oeuvre de Racine. Paris, 1959.
38585.16.305 Coenen, Hans Georg. Elemente der Racineschen Dialoglechnik. Münster, 1961.
38585.16.310 Stapfer, Paul. Racine et Victor Hugo. 6. éd. Paris, 1897.
38585.16.315 Bady, René. Portrait de Jean Racine. Fribourg, 1940.
38585.16.320 Blum, M. Le thème symbolique dans le théâtre de Racine. Paris, 1962. 2v.
38585.16.325 Weinberg, B. The art of Jean Racine. Chicago, 1963.
38585.16.330 Barthes, R. Sur Racine. Paris, 1963.
38585.16.331 Barthes, R. On Racine. 1. ed. N.Y., 1964.
38585.16.335 Congrès international Racinien. Actes du 1er congrès international Racinien. Uzès, 1962.
38585.16.340 Vivaver, E. Racine et la poésie tragique. 2. éd. Paris, 1963.
38585.16.345 Stone, John A. Sophocles and Racine. Genève, 1964.
38585.16.350 Baudouin, Charles. Jean Racine, l'infant du desert. Paris, 1963.
38585.16.355 Vaunois, Louis. L'enfance et la jeunesse de Racine. Paris, 1964.
38585.16.360 France, Peter. Racine's rhetoric. Oxford, 1965.
38585.16.365 Montifaud, Marc de. Racine et la voisin. Paris, 1878.
38585.16.370 Tilley, Arthur. Three French dramatists: Racine, Marivaux, Musset. N.Y., 1967.
38585.16.375 Paganelli, Don Sauveur. Jean Racine, essai. Uzès, 1966.
38585.16.380 Bibliothèque nationale, Paris. Jean Racine, Paris, 1967. Paris, 1967.
38585.16.385 Spillebout, Gabriel. Le vocabulaire, biblique dans les tragédies sacrées de Racine. Genève, 1968.
38585.16.390 Knight, Roy Clement. Racine. London, 1969.
38585.16.395 Fingerhut, Margret. Racine in deutschen Übersetzungen des neunzehnten und zwanzigsten Jahrhunderts. Bonn, 1970.
38585.16.401 Bowra, Cecil Maurice. The simplicity of Racine. Folcroft, 1970.
38585.16.410 Besançon, France. Université. Laboratoire d'analyse lexicologique. J. Racine, "Andromanque." Paris, 1970.
38585.16.415 Ambroze, Anna. Racine, poète du sacrifice. Paris, 1970.
38585.17 Masson-Forestier, Alfred. Autour d'un Racine ignoré. Paris, 1910.
38585.18.35 Racine, Jean. Andromaque....with English translation. N.Y., 1855.
38585.18.60 Picard, Raymond. La carrière de Jean Racine. 3. éd. Paris, 1956.
38585.18.60.5 Picard, Raymond. La carrière de Jean Racine d'après les documents contemporains. Thèse. Paris, 1956.
38585.18.60.10 Picard, Raymond. La carrière de Jean Racine. Paris, 1961.
38585.18.65 Picard, Raymond. Corpus Racinianum. Paris, 1956.
38585.18.65.2 Picard, Raymond. Corpus Racinianum. Supplement. Paris, 1961.
38585.18.70 Picard, Raymond. Corpus Racinianum. Thèse. Paris, 1956.
38585.18.75 Picard, Raymond. Racine polémiste. Paris, 1967.

38585.19 - .54 Individual authors, etc. - 1661-1715 - Drama - Racine - Individual works

NEDL 38585.19 Racine, Jean. Andromaque. Paris, 1886.
38585.19.1 Racine, Jean. Chefs-d'oeuvre de Jean Racine. Andromaque. Les plaideurs. Paris, 1874.
38585.19.1.3 Racine, Jean. Andromaque. Les plaideurs. Paris, 1887.
38585.19.1.5 Racine, Jean. Andromaque; tragédie. Paris, 1884.
38585.19.2 Racine, Jean. Andromaque. London, 1889.
38585.19.4 Racine, Jean. Andromaque, tragédie. London, 1893.
38585.19.5 Racine, Jean. Andromaque. Paris, 1896.
38585.19.6 Racine, Jean. Andromaque. Boston, 1910.
38585.19.7 Racine, Jean. Andromaque. Strasbourg, n.d.
38585.19.8 Racine, Jean. Andromaque, tragédie. Paris, 18- .
38585.19.9 Racine, Jean. Andromaque. Iphigénie. Athalie. Paris, 1900. 2v.
38585.19.9.5 Racine, Jean. Andromaque. Paris, 1945.
38585.19.9.8 Racine, Jean. Andromaque. Paris, 1961.
38585.19.9.10 Racine, Jean. Andromaque. Paris, 1962.
Htn 38585.19.10* Racine, Jean. The distrest mother. London, 1712.
38585.19.10.5 Racine, Jean. Andrómaca; tragédia en cincos actos. Nueva York, 1855.
38585.19.11 Racine, Jean. Andromache eller ett oint Moders-Hierta. Stockholm, 1723.
38585.19.50 Racine, Jean. Athalie. N.Y., 1871.
38585.19.51 Racine, Jean. Athalie. N.Y., 1871.
38585.19.60 Racine, Jean. Athalie; tragédie. 10th éd. London, 1885.
38585.20 Racine, Jean. Athalie. Paris, 1887.
38585.20.2 Racine, Jean. Athalie. London, 1893.
38585.20.4 Racine, Jean. Athalie. London, 1896.
38585.20.5A Racine, Jean. Athalie. Paris, 1896.
38585.20.5B Racine, Jean. Athalie. Paris, 1896.
38585.20.6 Racine, Jean. Athalie. Boston, 1898.
38585.20.9 Racine, Jean. Athalie. Paris, 1905.
38585.20.9.5 Racine, Jean. Athalie. London, 1908.
38585.20.10 Racine, Jean. Athalie. Strasbourg, n.d.
38585.20.11 Racine, Jean. Athalie. Paris, 1962.
38585.20.12 Racine, Jean. Athalie. Paris, 1920.

38585.19 - .54 Individual authors, etc. - 1661-1715 - Drama - Racine - Individual works - cont.

38585.20.13 Racine, Jean. Athalie. Paris, 1952.
Htn 38585.20.15* Racine, Jean. Athaliah. London, 1722.
38585.20.16A Racine, Jean. Athalie. Cambridge, 1897.
38585.20.16B Racine, Jean. Athalie. Cambridge, 1897.
38585.20.16C Racine, Jean. Athalie. Cambridge, 1897.
38585.20.17 Racine, Jean. Athaliah. Edinburgh, 1815.
38585.21 Racine, Jean. Esther. Tragôdia. En Hermoupolie, 1851.
38585.22 Racine, Jean. Bajazet. Paris, 18- .
38585.23 Racine, Jean. Bajazet. Paris, 1898.
38585.23.30 Racine, Jean. Bajazet. Neuva-York, 1855.
38585.23.40 Racine, Jean. Bajazet. Paris, 1947.
38585.23.45 Racine, Jean. Bajazet. London, 1964.
38585.23.48 Racine, Jean. Bajazet. London, 1968.
38585.23.75 Scherer, Jacques. Racine. v.1-2. Paris, 1956.
38585.24 Racine, Jean. Two tragedies. London, 1714.
38585.25.10 Racine, Jean. Britannicus. 3e éd. Bielefeld, 1869.
38585.25.25 Racine, Jean. Britannicus. Paris, 1882.
38585.26 Racine, Jean. Britannicus. Paris, 1889.
38585.27 Racine, Jean. Britannicus. London, 1886.
38585.27.9 Racine, Jean. Britannicus. N.Y., 1925.
38585.27.15 Racine, Jean. Britannicus. Cambridge, 1967.
Htn 38585.28* Racine, Jean. Esther. Paris, 1689.
38585.28.5 Racine, Jean. Esther. N.Y., 1883.
38585.29 Racine, Jean. Esther. Paris, 1889.
38585.29.5 Racine, Jean. Esther; tragédie, 1689. Heitz, 19- .
38585.30.15 Racine, Jean. Die uneinigen Brüder. Berlin, 1756?
38585.32 Racine, Jean. Ifigenia in Aulis. Amsterdam, 1781.
38585.33 Racine, Jean. Iphigénie. Paris, 1888.
38585.34 Racine, Jean. Iphigénie. London, 1886.
38585.34.15 Racine, Jean. Iphigénie. Paris, 1890.
38585.34.25 Racine, Jean. Iphigénie. 8. éd. Paris, 1906.
38585.35 Racine, Jean. Iphigénie. Paris, 1910.
38585.35.10 Racine, Jean. Iphigénia. Harmondsworth, 1963.
38585.38 Racine, Jean. Mithridate; tragédie. Paris, 1760.
38585.39 Racine, Jean. Mithridate. Paris, 1760.
38585.40A Racine, Jean. Mithridate. Chicago, 1921.
38585.40B Racine, Jean. Mithridate. Chicago, 1921.
38585.40.15 Racine, Jean. Mithridate; tragédie. Chicago, 1922.
38585.40.50A Racine, Jean. Mithridate. Medford, 1926.
38585.40.50B Racine, Jean. Mithridate. Medford, 1926.
38585.42 Racine, Jean. Phèdre. Strasbourg, n.d.
38585.42.6 Racine, Jean. Fedra. Neuva-York, 1855.
38585.43 Racine, Jean. Phèdre. London, 1892.
38585.43.3 Racine, Jean. Phèdre, tragédie en cinq actes. London, 1897.
38585.43.4 Racine, Jean. Phaedre. N.Y., 1866.
38585.43.4.12 Racine, Jean. Phaedre. Boston, 1910.
38585.43.5 Racine, Jean. Phèdre. N.Y., 188-?
38585.43.6 Racine, Jean. Phaedra. N.Y., 1905?
NEDL 38585.43.7 Racine, Jean. Phaedra. N.Y., 1896?
38585.43.7.5 Racine, Jean. Phaedra. N.Y., 1880.
38585.43.8 Racine, Jean. Phèdre. Manchester, 1943.
38585.43.9 Dreyfus-Brisac, E. Phèdre et Hippolyte ou Racine moraliste. Paris, 1902.
38585.43.10 Schlegel, A.W. Comparaison entre la Phèdre de Racine et celle d'Euripide. Paris, 1807.
38585.43.12 Lugli, Vittorio. Interpretazione di Phèdre. Rocca san Casciano, 1958.
38585.43.15 Racine, Jean. Phaedra. Great Neck, 1958.
38585.43.17 Racine, Jean. Phaedra. San Francisco, 1958.
38585.43.18 Racine, Jean. Phaedra. N.Y., 1959.
38585.43.20 Racine, Jean. Phaedra (Racine's Phèdre). N.Y., 1961.
38585.43.22 Racine, Jean. Phèdre. N.Y., 1962.
38585.43.24 Mauron, Charles. Phèdre. Paris, 1968.
38585.43.45 Racine, Jean. Les plaideurs. Leipzig, 1854.
38585.43.50 Racine, Jean. Les plaideurs. N.Y., 1885.
38585.43.55 Racine, Jean. Phèdre. London, 1961.
38585.43.60 Racine, Jean. Fedra. Milano, 1959.
38585.43.61 Racine, Jean. Fedra. 2. éd. Milano, 1963.
38585.43.65 Maulnier, Picary. Lecture de "Phèdre". Paris, 1967.
38585.44 Racine, Jean. Les plaideurs. Paris, 1887.
38585.44.3 Racine, Jean. Les plaideurs. London, 1872.
38585.44.5 Racine, Jean. Les plaideurs. London, 1895.
38585.44.9 Racine, Jean. Les plaideurs. Boston, 1906.
38585.44.15 Racine, Jean. The litigants. London, 1928.
38585.44.20 Tüchert, Aloys. Racine und Heliodor. Zweibrücken, 1889.
38585.45 Racine, Jean. Jule Cesar. Paris, 1962.
38585.46 Racine, Jean. The suitors. Detroit, 1862. 2v.
38585.46.5 Racine, Jean. The suitors. N.Y., 1871.
38585.47.10 Racine, Jean. Bérénice. N.Y., 1815.
38585.47.15 Racine, Jean. Bérénice. Manchester, 1929.
38585.47.16 Racine, Jean. Bérénice. London, 1965.
38585.48 Racine, Jean. Principes de la tragédie en marge de la poétique d'Aristote. Manchester, 1944.
38585.49 Racine, Jean. Théâtre complet. Paris, 1892.
38585.52 Racine, Jean. Confessions. London, 1956.
38585.53 Racine, Jean. Théâtre. Paris, 1880. 3v.

38585.55 - .89 Individual authors, etc. - 1661-1715 - Drama - Racine - Criticism [Discontinued]

38585.57 Pommier, Jean. Tradition litteraire et modeles vivants dans l'Andromaque. Cambridge, 1962.
38585.58 Besançon, France. Université. Centre d'étude du vocabulaire français. Jean Racine, Phèdre. Concordances. Paris, 1966.
38585.59 Dédéyan, Charles. Racine et sa Phèdre. Paris, 1965.
38585.60 Cambier, Maurice. Racine et Madame de Maintenon. Bruxelles, 1949.
38585.62 Edwards, Michael. La Thébaide de Racine. Paris, 1965.
38585.63 Mourques, Odette de. Racine; or, The triumph of relevance. Cambridge, 1967.
38585.64 Strarre, Evert van der. Racine et le théâtre de l'ambiquité. Leiden, 1966.
38585.66 Mercanton, Jacques. Racine. Paris, 1966.
38585.68 Mourques, Odette de. Autonomie de Racine. Paris, 1967.
38585.70 Biermann, Karlheinrich. Selbstentfremdung und Missverstandnis in den Tragödien Racines. Bad Homburg, 1969.
38585.72 Guibert, Albert Jean. Bibliographie des oeuvres de Jean Racine publiées au XVIIIe siècle. Paris, 1968.
38585.74 Gutwirth, Marcel. Jean Racine; un itineraire poétique. Montréal, 1970.
38585.76 Champseix, P.G. Considération générales sur Phèdre et le théâtre. Lausanne, 1853.
38585.78 Delcroix, Maurice. Le sacré dans les tragédies profanes de Racine. Paris, 1970.

38585.55 - .89 Individual authors, etc. - 1661-1715 - Drama - Racine - Criticism [Discontinued] - cont.

38585.80 Elliot, Revel. Mythe et legende dans le théâtre de Racine. Paris, 1969.

38587.1 - .19 Individual authors, etc. - 1661-1715 - Drama - Other dramatists - Regnard

38587.3.25 Regnard, Jean François. Oeuvres. v.2. Amsterdam, 1971.
38587.4 Oeuvres de Regnard. Paris, 1778. 4v.
38587.4.10 Regnard, Jean François. Oeuvres. Paris, 1789-90. 4v.
38587.6 Regnard, Jean François. Oeuvres. v.4. Paris, 1810.
38587.6.5 Regnard, Jean François. Oeuvres. v.1-5. Paris, 1817-1901. 3v.
38587.7 Regnard, Jean François. Oeuvres. Paris, 1820. 6v.
38587.8 Regnard, Jean François. Oeuvres complètes de Regnard. Paris, 1826. 6v.
38587.8.5 Regnard, Jean François. Oeuvres complètes avec notice et de nombreuses notes critiques. Paris, 1854. 2v.
38587.8.6 Regnard, Jean François. Le joueur; comédie en cinq actes. Paris, 1874.
38587.8.7 Regnard, Jean François. Le joueur, comédie en cinq actes. London, 1884.
38587.8.9 Regnard, Jean François. Les joueur. Les folies amoureuses. Paris, 1887.
38587.8.14 Regnard, Jean François. Le légataire universel, le bal. Paris, 1886.
38587.8.15 Regnard, Jean François. Le légataire universel. Austin, 1912.
38587.8.20 Regnard, Jean François. Le légataire universel. Manchester, 1927.
38587.8.80 Calame, Alexandre. Regnard, sa vie et son oeuvre. Paris, 1960.
38587.9 Théâtre de Regnard. Paris, 1845.
38587.9.4 Regnard, Jean François. Théâtre de Regnard, suivi de ses voyages en Laponie. Paris, 1851.
38587.9.5A Regnard, Jean François. Théâtre. Paris, n.d.
38587.9.5B Regnard, Jean François. Théâtre. Paris, n.d.
38587.9.6 Regnard, Jean François. Théâtre de Jean François Regnard. Paris, 1876. 2v.
38587.9.10 Regnard, Jean François. Chefs d'oeuvres dramatiques. Paris, 1921?
38587.10 Regnard, Jean François. Democrite, comédie. Amsterdam, 1702.
38587.10.10 Regnard, Jean François. La provençale. Paris, 1920.
38587.10.20 Regnard, Jean François. Les folies amoureuses. Paris, 1911.
38587.15 Menasci, G. Nuovi saggi di letterature francese. Regnard. Livorno, 1908.
38587.15.10 Juyot, Joseph. Le poete Jean François Regnard en son chateau de Quelon. Paris, 1907.
38587.16 La folle querelle ou La critique d'Andromaque. Paris, 1881.

38587.21 - Individual authors, etc. - 1661-1715 - Drama - Other dramatists - Hardy, A.

Htn 38587.22* Hardy, Alexandre. Théâtre. Paris, 1624-28. 5v.
38587.23 Hardy, Alexandre. Théâtre. v.1-5. Marburg, 1883. 4v.
Htn 38587.24* Hardy, Alexandre. Les chastes et loyal amours de Théagène et Cariclée. Paris, 1623.
38587.28 Rigal, Eugène. Alexandre Hardy. Paris, 1889.
38587.29 Kownatzki, F.A. Essai sur Hardy. Tilsit, 1885.
NEDL 38587.30 Beraneck, Jules. Senèque et Hardy. Leipzig, 1890.
38587.31 Sirich, Edward Hinman. Study in syntax of Alexandre Hardy. Baltimore, 1915.
38587.32 Kranzfelder, H.R. Die Hirtendichtung und die dramiatischen Pastoralen Alexandre Hardy's. Inaug. Diss. Würzburg, 1933.
38587.33 Garscha, Karsten. Hardy als Barockdramatiker. Frankfurt, 1971.

38588.1 - .29 Individual authors, etc. - 1661-1715 - Drama - Other dramatists - Poisson; Quinault; Dufresny; etc.

38588.9 Oeuvres de Raimond et Philippe Poisson. Paris, 1812.
38588.11 Poisson, Raymond. Oeuvres. Paris, 1623.
Htn 38588.12* Quinault, Philippe. Oeuvres. Paris, 1656.
38588.13 Quinault, Philippe. Le théâtre. Paris, 1739. 5v.
38588.14 Quinault, Philippe. Chefs-d'oeuvre de Quinault. Paris, 1810.
38588.15 Quinault, Philippe. Oeuvres choisies de Quinault. Paris, 1824. 2v.
38588.16 Quinault, Philippe. Théâtre choisi. Paris, 1882.
38588.16.1 Quinault, Philippe. La mère coquette ou Les amants brouillés. Thèse. Paris, 1926.
38588.16.2 Quinault, Philippe. La mère coquette. Paris, 1926.
Htn 38588.16.3* Quinault, Philippe. Les coups de l'amour et de la fortune. Rouen, 1660. 5 pam.
Htn 38588.16.5* Quinault, Philippe. Alceste ou Le triomphe d'Alcide. Paris, 1687.
Htn 38588.16.6* Quinault, Philippe. Le fantasme amoureux. Paris, 1656.
Htn 38588.16.7* Quinault, Philippe. La genereuse ingratitude. Paris, 1657.
Htn 38588.16.8* Quinault, Philippe. Astrate. Paris, 1665.
Htn 38588.16.9* Quinault, Philippe. Amalasonte, tragi-comédie. Paris, 1661.
38588.16.10 Quinault, Philippe. La mère coquette, ou Les amans brouillez. Paris, 1705.
38588.16.11 Quinault, Philippe. Les coups de l'amour et de la fortune. Paris, 1708.
38588.16.13 Quinault, Philippe. Sceaux, poeme en deux chants. Paris? 18- .
Htn 38588.16.15* Quinault, Philippe. Thesée; tragédie en musique. Paris, 1687.
Htn 38588.16.20* Quinault, Philippe. Amadis; tragédie en musique. Amsterdam, 1684.
Htn 38588.16.25* Quinault, Philippe. Agrippa, roy d'Abbe, ou Le faux Tiberinus. Paris, 1663.
38588.16.30 Quinault, Philippe. Cadmus et Hermione; tragédie en musique. n.p., n.d.
38588.17 Lindemann, F. Die Operntexte Philippe Quinaults. Leipzig, 1904.
38588.17.5 Richter, Erich. Philippe Quinault sein Leben. Leipzig, 1910.
38588.17.8 Gros, Etienne. Philippe Quinault; sa vie et son oeuvre. Thèse. Paris, 1926.
38588.17.10 Gros, Etienne. Philippe Quinault; sa vie et son oeuvre. Thèse. Paris, 1926.

38588.1 - .29 Individual authors, etc. - 1661-1715 - Drama - Other dramatists - Poisson; Quinault; Dufresny; etc. - cont.

38588.17.15 Buijtendorp, Johannes B.A. Philippe Quinault; sa vie, ses tragédies et ses tragi-comédies. Amsterdam, 1928.
38588.18 Pamphlet box. Dufresny.
38588.18.5 Dufresny, Charles Rivière. Théâtre. Paris, 1694.
38588.18.10 Dufresny, Charles Rivière. Oeuvres. Paris, 1747. 4v.
38588.19 Théâtre de Dufresny. Paris, 1882.
38588.20 Dufresny, Charles Rivière. Entretiens, ou Amusements. Paris, 1869.
38588.20.5 Dufresny, Charles Rivière. Amusements sèrieux et comiques. 6. éd. Amsterdam, 1629[1729]
38588.20.7 Dufresny, Charles Rivière. Petit voyage dans le grand monde. Paris, 1801.
38588.20.15 Dufresny, Charles Rivière. Amusements sérieux et comiques. Paris, 1921.
38588.21 Lemaitre, Jules. La comédie après Molière et le théâtre de Dancourt. Paris, 1882.
38588.22 Fournel, Victor. Petites comédies, rare et curieuses de 17e siècle. Paris, 1884. 2v.

38588.31 - Individual authors, etc. - 1661-1715 - Drama - Anonymous plays

38588.33 Bernhard, A. Die Parodie..."Chapelain decoiffée". Leipzig, 1910.
38588.34 Bernhard, A. Die Parodie..."Chapelain decoiffée". Inaug. Diss. Naumberg, 1910.
38588.48 Yvernaud. Le martyre de Sainete Valerie. Limoges, 1669.

39524 Individual authors, etc. - 1661-1715 - Poetry, humor, etc. - La Fontaine - Folios [Discontinued]

39524.4F La Fontaine, Jean de. The fables. London, 1872.
Htn 39524.5* La Fontaine, Jean de. Fables. Paris, 1886-87. 4v.
39524.7 La Fontaine, Jean de. Fables. Paris, n.d.
39524.7.5 La Fontaine, Jean de. Fables. Paris, 1927. 2v.
39524.7.15F La Fontaine, Jean de. Fables. Paris, 1883. 2v.

39525 Individual authors, etc. - 1661-1715 - Poetry, humor, etc. - La Fontaine - Complete and Selected works

Htn 39525.2* La Fontaine, Jean de. Oeuvres postumes. Bordeaux, 1696.
39525.4 La Fontaine, Jean de. Oeuvres diverses. Paris, 1729. 3v.
39525.5 La Fontaine, Jean de. Oeuvres diverses. Paris, 1894.
39525.5.10 La Fontaine, Jean de. Oeuvres diverses. v.2. Paris, 1942.
39525.5.15 La Fontaine, Jean de. Oeuvres complètes. Paris, 1814. 6v.
39525.6 La Fontaine, Jean de. Oeuvres complètes. Paris, 1826. 6v.
39525.13A La Fontaine, Jean de. Oeuvres. Paris, 1875-79. 7v.
39525.13B La Fontaine, Jean de. Oeuvres. Paris, 1875-79. 2v.
39525.14 La Fontaine, Jean de. Oeuvres. v.1-11 and album. Paris, 1883. 12v.
39525.15 La Fontaine, Jean de. Contes et nouvelles en vers. Paris, 1934. 2v.
39525.15.2A La Fontaine, Jean de. Fables choisies, mises en vers. Paris, 1934. 2v.
39525.15.2B La Fontaine, Jean de. Fables choisies, mises en vers. Paris, 1934. 2v.
39525.15.5 La Fontaine, Jean de. Fables choisies, mises en vers. Paris, 1946.
39525.15.25 La Fontaine, Jean de. Fables, contes et nouvelles. Paris, 1932.
39525.16 La Fontaine, Jean de. Contes et nouvelles en vers. v.1-2. Paris, 1875?
39525.17 La Fontaine, Jean de. Oeuvres inédites par P. Lacroix. Paris, 1863.
39525.19.5 La Fontaine, Jean de. Oeuvres: théâtre, fables, poésies. Paris, 1877.
39525.20 La Fontaine, Jean de. Oeuvres complètes. Paris, 1826.

39526 Individual authors, etc. - 1661-1715 - Poetry, humor, etc. - La Fontaine - Miscellany [Discontinued]

39526.2 Hamel, Frank. Jean de la Fontaine. London, n.d.
39526.2.8 Pamphlet box. La Fontaine.
39526.3 Guillon, M.N.S. La Fontaine et tous les fabulistes. Paris, 1803. 2v.
39526.4A Robert, A.C.M. Fables inédites der XII, XIII et XIV siècles, et de La Fontaine. Paris, 1825. 2v.
39526.4B Robert, A.C.M. Fables inédites der XII, XIII et XIV siècles, et de La Fontaine. Paris, 1825. 2v.
39526.5 Girardin, Saint-Marc. La Fontaine et les fabulistes. Paris, 1882. 2v.
39526.5.2 Collins, W. Lucas. La Fontaine and other French fabulists. Edinburgh, 1882.
39526.6 Lorin, Théodore. Vocabulaire pour...La Fontaine. Paris, 1852.
39526.8 Cocheris, Hippolyte. Premier livre des fables de La Fontaine. Paris, 1874-75.
39526.10 Joly, Aristide. Histoire de deux fables de La Fontaine. Paris, 1877.
39526.23 Moland, Louis. Oeuvres complètes de La Fontaine. Paris, 1872-76. 7v.
NEDL 39526.24 Moland, Louis. Oeuvres complètes de La Fontaine. Paris, 1874-75. 2v.
Htn 39526.26* La Fontaine, Jean de. Les bombous. Fort-Royal, 1846.
39526.27 Nodier, Charles. Fables de La Fontaine. Paris, 1818. 2v.
39526.27.15 La Fontaine, Jean de. Fables de La Fontaine. 3e éd. Cambridge, 1851.
39526.28 Faguet, Emile. La Fontaine. Paris, 1889.
39526.29 Jannet, Pierre. Fables de La Fontaine. v.1-2. Paris, 1880.
39526.29.4 La Fontaine, Jean de. Fables. Paris, 1880.
39526.29.9 La Fontaine, Jean de. Fables. Paris, 1842-43. 2v.
39526.29.12 La Fontaine, Jean de. Fables. Boston, 1861. 2v.
39526.29.15 La Fontaine, Jean de. Fables. Paris, 1926.
39526.29.20 La Fontaine, Jean de. Fables choisies. Paris, 1778.
39526.30 Wright, Elizur. Fables of La Fontaine. Boston, 1841. 2v.
39526.30.10 La Fontaine, Jean de. Fables. 2d ed. Boston, 1841.
39526.30.20A La Fontaine, Jean de. Fables. 3d ed. Boston, 1842. 2v.
39526.30.20B La Fontaine, Jean de. Fables. 3d ed. Boston, 1842. 2v.
39526.30.20C La Fontaine, Jean de. Fables. 3d ed. v.2. Boston, 1842.
39526.30.45 La Fontaine, Jean de. Fables. London, 1882.

39526 Individual authors, etc. - 1661-1715 - Poetry, humor, etc. - La Fontaine - Miscellany [Discontinued] - cont.

Htn 39526.31* La Fontaine, Jean de. Fables of La Fontaine. Boston, 1884.
39526.31.5 La Fontaine, Jean de. Fables, précédées d'une notice biographique. Paris, 1888.
39526.31.10 La Fontaine, Jean de. Fables. London, 1895.
39526.31.12F La Fontaine, Jean de. Fables. Tours, 1897.
39526.32 La Fontaine, Jean de. Fables of La Fontaine. London, 1853.
39526.32.5 La Fontaine, Jean de. Fables. Paris, 1858.
39526.32.10 La Fontaine, Jean de. Fables et oeuvres diverses. Paris, 1859.
39526.32.25 La Fontaine, Jean de. Fables et oeuvres diverses. Paris, 1865.
39526.33 La Fontaine, Jean de. Fables. Paris, 1868.
39526.33.5 La Fontaine, Jean de. Fables. Paris, 1869.
39526.33.10 La Fontaine, Jean de. Fables. Paris, 1883.
39526.33.27F La Fontaine, Jean de. Douze fables. Agen, 1946.
39526.33.30 La Fontaine, Jean de. Fables vom Jean de la Fontaine. Friburg, 1947.
Htn 39526.34* La Fontaine, Jean de. Contes et nouvelles. Paris, 1839.
39526.35 Kulpe, Wilhelm. La Fontaine sein Leben und seine Fabelen. Leipzig, 1882.
39526.36 Contance, A. La Fontaine et la philosophie naturelle. Paris, 1882.
39526.37 Noelle, A. Beiträge zum Studium der Fabel. Cuxhaven, 1893.
39526.40 Fischer, W.P. The literary relations between La Fontaine and the "Astrée" of Honoré d'Urfé. Philadelphia, 1913.
39526.41 Netter, Abraham. La Fontaine et Descartes, ou Les deux rats. Paris, 1886.
39526.44 Boulvé, Leon. De Fontanio Platonis studioso. Thesim. Paris, 1897.
39526.47 Arnould, Louis. La terre de France chez La Fontaine, bêtes et gens. Tours, 1924.
39526.50 Boillot, Félix. Les impressions sensorielles chez La Fontaine. Paris, 1926.
39526.55 Borri, Vittorio Ferruccio. Le novelle del Decameron, imitate da La Fontaine. Trieste, 1914.
39526.58 Nohain, Franc. La vie amoureuse de Jean de La Fontaine. Paris, 1928.

39527.1 - .7 Individual authors, etc. - 1661-1715 - Poetry, humor, etc. - La Fontaine - Biography and criticism

39527.1A Walckenaer, C.A. Histoire de la vie de La Fontaine. Paris, 1824.
39527.1B Walckenaer, C.A. Histoire de la vie de La Fontaine. Paris, 1824.
39527.2.2 Lafenestre, Georges. La Fontaine. Paris, 1895.
39527.2.3 Lafenestre, Georges. La Fontaine. 5e éd. Paris, 1922.
39527.2.5 Broc, V. de. La Fontaine moraliste. Paris, 1896.
39527.2.6 Delaporte, Louis. La philosophie de La Fontaine. Paris, 1896.
39527.3 Leveaux, Alphonse. De la poesie dans...La Fontaine. Paris, 1873.
39527.4.5 Soullié, P. La Fontaine et ses devanciers ou Histoire de l'Apologue. Paris, 1861.
39527.4.9A Taine, H.A. La Fontaine et ses fables. Paris, 1861.
39527.4.9B Taine, H.A. La Fontaine et ses fables. Paris, 1861.
39527.4.12 Uhlemayr, B. Der Einfluss La Fontaine's auf die Englische Fabeldichtung der 18. Jahrhundert. Nürnberg, 1900.
39527.4.13 Jahnow, Alfred. Beobachtungen über La Fontaine's Fabeln. Strehlen, 1894. 2v.
39527.4.14 De Rochambeau, Achille Lacroix. Bibliographie des oeuvres de La Fontaine. Paris, 1911.
39527.4.15 Roche, Louis. La vie de Jean de La Fontaine. 2. éd. Paris, 1913.
39527.4.16 Michant, G. La Fontaine. Paris, 1913. 2v.
39527.4.17A Faguet, E. La Fontaine. Paris, 1913.
39527.4.17B Faguet, E. La Fontaine. Paris, 1913.
39527.4.18 Richter, R. La Fontaine et Lamolle. Elbogen, 1904.
39527.4.20 Godchot, Simon. La Fontaine et St. Augustin. Paris, 1919.
39527.4.22 Godchot, Simon. La Fontaine et Sénèque. Saint-Cloud, 1930.
39527.4.25 Nicolardot, Louis. La Fontaine et la comédie humaine suivi du langage des animaux. 2e éd. Paris, 1885.
39527.4.30 Berèrne, Tristan. Sous les troènes du Beárn. St. Felicien, 1928.
39527.4.35 Gohin, Ferdinand. L'art de La Fontaine dans ses fables. St. Vivarais, 1929.
39527.4.37 Gohin, Ferdinand. La Fontaine. Paris, 1937.
39527.4.40 Soullié, Prosper. Études sur les fables de La Fontaine. Reims, 1881.
39527.4.42 Soullié, Prosper. Critique comparative des fables de La Fontaine. Reims, 1881.
39527.4.45 Cacudi, N. La Fontaine, imitateur de Boccace. Bari, 1922.
39527.4.50 Gohin, Ferdinand. Les comédies attribuées à La Fontaine. Paris, 1935.
39527.4.55 Bailly, A. La Fontaine. Paris, 1937.
39527.4.60A Giraudoux, Jean. Les cinq tentations de La Fontaine. Paris, 1938.
39527.4.60B Giraudoux, Jean. Les cinq tentations de La Fontaine. Paris, 1938.
39527.4.62 Giraudoux, Jean. Les cinq tentations de La Fontaine. 20e éd. Paris, 1938.
39527.4.65 Garnier, L. La vie de notre Bon Jehan de La Fontaine contée par l'image. Château-Thierry, 1937.
39527.4.70 Boissonade, Gustave. La Fontaine, économiste. Paris, 1872.
39527.4.75 Vianey, Joseph. La psychologie de La Fontaine. Paris, 1939.
39527.4.80 Pradier, M. La vie de Jean de La Fontaine. Paris, 1946.
39527.4.85A Clarac, Pierre. La Fontaine. Paris, 1947.
39527.4.85B Clarac, Pierre. La Fontaine. Paris, 1947.
39527.4.85.2 Clarac, Pierre. La Fontaine. Paris, 1959.
39527.4.86 La Fontaine, Jean de. La Fontaine par lui même. Paris, 1961.
39527.4.90 Hamel, Frank. Jean de La Fontaine. N.Y., 1912.
39527.4.95 Siegfried, André. La Fontaine, machiavel français. Paris, 1950.
39527.4.100 Guillet, L. Divers visages de La Fontaine. Paris, 1948.
39527.4.105A Wadsworth, P.A. Young La Fontaine. Evanston, 1952.
39527.4.105B Wadsworth, P.A. Young La Fontaine. Evanston, 1952.
39527.4.110 Sutherland, M. La Fontaine. London, 1953.
39527.4.115 Petit, Léon. La Fontaine et Saint-Evremond. Toulouse, 1953.
39527.4.120 Siegfried, André. La Fontaine. Paris, 1955.

39527.1 - .7 Individual authors, etc. - 1661-1715 - Poetry, humor, etc. - La Fontaine - Biography and criticism - cont.

39527.4.125 Couton, Georges. La poétique de La Fontaine. 1. éd. Paris, 1957.
39527.4.130 Couton, Georges. La politique de La Fontaine. Paris, 1959.
39527.4.135 Murques, Oditte. La Fontaine. Fables. London, 1960.
39527.4.140 Guiton, Margaret. La Fontaine. New Brunswick, 1961.
39527.4.145 Blavier-Paguot, Simone. La Fontaine. Paris, 1961.
39527.4.150 Jasinski, René. La Fontaine et le premier recueil des Fables. Paris, 1965-66. 2v.
39527.5 Taine, Hippolyte. La Fontaine et ses fables. 5e éd. Paris, 1870.
39527.5.1 Taine, Hippolyte. La Fontaine et ses fables. 6e éd. Paris, 1875.
39527.5.2A Taine, Hippolyte. La Fontaine et ses fables. 11e éd. Paris, 1888.
39527.5.2B Taine, Hippolyte. La Fontaine et ses fables. 11e éd. Paris, 1888.
39527.5.6 Taine, Hippolyte. La Fontaine et ses fables. Paris, 1875.
39527.5.10 Taine, Hippolyte. La Fontaine et ses fables. 13e éd. Paris, 1895.
39527.5.15 Biard, Jean Dominique. The style of La Fontaine's fables. Oxford, 1966[1967]
39527.6 Delboulle, A. Les fables de La Fontaine. Paris, 1891.
39527.6.5 Disprés, Armand. Les éditions illustrées des fables de La Fontaine. Paris, 1892.
39527.6.10 Hédé-Haüy, A. Les illustrations des contes de La Fontaine. Paris, 1893.
39527.7 Solvet, P.L. Études sur La Fontaine. Paris, 1812.
39527.7.5 Vossler, Karl. La Fontaine und sein Fabelwirk. Heidelberg, 1919.
39527.7.10 Hallays, André. Jean de La Fontaine. Paris, 1922.

39527.8 - .59 Individual authors, etc. - 1661-1715 - Poetry, humor, etc. - La Fontaine - Individual works

Htn 39527.8.3* La Fontaine, Jean de. Contes et nouvelles en vers. Amsterdam, 1685.
39527.8.7 La Fontaine, Jean de. Contes et nouvelles en vers. London, 1781.
Htn 39527.8.15* La Fontaine, Jean de. Contes et nouvelles en vers. Amsterdam, 1762.
Htn 39527.8.20* La Fontaine, Jean de. Contes et nouvelles en vers. Paris, 1795.
39527.8.25 La Fontaine, Jean de. Contes et nouvelles en vers. Paris, 1961.
Htn 39527.8.30* La Fontaine, Jean de. La Fontaine en estamps. Paris, 1821.
39527.9 La Fontaine, Jean de. Contes et nouvelles en vers. Paris, 1800.
39527.10.10 La Fontaine, Jean de. Contes et nouvelles. Paris, 1959-60. 2v.
39527.10.20 La Fontaine, Jean de. Nouvelles en vers, tirée de Bocace et de l'Ariosle. Paris? 1935.
Htn 39527.10.50* La Fontaine, Jean de. La Fontaine's tales. London, 1814. 2v.
Htn 39527.10.60* La Fontaine, Jean de. Tales and novels. London, 19- .
39527.10.65 La Fontaine, Jean de. Tales and novels. N.Y., 1929.
39527.11 La Fontaine, Jean de. Fables. Paris, 1799. 2v.
39527.11.2 La Fontaine, Jean de. Fables. Paris, 1799.
Htn 39527.11.5* La Fontaine, Jean de. Fables. Paris, 1796. 4v.
39527.11.10 La Fontaine, Jean de. Fables et epitres. Paris, 18- .
39527.12 La Fontaine, Jean de. Fables. Agen, 1801.
39527.12.5 La Fontaine, Jean de. Fables. Paris, 1803.
Htn 39527.13* La Fontaine, Jean de. Fables de La Fontaine. Paris, 1811. 2v.
39527.14 La Fontaine, Jean de. Fables de La Fontaine. Paris, 1817.
39527.15 La Fontaine, Jean de. Fables choisies de La Fontaine. N.Y., 1810.
39527.16 La Fontaine, Jean de. Fables de La Fontaine. Paris, 1818.
39527.16.5 La Fontaine, Jean de. Oeuvres complètes. v.3. Paris, 1820.
39527.16.10 La Fontaine, Jean de. Oeuvres. Paris, 1822.
39527.17 La Fontaine, Jean de. Fables de La Fontaine. Paris, 1828.
39527.17.10 La Fontaine, Jean de. Fables. v.1-2. Paris, 1829.
39527.18 La Fontaine, Jean de. Choix de fables de La Fontaine. Paris, 1831.
39527.18.3F La Fontaine, Jean de. Fables. v.1-2. Paris, 1834.
39527.18.5 La Fontaine, Jean de. Fables, avec des notes...par Francis Sales. 2e éd. Boston, 1841.
NEDL 39527.19 Sales, F. Fables de La Fontaine. Cambridge, 1851.
39527.20 La Fontaine, Jean de. Fables. Paris, 1838. 2v.
39527.20.10 La Fontaine, Jean de. Fables, avec des notes par Francis Sales. Boston, 1838.
39527.20.15 La Fontaine, Jean de. Fables. 5. ed. v.1-2. Boston, 1842.
39527.22 Colincamp, Ferdinand. Fables de La Fontaine. Paris, 1863.
39527.22.5 La Fontaine, Jean de. Fables. Tours, 1864.
39527.23 La Fontaine, Jean de. Fables de La Fontaine. Boston, 1870.
39527.23.4 La Fontaine, Jean de. Fables. Paris, 1874.
39527.23.5A La Fontaine, Jean de. Fables. Paris, 1875.
39527.23.5B La Fontaine, Jean de. Fables. Paris, 1875.
39527.24 Closset, A. de. Fables choisies de Jean de La Fontaine. Brussels, 1867.
39527.25 Sauveur, L. Fables de La Fontaine. N.Y., 1877.
39527.25.10 La Fontaine, Jean de. Fables choisies. N.Y., 1898?
39527.26 Buffon, George L. de. Fables de La Fontaine. Paris, n.d.
39527.26.10 Brays, René. Les fables de La fontaine aves un index de tous les noms cités. Paris, 1929.
39527.27 Desandré, J. Fables de Jean de La Fontaine. Paris, 1877.
39527.27.10 La Fontaine, Jean de. Fables. Tours, 1877.
39527.28 Aubertin, Charles. Fables de La Fontaine. Paris, 1887.
39527.28.8 Tarver, Francis. Fables de La Fontaine. London, n.d.
39527.29 Tarver, Francis. Fables de La Fontaine. London, 1886.
39527.29.2 La Fontaine, Jean de. Fables. London, 1890.
39527.29.3 La Fontaine, Jean de. Fables de La Fontaine. v.1-2. Paris, 1930.
39527.29.5 Lemaistre, Felix. Fables de La Fontaine. Paris, n.d.
39527.29.7 La Fontaine, Jean de. Fables. London, 1892.
39527.29.10 La Fontaine, Jean de. La Fontaine: récits et dialogues. Paris, 1938. 2v.
39527.29.15 La Fontaine, Jean de. Fables choisies. Paris, 192-?
39527.29.20 La Fontaine, Jean de. Choix de fables. Paris, 1925.
39527.29.23 La Fontaine, Jean de. Fables. London, 1903.
39527.29.25 La Fontaine, Jean de. Fifty fables. N.Y., 1903.
39527.29.26 La Fontaine, Jean de. Fables. Paris, 1913.
39527.29.27 La Fontaine, Jean de. Fables. N.Y., 1930.
39527.29.30 La Fontaine, Jean de. Fables. N.Y., 1954.

39527.8 - .59 Individual authors, etc. - 1661-1715 - Poetry, humor, etc. - La Fontaine - Individual works - cont.

39527.29.35 La Fontaine, Jean de. Fables à calorier. pt. 1-3,4-6. Montréal, 1943. 2v.
39527.29.50 La Fontaine, Jean de. Fables, contes et nouvelles. Paris, 1940.
39527.29.55 La Fontaine, Jean de. Fables. Londres, 1946.
39527.29.60 La Fontaine, Jean de. Fables. Paris, 1948.
39527.29.63 La Fontaine, Jean de. Le songe de vaux. Paris, 1924.
39527.29.63.5 La Fontaine, Jean de. Le songe de vaux. Genève, 1967.
39527.29.70 La Fontaine, Jean de. Fables. Paris, 1958-59. 2v.
39527.29.89 La Fontaine, Jean de. Fables de La Fontaine; cent fables choisies. Paris, 1925.
39527.29.90 La Fontaine, Jean de. Fables choisies. Paris, 1967.
39527.30 La Fontaine, Jean de. Fables choisies de La Fontaine. Morlaix, 1836.
NEDL 39527.31 La Fontaine, Jean de. Traducção livre das melhores fabulas. Lisboa, 1820.
39527.31.50 La Fontaine, Jean de. Fabulas escolhidas. v.1-2. Lisboa, 1814-15.
Htn 39527.31.125* La Fontaine, Jean de. Fables en vers gascouns. Bayoune, 1776.
39527.32 La Fontaine, Jean de. La Fountaines Fabler. København, 1918.
Htn 39527.33* La Fontaine, Jean de. Les amours de Psyché et de Cupidon. Paris, 1669.
39527.33.5 La Fontaine, Jean de. Les amours de psyché et de cupidon. Paris, 1810.
39527.33.26 La Fontaine, Jean de. Les amours de psyché, opuscules et lettres. Paris, 1926.
39527.34 La Fontaine, Jean de. The loves of cupid and psyche. London, 1744.
39527.35 La Fontaine, Jean de. Psyché. Paris, 1913.
39527.36 La Fontaine, Jean de. L'amour et psyché. Paris, 1892.
39527.36.5 La Fontaine, Jean de. Luibov' psikhei i kupidona. London, 1964.
39527.37 Marchain, R. Les distractions de La Fontaine. Paris, 1898.
39527.41 La Fontaine, Jean de. Poëme du Quinquina. Paris, 1682.
39527.42 La Fontaine, Jean de. Discours à Madame de la Sablière. Paris, 1938.
39527.42.5 La Fontaine, Jean de. Discours à Madame de la Sablière sur l'âme des animaux. Genève, 1950.
39527.42.10 La Fontaine, Jean de. Lettres de Jean de La Fontaine à sa femme sur un voyage des Paris en limosin. Paris, 1920.
39527.42.15 La Fontaine, Jean de. Voyage de Paris en limosin. Paris, 1969.
39527.43 La Fontaine. Paris, 1912.
Htn 39527.45* La Fontaine, Jean de. Les oeuvres postumes. Paris, 1646.
39527.50 Mandeville, Bernard de. Some fables after the easie and familiar method of M. de La Fontaine. London, 1703.
39527.54 La Fontaine, Jean de. Théâtre. Paris, 1804.
39527.58 La Fontaine, Jean de. Bajky. Praha, 1959.

39527.60 - .89 Individual authors, etc. - 1661-1715 - Poetry, humor, etc. - La Fontaine - Criticism [Discontinued]

39527.60 Kohn, R. Le goût de La Fontaine. Paris, 1962.
39527.61 Mourques, O. de. O Muse, fuyante proie. Paris, 1962.
39527.63 Clarac, Pierre. Jean de La Fontaine. Paris, 1965.
39527.65 Lugli, Vittorio. Il prodigio di La Fontaine. Messina, 1939.
39527.67 Mayer, Gerd Reiner. Die Funktion mythologischer Namen und Anspielungen in La Fontaines Fabelens. Bonn, 1969.
39527.70 Macé, Alcide. La Fontaine et Horace. Rennes, 1944.
39527.75 Collinet, Jean Pierre. Le monde littéraire de La Fontaine. Paris, 1970.
V39527.80 Lent, P. Van. Recueil de fables de La Fontaine. Rotterdam, 1838.

39531 Individual authors, etc. - 1661-1715 - Poetry, humor, etc. - Other poets and humorists, etc. - Folios [Discontinued]

Htn 39531.5* Oeuvres diverses de Jean Baptiste Rousseau. London, n.d. 2v.
39531.7 Oeuvres de Jean Baptiste Rousseau. Brussels, n.d. 3v.
39531.14 Chardon, H. Scarron inconnu. Paris, 1903. 2v.
39531.17 Fabre, A. Les ennemis de Chapelain. Paris, 1888.
39531.17.2 Fabre, A. Les ennemis de Chapelain. Paris, 1897.
39531.17.9 Furetière, A. The poésies diverses. Baltimore, 1908.
39531.18 Mühlan, Alois. Jean Chapelain als litterarischer Kritiker. Strassburg, 1892.
39531.18.10 Fischer, H. Antoine Funetière, 1619-1688. Berlin, 1937.
39531.20 Morisot, C.B. Pervirana. Divion, 1645.
39531.28 Martin de Pinchesne, E. La chronique des Chapons et des Gélinottes du Mans. Paris, 1907.

39532.1 - .4 Individual authors, etc. - 1661-1715 - Poetry, humor, etc. - Other poets and humorists, etc. - Rousseau, Jean Baptiste

39532.2.9 Rousseau, J.B. Les oeuvres. Rotterdam, 1712. 2v.
Htn 39532.2.10* Rousseau, J.B. Anti-Rousseau. Rotterdam, 1712.
39532.2.11 Rousseau, J.B. Anti-Rousseau Histoire satyrique de la vie...de Rousseau. Paris, 1716.
39532.2.19 Rousseau, J.B. Oeuvres. Paris, 1795. 4v.
39532.3 Latour, Antoine de. Oeuvres de J.B. Rousseau. Paris, 1869.
39532.3.5 Rousseau, J.B. Oeuvres diverses. Soleure, 1712.
39532.4.9 Rousseau, J.B. Lettres. Genève, 1749. 5v.
39532.4.15 Rousseau, J.B. Correspondance de J.B. Rousseau et de Brossette. Paris, 1910. 2v.
39532.4.45 Hyrvoix de Landosle, A. Jean-Baptiste Rousseau. Paris, 1911.
39532.4.50 Grubbs, H.A. Jean-Baptiste Rousseau. Paris, 1941.

39532.5 - .15 Individual authors, etc. - 1661-1715 - Poetry, humor, etc. - Other poets and humorists, etc. - Hamilton, A.

Htn 39532.5* Hamilton, Anthony. Memoires de la vie du comte de Grammont. Cologne, 1713.
39532.5.2 Hamilton, Anthony. Memoires du comte de Grammont. London, 1783.
39532.5.3 Hamilton, Anthony. Memoires du comte de Grammont. London, 1793.
39532.5.7 Hamilton, Anthony. Mémoires du chevalier de Grammont. Paris, 1883.
39532.5.8 Hamilton, Anthony. Der Chevalier von Grammont. München, 1911. 2v.
39532.5.9 Hamilton, Anthony. Oeuvres complètes d'Hamilton. Paris, 1805. 3v.
39532.6 Hamilton, Anthony. Oeuvres du comte Hamilton. Paris, 1825. 2v.

39532.5 - .15 Individual authors, etc. - 1661-1715 - Poetry, humor, etc. - Other poets and humorists, etc. - Hamilton, A. - cont.

39532.7 Hamilton, Anthony. Drei Hübsche, kurzweilige Märlein. n.p., n.d.
39532.7.5 Hamilton, Anthony. Contes d'Hamilton. Paris, 1873. 2v.
39532.7.9 Hamilton, Anthony. Fairy tales and romances. London, 1849.
39532.7.10 Hamilton, Anthony. Four Facardins. London, 1899.
39532.8 Hamilton, Anthony. Mémoires du Chevalier de Grammont. Paris, 1875.
39532.11.5 Hamilton, Anthony. Le Belier, conte. n.p., 1749.
39532.11.10 Hamilton, Anthony. Histoire de fleur d'epine. n.p., 1749.
39532.11.15 Hamilton, Anthony. Les quatre Facardins, conte. Paris? 1749.
39532.12 Hamilton, Anthony. Memoires of the life of Count de Grammont. London, 1714.
Htn 39532.12.15* Hamilton, Anthony. Memoires of the life of Count de Grammont. 2d ed. London, 1809. 3v.
39532.12.20 Hamilton, Anthony. Memorie del conte di Grammont. Milano, 1814. 2v.
39532.13 Hamilton, Anthony. Memoires of Count Grammont. London, 1828. 2v.
39532.13.4A Hamilton, Anthony. Memoires of the court of Charles the second, by Count Grammont. London, 1846.
39532.13.4B Hamilton, Anthony. Memoires of the court of Charles the second, by Count Grammont. London, 1846.
39532.13.4C Hamilton, Anthony. Memoires of the court of Charles the second, by Count Grammont. London, 1846.
39532.13.4D Hamilton, Anthony. Memoires of the court of Charles the second, by Count Grammont. London, 1846.
39532.13.6 Hamilton, Anthony. Memoires of the court of Charles the second by Count Grammont. London, 1853.
39532.13.8 Hamilton, Anthony. Memoires of the Count de Grammont. London, 1889. 2v.
39532.13.9A Hamilton, Anthony. Memoires of Count Grammont. London, 1903.
39532.13.9B Hamilton, Anthony. Memoires of Count Grammont. London, 1903.
39532.13.12 Hamilton, Anthony. Memoires of Count Grammont. Edinburgh, 1908. 2v.
39532.13.13 Hamilton, Anthony. Memoires of the court of Charles II, by Count de Grammont. Memoires of the courts of Europe. v.4. N.Y., 1910.
39532.13.15 Hamilton, Anthony. Memoires of Count Grammont. London, 1928.
39532.13.16 Hamilton, Anthony. Memoires of the comte de Grammont. London, 1965.
39532.13.17 Hamilton, Anthony. Mémoires du comte de Grammont. Paris, 1965.
39532.13.20 Hamilton, Anthony. History of May-Flower. 2e ed. Salisbury, 1796.
39532.15 Clark, Ruth. Anthony Hamilton. London, 1921.
39532.15.5 Kissenberth, Wilhelm. Antoine d'Hamilton; sein Leben und seine Werke. Berlin, 1907.

39532.16 Individual authors, etc. - 1661-1715 - Poetry, humor, etc. - Other poets and humorists, etc. - Chaulieu

39532.16 Chaulieu, G.A. de. Poésies. Paris, 1825.
39532.16.02 Chaulieu, G.A. de. Poésies de Chaulieu. Paris, 1803.
39532.16.05 Chaulieu, G.A. de. Oeuvres. La Haye, 1777. 2v.
39532.16.9 Chaulieu, G.A. de. Lettres inédites. Paris, 1850.

39532.17 Individual authors, etc. - 1661-1715 - Poetry, humor, etc. - Other poets and humorists, etc. - La Monnoye

39532.17 Peignot, Gabriel. Nouvelles recherches sur la vie et les ouvrages de Bernard de La Monnoye. Dijon, 1832.
39532.17.5 La Monnoye, Bernard de. Lettres inédites de Bernard de La Monnoye addressées à son fils le R.P. de La Monnoye. Dijon, 1856.

39532.18 - .20 Individual authors, etc. - 1661-1715 - Poetry, humor, etc. - Other poets and humorists, etc. - Loret

39532.18 Loret, Jean. Muse historique. Paris, 1857-78. 4v.
39532.18.5 Loret, Jean. La muse historique. Index. Paris, 1891.
39532.20 Rothschild, James de. Les continuateurs de Loret. Paris, 1881. 2v.

39532.24 - .26 Individual authors, etc. - 1661-1715 - Poetry, humor, etc. - Other poets and humorists, etc. - Lacroix

39532.24 Lacroix, Paul. Paris ridicule et burlesque. Paris, 1859.
39532.24.5 Lacroix, Paul. Paris ridicule et burlesque. Paris, 1878.
Htn 39532.25* Travers, Émile. Une promenade dans Paris en 1650 avec un poëte burlesque. Caen, 1877.

39532.28 - .30 Individual authors, etc. - 1661-1715 - Poetry, humor, etc. - Other poets and humorists, etc. - Menage

Htn 39532.28* Ménage, Gilles. Menagiana ou Bon mots. 3. éd. Amsterdam, 1713. 4v.
39532.28.5 Ménage, Gilles. Menagiana ou Les bons mots. Paris, 1715. 4v.
39532.28.10 Ménage, Gilles. Menagiana ou Les bons mots. Paris, 1729. 4v.
Htn 39532.29* Aegidii Menagii miscellanea. Paris, 1652.
39532.29.5 Ménage, Gilles. Mescolanza d'Egidio Menagio. Venezia, 1736.
NEDL 39532.30 Samfiresco, Elvire. Ménage. Paris, 1902.
39532.30.5 Baret, Eugene. Menage, sa vie et ses écrits. Lyon, 1859.

39532.32 - .33 Individual authors, etc. - 1661-1715 - Poetry, humor, etc. - Other poets and humorists, etc. - Patin [Discontinued]

39532.32 Reveillé-Parise, J.H. Lettres de Guy Patin. Paris, 1846. 3v.
39532.33 Triaire, P. Lettres de Gui Patin, 1630-1672. Paris, 1907.

39532.34 Individual authors, etc. - 1661-1715 - Poetry, humor, etc. - Other poets and humorists, etc. - Perrot

Htn 39532.34* Bible. O.T. Psalms. French, 1577. Perles d'eslite...François Perrot. Genève, 1577.

39532.36 - .39 Individual authors, etc. - 1661-1715 - Poetry, humor, etc. - Other poets and humorists, etc. - Gacon

Htn 39532.36* Gacon, François. Le poète sans fard. Contenant. Libreville, 1648.
39532.38 Gacon, François. Homere vengé. Paris, 1715.

39533.2 - .4 Individual authors, etc. - 1661-1715 - Poetry, humor, etc. - Other poets and humorists, etc. - Hamilton [Discontinued]

39533.2 Hamilton, Anthony. Memoires....de Grammont. n.p., 1760. 2v.
39533.3 Hamilton, Anthony. Memoires....de Grammont. Paris, 1816. 2v.
39533.3.5 Hamilton, Anthony. Memoires du comte de Grammont. Paris, 1832.
39533.4 Hamilton, Anthony. Memoires...de Grammont. v.1-2. Paris, 1874.

39533.6 - .8 Individual authors, etc. - 1661-1715 - Poetry, humor, etc. - Other poets and humorists, etc. - Chapelain

39533.6.9 Searles, C. Catalogue de tous les livres de feu M. Chapelain. Stanford, 1912.
39533.7 Chapelain, Jean. Les douze derniers chants du poème de La Pucelle. Orleans, 1882.
39533.7.5 Chapelain, Jean. De la lecture des vieux romans. Paris, 1870.
39533.8 Chapelain, Jean. La Pucelle ou La France delivrée. Paris, 1657.
39533.8.2 Émile de Molènes. La Pucelle ou La France delivrée. Paris, 1891. 2v.
Htn 39533.8.10F* Chapelain, Jean. La Pucelle; ou La France delivrée. Paris, 1656.
39533.8.15 Chapelain, Jean. Opuscules critiques publiés. Paris, 1936.
39533.8.20 Chapelain, Jean. Soixante-dix-sept lettres inédites à Nicolas Heinsius, 1649-1658. La Haye, 1966.
39533.8.30 Fabre, Antonin. Lexique de la langue de Chapelain. Paris, 1889.
39533.8.31 Fabre, Antonin. Lexigue de la langue de Chapelain. Genève, 1971.
39533.8.33 Hunter, Alfred. Lexique de la langue de Jean Chapelain. Genève, 1967.
39533.8.35 Van Roosbroeck, G.L. Chapelain décoiffe. Baltimore, 1924.
39533.8.37 Van Roosbroeck, G.L. Chapelain décoiffe. N.Y., 1932.

39533.9 Individual authors, etc. - 1661-1715 - Poetry, humor, etc. - Other poets and humorists, etc. - Chapelle

39533.9 Chapelle, C.E.L. Oeuvres de Chapelle et de Bachaumont. Paris, 1854.
39533.9.3 Chapelle, C.E.L. Voyage de Messieures Chapelle et Bachaumont. La Haye, 1742.
39533.9.4 Chapelle, C.E.L. Voyage de Chapelle et Bachaumont. Genève, 1777.
39533.9.5 Chapelle, C.E.L. Voyage d'Encausse. Caen, 1902.

39533.10 - .12 Individual authors, etc. - 1661-1715 - Poetry, humor, etc. - Other poets and humorists, etc. - Miscellany

39533.10 Michel, F. Extrait abrégé de vieux mémoriaux. Paris, 1853-57.
Htn 39533.11.50* Labadie, Jean de. Le chant royal du grand roy Jesus. Amsterdam, 1670.
Htn 39533.12* Le Laboureur, Louis. Charlemagne, poëme heroïque. Paris, 1664.

39533.13 Individual authors, etc. - 1661-1715 - Poetry, humor, etc. - Other poets and humorists, etc. - Blainville

39533.13 Blainville, J. de. Oeuvres diverses. Paris, 1713.

39533.15 - .16 Individual authors, etc. - 1661-1715 - Poetry, humor, etc. - Other poets and humorists, etc. - Segrais

NEDL 39533.15 Segrais, Jean R. Oeuvres diverses. Amsterdam, 1723.
39533.15.2 Segrais, Jean R. Oeuvres diverses. v.1-2. Amsterdam, 1723.
39533.15.5 Segrais, Jean R. Oeuvres. Paris, 1755. 2v.
39533.15.10 Segrais, Jean R. Five novels. London, 1725.
Htn 39533.15.20* Segrais, Jean R. Diverses poesies. Paris, 1659.
Htn 39533.15.30* Segrais, Jean R. Berenice. Paris, 1648-50. 2v.
39533.15.35 Segrais, Jean R. Le Toledan. v.1-5. Paris, 1648-55. 10v.
39533.15.40 Raynal, Marie-Aline. La nouvelle française de Segrais à Mme. de la Fayette. Thèse. Paris, 1926.
39533.15.50 Tipping, W.M. Jean Regnaud de Segrais. Thèse. Paris, 1933.
39533.15.55 Tipping, W.M. Jean Regnaud de Segrais, l'homme et son oeuvres. Paris, 1933.
39533.16 Bredif, M. Segrais, sa vie et ses oeuvres. Paris, 1863.

39533.17 Individual authors, etc. - 1661-1715 - Poetry, humor, etc. - Other poets and humorists, etc. - Sénecé

39533.17 Chasles, Émile. Oeuvres choisies de Sénecé. Paris, 1855.

39533.18 Individual authors, etc. - 1661-1715 - Poetry, humor, etc. - Other poets and humorists, etc. - Cotin

39533.18 Cotin, Charles. La satyre des satyres. Paris, 1883.

39533.19 - .19.10 Individual authors, etc. - 1661-1715 - Poetry, humor, etc. - Other poets and humorists, etc. - Chéron

39533.19 Chéron, E.S. La coupe du Val de Grace. Paris, 1880.
Htn 39533.19.9* Cyrano de Bergerac. Oeuvres. Paris, 1676.
Htn 39533.19.10* Chéron, E.S. Essay de pseaumes et cantiques mis en vers. Paris, 1694.

39533.19.11 - .20 Individual authors, etc. - 1661-1715 - Poetry, humor, etc. - Other poets and humorists, etc. - Cyrano de Bergerac

39533.19.12 Cyrano de Bergerac. Oeuvres. Amsterdam, 1709. 2v.
Htn 39533.20* Lacroix, Paul. Oeuvres...de Cyrano de Bergerac. Paris, 1858.
39533.20.2 Cyrano de Bergerac. Oeuvres diverses. Paris, 1933.
Htn 39533.20.3* Cyrano de Bergerac. Satyrical characters and handsome descriptions. London, 1658.
Htn 39533.20.3.2* Cyrano de Bergerac. The agreement...dream. n.p., 1756.
Htn 39533.20.3.25* Cyrano de Bergerac. The comical history of the states and empires of the worlds of the moon and sun. v.1-2. London, 1687.
39533.20.4A Cyrano de Bergerac. Histoire comique des etats...de la lune et du soleil. Paris, 1858.
39533.20.4B Cyrano de Bergerac. Histoire comique des etats...de la lune et du soleil. Paris, 1858.
39533.20.4.5 Cyrano de Bergerac. L'autre monde ou Les états et empires de la lune. Dresden, 1910.
39533.20.4.10 Cyrano de Bergerac. Histoire comique, contenant les états et l'empire de la lune et du soleil. Paris, 1961.
39533.20.4.12 Cyrano de Bergerac. Histoire comique des états et empires de la lune. Paris, 1962.
39533.20.4.15 Cyrano de Bergerac. Voyage dans la lune. Paris, 1970.

39533.19.11 - .20 Individual authors, etc. - 1661-1715 - Poetry, humor, etc. - Other poets and humorists, etc. - Cyrano de Bergerac - cont.

39533.20.5 Cyrano de Bergerac. Voyage to the moon. N.Y., 1899.
39533.20.7 Cyrano de Bergerac. Voyages to the moon and the sun. London, 1927.
39533.20.8 Cyrano de Bergerac. Voyages to the moon and the sun. N.Y., 1962.
39533.20.9A Cyrano de Bergerac. Le pedant joué. Boston, 1899.
39533.20.9B Cyrano de Bergerac. Le pedant joué. Boston, 1899.
39533.20.10 Cyrano de Bergerac. Le pedant joué. Paris, 1908.
39533.20.11 Cyrano de Bergerac. Oeuvres comiques. Paris, 1962.
39533.20.12 Cyrano de Bergerac. Lettres d'amour. Paris, 1905.
39533.20.13 Cyrano de Bergerac. L'autre monde. Paris, 1959.
39533.20.14 Cyrano de Bergerac. Other Worlds. London, 1965.
39533.20.15 Cyrano de Bergerac. Lettres. Milano, 1965.
NEDL 39533.20.15 Brun, P.A. Savinien de Cyrano de Bergerac, sa vie et ses oeuvres. Paris, 1893.
39533.20.16 Dübi, H. Cyrano de Bergerac (1619-1655) sein Leben. Bern, 1906.
39533.20.18 Normano, J.F. A neglected Utopian::Cyrano de Bergerac, 1619-1655. n.p., 1931.
Htn 39533.20.20* Russen, David. Iter lunare; or A voyage to the moon. London, 1707.
39533.20.22 Meder, Maria. Das Weltbild in Cyrano de Bergeracs Roman L'autremonde. Mannheim, 1940.
39533.20.25 Pujos, Charles. Le double visage de Cyrano de Bergerac. Agen, 1951.
39533.20.30 Brandwajn, R. Cyrano de Bergerac. Warszawa, 1960.
39533.20.35 Mongredien, Georges. Cyrano de Bergerac. Paris, 1964.
39533.20.40 Lanius, Edward W. Cyrano de Bergerac and the universe of the imagination. Genève, 1967.
39533.20.45 Harth, Erica. Cyrano de Bergerac and the polemics of modernity. N.Y., 1970.
39533.20.50 Ezba, Luciano. Magia e invenzione. Milano, 1967.
39533.20.55 Alcover, Madeleine. La pensée philosophique et scientifique de Cyrano de Bergerac. Genève, 1970.

39533.21 Individual authors, etc. - 1661-1715 - Poetry, humor, etc. - Other poets and humorists, etc. - Vitu

39533.21 Vitu, Auguste. La mort d'Agrippine. Paris, 1875.

39533.22 Individual authors, etc. - 1661-1715 - Poetry, humor, etc. - Other poets and humorists, etc. - Sorel

39533.22 Sorel, Charles. Vraie Histoire....de Francion. Paris, 1858.
39533.22.5 Sorel, Charles. La jeunesse de Francion, texte de 1626. Paris, 1922.
39533.22.15 Sorel, Charles. Histoire comique de Francion. Photoreproduction. Paris, 1924-31. 4v.
39533.22.16 Sorel, Charles. Histoire comique de Francion. Paris, 1965.
39533.22.20 Sorel, Charles. Oeuvres galante. Paris, 1924.
39533.22.81 Loch, Philipp. Charles Sorel als literarischer Kritiker. Inaug. Diss. Würzburg, 1933.
39533.22.85 Letsch, Karl. La vraie histoire comique de Francion von Charles Sorel. Inaug. Diss. Bielefeld, 1936.
39533.22.90 Sutcliffe, Frank. Le réalisme de Charles Sorel. Paris, 1965.
39533.22.95 Goebel, Gerhard. Zur Erzahltechnik in den "Histoires comigues" des 17. Jahrhunderts. Berlin, 1965.

39533.23 Individual authors, etc. - 1661-1715 - Poetry, humor, etc. - Other poets and humorists, etc. - Lignières

39533.23 Magne, Émile. Un ami de Cyrano de Bergerac, le chavalier de Lignières. Paris, 1920.

39533.24 Individual authors, etc. - 1661-1715 - Poetry, humor, etc. - Other poets and humorists, etc. - Assouey

Htn 39533.24* Laurent, Émile. Aventures....de D'Assoucy. Paris, 1858.
39533.24.5 Assoucy, Charles. Les amours d'Apollon et de Daphné. Genève, 1969.

39533.25 Individual authors, etc. - 1661-1715 - Poetry, humor, etc. - Other poets and humorists, etc. - Pecquet

39533.25 Pecquet, A. Memoires secrets pour servir à l'histoire de Perse. Amsterdam, 1745.
39533.25.5 Pecquet, A. Memoires secrets pour servir à l'histoire de Perse. Amsterdam, 1746.
39533.25.9 Pecquet, A. The secret history of Persia. London, 1745.

39533.27 Individual authors, etc. - 1661-1715 - Poetry, humor, etc. - Other poets and humorists, etc. - Lauvergne

Htn 39533.27* Lauvergne, (Mme.) de. Recueil de poesies. Paris, 1680.

39533.28 Individual authors, etc. - 1661-1715 - Poetry, humor, etc. - Other poets and humorists, etc. - Durand

39533.28 Durand, M. Laurent. Nouvelle édition des Cantiques de l'ame devoti. Lyon, n.d.

39533.30 Individual authors, etc. - 1661-1715 - Poetry, humor, etc. - Other poets and humorists, etc. - Renoult

Htn 39533.30* Renoult, J.B. Avantures de la Madona. Amsterdam, 1701.

39533.32 - .34 Individual authors, etc. - 1661-1715 - Poetry, humor, etc. - Other poets and humorists, etc. - Patin

39533.32 Lettres de....Guy Patin. n.p., n.d.
39533.32.5 Patin, Guy. Correspondance. Paris, 1901.
39533.33 Lettres choisies de Guy Patin. Cologne, 1691. 3v.
39533.33.15 Patin, Guy. Nouvelle lettres de feu Mr. Gui Patin. v.2. Amsterdam, 1718.
39533.34 Pic, P. Guy Patin. Paris, 1911.

39533.35 Individual authors, etc. - 1661-1715 - Poetry, humor, etc. - Other poets and humorists, etc. - Sainte Garde

Htn 39533.35* Carel, Jacques. Les Sarrazins chassez de France; poeme heroïque. Paris, 1667.

39533.45 Individual authors, etc. - 1661-1715 - Poetry, humor, etc. - Other poets and humorists, etc. - Morillon

39533.45 Morillon, Gatien de. Joseph, ou L'esclave fidele. Turin, 1679.

39534.1 - .5 Individual authors, etc. - 1661-1715 - Poetry, humor, etc. - Other poets and humorists, etc. - Bussy-Rabutin

39534.1.9 Bussy-Rabutin. Discours...sur le bon usage des adversitez. Paris, 1701.
Htn 39534.1.13* Bussy-Rabutin. La France galante ou Histoires. Cologne, 1689.
Htn 39534.1.15* Bussy-Rabutin. Histoire amoureuse des Gaules. n.p., 1754.
39534.1.20 Bussy-Rabutin. Histoire amoureuse des Gaules. Paris, 1857. 2v.
39534.1.30 Bussy-Rabutin. Histoire amoureuse des Gaules. Paris, 1930. 2v.
39534.1.32 Bussy-Rabutin. Histoire amoureuse des Gaules. Paris, 1961.
39534.2 Bussy-Rabutin. Histoire amoureuse des Gaules. 2. éd. Paris, 1857-58. 2v.
Htn 39534.3* Bussy-Rabutin. Histoire amoureuse de Gaules. Paris, n.d. 2v.
39534.4 Bussy-Rabutin. Histoire amoureuse de Gaules. Paris, n.d. 2v.
39534.4.9 Bussy-Rabutin. Lettres, avec les réponses. Paris, 1714. 5v.
39534.4.20 Bussy-Rabutin. The amorous history of the Gauls. London, 1725.
39534.5 Bussy-Rabutin. Lettres. Amsterdam, 1738.
39534.5.4 Bussy-Rabutin. Correspondance de Roger de Rabutin. Paris, 1858-59. 6v.
39534.5.9 Gérard-Gailly, E. Bussy-Rabutin; sa vie, ses oeuvres. Paris, 1909.

39534.6 - .7 Individual authors, etc. - 1661-1715 - Poetry, humor, etc. - Other poets and humorists, etc. - Benserade

Htn 39534.6* Benserade, Isaac de. Les oeuvres. Paris, 1697. 2v.
Htn 39534.6.5* Benserade, Isaac de. La Cleopatra. Paris, 1636-41. 5 pam.
39534.7 Uzanne, Octave. Poésies de Benserade. Paris, 1875.
39534.7.9 Silin, Charles I. Benserade and his Ballets de cour. Diss. Baltimore, 1940.
39534.7.10A Silin, Charles I. Benserade and his Ballets de cour. Baltimore, 1940.
39534.7.10B Silin, Charles I. Benserade and his Ballets de cour. Baltimore, 1940.

39534.10 - .12 Individual authors, etc. - 1661-1715 - Poetry, humor, etc. - Other poets and humorists, etc. - Vairasse

Htn 39534.10* Vairasse, Denis. Histoire des Sevarambes. Amsterdam, 1702.
Htn 39534.11* Vairasse, Denis. History of the Sevarites. London, 1675.
39534.12 Vairasse, Denis. The history of the Sevarambians. London, 1738.
39534.12.5 Vairasse, Denis. A. Roberts Historie der Neu-gefundenen Völcker Severambes. Nürnberg, 1717.
39534.12.25 Mühll, E. von der. Denis Veiras et son histoire des Sévarambes, 1677-1679. Diss. Paris, 1938.

39534.15 Individual authors, etc. - 1661-1715 - Poetry, humor, etc. - Other poets and humorists, etc. - Drelincourt

39534.15 Drelincourt, Laurent. Sonnets chrétiens. Amsterdam, 1731.
Htn 39534.17* Ferrand, David. Les l'armes et complaintes de la reyne d'Angleterre. Paris, 1649.
Htn 39534.18* Ferrand, David. Inventaire de la Muse Normande. Rouen, 1655.

39534.19 - .22 Individual authors, etc. - 1661-1715 - Poetry, humor, etc. - Other poets and humorists, etc. - Furetière

39534.19.5 Furetière, Antoine. Roman bourgeois, ouvrage comique. Amsterdam, 1704.
39534.19.7 Furetière, Antoine. Roman bourgeois. Nancy, 1712.
39534.19.9 Furetière, Antoine. Le Roman bourgeois. Paris, 1854.
39534.20 Furetière, Antoine. Le Roman bourgeois, ouvrage comique. Paris, 1878.
39534.20.10 Furetière, Antoine. Le Roman bourgeois. Paris, 1955?
39534.20.15 Furetière, Antoine. Le Roman bourgeois. Paris, 1968.
Htn 39534.21* Furetière, Antoine. Scarron's city romance made English. Savoy, 1671.
39534.22.9 Furetière, Antoine. Unsere biederen stadtleut...Deutsch von E. Meyer. Leipzig, 1905.
Htn 39534.22.15* Furetière, Antoine. Nouvelle allegorique. Paris, 1659.
Htn 39534.22.20* Furetière, Antoine. Furetieriana ou Les mots et les remarques d'histoire. Brusselles, 1696.
39534.22.50 Leuschner, Kurt. Antoine Furetière. Inaug. Diss. Erlangen, 1915.
39534.22.80 Gegou, Fabienne. Antoine Furetière. Paris, 1962.

39534.23 Individual authors, etc. - 1661-1715 - Poetry, humor, etc. - Other poets and humorists, etc. - Laurent

39534.23.1 Laurent, Émile. La journee des Madrigaux. Genève, 1971.

39534.24 - .25 Individual authors, etc. - 1661-1715 - Poetry, humor, etc. - Other poets and humorists, etc. - Deshoulières

39534.24.15 Deshoulières, A. du L. del G. (Mme.). Poésies. v.2. Brusselles, 1707.
39534.24.20 Deshoulières, A. du L. del G. (Mme.). Poésies de Madame et Mlle. Deshoulières. Bruxelles, 1740.
39534.25 Deschoulières, A. du L. del G. (Mme.). Oeuvres. Paris, 1764. 2v.
39534.25.5A Deshoulières, A. du L. del G. (Mme.). Oeuvres. Paris, 1799. 2v.
39534.25.5B Deshoulières, A. du L. del G. (Mme.). Oeuvres. Paris, 1799. 2v.
39534.25.10 Deshoulières, A. du L. del G. (Mme.). Oeuvres. Paris, 1810.

39534.26 - .36 Individual authors, etc. - 1661-1715 - Poetry, humor, etc. - Other poets and humorists, etc. - Scarron

39534.26.5 Scarron, Paul. Théâtre complet. Paris, 1879.
39534.26.7 Scarron, Paul. Oeuvres reveues. Paris, 1668. 2v.
39534.26.9 Scarron, Paul. Les nouvelles oeuvres tragi-comiques. Amsterdam, 1675.
39534.26.15 Scarron, Paul. Les dernières oeuvres. Amsterdam, 1713.
Htn 39534.26.20* Scarron, Paul. Les dernières oeuvres. v.1-2. La Haye, 1730.
39534.27 Scarron, Paul. Oeuvres. Paris, 1786. 7v.
39534.27.3 Scarron, Paul. The whole comical works of M. Scarron. London, 1759. 2v.
Htn 39534.27.5* Scarron, Paul. Oeuvres. Rouen, 1659.
Htn 39534.27.10* Scarron, Paul. Recueil des oeuvres burlesques. Paris, 1648. 6 pam.
39534.27.15 Scarron, Paul. Poesies diverses. v.2. Paris, 1960[1961]

39534.26 - .36 Individual authors, etc. - 1661-1715 - Poetry, humor, etc. - Other poets and humorists, etc. - Scarron - cont.

39534.28 Scarron, Paul. Oeuvres. Paris, 1877. 2v.
39534.28.2 Scarron, Paul. Le romant comique. Paris, 1706.
39534.28.3 Scarron, Paul. Les oeuvres de M. Scarron. v.1-2. Paris, 1709.
39534.28.5 Scarron, Paul. Le romant comique. Amsterdam, 1717.
Htn 39534.28.6* Scarron, Paul. Le roman comique. pt.1-3. Roterdam, 1727-30. 2v.
39534.28.7 Scarron, Paul. Le roman comique. Paris, 1846.
39534.28.9 Scarron, Paul. Le roman comique. Paris, 1857. 2v.
39534.28.12A Scarron, Paul. Le roman comique de M. Scarron. Paris, 1866.
39534.28.12B Scarron, Paul. Le roman comique de M. Scarron. Paris, 1866.
39534.29 Scarron, Paul. Le roman comique. Paris, 1880. 2v.
39534.29.5 Scarron, Paul. Le roman comique. v.1-3. Paris, n.d.
39534.29.6 Scarron, Paul. Le roman comique. Paris, 1880. 3v.
Htn 39534.29.9* Scarron, Paul. Typhon. The Gyant's war with the gods. London, 1665.
39534.30 Scarron, Paul. Virgile travesti. Oppeln, 1883.
39534.30.7 Scarron, Paul. Virgile travesty. Amsterdam, 1712. 2v.
39534.30.9 Scarron, Paul. Le virgile travesty en vers burlesque. Amsterdam, 1595.
39534.30.11 Scarron, Paul. Le virgile travesty en vers burlesque. Paris, 1675. 2v.
Htn 39534.30.25* Scarron, Paul. L'heritier ridicule, ou La dame interessée. Paris, 1650.
39534.31 Scarron, Paul. Virgile travesti. Paris, n.d.
39534.31.3 Scarron, Paul. Virgile travesti. Paris, 1858.
X Cg 39534.32 Scarron, Paul. Le roman comique. Paris, 1882.
39534.32.4 Cadorel, Raymond. Le roman comique. Paris, 1938.
39534.32.4.5 Scarron, Paul. Le roman comique. v.1-2. Paris, 1951.
39534.32.4.10 Cadorel, Raymond. Scarron et la nouvelle espagnole dans le Roman comique. Aix-en-Provence, 1960.
39534.32.5A Scarron, Paul. The comical romance and other tales. London, 1892. 2v.
39534.32.5B Scarron, Paul. The comical romance and other tales. London, 1892. 2v.
39534.32.5.2 Scarron, Paul. The comical romance. N.Y., 1968.
Htn 39534.32.6* Scarron, Paul. The comical romance and other tales. London, 1892. 2v.
Htn 39534.32.7* Scarron, Paul. The whole comical works of Paul Scarron. London, 1700.
39534.32.20 Scarron, Paul. Le marquis ridicule. Paris, 1670. 4 pam.
Htn 39534.32.50* Scarron, Paul. Comical romance. London, 1676.
39534.33 Scarron, Paul. Jodelet Duelliste und seine spanischen Quellen. Erlangen, 1893.
39534.33.7 Scarron, Paul. Le Jodelet, duelliste. Paris, 1668.
39534.33.12 Scarron, Paul. Le Jodelet, duelliste. Paris, 1668.
39534.34 Scarron, Paul. Poésies diverses. Paris, 1908.
39534.34.10 Scarron, Paul. Poésies diverses. Paris, 1947- 2v.
Htn 39534.35* Scarron, Paul. Les nouvelles tragi-comiques. Paris, 1656.
39534.35.20 Scarron, Paul. Scarron et sa Gazette Burlesque. Paris, 1929.
39534.36 Toldo, Pierre. Ce que Scarron doit aux auteurs burlesques d'Italie. Paris, 1893.
39534.36.05 Magne, Émile. Bibliographie générale des oeuvres de Scarron. Paris, 1924.
39534.36.2 Roy, Émile. La vie et les oeuvres de Charles Soral. Paris, 1891.
39534.36.5 Magne, Émile. Scarron et son milieu. Paris, 1905.
39534.36.7 Magne, Émile. Scarron et son milieu. Paris, 1924.
39534.36.9 Janicki, J. Les comedies de Paul Scarron. Posen, 1907.
39534.36.10 Pamphlet box. Scarron, Paul.
39534.36.15 Jéramec, Jacques. La vie de Scarron. 4th éd. Paris, 1929.
39534.36.20 Richardson, L.T. Lexique de la langue des oeuvres burlesques de Scarron. Thèse. Aix-en-Provence, 1930.
39534.36.25 Phelps, N.F. The queen's invalid. Baltimore, 1951.
39534.36.30 Marillot, Paul. Scarron. Thèse. Paris, 1888.

39534.37 - .40 Individual authors, etc. - 1661-1715 - Poetry, humor, etc. - Other poets and humorists, etc. - Brébeuf

Htn 39534.37* Brébeuf, Georges de. Lucain Travesty ou Les guerres civiles. Paris, 1656.
Htn 39534.37.40* Brébeuf, Georges de. Entretiens solitaires. Paris, 1660.
39534.38 Brébeuf, Georges de. Entretiens solitaires. Paris, 1912.
Htn 39534.39* Brébeuf, Georges de. Poésies diverses. Paris, 1658.
Htn 39534.39.5* Brébeuf, Georges de. Poésies diverses. Rouen, 1662.
39534.40 Harmaud, R. Essai sur la vie et les oeuvres de Georges de Brébeuf, 1617?-1661. Paris, 1897.

39534.43 - .45 Individual authors, etc. - 1661-1715 - Poetry, humor, etc. - Other poets and humorists, etc. - Gaultier Garguille

39534.43 Sansrefus, G. Gaultier Garguille. Caen, 1908.
39534.44A Gaultier, Garguille. Chansons. Paris, 1858.
39534.44B Gaultier, Garguille. Chansons. Paris, 1858.
39534.45 Gaultier, Garguille. Comédien. Paris, n.d.

39534.46 - .59 Individual authors, etc. - 1661-1715 - Poetry, humor, etc. - Other poets and humorists, etc. - Miscellany

39534.46 Marolles, Michel de. Le livre des peintres et graveurs. Poetry. Paris, 1855.
39534.47 Montreüil, M. Les oeuvres. Paris, 1671.
39534.48 Nicole, Claude. Les oeuvres. Paris, 1662.
39534.49 La Suze, Henriette de Coligny. Recueil de pieces galantes en prose et en vers. Paris, 1684. 4v.
39534.52 Bruslé de Montpleinchamp, Jean. Le diable bossu. Nancy, 1708.

39534.60 - Individual authors, etc. - 1661-1715 - Poetry, humor, etc. - Other poets and humorists, etc. - Anonymous works

Htn 39534.60* L'inconstant vaincu. Paris, 1661.

39535 Individual authors, etc. - 1661-1715 - Poetry, humor, etc. - Satirists and epigrammatists

39535.3 La grande confrairie des saouls d'ouvrer. Rouen, 1735. 4 pam.
39535.5 Le Roy, A. de. Le Momus François ou Les avantures. Cologne, 1759.
39535.5.5 Le Roy, A. de. Le Momus François ou Les avantures. Cologne, 1761.
Htn 39535.6* Naude, G. Naudaeana et Patiniana. Paris, 1701.
39535.7 Naude, G. Naudaeana et Patiniana ou Singularitez. Amsterdam, 1703.
39535.9 Pamphlet box. Naudé, Gabriel.

39535 Individual authors, etc. - 1661-1715 - Poetry, humor, etc. - Satirists and epigrammatists - cont.

39535.10 Callières, François de. Recueil des bons contes et de bons mots. Paris, 1693.

39535.11 Callières, François de. Recueil des bons contes et de bons mots. Utrecht, 1730.

Htn 39535.12* Callières, François de. Characters and criticisms upon the ancient orators. London, 1705.

39535.12.5 Callières, François de. Nouvelles amoureuses et galantes. Paris, 1678.

39535.13.7 Matanasiana, ou Memoires litteraires, historiques, et critiques du...Matanasius. La Haye, 1740.

39535.14 Neretti, Filippo. Dialogues et historiettes diverses. Venise, 1702.

Htn 39535.15* Sorbiere, S. Sorberiana ou Bon mots. Paris, 1694.

Htn 39535.16* Sorbiere, S. Sorberiana sive excerpta. Tolosae, 1694.

39535.18 Colnet du Ravel, C.J.A.M. de. Satiriques du 18e siècle. Paris, 1800. 7v.

39535.22 Roger Bontems, en belle humeur. 4th éd. Cologne, 1731.

39535.25 Du Cerceau, Jean Antoine. Recueil de poésies diverses. 3e éd. Paris, 1726.

39535.29 Garon, L. Le chasse ennuy, ou L'honneste. 4th éd. Paris, 1645.

39535.33 L'enclos, Anne. The memoirs of Anne L'enclos. London, 1776.

39535.33.5 Dauxménil. Mémoires pour servir à l'histoire. Paris, 1908.

Htn 39535.35* L'enclos, Anne. Portrait ou Le veritable caractere de le Coquette. Paris, 1701.

39535.37 L'enclos, Anne. Lettres de Ninon de L'enclos. Paris, 1928.

39535.40 Cypriot, O. Almanach d'amour. n.p., 1665.

39535.45 Bernier, J. Reflexions, pensées. Paris, 1696.

39535.50 Aubignae, F.H. Les conseils d'Ariste à Celimene. La Haye, 1687.

39535.55 Pauckoucke, A.J. L'arte de Desoppiler La Rote. n.p., n.d.

39535.57 Pringy, de Marenville de (Mme.). Les differens caractères des femmes du siècle. 2e éd. Paris, 1699.

39535.58 L'Art plumer la poule sans crier. Cologne, 1710.

39535.60 Grécourt, Jean B.J.W. de. Maranzakiniana. Paris, 1875.

39535.62A Le cabinet satyrique. Paris, 1924. 2v.

39535.62B Le cabinet satyrique. Paris, 1924. 2v.

Htn 39535.64* Berthod, François. La ville de Paris. Paris, 166-?

Htn 39535.66* Le mercure burlesque. Amsterdam.

39535.67.5 Lettres choisies de messieurs de l'Academie française. Paris, 1709.

39535.68 L'ombre d'Amarante. Montpellier, 1959.

39535.70 Trotti de la Chélardie. Maximes sur la cour. Amsterdam, n.d.

39536 - 39542 Individual authors, etc. - 1715-1799 - Voltaire - Complete and Selected works - Folios, etc. [Discontinued]

39536.32 Voltaire, François Marie Arouet de. Oeuvres complètes. 2d ed. Paris, 1825-28.

39536.33 Longchamp, Sebastian G. Mémoires sur Voltaire. Paris, 1826. 2v.

39536.34 Voltaire, François Marie Arouet de. Oeuvres. Paris, 1834-39. 74v.

Htn 39541.1* Voltaire, François Marie Arouet de. The maid of Orleans. London, 1780.

39541.2 Voltaire, François Marie Arouet de. Oeuvres de Voltaire. Paris, 1792. 55v.

39541.5 Voltaire, François Marie Arouet de. La Henriade. Neuchâtel, 1772.

39541.5.2 Voltaire, François Marie Arouet de. Théâtre. Neuchâtel, 1783. 8v.

39541.5.4 Voltaire, François Marie Arouet de. Essais sur les moeurs et l'esprit des nations. Neuchâtel, 1773. 8v.

39541.5.6 Voltaire, François Marie Arouet de. Mélanges philosophiques. Neuchâtel, 1773. 6v.

39541.5.8 Voltaire, François Marie Arouet de. Questions sur l'encyclopedie. Neuchâtel, 1777.

39541.5.10 Voltaire, François Marie Arouet de. Siècle de Louis XIV. Neuchâtel, 1783. 4v.

39541.5.12 Voltaire, François Marie Arouet de. Mélanges de poésies. Neuchâtel, 1773.

39541.5.14 Voltaire, François Marie Arouet de. Romans. Londres, 1776. 2v.

39541.5.16 Voltaire, François Marie Arouet de. Histoire de Charles XII. n.p., 1772. 2v.

Htn 39541.5.18* Voltaire, François Marie Arouet de. Histoire de l'empire de Russie sous Pierre le Grand. n.p., 1759-63. 2v.

39542.30 Voltaire, François Marie Arouet de. Oeuvres complètes. Hamburg, 1792. 18v.

39542.31 Voltaire, François Marie Arouet de. Oeuvres choisies. Paris, 1878.

39542.31.5 Voltaire, François Marie Arouet de. Oeuvres choisies. Paris, 188-.

39542.32 Voltaire, François Marie Arouet de. Chef-d'oeuvres dramatique. Paris, 1800? 4v.

39542.32.10 Voltaire, François Marie Arouet de. Théâtre de Voltaire. Paris, 1868.

39542.32.15 Voltaire, François Marie Arouet de. Théâtre de Voltaire. Paris, 1927. 2v.

39542.35 Voltaire, François Marie Arouet de. Contes et romans. Paris, 1930. 4v.

39542.35.15 Voltaire, François Marie Arouet de. Voltaire and the enlightenment. N.Y., 1931.

39543.1 - .799 Individual authors, etc. - 1715-1799 - Voltaire - Complete and Selected works - Other editions

39543.2 Voltaire, François Marie Arouet de. Collection complette des oeuvres. Genèva, 1764. 21v.

Htn 39543.3* Voltaire, François Marie Arouet de. Histoire de l'empire de Russie. Genèva, 1759-65. 2v.

39543.4 Voltaire, François Marie Arouet de. Traité sur la tolérance. Genèva, 1763.

Htn 39543.4.5* Voltaire, François Marie Arouet de. Traité sur la tolérance. Genèva, 1763. 3 pam.

Htn 39543.6* Voltaire, François Marie Arouet de. La philosophie de l'histoire. Genèva, 1765.

Htn 39543.7* Voltaire, François Marie Arouet de. Lettres secrettes. Genèva, 1765.

39543.15 Voltaire, François Marie Arouet de. Works. London, 1779-80. 5v.

39543.16 Voltaire, François Marie Arouet de. The works of Voltaire. Paris, 1901. 42v.

39543.1 - .799 Individual authors, etc. - 1715-1799 - Voltaire - Complete and Selected works - Other editions - cont.

39543.17 Voltaire, François Marie Arouet de. Oeuvres complètes de Voltaire. v.1-32,34-35,37-46,48-70. Kehl, 1785-89. 67v.

39543.18 Voltaire, François Marie Arouet de. Choix de contes. Cambridge, Eng., 1951.

39543.19 Voltaire, François Marie Arouet de. Romans et contes. Paris, 1950.

39543.20 Voltaire, François Marie Arouet de. Oeuvres complètes. v.4, 6-7. Paris, 1820-21. 3v.

39543.22 Voltaire, François Marie Arouet de. Les oeuvres complètes. Genève, 1968- 24v.

39543.25 Voltaire, François Marie Arouet de. Oeuvres historiques. Paris, 1957.

39543.30 Voltaire, François Marie Arouet de. Filosofia. Madrid, 1822.

39543.35 Voltaire, François Marie Arouet de. Les pages immortelles de Voltaire. Paris, 1961.

39543.40 Voltaire, François Marie Arouet de. Fragments on India. Lahore, 1937.

39543.45 Voltaire, François Marie Arouet de. Esprit de Voltaire. Paris, 1855.

39543.50 Voltaire, François Marie Arouet de. The whole prose romances. Philadelphia, 1897-98. 3v.

39543.51 Voltaire, François Marie Arouet de. The complete romances of Voltaire. N.Y., 1927.

39543.55 Voltaire, François Marie Arouet de. Mélanges. Paris, 1961.

39543.60 Voltaire, François Marie Arouet de. The portable Voltaire. N.Y., 1949.

39543.65 Vail, F. Voltaire, sa vie et son oeuvre, avec textes complèts annotés. Paris, 1953.

39543.66 Voltaire, François Marie Arouet de. Politique de Voltaire. Paris, 1963.

39543.67 Voltaire, François Marie Arouet de. The age of Louis XIV. N.Y., 1965.

39543.68 Voltaire, François Marie Arouet de. Voltaire: seine Persönlichkeit in seinen Werken. Stuttgart, 1906.

39543.70 Voltaire, François Marie Arouet de. Mélanges philosophiques. Paris, 1971.

39543.800 - .999 Individual authors, etc. - 1715-1799 - Voltaire - Bibliographies

39543.800 Bengescu, G. Voltaire; bibliographie de ses oeuvres. Paris, 1882-90. 4v.

39543.802 Barr, Mary M.H. A century of Voltaire study...1825-1925. N.Y., 1929.

39543.802.5 Barr, Mary M.H. Quarante années d'études Voltairiennes...1926-1965. Paris, 1968.

39544 Individual authors, etc. - 1715-1799 - Voltaire - Biography and criticism

39544.01 Pamphlet box. Voltaire.

39544.1 Gibert, M.E. Obiero sur les écrits de M. de Voltaire. London, 1788. 2v.

39544.2 Linguet, Simon N.H. Critical analysis...of Voltaire's works. London, 1790.

39544.2.9 Pamphlet vol. Oeuvres de Voltaire et Rousseau - 1817-1821. 16 pam.

39544.2.15 Boulogne, Étienne Antoine de. Istruzione pastorale sopra la pubblicazione de'cattivi libri. Firenze, 1822.

39544.3 Meusnier de Querlon, Anne Gabriel. Testament littéraire de Pierre-François Guyot. La Haye, 1746.

39544.4 Houssaye, Arsène. Le Roi Voltaire. Paris, 1858.

39544.5 Houssaye, Arsène. Le Roi Voltaire. Paris, 1858.

39544.5.5 Houssaye, Arsène. Le Roi Voltaire. Paris, 1860.

39544.6 Bavoux, Evariste. Voltaire a Ferney. Sa correspondance. Paris, 1860.

39544.7 Flottes, J.B.M. Introduction aux ouvrages de Voltaire. Montpellier, 1816.

39544.8 Beaune, Henri. Voltaire au collége. Paris, 1867.

X Cg 39544.9 Adolph, Carl. Voltaire et le théâtre de Shakespeare. Sorau, 1883.

39544.10 Foisset, M.T. Voltaire et le président de Brosses. Paris, 1853.

39544.10.6 Cunisset-Carnot, Paul. La querelle du président de Brosses, avec Voltaire. Dijon, 1888.

39544.11 Maynard, Michel U. Voltaire, sa vie. Paris, 1868. 2v.

39544.11.2 Strauss, D.F. Voltaire. Leipzig, 1870.

39544.12 Strauss, D.F. Voltaire. Leipzig, 1872.

39544.13 Strauss, D.F. Voltaire. Six Conférences. Paris, 1876.

39544.14 Mahrenholtz, R. Voltaire - Studien. Oppeln, 1882.

39544.14.3 Mahrenholtz, R. Voltaire - Studien. Wien, 1879.

39544.14.5 Vita del Signor di Voltaire...di lui opere. Londra, 1779.

39544.15 Desnoiresterres, G. Jeunesse de Voltaire. Paris, 1867.

39544.16 Desnoiresterres, G. Voltaire au Chateau de Cirey. Paris, 1868.

39544.17 Desnoiresterres, G. Voltaire a la cour. Paris, 1869.

39544.18 Desnoiresterres, G. Voltaire et Frédéric. Paris, 1870.

39544.19 Desnoiresterres, G. Voltaire aux Délices. Paris, 1873.

39544.20 Desnoiresterres, G. Voltaire et J.J. Rousseau. Paris, 1874.

39544.21 Desnoiresterres, G. Voltaire et Genève. Paris, 1875.

39544.22 Desnoiresterres, G. Voltaire, son retour et sa mort. Paris, 1876.

39544.23 Saint-René Taillandier, René. La Suisse chrétienne et le dix-huitième siècle. Pages inédites de Voltaire et de Rousseau. Genève, 1862.

X Cg 39544.24 Maugras, Gaston. Voltaire et J.J. Rousseau. Paris, 1886.

39544.24.5 Allier, Raoul. Voltaire et Calas. Paris, 1898.

39544.24.15 Maugras, Gaston. Voltaire et J.J. Rousseau. Wien, 1895.

39544.25 Maugras, Gaston. La vie de Voltaire. Paris, 1885.

39544.25.3 Renard, Georges. Vie de Voltaire. Paris, 1883.

39544.25.5 Voltaire, François Marie Arouet de. Memoirs of the life of Voltaire. London, 1784.

39544.25.10 Voltaire, François Marie Arouet de. Mémoires pour servir à la vie. Paris, 1945.

39544.25.15 Voltaire, François Marie Arouet de. Mémoires pour servir à la vie. Paris, 1965.

39544.26 Courtat, Félix-Titus. Défense de Voltaire. Paris, 1872.

39544.27 Courtat, Félix-Titus. Vraies lettres de Voltaire. Paris, 1875.

39544.27.2 Voltaire, François Marie Arouet de. Correspondance avec P.M. Hennin. Paris, 1825.

39544.27.3 Voltaire, François Marie Arouet de. Lettres choisies. 6th ed. Paris, 1891.

Classified Listing

39544 Individual authors, etc. - 1715-1799 - Voltaire - Biography and criticism - cont.

	39544.27.3.3	Voltaire, François Marie Arouet de. Lettres choisies. 18e éd. Paris, 1934.
	39544.27.3.5	Voltaire, François Marie Arouet de. Lettres choisies. Paris, 18- ? 2v.
	39544.27.3.7	Voltaire, François Marie Arouet de. Lettres d'amour...Louis Malard. Paris, 1888. 2v.
	39544.27.3.9	Voltaire, François Marie Arouet de. Lettres inédites aux Tranchin. v.1,2-3. Genève, 1950. 2v.
	39544.27.3.10	Voltaire, François Marie Arouet de. Voltaire. Paris, 1955.
	39544.27.3.12	Voltaire, François Marie Arouet de. Lettres d'amour de Voltaire à sa nièce. Paris, 1957.
	39544.27.4	Wege, Bernhard. Der Prozess Calas im Briefwechsel Voltaires. Berlin, 1896.
	39544.27.9	Foulet, L. Correspondance de Voltaire. Paris, 1913.
	39544.27.10A	Voltaire, François Marie Arouet de. Voltaire in his letters. N.Y., 1919.
	39544.27.10B	Voltaire, François Marie Arouet de. Voltaire in his letters. N.Y., 1919.
	39544.27.11	Charrot, C. Quelques notes sur la "Correspondance" de Voltaire. Paris, 1913.
	39544.27.13	Voltaire, François Marie Arouet de. Lettres d'Alsace à sa nièce Madame Denis. Paris, 1938.
Htn	39544.27.15*	Voltaire, François Marie Arouet de. Lettres de Voltaire et de J.J. Rousseau à C.J. Panckoucke. Paris, 1828.
Htn	39544.27.18*	Voltaire, François Marie Arouet de. Lettres ecrites de Londres sur les Anglois. Amsterdam, 1736.
	39544.27.21	Voltaire, François Marie Arouet de. Lettres. N.Y., 1927.
	39544.27.22	Voltaire, François Marie Arouet de. The love letters of Voltaire to his niece. London, 1958.
	39544.27.25	Voltaire, François Marie Arouet de. Voltaire's England. London, 1950.
	39544.27.28	Voltaire, François Marie Arouet de. Correspondance avec les Tondrin. Paris, 1950.
	39544.27.30A	Voltaire, François Marie Arouet de. A letter to James Boswell...Feb. 11, 1765. N.Y., 1927.
	39544.27.30B	Voltaire, François Marie Arouet de. A letter to James Boswell...Feb. 11, 1765. N.Y., 1927.
	39544.27.32	Voltaire, François Marie Arouet de. Select letters of Voltaire. London, 1963.
	39544.28	Voltaire, François Marie Arouet de. Lettres choisies. Paris, 1881.
	39544.28.3	Delattre, A. Répertoire chronologique des lettres de Voltaire. Chapel Hill, 1952.
	39544.28.5	Voltaire, François Marie Arouet de. Lettres choisies. Paris, 1893. 2v.
	39544.28.15	Voltaire, François Marie Arouet de. Lettres choisies. v.1-2. Paris, 1946.
	39544.28.16	Voltaire, François Marie Arouet de. Les peus belles lettres de Voltaire. Paris, 1961.
	39544.28.20	Voltaire, François Marie Arouet de. Lettre philosophique. Paris, 1818.
	39544.28.30	Voltaire, François Marie Arouet de. Lettres philosophiques. v.1-2. éd. Paris, 1915-
Htn	39544.28.35*	Voltaire, François Marie Arouet de. Lettre philosophique. Berlin, 1774.
	39544.28.40	Voltaire, François Marie Arouet de. Lettres philosophiques. Paris, 1964. 2v.
	39544.28.50	Voltaire, François Marie Arouet de. Lettres philosophiques. Paris, 1939.
	39544.28.60	Voltaire, François Marie Arouet de. Lettres philosophiques. Oxford, 1943.
	39544.28.65	Voltaire, François Marie Arouet de. Lettres philosophiques. Oxford, 1946.
	39544.28.70	Tribolati, F. Sill'epistolario italiano del Voltaire. Pisa, 1878.
	39544.28.75A	Voltaire, François Marie Arouet de. Correspondance. Genève, 1953-64. 107v.
	39544.28.75B	Voltaire, François Marie Arouet de. Correspondance. v.4-6. Genève, 1953-64. 3v.
	39544.28.80	Voltaire, François Marie Arouet de. Voltaire. Genève, 1952.
	39544.28.85	Voltaire, François Marie Arouet de. Lettres inédites à Constant d'Hermenches. Paris, 1956.
	39544.28.90	Voltaire, François Marie Arouet de. Lettres. Textes nouveaux de la correspondance de Voltaire. Moscou, 1956. 2v.
	39544.28.95	Voltaire, François Marie Arouet de. Lettres anglaises. Paris, 1964.
	39544.28.100	Voltaire, François Marie Arouet de. Voltaires Briefwechsel mit Friedrich dem Grossen. Berlin, 1944.
	39544.29	Grimm, Hermann. Voltaire und Frankreich. n.p., n.d.
	39544.30	Standish, F.H. Life of Voltaire. London, 1821.
	39544.31	Faguet, Émile. Voltaire. Paris, 1895.
	39544.32.1	Morley, John. Voltaire. N.Y., 1872.
X Cg	39544.32.3	Morley, John. Voltaire. London, 1872.
	39544.32.4A	Morley, John. Voltaire. 2d ed. N.Y., 1872.
	39544.32.4B	Morley, John. Voltaire. 2d ed. N.Y., 1872.
	39544.32.7	Morley, John. Voltaire. London, 1903.
	39544.32.8	Morley, John. Voltaire. London, 1913.
	39544.32.10A	Morley, John. Voltaire. London, 1923.
	39544.32.10B	Morley, John. Voltaire. London, 1923.
	39544.33A	Parton, James. Life of Voltaire. Boston, 1881. 2v.
	39544.33B	Parton, James. Life of Voltaire. Boston, 1881. 2v.
	39544.33C	Parton, James. Life of Voltaire. Boston, 1881. 2v.
	39544.33D	Parton, James. Life of Voltaire. Boston, 1881. 2v.
	39544.33.2	Parton, James. Life of Voltaire. 4th ed. Boston, 1884. 2v.
	39544.33.3	Parton, James. Life of Voltaire. 6. ed. Boston, 1889. 2v.
	39544.33.4	Parton, James. Life of Voltaire. 7. ed. Boston, 1892. 2v.
	39544.34	Mahrenholtz, R. Voltaires Leben und Werke. Oppeln, 1885.
	39544.35	Champion, E. Voltaire. Études critiques. Paris, 1893.
	39544.36A	Nourrisson, Jean Félix. Voltaire et le Voltairianisme. Paris, 1896.
	39544.36B	Nourrisson, Jean Félix. Voltaire et le Voltairianisme. Paris, 1896.
	39544.37	Vernier, Léon. Étude sur Voltaire Grammairien. Thèse. Paris, 1888.
	39544.38	Pompery, E. de. La vie de Voltaire. Paris, 1878.
	39544.39	Popper, Josef. Voltaire. Dresden, 1905.
	39544.40	Crouslé, L. La vie et les oeuvres de Voltaire. Paris, 1899. 2v.
	39544.42	Brougham, H.B. Lives of men of letters. Voltaire, Rousseau, etc. London, 1855.

39544 Individual authors, etc. - 1715-1799 - Voltaire - Biography and criticism - cont.

	39544.42.5	Brougham, H.B. Voltaire et Rousseau. London, 1845.
	39544.43	Desnoiresterres, G. Voltaire et J.J. Rousseau. Paris, 1875.
	39544.44	Bruce, H.L. Voltaire on the English stage. Berkeley, 1918.
	39544.44.20	Fenger, H. Voltaire et le théâtre anglais. Copenhague, 1949.
	39544.45	Hagmann, J.G. Ueber Voltaires "Essai sur les moeurs". Leipzig, 1883.
	39544.46.10	Lanson, Gustave. Voltaire. 2. éd. Paris, 1910.
	39544.46.15	Lanson, Gustave. Voltaire. Paris, 1960.
	39544.46.16	Lanson, Gustave. Voltaire. N.Y., 1966.
	39544.47	Mangold, Wilhelm. Voltaires Rechtsstreit mit dem Könglichen Schutzjuden Hirschel 1751. Berlin, 1905.
	39544.48A	Pellissier, G. Voltaire, philosophe. Paris, 1908.
	39544.48B	Pellissier, G. Voltaire, philosophe. Paris, 1908.
	39544.49	Labriola, A. Voltaire e la filosofia della liberazione. Napoli, 1926.
	39544.50A	Collins, J.C. Voltaire, Montesquieu and Rousseau in England. London, 1908.
	39544.50B	Collins, J.C. Voltaire, Montesquieu and Rousseau in England. London, 1908.
	39544.52	Lachèore, F. Voltaire mourant. Paris, 1908.
	39544.53	Muller, D. Les rentes viagères. Paris, 1920.
	39544.53.15	Ellissen, O.A. Voltaire als Denker. v.3. Leipzig, 1924.
	39544.54	Findlay, Robert. A vindication of the sacred books and of Josephus. Glasgow, 1770.
	39544.55	Hurn, A.S. Voltaire et Balingbroke. Thèse. Paris, 1915.
	39544.56A	Thaddeus, V. Voltaire, genius of mockery. N.Y., 1928.
	39544.56B	Thaddeus, V. Voltaire, genius of mockery. N.Y., 1928.
	39544.57.2	Guénée, Antoine. Lettres de quelques juifs portugais et allemands. 2e éd. Paris, 1769.
	39544.58	Guénée, Antoine. Lettres de quelques juifs portugais. 3e éd. Paris, 1772. 2v.
	39544.58.35	Guénée, Antoine. Letters of certain Jews to Monsieur de Voltaire. Dublin, 1777. 2v.
	39544.58.40	Guénée, Antoine. Letters of certain Jews to Monsieur Voltaire. Paris, 1845.
Htn	39544.58.40*	Guénée, Antoine. Letter of certain Jews to Monsieur Voltaire. Philadelphia, 1795.
	39544.59	Sonet, E. Voltaire et l'influence anglaise. Thèse. Rennes, 1926.
Htn	39544.60*	Pamphlet vol. Voltaire. 13 pam.
	39544.61	Pamphlet vol. Dupanloup. Lettres sur le centinaire de Voltaire. 3 pam.
	39544.61.3	Pamphlet vol. Dupanloup. Lettres sur le centinaire de Voltaire. 2 pam.
	39544.62	Nonnotte, C.F. Les erreurs de Voltaire. 3e éd. Lyon, 1767. 2v.
	39544.62.5	Hajdu, Pál. Egy fejezet a Jézus Tarsaság Voltaire elleni Küzdelméböl. Budapest, 1935.
	39544.62.10	Breuer, J. Claude François Nonnott S.J. Inaug. Diss. Werl, 1933.
	39544.64A	Minderhoud, H.J. La Henriade. Proefschrift. Paris, 1927.
	39544.64B	Minderhoud, H.J. La Henriade. Proefschrift. Paris, 1927.
	39544.65	Brandes, Georg. Voltaire in seinem Verhältnis zu Friedrich dem Grossen. Berlin, 1909.
	39544.65.10	Brandes, Georg. François de Voltaire. Kjøbenhavn, 1916-17. 2v.
	39544.68	Valles, Charles de. La propriété du coeur de Voltaire. Paris, 1922.
	39544.70	Meinhardt, G. Voltaire und seine Sekretäre. Inaug. Diss. Berlin, 1915.
	39544.72	Herman, G. Voltaires dramatische Arbeitsweise. Inaug. Diss. Erfurt, 1925.
	39544.75	DuBois-Reymond, E. Voltaire in seiner Beziehung zur Naturwissenschaft. Berlin, 1868.
	39544.76	Damilaville, Edouard. Voltaire à Paris. Paris, 1878.
	39544.77	Tochander, R. Fremdes Sprachgut im Wortschatze Voltaires. Paris, 1920.
	39544.78	Desnoiresterres, G. Inconographie voltairienne. Paris, 1879.
	39544.80	Ceballos, F. Juicio final de Voltaire. v.1-2. Sevilla, 1856.
	39544.82	Aldington, Richard. Voltaire; the republic of letters. London, 1925.
	39544.84A	Chase, C.B. Young Voltaire. N.Y., 1926.
	39544.84B	Chase, C.B. Young Voltaire. N.Y., 1926.
	39544.85	Tabaraud, M.M. De la philosophie de la Henriade. Paris, 1824.
	39544.85.10	De la philosophie de la Henriade. Paris, 1805.
	39544.88	Maestro, Marcello T. Voltaire and Beccaria as reformers of criminal law. Thesis. N.Y., 1942.
	39544.90	Torrey, N.L. Voltaire and the English deists. New Haven, 1930.
	39544.90.5	Torrey, N.L. The spirit of Voltaire. N.Y., 1938.
	39544.92	Kozminski, L. Voltaire, financier. Thèse. Paris, 1929.
	39544.94.5A	Brandes, Georg. Voltaire. N.Y., 1930. 2v.
	39544.94.5B	Brandes, Georg. Voltaire. N.Y., 1930. 2v.
	39544.96	Celarié, H. Monsieur de Voltaire. Paris, 1928.
	39544.98	Henriot, É. Voltaire et Frederic II. Paris, 1927.
	39544.100	Prod'homme, J.G. Voltaire raconté par ceux qui l'ont vu. Paris, 1929.
	39544.102	Price, W.R. Symbolism of Voltaire's novels. N.Y., 1911.
	39544.104A	Ballantyne, A. Voltaire's visit to England, 1726-1729. London, 1919.
	39544.104B	Ballantyne, A. Voltaire's visit to England, 1726-1729. London, 1919.
	39544.104C	Ballantyne, A. Voltaire's visit to England, 1726-1729. London, 1919.
	39544.106A	Bellessort, A. Essai sur Voltaire; cours professé à la Société des conférences. Paris, 1925.
	39544.106B	Bellessort, A. Essai sur Voltaire; cours professé à la Société des conférences. Paris, 1925.
	39544.108	Emmrich, Hanna. Zur Behandlung des Judentums bei Voltaire. Inaug. Diss. Breslau, 1930.
	39544.110	Engemann, W. Voltaire und China. Inaug. Diss. Leipzig, 1932.
	39544.112A	McGhee, D.M. Voltairian narrative devices as considered in author's Contes philosophiques. Menasha, 1933.
	39544.112B	McGhee, D.M. Voltairian narrative devices as considered in author's Contes philosophiques. Menasha, 1933.
	39544.114	Crist, C.M. The dictionnaire philosophique portatif and the early French deists. Brooklyn, 1934.
	39544.116	Fischer, E. Voltaire als Paedagoge. Inaug. Diss. Leipzig, 1934.

39544 Individual authors, etc. - 1715-1799 - Voltaire - Biography and criticism - cont.

39544.118 Libby, M.S. The attitude of Voltaire to magic and the sciences. N.Y., 1935.
39544.119 Obser, Karl. Voltaires Beziehungen zu der Markgräfen Karoline Luise von Baden-Durlach und dem Karlsruber Hofe. Heidelberg, 1902.
39544.120 Horn, Georg. Voltaire und die Markgräfin von Baireuth. Berlin, 1865.
39544.122 Fitch, R.E. Voltaire's philosophic procedure. Thesis. Forest Grove, 1935.
39544.123.5 Maurois, André. Voltaire. London, 1932.
39544.124A Maurois, André. Voltaire. 60e éd. Paris, 1935.
39544.124B Maurois, André. Voltaire. 60e éd. Paris, 1935.
39544.124.10 Maurois, André. Voltaire. N.Y., 1938.
39544.124.20 Maurois, André. Voltaire. London, 1952.
39544.126 Lowenstein, R. Voltaire. Diss. Baltimore, 1935.
39544.128A Naves, Alfred. Voltaire. N.Y., 1936.
39544.128B Naves, Alfred. Voltaire. N.Y., 1936.
X Cg 39544.130 Carré, J.R. Réflexions sur l'Anti-Pascal de Voltaire. Paris, 1935.
39544.130.10 Carré, J.R. Consistance de Voltaire. Paris, 1938.
39544.132 Morehouse, A.R. Voltaire and Jean Meslier. New Haven, 1936.
39544.136 Crouvezier, G. La vie de Voltaire. Paris, 1937.
39544.138 Pignet, G. La vérité sur la vie amoureuse de M. de Voltaire. Paris, 1938.
39544.140 Stern, Jean. Belle et Bonne, une fervente amie de Voltaire, 1757-1822. Paris, 1938.
39544.140.5 Stern, Jean. Voltaire et sa nièce. Paris, 1957.
39544.142 Rochwood, R.O. The cult of Voltaire to 1791; a revolutionary deity, 1789 - May 30, 1791. Chicago, 1937.
39544.144 Charpentier, J. Voltaire. Paris, 1938.
39544.145 Naves, Raymond. Le goût de Voltaire. Thèse. Paris, 1938?
39544.147 Naves, Raymond. Voltaire et l'encyclopédie. Paris, 1938.
39544.147.7 Naves, Raymond. Voltaire, l'homme et l'oeuvre. Paris, 1942.
39544.150 Amato, J. La grammaire et le lexique de Voltaire. Palermo, 1937?
39544.155 Hall, Evelyn B. The life of Voltaire. 3d ed. N.Y., 1905.
39544.155.2 Hall, Evelyn B. The life of Voltaire. 3d ed. N.Y., 19- . 2v.
39544.155.5 Hall, Evelyn B. The life of Voltaire. 3d ed. N.Y., 1905?
39544.155.10 Hall, Evelyn B. The life of Voltaire. 3d ed. N.Y., 1907.
39544.155.15 Hall, Evelyn B. The life of Voltaire. 3d ed. N.Y., 1910.
39544.155.20 Hall, Evelyn B. The life of Voltaire. 3d ed. N.Y., 1903.
39544.160 Harper, H.H. Voltaire. Boston, 1934?
39544.165 A brief sketch of the life and writings of M. de Voltaire. London, 18- ?
39544.167 Wheeler, J.M. Voltaire; a sketch of his life and work with selections from his writings. London, 1894.
39544.170 Dubas, V. Voltaire. Kaunas, 1932.
39544.175 Spitzer, Leo. Einige Voltaire-Interpretationen. Marburg, 1931.
39544.180 Steiner, Rudolf. Voltaire vom Gesichtspunkte der Geisteswissenschaft. Berlin, 1914.
39544.186 Meyer, A.E. Voltaire: man of justice. N.Y., 1945.
39544.186.3 Meyer, A.E. Voltaire. London, 1951.
39544.187 Waterman, Mina. Voltaire, Pascal and human destiny. Thesis. N.Y., 1942.
39544.189 Ingersoll, R.G. Oration on Voltaire. London, 1892.
39544.190 O'Flaherty, K. Voltaire. Cork, 1945.
39544.195 Trudel, Marcel. L'influence de Voltaire au Canada. Montreal, 1945. 2v.
39544.200 Russell, Trusten Wheeler. Voltaire, Dryden and heroic tragedy. N.Y., 1946.
39544.210 Francis, L. La vie privée de Voltaire. Paris, 1948.
39544.215 Crésson, André. Voltaire. Paris, 1948.
39544.220 Michelmore, G. and Co. Voltaire. London, 1923.
39544.225 Schilling, B.N. Conservative England and the case against Voltaire. N.Y., 1950.
39544.230 Donvez, J. De quoi vivait Voltaire. Paris, 1949.
39544.235 Lewis, J. Voltaire. N.Y., 1929.
39544.240 Roulet, L.E. Voltaire et les Bernois. Neuchâtel, 1950.
39544.245 Auger, L.S. Notice sur la vie et les ouvrages de Voltaire. Paris? 18- .
39544.250 Besterman, Theodore. Travaux sur Voltaire. Genève, 1955- 88v.
39544.252 Besterman, Theodore. Voltaire essays. London, 1962.
39544.255 Flowers, Ruth C. Voltaire's stylistic transformation of Rabelaisian satirical devices. Washington, 1951.
39544.260 Rowe, Constance. Voltaire and the state. N.Y., 1955.
39544.265 Straeten, E. Voltaire. Paris, 1878.
39544.270 Nicolardot, L. Ménage et finances de Voltaire. Paris, 1887. 2v.
39544.275 Pomeau, René. La religion de Voltaire. Paris, 1956.
39544.275.2 Pomeau, René. La religion de Voltaire. Thèse. Paris, 1956.
39544.275.4 Pomeau, René. La religion de Voltaire. Paris, 1969.
39544.280 Ceitac, Jane. Voltaire et l'affaire des natifs. Genève, 1956.
39544.285 Addamiano, Natale. Voltaire. Roma, 1956.
39544.290 Duvernet, T.I. La vie de Voltaire. Genève, 1786.
39544.295 Mitford, Nancy. Voltaire in love. London, 1957.
39544.300 Brumfitt, J.H. Voltaire. London, 1958.
39544.305 Carel, George. Voltaire und Goethe als Dramatiker. v.1-2. Berlin, 1889-98.
39544.310 Leningrad. Universitet. Vol'ter. Leningrad, 1947.
39544.315 Dédéyan, Charles. Voltaire et la pensée anglaise. Paris, 1956.
39544.320 Diaz, F. Voltaire storico. Torino, 1958.
39544.325 Gay, Peter. Voltaire's politics. Princeton, 1959.
39544.330 Sokolov, V.V. Vol'ter. Moskva, 1956.
39544.335 Waldinger, René. Voltaire and reform in the light of the French revolution. Genève, 1959.
39544.340 Girnus, Wilhelm. Voltaire. Berlin, 1958.
39544.345 Gielly, L.J. Voltaire. Genève, 1948.
39544.347 Bellugou, Henri. Voltaite et Frédéric II au temps de la Marquise du Châtelet. Paris, 1962.
39544.350 Leithaeuser, J.G. Er Nannte sich Voltaire. Stuttgart, 1961.
39544.351 Lauer, R.Z. The mind of Voltaire. Westminster, Md., 1961.
39544.352 Havens, George R. Voltaire's marginalia on the pages of Rousseau. Columbus, 1933.
39544.354 Liubbinskii, V.S. Voltaire - Studien. Berlin, 1961.
39544.355 Cousin d'Avallon, Charles Ives Cousin. Voltairiana. 3. ed. Paris, 1809?
39544.356 Snethlage, Jacob. Voltaire. Den Haag, 1961.

39544 Individual authors, etc. - 1715-1799 - Voltaire - Biography and criticism - cont.

39544.357 Rihs, Charles. Voltaire. Genève, 1962.
39544.358 Séguin, J.A.R. Voltaire and the gentleman's magazine, 1731-1868. N.Y., 1962.
39544.359 Mason, H.T. Pierre Bayle and Voltaire. London, 1963.
39544.360 Guiragossian, D. Voltaire's facéties. Genève, 1963.
39544.361 Brailsford, H.N. Voltaire. London, 1963.
39544.362 Iazykov, D.D. Vol'ter v russkoi literature, Sankt Peterburg, 1879. Ann Arbor, 1964.
39544.363 Brooks, R.A. Voltaire and Leibniz. Genève, 1964.
39544.364 Kuznetsov, Vitalii N. Vol'ter i filosofiia frantsuzskogo prosveshheniia XVIII veka. Moskva, 1965.
39544.365 La Roche de Maine, Jean Pierre. Histoire littéraire de Monsieur de Voltaire. Cassel, 1780. 3v.
39544.365.5 Alatri, Paolo. Voltaire, Diderot e il "partito filosofico". Messina, 1965.
39544.366 Dassen, Julio. Voltaire, defensor de Juan Calas. Buenos Aires, 1963.
39544.367 Zabuesnig, Johann Christoph von. Historische und kritische Nachrichten von dem Leben und den Schriften des Herrn von Voltaire und anderer Neuphilosophen unserer Zeiten. Augsburg, 1777. 2v.
39544.368 Ceitac, Jane. L'affaire des natifs et Voltaire. Genève, 1956.
39544.369 Orieux, Jean. Voltaire; ou, La royauté de l'esprit. Paris, 1966.
39544.370 Miró, César. Alzire et Candide, ou L'image de Perou chez Voltaire. Paris, 1967.
39544.371 Kotta, Nuçi. L'homme aux quarante écus; a study of Voltairian themes. The Hague, 1966.
39544.372 Trousson, Raymond. Socrate devant Voltaire, Diderot et Rousseau. Paris, 1967.
39544.373 Eberle, Josef. Voltaires Pucelle. Die Geschichte eines Gedichte. Aschaffenburg, 1966.
39544.374 Heuvel, Jacques van den. Voltaire dans ses contes. Paris, 1967.
39544.375 Sareil, Jean. Essai sur Candide. Genève, 1967.
39544.376 Fontius, Martin. Voltaire in Berlin. Berlin, 1966.
39544.378 Bo, Carlo. Voltaire e dopo Voltaire. Milano, 1968.
39544.380 Besterman, Theodore. Voltaire. 1st American ed. N.Y., 1969.
39544.381 Adamski, Jerzy. Sekrety wieku oświecenia. Krakow, 1969.
39544.382 Wade, Ira Owen. The intellectual development of Voltaire. Princeton, N.J., 1969.
39544.384 Centre Culturel Portugais, Paris. Voltaire et la culture portugaise. Paris, 1969.
39544.386 Schick, Ursula. Zur Erzähltechnik in Voltaires "Contes." München, 1968.
39544.388 Vulliamy, Glwyn Edward. Voltaire. Port Washington, N.Y., 1970.
39544.390 Giacomelli Deslex, Marcella. L'aggettivazione nei "contes" di Voltaire da Zadig a Candide. Torino, 1968.
39544.392A Noël, Eugene. Voltaire. Paris, 1855.
39544.392B Noël, Eugene. Voltaire. Paris, 1855.
39544.394 Schwarzbach, Bertram Eugene. Voltaire's Old Testament criticism. Genève, 1971.
39544.396 Bottiglia, William F. Voltaire; a collection of critical essays. Englewood Cliffs, N.J., 1968.
39544.398 Bouvy, Eugène. Voltaire et l'Italie. Genève, 1970.
39544.400 Holmsten, Georg. Voltaire in Selbstzeugnissen und Bilddokumenten. Reinbek, 1971.
39544.403 Morize, André. L'apologie du luxe au XVIIIe siècle et "Le mondain" de Voltaire. Genève, 1970.

39545.1 - .22 Individual authors, etc. - 1715-1799 - Voltaire - Criticism [Discontinued]

39545.1 Bungener, F. Voltaire et son temps. Paris, 1851. 2v.
39545.2 Gaberel, J. Voltaire et les Genevois. Paris, 1857.
39545.2.3 Comparet, J.A. La vérité, ode à M. de Voltaire, suivie d'une dissertation sur la gouvernement de Genève. Londres, 1765.
39545.2.5 Condorcet, Marie Jean A.N.C. Vie de Voltaire. Paris, 1895.
39545.3 Condorcet, Marie Jean A.N.C. Life of Voltaire. v.2. London, 1790.
39545.4 Havard, J.A. Voltaire et Mme. du Chatelet. Paris, 1863.
39545.4.2 Lepan, E.M.J. Vie politique. 2d ed. Paris, 1819.
39545.4.5 Lepan, E.M.J. Vie politique littéraire de Voltaire. 3d ed. Paris, 1823.
39545.4.10 Wade, Ira Owen. Voltaire and Madame du Chatelet. Princeton, 1941.
39545.4.11 Wade, Ira Owen. Voltaire and Candide. Princeton, 1959.
39545.4.12 Wade, Ira Owen. Studies on Voltaire. Princeton, 1947.
39545.4.15 Coptrajanov, Djordje. Essai sur Candide. Skopie, 1943.
39545.4.16A Barber, William. Voltaire. London, 1960.
39545.4.16B Barber, William. Voltaire. London, 1960.
39545.5 Noël, Eugène. Voltaire. Paris, 1878.
39545.5.5 Noël, Eugène. Voltaire et Rousseau. Paris, 187-?
39545.5.6 Mohr, L. Les centenaires de Voltaire et Rousseau. n.p., n.d.
39545.6 Hugo, Victor. Oration on Voltaire. N.Y., 1883.
39545.6.3 Hugo, Victor. Oration on Voltaire. Portland, Me., 1899.
39545.6.5 Hugo, Victor. Voltaire oration. Chicago, 1901.
39545.7 Espinasse, F. Life of Voltaire. London, 1892.
39545.9 Griswold, G.C. Voltaire als Historiker. Halle, 1878.
39545.10 Léouzon le Duc, L. Voltaire et la Police. Paris, 1857.
39545.11 Canssy, F. Voltaire Seigneur de village. Paris, 1912.
39545.12 Thiérist, A. Voltaire en Prusse. Paris, 1878.
39545.12.5 Gröschl, K. Die Deutschen Übersetzungen Voltaire'schen Tragöden. Prag, 1912.
39545.13 Petkovic, J. Voltaire's Tragödie, "La morte de César verglichen mit Shakespere" Julius Cäsar. Wien, 1909.
39545.14 Jacquot, C.J.B. La queue de Voltaire. Paris, 1864.
39545.15 Morize, A. L'apologie du Luxe au XVIIIe siècle. "Le mondain et ses sources". Paris, 1909.
39545.16 Meyer, J.B. Voltaire und Rousseau. Berlin, 1856.
39545.17 Dupanloup, F.A.P. Lettres à les membres du conseil municipal de Paris "centenaire de Voltaire." Paris, 1787.
39545.17.25 Ehrenborg, M. Reponse à la lettre qu'un citoyen. Lund, 1783.
39545.18.2 Hamley, E.B. Voltaire. Edinburgh, 1911.
39545.18.5 Klemperer, W. Voltaire und die Judin. Berlin, 1894.
39545.19.5 Boissier, R. La mort de Voltaire. Thèse. Paris, 1916.
Htn 39545.20* Bengesco, G. Voltaire. Bibliographie de ses oeuvres. Paris, 1882. 4v.
39545.20.5 Castex, Pierre. Voltaire. Paris, 1961.

39545.1 - .22 Individual authors, etc. - 1715-1799 - Voltaire - Criticism [Discontinued] - cont.

39545.21 Mahrenholtz, R. Voltaire im Urteile der Zeitgenossen. Oppeln, 1883.
39545.21.2 Pierron, Alexis. Voltaire et ses maitres. Paris, 1866.
39545.21.3A Tallentyre, S.G. The friends of Voltaire. N.Y., 1907.
39545.21.3B Tallentyre, S.G. The friends of Voltaire. N.Y., 1907.
39545.21.4 Chabrillan, A. Une amie de Voltaire; madame de Saint-Julien. Paris? 1923.
39545.21.5 Baumgärtner, G. Voltaire auf der englischen Bühne des 18 Jahrhunderts. Strassburg, 1913.
39545.21.9 Voltaire, François Marie Arouet de. Théâtre. Amsterdam, 1770. 6v.
39545.21.15 Delattre, André. Voltaire l'impétueux essai presenté par R. Pomeau. Paris, 1957.
39545.22 Deschanel, E. Le théâtre de Voltaire. Paris, 1866.
39545.22.5 Leon, Henri. Les tragédies de Voltaire. Paris, 1895.
39545.22.6 Olivier, J.J. Voltaire et les comédiens. Paris, 1900.
39545.22.10 Treich, Léon. L'esprit de Voltaire. Paris, 1927.
39545.22.15 Moench, W. Voltaire und Friedrich der Grosse. Stuttgart, 1943.
39545.22.20 Folman, Michel. Voltaire et Madame Denis. Genève, 1957.

39545.23 - .34 Individual authors, etc. - 1715-1799 - Voltaire - Collected and Selected plays or tales

39545.23 Voltaire, François Marie Arouet de. Chefs-d'oeuvre dramatiques. v.1-4. Paris, 1825. 2v.
39545.23.3 Voltaire, François Marie Arouet de. Chefs-d'oeuvre dramatiques. v.3. Paris, 1810.
39545.23.3.5 Voltaire, François Marie Arouet de. Chefs-d'oeuvre dramatiques. v.2-4. Paris, 1820. 4v.
39545.23.4 Voltaire, François Marie Arouet de. Chefs-d'oeuvre dramatiques. Paris, 1823. 3v.
39545.23.6 Voltaire, François Marie Arouet de. Chefs-d'oeuvre. Paris, 1822.
39545.23.7 Voltaire, François Marie Arouet de. Chefs-d'oeuvre dramatiques de Voltaire. Paris, 1828. 4v.
39545.24.3 Voltaire, François Marie Arouet de. The works of Voltaire. London, 1780. 10v.
39545.24.5 Théâtre de Voltaire. v.1-12. Paris, 1813. 6v.
39545.24.9 Voltaire, François Marie Arouet de. Oeuvres complètes. Paris, 1835-38. 13v.
39545.24.11 Voltaire, François Marie Arouet de. Théâtre. Paris, 1843.
39545.24.12 Voltaire, François Marie Arouet de. Théâtre. Paris, 1849.
39545.25 Théâtre de Voltaire. Paris, 1853.
39545.25.3 Théâtre de Voltaire. Paris, 1856.
Htn 39545.25.5* Voltaire, François Marie Arouet de. Tancréde, tragédie en vers croisés. Paris, 1761.
Htn 39545.25.6* Voltaire, François Marie Arouet de. Tancréde, tragédie en vers croisés. Genève, 1761.
39545.25.7 Voltaire, François Marie Arouet de. Dramatic works. v.1-2, 4. London, 1761-62. 2v.
39545.25.10 Voltaire, François Marie Arouet de. Tancrède. Strassburg, n.d.
Htn 39545.26* Voltaire, François Marie Arouet de. Miscellanies. Philadelphia, 1778.
39545.26.5 Voltaire, François Marie Arouet de. Oeuvres inédites. Paris, 1914.
39545.26.50 Voltaire, François Marie Arouet de. Essays and criticisms. N.Y., 1899.
Htn 39545.27* Voltaire, François Marie Arouet de. Micromégas. London, 1753.
39545.27.10 Voltaire, François Marie Arouet de. Voltaire's micromégas. Princeton, 1950.
Htn 39545.28* Voltairiana, ou Eloges amphigouriques de M. Arouet. Paris, 1748.
39545.29 Cousin d'Avallon, Charles Ives Cousin. Voltairiana, ou Recueil...de Voltaire. Paris, 181-.
39545.29.3 Voltaire, François Marie Arouet de. Prayers, sermons and religious thoughts. Philadelphia, 1878.
39545.29.4 Voltaire, François Marie Arouet de. A new system of theology. n.p., n.d.
39545.29.5 Despréaux de la Condamine Simien. Soirées de Ferney, ou Confidences de Voltaire. Paris, 1802.
39545.29.10 Voltaire, François Marie Arouet de. Voltairiana. Paris, 1749. 2v.
39545.29.15 Vezinet, F. Autour de Voltaire. Paris, 1925.
39545.29.20 Cousin d'Avallon, Charles Ives Cousin. Voltairians. 2. ed. Paris, 1801.
39545.30 Voltaire, François Marie Arouet de. Romans de Voltaire. v.3-4. Paris, 1833.
39545.30.5 Voltaire, François Marie Arouet de. Romans de Voltaire. Paris, 1866.
39545.30.25 Voltaire, François Marie Arouet de. Romans et contes. London, 1781. 4v.
Htn 39545.31* Voltaire, François Marie Arouet de. Romans et contes. Paris, 1802. 2v.
39545.32 Voltaire, François Marie Arouet de. Pages choisies. Paris, 1903.
39545.32.15 Voltaire, François Marie Arouet de. Selections from Voltaire with explanatory comment. N.Y., 1925.
39545.32.17 Voltaire, François Marie Arouet de. Selections from Voltaire. N.Y., 1930.
39545.32.20 Voltaire, François Marie Arouet de. Zadig and other romances. London, 19- .
39545.32.25 Voltaire, François Marie Arouet de. Zadig and other tales. London, 1891.
39545.32.27 Voltaire, François Marie Arouet de. Zadig, an Oriental history. Photoreproduction. Cincinnati, 1925.
39545.32.30 Voltaire, François Marie Arouet de. Zadig and other tales. London, 1901.
39545.32.35 Voltaire, François Marie Arouet de. Zadig and other stories. Boston, 1905.
39545.32.37 Voltaire, François Marie Arouet de. Zadig. N.Y., 1929.
39545.32.40 Voltaire, François Marie Arouet de. Zadig; ou La destinée. Paris, 1946.
39545.32.45 Voltaire, François Marie Arouet de. Zadig, ou La destinée. Genève, 1956.
39545.33 Voltaire, François Marie Arouet de. Pièces fugitives de Voltaire. London, 1782.
Htn 39545.33.3* Voltaire, François Marie Arouet de. Recueil de pièces. Fugitives en prose et en vers. Paris, 1740.
39545.33.4 Voltaire, François Marie Arouet de. Voltaire's prose. Boston, 1897.
39545.33.5 Nagel, C. Voltaire et la revolution française, 1789-1830. Paris, 1839.
39545.33.25 Voltaire, François Marie Arouet de. Voltaire and the enlightenment selections. N.Y., 1931.

39545.23 - .34 Individual authors, etc. - 1715-1799 - Voltaire - Collected and Selected plays or tales - cont.

39545.34 Poemes...de Voltaire. Paris, 1800.
39545.34.3 Voltaire, François Marie Arouet de. Contes. I. Paris, 1939.
39545.34.5 Voltaire, François Marie Arouet de. Contes en vers, satires et poesies melées. Paris, 1801.
39545.34.6 Voltaire, François Marie Arouet de. Contes, satires, epitrus. Paris, 1842.
39545.34.7 Voltaire, François Marie Arouet de. Epitres, stances et odes. Paris, 1800.
39545.34.8 Voltaire, François Marie Arouet de. Cuentos y satiras. N.Y., 1825.
39545.34.9 Voltaire, François Marie Arouet de. La Doncella de Orleans. Madrid, n.d.
Htn 39545.34.15* Marchand, J.H. Requete du Curé de Fontemy au Roy. n.p., 1745.

39545.35 - Individual authors, etc. - 1715-1799 - Voltaire - Individual works

39545.35 Advielle, M.V. Voltaire. Lettres er poesies. Paris, 1872.
Htn 39545.35.5* Voltaire, François Marie Arouet de. Alzire, ou Les Americains. Paris, 1736.
Htn 39545.35.5.48* Voltaire, François Marie Arouet de. Candide, ou L'optimisme. Genève, 1759.
Htn 39545.35.5.50* Voltaire, François Marie Arouet de. Candide, ou L'optimisme. n.p., 1759.
Htn 39545.35.7* Voltaire, François Marie Arouet de. Alzire, of de Amerikanen. Amsterdam, 1781.
Htn 39545.35.8* Voltaire, François Marie Arouet de. Amelie, ou Le duc de foix. London, 1753.
39545.35.8.9 Voltaire, François Marie Arouet de. Astérite, ou Les loix de minos. Genève, 1773.
39545.35.9 Voltaire, François Marie Arouet de. Candide, ou L'optimisme. Azwickau, 1819.
39545.35.10 Voltaire, François Marie Arouet de. Candide. N.Y., 1966.
39545.35.15 Voltaire, François Marie Arouet de. Candide, ou L'optimisme. Paris, 1913.
39545.35.20 Voltaire, François Marie Arouet de. Candide. N.Y., 1929.
39545.35.25 Voltaire, François Marie Arouet de. Candide. N.Y., 194-?
39545.35.40 Voltaire, François Marie Arouet de. Candide. Oxford, 1945.
39545.35.42 Voltaire, François Marie Arouet de. Candido. Trodotto, 1955.
39545.35.47A Voltaire, François Marie Arouet de. Candide, ou L'optimisme. N.Y., 1947.
39545.35.47B Voltaire, François Marie Arouet de. Candide, ou L'optimisme. N.Y., 1947.
39545.35.50 Voltaire, François Marie Arouet de. Candide. N.Y., 1956.
39545.35.52 Voltaire, François Marie Arouet de. Candide. Paris, 1957.
39545.35.55 Voltaire, François Marie Arouet de. Candide. London, 1958.
39545.35.60 Voltaire, François Marie Arouet de. Candide. Paris, 1959.
39545.35.70 Voltaire, François Marie Arouet de. Candide, vollständiger Text. Frankfurt, 1963.
39545.35.80 Voltaire, François Marie Arouet de. Candide. London, 1966.
39545.35.90 Voltaire, François Marie Arouet de. Candide, ou L'optimisme. Genève, 1968.
Htn 39545.36* Voltaire, François Marie Arouet de. Candidus, or All for the best. Berwick, 1795.
Htn 39545.36.5* Voltaire, François Marie Arouet de. Candidus, or All for the best. London, 1773.
Htn 39545.36.10* Voltaire, François Marie Arouet de. Candid. 2d ed. London, 1759.
39545.36.25 Voltaire, François Marie Arouet de. Candide, Zadig, and selected short stories. Bloomington, 1961.
39545.37.6 Voltaire, François Marie Arouet de. Candide, or The optimist. London, 1888.
Htn 39545.37.8* Voltaire, François Marie Arouet de. Candide. London, n.d.
Htn 39545.37.9* Voltaire, François Marie Arouet de. The coffee house, or Fair fugitive. London, 1760.
39545.37.10 Voltaire, François Marie Arouet de. Voltaire, Candide. N.Y., 19- ?
Htn 39545.37.13* Voltaire, François Marie Arouet de. Le dépositaire. Genève, 1772.
39545.37.14 Voltaire, François Marie Arouet de. Dialogues et entretiens philosophiques. Paris, 1820. 2v.
39545.37.14.5 Voltaire, François Marie Arouet de. Dialogues et anecdotes philosophiques. Paris, 1966.
Htn 39545.37.15* Voltaire, François Marie Arouet de. Diatribe du Docteur Akakia. Rome, 1753.
39545.37.18.30 Voltaire, François Marie Arouet de. Satirical dictionary of Voltaire. Mt. Vernon, N.Y., 1946.
39545.37.19 Voltaire, François Marie Arouet de. Le duc d'Alencon. Paris, 1829.
Htn 39545.37.20F* Voltaire, François Marie Arouet de. Epistle from M. Voltaire to king of Prussia. London, 1757.
Htn 39545.37.20.5* Voltaire, François Marie Arouet de. Eriphile. Paris, 1779.
39545.37.21 Voltaire, François Marie Arouet de. Evangile du jour. London, 1769. 4 pam.
Htn 39545.37.23* Voltaire, François Marie Arouet de. An essay upon the civil wars of France. London, 1727.
39545.37.30 Voltaire, François Marie Arouet de. Extraits. Paris, 1930.
Htn 39545.37.32* Voltaire, François Marie Arouet de. L'enfant prodigue. Paris, 1773.
39545.38 Voltaire, François Marie Arouet de. La Henriade. Paris, 1801.
Htn 39545.38.5* Voltaire, François Marie Arouet de. La ligne, ou Henry le Grande. Genève, 1723.
39545.39 Voltaire, François Marie Arouet de. La Henriade. London, 1800.
39545.39.5 Voltaire, François Marie Arouet de. La Henriade. Paris, 1804.
39545.40 Voltaire, François Marie Arouet de. La Henriade. Paris, 1813.
39545.41 Voltaire, François Marie Arouet de. La Henriade. Paris, 1810.
39545.41.5 Voltaire, François Marie Arouet de. La Henriade. Paris, 1820.
39545.42 Voltaire, François Marie Arouet de. La Herniade. Boston, 1852.
39545.43 Voltaire, François Marie Arouet de. La Henriade. Paris, 1820.
39545.43.5 Voltaire, François Marie Arouet de. La Henriade. Paris, 1833.

39545.35 - Individual authors, etc. - 1715-1799 - Voltaire - Individual works - cont.

39545.43.9 Voltaire, François Marie Arouet de. La Henriade. Paris, 1854.
39545.43.14 Voltaire, François Marie Arouet de. La Henriade. Paris, 1805.
39545.43.15 Voltaire, François Marie Arouet de. La Henriade. London, 1835.
39545.43.20 Voltaire, François Marie Arouet de. La Henriade. Paris, 1836.
39545.44 Voltaire, François Marie Arouet de. La Henriade. Paris, 1874.
39545.44.15 Voltaire, François Marie Arouet de. The Henriade. Mobile, 1834.
39545.45 Voltaire, François Marie Arouet de. La Henriada. Alais, 1816.
Htn 39545.45.25* Voltaire, François Marie Arouet de. L'Enriade. Augusta, 1779.
39545.46 Voltaire, François Marie Arouet de. La Henriade. Charlestown, 1836.
Htn 39545.46.3* Voltaire, François Marie Arouet de. L'ingénu. Utrecht, 1767.
Htn 39545.46.3.6* Voltaire, François Marie Arouet de. L'ingénu. 1st ed. Paris, 1767.
39545.46.3.8 Voltaire, François Marie Arouet de. L'ingénu. Paris, 1927.
39545.46.3.10 Voltaire, François Marie Arouet de. L'ingénu. Paris, 1936.
39545.46.3.15 Voltaire, François Marie Arouet de. L'ingénu. Paris, 1955.
39545.46.3.20 Voltaire, François Marie Arouet de. L'ingénu. Genève, 1957.
39545.46.5 Voltaire, François Marie Arouet de. Lord Chesterfield's ears. London, 1826.
39545.46.10 Voltaire, François Marie Arouet de. Mahomet the prophet. N.Y., 1964.
39545.46.25 Voltaire, François Marie Arouet de. Merope; tragedia francesa puesta en español par D.M. de B. Madrid, 1815.
Htn 39545.47* Voltaire, François Marie Arouet de. La mort de César. Paris, 1736.
39545.48 Voltaire, François Marie Arouet de. Voltaires orphelin de la Chine. Dresden, 1913.
Htn 39545.48.5* Voltaire, François Marie Arouet de. The orphan of China. London, 1756.
Htn 39545.48.15* Voltaire, François Marie Arouet de. The orphan of China. Dublin, 1756.
Htn 39545.48.17* Voltaire, François Marie Arouet de. La pucelle d'Orleans. Louvain, 1755.
39545.48.19 Voltaire, Franç3is Marie Arouet de. La pucelle d'Orleans. London, 1775.
39545.48.25 Voltaire, François Marie Arouet de. La pucelle d'Orleans. Genève, 1793.
39545.49 Voltaire, François Marie Arouet de. La pucelle. Paris, 1801.
39545.50 Voltaire, François Marie Arouet de. La pucelle. Paris, 1814.
Htn 39545.52* Voltaire, François Marie Arouet de. La pucelle...d'Orleans. n.p., n.d.
Htn 39545.53.15* Voltaire, François Marie Arouet de. La pucelle: or the maid of Orleans. Dublin, 1796-97. 2v.
39545.54A Voltaire, François Marie Arouet de. La pucelle, the maid of Orleans. London, 1899. 2v.
39545.54B Voltaire, François Maire Arouet de. La pucelle, the maid of Orleans. London, 1899. 2v.
39545.55 Voltaire, François Marie Arouet de. La pucelle d'Orleans. Monte-Carlo, 1959?
39545.55.2 Voltaire, François Marie Arouet de. La pucelle d'Orleans. Genève, 1777.
39545.55.5 Voltaire, François Marie Arouet de. Orleanskais devstvennitsa. Moskva, 1924. 2v.
39545.56 Die Jungfrau von Orleans. Boston, 1905.
Htn 39545.58* Voltaire, François Marie Arouet de. Rome sauvée. Berlin, 1752.
39545.58.10 Voltaire, François Marie Arouet de. Saul; a drama. London, 1820.
39545.60 Refutation du sermon des cinquante. n.p., 17- ?
39545.60.11 Voltaire, François Marie Arouet de. The sermon of the fifty. Jersey City, 1963.
Htn 39545.61* Voltaire, François Marie Arouet de. Religion naturelle, poeme. Genève, 1756.
39545.61.33 Voltaire, François Marie Arouet de. Le temple du goût. Paris, 1938.
39545.61.33.2 Voltaire, François Marie Arouet de. Le temple du goût. 2. éd. Genève, 1953.
Htn 39545.62* Voltaire, François Marie Arouet de. Zadig et voyage de St. Cloud. n.p., 1748.
39545.64 Voltaire, François Marie Arouet de. Zadig. Paris, 1885.
39545.65 Voltaire, François Marie Arouet de. Zadig. London, 1749.
39545.65.5 Voltaire, François Marie Arouet de. Zadig. Strasbourg, 1909.
39545.65.8 Voltaire, François Marie Arouet de. Zadig ou la destinée. Oxford, 1926.
39545.65.10 Voltaire, François Marie Arouet de. Zadig. Thèse. v.1-2. Paris, 1929.
39545.66 Voltaire, François Marie Arouet de. Zayre-Alzire. La Henriade de Voltaire. Breslau, n.d.
39545.66.75 Voltaire, François Marie Arouet de. Zadig: or, The book of fate. London, 1794?
39545.66.80 Voltaire, François Marie Arouet de. Zadig et micrimégas. London, 1894.
39545.67 Voltaire, François Marie Arouet de. Zaire. Paris, 1889.
39545.67.5 Voltaire, François Marie Arouet de. Zaire; tragédie. London, 1889.
39545.67.8A Voltaire, François Marie Arouet de. Zadig and other stories. Boston, 1905.
39545.67.8B Voltaire, François Marie Arouet de. Zadig and other stories. Boston, 1905.
39545.68 Voltaire, François Marie Arouet de. Chefs d'oeuvres dramatiques. Paris, 1833-
39545.69 Voltaire, François Marie Arouet de. Zaïre-Mérope. Chefs-d'oeuvre dramatiques. Paris, 1890.
39545.69.5 Voltaire, François Marie Arouet de. Zayre. Leipzig? 1778.
39545.70 Voltaire, François Marie Arouet de. Le Sottisier. Paris, 1880.
Htn 39545.71* Voltaire, François Marie Arouet de. Histoire de Jenni, ou Le sage et l'Athée par Sherloc (pseud.). Londres, 1776.
Htn 39545.73* Voltaire, François Marie Arouet de. Oreste; tragédie. Paris, 1750.

39545.35 - Individual authors, etc. - 1715-1799 - Voltaire - Individual works - cont.

39545.74 Voltaire, François Marie Arouet de. Les lettres d'Amabed de Voltaire. Paris, 1961.
39545.75 Voltaire, François Marie Arouet de. Un accte inédit d'un opéra de Voltaire. Upsala, 1905.
Htn 39545.76* Voltaire, François Marie Arouet de. Les loix de Minos. Genève, 1773.
Htn 39545.78* Voltaire, François Marie Arouet de. Les scythes, tragédie. Paris, 1767.
39545.80 Voltaire, François Marie Arouet de. The white bull. London, 1929.
39545.86 Voltaire, François Marie Arouet de. Romans et contes de Voltaire. Paris, 1967.
39545.90 Voltaire, François Marie Arouet de. Contes choisis. London, 1907.
39545.92 Voltaire, François Marie Arouet de. Contes choisis. Paris, 1918.
39545.95 Voltaire, François Marie Arouet de. An essay upon the civil wars of France. Westport, 1928.
Htn 39545.100* Voltaire, François Marie Arouet de. Pensées, remarques et observations. Paris, 1802.
39545.102 Voltaire, François Marie Arouet de. Bog i luedi, stat'i, pamflety, pis'ma. Moskva, 1967. 2v.
39545.105 Voltaire, François Marie Arouet de. Das lächeln Voltaires, ein Buch in dise Zeit. Leipzig, 1921.
39545.110 Voltaire, François Marie Arouet de. Sémiramis; tragédie. Paris, 1946.
39545.115 Voltaire, François Marie Arouet de. La princesse de Babylone. Paris, 1927.
39545.120 Voltaire, François Marie Arouet de. Notebooks. Genève, 1952. 2v.
39545.125 Voltaire, François Marie Arouet de. Le taureau blanc. Lyon, 1956.
39545.125.2 Voltaire, François Marie Arouet de. Le taureau blanc. Paris, 1956.
39545.126 Le Brun. Remarques historiques, politiques, mythologiques et critiques, sur la Henriade de Mr. de Voltaire. La Haye, 1741. 3 pam.
39545.130 Voltaire, François Marie Arouet de. Sermon du rabin akib. Jersey City, 1963.
39545.131 Voltaire, François Marie Arouet de. The philosophy of history. N.Y., 1965.
39545.132 Voltaire, François Marie Arouet de. Essai sur les moeurs et l'esprit des nations et sur les principaux faits de l'histoire depuis Charlemagne jusqu'à Louis XIII. Paris, 1963. 2v.
39545.132.2 Voltaire, François Marie Arouet de. Essai sur les moeurs et l'esprit des nations. Paris, 1962.

39551 Individual authors, etc. - 1715-1799 - Voltaire - Miscellaneous complete works [Discontinued]

39551.3 Voltaire, François Marie Arouet de. Oeuvres complètes. n.p., 1784. 72v.
39551.5 Voltaire, François Marie Arouet de. Oeuvres complètes. n.p., 1785. 92v.
39551.30A Voltaire, François Marie Arouet de. Oeuvres complètes. n.p., 1877-85. 52v.
39551.30B Voltaire, François Marie Arouet de. Oeuvres complètes. n.p., 1877-85. 52v.
39551.30C Voltaire, François Marie Arouet de. Oeuvres complètes. v.34-52. Paris, 1877-85. 19v.

39561 - 39563 Individual authors, etc. - 1715-1799 - Diderot - Complete and selected works - Folios, etc. [Discontinued]

39561.20A Diderot, Denis. Oeuvres complètes. Paris, 1875-77. 20v.
39561.20B Diderot, Denis. Oeuvres complètes. Paris, 1875-77. 20v.
Htn 39562.2* Diderot, Denis. Oeuvres. Paris, 1798. 15v.
39562.3 Diderot, Denis. Oeuvres. Paris, 1800. 15v.
39563.3A Diderot, Denis. Oeuvres. Paris, 1818-19. 12v.
39563.3B Diderot, Denis. Oeuvres. Paris, 1818-19. 12v.
39563.4A Diderot, Denis. Supplément aux oeuvres. Paris, 1819.
39563.4B Diderot, Denis. Supplément aux oeuvres. Paris, 1819.
39563.5 Diderot, Denis. Collection...des oeuvres. London, 1773. 5v.
39563.6 Diderot, Denis. Oeuvres. Paris, 1951.
39563.8 Diderot, Denis. Oeuvres philosophiques et dramatiques. Amsterdam, 1772. 6v.

39564.1 - .8 Individual authors, etc. - 1715-1799 - Diderot - Complete and selected works - Other editions

39564.3 Diderot, Denis. Oeuvres. Paris, 1821. 20v.
39564.3.5 Diderot, Denis. Oeuvres complètes. Paris, 1969- 12v.
39564.4 Diderot, Denis. Oeuvres inédites. Paris, 1821.
39564.4.10 Diderot, Denis. Oeuvres romanesques de Denis Diderot. Paris, 1968-69. 2v.
39564.5 Naigeon, J.A. Mémoires sur la vie de Diderot. Paris, 1821.
39564.6 Diderot, Denis. Lectures choisies par H. Parigot. Paris, 1892.
39564.6.5 Diderot, Denis. Extraits. Paris, 1897.
39564.6.9 Diderot, Denis. Extraits. Paris, 1909.
39564.6.15 Diderot, Denis. Diderot. London, 1937.
Htn 39564.6.17* Diderot, Denis. Jacques le fataliste et son maître. Paris, 1796-97. 2v.
39564.7 Diderot, Denis. Morceaux choisis. Paris, 1881.
39564.7.2 Diderot, Denis. Morceaux choisis. Paris, n.d.
39564.7.4 Diderot, Denis. Oeuvres romanesques. Paris, 1951.
39564.7.6 Diderot, Denis. Oeuvres choisies. Paris, 1847. 2v.
39564.7.10 Diderot, Denis. Oeuvres choisies. Paris, 1862. 2v.
39564.7.15 Diderot, Denis. Oeuvres choisies. Paris, 1877-79. 6v.
39564.7.20A Diderot, Denis. Textes choisis. v.1-3, 6. Paris, 1952- 4v.
39564.7.20B Diderot, Denis. Textes choisis. Paris, 1952- 2v.
39564.8 Diderot, Denis. Oeuvres choisies. Paris, 1884.
39564.8.2 Diderot, Denis. Oeuvres choisies. Paris, 1908. 2v.
39564.8.3 Diderot, Denis. Pages choisies des grands ecrivains. Paris, n.d.
39564.8.5 Diderot, Denis. Le paradoxe sur le comédien le neveu de Rameau. Strassburg, n.d.
39564.8.7 Diderot, Denis. Pensées philosophiques. Genève, 1950.
39564.8.8 Diderot, Denis. Ecrits philosophiques. Paris, 1964.
39564.8.9A Diderot, Denis. Diderot pensées philosophiques le nevue de Rameau. Paris, 1914.

564.1 - .8 Individual authors, etc. - 1715-1799 - Diderot - Complete and selected works - Other editions - cont.

39564.8.9B Diderot, Denis. Diderot pensées philosophiques le nevue de Rameau. Paris, 1914.
39564.8.10 Diderot, Denis. Philosophische Schriften. Berlin, 1961. 2v.
39564.8.12 Diderot, Denis. Diderot. Notice de Jacques Marlord. Paris, 1914.
39564.8.15 Diderot, Denis. Diderot's writings on the theatre. Cambridge, Eng., 1936.
39564.8.20 Diderot, Denis. Diderot par lui-même. Paris, 1953.
39564.8.22 Diderot, Denis. Oeuvres esthétiques. Paris, 1959.
39564.8.23 Diderot, Denis. Oeuvres esthétiques de Diderot. Paris, 1968.
39564.8.25 Diderot, Denis. Mystification. Paris, 1954.
39564.8.30 Diderot, Denis. Oeuvres politiques. Paris, 1963.
39564.8.50 Diderot, Denis. Romans et contes. Paris, 1864.
39564.8.65 Diderot, Denis. Contes. London, 1963.
39564.8.70 Diderot, Denis. Quatres contes. Genève, 1964.

564.9 - .23 Individual authors, etc. - 1715-1799 - Diderot - Individual works

39564.9.5 Diderot, Denis. Lettres à Sophie Volland. Paris, 1930. 3v.
39564.9.10 Diderot, Denis. Lettre sur les avengles. Genève, 1951.
39564.9.15 Diderot, Denis. Lettre adressée à un magistrat sur le commerce de la librairie. Paris, 1937.
39564.9.20 Diderot, Denis. Le pour et le contre. Paris, 1958.
tn 39564.10* Diderot, Denis. Les bijoux indescrets. Paris, 1748. 2v.
39564.10.18 Diderot, Denis. Le rêve le d'Alembert. Thèse. Paris, 1951.
39564.10.20 Diderot, Denis. Le rêve le d'Alembert. Paris, 1951.
tn 39564.10.50* Diderot, Denis. Pensées sur l'interpretation de la nature. Paris, 1754.
39564.10.75A Diderot, Denis. Supplément au voyage de Bougainville. Paris, 1935.
39564.10.75B Diderot, Denis. Supplément au voyage de Bougainville. Paris, 1935.
39564.10.76 Diderot, Denis. Supplément au voyage de Bougainville. Genève, 1955.
39564.10.78 Diderot, Denis. Nachtrag zu Bougainvilles Reise. Frankfurt, 1965.
39564.10.90 Diderot, Denis. Les pages immortelles de Diderot. Paris, 1949.
39564.11 Diderot, Denis. La religieuse. Paris, 1822.
39564.11.10 Diderot, Denis. La religieuse. Paris, 1913.
39564.11.15 Diderot, Denis. La religieuse. Paris, 1916.
39564.11.20 Diderot, Denis. La religieuse. Paris, 1947.
39564.11.30 Diderot, Denis. La religieuse. London, 1959.
39564.11.40 Diderot, Denis. Mémoires pour Catherine II. Paris, 1966.
39564.12 Diderot, Denis. La religiosa. Paris, 1916.
39564.13 Diderot, Denis. Le nevue de Rameau. Paris, 1884.
39564.13.5 Diderot, Denis. Le neveu de Rameau. Paris, 1862.
39564.13.10 Diderot, Denis. Rameau's nephew, and d'Alembert's dream. Harmondsworth, 1966.
Cg 39564.14 Diderot, Denis. Rameau's nephew, and d'Alembert's dream. Paris, 1891.
39564.15 Diderot, Denis. Le nevue de Rameau. Paris, 1947.
39564.15.5 Diderot, Denis. Le nevue de Rameau. Paris, 1957.
39564.15.10 Diderot, Denis. Le nevue de Rameau. Genève, 1950.
39564.15.11 Diderot, Denis. Le nevue de Rameau. Thèse. Genève, 1950.
39564.15.15A Diderot, Denis. Le siècle des lumières. Paris, 1957.
39564.15.15B Diderot, Denis. Le siècle des lumières. Paris, 1957.
39564.15.20 Diderot, Denis. Opinions et paradoxes. Paris, 1963.
39564.15.50 Diderot, Denis. Eléments de physiologie. Paris, 1964.
tn 39564.16* Diderot, Denis. Rameau's Neffe...Übersetzt von Goethe. Leipzig, 1805.
39564.17 Diderot, Denis. Rameau's Neffe...Studien in Goethes Übersetzung. Berlin, 1900.
39564.17.5 Diderot, Denis. Entretien entre d'Alembert et Diderot. Paris, 1921.
39564.17.6 Diderot, Denis. Entretien entre d'Alembert et Diderot. Paris, 1965.
39564.17.10 Diderot, Denis. Selected writings. N.Y., 1943.
39564.17.20 Encyclopédie of Diderot. The encyclopédie of Diderot. Cambridge, Eng., 1954.
39564.18 Tolemache, B.L. Diderot's thoughts on art and style. London, 1893.
39564.19A Diderot, Denis. Salons. Oxford, 1957- 4v.
39564.19B Diderot, Denis. Salons. Oxford, 1957- 4v.
tn 39564.20* Diderot, Denis. Dorval; or The test of virtue. London, 1767.
39564.20.5 Diderot, Denis. Regrets sur ma vieille robe et Lettre à une jeune mariée. 's-Gravenhage, 1959.
39564.20.105 Diderot, Denis. Jacques, le fataliste, et son maîte. Paris, 1947.
39564.20.110 Diderot, Denis. Jacques, le fataliste, et son maîte. Paris, 1953.
39564.20.115 Diderot, Denis. Jacques, the fatlist and his master. N.Y., 1959.
39564.21.10 Diderot, Denis. The nun. Dublin, 1797.
39564.21.50 Diderot, Denis. Tratado de lo bello. La Plate? 1962.
39564.22 Diderot, Denis. Diderot et l'abbé Barthélemy. Paris, 1921.
39564.23 Diderot, Denis. Ist er gut? Ist er böse? Dresden, 1922.
39564.23.10 Diderot, Denis. Sur l'art et les artistes. Paris, 1967.

39564.24 - .49 Individual authors, etc. - 1715-1799 - Diderot - Criticism [Discontinued]

39564.24 Tourneux, M. Diderot et Catherine II. Paris, 1899.
39564.25 Leo, Werner. Diderot als Kunstphilosophie. Inaug. Diss. Erlangen, 1918.
39564.27 Busnelli, Manlio D. Diderot et l'Italie. Thèse. Paris, 1925.
39564.28 Busnelli, Manlio D. Diderot et l'Italie. Paris, 1925.
39564.29 Hermand, Pierre. Les idées morales de Diderot. Paris, 1923.
39564.29.5 Corday, Michel. La vie amoureuse de Diderot. Paris, 1928.
39564.29.7 Hirn, Yrjö. Diderot. Stockholm, 1917.
39564.29.10 Salverte, Eugsèbe. Éloge philosophique de Denis Diderot. Paris, 1800-01.
39564.30 Nedergaard, Leif. Diderot, filosoffens liv og virke. København, 1953.
39564.33 Morley, John M. Diderot and the encyclopaedists. N.Y., 1879.
39564.35 Lefebure, H. Diderot. Paris, 1949.

39564.24 - .49 Individual authors, etc. - 1715-1799 - Diderot - Criticism [Discontinued] - cont.

39564.40 Kazarin, A.I. Ekonomicheskie vozzreniia Deni Didro. Moskva, 1960.
39564.42 Mayer, Jean. Diderot, homme de science. Rennes, 1959.

39564.60 - .69 Individual authors, etc. - 1715-1799 - Diderot - Letters

39564.61 Diderot, Denis. Correspondance inédite. Paris, 1931. 2v.
39564.61.5 Diderot, Denis. Correspondance. Paris, 1955. 16v.
39564.61.10 Diderot, Denis. Diderot et Falconet correspondance. Frankfurt, 1959.

39566 Individual authors, etc. - 1715-1799 - Diderot - Biography and criticism

39566.3 Diderot, Denis. Mémoires. Paris, 1830-31. 4v.
39566.4 Diderot, Denis. Mémoires. Paris, 1841. 2v.
39566.6.2 Collignon, Albert. Diderot, sa vie et ses oeuvres, sa correspondance. Paris, 1895.
39566.7A Ducros, Louis. Diderot - l'homme et l'écrivain. Paris, 1894.
39566.7B Ducros, Louis. Diderot - l'homme et l'écrivain. Paris, 1894.
39566.8A Reinach, Joseph. Diderot. Paris, 1894.
39566.8B Reinach, Joseph. Diderot. Paris, 1894.
39566.9 Avezac-Lavigne, C. Diderot et Baron d'Holbach. Paris, 1875.
39566.9.1 Avezac-Lavigne, C. Diderot et la société du Baron d'Holbach. Paris, 1970.
39566.12.2 Morley, John. Diderot and the encyclopaedists. London, 1878. 2v.
39566.12.3 Morley, John. Diderot and the encyclopaedists. London, 1886. 2v.
39566.12.4 Morley, John. Diderot and the encyclopaedists. London, 1891. 2v.
39566.12.5A Paris. Bibliothèque nationale. Diderot et l'encyclopédie. Paris, 1951.
39566.12.5B Paris, Bibliothèque nationale. Diderot et l'encyclopédie. Paris, 1951.
39566.13A Scherer, E. Diderot. Paris, 1880.
39566.13B Scherer, E. Diderot. Paris, 1880.
39566.14 Bersot, Enrest. Études sur Diderot. Paris, 1851.
39566.16A Rosenkranz, Karl. Diderot's Leben und Werke. v.1-2. Leipzig, 1866.
39566.16B Rosenkranz, Karl. Diderot's Leben und Werke. v.1-2. Leipzig, 1866.
39566.17 Kempf, R. Diderot et le roman ou Le démon de la presence. Paris, 1964.
39566.22 Leyds, J.J.C. Principaux écrits religieuse à la personne...de Diderot. Paris, 1887.
39566.22.5 Le Gras, Joseph. Diderot er l'encyclopédie. Amiens, 1928.
39566.22.8 Rzadkowska, E. Encyklopedia i Diderot w polskiem oświeceniu. Wrocław, 1955.
39566.22.10 Barker, J.E. Diderot's treatment of the Christian religion in the encyclopédia. N.Y., 1941.
39566.26 Ipsen, Knud. Diderot, hans liv og hans gerning. København, 1891.
39566.28 Kassner, R. Denis Diderot. Berlin, 1908.
39566.31 Voss, K.J. von. Diderots Moralphilosophie. Halle, 1909.
39566.33 Murobian, A. Les conceptions pédagogiques de Diderot. Paris, n.d.
39566.35A Cru, Robert L. Diderot as a disciple of English thought. N.Y., 1913.
39566.35B Cru, Robert L. Diderot as a disciple of English thought. N.Y., 1913.
39566.35C Cru, Robert L. Diderot as a disciple of English thought. N.Y., 1913.
39566.36 Dieckmann, H. Stand und Probleme der Diderot-Forschung. Bonn, 1931.
39566.37 Billy, André. Diderot. Paris, 1932.
39566.37.5 Billy, André. Vie de Diderot. Paris, 1943.
39566.38 Johansson, J.V. Études sur Denis Diderot. Göteborg, 1927.
39566.39 Johansson, J.V. Sur la correspondance littéraire. Göteborg, 1960.
39566.40 Beck, Fritz. Die dramatischen Entwürfe Denis Diderots. Inaug. Diss. Kallmünz, 1932.
39566.41 Engelmayer, Otto. Romantische Lendenzen im Künstlerischen. Inaug. Diss. München, 1933.
39566.42 Scheyer, Alice. Diderot als universaler Denker. Inaug. Diss. Berlin, 1932.
39566.43 Luppol, I.K. Diderot. Paris, 1936.
39566.44 Brugmans, H. Diderot, 1710-1784. Amsterdam, 1937.
39566.45 Luc, Jean. Diderot, l'artiste et le philosophe. Paris, 1938.
39566.46 Gillot, H. Denis Diderot. Paris, 1937.
39566.48 Thomas, Jean. L'humanisme de Diderot. 2e éd. Paris, 1938.
39566.50 Venturi, F. Jeunesse de Diderot, 1713-1753. Paris, 1939.
39566.51 Oestreicher, Jean. La pensée politique. Vincennes, 1936.
39566.52 Allison, J.M.S. Concerning the education of a prince. New Haven, 1941.
39566.54 Steel, Eric M. Diderot's imagery. Thesis. N.Y., 1941.
39566.56 Charles, M.L. The growth of Diderot's fame in France from 1784 to 1875. Thesis. Bryn Mawr, 1942.
39566.58 Mornet, Daniel. Diderot; l'homme et l'oeuvre. Paris, 1941.
39566.60 Seillière, Ernest. Diderot. Paris, 1944.
39566.65 Cresson, A. Diderot. Paris, 1949.
39566.70 Lücke, T. Denis Diderot. Berlin, 1949.
39566.72 Mortier, Roland. Diderot en Allemagne, 1750-1850. 1. éd. Paris, 1954.
39566.72.5 Mortier, Roland. Diderot in Deutschland, 1750-1850. Stuttgart, 1967.
39566.75 Diderot studies. Syracuse, N.Y., 1949-52. 13v.
39566.80 Loy, J.R. Diderot's determined fatalist. N.Y., 1950.
39566.85 Belavel, Y. L'esthétique sans paradox de Diderot. Paris, 1950.
39566.90 May, Georges C. Quatre visages de Denis Diderot. Paris, 1951.
39566.92 May, Georges C. Diderot et la religieuse. 11. éd. New Haven, 1954.
39566.95 Dieckmann, H. Inventaire du fonds vandeul et inédits de Diderot. Genève, 1951.
39566.96 Séché, A. Diderot. Paris, 1909?
39566.97 Les Cahiers Haut-Marnais. Cahier Diderot. Chaumont, 1951.
39566.100 Crocker, L.G. Two Diderot studies. Baltimore, 1952.
39566.105 Mesnard, P. Le cas Diderot. Paris, 1952.
39566.110 Crocker, L.G. The embattled philosopher. East Lansing, 1954.

39566 Individual authors, etc. - 1715-1799 - Diderot - Biography and criticism - cont.

39566.115 Fredman, A.G. Diderot and Sterne. N.Y., 1955.
39566.120 Diderot; célébration à Langres. Langres, 1879.
39566.125 François, L. Lettres à M. Bizot de Fonteny. Langres, 1884.
39566.130 Marcel, Louis. La mort de Diderot. Paris, 1925.
39566.140 Goll, Iwan. Die drei guten Geister Frankreichs. 2. Aufl. Berlin, 1919.
39566.150 Saenger, H. Juden und Altes Testament bei Diderot. Wertheim, 1933.
39566.160A Wilson, A.M. Diderot. N.Y., 1957.
39566.160B Wilson, A.M. Diderot. N.Y., 1957.
39566.161 Wilson, Arthur McCandless. Diderot. N.Y., 1972.
39566.165 Seznec, Jean. Essais sur Diderot et l'antiquite. Oxford, 1957.
39566.170 Hinterhaeuser, Hans. Utopie und Wirklichkeit bei Diderot. Heidelberg, 1957?
39566.175 Luppol, I.K. Deni Didro. Moskva, 1960.
39566.180 Doolittle, J. Rameau's nephew. Genève, 1960.
39566.181 Duchet, Michèle. Entretiens sur "Le neveu de Rameau." Paris, 1969.
39566.185 Gachev, D.I. Esteticheskie vzgeiady Didro. 2. izd. Moskva, 1961.
39566.190 Beaurepaire, Edmond. Les logis de Diderot. Photostat of an article in Revue de français. v.17. n.p., 1913.
39566.192 Pommier, Jean. Diderot avant Vincennes. Paris, 1939.
39566.194 Proust, Jacques. Diderot et l'encyclopédie. Paris, 1962.
39566.196 Bonfantini, Mario. Introduzione alla lettura di Diderot. Torino, 1963.
39566.197 Laidlaw, G.N. Elysian encounter. Syracuse, N.Y., 1963.
39566.198 Schroeder, E. Diderot und die literarästhetische Tradition. Marburg, 1963.
39566.200 Akimova, A.A. Didro. Moskva, 1963.
39566.201 French, John. Diderot's treatment of dramatic representation in theater and painting. Ann Arbor, 1962.
39566.202 Desne, Roland. Diderot et le neveu de Rameau. Paris, 1964?
39566.202.5 Josephs, Herbert. Diderot's dialogue of language? Columbus, 1969.
39566.203 Mornet, Daniel. Les cours de lettres, 1964-65. Paris, 1964.
39566.204 Smietanski, Jacques. Le réalisme dans Jacques le fataliste. Paris, 1965.
39566.205 Booy, J.T. de. Histoire d'un manuscript de Diderot. Frankfurt, 1964.
39566.206 Bonneville, Douglas A. Diderot's Vie de Sénèque. Gainesville, 1966.
39566.207 Schwartz, Jerome. Diderot and Montaigne. Genève, 1966.
39566.208 Tierno, Galvanl Enrique. Diderot como pretexto. Madrid, 1965.
39566.209 Roy, Marie L. Die Poetik Denis Diderots. München, 1966.
39566.210 Moelbjerg, Hans. Aspects de l'esthetique de Diderot. København, 1964.
39566.212 Vernière, Paul. Diderot, ses manuscrits et ses copistes. Paris, 1967.
39566.215 Aquino, Pasquale d'. L'enciclopedismo e l'etica del Diderot. Salerno, 1965.
39566.220 Joly, Raymond. Deux études sur la préhistorie du réalisme: Diderot. Québec, 1969.
39566.225 Shackleton, Robert. The encyclopédie and the clerks. Oxford, 1970.
39566.230 Pruner, Francis. L'unite' secréte de "Jacques le fataliste." Paris, 1970.
39566.235 Lough, John. The encyclopédie in eighteenth-century England, and other studies. Newcastle, 1970.
39566.240 O'Gorman, Donal. Diderot, the satirist. Toronto, 1971.
39566.245 Bénot, Yves. Diderot: de l'athéisme à l'antecolonialisme. Paris, 1970.
39566.250 Gorny, Léon. Diderot, un grand européen. Paris, 1971.
39566.255 Catrysse, Jean. Diderot et la mystification. Paris, 1970.
39566.260 May, Gita. Diderot et Boudelaire, critiques d'art. Genève, 1957.
39566.260.2 May, Gita. Diderot et Boudelaire, critiques d'art. 2e ed. Genève, 1967.
39566.265 Paitre, Fernand. Diderot biologiste. Genève, 1971.

39567 - 39568 Individual authors, etc. - 1715-1799 - Diderot - Correspondence with F.M. Grimm

39567.3 Grimm, F.M. von. Correspondance. Paris, 1812-14. 17v.
Htn 39567.3.5* Grimm, F.M. von. Correspondance. pt.1. Paris, 1813. 5v.
Htn 39567.3.6* Grimm, F.M. von. Correspondance. pt.2. Paris, 1812. 5v.
Htn 39567.3.7* Grimm, F.M. von. Correspondance. pt.3. v.1-5. Paris, 1813.
39567.4 Grimm, F.M. von. Correspondance littéraire. Paris, 1829-31. 15v.
39567.5 Grimm, F.M. von. Correspondance littéraire. Paris, 1877-79. 16v.
39567.9 Rubensohn, Georg. Die "Coresspondance littéraire". Inaug. Diss. Berlin, 1917.
39567.15 Krakeur, L.G. La correspondance de Diderot. N.Y., 1939.
39568.5A Correspondance inédits de Grimm et Diderot. Paris, 1829.
39568.5B Correspondance inédits de Grimm et Diderot. Paris, 1829.
39568.5.5 Grimm, F.M. von. Correspondance inédite de Grimm et de Diderot. Paris, 1829.
39568.6 Grimm, F.M. von. Correspondance inédite, 1794-1801...au comte de Findlater. Paris, 1934.
39568.6.2 Grimm, F.M. von. Correspondance inédite, 1794-1800 du Baron Grimm au comte de Findlater. Thèse. Paris, 1934.
39568.6.25 Grimm, F.M. von. Esquisses européennes, commencées en 1798, et finies en 1815. Paris, 1818.
39568.6.30 Grimm, F.M. von. Freiherr Grimm's und Diderot's Correspondenz, von 1753 bis 1790. Brandenburg, 1820.
39568.7 Gazette littéraire de Grimm. Paris, 1854.
39568.10 Sbornik russkago istoricheskago obshchestva. Sankt Peterburg, 1881.
39568.16 Torneaux, M. Grimm; la bibliothèque et les papiers. Paris, 1882.
39568.19 Georges, Karl A. Friedrich Melchior Grimm als Kritiker. Leipzig, 1904.
39568.20 Scherer, E. Melchior Grimm. Paris, 1887.
39568.23 Jones, A.C. Friederich Melchior Grimm. Wiesbaden, 1920.
39568.23.8 Cazes, André. Grimm et les encyclopédistes. Thèse. Paris, 1933.
39568.23.10 Cazes, André. Grimm et les encyclopédistes. Paris, 1933.

39567 - 39568 Individual authors, etc. - 1715-1799 - Diderot - Correspondence with F.M. Grimm - cont.

39568.23.15 Juettner, Siegfried. Grundtendenzen der Theaterkritik von Friedrich-Melchior Grimm (1753-1773). Wiesbaden, 1969.
39568.25 Monty, Jeanne R. La critique littéraire de Melchior Grimm. Genève, 1961.

39571 - 39572.19 Individual authors, etc. - 1715-1799 - Other philosophers - Condillac - Writings

39571.25 Condillac, E.B. de. Oeuvres. Paris, 1798. 7v.
39571.30 Condillac, E.B. de. Lettres inédites à Gabriel Cramer. 1. éd. Paris, 1953.
39572.3 Condillac, E.B. de. Oeuvres. Paris, 1798. 16v.

39572.20 - Individual authors, etc. - 1715-1799 - Other philosophers - Condillac - Works about

39572.25 Grases, Pedro. Notas sobre filologia. Caracas, 1943.

39574.1 - .28 Individual authors, etc. - 1715-1799 - Other philosophers - Alembert - Writings

39574.16 Alembert, J. Le Rond d'. Oeuvres. Paris, 1805. 18v.
39574.19 Alembert, J. Le Rond d'. Oeuvres. Paris, 1821-22. 5v.
39574.20 Alembert, J. Le Rond d'. Oeuvres posthumes. Berlin, 1799. 2v.
39574.21 Alembert, J. Le Rond d'. Oeuvres posthumes. Paris, 1799.
39574.23 Condorcet, J.M. de. Oeuvres de d'Alembert. Paris, 1853.
39574.25.1 Alembert, J. Le Rond d'. Oeuvres et correspondance inédites de d'Alembert. Genève, 1967.
Htn 39574.26* Alembert, J. Le Rond d'. Mélanges de littérature. Amsterdam, 1764. 4v.
39574.26.15 Alembert, J. Le Rond d'. Mélanges de littérature. v.2. Berlin, 1753.
39574.27.2 Alembert, J. Le Rond d'. Discours préliminaire de l'encyclopédie. Paris, 1893.
39574.27.3 Alembert, J. Le Rond d'. Discours préliminaire de l'encyclopédie. Paris, 1894.
39574.27.5 Alembert, J. Le Rond d'. Discours préliminaire de l'encyclopédie. 5e éd. Paris, 1929.
39574.27.10 Alembert, J. Le Rond d'. Discours préliminaire de l'encyclopédie. Paris, 1966.
39574.27.20 Alembert, J. Le Rond d'. Einleitung in die französische Enzyklopädie von 1751. Leipzig, 1912.
39574.27.25 Alembert, J. Le Rond d'. Einleitung zur Enzyklopädie von 1751. Hamburg, 1955.
39574.27.30 Alembert, J. Le Rond d'. Einleitende Abhandlung zur Enzyklopädie, 1751. Berlin, 1958.
39574.28 Alembert, J. Le Rond d'. Discours sur la philosophie prononcé par d'Alembert le 3 decembre 1768. N.Y., 1928.

39574.29 - Individual authors, etc. - 1715-1799 - Other philosophers - Alembert - Works about

NEDL 39574.29 Bertrand, Joseph. D'Alembert. Paris, 1889.
39574.30 Förster, Max. Beiträge zur Kenntnis des Characters und der Philosophie d'Alemberts. Hamburg, 1892.
39574.31 Damiron, J.P. Mémoire sur d'Alembert. Paris, 1854.
39574.32 Muller, Maurice. Essai sur la philosophie de Jean d'Alembert. Thèse. Paris, 1926.
39574.33 Muller, Maurice. Essai sur la philosophie de Jean d'Alembert. Paris, 1926.
39574.34 Grimsley, R. Jean d'Alembert, 1717-83. Oxford, 1963.

39576.1 - .2 Individual authors, etc. - 1715-1799 - Other philosophers - Argens - Works about

39576.2 Johnston, Elsie. Le marquis d'Argens, sa vie et ses oeuvres. Paris, 1928.
39576.2.5 Johnston, Elsie. Le marquis d'Argens, sa vie et ses oeuvres. Thèse. Paris, n.d.
39576.2.10 Argens, Jean Baptiste de Boyer. Mémories secrets de la république de lettres. Genève, 1967.

39576.3 - .12 Individual authors, etc. - 1715-1799 - Other philosophers - Argens - Writings

Htn 39576.3* Argens, Jean Baptiste de Boyer. Man, a machine. London, 1749.
39576.4 Argens, Jean Baptiste de Boyer. New mémoirs. London, 1747. 2v.
39576.5 Argens, Jean Baptiste de Boyer. Mémoirs du comte de Vaxère. Amsterdam, 1737.
39576.5.10 Argens, Jean Baptiste de Boyer. La fortune Florentin; ou Le mémoirs du comte della Valle. Amsterdam, 17- ?
39576.6 Argens, Jean Baptiste de Boyer. Mémoires de madmoiselle de Mainville. La Haye, 1736.
39576.7 Argens, Jean Baptiste de Boyer. Lettres juives. La Haye, 1764. 8v.
39576.7.15 Argens, Jean Baptiste de Boyer. The Jewish spy. London, 1739. 5v.
39576.7.20 Argens, Jean Baptiste de Boyer. The Jewish spy. 2. ed. London, 1744. 5v.
39576.7.25 Argens, Jean Baptiste de Boyer. Jewish letters. Newcastle, 1746. 4v.
39576.8 Argens, Jean Baptiste de Boyer. Jewish letters. London, 1766. 5v.
39576.9 Argens, Jean Baptiste de Boyer. Lettres cabalistiques. La Haye, 1737. 4v.
39576.10 Argens, Jean Baptiste de Boyer. Lettres cabalistiques. La Haye, 1754-70. 7v.
39576.11 Argens, Jean Baptiste de Boyer. Lettres cabalistiques. La Haye, 1754. 7v.
39576.12 Argens, Jean Baptiste de Boyer. Chinese letters. London, 1741.
39576.12.5 Argens, Jean Baptiste de Boyer. Lettres morales et critiques sur les differens états. Amsterdam, 1737.
39576.12.6 Argens, Jean Baptiste de Boyer. Lettres chinoises, ou Correspondance philosophique. La Haye, 1766. 6v.

39576.13 - .14 Individual authors, etc. - 1715-1799 - Other philosophers - Gondar

39576.13 Gondar, Ange. The Chinese spy. Paris, 1765. 6v.
39576.14 Gondar, Ange. L'espion chinois. Cologne, 1764. 6v.
39576.14.5 Gondar, Ange. L'espion chinois. v.1-6. Cologne, 1765. 3v.

Classified Listing

39576.15 - Individual authors, etc. - 1715-1799 - Other philosophers - Miscellany

39576.15 Henrion, Charles. Mémoires philosophiques. Paris, n.d.
39576.17 Coyer, G.F. Bagatelles morales et dissertations. London, 1759.
Htn 39576.18* Desnoiresterres, F.H. Sacre bouquet de differentes fleurs d'Hyacinte. Caen, 1722.
39576.20 Maimieux, J. Éloge...de l'impertinence. Abdère, 1788.
39576.21 Maimieux, J. Souvenirs d'un homme du monde. v. 1-2. Leipzig, 1789.
Htn 39576.23.6* Mes pensées. Supplement. Berlin, 1761.
39576.24 Chicaneau de Neuville, Didier R. Dictionnaire philosophique. Londres, 1751.
39576.25 Bérenger, L.P. Le mentor vertueux. Paris, 1808.
39576.25.10 Bérenger, L.P. La morale en action et en exemples. Lyon, 1804. 3v.
39576.25.15 Bérenger, L.P. La morale en action. Paris, 1810.
Htn 39576.26* Bernard, J.F. Dialogue critiques et philosophiques. Amsterdam, 1730.
39576.27.2 Éloge de l'enfer. 2. éd. London, 1777.
39576.28 Bernard, J.F. The praise of Hell. London, 1760. 2v.
39576.30 Ruplingen, André. Un representant provincial de l'esprit philosophique au XIIIe siècle...C. Bordes. Lyon, 1915.
39576.31 Friedrich II, der Grosse.al guerra...tratta dal poema francese. In Parigi, 1761.
39576.32 Friedrich II, der Grosse. Examen de l'essai sur les préjugés. London, 1770.
39576.37 Benouville, de (Mme.). Les pensées errantes. London, 1758.
39576.40 Verzure, de (Mme.). Réflexions hazardées d'une femme ignorante. Amsterdam, 1766.
39576.45 Le cocq ou Mémoires de chevalier de V. Amsterdam, 1742.
39576.46 L'hermite philosophie, ou Lettres et réflexions. n.p., 1785.
39576.50 Godard d'Aucour, C. Mémoires turcs ou Histoire galente. Francfort, 1750.
39576.51 Godard d'Aucour, C. Mémoires turcs ou Histoire galente. Amsterdam, 1767. 2v.
39576.55 Blondel, J. Des hommes tels qu'ils sont et doivent etre. Hamburg, 1760.
39576.60 Brusnoy, Pierre. Recueil de divers ouvrages en prose et en vers. Paris, 1741. 3v.
39576.65 Valentin. Instruction tirée des saintes ecritures sur l'ordre social. Venise, 1799.

39577.1 - .79 Individual authors, etc. - 1715-1799 - Other philosophers - Condorcet - Writings

39577.3 Condorcet, Marie Jean Antoine. Oeuvres complètes. Paris, 1804. 21v.
39577.5 Condorcet, Marie Jean Antoine. Oeuvres complètes. Paris, 1747-49. 12v.
39577.6 Condorcet, Marie Jean Antoine. Oeuvres. Stuttgart, 1968. 12v.
39577.8 Condorcet, Marie Jean Antoine. Éloges des academiciens. Brunswick, 1799. 5v.

39577.80 - Individual authors, etc. - 1715-1799 - Other philosophers - Condorcet - Works about

39577.80 Ellis, Henry. The centenary of Condorcet. London, 1894?

39578.3 - .4 Individual authors, etc. - 1715-1799 - Other philosophers - Du Chatelet - Works about

39578.3 Hamel, Frank. An eighteenth century marquise. London, 1910.
39578.3.25 Maurel, André. La marquise de Châtelet, amie de Voltaire. Paris, 1930.
39578.4 Capfigue, M. La marquise du Chatelet. Paris, 1868.

39578.5 - .6 Individual authors, etc. - 1715-1799 - Other philosophers - Du Chatelet - Writings

39578.5 Du Châtelet, G.É. Lettres inédites...correspondance de Voltaire. Paris, 1818.
39578.6 Asse, Eugène. Lettres de le Marquise de Châtelet. Paris, 1878.
39578.6.5 Du Châtelet, G.É. Lettres. Genève, 1958. 2v.
39578.6.10 Du Châtelet, G.É. Discours sur le bonheur. Paris, 1961.

39578.7 - .8.29 Individual authors, etc. - 1715-1799 - Other philosophers - Vauvenargues - Works about

39578.7 Bore, Léon. Étude sur Vauvenargues. Paris, 1858.
39578.7.5 Reyher, Gustave. Essai sur Vauvenargues et sa morale. Neustadt, 1872.
39578.8 Paléologue, Maurice. Vauvenargues. Paris, 1890.
39578.8.5A Wallas, May. Luc de Clapiers, marquis de Vauvenargues. Cambridge, 1928.
39578.8.5B Wallas, May. Luc de Clapiers, marquis de Vauvenargues. Cambridge, 1928.
39578.8.5C Wallas, May. Luc de Clapiers, marquis de Vauvenargues. Cambridge, 1928.
39578.8.10 Lanson, Gustave. Le marquis de Vauvenargues. Genève, 1970.
39578.8.11 Rabow, Hans. Die zehn Schaffensjahre des Vauvenargues. Inaug. Diss. Berlin, 1931.
39578.8.13 Richard, Pierre. La vie de Vauvenargues. 5th ed. Paris, 1930.
39578.8.15 Norman, S.M. Vauvenargues d'après sa corrrespondance. Toulouse, 1929.
39578.8.20 Rabow, Hans. Die zehn Schaffensjahre des Vauvenargues. Berlin, 1932.
39578.8.25 Saintville, G. Quelques notes sur Vauvenargues. Paris, 1931.
39578.8.27 Vial, F. Une philosophie et une morale du sentiment, Luc de Clapiers, marquis de Vauvenargues. Paris, 1938.

39578.8.30 - .9 Individual authors, etc. - 1715-1799 - Other philosophers - Vauvenargues - Writings

39578.8.30 Vauvenagues, L. de C. Lettres inédites de Vauvenargues et de son frère Cadet. Paris, 1933.
39578.8.38 Vauvenargues, L. de C. Réflexions et maximes. Paris, 1934.
39578.8.40 Vauvenargues, L. de C. Réflexions et maximes. Cambridge, Eng., 1936.
39578.8.42 Vauvenargues, L. de C. The reflections and maxims. London, 1940.
39578.8.43 Vauvenargues, L. de C. Oeuvres complètes de Vauvenargues. Paris, 1827.
39578.8.44 Vauvenargues, L. de C. Oeuvres posthumes de Vauvenargues. Paris, 1827.

39578.8.30 - .9 Individual authors, etc. - 1715-1799 - Other philosophers - Vauvenargues - Writings - cont.

39578.8.44.5 Vauvenargues, L. de C. Oeuvres choisies de Vauvenargues. Paris, 1942.

39578.10 - Individual authors, etc. - 1715-1799 - Other philosophers - Miscellany

39578.10 Voyer, René Louis. Essays. Worcester, 1797.
39578.11 Eggli, Edmond. L'érotique comparée de C. de Villers, 1806. Thèse. Paris, 1927.
39578.12 Eggli, Edmond. L'érotiques comparée de C. de Villers, 1806. Paris, 1927.
39578.13 Du Marsais, César C. Oeuvres. Paris, 1797. 7v.
39578.14 Gerando, J.M. Éloge de Du Marsais. Paris, 1805.
39578.15 Escherny, F.L. Mélanges de littérature, d'histoire. Paris, 1811. 3v.
39578.17 Lambert, Anne Thérèse. Oeuvres. Lausanne, 1750.
39578.17.5 Lambert, Anne Thérèse. The works of the Marchioness de Lambert. London, 1769. 2v.
39578.18 Necker, S.C. (Mme.). Nouveaux mélanges extraits des manuscrits. Paris, 1801. 2v.
Htn 39578.34* Saint-Martin, Louis Claude. Le crocodile, ou La guerre du bien et du mal. Paris, 1799.
39578.35 Saint-Martin, Louis Claude. Le crocodile, ou La guerre du bien et du mal. Paris, 1962.

39579 Individual authors, etc. - 1715-1799 - Other philosophers - Anonymous works (99 scheme, A-Z by title)

39579.14 Congo, ou Nouvelle histoire politique et morale de la cacomonade. Aux Pays-Bas, 1777.
39579.24 An essay on laughter. London, 1769.

39581 - 39582.9 Individual authors, etc. - 1715-1799 - History, criticism, etc. - Mably

39581.3 Mably. Collection...des oeuvres de...Mably. Paris, 1794-95. 15v.
39581.20 Mably. Collection...des oeuvres de...Mably. Paris, 1794-95. 15v.
39582.4 Oeuvres complètes de Mably. v.1-24. Paris, n.d. 12v.

39582.10 - .11 Individual authors, etc. - 1715-1799 - History, criticism, etc. - Maury

39582.10 Maury, J.S. Oeuvres choisies. Paris, 1827. 5v.
39582.10.15 Maury, J.S. Esprit, pensées et maximes de l'abbé Maury. Paris, 1791.

39582.12 - .13 Individual authors, etc. - 1715-1799 - History, criticism, etc. - Morellet

39582.12 Morellet, André. Mélanges de littérature. Paris, 1818. 4v.

39582.15 - Individual authors, etc. - 1715-1799 - History, criticism, etc. - Arnaud

39582.15 Arnaud, F.T.M. de B. Oeuvres. Paris, 1770. 12v.
39582.17 Arnaud, F.T.M. de B. Oeuvres. Paris, 1808.
39582.23 Arnaud, F.T.M. de B. Euphémie. Paris, 1768.
39582.23.10 Arnaud, F.T.M. de B. Les amans malheureux. Avignon, 1793.
39582.24.5 Arnaud, F.T.M. de B. Lorimon, or Man in every stage of life. London, 1803. 2v.
39582.25 Arnaud, F.T.M. de B. Warbeck. London, 1786. 2v.
39582.27 Arnaud, F.T.M. de B. Les matinées, nouvelles anecdotes par d'Arnaud. Paris, 1799. 3v.
39582.30 La Villeherve, Bertran de. Francois-Thomas de Baculard d'Arnaud. Paris, 1920.
39582.31 Inklaar, Derk. François-Thomas de Baculard d'Arnaud. 's-Gravenhage, 1925.

39583.1 - .9 Individual authors, etc. - 1715-1799 - History, criticism, etc. - Thomas, A.

39583.2 Micard, Étienne. Un écrivain académique au XVIIIe siècle. Paris, 1924.
39583.2.5 Micard, Étienne. Écrivain académique au XVIIIe siècle, Antoine L. Thomas. Thèse. Paris, 1924.
39583.3 Thomas, Antoine L. Oeuvres. Paris, 1773. 4v.
39583.4 Thomas, Antoine L. Oeuvres. Paris, 1819. 4v.
39583.5 Thomas, Antoine L. Oeuvres. Paris, 1825. 6v.
39583.6 Thomas, Antoine L. Oeuvres diverses. Lyon, 1767-71. 2v.

39583.11 - .17 Individual authors, etc. - 1715-1799 - History, criticism, etc. - Servan

39583.12 Portets, Xavier de. Oeuvres choisies de Servan. Paris, 1822. 5v.

39583.18 - Individual authors, etc. - 1715-1799 - History, criticism, etc. - Trublet

39583.18 Jacquart, Jean. L'abbé Trublet, critique et moraliste, 1697-1770. Thèse. Paris, 1926.
39583.19 Trublet, N.C.J. Essais. Amsterdam, 1755-60. 4v.
39583.20 Trublet, N.C.J. Essais sur divers sujets. v.1,3-4. Paris, 1744-60. 3v.
39583.20.5 Jacquart, Jean. La correspondance de l'abbé Trublet. Thèse. Paris, 1926.
39583.23 Jacquart, Jean. La correspondance de l'abbé Trublet. Thèse. Paris, 1926.
39583.30 Jacquart, Jean. L'abbé Trublet, critique et moraliste, 1697-1770. Paris, 1926.

39584.1 - .20 Individual authors, etc. - 1715-1799 - History, criticism, etc. - La Harpe

39584.4 La Harpe, Jean François de. Oeuvres. Yverdon, 1777. 3v.
39584.6 La Harpe, Jean François de. Oeuvres. Paris, 1778. 6v.
39584.7 La Harpe, Jean François de. Oeuvres choisies et posthumes. Paris, 1806. 4v.
39584.8 La Harpe, Jean François de. Correspondance inédite de Jean-François de La Harpe. Paris, 1965.
39584.10 La Harpe, Jean François de. Correspondance littéraire. Paris, 1804.
39584.20 Pamphlet box. La Harpe, Jean François.
39584.20.5 Palissot de Montevoy, C. Étrennes à M. de La Harpe. Paris, 1802.
39584.20.10 Chazet, A.R.P.A. de. Éloge de La Harpe. Paris, 1805.
39584.20.15 Boulard, A.M.H. Lettre adressée au rédacteur du moniteur. Paris, 1814.
39584.20.20 Saint-Surin, P.T. de. Notice sur La Harpe. Paris, 1822.

39584.1 - .20 Individual authors, etc. - 1715-1799 - History, criticism, etc. - La Harpe - cont.

	39584.20.25	Sproull, G.M. The critical doctrine of Jean-François de La Harpe. Chicago, 1939.

39584.30 - .39 Individual authors, etc. - 1715-1799 - History, criticism, etc. - Saint Foix

	39584.30	Saint Foix, G.F.P. de. Lettres turques. Cologne, 1750.
	39584.31	Saint, Foix, G.F.P. de. Lettres turques. Amsterdam, 1750. 2v.
	39584.32	Saint, Foix, G.F.P. de. Lettres turques. Paris, 1869.
	39584.35	Saint Foix, G.F.P. de. Oeuvres complètes. Paris, 1778. 6v.
	39584.36	Saint Foix, G.F.P. de. Oeuvres de théâtre. Paris, 1762. 4v.
	39584.39	Wright, Katheryn Thorne. Germain François Poullain de Saint Foix. Cleveland, 1928.

39585.1 Individual authors, etc. - 1715-1799 - History, criticism, etc. - Chevrier

	39585.1	Chevrier, F.A. Le Colporteur. London, 1753. 2 pam.
	39585.1.10A	Chevrier, F.A. Un roman satyrique du XVIIIe siècle: Le Colporteur. Paris, 1914.
	39585.1.10B	Chevrier, F.A. Un roman satyrique du XVIIIe siècle: Le Colporteur. Paris, 1914.

39585.2 Individual authors, etc. - 1715-1799 - History, criticism, etc. - Miscellany

	39585.2	Chomel. Aménités littéraires et recueil d'anecdotes. Amsterdam, 1773.
	39585.2.15	Clement, Pierre. Les cinq années littéraires, ou Lettres...1748-52. Berlin, 1756. 2v.

39585.3 - .5 Individual authors, etc. - 1715-1799 - History, criticism, etc. - Dulaurens

	39585.3	Dulaurens, H.J. Le compère Mathieu. Paris, 1792. 3v.
	39585.4	Dulaurens, H.J. Le compère Mathieu. n.p., 1796. 3v.
	39585.4.2	Dulaurens, H.J. Le compère Mathieu. Paris, 1796. 3v.
	39585.4.5	Dulaurens, H.J. Le compère Mathieu. v.1-4. Paris, 1797. 2v.
	39585.5	Dulaurens, H.J. Le porte-feuille d'un philosophe. Cologne, 1770. 2v.
	39585.5.10	Dulaurens, H.J. L'Arretin. v.1-2. Rouen, 1923.
	39585.5.25	Dulaurens, H.J. La chandelle d'Arras; poéme. Paris, 1807.
	39585.5.80	Schnelle, K. Aufklärung und klerikale Reaktion. Berlin, 1963.

39585.6 - .11 Individual authors, etc. - 1715-1799 - History, criticism, etc. - Saint Hyacinthe

	39585.6	St. Hyacinthe, H.C. Le chef d'oeuvre d'un inconnu. La Haye, 1714.
	39585.7	St. Hyacinthe, H.C. Le chef d'oeuvre d'un inconnu. 8. éd. La Haye, 1745. 2v.
	39585.8	Lettres d'un inconnu. n.p., 1750.
	39585.10	St. Hyacinthe, H.C. Le chef d'oeuvre d'un inconnu. La Haye, 1744. 2v.

39585.12 - .14 Individual authors, etc. - 1715-1799 - History, criticism, etc. - Orbessan

	39585.12	Orbessan, Anne Marie d'Aignon. Mélanges historiques...de physique, de littérature et de poésie. v.3. Paris, 1778.

39585.17 - .18 Individual authors, etc. - 1715-1799 - History, criticism, etc. - Suard

	39585.17	Suard, J.B.A. Mélanges de littérature. 2. éd., v.1-3; 3. éd., v.4-5. Paris, 1804-06. 5v.
	39585.17.50	Hunter, Alfred C. J.B.A. Suard; un introducteur de la littérature anglaise en France. Thèse. Paris, 1925.
	39585.18	Hunter, Alfred C. J.B.A. Suard; un introducteur de la littérature anglaise en France. Paris, 1925.
	39585.18.10	Suard, Amelie. Essais de mémoires sur M. Suard. Paris, 1920.
	39585.18.20	Suard, Jean. Lettres inédites de Suard à Wilkes. Berkeley, 1932.

39585.19 - .20 Individual authors, etc. - 1715-1799 - History, criticism, etc. - Bruhier d'Ablaincourt

	39585.19.25	Bruhier d'Ablaincourt, J. Caprices d'imagination. Paris, 1740.
	39585.20	Bruhier d'Ablaincourt, J. Caprices d'imagination. Amsterdam, 1741.

39585.21 - .22 Individual authors, etc. - 1715-1799 - History, criticism, etc. - Caraccioli

Htn	39585.21*A	Caraccioli, L.A. Le livre de quatre couleurs. Paris, 1760.
Htn	39585.21*B	Caraccioli, L.A. Le livre de quatre couleurs. Paris, 1760.
Htn	39585.21.5*	Caraccioli, L.A. Le livre à la mode. n.p., n.d.
	39585.21.10	Caraccioli, L.A. L'esprit de monsieur le marquis Caraccioli. Liège, 1763.
	39585.22	Caraccioli, L.A. Dictionnaire critique. Lyon, 1768. 3v.
	39585.22.5	Caraccioli, L.A. Entretiens du Palais-Royal. Utrecht, 1787. 2v.
	39585.22.7	Caraccioli, L.A. Le tableau de la mort. Paris, 1767.
	39585.22.9	Caraccioli, L.A. Lettres récréatives et morales. Paris, 1767-68. 4v.
	39585.22.10	Caraccioli, L.A. La grandeur d'ame. Paris, 1764.
	39585.22.15	Caraccioli, L.A. Les derniers adieux de la Maréchale de *** à des enfans. Paris, 1769.
	39585.22.20	Caraccioli, L.A. La conversation aves soi-même. 9. éd. Liège, 1760.

39585.23 - Individual authors, etc. - 1715-1799 - History, criticism, etc. - Miscellany

	39585.23	Sablier, M. Variétés sérieuses et amusantes. Amsterdam, 1769. 3v.
Htn	39585.24*	Charpentier, F. Carpentariana ou Remarques d'histoire. Paris, 1724.
	39585.24.2	Charpentier, F. Carpentariana. Paris, 1741.
	39585.25	Arnaud, F. Variétés littéraires. Paris, 1804. 4v.
	39585.26	Chassaigon, J.M. Cataractes de l'imagination. n.p., 1779. 3v.

39585.23 - Individual authors, etc. - 1715-1799 - History, criticism, etc. - Miscellany - cont.

	39585.27	Delacroix, J.V. Peinture des moeurs du siècle. Amsterdam, 1777. 2v.
	39585.30	La Fargue, de. Oeuvres mélées. Paris, 1765. 2v.
	39585.32	Lormberg, J.M. de. Mémorial d'un mondain. London, 1776.
Htn	39585.34*	Mirabaud, Jean Baptiste. Réflexions impartiales sur l'évangile. London, 1769.
	39585.35	Ducatiana ou Remarques de feu M.C. Duchat. Amsterdam, 1738. 2v.
	39585.38	Puisieux, M. d'A. de. Le caractères. London, 1750.
	39585.40	Dreux du Radier, J.F. Récréations historiques, critiques, morales. Paris, 1767. 2v.
	39585.43	Dreux du Radier, J.F. Essai...sur les lanternes, leur origin. Dôle, 1755.
	39585.45	St. Martin de Chassonville. Les delassemens d'un galant-homme. Amsterdam, 1742.

39586.1 - .7 Individual authors, etc. - 1715-1799 - History, criticism, etc. - Bachaumont

	39586.2	Bachaumont, Louis Petit de. Mémoires secrets. v.1-36. London, 1780-89. 18v.
	39586.2.2	Bachaumont, Louis Petit de. Mémoires secrets. Table. Bruxelles, 1866.
	39586.3	Bachaumont, Louis Petit de. Mémoires secrets...des lettres en France. London, 1783.
	39586.6	Bachaumont, Louis Petit de. Mémoires secrets. Paris, 1874.
	39586.7	Gay, Jean. Anecdotes piquantes de Bachaumont. Bruxelles, 1881.

39586.8 - .9 Individual authors, etc. - 1715-1799 - History, criticism, etc. - Bondeli

	39586.8.60	Bondeli, Julie von. Die Briefe von Julie Bondeli an J.G. Zimmermann. Leipzig, 1930.
	39586.9	Bodemann, E. Julie von Bondeli und ihr Freundeskreis. Hannover, 1874.

39586.10 - .12 Individual authors, etc. - 1715-1799 - History, criticism, etc. - Boulanger

	39586.10	Boulanger, N.A. Oeuvres. Paris, 1792-93.
	39586.10.10	Le Gros, C.F. Analyse et examen de l'antiquité devoilée. Genève, 1788.
Htn	39586.11*	Boulanger, N.A. Dissertation sur Elie et Enoch. n.p., 1764.
Htn	39586.11.2*	Boulanger, N.A. Dissertation sur Elie et Enoch. n.p., 1762.
	39586.11.4	Hampton, John. Nicolas Antoine Boulanger et la science de son temps. Genève, 1955.
	39586.12	Venturi, Franco. Antichità svelata e l'idea del progresso in N.A. Boulanger, 1722-1759. Bari, 1747.

39586.14 Individual authors, etc. - 1715-1799 - History, criticism, etc. - Miscellany

	39586.14	Faulcon, Félix. Fruits de la solitude et du malheur. Paris, 1795-96. 3 pam.

39586.16 - .19 Individual authors, etc. - 1715-1799 - History, criticism, etc. - Chamfort

	39586.16	Chamfort, S.R.N. Oeuvres, recueillies et publiées par un ami. Paris, 1795. 4v.
	39586.17	Chamfort, S.R.N. Oeuvres. Paris, 1824-25. 5v.
	39586.18	Chamfort, S.R.N. Oeuvres. Paris, 1884.
	39586.18.10	Chamfort, S.R.N. Oeuvres choisies. Paris, 1883-85. 3v.
	39586.18.15	Chamfort, S.R.N. Le marchand de Smyrne. Paris, 1770.
	39586.19	Chamfort, S.R.N. Pensées - maximes - anecdotes - dialogues. Paris, 1900.
	39586.19.1	Chamfort, S.R.N. Maximes et pensées de Chamfort. Paris, 1922.
	39586.19.2	Chamfort, S.R.N. Chamfort; produits de la civilization perfectionnes. 10e éd. Paris, 1923?
	39586.19.3.5	Chamfort, S.R.N. Maximes et pensées caractères, ancedotes. Paris, 1953. 2v.
	39586.19.3.6	Chamfort, S.R.N. Maximes et pensées: caractéres et anecdotes. Paris, 1970.
	39586.19.3.10	Chamfort, S.R.N. Maximes et pensées. Suivies de mélanges de littérature et d'histoire. Paris, 1970.
	39586.19.3.25	Chamfort, S.R.N. Maksimy i mysli, kharaktery i anekdoty. Leningrad, 1966.
	39586.19.4	Chamfort, S.R.N. La jeune Indienne. Paris, 1774.
	39586.19.5	Chamfort, S.R.N. La jeune Indienne. Paris, 1787.
	39586.19.6	Chamfort, S.R.N. La jeune Indienne. Princeton, 1945.
	39586.19.7	Chamfort, S.R.N. Caractères et anecdotes. Paris, 1924.
	39586.19.9	Pellisson, M. Chamfort. Paris, 1895.
	39586.19.10	Teppe, Julien. Chamfort; sa vie, son oeuvre, sa pensée. Paris, 1950.
	39586.19.15	Gabor, Georg. Die Misanthropie Chamforts. Inaug. Diss. Berlin, 1928.
	39586.19.16	List-Marzolff, Renate. Sebastien-Roch Nicolas Chamfort. München, 1966.

39586.20 Individual authors, etc. - 1715-1799 - History, criticism, etc. - Constant de Rebeque, San

	39586.20	Constant de Rebecque, Samuel. Laure. v.6. Genève, 1786.

39586.21 Individual authors, etc. - 1715-1799 - History, criticism, etc. - Miscellany

	39586.21	Fréron, Elie Catharine. Les confessions de Fréron (1719-1776). Paris, 1876.
	39586.21.3	Fréron, Elie Catharine. Lettres sur quelques écrits de ce temps. London, 1751-54. 13v.
	39586.21.5	Monselet, C. Fréron ou L'illustre critique. Paris, 1864.
	39586.21.6	Cornou, François. Elie Fréron, 1718-1776. Paris, 1922.
	39586.21.9	Duchannavie neologique. 2. éd. n.p., 1727.
	39586.21.10	Duchannavie neologique. Amsterdam, 1748.
	39586.21.30	Myers, Robert. The dramatic theories of Elie-Catharine Fréron. Genève, 1962.
	39586.21.150	Pamphlet vol. Mullot, François Valentin. Mélanges. 18 pam.
	39586.21.300	Finke, Hans. Les fréres parfaict. Inaug. Diss. Dresden, 1936.
	39586.21.500	Desfontaines, P.F.G. L'esprit de l'abbé Desfontaines. Londres, 1754-57. 4v.
	39586.21.580	Mormile, Mario. Desfontaines et la crise néologique. Roma, 1967.

39586.22 Individual authors, etc. - 1715-1799 - History, criticism, etc. - Grimod de la Reynière

39586.22 Desnoiresterres, G. Grimod de la Reynière et son groupe. Paris, 1877.
39586.22.5 Béarn, P. Grimod de la Reynière. 4. éd. Paris, 1930.

39586.23 - .25 Individual authors, etc. - 1715-1799 - History, criticism, etc. - Rivarol - Writings

39586.23 Sainte-Beuve. Oeuyres de Rivarol. Paris, 1852.
39586.23.10 Rivarol, Antoine. Ecrits politiques et littéraires. Paris, 1956.
39586.23.15 Rivoral, Antoine. Esprit de Rivarol. Paris, 1808.
39586.23.20 Rivarol, Antoine. Rivarol, par Jean Dutour. Paris, 1963.
39586.25 Rivarol, Antoine. Oeuvres choisis de A. Rivarol. Paris, 1880. 2v.
39586.25.5 Rivarol, Antoine. Discours préliminaire du nouveau dictionnaire de la lanque française. Paris, 1797.

39586.26 - .27 Individual authors, etc. - 1715-1799 - History, criticism, etc. - Rivarol - Works about

39586.26 Lescure, M. de. Rivarol et la société française. Paris, 1883.
39586.27 Le Breton, André. Rivarol; sa vie, ses idées, son talent. Paris, 1895.
39586.27.5 Latzarus, L. La vie paresseuse de Rivarol. Paris, 1926.
39586.27.10 Treich, Léon. L'esprit de Rivarol. Paris, 1926.
39586.27.15 Vadasz, E.B. Studien zu Rivarol. Inaug. Diss. Berlin, 1933.
39586.27.20 Rochery, Paul. Rivarol, sa vie et des écrits. n.p., n.d.
39586.27.25 Harris, G.W. Antoine Rivarol, journalist of the French revolution. Oxford, 1940.
39586.27.30 Juenger, Ernst. Rivarol. Frankfurt, 1956.
39586.27.35 Loiseau, Yoan. Rivarol, suivi de Le vrai Laches. Paris, 1961.
39586.27.40 Curnier, Léonce. Rivarol, sa vie et ses oeuvres. Nîmes, 1858.

39586.29 - Individual authors, etc. - 1715-1799 - History, criticism, etc. - Miscellany

39586.29 Rustaut, Christophe. Le nogzag. Amsterdam, 1771.
39586.30 Stael-Holstein, A.L. Memoirs of the private life of my father. London, 1818.
39586.31 Sabatier, Antoine de Castres. Considérations politiques sur les gens d'esprit et de talent, tirées d'un ouvrage inédit de...S. de Castres. Paris, 1804.
39586.32 Scherer, Edmond H.A. Études sur la littérature au XVIIIe siècle. Paris, 1891.
39586.34 Grosley, P.J. Mémoires de l'académie des sciences...satire. Troyes, 1787.
39586.34.5 Grosley, P.J. Mémoires de l'académie des sciences...satire. 2. ed. v.1-2. Troyes, 1756.
39586.34.6 Grosley, P.J. Mémoires de l'académie des sciences...satire. Troyes, 1756.
39586.36.1 Chastellux, François Jean. Essai sur l'union de la poésie et de la musique. Genève, 1970.

39591 Individual authors, etc. - 1715-1799 - History, criticism, etc. - Montesquieu - Folios [Discontinued]

39591.4 Montesquieu, C.L. de S. Oeuvres. London, 1767. 3v.
39591.6 Montesquieu, C.L. de S. Oeuvres complètes. Paris, 1855.
39591.7 Montesquieu, C.L. de S. Oeuvres. Paris, 1838.
39591.10 Montesquieu, C.L. de S. Oeuvres. Paris, 1826. 8v.
39591.12 Montesquieu, C.L. de S. Oeuvres complètes. Paris, 1846.
Htn 39591.15* Montesquieu, C.L. de S. De l'esprit des loix. Genève, 1748? 2v.
39591.15.5 Montesquieu, C.L. de S. De l'esprit des loix. Genève, 1750. 3v.
39591.18A Montesquieu, C.L. de S. Correspondance. Paris, 1914. 2v.
39591.18B Montesquieu, C.L de S. Correspondance. Paris, 1914. 2v.
39591.20 Vian, Louis. Histoire de Montesquieu. Paris, 1879.
39591.21 Schwarcz, J. Montesquieu und die Verantwortlichkeit der Räthe des Monarchen. Leipzig, 1901.
39591.22 Dedieu, J. Montesquieu. Paris, 1913.
39591.23 Lypschutz, Michael. Montesquieu als Geschichtsphilosophie. Inaug. Diss. Strasbourg, 1927.

39592 Individual authors, etc. - 1715-1799 - History, criticism, etc. - Montesquieu - Complete works

39592.2 Montesquieu, C.L. de S. Oeuvres. Copenhagen, 1759-61. 6v.
39592.3 Montesquieu, C.L. de S. Oeuvres. Paris, 1795. 5v.
39592.3.5 Montesquieu, C.L. de S. Oeuvres. Amsterdam, 1773. 6v.
39592.4 Montesquieu, C.L. de S. Oeuvres. Paris, 1798. 5v.
39592.5 Montesquieu, C.L. de S. Oeuvres. Paris, 1817.
39592.6 Montesquieu, C.L. de S. Oeuvres complètes. Paris, 1816. 6v.
39592.7 Montesquieu, C.L. de S. Oeuvres complètes. Paris, 1875-79. 7v.
39592.8.20 Montesquieu, C.L. de S. Oeuvres. Amsterdam, 1758. 3v.
39592.9 Montesquieu, C.L. de S. Oeuvres. Amsterdam, 1769.
39592.10 Montesquieu, C.L. de S. Complete works. v.2-4. Dublin, 1777. 3v.
Htn 39592.12* Montesquieu, C.L. de S. Oeuvres posthumes. London, 1783.
39592.13 Montesquieu, C.L. de S. Oeuvres. v.1-8. Deux-Ponts, 1784. 5v.
39592.15 Montesquieu, C.L. de S. Oeuvres complètes. Basle, 1799. 8v.
39592.20 Montesquieu, C.L. de S. Oeuvres complètes. Paris, 1950. 3v.
39592.21 Montesquieu, C.L. de S. Oeuvres complètes. Paris, 1949-51. 2v.
39592.22 Montesquieu, C.L. de S. Oeuvres complètes. Paris, 1964.

39593 Individual authors, etc. - 1715-1799 - History, criticism, etc. - Montesquieu - Selections

39593.10 Montesquieu, C.L. de S. Montesquieu. Paris, 1929.
39593.15 Montesquieu, C.L. de S. Montesquieu, 1689-1755. Genève, 1947.
39593.20A Montesquieu, C.L. de S. Montesquieu par lui-même. Paris, 1953.
39593.20B Montesquieu, C.L. de S. Montesquieu par lui-même. Paris, 1953.
39593.30 Montesquieu, C.L. de S. Pensées et fragments inédits de Montesquieu. Bordeaux, 1899.

39593 Individual authors, etc. - 1715-1799 - History, criticism, etc. - Montesquieu - Selections - cont.

39594.08 Montesquieu, C.L. de S. Catalogue de la bibliothèque de Montesquieu. Genève, 1954.

39594.1 - .14 Individual authors, etc. - 1715-1799 - History, criticism, etc. - Montesquieu - Individual works

39594.1 Montesquieu, C.L. de S. De l'esprit des loix. Genève, 1749.
39594.1.10 Montesquieu, C.L. de S. De l'esprit des loix. Amsterdam, 1749.
39594.1.35 Montesquieu, C.L. de S. Oeuvres. v.2-4. Londres, 1769. 3v.
39594.2 Montesquieu, C.L. de S. De l'esprit des lois. Paris, 1832. 3v.
39594.2.2 Montesquieu, C.L. de S. Esprit des lois par Montesquieu. Paris, 1844.
39594.2.3 Montesquieu, C.L. de S. Esprit des lois par Montesquieu. Paris, 1872.
39594.2.5 Montesquieu, C.L. de S. Extraits de l'esprit des lois. Paris, 1896.
39594.2.10 Montesquieu, C.L. de S. De l'esprit des lois. Paris, 1962. 2v.
39594.2.15 Montesquieu, C.L. de S. Montesquieu. Paris, 1932.
39594.2.25 Montesquieu, C.L. de S. Extraits sur la loi, la liberté et le gouvernment anglais. Princeton, 1944.
39594.2.30 Montesquieu, C.L. de S. De l'esprit des lois. Paris, 1944-45.
39594.2.32 Montesquieu, C.L. de S. De l'esprit des lois. Paris, 1950- 2v.
39594.2.34 Montesquieu, C.L. de S. Vom Geist der Gesetze. n.p., 1951. 2v.
39594.3 Montesquieu, C.L. de S. De l'esprit des lois. v.3-5. Paris, 1803. 2v.
39594.3.2 Montesquieu, C.L. de S. Spirit of laws. 2. ed. v.2. London, 1752.
39594.3.3 Montesquieu, C.L. de S. The spirit of laws. London, 1758. 2v.
39594.3.4 Montesquieu, C.L. de S. The spirit of laws. 5. ed. London, 1794. 2v.
39594.3.5 Montesquieu, C.L. de S. The spirit of laws. Philadelphia, 1802. 2v.
39594.3.7 Montesquieu, C.L. de S. The spirit of laws. N.Y., 1899. 2v.
39594.3.8 Montesquieu, C.L. de S. The spirit of the laws. v.1-2. N.Y., 1949.
39594.3.13 Montesquieu, C.L. de S. Werk von den Gesetzen. Frankfurt, 1753. 3v.
39594.3.15 Montesquieu, C.L. de S. Der Geist der Gesetze von Montesquieu. Leipzig, 1891.
39594.3.19 Montesquieu, C.L. de S. Defense de l'esprit des lois. Genève, 1750.
39594.3.20 La Roche, J.B.L. Critique de l'esprit des loix. Genève, 1750. 2 pam.
39594.3.23 Bonnaire, L. de. L'esprit des lois quintessencié par...lettres. n.p., 1751. 2v.
39594.3.25 Laporte, J. de. Obserbations sur l'esprit des loix. 2. ed. Amsterdam, 1751.
39594.3.28 Destutt de Tracy, A.L.C. Commentaire sur l'esprit des lois de Montesquieu. Liège, 1817.
39594.3.29 Destutt de Tracy, A.L.C. Commentaire sur l'esprit des loix de Montesquieu. Paris, 1828.
39594.3.30 Destutt de Tracy, A.L.C. Commentary and review... spirit of laws. Philadelphia, 1811.
39594.3.31 Barckhausen, Henri. Montesquieu, l'esprit des loix et les archives. Bordeaux, 1904.
39594.3.32 Marat, J.P. Eloge de Montesquieu. Libourne, 1883.
39594.3.35 Pietsch, Theodor. Über das Verhältnis der politischen Theorie, Locke's zu Montesquieu. Breslau, 1887.
39594.3.40 Levi, L.M. The political doctrine of Montesquieu's Esprit des lois. N.Y., 1936.
39594.3.45 Fletcher, F.T.H. Montesquieu and English politics, 1750-1800. London, 1939.
39594.3.50 Durkheim, É. Quid secundatus politicae scientiae. Burdigalae, 1892.
39594.3.50.5A Durkheim, É. Montesquieu et Rousseau. Paris, 1953.
39594.3.50.5B Durkheim, É. Montesquieu et Rousseau. Paris, 1953.
39594.3.50.10 Durkheim, É. Montesquieu and Rousseau. Ann Arbor, 1960.
39594.3.55 Morgan, Charles. The liberty of thought and the separation of powers. Oxford, 1948.
39594.4 Montesquieu, C.L. de S. Lettres persanes. Paris, 1803.
39594.5 Montesquieu, C.L. de S. Oeuvres mélées et posthumes. Paris, 1807. 12v.
X Cg 39594.5.9 Montesquieu, C.L. de S. Considérations sur...des Romains. Paris, 1828.
39594.6 Montesquieu, C.L. de S. Considérations sur...des Romains. Paris, 1830.
39594.6.8 Montesquieu, C.L. de S. Grandeur et décadence des Romains. Paris, 1843.
39594.6.10 Montesquieu, C.L. de S. Grandeur et décadence des Romains. Paris, 1851.
39594.6.25 Montesquieu, C.L. de S. Grandeur et décadence...politique...dialogue de Sylla et d'Eucrate...et temple de Gnide. Paris, 1866.
39594.6.45 Montesquieu, C.L. de S. Considérations sur les causes...décadence. 4e éd. Paris, 1917.
39594.7.5 Montesquieu, C.L. de S. Der Geist des herrn von Montesquieu. Basel, 1788.
39594.8 Montesquieu, C.L. de S. The temple of Gnidus and Arsaces and Ismenia. London, 1797.
39594.9 Montesquieu, C.L. de S. Mélanges inédits de Montesquieu. Bordeaux, 1892.
39594.9.40 Montesquieu, C.L. de S. Essai sur le gout. 1. éd. Genève, 1967.
Htn 39594.9.50* Montesquieu, C.L. de S. Lettres familières. Florence, 1767.
39594.9.55 Montesquieu, C.L. de S. Lettres familières à divers amis d'Italie. Rome, 1773.
39594.9.60 Montesquieu, C.L. de S. Politique et Montesquieu. Paris, 1965.
Htn 39594.9.75* Montesquieu, C.L. de S. Lettres persanes. v.1-2. Amsterdam, 1721.
Htn 39594.9.77* Montesquieu, C.L. de S. Lettres persanes. Amsterdam, 1721.
Htn 39594.10* Montesquieu, C.L. de S. Lettres persanes. Cologne, 1744.
39594.11 Montesquieu, C.L. de S. Lettres persanes. Amsterdam, 1761.
39594.11.6 Montesquieu, C.L. de S. Lettres persanes. Paris, 1833.

39594.1 - .14 Individual authors, etc. - 1715-1799 - History, criticism, etc. - Montesquieu - Individual works - cont.

X Cg 39594.11.20 Montesquieu, C.L. de S. Lettres persanes. London, 1784. 2v.
39594.12A Montesquieu, C.L. de S. Lettres persanes. Paris, n.d.
39594.12B Montesquieu, C.L. de S. Lettres persanes. Paris, n.d.
39594.12.7 Montesquieu, C.L. de S. Lettres persanes. Paris, 1873.
39594.12.9 Barckhausen, Henri. Montesquieu; Lettres persanes. Paris, 1913. 2v.
39594.13.2 Montesquieu, C.L. de S. Lettres persanes. v.1-2. Paris, 1880-
39594.13.3 Persian and Chinese letters; being the lettres persanes. Washington, 1901.
39594.13.5 Montesquieu, C.L. de S. Lettres persanes. Paris, 1904.
39594.13.7 Montesquieu, C.L. de S. Lettres persanes. Paris, 1929. 2v.
39594.13.35 Montesquieu, C.L. de S. Lettres persanes. Paris, 1945.
39594.13.40 Montesquieu, C.L. de S. Lettres persanes. Paris, 1946.
39594.13.45 Montesquieu, C.L. de S. Lettres persanes. Genève, 1954.
39594.13.50 Montesquieu, C.L. de S. Lettres persanes de Montesquieu. Paris, 1969.
39594.13.80 Cadalso, José. Defensa de la nación española contra la Carta persiana LXXVIII de Montesquieu. Toulouse, 1970.
39594.14 Montesquieu, C.L. de S. Persian letters. 6th ed. Edinburgh, 1773.
39594.14.2 Montesquieu, C.L. de S. Persian letters. London, 1923.
Htn 39594.14.3* Montesquieu, C.L. de S. The Persian letters. London, 1892. 2v.
39594.14.4A Montesquieu, C.L. de S. The Persian letters. London, 1892. 2v.
39594.14.4B Montesquieu, C.L. de S. The Persian letters. London, 1892. 2v.
39594.14.4.5 Montesquieu, C.L. de S. The Persian letters. N.Y., 1961.
Htn 39594.14.5* Montesquieu, C.L. de S. Histoire veritable publiée d'après un nouveau manuscrit. Bordeaux, 1902.
Htn 39594.14.10* Montesquieu, C.L. de S. Histoire veritable. Lille, 1948.
39594.14.20 Montesquieu, C.L. de S. Considérations sur les richesses de l'Espagne. Paris, 1929.
39594.14.25 Montesquieu, C.L. de S. Cahiers (1716-1755). 22. ed. Paris, 1941.
39594.14.30 Montesquieu, C.L. de S. Le spicilège, un carnet inédit. Paris, 1944.

39594.15 Individual authors, etc. - 1715-1799 - History, criticism, etc. - Montesquieu - Bibliographies

39594.15 Heemskerk, J. Speciminis inauguralis de Montesquiro pars prior. Amsterdam, 1839.
39594.15.5 Cabeen, David Clark. Montesquieu: a bibliography. N.Y., 1947.
39594.15.20 Shackleton, R. Montesquieu. London, 1961.
39594.15.25 Montesquieu, C.L. de S. Manuscrits de Montesquieu. Paris, 1939.

39594.16 - .19 Individual authors, etc. - 1715-1799 - History, criticism, etc. - Montesquieu - Biography and criticism

39594.17 Sorel, Albert. Montesquieu. London, 1887.
39594.17.3 Sorel, Albert. Montesquieu. Chicago, 1888.
39594.17.4 Sorel, Albert. Montesquieu. 2. éd. Paris, 1889.
39594.17.5 Sorel, Albert. Montesquieu. Deutsch von Adolf Kressner. Berlin, 1896.
39594.18 Zévort, Edgar. Montesquieu. London, 1888.
39594.18.5A Dargan, E.P. The aesthetic doctrine of Montesquieu. Baltimore, 1907.
39594.18.5B Dargan, E.P. The aesthetic doctrine of Montesquieu. Baltimore, 1907.
39594.18.9A Archambault, P. Montesquieu. Paris, n.d.
39594.18.9B Archambault, P. Montesquieu. Paris, n.d.
39594.19 Marcus, W. Die Darstellung der französische Zustände in Montesquieus Lettres persanes...der Wirklichkeit. Breslau, 1902.
39594.19.2 Bremer, Klaus-Jürgen. Montesquieus Lettres persanes und Cadalsos Cartas marruecas. Thesis. Heidelberg, 1971.
39594.19.3 Gäbler, H. Studien zu Montesquieus Persischen Briefen. Chemnitz, 1898.
39594.19.5 Tchernoff, J. Montesquieu et J.J. Rousseau. Paris, 1903.
39594.19.9.1 Barckhausen, Henri. Montesquieu, ses idées et ses oeuvres d'après les papiers de la Brède. Genève, 1970.
39594.19.11 Dedieu, J. Montesquieu et la tradition politique. Paris, 1909.
39594.19.11.5 Dedieu, J. Montesquieu; l'homme et l'oeuvre. Paris, 1943.
39594.19.12 Tournyol du Clos, Jean. Les idées financières de Montesquieu. Paris, 1912.
39594.19.13 Chevalley, E. La théorie de différents ordres de lois. Le Caire, n.d.
39594.19.14 Klemperer, Victor. Montesquieu. Heidelberg, 1914-15. 2v.
39594.19.15 Leir-Malvano, E. Montesquieu et Machiavelli. Paris, 1912.
39594.19.17 Michel, Ernst Friedrich. Die anthropogeographischen Anschauung Montesquieus. Inaug. Diss. Heidelberg, 1915.
39594.19.21 Holmes, Oliver W. Montesquieu. N.Y., 1900.
39594.19.23 Doods, Muriel. Les récits de voyages. Thèse. Paris, 1929.
39594.19.23.5 Doods, Muriel. Les récits de voyages. Thèse. Paris, 1929.
39594.19.27 Petersen, Karl. Die Satzverbindung bei Montesquieu. Inaug. Diss. n.p., 1931.
39594.19.33 Struck, Walter. Montesquieu als Politiker. Berlin, 1933.
39594.19.42 Assollant, G. Montesquieu; les lettres persanes. Paris, 1931.
39594.19.45 Spurlin, P.M. Montesquieu in America, 1760-1801. University, La., 1940.
39594.19.48 Smoleński, W. Monteskjusz w polsce w XVIII. Warszawa, 1927.
39594.19.49 Bordeaux. Bibliothèque Municipale. Exposition des manuscrits de Montesquieu acguis à la vente du 23 février 1939 accompagnés d'un choix de livres. Bordeaux, 1939.
39594.19.50 Bordeaux. Bibliothèque Municipale. Montesquieu et l'esprit des lois. Bordeaux, 1948.
39594.19.53 Bordeaux. Bibliothèque Municipale. Montesquieu. Bordeaux, 1955.
39594.19.55 Cotta, S. Montesquieu e la scienza della società. Tornio, 1953.
39594.19.57 Oudin, Charles. Le spinozisme de Montesquieu. Genève, 1971.
39594.19.60 Eyland, J.M. Montesquieu chez ses notaires de la Brede. Bordeaux, 1956.
39594.19.65 Berlin, Isaiah. Montesquieu. London, 1955?
39594.19.70 Loehring, Martin. Montesquieu. Wiesbaden, 1950.
39594.19.75 Congrès Montesquieu, Bordeaux. Actes du congrès. Bordeaux, 1956.

39594.16 - .19 Individual authors, etc. - 1715-1799 - History, criticism, etc. - Montesquieu - Biography and criticism - cont.

39594.19.80 Rombaut, M.W. La conception stoïcienne du bonheur chez Montesquieu et chez quelques-uns de ses contemporains. Leiden, 1958.
39594.19.85 Althusser, Louis. Montesquieu. Paris, 1959.
39594.19.90 Kassem, Badreddine. Décadence et absolutisme. Droz, 1960.
39594.19.95 Stark, Werner. Montesquieu. London, 1960.
39594.19.100 Polska Akademii Nauk. Komitet Nauk Prawnych. Monteskiusz i jegodzieło. Wrocław, 1956.
39594.19.105 Baskin, Mark P. Montesk'e. Moskva, 1965.
39594.19.110 Snethage, Jacob Leonard. Montesquieu. Den Haag, 1964.
39594.19.115 Gentile, Francesco. L'esprit classique nel pensiero del Montesquieu. Padova, 1965.
39594.19.120 Loy, John Robert. Montesquieu. N.Y., 1968.
39594.19.125 Dédéyan, Charles. Montesquieu et l'Angleterre. Paris, 1958.
39594.19.130 Rosso, Corrado. Montesquieu moralista, dalle leggi al "Bonheur." Pisa, 1965.
39594.19.132 Rosso, Corrado. Intorno a Montesquieu. Pisa, 1970.
39594.19.135 Merry, Henry J. Montesquieu's system of natural government. West Lafayette, 1970.
39594.19.140 Devletoglou, Nicos E. Montesquieu and the wealth of nations. Athens, 1963.
39594.19.145 Waddicor, Mark H. Montesquieu and philosophy of natural law. The Hague, 1970.
39594.19.150 Cattaneo, Mario A. Le dottrine politiche de Montesquieu e di Rousseau. Milano, 1964.
39594.19.155 Ehrard, Jean. Montesquieu, critique d'art. Paris, 1965.
39594.19.160 Mas, Enrico de. Montesquieu, Genovesi e le edizioni italiane dello Spirito delle leggi. Firenze, 1971.

39594.20 - .39 Individual authors, etc. - 1715-1799 - Fiction - Saint Pierre - Folios, etc. [Discontinued]

39594.20 St. Pierre, J.H.B. de. La chaumière indienne. Paris, 1807.
Htn 39594.20.07* St. Pierre, J.H.B. de. La chaumière indienne. London, 1792.
39594.22 St. Pierre, J.H.B. de. La chaumière indienne. Paris, 1828.
39594.24 St. Pierre, J.H.B. de. La caboña indiana. Madrid, 1820.
Htn 39594.26* St. Pierre, J.H.B. de. Paul et Virginie. Paris, 1838.
Htn 39594.26.4* St. Pierre, J.H.B. de. Paul et Virginie. Paris, 18- ?
Htn 39594.26.5* St. Pierre, J.H.B. de. Paul et Virginie. Paris, 18- .
39594.27 St. Pierre, J.H.B. de. Paul et Virginie. Paris, 1819.
39594.27.5 St. Pierre, J.H.B. de. Paul et Virginie. London, 1824.
39594.27.8 St. Pierre, J.H.B. de. Paul et Virginie. Paris, 1828.
39594.27.12 St. Pierre, J.H.B. de. Paul et Virginie. Paris, 1834.
39594.28.5 St. Pierre, J.H.B. de. Paul et Virginie. London, 1839.
39594.29.5 St. Pierre, J.H.B. de. Paul et Virginie suivi de La chaumière indienne. Paris, 1860.
39594.30 St. Pierre, J.H.B. de. Paul et Virginie suivi de La chaumière indienne. Paris, 1863.
39594.30.3 St. Pierre, J.H.B. de. Paul et Virginie. Paris, 1863.
39594.30.5 St. Pierre, J.H.B. de. Paul et Virginie et La chaumière indienne. N.Y., 1869.
39594.30.6 St. Pierre, J.H.B. de. Paul and Virginia. Boston, 1883.
39594.30.7 St. Pierre, J.H.B. de. Paul et Virginie. Paris, 1886.
39594.30.10 St. Pierre, J.H.B. de. Paul et Virginie. Paris, 1930.
39594.30.12 St. Pierre, J.H.B. de. Paul et Virginie. N.Y., 1937.
Htn 39594.31* St. Pierre, J.H.B. de. Paolo e Virginia. n.p., 1791.
39594.31.5 St. Pierre, J.H.B. de. Pablo y Virginia. Paris, 1822.
39594.32 St. Pierre, J.H.B. de. Paulo e Virginia. Paris, 1834.
Htn 39594.32.10* St. Pierre, J.H.B. de. Paul and Mary. Dublin, 1789.
39594.33 St. Pierre, J.H.B. de. Paul and Virginia. 2. ed. London, 1796.
39594.34 St. Pierre, J.H.B. de. Paul and Virginia. London, 1800.
Htn 39594.34.10* St. Pierre, J.H.B. de. Paul and Virginia. London, 1819.
39594.34.15 St. Pierre, J.H.B. de. Paul and Virginia. Boston, 1834.
39594.34.20 St. Pierre, J.H.B. de. Paul and Virginia. Philadelphia, 1856.
39594.34.23 St. Pierre, J.H.B. de. Paul and Virginia. N.Y., 1857.

39595.1 - .17 Individual authors, etc. - 1715-1799 - Fiction - Saint Pierre - Complete and Selected works

39595.5 St. Pierre, J.H.B. de. Oeuvres. Paris, 1826. 12v.
39595.11 St. Pierre, J.H.B. de. Oeuvres complètes. Paris, 1820. 2v.
39595.12 St. Pierre, J.H.B. de. Oeuvres choisies. Paris, 1878.
39595.13 St. Pierre, J.H.B. de. Oeuvres choisies. Paris, 1866.
39595.13.5A St. Pierre, J.H.B. de. Oeuvres choisies. Paris, 1867.
39595.13.5B St. Pierre, J.H.B. de. Oeuvres choisies. Paris, 1867.
39595.14 St. Pierre, J.H.B. de. Oeuvres choisies. Paris, 1846.
39595.14.3 St. Pierre, J.H.B. de. Oeuvres choisies. Paris, 1843.
39595.15 St. Pierre, J.H.B. de. Oeuvres choisies. Paris, 1848.
39595.16 St. Pierre, J.H.B. de. Works. London, 1846. 2v.
39595.17 St. Pierre, J.H.B. de. Correspondance. Paris, 1826. 3v.
39595.17.2 Martin, L.A. Mémoire sur la vie...de J.H. Bernardin de St. Pierre. Paris, 1826.

39595.18 - Individual authors, etc. - 1715-1799 - Fiction - Saint Pierre - Paul et Virginie

39595.18 St. Pierre, J.H.B. de. Paul et Virginie. N.Y., 1852.
39595.19 St. Pierre, J.H.B. de. The shipwreck of Paul and Virginia. London, 18- .
39595.20.15 St. Pierre, J.H.B. de. Paul et Virginie. Paris, 1849.
39595.20.50 St. Pierre, J.H.B. de. Paul and Virginia. N.Y., 1892.
39595.22 St. Pierre, J.H.B. de. Paul et Virginie. Strasbourg, n.d.
39595.22.5 St. Pierre, J.H.B. de. Paul and Virginia. Boston, 19- .
39595.22.7 St. Pierre, J.H.B. de. Paul et Virginie. London, 1905.
39595.22.8 St. Pierre, J.H.B. de. Paul et Virginie. Boston, 1906.
39595.22.10A St. Pierre, J.H.B. de. Paul and Virginia. N.Y., 1929.
39595.22.10B St. Pierre, J.H.B. de. Paul and Virginia. N.Y., 1929.
39595.22.13 St. Pierre, J.H.B. de. Paul et Virginie. Paris, 19- .
39595.22.15 St. Pierre, J.H.B. de. Paul et Virginie. Paris, 1930.
39595.22.20 St. Pierre, J.H.B. de. Paul et Virginie suivi de La chaumière indienne. Paris, 1934.
39595.22.30 St. Pierre, J.H.B. de. Paul et Virginie suivi de La chaumière indienne. Manchester, 1942.
39595.23 St. Pierre, J.H.B. de. Paul et Virginie suivi de La chaumière indienne. Paris, 1911?
Htn 39595.25* St. Pierre, J.H.B. de. Paul et Virginie. Paris, 18- .
39595.26 St. Pierre, J.H.B. de. Pablo y Virginia. Philadelphia, 1808.
39595.27 St. Pierre, J.H.B. de. Pablo y Virginia. Paris, 1826.
39595.30 St. Pierre, J.H.B. de. Paolo e Virginia. Firenze, 1795.

Classified Listing

39596.1 - .19 Individual authors, etc. - 1715-1799 - Fiction - Saint Pierre - Other individual works

39596.6 St. Pierre, J.H.B. de. Étude de la nature. Paris, 1792. 5v.
39596.7 St. Pierre, J.H.B. de. Studies of nature. Worcester, 1797. 3v.
39596.8 St. Pierre, J.H.B. de. Studies of nature. Worcester, 1797. 3v.
39596.9 St. Pierre, J.H.B. de. Beauties of the studies of nature. London, 1799.
39596.10 St. Pierre, J.H.B. de. Studies of nature. Philadelphia, 1808. 3v.
39596.12 St. Pierre, J.H.B. de. Harmonies of nature. Sequel to Studies of nature. London, 1815. 3v.
Htn 39596.14* St. Pierre, J.H.B. de. Voeux d'un solitaire, pour servir de suite aux Études de la nature. Paris, 1789.
Htn 39596.16* St. Pierre, J.H.B. de. La chaumière indienne. Paris, 1791.
39596.18 St. Pierre, J.H.B. de. Voyages of Amasis. Boston, 1795.
39596.18.5 St. Pierre, J.H.B. de. Amasis. London, 1799.

39596.20 - Individual authors, etc. - 1715-1799 - Fiction - Saint Pierre - Biography and criticism

39596.20 Pamphlet box. Jacques Henri Bernardin de St. Pierre.
39596.21 Barine, Arvède. Bernardin de St. Pierre. Paris, 1891.
39596.21.2 Barine, Arvède. Bernardin de St. Pierre. Paris, 1904.
39596.22 Lescure, M. de. Bernardin de St. Pierre. Paris, 1892.
39596.23 Maury, Fernand. Étude sur la vie et les oeuvres de Bernardin de St. Pierre. Paris, 1892.
39596.26 Hawkins, Richmond L. Bernardin de St. Pierre and Peale's Philadelphia Museum. n.p., 1929.
39596.30 Duchêne, Albert. Les rêveries de Bernardin de St. Pierre. Paris, 1935.
39596.31 Toinet, P. Paul et Virginie. Paris, 1963.
39596.32 Baridon, Silvio F. Le harmonies de la nature di Bernardin de St. Pierre. Milano, 1958. 2v.
39596.33 Simon, Jean Jacques. Bernardin de St. Pierre ou Le triomphe de Flore. Paris, 1967.

39597 Individual authors, etc. - 1715-1799 - Fiction - Marmontel - Complete and Selected works

39597.3 Marmontel, J.F. Oeuvres complètes. Paris, 1787. 17v.
39597.7 Marmontel, J.F. Poetique françoise. Paris, 1763. 2v.
39597.9 Marmontel, J.F. Contes moraux. Paris, 1775. 3v.
39597.10 Marmontel, J.F. Contes moraux. Amsterdam, 1779. 3v.
39597.11 Marmontel, J.F. Contes moraux. Deux-Ponts, 1793.
39597.13 Marmontel, J.F. Contes moraux, anciens et nouveaux. Paris, 1804. 8v.
39597.14 Marmontel, J.F. Contes moraux. v.1-2,3,4. Paris, 1822. 3v.
39597.18 Marmontel, J.F. Nouveaux contes moraux. Paris, 1816-17. 4v.
39597.23 Marmontel, J.F. Oeuvres posthumes. Paris, 1804. 4v.
39597.26 Marmontel, J.F. Regence du duc d'Orléans. Paris, 1805. 2v.
39597.29 Marmontel, J.F. Oeuvres posthumes. Paris, 1804. 4v.
39597.30 Marmontel, J.F. Mémoires. Paris, 1805. 4v.

39598.1 - .36 Individual authors, etc. - 1715-1799 - Fiction - Marmontel - Individual works

39598.3 Marmontel, J.F. Memoirs. London, 1805. 4v.
39598.5 Marmontel, J.F. Memoirs. v.1-2. Philadelphia, 1807.
39598.6 Marmontel, J.F. Memoirs. London, 1830. 2v.
39598.7 Marmontel, J.F. Memoirs. Boston, 1878. 2v.
39598.8 Marmontel, J.F. Memoirs. Paris, 1891. 3v.
39598.8.5 Marmontel, J.F. Memoirs. Paris, 1891.
39598.9A Marmontel, J.F. Memoirs. London, 1895. 2v.
39598.9B Marmontel, J.F. Memoirs. London, 1895. 2v.
39598.9.5 Marmontel, J.F. Memoirs of Marmontel. Paris, 1903.
39598.9.15 Marmontel, J.F. Tales, selected. London, 1799.
39598.9.20 Marmontel, J.F. Moral tales. London, 1795? 2v.
39598.9.25 Marmontel, J.F. Moral tales. London, 1800.
39598.10 Marmontel, J.F. Moral tales. N.Y., 1813.
39598.11A Marmontel, J.F. Moral tales. London, 1895.
39598.11B Marmontel, J.F. Moral tales. London, 1895.
Htn 39598.13* Marmontel, J.F. Select translations and imitations from the French. N.Y., 1801.
39598.13.15 Marmontel, J.F. Contos morals. Lisboa, 1769.
39598.14 Marmontel, J.F. Nowe powiesci moralne. Warszawie, 1794.
Htn 39598.15* Marmontel, J.F. Belisaire. Paris, 1767.
39598.15.6 Marmontel, J.F. Bélisaire. Paris, 1767.
39598.16 Marmontel, J.F. Bélisarius. Brussels, 1792. 2v.
39598.18 Marmontel, J.F. Bélisaire. Paris, 1808.
39598.23 Marmontel, J.F. Bélisarius. London, 1768.
39598.24 Marmontel, J.F. Bélisarius. London, 1794.
39598.25 Marmontel, J.F. Bélisarius. Newburyport, 1796.
39598.27 Marmontel, J.F. Bélisaire. Paris, 1816.
39598.27.5 Marmontel, J.F. Bélisaire. London, 1818.
39598.28 Marmontel, J.F. Bélisario. 2. ed. Burdeos, 1820.
39598.29 Marmontel, J.F. Bélisaire. Paris, 1821.
39598.29.75 Marmontel, J.F. Les incas. Paris, 1794. 3v.
39598.30 Marmontel, J.F. Les Incas. Parris, 1817.
39598.31 Marmontel, J.F. Principes d'éloquence de Marmontel. Paris, 1809.
39598.33 Marmontel, J.F. Trial of friendship. Boston, 1802.
39598.34 Marmontel, J.F. Lucile. Besançon, 1769.
39598.36 Marmontel, J.F. The widow of the village. Hartford, 1815.

39598.37 - Individual authors, etc. - 1715-1799 - Fiction - Marmontel - Biography and criticism

39598.37 Pamphlet box. Marmontel.
39598.40 Lenel, S. Un homme de lettres au XVIIIe siècle. Marmontel. Paris, 1902.
39598.42 Freund, Max. Die moralischen Erzählungen Marmontels. Halle, 1904.
39598.42.5 Bauer, H. Jean-François Marmontel als Literarkritiker. Inaug. Diss. Dresden, 1937.
39598.43 Body, Albin. Annette et Lubin. 2e ed. Bruxelles, 1872.
39598.44A Price, Lawrence M. The vogue of Marmontel on the German stage. Berkeley, 1944.
39598.44B Price, Lawrence M. The vogue of Marmontel on the German stage. Berkeley, 1944.
39598.50 Ehrard, Jean. De l'encyclopédie à la contre-révolution; Jean-François Marmontel, 1723-1799. Clermont-Ferrand, 1970.

40511 Individual authors, etc. - 1715-1799 - Fiction - Le Sage - Folios [Discontinued]; Complete and Selected works

40511.01 Pamphlet box. French readers.
40511.2 LeSage, Alain René. Bibliographical notes upon an unique set of his editions. London, n.d.
40511.3 LeSage, Alain René. Oeuvres choisies. Paris, 1810. 16v.
40511.6 LeSage, Alain René. Oeuvres. Paris, 1840.
40511.9 LeSage, Alain René. Pages choisies. Paris, 1896.
40511.21 LeSage, Alain René. Théâtre. Paris, 1877.
40511.22 LeSage, Alain René. Théâtre choisi. Paris, 1830.
40511.24 LeSage, Alain René. Aventuras de Gil Blas de Santillana. Madrid, 1799. 5v.
40511.25 LeSage, Alain René. Adventures of Gil Blas. London, 1809. 2v.
40511.28 LeSage, Alain René. The adventures of Gil Blas. Hartford, 1831.
40511.29 LeSage, Alain René. The history of Gil Blas of Santillana. Philadelphia, 1898. 3v.
40511.31 LeSage, Alain René. Historia de Gil Blas. Paris, 1835.
40511.31.2 LeSage, Alain René. Histoire de Gil Blas. Paris, 1835.
40511.32 LeSage, Alain René. Historia de Gil Blas. Paris, 1855.
40511.35 LeSage, Alain René. Histoire de Gil Blas. Paris, 1838.

40512 Individual authors, etc. - 1715-1799 - Fiction - Le Sage - Individual works

40512.2 LeSage, Alain René. Le diable boiteux. Amsterdam, 1739. 2v.
40512.2.25 LeSage, Alain René. Le diable boiteux. v.1-2. Paris, 1779.
40512.2.40 LeSage, Alain René. The devil upon two sticks. London, 179-.
40512.3 LeSage, Alain René. Le diable boiteux. Paris, 1819. 2v.
40512.3.5 LeSage, Alain René. Le diable boiteux. v.1-2. Paris, 1830.
40512.3.7 LeSage, Alain René. Le diable boiteux. Paris, 1876. 2v.
40512.3.12 LeSage, Alain René. Le diable boiteux. Paris, 1928.
40512.3.18 LeSage, Alain René. Le diable boiteux. London, 1708.
40512.3.20 LeSage, Alain René. Le diable boiteux. 2. éd. Paris, 1970.
Htn 40512.3.25* LeSage, Alain René. Asmodeus. London, 1841.
40512.3.50 LeSage, Alain René. Diavolul schiop. Bucuresti, 1924.
40512.4A LeSage, Alain René. Histoire de Gil Blas. Paris, 1824. 3v.
40512.4B LeSage, Alain René. Histoire de Gil Blas. Paris, 1824. 3v.
40512.4.5 LeSage, Alain René. Histoire de Gil Blas de Santillane. Paris, 1818. 4v.
40512.5 LeSage, Alain René. Histoire de Gil Blas. v.2-4. Paris, 1824. 3v.
40512.6 LeSage, Alain René. Histoire de Gil Blas. London, 1826. 2v.
Htn 40512.7* LeSage, Alain René. The adventures of Gil Blas of Santillane. London, 1826. 2v.
40512.8 LeSage, Alain René. Histoire de Gil Blas de Santillane. Paris, 1829. 4v.
40512.8.7 LeSage, Alain René. Histoire de Gil Blas de Santillane. Paris, 1852.
40512.8.9 LeSage, Alain René. Histoire de Gil Blas de Santillane. Paris, 1854.
40512.8.12 LeSage, Alain René. Histoire de Gil Blas de Santillane. Paris, 1870.
40512.9 LeSage, Alain René. Aventures de Gil Blas de Santillane. Paris, 1875.
40512.9.15 LeSage, Alain René. Aventures de Gil Blas de Santillane. London, 1870.
40512.10.5 LeSage, Alain René. Adventures of Gil Blas. v.1-2,3-4. N.Y., 1814. 2v.
Htn 40512.10.15* LeSage, Alain René. Aventures de Gil Blas de Santillane. London, 1819. 3v.
40512.11 LeSage, Alain René. Adventures of Gil Blas. Hartford, 1847. 3v.
40512.11.5 LeSage, Alain René. Adventures of Gil Blas. London, 1774. 2v.
40512.11.6 LeSage, Alain René. Adventures of Gil blas. v.1-2. London, 1744.
40512.12 LeSage, Alain René. Adventures of Gil Blas. Boston, 1864. 3v.
40512.12.1 LeSage, Alain René. Adventures of Gil Blas of Santillane. London, 1881. 3v.
40512.12.3 LeSage, Alain René. Adventures of Gil Blas of Santillane. London, 1878?
40512.12.4A LeSage, Alain René. Adventures of Gil Blas of Santillane. Edinburgh, 1886. 3v.
40512.12.4B LeSage, Alain René. Adventures of Gil Blas of Santillane. Edinburgh, 1886. 3v.
40512.12.5A LeSage, Alain René. Adventures of Gil Blas of Santillane. v.2. London, 1907.
40512.12.5B LeSage, Alain René. Adventures of Gil Blas of Santillane. London, 1907. 2v.
40512.12.7 LeSage, Alain René. The adventures of Gil Blas. London, 1904. 4v.
40512.13 LeSage, Alain René. Adventures of Gil Blas of Santillane. Leominster, 1810.
40512.14 LeSage, Alain René. Aventuras de Gil Blas. London, 1808. 4v.
40512.14.2 LeSage, Alain René. Histoire de Gil Blas de Santillane. London, 1809. 4v.
40512.15 LeSage, Alain René. Aventuras de Gil Blas. London, 1815. 4v.
40512.25.5 LeSage, Alain René. Aventuras de Gil Blas de Santillana. Madrid, 1800. 5v.
40512.25.18 LeSage, Alain René. De Gil Blas de Santillana. Valencia, 1812. 6v.
40512.25.30 LeSage, Alain René. Historia de Gil Blas de Santillana. Paris, 1838.
40512.26A LeSage, Alain René. Histoire de Gil Blas. Paris, 1865.
40512.26B LeSage, Alain René. Histoire de Gil Blas. Paris, 1865.
40512.27.10 LeSage, Alain René. Histoire de Gil Blas. Boston, 1929.
40512.28 LeSage, Alain René. Histoire de Gil Blas de Santillana. Leipzig, 1870. 2v.
40512.29 LeSage, Alain René. Histoire de Gil Blas de Santillana. Paris, 1844.
40512.30 LeSage, Alain René. Histoire de Gil Blas de Santillana. Barcelona, 1840-41. 2v.

40512 Individual authors, etc. - 1715-1799 - Fiction - Le Sage - Individual works - cont.

40512.31 LeSage, Alain René. Histoire de Gil Blas de Santillana. Barcelona, 1840.
40512.31.5 LeSage, Alain René. Histoire de Gil Blas de Santillana. Madrid, 18- .
40512.32 LeSage, Alain René. Gil Blas di Santillano. London, 1809. 4v.
40512.33 LeSage, Alain René. Historia de Gil Blas de Santillana. Paris, 1864.
40512.33.3 LeSage, Alain René. Historia de Gil Blas de Santillana. Paris, 1873.
40512.33.5 LeSage, Alain René. Historia de Gil Blas de Santillana. N.Y., 1889.
40512.34 LeSage, Alain René. Historia de Gil Blas de Santillana. N.Y., 1890.
40512.34.2 LeSage, Alain René. Historia de Gil Blas de Santillana. N.Y., 1880.
40512.34.4 LeSage, Alain René. Historia de Gil Blas de Santillana. N.Y., 1886.
40512.36 LeSage, Alain René. The bachelor of Salamanca. Boston, 1901.
40512.37 LeSage, Alain René. The bachelor of Salamanca. Paris, 1837. 4v.
40512.38 LeSage, Alain René. LeSage: Historia de Gil Blas de Santillana. Boston, 1923.
40512.39 LeSage, Alain René. Avventure di Gil Blas di Santillana. Milano, 1876.
40512.42 LeSage, Alain René. Histoire de Gil Blas de Santillane. Paris, 1850.
40512.43 LeSage, Alain René. Histoire de Gil Blas de Santillane. Chicago, 1916.
40512.44 LeSage, Alain René. Histoire de Gil Blas de Santillane. v.1-2. Paris, 1942.
40512.44.2 LeSage, Alain René. Gil Blas. Paris, 1932.
40512.44.3 LeSage, Alain René. Histoire de Gil Blas de Santillane. Paris, 1935. 2v.
40512.44.5 LeSage, Alain René. Histoire de Gil Blas de Santillane. Paris, 1969. 2v.
40512.46 LeSage, Alain René. Aventuras de Gil Blas de Santillana. Barcelona, 1960.
40512.47 LeSage, Alain René. Gil Blas von Santillana. Berlin, 1779. 6v.
40512.48 LeSage, Alain René. The adventures of Gil Blas of Santillane. N.Y., 1913.
40512.49 LeSage, Alain René. Oeuvre. Paris, 1821. 12v.
40512.50 LeSage, Alain René. Historia d'Estevenho Goncalves. Paris, 1837.
40512.55 LeSage, Alain René. The comical history and humorous adventures of Estevanille Gonzalez. 2. ed. London, 1737.
40512.57 LeSage, Alain René. Le bachelier de Salamanque. Paris, 1820.
Htn 40512.58* LeSage, Alain René. The bachelor of Salamanca. London, 1737-39. 2v.
40512.58.9 LeSage, Alain René. The bachelor of Salamanca. Philadelphia, 1854. 2v.
40512.58.15 LeSage, Alain René. The bachelor of Salamanca. N.Y., 1908.
40512.59 LeSage, Alain René. El bachiller de Salamanca. Madrid, 1821. 2v.
40512.60.1 LeSage, Alain René. Turcaret. London, 1969.
40512.65 LeSage, Alain René. Les aventures du flibustier Beauchêne. N.Y., 1926.
40512.80 LeSage, Alain René. Crispin, rival of his master. N.Y., 1915.

40513 Individual authors, etc. - 1715-1799 - Fiction - Le Sage - Biography and criticism

40513.1 Cordier, Henri. Essai bibliographique sur les oeuvres d'Alain René LeSage. Paris, 1910.
40513.7 Llorente, J.A. Obeservations critiques...Gil Blas de Santillane. Paris, 1822.
40513.8 Llorente, J.A. Observaciones criticas...Gil Blas de Santillana. Madrid, 1822.
40513.9 Llorente, J.A. Observaciones criticas sobre el romance de Gil Blas de Santillana. Barcelona, 1837.
40513.10 Haack, Gustav. Untersuchungen zur Quellenkunde von LeSage's "Gil Blas." Kiel, 1896.
40513.12 Heinz, Hans. Gil Blas und das zeitgenossische Leben in Frankreich. Inaug. Diss. Erlangen, 1914.
40513.14 La vie de Don Alphonse Blas de Lirias, fils de Gil Blas de Santillane. Amsterdam, 1744.
40513.16 Barberet, V. LeSage et le théâtre de la foire. Nancy, 1887.
40513.18 Barao y Clemente, Gerónimo. LeSage y su ncareful novéla de costumbres Gil Blas de Santillana. Barcelona, 1867.
X Cg 40513.26 Claretie, Leo. LeSage. Paris, 1894.
40513.27 Claretie, Leo. LeSage. Paris, 1890.
40513.28A Lintilhac, E. LeSage. Paris, 1893.
40513.28B Lintilhac, E. LeSage. Paris, 1893.
40513.29 Pierson, O.P. The dramatic works of Alain-René LeSage and analytical and comparative study. Urbana, 1930.
40513.38 Dédéyan, Charles. A.R. LeSage. v.1-2. Paris, 1956.
40513.38.5 Dédéyan, Charles. LeSage et Gil Blas. Paris, 1965. 2v.
40513.40 Laufer, Roger. Lesage. Paris, 1971.

40515.1 - .2 Individual authors, etc. - 1715-1799 - Fiction - Miscellany

40515.1 Albert, Mlle. d'. Les confidences d'une jolie femme. pt. 1-4. Francfort, 1775.
X Cg 40515.1.30 Belin de Ballu, J.N. Le prêtre. Paris, 1802.
40515.2.4 Bitaubé, P.J. Joseph. 4. éd. Paris, 1786.
40515.2.10 Bitaubé, P.J. José. pt. 1-2. Lisboa, 1792.
40515.2.25 Charrière, Isabella A. Four tales by Zélide. London, 1925.
40515.2.26 Charrière, Isabella A. Four tales by Zélide. N.Y., 1925.
40515.2.34 Farnum, Dorothy. The Dutch divinity. London, 1959.
40515.2.35 Godet, Philippe. Madame de Charrière et ses amis (1740-1805). Lausanne, 1927.
40515.2.36 Kimstedt, C. Frau von Charrière, 1740-1805; ihre Gedankenwelt und ihre Beziehungen zur französischen und deutschen Literatur. Berlin, 1938.
40515.2.36.2 Kimstedt, C. Frau von Charrière, 1740-1805. Inaug. Diss. Berlin, 1938.
40515.2.36.4A Scott, Geoffrey. The portrait of Zélide. N.Y., 1927.
40515.2.36.4B Scott, Geoffrey. The portrait of Zélide. N.Y., 1927.
40515.2.36.5 Scott, Geoffrey. The portrait of Zélide. N.Y., 1959.

40515.1 - .2 Individual authors, etc. - 1715-1799 - Fiction - Miscellany - cont.

40515.2.36.6 Scott, Geoffrey. The portrait of Zélide. N.Y., 1926.
40515.2.36.10 Riccioli, Giovanni. L'esprit di Madame de Charrière. Bari, 1967.
40515.2.49 Denon, Vivant. Point de lendemain. Strasbourg, 1861.
40515.2.50 Denon, Vivant. Point de lendemain. Rouen, 1879.
40515.2.60 Nowinski, Judith. Baron Dominique Vivant Denon (1747-1825). Rutherford, 1970.
40515.2.80 Duperron de Castéra, L. La pierre philosophale des dames. n.p., 1753.
Htn 40515.2.85* Duperron de Castéra, L. Entretiens litteraires et galans. Amsterdam, 1738. 2v.

40515.3 - .6 Individual authors, etc. - 1715-1799 - Fiction - Épinay

40515.3 D'Épinay, Louise F. Mémoires et correspondence. Paris, 1818. 3v.
40515.4 D'Épinay, Louise F. Mémoires et correspondence. Paris, 1818. 3v.
40515.4.5A D'Épinay, Louise F. Mémoires. Paris, n.d. 2v.
40515.4.5B D'Épinay, Louise F. Mémoires. Paris, n.d. 2v.
40515.4.9 Campardon, Émile. Les prodigalités d'un fermier général. Paris, 1882.
40515.5 D'Épinay, Louise F. Oeuvres. Paris, 1869. 2v.
40515.5.10 D'Épinay, Louise F. Lettere inedite, 1769-1772. Bari, 1929.
40515.5.30 D'Épinay, Louise F. Les conversations d'Émilie. Paris, 1782. 2v.
40515.5.32 D'Épinay, Louise F. Gli ultimi anni della signora d'Épinay. Bari, 1933.
40515.5.35 D'Épinay, Louise F. Histoire de Madame de Montbrillant. 1. éd. Paris, 1951. 3v.
40515.5.85 Herpin, C.A.L. Une femme du monde au XVIIIe siècle. La jeunesse de Madame d'Épinay. Paris, 1882.
40515.5.85.4 Herpin, C.A.L. Une femme du monde au XVIIIe siècle. La jeunesse de Madame d'Épinay. 4e éd. Paris, 1883.
40515.5.85.7 Herpin, C.A.L. Une femme du monde au XVIIIe siècle. La jeunesse de Madame d'Épinay. 7e éd. Paris, 1898.
40515.5.86 Herpin, C.A.L. Une femme du monde au XVIIIe siècle; dernières années de Madame d'Épinay. Paris, 1883.
40515.5.86.2 Herpin, C.A.L. Une femme du monde au XVIIIe siècle; dernières années de Madame d'Épinay. 2e éd. Paris, 1883.
40515.5.86.3 Herpin, C.A.L. Une femme du monde au XVIIIe siècle; dernières années de Madame d'Épinay. 3e éd. Paris, 1883.
40515.5.86.5 Herpin, C.A.L. Une femme du monde au XVIIIe siècle; dernières années de Madame d'Épinay. 5e éd. Paris, 1884.
40515.5.90 Legros, A. Madame d'Épinay, valenciennoise. Valenciennes, 1920.
40515.5.95 Valentino, Henri. Madame d'Épinay, 1726-1783. Paris, 1952.
Htn 40515.6* Desfontaines, P.F.G. Le nouveau Gulliver. Paris, 1730.

40515.7 - .13 Individual authors, etc. - 1715-1799 - Fiction - Espinasse - Writings

Htn 40515.7* Lespinasse, J.J.E. de. Lettres, 1773-1776. Paris, 1809. 3v.
40515.8 Lespinasse, J.J.E. de. Lettres. Paris, 1815. 2v.
40515.8.5 Lespinasse, J.J.E. de. Lettres. Paris, 1876.
40515.8.15 Lespinasse, J.J.E. de. Lettres. Paris, 1903.
40515.9 Lespinasse, J.J.E. de. Lettres. Paris, 1887.
40515.9.9 Lespinasse, J.J.E. de. Lettres. Paris, 1906.
40515.9.9.5 Lespinasse, J.J.E. de. Lettres. Paris, 1906.
40515.9.10 Asse, E. Mlle. de L'Espinasse et la marquise du Deffand. Paris, 1877.
40515.9.15 Lespinasse, J.J.E. de. Coresspondance entre Mlle. de Lespinasse et le comte de Guibert. Paris, 1906.
40515.10 Lespinasse, J.J.E. de. Nouvelles lettres. Paris, 1820.
40515.11A Lespinasse, J.J.E. de. Lettres. Paris, 1903.
40515.11B Lespinasse, J.J.E. de. Lettres. Paris, 1903.
40515.12 Lespinasse, J.J.E. de. Die Liebesbriefe der Julie, 1773-1776. München, 1908.

40515.14 - .15 Individual authors, etc. - 1715-1799 - Fiction - Espinasse - Works about

40515.14 Ségur, Pierre. Julie de Lespinasse. Paris, 1905.
40515.14.3 Ségur, Pierre. Julie de Lespinasse. Paris, 1907?
40515.14.8 Ségur, Pierre. Julie de Lespinasse. N.Y., 1927.
40515.14.15 Élica, G. Un après-midi chez Julie de Lespinasse. 2e éd. Paris, 1912.
40515.14.20 Ehmer, Gisela. Die sensible Selbstdarstellung bei Julie de Lespinasse. Berlin, 1957.
40515.15 Jebb, Camilla. A star of the salons. London, 1908.
40515.15.4 Jebb, Camilla. A star of the salons. N.Y., 1908.
40515.15.7 Beaunier, André. La vie amoureuse de Julie de Lespinasse. Paris, 1925.
40515.15.8 Mitchener, Margret. A muse in love. London, 1962.
40515.15.9 Bouissounouse, J. Julie de Lespinasse. Paris, 1958.
40515.15.10 Royde-Smith, N. The double heart. N.Y., 1931?

40515.16 - .48 Individual authors, etc. - 1715-1799 - Fiction - Florian - Writings

40515.16 Florian, Jean P.C. de. Oeuvres. Paris, 1838. 7v.
NEDL 40515.16.10 Florian, Jean P.C. de. Oeuvres complèttes. v.2,4. Paris, 1803. 2v.
40515.16.50 Florian, Jean P.C. de. Oeuvres posthumes. Paris, 1799?
40515.17 Florian, Jean P.C. de. Oeuvres posthumes. Paris, 1837. 5v.
40515.17.50 Florian, Jean P.C. de. Lettres au Marquis A. de Florian, 1779-1793. Paris, 1957.
Htn 40515.18.20* Bignon, Jean P. The adventures of Abdalla. London, 1729.
Htn 40515.18.50* Florian, Jean P.C. de. Les six nouvelles de M. de Florian. Paris, 1784.
40515.18.53 Florian, Jean P.C. de. Les six nouvelles de M. de Florian. 3e éd. Genève, 1787.
40515.19 Florian, Jean P.C. de. Nouvelles nouvelles. Paris, 1792.
40515.19.5 Florian, Jean P.C. de. Nouvelles nouvelles. Paris, 1792.
40515.20 Florian, Jean P.C. de. Nouvelles. Paris, 1812.
40515.20.5 Florian, Jean P.C. de. Nouvelles. v.1-2. Paris, 1831.
40515.21 Florian, Jean P.C. de. Mélanges de poésies et de littérature. Paris, 1786.
Htn 40515.21.3* Florian, Jean P.C. de. Mélanges de poésies et de littérature. Paris, 1787.
40515.21.5 Florian, Jean P.C. de. Mélanges de poésies et de littérature. Genève, 1787.
40515.22 Florian, Jean P.C. de. Fables. Paris, 1812.
40515.22.5 Florian, Jean P.C. de. Fables. Paris, 1811.
40515.24 Florian, Jean P.C. de. Fables. Paris, n.d.
40515.24.5 Florian, Jean P.C. de. Fables. Paris, 1792.

Classified Listing

40515.16 - .48 Individual authors, etc. - 1715-1799 - Fiction - Florian - Writings - cont.

40515.28 Florian, Jean P.C. de. Fables. Paris, 1820.
40515.29 Florian, Jean P.C. de. Fables. 2e éd. Paris, 1829.
40515.29.4 Florian, Jean P.C. de. Fables. Paris, 1839.
Htn 40515.30* Florian, Jean P.C. de. Fables. Paris, 1843.
40515.30.2A Florian, Jean P.C. de. Fables de Florian. Paris, 1846.
40515.30.2B Florian, Jean P.C. de. Fables de Florian. Paris, 1856.
40515.30.5 Florian, Jean P.C. de. Fables de Florian. Paris, 1857.
40515.30.35 Florian, Jean P.C. de. Fables, précédées d'un étude sur la fable suivies de Tuth et de Tobie. Paris, 1920.
Htn 40515.30.50* Florian, Jean P.C. de. Fabulas de Florian. Madrid, 1831.
40515.30.75 Florian, Jean P.C. de. Les arlequinades. Strasbourg, 192-.
40515.31 Florian, Jean P.C. de. Éliezer. Paris, 1812.
40515.31.1 Florian, Jean P.C. de. Eliezer et Nephtaly. Paris, 1803.
40515.31.5 Florian, Jean P.C. de. Eleazar and Naphtaly. London, 1827.
X Cg 40515.31.7 Florian, Jean P.C. de. Galatée. Genève, 1784.
Htn 40515.32* Florian, Jean P.C de. Galatea. Boston, 1798.
40515.32.5 Florian, Jean P.C. de. La Galatea de Miguel de Cervantes. Perpignan, 1804.
40515.32.9 Florian, Jean P.C. de. Gonzalve de Cordoue. v.1-2. Paris, 1820.
40515.32.11 Florian, Jean P.C. de. Gonzalve de Cordoue. v.1-2. Paris, 1820.
40515.32.17 Florian, Jean P.C. de. Gonzalve de Cordoue. v.1-2. Paris, 1842.
40515.33 Florian, Jean P.C. de. Gonzalve de Cordoue. v.1-3. Paris, 1828.
40515.33.5 Florian, Jean P.C. de. Gonzalve de Cordoue. v.1-2. Paris, 1836.
40515.33.7 Florian, Jean P.C. de. Gonzalve de Cordoue. v.1-2. Paris, 1836.
40515.34 Florian, Jean P.C. de. Gonzalve de Cordoue. Paris, 1810. 3v.
40515.35 Florian, Jean P.C. de. Gonzalo de Cordoba. Perpignan, 1811. 2v.
40515.35.5 Florian, Jean P.C. de. Gonzalo de Cordoba. v.1-2. Madrid, 1821.
40515.35.10 Florian, Jean P.C. de. Gonzalo de Cordoba. Perpignan, 1828.
40515.36A Florian, Jean P.C. de. Gonzalva of Cordova. Dublin, 1793. 2v.
40515.36B Florian, Jean P.C. de. Gonzalva of Cordova. Dublin, 1793. 2v.
40515.36.2 Florian, Jean P.C. de. Gonsalve de Cordoue. 2e éd. Paris, 1792. 3v.
40515.36.5 Florian, Jean P.C. de. Gonsalve de Cordoue. London, 1808.
40515.36.50 Florian, Jean P.C. de. Gonsalve de Cordoue ou Grenade reconquise. 2. éd. Paris, 1792. 3v.
40515.37 Florian, Jean P.C. de. Gonsalve de Cordoue. v.1-2. Paris, 1812.
40515.37.2 Florian, Jean P.C. de. Guillaume Tell. Paris, 1810.
40515.37.5 Florian, Jean P.C. de. Guillaume Tell. Paris, 1812.
40515.37.10 Florian, Jean P.C. de. Guillaume Tell ou La Suisse libre. Paris, 1820.
40515.38 Florian, Jean P.C. de. Guilherme Tell. Paris, 1830.
40515.39 Florian, Jean P.C. de. Guilherme Tell. Greenfield, 1836.
40515.39.5 Florian, Jean P.C. de. Guillaume Tell ou La Suisse libre. Boston, 1849.
NEDL 40515.39.8 Florian, Jean P.C. de. William Tell, or Swisserland delivered. Baltimore, 1810.
40515.40 Florian, Jean P.C. de. William Tell. Boston, 1820.
40515.40.10 Florian, Jean P.C. de. William Tell. Concord, 1843.
40515.42 Florian, Jean P.C. de. Look before you leap. London, 1788.
40515.42.3 Florian, Jean P.C. de. Look before you leap. Dublin, 1789.
40515.42.5 Florian, Jean P.C. de. Numa Pompelius, second roi de Rome. Paris, 1786. 2v.
40515.42.9 Florian, Jean P.C. de. The adventures of Numa Pompelius. Brussels, 1790.
40515.43 Florian, Jean P.C. de. Numa Pompelius. Paris, 1812.
40515.43.2 Florian, Jean P.C. de. Numa Pompelius, second roi de Rome. v.1-2. Paris, 1814.
40515.43.5 Florian, Jean P.C. de. Numa Pompelius. Paris, 1820.
40515.44 Florian, Jean P.C. de. Numa Pompelius. Paris, 1830.
40515.45 Florian, Jean P.C. de. Numa Pompelius. v.1-2. Paris, 1833.
40515.45.5 Florian, Jean P.C. de. Numa Pompelius. Paris, 1842.
40515.46 Florian, Jean P.C. de. Numa Pompelius. Boston, 1850.
40515.47A Florian, Jean P.C. de. Mémoires d'un jeune Espagnol...lettres à Mme. de La Briche. Paris, 1923.
40515.47B Florian, Jean P.C. de. Mémoires d'un jeune Espagnol...lettres à Mme. de La Briche. Paris, 1923.
40515.47.5 Florian, Jean P.C. de. Six nouvelles. Mémoires d'un jeune Espagnol. Paris, 1971.
40515.48.5 Florian, Jean P.C. de. Estelle. Genève, 1795.
40515.48.7 Florian, Jean P.C. de. Estelle, pastorale. Paris, 1798.
40515.48.8 Florian, Jean P.C. de. Estelle. v.1-2. London, 1798.
40515.48.9 Florian, Jean P.C. de. Estelle. Paris, 1820.
40515.48.10 Florian, Jean P.C. de. Théâtre. Genève, 1787. 3v.

40515.49 - Individual authors, etc. - 1715-1799 - Fiction - Florian - Works about

40515.49 Pamphlet box. Florian.
40515.50 Schwenke, Walter. Florians Beziehungen zur deutschen Literatur. Weida, 1908.
40515.51 Claretie, Léo. Florian. Paris, 1888.
40515.52 Saillard, G. Florian, sa vie - son oeuvre. Toulouse, 1912.
40515.52.5 Pourrat, Henri. Le bosquet pastoral. Florian. 6. éd. Paris, 1931.
40515.54 Falconet, Ambroise. Le début. London, 1770.
Htn 40515.55* Fauques, Marianne Agnès de. The Vizirs. London, 1774. 3v.
40515.55.8 Fauques, Marianne Agnès de. Oriental anecdotes, or The history of Haroun Alrachid. London, 1764. 2v.
40515.56 Rühfel, Fritz. Florians Bearbeitung der Galatea des Cervantes. Inaug. Diss. München, 1928.
40515.57 Günther, E. Die Quellen der Fabeln Florians. Plauen, 1900.
40515.57.5 Mueller, H.W. Der Fabeldichter Florian. Wesel, 1925.

40516.1 - .3 Individual authors, etc. - 1715-1799 - Fiction - Miscellany

40516.1 Carra, J.L. Odazir ou le jeune Syrien. La Haye, 1772.
40516.2 Charpentier, L. Nouveaux contes moraux. Amsterdam, 1767. 3 pam.

40516.4 Individual authors, etc. - 1715-1799 - Fiction - Ducray-Dumenil

40516.4 Ducray-Duminil, F.G. Victor, ou L'enfant de la forêt. Paris, 1814. 4v.
Htn 40516.4.5* Ducray-Duminil, F.G. Alexis: or The cottage in the woods. Boston, 1796.
40516.4.10 Ducray-Duminil, F.G. Carlos y Fanny, o aventuras de dos niños abandonados em una isla desierta. México, 1844. 2v.
40516.4.15 Ducray-Duminil, F.G. Las tardes de la Granja. Madrid, 1935.

40516.5 - .6 Individual authors, etc. - 1715-1799 - Fiction - Cazotte

40516.5 Cazotte, Jacques. Oeuvres badines et morales, historiques et philosophiques. 1e éd. Paris, 1817. 4v.
40516.6 Cazotte, Jacques. Contes de J. Cazotte. Paris, 1880.
40516.6.1 Cazotte, Jacques. Plates. Paris, 1882.
40516.6.1.2 Cazotte, Jacques. Contes de J. Cazotte. Paris, 1880.
Htn 40516.6.2* Cazotte, Jacques. The devil in love. Boston, 1830.
40516.6.5 Cazotte, Jacques. Le diable amoureux. Paris, 1871.
40516.6.6 Cazotte, Jacques. Le diable amoureux. Paris, 1880.
40516.6.7 Cazotte, Jacques. Amores do diabo; romance. 2. ed. Porto, 19- .
40516.6.8 Cazotte, Jacques. Le diable amoureux. Paris, 1921.
40516.6.10 Bourgeois, Armand. Pages inédites ou ignorées sur Cazotte. Paris, 1911.
40516.6.80A Shaw, E.P. Jacques Cazotte, 1719-1792. Cambridge, 1942.
40516.6.80B Shaw, E.P. Jacques Cazotte, 1719-1792. Cambridge, 1942.
40516.6.82 Trintzius, R. Jacques Cazotte. 2. éd. Paris, 1944.
40516.6.85 Rieger, Dietmar. Jacques Cazotte. Heidelberg, 1969.

40516.7 - .11 Individual authors, etc. - 1715-1799 - Fiction - Miscellany

40516.7 Le soupe des petits-maitres ouvrage moral. Bruxelles, n.d.
40516.8 Menin, Nicolas. Cleodamis et Lelex. La Haye, 1746.
40516.9 Saint-Clair. Les égaremens d'un philosophe. Genève, 1787. 2v.
40516.11.35 Galli de Bibiena, J. The fairy doll. London, 1925.

40516.12 Individual authors, etc. - 1715-1799 - Fiction - Gudin

40516.12 Gudin, Paul-Phillippe. Contes. Paris, 1806. 2v.
40516.12.5 Gudin, Paul-Phillippe. Le royaume mis en interdit. n.p., n.d.

40516.13 Individual authors, etc. - 1715-1799 - Fiction - Cointreau

40516.13 Cointreau. L'amant Salamendre. London, 1756.

40516.15 Individual authors, etc. - 1715-1799 - Fiction - Coquelet

40516.15 Coquelet, L. Le triomphe de la charlatanerie dédié au Grand T***.Paris, 1730.
40516.15.5 Coquelet, L. L'eloge de quelque chose dédié à quelqu'un. Paris, 1730. 2 pam.
40516.15.7 Coquelet, L. Eloge de la goute. Paris, 1727.
40516.15.15 Cobb, Lillian. Pierre-Antoine de La Place, sa vie et son oeuvre (1707-1793). Thèse. Paris, 1928.

40516.16 - .17 Individual authors, etc. - 1715-1799 - Fiction - Miscellany

Htn 40516.16* Masson, Alexandre F.J. de. Les tableaux. Amsterdam, 1771.
NEDL 40516.17 Mayer, Charles Joseph de. Geneviève de Cournouailles et le damoisel sans nom. London, 1786.

40516.18 - .19 Individual authors, etc. - 1715-1799 - Fiction - Fromaget

40516.18 Fromaget, N. Le cousin de Mahomet. Constantin, 1781. 2v.
40516.19 Fromaget, N. Kara Mustapha et Basch-Savi. Amsterdam, 1750.
Htn 40516.19.10* Fromaget, N. Mirima, Impératrice du Japon. La Haye, 1745.

40516.20 - .21 Individual authors, etc. - 1715-1799 - Fiction - Godard d'Aucour

40516.20 Godard d'Aucour, Claude. Contes de Godard d'Aucour. Paris, 1883.
40516.20.2 Eaux fortes pour illustrer les contes. Paris, 1883.
40516.20.10 Godard d'Aucour, Claude. Themidor. Heidenheim, 1951.

40516.22 Individual authors, etc. - 1715-1799 - Fiction - Jouin

40516.22 Jouin, Nicolas. Remonstrances. n.p., n.d.
40516.22.5 Jouin, Nicolas. Le vrai recueil de Sarcelles. Amsterdam, 1764. 2v.
40516.22.10 Annecdotes jesuitiques. La Haye, 1740. 3v.

40516.23 - .25.8 Individual authors, etc. - 1715-1799 - Fiction - Deslandes

Htn 40516.23* Deslandes, A.F.B. Réflexions sur les grands hommes. Rochefort, 1714.
40516.24 Deslandes, A.F.B. Réflexions sur les grands hommes. Amsterdam, 1732.
40516.25 Deslandes, A.F.B. Réflexions sur les grands hommes. Amsterdam, 1776.

40516.25.9 - .27 Individual authors, etc. - 1715-1799 - Fiction - Miscellany

40516.25.9 Guiard de Servigné, J. Les sonnettes, ou Mémoires de M. le Marquis. Bruxelles, 1882.
Htn 40516.25.20* Gourdan, Alexandrine E. Correspondance de Madame Gourdan. Bruxelles, 1883.
40516.25.30 Defrance, Eugène. La maison de Madame Gourdan. Paris, 1908.
40516.26 Jonval, de. Les erreurs instructives. pt.1-3. London, 1765.
Htn 40516.27* Lavallée, Joseph. The negro equalled by few Europeans. Philadelphia, 1801. 2v.

40516.28 Individual authors, etc. - 1715-1799 - Fiction - Louvet de Couvrai

40516.28 Louvet de Couvral, J.B. Vie du chevalier de Faublas. Londres, 1791. 7v.
40516.28.2 Louvet de Couvral, J.B. Vie du chevalier de Faublas. pt.1-13. Paris, 1793. 6v.
40516.28.4 Louvet de Couvral, J.B. Vie du chevalier de Faublas. v.1-8. Paris, 1821-22. 4v.

40516.28 Individual authors, etc. - 1715-1799 - Fiction - Louvet de Couvrai - cont.

40516.28.6 Louvet de Couvral, J.B. Les aventures du chevalier de Faublas. Paris, 1842. 2v.
40516.28.6.2 Louvet de Couvral, J.B. Les aventures du chevalier de Faublas. v.1-4. Bruxelles, 1883. 2v.
40516.28.10 Louvet de Couvral, J.B. Émilie de Varmont ou le divorce nécessaire. Paris, 1791. 3v.

40516.29 - .35 Individual authors, etc. - 1715-1799 - Fiction - Miscellany

40516.29 Vasse, C.P.B.W. de. L'art de corriger...les hommes. London, 1783.
40516.31 Vernes, Jacob. Confidence philosophique. Genève, 1776.
40516.33 Confessions d'un courtisane. London, 1784.
40516.35 Pechméja, Jean de. Télèphe. Paris, 1795. 2v.

40516.36 - .39 Individual authors, etc. - 1715-1799 - Fiction - Ramsay

40516.36 Ramsay, A.M. de. Voyages de Cyrus. Amsterdam, 1728.
40516.37 Ramsay, A.M. de. A new cyropaedia. Edinburgh, n.d.
40516.38 Ramsay, A.M. de. Travels of Cyrus. London, 1763.
40516.38.1 Ramsay, A.M. de. Travels of Cyrus. 4th ed. London, 1730.
40516.39 Ramsay, A.M. de. Travels of Cyrus. London, 1795.

40516.40 - .46 Individual authors, etc. - 1715-1799 - Fiction - Miscellany

40516.40 Charrière, P.A.C. de. Caliste. Paris, 1845.
40516.41 Reinhäckel, R.P. Madame de Charriere. Weida, 1906.
40516.44 Doray de Longrais, Jean Paul. Faustin. Amsterdam, 1784.
40516.45 Guerle, J.N.M. Eloge des Perrugues. Paris, 1798.
40516.46 Lassay, A.L. de. Recueil de différentes chose. Lausanne, 1756. 4v.

40516.47 - .59 Individual authors, etc. - 1715-1799 - Fiction - Mercier

40516.47 Mercier, Louis S. Mon bonnet de nuit. Amsterdam, 1784. 2v.
40516.48 Mercier, Louis S. Théâtre complet. Amsterdam, 1778-1784. 4v.
40516.49.50 Mercier, Louis S. L'an deux mille quatre cent quarante. Amsterdam, 1771.
40516.50 Mercier, Louis S. L'an deux mille quatre cent quarante. London, 1772.
40516.50.2 Mercier, Louis S. L'an deux mille quatre cent quarante. London, 1773.
40516.50.4 Mercier, Louis S. L'an deux mille quatre cent quarante. Londres, 1775.
40516.50.10 Mercier, Louis S. L'an deux mille quatre cent quarante. n.p., 1786. 3v.
40516.50.21 Mercier, Louis S. Du théâtre; ou Nouvel essai sur l'art dramatique. Genève, 1970.
40516.51 Mercier, Louis S. La brouette vinaigrier. Avignon, 1792.
Htn 40516.52* Mercier, Louis S. Memoirs of the year 2500. Philadelphia, 1795.
40516.52.5 Mercier, Louis S. Memoirs of the year 2500. Liverpool, 1802.
Htn 40516.53* Mercier, Louis S. L'indigent; drame en quatre actes en prose. La Haye, 1772.
40516.53.5 Mercier, Louis S. Jean Hennuyer, bishop of Lizieux. London, 1773.
40516.53.15 Mercier, Louis S. Charles II, roi d'Angleterre en certain lieu. Venise, 1789.
40516.53.30 Mercier, Louis S. Le ci-devant noble. Paris, 1792.
40516.54 Mercier, Louis S. Eloges et discours philosophiques. Amsterdam, 1776.
40516.55 Mercier, Louis S. Fictions; morales. Paris, 1792. 3v.
40516.56 Mercier, Louis S. Voyage philosophique dans l'Amérique. Paris, 1829.
40516.57 Pamphlet box. Louis Sébastien Mercier.
40516.58 Béclard, S. Sébastien Mercier, sa vie, son oeuvre, son temps. Paris, 1903.
40516.59 San-Giorgiu, J. Sébastien Merciers dramaturgische Ideen im "Sturm und Drang." Inaug. Diss. Basel, 1921.
40516.59.10 Zollinger, Oskar. Louis Sébastien Mercier als Dramatiker und Dramaturg. Strassburg, 1899.
40516.59.25 Pusey, W.W. Louis-Sébastien Mercier in Germany. N.Y., 1939.

40516.60 Individual authors, etc. - 1715-1799 - Fiction - Sade

40516.60 Sade, D.A.F. de. Idée sur les romans. Paris, 1878.
40516.60.5 Sade, D.A.F. de. Idée sur les romans. 4. ed. Paris, 1947.
40516.60.5.5 Sade, D.A.F. de. Idée sur les romans. Paris, 1970.
X Cg 40516.60.20 Sade, D.A.F. de. La nouvelle justine. Hollande, 1797. 4v.
40516.60.22 Sade, D.A.F. de. De Sade quartet. London, 1963.
40516.60.24 Sade, D.A.F. de. Selected letters. N.Y., 1966.
40516.60.25 Sade, D.A.F. de. Schriften aus der Revolutionszeit (1788-1795). Frankfurt, 1969.
40516.60.30 Sade, D.A.F. de. Morceaux choisis. Paris, 1948.
40516.60.38 Sade, D.A.F. de. Français. Paris, 1965.
40516.60.41 Sade, D.A.F. de. Les infortunes de la vertu. Paris, 1969.
40516.60.42 Sade, D.A.F. de. Voyage d'Italie, précédé des premières oeuvres, suivi de opuscules sur le théâtre. Paris, 1967.
40516.60.45 Sade, D.A.F. de. Adelaide of Brunswick. Washington, 1954.
40516.60.48 Sade, D.A.F. de. Justine. N.Y., 1966.
40516.60.50 Sade, D.A.F. de. Cahiers personnels, 1803-1804. Paris, 1953.
40516.60.52 Sade, D.A.F. de. Gesprek tussen een priester en een stervende, en andere teksten. Brugge, 1965.
40516.60.55 Sade, D.A.F. de. Histoire secrète d'Isabelle de Bavière. Paris, 1953.
40516.60.57 Sade, D.A.F. de. Journal inédit. Paris, 1970.
40516.60.60 Sade, D.A.F. de. Monsieur le 6. Paris, 1954.
40516.60.65 Sade, D.A.F. de. Le carillon de Vincennes. Paris, 1953.
40516.60.70 Sade, D.A.F. de. La Marquise de Gange. Paris, 1957.
40516.60.75 Sade, D.A.F. de. Nouvelles exemplaires. Paris, 1958.
40516.60.76 Sade, D.A.F. de. Lettres choisies. Paris, 1963.
40516.60.78 Sade, D.A.F. de. Corespondance inédite du Marquis de Sade. Paris, 1929.
40516.60.79 Sade, D.A.F. de. Juliette. 1st American ed. N.Y., 1968.
40516.60.80 Heine, Maurice. Le Marquis de Sade. Paris, 1950.
40516.60.82 Beauvoir, S. de. Must we burn De Sade? London, 1953.
40516.60.84 Gorer, G. The life and ideas of the Marquis de Sade. London, 1953.
40516.60.84.5 Gorer, G. The devil's disciple. Paris, 193-?

40516.60 Individual authors, etc. - 1715-1799 - Fiction - Sade - cont.

40516.60.86 Lély, Gilbert. Vie du Marquis de Sade. 2. éd. Paris, 1952.
40516.60.87 Lély, Gilbert. The Marquis de Sade. London, 1961.
40516.60.90 Jacobus X (pseud.). Le Marquis de Sade et son oeuvre devant la science. Paris, 1901.
40516.60.95 Klossowski, P. Sade mon prochain. Paris, 1947.
40516.60.100 Gyser, René. De slecht befaande markies de Sade. Amsterdam, 1961.
40516.60.105 Pauvert, J.J. L'affaire Sade. Paris, 1963.
40516.60.110 Pauvert, J.J. L'affaire Sade. Paris, 1957.
40516.60.115 Lély, Gilbert. Vie du Marquis de Sade. Paris, 1965.
40516.60.117 Lély, Gilbert. Sade. Études sur sa vie. Paris, 1967.
40516.60.120 Brochier, Jean Jacques. Sade. Paris, 1966.
40516.60.125 Brochier, Jean Jacques. Le Marquis de Sade et la conquête de l'unique. Paris, 1966.
40516.60.130 Favre, Pierre. Sade, utopiste. 1. éd. Paris, 1967.
40516.60.135 Pappot, G. De Markies de Sade. Amsterdam, 1967.
40516.60.140 Le Marquis de Sade. Paris, 1968.
40516.60.145 Delpech, Jeanine. La passion de la Marquise de Sade. Paris, 1970.

40516.61 - .63 Individual authors, etc. - 1715-1799 - Fiction - Kruedener

40516.61 Kruedener, B.J. Valérie. Paris, 1840.
40516.61.5 Kruedener, B.J. Valérie. Paris, 1878.
40516.62 Jacob, P.L. Madame de Kruedener. Paris, 1881.
40516.63A Ford, Clarence. The life and letters of Madame de Kruedener. London, 1893.
40516.63B Ford, Clarence. The life and letters of Madame de Kruedener. London, 1893.
40516.63.10 Turquan, Joseph. La baronne de Kruedener (1766-1824) d'après des documents inédits. Paris, 19- .
40516.63.15 Drygalski, Irma von. Juliane von Krüdener; der Roman eines Lebens. Jena, 1928.
40516.63.20 Hermant, A. Madame de Kruedener. Paris, 1934.
40516.63.25 Ley, Francis. Madame de Kruedener et son temps. Paris, 1961.

40516.64 - .69 Individual authors, etc. - 1715-1799 - Fiction - Miscellany

40516.64 Voyage merveilleux du prince Fan Feredin dans la romancie. Paris, 1735.
Htn 40516.65* Bougeant, G.H. Wonderful travels of Prince Fan Feredin. Northhampton, n.d.
40516.66 Le Givre de Richebourg, Mme. Avantures de Don Ramire de Roxas et de Dona Leonor de Mendoce. pt.1-2. Paris, 1737.
40516.67 St. Quenain, de. Le Hollandois raisonnable; ou Sort digne d'envie. Amsterdam, 1741. 3v.
40516.68 Maquin. Je ne sçais quoi. n.p., 1780.

40516.70 - .74 Individual authors, etc. - 1715-1799 - Fiction - Marin

40516.70 Marin, R.P.M.A. La marquise de los Valientes. Avignon, 1767. 2v.

40516.75 - Individual authors, etc. - 1715-1799 - Fiction - Miscellany

40516.75 Bastide, J.F. La trentaine de Cithere. London, 1753.
40516.75.10 Bastide, J.F. L'etre pensant. pt. 1-2. Amsterdam, 1755.
40516.76 La Vieuville d'Orville, A. Les avantures du Prince Jakaya. Paris, 1732. 2v.
40516.77 Laveaux, J.C.T. de. Euseb. Wien, 1790.
40516.80 Frenais, Joseph Pierre. Histoire d'Agathe de St. Bohaire. v.1-2. Amsterdam, 1769.
40516.85 La Barre de Beaumarchais, A. de. La retraite de la marquise de Gozanne. Amsterdam, 1735.
40516.90 Ducas de Bois St. Just, J.L.M. Les sires de Beaujeu. Lyon, 1810. 2v.
40516.95 Desboulmiers, J.A.J. Kerwald Castle, or Memoirs of the Marquis de Solanges. Maidstone, 1803.

40517.1 Individual authors, etc. - 1715-1799 - Fiction - Caylus

40517.1 Caylus, Anne C.P. Oeuvres badines complettes. Amsterdam, 1787.
40517.1.7 Nisard, C. Le comte de Caylus. Paris, 1877.
40517.1.9 Caylus, Anne C.P. Correspondance inédite. Paris, 1887. 2v.
40517.1.15 Caylus, Anne C.P. Mémoires et réflexions. Paris, 1874.
40517.1.17 Caylus, Anne C.P. Oeuvres badines et galantes du Conte de Caylus. Paris, 1920.
40517.1.20 Cochin, C.N. Mémoires inédits de Charles Nicolas Cochin sur le comte de Caylus. Paris, 1880.

40517.2 - .3 Individual authors, etc. - 1715-1799 - Fiction - Miscellany

40517.2 Martorell, Joannot. Histoire du vaillant chevalier Tiran le Blanc. London, 1737. 2v.
40517.2.5 Godard d'Aucour, C. Lettres du Chevalier Danteuil et de mademoiselle de Thelis. n.p., 1742.

40517.4 Individual authors, etc. - 1715-1799 - Fiction - Challes

40517.4 Challes, Robert. Les illustres françoises. Paris, 1725. 4v.
40517.4.5A Challes, Robert. Les illustres françaises. Paris, 1959. 2v.
40517.4.5B Challes, Robert. Les illustres françaises. Paris, 1959. 2v.
40517.4.80 Knapp-Tepperberg, Eva Maria. Robert Challes Illustres françaises. Heidelberg, 1970.
40517.4.85 Forno, Lawrence J. Robert Challe: intimations of the Enlightenment. Rutherford, N.J., 1972.

40517.5 Individual authors, etc. - 1715-1799 - Fiction - Beauharnais

40517.5 Beauharnais, F.M. de C. Le somnambule. Paris, 1786.
40517.5.5A Beauharnais, F.M. de C. L'ile de la félicité ou Anaxis et Théoni. Paris, 1801.
40517.5.5B Beauharnais, F.M. de C. L'ile de la félicité ou Anaxis et Théoni. Paris, 1801.
40517.5.7 Beauharnais, F.M. de C. L'Abailard supposé, ou sentiment à l'épreuve. Amsterdam, 1780.
40517.5.9 Beauharnais, F.M. de C. L'Abailard supposé. Lyon, 1791.
40517.5.15 Beauharnais, F.M. de C. Lettres de Stéphanie. Paris, 1778. 3v.
40517.5.20 Beauharnais, F.M. de C. Mélange de poésies fugitives et de prose sans conséquence. Amsterdam, 1776.
40517.5.25 Beauharnais, F.M. de C. La marmote philosophie, ou La philosophie en domino. Paris, 1811. 3v.
40517.5.35 Beauharnais, F.M. de C. L'aveugle par amour. Paris, 1781.

Classified Listing

40517.5 Individual authors, etc. - 1715-1799 - Fiction - Beauharnais - cont.

40517.5.45 Beauharnais, F.M. de C. Les amans l'autrefois. Paris, 1787. 3v.
40517.5.55 Beauharnais, F.M. de C. La fausse inconstance, ou Le triomphe de l'honnêteté. Paris, 1787.

40517.6 Individual authors, etc. - 1715-1799 - Fiction - Baret

40517.6 Baret, Paul. Le grelot. Paris, 1754.

40517.7 - .7.49 Individual authors, etc. - 1715-1799 - Fiction - Aulnoy

40517.7 Aulnoy, Marie C.J. de B. Histoire d'Hypolite comte de Duglas. v.1-2. Paris, 1733.
40517.7.1 Aulnoy, Marie C.J. de B. Histoire de Jean de Bourbon, prince de Carency. La Haye, 1704.
NEDL 40517.7.2 Aulnoy, Marie C.J. de B. The history of Hypolitus, earl of Douglas. London, 1741.
40517.7.3 Aulnoy, Marie C.J. de B. The earl of Douglas. 2. ed. v.1-3. Lyon, 1778.
40517.7.3.10 Aulnoy, Marie C.J. de B. Contes de Saphir. Paris, 1957.
Htn 40517.7.4* Aulnoy, Marie C.J. de B. The prince of Carency, a novel. London, 1719.
40517.7.5 Aulnoy, Marie C.J. de B. The history of John of Bourbon, Prince of Carency. 2. ed. London, 1724.
40517.7.35 Bergmann, H. Madame d'Aulnoy und Spanien. Inaug. Diss. Würzburg, 1934.

40517.7.50 - .7.99 Individual authors, etc. - 1715-1799 - Fiction - Beaurieu

40517.7.50 Pamphlet box. Beaurieu, G.G. de.
40517.7.55 Beaurieu, G.G. de. Eleve de la nature. Amsterdam, 1771. 3v.

40517.8 - .17 Individual authors, etc. - 1715-1799 - Fiction - Berquin

Htn 40517.8* Berquin, Arnaud. Oeuvres complètes. Paris, 1802. 10v.
40517.9 Pamphlet vol. Berquin, Arnaud. Recueil complet des idylles. 2 pam.
Htn 40517.10* Berquin, Arnaud. L'ami des enfans. London, 1782-83. 12v.
40517.11 Berquin, Arnaud. L'ami des enfans. Paris, 1808. 12v.
40517.12 Berquin, Arnaud. Abregé de l'ami des enfans. v.1-4. Paris, 1834. 2v.
40517.13 Berquin, Arnaud. L'ami des enfans. v.4. Lausanne, 1794.
40517.14 Berquin, Arnaud. L'ami de l'adolescence. Paris, 1789.
40517.15 Berquin, Arnaud. L'amico de fanciulli. London, 1788-89. 4v.
40517.16 Berquin, Arnaud. Childrens' fireside book. Philadelphia, 1840.
40517.17 Berquin, Arnaud. The childrens' friend. Newburyport, n.d. 2v.

40517.18 Individual authors, etc. - 1715-1799 - Fiction - Benseval

40517.18.9 Besenval, Pierre V. de. Erzählungen. Leipzig, 1906.
40517.18.9.5 Besenval, Pierre V. de. Spleen. London, 1928.

40517.19 - .21 Individual authors, etc. - 1715-1799 - Fiction - Miscellany

40517.19 Bossigny, Louise de. Les chevaliers errans et le genie familier. Amsterdam, 1710.
40517.19.110 Daubenton, M. Zelia in the desert. New Haven, 1812.
40517.20 Drouet de Maupertuis. Les aventures d'Euphormion. Anvers, 1711. 3v.
40517.21 G*** de la Bataille. Jeannette Seconde. Amsterdam, 1757.

40517.22 - .23.6 Individual authors, etc. - 1715-1799 - Fiction - Delaunay

Htn 40517.22* Delaunay. Histoire d'un pou françois. 4. ed. Paris, 1779.
Htn 40517.23* Delaunay. Histoire d'un pou françoise. Paris, 1781.
Htn 40517.23.5* Delaunay. History of a French louse. London, 1779.
Htn 40517.23.5.2* Delaunay. History of a French louse. 4. ed. London, 1779.

40517.23.7 - .23.199 Individual authors, etc. - 1715-1799 - Fiction - Duclos

40517.23.7 Duclos, C.P. Oeuvres complètes. Paris, 1820-21. 9v.
40517.23.9 Duclos, C.P. Acajou et Zirphile, conte. Paris, 1744.
Htn 40517.23.10* Duclos, C.P. Les confessions du Comte de ***. 4. ed. Amsterdam, 1742.
40517.23.12 Duclos, C.P. Les confessions du Comte de ***. Paris, 1969.
40517.23.15 Duclos, C.P. A course of gallantries. v.1-2. London, 1775.
40517.23.20 Duclos, C.P. Morceaux choisis ou Recueil de pensées, remarques. Paris, 1810. 2v.
40517.23.25 Duclos, C.P. The pleasures of retirement preferable to the joys of dissipation. London, 1774.
40517.23.26 Duclos, C.P. Correspondance de Charles Duclos, 1704-1722. Saint Brieuc, 1970.
40517.23.30 Duclos, C.P. Considerations sur les moeurs de ce siècle. Paris, 1751.
40517.23.50 Heilmann, E. Charles Pinot Duclos, ein Literat des 18. Jahrhunderts und seine Beziehungen zu Rousseau. Inaug. Diss. Würzburg, 1936.
40517.23.80 Meister, Paul. Charles Duclos. Genève, 1956.
40517.23.82 Meister, Paul. Charles Duclos. Genève, 1956.

40517.24 Individual authors, etc. - 1715-1799 - Fiction - Feutry

40517.24 Feutry, M. Choix d'histoires tirées. London, 1779. 2v.

40517.25 - .28 Individual authors, etc. - 1715-1799 - Fiction - Gomez

40517.25 Gomez, M.A.P. de. La belle assemblée. 6. ed. London, 1749. 4v.
40517.25.2 Gomez, M.A.P. de. La belle assemblée. 6. ed. et 7. ed. London, 1754- 4v.
40517.26 Gomez, M.A.P. de. Les cent nouvelles nouvelles. La Haye, 1733. 20v.
40517.27 Gomez, M.A.P. de. The memoires of Baron Du Tan. London, 1744.
40517.27.15 Gomez, M.A.P. de. Anecdotes, ou histoire secrette de la maison ottomane. Amsterdam, 1740.
40517.27.25 Gomez, M.A.P. de. Persian anecdotes. London, 1730.
40517.27.35 Gomez, M.A.P. de. Select novels. London, 1745.

40517.29 - .30 Individual authors, etc. - 1715-1799 - Fiction - La Roche

40517.29 La Roche du Maint, J.P.L. de. Olinde. n.p., 1784.
40517.30 La Roche du Maint, J.P.L. de. Mémoires de Madame de Baudéon. Strassbourg, 1786.
40517.30.5 La Roche du Maint, J.P.L. de. Analyse raisonnée de la sagesse de Charron. London, 1789. 2v.
NEDL 40517.30.10 La Roche du Maint, J.P.L. de. Le vicomte de Barjac. v.1-2. Paris, 1784.

40517.31 Individual authors, etc. - 1715-1799 - Fiction - Le Prince de Beaumont

40517.31 Le Prince de Beaumont, M. Le magasin de enfans. v.1-4. Paris, 1797. 2v.
40517.31.3 Le Prince de Beaumont, M. Magasin de enfans. v.1-4. Paris, 1809. 2v.
40517.31.5 Le Prince de Beaumont, M. The young misses' magazine. v.1-2. N.Y., 1819.
40517.31.7 Le Prince de Beaumont, M. Magasin des enfans. Paris, 1883. 2v.
40517.31.8 Le Prince de Beaumont, M. Magasin des adolescentes. v.1-4. Bruxelles, 1789. 2v.
40517.31.10 Le Prince de Beaumont, M. Le magasin des adolescentes. Paris, 1810.
Htn 40517.31.15* Le Prince de Beaumont, M. The farmers, mechanics, and servants' magazine. N.Y., 1812.
40517.31.30 Le Prince de Beaumont, M. The triumph of truth, or Memoirs of Mr. de la Villette. London, 1775. 2v.
40517.31.45 Ginguené, Pierre Louis. P.L. Ginguené journaliste et critique littéraire. Torino, 1968.
40517.31.50 Hazard, Paul. Journal de Ginguené, 1807-1808. Paris, 1910.

40517.32 - .39 Individual authors, etc. - 1715-1799 - Fiction - Gueullette

40517.32 Gueulette, T.S. Les milles et une heure; contes peruviens. v.1-2. Paris, 1734.
40517.32.9 Gueulette, T.S. Peruvian tales. Dublin, 1734. 2v.
40517.33 Gueulette, T.S. Peruvian tales. London, 1817.
40517.34 Gueulette, T.S. Tausend und eine Viertelstunde. Erlangen, 1844. 2v.
40517.35 Gueulette, T.S. Tartarian tales. London, 1759.
40517.35.50 Gueulette, T.S. Les Sultanes de Guzarate, ou Les songes des hommes eveillés. Paris, 1733. 3v.
40517.36 Gueulette, T.S. Mogul tales. London, 1736. 2v.
40517.37 Gueulette, T.S. Chinese tales. London, 1817.
40517.37.10 Gueulette, T.S. Parades inédites. Paris, 1885.
40517.38 Gueulette, T.S. Transmigrations of the Mandarin Fum-Hoam. London, 1894.
40517.38.2 Gueulette, T.S. Transmigrations of the Mandarin Fum-Hoam. London, 1894.
40517.38.5 Gueulette, T.S. Chinese tales. 3. ed. London, 1745.
40517.38.8 Gueulette, T.S. Thousand and one quarters of an hour. London, 1893.
40517.38.12 Gueulette, T.S. The thousand and one quarters of an hour. N.Y., 1897.
40517.39.5 Coderre, A.D. L'oeuvre romanesque de Thomas Simon Gueullette (1683-1766. Thèse. Montpellier, 1934.
40517.39.14 Gueulette, J.E. Un magistrat du XVIIIe siècle. Thèse. Paris, 1938.
40517.39.15 Gueulette, J.E. Un magistrat du XVIIIe siècle. Paris, 1938.

40517.40 - .42 Individual authors, etc. - 1715-1799 - Fiction - Miscellany

40517.40 Gueuderville, N. Histoire abregée. Amsterdam, 1744.
Htn 40517.42* Hecquet, Mme. The history of a slave girl. London, 176-?
40517.42.7 Hecquet, Mme. Histoire d'une jeune fille sauvage. Paris, 1755.
40517.42.50 Jussy, de. Lettres de Mademoiselle de Jussy. Amsterdam, 1765.

40517.43 Individual authors, etc. - 1715-1799 - Fiction - Lambert

40517.43 Lambert, C.F. Mémoires et avantures. Francfort, 1740. 3v.
40517.43.5 Lambert, C.F. Le nouveau Telemaque. La Haye, 1741. 3v.

40517.44 Individual authors, etc. - 1715-1799 - Fiction - Choderlos de Laclos

40517.44 Choderlos de Laclos, Pierre A.F. Poesies. Paris, 1908.
40517.44.2 Choderlos de Laclos, Pierre A.F. Oeuvres complètes. 2. éd. Paris, 1943.
Htn 40517.44.3* Choderlos de Laclos, Pierre A.F. Les liaisons dangereuses. pt.1-4. Amsterdam, 1782. 2v.
40517.44.5 Choderlos de Laclos, Pierre A.F. Les liaisons dangereuses. 17. éd. Paris, 1919.
40517.44.6 Choderlos de Laclos, Pierre A.F. Les liaisons dangereuses. Paris, 1958.
40517.44.7 Choderlos de Laclos, Pierre A.F. Les liaisons dangereuses. Paris, 1932.
40517.44.8 Choderlos de Laclos, Pierre A.F. Dangerous acquaintances. London, 1924.
40517.44.10A Choderlos de Laclos, Pierre A.F. Dangerous acquaintances. Norfolk, Conn., 1952.
40517.44.10B Choderlos de Laclos, Pierre A.F. Dangerous acquaintances. Norfolk, Conn., 1952.
40517.44.10C Choderlos de Laclos, Pierre A.F. Dangerous acquaintances. Norfolk, Conn., 1952.
40517.44.12 Choderlos de Laclos, Pierre A.F. Dangerous acquaintances. Norfolk, Conn., 1957.
40517.44.14 Choderlos de Laclos, Pierre A.F. Les liaisons dangereuses. London, 1962.
40517.44.15 Choderlos de Laclos, Pierre A.F. Les liaisons dangereuses. N.Y., 1960.
40517.44.20 Choderlos de Laclos, Pierre A.F. Las amistades peligrosas. Madrid, 1822. 3v.
40517.44.21 Choderlos de Laclos, Pierre A.F. Opasnye sviazi. Leningrad, 1965.
40517.44.25 Choderlos de Laclos, Pierre A.F. Laclos, par lui-même. Paris, 1953.
40517.44.80 Seylaz, Jean Luc. Les liaisons dangereuses et la creation romanesque chez Laclos. Genève, 1958.
40517.44.85 Koppen, Erwin. Laclos Liaisons dangereuses in der Kritik. Wiesbaden, 1961.
40517.44.90 Thelander, D.R. Laclos and the epistolary novel. Genève, 1963.

40517.44 Individual authors, etc. - 1715-1799 - Fiction - Choderlos de Laclos - cont.

40517.44.95 Delmas, André A. À la recherche des liaisons dangereuses. Paris, 1964.
40517.44.105 Ungarelli, Augusto. Un grande romanzo del settecento. Roma, 1965.
40517.44.110 Knufmann, Helmut. Das Böse in der Liaisons dangereuses des Choderlos de Laclos. München, 1965.
40517.44.115 Versini, Laurent. Laclos et la tradition. Paris, 1968.
40517.44.120 Daniel, Georges. Fatalité du secret et fatalité du bavardage au 18e siècle. Paris, 1966.
40517.44.125 Thody, Philip M.W. Laclos: Les liaisons dangereuses. London, 1970.
40517.44.130 Malraux, André. Le triangle noir. Paris, 1970.

40517.45 - .48 Individual authors, etc. - 1715-1799 - Fiction - Miscellany

40517.46 Le Gouz de Gerland, B. Histoire de Lates. Corinthe, 1774.
40517.48.5 Montjoie, C.F.L. D'Aveyro, or The head in the glass cage. v.1-4. London, 1813. 2v.

40517.49 - .51 Individual authors, etc. - 1715-1799 - Fiction - La Morlière

X Cg 40517.50 Lamorlière, J.R. de. Angola. Histoire indienne. London, 1786. 2v.
40517.50.10 Lamorlière, J.R. de. Angola: an Eastern tale. London, 1926.
40517.51 Lamorlière, J.R. de. Contes du chevalier de la Morlière. Paris, 1879.

40517.52 - .53 Individual authors, etc. - 1715-1799 - Fiction - Mouhy

Htn 40517.52* Mouhy, Charles de F. Les mille et une faveurs. London, 1783. 5v.
40517.53 Mouhy, Charles de F. Le masque de fer. v.1-5. La Haye, 1750.
40517.53.4 Mouhy, Charles de F. La paysame parvenue. Amsterdam, 1777. 4v.
40517.53.7 Mouhy, Charles de F. The fortunate country maid. London, 1782.

40517.54 Individual authors, etc. - 1715-1799 - Fiction - La Place

40517.54 La Place, P.A. de. L'orpheline angloise, ou Histoire de Charlotte Summers. London, 1752. 4v.
40517.54.10 La Place, P.A. de. Le supplice des cloches. n.p., 178-?
40517.54.25 Cobb, Lillian. Pierre-Antoine de la Place, sa vie, et son oeuvre, 1707-1793. Paris, 1928.

40517.55 Individual authors, etc. - 1715-1799 - Fiction - Pajon

40517.55 Pajon, H. Histoire des trois fils d'Hal i-Bassa. Constantinople, 1748.

40517.56 - .57 Individual authors, etc. - 1715-1799 - Fiction - Poujens

Htn 40517.56* Porée, C.G. Histoire de D. Ranucio d'Aletes. Venise, 1758. 2v.
40517.56.25 Pougens, Marie C. Abel, ou Les trois frères. Paris, 1826.
40517.56.35 Pougens, Marie C. Julie ou La religieuse de Nismes. Paris, 1796.
40517.57 Pougens, Marie C. Jocko; précédé d'une notice par Anatole France. Paris, 1881.

40517.58 - .60 Individual authors, etc. - 1715-1799 - Fiction - Miscellany

40517.58 Pernetti, J. Le repos de Cyrus. Paris, 1732.
40517.59 Pagès, François. La France républicaine. 2e éd. Paris, 1793.
40517.60 Panard, C.F. Alzirette; an unpublished parody of Voltaire's Alzire. N.Y., 1929.

40517.61 - .62 Individual authors, etc. - 1715-1799 - Fiction - Tiphaigne de la Roche

40517.61 Tiphaigne de la Roche, C.F. Amilec, ou La graine d'hommes qui sert a peuple les planetes. 3. ed. pt.1-2. Luneville, 1754?
Htn 40517.62* Tiphaigne de la Roche, C.F. Giphantie. Babylone, 1760. 2 pam.
Htn 40517.62.5* Tiphaigne de la Roche, C.F. Giphantie. London, 1761. 2 pam.

40517.63 - .75 Individual authors, etc. - 1715-1799 - Fiction - Miscellany

NEDL 40517.63 Voisenon, C.H.F. Contes de l'abbé de Voisenon. Paris, 1878.
Htn 40517.65* Les amours de Sainfroid Jesuite et d'Eulalie. La Haye, 1729.
40517.70 Soliman ou Les aventures de Macanet. Amsterdam, 1750.
40517.75 Hilliard d'Auberteud, M.R. Miss McCrea. 1784. Gainesville, Fla., 1958.

40517.80 Individual authors, etc. - 1715-1799 - Fiction - Caumont de la Force

Htn 40517.80* Caumont de la Force, Charlotte R. de. Anecdote galante. Nancy, 1703.
40517.80.10 Caumont de la Force, Charlotte R. de. Histoire secrete de Bourgogne. Paris, 1782. 3v.

40517.86 - .88 Individual authors, etc. - 1715-1799 - Fiction - Bedacier

40517.86 Bédacier, C.D. La comtesse de Mortane. La Haye, 1700.
40517.86.10 Bédacier, C.D. Les avantures galantes du Chevalier de Tre. Lion, 1706.
40517.88 Bédacier, C.D. Histoire des amours de Gregoire VII. Cologne, 1700.

40521 Individual authors, etc. - 1715-1799 - Fiction - Prévost - Folios [Discontinued]; Complete and Selected works

40521.2 Prévost, Antoine F. Oeuvres choisies. Paris, 1810-16. 39v.
Htn 40521.9F* Prévost, Antoine F. Histoire de Manon Lescaut et du chevalier des Grieux. Paris, 1885.

40522.1 - .9 Individual authors, etc. - 1715-1799 - Fiction - Prévost - Individual works

40522.4.5 Prévost, Antoine F. Geschichte einer Neugriechin. Leipzig, 1906.
Htn 40522.5.5* Prévost, Antoine F. The Dean of Coleraine. A moral history. London, 1742. 3v.

40522.1 - .9 Individual authors, etc. - 1715-1799 - Fiction - Prévost - Individual works - cont.

40522.5.10 Prévost, Antoine F. Le doyen de Killerine, histoire morale. La Haye, 1760. 2v.
40522.5.20 Prévost, Antoine F. Mémoires pour servir à l'histoire de Malte. pt.1-2. Amsterdam, 1741.
40522.5.22 Prévost, Antoine F. Memoirs of a man of honour. v.1-2. London, 1747.
40522.5.25 Prévost, Antoine F. Memoires of a man of quality. London, 1770. 2v.
40522.6 Prévost, Antoine F. Mémoires. La Haye, 1772. 2v.
40522.6.15 Prévost, Antoine F. L'abbé Prévost, mémoires et avantures d'un homme de qualité qui s'est retiré du monde. Paris, 1927.
40522.6.16 Prévost, Antoine F. Mémoires et avantures d'un homme de qualité qui s'est retiré de monde. Paris, 1927.
40522.7 Prévost, Antoine F. P. Angloise ou Histoire de M. Cleveland. London, 1777. 6v.
40522.7.9 Prévost, Antoine F. Histoire de Manon Lescaut et du chevalier des Grieux. Paris, 1781. 2v.
40522.8 Prévost, Antoine F. Histoire de Manon Lescaut et du chevalier des Grieux. Paris, 1832.
40522.9 Prévost, Antoine F. Histoire de Manon Lescaut. Paris, 1858.
40522.9.2 Prévost, Antoine F. Histoire de Manon Lescaut et du chevalier des Grieux. Paris, 1860.
40522.9.5 Prévost, Antoine F. Histoire de Manon Lescaut et du chevalier des Grieux. Paris, 1881.
40522.9.6 Prévost, Antoine F. The story of Manon Lescaut. N.Y., 1886.
40522.9.7 Prévost, Antoine F. Manon Lescaut. London, 1886.
40522.9.8 Prévost, Antoine F. Manon Lescaut. Paris, 1892.
40522.9.9 Prévost, Antoine F. Manon Lescaut. Boston, 1893. 2v.
40522.9.10 Prévost, Antoine F. Histoire du chevalier des Grieux et de Manon Lescaut. Paris, 1885.
Htn 40522.9.12* Prévost, Antoine F. Histoire de Manon Lescaut et de chevalier des Grieux. Paris, 1875.
40522.9.13 Prévost, Antoine F. Histoire de Manon Lescaut et du chevalier des Grieux. Paris, 1895.
40522.9.14 Prévost, Antoine F. Histoire de Manon Lescaut et du chevalier des Grieux. Vienne, 19- ?
40522.9.14.5 Prévost, Antoine F. Manon Lescaut. Strasbourg, 1907.
40522.9.15 Prévost, Antoine F. Manon Lescaut. Paris, 1912.
40522.9.17 Prévost, Antoine F. Manon Lescaut. Paris, 1912?
40522.9.19 Prévost, Antoine F. Histoire du chevalier des Grieux et de Manon Lescaut. Paris, 188-?
40522.9.20 Prévost, Antoine F. Histoire du chevalier des Grieux et de Manon Lescaut. N.Y., 1930.
40522.9.30 Prévost, Antoine F. Histoire du chevalier des Grieux et de Manon Lescaut. Paris, 1946.
40522.9.35 Prévost, Antoine F. Histoire du chevalier des Grieux et de Manon Lescaut. Paris, 1952.
40522.9.36 Prévost, Antoine F. Histoire du chevalier des Grieux et de Manon Lescaut. Genève, 1953.
40522.9.40 Prévost, Antoine F. Histoire du chevalier des Grieux et de Manon Lescaut. Bordeaux, 1954.
40522.9.41 Prévost, Antoine F. Histoire du chevalier des Grieux et de Manon Lescaut. Paris, 1957.
40522.9.42 Prévost, Antoine F. Histoire du chevalier des Grieux et de Manon Lescaut. London, 1963.
Htn 40522.9.50* Prévost, Antoine F. Manon Lescaut. London, 1841.
40522.9.52 Prévost, Antoine F. The history of Manon Lescaut. v.1-3. Edinburgh, 1886.
40522.9.53 Prévost, Antoine F. The history of Manon Lescaut. N.Y., 1931.
40522.9.55 Prévost, Antoine F. Manon Lescaut. N.Y., 1935.
40522.9.60 Prévost, Antoine F. Manon Lescaut. Oxford, 1943. 2v.
40522.9.65 Prévost, Antoine F. Manon Lescaut. Harmondsworth, 1951.
40522.9.70 Prévost, Antoine F. Manon Lescaut. Paris, 1958.
40522.9.74 Prévost, Antoine F. Istoriia kavalera de Grie i Manon Lesko. Moskva, 1964.
40522.9.75 Prévost, Antoine F. Histoire du chevalier des Grieux et de Manon Lescaut. Paris, 1965.
40522.9.77 Prévost, Antoine F. The history of the chevalier des Grieux and of Manon Lescaut. London, 1931.

40522.10 Individual authors, etc. - 1715-1799 - Fiction - Prévost - Bibliographies

40522.10 Harrisse, Henry. Bibliographie de Manon Lescaut. Paris, 1877.
40522.10.5 Bibliothèque nationale, Paris. Manon Lescaut à travers deux siècles. Paris, 1963.

40522.11 - Individual authors, etc. - 1715-1799 - Fiction - Prévost - Biography and criticism

40522.11.25 Pamphlet box. Abbé Prévost.
40522.12 Harrisse, Henry. L'Abbé Prévost. Histoire de sa vie et ses oeuvres. Paris, 1896.
40522.14 Schroeder, V. L'Abbé Prévost. Sa vie - ses romans. Paris, 1898.
40522.16 Heinrich, P. L'Abbé Prévost et la Louisiane. Paris, n.d.
40522.17A Hazard, Paul. Études critiques sur Manon Lescaut. Chicago, 1929.
40522.17B Hazard, Paul. Études critiques sur Manon Lescaut. Chicago, 1929.
40522.18 Pauli, F. Die philosophischen Grundanschauungen in den Romanen des Abbé Prévost. Marburg, 1912.
40522.19 Friedrich, Hugo. Abbé Prévost in Deutschland. Heidelburg, 1929.
40522.20 Havens, G.R. The Abbé Prévost and English literature. Baltimore, 1921.
40522.20.5 Havens, G.R. The Abbé Prévost and English literature. Princeton, 1921.
40522.20.12 Müller, W. Die Grundbegriffe der gesellschaftlichen Welt in den Werken des Abbé Prévost. Marburg, 1938.
40522.21 Engel, Claire E. Figures et aventures du XVIIIe siècle. Paris, 1939.
40522.22 Roddier, Henri. L'Abbé Prévost. Paris, 1955.
40522.24 Billy, André. L'Abbé Prévost, auteur de Manon Lescaut. Paris, 1969.
40522.26 Josephsohn, Mirjam. Die Romane des Abbé Prévost als Spiegel des 18. Jahrhunderts. Thesis. Winterthur, 1966.
40522.28 Sgard, Jean. Prévost romancier. Paris, 1968.
40522.30 Engel, Claire E. Le véritable Abbé Prévost. Monaco, 1958.

Classified Listing

40524.1 - .2 Individual authors, etc. - 1715-1799 - Fiction - Tencin

40524.1 Tencin, Claudine A.G de. Mémoires du Comte de Comminge. London, 1784.
40524.1.15 Tencin, Claudine A.G. de. Mémoires du Comte de Comminge. La Haye, 1735.
40524.1.17 Tencin, Claudine A.G. de. Mémoires du Comte de Comminge. Lille, 1969.
Htn 40524.2* Tencin, Claudine A.G. de. Mémoires du Comte de Comminges. Paris, 1885.
40524.2.5 Tencin, Claudine A.G. de. Les malheurs de l'amour. Amsterdam, 1766.
40524.2.6 Tencin, Claudine A.G. de. Louise de Valrose; ou Mémoires d'une autrichienne. v.1-2. Paris, 1789.
40524.2.8 Tencin, Claudine A.G de. The female adventurers. v.1-2. Dublin, 1766.
40524.2.10 Tencin, Claudine A.G. de. The siege of Calais. London, 1740.

40524.14 Individual authors, etc. - 1715-1799 - Fiction - La Fite

40524.14 La Fite, M. Entretiens et contes moraux. v.1-2,4. Paris, 1820. 2v.

40524.15 Individual authors, etc. - 1715-1799 - Fiction - Fontaines

40524.15 Fontaines, M.L.C. Oeuvres. Paris, n.d.
40524.15.5 Fontaines, M.L.C. Histoire d'Amenophis. Paris, 1728.

40524.16 - .16.19 Individual authors, etc. - 1715-1799 - Fiction - Elie de Beaumont

40524.16 Elie de Beaumont, A.L. Oeuvres. Paris, 1865.
40524.16.5 Elie de Beaumont, A.L. Lettres du Marquis de Roselle. London, 1764.
40524.16.6 Elie de Beaumont, A.L. Lettres de Sophie et du chevalier de **. Londres, 1765. 2v.
40524.16.7 Elie de Beaumont, A.L. History of the Marquis de Roselle. London, 1765. 2v.

40524.16.20 - .17.39 Individual authors, etc. - 1715-1799 - Fiction - Fiévée

40524.16.25 Fiévée, Joseph. Oeuvres. Paris, 1843.
40524.17 Fiévée, Joseph. La dot de Suzette...Histoire de Mme. de Senneterre. Paris, 1798.
40524.17.5 Fiévée, Joseph. Suzette's marriage portion; a novel. Dublin, 1802.
40524.17.20 Fiévée, Joseph. Le divorce, Le faux revolutionnaire, et L'héroïsme des femmes. London, 1802.

40524.17.40 - .20 Individual authors, etc. - 1715-1799 - Fiction - Miscellany

40524.17.50 Mainvilliers, G.S. The beau-philosopher. London, 1751.
40524.17.54 Maubert de Gouvest, J.H. Lettres iroquoises. Irocopolis, 1755.
40524.17.57 Maubert de Gouvest, J.H. Lettres cherakusiennes. Rome, 1769.
Htn 40524.17.65* Nogaret, François Félix. Le fond du sac. Paris, 1866.
40524.17.65.5 Nogaret, François Félix. Le fond du sac. Rouen, 1879. 2v.
40524.17.80 Nogaret, François Félix. Profession de foi. n.p., n.d. 2 pam.
40524.17.300 Nerciat, A.R. Oeuvre. Paris, 1927. 2v.
40524.18 Perreau, J.A. Le roi voyageur. London, 1784.
40524.19 Poinsinette de Sivry, Louis. Le phasma, ou L'apparition. Paris, 1772.
Htn 40524.19.50* Raby. Le viellard abyssin rencontré. Paris, 1779.
40524.20 Rustaing de Saint-Jory, Louis. Avantures secretes arrivées au siege de Constantinople. Paris, 1711.

40524.21 - .25 Individual authors, etc. - 1715-1799 - Fiction - Riccoboni

40524.21 Riccoboni, M.J.L. de (Mme.). Oeuvres complettes. v.1-2,4-8. Paris, 1786. 7v.
40524.22 Riccoboni, M.J.L. de (Mme.). Oeuvres. Paris, 1865.
40524.23 Riccoboni, M.J.L. de (Mme.). Histoire de Christine, reine de Suabe; et celle d'Aloise de Livarot. Histoire d'Enguerrand et celle des amours de Gertrude. Paris, 1783.
40524.23.15 Riccoboni, M.J.L. de (Mme.). The history of Christina, princess of Swabia. London, 1784. 2v.
40524.23.25 Crosby, Emily A. Une romancière oubliée, Mme. Riccoboni. Thèse. Paris, 1924.
40524.23.27 Crosby, Emily A. Une romancière oubliée, Mme. Riccoboni...ses oeuvres. Paris, 1924.
40524.24 Riccoboni, M.J.L. de (Mme.). Lettres de Milady G. Catesby à H. Campley. Amsterdam, 1759.
40524.24.5 Riccoboni, M.J.L. de (Mme.). Letters from Juliet Lady Catesby, to her friend, Lady Henrietta Campley. London, 1760.
40524.24.10 Riccoboni, M.J.L. de (Mme.). Letters from Elizabeth Sophia de Valiere to her friend Louisa Hortensia de Canteleu. London, 1772. 2v.
40524.24.15 Riccoboni, M.J.L. de (Mme.). Letters from Lord Rivers to Sir Charles Cardigan. London, 1778. 2v.

40524.27 - .27.49 Individual authors, etc. - 1715-1799 - Fiction - Restif de la Bretonne - Bibliographies

Htn 40524.27* Jacob, P.L. Bibliographie et iconographie...de Restif de la Bretonne. Paris, 1875.

40524.27.50 - .27.999 Individual authors, etc. - 1715-1799 - Fiction - Restif de la Bretonne - Complete and Selected works

Htn 40524.27.50* Restif de la Bretonne, Nicolas E. L'oeuvre. Paris, 1930-32. 9v.
40524.27.51 Restif de la Bretonne, Nicolas E. L'oeuvre de Restif de la Bretonne. Paris, 1930-32. 9v.
40524.27.55 Restif de la Bretonne, Nicolas E. Oeuvre. Paris, 1911-22. 2v.

40524.28 - .31 Individual authors, etc. - 1715-1799 - Fiction - Restif de la Bretonne - Individual works

Htn 40524.28.2* Restif de la Bretonne, Nicolas E. Les contemporaines. v.1-42. Leipzip, 1781-92. 21v.
40524.28.2.5 Restif de la Bretonne, Nicolas E. Les contemporaines du commun. Paris, 18- .
Htn 40524.28.3* Restif de la Bretonne, Nicolas E. Les contemporaines. Paris, 1875? 2v.
Htn 40524.28.5* Restif de la Bretonne, Nicolas E. Les contemporaines mêlées. Paris, n.d.
40524.28.6 Restif de la Bretonne, Nicolas E. Les contemporaines. Paris, 1875-76. 3v.

40524.28 - .31 Individual authors, etc. - 1715-1799 - Fiction - Restif de la Bretonne - Individual works - cont.

40524.28.7 Restif de la Bretonne, Nicolas E. El Descubrimiento Austral por un Hombre Volador o y Dedalo Francés. Santiago de Chile, 1962.
40524.28.8 Restif de la Bretonne, Nicolas E. Les nuits de Paris. Paris, 1960.
Htn 40524.28.10* Restif de la Bretonne, Nicolas E. Monsieur Nicolas. Paris, 1794-97. 7v.
40524.28.12 Restif de la Bretonne, Nicolas E. Le plus fort des pamphlets. Paris, 1967.
40524.28.15 Restif de la Bretonne, Nicolas E. Monsieur Nicolas. Paris, 1959. 6v.
Htn 40524.28.20* Restif de la Bretonne, Nicolas E. Monsieur Nicolas. Paris, 1883. 14v.
Htn 40524.28.30* Restif de la Bretonne, Nicolas E. Monsieur Nicolas. Paris, 1924-25. 4v.
40524.28.75 Restif de la Bretonne, Nicolas E. Monsieur Nicolas. London, 1930-31. 6v.
40524.28.80 Restif de la Bretonne, Nicolas E. L'Anti-Justine de Rétif de La Bretonne. Paris, 1969.
40524.28.100 Restif de la Bretonne, Nicolas E. Mes inscripions journal intime de Restif de la Bretonne, (1780-1787). Paris, 1889.
40524.29 Restif de la Bretonne, Nicolas E. L'an 2000. Strasbourg, n.d.
Htn 40524.29.5* Restif de la Bretonne, Nicolas E. La decouverte australe par un homme volant. Leipzig, 1781. 4v.
Htn 40524.30* Restif de la Bretonne, Nicolas E. La paysan perverti. v.1-4. Amsterdam, 1776. 2v.
40524.31 Restif de la Bretonne, Nicolas E. La vie de mon père. Paris, 1884.
40524.31.25 Restif de la Bretonne, Nicolas E. La vie de mon père. Paris, 1924.
40524.31.30 Restif de la Bretonne, Nicolas E. La vie de mon père. Paris, 1962.
40524.31.35 Restif de la Bretonne, Nicolas E. Les contemporaines. Paris, 1962. 3v.

40524.32 Individual authors, etc. - 1715-1799 - Fiction - Restif de la Bretonne - Biography and criticism

40524.32 Dühren, E. Rétif de la Bretonne. Berlin, 1906.
40524.32.5A Funck-Bretano, F. Restif de la Bretonne. Paris, 1928.
40524.32.5B Funck-Bretano, F. Restif de la Bretonne. Paris, 1928.
40524.32.10 Naughton, A. Le tableau des moeurs dans les romans de Restif de la Bretonne. Thèse. Paris, 1929.
40524.32.15 Courbin, Jean Claude. Restif et son oeuvre. Paris, 1961.
40524.32.20 Tabarant, A. Le vrai visage de Restif de la Bretonne. Paris, 1936.
40524.32.25 Monselet, Charles. Restif de la Bretonne. Paris, 1858.
40524.32.30 Dawes, C.R. Restif de la Bretonne, 1734-1806. London, 1946.
40524.32.35 Childs, J. Restif de la Bretonne. Paris, 1949.
40524.32.40 Bégue, A. État présent des études sur Restif de la Bretonne. Paris, 1948.
40524.32.45 Grasilier, Leonce. Restif de la Bretonne. Paris, 1927.
40524.32.50 Chadourne, Marc. Restif de la Bretonne. Paris, 1958.
40524.32.55 Porter, Charles Allan. Restif's novels; or, An autobiography in search of an author. New Haven, 1967.
40524.32.60A Karmel, Alex. My revolution; promenades in Paris, 1789-1794, being the diary of Restif de la Bretonne. 1st ed. N.Y., 1970.
40524.32.60B Karmel, Alex. My revolution; promenades in Paris, 1789-1794, being the diary of Restif de la Bretonne. 1st ed. N.Y., 1970.

40524.33 - .99 Individual authors, etc. - 1715-1799 - Fiction - Miscellany

40524.35 Voisenon, Claude Henri. Contes légers. Paris, 1885.
40524.40 Lentier, E.F. de. Voyages d'Antenor en Grèce et en Asie. 5e éd. Paris, 1802. 3v.
40524.41 Garouville, de. L'amant oisif. v.1-3. Bruxelles, 1711.
40524.42 Lecoq-Madeleine. La fidelité couronnée. Bruxelles, 1717.
40524.44 Siret, Louis Pierre. L'homme au latin; ou, La destinée des savans. Genève, 1769.
40524.46 Sentilly, de. Le rideau levé. v.1-2. Cythère, 1964.
40524.48.5 Marat, Jean Paul. Przygody młodego hrabiego Potowskiego. wyd. 1. Warszawa, 1969.

40525.1 - .2 Individual authors, etc. - 1715-1799 - Fiction - Sénac de Meilham

40525.1 Sénac de Meilhan, G. L'émigré. Paris, 1904.
40525.2 Sénac de Meilhan, G. Portraits et caractères de personnages distingué de la fin du dix-huitième siècle. Paris, 1813.
40525.2.25 Sénac de Meilhan, G. Portraits et caractères. Paris, 1945.
40525.2.80 Stavan, Henry A. Gabriel Sénac de Meilhan. Paris, 1968.
40525.2.85 Monsembernard, Guy de. Sénac de Meilhan, 1736-1803. Auch, 1969.

40525.3 - .4 Individual authors, etc. - 1715-1799 - Fiction - Miscellany

Htn 40525.3* Terrasson, Jean. The life of Sathos. London, 1732. 2v.

40525.5 - .8 Individual authors, etc. - 1715-1799 - Fiction - Tressan - Writings

40525.5 Tressan, L.E. Oeuvres. Paris, 1822-23. 10v.
40525.5.2 Tressan, L.E. Oeuvres. Paris, 1822-23. 10v.
40525.5.7 Tressan, L.E. Oeuvres diverses. Amsterdam, 1776.
40525.6 Tressan, L.E. Souvenirs de comte de Tressan. Versailles, 1897.
40525.7 Tressan, L.E. Le chevalier Robert, surnommé le Brave. Paris, 1800.
NEDL 40525.8 Tressan, L.E. Histoire de Huon de Bordeaux. Paris, n.d.

40525.9 - .12 Individual authors, etc. - 1715-1799 - Fiction - Tressan - Works about

40525.9 Wespy, Paul. Der graf Tressan. Leipzig, 1888.
40525.11 Jacoubet, Henri. Le comte de Tressan et les origines du genre troubadour. Thèse. Paris, 1923.
40525.11.2 Jacoubet, Henri. Le comte de Tressan et les origines du genre troubadour. Thèse. Paris, 1923.

40525.15 - .17 Individual authors, etc. - 1715-1799 - Fiction - Moncrif - Writings

40525.15 Uzanne, Octave. Contes de A.P. de Moncrif. Paris, 1879.
40525.17 Moncrif, François A.P. de. Les ames rivales. Histoire fabulense. London, 1738.
40525.17.10 Moncrif, François A.P. de. Les aventures de Zeloïde et d'Amangarifdine. Paris, 1717.
40525.17.20 Moncrif, François A.P. de. Cats. London, 1961.

40525.18 Individual authors, etc. - 1715-1799 - Fiction - Moncrif - Works about

40525.18 Shaw, Edward Pease. François-Augustin Paradis de Moncrif, 1687-1770. N.Y., 1958.

40525.20 - Individual authors, etc. - 1715-1799 - Fiction - Anonymous novels

40525.22 Les faits et gestes du vicomte de Nantel: ma vie de garçon. Paris, 1910.
40525.24 Adolphus. Histoire des diables modernes. Cleves, 1771.
40525.26 Aventures singulieres d'un voyageur aérien mises au jour par M. J***. v.1-2. Londres, 1785.
40525.28 L'amour magot. Les tisons. London, 1738.
Htn 40525.30* Candide en Dannemarc. Genève, 1769.
40525.31 Cleandre et Caliste ou L'amour veritable. Amsterdam, 1722.
Htn 40525.32* L'art de Peter. Westphalie, 1751. 2 pam.
40525.34 Nouvelles folies sentimentales. Paris, 1786.
40525.35 Promenades de Mr. de Clairenville. Cologne, 1743.
Htn 40525.36* Oderahi, histoire américaine. Paris, 1801.
40525.36.5 Une soeur aînée d'Atala: Odérahi, histoire américaine. Paris, 1950.
X Cg 40525.37 Les partisans demasquez. Cologne, 1709.
40525.38 Les matinées du Palais royal. Paris, 1772.
40525.40 Les amours d'Eumène et de Flora. Cologne, 1707.
40525.42.1 Chevalier de la Marmotte. Les songes du Chevalier de la Marmotte. pt.1. Paris, 1970.
40525.45 Mackrodt, J. Die Romanze vom sire de Criqui. Halle, 1905.
40525.51 Gaudriole; conte. La Haye, 1746.

40526.1 - .3 Individual authors, etc. - 1715-1799 - Poetry - Blin de Sainmore, Berchoux, etc.

40526.1 Blin de Sainmore, A.M.H. Lettre de Biblis à Caunus son frère. 3e éd. Paris, 1767.
40526.1.5 Blin de Sainmore, A.M.H. Lettre de la duchesse de La Valliere à Louis XIV. London, 1773.
40526.1.25 Berchoux, J. de. La danse, ou Les dieux de l'opera, poëme. Paris, 1806.
40526.1.30 Berchoux, J. de. Voltaire ou Le triomphe de la philosophie moderne. Lyon, 1814.
40526.2 Boccage, Marie Anne F. du. Recueil des oeuvres. Lyon, 1762. 3v.
40526.3 Maillard, Porges. Oeuvres nouvelles. Nantes, 1882. 2v.

40526.4 - .7 Individual authors, etc. - 1715-1799 - Poetry - André Chénier - Writings

40526.4.5 Chénier, André. Oeuvres complètes. Paris, 1908-20. 3v.
40526.4.20 Chénier, André. Oeuvres complètes. Paris, 1940.
40526.4.23 Chénier, André. Oeuvres complètes. Paris, 1950.
40526.4.25 Chénier, André. Les chefs d'oeuvre lyriques. 2e éd. N.Y., 1908.
40526.5 Chénier, André. Oeuvres anciennes. Paris, 1826.
40526.6 Chénier, André. Oeuvres posthumes. Paris, 1826.
40526.7A Chénier, André. Oeuvres poétiques. Paris, 1899. 2v.
40526.7B Chénier, André. Oeuvres poétiques. Paris, 1899. 2v.
40526.7.2 Chénier, André. Oeuvres poétiques. Paris, 1924. 2v.
40526.7.6 Chenier, André. Poésies choisies. 2e éd. Paris, 1889.
40526.7.7 Chénier, André. Poésies choisies. Oxford, 1907.
40526.7.8 Chénier, André. Poésies. Paris, 1901.
40526.7.10 Chénier, André. Poésies. Lyon, 1919.
40526.7.95 Chénier, André. André Chénier. Paris, 1958.

40526.8 Individual authors, etc. - 1715-1799 - Poetry - André Chénier - Works about

40526.8 Morillot, Paul. André Chénier. Paris, 1894.
40526.8.5 Bertheroy, J. Eloge de André Chénier. Paris, 1901.
40526.8.9 Zyromski, E. De A. Chenerio poeta. Paris, 1897.
40526.8.10 Hildebrandt, P. Bemerkungen zu André Chénier. Berlin, 1897.
40526.8.12 Kramer, C. André Chénier et la poésie parnassiene - Leconte de Lisle. Paris, 1925.
Htn 40526.8.15* Collé, Charles. Chansons joyeuses, mises au jour. Paris, 1765.
40526.8.20 Hülsen, R. André Chénier. Berlin, 1885.
40526.8.25 Loggins, Vernon. André Chénier. Athens, 1965.
40526.8.30 Walter, Gérard. André Chénier. 10. éd. Paris, 1947.
40526.8.35 Galzy, Jeanne. Vie intime d'André Chénier. Paris, 1947.
40526.8.40 Gaiffe, Felix. Chénier: les bucoliques. Paris, 1961.
40526.8.45 Aubarède, Gabriel d'. André Chénier. Paris, 1970.
40526.8.50 Bibliothèque nationale, Paris. André Chénier, 1762-1794. Paris, 1962.
40526.8.55 Fabre, Jean. André Chénier, l'homme et l'oeuvre. Paris, 1955.
40526.8.60 Dimoff, Paul. La vie et l'oeuvre d'André Chénier jusqu'à la révolution française, 1762-1790. Thèse. Paris, 1936. 2v.
40526.8.61 Dimoff, Paul. La vie et l'oeuvre d'André Chénier jusqu'à la révolution française, 1762-1790. Paris, 1936. 2v.
40526.8.65 Gausseron, Jacques. André Chénier et le drame de la pensée moderne. Paris, 1963.
40526.8.70 Scarfe, Francis. André Chénier, his life and work. Oxford, 1965.

40526.9 - .17 Individual authors, etc. - 1715-1799 - Poetry - Gresset

40526.9 Gresset, Jean B. Oeuvres. London, 1758. 2v.
40526.9.2 Gresset, Jean B. Oeuvres. Londres, 1765. 2v.
40526.9.3 Gresset, Jean B. Oeuvres. London, 1785. 2v.
40526.9.5 Gresset, Jean B. Oeuvres. Rouen, 1788. 2v.
40526.10 Gresset, Jean B. Oeuvres. London, 1779.
40526.10.2 Gresset, Jean B. Oeuvres choisies. Paris, 1796.
40526.11 Gresset, Jean B. Oeuvres choisies. Paris, 1813.
40526.12 Gresset, Jean B. Oeuvres choisies. Paris, 1817. 2v.
40526.13 Gresset, Jean B. Oeuvres choisies. Paris, 1878.
40526.13.2 Gresset, Jean B. Oeuvres choisies. Paris, 1877.
40526.14 Gresset, Jean B. Oeuvres. Paris, n.d.

40526.9 - .17 Individual authors, etc. - 1715-1799 - Poetry - Gresset - cont.

40526.15 Gresset, Jean B. Oeuvres. Paris, 1811. 2v.
40526.15.5 Gresset, Jean B. Les poésies. n.p., n.d. 2v.
40526.16 Gresset, Jean B. Le Parrain Magnifique. Paris, 1810.
40526.17 Gresset, Jean B. Ver-Vert. W. Briné, 1817.
40526.17.3 Gresset, Jean B. Ver-Vert. London, 1759.
40526.17.5 Gresset, Jean B. Vert-vert. London, 1840.
40526.17.80 Cayrol, Louis Nicolas Jean Joachim de. Essai historique sur la vie et les ouvrages de Gresset. v.1-2. Amiens, 1844.

40526.18 - .21 Individual authors, etc. - 1715-1799 - Poetry - La Grange-Chancel

40526.18 La Grange-Chancel, Joseph de. Oeuvres. Paris, 1758. 5v.
40526.19 La Grange-Chancel, Joseph de. Les Philippiques Odes. Paris, 1875.
40526.20 La Grange-Chancel, Joseph de. Les Philippiques Odes. Paris, 1858.
Htn 40526.21* La Grange-Chancel, Joseph de. Recueil des tragédies. Paris, 1699-1700.
40526.21.5 La Grange-Chancel, Joseph de. Poésies inédites. Paris, 1878.
40526.21.80 Nietzelt, Otto. La Grange-Chancel als Tragiken. Inaug. Diss. Leipzig, 1908.

40526.22 Individual authors, etc. - 1715-1799 - Poetry - Malfilâtre

40526.22 Malfilâtre, J.C.L. de C. de. Poésies. Paris, 1884.
X Cg 40526.22.3 Malfilâtre, J.C.L. de C. de. Oeuvres. Paris, 1829.
40526.22.5 Malfilâtre, J.C.L. de C. de. Narcisse dans l'Isle de Vénus. Paris, 1795.
40526.22.12 Bandre, M. de. Discours sur la vie...de Malfilâtre. Caen, 1825.

40526.23 - .26 Individual authors, etc. - 1715-1799 - Poetry - Gilbert

40526.23 Gilbert, N.J.L. Oeuvres complètes. Paris, 1823.
40526.25 Gilbert, N.J.L. Oeuvres complètes. v.2. Paris, 1805.
40526.26 Gilbert, N.J.L. Oeuvres. Paris, n.d.

40526.27 - .28 Individual authors, etc. - 1715-1799 - Poetry - Miscellany

40526.27 Josz, V. Clavel d'Haurimonts. Paris, 1901.
40526.28 Guyétand, M. Poésies diverses. Paris, 1790.
40526.28.20 Grandval, Nicolas Racot de. Le vice puni, ou Cartouche. Paris, 1726.

40526.29 - .31 Individual authors, etc. - 1715-1799 - Poetry - Boufflers

40526.29 Boufflers, Stanislas de. Oeuvres. Paris, 1813. 2v.
40526.29.5 Boufflers, Stanislas de. Oeuvres. Londres, 1782.
40526.30 Boufflers, Stanislas de. Oeuvres choisies. Paris, 1892.
40526.30.35 Boufflers, Stanislas de. The queen of Golconda. London, 1926.
40526.31 Webster, Nestor H. (Mrs.). Chevalier de Boufflers. London, 1925.
40526.31.5A Webster, Nestor H. (Mrs.). The chevalier de Boufflers. N.Y., 1925.
40526.31.5B Webster, Nestor H. (Mrs.). The chevalier de Boufflers. N.Y., 1925.
40526.31.10 Webster, Nestor H. (Mrs.). The chevalier de Boufflers. N.Y., 1923.

40526.32 - .33 Individual authors, etc. - 1715-1799 - Poetry - Bernis, etc.

40526.32 Bernis, François Joachim de Pierre de. La religion vengée. Paris, 1805.
40526.32.5 Bernis, François Joachim de Pierre de. La religion vengée. n.p., 1796.
40526.32.6 Bernis, François Joachim de Pierre de. Oeuvres complettes. Londres, 1779. 2v.
40526.32.10 Schäfer, K. François Joachim de Pierre. Inaug. Diss. Dresden, 1939.
40526.32.11 Vailland, Roger. Eloge du cardinal de Bernis. Paris, 1956.
40526.32.12 Cheke, Marcus. The cardinal de Bernis. London, 1958.
40526.32.20 Blandurel, Antoine. La lyre chrétienne. Beauvais, 1804.
40526.32.40 Cubières, Michel de. Le calendrier républicain, poëme. Paris, 1799.
40526.32.45 Cubières, Michel de. La mort de Caton, tragédie. Paris, 1804.
40526.33 Tamisier, F. Étude biographique sur Pierre Dorange. Marseille, 1859.

40526.34 Individual authors, etc. - 1715-1799 - Poetry - Dorat

40526.34 Desnoiresterres, G. Le chevalier Dorat. Paris, 1887.
Htn 40526.34.5* Dorat, C.J. Lettres envers et oeuvres mêlées. Paris, 1767. 2v.
Htn 40526.34.9* Régulus, tragédie et la feinte par amour. Paris, 1773.
40526.34.10 Dorat, C.J. La feinte par amour. Troyes, 1799?
40526.34.11 Dorat, C.J. Les sacrifices de l'amour. Avignon, 1793. 3v.
40526.34.20 Dorat, C.J. Poésies. Genève, 1777. 4v.
40526.34.31 Dorat, C.J. The fatal effects of inconstancy. London, 1774. 2v.
40526.34.35 Dorat, C.J. Mélanges de poésies fugitives. Paris, 1780.
40526.34.50 Dorat, C.J. The kisses. London, 1888.
40526.34.60 Dorat, C.J. Amilka, ou Pierre-le-grand, tragédie. Paris, 1767.
40526.34.70 Dorat, C.J. Les malheurs de l'inconstance. Neuchâtel, 1776.
40526.34.80 Raitière, Anna. L'art de l'acteur selon Dorat et Samson, 1766-1863/65. 1. éd. Genève, 1969.

40526.35 - .38 Individual authors, etc. - 1715-1799 - Poetry - Miscellany

40526.35 Dougados, Jean. Oeuvres. Paris, 1810.

40526.39 - .40 Individual authors, etc. - 1715-1799 - Poetry - Monbron

40526.39 Fougeret de Monbron, Louis Charles. La Henriade travestie. Berlin, 1745.
40526.40 Fougeret de Monbron, Louis Charles. La Henriade travestie. Amsterdam, 1771.

Classified Listing

40526.41 Individual authors, etc. - 1715-1799 - Poetry - Miscellany
40526.41 Le pot-pourri. London, 1783.

40526.42 - .44 Individual authors, etc. - 1715-1799 - Poetry - Louis Racine
40526.42.4 Racine, Louis. Oeuvres. 6e éd. Amsterdam, 1750. 6v.
40526.42.5 Racine, Louis. Oeuvres. Paris, 1808. 6v.
40526.42.15 Racine, Louis. Die Religion entworfen von Herren Racine. Frankfurt, 1752.
40526.42.25 Racine, Louis. La religion, poëme. Paris, 1742.
40526.43 Racine, Louis. Le religion, poëme. Paris, 1821.
40526.44 Racine, Louis. Correspondance littéraire inédite de Louis Racine avec René Chevaye. Paris, 1858.

40526.47 Individual authors, etc. - 1715-1799 - Poetry - Bourgeois
40526.47.2 Bourgeois, N. Christophe Colombe. Paris, 1773. 2v.

40526.48 - .50 Individual authors, etc. - 1715-1799 - Poetry - Duboccage - Writings
40526.48 Boccage, Marie Anne F. du. La Colombiade. Paris, 1756.
Htn 40526.49* Boccage, Marie Anne F. du. La Colombiade. Paris, 1756.
40526.50 Boccage, Marie Anne F. du. La Colombiade. Paris, 1756.

40526.51 Individual authors, etc. - 1715-1799 - Poetry - Duboccage - Works about
40526.51 Boccage, Marie Anne F. du. La Colombiade. Milan, 1771.
40526.51.50 Boccage, Marie Anne F. du. La Colombiade. Lisboa, 1893.
40526.51.100 Gill-Mark, Grace. Une femme de lettres au XVIIIe siècle, Anne-Marie du Boccage. Thèse. Paris, 1927.
40526.51.105 Gill-Mark, Grace. Une femme de lettres au XVIIIe siècle, Anne Marie du Boccage. Paris, 1927.

40526.52 - .57 Individual authors, etc. - 1715-1799 - Poetry - Le Suire
40526.52 Le Suire, Robert M. Le philosophe parvenu. London, 1787.
40526.56 Le Suire, Robert M. Le nouveau monde. Paris, 1800.

40526.58 - .59 Individual authors, etc. - 1715-1799 - Poetry - Fontanes - Writings
40526.58 Oeuvres de M. de Fontanes. Paris, 1859. 2v.
40526.59 Fontanes, Louis. Collection complète des discours de M. de Fontanes. Paris, 1821.
40526.59.10 Fontanes, Louis. Correspondance de Louis de Fontanes et de Joseph Joubert. Paris, 1943.

40526.60 Individual authors, etc. - 1715-1799 - Poetry - Fontanes - Works about
40526.60 Wilson, Aileen. Fontanes, 1757-1821. Thèse. Paris, 1928.
40526.60.5 Wilson, Aileen. Fontanes, 1757-1821. Paris, 1928.

40526.61 - .66 Individual authors, etc. - 1715-1799 - Poetry - Miscellany
40526.61 Cerutti, G.A.G. L'aigle et le hibou. Glascow, 1783.
40526.61.100 Gallet, Pierre. Dieu; poëme épique en huit chants. Paris? 1799.
40526.61.150 Gence, J.B.M. Dieu, l'être infini. Paris, 1806.
40526.61.175 Vallier, Gustave. Notes sur l'Abbé Guilloud. Vienne, 1877.
40526.61.200 Henriquez, L.M. Les graces à confesse, poëme. Paris, 1804.
40526.61.300 Isnard, Maximin. Dithyrambe sur l'immortalité de l'âme. Paris, 1805.
40526.62 Laignel, Jean B.J. La fête de Louisee. Rouen, 1905.
40526.63 Kerby, W.M. The life, diplomatic career and literary activities of Nicolas Germain Léonard. Paris, 1925.
40526.64 Lalanne, Jean B. Le potager. Paris, 1800.
40526.65 Le Laé, Claude Marie. La vie les oeuvres comiques. Paris, 1921.
40526.66 Luchet, Mary de. Recueuil de poésies. London, 1777.
40526.66.100 Ramier, J.D. La lyre protestante consacrée aux partisans de la bonne cause. 2e éd. n.p., 1760?

40526.67 - .69 Individual authors, etc. - 1715-1799 - Poetry - Vadé - Writings
40526.67 Vadé, Jean Joseph. Oeuvres complettes. Troyes, 1798. 6v.
40526.67.5 Vadé, Jean Joseph. Oeuvres complettes. Genève, 1777. 4v.
40526.68 Vadé, Jean Joseph. Oeuvres choisies. Paris, 1834.
40526.69 Vadé, Jean Joseph. La pipe casée. Rouen, 1879.
40526.69.5 Vadé, Jean Joseph. La pipe casée. Paris, 1882.
40526.69.50 Vadé, Jean Joseph. Jerosme et Franchonnette. Paris, 1764.
40526.69.70 Vadé, Jean Joseph. Nicaise. Paris, 1756.
40526.69.90 Vadé, Jean Joseph. Le suffisant. Paris, 1761.
40526.69.110 Vadé, Jean Joseph. Les troqueurs. Paris, n.d. 3 pam.

40526.70 Individual authors, etc. - 1715-1799 - Poetry - Vadé - Works about
40526.70 Müller, Max. Jean Joseph Vadé (1719-1757) und das Vaudeville. Griefswald, 1911.

40526.72 - .99 Individual authors, etc. - 1715-1799 - Poetry - Miscellany
40526.74.2 Campion, Charles Michel. Oeuvres de Charles Michel Campion. Bloomington, 1945.
40526.76 Guérin, François Nicolas. La victoire de Fontenoy, poëme. Paris, 1746.
40526.78 Giraud, Claude Marie. Vision de Silvius Graphalètes. v.2. Londres, 1767.
40526.80 Affolter, Hans. Un jurisconsulte bernois, poète français, Sigismond Louis de Lerber. Bienne, 1947.
40526.82 Boisard, Jean Jacques François Marius. Fables. Paris, 1779.
40526.84 Cassier, François. Un poète nivernais de XVIII siècle: l'Abbé François Cassier, 1721-1772. Nevers, 1928.

40527.1 - .2 Individual authors, etc. - 1715-1799 - Poetry - L'Attaignant
40527.2 L'Attaignant, Gabriel Charles de. Cantiques spirituels. Paris, 1762.

40527.3 - .7 Individual authors, etc. - 1715-1799 - Poetry - Bernard
40527.3 Bernard, Pierre Joseph. Oeuvres complètes. n.p., 17- ?
40527.4.5 Bernard, Pierre Joseph. Oeuvres. Paris, 1803. 2v.
40527.5 Bernard, Pierre Joseph. Oeuvres choisies. Paris, 1811.
40527.6 Bernard, Pierre Joseph. Oeuvres. Paris, 1823.
40527.7 Bernard, Pierre Joseph. Oeuvres complètes. Paris, 180-?

40527.8 - .19 Individual authors, etc. - 1715-1799 - Poetry - Chénier [Discontinued]
40527.8 Becq de Fouquières, L. Documents nouveaux sur André Chenier. Paris, 1875.
40527.9 Becq de Fouquières, L. Lettres critiques sur la vie, d'André Chenier. Paris, 1881.
40527.14 Chenier, André. Oeuvres en prose. Paris, 1872.
40527.15 Chenier, André. Poésies. Paris, 1870.
40527.16A Chenier, André. Poésies. 2e éd. Paris, 1872.
40527.16B Chenier, André. Poésies. 2e éd. Paris, 1872.
40527.16.5 Chenier, André. Poésies. Paris, 1884.
40527.16.8 Chenier, André. Oeuvres poétiques. Paris, 1885.
40527.17 Chenier, André. Oeuvres inédites. Paris, 1914.
40527.18 Harassti, Jules. La poésie d'André Chenier. Paris, 1892.
40527.18.5 Lewy, Fritz. Zur Verbalmmetapher bie André Chenier. Inaug. Diss. Strassburg, 1913.
40527.19 Glachant, Paul. André Chenier Critique et critiqué. Paris, 1902.
40527.19.5 Faguet, E. André Chenier. Paris, 1902.
40527.19.6 Pamphlet box. André Chenier.
40527.19.10 Kramer, Cornelie. André Chenier et la poésie parnassienne. Reims, 1925.
40527.19.15 Venzac, Géraud. Jeux d'ombre et de lumière sur la jeunesse d'André Chenier. 6. éd. Paris, 1957.
40527.19.20 Toens, Ulrich. Studien zur Dichtung André Chéniers. Münster, 1970.
40527.19.100 Kerviler, R. Olivier Morvan, 1754-1794. St. Brieuc, 1888.

40527.20 Individual authors, etc. - 1715-1799 - Poetry - Robbé de Beauveset
Htn 40527.20* Robbé de Beauveset, P.H. Oeuvres badines. London, 1801. 2v.
40527.20.10 Robbé de Beauveset, P.H. Les victimes du despotisme episcopal. Paris, 1792.

40527.21 Individual authors, etc. - 1715-1799 - Poetry - Miscellany
40527.21 Roucher, M. Maximilien-Jules-Leopold Duc de Brunswick-Lunebourg. Paris, 1786.
40527.21.10 Roucher, Jean Antoine. Les mois; poëme en douze chants. Paris, 1779. 2v.

40527.22 - .24 Individual authors, etc. - 1715-1799 - Poetry - Saint-Lambert
40527.22 Saint-Lambert, Jean F. Poésies. Paris, 1826.
Htn 40527.22.15* Saint-Lambert, Jean F. Les saisons. 7. éd. Amsterdam, 1775.
40527.23 Saint-Lambert, Jean F. Les saisons, poëme. Paris, 1795.
40527.24 Saint-Lambert, Jean F. Oeuvres mêlées. Paris, 1795.
40527.24.15 Saint-Lambert, Jean F. Sara Th. Paris? 1765?
40527.24.80 Nardis, L. de. Saint-Lambert. Roma, 1961.

40527.25 - .29 Individual authors, etc. - 1715-1799 - Poetry - Miscellany
40527.25 Verny, Pierre. Oeuvres poétiques. Paris, 1826.
Htn 40527.26* Quesnel, Pierre. Almanach du diable. Enfers, n.d.
40527.27 Demachy, Jacques François. Histoires et contes. Paris, 1907.
40527.28 Le Brun, Ponce Denis Ecouchard. Oeuvres. Paris, 1811. 4v.

40527.30 - .99 Individual authors, etc. - 1715-1799 - Poetry - Anonymous poems
40527.30 Mélanges de Poezie. La Haye, 1751- 2v.
40527.32 Collection ó Héroïdes. Frankfurt, 1771-76. 12v.
40527.34 Guimonde de la Touche, Claude. Les soupirs du cloitre. London, 1770.
40527.34.5 Guimonde de la Touche, Claude. Les soupirs du cloitre. London, 1766.
40527.36 Poëmes sur des sujets pris de l'histoire de notre tems. Liège, 1758. 2v.
40527.40 Les charmes de mon exil. 2e éd. En Allemagne, 1804.
40527.45 L'immaculée conception de la très-sainte vierge. Rome, 1796.
40527.50 Poésie sacrée. 2e éd. n.p., 1800. 2 pam.
40527.55 Mes j'ai vu, ou Les prédictions accomplies dans ces derniers tems. Babylone, 1794.
40527.58 La Crèche. Besançon, 1969.

40528 Individual authors, etc. - 1715-1799 - Poetry - Petites Poètes du XVIIIe Siècle
40528.2 Vadé, Jean Joseph. Poésies. Paris, 1879.
40528.3 Piron, Alexis. Poésies choisies. Paris, 1879.
40528.4 Bertin, Antoine. Poésies. Paris, 1879.
40528.5 Desforges-Maillard, Paul. Poésies diverses. Paris, 1880.
40528.6 L'Attaignant, Gabriel Charles de. Poésies diverses. Paris, 1881.
40528.7 Gilbert. Poésies diverses. Paris, 1882.
40528.8 De Bernis, C. Poésies diverses. Paris, 1882.
40528.9 Gresset, Jean B. Poésies choisies. Paris, 1883.
40528.10 Bernard, Pierre Joseph. Poésies choisies. Paris, 1884.
40528.11 Malfilâtre, J.C.L. de C. de. Poésies. Paris, 1884.
40528.12 De Bonnard, C. Poésies diverses. Paris, 1884.
40528.13 Boufflers, S. de. Poésies diverses. Paris, 1886.
40528.20A Raunie, Émile. Chansonniers historiques du XVIIIe siècle. Paris, 1879-84. 10v.
40528.20B Raunie, Émile. Chansonniers historiques du XVIIIe siècle. Paris, 1879-84. 10v.

40529 Individual authors, etc. - 1715-1799 - Poetry - Satirists and epigrammatists
40529.1 Ana, ou Collection de bons mots. Amsterdam, n.d. 10v.
40529.5 Lettres infernales et les tisons. Paris? 1740.
Htn 40529.6* Bazin, Gilles A. Le livre jaune. Bâle, 1748.
40529.8 Boudouin de Guemadene. L'espion de balisé. London, 1783.
40529.13 Beausobre, L. de. Le Pirrhonisme du Sage. Berlin, 1754.
40529.15 Bièvre, François Georges Maréchal. Bièvriana, ou Jeux de mots. Paris, n.d.
40529.15.3 Bièvre, François Georges Maréchal. Bièvriana, ou Jeux de mots. Paris, 1800.
Htn 40529.15.10* Bièvre, François Georges Maréchal. Vercingentarixe, tragedie, oeuvre posthume du sieur de Bois-Flotte. Paris, 1770.
40529.17 Bordelon, L. Les coudées franches. Paris, 1712. 2 pam.
40529.18 Bordelon, L. Les solitaires en belle humeur. Paris, 1723. 2v.
40529.18.5 Bordelon, L. Les solitaires en belle humeur. Utrecht, 1741. 3v.

40529 Individual authors, etc. - 1715-1799 - Poetry - Satirists and epigrammatists - cont.

Htn 40529.19* Etrennes gaillades. Lampsaque, 1782.
40529.20 Gayot, F. Heures perdues du chevalier de Rior. Paris, 1715.
40529.24 Marchadier. L'isle de France, ou La nouvelle colonie de Venus. Amsterdam, 1752.
40529.25 Rémond de Saint Mard, J. Lettres galantes et philosophiques. Cologne, 1721.
40529.26.4 Maréchal, Nicolas. La renaissance de la religion en France. 4e éd. Blois, 1800.
40529.27 Maréchal, Pierre S. Le jujement dernier des rois. Paris, 1794.
40529.28 Maréchal, Pierre S. Dieu et la prêtres. Paris, 1794?
40529.28.10 Maréchal, Pierre S. Izbrannye ateist proizved. Moskva, 1958.
40529.29 Maréchal, Pierre S. Projet d'une loi portant defense d'apprendre à lire aux femmes. Lille, 1841.
Htn 40529.29.2* Maréchal, Pierre S. Projet d'une loi portant defense d'apprendre à lire aux femmes. Paris, 1801.
40529.29.3 Maréchal, Pierre S. Projet d'une loi portant defense d'apprendre à lire aux femmes. Paris, 1801.
40529.30 Maréchal, Pierre S. Le temple de l'Hymen, de dié à l'amour. Paris, 1771.
40529.31 Maréchal, Pierre S. Ad majorem gloriam virtutis. Atheopolis, 1781.
40529.31.5 Maréchal, Pierre S. La femme abbé. Paris, 1801.
40529.31.10 Maréchal, Pierre S. Nouvelle légende dorée, ou Dictionnaire des saintes. Rome, 1790. 2v.
40529.31.25 Maréchal, Pierre S. De la vertu. Paris, 1807.
40529.31.85 Fusil, Casimir Alexandre. Sylvain Maréchal. Paris, 1936.
40529.31.90 Dommanget, M. Sylvain Maréchal. Paris, 1950.
40529.32 Campan. Le mot et la chose. n.p., 1752.
40529.36 Les sotises du tems, ou Memoires. La Haye, 1754.
40529.40 Junquieres, J.B. de. Caquet-Bonbec, la poule à ma tante. n.p., 1785.
40529.45 Amusmens de Beau-Sexe ou Nouvelles histoire et avantures. v.1-2. La Haye, 1740.
40529.50 M***, de. Le carnaval de la Barbarie et le temple d'Yurognes. Barbarie, 1765.
40529.52 Contes et épigrammes en vers. 2e éd. Paris, 1802.
40529.60 Sélis, Nicolas J. L'inoculation du bon sens. Oxfort, 1766.
40529.75 Clément, Jean Marie B. Satires. Amsterdam, 1786.
40529.75.10 Clément, Jean Marie B. Satire sur la fausse philosophie. n.p., 1778.
40529.75.20 Clément, Jean Marie B. Le cri d'un citoyen, satire. Paris, 1784.
40529.80 Maurepas, J.F.P. Recueil dit de Maurepas. v.1-6. Leyde, 1865. 3v.
40529.81 Graaft, de. Avantures secrettes et plaisantes. Brusselles, 1706.
40529.82 Le Plat du Temple, Victor Alexandre Chretien. Virgile en France, ou La nouvelle Enéide. Bruxelles, 1807-08. 2v.

40531.1 - .2 Individual authors, etc. - 1715-1799 - Drama - Aignan, Amar, etc.

40531.2 Aignan, Étienne. La mort de Louis XVI. Paris, 1793.
40531.2.4 Aignan, Étienne. La mort de Louis XVI. Paris, 1793.
40531.2.5 Aignan, Étienne. La mort de Louis XVI. Paris, 1796.
40531.2.9 Allainval, L.J.C. de. L'Embarras des richesses. London, 1733.
40531.2.12 Amar, A.D. Le double divorce. Paris, 1798.
40531.2.15 Andrews, James P. The inquisitor, tragedy in 5 acts. London, 1798.
Htn 40531.2.20* Annet, Peter. Saul et David. London, 1760.

40531.3 Individual authors, etc. - 1715-1799 - Drama - Anseaume

40531.3 Pamphlet box. Anseaume, Louis.
40531.3.100 Anseaume, Louis. Théâtre de M. Anseaume. Paris, 1766. 3v.

40531.4 - .5 Individual authors, etc. - 1715-1799 - Drama - Armault

40531.4 Arnault, A.Y. Oeuvres. Paris, 1824-27. 8v.
40531.4.15 Arnault, A.Y. Les loisirs d'un banni. Paris, 1823. 2v.
40531.4.50 La confession générale d'Audinot. Rouen, 1880.

40531.6.1 - .6.99 Individual authors, etc. - 1715-1799 - Drama - Barthès de Marmorières

40531.6.25 Barthès de Marmorieres, Antoine. Le martyre de Marie-Antoinette. Amsterdam, 1794.
40531.6.28 Barthès de Marmorieres, Antoine. Le martyre de Marie-Antoinette. n.p., 179-?
40531.6.30 Barthès de Marmorieres, Antoine. Le martyre de Marie-Antoinette. Paris, 1796.
40531.6.35 Barthès de Marmorieres, Antoine. La mort de Marie-Antoinette. Paris, 1814.

40531.6.100 - .6.199 Individual authors, etc. - 1715-1799 - Drama - Beaunoir

40531.6.100 Beaunoir, A.L.B.R. de. Les couronnes. Paris, 1810.

40531.7 Individual authors, etc. - 1715-1799 - Drama - Bizet

40531.7 Bizet. Les boites. Paris, 1796.

40531.10 Individual authors, etc. - 1715-1799 - Drama - Bergasse

40531.10 Puységur, Armand Marie Jacques de Chastenet. La journée des dupes. n.p., 1790.
40531.10.5 Puységur, Armand Marie Jacques de Chastenet. La journée des dupes. n.p., 1790.

40531.14 - .16 Individual authors, etc. - 1715-1799 - Drama - Miscellany

40531.14 Bonneville, N. de. L'année, MDCCLXXIX. Paris, 1789?
40531.15 Boutillier, Maximilien Jean. Le souper d'Henri IV. Paris, 1789.
40531.15.200 Boyer. Le bienfait récompensé. Paris, 1795.
40531.15.250 Brizard, Gabriel. La destruction de l'Aristocratisme. Chantilly, 1789.
40531.15.255 Brizard, Gabriel. Les imitateurs de Charles Neuf. Paris, 1790.
40531.16 Dutrait, Maurice. Étude sur la vie de Crébillon (1674-1762). Bordeaux, 1895.

40531.20 - .30 Individual authors, etc. - 1715-1799 - Drama - Folios [Discontinued]

40531.21 Marchand, J.H. Le vindangeur sensible. L'assommoire du XVIII siècle. Paris, 1880.
40531.30 Marivaux, Pierre Carlet de Chamblain de. Oeuvre. Paris, 1878.

40532.1 - .2 Individual authors, etc. - 1715-1799 - Drama - Beaumarchais - Bibliographies

40532.1 Cordier, Henri. Bibliographie des oeuvres de Beaumarchais. Paris, 1883.
40532.2 Macpherson, Harriet D. Editions of Beaumarchais in New York City. N.Y., 1925.

40532.3 Individual authors, etc. - 1715-1799 - Drama - Beaumarchais - Collected and Selected works

40532.3 Beaumarchais, Pierre A.C. de. Oeuvres complètes. Paris, 1809. 7v.
40532.3.10 Beaumarchais, Pierre A.C. de. Oeuvres complètes. Paris, 1874.
40532.3.40 Beaumarchais, Pierre A.C. de. Beaumarchais. Montréal, 1945.
40532.3.45 Beaumarchais, Pierre A.C. de. Beaumarchais par lui-même. Paris? 1960.

40532.4 - .17 Individual authors, etc. - 1715-1799 - Drama - Beaumarchais - Individual works

Htn 40532.4* Beaumarchais, Pierre A.C. de. Le barbier de Séville. n.p., 1775. 3 pam.
40532.4.15A Beaumarchais, Pierre A.C. de. Le barbier de Séville. Paris, 1871.
40532.4.15B Beaumarchais, Pierre A.C. de. Le barbier de Séville. Paris, 1871.
40532.4.20 Beaumarchais, Pierre A.C. de. Le barbier de Séville. Paris, 1884.
40532.4.25 Beaumarchais, Pierre A.C. de. Le barbier de Séville. Paris, 189-.
40532.5 Beaumarchais, Pierre A.C. de. Le barbier de Séville. Boston, 1898.
40532.5.3 Beaumarchais, Pierre A.C. de. Le barbier de Séville. Ann Arbor, 1909.
40532.5.7A Beaumarchais, Pierre A.C. de. The barber of Seville. London, 1905.
40532.5.7B Beaumarchais, Pierre A.C. de. The barber of Seville. London, 1905.
40532.5.10 Beaumarchais, Pierre A.C. de. Le barbier de Séville. Firenze, 1964.
Htn 40532.6* Beaumarchais, Pierre A.C. de. La folle journée, ou Le mariage de Figaro. n.p., 1785.
Htn 40532.6.2* Beaumarchais, Pierre A.C. de. La folle journée, ou Le mariage de Figaro. n.p., 1785.
Htn 40532.6.4* Beaumarchais, Pierre A.C. de. La folle journée, ou Le mariage de Figaro. Paris, 1785.
40532.6.5 Beaumarchais, Pierre A.C. de. La folle journée, ou Le mariage de Figaro. Paris, 1957.
40532.6.20 Beaumarchais, Pierre A.C. de. Die Hochzeit des Figaro. Frankfurt, 1965.
40532.7A Beaumarchais, Pierre A.C. de. Le mariage de Figaro. Paris, n.d.
40532.7B Beaumarchais, Pierre A.C. de. Le mariage de Figaro. Paris, n.d.
40532.7.9 Beaumarchais, Pierre A.C. de. Le mariage de Figaro. Paris, 1872.
40532.7.15 Beaumarchais, Pierre A.C. de. Le mariage de Figaro. Paris, 1893?
40532.7.20 Jasinski, René. Le mariage de Figaro. v.1-3. Paris, 1948.
40532.7.30 Beaumarchais, Pierre A.C. de. El casamiento de Figaro. N.Y., 1888.
40532.7.35 Beaumarchais, Pierre A.C. de. Le mariage de Figaro. Paris, 1953.
40532.7.40 Beaumarchais, Pierre A.C. de. Essai sur le genre dramatique. Paris, 19- ?
40532.8 Beaumarchais, Pierre A.C. de. Tarare, an opera. London, 1787.
40532.9 Beaumarchais, Pierre A.C. de. Les deux amis. Paris, 1796.
40532.9.10 Beaumarchais, Pierre A.C. de. L'autre tartuffe. Avignon, 1799.
40532.10A Beaumarchais, Pierre A.C. de. Théâtre. Paris, 1844.
40532.10B Beaumarchais, Pierre A.C. de. Théâtre. Paris, 1844.
40532.11A Beaumarchais, Pierre A.C. de. Théâtre. Paris, 1846.
40532.11B Beaumarchais, Pierre A.C. de. Théâtre. Paris, 1846.
40532.12 Beaumarchais, Pierre A.C. de. Théâtre. Paris, n.d.
40532.14 Beaumarchais, Pierre A.C. de. Théâtre complet. Paris, 1869-71. 4v.
40532.14.2 Beaumarchais, Pierre A.C. de. Théâtre complet. Paris, 1869-71. 4v.
40532.14.5A Beaumarchais, Pierre A.C. de. Théâtre. Paris, 186-.
40532.14.5B Beaumarchais, Pierre A.C. de. Théâtre. Paris, 186-.
40532.14.10 Beaumarchais, Pierre A.C. de. Théâtre illustré. Bibliothèque Larousse. Paris, 1911?
40532.14.15 Beaumarchais, Pierre A.C. de. Théâtre choisi. Paris, 19- ?
40532.14.25 Beaumarchais, Pierre A.C. de. Théâtre. Paris, 1934.
40532.14.30 Beaumarchais, Pierre A.C. de. Théâtre de Beaumarchais: Le barbier de Séville. Paris, 1964.
40532.15 Beaumarchais, Pierre A.C. de. Notes et reflexiones. Paris, 1961.
40532.16A Beaumarchais, Pierre A.C. de. Lettres inédites de Beaumarchais. Paris, 1929.
40532.16B Beaumarchais, Pierre A.C. de. Lettres inédites de Beaumarchais. Paris, 1929.
40532.16.5 Beaumarchais, Pierre A.C. de. Correspondance. Paris, 1969- 2v.
40532.17 Beaumarchais, Pierre A.C. de. Lettres à Madame de Godeville, 1777-79. Paris, 1928.

40532.18 - Individual authors, etc. - 1715-1799 - Drama - Beaumarchais - Biography and criticism

40532.18 Pamphlet vol. Beaumarchais, Pierre Augustin Caronde. Miscellaneous pamphlets.
40532.19.1 Lintilhac, Eugène. Beaumarchais et ses oeuvres. Genève, 1970.
40532.25 Chévrier, Maurice. Discours sur Beaumarchais. Paris, 1886.
40532.25.6 Dalséme, René. La vie de Beaumarchais. 6. éd. Paris, 1928.
40532.25.7 Dalséme, René. Beaumarchais. 1. American ed. N.Y., 1929.
40532.25.10 Latzarus, Louis. Beaumarchais. Paris, 1930.

Classified Listing

40532.18 - Individual authors, etc. - 1715-1799 - Drama - Beaumarchais - Biography and criticism - cont.

40532.25.15 Lafon, Roger. Beaumarchais, le brillant armateur. Paris, 1928.
40532.25.20 Frischauser, Paul. Beaumarchais. N.Y., 1935.
40532.25.22 Frischauser, Paul. Beaumarchais, adventurer in the century of women. Port Washington, 1970.
40532.25.25 Frischauser, Paul. Beaumarchais, Wegbereiter der grossen Revolution. Hamburg, 1961.
40532.25.30 Bailly, Auguste. Beaumarchais. 12. éd. Paris, 1945.
40532.30 Castil-Blare, F.H.J. Barbier de Séville. Boston, 1831.
40532.34 Jones, Florence N. Beaumarchais and Plautus the sources of the Barbier de Séville. Chicago, 1908.
40532.36 Scherer, J. La dramaturgie de Beaumarchais. Paris, 1954.
40532.38 Filippini, F. Figaro. n.p., 1952.
40532.40 Pomeau, R. Beaumarchais. Paris, 1956.
40532.42 Pooschwitz, G. von. Introduction à l'étude du vocabulaire de Beaumarchais. Stockholm, 1956.
40532.44 Arneth, A. Ritter von. Beaumarchais und Sonnenfels. Wien, 1868.
40532.46 Pollitzer, Marcel. Beaumarchais. Paris, 1957.
40532.48 Ratermanis, J.B. The comic style of Beaumarchais. Seattle, 1961.
40532.50 Gaiffe, Felix. Beaumarchais. Paris, 1961.
40532.52 Cox, Cynthia. The real Figaro. London, 1962.
40532.53 Kerdik, Frjts. Terloops ook drukker. 's-Gravenhage, 1961.
40532.54 Arnould, Emile Jules François. La genèse du Barbier de Séville. Dublin, 1965.
40532.56 Giudici, Enzo. Beaumarchais nel suo e nel nostro tempo. Roma, 1964.
40532.58 Thomasset, René. Beaumarchais, écrivain et aventurier. Paris, 1966.
40532.59 Niklaus, Robert. Beaumarchais: Le barbier de Séville. London, 1968.
40532.60 Pugh, Anthony Roy. A critical commentary on Beaumarchais's Le mariage de Figaro. London, 1968.

40534.1 - .9 Individual authors, etc. - 1715-1799 - Drama - Anthologies [Discontinued]

40534.1 Pamphlet vol. Théâtre de second ordre. 37 pam.
40534.2 Théâtre des auteurs du second ordre. v.37. Paris, 1810.
40534.4 Opéras-comiques. Paris, 1781-1827.
40534.5 Chefs-d'oeuvre dramatiques du XVIIIe siècle. Paris, 1872.

40534.10 Individual authors, etc. - 1715-1799 - Drama - Belloy - Writings

40534.10 Belloy, Pierre L.B. Oeuvres complètes. Paris, 1787. 6v.
40534.10.9 Belloy, Pierre L.B. Le siege de Calais. Paris, 1787.
40534.10.12 Belloy, Pierre L.B. The siege of Calais. London, 1765.
40534.10.15 Belloy, Pierre L.B. La Gabriela. Barcelona, 17- .

40534.11 Individual authors, etc. - 1715-1799 - Drama - Belloy - Works about

40534.11 Zimmermann, Erich. Pierre-Laurent Buirette de Belloy, sein Leben und seine Tragödien. Leipzig, 1911.

40534.13 - .17 Individual authors, etc. - 1715-1799 - Drama - Miscellany, B-C

40534.13 Bièvre, G. Mareschal de. Le marquis de Bièvre. Paris, 1910.
40534.14 Billard-Dumonceau, Edme. Voltaire apprécié; comédie. n.p., 1779?
Htn 40534.15* Billardon, Louis E. Hirra. Paris, 1767.
40534.15.25 Billardon, Louis E. Vashington, ou La liberté du Nouveau Monde. Princeton, N.J., 1941.
40534.15.100 Keys, Allwyn Charles. Antoine Bret, 1717-92. Auckland, 1959.
40534.16 Du Boccage, Marie Anne (Le Page) Fiquet (Mme.). Le amazzoni. Tragedia. Venezia, 1756.
40534.16.3 Boissy, Louis de. Oeuvres de théâtre. Paris, 1766. 9v.
40534.16.5 Chamfort, Sebastian. Mustapha et Zéangir. Paris, 1778.
Htn 40534.16.7* Cahusac, Louis de. Grigri. Pt.1-2. Paris? 1739.
Htn 40534.16.9* Cailhava d'Estendoux, J.F. Théâtre. Paris, 1781-82. 2v.
Htn 40534.16.10* Cailhava d'Estendoux, J.F. Les Menechmes grecs. Paris, 1791.
40534.16.11 Cailhava d'Estendoux, J.F. Ziste et zeste. Paris, 1797.
40534.16.12 Cailleau, A.C. Clef du grand oeuvre, ou Lettres du Sancelrien Tourangeau. Corinte, 1777.
40534.16.15 Cammaille-Saint-Aubin, M.C. L'ami du peuple. Paris, 1793.
40534.16.17.5 Candeille, Julie. Catherine. Paris, 1793.
40534.16.17.8 Candeille, Julie. Catherine. Paris, 1793.
40534.16.17.9 Candeille, Julie. Catherine. Paris, 1805.
40534.16.17.11 Candeille, Julie. Le commissionaire. Paris, 1795.
40534.16.19 Carmontelle, L.G. Proverbes dramatiques. Paris, 1822. 4v.
40534.16.20 Carmontelle, L.G. Proverbes et comédies posthumes. Paris, 1825. 3v.
40534.16.22 Friedrich, Kurt. Carmontelle und seine Proverbes dramatiques. Inaug. Diss. Halle, 1914.
40534.16.24 Herrmann, Michael. Das Gesellschaftstheater des Louis Carrogis de Carmontelle. Meisenheim, 1968.
40534.16.25 Urschlecter, Hans. Die vornehme französische Frau des XVIII Jahrhunderts...Proverbes dramatiques. n.p., 1909.
40534.16.28 Donnard, Jean Hervé. Le théâtre de Carmontelle. Paris, 1967.
40534.16.30 Chateaubrun, Jean B.V. de. Oeuvres choisis de Chateaubrun et de Guimond de la Touche. Paris, 1814.
40534.16.35 Chateaubrun, Jean B.V. de. The text and sources of Chateaubrun's lost Ajax. Frankfurt, 1969.
40534.16.75 Charlemagne, A. Le souper des Jacobins. Paris, 1796-97.
40534.16.80 Charlemagne, A. Le souper des Jacobins. Paris, 1795.
Htn 40534.16.100* Puységur, Armand Marie Jacques de Chastenet. L'intérieur d'un ménage republicain. Paris, 1794.
40534.17.9 Cizos, François. Adieux à l'univers. Comédies. Toulouse, 1815.
40534.17.10 Bonnay, François. La prise des annonciades. Hamburg, 1796.
40534.17.10.5 Bonnay, François. La prise des annonciades. Paris? 1789?
40534.17.10.7 Bonnay, François. La prise des annonciades. v.1-2. Paris? 1789?
40534.17.10.9 Bonnay, François. Expedition du général Lamethore. La prise des annonciades. Paris? 179-.
40534.17.10.12 Bonnay, François. La prise des annonciades. 2. éd. Paris? 1790?
40534.17.10.15 Bonnay, François. La prise des annonciades. 5. éd. Paris? 179-?

40534.13 - .17 Individual authors, etc. - 1715-1799 - Drama - Miscellany, B-C - cont.

40534.17.12 Cizos, François. Les peuples et les rois. Paris, 1794.

40534.18 - .19.149 Individual authors, etc. - 1715-1799 - Drama - Colardeau

40534.18 Colardeau, Charles P. Oeuvres choisies. Paris, 1811.
40534.19 Colardeau, Charles P. Oeuvres choisies. Paris, 1779. 2v.
40534.19.50 Bouvier, Armand. Le poete Colardeau, 1732-1776. Orléans, 1925.

40534.19.150 - Individual authors, etc. - 1715-1799 - Drama - Carolet

40534.19.150 Levy, Bernard. The unpublished plays of Carolet. N.Y., 1931.

40534.20 Individual authors, etc. - 1715-1799 - Drama - Collé

40534.20 Collé, Charles. Correspondance inédite. Paris, 1864.
40534.20.25 Collé, Charles. Théâtre de société. Paris, 1777. 3v.

40534.21 - .23.79 Individual authors, etc. - 1715-1799 - Drama - Collin d'Harleville - Writings

40534.21 Collin d'Harleville, J.F. Théâtre. Paris, 1877.
40534.22 Collin d'Harleville, J.F. Le vieux célibataire. Paris, 1801.
40534.22.3 Collin d'Harleville, J.F. Le vieux célibataire. Paris, 1888.
40534.22.5 Collin d'Harleville, J.F. Le vieillard et les jeunes gens. Paris, 1803.
40534.22.15 Collin d'Harleville, J.F. Rose et Picara. Paris, 1795.
40534.22.19 Collin d'Harleville, J.F. Les moeurs du jour. Paris, 1800.
40534.23 Collin d'Harleville, J.F. Oeuvres. Paris, 1828. 4v.

40534.23.80 - .23.249 Individual authors, etc. - 1715-1799 - Drama - Collin d'Harleville - Works about

40534.23.81 Skinner, L.H. Collin d'Harleville, 1755-1806. N.Y., 1933.
40534.23.85 Tissier, André. Collin d'Harleville, 1755-1806. Paris, 1964-65. 2v.

40534.23.250 - Individual authors, etc. - 1715-1799 - Drama - Collot d'Herbois

40534.23.250 Collot d'Herbois, J.M. Les porte-feuilles comedie. Paris, 1791.
40534.23.255 Collot d'Herbois, J.M. La famille patriote. Paris, 1790.
40534.23.260 Collot d'Herbois, J.M. Le paysan magistrat. Paris, 1790.
40534.23.265 Collot d'Herbois, J.M. La famille patriote. Paris, 1790.
40534.23.301 Collot d'Herbois, J.M. Théâtre. n.p., n.d. 2v.

40534.24 - .29 Individual authors, etc. - 1715-1799 - Drama - Crébillon, P.J. - Writings

40534.24 Crébillon, Prosper Jolyot de. Oeuvres. Paris, 1743. 2v.
40534.24.5 Crébillon, Prosper Jolyot de. Oeuvres. Paris, 1754. 2v.
40534.24.10 Crébillon, Prosper Jolyot de. Oeuvres. Paris, 1772. 2v.
Htn 40534.25* Crébillon, Prosper Jolyot de. Oeuvres complètes. Paris, 1785. 3v.
40534.26 Crébillon, Prosper Jolyot de. Oeuvres. Paris, 1802.
40534.26.2 Crébillon, Prosper Jolyot de. Oeuvres. Paris, 1802.
40534.27A Crébillon, Prosper Jolyot de. Oeuvres. Paris, 1812. 3v.
40534.27B Crébillon, Prosper Jolyot de. Oeuvres. Paris, 1812. 3v.
40534.28 Crébillon, Prosper Jolyot de. Oeuvres. Paris, 1818. 2v.
40534.28.2 Crébillon, Prosper Jolyot de. Oeuvres. Paris, 1822. 3v.
40534.28.5 Crébillon, Prosper Jolyot de. Oeuvres. Paris, 1828. 2v.
40534.28.6 Crébillon, Prosper Jolyot de. Oeuvres. Paris, 1828. 2v.
40534.29 Crébillon, Prosper Jolyot de. Théâtre complet. Paris, 1885.
40534.29.12 Crébillon, Prosper Jolyot de. Radamisto e Zenobia. Paris, 1798.
40534.29.15 Crébillon, Prosper Jolyot de. Rhadamiste et Zenobie. Paris, 1800.

40534.30 Individual authors, etc. - 1715-1799 - Drama - Crébillon, P.J. - Works about

40534.30.5 Ciureanu, Petre. Crébillon. Genova, 1965.

40534.31 - .35 Individual authors, etc. - 1715-1799 - Drama - Crébillon, C.P.J. - Writings

40534.31 Crébillon, Claude Prosper Jolyot de. L'oeuvre de Crébillon le fils: Tableau des moeurs du temps dans les différents ages de la vie. Paris, 1921.
Htn 40534.32* Crébillon, Claude Prosper Jolyot de. Lecumoire. Histoire japonoise. v.1-2. London, 1735.
40534.32.5 Crébillon, Claude Prosper Jolyot de. L'ecumoire. Bruxelles, 1733-1884.
40534.32.10 Crébillon, Claude Prosper Jolyot de. Crébillon fils. Paris, 1964.
40534.33 Crébillon, Claude Prosper Jolyot de. Les egaremens. Paris, 1815.
40534.33.5 Crébillon, Claude Prosper Jolyot de. Les egaremens du coeur et de l'esprit, ou Memoires de Mr. De Meilsour. La Haye, 1748.
40534.33.6 Crébillon, Claude Prosper Jolyot de. Les égarements du coeur et de l'esprit. Paris, 1961.
40534.33.9 Crébillon, Claude Prosper Jolyot de. Nuit et le moment ou Les matins de Cynthère. Bruxelles, 1881.
X Cg 40534.33.9.2 Crébillon, Claude Prosper Jolyot de. La nuit et le moment. Paris, 1966.
40534.34 Crébillon, Claude Prosper Jolyot de. Das Spiel des Zufalls am Kaminfeuer. Leipzig, 1905.
Htn 40534.34.5* Le hazard du coin du feu, dialogue moral. La Haye, 1763.
40534.34.7 Crébillon, Claude Prosper Jolyot de. Le hazard du coin du feu. Bruxelles, 1880.
40534.34.9 Crébillon, Claude Prosper Jolyot de. Le sopha, conte moral. Bruxelles, 1881.
40534.34.13 Crébillon, Claude Prosper Jolyot de. The sofa; a moral tale. London, 1927.
40534.34.15 Crébillon, Claude Prosper Jolyot de. Letters from Marchioness de M***. London, 1735.

40534.31 - .35 Individual authors, etc. - 1715-1799 - Drama - Crébillon, C.P.J. - Writings - cont.

40534.34.15B Crébillon, Claude Prosper Jolyot de. Letters from Marchioness de M***. London, 1735.
40534.34.20A Crébillon, Claude Prosper Jolyot de. Lettres de la Marquise de M*** au comte de R***. Paris, 1930.
40534.34.20B Crébillon, Claude Prosper Jolyot de. Lettres de la Marquise de M*** au comte de R***. Paris, 1930.

40534.36 Individual authors, etc. - 1715-1799 - Drama - Crébillon, C.P.J. - Works about

40534.36 Pamphlet box. Crébillon, Claude Prosper Jolyot de.
40534.36.10 Cherpack, Clifton. An essay on Crébillon, fils. Durham, 1962.
40534.36.15 Sturm, Ernest. Crébillon fils et le libertinage au dix-huitième siècle. Paris, 1970.

40534.37 - .99 Individual authors, etc. - 1715-1799 - Drama - Miscellany, C

40534.40 Tissier, André. M. de Crac, gentilhomme garcon. Paris, 1959.
40534.43.30 Caigniez, Louis. Le mandarin Houng-Pouf. Paris, 1821.

40535.1 - .3 Individual authors, etc. - 1715-1799 - Drama - Miscellany, D

40535.1.25 Dampierre de La Salle. Le bienfait rendu, ou Le négociant. Paris, 1763.
40535.2 Danchet, M. Théâtre. Paris, 1751. 4v.
40535.2.5 Boissy, Louis de. The Frenchman in London. London, 1755.
40535.2.7 Defauconpret, A.J.B. La papesse Jeanne. Paris, 1793.
40535.2.8 Desfontaines, F.G. Fouques. La chaste Suzanne. Paris, 1793.
40535.2.8.3 Desfontaines, F.G. Fouques. La chaste Suzanne. Paris, 1793.
40535.2.8.7 Desfontaines, F.G. Fouques. Le divorce. Paris, 1793-94.
40535.2.9 Desforges, Pierre Jean Baptiste. Le sourd, ou L'auberge pleine. Paris, 1794.
Htn 40535.2.15* Desforges, Pierre Jean Baptiste. Le poéte. Hambourg, 1798. 4v.
40535.2.16 Desforges, Pierre Jean Baptiste. Mémoires du poète libertin (1798). Paris, 1912.
40535.2.20 Delaunay. Le paresseux, comédie en vers. Paris, 1733.
40535.2.25 Humbert, H. Delisle de la Drévetière. Berlin, 1904.
40535.2.30 Demautort, J.B. Vadé chez lui. Paris, 1800.
40535.2.40 Déniot. Le français a Burgos. Paris? 1796.
40535.2.50 Demonstier, C.A. Le conciliateur. Paris, 1794.
40535.2.55 Demonstier, C.A. Le divorce. Paris, 1795.
40535.2.60 Demonstier, C.A. Le tolérant. Paris, n.d.
40535.2.65 Demonstier, C.A. Alceste à la campagne. Paris, 1798.
40535.3 Desmahis, J.F.E. Oeuvres choisies. Paris, 1813.
40535.3.30 Deschamps, F.M.C. La religion defendue. Rotterdam, 1733.
40535.3.60 Desorgues, Théodore. Rousseau ou l'enfance. Paris, 1794?

40535.4 - .5 Individual authors, etc. - 1715-1799 - Drama - Destouches - Writings

40535.4 Destouches, Philippe Néricault. Oeuvres dramatiques. Paris, 1811. 6v.
40535.4.5 Destouches, Philippe Néricault. Der poetische Dorfjunker...Ein Lustspiel in 5 Aufzügen. Wien, 1761.
40535.5 Destouches, Philippe Néricault. Oeuvres choisies. Paris, 1826. 3v.
40535.5.21 Destouches, Philippe Néricault. Théâtre choisi. Paris, 1884.
40535.5.25 Destouches, Philippe Néricault. Deux comédies de Destouches. Cambridge, Eng., 1929.

40535.6 - .7 Individual authors, etc. - 1715-1799 - Drama - Destouches - Works about

40535.6 Defrémery, Charles. Note bibliographique et littéraire. Destouches Le Philosophe marié. Paris, 1880.
40535.7 Graziano, Joseph. Essai sur la vie et les oeuvres de Destouches. Frauenfeld, 1889.
40535.7.3 Schoepke, P.T. Philippe Nericault Destouches et son théâtre. Leipzig, 1886.

40535.8 Individual authors, etc. - 1715-1799 - Drama - Miscellany, D

40535.8 Dorvigny, Louis A. De witte-neger; blyspel. Amsteldam? 1777.
40535.8.5 Dorvigny, Louis A. Les noces du pere Duchesne. Paris, 1789.
40535.8.9 Dubuisson, M. La parfaite égalité ou Les tu et toi. Paris, 1794.
40535.8.14 Dorvigny, Louis A. L'hospitalité. Paris, 1795.
40535.8.50 Dorvo, H. Figaro de retour à Paris. Paris, 1795.
40535.8.55 Dorvo, H. Le faux député. Paris, 1795.
40535.8.100 Dubuisson, P.N. Trasime et timagene. Paris, 1787.
40535.8.150 Ducancel, Charles Pierre. L'interieur des comités révolutionnaires. Paris, 1797.
40535.8.155 Ducancel, Charles Pierre. Le hableur. Paris, 1795.
40535.8.170 Duchaume. L'hiver, ou Les deux moulins. Paris, 1793.
40535.8.200 Dugazon, J.B.H.G. Le modéré. Paris, 1794.

40535.9 - .11 Individual authors, etc. - 1715-1799 - Drama - Ducis - Writings

40535.9 Ducis, Jean F. Oeuvres. Paris, 1826. 3v.
40535.10 Ducis, Jean F. Oeuvres. Paris, 1826.
40535.11 Ducis, Jean F. Hamlet. Paris, 1826.
40535.11.5 Ducis, Jean F. Le roi Lear. Paris, 1784.
40535.11.19 Ducis, Jean F. Othello, ossia il moro di Venezia. Firenze, n.d.
40535.11.20 Ducis, Jean F. Othello, ou le more de Venise. Paris, 1800.
Htn 40535.11.30* Ducis, Jean F. Romeo et Juliette, tragédie. Paris, 1772.

40535.12 - .12.149 Individual authors, etc. - 1715-1799 - Drama - Ducis - Works about

40535.12 Ducis, Jean F. Lettres. Paris, 1879.
40535.12.9 Leroy, Onésime. Études morales et litteraires sur...J.F. Ducis. Paris, 1832.
40535.12.10 Campenon, Vincent. Essais de mémoires...de J.F. Ducis. Paris, 1824.
40535.12.11 Leroy, Onésime. Études sur la personne et les écrits de J.F. Ducis. 3. éd. Paris, 1836.
40535.12.15 Ducis, Jean F. Hamlet. Paris, 1815.

40535.12.150 - .13.8 Individual authors, etc. - 1715-1799 - Drama - Miscellany, D

40535.12.150 Duclos, P.G. La prise de Paris. Paris, 1795.
40535.12.180 Dufresnes. Idylles et pièces fugitives. Paris, 1781.
40535.12.200 Dupuis. L'artiste patriote. Paris, 1791.
40535.13 Duveyrier, H. La cour pléniére. Paris, 1788.
40535.13.2 Duveyrier, H. La cour pléniére. Paris, 1788.
40535.13.5 Duveyrier, H. La cour pléniére. Paris, 1788.
40535.13.7 Duveyrier, H. Supplément à la cour pléniére. Baville, 1788.

40535.13.9 Individual authors, etc. - 1715-1799 - Drama - Faur

40535.13.9.5 Faur, Louis F. L'amour à l'épreuve. Paris, 1784.
40535.13.9.10 Faur, Louis F. La fête de la cinquantaine. Paris, 1796.

40535.13.10 - .13.99 Individual authors, etc. - 1715-1799 - Drama - Falbaire de Quingey

40535.13.10 Falbaire de Quingey, C.G. Fenouillot de. Les Jammabos, ou Les moines japonais. Londres, 1778?
40535.13.12 Falbaire de Quingey, C.G. Fenouillot de. L'honnête criminel. 2. éd. Amsterdam, 1768.
40535.13.25 Falbaire de Quingey, C.G. Fenouillot de. L'école des moeurs. Paris, 1776.
40535.13.30 Falbaire de Quingey, C.G. Fenouillot de. Les deux avares. Paris? 1770.
40535.13.50 Dénonciation au public à l'occasion quelques écrits anonymes. Paris, 1788.

40535.14 - .14.19 Individual authors, etc. - 1715-1799 - Drama - Fabré d'Eglantine

40535.14.5 Fabre d'Eglantine, P.F.N. Oeuvres mêlées et posthumes. Paris, 1802. 2v.
40535.14.9 Fabre d'Eglantine, P.F.N. Théâtre. Le Présomptueux. Paris, 1790. 5 pam.
40535.14.10 Fabre d'Eglantine, P.F.N. Les précepteurs. Paris, 1799-1800.
40535.14.11 Fabre d'Eglantine, P.F.N. Le convalescent de qualité. Paris, 1791.
40535.14.15 Almeras, H. de. Fabre d'Eglantine. Paris, n.d.
40535.14.17 Fabre d'Eglantine, P.F.N. Le collatéral. Paris, 1791.

40535.14.20 - .14.99 Individual authors, etc. - 1715-1799 - Drama - Fagan

40535.14.25 Fagan, C.B. La pupile. Paris, 1742.
40535.14.28 Ulrich, Erich. Charles B. Fagan's Lustspiele. Inaug. Diss. Dresden, 1915.

40535.14.500 - .15.12 Individual authors, etc. - 1715-1799 - Drama - Favart

40535.14.505 Iacuzzi, Alfred. The European vogue of Favart. N.Y., 1930.
40535.14.510 Salvatore, P.J. Favart's unpublished plays. N.Y., 1935.
40535.15.2 Font, Auguste. Favart l'opéra comique. Paris, 1894.
40535.15.3A Favart, Charles S. Polichinelle, comte de Paonfier. Paris, 1924.
40535.15.3B Favart, Charles S. Polichinelle, comte de Paonfier. Paris, 1924.
40535.15.3.5 Favart, Charles S. Polichinelle, comte de Paonfier. N.Y., 19- .
40535.15.4 Favart, Charles S. Les jeunes mariés. Paris, 1778? 3 pam.
40535.15.4.5 Favart, Charles S. Soliman Second; comédie. n.p., n.d.
40535.15.5 Favart, Charles S. Memoires et correspondance littéraires. Paris, 1808. 3v.
40535.15.7 Favart, Charles S. La chercheuse d'esprit. Paris, 1741.
Htn 40535.15.8* Favart, Charles S. La fée urgele. Paris, 1765.
40535.15.9 Favart, Charles S. L'empirique. N.Y., 1929.
40535.15.10 Favart, Charles S. Soliman Second. Avignon, 1774.
40535.15.11 Favart, Charles S. A cajou. Avignon, 1767.
40535.15.12 Favart, Charles S. Théâtre, ou Recueil des comédies, parodies et opera-comiques. Paris, 1763. 8v.

40535.15.13 - .15.999 Individual authors, etc. - 1715-1799 - Drama - Miscellany, F

40535.15.13 Favart, M.J.B.D. (Mme.). Annette et Lubin. Paris, 1770.
40535.15.14 Forgeot, Nicolas. Les dettes; comedie. Paris, 1787.
40535.15.18 Favières, Edme G.F. de. Les espiègleries de Garnison. Paris, 1792.
40535.15.19 Fuzelier, Louis. Momus turned fabulist. London, 1729.
40535.15.25 Carbon Flins des Oliviers, C.M.L.E. Le reveil d'épiménide, à Paris. Toulouse, 1790.
40535.15.29 Carbon Flins des Oliviers, C.M.L.E. Le mari directeur. Paris, 1791.
40535.15.32 Carbon Flins des Oliviers, C.M.L.E. La jeune hôtesse. Paris, 1792.
40535.15.50 Fonvielle, B.F.A. Collot dans Lyon. n.p., 1795.
40535.15.110 Marivaux, Pierre Carlet de Chamblain. Journaux et oeuvres diverses. Paris, 1969.

40535.16 Individual authors, etc. - 1715-1799 - Drama - Miscellany, G

40535.16 Gardel, Pierre Gabriel. Télémaque dans l'Isle de Calipso. Paris, 1790.
40535.16.5 Gardel, Pierre Gabriel. La rociere. n.p., 1798?
40535.16.9 Gobemouche, Leonard. I.K.L. Essai dramatique. Montmartre, 1776.
40535.16.25 Godard D'Aucour de Saint Just, Claude. L'heureuse nouvelle. Paris, 1797.
40535.16.40 Godard, Louis. Poesie di Cimante Micenis. Roma, 1823.
40535.16.45 Gorsas, A.J. Le grand-bailliage. Harcourt, 1788.
40535.16.50 Gouges, M.O. de. (Mme.). Le convent. Paris, 1792.
40535.16.100 Gueroult, Jean F. La journée de Marathon. Paris, 1796.

40535.17 - .19.18 Individual authors, etc. - 1715-1799 - Drama - Graffigny

40535.17 Graffigny, Françoise d'Issembourg d'Happoncourt de. Oeuvres complètes. Paris, 1821.
40535.18 Graffigny, Françoise d'Issembourg d'Happoncourt de. Lettres. Paris, 1883.
40535.19 Graffigny, Françoise d'Issembourg d'Happoncourt de. Lettere d'una peruviana. Avignone, 1817.
40535.19.2 Graffigny, Françoise d'Issembourg d'Happoncourt de. Lettere d'una peruviana. Londres, 1821.
40535.19.3 Graffigny, Françoise d'Issembourg d'Happoncourt de. Lettres d'une peruvienne. Paris, 1756. 2v.
40535.19.4 Graffigny, Françoise d'Issembourg d'Happoncourt de. Lettres d'une peruvienne. Genève, 1777.
40535.19.5 Graffigny, Françoise d'Issembourg d'Happoncourt de. Lettres d'une peruvienne. Paris, 1822.

40535.17 - .19.18 Individual authors, etc. - 1715-1799 - Drama - Graffigny - cont.

40535.19.9 Graffigny, Françoise d'Issembourg d'Happoncourt de. Letters written by a Peruvian princess. London, 1748.

40535.19.15 Graffigny, Françoise d'Issembourg d'Happoncourt de. The Peruvian letters. London, 1774.

40535.19.17 Noël, Georges. Madame de Grafigny, 1695-1758. Paris, 1913.

40535.19.19 - .25.8 Individual authors, etc. - 1715-1799 - Drama - Miscellany, G-M

Htn 40535.19.19* Griffet de la Baume, A. La messe de Gnide. Paris, 1794.

40535.19.23 LaHarpe, J.F. de. Le triomphe de la religion. Paris, 1814.

40535.19.25 LaHarpe, J.F. de. Le comte de Warwik. Paris, 1764.

40535.19.27 LaHarpe, J.F. de. Mélanie. Paris, 1792.

40535.19.28 LaHarpe, J.F. de. Mélanie. Paris, 1804.

40535.19.30 Imbert, B. Marie de Brabant. Paris, 1790.

Htn 40535.19.32* Imbert, B. Le jugement de Paris. Amsterdam, 1772.

40535.19.35.3 Jacquelin, J.A. L'amour à l'anglaise. 2. éd. Paris, 1816.

40535.19.40 Joigny. Le siège de Lille. Paris, 1794.

40535.19.45 Jars, Antoine G. Les confidences. Paris, 1803.

40535.19.50 Hele, T. Les événements imprevus. Paris, 1780.

40535.19.60 La Chabeaussière, A.E.T.P. de. Apologues moreaux. Paris, 1814? 2 pam.

40535.19.63 La Chabeaussière, A.E.T.P. de. Oeuvres diverses. Paris, 1801.

40535.19.75 La Chaussée, Pierre Claude Nivelle de. Oeuvres. Paris, 1777. 5v.

40535.19.77 La Chaussée, Pierre Claude Nivelle de. Diana en Endimion. Amsterdam, 1742.

40535.19.80 La Chaussée, Pierre Claude Nivelle de. La fausse antipathie. Paris, 1735.

40535.19.85 La Chaussée, Pierre Claude Nivelle de. De tover - buryloft, of het huwelyk door tovery. Amsterdam, 1743.

40535.19.90 La Chaussée, Pierre Claude Nivelle de. Le préjuge à la mode. Paris, 1773.

40535.19.100 La Chaussée, Pierre Claude Nivelle de. Freundeschule. Naumburg, 1902.

40535.19.200 Lanson, Gustave. Nivelle de La Chaussée et la comédie larmoyante. Paris, 1887.

40535.19.202 Lanson, Gustave. Nivelle de La Chaussée et la comédie larmoyante. 2. éd. Genève, 1970.

40535.19.800 Landois, Paul. The first French tragédie bourgeoise Silvie. Baltimore, 1954.

40535.19.805 Landois, Paul. Serena. Photoreproduction. Frankfurt, 1764.

40535.20 Sally-Tolendal, T.A. Le comte de Strafford: tragédie. London, 1795.

40535.20.9 Leblanc de Guillet, Antoine Blanc. Les druides; tragédie. Saint-Petersbourg, 1783.

40535.20.15 Leblanc de Guillet, Antoine Blanc. Le clergé dévoilé. Paris, 1791.

40535.21 Le Blanc de Villeneufve. La fête du petit blé. New Orléans, 1814.

40535.21.25 Duffo, F.A. J.J. Lefranc, poète et magistrat. Thèse. Paris, 1913.

40535.21.50 LeFranc-Ponteuil, N. L'école des frères, ou L'incertitude. Lyon, 1792.

40535.22 Legrand, Marc Antoine. Cartouche, or The robbers. London, 1722.

40535.22.2 Legrand, Marc Antoine. Théâtre. Paris, 1731. 4v.

40535.22.5 Segitz, Conrad. Marc Antoine Le Grand. Erlangen, 1910.

40535.22.6 Burnet, M.S. Marc Antoine Legrand...1673-1728. Thèse. Paris, 1938.

40535.22.8 Burnet, M.S. Marc Antoine Legrand...1673-1728. Paris, 1938.

40535.22.9 Burnet, M.S. Marc Antoine Legrand. Paris, 1938.

40535.22.19 Le Maingre de Bonciqualt, Louis. Les Amazones revoltées. Rotterdam, 1730.

40535.22.50 Le Grand, Jérôme. Louis XIV et le masque der fer. Paris, 1791.

40535.22.53 Le Grand, Jérôme. Louis XIV et le masque de fer. Paris, 1792.

40535.23 Le Mierre, A.M. Oeuvres. Paris, 1810. 3v.

40535.23.5 Le Mierre, A.M. Barnevelt. Paris, 1791.

40535.23.7 Le Mierre, A.M. Artaxerce; tragédie. Paris, 1770.

40535.23.9 Wienhold, Hans. Lemierre's Tragödien. Leipzig, 1905.

40535.23.12 Harny de Guerville. Le petit maître en province. Paris, 1765.

40535.23.13 Henriet, Maurice. Letellier, auteur dramatique forain. Château-Thierry, 1904.

40535.23.15 Lougueil. L'orphelin anglais. Toulouse, 1787.

40535.24 Henault, Charles. Pièces de théâtre. n.p., 1770.

40535.24.10 Huvier des Fontenelles, Pierre M.F. La targetade, tragédie un peu burlesque. Paris? 1791.

Htn 40535.25* Henault, Charles. Cornélie. Vestale. Strawberry-Hill, 1768.

40535.25.2 Maillet-Duclairon, A. Cromwell; tragédie en cinq actes. Paris, 1764.

Htn 40535.25.3* Marivaux, Pierre Carlet de Chamblain de. Oeuvres choisies. Le jeu de l'amour. Paris, 1741-73. 3 pam.

40535.25.7 Maillot, A.F.E. Madame Angot. Paris, 1797.

40535.25.8 Marchant, François. La constitution en vaudevilles, Paris 1792. Paris, 1872.

40535.25.8.10 Marchant, François. Fénélon; poème. 2. éd. Cambrai, 1804.

40535.25.9 - .27 Individual authors, etc. - 1715-1799 - Drama - Marivaux - Complete and Selected works

40535.25.9 Marivaux, Pierre Carlet de Chamblain de. Oeuvres complettes. Paris, 1781. 12v.

40535.25.20 Marivaux, Pierre Carlet de Chamblain de. Le paysan parvenu. London, 1735.

40535.25.30 Marivaux, Pierre Carlet de Chamblain de. Oeuvres choisies. Paris, 1890.

40535.26 Marivaux, Pierre Carlet de Chamblain de. Théâtre. Paris, 1863.

40535.26.5 Marivaux, Pierre Carlet de Chamblain de. Théâtre. Paris, 1870.

40535.27 Marivaux, Pierre Carlet de Chamblain de. Théâtre choisi. Paris, 1883.

40535.27.3 Marivaux, Pierre Carlet de Chamblain de. Théâtre. Paris, 1881. 2v.

40535.27.5 Marivaux, Pierre Carlet de Chamblain de. Théâtre choisi. Paris, n.d.

40535.27.6 Marivaux, Pierre Carlet de Chamblain de. Théâtre. Paris, 191-? 2v.

40535.25.9 - .27 Individual authors, etc. - 1715-1799 - Drama - Marivaux - Complete and Selected works - cont.

40535.27.7 Marivaux, Pierre Carlet de Chamblain de. Théâtre. Paris, 1916-17. 2v.

40535.27.10 Marivaux, Pierre Carlet de Chamblain de. Théâtre. Paris, 1935. 2v.

40535.27.15 Marivaux, Pierre Carlet de Chamblain de. Les chefs-d'oeuvre de Marivaux. Rio de Janeiro, 1945.

40535.27.20 Marivaux, Pierre Carlet de Chamblain de. Théâtre complet. v.1-2. Paris, 1946.

40535.27.25 Marivaux, Pierre Carlet de Chamblain de. Théâtre complet. Paris, 1949.

40535.27.30 Marivaux, Pierre Carlet de Chamblain de. Théâtre choisi. Firenze, 1959-60. 2v.

40535.27.33 Marivaux, Pierre Carlet de Chamblain de. Théâtre. Paris, 1961-62. 4v.

40535.27.35 Marivaux, Pierre Carlet de Chamblain de. Théâtre complet. Paris, 1968. 2v.

40535.27.50 Marivaux, Pierre Carlet de Chamblain de. Marivaux narratore e moralista. Napoli, 1958.

40535.27.55 Marivaux, Pierre Carlet de Chamblain de. Marivaux, par lui-même. Paris, 1954.

40535.28 - .30 Individual authors, etc. - 1715-1799 - Drama - Marivaux - Individual works

Htn 40535.28* Marivaux, Pierre Carlet de Chamblain de. Le petit maître corrigé. Paris, 1739.

40535.28.3 Marivaux, Pierre Carlet de Chamblain de. Le petit-maître corrigé. Genève, 1955.

40535.28.5 Marivaux, Pierre Carlet de Chamblain de. La surprise de l'amour français; comédie. Paris, 1785.

Htn 40535.29* Marivaux, Pierre Carlet de Chamblain de. Les fausses confidences; comédie. Paris, n.d.

40535.29.2 Marivaux, Pierre Carlet de Chamblain de. Les fausses confidences; comédie. London, 192-?

40535.29.4 Marivaux, Pierre Carlet de Chamblain de. Les fausses confidences; comédie. L'épreuve; comédie. Paris, 1932?

Htn 40535.29.7* Marivaux, Pierre Carlet de Chamblain de. Le jeu de l'amour. Paris, 1919?

40535.29.9 Marivaux, Pierre Carlet de Chamblain de. Le paysan parvenu. La Haye, 1779.

40535.29.10 Marivaux, Pierre Carlet de Chamblain de. Le paysan parvenu. v.1-8. Paris, 1756. 4v.

40535.29.12 Marivaux, Pierre Carlet de Chamblain de. Le paysan parvenu. Paris, 1959.

40535.29.14 Marivaux, Pierre Carlet de Chamblain de. Udachlivyi krest'ianin, ili mennary 6-na. Moskva, 1970.

40535.29.15 Marivaux, Pierre Carlet de Chamblain de. Le spectateur français. Paris, 1921.

40535.29.17 Marivaux, Pierre Carlet de Chamblain de. La provinciale. Genève, 1922.

40535.29.19 Marivaux, Pierre Carlet de Chamblain de. La fause suivante. Paris, 1762.

40535.29.30 Marivaux, Pierre Carlet de Chamblain de. The life of Marianne. London, 1736.

40535.29.35 Marivaux, Pierre Carlet de Chamblain de. The virtuous orphan. Carbondale, 1965.

40535.29.40 Marivaux, Pierre Carlet de Chamblain de. Le Télémaque travesti. Genève, 1956.

40535.29.45 Marivaux, Pierre Carlet de Chamblain de. L'Iliade en vers burlesques. Paris, 1765.

40535.30 Marivaux, Pierre Carlet de Chamblain de. La vie de Marianne. Paris, n.d. 2v.

40535.30.5 Pamphlet box. Marivaux, Pierre Carlet de Chamblain de.

40535.30.15 Marivaux, Pierre Carlet de Chamblain de. La vie de Marianne. London, 1778. 4v.

40535.30.35 Marivaux, Pierre Carlet de Chamblain de. La vie de Marianne. Paris, 1947.

40535.30.40 Marivaux, Pierre Carlet de Chamblain de. La vie de Marianne. Paris, 1957.

40535.30.45 Marivaux, Pierre Carlet de Chamblain de. Pharsamond. London, 1750. 2v.

40535.30.50 Marivaux, Pierre Carlet de Chamblain de. Le legs. Paris, 1788.

40535.30.55 Marivaux, Pierre Carlet de Chamblain de. Romans. Paris, 1949.

40535.30.70 Desvignes-Parent, Lucette. Marivaux et l'Angleteer. Paris, 1970.

40535.30.76 Marivaux, Pierre Carlet de Chamblain de. Le cabinet du philosophe. Genève, 1970.

40535.31 - .32 Individual authors, etc. - 1715-1799 - Drama - Marivaux - Biography and criticism

40535.31 Larroumet, Gustave. Marivaux, sa vie et ses oeuvres. Paris, 1882.

40535.31.5 Gossot, Emile. Marivaux moraliste. Paris, 1881.

40535.31.9 Printzen, W. Marivaux. Sein Leben, sein Werke. Münster, 1885.

X Cg 40535.31.10 Larroumet, Gustave. Marivaux. Paris, 1894.

40535.31.15 Bonaccorso, Giovanni. Gli anni difficili di Marivaux. Messina, 1964.

40535.31.20 Brady, Valentini Papadopoulow. Love in the theatre of Marivaux; a study of the factors influencing its birth, development, and expression. Genève, 1970.

40535.31.25 Muehlemann, Suzanne. Ombres et lumières dans l'oeuvre de Pierre Carlet de Chamblain de Marivaux. Berne, 1970.

40535.31.30 Meister, Anna. Zur Entwicklung Marivaux. Diss. Bern, 1955.

40535.31.35 Meyer, Marlyse M. La convention dans le théâtre d'amour de Marivaux. São Paulo, 1961.

40535.31.40 Ratermanis, J.B. Étude sur le comique dans le théâtre de Marivaux. Genève, 1961.

40535.31.45 Schaad, Harold. Le thème de l'être et du paraître dans l'oeuvre de Marivaux. Zürich, 1969.

40535.31.50 Friedrichs, Friedhelm Alfred. Untersuchungen zur Handlungs- und Vorgangsmotivik im Werk Marivaux. Inaug. Diss. Heidelberg? 1965.

40535.32A Fleury, Jean. Marivaux et le Marivaudage. Paris, 1881.

40535.32B Fleury, Jean. Marivaux et le Marivaudage. Paris, 1881.

40535.32.5A Deschampe, Gaston. Marivaux. Paris, 1897.

40535.32.5B Deschampe, Gaston. Marivaux. Paris, 1897.

40535.32.9 Golubev, Viktor. Marivaux' Lustspiele in deutschen Übersetzungen des 18. Jahrhunderts. Heidelberg, 1904.

40535.32.12 Meyer, E. Marivaux. Paris, 1929.

40535.32.15 Holzbecher, Karl. Denkart und Denkform von Pierre de Marivaux. Inaug. Diss. Berlin, 1936.

40535.32.20 Michaut, G. Marivaux; Jeu de l'amour et du hasard. Paris, 1939.

Classified Listing

40535.31 - .32 Individual authors, etc. - 1715-1799 - Drama - Marivaux - Biography and criticism - cont.

40535.32.25 Jamieson, Ruth K. Marivaux. Morningside Hts., N.Y., 1941.
40535.32.30 Roy, Claude. Lire Marivaux. Neuchâtel, 1947.
40535.32.32 Arland, M. Marivaux. 4. éd. Paris, 1950.
40535.32.35 Deloffre, Frédéric. Une préciosité nouvelle. Paris, 1955.
40535.32.36 Deloffre, Frédéric. Une préciosité nouvelle, Marivaux et le Marivaudage. Thèse. Paris, 1955.
40535.32.38 Deloffre, Frédéric. Marivaux et le Marivaudage. 2. éd. Paris, 1971.
40535.32.40 McKee, K.N. The theater of Marivaux. N.Y., 1958.
40535.32.45 Durry, Marie J. A propos de Marivaux. Paris, 1960.
40535.32.50 Matucci, M. L'opera narrativa di Marivaux. Napoli, 1962.
40535.32.55 Luethi, K. Les femmes dans l'oeuvre de Marivaux. Bienne, 1943.
40535.32.60 Greene, Edward J. Marivaux. Toronto, 1965.
40535.32.65 Rigault, Claude. Les domestiques dans le théâtre de Marivaux. Sherbrooke, 1968.

40535.33 - .34 Individual authors, etc. - 1715-1799 - Drama - La Motte - Writings

40535.33.5 La Motte, Antoine Houdar de. Oeuvres. v.1-10. Paris, 1754. 11v.
40535.34.5 La Motte, Antoine Houdar de. Fables nouvelles. Paris, 1719.
40535.34.7 La Motte, Antoine Houdar de. Fables nouvelles. 3. éd. Paris, 1719.
Htn 40535.34.15* La Motte, Antoine Houdar de. One hundred new court fables. London, 1721.
40535.34.50 La Motte, Antoine Houdar de. Odes. 5. éd. Amsterdam, 1719. 3v.

40535.35 Individual authors, etc. - 1715-1799 - Drama - La Motte - Works about

NEDL 40535.35 Dupont, Paul. Houdar de La Motte. Paris, 1898.
40535.35.5 Dost, G. Houdar de La Motte...Theoretiker. Weida, 1909.

40535.36 - .99 Individual authors, etc. - 1715-1799 - Drama - Miscellany, M

40535.40 Mayeur de Saint Paul, François Marie. Jeanne Hachette, ou Le siège de Beauvais. Paris, 1784.
40535.45 Oláh, Liliane. Une grande dame, auteur dramatique et poète au XVIIIe siècle, Madame de Montesson. Paris, 1928.
40535.45.1 Oláh, Liliane. Une grande dame, auteur dramatique et poète au XVIIIe siècle, Madame de Montesson. Thèse. Paris, 1928.
40535.50.3 Mignan. L'enrôlement supposé. Paris, 1797.
40535.60.9 Milcent, Jean B.G.M. de. Lord Davenant. Valencia, 1830.
40535.60.10 Milcent, Jean B.G.M. de. Hécube; tragédie-lyrique en quatre actes. Paris, 1800.
40535.65 Monvel, Jacques Marie Boutet de. Les victimes cloitrées. Bordeaux, 1792.
40535.65.2 Monvel, Jacques Marie Boutet de. Les victimes cloitrées. Paris, 1803.
40535.65.3 Monvel, Jacques Marie Boutet de. De slacht-offers van kloosterdwang. Amsterdam, 1796.
40535.65.5 Monvel, Jacques Marie Boutet de. Junius. Paris, 1797.
40535.68 Morel. L'intérieur d'un comité révolutionnaire. Paris, 1799-1800.
40535.72 Guyot de Merville, M. Les mascarades amoureuses. Amsterdam, 1737.
40535.73 Desaudras. Minuit, comédie en un acte. Bordeaux, 1798.
40535.74 Du Berry. Les rivaux indiscrets. La Haye, 1738.
40535.80 Orvigny. On fait ce qu'on peut, et non pas ce qu'on veut. Toulouse, 1793.

40536.1 - .10 Individual authors, etc. - 1715-1799 - Drama - Miscellany, L-O

40536.2 Larnac, François. Thémistocle. Paris, 1798.
40536.2.100 Laya, Jean L. Les dangers de l'opinion. Paris, 1790.
40536.2.105 Laya, Jean L. Jean Calas. Paris, 1791.
40536.2.110 Laya, Jean L. L'ami des loix. Paris, 1793.
40536.2.112 Laya, Jean L. L'ami des loix. Paris, 1793.
40536.2.115 Laya, Jean L. L'ami des loix. Paris, 1793.
40536.2.118 Laya, Jean L. L'ami des loix. Paris, 1794?
40536.3 Le Blanc, J.B. Aben-said, empereur des Mogols. 2. éd. Paris, 1743.
40536.4 Le Blanc, J.B. Manco-Capac, premier ynca du Pérou. Paris, 1782.
40536.4.40 Le Blanc, J.B. Un voyageur-philosophe au XVIIIe siècle; l'abbé Jean-Bernard Le Blanc. Cambridge, 1941.
40536.4.50 Mühlhofer, L. Abbé Jean Bernard Le Blanc, seine Leben und Werke. Inaug. Diss. Würzburg, 1936.
40536.4.75 Lebeau de Schosne, A.T.V. L'assemblée. Paris? 179-.
40536.5 Leroy, Onésime. L'irresolu. Paris, 1849.
40536.7 La Marteliere, J.H.F. Robert chef de brigands. Paris, 1793.
40536.7.5 La Marteliere, J.H.F. Le tribunal redoutable ou La suite de Robert chef de brigands. Paris, 1793.
40536.7.10 La Marteliere, J.H.F. Les trois espiègles. Paris, 1798.
40536.7.15 La Marteliere, J.H.F. Le testament, ou Les mysteres d'Udolphe. Paris, 1798.
40536.7.30 Doberenz, Heinrich. La Marteliere und seine Bearbeitung Schillerscher Dramen auf den Theater der französischen Revolution. Löbau, 1883.
40536.7.150 Mathelin, Nicolas B. Marat dans le soutterrain des Cordeliers. Paris, 1794.
40536.10 Laujon, Pierre. Silvie. Opera en trois actes. Stockholm, 1774.
40536.10.5 Laujon, Pierre. Oeuvres choisies. Paris, 1811. 4v.
40536.10.9 La Porte, J. de. L'antiquaire; comédie en trois actes (1751). Paris, 1870.
Htn 40536.10.19* Noverre, J.G. Historical account of Adela of Ponthieu. London, 1782.
40536.10.30 Laugier, Marie. Les épreuves du républicain. Paris, 1794.
40536.10.50 Laus DeBoissy, L. de. La tete sans cervelle. Paris, 1794.
40536.10.100 Lebrun-Tossa, J.A. Arabelle et vascos. Paris, 1795.
40536.10.103 Lebrun-Tossa, J.A. La folie de Georges. Paris, 1793.
40536.10.200 Lavallé, J. Manlius Torquatus. Paris, 1794.
40536.10.250 Léger, F.P.A. La gageure inutile. Paris, 1793.
40536.10.255 Léger, F.P.A. Le dédit mal gardé. Paris, 1793.
40536.10.260 Léger, F.P.A. Georges et gros-Jean. Paris, 1793.
40536.10.265 Léger, F.P.A. La papesse Jeanne. Paris, 1793.
40536.10.267 Léger, F.P.A. Il faut un état. Paris, 1799.
40536.10.270 Léger, F.P.A. Il faut un état. Paris, 1799.
40536.10.273 Léger, F.P.A. La journée de Saint-Cloud. Paris, 1800.
40536.10.290 Barts, E. Gabriel Jean-Baptiste Legouvé, ein vergessener Dichter der Revolutionszeit. Berlin, 1939.

40536.1 - .10 Individual authors, etc. - 1715-1799 - Drama - Miscellany, L-O - cont.

40536.10.300 Legouvé, Gabriel. La mort de Henri quatre, roi de France. Paris, 1806.
40536.10.304 Legouvé, Gabriel. Epicharis et Néron. Paris, 1800.
40536.10.305 Legouvé, Gabriel. Epicharis et Neron. Paris, 1794.
40536.10.310 Legouvé, Gabriel. La mort d'Abel. Paris, 1793.
40536.10.315 Legouvé, Gabriel. Étéocle. Paris, 1800.
40536.10.320 Legouvé, Gabriel. Quintus Fabius. Paris, 1796.
40536.10.500 Lessieur. Les déguisemens villageois. Paris, 1797.
40536.10.600 Ligier, F. Grécourt, ou La dinée de la diligence. Paris, 1800.
40536.10.800 Lourdet de Santerre, J.B. Ziméo. Paris, 1800.
40536.10.1100 Mazoïer, F. Thesée. Paris, 1801.

40536.11 - .12 Individual authors, etc. - 1715-1799 - Drama - Miscellany, P

40536.11 Pain, M.J. L'appartement à louer. Paris, 1799.
40536.11.30 Patissier de la Foretille. La culte du vrai Dieu rétable. Berne, 1798.
40536.11.50 Patrat, Joseph. L'orpheline. Paris, 1796.
40536.11.60 Patrat, Joseph. L'heureuse erreur. Paris, 1817.

40536.13 Individual authors, etc. - 1715-1799 - Drama - Palissot - Works about

40536.13 Delfarge, D. La vie et l'oeuvre de Palissot. Paris, 1912.

40536.14 - .17 Individual authors, etc. - 1715-1799 - Drama - Palissot - Writings

40536.14 Palissot de Montenoy, Charles. Oeuvres. Paris, 1788. 4v.
40536.14.5 Palissot de Montenoy, Charles. Oeuvres complètes. London, 1779. 7v.
40536.15 Palissot de Montenoy, Charles. L'écueil des moeurs, comédie. Paris, 1782.
40536.16 Palissot de Montenoy, Charles. La dunciade. Chelsea, 1764.
40536.17 Palissot de Montenoy, Charles. La dunciade. v.1-2. Londres, 1771.
40536.17.80 Palissot de Montenoy, Charles. Mémoires pour servir à l'histoire de notre littérature. Paris, 1803. 2v.

40536.18 - .19 Individual authors, etc. - 1715-1799 - Drama - Miscellany, P-R

40536.18 Pannard, Charles François. Théâtre et oeuvres diverses. Paris, 1763. 4v.
40536.18.15 Junge, Ernest. Charles François Panard. Leipzig, 1911.
40536.18.50 Patrat, Joseph. L'anglais. Paris, 1919.
40536.18.100 Pelletier-Volméranges, B. Le mariage du Capucin. Paris, 1799.
40536.18.105A Pelletier-Volméranges, B. Le mariage du Capucin. Marseille, 1799.
40536.18.105B Pelletier-Volméranges, B. Le mariage du Capucin. Marseille, 1799.
40536.19 Perrin, J.B. Pièces dramatiques. Lons-le-Saunier, 1842.
40536.19.50 Pessey, H. Ortalbano. Paris, 1802.
40536.19.75 Petitot, C.B. Géta. Paris, 1797.
40536.19.76 Petitot, C.B. Laurent de Médicis. Paris, 1799.
40536.19.100 Piis, Augustin. La nourrice républicaine. Paris, 1794.
40536.19.105 Piis, Augustin. La saint Deniche, ou La saint Nicolas d'été. Paris, 1793.
40536.19.200 Pillet, Fabien. Wenzel. Paris, 1794.
40536.19.800 Radet, Jean B. La soirée orageuse. Paris, 1791.
40536.19.805 Radet, Jean B. Arlequin afficheur. 2. éd. Paris, 1792.
40536.19.810 Radet, Jean B. Encore un curé, fait historique et patriotique. Paris, 1793-94.
40536.19.815 Radet, Jean B. Le faucon. Paris, 1794.
40536.19.820 Radet, Jean B. Le noble roturier. Paris, 1795.
40536.19.825 Radet, Jean B. Pauline. Paris, 1797.
40536.19.830 Radet, Jean B. Pauline. Paris, 1797.
40536.19.835 Radet, Jean B. Honorine, ou La femme difficile a vivre. Paris, 1797.
40536.19.900 Raffard-Brienne, Jean S. Le retour du père Gérard a sa ferme. Lille, 1792.
40536.19.2000 Ravrio, A.A. Arlequin journaliste. Paris, 1797.
40536.19.2500 Révéroni St. Cyr, J.A. Le délire. Paris, 1800.
40536.19.2505 Révéroni St. Cyr, J.A. Le vaisseau amiral. Paris, 1805.
40536.19.3000 Rézicourt. Les vrais sans-culottes. Avignon, 1795.
40536.19.3002 Rézicourt. Les vrais sans-culottes. Paris, 1793.

40536.20 - .20.149 Individual authors, etc. - 1715-1799 - Drama - Piron

40536.20 Piron, Alexis. Oeuvres complettes. Paris, 1776. 7v.
40536.20.07 Piron, Alexis. Oeuvres choisis de Piron. Genève, 1777. 2v.
40536.20.1 Piron, Alexis. Oeuvres choisies. Paris, 1810. 2v.
40536.20.2 Piron, Alexis. Oeuvres choisies. Paris, 1817.
40536.20.3 Piron, Alexis. Oeuvres choisies. Paris, 1869.
40536.20.4 Piron, Alexis. Gustave. Paris, 1733.
40536.20.5 Piron, Alexis. La métromanie. Paris, 1853.
40536.20.5.8 Piron, Alexis. La métromanie. Cambridge, 1875.
40536.20.10 Piron, Alexis. Oeuvres inédites. Paris, 1859.
40536.20.11 Piron, Alexis. Complément de ses oeuvres inédites. Paris, 1866.
40536.20.20 Piron, Alexis. Voyage à Beaune. Dijon, 1847.
40536.20.25 Piron, Alexis. Voyage à Beaune. Paris, 1884.
40536.20.30 Piron, Alexis. Poésies libres et joyeuses. n.p., 1800?
40536.20.80 Hagen, Diedrich. Alexis Pirons Dramen. Inaug. Diss. Leipzig, 1904.
40536.20.85 Chaponnière, Paul. Piron; sa vie et son oeuvre. Genève, 1910.
40536.20.90 Pamphlet box. Piron.

40536.20.150 - .23 Individual authors, etc. - 1715-1799 - Drama - Miscellany, P-R

40536.20.150 Plancher-Valcour, P.A.L.P. Les petits montagnards. Paris, 1794.
40536.20.160 Plancher-Valcour, P.A.L.P. La république; poème. n.p., 1799.
40536.20.165 Plancher-Valcour, P.A.L.P. Le consistoire; poème. Paris, 1799.
40536.20.170 Plancher-Valcour, P.A.L.P. Eginard et Imnia. Paris, 1807.
40536.20.200 Planterre, Berthelemi Ambroise. La famille indigente, fait historique. Paris, 1796.
40536.20.500 Prevost-Montfort, P. L'esprit des prètres. Paris, 1794.
40536.20.505 Prevost-Montfort, P. Ténais et zeliska. Paris, 1798.
40536.20.600 Privat, Jean F. Demonville. Perpignan, 1798.
40536.21 Poisson, Philippe. Les ruses d'amour. La Haye, 1748.

40536.20.150 - .23 Individual authors, etc. - 1715-1799 - Drama - Miscellany, P-R - cont.

40536.21.5 Poinsinet de Sivry, M. Caton d'utique. Paris, 1789.
40536.21.7 Poinsinet de Sivry, M. La berlue. Paris, 1759.
40536.21.9 Renou, M. Térée et Philomele. Amsterdam, 1773.
40536.21.15 Martelly, Honoré François Richaud de. Les deux Figaro. La Haye, 1791.
40536.21.16 Martelly, Honoré François Richaud de. L'intrigant dupé par lui-même. Paris, 1803.
40536.21.18 Roger, Jean François. Oeuvres. Paris, 1835. 2v.
40536.21.19 Roger, Jean François. La dupe de soi-même. Paris, 1799.
40536.21.20 Roger, Jean François. Le valet de deux maîtres. 2. éd. Paris, 1801.
40536.21.22 Roger, Jean François. Caroline, ou Le tableau. Paris, 1800.
40536.21.27 Richard, Achille. Judas. Paris, 1914.
40536.21.30 Richard, Achille. Les suppliants. Paris, 1911.
40536.21.50 Rochon de Chabannes, Marc Antoine Jacques. Théâtre, suivi de quelques pièces fugitives. Paris, 1786. 2v.
40536.21.55 Rochon de Chabannes, Marc Antoine Jacques. La tribu. Strasbourg, 1781.
40536.21.75 Rolland. Arlequin Perruquier. Paris, 1795.
40536.22 Ronsin, Charles P. Théâtre. Paris, 1786.
40536.22.5 Ronsin, Charles P. Arétaphile. Toulouse, 1793.
40536.22.8 Rosoy, B.F. de. Le réduction de Paris. Paris, 1778.
40536.22.9 Rosoy, B.F. de. Richard III. Paris, 1782.
40536.22.10 Ronsin, Charles P. La ligne des fanatiques et des tyrans. Paris, 1791.
40536.22.25 Randon de Malboissière, G.F. Laurette de Malboissière. Lettres d'une jeune fille au temps de Louis XV, 1761-1766. Paris, 1866.
40536.22.29 Randon de Malboissière, G.F. Lettres de Geneviève de Malboissière à Adélaïde Méliand, 1761-1766. Thèse. Paris, 1924.
40536.22.30 Randon de Malboissière, G.F. Une jeune fille au XVIIIe siècle. Lettres...à Adélaïde Méliand, 1761-1766. Paris, 1925.
40536.22.180A Palinger, E.H. Pierre Charles Roy, playwriter. N.Y., 1930.
40536.22.180B Palinger, E.H. Pierre Charles Roy, playwriter. N.Y., 1930.
40536.23 Laservière, Joseph de. Un professeour d'ancien régime le Père Charles Porée (1676-1741). Paris, 1899.

40536.24 Individual authors, etc. - 1715-1799 - Drama - Ramond

40536.24.5 Ramond de Carbonnierès, L.F.E. La guerre d'Alsace pendant le grand schisme d'occident. Basle, 1780.
40536.24.10 Girdlestone, Cuthbert Morton. Louis François Ramond, 1755-1827. Paris, 1968.
40536.24.15 Reboul, Jacques. Un grand précurseur des romantiques, Ramond, 1755-1827. Nice, 1910.
40536.24.20 Orlando, Francesco. L'opera di Louis Ramond. Milano, 1960.
40536.24.25 Lourdes. Musée Pyrénéen. Exposition L.F.E. Ramond, 1755-1827, Lourdes, 1953. Pau, 1953.
40536.24.30 Lourdes. Musée Pyrénéen. Bibliothèque. Catalogue des ouvrages constituant la bibliothèque de Louis-François-Elisabeth Ramond, 1755-1827. Lourdes, 1968.
40536.24.75 Chevalier, A. Rulhière, Jean-Jacques Rousseau et la comédie de caractere de 1770 à 1778. Thèse. Paris, 1939.

40536.25 - .27 Individual authors, etc. - 1715-1799 - Drama - Miscellany, S

40536.25 Salles, Jean Baptiste. Charlotte Corday. Paris, 1864.
40536.25.75 Saint Firmin. La jeune esclave. Paris, 1793.
40536.26 Saint Romain. Louis XVI. En Allemagne, 1793.
40536.27 Saint-Marc, J.P.A. Oeuvres. Paris, 1781. 3v.
40536.27.3 Sanchaman, J.J. Les décemvirs. Paris, 1795.
40536.27.5 Saurin, Bernard J. L'orpheline lé guée. Paris, 1765. 3 pam.
40536.27.7 Saurin, Bernard J. Spartacus; tragédie. Paris, 1801.
40536.27.9 Mühle, M. B.J. Saurin. Sein Leben und seine Werke. Inaug. Diss. Dresden, 1913.
40536.27.15 Saurin, Bernard J. Spartacus. Paris, 1792.
40536.27.35 Saurin, Bernard J. Mirza and Fatima. London, 1954.
40536.27.60 Saulnier, G. Le siége de Thionville, drame lyrique en deux actes. Paris, 1793?
40536.27.150 La Noue, Jean Sauvé de. Oeuvres de théatre de M. de la Noue. Paris, 1765.

40536.28 - .31 Individual authors, etc. - 1715-1799 - Drama - Sedaine - Writings

40536.28 Sedaine, Michel Jean. Recueil de poesies. 2. éd. London, 1760.
40536.28.10 Sedaine, Michel Jean. Oeuvres choisies. Paris, 1813. 3v.
40536.28.21 Sedaine, Michel Jean. Théâtre. Genève, 1970.
40536.29 Sedaine, Michel Jean. Le deserteur. Avignon, 1791.
40536.29.3 Sedaine, Michel Jean. Le deserteur. 2. éd. Paris, 1770.
40536.29.5 Sedaine, Michel Jean. Le diable à quatre. La Haye, 1760.
40536.30 Sedaine, Michel Jean. Aucassin et Nicolette. Paris, 1782.
40536.30.5 Sedaine, Michel Jean. Felix, ou L'enfant trouvé. Paris, 1777.
40536.30.6 Sedaine, Michel Jean. A key to the lock. London, 1788.
40536.30.7 Sedaine, Michel Jean. La gageure imprévue; comedie. Paris, 1809.
40536.31A Sedaine, Michel Jean. Guillaume Tell drame. Paris, n.d.
40536.31B Sedaine, Michel Jean. Guillaume Tell drame. Paris, n.d.
40536.31.5 Sedaine, Michel Jean. L'huitre et les plaideurs. Paris, 1767.
40536.31.7 Sedaine, Michel Jean. Le philosophe sans le scavoir. N.Y., 1914.
40536.31.9 Sedaine, Michel Jean. L'anneau perdu et retrouvé. Paris, 1769.
40536.31.12 Sedaine, Michel Jean. Guillame Tell. Paris, 1794.

40536.32 - .33.8 Individual authors, etc. - 1715-1799 - Drama - Sedaine - Works about

40536.32 Günther, L. L'oeuvre dramatique de Sedaine. Thèse. Paris, 1908.
40536.32.5 Arnoldson, Louise Parkinson. Sedaine et les musiciens de son temps. Thèse. Paris, 1934.
40536.33 Rey, A. La vieillesse de Sedaine. Paris, 1906.
40536.33.5 Guieysse-Frère, E. Sedaine, ses protecteurs et ses amis. Paris, n.d.
40536.33.7 Pipelet, C.D.T. Eloge historique de M.J. Sédaine. n.p., 1797.

40536.33.9 - .99 Individual authors, etc. - 1715-1799 - Drama - Miscellany, S-Z

40536.33.9 Pujoulx, Jean B. L'anti-célibataire. Paris, 1794.
40536.33.10 Pujoulx, Jean B. L'école des parvenus. Paris, 1797?
40536.33.15 Pujoulx, Jean B. Les montagnards. Paris, 1793-94.
40536.33.50 Sequier, A.L.M. Le Marechal Ferrant de la ville d'Anvers. Paris, 1799.
40536.33.75 Souriguere de St. Marc, J.M. Cécile. Paris, 1796.
40536.33.100 Tannevot, Alex. Adam et Eve. Amsterdam, 1743.
40536.34 Tronchin, François. Le Conseiller François Tronchin et ses amis. (1704-1798). Paris, 1895.
40536.34.40 Le Vendemie; drama giocoso in tre atti. Paris, 1791.
Htn 40536.34.50* Vieillard De Boismartin, A. Theraméne. Saint Lo, 1797.
Htn 40536.34.55* Vieillard De Boismartin, A. Blanchard. Saint Lo, 1793.
40536.34.75 Vigée, L.J.B.E. La matinée d'une jolie femme, comédie en un acte. n.p., 1792.
40536.35 Villemain d'Abancourt, J.F. Proverbes dramatiques. Berlin, 1781.
40536.35.5 Villemain d'Abancourt, J.F. La bienfaisance de Voltaire. Paris, 1791.
40536.37 Villeneuve, (Mdme.). Les crimes de la noblesse. Paris, 1794-95.
40536.39 Viller. Cange. Paris, 1793.
40536.42 Serieys, Antoine. La mort de Robespierre. Paris, 1800-01.
40536.42.1 Serieys, Antoine. La mort de Robespierre. Paris, 1801.
40536.44 Saint-Chamond, Claire Marie. Les amants sans le sçavoir. Paris, 1771.

40537 Individual authors, etc. - 1715-1799 - Drama - Chénier, M.J.

40537.6 Chénier, Marie Joseph. Oeuvres. Paris, 1826. 5v.
40537.6.5 Chénier, Marie Joseph. Théâtre de M.J. de Chénier. Paris, 1818. 3v.
40537.7 Chénier, Marie Joseph. Oeuvres posthumes. Paris, 1824. 3v.
40537.8 Chénier, Marie Joseph. Oeuvres diverses et inédites. Bruxelles, 1816.
40537.10 Chénier, Marie Joseph. Les miracles. 4. éd. Paris, 1802.
40537.11 Chénier, Marie Joseph. Timoléon. Paris, 1795.
40537.11.5 Chénier, Marie Joseph. Jean Calas. Paris, 1793.
40537.11.9 Chénier, Marie Joseph. Cains Gracchus. Paris, 1793.
40537.11.12 Chénier, Marie Joseph. Charles IX ou L'école des rois. Beaucaire, 1790.
40537.11.25 Pamphlet vol. Chénier, Marie Joseph. Épitre à Voltaire. 7 pam.
40537.11.27 Chénier, Marie Joseph. Épitre à Voltaire. Paris, 1806.
40537.11.30 Pamphlet vol. Chénier, Marie Joseph. Les Nouveaux Saints. 10 pam.
40537.11.35 Chénier, Marie Joseph. Fénelon...tragédie. Paris, 1793.
40537.11.39 Chénier, Marie Joseph. Fénelon...tragédie. Paris, 1802.
40537.11.41 Chénier, Marie Joseph. Fénelon...tragédie. 4. éd. Paris, 1802.
40537.12 Pamphlet vol. Chénier, Marie Joseph. Pie VI et Louis XVIII. 4 pam.
40537.12.5 Dialogue entre l'ex-pape Pie VI et le roi très-chrétien, Louis XVIII. n.p., 1799?
40537.13 Sieby, A. Etude sur le théâtre de Marie Joseph Chénier. Paris, 1901.
40537.14 Peters, Ernst. Marie Joseph Chénier als Kritiker. Leipzig, 1911.
40537.15A Daunou, Pierre C.F. Notice sur La vie et les ouvrages de M.J. de Chénier. Paris, 1811.
40537.15B Daunou, Pierre C.F. Notice sur La vie et les ouvrages de M.J. de Chénier. Paris, 1811.
40537.16 Roederer, A.L. Lettre à Adrien Lézay sur Chénier. Paris, n.d.
40537.17 Pyat, Félix. Marie Joseph Chénier et le prince des critiques. Paris, 1844.
40537.37 Les confidences aux états généraux. n.p., 1790.
40537.38 L'attentat de Versailles. Genève, 1790.
40537.39 La chasse a la grand bête. Mayence, 1789.
40537.40 Charlotte Corday. Caen, 1797.
40537.41 La journée des dupes. n.p., 1790.
40537.42 Le grand denouement de la constitution. Bruxelles, 1791.
40537.43 Naissance de très-haute, très-puissante et très-désirée madame constitution. n.p., 1790.
40537.44 Le Vicomte de Barjolean. n.p., 179-?
40537.45 Tactique des cannibales. Paris, 1795.
40537.46 Théroigne et populus. London, 1790.
40537.47 Les quatres préjugés du ministre. n.p., 1790.
40537.48 Le lever de Bâville. Rome, 1788.
40537.49 Le triomphe du tiers-état. n.p., 1789.
40537.52 La foi couronée...poëme en cinq chants. Londres, 1799.
40537.53 Le Vatican...tragédie. Paris, 1798.
40537.54 Fouéré-Macé, M.E. Époque révolutionnaire; curiosités historiques. Rennes, 1894.
40537.55 The force of education. London, 1751.
40537.58 Le mariage de la princesse du L'anturelu. n.p., n.d.
40537.60 La disolation des procureurs. Paris, 1789.
40537.65 Harlequin, vivandier à l'armée françois au Lord de la mer; comédie. London, 1757.
40537.67 Les moines. Rouen, 1880.
40537.70 Eloisa de Clairville. London, 1790. 2v.
40537.71 Academie galante contenant diverses histoires très curieuses. Amsterdam, 1732.
40537.72 Memoirs of a traveller now in retirement. London, 1806. 5v.

40538 Individual authors, etc. - 1715-1799 - Drama - Anonymous dramas

40538.5 La Blanchisseuse de Mousseaux. Paris, 1791.
40538.10 Chimère et réalité. Paris, 1803.
40538.15 La femme jalouse; comedie. Paris? 1727?
40538.20 Frédegonde et Brunehaut. Paris, 1795.
40538.25 Une matinée du Luxembourg. Paris, 179-.
40538.30 Les moeurs de Londres. Paris, 1807.

40539 Individual authors, etc. - 1715-1799 - Miscellaneous works

40539.5 Rosny, Joseph de. La réve d'un philosophe, ou Voici toute mon ambition! Rodez, 1800.
40539.10 Cellier, Léon. Fabre d'Olivet. Thèse. Paris, 1953.
40539.15 Potocki, Jan. Manuscript trouvé à Saragosse. Paris, 1958.
40539.15.5 Potocki, Jan. The Saragossa manuscript. 1st American ed. N.Y., 1960.
40539.15.10 Potocki, Jan. Die Handschrift von Saragossa. Frankfurt, 1961.
40539.15.13 Potocki, Jan. Rękopis znaleziony w Saragossie. Warszawa, 1950. 3v.
40539.15.14 Potocki, Jan. Rękopis znaleziony w Saragossie. Warszawa, 1956.

40539 Individual authors, etc. - 1715-1799 - Miscellaneous works - cont.

40539.15.15 Potocki, Jan. Rękopis znaleziony w Saragossie. Warszawa, 1965.
40539.15.20 Brückner, Alexander. Jana hr. Potockiego i zasługi naukowe. Warszawa, 1911.
40539.15.25 Kotwicz, Władysław. Jan hr. Potocki i jego podróz do Chin. Wilno, 1935.
40539.15.30 Potocki, Jan. Parady. Warszawa, 1966.
40539.15.35 Potocki, Jan. El manuscrito hallado en Zaragoza. Barcelona, 1968.
40539.15.40 Potocki, Jan. Rukopis', naidennaia v Saragose. Moskva, 1968.
40539.15.47 Potocki, Jan. Voyage en Turquia et en Egypte. 2. éd. Varsovie, 1889.
40539.15.80 Krakowski, E. Le comte Jean Potocki. Paris, 1963.
40539.20 Mercier, Barthelemy. Merceriana. Paris, 1893.
40539.22 Joubert de la Rue, J. Lettres d'un Sauvage Depaysé. Amsterdam, 1746. 2v.
40539.24 Pamphlet vol. Memoires pour servir à l'histoire de la callotte et 2 comedies. 3 pam.

40541 Individual authors, etc. - 1800-1849 - History - Roederer

40541.5 Roederer, Pierre L. Oeuvres. Paris, 1853-59. 8v.

40542.1 - .15 Individual authors, etc. - 1800-1849 - History - Ozanam - Writings

40542.5 Ozanam, Antoine P. La civilisation au cinquième siècle. Paris, 1862. 2v.
40542.6 Ozanam, Antoine P. Les germains avant le christianisme. n.p., 1861.
40542.6.5 Ozanam, Antoine P. Les germains avant le christianisme. Liège, 1850.
40542.7 Ozanam, Antoine P. La civilisation chrétienne. n.p., 1861.
40542.7.50 Ozanam, Antoine P. Les poètes franciscains en Italie au treizième siècle. Paris, 1852.
40542.9 Ozanam, Antoine P. Dante. n.p., 1859.
40542.10 Ozanam, Antoine P. Mélanges. n.p., 1859. 2v.
40542.11 Ozanam, Antoine P. Le purgatoire de Dante. n.p., 1862.
40542.13 Ozanam, Antoine F. Una peregrinación al país del Cid. Buenos Aires, 1950.
40542.14 Ozanam, Antoine F. Deux oeuvres de jeunesse de F. Ozanam. Lyon, 1913.
40542.15 Ozanam, Antoine F. Oeuvres choisies. Paris, 1859.

40542.16 - Individual authors, etc. - 1800-1849 - History - Ozanam - Works about

40542.16 Auge, Thomas E. Frederic Ozanam and his world. Milwaukee, 1966.
40542.17 Pativilca (pseud.). Federico Ozanam. Bilbao, 1958.
40542.18 Auer, Heinrich. Friedrich Ozanam, der Gründer des Vinzenz-Vereins. Freiburg, 1913.
40542.20 Girard, H. Un catholique romantique: F. Ozanam. Paris, 1930.
40542.23 Galopin, Eugène. Essai de bibliographie chronologique sur Antoine-Frédéric Ozanam. Paris, 1933.
40542.25 Chauveau, Pierre. Frédéric Ozanam. Montréal, 1887.
40542.28 Baudrillart, Alfred. Frédéric Ozanam. Paris, 1912.
40542.30 Goyau, Georges. Frédéric Ozanam. Paris, 1925.
40542.31 Mejecaze, F. Frédéric Ozanam et l'eglise catholique. Lyon, 1932.
40542.31.10 Mejecaze, F. Essai de synthèse des idées. Lyon, 1932.
40542.33 O'Meara, Kathleen. Frederic Ozanam, his life and works. 3. American ed. N.Y., 1883.
40542.33.5 O'Meara, Kathleen. Frederic Ozanam. N.Y., 190-?
40542.34 Schimberg, Albert P. The great friend: Frederick Ozanam. Milwaukee, 1946.
40542.35 Cassidy, J.F. Frederic Ozanam; a study in sanctity and scholarship. Dublin, 1943.
40542.36 Camus, L.Y. Frédéric Ozanam. Paris, 1953.
40542.37 Celier, Léonce. Frédéric Ozanam. Paris, 1956.
40542.37.5 Celier, Léonce. Federico Ozanam. 5. ed. Roma, 1958.
40542.40 Louvain. Université catholique. Foundation Jules Besucci. Frédéric Ozanam. Louvain, 1954.
40542.45 Romero Carranza, A. Ozanam e i suoi contemporanei. Firenze, 1956.

40543 Individual authors, etc. - 1800-1849 - History - Ségur - Complete works

40543.3 Ségur, Louis P. de. Oeuvres complètes. Paris, 1824-27. 34v.
40543.6 Ségur, Louis P. de. Mélanges. Paris, 1873.
40543.10 Segur, Alexandre Joseph Pierre. Les vieux fous. Paris, 1796.
40543.15 Segur, Alexandre Joseph Pierre. La portrait de Fielding. Paris, 1800.
40543.20 Segur, Alexandre Joseph Pierre. Le parti le plus gai. Paris, 1796.

40545 Individual authors, etc. - 1800-1849 - History - Miscellany, A-Z

40545.5 Bazin, M.A. Etudes d'histoire et de biographie. Paris, 1844.
40545.7 Custine, A. Lettres inédites au Marquis de la Grange. Paris, 1925.
40545.7.5 Custine, Astolphe. Aloys; ou, Le religieux du Mont Saint-Bernard. Paris, 1971.
40545.8 Genonde, Eugène de. Considérations sur les grecs et les turcs. Paris, 1821.
40545.10 Guizot, M. François. Discours académiques. Paris, 1862.
40545.13 Lauraguais, L.B. Lettres à Madame ***. Paris, 1802.
40545.14 Lemontey, P.E. Oeuvres. Paris, 1829. 5v.
40545.16 Bazin, Rigomer. Le lynx; coup-d'oeil et réflexions libres sur les écrits. Mans, 1817.
40545.19 Fauriel, C.C. Fauriel in Italy. Roma, 1962.
40545.20 Galley, J.B. Claude Fauriel. Saint-Etienne, 1909.
40545.20.10 Gubernatis, A. de. Il Manzoni ed il Fauriel. Roma, 1880.
40545.21 De Mohl, O. Correspondance de Fauriel et Mary Clarke. Paris, 1911.
40545.24 Simonde de Sismondi, Jean Charles Léonard. Fragments de son journal et correspondance. Genève, 1857.
40545.26.2 Touchard-Lafosse, Georges. Le lutin couleur de feu. 2. éd. Paris, 1821.
40545.28 Côte, Léon. Achille, allier, historien, conteur, imagier bourbonnais, 1807-1836. Thèse. Moulins, 1942.
Htn 40545.30.81* Contades, Gerard de. Armand Malitourne. Argentan, 1886.

40546.1 - .8 Individual authors, etc. - 1800-1849 - History - Courier - Writings

40546.5 Courier de Méré, Paul Louis. Oeuvres complètes. Bruxelles, 1833.
40546.5.5 Courier de Méré, Paul Louis. Oeuvres. Paris, 186-?
40546.5.10 Courier de Méré, Paul Louis. Oeuvres complètes. Paris, n.d.
40546.6 Courier de Méré, Paul Louis. Oeuvres. Paris, 1845.
40546.6.9 Courier de Méré, Paul Louis. Oeuvres. Paris, 1855.
40546.7 Courier de Méré, Paul Louis. Oeuvres. Paris, 1865.
40546.7.5 Courier de Méré, Paul Louis. Collection complète des pamphlets politiques. Bruxelles, 1826.
40546.7.10 Courier de Méré, Paul Louis. Pamphlets politiques choisis. Paris, 1961.
40546.7.15 Courier de Méré, Paul Louis. Pamphlets. Paris, 1966.
40546.8 Caussade, François de. Oeuvres de P.L. Courier. Paris, 1880.
40546.8.9 Courier de Méré, Paul Louis. Paul Louis Courier; a selection from the works. Manchester, 1920.
40546.8.61 Courier de Méré, Paul Louis. Lettres et pamphlets. Paris, 1917?

40546.9 - .10 Individual authors, etc. - 1800-1849 - History - Courier - Works about

40546.9 Gaschet, R. Paul Louis Courier et la restauration. Paris, 1913.
40546.9.10 Gaschet, R. Les aventures d'un écrivain, Paul Louis Courier. Paris, 1928.
40546.9.15 Axthelm, M.S. Paul Louis Courier. Inaug. Diss. Jena, 1937.
40546.9.20 Lelarge, André. Paul Louis Courier. Paris, 1925.
40546.9.25 Desternes, Louis. Paul Louis Courier et les Bourbons. Moulin, n.d.

40546.11 - .24 Individual authors, etc. - 1800-1849 - History - Toqueville - Writings

40546.11 Schemann, L. Alexis de Tocqueville. Stuttgart, 1911.
40546.12 Tocqueville, Alexis de. De la démocratie en Amérique. Paris, 1868. 3v.
40546.13 Tocqueville, Alexis de. L'ancien régime et la revolution. Paris, 1866.
40546.14 Tocqueville, Alexis de. Correspondance et oeuvres posthumes. Paris, 1866.
40546.15 Tocqueville, Alexis de. Correspondance. Paris, 1867.
40546.16 Tocqueville, Alexis de. Nouvelle correspondance. Paris, 1866.
40546.17 Tocqueville, Alexis de. Mélanges. Paris, 1865.
40546.18 Tocqueville, Alexis de. Études économiques. Paris, 1866.
40546.19A Tocqueville, Alexis de. Oeuvres et correspondance inédites. Paris, 1861. 2v.
40546.19B Tocqueville, Alexis de. Oeuvres et correspondance inédites. Paris, 1861. 2v.
40546.20 Tocqueville, Alexis de. Oeuvres complètes publiées. v.4, 7-8. Paris, 1866- 3v.
40546.20.10 Tocqueville, Alexis de. Oeuvres. Paris, 1951-53. 15v.
40546.20.15 Tocqueville, Alexis de. L'ancien régime et la révolution. Paris, 1960?
40546.21 Tocqueville, Alexis de. Correspondance...et A. de Gobinean, 1843-1859. Paris, 1909.
40546.22 Tocqueville, Alexis de. De la democratie en Amérique. 14. éd. Paris, 1864. 3v.
40546.24 Tocqueville, Alexis de. Recollections. London, 1948.
40546.24.5 Tocqueville, Alexis de. The European revolution and correspondence. Garden City, 1959.

40546.25 - Individual authors, etc. - 1800-1849 - History - Toqueville - Works about

40546.27 France. Centre National de la Recherche Scientifique. Alexis de Tocqueville. Paris, 1960.
40546.28 Brunius, Teddy. Alexis de Tocqueville. Uppsala, n.d.
40546.29A Drescher, S. Tocqueville and England. Cambridge, 1964.
40546.29B Drescher, S. Tocqueville and England. Cambridge, 1964.
40546.32 Zeitlin, Irving M. Liberty, equality and revolution in Alexis de Tocqueville. Boston, n.d.

40547 Individual authors, etc. - 1800-1849 - History - Michelet

40547.14 Michelet, Jules. Pages choisies. Paris, n.d.
40547.14.10 Michelet, Jules. Pages littéraires. Paris, 1936.
40547.14.15 Michelet, Jules. Michelet. Genève, 1946.
40547.14.17 Michelet, Jules. Pages choisies des grands écrivains. 9. éd. Paris, 1906.
40547.14.20 Michelet, Jules. Pages choisies. v.1-2. Paris, 1947.
40547.14.80 Kuhn, Hildegard. Michelets Landschaft in La Mer und La Montagne. Wertheim, n.d.
40547.16 Michelet, Jules. The sea. N.Y., 1861.

40551 Individual authors, etc. - 1800-1849 - Philosophy, etc. - Bonald

40551.3 Bonald, L.G.A. de. Essai analytique. Oevres I. Paris, 1817.
40551.4 Bonald, L.G.A. de. Législation primitive. Oevres II-IV. Paris, 1817. 3v.
40551.5 Bonald, L.G.A. de. Du divorce. Oevres V. Paris, 1818.
40551.6 Bonald, L.G.A. de. Pensées. Oevres VI-VII. Paris, 1817. 2v.
40551.7 Bonald, L.G.A. de. Recherches philosophiques. Oevres VIII-IX. Paris, 1818. 2v.
40551.8 Bonald, L.G.A. de. Mélanges littéraires. Oevres X-XI. Paris, 1819. 2v.
40551.9 Bonald, L.G.A. de. Démonstration philosophique. Oevres XII. Paris, 1830.
40551.12 Bonald, L.G.A. de. Essai analytique. Oevres I. Paris, 1817.
40551.13 Bonald, L.G.A. de. Législation primitive. Oevres II-IV. Paris, 1817. 3v.
40551.14 Bonald, L.G.A. de. Du divorce. Oevres V. Paris, 1818.
40551.15 Bonald, L.G.A. de. Pensées. Oevres VI-VII. Paris, 1817. 2v.
40551.16 Bonald, L.G.A. de. Recherches philosophiques. Oevres VIII-IX. Paris, 1826. 2v.
40551.17 Bonald, L.G.A. de. Mélanges littéraires. Oevres X-XI. Paris, 1819. 2v.
40551.18 Bonald, L.G.A. de. Démonstration philosophique. Oevres XII. Paris, 1840.
40551.19 Bonald, L.G.A. de. Théorie du pouvoir. Oevres XIII-XV. Paris, 1843. 3v.
Htn 40551.19.25* Bonald, L.G.A. de. Théorie du pouvoir politique et religieux. Constance, 1796. 3v.

40551 Individual authors, etc. - 1800-1849 - Philosophy, etc. - Bonald - cont.

40551.20 Moulinié, Henri. Lettres inédites du Vicomte de Bonald...à Madame Victor de Sèze. Thèse. Paris, 1915.
40551.21 Bonald, L.G.A. de. Oeuvres complètes. Paris, 1859. 3v.
40551.22 Bonald, L.G.A. de. En marge de la Sainte-Alliance, lettres de Bonald au Comte de Senfft. Paris, 1967.
40551.24 Des conséquences funestes des principes philosophiques de M. de Bonald et de M. l'abbé de la Mennais. Paris, 1825.
40551.24.5 Bonald, Henri. Notice sur le vicomte de Bonald. Paris, 1841.
40551.25.5 Moulinié, Henri. De Bonald. Thèse. Paris, 1915.
40551.26 Bourget, Paul. Bonald. Paris, 18- .
40551.27 Spaemann, Robert. Der Ursprung der Soziologie aus dem Geist der Restauration. München, 1959.
Htn 40551.30* Constant, B. Lettres à Madame Récamier 1807-1830. Paris, 1882.

40552 Individual authors, etc. - 1800-1849 - Philosophy, etc. - Miscellany, A-C

40552.2 Baudouin, Alexandre. The man of the world's dictionary. London, 1822.
40552.4 Beaulieu, Camille. Vie et travaux de Burgaud des Marets, philologue, bibliophile et poète saintongeais. La Rochelle, 1928.
40552.17 Castel, P. Esprit, Saillies et Singularités. Amsterdam, 1763.

40553.1 - .9 Individual authors, etc. - 1800-1849 - Philosophy, etc. - Constant de Rebecque - Writings

Htn 40553.3* Constant de Rebecque, Benjamin. Wallstein. Paris, 1809.
40553.3.5 Constant de Rebecque, Benjamin. Wallstein, tragédie en 5 actes et en vers. Paris, 1965.
40553.4 Constant de Rebecque, Benjamin. Adolphe. Paris, 1845.
40553.4.15 Constant de Rebecque, Benjamin. Adolphe. Paris, 1867.
40553.4.80 Constant de Rebecque, Benjamin. Benjamin Constant par lui-même. Paris, 1968.
40553.5 Constant de Rebecque, Benjamin. Adolphe. Paris, 1868.
40553.5.25 Constant de Rebecque, Benjamin. Adolphe. Paris, 191-?
40553.7 Constant de Rebecque, Benjamin. Adolphe. Paris, n.d.
40553.7.6 Constant de Rebecque, Benjamin. Adolphe. Manchester, 1941.
40553.7.10 Constant de Rebecque, Benjamin. Adolphe. Le cahier rouge. Paris, 1931.
40553.7.15 Constant de Rebecque, Benjamin. Adolphe; suivi de lettres choisies de Benjamin Constant. Paris, 1929.
40553.7.18A Constant de Rebecque, Benjamin. Le romantisme. Paris, 1957.
40553.7.18B Constant de Rebecque, Benjamin. Le romantisme. Paris, 1957.
40553.7.20 Constant de Rebecque, Benjamin. Adolfo. Bruxelles, 1930.
40553.7.25 Constant de Rebecque, Benjamin. Adolphe. Paris, 1946.
40553.7.27 Murry, J.M. The conquest of death. London, 1951.
40553.7.30 Constant de Rebecque, Benjamin. Cecile. Paris, 1951.
40553.7.30.2 Constant de Rebecque, Benjamin. Çecile. London, 1952.
40553.7.35 Constant de Rebecque, Benjamin. Ecrits et discours politiques. Paris, 1964. 2v.
40553.7.40 Congrès Benjamin Constant, Lausanne, 1967. Benjamin Constant. Paris, 1968.
40553.7.80 Bastid, Paul. Benjamin Constant et sa doctrine. Paris, 1966. 2v.
40553.8 Constant de Rebecque, Benjamin. Mélanges de littérature et de politique. Bruxelles, 1829.
40553.8.25 Constant de Rebecque, Benjamin. Les chevaliers. Paris, 1927.
40553.8.50 Constant de Rebecque, Benjamin. Cecile. Norfolk, 1953.
40553.9 Constant de Rebecque, Benjamin. Lettres. Paris, 1888.
40553.9.5 Constant de Rebecque, Benjamin. Lettres à Bernadotte. Genève, 1952.
40553.9.7 Constant de Rebecque, Benjamin. Lettres de Benjamin Constant à sa famille. Paris, 1931[1932]
40553.9.10 Constant de Rebecque, Benjamin. Choix de textes politiques. Utrecht, 1965.
40553.9.10 Constant de Rebecque, Benjamin. Lettres à un ami; Benjamin Constant et Madame de Staël. Neuchâtel, 1949.
40553.9.12 Constant de Rebecque, Benjamin. Correspondance de Benjamin Constant et d'Anna Lindsay. Paris, 1933.
40553.9.15 Constant de Rebecque, Benjamin. Lettres de Benjamin Constant à Madame Récamier, 1807-1830. Paris, 1882.
40553.9.45 Constant de Rebecque, Benjamin. Journal intime et lettres à sa famille et à ses amis. Paris, 1895.
40553.9.50 Constant de Rebecque, Benjamin. Journal intime, 1804-1816. Paris, 1928.
40553.9.55 Constant de Rebecque, Benjamin. Journal intime. 2. éd. Monaco, 1945.
40553.9.60 Constant de Rebecque, Benjamin. Journaux intimes. Paris, 1952.
40553.9.64.3 Constant de Rebecque, Benjamin. Adolphe. Paris, 1913.
40553.9.65 Constant de Rebecque, Benjamin. Adolphe. Paris, 1955.
40553.9.67 Constant de Rebecque, Benjamin. Adolphe and The red note-book. London, 1959.
40553.9.70 Constant de Rebecque, Benjamin. Benjamin et Rosalie de Constant. Paris, 1955.
40553.9.75 Constant de Rebecque, Benjamin. Oeuvres. Paris, 1957.
40553.9.80 Constant de Rebecque, Benjamin. Le cahier rouge. Paris, 1957.
40553.9.81 Holdheim, William W. Benjamin Constant. London, 1961.

40553.10 Individual authors, etc. - 1800-1849 - Philosophy, etc. - Constant de Rebecque - Works about

40553.10 Sauris, Georges de. Benjamin Constant et les idées libérales. Paris, 1904.
40553.10.4 Ullmann, Helene. Benjamin Constant und seine Beziehungen zum deutschen Geistesleben. Inaug. Diss. Marburg, 1915.
40553.10.5 Ullmann, Helene. Benjamin Constant und seine Beziehungen zum deutschen Geistesleben. Marburg, 1915.
40553.10.8 Dumont-Wilden, L. La vie de Benjamin Constant. 11. éd. Paris, 1930.
40553.10.10 Gougelot, Henri. L'idée de liberté. Thèse. Melun, 1942.
40553.10.12 Romieu, André. Benjamin Constant et l'esprit européen. Thèse. Paris, 1933.
40553.10.15 Luzi, Mario. Lo stile de Constant. Milano, 1962.
40553.10.20 Talma, Julie C. (Mme.). Lettres de Julie Talma à Benjamin Constant. Paris, 1933.
40553.10.22 Talma, Julie C. (Mme.). Erotisch schimmenspel. Amsterdam, 1962.
40553.10.25 Bach, W. Benjamin Constant und die Politik, 1767-1802. Inaug. Diss. Engelsdorf, 1936.

40553.10 Individual authors, etc. - 1800-1849 - Philosophy, etc. - Constant de Rebecque - Works about - cont.

40553.10.30 Luz León, José de la. Benjamin Constant o El donjuanismo intelectual. Habana, 1937.
40553.10.33 Deguise, Pierre. Benjamin Constant méconnu. Genève, 1966.
40553.10.35 Léon, Paul L. Benjamin Constant. Paris, 1930.
40553.10.40 Fabre-Luce, A. Benjamin Constant. Paris, 1939.
40553.10.45 Kerchove, Arnold de. Benjamin Constant. Bruxelles, 1941.
40553.10.46 Kerchove, Arnold de. Benjamin Constant. Paris, 1950.
40553.10.48 Levaillant, Maurice. Les amours de Benjamin Constant. Paris, 1958.
40553.10.49 Nicolson, H.G. Benjamin Constant. Garden City, 1949.
40553.10.50 Nicolson, H.G. Benjamin Constant. London, 1949.
40553.10.55 Hasselrot, Bengt. Nouveaux documents sur Benjamin Constant et Mme de Staël. Copenhague, 1952.
40553.10.60 Guillemin, Henri. Benjamin Constant muscadin, 1795-1799. Paris, 1958.
40553.10.65 Hogue, Helen H.S. Of changes in Benjamin Constant's books on religions. Genève, 1964.
40553.10.70 Tambour, Ernest. Benjamin Constant à Luzarches. Versailles, 1906.
40553.10.75 Baelen, Jean. Benjamin Constant et Napoléon. Paris, 1965.
40553.10.80 Lausanne. Bibliothèque cantonale et universitaire. Benjamin Constant, 1767-1830. Lausanne, 1967.
40553.10.85 Bibliothèque nationale. Benjamin Constant. Paris, 1967.
40553.10.90 Cahiers Benjamin Constant. Ser. 1, no. 4. Lausanne. 1967
40553.10.95 Gouhier, Henri. Benjamin Constant. Paris, 1967.
40553.10.100 Jasinski, Béatrice W. L'engagement de Benjamin Constant. Paris, 1971.
40553.10.105 Zampogna, Domenico. Benjamin Constant et Belle de Charrière. Messina, 1969.
40553.10.110 Oliver, Andrew. Benjamin Constant, écriture et conquète du moi. Paris, 1970.

40553.11 - .12 Individual authors, etc. - 1800-1849 - Philosophy, etc. - Cousin d'Avalon

40553.11 Cousin d'Avallon, Charles Yves Cousin. Le nouveau tambour du monde. Paris, 1801.
40553.12 Wallon, J. Cousin. Paris, 1859.

40553.15 - .29 Individual authors, etc. - 1800-1849 - Philosophy, etc. - Cousin, Victor - Folios [Discontinued]

40553.15 Cousin, Victor. Cours de l'histoire de la philosophie moderne. Paris, 1846. 5v.
40553.16 Cousin, Victor. Cours de l'histoire de la philosophie moderne. Paris, 1847. 3v.
40553.17 Cousin, Victor. Fragments philosophiques. Paris, 1847. 4v.
40553.18 Cousin, Victor. Littérature. Paris, 1849. 3v.
40553.19 Cousin, Victor. Instruction publique. Paris, 1850. 3v.
40553.20 Cousin, Victor. Discours politiques. Paris, 1851.
40553.21.5 Cousin, Victor. Fragments philosophiques. 5. éd. Paris, 1865-66. 5v.
40553.25 Cahiers Benjamin Constant. Ser. 1, no. 1. Lausanne. 1955

40554.1 - .15 Individual authors, etc. - 1800-1849 - Philosophy, etc. - Cousin, Victor - Writings

40554.8 Cousin, Victor. Fragments et souvenirs. Paris, 1857.
40554.11 Cousin, Victor. Fragments littéraires. Paris, 1843.
40554.14 Cousin, Victor. Pages choisies. Paris, 1898.
40554.15 Cousin, Victor. Gasconiana. Paris, 1809.

40554.16 - Individual authors, etc. - 1800-1849 - Philosophy, etc. - Cousin, Victor - Works about

40554.17 Simon, Jules. Victor Cousin. Paris, 1887.
40554.19 Simon, Jules. Victor Cousin. Chicago, 1888.
40554.21 Barthélemy-Saint Hilaire, J. Victor Cousin, sa vie, sa correspondance. Paris, 1895. 3v.
40554.22 Knoop, B. Victor Cousin, Hegel und die französische Romantik. Inaug. Diss. Oberviechtach, 1932.

40555 Individual authors, etc. - 1800-1849 - Philosophy, etc. - Miscellany, D-Z

40555.3 Dutens, M. Mémoires d'un voyageur qui se repose. Paris, 1806. 3v.
40555.12 Muravef, graf. 4 numeros du livre sans titre. Paris, 1839.
40555.20 Stapfer, M.P.A. Mélanges. Paris, 1844. 2v.
40555.31 Wittmer, L. Charles de Villers, 1765-1815. Genève, 1908.
40555.31.5 Ulrich, O. Charles de Villers. Leipzig, 1899.

40556.1 - .6 Individual authors, etc. - 1800-1849 - Philosophy, etc. - Deschamel

40556.4 Deschanel, Émile. Causeries de Quinzaine. Paris, 1861.
40556.5 Deschanel, Émile. Physiologie des écrivains. Paris, 1864.

40556.7 - .11 Individual authors, etc. - 1800-1849 - Philosophy, etc. - Droz

40556.7 Droz, Gustave. Betsy's profile. N.Y., 1879.
40556.7.5 Droz, Gustave. Diplomacy. N.Y., n.d.
40556.8 Droz, Gustave. Oeuvres. Paris, 1826. 3v.

40556.12 - .14 Individual authors, etc. - 1800-1849 - Philosophy, etc. - Miscellany

40556.12 Combes de Patris, B. Une muse romantique, Pauline de Flaugerques et son oeuvre. Paris, 1927.
40556.13 Fénélon, C.E. de Salignac. Un mot a tout le monde, ou Gros Jean qui prêche son curé. Paris, 1815.
40556.14 Frayssinous, Denis L. Conférences et discours inédits. 2. éd. Paris, 1843.
40556.14.2 Frayssinous, Denis L. Conférences et discours inédits. Paris, 1851.

40556.18 - .21 Individual authors, etc. - 1800-1849 - Philosophy, etc. - Joubert - Writings

40556.18.25 Joubert, Joseph. Joubert; textes choisis. Paris, 1914.
40556.18.80 Condamin, J. Essai sur les pensées de J. Joubert. Thèse. Paris, 1877.
40556.19 Joubert, Joseph. Pensées, essais, et maximes. Paris, 1842. 2v.
40556.19.8 Joubert, Joseph. Pensées. 3. éd. Paris, 1862.
40556.20 Joubert, Joseph. Pensées. Paris, 1869. 2v.
40556.20.2 Joubert, Joseph. Joubert, 1754-1824. (Maximes et pensées). Paris, 1961.
40556.20.5 Joubert, Joseph. Pensées. Paris, 1966.
40556.20.7 Joubert, Joseph. Lettres à Madame de Vintimille. Paris, 1921.

40556.18 - .21 Individual authors, etc. - 1800-1849 - Philosophy, etc. - Joubert - Writings - cont.

40556.20.9 Joubert, Joseph. Pensées. Paris, 1909.
40556.20.15 Joubert, Joseph. Pensées of Joubert. London, 1877.
40556.20.18 Joubert, Joseph. Pensées of Joubert. Paris, 1885. 2v.
40556.20.20 Joubert, Joseph. Some of the "Thoughts". Boston, 1867.
40556.21A Raynal, Paul de. Les correspondents de J. Joubert, 1785-1822. Paris, 1883.
40556.21B Raynal, Paul de. Les correspondents de J. Joubert, 1785-1822. Paris, 1883.
40556.21.5 Raynal, Paul de. Correspondance de J. Joubert. 9. éd. Paris, 1895.
40556.21.10 Joubert, Joseph. Pensées de J. Joubert précédées de sa correspondance. 4. éd. Paris, 1864.
40556.21.15 Joubert, Joseph. Les carnets de Joseph Joubert. Paris, 1938.

40556.22 - .23 Individual authors, etc. - 1800-1849 - Philosophy, etc. - Joubert - Works about

40556.22 Bibliothèque National. Paris. Joseph Joubert. Paris, 1954.
40556.23 Beaunier, André. La jeunesse de Joseph Joubert. Paris, 1900.
40556.23.5 Beaunier, André. Joseph Joubert et la révolution. Paris, 1918.
40556.23.9 Beaunier, André. Le roman d'une amitié. 3. éd. Paris, 1924.
40556.23.15 Tessoneau, Rémy. Joseph Joubert. Thèse. Paris, 1944.
40556.23.20 Evans, Joan. The unselfish egoist; a life of Joseph Joubert. London, 1947.
40556.23.25 Halda, Bernard. Joseph Joubert, ou De la perfection. Paris, 1954.
40556.23.30 Billy, André. Joubert, énigmatique et délicieux. Paris, 1969.
40556.23.35 Pailhès, Gabriel. Du nouveau sur J. Joubert. Paris, 1900.
40556.23.40 Thévenaz-Schmalenbach, Cornelia. Joseph Joubert. Inaug. Diss. Genève, 1956.

40556.24 - .26 Individual authors, etc. - 1800-1849 - Philosophy, etc. - Maistre, Joseph de - Works about [Discontinued]

40556.24 Pamphlet box. Joseph de Maistre.
40556.24.5 Gignoux, Claude Joseph. Joseph de Maistre; prophète du passé. Paris, 1963.
40556.25 Barthelémy, Charles. L'esprit du Comte Joseph de Maistre. Paris, 1859.
40556.26 Moreau, Louis. Joseph de Maistre. Paris, 1879.
40556.26.5 Goyau, Georges. La pensée religieuse de Joseph de Maistre. Paris, 1921.
40556.26.50 Dermenghem, E. Joseph de Maistre, mystique. Paris, 1923.
40556.26.52 Dermenghem, E. Joseph de Maistre, mystique. Paris, 1946.
40556.26.55 Rheinlaender, Eduard. Die Geschichtsphilosophie des Grafen Joseph de Maistre. Inaug. Diss. Elberfeld, 1926.
40556.26.60 Gianturco, Elio. Joseph de Maistre and Giambattista Vico (Italian roots of De Maistre's political culture). Washington, 1937.
40556.26.65 Maistre, Joseph de. Du pape. Paris, 1964.

40556.27 - .28 Individual authors, etc. - 1800-1849 - Philosophy, etc. - Maistre, Joseph de - Writings

40556.27 Maistre, Joseph de. Oeuvres. Bruxelles, 1838. 7v.
40556.27.3 Maistre, Joseph de. Oeuvres. Paris, 1841.
40556.27.5 Maistre, Joseph de. Oeuvres complètes. Lyon, 1884. 14v.
40556.27.9 Maistre, Joseph de. Oeuvres. Paris, 1845-60. 13v.
40556.27.11 Maistre, Joseph de. Oeuvres inédites. Paris, 1870.
40556.27.50 Maistre, Joseph de. Works. N.Y., 1965.
40556.27.100 Maistre, Joseph de. Die Werke des Grafen. v.1-2, 3-5. Frankfurt, 1822-25. 4v.
40556.27.115 Maistre, Joseph de. Une politique expérimentale. Paris, 1940.
40556.28 Maistre, Joseph de. Lettres et opuscules inédits. Paris, 1853. 2v.
40556.28.3 Maistre, Joseph de. Lettres et opuscules inédits. 6. éd. Paris, 1873. 2v.
40556.28.4 Maistre, Joseph de. Lettres inédits. St. Petersbourg, 1858.
40556.28.5 Maistre, Joseph de. Les carnets. Lyon, 1923.
40556.28.6 Maistre, Joseph de. Pages choisies. Paris, 1901.
40556.28.8 Maistre, Joseph de. Les soirées de Saint Petersbourg. 5. éd. Lyon, 1845. 2v.
40556.28.9 Maistre, Joseph de. Textes choisis et présentés par E.M. Cioran. Monaco, 1957.
40556.28.80 Huber, Max. Die Staatsphilosophie von Joseph de Maistre in Lichte des Thomesmus. Basel, 1958.

40556.29 - Individual authors, etc. - 1800-1849 - Philosophy, etc. - Maistre, Joseph de - Works about

40556.29 Margerie, Amédée de. Le Comte Joseph de Maistre. Paris, 1882.
40556.30 Sybel, H. von. Graf Joseph de Maistre. München, 1869.
40556.31 Descostes, François. Joseph de Maistre. Paris, 1893. 2v.
40556.31.2 Descostes, François. Joseph de Maistre pendant la révolution. Tours, 1895.
40556.32A Paulhan, F. Joseph de Maistre. Paris, 1893.
40556.32B Paulhan, F. Joseph de Maistre. Paris, 1893.
40556.33 Lescure, M. de. Le Comte Joseph de Maistre et sa famille. Paris, 1892.
40556.34 Cogordan, G. Joseph de Maistre. Paris, 1894.
40556.35 Paillette, C. La politique de Joseph de Maistre. Paris, 1895.
40556.35.10A Vulliaud, Paul. Joseph de Maistre, franc-maçon. Paris, 1926.
40556.35.10B Vulliaud, Paul. Joseph de Maistre, franc-maçon. Paris, 1926.
40556.35.20 Laurent, Jules. Joseph de Maistre. Monte-Carlo, 1951.
40556.36 Joseph de Maistre et Blacas. Paris, 1908.
40556.37 Chavanne, Paul. Les idées de Joseph de Maistre. Angers, 1901.
40556.37.5 Montmasson, J. L'idée de Providence d'après Joseph de Maistre. Thèse. Lyon, 1928.
40556.38 Wandoul, J. Un homme d'état Italien. Joseph de Maistre. Paris, n.d.
40556.39 Albalat, A. Joseph de Maistre. Lyon, 1914.
40556.39.5 Cordelier, Jean P. La théorie constitutionnelle de Joseph Maistre. Paris, 1965.

40556.29 - Individual authors, etc. - 1800-1849 - Philosophy, etc. - Maistre, Joseph de - Works about - cont.

40556.39.10 Baussan, Charles. Joseph de Maistre et l'idée de l'orde. Paris, 1921.
40556.39.15 Vermale, François. Notes sur Joseph de Maistre inconnu. Chambéry, 1921.
40556.39.20 Ostrogorsky, C. Joseph de Maistre and seine Lehre von der Höchseten Macht und ihren Trägern. Helsingfors, 1932.
40556.39.24 Holdsworth, F. Joseph de Maistre et l'Angleterre. Thèse. Paris, 1935.
40556.39.25 Holdsworth, F. Joseph de Maistre et l'Angleterre. Paris, 1935.
40556.39.27 Omodeo, A. Un reazionario, il conte J. de Maistre. Bari, 1939.
40556.39.33 Mary Alphonsus, mother. The influence of Joseph de Maistre on Baudelaire. Thesis. Bryn Mawr, 1943.
40556.39.40 Bayle, Francis. Les idées politiques de Joseph de Maistre. Paris, 1945.
40556.40 Ménégault, A.P.F. Dictionnaire amusant et instructif. Paris, 1809. 2v.
40556.40.10 Ménégault, A.P.F. L'impiété. 3. éd. Lyon, 1823.
40556.41 Maître, Pierre. Le savant de village. Paris, 1831-33. 3v.
40556.42 Senli, Piérre-Elie. Purgatoire de feu M. le comte Joseph de Maistre. Paris, 1823.
40556.42.2 Senli, Piérre-Elie. Purgatoire de feu M. le comte Joseph de Maistre. Paris, 1823.
40556.45 Treves, P. Joseph de Maistre. Milano, 1936.
40556.47 Caponigri, A.R. Some aspects of the philosophy of Joseph de Maistre. Chicago, 1945.
40556.48 Triomphe, Robert. Joseph de Maistre; étude sur la vie et sur la doctrine d'un matérialiste mystique. 1. éd. Thèse. Genève, 1968.
V40556.48.5 Trybusiewicz, Janusz. De Maistre. 1. wyd. Wernava, 1968.
40556.48.10 Brunello, Bruno. Joseph De Maistre: politico e filosofo. Bologna, 1967.
40556.50 Lebrun, Richard Allen. Throne and altar. Ottawa, 1965.

40557 Individual authors, etc. - 1800-1849 - Philosophy, etc. - Montalembert

40557.5 Montalembert, Charles F.R. Discours. Paris, 1860. 3v.
40557.6 Montalembert, Charles F.R. Oeuvres polémiques. n.p., 1860. 3v.
40557.7 Montalembert, Charles F.R. Mélanges. n.p., 1861.
40557.8 Montalembert, Charles F.R. Histoire de Sainte Elisabeth de Hongrie. n.p., 1861. 2v.
40557.85 Monsieur de Montalembert. Paris, 1859.

40561 Individual authors, etc. - 1800-1849 - Criticism, etc. - Folios [Discontinued]

NEDL 40561.4 Montalembert, Charles F.R. Memoir of the Abbe Lacordaire. London, 1863.
40561.20 Janin, Jules. Un hiver à Paris. Paris, 1843.
40561.22 Janin, Jules. L'été à Paris. Paris, n.d.
40561.24 Janin, Jules. Les symphonies. Paris, 1858.

40562.1 - .12 Individual authors, etc. - 1800-1849 - Criticism, etc. - Lacordaire - Writings

40562.4 Lacordaire, Jean Baptiste Henri. Vie de Saint Domenique. Paris, 1871.
40562.5 Lacordaire, Jean Baptiste Henri. Conférences de Notre-Dame de Paris. Paris, 1872. 5v.
40562.6 Lacordaire, Jean Baptiste Henri. Oeuvres philosophiques. Paris, 1872.
40562.7 Lacordaire, Jean Baptiste Henri. Notices et panegyriques. Paris, 1872.
40562.8 Lacordaire, Jean Baptiste Henri. Mélanges. Paris, 1872.
40562.9 Lacordaire, Jean Baptiste Henri. Correspondence inédite de R.P. Lacordaire. Paris, 1914.
40562.10 Lacordaire, Jean Baptiste Henri. Pages choisies. 7. éd. Paris, 1926?

40562.13 - Individual authors, etc. - 1800-1849 - Criticism, etc. - Lacordaire - Works about

40562.13 Pamphlet vol. Le père Lacordaire. 15 pam.
40562.13.2 Pamphlet box. Le père Lacordaire. Miscellaneous pamphlets.
40562.14 Chocarne, B. Le R.P.H.D. Lacordaire...sa vie intime et religieuse. Paris, 1867. 2v.
40562.14.2 Chocarne, B. Le R.P.H.D. Lacordaire...sa vie intime et religieuse. Paris, 1866. 2v.
40562.14.4 Chocarne, B. The inner life of Père Lacordaire. Dublin, 1867.
40562.15 Lear, H.L. Sidney. Henri Dominique Lacordaire. London, 1882.
40562.16 Ricard, Antoine l'abbé. Lacordaire. Paris, 1888.
40562.17 Haussonville, Gabriel Paul Othenin de Cléron. Lacordaire. Paris, 1895.
40562.18 Montalembert, Charles F.R. Le testament du P. Lacordaire. Paris, 1870.
40562.19 Jacquot, C.J.B. Les contemporains - Lacordaire. Paris, 1855.
NEDL 40562.20 Noble, P.H.D. Le P. Lacordaire. Paris, 1910.
40562.21 Greenwell, Dora. Lacordaire. Edinburgh, 1867.
40562.22 Beslay, François. Lacordaire. Paris, 1862.
Htn 40562.24* Falloux, C. de. Correspondance du R.P. Lacordaire et de Mme. Swetchine. Paris, 1872.
40562.25 Lacordaire, Jean Baptiste Henri. Le Père Lacordaire et son ordre. 2. ed. Paris, 1865.
40562.26 Lacordaire, Jean Baptiste Henri. Oeuvres du R.P.H.D. Lacordaire. Paris, 1872.
40562.27 Lacordaire, Jean Baptiste Henri. Le Père Lacordaire. Paris, 1889.
40562.28 Lacordaire, Jean Baptiste Henri. Mgr. d'Hulst et le P. Lacordaire. Paris, 1897.
40562.30 Vaast, E. Lacordaire et ses conférences de Notre Dame. Paris, 1937.
40562.32 Fesch, P. Lacordaire journaliste, 1830-1848. Paris, 1897.
40562.34 Foisset, T. Vie du r.p. Lacordaire. Paris, 1870. 2v.
40562.40 Mauriac, François. Lacordaire et nous. 24e éd. Paris, 1940.
40562.45 Ridel, Jean. Lacordaire. Rennes, 1955.
40562.45.5 Ridel, Jean. Lacordaire et Madame Swetchine. Dijon, 1956.
40562.45.6 Ridel, Jean. Une amitié féminine de Lacordaire. Dijon, 1956.
40562.45.10 Zeller, Renée C.T. Lacordaire. Paris, 1932.
40562.45.15 Folghera, J.D. L'apologétique de Lacordaire. Paris, 1911.
40562.47 Langle de Cary, M. Prophète en son pays, Lacordaire, 1802-1861. Paris, 1961.

Classified Listing

40562.13 - Individual authors, etc. - 1800-1849 - Criticism, etc. - Lacordaire - Works about - cont.
40562.50 Nujens, Alvarus. Getuige voor de vrijheid. Lien, 1967.

40563.1 - .14 Individual authors, etc. - 1800-1849 - Criticism, etc. - Ampère - Writings
40563.5 Ampère, Jean J. Heures de poésie. Paris, 1863.
40563.8 Ampère, Jean J. Litterature et voyages. Paris, 1833.
40563.11 Ampère, Jean J. Mélanges d'histoire littéraire. Paris, 1867. 2v.
40563.13 Ampère, Jean J. La science et les lettres en Orient. Paris, 1865.

40563.15 - .19 Individual authors, etc. - 1800-1849 - Criticism, etc. - Ampère - Works about
40563.15 Haufe, Heinz. Jean-Jacques Ampère, 1800-1864. Inaug. Diss. Dresden, 1935.

40563.21 Individual authors, etc. - 1800-1849 - Criticism, etc. - Allier
40563.21 Allier, Achille. Illusions et realités. n.p., n.d.

40563.22 - .23 Individual authors, etc. - 1800-1849 - Criticism, etc. - Ballanche - Writings
40563.22 Ballanche, Pierre Simon. Oeuvres. Paris, 1830. 4v.
40563.22.5 Ballanche, Pierre Simon. Oeuvres. Paris, 1833. 6v.
40563.22.10 Ballanche, Pierre Simon. La vielle des expiations (livres IV à VII). Paris, 1926.
40563.22.15 Ballanche, Pierre Simon. La théodicée et la Virginie romaine. Genève, 1959.
40563.22.20 Ballanche, Pierre Simon. La vision d'Hébal. Genève, 1969.

40563.24 - .29 Individual authors, etc. - 1800-1849 - Criticism, etc. - Ballanche - Works about
40563.24A Bredin, Claude Julien. Un ami de Ballanche. Correspondence...avec Ballanche. Thèse. Paris, 1928.
40563.24B Bredin, Claude Julien. Un ami de Ballanche. Correspondence...avec Ballanche. Thèse. Paris, 1928.
NEDL 40563.26 Marquiset, Alfred. Ballanche et Mme. d'Hautefeuille. Lettres inédites. Paris, 1912.
40563.27 Mauduit, Roger. Ballanche le vieillard et le jeune homme. Thèse. Paris, 1928.
40563.28 George, Albert J. Pierre-Simon Ballanche. Syracuse, 1945.

40563.30 - .34 Individual authors, etc. - 1800-1849 - Criticism, etc. - Boissonade - Writings
40563.30 Boissonade, Jean F. Critique littéraire. Paris, 1863. 2v.

40564.1 - .9 Individual authors, etc. - 1800-1849 - Criticism, etc. - Barante - Writings
40564.5 Barante, A.G.P. de. Études littéraires. Paris, 1859. 2v.
40564.8 Mélanges. Brussels, 1835. 3v.

40564.15 - .33 Individual authors, etc. - 1800-1849 - Criticism, etc. - Chasles - Writings
40564.20 Chasles, Philarète. Études contemporaines. Paris, 1866. 2v.
40564.21 Chasles, Philarète. Encore sur les contemporaines. Paris, 1869.
40564.23 Chasles, Philarète. Questions du temps. n.p., 1867.
40564.23.9 Chasles, Philarète. Scènes des camps et des Bivouacs Hongrois. Paris, 1879.
40564.24 Chasles, Philarète. Voyages d'un critique. n.p., 1865. 2v.
40564.29 Chasles, Philarète. Études sur les hommes et les moeurs au XIXe siècle. Paris, 1850.
40564.30 Chasles, Philarète. Notabilities in France and England. N.Y., 1853.
40564.33 Chasles, Philarète. The legacy of Philarète Chasles. Chapel Hill, N.C., 1957.

40564.35 Individual authors, etc. - 1800-1849 - Criticism, etc. - Chauvet
40564.35 Chauvet, Victor. Manzoni, Stendhal. Catania, 1958.
40564.35.10 Cordié, Carlo. Romanticismo e classicismo nell'opera di Victor Chauvet. Messina, 1958.

40565.1 - .29 Individual authors, etc. - 1800-1849 - Criticism, etc. - Cuvillier-Fleury - Writings
40565.17 Cuvillier-Fleury, A.A. Journal intime. Paris, n.d. 2v.
40565.20 Cuvillier-Fleury, A.A. Études historiques et littéraires. Paris, 1854. 2v.
40565.21 Cuvillier-Fleury, A.A. Nouvelles études historiques et littéraires. Paris, 1855.
40565.22 Cuvillier-Fleury, A.A. Derniers études historiques et littéraires. Paris, 1859. 2v.
40565.23 Cuvillier-Fleury, A.A. Études et portraits. Paris, 1865. 2v.
40565.24 Cuvillier-Fleury, A.A. Historiens, poétes et romanciers. Paris, 1863. 2v.
40565.25 Cuvillier-Fleury, A.A. Posthumes et revenants. Paris, 1879.

40565.75 Individual authors, etc. - 1800-1849 - Criticism, etc. - Deplace
Htn 40565.75* Collombet, F.Z. Notice sur Guy-Marie Deplace. Lyon, 1843.

40566.1 - .5 Individual authors, etc. - 1800-1849 - Criticism, etc. - Doudan - Writings
40566.3 Doudan, Ximénès. Pensées, essais et maximes. Paris, 1880.
40566.3.5 Doudan, Ximénès. Pensées et fragments. Paris, 1881.
40566.4 Doudan, Ximénès. Mélanges et lettres. Paris, 1876-77. 4v.
40566.4.5A Doudan, Ximénès. Mélanges et lettres. Paris, 1878. 4v.
40566.4.5B Doudan, Ximénès. Mélanges et lettres. Paris, 1878. 4v.
40566.4.11 Doudan, Ximénès. Lettres. Paris, 1879. 4v.
40566.5 Doudan, Ximénès. Des révolutions du gout. Paris, 1924.

40566.6 Individual authors, etc. - 1800-1849 - Criticism, etc. - Doudan - Works about
40566.6.100 Witmeur, Claire. Ximénès Doudan, sa vie et son oeuvre. Liège, 1934.

40566.7 Individual authors, etc. - 1800-1849 - Criticism, etc. - Miscellany, D
40566.7 Dubois, P.F. Fragments littéraires. Paris, 1879. 2v.
40566.7.5 Gerbod, Paul. Paul François Dubois, universitaire, journaliste et homme politique, 1793-1874. Thèse. Paris, 1967.
40566.7.9 Du Meril, E. Mélanges archéologiques et littéraires. Paris, 1830.

40566.8 Individual authors, etc. - 1800-1849 - Criticism, etc. - Dussault
40566.8 Dussault, Jean J. Annales littéraires. Paris, 1818-24. 5v.

40566.9 Individual authors, etc. - 1800-1849 - Criticism, etc. - Félitz
40566.9.5 Félitz, C.M. de. Melanges de philosophie. Paris, 1828-30. 6v.

40566.10 Individual authors, etc. - 1800-1849 - Criticism, etc. - Fontaney
40566.10 Fontaney, Antoine. Journal intime. Paris, 1925.
40566.10.10 Jasinski, René. Une amitié amoureuse; Marie Nodier et Fontaney. Paris, 1925.

40566.13 Individual authors, etc. - 1800-1849 - Criticism, etc. - Guizot
40566.13 Guizot, François Pierre Guillaume. Le temps passé. Paris, 1887. 2v.

40566.18 - .31 Individual authors, etc. - 1800-1849 - Criticism, etc. - Janin - Folios [Discontinued]
40566.18 Janin, Jules. Les gaités champêtres. Paris, 1851. 2v.
40566.19 Janin, Jules. La fin d'un monde. Paris, 1861.
Htn 40566.23* Janin, Jules. La réligieuse de Toulouse. Paris, 1850. 2v.
40566.30 Janin, Jules. Le livre. Paris, 1870.

40567.1 - .39 Individual authors, etc. - 1800-1849 - Criticism, etc. - Janin - Writings
40567.2 Piedagnel, A. Jules Janin. Paris, 1884.
40567.6 Janin, Jules. Les amours du Chevalier de Fosseuse. Paris, 1867.
40567.6.5 Janin, Jules. L'ane mort. Paris, 1842.
40567.6.9 Janin, Jules. L'ane mort. Paris, 1860.
40567.7 Janin, Jules. L'ane mort. n.p., 1865.
40567.9 Janin, Jules. Barnave. n.p., 1860.
40567.9.5 Janin, Jules. Barnave. v.1-2. Paris, 1878.
40567.10 Janin, Jules. Les catacombes. II. Paris, 1839.
40567.11 Janin, Jules. Le chemin de traverse. n.p., 1870.
40567.12 Janin, Jules. The cross roads. London, 1841.
40567.13 Janin, Jules. Un coeur pour deux amours. Paris, 1870.
40567.15 Janin, Jules. La confession. n.p., 1861.
40567.16 Janin, Jules. Contes fantastiques. n.p., 1863.
40567.17 Janin, Jules. Contes non estampillés. Paris, n.d.
40567.20 Janin, Jules. L'interné. n.p., 1869.
40567.23 Janin, Jules. La semaine des trois jeudis. n.p., n.d.
40567.24 Janin, Jules. La Sorbonne et les gazetiers. Paris, 1867.
40567.26 Janin, Jules. Les petits bonheurs. n.p., n.d.
40567.27 Janin, Jules. Petits romans. n.p., 1869.
40567.30 Janin, Jules. Histoire de la littérature dramatique. n.p., 1853-58. 6v.
40567.32 Janin, Jules. Deux discours. Paris, 1872.
40567.33 Janin, Jules. Discours de réceptions a la porte de l'académie française. Paris, 1865.
40567.34 Janin, Jules. Lamartine. Paris, 1869.
40567.36 Janin, Jules. Confession. Paris, 1830.

40567.40 - Individual authors, etc. - 1800-1849 - Criticism, etc. - Janin - Works about
40567.40.3 Piedagnel, Alexander. Jules Janin. 3. éd. Paris, 1884.

40571 Individual authors, etc. - 1800-1849 - Criticism, etc. - K-Mi
40571.4 Labitte, Charles. Études littéraires. Paris, n.d. 2v.
40571.4.50 Remise d'une epée d'academicien à M.A. Lefranc. Nogent-le-Rotrou, 1929.
40571.5 Levallois, Jules. Critique militante. Paris, 1863.
40571.6 Pamphlet box. Le Roux de Lincy.
40571.7 Maignien, E.A.N. Études littéraires et philosophiques. Paris, n.d.
40571.9 Magnin, Charles. Causeries et meditations. Paris, 1843. 2v.
40571.20 Maillet-Lacoste, P.L. Oeuvres. Paris, 1822.
40571.25 Lobinger, M. Un précurseur de la littérature comparée; Nicolas Martin. Szeged, 1937.

40572.2 Individual authors, etc. - 1800-1849 - Criticism, etc. - Montlaur
40572.2 Montlaur, Eugène de. Essais littéraires. Paris, 1844.
40572.2.20 Montlaur, Eugène de. De l'Italie et de l'Espagne. Paris, 1852.

40572.5 - .9 Individual authors, etc. - 1800-1849 - Criticism, etc. - Muret
40572.5 Muret, Théodore. Mademoiselle de Montpensier. Brusselles, 1836. 2v.
40572.8 Muret, Théodore. Souvenirs et causeries d'un journaliste. Paris, 1862. 2v.

40572.20 - .34 Individual authors, etc. - 1800-1849 - Criticism, etc. - Nisard - Writings
40572.24 Nisard, Désiré. Études de la critique littéraire. Paris, 1858.
40572.25 Nisard, Désiré. Études d'histoire de la littérature. Paris, 1856.
40572.27 Nisard, Désiré. Nouvelles études d'histoire et de littérature. Paris, 1864.
40572.29 Nisard, Désiré. Mélanges d'histoire et de littérature. Paris, 1868.
40572.30 Nisard, Désiré. Portraits et études. Paris, 1875.
40572.31 Nisard, Désiré. Oegrè somnia. Paris, 1889.

40572.45 Individual authors, etc. - 1800-1849 - Criticism, etc. - Ozenne
40572.45 Ozenne, Louise. Mélanges critiques et littéraires. Paris, 1843.

40573.1 - .3 Individual authors, etc. - 1800-1849 - Criticism, etc. - Peignot - Writings

Htn 40573.1* Peignot, Gabriel. Opuscules philosophiques et poétiques. Paris, 1796.
40573.1.5 Peignot, Gabriel. Quelques recherches sur...l'oraison domenicale. Dijon, 1835-39. 4 pam.
40573.1.6 Peignot, Gabriel. Moeurs et usage au moyen-âge. Paris, 1836.
40573.2 Peignot, Gabriel. Le livre des singularités. Dijon, 1841.
40573.2.10 Peignot, Gabriel. Mélanges littéraires. v.1-4. Lyon, 1828.
40573.3 Peignot, Gabriel. Predicatoriana, ou revélations singulières. Dijon, 1841.
40573.3.30 Peignot, Gabriel. Recherches historiques et philosophiques sur la philatesie ou usage de boire à la santé. Dijon, 1835.
40573.3.50 Peignot, Gabriel. Lettres inédites. Dijon, 1884.
40573.3.55 Peignot, Gabriel. Lettres inédites au Docteur Bourée. Dijon, 1885.

40573.4 Individual authors, etc. - 1800-1849 - Criticism, etc. - Peignot - Works about

40573.4 Simonnet, Jules. Essai sur la vie et les ouvrages de Gabriel Peignot. Paris, 1863.
40573.4.25 Milsand, P. Catalogue par ordre alphabétique des ouvrages imprimés de Gabriel Peignot. Supplement. Paris, 1861.

40573.5 - .13 Individual authors, etc. - 1800-1849 - Criticism, etc. - Planche - Writings

40573.5 Planche, Gustave. Études sur les arts. Paris, 1855.
40573.6 Planche, Gustave. Études sur l'école française. Paris, 1855. 2v.
40573.8 Planche, Gustave. Études littéraires. Paris, 1855.
40573.9 Planche, Gustave. Portraits d'artistes. Paris, 1853. 2v.
40573.10 Planche, Gustave. Portraits littéraires. Paris, 1848. 2v.
40573.12 Planche, Gustave. Nouveaux portraits littéraires. Paris, 1854. 2v.

40573.14 Individual authors, etc. - 1800-1849 - Criticism, etc. - Planche - Works about

40573.14 Regard, Maurice. L'adversaire des romantiques. Paris, 1956. 2v.

40573.18 - .22 Individual authors, etc. - 1800-1849 - Criticism, etc. - Pyat - Writings

40573.19 Pyat, Félix. Les deux serruriers. Paris, 1841.
40573.22 Pyat, Félix. The rag-picker of Paris. 4. ed. N.Y., 1893.

40573.25 - .29 Individual authors, etc. - 1800-1849 - Criticism, etc. - Rémusat - Writings

40573.25 Rémusat, Charles de. Critiques et études littéraires. Paris, 1857. 2v.
40573.26 Rémusat, Charles de. La Saint-Barthélemy, drame inédit. Paris, 1878.
40573.26.7 Rémusat, Charles de. Abélard; drame inédit. 2. éd. Paris, 1877.
40573.26.8 Rémusat, Charles de. Abélard; drame inédit. 3. éd. Paris, 1877.
40573.29 Rémusat, Charles de. Passé et présent, Mélanges. Paris, 1847. 2v.

40573.34 Individual authors, etc. - 1800-1849 - Criticism, etc. - Rigault

40573.34 Rigault, H. Oeuvres. Paris, 1859. 4v.

40573.45 Individual authors, etc. - 1800-1849 - Criticism, etc. - Salgues

40573.45 Salgues, J.B. De Paris, des moeurs, de la littérature. Paris, 1813.

40575.01 - .099 Individual authors, etc. - 1800-1849 - Criticism, etc. - Saint Beuve - Pamphlet volumes

40575.01 Pamphlet box. French literature. 19th century. Miscellaneous pamphlets.

40575.1 Individual authors, etc. - 1800-1849 - Criticism, etc. - Saint Beuve - Bibliographies

40575.1.4 Sainte-Beuve, C.A. Vie. Paris, 1957.
40575.1.5 Jacquol, Eugene de Mirecourt. Sainte-Beuve. Paris, 1856.
40575.1.10 Bonnerot, Jean. Bibliographie de l'oeuvre de Sainte-Beuve. Paris, 1937- 3v.
40575.1.12 Bonnerot, Jean. Un demi-siècle d'études sur Sainte-Beuve, 1904-1954. Paris, 1957.

40575.2 - .5 Individual authors, etc. - 1800-1849 - Criticism, etc. - Saint Beuve - Biography and criticism

40575.2 Lavallon, Jules. Sainte-Beuve. Paris, 1872.
40575.2.5 Voizard, F. Sainte-Beuve l'homme et l'oeuvre. Paris, 1911.
40575.3 Haussonville, Gabriel Paul Othenin de Cléron. E.A. Sainte-Beuve. Paris, 1875.
40575.3.5 Académie Française, Paris. Inauguration du monument élève à la memoire de Sainte-Beuve. Paris, 1898. 2 pam.
40575.4 Morel, L. Études littéraires Sainte-Beuve...Pascal. Zurich, 1898.
40575.5 Morand, François. Les jeunes annees de C.A. Sainte-Beuve. Paris, 1872.
40575.5.3 Faguet, E. La jeunesse de Sainte-Beuve. Paris, 1914.
40575.5.4 Grojean, Oscar. Sainte-Beuve a Liege. Lettres et documents inédits. Bruxelles, 1905.
40575.5.5 Spoelberch de Lovenjoul, V. de. Sainte-Beuve inconnu. Paris, 1901.
40575.5.9 Michaut, G. Sainte-Beuve avant Les "Lundis". Paris, 1903.
40575.5.9.2 Michaut, G. Sainte-Beuve avant Les "Lundis". Fribourg, 1903.
40575.5.10 Michaut, G. Études sur Sainte-Beuve. Paris, 1905.
40575.5.11 Michaut, G. Sainte-Beuve. Paris, 1921.
40575.5.13 Séché, Leon. Sainte-Beuve. Paris, 1904. 2v.
40575.5.14A Harper, George M. Charles Augustin Sainte-Beuve. Philadelphia, 1909.
40575.5.14B Harper, George M. Charles Augustin Sainte-Beuve. Philadelphia, 1909.
40575.5.15 Séché, Leon. Madame d'Arbouville...1846-1850. Paris, 1909.
40575.5.17 MacClintock, Lauder. Sainte-Beuve's critical theory and practice after 1849. Chicago, 1920.
40575.5.18 MacClintock, Lauder. Sainte-Beuve's critical theory and practice after 1849. Chicago, 1920.

40575.2 - .5 Individual authors, etc. - 1800-1849 - Criticism, etc. - Saint Beuve - Biography and criticism - cont.

40575.5.20 Pailleron, M.L. (Mme.). Sainte-Beuve à seize ans. Paris, 1927.
40575.5.25 Choisy, Louis F. Sainte-Beuve, l'homme et la poète. 4. éd. Paris, 1921.
40575.5.27 Michaut, G. Le livre d'amour de Sainte-Beuve. Paris, 1905.
40575.5.29 Troubat, Jules. La salle à manger de Sainte-Beuve. Paris, 1910.
40575.5.35 Benoit-Levy, Edmond. Sainte-Beuve et Mme. Victor Hugo. Paris, 1926.
40575.5.37 Bellessort, A. Sainte-Beuve et le 19te siècle. Paris, 1927.
40575.5.40 Lemaitre, Jules. Les péchér de Sainte-Beuve. Paris, 1913.
40575.5.50 Morin, Georges. Sainte-Beuve, etudiant en medecine. Thèse. Lyon, 1928.
40575.5.60 Deschamps, Jules. Sainte-Beuve et les sillage de Napoleon. Liège, 1922.
40575.5.70 Seilliere, Ernest. Saint-Beuve agent, juge et complice de l'evolution romantique. Paris, 1921.
40575.5.80 Giese, William F. Sainte-Beuve, a literary portrait. Madison, 1931.
40575.5.85A Mott, L.F. Saint-Beuve. N.Y., 1925.
40575.5.85B Mott, L.F. Saint-Beuve. N.Y., 1925.
40575.5.90 Giraud, V. La vie secrète de Sainte-Beuve. Paris, 1935.
40575.5.95 Bray, René. Sainte-Beuve à l'Académie de Lausanne. Paris, 1937.
40575.5.100 Thomas, Jean. Sainte-Beuve et l'école normale, 1834-1867. Paris, 1936.
40575.5.105 Kötz, Kurt. Das Frankreichbild im Werke Sainte-Beuve's. Inaug. Diss. Bochum-Langendreer, 1937.
40575.5.110 Combe, T.G.S. Sainte-Beuve poète et les poètes anglais. Thèse. Bordeaux, 1937.
40575.5.115 Pons, A.J. Sainte-Beuve et ses inconnues. Paris, 1879.
40575.5.120 Leroy, Maxime. La pensée de Sainte-Beuve. Paris, 1940.
40575.5.123 Leroy, Maxime. La politique de Sainte-Beuve. Paris, 1941.
40575.5.124 Leroy, Maxime. Vie de Sainte-Beuve. Paris, 1947.
40575.5.125 Mahieu, Robert G. Sainte-Beuve aux Etats-Unis. Princeton, 1945.
40575.5.127 Decreus-Van Liefland, Juliette. Sainte-Beuve et la critique des auteurs féminins. Paris, 1949.
40575.5.130 Grosclaude, P. Sainte-Beuve et Marceline Desbordes-Valmore. Paris, 1948.
40575.5.132A Billy, A. Sainte-Beuve. Paris, 1952- 2v.
40575.5.132B Billy, A. Sainte-Beuve. Paris, 1952- 2v.
40575.5.135 LeHir, Yves. L'originalité littéraire de Sainte-Beuve dans Volupte. Paris, 1953.
40575.5.140 Zweig, Stefan. Sainte-Beuve. Frankfurt, 1923.
40575.5.145 Allem, Maurice. Portrait de Sainte-Beuve. Paris, 1954.
40575.5.147 Allem, Maurice. Sainte-Beuve et "Volupte". Paris, 1935.
40575.5.150 Nicolson, H.G. Saint-Beuve. London, 1957.
40575.5.155 Regard, Maurice. Sainte-Beuve. Paris, 1959.
40575.5.160 Lausanne. Université. Hommage à Sainte-Beuve. Lausanne, 1938.
40575.5.165 Bo, Carlo. Delle imagini giovanili di Sainte-Beuve. Firenze, 1938.
40575.5.170 Lehmann, A.G. Sainte-Beuve. Oxford, 1962.
40575.5.175 Moreau, Pierre. La critique selon Sainte-Beuve. Paris, 1964.
40575.5.180 Bibliothèque nationale, Paris. Sainte-Beuve. Paris, 1955.
40575.5.185 Sainte-Beuve, Lamartine; colloques, 8 novembre, 1968. Paris, 1970.
40575.5.190 Lejeune-Dehousse, Rita. Sainte-Beuve et l'Université de Liège. Liège, 1969.

40575.6 - .9 Individual authors, etc. - 1800-1849 - Criticism, etc. - Saint Beuve - Correspondence

40575.6A Sainte-Beuve, Charles A. Correspondance. Paris, 1877. 2v.
Htn 40575.6*B Sainte-Beuve, Charles A. Correspondance. Paris, 1877-78. 2v.
40575.6.5 Sainte-Beuve, Charles A. Correspondance. Paris, 1877-99. 2v.
40575.7A Sainte-Beuve, Charles A. Nouvelle correspondance. Paris, 1880.
40575.7B Sainte-Beuve, Charles A. Nouvelle correspondance. Paris, 1880.
40575.7.5 Sainte-Beuve, Charles A. Lettres inédites. Paris, 1903.
40575.7.7 Sainte-Beuve, Charles A. Correspondance inédite de Sainte-Beuve avec M. et Mme. Juste Olivier. 3. éd. Paris, 1904.
40575.7.15 Sainte-Beuve, Charles A. Correspondance littéraire. Paris, 1929.
40575.7.20 Sainte-Beuve, Charles A. Correspondance générale recueillie classée. Paris, 1935-58. 16v.
40575.7.25 Sainte-Beuve, Charles A. Sainte Beuve et Alfred de Vigny; lettres. Paris, 1929.
40575.7.35 Sainte-Beuve, Charles A. Lettres inédites de Sainte-Beuve à Charles Labitte, 1834-45. Paris, 1911.
40575.7.40 Sainte-Beuve, Charles A. Lettres à deux amies. Paris, 1948.
40575.8 Sainte-Beuve, Charles A. Lettres à la princesse. Paris, 1873.
40575.9A Sainte-Beuve, Charles A. Souvenirs et indiscrétions. Paris, 1872.
40575.9B Sainte-Beuve, Charles A. Souvenirs et indiscrétions. Paris, 1872.

40575.10 - Individual authors, etc. - 1800-1849 - Criticism, etc. - Saint Beuve - Collected and Selected works

40575.10 Sainte-Beuve, Charles A. Poésies complètes. Paris, 1840.
40575.10.3 Sainte-Beuve, Charles A. Poésies complètes. Paris, 1869.
40575.10.5 Sainte-Beuve, Charles A. Poésies complètes. Paris, 1910.
40575.11 Sainte-Beuve, Charles A. Les cahiers. Paris, 1876.
40575.11.5 Sainte-Beuve, Charles A. Cahier de notes grecques. Chapel Hill, 1955.
40575.12 Sainte-Beuve, Charles A. Mes poisons, cahiers intunes inédits. Paris, 1926.
40575.13 Sainte-Beuve, Charles A. Chroniques parisiennes. Paris, 1876.
Htn 40575.14* Sainte-Beuve, Charles A. Le clou d'or la pendule. Paris, 1880.
40575.15 Sainte-Beuve, Charles A. Le livre d'or de Sainte-Beuve. Paris, 1904.
40575.16A Sainte-Beuve, Charles A. English portraits. N.Y., 1875.
40575.16B Sainte-Beuve, Charles A. English portraits. N.Y., 1875.
40575.16.5 Sainte-Beuve, Charles A. Profils anglais. London, 1905.

40575.10 - Individual authors, etc. - 1800-1849 - Criticism, etc. - Saint Beuve - Collected and Selected works - cont.

40575.16.10 Sainte-Beuve, Charles A. Profils anglais. 2. ed. London, 1907.
40575.18A Sainte-Beuve, Charles A. Portraits of the seventeenth century. N.Y., 1904. 2v.
40575.18B Sainte-Beuve, Charles A. Portraits of the seventeenth century. N.Y., 1904. 2v.
40575.18C Sainte-Beuve, Charles A. Portraits of the seventeenth century. N.Y., 1904. 2v.
40575.18D Sainte-Beuve, Charles A. Portraits of the seventeenth century. N.Y., 1904. 2v.
40575.18.8 Sainte-Beuve, Charles A. Portraits of the seventeenth century. N.Y., 1904.
40575.18.9 Sainte-Beuve, Charles A. Portraits of the seventeenth century. N.Y., 1964. 2v.
40575.18.10 Sainte-Beuve, Charles A. Portraits of the 18th century, historic and literary. v.1-2. N.Y., 1905.
40575.18.15 Sainte-Beuve, Charles A. Portraits of the 18th century, historic and literary. N.Y., 1905. 2v.
40575.18.20 Sainte-Beuve, Charles A. Portraits of the 18th century. N.Y., 1905.
40575.18.22 Sainte-Beuve, Charles A. Portraits of the 18th century. N.Y., 1906. 2v.
40575.18.24 Sainte-Beuve, Charles A. Portraits of the 18th century, historic and literary. N.Y., 1964. 2v.
40575.19 Sainte-Beuve, Charles A. Portraits de femmes. Paris, 1876.
40575.19.05 Sainte-Beuve, Charles A. Portraits de femmes. Paris, 1869.
40575.19.7 Sainte-Beuve, Charles A. Portraits de femmes. Paris, 1858.
40575.20 Sainte-Beuve, Charles A. Portraits of celebrated women. Boston, 1868.
40575.20.7 Sainte-Beuve, Charles A. Portraits of women. London, 1891.
40575.20.10 Sainte-Beuve, Charles A. Galerie de femmes célèbres tirée des causeries des lundi. Paris, 1862.
40575.20.11 Sainte-Beuve, Charles A. Galerie des femmes célèbres. Evreux, 1970?
40575.21 Sainte-Beuve, Charles A. Portraits of men. London, 1891.
40575.22 Sainte-Beuve, Charles A. Madame Desbordes-Valmore. Paris, 1870.
40575.22.5 Sainte-Beuve, Charles A. Memoirs of Madame Desbordes-Valmore. Boston, 1873.
40575.22.20 Sainte-Beuve, Charles A. Madame de Pontivy. Paris, 1920.
40575.23 Sainte-Beuve, Charles A. Literarische Portraits aus dem Frankreich. Frankfurt, 1923. 2v.
40575.25 Sainte-Beuve, Charles A. Pensées d'Août. Bruxelles, 1838.
40575.26 Sainte-Beuve, Charles A. Volupté. Bruxelles, 1834.
40575.26.4 Sainte-Beuve, Charles A. Volupté. v.1-2. Bruxelles, 1835.
40575.26.10 Sainte-Beuve, Charles A. Volupté. 10. éd. Paris, 1881.
40575.26.15 Sainte-Beuve, Charles A. Volupté. Paris, 1927. 2v.
40575.26.20 Sainte-Beuve, Charles A. Volupté. Paris, 1969.
40575.29 Sainte-Beuve, Charles A. Monday-chats. Chicago, 1877.
40575.31 Sainte-Beuve, Charles A. Portraits contemporains. Paris, 1846-47. 3v.
40575.31.5 Sainte-Beuve, Charles A. Portraits contemporains. Paris, 1852. 3v.
40575.32 Sainte-Beuve, Charles A. Portraits contemporains. Paris, 1870-71. 5v.
40575.33 Sainte-Beuve, Charles A. Portraits littéraires. Paris, 1876-78. 3v.
40575.33.5A Sainte-Beuve, Charles A. Portraits littéraires. Paris, 1864? 3v.
40575.33.5B Sainte-Beuve, Charles A. Portraits littéraires. Paris, 1864? 3v.
40575.34 Sainte-Beuve, Charles A. Derniers portraits. Paris, 1858.
40575.36.2 Sainte-Beuve, Charles A. Premiers lundis. Paris, 1874-75. 3v.
40575.37 Sainte-Beuve, Charles A. Premiers lundis. Paris, 1878-82. 3v.
40575.37.10 Sainte-Beuve, Charles A. Premiers lundis. Paris, 1886-94. 3v.
40575.38 Sainte-Beuve, Charles A. Essays. London, 1892.
40575.39A Sainte-Beuve, Charles A. Selected essays. Boston, 1896.
40575.39B Sainte-Beuve, Charles A. Selected essays. Boston, 1896.
40575.39.5 Sainte-Beuve, Charles A. Selected essays. 1. ed. Garden City, 1963.
40575.41 Sainte-Beuve, Charles A. Oeuvres. Paris, 1949. 2v.
40575.45 Sainte-Beuve, Charles A. Sainte-Beuve; textes choisis. Neuchâtel, n.d.
40575.50 Sainte-Beuve, Charles A. Literary criticism of Sainte-Beuve. Lincoln, 1971.

40576 Individual authors, etc. - 1800-1849 - Criticism, etc. - Saint Beuve - Individual works

40576.3 Sainte-Beuve, Charles A. Causeries du lundi. Paris, 1857-62. 15v.
40576.3.5 Sainte-Beuve, Charles A. Causeries du lundi. 3. éd. Paris, 1894.
40576.3.7 Sainte-Beuve, Charles A. Causeries du lundi. v.7. 3. éd. Paris, 18- .
40576.3.9 Sainte-Beuve, Charles A. Causeries du lundi. Paris, 1900.
40576.3.10 Sainte-Beuve, Charles A. Causeries du lundi. Paris, 18- . 15v.
40576.3.11 Sainte-Beuve, Charles A. Causeries du lundi; table générale et analytique. Paris, 188-?
40576.3.12 Sainte-Beuve, Charles A. Causeries du lundi. 3. éd. Paris, 1857?-83. 15v.
40576.4.5 Sainte-Beuve, Charles A. Seven of the Causeries du lundi. N.Y., 1897.
40576.4.15 Sainte-Beuve, Charles A. Causeries du lundi. London, 1909-11. 8v.
40576.4.20 Sainte-Beuve, Charles A. Nouvelle gallerie de femmes célèbres tirée des Causeries du lundi. Paris, 1865.
40576.5 Sainte-Beuve, Charles A. Nouveaux lundis. Paris, 1870. 13v.
40576.7 Sainte-Beuve, Charles A. Les grands écrivains français. (XVIe siècle). Paris, 1926. 2v.
40576.8 Sainte-Beuve, Charles A. Les grands écrivains français (XVIIe siècle). Paris, 1927-30. 5v.
40576.9 Sainte-Beuve, Charles A. Romanciers et moralistes. Paris, 1930.
40576.9.5 Sainte-Beuve, Charles A. Auteurs dramatiques et poètes. Paris, 1930.

40576 Individual authors, etc. - 1800-1849 - Criticism, etc. - Saint Beuve - Individual works - cont.

40576.10 Sainte-Beuve, Charles A. Philosophes et essayistes. Paris, 1930. 3v.
40576.12 Sainte-Beuve, Charles A. Livre d'amour. Paris, 1906.

40577 - 40578 Individual authors, etc. - 1800-1849 - Criticism, etc. - Saint Beuve - Folios, etc. [Discontinued]

40577.4 Sainte-Beuve, Charles A. Causeries du lundi. 3. éd. Paris, n.d. 15v.
40577.5 Pierrot, Charles. Causeries du lundi...Table générale. Paris, 1881.
40577.6 Sainte-Beuve, Charles A. Nouveau lundis. v.1, 3. éd. v.2-5, 2. éd. Paris, 1866-72. 13v.
40577.10 Sainte-Beuve, Charles A. Portraits contemporains. Paris, 1881-82. 5v.
40578.4 Sainte-Beuve, Charles A. Causeries du lundi. Paris, n.d. 16v.

40582.1 - .4 Individual authors, etc. - 1800-1849 - Criticism, etc. - Stendhal, i.e. H. Beyle - Complete works

40582.2.5 Cordier, Henri. Bibliographie Stendhalienne. Paris, 1914.
40582.2.10 Beyle, Henry. Vie de H. Brulard. Paris, 1913. 2v.
40582.2.15 Beyle, Henri. Journal. Paris, 1923.
40582.2.16 Beyle, Henri. Journal. Paris, 1923.
40582.2.25 Beyle, Henri. Vies de Haydn de Mozart et de Métastase. Paris, 1914.
40582.2.30 Beyle, Henri. Rome, Naples. Paris, 1919. 2v.
40582.2.35 Beyle, Henri. Le rouge et le noir. Paris, 1923. 2v.
40582.2.40 Beyle, Henri. Vie du Rossini. Paris, 1922. 2v.
40582.2.43 Beyle, Henri. Histoire de la peinture en Italie. Paris, 1924. 2v.
40582.2.45 Beyle, Henri. Armance, ou Quelques scènes d'un salon de Paris en 1827. Paris, 1925.
40582.2.47 Beyle, Henri. Racine et Shakspeare. Paris, 1925. 2v.
40582.2.50 Beyle, Henri. De l'amour. Paris, 1926. 2v.
40582.2.55 Beyle, Henri. Lucien Leuwen. Paris, 1926-27. 4v.
40582.2.60 Beyle, Henri. Napoléon. Paris, 1929. 2v.
40582.2.65 Beyle, Henri. Mémoires d'un touriste. Paris, 1932-33. 3v.
40582.2.110 Paupe, Adolphe. La vie littéraire de Stendhal. Paris, 1914.
40582.2.115 Arbelet, P. La jeunesse de Stendhal. Paris, 1919. 2v.
40582.3.3 Beyle, Henri. La chartreuse de Parme. Paris, 1927. 2v.
40582.3.5 Beyle, Henri. Correspondance. Paris, 1933-34. 10v.
40582.3.6 Beyle, Henri. Çourrier anglais. Paris, 1935-36. 5v.
40582.3.8 Beyle, Henri. Écoles italiennes de peinture. Paris, 1932. 3v.
40582.3.9 Beyle, Henri. Histoire de la peinture en Italie. Paris, 1929. 2v.
40582.3.10 Beyle, Henri. Journal. Paris, 1937. 5v.
40582.3.13 Beyle, Henri. Lucien Leuwen. Paris, 1929. 3v.
40582.3.13.5 Beyle, Henri. Lucien Leuwen. N.Y., 1961.
40582.3.14 Beyle, Henri. Mélanges d'art. Paris, 1932.
40582.3.15 Beyle, Henri. Mélanges de littérature. Paris, 1933. 3v.
40582.3.16 Beyle, Henri. Mélanges de politique et d'histoire. Paris, 1933. 2v.
40582.3.17 Beyle, Henri. Mélanges intimes et Marginalia. Paris, 1936. 2v.
40582.3.19 Beyle, Henri. Molière. Paris, 1930.
40582.3.20 Beyle, Henri. Napoléon. Paris, 1930. 2v.
40582.3.22 Beyle, Henri. Pensées. Paris, 1931. 2v.
40582.3.24 Beyle, Henri. Racine et Shakespeare. Paris, 1928.
40582.3.25 Beyle, Henri. Romans et nouvelles. Paris, 1928. 2v.
40582.3.25.2 Beyle, Henri. Romans et nouvelles. Bottin, 1952. 2v.
40582.3.25.5 Beyle, Henri. Romans. Paris, 1969. 2v.
40582.3.27 Beyle, Henri. Le rouge et le noir. Paris, 1927. 2v.
40582.3.29 Beyle, Henri. Théâtre. Paris, 1931. 3v.
40582.3.30A Beyle, Henri. Vie de Henri Bruland. Paris, 1927. 2v.
40582.3.30B Beyle, Henri. Vie de Henri Brulard. Paris, 1927. 2v.
40582.3.31 Beyle, Henri. Vie de Rossini. Paris, 1929. 2v.
40582.3.32 Beyle, Henri. Vies de Haydn, de Mozart. Paris, 1928.
40582.3.33 Beyle, Henri. Voyage dans le midi de la France. Paris, 1930.
40582.3.34 Beyle, Henri. Travels in the South of France. London, 1971.
40582.3.40 Beyle, Henri. Lettres à Stendhal. Paris, 1943. 2v.
40582.3.42 Beyle, Henri. Cent soixante-quatorze lettres à Stendhal. Paris, 1947. 2v.
40582.3.45 Constantin, Abraham. Idées italiennes sur quelques tableaux célèbres. 2. éd. Paris, 1931.
40582.4.130 Beyle, Henri. Oeuvres complètes. Paris, 1951-56. 25v.
40582.4.150F Beyle, Henri. Oeuvres complètes de Stendhal. Paris, 1851?
40582.4.155A Beyle, Henri. Oeuvres intimes de Stendhal. Paris, 1955.
40582.4.155B Beyle, Henri. Oeuvres intimes de Stendhal. Paris, 1955.

40582.5 - .7 Individual authors, etc. - 1800-1849 - Criticism, etc. - Stendhal, i.e. H. Beyle - Selected works

40582.5 Beyle, Henri. Cent y soixante petits faits vrais. Paris, 1946.
40582.5.5 Beyle, Henri. Feuillets inédits. Paris, 1957.
40582.6.5 Beyle, Henri. To the happy few; selected letters. London, 1952.
40582.6.10 Beyle, Henri. Selected journalism from the English reviews. London, 1959.
40582.7.5 Beyle, Henri. Stendhal (Henri Beyle). 4. éd. Paris, 1908.
40582.7.25 Beyle, Henri. Stendhal (Henri Beyle). 2. éd. Paris, 1922.
40582.7.30 Beyle, Henri. Stendhal. 4. éd. Paris, 1938.
40582.7.40 Beyle, Henri. Stendhal par lui même. Paris, 1951.

40582.8 - Individual authors, etc. - 1800-1849 - Criticism, etc. - Stendhal, i.e. H. Beyle - Individual works

40582.8.3 Beyle, Henri. De l'amour. Paris, 1864.
40582.8.3.50 Beyle, Henri. De l'amour. Paris, 1857.
40582.8.4 Beyle, Henri. De l'amour. Paris, 1924.
40582.8.4.10 Beyle, Henri. De l'amour. Paris, 1948.
40582.8.4.12 Beyle, Henri. De l'amour. Paris, 1957.
40582.8.4.13 Beyle, Henri. De l'amour. Paris, 1970.
40582.8.4.15 Beyle, Henri. On love. N.Y., 1927.
40582.8.4.20 Beyle, Henri. On love. N.Y., 1947.
40582.8.5 Beyle, Henri. Chartreuse de Parme. Paris, 1857.
40582.8.7 Beyle, Henri. La chartreuse de Parme. Paris, 1885.

40582.8 - Individual authors, etc. - 1800-1849 - Criticism, etc. - Stendhal, i.e. H. Beyle - Individual works - cont.

Htn 40582.8.8* Beyle, Henri. Chartreuse de Parme. N.Y., 1895. 3v.
40582.8.8.2 Beyle, Henri. Chartreuse de Parme. N.Y., 1895. 3v.
40582.8.9 Beyle, Henri. Chartreuse de Parme. Paris, 1916.
Htn 40582.8.10* Beyle, Henri. La chartreuse de Parme. Paris, 1921. 3v.
40582.8.15 Beyle, Henri. La chartreuse de Parme. Paris, 1930.
40582.8.17 Beyle, Henri. La chartreuse de Parme. v.1-2. Paris, 1933.
40582.8.20 Beyle, Henri. La charteuse de Parme. Paris, 1936.
40582.9 Beyle, Henri. Chartreuse de Parme. Paris, 1869.
40582.9.5 Beyle, Henri. Chartreuse de Parme. Paris, 1864.
40582.9.15 Beyle, Henri. La chartreuse de Parme. N.Y., 1937.
40582.9.16 Beyle, Henri. The chartreuse of Parma. N.Y., 1901.
40582.9.17 Beyle, Henri. The chartreuse of Parma. N.Y., 1901.
40582.9.18 Beyle, Henri. La chartreuse de Parme. Paris, 1939.
40582.9.20A Beyle, Henri. Chartreuse of Parma. London, 1923.
40582.9.20B Beyle, Henri. Chartreuse of Parma. London, 192-?
40582.9.25 Beyle, Henri. The charterhouse of Parma. N.Y., 1925.
40582.9.26 Beyle, Henri. The charterhouse of Parma. N.Y., 1925. 2v.
40582.9.28 Beyle, Henri. The charterhouse of Parma. N.Y., 1937.
40582.9.30 Beyle, Henri. La chartreuse de Parme. Paris, 1961.
40582.9.40 Beyle, Henri. La chartreuse de Parme. Paris, 1946.
40582.9.45 Beyle, Henri. The charterhouse of Parma. N.Y., 1960.
40582.10 Beyle, Henri. Chroniques italiennes. Paris, n.d.
40582.10.5 Beyle, Henri. Chroniques italiennes. Paris, 1946.
40582.10.10 Beyle, Henri. Chroniques italiennes. Paris, 1947.
40582.11 Beyle, Henri. Correspondence inédite. Paris, n.d. 2v.
40582.11.5 Beyle, Henri. Lettres intimes. 2. éd. Paris, 1892.
40582.11.20 Beyle, Henri. The private journals of Stendhal. Kentfield, Calif., 1954.
40582.11.25 Beyle, Henri. Correspondence. Paris, 1962. 3v.
40582.12 Beyle, Henri. La chasse au bonheur. Paris, 1912.
40582.12.45 Beyle, Henri. Armance. Paris, 1919.
40582.12.50 Beyle, Henri. Armance. N.Y., 1928.
40582.12.53 Beyle, Henri. Armance. Paris, 1946.
40582.12.55 Beyle, Henri. Armance. Paris, 1947.
40582.12.56 Beyle, Henri. Armance. Paris, 1962.
40582.12.57 Beyle, Henri. Armance, ou Quelques scènes d'un salon de Paris en 1827. Paris, 1950.
40582.12.70 Beyle, Henri. Armance; or Scenes from a Parisian salon in 1827. London, 1960.
40582.13 Beyle, Henri. Lamiel. Paris, 1889.
40582.13.50A Beyle, Henri. Lamiel. N.Y., 1929.
40582.13.50B Beyle, Henri. Lamiel. N.Y., 1929.
40582.13.55 Beyle, Henri. Lamiel. London, 1951.
40582.13.57 Beyle, Henri. Lamiel. Norfolk, 1952.
40582.13.60 Prevost, Jean. Essai sur les sources de Lamiel. Lyon, 1942.
40582.13.65 Beyle, Henri. Lamiel. Paris, 1947.
40582.13.70 Beyle, Henri. Lamiel. Paris, 1948.
40582.14 Beyle, Henri. Lucien Leuwen. Photoreproduction. Paris, n.d.
40582.14.12 Beyle, Henri. Lucien Leuwen. Monaco, 1945. 2v.
40582.14.15 Beyle, Henri. Lucien Leuwen. Paris, 1950.
40582.15 Beyle, Henri. Mélanges...de littérature. Paris, 1867.
40582.16 Beyle, Henri. Mémoires d'un touriste. Paris, 1854. 2v.
40582.16.5 Beyle, Henri. Mémoires d'un touriste. Paris, 1953. 2v.
40582.17 Beyle, Henri. Mémoires d'un touriste. Oxford, 1905.
40582.18 Beyle, Henri. Nouvelles inédites. Paris, 1855.
40582.18.5 Beyle, Henri. Nouvelles inédites. Paris, n.d.
40582.19 Beyle, Henri. Promenades dans Rome. Paris, 1806. 2v.
Htn 40582.19.3* Beyle, Henri. Promenades dans Rome. Paris, 1829. 2v.
40582.19.5 Beyle, Henri. Promenades dans Rome. Paris, 1858. 2v.
40582.19.8 Beyle, Henri. Promenades dans Rome. v.1-2. Paris, 1873.
40582.19.15 Beyle, Henri. Promenades dans Rome. Paris, 1938-40. 3v.
40582.19.20 Beyle, Henri. A Roman journal. N.Y., 1957.
40582.19.22 Beyle, Henri. A Roman journal. London, 1959.
40582.20.25 Beyle, Henri. Roma. 1. ed. Roma, 1906.
40582.21 Beyle, Henri. Racine et Shakespeare. Paris, 1854.
40582.21.5A Beyle, Henri. Racine et Shakespeare. Oxford, 1907.
40582.21.5B Beyle, Henri. Racine et Shakespeare. Oxford, 1907.
40582.21.15 Beyle, Henri. Racine and Shakespeare. N.Y., 1962.
40582.21.16 Beyle, Henri. Racine et Shakespeare. Paris, 1965.
40582.22 Beyle, Henri. Romans et nouvelles. Paris, 1854.
40582.23 Beyle, Henri. Rome, Naples, et Florence. Paris, 1865.
40582.23.25 Beyle, Henri. Rome. Paris, 1956.
40582.23.30 Beyle, Henri. Rome. Paris, 1927.
40582.23.35 Beyle, Henri. Rome, Naples and Florence. London, 1959.
40582.24 Beyle, Henri. Le rouge et le noir. Paris, 1870.
40582.24.2 Beyle, Henri. Le rouge et le noir. Paris, 1895. 2v.
40582.24.6 Beyle, Henri. Le rouge et le noir. Paris, 1884. 3v.
40582.25 Beyle, Henri. Le rouge et le noir. v.1-2. Paris, 1876.
40582.25.5 Beyle, Henri. Le rouge et le noir. Strassbourg, n.d.
40582.25.8 Beyle, Henri. Le rouge et le noir. Paris, 1929. 2v.
40582.25.9A Beyle, Henri. Le rouge et le noir. N.Y., 1930.
40582.25.9B Beyle, Henri. Le rouge et le noir. N.Y., 1930.
40582.25.10 Beyle, Henri. Le rouge et le noir. N.Y., 1931.
40582.25.12 Beyle, Henri. Le rouge et le noir. Paris, 1932.
40582.25.15 Beyle, Henri. Le rouge et le noir. v.1-2. Paris, 1937.
40582.25.17 Beyle, Henri. Le rouge et le noir. Paris, 1957. 2v.
40582.25.19 Beyle, Henri. Le rouge et le noir. Paris, 1959.
40582.25.29 Beyle, Henri. The red and the black. N.Y., 1953.
40582.25.31 Beyle, Henri. The red and the black. N.Y., 1953.
40582.25.35 Beyle, Henri. Scarlet and black. London, 1938. 2v.
40582.25.38 Beyle, Henri. The red and the black. N.Y., 1958.
40582.25.40 Beyle, Henri. Stendhal's The red and the black. Philadelphia, 1949.
40582.25.45 Beyle, Henri. The red and the black. London, 1916.
40582.25.70 Beyle, Henri. Il rosso e il nero. Roma, 1957. 2v.
40582.25.75 Beyle, Henri. Scarlet and black. London, 1965.
40582.25.80 Beyle, Henri. Red and black. N.Y., 1969.
40582.26 Beyle, Henri. Vies de Haydn, de Mozart. Paris, 1872.
40582.27 Beyle, Henri. Vie de Rossini. Paris, 1864.
NEDL 40582.29 Beyle, Henri. L'abbesse de Castro. Paris, 1912.
40582.30A Beyle, Henri. Chronique et nouvelles. Paris, 1855.
40582.30B Beyle, Henri. Chronique et nouvelles. Paris, 1855.
40582.31 Beyle, Henri. Journal de Stendhal. Paris, 1908.
40582.32 Beyle, Henri. Journal d'Italie. Paris, 1911.
40582.33 Beyle, Henri. Correspondance of Stendhal (1800-1842). Paris, 1908. 3v.
40582.33.5 Beyle, Henri. Les plus belles lettres de Stendhal. Paris, 1962.

40582.8 - Individual authors, etc. - 1800-1849 - Criticism, etc. - Stendhal, i.e. H. Beyle - Individual works - cont.

40582.34 Beyle, Henri. Stendhal, lettres à Pauline. Paris, 1921.
40582.34.5 Beyle, Henri. The private diaries of Stendhal. Garden City, 1954.
40582.34.6 Beyle, Henri. The private diaries of Stendhal. London, 1955.
40582.36 Beyle, Henri. Une position sociale. Paris, 1927.
40582.38 Beyle, Henri. Souvenirs d'égotisme. Paris, 1892.
40582.38.5 Beyle, Henri. Souvenirs d'égotisme. Paris, 1948.
40582.38.25 Beyle, Henri. Memoirs of egotism. N.Y., 1949.
40582.38.70 Beyle, Henri. Memoirs of an egotist. London, 1949.
40582.38.75 Beyle, Henri. Souvenirs d'égotisme. Paris, 1950.
40582.38.80A Beyle, Henri. Memoirs of a tourist. Evanston, 1962.
40582.38.80B Beyle, Henri. Memoirs of a tourist. Evanston, 1962.
40582.40 Beyle, Henri. Vie de Henri Brulard, autobiographie. Paris, 1890.
40582.40.2 Beyle, Henri. Vie de Henry Brulard. Paris, 1949. 2v.
40582.40.5 Beyle, Henri. Vie de Henry Brulard. Paris, 1953.
40582.40.10 Beyle, Henri. The life of Henri Brulard. London, 1958.
40582.41.2 Beyle, Henri. Life of Rossini. N.Y., 1970.
40582.65 Beyle, Henri. Féder. London, 1960.

40583 Individual authors, etc. - 1800-1849 - Criticism, etc. - Stendhal, i.e. H. Beyle - Biography and criticism

40583.1 Pamphlet box. Stendhal-Beyle.
40583.1.5F Pamphlet box. Henri Beyle.
40583.1.25 Silomon, Karl H. Stendhal in Deutschland; ein bibliographischer Versuch. Murnau, 1939.
40583.2 Collignon, Albert. L'art et la vie de Stendhal. Paris, 1868.
40583.3 Paton, A.A. Henry Beyle. London, 1874.
40583.4 Benedetto, L.F. Arrigo Beyle milanese. Firenze, 1942.
40583.4.10 Benedetto, L.F. La Parma di Stendhal. Firenze, 1950.
40583.5 Bougy, Alfred de. Stendhal, sa vie. Paris, 1868.
40583.6 Cordier, H. Stendhal et ses amis. Evreux, 1890.
40583.7 Rod, Edouard. Stendhal. Photoreproduction. Paris, 1892.
40583.10 Brun, Pierre. Henry Beyle-Stendhal. Grenoble, 1900.
40583.11 Comment a vécu Stendhal. Paris, 1900.
40583.12 Chuquet, A. Stendhal-Beyle. Paris, 1902.
40583.13 Brombert, V.H. Stendhal et la voie oblique. New Haven, 1954.
40583.13.5 Brombert, V.H. Stendhal. 1. ed. Englewood Cliffs, 1962.
40583.13.10 Brombert, Victor H. Stendhal: fiction and the themes of freedom. N.Y., 1968.
40583.15A Mélia, Jean. La vie amoureuse de Stendhal. Paris, 1909.
40583.15B Mélia, Jean. La vie amoureuse de Stendhal. Paris, 1909.
40583.18 Gunnel, D. Stendhal et l'Angleterre. Paris, 1909.
40583.21 Stryienski, C. Histoire des oeuvres de Stendhal. Paris, 1903.
40583.23 Mélia, Jean. Stendhal et ses commentateurs. Paris, 1911.
40583.24 Mélia, Jean. Les idées de Stendhal. Paris, 1910.
40583.26 Farges, Louis. Stendhal diplomate. Paris, 1892.
40583.28 Mino, F. Saggio di uno studio su lo Stendhal. Napoli, 1911.
40583.33 Blum, Léon. Stendhal et le beylisme. Paris, 1914.
40583.33.3 Blum, Léon. Stendhal et le beylisme. 3. éd. Paris, 1947.
40583.34 Arbelet, Paul. La jeunesse de Stendhal. Paris, 1914.
40583.36 Delacroix, Henri. La psychologie de Stendhal. Paris, 1918.
40583.37 Martineau, Henri. Litinéaire de Stendhal. Paris, 1912.
40583.37.5 Martineau, Henri. L'oeuvre de Stendhal. Paris, 1945.
40583.37.6 Martineau, Henri. L'oeuvre de Stendhal. Paris, 1966.
40583.37.10 Martineau, Henri. Le calendrier de Stendhal. Paris, 1950.
40583.37.15 Martineau, Henri. Nouvelles soirées du Stendhal-club. Paris, 1950.
40583.39 Stryienski, Casimir. Soirées du Stendhal club. Paris, 1905.
40583.40 Stryienski, Casimir. Soirées du Stendhal Club. 2. éd. Paris, 1905-08. 2v.
40583.45 La revue critique des idées et des livres. v.20. Paris, 1913.
40583.50 Bourget, Paul. Stendhal. Paris, 1920.
40583.53 Burger, Jakob. Stendhal-Beyle und die französische Romantik. Marburg, 1913.
40583.55 Champion, Edouard. Hommage à Stendhal. Abbeville, 1920.
40583.60 Faure, Gabriel. Au pays de Stendhal. Grenoble, 1920.
40583.65 Sabatier, Pierre. Equisse de la morale de Stendhal. Paris, 1920.
40583.72 Trompeo, Pietro Paolo. Nell'Italia romantica sulle orme di Stendhal. Roma, 1924.
Htn 40583.75* Suarès, André. Stendhal, Verlaine, Baudelaire, Gérard de Nerval et autres gueux. Paris, 1923.
40583.77 Henriot, Emile. Stendhaliana. Paris, 1924.
40583.79 Giglio, A. Stendhal e la letteratura italiana. Milano, 1925.
40583.81 Novati, Francesco. Stendhal e l'anima italiana. Milano, 1925.
40583.85 Arbelet, Paul. Stendhal épicier. Paris, 1926.
40583.86 Arbelet, Paul. Stendhal du pays des comédiennes. Grenoble, 1934.
40583.90B Bonnard, Abel. La vie amoureuse d'Henri Beyle (Stendhal). Paris, 1926.
40583.95.3 Hazard, Paul. La vie de Stendhal. 25. éd. Paris, 1927.
40583.102 Hazard, Paul. Stendhal (Henri Beyle). N.Y., 1929.
40583.107 Lebègue, Raymond. Etude bibliographique sur armance. Paris, 1923.
40583.110 Leroy, Maxime. Stendhal politique. Paris, 1929.
40583.112 Faure, Gabriel. Stendhal, compagnon d'Italie. Paris, 1931.
40583.114 Charlier, Gustave. Stendhal et ses amis belges. Paris, 1931.
40583.116 Jourda, Pierre. Stendhal raconté par ceux qui l'ont vu. Paris, 1931.
40583.118 David, Maurice. Stendhal; sa vie, son oeuvre. Paris, 1931.
40583.120 Fineshriber, William H. Stendhal, the romantic rationalist. Princeton, 1932.
40583.122 Marsan, Jules. Stendhal. Paris, 1932.
40583.124 Brussaly, Manuel. The political ideas of Stendhal. N.Y., 1933.
40583.126 Wagner, Wolfgang. Stendhals Beziehung zum 18. Jahrhundert und sein Werk. Inaug. Diss. Dresden, 1933.
40583.128 The life and writings of M. de Stendhal (Henri Beyle). London, 1856.
40583.130 Thihaudet, Albert. Stendhal. Paris, 1931.

583 Individual authors, etc. - 1800-1849 - Criticism, etc. - Stendhal, i.e. H. Beyle - Biography and criticism - cont.

40583.132 Le Breton, André V. Le rouge et le noir de Stendhal. Paris, 1933?
40583.132.5 Le Breton, André. Le rouge et le noir de Stendhal. Paris, 1950.
40583.134 Boylesve, René. Réflexions sur Stendhal. Paris, 1929.
40583.136 Dumolard, Henry. Autour de Stendhal. Grenoble, 1932.
40583.140 Enste, Egon. Stendhal als Schilderer der Sitten seiner Zeit. Inaug. Diss. Bochum-Langendrer, 1934.
40583.142 Caraccio, Armand. Stendhal et les promenades dans Rome. Thèse. Paris, 1934.
40583.142.5 Caraccio, Armand. Stendhal, l'homme et l'oeuvre. Paris, 1951.
40583.142.6 Caraccio, Armand. Stendhal. N.Y., 1965.
40583.142.10 Caraccio, Armand. Variétés Stendhaliennes. Grenoble, 1947.
40583.144 Martino, Pierre. Stendhal. Paris, 1934.
40583.146 Chartier, E. Stendhal. Paris, 1935.
40583.148 Bosselaers, R. Le cas Stendhal, une mise au point. Paris, 1938.
40583.148.5 Bosselaers, R. Le cas Stendhal, une mise au point. Paris, 1938.
40583.150 Wurm, J. Die Kunstanschauung von Henri Beyle-Stendhal. Inaug. Diss. Battrop, 1938.
40583.152 Madini, P. Stendhal a Milano e il Casino degli Andeghee. Milano, 1933.
40583.155.1 Green, Frederick Charles. Stendhal. N.Y., 1970.
40583.158 Tiltoni, T. Arrigo Beyle (Stendhal). Torino, 1925.
40583.160 Alciatore, J. Stendhal et Helvetius. Thesis. Chicago, 1941.
40583.160.5 Alciatore, J. Stendhal et Helvetius. Genève, 1952.
40583.162 Ravel, Louis. Stendhal, curieux homme. Avignon, 1941.
40583.164 Raya, Gino. Stendhal. Modena, 1943.
40583.167 Jacoubet, Henri. Stendhal. Paris, 1943.
40583.170 Poppe, Roger. Stendhal à Rome. Paris, 1944.
40583.172 Josephson, Matthew. Stendhal. Garden City, 1946.
40583.175 Prévost, Juan. La création chez Stendhal. Sagittaire, 1942.
40583.176A Bardèche, M. Stendhal Romancier. Paris, 1947.
40583.176B Bardèche, M. Stendhal Romancier. Paris, 1947.
40583.178 Litto, Victor del. Bibliographie stendhalienne, 1938-1943. Grenoble, 1945. 6v.
40583.178.5 Litto, Victor del. En marge des manuscrits de Stendhal. Paris, 1955.
40583.178.10 Litto, Victor del. La vie intellectuelle de Stendahl. Paris, 1959.
40583.178.12 Litto, Victor del. La vie intellectuelle de Stendhal. 2. éd. Thèse. Paris, 1962.
40583.178.15 Litto, Victor del. La vie de Stendhal. Paris, 1965.
40583.178.20 Litto, Victor del. Album Stendhal. Paris, 1966.
40583.180 Martineau, H. Petit dictionnaire stendhalien. Paris, 1948.
40583.185 Flake, Otto. Versuch über Stendhal. München, 1947.
40583.187 Mérimée, Prosper. H.B. par un des quarante. Paris, 1920.
40583.190 Dollot, René. Stendhal, journaliste. Paris, 1948.
40583.195 Mérimée, Prosper. H.B. Texte de l'édition originale de 1850. Paris, 1948.
40583.200 Chartier, E. Stendhal. Paris, 1948.
40583.202 Tusero, Clemente. Stendhal. 1. ed. Verona, 1949.
40583.204 Clewes, Howard. Stendhal. London, 1950.
40583.206 Liprandi, Claude. Stendhal. Avignon, 1949.
40583.206.5 Liprandi, Claude. Sur un personnage du Rouge et le noir. Lausanne, 1959.
40583.206.10 Liprandi, Claude. Au coeur du Rouge. Lausanne, 1961.
40583.208 Debraye, H. Stendhal. Genève, 1950.
40583.212 Martineau, Henri. Le coeur de Stendhal. Paris, 1952. 2v.
40583.214 François-Poncet, Andre. Stendhal in Braunschweig. Mainz, 1951.
40583.214.5 François-Poncet, Andre. Stendhal en Allemagne. Paris, 1967.
40583.215 François-Poncet, Andre. Stendhal a Genève. Neuchâtel, 1954.
40583.220 Aragon, L. La lumière de Stendhal. Paris, 1954.
40583.225 DuParc, Yves. Dans le sillage de Stendhal. Lyon, 1955.
40583.225.5 DuParc, Yves. Quand Stendhal relisait les Promenades. Lausanne, 1959.
40583.230 Marill, Francine. Le naturel chez Stendhal. Paris, 1956.
40583.231 Marill, Francine. Le naturel chez Stendhal. Thèse. Paris, 1956.
40583.235 Marill, Francine. Stendhal et le sentiment religieux. Paris, 1956.
40583.236 Marill, Francine. Stendhal et le sentiment. Thèse. Paris, 1956.
40583.238 Marill, Francine. Stendhal. Paris, 1959.
40583.240 Journées Stendhaliennes internationales. Journées Stendhaliennes internationales de Grenoble. Paris, 1956.
40583.245 Billy, André. Ce cher Stendhal. Paris, 1958.
40583.250 Michel, Francois. Études stendhaliennes. Paris, 1958.
40583.250.5F Michel, François. Fichier stendhalien. Boston, 1964. 3v.
40583.255 De'de'yuan, Charles. Stendhal et les chroniques italiennes. Paris, 1956.
40583.260 Blin, Georges. Stendhal et les problémes du roman. Paris, 1954.
40583.260.5 Blin, Georges. Stendhal et les problèmes de la personnalité. Paris, 1958.
40583.265 Stendhal club. Lausanne. 1,1958+ 10v.
40583.270 Frid, Iakov V. Stendal'. Moskva, 1958.
40583.270.2 Frid, Iakov V. Stendal'. Izd. 2. Moskva, 1967.
40583.275 Bonfantini, M. Stendhal e il realismo. 1. ed. Milano, 1958.
40583.280 Adams, Robert M. Stendhal. N.Y., 1959.
40583.285 Vianu, Tudor. Ideile lui Stendhal. Bucuresti, 1959.
40583.290 Dutourd, Jean. L'âme sensible. 11. éd. Paris, 1959.
40583.290.5 Dutourd, Jean. The man of sensibility. N.Y., 1961.
40583.295 Feuillade, J.H. Notes sur Stendhal. Paris, 1955.
40583.299 Vinogradov, Anatolii K. Stendal' i ego vremia. Moskva, 1938.
40583.300 Vinogradov, Anatolii K. Stendal' i ego vremia. 2. izd. Moskva, 1960.
40583.305 Parma (City). Biblioteca palatina. Mostra Stendhaliana. Parma, 1959.
40583.310 Moscow. Vsesoiuznaia gosudarstvennaia biblioteka innostrannykh literatury. Stendal'; bibliografiia russkikh perevodov i kriticheskikh literatury na russkom iazyke. Moskva, 1961.

40583 Individual authors, etc. - 1800-1849 - Criticism, etc. - Stendhal, i.e. H. Beyle - Biography and criticism - cont.

40583.315 Durand, Gilbert. Le décor mythique de la chartreuse de Parme. Paris, 1961.
40583.320 Dédéyan, Charles. Stendhal chroniqueur. Paris, 1962.
40583.320.5 Dédéyan, Charles. L'Italie dans l'oeuvre romanesque de Stendhal. Paris, 1963. 2v.
40583.322 Arbelet, Paul. Premier voyage de Stendhal au pays des comediennes. Paris, 1928.
40583.324 Klostermann, Wolf. Der Wandel des Stendhalbildes. Kiel, 1961.
40583.326 Maquet, Albert. Deux amis italiens de Stendhal. Lausanne, 1963.
40583.327 Jones, Grahame C. L'ironie dans les romans de Stendhal. Lausanne, 1966.
40583.328 Pellegrini, C. Stendhal e la Toscana. Firenze, 1962.
40583.329 Davray, J. Notre Stendhal. Paris, 1949.
40583.330 Souka, Fatma. Les idées de Stendhal en matière d'art littéraire. Le Caire, 1962.
40583.331 Hemmings, F.W.J. Stendhal, a study of his novels. Oxford, 1964.
40583.332 Berges, Consuelo. Stendhal, su vida, su mundo, su obra. Madrid, 1962.
40583.333 Dechamps, J. Amities stendhaliennes en Belgique. Bruxelles, 1963.
40583.334 Atherton, J.H. Stendhal. London, 1964.
40583.335 Baumann, Carl. Literatur und intellektueller Kitsch. Heidelberg, 1964.
40583.336 Stendhal-Club. Première journée du Stendhal Club par Ernest Abravanel. Lausanne, 1965.
40583.337 Delfini, Antonio. Modena 1831. Milano, 1962.
40583.338 Trompeo, Pietro Paolo. Incontri di Stendhal. Napoli, 1963.
40583.339 Fischer, Jan O. Stendhal, první soudce kapitalismu. Praha, 1951.
40583.340 Pieyre de Mandiargues, André. Beylamour. Paris, 1965.
40583.341 Gilman, Stephen. The tower as emblem. Frankfurt, 1967.
40583.345 Castex, Pierre. Le rouge et le noir de Stendhal. Paris, 1967.
40583.350 Strauss, André. La fortune de Stendhal en Angleterre. Paris, 1966.
40583.352 Colesanti, Massimo. Stendhal; la realtà e il ricordo. Roma, 1966.
40583.354 Rude, Fernand. Stendhal et la pensée sociale de son temps. Paris, 1967.
40583.356 Drevet, Camille. Le dauphiné de Stendhal. Gap, 1954.
40583.358 Maione, Italo. Due profili: Stendhal, G. de Nerval. Napoli, 1954.
40583.360 Imbert, Henri François. Les métamorphoses de la liberté. Paris, 1967.
40583.360.5 Imbert, Henri François. Stendhal et la tentation jauséniste. Genève, 1970.
40583.362 Reizov, Boris G. Stendal'. Leningrad, 1968.
40583.364 McWatters, K.G. Stendhal, lecteur des romanciers anglais. Lausanne, 1968.
40583.366 Pincherle, Bruno. In compagnia di Stendhal. (Beyle). Milano, 1967.
40583.368 Grün, Ruth. Hommes-copies, dandies and fausses passions. Genève, 1967.
40583.370 Doyon, André. Amitiés parisiennes de Stendhal. Lausanne, 1969.
40583.372 Montello, Josué. Un maître oublie de Stendhal. Paris, 1970.
40583.375 Fowlie, Wallace. Stendhal. N.Y., 1969.
40583.378 Dramińska-Joczowa, Maria. Wpływ ideologów na młodego Stendhala. Wrocław, 1970.
40583.380 Heisler, Marcel. Stendhal et Napoléon. Paris, 1969.
40583.382 Arbelet, Paul. Les amours romantiques de Stendhal et de Victorine. Paris, 1924.
40583.384 Weber, Jean Paul. Stendhal; les structures thématiques de l'oeuvre et du destin. Paris, 1969.
40583.386 Congrès stendhalien, 4th. Civitavecchia and Rome, 1964. Communications présentées au Congrès stendhalien de Civitavecchia. Firenze, 1966.
40583.388 Trout, Paulette. La vocation romanesque de Stendhal. Paris, 1970.
40583.390 Bolster, Richard. Stendhal, Balzac, et le féminisme romantique. Paris, 1970.
40583.392 Gutwirth, Marcel Marc. Stendhal. N.Y., 1971.
40583.394 Boncompain, Claude. Stendhal; ou, La double vie de Henri Beyle. Paris, 1955.
40583.396 Schwyn, Walter. La musique comme catalyseur de l'émotion stendhalienne. Thèse. Zürich, 1968.
40583.398 Tillett, Margaret G. Stendhal. London, 1971.
40583.400 Wood, Michael. Stendhal. London, 1971.

40584.5 Individual authors, etc. - 1800-1849 - Criticism, etc. - Vanderbourg

40584.5.80 Mortier, Roland. Un précurseur de Madame de Staël: Charles Vanderbourg, 1765-1827. Paris, 1955.

40584.10 Individual authors, etc. - 1800-1849 - Criticism, etc. - Vinet

40584.10.80 Beichel, Ursula. Alexandre Vinet. 1. Aufl. München, 1969.

40584.13 Individual authors, etc. - 1800-1849 - Criticism, etc. - Villemain - Works about

40584.13 Vauthier, G. Villemain. 1790-1870. Paris, 1913.
40584.13.10 Castille, H. M. Villemain. Paris, 1859.

40584.15 - .20 Individual authors, etc. - 1800-1849 - Criticism, etc. - Villemain - Writings

40584.17 Villemain, Abel L. Discours et mélanges littéraires. 3. éd. Paris, 1825.
40584.18 Villemain, Abel L. Discours et mélanges. Paris, 1846.
40584.18.5 Villemain, Abel L. Discours et mélanges littéraires. Paris, 1850.
40584.19 Villemain, Abel L. Mélanges. Brussels, 1829.
40584.19.3 Villemain, Abel L. Mélanges. Paris, 1827.
40584.19.5 Villemain, Abel L. Nouveaux mélanges historiques et littéraires. Paris, 1827.
40584.20 Villemain, Abel L. Études de littérature ancienne et etrangère. Paris, 1849.
40584.20.3 Villemain, Abel L. Études de littérature ancienne et etrangère. Paris, 1854.
40584.20.5 Villemain, Abel L. Études d'histoire moderne. Paris, 1848.

40584.21 - .30 Individual authors, etc. - 1800-1849 - Criticism, etc. - Vitet - Writings

40584.21 Vitet, L. Essais historiques. Paris, 1862.
40584.22 Vitet, L. Les états d'Orléans. Paris, 1849.
40584.23 Vitet, L. Étude sur...l'art. Paris, 1867-68. 4v.
40584.24 Vitet, L. La mort de Henri III. Bruxelles, 1829.
40584.25 Vitet, L. Les barricades. Scènes historiques. 4. éd. Paris, 1830.
40584.25.3 Vitet, L. Les barricades. Scènes historiques. 4. éd. Bruxelles, 1833.
40584.26 Vitet, L. Les états de Blois, ou La mort de Mme. de Guise. Bruxelles, 1829.
40584.28 Vitet, L. La ligue precédée des États d'Orléans. Paris, 1872. 2v.
40584.28.10 Vitet, L. Les états d'Orléans; scenes historiques. Paris, 1849.
40584.30 Vitet, L. Études philosophiques et littéraires. Paris, 1875.

40584.35 - Individual authors, etc. - 1800-1849 - Criticism, etc. - Anonymous works

40584.35 Aufzeichnungen eines nachgeborenen Prinzen. Stuttgart, 1841.

40585.1 Individual authors, etc. - 1800-1849 - Fiction - Chateaubriand, F.A.R. - Bibliographies

40585.1.5 Chateaubriand en Amérique; essai de bibliographie. n.p., 1949?

40585.2 - .399 Individual authors, etc. - 1800-1849 - Fiction - Chateaubriand, F.A.R. - Complete works

40585.3 Chateaubriand, F.A.R. Oeuvres complètes. v.1-28. Paris, 1826-31. 31v.
40585.5 Chateaubriand, F.A.R. Oeuvres complètes. Paris, 1830-31. 20v.
40585.10 Chateaubriand, F.A.R. Oeuvres complètes. Paris, 1843. 5v.

40585.400 - Individual authors, etc. - 1800-1849 - Fiction - Chateaubriand, F.A.R. - Selected works

40585.402 Chateaubriand, F.A.R. Oeuvres romanesques et voyages. Paris, 1969-
40585.410 Chateaubriand, F.A.R. Pages choisies. Paris, 1896.
40585.412 Chateaubriand, F.A.R. Pages choisies: La correspondance. Paris, 1911.
40585.415 Chateaubriand, F.A.R. François René de Chateaubriand: Choix de textes. Monaco, 1948.
40585.420 Chateaubriand, F.A.R. Lectures choisies de Chateaubriand. Paris, 1895.
40585.430 Chateaubriand, F.A.R. Chateaubriand, par lui-même. Paris, 1965.

40586 Individual authors, etc. - 1800-1849 - Fiction - Chateaubriand, F.A.R. - Individual works

40586.4 Chateaubriand, F.A.R. Oeuvres complètes. Paris, n.d. 12v.
40586.5.5 Chateaubriand, F.A.R. Atala. Paris, n.d.
40586.5.15 Chateaubriand, F.A.R. Itinéraire de Paris à Jérusalem. Paris, n.d.
40586.5.16 Chateaubriand, F.A.R. Voyages en Amérique, en Italie. Paris, 1829.
40586.5.18 Chateaubriand, F.A.R. Voyage en Italie. Paris, 1968.
40586.5.20 Chateaubriand, F.A.R. Voyages en Amérique, en Italie. Paris, 1860.
40586.5.22 Chateaubriand, F.A.R. Voyage en Amérique. Paris, 1964. 2v.
40586.5.23 Chateaubriand, F.A.R. Travels in America. Lexington, 1969.
40586.6 Chateaubriand, F.A.R. Oeuvres, v. XXI. Atala, René et les Abencérages. Brussels, 1826.
40586.6.5 Chateaubriand, F.A.R. Atala. Paris, 1851.
40586.7 Chateaubriand, F.A.R. Nouvelles. Paris, 1831. 3v.
40586.8 Chateaubriand, F.A.R. Pensées. Paris, 1914.
40586.9 Chateaubriand, F.A.R. Atala. Boston, 1802.
40586.10.2 Chateaubriand, F.A.R. Atala. Valencia, 1803.
Htn 40586.10.5* Chateaubriand, F.A.R. Atala. Paris, 1805.
40586.11 Chateaubriand, F.A.R. Atala. London, 1818.
40586.11.5 Chateaubriand, F.A.R. Atala. 2. ed. Boston, 1814.
X Cg 40586.11.5 Chateaubriand, F.A.R. Atala. 2. ed. Boston, 1814.
40586.11.15 Chateaubriand, F.A.R. Atala. Paris, 1849.
40586.11.20 Chateaubriand, F.A.R. Atala. Paris, 1859.
40586.11.25 Chateaubriand, F.A.R. Atala. Porto, 1878.
40586.11.27 Chateaubriand, F.A.R. Atala, René, Le dernier Abencérage. Paris, 1883.
40586.11.30F Chateaubriand, F.A.R. Atala. N.Y., 1884.
40586.12 Chateaubriand, F.A.R. Atala. Paris, n.d.
40586.13 Chateaubriand, F.A.R. Atala. Paris, 1889.
40586.13.5 Chateaubriand, F.A.R. Atala. Paris, 1892.
40586.13.10 Chateaubriand, F.A.R. Atala and René. Chicago, 1901.
40586.13.12 Chateaubriand, F.A.R. Atala. Boston, 1905.
40586.13.15 Chateaubriand, F.A.R. Atala. Paris, 1934.
40586.13.20 Chateaubriand, F.A.R. Atala. Paris, 1950.
40586.13.25 Chateaubriand, F.A.R. Atala. Berkeley, 1957.
NEDL 40586.14 Chateaubriand, F.A.R. Atala. Paris, 1906.
NEDL 40586.14.3 Chateaubriand, F.A.R. Atala, René, Le dernier Abencérage. Paris, 1907?
40586.14.3.5 Chateaubriand, F.A.R. Atala, René, Le dernier Abencérage. 3. ed. London, 1908.
40586.14.5 Chateaubriand, F.A.R. Atala, or The love and constancy of two savages in the desert. Stanford, 1930.
40586.14.10 Chateaubriand, F.A.R. Atala, René. Paris, 1930.
40586.14.20 Chateaubriand, F.A.R. Atala et ses critiques. n.p., n.d.
40586.14.50 Morellet, A. Observations critiques sur le roman intitulé Atala. Paris, 1801.
40586.14.60 Clément, J.M.B. Roman poétique: Atala. Paris, 1801.
40586.15 Chateaubriand, F.A.R. Recollections of Italy, England and America. Philadelphia, 1816.
40586.15.9 Chateaubriand, F.A.R. Travels in Greece, Palestine, Egypt. London, 1812. 2v.
40586.16 Chateaubriand, F.A.R. Travels in Greece, Palestine, Egypt and Barbary. Philadelphia, 1813.
40586.16.3 Chateaubriand, F.A.R. Travels in Greece, Palestine, Egypt and Barbary. N.Y., 1814.
40586.17 Chateaubriand, F.A.R. Itinerario da Parigi a Gerusalemme. v. 6. Naples, 1836.
40586.17.6 Chateaubriand, F.A.R. Itinéraire de Paris à Jérusalem. 2. éd. Paris, 1812. 2v.

40586 Individual authors, etc. - 1800-1849 - Fiction - Chateaubriand, F.A.R. - Individual works - cont.

40586.17.10 Chateaubriand, F.A.R. Itinéraire de Paris à Jérusalem. Paris, 1852. 2v.
40586.17.15 Chateaubriand, F.A.R. Itinéraire de Paris à Jérusalem. Baltimore, 1946. 2v.
40586.17.20 Chateaubriand, F.A.R. Journal de Jérusalem. Paris, 1950.
40586.17.25 Chateaubriand, F.A.R. Itinéraire de Paris à Jérusalem. Paris, 1963.
40586.17.35 Chateaubriand, F.A.R. Travels to Jerusalem and the Holy Land. 3. ed. London, 1835. 2v.
40586.18.6 Julien, servant of Chateaubriand. Itinéraire de Paris à Jérusalem. 3. éd. Paris, 1904.
40586.18.9 Julien, servant of Chateaubriand. Itinéraire de Paris à Jérusalem. Paris, 1904.
Htn 40586.18.10* Chateaubriand, F.A.R. Génie du Christianisme. Paris, 1802. 5v.
Htn 40586.18.10.7* Chateaubriand, F.A.R. Génie du Christianisme. 2. éd. Paris, 1809. 2v.
40586.18.11.2 Chateaubriand, F.A.R. Génie du Christianisme. v.1-4. Paris, 1830. 2v.
40586.18.12 Chateaubriand, F.A.R. Génie du Christianisme. Paris, 18-? 2v.
40586.18.12.3 Chateaubriand, F.A.R. Le génie du Christianisme. Paris, 1852. 2v.
40586.18.12.5 Chateaubriand, F.A.R. Le génie du Christianisme. Paris, 1871. 2v.
40586.18.12.7 Chateaubriand, F.A.R. Le génie du Christianisme. Tours, 1877.
NEDL 40586.18.13 Chateaubriand, F.A.R. Génie du Christianisme. v.1-2. Paris, 1894.
40586.18.14 Chateaubriand, F.A.R. O genio do Christianismo. 6a ed. Porto, 1910. 2v.
40586.18.25 Coup-d'oeil rapide sur le génie du Christianisme. Paris, 1802.
40586.18.28 Notes critiques...sur le Génie du Christianisme. Paris, 1803.
Htn 40586.18.30* Chateaubriand, F.A.R. Défense du génie du Christianisme. Paris, 1803.
40586.18.40 Fontanes, Louis. Extraits critiques du génie du Christianisme. Paris, 1803.
40586.18.50 Extrait de différens écrits sur le génie du christianisme. n.p., n.d.
40586.18.60 Lettre à M. de Chateaubriand, sur deux chapitres du Génie du Christianisme. Gèneve, 1806.
40586.18.100 Chateaubriand, F.A.R. The martyrs. N.Y., 1812. 3v.
40586.19 Chateaubriand, F.A.R. Les martyrs. Paris, 1830. 2v.
40586.19.5 Chateaubriand, F.A.R. Les martyrs. Paris, 18- ?
40586.19.50 Chateaubriand, F.A.R. The martyrs. N.Y., 1859.
40586.20 Chateaubriand, F.A.R. Les martyrs. Paris, 1891.
40586.20.10 Chateaubriand, F.A.R. Les martyrs. Paris, 1936.
40586.20.20A Chateaubriand, F.A.R. Les martyres de Dioclétien. Paris, 1951.
40586.20.20B Chateaubriand, F.A.R. Les martyres de Dioclétien. Paris, 1951.
40586.20.40.3 Chateaubriand, F.A.R. Os martyres. 3. ed. Lisboa, 1908. 2v.
40586.20.50 Deplace, Guy M. Examen de la critique des Martyrs, insérée dans le Journal de l'empire. n.p., n.d.
40586.20.55 Andlau, Beatrix. Chateaubriand et Les martyrs. Thèse. Paris, 1952.
40586.21 Chateaubriand, F.A.R. Moyse. St. Germain, n.d.
40586.21.10 Chateaubriand, F.A.R. René. Paris, 1935.
40586.21.12 Chateaubriand, F.A.R. René. Lille, 1947.
40586.21.13 Chateaubriand, F.A.R. René. Genève, 1970.
40586.21.14 Chateaubriand, F.A.R. Atala, René. Paris, 1966.
40586.21.15 Chateaubriand, F.A.R. Renato. Bruxelles, 1929.
40586.21.18 Chateaubriand, F.A.R. Congres de Vérone. Paris, 1838. 2v.
40586.21.25 Chateaubriand, F.A.R. The Congress of Verona. London, 1838. 2v.
40586.21.50 Chateaubriand, F.A.R. Les Natchez. Baltimore, 1932.
40586.21.75 Chateaubriand, F.A.R. Vie de Rancé. Paris, 1971.
40586.22 St. Beuve, C.A. Chateaubriand et son groupe littéraire sous l'Empire. Paris, 1861. 2v.
40586.22.3 St. Beuve, C.A. Chateaubriand et son groupe littéraire sous l'Empire. Paris, 1872. 2v.
40586.22.7A St. Beuve, C.A. Chateaubriand et son groupe littéraire sous l'Empire. Paris, 1878. 2v.
40586.22.7B St. Beuve, C.A. Chateaubriand et son groupe littéraire sous l'Empire. Paris, 1878. 2v.
40586.24.60 Chateaubriand, F.A.R. Essai historique, politique et moral. v.1-2. Londres, 1814.
40586.24.75A Chateaubriand, F.A.R. Essai historique, politique et moral. Londres, 1820.
40586.24.75B Chateaubriand, F.A.R. Essai historique, politique et moral. Londres, 1820.
40586.24.80 Variantes de l'édition de 1797. n.p., n.d.
40586.24.100 Spring, H.P. Chateaubriand at the crossways. N.Y., 1924.
40586.25 Chateaubriand, F.A.R. Études ou Discours historiques. Paris, 1834. 4v.
40586.25.5 Chateaubriand, F.A.R. Études historiques. v.2. Paris, 1872.
40586.25.30 Chateaubriand, F.A.R. Mélanges politiques. Paris, 1861.
40586.25.50 Chateaubriand, F.A.R. Politique. Paris, 1862.
40586.27 Chateaubriand, F.A.R. Mémoires d'outre-tombe. Paris, 1826-28. 6v.
40586.27.5 Chateaubriand, F.A.R. Mémoires d'outre-tombe. Bruxelles, 1859-60. 6v.
Htn 40586.27.10* Chateaubriand, F.A.R. Mémoires d'outre-tombe. N.Y., 1848-49. 2v.
40586.27.20 Chateaubriand, F.A.R. Mémoires d'outre-tombe. Paris, 1860. 6v.
40586.28 Chateaubriand, F.A.R. Memoires d'outre-tombe. v.1-4,6. Paris, 1899. 5v.
40586.28.5 Chateaubriand, F.A.R. Mémoires d'outre-tombe. Paris, 19- 6v.
40586.28.7 Chateaubriand, F.A.R. Mémoires d'outre-tombre, 1814-1815. Oxford, 1906.
40586.28.10 Chateaubriand, F.A.R. Mémoires de ma vie. Paris, 1948.
40586.28.12 Chateaubriand, F.A.R. Mémoires d'outre-tombe. Paris, 1911.
40586.28.50 Chateaubriand, F.A.R. En marge des mémoires d'outre-tombe. Thèse. Paris, 1933.
40586.28.55 Chateaubriand, F.A.R. En marge des mémoires d'outre-tombe. Paris, 1933.
40586.28.63 Levaillant, M. Deux livres des mémoires d'outre-tombe. Paris, 1936. 2v.

Classified Listing

)586 Individual authors, etc. - 1800-1849 - Fiction - Chateaubriand, F.A.R. - Individual works - cont.

40586.28.64 Gautier, Jean Maurice. L'exotisme américain dans l'oeuvre de Chateaubriand. Manchester, 1951.
40586.28.64.5 Gautier, Jean Maurice. Le style des mémoires d'outre-tembe de Chateaubriand. Genève, 1959.
40586.28.64.7 Gautier, Jean Maurice. Le style des mémoires d'outre-tombe de Chateaubriand. Genève, 1959.
40586.28.64.9 Gautier, Jean Maurice. Le style des mémoires d'outre-tombe de Chateaubriand. Genève, 1964.
40586.28.65 Chateaubriand, F.A.R. Deux livres des mémoires d'outre-tombe. Paris, 1936. 2v.
40586.28.75 Chateaubriand, F.A.R. Mémoires d'outre-tombe. Paris, 1945.
40586.28.82 Chateaubriand, F.A.R. Mémoires d'outre-tombe. Paris, 1948.
40586.28.84 Chateaubriand, F.A.R. Mémoires d'outre-tombe. 2. éd. Paris, 1949-50. 2v.
40586.28.85 Chateaubriand, F.A.R. Incidences, digression philosophique. Paris, 1947.
40586.28.86 Chateaubriand, F.A.R. Mémoires d'outre-tombe. v.2. Paris, 1958.
40586.28.90 Chateaubriand, F.A.R. Mémoires d'outre-tombe. Lausanne, 1963. 4v.
40586.28.92 Chateaubriand, F.A.R. Mémoires d'outre-tombe. 3. éd. Paris, 1966.
IEDL 40586.29 Chateaubriand, F.A.R. Memoirs of...Chateaubriand. London, 1902. 6v.
40586.29.5 Chateaubriand, F.A.R. Memoirs. N.Y., 1961.
40586.30 Chateaubriand, F.A.R. Memorias de ultra-tumba. Madrid, 1848-50. 4v.
Htn 40586.31* Lenormant, Charles. M. de Chateaubriand et les Mémoires d'outre-tombe. Paris, 1850.
Htn 40586.31.20* Lectures des Mémoires de m. de Chateaubriand. Paris, 1834.
40586.32 Chateaubriand, F.A.R. Correspondance générale. Paris, 1912-1924. 5v.
40586.33 Chateaubriand, F.A.R. Discours de réception à l'Académie Française. Paris, 1815.
40586.34 Chateaubriand, F.A.R. Un dernier amour de René; correspondance. Paris, 1903.
40586.35 La correspondance de Chateaubriand avec sa femme. Paris, 1908.
40586.35.10 Chateaubriand, F.A.R. Lettre à M. de Fontanes sur la campagne romaine. Genève, 1951.
40586.35.10.5 Chateaubriand, F.A.R. Lettre à M. de Fontanes sur la campagne romaine. Genève, 1961.
40586.36 Chateaubriand, F.A.R. A propos de la naissance du duc de Chateaubriand (Bordeaux). Paris, 1917.
40586.40 Chateaubriand, F.A.R. Chateaubriand. Grenoble, 1941.
40586.45 Chateaubriand, F.A.R. Las aventuras del ultimo Abencerrage. Paris, 1827.
40586.45.25 Chateaubriand, F.A.R. Les aventures du dernier Abencérage. Strasbourg, 1924?
40586.45.28 Chateaubriand, F.A.R. Les aventures du dernier Abencérage. Paris, 1926. 2v.
40586.50 Chateaubriand, F.A.R. Voyage au Mont-Blanc. Grenoble, 1920.
40586.55 Chateaubriand, F.A.R. Amour et vieillesse. Paris, 1922.
40586.63 Chateaubriand, F.A.R. The beauties of Christianity. Philadelphia, 1815.
40586.66 Chateaubriand, F.A.R. La jeunesse de Chateaubriand. Oxford, 1907.
40586.70 Observations critiques sur l'ouvrage intitulé: La Génie du Christianisme. Paris, 1817.

40587.1 - .899 Individual authors, etc. - 1800-1849 - Fiction - Chateaubriand, F.A.R. - Biography and criticism

40587.1 Pamphlet box. Chateaubriand.
40587.1.5 Pamphlet vol. Chateaubriand. 6 pam.
40587.1.7 Pamphlet vol. Chateaubriand. 4 pam.
40587.1.8 Pamphlet vol. Chateaubriand. 5 pam.
40587.1.10 Société Chateaubriand. Bulletin. Chatenay-Malabry. 1930+ 6v.
40587.2 Ancelot, Jacques A.F.P. Vie de Chateaubriand. Paris, 1860.
40587.3 Clergeau, l'abbé. Chateaubriand. Paris, 1860.
40587.3.2 Clergeau, l'abbé. Chateaubriand. 2. éd. Paris, 1860.
40587.4 Benoit, Charles. Chateaubriand, sa vie et ses oeuvres. Paris, 1865.
40587.4.2 Benoit, Charles. Éloge de Chateaubriand. Cuttings. n.p., 1864. 2 pam.
40587.5 Bona, Félix de. Chateaubriand, sa vie et ses écrits. Lille, 1885.
40587.6 Lenormant, C. Souvenirs d'enfance et de jeunesse de Chateaubriand. Paris, 1874.
40587.7 Lescure, M.F.A. de. Chateaubriand. Paris, 1892.
40587.8 Bardoux, A. Chateaubriand. Paris, 1893.
40587.8.5 Pailhès, G. Chateaubriand: sa femme et ses amis. Bordeaux, 1896.
40587.9 Roche, A. Chateaubriand et Madame de Staël. Paris, 1878.
40587.9.5 Gautier, P. Qua familiaritate Chateaubriand. Andigavis, 1902.
40587.11 Giraud, Victor. Chateaubriand. Paris, 1904.
40587.11.10 Giraud, Victor. Chateaubriand. Paris, 1932.
40587.12 Latreille, C. Chateaubriand. Paris, 1905.
40587.13A Lemaître, J. Chateaubriand. Paris, n.d.
40587.13B Lemaître, J. Chateaubriand. Paris, n.d.
40587.13C Lemaître, J. Chateaubriand. Paris, n.d.
40587.13D Lemaître, J. Chateaubriand. Paris, n.d.
40587.14 Le Braz, A. Au pays d'exil de Chateaubriand. Paris, 1909.
40587.14.2 Le Braz, A. Au pays d'exil de Chateaubriand. 2. éd. Paris, 1909.
40587.15 Giraud, Victor. Nouvelles études sur Chateaubriand. Paris, 1912.
40587.16 Essai sur Chateaubriand. Paris, 1866.
40587.17 Maurel, Andre. Essai sur Chateaubriand. Paris, 1898.
40587.18 Biro, E. Les dernières années de Chateaubriand. Paris, n.d.
40587.19 Sainte-Beuve, Charles. Chateaubriand. Paris, 1889. 2v.
40587.19.10 Sainte-Beuve, Charles. Chateaubriand et son groupe littéraire. Paris, 1948.
40587.20 Nantes, France. Société des Bibliophiles Bretons. Le cinquantenaire des funérailles de Chateaubriand. Nantes, 1899.
40587.22 Bertrin, G. La sincérité religieuse de Chateaubriand. Paris, 1900.

40587.1 - .899 Individual authors, etc. - 1800-1849 - Fiction - Chateaubriand, F.A.R. - Biography and criticism - cont.

40587.23 Souriau, Maurice. Les idées morales de Chateaubriand. 2. éd. Paris, 1909.
40587.24 Maurras, Charles. Chateaubriand, Michelet, Saint-Beuve. Paris, 1912.
40587.25 Lescure, M.F.A. de. Chateaubriand. Paris, 1908.
40587.25.7 Lescure, M.F.A. de. Chateaubriand. 7. éd. Paris, 1924?
40587.26 Michel, E. Chateaubriand. Paris, 1911. 2v.
40587.27 Potiquet, François Albert. Chateaubriand; l'anatomie de ses formes et ses amies. Paris, 1912.
40587.28 Körding, Hermann. Chateaubriand als Versdichter. Berlin, 1913.
40587.29 Noailles, M. de. Discours...le 6 décembre 1849. Paris, 1849.
Htn 40587.31* Senancour, E.P. Observations critiques sur les Génie du christianisme. Paris, 1816.
40587.32 Dick, Ernst. Plagiats de Chateaubriand. Bern, 1905.
Htn 40587.34* Gribble, Francis. Chateaubriand and his court of women. N.Y., 1909.
40587.34.2 Gribble, Francis. Chateaubriand and his court of women. N.Y., 1909.
40587.35 Audwin, M. Supernaturalism and satanism in Chateaubriand. Chicago, 1922.
40587.36 Beaunier, André. Trois amies de Chateaubriand. Paris, 1910.
40587.36.5 Courteuge, Charles. Touchante Pauline, amoureuse de Chateaubriand. Paris, 1965.
40587.37 Giraud, Victor. Passions et romans d'autrefois. Paris, 1925.
40587.38 Damaze de Raymond. Réponse aux attaques dirigées contre M. de Chateaubriand. Paris, 1812.
40587.39 Duclos, H.L. Éloge funèbre de M. Chateaubriand. Paris, 1848.
40587.40 Chinard, Gilbert. L'exotisme américain dans l'oeuvre de Chateaubriand. Photoreproduction. Paris, 1918.
40587.42 Levaillant, Maurice. Splendeurs et misères de Chateaubriand. 3. éd. Paris, 1922.
40587.42.8 Levaillant, Maurice. Chateaubriand, Madame Récamier et les mémoires d'outre-tombe, 1830-1850. Thèse. Paris, 1936.
40587.42.10 Levaillant, Maurice. Chateaubriand, Madame Récamier et les mémoires d'outre-tombe. Paris, 1936.
40587.42.12 Levaillant, Maurice. Chateaubriand. 2. éd. Paris, 1939.
40587.42.15 Levaillant, Maurice. Chateaubriand. Paris, 1960.
40587.44 Blennerhassett, C. Chateaubriand. Mainz, 1903.
40587.45 Carne, Louis. Études sur la vie et les ouvrages de M. de Chateaubriand. Paris, 1874.
40587.47 Miller, Meta Helena. Chateaubriand and English literature. Baltimore, 1925.
40587.47.5 Marcellus, M.L. Chateaubriand et son temps. Paris, 1859.
40587.50 Danielo, Julien. Les conversations de M. de Chateaubriand. Paris, 1864.
40587.53 Kervile, René. Essai d'une bio-bibliographie de Chateaubriand. Vannes, 1895.
40587.54 His, Charles. Lettre à M. le Comte de B***. Paris, 1812.
40587.55 Quillemin, Henri. L'homme des "Mémoires d'outre-tombe". Paris, 1965.
40587.56 Cantù, Cesare. Chateaubriand; discorso. Milano, 1835.
40587.57 Giraud, Victor. Le christianisme de Chateaubriand. Paris, 1925. 2v.
40587.60 Montgaillard, Jean G.M.R. de. Esprit, maximes et principes de M. François Auguste de Chateaubriand. Paris, 1815.
40587.65 Hart, Charles R. Chateaubriand and Homer. Baltimore, 1928.
40587.66 Moreau, Pierre. Chateaubriand, l'homme et l'oeuvre. Paris, 1956.
40587.66.5 Moreau, Pierre. Chateaubriand, l'homme et la vie. Paris, 1927.
40587.70 Briod, Blaisé. L'homérisme de Chateaubriand. Paris, 1928.
40587.75 Dempsey, Madeleine. A contribution to the study of the sources of the "Génie du christianisme". Thèse. Paris, 1928.
40587.80 Rouff, Marcel. La vie de Chateaubriand. 3. éd. Paris, 1929.
40587.82 Napione, T. Studi sulla fortuna di Chateaubriand nella letteratura e nell'arte italiana. Torino, 1928.
40587.86 Poirier, Alice. Les idées artistiques de Chateaubriand. Thèse. Paris, 1930.
40587.88 Poirier, Alice. Les notes critiques d'Avramiotti sur le voyage en Grèce de Chateaubriand. Thèse. Paris, 1929.
40587.90 Servien, Pius. Lyrisme et structures sonores. Thèse. Paris, 1930.
40587.91 Servien, Pius. Lyrisme et structures sonores. Thèse. Paris, 1930.
X Cg 40587.92 Dollinger, Albert. Les études historiques de Chateaubriand. Paris, 1932.
40587.92.5 Dollinger, Albert. Les études historiques de Chateaubriand. Thèse. Strasbourg, 1932.
40587.93 Döhner, Kurt. Zeit und Ewigkeit bei Chateaubriand. Inaug. Diss. Marburg, 1931.
40587.94 Durry, M.J. La vieillesse de Chateaubriand, 1830-1848. Thèse. Paris, 1933. 2v.
40587.94.5 Durry, M.J. La vieillesse de Chateaubriand, 1830-1848. Paris, 1933. 2v.
40587.95 Gillot, Hubert. Chateaubriand; ses idées, son action, son oeuvre. Paris, 1934.
40587.96 Deschamps, Jules. Chateaubriand en Angleterre. Paris, 1934.
40587.97 Moreau, Pierre. La conversion de Chateaubriand. Paris, 1933.
40587.97.5 Moreau, Pierre. Chateaubriand. Bruges, 1965.
40587.98 Longi, Olga. La terre et les morts dans l'oeuvre de Chateaubriand. Thèse. Baltimore, 1934.
40587.99 Diem, Heidi. Das Bild Deutschlands in Chateaubriands Werk. Bern, 1935.
40587.100 Vallese, R.E. (Mme.). Le thème de la mer dans l'oeuvre de Chateaubriand. Thèse. Milano, 1934.
40587.101 André-Vincent, P. Les idées politiques de Chateaubriand. Montpellier, 1936.
40587.102 André-Vincent, P. Les idées politiques de Chateaubriand. Montpellier, 1936.
40587.103 Hey, Paula. Chateaubriand und Pascal. Inaug. Diss. Würzburg, 1937.
40587.105 Bérenger, Henry. Chateaubriand; héros de l'aventure romantique. Paris, 1931.
40587.108 Duchemin, Marcel. Chateaubriand; essais de critique et d'histoire littéraire. Paris, 1938.

40587.1 - .899 Individual authors, etc. - 1800-1849 - Fiction - Chateaubriand, F.A.R. - Biography and criticism - cont.

40587.110.5A Maurois, André. Chateaubriand, poet, statesman, lover. N.Y., 1938.
40587.110.5B Maurois, André. Chateaubriand, poet, statesman, lover. N.Y., 1938.
40587.110.6A Maurois, André. Chateaubriand. Paris, 1938.
40587.110.6B Maurois, André. Chateaubriand. Paris, 1938.
40587.110.7 Maurois, André. Chateaubriand. Paris, 1939.
40587.110.8 Maurois, André. Chateaubriand. N.Y., 1958?
40587.110.9 Maurois, André. René. Paris, 1956.
40587.115 Evans, J. Chateaubriand; a biography. London, 1939.
40587.120 Pigasse, J. L'Occitanienne et sa soeur. Albi, 1940.
40587.125 Fauré, Gabriel. Essais sur Chateaubriand. Grenoble, 1946.
40587.126 Fauré, Gabriel. Les amours de Chateaubriand et de Madame de Vichet. Saint-Félicien-en-Vivarais, 1921.
40587.127 Fauré, Gabriel. Chateaubriand en Italie. Roma, n.d.
40587.128 Fauré, Gabriel. Chateaubriand et l'Occitanienne. Paris, 1920.
40587.130 Séchelles, R. Chateaubriand et l'âme celte. St. Brieuc, 1948.
40587.135 Trancia, Ennio. Chateaubriand. Brescia, 1958.
40587.138 Sekrecka, M. Chateaubriand; jako teoretyk i krytyk literacki. Lublin, 1958.
40587.140 Sieburg, Friedrich. Chateaubriand. Stuttgart, 1959.
40587.140.5 Sieburg, Friedrich. Chateaubriand. N.Y., 1962.
40587.145 Lathion, Lucien. Chateaubriand et Goethe en Valais. Sierre, 1944.
40587.150 Salonne, M.P. Chateaubriand et les Dames de Plancoët. 2. éd. St. Brieuc, 1960.
40587.152 Walker, Thomas Capell. Chateaubriand's natural scenery. Baltimore, 1946.
40587.155 Christophorov, Petr. Sur les pas de Chateaubriand en exil. Paris, 1961.
40587.156 Zdziechowski, M. Chateaubriand i Napoleon. Wilno, 1932.
40587.157 Zdziechowski, M. Chateaubriahd i Bourbonowie. Wilno, 1934.
40587.158 Diéguez, Manuel de. Chateaubriand. Paris, 1963.
40587.159 Mourot, J. Études sur les premières oeuvres de Chateaubriand. Paris, 1962.
40587.160 Vial, André. Chateaubriand et le Temps Perdu. Paris, 1963.
40587.160.5 Vial, André. Chateaubriand et une dame de Pierreclau. Paris, 1967.
40587.165 Richard, Jean-Pierre. Paysage de Chateaubriand. Paris, 1967.
40587.170 Bibliothèque Nationale. Chateaubriand, le voyageur et l'homme politique. Paris, 1969.
40587.175 Martin-Chauffer, Louis. Chateaubriand. Paris, 1968.
40587.178 Cordiè, Carlo. Chateaubriand politico. Messina, 1959.
40587.180 Bazin, Christian. Chateaubriand en Amérique. Paris, 1969.
40587.182 Bassan, Fernande. Chateaubriand et la Terre-Sainte. Thèse. Paris, 1959.
40587.182.1 Bassan, Fernande. Chateaubriand et la Terre-Sainte. Paris, 1959.
40587.185 Chateaubriand today; proceedings of the commemoration of the bicentenary of the birth of Chateaubriand, 1968. Madison, 1970.
40587.190 Switzer, Richard. Chateaubriand. N.Y., 1971.
40587.195 Bicentenaire de Chateaubriand. Paris, 1971.
40587.230 Mourot, Jean. Chateaubriand. Paris? 1960.
40587.231 Mourot, Jean. Le génie d'un style: Chateaubriand. Paris, 1960.
40587.231.2 Mourot, Jean. Le génie d'un style: Chateaubriand. Paris, 1969.
40587.232 Grevlund, Merete. Paysage intérieur et paysage extérieur dans les Mémoires d'outre-tombe. Paris, 1968.

40587.900 - .949 Individual authors, etc. - 1800-1849 - Fiction - Caud, Lucile (Chateaubriand's sister)

40587.902 Caud, Lucile (de Chateaubriand) de (Mme.). Oeuvres de Lucile de Chateaubriand. Paris, 1912.
40587.906 Caud, Lucile (de Chateaubriand) de (Mme.). Ses contes, ses poèmes, ses lettres. Paris, 1879.
40587.930 Cahuet, Albéric. Lucile de Chateaubriand. Paris, 1935.

40587.950 - .999 Individual authors, etc. - 1800-1849 - Fiction - Chateaubriand, Celeste B. (his wife)

40587.952 Chateaubriand, Celeste Buisson (de Lavigne) (Mme.). Cahiers. Paris, 1909.
40587.955 Chateaubriand, Celeste Buisson (de Lavigne) (Mme.). Lettres inédites à M. Clausel de Coussergues. Bordeaux, 1888.

40588.01 - .099 Individual authors, etc. - 1800-1849 - Fiction - Cottin - Complete and Selected works

40588.01.2 Cottin, Marie R. (Mme.). Oeuvres complètes. Paris, 1824. 12v.
40588.01.3 Cottin, Marie R. (Mme.). Oeuvres complètes. v.1-3. Paris, 1838.
40588.01.4 Cottin, Marie R. (Mme.). Oeuvres complètes. Paris, 1823. 8v.

40588.1 - .6 Individual authors, etc. - 1800-1849 - Fiction - Cottin - Individual works

40588.1 Cottin, Marie R. (Mme.). Elizabeth. London, n.d.
40588.1.2 Cottin, Marie R. (Mme.). Elizabeth. Carlisle, 1809.
Htn 40588.1.3* Cottin, Marie R. (Mme.). Elizabeth, or Exiles of Siberia. Philadelphia, 1808.
Htn 40588.1.6* Cottin, Marie R. (Mme.). Elizabeth, or Exiles of Siberia. N.Y., 1812.
40588.1.10 Cottin, Marie R. (Mme.). Elizabeth. London, 1814.
40588.2 Cottin, Marie R. (Mme.). Elizabeth. Paris, 1816.
40588.2.3 Cottin, Marie R. (Mme.). Elizabeth, or The exiles of Siberia. N.Y., 18- .
40588.2.5 Cottin, Marie R. (Mme.). Elizabeth, or Exiles of Siberia. London, 1822.
40588.2.5.4 Cottin, Marie R. (Mme.). Elizabeth, or Exiles of Siberia. Boston, 1828.
40588.2.5.5 Cottin, Marie R. (Mme.). Elizabeth, or The exiles of Siberia. Boston, 1828.
40588.2.6 Cottin, Marie R. (Mme.). Elisabetta, ossia Gli esiliati nella Siberia. 2a ed. Londra, 1821.
40588.2.6.50 Cottin, Marie R. (Mme.). Élisabeth. Paris, 1835.
40588.2.7 Cottin, Marie R. (Mme.). Élisabeth, ou Les exilés de Sibérie. Paris, 1836.
40588.2.9 Cottin, Marie R. (Mme.). Élisabeth, ou Les exilés de Sibérie. Paris, 1838.

40588.1 - .6 Individual authors, etc. - 1800-1849 - Fiction - Cottin - Individual works - cont.

40588.3 Cottin, Marie R. (Mme.). Élizabeth. Boston, 1840.
40588.3.5 Cottin, Marie R. (Mme.). Élisabeth, ou Les exilés de Sibérie. Paris, 1841?
40588.3.10 Cottin, Marie R. (Mme.). Élizabeth ou Les exilés de Sibérie. Paris, 1852.
40588.4 Cottin, Marie R. (Mme.). Isabel. Paris, 1827.
40588.4.10 Cottin, Marie R. (Mme.). Amélie Mansfield. v.1-3. Paris, 1836.
40588.5 Cottin, Marie R. (Mme.). Malvina. Paris, 1801. 4v.
40588.5.10 Cottin, Marie R. (Mme.). The Saracen, or Matilda and Malek Adhel. N.Y., 1810. 2v.
40588.6 Cottin, Marie R. (Mme.). Malvina. v.1-3. Paris, 1836.
40588.6.9 Cottin, Marie R. (Mme.). Mathilde. Paris, 1823. 3v.

40588.7 - .7.49 Individual authors, etc. - 1800-1849 - Fiction - Cottin - Biography and criticism

40588.7.10 Cardaillac, Ferdnand de. Madame Cottin à Bigoire. Paris, 1909.
40588.7.20 Rösler, G. Beiträge zur Kenntnis von Mme. Cottin. Inaug. Diss. Leipzig, 1908.
40588.7.30 Sykes, L.C. Madame Cottin. Oxford, 1949.

40588.7.50 - .7.999 Individual authors, etc. - 1800-1849 - Fiction - Miscellany, A-C

40588.7.103 Belloc, Louise Swauton. Pierre et Pierrette. 3. éd. Paris, 1838.
40588.7.150 Cronbach, Louise. Jeune fille du peuple. 2. éd. Paris, 184-.

40588.8 Individual authors, etc. - 1800-1849 - Fiction - Miscellany, D

40588.8.5 Des Essars, Eugène. Catherine de Lescun. v.1-2. Paris, 1839.
40588.8.200 Des Essarts, Alfred. La muger del espia. v.1-2. Matanzas, 1854.

40588.9 - .21 Individual authors, etc. - 1800-1849 - Fiction - Genlis - Writings

40588.9.8 Genlis, S.F.D. de St. Les mères rivales, ou La calomnie. Berlin, 1800. 3v.
40588.9.9 Genlis, S.F.D. de St. Dwie matki jednego dzieciétcia, czyli Matki rywalki. Warszawie, 1805. 2v.
40588.9.12 Genlis, S.F.D. de St. Herbier moral. Paris, 1801.
40588.9.14 Genlis, S.F.D. de St. La philosophie chrétienne. Paris, 1802.
40588.9.16 Genlis, S.F.D. de St. Les petits émigrés. 3. éd. Paris, 1803. 2v.
40588.9.18 Genlis, S.F.D. de St. Le petit La Bruyère. 2. éd. Paris, 1804.
40588.9.20 Genlis, S.F.D. de St. Adèle et Théodore. 4. éd. Paris, 1804. 4v.
40588.9.22 Genlis, S.F.D. de St. Nouveaux contes moraux. Paris, 1804. 3v.
40588.9.24 Genlis, S.F.D. de St. Les veillées du chateau. v.2,3. Paris, 1804. 2v.
40588.9.26 Genlis, S.F.D. de St. Les annales de la vertu. v.2,5. Paris, 1806. 2v.
40588.9.28 Genlis, S.F.D. de St. La duchesse de la Vallière. 8. éd. Paris, 1806. 2v.
40588.10 Genlis, S.F.D. de St. Theatre of education. London, 1781. 4v.
40588.11 Genlis, S.F.D. de St. Théâtre à l'usage des jeunes personnes. v.4. Paris, 1783.
40588.12 Genlis, S.F.D. de St. Souvenirs de Félicie. Paris, 1879.
40588.13 Genlis, S.F.D. de St. Les veillées du chateau. Paris, 1852. 2v.
40588.13.2 Genlis, S.F.D. de St. Les veillées du chateau. Paris, 1851.
40588.13.5 Genlis, S.F.D. de St. Les veillées du chateau. Paris, 1847. 2v.
40588.14 Genlis, S.F.D. de St. Tales of the the castle. 3. ed. London, 1787. 5v.
40588.14.5 Genlis, S.F.D. de St. Tales of the castle. London, 1817.
40588.14.25 Genlis, S.F.D. de St. The knights of the swan. Dublin, 1797. 2v.
40588.15 Genlis, S.F.D. de St. Jane of Paris. v.1-2. Boston, 1817.
40588.16 Genlis, S.F.D. de St. Juvenile theatre. N.Y., 1807.
40588.17 Genlis, S.F.D. de St. Mademoiselle de Clermont. Paris, 1844.
40588.17.5 Genlis, S.F.D. de St. Mademoiselle de la Fayette. 1st American ed. v.1-2. Baltimore, 1814.
40588.17.50 Genlis, S.F.D. de St. The siege of Rochelle. London, 1808. 3v.
40588.18 Genlis, S.F.D. de St. Le siège de la Rochelle. N.Y., 1857.
40588.18.3 Genlis, S.F.D. de St. Le siège de la Rochelle. Paris, 1847.
40588.18.4 Genlis, S.F.D. de St. Le siège de la Rochelle. Paris, 1843.
40588.18.5 Genlis, S.F.D. de St. Le siège de la Rochelle. N.Y., 1851.
40588.18.10 Genlis, S.F.D. de St. Le siège de la Rochelle. N.Y., 19-
40588.19 Genlis, S.F.D. de St. Théâtre de société. Dublin, 1783.
40588.20 Genlis, S.F.D. de St. Sacred dramas. Fredericksburg, 1797.
40588.20.5 Genlis, S.F.D. de St. Sacred dramas. London, 1786.
40588.21 Genlis, S.F.D. de St. Las veladas de la quinta. Madrid, 1791. 3v.
40588.21.5 Genlis, S.F.D. de St. Zuma, or The tree of health. London, 1818.
40588.21.10 Genlis, S.F.D. de St. The new aera. London, 1819. 4v.
40588.21.15 Genlis, S.F.D. de St. La Bruyère the less. London, 1800.
40588.21.16 Genlis, S.F.D. de St. La Bruyère the less. Dublin, 1801.
40588.21.50 Genlis, S.F.D. de St. Dernières lettres d'amour. Paris, 1954.
40588.21.75 Genlis, S.F.D. de St. Lettres inédites de Mme. de Genlis à son fils. Paris, 1902.
40588.21.80 Genlis, S.F.D. de St. The Duke of Lauzun. London, 1808. 2v.
40588.21.85 Genlis, S.F.D. de St. Petrarch and Laura. London, 1820.
40588.21.90 Genlis, S.F.D. de St. Rash vows. Dublin, 1799. 2v.
Htn 40588.21.95* Genlis, S.F.D. de St. Belisaire. v.1-2. Paris, 1808.
40588.21.100 Genlis, S.F.D. de St. Belisarius; an historical romance. London, 1809. 2v.

40588.9 - .21 Individual authors, etc. - 1800-1849 - Fiction - Genlis - Writings - cont.

Htn 40588.21.110* Genlis, S.F.D. de St. Madame de Maintenon. London, 1806. 2v.
Htn 40588.21.120* Genlis, S.F.D. de St. Sainclair, or the victim of the arts and sciences. N.Y., 1813.
40588.21.805 Laborde, Alice M. L'oeuvre de Madame de Genlis. Paris, 1966.

40588.22 Individual authors, etc. - 1800-1849 - Fiction - Genlis - Works about

40588.22 Bertaut, Jules. Madame de Genlis. Paris, 1941.

40588.24 - .28 Individual authors, etc. - 1800-1849 - Fiction - Montolieu

40588.24 Montolieu, I.P. de. Caroline de Lichtfield. Londres, 1787. 2v.
40588.25 Montolieu, I.P. de. Caroline de Lichtfield. Londres, 1786. 2v.
40588.27 Montolieu, I.P. de. Caroline of Litchfield; a novel. Dublin, 1795. 2v.
40588.27.75 Montolieu, I.P. de. The enchanted plants. 2. ed. London, 1801.
40588.28A Montolieu, I.P. de. The enchanted plants. N.Y., 1803.
40588.28B Montolieu, I.P. de. The enchanted plants. N.Y., 1803.
40588.28.50 Montolieu, I.P. de. Tales. London, 1805. 3v.

40588.29 - .30 Individual authors, etc. - 1800-1849 - Fiction - Souza, Mme de

40588.29 Sousa Botelho Mourão e Vasconcellos, A.M.E.F. Oeuvres complètes. Paris, 1821-22. 12v.
40588.30 Sousa Botelho Mourão e Vasconcellos, A.M.E.F. Oeuvres complètes. Paris, 1865.
40588.30.35 Sousa Botelho Mourão e Vasconcellos, A.M.E.F. A peep into the Thuilleries, or Parisian manners. London, 1811. 2v.
40588.30.125 Hundrup, M.A. Die Romane der Mme de Souza in problemgeschichtlicher Schau. Inaug. Diss. Emsdetten, 1937.

40588.33 - .40 Individual authors, etc. - 1800-1849 - Fiction - Maistre, Xavier de - Complete and Selected works

40588.33 Maistre, Xavier. Oeuvres complètes. Paris, 18- .
40588.34 Maistre, Xavier. Oeuvres complètes. Paris, 1853.
40588.35 Maistre, Xavier. Oeuvres complètes. Leipzig, 1847.
40588.37 Maistre, Xavier. Oeuvres complètes. Paris, 1858.
40588.38 Maistre, Xavier. Oeuvres complètes. Paris, n.d.
40588.39 Maistre, Xavier. Oeuvres complètes. Paris, 1872.
40588.39.5 Maistre, Xavier. Oeuvres complètes. Paris, 1872.
40588.39.15 Maistre, Xavier. Oeuvres complètes. Paris, 1909.
40588.40 Maistre, Xavier. Oeuvres complètes. Boston, n.d.

40588.41 - .69 Individual authors, etc. - 1800-1849 - Fiction - Maistre, Xavier de - Individual works

40588.41 Maistre, Xavier. La jeune sibérienne. Cambridge, 1885.
40588.41.2 Maistre, Xavier. La jeune sibérienne. London, 1885.
40588.41.10 Maistre, Xavier. La jeune sibérienne. Boston, 1912.
40588.42 Maistre, Xavier. Voyage autour de ma chambre. Boston, 1821.
40588.43 Maistre, Xavier. Voyage autour de ma chambre. Boston, 1861.
40588.43.5 Maistre, Xavier. Voyage autour de ma chambre. 1. édition américaine. N.Y., 1875?
40588.43.15A Maistre, Xavier. Voyage autour de ma chambre. Cambridge, 1901.
40588.43.15B Maistre, Xavier. Voyage autour de ma chambre. Cambridge, 1901.
40588.45 Maistre, Xavier. Journey round my room. Philadelphia, 1829.
40588.46 Maistre, Xavier. Journey round my room. London, 1845.
40588.46.2 Maistre, Xavier. Journey round my room. N.Y., 1871.
40588.47 Maistre, Xavier. Journey round my room. Edinburgh, 1885.
40588.47.1 Maistre, Xavier. Journey round my room. Edinburgh, 1885.
40588.48 Maistre, Xavier. Les prisonniers du Caucase. Boston, 1865.
40588.49 Maistre, Xavier. A nocturnal expedition round my room. Edinburgh, 1886.
40588.49.1 Maistre, Xavier. A noctural expedition round my room. Edinburgh, 1886.
40588.50.10 Maistre, Xavier. The leper of the city of Aoste. London, 1817.
40588.51 Maistre, Xavier. The Leper of Aost. Boston, 1825.
40588.55 Maistre, Xavier. Chapitre inédit d'histoire littéraire et bibliographique. Genève, 1895.

40588.70 - Individual authors, etc. - 1800-1849 - Fiction - Maistre, Xavier de - Biography and criticism

40588.70 Berthier, Alfred. Xavier Maistre. Thèse. Lyon, 1918?
40588.70.2 Berthier, Alfred. Xavier de Maistre. Lyon, 1918.
40588.72 Académie...Chambery. Xavier de Maistre. Chambéry, 1952.

40591 Individual authors, etc. - 1800-1849 - Fiction - Folios [Discontinued]

40591.9 Balzac, Honoré de. Oeuvres illustrées. Paris, 1851-54. 3v.
40591.15 Balzac, Honoré de. Paris Marié. Paris, 1851.
Htn 40591.20* Balzac, Honoré de. Les chouans. Paris, 1889.

40592.1 Individual authors, etc. - 1800-1849 - Fiction - Staël, Mme de - Bibliographies

40592.1.5A Schazmann, Paul E. Bibliographie des oeuvres de Mme. de Staël. Paris, 1938.
40592.1.5B Schazmann, Paul E. Bibliographie des oeuvres de Mme. de Staël. Paris, 1938.

40592.2 - .20 Individual authors, etc. - 1800-1849 - Fiction - Staël, Mme de - Complete works

40592.3 Oeuvres complètes de Mme. de Staël. Paris, 1820-21. 17v.
40592.5 Oeuvres complètes de Mme. de Staël. v.1-17. Bruxelles, 1830. 10v.

40592.21 - .39 Individual authors, etc. - 1800-1849 - Fiction - Staël, Mme de - Corinne

Htn 40592.21* Staël Holstein, Anne Louise. Corinne. Paris, 1807. 3v.
40592.21.3 Staël Holstein, Anne Louise. Corinne. Paris, 1831. 2v.
40592.21.4 Staël Holstein, Anne Louise. Corinne, ou l'Italie. Paris, 1836. 2v.

40592.21 - .39 Individual authors, etc. - 1800-1849 - Fiction - Staël, Mme de - Corinne - cont.

40592.21.5 Staël Holstein, Anne Louise. Corinne, ou l'Italie. Paris, 1847.
40592.22 Staël Holstein, Anne Louise. Corinne, ou l'Italie. Paris, 1850.
40592.22.5 Staël Holstein, Anne Louise. Corinne, ou l'Italie. N.Y., 1852.
40592.23 Staël Holstein, Anne Louise. Corinne. Paris, 1853.
40592.23.2 Staël Holstein, Anne Louise. Corinne. N.Y., 1854.
40592.23.3 Staël Holstein, Anne Louise. Corinne. N.Y., 1853.
40592.23.5 Staël Holstein, Anne Louise. Corinne. N.Y., 185-?
40592.24.10 Staël Holstein, Anne Louise. Corinne. Paris, 1857.
40592.24.15 Staël Holstein, Anne Louise. Corinne. Paris, 1861.
40592.24.20A Staël Holstein, Anne Louise. Corinne. Paris, 1871.
40592.24.20B Staël Holstein, Anne Louise. Corinne. Paris, 1871.
40592.24.25 Staël Holstein, Anne Louise. Corinne. N.Y., 1873.
40592.25 Staël Holstein, Anne Louise. Corinne. Paris, 1875.
40592.25.5 Staël Holstein, Anne Louise. Corinne, ou l'Italie. Paris, 18- ?
40592.26 Staël Holstein, Anne Louise. Corinne. Paris, n.d.
40592.26.5 Staël Holstein, Anne Louise. Corinne. Paris, 1876.
Htn 40592.27* Staël Holstein, Anne Louise. Corinne. Boston, 1808. 2v.
40592.27.2 Staël Holstein, Anne Louise. Corinne, or Italy. N.Y., 18-
40592.27.5 Staël Holstein, Anne Louise. Corinne, or Italy. Philadelphia, 1808.
Htn 40592.27.6* Staël Holstein, Anne Louise. Corinne, or Italy. Philadelphia, 1808. 2v.
40592.28 Staël Holstein, Anne Louise. Corinne, or Italy. London, 1850.
40592.29 Staël Holstein, Anne Louise. Corinne, or Italy. London, 1847.
40592.29.5 Staël Holstein, Anne Louise. Corinne, or Italy. Philadelphia, 1854.
40592.30 Staël Holstein, Anne Louise. Corinne. N.Y., 1876.
40592.32 Staël Holstein, Anne Louise. Corinne, or Italy. Philadelphia, 1894. 2v.
40592.33 Staël Holstein, Anne Louise. Corinne, or Italy. N.Y., 190-.
40592.34 Staël Holstein, Anne Louise. La Corinna. Firenze, 1808. 2v.
40592.35 Staël Holstein, Anne Louise. Corinna, ossia l'Italia. Venezia, 1820. 2v.
40592.35.5 Staël Holstein, Anne Louise. Corinna, oder Italien. Berlin, 1807. 4v.
Htn 40592.36* Staël Holstein, Anne Louise. Delphine. Paris, 1803. 3v.
40592.37 Staël Holstein, Anne Louise. Korinna ili Italiia. Moskva, 1969.

40592.40 - .59 Individual authors, etc. - 1800-1849 - Fiction - Staël, Mme de - Correspondence

40592.40 Staël Holstein, Anne Louise. Madame de Staël. London, 1964.
40592.41 Staël Holstein, Anne Louise. Madame de Staël et le duc de Wellington; correspondance inédite, 1815-1817. Paris, 1962.
40592.41.5 Staël Holstein, Anne Louise. The unpublished correspondence of Madame de Staël and the Duke of Wellington. London, 1965.
40592.42 Staël Holstein, Anne Louise. Madame de Staël et J.B.A. Sward; correspondance inédite (1786-1817). Genève, 1970.
40592.43A Staël Holstein, Anne Louise. Lettres de Mme. de Staël. 2. vyd. Prague, 1960.
40592.43B Staël Holstein, Anne Louise. Lettres de Mme. de Staël. 2. vyd. Prague, 1960.
40592.44 Staël Holstein, Anne Louise. De Staël-Du Pont letters. Madison, 1968.
40592.45 Staël Holstein, Anne Louise. Lettres à Ribbing. Paris, 1960.
40592.47 Staël Holstein, Anne Louise. Lettres à Narbonne. Paris, 1960.
40592.48 Staël Holstein, Anne Louise. Correspondance générale. Paris, 1960. 3v.
40592.50A Staël Holstein, Anne Louise. Lettres à B. Constant. Paris, 1928.
40592.50B Staël Holstein, Anne Louise. Lettres à B. Constant. Paris, 1928.
40592.52 Staël Holstein, Anne Louise. Lettres inédites à Juste Constant de Rebecque. Paris, 1937.
40592.54 Staël Holstein, Anne Louise. Lettres de Madame de Staël à Madame Récamier. Paris, 1952.

40592.60 - .99 Individual authors, etc. - 1800-1849 - Fiction - Staël, Mme de - Criticism [Discontinued]

40592.60 Nolde, Elizabeth. Madame de Staël and Benjamin Constant. N.Y., 1907.
40592.80 Gennari, G. Le premier voyage de Madame de Staël en Italie et la genèse de Corinne. Thèse. Paris, 1947.
40592.80.5 Gennari, G. Le premier voyage de Madame de Staël en Italie. Paris, 1947.
40592.82 Levaillant, M. Une amitié amoureuse. Paris, 1956.
40592.82.5 Levaillant, M. The passionate exiles. N.Y., 1958.
40592.84 Herold, J. Christopher. Mistress to an age. 1st ed. Indianapolis, 1958.
40592.86 Lang, André. Une vie d'orages. Paris, 1958.
40592.88 Onerva, L. (pseud.). Madame de Staël. Porvoossa, 1920.
40592.90 Villa-Urrutia, W.R. Mujeres de antaño. Madame de Staël. Madrid, 1930.
40592.92 Forsberg, R.J. Madame de Staël and freedom today. N.Y., 1963.
40592.94 Luppé, Robert de. Les idées littéraires de Madame de Staël et l'héritage des lumières (1795-1800). Paris, 1969.

40593.1 - .14 Individual authors, etc. - 1800-1849 - Fiction - Staël, Mme de - Selected works

40593.3 Staël Holstein, Anne Louise. Oeuvres inédites de Mme. de Staël. Paris, 1821. 3v.
40593.12 Staël Holstein, Anne Louise. Pages choisies des grands écrivains. Paris, n.d.

40593.15 - .25 Individual authors, etc. - 1800-1849 - Fiction - Staël, Mme de - Individual works

40593.18 Staël Holstein, Anne Louise. Treatise on...literature. London, 1803. 2v.
40593.21 Staël Holstein, Anne Louise. Influence of literature on society. v.2. Boston, 1813.
40593.22 Staël Holstein, Anne Louise. De la littérature considérée dans ses rapports avec les institutions sociales. Paris, 1872.
40593.22.5 Staël Holstein, Anne Louise. De la littérature considéreé dans ses rapports avec les institutions sociales. v.1-2. Genève, 1959.
Htn 40593.25* Staël Holstein, Anne Louise. Réflexions sur le suicide. Paris, 1814.

40593.26 - .899 Individual authors, etc. - 1800-1849 - Fiction - Staël, Mme de - Criticism

40593.27 Grahl-Schulze, Elisabeth. Die Anschauungen der Frau von Staël über das Wesen und die Aufgaben der Dichtung. Inaug. Diss. Neuminster, 1912.
40593.28 Canat, René. Quae de Graecis Mme. de Staël scripserit. Andegavis, 1904.
40593.29 Gibelin, Jean. L'esthétique de Schelling et l'Allemagne de Madame de Staël. Paris, 1934.
40593.29.5 Gibelin, Jean. L'esthétique de Schelling et l'Allemagne de Madame de Staël. Thèse. Clermont-Ferrand, 1934.
40593.32 Pellegrini, C. Madame de Staël. Firenze, 1938.
40593.35 Lacretelle, P. Madame de Staël et les hommes. Paris, 1939.
40593.37 Chanson, P. Le mariage d'amour selon Madame de Staël. Paris, 1947.
40593.39 Jaeck, Emma Gertrude. Madame de Staël. N.Y., 1915.
40593.40 Escarpit, R. L'Angleterre dans l'oeuvre de Madame de Staël. Paris, 1954.
Htn 40593.43* Lonchamp, F.C. L'oeuvre imprimé de Madame Germaine de Staël. Genève, 1949.
40593.45 Pange, P.L.M. de B. Le dernier amour de Madame de Staël d'après des documents inédites. Genève, 1944.
40593.45.5 Pange, P.L.M. de B. Madame de Staël et la découverte de l'Allemagne. n.p., n.d.
40593.46 Andrews, W. Germaine. 1. ed. N.Y., 1963.
40593.47 Cahiers staeliens. Paris. 1,1962+
40593.48 Haussonville, Gabriel Paul Othenin de Cléron. Le Prince Auguste de Prusse, Madame de Staël, et Madame Récamier. Paris, 1913.

40593.900 - .999 Individual authors, etc. - 1800-1849 - Fiction - Staël-Holstein, August L.

40593.905 Staël Holstein, Auguste Louis. Oeuvres diverses. Paris, 1829. 3v.

40594 - 40595 Individual authors, etc. - 1800-1849 - Fiction - Balzac - Folios [Discontinued]

40594.1 Balzac, Honoré de. Vie privée. La maison du Chat-qui-Pelote. Paris, 1884.
40594.2 Balzac, Honoré de. Vie privée. Mémoires de deux jeunes mariées. Paris, 1887.
40594.3 Balzac, Honoré de. Vie privée. Le contract de mariage. Paris, 1883.
40594.4 Balzac, Honoré de. Vie privée. Beatrix. Honorine. Paris, 1884.
40594.5 Balzac, Honoré de. Vie de province. Ursule Mirouët. Eugène Grandet. Paris, 1886.
40594.6 Balzac, Honoré de. Vie de province. Les célibataires. v.12.- Paris, 1884.
40594.7 Balzac, Honoré de. Vie de province. Les parisiens en province. Paris, 1885.
40594.8 Balzac, Honoré de. Vie de province. Illusions perdues. v.1-2. Paris, 1884.
40594.9 Balzac, Honoré de. Vie parisienne. Les courtisanes. Vautrin. Paris, 1887.
40594.11 Balzac, Honoré de. Vie parisienne. César Berotteau. La maison Nuchingen. Paris, 1884.
40594.12 Balzac, Honoré de. Vie parisienne. Les parents pauvres. Paris, 1887.
40594.13 Balzac, Honoré de. Vie politique. Une ténèbreuse affaire. Paris, 1882.
40594.14 Balzac, Honoré de. Vie politique. Le député d'Arcis. Paris, 1887.
40594.15 Balzac, Honoré de. Vie de campagne. Le médecin de campagne. Paris, 1884.
40594.16 Balzac, Honoré de. Études philosophiques. La peau de chagrin. Paris, 1884.
40594.17 Balzac, Honoré de. Études philosophiques. L'enfant maudit. Les Marana. Paris, 1886.
40594.18 Balzac, Honoré de. Études philosophiques. Sur Catherine de Médici. Louis Lambert. Paris, 1884.
40594.19 Balzac, Honoré de. Études analytiques. Physiologie du mariage. Paris, 1886.
40594.20 Balzac, Honoré de. Les contes drolatiques. v. 1-3. Paris, 1885.
40594.21 Balzac, Honoré de. Oeuvres de jeunesse. Argon le pirate. Jame la pale. Paris, 1884.
40594.22 Balzac, Honoré de. Oeuvres de jeunesse. La dernière fée. Paris, 1876.
40594.23 Balzac, Honoré de. Oeuvres de jeunesse. Dom Gigadas. L'excommunié. Paris, 1876.
40594.24 Balzac, Honoré de. Oeuvres de jeunesse. L'héritière de biraque. Paris, 1884.
40594.25 Balzac, Honoré de. Oeuvres de jeunesse. Jean Louis. L'Israélite. Paris, 1876.
40595.3 Oeuvres complètes de H. de Balzac. Paris, 1869-76. 24v.
40595.5 Balzac, Honoré de. Oeuvres complètes. Paris, 1874. 20v.
40595.7 Balzac, Honoré de. Oeuvres complètes. Paris, 1900-02. 49v.
40595.10 Balzac, Honoré de. Works. v.11 lost 1966. Boston, 1901. 34v.

40596 Individual authors, etc. - 1800-1849 - Fiction - Balzac - Complete and Selected words

40596.3 Balzac, Honoré de. Oeuvres. Bruxelles, 1837. 4v.
40596.4 Balzac, Honoré de. Oeuvres complètes. Paris, 1855. 20v.
40596.4.10 Balzac, Honoré de. Oeuvres complètes. Paris, 1873-79. 24v.

40596 Individual authors, etc. - 1800-1849 - Fiction - Balzac - Complete and Selected words - cont.

40596.4.11 Spoelberch de Lovenjoul, Charles. Histoire des oeuvres de H. de Balzac. 3. éd. Paris, 1888.
40596.4.12 Cerfberr, Anatole. Répertoirs de la Comédie humaine de H. de Balzac. Paris, 1893.
40596.5 Balzac, Honoré de. Oeuvres complètes. Paris, 1877. 20v.
40596.6 Balzac, Honoré de. L'oeuvre de Balzac. Paris, 1949-53. 16v.
40596.7.2 Balzac, Honoré de. Oeuvres. n.p., 1955-63. 28v.
40596.7.4 Balzac, Honoré de. Oeuvres complètes. Paris, 1965. 24v.
40596.7.4.1 Balzac, Honoré de. Lettres à Madame Hanska. Paris, 1967. 4v.
40596.7.4.5 Balzac, Honoré de. Oeuvres complètes. Paris, 1968-71. 24v.
40596.7.5A Balzac, Honoré de. Balzac par lui-même. Paris, 1956.
40596.7.5B Balzac, Honoré de. Balzac par lui-même. Paris, 1956.
40596.8 Balzac, Honoré de. Comédie humaine. Études de moeurs. Scènes de la vie privée. Paris, 1912-13. 7v.
40596.8.2 Balzac, Honoré de. Comédie humaine. Études de moeurs. Scènes de la vie de province. Paris, 1913. 5v.
40596.8.3 Balzac, Honoré de. Comédie humaine. Études de moeurs. Scènes de la vie parisienne. Paris, 1913-14. 8v.
40596.8.4 Balzac, Honoré de. Comédie humaine. Études de moeurs. Scénes de la vie politique. Paris, 1914.
40596.8.5 Balzac, Honoré de. Comédie humaine. Études de moeurs. Scènes de la vie militaire. Paris, 1920.
40596.8.6 Balzac, Honoré de. Comédie humaine. Études de moeurs. Scènes de la vie de campagne. Paris, 1922-23. 4v.
40596.8.7 Balzac, Honoré de. Comédie humaine. Études philosophiques. Paris, 1925-27. 5v.
40596.8.8 Balzac, Honoré de. Comédie humaine. Études analytiques. Paris, 1927. 2v.
40596.8.10 Balzac, Honoré de. Théâtre. Paris, 1929. 2v.
40596.8.12 Balzac, Honoré de. Contes drolatiques. Paris, 1930. 2v.
40596.8.14 Balzac, Honoré de. Oeuvres diverses. Paris, 1935-38. 3v.
40596.8.25 Balzac, Honoré de. La comédie humaine. Paris, 1935-37. 10v.
40596.8.30 Balzac, Honoré de. La comédie humaine. v.4-6,8,10-15,20. Paris, 1947. 11v.
40596.8.50 Balzac, Honoré de. Napoléon par Balzac; récits et épisodes du Premier Empire tirés de la "Comédie Humaine". Paris, 1913.
40596.8.74A Balzac, Honoré de. Cinq scènes de la comédie humaine. Boston, 1901.
40596.8.74B Balzac, Honoré de. Cinq scènes de la comédie humaine. Boston, 1901.
40596.9 Balzac, Honoré de. Oeuvres posthumes. Lettres à l'étrangère (1833-1842). Paris, 1899. 2v.
40596.9.10 Balzac, Honoré de. Lettres à l'étrangère. Paris, 1930. 4v.
40596.10.5 Balzac, Honoré de. Letters to Mme. Hanska. Boston, 1900.
40596.10.7A Balzac, Honoré de. Honoré de Balzac. Boston, 1900.
40596.10.7B Balzac, Honoré de. Honoré de Balzac. Boston, 1900.
40596.11 Balzac, Honoré de. Love letters. London, 1901. 2v.
40596.11.25 Balzac, Honoré de. Balzac and Souverain. An unpublished correspondence. Garden City, 1927.
40596.11.30 Balzac, Honoré de. Correspondance avec Zulma Carraud. 5. éd. Paris, 1951.
40596.11.35 Balzac, Honoré de. Letters to his family, 1809-1850. Princeton, 1934.
40596.11.40 Balzac, Honoré de. Lettres à sa famille, 1809-1850. Paris, 1950.
40596.11.45 Balzac, Honoré de. Correspondance inédite avec Madame Zulma Carraud (1829-1850). Paris, 1935.
40596.12 Balzac, Honoré de. About Catherine de Medici. London, 1897.
40596.12.2 Balzac, Honoré de. At the sign of the cat and racket. London, 1895.
40596.12.3A Balzac, Honoré de. The atheist's mass. London, 1896.
40596.12.3B Balzac, Honoré de. The atheist's mass. London, 1896.
40596.12.4A Balzac, Honoré de. A bachelor's establishment. London, 1896.
40596.12.4B Balzac, Honoré de. A bachelor's establishment. London, 1896.
40596.12.5 Balzac, Honoré de. Beatrix. London, 1896.
40596.12.6 Balzac, Honoré de. The rise and fall of César Biroteau. London, 1896.
40596.12.7 Balzac, Honoré de. The Chouans. London, 1895.
40596.12.9 Balzac, Honoré de. The country parson. London, 1896.
40596.12.10 Balzac, Honoré de. Cousin Betty. London, 1897.
40596.12.11 Balzac, Honoré de. Cousin Pons. London, 1897.
40596.12.12 Balzac, Honoré de. A daughter of Eve. London, 1897.
40596.12.13 Balzac, Honoré de. A distinguished provinicial at Paris. London, 1897.
40596.12.14A Balzac, Honoré de. Eugénie Grandet. London, 1895.
40596.12.14B Balzac, Honoré de. Eugénie Grandet. London, 1895.
40596.12.15 Balzac, Honoré de. A father's curse. London, 1898.
40596.12.16 Balzac, Honoré de. A Gondreville mystery. London, 1898.
40596.12.17 Balzac, Honoré de. La grande Bretêche and other stories. London, 1896.
40596.12.18 Balzac, Honoré de. A harlot's progress. London, 1896. 2v.
40596.12.19 Balzac, Honoré de. The jealousies of a country town. London, 1898.
40596.12.20 Balzac, Honoré de. The lily of the valley. London, 1897.
40596.12.21 Balzac, Honoré de. Lost illusions. London, 1897.
40596.12.22 Balzac, Honoré de. A marriage settlement. London, 1897.
40596.12.23 Balzac, Honoré de. The member for Arcis. London, 1898.
40596.12.24 Balzac, Honoré de. The middle classes. London, 1898.
40596.12.25A Balzac, Honoré de. Modeste Mignon. London, 1896.
40596.12.25B Balzac, Honoré de. Modeste Mignon. London, 1896.
40596.12.26 Balzac, Honoré de. Old Goriot. Photoreproduction. London, 1896.
40596.12.27 Balzac, Honoré de. Parisians in the country. London, 1898.
40596.12.28A Balzac, Honoré de. The peasantry. London, 1896.
40596.12.28B Balzac, Honoré de. The peasantry. London, 1896.
40596.12.29A Balzac, Honoré de. Pierrette and the Abbé Birotteau. London, 1896.
40596.12.29B Balzac, Honoré de. Pierrette and the Abbé Birotteau. London, 1896.
40596.12.30 Balzac, Honoré de. A princess's secrets. London, 1898.

40596 Individual authors, etc. - 1800-1849 - Fiction - Balzac - Complete and Selected words - cont.

40596.12.31A Balzac, Honoré de. The guest of the absolute. London, 1895.
40596.12.31B Balzac, Honoré de. The guest of the absolute. London, 1895.
40596.12.32 Balzac, Honoré de. The seamy side of history. London, 1897.
40596.12.33 Balzac, Honoré de. Seraphita and other stories. London, 1897.
40596.12.34 Balzac, Honoré de. The thirteen. London, 1898.
40596.12.35 Balzac, Honoré de. The unconscious mummers. London, 1897.
40596.12.36 Balzac, Honoré de. The unknown masterpiece and other stories. London, 1896.
40596.12.37 Balzac, Honoré de. Ursule Mirouet. London, 1895.
40596.12.38 Balzac, Honoré de. The wild ass's skin. London, 1895.
40596.12.39 Balzac, Honoré de. A woman of thirty. London, 1897.
40596.13 Wormeley, K.P. A memoir of Honoré de Balzac. Boston, 1894.
40596.13.2 Balzac, Honoré de. Albert Savarus. Boston, 1892.
40596.13.4 Balzac, Honoré de. The alkahest. Boston, 1887.
40596.13.6 Balzac, Honoré de. Béatrix. Boston, 1895.
40596.13.8 Balzac, Honoré de. The brotherhood of consolation. Boston, 1893.
40596.13.10 Balzac, Honoré de. Bureaucracy. Boston, 1889.
40596.13.12 Balzac, Honoré de. Cathérine de Médici. Boston, 1894.
40596.13.14 Balzac, Honoré de. César Birotteau. Boston, 1886.
40596.13.18 Balzac, Honoré de. The country doctor. Boston, 1887.
40596.13.20 Balzac, Honoré de. Cousin Bette. Boston, 1888.
40596.13.22 Balzac, Honoré de. A daughter of Eve. Boston, 1895.
40596.13.24 Balzac, Honoré de. The deputy of Arcis. Boston, 1896.
40596.13.26 Balzac, Honoré de. The Duchess de Langeais. Boston, 1885.
40596.13.28 Balzac, Honoré de. Fame and sorrow. Boston, 1890.
40596.13.30 Balzac, Honoré de. The gallery of antiquities. Boston, 1896.
40596.13.32 Balzac, Honoré de. Gabseck. Boston, 1896.
40596.13.34 Balzac, Honoré de. Eugénie Grandet. Boston, 1886.
40596.13.36 Balzac, Honoré de. A great man of the provinces in Paris. Boston, 1893.
40596.13.38 Balzac, Honoré de. An historical mystery. Boston, 1891.
40596.13.40 Balzac, Honoré de. Juana. Boston, 1896.
40596.13.42 Balzac, Honoré de. The lily of the valley. Boston, 1894.
40596.13.44 Balzac, Honoré de. Lost illusions. Boston, 1893.
40596.13.46 Balzac, Honoré de. Lucien de Rubempré. Boston, 1895.
40596.13.50 Balzac, Honoré de. The marriage contract. Boston, 1895.
40596.13.52 Balzac, Honoré de. Modeste Mignon. Boston, 1888.
40596.13.56 Balzac, Honoré de. Seraphita. Boston, 1889.
40596.13.58 Balzac, Honoré de. Sons of the soil. Boston, 1890.
40596.13.60 Balzac, Honoré de. A start in life. Boston, 1895.
40596.13.62 Balzac, Honoré de. The two brothers. Boston, 1887.
40596.13.64 Balzac, Honoré de. Memoirs of two young married women. Boston, 1894.
40596.13.66A Balzac, Honoré de. Ursula. Boston, 1891.
40596.13.66B Balzac, Honoré de. Ursula. Boston, 1891.
40596.13.68 Balzac, Honoré de. The village rector. Boston, 1893.
40596.13.70 Balzac, Honoré de. Sons of the soil. Boston, 1895.
40596.13.72 Balzac, Honoré de. César Birotteau. Boston, 1894.
40596.13.73 Balzac, Honoré de. Cousin Pons. Boston, 1898.
40596.13.74 Balzac, Honoré de. Pére Goriot. Boston, 1886.
40596.13.76 Balzac, Honoré de. The lily of the valley. Boston, 1895.
40596.13.78 Balzac, Honoré de. Ursula. Boston, 1893.
40596.13.80.5 Balzac, Honoré de. A start in life. Boston, 1899.
40596.13.80.9 Balzac, Honoré de. The lily of the valley. Boston, 1900.
40596.13.80.10 Balzac, Honoré de. Ursula. Boston, 1917.
40596.13.80.18 Balzac, Honoré de. Cousin Bette. Boston, 1900.
40596.13.80.19 Balzac, Honoré de. Cousin Pons. Boston, 1899.
40596.13.80.20 Balzac, Honoré de. The chouans. Boston, 1900.
40596.13.80.24 Balzac, Honoré de. The country doctor. Boston, 1900.
40596.13.80.26 Balzac, Honoré de. Sons of the soil. Boston, 1900.
40596.13.80.27 Balzac, Honoré de. Catherine de Medici. Boston, 1899.
40596.13.80.31 Balzac, Honoré de. Juana, and other stories. Boston, 1899.
40596.13.80.32 Balzac, Honoré de. Balzac, a memoir. Boston, 1900.
40596.13.80.34 Balzac, Honoré de. Letters to Madame Hanska. Boston, 1900.
40596.13.100 Balzac, Honoré de. Honoré de Balzac. v.1-49,51-53. Philadelphia, 1895-1900. 52v.
40596.13.110 Balzac, Honoré de. Comédie humaine. London, 1895-98. 40v.
40596.13.112 Balzac, Honoré de. La comédie humaine. Philadelphia, 1896-1900. 45v.
40596.13.114 Balzac, Honoré de. Novels. Philadelphia, 1895-1900. 50v.
40596.13.120 Balzac, Honoré de. The works. N.Y., n.d. 17v.
40596.13.121 Balzac, Honoré de. The works of Honoré de Balzac. N.Y., 190-. 16v.
40596.13.122 Balzac, Honoré de. Works. N.Y., 19- . 6v.
40596.13.125 Balzac, Honoré de. Honoré de Balzac. N.Y., 1900. 22v.
40596.13.126 Balzac, Honoré de. Honoré de Balzac. N.Y., 1903.
40596.13.126.5 Balzac, Honoré de. Honoré de Balzac. N.Y., 1903.
40596.13.130 Balzac, Honoré de. La comédie humaine. N.Y., 1909. 7v.
40596.13.130.1 Balzac, Honoré de. The comédie humaine. N.Y., 1904. 5v.
40596.13.130.2 Balzac, Honoré de. The comédie humaine. N.Y., 1911. 4v.
40596.13.131 Balzac, Honoré de. La comédie humaine. N.Y., 1906. 7v.
40596.13.132 Balzac, Honoré de. La comédie humaine. v.7A lost 1947. N.Y., 1908. 13v.
40596.13.135 Balzac, Honoré de. The human comedy. N.Y., 1893. 3v.
40596.13.140 Balzac, Honoré de. La comédie humaine. Paris, 1958. 11v.
40596.13.142 Balzac, Honoré de. Contes drolatiques. 2. éd. Paris, 1964.
40596.14A Balzac, Honoré de. After-dinner stories. N.Y., 1888.
40596.14B Balzac, Honoré de. After-dinner stories. N.Y., 1888.
40596.14.5 Balzac, Honoré de. After-dinner stories. N.Y., 1886.
40596.15B Balzac, Honoré de. Shorter stories of Balzac. London, 1890.
40596.15.3 Balzac, Honoré de. A daughter of Eve and Letters of two brides. London, 1897.
40596.15.5 Balzac, Honoré de. A daughter of Eve and other stories. N.Y., 1901.
40596.15.10 Balzac, Honoré de. Short stories. N.Y., 1920.
40596.15.12 Balzac, Honoré de. Short stories. N.Y., 19- .

40596 Individual authors, etc. - 1800-1849 - Fiction - Balzac - Complete and Selected words - cont.

40596.15.14 Balzac, Honoré de. Short stories. N.Y., 19- .
40596.15.20 Balzac, Honoré de. Morceaux choisis. Paris, 1912.
40596.15.25 Balzac, Honoré de. Contes choisis. London, 1905.
40596.16 Balzac, Honoré de. Pages choisies. Paris, 1895.
40596.16.10 Balzac, Honoré de. Pages sociales et politiques. Paris, 1910.
40596.16.50 Balzac, Honoré de. Sténie ou les erreurs philosophiques. Paris, 1936.
40596.17.5 Balzac, Honoré de. Le curé de Tours. Boston, 1899.
40596.17.10 Balzac, Honoré de. Le curé de Tours. Tours, 1946.
40596.17.30 Balzac, Honoré de. The vicar of Tours. London, 1950.
40596.18.10 Balzac, Honoré de. Le théâtre inédit de Honoré de Balzac. Thèse. Paris, 1930.
40596.18.12 Balzac, Honoré de. Le théâtre inédit de Honoré de Balzac. Paris, 1930.
40596.19 Balzac, Honoré de. The dramatic works. Chicago, 1901. 2v.
40596.21 Balzac, Honoré de. Les chouans. Paris, 189-?
40596.21.8 Balzac, Honoré de. The chouans. Chicago, 1891.
40596.21.10 Balzac, Honoré de. The chouans. Chicago, 19- ?
40596.21.12 Balzac, Honoré de. The chouans. Boston, 1905.
40596.22 Balzac, Honoré de. Père Goriot. Boston, 1907.
40596.22.5A Balzac, Honoré de. Le père Goriot. N.Y., 1928.
40596.22.5B Balzac, Honoré de. Le père Goriot. N.Y., 1928.
40596.22.5C Balzac, Honoré de. Le père Goriot. N.Y., 1928.
40596.23 Balzac, Honoré de. Balzac; sein Weltbild aus den Werken. Stuttgart, 1908.
40596.24 Balzac, Honoré de. The country doctor. N.Y., 1892.
40596.25 Balzac, Honoré de. Contes philosophiques. London, 1913?
40596.26 Balzac, Honoré de. The best of Balzac. N.Y., 1902.
40596.27A Balzac, Honoré de. Complete novelettes. N.Y., 1926.
40596.27B Balzac, Honoré de. Complete novelettes. N.Y., 1926.
40596.28 Frary, Léon. Selon Balzac; le coeur humain. Paris, 1913.
40596.30 Balzac, Honoré de. Parisian life. N.Y., 1901. 9v.
40596.31 Balzac, Honoré de. Le curé de ville. Montréal, 1946.
40596.33 Balzac, Honoré de. Le curé de village. Paris, 1960.
40596.34 Balzac, Honoré de. Le curé de village. Bruxelles, 1961.
40596.35 Balzac, Honoré de. Ferragus. Boston, 1940.
40596.36 Balzac, Honoré de. The student's Balzac. N.Y., 1937.
40596.38 Balzac, Honoré de. Balzac's Le message. Cambridge, Mass., 1940.
40596.40 Balzac, Honoré de. Le centenaire, ou Les deux Béringheld. Bruxelles, 1837. 2v.
40596.40.5 Balzac, Honoré de. Le centenaire, ou Les deux Béringheld. Paris, 1962. 2v.
40596.43 Balzac, Honoré de. Les idées de Balzac. Genève, 1949-50. 2v.
40596.45 Balzac, Honoré de. Le député d'Arcis. Paris, 1908.
40596.47 Balzac, Honoré de. Le chef-d'oeuvre inconnu. Genève, 1945.
40596.50 Balzac, Honoré de. About Catherine de Médici. N.Y., 1901.
40596.51 Balzac, Honoré de. The Chouans. N.Y., 1901.
40596.53 Balzac, Honoré de. A distinguished provincial at Paris. N.Y., 1901.
40596.54 Balzac, Honoré de. Eugénie Grandet. N.Y., 1901.
40596.55 Balzac, Honoré de. The lily of the valley. N.Y., 1901.
40596.56 Balzac, Honoré de. Old Goriot. N.Y., 1901.
40596.57 Balzac, Honoré de. Lost illusions. N.Y., 1901.
40596.58 Balzac, Honoré de. A princess's secrets. N.Y., 1901.
40596.59 Balzac, Honoré de. Ursule Mirouëtt. N.Y., 1901.
40596.101 Balzac, Honoré de. The rise and fall of César Birotteau. Boston, 1901.
40596.102 Balzac, Honoré de. At the sign of the cat and racket. Boston, 1901.
40596.103 Balzac, Honoré de. Scenes from a courtesans's life. Boston, 1901.
40596.104 Balzac, Honoré de. The magic skin. Boston, 1901.
40596.105 Balzac, Honoré de. Eugénie Grandet. Boston, 1901.
40596.106 Balzac, Honoré de. The lily of the valley. Boston, 1901.
40596.107 Balzac, Honoré de. A daughter of Eve. Boston, 1901.
40596.108 Balzac, Honoré de. The thirteen. Boston, 1901.
40596.109 Balzac, Honoré de. The member for Arcis. Boston, 1901.
40596.110 Balzac, Honoré de. A marriage settlement. Boston, 1901.
40596.111 Balzac, Honoré de. Cousin Betty. Boston, 1901.
40596.112 Balzac, Honoré de. Lost illusions. Boston, 1901.
40596.112.5 Balzac, Honoré de. Lost illusions. N.Y., 1967.
40596.113 Balzac, Honoré de. The dramas. Boston, 1901.
40596.114 Balzac, Honoré de. About Catherine de Medici. Boston, 1901.
40596.115 Balzac, Honoré de. Béatrix. Boston, 1901.
40596.116 Balzac, Honoré de. The Chouans. Boston, 1901.
40596.117 Balzac, Honoré de. The country parson. Boston, 1901.

40597 - 40597.099 Individual authors, etc. - 1800-1849 - Fiction - Balzac - Pamphlet volumes

40597 Pamphlet box. Balzac, Honoré de.
40597.01 Pamphlet box. Balzac, Honoré de.
40597.04 Perre, P. Les préfacons belges. Bruxelles, 1940.
40597.05 Royce, W.H. A Balzac bibliography. Chicago, 1929.
40597.05.2 Royce, W.H. A Balzac bibliography. Indexes. Chicago, 1930.
40597.06 Korwin-Piotrowska, S. Balzac en Pologne. Paris, 1933.
40597.06.5 Korwin-Piotrowska, S. Balzac en Pologne. Thèse. Paris, 1933.

40597.1 - .9 Individual authors, etc. - 1800-1849 - Fiction - Balzac - Biography and criticism

40597.1 Saltres, Edgar E. Balzac. Boston, 1888.
40597.1.2 Barbery, B. Henry de Balzac, ou une double famille. Paris, 1938.
40597.1.5 Werdet, E. Portrait intime de Balzac, sa vie, son humeur et son caractère. Paris, 1859.
40597.1.5.1 Werdet, Edmond. Portrait intime de Balzac. Paris, 1970?
40597.1.6 Surville, L. A une amie de province, lettres. Paris, 1932.
40597.1.7 Surville, L. Balzac, sa vie et ses oeuvres. Paris, 1858.
40597.1.8 Ruxton, G. La dilecta de Balzac. Paris, 1909.
40597.1.9 Sattler, Hermann. H. de Balzacs Roman La peau de chagrin. Halle, 1912.
40597.1.12 Floyd, J.H. Women in the life of Balzac. N.Y., 1921.
40597.1.95 Baschet, Armand. Honoré de Balzac. Paris, 1852.
40597.2 Baschet, Armand. Honoré de Balzac. 2. éd. Paris, 1852.
40597.2.2 Lemer, Julien. Balzac. Paris, 1892.
40597.2.3 Balzac à Saché. Tours.
40597.2.5 Bire, Edmond. Honoré de Balzac. Paris, 1897.

40597.1 - .9 Individual authors, etc. - 1800-1849 - Fiction - Balzac - Biography and criticism - cont.

40597.2.6 Spoelberch de Lovenjoul, Charles. Autour de Honoré de Balzac. Paris, 1897.
40597.2.7 Spoelberch de Lovenjoul, Charles. Un roman d'amour. Paris, 1896.
40597.2.8 Spoelberch de Lovenjoul, Charles. La genése d'un roman de Balzac: Les paysans. Paris, 1901.
40597.2.8.10 Spoelberch de Lovenjoul, Charles. Un dernier chapitre de l'histoire des oeuvres de H. de Balzac. Paris, 1880.
40597.2.9 Wright, T.F. Balzac and Swedenborg. Boston, 1896.
40597.2.10 Hanotaux, Gabriel. La jeunesse de Balzac. Paris, 1903.
40597.2.10.5 Hanotaux, Gabriel. La jeunesse de Balzac. Paris, 1921.
40597.2.11 Sandars, Mary F. Honoré de Balzac. His life and writings. N.Y., 1905.
40597.2.12 Le Breton, A. Balzac; l'homme et l'oeuvre. Paris, 1905.
40597.2.13 Bruntière, F. Honoré de Balzac. 1799-1850. Paris, 1906.
40597.2.13A Brunetière, F. Honoré de Balzac. 1799-1850. Paris, 1906.
40597.2.13B Brunetière, F. Honoré de Balzac. 1799-1850. Paris, 1906.
40597.2.13.2 Brunetière, F. Honoré de Balzac. 1799-1850. Philadelphia, 1906.
40597.2.13.5 Brunetière, F. Honoré de Balzac. N.Y., 19- .
40597.2.14 Canabès, Augustin. Balzac ignoré. 2. éd. Paris, 190-?
40597.2.15 Lawton, Fred. Balzac. London, 1910.
40597.2.16 Fagnet, E. Balzac. Paris, 1913.
40597.2.17 Haas, J. H. Balzacs Scènes de la vie privée von 1830. Halle, 1912.
40597.2.18 Bernheim, P. Balzac und Swedenborg. Berlin, 1914.
40597.2.19 Royaumont, Louis de. Balzac et la société des gens de lettres 1833-1913. Paris, 191-?
NEDL 40597.2.20 Roux, Fernand. Balzac, jurisconsulte et criminaliste. Paris, 1906.
40597.2.21 Calippe, Charles. Balzac, ses idées sociales. Reims, 19-?
40597.2.23 Schätzle, Anselm. Balzac als Naturalist. Inaug. Diss. Heidelberg, 1914.
40597.2.25 Burton, John M. Honoré de Balzac and his figures of speech. Baltimore, 1921.
40597.2.26 Burton, John M. Honoré de Balzac and his figures of speech. Princeton, N.J., 1921.
40597.2.28 Fees, Gilbert M. The correspondence of physical and material factors with character in Balzac. Thesis. Philadelphia, 1924.
40597.2.30 Wormeley, K.P. A memoir of Honoré de Balzac. Boston, 1892.
40597.2.32 Bellessort, A. Balzac et son oeuvres. 6. éd. Paris, 1924.
40597.2.34 Arrigon, L.J. Les débuts littéraires d'Honoré de Balzac. 2. éd. Paris, 1924.
40597.2.36 Parran, A. Romantique. Paris, 1881.
40597.2.37 Guérard, A.L. Honoré de Balzac et la Comédie Humaine. Houston, 1923?
40597.2.38 Barnes, Helen E. A study of the variations between the original and the standard editions of Balzac's Les Chouans. Chicago, 1923.
40597.2.40 Joseph, S.D.L. Les souvenirs et l'esprit napoléoniens chez Balzac. Thèse. Paris, 1924.
40597.2.42A Benjamin, René. La prodigieuse vie d'Honoré de Balzac. Paris, 1925.
40597.2.42B Benjamin, René. La prodigieuse vie d'Honoré de Balzac. Paris, 1925.
40597.2.42C Benjamin, René. La prodigieuse vie d'Honoré de Balzac. Paris, 1925.
40597.2.42.2 Benjamin, René. La prodigieuse vie d'Honoré de Balzac. Paris, 1925.
40597.2.43 Benjamin, René. La prodigieuse vie d'Honoré de Balzac. Paris, 1937.
40597.2.44 Benjamin, René. La prodigieuse vie d'Honoré de Balzac. Paris, 1958.
40597.2.44.2 Benjamin, René. La vie prodigieuse de Balzac. Paris, 1962.
40597.2.48 Baldensperger, F. Orientations étrangères chez Honoré de Balzac. Paris, 1927.
40597.2.50 Preston, E. Recherches sur la technique de Balzac. Paris, 1927.
40597.2.55 Altszyler, Hélène. La genèse et le plan des caractères dans l'oeuvre de Balzac. Paris, 1928.
40597.2.57 Altszyler, Hélène. La genèse et le plan des caractères dans l'oeuvre de Balzac. Paris, 1928.
40597.2.59 Takayama, Tetsuo. Les oeuvres romanesques avortées de Balzac, 1829-1842. Tokyo, 1966.
40597.2.60 Duviard, Ferdinand. Un prédécesseur de Ferdinand Fabre. Cahors, 1926.
40597.2.62 Cantù, C. Di Onorato Balzac e delle sue opere. Milano, 1838.
40597.2.65 Balzac mis à nu. Paris, 1928.
40597.2.69 Segar, Friéderic. Un maitre de Balzac. Paris, 1928.
40597.2.73 Milatchitch, Douchan Z. Le théatre de Honoré de Balzac d'après des documents nouveaux et inédits. Thèse. Paris, 1930.
40597.2.74 Milatchitch, Douchan Z. Le théâtre de Honoré de Balzac d'après des documents nouveaux et inèdits. Paris, 1930.
40597.2.77 Serval, M. Autor d'Eugénie Grandet d'après des documents inédits. Paris, 1924.
40597.2.78 Serval, M. Une amie de Balzac. Paris, 1925.
40597.2.80 Bouvier, René. Balzac, homme d'affaires. Paris, 1930.
40597.2.83 Jarblum, J. Balzac et la femme étrangère. Paris, 1930.
40597.2.84 Leathers, V.L. L'Espagne et les Espagnols dans l'oeuvre d'Honoré de Balzac. Thèse. Paris, 1931.
40597.2.85 Leathers, V.L. L'Espagne et les Espagnols dans l'oeuvre d'Honoré de Balzac. Paris, 1931.
40597.2.87 Buttke, Erika. Balzac als Dichter des modernen Kapitalismus. Inaug. Diss. Berlin, 1931.
40597.2.88 Buttke, Erika. Balzac als Dichter des modernen Kapitalismus. Berlin, 1932.
40597.2.89 Blanchard, Marc. La champagne et ses habitants dans l'oeuvre de Honoré de Balzac. Thèse. Paris, 1931.
40597.2.91 Blanchard, Marc. Témoignages et jugements sur Balzac. Thèse. Paris, 1931.
40597.2.93 Jarblum, Irène. Balzac et la femme étrangère. Thèse. Paris, 1930.
40597.2.95 Griffith, B. Balzac aux Etats-Unis. Thèse. Paris, 1930?
40597.2.97 Meissner, Emmy. Die soziologische Fragestellung bei Balzac. Inaug. Diss. Darmstadt, 193-.
40597.2.99 Drucker, P. The critical doctrine of Honoré de Balzac. Colorado Springs, 1932.
40597.2.100 Korwin-Piotrowska, S. Balzac et le monde slave. Thèse. Paris, 1933.

40597.1 - .9 Individual authors, etc. - 1800-1849 - Fiction - Balzac - Biography and criticism - cont.

40597.2.101 Korwin-Piotrowska, S. Balzac et le monde slave. Paris, 1933.
40597.2.102 Korwin-Piotrowska, S. L'etrangère, Eveline Hanska de Balzac. Paris, 1938.
40597.2.103 Schöll, Erwin. César Birotteau. Inaug. Diss. Wertheim, 1932.
40597.2.103.2 Schöll, Erwin. César Birotteau. Wertheim, 1932.
40597.2.106 Curtius, E.R. Balzac. Paris, 1933.
40597.2.106.5 Curtius, E.R. Balzac. 2. Aufl. Bern, 1951.
40597.2.107 Grafe, Hans. Die Frauengestalten im Werke Honoré de Balzac's. Inaug. Diss. Zeulenroda, 1934.
40597.2.109 Büchsenschütz, Heinz. Balzac im Spiegel seines Briefwechsels. Inaug. Diss. Marburg, 1934.
40597.2.110 Ferguson, M.B. La volonté dans la "Comedie humaine" de Balzac. Paris, 1933.
40597.2.111 Ferguson, M.B. La volonté dans la "Comedie humaine" de Balzac. Thèse. Paris, 1935.
40597.2.112 Priault, A. Balzac avant la Comédie humaine, 1818-1829. Thèse. Paris, 1936.
40597.2.113 Priault, A. Balzac avant la Comédie humaine, 1818-1829. Paris, 1936.
40597.2.114 Saint-Germès, M. Balzac considéré comme historien du droit. Thèse. Besançon, 1936.
40597.2.115 Saint-Germès, M. Balzac considéré comme historien du droit. Besançon, 1927.
40597.2.117A Grib, V. Balzac. N.Y., 1937.
40597.2.117B Grib, V. Balzac. N.Y., 1937.
40597.2.119 Louis, Paul. Les types sociaux chez Balzac et Zola. Paris, 1925.
40597.2.121 Scott, Mary W. Art and artists in Balzac's Comédie humaine. Chicago, 1937.
40597.2.123 Wenger, Jared. The Province and the provinces in the work of Honoré de Balzac. Diss. Princeton, 1937.
40597.2.124 Stevenson, N.W. Paris dans la Comédie humaine de Balzac. Thèse. Paris, 1938.
40597.2.125 Stevenson, N.W. Paris dans la Comédie humaine de Balzac. Paris, 1938.
40597.2.128 Bouvier, R. Les comptes dramatiques de Balzac. Paris, 1938.
40597.2.130 Gillot, H. Balzac, le médecin de campagne. Paris, 1938.
40597.2.132 Césari, P. Étude critique des passions dans l'oeuvre de Balzac. Thèse. Paris, 1938.
40597.2.133 Césari, P. Étude critique des passions dans l'oeuvre de Balzac. Paris, 1938.
40597.2.134 Dargan, Edwin P. The evolution of Balzac's Comédie humaine. Chicago, 1942.
40597.2.135A Dargan, Edwin P. Studies in Balzac's realism. Chicago, 1932.
40597.2.135B Dargan, Edwin P. Studies in Balzac's realism. Chicago, 1932.
40597.2.136A Dargan, Edwin P. Honoré de Balzac. Chicago, 1932.
40597.2.136B Dargan, Edwin P. Honoré de Balzac. Chicago, 1932.
40597.2.137 Bowen, R.P. The dramatic construction of Balzac's novels. Eugene, 1940.
40597.2.139 Aubrée, E. Balzac à fougères. Paris, 1939.
40597.2.142 Faillettaz, E. Balzac et le monde des affaires. Diss. Lausanne, 1932.
40597.2.144A Chartier, Émile. Avec Balzac. 7. éd. Paris, 1937.
40597.2.144B Chartier, Émile. Avec Balzac. 5. éd. Paris, 1937.
40597.2.145 Garrett, H.T. Clothes and character. Philadelphia, 1941.
40597.2.146 Saba, Jean. Balzac as a social historian. Urbana, 1941.
40597.2.147 Crain, William L. An introduction to a critical edition of Le secret des Ruggieri. Chicago, 1942.
40597.2.148 Wilson, Rachel. Variations in Le cure de Tours. Chicago, 1942.
40597.2.149 Bettelheim, A. Balzac, eine Biografie. München, 1926.
40597.2.151 Gilbert, E. Balzac à vingt ans. Bruxelles, 1904.
40597.2.153 Billy, André. Vie de Balzac. Paris, 1944. 2v.
40597.2.155 Tours, France. Statue de Honoré de Balzac à Tours. Paris, 1887.
40597.2.157 Dedinsky, B.H. Development of the scheme of the Comédie humaine. Chicago, 1943.
40597.2.159.1 Bardèche, Maurice. Balzac, romancier. Genève, 1967.
40597.2.159.2 Bardèche, Maurice. Balzac, romancier. Bruxelles, 1944.
40597.2.162 Arrault, Albert. Madame de Berny; éducatrice de Balzac. Tours, 1945.
40597.2.163 Arrault, Albert. La Touraine de Baleac. Tours, 1947.
40597.2.163.5 Arrault, Albert. Madame de Berny; le premier amour de Balzac. Tours, 1948.
40597.2.164 Zweig, Stefan. Balzac. Stockholm, 1946.
40597.2.165A Zweig, Stefan. Balzac. N.Y., 1946.
40597.2.165B Zweig, Stefan. Balzac. N.Y., 1946.
40597.2.167 Abraham, Pierre. Balzac. Paris, 1929.
40597.2.169 Royce, William H. Balzac as he should be read. N.Y., 1946.
40597.2.171 Bertault, Philippe. Balzac et la religion. Thèse. Paris, 1942.
40597.2.173 Mauriac, Claude. Aimer Balzac. Paris, 1945.
40597.2.174 Mauriac, Claude. Aimer Balzac. Liege, 1945.
40597.2.175 Béguin, Albert. Balzac visionnaire, Propositions. Genève, 1946.
40597.2.180 Mayer, Gilbert. La qualification affective dans les romans d'Honoré de Balzac. Thèse. Paris, 1940.
40597.2.185A Levin, Harry. Toward Balzac. Norfolk, 1947.
40597.2.185B Levin, Harry. Toward Balzac. Norfolk, 1947.
40597.2.185C Levin, Harry. Toward Balzac. Norfolk, 1947.
40597.2.190A Bertault, Philippe. Balzac, l'homme et l'oeuvre. Paris, 1946.
40597.2.190B Bertault, Philippe. Balzac, l'homme et l'oeuvre. Paris, 1946.
40597.2.191 Bertault, Philippe. Balzac et la musique religieuse. Paris, 1929.
40597.2.195 Hirschfell, G.J. Balzac und Delacroix. Inaug. Diss. Saint-Louis, 1946.
40597.2.200A Guyon, Bernard. La pensée politique et sociale de Balzac. Paris, 1947.
40597.2.200B Guyon, Bernard. La pensée politique et sociale de Balzac. Thèse. Paris, 1947.
40597.2.200C Guyon, Bernard. La pensée politique et sociale de Balzac. Paris, 1947.
40597.2.200.2 Guyon, Bernard. La pensée politique et sociale de Balzac. 2. éd. Paris, 1967.
40597.2.202 Guyon, Bernard. La création littéraite chez Balzac. Paris, 1951.
40597.2.205 Grossman, L.P. Balzac en Russie. Paris, 1946.
40597.2.210 Chartier, Émile. En lisant Balzac. Paris, 1935.

40597.1 - .9 Individual authors, etc. - 1800-1849 - Fiction - Balzac - Biography and criticism - cont.

40597.2.215 Bernes, Pierre. Exposition commemorative du cent cinquantieme anniversaire de Balzac. Paris, 1949.
40597.2.220 Rosny, J.H. La vie amoureuse de Balzac. Paris, 1930.
40597.2.225 Pfeiffer, C.L. Taste and smell in Balzac's novels. Tucson, 1949.
40597.2.230 Gribble, F. Balzac, the man and the lover. London, 1930.
40597.2.235 Bertaut, Jules. La vie privée de Balzac. Paris, 1950.
40597.2.240 Bouteron, M. La véritable image de Madame Hanska. Paris, 1929.
40597.2.245 Emery, Leon. Balzac. Paris, 1943.
40597.2.246 Emery, Leon. Balzac en sa création. Lyon, 1952?
40597.2.250 Helm, W. Aspects of Balzac. N.Y., 1905.
40597.2.255 Jarry, P. Le dernier logis de Balzac. Paris, 1924.
40597.2.260 Descaves, Pierre. Les centjours de M. de Balzac. Paris, 1950.
40597.2.262 Descaves, Pierre. Balzac. Paris, 1960.
40597.2.265 Tersteeg, J. Honoré de Balzac en drie vrouwen. 's Gravenhage, 1949.
40597.2.270 Noiset, L. Balzac et les femmes. Paris, 1932.
40597.2.275 Bonnet-Roy, F. Balzac, les médecins. Paris, 1944.
40597.2.280 Fernandez, R. Balzac. Paris, 1943.
40597.2.285 Forest, H. L'esthétique du roman balzacien. Paris, 1950.
40597.2.290 Guignard, R. Balzac et Issoudun. Issoudun, 1949
40597.2.295 Léger, C. Eve de Balzac d'après des documents. Paris, 1926.
40597.2.300 Du Pontavice de Heussey, Robert. Balzac en Bretagne. Rennes, 1885.
40597.2.305 Cazenove, M. Le drame de Balzac. Paris, 1950.
40597.2.310 Arüss, A. Le joli page de Balzac. Paris, 1924.
40597.2.315 Spitzer, Márta. Les juifs de Balzac. Budapest, 1939.
40597.2.320 Ponceau, A. Paysages et destins balzaciens. Paris, 1950.
40597.2.325 Paris. Bibliotheque nationale. Honoré de Balzac. Paris, 1950.
40597.2.330 U.N.E.S.C.O. Hommage à Balzac. Paris, 1950.
40597.2.335 Taine, H.A. Balzac. Leipzig, 1913.
40597.2.340 Peytel, A. Balzac. Paris, 1950.
40597.2.345 Lamartine, A. de. Balzac et ses oeuvres. Paris, 1866.
40597.2.350 Les études balzaciennes. Paris. 1-10,1951-1960 2v.
40597.2.352 L'année balzacienne. Paris. 1961+ 10v.
40597.2.355 Lukács, G. Balzac und der Französische Realismus. Berlin, 1952.
40597.2.360 Balzac, le livre du centenaire. Paris, 1952.
40597.2.365 Rogers, S. Balzac and the novel. Madison, 1953.
40597.2.370 Desnoiresterres, G. M. De Balzac. Paris, 1831.
40597.2.375 Evans, Henri. Louis Lambert et la philosophie de Balzac. Paris, 1951.
40597.2.380 Durry, M.J. Balzac, un début dans la vie. Paris, 1953.
40597.2.385 Marceau, F. Balzac et son monde. 6. ed. Paris, 1955.
40597.2.390 Weigand, W. Stendhal und Balzac; essays. Leipzig, 1911.
40597.2.395 Pradalié, G. Balzac historien. 1. éd. Paris, 1955.
40597.2.400 Dagneud, R. Les éléments populaires dans le lexique de la comédie humaine d'Honoré de Balzac. Paris, 1954.
40597.2.405 Bouteron, M. Études balzaciennes. Paris, 1954.
40597.2.410 Weith, Otto. Romantisches im Theater Honoré de Balzac's. Wertheim, 1931.
40597.2.415 Hunt, Herbert James. Honoré de Balzac. London, 1957.
40597.2.417 Hunt, Herbert James. Balzac's Comédie humaine. London, 1959.
40597.2.418 Hunt, Herbert James. Balzac's Comédie humaine. London, 1964.
40597.2.420 Lecuyer, Maurice A.F. Balzac et Rabelais. Paris, 1956.
40597.2.425 Vouga, Daniel. Balzac malgré lui. Paris, 1957.
40597.2.450 Gozlan, Léon. Balzac intime. Paris, 1886.
40597.2.455 Griftsov, B.A. Kak rabotal Bal'zak. Moskva, 1958.
40597.2.460 Teuler, Gabriel. Du côté de Balzac. Paris, 1959.
40597.2.465 Pommier, Jean. L'invention et l'ecriture dans la Torpille d'Honoré de Balzac. Genève, 1957.
40597.2.470 Borel, Jacques. Personnages et destins balzaciens. Paris, 1958.
40597.2.475 Oliver, Edward. Balzac the European. London, 1959.
40597.2.480 Kuhn-Meierhans, Doris. Le curé de Tours. Zürich, 1958.
40597.2.485 Folman, Michel. Honoré de Balzac. Genève, 1959.
40597.2.490 George, Albert. Books by Balzac. Syracuse, N.Y., 1960.
40597.2.495 Billy, André. Balzac. Paris, 1959.
40597.2.500 Torres Bodet, J. Balzac. México, 1959.
40597.2.505 Reizov, Boris G. Bal'zak. Leningrad, 1960.
40597.2.510 Syracuse University. Honoré Balzac. Syracuse, 1960.
40597.2.515 Le Yaouanc, M. Nosographie de l'humanité balzacienne. Paris, 1959.
40597.2.520 Smith, Stephen R.B. Balzac et l'Angleterre. Londres, 1953.
40597.2.525 Donnard, J.H. La vie économique et les classes sociales dans l'oeuvre de Balzac. Paris, 1961.
40597.2.527 Donnard, J.H. Balzac; les réalités économiques. Paris, 1961.
40597.2.530 Richard, Max. Louis Lambert et la métaphysique balzacienne. Paris, 1960.
40597.2.535 Ablomievskii, D.D. Bal'zak. Moskva, 1961.
40597.2.540 Delattre, G. Les opinions littéraires de Balzac. Paris, 1961.
40597.2.545 Borel, Jacques. Le Lys dans la vallée et les sources profondes de la création balzacienne. Paris, 1961.
40597.2.550 Laubriet, Pierre. Un catechisme esthétique. Paris, 1961.
40597.2.552 Laubriet, Pierre. L'intelligence de l'art chez Balzac. Paris, 1961.
40597.2.555A Bérand, S.J. La genese d'un roman de Balzac. Paris, 1961. 2v.
40597.2.555B Bérand, S.J. La genese d'un roman de Balzac. Paris, 1961. 2v.
40597.2.560 Ducourneau, Jean. Album Balzac. Paris, 1962.
40597.2.565 Mancisidor, José. Balzac. México, 1952.
40597.2.570 Eaubonne, F. d'. Balzac que voici. Paris, 1962.
40597.2.575 Bertault, Philippe. Balzac and the human comedy. N.Y., 1963.
40597.2.580 Gun, Willem H. van der. La courtisane romantique et son rôle dans la Comédie humaine de Balzac. Assen, 1963.
40597.2.585 Oliver, E.J. Honoré de Balzac. N.Y., 1964.
40597.2.590 Wurmser, André. La comédie inhumaine. Paris, 1964.
40597.2.591 Wurmser, André. La comédie inhumaine. Paris, 1970.
40597.2.595 Gillette, Fredericka B. Title index to the works of Honoré de Balzac. Boston, 1909.
40597.2.600 Bardèche, Maurice. Une lecture de Balzac. Paris, 1964.
40597.2.605 Raser, George Bernard. Guide to Balzac's Paris. Choisy-le-Roi, 1964.
40597.2.610 Descaves, Pierre. Le president Balzac. Paris, 1951.
40597.2.615 Gigli, Guiseppe. Balzac in Italia. Milano, 1920.

40597.1 - .9 Individual authors, etc. - 1800-1849 - Fiction - Balzac - Biography and criticism - cont.

40597.2.620 Bertaut, Jules. Balzac anecdotique. Paris, 1908.
40597.2.625 Maurois, André. Prométhée; ou, La vie de Balzac. Paris, 1965.
40597.2.625.1 Maurois, André. Prométhée; ou, La vie de Balzac. Lausanne, 1965. 2v.
40597.2.626A Maurois, André. Prometheus. 1. ed. N.Y., 1966.
40597.2.626B Maurois, André. Prometheus. 1. ed. N.Y., 1966.
40597.2.670 Warneńska, Monika. Romantyczna podróż pana Honoriusza. Warszawa, 1965.
40597.2.675 Barbéris, Pierre. Aux sources de Balzac. Paris, 1965.
40597.2.680 Allemand, André. Honoré de Balzac. Paris, 1965.
40597.2.700 Métadier, Paul. Balzac au petit matin. Paris, 1964.
40597.2.705 Petrova, Evgeniia A. Stanovlenie realizma Bal'zaka. Saratov, 1964.
40597.2.707 Adamson, Donald. The genesis of Le cousin Pons. London, 1966.
40597.2.710 Hoffman, Léon-François. Repertoire geographique de la Comédie humaine. Paris, 1965. 2v.
40597.2.715 Nykrog, Per. La pensée de Balzac dans la Comédie humaine. Copenhague, 1965.
40597.2.720 Béguin, Albert. Balzac lu et relu. Paris, 1965.
40597.2.725 Allemand, André. Unité et structure de l'univers balzacien. Paris, 1965.
40597.2.730 Affron, Charles. Patterns of failure in La comédie humaine. New Haven, 1966.
40597.2.735 Moscow. Vsesoiuznaia gosudarstvennaia biblioteka inostrannoi literatury. Onore de Bal'zak. Moskva, 1965.
40597.2.740 Ford, Mary Hanford Finney. Balzac's Seraphita; the mystery of sex. Chicago, 1897.
40597.2.745 Mount, Alan John. The physical setting in Balzac's "Comédie Humaine". Hull, 1966.
40597.2.750 Lock, Peter W. Balzac: Le père Goriot. London, 1967.
40597.2.755 Des Loges, Stéphanie. L'art structural de la narration dans la nouvelle de Balzac. Wrocław, 1967.
40597.2.760 Martínez Estrada, Ezequiel. Realidad y fantasía en Balzac. Bahía Blanca, 1964.
40597.2.765 Lecour, Charles. Les personnages de la Comédie humaine. Paris, 1966. 2v.
V40597.2.770 Karczewska-Markiewicz, Zofia. Ojciec Goriot Honoriusza Balzaka. Warszawa, 1968.
40597.2.775 Hemmings, Frederick William John. Balzac; an interpretation of La comédie humaine. N.Y., 1967.
40597.2.780 Faillie, Marie-Henriette. La femme et le Code civil dans La comédie humaine d'Honoré de Balzac. Paris, 1968.
40597.2.785 Schilling, Bernard Nicholas. The hero as failure; Balzac and the Rubempré cycle. Chicago, 1968.
40597.2.790 Fargeaud, Madeleine. Balzac et la Recherche de l'absolu. Paris, 1968.
40597.2.796 Bertault, Philippe. Balzac. Paris, 1967.
40597.2.800 Besser, Gretchen R. Balzac's concept of genius. Genève, 1969.
40597.2.805 Schneiderbauer, Anna Maria. Das Element des Daemonischen in Honoré de Balzacs Comédie humaine. München? 1967?
40597.2.810 Reboussin, Marcel. Balzac et le mythe de Foedora. Paris, 1966.
40597.2.815 Trost, Sigrid. Die Persönlichkeit im Umschwung der politischen Macht nach Balzacs Comédie humaine. Bern, 1969.
40597.2.820 Reizov, Boris G. Tvorchestvo Bal'zaka. Leningrad, 1939.
40597.2.825 Kuchborskaia, Elizaveta P. Tvorchestvo Bal'zaka. Moskva, 1970.
40597.2.830 Bonard, Olivier. La peinture dans la création balzacienne. Thèse. Genève, 1969.
40597.2.835 Barbéris, Pierre. Balzac et le mal du siècle. Paris, 1970. 2v.
40597.2.840 Bakhmutskii, Vladimir Ia. "Otets Gorio" Balzaka. Moskva, 1970.
40597.2.845 Borel, Jacques. "Seraphita" et le mysti cisme balzacien. Paris, 1967.
40597.2.850 Raser, George Bernard. The heart of Balzac's Paris. Choisy-le-Roi, 1970.
40597.2.855 Denizot, Philippe M. Catalogue de la "Comédie humaine" de Balzac. Chinon, 1969.
40597.2.860 Spitzer, Márta. Balzac zsidó alakjai. Budapest, 1939.
40597.2.865 Toulouse. Musée Paul Dupuy. La comedie humaine et ses objets. Toulouse, 1970.
40597.2.870 Bilodeau, François. Balzac et le jeu des mots. Montréal, 1971.
40597.2.875 Jacques, Georges. Le doigt de Dieu. Louvain, 1970.
40597.2.880 Galantaris, Christian. Les portraits de Balzac connus et inconnus, février-avril 1971. Paris, 1971.
40597.3 Gozlan, Léon. Balzac chez lui. Paris, 1862.
40597.3.2 Gozlan, Léon. Balzac chez lui. Paris, 1863.
40597.3.12 Gozlan, Léon. Balzac en pantoufles. Paris, 1941?
40597.3.15 Gozlan, Léon. Balzac in slippers. N.Y., 1929.
40597.4 Fleury, Jules. Documents pour servir à la biographie de Balzac. Paris, 1875-79. 3 pam.
40597.5 Spoelberch de Lovenjoul, Charles. Histoire des oeuvres de Honoré de Balzac. Paris, 1886.
40597.5.1.2A Spoelberch de Lovenjoul, Charles. Histoire des oeuvres de Honoré de Balzac. Paris, 1879.
40597.5.1.2B Spoelberch de Lovenjoul, Charles. Histoire des oeuvres de Honoré de Balzac. Paris, 1879.
40597.5.2 Barriere, Marcel. L'oeuvre de Honoré de Balzac. Paris, 1890.
40597.5.5 Barriere, P. Honoré de Balzac. Thèse. Paris, 1928. 2 pam.
40597.6A Correspondance de Honoré de Balzac. Paris, 1876. 2v.
40597.6B Correspondance de Honoré de Balzac. Paris, 1876. 2v.
40597.6.1A Balzac, Honoré de. Correspondance. Paris, 1960-64. 5v.
40597.6.1B Balzac, Honoré de. Correspondance. Paris, 1960-64. 5v.
40597.6.2 Gautier, T. Honoré de Balzac. Paris, 1859.
40597.6.15 Keim, A. Balzac. (Los grandes hombres). Paris, 191-?
Htn 40597.7* Laporte, Antoine. Honoré de Balzac. Étude bibliographique. Paris, 1884.
40597.8A Cerfberr, Anatole. Répertoire de la comédie humaine de H. de Balzac. Paris, 1887.
40597.8B Cerfberr, Anatole. Répertoire de la comédie humaine de H. de Balzac. Paris, 1887.
40597.8.3 Cerfberr, Anatole. Repertory of la comédie humaine de H. de Balzac. N.Y., 1900.
40597.8.4 Cerfberr, Anatole. Compendium. Honoré de Balzac's Comédie humaine. Philadelphia, 1900.

40597.1 - .9 Individual authors, etc. - 1800-1849 - Fiction - Balzac - Biography and criticism - cont.

40597.8.5 Lhomer, J. Balzac dans l'intimité et les types de la comédie humaine. Paris, 1904.
Htn 40597.8.6* James, Henry. The question of our speech. Boston, 1905.
40597.8.10 Hastings, Walter Scott. The drama of Honoré de Balzac. Menasha, Wis., 1920.
40597.8.15 Seillière, Ernest. Balzac et la morale romantique. Paris, 1922.
40597.9A Wedmore, F. Life of H. de Balzac. London, 1890.
40597.9B Wedmore, F. Life of H. de Balzac. London, 1890.
40597.9.1 Wedmore, F. Life of H. de Balzac. London, 1890.
40597.9.2 Flat, Paul. Essais sur Balzac. Paris, 1893.
40597.9.5 Arrigon, L.J. Les années romantiques de Balzac. Paris, 1927.
40597.9.8 Arrigon, L.J. Balzac et la "contessa". Paris, 1932.
40597.9.10 Léger, Charles. A la recherche de Balzac. Paris, 1927.
40597.9.12 Wormeley, K.P. A memoir of Honoré de Balzac. Boston, 1895.
40597.9.15 Lotte, F. Dictionnaire biographique des personnages fictifs de La Comédie humaine. Paris, 1952.
40597.9.20 Lorant, André. Les parents pauvres d'Honoré de Balzac. Thèse. Genève, 1967. 2v.

40597.10 - Individual authors, etc. - 1800-1849 - Fiction - Balzac - Individual works

Htn 40597.10* Balzac, Honoré de. Droll stories. London, 1874.
40597.11 Balzac, Honoré de. Beatrix. Contract du mariage. Paris, 1873-74.
40597.11.10 Balzac, Honoré de. Beatrix. Paris, 1892.
40597.11.20 Balzac, Honoré de. Beatrix. Paris, 1960.
40597.12 Balzac, Honoré de. Histoire de...César Birotteau. Paris, 1838.
40597.12.60 Balzac, Honoré de. Nevedomyi shedevr. Moskva, 1966.
40597.13 Balzac, Honoré de. Les chouans. Paris, 1898.
40597.13.2 Balzac, Honoré de. The Chouans. N.Y., 1900.
Htn 40597.13.5* Balzac, Honoré de. Les fantaisies de Claudine. Paris, 1853.
40597.14 Balzac, Honoré de. The greatness of César Birotteau. N.Y., 1860.
40597.14.4 Balzac, Honoré de. César Birotteau. N.Y., 19- .
40597.14.6 Balzac, Honoré de. César Birotteau. N.Y., 1900.
40597.14.6.10 Balzac, Honoré de. César Birotteau. London, 19- .
40597.14.6.15 Balzac, Honoré de. César Birotteau. Montréal, 1945.
40597.14.6.18 Balzac, Honoré de. César Birotteau. N.Y., 1955.
40597.14.6.20 Balzac, Honoré de. Histoire de la grandeur et la décadence de César Birotteau. Paris, 1930.
40597.14.6.205 istoire de la grandeur et la décadence de César Birotteau. Paris, 1930.' 35fv.
40597.14.6.21 Balzac, Honoré de. César Birotteau. Paris, 1961.
40597.14.6.22 Balzac, Honoré de. Histoire de la grandeur et de la decadence de César Birotteau. Paris, 1964.
40597.14.7.1 Balzac, Honoré de. César Birotteau. Boston, 1888.
40597.14.7.2 Balzac, Honoré de. César Birotteau. Boston, 1889.
40597.14.7.5 Balzac, Honoré de. César Birotteau. Boston, 1898.
Htn 40597.14.12* Balzac, Honoré de. Les contes drolatiques. 7. éd. Paris, 1867.
40597.14.16 Balzac, Honoré de. Les contes drolatiques. Paris, 1926.
40597.14.40 Balzac, Honoré de. Droll stories. London, 187-? 2v.
X Cg 40597.14.50 Balzac, Honoré de. Droll stories. London, 1874. 2v.
Htn 40597.14.53* Balzac, Honoré de. Les contes drolatiques. Paris, 1873.
40597.14.54 Balzac, Honoré de. Les contes drolatiques. Paris, 1925. 2v.
40597.14.55A Balzac, Honoré de. Droll stories. London, 1874.
40597.14.55B Balzac, Honoré de. Droll stories. London, 1874.
40597.14.56 Balzac, Honoré de. Droll stories. London, 1874.
40597.14.58 Balzac, Honoré de. Droll stories. N.Y., 1874. 2v.
40597.14.58A Balzac, Honoré de. Droll stories. N.Y., 1874.
40597.14.58B Balzac, Honoré de. Droll stories. N.Y., 1874.
40597.14.61 Balzac, Honoré de. Droll stories. N.Y., 192-.
40597.14.67 Balzac, Honoré de. Droll stories; thirty tales. N.Y., 1932. 3v.
40597.14.68 Balzac, Honoré de. Droll stories; thirty tales. N.Y., 1965.
40597.14.70 Balzac, Honoré de. Short stories. Little French masterpieces. N.Y., 1909.
40597.14.75 Balzac, Honoré de. Short stories. N.Y., 1920?
40597.14.80 Balzac, Honoré de. Domestic peace, and other stories. Harmondsworth, 1958.
40597.15.5 Balzac, Honoré de. Le cousin Pons. Paris, 1908.
40597.15.6 Balzac, Honoré de. Le cousin Pons. Paris, 1885.
40597.15.7 Balzac, Honoré de. Le cousin Pons. Paris, 1873.
40597.15.101 Balzac, Honoré de. Le cousin Pons. N.Y., n.d.
40597.15.105 Balzac, Honoré de. Le cousin Pons. Boston, 1902.
40597.15.110 Balzac, Honoré de. Le cousin Pons. N.Y., 190- .
40597.15.125 Balzac, Honoré de. Le cousin Pons. Paris, 1949.
40597.16 Balzac, Honoré de. David Séchard. Brussels, 1844.
40597.16.61 Balzac, Honoré de. Don Juan. N.Y., n.d.
40597.17 Balzac, Honoré de. L'amour masqué ou imprudence et bonheur. Paris, n.d.
40597.19 Balzac, Honoré de. Eugénie Grandet. Paris, 1873.
40597.19.1.5 Balzac, Honoré de. Eugénie Grandet. Paris, 1868.
40597.19.2 Balzac, Honoré de. Eugénie Grandet. Paris, 1881.
40597.19.3 Balzac, Honoré de. Eugénie Grandet. Paris, 1891.
40597.19.7 Balzac, Honoré de. Eugénie Grandet. Philadelphia, 1897.
40597.19.15 Balzac, Honoré de. Eugénie Grandet. N.Y., 1895.
40597.19.18 Balzac, Honoré de. Eugénie Grandet. Paris, 1901?
40597.19.22 Balzac, Honoré de. Eugénie Grandet. Paris, 1911.
40597.19.25 Balzac, Honoré de. Eugénie Grandet. Paris, 1929.
40597.19.30 Balzac, Honoré de. Eugénie Grandet. London, 1910.
40597.19.35 Balzac, Honoré de. Eugénie Grandet. Tours, 1947.
40597.19.40 Balzac, Honoré de. Eugénie Grandet. Paris, 1959.
40597.19.45 Balzac, Honoré de. Evgeniia Grande. Moskva, 1935.
40597.19.50 Balzac, Honoré de. Eugénie Grandet. Paris, 1965.
40597.19.55 Balzac, Honoré de. Eugénie Grandet. Paris, 1934. 2v.
40597.20.3 Balzac, Honoré de. Eugénie Grandet. Boston, 1889.
40597.20.4 Balzac, Honoré de. Eugénie Grandet. London, 19- .
40597.20.5 Balzac, Honoré de. Eugénie Grandet. Boston, 1914.
40597.20.6 Balzac, Honoré de. Eugénie Grandet. Strassbourg, 1910.
40597.20.7 Balzac, Honoré de. Eugénie Grandet. N.Y., 1914.
40597.20.19 Balzac, Honoré de. Eugénie Grandet. N.Y., 1914.
40597.20.25A Balzac, Honoré de. Eugénie Grandet. N.Y., 1932.
40597.20.25B Balzac, Honoré de. Eugénie Grandet. N.Y., 1932.
40597.20.29 Balzac, Honoré de. Eugénie Grandet. Boston, 1930.
40597.21 Balzac, Honoré de. Revue Parisienne. Paris, 1840.
40597.21.10 Balzac, Honoré de. Les parisiens comme ils sont, 1830-1846. Genève, 1947.

40597.10 - Individual authors, etc. - 1800-1849 - Fiction - Balzac - Individual works - cont.

40597.22 Balzac, Honoré de. Une fille d'Eve. Paris, n.d.
Htn 40597.23* Balzac, Honoré de. Histoire de l'Empereur. Paris, 1842.
40597.23.101 Balzac, Honoré de. An historical mystery. Boston, 1904.
40597.24 Balzac, Honoré de. Histoire des Treize. Paris, 1876.
40597.24.5 Balzac, Honoré de. Histoire des Treize. Paris, 1892.
40597.24.10 Balzac, Honoré de. Histoire des Treize. Ferragus. Paris, 1966.
40597.24.50A Balzac, Honoré de. The lily of the valley. Boston, 1891.
40597.24.50B Balzac, Honoré de. The lily of the valley. Boston, 1891.
40597.25 Balzac, Honoré de. Le livre mystique. Brussels, 1836.
40597.26A Balzac, Honoré de. Louis Lambert. Boston, 1889.
40597.26B Balzac, Honoré de. Louis Lambert. Boston, 1889.
40597.28 Balzac, Honoré de. Le lys dans la vallée. Paris, 1860.
40597.28.2 Balzac, Honoré de. Le lys dans la vallée. Paris, 1878.
40597.28.4 Balzac, Honoré de. Le lys dans la vallée. Paris, 1891.
40597.28.5 Balzac, Honoré de. Le lys dans la vallée. Paris, 1891.
40597.28.7 Balzac, Honoré de. La maison du chat-qui-pelote. Paris, 1898.
40597.28.20 Balzac, Honoré de. Le lys dans la vallée. Tours, 1947.
40597.28.20.5 Balzac, Honoré de. Le lys dans la vallée. Paris, 1966.
40597.29 Balzac, Honoré de. La maison du chat-qui-pelote. La paix du ménage. London, 1874-75.
40597.29.1.3 Balzac, Honoré de. La maison du chat-qui-pelote. Paris, 1901.
40597.29.1.4 Balzac, Honoré de. La maison du chat-qui-pelote. Montréal, 1946?
40597.29.1.5 Balzac, Honoré de. The cat and battledore. Chicago, 1879.
40597.29.1.10A Balzac, Honoré de. At the sign of the cat and racket. N.Y., 1914.
40597.29.1.10B Balzac, Honoré de. At the sign of the cat and racket. N.Y., 1914.
40597.29.1.20 Balzac, Honoré de. La maison du chat-qui-pelote. Paris, 1963.
40597.29.2 Balzac, Honoré de. La maison Nucingen. Paris, 1875.
40597.29.3 Balzac, Honoré de. Un ménage de garçon. Paris, 1926.
40597.29.3.80 Balzac, Honoré de. Père Goriot. The marriage contract. Boston, 1901.
40597.29.4 Balzac, Honoré de. Le père Goriot. Paris, 1924.
40597.29.4.3 Balzac, Honoré de. Père Goriot. Paris, 1885.
40597.29.4.4 Balzac, Honoré de. Le père Goriot. Paris, 1885.
40597.29.4.10 Balzac, Honoré de. Le père Goriot. Paris, 1930.
40597.29.4.12 Balzac, Honoré de. Father Goriot. N.Y., 1914.
40597.29.4.15 Balzac, Honoré de. Père Goriot. N.Y., 1931.
40597.29.4.20 Balzac, Honoré de. Père Goriot. Paris, 1913.
40597.29.4.25 Balzac, Honoré de. Old Goriot. London, 1918.
40597.29.4.45 Balzac, Honoré de. Père Goriot. N.Y., 1886.
40597.29.4.50 Balzac, Honoré de. Père Goriot. N.Y., 1887.
40597.29.4.55 Balzac, Honoré de. Père Goriot. Washington, 1932.
40597.29.4.57 Balzac, Honoré de. Père Goriot and Eugénie Grandet. 1. ed. N.Y., 1946.
40597.29.4.60 Balzac, Honoré de. Old Goriot. N.Y., 19- .
40597.29.4.65 Balzac, Honoré de. Father Goriot. N.Y., 1915.
40597.29.4.75 Balzac, Honoré de. Père Goriot. Boston, 1885.
40597.29.4.80 Balzac, Honoré de. Père Goriot. Boston, 1927.
40597.29.4.85 Balzac, Honoré de. Le père Goriot. Paris, 1957.
40597.29.4.90 Balzac, Honoré de. Le père Goriot. Paris, 1960.
40597.29.4.95 Balzac, Honoré de. Le père Goriot. London, 1967.
40597.29.5.3A Balzac, Honoré de. Father Goriot. London, 1913.
40597.29.5.3B Balzac, Honoré de. Father Goriot. London, 1913.
40597.29.5.6 Balzac, Honoré de. Old Goriot. London, 1926.
40597.29.5.8 Balzac, Honoré de. Old Goriot. London, 1931.
40597.29.5.10A Balzac, Honoré de. Old Goriot. London, 1940.
40597.29.5.10B Balzac, Honoré de. Old Goriot. London, 1940.
40597.29.5.10C Balzac, Honoré de. Old Goriot. London, 1940.
40597.29.5.10D Balzac, Honoré de. Old Goriot. London, 1940.
40597.29.5.10E Balzac, Honoré de. Old Goriot. London, 1940.
40597.29.25 Balzac, Honoré de. Petites misères de la vie conjugale. Paris, n.d.
40597.30 Balzac, Honoré de. Petty annoyances of married life. N.Y., 1861.
40597.30.15 Balzac, Honoré de. Petites misères de la vie conjugale. Paris, 1881.
40597.31 Balzac, Honoré de. Memoires de deux jeunes mariées. La femme de 30 ans. London, 1873-75.
40597.31.2 Balzac, Honoré de. La femme de trente ans. Paris, 1948.
40597.31.3 Balzac, Honoré de. Memoires de deux jeunes mariées. Paris, 1903?
40597.31.5 Balzac, Honoré de. The two young brides. London, 19- .
40597.31.6 Balzac, Honoré de. Memoires of two young brides. N.Y., 1902. 2v.
40597.31.8 Balzac, Honoré de. The comédie humaine: Memoirs of two young married women and Albert Savarus. Boston, 1904.
40597.31.10 Balzac, Honoré de. Modeste Mignon. Paris, 1881.
40597.32 Balzac, Honoré de. Les parents. London, 1875.
40597.32.4 Balzac, Honoré de. La peau de chagrin. Paris, 1884.
40597.32.4.5 Balzac, Honoré de. La peau de chagrin. Paris, 1891.
40597.32.4.10 Balzac, Honoré de. La peau de chagrin. Paris, 1900.
40597.32.6 Balzac, Honoré de. The wild ass's skin. London, 1906.
40597.32.6.5 Balzac, Honoré de. The wild ass's skin. N.Y., 19- .
40597.32.6.10 Balzac, Honoré de. The wild ass's skin. London, 1908.
40597.32.6.50 Balzac, Honoré de. The magic skin. The hidden masterpiece. Boston, 1902.
40597.32.7 Balzac, Honoré de. The magic skin. N.Y., 1915.
40597.32.8 Balzac, Honoré de. The magic skin. N.Y., 1914.
Htn 40597.32.9* Balzac, Honoré de. Physiologie du mariage. Paris, 1830. 2v.
40597.32.10 Balzac, Honoré de. The fatal skin. London, 1949.
Htn 40597.32.11* Balzac, Honoré de. The fatal skin. v.1-2. Paris, 1834.
40597.32.13.5 Balzac, Honoré de. The physiology of marriage. London, 1904.
40597.32.13.6 Balzac, Honoré de. The physiology of marriage. London, 1925.
Htn 40597.32.13.7* Balzac, Honoré de. The physiology of marriage. London, 1904.
40597.32.13.9 Balzac, Honoré de. The physiology of marriage. Boston, 1901.
40597.32.13.15 Balzac, Honoré de. Physiologie du mariage. Paris, 1940.
40597.32.15 Balzac, Honoré de. Scenes de la vie de province. 2 series. Paris, 1839. 2v.
40597.32.30 Balzac, Honoré de. Jean Louis, ou La fille trouvée. v.1-4. Paris, 1822. 2v.
40597.32.55 Balzac, Honoré de. A harlot's progress. N.Y., 19-
40597.32.75 Balzac, Honoré de. La Rabouilleuse. Paris, 1923.
40597.32.80 Balzac, Honoré de. La Rabouilleuse. Paris, 1932.
40597.32.85 Balzac, Honoré de. La rabouilleuse. Paris, 1966.
40597.33 Balzac, Honoré de. Alchemist. N.Y., 1861.

40597.10 - Individual authors, etc. - 1800-1849 - Fiction - Balzac - Individual works - cont.

40597.33.5 Balzac, Honoré de. La recherche de l'absolu. Paris, 19- .
Htn 40597.33.9* Balzac, Honoré de. Les cahiers balzaciens. v.1-4, 5-8. Paris, 1923-28. 2v.
40597.33.10 Balzac, Honoré de. Balzaciand. Paris. 1,1925
40597.34A Balzac, Honoré de. Les rivalités. Paris, 1876.
40597.34B Balzac, Honoré de. Les rivalités. Paris, 1876.
40597.34.2 Balzac, Honoré de. Une ténébreuse affaire. Paris, 1892.
40597.34.3 Balzac, Honoré de. Une ténébreuse affaire. Paris, 1882.
40597.34.4 Balzac, Honoré de. Une ténébreuse affaire. Paris, 1958.
40597.34.5 Balzac, Honoré de. Ursule Mirouet. Paris, 18- .
40597.34.5.5 Balzac, Honoré de. Ursule Mirouet. Paris, 1944.
40597.34.5.20 Balzac, Honoré de. Ursule Mirouet. Paris, 1891.
40597.34.6 Balzac, Honoré de. Ursula. Paris, 1896.
40597.34.7 Balzac, Honoré de. Ursula. The vicar of Tours. Boston, 1906.
40597.34.8 Balzac, Honoré de. Ursula. The vicar of Tours. Boston, 1907.
40597.35 Balzac, Honoré de. Vendetta. Boston, 1864.
40597.35.5 Balzac, Honoré de. Le vicaire des Ardennes. Paris, 1836. 2v.
40597.35.7 Balzac, Honoré de. Le vicaire des Ardennes. Paris, 1962. 2v.
40597.35.8 Balzac, Honoré de. Annette et le criminel. v.1-4. Paris, 1824. 2v.
40597.35.10 Balzac, Honoré de. Louis Lambert. Paris, 1954.
40597.35.61 Balzac, Honoré de. A tragedy by the sea and other stories. N.Y., n.d.
40597.35.65 Balzac, Honoré de. A tragedy by the sea and other stories. N.Y., n.d.
40597.35.70 Balzac, Honoré de. Catherine de Medici. N.Y., 19- .
40597.35.72 Balzac, Honoré de. About Catherine de Medici and Gambara. Boston, 1901.
40597.35.80 Balzac, Honoré de. Le médecin de campagne. Paris, 1931.
40597.35.81 Balzac, Honoré de. Le médecin de campagne. Paris, 1951.
40597.35.82 Balzac, Honoré de. Le médecin de campagne. Paris, 1960.
40597.35.83 Balzac, Honoré de. Le médecin de campagne. Paris, 1965.
40597.35.84 Balzac, Honoré de. Le médecin de campagne. Paris, 1967.
40597.35.85 Balzac, Honoré de. Les illusions perdues. Paris, 1946.
40597.35.85.1 Balzac, Honoré de. Lost illusions. A distinguished provincial at Paris. Boston, 1901.
40597.35.86 Balzac, Honoré de. Illusions perdues. Paris, 1959.
40597.35.87 Balzac, Honoré de. Illusions perdues. v.1-2. Paris, 1958.
40597.35.88 Balzac, Honoré de. Illusions perdues. Paris, 1967.
40597.35.90 Balzac, Honoré de. La duchesse de Langeais. Paris, 1949.
40597.35.91 Balzac, Honoré de. La duchesse de Langeais. Paris, 1949.
40597.35.95 Balzac, Honoré de. Maître Cornélius. Tours, 1947.
40597.35.100 Balzac, Honoré de. La femme et l'amour. 2. éd. Paris, 1888.
40597.35.101 Balzac, Honoré de. La femme et l'amour. Paris, 1912.
40597.35.105 Balzac, Honoré de. Le colonel Chabert. Paris, 1932.
40597.35.106 Balzac, Honoré de. Le colonel Chabert. Paris, 1902.
40597.35.107 Balzac, Honoré de. Le colonel Chabert. Paris, 1961.
40597.35.107.2 Balzac, Honoré de. Le colonel Chabert. Paris, 1961.
40597.35.110 Balzac, Honoré de. Albert Savarus. Oran, 1946.
40597.35.115 Balzac, Honoré de. Mademoiselle du Vissard. Paris, 1950.
40597.35.120 Balzac, Honoré de. L'illustre Gaudissart. Tours, 1947.
40597.35.124 Balzac, Honoré de. L'illustre Gaudissart. La muse du département. Paris, 1970.
40597.35.125 Balzac, Honoré de. Le rendez-vous. Tours, 1946.
40597.35.130 Balzac, Honoré de. L'eglise. Paris, 1947.
NEDL 40597.35.131 Balzac, Honoré de. L'eglise. Paris, 1947.
40597.35.140 Balzac, Honoré de. Splendeurs et misères des courtisanes. Paris, 1900. 2v.
40597.35.142 Balzac, Honoré de. Splendeurs et misères des courtisanes. Paris, 1958.
40597.35.144 Balzac, Honoré. Splendeurs et misères des courtisanes. Paris, 1958. 2v.
40597.35.145 Balzac, Honoré de. Un inédit de Balzac. Paris, 1933.
40597.35.146 Balzac, Honoré de. A harlot high and low. Harmondsworth, Eng., 1970.
40597.35.155 Balzac, Honoré de. Falthurne. Paris, 1950.
40597.35.160 Balzac, Honoré de. La vieille fille. Paris, 1957.
40597.35.163 Balzac, Honoré de. La cousine Bette. Paris, 1949.
40597.35.164 Balzac, Honoré de. Cousin Bette. N.Y., 1958.
40597.35.165 Balzac, Honoré de. La cousine Bette. Paris, 1959.
40597.35.166 Balzac, Honoré de. Cousin Bette. Boston, 1889.
40597.35.170 Balzac, Honoré de. L'envers de l'histoire contemporaine. Paris, 1959.
40597.35.175 Balzac, Honoré de. La cabinet des antiques. Paris, 1958.
40597.35.180 Balzac, Honoré de. La dernière fée. v.1-2. Paris, 1823.
40597.35.190 Balzac, Honoré de. Wann-Chlore. v.1-4. Paris, 1825. 2v.
40597.35.200A Balzac, Honoré de. Un début dans la vie. Genève, 1950.
40597.35.200B Balzac, Honoré de. Un début dans la vie. Genève, 1950.
40597.35.210 Balzac, Honoré de. Monographie de la presse parisienne. Paris, 1943.
40597.35.211 Balzac, Honoré de. Monographie de la presse parisienne. Paris, 1964.
40597.35.220 Balzac, Honoré de. Les paysans. Paris, 1964.
40597.35.230 Balzac, Honoré de. Clotilde de Lausignan. Paris, 1962. 2v.
40597.35.240 Balzac, Honoré de. Massimilla Doni. Thèse. Paris, 1964.
40597.35.250 Balzac, Honoré de. Le secret des Ruggieri. Columbia, 1970.
40597.35.260 Balzac, Honoré de. Gambara. Paris, 1964.
40597.36 Balzac, Honoré de. Une page perdue. Paris, 1903.
40597.36.5 Balzac, Honoré de. Traité de la vie elegante suivi de la théorie de la démarche. Paris, 1922.
40597.36.7 Balzac, Honoré de. Traité de la prière. Thèse. Paris, 1942.
40597.36.9 Balzac, Honoré de. Les Parisiens en Province. Paris, 1885.
40597.36.12A Balzac, Honoré de. Théâtre II. La maratre. Le faiseur. Paris, 1928.
40597.36.12B Balzac, Honoré de. Théâtre II. La maratre. Le faiseur. Paris, 1928.
40597.36.12C Balzac, Honoré de. Théâtre II. La maratre. Le faiseur. Paris, 1928.
40597.37 Balzac, Honoré de. At the sign of the cat and racket. London, 1895.
40597.38 Balzac, Honoré de. The chouans. London, 1895.
40597.39 Balzac, Honoré de. The wild ass's skin. London, 1895.
40597.40 Balzac, Honoré de. The country doctor. London, 1895.
40597.42 Balzac, Honoré de. The quest of the absolute. London, 1895.
40597.43 Balzac, Honoré de. Ursule Mirouet. London, 1895.

40597.10 - Individual authors, etc. - 1800-1849 - Fiction - Balzac - Individual works - cont.

40597.45 Balzac, Honoré de. The Atheist's mass. London, 1896.
40597.46 Balzac, Honoré de. La grande Bretêche. London, 1896.
40597.47 Balzac, Honoré de. A bachelor's establishment. London, 1896.
40597.47.5 Balzac, Honoré de. A bachelor's establishment. London, 1951.
40597.47.10 Balzac, Honoré de. The bachelor's house. N.Y., 1956.
40597.49 Balzac, Honoré de. Modeste Mignon. N.Y., 1956.
40597.50 Balzac, Honoré de. The country parson. N.Y., 1956.
40597.51 Balzac, Honoré de. Béatrix. N.Y., 1956.
40597.52 Balzac, Honoré de. The unknown masterpiece. London, 1896.
40597.53 Balzac, Honore de. Pierrette and The Abbé Birotteau. London, 1896.
40597.54 Balzac, Honoré de. The peasantry. London, 1896.
40597.55 Balzac, Honoré de. A Harlot's progress. London, 1896. 2v.
40597.56 Balzac, Honoré de. A distinguished provincial at Paris. London, 1897.
40597.57 Balzac, Honoré de. About Catherine de Medici. London, 1897.
40597.58 Balzac, Honoré de. The lily of the valley. London, 1897.
40597.59 Balzac, Honoré de. Lost illusions. London, 1897.
40597.61 Balzac, Honoré de. The seamy side of history. London, 1897.
40597.62 Balzac, Honoré de. Seraphita. London, 1897.
40597.63 Balzac, Honoré de. A woman of thirty. London, 1897.
40597.64 Balzac, Honoré de. Cousin Pons. London, 1897.
40597.66 Balzac, Honoré de. The unconscious mummers. London, 1897.
40597.67 Balzac, Honoré de. Parisians in the country. London, 1898.
40597.68 Balzac, Honoré de. A marriage settlement. London, 1897.
40597.69 Balzac, Honoré de. The jealousies of a country town. London, 1898.
40597.70 Balzac, Honoré de. The thirteen. London, 1898.
40597.71 Balzac, Honoré de. A father's curse and other stories. London, 1898.
40597.72A Balzac, Honoré de. The member for Arcis. London, 1898.
40597.72B Balzac, Honoré de. The member for Arcis. London, 1898.
40597.73 Balzac, Honoré de. A gondreville mystery. London, 1898.
40597.74 Balzac, Honoré de. A princess's secrets. London, 1898.
40597.75 Balzac, Honoré de. The middle classes. London, 1898.
40597.75.10 Balzac, Honoré de. The middle classes. Boston, 1901.
40597.75.15 Balzac, Honoré de. Les petits bourgeois. Paris, 1960.
40597.77A Balzac, Honoré de. Ferragus, chief of the Devorants. Boston, 1895.
40597.77B Balzac, Honoré de. Ferragus, chief of the Devorants. Boston, 1895.
40597.79 Balzac, Honoré de. Cromwell. v.1-2. Paris, 1925.
40597.81 Balzac, Honoré de. Gobseck et Jésus Christ en Flandre. N.Y., 1913.
40597.83 Balzac, Honoré de. Sténie ou Les erreurs philosophiques. Paris, 1936.
40597.84.1 Balzac, Honoré de. Seraphita. Boston, 1898.
40597.85 Balzac, Honoré de. Vautrin. Paris, 1947.
40597.86 Balzac, Honoré de. The stepmother. London, 1958.
40597.87 Balzac, Honoré de. L'heritière de Birague. Paris, 1961.
40597.90 Balzac, Honoré de. The celibates. Philadelphia, 1899.
40597.91 Balzac, Honoré de. César Birotteau. Philadelphia, 1899.
40597.92 Balzac, Honoré de. The country doctor. Philadelphia, 1899.
40597.93 Balzac, Honoré de. Cousin Betty. Philadelphia, 1899.
40597.94A Balzac, Honoré de. The deputy for Arcis. Philadelphia, 1899.
40597.94B Balzac, Honoré de. The deputy for Arcis. Philadelphia, 1899.
40597.95 Balzac, Honoré de. A distinguished provincial at Paris. Philadelphia 1899.
40597.96 Balzac, Honoré de. Eugénie Grandet. Philadelphia, 1899.
40597.98 Balzac, Honoré de. The harlot's progress. Philadelphia, 1899.
40597.99 Balzac, Honoré de. The jealousies of a country town. Philadelphia, 1899.
40597.100 Balzac, Honoré de. Modeste Mignon. Philadelphia, 1899.
40597.101A Balzac, Honoré de. Muse of the department. Philadelphia, 1899.
40597.101B Balzac, Honoré de. Muse of the department. Philadelphia, 1899.
40597.102A Balzac, Honoré de. The peasantry. Philadelphia, 1899.
40597.102B Balzac, Honoré de. The peasantry. Philadelphia, 1899.
40597.103 Balzac, Honoré de. Seraphita. Philadelphia, 1899.
40597.104 Balzac, Honoré de. The wild ass's skin. Philadelphia, 1899.
40597.105 Balzac, Honoré de. A woman of thirty. Philadelphia, 1899.
40597.200 Balzac, Honoré de. Jesus Christus in Flandern. Potsdam, 1921.

41522.1 - .2 Individual authors, etc. - 1800-1849 - Fiction - Barbey d'Aurevilly - Writings

41522.1 Barbey d'Aurevilly, Jules. Un prêtre marié. Paris, 1881. 2v.
41522.1.1 Barbey d'Aurevilly, Jules. Un prêtre marié. Paris, 1881. 2v.
41522.1.1.5 Barbey d'Aurevilly, Jules. Un prêtre marié. Paris, 1926. 2v.
41522.1.2 Barbey d'Aurevilly, Jules. Une histoire sans nom. Paris, 1889.
41522.1.3 Barbey d'Aurevilly, Jules. Une histoire sans nom. Paris, 1882.
41522.1.3.5 Barbey d'Aurevilly, Jules. L'amour impossible. Paris, 1859.
41522.1.3.9 Barbey d'Aurevilly, Jules. Amour et haine. Paris, 1833.
41522.1.3.10 Barbey d'Aurevilly, Jules. Poussieres. Paris, 1909.
41522.1.4 Barbey d'Aurevilly, Jules. Le chevalier des Touches. Paris, 1893.
41522.1.4.2 Barbey d'Aurevilly, Jules. Le chevalier des Touches. Paris, 1886.
41522.1.5 Barbey d'Aurevilly, Jules. Les diaboliques. Paris, n.d.
41522.1.5.5 Barbey d'Aurevilly, Jules. Les diaboliques. Paris, 188-?
41522.1.6 Barbey d'Aurevilly, Jules. Les diaboliques. Paris, 1934.
41522.1.7 Barbey d'Aurevilly, Jules. The diaboliques. N.Y., 1925.
41522.1.8 Barbey d'Aurevilly, Jules. Les diaboliques. Paris, 1963.
41522.1.9 Barbey d'Aurevilly, Jules. The she-devils. London, 1964.
41522.1.10.15 Barbey d'Aurevilly, Jules. Poussières. Paris, 1918.
Htn 41522.2* Barbey d'Aurevilly, Jules. Lettres à Trebutien. Paris, 1908. 2v.

41522.1 - .2 Individual authors, etc. - 1800-1849 - Fiction - Barbey d'Aurevilly - Writings - cont.

41522.2.3 Barbey d'Aurevilly, Jules. Oeuvres romanesques complètes. Paris, 1964-66. 2v.
41522.2.5 Barbey d'Aurevilly, Jules. Pensées détachées. Paris, 1889.
41522.2.9 Barbey d'Aurevilly, Jules. Polemiques d'hier. 2. éd. Paris, 1889.
41522.2.12 Barbey d'Aurevilly, Jules. Dernières polémiques. 2. éd. Paris, 1891.
41522.2.15 Barbey d'Aurevilly, Jules. Letteres à une amie, 1880-1887. Paris, 1907.
41522.2.16 Barbey d'Aurevilly, Jules. Lettres et fragments. Paris, 1958.
41522.2.20 Barbey d'Aurevilly, Jules. Lettres à Léon Bloy. Paris, 1902.
41522.2.21 Barbey d'Aurevilly, Jules. Le cachet d'onyx. Lea, 1831-1832. Paris, 1919.
41522.2.23 Barbey d'Aurevilly, Jules. Ce qui ne meurt pas. Paris, 1888. 2v.
41522.2.25 Barbey d'Aurevilly, Jules. Les ridicules du temps. 5. éd. Paris, 1883.
Htn 41522.2.27* Barbey d'Aurevilly, Jules. Amaidée: poeme en prose. Paris, 1890.
41522.2.30 Barbey d'Aurevilly, Jules. Fragment à mettre en tête du Joseph Delorme que je dois donner. Paris, 1912.
41522.2.33 Barbey d'Aurevilly, Jules. Memorandum. Caen, 1856.
41522.2.34 Barbey d'Aurevilly, Jules. Premier memorandum, 1836-1838. 3. éd. Paris, 1900.
41522.2.35 Barbey d'Aurevilly, Jules. Memoranda. Paris, 1883.
41522.2.38 Barbey d'Aurevilly, Jules. Deuxième memorandum (1838) et quelques pages de 1864. Paris, 1906.
41522.2.39 Barbey d'Aurevilly, Jules. Journal (memoranda). Paris, 1947.
41522.2.40 Barbey d'Aurevilly, Jules. Voyageurs et romanciers. Paris, 1908.
41522.2.42 Barbey d'Aurevilly, Jules. Disjesta membra. Paris, 1925.
41522.2.45 Barbey, d'Aurevilly, Jules. Poésie et poètes. 3. éd. Paris, 1906.
41522.2.47 Barbey d'Aurevilly, Jules. Poésies. Bruxelles, 1870.
41522.2.50 Barbey d'Aurevilly, Jules. A côté de la grande histoire. Paris, 1870.
41522.2.52 Barbey d'Aurevilly, Jules. Une vieille maîtresse. Paris, 1928. 2v.
41522.2.53 Barbey d'Aurevilly, Jules. Une vieille maîtresse. 2. éd. Paris, 1866.
41522.2.54 Barbey d'Aurevilly, Jules. Une vieille maîtresse. Paris, 1926. 2v.
41522.2.55 Barbey d'Aurevilly, Jules. Critiques diverses. 3. éd. Paris, 1909.
Htn 41522.2.58* Barbey d'Aurevilly, Jules. Disjecta membra. Paris, 1920.
41522.2.60 Barbey d'Aurevilly, Jules. L'ensorcelée. Paris, 1916.
41522.2.61 Barbey d'Aurveilly, Jules. L'ensorcelée. Paris, 1928.
41522.2.63 Barbey d'Aurevilly, Jules. Rhythmes oubliés. Paris, 1897.
41522.2.65 Barbey d'Aurevilly, Jules. Romanciers d'hier et d'avant hier. Paris, 1904.
Htn 41522.2.68* Barbey d'Aurevilly, Jules. Les dédicaces a la main de J. Barbey d'Aurevilly. Paris, 1908.
41522.2.70 Barbey d'Aurevilly, Jules. Du dandysme et de G. Brummell. Memoranda. Paris, 19- ?
41522.2.70.5 Barbey d'Aurevilly, J.A. Du dandysme et de G. Brummell. Caen, 1845.

41522.3 Individual authors, etc. - 1800-1849 - Fiction - Barbey d'Aurevilly - Works about

41522.3 La Porte, Antonio. Barbey d'Aurevilly et ses oeuvres. Paris, 1884.
41522.3.9 Grele, Eugene. Jules Barbey d'Aurevilly, sa vie et son oeuvre. Caen, 1904. 2v.
41522.3.10 Seillière, E. Barbey d'Aurevilly. Paris, 1910.
41522.3.10.5 Seillière, E. Barbey d'Aurevilly. Halle, 19- .
41522.3.11 Laurentie, F. Sur Barbey d'Aurevilly. 2. éd. Paris, 1912.
41522.3.12 Maffre de Baugé, Achille. J. Barbey d'Aurevilly. Toulouse, 1889.
41522.3.15 Bordeaux, Henry. Le Walter Scott Normand. Paris, 1925.
41522.3.19 Doyon, R.L. Barbey d'Aurevilly, amoureux et dupe. Paris, 1934.
41522.3.22 Werner, J. Die aristokratische Lebensanschauung von Jules Barbey d'Aurevilly. Inaug. Diss. Berlin, 1935.
41522.3.25 Merz, F. Das psychologisch-problematische bei Barbey d'Aurevilly und seine Wurzeln. Inaug. Diss. Bielefeld, 1935.
41522.3.26 Canu, Jean. Barbey d'Aurevilly. 7. éd. Paris, 1945.
41522.3.28 Pinthus, H. Die Normandie in Barbey d'Aurevillys Romanen. Jena, 1937.
41522.3.31 Creed, Elizabeth. Le dandysme de Jules Barbey d'Aurevilly. Thèse. Paris, 1938.
41522.3.32 Creed, Elizabeth. Le dandysme de Jules Barbey d'Aurevilly. Paris, 1938.
41522.3.34 Martineau, R. Aspects méconnus de Barbey d'Aurevilly. Paris, 1938.
41522.3.37 LaVarende, J. de. Grands normands. Rouen, 1939.
41522.3.40 Le Corbeille, A. Les diaboliques de Barbey d'Aurevilly. Paris, 1939.
41522.3.42 Quéru, Hermann Albert. Le dernier grand seigneur. Paris, 1946.
41522.3.45 Clermont-Tonnerre, Élisabeth de. Barbey d'Aurevilly. Paris, 1946.
41522.3.50 Seguin, J.P. Barbey d'Aurevilly. Avranches, 1948.
41522.3.55 Bonnes, J.P. Le bonheur du masque. Tournai, 1947.
41522.3.60 Bésus, Roger. Barbey d'Aurevilly. Paris, 1958.
41522.3.65 Chastain, André. Un convive du Dîner d'athées de Barbey d'Aurevilly. Coutances, 1958.
41522.3.70 Leberruyer, Pierre. au pays de J. Barbey d'Aurevilly. Coutances, 1960.
41522.3.75 Schuetz, Günther. Barbey d'Aurevilly als Kritiker. Mainz, 1959.
41522.3.80 Yarrow, Philip J. La pensée politique et religieuse. Genève, 1961.
41522.3.85 Gautier, Jean. J. Barbey d'Aurevilly, ses amours, son romantisme. Paris, 1961.
41522.3.90 Seguin, Jean P. Iconographie de Barbey d'Aurevilly. Genève, 1961.
41522.3.95 Corbière-Gille, Gizele. Barbey d'Aurevilly. Genève, 1962.
41522.3.100 Rogers, Brian G. The novels and stories of Barbey d'Aurevilly. Genève, 1967.
41522.3.105 Borneque, Jacques Henry. Paysages extérieurs et monde intérieur dans l'oeuvre de Barbey d'Aurevilly. Caen, 1968.

41522.3 Individual authors, etc. - 1800-1849 - Fiction - Barbey d'Aurevilly - Works about - cont.

41522.3.110 Risolo, Michel. Barbey d'Aurevilly. Napoli, 1923.
41522.3.115 Colla, Pierre. L'univers tragique de Barbey d'Aurevilly. Bruxelles, 1965.
41522.3.120 Schwartz, Helmut. Idéologie et art romanesque chez Jules Barbey d'Aurevilly. München, 1971.

41522.4 - .5 Individual authors, etc. - 1800-1849 - Fiction - Baudelaire, C. - Complete and Selected works

41522.4.5 Baudelaire, Charles. Baudelaire choisie, poésie. Lyon, 1918.
41522.4.5.8 Baudelaire, Charles. Morceaux choisis; poëmes et proses. 8. éd. Paris, 1929.
41522.4.6 Baudelaire, Charles. J. Barbey d'Aurevilly prose. Paris, 1918.
41522.4.7 Baudelaire, Charles. Selected critical studies. Cambridge, Eng., 1949.
41522.4.8 Baudelaire, Charles. Novellen und kleine Dichtungen in Prosa. Minden in Westfalen, 1904.
41522.4.9 Baudelaire, Charles. Oeuvres posthumes et correspondances inédites. Paris, 1887.
41522.4.9.2 Baudelaire, Charles. Oeuvres posthumes et correspondances inédites. Paris, 1908.
41522.4.10 Baudelaire, Charles. Lettres inédites a sa mère. Paris, 1918.
41522.4.15 Baudelaire, Charles. Lettres à sa mère. Paris, 1932.
41522.4.20 Baudelaire, Charles. Correspondance générale. Paris, 1947-53. 6v.
41522.5 Baudelaire, Charles. Les fleurs du mal. Paris, 1869. 4v.
41522.5.10 Baudelaire, Charles. Werke. Minden in Westfalen, 1904-10. 5v.
41522.5.15 Baudelaire, Charles. Oeuvres. Paris, 1948.
41522.5.20 Baudelaire, Charles. Oeuvres complètes. Paris, 1955. 2v.
41522.5.22 Baudelaire, Charles. Oeuvres. Paris, 1958.
41522.5.25A Baudelaire, Charles. Oeuvres complètes. Paris, 1961.
41522.5.25B Baudelaire, Charles. Oeuvres complètes. Paris, 1961.
41522.5.28 Baudelaire, Charles. Oeuvres complètes. Paris, 1966. 3v.
41522.5.30 Baudelaire, Charles. Juvenilia; oeuvres posthumes. Paris, 1939-52. 3v.

41522.6 - .15 Individual authors, etc. - 1800-1849 - Fiction - Baudelaire, C. - Individual works

41522.6 Baudelaire, Charles. Les fleurs du mal. Paris, 1922.
41522.6.2 Baudelaire, Charles. Quelques-uns de mes contemporains. Paris, 1923.
41522.6.4A Baudelaire, Charles. L'art romantique. Paris, 1925.
41522.6.4B Baudelaire, Charles. L'art romantique. Paris, 1925.
41522.6.5 Baudelaire, Charles. L'art romantique, littérature et musique. Paris, 1968.
41522.6.6 Baudelaire, Charles. Petits poèmes en prose. Oeuvres complètes. Paris, 1926.
41522.6.7 Baudelaire, Charles. The mirror of art. London, 1955.
41522.6.8 Baudelaire, Charles. Les paradis artificiels. Paris, 1928.
41522.6.10 Baudelaire, Charles. Les paradis artificiels suivis des journeaux intimes. Lausanne, 1946.
41522.6.11 Baudelaire, Charles. Les paradis artificiels. Paris, 1961.
41522.6.12 Poe, Edgar Allan. Nouvelles historiques extraordinaires. Paris, 1933.
41522.6.14 Poe, Edgar Allan. Aventures d'Arthur Gordon Pym. Paris, 1934.
41522.6.16 Poe, Edgar Allan. Eureka, La Genèse d'un poème. Paris, 1936.
41522.6.18 Poe, Edgar Allan. Histoires grotesques et sérieuses. Paris, 1937.
41522.6.20 Poe, Edgar Allan. Histoires extraordinaires. Oeuvres complètes de Charles Baudelaire. Paris, 1932.
41522.6.25 Bandy, William T. A word index to Baudelaire's poems. Madison, 1939.
41522.6.30 Baudelaire, Charles. Výbor z malých básní v prose. Praha, 1898.
41522.6.35 Baudelaire, Charles. Jugendbriefe. Lettres inédites aux siens. Olten, 1969.
41522.12.10 Baudelaire, Charles. Oeuvres en collaboration. Paris, 1932.
41522.12.13 Baudelaire, Charles. Pensées de Baudelaire. Paris, 1951.
41522.12.15 Baudelaire, Charles. Baudelaire, prose and poetry. N.Y., 1926.
41522.12.17 Baudelaire, Charles. Gedichte in Vers und Prosa. Leipzig, 1902.
41522.12.20 Baudelaire, Charles. Selected poems. London, 1946.
41522.13A Baudelaire, Charles. Poems. London, 1906?
41522.13B Baudelaire, Charles. Poems. London, 1906?
41522.13.3 Baudelaire, Charles. Poèmes. Paris, 1946.
41522.13.4 Baudelaire, Charles. Les fleurs du mal. Paris, 1906.
41522.13.5 Baudelaire, Charles. Les fleurs du mal. Paris, 1917.
41522.13.6 Baudelaire, Charles. Les fleurs du mal. Paris, 1918.
41522.13.7 Baudelaire, Charles. Les fleurs du mal. Paris, 1919.
41522.13.8 Baudelaire, Charles. Les fleurs du mal. Paris, 1921.
X Cg 41522.13.8.3 Baudelaire, Charles. Les fleurs du mal. Paris, 1921.
41522.13.8.4 Baudelaire, Charles. Les fleurs du mal. Münich, 1922.
41522.13.8.10 Baudelaire, Charles. Les fleurs du mal. Paris, 1929.
41522.13.8.25 Baudelaire, Charles. Les fleurs du mal. Paris, 1941.
41522.13.8.30 Baudelaire, Charles. Les fleurs du mal. Buenos Aires, 1943.
41522.13.8.38 Baudelaire, Charles. The essence of laughter. N.Y., 1956.
41522.13.8.40 Baudelaire, Charles. Les fleurs du mal. London, 1952.
41522.13.8.50 Baudelaire, Charles. Les fleurs du mal; 14 poems. Baltimore, 1955.
41522.13.8.70 Baudelaire, Charles. Les fleurs du mal. N.Y., 1926.
41522.13.8.72A Baudelaire, Charles. Flowers of evil. N.Y., 1931.
41522.13.8.72B Baudelaire, Charles. Flowers of evil. N.Y., 1931.
41522.13.8.78 Baudelaire, Charles. Flowers of evil. 3. ed. N.Y., 1936.
41522.13.8.85 Morgan, Edwin. Flower of evil. N.Y., 1943.
41522.13.8.86 Morgan, Edwin. Flower of evil, a life of Charles Baudelaire. London, 1944.
41522.13.8.90 Baudelaire, Charles. Flowers of evil. Norfolk, 1946.
41522.13.8.92 Baudelaire, Charles. The flowers of evil. N.Y., 1950.
41522.13.8.95 Baudelaire, Charles. Paris spleen, 1869. N.Y., 1947.
41522.13.8.96 Baudelaire, Charles. Poems. London, 1952.
41522.13.8.98 Baudelaire, Charles. Baudelaire. London, 1960.
41522.13.9.6 Baudelaire, Charles. Les fleurs du mal. Paris, 1888.
41522.13.9.8 Baudelaire, Charles. Les fleurs du mal. Paris, 1894.

41522.6 - .15 Individual authors, etc. - 1800-1849 - Fiction - Baudelaire, C. - Individual works - cont.

41522.13.9.10	Baudelaire, Charles. Les fleurs du mal. Leipzig, n.d.
41522.13.9.15	Baudelaire, Charles. Les fleurs du mal. Oxford, 1942.
41522.13.9.17A	Baudelaire, Charles. Les fleurs du mal. 2. éd. Paris, 1942.
41522.13.9.17B	Baudelaire, Charles. Les fleurs du mal. 2. éd. Paris, 1942.
41522.13.9.18	Baudelaire, Charles. Les fleurs du mal. Paris, 1968-
41522.13.9.20	Baudelaire, Charles. Flores das "Flores do mal". Rio de Janeiro, 1944.
41522.13.9.21	Baudelaire, Charles. Květy zla. Praha, 1964.
41522.13.9.22	Baudelaire, Charles. Květy zla. Praha, 1962.
41522.13.9.23	Baudelaire, Charles. Les fleurs du mal. Paris, 1959.
41522.13.9.24	Baudelaire, Charles. Les fleurs du mal. Paris, 1957.
41522.13.9.25	Baudelaire, Charles. Las flores del mal. México, 1944.
41522.13.9.26A	Baudelaire, Charles. Les fleurs du mal. Paris, 1957.
41522.13.9.26B	Baudelaire, Charles. Les fleurs du mal. Paris, 1957.
41522.13.9.27	Baudelaire, Charles. Les fleurs du mal. Paris, 1945.
41522.13.9.28	Baudelaire, Charles. The flowers of evil. Norfolk, 1955.
41522.13.9.29	Baudelaire, Charles. Flowers of evil. N.Y., 1933.
41522.13.9.30	Baudelaire, Charles. Blumen des Bösen. Leipzig, 1907.
41522.13.9.31	Baudelaire, Charles. The flowers of evil. N.Y., 1958.
41522.13.9.32	Besancon, France. Baudelaire. Les fleurs du mal. Concordances. Paris, 1965.
41522.13.9.33	Baudelaire, Charles. The flowers of evil. N.Y., 1958.
41522.13.9.38	Baudelaire, Charles. The flowers of evil, and other poems. Charlottesville, 1961.
41522.13.9.40	Baudelaire, Charles. Les fleurs du mal. Paris, 1960.
41522.13.9.45	Baudelaire, Charles. Hořké propasti. Praha, 1966.
41522.13.9.50	Baudelaire, Charles. La floraj de l'malbono. La Laguna, 1957.
41522.13.9.58	Baudelaire, Charles. Tsvety zla. 3. izd. Moskva, 1970.
41522.13.9.60	Baudelaire, Charles. Les fleurs du mal. Paris, 1968.
41522.13.9.61	Pommier, Jean. Autour de l'édition originale des Fleurs du mal. Genève, 1968.
41522.13.10	Baudelaire, Charles. La fanfarlo. Monaco, 1957.
41522.13.12	Baudelaire, Charles. Journaux intimes. Paris, 1920.
41522.13.12.5	Baudelaire, Charles. Intimate journals. Hollywood, 1947.
41522.13.12.10	Baudelaire, Charles. Écrits intimes. Paris, 1946.
41522.13.12.15	Baudelaire, Charles. Journaux intimes. Paris, 1949.
41522.13.14	Baudelaire, Charles. Baudelaire par lui-même. Paris, 1952.
41522.13.14.5	Baudelaire, Charles. Baudelaire. Paris, 1954.
41522.13.14.6	Baudelaire, Charles. Charles Baudelaire in Selbstzeugnissen und Bilddokumenten. Reinbek, 1967.
41522.13.14.10	Baudelaire, Charles. Baudelaire. London, 1957.
41522.13.25	Baudelaire, Charles. Curiosités esthétiques. Lausanne, 1956.
41522.13.26	Baudelaire, Charles. Curiosités esthétiques. Paris, 1962.
41522.13.27	Baudelaire, Charles. Curiosités esthétiques et autres écrits sur l'art. Paris, 1968.
41522.13.28	Baudelaire, Charles. Ausgewählte Gedichte. 1. Aufl. Frankfurt, 1970.
41522.13.30	Baudelaire, Charles. Baudelaire critique d'art. Paris, 1956.
41522.13.32	Baudelaire, Charles. Douze poèmes. Paris, 1917.
41522.13.35	Baudelaire, Charles. Petits poèmes en prose (Le spleen de Paris). Paris, 1934.
41522.13.36	Baudelaire, Charles. Petits poèmes en prose. Paris, 1969.
41522.13.37	Baudelaire, Charles. Petits poèmes en prose. Paris, 1968.
41522.13.40	Baudelaire, Charles. Mon coeur mis à nu. Mexico, 1945.
41522.13.45	Bandelaire, Charles. Ecrits intimes. Paris, 1946.
41522.13.50	Baudelaire, Charles. Le spleen de Paris. Paris, 1947.
41522.14.10	Baudelaire, Charles. Poèmes d'amour de Baudelaire. Paris, 1927.
41522.14.25	Baudelaire, Charles. Le salon de 1845 de Charles Baudelaire. Thèse. Toulouse, 1933.
41522.14.30	Baudelaire, Charles. The mirror of Baudelaire. Norfolk, Conn., 1942.
41522.14.35	Baudelaire, Charles. My heart laid bare. London, 1950.
41522.14.40	Baudelaire, Charles. Conseils aux jeunes litterateurs. Paris, 1929.
41522.14.45	Baudelaire, Charles. Baudelaire as a literary critic. University Park, Penn., 1969.
41522.14.50	Baudelaire as a love poet and other essays commemorating the centenary of the death of the poet. University Park, Penn., 1969.
41522.15	Baudelaire, Charles. Lettres 1841-1866. Paris, 1906.
41522.15.5	Baudelaire, Charles. Lettres inédites aux siens. Paris, 1967.

41522.16 - .18 Individual authors, etc. - 1800-1849 - Fiction - Baudelaire, C. - Biography and criticism

41522.16	Patterson, Arthur S. L'influence d'Edgar Poe sur Charles Baudelaire. Thèse. Grenoble, 1903.
41522.16.5	Pamphet box. Charles Baudelaire.
41522.16.10	Bibliothèque national, Paris. Charles Baudelaire. Exposition. Paris, 1957.
41522.16.15	Aggeler, William F. Baudelaire, judged by Spanish critics, 1857-1957. Athens, Georgia, 1971.
41522.17A	Holitscher, A. Charles Baudelaire. Berlin, n.d.
41522.17B	Holitscher, A. Charles Baudelaire. Berlin, n.d.
41522.17.5	La Fizelière, A. de. Bibliographie de Charles Baudelaire. Paris, 1868.
41522.17.7	Gautier, T. Charles Baudelaire. N.Y., 1915.
41522.17.8	Laporte, A. Baudelaire et Roger de Beauvoir; bibliographie. Paris, 1884.
41522.17.8.15	Maggs Bros., London. Éditions originales et autographes de Charles Baudelaire, Paul Verlaine. Paris, 1937.
41522.17.9A	Aubry, G. Jean. Baudelaire et Honfleur. Paris, 1917.
41522.17.9B	Aubry, G. Jean. Baudelaire et Honfleur. Paris, 1917.
41522.17.10	Vandérem, Fernand. Baudelaire et Sainte-Beuve. Paris, 1917.
41522.17.11	Van Roosbroek, Gustava. Charles Baudelaire. Haarlem, n.d.
41522.17.12	Le cinquantenaire de Charles Baudelaire. Paris, 1917.
41522.17.13	Barthou, Louis. Autour de Baudelaire. Paris, 1917.
41522.17.14	Mauclair, Camille. Charles Baudelaire, sa vie. Paris, 1917.
41522.17.20	Raynaud, Ernest. Baudelaire et la religion du Dandysme. Paris, 1918.
41522.17.23	Porché, François. La vie douloureuse de Charles Baudelaire. Paris, 1926.
41522.17.23.10	Porché, François. Baudalaire et la présidente. Genève, 1941.
NEDL 41522.17.23.15	Porché, François. Baudelaire. Paris, 1946.
41522.17.23.20	Mermaz, Louis. Madame Sabatier. Lausanne, 1967.

41522.16 - .18 Individual authors, etc. - 1800-1849 - Fiction - Baudelaire, C. - Biography and criticism - cont.

41522.17.25	Rougemout, Edouard de. Commentaires graphologiques sur Charles Boudelaire. Paris, 1922.
41522.17.33	Fumet, Stanislas. Notre Baudelaire. Paris, 1926.
41522.17.35A	Flottes, Pierre. Baudelaire. Paris, 1922.
41522.17.35B	Flottes, Pierre. Baudelaire. Paris, 1922.
41522.17.40	Cerini, Matteo. La poesia di Carlo Baudelaire. Catania, 1922.
41522.17.42	Barrès, Maurice. La folie de Charles Baudelaire. Paris, 1926.
41522.18	Turquet-Milnes, G. The influence of Baudelaire in France and England. London, 1913.
41522.18.10	Symons, Arthur. Charles Baudelaire; a study.. N.Y., 1920.
41522.18.12	Raynaud, Ernest. Charles Baudelaire. Paris, 1922.
41522.18.15	Baudelaire, Charles. Dernières lettres inédites à sa mère. Paris, 1926.
41522.18.20	Mauclair, Camille. La vie amoureuse de Charles Baudelaire. Paris, 1927.
41522.18.25	Freund, Cayetan. Der Vers Baudelaires. Inaug. Diss. München, 1927.
41522.18.35	Bonfantini, Mario. Vita, opere e pensieri di Charles Baudelaire. 2. ed. Novara, 1928.
41522.18.36	Bonfantini, Mario. Baudelaire. 3. ed. Torino, 1962.
41522.18.40	Wright, Malcolm. The role of the auditive sense in Baudelaire's works. Thesis. Philadelphia, 1929.
41522.18.45A	Vivier, Robert. L'originalité de Baudelaire. Bruxelles, 1926.
41522.18.45B	Vivier, Robert. L'originalité de Baudelaire. Bruxelles, 1926.
41522.18.48	Vivier, Robert. L'originalité de Baudelaire. Bruxelles, 1952.
41522.18.50	Loving, Pierre. Gardener of evil. N.Y., 1931?
41522.18.53	Laforque, R. L'échec de Baudelaire. Paris, 1931.
41522.18.54	Laforgue, R. L'échec de Baudelaire. Genève, 1964.
41522.18.55	Laforgue, R. The defeat of Baudelaire. London, 1932.
41522.18.60	Dufay, Pierre. Autour de Baudelaire. Paris, 1931.
41522.18.65	Seillière, E. Baudelaire. Paris, 1931.
41522.18.70	Pommier, J. La mystique de Baudelaire. Paris, 1932.
41522.18.72	Pommier, J. Dans les chemins de Boudelaire. Paris, 1945.
41522.18.75	Bandy, W.T. Baudelaire judged by his contemporaries, 1845-1867. N.Y., 1933.
41522.18.76	Bandy, W.T. Baudelaire devant ses contemporains. Monaco, 1957.
41522.18.79	Ferran, André. L'esthetique de Baudelaire. Thèse. Paris, 1933.
41522.18.80	Ferran, André. L'esthetique de Baudelaire. Paris, 1933.
41522.18.85	Schröer, C. Les petits poèmes en prose von Baudelaire. Inaug. Diss. Leipzig, 1935.
41522.18.90	Starkie, Enid. Baudelaire. N.Y., 1933.
41522.18.90.3	Starkie, Enid. Baudelaire. Norfolk, 1958.
41522.18.96	Thibaudet, Albert. Intérieurs. 6. éd. Photoreproduction. Paris, 1924.
41522.18.100	Charpentier, John. Baudelaire. Paris, 1937.
41522.18.105	Soupault, P. Baudelaire. Paris, 1938.
41522.18.110	Porché, F. Der Leidensweg des Dichters Baudelaire. Berlin, 1930.
41522.18.115	Klassen, P. Baudelaire; weet und gegenwelt. Weimar, 1931.
41522.18.120	Rechert, E. Charles Baudelaire und die Modernen. Wien, 1895.
41522.18.125	Seguin, M. Génie des fleurs du mal. Paris, 1938.
41522.18.130	Shanko, L.P. Baudelaire flesh and spirit. Boston, 1930.
41522.18.135	Feuillerat, A. Baudelaire et la belle aux cheveux d'or. New Haven, 1941.
41522.18.137	Feuillerat, A. Baudelaire et sa mère. Montréal, 1944.
41522.18.140	Adriani, B. Baudelaire und Georges. Berlin, 1939.
41522.18.145	Gilman, M. Baudelaire, the critic. N.Y., 1943.
41522.18.150	Fleury, René Albert. Huit ans de lutte pour le buste de Baudelaire. Paris, 1942.
41522.18.155	Massin, Jean. Baudelaire "Entre Dieu et Satan". Paris, 1945.
41522.18.157	Massin, Jean. Baudelaire devant la donleur. Paris, 1944.
41522.18.160	Mouquet, Jules. Baudelaire en 1848. Paris, 1946.
41522.18.162	Macchia, Giovanni. Baudelaire critico. Firenze, 1939.
41522.18.165	Macchia, Giovanni. Baudelaire e la poetica della Malinconia. Napoli, 1946.
41522.18.167	Macchia, Giovanni. La poetica di Baudelaire. Roma, 1960.
41522.18.170	Arnold, Paul. Le Dieu de Baudelaire. Paris, 1947.
41522.18.175	Sarte, Jean Paul. Baudelaire. 17. éd. Paris, 1947.
41522.18.180A	Aressy, Lucien. Les dernières années de Baudelaire. Paris, 1947.
41522.18.180B	Aressy, Lucien. Les dernières années de Baudelaire. Paris, 1947.
41522.18.190	Fondane, B. Baudelaire et l'experience du Gouffre. Paris, 1947.
41522.18.195	Blin, Georges. Le sadisme de Baudelaire. Paris, 1948.
41522.18.200	Messiaen, Pierre. Sentiment chrétien et poésie française. Baudelaire, Verlaine, Rimbaud. Paris, 1947.
41522.18.205	Landa, M.T. de. Charles Baudelaire. México, 1947.
41522.18.210A	Sartre, J.P. Baudelaire. London, 1949.
41522.18.210B	Sartre, J.P. Baudelaire. London, 1949.
41522.18.215	Chérix, Robert B. Commentaire des Fleurs du mal. Genève, 1949.
41522.18.216	Chérix, Robert B. Commentaire des Fleurs du mal. 2. éd. Genève, 1962.
41522.18.217	Chérix, Robert B. Commentaire des Fleurs du mal. 2. éd. Genève, 1962.
41522.18.220	Ratermanis, J.B. Étude sur le style de Baudelaire. Bade, 1949.
41522.18.225	Turnell, M. Baudelaire. London, 1953.
41522.18.226	Turnell, M. Baudelaire. Norfolk, Conn., 1953.
41522.18.230	Cladel, Judith. Maître et disciple. Paris, 1951.
41522.18.235	Jones, Percy Mancell. Baudelaire. Cambridge, 1952.
41522.18.240	Eigeldinger, Marc. Le platonisme de Baudelaire. Neuchâtel, 1952.
41522.18.245	Hamelin, Jacques. La réhabilitation judiciaire de Baudelaire. Paris, 1952.
41522.18.250	Jouanne, R. Baudelaire et Poulet-Malassis. Alençon, 1952.
41522.18.255A	Hubert, Judd David. L'ésthétique des Fleurs du mal. Genève, 1953.
41522.18.255B	Hubert, Judd David. L'ésthétique des Fleurs du mal. Genève, 1953.
41522.18.260	Prévost, Jean. Baudelaire. Paris, 1953.
41522.18.265	Sugar, L. de. Baudelaire et R.M. Rilke. Paris, 1954.
41522.18.270	Peyre, Henri. Connaissance de Baudelaire. Paris, 1951.
41522.18.275	Asselineau, Charles. Baudelaire et Asselineau. Paris, 1953.
41522.18.280	Guex, André. Art baudelairien. Lausanne, 1955.

41522.16 - .18 Individual authors, etc. - 1800-1849 - Fiction - Baudelaire, C. - Biography and criticism - cont.

41522.18.285	Ruff, Marcel A. Baudelaire. Paris, 1955.
41522.18.290	Ruff, Marcel A. L'esprit du mal et l'esthétique baudelairienne. Paris, 1955.
41522.18.291	Ruff, Marcel A. L'esprit du mal et l'esthétique baudelairienne. Paris, 1955.
41522.18.295	Austin, L.J. L'univers poétique de Baudelaire. Paris, 1956.
41522.18.300	Grava, Arnolds. L'aspect metaphysique du mal dans l'oeuvre littéraire de Charles Baudelaire et d'Edgar Alleunde. Lincoln, 1956.
41522.18.305	Horner, Lucie. Baudelaire. Genève, 1956.
41522.18.310	Crépet, Jacques. Propos sur Baudelaire. Paris, 1957.
41522.18.315	Manoll, Michel. La vie passionnée de Charles Baudelaire. Paris, 1957.
41522.18.320	Aguettant, Louis. Lecture de Baudelaire. Paris, 1957.
41522.18.325	Vouga, Daniel. Baudelaire et Joseph de Maistre. Paris, 1957.
41522.18.330	Wisconsin. University. Memorial Library. Baudelaire. Madison, 1957.
41522.18.335	Samuel, Paul de. Baudelaire. Brussel, 1934.
41522.18.340	Porché, François. Baudelaire et la presidente. 2. éd. Paris, 1959.
41522.18.342	Porché, François. Baudelaire. Paris, 1947.
41522.18.345	The centennial celebration of Baudelaire's Les fleurs du mal. Austin, 1958.
41522.18.350	Bonzon, Alfred. La degradation des images dans la poésie Baudelairienne. São Paulo, 1958.
41522.18.355	Sartre, J.P. Baudelaire. Norfolk, 1950.
41522.18.357	Sartre, J.P. Baudelaire. Paris, 1963.
41522.18.360	Séché, Alphonse. La vie des Fleurs du mal. Amiens, 1928.
41522.18.365	Fairlie, Alison. Baudelaire. London, 1960.
41522.18.370	Arnold, Paul. Das Geheimnis Baudelaires. Berlin, 1958.
41522.18.375	Butor, Michel. Histoire extraordinaire. Paris, 1961.
41522.18.376	Butor, Michel. Histoire extraordinaire. London, 1969.
41522.18.380	Giacomelli Deslex, M. Appunti su Charles Baudelaire. Torino, 1960.
41522.18.385	Pichois, C. Iconographie de Charles Baudelaire. Genève, 1960.
41522.18.390	Borgal, Clément. Baudelaire. Paris, 1961.
41522.18.392	Borgal, Clément. Charles Baudelaire. Paris, 1967.
41522.18.395	Anhegger, G. Der Spleen bei Charles Baudelaire. Zürich, 1937.
41522.18.400	Mossop, D.J. Baudelaire's tragic hero. London, 1961.
41522.18.405A	Dérieux, H. Baudelaire; trois essais. Bale, 1917.
41522.18.405B	Dérieux, H. Baudelaire; trois essais. Bale, 1917.
41522.18.410	Lemonnier, Léon. Enquêtes sur Baudelaire. Paris, 1929.
41522.18.415	Peyre, Henri. Baudelaire; a collection of critical essays. Englewood, 1962.
41522.18.425	Wetherill, P.M. Charles Baudelaire et la poésie d'Edgar Allan Poe. Paris, 1962.
41522.18.430	Brunelli, G.A. Charles Baudelaire e i Limbes 1851. Milano, 1962.
41522.18.435	Séché, A. Charles Baudelaire. Paris, 1925.
41522.18.440	Carter, A.E. Baudelaire et la critique française, 1868-1917. Columbia, 1963.
41522.18.445	Accaputo, N. L'estetica di Baudelaire e le sue fonti germaniche. Torino, 1961.
41522.18.455	Nicoletti, G. Poesia in Baudelaire. Venezia, 1961.
41522.18.460	Barlow, N.H. Sainte-Beuve to Baudelaire. Durham, N.C., 1964.
41522.18.465	Bopp, L. Psychologie des Fleurs du mal. v.1-2,3,4, pt.1-2. Genève, 1964. 5v.
41522.18.466	Rouger, Jean. Baudelaire et la vérité littéraire des Fleurs du mal. Paris, 1970.
41522.18.470	Bertocci, A.P. From symbolism to Baudelaire. Carbonade, 1964.
41522.18.475	Cargo, Robert. Concordance to Baudelaire's Les fleurs du mal. Chapel Hill, 1965.
41522.18.480	Lang, Georges E. Charles Baudelaire jugé par Ernest Feydeay. Paris, 1921.
41522.18.485	Thomas, Louis. Curiosités sur Baudelaire. Paris, 1912.
41522.18.490	Bulletin baudelairien. Nashville. 1,1965+
41522.18.495	Nies, Fritz. Poesie in prosaischer Welt. Heidelberg, 1964.
41522.18.500	Mauron, Charles. Le dernier Baudelaire. Paris, 1966.
41522.18.505	Milner, Max. Baudelaire; enfer ou ciel, qu'importe! Paris, 1967.
41522.18.510	Emmanuel, Pierre. Baudelaire. Paris, 1967.
41522.18.515	Melançon, Joseph. Le spiritualisme de Baudelaire. Montréal, 1967.
41522.18.520	Baudelaire. Paris, 1967.
41522.18.525	Kies, Albert. Études baudelairiennes. Louvain, 1967.
41522.18.530	Brussels. Bibliothéque royale. Baudelaire en Belgique, avril 1864-juillet 1866. Bruxelles, 1967.
41522.18.535	Pichois, Claude. Baudelaire. Études et témoignages. Neuchâtel, 1967.
41522.18.540	Belleli, Maria Luisa. Introduzione alla lettura di Baudelaire. Torino, 1967. 4v.
41522.18.545	Cargo, Robert T. Baudelaire criticism, 1950-1967; a bibliography. University, 1968.
41522.18.550	Daniel, Frank. Die Frau bei Baudelaire. Erlangen, 1965?
41522.18.555	Journées Baudelaire, Namur and Brussels, 1967. Journées Baudelaire. Actes du Colloque. Bruxelles, 1968.
41522.18.560	Baudelaire, Charles. Letters from his youth. Garden City, N.Y., 1970.
41522.18.565	Bennett, Joseph D. Baudelaire, a criticism. Princeton, 1924.
41522.18.570	Benjamin, Walter. Charles Baudelaire. Frankfurt, 1969.
41522.18.575	Études baudelairiennes. Neuchâtel. 1,1969+ 2v.
41522.18.580	Macchia, Giovanni. La critica letteraria di Baudelaire. Roma, 1969.
41522.18.585	Urruty, Jean. Le voyage de Baudelaire aux Mascareignes. Port-Louis, 1968.
41522.18.590	Baudelaire. Petit Palais. 23 novembre 1968-17 mars 1969. Paris, 1968.
41522.18.595	Marchand, Jean José. Sur Mon coeur mis à nu de Baudelaire. Paris, 1970.
41522.18.600	Galand, René M. Baudelaire; poétiques et poésie. Paris, 1969.
41522.18.605	Le cramérien; bulletin d'information des amis de Samuel Cramer. Paris. 1,1969+
41522.18.610	Leakey, F.W. Baudelaire and nature. N.Y., 1969.
41522.18.615	Planche, Henry. La recherche de Baudelaire. Aix-les-Bains, 1968.
41522.18.620	Capasso, Aldo. Baudelaire quasi sconosciuto. Roma, 1967.
41522.18.625	Flavien, Jean. D'un Baudelaire à l'autre. Paris, 1969.

41522.16 - .18 Individual authors, etc. - 1800-1849 - Fiction - Baudelaire, C. - Biography and criticism - cont.

41522.18.630	Cellier, Léon. Baudelaire et Hugo. Paris, 1970.
41522.18.635	Genovali, Sandro. Baudelaire, o della dissonanza. Firenze, 1971.

41522.19 Individual authors, etc. - 1800-1849 - Fiction - Beaumont-Vassy

41522.19	Beaumont-Vassy, E.F. Le fils de la polonaise. Paris, 1873.
41522.19.5	Beaumont-Vassy, E.F. Papiers curieux d'un homme de cour, 1770-1870. Paris, 1875.

41522.20 Individual authors, etc. - 1800-1849 - Fiction - Beauvoir

41522.20.5	Beauvoir, E. Roger de. Le chevalier de Saint-Georges. Paris, 1875.
41522.20.10	Beauvoir, E. Roger de. L'ecolier de Cluny, ou le sophisme, 1315. Paris, 1832.
41522.20.15	Beauvoir, E. Roger de. Les enfers de Paris, cinq actes mêlés de chant. Paris, 1853.
41522.20.30	Beauvoir, E. Roger de. Les soupeurs de mon temps. Paris, 1868.
41522.20.80	Schmook, Gerard. Ein parijse beau onder Antwerpse jolikes. Gent, 1959.

41522.21 Individual authors, etc. - 1800-1849 - Fiction - Badon

41522.21	Badon, Edmond. Montbrun, ou Les Huguenots en Dauphiné. Paris, 1838. 2v.

41522.23 Individual authors, etc. - 1800-1849 - Fiction - Bellin de la Liborlière

41522.23	Bellin de La Liborlière, L. Voyage de M. Candide fils. Paris, 1803. 2v.
41522.23.10	Bellin de La Liborlière, L. Travels of young Candid. v.1-3. London, 1804.
41522.23.20	Bellin de La Liborlière, L. The hero. London, 1817. 2v.

41522.24 - .25 Individual authors, etc. - 1800-1849 - Fiction - Belot

41522.24	Belot, Adolphe. L'article 47. Paris, 1870.
41522.25	Belot, Adolphe. Le testament de César Girodot. Paris, n.d.

41522.27 - .55 Individual authors, etc. - 1800-1849 - Fiction - Bernard, Charles de - Writings

41522.27	Bernard, Charles de. Poésies et théâtre. Paris, 1855.
41522.30	Bernard, Charles de. Les ailes d'icare. Paris, 1871.
41522.30.2	Bernard, Charles de. Les ailes d'icare. Bruxelles, 1839.
41522.32	Bernard, Charles de. Un beau-père. Bruxelles, 1868. 2v.
41522.33	Bernard, Charles de. Un beau-père. Bruxelles, 1875-85. 2v.
41522.34	Bernard, Charles de. La chasse aux amants. Bruxelles, 1840.
41522.35	Bernard, Charles de. L'écueil. Paris, 1869.
41522.36	Bernard, Charles de. L'écueil. Paris, 1872.
41522.36.5	Bernard, Charles de. L'écueil. Paris, 1876.
41522.37	Bernard, Charles de. Le gentilhomme Campagnard. Paris, 1872. 2v.
41522.37.2	Bernard, Charles de. Le gentilhomme Campagnard. Paris, 1864. 2v.
41522.38	Bernard, Charles de. Gerfaut. Paris, 1870.
41522.38.2	Bernard, Charles de. Gerfaut. Paris, 1867.
41522.38.5	Bernard, Charles de. Gerfaut. Paris, 1874.
41522.38.10	Bernard, Charles de. Gerfaut. Paris, 1886.
41522.39	Bernard, Charles de. Un homme sérieux. Paris, 1870.
41522.39.4	Bernard, Charles de. Un homme sérieux. Paris, 1857.
41522.40	Bernard, Charles de. Un homme sérieux. Paris, 1865.
41522.41	Bernard, Charles de. Le noeud gordien. Paris, 1860.
41522.42	Bernard, Charles de. Le noeud gordien. Paris, 1885.
41522.43	Bernard, Charles de. Le noeud gordien. Bruxelles, 1859. 2v.
41522.44	Bernard, Charles de. Nouvelles et mélanges. Paris, 1854.
41522.45	Bernard, Charles de. Le paravent. Bruxelles, 1839. 2v.
41522.46	Bernard, Charles de. Le paravent. Bruxelles, 1858.
41522.47	Bernard, Charles de. Le paravent. Paris, 1870.
41522.48	Bernard, Charles de. Le paravent. Paris, 1875.
41522.49	Bernard, Charles de. Le paratonnerre. Paris, 1864.
41522.54	Bernard, Charles de. La peau du lion. Bruxelles, 1840.
41522.55	Bernard, Charles de. La peau du lion. Paris, 1858.

41522.56 Individual authors, etc. - 1800-1849 - Fiction - Bernard, Charles de - Works about

41522.56	Wal, Jan S. van der. Charles de Bernard, 1804-1850. Purmerend, 1940.
41522.56.5	Piépape, Léonce de. Charles de Bernard sa vie, ses oeuvres. Paris, 1885.

41522.58 Individual authors, etc. - 1800-1849 - Fiction - Bertrand, Louis - Writings

41522.58.5	Bertrand, Louis. Gaspard de la nuit. Paris, 1902.
41522.58.8	Bertrand, Louis. Gaspard de la nuit. Monte-Carlo, 1959?
41522.58.10	Bertrand, Louis. Gaspard de la nuit. 8. éd. Monte-Carlo, 1920.
41522.58.12	Bertrand, Louis. Le keepsake fantastique. Paris, 1923.
41522.58.15	Bertrand, Louis. Le keepsake fantastique. Paris, 19- .
41522.58.17	Bertrand, Louis. Gaspard de la nuit. Paris, 1943.
41522.58.18	Bertrand, Louis. Gaspard de la nuit. Paris, 1965.
41522.58.20	Bertrand, Louis. Oeuvres poétiques. Paris, 1926.
41522.58.22	Bertrand, Louis. Oeuvres poétiques. Thèse. Paris, 1926.

41522.59 - .60 Individual authors, etc. - 1800-1849 - Fiction - Bertrand, Louis - Works about

41522.59	Sprietsma, Cargill. Louis Bertrand dit Aloysius Bertrand, 1807-1841. Paris, 1926.
41522.59.2	Sprietsma, Cargill. Louis Bertrand dit Aloysius Bertrand, 1807-1841. Thèse. Paris, 1926.
41522.60	Banner, F. Aloysius Bertrand's Gaspard de la nuit als Wortkunstwerk. Inaug. Diss. Augsburg, 1931.

41522.64 - .66 Individual authors, etc. - 1800-1849 - Fiction - Borel d'Hauterive - Writings

41522.64	Borel d'Hauterive, Petrus. Champavert. Bruxelles, 1872.
41522.64.40	Borel d'Hauterive, Petrus. Champavert. Paris, 1922.
41522.64.45	Borel d'Hauterive, Petrus. Champavert. Chicago, 1959.
41522.64.50	Borel d'Hauterive, Petrus. Shampaver. Leningrad, 1971.
41522.65.2	Borel, d'Hauterive, Petrus. Rapsodies. Bruxelles, 1868.

41522.64 - .66 Individual authors, etc. - 1800-1849 - Fiction - Borel d'Hauterive - Writings - cont.
41522.65.5 Borel, d'Hauterive, Petrus. Rapsodies. Avec une eau-forte d'Adrien Aubry. Bruxelles, 1884.
41522.66.2 Borel, d'Hauterive, Petrus. Madame Putiphar. v.1-2. Genève, 1967.

41522.67 Individual authors, etc. - 1800-1849 - Fiction - Borel d'Hauterive - Works about
41522.67.30 Borel d'Hauterive, Petrus. Rhapsodies. Paris, 1922.
41522.67.80 Marie, Aristide. Petrus Borel, le lycanthrope. Paris, 1922.
41522.67.82 Starkie, E. Petrus Borel. London, 1954.
41522.67.83 Starkie, E. Petrus Borel. Norfolk, 1954.
41522.67.90 Claretie, Jules. Pétrus Borel le lycanthrope. Paris, 1865.

41522.68 Individual authors, etc. - 1800-1849 - Fiction - Bouis
Htn 41522.68* Bouis, A.T. Whip-poor-will. Paris, 1847.

41522.69 - .70 Individual authors, etc. - 1800-1849 - Fiction - Miscellany, B-C
41522.69 Breton, Louis Julien. A lala. 3. é. Paris, 1801.
41522.69.5 Breton, Louis Julien. A lala. Au grand Village, 1801. 2 pam.
41522.69.105 Briffaulk, E. Le secret de Rome au XIXme siècle. Paris, 1846.
41522.69.150 Bruno, Louis de. Lioncel, ou l'émigré, nouvelle historique. Paris, 1800.
41522.69.250 Blaze, Henri Sebastien. Julien, ou le prêtre. pts.1-2. Paris, 1805.
41522.69.500 Careñou, A. Le sire de Montpegat. Montauban, 1843.
41522.69.528 Carraud, Z.T. (Mme.). Une servante d'autrefois. 2. éd. Paris, 1869.
41522.69.600 Charlieu, H. de. La marseillaise. Paris, 1910.
41522.70 Clarke, M.L. Olésia, ou la Pologne. Paris, 1827.

41522.72 Individual authors, etc. - 1800-1849 - Fiction - Chevalier, Pierre
41522.72 Chevalier, Pierre M.F. Michel Columb, le tailleur d'images; epoque des arts et de la décadence: 1490, règnes de Charles VIII et de Louis XII. v.1-2. Paris, 1841.
41522.72.7 Chevalier, Pierre M.F. Aliénor, prieure de Lok Maria; de la ligne: 1594, règne de Henri IV. 2. éd. v.1-2. Paris, 1842.
41522.72.10 Chevalier, Pierre M.F. Jeanne de Montfort; epoque guerrière: 1342; régne de Philippe de Valois. v.1-2. Paris, 1840.

41522.75 - .78 Individual authors, etc. - 1800-1849 - Fiction - Cordellier-Delanoue
41522.75 Cordellier-Delanoue, A. Jacques Coeur. Tours, 1847.
41522.76 Cordellier-Delanoue, A. Jacques Coeur. Tours, 1866.
41522.77 Cordellier-Delanoue, A. Cronwell; A drama. Paris, 1835.

41522.100 Individual authors, etc. - 1800-1849 - Fiction - Dondey
41522.100.21 Dondey, T. Oeuvres en prose. Paris, 1878.
41522.100.25 Dondey, T. Poésies posthumes de Philothée O'Neddy. Paris, 1877.
41522.100.81 Havet, Ernest. Notice sur Philothée O'Neddy. Paris, 1877.
41522.100.85 Larbaud, Valery. Théophile Dondey de Santeny. Tunis, 1935.

41522.150 - .155 Individual authors, etc. - 1800-1849 - Fiction - Drouineau
41522.150 Drouineau, Gustave. Le manuscrit vert. 2. éd. Paris, 1832. 2v.
41522.152 Drouineau, Gustave. Résignée. Paris, 1833. 2v.

41523 - 41528 Individual authors, etc. - 1800-1849 - Fiction - Dumas père - Complete works - Paris edition in French [Discontinued]
41523.1 Pamphlet box. Alexander Dumas. Miscellaneous pamphlets.
41523.2.10 Dumas, Alexandre. Oeuvres. Bruxelles, 1838-43. 6v.
41523.3 Dumas, Alexandre. Acté. Paris, 1881.
41523.4 Dumas, Alexandre. Amaury. Paris, 1882.
41523.5 Dumas, Alexandre. Ange Pitou. Paris, 1873.
41523.5.2 Dumas, Alexandre. Ange Pitou. v.1-2. Bruxelles, 1866.
41523.6 Dumas, Alexandre. Ascanio. Paris, 1881.
41523.6.2 Dumas, Alexandre. Aventure d'amour. Paris, 1873.
41523.7 Dumas, Alexandre. Aventure d'amour. Paris, 1881.
41523.8 Dumas, Alexandre. Aventures de John Davys. Paris, 1872.
41523.9 Dumas, Alexandre. Les baleiniers. Paris, 1877.
41523.10 Dumas, Alexandre. Le bâtard de Mauléon. Paris, 1877.
41523.11 Dumas, Alexandre. Black. Paris, 1875.
41523.12 Dumas, Alexandre. Les blancs et les bleus. Paris, 1870. 3v.
41523.13 Dumas, Alexandre. La bouillie de la comtesse Berthe. Paris, 1881.
41523.14 Dumas, Alexandre. La boule de Neige. Paris, 1879.
41523.15 Dumas, Alexandre. Bric-a-Brac. Paris, 1881.
41523.16 Dumas, Alexandre. Cadet de famille. Paris, 1874.
41523.17A Dumas, Alexandre. Capitaine Pamphile. Paris, 1881.
41523.17B Dumas, Alexandre. Capitaine Pamphile. Paris, 1881.
41523.18 Dumas, Alexandre. Capitaine Paul. Paris, 1881.
41523.19 Dumas, Alexandre. Capitaine Rhino. Paris, 1876.
41523.20 Dumas, Alexandre. Capitaine Richard. Paris, 1882.
41523.21 Dumas, Alexandre. Catherine Blum. Paris, 1873.
41523.22 Dumas, Alexandre. Canseries. Paris, 1860.
41523.23 Dumas, Alexandre. Cécile. Paris, 1881.
41523.24 Dumas, Alexandre. Charles le téméraire. Paris, 1871.
41523.25 Dumas, Alexandre. Chasseur de sauvagine. Paris, 1872.
41523.26 Dumas, Alexandre. Château d'Eppstein. Paris, 1879.
41523.27 Dumas, Alexandre. Chevalier d'Harmental. Paris, 1873.
41523.28 Dumas, Alexandre. Chevalier de Maison-Rouge. Paris, 1872.
41523.29 Dumas, Alexandre. Collier de la reine. Paris, 1873. 3v.
41523.30 Dumas, Alexandre. Colomba. Paris, 1871.
41523.31 Dumas, Alexandre. Compagnons de Jéhu. Paris, 1876.
41524.3 Dumas, Alexandre. Comte de Monte Cristo. v.1-6. Paris, 1887. 3v.
41524.6 Dumas, Alexandre. Comtesse de Salisbury. Paris, 1878.
41524.7 Dumas, Alexandre. Confessions de la marquise. Paris, 1875.
41524.8 Dumas, Alexandre. Conscience l'innocent. Paris, 1861.
41524.9 Dumas, Alexandre. Docteur mystérieux. v.1-2. Paris, 1875.
41524.10 Dumas, Alexandre. La fille du marquis. v.1-2. Paris, 1875.

41523 - 41528 Individual authors, etc. - 1800-1849 - Fiction - Dumas père - Complete works - Paris edition in French [Discontinued] - cont.
41524.11 Dumas, Alexandre. Dame de Monsoreau. Paris, 1872. 2v.
41524.11.8 Dumas, Alexandre. Dame de Monsoreau. Paris, 1903.
41524.12 Dumas, Alexandre. Dame de Volupté. Paris, 1875.
41524.13 Dumas, Alexandre. Les deux Diane. v.1-2,3. Paris, 1882. 2v.
41524.14 Dumas, Alexandre. Deux reines. Paris, 1875.
41524.15 Dumas, Alexandre. Dieu dispose. Paris, 1879.
41524.16 Dumas, Alexandre. Drame de quatre-vingt-treize. Paris, 1875.
41524.17 Dumas, Alexandre. Drames de la mer. Paris, 1873.
41524.18 Dumas, Alexandre. Drames galants. Paris, 1876.
41524.19 Dumas, Alexandre. Emma Lyonna. v.1-2,3,4-5. Paris, 1876. 3v.
41524.20 Dumas, Alexandre. Femme au Collier de Velours. Paris, 1881.
41524.21 Dumas, Alexandre. Fernande. Paris, 1881.
41525.1 Dumas, Alexandre. Une fille du régent. Paris, 1873.
41525.3 Dumas, Alexandre. Le fils du forçat. Paris, 1881.
41525.4 Dumas, Alexandre. Les frères corses. Paris, 1867.
41525.5 Dumas, Alexandre. Gabriel Lambert. Paris, 1874.
41525.6 Dumas, Alexandre. Les Garibaldiens. Paris, 1868.
41525.7 Dumas, Alexandre. Gaule et France. Paris, 1875.
41525.8 Dumas, Alexandre. Georges. Paris, 1881.
41525.9 Dumas, Alexandre. Un Gil-Blas in Californie. Paris, 1872.
41525.10 Dumas, Alexandre. Les grands hommes en robe de Chambre. César. Paris, 1866.
41525.11 Dumas, Alexandre. Les grands hommes en robe de Chambre. Henri IV. Paris, 1877.
41525.12 Dumas, Alexandre. La guerre des femmes. Paris, 1878.
41525.13 Dumas, Alexandre. Histoire d'un Casse-Noisette. Paris, 1871.
41525.14 Dumas, Alexandre. L'homme aux Contes. Paris, 1878.
41525.15 Dumas, Alexandre. Les hommes de Fer. Paris, 1875.
41525.16 Dumas, Alexandre. L'horoscope. Paris, 1875.
41525.17 Dumas, Alexandre. L'île de feu. Paris, 1870.
41525.18 Dumas, Alexandre. Impressions de voyage. Une année à Florence. Paris, 1867.
41525.19 Dumas, Alexandre. Impressions de voyage. L'Arabie heureuse. Paris, 1860. 3v.
41525.20 Dumas, Alexandre. Impressions de voyage. Excursions sur les bords du Rhin. Paris, 1894.
41525.21 Dumas, Alexandre. Impressions de voyage. Le capitaine Aréna. Paris, 1870.
41525.22 Dumas, Alexandre. Impressions de voyage. Voyage au Caucase. Paris, 1865. 3v.
41525.23 Dumas, Alexandre. Impressions de voyage. Le corricolo. Paris, 1872.
41525.24 Dumas, Alexandre. Impressions de voyage. Midi de la France. Paris, 1865.
41525.25 Dumas, Alexandre. Impressions de voyage. De Paris à Cadix. Paris, 1870.
41525.26 Dumas, Alexandre. Impressions de voyage. Quinze jours au Sinai. Paris, 1868.
41525.27 Dumas, Alexandre. Impressions de voyage. En Russie. v.1,2,3-4. Paris, 1865. 3v.
41525.28 Dumas, Alexandre. Impressions de voyage. Suisse. Paris, 1868. 3v.
41525.29 Dumas, Alexandre. Impressions de voyage en Suisse. N.Y., 1948.
41526.1 Dumas, Alexandre. Impressions de voyage. Le spéronare. Paris, 1873.
41526.2 Dumas, Alexandre. Impressions de voyage. Le véloce. Paris, 1871.
41526.3 Dumas, Alexandre. Impressions de voyage. La villa Palmieri. Paris, 1865.
41526.4 Dumas, Alexandre. Ingénue. Paris, 1873.
41526.5 Dumas, Alexandre. Isaac Laguedem. v.1-2. Paris, 1878.
41526.6 Dumas, Alexandre. Isabel de Bavière. Paris, 1872.
41526.7 Dumas, Alexandre. Italiens et Flamands. Paris, 1862.
41526.8 Dumas, Alexandre. Ivanhoe par Walter Scott. v.1-2. Paris, 1874.
41526.9 Dumas, Alexandre. Jacques Ortis. Paris, 1881.
41526.10 Dumas, Alexandre. Jane. Paris, 1860.
41526.11 Dumas, Alexandre. Jane. Paris, 1879.
41526.12 Dumas, Alexandre. Jehanne la Pucelle. Paris, 1874.
41526.13 Dumas, Alexandre. Louis XIV et son siècle. Paris, 1882. 2v.
41526.15 Dumas, Alexandre. Louis XVI et la révolution. Paris, 1875.
41526.16 Dumas, Alexandre. Les louves de Machecoul. Paris, 1877. 3v.
41526.17 Dumas, Alexandre. Madame de Chamblay. Paris, 1881.
41526.18 Dumas, Alexandre. La maison de Glace. Paris, 1867.
41526.19 Dumas, Alexandre. Le maitre d'Armes. Paris, 1881.
41526.20 Dumas, Alexandre. Les mariages du Père Olifus. Paris, 1877.
41526.21 Dumas, Alexandre. Les médicis. Paris, 1872.
41526.22 Dumas, Alexandre. Mes mémoires. v.1-10. Paris, 1865. 5v.
41526.24 Dumas, Alexandre. Mémoires d'une aveugle. Paris, 1867.
41527.2 Dumas, Alexandre. Le meneur de loups. Paris, 1868.
41527.3 Dumas, Alexandre. Les mille et un fontomes. Paris, 1881.
41527.4 Dumas, Alexandre. Les mohicans de Paris. v.1-4. Paris, 1874. 2v.
41527.5 Dumas, Alexandre. Les morts vont vite. Paris, 1879.
41527.6 Dumas, Alexandre. Napoléon. Paris, 1881.
41527.7 Dumas, Alexandre. Une nuit à Florence. Paris, 1877.
41527.8 Dumas, Alexandre. Olympe de Clèves. Paris, 1872.
41527.9 Dumas, Alexandre. Le page du Duc de Savoie. Paris, 1876.
41527.10 Dumas, Alexandre. Parisiens et provinciaux. Paris, 1868.
41527.11 Dumas, Alexandre. Le pasteur d'Ashbourn. Paris, 1860.
41527.12 Dumas, Alexandre. Pauline et Pascal Bruno. Paris, 1874.
41527.13 Dumas, Alexandre. Un pays inconnu. Paris, 1873.
41527.14 Dumas, Alexandre. Le Père Gigogne. Paris, 1860.
41527.15 Dumas, Alexandre. Le Père la Ruine. Paris, 1875.
41527.16 Dumas, Alexandre. Le prince des voleurs. v.1-2. Paris, 1882.
41527.17 Dumas, Alexandre. La princesse Flora. Paris, 1877.
41527.18 Dumas, Alexandre. La princesse de Monaco. Paris, 1874.
41527.19 Dumas, Alexandre. Propos d'art et de cuisine. Paris, 1877.
41527.20 Dumas, Alexandre. Quarante-Cinq. Paris, 1873. 3v.
41527.21 Dumas, Alexandre. La régence. Paris, 1881.
41527.22 Dumas, Alexandre. La reine-Margot. Paris, 1873.

41523 - 41528 Individual authors, etc. - 1800-1849 - Fiction - Dumas père - Complete works - Paris edition in French [Discontinued] - cont.

41527.23 Dumas, Alexandre. Robin Hood. Le proscrit. v.1-2. Paris, 1874.
41527.24 Dumas, Alexandre. La route de Varennes. Paris, 1869.
41527.25 Dumas, Alexandre. Le salteador. Paris, 1877.
41527.26 Dumas, Alexandre. Salvator. v.1-2, 3-5. Paris, 1873. 2v.
41528.1 Dumas, Alexandre. La San-Filia. v.1-4. Paris, 1876. 2v.
41528.1.2 Dumas, Alexandre. Souvenirs d'Antony. Paris, 1877.
41528.2 Dumas, Alexandre. Souvenirs d'une favorite. v.1-4. Paris, 1877. 2v.
41528.3 Dumas, Alexandre. Les Stuarts. Paris, 1872.
41528.4 Dumas, Alexandre. Sultanetta. Paris, 1879.
41528.5 Dumas, Alexandre. Sylvandire. Paris, 1881.
41528.6 Dumas, Alexandre. La terreur prussienne. Paris, 1872.
41528.7 Dumas, Alexandre. Le testament de M. Chavelin. Paris, 1879.
41528.9 Dumas, Alexandre. Trois maitres. Paris, 1878.
41528.10.2 Dumas, Alexandre. Trois mousquetaires. Paris, 1846.
41528.11 Dumas, Alexandre. Le trou de l'enfer. Paris, 1873.
41528.12 Dumas, Alexandre. La tulipe noire. Paris, 1872.
41528.13 Dumas, Alexandre. Le vicomte de Bragelonne. v.1-6. Paris, 1872. 3v.
41528.14 Dumas, Alexandre. La vie au désert. Paris, 1869.
41528.15 Dumas, Alexandre. Une vie d'artiste. Paris, 1874.
NEDL 41528.17 Dumas, Alexandre. Vingt ans après. Paris, 1888. 3v.

41529 Individual authors, etc. - 1800-1849 - Fiction - Dumas père - Complete works - Boston and N.Y. editions in English [Discontinued]

41529.1A Dumas, Alexandre. The three musketeers. Boston, 1897. 2v.
41529.1B Dumas, Alexandre. The three musketeers. v.2. Boston, 1897.
41529.2A Dumas, Alexandre. Twenty years after. Boston, 1897.
41529.2B Dumas, Alexandre. Twenty years after. Boston, 1897. 2v.
41529.3 Dumas, Alexandre. Vicomte de Bragelonne; or, Ten years later. v.3-6. v.1 lost 1931. Boston, 1897.
41529.4 Dumas, Alexandre. The count of Monte Cristo. v.3-4. v.1-2 lost 1931. Boston, 1897. 2v.
41529.50 Dumas, Alexandre. Romances. Boston, 1893-95. 54v.
41529.51 Dumas, Alexandre. Works. N.Y., 190-? 18v.
41529.55 Dumas, Alexandre. The celebrated crimes of history. N.Y., 1895. 8v.
41529.57 Dumas, Alexandre. Celebrated crimes. N.Y., 1910. 8v.
41529.76 Dumas, Alexandre. The duke's page. Boston, 1894. 2v.
41529.77 Dumas, Alexandre. Olympe de Clèves. Boston, 1894. 2v.
41529.78 Dumas, Alexandre. The two Dianas. Boston, 1894. 3v.
41529.85 Dumas, Alexandre. Ascanio. Boston, 1895. 2v.
41529.85.20A Dumas, Alexandre. Black. The story of a dog. Boston, 1895.
41529.85.20B Dumas, Alexandre. Black. The story of a dog. Boston, 1895.
41529.86 Dumas, Alexandre. Sylvandire. Boston, 1897.
41529.90 Dumas, Alexandre. Ange Pitou. Boston, 1895. 2v.
41529.91 Dumas, Alexandre. Memoirs of a physician. v.2-3. v.1 lost 1931. Boston, 1895. 2v.
41529.100 Dumas, Alexandre. The companions of Jehu. Boston, 1895. 2v.
41529.100.3 Dumas, Alexandre. The company of Jehu. Boston, 1894. 2v.
41529.101 Dumas, Alexandre. The whites and the blues. Boston, 1895. 2v.
41529.101.10 Dumas, Alexandre. The first republic. Boston, 1894. 2v.
41529.105.1A Dumas, Alexandre. The three guardsmen. N.Y., 19- .
41529.105.1B Dumas, Alexandre. The three guardsmen. N.Y., 19- .
41529.105.2 Dumas, Alexandre. Twenty years after. N.Y., 19- .
41529.105.4.5 Dumas, Alexandre. Ten years later. N.Y., 1899.
41529.105.6A Dumas, Alexandre. The man in the iron mask. N.Y., 19- .
41529.105.6B Dumas, Alexandre. The man in the iron mask. N.Y., 19- .
41529.107.1 Dumas, Alexandre. Joseph Balsamo. N.Y., 19- .
41529.107.2A Dumas, Alexandre. The memoirs of a physician. N.Y., 19- .
41529.107.2B Dumas, Alexandre. The memoirs of a physician. N.Y., 19- .
41529.107.2.3 Dumas, Alexandre. The memoirs of a physician. London, 1879.
41529.107.3 Dumas, Alexandre. The queen's necklace. N.Y., 19- .
41529.107.4 Dumas, Alexandre. Taking the Bastile (Ange Pitou). N.Y., 19- .
41529.107.4.2 Dumas, Alexandre. Taking the Bastile (Ange Pitou]. v.1-2. N.Y., 1896?
41529.107.5 Dumas, Alexandre. The countess de Charny. N.Y., 19- .
41529.107.6 Dumas, Alexandre. The chevalier de Maison Rouge. N.Y., 19- .
41529.109.1 Dumas, Alexandre. Marguerite de Valois. N.Y., 19- .
41529.109.2 Dumas, Alexandre. Chicot, the jester (La dame Monsoreau). N.Y., 19- .
41529.109.3 Dumas, Alexandre. The forty-five guardsmen. N.Y., 19- .
41529.111.2A Dumas, Alexandre. The black tulip. N.Y., 19- .
41529.111.2B Dumas, Alexandre. The black tulip. N.Y., 19- .
41529.111.4 Dumas, Alexandre. The page of the Duke of Savoy. N.Y., 19- .
41529.111.5 Dumas, Alexandre. The page of the duke of Savoy. N.Y., 19- .
41529.111.6 Dumas, Alexandre. The two Dianas. N.Y., 19- .
41529.111.7 Dumas, Alexandre. The two Dianas. N.Y., 19- .
41529.111.8 Dumas, Alexandre. The conspirators or The chevalier d'Harmental. N.Y., 19- .
41529.111.9 Dumas, Alexander. The regent's duaghter. N.Y., 19- .
41529.112 Dumas, Alexandre. The Chevalier d'Harmental. Boston, 19-
41529.112.2 Dumas, Alexandre. The count of Monte Cristo. v.1-4. Boston, 19- . 2v.
41529.112.4 Dumas, Alexandre. La dame de Monsoreau. v.1-2. Boston, 19- .
41529.112.6 Dumas, Alexandre. The forty-five. v.1-2. Boston, 19- .
41529.112.8 Dumas, Alexandre. Marguerite de Valois. Boston, 19- .
41529.112.10 Dumas, Alexandre. The regent's daughter. The black tulip. Boston, 19- .
41529.112.12 Dumas, Alexandre. Twenty years after. Boston, 19- .
41529.112.14 Dumas, Alexandre. The vicomte de Bragelonne. v.1,2-5. Boston, 19- . 3v.

41530.300 - .499 Individual authors, etc. - 1800-1849 - Fiction - Dumas père - Complete works - Other English editions

41530.300 Dumas, Alexandre. Works. v.1, 3-7. N.Y., 1908.
41530.310 Dumas, Alexandre. On board the Emma. London, 1929.
41530.315 Dumas, Alexandre. The romances of Alexandre Dumas. Boston, 1892-97. 45v.
41530.320 Dumas, Alexandre. The first republic. Boston, 1894.
41530.321 Dumas, Alexandre. The company of Jehu. Boston, 1894.
41530.322 Dumas, Alexandre. The regent's daughter. Boston, 19- ?
41530.323 Dumas, Alexandre. The three musketeers. Boston, 19- ?
41530.324 Dumas, Alexandre. The count of Monte Christo or, the adventures of Edmond Dantes. v.1-4. Boston, 19- ? 2v.
41530.331 Dumas, Alexandre. The regent's daughter. Boston, 1891.
41530.332 Dumas, Alexandre. Le chevalier d'Harmental. Boston, 1891.
41530.333 Dumas, Alexandre. The black tulip. Boston, 1891.
41530.334 Dumas, Alexandre. The page of the duke of Savoy. Boston, 1891. 2v.
41530.335 Dumas, Alexandre. The two Dianas. Boston, 1891. 3v.
41530.336 Dumas, Alexandre. The companions of Jehu. Boston, 1894. 2v.
41530.337 Dumas, Alexandre. The Whites and the Blues. Boston, 1894. 2v.
41530.338 Dumas, Alexandre. The she-wolves of Machecoul. Boston, 1894. 2v.
41530.339 Dumas, Alexandre. Olympe de Clèves. Boston, 1893. 2v.
41530.345 Dumas, Alexandre. The alchemist. San Francisco, 1940.

41538 Individual authors, etc. - 1800-1849 - Fiction - Dumas père - Individual works

41538.2.5 Dumas, Alexandre. Ange Pitou. v.1-2. Paris, 1869.
41538.2.6 Dumas, Alexandre. Ange Pitou. v.1-2. Boston, 1890.
41538.2.7 Dumas, Alexandre. Ange Pitou. Boston, 1894. 2v.
Htn 41538.3* Dumas, Alexandre. The comtesse de Saint-Géran. N.Y., 19-
Htn 41538.3.5* Dumas, Alexandre. The comtesse de Saint-Géran. N.Y., 19- ?
41538.4 Dumas, Alexandre. Iza's love letters. N.Y., 1890.
41538.5.10 Dumas, Alexandre. Ascanio. Paris, 1848.
41538.5.15 Dumas, Alexandre. Ascanio. Boston, 1895.
41538.5.16 Dumas, Alexandre. Ascanio. Boston, 1895.
41538.5.20 Dumas, Alexandre. Ascanio. v.1-2. Boston, 1896.
41538.5.50 Dumas, Alexandre. The ball of snow, to which is added Sultanetta. Boston, 1895.
41538.6 Dumas, Alexandre. Cherubino y Celestini. Madrid, 1897.
41538.8A Dumas, Alexandre. The memoirs. London, 1891. 2v.
41538.8B Dumas, Alexandre. The memoirs. London, 1891. 2v.
41538.9A Dumas, Alexandre. The road to Monte Cristo. N.Y., 1956.
41538.9B Dumas, Alexandre. The road to Monte Cristo. N.Y., 1956.
41538.10 Dumas, Alexandre. The chevalier d'Harmental. Boston, 18-
41538.10.5 Dumas, Alexandre. The chevalier d'Harmental. Boston, 1893.
41538.10.6 Dumas, Alexandre. The chevalier d'Harmental. Boston, 1893.
41538.10.8 Dumas, Alexandre. The chevalier d'Harmental. Boston, 1894?
41538.10.10 Dumas, Alexandre. The chevalier d'Harmental. Boston, 19- ?
41538.11.5 Dumas, Alexandre. Chicot the jester. N.Y., 1904.
41538.11.10 Dumas, Alexandre. Chicot the jester. London, 1912.
41538.12 Dumas, Alexandre. Pages choisies des grands écrivains. Paris, 1897.
41538.13 Dumas, Alexandre. Acte of Corinth. N.Y., 1852.
41538.14 Dumas, Alexandre. Caligula; drama. Madrid, 1839.
41538.14.5 Dumas, Alexandre. Le collier de la reine. Paris, 1882. 2v.
41538.14.10 Dumas, Alexandre. Le collier de la reine. Paris, 1896. 3v.
41538.16 Dumas, Alexandre. Comte de Monte-Cristo. v.1-4. Paris, 1882. 2v.
41538.16.1 Dumas, Alexandre. Count of Monte-Cristo. London, 187-?
41538.16.2 Dumas, Alexandre. Count of Monte Cristo. N.Y., 187-?
41538.16.3.10 Dumas, Alexandre. Count of Monte Cristo. N.Y., 18- .
41538.16.3.20 Dumas, Alexandre. Le comte de Monte-Cristo. Paris, 1877. 5v.
41538.16.4.2 Dumas, Alexandre. The count of Monte Cristo. Boston, 1889. 4v.
41538.16.4.3 Dumas, Alexandre. Le comte de Monte Cristo. Paris, 1892.
41538.16.5A Dumas, Alexandre. Count of Monte Cristo. Boston, 1894. 3v.
41538.16.5B Dumas, Alexandre. Count of Monte Cristo. Boston, 1894. 3v.
41538.16.6 Dumas, Alexandre. Count of Monte Cristo. Boston, 1894. 3v.
41538.16.6.5 Dumas, Alexandre. Count of Monte Cristo. N.Y., 1894. 2v.
41538.16.7 Dumas, Alexandre. Count of Monte Cristo. Boston, 1890. 4v.
41538.16.8.3 Dumas, Alexandre. The count of Monte Cristo. Boston, 1899. 2v.
41538.16.8.5 Dumas, Alexandre. Count of Monte Cristo. N.Y., 1915. 2v.
41538.16.8.43 Dumas, Alexandre. La comtesse de Charny. Boston, 1890. 4v.
41538.16.8.48 Dumas, Alexandre. Comtesse de Charny. Boston, 1894. 3v.
41538.16.8.50 Dumas, Alexandre. The countess de Charny. N.Y., 1903.
41538.16.9 Dumas, Alexandre. Countess of Monte Cristo. Philadelphia, 1871.
41538.16.11 Dumas, Alexandre. Il conte di Monte Cristo. Milano? 1852.
41538.16.12 Dumas, Alexandre. Edmond Dantès. Chicago, 19- .
41538.16.15 Dumas, Alexandre. Edmond Dantès. N.Y., 1911.
41538.16.16 Dumas, Alexandre. Il conte di Morcerf ed il conte di Monte Cristo. Milano? 185-?
41538.16.20 Dumas, Alexandre. Le comte de Monte Cristo. Paris, 1968. 2v.
41538.17 Dumas, Alexandre. Monsieur de Chauvelin's will; The woman with the velvet necklace. Boston, 1897.
41538.17.2 Dumas, Alexandre. Monsieur de Chauvelin's will; The woman with the velvet necklace. Boston, 1897.
41538.17.3 Dumas, Alexandre. Chauvelin's will; The woman with the velvet necklace, Blanche de Beaulieu. Boston, 1897.
41538.17.5A Dumas, Alexandre. Countess of Salisbury. N.Y., 1851.
41538.17.5B Dumas, Alexandre. Countess of Salisbury. N.Y., 1851.
41538.18 Senotre, G. Le vrai chevalier de Maison-Rouge. Paris, 1903.

41538 Individual authors, etc. - 1800-1849 - Fiction - Dumas père - Individual works - cont.

41538.18.5 Dumas, Alexandre. Le chevalier de Maison-Rouge. N.Y., 1903.
41538.18.10 Dumas, Alexandre. Le chevalier de Maison-Rouge. Boston, 1894.
41538.19 Dumas, Alexandre. The bird of fate, a modern Gil Blas. London, n.d.
41538.19.5 Dumas, Alexandre. La conscience, drame en cinq actes en six tableaux. Paris, 1854.
41538.19.9 Dumas, Alexandre. Conscience. London, 1854.
41538.19.15 Dumas, Alexandre. Dame de volupte. v.1-3. Bruxelles, 1857.
41538.20 Dumas, Alexandre. La dame de volupté. v.1-2. Paris, 1886.
41538.20.2 Dumas, Alexandre. Les demoiselles de St. Cyr. London, 1886.
41538.20.5 Dumas, Alexandre. Les deux Diane. Bruxelles, 1847. 3v.
41538.20.6 Dumas, Alexandre. Les deux Diane. Paris, 1893. 3v.
41538.20.7F Dumas, Alexandre. La dame de Monsoreau. Paris, 1852.
41538.20.8.3 Dumas, Alexandre. The forty five. Boston, 1889. 2v.
41538.20.8.5 Dumas, Alexandre. The forty five. Boston, 1893.
41538.20.8.7 Dumas, Alexandre. The forty five. Boston, 1893.
41538.20.8.10 Dumas, Alexandre. La dame de Monsoreau. v.1-2. Boston, 1894?
41538.20.8.15 Dumas, Alexandre. The forty five. Boston, 1897. 2v.
41538.20.8.20A Dumas, Alexandre. La dame de Monsoreau. N.Y., 1900.
41538.20.8.20B Dumas, Alexandre. La dame de Monsoreau. N.Y., 1900.
41538.20.8.23 Dumas, Alexandre. La dame de Monsoreau. Boston, 1900.
41538.20.8.25 Dumas, Alexandre. La dame de Monsoreau. v.1-2. Boston, 19- ?
41538.20.9 Dumas, Alexandre. Le drame de quatre-vingt-treize. Bruxelles, 1851.
41538.20.25 Dumas, Alexandre. The forty-five guardsmen, a sequel to La dame de Monsoreau. N.Y., 188-?
41538.20.28 Dumas, Alexandre. The forty-five. Boston, 1889. 2v.
41538.20.30A Dumas, Alexandre. The forty-five. v.1-2. Boston, 1893.
41538.20.30B Dumas, Alexandre. The forty-five. v.1-2. Boston, 1893.
41538.20.30C Dumas, Alexandre. The forty-five. v.1-2. Boston, 1893.
41538.20.32 Dumas, Alexandre. The forty-five. v.1-2. Boston, 1894?
41538.20.45 Dumas, Alexandre. The forty-five guardsmen. N.Y., 1900.
41538.20.50 Dumas, Alexandre. The forty-five. v.1-2. Boston, 19- ?
41538.21 Dumas, Alexandre. La bouillie de la comtesse Berthe. London, 1889.
41538.21.9 Dumas, Alexandre. Edmund Kean. London, 1847.
41538.21.10 Dumas, Alexandre. Edmund Kean. n.p., 1881.
41538.22 Dumas, Alexandre. Episodes from Pepin et Charlemagne. London, 1889.
41538.23 Dumas, Alexandre. Episodes from Aventures de Lyderic. London, 1890.
41538.24.2 Dumas, Alexandre. Episodes from Monte-Cristo. London, 1901. 2v.
41538.24.9 Dumas, Alexandre. La hija del regente; comedia. Madrid, 1846.
41538.24.26 Dumas, Alexandre. The regent's daughter. Boston, 1893.
41538.24.28 Dumas, Alexandre. The regent's daughter. Boston, 1899.
41538.24.30 Dumas, Alexandre. The regent's daughter. N.Y., 19- ?
41538.25 Dumas, Alexandre. The foresters. N.Y., 1854.
41538.26 Dumas, Alexandre. Lièvre de mon grand-père. Paris, 1856.
41538.28 Dumas, Alexandre. Impressions de voyage. Paris, 1842.
41538.28.5F Dumas, Alexandre. Impressions de voyage. Paris, 185-?
41538.28.9.5 Dumas, Alexandre. Impressions de voyage. v.1-3. Paris, 1853-54.
41538.28.10 Dumas, Alexandre. Travels in Switzerland. London, 1958.
41538.28.12 Dumas, Alexandre. From Paris to Cadiz. London, 1958.
41538.28.15 Dumas, Alexandre. Journeys with Dumas. Boston, 1902.
41538.28.50 Dumas, Alexandre. The last Vendée. Boston, 1894.
41538.28.52 Dumas, Alexandre. The last Vendée. Boston, 1894.
41538.28.54 Dumas, Alexandre. The last Vendée. v.1-2. Boston, 1894.
41538.29 Dumas, Alexandre. La maison de glace. Paris, 1860. 2 pam.
41538.29.2 Dumas, Alexandre. Marguerite de Valois. London, 1846.
41538.29.2.3 Dumas, Alexandre. Marguerite de Valois. Boston, 1889. 2v.
41538.29.2.5A Dumas, Alexandre. Marguerite de Valois. Boston, 1893.
41538.29.2.5B Dumas, Alexandre. Marguerite de Valois. Boston, 1893.
41538.29.3 Dumas, Alexandre. Marguerite de Valois. Boston, 1893.
41538.29.3.8 Dumas, Alexandre. Marguerite de Valois. Boston, 1897. 2v.
41538.29.3.15 Dumas, Alexandre. Marguerite de Valois. N.Y., 1900.
41538.29.3.18 Dumas, Alexandre. Marguerite de Valois. N.Y., 1900.
41538.29.3.20 Dumas, Alexandre. Marguerite de Valois. Boston, 19- ?
41538.29.5 Dumas, Alexandre. Margarita de Borgona; drama. Madrid, 1874.
41538.29.9 Dumas, Alexandre. A marriage of convenience. London, 1899.
41538.29.11 Dumas, Alexandre. A marriage of convenience. N.Y., 1899.
41538.29.15 Dumas, Alexandre. Un mariage sous Louis XV. Paris, 1861.
41538.30 Dumas, Alexandre. Pauline, Pascal Bruno and Boutekoe. London, n.d.
41538.30.10 Dumas, Alexandre. Pauline. Paris, 1947.
41538.31 Dumas, Alexandre. Pascal Bruno. London, 1837.
41538.32 Dumas, Alexandre. Quarante-cinq. Paris, 1850.
41538.34 Dumas, Alexandre. Sketches of Naples. Philadelphia, 1845.
41538.35 Dumas, Alexandre. Père la ruine. London, n.d.
41538.36 Dumas, Alexandre. Mademoiselle de belle-isle. N.Y., 1855.
41538.36.5 Dumas, Alexandre. Mademoiselle de belle-isle. N.Y., 1855.
41538.36.8 Dumas, Alexandre. Mademoiselle de belle-isle. Paris, 185-?
41538.37 Dumas, Alexandre. Gabrielle de belle-isle. N.Y., 1891.
41538.38.10 Dumas, Alexandre. Acté. Bruxelles, 1839. 2v.
41538.40 Dumas, Alexandre. L'alchimista, dramma in cinque atti. n.p., 1853.
41538.42 Dumas, Alexandre. Celebrated crimes. Philadelphia, 1895. 8v.
Htn 41538.43* Dumas, Alexandre. Canaris. Paris, 1826.
41538.45 Dumas, Alexandre. Captain Paul Jones. London, 18- .
41538.45.5 Dumas, Alexandre. Paul Jones. Philadelphia, 1839.
41538.45.15 Dumas, Alexandre. Paul Jones. London, 187-?
41538.46 Dumas, Alexandre. Catharine of Clèves. London, 1831.
41538.47 Dumas, Alexandre. Henri III et sa cour. Paris, 18- .
Htn 41538.47.5* Dumas, Alexandre. Henri et sa cour. Paris, 1829.
41538.47.8A Dumas, Alexandre. Henri III et sa cour. Paris, 1928.
41538.47.8B Dumas, Alexandre. Henri III et sa cour. Paris, 1928.
41538.47.10 Dumas, Alexandre. The king's gallant. N.Y., 1902.
41538.47.24 Albertin. Edition critique d'une mise en scène romantique. Paris, 1938.

41538 Individual authors, etc. - 1800-1849 - Fiction - Dumas père - Individual works - cont.

41538.47.25 Albertin. Edition critique d'une mise en scène romantique. Paris, 1938.
41538.48 Dumas, Alexandre. The history of a nutcracker. London, 1873.
41538.48.15 Dumas, Alexandre. The two Dianas. London, 18- .
41538.48.20 Dumas, Alexandre. The two Dianas. Boston, 1892. 2v.
Htn 41538.49* Dumas, Alexandre. Stockholm. Paris, 1830.
41538.50 Dumas, Alexandre. Théâtre complet. Paris, 1864.
41538.51 Dumas, Alexandre. Théâtre complet. v.3-25. Paris, 1883. 11v.
41538.51.3 Dumas, Alexandre. Théâtre complet. v.8. Paris, 1883.
41538.51.5 Dumas, Alexandre. Théâtre complet. Paris, 1874. 25v.
41538.52 Dumas, Alexandre. Théâtre complet. v.8. Paris, 1887.
41538.52.9 Dumas, Alexandre. Don Juan de Marana; Kean; Riquillo. Paris, 1899.
41538.53A Dumas, Alexandre. Les trois mousquetaires. Boston, 1890.
41538.53B Dumas, Alexandre. Les trois mousquetaires. Boston, 1890.
41538.53.1 Dumas, Alexandre. Les trois mousquetaires. Boston, 1889.
41538.53.5F Dumas, Alexandre. Les trois mousquetaires. Paris, 1894. 2v.
41538.53.8 Dumas, Alexandre. Les trois mousquetaires. Paris, 19- .
41538.53.10 Dumas, Alexandre. Les trois mousquetaires. Paris, 1909.
41538.53.14A Dumas, Alexandre. Les trois mousquetaires. N.Y., 1926.
41538.53.14B Dumas, Alexandre. Les trois mousquetaires. N.Y., 1926.
41538.53.20 Dumas, Alexandre. The three guardsmen. N.Y., 1846. 2 pam.
41538.53.22 Dumas, Alexandre. The three guardsmen. Philadelphia, 1873.
41538.53.23 Dumas, Alexandre. The three guardsmen. Philadelphia, 188-?
41538.53.24 Dumas, Alexandre. The three musketeers. Boston, 1890. 2v.
41538.53.24.3 Dumas, Alexandre. The three musketeers. Boston, 1889. 2v.
41538.53.24.5 Dumas, Alexandre. The three musketeers. N.Y., 189-?
41538.53.25 Dumas, Alexandre. The three musketeers. Boston, 1893. 2v.
41538.53.26 Dumas, Alexandre. The three musketeers. N.Y., 1892.
41538.53.27F Dumas, Alexandre. The three musketeers. N.Y., 1894. 2v.
41538.53.32 Dumas, Alexandre. The three musketeers. v.1-2. N.Y., 1896.
41538.53.32.10 Dumas, Alexandre. The three musketeers. N.Y., 1899.
41538.53.33 Dumas, Alexandre. The three guardsmen. N.Y., 19- ?
41538.53.33.5 Dumas, Alexandre. The three guardsmen. N.Y., 19- .
41538.53.34 Dumas, Alexandre. The three musketeers. N.Y., 19- . 2v.
41538.53.35 Dumas, Alexandre. The three musketeers. London, 19- .
41538.53.36A Dumas, Alexandre. The three guardsmen. N.Y., 1901.
41538.53.36B Dumas, Alexandre. The three guardsmen. N.Y., 1901.
41538.53.37 Dumas, Alexandre. The three musketeers. N.Y., 1900.
41538.53.40 Dumas, Alexandre. The three musketeers. London, 1906.
41538.53.45 Dumas, Alexandre. The three musketeers. N.Y., 1915.
41538.53.51 Dumas, Alexandre. The three musketeers. N.Y., 192-?
41538.53.57 Fairbanks, Douglas. The three musketeers. N.Y., 1921.
41538.53.60 Dumas, Alexandre. The three musketeers. Harmondsworth, 1952.
41538.53.65 Dumas, Alexandre. Les trois mousquetaires. Paris, 1966.
41538.53.75 Dumas, Alexandre. De tre musketerer. Kjøbenhavn, 1884.
41538.53.95 Dumas, Alexandre. Twenty years after. Boston, 1888. 2v.
41538.53.100 Dumas, Alexandre. Twenty years after. Boston, 1890.
41538.53.102 Dumas, Alexandre. Twenty years after. N.Y., 188-?
41538.53.103 Dumas, Alexandre. Twenty years after. Boston, 1893. 2v.
41538.53.104 Dumas, Alexandre. Twenty years after. N.Y., 1901.
41538.53.105 Dumas, Alexandre. Twenty years after. N.Y., 1901.
41538.53.110 Dumas, Alexandre. Twenty years after. N.Y., 191-?
41538.53.112 Dumas, Alexandre. Twenty years after. London, 1930.
41538.53.114 Dumas, Alexandre. Twenty years after. v.1-2. Boston, 19- ?
41538.53.123 Dumas, Alexandre. Ten years later. N.Y., 189-?
41538.53.125 Dumas, Alexandre. Ten years later. N.Y., 19- .
41538.54 Dumas, Alexandre. The iron mask. Philadelphia, 1850.
41538.54.1 Dumas, Alexandre. Man in the iron mask. N.Y., 188-?
41538.54.2 Dumas, Alexandre. The iron mask. Philadelphia, n.d.
41538.54.20 Dumas, Alexandre. The man in the iron mask. London, 19- ?
41538.54.25 Dumas, Alexandre. The man in the iron mask. N.Y., 1904.
41538.55 Dumas, Alexandre. Vicomte de Bragelonne. Paris, 1852.
41538.55.15 Dumas, Alexandre. Bragelonne. N.Y., 188-?
41538.55.17 Dumas, Alexandre. Le vicomte de Bragelonne. v.1-6. Paris, 1883. 3v.
41538.55.19 Dumas, Alexandre. The vicomte de Bragelonne. Boston, 1889. 6v.
41538.55.20 Dumas, Alexandre. Vicomte de Bragelonne; or Ten years later. Boston, 1890.
41538.55.22 Dumas, Alexandre. Le vicomte de Bragelonne. v.1-6. Paris, 1890. 3v.
41538.55.25 Dumas, Alexandre. The vicomte de Bragelonne. N.Y., 19- ?
41538.55.30 Dumas, Alexandre. Le vicomte de Bragelonne, ou Dix ans plus tard. Paris, 191-? 5v.
41538.55.35 Dumas, Alexandre. The vicomte de Bragelonne. v.1,2-3,4-5. Boston, 19- . 3v.
41538.56.10 Dumas, Alexandre. Louise La Vallière. Philadelphia, 1851.
41538.56.20 Dumas, Alexandre. Louis XV et sa cour. Paris, 1888. 2v.
41538.57 Dumas, Alexandre. Louisa, or the adventures of a French milliner. Cincinnati, 1854.
41538.59 Dumas, Alexandre. Kean o sia genio e sregolatezza. n.p., 1851.
41538.60 Dumas, Alexandre. Le mari de la veuve. n.p., n.d.
41538.61.5A Dumas, Alexandre. Mèmoires d'un médecin, Joseph Balsamo. Paris, 1888-89. 5v.
41538.61.5B Dumas, Alexandre. Mèmoires d'un médecin, Joseph Balsamo. Paris, 1888-89. 3v.
41538.61.10 Dumas, Alexandre. Memoirs of a physician. N.Y., 1912.
41538.61.15 Dumas, Alexandre. Memoirs of a physician. Chicago, 189-.
41538.61.16 Dumas, Alexandre. Memoirs of a physician. N.Y., 1898.
41538.61.18 Dumas, Alexandre. Memoirs of a physician. Boston, 1893. 3v.
41538.61.20 Dumas, Alexandre. Joseph Balsamo. Chicago, 1894.
41538.61.25 Dumas, Alexandre. Joseph Balsamo. Chicago, 19- ?
41538.61.30 Dumas, Alexandre. Joseph Balsamo. N.Y., 1903.
41538.62 Dumas, Alexandre. Napoléon Bonaparte. Paris, 1831.
41538.63.10 Dumas, Alexandre. Napoléon. N.Y., 1864.

41538 Individual authors, etc. - 1800-1849 - Fiction - Dumas père - Individual works - cont.

41538.63.25 Dumas, Alexandre. The queen's necklace. London, 18- .
41538.63.30 Dumas, Alexandre. The queen's necklace. N.Y., 1850. 2 pam.
41538.63.31 Dumas, Alexandre. The queen's necklace. Boston, 1893. 2v.
41538.63.32 Dumas, Alexandre. The queen's necklace. Boston, 1890. 2v.
41538.63.33 Dumas, Alexandre. The queen's necklace. N.Y., 1903.
41538.63.34 Dumas, Alexandre. The queen's necklace. N.Y., 1904.
41538.63.35 Dumas, Alexandre. The queen's necklace. London, 1915.
41538.63.50A Dumas, Alexandre. Taking the Bastile, or Six years later. London, 188-.
41538.63.50B Dumas, Alexandre. Taking the Bastile, or Six years later. London, 188-.
41538.63.60 Dumas, Alexandre. Six years later, or Taking the Bastile. N.Y., 1896.
41538.64 Dumas, Alexandre. Oi treis somatophylakes. En Athenais, 1884. 2v.
41538.65 Dumas, Alexandre. The conscript. N.Y., 1874.
41538.66 Dumas, Alexandre. The son of Porthos or The death of Aramis. N.Y., 1892.
41538.66.10 Dumas, Alexandre. The son of Porthos or The death of Aramis. N.Y., 1892.
41538.68 Dumas, Alexandre. The countess de Charny. London, 18- ?
41538.68.30 Dumas, Alexandre. La comtesse de Charny. v.1-6. Paris, 1887. 3v.
41538.69 Dumas, Alexandre. The chevalier de Maison Rouge. London, 18- .
41538.69.5 Dumas, Alexandre. Le Chevalier de Maison Rouge. N.Y., n.d.
41538.69.15 Dumas, Alexandre. Le Chevalier de Maison Rouge. Paris, 1889. 2v.
41538.69.20 Dumas, Alexandre. The Chevalier de Maison-Rouge. Boston, 1890.
41538.69.25 Dumas, Alexandre. Le Chevalier de Maison-Rouge. Paris, 1892. 2v.
41538.70 Dumas, Alexandre. The Chevalier de Maison-Rouge. Paris, 1894. 2v.
41538.70.85 Dumas, Alexandre. The black tulip. Boston, 1895.
41538.70.90 Dumas, Alexandre. La tulipe noire. Paris, 19- ?
41538.71 Dumas, Alexandre. La tulipe noire. N.Y., 1903?
41538.71.5 Dumas, Alexandre. The black tulip. N.Y., 1902.
41538.72 Dumas, Alexandre. Romans et nouvelles. N.Y., n.d.
41538.73 Dumas, Alexandre. Antony; drame en cinq actes. Paris, 1930.
41538.75A Dumas, Alexandre. The brigand. Boston, 1897.
41538.75B Dumas, Alexandre. The brigand. Boston, 1897.
41538.77 Dumas, Alexandre. Andree de Javerney, or The downfall of French monarchy. N.Y., 18- .
41538.80 Dumas, Alexandre. The journal of Madame Giovanni. N.Y., 1944.
41538.83 Dumas, Alexandre. The whites and the blues. Boston, 1894. 2v.
41538.85 Dumas, Alexandre. The whites and the blues. N.Y., 19- ?
41538.85.10 Dumas, Alexandre. The whites and the blues. N.Y., 1904.
41538.86 Dumas, Alexandre. Isabel of Bavaria. London, 1846.
41538.90 Dumas, Alexandre. Agénor de Mauléon. Boston, 1897. 2v.
41538.91 Dumas, Alexandre. Agénor de Mauléon. London, 1906. 2v.
41538.95 Dumas, Alexandre. The war of women. Boston, 1895.
41538.96 Dumas, Alexandre. La guerre des femmes. Paris, 1895. • 2v.
41538.100 Dumas, Alexandre. Tales of the Caucasus. Boston, 1895.
41538.105 Dumas, Alexandre. Sylvandire. Boston, 1897.
41538.110 Dumas, Alexandre. The page of the duke of Savoy. Boston, 1893. 2v.
41538.115 Dumas, Alexandre. Olympe de Cleves. Boston, 1893. 2v.
41538.120 Dumas, Alexandre. The she-wolves of Machecoul and The Corsican brothers. Boston, 1894. 2v.
41538.125 Dumas, Alexandre. The companions of Jehu. Boston, 1894. 2v.
41538.130 Dumas, Alexandre. Ma revolution de 1830. Paris, 1946.
41538.135 Dumas, Alexandre. Une nuit a Florence. Paris, 1947.
41538.140 Dumas, Alexandre. The first republic. v.1-2. Boston, 1894.
41538.145 Dumas, Alexandre. A life's ambition. Philaldelphia, 1925?
41538.150 Dumas, Alexandre. The company of Jehu. Boston, 1894.
41538.160 Dumas, Alexandre. The wolf leader. Philadelphia, 1950.
41538.170 Dumas, Alexandre. Marie Stuart à Lochleven. N.Y., 1900.
41538.185 Dumas, Alexandre. Captain Marion. Christchurch, N.Z., 1949.
41538.190 Dumas, Alexandre. La tour de Nesle. Bruxelles, 1842.
41538.195 Dumas, Alexandre. Tangier to Tunis. London, 1959.
41538.200 Dumas, Alexandre. Voyage en Russie. Paris, 1960.
41538.205 Dumas, Alexandre. The flight to Varennes. London, 1962.
41538.210 Dumas, Alexandre. Quinze jours au Sinai. v.1-2. Bruxelles, 1839.

41539 Individual authors, etc. - 1800-1849 - Fiction - Dumas père - Biography and criticism

41539.05 Reed, Frank W. A bibliography of Alexandre Dumas père. London, 1933.
41539.1A Davidson, Arthur F. Alexandre Dumas, (père) his life and works. Philadelphia, 1902.
41539.1B Davidson, Arthur F. Alexandre Dumas, (père) his life and works. Philadelphia, 1902.
41539.1C Davidson, Arthur F. Alexandre Dumas, (père) his life and works. Philadelphia, 1902.
41539.1.5 Spurr, H.A. The life and writings of Alexandre Dumas, 1802-70. London, 1902.
41539.1.6 Spurr, H.A. The life and writings of Alexandre Dumas, 1802-70. N.Y., 1902.
41539.2 Lecomte, L. Henry. Alexandre Dumas, 1802-70, sa vie intime, ses oeuvres. Paris, 1903.
41539.3 Fitzgerald, Percy. Alexandre Dumas, life and adventures. London, 1873. 4v.
41539.4A Blaze Bury, H. Alexandre Dumas, sa vie, son temps, son oeuvre. Paris, 1885.
41539.5 Glinel, Charles. Alexandre Dumas et son oeuvre. Reims, 1884. 2v.
41539.6 Parigot, Hippolyte. Le drame d'Alexandre Dumas. Paris, 1899.
41539.7 Parigot, Hippolyte. Alexandre Dumas père. Paris, 1902.
41539.8 Mansfield, M.F. Dumas' Paris,. Boston, 1908.

41539 Individual authors, etc. - 1800-1849 - Fiction - Dumas père - Biography and criticism - cont.

41539.8.2 Mansfield, M.F. Dumas' Paris. Boston, 1905.
41539.9 Simon, Gustave. Histoire d'une collaboration. Paris, 1919.
41539.10 Dumas, Alexandre. Le monument de Alexandre Dumas, oeuvre de Gustave Doré. Paris, 1884.
41539.12 Dumas, Alexandre. My memoirs. N.Y., 1907-09. 6v.
41539.13 Lucas-Dubreton, Jean. La vie d'Alexandre Dumas. 15. éd. Paris, 1928.
41539.13.10 Lucas-Dubreton, Jean. The fourth musketeer. N.Y., 1928.
41539.13.12 Lucas-Dubreton, Jean. The fourth musketeer. N.Y., 1928.
41539.15 Wilke, Heinz. Alexandre Dumas, père, als Dramatiker. Inaug. Diss. München, 1927.
41539.17 Gribble, F.H. Dumas, father and son. London, 1930.
41539.19 Döling, Erich. Alexandre Dumas pères Subjektivismus in seinen Dramen aus der Zeit der Romantik. Inaug. Diss. Halle, 1931.
41539.20 Davidson, A.F. Alexandre Dumas (père) his life and works. Westminster, 1902.
41539.21 Pearce, G.R. Dumas Père. London, 1934.
41539.22 Gorman, H.S. The incredible marquis, Alexandre Dumas. N.Y., 1929.
41539.23 Thompson, J.A. Alexandre Dumas père and Spanish romantic drama. University, La., 1938.
41539.25 Todd, R. The laughing mulatto. London, 1940?
41539.27 Constantin-Weyer, Maurice. L'aventure vécue de Dumas père. Genève, 1944.
41539.30 Duriline, S. Alexander Dumas Perè en Russie. Paris, 1947.
41539.33 Bell, A. Alexandre Dumas. London, 1950.
41539.36 Saunders, E. The prodigal father. London, 1951.
41539.38 Gaillard, Robert. Alexandre Dumas. Paris, 1953.
41539.40 Maurois, André. Alexandre Dumas. 1. ed. N.Y., 1955.
41539.40.5 Maurois, Andre. Three musketeers. London, 1957.
41539.40.10 Maurois, André. Les trois Dumas. Paris, 1957.
41539.42 Clanard, Henri. Alexandre Dumas. Paris, 1955.
41539.44 The dumasian; the magazine of the Dumas Association. Keighley, Eng. 1956-60

41540.2 Individual authors, etc. - 1800-1849 - Fiction - Dumesnil, P.

41540.2.10 Dumesnil, Pierre. Alain Blauchart; chronique normande. pt.1-2. Paris, 1849.

41540.4 Individual authors, etc. - 1800-1849 - Fiction - Fazy

41540.4 Fazy, James. Jean d'Yvoire au bras de fer. Paris, 1840.

41540.15 Individual authors, etc. - 1800-1849 - Fiction - Féré

41540.15 Fére, Octave. Les mystères de Rouen. 3. éd. Rouen, 1861.

41540.50 Individual authors, etc. - 1800-1849 - Fiction - Ferrière

41540.50 Ferrière, Théophile de. Il vivere par Samuel Bach. Paris, 1836.
41540.50.32 Ferrière, Théophile de. Les romans et le mariage. v.2. v.1 lost 1965. Paris, 1737.

41540.75 Individual authors, etc. - 1800-1849 - Fiction - Floquet

41540.75.32 Floquet, A. Louis XI et la Normande; anecdote rouennaise du XVe siècle. Rouen, 1832.

41540.125 Individual authors, etc. - 1800-1849 - Fiction - François de Nantes, A.

41540.125 Francois de Nantes, Antoine. Recueil de fadaises. Paris, 1826. 2v.

41541.1 - .4 Individual authors, etc. - 1800-1849 - Fiction - Folios [Discontinued]

41541.1 Flint, Timothy. The bachelor reclaimed. Philadelphia, 1834.
41541.2 Spoelberch de Lovenjoul, Charles. Histoire des oeuvres de Théophile Gautier. Paris, 1887. 2v.
Htn 41541.4* Gautier, Théophile. Une nuit de Cléopatre. Paris, 1894.
Htn 41541.4.6* Gautier, Théophile. Le roi Candaule. Paris, 1893.

41541.5 Individual authors, etc. - 1800-1849 - Fiction - Girardin, Emile de

41541.5.30 Girardin, Émile de. La fille du millionnaire. Paris, 1858.
41541.5.80 Iraizoz y de Villar, Antonio. Emilio de Girardin y el periodismo moderno. Habana, 1940.

41541.6 - .17 Individual authors, etc. - 1800-1849 - Fiction - Girardin, Delphine - Writings

41541.6 Girardin, Delphine Gay. Oeuvres complètes. Paris, 1860.
41541.6.15 Girardin, Delphine Gay. Choix de lettres parisiennes. Oxford, 1906.
41541.7 Girardin, Delphine Gay. Le dernier jour de Pompei. 2. ed. Paris, 1829.
41541.8 Girardin, Delphine Gay. La joie fait peur, comédie en un acte et en prose. Paris, 1854.
41541.8.5 Girardin, Delphine Gay. La joie fait peur. Boston, 1864.
41541.8.6 Girardin, Delphine Gay. La joie fait peur. 5. éd. N.Y., 1864.
41541.8.10 Girardin, Delphine Gay. La joie fait peur. Boston, 1866.
41541.8.12 Girardin, Delphine Gay. La joie fait peur. Paris, 1877.
41541.8.13 Girardin, Delphine Gay. La joie fait peur. Paris, 1883.
41541.8.15 Girardin, Delphine Gay. La joie fait peur. Bielefeld, 1922.
41541.9 Girardin, Delphine Gay. Nouvelles. Paris, 1859.
41541.9.5 Girardin, Delphine Gay. Nouvelles. Paris, 1856.
41541.10 Girardin, Delphine Gay. Il cappello dell'Orinolojo. Milano, n.d.
41541.10.5 Girardin, Delphine Gay. La gioia fa paura. Milano, 1855.
41541.11 Girardin, Delphine Gay. Lady Tartuffe. Paris, 1853.
41541.11.5 Girardin, Delphine Gay. Lady Tartuffe. N.Y., 1855.
41541.11.10 Girardin, Delphine Gay. Lady Tartuffe. N.Y., 1855.
41541.12 Girardin, Delphine Gay. Contes d'une vieille fille à ses neveux. Paris, 1857.
41541.13 Girardin, Delphine Gay. La croix de Berny. Paris, 1855.
41541.13.2 Girardin, Delphine Gay. The cross of Berny. Philadelphia, 1873.
41541.13.5 Girardin, Delphine Gay. Le chapeau d'un horloger. Paris, 1859.
41541.13.10 Girardin, Delphine Gay. Le chapeau d'un horloger. Paris, 1877.
41541.13.12 Girardin, Delphine Gay. The clockmaker's hat. N.Y., 184-.
41541.13.15 Girardin, Delphine Gay. Poésies complètes. Paris, 1842.
41541.14 Girardin, Delphine Gay. Judith. Paris, 1843.

Classified Listing

41541.6 - .17 Individual authors, etc. - 1800-1849 - Fiction - Girardin, Delphine - Writings - cont.

41541.15 Girardin, Delphine Gay. Marguerite ou deux amours. Paris, 1865.
41541.16 Girardin, Delphine Gay. Marguerite. N.Y., 1862.
41541.17.5 Girardin, Delphine Gay. Marguerite. Paris, 1874.

41541.18 - .20.99 Individual authors, etc. - 1800-1849 - Fiction - Girardin, Delphine - Works about

41541.19 Séché, L. Delphine Gay, Mme. de Girardin. Paris, 1910.
41541.20 D'Heilly, G. Madame E. de Girardin. Paris, 1869.
41541.20.5 Malo, Henri. La gloire de Vicomte de Launay. Paris, 1925.
41541.20.15 Malo, Henri. Une muse et sa mère, Delphine Gay de Girardin. Paris, 1924.
41541.20.21 Bondy, François de. Une femme d'esprit en 1830, madame de Girardin. Paris, 1928.

41541.20.100 - Individual authors, etc. - 1800-1849 - Fiction - Folios [Discontinued]

41541.20.100 Girardin, Francois. Le supplice d'une femme. Paris, 1869.
41541.20.125 Le Rousseau, Julien. Progrès de la littérature dramatique. Paris, 1865.
41541.21 Kerardven, L. Guionrac'h. Chronique bretonne. Nantes, 1890.
41541.25 Gozlan, Léon. Oeuvres. Paris, 1846.
X Cg 41541.36 Cartier, J. Un intermediaire entre la France et l'Allemagne, G. de Nerval. Genève, 1904.

41542.1 - .4 Individual authors, etc. - 1800-1849 - Fiction - Gautier - Biography and criticism

41542.1 Pamphlet box. French literature. 19th century.
41542.2 Bibliothèque nationale, Paris. Théophile Gautier, 1811-72. Paris, 1961.
41542.3 Feydeau, Ernst. Théophile Gautier. Paris, 1874.
41542.4 Du Camp, Maxime. Théophile Gautier. Paris, 1890.
41542.4.3 Dillingham, L.B. The creative imagination of Théophile Gautier. Diss. Bryn Mawr, 1927?
41542.4.3.9 Bergerat, Émile. Théophile Gautier, peintre. Paris, 1877.
41542.4.4 Bergerat, Émile. Théophile Gautier. 2. éd. Paris, 1879.
41542.4.5 Bergerat, Émile. Théophile Gautier. Paris, 1879.
41542.4.6 Luitz, Friedrich. Die Asthetik von Théophile Gautier. Inaug. Diss. Freiburg, 1913.
41542.4.10 Patch, Helen E. The dramatic criticism of Théophile Gautier. Diss. Bryn Mawr, 1922.
Htn 41542.4.15* Lemerre, Alphonse. Le tombeau de Théophile Gautier. Paris, 1873.
41542.4.20 Velthius, H.E.A. Théophile Gautier; l'homme - l'artiste. Middelburg, 1924.
41542.4.25 Jasinski, René. Les années romantiques de Théophile Gautier. Paris, 1929.
41542.4.26 Jasinski, René. Les années romantiques de Théophile Gautier. Thèse. Paris, 1929.
41542.4.30 Palache, John. Gautier and the romantics. London, 1927.
41542.4.35 Payr, B. Théophile Gautier und E.T.A. Hoffmann. Berlin, 1932.
41542.4.40 Schulz, Agnes. Die Sprachkunst Théophile Gautiers. Inaug. Diss. Bochum-Langendreer, 1934.
41542.4.44 Tuin, H. van der. L'évolution psychologique, esthétique et littéraire de T. Gautier. Thèse. Amsterdam, 1933.
41542.4.45 Tuin, H. van der. L'évolution psychologique, esthétique et littéraire de T. Gautier. Amsterdam, 1933.
41542.4.50 Boschot, Adolphe. Théophile Gautier. Paris, 1933.
41542.4.55 Guillaumie-Reicher, G. Théophile Gautier et l'Espagne. Thèse. Ligugé, 1936.
41542.4.60 Weiss, Edith. Natur und Landschaft bei Théophile Gautier. Inaug. Diss. Würzburg, 1937.
41542.4.65 Marcel, H. Essai sur Théophile Gautier. Paris, 1903.
41542.4.70 Boucher, Henri. Iconographie générale de Théophile Gautier. Paris, 1912.
41542.4.80A Matoré, G. Le vocabulaire et la société sous Louis-Philippe. Genève, 1951.
41542.4.80B Matoré, G. Le vocabulaire et la société sous Louis-Philippe. Genève, 1951.
41542.4.80.10 Matoré, G. Le vocabulaire de la prose littéraire de 1833 à 1845. Thèse. Genève, 1951.
41542.4.85 Richardson, Joanna. Theóphile Gautier. London, 1958.
41542.4.90 Larguier, Léo. Théophile Gautier. Paris, 1948.
41542.4.95 Derosier, Marcel. Le souvenir de Théophile Gautier en Bigorre. Tarbes, 1963.
41542.4.100 Tarbes, France. Musée Massey. Exposition Théophile Gautier, 1811-1872. Tarbes, 1963.
41542.4.105 Delvaille, Bernard. Théophile Gautier. Paris, 1968.
41542.4.110 Smith, Albert Brewster. Ideal and reality in the fictional narratives of Théophile Gautier. Gainsville, 1969.
41542.4.115 Benesch, Rita. Le regard de Théophile Gautier. Thèse. Zurich, 1969.
41542.4.120 Rizza, Cecilia. Théophile Gautier, critico letterario. Torino, 1971.

41542.5 Individual authors, etc. - 1800-1849 - Fiction - Gautier - Collected and Selected works

41542.5 Gautier, Théophile. Works of Théophile Gautier. N.Y., 1900-03. 24v.
41542.5.2 Gautier, Théophile. Oeuvres. Paris, 1890. 3v.
41542.5.5 Gautier, Théophile. Lectures littéraires. Pages choisies des grands écrivains. Paris, 1895.
41542.5.7 Gautier, Théophile. Stories. N.Y., 1908.
41542.5.25 Gautier, Théophile. Théophile Gautier. N.Y., 1903.
41542.5.27 Gautier, Théophile. Théophile Gautier. N.Y., 1903.

41542.6 - .37 Individual authors, etc. - 1800-1849 - Fiction - Gautier - Individual works

41542.6 Gautier, Théophile. Le capitaine Fracasse. Paris, 1871. 2v.
41542.6.5 Gautier, Théophile. Le capitaine Fracasse. N.Y., 1864.
41542.7.5 Gautier, Théophile. Captain Fracasse. N.Y., 1902.
41542.7.8 Gautier, Théophile. Captain Fracasse. Boston, 1916.
41542.7.10 Gautier, Théophile. Le capitaine Fracasse. Paris, 1930. 2v.
41542.7.13 Gautier, Théophile. Le capitaine Fracasse. Lausanne, 1963.
41542.7.15 Gautier, Théophile. Le capitaine Fracasse. N.Y., 1930.
41542.7.65 Bruneau, Charles. Explication de Théophile Gautier: Emaux et camées. Paris, 1939.
41542.8 Gautier, Théophile. Émaux et camées. Paris, 1872.
41542.8.3 Gautier, Théophile. Émaux et camées. Paris, 1910.
41542.8.5 Gautier, Théophile. Émaux et camées. Paris, 1927.
Htn 41542.8.6* Gautier, Théophile. Émaux et camées. 2. éd. Paris, 1858.

41542.6 - .37 Individual authors, etc. - 1800-1849 - Fiction - Gautier - Individual works - cont.

X Cg 41542.8.7 Gautier, Théophile. Émaux et camées. Paris, 1894.
41542.8.10 Gautier, Théophile. Émaux et camées. Paris, 1895.
41542.8.25 Gautier, Théophile. Émaux et camées. Lille, 1947.
41542.9.4 Gautier, Théophile. Émaux et camées. Paris, 1929.
X Cg 41542.9.5 Gautier, Théophile. Fortunio. Paris, 1897.
41542.9.8 Gautier, Théophile. Fortunio et autres nouvelles...1833-1849. Paris, 1930.
41542.9.11 Gautier, Théophile. Les grotesques. Paris, 1859.
41542.10 Gautier, Théophile. Les grotesques. Paris, 1871.
41542.10.90 Gautier, Théophile. Mademoiselle de Maupin. Paris, 1873.
41542.11.3 Gautier, Théophile. Mademoiselle de Maupin. Paris, 1885.
41542.11.5 Gautier, Théophile. Mademoiselle de Maupin. Paris, 1892.
41542.11.6 Gautier, Théophile. Mademoiselle de Maupin. Paris, 19- ?
X Cg 41542.11.7 Gautier, Théophile. Mademoiselle de Maupin. Paris, 1907.
41542.11.8 Gautier, Théophile. Mademoiselle de Maupin. Philadelphia, 1897. 2v.
41542.11.12 Gautier, Théophile. Mademoiselle de Maupin. N.Y., 1918.
41542.11.13 Gautier, Théophile. Mademoiselle de Maupin. N.Y., 1918.
41542.11.15 Gautier, Théophile. Mademoiselle de Maupin. Paris, 1930.
41542.11.17 Gautier, Théophile. Mademoiselle de Maupin. Paris, 1905.
41542.11.50 Gautier, Théophile. Mademoiselle de Maupin. London, 1887.
41542.11.75 Gautier, Théophile. La préface de Mademoiselle de Maupin. Paris, 1946.
41542.12 Gautier, Théophile. Histoire du romantisme. Paris, 1874.
41542.13 Gautier, Theophile. Portraits et souvenirs. Paris, 1875.
41542.14 Gautier, Theophile. Portraits contemporains. Paris, 1874.
41542.14.2 Gautier, Théophile. Portraits contemporains. Paris, 1886.
41542.14.25 Gautier, Théophile. Souvenirs romantiques. Paris, 1929.
41542.15 Gautier, Théophile. Premières poésies. Paris, 1870.
41542.16 Gautier, Théophile. Souvenirs de théâtre. Paris, 1883.
41542.17 Gautier, Théophile. Voyage en Espagne. Paris, 1873.
41542.17.5 Gautier, Théophile. Voyage en Espagne. Paris, 1856.
41542.18.5A Gautier, Théophile. Voyage en Espagne. Paris, 1879.
41542.18.5B Gautier, Théophile. Voyage en Espagne. Paris, 1879.
41542.18.7 Gautier, Théophile. Voyage en Espagne. Paris, 1883.
NEDL 41542.18.15 Gautier, Théophile. L'España de T. Gautier. Thèse. Paris, 1929.
41542.19.5 Gautier, Théophile. Voyage en Russie. Paris, 1875.
41542.19.10 Gautier, Théophile. Voyage en Russie. Paris, 1961.
41542.20 Gautier, Théophile. Nouvelles. Paris, 1845.
41542.20.5 Gautier, Théophile. Nouvelles. 11. éd. Paris, 1874.
41542.20.10 Gautier, Théophile. Nouvelles. Paris, 1917.
41542.21 Gautier, Théophile. Spirite. Paris, 1877.
41542.21.5 Gautier, Théophile. Spirite. N.Y., 1877.
41542.21.10 Gautier, Théophile. Stronger than death, or Spirite. Chicago, 189-.
41542.22 Gautier, Théophile. Fusains et eaux-fortes. Paris, 1880.
41542.23 Gautier, Théophile. Loin de Paris. Paris, 1881.
41542.24 Gautier, Théophile. Théâtre, mystère, comédies et ballets. Paris, 1882.
41542.25 Gautier, Théophile. L'Orient. Paris, 1884. 2v.
41542.26 Gautier, Théophile. Caprices et zigzags. Paris, 1884.
41542.26.9 Gautier, Théophile. Les jeunes-France. Paris, 1873.
X Cg 41542.26.12 Gautier, Théophile. Les jeunes-France. Paris, 1881.
41542.28 Gautier, Théophile. Les vacances du Lundi. Paris, 1888.
41542.29.5 Gautier, Théophile. Un trio de romans. Paris, 1916.
41542.30 Gautier, Théophile. Partie carrée. Paris, 1889.
41542.30.85 Gautier, Théophile. Poésies complètes. Paris, 1882. 2v.
41542.30.90 Gautier, Théophile. Poésies complètes. Paris, 1884-85. 2v.
41542.31A Gautier, Théophile. Poésies complètes. Paris, 1889-90. 2v.
41542.31B Gautier, Théophile. Poésies complétes. v.2. v.1 lost 1947. Paris, 1889-90.
41542.31.2 Gautier, Théophile. Poésies complètes de Théophile Gautier. Paris, 1970. 3v.
41542.31.5 Gautier, Théophile. Poésies complètes de T. Gautier. v.1-3. Paris, 1932.
Htn 41542.31.10* Gautier, Théophile. Poésies de T. Gautier qui ne figureront pas dans ses oeuvres. n.p., 1873.
41542.31.25 Gautier, Théophile. Gentle enchanter. London, 1960.
41542.31.30 Gautier, Théophile. Les plus belles lettres de T. Gautier. Paris, 1962.
41542.32 Gautier, Théophile. La nature chez elle et ménagerie intime. Photoreproduction. Paris, 1891.
41542.33.10 Gautier, Théophile. Romans et contes. Paris, 1923.
41542.34 Gautier, Théophile. Voyage en Italie. Paris, 1892.
41542.34.10 Gautier, Théophile. Italia. 2. éd. Paris, 1855.
41542.35.5 Gautier, Théophile. Le roman de la momie. Paris, 190-.
41542.35.10 Gautier, Théophile. Le roman de la momie. Paris, 1927.
41542.35.15 Gautier, Théophile. Le roman de la momie. Paris, 1934.
41542.36 Gautier, Théophile. The romance of the mummy. N.Y., 1863.
X Cg 41542.37 Gautier, Théophile. Mademoiselle Dafué. Paris, n.d.
41542.37.2 Gautier, Théophile. La peau de Tigre. Paris, 1866.
41542.37.3 Gautier, Théophile. Théâtre de poche. Paris, 1855.
41542.37.4 Gautier, Théophile. Quand on voyage. Paris, 1865.
41542.37.5 Gautier, Théophile. La belle Jenny. Paris, 1868.
41542.37.7 Gautier, Théophile. My household of pets. Boston, 1882.
41542.37.8.5 Gautier, Théophile. One of Cleopatra's nights. N.Y., 1906.
41542.37.9 Gautier, Théophile. One of Cleopatra's nights. N.Y., 1910.
41542.37.11 Gautier, Théophile. One of Cleopatra's nights. N.Y., 1882.
41542.37.12 Gautier, Théophile. One of Cleopatra's nights. N.Y., 1927.
Htn 41542.37.13* Gautier, Théophile. Paul d'Aspremont. Paris, 1857.
Htn 41542.37.15* Gautier, Théophile. Un trio de Romans. Paris, 1852.
Htn 41542.37.18* Gautier, Théophile. La mille et deuxième nuit. Paris, 1898.

41542.38 - .79 Individual authors, etc. - 1800-1849 - Fiction - Gozlan - Writings

41542.38 Gozlan, Léon. Aristide Froissart. Paris, 1880.
41542.40 Gozlan, Léon. Balzac en Pantoufles. Paris, 1865.
41542.42 Gozlan, Léon. Comédie des comédiens. Paris, 1863.
41542.45 Gozlan, Léon. Les Méandres. Bruxelles, 1837. 2v.
41542.46F Gozlan, Léon. Louise de Nanteuil. Paris, 18- .
41542.48 Gozlan, Léon. Le notaire. Bruxelles, 1836. 2v.
41542.51 Gozlan, Léon. Un petit bout d'oreille; comédie. Paris, 1858.
41542.53 Gozlan, Léon. La pluie et le beau temps. Paris, 1875.
41542.54 Gozlan, Léon. La pluie et le beau temps. Paris, 1878.
41542.56 Gozlan, Léon. La pluie et le beau temps. Paris, 1880.

41542.80 Individual authors, etc. - 1800-1849 - Fiction - Gozlan - Works about

41542.80 Lader, M.K. The life and novels of Léon Gozlan. Philadelphia, 1943.
41542.80.6 Audebrand, Philibert. Léon Gozlan: scènes de la vie littéraire, 1828-1865. Genève, 1970.

41542.81 - Individual authors, etc. - 1800-1849 - Fiction - Miscellany, G

41542.81.30 Germaine. La petite fille de Robinson. Paris, 1848.
41542.83.30 Guérin, Eugène Louis. Le testament d'un gueux. v.1-2. Bruxelles, 1857.
41542.85.100 Guillot, Henry. Le cousin germain de Vadé. Paris, 1829.
41542.98.102 Guyot-Duvigneul, T. Etrennes aux B ... nois. 2. éd. Paris, 1811.

41543.1 - .5 Individual authors, etc. - 1800-1849 - Fiction - Gérard de Nerval - Complete works

41543.4 Nerval, Gerard de. Oeuvres complètes. Paris, 1868-73. 4v.
41543.4.5 Nerval, Gerard de. Oeuvres. Paris, 1952. 2v.
41543.4.7A Nerval, Gerard de. Oeuvres. Paris, 1958. 2v.
41543.4.7B Nerval, Gerard de. Oeuvres. v.2. Paris, 1958.
41543.4.8 Nerval, Gerard de. Oeuvres. Paris, 1958.
41543.4.9 Nerval, Gerard de. Oeuvres. 4. éd. Paris, 1966-
41543.4.25 Marie, Aristide. Bibliographie des oeuvres de Gerard de Nerval. Paris, 1926.
41543.4.27 Nerval, Gerard de. Petits chateaux de bohême. Paris, 1926.
41543.4.29 Goethe, J.W. von. Les deux Faust de Goethe. Paris, 1932.
41543.4.30 Nerval, Gerard de. La Pandora. Paris, 1925.
41543.4.32 Guillaume, Jean. Gérard de Nerval: Pandora. Namur, 1968.
41543.5.1 Audiat, Pierre. L'Aurelia de Gerard de Nerval. Paris, 1926.

41543.6 - .7 Individual authors, etc. - 1800-1849 - Fiction - Gérard de Nerval - Selected works

41543.6 Nerval, Gerard de. Poésie et théâtre. Paris, 1928.
41543.6.5 Nerval, Gerard de. Poésies. Paris, 1947.
41543.6.10 Nerval, Gerard de. Poésies. 2. éd. Mermod, 1947.
41543.6.20 Nerval, Gerard de. Les poètes du XVIe siècle. Cambridge, 1959.
41543.6.80A Richard, J.P. Poésie et profondeur. Paris, 1955.
41543.6.80B Richard, J.P. Poésie et profondeur. Paris, 1955.
41543.7.5 Nerval, Gerard de. Gerard de Nerval. 10e éd. Paris, 1931.
41543.7.10 Nerval, Gerard de. Selected writings. N.Y., 1957.
41543.7.11 Nerval, Gerard de. Selected writings. Ann Arbor, 1970.
41543.7.15 Nerval, Gerard. Oeuvres complémentaires. Paris, 1959- 4v.
41543.7.20 Nerval, Gerard de. Oeuvres. v.2. v.1 lost. Paris, 1960.

41543.8 - .18 Individual authors, etc. - 1800-1849 - Fiction - Gérard de Nerval - Individual works

41543.8 Nerval, Gerard de. La bohème galante. Paris, 1866.
41543.8.10 Nerval, Gerard de. La bohème galante. Paris, 1921.
41543.8.12 Nerval, Gerard de. La bohème galante. Paris, 1931.
41543.8.15 Nerval, Gerard de. La bohème galante. Paris, 1954.
41543.9 Nerval, Gerard de. Contes et facéties. Paris, 1852.
41543.10 Nerval, Gerard de. De Paris à Cythère. Paris, 1920.
41543.10.10 Nerval, Gerard de. La sonate du diable. Paris, 1927.
41543.10.20 Nerval, Gerard de. Le cabaret de la mère Saguet. Paris, 1927.
41543.10.30 Nerval, Gerard de. Lorely. Paris, 1929.
41543.10.40 Nerval, Gerard de. Le marquis de Fayolle. Paris, 1930.
Htn 41543.11* Nerval, Gerard de. Sylvie: Souvenirs du Valois. Portland, 1896.
41543.11.7 Nerval, Gerard de. Sylvie, souvenirs du Valois. Paris, 1946.
41543.11.9 Nerval, Gerard de. Sylvie. Montréal, 1946.
41543.11.12 Nerval, Gerard de. Sylvie. Monaco, 1946.
41543.11.15 Nerval, Gerard de. Sylvie. Paris, 1947.
41543.12 Nerval, Gerard de. Voyage en Orient. Paris, 1875. 2v.
41543.12.3 Nerval, Gerard de. Voyage en Orient. Paris, 1927-30. 3v.
41543.12.5 Nerval, Gerard de. Voyage en Orient. v.1-4. Paris, 1950. 2v.
41543.12.6 Nerval, Gerard de. Voyage en Orient. Paris, 1964.
41543.12.10 Nerval, Gerard de. Aurélia. Paris, 1927.
41543.12.12 Nerval, Gerard de. Aurélia, ou Le rêve et la vie. Paris, 1930.
41543.12.13 Nerval, Gerard de. Aurélia. Paris, 1965.
41543.12.15 Nerval, Gerard de. Nouvelles et fantaisies. Paris, 1928.
41543.13 Nerval, Gerard de. Jemmy. London, 1925.
41543.14.5A Nerval, Gerard de. Les chimères. Bruxelles, 1966.
41543.14.5B Nerval, Gerard de. Les chimères. Bruxelles, 1966.
41543.15 Nerval, Gerard de. Les illuminés. Paris, 1929.
41543.15.5 Nerval, Gerard de. Les illuminés. Paris, 1929.
41543.15.10 Nerval, Gerard de. L'Academie ou Les membres introuvables. Cambridge, 1961.
41543.16 Nerval, Gerard de. Correspondance (1830-1855). Paris, 1911.
41543.17 Nerval, Gerard de. Les filles du feu. Paris, 1931. 2v.
41543.17.2 Nerval, Gerard de. Les filles du feu. Le rêve et la vie. Paris, 1931.
41543.17.3 Nerval, Gerard de. Les filles du feu. Paris, 1957.
41543.17.4 Nerval, Gerard de. Les filles du feu. Paris, 1928.
41543.17.25 Nerval, Gerard de. Daughters of fire. N.Y., 1922.
41543.18 Nerval, Gerard de. Fortune's fool. London, 1959.
41543.18.20 Guillaume, Jean. Gérard de Nerval: Pandora. Namur, 1968.

41543.19 - .22 Individual authors, etc. - 1800-1849 - Fiction - Gérard de Nerval - Biography and criticism

41543.19 Delvan, A. Gerard de Nerval. Paris, 1865.
41543.20 Audiat, Pierre. L'Aurélia de Gerard de Nerval. Thèse. Paris, 1925.
41543.21 Ferrières, G. Gerard de Nerval, la vie et l'oeuvre, 1808-1855. Paris, 1906.
41543.21.80 Bibliothèque nationale, Paris. Gerard de Nerval. Paris, 1955.
41543.22 Marie, Aristide. Gerard de Nerval, le poète, l'homme. Paris, 1914.
41543.22.5 Bizet, René. La double vie de Gerard de Nerval. Paris, 1928.
41543.22.10 Boulenger, Jacques. Au pays de Gerard de Nerval. Paris, 1914.

41543.19 - .22 Individual authors, etc. - 1800-1849 - Fiction - Gérard de Nerval - Biography and criticism - cont.

41543.22.15 Clouard, Henri. La destinée tragique de Gerard de Nerval. Paris, 1929.
41543.22.20 Beguin, Albert. Gerard de Nerval. Paris, 1936.
41543.22.23A Beguin, Albert. Gerard de Nerval. Paris, 1945.
41543.22.23B Beguin, Albert. Gerard de Nerval. Paris, 1945.
41543.22.25 Haedens, Kleber. Gerard de Nerval; ou La sagesse romantique. Paris, 1939.
41543.22.30 Nerval, Gerard de. Lettres d'amour à Jenny Colon. Bruxelles, 1943.
41543.22.35 Richer, Jean. Gerard de Nerval et les doctrines ésotériques. Paris, 1947.
41543.22.40 Sebillotte, L. Le secret de Gerard de Nerval. Paris, 1948.
41543.22.43A Ducray, C. Gerard de Nerval. Paris, 1946.
41543.22.43B Ducray, C. Gerard de Nerval. Paris, 1946.
41543.22.45 Rhodes, Solomon. Gerard de Nerval. N.Y., 1951.
41543.22.47 Rhodes, Solomon. Gerard de Nerval, 1808-1855. London, 1952.
41543.22.50 Borgal, C. De quoi vivait Gerard de Nerval. Paris, 1950.
41543.22.51 Cellier, Léon. Gerard de Nerval. Paris, 1956.
41543.22.52 Cellier, Léon. Gerard de Nerval. Paris, 1963.
41543.22.55 Dédéyan, Charles. Gerard de Nerval et l'Allemagne. Paris, 1957. 3v.
41543.22.60 Durry, M.J. Gerard de Nerval et le mythe. Paris, 1956.
41543.22.65 Aunos y Pérez, Eduardo. Gerard de Nerval et ses énigmes. Paris, 1956.
41543.22.70 Gaulmier, Jean. Gerard de Nerval et Les filles du feu. Paris, 1956.
41543.22.75 Sénelier, Jean. Gerard de Nerval. Paris, 1959.
41543.22.75.5 Sénelier, Jean. Bibliographie nervalienne, 1960-67, et compléments antérieurs. Paris, 1968.
41543.22.78 Sénelier, Jean. Un amour inconnu de Gerard de Nerval, avec des documents et des estampes inédits. Paris, 1966.
41543.22.80 Marill, René. Gerard de Nerval. Paris, 1955.
41543.22.85 La Tour Saint-Jacques. Gerard de Nerval. Paris, 1958.
41543.22.90 Vivier, M. Gerard de Nerval. Paris, 1963.
41543.22.100 Richer, Jean. Nerval. Paris, 1963.
41543.22.102 Richer, Jean. Nerval, expérience et création. 2e éd. Paris, 1970.
41543.22.105 Nerval, Gerard de. Nerval, par lui-même. Paris, 1964.
41543.22.110 Dubruck, Alfred. Gerard de Nerval and the German heritage. The Hague, 1965.
41543.22.115 Peyrouzet, Edouard. Gerard de Nerval inconnu. Paris, 1965.
41543.22.120 Krüger, Manfred. Gerard de Nerval. Stuttgart, 1966.
41543.22.125 Dédéyan, Christian. Nerval, pèlerin de la nuit, essai. Avignon, 1966.
41543.22.130 Moreau, Pierre. Sylvie et ses soeurs nervaliennes. Paris, 1966.
41543.22.135 Carofiglio, Vito. Nerval e il mito della Puretè. 1. ed. Firenze, 1966.
41543.22.140 Schaeffer, Gérald. Le Voyage en Orient de Nerval. Neuchâtel, 1967.
41543.22.145 Villas, James. Gerard de Nerval; a critical bibliography, 1900 to 1967. Columbia, Mo., 1968.
41543.22.150 Chambers, Ross. Gerard de Nerval et la poétique du voyage. Paris, 1969.
41543.22.155 Girolamo, Nicola di. Miti e simboli napoletani nell'opera di Nerval. Bologna, 1964.
41543.22.160 Schaerer, Kurt. Thematique de Gerard de Nerval. Paris, 1968.
41543.22.165 Messiaen, Pierre. Gerard de Nerval. Paris? 1945.
41543.22.170 Benichou, Paul. Nerval et la chanson folklorique. Paris, 1970.
41543.22.175 Stierle, Karlheinz. Dunkelheit und Form in Gerard de Nervals "Chimères". München, 1967.
41543.22.180 Humphrey, George René. L'esthétique de la poésie de Gerard de Nerval. Paris, 1969.
41543.22.185 Girolamo, Nicola di. Nerval e la tematica delle Figlie del fuoco. Bologna, 1970.
41543.23 Pamphlet box. Gerard de Nerval.

41543.27 - .33 Individual authors, etc. - 1800-1849 - Fiction - Guiraud - Writings

41543.27 Guiraud, Alexandre. Oeuvres. v.1-2,3. Paris, 1845. 2v.
41543.27.10 Guiraud, Alexandre. Flavien ou De Rome au désert. Paris, 1835. 3v.
41543.29 Guiraud, Alexandre. Poëmes et chants elegiaques. Paris, 1824.
41543.30 Guiraud, Alexandre. Virginie. Paris, 1827.
41543.32 Guiraud, Alexandre. Pélage. Paris, 1938.

41543.35 - .38 Individual authors, etc. - 1800-1849 - Fiction - Grandville - Writings

41543.35 Grandville, J.I.I.G. Un autre monde. Paris, n.d.
41543.35.25 Grandville, J.I.I.G. Bilder aus dem Staats- und Familienleben der Thiere. Leipzig, 1846. 2v.
41543.35.30 Grandville, J.I.I.G. Aus einer anderen Welt. Dresden, 1961.
41543.36.5 Cleaveland, Nehemiah. The flowers personified. N.Y., 1847.
41543.36.6 Delord, Taxile. The flowers personified. N.Y., 1849.
41543.37 Grandville, J.I.I.G. Les metamorphoses du jour par Grandville. Paris, 1869.

41544 - 41545.79 Individual authors, etc. - 1800-1849 - Fiction - Karr, Alphonse - Writings

41544.2 Karr, Alphonse. Agathe et Cécile. Clovis Gosselin. Paris, 1867.
41544.3 Karr, Alphonse. Les cailloux blancs du Petit Poucet. Paris, 1881.
41544.4 Karr, Alphonse. Contes et nouvelles. Paris, 1869.
41544.6 Karr, Alphonse. La famille Alain. Paris, 1866.
41544.6.3 Karr, Alphonse. La famille Alain. Paris, 1861.
41544.6.9 Karr, Alphonse. Les femmes. Paris, 1857.
41544.6.10 Karr, Alphonse. Encore les femmes. 2. éd. Paris, 1888.
41544.7 Karr, Alphonse. Les femmes. Encore les femmes. Paris, 1871.
41544.7.5 Karr, Alphonse. Les femmes. Paris, 1853.
41544.7.9 Karr, Alphonse. Las mujeres. Madrid, 1864.
41544.8 Karr, Alphonse. Feu Bressier. Menus propos. Paris, 1872.
41544.11 Karr, Alphonse. Les guêpes. Paris, 1867-69. 6v.
41544.11.5 Karr, Alphonse. Les guêpes. Paris, 1858. 3v.
41544.12 Karr, Alphonse. Une heure trop tard. Paris, 1871.

41544 - 41545.79 Individual authors, etc. - 1800-1849 - Fiction - Karr, Alphonse - Writings - cont.

41544.13 Karr, Alphonse. Histoire de Rose et de Jean Duchemin-Clotilde. Paris, 1869.
41544.14 Karr, Alphonse. Notes de voyage d'un casanier. Paris, 1877.
41544.15 Karr, Alphonse. Midi à quatorze heures. Paris, 1865.
41544.16 Karr, Alphonse. La pêche. Les fleurs. Paris, 1860.
41544.17 Karr, Alphonse. La pénélope normande. Les Soirées de Sainte-Adresse. Paris, 1866.
41544.18 Karr, Alphonse. Une poignée de vérités. Raoul. Paris, 1871.
41544.19 Karr, Alphonse. Promenades hors de mon jardin. Sous les orangers. Paris, 1872.
41544.19.2 Karr, Alphonse. Promenades hors de mon jardin. Sous les orangers. Paris, 1862.
41544.20 Karr, Alphonse. Roses noires et roses bleues. Paris, 1859.
41544.24 Karr, Alphonse. De loin et de près. Paris, 1862.
41544.25 Karr, Alphonse. Les dents du dragon. Paris, 1869.
41544.26 Karr, Alphonse. En fumant. Paris, 1862.
41544.27 Karr, Alphonse. Les gaietés romaines. Paris, 1870.
41544.28 Karr, Alphonse. Lettres écrites de mon jardin. Paris, 1853.
41544.29 Karr, Alphonse. La maison close. Paris, 1870.
41544.31 Karr, Alphonse. La queue d'or. Paris, 1871.
41544.32 Karr, Alphonse. Sur la plage. Paris, 1865.
41544.34 Karr, Alphonse. Voyage autour de mon jardin. Paris, n.d.
41544.34.5 Karr, Alphonse. Voyage autour de mon jardin. Paris, 1857.
41544.35 Karr, Alphonse. Voyage autour de mon jardin. Paris, 1876.
41544.36 Karr, Alphonse. A tour round my garden. London, 1855.
41545.5 Karr, Alphonse. Le chemin le plus court. Bruxelles, 1836. 2v.
41545.10 Karr, Alphonse. Geneviève. Paris, 1857.
41545.12 Karr, Alphonse. Hortense. Feu Bressier. Paris, 1857.
41545.13 Karr, Alphonse. Histoire invraisemblable. v.2. Bruxelles, 1844.
41545.14 Karr, Alphonse. Histoires normandes. Paris, 1855.
41545.20 Karr, Alphonse. Sous les Tilleuls. Paris, 1832. 2v.

41545.80 - Individual authors, etc. - 1800-1849 - Fiction - Karr, Alphonse - Works about

41545.80 Scales, Derek P. Alphonse Karr. Genève, 1959.

41547.1 - .14 Individual authors, etc. - 1800-1849 - Fiction - Pigault-Lebrun - Writings

41547.5 Pigault-Lebrun, C.A.G.R. de. Oeuvres complètes. Paris, 1822-29. 21v.
41547.6 Pigault-Lebrun, C.A.G.R. de. Adelaide de Meran. Paris, 1815. 4v.
41547.7 Pigault-Lebrun, C.A.G.R. de. Les barons de Felsheim. Pts. 1,3,4. Paris, 1802.
41547.8 Pigault-Lebrun, C.A.G.R. de. Le citateur. Pt.1-2. Paris, 1803.
41547.8.2 Pigault-Lebrun, C.A.G.R. de. Le citateur. Hamborg, 1803. 2v.
41547.8.25 Pigault-Lebrun, C.A.G.R. de. O citader. Paris, 1834. 2v.
41547.9 Pigault-Lebrun, C.A.G.R. de. Jérôme. Paris, 1812. 4v.
41547.10 Pigault-Lebrun, C.A.G.R. de. Le mouchard. Paris, 1875.
41547.11 Pigault-Lebrun, C.A.G.R. de. La folie espagnole. Paris, 1801. 4v.
41547.11.5 Pigault-Lebrun, C.A.G.R. de. La folie espagnole. Paris, 1891.
41547.12 Pigault-Lebrun, C.A.G.R. de. Une macédoine. Paris, 1811. 4v.
41547.13.5 Pigault-Lebrun, C.A.G.R. de. Les dragons et les bénédictines. Paris, 1794.
41547.13.7 Pigault-Lebrun, C.A.G.R. de. Les dragons et les bénédictines. Paris, 1794.
41547.13.15 Pigault-Lebrun, C.A.G.R. de. Les dragons en cantonnement. Paris, 1830.
41547.13.17 Pigault-Lebrun, C.A.G.R. de. Les dragons en cantonnement. Paris, 1830.
41547.13.20 Pigault-Lebrun, C.A.G.R. de. Les moeurs, ou Le divorce. Paris, 1795.
41547.13.25 Pigault-Lebrun, C.A.G.R. de. Les empiriques. Paris, 1795.
41547.13.30 Pigault-Lebrun, C.A.G.R. de. L'orphelin. Paris, 1794.
41547.13.40 Pigault-Lebrun, C.A.G.R. de. Les sabotiers. Paris, 1796.
41547.13.45 Pigault-Lebrun, C.A.G.R. de. My uncle Thomas. London, 1801. 4v.
41547.13.50 Pigault-Lebrun, C.A.G.R. de. Le cordonnier de Damas. Paris, 1798.

41547.17 - .19 Individual authors, etc. - 1800-1849 - Fiction - Privat d'Anglemont - Writings

41547.17 Privat d'Anglemont, A. Paris inconnu. Paris, 1875.
41547.19 Privat d'Anglemont, A. Paris anecdote. Paris, 1854.
41547.19.2 Privat d'Anglemont, A. Paris anecdote. Paris, 1860.

41548.10 Individual authors, etc. - 1800-1849 - Fiction - Kérardven

41548.10 Kérardven, L. Guionvach. Études sur la Bretagne. 2e éd. Paris, 1835.

41548.25 Individual authors, etc. - 1800-1849 - Fiction - Kératry

41548.25 Kératry, A.H. de. La baronne de Kerléya. v.1-2. Bruxelles, 1843.

41548.50 Individual authors, etc. - 1800-1849 - Fiction - Kermel

41548.50 Kermel, A. Une ame en peine. Paris, 1834.

41551 Individual authors, etc. - 1800-1849 - Fiction - Folios [Discontinued]

41551.3 Kock, Paul de. L'enfant de ma femme. Paris, n.d.
41551.4 Kock, Paul de. Les femmes, le jeu, le vin. Paris, n.d.
41551.5 Kock, Paul de. Mon ami Piffard. Paris, n.d.
41551.6 Kock, Paul de. Une fête aux environs de Paris. Paris, n.d.
41551.7 Lacroix, Paul. Contes du bibliophile Jacob. Paris, 1880.
41551.10 Lacroix, Paul. Romans relatifs à l'histoire de France. Paris, 1838.
41551.11 Lacroix, Paul. Les deux fous. Paris, 1845.
41551.15 Nodier, Charles. Le génie bonhomme. Paris, 1873.
41551.25 Wiese, Oskar. Kritische Beiträge zur Geschichte der Jugend und Jugendwerke. Olenburg, 1904.

41552 - 41553.99 Individual authors, etc. - 1800-1849 - Fiction - Kock, C.P. de - Writings

41552.4 Kock, Charles Paul de. L'amant de la lune. Paris, n.d. 3v.
41552.5 Kock, Charles Paul de. L'amoureux transi. Paris, n.d.
41552.6 Kock, Charles Paul de. André le Savoyard. Paris, 1869.
41552.7 Kock, Charles Paul de. L'ane à M. Martin. Paris, 1872.
41552.8.15 Kock, Charles Paul de. La baronne Blaguiskof. Paris, 1866.
41552.9 Kock, Charles Paul de. Un bon enfant. Paris, 1873.
41552.10 Kock, Charles Paul de. La bouqutière du chateau d'eau. Paris, n.d. 2v.
41552.11 Kock, Charles Paul de. Carotin. Paris, n.d.
41552.12 Kock, Charles Paul de. Ce monsieur. Paris, n.d.
41552.13 Kock, Charles Paul de. Cerisette. Paris, n.d.
41552.14 Kock, Charles Paul de. La demoiselle du cinquième. Paris, 1873.
41552.15 Kock, Charles Paul de. Les demoiselles de magasin. Paris, n.d.
41552.16 Kock, Charles Paul de. Une drôle de maison. Paris, n.d.
41552.17 Kock, Charles Paul de. Les étuvistes. Paris, n.d.
41552.19 Kock, Charles Paul de. La femme à trois visages. Paris, n.d.
41552.20 Kock, Charles Paul de. Les femmes, le jeu et le vin. Paris, n.d.
41552.21 Kock, Charles Paul de. La fille aux trois jupons. Paris, n.d.
41552.22 Kock, Charles Paul de. Friquette. Paris, n.d.
41552.23 Kock, Charles Paul de. Une gaillarde. Paris, n.d.
41552.24 Kock, Charles Paul de. La grande ville. Paris, n.d.
41552.25 Kock, Charles Paul de. Une grappe de groseille. Paris, n.d.
41552.26 Kock, Charles Paul de. Un homme à marier. Paris, 1843.
41552.27 Kock, Charles Paul de. L'homme de la nature. Paris, 1866.
41552.28 Kock, Charles Paul de. L'homme aux trois culottes. Paris, 1877.
41552.29 Kock, Charles Paul de. Les intrigants. Paris, n.d. 2v.
41553.4 Kock, Charles Paul de. Un jeune homme charmant. Paris, 1870.
41553.5 Kock, Charles Paul de. Un jeune homme mystérieux. Paris, n.d.
41553.6 Kock, Charles Paul de. La jolie fille du faubourg. Paris, n.d.
41553.7 Kock, Charles Paul de. La laitière de Montfermeil. Paris, 1870.
41553.8 Kock, Charles Paul de. Madame de Montflanquin. Paris, n.d.
41553.9 Kock, Charles Paul de. Madame Pantalon. Paris, n.d.
41553.10 Kock, Charles Paul de. Madame Papin. Paris, n.d.
41553.11 Kock, Charles Paul de. Madeleine. Paris, 1869.
41553.12 Kock, Charles Paul de. La maison blanche. Paris, 1870.
41553.13 Kock, Charles Paul de. Un mari perdu. Paris, 1869.
41553.14 Kock, Charles Paul de. La mariée de Fontenay-aux-Roses. Paris, n.d.
41553.15 Kock, Charles Paul de. Mon ami Piffard. Paris, n.d.
41553.17 Kock, Charles Paul de. Monsieur Choublanc. Paris, n.d.
41553.18 Kock, Charles Paul de. Moustache. Paris, 1868.
41553.19 Kock, Charles Paul de. Papa beau-père. Paris, n.d.
41553.20 Kock, Charles Paul de. Le petit bonhomme du coin. Paris, 1874.
41553.21 Kock, Charles Paul de. La petite Lise. Paris, n.d.
41553.22 Kock, Charles Paul de. Les petits ruisseaux. Paris, n.d.
41553.23 Kock, Charles Paul de. La prairie aux coquelicots. Paris, n.d.
41553.24 Kock, Charles Paul de. Le professeur Ficheclaque. Paris, n.d.
41553.25 Kock, Charles Paul de. Sans cravate. Paris, n.d.
41553.26 Kock, Charles Paul de. Le sentier aux prunes. Paris, n.d.
41553.27 Kock, Charles Paul de. Un tourlonrou. Paris, 1866.
41553.29 Kock, Charles Paul de. Zizine. Paris, 1864.
41553.30 Kock, Charles Paul de. Gustave ou le mauvais sujet. Paris, 1842.
41553.30.25 Kock, Charles Paul de. Gustave. Boston, 1904.
41553.32 Kock, Charles Paul de. La jolie fille du faubourg. Bruxelles, 1840.
41553.33 Kock, Charles Paul de. Le sentier aux prunes. Paris, 1865.
41553.33.5 Kock, Charles Paul de. Soeur Anne. Paris, 1842.
41553.33.7 Kock, Charles Paul de. Sister Anne. Boston, 1902.
41553.33.8 Kock, Charles Paul de. Sister Anne. Boston, 1902. 2v.
41553.34 Kock, Charles Paul de. Andrew the Savoyard. Philadelphia, 1836. 2v.
41553.34.5 Kock, Charles Paul de. André the Savoyard. N.Y., 1904.
41553.35 Kock, Charles Paul de. Madame Saint Lambert. Paris, n.d.
41553.38 Kock, Charles Paul de. Le barbier de Paris. Paris, 188-.
41553.38.1 Kock, Charles Paul de. Le barbier de Paris. Paris, 1873.
41553.38.5 Kock, Charles Paul de. The barber of Paris. v.1-2. Boston, 1903.
41553.40 Kock, Charles Paul de. Un bon enfant. Paris, 188-.
41553.42 Kock, Charles Paul de. Le concierge de la rue de Bac. Paris, 188-.
41553.46 Kock, Charles Paul de. La femme, le mari et l'amant. Paris, 188-.
41553.48 Kock, Charles Paul de. Les femmes de jeu et le vin. Paris, 188-.
41553.50 Kock, Charles Paul de. Frère Jacques. Paris, 188-.
41553.52 Kock, Charles Paul de. Georgette. Paris, 188-.
41553.54 Kock, Charles Paul de. Un jeune homme mystérieux. Paris, 188-.
41553.56 Kock, Charles Paul de. Un mari perdu, l'homme à marier. Paris, 188-.
41553.58 Kock, Charles Paul de. Mon voisin Raymond. Paris, 188-.
41553.60 Kock, Charles Paul de. Monsieur Dupont. Paris, 188-.
41553.62 Kock, Charles Paul de. La pucelle de Belleville. Paris, 188-.
41553.65 Kock, Charles Paul de. The child of my wife. Boston, 1903.
41553.68 Kock, Charles Paul de. Mémoires. Paris, 1873.
41553.70 Kock, Charles Paul de. La demoiselle du cinquième. Paris, 1909.

41553.100 - Individual authors, etc. - 1800-1849 - Fiction - Kock, C.P. de - Works about

41553.100 Trimm, T. La vie de Charles Paul de Kock. Paris, 1873.
41553.110 Clement, J. Charles Paul de Kock and the Bourgeoisie of Paris,. n.p., 19- ?
41553.115 Beyer, Friedrich. Der Romanschriftsteller Charles Paul de Kock und seine Welt. Inaug. Diss. Barmen, 1928.

41554.3 Individual authors, etc. - 1800-1849 - Fiction - Labutte

41554.3 Labutte, Augustine. Chronique du jour des morts. Paris, 1833.

41554.5 - .11 Individual authors, etc. - 1800-1849 - Fiction - Lacroix, Jules - Writings

41554.5 Lacroix, Jules. Oeuvres. Théâtre. Paris, 1874. 3v.
41554.9 Lacroix, Jules. La justice des hommes. Bruxelles, 1837.
41554.11 Lacroix, Jules. Le testament de César. Paris, 1849.

41554.12 - .28 Individual authors, etc. - 1800-1849 - Fiction - Lacroix, Paul - Writings

41554.12 Lacroix, Paul. Le bon vieux temps. n.p., n.d.
41554.13 Lacroix, Paul. Les catacombes de Rome. v.1-2. Bruxelles, 1845.
41554.15 Lacroix, Paul. La danse maccabre. Bruxelles, 1832.
41554.15.10 Lacroix, Paul. My republic. Chicago, 1936.
41554.22 Lacroix, Paul. Pignerol. Bruxelles, 1836. 2v.
41554.24 Lacroix, Paul. De près et de loin. Bruxelles, 1857. 2v.

41554.34 Individual authors, etc. - 1800-1849 - Fiction - Lacroix, Appoline

41554.34 Lacroix, Appoline. Falcone. Bruxelles, 1856.

41554.35 Individual authors, etc. - 1800-1849 - Fiction - Lambert de Saumery

41554.35.105 Lambert de Saumery, P. The Devil turn'd hermit, or The adventures of Astaroth banish'd hell. London, 1741.

41554.36 Individual authors, etc. - 1800-1849 - Fiction - Lanjiunais, S.J.

41554.36 Lanjiunais, J.D. Oeuvres, avec une notice biographique. Paris, 1832. 4v.
41554.36.50 Lanjiunais, Victor. Notice historique sur la vie et les ouvrages du Comte Lanjiunais. 2. éd. Paris, 1855.

41554.37 Individual authors, etc. - 1800-1849 - Fiction - Lassailly

41554.37 Lassailly, Charles. Les roueries de Trialph. Paris, 1833.
41554.37.80 Kaye, Eldon. Charles Lassailly, 1806-1843. Genève, 1962.

41554.38 Individual authors, etc. - 1800-1849 - Fiction - Lebras

41554.38 Lebras, Auguste. Les Armoricaines. Paris, 1830.

41554.39 Individual authors, etc. - 1800-1849 - Fiction - Lebrun

Htn 41554.39* Le Brun, P. The history of Tekeli. Albany, 1815.

41554.41 Individual authors, etc. - 1800-1849 - Fiction - Lourdoueix

41554.41.50 Lourdoueix, H. Les seductions politiques. Paris, 1822.

41554.45 Individual authors, etc. - 1800-1849 - Fiction - Manceau

41554.45 Manceau, A.V.A. (Mme.). Céline. Paris, n.d.

41554.50 Individual authors, etc. - 1800-1849 - Fiction - Maydieu

41554.50 Maydieu, Jean. Histoire de la vertueuse portugaise. Besançon, 1824.

41554.54 Individual authors, etc. - 1800-1849 - Fiction - Mercey

41554.54 Mercey, Frédéric. Tiel, le rodeur; romans et tableaux de genre. Paris, 1834. 2v.

41554.58 Individual authors, etc. - 1800-1849 - Fiction - Laponneraye

41554.58 Laponneraye, A. Stéphanowa; histoire russe. Paris, 1840.

41555.01 - .099 Individual authors, etc. - 1800-1849 - Fiction - Mérimée - Pamphlet volumes

41555.01 Pamphelt box. Mérimée, Prosper. Miscellaneous pamphlets.

41555.1 Individual authors, etc. - 1800-1849 - Fiction - Mérimée - Complete works

41555.1 Mérimée, Prosper. Premiers essais (1823-1824) théâtre de Clara Gazul (1825-1830). Paris, 1927.
41555.1.3 Mérimée, Prosper. Carmen, Arsène Guillot, L'abbé Aubain. Paris, 1927.
41555.1.5 Mérimée, Prosper. Dernières nouvelles. Paris, 1929.
41555.1.7 Mérimée, Prosper. Portraits historiques et littéraires. Paris, 1928.
41555.1.10 Mérimée, Prosper. Lettres à Francisque Michel (1848-1870). Journal de Prosper Mérimée (1860-1868). Paris, 1930.
41555.1.12 Mérimée, Prosper. Lettres a Viollet-le-duc (documents inédits), 1839-1870. Paris, 1927.
41555.1.14 Mérimée, Prosper. Études anglo-américaines. Paris, 1930.
41555.1.16 Mérimée, Prosper. Études de littérature russe. Paris, 1931-32. 2v.
41555.1.18 Mérimée, Prosper. La Jaquerie suivie de La famille de Carvajal. Paris, 1931.
41555.1.25 Mérimée, Prosper. Oeuvres en trois volumes. Paris, 1927. 3v.

41555.2 - .19 Individual authors, etc. - 1800-1849 - Fiction - Mérimée - Selected works, Letters

41555.2 Mérimée, Prosper. Ausgewählte Novellen. Leipzig, 1906.
41555.2.10 Mérimée, Prosper. Contes et nouvelles. Oxford, 1907.
41555.2.15 Mérimée, Prosper. Romans et nouvelles. Paris, 1957.
41555.2.18 Mérimée, Prosper. Romans et nouvelles. Paris, 1967. 2v.
41555.3 Mérimée, Prosper. Les deux héritages. Paris, 1867.
41555.4 Mérimée, Prosper. Lettres à une autre inconnue. Paris, 1875.
Htn 41555.5.5* Mérimée, Prosper. Lettres à une inconnue. Paris, 1874. 2v.
41555.6 Mérimée, Prosper. Lettres à une inconnue. 9. éd. Paris, 1874. 2v.
41555.6.2 Mérimée, Prosper. Lettres à une inconnue. 10. éd. Paris, 1876. 2v.
41555.6.15 Mérimée, Prosper. Lettres à une inconnue. Paris, 1899. 2v.
41555.7A Mérimée, Prosper. Letters to an incognita. N.Y., 1874.
41555.7B Mérimée, Prosper. Letters to an incognita. N.Y., 1874.

41555.2 - .19 Individual authors, etc. - 1800-1849 - Fiction - Mérimée - Selected works, Letters - cont.

41555.7.5 Mérimée, Prosper. Prosper Mérimée's letters to an incognita. N.Y., 1875.
41555.7.10 Mérimée, Prosper. Letters to an incognita. N.Y., 1889.
41555.7.40 Mérimée, Prosper. Correspondance générale. Paris, 1941. 17v.
41555.7.50 Mérimée, Prosper. Lettres de Prosper Mérimée à la comtesse de Montijó. Paris, 1930. 2v.
41555.7.60 Mérimée, Prosper. Lettres de Mérimée à la famille Delessert publiées. Paris, 1931.
41555.7.70 Mérimée, Prosper. Lettres à M. Panizzi, 1850-1870. 5. éd. Paris, 1881. 2v.
41555.7.72 Mérimée, Prosper. Lettres à M. Panizzi, 1850-1870. 5. éd. Paris, 1881. 2v.
41555.7.74 Mérimée, Prosper. Lettres à M. Panizzi, 1850-1870. 2. éd. Paris, 1881. 2v.
41555.7.78 Mérimée, Prosper. Letters of Prosper Mérimée to Panizzi. London, 1881. 2v.
41555.7.80 Mérimée, Prosper. Lettres à Edward Ellice, 1857-1863. Paris, 1963.
41555.7.90 Mérimée, Prosper. Lettere di Prospero Mérimée ad Antonio Panizzi. Bolongna, 1881. 2v.
41555.7.110 Mérimée, Prosper. Lettres de Mérimée à Ludovic Vitet. Paris, 1934.
41555.7.120 Mérimée, Prosper. Lettres de Prosper Mérimée à la comtesse de Boigne. Paris, 1933.
41555.7.130 Mérimée, Prosper. Lettres de Prosper Mérimée à madame de Beaulaincourt, 1866-1870. Paris, 1936.
41555.7.140 Mérimée, Prosper. Lettres aux antiquaires de l'Ouest, 1836-1869. Poitiers, 1937.
41555.7.150 Mérimée, Prosper. Merime v pis'makh k Dubenskoi. Moskva, 1937.
41555.7.160 Mérimée, Prosper. Lettres à Fanny Lagden. Paris, 1938.
41555.7.180 Mérimée, Prosper. Lettres à la duchesse de Castiglione-Colonna. Paris, 1938.
41555.7.190 Mérimée, Prosper. Une amitié littéraire. Paris, 1952.
41555.8 Mérimée, Prosper. Mélanges historiques et littéraires. Paris, 1868.
41555.9 Mérimée, Prosper. Nouvelles. Paris, 1872.
41555.9.20 Mérimée, Prosper. Romans et nouvelles. Paris, 1934.
41555.10 Mérimée, Prosper. Derniers nouvelles. 7. éd. Paris, 1874.
41555.10.5 Mérimée, Prosper. Derniers nouvelles. 6. éd. Paris, 1874.
41555.12 Mérimée, Prosper. Portraits historiques et littéraires. Paris, 1874.
41555.12.5 Mérimée, Prosper. La guzla, ou choix de poésies illyriques. Paris, 1827.
41555.12.10 Mérimée, Prosper. La guzla, ou choix de poésies illyriques. Strasbourg, 1926?
41555.16 Mérimée, Prosper. Notes d'un voyage dans le midi de la France. Bruxelles, 1835.
41555.18 Mérimée, Prosper. Prosper Mérimée. N.Y., 1903.
41555.18.2 Mérimée, Prosper. Prosper Mérimée. N.Y., 1903.

41555.20 - .35 Individual authors, etc. - 1800-1849 - Fiction - Mérimée - Individual works

41555.20 Mérimée, Prosper. Carmen. 9. éd. Paris, 1875.
41555.20.3 Mérimée, Prosper. Carmen. 13. éd. Paris, 1883. 7 pam.
41555.20.4 Mérimée, Prosper. Carmen. Boston, 1896.
41555.20.7A Mérimée, Prosper. Carmen. Boston, 1907.
41555.20.7B Mérimée, Prosper. Carmen. Boston, 1907.
41555.20.8 Mérimée, Prosper. Carmen. N.Y., 1903.
41555.20.20 Mérimée, Prosper. Carmen. Arsène Guillot. Paris, 1927.
41555.20.21 Mérimée, Prosper. Carmen. Arsène Guillot. Paris, 1930.
41555.20.25 Mérimée, Prosper. Carmen et autres nouvelles. Boston, 1930.
41555.20.70 Mérimée, Prosper. Carmen. Philadelphia, 189-?
41555.20.75 Mérimée, Prosper. Carmen based on Prosper Mérimée's story. N.Y., 1915.
41555.20.85 Mérimée, Prosper. Carmen based on Prosper Mérimée's story. N.Y., 1931.
41555.20.95 Mérimée, Prosper. Carmen. Gand, 1932.
41555.20.105 Mérimée, Prosper. Carmen. Monaco, 1945.
41555.20.110 Mérimée, Prosper. Carmen. Paris, 1947.
41555.21 Mérimée, Prosper. Crónica del reinado de Carlos IX. Valparaíso, 1895.
41555.22 Mérimée, Prosper. Chronique du règne de Charles IX. Paris, 1873.
41555.22.1.3 Mérimée, Prosper. Chronique du règne de Charles IX. Paris, 1889.
41555.22.1.5 Mérimée, Prosper. Chronique du règne de Charles IX. Boston, 1899.
41555.22.1.15 Mérimée, Prosper. Chronique du règne de Charles IX. Paris, 1933.
41555.22.2 Mérimée, Prosper. A chronicle of the reign of Charles IX. London, 1890.
41555.22.15 Mérimée, Prosper. Colomba. Paris, 1886.
41555.23 Mérimée, Prosper. Colomba. Paris, 1862.
41555.23.1 Mérimée, Prosper. Colomba. Paris, 1880.
41555.23.2 Mérimée, Prosper. Colomba. London, 1890.
41555.23.2.5 Mérimée, Prosper. Colomba. London, 1894.
41555.23.3 Mérimée, Prosper. Colomba. N.Y., 1894.
41555.23.5 Mérimée, Prosper. Colomba. Boston, 1899.
41555.23.6 Mérimée, Prosper. Colomba. Paris, n.d.
41555.23.9 Mérimée, Prosper. Colomba. Gotha, 1904.
41555.23.10 Mérimée, Prosper. Colomba. London, 1905.
41555.23.12 Mérimée, Prosper. Colomba. Boston, 1916.
41555.23.15 Mérimée, Prosper. Mateo Falcone. Colomba. Paris, 1927.
41555.23.20 Mérimée, Prosper. Colomba. Paris, 1958.
41555.23.25 Mérimée, Prosper. Colomba. N.Y., 1931.
41555.23.30 Mérimée, Prosper. Colomba, suivi de la mosaique. Paris, 1874.
41555.23.35 Mérimée, Prosper. Colomba. Paris, 1947.
41555.23.70 Mérimée, Prosper. Colomba. N.Y., 1897.
41555.23.73A Mérimée, Prosper. Colomba and Carmen. The French classical romances. N.Y., 1901.
41555.23.73B Mérimée, Prosper. Colomba and Carmen. The French classical romances. N.Y., 1901.
41555.23.78 Mérimée, Prosper. Colomba. N.Y., 1920.
41555.24.15 Mérimée, Prosper. Mosaique. Paris, 1933.
41555.25 Mérimée, Prosper. The venus of Ille, and other stories. London, 1966.
41555.26.5 Mérimée, Prosper. Stat'i o russkikh pisateliakh. Moskva, 1958.
41555.27 Mérimée, Prosper. Théâtre de Clara Gazul. Paris, 1870.
41555.27.5 Mérimée, Prosper. Plays of Clara Gazul. London, 1825.
41555.27.20 Mérimée, Prosper. Théâtre de Clara Gazul. Paris, 1929.

41555.20 - .35 Individual authors, etc. - 1800-1849 - Fiction - Mérimée - Individual works - cont.

41555.29 Mérimée, Prosper. Episodes from Mateo Falcone. London, 1890.
41555.29.5 Mérimée, Prosper. Mateo Falcone. Strasbourg, 19- ?
41555.29.10 Mérimée, Prosper. Mateo Falcone and other stories. London, 1908.
41555.29.25 Mérimée, Prosper. The house of a traitor. London, 189-.
41555.29.30 Mérimée, Prosper. Helmiä. Helsingissä, 1895.
41555.31 Mérimée, Prosper. The slave ship. Evanston, 1934.
41555.32 Mérimée, Prosper. La double méprise. Bruxelles, 1833.
41555.32.5 Mérimée, Prosper. 1572. N.Y., 1830.
41555.34 Mérimée, Prosper. Pages choisies. Paris, 1926.

41555.36 Individual authors, etc. - 1800-1849 - Fiction - Mérimée - Bibliographies

41555.36 Bibliothéque nationale, Paris. Prosper Mérimée; exposition. Paris, 1953.
41555.36.5 Trahard, Pierre. Bibliographie des oeuvres de Prosper Mérimée. Paris, 1929.
41555.36.10 Paevska, Anastasia V. Prosper Merime; bibliografiia. Moskva, 1968.

41555.37 - .54 Individual authors, etc. - 1800-1849 - Fiction - Mérimée - Biography and criticism

41555.37 Filon, A. Mérimée et ses amis. Paris, 1894.
41555.38 Filon, A. Mérimée et ses amis. Paris, 1898.
41555.39 Chambon, F. Notes sur Prosper Mérimée. Paris, 1902.
41555.39.5 Haussonville, Gabriel Paul. Prosper Mérimée. Paris, 1885.
41555.39.10 Du Bos, Charles. Notes sur Mérimée. Paris, 1920.
41555.40 Pinvert, L. Sur Mérimée. Paris, 1908.
41555.41 Tourneux, M. Prosper Mérimée. Paris, 1879.
41555.42 Falke, E. Die romantischen Elemente in Prosper Mérimées Roman und Novellen. Halle, 1915.
41555.42.5 Lyon, Sylvia. The life and times of Prosper Mérimée. N.Y., 1948.
41555.43 Lefebvre, Alphonse. La célèbre inconnue de Prosper Mérimée. Paris, 1908.
41555.43.15 Mart'ianova, Elizaveta P. Ob otrazhenii russko-frantsuzskikh kulturnykh sviazei vo frantsuzskom iazyke i literature XIX veka. Khar'kov, 1960.
41555.43.25 Trahard, Pierre. La jeunesse de Prosper Mérimée. Thèse. Paris, 1924.
41555.43.26 Trahard, Pierre. Prosper Mérimée de 1834 à 1853. Paris, 1928.
41555.43.27 Trahard, Pierre. La vieillesse de Prosper Mérimée, 1854-1870. Paris, 1930.
41555.43.30 Hovenkamp, Jan W. Mérimée et la couleur locale. Nijmegen, 1928.
41555.43.40 Luppé, A.M.P. Mérimée. Paris, 1945.
41555.43.45 Billy, André. Mérimée. Paris, 1959.
41555.43.50 Baschet, Robert. Mérimée, 1803-1870. Paris, 1958.
41555.43.55 Raitt, Alan William. Prosper Mérimée. London, 1970.
41555.44.5 Roger, G. Prosper Mérimée et la Corse. Alger, 1945.
41555.44.15 Dale, R.C. The poetics of Prosper Mérimée. The Hague, 1966.
41555.45 Dupouy, Auguste. Carmen de Mérimée. Paris, 1930.
41555.46 Johnstone, G.H. Prosper Mérimée, a mask and a face. London, 1926.
41555.47 Séché, L. Hortense Allart de Méritens. Paris, 1908.
41555.47.5 Billy, Andre. Hortense et ses amantes. Paris, 1961.
41555.48 Yu, Hous Jali. Prosper Mérimée, romancier et nouvelliste. Thèse. Lyon, 1935.
41555.48.10 Kosko, Marja. Le thème de Mateo Falcone. Paris, 1960.
41555.49 Bac, F. Mérimée inconnu. Paris, 1939.
41555.51 Allart de Méritens, Hortense. Les nouveaux enchantements. Paris, 1873.
41555.52 Healy, Dennis M. Mérimée et les Anglais. Thèse. Paris, 1946?
41555.53 Léon, Paul. Mérimée et son temps. Paris, 1962.
41555.54 Loennbohm, K. Prosper Mérimée. Helsingissä, 1895.
41555.54.6 Meier, Harri. La carroza del santo sacramento de Próspero Merimé. Lima, 1965.

41555.55 Individual authors, etc. - 1800-1849 - Fiction - Meritens, Mme. H. Allart de

41555.55.20 Allart de Méritens, Hortense. Lettere inedite a Gino Capponi. Genova, 1961.
41555.55.22 Allart de Méritens, Hortense. Nouvelles lettres à Sainte-Beuve, 1832-1864. Genève, 1965.
41555.55.30 Allart de Méritens, Hortense. Les enchantements de Prudence. Paris, 1877.

41555.56 Individual authors, etc. - 1800-1849 - Fiction - Moine

41555.56.81 Galley, Jean B. Un romantique oublié, Antonin Moine, 1796-1849. Saint-Etienne, 1898.

41555.58 Individual authors, etc. - 1800-1849 - Fiction - Moke

41555.58 Moke, Henri G. Herman of Natuur en beschaving. v.1-2. Amsterdam, 1833.

41555.62 Individual authors, etc. - 1800-1849 - Fiction - Montbrun

41555.62 Montbron, J.C. de. Essais sur la littérature des Hébreux. v.1-3. Paris, 1819. 2v.

41555.63 - .68 Individual authors, etc. - 1800-1849 - Fiction - Montgolfier - Writings

41555.65 Montgolfier, Adelaide. Piccolissima. 2. éd. Paris, n.d.
41555.66 Montgolfier, Adelaide. Barnabé, conte vrai. 2. éd. Paris, n.d.
41555.67 Montgolfier, Adelaide. Contes devenues histoires. Paris, 18- .

41556.6 - .14 Individual authors, etc. - 1800-1849 - Fiction - Nodier - Collected and Selected works

41556.6 Nodier, Charles. Oeuvres. v.5,8,9. Paris, 1832. 3v.
41556.10.5 Nodier, Charles. Contes. Paris, 1859.
41556.10.10 Nodier, Charles. Contes, avec des textes et des documents inédits. Paris, 1961.
41556.11 Nodier, Charles. Contes fantastiques. Paris, 1869.
41556.11.5 Nodier, Charles. Contes fantastiques. Paris, 191-?
41556.11.6 Nodier, Charles. Contes fantastiques. Paris, 1957. 2v.
41556.12 Nodier, Charles. Contes de la veillée. Paris, 1872.
41556.13 Nodier, Charles. Nouvelles. Paris, 1871.
41556.14 Nodier, Charles. Romans. Paris, 1862.

41556.15 - .33 Individual authors, etc. - 1800-1849 - Fiction - Nodier - Individual works

Htn 41556.15* Nodier, Charles. Histoire du roi de Bohême. Paris, 1830.
41556.16 Nodier, Charles. Les sept chateaux. Paris, 1852.
41556.17 Nodier, Charles. Souvenirs de jeunesse. Paris, 1862.
41556.18 Nodier, Charles. Souvenirs de la révolution. Paris, 1872. 2v.
41556.18.5 Nodier, Charles. The luck of the bean-rows. London, 1921.
41556.22 Nodier, Charles. Trilby, the fairy of Argyle. 1st ed. Boston, 1895.
41556.24 Nodier, Charles. Thérèse Aubert. Paris, 1819.
41556.25 Nodier, Charles. Trésor des Feves et Fleur des Pois. Paris, 1844. 3 pam.
41556.26 Nodier, Charles. Trésor des Feves et Fleur des Pois. Paris, 1853.
41556.28 Nodier, Charles. Moi-même. Paris, 1921.
Htn 41556.29* Nodier, Charles. Les tristes. Paris, 1806.
41556.30 Nodier, Charles. Inès de las Sierras. Paris, 1894.
41556.31 Nodier, Charles. La neuvaine de la Chandeleur. Paris, 1896.

41556.34 Individual authors, etc. - 1800-1849 - Fiction - Nodier - Bibliographies

41556.34 Larat, Jean. La tradition et l'exotisme dans l'oeuvre de Charles Nodier, 1780-1844. Thèse. Paris, 1923.
41556.34.2 Larat, Jean. Biblioographie critique des oeuvres de Charles Nodier. Thèse. Paris, 1923.
NEDL 41556.34.3 Larat, Jean. La tradition et l'exotisme dans l'oeuvre de Charles Nodier. Paris, 1923.
41556.34.4 Larat, Jean. Bibliographie critique des oeuvres de Charles Nodier. Paris, 1923.

41556.35 - Individual authors, etc. - 1800-1849 - Fiction - Nodier - Biography and criticism

41556.35 Salomon, Michel. Charles Nodier et le groupe romantique. Paris, 1908.
41556.36 Nodier, M. (Mme.). Charles Nodier. Paris, 1867.
41556.37 Fach, Theodor. Naturschilderung bei Charles Nodier. Halle, 1912.
41556.38 Pinquad, Léonce. La jeunesse de Charles Nodier. Besançon, 1914.
41556.39 Juin, Hubert. Charles Nodier. Paris, 1970.
41556.40 Pamphlet box. Nodier, Charles.
41556.41 Vodoz, Jules. "Les fes aux miettes." Paris, 1925.
41556.42 Stadelmann, J. Charles Nodier im Urteil seiner Zeitgenossen. Inaug. Diss. n.p., 1929.
41556.43 Henry-Rosier, M. La vie de Charles Nodier. 2e éd. Paris, 1931.
41556.44 Mönch, Walter. Charles Nodier, Zusammenhang von Erlebnis - Übertragung. Inaug. Diss. Berlin, 1931.
41556.45 Mönch, Walter. Charles Nodier und die deutsche und englische Literatur. Berlin, 1931.
41556.46 Held, Mariette. Charles Nodier. Bienne, 1949.
41556.47 Maixner, Rudolf. Charles Nodier et l'Illyrie. Paris, 1960.
41556.48 Oliver, Alfred R. Charles Nodier. Syracuse, N.Y., 1964.
41556.50 Schulze, Joachim. Enttäuschung und Wahnwelt; Studien zu Charles Nodiers Erzählungen. München, 1968.

41557.2 Individual authors, etc. - 1800-1849 - Fiction - Miscellany, P

41557.2 Perrin, Max. Le secret de Madame. Paris, 1862.
41557.2.25 Picquemard, Jean B. Zoflora. London, 1804. 2v.

41557.3 Individual authors, etc. - 1800-1849 - Fiction - Ropartz

41557.3 Ropartz, S. Récits bretons. St. Brieuc, 18- .

41557.4 - .6 Individual authors, etc. - 1800-1849 - Fiction - Reybaud, Louis - Writings

41557.4 Reybaud, Louis. Le dernier des commis voyageurs. Paris, 1856.
41557.4.20 Reybaud, Louis. César Falempin. Paris, 1861.
41557.4.30 Reybaud, Louis. Pierre Mouton. Paris, 1861.
41557.5 Reybaud, Louis. Jérôme Paturot. Paris, 1848. 4v.
41557.5.2 Reybaud, Louis. Jérôme Paturot. v.1-4. Paris, 1848. 2v.
41557.5.3 Reybaud, Louis. Jérôme Paturot. 4e éd. Paris, 1844.
41557.5.5 Reybaud, Louis. Jérôme Paturot. Paris, 1849.
41557.5.10 Reybaud, Louis. Jérôme Paturot à la recherche. Paris, 1965.
41557.6 Reybaud, Louis. Jérôme Paturot. Paris, 1870.

41557.7 Individual authors, etc. - 1800-1849 - Fiction - Reybaud, Louis - Works about

41557.7 Reybaud, Louis. Jérôme Paturot. v.1-4. Paris, 1849. 2v.
41557.7.9 Reybaud, Louis. Geronimo Paturot. Habana, 1853.
41557.7.80 Mireaux, Emile. Un témoin critique de la monarchie bourgeoise et de la Révolution de 1848: Louis Reybaud. Paris, 1964.
41557.7.81 Schüler, Helene. Louis Reybauds Roman: "Jérôme Paturot à la recherche d'une position sociale" im Spiegel seiner Zeit. Inaug. Diss. Würzhurg, 1937.

41557.8 - .8.39 Individual authors, etc. - 1800-1849 - Fiction - Miscellany, R-Sa

41557.8 Robert, Clémence. Les mendiants de la mort. Paris, 1874.
41557.8.10 Rome, Marne de Morville de (Mme.). Eulalie. Paris, 1799.
41557.8.10.5 De Rome. (Mme.). Pélage. Paris, 1818.
41557.8.15.5 Roy, Just J.E. The recluse of Rambouillet. N.Y., 1896.
41557.8.15.13 Roy, Just J.E. Solange de Chateaubrun. 3. éd. Tours, 1863.
41557.8.30 Saint-Félix, Jules de. Cléopatre, reine d'Egypte. v.1-2. Bruxelles, 1855.

41557.8.40 - .8.999 Individual authors, etc. - 1800-1849 - Fiction - Sand, George, pseud. - Collected and Selected works

41557.8.45 Sand, George. Oeuvres illustrées. v.1-9. Paris, 1852-56. 3v.
41557.8.50 Sand, George. Les amours de l'Age d'or. Paris, 1871.
41557.8.50.5 Sand, George. Les amours de l'Age d'or. Paris, 1889.
41557.8.51 Sand, George. André. Paris, 1868.
41557.8.53 Sand, George. Autour de al table. Paris, 1875.
41557.8.54 Sand, George. Le Beau Laurence. 2e éd. Paris, 1870.
41557.8.54.5 Sand, George. Le Beau Lawrence. Paris, 1870.
41557.8.55 Sand, George. Beaux messieurs de Bois-Doré. Paris, 1868. 2v.
41557.8.56 Sand, George. Cadio. Paris, 1868.
41557.8.57 Sand, George. Cesarine Dietrich. 3e éd. Paris, 1872.

41557.8.40 - .8.999 Individual authors, etc. - 1800-1849 - Fiction - Sand, George, pseud. - Collected and Selected works - cont.

41557.8.58 Sand, George. Contes d'une grand'mere. 3e éd. Paris, 1874.
41557.8.59 Sand, George. Le chateau des Desertes. Paris, 1866.
41557.8.60 Sand, George. Le Chêne parlant. Paris, 1876.
41557.8.61 Sand, George. Le compagnon du tour de France. Paris, 1861. 2v.
41557.8.61.10 Sand, George. Le compagnon du tour de France. Paris, 1885. 2v.
41557.8.62 Sand, George. La comtesse de Rudolstadt. v.1-2. Paris, 1857.
41557.8.63A Sand, George. La confession d'une jeune fille. 2. éd. Paris, 1865. 2v.
41557.8.63B Sand, George. La confession d'une jeune fille. 2. éd. v.1-2. Paris, 1865.
41557.8.64 Sand, George. Constance Verrier. Paris, 1860.
41557.8.65 Sand, George. Consuelo. Paris, 1856. 3v.
41557.8.66 Sand, George. La coupe; Lupo Liverani; Le toast. 2e éd. Paris, 1876.
41557.8.67 Sand, George. Les dames vertes. Paris, 1870.
41557.8.68 Sand, George. La Daniella. Paris, 1869. 2v.
41557.8.69 Sand, George. La derniere Aldini. Paris, 1866.
41557.8.69.3 Sand, George. La Derniere Aldini. Paris, 1843.
41557.8.70 Sand, George. Le dernier amour. Paris, 1867.
41557.8.71 Sand, George. Les deux frères. Paris, 1875.
41557.8.72 Sand, George. Le diable aux champs. Paris, 1867.
41557.8.73 Sand, George. Elle et lui. 6e éd. Paris, 1869.
41557.8.74 Sand, George. La famille de Germandre. 3e éd. Paris, 186-.
41557.8.74.5 Sand, George. La famille de Germandre. 3e éd. Paris, 1861.
41557.8.75 Sand, George. La filleule. Paris, 1869.
41557.8.76 Sand, George. Flamarande. 6e éd. Paris, 1875.
41557.8.77 Sand, George. Flavie. Les majoliques florentines. Paris, 1872.
41557.8.78 Sand, George. Francia. Un bienfait n'est jamais perdu. 3e éd. Paris, 1872.
41557.8.79 Sand, George. L'homme de neige. Paris, 1869. 3v.
41557.8.79.5 Sand, George. L'homme de neige. Paris, 18- . 2v.
41557.8.80 Sand, George. Un hiver à Majorque. Spiridion. Paris, 1867.
41557.8.81 Sand, George. Horace. Paris, 1869.
41557.8.82 Sand, George. Impressions et souvenirs. Paris, 1873.
41557.8.83 Sand, George. Indiana. Paris, 1869.
41557.8.83.2 Sand, George. Indiana. Paris, 1838. 2v.
41557.8.84 Sand, George. Isidora. Paris, 1869.
41557.8.84.10 Sand, George. Isidora. Paris, 1880.
41557.8.85 Sand, George. Jacques. Paris, 1857.
41557.8.85.5 Sand, George. Jacques. Paris, 1856.
41557.8.86 Sand, George. Jean de la Roche. Paris, 186-.
41557.8.86.5 Sand, George. Jean de la Roche. Paris, 1860.
41557.8.87 Sand, George. Jacques. Paris, 1866.
41557.8.88 Sand, George. Jean Zyska. Gabriel. Paris, 1867.
41557.8.89 Sand, George. Jeanne. Paris, 1867.
41557.8.90 Sand, George. Journal d'un voyageur pendant la guerre. Paris, 1871.
41557.8.91 Sand, George. Laura. Voyages et impressions. Paris, 1865.
41557.8.92 Sand, George. Lélia. Paris, 1869. 2v.
41557.8.93 Sand, George. Lettres d'un voyageur. Paris, 1869.
41557.8.93.3 Sand, George. Lettres d'un voyageur. Paris, 1869.
41557.8.93.5 Sand, George. Lucie. Paris, 1856.
41557.8.94 Sand, George. Lucrezia Floriani. Lavinia. Paris, 1869.
41557.8.94.3 Sand, George. Lucrezia Floriani. Paris, 1857.
41557.8.95 Sand, George. Mademoiselle la Quintinie. 5e éd. Paris, 1871.
41557.8.96 Sand, George. Mademoiselle Merquem. 3e éd. Paris, 187-.
41557.8.97 Sand, George. Les maîtres mosaistes. Paris, 1883.
41557.8.97.5 Sand, George. Les maîtres mosaistes. Paris, 1864.
41557.8.98 Sand, George. Les maîtres sonneurs. Paris, 186-.
41557.8.100 Sand, George. Les maîtres sonneurs. Paris, 1869. 2v.
41557.8.101 Sand, George. Malgrétout. 3e éd. Paris, 1870.
41557.8.102 Sand, George. La mare au diable. Paris, 1869.
41557.8.102.3 Sand, George. La mare au diable. Paris, 1884.
41557.8.103 Sand, George. La mare au diable. Paris, 1888.
41557.8.103.5 Sand, George. La petite Fadette. Paris, 1869.
41557.8.104 Sand, George. Le marquis de Villemer. Paris, 1869.
41557.8.105 Sand, George. Le marquis de Villemer. Paris, 1890.
41557.8.105.5 Sand, George. Le marquis de Villemer. Paris, 1898.
41557.8.105.15 Sand, George. Le marquis de Villemer. 2. éd. Paris, 1864.
41557.8.106 Sand, George. Le marquis de Villemer. 2. éd. Paris, 1865.
41557.8.107 Sand, George. Ma soeur Jeanne. Paris, 1874.
41557.8.107.3 Sand, George. Mauprat. Paris, 1869.
41557.8.107.5 Sand, George. Mauprat. Paris, 1856.
41557.8.108 Sand, George. Le meunier d'Angibault. Paris, 1869.
41557.8.108.5 Sand, George. Le meunier d'Angibault. Paris, 1853.
41557.8.109 Sand, George. Le meunier d'Angibault. Paris, 1879.
41557.8.110 Sand, George. Monsieur Sylvestre. Paris, 1866.
41557.8.111 Sand, George. Mont-Revêche. Paris, 1855.
41557.8.112 Sand, George. Nanon. Paris, 1878.
41557.8.112.10 Sand, George. Nanon. Paris, 1891.
41557.8.113 Sand, George. Narcisse. Paris, 1869.
41557.8.113.10 Sand, George. Narcisse. Paris, 1897.
41557.8.114 Sand, George. Nouvelles. Paris, 1861.
41557.8.115 Sand, George. Pauline. Paris, 1870.
41557.8.117 Sand, George. Le peche de monsieur Antoine. Paris, 1869. 2v.
41557.8.117.10 Sand, George. Le peche de monsieur Antoine. Paris, 1896. 2v.
41557.8.118 Sand, George. Le Piccinino. Paris, 1869. 2v.
41557.8.119 Sand, George. Pierre qui roule. 2e ed. Paris, 1870.
41557.8.120 Sand, George. Promenades autour d'un village. Paris, 1869.
41557.8.121 Sand, George. Le secrétaire intime. Paris, 1868.
41557.8.122 Sand, George. Les sept cordes de la lyre. Paris, 1869.
41557.8.123 Sand, George. Simon. La marquis. Paris, 1869.
41557.8.123.2 Sand, George. Simon. Paris, 1838.
41557.8.124 Sand, George. Tamaris. 3e éd. Paris, 1867.
41557.8.125 Sand, George. Teverino. Leone Leoni. Paris, 1868.
41557.8.126 Sand, George. La tour de Percemont. 5e éd. Paris, 1877.
41557.8.127 Sand, George. L'Uscoque. Paris, 1869.
41557.8.128 Sand, George. Valentine. Paris, 1869.
41557.8.129 Sand, George. Valvèdre. Paris, 1863.
41557.8.130 Sand, George. La ville noire. 3e éd. Paris, 1862.
41557.8.130.2 Sand, George. La ville noire. 2. éd. Paris, 1861.
41557.8.131 Sand, George. Théâtre complet. Paris, 1866-67. 4v.

41557.8.40 - .8.999 Individual authors, etc. - 1800-1849 - Fiction - Sand, George, pseud. - Collected and Selected works - cont.

41557.8.132 Sand, George. Théâtre de Nohant. Paris, 1865.
41557.8.133 Sand, George. Questions d'art et de littérature. Paris, 1878.
41557.8.134 Sand, George. Thoughts and aphorisms from her work. London, 1911.
41557.8.135 Sand, George. Germain's marriage. N.Y., 1892.
41557.8.140 Sand, George. Oeuvres autobiographiques. Paris, 1970- 2v.

41557.9 Individual authors, etc. - 1800-1849 - Fiction - Sand, George, pseud. - Individual works

41557.9.5 Sand, George. Pages choisies des Grands Écrivains. Paris, 1894.
41557.9.15 Sand, George. Adriani. Paris, 1880.
41557.9.19 Sand, George. Les Beaux Messieurs. Paris, n.d. 2v.
41557.9.20A Sand, George. Cesarine Dietrich. Boston, 1871.
41557.9.20B Sand, George. Cesarine Dietrich. Boston, 1871.
41557.9.21 Sand, George. Consuelo. Bruxelles, 1842. 2v.
41557.9.22.20 Sand, George. Consuelo. Paris, 1822. 3v.
41557.9.23A Sand, George. Consuelo. Boston, 1846. 2v.
41557.9.23B Sand, George. Consuelo. Boston, 1846. 2v.
41557.9.23C Sand, George. Consuelo. Boston, 1846. 2v.
41557.9.24 Sand, George. Consuelo. N.Y., 1851.
41557.9.24.7 Sand, George. Consuelo. Philadelphia, 1870.
41557.9.24.20 Sand, George. Consuelo. Boston, 1897. 2v.
41557.9.24.25 Sand, George. Consuelo. N.Y., 19- .
41557.9.24.50 Sand, George. La comtesse de Rudolstadt. v.1-2. Paris, 1845.
41557.9.25 Sand, George. The countess of Rudolstadt. Philadelphia, n.d.
Htn 41557.9.25.5* Sand, George. The countess of Rudolstadt. v.1-2. Boston, 1847.
41557.9.25.10 Sand, George. The countess of Rudolstadt. Philadelphia, 1870.
41557.9.26 Sand, George. The countess of Rudolstadt. N.Y., 1894.
41557.9.27 Sand, George. Les dames vertes. Paris, 1873.
Htn 41557.9.27.9* Sand, George. Elle et lui. Paris, 1859.
41557.9.28 Sand, George. Elle et lui. 2d éd. Paris, 1860.
41557.9.28.3 Sand, George. Elle et lui. 6e ed. Paris, 1869.
41557.9.28.10 Sand, George. Elle et lui. 6e éd. Paris, 1909.
41557.9.28.15 Sand, George. Elle et lui. Neuchâtel, 1963.
41557.9.29 Sand, George. Evenor et Leucippe. Paris, 1856.
41557.9.30 Sand, George. Fadette. A domestic story. 2e ed. N.Y., 1851.
NEDL 41557.9.30.4 Sand, George. Fadette. N.Y., 1896.
41557.9.30.5 Sand, George. Little Fadette. A domestic story. London, 18- ?
41557.9.30.10 Sand, George. Little Fadette. A domestic story. N.Y., 1928.
41557.9.30.50 Sand, George. La petite Fadette. N.Y., 1865.
41557.9.31 Sand, George. La petite Fadette. Boston, 1866.
41557.9.31.3 Sand, George. La petite Fadette. 5. ed. Boston, 1869.
41557.9.31.4 Sand, George. La petite Fadette. Paris, 1883.
41557.9.31.5 Sand, George. La petite Fadette. N.Y., 1899.
41557.9.31.7 Sand, George. La petite Fadette. N.Y., 1900.
41557.9.31.10 Sand, George. La petite Fadette. N.Y., 1929.
41557.9.31.15 Sand, George. La petite Fadette. Paris, 1967.
41557.9.32 Sand, George. La famille de Germandre. Paris, 1872.
41557.9.32.5 Sand, George. La petite Fadette. 5e éd. Paris, 1872.
41557.9.32.8 Sand, George. La petite Fadette. Boston, 1895.
41557.9.33 Sand, George. Fanchon the Cricket. N.Y., 1863.
41557.9.33.2 Sand, George. Fanchon the Cricket. N.Y., 1864.
41557.9.34 Sand, George. Histoire de ma vie. Paris, 1854. 10v.
41557.9.34.5 Sand, George. Histoire de ma vie. Paris, 1855. 4v.
41557.9.35 Sand, George. Histoire de ma vie. Paris, 1879. 4v.
41557.9.35.5 Sand, George. Histoire de ma vie. Paris, 1879. 4v.
41557.9.35.10 Sand, George. Histoire de ma vie. Paris, 1945.
41557.9.36 Sand, George. Convent life of George Sand. Boston, 1893.
41557.9.37 Sand, George. Histoire du véritable Gribonille. Paris, 1851.
41557.9.38 Sand, George. Impressions and reminiscences. Boston, 1877.
41557.9.39A Sand, George. Jacques. N.Y., 1847.
41557.9.39B Sand, George. Jacques. v.1-2. N.Y., 1847.
41557.9.40 Sand, George. The last Aldini. A love story. Philadelphia, n.d.
41557.9.41 Sand, George. Oeuvres de George Sand. Paris, 1842.
41557.9.42 Sand, George. Lettres à Alfred de Musset et à St. Beuve. Paris, 1897.
41557.9.42.5A Sand, George. Correspondance; publiée intégralement. Bruxelles, 1904.
41557.9.42.5B Sand, George. Correspondance; publiée intégralement. Bruxelles, 1904.
41557.9.42.7 Sand, George. Correspondance de George Sand et d'Alfred de Musset. Bruxelles, 1904.
41557.9.42.15 Sand, George. Correspondance, 1812-1876. Paris, 1822-84. 6v.
41557.9.42.25 Sand, George. Correspondance, 1812-1876. 4. ed. Paris, 1883-92. 6v.
41557.9.42.30 Sand, George. Lettres à Alfred de Musset et Gustave Flaubert. Paris, 1970.
41557.9.43 Sand, George. Lettres d'un voyageur. Bruxelles, 1838.
41557.9.43.9 Sand, George. Maître Favilla. Paris, 1855.
41557.9.43.15 Sand, George. Lettres inédites de George Sand et de Pauline Viardat. Paris, 1959.
41557.9.44 Sand, George. Les maîtres mosaistes. Bruxelles, 1842. 2v.
41557.9.44.20 Sand, George. Les maîtres sonneurs. Oxford, 1910.
41557.9.44.25 Sand, George. Les maîtres sonneurs. Paris, 1968.
Htn 41557.9.45* Sand, George. Les maîtres sonneurs. Bruxelles, 1853.
41557.9.45.10 Sand, George. La mare au diable. Cambridge, 18- .
41557.9.45.25 Sand, George. La mare au diable. Paris, 1850.
41557.9.46 Sand, George. La mare au diable. N.Y., 1886.
41557.9.46.2 Sand, George. La mare au diable. N.Y., 1885.
41557.9.46.3 Sand, George. La mare au diable. London, 1885.
41557.9.46.5 Sand, George. La mare au diable. London, 1893.
41557.9.46.10 Sand, George. La mare au diable. N.Y., 1890.
41557.9.47 Sand, George. La mare au diable. Boston, 1892.
41557.9.48 Sand, George. La mare au diable. Boston, 1892.
41557.9.48.4 Sand, George. The haunted pool. N.Y., 1890.
41557.9.48.7 Sand, Goerge. The haunted pool. N.Y., 1893.
41557.9.48.8 Sand, George. The haunted pool. N.Y., 1895.
41557.9.48.9 Sand, George. La mare au diable. N.Y., 1916.
41557.9.48.10A Sand, George. The devil's pool. London, 1929.
41557.9.48.10B Sand, George. The devil's pool. London, 1929.
41557.9.48.12 Sand, George. The devil's pool. London, 1930.

41557.9 Individual authors, etc. - 1800-1849 - Fiction - Sand, George, pseud. - Individual works - cont.

41557.9.48.13 Sand, George. La mare au diable. Paris, 1966.
41557.9.48.14 Sand, George. The devil's pool. Boston, 1896.
41557.9.48.15 Sand, George. La mare au diable. Paris, 1930.
41557.9.48.16 Sand, George. La mare au diable. François le Champi. Evreux, 1969.
41557.9.49 Sand, George. Le marquis de Villemer. Paris, 1860.
41557.9.49.2 Sand, George. The marquis de Villemer. Boston, 1871.
41557.9.49.5 Sand, George. Nanon. 6e éd. Paris, 1873.
41557.9.49.10 Sand, George. Le marquis de Villemer. Paris, 1948.
41557.9.50 Sand, George. The rolling stone. Boston, 1871.
41557.9.51 Sand, George. Handsome Lawrence. Boston, 1871.
Htn 41557.9.52* Sand, George. Les sept cordes de la Lyre. Bruxelles, 1859.
41557.9.53 Sand, George. Souvenirs et idées. Paris, 1904.
Htn 41557.9.54* Sand, George. Spiridion. Paris, 1839.
41557.9.55A Sand, George. Teverino; a romance. N.Y., 1855.
41557.9.55B Sand, George. Teverino; a romance. N.Y., 1855.
41557.9.58 Sand, George. Le voyage à Majorque de George Sand et seduc Chopin. Paris, 1959.
41557.9.60 Sand, George. François le Champi. N.Y., 1914.
41557.9.62 Sand, George. François le Champi. Paris, 1898.
41557.9.64 Sand, George. François the waif. N.Y., 1894.
41557.9.65 Sand, George. The country waif. London, 1930.
41557.9.66 Sand, George. François the waif. N.Y., 1894.
41557.9.67 Sand, George. François the Champi. Oxford, 1910.
41557.9.68 Sand, George. Souvenirs de 1848. Paris, 1880.
41557.9.69 Sand, George. The bagpipers. Boston, 1890.
41557.9.70 Biblioteque nationale, Paris. George Sand. Paris, 1954.
41557.9.71 Sand, George. George Sand et Alfred de Musset. Monaco, 1956.
41557.9.72 Sand, George. Les lettres de George Sand à Sainte-Beuve. Genève, 1964.
41557.9.73 Sand, George. Indiana. Paris, 1962.
41557.9.73.2 Sand, George. Indiana. Paris, 1948.
41557.9.74 Sand, George. Indiana. Philadelphia, 1888.
41557.9.75 Parturier, Maurice. Une expérience of Lélia. Paris, 1934.
41557.9.80 Sand, George. Marianne. Boston, 18- .
41557.9.81A Sand, George. Marianne. N.Y., 1893.
41557.9.81B Sand, George. Marianne. N.Y., 1893.
41557.9.85 Sand, George. Lélia. Paris, 1960.
41557.9.90 Sand, George. Antonia. Boston, 1870.
41557.9.90.5 Sand, George. Antonia. Boston, 1902.
41557.9.94.2 Sand, George. Mauprat. Paris, 1904.
41557.9.94.5 Sand, George. Mauprat. Paris, 1913.
41557.9.95 Sand, George. Mauprat. Boston, 1870.
41557.9.95.2 Sand, George. Mauprat. Boston, 1899.
41557.9.96A Sand, George. Mauprat. N.Y., 1902.
41557.9.96B Sand, George. Mauprat. N.Y., 1902.
41557.9.100A Sand, George. My sister Jeannie. Boston, 1874.
41557.9.100B Sand, George. My sister Jeannie. Boston, 1874.
41557.9.105 Sand, George. The miller of Angibault. Boston, 1871.
41557.9.110 Sand, George. Mlle. Merguem. N.Y., 1868.
41557.9.115 Sand, George. Monsieur Sylvestre. Boston, 1870.
41557.9.120 Sand, George. The snow man. Boston, 1871.
41557.9.125 Sand, George. The tower of Percemont. N.Y., 1877.
41557.9.130 Sand, George. Winter in Majorca. 2d ed. London, 1956.

41557.10 Individual authors, etc. - 1800-1849 - Fiction - Sand, George, pseud. - Biography and criticism

41557.10.01 Pamphlet box. George Sand.
41557.10.5 Thomas, Bertha. George Sand. Boston, 1883.
41557.10.6A Caro, Elme. George Sand. Paris, 1887.
41557.10.6B Caro, Elme. George Sand. Paris, 1887.
41557.10.6.5 Caro, Elme. George Sand. Chicago, 1888.
41557.10.7 Revon, Michel. George Sand. Paris, 1896.
41557.10.8 Rocheblave, S. George Sand et sa fille, d'après leur correspondance inédite. Paris, 1905.
41557.10.8.5 Rocheblave, S. George Sand et sa fille. Paris, 1905.
41557.10.9 Plauchut, Edmond. Autour de Nohant. Lettres de Barbes à George Sand. Paris, 1897.
41557.10.10 Spoelberch de Lovenjoul, Charles. La veritable histoire de "Elle et lui". Paris, 1897.
41557.10.11 Born, Max. George Sand's Sprache in dem Romane Les maîtres sonneurs. Berlin, 1901.
41557.10.12 Born, Max. George Sand's Sprache in dem Romane Les maîtres sonneurs. Teil 1. Berlin, 1900.
41557.10.13 Le Roy, Albert. George Sand et ses amis. 2e éd. Paris, 1903.
41557.10.14 Caro, Elme. George Sand. London, 1888.
41557.10.15 Devaux, A. George Sand; étude à laquelle l'académie française a décerneé le prix d'éloquence en 1894. Paris, 1895.
41557.10.16A Komarova, V.D. George Sand, sa vie et ses oeuvres 1804-1876. Paris, 1899-1926. 4v.
41557.10.16B Komarova, V.D. George Sand, sa vie et ses oeuvres 1804-1876. v.3. Paris, 1899-1926.
41557.10.17 Lumbroso, A. Gli amanti di Venezia, Georgio Sand e Alfredo de Musset. Roma, 1903.
41557.10.17.5 Maurras, C. Les amants de Venise, George Sand et Musset. Paris, 1917.
41557.10.17.10 Adam, A. Le secret de l'aventure vénitienne. Paris, 1938.
41557.10.18 Sand, George. Correspondance...Gustave Flaubert. 5e éd. Paris, 1904.
41557.10.18.3 Sand, George. Correspondance entre George Sand et Gustave Flaubert. Paris, 1904.
41557.10.18.5 Sand, George. Correspondance entre George Sand et Gustave Flaubert. Paris, 1904.
41557.10.18.10 Sand, George. Correspondance inédite. 8. éd. Paris, 1953.
41557.10.18.15 David, Henri C.E. Flaubert and George Sand in their correspondance. Chicago, 1924.
41557.10.18.20 Sand, George. Correspondance. Paris, 1964. 8v.
41557.10.19 Pompery, A. de. Un ami de George Sand. Paris, 1897.
41557.10.20 Vincent, L. George Sand et l'amour. Paris, 1917.
41557.10.21 Sand, George. La langue et le style rustique de George Sand dans les champêtres. Paris, 1916.
41557.10.22 Sand, George. George Sand et le Berry. Paris, 1919. 2v.
41557.10.23 Doumic, René. George Sand. Paris, 1909.
41557.10.23.2 Doumic, René. George Sand. Paris, 1922.
41557.10.24 Seillière, Ernest. George Sand. Paris, 1920.
41557.10.26 Bertaut, Jules. Une amitie romantique. Paris, 1922?
41557.10.27 Owen, E.T. Notes on the Petite Fadette of George Sand. Madison, 1885.
41557.10.31 Schutz, A.H. Peasant vocabulary in works of George Sand. Columbia, 1927.
41557.10.35 Sand, George. Journal intime. Paris, 1926.

41557.10 Individual authors, etc. - 1800-1849 - Fiction - Sand, George, pseud. - Biography and criticism - cont.

41557.10.40 Raya, Maurace. George Sand. Paris, 1928.
41557.10.45 Langlade, J. La dernière manière de George Sand. Paris, 1925.
41557.10.49 Rouget, M.T. George Sand "socialiste." Thèse. Lyon, 1931.
41557.10.50 Rouget, M.T. George Sand "socialiste." Lyon, 1931.
41557.10.55 Rouget, M.T. George Sand et l'Italie. Thèse. Lyon, 1939.
41557.10.57 Rouget, M.T. Essai sur l'évolution psychologique et littéraire de George Sand. Thèse. Lyon, 1939.
41557.10.60 Ruggeberg, J. Die Persönlichkeit George Sands in ihren Werken. Inaug. Diss. Bonn, 1912.
41557.10.65 Brugger, Irene. Frauentypen bei George Sand. Inaug. Diss. Ochsenfurt, 1934.
41557.10.70 Toesca, Maurice. Le plus grand amour de George Sand. Thèse. Paris, 1933.
41557.10.72 Toesca, Maurice. The other George Sand. London, 1947.
41557.10.73 Toesca, Maurice. Une autre George Sand. Paris, 1945.
41557.10.74 Toesca, Maurice. Le plus grand amour de George Sand. Paris, 1965.
41557.10.75 Fahmy, Dorrya. George Sand, auteur dramatique. Thèse. Paris, 1934.
41557.10.80 Lüdicke, Heinz. George Sand als Heimatdichterin. Inaug. Diss. Leipzig, 1935.
41557.10.85 Moret, M.M. Le sentiment religieux chez George Sand. Thèse. Paris, 1936.
41557.10.90A Pailleron, M.L. George Sand; histoire de sa vie. Paris, 1938. 3v.
41557.10.90B Pailleron, M.L. George Sand; histoire de sa vie. v.2. Paris, 1938.
41557.10.95 Seyd, Felizia. Romantic rebel. N.Y., 1940.
41557.10.100 Ferra, Bartomeu. Chopin and George Sand in Majorca. Palma de Mallorca, 1935.
41557.10.102 Ferra, Bartomeu. Chopin y George Sand en Mallorca. Palma de Mallorca, 1949.
41557.10.105 Viens, Claude P. George Sand and Gustave Planche: unpublished correspondence. Providence, 1944.
41557.10.110 Schermerhorn, E.W. The seven strings of the lyre...George Sand. Boston, 1927.
41557.10.120 Charpentier, J. George Sand. 11. ed. Paris, 1936.
41557.10.125A Howe, M.J. George Sand. N.Y., 1927.
41557.10.125B Howe, M.J. George Sand. N.Y., 1927.
41557.10.125C Howe, M.J. George Sand. N.Y., 1927.
41557.10.130 Grebanier, F.V. The life of the heart. N.Y., 1945.
41557.10.132A Grebanier, F.V. The life of the heart. 4. ed. N.Y., 1945.
41557.10.132B Grebanier, F.V. The life of the heart. 2. ed. N.Y., 1945.
41557.10.135 L'Hopital, Madeleine. La notion d'artiste chez George Sand. Paris, 1946.
41557.10.140 Paillou, Paul H. La vie émouvante de George Sand. Paris, 1946.
41557.10.145 Paz, Magdeleine L. La vie d'un grand homme George Sand. Paris, 1947.
41557.10.150 Galzy, J. George Sand. Paris, 1950.
41557.10.155 Larnac, Jean. George Sand révolutionnaire. Paris, 1948.
41557.10.160 Mariéton, Paul. Une histoire d'amour. 38. éd. Paris, 1903.
41557.10.165 Maurois, André. Lélia. 80. éd. Paris, 1952.
41557.10.168 Maurois, André. Lélia. N.Y., 1953.
41557.10.170 Dolléans, E. George Sand. Paris, 1951.
41557.10.175 Ferra, Bartomen. Chopin i George Sand a la Cartoixa de Valldemossa. Ciutat de Mallorca, 1930.
41557.10.180 Boury, F. De quoi vivait George Sand. Paris, 1952.
41557.10.185 Salomon, P. George Sand. Paris, 1953.
41557.10.190 Roger, G. Les maîtres sonneurs de George Sand. Paris, 1954.
41557.10.195 Varilhe, Jean de. Les années d'adolescence de George Sand. Guéret, 1956.
41557.10.200 Kirpichnikov, A.I. Dve biografii: Zhorzh Zand i Genrikh Geinc. Moskva, 1886.
41557.10.205 Thomas, Edith. George Sand. Paris, 1959.
41557.10.210 Haussonville, Gabriel Paul Othenin de Cléron. George Sand, sa vie et ses oeuvres. Paris, 1878.
41557.10.215 Poli, Annarosa. L'Italie dans la vie et dans l'oeuvres de George Sand. Paris, 1960.
41557.10.220 Davray, Jean. George Sand et les amants. Paris, 1935.
41557.10.225 Södergård, Ö. Essais sur la création littéraire de George Sand. Uppsala, 1962.
41557.10.230 Codroc'h, M. Répertoire des lettres publiées de George Sand. Paris, 1962.
41557.10.240 Colin, Georges Emile. Bibliographie des premières publications des romans de George Sand. Bruxelles, 1965.
41557.10.245 Venskstern, Nataliia. Zhorzh Sand. Moskva, 1933.
41557.10.250 Pommier, Jean J.M. George Sand et le rêje monastique, "Spiridion". Paris, 1966.
41557.10.255 Poli, Annarosa. George Sand vue par les italiens. Firenze, 1965.
41557.10.260 Trepeznikova, Nataliia S. Zhorzh Sand - redaktor i sotrudnik zhurnala "Revue indépendante". Kazan, 1966.
41557.10.265 Hommage à George Sand. Paris, 1969.
41557.10.270 Dussault, Louis. George Sand. Montréal, 1970.
41557.10.275 Spire, Thérèse M. Les romantiques et la musique: le cas George Sand. Paris, 1955.
41557.10.280 Ryelandt, Christophe. Malgrétout. George Sand et les Ardennes. Mézières, 1953.
41557.10.285 Gerson, Noel Bertram. George Sand; a biography of the first modern, liberated woman. N.Y., 1972.
41557.10.290 Carrère, Casimir. George Sand amoureuse. Paris, 1967.

41557.11 - .32 Individual authors, etc. - 1800-1849 - Fiction - Sandeau - Writings

41557.11 Sandeau, Jules. Catherine. Paris, 1869.
41557.12 Sandeau, Jules. Un début dans la magistrature. Paris, 1863.
41557.13 Sandeau, Jules. Le docteur Herbeau. Paris, 1872.
41557.13.5 Sandeau, Jules. El doctor Herbeau. v.1-2. Habana, 1843.
41557.15 Sandeau, Jules. Fernand Vallaince Richard. Paris, 1868.
41557.16 Sandeau, Jules. Un héritage. Paris, 1855.
41557.18 Sandeau, Jules. Jean de Thommeray. Paris, 1873.
Htn 41557.18.5* Sandeau, Jules. Mlle. de la Seiglière. 4e éd. Paris, 1854.
41557.18.9 Sandeau, Jules. Mademoiselle de la Seiglière. Paris, 1858.
41557.19.2 Sandeau, Jules. Mademoiselle de la Seiglière. Paris, 1876.
41557.19.3 Sandeau, Jules. Helena de la Seiglière. N.Y., 1888.
41557.19.4 Sandeau, Jules. Mademoiselle de la Seiglière. 5. ed. N.Y., 1865.
41557.19.5 Sandeau, Jules. Helena de la Seiglière. N.Y., 1888.

Classified Listing

41557.11 - .32 Individual authors, etc. - 1800-1849 - Fiction - Sandeau - Writings - cont.

41557.19.10 Sandeau, Jules. Mademoiselle de la Seiglière. 7. ed. Bielefeld, 1879.
41557.19.12 Sandeau, Jules. Mademoiselle de la Seiglière. 7. ed. London, 1892.
41557.19.15 Sandeau, Jules. Mademoiselle de la Seiglière. London, 1894.
41557.19.18 Sandeau, Jules. Mademoiselle de la Seiglière. Paris, 1874.
41557.19.21 Sandeau, Jules. Mademoiselle de la Seiglière. 5. ed. London, 1887.
41557.19.23 Sandeau, Jules. Mademoiselle de la Seiglière. Boston, 1891.
41557.20 Sandeau, Jules. Madame de Sommerville. Paris, 1868.
41557.21 Sandeau, Jules. Mademoiselle de Keronare. Paris, 1870.
41557.22 Sandeau, Jules. La maison de Penarvan. Paris, 1867.
41557.22.5 Sandeau, Jules. La maison de Penarvan. Boston, 1865.
41557.23 Sandeau, Jules. Marianna. Paris, 1871.
41557.23.6 Sandeau, Jules. Marianna. 14e éd. Paris, 1883.
41557.24 Sandeau, Jules. Nouvelles. Paris, 1870.
41557.26 Sandeau, Jules. La Roche aux Mouettes. Paris, 1872.
41557.26.4 Sandeau, Jules. La Roche aux Mouettes. 25e ed. Paris, n.d.
41557.27 Sandeau, Jules. Sacs et parchemins. Paris, 1870.
41557.27.3 Sandeau, Jules. Sacs et parchemins. Paris, 1856.
41557.27.4 Sandeau, Jules. Sacs et parchemins. Paris, 1856.
41557.27.5 Sandeau, Jules. Money bags and titles. Philadelphia, 1850.
41557.27.15 Sandeau, Jules. Tears! Idle tears! n.p., n.d.
41557.28 Sandeau, Jules. Valcreuse. Paris, 1869.
41557.28.5 Sandeau, Jules. Valcreuse. Paris, 1862.
NEDL 41557.29.10 Sandeau, Jules. Madeleine. Paris, 1910.
41557.30 Sandeau, Jules. Madeleine: a story of French love. Chicago, 1881.
41557.30.5 Sandeau, Jules. Madeleine. Chicago, 1879.
41557.30.10 Sandeau, Jules. Madeleine: a story of French love. Chicago, 1899.
41557.31 Sandeau, Jules. Mademoiselle de la Seiglière. Paris, 1852.
41557.31.2 Sandeau, Jules. Mademoiselle de la Seiglière. Bielefeld, 1858.
41557.32 Sand, George. Madame de Sommerville. n.p., n.d.

41557.33 Individual authors, etc. - 1800-1849 - Fiction - Sandeau - Works about

41557.33.10 Silver, Mabel. Jules Sandeau; l'homme et la vie. Thèse. Paris, 1936. 10v.

41557.34 - .44 Individual authors, etc. - 1800-1849 - Fiction - Sarrazin - Writings

41557.34 Sarrazin, Adrien de. Bardouc. Paris, 1825.
41557.34.2 Sarrazin, Adrien de. Bardouc. Boston, 1850.
41557.35 Sarrazin, Adrien de. La caravanserail. Paris, 1850. 2v.
41557.36 Sarrazin, Adrien de. Contes nouveaux. Paris, 1850. 3v.

41558.1 - .29 Individual authors, etc. - 1800-1849 - Fiction - Soulié - Writings

41558.2 Soulié, Frédéric. Au jour le jour. v.1-2. Bruxelles, 1844.
41558.3 Soulié, Frédéric. Beltram el napolitano; drama. Madrid, 1844.
41558.4 Soulié, Frédéric. Le comte de Toulouse. Paris, 1870.
41558.5 Soulié, Frédéric. Les deux cadavres. Paris, 1870.
41558.6 Soulié, Férdéric. Le lion amoureux. Paris, 1872.
41558.6.25 Soulié, Frédéric. La lionne. Oeuvres complètes. Paris, 1856.
41558.8 Soulié, Frédéric. Les mémoirs du diable. Paris, 1869. 3v.
41558.11 Soulié, Frédéric. Olivier Duhamel. Paris, 1858.
41558.12 Soulié, Frédéric. Sathaniel. Paris, 1859.
41558.15 Soulié, Frédéric. Le vicomte de Bréziers. Paris, 1869.
41558.18 Soulié, Frédéric. La chambière. Paris, 1840.
41558.20 Soulié, Frédéric. Marguerite. Bruxelles, 1842. 2v.
41558.21 Soulié, Frédéric. El proscripto; drama. Madrid, 1839.
41558.22 Soulié, Frédéric. Les quatre soeurs. Paris, 1863.
41558.25 Soulié, Frédéric. Si jeunesse savait, si vieillesse pouvait. Paris, 1867. 2v.
41558.26 Soulié, Frédéric. Aventures d'un jeune cadet de famille. Paris, 1884.
41558.27 Soulié, Frédéric. La claserie des genêts. Paris, 18- .

41558.30 Individual authors, etc. - 1800-1849 - Fiction - Soulié - Works about

41558.30A March, Harold. Frédéric Soulié, novelist and dramatist. New Haven, 1931.
41558.30B March, Harold. Frédéric Soulié, novelist and dramatist. New Haven, 1931.
41558.30.5 Reinholdt, H. Die moralischen, religiösen und sozialen Ideen in den Romanen Frédéric Souliés. Inaug. Diss. Münster, 1935.

41558.40 - .89 Individual authors, etc. - 1800-1849 - Fiction - Souvestre - Writings

41558.40 Souvestre, Émile. Les anges du foyer. Paris, 1868.
41558.40.10 Souvestre, Émile. Brittany and La Vendée. N.Y., 1857.
41558.41 Souvestre, Émile. Causeries historiques littéraires. Genève, 1854. 2v.
41558.42 Souvestre, Émile. Chroniques de la mer. Paris, 1859.
41558.42.25 Souvestre, Émile. Claude Rionel; suivi de Une femme célèbre. Bruxelles, 1842.
41558.43 Souvestre, Émile. Au coin du feu. Paris, 1856.
41558.44 Souvestre, Émile. Au coin du feu. Paris, 1861.
41558.44.9 Souvestre, Émile. Au coin du feu. London, 1886.
41558.45 Souvestre, Émile. Les derniers Bretons. v.1-2. Paris, 1858.
41558.46 Souvestre, Émile. Les derniers Bretons. Paris, 1866. 2v.
41558.48 Souvestre, Émile. Les derniers paysans. Paris, 1871.
41558.48.5 Souvestre, Émile. Les derniers paysans. Paris, 1856. 2 pam.
41558.49F Souvestre, Émile. Deux misères. Paris, 1861.
41558.50 Souvestre, Émile. Dans la prairie. Paris, 1852.
41558.51.5 Souvestre, Émile. Histoires d'autrefois. Paris, 1859.

41558.40 - .89 Individual authors, etc. - 1800-1849 - Fiction - Souvestre - Writings - cont.

41558.52 Souvestre, Émile. Leaves from a family journal. N.Y., 1855.
41558.54 Souvestre, Émile. The lake shore. Boston, 1855.
41558.55 Souvestre, Émile. Loterie de Francfort . N.Y., 1865.
41558.56 Souvestre, Émile. Le mari de Madame de Solange. Boston, 1900.
41558.56.5 Souvestre, Émile. Le mari de Madame de Solange suivi de Les préventions. La Haye, 1841.
41558.57 Souvestre, Émile. La goutte d'eau. Bruxelles, 1842. 2v.
41558.57.5 Souvestre, Émile. La goutte d'eau. Paris, 1857.
41558.58 Souvestre, Émile. L'homme et l'argent. Paris, 1861.
41558.59 Souvestre, Émile. Le monde tel qu'il sera. Paris, n.d.
41558.61 Souvestre, Émile. Le mendiant de Saint-Roch. Paris, 1853.
41558.62 Souvestre, Émile. Le mémorial de famille. Paris, 1854.
41558.62.5 Souvestre, Émile. Le mémorial de famille. Paris, 1883.
41558.63 Souvestre, Émile. Riche et pauvre. Bruxelles, 1836.
41558.63.5 Souvestre, Émile. Riche et pauvre. Paris, 1848.
41558.64 Souvestre, Émile. Pendant la moisson. Paris, 1859.
41558.65 Souvestre, Émile. Un philosophe sous les toits. Paris, 1869.
41558.65.1 Souvestre, Émile. Un philosophe sous les toits. 6e éd. Paris, 1853.
41558.65.2 Souvestre, Émile. Un philosophe sous les toits. 8e éd. Paris, 1855.
41558.65.3 Souvestre, Émile. Un philosophe sous les toits. Paris, 1857.
41558.65.5 Souvestre, Émile. Un philosophe sous les toits. N.Y., 1868.
41558.66 Souvestre, Émile. Un philosophe sous les toits. London, 1874.
41558.66.10 Souvestre, Émile. Un philosophe sous les toits. London, 1895.
41558.66.15 Souvestre, Émile. Un philosophe sous les toits. Paris, 191-?
41558.66.16 Souvestre, Émile. Un philosophe sous les toits. Paris, 191-?
41558.67 Souvestre, Émile. An attic philosopher in Paris. N.Y., 1856.
41558.67.5 Souvestre, Émile. An attic philosopher in Paris. N.Y., 1854.
41558.67.8 Souvestre, Émile. An attic philosopher in Paris. N.Y., 1888.
41558.67.10 Souvestre, Émile. An attic philosopher in Paris. N.Y., 1892.
41558.68A Souvestre, Émile. An attic philosopher in Paris. N.Y., 1893.
41558.68B Souvestre, Émile. An attic philosopher in Paris. N.Y., 1893.
41558.68.5 Souvestre, Émile. An attic philosopher in Paris. N.Y., 1898.
41558.68.20 Souvestre, Émile. An attic philosopher in Paris. N.Y., 1910.
41558.69F Souvestre, Émile. Pierre Landais. Paris, 1861.
41558.70 Souvestre, Émile. Scènes et récits des Alpes. Paris, 1877.
41558.71 Souvestre, Émile. Théâtre de la jeunesse. Paris, 1878.
41558.72F Souvestre, Émile. Souvenirs d'un Bas-Breton. Paris, 18- .
41558.73 Souvestre, Émile. Le serf. Cambridge, 1895.
41558.81 Souvestre, Émile. Mrs. Willis's will; a comic drama. Boston, 18- .
41558.85 Souvestre, Émile. A slight mistake, a comedy. Boston, 18-

41561 Individual authors, etc. - 1800-1849 - Fiction - Folios [Discontinued]

41561.2.5 Sue, Eugène. Arthur. Paris, 19- . 2v.
41561.2.10 Sue, Eugène. The knight of Malta. Paris, 19- .
41561.2.15 Sue, Eugène. The mysteries of Paris. Paris, 19- .
41561.2.20 Sue, Eugène. The seven cardinal sins, avarice and anger. Paris, 19- .
41561.2.25 Sue, Eugène. The seven cardinal sins, envy. Paris, 19- .
41561.2.30 Sue, Eugène. The seven cardinal sins, luxury and gluttony. Paris, 19- .
41561.2.35 Sue, Eugène. The seven cardinal sins, pride. Paris, 19- . 2v.
41561.2.40 Sue, Eugène. The wandering Jew. Paris, 19- . 3v.
41561.5F Louvet, Jean Baptiste. Histoire du chevalier de Faublas. Paris, 1859.
41561.6 Sue, Eugène. Colonel de Surville. N.Y., 1846.
41561.7 Sue, Eugène. Deux histoires: Aventures d'Hercule Hardi, le colonel de Surville. Paris, 1851.
41561.8 Sue, Eugène. Le Juif errant. Paris, 1845. 2v.
41561.9 Sue, Eugène. Le Juif errant. Bruxelles, 1846. 3v.
41561.10 Sue, Eugène. Le Juif errant. Paris, 1851.
41561.11 Sue, Eugène. Le Juif errant. Paris, 1888.
41561.12 Sue, Eugène. El judio errante. Madrid, 1845. 4v.
41561.13A Sue, Eugène. Wandering Jew. N.Y., 1846. 2v.
41561.13B Sue, Eugène. Wandering Jew. N.Y., 1846. 2v.
41561.15 Sue, Eugène. Wandering Jew. N.Y., 1846.
41561.15.2 Sue, Eugène. Wandering Jew. N.Y., 1844-45.
41561.15.5 Sue, Eugène. Wandering Jew. N.Y., 1845.
41561.15.10 Sue, Eugène. Wandering Jew. London, 1844-45. 2v.
41561.15.20 Sue, Eugène. Wandering Jew. London, 1873?
41561.15.22 Sue, Eugène. Wandering Jew. London, 1889. 3v.
41561.16 Sue, Eugène. Les mystères du peuple. Boston, 1857.
41561.17 Sue, Eugène. Mysteries of the people. N.Y., 1867.
41561.18 Sue, Eugène. The knight of Malta. N.Y., 1900.
41561.21 Tchernychev, A. Oeuvres choisies. Paris, 1892.
41561.23 Toepffer, Rodolphe. Premiers voyages en zigzag. 5e éd. Paris, 1859.
41561.23.2 Toepffer, Rodolphe. Nouveaux voyages en zigzag. 2e éd. Paris, 1858.
41561.24 Toepffer, Rodolphe. Premiers voyages en zigzag. Paris, 1868.
41561.25 Toepffer, Rodolphe. Nouveaux voyages en zigzag. Paris, 1870.
41561.27 Blondel, A. Rodolphe Toepffer, l'écrivain, l'artiste et l'homme. Paris, 1886.

41562 Individual authors, etc. - 1800-1849 - Fiction - Sue - Complete and Selected works

41562.2 Sue, Eugène. Oeuvres choisies. Paris, n.d.
41562.3 Sue, Eugène. L'alouette de casque - Adèle Verneuil. Paris, 1866.
41562.4 Sue, Eugène. Arthur. Paris, 1869.
41562.5 Sue, Eugène. La bonne aventure. Paris, 1861.

41562 Individual authors, etc. - 1800-1849 - Fiction - Sue - Complete and Selected works - cont.

41562.6 Sue, Eugène. Eugène Sue photographié par lui-même. Genève, 1858.
41562.7 Sue, Eugène. Clémence Hervé. Jeanne Darc. Paris, 1866.
41562.8 Sue, Eugène. La coucaratcha. Latréaumont. Paris, 1858.
41562.9 Sue, Eugène. Les enfants de l'amour. Paris, n.d.
41562.11 Sue, Eugène. La famille Jouffroy. Paris, 1868. 3v.
41562.12 Sue, Eugène. La faucille d'or. La croix d'argent. Le collier de fer. Paris, 1866.
41562.13 Sue, Eugène. Les fils de famille. Paris, 1869.
41562.14 Sue, Eugène. Les fils de famille. Paris, 1861.
41562.15 Sue, Eugène. Gilbert et Gilberte. Paris, 1860. 3v.
41562.16 Sue, Eugène. Le diable médecin: La grande dame, Henriette Dumesnil. Paris, 1866.
41562.18 Sue, Eugène. Le Juif errant. Paris, 1869. 2v.
41562.19 Sue, Eugène. Le juif errant. v.1-4. Paris, 1881. 2v.
41562.20 Sue, Eugène. Mémoires d'un mari. Paris, 1874. 2v.
41562.21 Sue, Eugène. Le morne-au-diable. Paris, 1874.
41562.22 Sue, Eugène. Les mystères de Paris. Paris, 1869. 2v.
41562.23 Sue, Eugène. Les mystères de Paris. Paris, 1843-44. 2v.
41562.24 Sue, Eugène. Paula Monti - Commandeur de Malte. Paris, 1858.
41562.25 Sue, Eugène. Plik et Plok. Atar Gull. Deux histoires, 1772-1870. Paris, 1865.
41562.28 Sue, Eugène. Les secrets de l'oreiller. Paris, 1865. 3v.
41562.29 Sue, Eugène. Les sept péchés capitaux, orgueil. Paris, 1870.
41562.30 Sue, Eugène. Les sept péchés capitaux, l'envie, la colère. Paris, 1872.
41562.31 Sue, Eugène. Les sept péchés capitaux, luxure, paresse, avarice, gourmandise. Paris, 1866.
41562.32 Sue, Eugène. Thérèse Dunoyer. Paris, 1874.
41562.34 Sue, Eugène. La vigie de Koat-Ven. Paris, 1861.

41563.1 - .17 Individual authors, etc. - 1800-1849 - Fiction - Sue - Individual works

41563.3 Sue, Eugène. Le fils de famille. Bruxelles, 1856. 7v.
41563.4 Sue, Eugène. Les sept péchés capitaux. La luxure. La paresse. Paris, 1851.
41563.4.5 Sue, Eugène. Les sept péchés capitaux. L'orgueil. Paris, 1851-82. 2v.
41563.4.10 Sue, Eugène. Les sept péchés capitaux. L'envie - La colère. Paris, 1854-78. 2v.
41563.6 Sue, Eugène. Jean Cavalier, ou Les fanatiques des Cévennes. Bruxelles, 1840.
41563.7 Sue, Eugène. The hotel Lambert. N.Y., 1845.
41563.8 Sue, Eugène. Atar-gull. Paris, 1958.
41563.9 Sue, Eugène. The Marquis of Létorière. Boston, 1873.
41563.10 Sue, Eugène. Mathilde. Paris, 1845. 3v.
41563.11 Sue, Eugène. Martin, or The foundling. N.Y., 1846?
Htn 41563.11.5* Sue, Eugène. The salamander. N.Y., 1844.
41563.11.6 Sue, Eugène. Martin the foundling. n.p., 18- .
41563.12 Sue, Eugène. Les mystères du monde. Berlin, 1861.
41563.13 Sue, Eugène. The pilgrim's shell. N.Y., 1904.
41563.15 Sue, Eugène. The mysteries of Paris. v.1-2. N.Y., 1843.
41563.16 Sue, Eugène. The mysteries of Paris. London, 1845-46.
41563.16.5 Sue, Eugène. The mysteries of Paris. v.1-3. London, 1873.
41563.16.15 Sue, Eugène. The mysteries of Paris. v.1-6. N.Y., 1903. 3v.
41563.16.20 Sue, Eugène. The mysteries of Paris. Boston, 19- . 3v.
41563.17 Sue, Eugène. Los misterios de Paris. Madrid, 1845. 4v.
41563.17.5 Sue, Eugène. Das Mährlein von Fletsch und Winzelchen. Frankfurt, 1844.

41563.18 Individual authors, etc. - 1800-1849 - Fiction - Sue - Biography and criticism

41563.18 Atkinson, Nora. Eugène Sue et le roman. Feuilleton. Thèse. Nemours, 1929.
41563.18.5 Atkinson, Nora. Eugène Sue et le roman. Feuilleton. Nemours, 1929.
41563.18.25 Edler, Erich. Eugène Sue und die deutsche Mysterienliteratur. Berlin, 1932.
41563.18.30 Moosy, John. Les idées sociales d'Eugène Sue. Thèse. Paris, 1938.
41563.18.35 Chaunu, P. Eugène Sue et la seconde République. 1. ed. Paris, 1948.
41563.18.40 Bory, Jean L. Eugène Sue. Paris, 1962.

41563.20 Individual authors, etc. - 1800-1849 - Fiction - Suberwick

41563.20 Suberwick, de (Mme.). Geheimnisse der Inquisition. Budapest, 1899.

41563.23 Individual authors, etc. - 1800-1849 - Fiction - Thibaudeau

41563.23 Thibaudeau, Antoine C. La Bohême. Paris, 1834. 2v.
41563.23.5 Thibaudeau, Antoine C. Böhmen in den Jahren 1600 bis 1621. Gotha, 1836. 2v.

41563.25 - .32 Individual authors, etc. - 1800-1849 - Fiction - Toepffer - Writings

41563.25 Toepffer, Rodolphe. Mélanges. Paris, 1852.
41563.25.10 Toepffer, Rodolphe. Mélanges sur les beaux-arts. Genève, 1953. 2v.
41563.26 Toepffer, Rodolphe. Nouvelles genevoises. Rosa et Gertrude. Paris, 1853.
41563.26.2 Toepffer, Rodolphe. Nouvelles genevoises. Paris, 1851.
41563.26.3 Toepffer, Rodolphe. Nouvelles genevoises. 2. ed. Bielefeld, 1860.
41563.26.5 Toepffer, Rodolphe. Nouvelles genevoises. 2. éd. Bielefeld, 1860.
41563.26.10 Toepffer, Rodolphe. Nouvelles genevoises. Paris, 1865. 3v.
41563.27 Toepffer, Rodolphe. Nouvelles genevoises. Paris, 1872.
41563.27.2 Toepffer, Rodolphe. Nouvelles genevoises. Paris, 1882.
41563.27.5 Toepffer, Rodolphe. Enter the comics. Lincoln, Nebr., 1965.
41563.28 Toepffer, Rodolphe. Nouvelles genevoises. 4. éd. Bielefeld, 1872.
41563.28.1.20 Toepffer, Rodolphe. Nouvelles. v.1,2-3. Genève, 1942. 2v.

41563.25 - .32 Individual authors, etc. - 1800-1849 - Fiction - Toepffer - Writings - cont.

41563.28.1.25 Toepffer, Rodolphe. Caricatures. Genève, 1843- 8v.
41563.28.2 Toepffer, Rodolphe. Le Presbytère. Paris, 1852.
41563.28.4 Toepffer, Rodolphe. Le Presbytère. Paris, 1878.
41563.28.10 Toepffer, Rodolphe. Elisa et Widmer. Genève, 1957.
41563.29 Toepffer, Rodolphe. The Presbytère. Paris, 1869.
41563.29.10 Toepffer, Rodolphe. Le Presbytère. Genève, 1944. 2v.
41563.29.30 Toepffer, Rodolphe. L'histoire véritable de Mr. Crépin. n.p., 1837.
41563.30 Toepffer, Rodolphe. Réflexions et menus proper. Paris, 1872.
41563.30.2 Toepffer, Rodolphe. Réflexions et menus propos. Paris, 1878.
41563.30.20 Toepffer, Rodolphe. Voyages et aventures du Docteur Festes. Paris, 1963.
41563.31 Toepffer, Rodolphe. Rosa et Gertrude. Paris, 1863.
41563.32 Toepffer, Rodolphe. Rosa et Gertrude. Paris, 1847.
41563.32.10 Toepffer, Rodolphe. Rosa et Gertrude. Genève, 1944.
41563.32.25 Toepffer, Rodolphe. Voyages en zigzag. Genève, 1945-52. 7v.

41563.33 Individual authors, etc. - 1800-1849 - Fiction - Toepffer - Works about

41563.33 Champonniere, Paul. Notre Toepffer. Lausanne, 1930.
41563.33.10 Relove, P.M. La vie et les oeuvres de Toepffer. Paris, 1886.
41563.33.15 Beaumont, Elie de. Mons. Cryptogame en zijn metamorphose. 's-Gravenhage, 1960.
41563.33.20 Kossmann, Friedrich K.H. Rodolphe Toepffer. Rotterdam, 1946.
41563.33.25 Gagnebin, Marianne. Rodolphe Toepffer. Neuchâtel, 1947.

41563.34 Individual authors, etc. - 1800-1849 - Fiction - Trognan

41563.34 Trognon, Auguste. Manuscrits de l'ancienne abbaye de Saint Julien, à Brioude. Paris, 1825.

41563.35 Individual authors, etc. - 1800-1849 - Fiction - Vanhove

41563.35 Vanhove, C.C.C. (Mlle.). L'ile des fées. Paris, 1822. 2v.

41563.50 Individual authors, etc. - 1800-1849 - Fiction - Vidocq

41563.50 Vidocq, Eugène François. Life in Paris. London, 1848.
41563.50.5 Vidocq, Eugène François. Les chauffeurs du nord. Paris, 1959.

41564.1 Individual authors, etc. - 1800-1849 - Fiction - Vigny - Complete works

41564.1 Vigny, Alfred de. Théâtre. Paris, 1916.
41564.1.2A Vigny, Alfred de. Poésies. Paris, 1916.
41564.1.2B Vigny, Alfred de. Poésies. Paris, 1916.
41564.1.2.5 Vigny, Alfred de. Poésies complètes. Paris, 1925.
41564.1.3 Vigny, Alfred de. Cinq Mars ou conjuration sous Louis XIII. Paris, 1914. 2v.
41564.1.4 Vigny, Alfred de. Daphné. Paris, 1913.
41564.1.4.10 Vigny, Alfred de. Daphné. Bologna, 1960.
41564.1.5 Vigny, Alfred de. Journal d'un poete. Paris, 1911.
41564.1.6 Vigny, Alfred de. Servitude et grandeur militaire. Paris, 1914.
41564.1.6.15 Vigny, Alfred de. Stello. 6e éd. Paris, 1852.
NEDL 41564.1.7 Vigny, Alfred. Stello. Paris, 1913.
41564.1.25A Vigny, Alfred de. Oeuvres complètes. Paris, 1948. 2v.
41564.1.25B Vigny, Alfred de. Oeuvres complètes. Paris, 1948. 2v.
41564.1.30 Vigny, Alfred de. Oeuvres complètes. Paris, 1913-14. 13v.
41564.1.35 Vigny, Alfred de. Oeuvres complètes. Paris, 1964. 2v.
41564.1.40 Vigny, Alfred de. Vigny par lui-même. Paris, 1964.

41564.2 Individual authors, etc. - 1800-1849 - Fiction - Vigny - Selected works

41564.2 Giraud, J. Alfred de Vigny oeuvres choisies. Paris, 1913.
41564.2.5 Vigny, Alfred de. Morceaux choisis. Paris, 1914.

41564.3 - .31 Individual authors, etc. - 1800-1849 - Fiction - Vigny - Individual works

41564.3 Vigny, Alfred de. La vie du Capitaine Renaud. Paris, 1867.
41564.3.50 Vigny, Alfred de. Cinq-Mars. v.1-2. 8e éd. Bruxelles, 1834.
41564.3.53 Vigny, Alfred de. Cinq-Mars. 11. éd. Paris, 1855.
41564.3.55 Vigny, Alfred de. Cinq-Mars. 2e éd. Paris, 1859.
41564.3.65A Vingy, Alfred de. Cinq-Mars. Boston, 1869.
41564.3.65B Vingy, Alfred de. Cinq-Mars. Boston, 1869.
41564.3.66 Vigny, Alfred de. Cinq-Mars. Boston, 1877.
41564.3.67 Vigny, Alfred de. Cinq-Mars. 14e éd. Paris, 1878.
41564.3.70 Vigny, Alfred de. Cinq-Mars. Boston, 1892. 3v.
41564.3.75 Vigny, Alfred de. Cinq-Mars. Paris, 1882. 2v.
41564.3.77 Vigny, Alfred de. Cinq-Mars. N.Y., 1883.
41564.3.80 Vigny, Alfred de. Cinq-Mars. v.1-2. London, 1887.
41564.3.85 Vigny, Alfred de. Cinq-Mars. Boston, 1889.
41564.4.9A Vigny, Alfred de. Cinq-Mars. London, 1892.
41564.4.9B Vigny, Alfred de. Cinq-Mars. London, 1892.
41564.5 Vigny, Alfred de. Cinq-Mars. London, 1893.
41564.5.5 Vigny, Alfred de. Cinq-Mars. Paris, 1899.
41564.5.7 Vigny, Alfred de. Cinq-mars. London, 1899.
41564.5.15 Vigny, Alfred de. Cinq-Mars. Paris, 1913.
41564.5.20 Vigny, Alfred de. Cinq-Mars. Paris, 1914-22.
41564.5.65 Vigny, Alfred de. Cinq-Mars. N.Y., 1923.
41564.6 Vigny, Alfred de. Laurette. Paris, 1867.
41564.7 Vigny, Alfred de. Servitude et grandeur militaires. 7. ed. Paris, 1857.
41564.7.5 Vigny, Alfred de. Servitude et grandeur militaires. Paris, 1914.
41564.7.7 Vigny, Alfred de. Servitude et grandeur militaires. Paris, 1965.
41564.7.10 Vigny, Alfred de. The military necessity. N.Y., 1953.
41564.7.15 Vigny, Alfred de. Nevolia i velichie soldata. Leningrad, 1968.
41564.8 Vigny, Alfred de. Nevolia i velichie soldata. Paris, 1872.
41564.8.5 Vigny, Alfred de. Military servitude and grandeur. N.Y., 1919.
41564.9.5 Vigny, Alfred de. Stello. Bruxelles, 1832.
41564.10 Vigny, Alfred de. Stello. 7. ed. Paris, 1856.

41564.3 - .31 Individual authors, etc. - 1800-1849 - Fiction - Vigny - Individual works - cont.

41564.10.5 Castex, P. Vigny: Stello, Servitude et grandeur militaires. Paris, 1963.
41564.10.20 Vigny, Alfred de. Stello. Montréal, 1963.
41564.11 Vigny, Alfred de. La veillée de Vincennes. Paris, 1867.
41564.14 Vigny, Alfred de. Journal d'un poète. Paris, 1867.
41564.14.10 Vigny, Alfred de. Le journal d'un poète. Paris, 1935.
41564.14.15 Vigny, Alfred de. Journal d'un poète. Paris, 1949.
41564.15.2 Vigny, Alfred de. Poésies complètes. Paris, n.d.
41564.15.5 Vigny, Alfred de. Poésies complètes. Paris, 1898.
41564.15.10 Vigny, Alfred de. Poésies complètes. Paris, 1913.
41564.15.20 Vigny, Alfred de. Poèmes: Livre mystique. Livre antique. Livre moderne. Poèmes philosophiques. Paris, 1914.
41564.16 Vigny, Alfred de. Poèmes. Bruxelles, 1834.
41564.16.5 Vigny, Alfred de. Poèmes antiques et modernes. Les meilleurs auteurs classiques, français et étrangers. Paris, 18- .
41564.16.9 Vigny, Alfred de. Poèmes antiques et modernes. 7. ed. Paris, 1859.
X Cg 41564.16.10 Vigny, Alfred de. Poèmes antiques et modernes. Paris, 1914.
41564.16.12 Vigny, Alfred de. Poèmes choisis. Manchester, 1918.
41564.18 Vigny, Alfred de. Théâtre complet. 7. éd. Paris, 1858.
41564.19 Vigny, Alfred de. Théâtre complet. Paris, 1882.
41564.20 Vigny, Alfred de. Théâtre complet. Paris, 1864.
41564.21 Vigny, Alfred de. Théâtre. Paris, 1926. 2v.
41564.22 Vigny, Alfred de. Héléna. Paris, 1907.
41564.23 Vigny, Alfred de. La canne de jonc. Cambridge, 1887.
41564.24 Vigny, Alfred de. Chatterton. Brussels, 1835.
41564.24.8 Vigny, Alfred de. Chatterton. Oxford, 1908.
41564.24.10 Vigny, Alfred de. Chatterton. Strasbourg, 1920.
41564.24.15 Vigny, Alfred de. Chatterton. Bologna, 1962.
41564.26 Vigny, Alfred de. Les destinées. Paris, 1924.
41564.27 Vigny, Alfred de. Les destinées. Paris, 1947.
41564.27.2 Vigny, Alfred de. Les destinées. Genève, 1961.
41564.28 Vigny, Alfred de. Imperial grandeur or the family. n.p., 1899.
41564.29 Vigny, Alfred de. Mémoires inédits. 3. éd. Paris, 1958.
41564.30 Vigny, Alfred de. Lettres inédites de Alfred Vigny au marquis. Paris, 1914.
41564.31 Sorrento, Luigi. Correspondance, 1816-1863. Paris, n.d.
41564.31.10 Sorrento, Luigi. Correspondance. Paris, 1933.
41564.31.20 Vigny, Alfred de. Lettres d'un dernier amour. Genève, 1952.
41564.31.30 Vigny, Alfred de. Lettres à Brizeux. Paris, 1954.
41564.31.40 Vigny, Alfred de. Lettres inédites d'Alfred de Vigny. Bordeaux, 1913.
41564.31.45 Vigny, Alfred de. Lettres à Philippe Soulet. Angoulême, 1965.
41564.31.50 Vigny, Alfred. Les destinées. Paris, 1964.

41564.32 - .55 Individual authors, etc. - 1800-1849 - Fiction - Vigny - Biography and criticism

41564.32 Charavay, Étienne. Alfred de Vigny et Charles Baudelaire. Paris, 1879.
41564.33 Paléologue, Maurice. Alfred de Vigny. Paris, 1891.
41564.33.5 Paléologue, Maurice. Alfred de Vigny. 2. ed. Paris, 1903.
41564.34 Dorison, Léon. Alfred de Vigny. Paris, n.d.
41564.35 Alfred de Vigny et la poésie politique. Paris, 1894.
41564.35.5 Flottes, Pierre. La pensée politique et sociale d'Alfred de Vigny. Paris, 1927.
41564.35.9 Flottes, Pierre. La pensée politique et sociale d'Alfred de Vigny. Thèse. Strasbourg, 1926.
41564.36 Lafond, Paul. Alfred de Vigny en Béarn. Photoreproduction. Paris, 1897.
41564.36.5 Lafond, Paul. Alfred de Vigny en Béarn. Pau, 1894.
41564.37 Séché, Léon. Alfred de Vigny et son temps. Paris, 1902.
41564.38 Sakellarides, Emma. Alfred de Vigny. Paris, 1903.
41564.39A Lauvrière, E. Alfred de Vigny, sa vie et son oeuvre. Paris, 1909.
41564.39B Lauvrière, E. Alfred de Vigny, sa vie et son oeuvre. Paris, 1909.
41564.39.5 Lauvrière, E. Alfred de Vigny, sa vie et son oeuvre. Paris, 1945. 2v.
41564.40 Hoegen, W. Die Menschheitsdichtungen der französichen Romantiker Vigny-Lamartine-Hugo. Darmstadt, 1908.
41564.41 Amis d'Alfred de Vigny. Bulletin. Paris. 1,1967?+
41564.42 Pamphlet box. Alfred de Vigny. 5 pam.
41564.44 Prudhomme, S. A Alfred de Vigny sonnet. Paris, 1898.
41564.45 Dupuy, Ernest. Alfred de Vigny. Paris, 1910-12. 2v.
41564.45.5 Dupuy, Ernest. Alfred de Vigny, la vie et l'oeuvre. Paris, 1913.
41564.46A Baldensperger, F. Alfred de Vigny. Paris, 1912.
41564.46B Baldensperger, F. Alfred de Vigny. Paris, 1912.
41564.46.5 Baldensperger, F. Alfred de Vigny. 7e éd. Paris, 1929.
41564.47 Aicard, J. Alfred de Vigny. Paris, n.d.
41564.48 Sorrento, Luigi. Lettura e illustrazione critica della poesia di Alfred de Vigny. Milano, 1945.
41564.50 Calvet, J. Alfred de Vigny. Paris, 1914.
41564.53 Huber, Richard. Alfred de Vigny als Philosoph. Marburg, 1913.
41564.54A Citoleux, Marc. Alfred de Vigny. Paris, 1924.
41564.54B Citoleux, Marc. Alfred de Vigny. Paris, 1924.
41564.54.5 Lednicki, W. Alfred de Vigny. Warszawa, 1923.
41564.55 Fierini, Mario. Alfred de Vigny; saggio critico. Bari, 1922.
41564.55.5 Brach, Paul. La destinée du comte Alfred de Vigny. Paris, 1927.
41564.55.15 Estève, E. Alfred de Vigny. Paris, 1929.
41564.55.16 Traz, Robert de. Alfred de Vigny. Paris, 1928.
41564.55.23 Summers, V.A. L'orientalisme d'Alfred de Vigny. Thèse. Paris, 1930.
41564.55.25 Summers, V.A. L'orientalisme d'Alfred de Vigny. Paris, 1930.
41564.55.30 Clarke, S.H. The works of Vigny judged by his contemporaries. Toulouse, 1932.
41564.55.33 Whitridge, A. Alfred de Vigny. London, 1933.
41564.55.35 Moreau, P. Les "destinées" d'Alfred de Vigny. Paris, 1936.
41564.55.40 Lebbin, E. Alfred de Vignys Beziehungen zu England und zur englischen Literatur. Inaug. Diss. Halle, 1936.
41564.55.45 Popova, I.M. L'orignilité de l'oeuvre d'Alfred de Vigny. Thèse. Toulouse, 1937.
41564.55.50 Le Clercq, J.G.C. L'inspiration biblique dans l'oeuvre poétique d'Alfred de Vigny. Thèse. Annemasse, 1937.

41564.32 - .55 Individual authors, etc. - 1800-1849 - Fiction - Vigny - Biography and criticism - cont.

41564.55.54 Schweitzer, A. Die Darstellungskunst in A. de Vignys historischem Roman Cinq-Mars. Inaug. Diss. Emsdetten, 1937.
41564.55.60 Bird, Charles W. Alfred de Vigny's Chatterton. Los Angeles, 1941.
41564.55.63 LaSalle, Bertrand de. Alfred de Vigny. Paris, 1939.
41564.55.65 LaSalle, Bertrand de. Alfred de Vigny. Paris, 1944.
41564.55.70 Dorval, Marie. Lettres à Alfred de Vigny. Paris, 1942.
41564.55.75 Bonnefoy, Georges. La pensée religieuse et moral. Paris, 1940.
41564.55.80 Bélanger, D. Les séjours d'Alfred de Vigny en Charante. Angoulême, 1948.
41564.55.85 Castex, Pierre. Vigny. Paris, 1952.
41564.55.87 Castex, Pierre. Vigny. Paris, 1957.
41564.55.90 Guillemin, Henri. M. de Vigny. 7. ed. Paris, 1955.
41564.55.95 Cesare, Raffaele de. Intorno a servitude et grandeur militaires di A. de Vigny. Arona, 1949.
41564.55.100 France, Anatole. Alfred de Vigny. Paris, 1923.
41564.55.105 Germain, François. L'imagination d'Alfred de Vigny. Paris, 1961.
41564.55.110 Teppe, J. Alfred de Vigny et ses amants. Paris, 1963.
41564.55.115 Bibliothèque nationale, Paris. Alfred de Vigny, 1797-1863. Paris, 1963.
41564.55.120 Eigeldinger, Marc. Alfred de Vigny: Un tableau synoptique de la vie et des oeuvres d'Alfred de Vigny et des événements artistiques. Paris, 1965.
41564.55.125 Doolittle, James. Alfred de Vigny. N.Y., 1967.
41564.55.130 Quebedeau, Denise Bonhomme. Le collier theosophique d'Alfred de Vigny. Silverton, 1968.
41564.55.135 Bartfeld, Fernande. Vigny et la figure de Moïse. Paris, 1968.
41564.55.140 Sungolowsky, Joseph. Alfred de Vigny et le dix-huitième siècle. Paris, 1968.
41564.55.145 Nitschke, Uwe. Studien zum Schicksalsgedanken und seiner dichterischen Gestaltung bei Alfred de Vigny. Hamburg, 1969.

41565 Individual authors, etc. - 1800-1849 - Fiction - Folios [Discontinued]

41565.3 Bibliothèque choisie. Paris, 1833-34. 4v.
41565.6 Albitte, Gustave. Une vie d'homme. Paris, 1831.
41565.8 D'Arlincourt, Victor. Les trois châteaux. Paris, 1840.
41565.9 D'Arlincourt, Victor. L'étoile polaire. Paris, 1843. 2v.
41565.23 Legrand, Alex A. Le philosophe crétien. Paris, 1846.
41565.27 St. Mars, G.A.C. de C. Mémoires des autres. Paris, 1804-72. 6v.
41565.28 St. Mars, G.A.C. de C. Mademoiselle Robespierre. v.1-2. Paris, 1855.
41565.29 St. Mars, G.A.C. de C. Le soupers de la régence. Paris, 1869.
41565.30 St. Mars, G.A.C. de C. Madame de la Sablière. Paris, 1840.
41565.30.5 St, Mars, G.A.C. de C. La jolie Bohémienne. Paris, 1870.
41565.31 St. Mars, G.A.C. de. C. Une rivale de la Pompadour. Paris, 1871.
41565.31.10 St. Mars, G.A.C. de C. La chambre bleue. Paris, 1864.
41565.32 Waldor, Mélanie. L'ecuyer Dauberon. Paris, 1832.
41565.34 Vacquerie, Auguste. Profils et grimances. 4. ed. Paris, 1864.
41565.35 Vacquerie, Auguste. Aujourd'hui et demain. 2. éd. Paris, 1875.
41565.36 Vacquerie, Auguste. Jean Baudry. Paris, 1880.
41565.37 Vacquerie, Auguste. Souvent homme varie. Paris, 1887.

41566.1 Individual authors, etc. - 1800-1849 - Fiction - Abrantes

41566.1 Abrantes, L. St.M.P.J. L'amirante de Castille. 2e éd. Paris, 1836.

41566.2 - .5 Individual authors, etc. - 1800-1849 - Fiction - Arlincourt

41566.2 Marquiset, A. Le vicomte d'Arlincourt. Paris, 1909.
41566.2.9 D'Arlincourt, Charles V.P. The brewer king. N.Y., 1844.
41566.2.10 D'Arlincourt, Charles V.P. El cervecero rey. Barcelona, 1834. 2v.
41566.3 D'Arlincourt, Charles V.P. Le renégat. Paris, 1823. 2v.
41566.3.9 D'Arlincourt, Charles V.P. Le solitaire. Paris, 1821. 2v.
41566.4 D'Arlincourt, Charles V.P. The solitary. N.Y., 1822.
41566.5 D'Arlincourt, Hippolyte. The recluse. n.p., n.d.
41566.5.5 D'Arlincourt, Charles V.P. Les écorcheurs ou l'usurpation et la peste. Bruxelles, 1833.
41566.5.15 D'Arlincourt, Charles V.P. La rosa di Firenze. Napoli, 1850.
41566.5.20 D'Arlincourt, Charles V.P. Nagy Károly. Pesten, 1834. 2v.

41566.6 - .7 Individual authors, etc. - 1800-1849 - Fiction - Arnould

41566.6 Arnould, Auguste. Adèle Launay. Bruxelles, 1841.
41566.7 Arnould, Auguste. La mère-folle. Bruxelles, 1840.

41566.8 Individual authors, etc. - 1800-1849 - Fiction - Auger

41566.8 Auger, Hippolyte Nicolas Just. Priesterlist über alles. v.1-2. Leipzig, 1835. 2v.

41566.9 Individual authors, etc. - 1800-1849 - Fiction - Barginet

41566.9 Barginet, A.P. La trente-deuxième demi-brigade. Bruxelles, 1832.

41566.11 Individual authors, etc. - 1800-1849 - Fiction - Bazot

41566.11 Bazot, Étienne F. Historiettes. Paris, 1825.

41566.12 - .13 Individual authors, etc. - 1800-1849 - Fiction - Bonnellier

41566.12 Bonnellier, Hippolyte. Matinées. Paris, 1837.
41566.12.5 Bonnellier, Hippolyte. Les vieilles femmes de l'Ile de Sein. v.1-2. Paris, 1826.
41566.13 Bonnellier, Hippolyte. Un malheur domestique. Bruxelles, 1837. 2v.

41566.14 Individual authors, etc. - 1800-1849 - Fiction - Bouilly

41566.14 Bouilly, Jean N. Contes à ma fille. Bruxelles, 1835.
41566.14.2 Bouilly, Jean N. Contes à mes petites amies. Paris, 1827?
41566.14.3 Bouilly, Jean N. Contes offerts aux enfans de France. 1Paris, 18- ? 2v.
41566.14.5 Bouilly, Jean N. Pavidky pro magi d ceru. V Praze, 1854.

41566.14 Individual authors, etc. - 1800-1849 - Fiction - Bouilly - cont.
41566.14.9 Bouilly, Jean N. Mes recapitulations. Paris, n.d. 3v.
41566.14.12 Bouilly, Jean N. Les encourgaments de la jeunesse. 2. éd. Paris, 1817.
41566.14.15 Bouilly, Jean N. Aguador de Paris. Valencia, 1822.
41566.14.20 Bouilly, Jean N. Haine aux femmes. Paris, 1808.
41566.14.23 Bouilly, Jean N. Causeries d'un vieillard. 2e éd. Paris, n.d.
41566.14.28 Bouilly, Jean N. L'abbé de l'épée; comédie historique. Paris, 1800.
41566.14.30 Bouilly, Jean N. The abbé de l'épée. Munich, 1859.

41566.15 Individual authors, etc. - 1800-1849 - Fiction - Chabot de Bouin
41566.15 Chabot de Bouin, Jules. Histoire de deux soeurs. Brusselles, 1835.

41566.16 - .16.49 Individual authors, etc. - 1800-1849 - Fiction - Bourgeois
41566.16 Bourgeois, A. Brins d'herbe et un tour à pied. Morlaux, 1857.

41566.16.50 - .16.99 Individual authors, etc. - 1800-1849 - Fiction - Brucker
41566.16.50 Bruckar, R. Le puritain de Seine et Marne. Bruxelles, 1832.

41566.17 - .18 Individual authors, etc. - 1800-1849 - Fiction - Buonaparte, L.
41566.17A Buonaparte, Louis. Maria. Boston, 1815. 2v.
41566.17B Buonaparte, Louis. Maria. Boston, 1815.
41566.18.9 Buonaparte, Louis. Poésies. Florence, 1831.

41566.19 Individual authors, etc. - 1800-1849 - Fiction - Cadet
41566.19.10 Cadet, Jêsus. (pseud.). Les aventures de Jêsus Cadet, par lui. Paris, 1802.
41566.20 Chapus, Eugène. Les chasses princières en France. Paris, 1853.

41566.22 Individual authors, etc. - 1800-1849 - Fiction - Choiseul
41566.22 Choiseul, Felicite de. Recreations morales et amusantes. Paris, 1817.

41566.24 Individual authors, etc. - 1800-1849 - Fiction - Corbière
41566.24 Corbière, Edouard. Les aspirans de marine. Bruxelles, 1835.

41566.26 - .27 Individual authors, etc. - 1800-1849 - Fiction - Craon
41566.26 Craon, princesse de. Henri Percy. Paris, 1835. 2v.
41566.27 Craon, princesse de. Thomas Morus. Paris, 1834.

41566.28 Individual authors, etc. - 1800-1849 - Fiction - Creuzé du Lesser
41566.28 Creuzé de Lesser, A. 1800 ans. Paris, 1837. 3v.

41566.30 Individual authors, etc. - 1800-1849 - Fiction - Daux
41566.30 Daux, curé de Vauxbuin. Les petits hommes, ou Recueil d'anecdotes sur les hommes de petite stature qui se sont fait un nom par leurs vertus. Paris, 1822. 2v.

41566.31 Individual authors, etc. - 1800-1849 - Fiction - Defontenay
41566.31 De Fontenay. Star ou de Cassiopée. Paris, 1854.

41566.33 Individual authors, etc. - 1800-1849 - Fiction - Delafaye-Brehier
41566.33 Delafaye-Brehier, J. Les Portugais d'Amérique. Paris, 1847.

41566.36 Individual authors, etc. - 1800-1849 - Fiction - Delécluze
41566.36 Delécluze, E.J. Souvenirs de soixante années. Paris, 1862.
41566.36.3 Delécluze, E.J. Journal de Delécluze. 2. ed. Paris, 1948.
41566.36.4 Delécluze, E.J. Two loves in Rome. Garden City, 1958
41566.36.5 Delécluze, E.J. Mademoiselle Justine de Liron. Paris, 1921.
41566.36.10 Delécluze, E.J. Impéressions romaines. Paris, 1942.
41566.36.15 Baschet, Robert. E.J. Delécluze, témoin de son temps, 1781-1863. Paris, 1942.
41566.36.20 Baschet, Robert. E.J. Delécluze. Thèse. Paris, 1942.

41566.58 Individual authors, etc. - 1800-1849 - Fiction - Bonnardot
41566.58.30 Bonnardot, Alfred. Fantaisies multicolores. Paris, 1859.

41567.5 Individual authors, etc. - 1800-1849 - Fiction - Delrieu
41567.5 Delrieu, Andre. Virginité. Bruxelles, 1837. 2v.

41567.8 Individual authors, etc. - 1800-1849 - Fiction - Dincourt
41567.8 Dinocourt, T. Mozanino. Paris, 1825. 4v.

41567.10 - .11 Individual authors, etc. - 1800-1849 - Fiction - Duras - Writings
41567.10 Duras, Claire de Durfort. Ourika. Boston, 1829.
41567.11 Duras, Claire de Durfort. Ourika. Paris, 1824.

41567.12 Individual authors, etc. - 1800-1849 - Fiction - Duras - Works about
41567.12 Bardoux, Agénor. Étude sociales et politiques, La duchesse de Duras. Paris, 1898.

41567.14 - .16 Individual authors, etc. - 1800-1849 - Fiction - Fouinet - Writings
41567.14 Fouinet, E. Les douze nations. Paris, 1844.
41567.15 Fouinet, E. L'ile des cinq. Tours, 1866.
41567.16 Fouinet, E. Roch le corsaire. Bruxelles, 1837. 2v.

41567.18 Individual authors, etc. - 1800-1849 - Fiction - Gay, M.F.S.
41567.18 Gay, M.F.S.N. de. L. Anatole. n.p., n.d.

41567.19 Individual authors, etc. - 1800-1849 - Fiction - Geoffroy
41567.19 Geoffroy, J. Louis. Napoléon apocryphe, 1812-1852. Paris, 1841.
41567.19.5 Geoffroy, J. Louis. Napoléon apocryphe, 1812-1852. Paris, 1896?

41567.20 Individual authors, etc. - 1800-1849 - Fiction - Grandfort
41567.20 Grandfort, Manoël de. L'autre monde. Paris, 1855.

41567.22 - .24 Individual authors, etc. - 1800-1849 - Fiction - Guizot, Mme de - Writings
41567.22 Guizot, Elizabeth C.P. de M. Caroline. Boston, 1835.
41567.23 Guizot, Elizabeth C.P. de M. Tales in French. Boston, 1835.
41567.23.2 Guizot, Elizabeth C.P. de M. Popular tales. Boston, 1854.
41567.23.4 Guizot, Elizabeth C.P. de M. Nouveaux contes. Paris, 1833. 2v.
41567.23.5 Guizot, Elizabeth C.P. de M. Nouveaux contes. Paris, 1834. 2v.
41567.23.10 Guizot, Elizabeth C.P. de M. Les enfans. pt. 1. 2e éd. Paris, 181-?
41567.23.15 Guizot, Elizabeth C.P. de M. The young student. N.Y., 1844.
41567.24 Guizot, Elizabeth C.P. de M. Cecilia. Boston, 1848.

41567.25 Individual authors, etc. - 1800-1849 - Fiction - Guizot, Mme de - Works about
41567.25.25 Hilarion, père. Le triomphe de l'amour conjugal. Paris, 1805.

41567.27 Individual authors, etc. - 1800-1849 - Fiction - Montpezat, Mme de
41567.27 Montpezat, Charles de (Mme.). Corisande de Mauléon. Bruxelles, 1835.

41567.28 Individual authors, etc. - 1800-1849 - Fiction - Herbster, Mme de
41567.28 Herbster, de (Mme.). The sisters of the cavern. Boston, 1823.

41567.30 Individual authors, etc. - 1800-1849 - Fiction - Jauffret
41567.30 Jauffret, Louis F. Travels of Rolando. London, 1853.
41567.30.80 Reboul, R.M. Louis François Jauffret. Paris, 1869.

41567.32 Individual authors, etc. - 1800-1849 - Fiction - Juno
41567.32 Junot, Laure. La duchesse de Valombrai. Bruxelles, 1839. 2v.

41567.34 Individual authors, etc. - 1800-1849 - Fiction - Lottin de Laval
41567.34 Lottin de Laval, René V. Robert le magnifique. Bruxelles, 1835.
41567.34.5 Lottin de Laval, René V. Maria von Medicis. Heidelberg, 1835.

41567.37 Individual authors, etc. - 1800-1849 - Fiction - Lorvergne
41567.37 Lorvergne A. de. Le comte de Mansfeldt. Bruxelles, 1840.

41567.40 Individual authors, etc. - 1800-1849 - Fiction - La Madelaine
41567.40 La Madelaine, Stephen. La grande-prieure de Malte. Bruxelles, 1835.

41567.42 Individual authors, etc. - 1800-1849 - Fiction - Manesca
41567.42 Manesca, J. Historiettes nouvelles. Philadelphia, 1815.
41567.42.5 Manesca, J. Historiettes nouvelles. N.Y., 1822.

41567.43 - .44 Individual authors, etc. - 1800-1849 - Fiction - Masson - Writings
41567.43 Masson, Michel. La femme du réfractaire. Paris, 1865.
41567.44 Masson, Michel. Thadéus le ressuscité. Bruxelles, 1833.
41567.44.15 Masson, Michel. Ne touchez pas à la reine. Bruxelles, 1837.
41567.44.25 Masson, Michel. La lampe de fer de Daniel le lapidaire. Bruxelles, 1835.

41567.47 - .48 Individual authors, etc. - 1800-1849 - Fiction - Philipon
41567.47 Philipon, C. Parodie du Juif errant. Bruxelles, 1845.
Htn 41567.48* Philipon, C. Parodie des ewingen Judens. Frankfurt, 1845.

41567.50 Individual authors, etc. - 1800-1849 - Fiction - Ponson du Terrail
41567.50 Ponson du Terrail. Le capitaine Curebourse. N.Y., 1864.
41567.60 Historiettes et contes à ma petite fille. Paris, n.d.

41568.1 Individual authors, etc. - 1800-1849 - Fiction - Rabbé
41568.1 Rabbé, Alphonse. Album d'un pessimiste. Paris, 1836.
41568.1.25 Rabbé, Alphonse. Album d'un pessimiste. Le centaure. Le naufrage. L'adolescence. Paris, 1924.
41568.1.75 Andrieux, Louis. Alphonse Rabbé. Thèse. Paris, 1927.
41568.1.80 Wieclawik, L. de. Alphonse Rabbé dans la mélée politique et littéraire de la restauration. Paris, 1963.

41568.6 - .7 Individual authors, etc. - 1800-1849 - Fiction - Reybaud, H.E.F. - Writings
41568.6 Reybaud, Charles (Mrs.). La pauvre paysanne. Bruxelles, 1840.
41568.6.5 Reybaud, Charles (Mrs.). Mademoiselle de Malepeire. Paris, 1856.
41568.7 Reybaud, Charles (Mrs.). Esther de Chazeuil. Habana, 1841.

41568.9 Individual authors, etc. - 1800-1849 - Fiction - Saint-Genois
41568.9 St. Genois, Ludger D.G. Hembyse. Habana, 1835. 2v.
41568.9.8 St. Genois, Jules. Le chateau de Wildenborg. 3e éd. Paris, 1861.

41568.10 - .12 Individual authors, etc. - 1800-1849 - Fiction - Saintine - Writings
41568.10 Saintine, Joseph Xavier Boniface. Les métamorphoses de la femme. Paris, 1859.
41568.10.5 Saintine, Joseph Xavier Boniface. Poèmes, odes, épitres, et poésie diverse. Paris, 1823.
41568.11 Saintine, Joseph Xavier Boniface. Picciola. 2d ed. Philadelphia, 1839.
41568.11.2 Saintine, Joseph Xavier Boniface. Picciola. Paris, 1843.
41568.11.2.1 Saintine, Joseph Xavier Boniface. Picciola, the prisoner of Fenestrella. 3. ed. Philadelphia, 1843.
41568.11.2.2 Saintine, Joseph Xavier Boniface. Picciola. Boston, 1846.
41568.11.2.3 Saintine, Joseph Xavier Boniface. Picciola, the prisoner of Fenestrella. Philadelphia, 1849.
41568.11.3 Saintine, Joseph Xavier Boniface. Picciola. Philadelphia, 1850.
41568.11.4 Saintine, Joseph Xavier Boniface. Picciola. N.Y., 1850.

41568.10 - .12 Individual authors, etc. - 1800-1849 - Fiction - Saintine - Writings - cont.

41568.11.5 Saintine, Joseph Xavier Boniface. Picciola. Bruxelles, 1845.
41568.11.5.10 Saintine, Joseph Xavier Boniface. Picciola. N.Y., 1862.
41568.11.6 Saintine, Joseph Xavier Boniface. Picciola. 3. ed. London, 1865.
41568.11.7 Saintine, Joseph Xavier Boniface. Picciola. N.Y., 1869.
41568.11.8 Saintine, Joseph Xavier Boniface. Picciola. 17. ed. Paris, 1851.
41568.11.9 Saintine, Joseph Xavier Boniface. Picciola. Philadelphia, 1851.
41568.11.12 Saintine, Joseph Xavier Boniface. Picciola. N.Y., 1866.
41568.11.13 Saintine, Joseph Xavier Boniface. Picciola. N.Y., 1866.
41568.11.15 Saintine, Joseph Xavier Boniface. Picciola. London, 1875.
41568.11.18 Saintine, Joseph Xavier Boniface. Picciola. Chicago, 1890.
41568.11.20 Saintine, Joseph Xavier Boniface. Picciola. N.Y., 1893.
41568.12 Saintine, Joseph Xavier Boniface. Un rossignol. Paris, 1860.
41568.12.5 Saintine, Joseph Xavier Boniface. The solitary of Juan Fernadez. Boston, 1851.

41568.14 - .14.49 Individual authors, etc. - 1800-1849 - Fiction - Saunders, M.J.

41568.14 Saunders, J. Les deux créoles. Tours, 1846.

41568.14.50 - .14.99 Individual authors, etc. - 1800-1849 - Fiction - Say, J.B.

41568.14.53 Say, Jean Baptiste. Petit volume contenant quelques aperçus des hommes et de la société. 3. éd. Paris, 1839.

41568.15 Individual authors, etc. - 1800-1849 - Fiction - Senancour - Works about

41568.15 Levallois, Jules. Un précurseur: Sénancour. Paris, 1897.
41568.15.5 Michaut, G. Sénancour, ses amis et ses ennemis. Paris, 1909.
41568.15.6 Merlant, G. Sénancour. Paris, 1907.
41568.15.7 Pizzorusso, A. Sénancour. Messina, 1950.
41568.15.8 Le Gall, Béatrice. L'imaginaire chez Sénancour. Paris, 1966. 2v.
41568.15.10 Raymond, Marcel. Sénancour; sensations et révélations. Paris, 1965.
41568.15.15 Fischler, Anita. Sensation ou raison, plaisir ou bonheur dans l'oeuvre d'Etienne Pivert de Sénancour. Thèse. Zürich, 1968.
41568.15.20 Sénelier, Jean. Hommage à Sénancour. Paris, 1970.
41568.15.25 Bouyer, Raymond. Obermann, précurseur et musicien. Paris, 1907.
41568.15.45 Pamphlet box. Sénancour.

41568.16 - .19 Individual authors, etc. - 1800-1849 - Fiction - Senancour - Writings

41568.16 Sénancour, Étienne Pivert de. Obermann. Bruxelles, 1837. 2v.
41568.17 Sénancour, Étienne Pivert de. Obermann. Paris, 1863.
NEDL 41568.17.1 Sénancour, Étienne Pivert de. Obermann. Paris, 1892.
NEDL 41568.17.1A Sénancour, Étienne Pivert de. Obermann. Paris, 1892.
41568.17.2 Sénancour, Étienne Pivert de. Obermann. Cambridge, 1901. 2v.
41568.17.3 Michaut, G. De Sénancour. Obermann. Paris, 1912. 2v.
41568.17.5A Sénancour, Étienne Pivert de. Obermann. London, 1903.
41568.17.5B Sénancour, Étienne Pivert de. Obermann. London, 1903.
41568.17.10 Sénancour, Étienne Pivert de. Obermann; texte original de 1804. Grenoble, 1947. 3v.
41568.17.12 Sénancour, Étienne Pivert de. Obermann. Paris, 1965.
41568.17.25 Sénancour, Étienne Pivert de. Aldomen. Paris, 1925.
41568.17.30 Sénancour, Étienne Pivert de. Sur les générations actuelles. Genève, 1963.
41568.17.35 Sénancour, Étienne Pivert de. Libres méditations. Genève, 1970.
41568.18 Sénancour, Étienne Pivert de. Isabelle. Paris, 1833.
Htn 41568.18.5* Sénancour, Étienne Pivert de. Libres méditations d'un solitaire inconnu. Paris, 1819.
41568.19.5 Sénancour, Étienne Pivert de. Rêveries. 3. éd. Paris, 1833.
41568.19.10 Sénancour, Étienne Pivert de. Rêveries sur la nature primitive de l'homme. Paris, 1939-40.

41568.20 - .21 Individual authors, etc. - 1800-1849 - Fiction - Sewrin - Writings

41568.20 Sewrin, C.A. Hilaire et Berthille. Paris, 1801.
41568.21 Serwin, C.A. La première nuit des mes noces. Paris, 1802. 2v.

41568.24 Individual authors, etc. - 1800-1849 - Fiction - Thenaisie

41568.24.6 Thenaisie, Charles. Le cornette; chronique de Bretagne, 1588-89. 2. éd. Paris, 1846.

41568.25 - .26.49 Individual authors, etc. - 1800-1849 - Fiction - Tillier - Writings

41568.25.50 Tillier, Claude. Oeuvres. Nevers, 1846. 4v.
41568.25.70 Tillier, Claude. De l'Espagne. Paris, 1925.
41568.26 Tiller, Claude. Mon oncle Benjamin. Strasbourg, n.d.
41568.26.3 Tillier, Claude. Mon oncle Benjamin. N.Y., 1928.
41568.26.4 Tillier, Claude. Mon oncle Benjamin. Paris, 1969.
41568.26.5 Tillier, Claude. Belle-Plante et Cornélius. Strasbourg, n.d.

41568.26.50 - .26.99 Individual authors, etc. - 1800-1849 - Fiction - Tillier - Works about

41568.26.50 Marx, Ludwig. Claude Tillier als Romanschriftsteller. Inaug. Diss. Heidelberg, 1916.
41568.26.60 O'Hara, F.P. Claude Tillier, sa vie et ses oeuvres. Thèse. Paris, 1939.
41568.26.70 Maple, H.L. Claude Tillier, 1801-1844. Genève, 1957.

41568.27 Individual authors, etc. - 1800-1849 - Fiction - Villiers

41568.27 Villiers, Pierre. Souvenirs d'un déporté. Paris, 1802.

41568.28 Individual authors, etc. - 1800-1849 - Fiction - Viollet-le-Duc

41568.28 Viollet-Le-Duc, E.L.N. Six mois de vie d'un jeune homme. Paris, 1853.

41568.29 Individual authors, etc. - 1800-1849 - Fiction - Wailly

41568.29 Wailly, Leon de. Angelica Kauffmann. Paris, 1859.

41568.32 Individual authors, etc. - 1800-1849 - Fiction - Waldor

41568.32 Waldor, Mélancé. Pages de la vie intime. Bruxelles, 1836. 2v.

41568.70 Individual authors, etc. - 1800-1849 - Fiction - Yvan

41568.70 Yvan, Melchior. Les déportés. Bruxelles, 1852.

41569 Individual authors, etc. - 1800-1849 - Fiction - Anonymous novels, etc.

41569.4 Les fous douteux et les fous sublimes. Paris, 1844.
41569.6 Maucheron, Claude Athanase. Omniana. Paris, 1808.
41569.8 Parafaragaramus, ou Croquiguole et sa famille. Paris, 1817.
41569.10 Le petit pélerin de Parme et de Plaisance. Parme, 1815.
41569.12 Historiettes et contes à ma petite fille et à mon petit garçon. Paris, n.d.
41569.14 Keepsake breton, par A.V.B.O. Paris, 1841.
41569.16 Le roman de mes fredaines. Bruxelles, 1887.
41569.18 T....., baroness de. Mystère. Bruxelles, 1887.
41569.20 Les sérails de Londres. Paris, 1911.
41569.22 T., A. of Rochefort. Adraste et Nancy V.Y., anecdote américaine. St. Maixent, 1794.
41569.24 The little mountaineers of Auvergne. London, 1801.
41569.30 Gamiani, ou deux nuits d'excès. Paris, 1970.

41571.1 - .4 Individual authors, etc. - 1800-1849 - Hugo, Victor - Complete works

41571.1 Hugo, Victor. Roman. Paris, 1904-24. 9v.
41571.1.3 Hugo, Victor. Poésie. Paris, 1905-35. 12v.
41571.1.5 Hugo, Victor. Théâtre. Paris, 1905-34. 6v.
41571.1.7 Hugo, Victor. En voyage. Paris, 1905-10.
41571.1.9 Hugo, Victor. Histoire. Paris, 1907. 2v.
41571.1.11 Hugo, Victor. Souvenirs. Paris, 1913. 2v.
41571.1.13 Hugo, Victor. Philosophie. Paris, 1934-37. 2v.
41571.1.15 Hugo, Victor. Actes et paroles. Paris, 1937-40. 3v.
41571.1.17 Hugo, Victor. Ocean and Tas de Pierres. Paris, 1942.
41571.1.19 Hugo, Victor. Correspondance. Paris, 1947-52. 4v.
41571.2 Hugo, Victor. Oeuvres de Victor Hugo. Paris, 1885-91. 29v.
41571.2.2 Pamphlet box. Covers, oeuvres de Victor Hugo, v.1-19,21-30. Paris, 1885-91.
41571.3.25 Hugo, Victor. L'oeuvre de Victor Hugo; poesie, prose, théâtre. Paris, 1931.
41571.3.26 Hugo, Victor. L'oeuvre de Victor Hugo. Paris, 1959.
41571.3.60 Hugo, Victor. Oeuvres. Bruxelles, 1836-37. 2v.
Htn 41571.3.75* Hugo, Victor. Oeuvres oratoires. Bruxelles, 1853.
41571.3.85 Hugo, Victor. Oeuvres. Paris, 1876. 4v.
41571.3.88 Hugo, Victor. Oeuvres choisies. Paris, 1950. 2v.
41571.3.90 Hugo, Victor. Poèmes choisis 1822-1865. London, 1909.
41571.3.95 Hugo, Victor. The poetry of Victor Hugo. Boston, 1911.
41571.3.100 Hugo, Victor. Poèmes choisis. Manchester, 1932.
41571.3.105 Hugo, Victor. Oeuvres poetiques complètes. Paris, 1961.
41571.3.108 Hugo, Victor. Oeuvres poetiques. Paris, 1964.
41571.3.110 Hugo, Victor. Oeuvres dramatiques complètes. Paris, 1963.
41571.3.115 Hugo, Victor. Oeuvres romanesques complètes. Paris, 1962.
41571.3.120 Hugo, Victor. Oeuvres. Lausanne, 1960-63. 24v.
41571.3.125 Hugo, Victor. Oeuvres politiques complètes. Paris, 1964.
41571.3.130 Hugo, Victor. Oeuvres complètes. Lausanne, 1966- 38v.
41571.4A Hugo, Adèle F. Victor Hugo. N.Y., 1863.
41571.4B Hugo, Adèle F. Victor Hugo. N.Y., 1863.

41571.5 Individual authors, etc. - 1800-1849 - Hugo, Victor - Bibliographies

41571.5 Méaulle, L.F. (Mme.). Victor Hugo 1802-1902. Paris, 1902.
41571.5.9 Alexandre, A. La maison de Victor Hugo. Paris, 1903.
41571.5.10 Dubois, P. Bio-bibliographie de Victor Hugo de 1802-25. Paris, 1913. 10v.
41571.5.12 Rudwin, M.J. Bibliographie de Victor Hugo. Paris, 1926.
41571.5.15 Michaux, F. Essais bibliographiques concernant les oeuvres de V. Hugo...pendant l'exil. Paris, 1930.
41571.5.17 Gregh, Fernand. Étude sur Victor Hugo. Paris, 1905.
41571.5.19 Bibliothèque nationale, Paris. Victor Hugo. Paris, 1952.

41571.6 - .49 Individual authors, etc. - 1800-1849 - Hugo, Victor - Folios [Discontinued]

41571.6 Hugo, Victor. Han d'Islande. Notre Dame de Paris. Paris, 1853.
41571.6.10 Hugo, Victor. Les misérables. Chicago, n.d. 3v.
41571.8 Hugo, Victor. L'homme qui rit. N.Y., 1869.
41571.10 Hugo, Victor. Les misérables. pts.3,4,5. N.Y., 1862. 3v.
41571.10.3 Hugo, Victor. Les misérables. N.Y., 1862. 2v.
41571.10.4 Hugo, Victor. Les misérables. N.Y., 18- . 2v.
41571.10.5 Hugo, Victor. Les misérables. 8. éd. Paris, 1862. 10v.
41571.10.15 Hugo, Victor. Les misérables. Paris, 1865.
41571.11 Hugo, Victor. Les misérables. Paris, 1872.
41571.12.2 Hugo, Victor. Les misérables. N.Y., 1888.
41571.12.4 Hugo, Victor. Les misérables. N.Y., 18- .
41571.15 Hugo, Victor. Les misérables. N.Y., 1862. 5v.
41571.15.3 Hugo, Victor. Les misérables. London, 1910.
41571.15.5 Hugo, Victor. Les misérables; a novel. London, 1913.
41571.15.10 Hugo, Victor. Les misérables. N.Y., 1862. 2v.
41571.16.1 Hugo, Victor. Les misérables. N.Y., 1887.
41571.16.2 Hugo, Victor. Les misérables. v.1 lost 1931. N.Y., 1892. 2v.
41571.16.3 Sozialistische Einheitsparti. Die Bedeutung der Arbeiten des Genossen Stalin. Berlin, 1952.
41571.16.5 Sozialistische Einheitsparti. Die Bedeutung der Arbeiten des Genossen Stalin. v.3-5. v.1-2 lost 1931. Boston, 1892. 5v.
41571.16.6 Hugo, Victor. Les misérables. Boston, 1887. 5v.
41571.16.7 Hugo, Victor. Les misérables. Boston, 189-? 5v.
41571.16.8 Hugo, Victor. Les misérables. N.Y., 19- . 2v.
41571.16.9 Hugo, Victor. Les misères. Paris, 1927. 2v.
41571.16.10 Hugo, Victor. Les misérables. v.1-5. Boston, 1910? 3v.
41571.16.13 Hugo, Victor. Les misérables. N.Y., 196-?
41571.16.15 Hugo, Victor. Les misérables. N.Y., 1943.
41571.16.20 Hugo, Victor. Les misérables. Garden City, 1947.
41571.16.25 Hugo, Victor. Les misérables. Paris, 1951.
41571.16.30 Hugo, Victor. Les misérables. Paris, 1957. 2v.
41571.16.35 Hugo, Victor. Les misérables. Paris, 1969. 2v.
41571.17 Hugo, Victor. Les misérables. v.1-5. N.Y., 1862.

Classified Listing

41571.6 - .49 Individual authors, etc. - 1800-1849 - Hugo, Victor - Folios [Discontinued] - cont.

41571.17.1 Hugo, Victor. Les misérables. Oeuvres complètes. Paris, 19- . 4v.
41571.17.5 Hugo, Victor. Les misérables. pt. 1, 2-3,4,5. Paris, 1912. 4v.
41571.17.10 Hugo, Victor. Les chandeliers de l'évêque; episodes des misérables de Victor Hugo. Boston, 1936.
41571.18 Hugo, Victor. Les chandeliers. pt.4. N.Y, 1864.
41571.18.5 Hugo, Victor. Illustrations to Les misérables. N.Y., 1863.
Htn 41571.19* Hugo, Victor. Les misérables. pt.1,3,4,5. Richmond, 1863-64.
41571.19.10 Hugo, Victor. Cosette et Marius. Boston, 1945.
41571.20 Hugo, Victor. Gavroche, from "Les misérables". Philadelphia, 1872.
41571.21 Hugo, Victor. Les chatiments. Paris, n.d.
41571.22 Hugo, Victor. Notre Dame de Paris. Paris, 1844.
41571.25 Hugo, Victor. Les travailleurs de la mer. N.Y., 1866.
Htn 41571.28* Hugo, Victor. Les quatre vents de l'esprit. Paris, 1881. 2v.
Htn 41571.29* Hugo, Victor. Quatre-vingt treize. Paris, n.d.
41571.30 Hugo, Victor. Les feuilles d'automne. Paris, n.d.
41571.30.2 Hugo, Victor. Les feuilles d'automne. Paris, 19- .
41571.30.5 Hugo, Victor. By order of the king. N.Y., 18- .
41571.30.8 Hugo, Victor. By order of the king. London, 1870. 3v.
41571.31 Hugo, Victor. The man who laughs. Boston, 189-? 2v.
41571.31.5A Hugo, Victor. The man who laughs. Boston, 1888. 2v.
41571.31.5B Hugo, Victor. The man who laughs. Boston, 1888. 2v.
41571.31.10 Hugo, Victor. The man who laughs. v.1-2. Boston, 1910?
41571.32.1 Hugo, Victor. The man who laughs. Boston, 1900. 2v.
41571.32.2 Hugo, Victor. Les misérables. v.1-4. v.5 lost 1921. Boston, 1887. 5v.
41571.32.3 Hugo, Victor. Ninety-three. Boston, 1888.
41571.32.3.2 Hugo, Victor. Ninety-three. Boston, 1888.
41571.32.3.3 Hugo, Victor. Ninety-three. London, 1886.
41571.32.3.5 Hugo, Victor. Ninety-three. v.1-2. Boston, 1910?
41571.32.4 Hugo, Victor. Notre-Dame de Paris. Boston, 1888. 2v.
41571.32.5 Hugo, Victor. The toilers of the sea. Boston, 1888. 2v.
41571.32.6 Hugo, Victor. The toilers of the sea. Chicago, 19- ?
41571.32.9 Hugo, Victor. The toilers of the sea. v.1-2. Boston, 18- .
41571.32.15 Hugo, Victor. Havets arbetare. Stockholm, 1927. 2v.
41571.40A Hugo, Victor. The man who laughs. London, 1889. 2v.
41571.40B Hugo, Victor. The man who laughs. London, 1889. 2v.
41571.40.15 Hugo, Victor. The laughing man. N.Y., 19- .
41571.41 Hugo, Victor. Les misérables. v.2-5. v.1 lost 1929. London, 1887. 5v.
41571.42A Hugo, Victor. Ninety-three. London, 1889. 2v.
41571.42B Hugo, Victor. Ninety-three. London, 1889. 2v.
41571.43A Hugo, Victor. The toilers of the sea. London, 1888. 2v.
41571.43B Hugo, Victor. The toilers of the sea. London, 1888. 2v.

41572 Individual authors, etc. - 1800-1849 - Hugo, Victor - Selected works

41572.2 Hugo, Victor. L'année terrible. Paris, 1872.
41572.2.10 Hugo, Victor. L'année terrible. Paris, 19- .
41572.4 Hugo, Victor. Bug-Jargal. Claude Gueux. Paris, 1871.
41572.4.2 Hugo, Victor. Jargal. N.Y., 1866.
41572.4.5 Hugo, Victor. Jargal. Oxford, 1904.
41572.4.8 Hugo, Victor. Bug-Jargal. Paris, 1912.
41572.4.10 Hugo, Victor. Claude Gueux. N.Y., 1869.
41572.7 Hugo, Victor. Han d'Islande. Paris, 1868. 2v.
41572.7.15 Hugo, Victor. Hans of Iceland. N.Y., 18- .
41572.7.17 Hugo, Victor. Hans of Iceland. Boston, 189-?
41572.7.18 Hugo, Victor. Hans of Iceland. Boston, 1894.
41572.7.19 Hugo, Victor. Hans of Iceland. Boston, 1891.
41572.7.20 Hugo, Victor. Han de Islandia. Barcelona, 1930.
41572.7.25 Hugo, Victor. Histoire d'un crime. Paris, 1877-78. 2v.
41572.8 Hugo, Victor. Histoire d'un crime. Paris, 1877-78. 2v.
41572.8.2 Hugo, Victor. Histoire d'un crime. Première journée et deuxième journée. 2e éd. Paris, 1877.
41572.8.3 Hugo, Victor. Histoire d'un crime. v.1. 4e éd. Paris, 1877-78. 2v.
41572.8.10 Hugo, Victor. Histoire d'un crime. N.Y., n.d.
41572.8.70 Hugo, Victor. History of a crime. N.Y., 1888.
41572.8.75 Hugo, Victor. History of a crime. N.Y., 19- ? 2v.
41572.8.76 Hugo, Victor. History of a crime. Boston, 19- ?
41572.8.77 Hugo, Victor. History of a crime. N.Y., 19- .
41572.9 Hugo, Victor. Notre-Dame de Paris. Paris, 1858. 2v.
41572.10 Hugo, Victor. Notre-Dame de Paris. Paris, 1871. 2v.
41572.12 Hugo, Victor. Littérature et philosophie mêlées. Paris, 1834. 2v.
41572.13 Hugo, Victor. Littérature et philosophie mêlées. Paris, 1868. 2v.
41572.14F Hugo, Victor. L'ârt d'être grand-père. Paris, 188-.
41572.16 Hugo, Victor. Le Rhin. Paris, 1869. 3v.
41572.17 Hugo, Victor. Le Rhin. Boston, 19- . 2v.
41572.18 Hugo, Victor. Napoléon le petit. Paris, n.d.
41572.19 Hugo, Victor. Victor Hugo, témoin de son siècle. Paris, 1962.
41572.20 Hugo, Victor. Quatre-vingt-treize. Paris, 1874. 2v.
41572.20.2 Hugo, Victor. Quatre-vingt-treize. Paris, 1874. 3v.
41572.20.5 Hugo, Victor. Quatre-vingt-treize. N.Y., 1888.
41572.20.10 Hugo, Victor. Quatre-vingt-treize. Paris, 1963.
41572.21 Hugo, Victor. Quatre-vingt-treize. Paris, 1890? 4v.
41572.22 Hugo, Victor. Quatre-vingt-treize. N.Y., 1892.
41572.23 Hugo, Victor. Les châtiments. Paris, n.d.
41572.23.5 Hugo, Victor. Les châtiments. Paris, 1875.
41572.23.10 Hugo, Victor. Les châtiments. Paris, 1932.
41572.24 Hugo, Victor. Les contemplations. Paris, 1872. 2v.
41572.24.5 Hugo, Victor. Les contemplations. Paris, 1869.
41572.24.7 Hugo, Victor. Les contemplations. 2e éd. Paris, 1856.
41572.24.8 Hugo, Victor. Les contemplations. 5e ed. Paris, 1858. 2v.
41572.24.9A Hugo, Victor. Les contemplations. Paris, 1922. 3v.
41572.24.9B Hugo, Victor. Les contemplations. Paris, 1922. 3v.
41572.24.10 Hugo, Victor. Les contemplations. Paris, 19- .
41572.24.12 Hugo, Victor. Les contemplations. Paris, 1969.
41572.24.15 Glotz, R. Les variantes des contemplations. Thèse. Paris, 1924.
41572.24.20 Hugo, Victor. Essai sur la psychologie des variantes des "Contemplations". Thèse. Paris, 1924.

41572 Individual authors, etc. - 1800-1849 - Hugo, Victor - Selected works - cont.

41572.24.40 Hugo, Victor. Pierres. Genève, 1951.
Htn 41572.25* Hugo, Victor. La légende des siècles. Paris, 1859. 2v.
41572.26 Hugo, Victor. La légende des siècles. Paris, 1871.
41572.26.10 Hugo, Victor. La légende des siècles. Paris, 188-?
41572.26.12 Hugo, Victor. La légende des siècles. v.2-3. Paris, 188-? 2v.
41572.28 Hugo, Victor. Les orientales. Paris, 1872.
41572.28.11 Hugo, Victor. Les orientales. Les feuilles d'automne. Les chants du crépuscule. Paris, 1881.
41572.28.15 Hugo, Victor. Les orientales. Les feuilles d'automne. Les chants du crépuscule. Paris, 1884.
41572.29 Hugo, Victor. Le roi s'amuse. Paris, 1832.
41572.29.2 Hugo, Victor. Le roi s'amuse; drame. Paris, 1832.
41572.29.3 Hugo, Victor. Le roi s'amuse. London, 1843.
41572.29.4 Hugo, Victor. Le roi s'amuse. Paris, 1853.
41572.29.5 Hugo, Victor. Le roi s'amuse. London, 1877.
41572.29.6 Hugo, Victor. Le roi s'amuse. Paris, 188-?
41572.29.7 Hugo, Victor. Le roi s'amuse. Paris, 1912.
41572.30 Hugo, Victor. Les voix interieures. Les rayons et les ombres. Paris, 1869.
41572.30.6 Hugo, Victor. Les voix interieures. Les rayons et les ombres. Paris, 1879.
41572.30.12 Hugo, Victor. Les voix intérieures. Les rayons et les ombres. Paris, 1884.
41572.32 Hugo, Victor. Théâtre. Marie Tudor. Paris, 1858.
41572.32.5 Hugo, Victor. Théâtre. Paris, 1858.
41572.32.10 Hugo, Victor. Théâtre. Paris, 1858. 2 pam.
41572.33 Hugo, Victor. Théâtre. v.1,2,4. Paris, 1872. 3v.
41572.33.5 Hugo, Victor. Théâtre. Paris, 1884. 3v.
41572.34 Hugo, Victor. Théâtre. Paris, 1872. 4v.
41572.34.10 Hugo, Victor. Théâtre. Paris, 187-.
41572.35F Hugo, Victor. Théâtre complète. Paris, 185-.
41572.36 Hugo, Victor. Théâtre complète. Paris, 1872.
41572.36.5 Hugo, Victor. Théâtre complète. Paris, 1963-64. 2v.
41572.40 Hugo, Victor. Les chansons des rues et des lois. Paris, 1884.
41572.42 Hugo, Victor. Avez-vous lu Victor Hugo? Paris, 1964.
41572.45 Hugo, Victor. Les contemplations. Paris, 1890? 2v.
41572.50 Hugo, Victor. Les quatre vents de l'esprit. Paris, 18- . 2v.
41572.52 Hugo, Victor. Pages d'amour de Victor Hugo. Paris, 1949.
41572.53 Hugo, Victor. La poésie. Paris, 1965.
41572.60 Hugo, Victor. Toute la lyre. Paris, 18- . 3v.
NEDL 41572.60.5 Hugo, Victor. La fin de Satan. Paris, 1897.
41572.60.10 Hugo, Victor. The last days of a condemned. London, 1897.
41572.70.10 Cahiers Victor Hugo. Paris. 1,1965+ 2v.

41573 Individual authors, etc. - 1800-1849 - Hugo, Victor - Individual works

41573.2 Hugo, Victor. Le conservateur littéraire 1819-1821. pt. 1,2. Paris, 1922-38. 4v.
41573.5 Hugo, Victor. Morceaux choisis. Paris, 1897.
41573.5.10 Hugo, Victor. Morceaux choisis. Paris, 1906?
41573.5.15 Hugo, Victor. Morceaux choisis. Paris, 1911.
41573.5.20 Hugo, Victor. Morceaux choisis. Paris, 1918.
41573.6 Hugo, Victor. Morceaux choisis. Paris, 1900.
41573.7 Hugo, Victor. Avez-vous lu Victor Hugo? Paris, 1952.
41573.8 Hugo, Victor. Rasgos de Victor Hugo por Manuel Delofen y Leonard. Habana, 1886.
41573.9 Hugo, Victor. Dessinateur. Paris, 1963.
41573.10 Hugo, Victor. Marion de Lorme. Bruxelles, 1831.
41573.10.2 Hugo, Victor. Marion de Lorme. Bruxelles, 1831.
41573.10.5 Hugo, Victor. Marion de Lorme. Paris, 18- .
41573.10.10 Hugo, Victor. Marion de Lorme. 3. éd. Paris, 1831.
41573.12 Hugo, Victor. Les chants du crépuscule. Paris, 18- .
41573.13 Hugo, Victor. Hoi Athlioi.' v.1-2,3-5. en Athènais, 1888. 2v.
41573.15 Berret, Paul. Le moyen age dans la légende des siècles et les sources de Victor Hugo. Paris, 19- .
41573.16 Hugo, Victor. The laughing man. London, 1908.
41573.16.5 Hugo, Victor. Les travailleurs de la mer. N.Y., 1890.
41573.16.10 Hugo, Victor. Les travailleurs de la mer. Paris, 1866. 2v.
41573.16.12 Hugo, Victor. Les travailleurs de la mer. N.Y., 1866.
41573.16.20 Hugo, Victor. Les travailleurs de la mer. v.1-2. 17e éd. Paris, 1869.
41573.17 Hugo, Victor. The toilers of the sea. London, 1908.
41573.17.2 Hugo, Victor. The toilers of the sea. London, 1896.
41573.17.3 Hugo, Victor. The toilers of the sea. Boston, 1888. 2v.
41573.17.4 Hugo, Victor. The toilers of the sea. Boston, 1888. 2v.
41573.17.5 Hugo, Victor. The toilers of the sea. London, 1913.
41573.17.6 Hugo, Victor. The toilers of the sea. Boston, 189-?
41573.17.7 Hugo, Victor. Things seen. N.Y., 19- .
41573.17.7.5 Hugo, Victor. Things seen. London, 1964.
41573.17.8A Hugo, Victor. Tristesse d'Olympio. Paris, 1928.
41573.17.8B Hugo, Victor. Tristesse d'Olympio. Paris, 1928.
41573.18A Hugo, Victor. Ninety-three. N.Y., 1874.
41573.18B Hugo, Victor. Ninety-three. N.Y., 1874.
41573.18.2 Hugo, Victor. Ninety-three. N.Y., 1874.
41573.18.4 Hugo, Victor. Ninety-three. Boston, 189-? 2v.
Htn 41573.18.11* Hugo, Victor. La légende des siècles. Paris, 1877. 2v.
NEDL 41573.18.12 Hugo, Victor. La légende des siecles. 1e série. Paris, 1884.
41573.18.15 Hugo, Victor. Legende des siècles. Paris, 1920-27. 6v.
41573.18.20 Hugo, Victor. La légende des siècles. Paris, 1950.
41573.18.25 Hugo, Victor. La légende des siècles. Paris, 1962.
41573.19 Hugo, Victor. Notre Dame de Paris. Bruxelles, 1840.
41573.21 Hugo, Victor. Notre Dame de Paris. v.1-4. Paris, 1837. 2v.
41573.21.5 Hugo, Victor. Notre Dame de Paris. Paris, 18- . 2v.
41573.21.20 Hugo, Victor. Notre Dame de Paris. Paris, 1873.
41573.21.30 Hugo, Victor. Notre Dame de Paris, 1482. Paris, 1912? 2v.
41573.22 Hugo, Victor. The hunchback of Notre Dame. Philadelphia, 1834.
41573.22.2 Hugo, Victor. Quatre-vingt-treize. Boston, 1892.
41573.22.3 Hugo, Victor. Quatre-vingt-treize. Boston, 1901.
41573.22.4 Hugo, Victor. Quatre-vingt-treize. N.Y., 1890.
41573.22.5 Hugo, Victor. Quatre-vingt-treize. Paris, 1967.
41573.23.1 Hugo, Victor. Notre Dame de Paris. v.1-2. Boston, 1888.
41573.23.3 Hugo, Victor. Notre Dame de Paris. Boston, 189-?

41573 Individual authors, etc. - 1800-1849 - Hugo, Victor - Individual works - cont.

41573.23.4 Hugo, Victor. Notre Dame de Paris. Boston, 1889. 2v.
41573.23.5.5A Hugo, Victor. Notre Dame de Paris. N.Y., 1902. 2v.
41573.23.5.5B Hugo, Victor. Notre Dame de Paris. N.Y., 1902. 2v.
41573.23.5.10 Hugo, Victor. Notre Dame de Paris. Oxford, 1906.
41573.23.6 Hugo, Victor. Notre Dame de Paris. London, 1908.
41573.23.6.3 Hugo, Victor. Notre Dame de Paris. v.1-2. Boston, 1910?
41573.23.6.5 Hugo, Victor. Notre Dame de Paris. London, 1921.
41573.23.7 Hugo, Victor. Notre Dame de Paris. London, 1908?
41573.23.8 Hugo, Victor. Notre Dame de Paris. N.Y., 1940.
41573.23.9 Hugo, Victor. The hunchback of Notre Dame. N.Y., 1862.
41573.23.10A Hugo, Victor. Notre Dame. Boston, 1888.
41573.23.10B Hugo, Victor. Notre Dame. Boston, 1888.
41573.23.11 Hugo, Victor. The hunchback of Notre Dame. Boston, 1899.
41573.23.12 Hugo, Victor. The hunchback of Notre Dame. Chicago, 19- .
41573.23.13A Hugo, Victor. Notre Dame de Paris. N.Y., 1902.
41573.23.13B Hugo, Victor. Notre Dame de Paris. N.Y., 1902.
41573.23.14 Hugo, Victor. The hunchback of Notre Dame. N.Y., 1923.
41573.23.15 Hugo, Victor. The story of Esmeralda; condensed from the hunchback. N.Y., n.d.
41573.23.17 Hugo, Victor. Notre Dame de Paris, 1492. London, 1928.
41573.23.20 Hugo, Victor. Notre Dame de Paris. v.1-2. N.Y., 1931.
41573.23.25 Hugo, Victor. The hunchback of Notre Dame. N.Y., 1939.
41573.24 Hugo, Victor. Cromwell. Bruxelles, 1835.
41573.24.5 Hugo, Victor. Cromwell. Paris, 188-?
41573.24.25 Hugo, Victor. Religions et religion. 12. éd. Paris, 1880.
NEDL 41573.25.3 Hugo, Victor. La préface de Cromwell. Paris, 1897?
41573.25.4 Hugo, Victor. La préface de Cromwell and Hernani. Chicago, 1900.
41573.25.4.2 Hugo, Victor. La préface de Cromwell and Hernani. Chicago, 1900.
41573.25.5 Hugo, Victor. La préface de Cromwell. Berlin, 1920.
41573.26 Hugo, Victor. Ruy Blas. N.Y., 1909.
41573.26.1 Hugo, Victor. Ruy Blas. N.Y., 1909.
41573.26.2 Hugo, Victor. The prompt book...drama of Ruy Blas. N.Y., 1878.
41573.26.9 Hugo, Victor. Ruy Blas. N.Y., 1886.
41573.26.10 Hugo, Victor. Ruy Blas. Paris, 1908?
41573.26.11 Hugo, Victor. Ruy Blas. Boston, 1909.
41573.26.12A Hugo, Victor. Ruy Blas. Paris, 188-.
41573.26.12B Hugo, Victor. Ruy Blas. Paris, 188-.
41573.26.15F Wogel, J. Grandes scèces de Ruy Blas. Paris, 1888.
41573.26.17 Hugo, Victor. Ruy Blas. Paris, 1894.
41573.26.30 Hugo, Victor. Ruy Blas, Les Burgraves, Marion de Lorme. Paris, 1913.
41573.26.31 Hugo, Victor. Ruy Blas. Paris, 1939.
41573.27 Hugo, Victor. Théâtre. Paris, 1858.
41573.28 Hugo, Victor. Torquemada drame. 5e éd. Paris, 1882.
41573.28.3 Hugo, Victor. Torquemada drame. 6e éd. Paris, 1882.
41573.28.5 Hugo, Victor. Torquemada drama. México, 1891.
41573.30.5 Hugo, Victor. Dramas. v.1-4. Boston, n.d. 2v.
41573.30.7 Hugo, Victor. Dramas. v.1-4. Boston, 1910. 2v.
41573.30.10 Hugo, Victor. Dramatic works. London, 1887.
41573.31 Hugo, Victor. Dernière gerbe. Paris, 1902.
41573.32.1A Hugo, Victor. Hernani. Paris, 18- .
41573.32.1B Hugo, Victor. Hernani. Paris, 18- .
Htn 41573.32.2* Hugo, Victor. Hernani. n.p., n.d.
41573.32.3 Hugo, Victor. Hernani. 2e éd. Paris, 1830.
41573.32.3.2 Hugo, Victor. Hernani. 3e éd. Paris, 1830.
41573.32.4 Hugo, Victor. Hernani. Paris, 1854.
41573.32.4.9 Hugo, Victor. Hernani. Paris, 1878.
41573.32.4.12 Hugo, Victor. Hernani. 5e éd. Bielefeld, 1872.
41573.32.4.15 Hugo, Victor. Hernani. 6e éd. Bielefeld, 1878.
41573.32.5 Hugo, Victor. Hernani. Paris, 1879.
41573.32.7.10 Hugo, Victor. Hernani. N.Y., 1880.
41573.32.8 Hugo, Victor. Hernani. N.Y., 1881?
41573.32.9 Hugo, Victor. Hernani. N.Y., 1887.
NEDL 41573.32.10 Hugo, Victor. Hernani. N.Y., 1894-
41573.32.11 Hugo, Victor. Hernani. Boston, 1891.
41573.32.14 Hugo, Victor. Hernani; a drama. London, 1898.
41573.32.15 Hugo, Victor. Hernani. 12. ed. London, 1899.
41573.32.16 Hugo, Victor. Hernani. Paris, 191-.
41573.32.17 Hugo, Victor. Hernani, Marion de Lorme. Paris, 1913-15.
41573.32.18 Hugo, Victor. Herani, ó el pundonor castellano. Habana, 1896.
41573.32.19 Hugo, Victor. Hernani. Paris, 1943.
41573.32.20 Hugo, Victor. Angelo. N.Y., 1855.
41573.32.23 Hugo, Victor. Marie Tudor. Angelo. Paris, 1836.
41573.32.25 Hugo, Victor. Angelo. N.Y., 1866.
41573.32.26 Hugo, Victor. Angelo. London, 1880.
41573.32.50 Hugo, Victor. Lucretia Borgia. N.Y., 1875.
41573.32.51A Hugo, Victor. Lucretia Borgia. N.Y., 1875.
41573.32.51B Hugo, Victor. Lucretia Borgia. N.Y., 1875.
41573.32.52 Hugo, Victor. Lucretia Borgia. New Orleans, n.d.
41573.32.70 Hugo, Victor. Carnets intimés, 1870-1871. 7. ed. Paris, 1953.
41573.32.75 Hugo, Victor. Claude Gueux. 1. ed. Paris, 1956.
41573.32.76 Hugo, Victor. Claude Gueux. Thèse. Paris, 1956.
41573.33 Hugo, Victor. Les orientales. Paris, 1859.
41573.33.5 Hugo, Victor. Les orientales. Paris, 1952. 2v.
41573.34 Hugo, Victor. Oeuvres poétiques. Odes. Paris, 1890.
41573.35 Hugo, Victor. Odes et ballades. Les orientales. Paris, 1875. 2v.
Htn 41573.35.3* Hugo, Victor. Odes et ballades. 5e éd. Paris, 1828. 2v.
41573.35.5 Hugo, Victor. Odes et ballades. Paris, 1880.
41573.35.10 Hugo, Victor. Odes et ballades. Paris, 18- .
41573.36 Hugo, Victor. Odes et ballades. Paris, 1878.
41573.36.3 Hugo, Victor. Odes et ballades. Paris, 191-.
41573.36.4 Hugo, Victor. Les feuilles d'automne. Paris, n.d.
41573.36.5 Hugo, Victor. Les feuilles d'automne. Chants du crépuscule. Paris, n.d.
41573.36.6 Hugo, Victor. Les feuilles d'automne. v.1-2. 3. éd. Paris, 1832.
41573.36.7 Hugo, Victor. Chefs-d'oeuvre lyriques. London, 1919.
41573.36.9 Hudson, William H. Victor Hugo and his poetry. London, 1918.
41573.36.10 Hugo, Victor. Dieu (L'océan d'en haut). Paris, 1960.
41573.36.15 Hugo, Victor. La petié suprème. Paris, 1879.
41573.36.30 Hugo, Victor. Les enfants. Paris, 18- .
41573.36.40 Hugo, Victor. Les années funestes, 1852-1870, Dernière Gerbe. Paris, 1941.
41573.37 Hugo, Victor. Translations from the poems of Victor Hugo. London, 1885.
41573.37.2 Hugo, Victor. Translations from the poems of Victor Hugo. 2d ed. London, 1887.
41573.37.3 Hugo, Victor. Translations from the poems of Victor Hugo. N.Y., 1887?
41573.37.9 Hugo, Victor. Poems. The history of a crime. Boston, 18-? 2 pam.
41573.37.10 Hugo, Victor. Poems. Boston, 190-?
Htn 41573.38* Hugo, Victor. Le Christ au Vatican. Bruxelles, n.d.
Htn 41573.39* Hugo, Victor. La voix de Guernesey. Bruxelles, 1867.
41573.39.25 Hugo, Victor. La Belgique vue par Victor Hugo. Bruxelles, 1945.
41573.39.26 Hugo, Victor. La Belgique selon Victor Hugo. Bruxelles, 1968.
41573.40.10 Hugo, Victor. L'oeuvre compléte de Victor Hugo; extraits. Paris, 1885.
41573.41 Hugo, Victor. Oeuvres complètes. v.1-23,25-48. v.24 lost 1963. Paris, 1880. 48v.
41573.42 Hugo, Victor. Oeuvres complètes. Paris, 1880. 48v.
41573.48 Hugo, Victor. Works. Boston, 1894.
41573.49 Hugo, Victor. Victor Hugo s'amuse. Paris, 1955.
NEDL 41573.50 Hugo, Victor. The novels of Victor Hugo. N.Y., 18- . 5v.
41573.51 Hugo, Victor. The works. Boston, 189-.
41573.53 Hugo, Victor. Works. N.Y., 1906. 7v.
41573.54A Hugo, Victor. Works. N.Y., 1908. 7v.
41573.54B Hugo, Victor. Works. N.Y., 1908. 7v.
41573.55 Hugo, Victor. Victor Hugo de la jeunesse. Paris, 1889.
41573.60 Hugo, Victor. La vie de Victor Hugo. Paris, 1958.
41573.65 Hugo, Victor. Les contemplations. Paris, 1964. 2v.
41573.66 Hugo, Victor. Dieu (Le seuil du gouffre). Paris, 1961.
41573.69 Hugo, Victor. Un carnet des misérables, octobre-decembre 1860. Paris, 1965.

41574.1 - .16 Individual authors, etc. - 1800-1849 - Hugo, Victor - Letters and journals

41574.7 Hugo, Victor. Oeuvres complètes. La fin de Satan. 2d ed. Paris, 1886.
41574.8 Hugo, Victor. Oeuvres complètes. Théâtre en liberté. Paris, 1886.
41574.8.5 Hugo, Victor. Oeuvres posthumes. Correspondance, 1815-1882. Paris, 1898. 2v.
41574.9 Hugo, Victor. Oeuvres inédites. Choses vues, 1815-35. Paris, 1887.
41574.10 Hugo, Victor. Oeuvres inédites. Dieu. Paris, 1891.
Htn 41574.11* Hugo, Victor. Oeuvres inédites. En voyage. Alps et Pyrénées. Paris, 1890.
41574.12 Hugo, Victor. Oeuvres inédites. En voyage. France et Belgique. Paris, 1892.
41574.13.5 Hugo, Victor. Memoirs. N.Y., 1899.
41574.13.6 Hugo, Victor. Memoirs. N.Y., 1899.
41574.13.20 Hugo, Victor. Souvenirs personnels. Paris, 1952.
41574.13.40 Hugo, Goerges Victor. Mon Grand-Père. Paris, 1902.
41574.14 Hugo, Victor. Post-scriptum de ma vie. Paris, 1901.
41574.14.20 Hugo, Victor. Victor Hugo par lui-même. Paris, 1951.
41574.14.25A Hugo, Victor. Victor Hugo's intellectual autobiography. N.Y., 1907.
41574.14.25B Hugo, Victor. Victor Hugo's intellecutal autobiography. N.Y., 1907.
41574.14.30 Hugo, Victor. Journal. Paris, 1954.
41574.14.35 Hugo, Victor. Post-scriptum de ma vie. Neuchâtel, 1961.
41574.15 Hugo, Victor. Lettres à la fiancée. 1820-1822. Paris, 1901.
41574.15.20 Hugo, Victor. Victor Hugo et ses correspondants. Paris, 1947.
41574.15.30 Hugo, Victor. The love letters of Victor Hugo. N.Y., 1901.
41574.16 Hugo, Victor. Victor Hugo's letters to his wife. Boston, 1895.
41574.16.5 Hugo, Victor. Letters of Victor Hugo to his family. Boston, 1896. 2v.
41574.16.8 Hugo, Victor. Juliette Drouet's love letters to V. Hugo. London, 1915.
41574.16.8.10 Drouet, Juliette. Juliette Drouet's love-letters to Victor Hugo. 2d ed. London, 1915.
41574.16.9 Hugo, Victor. Le roman de Juliette et de Victor Hugo. Paris, n.d.
41574.16.10A Wack, Henry W. The romance of Victor Hugo and Juliette Drouet. N.Y., 1905.
41574.16.10B Wack, Henry W. The romance of Victor Hugo and Juliette Drouet. N.Y., 1905.
41574.16.15 Drouet, Juliette. Autour de "Ruy Blas"; lettres inédites de Juliette Drouet à Victor Hugo. Paris, 1939.
41574.16.25 Hugo, Victor. Lettres à Juliette Drouet, 1833-1883. Paris, 1964.
41574.16.30 Hugo, Victor. Victor Hugo publie Les miserables. Paris, 1970.

41574.17 - Individual authors, etc. - 1800-1849 - Hugo, Victor - Biography and criticism

41574.17 Hugo, A.F. (Mme.). Victor Hugo raconté par un temoin de sa vie. Photoreproduction. Paris, 1868. 2v.
41574.17.5 Laube, Herbert David. The story of Jean Valjean. Geneva, N.Y., 1928.
41574.17.10 Ouayle, W.A. A hero. Jean Valjean. Cincinnati, 1902.
41574.20 Rivet, Gustave. Victor chez lui. Paris, 1878.
X Cg 41574.21 Biré, Edmond. Victor Hugo avant 1830. Paris, 1883.
41574.21.2 Biré, Edmond. Victor Hugo après 1830. Paris, 1891. 2v.
41574.21.3 Biré, Edmond. Victor Hugo après 1852. Paris, 1894.
41574.22 Barbou, Alfred. Victor Hugo. Paris, 1880.
41574.22.4 Barbou, Alfred. Victor Hugo et son temps. Paris, 1881.
41574.22.5 Barbou, Alfred. Victor Hugo; his life and works. Chicago, 1881.
41574.22.6 Barbou, Alfred. Victor Hugo and his time. N.Y., 1882.
41574.23 Hartmann, K.A.M. Victor Hugo. Leipzig, 1884.
41574.24 A memento of Victor Hugo. n.p., 1886.
41574.25.2A Marzials, Frank T. Life of Victor Hugo. London, 1888.
41574.25.2B Marzials, Frank T. Life of Victor Hugo. London, 1888.
41574.26 Swinburne, A.C. A study of Victor Hugo. London, 1886.
41574.27 Daudet, Alphonse. Victor Hugo. N.Y., 1882.
41574.27.10 Daudet, Léon. La tragique existence de Victor Hugo. Paris, 1937.
NEDL 41574.28 Renouvier, Charles. Victor Hugo. Paris, 1893.
41574.28.5 Renouvier, Charles. Victor Hugo. 5. ed. Paris, 1907.
41574.29 Hartmann, K.A.M. Zeittafel zu Victor Hugos Leben und Werken. Oppeln, 1886.
41574.30 Mailleau, L. Victor Hugo. Paris, 1893.
41574.30.5 Mabilleau, L. Victor Hugo. Paris, 1902.

1574.17 - Individual authors, etc. - 1800-1849 - Hugo, Victor - Biography and criticism - cont.

41574.30.10 Comitato italiano per celebrazioni il centenario di Victor Hugo. Il centenario di Victor Hugo a Roma. Roma, 1902.
41574.32 Dupuy, Ernest. Victor Hugo. Paris, 1890.
41574.33 Dupuy, Ernest. Victor Hugo. Paris, 1890.
41574.34 Pellier, H. La philosophie de Victor Hugo. Paris, 1904.
41574.34.5 Heugel, Jacques. Essai sur la philosophie de Victor Hugo. Paris, 1922.
41574.34.10 Heugel, J. Essai sur la philosophie de Victor Hugo. Paris, 1930.
41574.34.15 Heugel, J. Hugo, et le génie latin. Paris, 1957.
41574.35 Renouvier, Charles. Victor Hugo le philosophe. Paris, 1900.
41574.36 Glachant, P. Papiers d'autrefois. Paris, 1899.
41574.37 Rigal, Eugène. Victor Hugo poète epique. Paris, 1900.
41574.38 Garson, J. L'évolution Napoléonienne de Victor Hugo sous la restauration. Paris, 1900.
41574.39 Sleumer, A. Die Dramen Victor Hugos. Berlin, 1901.
41574.39.5 Mrodzinsky, Rektor Carl. Die deutschen Übersetzungen der dramatischen Hauptwerke Victor Hugos. Inaug. Diss. Halle, 1915.
41574.40 Claretie, Jules. Victor Hugo. Paris, 1902.
41574.41A Brunetière, F. Victor Hugo. Paris, 1902. 2v.
41574.41B Brunetière, F. Victor Hugo. Paris, 1902. 2v.
41574.42 Legay, T. Victor Hugo jugé par son siècle. Paris, 1902.
41574.42.5 Dupuy, E. La jeunesse des romantiques. Paris, 1905.
41574.43.5 Simon, G. L'enfance de Victor Hugo. Paris, 1904.
41574.44 Roedel, P. Victor Hugo und der conservateur littéraire. Heidelberg, 1902.
41574.45 Chenay, P. Victor Hugo à Guernesey. Paris, n.d.
41574.45.5 Stapfer, Paul. Victor Hugo à Guernesey. Paris, 1905.
41574.45.10 Stapfer, Paul. Victor Hugo et la grande poésie satirique en France. Paris, 1901.
41574.46 Glanchant, P. Essai critique sur le théâtre de Victor Hugo. Les drames en vers. Paris, 1902.
41574.46.2 Glachant, P. Essai critique sur le théâtre de Victor Hugo. Les drames en prose. Paris, 1903.
41574.47 Lesclide, Richard (Mme.). Victor Hugo intime. Paris, n.d.
41574.48 Hugo, Victor. Propos de table recueillis par R. Lesclide. 3e éd. Paris, 1885.
41574.48.2 Lesclide, Richard. Propos de table de Victor Hugo. 4e éd. Paris, 1885.
41574.49 Allais, G. Les debuts dramatiques de Victor Hugo. Paris, 1903.
41574.50 Blanchard, Alexandre. Le théâtre de Victor Hugo et la parodie. Amiens, 1904.
41574.51 Huguet, E. Le sens de la forme dans les métaphores de Victor Hugo. Paris, 1904.
41574.51.2 Huguet, E. La couleur...et l'ombre dans les métaphores de Hugo. Paris, 1905.
41574.52 Fréminet, E. Les sources grecques des trois cents. Paris, 1906.
41574.53 Rochette, A. L'alexandrin chez Victor Hugo. Paris, 1911.
41574.54 Davidson, Arthur F. Victor Hugo; his life and work. Philadelphia, 1912.
41574.55 Guiard, A. Virgile et Victor Hugo. Paris, 1910.
41574.56 Guimbaud, Louis. Victor Hugo et Juliette Drouet. Paris, 1914.
41574.56.2 Guimbaud, Louis. Les orientales de Victor Hugo. Amiens, 1928.
41574.56.3 Haggard, A.C.P. Victor Hugo; his work and his love. N.Y., 1923.
41574.57 Reuve, Paul. Victor Hugo. Paris, 1902.
41574.58 Pamphlet box. Hugo, Victor. 7 pam.
41574.59 Barthou, Louis. Les amours d'un poète. Paris, 1919.
41574.60 Moell, O. Beiträge zur Geschichte...der "Orientales" von Victor Hugo. Mannhein, 1901.
41574.63 Stange, Paul. Le Cid dans la poèsie lyrique de Victor Hugo. Erfurt, 1903.
41574.65 Dufay, P. Victor Hugo à vingt ans. Paris, 1909.
41574.67 Stölten, O. Die Entwicklung des bildlichen Ausdrucks in der Sprache Victor Hugos. Jena, 1911.
41574.68 Séché, L. Victor Hugo et les poètes. Paris, 1912. 2v.
41574.70 Saint-Victor, P. de. Victor Hugo. Paris, 1892.
41574.71 Duclaux, A.M.F. (Mrs.). Victor Hugo. London, 1921.
41574.72 Dubois, P. Victor Hugo, ses idées religieuses, 1802-25. Paris, 1913.
41574.73 Prensa associada de Santo Domingo. Victor Hugo. Santo Domingo, 1885.
41574.75 Schenck, E.M. La part de Charles Nodier de la formation des idées de Victor Hugo. Paris, 1914.
41574.77 Hugo, Adele. Victor Hugo. N.Y., 1887.
41574.78 Courtat, Félix-Titus. Discours de successeur de Victor Hugo. Paris, 1877.
41574.79 Bouvenne, Aglaus. Victor Hugo, ses portraits et ses charges. Paris, 1879.
41574.80 Lalanne, M. Maxime. Chez Victor Hugo. Paris, 1864.
41574.82 Bersaucourt, Albert. Les pamphlets contre Victor Hugo. Paris, 1912.
41574.83 Seilliere, Ernest. Du quiétisme au socialisme romantique. Paris, 1925.
Htn 41574.85* Swinburne, Algernon C. A study of Victor Hugo's "Les Misérables". London, 1914.
41574.87 Hofmannsthal, Hugo. Victor Hugo. Berlin, 1904.
41574.88 Cüppers, Franz Maria. Der Gottesgedanke bei Victor Hugo. Inaug. Diss. Marburg, 1918.
41574.89 Poinsot, Maffeo C. Auprès de Victor Hugo. Paris, 1919.
41574.91 Vodoz, J. "Roland". Paris, 1920.
41574.93 Joussain, André. Le pittoresque dans le lyrisme et et dans l'épopée. Thèse. Paris, 1915.
41574.93.2 Joussain, André. Le pittoresque dans l'esthétique de Victor Hugo. Paris, 1920.
41574.95 Clement-Janin, Noël. Victor Hugo en exil. 5e éd. Paris, 1922.
41574.97 Ditchy, Jay Karl. La mer dans l'oeuvre littéraire de Victor Hugo. Inaug. Diss. Paris, 1925.
41574.97.5 Ditchy, Jay Karl. La mer dans l'oeuvre littéraire de Victor Hugo. Paris, 1925.
41574.99 Yperloon, J.C. Les traductions hollandaises des poésies lyriques de Victor Hugo jusqu'en 1885. Bussum, 1925.
41574.102 Giese, W.F. Victor Hugo, the man and the poet. N.Y., 1926.
41574.105 Martin, Eugène-Louis. Les symétries de la prose dans les principaux romans de Victor Hugo. Thèse. Paris, 1925.
41574.107 Guiard, Amédée. La fonction du poète; étude sur Victor Hugo. Thèse. Paris, 1910.

41574.17 - Individual authors, etc. - 1800-1849 - Hugo, Victor - Biography and criticism - cont.

Htn 41574.109* Hofmannsthal, H. Versuch über Victor Hugo. München, 1925.
41574.115A Escholier, Raymond. Victor Hugo, artiste. Paris, 1926.
41574.115B Escholier, Raymond. Victor Hugo, artiste. Paris, 1926.
41574.120 Guimbaud, Louis. Victor Hugo et Madame Biard. Paris, 1927.
41574.120.10 Guimbaud, Louis. La mère de Victor Hugo, 1772-1821. Paris, 1930.
41574.120.15 Guimbaud, Louis. En cabriolet vers l'Académie. Paris, 1947.
41574.122 Simon, Gustave. La vie d'une femme. 2e éd. Paris, 1914.
41574.122.10 Simon, Gustave. Visite à la maison de Victor Hugo. 4e éd. Paris, 1904.
41574.123 Constans, Charles. Leopoldine Hugo. Beziers, 1931.
41574.124 Constans, Charles. Leopoldine Hugo. Beziers, 1931.
41574.125 Berret, Paul. Victor Hugo. Paris, 1927.
41574.125.6 Berret, Paul. La philosophie de Victor Hugo (1854-1859). Paris, 1910.
41574.128 Rudwin, Maximilien. Satan et le satanisme dans l'oeuvre de Victor Hugo. Thèse. Paris, 1926.
41574.128.5 Rudwin, Maximilien. Satan et le satanisme dans l'oeuvre de Victor Hugo. Paris, 1926.
41574.130 Robertson, Mysie E.I. L'epithète dans les oeuvres lyriques de Victor Hugo. Paris, 1926.
41574.135 Weil, Felix. Victor Hugo et Richard Wagner. Thèse. Zofingue, 1926.
41574.137 Saurat, Denis. La religion de Victor Hugo. Paris, 1929.
41574.139 Bellesart, André. Victor Hugo. Paris, 1930.
41574.140 Le Breton, André Victor. La jeunesse de Victor Hugo. Paris, 1928.
41574.143A Escholier, Raymond. La vie glorieuse de Victor Hugo. Paris, 1928.
41574.143B Escholier, Raymond. La vie glorieuse de Victor Hugo. Paris, 1928.
41574.143.15 Escholier, Raymond. Victor Hugo raconté par ceux qui l'ont vu. Paris, 1931.
41574.145 Pelletan, Camille. Victor Hugo, homme politique. Paris, 1891.
41574.147 Ulbach, Louis. La vie de Victor Hugo. Paris, 1886.
41574.149 Boulanger, Louis. Costumes dessinés par Louis Boulanger pour La Esmeralda. Paris, 1888.
41574.152 Lacretelle, Pierre de. Vie politique de Victor Hugo. Paris, 1928.
41574.157 Grillet, Claudius. Victor Hugo spirite. Lyon, 1929.
41574.158 Grillet, Claudius. Le Bible dans Victor Hugo d'après de nombreux tableaux de concordance. Lyon, 1910.
41574.160 Lacretelle, Pierre de. La véritable édition originale des Châtiments. Paris, 1922.
41574.162 Flemming, Hans. Mit Victor Hugo im alten Paris. Inaug. Diss. Berlin, 1929.
41574.164 Flutre, Fernand. Victor Hugo. Paris, 1927.
41574.170 Chesnier du Chessne, A. Le "Ronsard" de Victor Hugo. Paris, 1929.
41574.172 Le Dû, M.A. Le groupement ternaire dans la prose de Victor Hugo. Thèse. Paris, 1929.
41574.172.5 Le Dû, M.A. La répétition symétrique dans l'Alexandrin de Victor Hugo. Thèse. Paris, 1929.
41574.175 Larroumet, Gustave. La maison de Victor Hugo. Paris, 1895.
41574.176 Tomov, T.S. Eziku i stilu vu "Legendata na věkovetě". Sofiia, 1928.
41574.177 Lote, Georges. En préface à "Hernani" cent ans d'après. Paris, 1930.
41574.179 Bohland, Werner. "Les rayons et les ombres" von Victor Hugo. Inaug. Diss. Berlin, 1930.
41574.181 Carli, Antoino de. L'Italia nell'opera di Victor Hugo. Torino, 1930.
41574.182 Rosso, A.T. L'ispirazione Hughiana nel Carducci. Torino, 1932.
41574.183 Benoît-Lévy, E. La jeunesse de Victor Hugo. Paris, 1928.
41574.185 Schenk, Rudolf. Die sprachmechanischen Grundlagen der Bildersprache in der Lyrik Victor Hugos. Würzburg, 1929.
41574.187 Heimbecher, H.J. Victor Hugo und die Ideen der grossen französischen Revolution. (Teildruck). Inaug. Diss. Berlin, 1931.
41574.187.5 Heimbecher, H.J. Victor Hugo und die Ideen der grossen französischen Revolution. Berlin, 1932.
41574.189 Gregoire, E. L'astronomie dans l'oeuvre de Victor Hugo. Liège, 1933.
41574.191 Hennig, E. Die ethische Wertung des Kindes hei Victor Hugo. Inaug. Diss. Charlottenburg, 1931.
41574.193 Turner, R.E. The sixteenth century in Victor Hugo's inspiration. N.Y., 1934.
41574.195 Blanchard, M. Marie-Tudor; essais sur les sources...avec notes...de Victor Hugo. Paris, 1934.
41574.197 Lyonnet, Henry. Les premières de Victor Hugo. Paris, 1930.
41574.199 Batault, G. Le pontéfe de la démagogie, Victor Hugo. Paris, 1934.
41574.200 Thomas, John H. L'Angleterre dans l'oeuvre de Victor Hugo. Thèse. Paris, 1933.
41574.201 Thomas, J.H. L'Angleterre dans l'oeuvre de Victor Hugo. Paris, 1934.
41574.203 Ascoli, G. Reponse à quelques détracteurs de Victor Hugo. Paris, 1935.
41574.205 Graef, Karl. Die wirkungsvollen Abschlüsse in der Lyrik Victor Hugos. Eine psychologische-genetische Stiluntersuchung. Gekrönte Preis. Wertheim, 1933.
41574.207 Reymann, E. Victor Hugos Stellung zur Frau. Inaug. Diss. Coburg, 1934.
41574.209 Grant, E.M. Victor Hugo during the second republic. Northampton, 1935.
41574.211 Matt, Hildegard. Das visuelle Element in der Kunst Victor Hugos betrachtet an seinen Bildern. Inaug. Diss. Freiburg, 1934.
41574.212 Bauer, H.F. Les "Ballades" de Victor Hugo. Thèse. Paris, 1935.
41574.213 Bauer, H.F. Les "Ballades" de Victor Hugo. Paris, 1936.
41574.215 Boer, J.P.C. Victor Hugo et l'enfant. Wassenaar, 1933.
41574.217 Ley-Deutsch, M. Le gueux chez Victor Hugo. Thèse. Paris, 1936.
41574.219 Spiegelberg, W.E. Einheit und Vielheit bei Victor Hugo. Inaug. Diss. Lengerich, 1937.
41574.221 Marsan, Jules. Le centenaire de Tristesse d'Olympio. Toulouse, 1938.
41574.223A Hooker, K.W. The fortunes of Victor Hugo in England. N.Y., 1938.

41574.17 - Individual authors, etc. - 1800-1849 - Hugo, Victor - Biography and criticism - cont.

41574.223B Hooker, K.W. The fortunes of Victor Hugo in England. N.Y., 1938.

41574.225 Maison de Victor Hugo, Paris. Victor Hugo raconte par l'image. Paris, 1930?

41574.225.5 Hugo, Paris Maison de Victor. Victor Hugo. Paris, 1956.

41574.227 Buchanan, D.W. Les sentiments religieux de Victor Hugo de 1825 à 1848. Thèse. Besançon, 1939.

41574.230 Ganser, F. Beiträge zur Beurteilung des Verhältnisses. Inaug. Diss. Heidelberg, 1900.

41574.232 Nuse, P. Victor Hugo als Dramatiker. Berlin, 1897.

41574.234 Dullaert, M. Victor Hugo à Bruxelles. Bruxelles, 1922.

41574.237 Josephson, Matthew. Victor Hugo. Garden City, 1942.

41574.239A Viatte, Auguste. Victor Hugo et les illuminés de son temps. Montreal, 1942.

41574.239B Viatte, Auguste. Victor Hugo et les illuminés de son temps. Montreal, 1942.

41574.241 O'Connor, M.I. A study of the sources of Han d'Islande and their significance in the literary development of Victor Hugo. Thesis. Washington, 1942.

41574.243 Baudouin, Charles. Psychoanalyse de Victor Hugo. Genève, 1943.

41574.245 Fecarotta, F. L'elemento storico del "Cromwell" di Victor Hugo. Palermo, 1939.

41574.250 Pendell, William D. Victor Hugo's acted dramas and the contemporary press. Baltimore, 1947.

41574.250.5 Pendell, William D. Victor Hugo's acted dramas. Thesis. Baltimore, 1947.

41574.255 Monteamor, H.H. Victor Hugo. Rosario, 1946.

41574.260 Froment-Guieysse, G. Victor Hugo. v.1-2. Paris, 1948.

41574.270 Audiat, Pierre. Ainsi vécut Victor Hugo. Paris, 1947.

41574.275 Zumthor, Paul. Victor Hugo. 7. éd. Paris, 1946.

41574.277 Delande, Jean. Victor Hugo à Hauteville House. Paris, 1947.

41574.280 Souchon, Paul. Les deux femmes de Victor Hugo. Paris, 1948.

41574.280.5 Souchon, Paul. Victor Hugo. Paris, 1949.

41574.280.10 Souchon, Paul. Claire Pradier et Victor Hugo. n.p., n.d.

41574.283 Barrère, Jean Bertrand. La fantaisie de Victor Hugo. Paris, 1949. 3v.

41574.283.5B Barrère, Jean Bertrand. Hugo, l'homme et l'oeuvre. Paris, 1952.

41574.283.10 Barrère, Jean Bertrand. Victor Hugo à l'oeuvre. Paris, 1966.

41574.283.15 Barrère, Jean Bertrand. Victor Hugo. Bruges, 1965.

41574.283.20 Barrère, Jean Bertrand. Hugo. Paris, 1970.

41574.285 Gregh, Fernand. L'oeuvre de Victor Hugo. Paris, 1933.

41574.287 Dubuc, A. Villeguier dans la vie et l'oeuvre de Victor Hugo. Rouen, 1946.

41574.290 Guillemin, H. L'humour de Victor Hugo. Neuchâtel, 1951.

41574.291 Guillemin, H. Hugo et la sexualité. Paris, 1959.

41574.292A Boussel, P. De quoi vivait Victor Hugo. Paris, 1952.

41574.292B Boussel, P. De quoi vivait Victor Hugo. Paris, 1952.

41574.294 Aragon, L. Hugo. Paris, 1952.

41574.298 Escholier, R. Un amant de génie. Paris, 1953.

41574.300 Drouet, J. Mille et une lettres d'amour à Victor Hugo. 4. éd. Paris, 1951.

41574.301 Maurois, André. Victor Hugo and his world. N.Y., 1966.

41574.302A Maurois, André. Olympio. Paris, 1954.

41574.302B Maurois, André. Olympio. Paris, 1954.

41574.303 Maurois, André. Victor Hugo. London, 1956.

41574.304 Gregh, F. Victor Hugo: sa vie, son oeuvre. Paris, 1954.

41574.306 Hawana. Oficina del Histanador de la Cuidad. Homenaje a Victor Hugo. La Habana, 1952.

41574.308 Celarie, H. Victor Hugo amoureux. Paris, 1952.

41574.310 Levaillant, M. La crise mystique de Victor Hugo (1843-1856) d'après des documents inédits. Paris, 1954.

41574.312 Venzac, Geraud. Les origines religieuses de Victor Hugo. Paris, 1955.

41574.315 Venzac, Geraud. Les premiers maîtres de Victor Hugo. Paris, 1955.

41574.320 Guyer, F.E. The Titan. N.Y., 1955.

41574.325 Revel, Bruno. Victor Hugo. Milano, 1955.

41574.330 Glauser, A.C. Hugo et la poésie pure. Genève, 1957.

41574.500 Castelnau, Jacques. Adèle Hugo. Paris, 1941.

41574.505 Escande de Messières, R. Le journal de l'exil d'Adèle Hugo. N.Y., 1952.

41574.507 Hugo, Adèle. Le journal d'Adèle Hugo. Paris, 1968- 2v.

41574.510 Gaudon, J. Victor Hugo. Paris, 1955.

41574.515 Savey-Casard, Paul. Le crime et la peine dans l'oeuvre de Victor Hugo. 1. éd. Paris, 1956.

41574.520 Moscow. Vsesoiuznaia gosudarstvennaia biblioteka inostrannoi literatury. Bibliografiia russkikh perevodov proizvedenii Viktora Giugo. Moskva, 1953.

41574.525 Flottes, Pierre. L'éveil de Victor Hugo, 1802-1822. 8. éd. Paris, 1957.

41574.530 Ciana, Albert. Victor Hugo. Genève, 1941.

41574.535 Nikolaev, V.N. V. Giugo. Moskva, 1955.

41574.540 Roos, Jacques. Les idées philosophiques de Victor Hugo. Paris, 1958.

41574.542 Miquel, Pierre. Hugo, touriste. Paris, 1958-

41574.544 Miquel, Pierre. Avec Victor Hugo. Lefort, 1960.

41574.545 Vincent, Paul. Victor Hugo entre les femmes et l'amour. Paris, 1958.

41574.550 Blum-Manderieux, Arlette. Juliette Drouet et Victor Hugo. Paris, 1960.

41574.555 Maurras, Charles. Lorsque Hugo eut les cent ans. Paris, 1927.

41574.560 Barbier, Henry. L'ame et dieu. Paris, 1935.

41574.565 Brunet, Georges. Victor Hugo. Paris, 1935.

41574.570 Levalley, Sylvie. Ruy Blas. Paris, 1960.

41574.575 Murav'eva, N.I. Guigo. Moskva, 1961.

41574.580 Treskunov, M.S. Viktor Guigo. Izd. 2. Moskva, 1961.

41574.582 Carneiro Leão, Antonio. Victor Hugo no Brasil. 1. éd. Rio de Janeiro, 1960.

41574.585 Rousselot, Jean. Le roman de Victor Hugo. Paris, 1961.

41574.587 Angrand, Pierre. Victor Hugo raconté par les papiers d'État. Paris, 1961.

41574.589 Born, Émile. Victor Hugo. Paris, 1962.

41574.590 Barbey d'Aurevilly, Jules. Les misérables de M.V. Hugo. Paris, 1862.

41574.592 Simaika, Raouf. L'inspiration épique dans les romans de Victor Hugo. Genève, 1962.

41574.593 Alexandre, M. En marge d'un voyage romantique. Saint-Louis, 1961.

41574.17 - Individual authors, etc. - 1800-1849 - Hugo, Victor - Biography and criticism - cont.

41574.594 Mallion, J. Victor Hugo et l'art architectural. Paris, 1962.

41574.595 Py, Albert. Les mythes grecs dans la poésie de Victor Hugo. Genève, 1963.

41574.596 Russell, O.W. Étude historique et critique des Burgraves de Victor Hugo. Paris, 1962.

41574.597 Cantú, Cesare. Di Vittore Hugo e del romanticismo in Frincia. Milano, 1834.

41574.598 Piroué, G. Victor Hugo romancier. Paris, 1964.

41574.599 Dédéyan, C. Victor Hugo et l'Allemagne. Paris, 1964. 2v.

41574.600 Delalande, J. Victor Hugo. Paris, 1964?

41574.601 Ecalle, Martine. Album Hugo. Paris, 1964.

41574.602 Garcia Lyon, Virgina. Centenario de Los miserables de Victor Hugo. Santiago, 1963.

41574.603 Journet, René. Le mythe du peuple dans Les misérables. Paris, 1964.

41574.603.5 Brakhman, Sel'ma R. "Otverzhennye" Viktora Giugo. Moskva, 1968.

41574.604 Albony, Pierre. La création mythologique chez Victor Hugo. Paris, 1963.

41574.605 Garson, Jules. L'évolution démocratique de Victor Hugo. Bruxelles, 1904.

41574.606 Romains, Jules. Inauguration du nouveau monument Victor Hugo à Paris...le mercredi 17 juin 1964. Paris, 1964.

41574.607 Barbey d'Aurevilly, Jules. Victor Hugo. Paris, 1922.

41574.609 Rousselot, Jean. Victor Hugo, phare ébloui. Paris, 1966.

41574.610 Maurois, André. Victor Hugo. Paris, 1965.

41574.612 Grant, Richard Bobson. The perilous quest. Durham, 1968.

41574.614 Coulmas, Danae. Das Apokalyptische im lyrischen Werk Victor Hugos. Hamburg, 1966.

41574.615 Nusinov, Isaak M. Problema istoricheskoqo romana; V. Giugo i A. Frans. Moskva, 1927.

41574.616 Mercié, Jean Luc. Victor Hugo et Julie Chenay, documents inédits. Paris, 1967.

41574.618 Gaudon, Jean. Le temps de la contemplation...Victor Hugo. Paris, 1969.

41574.620 Gely, Claude. Victor Hugo, poète de l'intimité. Paris, 1969.

41574.622 Georgel, Pierre. Léopoldine Hugo, une jeune fille romantique. Villequier, 1967.

41574.624 Huas, Jeanine. Juliette Drouet; ou, La passion romantique. Paris, 1970.

41574.626 Van Tieghem, Philippe. Dictionnaire de Victor Hugo. Paris, 1969.

41574.628 Delteil, Yvan. La fin tragique du voyage de Victor Hugo en 1843. Paris, 1970.

41574.630 Gerson, Noel Bertram. Victor Hugo: a tumultuous life. N.Y., 1971.

41574.632 Villiers, Charles. L'univers métaphysique de Victor Hugo. Paris, 1970.

41574.634 Lebreton-Savigny, Monique. Victor Hugo et les Américains (1825-1885). Paris, 1971.

41574.636 Guillaumie-Reicher, Gilberte. Le voyage de Victor Hugo en 1843: France, Espagne, Pays basque. Paris, 1936.

41574.638 Chételat, Emmanuel J. Les occidentales; ou, Lettres critiques sur Les Orientales de M. Victor Hugo. Paris, 1829. Paris, 1970.

41576 - 41577.11 Individual authors, etc. - 1800-1849 - Lamartine - Complete works

41576.3 Lamartine, Alphonse de. Méditations poétiques. (Oeuvres comp.1). Paris, 1862.

41576.4 Lamartine, Alphonse de. Harmonies poétiques. (Oeuvres comp.2 + 3). Paris, 1862. 2v.

41576.5 Lamartine, Alphonse de. Jocelyn. (Oeuvres comp.4). Paris, 1862.

41576.6 Lamartine, Alphonse de. Recueillements poétiques. (Oeuvres comp.5). Paris, 1862.

41576.7 Lamartine, Alphonse de. Voyage en Orient, 1832-1833. (Oeuvres comp.6-8). Paris, 1862. 3v.

41576.8 Lamartine, Alphonse de. Histoire des Girondins. (Oeuvres comp.9-15). Paris, 1861-1862. 7v.

41576.9 Lamartine, Alphonse de. La chute d'un ange. (Oeuvres comp.16). Paris, 1861.

41576.10 Lamartine, Alphonse de. Histoire de la Restauration. (Oeuvres comp.17-22). Paris, 1861-1862. 10v.

41576.11 Lamartine, Alphonse de. Histoire de la Turquie. (Oeuvres comp.23-25). Paris, 1862. 3v.

41577.1 Lamartine, Alphonse de. Histoire de la Turquie. v.4-6. (Oeuvres comp.26-28). Paris, 1862. 3v.

41577.2 Lamartine, Alphonse de. Nouvelles confidences. (Oeuvres comp.29-30). Paris, 1863. 2v.

41577.3 Lamartine, Alphonse de. Histoire de la Russie. (Oeuvres comp.31). Paris, 1863.

41577.4 Lamartine, Alphonse de. Toussaint Louverture. (Oeuvres comp.32). Paris, 1863.

41577.5 Lamartine, Alphonse de. Nouveau voyage en Orient (1850). (Oeuvres comp.33). Paris, 1863.

41577.6 Lamartine, Alphonse de. Vies de quelques hommes illustres. (Oeuvres comp.34-36). Paris, 1863. 3v.

41577.7 Lamartine, Alphonse de. Mémoires politiques. (Oeuvres comp.37-40). Paris, 1863. 4v.

41577.8 Lamartine, Alphonse de. Fior d'Aliza. (Oeuvres complètes 41). Paris, 1866.

Htn 41577.10* Lamartine, Alphonse de. Oeuvres. Paris, 1832. 4v.

41577.10.12 Lamartine, Alphonse de. Oeuvres. Paris, 1836.

41577.11 Lamartine, Alphonse de. Oeuvres. Bruxelles, 1836.

41577.11.5 Lamartine, Alphonse de. Oeuvres. Bruxelles, 1841.

41577.11.35 Lamartine, Alphonse de. Chefs-d'oeuvre poétiques. Paris, 19- .

41577.11.40A Lamartine, Alphonse de. Oeuvres poétiques complètes. Paris, 1963.

41577.11.40B Lamartine, Alphonse de. Oeuvres poétiques complètes. Paris, 1963.

41577.12 Individual authors, etc. - 1800-1849 - Lamartine - Selected works

41577.12 Lamartine, Alphonse de. Recueillements poétiques. Paris, 1907.

41577.12.3 Lamartine, Alphonse de. Recueillements poétiques. Paris, 1872.

41577.12.5 Lamartine, Alphonse de. Recueillements poétiques. Boston, 19- ?

41577.12.10 Lamartine, Alphonse de. Recueillements poétiques. Paris, 1925.

41577.12 Individual authors, etc. - 1800-1849 - Lamartine - Selected works - cont.

41577.12.55 Lamartine, Alphonse de. Lectures pour tous. 2e éd. Paris, 1855.

41577.13 - Individual authors, etc. - 1800-1849 - Lamartine - Letters and memoirs

41577.13 Lamartine, Alphonse de. Correspondance. Paris, 1881.
41577.13.5 Lamartine, Alphonse de. Correspondance générale de 1830 à 1848. Paris, 1943- 2v.
41577.14 Doumic, R. Lettres d'Elvire à Lamartine. Paris, 1905.
41577.14.5 B., Th. Lettres à M. de Lamartine. Paris, n.d.
41577.14.10 Lamartine, Alphonse de. Lettres des années sombres, 1853-1867. Fribourg, 1942.
41577.14.15 Lamartine, Alphonse de. Lettres inédites, 1821-1851. 7. éd. Porrentruy, Switzerland, 1944.
41577.15 Lamartine, Alphonse de. Les confidences. N.Y., 1849.
41577.15.10 Lamartine, Alphonse de. Les confidences. Paris, 1856. 2 pam.
41577.15.14 Lamartine, Alphonse de. Les confidences. Boston, 18- . 2v.
41577.21 Lamartine, Alphonse de. Mémoires inédits de Lamartine, 1790-1815. Paris, 1881.
41577.22 Lamartine, Alphonse de. Memoirs of my youth. N.Y., 1849.

41578.1 - .35 Individual authors, etc. - 1800-1849 - Lamartine - Individual works

41578.1 Lamartine, Alphonse de. La chute d'un ange. Paris, 1910.
41578.1.5 Lamartine, Alphonse de. La chute d'un ange. Genève, 1954.
41578.1.6 Lamartine, Alphonse de. La chute d'un ange. Thèse. Genève, 1954.
41578.2 Lamartine, Alphonse de. Cours familier de littérature. Paris, 1856-69. 28v.
41578.4 Lamartine, Alphonse de. Harmonies. Tome 2. Paris, 1838.
41578.5 Lamartine, Alphonse de. Harmonies. Paris, 1840. 2v.
41578.5.5 Lamartine, Alphonse de. Harmonies poétiques et religieuses. Paris, 1886.
41578.5.10 Lamartine, Alphonse de. Harmonies poétiques et religieuses. Paris, 1893.
41578.5.11 Lamartine, Alphonse de. Harmonies poétiques et religieuses. Boston, 18- ?
41578.5.12 Lamartine, Alphonse de. Harmonies poétiques et religieuses. Paris, 1911.
41578.5.13 Lamartine, Alphonse de. Harmonies poétiques et religieuses. Paris, 1897.
41578.5.14 Lamartine, Alphonse de. Harmonies poétiques et religieuses. Paris, 1925.
41578.5.15 Lamartine, Alphonse de. Les harmonies. Paris, 1859.
41578.6 Lamartine, Alphonse de. Méditations poétiques. v.1-2. Stuttgart, 1828.
Htn 41578.6.10* Lamartine, Alphonse de. Oeuvres. Méditations. Bruxelles, 1833.
41578.6.20 Lamartine, Alphonse de. Premières méditations poétiques. Paris, 1903.
41578.7A Lamartine, Alphonse de. Premières méditations poétiques. Paris, 1886.
41578.7B Lamartine, Alphonse de. Premières méditations poétiques. Paris, 1886.
41578.7.2A Lamartine, Alphonse de. Premières méditations poétiques. Paris, 1900.
41578.7.2B Lamartine, Alphonse de. Premières méditations poétiques. Paris, 1900.
41578.7.3 Lamartine, Alphonse de. Premières méditations poétiques. Paris, 1897.
41578.7.4 Lamartine, Alphonse de. Premières mèditations poétiques. Strasbourg, 1907?
41578.7.5 Lamartine, Alphonse de. Méditations poétiques. Boston, 18- ?
41578.7.9 Lamartine, Alphonse de. Méditations poétiques. Paris, 1915. 2v.
41578.7.15 Lamartine, Alphonse de. Méditations poétiques. Paris, 1925.
41578.8 Lamartine, Alphonse de. Nouvelles méditations poétiques. v.2. Paris, 1856.
41578.9 Lamartine, Alphonse de. Nouvelles méditations poétiques. Paris, 1886.
41578.9.5 Lamartine, Alphonse de. Nouvelles méditations poétiques. Paris, 1892.
41578.9.6 Lamartine, Alphonse de. Nouvelles méditations poétiques. Paris, 1898.
41578.9.7 Lamartine, Alphonse de. Nouvelles méditations poétiques. Paris, 1900.
X Cg 41578.9.10 Lamartine, Alphonse de. Nouvelles méditations poétiques. Paris, 1914.
X Cg 41578.10 Lamartine, Alphonse de. Poetic meditations. London, 1848.
41578.10.5 Lamartine, Alphonse de. Translations from the meditations of Lamartine. N.Y., 1852.
41578.12 Lamartine, Alphonse de. Auserlesene Gedichte. Stuttgart, 1826.
41578.13 Lamartine, Alphonse de. Poésies inédites de Lamartine. Photoreproduction. Paris, 1873.
41578.14 Lamartine, Alphonse de. Poèmes choisies. Manchester, 1921.
41578.15 Lamartine, Alphonse de. Dos perlas literarias del célebre Adolfo de Lamartine. Madrid, 1853.
41578.16 Lamartine, Alphonse de. Les confidences. Paris, 1857.
41578.18A Lamartine, Alphonse de. Les confidences. Confidential disclosures. N.Y., 1849.
41578.18B Lamartine, Alphonse de. Les confidences. Confidential disclosures. N.Y., 1849.
41578.19 Lamartine, Alphonse de. Les confidences. Confidential disclosures. N.Y., 1859.
41578.20 Lamartine, Alphonse de. Prosper Mérimée's letters...with recollections by Lamartine. N.Y., 1874.
41578.21 Lamartine, Alphonse de. Milly o La terra natale. Trieste, 1866.
41578.22 Lamartine, Alphonse de. Voyage en Orient. Paris, 1875. 2v.
41578.23 Lamartine, Alphonse de. Le manuscrit de ma mère. Paris, 1907.
41578.24 Lamartine, Alphonse de. Fior d'Aliza. N.Y., 1868.
Htn 41578.25* Lamartine, Alphonse de. Nouveau voyage en Orient. Paris, 1851. 2 pam.
Htn 41578.26* Lamartine, Alphonse de. Le conseiller du peuple. Paris. 1-3,1849-1851 3v.
Htn 41578.26.3* Lamartine, Alphonse de. Le conseiller du peuple. Paris. 4,1850

41578.1 - .35 Individual authors, etc. - 1800-1849 - Lamartine - Individual works - cont.

41578.27 Lamartine, Alphonse de. Geneviève, histoire d'une servante. Paris, 1851.
41578.27.5 Lamartine, Alphonse de. Geneviève, histoire d'une servante. Paris, 1855.
41578.27.6 Lamartine, Alphonse de. Geneviève. Paris, 1972.
41578.28 Lamartine, Alphonse. Jocelyn. Paris, 1892.
41578.28.5 Lamartine, Alphonse. Jocelyn. Paris, 1897.
41578.28.10 Lamartine, Alphonse. Jocelyn. Paris, 1925.
41578.28.15 Lamartine, Alphonse. Jocelyn, épisode. Paris, 1967.
41578.29 Lamartine, Alphonse. Josselin inédit. Paris, 1909.
41578.29.5 Lamartine, Alphonse. Jocelyn. Paris, 1837.
Htn 41578.29.10* Lamartine, Alphonse. Jocelyn. v.1-2. Paris, 1836.
41578.29.48 Lamartine, Alphonse. Les visions. Thèse. Paris, 1936.
41578.29.50 Lamartine, Alphonse. Les visions. Paris, 1936.
41578.30 Lamartine, Alphonse. The stone-mason of Saint Point. N.Y., 1859.
41578.30.3 Lamartine, Alphonse. Raphael. Paris, 1859.
41578.30.4 Lamartine, Alphonse. Raphael. Paris, 1885.
41578.30.5 Lamartine, Alphonse. Le tailleur de pierre de Saint-Point. Paris, 1882.
41578.32 Lamartine, Alphonse. Graziella. Paris, 1888.
41578.32.4 Lamartine, Alphonse. Graziella. Chicago, 1898.
41578.32.5 Lamartine, Alphonse. Graziella. Boston, 1900.
41578.32.7 Lamartine, Alphonse. Graziella. Paris, 1927.
41578.32.10 Lamartine, Alphonse. Graziella. Campobasso, 1935.
41578.32.12 Lamartine, Alphonse. Graziella. Chicago, 1892.
41578.32.15 Lamartine, Alphonse. Graziella. Chicago, 1905.
41578.33 Lamartine, Alphonse. Saül, tragédie. Paris, 1918.
41578.34 Lamartine, Alphonse. Raphael. N.Y., 1849.
41578.34.2 Lamartine, Alphonse. Raphael. Paris, 19- .
41578.34.3 Lamartine, Alphonse. Raphäel; notices et annotations par Georges Roth. Paris, 1925.
41578.34.4 Lamartine, Alphonse. Raphäel. Neuchâtel, 1962. 2v.
41578.34.5 Lamartine, Alphonse. Philosophie et littérature. Paris, 1894.
41578.35 Lamartine, Alphonse. Toussaint Louverture. Bruxelles, 1850.
Htn 41578.35.10* Lamartine, Alphonse. Sur la politique rationelle. Paris, 1831.
Htn 41578.35.15* Lamartine, Alphonse. Discours sur la dette americaine, 1 avril 1834. Paris, 1834.
Htn 41578.35.70* Lamartine, Alphonse. Discours prononcé à l'Assemblée nationale sur le projet de constitution. Paris, 1848.
41578.35.70.5 Lamartine, Alphonse. Discours prononcé à l'Assemblée nationale sur le projet de constutution. Paris, 1848,
Htn 41578.35.90* Lamartine, Alphonse. Antoniella. Paris, 1867.
Htn 41578.35.95* Lamartine, Alphonse. Discours prononcé dans la séance du 15 février 1834 sur les frères des écoles chrétiennes. n.p., 18- .
Htn 41578.35.100* Lamartine, Alphonse. La presidence. Paris, 1848.
Htn 41578.35.110* Lamartine, Alphonse. Heloïse et Abélard. Paris, 1853.
41578.35.115 Lamartine, Alphonse. Antar. Paris, 1864.
41578.35.125 Lamartine, Alphonse. Lamartine on atheism. Boston, 1850.
41578.35.127 Lamartine, Alphonse. England in 1850. N.Y., 1851.
Htn 41578.35.135* Per le nozze Grancini Lamarre. Firenze, 1901.
41578.35.140 Lamartine, Alphonse de. Alphonse de Lamartine ve Istanbul yazilari. Istanbul, 1971.

41578.36 - Individual authors, etc. - 1800-1849 - Lamartine - Biography and criticism

41578.36 Alexandre, Charles. Souvenirs sur Lamartine. Paris, 1884.
41578.37 Lacretelle, Henri de. Lamartine et ses amis. Paris, 1878.
41578.38 Rod, Edouard. Lamartine. Paris, 1893.
41578.39 Mazade, Charles de. Lamartine. Paris, 1872.
41578.40 Legouvé, Ernest. Lamartine. Paris, 1876.
41578.40.10 Latreille, Camile. Lamartine, poète politique. Lyon, 1924.
41578.40.15 Roth, Georges. Lamartine et la Savoie, extraits situés et commentés. Chambéry, 1927.
41578.40.20 Hazard, Paul. Lamartine. Paris, 1925.
41578.40.25 Fournet, Charles. Lamartine et ses amis suisses. Paris, 1928.
41578.40.27 Fournet, Charles. Lamartine-Roi. Neuchatel, 1942.
41578.40.30 Lima-Barbosa, Mario de. Lamartine et le Brésil. Paris, 1927.
41578.40.39 Schwabbauer, W. Lamartines "Graziella". Inaug Diss. Bielefeld, 1934.
41578.40.43 Charlier, G. Aspects de Lamartine. Paris, 1937.
41578.40.45 George, A.J. Lamartine and romantic unanimism. N.Y., 1940.
41578.40.48 Bert, Paul. Lamartine "homme social", son action dans la région natale. Paris, 1947.
41578.40.49 Bert, Paul. Lamartine, homme sociale. Paris, 1924.
41578.40.51 Dupouy, Auguste. Elvire. Paris, 1944.
41578.41 Soullié, P. Études morales et littéraires sur la poésie lyrique en France. Paris, 1854.
41578.44 Reyssié, Félix. La jeunesse de Lamartine. Paris, 1892.
41578.45 France, A. L'Elvire de Lamartine. Paris, 1893.
41578.46 Zyromski, E. Lamartine, poète lyrique. Paris, 1897.
41578.47 Quentin-Bauchart, P. Lamartine homme politique. Paris, 1903.
41578.47.10 Quentin-Bauchart, P. Lamartine et la politique étrangère de la révolution de février. Paris, 1913.
41578.48 Mehnert, K. Ueber Lamartines politische Gedichte. Erlangen, 1902.
41578.49 Poplawsky, T.A. von. L'influence d'Ossian sur l'oeuvre de Lamartine. Heidelberg, 1905.
41578.50 Séché, Léon. Lamartine de 1816 à 1830. Paris, 1906.
41578.51A Marechal, Christian. Le véritable "Voyage en Orient" de Lamartine d'après manuscrits. Paris, 1908.
41578.51B Marechal, Christian. Le véritable "Voyage en Orient" de Lamartine d'après manuscrits. Paris, 1908.
41578.52 Sanvert, P.A. Notes sur la poésie religieuse de Lamartine. Macon, 1880.
41578.53 Séché, Léon. Le roman de Lamartine. Paris, n.d.
41578.54 Sugier, S. Lamartine - étude morale. Paris, 1910.
41578.55 Chamborant de Périssat, Albert. Lamartine inconnu. Paris, 1891.
41578.56 Combes, A. Mes souvenirs sur Lamartine. Castres, 1869.
41578.57 Olliver, M.T.E. Valentine de Lamartine. Paris, 1908.
41578.58 Deschanel, E. Lamartine. Paris, n.d. 2v.
41578.59 Mélanges sur Lamartine. n.p., n.d.
41578.60 Alphonse Lamartine. Angers, 1869.
41578.61 Alexandre, Charles. Madame de Lamartine. Paris, 1887.
41578.61.5 Lebailly, Armand. Madame de Lamartine. Paris, 1864.

41578.36 - Individual authors, etc. - 1800-1849 - Lamartine - Biography and criticism - cont.

41578.61.10 Lamartine, Alix. Les confidences de Madame de Lamartine. Paris, 1957.
41578.62 Séché, Léon. Les amitiés de Lamartine. 1e série. Paris, 1911.
41578.63 Lacretelle, Pierre de. Les origines et la jeunesse de Lamartine. 1790-1812. Paris, 1911.
41578.64 Doumic, R. Les grands écrivains français, Lamartine. Paris, 1912.
41578.65 Cochin, Henry. Lamartine et la Flandre. Paris, 1912.
41578.66 Cognets, Jean des. La vie intérieure de Lamartine. Paris, 1913.
41578.67 Barrès, Maurice. L'abdication du poète. Paris, 1914.
41578.68 Rolla, C. Lamartine et l'Italie. Novare, 1913.
41578.68.5 Saint-Victor, P. Lamartine. Paris, 1869.
41578.68.15 Cenzatti, G. Alfonso de Lamartine et l'Italie. Livorno, 1903.
41578.68.25 Artensi, M. Lamartine, le poète et l'Italie. Città de Castello, 1909.
41578.68.35 Mengin, U. Lamartine à Florence, 1825-1828. Grenoble, 1925.
41578.68.45 Mirecourt, E. de. Lamartine. 7. éd. Paris, 1856.
41578.70 Pamphlet box. Lamartine.
41578.71 Kool, Jacob Heye. Les premières meditations en Hollande. Paris, 1920.
41578.72 Sachs, Eva. Les idées sociales de Lamartine jusqu'a 1848. Thèse. Paris, 1915.
41578.73 Bouchard, Marcel. Lamartine; ou, Le sens de l'amour. Paris, 1940.
41578.74 Jacquemin, Juliette. Lamartine, ses origins Franc-comtoises. Lyon, 1926.
41578.75 Barthow, Louis. Lamartine, orateur. Paris, 1916.
41578.76A Whitehouse, Henry R. The life of Lamartine. Boston, 1918.
41578.77 Masson, Pierre M. Lamartine. Paris, 1911.
41578.79 Marie, Margueritte. Le roman d'une grande âme. Paris, 1920.
41578.81 Lamartine, Alphonse. Lettere inedite di Alphonse de Lamartine alla marchesa di Barolo. Torino, 1926.
41578.85 Lamartine, Alphonse. Lamartine. Genève, 1958.
41578.87 Barthou, Louis. Autour de Lamartine. Paris, 1925.
41578.88 Larguier, Leo. Alphonse de Lamartine. Paris, 1929.
41578.89 Raronneaux, Alfred. Lamartine, romancier populaire et social. Thèse. Lyon, 1929.
41578.90 Lasbordes, Henriette. La poèsie des souvenirs d'enfance chez Lamartine. Thèse. Paris, 1929.
41578.90.5 Lasbordes, Henriette. La poèsie des souvenirs d'enfance chez Lamartine. Thèse. Paris, 1929.
41578.91 Roustan, Marius. Lamartine et les Calhaliques Lyonnais. Paris, 1906.
41578.93 Pirazzini, Agide. The influence of Italy on the literary career of Alphonse de Lamartine. N.Y., 1917.
41578.95 Brimont, R. de B. Autour de "Graziella". Paris, 1931.
41578.97 Schulz, J. Lamartines Jugend und Bildungsgang. Inaug. Diss. München, 1930.
41578.99 Hinrichs, M.S. Étude sur le cours familier de littérature de Lamartine. Thèse. Strasbourg, 1930.
41578.101 Harris, Ethel. Lamartine et le peuple. Thèse. Paris, 1932.
41578.103 Antoir, J. Les manuscrits d'Antoir, l'ami Lamartine. Paris, 1925.
41578.105 Lamartine; memorie particolari e segrete. Italia, 1850.
41578.107 Assollant, Georges. Lamartine, premières meditations poetiques. Paris, 1931.
41578.109 Kaiser, P. Lamartine und die Musik. Inaug. Diss. München, 1936.
41578.111 Guillemin, H. Le Jocelyn de Lamartine. Thèse. Paris, 1936.
41578.112 Viallaneix, Paul. Lamartine. Paris, 1971.
41578.113 Boeniger, Y. Lamartine et le sentiment de la nature. Paris, 1934.
41578.114 Michaud-Lapeyre, M.R. Lamartine à Tresserve. Chambéry, 1927.
41578.115 Michaud-Lapeyre, M.R. Itinéraire des sites Lamartiniens de Savoie. Chambéry, 1937.
41578.117A Dérieux, H. Lamartine, raconté par ceux qui l'ont vu. Paris, 1938.
41578.117B Dérieux, H. Lamartine, raconté par ceux qui l'ont vu. Paris, 1938.
41578.118 Grillet, C. La Bible dans Lamartine. Lyon, 1938.
41578.119 Guillemin, H. Connaissance de Lamartine. Fribourg, 1942.
41578.120A Guillemin, H. Lamartine, l'homme et l'oeuvre. Paris, 1940.
41578.120B Guillemin, H. Lamartine, l'homme et l'oeuvre. Paris, 1940.
41578.121 Guillemin, H. Lamartine et la question sociale (documents inédits). Genève, 1946.
41578.121.10 Guillemin, H. Lamartine en 1848. 1. éd. Paris, 1948.
41578.122 Bertrand, L. Lamartine. Paris, 1940.
41578.123 Bertrand, L. Lamartine. Paris, 1944.
41578.124 Lecomte, G. Lamartine. Abbeville, 1927.
41578.126 Barthou, Louis. Victor Hugo. Abbeville, 1925.
41578.128 Harcourt, B. Lamartine, Barbey d'Aurevilly et Paul de Saint Victor en 1848. Paris, 1948.
41578.130 Dumont, F. De guoi vivait Lamartine. Paris, 1952.
41578.132 Jallaguier, B. Les idées politiques et sociales d'Alphonse de Lamartine. Montpellier, 1954.
41578.134 Magnien, Emil. Dans l'intimité de Lamartine. Macon, 1955.
41578.135 Magnien, Emil. Lamartine et le Pelerinage Lamartinien en Maconnais. Macon, 1957.
41578.136 Guyard, M.F. Alphonse de Lamartine. Paris, 1956.
41578.138 Lebey, André. Lamartine dans ses horizons. Paris, 1929.
41578.140 Puls, Hans. Die Musikauffassung der französischen Romantiker. Saarbrücken? 1956?
41578.145 Fréjaville, Gustave. Les méditations de Lamartine. Paris, 1931.
41578.150 Luppe Albert, M.P. Les travaux et les jours d'Alphonse de Lamartine. Paris, 1948.
41578.152 Citoleux, Marc. La poésie philosophique au XIXe siècle; Lamartine. Thèse. Paris, 1905.
41578.155 Lucas-Dubreton, Jean. Lamartine. Paris, 1951.
41578.156 Charvot, Louis. Aux confins du Dauphiné et de la Savoie. Montfleury, 1970.
41578.160 Jussieu de Senevier, Charles B. En marge de la vie de Lamartine. Paris, 19- .
41578.165 Cerf, Léon. Le reliquaire de Lamartine. Paris, 1925.
41578.166 Journées européennes d'études Lamartiniennes. Actes du congrès. Macon, 1961- 3v.

41578.36 - Individual authors, etc. - 1800-1849 - Lamartine - Biography and criticism - cont.

41578.167 Verdiers, Abel. Les amours italiennes de Lamartine. Paris, 1963.
41578.168 Olivier, Émile. Lamartine. Paris, 1874.
41578.170 Domange, Michel. Le Petit monde de Lamartine. Evian, 1968.
41578.175 Toesca, Maurice. Lamartine ou l'amour de la vie. Paris, 1969.
41578.180 Ireson, J.C. Lamartine: a revolution. Hull, England, 1969.
41578.185 Hirdt, Willi. Studien zur Metaphorik Lamartines. München, 1967.
41578.190 Bibliothèque Nationale, Paris. Lamartine; le poète et l'homme d'État. Paris, 1969.
41578.195 Musée Lamartine. Sur les pas de Lamartine, Mâcon, Musée Lamartine. Mâcon, 1969.

41581.1 - .28 Individual authors, etc. - 1800-1849 - Drama - Folios [Discontinued]

41581.3 Saintine, X.B. Oeuvres complètes de M. Ancelot. Paris, 1838.
41581.5 Bourgeois, A. Théâtre. Paris, n.d. 9 pam.
41581.7 Delavigne, C. Oeuvres complètes. Paris, 1836.
Htn 41581.17* Virely, A. René-Charles Guilbert de Pixerécourt, 1773-1844. Paris, 1909.
41581.25 Scribe, Augustin E. Théâtre. N.Y., 1844-1858.

41581.29 - .49 Individual authors, etc. - 1800-1849 - Drama - Pamphlet volumes

41581.29 Pamphlet vol. Repertoire dramatique. 5 pam.
41581.30 Pamphlet vol. Various French plays.
41581.31 Pamphlet vol. Théâtre français. Paris, 1780-1821. 8 pam.
41581.32 Pamphlet vol. Théâtre français. Paris, 1828-34. 4 pam.
41581.33 Pamphlet vol. Théâtre français. Paris, 1826-1839. 8 pam.
41581.34 Pamphlet vol. Théâtre français. Paris, 1828. 8 pam.
41581.35 Pamphlet vol. Théâtre français. 19 pam.
41581.36 Pamphlet vol. Théâtre français. 23 pam.
41581.38 Pamphlet vol. Théâtre français. 18 pam.
41581.39 Pamphlet vol. Théâtre français. 22 pam.
41581.40 Pamphlet vol. Théâtre français. 31 pam.
41581.41 Pamphlet vol. French plays. 16 pam.
41581.41.5 Pamphlet vol. French plays. 15 pam.
41581.42 Pamphlet vol. French plays. 7 pam.
41581.43 Pamphlet vol. French comedies. Paris, 1806-1810. 7 pam.
41581.44 Pamphlet vol. Mélanges. Paris, 1825- 5 pam.
41581.45 Pamphlet vol. Théâtre varié. Paris, 1803. 10 pam.
41581.46 Pamphlet vol. Théâtre varié. Paris, 1846- 13 pam.
41581.47 Pamphlet vol. French plays. 11 pam.
41581.48 College series of modern French plays. Boston. 1-8 2v.
41581.49 College series of modern French plays. N.Y. 1-9 2v.

41583.2 Individual authors, etc. - 1800-1849 - Drama - Adamoli

41583.2 Adamoli, Luigi. Les deux chaises de poste. Genève, 1850.

41583.3 Individual authors, etc. - 1800-1849 - Drama - Antier

41583.3 Antier, Benjamin. L'Auberge des Adrets. Grenoble, 1966.

41583.4 Individual authors, etc. - 1800-1849 - Drama - Ancelot

41583.4 Ancelot, Marguerite Louise Virginie (Chardon). Théâtre complet. Paris, 1848.
41583.4.5 Ancelot, Marguerite Louise Virginie (Chardon). Tragédies. Paris, n.d. 4 pam.

41583.6 Individual authors, etc. - 1800-1849 - Drama - Andrieux - Writings

41583.6 Andrieux, François G.J.S. Les contes en vers d'Andrieux. Paris, 1882.
41583.6.5 Andrieux, François G.J.S. L'enfance de Jean-Jacques Rousseau. Paris, 1794.
41583.6.10 Andrieux, François G.J.S. Contes et opuscules. Paris, 1800.
41583.6.15 Andrieux, François G.J.S. Oeuvres de F.G.J.S. Andrieux. Paris, 1818-23. 4v.

41583.7 Individual authors, etc. - 1800-1849 - Drama - Artois

41583.7.100 Artois, Armand d'. Papa flirt. Paris, 1913.

41583.8 - .8.9 Individual authors, etc. - 1800-1849 - Drama - Arago

41583.8 Arago, E. C'est demain le treise. Paris, 1826.
41583.8.5 Arago, E. Les quatres artistes. Paris, 1827.
41583.8.6 Arago, E. 27, 28 et 29 juillet. Paris, 1830.

41583.8.20 Individual authors, etc. - 1800-1849 - Drama - Arnault, A.

41583.8.20 Arnault, A. Les Casaques. Paris, 1853.

41583.8.25 Individual authors, etc. - 1800-1849 - Drama - Arnoult, S.

41583.8.25 Arnoult, S. Proverbes anecdotiques. Paris, 1835.

41583.8.40 Individual authors, etc. - 1800-1849 - Drama - Aude

41583.8.40 Aude, Joseph. La veille d'une grande fête. Paris, 1808.

41583.9 Individual authors, etc. - 1800-1849 - Drama - Barré

41583.9 Barré, Pierre y. Santara. Paris, 1809.
41583.9.2 Barré, Pierre y. Des deux lions. Paris, 1810.
41583.9.5 Barré, Pierre y. L'heureuse décade. 2e éd. Paris, 1793-1794.
41583.9.8 Barré, Pierre y. Gessner. Paris, 1800.
41583.9.11 Barré, Pierre y. Favart aux Champs-Élysées. Paris, 1793.
41583.9.15 Barré, Pierre y. La chaste Suzanne. Paris? 179-.
41583.9.15.2 Barré, Pierre y. La chaste Suzanne. Paris, 1793.
41583.9.15.4 Barré, Pierre y. La chaste Suzanne. Paris, 1793.

41583.10 Individual authors, etc. - 1800-1849 - Drama - Aumer

41583.10 Aumer, Pierre. Jemry, ou Le mariage secret. Paris, 1806.

41583.11 Individual authors, etc. - 1800-1849 - Drama - Barthelmy-Hadot; Basté; Bawr; Bazin

41583.11.2 Barthelemy-Hadot, M.A. (Mme.). Jules, ou Le toit paternel. Paris, 1806.
41583.11.2.5 Barthelemy-Hadot, M.A. (Mme.). Cosme de Médicis. Paris, 1809.
41583.11.3 Basté, Eugène Pierre. Les frères corses. London, 18- ?

Classified Listing

583.11 Individual authors, etc. - 1800-1849 - Drama - Barthelmy-Hadot; Basté; Bawr; Bazin - cont.
41583.11.4 Basté, Eugène Pierre. The Corsican brothers. N.Y., 185-. 4 pam.
41583.11.4.5 Basté, Eugène Pierre. The Corsican brothers. N.Y., 1850?
41583.11.5 Basté, Eugène Pierre. Les domestiques. Paris, 1875.
41583.11.50 Bawr, A.S. (Goury de Champgrand). La suite d'un bal masque. Paris, 1818.
41583.11.55 Bawr, A.S. (Goury de Champgrand). Mes souvenirs. 2e éd. Paris, 1853.
41583.11.60 Bawr, A.S. (Goury de Champgrand). Nouvelles. Paris, 1854.
41583.11.250 Bazin, Rigomer. Jacqueline d'Olzebourg. Paris, 1803.

583.12 Individual authors, etc. - 1800-1849 - Drama - Bayard; Beffroy de Reigny; Belfort; etc.
41583.12 Bayard, Jean F.A. El articulo V. Habana, 1844.
41583.12.3 Beffroy De Reigny, L.A. La petite Nannette. Paris, 1796.
41583.12.5 Beffroy De Reigny, L.A. Jean Baptiste. Paris, 1798.
41583.12.7 Beffroy De Reigny, L.A. Nicodème dans la lune. Paris, 1791.
41583.12.9 Beffroy De Reigny, L.A. Le club des bonnes-gens. Paris, 1791.
41583.12.11 Beffroy De Reigny, L.A. Le club des bonnes-gens. Paris, 1792.
41583.12.12 Beffroy De Reigny, L.A. Le club des bonnes-gens. Paris, 1795.
41583.12.13 Beffroy De Reigny, L.A. Toute la Grèce. Paris, 1794.
41583.12.14 Beffroy De Reigny, L.A. Testament d'un électeur de Paris. Paris, 1796.
41583.12.15 Beffroy De Reigny, L.A. Allons, ça va, ou Le quaker en France. 2e éd. Paris, 1793.
41583.12.17 Belfort. Hommage à Louis XVIII; scène lyrique. Montpellier, 1814.
41583.12.19 Benjamin, A. Le jeune médecin. Paris, 1829.
41583.12.35 Bernos, Alexandre. Le siège du clocher. Paris, 1809.
41583.12.50 Bertrand, Leon. Oliver Cromwell. Paris, 1841.
41583.12.100 Bignon, E.A. Les chevaliers du soleil. Paris, 1801.

583.13 Individual authors, etc. - 1800-1849 - Drama - Blache; etc.
41583.13 Blache, M. Polichinel vampire. Paris, 1823.

1583.14 Individual authors, etc. - 1800-1849 - Drama - Boirie; Bonel; etc.
41583.14 Boirie, E.C. de. La jeunesse du Grand Frédéric. Paris, 1817.
41583.14.5 Boirie, E.C. de. Le couvrier de Naples. Paris, 1822.
41583.14.7 Boirie, E.C. de. La caverne de Sonabe. Paris, 1806.
41583.14.9 Boirie, E.C. de. La fille maudite. Paris, 1818.
41583.14.19 Bonel, P.G.A. La tour du sud. Paris, 1804.
41583.14.22 Bonel, P.G.A. L'auberge de Calais. Paris, 1802.
41583.14.50 Baudouin, Théodore. Les inseparables. Paris, 1823.
41583.14.55 Baudouin, Théodore. Le pauvre berger. Paris, 1823.
41583.14.60 Baudouin, Théodore. Démétrius. Paris, 1797.

1583.15 Individual authors, etc. - 1800-1849 - Drama - Bonjour; Bouchardy; Bourgeois; etc.
41583.15 Bonjour, Casimir. Théâtre. Paris, 1901. 3v.
41583.15.5 Bonjour, Casimir. L'education, ou Les deux cousines. Paris, 1823.
41583.15.6 Bonjour, Casimir. Oeuvres. Paris, 1901.
41583.15.9 Bouchardy, Joseph. Cristobal el Señador. Madrid, 1840.
41583.15.10 Bouchardy, Joseph. El hijo de la tempestad. Madrid, 1841.
41583.15.12 Bourgeois, Anicet. Napoleon, pièce historique. Paris, 1830.
41583.15.13 Bourgeois, Anicet. The black doctor. London, 18- ?
41583.15.14 Bourgeois, Anicet. The duke's daughter. N.Y., n.d.
41583.15.14.3 Bourgeois, Anicet. The duke's daughter. N.Y., 186-?
41583.15.14.5 Bourgeois, Anicet. The duke's daughter. N.Y., 18- ?
41583.15.14.7 Bourgeois, Anicet. Clarisse. Paris, 1829.
41583.15.15 Bourgeois, Anicet. Marthe et Marie. Paris, 1852.
41583.15.16 Bonnechose, Emile. Rosemonde; tragédie. Paris, 1826.
41583.15.25 Pamphlet box. Bonjour, Casimir.
41583.15.40 Bonnais, Henri. Le 9 thermidor, ou La mort de Robespierre. Paris, 1831.
41583.15.150 Boullault, M.J. La mort de Cadet-Roussel. Paris, 1798.
41583.15.250 Bouquier, G. La réunion du dix août. Paris, 1802.
41583.15.300 Boutroux, L.A. de Montargis. La mort de Charles Ier. Paris, 1820.

1583.16 Individual authors, etc. - 1800-1849 - Drama - Brazier
41583.16 Brazier, Dumersan. Les filles de Vulcain. Paris, 1826.
41583.16.5 Brazier, Dumersan. Tony, ou Cinq années en deux heures. Paris, 1827.
41583.16.6 Brazier, Dumersan. L'école de village. Paris, 1818.
41583.16.7 Brazier, Nicholas. Catharine, ou La croix d'or. Paris, 18- ?

1583.17 Individual authors, etc. - 1800-1849 - Drama - Brifaut
41583.17 Brifaut, Charles. Oeuvres. Paris, 1858. 6v.
41583.17.50 Brifaut, Charles. Souvenirs d'un académicien. Paris, 1921. 2v.

1583.18 Individual authors, etc. - 1800-1849 - Drama - Brisebarre; Brunneaux; Caigniez; Chazet; etc.
41583.18 Brisebarre, Édouard. Monsieur de la Raclée. Paris, 1862.
41583.18.5 Brisebarre, Édouard. Adrienne de Carotteville. Paris, 1849.
41583.18.9 Broban, Augustine S. Compter sans son hote; proverbe. Paris, 1849.
41583.18.12 Brunneaux, Jean. Pyrame et Thisbé. Tragédie. Paris, 1823.
41583.18.13 Brunneaux, Jean. Ulysse. Tragédie. Paris, 1823.
41583.18.19 Caigniez, Louis Charles. La pie voleuse. Paris, 1815.
41583.18.20 Caigniez, Louis Charles. The maid and the magpic, or Who is the thief? London, 1815.
41583.18.20.3A Caigniez, Louis Charles. The magpie. Boston, 1822.
41583.18.20.3B Caigniez, Louis Charles. The magpie. Boston, 1822.
41583.18.20.6 Caigniez, Louis Charles. La belle-mère et les deux orphelins. Paris, 1808.
41583.18.20.9 Caigniez, Louis Charles. La forêt d'Hermanstad. Paris, 1806.
41583.18.21 Carmouche, P.F.A. Le marquis de Lauzun. Paris, 1848.
41583.18.22 Carmouche, P.F.A. N.i.ni, ou Le danger des Castilles. Paris, 1830.
41583.18.23 Cavaignac, Godefroy. Dubois cardinal, proverbe historique. Paris, 1831.
41583.18.25 Charrin, P.J. Le lion parlant. Paris, 1806.
41583.18.35 Chateauneuf, A. L'infidelité conjugale. Paris, 1834.

41583.18 Individual authors, etc. - 1800-1849 - Drama - Brisebarre; Brunneaux; Caigniez; Chazet; etc. - cont.
41583.18.50 Chaussier, Hector. Maria ou La forête de Limberg. Paris, 1800.
41583.18.50.5 Chaussier, Hector. Les prestiges, ou Amine et Sohi. Paris, 1801.
41583.18.53 Chazet, André René P.A. Philippe le Savoyard, ou L'origine des ponts neufs. Paris, 1801.
41583.18.53.5 Chazet, André René P.A. Les français à Cythère. Paris, 1798.
41583.18.53.10 Chazet, André René P.A. L'officier de quinze ans. Paris, 1811.
41583.18.54 Claude Macée, frère. Pastorale sur la naissence de Jesus-Christ. Rennes, 1821.
41583.18.55 Coquatrix. Italie. Paris, 1834.
41583.18.75 Crosnier, Edmond. Le contrebandier. 2e éd. Paris, 1823.

41583.19 Individual authors, etc. - 1800-1849 - Drama - Cuvelier
41583.19 Cuvelier de Trie, J.G.A. Bélisaire. Paris, 1815.
41583.19.5 Cuvelier de Trie, J.G.A. La fille hussard, ou Le sergent suédois. Paris, 1805.
41583.19.6 Cuvelier de Trie, J.G.A. La bataille d'Aboukir. Paris, 1808.
41583.19.9 Cuvelier de Trie, J.G.A. Le petit poucet. Paris, 1820.
41583.19.12 Cuvelier de Trie, J.G.A. La fille mendiante. Paris, 1809.
41583.19.15 Cuvelier de Trie, J.G.A. Le petit poucet. Paris, 1798.
41583.19.20 Cuvelier de Trie, J.G.A. L'enfant du malheur. Paris, 1796-97.
41583.19.25 Cuvelier de Trie, J.G.A. La mort de Kléber. Paris, 1819.
41583.19.30 Cuvelier de Trie, J.G.A. Macbeth, ou les sorcières de la forêt. Paris, 1817.

41583.20 - .31 Individual authors, etc. - 1800-1849 - Drama - Delavigne, Casimir - Writings
41583.20 Delavigne, Casimir. Oeuvres complètes. Paris, 1850. 6v.
41583.20.5 Delavigne, Casimir. Théâtre. Paris, 1826. 4v.
41583.20.10 Delavigne, Casimir. Théâtre. Paris, 1857. 3v.
41583.21 Delavigne, Casimir. Oeuvres complètes. v.3. Bruxelles, 1832.
41583.22 Delavigne, Casimir. Oeuvres complètes. Paris, 1855. 6v.
41583.22.15 Delavigne, Casimir. Oeuvres complètes. Paris, 1881. 3v.
41583.23 Delavigne, Casimir. Théâtre français. Paris, n.d.
41583.24 Delavigne, Casimir. Théâtre français. Paris, n.d. 5 pam.
41583.25 Delvaigne, Casimir. Théâtre français. Paris, n.d. 3 pam.
41583.27 Delavigne, Casimir. Les enfans d'Édouard. Paris, 1833.
41583.27.15 Delavigne, Casimir. Les enfans d'Édouard. Cambridge, 1895.
41583.27.20 Delavigne, Casimir. Les enfants d'Édouard. London, 1880?
41583.28 Delavigne, Casimir. Une famille au temps de Luther. Paris, 1836.
41583.28.3 Delavigne, Casimir. Louis XI. N.Y., n.d.
41583.28.5 Delavigne, Casimir. Louis XI. N.Y., 188-.
41583.28.9 Delavigne, Casimir. Louis XI. London, 1894.
41583.28.12 Delavigne, Casimir. Louis XI. London, 1909.
41583.28.15 Delavigne, Casimir. El paria. Nueva Orleans, 1847.
41583.29 Delavigne, Casimir. Marino Faliero. Paris, 1829.
41583.30 Delavigne, Casimir. Messéniennes et chants populairs. Paris, 1840.
41583.30.3 Delavigne, Casimir. Messéniennes et poésies diverses. 6e éd. Paris, 1823.
41583.30.5 Delavigne, Casimir. Sept messéniennes nouvelles. Paris, 1827.
41583.30.10 Delavigne, Casimir. Messénienne sur Lord Byron. 2e éd. Paris, 1824.
41583.30.19 Delavigne, Casimir. Messéniennes et poesies nouvelles. 5. éd. Paris, 1824.
41583.31 Delavigne, Casimir. Trois messéniennes, sur les malheurs de la France. 5e éd. Paris, 1822.

41583.32 Individual authors, etc. - 1800-1849 - Drama - Delavigne, Casimir - Works about
41583.32 Fauchier Delavigne, M. Casimir Delavigne intime. Paris, 1907.
41583.32.15 Wetzig, Reinold. Studie über die Tragödien Casimir Delavignes. Leipzig, 1900.
41583.32.20 Vuacheux, Ferdinand. Casimir Delavigne. Havre, 1893.
41583.32.25 Klinger, Ludwig. Über die Tragödien Casimir Delavignes. pt.1-3. Waldenburg, 1899-1907.

41583.34 Individual authors, etc. - 1800-1849 - Drama - Delavigne, G.
41583.34 Delavigne, G. La muette de Portici. Paris, 1828.

41583.45 Individual authors, etc. - 1800-1849 - Drama - Désnoyer
41583.45 Désnoyer, C. L'ombre de Nicolet. Paris, 1837.

41584.2 Individual authors, etc. - 1800-1849 - Drama - Debraux
41584.2 Debraux, Paul Émile. Les barricades de 1830. Paris, 1830.

41584.3 Individual authors, etc. - 1800-1849 - Drama - Delisle de Sales
41584.3 Delisle de Sales, J.C. Oeuvres dramatiques et littéraires. Paris, 1809. 2v.

41584.4 Individual authors, etc. - 1800-1849 - Drama - Delaunay
41584.4 Delaunay, A.J. L'un pour l'autre. Paris, 1805.

41584.5 Individual authors, etc. - 1800-1849 - Drama - Demoustier
41584.5 Demoustier, Charles A. Théâtre de C.A. Demoustier. Paris, 1804. 2v.

41584.6 Individual authors, etc. - 1800-1849 - Drama - Desprey
41584.6 Desprez, C.A. L'espoir realisé. Paris, 1811.
41584.6.5 Desprez, C.A. L'allarmiste, impromptu, républicain. Paris, 1794.

41584.7 Individual authors, etc. - 1800-1849 - Drama - Dieu-la-Foy
41584.7 Dieu-La-Foy, J.M.A.M. La revue de l'an huit, suite de la revue de l'an six. Paris, 1801.

41584.8 Individual authors, etc. - 1800-1849 - Drama - Goubaux (Denaux)
41584.8.5 Gonbaux, Prosper Parfait. Louise de Lignerolles. London, 18- ?

41584.15 - .18 Individual authors, etc. - 1800-1849 - Drama - Doucet - Writings
41584.15 Doucet, Camille. Oeuvres complètes. Paris, 1874. 2v.
41584.15.10 Pamphlet vol. Pièces de théâtre. 4 pam.
41584.16 Doucet, Camille. La consideration. Paris, 1860.
41584.17 Doucet, Camille. Le fruit défendu. Paris, 1858.

41584.23 Individual authors, etc. - 1800-1849 - Drama - Dittmer
41584.23 Dittmer, Antoine D.A. Les soirées de Neuilly. Paris, 1827. 2v.

41584.26 Individual authors, etc. - 1800-1849 - Drama - Drague
41584.26 Drague, Joseph. Que deviendra-t-elle? Paris, 1835.
41584.26.9 Drague, Joseph. Urbain-Grandier. Dijon, 1834.

41584.27 Individual authors, etc. - 1800-1849 - Drama - Druancel; Ducange; Dupetit; etc.
41584.27 Druancel, P.C. Esquisses dramatiques du gouvernement Révolutionnaire de France. Paris, 1830.
41584.27.5 Drichatellier, A. Théâtre historique de la Révolution. v.2. Paris, 1829.
41584.27.9 Dufresny, C. Les deux jaloux. Paris, 1813.
41584.27.12 Dupaty, Emmanuel. La jeune prude. Paris, 1804.
41584.27.15 Dumaniant, A.J. Le soeur rival. Paris, 1818.
41584.27.16 Dumaniant, A.J. Diamond cut diamond. London, 1787.
41584.27.20 Dumaniant, A.J. Le soldat Prussien. Paris, 1791.
41584.27.21 Dumersan, Théophile Marion. Le tyran peu délicat. 2e éd. Paris, 1814.
41584.27.22 Dumersan, Théophile Marion. Jocrisse grand-père, Jocrisse fils, et Jocrisse petit-fils. Paris, 1816.
41584.27.25 Dumaniant, A.J. Isaure et gernance. Paris, 1795.
41584.27.30 Dupin, Jean Henri. Tigresse; mort-aux-rats. Paris, 1833.
41584.27.50 Ducange, Victor. Le diamant. Paris, 1824.
41584.27.55 Ducange, Victor. Palmérin. Paris, 1813.
41584.27.60 Ducange, Victor. Adolphe et Sophie. Paris, 1816.
41584.27.63 Ducange, Victor. Trente ans. Paris, 1856.
41584.27.75 Dupetit-Méré, F. Aurengzeb, ou La famille indienne. Paris, 1817.
41584.27.80 Dupetit-Méré, F. L'isle des mariages. Paris, 1809.
41584.27.85 Dupetit-Méré, F. Minuit, ou La révélation. Paris, 1824.
41584.27.90 Dupetit-Méré, F. A Spandau, ou le libelle. Paris, 1806.
41584.27.150 Duval, George. Ildamor et Tubéma. Paris, 1805.

41584.28 - .29 Individual authors, etc. - 1800-1849 - Drama - Duval, A.
41584.28 Duval, A. Oeuvres. Paris, 1822. 9v.
41584.29 Duval, A. Charles II, ou Le Labyrinthe de Woodstock. Paris, 1828.
41584.29.5 Duval, A. Le misantrope du Marais. Paris, 1832.
41584.29.19 Duval, A. Shakespeare enamorado; comedia. 2a ed. Madrid, 1843.
41584.29.21 Duval, A. La jeunesse du duc de Richelieu. Paris, 1797.
41584.29.22 Duval, A. Invloed der gelijkenis of gewaande. Amsterdam, 1814.
41584.29.25 Duval, A. Die Jugend Heinrichs. Wien, 1807.
41584.29.28 Duval, A. Le souper imprévu. Paris, 1798.
41584.29.40 La Borderie, Arthur de. Une illustration rennaise. Rennes, 1893.
41584.29.80 Bellier-Dumaine, C. Alexandre Duval et son oeuvre dramatique. Paris, 1905.

41584.30 Individual authors, etc. - 1800-1849 - Drama - Duvert
41584.30 Duvert, F.A. Théâtre choisi. Paris, 1877-1879. 6v.

41584.32 Individual authors, etc. - 1800-1849 - Drama - Duveyrier
41584.32.20 Duveyrier, A.H.J. Le chevalier de St. George. London, 18- ?
41584.32.25 Duveyrier, A.H.J. Les Mexicains. Paris, 1819.
41584.32.33 Duveyrier, A.H.J. Sullivan. N.Y., 1873.
41584.32.34 Duveyrier, A.H.J. Sullivan. N.Y., 1880.
41584.32.36 Duveyrier, A.H.J. Le chateau de Paluzzi. Paris, 1818.
41584.32.39 Duveyrier, A.H.J. Les vieux péchés. Paris, 1833.
41584.32.45 Duveyrier, A.H.J. Michel Perrin. Paris, 1844.

41584.33 Individual authors, etc. - 1800-1849 - Drama - Dumolard
41584.33 Dumolard, Henri François. Vincent de Paul; drame. Paris, 1804.
41584.33.5 Dumolard, Henri François. Le Philinte de Destouches. Paris, 1803.

41584.34 Individual authors, etc. - 1800-1849 - Drama - Dubois
41584.34 Dubois, Jean B. La fausse marquise. Paris, 1805.

41584.35 - .36 Individual authors, etc. - 1800-1849 - Drama - Etienne, C.G. - Works about
41584.35 Le Senne, C. Charles Guillaume Étienne. Paris, 1913.
41584.35.10 Wicks, C.B. Charles-Guillaume Étienne. Baltimore, 1940.
41584.36 Thiesse, Léon. M. Étienne. Paris, 1853.

41584.37 - .39 Individual authors, etc. - 1800-1849 - Drama - Etienne, C.G. - Writings
41584.37 Étienne, Charles Guillaume. Oeuvres. Paris, 1846. 5v.
41584.38 Étienne, Charles Guillaume. Works. Paris, 1824. 2v.
41584.39 Étienne, Charles Guillaume. Conaxa ou les Gendres Dupés. Paris, 1812.
41584.39.2 Étienne, Charles Guillaume. Conaxa ou les Gendres Dupés. Paris, 1815.
41584.39.8 Étienne, Charles Guillaume. Conaxa ou les Gendres Dupés. Comédie. Paris, 1812. 9 pam.

41584.40 Individual authors, etc. - 1800-1849 - Drama - Eustache
41584.40 Eustache, A.J.R. Les filles savantes. Paris, 1838.

41584.41 Individual authors, etc. - 1800-1849 - Drama - Fezet-Mougest; Flareau; etc.
41584.41.3 Cim, A. En pleine gloire; histoire d'une mystification. Paris, 1893.
Htn 41584.41.9* Flareau. The ocean spectre. n.p., 18- .

41584.42 Individual authors, etc. - 1800-1849 - Drama - Fontan
41584.42 Fontan, Louis Marie. Bergami et la reine d'Angleterre. Paris, 1833.

41584.43 Individual authors, etc. - 1800-1849 - Drama - Forneret
41584.43.5 Forneret, Xavier. Le diamant de l'herbe. Paris, 1955.
41584.43.25 Kaye, Eldon. Xavier Forneret dit "L'homme noir" (1809-1884). Genève, 1971.

41584.44 Individual authors, etc. - 1800-1849 - Drama - Fougher
41584.44 Fougher, P. Yseult Raimbaud. Paris, 1830.

41584.47 Individual authors, etc. - 1800-1849 - Drama - Francis
Htn 41584.47* Allarde, M.F.D.T.L.R. L'imprimeur sans caractère. Paris, 1824.

41584.49 Individual authors, etc. - 1800-1849 - Drama - Ferrand; Friedalle; etc.
41584.49 Ferrand of Rouen. Le savetier de Péronne. Rouen, 1801.
41584.49.150 Friedelle, A. Amélie, ou Le protecteur mystérieux. Paris, 1807.

41584.50 Individual authors, etc. - 1800-1849 - Drama - Gaillardet; Gain-Montaignac
41584.50.5 Gaillardet, Frédéric. La tour de Nesle. N.Y., 1853.
41584.50.8 Gaillardet, Frédéric. La tour de Nesle. N.Y., 1853?
41584.50.15 Gaillardet, Frédéric. La tour de Nesle. Paris, 1908.
41584.50.25 Gain-Montaignac, J.R. Théâtre. Paris, 1820.

41584.51 Individual authors, etc. - 1800-1849 - Drama - Gardy; Germeau; Gibelin; etc.
41584.51 Lurieu, Gabriel de. Jocko, ou Le singe du Brésil. 3e éd. Paris, 1825.
41584.51.10 Gardy, J.A. Gilles bon ami. Paris, 1801.
41584.51.12 Gardy, J.A. Celestine, ou La fille alcade. Paris, 1799.
41584.51.25 Germeau. La reforme en 1560, ou Le tumulte d'Amboise. Paris, 1829.
41584.51.150 Gibelin, A.E. Epitre aus chretiens de toutes les communions. London, 1808.

41584.52 Individual authors, etc. - 1800-1849 - Drama - Gibert
41584.52 Gibert, B. Rozélina. Paris, 1800.

41584.53 Individual authors, etc. - 1800-1849 - Drama - Gosse
41584.53 Gosse, Etienne. Proverbes dramatiques. Paris, 1819. 2v.

41584.54 Individual authors, etc. - 1800-1849 - Drama - Gouffe
41584.54 Gouffe, Armand. Le duel et le Dejeuner. Paris, 1818.

41584.55 Individual authors, etc. - 1800-1849 - Drama - Gougibus; Guénard; Grévin; etc.
41584.55 Gougibus, J.T. L'homme d'Airain. Paris, 1804.
41584.55.9 Guénard, Elisabeth. La jolie ferme. Paris, 1822.
41584.55.12 Guénard, Elisabeth. Vie et aventures de Marion de Lorme. 3e éd. v.1-2,3-4. Paris, 1828. 2v.
41584.55.150 Maloigne, M. Jacques Grévin, sa vie, son oeuvre. Laval, 1926.
41584.55.200 Nézel, Théodore. Cartouche. 2e éd. Paris, 1827.
41584.55.700 Guilleau de Formont. Jean de Bourgogne. Paris, 1820.

41584.56 Individual authors, etc. - 1800-1849 - Drama - Hapdé; Henrion; etc.
41584.56 Hapdé, J.B. La naissance d'Arlequin. Paris, 1813.
41584.56.5 Hapdé, J.B. La guerrière des sept Montagnes. Paris, 1805.
41584.56.10 Hapdé, J.B. Le pont du diable. Paris, 1806.
41584.56.50 Henrion, Charles. Les persécutions diaboliques. Liège, 1805.

41584.57 - .58 Individual authors, etc. - 1800-1849 - Drama - Hoffman, F.B. - Writings
41584.57 Hoffman, F.B. Oeuvres. Paris, 1829-34. 10v.
41584.58 Hoffman, F.B. Le brigand. Paris, n.d.
41584.58.5 Hoffman, F.B. Stratonice. Lyon, 1792.
41584.58.7 Hoffman, F.B. Callais. Paris, 1795.
41584.58.9 Hoffman, F.B. Euphrosine. Paris, 1791.
41584.58.10 Hoffman, F.B. L'original comédie. Paris, 1797.
41584.58.11 Hoffman, F.B. Le jeune sage et le vieux fou. Paris, 1801-02.

41585.2 Individual authors, etc. - 1800-1849 - Drama - Imbert de Saint Armand
41585.2 Imbert de Saint-Armand. Le Réveillon dramatique. Paris, 1835.

41585.5 - .18 Individual authors, etc. - 1800-1849 - Drama - Jouy - Writings
41585.5 Jouy, Étienne. Oeuvres complètes. Paris, 1823-28. 27v.
41585.10 Jouy, Étienne. Bélisaire. 3e éd. Paris, 1825.
41585.16 Jouy, Étienne. Sylla. 2e éd. Paris, 1822. 6 pam.
41585.17 Jouy, Étienne. Sylla, a tragedy. N.Y., 1826.

41585.24 Individual authors, etc. - 1800-1849 - Drama - Dulong, J. (M. Jules)
41585.24 Dulong, Jules. La prise de tarifa. Paris, 1824.

41585.31 Individual authors, etc. - 1800-1849 - Drama - La Gleyenhaye
41585.31 La Gleyenhaye, L.T. de. La loi singuliere. Paris, 1811.

41585.35 Individual authors, etc. - 1800-1849 - Drama - Laloue
41585.35 Laloue, Ferdinand. Le commissionnaire. Paris, 1824.

41585.36 Individual authors, etc. - 1800-1849 - Drama - Lamey
41585.36 Lamey, Auguste. Elvérine de Wertheim. Paris, 1808.
41585.36.5 Lamey, Auguste. Dekadische Lieder für die Franken am Rheim. Strassburg, 1794-95. 2 pam.
41585.36.10 Lamey, Auguste. Gedichte eines Franken an Rheinstrom. Strassburg, 1791.

41586.1 Individual authors, etc. - 1800-1849 - Drama - La Roche; La Rochefoucauld-Liancourt
41586.1 La Roche, Philippe J. de. Gustave, ou Le Napolitain. Paris, 1825.
41586.1.5 La Roche, Philippe J. de. Ramire, ou Le fils naturel. 2e éd. Paris, 1805.
41586.1.9 La Roche, Philippe J. de. Le faux martinguerre. Paris, 1813.

41586.1 Individual authors, etc. - 1800-1849 - Drama - La Roche; La Rochefoucauld-Liancourt - cont.

41586.1.12 La Roche, Philippe J. de. Clara. Paris, 1808.
41586.1.14 La Roche, Philippe J. de. Rodolphe, ou La tour de Falkenstein. Paris, 1812.
41586.1.18 La Roche, Philippe J. de. Amélasis, ou Amour et ambition. Paris, 1811.
41586.1.100 La Rochefoucauld-Liancourt, F.G. La révolution française et Bonaparte. Paris, 1818.

41586.2 Individual authors, etc. - 1800-1849 - Drama - Latour

41586.2 Latour, Isidore. Virginie. N.Y., 1855.

41586.3 Individual authors, etc. - 1800-1849 - Drama - Latouche, H. de; Laurençot; etc.

41586.3 Latouche, Henri de. La reine d'Espagne. Paris, 1831.
41586.3.5 Latouche, Henri de. La reine d'Espagne. Paris, 1928.
41586.3.6 Latouche, Henri de. Clement XIV et Carlo Bertinazzi, correspondance inédite. Paris, 1844.
41586.3.9 Ségu, Fréderic. H. de Latouche, 1785-1851. Paris, 1931.
41586.3.10A Ségu, Fréderic. H. de Latouche et son intervention dans les arts. Paris, 1931.
41586.3.10B Ségu, Fréderic. H. de Latouche et son intervention dans les arts. Paris, 1931.
41586.3.11 Ségu, Fréderic. Un maitre de Balzac méconnu, H. de Latouche. Paris, 1928.
41586.3.12 Laurençot, Charles H.L. Toma y daga, ó Que se queje aquel que pierda, comedia. Madrid, 1840.
41586.3.19 Laverpillière, A. L'homme et ses écrits. Paris, 1833.

41586.4 Individual authors, etc. - 1800-1849 - Drama - La Ville de Mirmont

41586.4 La Ville de Mirmont, Alexandre Jean Joseph. L'intrigue et l'amour. Paris, 1826.
41586.4.5 La Ville de Mirmont, Alexandre Jean Joseph. Oeuvres dramatiques. Paris, 1846. 4v.
41586.4.10 La Ville de Mirmont, Alexandre Jean Joseph. Le roman, comédie en cinq actes. Paris, 1825.

41586.5 - .8 Individual authors, etc. - 1800-1849 - Drama - Laya, L. - Writings

41586.5 Laya, Léon. Les coeurs d'or. Paris, 1869.
41586.6 Laya, Léon. Un coup de Lansquenet. Paris, 1862.
41586.7 Laya, Léon. Les jeunes gens. Paris, 1861.
41586.8 Laya, Léon. Le duc job. Paris, 1860.
41586.8.5 Laya, Léon. Le duc job; comédie en quatre actes et en prose. Paris, 1894.
41586.8.10 Laya, Léon. Madame Desroches. Paris, 1868.

41586.10 Individual authors, etc. - 1800-1849 - Drama - Leblanc; etc.

41586.10.250 Leblanc de Ferrière, A. Archambaud. Paris, 1813.

41586.11 Individual authors, etc. - 1800-1849 - Drama - Leclercq

41586.11 Leclercq, Théodore. Proverbs dramatiques. Paris, 1835. 8v.
41586.11.5 Leclercq, Théodore. Nouveaux proverbes dramatiques. Paris, 1830.
41586.11.8 Leclercq, Théodore. Trois proverbes. Boston, 1865.
41586.11.10 Leclercq, Théodore. Trois proverbes dramatiques. 2e éd. Bielefeld, 1879.

41586.12 Individual authors, etc. - 1800-1849 - Drama - Le Feure; Le Hoc; etc.

41586.12.3 Le Feure, Pierre. Zuma, a tragedy. London, 1800.
41586.12.9 Le Hoc, M. Pyrrhus, ou les Aeacides. Paris, 1807.

41586.13 - .15 Individual authors, etc. - 1800-1849 - Drama - Lemercier, N.L.

41586.13 Lemercier, N.L. Clovis, tragédie. Paris, 1820.
41586.13.5 Lemercier, N.L. Ophis. Paris, 1798-1799.
41586.14 Lemercier, N.L. Comédies historiques. Paris, 1828.
41586.15 Lemercier, N.L. Louis IX en Egypte. Paris, 1821.
41586.15.2A Lemercier, N.L. Agamemnon, tragédie en 5 actes. Paris, 1796-1797.
41586.15.2B Lemercier, N.L. Agamemnon, tragédie en 5 actes. Paris, 1796-1797.
41586.15.2.30 Lemercier, N.L. Agamenon. Madrid, 1800.
41586.15.3 Lemercier, N.L. La démence de Charles VI; tragédie en 5 actes. Paris, 1820.
41586.15.4 Lemercier, N.L. Les deux filles spectres; mélodrame 3 actes en prose. Paris, 1827.
41586.15.4.15 Lemercier, N.L. Frédégonde et Brunehaut. Cambridge, 1876.
41586.15.5 Lemercier, N.L. L'héroine de Montpellier; mélodrame en 5 actes. Paris, 1835.
41586.15.6 Lemercier, N.L. Isule et Orovèse; tragédie en 5 actes. Paris, 1803.
41586.15.7 Lemercier, N.L. Richard III et Jeanne Shore; drame historique en vers. Paris, 1824.
41586.15.8 Lemercier, N.L. Charlemagne; tragédie en 5 actes. Paris, 1816.
41586.15.9 Lemercier, N.L. Christopher Colomb. Paris, 1809.
41586.15.12 Lemercier, N.L. Pinto, ou La journée d'une conspiration. Paris, 1800.
41586.15.80 Rousseau, Laurier. Le Pinto de Népomucène Lemercier et la censure. Mayenne, 1958.
41586.15.85 Vauthier, Gabriel. Essai sur la vie et les oeuvres de Népomucène Lemercier. Thèse. Photoreproduction. Toulouse, 1886.

41586.16 Individual authors, etc. - 1800-1849 - Drama - Le Riche; Leroy; Loaisel; etc.

41586.16.12 Le Riche, Mlle. Caroline et Storm. Paris, 1811.
41586.16.13 Leroy, Onésime. Les deux candidats. Paris, 1821.
41586.16.14 Leroy, Onésime. Le méfiant. Paris, 1814.
41586.16.15 Leroy, Onésime. Une première représentation. Paris, 1825.
41586.16.19 Loaisel-Tréogate, J.M. Le grand chasseur. Paris, 1804.
41586.16.20 Loaisel-Tréogate, J.M. La bisarrerie de la fortune. Paris, 1793.
41586.16.23 Loaisel-Tréogate, J.M. Le chateau du diable. Paris, 1793.
41586.16.75 Lacoste, A. Le platrier. Paris, 1824.

41586.17 Individual authors, etc. - 1800-1849 - Drama - Lombard; Lucas; etc.

41586.17 Lombard, V. de Langires. Le meunier de Sans-Souci. Paris, n.d.
41586.17.9 Leuven, Adolphe de. La poupee de Nuremberg. Paris, 1883.
41586.17.50 Lucas, Hyppolite. Rachel; drama em 4 actos, em verso. Lisboa, 1895.

41586.17 Individual authors, etc. - 1800-1849 - Drama - Lombard; Lucas; etc. - cont.

41586.17.150 Luce de Lancival, J.C.J. Hector; a tragedy in five acts. London, 1810.

41586.18 Individual authors, etc. - 1800-1849 - Drama - Luchet; etc.

41586.18 Luchet, A. Ango. Paris, 1835.

41586.19 Individual authors, etc. - 1800-1849 - Drama - Marie; Marsollier; Martainville; etc.

41586.19 Marie, M. Paul Morin. Paris, 1829.
41586.19.9 Marsollier des Vivetières, B.J. Gulnare, ou L'esclave Persane. Paris, 1820.
41586.19.9.5 Marsollier des Vivetières, B.J. Les détenus. Paris, 1794-95.
41586.19.9.12 Marsollier des Vivetières, B.J. La pauvre femme. 4e éd. Paris, 1796-1777.
41586.19.9.15 Marsollier des Vivetières, B.J. Camille. Paris, 1791.
41586.19.9.18 Marsollier des Vivetières, B.J. Alexis, ou L'erreur d'un bon père. Paris, 1802.
41586.19.9.22 Marsollier des Vivetières, B.J. La pauvre femme. Paris, 1795.
41586.19.12 Martainville, Alphonse Louis Dieudonné. Le suicide de Falaise. Paris, 1803.
41586.19.12.5 Martainville, Alphonse Louis Dieudonné. Buonabarte, ou L'abus de l'abdication. 2. éd. Paris, 1815.
41586.19.12.10 Martainville, Alphonse Louis Dieudonné. Grivoisiana, ou Recueil facétieux. 3. éd. Paris, 1807.
41586.19.19 Martin, Pierre Henri. La vielle Fronde, 1648. Paris, 1832.
41586.19.20 Martin, Pierre Henri. Les roueries du Marquis de Lansac. Paris, 1840? 2 pam.
41586.19.50 Marie, Hyppolite. Dialogue mêlé de complets sur la naissance du roi de Rome. Paris, 1811.

41586.20 - .21 Individual authors, etc. - 1800-1849 - Drama - Mazères

41586.20 Mazères, Edouard Joseph E. Comédies et souvenirs. Paris, 1858. 3v.
41586.21 Mazères, Edouard Joseph E. Le fin du mois. Paris, 1826.
41586.21.5 Mazères, Edouard Joseph E. La demoiselle de campagnie. Paris, 1826.
41586.21.80 Sessler, Georg. Die Komödien Mazères'. Diss. Heidelberg, 1912.

41586.22 Individual authors, etc. - 1800-1849 - Drama - Mélesville; Merle; etc.

41586.22.9 Duveyrier, A.H.J. Mort civilement. Bruxelles, 1846.
41586.22.45 Merle, Jean T. Crispin financier. Paris, 1813.
41586.22.50 Merle, Jean T. Le monstre et le magicien. Paris, 1826.

41586.23 Individual authors, etc. - 1800-1849 - Drama - Merville; Méry; etc.

41586.23 Merville, P.F.C. La prèmiere affaire. Paris, 1827.
41586.23.3 Merville, P.F.C. Les deux anglais. Paris, 1827.
41586.23.9 Méry, Joseph. L'assassinat; scènes méridionales de 1815. Paris, 1832.
41586.23.15 Méry, Joseph. Peyronnéide. Paris, 1827.
41586.23.20 Méry, Joseph. Quatre nouvelles humoristiques. Paris, 1922.
41586.23.25 Méry, Joseph. Le congrès des ministres. 8e éd. Paris, 1827.
41586.23.30 Méry, Joseph. Poésies intimes; mélodies. Paris, 1864.
41586.23.35 Méry, Joseph. Les nuits italiennes. Paris, 1868.
41586.23.40 Méry, Joseph. Les nuits anglaises. Paris, 1866.
41586.23.45 Méry, Joseph. André Chénier. Paris. 1856.
41586.23.48 Méry, Joseph. Through thick and thin. N.Y., 1874.

41586.24 Individual authors, etc. - 1800-1849 - Drama - Maurice

41586.24 Maurice-Descombes, Charles. Histoire anecdotique du théatre de la littérature. Paris, 1856. 2v.
41586.24.5 Maurice-Descombes, Charles. Epaves, théâtre, histoire, anecdotes, mots. Paris, 1865.

41586.25 Individual authors, etc. - 1800-1849 - Drama - Monbion

41586.25 Monbrion, M. Le Siége de Grenade. Paris, 1834.

41586.26 Individual authors, etc. - 1800-1849 - Drama - Monperlier; Moreau; Ourliac; etc.

41586.26 Monperlier, J.A.M. Le prince et le soldat. Paris, 1814.
41586.26.5 Monperlier, J.A.M. Les chevaliers de Malte. Paris, 1813.
41586.26.100 Moreau. La femme du sous-préfélt. 2e éd. Paris, 1821.
41586.26.210 Ourliac, Edouard. Théâtre du seigneur croquignole. Paris, 1866.
41586.26.231 Ourliac, Edouard. Proverbes et scènes Bourgeoises. Paris, 1868.
41586.26.281 Hupperts, F.D. Edouard Ourliac, 1813-1848. Groningen, 1934.

41586.27 Individual authors, etc. - 1800-1849 - Drama - Outrepont; Perin; Petit; etc.

41586.27.6 Outrepont, Chardles d'. La mort de Henri III. Paris, 1826.
41586.27.7 Outrepont, Charles d'. Le Saint-Barthélemi; drame. Paris, 1826.
41586.27.8 Perin, René. Fitz-Henri, ou maison des fous. n.p., n.d.
41586.27.9 Perin, René. Itinéraire de Pautin au Mont Clavaire. Paris, 1811.
41586.27.11 Perin, René. Isabelle de Levanzo ou La fille écuyer. Paris, 1821.
41586.27.15 Perin, René. La grande ville. Paris, 1802.
41586.27.75 Mourier, J.F. Zara, ou La soeur de l'Arabe. Paris, n.d.
41586.27.150 Pitt. Les bandoléros. Paris, 1805.
41586.27.200 Petit, P.A.S. L'Anglais à Berlin. Paris, 1802.

41586.28 Individual authors, etc. - 1800-1849 - Drama - Pixerécourt; Pourchel; etc.

41586.28 Pixerécourt, R.C.G. de. Les petits Auvergnats. Paris, n.d.
41586.28.5 Pixerécourt, R.C.G. de. L'abbaye aux Bois. Paris, 1832.
41586.28.6 Pixerécourt, R.C.G. de. Tékéli, ou le siège de Montgatz. Paris, 1804.
41586.28.6.5 Pixerécourt, R.C.G. de. Adelaide. London, 18- ?
41586.28.7 Pixerécourt, R.C.G. de. Christophe Colomb. Paris, 1815.
41586.28.8 Pixerécourt, R.C.G. Les natchez. Paris, 1827.
41586.28.9 Hartog, W.G. Guilbert de Pixerécourt, sa vie, son mélodrame. Thèse. Paris, 1912.
41586.28.10 Hartog, W.G. Guilbert de Pixerécourt, sa vie, son mélodrame. Paris, 1913.

41586.28 Individual authors, etc. - 1800-1849 - Drama - Pixerécourt; Pourchel; etc. - cont.

41586.28.11	Lacey, Alexander. Pixerécourt and the French romantic drama. Toronto, 1928.
41586.28.12	Heel, Franz. Guilbert de Pixerécourt. Erlangen, 1912.
41586.28.15	Pixerécourt, R.C.G. de. Robinson Crusoé. Paris, 1805.
41586.28.20	Pixerécourt, R.C.G. de. Le solitaire de la roche noir. Paris, 1806.
41586.28.25	Pixerécourt, R.C.G. de. Les ruines de Babylone. Paris, 1810.
41586.28.30	Pixerécourt, R.C.G. de. Le fanal de Messive. Paris, 1812.
41586.28.35	Pixerécourt, R.C.G. de. La fille de l'exilé. Paris, 1819.
41586.28.40	Pixerécourt, R.C.G. de. Le petit carillonneur. Paris, 1812.
41586.28.45	Pixerécourt, R.C.G. de. Le château de Loch-Leven. Paris, 1822.
41586.28.50	Pixerécourt, R.C.G. de. Guillaume Tell. Paris, 1828.
41586.28.55	Pixerécourt, R.C.G. de. La tête de mort. Paris, 1828.
41586.28.60	Pixerécourt, R.C.G. de. Valentine. Paris, 1822.
41586.28.65	Pixerécourt, R.C.G. de. Le pélerin blanc. Paris, 1801.
41586.28.100	Pixerécourt, R.C.F. de. Polder, o El verdugo de Amsterdam. Madrid, 1844.
41586.28.300	Pourchel, Alfred. Une Chrétienne et Néron. Paris, 1835.

41586.29 Individual authors, etc. - 1800-1849 - Drama - Pyat; Revoil; Saulnier; etc.

41586.29	Pyat, F. Le brigand et le philosophe. Paris, 1834.
41586.29.5	Guilbert, R.C. Le Belvéder. Paris, 1818.
41586.29.50	Reynery. Les conscrits, ou Le triomphe de la vertu. Lyon, 1803.
41586.29.75	Revoil, P.H. Sterne à Paris. Paris, 1800.
41586.29.100	Saulnier, G. Mahomet II. Paris, 1803.

41586.30 - .31 Individual authors, etc. - 1800-1849 - Drama - Soumet, A. - Writings

41586.30	Soumet, A. Elisabeth de France. Paris, 1828.
41586.30.2	Soumet, A. Cléopatre, tragédie. Paris, 1825.
41586.30.3	Soumet, A. Clytemnestre, tragédie en 5 actes. 2e éd. Paris, 1822.
41586.30.3.2	Soumet, A. Clytemnestre, tragédie en 5 actes. 2e éd. Paris, 1822.
41586.30.4	Soumet, A. David, opera en 3 actes. Paris, 1846.
41586.30.5	Soumet, A. La France dramatique au 19 siècle. Paris, 1834.
41586.30.6	Soumet, A. Un soirée du théâtre-français, 24 avril 1841. Paris, 1841.
41586.30.7	Soumet, A. Jane Grey, tragédie en 5 actes et en vers. Paris, 1844.
41586.30.8	Soumet, A. Pharamond. Paris, 1825.
41586.30.9	Soumet, A. Norma. Paris, 1831.
41586.30.10	Soumet, A. Une fête de Néron. Paris, 1830.
41586.30.11	Soumet, A. Ode sur les drapeaux. Paris, 1810.
41586.30.12	Soumet, A. The gladiator...performed by Salvini. N.Y., 1873.
41586.30.12.2	Soumet, A. The gladiator...performed by Salvini. N.Y., 1880.
41586.30.12.3	Soumet, A. The gladiator...performed by Salvini. N.Y., 1881.
41586.30.12.4	Soumet, A. The gladiator...performed by Salvini. N.Y., 1882.
41586.30.12.5	Soumet, A. The gladiator...performed by Salvini. N.Y., 1885.
41586.30.12.6	Soumet, A. The gladiator...performed by Salvini. N.Y., 1889.
41586.31	Soumet, A. L'incrédulité. Paris, 1810.

41587.5 - .18.79 Individual authors, etc. - 1800-1849 - Drama - Picard, L.B. - Writings

41587.5	Picard, Louis Benoît. Oeuvres. Paris, 1821. 10v.
41587.6	Picard, Louis Benoît. Les visitandines. Paris, 1793.
41587.6.2	Picard, Louis Benoît. Les visitandines. Paris, 1792.
41587.6.3	Picard, Louis Benoît. Les visitandines. Paris, 1793.
41587.6.7	Picard, Louis Benoît. Les visitandines. Paris, 1794.
41587.6.10	Picard, Louis Benoît. Les visitandines. Paris, 1797.
41587.7	Picard, Louis Benoît. Le cousin de tout le monde. Paris, 1793.
41587.7.5	Picard, Louis Benoît. Encore des menechmes. Paris, 1802.
41587.7.15	Picard, Louis Benoît. Médiocre et rampant. Paris, 1797.
41587.7.20	Picard, Louis Benoît. Les comédies ambulans. Paris, 1799.
41587.7.25	Picard, Louis Benoît. La moitié du chemin. Paris, 1794.
41587.7.30	Picard, Louis Benoît. Le conteur, ou Les deux postes. Paris, 1794-1795.
41587.7.35	Picard, Louis Benoît. Arlequin friand. Paris, 1793.
41587.7.40	Picard, Louis Benoît. Les conjectures. Paris, 1795.
41587.7.45	Picard, Louis Benoît. L'entrée dans le monde. 2e éd. Paris, 1802.
41587.7.55	Picard, Louis Benoît. Les provinciaux a Paris. Paris, 1802.
41587.7.60	Picard, Louis Benoît. La petite ville. Paris, 1801.
41587.7.65	Picard, Louis Benoît. La Saint-Jean. n.p., 1802.
41587.7.70	Picard, Louis Benoît. Les tracasseries. Paris, 1804.
41587.7.75	Picard, Louis Benoît. Les trois maris. Paris, 1800.
41587.7.80	Picard, Louis Benoît. Le vieux comédien. Paris, 1803.
41587.7.85	Picard, Louis Benoît. Les voisins. Paris, 1799?
41587.7.90	Pamphlet vol. Picard, Louis Benoît. Plays. 3 pam.
41587.8.5	Picard, Louis Benoît. Duhautcours; ou Le contrat d'union. Paris, 1801.
41587.13	Picard, Louis Benoît. Mediocre et rampant. Paris, 1802.
41587.13.25	Picard, Louis Benoît. Mediocre et rampant. Halle, 1888.
41587.13.40	Picard, Louis Benoît. Le Gilblas de la revolution. Paris, 1824.
41587.13.45	Picard, Louis Benoît. The Gil Blas of the revolution. London, 1825. 3v.
41587.14	Picard, Louis Benoît. Oeuvres choisies. N.Y., 1830.
41587.15	Picard, Louis Benoît. Théâtre républicain, posthume et inédit. Paris, 1832.
41587.16	Picard, Louis Benoît. Théâtre. Paris, 1877.
41587.16.5	Picard, Louis Benoît. Théâtre. Paris, 1812. 5v.
41587.17	Picard, Louis Benoît. L'honnête homme. 2e éd. Paris, 1825. 3v.
41587.17.5	Picard, Louis Benoît. La perruque blonde. Paris, 1796?
41587.17.7	Picard, Louis Benoît. Les prometteurs. Paris, 1812.
41587.17.9	Picard, Louis Benoît. L'absence. Paris, 1823.
41587.17.10	Picard, Louis Benoît. Le jeune médecin. Paris, 1807.
41587.17.11	Picard, Louis Benoît. Le mariage des grenadiers. Paris, 1807.

41587.5 - .18.79 Individual authors, etc. - 1800-1849 - Drama - Picard, L.B. - Writings - cont.

41587.17.13	Picard, Louis Benoît. L'exalté. 3e éd. Bruxelles, 1824. 3v.
41587.17.20	Picard, Louis Benoit. Les marionnettes. London, 1925.
41587.18	Picard, Louis Benoît. Les trois quartiers. Paris, 1827.
41587.18.5	Picard, Louis Benoît. Les deux ménages. Paris, 1884.
41587.18.9	Picard, Louis Benoît. Un jeu de bourse. Paris, 1821.
41587.18.10	Picard, Louis Benoît. Les suspects. Paris, 1797.
41587.18.11	Picard, Louis Benoît. L'album. Paris, 1830.
41587.18.15	Picard, Louis Benoît. L'impostore o L'arte di far Fortuna. Firenze, 1865.
41587.18.17	Picard, Louis Benoît. Der Parasit. Stuttgart, 1860.
41587.18.18	Picard, Louis Benoît. The parasite. Leipzig, 1856.
41587.18.20	Pamphlet box. Picard.
41587.18.30	Picard, Louis Benoît. Le mari ambitieux. Paris, 1803.

41587.19 Individual authors, etc. - 1800-1849 - Drama - Pompigny; Ponet; Pradel; etc.

41587.19.50	Pompigny, M. de. La princesse de Jérusalem. Paris, 1812.
41587.19.54	Pompigny, M. de. Le franc marin. Paris, 1795.
41587.19.55	Pompigny, M. de. Le franc marin. Paris, 1796-1797.
41587.19.60	Pompigny, M. de. L'époux républicain. Paris, 1794.
41587.19.70	Ponet, Louis. Le pâtre. Paris, 1823.
41587.19.75	Ponet, Louis. Les hussards. Paris, 1824.
41587.19.100	Pradel, H. Le contrariant, comédie en cinq actes et en vers. Paris, 1804.
41587.19.150	Prévost, Augustin. La vengeance inattendue. 2e éd. Paris, 1803.

41587.20 Individual authors, etc. - 1800-1849 - Drama - Raimond; Ratier; Rousseau, P.J.; etc.

	41587.20	Raimond, M. Bertram, ou le Pirate. Paris, 1822.
	41587.20.5	Regmer d'Estourbet, H. Les septembriseurs. 2e éd. Paris, 1829.
	41587.20.9	St. Esteben. La mort de Coligny ou la nuit de Saint-Barthelemy, 1572. Paris, 1830.
	41587.20.75	Ratier, Victor. Le Te-Deum et le De Profundis. Paris, 1832.
Htn	41587.20.80*	Romieu, Auguste. Proverbes romantiques. Paris, 1827.
	41587.20.100	Rousseau, E. Herminie. Paris, 1812.
	41587.20.150F	Rousseau, Pierre Joseph. La mort de Bucéphale. Paris, 1864.
	41587.20.160	Rousseau, Pierre Joseph. Die Portierfrau. Berlin, 1921.
	41587.20.170	Rousseau, Pierre Joseph. Robert-Macaire, der unsterbliche Betrüger. Berlin, 1840.

41587.21 Individual authors, etc. - 1800-1849 - Drama - Saint-Georges

41587.21	Saint-Georges, J.H.V. de. L'ombre. Paris, 1870. 4 pam.
41587.21.5	Saint-Georges, J.H.V. de. Fanchonette; opéra comique en trois actes. Paris, 1856.

41587.22 Individual authors, etc. - 1800-1849 - Drama - Saint-Hilaire

41587.22	Saint-Hilaire, Amable Villain de. Valentine ou La chute des feuilles. Paris, 1828.

41587.25 Individual authors, etc. - 1800-1849 - Drama - Saint-Just

41587.25	Saint-Just, Antoine. Essais littéraires. Paris, 1826. 2v.

41587.26 Individual authors, etc. - 1800-1849 - Drama - Saint-Maurice; Sadler; etc.

41587.26	Saint-Maurice, C.R.E. Rome, Londres et Paris. Scènes contemporaines. Paris, 1830.
41587.26.9	Sadler, P. Fifty years...an allegorical play. Paris, 1832.

41587.27 Individual authors, etc. - 1800-1849 - Drama - Salverte; Sidony; etc.

41587.27	Salverte, E. Phédosie. Tragédie en cinq actes. Paris, 1813.
41587.27.75	Sassernò, A.S. Glorie e sventure. Turin, 1852. 2v.
41587.27.150	Sidoni. Cadet Roussel. Paris, 1805.
41587.27.160	Sidony. Jocrisse suicide. 2e éd. Paris, 1809.

41587.29 - Individual authors, etc. - 1800-1849 - Drama - Scribe, E. - Complete works

41587.29	Scribe, Eugène. Le chanoinesse. Paris, 1834. 9 pam.
41587.30	Scribe, Eugène. Le charlataniseme. 2e éd. Paris, 1825. 11 pam.
41587.31	Scribe, Eugène. Dix ans de la vie d'une femme. Paris, 1832. 6 pam.
41587.32	Scribe, Eugène. Le colonel. Paris, 18- ?
41587.33	Scribe, Eugène. La chatte métamorphosée en femme. Paris, 1827. 10 pam.
41587.91	Scribe, Eugène. Oeuvres complètes. Serie I. Paris, 1874. 9v.
41587.92	Scribe, Eugène. Oeuvres complètes. Serie II. Paris, 1876. 33v.
41587.93	Scribe, Eugène. Oeuvres complètes. Serie III. Paris, 1875. 6v.
41587.94	Scribe, Eugène. Oeuvres complètes. Serie IV. Paris, 1877. 20v.
41587.95	Scribe, Eugène. Oeuvres complètes. Serie V. Paris, 1874. 8v.

41588.1 - .15.8 Individual authors, etc. - 1800-1849 - Drama - Scribe, E. - Selected works; Individual works

	41588.1	Scribe, Eugène. Le secrétaire et le cuisinier. Paris, 1829.
	41588.2	Scribe, Eugène. La lune de miel. Paris, 1830.
	41588.3	Scribe, Eugène. Les grisettes. Paris, 1830.
	41588.3.2	Scribe, Eugène. Louise. Paris, 1831.
	41588.3.4	Scribe, Eugène. Adrienne Lecouvreur. Bielefeld, 1887.
	41588.3.4.5	Scribe, Eugène. Adrienne Lecouvreur. Paris? 1849?
	41588.3.4.10	Scribe, Eugène. Adrienne Lecouvreur. Paris, 1851.
	41588.3.5	Scribe, Eugène. Adrienne Lecouvreur. N.Y., 1855.
	41588.3.5.6	Scribe, Eugène. Adriana Lecouvreur. N.Y., 1855.
	41588.3.5.10	Scribe, Eugène. Adriana Lecouvreur. N.Y., 1866.
	41588.3.6	Scribe, Eugène. Adrienne Lecouvreur. N.Y., 1867.
	41588.3.7	Scribe, Eugène. Adrienne Lecouvreur. N.Y., 1880.
	41588.3.8	Scribe, Eugène. Le charlatanisme. 2e éd. Paris, 1825.
	41588.3.9	Scribe, Eugène. Los cuentos de la reina de Navarra. Santiago, 1859.
	41588.3.12	Scribe, Eugène. Une chaîne. London, 1895.
Htn	41588.3.14*	Scribe, Eugène. La dame blanche, or The white lady. Baltimore, 1831.

Classified Listing

41588.1 - .15.8 Individual authors, etc. - 1800-1849 - Drama - Scribe, E. - Selected works; Individual works - cont.

41588.3.15 Scribe, Eugène. Les doigts de fée. Strassburg, n.d.
41588.3.16 Scribe, Eugène. Les doigts de fée. N.Y., 1865.
41588.3.17 Scribe, Eugène. Les doigts de fée. N.Y., 1865.
41588.3.19 Scribe, Eugène. La grande aventure. Paris, 1832.
41588.3.20 Scribe, Eugène. I ciarlatani in Ispagna. n.p., 18- ?
41588.4 Scribe, Eugène. Théâtre. 1e série. Paris, 1856.
41588.5 Scribe, Eugène. Théâtre. 2e série. Paris, 1856.
41588.5.2 Scribe, Eugène. Théâtre. Paris, 1857.
X Cg 41588.6 Scribe, Eugène. Théâtre. 6e série. Paris, 1857.
41588.7 Scribe, Eugène. Théâtre. 7e série. Paris, 1857.
41588.7.5 Scribe, Eugène. Théâtre complet. 2e éd. Paris, 1834-42. 24v.
41588.8A Scribe, Eugène. Oeuvres choisies. Paris, 1845. 5v.
41588.8B Scribe, Eugène. Oeuvres choisies. Paris, 1845. 5v.
41588.10 Scribe, Eugène. Historiettes et proverbes. Paris, 1858.
41588.11 Scribe, Eugène. Nouvelles. Paris, 1856.
41588.12.5 Scribe, Eugène. Mon étoile. Bielefeld, 1920.
41588.12.9 Scribe, Eugène. Tu amor, o La muerte! Comedia en un acto. Madrid, 1836.
41588.13 Scribe, Eugène. Théâtre. n.p., n.d.
41588.13.5 Scribe, Eugène. Teatro italiano. Montepulciano, 1838. 4 pam.
41588.13.9 Scribe, Eugène. La calumnia. Milano, 1842.
41588.13.10 Scribe, Eugène. La calumnia; comedia. Madrid, 1844.
41588.13.15 Scribe, Eugène. La camera verde. n.p., n.d.
41588.13.19 Scribe, Eugène. Las capas; comedia. Madrid, 1833.
41588.13.25 Scribe, Eugène. El diplomático, comedia. Madrid, 1844.
41588.14 Scribe, Eugène. Théâtre. n.p., n.d. 6 pam.
41588.14.1 Scribe, Eugène. Le verre d'eau. 4e éd. Leipzig, 1852.
41588.14.1.5 Scribe, Eugène. Le verre d'eau. Bielefeld, 1868.
41588.14.3 Scribe, Eugène. Le verre d'eau. Bielefeld, 1874.
41588.14.6 Scribe, Eugène. Le verre d'eau. Strasbourg, n.d.
41588.14.7F Scribe, Eugène. Le verre d'eau. Paris, 1840?
41588.14.8 Scribe, Eugène. Le verre d'eau. Cambridge, 1880.
41588.14.9 Scribe, Eugène. Das Glas Wasser. 2. ed. Hamburg, 18- .
41588.14.10 Scribe, Eugène. Das Glas Wasser, oder Ursachen und Wirkungen. Leipzig, 189-.
41588.14.15 Scribe, Eugène. Maitre Jean, ou la Comédie a la Cour. Bruxelles, 1847.
41588.14.20 Scribe, Eugène. Tonadillas. Paris, 1838. 2v.
41588.14.30 Scribe, Eugène. Marie Jobard, imitation burlesque, en six actes et en vers. Paris, 1820.
41588.14.35 Scribe, Eugène. L'intérieur d'un bureau. Bruxelles, 18- .
41588.14.40 Scribe, Eugène. La protégée sans le savoir. Bruxelles, 1847.
41588.15 Scribe, Eugène. Valérie. Bielefeld, 1860. 8 pam.
41588.15.1 Scribe, Eugène. Valérie. London, 1828.
41588.15.2.2 Scribe, Eugène. Contes de la Reine de Navarre. Bielefeld, 1897.
41588.15.3 Scribe, Eugène. Feu Lionel. Paris, 1858.
41588.15.7 Scribe, Eugène. La fille de trente ans. Comédie. Paris, 1860.
41588.15.8 Scribe, Eugène. Avant, pendant et après. Paris, 1830.
41588.15.8.3 Scribe, Eugène. La bataille de dames. 5e éd. N.Y., 1864.
41588.15.8.4 Scribe, Eugène. La bataille de dames. N.Y., 1864.
41588.15.8.5 Scribe, Eugène. La bataille de dames...notes by F. Bôcher. Boston, 1870.
41588.15.8.6 Scribe, Eugène. The ladies' battle. N.Y., 1855? 9 pam.
41588.15.8.7 Scribe, Eugène. The ladies' battle. Boston, 1855? 2 pam.
41588.15.8.9 Scribe, Eugène. Toujours, ou L'avenir d'un fils. Paris? 1832?
41588.15.8.10 Scribe, Eugène. Bataille de dames, ou Un duel en amour. 2. éd. London, 1890.
41588.15.8.15 Scribe, Eugène. La somnambule. N.Y., 1837.

41588.15.9 - .15.999 Individual authors, etc. - 1800-1849 - Drama - Scribe, E. - Biography and criticism

41588.15.9 Mirécourt, Eugène de. Scribe. Paris, 1856.
41588.15.10 Rolland, J. Les comédies politiques d'Eugène Scribe. Paris, 1912.
41588.15.12 Pamphlet box. Scribe.
41588.15.15 Arvin, Neil Cole. Eugène Scribe and the French theatre, 1815-1860. Cambridge, 1924.

41588.16 - .18 Individual authors, etc. - 1800-1849 - Drama - Scribe, A.

41588.16 Scribe, Augustin E. French plays. Paris, n.d. 7 pam.
41588.17 Scribe, Eugène. French drama. Paris, 1799-1850. 3 pam.
41588.18 Pamphlet vol. Théâtre français. 8 pam.
41588.18.5 Pamphlet vol. Théâtre français. 13 pam.
41588.18.10 Pamphlet vol. Théâtre français. 6 pam.

41588.19 Individual authors, etc. - 1800-1849 - Drama - Arlincourt

41588.19 D'Arlincourt, Victor. La siége de Paris. Paris, 1826.

41588.20 Individual authors, etc. - 1800-1849 - Drama - Barthet

41588.20 Barthet, Armand. Le moineau de Lesbie. Paris, 1849.
41588.20.3 Barthet, Armand. The sparrow of Lesbia. N.Y., 1855.

41588.23 Individual authors, etc. - 1800-1849 - Drama - Loeve-Weimars

41588.23 Loeve-Weimars, A. Scènes contemporaines. Paris, 1828-30. 2v.

41588.24 Individual authors, etc. - 1800-1849 - Drama - Sewrin

41588.24 Sewrin, C.A. Les Anglais pour Rire. 2e éd. Paris, 1817. 2 pam.

41588.25 Individual authors, etc. - 1800-1849 - Drama - Gallois

41588.25 Gallois, Léonard. Le vingt-mars. Bruxelles, 1829.
41588.25.5 Gallois, Léonard. Le citateur dramatique. 5e éd. Paris, 1829.
41588.25.9 Gallois, Léonard. Trois actes d'un grand drame. Paris, 1829.

41588.26 Individual authors, etc. - 1800-1849 - Drama - Geoffrey, M.

41588.26 Geoffrey, M. Théâtre des jeunes étudiants. Paris, 1846.

41588.28 Individual authors, etc. - 1800-1849 - Drama - Quinet

41588.28 Quinet, Edgar. Prométhée. Paris, 1838.

41588.29 Individual authors, etc. - 1800-1849 - Drama - Séjour; Servières; Simonnin; etc.

41588.29.2 Séjour, Victor. La tireuse de cartes. Drame. 2. éd. Paris, 1860.
41588.29.4 Séjour, Victor. Richard III. 2e éd. Paris, 1852.
41588.29.5 Séjour, Victor. The outlaw of the Adriatic. London, n.d.
41588.29.6 Servières, Joseph. Alphonsine, ou La tendresse maternelle. Paris, 1806.
41588.29.7 Servières, Joseph. Toujours le même. Paris, 1804.
41588.29.8 Servières, Joseph. Le dansomane de la rue Quincampoix. Paris, 1804.
41588.29.8.10 Servières, Joseph. La martingale, ou Le secret de Gagner au jeu. Paris, 1801.
41588.29.9 Lockroy, Joseph P.S. Un duel sous le Cardinal de Richelieu. Paris, 1832.
41588.29.9.5 Lockroy, Joseph P.S. Un duel sous le Cardinal de Richelieu. Paris, 1842.
41588.29.10 Lockroy, Joseph P.S. Good night, Signor Pantaloon. London, 18- ?
41588.29.15 Lockroy, Joseph P. Pourquoi? 2e éd. Bielefeld, 1858.
41588.29.75 Simonnin, A.J.B. Caroline de Lichtfield. Paris, 1807.
41588.29.80 Simonnin, A.J.B. La jardinière de Vincennes. Paris, 1807.
41588.29.82 Simmonin, A.J.B. Parlez pour moi. Paris, 1803.
41588.29.85 Simonnin, A.J.B. Tricotinet, ou Parlez pour mai. Paris, 1803.
41588.29.90 Simonnin, A.J.B. Lisette toute seule, ou Ils se trompent tous deux. Paris, 1803.
41588.29.95 Simonnin, A.J.B. Danières à gonesse. Paris, 1805.

41588.30 Individual authors, etc. - 1800-1849 - Drama - Superville

41588.30 Humbert de Superville. Jésus. Leide, 1812.

41588.33 Individual authors, etc. - 1800-1849 - Drama - Passard

41588.33 Passard, L. Petit théâtre bouffon. Paris, 1859.

41588.37 Individual authors, etc. - 1800-1849 - Drama - Tardif

41588.37 Tardif, A. Essais dramatiques. Paris, 1835.
41588.37.25 Tardif, Marc Louis de. Fables et tragédies. Paris, 1847.

41588.38 Individual authors, etc. - 1800-1849 - Drama - Theaulon

41588.38 Théaulon de Lambert, Marie Emmanuel G.M. Le petit chaperon rouge. Baltimore, 1831.
41588.38.3 Théaulon de Lambert, Marie Emmanuel G.M. Le petit chaperon rouge. Baltimore, 1831.
41588.38.5 Théaulon de Lambert, Marie Emmanuel G.M. Jeanne d'Arc. Paris, 1821.

41588.39 Individual authors, etc. - 1800-1849 - Drama - Lambert-Thiboust

41588.39 Théaulon de Lambert, Marie Emmanuel G.M. Un mari dans du Coton. Paris, 1876.

41588.40 Individual authors, etc. - 1800-1849 - Drama - Trouvé, C.J.

41588.40.20 Trauvé, Claude Joseph. Pausanias. Carcassonne, 1810.

41588.41 Individual authors, etc. - 1800-1849 - Drama - Vander-Burch

41588.41 Vanderburch, Émile. Le barbier de Paris. Paris, 1827.
41588.41.5 Vanderburch, Émile. Théâtre de l'enfance. Paris, 1841. 2v.
41588.41.10 Vanderburch, Émile. Henri IV en famille. Paris, 1828.

41588.42 Individual authors, etc. - 1800-1849 - Drama - Verez

41588.42.75 Verez, E.F. La fille coupable, repentante. Paris, 1812.

41588.43 Individual authors, etc. - 1800-1849 - Drama - Victor, M.

41588.43 Victor, M. Le prince de Norwège. Paris, 1818.

41588.47 Individual authors, etc. - 1800-1849 - Drama - Villemontez

41588.47.250 Villemontez, Bidon de. Ovinska, ou Les exilés en Sybérie. Paris, 1801.

41588.48 Individual authors, etc. - 1800-1849 - Drama - Villeterque

41588.48 Villeterque, A.L. de. Enguerrand sire de Rosemont. Paris, 1793.

41588.49 - .50 Individual authors, etc. - 1800-1849 - Drama - Wafflard - Writings

41588.49 Wafflard, A.J.M. Un moment d'imprudence. n.p., 18- ?
41588.50 Wafflard, A.J.M. Le voyage a Dieppe. Paris, 1821.
41588.50.3 Wafflard, A.J.M. Le voyage a Dieppe. Liepsic, 1849?
41588.50.5 Wafflard, A.J.M. Théatre français...Le voyage a Dieppe. 5e éd. Bielefeld, 1855.

41588.52 Individual authors, etc. - 1800-1849 - Drama - Wailly

41588.52 Wailley, G. de. Amour et intrigue. Paris, 1826.

41588.60 - Individual authors, etc. - 1800-1849 - Drama - Anonymous dramas

41588.60 Les Hussietes, ou Le siége de Neurnbourg. n.p., n.d.
41588.61 L'influence des femmes sur les moeurs. Paris, 1814.
41588.62 Les Marchandes de Modes. Paris, 1825.
41588.65 Le vampire. Paris, 1820.
41588.65.5 Le fantôme de Bérezule. Paris, 1805.
41588.67 La mort du duc d'Enguien; tragédie. Paris, 1820.
41588.69 Mellinet, Anne François. Le muette de sénès. Paris, 1805.
41588.70 La Passion de N.S. Jésus-Christ. Jerusalem, 18- ?

41591 Individual authors, etc. - 1800-1849 - Poetry - Folios [Discontinued]

41591.05 Alhoy, Louis. Les hospices; poëme. Paris, 1804.
41591.1 Arnassant, M.L. Atala, poëme en six chants. Lyon, 1810.
41591.2 Astouin, L. Ephémérides ou Loisirs poetiques. Paris, 1846.
41591.2.9 Aveline, Alexandre. Poésies. v.1-2. La Havane, 1864.
41591.3A Béranger, P.J. de. Oeuvres complètes. Paris, 1847-52. 2v.
41591.3B Béranger, P.J. de. Oeuvres complètes. Paris, 1847-52. 2v.
41591.3.2 Béranger, P.J. de. Oeuvres ccomplètes. Paris, 1840.
41591.3.3 Béranger, P.J. de. Oeuvres complètes. Paris, 1845. 2v.
41591.3.5 Béranger, P.J. de. Oeuvres complètes. Paris, 1846. 2v.
41591.3.7A Béranger, P.J. de. Oeuvres complètes. v.2. Paris, 1858.
41591.3.7B Béranger, P.J. de. Oeuvres complètes. v.1-2. Paris, 1858.
41591.4 Béranger, P.J. de. Oeuvres. Paris, 1867. 2 pam.
41591.4.5 Béranger, P.J. de. Oeuvres. Paris, 1876. 2v.
41591.6 Béranger, P.J. de. Dernières chansons. Paris, 18- .
41591.7 Béranger, P.J. de. Musique. Paris, 1868.
41591.8 Béranger, P.J. de. Ma biographie. Paris, 1868.

41591 Individual authors, etc. - 1800-1849 - Poetry - Folios [Discontinued] - cont.

	41591.9	Béranger, P.J. de. Ma biographie. Paris, 1860.
	41591.11	Béranger, P.J. de. Chansons. Paris, 1869. 2v.
	41591.12	Béranger, P.J. de. Dernières chansons. Paris, n.d.
	41591.13	Béranger, P.J. de. Musique. Paris, n.d.
	41591.13.50	Béranger, P.J. de. Ma biographie, ouvrage posthume. Paris, 1857.
	41591.13.52	Béranger, P.J. de. Ma biographie. 2. éd. Paris, 1859.
	41591.14	Béranger, P.J. de. Ma biographie. Paris, 1868.
	41591.15	Béranger, P.J. de. Correspondance. Paris, n.d. 4v.
	41591.20	Bonaparte, Lucien. Charlemagne. Rome, 1814. 2v.
	41591.20.10	Bonaparte, Lucien. Charlemagne. Paris, 1815. 2v.
	41591.24	Delille, Jacques. Oeuvres complètes. Paris, 1865.
	41591.24.25	Delille, Jacques. L'imagination, poëme. Paris, 1806. 2v.
Htn	41591.24.30*	Delille, Jacques. L'homme des champs. Strasbourg, 1802.
	41591.24.40	Rimpler, Karl. Jacques Delille als beschreibend-didaktischer Dichter. Inaug. Diss. Weida, 1913.
	41591.28	Gonzalle, J.L. L'Enménide. Paris, 1848.
	41591.55	Tastu, A. (Mme.). Poésies. Paris, 1826.

41592.01 Individual authors, etc. - 1800-1849 - Poetry - Agnant; etc.

	41592.01.9	Agnant, A. Gusman ou l'expiation. Paris, 1843.

41592.1 Individual authors, etc. - 1800-1849 - Poetry - Alletz; Allo; Arnould; etc.

	41592.1	Alletz, E. La nouvelle messiade. Paris, 1831.
	41592.1.50	Allo, Marie. Bretons d'après nature. Paris, 1820.
	41592.1.75	Schuré, M. Étude sur les sonnets d'Edmond Arnould. Paris, 1863.

41592.2 Individual authors, etc. - 1800-1849 - Poetry - Arvers

	41592.2	Aigoin, L. Notice sur Félix Arvers. Paris, 1897.
	41592.2.5	Arvers, Félix. Poésies. Paris, 1900.
	41592.2.31	Arvers, Félix. Mes heures perdues. Paris, 1878.

41592.3 - .10 Individual authors, etc. - 1800-1849 - Poetry - Béranger, P.J. - Works about

	41592.3	Travers, Julien. Béranger. Paris, 1861.
	41592.4	Silbergleit, L.G. Béranger als Bonapartist. n.p., n.d.
	41592.5	Brivois, Jules. Bibliographie de l'oeuvre de P.J. de Béranger. Paris, 1876.
	41592.5.5	Pamphlet box. Almanach de Béranger pour 1862.
	41592.6	Pamphlet box. Béranger, Pierre J. de.
	41592.7	Arnould, Arthur. Béranger. Paris, 1864. 2v.
	41592.8	Rowland, John Thomas. Lecture on Béranger. Drogheda, 1858.
	41592.8.5	Bernard, Joseph. Béranger et ses chansons. Paris, 1858.
	41592.8.10	Fischer, Jan O. Pierre-Jean de Béranger. 1. Aufl. Berlin, 1960.
	41592.9	Janin, Jules. Béranger et son temps. Paris, 1866.
	41592.10	Causeret, Charles. Béranger. Paris, 1895.
	41592.10.10	Des Vallieres, Jean. Cannaissez-vous ce bon M. de Béranger. Paris, 1958.
	41592.10.15	Faur, Léon. La vie en chansons de Béranger. Paris, 1930.
	41592.10.20	Lucas-Dubreton, J. Béranger. Paris, 1934.
	41592.10.25	Staritsyna, Z.A. Beranzhe v Rossii XIX vek. Moskva, 1969.
	41592.10.30	Touchard, Jean. La gloire de Béranger. Paris, 1968. 2v.
	41592.10.35	Boiteau, Paul. Vie de Béranger, 1780-1857. Paris, 1861.
	41592.10.40	Danilin, Iurii I. Beranzhe i ego pesni. Moskva, 1958.
	41592.10.45	Murav'eva, Natal'ia I. Beranzhe. Moskva, 1965.

41592.11 - Individual authors, etc. - 1800-1849 - Poetry - Béranger, P.J. - Writings

	41592.11	Lettres inédites de Béranger à Dupont de l'Eure. Paris, n.d.
	41592.11.5	Béranger, P.J. de. Memoirs of Béranger. London, 1858.
	41592.11.7	Béranger, P.J. de. Memoirs of Béranger. 2nd ed. London, 1858.
	41592.11.10	Béranger, P.J. de. Le Béranger des familles. Paris, 18- .
	41592.11.12	Béranger, P.J. de. Oeuvres complétes de P.J. de Béranger. Paris, 1856. 2v.
	41592.12	Colet, Louise. Quarante-cinq letters de Béranger. Paris, 1857.
Htn	41592.13*	Béranger, P.J. de. Chansons. Paris, 1821.
Htn	41592.13.5*	Béranger, P.J. de. Chansons. v.1-4. Paris, 1826. 2v.
	41592.14	Béranger, P.J. de. Chansons inédites. Paris, 1828.
	41592.15	Béranger, P.J. de. Chansons. v.1-4. Paris, 1829-33. 3v.
	41592.16A	Béranger, P.J. de. Chansons. Bruxelles, 1832-1833. 4v.
	41592.16B	Béranger, P.J. de. Chansons. v.3-4. Bruxelles, 1832-1833. 2v.
Htn	41592.16.2*	Béranger, P.J. de. Chansons. v.1. Bruxelles, 1832.
NEDL	41592.16.5	Béranger, P.J. de. Chansons nouvelles et dernières. Bruxelles, 1833.
	41592.16.10	Béranger, P.J. de. Chansons. Paris, 1859. 2v.
	41592.17	Béranger, P.J. de. Chansons. Paris, 1861.
	41592.17.5	Béranger, P.J. de. Chansons. Paris, 1866.
	41592.18	Béranger, P.J. de. Chansons, 1815-1834. Paris, 1858.
	41592.18.5	Béranger, P.J. de. Dernières chansons, 1834-1851. Paris, 1859. 2 pam.
	41592.18.7	Béranger, P.J. de. Dernières chansons de Béranger de 1834-1851. Paris, 1860.
	41592.18.10	Béranger, P.J. de. Dernières chansons de 1834 à 1851. Frankfurt, 1842.
	41592.18.14A	Béranger, P.J. de. Dernières chansons. Paris, 1857.
	41592.18.14B	Béranger, P.J. de. Dernières chansons. Paris, 1857.
	41592.19	Béranger, P.J. de. Les chansons de Béranger, morceaux choisis. London, 1911.
	41592.23	Béranger, P.J. de . Hundert-drei Lieder. Braunschweig, 1839.
	41592.27	Béranger, P.J. de. Songs of France. Philadelphia, 1895.
	41592.29	Béranger, P.J. de. Songs. London, n.d.
	41592.29.25	Béranger, P.J. de. One hundred songs of Pierre-Jean de Béranger. London, 1947.
	41592.30	Béranger, P.J. de. Songs. London, 1856.
	41592.30.15A	Béranger, P.J. de. Béranger, two hundred of his lyrical poems. N.Y., 1850.
	41592.30.15B	Béranger, P.J. de. Béranger, two hundred of his lyrical poems. N.Y., 1850.
	41592.30.15.2	Béranger, P.J. de. Béranger, two hundred of his lyrical poems. N.Y., 1850.
	41592.31	Béranger, P.J. de. Two hundred lyrical poems. N.Y., 1857.

41592.11 - Individual authors, etc. - 1800-1849 - Poetry - Béranger, P.J. - Writings - cont.

NEDL	41592.31.2	Béranger, P.J. de. Béranger, two hundred of his lyrical poems. 4. ed. N.Y., 1869.
	41592.31.4	Béranger, P.J. de. Béranger's poems. Philadelphia, 1889.
	41592.31.5A	Betts, Craven L. Songs from Béranger. N.Y., 1888.
	41592.31.5B	Betts, Craven L. Songs from Béranger. N.Y., 1888.
	41592.31.10	Béranger, P.J. de. Sochineniia. Moskva, 1957.
	41592.34	Béranger, P.J. de. Oeuvres inédites. Paris, 1909.
	41592.35	Béranger, P.J. de. Oeuvres posthumes de...dernières chansons. Paris, 1858.

41593.3 Individual authors, etc. - 1800-1849 - Poetry - Baour-Lormian

	41593.3	Baour-Lormian, P.M.L. Légendes, ballades et fabliaux. Paris, 1829.
	41593.3.5	Baour-Lormian, P.M.L. Satire. Paris, 1826.
	41593.3.6	Baour-Lormian, P.M.L. Le classique et le romantique. Paris, 1825.
	41593.3.10	Baour-Lormian, P.M.L. Recueil de poésies diverses. Bordeaux, 1803.
	41593.3.80	Gallagher, M. Baour-Lormian. Diss. Philadelphia, 1938.

41593.5 - .8 Individual authors, etc. - 1800-1849 - Poetry - Barthélemy

	41593.5	Barthélemy, Auguste Marseille. Oeuvres. Paris, 1831. 2v.
	41593.5.5	Barthélemy, Auguste Marseille. Une soirée chez M. de Peyronnet. Paris, 1827.
	41593.5.10	Barthélemy, Auguste Marseille. Napoléon en Egypte. Paris, 1829.
	41593.5.30	Barthélemy, Auguste Marseille. Rome à Paris, poëme. 8. éd. Paris, 1827.
	41593.6	Barthélemy, Auguste Marseille. Douze journées de la révolution. Poèmes. Paris, 1832.
	41593.6.3	Barthélemy, Auguste Marseille. Douze journées de la révolution. Poèmes. Paris, 1835.
	41593.6.4	Barthélemy, Auguste Marseille. Némésis. Paris, 1831-1832.
	41593.6.5	Barthélemy, Auguste Marseille. Némésis. Satire hebdomadaire. 7. éd. Paris, 1845.
	41593.6.9	Barthélemy, Auguste Marseille. Nouvelle Némésis. Paris, 1845.
	41593.6.20	Barthélemy, Auguste Marseille. L'insurrection, poème. Bruxelles, 1830.
	41593.6.30	Barthélemy, Auguste Marseille. A sa sainteté Pie IX. Paris, 1846.
	41593.6.40	Barthélemy, Auguste Marseille. Waterloo al generale Bourmont. Lugano, 1829.
	41593.6.50	Barthélemy, Auguste Marseille. A Léopold II. Paris, 1847.
	41593.7	Mery, Joseph. Le fils de l'homme. Bruxelles, 1829.
	41593.8	Mery, Joseph. Le fils de l'homme. Bruxelles, 1829.
	41593.8.1	Mery, Joseph. Le fils de l'homme. Bruxelles, 1829.
	41593.8.2	Mery, Joseph. Le fils de l'homme. Bruxelles, 1829.
	41593.8.10	Mery, Joseph. Il figlio dell'uomo. Brusselles, 1829.

41593.9 Individual authors, etc. - 1800-1849 - Poetry - Boucher de Perthes; Boussot; Brad; etc.

	41593.9.7	Boucher de Crèvecoeur de Perthes, Jacques. Romances, ballads et légendes. Paris, 1830.
	41593.9.8	Boucher de Crèvecoeur de Perthes, Jacques. Satires, contes et chansonnettes. Paris, 1833.
	41593.9.10	Bourlier, Louis. La prêtréxide, poème. Paris, 1832.
	41593.9.12	Boussot, P.L. Le triomphe de la religion catholique. Dithyrambe. Aix-la-Chapelle, 1814.
	41593.9.15	Bouzon de Mairet, E. Le testament du diable. Paris, 1822.
	41593.9.60	Brad, J.L. L'Italie, poème. Alexandrie, n.d.

41593.10 - .11 Individual authors, etc. - 1800-1849 - Poetry - Brizeux - Writings

	41593.10	Brizeux, Auguste. Oeuvres complètes. Paris, 1860. 2v.
	41593.11	Brizeux, Auguste. Oeuvres. Paris, n.d. 4v.
	41593.11.20	Brizeux, Auguste. Racine. Paris, 1828.

41593.12 Individual authors, etc. - 1800-1849 - Poetry - Brizeux - Works about

	41593.12	Lecigne, C. Brizeux. Sa vie et ses oeuvres. Paris, 1898.
	41593.12.5	Quellien, Narcisse. Bardit lu sur la tombe de Brizeux au cimetière du Barnel. Paris, 1888.
	41593.12.7	Le Mouel, Eugène. Stances à Brizeux. Paris, 1888.
	41593.12.9	Le Mouel, Eugène. Kèmenes. Paris, 1894.
	41593.12.15	Le Mouel, Eugène. Bonnes gens de Bretagne. Paris, 1887.
	41593.12.20	Bernard, D. Autour de Brizeux. Quimper, 1931.
	41593.12.25	Duchesne, Julien. Étude sur Auguste Brizeux. Rennes, 1879.
	41593.12.30	Augier, E. Brizeux et Mistral. Brest, 1888.

41593.13 Individual authors, etc. - 1800-1849 - Poetry - Boulay-Paty; Boyer d'Agen; etc.

	41593.13	Berquin-Duvallon. Recueil de poésies d'un colon de St. Domingue. Brest, 1802.
	41593.13.3	Boulay-Paty, Évariste. Sonnets de la vie humaine. Brest, 1852.
	41593.13.4	Boulay-Paty, Évariste. Odes. Brest, 1844.
	41593.13.4.10	Boulay-Paty, Évariste. Elie Mariaker. Paris, 1834.
	41593.13.5	Bourlet-Delavallée, E. Derniers chants du soir. Paris, 1833.
	41593.13.230	Boyer d'Agen, J.A.B. Les sept paraliponienes à la Divine Comédie. Paris, 1919.

41593.14 Individual authors, etc. - 1800-1849 - Poetry - Brifant; Buchon; etc.

	41593.14	Brifant, Charles. Dialogues, contes et autres poésies. Paris, 1824. 2v.
	41593.14.30	Frey, Hugo. Max Buchon et son oeuvre. Thèse. Besancon, 1940.

41593.15 Individual authors, etc. - 1800-1849 - Poetry - Chalette; Chatelain; etc.

	41593.15	Chalette. La joinvilleide, poème héroïque. Châlons, 1838.
	41593.15.3	Chapais de Monval. Cantate à l'occasion de la naissance du roi de Rome. Rouen, 1811?
	41593.15.4	Charles, V. La revolution de fevrier, poème. Pt. 1. Paris, 1849.
	41593.15.5	Charron, J. Pocancy, stances à M***. Châlons, 18- .
	41593.15.9	Chatelain, J. La première parole du coeur. Epinal, 1843.

41593.16 Individual authors, etc. - 1800-1849 - Poetry - Chênedollé; Chevigné; Clément, R.; etc.

Htn 41593.16* Chênedollé, C. de. Études poétiques. Paris, 1820.
Htn 41593.16.2* Chênedollé, C. de. Études poétiques. 2. éd. Paris, 1822.
Htn 41593.16.3* Chênedollé, C. de. Etudes poétiques. 2. éd. Bruxelles, 1822.
41593.16.5 Oeuvres complètes de Charles de Chênedollé. Paris, 1864.
41593.16.10 Samie, Lucy. A l'aube du romanticisme, Chênedollé and Extraits du journal de Chênedollé. Thèse. v.1-2. Caen, 1922.
41593.16.11.15 Cherpilloud, J. La nouvelle Helvétie, ou Les regrets et l'espérance. Londres, 1818.
41593.16.12 Chevigné, L. de. Les contes Rémois. 3. éd. Paris, 1858.
41593.16.13 Chevigné, L. de. Les contes Rémois. 3. éd. Paris, 1858.
41593.16.15 Chevremont, Alexander. La destinée du pauvre. Rennes, 1846.
41593.16.17 Clemenceau. Le vengeur des rois, poème. Londres, 1801.
41593.16.19 Clément, René. Albert-love, ou L'enfer. 2. éd. Paris, 1837.

41593.17 Individual authors, etc. - 1800-1849 - Poetry - Colet; Coquerel; Daru; etc.

41593.17 Colet, Louise. Lui. Paris, 1880.
41593.17.2 Colet, Louise. Poésies complètes. Paris, 1844.
41593.17.3 Colet, Louise. Quatre poèmes. Paris, 1855.
41593.17.3.50 Jackson, J.F. Louise Colet et ses amis littéraires. New Haven, 1937.
41593.17.3.55 Enfield, D.E. A lady of the salons. The story of Louise Colet. London, 1922.
41593.17.3.60 Gérard-Gailly, E. Autour de Gustave Flaubert, les véhémences de Louise Colet. Paris, 1934.
41593.17.4.5 Collot, J.P. La chute de Napoléon. Paris, 1846.
41593.17.4.10 Collot, J.P. Prédictions de Napoléon. Paris, 1849.
41593.17.5 Coquerel, Athan. Le calendrier. 2. éd. Paris, 1840.
41593.17.8.50 Cormenin, L.M. de L. Odes, précédées de réflexions sur la poésie lyrique. Paris, 1811.
41593.17.9 Daru, P. La Cléopédie. Paris, n.d.
41593.17.10 Daru, P. Epitre à M. le Duc de la Rochefoucauld. Paris, 1824.
41593.17.20 Sainte-Beuve, C.A. M. Daru. Cambridge, 1879.
41593.17.50 Debuire du Buc, L. Les lilloises. Lille, 1856-1859. 2 pam.

41593.18 Individual authors, etc. - 1800-1849 - Poetry - DeFoudras

41593.18 De Foudras. Chants pour Tous. Poésies. Paris, 1842.

41593.19 Individual authors, etc. - 1800-1849 - Poetry - Delasalle; Delaurel; etc.

41593.19 Delasalle, Paul. Fleurs de Pommier. Paris, 1839.
41593.19.200 Delaurel, S. Chant épique sur la naissance du roi de Rome. Rome, 1811?

41593.20 Individual authors, etc. - 1800-1849 - Poetry - Delille, J. - Complete and Selected works

41593.20.8 Delille, J. Oeuvres. Paris, 1824. 16v.
41593.20.9 Delille, J. Oeuvres. Paris, 1825.
41593.20.25 Delille, J. Poésies fugitives. Paris, 1802-1805. 8v.
41593.20.27 Delille, J. Poésies fugitives et morceaux choisis. Paris, 1802.

41593.21 - .26 Individual authors, etc. - 1800-1849 - Poetry - Delille, J. - Individual works

41593.21 Delille, J. L'homme des Champs. Basle, 1800.
41593.22 Delille, J. L'homme des Champs. Paris, 1805.
41593.22.5 Delille, J. L'homme des Champs. Paris, 1820.
Htn 41593.23* Delille, J. The rural philosopher. Newbern, North Carolina, 1804.
Htn 41593.24* Delille, J. The rural philosopher. London, 1801.
41593.26 Delille, J. Le malheur et la pitié. London, 1803.
41593.26.5 Delille, J. The garden. London, 1789.
41593.26.6 Delille, J. Les jardins. Paris, 1813.
41593.26.7 Delille, J. La conversation, poème. Paris, 1812.
41593.26.7.5 Delille, J. La conversation, poème. Paris, 1812.
41593.26.8 Delille, J. La pitié, poème. Paris, 1803.
41593.26.9 Delille, J. La pitié, poème. Paris, 1803.
41593.26.10 Delille, J. La pitié, poème. Paris, 1805.
41593.26.11 Delille, J. La pitié, poème. Paris, 1822.
41593.26.15 Delille, J. L'imagination, poème. 2. éd. Paris, 1819. 2v.
41593.26.17 Delille, J. Les jardins, poème. Paris, 1820.
41593.26.50 Delille, J. Dithyrambe sur l'immortalité de l'âme. Paris, 1802.

41593.27 Individual authors, etc. - 1800-1849 - Poetry - Delille, J. - Biography and criticism

41593.27 Kremer, A.R. Sprachliche Untersuchungen über J.M. Delille. Bonn, 1896.
41593.27.5 Berthaoldt, Ludwig. Jacques Delille. Inaug. Diss. Nürnberg, 1914.
41593.27.10 Zatuska, A. Poezja opisowa Delille a w Polsce. Kraków, 1934.
41593.27.20 Chaussard, P.J.B. Examen de l'homme des champs. Paris, 1801.
41593.27.30 Dupuy des Islets. Examen critique du poème de La Pitié de Jacques Delille. Paris, 1803.
41593.27.40 Fayolle. Pour et contre Delille. Paris, 1817.
41593.27.50 Villeneuve, M.T. de. Éloge de Jacques Delille. Toulouse, 1856.
41593.27.60 Delille, est-il mort? Clermont-Ferrand, 1967.

41593.28 Individual authors, etc. - 1800-1849 - Poetry - Delonne; Dénoix des Vergnes; etc.

41593.28 Delonne, Joseph. Vie, poésies et pensées. Bruxelles, 1837.
41593.28.5 Moll, J.J. de. La liberté en Belgique. Bruxelles, 1839.
41593.28.9 Dénoix des Vergnes, F. Guerrières et sentimentales. Poésies. Paris, 1841.

41593.29 Individual authors, etc. - 1800-1849 - Poetry - Désaugiers; Desbordes-Valmore; Deschamps; etc.

41593.29 Désaugiers, M.A. Chansons et poésies diverses. Paris, 1827. 4v.
41593.29.2 Désaugiers, M.A. Théâtre. Paris, 1887.
41593.29.2.3 Désaugiers, M.A. Le mari intrigué. Paris, 180(.
41593.29.2.4 Désaugiers, M.A. Le valet d'emprunt. Paris, 1807.
41593.29.2.5 Désaugiers, M.A. Un diner par victoire. Paris, 1807.

41593.29 Individual authors, etc. - 1800-1849 - Poetry - Désaugiers; Desbordes-Valmore; Deschamps; etc. - cont.

41593.29.3.1 Desbordes-Valmore, Marceline. Poésies complètes. Paris, 1931-1932. 2v.
41593.29.3.3 Desbordes-Valmore, Marceline. Poésies. Paris, 1842.
41593.29.3.4 Desbordes-Valmore, Marceline. Choix de poésies. Paris, 1933.
41593.29.3.5 Desbordes-Valmore, Marceline. Lettres inedites. 1812-1857. Paris, 1911?
41593.29.3.6 Desbordes-Valmore, Marceline. Poèmes choises. Paris, 1950.
41593.29.3.7 Desbordes-Valmore, Marceline. Les greniers et la guitare de Marceline. Paris, 1931.
41593.29.3.8 Desbordes-Valmore, Marceline. Oeuvres poétiques. Paris, 1886?-1922. 4v.
Htn 41593.29.3.10* Desbordes-Valmore, Marceline. Correspondance intime de Marceline Desbordes-Valmore. Paris, 1896. 2v.
41593.29.3.12 Desbordes-Valmore, Marceline. Lettres de Marceline. Paris, 1924. 2v.
41593.29.3.15 Desbordes-Valmore, Marceline. Marceline Desbordes-Valmore et ses amis lyonnais. Paris, 1923.
41593.29.3.16 Desbordes-Valmore, Marceline. Albums à Pauline. Oeuvres manuscrites. Paris, 1921.
41593.29.3.20 Desbordes-Valmore, Marceline. Poèmes et proses. Paris, 1928.
41593.29.3.25 Desbordes-Valmore, Marceline. Poésies. Paris, 1925.
41593.29.3.50 Pougin, Arthur. La jeunesse de Mme. Desbordes-Valmore. Paris, 1898.
41593.29.3.55 Boulenger, Jacques. Marceline Desbordes-Valmore. Paris, 1926.
41593.29.3.56 Boulenger, Jacques. Marceline Desbordes-Valmore d'après ses papiers inédits. Paris, 1909?
41593.29.3.59 Descaves, Lucien. La vie amoureuse de Marceline Desbordes-Valmore. Paris, 1925.
41593.29.3.63 Zweig, Stefan. Marceline Desbordes-Valmore. Leipzig, 1927.
41593.29.3.65 Zweig, Stefan. Marceline Desbordes-Valmore, son oeuvre. Paris, 1928.
41593.29.3.68 Bibliothèque nationale, Paris. Marceline Desbordes-Valmore. Paris, 1959.
41593.29.3.70 Jasenas, Eliane. Marceline Desbordes-Valmore devant la critique. Genève, 1962.
41593.29.5 Deschamps, E. Oeuvres complètes. Poésie. Prose. Théâtre. Paris, 1872. 6v.
41593.29.9 Deschamps, E. Études françaises et étrangères. Paris, 1829.
41593.29.9.50 Girard, Henri. Bourgeois dilettante...E. Deschamps. Paris, 1921.
41593.29.9.51 Girard, Henri. Un bourgeois dillettante...Émile Deschamps. Thèse. Paris, 1921. 2 pam.
41593.29.10 Deschamps, E. Un manifeste du romantisme. Paris, 1923.
41593.29.15 De Selves, A. Catou, ou La guerre electorale. Paris, 1823.
41593.29.25 Deshayes, Valentin. Hymne national, liberté, egalité, fraternité. Paris, 18- ?
41593.29.50 Desquiron de Saint-Agnan, Antoine Toussaint. Solyme conquise. Paris, 1819. 2v.
41593.29.80 Deshayes, Adrien. Étude historique et littéraire sur Madame de Maintenon. St. Petersbourg, 1865.

41593.30 Individual authors, etc. - 1800-1849 - Poetry - Direy; etc.

41593.30 Direy, Louis. Les orphelines. Paris, 1838.

41593.31 Individual authors, etc. - 1800-1849 - Poetry - Dierx, L.; etc.

41593.31.10 Dierx, Léon. Oeuvres complètes. Paris, 1925. 2v.
Htn 41593.31.20* Dierx, Léon. Les paroles du vaincu. Paris, 1871.
41593.31.81 Camus-Clavier, M.L. Le poète Léon Dierx, 1838-1912. Thèse. Moret-sur-Loing, 1942.

41593.32 Individual authors, etc. - 1800-1849 - Poetry - Miscellany, Du-Gu

41593.32 Duchapt, Théophile. Fables. Paris, 1850.
41593.32.3 Dupont, Pierre. Les deux anges. Provins, 1844.
41593.32.4 Dupont, Pierre. Études littéraires, vers et prose. Paris, 1859.
41593.32.5 Dupont, Pierre. Chants et poésies. Paris, 1875.
41593.32.5.5 Dupont, Pierre. Muse populaire. Chants et poésies. 9. éd. Paris, 1875.
41593.32.6 Dupont, Pierre. Chants et chansons. Paris, 1851-1862. 4v.
41593.32.8 Dupont, Pierre. Dix églogues, poèmes bycoliques. Lyon, 1864.
41593.32.8.15 Dupont, Pierre. Le siècle. Paris, 1845?
41593.32.8.80 Bailly, Antoine. Pierre Dupont. Lyon, 1959.
41593.32.9 Ducos, Florentin. Epopée toulousaine, ou Guerre des Albigeois. Toulouse, 1850. 2v.
41593.32.10 Durand, J.B.A. La forêt de Fontainebleau, poème. Paris, 1836.
41593.32.10.50 Durand, Claude. La chanson des Vignerons. Niort, 1886.
41593.32.12 Esménard, J. La navigation. Poème. Paris, 1806.
41593.32.13 Fabre, J.R.A. La Calédonie. Poème. Paris, 1823.
Htn 41593.32.14* Fantelin. Ode à S.M. Alexander I. Rouen, 1814?
41593.32.15 Favier, Eulalie. Poésies de l'ame. Paris, 1835.
41593.32.17 Garnier, J.H. Mélancolies et miscellanées. Paris, 1839.
41593.32.18 Gaudy-Le Fort, Jean A. Esquisses genevoises. Genève, 1829.
41593.32.20 Gaudois, G. Les romantiques. Satire. Paris, 1830.
41593.32.40 Gerando, Joseph Marie de. Le fabuliste des familles. Strasbourg, 1855.
41593.32.50 Pamphlet box. Gerand, Edmond.
41593.32.55 Germigny, Paul. Une lyre a l'atelier. 2. éd. Orléans, 1843.
41593.32.75 Feburel, Edmond. Fleurettes. Strasbourg, 1864. 2 pam.
41593.32.150 Godard-Lange. La congrégation. Paris, 1846.
41593.32.200 Grobert, Joseph. Napoleone al Danubio, canzone. Parigi, 1805.
41593.32.300 Guérin, Amand. Bretagne. Paris, 1842.

41593.33 - .36.9 Individual authors, etc. - 1800-1849 - Poetry - Guérin, M. de - Writings

41593.33.50 Guérin, Maurice de. Oeuvres. Paris, 1930. 2v.
41593.33.55 Guérin, Maurice de. Oeuvres complètes. v.1-2. Paris, 1947.
41593.33.60 Guérin, Maurice de. Maurice et Eugenié de Guérin. Paris, 1965.
41593.33.85 Guérin, Maurice de. Le centaure. 7. éd. Paris, 1923.
41593.34 Guérin, Maurice de. Journal, lettres et poèmes. Paris, 1862.

41593.33 - .36.9 Individual authors, etc. - 1800-1849 - Poetry - Guérin, M. de - Writings - cont.

41593.34.2 Guérin, Maurice de. Journal, lettres et poèmes. Paris, 1863.
41593.34.2.5 Guérin, Maurice de. Journal, lettres et poèmes. 6. éd. Paris, 1864.
41593.34.3 Guérin, Maurice de. Journal, lettres et poèmes. 9. éd. Paris, 1866.
41593.34.5 Guérin, Maurice de. Journal, lettres et poèmes. Strasbourg, n.d.
41593.34.17 Guérin, Maurice de. Maurice de Guérin; Journal, lettres et poèmes. Paris, 1882.
41593.34.22 Guérin, Maurice de. Journal, lettres et poèmes avec l'assentiment. 22. éd. Paris, 1898.
41593.34.25 Guérin, Maurice de. Journal, lettres et poèmes. 25. éd. Paris, 1911.
41593.34.40 Guérin, Maurice de. Le cahier vert. Paris, 1921.
41593.34.50 Guérin, Maurice de. Pages choisies. Manchester, 1965.
41593.35 Guérin, Maurice de. Journal. N.Y., n.d.
41593.35.5 Guérin, Maurice de. Journal. N.Y., 1867.
41593.36 Guérin, Maurice de. Le centaure, la bacchante, glaucus. Paris, 1909.
41593.36.2 Guérin, Maurice de. Der Kentauer. Leipzig, 1919.
41593.36.3 Guérin, Maurice de. Le centaure et la bacchante. Thèse. Paris, 1932.
41593.36.6 Guérin, Maurice de. La centaure, la bacchante. Lausanne, 1947.
41593.36.7 Guérin, Maurice de. From centaur to cross. N.Y., 1929.
41593.36.8 Guérin, Maurice de. Der Kentauer. Leipzig, 1940.
41593.36.9 Guérin, Maurice de. Der Kentauer. Wiesbaden, 1950.

41593.36.10 - .42 Individual authors, etc. - 1800-1849 - Poetry - Guérin, M. de - Works about

41593.36.10 Zyromski, Ernest. Maurice de Guérin. Paris, 1921.
41593.36.15 Brodnitz, Lili-Charlotte. Maurice de Guérin. Inaug. Diss. Jena, 1929.
41593.36.25 Harcourt, B. Maurice de Guérin et le poème en prose. Paris, 1932.
41593.36.30 Decahors, E. Maurice de Guérin. Paris, 1932.
41593.36.32 Decahors, E. Maurice de Guérin, essai de biographie psychologique. Thèse. Paris, 1932.
41593.36.35 Wouden-Veldkamrp, J.M. von. Maurice de Guérin. Proefschrift. Amsterdam, 1932.
41593.36.40 Wauner, M. Versuch über den Stil Maurice de Guérins. Wädenswil, 1937.
41593.36.45 Heuschele, Otto. Maurice de Guérin, Leben und Werk, eines Dichter. Bühl, 1947.
41593.36.80 Schaerer-Nussberger, Maya. Maurice de Guérin. Paris, 1965.
41593.41 Lefranc, A. Maurice de Guérin d'après des documents inedits. Paris, 1910.
41593.42 Schneegans, F. Maurice de Guérin. Strassburg, 1914.

41593.45 - .49 Individual authors, etc. - 1800-1849 - Poetry - Guttinguer

41593.45 Guttinguer, Ulric. Nadir, lettres orientales. Paris, 1822.
41593.46 Guttinguer, Ulric. Mélanges poétiques. Paris, 1824.
41593.47 Guttinguer, Ulric. Poèmes et poésies nouvelles. Paris, 1827.
41593.48 Guttinguer, Ulric. Arthur. Rouen, 1834.
41593.48.10 Guttinguer, Ulric. Arthur. Paris, 1925.
41593.49 Guttinguer, Ulric. Les deux ages du poétes. 2. éd. Paris, 1846.
41593.49.5 Guttinguer, Ulric. Jumiéges, prose et vers et poésies diverses. Rouen, 1839.
41593.49.25 Bremond, Henri. Le roman et l'histoire d'une conversion. Paris, 1925.

41593.60 Individual authors, etc. - 1800-1849 - Poetry - Halma

41593.60.5 Halma, N. La maltéide ou Le siége de Malte. Paris, 1811.

41593.70 Individual authors, etc. - 1800-1849 - Poetry - Hugo, E.

41593.70.80 Dufay, Pierre. Celui dout ou ne parle pas, Eugène Hugo, sa vie, sa folie, ses oeuvres. Paris, 1924.

41593.92 Individual authors, etc. - 1800-1849 - Poetry - Jouin

41593.92 Jouin, Henri A. L'Ardoisé, poésie. Paris, 1883.

41593.125 Individual authors, etc. - 1800-1849 - Poetry - Jullien

41593.125 Jullien, M.A. La France en 1825, ou Mes regrets et mes espérances. Paris, 1825.

41593.170 Individual authors, etc. - 1800-1849 - Poetry - Collet

41593.170.5 Collet, L. Josué, ou La conquête de la terre promise. Bourg, 1807.

41593.175 Individual authors, etc. - 1800-1849 - Poetry - Corday

41593.175.5 Corday, Aglaé de. Les fleurs neustriennes. Mortagne, 1855-1857. 2v.

41593.190 Individual authors, etc. - 1800-1849 - Poetry - Croiszetière

41593.190.5 Croiszetière, G.J.C. Poésies morales et philosophiques. Paris, 1801.

41593.225 Individual authors, etc. - 1800-1849 - Poetry - Flamen

41593.225.5 Flamen, P. Paris, ou Nouvelle mission de Belphégor. Paris, 1838.

41593.240 Individual authors, etc. - 1800-1849 - Poetry - Forget

41593.240.5 Forget. La France nouvelle. Paris, 1830.

41595.1 Individual authors, etc. - 1800-1849 - Poetry - Lacan

41595.1.5 Lacan, E. La mort de l'archevêque de Paris. 2. éd. Paris, 1849.

41595.2 Individual authors, etc. - 1800-1849 - Poetry - Lacenaire

41595.2.10 Lacenaire, Pierre François. Memoirs. London, 1952.
41595.2.15 Lacenaire, Pierre François. Memoire de Lacenaire. Paris, 1968.
41595.2.80 Lapaquellerie, Yvon. Lacenaire. Paris, 1934.
41595.2.81 Marseille-Lansiart, Monique. Lacenaire. Bourgoin, 1965.
41595.2.82 Lucas-Dubreton, Jean. Lacenaire, ou Le romantisme de l'assassinat. Paris, 1930.

41595.4 Individual authors, etc. - 1800-1849 - Poetry - Lapointe

41595.4 Lapointe, S. Une voix d'en bas. Poésies. Paris, 1844.

41595.5 Individual authors, etc. - 1800-1849 - Poetry - Le Poitevin

41595.5 Le Poittevin, Alfred. Oeuvres inédites. Paris, 1909.
41595.5.10 Le Poittevin, Alfred. Une promenade de Belial et oeuvres inédites. Paris, 1924.
41595.5.50 Le dix-neuf brumaire. Paris? 1832.

41595.6 Individual authors, etc. - 1800-1849 - Poetry - Lebrèton

41595.6 Lebrèton, T. Heures de repos d'un ouvrier. Rouen, 1857.

41595.7 - .9 Individual authors, etc. - 1800-1849 - Poetry - Lebrun, Pierre - Writings

41595.7 Lebrun, Pierre. Oeuvres. Théâtre. Poésies. Discours. Paris, n.d. 4v.
41595.9 Lebrun, Pierre. Marie Stuart, tragédie en cinq actes. Paris, 1820.
41595.9.2 Lebrun, Pierre. Marie Stuart, tragédie en cinq actes. 2. éd. Paris, 1820.
41595.9.5 Lebrun, Pierre. Maria Stuardo. N.Y., 1855.

41595.10 - .11 Individual authors, etc. - 1800-1849 - Poetry - Lebrun, Pierre - Works about

41595.10 Pamphlet box. Lebrun, Pierre.
41595.10.15 Beranger, Alphonse. Lettres inédites à Pierre Lebrun et à Mme. Lebrun. Paris, 1913.
41595.11 Szwarc, Herc. Un précurseur du romantisme. Thèse. Dijon, 1928.

41595.12 - .16 Individual authors, etc. - 1800-1849 - Poetry - Le Fevre-Deumier - Writings

41595.12 Le Fevre-Deumier, J. Poésies. Paris, 1844.
41595.13 Le Fevre-Deumier, J. Le couvre-feu. Paris, 1857.
41595.14 Le Fevre-Deumier, J. Le clocher de Saint-Marc. Paris, 1825.
41595.15 Le Fevre-Deumier, J. Les vespres de l'abbaye du val. Paris, 1924.
Htn 41595.16* Le Fevre-Deumier, J. Confidences. Paris, 1833.

41595.18 Individual authors, etc. - 1800-1849 - Poetry - Léon, Louis de

41595.18 Léon, Louis de. La tragédie du monde. Paris, 1843.

41595.19 Individual authors, etc. - 1800-1849 - Poetry - Lesseps

41595.19 Lesseps, M. Ode aux français residant a Livourne pour le jour de la fête de St. Napoléon. Livourne, 1807?

41595.20 Individual authors, etc. - 1800-1849 - Poetry - Luce de Lancival

41595.20 Luce de Lancival, J.C.J. Achille. Paris, 1807.
41595.20.5 Luce de Lancival, J.C.J. Oeuvres. Paris, 1826. 2v.

41595.22 Individual authors, etc. - 1800-1849 - Poetry - Magalon; Magu; Martin-Maillefer; etc.

41595.22 Magalon, J.D. Souvenirs poétiques de deux prisonniers. Paris, 1823.
41595.22.9 Magu. Poésies. Paris, 1840.
41595.22.25 Martin-Maillefer, P.D. Les fiancés de Caracas. Paris, 1829.
41595.22.26 Martin-Maillefer, P.D. Los novios de Caracas, poema eclectico en dos cantos. Caracas, 1954.

41595.23 Individual authors, etc. - 1800-1849 - Poetry - Massas; Mirecourt; Michaud; etc.

41595.23 Massas, Charles. Dithyrambes et poésies diverses. Paris, 1826.
41595.23.3 Maury, François. Le concile de Paris. Clermont-Ferrand, 1839.
41595.23.5 Mirecourt, E. de. Méry. 4. éd. Paris, 1855.
41595.23.5.2 Mirecourt, E. de. Méry. Paris, 1867.
41595.23.5.3 Mirecourt, E. de. Méry. 3. éd. Paris, 1869.
41595.23.5.8 Mayer, G. Eugène de Mirecourt. Paris, 1855.
41595.23.5.9 Deschamps, Théophile. Biographie de Jaquot dit de Mirecourt. 3. éd. Paris, 1857.
41595.23.5.10 Mazerolle, Pierre. Confession d'un biographe. Paris, 1857.
41595.23.9 Michaux, Clovis. Poésies posthumes. Paris, 1875.
41595.23.150 Michaud, Joseph. Le printemps d'un proscrit. 7. éd. Paris, 1814. 2v.

41595.24 - .29 Individual authors, etc. - 1800-1849 - Poetry - Millevoye - Writings

41595.24 Millevoye, Charles H. Oeuvres complètes. Paris, 1822. 4v.
41595.25 Millevoye, Charles H. Oeuvres complètes. Bruxelles, 1823. 2v.
41595.27 Millevoye, Charles H. Oeuvres. Paris, 1874.

41595.30 Individual authors, etc. - 1800-1849 - Poetry - Millevoye - Works about

41595.30 Ladoué, Pierre. Millevoye. 1782-1816. Paris, 1912.
41595.30.2 Ladoué, Pierre. Millevoye. La vie et l'oeuvre. Paris, 1912.
41595.30.5 Wirthwein, Theodora. Die Elegie bei Millevoye. Diss. Darmstadt, 1912.

41595.31 Individual authors, etc. - 1800-1849 - Poetry - Larrebat; Mercoeur; Mollevant; etc.

41595.31.50 Larrebat, J. Poesies Gasconnes. Paris, 1926.
41595.31.75 Loynes d'Autroche, Claude de. Ode au pape Pie VII. Paris?, 1822?
41595.31.85 Mercoeur, Elisa. Oeuvres complètes d'Elisa Mercoeur de Nantes. Paris, 1843. 3v.
41595.31.100 Mollevant, C.L. Ode sur le 18 brumaire. n.p., n.d.

41595.32 - .35 Individual authors, etc. - 1800-1849 - Poetry - Moreau, Hegesippe - Complete and Selected works

41595.32 Moreau, Hégésippe. Oeuvres complètes. Paris, 1861.
41595.33 Moreau, Hégésippe. Oeuvres complètes. Paris, 1890. 2v.
41595.34 Moreau, Hégésippe. Contes. Paris, 1881.
41595.35 Moreau, Hégésippe. Oeuvres. Selections. Paris, 1870.

41595.50 Individual authors, etc. - 1800-1849 - Poetry - Moreau, Hegesippe - Biography and criticism

41595.50 Lhuillier, T. Hégésippe Moreau et son Diogenè. Paris, 1881.

Classified Listing

41595.55 Individual authors, etc. - 1800-1849 - Poetry - Montlivault

41595.55.80 Philippon, Albert. Les albums de Sophie-Aimée-Arménide de Montlivault. Tours, 1968.

41595.60 Individual authors, etc. - 1800-1849 - Poetry - Moussard

41595.60.2 Moussard, P. Les prêtres tels qu'ils devraient être. Paris, 1819.

41595.70 Individual authors, etc. - 1800-1849 - Poetry - Manso

41595.70.100 Manso, C. Sonnets d'automne. Paris, 1885.

41596.01 - .099 Individual authors, etc. - 1800-1849 - Poetry - Musset, Alfred de - Pamphlet volumes

41596.01 Pamphlet box. Alfred de Musset.
41596.02 Pamphlet box. Alfred de Musset.

41596.1 - .4 Individual authors, etc. - 1800-1849 - Poetry - Musset, Alfred de - Biography and criticism

41596.1 Lindan, Paul. Alfred de Musset. Berlin, 1877.
41596.1.2 Barine, Arvède. Alfred de Musset. Paris, 1893.
41596.1.5 Vincens, Cécile. Alfred de Musset. 3. éd. Paris, 1900.
41596.2 Étude critique et bibliographique des oeuvres de Alfred de Musset. Paris, 1867.
41596.2.5 Le Mussetiste. Ann. 1-12. v.1-2. Paris, 1907-1918.
41596.2.10 Clouard, Maurice. Bibliographie des oeuvres d'Alfred de Musset. Paris, 1883.
41596.2.15 Clouard, Maurice. Documents inedits sur Alfred de Musset. Paris, 1900.
41596.2.20 Bibliothèque nationale, Paris. Alfred de Musset, 1810-1857. Paris, 1957.
41596.3 Nienkirchen, Friedrich. Alfred de Mussets Gedicht::Sur la Paresse. Inaug. Diss. Berlin, 1889.
41596.3.2 Werner, Moritz. Kleine Beiträge zur Würdigung Alfred de Mussets. Berlin, 1896.
41596.4 Janzé, Alix C.C. Étude et récits sur Alfred de Musset. Paris, 1891.
41596.4.2 Claveau, A. Alfred de Musset. Paris, 1894.
41596.4.3 Oliphant, Cyril F. Alfred de Musset. Edinburgh, 1890.
41596.4.7 Donnay, Maurice C. La vie amoureuse d'Alfred de Musset. Paris, 1926.
41596.4.9 Teissier, O. Alfred de Musset. Documents généalogiques. Draguignan, 1903.
41596.4.12 Séché, L. Alfred de Musset. Paris, 1907. 2v.
41596.4.13 Martellet, Adèle C. Dix ans chez Alfred de Musset. Paris, 1899.
41596.4.15 Dumoulin, M. Les ancêtres d'Alfred de Musset. Paris, 1911.
41596.4.17 Donnay, Maurice. Alfred de Musset. Paris, 1914.
41596.4.19 Betheder-Matibet, M. L'influence de Shakespeare sur Musset. Paris, 1921.
41596.4.21 Moroncine, E. Alfred de Musset e l'Italia. Milano, 1921.
41596.4.25 Hendreich, Otto. Alfred de Musset, ein Vertreter des "esprit gaulois". Berlin, 1899.
41596.4.29 Lyonnet, Henry. Les "premières" de Alfred de Musset. Paris, 1927.
NEDL 41596.4.35 Henriot, Emile. Alfred de Musset. Paris, 1928.
41596.4.38 Henriot, Emile. L'enfant du siècle, Alfred de Musset. Paris, 1953.
41596.4.40 Sedgwick, H.D. Alfred de Musset, 1810-1857. Indianapolis, 1931.
41596.4.47 Gastinel, Pierre. Le romantisme d'Alfred de Musset. Paris, 1933.
41596.4.50 Rickey, H. Wynn. Musset Shakespearien. Thèse. Bordeaux, 1932.
41596.4.55 Tuong, N.M. Essai sur la valeur dramatique du théâtre d'Alfred de Musset. Thèse. Montpellier, 1932.
41596.4.60 Steis, Alois. Das Motiv des Ennui bei Alfred de Musset. Inaug. Diss. Würzburg, 1933.
41596.4.65 Brunet, V. Le lyrisme d'Alfred de Musset. Thèse. Toulouse, 1932.
41596.4.70 Bock, M. Symbolistisches in den Dramen von Alfred de Musset. Inaug. Diss. Berlin, 1936.
41596.4.75 Charpentier, J. Alfred de Musset. Paris, 1938.
41596.4.80 Villiers, André. La vie privée d'Alfred de Musset. Paris, 1939.
41596.4.85 Van Tieghem, Philippe. Musset, l'homme et l'oeuvre. Paris, 1944.
41596.4.86 Van Tieghem, Philippe. Musset. Paris, 1969.
41596.4.90 Pommier, Jean. Variétés sur Alfred de Musset et son théâtre. Paris, 1944?
41596.4.92 Pommier, Jean. Autour du drame de Venise: G. Sand et A. de Musset au lendemain de "Lorenzaccio". Paris, 1958.
41596.4.95 Allem, M. Alfred de Musset. Grenoble, 1948.
41596.4.100 Blum, Arlette. L'expression poetique des souvenirs chez Alfred de Musset. Paris, 1954.
41596.4.105 Lefebvre, Henri. Alfred de Musset. Paris, 1955.
41596.4.107 Lefebvre, Henri. Musset; essai. 2. éd. Paris, 1970.
41596.4.110 Pommier, Jean. Alfred de Musset. Oxford, 1957.
41596.4.115 Merlant, J.C. Le moment de Lorenzaccio dans le destin de Musset. Athènes, 1955.
41596.4.120 Meunier, Micheline. Trente-deux variations autour du nom d'Alfred de Musset. Paris, 1959.
41596.4.125 Koskenniemi, V.A. Alfred de Musset. Porvoo, 1918.
41596.4.130 Prestreau, Georges. Alfred de Musset, sa famille et l'anjon. Angers, 1958.
41596.4.135 Lebois, André. Vues sur le théâtre de Musset. Avignon, 1966.
41596.4.140 Gochberg, Herbert S. Stage of dreams. The dramatic art of Alfred de Musset. Genève, 1967.
41596.4.145 Ganne, Gilbert. Alfred de Musset, sa jeunesse et la nôtre. Paris, 1970.
41596.4.150 Tonge, Frederich. L'art du dialogue dans les comédies en prose d'Alfred de Musset. Paris, 1967.
41596.4.155 Toesca, Maurice. Alfred de Musset, ou L'amour de la mort. Paris, 1970.
41596.4.161A Musset, Paul. The biography of Alfred de Musset. Boston, 1877.
41596.4.161B Musset, Paul. The biography of Alfred de Musset. Boston, 1877.
41596.4.165 Haldane, Charlotte F. Alfred; the passionate life of Alfred de Musset. London, 1960.
41596.4.170 Suarès, André. Alfred de Musset au théâtre. Abbeville, 1923.
41596.4.175 Lietz, Jutta. Studien zu den Novellen Alfred de Mussets. Hamburg, 1971.
41596.4.180 Rees, Margaret A. Alfred de Musset. N.Y., 1971.

41596.5 - .8 Individual authors, etc. - 1800-1849 - Poetry - Musset, Alfred de - Complete and Selected works

41596.5 Musset, Paul de. Biographie de Alfred de Musset. Paris, 1877.
41596.6 Musset, Paul de. Biographie de Alfred de Musset. Paris, 1877.
41596.6.4 Musset, Paul de. Biographie de Alfred de Musset. Paris, 1881.
41596.6.5 Musset, Alfred de. Oeuvres complètes de Alfred de Musset. Paris, 1866. 10v.
41596.6.6 Musset, Alfred de. Oeuvres complètes. Paris, 1881. 9v.
41596.6.9 Musset, Alfred de. Oeuvres complètes de Alfred de Musset. Paris, 1876. 10v.
41596.7 Musset, Alfred de. Oeuvres complètes. Paris, 1876. 10v.
41596.8 Musset, Alfred de. Oeuvres complètes. Paris, 1877. 10v.
41596.8.6 Musset, Alfred de. Poésies complètes. Paris, 1962.
41596.8.9 Musset, Alfred de. Les chefs-d'oeuvre lyriques. Paris, 1912.
41596.8.15 Musset, Alfred de. Oeuvres complètes. Paris, 1926-1935. 4v.
41596.8.16 Musset, Alfred de. Premières poésies, 1828-1833. Paris, 1922.
41596.8.16.2 Musset, Alfred de. Poésies. Strasbourg, 1909.
41596.8.17 Musset, Alfred de. Poésies nouvelles, 1833-1852. Paris, 1923.
41596.8.18 Musset, Alfred de. La confession d'un enfant du siècle. Paris, 1937.
41596.8.20 Musset, Alfred de. La confession d'un enfant du siècle. Lille, 1945.
41596.8.22 Musset, Alfred de. La confession d'un enfant du siècle. Paris, 1968.

41596.9 Individual authors, etc. - 1800-1849 - Poetry - Musset, Alfred de - Correspondence

41596.9 Musset, Alfred de. Correspondance. 1827-1857. Paris, 1907.
41596.9.2 Musset, Alfred de. Correspondance. 1827-1857. Paris, 1907. 2v.
41596.9.4A Musset, Alfred de. Lettres d'amour à Aimée d'Alton. Paris, 1910.
41596.9.4B Musset, Alfred de. Lettres d'amour à Aimée d'Alton. Paris, 1910.

41596.10 - .38 Individual authors, etc. - 1800-1849 - Poetry - Musset, Alfred de - Individual works

41596.10 Musset, Alfred de. Premières poésies. Paris, 1865.
41596.10.5 Musset, Alfred de. Premières poésies. Paris, 1858.
41596.10.7 Musset, Alfred de. Premières poésies. 1829-1835. Paris, 1867.
41596.12 Musset, Alfred de. Poésies nouvelles. Paris, 1867.
41596.12.2 Musset, Alfred de. Poésies. Paris, 1867.
Htn 41596.12.3* Musset, Alfred de. Premières poésies. 1829-1835. Paris, 1879.
41596.12.4 Musset, Alfred de. Premières poésies. Paris, 1881.
41596.12.5A Musset, Alfred de. Premières poésies. 1829-1835. Paris, 1884.
41596.12.5B Musset, Alfred de. Premières poésies. 1829-1835. Paris, 1884.
41596.12.7 Musset, Alfred de. Poésies nouvelles. 1836-1852. Paris, 1882.
41596.12.8A Musset, Alfred de. Poésies nouvelles. 1836-1852. Paris, 1885.
41596.12.8B Musset, Alfred de. Poésies nouvelles. 1836-1852. Paris, 1885.
X Cg 41596.12.9 Musset, Alfred de. Poésies nouvelles. 1836-1852. Paris, 1886.
41596.12.10 Musset, Alfred de. Premières poésies. 1829-1835. Paris, 1887.
41596.12.12 Musset, Alfred de. Premières poésies, 1829-1835. Paris, 1887.
41596.12.80 Cassou, Jean. Les nuits de Musset. Paris, 1930.
41596.13 Musset, Alfred de. Premières poésies. 1829-1835. Paris, 1890.
41596.13.1A Musset, Alfred de. Poésies. Paris, 189-?
41596.13.1B Musset, Alfred de. Poésies. Paris, 189-?
41596.13.2 Musset, Alfred de. Poésies nouvelles. 1836-1852. Paris, 1891.
41596.13.4 Musset, Alfred de. Premières poésies. Paris, 1896.
41596.13.5 Musset, Alfred de. Premières poésies, 1829-1835. Paris, 1899.
41596.13.7 Musset, Alfred de. Poésies nouvelles, 1836-1852. Paris, 1899.
41596.13.8 Musset, Alfred de. Premières poésies. Paris, 19- ?
41596.13.9 Musset, Alfred de. Poésies nouvelles. Londres, 1913.
41596.13.10 Musset, Alfred de. Poésies nouvelles. Paris, 19- ?
41596.13.11A Musset, Alfred de. Poésies nouvelles. Paris, 1906.
41596.13.11B Musset, Alfred de. Poésies nouvelles. Paris, 1906.
41596.13.13 Musset, Alfred de. Poésies choisies. Oxford, 1906.
41596.13.15 Musset, Alfred de. Poèmes choisies. Manchester, 1931.
41596.14 Musset, Alfred de. Oeuvres posthumes. Paris, 1860.
41596.14.3 Musset, Alfred de. Oeuvres posthumes. Paris, 1881.
41596.14.5 Musset, Alfred de. Oeuvres posthumes. Paris, 1887.
41596.14.10 Musset, Alfred de. Oeuvres posthumes. Paris, 1897.
41596.14.15 Musset, Alfred de. Oeuvres posthumes. Paris, 19- ?
41596.16 Musset, Alfred de. Mélanges de littérature. Paris, 1867.
41596.16.10 Musset, Alfred de. Mélanges de littérature. Paris, 1894.
41596.16.15 Musset, Alfred de. Mélanges de littérature et de critique. Paris, 19- ?
41596.16.25 Musset, Alfred de. Oeuvres complètes en prose. Paris, 1938.
41596.16.50 Musset, Alfred de. Comédies et nuits. N.Y., 1932.
41596.17 Musset, Alfred de. Comédies et proverbes. Paris, 1881. 3v.
41596.17.3 Musset, Alfred de. Comédies et proverbes. v.2. Paris, 1882.
41596.17.5 Musset, Alfred de. Comédies et proverbes. Paris, 1850.
41596.17.10 Musset, Alfred de. Comédies et proverbes. Paris, 1878. 3v.
41596.17.15 Musset, Alfred de. Comédies et proverbes. Paris, 1897-1899. 3v.
41596.17.25 Musset, Alfred de. Alfred de Musset. v.1-2. Lyon, 1946.
41596.18 Musset, Alfred de. Comédies et proverbes. Paris, 1856. 2v.
NEDL 41596.18.3A Musset, Alfred de. Comedies. London, 1890.
41596.18.3B Musset, Alfred de. Comedies. London, 1890.

41596.10 - .38 Individual authors, etc. - 1800-1849 - Poetry - Musset, Alfred de - Individual works - cont.

41596.18.5 Musset, Alfred de. Comédies et proverbes. Paris, 1867. 2v.
41596.18.5.5 Musset, Alfred de. Barberine. Lorenzaccio. Strassburg, n.d.
41596.18.5.10 Musset, Alfred de. Barberine. Paris, 1917.
41596.18.5.15A Musset, Alfred de. A selection from the poetry and comedies of Alfred de Musset. Boston, 1895.
41596.18.5.20 Musset, Alfred de. Selections from the prose and poetry of Alfred de Musset. N.Y., 1870.
41596.18.6A Musset, Alfred de. Selection from poetry and comedies. Boston, 1895.
41596.18.6B Musset, Alfred de. Selection from poetry and comedies. Boston, 1895.
41596.18.6.5 Musset, Alfred de. Comédies et proverbes. Paris, 1895. 3v.
41596.18.6.10 Musset, Alfred de. Comédies et proverbes. Paris, 19- ? 2v.
41596.18.7 Musset, Alfred de. A selection from the poetry and comedies. Boston, 1903.
41596.18.7.5 Musset, Alfred de. Comédies et proverbes. Paris, 1907.
41596.18.8 Musset, Alfred de. Morceaux choisis. Paris, 1917.
NEDL 41596.18.8.25 Musset, Alfred de. Comédies et proverbes. v.2. Paris, 1917?
41596.18.9F Musset, Alfred de. Oeuvres. Paris, 1883.
41596.18.10 Musset, Alfred de. Les chefs-d'oeuvre lyriques. Paris, 1907.
41596.18.12 Musset, Alfred de. Les chefs-d'oeuvre lyriques. Paris, 1867.
41596.18.13 Musset, Alfred de. Three novelettes and Valentine's wager, a comedy. Photoreproduction. N.Y., 1888.
41596.18.14 Musset, Alfred de. Three plays. Fantasio. On ne badine pas avec l'amour. Carmosine. London, 19- ?
41596.18.15A Musset, Alfred de. Trois comédies: Fantasio, On ne badine pas avec l'amour, Il faut qu'une porte soit ouverte ou fermée. Boston, 1901.
41596.18.15B Musset, Alfred de. Trois comédies: Fantasio, On ne badine pas avec l'amour, Il faut qu'une porte soit ouverte ou fermée. Boston, 1901.
41596.18.16 Musset, Alfred de. Trois comédies: Fantasio, On ne badine pas avec l'amour, Il faut qu'une porte soit ouverte ou fermée. Boston, 1901.
41596.18.17 Musset, Alfred de. Textes dramatiques inedits. Paris, 1953.
41596.18.25 Musset, Alfred de. Comédies et proverbes. Paris, 1931. 2v.
41596.18.28 Musset, Alfred de. Comédies et proverbes. Paris, 1934.
41596.18.29 Musset, Alfred de. Comédies et proverbes. Paris, 1934. 2v.
41596.18.35 Musset, Alfred de. Théâtre complete; comédies et proverbes. Paris, 1934.
41596.18.40 Musset, Alfred de. Théâtre. Paris, 1889-1891. 4v.
41596.18.45 Musset, Alfred de. Le théâtre d'Alfred de Musset. Strasbourg, 1908.
41596.19 Musset, Alfred de. Nouvelles. London, 1867.
41596.19.2 Musset, Alfred de. Nouvelles. Paris, 1857.
X Cg 41596.19.5 Musset, Alfred de. Nouvelles et contes. Paris, 1883.
41596.19.7 Musset, Alfred de. Nouvelles. Paris, 19- ?
41596.19.10 Musset, Alfred de. Nouvelles. Paris, 1896.
41596.19.12 Musset, Alfred de. Nouvelles. Lille, 1946.
41596.19.12.5 Musset, Alfred de. Novelleja. Helsinki, 1907.
41596.19.15 Musset, Alfred de. Contes. Paris, 1897.
41596.20 Musset, Alfred de. Contes. Paris, 1867.
41596.20.5 Musset, Alfred de. Contes. Paris, 19- ?
41596.20.10 Musset, Alfred de. Contes et nouvelles. Paris, 1902.
41596.20.90 Musset, Alfred de. La confession d'un enfant du siècle. Paris, 1859.
41596.21 Musset, Alfred de. La confession d'un enfant du siècle. Paris, 1865.
41596.22 Musset, Alfred de. La confession d'un enfant du siècle. Paris, 1867.
41596.22.5 Musset, Alfred de. La confession d'un enfant du siècle. Paris, 1884.
41596.22.7 Musset, Alfred de. La confession d'un enfant du siècle. Paris, 19- ?
41596.22.10 Musset, Alfred de. La confession d'un enfant du siècle. Paris, 1899.
41596.22.15 Musset, Alfred de. La confession d'un enfant du siècle. Paris, 1934.
41596.22.75 Musset, Alfred de. The confession of a child of the century. N.Y., 1908.
41596.23A Musset, Alfred de. Histoire d'un merle blanc. Cambridge, 18- ?
41596.23B Musset, Alfred de. Histoire d'un merle blanc. Cambridge, 18- ?
Htn 41596.23.25* Morley, Christopher. Two fables. Garden City, N.Y., 1925.
41596.23.30 Musset, Alfred de. A comedy and two proverbs. London, 1957.
41596.23.32 Musset, Alfred de. Comédies et proverbes. Paris, 1958. 2v.
41596.23.35 Musset, Alfred de. Comédies et proverbes. Paris, 1960.
41596.24.5 Musset, Alfred de. On ne badine pas avec l'amour. Evanston, 1928.
41596.25 Musset, Alfred de. Frédéric et Bernerette. Paris, 1893.
NEDL 41596.26 Musset, Alfred de. Lorenzaccio, drame. Paris, 1898.
41596.26.5 Musset, Alfred de. Lorenzaccio. Manchester, 1941.
41596.26.9 Musset, Alfred de. La genèse de Lorenzaccio. Thèse. Paris, 1936.
41596.26.10 Musset, Alfred de. La genèse de Lorenzaccio. Paris, 1936.
41596.27 Musset, Alfred de. Il ne faut jurer de rien. Paris, 1947.
41596.28 Musset, Alfred de. Un caprice. Paris, 1848.
41596.29A Musset, Alfred de. Un caprice. N.Y., 1869.
41596.29B Musset, Alfred de. Un caprice. N.Y., 1869.
41596.29.3 Musset, Alfred de. Un caprice. Boston, 186-?
41596.29.5 Musset, Alfred de. A good little wife, from "Un caprice". London, 18- ?
41596.30 Musset, Alfred de. A good little wife, from "Un caprice". London, 18- ?
41596.30.25 Musset, Alfred de. El capricho. Madrid, 1864.
41596.31 Musset, Alfred de. Mademoiselle Mimi Pinson. Paris, 1853.
41596.32 Musset, Alfred de. Les deux "André del Sarto". Thèse. Rouen, 1933.
41596.32.10F Musset, Alfred de. La nuit venitienne. Paris, 1913.
Htn 41596.33* Musset, Alfred de. Voyage ou Il vous plaira. Paris, 1843.
41596.34 Foss, Ernst. Die "Nuits" von Alfred de Musset. Berlin, 1902.
41596.34.15 Musset, Alfred de. The poet and the muse. London, 1880.

41596.10 - .38 Individual authors, etc. - 1800-1849 - Poetry - Musset, Alfred de - Individual works - cont.

41596.35.2 Musset, Alfred de. Il faut qu'une porte soit ouverte ou fermée. Paris, 1906.
41596.35.5 Musset, Alfred de. Il faut qu'une porte soit ouverte ou fermée. London, 1910.
41596.35.6 Musset, Alfred de. Il faut qu'une porte soit ouverte ou fermée. London, 1910.
41596.37 Musset, Alfred de. Le chandelier. Paris, 1946.
41596.37.5 Musset, Alfred de. O castiçal, e dois provérbios. Pôrto Alegre, 1968.
41596.37.55 Dolder, Charlotte. Le thème de l'être et du paraître dans l'itinéraire spirituel d'Alfred de Musset. Zürich, 1968.

41596.39 - .40 Individual authors, etc. - 1800-1849 - Poetry - Moyria

41596.39 Moyria, G. de. Esquisses poétiques du département de l'Ain. Bourg, 1841.
41596.40 Moyria, G. de. Le malheur, poème. Paris, 1820.

41596.41 Individual authors, etc. - 1800-1849 - Poetry - Norvins

41596.41 Norvins, J.M. de. Napoléon et Pie IX, poème. Paris, 1847.

41596.42 Individual authors, etc. - 1800-1849 - Poetry - Olivier; Ourry; etc.

41596.42 Olivier, Juste. Les chansons lointaines. Lausanne, 1847.
41596.42.5 Delhorbe, C. Juste et Caroline Olivier. Neuchâtel, 1935.
41596.42.9 Ourry, E.T.M. Bourbons et la France. Paris, 1826.

41596.43 Individual authors, etc. - 1800-1849 - Poetry - Paillet

41596.43 Paillet, M. Oromaze. Paris, 1832.
41596.43.5 Paillet, M. Epitres et poésies diverses. Paris, 1828.
41596.43.10 Paillet, Julien. Le panthéon dijonnais. Dijon, 1805.

41596.44 Individual authors, etc. - 1800-1849 - Poetry - Pécontal

41596.44 Pécontal, Simeon. Ballades et légendes. Paris, 1846.

41596.45 Individual authors, etc. - 1800-1849 - Poetry - Poncy

41596.45 Poncy, Charles. Poésies. Paris, 1846.
41596.45.81 Fahmy, Dorrya. Charles Poncy: poète-macon, 1821-1891. Thèse. Paris, 1934.

41596.46 - .48 Individual authors, etc. - 1800-1849 - Poetry - Parny

Htn 41596.46.2* Parny, Évariste. La guerre des dieux. Paris, 1799.
41596.46.5 Parny, Évariste. La guerre des dieux anciens et modernes. 2. éd. Paris, 1799.
41596.46.10 Parny, Évariste. La guerre des dieux. Paris, 1799.
41596.46.25 Parny, Évariste. La guerre des dieux. Paris, 1807.
41596.46.30 Parny, Évariste. Voina bogov. Leningrad, 1970.
41596.47 Parny, Évariste. Porte-feuille volé. Paris, 1805.
41596.48 Parny, Évariste. Oeuvres choisies. Paris, 1827.

41596.49 Individual authors, etc. - 1800-1849 - Poetry - Parseval; Pellet; Périn; Popelin; etc.

Htn 41596.49* Parny, Évariste. Oeuvres complètes. Paris, 1831. 4v.
41596.49.7 Parseval, F.A. Philippe-Auguste. Poème héroïque. Paris, 1829.
41596.49.12 Pellet, D'Epinal. Le barde des vosages. Paris, 1828.
41596.49.19 Périn, F.C. Nuits poétiques. Paris, 1835.
41596.49.30 Peyre-Terry, F. Conseils de l'esprit d'un vieillard septuagenaire. Philadelphia, 1831.
41596.49.100 Popelin, Claudius. Un cent de Strophes à Pailleron. Paris, 1881.

41596.50 Individual authors, etc. - 1800-1849 - Poetry - Pommier

41596.50.7 Pommier, A. Poésies. n.p., n.d.
41596.50.9 Pommier, A. Les assassins. Paris, 1837.
41596.50.10 Pommier, A. La république ou le livre de sang. Paris, 1837.
41596.50.11 Pommier, A. Colères. Paris, 1844.

41596.51 Individual authors, etc. - 1800-1849 - Poetry - Porchat; Pottier; Raynouard; etc.

41596.51 Porchat, Jacques. Trois mois sous la neige. N.Y., 1869.
41596.51.2 Porchat, Jacques. Trois mois sous la neige. N.Y., n.d.
41596.51.5 Porchat, Jacques. Trois mois sous la neige. Philadelphia, 1864.
41596.51.7 Porchat, Jacques. Trois mois sous la neige. N.Y., 1866.
41596.51.15 Pottier, Eugène. Oeuvres complètes rassemblées, présentées et annotées par Pierre Brochon. Paris, 1966.
41596.51.20 Pottier, Eugène. Pesni, stikhi, poemy. Moskva, 1966.
41596.51.25 Pottier, Eugène. Chants révolutionnaires. Paris, 1937.
41596.51.30 Ezhen Pot'e, sozdatel' gimna internatsional. Moskva, 1966.
41596.51.35 Zévaès, A.B. Eugène Pottier et "L'International". Paris, 1936.
41596.51.37 Pottier, Eugène. Internatsional. Moskva, 1939.
41596.51.40 Tersen, Émile. L'Internationale. Paris, 1962.
41596.51.45 Dmitriev, Valentin G. Poet-kommunar. Moskva, 1966.
41596.51.50 Lafond, Paul. L'aube romantique. 2. éd. Paris, 1910.
41596.51.60 Puycousin, E. de. Poésies maritimes et fantastiques. Toulon, 1834.
41596.51.75 Pamphlet box. Raynouard, F.M.J.

41596.52 Individual authors, etc. - 1800-1849 - Poetry - Reynaud; Richard; etc.

41596.52 Reynaud, Charles. Epitres, contes et pastorales. Paris, 1853.
41596.52.75.3 Richard, C. Le bon Célime; poème anodin. Paris, 1867.

41596.53 Individual authors, etc. - 1800-1849 - Poetry - Rouget de Lisle

Htn 41596.53.2* Rouget de Lisle, Joseph. Essais en vers et en prose. Paris, 1796.
41596.53.30 Delfolie, Valéry. La Marseillaise. Montmorillon, 1956.
41596.53.50 Société d'emulation du Jura. Les cérémonies du deuxième centenaire de la naissance de Rouget de Lisle. Lons-le-Saunier, 1960.
41596.53.55 Le Roy de Sainte Croix, François Noël. Le chant de guerre pour l'armée du Rhin ou la Marseillaise. Strasbourg, 1880.

41596.56 - .57 Individual authors, etc. - 1800-1849 - Poetry - Rouquette

41596.56 Rouquette, Adrien E. Les savanes. Paris, 1841.
Htn 41596.56.2* Rouquette, Adrien E. Les savanes. Paris, 1841.
Htn 41596.57* Rouquette, Adrien E. La nouvelle Atala. New Orleans, 1879.
41596.57.10 Lebreton, Dagmar R. Chahta-Ima. Baton Rouge, 1947.

41596.58 Individual authors, etc. - 1800-1849 - Poetry - Salm-Rufferscheid

41596.58 Salm-Rufferscheid-Dyck, C. Poésies. 2. éd. Paris, 1817.
41596.58.10 Salm-Rufferscheid-Dyck, C. Sapho. Paris, 1794.

41596.59 Individual authors, etc. - 1800-1849 - Poetry - Ségur, Anatole

41596.59 Ségur, Anatole de. Fables. Paris, n.d.

41596.60 Individual authors, etc. - 1800-1849 - Poetry - Servan de Sugny

41596.60 Servan de Sugny, P.F.J. Satires contemporaines et mélanges. Paris, 1832.

41596.63 Individual authors, etc. - 1800-1849 - Poetry - Tastu

41596.63 Tastu, Amable. Poésies. 4. éd. Paris, 1827.
41596.63.5 Tastu, Amable. Poésies nouvelles. Paris, 1835.

41596.64 Individual authors, etc. - 1800-1849 - Poetry - Treneuil; Tellier; etc.

41596.64.3 Treneuil, Joseph. Les tombeaux de Saint-Denis. Paris, 1808.
Htn 41596.64.5* Treneuil, Joseph. Les tombeaux de Saint-Denis. 5. éd. Paris, 1810.
41596.64.20 Treneuil, Joseph. Le martyre de Louis XVI. Paris, 1815.
41596.64.30 Treneuil, Joseph. La princesse Amélie, élégie. Paris, 1808.
41596.64.800 Müller, P.O. Jules Tellier. Appenzell, 1939.

41596.65 Individual authors, etc. - 1800-1849 - Poetry - Urbain

41596.65.75 Urbain, Charles. Simples vérités. Bruxelles, 1848.

41596.66 Individual authors, etc. - 1800-1849 - Poetry - Veyrat

41596.66 Berthier, Alfred. Le poète savoyard Jean-Pierre Veyrat, 1810-1844. Thèse. Paris, n.d.
41596.66.2 Berthier, Alfred. Le poète savoyard Jean-Pierre Veyrat, 1810-1844. Paris, 1920.
Htn 41596.66.3* Berthier, Alfred. Le poète savoyard Jean-Pierre Veyrat. Paris, 1920.
41596.66.10 Berthier, Alfred. Le désaccord Veyrat-Raymond, 1841-1843. Paris, 1922.

41596.67 - .69 Individual authors, etc. - 1800-1849 - Poetry - Viennet

41596.67 Viennet, J.P.G. Epître à empereur Nicolas, en faveur des grecs. Paris, 1826.
41596.67.10 Viennet, J.P.G. Journal. Paris, 1955.
41596.69 Viennet, J.P.G. Franciade; poëme en dix chants. Paris, 1863.

41596.71 Individual authors, etc. - 1800-1849 - Poetry - Violeau

41596.71 Violeau, Hippolyte. Loisirs; poétiques. 2. éd. Paris, 1844.

41596.80 Individual authors, etc. - 1800-1849 - Poetry - Weustenraad

41596.80 Weustenraad, T. Poésies lyriques. Bruxelles, 1848.

41596.100 Individual authors, etc. - 1800-1849 - Poetry - Yvaren

41596.100 Yvaren, Prosper. Cromwel; ode. n.p., 1834.

41596.120 Individual authors, etc. - 1800-1849 - Poetry - Valori

41596.120 Valori, F. Odes choisies. Paris, 1819.

41597 Individual authors, etc. - 1800-1849 - Poetry - Anonymous works

41597.20 Appoloniana, ou Recueil de pieces fugitives en vers. Lille, 18- ?
41597.26 Les Échecs. Poëme. n.p., n.d.
41597.27 Roman, J.J.T. Les Échecs. Poëme. Paris, 1807.
41597.28 Le Caveau. Paris, 1852.
41597.29 L'écho des bardes. Année 5. Paris, 1819.
41597.31 Annales poétiques. Paris, 1807. 2v.
41597.40 L'hymen et la naissance. Paris, 1812.
41597.40.5 L'hymen et la naissance. Paris, 1812.
41597.45 Ode à sa majesté imperiale et royale Napoléon à l'occasion de son mariage. Paris, 1810.
Htn 41597.46* Couronne poétique de Napoléon-le-Grand. Paris, 1807.
41597.47 Le regard de Dieu sur la France. Paris, 1802.
Htn 41597.50* Le mystère du chevalier. Paris, 1800.
41597.53 Les soupers lyriques. 2. année. v.1-2. Paris, 1820.
41597.56 Poirié Saint-Aurèle. Les veillées françaises. Paris, 1826.
41597.58.3 Lanusse, A. Creole voices; poems in French by free men of color. Washington, 1945.
41597.65 Recueil de cantiques à l'usage des missions de France. Bordeaux, 1817. 2 pam.

41598 Individual authors, etc. - 1800-1849 - Poetry - Satirical and epigrammatic works

41598.3 Album drôlatique. Paris, 18- ?
Htn 41598.6F* Huart, Louis. Les physiologies parisiennes. Paris, 184-?
41598.7 Rousseau, T.J. Physiologie de la portière. v.1-5. Paris, 1841.
41598.8 Blague-en-Main, M. Nouveau catechisme Poissard. Paris, 1849.
41598.9 Ourliac, Édouard. Physiologie de l'écolier. Paris, 1841? 4 pam.
41598.9.2 Saint-Hilaire, E.M.H. Physiologie du troupier. Paris, 1841. 4 pam.
41598.9.3 Huart, Louis. Physiologie du tailleur. Paris, 1841. 4 pam.
41598.9.3.25 Huart, Louis. The student at Paris. N.Y., 1844.
41598.9.4 Huart, Louis. Physiologie de l'étudiant. Paris, 1841. 4 pam.
41598.9.5 Physiologie de l'homme de loi. Paris, 1841? 4 pam.
41598.9.6 Delord, Taxile. Physiologie de la parisienne. Paris, 1841. 4 pam.
41598.10 L'épicurien normand. Rouen, n.d.
41598.12 Le nouvel Angotiana. Lille, 1813.
41598.14 Brochon, Pierre. Béranger et son temps. Paris, 1956. 2v.
41598.16 Une academie en province, par un étudiant. Paris, 1865.

42511 Individual authors, etc. - 1850-1899 - History, philosophy, etc. - Folios [Discontinued]

42511.5 Sand, G. Le diable à Paris. Paris et les Parisiens. Paris, 1853.
42511.10 Laboulaye, Édourd. Nouveaux contes bleus. Paris, 1868.
42511.13 Laboulaye, Édourd. Abdallah. Nashville., n.d.
42511.13.5 Laboulaye, Édourd. Abdallah. 9. ed. London, n.d.
42511.13.10 Laboulaye, Édourd. Abdallah. London, 1868.

42511 Individual authors, etc. - 1850-1899 - History, philosophy, etc. - Folios [Discontinued] - cont.

42511.20 Poujoulat, M. Souvenirs d'histoire et de littérature. Lille, 1875.
42511.21 Poujoulat, M. Variétés littéraires. Lille, n.d.

42512.3 Individual authors, etc. - 1850-1899 - History, philosophy, etc. - Albert, P.

42512.3 Albert, Paul. Poètes et poésies. Paris, 1881.
42512.3.5 Albert, Paul. Variétés morales et litteraires. Paris, 1879.

42512.4 Individual authors, etc. - 1850-1899 - History, philosophy, etc. - Amis

42512.4.9 Amis, Henri. Jours passés. Paris, 1908.

42512.6 Individual authors, etc. - 1850-1899 - History, philosophy, etc. - Bernard-Derosne

42512.6 Bernard-Derosne, Léon. Types et travers. Paris, 1883.

42512.7 Individual authors, etc. - 1850-1899 - History, philosophy, etc. - Bois

42512.7 Bois, Georges. Souvenirs et fantaisies. Causeries du Dimanches. 2. ser. Paris, 1898.
42512.7.3 Bois, Georges. Au temps de la ballade. Paris, 1889.

42512.8 - .19 Individual authors, etc. - 1850-1899 - History, philosophy, etc. - Broglie

42512.8 Broglie, Albert de. Questions de religion et d'histoire. Paris, 1860. 2v.
42512.11 Broglie, Albert de. Nouvelles études de littérature. Paris, 1869.
42512.14 Broglie, Albert de. Histoire et diplomatie. Paris, 1889.
42512.16 Broglie, Albert de. Histoire et politique. Paris, 1897.

42513.3 Individual authors, etc. - 1850-1899 - History, philosophy, etc. - Darmesteter

42513.3 Darmesteter, James. Selected essays. Boston, 1895.

42513.5 Individual authors, etc. - 1850-1899 - History, philosophy, etc. - Delepierre, O.

42513.5.80 Trübner, Nikolaus. Joseph Octave Delepierre. Edinburgh, 1879.

42513.7 Individual authors, etc. - 1850-1899 - History, philosophy, etc. - Denis, F.

42513.7 Denis, F. Journal (1829-1848) publié avec une introduction et des notes par Pierre Moreau. Fribourg, n.d.
42513.7.5 McNeil, P.A. Notes on the works of F. Denis, 1798-1890. Washington, 1941.

42513.10 Individual authors, etc. - 1850-1899 - History, philosophy, etc. - Despois

42513.10 Despois, Eugene. Les lettres et la liberté. Paris, 1865.

42513.16 Individual authors, etc. - 1850-1899 - History, philosophy, etc. - Diane

42513.16 Beausacq, Marie Josephine. Maximes de la vie. Paris, 1884.

42513.22 Individual authors, etc. - 1850-1899 - History, philosophy, etc. - Didon

42513.22 Didon, Henri. Lettres du R.P. Didon de l'Ordre prêcheurs à Mlle. Thérèse Vianzane. Paris, 1904.

42513.23 Individual authors, etc. - 1850-1899 - History, philosophy, etc. - Dollfus

42513.23.79 Martin, René. Bibliographie de Charles Dollfus (Mulhouse, 1827. Paris, 1913.) Thèse. Gap, 1934.
42513.23.81 Martin, René. La vie et l'oeuvre de Charles Dollfus. Mulhouse, 1827. Paris, 1913. Thèse. Gap, 1934.

42513.25 Individual authors, etc. - 1850-1899 - History, philosophy, etc. - DuLaz

42513.25.80 Baudry, Joséphine. Une Bretonne de lettres; la comtesse Jégou Du Laz. Heunebont, 1909.

42513.26 Individual authors, etc. - 1850-1899 - History, philosophy, etc. - Esquiros

42513.26.80 Linden, Jacobus Petrus van der. Alphonse Esquiros. Heerlem, 1948.

42513.27 - .30 Individual authors, etc. - 1850-1899 - History, philosophy, etc. - Favre, Jules

42513.27 Favre, Jules. Discours de M. Jules Favre prononcé à sa réception à l'academie francaise, le 23 avril 1868. Paris, 1868. 2 pam.
42513.29 Favre, Jules. Conferences et discours littéraires. Paris, 1873.
42513.30 Favre, Jules. Quatre conférences. Paris, 1874.
42513.30.30 Favre, Jules. Henry Belval. Paris, 1880.

42513.33 - .40 Individual authors, etc. - 1850-1899 - History, philosophy, etc. - Gasparin

42513.33 Gasparin, V.B.C. de. Les horizons prochains. Paris, 1872.
42513.34 Gasparin, V.B.C. de. Les horizons célestes. Paris, 1868.
42513.35 Gasparin, V.B.C. de. Vesper. Paris, 1862.
42513.36 Gasparin, V.B.C. de. Les tristesses humaines. Paris, 1864.
42513.37 Gasparin, V.B.C. de. Au bord de la mer. 2. éd. Paris, 1866.
42513.38 Gasparin, V.B.C de. Near and heavenly horizons. N.Y., 1862.
42513.38.5 Gasparin, V.B.C. de. Near and heavenly horizons. N.Y., 1863.
42513.39 Gasparin, V.B.C. de. Near and heavenly horizons. N.Y., 1864.
42513.39.15 Gasparin, V.B.C. de. Under French skies. N.Y., 1888.

42513.42 Individual authors, etc. - 1850-1899 - History, philosophy, etc. - Guyau

42513.42 Guyau, J.M. Pages choisies. Paris, 1912.
42513.42.5 Guyau, M. Vers d'un philosophe. 9. éd. Paris, 1917.
42513.42.9 Kiesow, Julius. Die philosophische Lyrik von Guyau und Lahor. Greifswald, 1916.

42513.43 Individual authors, etc. - 1850-1899 - History, philosophy, etc. - Guizot

42513.43 Guizot, F.P.G. Mélanges biographiques et littéraires. Paris, 1868.

42513.43.10 Guizot, F.P.G. Un projet de mariage royal. Paris, 1863.

42513.44 Individual authors, etc. - 1850-1899 - History, philosophy, etc. - Hauréau

42513.44.5 Haureau, Barthélemy. Singularités historiques et littéraires. Paris, 1861.

42513.45 Individual authors, etc. - 1850-1899 - History, philosophy, etc. - Jusserand

42513.45.50A Jusserand, J.J. The school for ambassadors. N.Y., 1925.

42513.45.50B Jusserand, J.J. The school for ambassadors. N.Y., 1925.

42513.45.50C Jusserand, J.J. The school for ambassadors. N.Y., 1925.

42513.46 Individual authors, etc. - 1850-1899 - History, philosophy, etc. - Kuhn, Emile

42513.46 Kuhn, Emile. La légende des rues; histoire de mon temps, politique critique et littéraire. Paris, 1869-70. 2v.

42513.47 Individual authors, etc. - 1850-1899 - History, philosophy, etc. - Adam, Juliette (Lamber) - Writings

42513.47 Adam, Juliette. Mes premières armes littéraires et politiques. Paris, 1904.

42513.47.5 Adam, Juliette. Après l'abandon de la revanche. Paris, 1910.

42513.47.10 Adam, Juliette. My literary life. N.Y., 1904.

42513.47.15 Adam, Juliette. My literary life. London, 1904.

42513.47.20 Adam, Juliette. Mon village. Paris, 1868.

42513.48 Individual authors, etc. - 1850-1899 - History, philosophy, etc. - Adam, Juliette (Lamber) - Works about

42513.48.9 Adam, Juliette. The romance of my childhood and youth. N.Y., 1902.

42513.48.10 Stephens, Winifred. Madame Adam. N.Y., 1917.

42513.48.15 Arndt, Dora. Juliette Adam. Inaug. Diss. Würzburg, 1933.

42513.48.20 Cormier, Manon. Madame Juliette Adam. Bordeaux, 1934.

42513.48.25 Eliott, A. Madame Adam (Juliette Lamber)...1870-71. Paris, 1922.

42513.48.30 Morcos, Saad. Juliette Adam. Thèse. Le Caire, 1961.

42513.48.31 Morcos, Saad. Juliette Adam. Beirut, 1962.

42513.49 Le Carpentier, P.H.M. Essais lipogrammatiques. Paris, 1858.

42513.50 Individual authors, etc. - 1850-1899 - History, philosophy, etc. - Lemoine

42513.50 Lemoinne, John. Nouvelles études critiques. Paris, 1863.

42513.60 Individual authors, etc. - 1850-1899 - History, philosophy, etc. - Laveleye

42513.60 Laveleye, Émile de. Études et essais. Paris, 1869.

42513.60.2 Laveleye, Émile de. Essais et études. 1st serie, 1861-75, 2d serie, 1875-82, 3d serie 1883-1892. Paris, 1894. 3v.

42513.73 - .89 Individual authors, etc. - 1850-1899 - History, philosophy, etc. - Leroy-Beaulieu - Writings

42513.74 Leroy-Beaulieu, A. Un homme d'etat Russe. Paris, 1884.

42513.75 Leroy-Beaulieu, A. La France, La Russie et l'Europe. Paris, 1888.

42513.76 Leroy-Beaulieu, A. Études Russes et européennes. Paris, 1897.

42513.77 Leroy-Beaulieu, A. La papauté. Paris, 1893.

42513.78 Leroy-Beaulieu, A. Un empereur, un roi, un pape. Paris, 1879.

42513.79 Leroy-Beaulieu, A. La revolution et le liberalisme. Paris, 1890.

42513.80 Leroy-Beaulieu, A. Les catholiques liberaux. Paris, 1885.

42513.82 Leroy-Beaulieu, A. L'antisémitisme. Paris, 1897.

42513.90 - .95 Individual authors, etc. - 1850-1899 - History, philosophy, etc. - Leroy-Beaulieu - Works about

42513.95 Leroy-Beaulieu, A. Discours prononcés à l'inauguration du monument. n.p., 1914.

42513.99 Individual authors, etc. - 1850-1899 - History, philosophy, etc. - Littré, E.

42513.99 Littré, Émile. Littérature et histoire. Paris, 1875.

42514.3 - .4 Individual authors, etc. - 1850-1899 - History, philosophy, etc. - Laboulaye - Works about

42514.3 Bigelow, John. Edward Laboulaye. N.Y., 1888.

42514.4 Bigelow, John. Some recollections of the late Edward Laboulaye. N.Y., n.d.

42514.4.10 Sbarbaro, Pietro. Laboulaye, un fonditore di caratteri. Rome, 1886.

42514.5 - .24 Individual authors, etc. - 1850-1899 - History, philosophy, etc. - Laboulaye - Writings

42514.5 Laboulaye, Édouard. Discours populaires. Paris, 1570.

42514.6 Laboulaye, Édouard. Études contemporaines sur l'Allemagne. Paris, 1865.

42514.7 Laboulaye, Édouard. Études contemporaines sur l'Allemagne. 3. éd. Paris, 1868.

42514.7.2 Laboulaye, Édouard. Études contemporaines sur l'Allemagne. 4. éd. Paris, 1872.

42514.8 Laboulaye, Édouard. Études morales. Paris, 1871.

42514.9 Laboulaye, Édouard. Études morales et politiques. Paris, 1862.

42514.11 Laboulaye, Edouard. Le parti libéral. Paris, 1871.

42514.12 Laboulaye, Edouard. La république - le progrès. Paris, 1871.

42514.16 Laboulaye, Edouard. Abdallah. Paris, 1871.

42514.16.7A Laboulaye, Edouard. Abdallah. Chicago, 1890.

42514.16.7B Laboulaye, Edouard. Abdallah. Chicago, 1890.

42514.17 Laboulaye, Edouard. Abdallah. N.Y., 1913.

42514.18 Laboulaye, Edouard. Contes bleus. Paris, 1869.

42514.18.5 Laboulaye, Edouard. Contes bleus. Boston, 1901.

42514.18.6 Laboulaye, Edouard. Contes bleus. Boston, 1903.

42514.18.7A Laboulaye, Edouard. Derniers contes bleus. Paris, 1884.

42514.18.7B Laboulaye, Edouard. Derniers contes bleus. Paris, 1884.

42514.18.9 Laboulaye, Edouard. Contes bleus. Boston, 1907.

42514.19 Laboulaye, Edouard. Contes et nouvelles. Paris, 1868.

42514.20 Laboulaye, Edouard. Contes choisis. Paris, 1891.

42514.21 Laboulaye, Edouard. Fairy tales. London, 1909.

42514.21.5 Laboulaye, Edouard. Laboulaye's fairy book. N.Y., 1868.

42514.5 - .24 Individual authors, etc. - 1850-1899 - History, philosophy, etc. - Laboulaye - Writings - cont.

42514.21.10 Laboulaye, Edouard. Finette; a legend of Brittany. Boston, 1867.

42514.22 Laboulaye, Edouard. Le prince-Caniche. Paris, 1868.

42514.22.2 Laboulaye, Edouard. The spaniel-prince. Liverpool, 1895.

42514.22.10 Laboulaye, Edouard. Prince charming. Polo, Ill., 1909.

42514.23 Laboulaye, Edouard. Souvenirs d'un voyageur. Paris, 1858.

42514.24 Laboulaye, Edouard. Souvenirs d'un voyageur. Paris, 1869.

42514.25 Individual authors, etc. - 1850-1899 - History, philosophy, etc. - Lamy

42514.25 Lamy, E. Au service des idées et des lettres. Paris, 1909.

42514.26 Individual authors, etc. - 1850-1899 - History, philosophy, etc. - Lanfrey

42514.26 Lanfrey, P. Correspondance. Paris, 1885. 2v.

42514.26.5 Lanfrey, P. Les lettres d'Éverard. Paris, 1880.

42514.27 Individual authors, etc. - 1850-1899 - History, philosophy, etc. - Lefébure; Lerne; Lomenie; etc.

42514.27.10 Mondor, Henri. Eugène Lefébure. 8. éd. Paris, 1951.

42514.27.11 Mondor, Henri. Alain. 9. éd. Paris, 1853.

42514.27.15 Lerne, E. de. Socières blondes. Paris, 1853.

42514.27.250 Lomenie, Louis de. Esquises en historiques et littéraires. Paris, 1879.

42514.28 Individual authors, etc. - 1850-1899 - History, philosophy, etc. - Maurras, Charles

42514.28.11 Maurras, Charles. Poesie et verite. Lyon, 1944.

42514.28.21 Maurras, Charles. Lettres passe-murailles. Paris, 1966.

42514.28.30 Maurras, Charles. Tragi-comédie de ma surdité. Aix-en-Provence, 1951.

42514.28.32 Maurras, Charles. Inscriptions. Paris, 1921.

42514.28.35 Maurras, Charles. La balance interieure. 3. éd. Lyon, 1952.

42514.28.38 Maurras, Charles. Ironie et poésie. St. Félicien-en-Vivarais, 1932.

42514.28.40 Maurras, Charles. Le guignon français. Roanne, 1952.

42514.28.45 Maurras, Charles. Les plus belles pages de Maurras. Paris, 1931.

42514.28.46 Maurras, Charles. Pascal puni. Paris, 1953.

42514.28.47 Maurras, Charles. Oeuvres capitales. Paris, 1954. 4v.

42514.28.48 Maurras, Charles. Votre bel aujourd'hui. Paris, 1953.

42514.28.49 Maurras, Charles. Principes. Paris, 1931.

42514.28.50 Maurras, Charles. Pages littéraires choisies. 5. éd. Paris, 1922.

42514.28.52 Maurras, Charles. De Demas à César. v.1-2. Paris, 1930.

42514.28.53 Maurras, Charles. Au signe de flore. Paris, 1931.

42514.28.54 Maurras, Charles. Prologue d'un essai sur la critique. Paris, 1932.

42514.28.58 Maurras, Charles. La deutelle du rempart, 1886-1936. Paris, 1937.

42514.28.59.50 Maurras, Charles. La musique intérieure. 50. éd. Paris, 1925.

42514.28.60 Maurras, Charles. Réponse à André Gide. Paris, 1948.

42514.28.65 Groos, René. Esquisses: Charles Maurras, M. Proust, G.B. Shaw. Paris, 1928.

42514.28.70 Benjamin, René. Charles Maurras, ce fils de la mer. Paris, 1932.

42514.28.70.2 Benjamin, René. Charles Maurras, ce fils de la mer. Paris, 1932.

42514.28.73 Chandet, Henriette. Le procés Maurras. Lyon, 1945.

42514.28.75 Clavière, M. Charles Maurras, ou la restauration des valeurs humaines. Paris, 1939.

42514.28.76 Maurras, Charles. Lettres de prison. Paris, 1958.

42514.28.77A Maurras, Charles. Le procès de Charles Maurras. Paris, 1946.

42514.28.77B Maurras, Charles. Le procès de Charles Maurras. Paris, 1946.

42514.28.78 Maurras, Charles. Le mont de saturne. n.p., 1950.

42514.28.79 Maurras, Charles. Inscriptions sur nos ruines. Paris, 1949.

42514.28.80 Massis, H. Maurras et notre temps. v.1-2. Paris, 1951.

42514.28.81 Massis, H. Maurras et notre temps. Paris, 1961.

42514.28.82 Mourre, M. Charles Maurras. Paris, 1953.

42514.28.84 Vallat, X.J. Charles Maurras. Paris, 1953.

42514.28.86 Charles Maurras. Paris, 1953.

42514.28.87 Cromier, Aristide. Mes entretiens de prêtre avec Charles Maurras. Paris, 1953.

42514.28.88 Cormier, Aristide. La vie interieure de Charles Maurras. Paris, 1956.

42514.28.89 Cormier, Aristide. Mes entretiens de prêtre avec Charles Maurras. Paris, 1970.

42514.28.90 Roudiez, L.S. Maurras jusqu'à l'action française. Paris, 1957.

42514.28.95 Hupin, Gérard. Charles Maurras. Paris, 1956.

42514.28.100 Boyer, Noél. Charles Maurras en prison. Paris, 1938?

42514.28.105 Descogs, Pedro. A travers l'oeuvre de M. Maurras. Paris, 1911.

42514.28.110 Beau de Loménie, Emanuel. Maurras et son système. Bourg, 1953.

42514.28.112 Beau de Loménie, Emanuel. Maurras et son système. Monsecret, Orne, 1965.

X Cg 42514.28.115 Truc, Gonzague. Charles Maurras et son temps. Paris, 1918.

42514.28.120 Roche, A.V. Les idées traditionalistes en France et le traditionisme de Charles Maurras. Urbana, 1935.

42514.28.125 Maurras, Charles. Le procès de Charles Maurras. Lyon, 1945.

42514.28.130 Charles Maurras; poèms, portraits. Aix-en-Provence, 1919.

42514.28.135 Arbellot, Simon. Maurras, homme d'action. Paris, 1937.

42514.28.140 Buthman, W.C. The rise of integral nationalism in France. N.Y., 1939.

42514.28.145 Daudet, Léon. Charles Maurras et son temps. Paris, 1928.

42514.28.150 Ségard, Achille. Les hommes d'action. Paris, 1919.

42514.28.155 Larpent, G. Pour connaître Charles Maurras. Paris, 1926.

42514.28.160 Roux, Marie. Charles Maurras et le nationalisme de l'action française. Paris, 1928.

42514.28.165 Maritain, Jacques. Une opinion sur Charles Maurras. Paris, 1926.

42514.28.170 Points et contrepoints. Hommage à Charles Maurras. Paris, 1953.

42514.28.175 Santos, Arlindo Veiga dos. Maurras. Sao Paulo, 195-?

42514.28.180 Liévre, Pierre. Maurras. Paris, 1925.

42514.28.185 Barko, I.P. L'esthétique littéraire de Charles Maurras. Genève, 1961.

42514.28 Individual authors, etc. - 1850-1899 - History, philosophy, etc. - Maurras, Charles - cont.

42514.28.190 Joseph, Roger. Le poète Charles Maurras. Paris, 1962.
42514.28.195 Cahiers Charles Maurras. Paris. 1,1960+ 4v.
42514.28.200 Gurian, Waldemar. Der integrale Nationalismus. Frankfurt, 1931.
42514.28.205 Maurras, Charles. Charles Maurras. Lisboa, 1960.
42514.28.210 Maurras, Charles. Charles Maurras et la critique des lettres. Paris, 1913.
42514.28.220 Oberson, Gabriel. La politique de Charles Maurras. Olten, 1929.
42514.28.225 Vandromme, Pol. Maurras, l'eglise de l'ordre. Paris, 1965.
42514.28.230 Fabrégues, Jean de. Charles Maurras et son action française. Paris, 1966.
42514.28.235 Maurras, Hélène. Souvenirs des prisons de Charles Maurras. Paris, 1965.
42514.28.240 Vaulx, Bernard de. Charles Maurras. Moulins, 1968.
42514.28.245 Detaille, Albert. Maurras en Provence. Marseille, 1968.
42514.28.250 Joseph, Roger. J'ai vu condamner un juste au bagne. (Charles Maurras). Orleans, 1966.
42514.28.260 Lubac, Paul de. Maurras face à Pascal. Privas, 1970.

42514.29 - .36 Individual authors, etc. - 1850-1899 - History, philosophy, etc. - Mignet - Writings

42514.29 Mignet, F.A.M. Éloges historiques. Paris, 1864.
42514.30 Mignet, F.A.M. Nouveaux éloges historiques. Paris, 1877.
42514.32 Mignet, F.A.M. Mémoires historiques. Paris, 1859.
42514.33 Mignet, F.A.M. Études historiques. Paris, 1877.
42514.34 Mignet, F.A.M. Portraits et notices. Paris, 1877. 2v.
42514.34.5 Mignet, F.A.M. Notices et portraits historiques et littéraires. 3. éd. Paris, 1854. 2v.
42514.35 Mignet, F.A.M. Lectures littéraires. Pages choisies des grands écrivains. Mignet. Paris, 1895.
42514.36 Mignet, F.A.M. Pages choisies de Mignet. Paris, 1896.

42514.37 Individual authors, etc. - 1850-1899 - History, philosophy, etc. - Mignet - Works about

42514.37 Roziere, E. de. Bibliographie des oeuvres de M. François Mignet. Paris, 1887.

42514.39 Individual authors, etc. - 1850-1899 - History, philosophy, etc. - Masson, F.

42514.39.2 Masson, Frédéric. Au jour le jour. 2. éd. Paris, 1910.

42515.10 Individual authors, etc. - 1850-1899 - History, philosophy, etc. - Pelletan, E.

42515.10.5 Pelletan, Eugene. La nouvelle Babylone. Paris, 1862.

42515.13 Individual authors, etc. - 1850-1899 - History, philosophy, etc. - Pichot

42515.13 Bisson, L.A. Amedée Pichot, a romantic Prometheus. Oxford, 1942.

42515.15 Individual authors, etc. - 1850-1899 - History, philosophy, etc. - Poulet-Malassis

Htn 42515.15* Poulet-Malassis, A. Bibliographie descriptive et anecdotique des ouvrages. Paris, 1883.
42515.15.5 Les Amitiés littéraires et artistiques. A. Poulet-Malassis. Alençon, 1957.

42515.17 Individual authors, etc. - 1850-1899 - History, philosophy, etc. - Pirmez

42515.17 Champagne, Paul. Nouvel essai sur Octane Pirmez. Gembloux, 1952.

42515.20 Individual authors, etc. - 1850-1899 - History, philosophy, etc. - Prevost-Paradol

42515.20.9 Prevost-Paradol, L.A.P. de. Essais de politique et de littérature. Paris, 1859.
42515.20.15 Prevost-Paradol, L.A.P. de. Essais de politique et de littérature. 2. éd. 2. ser. Paris, 1863.

42515.22 Individual authors, etc. - 1850-1899 - History, philosophy, etc. - Primoli

42515.22 Primoli, Joseph Napoléon. Pages inédites. Roma, 1959.
NEDL 42515.23 Reinach, Joseph. Études de littérature et d'histoire. Paris, 1889.

42515.25 Individual authors, etc. - 1850-1899 - History, philosophy, etc. - Renan - Complete and Selected works

42515.25.5 Renan, Ernest. Oeuvres complètes. Paris, 1947-49. 10v.
42515.25.10 Renan, Ernest. Pages choisies. Paris, 1890.
42515.25.14 Renan, Ernest. Pages choisies. 9. éd. Paris, 1894.
42515.25.24 Renan, Ernest. Páginas escogidas. 2a. ser. San José, 1921.
42515.25.25 Renan, Ernest. Páginas escogidas. 3a. ser. San José, 1925.
42515.25.30 Renan, Ernest. Fragments intimes et romanesques. Paris, 1914.
42515.25.40 Renan, Ernest. Pages françaises. Paris, 1921.
42515.25.50 Renan, Ernest. Travaux de jeunesse, 1843-1844. Paris, 1931.
42515.25.60 Renan, Ernest. Cahiers de jeunesse. 2. éd. Paris, 1906. 2v.
42515.25.70 Renan, Ernest. Ernest Renan et l'Allemagne. N.Y., 1945.

42515.27 Individual authors, etc. - 1850-1899 - History, philosophy, etc. - Renan - Histoire des origines du Christianisme - Complete editions

42515.27.6A Renan, Ernest. Histoire des origines du christianisme. Index général. Paris, 1883.
42515.27.6B Renan, Ernest. Histoire des origines du christianisme. Index général. Paris, 1883.
42515.27.6C Renan, Ernest. Histoire des origines du christianisme. Index général. Paris, 1883.
42515.27.8 Renan, Ernest. Histoire des origines du christianisme. v.2. Paris, 1894.
42515.27.10A Renan, Ernest. Histoire des origines du christianisme. Paris, 1866-77. 7v.
42515.27.10B Renan, Ernest. Histoire des origines du christianisme. v.1,7. v.2 lost 1947. Paris, 1866-77. 2v.

42515.29 Individual authors, etc. - 1850-1899 - History, philosophy, etc. - Renan - Histoire des origines du Christianisme - Separate volumes

42515.29.2 Renan, Ernest. Vie de Jésus. Paris, 1863.
Htn 42515.29.2.5* Renan, Ernest. Vie de Jésus. Paris, 1863.
42515.29.2.8 Renan, Ernest. Vie de Jésus. 5. éd. Paris, 1863.
42515.29.3 Renan, Ernest. Jésus. 3. éd. Paris, 1864.
42515.29.5 Renan, Ernest. Vie de Jésus. 7. éd. Paris, 1864.
42515.29.7 Renan, Ernest. Jésus. 16. éd. Paris, 1864.
42515.29.12 Renan, Ernest. Vie de Jésus. 12. éd. Boston, 1866.
42515.29.15 Renan, Ernest. Vie de Jésus. 13. éd. Paris, 1867.
42515.29.18 Renan, Ernest. Vie de Jésus. Paris, 1870.
42515.29.19 Renan, Ernest. Vie de Jésus. Paris, 1870.
42515.29.20 Renan, Ernest. Vie de Jésus. 16. éd. Paris, 1879.
42515.29.25 Renan, Ernest. Vie de Jésus. 17. éd. Paris, 1882.
42515.29.30A Renan, Ernest. Vie de Jésus. 19. éd. Paris, 1888.
42515.29.30B Renan, Ernest. Vie de Jésus. 19. éd. Paris, 1888.
42515.29.35 Renan, Ernest. Vie de Jésus. 23. éd. Paris, 1893.
42515.29.45 Renan, Ernest. Vie de Jésus. 58. éd. Paris, 1895.
42515.29.75 Renan, Ernest. Vie de Jésus. 101. éd. Paris, 1906?
42515.29.100 Renan, Ernest. Life of Jesus. London, 1864.
42515.29.250 Renan, Ernest. The apostles. N.Y., 1866.
42515.29.252 Renan, Ernest. Les apotres. Paris, 1866.
42515.29.255 Renan, Ernest. The apostles. London, 1869.
42515.29.257 Renan, Ernest. Les apostles. N.Y., 1869.
42515.29.270 Renan, Ernest. Les apotres. Paris, 1889.
42515.29.280A Renan, Ernest. The apostles. Boston, 1898.
42515.29.280B Renan, Ernest. The apostles. Boston, 1898.
42515.29.345 Renan, Ernest. Saint Paul. Paris, 1869.
42515.29.350 Renan, Ernest. Saint Paul. N.Y., 1869.
42515.29.369 Renan, Ernest. Saint Paul. Paris, 1888.
42515.29.370 Renan, Ernest. Saint Paul. 13. éd. Paris, 1893.
42515.29.401A Renan, Ernest. L'antéchrist. Paris, 1873.
42515.29.401B Renan, Ernest. L'antéchrist. Paris, 1873.
42515.29.410A Renan, Ernest. L'antéchrist. 5. éd. Paris, 1893.
42515.29.410B Renan, Ernest. L'antéchrist. 5. éd. Paris, 1893.
42515.29.475 Renan, Ernest. Antichrist. Boston, 1897.
42515.29.501A Renan, Ernest. Les évangiles et la seconde génération. Paris, 1877.
42515.29.501B Renan, Ernest. Les évangiles et la seconde génération. Paris, 1877.
42515.29.503 Renan, Ernest. Les évangiles et la seconde génération chrétienne. 3. éd. Paris, 1877.
42515.29.600 Renan, Ernest. L'église chrétienne. 4. éd. Paris, 1879.
42515.29.601A Renan, Ernest. L'église chrétienne. Paris, 1879.
42515.29.601B Renan, Ernest. L'église chrétienne. Paris, 1879.
42515.29.702 Renan, Ernest. Marc-Auréle et la fin du monde antique. 2. éd. Paris, 1882.
42515.29.704 Renan, Ernest. Marc-Aurèle et la fin du monde antique. 4. éd. Paris, 1882.
42515.29.707 Renan, Ernest. Marc-Aurèle et la fin du monde antique. 5. éd. n.p., 1885.
42515.29.710 Renan, Ernest. Marc-Aurèle et la fin du monde antique. 6. éd. Paris, 1891.
42515.29.715 Renan, Ernest. Marcus Aurelius. London, 1903.
42515.29.720 Renan, Ernest. Vie de Jésus. Paris, 1938.

42515.30 Individual authors, etc. - 1850-1899 - History, philosophy, etc. - Renan - Other individual works

42515.30.5 Renan, Ernest. L'abbesse de Jouarre. 21. éd. Paris, 1886.
42515.30.20 Renan, Ernest. L'abbesse de Jouarre. London, 18- ?
42515.30.35 Renan, Ernest. L'avenir de la science. Pensées de 1848. 4. éd. Paris, 1890.
42515.30.40 Renan, Ernest. Voyages; Italie, 1849. Paris, 1927.
42515.30.51 Renan, Ernest. The future of science. Boston, 1891.
42515.30.54 Renan, Ernest. The future of science. London, 1891.
42515.30.60 Renan, Ernest. Caliban. Paris, 1878.
42515.30.61 Renan, Ernest. Caliban. Paris, 1878. 2 pam.
42515.30.63 Renan, Ernest. Caliban, suite de La tempète. 2. éd. Paris, 1878.
42515.30.80 Renan, Ernest. Caliban. N.Y., 1896.
42515.30.96 Renan, Ernest. Le cantique des cantiques. 6. éd. Paris, 1891.
42515.30.120 Renan, Ernest. La chaire d'hébreu au college de France. 4. éd. Paris, 1862.
42515.30.130 Renan, Ernest. Conférences d'Angleterre Rome et le Christianisme Marc-Aurèle. Paris, 1880.
42515.30.132 Renan, Ernest. Conférences d'Angleterre Rome et le Christianisme Marc-Aurèle. 2. éd. Paris, 1880.
42515.30.150A Renan, Ernest. Lectures on the influence of the institutions. London, 1880.
42515.30.150B Renan, Ernest. Lectures on the influence of the institutions. London, 1880.
42515.30.151 Renan, Ernest. Lectures on the influence of the institution...of Rome. 4. ed. London, 1898.
42515.30.152A Renan, Ernest. English conferences. Boston, 1880.
42515.30.152B Renan, Ernest. English conferences. Boston, 1880.
Htn 42515.30.174* Renan, Ernest. De la part des peuples sémitiques dans l'histoire de la civilisation. Paris, 1862.
42515.30.175 Renan, Ernest. De la part des peuples sémitiques dans l'histoire de la civilisation. 5. éd. Paris, 1862.
42515.30.190 Renan, Ernest. Dialogues et fragments philosophiques. Paris, 1876.
42515.30.193 Renan, Ernest. Dialogues et fragments philosophiques. Paris, 1886.
42515.30.210 Renan, Ernest. Discours. Paris, 1879.
42515.30.220 Renan, Ernest. Discours et conférences. Paris, 1887.
42515.30.222 Renan, Ernest. Discours et conférences. 2. éd. Paris, 1887.
42515.30.250A Renan, Ernest. Drames philosophiques. Paris, 1888.
42515.30.250B Renan, Ernest. Drames philosophiques. Paris, 1888.
42515.30.310 Renan, Ernest. Ecclésiaste. Paris, 1882.
42515.30.313 Renan, Ernest. L'ecclésiaste. 3. éd. Paris, 1890.
42515.30.330 Renan, Ernest. Essai psychologique sur Jésus-Christ. Paris, 1921.
42515.30.350 Renan, Ernest. Essais de morale et de critique. Paris, 1859.
42515.30.351A Renan, Ernest. Essais de morale et de critique. Paris, 1860.
42515.30.351B Renan, Ernest. Essais de morale et de critique. Paris, 1860.
42515.30.380 Renan, Ernest. Études d'histoire religieuse. 4. éd. Paris, 1858.
42515.30.385 Renan, Ernest. Études d'histoire religieuse. 5. éd. Paris, 1862.
42515.30.400A Renan, Ernest. Studies of religious history and criticism. N.Y., 1864.
42515.30.400B Renan, Ernest. Studies of religious history and criticism. N.Y., 1864.

42515.30 Individual authors, etc. - 1850-1899 - History, philosophy, etc. - Renan - Other individual works - cont.

42515.30.404 Renan, Ernest. Studies in religious history. 2. ser. London, 1893?
42515.30.405 Renan, Ernest. Studies of religious history. London, 1893.
42515.30.410 Renan, Ernest. Nouvelles études d'histoire religieuse. Paris, 1884.
42515.30.435 Renan, Ernest. Feuilles détachées. 8. éd. Paris, 1892.
42515.30.438 Renan, Ernest. Feuilles détachées. 13. éd. Paris, 1892.
42515.30.452 Renan, Ernest. L'islamisme et la science. 2. éd. Paris, 1883.
42515.30.490 Renan, Ernest. Le judaisme et le christianisme. Paris, 1883. 2 pam.
42515.30.495 Renan, Ernest. Le judaisme comme race et comme religion. Paris, 1883. 3 pam.
42515.30.512 Renan, Ernest. Le livre de Job. Paris, 1860.
42515.30.520 Renan, Ernest. Le livre de Job. 4. éd. Paris, 1882.
42515.30.535 Renan, Ernest. Ma soeur Henriette. Paris, 1895.
42515.30.545 Renan, Ernest. My sister Henrietta. Boston, 1895.
42515.30.546 Renan, Ernest. Ma soeur Henriette. Paris, 1964.
42515.30.550 Renan, Ernest. Melanges d'hisoire et de voyages. Paris, 1890.
Htn 42515.30.570* Renan, Ernest. 1802; dialogue des morts. Paris, 1886.
42515.30.615 Renan, Ernest. Le prêtre de Nemi. 6. éd. Paris, 1886.
42515.30.615.2 Renan, Ernest. Le prêtre de Nemi. 3. éd. Paris, 1886.
42515.30.630 Renan, Ernest. Prière sur l'acropole. Paris, 1899.
42515.30.634 Renan, Ernest. Prière sur l'acropole. Manchester, 1934.
42515.30.650 Renan, Ernest. Qu'est-ce qu'une nation? Paris, 1882.
42515.30.660 Renan, Ernest. Questions contemporaines. Paris, 1868.
42515.30.662A Renan, Ernest. Questions contemporaines. 2. éd. Paris, 1868.
42515.30.662B Renan, Ernest. Questions contemporaines. 2. éd. Paris, 1868.
42515.30.683 Renan, Ernest. La réforme intellectuelle et morale. 3. éd. Paris, 1872.
42515.30.685 Renan, Ernest. La réforme intellectuelle et morale. Cambridge, 1950.
42515.30.695 Renan, Ernest. Les sciences de la nature et les sciences historiques. Princeton, 1944.
42515.30.710 Renan, Ernest. Souvenirs d'enfance et de jeunesse. Paris, 1883.
42515.30.718 Renan, Ernest. Souvenirs d'enfance et de jeunesse. Paris, 1893.
42515.30.720 Renan, Ernest. Souvenirs d'enfance et de jeunesse. 26. éd. Paris, 1893.
42515.30.728A Renan, Ernest. Souvenirs d'enfance et de jeunesse. Boston, 1902.
42515.30.728B Renan, Ernest. Souvenirs d'enfance et de jeunesse. Boston, 1902.
42515.30.728C Renan, Ernest. Souvenirs d'enfance et de jeunesse. Boston, 1902.
42515.30.728D Renan, Ernest. Souvenirs d'enfance et de jeunesse. Boston, 1902.
42515.30.729A Renan, Ernest. Souvenirs d'enfance et de jeunesse. Boston, 1909.
42515.30.729B Renan, Ernest. Souvenirs d'enfance et de jeunesse. Boston, 1909.
42515.30.729.10 Renan, Ernest. Souvenirs d'enfance et de jeunesse. Paris, 1959.
42515.30.729.15 Renan, Ernest. Souvenirs d'enfance et de jeunesse. Lausanne, 1961.
42515.30.730 Renan, Ernest. Sur Corneille, Racine et Bossuet. Paris, 1926.
42515.30.731 Renan, Ernest. Recollections of my youth. N.Y., 1883.
42515.30.732 Renan, Ernest. Recollections of my youth. London, 1883.
42515.30.733 Renan, Ernest. The poetry of the Celtic races. London, 1896.

42515.32 Individual authors, etc. - 1850-1899 - History, philosophy, etc. - Renan - Bibliographies

42515.32.5 Girard, Henri. Bibliographie des oeuvres de Ernest Renan. Paris, 1923.
42515.32.10 Novak, O. Renanova theorie slohu. Praha, 1946.

42515.33 Individual authors, etc. - 1850-1899 - History, philosophy, etc. - Renan - Pamphlet volumes

42515.33.3 Pamphlet vol. Renan. Mélanges religieux. 1860. 13 pam.
42515.33.5 Pamphlet vol. Renan. Mélanges religieux. 1863. 16 pam.
42515.33.7 Pamphlet vol. Piecès diverses sur Renan. 20 pam.
42515.33.9 Pamphlet vol. Piecès diverses sur Renan. 4 pam.
42515.33.11 Articles de journeaux relatifs à la vie de M. Renan. n.p., n.d.
42515.33.25 Pamphlet vol. Ernest Renan.

42515.34 Individual authors, etc. - 1850-1899 - History, philosophy, etc. - Renan - Correspondence

42515.34.5 Renan, Ernest. Lettres du séminaire, 1838-1846. 3. éd. Paris, 1902.
42515.34.10 Renan, Ernest. Lettres intimes, 1842-1845. 3. éd. Paris, 1896.
42515.34.15 Renan, Ernest. Nouvelles lettres intimes, 1846-1850. Paris, 1923.
42515.34.20A Renan, Ernest. Brother and sister. N.Y., 1896.
42515.34.20B Renan, Ernest. Brother and sister. N.Y., 1896.
42515.34.25 Renan, Ernest. E. Renan et M. Berthelot. Paris, 1898.
42515.34.30 Renan, Ernest. Lettre à un ami d'Allemagne. Paris, 1879.
42515.34.35 Renan, Ernest. Correspondence, 1846-1871. Paris, 1926. 2v.
42515.34.40 Renan, Ernest. Lettres familières, 1851-1871. Paris, 1947.
42515.34.45 Renan, Ernest. Renan, Taine et Brunetière à quelques amis italiens. Florence, 1956.
42515.34.50 Renan, Ernest. Lettres à son frère Alain. Paris, 1925.
42515.34.75 Renan, Ernest. Recollections and lettres of Ernest Renan. N.Y., 1892.

42515.35 Individual authors, etc. - 1850-1899 - History, philosophy, etc. - Renan - Biography and criticism - General works (299 scheme minus 100]

42515.35.8 Allier, Raoul. La philosophie d'Ernest Renan. Paris, 1895.
42515.35.18 Auzies, Célestin. Les origines de la Bible et M. Ernest Renan. Paris, 1889.
42515.35.26 Barrès, Maurice. Ernest Renan. Abbeville, 1923.
42515.35.26.2 Barrès, Maurice. Huit jours chez M. Renan. 2. éd. Paris, 1890.
42515.35.26.5A Barrès, Maurice. Huit jours chez M. Renan. Paris, 1913.

42515.35 Individual authors, etc. - 1850-1899 - History, philosophy, etc. - Renan - Biography and criticism - General works (299 scheme minus 100] - cont.

42515.35.26.5B Barrès, Maurice. Huit jours chez M. Renan. Paris, 1913.
42515.35.26.10 Barrès, Maurice. Huit jours chez M. Renan. Paris, 1965.
42515.35.27 Barry, William. Ernest Renan. London, 1905.
42515.35.27.2A Barry, William. Ernest Renan. N.Y., 1905.
42515.35.27.2B Barry, William. Ernest Renan. N.Y., 1905.
42515.35.28 Bauer, Bruno. Philo, Straus und Renan und das Urchristenthum. Berlin, 1874.
42515.35.40 Brauer, H.G.A. The philosophy of Ernest Renan. Madison, 1903.
42515.35.42 Brunetière, Ferdinand. Cinq lettres sur Ernest Renan. Paris, 1910.
42515.35.51 Castro y Rossi, Adolfo de. Ernesto Renan ante la erudición sagrada y profana. Cadiz, 1864.
42515.35.71 Delaporte, V. L'"Apothéose" de Renan. Paris, 1893.
42515.35.72 Desportes, Henri. Ernest Renan, sa vie et son oeuvre. Paris, 1893.
42515.35.76 Duclaux, A.M.F.R. La vie de Ernest Renan. Paris, 1898.
42515.35.77 Duclaux, A.M.F.R. The life of Ernest Renan. Boston, 1897.
42515.35.78 Duclaux, A.M.F.R. The life of Ernest Renan. 2. ed. London, 1898.
42515.35.80 Duclaux, A.M.F.R. The life of Ernest Renan. Boston, 1899.
42515.35.82 Dussaud, R. L'oeuvre scientifique d'Ernest Renan. Paris, 1951.
42515.35.89A Espinasse, Francis. Life of Ernest Renan. London, 1895.
42515.35.89B Espinasse, Francis. Life of Ernest Renan. London, 1895.
42515.35.105 France, Anatole. Discours prononcé à l'inauguration de la statue d'Ernest Renan. Paris, 1903.
42515.35.112 Gerbert, Philippe. La stratégie de M. Renan. 2. éd. Paris, 1866.
42515.35.122A Grant Duff, M.E. Ernest Renan. London, 1893.
42515.35.122B Grant Duff, M.E. Ernest Renan. London, 1893.
42515.35.124 Guilloux, Pierre. L'esprit de Renan. Paris, 1920.
42515.35.126 Guisan, Gilbert. Ernest Renan et l'art d'écrire. Genève, 1962.
42515.35.127 Harrisse, Henry. M. Ernest Renan. Paris, 1864.
42515.35.128 Hello, Ernest. M. Renan. Paris, 1859.
42515.35.131 Huré, Anne. Entretiens avec Monsieur Renan. Paris, 1962.
42515.35.145 Jaspar, M.H. Ernest Renan et sa republique. Paris, 1934.
42515.35.147 Jaspar, M.H. Le genie liberal de la France. N.Y., 1942.
42515.35.155 Lasserre, Pierre. La jeunesse d'Ernest Renan. Paris, 1925-32. 3v.
42515.35.155.5 Lasserre, Pierre. Renan et nous. Paris, 1923.
42515.35.157 LeRoy, Ernest. Réponse d'un poète à E. Renan. Paris, 1863.
42515.35.158 Le livre d'or de Renan. Paris, 1903.
42515.35.159 Lefrance, A. Ernest Renan en Italie. Paris, 1938.
42515.35.167 Marriot, Maurice. La vie de Renan suite à la vie de Jésus. 4. éd. Toulouse, 1863.
42515.35.168 Félix, Célestin Joseph. M. Renan et sa vie de Jésus. Paris, 1863. 3 pam.
42515.35.169 Massis, Henri. Jugements. 1. ser. Paris, 1923.
42515.35.169.5A Massis, Henri. Jugements. 2. sér. Paris, 1924.
42515.35.169.5B Massis, Henri. Jugements. 2. sér. Paris, 1924.
42515.35.172 Michaelis, Paul. Philosophie und Dichtung bei Ernest Renan. Berlin, 1913.
42515.35.172.5 Millepierres, François. La vie d'Ernest Renan. Paris, 1961.
42515.35.173 Mirville, J.E. Le vrai secret de M. Renan. Paris, 1864.
42515.35.177 Mott, Lewis F. Ernest Renan. N.Y., 1921.
42515.35.204 Parigot, Hippolyte. Renan. Paris, 1909.
42515.35.208 Pavy, L.C. Conférence contre le livre de M. Renan. 2. éd. Constantine, 1863.
42515.35.211 Plasman, L. Les Strauss français....Littré et Renan. Paris, 1858.
42515.35.213 Platzhoff, L.E. Ernest Renan. Dresden, 1900.
42515.35.214 Poincaré, Raymond. Ernest Renan. Paris, 1923.
42515.35.214.5 Poincaré, R. Ernest Renan. Abbeville, 1923.
42515.35.215 Pommier, Jean. Renan d'après des documents inédits. Paris, 1923.
42515.35.215.5 Pommier, Jean. La jeunesse cléricale d'Ernest Renan. Thèse. Strasbourg, 1933.
42515.35.215.7 Pommier, Jean. La jeunesse cléricale d'Ernest Renan. Paris, 1933.
42515.35.216 Psichari, Jean. Ernest Renan. Paris, 1925.
42515.35.217A Psichari, H. Renan d'après lui-même. Paris, 1937.
42515.35.217B Psichari, H. Renan d'après lui-même. Paris, 1937.
42515.35.217.5 Psichari, H. Renan et la guerre de 70. Paris, 1947.
42515.35.223 Perraud, A. A propos de la mort et des funérailles de M. Ernest Renan. 2. éd. Paris, 1893.
42515.35.224 Renard, Edmond. Renan; les étapes de sa pensée. Paris, 1928.
42515.35.226 Roberto, Diego de. Renan. Torino, 1911.
42515.35.234 Saquet, J. Ernest Renan et ses oeuvres. Rodez, 1864.
42515.35.237 Séailles, G. Ernest Renan. Paris, 1895.
42515.35.240 Société des études renaniennes. Bulletin. Paris. 1,1970+
42515.35.243 Soman, Mariette. La formation philosophique d'Ernest Renan. Thèse. Paris, 1914.
42515.35.244 Sorel, Georges. Le système historique de Renan. Paris, 1906.
42515.35.252 Tielrooy, J.B. Ernest Renan. Amsterdam, 1948.
42515.35.259 Tronchon, Henri. Ernest Renan et l'étranger. Paris, 1928.
42515.35.275 Van Jieghem, Philippe. Renan. Paris, 1948.
42515.35.285 Weiler, Maurice. La pensée de Renan. Grenoble, 1945.
42515.35.285.10 Wardman, H.W. Ernest Renan; a critical biography. London, 1964.
42515.35.293 Ys, René d'. Ernest Renan en Bretagne d'après des documents nouveaux. 3. éd. Paris, 1904.
42515.35.299F Ernest Renan, 1823-1892. Paris, 1892.

42515.36 Individual authors, etc. - 1850-1899 - History, philosophy, etc. - Renan - Biography and criticism - Criticism of individual works (299 scheme minus 100, A-Z by author)

42515.36.02 Pamphlet vol. Renan's Vie de Jésus. 11 pam.
42515.36.3 Milsand, P. Bibliographie des publications relatives au livre de M. Renan Vie de Jésus. Paris, 1864.
42515.36.8 Alfaric, Prosper. Les manuscrits de la Vie de Jésus. Paris, 1939.
42515.36.10 Renan, Ernest. Valentine de Milan; Christene de Suède. Abbeville, 1923.
42515.36.40 Bourgade, F. Lettre à M.E. Renan à l'occasion de son ouvrage intutulé, Vie de Jésus. Paris, 1864.
42515.36.43 Brunner, Sebastian. Der Atheist Renan und sein Evangelium. Regensburg, 1864.
42515.36.55 Chauvelot, Barnabé. À M. Ernest Renan. Paris, 1863.

Classified Listing

42515.36 Individual authors, etc. - 1850-1899 - History, philosophy, etc. - Renan - Biography and criticism - Criticism of individual works (299 scheme minus 100, A-Z by author) - cont.

42515.36.56 Cheret. Lettres d'un curé de campagne à M. Renan sur sa Vie de Jésus. Paris, 1863.
42515.36.62 Colani, T. Examen de La vie de Jésus de M. Renan. 2. éd. Strassburg, 1864.
42515.36.66 Crelier, H.J. M.E. Renan trahissant le Christ par un roman. 2. ed. Paris, 1864.
42515.36.70 Daspers, L. Le Christ de l'histoire en face du Christ de M. Renan. Paris, 1864.
42515.36.72 Delaunay, F. de F. Le Vme Évangile de M. Renan. Paris, 1863.
42515.36.73 Deshaires, G. La vie de Jésus, les évangiles et M. Renan. Paris, 1863.
42515.36.96 Felix, C.J. M. Renan et sa Vie de Jésus. 4. éd. Paris, 1863.
42515.36.105 Fregier, J.C. Jésus devant le droit. Paris, 1864.
42515.36.106 Freppel, C.E. Examen critique de la Vie de Jésus de M. Renan. 6. éd. Paris, 1863.
42515.36.110 Furness, W.H. Remarks on Renan's Life of Jésus. Philadelphia, 1865.
42515.36.116 Ginoulhiac, Jacques Marie Achille. Lettre de monseigneur l'évêque de Grenoble à l'un de ses vicaires généraux sur la Vie de Jésus. Grenoble, 1863.
42515.36.154 Larroque, Patrice. Opinion des déistes rationalistes sur la Vie de Jésus selon M. Renan. 2. éd. Paris, 1863.
42515.36.155 Lasserre, Henri. Evangelho segundo Renan. 25. éd. Porto, 1873.
42515.36.155.4 Lasserre, Henri. L'évangile selon Renan. 5. éd. Paris, 1863.
42515.36.156 Laurentie, P.S. L'athéisme scientifique. Paris, 1862. 2 pam.
42515.36.161 Loyseau, Jean. Lettres sur la vie d'un nommé Jésus selon M. E. Renan. Paris, 1863.
42515.36.162 Loyson, Jules T. Une prétendue vie de Jésus ou Ernest Renan. 3. éd. Paris, 1863.
42515.36.169A Massis, Henri. Jugements. Paris, 1923.
42515.36.169B Massis, Henri. Jugements. Paris, 1923.
42515.36.170 Meignan, G. M. Renan réfuté par les rationalistes allemands. Paris, 1863.
42515.36.184 Nicolas, A. Renan et sa Vie de Jésus sous les rapports moral, légal et littéraire. Paris, 1864.
42515.36.195 Orth, Jacques. La Vie de Jésus selon M. Renan. Mulhouse, 1863.
42515.36.204 Passaglia, Carlo. Étude sur la Vie de Jésus de Ernest Renan. 2. éd. Paris, 1864.
42515.36.211 Pinard, C. Notes à l'usage des lecteurs du Jésus de M. Renan. Paris, 1863.
42515.36.212 Plasman, L.C. de. M. Renan, peint par ses oeuvres. Paris, 1879.
42515.36.213 Plantier, C.H.A. Instruction pastorale de Mgr. Plantier. 2. éd. Paris, 1863.
42515.36.213.2 Plantier, C.H.A. La vraie vie de Jésus. 2. éd. Paris, 1864.
42515.36.214 Potrel, Eugène. Vie de N.S. Jésus-Christ. Paris, 1863.
42515.36.216 Pressense, E. L'école critique et Jésus-Christ à propos de la vie de Jésus de M. Renan. 3. éd. Paris, 1863.
42515.36.217 Psichari, Henriette. La prière sur l'Acropole et ses mystères. Paris, 1956.
42515.36.220 Ratiolisme étudie dans la vie de Jésus de E. Renan par un catholique. Besançon, 1869.
42515.36.231 Sabatier, Auguste. Essai sur les sources de la Vie de Jésus. Paris, 1866.
42515.36.261 Tullock, John. The Christ of the Gospels and the Christ of modern criticism. London, 1864.

42515.37 - .38 Individual authors, etc. - 1850-1899 - History, philosophy, etc. - Renan - Biography and criticism - Special topics

42515.37.5 Freppel, C.E. Examen critique des apôtres de M. Renan. Paris, 1866.
42515.37.10 Meissas, A.F.N. M. Renan, apologiste malgré lui. Paris, 1879.
42515.37.15 Le Nordez, Albert. M. Renan d'après lui-même...La reforme intellectuelle et morale de la France. Coutances, 1872.
42515.37.20 Inauguration du Musée Renan. Paris, 1948.
42515.37.25 Cresson, A. Ernest Renan. Paris, 1949.
42515.37.30 Vié, L. Renan, la guerre de 70. Paris, 1949.
42515.37.35 Galaud, René M. L'âme celtique de Renan. 1. ed. New Haven, 1958.
42515.38 Chaix-Ruy, J. Ernest Renan. Paris, 1956.
42515.38.5 Chadbourne, Richard MClain. Ernest Renan as an essayist. Ithaca, N.Y., 1957.
42515.38.8 Chadbourne, Richard McClain. Ernest Renan. N.Y., 1968.
42515.38.10 Massis, Henri. Portrait de Monsieur Renan. Paris, 1949.
42515.38.15 France. Institut pédagogique national. Exposition Ernest Renan. Paris, 1959.
42515.38.20 Paganelli, Don Sauveur. Ernest Renan, essai. Uzès, 1966.
42515.38.25 La Ferla, Guiseppe. Renan, politico. Torino, 1953.
42515.38.30 Dubreuil, Léon. Rosmapamon. [Renan, E.]. Paris, 1946.
42515.38.35 Fini, Salvatore. Renan e l'Italia. San Severo, 1965.

42515.39 - .44 Individual authors, etc. - 1850-1899 - History, philosophy, etc. - Quinet, Edgar - Biography and criticism

42515.39 Chassin, C.L. Edgar Quinet. Paris, 1859.
42515.40 Quinet, E. (Mme.). Edgar Quinet avant l'exil. Paris, 1887.
42515.40.2 Quinet, E. (Mme.). Edgar Quinet avant l'exil. Paris, 1888.
42515.41 Quinet, E. (Mme.). Edgar Quinet avant l'exil. Paris, 1889.
42515.41.5 Wenderoth, O. Der junge Quinet und seine Übersetzungen und...Ideen. Erlangen, 1906.
42515.42 Heath, Richard. Edgar Quinet. London, 1881.
42515.42.9 Seillière, Ernest. Edgar Quinet et le mysticisme démocratique. Paris, 1919.
42515.42.11 Bär, Georg. Edgar Quinets Ahasvérus und seine Beziehungen zu Quinets Geschichtsphilosophie. Inaug. Diss. Rostock, 1917.
42515.43 Dufour, Théophile. Lettres à Quinet sous l'empire. 1849-1866. Paris, 1883.
42515.44 Quinet, E. (Mme.). Cinquante ans d'amitié. Paris, 1899.
42515.44.5 Quinet, E. (Mme.). Mémoires d'exil (Bruxelles-Oberland). Paris, 1869.
42515.44.6 Quinet, E. (Mme.). Mémoires d'exil. L'amniste. Suisse orientale. Bords du Leman. 2. éd. Paris, 1870.
42515.44.10 Gaetani-Tamburini, N. Edgardo Quinet; studi. 2. ed. Milano, 1865.

42515.39 - .44 Individual authors, etc. - 1850-1899 - History, philosophy, etc. - Quinet, Edgar - Biography and criticism - cont.

42515.44.20 Pellegrini, Carlo. Edgar Quinet e l'Italia. Roma, 1915.
42515.44.22F Pellegrini, Carlo. Edgar Quinet e la litteratura italiana. Pisa, 1915.
42515.44.30 Tronchon, Henri. Le jeune Edgar Quinet. Paris, 1937.
42515.44.35A Powers, Richard H. Edward Quinet. Dallas, 1951.
42515.44.35B Powers, Richard H. Edward Quinet. Dallas, 1951.
42515.44.40 DuPasquier, Marcel. Edgar Quinet en Suisse. Neuchâtel, 1959.
42515.44.45 Vabre Pradal, Georgette. La dimension historique de l'homme. Paris, 1961.

42515.45 - .68 Individual authors, etc. - 1850-1899 - History, philosophy, etc. - Quinet, Edgar - Complete works

42515.46 Quinet, Edgar. Le Jésuits. (Oeuvres complètes, 2). Paris, n.d.
42515.47 Quinet, Edgar. Christianisme et la revolution française. (Oeuvres complètes, 3). Paris, n.d.
42515.48 Quinet, Edgar. Les révolutions d'Italie. (Oeuvres complètes, 4). Paris, n.d.
42515.49 Quinet, Edgar. Marnix de Sainte-Aldegonde. (Oeuvres complètes, 5). Paris, n.d.
42515.50 Quinet, Edgar. Les roumains. (Oeuvres complètes, 6). Paris, n.d.
42515.51 Quinet, Edgar. Ahasvérus. (Oeuvres complètes, 7). Paris, n.d.
42515.52 Quinet, Edgar. Prométhie, les esclaves. (Oeuvres complètes, 8). Paris, n.d.
42515.52.5 Quinet, Edgar. Mes vacances en Espagne. (Oeuvres complètes, 9). Paris, n.d.
42515.53 Quinet, Edgar. Histoire de mes idées. (Oeuvres complètes, 10). Paris, n.d.
42515.54 Quinet, Edgar. L'enseignement du peuple. (Oeuvres complètes, 11). Paris, n.d.
42515.55 Quinet, Edgar. La révolution. (Oeuvres complètes, 12-14). Paris, n.d. 3v.
42515.56 Quinet, Edgar. Histoire de la campagne de 1815. (Oeuvres complètes, 15). Paris, n.d.
42515.57 Quinet, Edgar. Merlin l'enchanteur. (Oeuvres complètes, 17, 18). Paris, n.d.
42515.58 Quinet, Edgar. Correspondance. Lettres à sa mere. (Oeuvres complètes, 19, 20). Paris, n.d. 2v.
42515.59 Quinet, Edgar. La création. (Oeuvres complètes, 21, 22). Paris, n.d. 2v.
42515.60 Quinet, Edgar. L'esprit nouveau. (Oeuvres complètes, 23). Paris, n.d.
42515.61 Quinet, Edgar. Le siège de Paris. (Oeuvres complètes, 24). Paris, n.d.
42515.62 Quinet, Edgar. La république. (Oeuvres completes, 25). Paris, n.d.
42515.63 Quinet, Edgar. Le livre de l'exilé. (Oeuvres complètes, 26). Paris, n.d.
42515.64 Quinet, Edgar. La Grèce moderne. (Oeuvres complètes, 27). Paris, n.d.
42515.65 Quinet, Edgar. Vie et mort du genie grec. (Oeuvres complètes, 28). Paris, n.d.
42515.66 Quinet, Edgar. Oeuvres complètes de Edgar Quinet. Paris, 1857-70. 11v.
42515.68 Quinet, Edgar. Le génie des religions. Paris, n.d.
42515.68.2 Quinet, Edgar. Les Jésuites. Paris, n.d.
42515.68.3 Quinet, Edgar. Le Christianisme et la revolution française. Paris, n.d.
42515.68.4 Quinet, Edgar. Les révolutions d'Italie. Paris, n.d. 2v.
42515.68.5 Quinet, Edgar. Marnix de Sainte-Aldegonde. 6. éd. Paris, n.d.
42515.68.6 Quinet, Edgar. Les roumains. Allemagne et Italie. Paris, n.d.
42515.68.7 Quinet, Edgar. Premiers travaux. Paris, n.d.
42515.68.8 Quinet, Edgar. La Grèce moderne. Paris, n.d.
42515.68.9 Quinet, Edgar. Mes vacances en Espagne. 5. éd. Paris, n.d.
42515.68.10 Quinet, Edgar. Ahasvérus. Paris, n.d.
42515.68.11 Quinet, Edgar. Prométhée. Paris, n.d.
42515.68.13 Quinet, Edgar. L'enseignement du peuple. Paris, n.d.
42515.68.14 Quinet, Edgar. Histoire de mes idées. Paris, n.d.
42515.68.15 Quinet, Edgar. Merlin l'enchanteur. Paris, n.d. 2v.
42515.68.16 Quinet, Edgar. La révolution précédée de la critique de la révolution. Paris, n.d. 3v.
42515.68.17 Quinet, Edgar. Histoire de la campagne de 1815. Paris, n.d.
42515.68.18 Quinet, Edgar. La création. Paris, n.d. 2v.
42515.68.19 Quinet, Edgar. Le livre de l'exilé. Paris, n.d.
42515.68.20 Quinet, Edgar. Le siège de Paris. Paris, n.d.
42515.68.21 Quinet, Edgar. La république. Paris, n.d.
42515.68.22 Quinet, Edgar. L'esprit nouveau. Paris, n.d.
42515.68.23 Quinet, Edgar. Vie et mort du génie grec. Paris, n.d.
42515.68.24 Quinet, Edgar. Correspondance. Lettres à sa mère. Paris, n.d. 2v.

42515.69 - Individual authors, etc. - 1850-1899 - History, philosophy, etc. - Quinet, Edgar - Individual works

42515.69 Quinet, Edgar. Lettera alla marchesa Arconati Visconti. Città di Castello, 1900.
42515.70 Quinet, Edgar. Allemagne et Italie. Paris, 1846. 2v.
42515.70.5A Quinet, Edgar. Allemagne et Italie. 2. éd. Paris, 1846. 2v.
42515.70.5B Quinet, Edgar. Allemagne et Italie. 2. éd. Paris, 1846. 2v.
42515.72 Quinet, Edgar. La creación. Madrid, 1871. 2v.
42515.74 Quinet, Edgar. France et Allemagne. Oxford, 1908.
42515.94 Aelberts, Alain V. Fatras; poèmes. Liège, 1964.

42516.6 Individual authors, etc. - 1850-1899 - History, philosophy, etc. - Schaeffer

42516.6 Schaeffer, Adolphe. Mélanges d'histoire. Neuchâtel, 1873.
42516.6.5 Schaeffer, Adolphe. Roses et épines. Colmar, 1878.

42516.9 Individual authors, etc. - 1850-1899 - History, philosophy, etc. - Secrétan

42516.9 Secrétan, Charles. Essais de philosophie et de littérature. Lausanne, 1896.

42516.16 - .17 Individual authors, etc. - 1850-1899 - History, philosophy, etc. - Sorel

42516.16 Sorel, Albert. Essais d'histoire et de critique. Paris, 1883.
42516.16.2 Sorel, Albert. Nouveaux essais d'histoire et de critique. Paris, 1898.
42516.17 Sorel, Albert. Pages normandes. Paris, 1908.

42521.1 - .2 Individual authors, etc. - 1850-1899 - History, philosophy, etc. - Veuillot, L. - Complete and Selected works

42521.2 Veuillot, Louis. Louis Veuillot; pages choisies. Paris, 1927.

42521.3 - .18 Individual authors, etc. - 1850-1899 - History, philosophy, etc. - Veuillot, L. - Individual works

42521.3 Veuillot, Louis. Correspondance. Paris, 1884. 9v.
42521.5 Veuillot, Louis. Mélanges. 1. série. Paris, 1860-61. 6v.
42521.11 Veuillot, Louis. Mélanges. 2. série. Paris, 1859-61. 6v.
42521.12 Veuillot, Louis. Le lendemain de la victoire vision. 2. éd. Paris, 1871.
42521.13 Veuillot, Louis. Les odeurs de Paris. Paris, 1867.
42521.15 Veuillot, Louis. Ca et la. Paris, 1891. 2v.
42521.15.5 Veuillot, Louis. Ca et la. v.2. 5. éd. Paris, 1865.
42521.17 Veuillot, Louis. Le fond de Giboyer. 5. éd. Paris, 1863.
42521.18.4 Veuillot, Louis. Les libres penseurs. 7. éd. Paris, 1886.

42521.19 - Individual authors, etc. - 1850-1899 - History, philosophy, etc. - Veuillot, L. - Biography and criticism

42521.19 Fernessole, Pierre. Les origines littéraires de Louis Veuillot, 1813-1843. Thèse. Paris, 1923.
42521.19.2 Fernessole, Pierre. Bio-biliographie de la jeunesse de Louis Veuillot, 1813-1843. Thèse. Tarbes, 1923.
42521.19.3 Fernessole, Pierre. Les origines littéraires de Louis Veuillot (1813-1843). Paris, 1922.
42521.19.10 Veuillot, E. Louis Veuillot. Paris, 1903. 3v.
42521.19.20 Gauthier, E. Le vrai Louis Veuillot. Paris, 1937.
42521.19.22 Gauthier, E. Le génie satirique de Louis Veuillot. Lyon, 1953.
42521.19.24 Casoli, Pier. Di Luigi Veuillot. Modena, 1884.
42521.21 Lasserre, Maurice. Essai sur les poésies de Louis Veuillot. Paris, 1957.
42521.22 Christophe, Lucien. Louis Veuillot. Paris, 1967.
42521.23 Renault, Jules. Louis Veuillot. Paris, 1928.
42521.24 Bontoux, G. Louis Veuillot et les mauvais maîtres des XVIe, XVIIe et XVIIIe siècles. Paris, 1919.
42521.25 Michaud, Eugène. Guignot et la révolution dans l'église romaine. Paris, 1872.
42521.26 Marconcini, Federico. Luigi Veuillot, atleta della penna, 1813-1883. Alba, 1947.

42522.1 - .22 Individual authors, etc. - 1850-1899 - History, philosophy, etc. - Vogüé, E.M. - Writings

Htn 42522.3* Régnier, H. de. Discours de réception à l'academie française. Paris, 1911.
42522.5 Vogüé, E.M. de. Regards historiques et littéraires. Paris, 1892.
42522.6 Vogüé, E.M. de. Spectacles contemporains. Paris, 1891.
42522.7 Vogüé, E.M. de. Le rappel des ombres. Paris, 1900.
42522.8 Vogüé, E.M. de. Devant le siècle. Paris, 1896.
42522.9 Vogüé, E.M. de. Heures d'histoire. Paris, n.d.
42522.10 Vogüé, E.M. de. Histoires d'hiver. Paris, 1885.
42522.10.2 Vogüé, E.M. de. Coeurs Russes. Paris, 1893.
42522.11 Vogüé, E.M. de. Histoires orientales. Paris, 1880.
42522.12 Vogüé, E.M. de. Souvenirs et vision. Paris, n.d.
42522.13 Vogüé, E.M. de. Jean d'Agrève. Paris, 1897.
42522.14 Vogüé, E.M. de. Histoire et poésie. Paris, 1898.
42522.15 Vogüé, E.M. de. Les morts qui parlent. Paris, n.d.
42522.16 Vogüé, E.M. de. Russian portraits. N.Y., 1895.
42522.17 Vogüé, E.M. de. Le maitre de la mer. Paris, n.d.
42522.18 Vogüé, E.M. de. Sous l'horizon. Paris, 1904.
42522.19 Vogüé, E.M. de. Pages choisies. Paris, 1912.
42522.20 Vogüé, E.M. de. Trois drames de l'histoire de Russie. Paris, 1911.

42522.23 Individual authors, etc. - 1850-1899 - History, philosophy, etc. - Vogüé, E.M. - Works about

42522.23 Le Meur, Léon. L'adolescence et la jeunesse d'Eugéne Melchior de Vogüé. Thèse. Paris, 1931.
42522.23.5 Tillmann, Erich. Eugène Melchior de Vogüé. Inaug. Diss. Bochum-Langendreer, 1934.

42522.25 Individual authors, etc. - 1850-1899 - History, philosophy, etc. - Vogüé, C.J.M.

42522.25.80 Cagnat, René. Notice sur la vie et les travaux de Charles Jean Melchior le marquis de Vogüé. Paris, 1918.

42522.32 Individual authors, etc. - 1850-1899 - History, philosophy, etc. - Warney

42522.32 Warney, H. Le chemin d'espérance. Paris, 1899.

42522.36 - .37 Individual authors, etc. - 1850-1899 - History, philosophy, etc. - Weyer

42522.36 Weyer, Sylvain van der. Choix d'opuscules. Bruxelles, 1863. 4v.
42522.36.2 Weyer, Sylvain van der. Choix d'opuscules. N.Y., 1863.
42522.37 Weyer, Sylvain van der. Lettres fur les Anglais qui ont écrit en français. London? 1854?

42524.7 Individual authors, etc. - 1850-1899 - Criticism - Alaux

42524.7 Alaux, Jules E. Études esthétiques. Paris, 1873.

42524.8 Individual authors, etc. - 1850-1899 - Criticism - Babou

42524.8 Babou, H. Lettres satiriques et critiques. Paris, 1860.

42524.9 Individual authors, etc. - 1850-1899 - Criticism - Baldensperger

42524.9 Baldensperger, F. Études d'histoire littéraire. 1. série. Paris, 1907.
42524.9.2A Baldensperger, F. Études d'histoire littéraire. 2d ser. Paris, 1910.
42524.9.2B Baldensperger, F. Études d'histoire littéraire. 2d ser. Paris, 1910.
42524.9.3 Baldensperger, F. Études d'histoire littéraire. 3. série. Paris, 1939.
42524.9.4 Baldensperger, F. Études d'histoire littéraire. 4. série. Paris, 1939.

42524.9 Individual authors, etc. - 1850-1899 - Criticism - Baldensperger - cont.

42524.9.81 Hergešić, I. Zapadmjački pogledi na književnost. Zagreb, 1935.

42524.10 Individual authors, etc. - 1850-1899 - Criticism - Bardoux

42524.10 Bardoux, A. Études d'un autre temps. Paris, 1889.

42524.12 Individual authors, etc. - 1850-1899 - Criticism - Bonneau; Bonnefou; Bredif; etc.

42524.12 Bonneau, A. Curiosa. Essais critiques de littérature. Paris, 1887.
42524.12.5 Bonnefou, Jean de. Dans les débris et sur les ruines. Paris, 1912.
42524.12.9 Brédif, L. Mélanges. Paris, 1910.

42524.13 - .18 Individual authors, etc. - 1850-1899 - Criticism - Brunetière - Writings

42524.13 Brunetière, F. L'art et la morale. Paris, 1898.
42524.13.3 Brunetière, F. Art and morality. N.Y., n.d.
42524.13.5 Brunetière, F. La renaissance de l'idéalisme. Paris, 1896.
42524.14 Brunetière, F. Histoire et littérature. Paris, 1884. 3v.
42524.15 Brunetière, F. Questions de critique. Paris, 1889.
42524.16 Brunetière, F. Nouvelles questions de critique. Paris, 1890.
42524.16.6 Brunetière, F. Discours académiques. Paris, 1901.
42524.16.8 Brunetière, F. Discours de combat. Paris, 1903.
42524.16.9 Brunetière, F. Discours de combat. Paris, 1907.
42524.16.9.2 Brunetière, F. Discours de combat. Paris, 1907.
42524.16.9.3 Brunetière, F. Discours de combat. Paris, 1907.
42524.16.10 Brunetière, F. Lettres de combat. Paris, 1912.
42524.16.12 Brunetière, F. Science et la religion. Paris, 1913.
42524.16.18 Brunetière, F. Variétés lietteraires. 2. éd. Paris, 1904.
42524.17 Brunetière, F. Le roman naturaliste. Paris, 1883.
42524.17.2 Brunetière, F. Le roman naturaliste. Paris, 1883.
42524.18 Brunetière, F. Le roman naturaliste. Paris, 1892.
42524.18.2 Brunetière, F. Le roman naturaliste. 7. éd. Paris, 1896.

42524.19 Individual authors, etc. - 1850-1899 - Criticism - Brunetière - Works about

42524.19.9 Richard, L.R. Ferdinand Brunetière. Paris, 1905.
42524.19.10 Delmont, T. Ferdinand Brunetière. Paris, n.d.
42524.19.12 Allard, Louis. Ferdinand Brunetière. n.p., 1918?
42524.19.15 Curtus, Ernst Robert. Ferdinand Brunetière. Strassburg, 1914.
42524.19.17 Bondy, Louis Joseph. Le classicisme de Ferdinand Brunetière. Diss. Baltimore, 1930.
42524.19.20 Giraud, Victor. Brunetière. Paris, 1932.
42524.19.25 Nanteuil, Jacques. Ferdinand Brunetière. Paris, 1933.
42524.19.30 Hacking, Elton. Ferdinand Brunetière. Madison, 1936.
42524.19.35 Clerk, J.G. La pensée de Ferdinand Brunètiere. Paris, 1954.

42524.20 Individual authors, etc. - 1850-1899 - Criticism - Büchner

42524.20 Büchner, Alexander. Considérations sur le roman moderne. n.p., n.d.

42524.22 Individual authors, etc. - 1850-1899 - Criticism - Capperon

42524.22 Capperon, J. Notes d'art et de littérature. Paris, 1897.

42524.24 - .25 Individual authors, etc. - 1850-1899 - Criticism - Circourt - Works about

42524.24A Huber-Saladin, J. Le comte de Circourt. Paris, 1881.
42524.24B Huber-Saladin, J. Le comte de Circourt. Paris, 1881.
42524.25 Huber-Saladin, J. Le comte de Circourt. Paris, 1881.

42524.26 - .27 Individual authors, etc. - 1850-1899 - Criticism - Circourt - Writings

42524.26 Circourt, Adolphe. Histoire des États Unis...par Bancroft. n.p., 1846-64.
42524.26.10 Circourt, Adolphe. Le mystère des Alpes. Dijon, 1838.
42524.27 Circourt, Adolphe. L'abbaye de Westminster. Paris, 1868. 2 pam.

42524.30 - .31 Individual authors, etc. - 1850-1899 - Criticism - Clement de Ris

42524.30 Clément de Ris, Louis. Portraits à la plume. Paris, 1853.
42524.31 Clément de Ris, Louis. Critiques d'art et de littérature. Paris, 1862.

42524.34 Individual authors, etc. - 1850-1899 - Criticism - Contades

42524.34 Contades, G. de. Portraits et fantaisies. Paris, 1887.
42524.34.10 Contades, G. de. Flers (souvenirs litteraires). Discours. Alençon, 1895.

42524.38 Individual authors, etc. - 1850-1899 - Criticism - Desjardins

42524.38 Desjardins, Paul. Esquisses et impressions. Paris, 1889.
42524.38.80 Heurgon-Desjardins, A. Paul Desjardins et les décades de Pontigny. Paris, 1964.

42524.40 Individual authors, etc. - 1850-1899 - Criticism - Doumic - Works about

42524.41 Beaufils, Edouard. René Doumic. Paris, 1909.

42524.42 Individual authors, etc. - 1850-1899 - Criticism - Doumic - Writings

42524.42 Doumic, René. La vie et les moeurs au jour le jour. Paris, 1895.

42524.50 Individual authors, etc. - 1850-1899 - Criticism - Duret

42524.50 Duret, T. Critique d'avant-garde. Paris, 1885.

42524.55 Individual authors, etc. - 1850-1899 - Criticism - Faguet

42524.55 Duval, Maurice. Émile Faguet. Le critique, le moraliste. Paris, 1911.

42524.58 Individual authors, etc. - 1850-1899 - Criticism - Foulché-Delbosc

42524.58.05 Foulché-Delbosc, Isabel. Bibliografia de Raymond Foulché-Delbosc (1864-1929). Madrid, 1931.
42524.58.81 Bourlaud, B.P. Raymond Foulché-Delbosc, 1864-1929. N.Y., 1933.

42524.60 - .62 Individual authors, etc. - 1850-1899 - Criticism - Frary
42524.60 Frary, Raoul. Essais de critique. Paris, n.d.
42524.61 Frary, Raoul. Mes tiroirs. Paris, 1886.
42524.62 Felix, Jozef. Modernita súčasnosti. 1. vyd. Bratislava, 1970.

42525.5 - .6 Individual authors, etc. - 1850-1899 - Criticism - Gautier
42525.5 Gautier, Leon. Portraits contemporains et questions actuelles. Paris, 1880.
42525.6 Gautier, Leon. Portraits littéraires. Paris, 1881.

42525.7 Individual authors, etc. - 1850-1899 - Criticism - Gazier; Grousset; etc.
42525.7 Gazier, A. Mélanges de littérature et d'histoire. Paris, 1904.
42525.7.19A Grousset, R. Oeuvres posthumes. Paris, 1886.
42525.7.19B Grousset, R. Oeuvres posthumes. Paris, 1886.

42525.8 Individual authors, etc. - 1850-1899 - Criticism - Hello
42525.8 Hello, Ernest. Le siècle, les hommes et les idées. Paris, 1896.
42525.8.81 Serre, J. Ernest Hello, l'homme, le penseur, l'écrivain. Paris, 1904?
42525.8.82 Fumet, Stanislas. Ernest Hello. Paris, 1945.
42525.8.84 Angwerd, P.M. L'oeuvre d'Ernest Hello. Thèse. Sarnen, 1947.
42525.8.86 Bertin, G.M. L'essere e il nulla in Ernest Hello. 1. ed. Milano, 1951.
42525.8.88 Hoh, Friedrich. Ernst Hello. München? 1958.

42525.9 Individual authors, etc. - 1850-1899 - Criticism - Hallays
42525.9 Hallays, A. En flânant. Paris, n.d.

42525.10 Individual authors, etc. - 1850-1899 - Criticism - Hugues
42525.10 Hugues, Edmond. Essais de littérature et d'histoire. Paris, 1880.

42525.22 Individual authors, etc. - 1850-1899 - Criticism - Jal
42525.22 Jal, A. Souvenirs d'un homme de lettres (1795-1873). Paris, 1877.

42526.3 Individual authors, etc. - 1850-1899 - Criticism - Lacour
42526.3 Lacour, Léopold. Trois théâtres. Paris, 1880.

42526.4 Individual authors, etc. - 1850-1899 - Criticism - Larroumet
42526.4 Larroumet, G. Petits portraits et notes d'art. Paris, 1897.

42526.5 Individual authors, etc. - 1850-1899 - Criticism - Lhomme
42526.5 Lhomme, F. La comédie d'aujourd'hui. Paris, 1904.
42526.5.5 Lhomme, F. La comédie d'aujourd'hui. Paris, 1898.

42526.6 - .7 Individual authors, etc. - 1850-1899 - Criticism - Lucas, H. - Writings
42526.6 Lucas, Hippolyte. Curiosités dramatiques. Paris, 1855.
42526.7 Lucas, Hippolyte. Chants de divers pays. Nantes, 1893.
42526.7.25 Lucas, Hippolyte. Portraits et souvenirs littéraires. Paris, 1890.

42526.8 Individual authors, etc. - 1850-1899 - Criticism - Lucas, H. - Works about
42526.8 Pamphlet box. Lucas.

42526.9 Individual authors, etc. - 1850-1899 - Criticism - Langlois
42526.9 Dupire, Noël. Bibliographie des travaux de Ernest Langlois. Paris, 1929.

42526.10 Individual authors, etc. - 1850-1899 - Criticism - Le Blond
42526.10.80 Renaud, Jacques. Maurice le blond. Paris, 193-?

42526.14 - .17 Individual authors, etc. - 1850-1899 - Criticism - Mauclair, C. - Writings
42526.14 Mauclair, C. L'art en silence. Photoreproduction. Paris, 1901.

42526.18 Individual authors, etc. - 1850-1899 - Criticism - Mauclair, C. - Works about
42526.18 Aubry, G.J. Camille Mauclair. Paris, 1905.

42531 - 42532 Individual authors, etc. - 1850-1899 - Criticism - Folios [Discontinued]
42531.20 Gastineau, Benjamin. H. Taine. Paris, 1867.
42532.10 Paris-Murcie. Paris, 1879.

42533.1 Individual authors, etc. - 1850-1899 - Criticism - Marchand
42533.1 Marchand, Alfred. Poetes et penseurs. Paris, 1892.

42533.2 Individual authors, etc. - 1850-1899 - Criticism - Mazade
42533.2 Mazade, C. de. Portraits d'histoire morale et politique. Paris, 1875.

42533.5 - .8 Individual authors, etc. - 1850-1899 - Criticism - Merlet, G. - Writings
42533.5 Merlet, Gustave. Portraits d'hier et d'aujourd'hui, antiques. Paris, 1863.
42533.6 Merlet, Gustave. Causeries sur les femmes et les livres. Paris, 1865.
42533.7 Merlet, Gustave. Hommes et livres. Paris, 1869.
42533.8 Merlet, Gustave. Réalistes et fantaisies. Paris, 1863.

42533.10 - .13 Individual authors, etc. - 1850-1899 - Criticism - Mézières
42533.10 Mézières, A. Pages d'automne. Paris, 1911.
42533.11A Mézières, A. En France XVIIIe et XIXe siècles. Paris, 1883.
42533.11B Mézières, A. En France XVIIIe et XIXe siècles. Paris, 1883.
42533.12 Mézières, A. Hors de France; Italie, Espagne. Paris, 1883.
42533.13 Mézières, A. Morts et vivants. Paris, 1897.

42533.14 - .16 Individual authors, etc. - 1850-1899 - Criticism - Montégut - Writings
42533.14.5 Montégut, Émile. Libres opinions morales et historiques. Paris, 1888.
42533.14.10 Montégut, Émile. Esquisses littéraires. Paris, 1893.
42533.15A Montégut, Émile. Nos morts contemporains. 1. sér. Paris, 1883.
42533.15B Montégut, Émile. Nos morts contemporains. 1. sér. Paris, 1883.
42533.16A Montégut, Émile. Nos morts contemporains. 2. sér. Paris, 1884.
42533.16B Montégut, Émile. Nos morts contemporains. 2. sér. Paris, 1884.

42533.17 Individual authors, etc. - 1850-1899 - Criticism - Montégut - Works about
42533.17.25 Laborde-Milau, A. Un essayiste, Emile Montégut, 1825-1895. Paris, 1922.
42533.17.27 Meunier, Pierre-Alexis. Émile Montégut. Thèse. Paris, 1925. 2 pam.
42533.17.28 Meunier, Pierre-Alexis. Émile Montégut. Paris, 1925.

42533.18 Individual authors, etc. - 1850-1899 - Criticism - Mortier
42533.18 Mortier, Arnold. Les soirées parisiennes. 1874-1884. Paris, n.d. 11v.

42533.19 Individual authors, etc. - 1850-1899 - Criticism - Milsand
42533.19.25 L'Hopital, Suzanne Aline. Joseph Milsand. Dijon, 1955.

42533.20 Individual authors, etc. - 1850-1899 - Criticism - Mockel
42533.20 Mockel, Albert. Esthétique du symbolisme. Bruxelles, 1962.
42533.20.5 Mockel, Albert. La correspondance entre Albert Mockel et Roger Desaise. Bruxelles, 1965.
42533.20.80 Warmoes, Jean. Albert Mockel, le centenaire de sa naissance. Bruxelles, 1966.
42533.20.85 Fondation Charles Plisnier. Catalogue de l'exposition Albert Mockel. Bruxelles, 1967.

42534.1 - .4 Individual authors, etc. - 1850-1899 - Criticism - Paris, Gaston - Works about
42534.1 Société Amicale Gaston, Paris. Bulletin. Paris, n.d.
42534.3 Bédier, J. Bibliographie des travaux de Gaston Paris. Paris, 1904.
42534.3.2 Bédier, J. Bibliographie des travaux de Gaston Paris. Paris, 1904.
42534.4 Bédier, J. Hommage à Gaston Paris. Paris, 1904.
42534.4.10 Rajna, Pio. Gaston Paris; discorso letto alla R. Accademia della Crusca. Firenze, 1904.

42534.12 Individual authors, etc. - 1850-1899 - Criticism - Pavie
42534.12.23 Pavie, V. Oeuvres choisies précédées d'une notice biographique par René Bazin. Paris, 1887. 2v.

42534.14 Individual authors, etc. - 1850-1899 - Criticism - Pons
42534.14.2 Pons, A.J. Coups de plume indépendants. 2. éd. Paris, 1880.

42534.15 - .35 Individual authors, etc. - 1850-1899 - Criticism - Pontmartin - Writings
42534.15 Pontmartin, A.F. de. Causeries littéraires. Paris, 1862.
42534.16 Pontmartin, A.F. de. Nouvelles causeries littéraires. Paris, 1859.
42534.17 Pontmartin, A.F. de. Derniers causeries littéraires. Paris, 1862.
42534.18 Pontmartin, A.F. de. La fin du procès. Paris, 1856.
42534.19 Pontmartin, A.F. de. Causeries du Samedi. Paris, 1859.
42534.20 Pontmartin, A.F. de. Nouvelles causeries du Samedi. Paris, 1860.
42534.21 Pontmartin, A.F. de. Derniers causeries du Samedi. Paris, 1866.
42534.22 Pontmartin, A.F. de. Les semaines littéraires. Paris, 1861.
42534.23 Pontmartin, A.F. de. Nouvelles semaines littéraires. Paris, 1863.
42534.24 Pontmartin, A.F. de. Derniers semaines littéraires. Paris, 1864.
42534.25 Pontmartin, A.F. de. Contes d'un planteur de choux. Paris, 1863.
42534.26 Pontmartin, A.F. de. Or et linquant. Paris, 1859.
42534.27 Pontmartin, A.F. de. Mémoires d'un notaire. Paris, 1856.
42534.28 Pontmartin, A.F. de. Nouveaux Samedis. Paris, 1872-80. 20v.
42534.29 Pontmartin, A.F. de. La filleul de Beaumarchais. Paris, 1872.
42534.30 Pontmartin, A.F. de. Le fond de la coupe. Paris, 1854.
42534.31 Pontmartin, A.F. de. Souvenirs d'un vieux critique. Paris, 1881-82. 10v.
42534.31.10 Pontmartin, A.F. de. Mes mémoires. Paris, 1885-86. 2v.
42534.32 Pontmartin, A.F. de. Derniers Samedis. Paris, 1891-92. 3v.
42534.33 Pontmartin, A.F. de. Souvenirs d'un vieux mélomane. Paris, 1879.
42534.34 Pontmartin, A.F. de. Le radeau de la méduse. Paris, 1871.
42534.35 Pontmartin, A.F de. Péchés de vieillesse. Paris, 1889.
42534.35.5 Pontmartin, A.F. de. Épisodes littéraires. Paris, 1890.
42534.35.10 Pontmartin, A.F. de. Les corbeaux du Gévaudan. Paris, 1868.
42534.35.15 Pontmartin, A.F. de. Contes et nouvelles. Paris, 1859.
42534.35.20 Pontmartin, A.F. de. Le mandarine. Paris, 1873.
42534.35.25 Pontmartin, A.F. de. Les jeudis de Madame Charbonneau. Paris, 1872.

42534.36 Individual authors, etc. - 1850-1899 - Criticism - Pontmartin - Works about
42534.36 Biré, E. A. de Pontmartin, sa vie et ses oeuvres. 1811-1890. Paris, 1904.

42535.3 Individual authors, etc. - 1850-1899 - Criticism - Romey
42535.3.5 Romey, Charles. Hommes et choses de divers temps. Paris, 1864.

42535.5 Individual authors, etc. - 1850-1899 - Criticism - Savine
42535.5 Savine, Albert. Les étapes d'un naturaliste. Paris, 1885.

42535.11 Individual authors, etc. - 1850-1899 - Criticism - Rambert
42535.11 Rambert, Eugène. Études de littérature alpestre. Lausanne, 1889.
42535.11.2 Rambert, Eugène. Études littéraires. Lausanne, 1890. 2v.
42535.11.4 Rambert, Eugène. Mélanges. Lausanne, 1890.

42535.15 - .19 Individual authors, etc. - 1850-1899 - Criticism - Ratisbonne
42535.15 Ratisbonne, Louis. Impressions littéraires. Paris, 1855.
42535.17 Ratisbonne, Louis. Morts et vivants. Paris, 1860.
42535.17.10 Ratisbonne, Louis. Hero et Léandre. Paris, 1859.
42535.18 Ratisbonne, Louis. Les figures jeunes. Paris, 1865.
42535.19 Ratisbonne, Louis. La comédie enfantine. Pt. 2. 77. éd. Paris, 18- .
42535.19.5 Ratisbonne, Louis. La comédie enfantine. Pt. 1. 91. éd. Paris, n.d.

42535.20 - .21 Individual authors, etc. - 1850-1899 - Criticism - Saint-Victor - Writings
42535.20 Saint-Victor, Paul de. Hommes et dieux. Paris, 1882.
42535.20.10 Saint-Victor, Paul de. Hommes et dieux. 9. éd. Paris, 1896.
42535.21 Saint-Victor, Paul de. Les deux masques. Paris, 1881-5. 3v.
42535.21.2 Saint-Victor, Paul de. Les deux masques. Paris, 1880-84. 3v.

42535.22 - .22.49 Individual authors, etc. - 1850-1899 - Criticism - Saint-Victor - Works about
42535.22 Saint-Victor, Paul de. Anciens et modernes. Paris, 1886.
42535.22.9 Delzant, A. Paul de Saint-Victor. Paris, 1886.
42535.22.12 Beuchat, Charles. Paul de Saint-Victor, sa vie, son oeuvre. Paris, 1937.

42535.22.50 - .22.99 Individual authors, etc. - 1850-1899 - Criticism - Scherer
42535.22.50 Scherer, Edmond. Études critiques sur la littérature contemporaine. Paris, 1863-95. 10v.
42535.22.55 Scherer, Edmond. Études critiques de littérature. Paris, 1876.
42535.22.60 Scherer, Edmond. Études sur la littérature contemporaine. Paris, 1885-95. 10v.
42535.22.85 Tremblay, Napoléon. La critique littéaire d'Edmond Scherer. Tuscon, 1932?
42535.22.85.5 Tremblay, Napoléon. La critique littéraire d'Edmond Scherer. Menasha, Wis., 1932.
42535.22.90 Seilliere, Ernest. Romantisme et démocratie romantique. Paris, 1930.
42535.22.95 Gréard, Octave. Edmond Scherer. Paris, 1890.

42535.23 Individual authors, etc. - 1850-1899 - Criticism - Segur, M. de
42535.23 Segur, M. de. Parmi les Cyprès et les Lauriers. Paris, 1912.

42535.24 Individual authors, etc. - 1850-1899 - Criticism - Silvestre
42535.24 Silvestre, Samuel U. Variétés littéraires. Paris, 1858. 2v.

42535.25 Individual authors, etc. - 1850-1899 - Criticism - Simon, P.M.
42535.25.31 Simon, P.M. Temps passé. 2e éd. Paris, 1896.

42535.27 Individual authors, etc. - 1850-1899 - Criticism - Spach
42535.27 Spach, Louis. Mélanges d'histoire et de critique littéraire. v.1-2,3-4,5. Strasbourg, 1864-70. 3v.

42535.30 - .35 Individual authors, etc. - 1850-1899 - Criticism - Stapfer
42535.30 Stapfer, Paul. Causeries guernesiaises. Guernesey, 1869.
42535.31 Stapfer, Paul. Études sur la littérature française. Paris, 1881.
42535.34 Stapfer, Paul. Des réputations littéraires. Paris, 1901. 2v.
42535.35 Stapfer, Paul. Variétés morales et littéraires. Paris, 1881.

42536.4 Individual authors, etc. - 1850-1899 - Criticism - Taillandier
42536.4 Taillandier, Saint-René. Études littéraires. Paris, 1881.

42536.8 - .24 Individual authors, etc. - 1850-1899 - Criticism - Taine - Writings
42536.9 Taine, Hippolyte. Nouveaux essais de critique et d'histoire. Paris, 1865.
42536.10 Taine, Hippolyte. Nouveaux essais. Paris, 1866.
42536.11 Taine, Hippolyte. Derniers essais de critique et d'histoire. Paris, 1894.
42536.11.5 Taine, Hippolyte. Essais de critique et d'histoire. Paris, 1858.
42536.11.7 Taine, Hippolyte. Essais de critique et d'histoire. 2. éd. Paris, 1866.
42536.12 Taine, Hippolyte. Essais de critique et d'histoire. Paris, 1896.
42536.15 Taine, Hippolyte. Vie et opinions de M. Graindorge. Paris, 1870.
42536.17A Taine, Hippolyte. Notes on Paris. N.Y., 1875.
42536.17B Taine, Hippolyte. Notes on Paris. N.Y., 1875.

42536.25 - .43 Individual authors, etc. - 1850-1899 - Criticism - Taine - Works about
42536.25 Weinstein, Leo. Hippolyte Taine. N.Y., 1972.
42536.26 Cresson, André. Hippolyte Taine. 1. éd. Paris, 1951.
42536.27 Boutmy, E. Taine, Scherer, Laboulaye. Paris, 1901.
42536.28 Giraud, V. Essai sur Taine; son oeuvre et son influence. Fribourg, 1901.
42536.28.5 Giraud, V. Essai sur Taine; son oeuvre et son influence. 7e éd. Paris, 1932.
42536.29 Giraud, V. Taine. Paris, 1902.
42536.30 Roe, F.C. Taine et l'Angleterre. Paris, 1923.
42536.31 Roe, F.C. Taine et l'Angleterre. Thèse. Paris, 1923.
42536.32 Taine, Hippolyte. Hippolyte Taine, sa vie et sa correspondance. Paris, 1902. 4v.
42536.32.50 Taine, Hippolyte. Life and letters of Hippolyte Taine 1828-1852. Westminster, 1902. 3v.
42536.32.52 Taine, Hippolyte. Life and letters of Hippolyte Taine 1828-52. Westminster, 1904-08. 2v.

42536.25 - .43 Individual authors, etc. - 1850-1899 - Criticism - Taine - Works about - cont.
42536.33 Taine, Hippolyte. Sein Leben in Briefen. v.1-2. Berlin, 1911.
42536.34 Lefèvre, E. Hippolyte Taine de l'Académie Française. Paris, 1904.
42536.34.6 Giraud, V. Hippolyte Taine; études et documents. Paris, 1928.
42536.34.10 Bailleu, Paul. Hippolyte Taine. n.p., 1893?
42536.34.20 Eustis, A.A. Hippolyte Taine and the classical genius. Berkeley, 1951.
42536.34.30 Kahn, S.J. Science and aesthetic judgment. London, 1953.
42536.34.30.2 Kahn, S.J. Science and aesthetic judgment. N.Y., 1953.
42536.35 Rosca, Dumitru D. L'influence de Hegel sur Taine théoricien de la connaissance et de l'art. Thèse. Paris, 1928.
42536.35.2 Rosca, Dumitru D. L'influence de Hegel sur Taine. Paris, 1928.
42536.35.5 Rosca, Dumitru D. Influenţa lui Hegel asupra lui Taine teoretician al cunoaşterii şi al artei. Bucureşti, 1968.
42536.36 Langwieler, W. Hippolyte Taine. Inaug. Diss. Heidelberg, 1935.
42536.37 Schaepdryner, K. de. Hippolyte Taine. Paris, 1938.
42536.37.5 Schaepdryner, C.J.R.B. de. Hippolyte Taine. Proefschrift. Paris, 1938.
42536.38 Chevrillon, André. Portrait de Taine. Paris, 1958.
42536.40 Jean-Desthieux, F. Taine, son oeuvre. Paris, 1923.
42536.42 Jeune, Simon. Poésie et système, Taine interprète de la Fontaine. Paris, 1968.

42536.45 - Individual authors, etc. - 1850-1899 - Criticism - Troubat
42536.45 Troubat, Jules. Essais critiques. Paris, 1902.
42536.48 Troubat, Jules. Plume et pinceau. Paris, 1878.
42536.49 Troubat, Jules. Le blason de la révolution. Paris, 1883.

42537.16 Individual authors, etc. - 1850-1899 - Criticism - Vayssière
42537.16 Vayssière, Georges André. Les prairies d'argent et le bosquet de la rime. Paris, 1902.

42537.20 Individual authors, etc. - 1850-1899 - Criticism - Weiss
42537.20 Weiss, J.J. Notes et impressions. Paris, 1902.

42537.25 Individual authors, etc. - 1850-1899 - Criticism - Wyzewa
42537.25 Duval, Elga J. Teodor de Wyzewa. Geneve, 1961.
42537.25.10 Delsemme, Paul. Teodor de Wyzewa et le cosmopolitisme littéraire en France à l'époque du symobolisme. Bruxelles, 1967?
42537.25.15 Girolamo, Nicola. Teodor de Wyzewa. Bologna, 1969.

42541.1 - .69 Individual authors, etc. - 1850-1899 - Drama - Folios [Discontinued]
42541.3 Rambeau, A. Augier's L'aventurière of 1848 and 1860. Boston, 1902.
42541.4 Augier, Émile. Paul Forestier. Paris, 1868.
Htn 42541.4.9* Augier, Émile. Les Fourchambault. N.Y., 1878.
42541.6 Banet-Rivet, L. La mort de Lincoln. Paris, 1867-68. 2v.
42541.6.5 Barbier, Paul Jules. Graziella. Paris, 1849.
42541.6.9 Bataille, Henry. Poliche. Paris, 1907.
42541.6.10 Bataille, Henry. L'enfant de l'amour. Paris, 1911.
42541.6.55 Stewart, Nancy. La vie et l'oeuvre d'Henri de Bornier. Thèse. Paris, 1935.
42541.7 Bornier, Henri de. Noces d'Attila. Fille de Roland. Paris, 1880.
42541.7.5 Bornier, Henri de. La fille de Roland. N.Y., 1886.
42541.7.7 Bornier, Henri de. La fille de Roland. Paris, 1897.
42541.7.9 Brieux, Eugène. La petite amie. Paris, n.d.
42541.7.11 Brieux, Eugène. La Française. Paris, 1907.
42541.7.12 Brieux, Eugène. La Française, comédie en trois actes. Paris, 1907.
42541.7.12.5 Brieux, Eugène. La Française. N.Y., 1927.
42541.7.15 Croisset, F. de. Paris - New York. Paris, 1907.
42541.8 Dumanior, P.F.P. Don Caesar de Bazan. N.Y., 1888.
42541.8.5 Dumanior, P.F.P. Don Caesar de Bazan. Paris, 1873.
42541.8.15 Dumanior, P.F.P. Les invalides du mariage. Paris, 1884.
42541.13.12 Fabre, Émile. La maison d'argile. Paris, 1907.
42541.13.15 Fabre, Émile. Timon d'Athenes. Paris, 1907.
42541.13.16 Fabre, Émile. La maison sous l'orage. Paris, 1920.
42541.13.35 Guirand, Edmond. Anna Karénine. Paris, 1907.
42541.16 Henneguy, Félix. Panthéia. Paris, 1874.
42541.17 Hennequin, Alfred. La femme à papa. N.Y., 1885.
42541.17.5 Hennequin, Alfred. Lili. Paris, 1886.
42541.18 Hermant, Abel. Souvenirs du Vte. de Courpière. Paris, n.d.
42541.18.2 Hermant, Abel. Monsieur de Courpière marié. Paris, n.d.
42541.18.5 Hermant, Abel. Les transatlantiques. Paris, 1905.
42541.18.5.2 Hermant, Abel. Les transatlantiques. Paris, 1905.
42541.18.6 Hermant, Abel. Les Jacobines. Paris, 1907.
42541.20 Legouvé, Ernest. Médée. Paris, 1856.
42541.20.9 Legouvé, Ernest. Soixante ans de souvenirs. Paris, 1886. 2v.
42541.21 Legouvé, Ernest. Soixante ans de souvenirs. Paris, 1887. 2v.
42541.21.12 Leroux, G. La maison des juges. Paris, 1907.
42541.21.17 Maeterlinck, M. Douze chansons. Paris, n.d.
42541.22 Monnier, Henry. Scènes populaires. Paris, n.d.
42541.22.5 Pailleron, Edouard. Le monde où l'on s'ennuie. Paris. 18-
42541.23 Pailleron, Edouard. Hélène. Drame en trois actes. Paris, 1873.
42541.24 Pailleron, Édouard. Le monde où l'on s'ennuie. Paris, 1883.
42541.24.5 Pailleron, Édouard. Le monde où l'on s'ennuie. Paris, 1881.
42541.24.6 Pailleron, Édouard. Le monde où l'on s'ennuie. 22e éd. Paris, 1882.
42541.24.10 Pailleron, Édouard. Le monde où l'on s'ennuie. Thèse. N.Y., 1887.
42541.25 Pailleron, Édouard. La souris. Paris, 1888.
42541.25.5A Pailleron, Édouard. La souris, comédie. 29e éd. Paris, 1909?
42541.25.5B Pailleron, Édouard. La souris, comédie. 29e éd. Paris, 1909?
42541.29 Ponsard, François. Oeuvres complètes. Paris, 1865. 2v.
42541.30 Ponsard, François. L'honneur et l'argent. N.Y., 1890.
42541.30.3 Ponsard, François. L'honneur et l'argent. Paris, 1855.
42541.30.5 Ponsard, François. L'honneur et l'argent. Paris, 1862.

Classified Listing

42541.1 - .69 Individual authors, etc. - 1850-1899 - Drama - Folios [Discontinued] - cont.

42541.30.7 Ponsard, François. L'honneur et l'argent. Paris, 1872.
42541.31 Ponsard, François. Le lion amoureux. London, 1886.
42541.31.9 Pottecher, Maurice. Le diable marchand de Goutte. Nancy, 1895.
42541.31.9.5 Pottecher, Maurice. Les spectacles du théâtre du peuple. v.1-4,5-7. n.p., n.d. 2 pam.
42541.31.15 Richepin, J. La marjolaine. pt. 1-2. Paris, 1907.
42541.31.25F Rostand, Edmond. La dernière nuit de Don Juan. Paris, 1921.
42541.32 Sardou, Victorien. Fernande. Patrie. Paris, 1869-70.
42541.34 Sardou, Victorien. Daniel Rochat. Paris, 1880.
42541.34.2 Sardou, Victorien. Daniel Rochat. 9. éd. Paris, 1880.
42541.35 Sardou, Victorien. Divorçons. N.Y., 1885.
42541.41 Jules, F. Un moment de Toute-Puissance. Paris, 1873.
Htn 42541.45* Villiers de l'Isle-Adam, A. Morgane. Saint-Brieuc, 1866.
42541.56 Wolff, Pierre. Le ruisseau. Paris, 1907.

42541.71 - .99 Individual authors, etc. - 1850-1899 - Drama - Pamphlet volumes

42541.71 Magasin théâtral illustré. Paris, 1856- 3v.
42541.73 Pamphlet vol. Théâtre varié. 6 pam.
42541.74 Pamphlet vol. Théâtre varié. 8 pam.
42541.75 Pamphlet vol. Théâtre varié. 6 pam.
42541.76 Pamphlet vol. Théâtre varié. 8 pam.
42541.77 Pamphlet vol. Théâtre varié. 7 pam.
42541.78 Pamphlet vol. Théâtre varié. 5 pam.
42541.79 Pamphlet vol. Théâtre varié. 6 pam.
42541.80 Pamphlet vol. Théâtre varié. 4 pam.

42542.1 Individual authors, etc. - 1850-1899 - Drama - Abraham; Ajalbert; Alexis; Ancey; Arnault; etc.

42542.1.2 Abraham, Émile. L'amour d'une ingénue. Paris, 1868.
42542.1.9 Adenis, E. Le chevalier qui donna sa femme au diable. Paris, 1903.
42542.1.11 Ajalbert, Jean. La fille Elisa. Paris, 1904.
42542.1.11.5 Ajalbert, Jean. A fleur de peau. Paris, 1901.
42542.1.11.19 Alexandre, André. Le sac. Paris, 1888.
42542.1.11.25 Alexandre, André. Le sonneur de Biniou. Paris, 1885.
42542.1.11.30 Ajalbert, Jean. Raffin Su-Su. Paris, 1911.
42542.1.11.35 Ajalbert, Jean. Maître Lacombasse. Paris, 1904.
42542.1.12 Alexis, Paul. La fin de Lucie Pellegrin. Paris, 1888.
42542.1.13 Alexis, Paul. Charles Demailly. Paris, 1893.
42542.1.13.5 Alexis, Paul. Celle qu'on n'épouse pas. Paris, 1898.
42542.1.13.10 Alexis, Paul. Monsieur Betey. Paris, 1890.
42542.1.15 Ancey, Georges. L'avenir. Paris, 1898.
42542.1.16.5 Ancey, Georges. La dupe. Paris, 1892.
42542.1.17 Ancey, Georges. Grand'mère. Paris, 1890.
42542.1.18 Ancey, Georges. Les inséparables. Paris, 1889.
42542.1.19 Ancey, Georges. Ces Messieurs. Paris, 1905.
42542.1.20 Ancey, Georges. Monsieur Lamblin. Paris, 1888.
42542.1.21 Ancey, Georges. L'ecole des veufs. Paris, 1889.
42542.1.24 Ancey, Georges. Théâtre. Paris, 1968.
42542.1.30 Arnault, L. Oeuvres dramatiques. Paris, 1865. 3v.
42542.1.35 Arnault, L. Attilio Regolo e Fiesco. Ferrara, 1930.
42542.1.75 Audouard, O. (Mme.). Il n'y a pas d'amour sans jalousie et de jalousie sans amour. Paris, 18- ?
42542.1.100 Albin de Cigala, Celestin. Le Christ-Roi. Paris, 1906.

42542.2 Individual authors, etc. - 1850-1899 - Drama - Augier - Biography and criticism

42542.2 Parigot, H. Émile Augier. Paris, 1890.
42542.2.5 Morillot, Paul. Émile Augier, 1820-1889. Grenoble, 1901.
42542.2.7 Saint-Victor, P. Le théâtre contemporaine, Émile Augier. Paris, 1889.
42542.2.9 Rainneville, J. Lettre d'un gentilhomme à Émile Augier. Paris, 1862.
42542.2.10 Gaillard de Champris, Henry. Émile Augier et la comédie sociale. Paris, 1910.
42542.2.15 Friedrich, W. Die Entwicklung Émile Augiers bis zu seinen Sittendramen. Inaug. Diss. Zwickau, 1931.

42542.3 Individual authors, etc. - 1850-1899 - Drama - Augier - Complete and Selected works

42542.3A Augier, Émile. Théâtre complet. Paris, 1876-78. 7v.
42542.3B Augier, Émile. Théâtre complet. Paris, 1876-78. 7v.
42542.3.5 Augier, Émile. Théâtre complet. v.3. lost 1947. Paris, 1883-86. 6v.
42542.3.7 Augier, Émile. Théâtre complet. Boston, 1897. 7v.

42542.4 - .26 Individual authors, etc. - 1850-1899 - Drama - Augier - Individual works

42542.4 Augier, Émile. L'aventurière. Paris, 1870.
42542.4.3 Augier, Émile. L'aventurière. Paris, 1880.
42542.4.5 Augier, Émile. The adventuress. N.Y., 1888.
42542.5 Augier, Émile. La cigue. Paris, 1868.
42542.5.15 Augier, Émile. Les effrontés. Paris, 1883.
42542.6 Augier, Émile. Le fils de Giboyer. Paris, 1870.
42542.6.3 Augier, Émile. Le fils de Giboyer. Paris, 1920?
42542.6.5A Augier, Émile. Compte-rendu de débats...fils de Giboyer. Toulouse, 1863.
42542.6.5B Augier, Émile. Compte-rendu de débats...fils de Giboyer. Toulouse, 1863.
42542.7 Augier, Émile. Un homme de bien. Paris, 1857.
42542.8 Augier, Émile. Maître Guérin. Paris, 1865.
42542.8.1 Augier, Émile. Maître Guérin. 2. éd. Paris, 1865.
42542.8.2A Augier, Émile. Maître Guérin. Paris, 1889.
42542.8.2B Augier, Émile. Maître Guérin. Paris, 1889.
42542.8.25 Augier, Émile. Maître Guérin. N.Y., 1924.
42542.9 Augier, Émile. Les méprises de l'amour. Paris, 1865-68.
42542.9.90 Augier, Émile. Le gendre de M. Poirier. 5. sér. Bielefeld, 1854.
42542.10.1 Augier, Émile. Le gendre de M. Poirier. Paris, 1874.
42542.10.2 Augier, Émile. Le gendre de M. Poirier. Paris, 1888.
42542.10.3 Augier, Émile. Le gendre de M. Poirier. 2e éd. Bielefeld, 1865.
42542.10.4 Augier, Émile. Le gendre de M. Poirier. 2. ed. London, 1889.
42542.10.5.9 Augier, Émile. Le gendre de M. Poirier. Boston, 1910.
42542.10.5.13 Augier, Émile. Le gendre de M. Poirier. Boston, 1926.
42542.10.5.15 Augier, Émile. Le gendre de M. Poirier. N.Y., 1936.
42542.10.5.17 Augier, Émile. Le gendre de M. Poirier. Boston, 1936.
42542.10.6 Augier, Émile. Il genero del signor Poirier. Milano, 1854.

42542.4 - .26 Individual authors, etc. - 1850-1899 - Drama - Augier - Individual works - cont.

42542.11 Augier, Émile. Madame Caverlet. Paris, 1876.
42542.12 Augier, Émile. Four plays. N.Y., 1915.
42542.13 Augier, Émile. Jean de Thommeray. 2. éd. Paris, 1874.
42542.14.5 Augier, Émile. La pietra del Paragone. Milano, 1854.
42542.15 Augier, Émile. Poésies complètes. Paris, 1865.
42542.15.5 Augier, Émile. Poésies complètes. Paris, 1857.
42542.16 Augier, Émile. Les Fourchambault. 11. éd. Paris, 1878.
42542.16.5 Augier, Émile. Les Fourchambault. 8. éd. Paris, 1878.
42542.17 Augier, Émile. Les Fourchambault. 15. éd. Paris, 1878.
42542.18 Augier, Émile. Les Fourchambault. 20. éd. Paris, 1879.
42542.18.5 Augier, Émile. Les Fourchambault. 23. éd. Paris, 1890.
42542.18.20 Augier, Émile. Haus Fourchambault. 2. Aufl. Leipzig, 187-?
42542.19 Augier, Émile. Gabrielle. Paris, 1850.
42542.19.5 Augier, Émile. Le jouer de flute. Paris, 1897.
42542.20 Augier, Émile. Gabrielle. Paris, 1856.
42542.21 Augier, Émile. Gabrielle. Paris, 1866.
42542.21.5 Augier, Émile. Home truths; a domestic drama. London, 1860.
42542.21.9 Augier, Émile. Good for evil. London, 18- ?
42542.22 Augier, Émile. Les lionnes pauvres. Paris, 1858.
42542.22.3 Augier, Émile. Les lionnes pauvres. 3. éd. Paris, 1859.
42542.22.7 Augier, Émile. Les lionnes pauvres. Paris, 1880.
42542.23 Augier, Émile. Le post-scriptum. Paris, 1886.
42542.24 Augier, Émile. Le mariage d'Olympe. Paris, 1855.
42542.25 Augier, Émile. La pierre de touche. London, 1897.
42542.26 Augier, Émile. Philiberte. 4. éd. Paris, 1853.
42542.26.1 Augier, Émile. Philiberte. 5. éd. Paris, 1853.

42542.27 Individual authors, etc. - 1850-1899 - Drama - Barbier; Barrière; Bayard; etc.

42542.27.15 Barbier, Jules. La fille du Maudit. Paris, 1864.
42542.27.17 Barbier, Jules. Le franc-tireur; chants de guerre, 1870-1871. Limoges, 1871.
42542.27.17.15 Barbier, Jules. Sous le même loit. Paris, 1872.
42542.27.19 Barrière, Théodore. Malheur aux vaincus. Paris, 1866.
42542.27.20 Barrière, Théodore. Une corneille qui abat des noix. 2. éd. Paris, 1869.
42542.27.20.5 Barrière, Théodore. Une corneille qui abat des noix. Paris, 1862.
42542.27.20.15 Barrière, Théodore. Un monsieur qui suit les femmes. Paris, 1850.
42542.27.21 Barrière, Théodore. Les filles de Marbre. Paris, 1853.
42542.27.21.5 Barrière, Théodore. Les faux bonshommes. Paris, 1856.
42542.27.21.7 Barrière, Théodore. Les faux bonshommes. 3. éd. Paris, 1857.
42542.27.21.9A Barrière, Théodore. Les faux bonshommes. 2. éd. Paris, 1857.
42542.27.21.9B Barrière, Théodore. Les faux bonshommes. 2. éd. Paris, 1857.
42542.27.21.11 Barrière, Théodore. Les faux bonshommes. 4. éd. Paris, 1858.
42542.27.21.13 Barrière, Théodore. Les faux bonshommes. Paris, 1858.
42542.27.21.15 Barrière, Théodore. Les faux bonshommes. Paris, 1906.
42542.27.22 Barrière, Théodore. Les jocrisses de l'amour. v.1-7. Paris, 1865.
42542.27.22.5 Barrière, Théodore. Le bout de l'an de l'amour. Paris, 1863.
42542.27.23 Barrière, Théodore. La vie en rose. Paris, 1854.
42542.27.23.50 Barrière, Théodore. Les bêtises du coeur. Paris, 1871.
42542.27.24 Barrière, Théodore. Le feu au couvent. Paris, n.d.
42542.27.25 Barrière, Théodore. La vie de Bohème. Paris, n.d.
42542.27.26 Barrière, Théodore. Aux crochets d'un gendre. Paris, 1874.
42542.27.26.5 Barrière, Théodore. The old house on the bridge. London, n.d.
42542.27.26.10 Barrière, Théodore. Zerstreut (Tête de linotte). Leipzig, 1893.
42542.27.26.100A Byam, E.C. Théodore Barrière. Baltimore, 1938.
42542.27.26.100B Byam, E.C. Théodore Barrière. Baltimore, 1938.
42542.27.26.105 Byam, E.C. Théodore Barrière. Thesis. Baltimore, 1938.
42542.27.26.200 Barrière, Théodore. A collection of reprints on Barrière. n.p., n.d.
42542.27.27 Barthet, Armand. Théâtre complète. Paris, 1861.
42542.27.50 Bayard, J.F.A. Théâtre. Paris, 1855-58. 12v.
42542.27.55 Bayard, J.F.A. Le gamin de Paris. Paris? 18- .
42542.27.56 Bayard, J.F.A. Le mari a la campagne. 6. éd. Bielfeld, 1871.
42542.27.57 Bayard, J.F.A. La reine de seize ans. 7. éd. Bielefeld, 1870.

42542.28 Individual authors, etc. - 1850-1899 - Drama - Becque

42542.28 Becque, Henri. Théatre complet. Paris, 1890.
NEDL 42542.28.05 Becque, Henri. Oeuvres complètes. Paris, 1924. 7v.
42542.28.2.10 Becque, Henri. Théâtre complet. Paris, 1922-24. 2v.
42542.28.2.12 Becque, Henri Théâtre complet. Paris, 1922. 2v.
42542.28.3 Becque, Henri. The vultures, The woman of Paris. N.Y., 1913.
42542.28.5 Becque, Henri. Les polichinelles. Paris, 1910.
42542.28.6 Becque, Henri. Les polichinelles. Paris, 1910.
42542.28.7 Becque, Henri. Le frisson; fantasie rimée. Paris, 1884.
42542.28.8 Becque, Henri. La parisienne. Paris, n.d.
42542.28.50 Got, Ambroise. Henry Becque, sa vie et son oeuvre. Paris, 1920.
42542.28.53 Dawson, E.A. Henry Becque, sa vie et son théâtre. Paris, 1923.
42542.28.55 Sée, Edmond. Henry Becque, ou Servitude et grandeur dramatiques. 4. éd. Paris, 1926.
42542.28.58 Arnaoutovich, A. Henry Becque; sa biographie, son observation, sa philosophie. Paris, 1927. 3v.
42542.28.60 Arnaoutovitch, A. Henry Becque. Thèse. Paris, 1927. 2v.
42542.28.61 Arnaoutovitch, A. Henry Becque devant ses contemporains et devant la postérite. Thèse. Paris, 1927.
42542.28.65 Blanchart, Paul. Henry Becque, son oeuvre. Paris, 1930.
42542.28.70 Damianov, H. L'oeuvre de Becque au théatre. Thèse. Grenoble, 1927.
42542.28.75 Schilling, Ida. Frauentypen in den Dramen von Henry Becque. Inaug. Diss. Würzburg, 1934.
42542.28.80 Behrens, A. Henry Becque als Kritiker. Inaug. Diss. Würzburg, 1935.
42542.28.85 Möller, G. Henry Becque und Eugène Brieux. Inaug. Diss. Breslau, 1937.
42542.28.90 Descotes, Maurice. Henry Becque et son théâtre. Paris, 1962.

42542.28 Individual authors, etc. - 1850-1899 - Drama - Becque - cont.

42542.28.95 Hyslop, Lois Boe. Henry Becque. N.Y., 1972.

42542.29 Individual authors, etc. - 1850-1899 - Drama - Benière; Bergerat; Bernard; Bernstein; Bisson; Bonnetain; Bornier; etc.

42542.29 Beniére, L, Papillon, dit Lyonnais le Juste. Paris, 1909.
42542.29.8 Bergerat, Émile. Théâtre. 2. éd. Paris, 1900.
42542.29.9 Bergerat, Émile. Le capitaine fracassé. Paris, 1896.
42542.29.10 Bergerat, Émile. Souvenirs d'un enfant de Paris. Paris, 1911. 2v.
42542.29.11 Bergerat, Émile. Séparés de corps. Paris, 1874.
Htn 42542.29.12* Bergerat, Émile. L'amour en république. Paris, 1889.
42542.29.13 Bergerat, Émile. Ours et fours; théâtre en chambre. Paris, 1886. 2v.
42542.29.14 Bergerat, Émile. La Pompadour. Paris, 1901.
42542.29.14.9 Bergerat, Émile. Plus que reine. 3. éd. Paris, 1899.
42542.29.14.15 Bergerat, Émile. Le livre de Caliban. Paris, 1887.
42542.29.14.20 Bergerat, Émile. A Châteaudin. Paris, 1871.
42542.29.15 Bernard, Tristan. L'anglais tel qu'on le parle. 25. éd. Paris, n.d.
42542.29.15.5 Bernard, Tristan. L'anglais tel qu'on le parle. Paris, 19- .
42542.29.16 Bernard, Tristan. Les jumeaux de Brighton. Paris, 1908.
42542.29.17 Bernard, Tristan. Le danseur inconnu. Paris, 1910.
42542.29.18 Bernard, Tristan. Le costand des Epinettes. Paris, 1910.
42542.29.20 Bernard, Tristan. L'accord parfait. Paris, 1912.
42542.29.21.5 Bernard, Tristan. Sa soeur; pièce en trois actes. Paris, 1907.
42542.29.22 Bernard, Tristan. On nait esclave. Paris, 1912.
42542.29.23 Bernard, Tristan. Le petit café. Paris, 1912.
42542.29.24 Bernard, Tristan. Les petites curieuses. Paris, 1920.
42542.29.25 Bernard, Tristan. Les phares soubigou. Paris, 1913.
42542.29.26 Bernard, Tristan. Jeanne Doré. Paris, 1914. 2 pam.
42542.29.27 Bernard, Tristan. Les deux Canards. Paris, 1914.
42542.29.27.5 Bernard, Tristan. Féerie bougeoise; roman. Paris, 1924.
42542.29.28 Bernard, Tristan. Théâtre. Paris, 1908-39. 7v.
42542.29.28.10 Bernard, Tristan. Too much of a good thing. Bangkok, 192-?
42542.29.28.15 Bernard, Tristan. My love, Mon amour. Paris, 1922.
42542.29.28.20 Bernard, Tristan. Le taxe fantôme. Paris, 1919.
42542.29.28.25 Bernard, Tristan. Autour du ring (tableau de la boxe). Paris, 1925.
42542.29.28.30 Bernard, Tristan. Un perdreau de l'année; comédie en trois actes. Paris, 1926.
42542.29.28.35 Bernard, Tristan. Sous toutes reserves. Paris, 1898.
42542.29.28.40 Bernard, Tristan. L'école des charlatans. Paris, 1930.
42542.29.28.45 Bernard, Tristan. Les moyens du bord. Paris, 1927.
42542.29.28.50 Bernard, Tristan. Triple patte. Paris, 1906.
42542.29.28.60 Bernard, Tristan. L'ecole des quinquagénaires. Paris, 1925. 3 pam.
42542.29.28.70 Bernard, Tristan. Jules, Juliette et Julien. Paris, 1929.
42542.29.28.80 Bernard, Tristan. Sketches radiophoniques. Paris, 1930.
42542.29.28.90 Bernard, Tristan. Langrevin père et fils. Paris, 1930.
42542.29.28.100 Bernard, Tristan. Un ami d'Argentine. Paris, 1931.
42542.29.28.110 Bernard, Tristan. Théâtre sans directeur. Paris, 1930.
42542.29.28.120 Bernard, Tristan. Le sauvage. Paris, 1932.
42542.29.28.130 Bernard, Tristan. Le sexe fort. Paris, 1932.
42542.29.28.140 Bernard, Tristan. Le prince charmant. v.1-2. Paris, 1933.
42542.29.28.145 Bernard, Tristan. Le voyage imprevu. Paris, 1928.
42542.29.28.150 Bernard, Tristan. L'intrús (Le danseur inconnu). Barcelona, 1911.
42542.29.28.160 Bernard, Tristan. Contes de Caliban. Paris, 1909.
42542.29.28.170 Bernard, Tristan. La partie de bridge. Paris, 1937.
42542.29.28.180 Bernard, Tristan. Mémoires. Paris, 1926.
42542.29.28.190 Bernard, Tristan. Franches lippées. Paris, 1899.
42542.29.28.800 Bernard, J.J. Mon père Tristan Bernard. Paris, 1955.
42542.29.29 Bernhardt, S. (Mme.). Adrienne. Paris, 1907.
42542.29.29.3 Bernhardt, S. (Mme.). L'aveu. Paris, 1888. 2v.
42542.29.29.5F Bernhardt, S. (Mme.). In the clouds. N.Y., 1880.
42542.29.29.7 Bernhardt, S. (Mme.). Un coeur d'homme. Paris, 1911. 2 pam.
42542.29.29.10 Bernhardt, S. (Mme.). Petit idole. Paris, 1920.
42542.29.30 Bernstein, H. La Rafael. Paris, 1906.
42542.29.31 Bernstein, H. Le Bercail. Paris, 1905.
42542.29.31.3 Bernstein, H. Le Bercail. Paris, 1905.
42542.29.32 Bernstein, H. Le détour. Paris, 1906.
42542.29.33 Bernstein, H. Joujou. Paris, 1903.
42542.29.34 Bernstein, H. Le marché. Paris, 1900.
42542.29.35 Bernstein, H. Samson. Paris, 1908.
42542.29.36 Bernstein, H. Israël. Paris, 1908.
42542.29.37 Bernstein, H. L'assaut. Paris, 1912.
42542.29.38 Bernstein, H. Le détour. Paris, 1912.
42542.29.39 Bernstein, H. La griffe. La marché. Paris, n.d.
42542.29.40 Bernstein, H. Le voleur. Paris, 1907.
42542.29.40.5 Bernstein, H. Le voleur. Paris, 1907.
42542.29.40.15 Bernstein, H. The thief. Garden City, 1915.
42542.29.41 Bernstein, H. La griffe. Paris, 1906.
42542.29.42 Bernstein, H. La rafale. Paris, 1905.
42542.29.43 Bernstein, H. Le secret. Paris, 1913.
42542.29.44 Bernstein, H. Élevation; piece en trois actes. Paris, 1917.
42542.29.45 Bernstein, H. Après moi. Paris, 1911.
42542.29.46 Bernstein, H. Le detour. Israel. Paris, 191-.
42542.29.48 Bernstein, H. Judith. Paris, 1922.
42542.29.49 Bernstein, H. Bakkarat; ein Stück in drei Aufzügen. Leipzig, 1908.
42542.29.50 Bernstein, H. La galerie des glaces, pièce en trois actes. Paris, 1925.
42542.29.52 Bernstein, H. Mélo. Paris, 1933.
42542.29.53 Bernstein, H. Le coeur. Paris, 1937.
42542.29.54 Bernstein, H. Espoir; pièce en cinq actes. Paris, 1936.
42542.29.55 Bernstein, H. Félix. Paris, 1929.
42542.29.55.10 Bernstein, H. Le voyage. Paris, 1938.
42542.29.55.15 Bernstein, H. Le cap des tempêtes. Paris, 1938.
42542.29.56 Bathille, Pierre. Henry Bernstein, son oeuvre. Paris, 1931.
42542.29.60 Berr, Georges. Monsieur Beverley. Paris, 1920.
42542.29.62 Berr, Georges. Miss France; comédie en quatre actes. Paris, 1930.
42542.29.65 Berr, Georges. Azais, comédie en trois actes. Paris, 1926.
42542.29.68 Berr, Georges. Les fontaines lumineuses. Paris, 1936.
42542.29.70 Berr, Georges. Maître Bolbec et son mari. Paris, 1927.
42542.29.72 Berr, Georges. Mon crime! Comédie en deux actes. Paris, 1934.
42542.29.73 Berr, Georges. Le train pour Venise. Paris, 1938.
42542.29.75 Berr de Turique, J. Comme ils sont tous. Paris, 1897.
42542.29.76 Berr de Turique, J. Lettres posthumes. Paris, 1904.

42542.29 Individual authors, etc. - 1850-1899 - Drama - Benière; Bergerat; Bernard; Bernstein; Bisson; Bonnetain; Bornier; etc. - cont.

42542.29.77 Berr de Turique, J. Madame Agnès. Paris, 1893.
42542.29.78 Berr de Turique, J. Le Maroquin. Paris, 1904.
42542.29.79 Berton, C.S. (Mme.). La diplomatie du ménage. Paris, 1860.
42542.29.80 Berton, Pierre. La rencontre. Paris, 1909.
42542.29.81 Berton, Pierre. Les jurons de Cadillac. Paris, 1889.
42542.29.90 Beudin, J.F. Pedro el negro. Madrid, 1885.
42542.29.94 Bilhaud, P. Le gaut. Paris, 1905.
42542.29.98 Bisson, Alexandre. Ma gouvernante; comédie. Paris, 1887.
42542.29.99 Bisson, Alexandre. Les plumes du Paon. Paris, 1907.
42542.29.101 Bisson, Alexandre. Nick Carter. Paris, 1910.
42542.29.102 Bisson, Alexandre. Le député de Bombignac. 2. éd. Paris, 1891.
42542.29.103 Bisson, Alexandre. Le député de Bombignac; comédie. Paris, 1904.
42542.29.104 Bisson, Alexandre. Le député de Bombignac; comédie. Paris, 1906.
42542.29.105 Bisson, Alexandre. Mariage d'etoile. Paris, 1908.
X Cg 42542.29.106 Bisson, Alexandre. Les surprises du divorce. Paris, 1911.
42542.29.110 Bisson, Alexandre. Chateau historique! 6. éd. Paris, 1913.
42542.29.115 Boniface, Maurice. La tante Léontine. 2. éd. Paris, 1895.
42542.29.120 Bonnetain, P. La pelote. Paris, 1889.
42542.29.121 Bonnetain, P. En mer. Paris, 1888.
42542.29.122 Bonnetain, P. Passagère. 7. éd. Paris, 1892.
42542.29.124 Bordise, S. Bureau de renseignements, ouvert à une heure. Paris, 1899.
42542.29.125 Stewart, Nancy. La vie et l'oeuvre d'Henri de Bornier. Paris, 1935.
42542.29.130 Pamphlet box. Bornier, Henri de.
42542.29.135 Bornier, Henri de. Poésies complètes (1850-1881). Paris, 1881.
42542.29.135.25 Bornier, Henri de. Oeuvres choisies. Paris, 1913.
42542.29.136 Bornier, Henri de. La fille de Roland. N.Y., 1895.
42542.29.136.4 Bornier, Henri de. La fille de Roland. 25. éd. Paris, 1875.
42542.29.136.5 Bornier, Henri de. La fille de Roland. 28. éd. Paris, 1875.
42542.29.137 Bornier, Henri de. La lizardière. Paris, 1883.
42542.29.138 Bornier, Henri de. France...d'abord! Paris, 1900.
42542.29.139 Bornier, Henri de. Les noces d'Attila. 3. ed. Paris, 1880.
42542.29.140 Bornier, Henri de. Agamemnon. Paris, 1868.
42542.29.145 Borrelli, V. Alain Chartier. Paris, 1889.
42542.29.175 Bernard, Tristan. Decadence et grandeur. Paris, 1928.

42542.30 Individual authors, etc. - 1850-1899 - Drama - Bouchor, M.

42542.30 Bouchor, Maurice. La dévotion à St. André. Paris, 1892.
42542.30.5 Bouchor, Maurice. Les chansons joyeuses poesies. Paris, 1874.
42542.30.6 Bouchor, Maurice. Poèmes et récits. Paris, 1899.
42542.30.7 Bouchor, Maurice. La légende de Sainte Cécile. Paris, n.d.
42542.30.8 Bouchor, Maurice. Les mystères d'Elensis. Paris, 1894.
42542.30.9 Bouchor, Maurice. Noël ou Le mystère de la nativité. Paris, 1890.
42542.30.9.15 Bouchor, Maurice. A Christmas tale, in one act. N.Y., 1915.
42542.30.10 Bouchor, Maurice. Tobie. Paris, 1899.
42542.30.11 Bouchor, Maurice. L'Aurore. Paris, 1884.
42542.30.12 Bouchor, Maurice. La première vision de Jeanne d'Arc. Paris, 1900.
42542.30.13 Bouchor, Maurice. Les symboles. Paris, 1895.
42542.30.17 Bouchor, Maurice. Cinq pièces, en un acte. Paris, 1908.
42542.30.20 Bouchor, Maurice. Les mystères d'Eleusis, en quatre tableaux, en vers. Paris, 1894.
42542.30.25 Bouchor, Maurice. Dieu le Vent. Paris, 1888.
42542.30.29 Bouchor, Maurice. Il faut mourir. Paris, 1908.
42542.30.35 Bouchor, Maurice. Le mariage de Papillonne. Paris, 1897.
42542.30.40 Bouchor, Maurice. Mystères bibliques et chrétiens. Paris, n.d.

42542.31 - .35 Individual authors, etc. - 1850-1899 - Drama - Bouilhet - Writings

42542.31 Bouilhet, Louis. Hélène Peyron. Paris, 1862.
42542.31.5 Bouilhet, Louis. Oeuvres. Paris, 1891.
42542.32 Bouilhet, Louis. L'oncle million. Paris, 1862.
42542.33 Bouilhet, Louis. Mademoiselle Aissé. Paris, 1872.
42542.34 Bouilhet, Louis. Mademoiselle Aissé. v.1-3. Paris, 1872.
42542.35 Bouilhet, Louis. Madame de Montarcy. Paris, 1856.
42542.35.5 Bouilhet, Louis. Melaenis. Paris, 1857.
42542.35.25 Bouilhet, Louis. Sous peine de mort. Thèse. Rouen, 1919.
42542.35.30 Bouilhet, Louis. Lettres à Louise Colet. Rouen, 1968?
42542.35.35 Bouilhet, Louis. Dernières chansons. Paris, 1872.

42542.36 Individual authors, etc. - 1850-1899 - Drama - Bouilhet - Works about

42542.36.100 Letellier, L. Louis Bouilhet, 1821-1869. Thèse. Rouen, 1919.

42542.37 Individual authors, etc. - 1850-1899 - Drama - Bois

42542.37 Bois, Jules. La furie. Paris, 1909.
42542.37.5 Bois, Jules. Nail. Paris, 1912.
42542.37.10 Bois, Jules. Hippolyte couronné. Paris, 1904.
42542.37.15 Bois, Jules. Les deux Hélène. Paris, 1911.

42542.42 Individual authors, etc. - 1850-1899 - Drama - Bouché, J.

42542.42.5 Bouché, Jacques. Gallet et le Caveau, 1698-1757. v.1-2. Paris, 1884.

42542.44 Individual authors, etc. - 1850-1899 - Drama - Bourdet

42542.44 Bourdet, Édouard. Le Rubicon. Paris, 1910. 2 pam.
42542.44.5 Bourdet, Édouard. L'heure du berger. Paris, 1922.
42542.44.7 Bourdet, Édouard. L'heure du berger. Paris, 1922.
42542.44.10 Bourdet, Édouard. L'homme enchaîné. Paris, 1923.
42542.44.25A Bourdet, Édouard. Captive. N.Y., 1926.
42542.44.25B Bourdet, Édouard. Captive. N.Y., 1926.
42542.44.29 Bourdet, Édouard. La prisonnière. Paris, 1926.
42542.44.30 Bourdet, Édouard. La prisonnière. 6. éd. Paris, 1926.
42542.44.31 Bourdet, Édouard. La prisonnière. Paris, 1926.
42542.44.32 Bourdet, Édouard. Vient de paraître. Paris, 1928.
42542.44.35 Bourdet, Édourd. Les temps difficiles. Paris, 1934.
42542.44.40 Bourdet, Édouard. Le sexe faible; pièce en trois actes. Paris, 1931.
42542.44.42 Bourdet, Édouard. Le sexe faible. 10. éd. v.1-9. Paris, 1931.

42542.45 Individual authors, etc. - 1850-1899 - Drama - Bourgeois

42542.45 Bourgeois, Anicet. Les petites Lachetes. Paris, 1858.

42542.46 Individual authors, etc. - 1850-1899 - Drama - Bourget

42542.46 Bourget, Paul. Un divorce; pièce en trois actes. Paris, 1908.
42542.46.2 Bourget, Paul. Un divorce; pièce en trois actes. Paris, 1908.
42542.46.5 Bourget, Paul. La barricade. Paris, 1910.
42542.46.7 Bourget, Paul. Un cas de conscience. Paris, 1910.

42542.47 Individual authors, etc. - 1850-1899 - Drama - Brieux; Bruno; Burani; Busnach; Cadol; Caillavet; etc.

42542.47 Brieux, Eugène. Les avaries. Paris, 1902.
42542.47.1 Brieux, Eugène. Théâtre complet. Paris, 1921-29. 9v.
42542.47.3 Brieux, Eugène. Damaged goods. N.Y., 1912.
42542.47.5 Brieux, Eugène. Le Berceau. 2. éd. Paris, 1902.
42542.47.5.2 Brieux, Eugène. Le Berceau. Paris, 1908.
42542.47.6 Brieux, Eugène. Blanchette. Paris, 1903.
42542.47.6.5 Brieux, Eugène. Blanchette. 14. éd. Paris, 1910.
42542.47.6.25 Brieux, Eugène. Les remplacantes. Paris, 1902.
42542.47.7 Brieux, Eugène. Les remplacantes. Paris, 1903.
42542.47.7.2 Brieux, Eugène. Les remplacantes. 8. éd. Paris, 1907.
42542.47.8.2 Brieux, Eugène. La robe rouge. Paris, 1913.
42542.47.9.2 Brieux, Eugène. Les trois filles de M. Dupont. 3. éd. Paris, 1910.
42542.47.9.3 Brieux, Eugène. Les trois filles de M. Dupont. 4. éd. Paris, 1913.
42542.47.10 Brieux, Eugène. Resultat des courses. Paris, 1898.
42542.47.11 Brieux, Eugène. Les Hannetons. Paris, 1906.
42542.47.12 Brieux, Eugène. L'armature. Paris, 1905.
42542.47.13 Brieux, Eugène. La couvée. Paris, 1904.
42542.47.14 Brieux, Eugène. L'ecole des belles-mères. Paris, 1902.
42542.47.15 Brieux, Eugène. L'engrenage. Paris, 1902.
42542.47.15.2 Brieux, Eugène. L'engrenage. Paris, 1910.
42542.47.16 Brieux, Eugène. La rose bleue. Paris, 1895.
42542.47.17 Brieux, Eugène. La déserteuse. Paris, 1904.
42542.47.18 Brieux, Eugène. Les bienfaiteurs. Paris, 1902.
42542.47.18.5 Brieux, Eugène. Les bienfaiteurs. 4. éd. Paris, 1910.
42542.47.19 Brieux, Eugène. L'evasion. Paris, 1905.
42542.47.20 Brieux, Eugène. Maternité. Paris, 1904.
42542.47.20.5 Brieux, Eugène. Maternité. 6. éd. Paris, 1904.
42542.47.21 Brieux, Eugène. Simone. Paris, 1908.
42542.47.22 Brieux, Eugène. Suzette. Paris, 1909.
42542.47.23 Brieux, Eugène. Argument of La robe rouge. N.Y., 1904.
42542.47.25A Brieux, Eugène. Three plays. London, 1911.
42542.47.25B Brieux, Eugène. Three plays. London, 1911.
42542.47.26 Brieux, Eugène. La foi. Paris, 1912.
42542.47.27 Brieux, Eugène. La femme seule. Paris, 1913.
42542.47.27.5 Brieux, Eugène. Woman on her own, False gods and The red robe. London, 1916.
42542.47.28 Brieux, Eugène. L'armature. Paris, 1905.
42542.47.30 Brieux, Eugène. Bernard Palissy. Paris, 1880.
42542.47.31 Brieux, Eugène. Les avaries. 33. éd. Paris, 1913.
42542.47.32 Brieux, Eugène. Bourgeois aux champs. Paris, 1914.
42542.47.32.5 Brieux, Eugène. Discours de réception à l'Académie Française. Paris, 1910.
42542.47.33A Brieux, Eugène. Blanchette and the escape. Boston, 1913.
42542.47.33B Brieux, Eugène. Blanchette and the escape. Boston, 1913.
42542.47.34 Brieux, Eugène. The plays of Eugène Brieux. Boston, 1915.
42542.47.35F Brieux, Eugène. Les americains chez nous. Paris, 1920.
42542.47.36 Brieux, Eugène. Artists' families. N.Y., 1918.
42542.47.37 Brieux, Eugène. L'avocat. Paris, 1922.
42542.47.38 Brieux, Eugène. L'enfant; comédie. Paris, 1923.
42542.47.39A Brieux, Eugène. Three plays; Maternity, Three daughters, Damaged goods. 7. ed. N.Y., 1913.
42542.47.39B Brieux, Eugène. Three plays; Maternity, Three daughters, Damaged goods. 7. ed. N.Y., 1913.
42542.47.39.3A Brieux, Eugène. Three plays. 6. ed. N.Y., 1913.
42542.47.39.3B Brieux, Eugène. Three plays. 6. ed. N.Y., 1913.
42542.47.39.3C Brieux, Eugène. Three plays. 6. ed. N.Y., 1913.
42542.47.39.5A Brieux, Eugène. Three plays. London, 1914.
42542.47.39.5B Brieux, Eugène. Three plays. London, 1914.
42542.47.39.10 Brieux, Eugène. Famille Lavolette. Paris, 1926.
42542.47.39.15A Brieux, Eugène. Three plays. N.Y., 1911.
42542.47.39.15B Brieux, Eugène. Three plays. N.Y., 1911.
42542.47.39.15C Brieux, Eugène. Three plays. N.Y., 1911.
42542.47.39.20 Brieux, Eugène. Three plays. 4. ed. N.Y., 1912.
42542.47.40 Bertrand, A. Eugène Brieux. Paris, 1910.
42542.47.41 Scheifley, W.H. Brieux and contemporary French history. N.Y., 1917.
42542.47.45 Bruno, W. Etudes shakespeariennes. 1. série. Paris, 1856.
42542.47.50 Burani, P. Le droit du seigneur. Paris, 1878.
42542.47.60 Burion, A. Une cause célèbre. Paris, n.d.
42542.47.65 Busnach, W. L'assommoir. Paris, 1894.
42542.47.70 Cadol, Édouard. La grand maman. Paris, n.d.
42542.47.71 Cadol, Édouard. Jaques Cernol. Paris, 1870.
42542.47.75 Caillavet, G.A. La Montansier. Paris, 1904.
42542.47.76.2 Caillavet, G.A. L'amour veille. Paris, 1908.
42542.47.77 Caillavet, G.A. Le roi. Paris, 1908.
42542.47.77.5 Caillavet, G.A. Le roi. 22. éd. Paris, 1908.
42542.47.78 Caillavet, G.A. Le bois sacré. Paris, 1910.
42542.47.79 Caillavet, G.A. Primerose. Paris, 1912.
42542.47.79.3 Caillavet, G.A. Primerose. Paris, 1911.
42542.47.80 Caillavet, G.A. La belle aventure. Paris, 1914.
42542.47.80.2 Caillavet, G.A. La belle aventure. Paris, 191-.
42542.47.90 Caillavet, G.A. La belle aventure. Paris, 1920?

42542.48 Individual authors, etc. - 1850-1899 - Drama - Capus; Carré; etc.

42542.48 Capus, Alfred. La bourse ou la vie. Paris, 1901.
42542.48.2 Capus, Alfred. La chatelaine. Paris, 1904.
42542.48.3 Capus, Alfred. Les deux ecoles. Paris, 1903.
42542.48.4 Capus, Alfred. Théâtre: Brignol et sa fille, et petites folles. Paris, 1905.
42542.48.5 Capus, Alfred. Monsieur Piégois. Paris, 1905.
42542.48.7 Capus, Alfred. Notre Jeunesse. Paris, 1905.
42542.48.8 Capus, Alfred. Les passagères. Paris, 1907.
42542.48.9 Capus, Alfred. Les deux hommes. Paris, 1908.
42542.48.10 Capus, Alfred. La veine. Paris, 1902.
42542.48.11 Capus, Alfred. Rosine. 2. éd. Paris, 1901.
42542.48.12A Capus, Alfred. L'oiseau blessé. Paris, 1909.
42542.48.12B Capus, Alfred. L'oiseau blessé. Paris, 1909.
42542.48.13 Capus, Alfred. Un auge. Paris, 1910.
42542.48.14 Capus, Alfred. Les deux écoles. Paris, 1910.
42542.48.15 Capus, Alfred. L'adversaire. Paris, 1904.
42542.48.16 Capus, Alfred. L'attentat. Paris, 1906.

42542.48 Individual authors, etc. - 1850-1899 - Drama - Capus; Carré; etc. - cont.

42542.48.17 Capus, Alfred. L'aventurier. Paris, 1910.
42542.48.18 Capus, Alfred. En garde. Paris, 1912.
42542.48.19 Capus, Alfred. Les favorites. Paris, 1912.
42542.48.20 Capus, Alfred. L'attentat. Paris, 1906.
42542.48.21 Capus, Alfred. Hélène Ardouin. Paris, 1913.
42542.48.22 Capus, Alfred. Ses passagères. Paris, 1906.
42542.48.23 Capus, Alfred. Monsieur Piegois. Paris, 1905.
42542.48.24 Capus, Alfred. Les moeurs du temps. Paris, 1912. 2v.
42542.48.24.5 Capus, Alfred. L'institut de beauté. Paris, 1914.
42542.48.24.10 Capus, Alfred. La traversée. Paris, 1920.
42542.48.25 Quet, E. Alfred Capus. Paris, 1904.
42542.48.26 Noel, C.M. Bourgeoisie française et l'oeuvre de M. A. Capus. n.p., n.d.
42542.48.27 Treich, Léon. L'esprit d'Alfred Capus. 3. éd. Paris, 1926.
42542.48.30 Caraguel, C. Le bougeoir. Paris, 1852.
42542.48.45 Carré, Michel. La courtisane de Corinthe. Paris, 1908.
42542.48.46 Carré, Michel. Faust and Marguerite. London, n.d. 2 pam.
42542.48.47 Carré, Michel. Faust and Marguerite. London, n.d.

42542.49 Individual authors, etc. - 1850-1899 - Drama - Céard

42542.49 Céard, Henry. Les résignés. Paris, 1889.
42542.49.5 Céard, Henry. Tout pour l'honneur. Paris, 1890.
42542.49.9 Céard, Henry. Terrains à vendre au bord de la mer. Paris, 1906.
42542.49.15 Céard, Henry. Sonnets de guerre, 1914-1918. Paris, 1919.
42542.49.25 Céard, Henry. Une belle journée. Genève, 1970.
42542.49.65 Céard, Henry. Lettres inédites à Émile Zola. Paris, 1958.
42542.49.81 Brand, R.F. Henry Céard. Ithaca, 1932.
42542.49.85 Frazee, R. Henry Céard, idéaliste de détrompé. Toronto, 1963.

42542.50 Individual authors, etc. - 1850-1899 - Drama - Chriecki

42542.50 Chriecki, K.E. Zephyrin Cazavan en Égpyte. Paris, 1880.

42542.52 Individual authors, etc. - 1850-1899 - Drama - Clairville

42542.52 Clairville, Louis François Nicolaïe. La corde sensible. Paris, 1863.
42542.52.3 Clairville, Louis François Nicolaïe. Les parisiens à Londres. n.p., n.d.
42542.52.5 Clairville, Louis François Nicolaïe. Les cloches de Corneville. 7. éd. Paris, 1877.
42542.52.9 Clairville, Louis François Nicolaïe. La fille de madame Angot. Paris, 1878.
42542.52.11 Clairville, Louis François Nicolaïe. Les petites misères de la vie humaine. Boston, 1865.
42542.52.12 Clairville, Louis François Nicolaïe. Les petites misères de la vie humaine. 3. éd. Boston, 1869.
42542.52.13 Clairville, Louis François Nicolaïe. Les petites misères de la vie humaine. 3. éd. N.Y., n.d.
42542.52.20 Clairville, Louis François Nicolaïe. La propriété c'est le vol. Paris, 1849.

42542.53 Individual authors, etc. - 1850-1899 - Drama - Coolus; Copeau; etc.

42542.53 Coolus, R. Antoinette Sabrier. Paris, 1906.
42542.53.5 Coolus, R. L'enfant malade. Paris, 1897.
42542.53.6 Coolus, R. Lucette. Paris, 1903.
42542.53.9 Coolus, R. Coeur à coeur. Paris, 1907.
42542.53.10 Coolus, R. Raphael. Paris, 1896.
42542.53.11 Coolus, R. Une femme passa. Paris, 1910.
42542.53.12 Coolus, R. Les amants de Sazy. Paris, 1901.
42542.53.13 Coolus, R. Coeurblette. Paris, 1899.
42542.53.14 Coolus, R. Le marquis de Carabas. Paris, 1900.
42542.53.15 Coolus, R. Les rendez-vous strasbourgeois, et autres. Paris, 1908.
42542.53.16 Coolus, R. L'enfant chérie. Paris, 1906.
42542.53.17 Coolus, R. L'autruche; comédie en 3 actes. Paris, 1923.
42542.53.19 Coolus, R. Pardon, madame, comédie en trois actes. Paris, 1930.
42542.53.22 Coolus, R. Les vacances de Paques Coeurblette. Paris, 1928.
42542.53.25 Coolus, R. Le menage Brésile. Paris, 1893.
42542.53.50 Copeau, Jacques. Les frères Karamazov. Paris, 1911.
42542.53.51 Copeau, Jacques. Les frères Karamazov. Paris, 1921.
42542.53.54A Copeau, Jacques. The brothers Karamazov. Garden City, N.Y., 1927.
42542.53.54B Copeau, Jacques. The brothers Karamazov. Garden City, N.Y., 1927.
42542.53.60 Copeau, Jacques. La maison natale. Paris, 1923.
42542.53.65 Copeau, Jacques. Le petit pauvre. 3. éd. Paris, 1946.
42542.53.74 Cologni, Franco. Jacques Copeau. Bologna, 1962.
42542.53.75 Corneau, André. Belle-petite; comédie. Paris, 1888.
42542.53.80 Anders, France. Jacques Copeau et le Cartel des Quatre. Paris, 1959.

42542.54 Individual authors, etc. - 1850-1899 - Drama - Cottinet; Crémieux; etc.

42542.54 Corneille, P. Richelieu. Paris, 1901.
42542.54.3 Cottinet, E. Le docteur Bourguibus. Paris, 1874.
42542.54.4 Courson de la Villeneuve, R. de. Théâtre. Paris, 1904.
42542.54.9 Crémieux, Hector. Le petit Faust. Paris, 1881.
42542.54.10 Crémieux, Hector. Orphée. Paris, 1860.
42542.54.11 Crémieux, Hector. Théâtre. Paris, 1860-61. 4 pam.
42542.54.75 Crisafulli, H. Le bonnet de coton. Paris, 1900.

42542.55 Individual authors, etc. - 1850-1899 - Drama - Croisset (Wiener)

42542.55 Croisset, Francis de. Théâtre. Paris, 1905. 2v.
42542.55.1 Croisset, Francis de. Théâtre. v.3. Paris, 1921?
42542.55.2 Croisset, Francis de. Le tour de main. Paris, 1906.
42542.55.5 Croisset, Francis de. Arsène Lupin. Paris, 1909.
42542.55.7 Croisset, Francis de. Le feu du voisin. Paris, 1910.
42542.55.8 Croisset, Francis de. Le coeur dispose. Paris, 1912.
42542.55.9F Croisset, Francis de. L'épervier. Paris, 1914.
42542.55.10 Croisset, Francis de. La bonne intention. Paris, 1906.
42542.55.15 Croisset, Francis de. Le docteur miracle. Paris, 1927.
42542.55.20 Croisset, Francis de. La livrée de M. le Comte. Paris, 1928.
42542.55.25 Croisset, Francis de. Les nouveaux messieurs. Paris, 1927.
42542.55.30 Croisset, Francis de. Pierre ou Jack. Paris, 1932.
42542.55.35 Croisset, Francis de. Il était une fais. Paris, 1932.
42542.55.40 Croisset, Francis de. Le vol nuptial. Paris, 1933.
42542.55.45 Croisset, Francis de. La côte de Jade. Paris, 1941.

42542.58 Individual authors, etc. - 1850-1899 - Drama - Curel - Writings

42542.58 Curel, François de. Théâtre complet. Paris, 1919-1922. 6v.
42542.58.5 Curel, François de. Le coup d'Aile. Paris, 1906.
42542.58.6 Curel, François de. L'envers d'une sainte. Paris, 1901.
42542.58.6.5 Curel, François de. L'envers d'une sainte. 4. éd. Paris, 1909.
42542.58.7 Curel, Francois de. La fille sauvage. Paris, 1902.
42542.58.8 Curel, François de. Le repas du Lion. Paris, 1903.
42542.58.9 Curel, François de. L'amour brode. Paris, 1893.
42542.58.10 Curel, François de. L'invitée. Paris, 1899.
42542.58.11 Curel, François de. A false saint. Garden City, 1916.
42542.58.12F Curel, François de. Le danse devant le miroir. Paris, 1914.
42542.58.13F Curel, François de. L'ame en folie. Paris, 1920.
42542.58.14 Curel, François de. La comédie du génie. Paris, 1921.
42542.58.16 Curel, François de. Le coup d'aile. Paris, 1922.
42542.58.18 Curel, François de. L'ivresse du sage. Paris, 1922.
42542.58.20 Curel, François de. Terre inhumaine. Paris, 1923.
42542.58.25 Curel, François de. La viveuse et le moribund; trois actes. Paris, 1926.
42542.58.30 Curel, François de. Les fossiles. Paris, 1900.
42542.58.35 Curel, Francois de. La nouvelle idole. Photoreproduction. Paris, 1899.
42542.58.37 Curel, François de. La nouvelle idole. 7. éd. Paris, 1912.
42542.58.38 Curel, François de. La nouvelle idole, pièce en trois actes. N.Y., 1924.
42542.58.40 Curel, François de. La figurante. Paris, 1896.
42542.58.45 Curel, François de. Orage mystique. Paris, 1927.

42542.59 Individual authors, etc. - 1850-1899 - Drama - Curel - Works about

42542.59.82 Gilbert de Voisins, Auguste. François de Curel. Paris, 1931.
42542.59.84 Richter, Kurt. François de Curel, ein Beitrag zur französischen dramatischen Literatur um die Jahrhundertwende. Inaug. Diss. Grimma, 1934.
42542.59.88 Pronier, Ernest. La vie et l'oeuvre de François de Curel. Paris, 1935.
42542.59.95 Braunstein, E. François de Curel et le théâtre d'idées. Genève, 1962.

42542.60 Individual authors, etc. - 1850-1899 - Drama - Darmont; Dartigues; Decourcelle, A.

42542.60.5 Darmont, A. Argument of the play of Pauline Blanchard. N.Y., 1890.
42542.60.9 Dartigues, L. Répudiée. Paris, 1908.
42542.60.10 Darmont, A. Argument of the play of Leah. N.Y., 1892.
42542.60.701 Decourcelle, Adrien. Les extrêmes se touchent. Paris, 1848.
42542.60.703 Decourcelle, Adrien. Fais ce que dois. Paris, 1856.

42542.61 Individual authors, etc. - 1850-1899 - Drama - Decourcelle, P.

42542.61 Decourcelle, P. Après le pardon. Paris, 1907.
42542.61.9 Decourcelle, P. Service secret. Paris, 1908.
42542.61.10 Decourcelle, P. La rue du Sentier. Paris, 1913.
42542.61.12 Decourcelle, P. Le roy sans royaume. Paris, 1909.
42542.61.14 Decourcelle, Adrien. Je dine chez ma mère. Paris, 1856.
42542.61.15 Decourcelle, Adrien. I dine with my mother. N.Y., 1904.
42542.61.17 Decourcelle, P. L'autre fils. Paris, 1922.

42542.62 Individual authors, etc. - 1850-1899 - Drama - Delacour

42542.62.25 Delacour, A. Le retour du Japon. N.Y., 1890.

42542.63 Individual authors, etc. - 1850-1899 - Drama - Délerot; Demesse; Denayrouze; etc.

42542.63 Délerot, E. Vercingétorix. Paris, 1864.
42542.63.2 Dellard, P. Un amour de Wateau. Valenciennes, 1884.
42542.63.3 Demesse, H. Les mères rivales. Paris, 1889.
42542.63.5 Denayrouze, L. La belle Paule. Paris, 1874.

42542.64 Individual authors, etc. - 1850-1899 - Drama - Déroulède; Descaves; Dieudonne; etc.

42542.64 Déroulède, Paul. La moabite. Paris, 1881.
42542.64.3 Déroulède, Paul. L'hetman. 15. éd. Paris, 1877.
42542.64.5 Déroulède, Paul. Histoire d'amour. Paris, 1890.
42542.64.6 Déroulède, Paul. Le mort de Hoche. Paris, 1897.
42542.64.9 Déroulède, Paul. Marches et sonneries. Paris, 1886.
42542.64.10 Déroulède, Paul. Messire du gueselin. 4. éd. Paris, 1896.
42542.64.12 Florent-Matter, Eugène. Paul Déroulède. Paris, 1909.
42542.64.13 Ducray, C. Paul Déroulède, 1846-1914. Paris, 1914.
42542.64.13.5 Tharaud, J. La morte de Paul Déroulède. Paris, 1914.
42542.64.13.10 Tharaud, J. Paul Déroulède. Paris, 1914.
42542.64.13.15 Chevé. Au chevet d'un héros. Paris, 1915.
42542.64.13.20 Plat, Armand. Paul Déroulède. Paris, 1965.
42542.64.13.35 Ligue des patriotes. La glorification de Déroulède à Metz. Paris, 1921.
42542.64.15 Descamps, E. Afrika; preisgekröntes Drama in fünf Aufzügen. Münster, 1894.
42542.64.18 Descaves, Lucien. La cage. Paris, 1898.
42542.64.19 Descaves, Lucien. L'imagier d'Epinal. 3. éd. Paris, 1919.
42542.64.19.10F Descaves, Lucien. L'humble Georgin. Paris, 1932.
42542.64.22 Descaves, Lucien. La maison anxieuse. Paris, 1961.
42542.64.25 Descaves, Lucien. La préférée. Paris, 1906.
42542.64.26 Descaves, Lucien. La saignée. Paris, 1913.
42542.64.27 Descaves, Lucien. Les chapons. Paris, 1890.
42542.64.27.5 Descaves, Lucien. La colonne. 4. éd. Paris, 1901.
42542.64.27.10 Descaves, Lucien. Le coeur ébloui. Paris, 1926.
42542.64.27.15 Descaves, Lucien. Les fruits de l'amour. Paris, 1928.
42542.64.27.20 Descaves, Lucien. Philémon, vieux de la vieille. 19. éd. Paris, 1913.
42542.64.27.80 Darien, Georges. Les vrais sous-offs; réponse à M. Descaves. Paris, 1890.
42542.64.28 Moselly, E. Lucien Descaves. Paris, n.d.
42542.64.40 Devore, G. La sacrifiée. Paris, 1907.
42542.64.55.80 Durantin, Armand. La moglie di un grand'uomo. n.p., 186-?
42542.64.60 Dieudonne, R. Messieurs les ronds-de-cuir. Paris, 1911.
42542.64.60.8 Dieudonne, R. La bonne aventure. Paris, 1919.
42542.64.1100 Descamps, Frederic. Le billet rose. Mons, 1880.

42542.65 Individual authors, etc. - 1850-1899 - Drama - Donnay; Doucet; etc.

42542.65.1 Donnay, Maurice. Théâtre. Paris, 1912. 6v.
42542.65.2 Donnay, Maurice. Le retour de Jérusalem. Paris, 1804.
42542.65.2.5 Donnay, Maurice. Le retour de Jérusalem. Paris, 1929.
42542.65.3 Donnay, Maurice. L'autre danger. Paris, 1904.
42542.65.4 Donnay, Maurice. La bascule. Paris, n.d.

42542.65 Individual authors, etc. - 1850-1899 - Drama - Donnay; Doucet; etc. - cont.

42542.65.5 Donnay, Maurice. La douloureuse. Paris, 1898.
42542.65.6 Donnay, Maurice. Paraitre. Paris, 1906.
42542.65.7 Donnay, Maurice. L'affranchie. Paris, 1905.
42542.65.8 Donnay, Maurice. Amants. 13. éd. Paris, 1907.
42542.65.8.5F Donnay, Maurice. Amants. Paris, 1921.
42542.65.9 Donnay, Maurice. Lysistrata. Paris, 1896.
42542.65.9.1 Donnay, Maurice. Lysistrata. Paris, 1905.
42542.65.9.2 Donnay, Maurice. Lysistrata. Paris, 1909.
42542.65.9.5 Donnay, Maurice. Lysistrata. Paris, 1919.
42542.65.10 Donnay, Maurice. Oiseaux de passage. Paris, 1904.
42542.65.11 Donnay, Maurice. Phryné. Paris, 1894.
42542.65.12 Donnay, Maurice. La Vrille. Paris, 1902.
42542.65.13 Donnay, Maurice. Le torrent. Paris, 1899.
42542.65.13.2 Donnay, Maurice. Le torrent, in four acts. N.Y., 1899.
42542.65.14 Donnay, Maurice. Education de prince. Paris, 1907.
42542.65.14.2 Donnay, Maurice. Education de prince. Paris, 1906.
42542.65.16A Donnay, Maurice. La patronne. Paris, 1908.
42542.65.16B Donnay, Maurice. La patronne. Paris, 1908.
42542.65.17 Donnay, Maurice. La clairière. Paris, 1909.
42542.65.18 Donnay, Maurice. Chères madames. Paris, 1908.
42542.65.18.5 Donnay, Maurice. Chères madames. 9. éd. Paris, 1928.
42542.65.19 Donnay, Maurice. Ailleurs. Paris, 1908.
42542.65.20 Donnay, Maurice. Les eclaireuses. Paris, 1913.
42542.65.21 Donnay, Maurice. L'escalade. Paris, 1904.
42542.65.22 Donnay, Maurice. L'impromptu du paquetage, pièce en un acte. Paris, 1916.
42542.65.23 Donnay, Maurice. Lovers; The free woman; They. N.Y., 1915.
42542.65.24 Donnay, Maurice. Le théatre aux armées. Paris, 1916.
42542.65.25 Donnay, Maurice. La chasse à l'homme. Paris, 1920.
42542.65.26 Donnay, Maurice. Dialogues d'hier. Paris, 1920.
42542.65.27 Donnay, Maurice. La belle angevine. Paris, 1922.
42542.65.28 Donnay, Maurice. Le roi Candaule. Paris, 1920.
42542.65.29 Donnay, Maurice. Le geste. Paris, 1924.
42542.65.30 Donnay, Maurice. Un homme léger. Paris, 1925.
42542.65.35 Donnay, Maurice. Autour du Chat Noir. Paris, 1926.
42542.65.36 Donnay, Maurice. Lettres à une dame blanche. Paris, 1917.
42542.65.37 Donnay, Maurice. L'ascension de Virginie. Paris, 1929.
42542.65.40 Donnay, Maurice. Mes débuts à Paris. 2. éd. Paris, 1937.
42542.65.42 Donnay, Maurice. Eux. Paris, 1891.
42542.65.50 Le Brun, R. Maurice Donnay. Paris, 1903.
42542.65.62 Treich, Léon. L'esprit de Maurice Donnay. Paris, 1926.
42542.65.64 Duvernois, Henri. Maurice Donnay. Paris, 1928.
42542.65.70 Bathilles, P. Maurice Donnay. Paris, 1932.
42542.65.90 Dorian, Tola. Mineur et soldat. Paris, 1896.
42542.65.100 Doucet, J. Notre ami Pierrot. Paris, 1900.
42542.65.110 Doucet, J. Tales of the spinner. N.Y., 1902.

42542.66 Individual authors, etc. - 1850-1899 - Drama - Dreyfus; Dugué; etc.

42542.66 Dreyfus, A. Jouons la comédie. Paris, 1887.
42542.66.5 Dreyfus, A. On his devoted head. N.Y., 1885.
42542.66.7 Dreyfus, A. La gifle. N.Y., 1890.
42542.66.10 Dreyfus, A. Scènes de la vie de théâtre. Paris, 1880.
42542.66.55 Dugué, Ferdinand. Théâtre complet. Paris, 1891-94. 10v.
42542.66.58 Dugué, Ferdinand. Le vol des heures; poésies. Paris, 1839.
42542.66.60 Dugué, Ferdinand. La semaine de Pâques. Paris, 1834.
42542.66.63 Dugué, Ferdinand. Horizons de la poésie. Paris, 1836.
42542.66.65 Dugué, Ferdinand. L'oasis. Paris, 1850.
42542.66.68 Dugué, Ferdinand. Ismène; comédie en vers. Paris, 1873.
42542.66.70 Dugué, Ferdinand. Théroigne; drame en 5 actes, en vers. Paris, 1887.
42542.66.200 DuGuillet, P. Rymes de gentile et vertueuse dame. Lyon, 1864.

42542.67 - .69 Individual authors, etc. - 1850-1899 - Drama - Dumanoir

42542.67 Dumanoir, M. Les femmes terribles. Paris, 1858.
42542.67.3 Dumanoir, M. Le code des femmes. Boston, 1863.
42542.68 Dumanoir, M. Les fanfarons de vices. Paris, 1856.
42542.68.5 Dumanoir, M. Smiles and tears. Boston, 1871.
42542.68.9 Dumanoir, M. Sous clé; comédie vaudeville. Paris, 1833.
42542.69 Dumanoir, M. Jeanne qui pleure et Jeanne qui rit. Paris, 1860.
42542.69.5 Dumanoir, M. Le gentilhomme pauvre. N.Y., 1883.
42542.69.6 Dumanoir, M. Le gentilhomme pauvre. N.Y., n.d.

42542.72 Individual authors, etc. - 1850-1899 - Drama - Duru

42542.72 Duru, A. La mascotte. Paris, 1881.
42542.72.3 Duru, A. La mascotte. Paris, 1882.
42542.72.5 Duru, A. La fille du Tambour major. Paris, 1880.
42542.72.7 Duru, A. Madame Favar; opera. Paris, 1879.

42543.1 Individual authors, etc. - 1850-1899 - Drama - Dumas fils - Biography and criticism

42543.1 Moreau, F. Le code civil et le théâtre contemporain. Paris, 1887.
42543.1.9 Vattier, F. Réponse à Alexandre Dumas fils à propos de la préface de l'ami des femmes. Paris, n.d.
42543.1.10 Noel, C.M. Les idées sociales dans le théâtre de Alexandre Dumas fils. Paris, 1912.
X Cg 42543.1.11 Bonney, M.T. Les idées morales dans le théâtre d'Alexandre Dumas fils. Thèse. Quimper, 1921.
42543.1.12 Seillière, E. L'évolution passionnelle dans le théâtre contemporain. Paris, 1921.
X Cg 42543.1.15 Pamphlet box. Alexandre Dumas fils.
42543.1.17 Moniquet, P. Les idées de Alexandre Dumas fils. Paris, 1888. 2 pam.
42543.1.20 Gros, Johannes. Une page du romantisme galant; A. Dumas et Marie Duplessis. Paris, 1923.
42543.1.23 Dyssord, J. La vie amoureuse de la dame aux camelias. Paris, 1930.
42543.1.25 Soreau, Georges. La vie de la dame aux camélias. Paris, 1898.
42543.1.28A Schwarz, H.S. Alexandre Dumas fils dramatist. N.Y., 1927.
42543.1.28B Schwarz, H.S. Alexandre Dumas fils dramatist. N.Y., 1927.
42543.1.28C Schwarz, H.S. Alexandre Dumas fils dramatist. N.Y., 1927.
42543.1.35 Lamy, Pierre. Le théâtre de Alexandre Dumas fils. Thèse. Paris, 1928.
42543.1.40 Gheorghin, O. Le théâtre de Dumas fils et la société contemporaine. Thèse. Nancy, 1931.
42543.1.43 Linge, Tore. La conception de l'amour dans le drame de Dumas fils et d'Ibsen. Thèse. Paris, 1935.

543.1 Individual authors, etc. - 1850-1899 - Drama - Dumas fils - Biography and criticism - cont.

42543.1.45 Linge, Tore. La conception de l'amour dans le drame de Dumas fils et d'Ibsen. Paris, 1935.
42543.1.50A Taylor, F.A. The theatre of Alexandre Dumas fils. Oxford, 1937.
42543.1.50B Taylor, F.A. The theatre of Alexandre Dumas fils. Oxford, 1937.

543.2 - .11 Individual authors, etc. - 1850-1899 - Drama - Dumas fils - Complete works

42543.2 Dumas, Alexandre. Théâtre complet. 3. éd. Paris, 1894. 2v.
EDL 42543.3 Dumas, Alexandre. Théâtre complet. 1. série. Paris, 1872-70.
EDL 42543.4 Dumas, Alexandre. Théâtre complet. 2. série. n.p., n.d.
EDL 42543.5 Dumas, Alexandre. Théâtre complet. 3. série. n.p., n.d.
EDL 42543.6 Dumas, Alexandre. Théâtre complet. 4. série. n.p., n.d.
EDL 42543.7 Dumas, Alexandre. Théâtre complet. 5. série. Paris, 1880.
EDL 42543.8 Dumas, Alexandre. Théâtre complet. 6. série. Paris, 1880.
EDL 42543.9 Dumas, Alexandre. Théâtre complet. 7. série. Paris, 1892.
EDL 42543.10 Dumas, Alexandre. Théâtre complet. 8. série. Paris, 1898.
42543.10.25 Dumas, Alexandre. Théâtre complet. série 1-4. v.1-2,3-4. Paris, 1868-70. 2v.
42543.11 Dumas, Alexandre. Théâtre complet. v.3-6. Paris, 1880-85. 4v.
42543.11.2 Dumas, Alexandre. Théâtre complet. v.7. Paris, n.d. 8v.
42543.11.2B Dumas, Alexandre. Théâtre complet. v.7. Paris, n.d.
tn 42543.11.5* Dumas, Alexandre. Théâtre complet. Paris, 1882-93. 7v.
EDL 42543.11.7 Dumas, Alexandre. Théâtre complet. Paris, 1893-96. 7v.

543.12 - .27 Individual authors, etc. - 1850-1899 - Drama - Dumas fils - Individual works

42543.12 Dumas, Alexandre. Antonine. Paris, 1860.
42543.12.10 Dumas, Alexandre. Entr'actes. Paris, 1878-79. 3v.
42543.12.15 Dumas, Alexandre. Nouveaux entr'actes. 5. éd. Paris, 1890.
42543.13 Dumas, Alexandre. Aventures de quatre femmes. Paris, 1856.
42543.13.7 Dumas, Alexandre. Aventuras de cuatro mugeres y un loro. v.1,4,5. Madrid, 1856-57. 3v.
42543.13.33 Dumas, Alexandre. Les idées de Mme. Aubray. 3. éd. Paris, 1867.
42543.13.50 Dumas, Alexandre. The Clemenceau case. N.Y., 1890.
42543.14 Dumas, Alexandre. Le demi-monde. 6. éd. Paris, 1855.
42543.14.2 Dumas, Alexandre. Le demi-monde. 6. éd. Paris, 1857.
42543.14.3 Dumas, Alexandre. Le demi-monde. Paris, 1875.
42543.14.5A Dumas, Alexandre. The "Demi-Monde". Philadelphia, 1858.
42543.14.5B Dumas, Alexandre. The "Demi-Monde". Philadelphia, 1858.
42543.14.9 Dumas, Alexandre. Demi-monde; comedia. Madrid, 1883.
42543.15 Dumas, Alexandre. La dame aux camélias. 6. éd. Paris, 1852.
42543.15.3 Dumas, Alexandre. La dame aux camélias. Paris, 1857.
42543.15.5 Dumas, Alexandre. La dame aux camélias. Paris, 1858.
42543.15.7 Dumas, Alexandre. La dame aux camélias. v.1-2. Paris, 1878.
42543.15.8 Dumas, Alexandre. Camille; or The fate of a coquette. N.Y., 1856?
42543.15.8.5 Dumas, Alexandre. Camille. N.Y., 189-.
42543.15.8.10 Dumas, Alexandre. Camille. Philadelphia, 189-.
42543.15.8.12 Dumas, Alexandre. The lady of the camellias. London, 1902.
42543.15.8.13A Dumas, Alexandre. The lady of the camellias. N.Y., 1902.
42543.15.8.13B Dumas, Alexandre. The lady of the camellias. N.Y., 1902.
42543.15.9B Dumas, Alexandre. Camille; play in five acts. Boston, 1907.
42543.15.10 Dumas Alexandre. Camille. Cincinnati, 1857.
42543.15.11 Dumas, Alexandre. Camille. Philadelphia, 1860.
42543.15.11.5 Dumas, Alexandre. The camelia-lady. Philadelphia, 1857.
42543.15.12A Dumas, Alexandre. La dame aux camélias. N.Y., 1880.
42543.15.15 Dumas, Alexandre. La dame aux camélias. Paris, 1896.
42543.15.18 Dumas, Alexandre. La dame aux camélias. Paris, 1898.
42543.16 Dumas, Alexandre. La dame aux camélias. Paris, 1883.
42543.16.2 Dumas, Alexandre. La dame aux perles. Paris, 1869.
42543.16.3 Dumas, Alexandre. La dame aux perles. Paris, 1878. 2 pam.
42543.16.4 Dumas, Alexandre. La dama de las perlas. 2a ed. Barcelona, 1859.
42543.16.5F Dumas, Alexandre. The lady with the camellias. London, 1887.
42543.16.5.5 Dumas, Alexandre. La dame aux camélias. Paris, 1881.
42543.16.6 Dumas, Alexandre. La dame aux camélias. N.Y., 1880.
42543.16.7A Dumas, Alexandre. La dame aux camélias. N.Y., 1880.
42543.16.7B Dumas, Alexandre. La dame aux camélias. N.Y., 1880.
42543.16.7.05 Dumas, Alexandre. La dame aux camélias. N.Y., 1891.
42543.16.7.08 Dumas, Alexandre. La dame aux camélias. N.Y., 1905.
42543.16.7.1 Dumas, Alexandre. La dame aux camélias. N.Y., 1911.
42543.16.7.2A Dumas, Alexandre. La dame aux camélias. (Camille). N.Y., 1880.
42543.16.7.2B Dumas, Alexandre. La dame aux camélias. (Camille). N.Y., 1880.
42543.16.7.25A Dumas, Alexandre. La dame aux camélias. N.Y., 1924.
42543.16.7.25B Dumas, Alexandre. La dame aux camélias. N.Y., 1924.
42543.16.8A Dumas, Alexandre. La signora dalle camelie. N.Y., 1896.
42543.16.8B Dumas, Alexandre. La signora dalle camelie. N.Y., 1896.
42543.16.9 Dumas, Alexandre. The lady of the camelias. London, 18- ?
42543.16.9.2 Dumas, Alexandre. The lady of the camelias; a tragic drama. London, 18- ?
42543.16.10 Dumas, Alexandre. Camille or The fate of a coquette. Philadelphia, 1880.
42543.16.10.5 Dumas, Alexandre. La dame aux camélias. N.Y., 1885.
42543.16.11 Dumas, Alexandre. Camille. Indianapolis, 1883.
42543.16.14 Dumas, Alexandre. Camille. N.Y., 1925.
42543.16.27.5 Korvin-Krukovskii, P. Les Danicheff. Paris, 1893.
42543.16.27.15 Korvin-Krukovskii, P. The Danicheffs. n.p., 187-?
42543.16.27.25 Korvin-Krukovskii, P. Die Danischeffs. Leipzig, 1886.
42543.16.30 Dumas, Alexandre. Denise; pièce en quatre actes. 3e éd. Paris, 1885.
42543.16.30.15 Dumas, Alexandre. Denise. 31. éd. Paris, 1888.
42543.16.30.20 Dumas, Alexandre. Denise. Paris, 1900.
42543.16.35 Dumas, Alexandre. Le démi-monde. Paris, 1926.
42543.17 Dumas, Alexandre. Diana de Lys. n.p., n.d.
42543.18 Dumas, Alexandre. Diane de Lys. Paris, 1856.
42543.18.5 Dumas, Alexandre. L'étrangère. Paris, 1877.
42543.19 Dumas, Alexandre. L'étrangère. Paris, 1878.

42543.12 - .27 Individual authors, etc. - 1850-1899 - Drama - Dumas fils - Individual works - cont.

42543.19.2 Dumas, Alexandre. L'étrangère. Paris, 1880.
42543.19.3 Dumas, Alexandre. L'étrangère. N.Y., 1881.
42543.19.9 Dumas, Alexandre. Les femmes qui tuent et les femmes qui votent. 22. éd. Paris, 1880.
42543.19.10 Dumas, Alexandre. La femme de Claude. Paris, 1873.
42543.19.12 Dumas, Alexandre. La femme de Claude. N.Y., 1905.
42543.19.15 Dumas, Alexandre. Filles, Lorettes et Courtisanes. Paris, 1881.
42543.19.19 Dumas, Alexandre. Le fils naturel. Paris, 1858.
42543.19.21 Dumas, Alexandre. Le fils naturel. London, 1879.
42543.19.30 Dumas, Alexandre. Francillon. 28e éd. Paris, 1887.
42543.19.35 Dumas, Alexandre. Francillon. 35. éd. n.p., n.d. 2 pam.
Htn 42543.20* Dumas, Alexandre. Ilka. Paris, 1896.
42543.20.5 Dumas, Alexandre. Un paquete de cartas. Habana, 1864.
42543.22 Dumas, Alexandre. La question d'argent. Paris, 1857.
42543.22.5 Dumas, Alexandre. La question d'argent. Boston, 1898.
42543.23 Dumas, Alexandre. L'homme-femme. Paris, 1872.
42543.23.2 Dumas, Alexandre. L'homme-femme. 27e éd. Paris, 1872.
42543.23.5 Dumas, Alexandre. Man-woman. Philadelphia, 1873.
42543.23.25 Charnace, Guy. Reponse à l'homme-femme de M. A. Dumas. Paris, 1872.
42543.24 Dumas, Alexandre. La princesse Georges. 5. éd. Paris, 1873.
42543.24.3 Dumas, Alexandre. La princesse Georges. N.Y., 1881.
42543.24.4 Dumas, Alexandre. La princesse Georges. Paris, 1882.
42543.24.5 Dumas, Alexandre. Le roman d'une femme. Paris, 1859.
42543.24.6 Dumas, Alexandre. Le roman d'une femme. Paris, 1855.
42543.25 Dumas, Alexandre. Trois hommes forts. Paris, 1855.
42543.25.15 Dumas, Alexandre. Une visite de noces. 10e éd. Paris, 1881.
42543.25.18 Dumas, Alexandre. Une visite de noces. Paris, 1912.
42543.26 Dumas, Alexandre. Le Dossier "Tue-la!". Avignon, 1969.
42543.27 Dumas, Alexandre. La vie à vingt ans. Paris, 1856.
42543.27.5 Dumas, Alexandre. La vie à vingt ans. v.1-2. Paris, 1880.

42543.28 Individual authors, etc. - 1850-1899 - Drama - Durantin; Empic; Ennes; Eudel; etc.

42543.28.15 Durantin, Armand. Héloise Paranquet. Paris, 1866.
42543.28.15.2 Durantin, Armand. Héloise Paranquet. n.p., n.d.
42543.28.19 Empic, A.S. Théâtre. Paris, 1840. 2v.
42543.28.25 Empic, A.S. Les six femmes de Henri VIII. Paris, 1854. 2v.
42543.28.29 Dennery, A.F. Le grace de Dieu. Paris, 1841.
42543.28.35 Ennes, Antonie. Un divorce: drame. Paris, 1878.
42543.28.1100 Eudel, Paul. Le mort récalcitrant. Paris, 1898.

42543.29 Individual authors, etc. - 1850-1899 - Drama - Erckmann; Eude

42543.29 Erckmann, Émile. L'ami Fritz. N.Y., 1889.
42543.29.5 Erckmann, Émile. L'ami Fritz. N.Y., 1886.
42543.29.50 Eude, Émile. Le nouveau mystère du siège d'Orléans. Orléans, 1894.
42543.29.55 Eude, Émile. Poëmes johanniques. Paris, 1892.

42543.30 Individual authors, etc. - 1850-1899 - Drama - Fournier, N.

42543.30 Fournier, Narcisse. La vie indépendante. Paris, 1861.
42543.30.3 Fournier, Narcisse. Les absences de monsieur. Paris, 1856.
42543.30.5 Fournier, Narcisse. Comedy and tragedy. N.Y., 185-?
42543.30.15 Fournier, Narcisse. Les nuits de la Seine. Paris, 1852.

42543.31 Individual authors, etc. - 1850-1899 - Drama - Fournier, M.; Fournier, E.

42543.31 Fournier, Marc. Le monde et la comédie. Paris, 1881.
42543.31.1100 Fournier, Edouard. L'hôtesse de Virgille. Paris, 1859.

42543.32 Individual authors, etc. - 1850-1899 - Drama - Fremy

42543.32 Fremy, Arnould. Les maitresses parisiennes. Paris, 1855.
42543.32.3 Fremy, Arnould. Les maitresses parisiennes. Paris, 1856.

42543.34 Individual authors, etc. - 1850-1899 - Drama - Foussier

42543.34 Foussier, E. La famille de Pluiméné. Paris, 1861.

42543.36 Individual authors, etc. - 1850-1899 - Drama - Fabins

42543.36 Fabius de Champville, G. Cyrano Farceur. Paris, 1900.

42543.37 - .38 Individual authors, etc. - 1850-1899 - Drama - Fabre, E.

42543.37 Fabre, Émile. Les vainqueurs. Paris, 1909.
42543.37.5 Fabre, Émile. Théâtre. v.1-2,4-5. Paris, 1920-21. 4v.
42543.38 Fabre, Émile. Les ventres dorés. Paris, 1905.
42543.38.5 Fabre, Émile. La vie publique. Paris, 1906.
42543.38.9 Fabre, Émile. L'argent, comédie en quatre actes. Paris, 1895.
42543.38.10 Fabre, Émile. César Birotteau. Paris, 1910.
42543.38.11 Fabre, Émile. Le bien d'Autrue. Paris, 1898.
42543.38.12 Fabre, Émile. Les sauterelles. Paris, 1911.
42543.38.13 Fabre, Émile. Les ventres dorés. Paris, 1905.
42543.38.14 Fabre, Émile. Un grand bourgeois. Paris, 1914.
42543.38.16 Fabre, Émile. Comme ils sont tous. Paris, 1894.
42543.38.18 Fabre, Émile. La rabouilleuse. Paris, 1936.
42543.38.29 Fabre, Joseph. Jeanne d'Arc. Paris, n.d.
42543.38.32 Fabre, Joseph. Jeanne d'Arc. Paris, 1890.

42543.39 Individual authors, etc. - 1850-1899 - Drama - Fallet

42543.39 Fallet, C. (Mme.). Théâtre de la jeunesse. Lyon, 1852.
42543.39.5 Fallet, C. (Mme.). Le coffret d'Ebène ou Les diamants de l'aieule. Rouen, 1859.

42543.40 Individual authors, etc. - 1850-1899 - Drama - Faramond; Ferrier; Fauchois

42543.40 Faramond, Maurice de. Monsieur Bonnet. Paris, n.d.
42543.40.5 Ferrier, Paul. Fabarin. Paris, 1875. 6 pam.
42543.40.7 Ferrier, Paul. Yvonic. Paris, 1913.
42543.40.9 Fauchois, R. Beethoven et la fille de Pilate. Paris, 1909.
42543.40.10 Fauchois, R. Rivoli. Paris, 1911.
42543.40.11 Fauchois, R. Louis XVII, drame en 5 actes. Paris, 1903.
42543.40.12 Fauchois, R. Mozart; comédie. Paris, 1924.
42543.40.15 Fauchois, R. Comédies. Paris, 1923. 2v.
42543.40.20 Fauchois, R. La leçon de Talma. Paris, 1927.

42543.41 Individual authors, etc. - 1850-1899 - Drama - Figuies; Feydeau, G.; Flers, P.L.

42543.41 Figuies, L. La science au théâtre, comédies. Paris, 1889. 2v.
42543.41.2 Figuies, L. La science au théâtre, drames. Paris, 1889.
42543.41.9 Feydeau, Georges. On purge Bébé! Paris, 1910.
42543.41.10 Feydeau, Georges. Occupe-toi d'Amélie! Paris, 1911.
42543.41.11 Feydeau, Georges. La dame de chez Maxim. v.1-2. Paris, 1914-19.
42543.41.13 Feydeau, Georges. Du mariage au divorce. Paris, 1959.
42543.41.20 Feydeau, Georges. Théâtre complet. v.1,2-3,4-5,6-7,8,9. Paris, 1948. 6v.
42543.41.30 Feydeau, Georges. Four farces. Chicago, 1970.
42543.41.80 Treich, Léon. L'esprit de Georges Feydeau. Paris, 1927.
42543.41.150 Flers, P.L. Le bon Désaugiers. Paris, 1927.

42543.42 Individual authors, etc. - 1850-1899 - Drama - Flers, R.

42543.42 Flers, Robert de. L'eventail. Paris, 1908.
42543.42.5 Flers, Robert de. L'ane de Buridan. Paris, 1909.
42543.42.6 Flers, Robert de. Papa. Comédie en trois actes. Paris, 1911.
42543.42.7 Flers, Robert de. L'habit vert. Paris, 1913.
42543.42.7.5 Flers, Robert de. L'habit vert; comédie. 4e éd. Paris, 1913. 2 pam.
42543.42.8F Flers, Robert de. Le retour; comédie. Paris, 1921.
42543.42.9 Flers, Robert de. Le roi. L'ange du foyer. Paris, 1912.
42543.42.10 Flers, Robert de. Monsieur Brotonneau. Paris, 1923.
42543.42.11 Flers, Robert de. Miquette et sa mère. Paris, 1911.
42543.42.12 Flers, Robert de. Les vignes du Seigneur; comédie. Paris, 1923.
42543.42.15 Flers, Robert de. Romance. Paris, 1926.
42543.42.20 Flers, Robert de. L'ane de Buridan; comédie en trois actes. Paris, 1909?

42543.43 Individual authors, etc. - 1850-1899 - Drama - Fonson; Galipaux

42543.43 Fonson, F. Le mariage de Mlle Beulemans. Paris, 1910.
42543.43.25 Galipaux, Felix. Confetti. Paris, n.d.

42543.44 Individual authors, etc. - 1850-1899 - Drama - Gandillot; Ganem; Gassier; etc.

42543.44 Gandillot, Leon. Vers l'amour. Paris, 1905.
42543.44.2 Gandillot, Leon. Vers l'amour. Paris, 1905.
42543.44.9 Ganem, C. Antar. Paris, 1910.
42543.44.15 Gassier, Alfred. Théâtre romantique. Paris, 1912.
42543.44.20 Gassier, Alfred. Alceste. Paris, 1891.
42543.44.50 Morens, Antonio de. Refutacion al drama de Alfredo Gassier "Juárez ó la guerra de Mexico". Mexico, 1887.

42543.45 Individual authors, etc. - 1850-1899 - Drama - Gavault

42543.45 Gavault, Paul. Le bonheur de Jacqueline. Paris, 1908.
42543.45.5 Gavault, Paul. La petite chocolatière. Paris, 1909.
42543.45.6 Gavault, Paul. Le bonheur sous la main. Paris, 1912.
42543.45.7 Gavault, Paul. L'idée de Françoise. Paris, 1912.
42543.45.8 Gavault, Paul. Mlle Josette, ma femme. Paris, 1907.
42543.45.8.2 Gavault, Paul. Mlle Josette, ma femme. Paris, 1907.
42543.45.9 Gavault, Paul. Le mannequin. Paris, 1914.
42543.45.10F Gavault, Paul. Ma tante d'Honfleur: comédie-bouffe. Paris, 1914.
42543.45.15 Gavault, Paul. Manu militari! Paris, 1923.
42543.45.20 Gavault, Paul. La dette. Paris, 1927.
42543.45.25 Gavault, Paul. Fin de rêve. Paris, 1904.
42543.45.30 Gavault, Paul. Family-hotel. Paris, 1911.
42543.45.35 Gavault, Paul. Les femmes de Paille. Paris, 1904.
42543.45.40 Gavault, Paul. La petite Madame Dubois. Paris, 1908.
42543.45.46 Gavault, Paul. Monsieur l'Adjoint. Paris, 1922.
42543.45.50 Gavault, Paul. Le petit Guignol. Paris, 1897.
42543.45.56 Gavault, Paul. Les Dupont. Paris, 1903.
42543.45.60 Gavault, Paul. Le passant. Paris, 1894.
42543.45.65 Gavault, Paul. Napoléon malgré lui. Paris, 1908.
42543.45.70 Gavault, Paul. Une affaire scandaleuse. Paris, 1905.
42543.45.75 Gavault, Paul. Plutus. Paris, 1896.
42543.45.80 Gavault, Paul. L'inconnue. Paris, 1903.
42543.45.85 Gavault, Paul. Madame Flirt. Paris, 191-.
42543.45.90 Gavault, Paul. L'enfant du miracle. Paris, 1903.

42543.46 Individual authors, etc. - 1850-1899 - Drama - Geffroy

42543.46 Geffroy, Gustave. L'apprentie. Paris, 1908.

42543.47 Individual authors, etc. - 1850-1899 - Drama - Giocosa

42543.47 Giocosa, J. Comme les feuilles. Paris, 1909.

42543.48 Individual authors, etc. - 1850-1899 - Drama - Giron

42543.48 Giron, A. Un soir des saturnales. Paris, 1901.

42543.49 Individual authors, etc. - 1850-1899 - Drama - Glatigny

42543.49 Glatigny, Albert. Théâtre. v.1-5. Paris, 1867-72.
42543.49.6 Glatigny, Albert. Poésies complètes. Paris, 1922?
42543.49.7 Glatigny, Albert. Lettres d'Albert Glatigny à Théodore de Bainville. Paris, 1923.
42543.49.8 Glatigny, Albert. Le bois. Paris, 1870.
42543.49.10 Glatigny, Albert. Le jour de l'an d'un vacabond. Paris, n.d.
42543.49.15 Glatigny, Albert. Lettres inédites. Rouen, 1932.
42543.49.18 Reymond, Jean. Albert Glatigny: la vie, l'homme, le poète. Thèse. Paris, 1936.
42543.49.20 Reymond, Jean. Albert Glatigny; la vie, l'homme, le poète. Paris, 1936.

42543.51 Individual authors, etc. - 1850-1899 - Drama - Gohier

42543.51 Gohier, Urbain. Spartacus. Paris, n.d.
42543.51.25 Gohier, Urbain. Spartacus. Paris, 1926.
42543.51.72 Gohier, Urbain. Mon jubilé, après cinquante années de journalisme, 1884-1934. 3e éd. Paris, 1937.

42543.53 - .55 Individual authors, etc. - 1850-1899 - Drama - Gondinet

42543.53A Gondinet, Edmond. Théâtre complet. Paris, 1897. 6v.
42543.53B Gondinet, Edmond. Théâtre complet. Paris, 1897. 6v.
42543.54 Gondinet, Edmond. La belle madame Donis. Paris, 1878.
42543.54.5 Gondinet, Edmond. Le club. Paris, 1878.
42543.54.6 Gondinet, Edmond. La cravate blanche. Paris, 1873.
42543.54.7 Gondinet, Edmond. Les grandes demoiselles. Paris, 1874.
42543.54.8 Gondinet, Edmond. Le homard. Paris, 1878.
42543.54.9 Gondinet, Edmond. Johathan. 2d éd. Paris, 1880.
42543.54.10 Gondinet, Edmond. Les tapageurs. Paris, 1879.
42543.54.11 Gondinet, Edmond. Le roi l'a dit. Paris, 1873.

42543.53 - .55 Individual authors, etc. - 1850-1899 - Drama - Gondinet - cont.

42543.54.12 Gondinet, Edmond. Gravaut Minard et cie; comédie. Paris, 1875.
42543.54.13 Gondinet, Edmond. Jean de Nivelle; opéra-comique. Paris, 1880.
42543.54.16 Gondinet, Edmond. Un parisien. Paris, 1886.
42543.55 Gondinet, Edmond. Sous cloche. Paris, 1864.
42543.55.81 Stolle, Hermann. Das Komische bei Gondinet. Inaug. Diss. Rostock, 1933.

42543.56 Individual authors, etc. - 1850-1899 - Drama - Grenet-Dancourt

42543.56.30 Grenet-Dancourt, Ernest. La scène à faire. Paris, 1890.

42543.57 Individual authors, etc. - 1850-1899 - Drama - Goury

42543.57 Goury, G. Vercingetorix. Paris, 1894.

42543.60 Individual authors, etc. - 1850-1899 - Drama - Grandmougin

42543.60 Grandmougin, Charles. Le Christ. Paris, 1892.
42543.60.3F Grandmougin, Charles. L'enfant Jésus. Paris, 1892.
42543.60.5 Grandmougin, Charles. Visions chrétiennes. Paris, 1899.
42543.60.8 Grandmougin, Charles. Prométhée. Paris, 1878.
42543.60.12 Grandmougin, Charles. Le sang du Calvaire. Paris, 1905.
42543.60.15 Grandmougin, Charles. Yvonne. Paris, 1885.
42543.60.16 Grandmougin, Charles. L'empereur 1807-1821. Paris, 1893.
42543.60.20 Grandmougin, Charles. Le réveillon. Paris, 1892.
42543.60.25 Grandmougin, Charles. Aryénis. Paris, 1891.

42543.61 Individual authors, etc. - 1850-1899 - Drama - Guinon; Guillemot

42543.61 Guinon, Albert. Décadence. Paris, 1904.
42543.61.5 Guinon, Albert. Deux pièces. Seul et À qui la faute? Paris, 1892.
42543.61.9 Guinon, Albert. Le partage. Paris, 1906.
42543.61.10 Guinon, Albert. Le bonheur. Paris, 1911.
42543.61.19 Guinon, Albert. Son père. Paris, 1907.
42543.61.150 Guillemot, Jules. Une heure en gare; comédie. Paris, 1875.

42543.62 Individual authors, etc. - 1850-1899 - Drama - Guiard; Guiraud; Haraucourt; Hennique; etc.

42543.62 Guinon, Albert. Les jobards. Paris, 1898.
42543.62.9 Guinon, Albert. Le jong. Paris, 1903.
42543.62.20 Guitry, Sacha. Le veilleur de nuit. Paris, 1911.
42543.62.23 Guiard, Émile. Mon fils. Paris, 1882.
42543.62.23.5 Guiard, Émile. Poésies. Paris, 1889.
42543.62.24 Guiard, Émile. Feu de paille. Paris, 1885.
42543.62.25 Guiraud, E. Marie-Victoire. Paris, 1911.
42543.62.26 Guiraud, E. Vautrin. Paris, 1923.
42543.62.27 Guiraud, E. Une femme. Paris, 1925.
42543.62.28 Guiraud, E. Le bonheur de jour. Paris, 1927.
42543.62.29 Haraucourt, Edmond. Héro et Léandre. Paris, 1902.
42543.62.30 Haraucourt, Edmond. La passion. Paris, 1904.
42543.62.31 Haraucourt, Edmond. Les Oberlé. Paris, 1905.
42543.62.32 Haraucourt, Edmond. Don Juan de Mañara. Paris, 1898.
42543.62.33 Haraucourt, Edmond. Le peur. Paris, 1907.
42543.62.34 Haraucourt, Edmond. Trumaille et Pélisson. Paris, 1909.
42543.62.35 Haraucourt, Edmond. L'ame nue. Paris, 1908.
42543.62.36 Haraucourt, Edmond. Seul. Paris, 1908.
42543.62.37 Haraucourt, Edmond. Les naufragés. Paris, 1902.
42543.62.38 Haraucourt, Edmond. Amis. Paris, 1887.
42543.62.39 Haraucourt, Edmond. Les Oberlé. Paris, 1905.
42543.62.40 Haraucourt, Edmond. Les Oberlé. Paris, 1905.
42543.62.45 Haraucourt, Edmond. Shylock. Paris, 1918.
Htn 42543.62.47* Haraucourt, Edmond. L'effort. Paris, 1894.
42543.62.50 Haraucourt, Edmond. Circé. Paris, 1907.
42543.62.52 Haraucourt, Edmond. Le livre de mon chien. Paris, 1939.
42543.62.52.5 Haraucourt, Edmond. Mémoires des jours et des gens. Paris, 1946.
42543.62.55 Heller, Louie R. André Chénier. N.Y., 1895.
42543.62.75 Hennequin, Maurice. Heureuse. Paris, 1903.
Htn 42543.62.85* Hennique, Léon. L'accident de Monsieur Hébert. Paris, 1884.
42543.62.88 Hennique, Léon. Benjamin Royes. Bruxelles, 18- ?
Htn 42543.62.89* Hennique, Léon. Les hauts faits de M. de Ponthau. Paris, 1880.
42543.62.90 Hennique, Léon. Jacques Damour. Paris, 1887.
42543.62.91 Hennique, Léon. Esther Brandès. Paris, 1887.
42543.62.92 Hennique, Léon. Amour. Paris, 1890.
42543.62.93 Hennique, Léon. Pierrot Sceptique. Paris, 1881.
42543.62.94 Hennique, Léon. Poeuf. Paris, 1887.
42543.62.96 Hennique, Léon. Minnie Brandon. Paris, 1899.
42543.62.100 Valentin, N. Mon père Léon Hennique. Paris, 1959.

42543.63 - .67 Individual authors, etc. - 1850-1899 - Drama - Hermant

42543.63 Hermant, Abel. La belle Madame Héber. Paris, 1905.
42543.63.3 Hermant, Abel. Chronique du cadet de Coutras. Paris, 1909.
42543.63.5 Hermant, Abel. Confession d'un homme d'aujourd'hui. Paris, 1904.
42543.63.7 Hermant, Abel. Coutras voyage. Paris, 1912.
42543.63.9 Hermant, Abel. La discorde. Paris, 1907.
42543.63.10 Hermant, Abel. La biche relancée. Paris, 1911.
42543.64 Hermant, Abel. Les grands bourgeois. Paris, 1906.
42543.64.5 Hermant, Abel. La carrière. Paris, 1894.
42543.64.10 Hermant, Abel. Théâtre des deux mondes. Paris, 1899.
42543.64.15A Hermant, Abel. Dernier et premier amour. Paris, 1923.
42543.64.15B Hermant, Abel. Dernier et premier amour. 2e éd. Paris, 1923.
42543.64.20 Hermant, Abel. Last and first love. N.Y., 1950.
42543.65 Hermant, Abel. L'empreinte. Paris, 1900.
42543.65.5 Hermant, Abel. L'esbroufe. Paris, n.d.
42543.65.6 Hermant, Abel. Le Fanbourg. Paris, 1900.
42543.65.6.25 Hermant, Abel. Le loyal serviteur. 17e éd. Paris, 1923.
42543.65.7 Hermant, Abel. La meute. Paris, 1896.
42543.65.7.10 Hermant, Abel. La meute, Sylvie. Paris, 1914.
42543.65.8 Hermant, Abel. Histoire amoureuse de Fanfan. Paris, 1917.
42543.65.9 Hermant, Abel. Monsieur de Courpière. Paris, 1907.
42543.65.10 Hermant, Abel. M. Rabosson. Paris, 1884.
42543.65.10.15 Hermant, Abel. Le proces du très honorable lord. 2e éd. Paris, 1923.
42543.65.11 Hermant, Abel. Le joyeux garçon. Paris, 1914.
42543.65.12 Hermant, Abel. L'autre aventure du joyeux garçon. Paris, 1916.
42543.65.13 Hermant, Abel. Le rival inconnu. Paris, 1918.
42543.65.14 Hermant, Abel. Heures de guerre de la famille Valadier. 18e éd. Paris, 1915.
42543.65.15 Hermant, Abel. Heures de guerre de la famille Valadier. 15e éd. Paris, 1915.

42543.63 - .67 Individual authors, etc. - 1850-1899 - Drama - Hermant - cont.

42543.65.17 Hermant, Abel. Le suborneur. 18e éd. Paris, 1923.
42543.65.19 Hermant, Abel. Trains de luxe. Paris, 1909.
42543.65.20 Hermant, Abel. Trains de luxe. Paris, n.d.
42543.65.25 Hermant, Abel. La journée brève. Paris, 1920.
42543.65.30 Hermant, Abel. Le crépuscule tragique. Paris, 1921.
42543.65.35 Hermant, Abel. L'aube ardente. 9e éd. Paris, 1919.
42543.65.37 Hermant, Abel. Les renards. Paris, 1912.
42543.65.39 Hermant, Abel. Histoires héroïques de mon ami Jean. Paris, 1917.
42543.65.50 Hermant, Abel. La fameuse comédienne. 7e éd. Paris, 1913?
42543.65.55 Hermant, Abel. Eddy et Paddy. Paris, 1931.
42543.65.60 Hermant, Abel. Chroniques de Lancelot du temps. (1933-1936). Paris, 1936-38. 2v.
42543.65.66 Hermant, Abel. Les épaves; roman. Paris, 1931.
42543.65.70 Hermant, Abel. Souvenirs de la vie mondaine. Paris, 1935.
42543.65.75 Hermant, Abel. Le fremier pas. Paris, 1910.
42543.66 Hermant, Abel. Essais de critique. Paris, 1912.
42543.67 Hermant, Abel. Les transatlantiques. Paris, 1898.

42543.68 Individual authors, etc. - 1850-1899 - Drama - Halévy, L.; Hennequin

42543.68 Halévy, Leon. Ce que fille veut. Paris, 1858.
42543.68.5 Halévy, Leon. Un mari, s'il vous plait. Paris, 1843.
42543.68.19 Hennequin, Alfred. Niniche: vaudeville en trois actes. Paris, 1878.
42543.68.20 Hennequin, Alfred. A woman of sense and a hair powder plot. N.Y., 1896.

42543.69 Individual authors, etc. - 1850-1899 - Drama - Hervieu; Hervilly; Humières; Ivry

42543.69 Hervieu, Paul. La course du flambeau. Paris, 1909.
42543.69.5 Hervieu, Paul. Connais-toi. Paris, 1909.
42543.69.7 Hervieu, Paul. Le dédale. Paris, n.d.
42543.69.7.15 Hervieu, Paul. The labyrinth. N.Y., 1913.
42543.69.8 Hervieu, Paul. The trail of the torch; play in 4 acts. N.Y., 1915. 2v.
42543.69.9 Hervieu, Paul. The trail of the torch; play in 4 acts. Garden City, 1917.
42543.69.12 Hervieu, Paul. Enchained, a play in 3 acts. n.p., 1910.
42543.69.13 Hervieu, Paul. Enchained, a play in 3 acts. n.p., 1909.
42543.69.14 Hervilly, Ernest. La belle saïnara. Paris, 1876.
42543.69.14.5 Hervilly, Ernest. Sayonava, or The testing of the poet. Brooklyn, 1912.
42543.69.14.10 Hervilly, Ernest. Le Harem. Paris, 1874.
42543.69.15 Hervilly, Ernest. Vent d'ouest, comédie, et La soupière. N.Y., 1883.
42543.69.16 Hervilly, Ernest. Carried by assault. N.Y., 1879.
42543.69.16.10 Hervilly, Ernest. Bric-a-brac. N.Y., 1879.
42543.69.16.25 Too windy for an umbrella. N.Y., 1879.
42543.69.75 Humières, Robert. Théâtre. Paris, 1923.
42543.69.100 Ivry, marquis d'. Les amants de Vérone; drame. Paris, 1878.

42543.70 Individual authors, etc. - 1850-1899 - Drama - Janvier

42543.70 Janvier, A. Théâtre. Paris, 1905. 4v.

42543.71 Individual authors, etc. - 1850-1899 - Drama - Jullien

42543.71 Jullien, Jean. Le théâtre vivant. Paris, 1892. 2v.

42543.73 Individual authors, etc. - 1850-1899 - Drama - Josz

42543.73 Josz, Virgile. Rembrandt. Paris, 1896.

42544.1 Individual authors, etc. - 1850-1899 - Drama - Keranbors

42544.1.75 Keranbars, Charles de. Velléda la druidesse de l'Ile de Sein. Vannes, 1902.

42544.2 Individual authors, etc. - 1850-1899 - Drama - Kistemaeckers

42544.2.4 Kistemaekers, Henry. Le flambée. Paris, 1912.
42544.2.5 Kistemaekers, Henry. La rivale. Paris, 1907.
42544.2.6 Kistemaekers, Henry. Le marchand de bonheur. Paris, 1910.
42544.2.7 Kistemaekers, Henry. Théâtre de rire et de larmes. Paris, 1905.
42544.2.8 Kistemaekers, Henry. La rivale. Paris, 1907.
42544.2.8.5 Moinaux, G. La conversion d'Alceste; et L'instinct par Henry Kistemaeckers. Paris, 1905.
42544.2.8.6 Kistemaekers, Henry. L'exilée. Paris, 1913.
42544.2.8.7 Kistemaekers, Henry. L'embuscade. Paris, 1913.
42544.2.8.8 Kistemaekers, Henry. L'occident. Paris, 1913.
42544.2.8.9 Kistemaekers, Henry. Monsieur Dupont Chauffeur. Paris, 1908.
42544.2.8.10 Kistemaekers, Henry. La passante. Paris, 1921.
42544.2.8.12 Kistemaekers, Henry. Le roi des palaces; comédie en 4 actes. Paris, 1923.
42544.2.8.14 Kistemaekers, Henry. L'esclave errante; pièce en 3 actes. Paris, 1923.
42544.2.8.16 Kistemaekers, Henry. L'amour. Paris, 1924.
42544.2.8.18 Kistemaekers, Henry. En bombe. Paris, 1923.
42544.2.8.20 Kistemaekers, Henry. La nuit est à nous. Paris, 1925.

42544.3 Individual authors, etc. - 1850-1899 - Drama - Lafont; Lapommeraye; Laroze; etc.

42544.3 Lafont, C. Le passé d'une femme. Paris, 1859.
42544.3.5 Lafont, C. Un cas de conscience. Paris, 1839.
42544.3.9 Lapommeraye, H. de. La critique de Francillon. Paris, 1887.
42544.3.25 Laroze, L. Le respect de l'amour. Paris, 1911.

42544.4 Individual authors, etc. - 1850-1899 - Drama - Launay

42544.4 Launay, Alphonse. Le supplice d'une mère. Paris, 1879.

42544.5 - .16 Individual authors, etc. - 1850-1899 - Drama - Legouvé, E.

42544.5 Legouvé, Ernest. Beatrix. Paris, 1861.
42544.5.5 Legouvé, Ernest. La cigale chez les fourmis. Boston, 1892.
42544.5.8 Legouvé, Ernest. La cigale chez les fourmis. Boston, 1902.
42544.6 Legouvé, Ernest. À deux jeu. Paris, 1869.
42544.7 Legouvé, Ernest. Médée. Paris, 1870.
42544.7.2 Legouvé, Ernest. Medea. N.Y., 1866.
42544.7.3 Legouvé, Ernest. Medea. N.Y., 1867.
42544.7.4 Legouvé, Ernest. Médée. Paris, 1856.
42544.7.6 Legouvé, Ernest. Medea. London, 18- ?
42544.7.7 Legouvé, Ernest. Medea. N.Y., 1857.
42544.8 Legouvé, Ernest. Les deux reines de France. Paris, 1873.

42544.5 - .16 Individual authors, etc. - 1850-1899 - Drama - Legouvé, E. - cont.

42544.8.2 Legouvé, Ernest. Il migliore amico della donna. Roma, 1898.
42544.11 Legouvé, Ernest. Beatrix. Paris, 1861.
42544.12 Legouvé, Ernest. Par droit de conquête. Paris, 1867.
42544.12.2 Legouvé, Ernest. Par droit de conquête. Paris, 1858.
42544.13 Legouvé, Ernest. À deux de jeu. Paris, 1869.
42544.16 Legouvé, Ernest. Édith de Falsen. Paris, 1852.
42544.16.5 Legouvé, Ernest. Medea. London, 1857.

42544.17 - .19 Individual authors, etc. - 1850-1899 - Drama - Legouvé, G.

42544.17 Legouvé, Gabriel. Le mérite des femmes. Poëme. Paris, 1850.
42544.17.2 Legouvé, Gabriel. Le mérite des femmes. Paris, 1824.
42544.17.4 Legouvé, Gabriel. Il merto delle donne. Paris, 1802.
42544.17.8A Legouvé, Gabriel. Nos filles et nos fils. 6e éd. Paris, 1879.
42544.17.8B Legouvé, Gabriel. Nos filles et nos fils. 11e éd. Paris, 1879.
42544.19 Legouvé, Gabriel. Conferences parisiennes. Paris, n.d.
42544.19.15 Bazin, René. Dicours de reception sur Ernest Legouvé. Paris, 1904.
42544.19.50 Barts, E. Gabriel-Jean-Baptiste Legouvé. Inaug. Diss. Berlin, 1938.

42544.20 Individual authors, etc. - 1850-1899 - Drama - Lengyel

42544.20 Lengyel, M. Le typhon. Paris, 1911.

42544.22 - .25 Individual authors, etc. - 1850-1899 - Drama - Lavedan

42544.22 Lavedan, Henri. Une famille. Paris, 1891.
42544.23 Lavedan, Henri. Inconsolables. (Fiction). Paris, n.d.
42544.23.5 Lavedan, Henri. Le bon temps. (Roman). Paris, 1906.
42544.23.6 Lavedan, Henri. Bon an, Malan. Paris, 1908. 7v.
42544.24.2 Lavedan, Henri. Le duel. Paris, 1905.
42544.24.2.2 Lavedan, Henri. Le duel. 30. éd. Paris, 1905.
42544.24.2.3 Lavedan, Henri. Le duel. 2. éd. Paris, 1906.
42544.24.2.4 Lavedan, Henri. Le duel. Paris, 1907.
42544.24.2.5 Lavedan, Henri. Le duel. N.Y., 1928.
42544.24.3 Lavedan, Henri. Les deux noblesses. (Drama). Paris, 1897.
42544.24.4 Lavedan, Henri. Catherine. Paris, n.d.
42544.24.5 Lavedan, Henri. Viveurs. (Drama). Paris, n.d.
42544.24.6 Lavedan, Henri. Le marquis de Priola. (Drama). Paris, n.d.
42544.24.6.5F Lavedan, Henri. Le marquis de Priola. (Drama). Paris, 1902.
42544.24.7 Lavedan, Henri. Le prince d'Aurec. Paris, n.d.
42544.24.7.3A Lavedan, Henri. Three modern plays from the French: The prince d'Aurec. N.Y., 1914.
42544.24.7.3B Lavedan, Henri. Three modern plays from the French: The prince d'Aurec. N.Y., 1914.
42544.24.7.5 Lavedan, Henri. La critique du prince d'Aurec. 2e éd. Paris, 1892.
42544.24.8 Lavedan, Henri. Les sacrifices. Paris, 1918.
42544.24.9 Lavedan, Henri. Le vieux marcheur. Paris, n.d.
42544.24.10 Lavedan, Henri. Sire. Paris, 1909.
42544.24.11 Lavedan, Henri. Le gout du vice. Paris, 1911.
42544.24.12 Lavedan, Henri. Servir. Paris, 1913.
42544.24.13 Lavedan, Henri. Le nouveau jeu. Paris, 1906.
Htn 42544.24.14* Lavedan, Henri. Le nouveau jeu. Paris, n.d.
42544.24.15 Lavedan, Henri. Les jeunes. Paris, 1897.
42544.24.16 Lavedan, Henri. Reine janvier. Paris, 1886.
42544.24.18 Lavedan, Henri. Le lit. Paris, 19- .
42544.24.20 Lavedan, Henri. Une cour. Paris, 1895.
42544.24.21 Lavedan, Henri. Leur beau physique. Paris, 1896.
42544.24.21.5 Lavedan, Henri. Leur beau physique. Paris, 1915.
42544.24.22 Lavedan, Henri. Petites fêtes. 9e éd. Paris, 1896.
42544.24.26 Lavedan, Henri. Les petites visites. 4e éd. Paris, 1896.
42544.24.30 Lavedan, Henri. Nocturnes. 12e éd. Paris, 1899.
42544.24.35 Lavedan, Henri. La haute. 20e éd. n.p., 1909.
42544.24.40 Lavedan, Henri. Le chemin du salut. I, Inène Olette. Paris, 1920.
42544.24.40.2 Lavedan, Henri. Le chemin du salut. II, Gaudias. v.1-2. Paris, 1921.
42544.24.40.3 Lavedan, Henri. Le chemin du salut. III, Panteau. v.1-2. Paris, 1923.
42544.24.45 Lavedan, Henri. La belle histoire de Geneviève. Paris, 1920.
42544.24.50 Lavedan, Henri. Leur coeur. 18e éd. Paris, 1895.
42544.24.52 Lavedan, Henri. Leurs soeurs. Paris, 1896.
42544.24.55 Lavedan, Henri. Bonne-étoile; roman. Pt.1-4. Paris, 1931.
42544.25 Lavedan, Henri. Verennes. Paris, 1904.
42544.25.81 Lavedan, Henri. Avant l'oubli; un enfant rêveur. Pt.1-3. Paris, 1933.
42544.25.83 Lavedan, Henri. Avant l'oubli écrire. Paris, 1934.
42544.25.85 Lavedan, Henri. Avant l'oubli. Paris, 1936.
42544.25.88 Lavedan, Henri. Avant l'oubli; les beaux soirs. Pt.1-3. Paris, 1938.
42544.25.90 Lavedan, Henri. Avant l'oubli. Paris, 1933-37. 3v.

42544.26 - .30 Individual authors, etc. - 1850-1899 - Drama - Labiche

42544.26.1 Labiche, Eugène. Théâtre complet. Paris, 1922-23. 10v.
42544.26.2 Labiche, Eugène. Le voyage de Monsieur Perrichon. N.Y., 1883.
42544.26.3 Labiche, Eugène. Le voyage de Monsieur Perrichon. 3e éd. N.Y., 1884.
42544.26.4 Labiche, Eugène. Le voyage de Monsieur Perrichon. London, 1885.
42544.26.5 Labiche, Eugène. Le voyage de Monsieur Perrichon. Boston, 1905.
42544.26.5.8 Labiche, Eugène. Le voyage de Monsieur Perrichon. Boston, 1908.
42544.26.6 Labiche, Eugène. Le voyage de Monsieur Perrichon. Boston, 1911.
42544.26.7 Labiche, Eugène. Le voyage de Monsieur Perrichon. Paris, 1912.
42544.26.20 Labiche, Eugène. Le voyage de Monsieur Perrichon. Boston, 1919.
42544.26.35 Labiche, Eugène. Le voyage de Monsieur Perrichon. Paris, 1930.
42544.26.40 Labiche, Eugène. Nouveau théâtre choisi. Paris, 1960.
42544.27 Labiche, Eugène. Un jeune homme pressé. Paris, 1897.
42544.27.9 Labiche, Eugène. La grammaire. Paris, 1879.
42544.27.12 Labiche, Eugène. La grammaire: comédie. N.Y., 1890.
42544.27.25 Labiche, Eugène. La grammaire, comédie-vaudeville. 5. éd. London, 1888.

42544.26 - .30 Individual authors, etc. - 1850-1899 - Drama - Labiche - cont.

42544.28 Labiche, Eugène. La grammaire. N.Y., 1883.
42544.28.2 Labiche, Eugène. La grammaire. N.Y., 1883.
42544.28.5 Labiche, Eugène. La poudre aux yeux. 4. éd. Boston, 1866.
42544.28.6 Labiche, Eugène. La poudre aux yeux. Boston, 1867.
42544.28.10 Labiche, Eugène. Un chapeau de paille d'Italie. Paris, 1888.
42544.28.15 Labiche, Eugène. The Italian straw hat, and The spelling mistakes. N.Y., 1967.
42544.28.20 Labiche, Eugène. La clé des champs. Paris, 1972.
42544.30 Labiche, Eugène. Moi. Comédie en trois actes. Boston, 1896.
42544.30.15 Labiche, Eugène. Monsieur Pickwick. Paris, 1911.
42544.30.20 Pamphlet box. Labiche.
42544.30.80 Gordon, Zina. Labiche et son oeuvre. Thèse. Toulouse, 1932.
42544.30.85 Soupault, Philippe. Eugène Labiche, sa vie, son oeuvre. Paris, 1945.
42544.30.86 Soupault, Philippe. Eugène Labiche. Paris, 1964.

42544.31 Individual authors, etc. - 1850-1899 - Drama - Lapointe; Lecomte; Legendre; etc.

42544.31 Lapointe, A. Le cousin César. Paris, 1883.
42544.31.3 Lapointe, A. Les rivalites. Paris, 1878.
42544.31.15 Lecomte, Jules. Un scandale littéraire. Paris, 1925.
42544.31.20 Lecomte, Georges. Les lettres au service de la patrie. Paris, 1917.
42544.31.25 Lecomte, Georges. Mirages. Paris, 1893.
42544.31.26 Lecomte, Georges. La meule. Paris, 1891.
42544.31.30 Lecomte, Jules. Le luxe. 2. éd. Paris, 1859.
42544.31.32 Delay, Jean Paul Louis. Discours de réception de M. Jean Delay à l'Academie Française et réponse de M. Pasteur Vallery-Radot. Paris, 1960.
42544.31.35 Lefebure, H. Conte bleu. Paris, 1893.
42544.31.40 Legendre, Louis. Pylade. Paris, 1909.

42544.32 - .33 Individual authors, etc. - 1850-1899 - Drama - Lemaître, J.

42544.32 Lamaître, Jules. Opinions à répandre. Paris, 1901.
42544.32.5A Lemaître, Jules. Moreaux choisis. Boston, 1896.
42544.32.5B Lemaître, Jules. Moreaux choisis. Boston, 1896.
42544.33 Lemaître, Jules. Le députe Leveau. Paris, 1891.
42544.33.6 Lemaître, Jules. En marge des vieux livres. Paris, 1905-08. 2v.
42544.33.7 Lemaître, Jules. En marge des vieux livres. Paris, 1906.
42544.33.7.10 Lamaître, Jules. En marge des vieux livres. v.1-2. Paris, 193-?
42544.33.8 Lemaître, Jules. On the margins of old books. N.Y., 1929.
42544.33.9 Lemaître, Jules. La massiere. Paris, n.d.
42544.33.12A Lemaître, Jules. Théâtre. Paris, n.d. 3v.
42544.33.12B Lemaître, Jules. Théâtre. Paris, n.d. 3v.
42544.33.12.3 Lemaître, Jules. Révoltée, Le député, Le veau, Mariage blanc, Flipote. Paris, 1906.
42544.33.12.5 Lemaître, Jules. Révoltée. Paris, 19- ?
42544.33.13 Lemaître, Jules. Bertrade. Paris, n.d.
42544.33.13.5 Lemaître, Jules. Bertrade. Paris, 1905.
42544.33.14F Lemaître, Jules. Bertrade. Paris, 1905.
42544.33.15F Lemaître, Jules. La massière. Paris, 1905.
42544.33.16F Lemaître, Jules. Kismet. Paris, 1913.
42544.33.17 Lemaître, Jules. La vieillesse d'Hélène. Paris, n.d.
42544.33.18F Lemaître, Jules. Le mariage de Telemaque. Paris, 1910.
42544.33.19 Lemaître, Jules. L'âge difficile. N.Y., 1895.
42544.33.20 Lemaître, Jules. Sérénus. Paris, 1886.
42544.33.20.5A Lemaître, Jules. Serenus and other stories. London, 1920.
42544.33.20.5B Lemaître, Jules. Serenus and other stories. London, 1920.
42544.33.21 Lemaître, Jules. Les rois. Paris, 1912.
42544.33.22 Lemaître, Jules. Myrrha, vierge et martyre. Paris, 19- .
42544.33.26 Lemaître, Jules. Quatre discours. Paris, 1902.
42544.33.28 Lemaître, Jules. Nouvel état d'esprit. Paris, 1903.
42544.33.29 Lemaître, Jules. La bonne Hélène. Paris, 1896.
42544.33.30 Lemaître, Jules. Mariage blanc. Paris, 1891.
42544.33.31 Durrière, G. Productions et variantes dramatiques inédites de Jules Lemaître. Thèse. Paris, 1934.
42544.33.35 Lemaître, Jules. Lettres à mon ami, 1909. Paris, 1910.
42544.33.50 Bordeaux, H. Jules Lemaître, avec huit gravures. Paris, 1920.
42544.33.52 Knopf, A. Jules Lemaître als Dramatiker. Inaug. Diss. Leipzig, 1926.
42544.33.55 Grimm, L. Lemaître als Kritiker des französischen Theaters. Inaug. Diss. Nürnberg, 1927.
42544.33.60 Hucke, S. Jules Lemâitre als Erzähler. Inaug. Diss. Schwelm, 1932.
42544.33.64 Lemaître, Jules. Jules Lemaître et le théâtre. Thèse. Paris, 1934.
42544.33.65 Durrière, G. Jules Lemaître et le théâtre. Paris, 1934.
42544.33.66 Parsell, J.R. L'esthetique de Jules Lemaître. Minneapolis, 1939.
42544.33.68 Harry, Myriam. La vie Jules Lemaître. Paris, 1946.
42544.33.70 Joseph, Roger. Pour les fidèles de Jules Lemaître. Orléans, 1969.
42544.33.80 Sansot-Orland, E. Jules Lemaître. Paris, 1903.
42544.33.100 Pamphlet box. Jules Lemaître.

42544.34 Individual authors, etc. - 1850-1899 - Drama - Lemercier; Lepelletier; Lomon; Lorde; Louys, P.; etc.

42544.34 Lemercier de Neuville, Louis. Nouveau théâtre des pupazzi. Paris, 1882.
42544.34.2A Lemercier de Neuville, Louis. Les tourniquets. Paris, 1862.
42544.34.2B Lemercier de Neuville, Louis. Les tourniquets. Paris, 1862.
42544.34.2.30 Lemercier de Neuville, Louis. Le passé. Lyon, 1874.
42544.34.5 Lepelletier, E. Madame Sans-Gêne. N.Y., 1895.
42544.34.6 Lepelletier, E. Madame Sans-Gêne. Boston, 1895.
42544.34.6.20 Lepelletier, E. Il giuramento d'Orsini. Milano, 1902.
42544.34.6.50F Leroy, Louis. Les pensionnaires du Louvre. Paris, 1880.
42544.34.7 Lomon, A. Théâtre et poésies diverses. Paris, 1867.
42544.34.9 Lomon, Charles. Jean Dacier. 2e éd. Paris, 1877.
42544.34.10 Lomon, Charles. Jean Dacier. 3e éd. Paris, 1877.
42544.34.19 Lorde, André de. Terre d'Epouvante. Paris, 1907.
42544.34.20 Lorde, André de. Théâtre d'Epouvante. Paris, 1909.
42544.34.21F Lorde, André de. Napoléonette. Paris, 1921.
42544.34.23 Lorde, André de. Théâtre de la peur. Paris, 1919.
42544.34.24 Lorde, André de. Théâtre rouge. 3e éd. Paris, 1922.
42544.34.25 Lorde, André de. Bagnes d'enfants. Paris, 1910.
42544.34.25.5 Lorde, André de. Cauchemars. Paris, 1912.
42544.34.25.10 Lorde, André de. Dans la nuit. Paris, 1898.
42544.34.25.15 Lorde, André de. Madame Blanchard. Paris, 1898.

42544.34 Individual authors, etc. - 1850-1899 - Drama - Lemercier; Lepelletier; Lomon; Lorde; Louys, P.; etc. - cont.

42544.34.25.20 Lorde, André de. Une leçon à la salpétrière. Tableau dramatique. Paris, 1908.
42544.34.25.25 Lorde, André de. Les drames célèbres du Grand-guignol. Paris, 1924.
42544.34.25.30 Lorde, André de. Monsieur, Madame et les autres. Paris, 1893.
42544.34.26 Lorde, André de. Mon curé chez les riches. Paris, 1928.
42544.34.27 Lorde, André de. Mon curé chez les pauvres. Paris, 1930.
42544.34.28 Louys, Pierre. Les chansons de Bilitis. 15. éd. Paris, 1898.
42544.34.28.2 Louys, Pierre. Les chansons de Bilitis. 14. éd. Paris, 1898.
42544.34.28.3 Louys, Pierre. Les chansons de Bilitis. Paris, 1901.
Htn 42544.34.28.5* Louys, Pierre. Les chansons de Bilitis. Paris, 1911.
42544.34.28.10 Louys, Pierre. Les chansons de Bilitis. Paris, 1930.
42544.34.28.15 Louys, Pierre. A vida amorosa de Bilitis. Lisboa, 1927.
Htn 42544.34.28.20* Louys, Pierre. The songs of Bilitis. n.p., 1920.
42544.34.28.25 Louys, Pierre. Les poëmes de Pierre Louys. Paris, 1945. 2v.
42544.34.28.30 Louys, Pierre. Collected works. N.Y., 1932.
Htn 42544.34.29* Louys, Pierre. La femme et le pantin. Paris, 1899.
42544.34.29.5 Louys, Pierre. La femme et le pantin. 20e éd. Paris, 1898.
42544.34.31 Louys, Pierre. La femme et le pantin. Paris, 1925.
42544.34.31.5 Louys, Pierre. La femme et le pantin. Paris, 1930.
42544.34.32.5 Louys, Pierre. Aphrodite. Paris, 1906.
42544.34.32.8 Louys, Pierre. Aphrodite. Paris, 1930.
42544.34.32.10 Louys, Pierre. Aphrodite. n.p., 1919.
42544.34.32.12 Louys, Pierre. Aphrodite; Ancient manners. N.Y., 1932.
Htn 42544.34.33* Louys, Pierre. L'homme de pourpre. Paris, 1901.
Htn 42544.34.39* Louys, Pierre. Lêda. Paris, 1893.
42544.34.42 Louys, Pierre. Mimes des courtisanes de Lucien. 6e éd. Paris, 1899.
42544.34.45 Louys, Pierre. Woman and puppet. N.Y., 1913.
42544.34.45.10 Louys, Pierre. Woman and puppet. N.Y., 1910.
42544.34.50 Louys, Pierre. Byblis, Leda, A new pleasure. N.Y., 1920.
42544.34.53.5A Louys, Pierre. Sanguines. Paris, 1903.
42544.34.53.5B Louys, Pierre. Sanguines. Paris, 1903.
Htn 42544.34.55* Louys, Pierre. The twilight of the nymphs. Philadelphia, 1927.
42544.34.60 Louys, Pierre. Les aventures du Roi Pausole. Paris, 1931.
42544.34.60.5A Louys, Pierre. Les aventures de Roi Pausole. Paris, 1901.
42544.34.60.5B Louys, Pierre. Les aventures de Roi Pausole. Paris, 1901.
42544.34.60.10 Louys, Pierre. Les aventures du Roi Pausole. Lausanne, 1947.
42544.34.65 Louys, Pierre. Psyché. Paris, 1927.
42544.34.70 Louys, Pierre. Contes choisis. Paris, 1931.
42544.34.80 Gaubert, E. Pierre Louys. 2e éd. Paris, 1904.
42544.34.85 Franke, Karl. Pierre Louys. Inaug. Diss. Bonn, 1937.
42544.34.87 Cardinne-Petit, R. Pierre Louys intime. Paris, 1942.
42544.34.90 Farrere, C. Mon ami Pierre Louys. Paris, 1953.

42544.35 Individual authors, etc. - 1850-1899 - Drama - Lurine, L.

42544.35 Lurine, Louis. La boite d'argent. Paris, 1858.

42544.36 Individual authors, etc. - 1850-1899 - Drama - Loyson

42544.36 Loyson, Paul H. L'apôtre. Paris, 1911.
42544.36.5 Loyson, Paul H. The apostle; modern tragedy in 3 acts. Garden City, 1916.
42544.36.9 Loyson, Paul H. L'apostolo; tragedia moderna. Milano, 1912.
42544.36.15 Loyson, Paul H. L'Évangile du Sang. 2e éd. Genève, 1900.
42544.36.20 Loyson, Paul H. Mystique du liberalisme. Paris, 1952.

42544.40 Individual authors, etc. - 1850-1899 - Drama - Lubac

42544.40 Lubac, Jules de. Les Français devant Pékin. Lyon, 1861.

42545.01 - .099 Individual authors, etc. - 1850-1899 - Drama - Maeterlinck - Complete and Selected works

42545.01 Maeterlinck, Maurice. Théâtre. Bruxelles, 1905-1908. 3v.
42545.01.5 Maeterlinck, Maurice. Théâtre. Bruxellles, 1911-12. 3v.
42545.05 Maeterlinck, Maurice. Poésies complètes. Bruxelles, 1965.
42545.010 Maeterlinck, Maurice. Morceaux choisis. Paris, 19- .

42545.1 - .3.349 Individual authors, etc. - 1850-1899 - Drama - Maeterlinck - Individual works

42545.1 Maeterlinck, Maurice. Les aveugles. Bruxelles, 1861.
42545.1.2 Maeterlinck, Maurice. Les aveugles. 3. éd. Bruxelles, 1892.
42545.1.9 Maeterlinck, Maurice. Blind. The intruders. Washington, 1891.
42545.2A Maeterlinck, Maurice. Les sept princesses. Bruxelles, 1891.
42545.2B Maeterlinck, Maurice. Les sept princesses. Bruxelles, 1891.
42545.3A Maeterlinck, Maurice. La princesse Maleine. 5e éd. Bruxelles, 1891.
42545.3B Maeterlinck, Maurice. La princesse Maleine. 8e éd. Bruxelles, 1891.
42545.3.1 Maeterlinck, Maurice. La princesse Maleine. 9e éd. Bruxelles, 1891.
42545.3.1.3 Maeterlinck, Maurice. Princess Maleine. N.Y., 1911.
42545.3.2 Maeterlinck, Maurice. Alladine et Palomides. 2e éd. Bruxelles, 1894.
42545.3.2.5 Maeterlinck, Maurice. Alladine et Palomides. 4e éd. Bruxelles, 1894.
42545.3.3.1 Maeterlinck, Maurice. Pélléas et Mélisande. 2e éd. Bruxelles, 1892.
42545.3.3.2 Maeterlinck, Maurice. Pélléas et Mélisande. 7e éd. Bruxelles, 1898.
42545.3.3.5 Maeterlinck, Maurice. Pélléas et Mélisande. N.Y., 1894.
42545.3.3.6A Maeterlinck, Maurice. Pélléas et Mélisande. N.Y., 1908.
42545.3.3.6B Maeterlinck, Maurice. Pélléas et Mélisande. N.Y., 1908.
42545.3.3.6C Maeterlinck, Maurice. Pélléas et Mélisande. N.Y., 1908.
42545.3.3.7 Maeterlinck, Maurice. Pélléas et Mélisande. N.Y., 1907.
42545.3.3.8 Maeterlinck, Maurice. Pélléas et Mélisande. Leipzig, 1902.
42545.3.3.9 Maeterlinck, Maurice. Pélléas and Mélisande, Alladine and Palomides, Home. N.Y., 1911.
42545.3.3.14 Maeterlinck, Maurice. Pélléas and Mélisande. N.Y., 1915.
42545.3.4 Maeterlinck, Maurice. Serres chaudes. Bruxelles, 1895.
42545.3.4.2 Maeterlinck, Maurice. Serres chaudes. Bruxelles, 1890.
42545.3.5 Maeterlinck, Maurice. Le trésor des humbles. 3e éd. Bruxelles, 1896.

2545.1 - .3.349 Individual authors, etc. - 1850-1899 - Drama - Maeterlinck - Individual works - cont.

42545.3.5.3 Maeterlinck, Maurice. Le trésor des humbles. 14e éd. Paris, 1898.
42545.3.5.4 Maeterlinck, Maurice. Le trésor des humbles. 33e éd. Paris, 1904.
42545.3.5.5 Maeterlinck, Maurice. The treasure of the humble. N.Y., 1897.
42545.3.5.6 Maeterlinck, Maurice. The treasure of the humble. N.Y., 1899.
42545.3.5.7 Maeterlinck, Maurice. The treasure of the humble. N.Y., 1900.
42545.3.5.9 Maeterlinck, Maurice. The treasure of the humble. London, 1911.
42545.3.5.10 Maeterlinck, Maurice. The treasure of the humble. N.Y., 1913.
42545.3.5.11 Maeterlinck, Maurice. Le trésor des humbles. 31. éd. Paris, 1902.
42545.3.5.20 Maeterlinck, Maurice. Der Schotz der Armen. 3. Aufl. Jena, 1906.
NEDL 42545.3.6 Maeterlinck, Maurice. Aglavaine et Selysette. Paris, 1896.
42545.3.6.2 Maeterlinck, Maurice. Aglavaine et Selysette. N.Y., 1911.
42545.3.6.3 Maeterlinck, Maurice. Aglavaine et Selysette. 7e éd. Paris, 1899.
42545.3.6.4 Maeterlinck, Maurice. Aglavaine and Selysette. London, 1897.
42545.3.6.5 Maeterlinck, Maurice. Aglavaine and Selysette. London, 1904.
42545.3.6.20 Maeterlinck, Maurice. Aglavaine and Selysette. Jena, 1911.
42545.3.7 Maeterlinck, Maurice. Alladine and Palomides. Interior. The death of Tintagiles. London, 1899.
42545.3.7.2 Maeterlinck, Maurice. Alladine and Palomides. Chicago, 1899.
42545.3.7.6 Maeterlinck, Maurice. Plays. Ser. 1. Chicago, 1894.
42545.3.7.7 Maeterlinck, Maurice. Plays. 2d ed. Chicago, 1895.
42545.3.7.8 Maeterlinck, Maurice. Plays. Ser. 2. Chicago, 1896.
42545.3.7.11 Maeterlinck, Maurice. Drei mystische Spiele. 2. Aufl. Leipzig, 1904.
42545.3.7.15 Maeterlinck, Maurice. Three plays. London, 1911.
42545.3.7.20 Maeterlinck, Maurice. The plays. Chicago, 1902. 2v.
42545.3.8.1 Maeterlinck, Maurice. Wisdom and destiny. N.Y., 1898.
42545.3.8.2 Maeterlinck, Maurice. Wisdom and destiny. N.Y., 1901.
42545.3.8.3A Maeterlinck, Maurice. Wisdom and destiny. N.Y., 1902.
42545.3.8.3B Maeterlinck, Maurice. Wisdom and destiny. N.Y., 1902.
42545.3.8.4 Maeterlinck, Maurice. Wisdom and destiny. N.Y., 1916.
42545.3.8.5 Maeterlinck, Maurice. Wisdom and destiny. N.Y., 1903.
42545.3.8.6 Maeterlinck, Maurice. Wisdom and destiny. N.Y., 1918.
42545.3.8.7 Maeterlinck, Maurice. Wisdom and destiny. N.Y., 1900.
42545.3.8.15 Maeterlinck, Maurice. La sagesse et la destinée. Paris, 1930.
42545.3.9A Maeterlinck, Maurice. Sister Beatrice and Ardiane and Barbe Bleue. N.Y., 1902.
42545.3.9B Maeterlinck, Maurice. Sister Beatrice and Ardiane and Barbe Bleue. N.Y., 1902.
42545.3.9.3 Maeterlinck, Maurice. Sister Beatrice and Ardiane and Barbe Bleue. N.Y., 1906.
42545.3.9.5 Maeterlinck, Maurice. Sister Beatrice and Ardiane and Barbe Bleue. N.Y., 1910.
42545.3.9.6 Maeterlinck, Maurice. Sister Beatrice and Ardiane and Barbe Bleue. N.Y., 1911.
42545.3.9.10 Maeterlinck, Maurice. Sister Beatrice and Ardiane and Barbe Bleue. N.Y., 1916.
42545.3.9.25 Maeterlinck, Maurice. Le Temple Enseveli. Paris, 1902.
42545.3.10A Maeterlinck, Maurice. The Buried temple. N.Y., 1902.
42545.3.10B Maeterlinck, Maurice. The Buried temple. N.Y., 1902.
42545.3.10C Maeterlinck, Maurice. The Buried temple. N.Y., 1902.
42545.3.10.5 Maeterlinck, Maurice. The Buried temple. N.Y., 1917.
42545.3.11 Maeterlinck, Maurice. Monna Vanna. Paris, 1902.
42545.3.11.2 Maeterlinck, Maurice. Monna Vanna. Paris, 1924.
42545.3.11.3 Maeterlinck, Maurice. Monna Vanna. N.Y., 1903.
42545.3.11.4 Maeterlinck, Maurice. Monna Vanna. N.Y., 1903.
42545.3.11.4.5 Maeterlinck, Maurice. Monna Vanna. N.Y., 1905.
42545.3.11.5A Maeterlinck, Maurice. Monna Vanna. N.Y., 1913.
42545.3.11.5B Maeterlinck, Maurice. Monna Vanna. N.Y., 1913.
42545.3.11.20 Maeterlinck, Maurice. Monna Vanna. Leipzig, 1903.
42545.3.11.22 Maeterlinck, Maurice. Monna Vanna. Jena, 1913.
42545.3.12.3A Maeterlinck, Maurice. The double garden. N.Y., 1904.
42545.3.12.3B Maeterlinck, Maurice. The double garden. N.Y., 1904.
42545.3.12.3C Maeterlinck, Maurice. The double garden. N.Y., 1904.
42545.3.12.3D Maeterlinck, Maurice. The double garden. N.Y., 1904.
42545.3.12.4 Maeterlinck, Maurice. The double garden. London, 1909.
42545.3.13 Maeterlinck, Maurice. La vie des abeilles. Paris, 1905.
42545.3.13.3 Maeterlinck, Maurice. The life of the bee. 4. ed. London, 1901.
42545.3.13.5 Maeterlinck, Maurice. The life of the bee. N.Y., 1902.
42545.3.13.7 Maeterlinck, Maurice. The life of the bee. N.Y., 1919.
42545.3.13.8 Maeterlinck, Maurice. The children's life of the bee. N.Y., 1919.
42545.3.13.9A Maeterlinck, Maurice. The swarm. N.Y., 1906.
42545.3.13.9B Maeterlinck, Maurice. The swarm. N.Y., 1906.
42545.3.13.10 Maeterlinck, Maurice. The life of the bee. N.Y., 1920.
42545.3.13.12 Maeterlinck, Maurice. The life of the bee. N.Y., 1912.
42545.3.14.5A Maeterlinck, Maurice. The measure of the hours. N.Y., 1907.
42545.3.14.5B Maeterlinck, Maurice. The measure of the hours. N.Y., 1907.
42545.3.14.5C Maeterlinck, Maurice. The measure of the hours. N.Y., 1907.
X Cg 42545.3.15 Maeterlinck, Maurice. Joyzelle. Paris, 1903.
X Cg 42545.3.15.4 Maeterlinck, Maurice. Joyzelle. Paris, 1903.
X Cg 42545.3.15.6 Maeterlinck, Maurice. Joyzelle. Paris, 1903.
42545.3.15.8 Maeterlinck, Maurice. Joyzelle. Leipzig, 1903.
42545.3.15.25 Maeterlinck, Maurice. Joyzelle. N.Y., 1911.
42545.3.15.30 Maeterlinck, Maurice. Joyzelle. Paris, 1927.
42545.3.15.32 Maeterlinck, Maurice. Joyzelle. N.Y., 1917.
42545.3.16.5 Maeterlinck, Maurice. Die Intelligenz der Blumen. Jena, 1907.
42545.3.18A Maeterlinck, Maurice. The blue bird. N.Y., 1909.
42545.3.18B Maeterlinck, Maurice. The blue bird. N.Y., 1909.
42545.3.18.1 Maeterlinck, Maurice. The blue bird. London, 1909.
42545.3.18.2 Maeterlinck, Maurice. The blue bird. London, 1910.
42545.3.18.3 Maeterlinck, Maurice. The blue bird. N.Y., 1910.
42545.3.18.5A Maeterlinck, Maurice. The blue bird. N.Y., 1911.
42545.3.18.5B Maeterlinck, Maurice. The blue bird. N.Y., 1911.
42545.3.18.22A Maeterlinck, Maurice. The betrothal. N.Y., 1918.
42545.3.18.22B Maeterlinck, Maurice. The betrothal. N.Y., 1918.

42545.1 - .3.349 Individual authors, etc. - 1850-1899 - Drama - Maeterlinck - Individual works - cont.

42545.3.18.25 Maeterlinck, Maurice. The betrothal. London, 1919.
42545.3.18.30 Maeterlinck, Maurice. The blue bird. London, 1911.
42545.3.18.40 Maeterlinck, Maurice. Der blaue Vogel. 6. Aufl. Berlin, 1910.
42545.3.19.15A Maeterlinck, Maurice. Macbeth. Paris, 1909.
42545.3.19.15B Maeterlinck, Maurice. Macbeth. Paris, 1909.
42545.3.20.3 Maeterlinck, Maurice. L'oiseau bleu. Paris, 1910.
X Cg 42545.3.20.5 Maeterlinck, Maurice. L'oiseau bleu. Paris, 1910.
42545.3.21 Maeterlinck, Maurice. L'oiseau bleu. Paris, 1911.
42545.3.21.5 Maeterlinck, Maurice. L'oiseau bleu. Paris, 1953.
42545.3.21.6 Maeterlinck, Maurice. Sininen lintu. Porvoossa, 1921.
42545.3.22 Maeterlinck, Maurice. Mary Magdalene. London, 1910.
42545.3.22.5A Maeterlinck, Maurice. Mary Magdalene. N.Y., 1910.
42545.3.22.5B Maeterlinck, Maurice. Mary Magdalene. N.Y., 1910.
42545.3.22.5C Maeterlinck, Maurice. Mary Magdalene. N.Y., 1910.
42545.3.22.10 Maeterlinck, Maurice. Mary Magdalene. Paris, 1922.
42545.3.23 Maeterlinck, Maurice. Marie-Magdeleine. Paris, 1913.
42545.3.23.5 Maeterlinck, Maurice. Marie-Magdeleine. Paris, 1913.
42545.3.26.5 Maeterlinck, Maurice. Our eternity. N.Y., 1914.
42545.3.28 Maeterlinck, Maurice. The intruder and other plays. N.Y., 1914.
42545.3.29 Maeterlinck, Maurice. The intruder and other plays. N.Y., 1914.
42545.3.30 Maeterlinck, Maurice. Le mort. Paris, 1913.
NEDL 42545.3.31 Maeterlinck, Maurice. Death. N.Y., 1912.
42545.3.32 Maeterlinck, Maurice. Death. 3d ed. London, 1911.
42545.3.33 Maeterlinck, Maurice. Les débris de la guerre. Paris, 1916.
42545.3.34 Maeterlinck, Maurice. Les débris de la guerre. Paris, 1916.
42545.3.35 Maeterlinck, Maurice. Les débris de la guerre. Paris, 1916.
42545.3.36 Maeterlinck, Maurice. Le miracle de Saint Antoine. Paris, 1919.
42545.3.37 Maeterlinck, Maurice. The miracle of St. Anthony. N.Y., 1918.
42545.3.37.10 Maeterlinck, Maurice. Das Wunder des heiligen Antonius. Jena, 1904.
42545.3.38 Maeterlinck, Maurice. Le bourgmestre de Stilmonde. Paris, 1919.
42545.3.39A Maeterlinck, Maurice. The burgomaster of Stilemonde. N.Y., 1919.
42545.3.39B Maeterlinck, Maurice. The burgomaster of Stilemonde. N.Y., 1919.
42545.3.40 Maeterlinck, Maurice. Deux contes: Le massacre des innocents. Onirologie. Paris, 1918.
42545.3.41 Maeterlinck, Maurice. The massacre of the innocents. London, 1914.
42545.3.42.5A Maeterlinck, Maurice. Les aveugles. 8e éd. Bruxelles, 1898.
42545.3.42.5B Maeterlinck, Maurice. Les aveugles. 7e éd. Bruxelles, 1898.
42545.3.43 Maeterlinck, Maurice. Blind. The Intruder. Washington, 1891.
42545.3.43.15 Maeterlinck, Maurice. Der Eindrinqling, die Blinden. Leipzig, n.d.
42545.3.44 Maeterlinck, Maurice. Les sentiers dans la montagne. Paris, 1919.
42545.3.45 Maeterlinck, Maurice. Mountain paths. N.Y., 1919.
42545.3.46 Maeterlinck, Maurice. Intérieur; pièce. Paris, 1918.
42545.3.47 Maeterlinck, Maurice. Interior. London, 1908.
42545.3.48 Maeterlinck, Maurice. L'hôte inconnu. Paris, 1921.
42545.3.49 Maeterlinck, Maurice. The cloud that lifted and the power of the dead. N.Y., 1923.
42545.3.50A Maeterlinck, Maurice. Chrysanthemums and other essays. N.Y., 1907.
42545.3.50B Maeterlinck, Maurice. Chrysanthemums and other essays. N.Y., 1907.
42545.3.52 Maeterlinck, Maurice. The life of space. London, 1928.
42545.3.60 Maeterlinck, Maurice. Our friend the dog. N.Y., 1913.
42545.3.70 Maeterlinck, Maurice. Pigeons and spiders (the water spider). N.Y., 1936.
42545.3.75 Pamphlet box. Maeterlinck, Maurice.
42545.3.80 Maeterlinck, Maurice. Le sablier. Paris, 1936.
42545.3.90 Maeterlinck, Maurice. Before the great silence. N.Y., 1936.
42545.3.93 Maeterlinck, Maurice. Vor dem grossen Schweigen. Berlin, 1935.
42545.3.100 Maeterlinck, Maurice. The hour-glass. N.Y., 1936.
42545.3.110 Maeterlinck, Maurice. L'ombre des ailes. Paris, 1936.
42545.3.115 Maeterlinck, Maurice. La grande porte. Paris, 1939.
42545.3.125 Maeterlinck, Maurice. The inner beauty. N.Y., 1911.
42545.3.127A Maeterlinck, Maurice. The inner beauty. Chicago, 1911.
42545.3.127B Maeterlinck, Maurice. The inner beauty. Chicago, 1911.
42545.3.128 Maeterlinck, Maurice. The inner beauty. London, 1910.
42545.3.135 Maeterlinck, Maurice. The great secret. N.Y., 1922.
42545.3.140 Maeterlinck, Maurice. La vida del espacio. Montevideo, 1928.
42545.3.150A Maeterlinck, Maurice. On Emerson. N.Y., 1912.
42545.3.150B Maeterlinck, Maurice. On Emerson. N.Y., 1912.
42545.3.155 Maeterlinck, Maurice. The great beyond. N.Y., 1947.
42545.3.160 Maeterlinck, Maurice. L'araignée de verre. Paris, 1932.
42545.3.170 Maeterlinck, Maurice. The unknown guest. N.Y., 1914.
42545.3.190 Maeterlinck, Maurice. Berniquel. Paris, 1929.
42545.3.200 Maeterlinck, Maurice. Le double jardin. Paris, 1904.
42545.3.205 Maeterlinck, Maurice. L'autre monde. N.Y., 1942.
42545.3.210 Maeterlinck, Maurice. La grande féerie. Paris, 1929.
42545.3.215 Maeterlinck, Maurice. Bulles bleues, souvenirs heureux. Monaco, 1948.

42545.3.350 - .4 Individual authors, etc. - 1850-1899 - Drama - Maeterlinck - Biography and criticism

42545.3.360 Pastore, A. Filosofia e poesia nell'opere di Maurizio Maeterlinck. Genova, 1915.
42545.3.365 Halls, W.D. Maurice Maeterlinck. Oxford, 1960.
42545.3.375 Lecat, Maurice. Bibliographie de Maurice Maeterlinck. Bruxelles, 1939.
42545.3.376 Lecat, Maurice. Maurice Maeterlinck en Pantoufles. Bruxelles, 1939.
42545.3.400 Bever, A. v. Maurice Maeterlinck. Paris, 1904.
42545.3.410 Schlaf, J. Maurice Maeterlinck. Berlin, 1908.
42545.3.419 Harry, Gérard. La vie et l'oeuvre de Maurice Maeterlinck. Paris, 1932.
42545.3.420 Harry, Gérard. Maurice Maeterlinck. London, 1910.
42545.3.430 Taylor, U. Maurice Maeterlinck; a critical study. N.Y., 1915.

42545.3.350 - .4 Individual authors, etc. - 1850-1899 - Drama - Maeterlinck - Biography and criticism - cont.

42545.3.440 Thomas, Edward. Maurice Maeterlinck. 2d ed. N.Y., 1912.
42545.3.440.2 Thomas, Edward. Maurice Maeterlinck. N.Y., 1911.
42545.3.450 Rose, Henry. On Maeterlinck. London, 1911.
42545.3.460 Heine, Selma. Maeterlinck. Berlin, 1905.
42545.3.470 Timmerman, B. Le Spinozisme de Maeterlinck. Proefschrift. Zalt-Bommel, 1924.
42545.3.480 Fidler, F. The bird that is blue. London, 1928.
42545.3.490 Bailly, A. Maeterlinck. Paris, 1931.
42545.3.500 Cartwright, F. (Mrs.). Amerikanische Gedanken in den literarischen Werken Maeterlincks. Inaug. Diss. n.p., 1935.
42545.3.510 Lecat, Maurice. Le Maeterlinckianisme. Bruxelles, 1937-
42545.3.515 Lecat, Maurice. L'ombre des Ailes de Maeterlinck. Bruxelles, 1937.
42545.3.525 Beachboard, R. Le théâtre de Maeterlinck aux États-Unis. 2. éd. Thèse. Paris, 1951.
42545.3.530 Gerardino, A. La théâtre de Maeterlinck. Thèse. Paris, 1934.
42545.3.535A Leblanc, Georgette. Souvenirs; my life with Maeterlinck. N.Y., 1932.
42545.3.535B Leblanc, Georgette. Souvenirs; my life with Maeterlinck. N.Y., 1932.
42545.3.536 Leblanc, Georgette. Souvenirs. Paris, 1931.
42545.3.540 Palleske, S.O. Maurice Maeterlinck en Allemagne. Thèse. Strasbourg, 1938.
42545.3.541 Palleske, S.O. Maurice Maeterlinck en Allemagne. Paris, 1938?
42545.3.545 Pasquier, Alexandre. Maurice Maeterlinck. Bruxelles, 1950.
42545.3.550 Compere, Gaston. Le théâtre de Maurice Maeterlinck. Bruxelles, 1955.
42545.3.555 Tille, Vaclav. Maurice Maeterlinck; analyticna studie. V Praze, 1910.
42545.3.815 Griggs, E.H. Maeterlinck. N.Y., 1916.
42545.3.820 Le Sidaner, Louis. Maurice Maeterlinck. Paris, 1929.
42545.3.830 Andrieu, Jean Marie. Maeterlinck. Paris, 1962.
42545.3.835A Doneux, Guy. Maurice Maeterlinck; une poésie, une sagesse, un homme. Bruxelles, 1961.
42545.3.835B Doneux, Guy. Maurice Maeterlinck; une poésie, une sagesse, un homme. Bruxelles, 1961.
42545.3.840 Warmoes, Jean. Maurice Maeterlinck. Bruxelles, 1962.
42545.3.845 Bibliothèque nationale, Paris. Maurice Maeterlinck, 1862-1949. Paris, n.d.
42545.3.850 Hanse, J. Maurice Maeterlinck, 1862-1962. Paris, 1962.
42545.3.860 Lerberghe, C. Pelléas et Mélisande. Liège, 1962.
42545.3.865 Fondation Maurice Maeterlinck. Annales. Gand. 1,1955+ 3v.
42545.3.870 Renard, R. Maurice Maeterlinck et l'Italie. Paris, 1959.
42545.3.875 Académie...Brussels. Académie royale de langue et littérature françaises. Bruxelles, 1964.
42545.3.880 Esch, Maximilian. L'oeuvre de Maurice Maeterlinck. Paris, 1912.
42545.3.885 Maenner, Peter Johannes. Maurice Maeterlinck; Theatralische Repräsentation einer Philosophie im Zusammenhang der modernen Dramaturgie. Diss. München, 1965.
42545.3.890 Postic, Marcel. Maeterlinck et le symbolisme. Paris, 1970.

42545.5 Individual authors, etc. - 1850-1899 - Drama - Manquat; Manuel; Maiziere; etc.

42545.5 Manquat, Maurice. Tout se pays. Paris, 1908.
42545.5.150 Manuel, Eugène. L'absent. Drame en un acte en vers. 4e éd. Paris, 1873.
42545.5.245 Maiziere, Anot de. Cromwell protecteur de la république anglaise. Paris, 1860-[1861]
42545.5.250 Maiziere, Anot de. Un coup d'etat ou Cromwell, tragédie en cinq actes et en vers. 2e éd. Paris, 1869.

42545.6 Individual authors, etc. - 1850-1899 - Drama - Mazel; Maques; Marot; etc.

42545.6 Mazel, Henri. La fin des dieux. Paris, 1892.
42545.6.35 Mazel, Henri. Le Khalife de Carthage. Paris, 1897.
42545.6.50 Mazel, Henri. Le serment, 1848-1852. Paris, 1937.
42545.6.151 Maques, Melville G. Gustave the professor. Boston, 1888.
42545.6.250 Martin, Alexis. Les débuts de Corneille. Paris, 1888.
42545.6.350 Marot, Gaston. Les Francais au Tonkin. Paris, 1885.

42545.7 - .8 Individual authors, etc. - 1850-1899 - Drama - Maquet

Htn 42545.7* Maquet, A. The double marriage. London, n.d.
42545.8 Maquet, A. Valéria. Paris, 1857.

42545.9 Individual authors, etc. - 1850-1899 - Drama - Martel de Janville

42545.9 Martel de Janville, S.G. Israel. Paris, 1898.
42545.9.2 Martel de Janville, S.G. Ces bons Normands. Paris, 1895.
42545.9.2.5 Martel de Janville, S.G. Ces bons Normands. 17e éd. Paris, 1895.
42545.9.3 Martel de Janville, S.G. Miquette. Paris, 1898.
42545.9.4 Martel de Janville, S.G. Napoléonette. Paris, n.d.
42545.9.5 Martel de Janville, S.G. Les flanchards. 14. éd. Paris, 1917.
42545.9.6 Martel de Janville, S.G. A professional lover. N.Y., 1896.
42545.9.7 Martel de Janville, S.G. Those good Normans. Chicago, 1896.
42545.9.8 Martel de Janville, S.G. Journal d'un grinchu. Paris, 1898.
42545.9.10 Martel de Janville, S.G. Ceux qui s'en f.... Paris, 1918.
42545.9.11 Martel de Janville, S.G. Le monde à côté. Paris, 1920.
42545.9.12 Martel de Janville, S.G. Les amoureux. Paris, 1920.
42545.9.13 Martel de Janville, S.G. Ces bons docteurs. Paris, 1930.
42545.9.14 Martel de Janville, S.G. Autour du mariage. 47e éd. Paris, 1884.
42545.9.16 Martel de Janville, S.G. Trop de chic. Paris, 1900.
42545.9.19 Martel de Janville, S.G. Chiffon's marriage. N.Y., 1895.
42545.9.20 Martel de Janville, S.G. Chiffon's marriage. 2d ed. N.Y., 1895.
42545.9.22 Martel de Janville, S.G. Le mariage de Chiffon. Paris, 1908.
42545.9.23 Martel de Janville, S.G. Le mariage de Chiffon. 36e éd. Paris, 1895.
42545.9.24 Martel de Janville, S.G. A Gallic girl. N.Y., 1895.
42545.9.25 Martel de Janville, S.G. Le joyeuse enfance de la IIIe République. Paris, 1931.
42545.9.26 Martel de Janville, S.G. Autour du divorce. Paris, 189-.
42545.9.30 Martel de Janville, S.G. Petit Bob. Paris, 189-.

42545.9 Individual authors, etc. - 1850-1899 - Drama - Martel de Janville - cont.

42545.9.35 Martel de Janville, S.G. Le coup du lapin. Paris, 1931.
42545.9.40 Martel de Janville, S.G. Un raté. 12. éd. Paris, 1891.
42545.9.45 Martel de Janville, S.G. Bijou. Paris, 1897.
42545.9.50 Martel de Janville, S.G. Souricette. Paris, 1922.

42545.10 - .18 Individual authors, etc. - 1850-1899 - Drama - Meilhac - Writings

42545.10 Meilhac, Henri. Le petit duc. Paris, 1878.
42545.10.5 Meilhac, Henri. Barbe-bleue. Paris, 1888.
42545.10.7 Meilhac, Henri. Les brigands. Paris, 1897.
42545.10.8 Meilhac, Henri. La grande-duchesse de Gérolstein. Paris, 1899.
42545.10.8.5 Meilhac, Henri. La grande-duchesse de Gérolstein. Paris, 1867.
42545.10.9 Meilhac, Henri. La vie Parisienne. Paris, 1889.
42545.10.9.3 Meilhac, Henri. La vie Parisienne. Paris, 1867.
42545.10.9.5 Meilhac, Henri. Pariser Leben; romische Operette. Berlin, 1867.
42545.10.10 Meilhac, Henri. La clé de Metella. 2. éd. Paris, 1863.
42545.10.10.9 Meilhac, Henri. Froufrou. Paris, 1870.
42545.10.11 Meilhac, Henri. Froufrou. 7. éd. Paris, 1873.
42545.10.11.2 Meilhac, Henri. Froufrou. N.Y., 1881.
42545.10.11.3 Meilhac, Henri. Froufrou. N.Y., 188-?
42545.10.11.4 Meilhac, Henri. Froufrou. N.Y., 188-?
42545.10.11.5 Meilhac, Henri. Froufrou. N.Y., 1880.
42545.10.11.6 Meilhac, Henri. Froufrou. 8. éd. Paris, 1880.
42545.10.11.7 Meilhac, Henri. Froufrou. Indianapolis, 1883.
42545.10.11.8 Meilhac, Henri. Froufrou. London, n.d.
42545.10.11.9 Meilhac, Henri. Froufrou. N.Y., 1880.
42545.10.12 Meilhac, Henri. Loulou. Paris, 1876.
42545.10.13 Meilhac, Henri. La petite marquise. Paris, 1874.
42545.10.14 Meilhac, Henri. Le fandango. Paris, 1877.
42545.10.15 Meilhac, Henri. Barbe-bleue. Paris, 1872.
42545.10.16 Meilhac, Henri. Les brigands. Paris, 1875.
42545.10.17 Meilhac, Henri. Le chateau à Toto. Paris, 1873.
42545.10.18 Meilhac, Henri. Janot. Paris, 1881.
42545.10.19 Meilhac, Henri. La diva. Paris, 1869.
42545.10.20 Meilhac, Henri. Ma camarade. Paris, 1894.
42545.10.21 Meilhac, Henri. Décoré. Paris, 1899.
42545.10.22 Meilhac, Henri. Rip. Paris, 1901.
42545.10.22.5 Meilhac, Henri. Rip Van Winkle. London, 1882.
42545.10.23 Meilhac, Henri. Le mari à Babette. Paris, 1882.
42545.10.24 Meilhac, Henri. L'autographe. Paris, 1913.
42545.10.25 Meilhac, Henri. Mam'zelle Nitouche. Paris, n.d.
42545.10.26 Meilhac, Henri. Gotte. Paris, 1894.
42545.10.29 Meilhac, Henri. Ma cousine. N.Y., 1895.
42545.10.30 Meilhac, Henri. L'été de la Saint-Martin. 2e éd. Paris, 1874.
42545.10.31 Meilhac, Henri. La périchole. London, 1870.
42545.10.33 Meilhac, Henri. Pepa. Paris, 1894.
42545.10.42 Meilhac, Henri. Panurge's sheep. N.Y., 1915.
42545.11 Meilhac, Henri. La duchesse Martin. Boston, 1885.
42545.11.10A Meilhac, Henri. Théâtre de Meilhac et Halévy. Paris, 1900. 8v.
42545.11.10B Meilhac, Henri. Théâtre de Meilhac et Halévy. Paris, 1900. 8v.
42545.11.10C Meilhac, Henri. Théâtre de Meilhac et Halévy. v.2,5. Paris, 1900. 2v.
42545.12 Meilhac, Henri. Théâtre. v.1. Paris, 1859-80.
42545.13 Meilhac, Henri. Théâtre. v.2. Paris, n.d.
42545.14 Meilhac, Henri. Théâtre. v.3. n.p., n.d.
42545.15 Meilhac, Henri. Théâtre. v.4. n.p., n.d.
42545.16 Meilhac, Henri. Théâtre. v.5. n.p., n.d.
42545.17 Meilhac, Henri. Théâtre. v.6. n.p., n.d.
42545.18 Meilhac, Henri. Théâtre. v.7. n.p., n.d.
42545.18.20 Meilhac, Henri. Ma cousine. Paris, 1902. 3 pam.

42545.20 Individual authors, etc. - 1850-1899 - Drama - Massonneau; Mazilier; etc.

42545.20.15 Massonneau, F. Étude sentimentale; coeurs blessés. N.Y., 1899.
42545.20.19 Mazilier, N. Aelia et Mysis. Paris, 1853.

42545.21 Individual authors, etc. - 1850-1899 - Drama - Méry; Méténier; etc.

42545.21 Méry, J. Herculanum. Paris, 1859.
42545.21.5 Méry, J. La bête féroce. Paris, 1908.
42545.21.9 Méténier, Oscar. En famille. Paris, n.d.
42545.21.10 Méténier, Oscar. La casserole. Paris, 1889.
42545.21.11 Méténier, Oscar. Demi-castors. Paris, 1894.
42545.21.12 Méténier, Oscar. Les voyous au théâtre. Bruxelles, 1891.
42545.21.14 Méténier, Oscar. Son poteau. Paris, 1901.

42545.22 - .24 Individual authors, etc. - 1850-1899 - Drama - Meurice

42545.22 Meurice, Paul. Paris. Paris, 1855.
42545.23 Meurice, Paul. Benvenuto Cellini. Paris, n.d.
42545.24 Meurice, Paul. Fanfan la Tulipe. Paris, 1892.
42545.24.5 Meurice, Paul. Louspillac et Beautrubin. Paris, 1854.

42545.26 Individual authors, etc. - 1850-1899 - Drama - Mercier; Michaud; etc.

42545.26 Mercier, P. Le roman du village. Paris, 1853.
42545.26.50 Michaud, H. Ma bonne. N.Y., 19- ?
42545.26.52 Michaud, H. Une héroïne. N.Y., 19- ?

42545.27 Individual authors, etc. - 1850-1899 - Drama - Mikhaël, Millanvoye

42545.27.5 Mikhaël, Ephraim. Le cor fleuri. Paris, 1888.
42545.27.9 Millanvoye, B. Le diner de Pierrot. 2e éd. Paris, 1883.

42545.28 - .28.8 Individual authors, etc. - 1850-1899 - Drama - Mirbeau

42545.28 Mirbeau, Octave. Les mauvais bergers. Paris, 1898.
42545.28.3 Mirbeau, Octave. Théâtre. Paris, 1921. 2v.
42545.28.6 Mirbeau, Octave. Les affaires sont les affaires. Paris, 1911.
42545.28.7A Mirbeau, Octave. Le foyer. Paris, 1908.
42545.28.7B Mirbeau, Octave. Le foyer. Paris, 1908.
42545.28.7.11 Mirbeau, Octave. La pipe et cidre. Paris, 1919.
42545.28.7.12 Mirbeau, Octave. La vache tachetée. Paris, 1918.
42545.28.7.13 Mirbeau, Octave. Chez l'illustre écrivain. Paris, 1919.
42545.28.7.14 Mirbeau, Octave. Un gentilhomme. Paris, 1920.
42545.28.7.16 Mirbeau, Octave. La guerre. Bruxelles, n.d.
42545.28.7.20 Mirbeau, Octave. Le jardin des supplices. Paris, 1929.
42545.28.7.21 Mirbeau, Octave. Le jardin des supplices. Paris, 1904.
42545.28.7.30A Mirbeau, Octave. Contes de la chaumiere. Paris, 1923.
42545.28.7.30B Mirbeau, Octave. Contes de la chaumiere. Paris, 1923.

2545.28 - .28.8 Individual authors, etc. - 1850-1899 - Drama - Mirbeau - cont.

42545.28.7.40 Mirbeau, Octave. La pipe de cidre. Paris, 1918.
42545.28.7.45 Mirbeau, Octave. Le journal d'une femme de chambre. Paris, 1906.
42545.28.7.50 Mirbeau, Octave. Les grimaces et quelques autres chroniques. Paris, 1927.
42545.28.7.70 Mirbeau, Octave. Diary of a chambermaid. N.Y., 1946.
42545.28.7.73 Mirbeau, Octave. Torture garden. N.Y., 1948.
42545.28.7.80 Revon, M. Octave Mirbeau, son oeuvre. Paris, 1924.
42545.28.7.85 Schwarz, Martin. Octave Mirbeau, vie et oeuvre. The Hague, 1966.
42545.28.8 Pilon, E. Octave Mirbeau. Paris, 1903.

2545.28.9 - .28.999 Individual authors, etc. - 1850-1899 - Drama - Moinaux (Courteline)

42545.28.9 Moinaux, Georges. Boubouroche. Paris, n.d.
Cg 42545.28.9.5 Moinaux, Georges. La paix chez soi. Paris, n.d. 8 pam.
EDL 42545.28.9.9 Moinaux, Georges. Théâtre. v.2. Paris, 1918.
42545.28.9.10 Moinaux, Georges. Théâtre. Paris, 1927. 2v.
42545.28.9.20 Moinaux, Georges. La vie de Caserne. Paris, 1896?
42545.28.9.32 Moinaux, Georges. Messieurs les ronds-de-cuir. Paris, 1937.
42545.28.9.35 Moinaux, Georges. Messieurs les ronds-de-cuir. n.p., 1948.
42545.28.9.38 Moinaux, Georges. The plays of Georges Courteline. London, 1961.
42545.28.9.40 Moinaux, Georges. La cruche. Paris, 1911.
EDL 42545.28.11 Moinaux, Georges. Théâtre. v.1. Paris, 1926.
42545.28.16 Moinaux, Georges. Un client sérieux. Paris, 19- ?
42545.28.19.5 Moinaux, Jules. Les deux sourds; comédie en un acte. Paris, 1922.
42545.28.20 Moinaux, Jules. Les deux aveugles. n.p., n.d.
42545.28.25 Moinaux, Georges. Les gaîtés de l'escadron. Paris, 1937.
42545.28.25.10 Moinaux, Georges. Les gaîtés de l'escadron. Paris, 1948.
42545.28.26 Moinaux, Georges. Les gaîtés de l'escadron. Paris, 19- .
42545.28.27 Moinaux, Georges. Les plus belles pages de Courteline. Paris, 1932.
42545.28.30 Moinaux, Jules. Les tribunaux comiques. Paris, 1881.
42545.28.40 Moinaux, Georges. Boubouroche. n.p., 1947.
42545.28.50 Moinaux, Georges. Un client sérieux. n.p., 1948.
42545.28.60 Moinaux, Georges. Les femmes d'amis. n.p., 1947.
42545.28.70 Moinaux, Georges. Le train de 8h. 47. n.p., 1948.
42545.28.80 Moinaux, Georges. Les linottes. n.p., 1948.
42545.28.90 Moinaux, Georges. Ah! Jeunesse et autres contes. Paris, 1948.
42545.28.100 Moinaux, Georges. La vie de ménage. Paris, 1949.
42545.28.110 Moinaux, Georges. Les balances. Paris, 1910?
42545.28.800 Dubeux, Albert. La curieuse vie de Georges Courteline. Paris, 1949.
42545.28.800.2 Dubeux, Albert. La curieuse vie de Georges Courteline. Paris, 1958.
42545.28.802 Le Brun, Roger. Georges Courteline. Paris, 1906.
42545.28.805 Richards, M.L. Le comique de Courteline. Montreal, 1950.
42545.28.805.2 Richards, M.L. Le comique de Courteline. Montreal, 1950.
42545.28.810 Portail, Jean. Georges Courteline, l'humoriste Français. Paris, 1928.
42545.28.815 Bornecque, Pierre Henry. Le théâtre de Georges Courteline. Thèse. Paris, 1969.

2545.29 - .38 Individual authors, etc. - 1850-1899 - Drama - Monnier, H.

42545.29 Monnier, Henry. Un détraqué. Paris, 1883.
42545.30 Monnier, Henry. Paris et la province. Paris, 1866.
Htn 42545.31* Monnier, Henry. Bas-fonds de la société. Amsterdam, 1866.
42545.32 Monnier, Henry. La religion des imbeciles. Paris, n.d.
42545.34 Monnier, Henry. Mémoires de M. Joseph Prudhomme. Paris, 1857. 2v.
42545.38 Monnier, Henry. Les Bourgeois aux champs. Paris, 1858.
42545.38.5 Monnier, Henry. Galerie d'originaux. Paris, 1858.
42545.38.10 Monnier, Henry. Les bourgeois de Paris. Paris, 1854.
42545.38.15 Monnier, Henry. Croquis à la plume. Paris, 1858.
42545.38.21 Monnier, Henry. Morceaux choisis. Paris, 1935.
42545.38.75 Wolerum, H. Das literarische Werk Henri Monnier's. Inaug. Diss. Lauf, 1930.
42545.38.80A Melcher, Edith. The life and times of Henry Monnier. Cambridge, 1950.
42545.38.80B Melcher, Edith. The life and times of Henry Monnier. Cambridge, 1950.
42545.38.90 Marash, J.G. Henry Monnier. London, 1951.

2545.39 - .42 Individual authors, etc. - 1850-1899 - Drama - Monselet

42545.39 Monselet, Charles. Les aveux d'un pamphlétaire. Paris, 1854.
42545.39.15 Monselet, Charles. Une troupe de comédiens. Paris, 1879.
42545.39.20 Monselet, Charles. Un carreau brisé. Bordeaux, 1844.
42545.41 Monselet, Charles. Théâtre de Figaro. Paris, 1861.
42545.42 Monselet, Charles. Panier fleuri prose et vers. Paris, 1873.
42545.42.5 Monselet, Charles. Le revue sans titre...1876. Paris, 1877.
42545.42.10 Monselet, Charles. Lettres de Monselet à Lesclide, juin-octobre, 1846. Thèse. Paris, 1927.
42545.42.50 Desfeuilles, P. Charles Monselet et la critique anecdotique. Thèse. Paris, 1927.

2545.43 - .44 Individual authors, etc. - 1850-1899 - Drama - Moreau; etc.

42545.43 Moreau, Émile. Théâtre. Paris, n.d. 2v.
42545.44 Moreau, Émile. Le procès de Jeanne d'Arc. Paris, 1909.
42545.44.2 Moreau, Émile. Le procès de Jeanne d'Arc. Paris, 1910.
42545.44.3 Moreau, Émile. Argument of the play Le procès de Jeanne d'Arc. N.Y., 1911.
42545.44.4 Moreau, Émile. Argument of the play Le procès de Jeanne d'Arc. N.Y., 191-?
42545.44.9 Moreau, Émile. Madame Margot. Paris, 1910.
42545.44.10 Moreau, Émile. Matapan; comédie en trois actes. Paris, 1886.
Htn 42545.44.15* Moreau, Eugène. The courier of Lyons. v.1-2. London, 1854?
42545.44.16 Moreau, Eugène. The courier of Lyons. v.1-2. London, n.d.
42545.44.22 Moreau, Pol. Nos alliées. Paris, 1882.
42545.44.30 Mullem, Louis. Une nouvelle école. Paris, 1890.

42545.45 Individual authors, etc. - 1850-1899 - Drama - Najac; Népoty; Nigond; etc.

42545.45 Najac, Émile de. La poule et ses poussins. Paris, 1861.
42545.45.5 Najac, Émile de. Babie; a comedy in three acts. Boston, 1880.
42545.45.6 Najac, Émile de. Babie; a comedy in three acts. Boston, 1889.
42545.45.7 Najac, Raoul de. Maman; drame zoologique en deux actes et un prologue. n.p., 1910.
42545.45.10 Népoty, L. L'Oreille. Fendue. Paris, 1908.
42545.45.11 Népoty, L. Les petits. Paris, 1912.
42545.45.11.3F Népoty, L. La cigale ayant aimé. Paris, 1921.
42545.45.13 Nigond, Gabriel. Théâtre. 2e éd. Paris, 1912.
42545.45.15 Nigond, Gabriel. L'Ombre des pins. Paris, 1904.
42545.45.16 Nigond, Gabriel. 1812. v.1-2. Paris, 1910.
42545.45.17F Nigond, Gabriel. Sophie Arnould. v.1-2. Paris, 1921.
42545.45.18 Nigond, Gabriel. Sophie Arnould. Paris, 1922.
42545.45.35 Nigond, Gabriel. Kéroubinos. Paris, 1909.
42545.45.40 Nigond, Gabriel. Perlot; pièce en un acte. Paris, 1911.
42545.45.50 Nigond, Gabriel. Nouveaux contes de la Limousine. Paris, 1907.
42545.45.80 Vesvre, Hilaire de. Gabriel Nigond. Verneuil-sur-Igneraie, 1947.

42545.46 Individual authors, etc. - 1850-1899 - Drama - Normand

42545.46 Normand, J. La muse qui trotte. Paris, 1894.
42545.46.5 Normand, J. Les drapeaux déployés. Paris, 1919.
42545.46.10 Normand, J. L'amiral. Paris, 1895.

42545.47 - .48 Individual authors, etc. - 1850-1899 - Drama - Nuitter de Beaumont

42545.47 Nuitter de Beaumont, E. La flute enchantée. Paris, 1865.
42545.48 Nuitter de Beaumont, E. Le coeur et main. Paris, 1882.

42545.50 Individual authors, etc. - 1850-1899 - Drama - Nus

42545.50 Nus, Eugène. Miss Multon. 3d ed. Paris, 1869.
42545.50.5 Nus, Eugène. Un mari brulé. Boston, 1863.

42545.62 - .68 Individual authors, etc. - 1850-1899 - Drama - Pailleron

42545.62 Pailleron, Edouard. Amours et haines. Paris, 1889.
42545.62.7 Pailleron, Edouard. Les faux menages. Paris, 1869.
42545.62.9 Pailleron, Edouard. L'autre motif. Paris, 1922.
42545.63.3 Pailleron, Edouard. Le monde ou l'on s'ennuie. 24. éd. Paris, 1882.
42545.63.5 Pailleron, Edouard. Le monde ou l'on s'ennuie. 38. éd. Paris, 1889.
42545.63.6 Pailleron, Edouard. Le monde ou l'on s'ennuie. 46. éd. Paris, 1890.
42545.63.7 Pailleron, Edouard. Le monde ou l'on s'ennuie. Boston, 1911.
42545.63.9 Pailleron, Edouard. Le monde ou l'on s'ennuie. 130e éd. Paris, 1919?
42545.63.12 Pailleron, Edouard. Prière pour la France. Paris, 1871.
42545.64 Pailleron, Edouard. Cabotins! La Poupée. Le Narcotique. Paris, 1882-97.
42545.65 Pailleron, Edouard. Théâtre. v.1. Paris, 1860.
42545.66 Pailleron, Edouard. Théâtre. v.2. Paris, 1873.
42545.68 Pailleron, Edouard. Le théâtre chez madame. Paris, 1881.
Htn 42545.68.2* Pailleron, Edouard. Le théâtre chez madame. Paris, 1881.
42545.68.5 Pailleron, Edouard. Le monde ou l'on s'amuse. 11e éd. Paris, n.d.
42545.68.15 Pailleron, Edouard. Pièces et morceaux. Paris, 1897.
42545.68.75 Paternostro, A.L. Edouard Pailleron, 1834-1899. Paris, 1931.

42545.69 Individual authors, etc. - 1850-1899 - Drama - Parodi; Pelletier; Petitdidier; Philippe d'Ennery; Pierron; etc.

42545.69.4.75 Parodi, A. Rome vaincue. 6. éd. Paris, 1876.
42545.69.4.80 Parodi, A. Rome vaincue. 10. éd. Paris, 1876.
42545.69.5 Parodi, A. Théâtre. Paris, 1893. 2v.
42545.69.6.10 Pelletier, Claude. Les hérétiques revolutionnaires-socialistes du XVème siècle. N.Y., 1867.
42545.69.7 Petit, Georges. La dame d'en face. Paris, 1872.
42545.69.9 Petitdidier, L.E. Théâtre légendaire. Paris, 1908.
42545.69.10 Petitdidier, L.E. Pour les inondés. Paris, 1875.
42545.69.12 Petit-Favre. Le drapeau. Epernay, 1907.
42545.69.13 Dennery, Adolphe Philippe. A celebrated case. N.Y., 18- ?
42545.69.13.3 Dennery, Adolphe Philippe. A celebrated case. N.Y., 18- .
42545.69.14 Dennery, Adolphe Philippe. Le Cid. Paris, 1886.
42545.69.15 Dennery, Adolphe Philippe. Les deux orphelines. Paris, 1907.
42545.69.16 Dennery, Adolphe Philippe. Les deux orphelines. Paris, 1875.
42545.69.17 Dennery, Adolphe Philippe. The two orphans. N.Y., n.d.
42545.69.18 Dennery, Adolphe Philippe. Ernestine. N.Y., 18- .
42545.69.19 Dennery, Adolphe Philippe. Marie-Jeanne. Paris, n.d.
42545.69.19.3 Dennery, Adolphe Philippe. Jocrisse, the juggler. London, 18- ?
42545.69.19.5 Dennery, Adolphe Philippe. Maria Giovanna, o La famiglia del Beone. Milano, 1853.
42545.69.19.20 Dennery, Adolphe Philippe. Sept merveilles du monde. Paris, 1853.
42545.69.19.25 Dennery, Adolphe Philippe. Si j'étais roi! ... opéra comique. Paris, 1852.
42545.69.20 Dennery, Adolphe Philippe. Martyre. Paris, 1907.
42545.69.25 Dennery, Adolphe Philippe. The sea of ice. London, 18- ?
42545.69.50 Pierron, Eugène. Book the third, chapter the first, a comedy. London, 18- ?
42545.69.60 Pierron, Eugène. Two can play at that game. v.1-2. N.Y., n.d.
42545.69.62A Pierron, Eugène. Two can play at that game. Boston, 1857?
42545.69.62B Pierron, Eugène. Two can play at that game. Boston, 1857?

42545.71 Individual authors, etc. - 1850-1899 - Drama - Piestre

42545.71 Piestre, P.E. La goton de Biranger. Paris, 1851.

42545.75 - .77 Individual authors, etc. - 1850-1899 - Drama - Picard

42545.75 Picard, André. L'ange gardien. Paris, 1910.
42545.75.30 Picard, André. Franchise. Paris, 1899.
42545.76 Picard, André. La fugitive. Paris, 1910.
42545.77 Picard, André. Jeunesse. Paris, 1906.

42545.78 Individual authors, etc. - 1850-1899 - Drama - Plouvier

42545.78.30 Plouvier, Édouard. Le sang-mêlé; drame en cinq actes, en prose. Paris, 1856.
42545.78.35 Plouvier, Édouard. Toute seule. Paris, 1860.

42545.80 Individual authors, etc. - 1850-1899 - Drama - Ply
42545.80 Ply, H. Les chevaliers d'Eppes. Chauny, 1898.

42545.82 - .83 Individual authors, etc. - 1850-1899 - Drama - Ponsard - Writings
42545.82 Ponsard, F. L'honneur et l'argent. 4. éd. Paris, 1853.
42545.82.3 Ponsard, F. L'honneur et l'argent. 4. éd. Bielefeld, 1865.
42545.83 Ponsard, F. Ce qui plait aux femmes. 2e éd. Paris, 1860.
42545.83.3 Ponsard, F. La bourse. 2e éd. Paris, 1856.
42545.83.5 Ponsard, F. Galilée. 3e éd. Paris, 1867.
42545.83.6 Ponsard, F. Études antiques. Paris, 1852.
42545.83.8 Ponsard, F. Lucrèce. 4e éd. Paris, 1843.
42545.83.10 Ponsard, F. La comtesse d'Agouet et François Ponsard. Paris, 1960.

42545.84 Individual authors, etc. - 1850-1899 - Drama - Ponsard - Works about
42545.84 Schrenker, H. Ponsard als Dramatiker und Lyriker. Inaug. Diss. Borna, 1913.
42545.84.5 Landström, A.R. Om François Ponsard som dramatisk skald. Stockholm, 1877.
42545.84.10 Inauguration de la statue de F. Ponsard. Vienne, 1870.
42545.84.15 Janin, J.G. F. Ponsard, 1814-67. Paris, 1872.

42545.85 - .88 Individual authors, etc. - 1850-1899 - Drama - Porto-Riche
42545.85 Porto-Riche, G. Théâtre d'amour. Paris, 1907.
42545.85.2 Porto-Riche, G. Théâtre d'amour. 19e éd. Paris, 192-?
42545.85.5 Porto-Riche, G. Théâtre complet. Paris, 1923. 2v.
42545.86 Porto-Riche, G. Amoureuse. Paris, 1908.
42545.87 Porto-Riche, G. Le vieil homme. Paris, 1911.
42545.88 Porto-Riche, G. Un drame sous Philippe II. Paris, 1912.
42545.88.5 Porto-Riche, G. Le passé; comédie. Paris, 1921.
42545.88.25 Porto-Riche, G. Les vrais dieux. Paris, 1930. 2 pam.
42545.88.35 Porto-Riche, G. Le marchand d'estampes. Paris, 1930.
42545.88.40 Porto-Riche, G. Anatomie sentimentale. Paris, 1920?
42545.88.43 Porto-Riche, G. Zubiri. Paris, 1912.
42545.88.47 Porto-Riche, G. Le vertige. Paris, 1873.
42545.88.50 Porto-Riche, G. Vanina. Paris, 1879.
42545.88.52 Porto-Riche, G. Tout n'est pas rose. Paris, 1877.
42545.88.55 Porto-Riche, G. L'infidèle. Paris, 1890.
42545.88.57 Porto-Riche, G. Les deux fautes. Paris, 1879.
42545.88.60 Porto-Riche, G. Bonheur manqué. Paris, 1903.
42545.88.100 Brugmans, H. Georges de Porto-Riche. Proefschrift. Paris, 1934.
42545.88.102 Brugmans, H. Georges de Porto-Riche. Paris, 1934.
42545.88.109 Müller, W. Georges de Porto-Riche, 1849-1930; l'homme, le poète, le dramaturge. Thèse. La Flèche, 1934.
42545.88.110 Müller, W. Georges de Porto-Riche, 1849-1930. Paris, 1934.
42545.88.115 Sée, Edmond. Porto-Riche. Paris, 1932.
42545.88.120 Rey, Étienne. Georges de Porto-Riche. Abbeville, 1924.
42545.88.130 Henry-Marx. Georges de Porto-Riche. Paris, 1924.
42545.88.135 Roger-Marx, Claude. G. de Porto-Riche. Paris, 1912.

42545.89 Individual authors, etc. - 1850-1899 - Drama - Potron
42545.89 Potron, C. A bad temper. N.Y., 1879?
42545.90 Aubrun, R.G. Péladan. Paris, 1904.

42545.95 Individual authors, etc. - 1850-1899 - Drama - Pottecher
42545.95 Pottecher, M. Le château de Hans. Paris, 1908.
42545.95.2 Pottecher, M. Le château de Hans. Paris, 1934?
42545.95.5 Pottecher, M. Le bourdon de Herlisheim. Paris, 1934.
42545.95.10 Pottecher, M. Le secret de la montagne. Paris, 1931?
42545.95.15 Pottecher, M. La passion de Jeanne d'Arc. Paris, 1904.
42545.95.20 Pottecher, M. La passion de Jeanne d'Arc. Paris, 193-?
42545.95.25 Pottecher, M. La clairière aux abeilles. Paris, 1910.
42545.95.30 Auvray, R. Le sotré de Noël. Remiremont, 1933?
42545.95.35 Pottecher, M. Jean de Calais. Paris, 1933.
42545.95.40 Pottecher, M. Le mystère de Judas Iscariote. Paris, 1911.
42545.95.45 Pottecher, M. T'es pris, Grillot! Paris, 1931?
42545.95.50 Pottecher, M. Un d'eux, nommé Jean. Paris, 1926.
42545.95.55 Pottecher, M. Les chants de la tourmente. Paris, 1916.
42545.95.60 Pottecher, M. L'appel des sirènes. Paris, 1930.

42545.100 - .101 Individual authors, etc. - 1850-1899 - Drama - Prével
42545.100 Prével, Jules. L'amour mouillé. Paris, 1887.
42545.101 Prével, Jules. Un mari qui pleure. Paris, 1876.

42545.105 Individual authors, etc. - 1850-1899 - Drama - Prévost
42545.105 Prévost, M. Pierre et Thérèse. Paris, 1910.

42546.4 Individual authors, etc. - 1850-1899 - Drama - Richard
42546.4 Richard, G. Les enfants. 2e ed. Paris, 1872.

42546.6 Individual authors, etc. - 1850-1899 - Drama - Ringal; Rivoire
42546.6.5 Ringal, Gustave. Le vidame. Paris, 1873.
42546.6.9 Rivoire, A. Mon ami Teddy. Paris, 1910.
42546.6.10 Rivoire, A. Mon ami Teddy. Paris, 1910.
42546.6.12 Rivoire, A. Pour vivre heureux. Paris, 1912.
42546.6.14 Rivoire, A. Le plaisir des jours. Paris, 1914.

42546.8 Individual authors, etc. - 1850-1899 - Drama - Rodenbach
42546.8 Rodenbach, G. Le voile. Paris, 1897.
42546.8.5 Rodenbach, G. Le mirage. Paris, 1901.
42546.8.9 Rodenbach, G. Bruges-la-Morte. Paris, n.d.
42546.8.15 Rodenbach, G. La vocation. Paris, 1895.
42546.8.35 Rodenbach, G. Die dramatischen Werke. München, 1913.
42546.8.40 Rodenback, G. Choix de poésies. Paris, 1949.
42546.8.41 Rodenbach, G. Oeuvres. Paris, 1923-25. 2v.
42546.8.79 Violato, Gabriella. Bibiographie de Georges Rodenbach et de Albert Samain en Italie. Firenze, 1965.
42546.8.80 Maes, Pierre. Georges Rodenbach. Gembloux, 1952.

42546.9 Individual authors, etc. - 1850-1899 - Drama - Rosier
42546.9 Rosier, Joseph Bernard. Brutus, lâche César comédie en un acte mêleé de chant. Paris, 1864.
42546.9.5 Rosier, Joseph Bernard. El secreto de la reina: Zarzuela en tres actos. Madrid, 1852.

42546.10 - .11 Individual authors, etc. - 1850-1899 - Drama - Rostand, Edmond - Writings
42546.10.2 Rostand, Edmond. Plays of Edmond Rostand. N.Y., 1921. 2v.
42546.10.4 Rostand, Edmond. L'aiglon. Paris, 1900.
42546.10.4.5 Rostand, Edmond. L'aiglon. Paris, 1900.
42546.10.5A Rostand, Edmond. L'aiglon. N.Y., 1900.
42546.10.5B Rostand, Edmond. L'aiglon. N.Y., 1900.
42546.10.5C Rostand, Edmond. L'aiglon. N.Y., 1900.
42546.10.5D Rostand, Edmond. L'aiglon. N.Y., 1900.
42546.10.5E Rostand, Edmond. L'aiglon. N.Y., 1900.
42546.10.5G Rostand, Edmond. L'aiglon. N.Y., 1900.
42546.10.6 Rostand, Edmond. L'aiglon. N.Y., 1900.
42546.10.8 Rostand, Edmond. L'aiglon. New Haven, 1927.
42546.11A Rostand, Edmond. L'aiglon. N.Y., 1900.
42546.11B Rostand, Edmond. L'aiglon. N.Y., 1900.
42546.11C Rostand, Edmond. L'aiglon. N.Y., 1900.
42546.11.2 Rostand, Edmond. L'aiglon. N.Y., 1901.
42546.11.5 Rostand, Edmond. L'aiglon. N.Y., 1900.
42546.11.6 Rostand, Edmond. L'aiglon. N.Y., 1901.
42546.11.15 Rostand, Edmond. L'aiglon, drame en six actes. N.Y., 1913.

42546.12 Individual authors, etc. - 1850-1899 - Drama - Rostand, Edmond - Biography and criticism
42546.12 Magne, Émile. Les erreurs de documentation de Cyrano de Bergerac. Paris, 1898.
42546.12.5 Strachey, L. Cyrano de Bergerac. n.p., n.d.
42546.12.9 Schenk, A. Études sur la Rime dans Cyrano de Bergerac. Kiel, 1900.
42546.12.10 Platow, Hans. Die Personen von Rostands Cyrano de Bergerac. Erlangen, 1902.
42546.12.12 Pamphlet box. Rostand Edmond.
42546.12.13F Pamphlet box. Rostand Edmond.
42546.12.19 Hangmard, L. Edmond Rostand. Paris, n.d.
42546.12.20 Rostand, Edmond. Discours de réception à l'Académie Française. Paris, 1903.
42546.12.21A Haraszti, J. Edmond Rostand. Paris, 1913.
42546.12.21B Haraszti, J. Edmond Rostand. Paris, 1913.
42546.12.23 Suberville, J. Le théâtre d'Edmond Rostand. Paris, 1919.
42546.12.25 Lautier, André. Edmond Rostand, son oeuvre, portrait et autographe. Paris, 1924.
42546.12.30 Bédier, Joseph. Discours de réception à l'Académie Française. Paris, 1921.
42546.12.35 Page, Dorothy. Edmond Rostand et la légende napoléonienne dans L'aiglon. Thèse. Paris, 1928.
42546.12.38 Lemke, Ottilie. Der historische Hintergrund. Inaug. Diss. Leipzig, 1929.
42546.12.40 Faure, Paul. Vingt ans d'intimite avec Edmond Rostand. Paris, 1928.
42546.12.43 Mügge, O. Edmond Rostand als Dramatiker. Friedeberg, 1903.
42546.12.44 Grieve, J.W. L'oeuvre dramatique d'Edmond Rostand. Thèse. Paris, 1931.
42546.12.45 Grieve, J.W. L'oeuvre dramatique d'Edmond Rostand. Paris, 1931.
42546.12.50 Premsela, M.J. Edmond Rostand. Amsterdam, 1933.
42546.12.55 Katz, Elly. L'esprit français dans le théâtre d'Edmond Rostand. Thèse. Paris, 1934.
42546.12.56 Gérard, R. Edmond Rostand. Paris, 1935.
42546.12.57 Ryland, H. The sources of the play Cyrano de Bergerac. N.Y., 1936.
42546.12.60 Lutgen, Odette. De pére en fils: Edmond et Jean. Paris, 1965.
42546.12.65 Daladie, Maité. Lettre à ma niece sur Edmond Rostand. Toulouse, 1970.

42546.13 - .15.18 Individual authors, etc. - 1850-1899 - Drama - Rostand, Edmond - Writings
42546.13 Rostand, Edmond. Cyrano de Bergerac. Paris, 1898.
42546.13.1.2 Rostand, Edmond. Cyrano de Bergerac. Paris, 1898.
42546.13.1.3 Rostand, Edmond. Cyrano de Bergerac. Paris, 1929.
42546.13.1.4 Rostand, Edmond. Cyrano de Bergerac. Paris, 1898.
42546.13.1.5 Rostand, Edmond. Cyrano de Bergerac. Paris, 1930.
42546.13.1.6 Rostand, Edmond. Cyrano de Bergerac. N.Y., 1898.
42546.13.1.7 Rostand, Edmond. Cyrano de Bergerac. Paris, 1898.
42546.13.1.10 Rostand, Edmond. Cyrano de Bergerac. Paris, 1938.
42546.13.1.15 Rostand, Edmond. Cyrano de Bergerac. Oxford, 1943.
42546.13.2.3 Rostand, Edmond. Cyrano de Bergerac. N.Y., 1898.
42546.13.3 Rostand, Edmond. Cyrano de Bergerac. N.Y., 1898.
42546.13.5 Rostand, Edmond. Cyrano de Bergerac. Paris, 1898.
42546.13.6 Rostand, Edmond. Cyrano de Bergerac. Paris, 1898.
42546.13.6.5 Rostand, Edmond. Cyrano de Bergerac. Paris, 1898.
42546.13.15 Rostand, Edmond. Cyrano de Bergerac. Mount Vernon, 1941.
42546.13.20 Rostand, Edmond. Cyrano de Bergerac. Milano, 1952.
42546.14A Rostand, Edmond. Cyrano de Bergerac. N.Y., 1898.
42546.14B Rostand, Edmond. Cyrano de Bergerac. N.Y., 1898.
42546.14.1.5A Rostand, Edmond. Cyrano de Bergerac. N.Y., 1898.
42546.14.1.5B Rostand, Edmond. Cyrano de Bergerac. N.Y., 1898.
42546.14.1.5C Rostand, Edmond. Cyrano de Bergerac. N.Y., 1898.
42546.14.2A Rostand, Edmond. Cyrano de Bergerac. N.Y., 1899.
42546.14.2B Rostand, Edmond. Cyrano de Bergerac. N.Y., 1899.
42546.14.3A Rostand, Edmond. Cyrano de Bergerac. Boston, 1898.
42546.14.3B Rostand, Edmond. Cyrano de Bergerac. Boston, 1898.
42546.14.3C Rostand, Edmond. Cyrano de Bergerac. Boston, 1898.
42546.14.4 Rostand, Edmond. Cyrano de Bergerac. N.Y., 18- .
42546.14.5.10 Rostand, Edmond. Cyrano de Bergerac. N.Y., 1919.
42546.14.5.50A Rostand, Edmond. Cyrano de Bergerac. N.Y., 1924.
42546.14.5.50B Rostand, Edmond. Cyrano de Bergerac. N.Y., 1924.
42546.14.5.50C Rostand, Edmond. Cyrano de Bergerac. N.Y., 1924.
42546.14.5.60 Rostand, Edmond. Cyrano de Bergerac. N.Y., 1921.
42546.14.5.62 Rostand, Edmond. Cyrano de Bergerac. Garden City, 1922.
42546.14.5.63 Rostand, Edmond. Cyrano de Bergerac. N.Y., 1923.
42546.14.5.70A Rostand, Edmond. Cyrano de Bergerac. N.Y., 1929.
42546.14.5.70B Rostand, Edmond. Cyrano de Bergerac. N.Y., 1929.
42546.14.5.73 Rostand, Edmond. Cyrano de Bergerac. Washington, 1933.
42546.14.5.75 Rostand, Edmond. Cyrano de Bergerac. N.Y., 1931.
42546.14.7 Rostand, Edmond. The story of Cyrano de Bergerac. N.Y., 1898.
42546.14.8.15 Rostand, Edmond. Cyrano von Bergerac. Stuttgart, 1922.
42546.14.8.75 Rostand, Edmond. Syrano de Mperzerak. en Peiraiei, 1898.
42546.14.9 Rostand, Edmond. The fantasticks. London, 1900.
42546.14.10 Rostand, Edmond. The fantasticks. N.Y., 1900.
42546.15 Rostand, Edmond. The romancers. N.Y., 1899.
42546.15.3.30 Rostand, Edmond. Chantecler. Paris, 1946.
42546.15.5 Rostand, Edmond. Les romanesques. Paris, 1899.
42546.15.6 Rostand, Edmond. Les romanesques. Boston, 1903.
42546.15.6.11 Rostand, Edmond. La princesse Lointaine. Paris, 1899.

2546.13 - .15.18 Individual authors, etc. - 1850-1899 - Drama - Rostand, Edmond - Writings - cont.

42546.15.6.12	Rostand, Edmond. La princesse Lointaine. Paris, 1900.
42546.15.7	Rostand, Edmond. La princesse Lointaine. Paris, 1905.
42546.15.7.2	Rostand, Edmond. La princesse Lointaine. Paris, 1905.
42546.15.7.5	Rostand, Edmond. La princesse Lointaine. Paris, 1911.
42546.15.7.6	Rostand, Edmond. La princesse Lointaine. Paris, 1911.
42546.15.7.10	Rostan,d Edmond. La princesse Lointaine. Paris, 1929.
42546.15.7.40	Rostand, Edmond. The far princess. Boston, 1935.
42546.15.7.42	Rostand, Edmond. The far princess. N.Y., 1925.
42546.15.8	Rostand, Edmond. La Samaritaine. Paris, 1905.
42546.15.8.2	Rostand, Edmond. La Samaritaine. Paris, 1905.
42546.15.8.5	Rostand, Edmond. La Samaritaine. Paris, 1903.
42546.15.9	Arnold, N. Edmond Rostands "Princesse Lointaine" und "Samaritaine". Arnstadt, 1901.
42546.15.10	Rostand, Edmond. Un soir à Hernani. Paris, 1902.
42546.15.11	Rostand, Edmond. Pour la Grèce. Paris, 1897.
42546.15.12	Rostand, Edmond. Chantecler. pts.1-4. Paris, 1910.
42546.15.13	Rostand, Edmond. Chantecler. Paris, 1910.
42546.15.13.1	Rostand, Edmond. Chantecler. Paris, 1910.
42546.15.13.2	Rostand, Edmond. Chantecler. Paris, 1910.
42546.15.13.3A	Rostand, Edmond. Chantecler. N.Y., 1910.
42546.15.13.3B	Rostand, Edmond. Chantecler. N.Y., 1910.
42546.15.13.3C	Rostand, Edmond. Chantecler. N.Y., 1910.
42546.15.13.4	Rostand, Edmond. Chantecler. Paris, 1910.
42546.15.13.5	Rostand, Edmond. Chantecler. Paris, 1910.
42546.15.13.6A	Rostand, Edmond. Chantecler. Paris, 1910.
42546.15.13.6B	Rostand, Edmond. Chantecler. Paris, 1910.
42546.15.13.7	Rostand, Edmond. Chantecler; pièce en quatre actes, en vers. Paris, 1910.
42546.15.13.25	Rostand, Edmond. The story of Chanticleer. N.Y., 1913.
42546.15.14	Rostand, Edmond. Les musardises. Paris, 1911.
42546.15.15A	Rostand, Edmond. La dernière nuit de Don Juan. Paris, 1921.
42546.15.15B	Rostand, Edmond. La dernière nuit de Don Juan. Paris, 1921.
42546.15.15.25	Rostand, Edmond. The last night of Don Juan. Yellow Springs, Ohio, 1929.
42546.15.16	Rostand, Edmond. Le cantique de l'aile. Paris, 1922.
42546.15.17	Rostand, Edmond. Die romanse oor die muur. Kaapstad, 1962.

42546.15.19 Individual authors, etc. - 1850-1899 - Drama - Rostand, Maurice

42546.15.19.5	Rostand, Maurice. Charlotte et Macimilien. Paris, 1945.

42546.15.20 - .15.99 Individual authors, etc. - 1850-1899 - Drama - Rothschild; Saint Geniès; Salandri; etc.

	42546.15.20	Rothschild, Henri de. La rampe et les deux visages. Paris, 1909.
	42546.15.20.3F	Rothschild, Henri de. Le caducée; pièce. Paris, 1921.
	42546.15.20.5	Rothschild, Henri de. Le grand patron. Paris, 1931.
	42546.15.20.6	Rothschild, Henri de. Un côeur sur le gril; pièce en quatre actes. Pôrto, 1944.
	42546.15.20.9	Saglier, Louis. Le théâtre en famille. 2e éd. Paris, 185-?
	42546.15.21	St. Geniès, Richard. Le club des Braconniers. Paris, 1887.
	42546.15.22	St. Geniès, Richard. Place au théâtre! 3e éd. Paris, 1894.
	42546.15.22.10	St. Geniès, Richard. L'amour sans phrases. Paris, 1904.
	42546.15.23	St. Georges de Bouhélier. La tragédie royale. Paris, 1909.
	42546.15.24	Le Blond, M. St. Georges de Bouhélier. Paris, 1909.
X Cg	42546.15.25	Salandri, Gaston. La prose. Paris, 1888.
	42546.15.26	Salandri, Gaston. La prose. Paris, 1888.
	42546.15.27	Salandri, Gaston. La ronçon. Paris, 1892.

42546.16 Individual authors, etc. - 1850-1899 - Drama - Sardou - Complete and Selected works

42546.16.5	Sardou, Victorien. Théâtre. Paris, 1884-98. 2v.
42546.16.10	Sardou, Victorien. Théâtre complet. Paris, 1934. 15v.

42546.17 - .30 Individual authors, etc. - 1850-1899 - Drama - Sardou - Individual works

42546.17	Sardou, Victorien. Nos bons villageois. Paris, 1867.
42546.17.3	Sardou, Victorien. La famille Benoiton. Paris, 1873. 3 pam.
42546.17.5	Sardou, Victorien. Nos bons villageois. Paris, 1867.
42546.18	Sardou, Victorien. Maison neuve. Paris, 1867.
42546.18.5	Sardou, Victorien. Maison neuve. Paris, 1867.
42546.19	Sardou, Victorien. Le dégel. Paris, 1864.
42546.19.5	Sardou, Victorien. Le dégel. Paris, 1864.
42546.20	Sardou, Victorien. Rabagas. Paris, 1872.
42546.20.2	Sardou, Victorien. Rabagas; comedie en 5 actes, en prose. Paris, n.d.
42546.20.5	Sardou, Victorien. Rabagas; comedia en cinco actos. Valparaiso, 1895.
42546.20.8	Sardou, Victorien. Rabagas. 28e éd. Paris, 1872.
42546.21.2	Sardou, Victorien. Séraphine. Paris, 1869.
42546.21.5	Sardou, Victorien. Séraphine. Paris, 1869.
42546.22	Sardou, Victorien. Les vieux garçons. 5e éd. Paris, 1865.
42546.22.5	Sardou, Victorien. Les vieux garçons. Paris, 1865.
42546.23	Sardou, Victorien. Andrea. Paris, 1880.
42546.23.5	Sardou, Victorien. Andrea; comedia. Madrid, 1886.
42546.23.30	Sardou, Victorien. Daniel Rochat. 4e ed. Paris, 1880.
42546.23.35	Sardou, Victorien. Daniel Rochat. 11e ed. Paris, 1887.
42546.24.2	Sardou, Victorien. Divorçons. Paris, 1883.
42546.24.4	Sardou, Victorien. Divorçons. N.Y., 1880.
42546.24.6	Sardou, Victorien. Divorçons! 22e éd. Paris, 1894.
42546.24.7	Sardou, Victorien. Divorçons. Chicago, 1909.
42546.24.9	Sardou, Victorien. Don Quichotte. Paris, 1878.
42546.25	Sardou, Victorien. L'ecureuil. Paris, 1885.
42546.25.30	Sardou, Victorien. Les ganaches. N.Y., 1863.
42546.25.35	Sardou, Victorien. Les ganaches. Paris, 1891.
42546.26	Sardou, Victorien. La haine. Paris, 1875.
42546.26.5	Sardou, Victorien. La papillonne. Paris, 1874.
42546.26.5.2	Sardou, Victorien. Flattersucht. Wien, 187-.
42546.26.6	Sardou, Victorien. Les pattes de mouche. Paris, 1877.
42546.26.6.08	Sardou, Victorien. Les pattes de mouche. Paris, 1870.
42546.26.6.1	Sardou, Victorien. Les pattes de mouche. Paris, 1868.
42546.26.6.2	Sardou, Victorien. Les pattes de mouche. N.Y., 1888.
42546.26.6.5	Sardou, Victorien. Les pattes de mouche. Paris, 1891.
42546.26.7	Sardou, Victorien. Les pommes du voisin. 3e ed. Paris, 1878.
42546.26.10	Sardou, Victorien. Les pommes du voisin. Paris, 1865.
42546.27	Sardou, Victorien. La sorcière. 12e éd. Paris, n.d.

42546.17 - .30 Individual authors, etc. - 1850-1899 - Drama - Sardou - Individual works - cont.

42546.27.5	Sardou, Victorien. La sorcière. Paris, 1904.
42546.27.6	Sardou, Victorien. La sorcière. Paris, 1904.
42546.27.8	Byrne, C.A. La sorcière. N.Y., 1905.
42546.27.9	Byrne, C.A. The sorceress. Boston, 1917.
42546.27.10	Sardou, Victorien. La sorcière. N.Y., 1905.
42546.28	Sardou, Victorien. L'oncle Sam. Paris, 1882.
42546.28.5	Sardou, Victorien. L'oncle Sam. Paris, 1875.
42546.29	Sardou, Victorien. La perle noire. N.Y., 1884.
42546.29.3	Sardou, Victorien. La perle noire. N.Y., 1884.
42546.29.5	Sardou, Victorien. La perle noire. 2d ed. Paris, 1869.
42546.29.8	Sardou, Victorien. La perle noire. Paris, 1882.
42546.29.10	Sardou, Victorien. La perle noire. N.Y., 1924.
42546.29.25	Sardou, Victorien. Argument of Gesmonda. N.Y., 1896.
42546.30	Sardou, Victorien. Argument of the play of La Tosca. Paris, 1890.
42546.30.5	Sardou, Victorien. Théodora. Paris, 1907.
42546.30.6	Sardou, Victorien. L'affaire des poisons. Paris, 1908.
42546.30.7	Sardou, Victorien. Fédora. Paris, 1908.
42546.30.7.3	Sardou, Victorien. Fédora. Milano, 1892.
42546.30.7.5	Sardou, Victorien. Fédora. Milano, n.d.
42546.30.7.7	Sardou, Victorien. Fédora. n.p., n.d.
42546.30.7.9	Sardou, Victorien. Fédora. N.Y., 1893.
42546.30.8	Sardou, Victorien. La Tosca. Paris, 1909.
42546.30.9	Sardou, Victorien. L'heure du spectacle. Paris, 1878. 4 pam.
42546.30.12	Sardou, Victorien. L'heure du spectacle. Paris, 1879.
42546.30.19	Sardou, Victorien. Madame Sans-Gêne. Paris, 1907.
42546.30.19.5	Sardou, Victorien. Madame Sans-Gêne. Milano, 1920.
42546.30.19.9	Sardou, Victorien. Madame Sans-Gêne. N.Y., 1895.
42546.30.19.10	Sardou, Victorien. Madame Sans-Gêne. N.Y., 1895.
42546.30.19.12	Sardou, Victorien. Madame Sans-Gêne. N.Y., 1901.
42546.30.20	Sardou, Victorien. Madame Sans-Gêne. London, 1901.
42546.30.20.1	Sardou, Victorien. Madame Sans-Gêne. N.Y., 1901.
42546.30.20.2	Sardou, Victorien. Arguments of the play of Mme. Sans-Gêne. N.Y., 1895.
42546.30.21	Sardou, Victorien. La piste. Paris, 1906.
42546.30.22	Sardou, Victorien. Thermidor. Paris, 1906.
42546.30.22.5	Sardou, Victorien. Argument of the play Thermidor. N.Y., 19- ?
42546.30.23	Pamphlet box. Thermidor and others.
42546.30.25A	Sardou, Victorien. Les femmes fortes, comédie. Paris, 1861.
42546.30.25B	Sardou, Victorien. Les femmes fortes, comédie. Paris, 1861.
42546.30.26	Sardou, Victorien. Les femmes fortes, comédie. Paris, 1896.
42546.30.29	Sardou, Victorien. Patrie! Paris, 1869.
42546.30.30	Sardou, Victorien. Patrie. Paris, 1887.
42546.30.31A	Sardou, Victorien. Patrie! Historical drama in five acts. Garden City, 1915.
42546.30.31B	Sardou, Victorien. Patrie! Historical drama in five acts. Garden City, 1915.
42546.30.33	Sardou, Victorien. Patrie. Paris, 1886.
42546.30.35	Sardou, Victorien. Les prés Saint Gervais; opéra bouffe en trois actes. Paris, 1875.
42546.30.39	Sardou, Victorien. Our boon companions. N.Y., n.d.
42546.30.40	Sardou, Victorien. Nos intimes! Paris, 1929.
42546.30.45	Sardou, Victorien. Carlin; roman. Paris, 1932.
42546.30.100	Pamphlet box. Collections of pamphlets relating to Victorien Sardou.
42546.30.105	Pamphlet vol. Collections of pamphlets relating to Victorien Sardou. 20 pam.

42546.31 Individual authors, etc. - 1850-1899 - Drama - Sardou - Biography and criticism

42546.31	Rebell, Hugues. Victorien Sardou. Paris, 1903.
42546.31.5	Hart, J.A. Sardou and the Sardou plays. Philadelphia, 1913.
42546.31.7	Macchetta, B.R. (Mrs.). Victorien Sardou, poet, author, and member of the Academy of France. London, 1892.
42546.31.8	Roosevelt, B. Victorien Sardou...a personal study. N.Y., n.d.
42546.31.10	Dante. London, 1903.
42546.31.12	Uchard, Mario. Un Jossier. La fiammina contre Odette. Paris, 1882.
42546.31.13	Castelfranco, A. Il teatro francese contemporaneo. Firenze, 1807.
42546.31.14	Julien, B. De da production indéfinie d'ouvrages dramatiques. n.p., n.d.
42546.31.16	Chadourne, A. La collaboration au théâtre. Paris, 1892.
42546.31.18	Deraismes, M. Le théâtre de M. Sardou. Paris, 1875.
42546.31.20	Vibert, P. Affaire Sardou. Paris, 1880.
42546.31.22	Les merveilleuses; analyse et notes. Paris, 1874.
42546.31.24	Cournier, J.M.J.J.M. Cournier contre Montigny et Sardou. Paris, 1873.
42546.31.27	Gastineau, B. Victorien Sardon. Paris, 1866.
42546.31.30	Mouly, Georges. Vie prodigieuse de Victorien Sardou. Paris, 1931.

42546.32 Individual authors, etc. - 1850-1899 - Drama - Sartène; Second; Sermet; etc.

42546.32	Sartène, Jean. Le hotteu. Paris, 1903.
42546.32.5	Second, Albéric. Les demoiselles du Ponçay. 7e éd. Paris, 1879.
42546.32.6	Second, Albéric. A mysterious kiss. Boston, 1870.
42546.32.9	Serment, Julien. Ki-Ki-ri-ki; japone-asmeria en un acto. Madrid, 1890.

42546.33 - .34 Individual authors, etc. - 1850-1899 - Drama - Silvestre

	42546.33	Silvestre, Armand. Grisélidis. Paris, 1891.
Htn	42546.33.2*	Silvestre, Armand. Grisélidis. Paris, 1891.
	42546.33.5	Silvestre, Armand. Le pays des roses. Paris, 1882.
	42546.33.9	Silvestre, Armand. Argument of "Izeyl". N.Y., 1895. 2v.
	42546.34	Silvestre, Armand. Contes incongrus et fantaisies galantes. Paris, 1887.
	42546.34.5	Silvestre, Armand. Fabliaux gaillards. Paris, 1888.
	42546.34.6	Silvestre, Armand. Les faceties de Cadet-Bitard. Paris, 1890.
	42546.34.7	Silvestre, Armand. Gauloiseries nouvelles. Paris, 1888.
	42546.34.8	Silvestre, Armand. Pour faire rire; gauloiseries contemporaines. Paris, 1883.
Htn	42546.34.9*	Silvestre, Armand. Le nu au champ de mars. Paris, 1889.
Htn	42546.34.10*	Silvestre, Armand. Le nu au salon de 1888-1890. v.1,2,4,5,10. Paris, 1888-92. 5v.

42546.33 - .34 Individual authors, etc. - 1850-1899 - Drama - Silvestre - cont.
42546.34.11 Silvestre, Armand. Les tendresses; poésies nouvelles. Paris, 1898.
42546.34.12 Silvestre, Armand. Les aurores lointaines; poésies nouvelles. Paris, 1896.
42546.34.13 Silvestre, Armand. Les tocasson. Paris, 1883.
42546.34.14 Silvestre, Armand. Madame Dandin et Mademoiselle Phryné. Paris, 1883.
42546.34.15 Silvestre, Armand. Les mélancolies d'un joyeux. Paris, 1883.
42546.34.16 Silvestre, Armand. Pour les amants. Paris, 1892?
42546.34.19 Silvestre, Armand. Les ailes d'or. Paris, 1891.
42546.34.21 Silvestre, Armand. Rimes, neuves et vieilles. Paris, 1866.
42546.34.23 Silvestre, Armand. Belles histoires d'amour. Paris, 1898.
42546.34.25 Silvestre, Armand. Au pays des souvenirs. 3. éd. Paris, 1887.
42546.34.28 Silvestre, Armand. Trente sonnets pour mademoiselle Bartet. Paris, 1896.

42546.39 Individual authors, etc. - 1850-1899 - Drama - Serret
42546.39 Serret, Ernest. Que dira le monde. 2e ed. Paris, 1854.

42546.40 Individual authors, etc. - 1850-1899 - Drama - Scholl
42546.40.100 Scholl, Aurélien. Jaloux du passé. Paris, 1861.
42546.40.110 Scholl, Aurélien. Denise. Paris, 1884.

42546.43 Individual authors, etc. - 1850-1899 - Drama - Siraudin
42546.43 Siraudin, Paul. Left the stage. London, n.d.
42546.43.3 Siraudin, Paul. Left the stage. London, 1852?

42546.46 Individual authors, etc. - 1850-1899 - Drama - Sorbets
42546.46 Sorbets, G. La Rencontre. Paris, 1908.

42546.47 Individual authors, etc. - 1850-1899 - Drama - Sonal
42546.47.30 Sonal, Marc. Le sonnet d'Arvers. Paris, 1884.

42547.1 Individual authors, etc. - 1850-1899 - Drama - Thalasso
Htn 42547.1* Thalasso, Adolphe. L'art. Paris, 1894.

42547.2 Individual authors, etc. - 1850-1899 - Drama - Thénard
42547.2 Thénard, J. (Mme.). Marie Antoinette et son cercle. Paris, 1901.

42547.4 Individual authors, etc. - 1850-1899 - Drama - Thomas; Thurner; Tourte; etc.
42547.4 Thomas, André. Le pamphlétaire. Paris, 1858.
42547.4.9 Thurner, Georges. Le passe partour. Paris, 1908.
42547.4.10 Thurner, Georges. Gaby. Paris, 1910.
42547.4.15 Thurwanger, Joseph. Quatre comédies. Paris, 1887.
42547.4.19 Tourte, Francis. Almanach du théâtre comique. Paris, n.d.

42547.5 Individual authors, etc. - 1850-1899 - Drama - Trarieux
42547.5 Trarieux, Gabriel. L'alibi. Paris, 1908.
42547.5.5 Trarieux, Gabriel. La dette, trois actes. Paris, 1909.
42547.5.9 Trarieux, Gabriel. La brebis perdue. Paris, 1911.
42547.5.10 Trarieux, Gabriel. Un soir. Paris, 1911.
42547.5.11A Trarieux, Gabriel. L'escapade. Paris, 1912.
42547.5.11B Trarieux, Gabriel. L'escapade. Paris, 1912.
42547.5.12 Trarieux, Gabriel. La lanterne de Diogène (notes sur le théâtre.). Paris, n.d.
42547.5.30 Trarieux, Gabriel. La guerre au village. Paris, 1903.
42547.5.40 Trarieux, Gabriel. Sur la foi des étoiles. Paris, 1901.

42547.6 Individual authors, etc. - 1850-1899 - Drama - Trézenik
42547.6 Trézenik, Léo. La ménage rousseau. Paris, n.d.

42547.7 - .8 Individual authors, etc. - 1850-1899 - Drama - Uchard
42547.7 Uchard, Mario. La fiammina. 3e éd. Paris, 1857.
42547.7.3 Uchard, Mario. La fiammina. Paris, 1857.
42547.7.4 Uchard, Mario. La fiammina. Paris, 1857.
42547.7.10 Uchard, Mario. La seconde jeunesse. Paris, 1859.
42547.7.15 Uchard, Mario. Mademoiselle Blaisot. 10e ed. Paris, 1884.
42547.8 Uchard, Mario. La fiammina. Paris, 1858.
42547.8.25 Uchard, Mario. La fiammina. Cienfuegos, 1857.

42547.10 Individual authors, etc. - 1850-1899 - Drama - Vacquerie; Vallette; Vandérem; etc.
42547.10.9 Vacquerie, Auguste. Théâtre complet. Paris, 1879. 2v.
42547.10.9.5 Vacquerie, Auguste. Jean Baudrey. Boston, 1867.
42547.10.15 Gaubert, Ernest. Rachilde. Paris, 1907.
42547.10.18 Vallette, Marguerite. La tour d'amour. Paris, 1916.
Htn 42547.10.20* Vallette, Marguerite. Théâtre. Paris, 1916.
42547.10.21 Vallette, Marguerite. Monieur Vénus. Bruxelles, 1884.
42547.10.22 Vallette, Marguerite. La jongleuse. 4e éd. Paris, 1900.
42547.10.23 Vallette, Marguerite. Les Rageac. Paris, 1921.
42547.10.24 Vallette, Marguerite. Le prisonnier. Paris, 1928.
42547.10.25 Vallette, Marguerite. L'heure sexuelle. Paris, 1898?
42547.10.26 Vallon-Colley, H.M. Garibaldis et François II. Lausanne, 1865.
42547.10.27 Vallette, Marguerite. Quand j'etais jeune. Paris, 1948.
42547.10.29 Vandérem, F. Cher maître. Paris, 1911.
42547.10.32 Vandérem, F. Les deux rives; roman. 18e éd. Paris, 19- .
42547.10.35 Vandérem, F. La bibliophile nouvelle. Paris, 1931-33. 2v.
42547.10.38 Vandérem, F. Gens de qualité. Paris, 1938.
42547.10.39 Vandérem, F. Le miroir de lettres. Paris, 1919-29. 8v.
42547.10.41 Letérrier, E. Le jour et la nuit. Paris, 1882.
42547.10.630 Valabrèque, D. Le quatorzième convive. 3. éd. Paris, 1897?

42547.11 Individual authors, etc. - 1850-1899 - Drama - Vaucaire
42547.11 Vaucaire, Maurice. Amoureuse Anitié. Paris, 1901.
42547.11.5 Vaucaire, Maurice. Les girouettes. Paris, 1899.
42547.11.9 Vaucaire, Maurice. La petite madame Bec et ougles. Paris, n.d.
42547.11.10 Vaucaire, Maurice. Mlle X...souris d'hôtel. Paris, n.d.
42547.11.11 Vaucaire, Maurice. Janne et Blanche. Paris, n.d.
42547.11.12 Vaucaire, Maurice. Petit chagrin. Paris, 1899.
42547.11.13 Vaucaire, Maurice. Valet de coeur. Paris, 1893.
42547.11.14 Vaucaire, Maurice. Un beau soir. Paris, 1892.
42547.11.15 Vaucaire, Maurice. Le poète et le financier. Paris, 1893.
42547.11.17 Vaucaire, Maurice. Arc-en-ciel. Paris, 1885.
42547.11.20 Vaucaire, Maurice. Le panier d'argenterie. Paris, 1895.

42547.12 Individual authors, etc. - 1850-1899 - Drama - Veber
42547.12 Veber, Pierre. Qui perd gagne, d'après le roman d'A. Capus. Paris, 1908.
42547.12.3 Veber, Pierre. Les grands. Paris, 1909.
42547.12.4 Veber, Pierre. La gamine. Paris, 1911.
42547.12.5 Veber, Pierre. Un fils d'Amérique; comédie. Paris, 1914.
42547.12.10 Veber, Pierre. Une passade. Paris, 1907.
42547.12.30 Veber, Pierre. L'aventure. Paris, 1926.

42547.13 Individual authors, etc. - 1850-1899 - Drama - Verhaeren [Discontinued]; Villemin
42547.13 Verhaeren, Émile. The dawn. London, 1898.
42547.13.2 Verhaeren, Émile. The dawn. Boston, 1915.
Htn 42547.13.75* Villemin, Eugène. Alfred le rimeur. Oréans, 1852.

42547.14 Individual authors, etc. - 1850-1899 - Drama - Villiers de l'Isle-Adam - Pamphlet volumes; Bibliographies
42547.14 Pamphlet box. Auguste, comte de Villiers de l'Isle Adam.

42547.15 Individual authors, etc. - 1850-1899 - Drama - Villiers de l'Isle-Adam - Works about [Discontinued]
42547.15 Chapoutot, H. Villiers de l'Isle Adam. Paris, 1908.
42547.15.5 Du Pontairce de Heussey, R. Villiers de l'Isle Adam. London, 1894.
42547.15.7 Kraemer, Alexio von. Villiers de l'Isle Adam. Thèse. Helsingfors, 1900.
42547.15.9 Bloy, Leon. La resurrection de Villiers de l'Isle Adam. Paris, 1906.
42547.15.12 Van der Meulen, C.J.C. L'idéalisme de Villiers de l'Isle Adam. Amsterdam, 1925.
NEDL 42547.15.15 Pierredon, Georges. Notes sur Villiers de l'Isle Adam. Paris, 1919.
42547.15.20 Daireaux, Max. Villiers de l'Isle Adam, l'homme et l'oeuvre. Paris, 1936.

42547.16 - .21 Individual authors, etc. - 1850-1899 - Drama - Villiers de l'Isle-Adam - Writings
42547.16 Villiers de l'Isle Adam, Auguste. Axel. Paris, 1890.
42547.16.3 Villiers de l'Isle Adam, Auguste. Axel. London, 1925.
42547.16.5 Villiers de l'Isle Adam, Auguste. Axel. Dublin, 1970.
42547.17 Villiers de l'Isle Adam, Auguste. Elën. Paris, 1896.
42547.17.20A Villiers de l'Isle Adam, Auguste. Correspondance générale de Villiers de l'Isle Adam et documents inédits. Paris, 1962. 2v.
42547.17.20B Villiers de l'Isle Adam, Auguste. Correspondance générale de Villiers de l'Isle Adam et documents inédits. Paris, 1962. 2v.
42547.17.25 Villiers de l'Isle Adam, Auguste. Réliqués. Paris, 1954.
42547.17.30 Villiers de l'Isle Adam, Auguste. Le prétendant. Paris, 1965.
42547.17.35A Villiers de l'Isle Adam, Auguste. Le nouveau monde. Paris, 1913.
42547.17.35B Villiers de l'Isle Adam, Auguste. Le nouveau monde. Paris, 1913.
42547.18 Villiers de l'Isle Adam, Auguste. Premières poésies 1856-1858. Bruxelles, 1893.
42547.18.5 Villiers de l'Isle Adam, Auguste. L'Eve future. Paris, 1902.
42547.18.5.2 Villiers de l'Isle Adam, Auguste. L'Eve future. Paris, 1960.
Htn 42547.18.6* Villiers de l'Isle Adam, Auguste. L'amour suprëme. Paris, 1886.
42547.18.7 Villiers de l'Isle Adam, Auguste. L'évasion; drame. 2e éd. Paris, 1910.
42547.18.9 Villiers de l'Isle Adam, Auguste. La révolte. Photoreproduction. Paris, 1897.
Htn 42547.18.9.2* Villiers de l'Isle Adam, Auguste. La révolte. Paris, 1870.
42547.18.10 Van der Meulen, C.J.C. The revolt and The escape. London, 1901.
42547.19.5 Villiers de l'Isle Adam, Auguste. Oeuvres. Paris, 1957.
42547.20 Villiers de l'Isle Adam, Auguste. Histoires insolites. Paris, n.d.
42547.20.3 Villiers de l'Isle Adam, Auguste. Isis. Paris, n.d.
Htn 42547.20.5* Villiers de l'Isle Adam, Auguste. Chez les passants. Paris, 1890.
42547.21 Villiers de l'Isle Adam, Auguste. Contes cruels. Paris, n.d.
42547.21.5 Villiers de l'Isle Adam, Auguste. Contes cruels. Paris, 1954-
42547.21.7 Villiers de l'Isle Adam, Auguste. Contes cruels. Paris, 1968.
42547.21.10 Villiers de l'Isle Adam, Auguste. Cruel tales. London, 1963.

42547.22 Individual authors, etc. - 1850-1899 - Drama - Villiers de l'Isle-Adam - Biography and criticism
42547.22 Villiers de l'Isle Adam, Auguste. Tribulst Bonhornet. Photoreproduction. Paris, 1896.
42547.22.15A Villiers de l'Isle Adam, Auguste. Correspondance générale. Paris, 1962. 2v.
42547.22.15B Villiers de l'Isle Adam, Auguste. Correspondance générale. Paris, 1962. 2v.
42547.22.25.2 Villiers de l'Isle Adam, Auguste. Axël. Paris, 1960.
42547.22.80 Rougemont, E. de. Villiers de l'Isle Adam, biographie et bibliographie. Paris, 1910.
42547.22.85 Palgen, R. Villiers de l'Isle Adam, auteur dramatique. Paris, 1925.
42547.22.87 Thomas, Louis. Le vrai Villiers de l'Isle Adam. Paris, 1944.
42547.22.90 Lanfredini, Dina. Villiers de l'Isle Adam (1838-1889) studio critico. Firenze, 1940.
42547.22.95 Deenen, M. Le merveilleux dans l'oeuvre de Villiers de l'Isle Adam. Paris, 1939.
42547.22.100 Lebais, A. Villiers de l'Isle Adam. Neuchâtel, 1952.
42547.22.105 Castex, Pierre. Contes cruels. Paris, 1956.
42547.22.110 Bollery, Joseph. La Bretagne de Villiers de l'Isle Adam. Saint-Brieuc, 1961.
42547.22.120 Raitt, Alan William. Villiers de l'Isle Adam et le mouvement symboliste. Paris, 1965.
42547.22.125 Buergisser, Peter. La double illusion de l'or et de l'amour chez Villiers de l'Isle Adam. Berne, 1969
42547.22.130 Gourévitch, Jean Paul. Villiers de l'Isle Adam. Paris, 1971.
42547.22.135 Aubry, Georges Jean. Une amitie exemplaire. Paris, 1942.

Classified Listing

42547.23 - .25 Individual authors, etc. - 1850-1899 - Drama - Weill

42547.23 Weill, Alexandre. Mon théâtre. Paris, 1885.
42547.25 Weill, Alexandre. Mes romans. Paris, 1886. 2v.

42547.28 - .48 Individual authors, etc. - 1850-1899 - Drama - Wolff, P. - Writings

42547.28 Wolff, Pierre. Théâtre. Paris, 1921.
42547.29 Wolff, Pierre. L'age d'aimer. Paris, 1905.
42547.29.5 Wolff, Pierre. L'age d'aimer. Paris, 1905.
42547.30 Wolff, Pierre. Le béguin. Paris, n.d.
42547.31 Wolff, Pierre. Le secret de Polichinelle. Paris, n.d.
42547.32 Wolff, Pierre. Celles qu'on respecte. Paris, 1903.
42547.33 Wolff, Pierre. Les marionnettes. Paris, 1910.
42547.34 Wolff, Pierre. Leurs filles. Paris, 1891.
42547.35 Wolff, Pierre. Le lys. Paris, 1909.
42547.35.10 Wolff, Pierre. Le lys. Paris, 1909.
42547.36 Wolff, Pierre. L'amour défendu. Paris, 1911.
42547.37 Wolff, Pierre. Jacques Bouchard. Paris, 1890.
42547.38 Wolff, Pierre. Les maris de leurs filles. Paris, 1892.
42547.40 Wolff, Pierre. Le voile déchiré. Paris, 1919.
42547.42 Wolff, Pierre. Le chemin de Damas. Paris, 1921.
42547.44 Wolff, Pierre. Les ailes brisées. Paris, 1921.
42547.46 Wolff, Pierre. Après l'amour. Paris, 1924.

42548.1 - .70 Individual authors, etc. - 1850-1899 - Drama - Miscellany [Discontinued]

42548.3 Barbier, J.P. Jeanne d'Arc. Paris, 1891.
42548.5 Bayard, J.F.A. La niaise de Saint Flour. Boston, 1865.
42548.5.10 Bayard, J.F.A. La niaise de Saint Flour. N.Y., 18- ?
42548.6 Bayard, J.F.A. Un fils de famille. Paris, 1853.
42548.8 Delair, Paul. Les contes d'à présent. Paris, 1884.
42548.8.5 Delair, Paul. Argument of La mégère apprivoisée. N.Y., n.d.
42548.10 Goetsehy, G. Pressé pour le salon. Paris, n.d.
42548.11 Labiche, Eugène. La cagnotte. Boston, 1865.
42548.11.3 Labiche, Eugène. La cagnotte. Boston, 1870.
42548.11.5 Labiche, Eugène. La cagnotte. N.Y., 18- ?
42548.13 Maltchycé, Marie de. La petite maman. Boston, 1864.
42548.13.2 Maltchycé, Marie de. La petite maman. 4. éd. N.Y., 1864. 2 pam.
42548.13.9 Madinier, Henry. Amour et typographie. Paris, 1856.
42548.14 Mazeres, E.J.E. Le collier de perles. Paris, 1865.
42548.16 Scribe, E. Valérie. Boston, 1865.
42548.17 Scribe, E. Valérie. N.Y., 1865.
42548.18 Siraudin, P. Les femmes qui pleurent. Boston, 1865.
42548.18.5 Siraudin, P. Les femmes qui pleurent. N.Y., 1865.
42548.18.6 Siraudin, P. Les femmes qui pleurent. N.Y., 18- ?
42548.20 Souvestre, Émile. Le testament. Boston, 1865.
42548.21 Souvestre, Émile. La vieille cousine. Boston, 1864.
42548.25 Girardin, Émile de. La joie fait peur. Boston, 1865.
42548.26 Scribe, E. La bataille de dames. Boston, 1865.
42548.26.2 Scribe, E. La bataille de dames. N.Y., 1873.
42548.26.5 Scribe, E. La bataille de dames. Paris, 1879.
42548.26.7 Scribe, E. La bataille de dames. Paris, 1882.
42548.26.9 Scribe, E. The ladies battle. N.Y., 1883.
42548.27 Sandeau, Jules. La maison de Penarvan. Boston, 1864.
42548.28 Labiche, Eugène. La poudre aux yeux. Boston, 1864.
42548.28.9 Labiche, Eugène. La poudre aux yeux. 5. éd. Boston, 1870.
42548.28.15 Labiche, Eugène. La poudre aux yeux. N.Y., n.d.
42548.28.20 Labiche, Eugène. La poudre aux yeux. N.Y., 1919.
42548.29 Labiche, Eugène. Les petits oiseaux. Boston, 1864.
42548.29.5 Labiche, Eugène. Les petits oiseaux. 5. éd. Boston, 1870.
42548.29.9 Labiche, Eugène. Les petis oiseaux. N.Y., 1924.
42548.30.2 Sandeau, Jules. Mademoiselle de la Seiglière. N.Y., 1865.
42548.32 Scribe, E. Les doigts de fée. Boston, 1865.
42548.39 Legouvé, Ernest. Théâtre de campagne. Tom. 1-3,5-8. Paris, 18- ? 7v.
42548.40 Legouvé, Ernest. Théâtre de campagne. ser. 1. Paris, 1876.
42548.41A Legouvé, Ernest. Théâtre de campagne. ser. 2. 3. ed. Paris, 1877.
42548.41B Legouvé, Ernest. Théâtre de campagne. ser. 2. 3. ed. Paris, 1877. 3v.
42548.42 Legouvé, Ernest. Théâtre de campagne. ser. 3. Paris, 1878.
42548.43 Legouvé, Ernest. Théâtre de campagne. ser. 4. Paris, 1878.
42548.44 Legouvé, Ernest. Théâtre de campagne. ser. 5. Paris, 1879.
42548.45 Legouvé, Ernest. Théâtre de campagne. ser. 6. Paris, 1880.
42548.46 Legouvé, Ernest. Théâtre de campagne. ser. 7. Paris, 1881.
42548.47 Legouvé, Ernest. Théâtre de campagne. ser. 8. Paris, 1882.
42548.48 Legouvé, Ernest. Théâtre de campagne. ser. 9. Paris, 1899.
42548.50 Newport, Rhode Island. Bellevue Drama Club. Plays for private acting. N.Y., 1878.
42548.50.5 Newport, Rhode Island. Bellevue Drama Club. Plays for private acting. N.Y., 1878.
42548.52 Verconsin, Eugène. Saynètes et comédies. Paris, 1882.
42548.53 Verconsin, Eugène. En wagon. Paris, 1869.
42548.54 Verconsin, Eugène. En wagon. Paris, 1877.
42548.55 Verconsin, Eugène. La matrone d'Éphèse. Paris, 1870.
42548.57 Xanrof, Léon. La mécanique de l'esprit. Paris, 1931.
42548.60 Barrière, Théodore. Les bourgeois gentilhommes. Paris, 1852-57.
42548.61 Pamphlet vol. Barbrec, et al. Plays.
42548.67 Voisine, A. Le moblot du 33e épisode de la guerre de 1870. Le Mans, 1896.
42548.69 Courteline, G. Les pièces à succès. Paris, n.d. 2v.
42548.70 Metenier, O. Les pièces à succès. Paris, n.d. 2v.

42548.71 - Individual authors, etc. - 1850-1899 - Drama - Anonymous plays

42548.71 Le Rubicon. Paris, 1893.
42548.71.10 Olympe Dunoyer ou La jeunesse de Voltaire. Paris, 1900.
42548.71.20 La demoiselle de compagnie. N.Y., 1899.
42548.71.30 L'école des biches ou Moeurs des petites dames de ce temps. Paris, 1969.
42548.72 Le fils Gibaugier. Paris, 1863.
42548.73 Les mendiantes. Cambridge, 1887.
42548.75 L'ingrat, comédie en cinq actes. Mss. n.p., n.d.
42548.76 St. Louis in chains; drama. Baltimore, 1883.
42548.77 Géraldine. 3e ed. London, 1876.

42548.71 - Individual authors, etc. - 1850-1899 - Drama - Anonymous plays - cont.

Htn 42548.78* L'ainé. Mss. n.p., n.d.

42551 - 42552 Individual authors, etc. - 1850-1899 - Poetry - Folios [Discontinued]

42551.7 Citoleux, Marc. Mme Ackermann. Paris, 1906.
42551.8 Ackermann, L. Oeuvres. Paris, n.d.
42551.15 Montaiglon, Anatole de. L'Aubepine et le Marronnier de Sannois. Paris, 1865. 5 pam.
42551.20 Serment, J.H. A Abraham Lincoln. Paris, 1865.

42553.2 - .3 Individual authors, etc. - 1850-1899 - Poetry - Ackermann

42553.2 Ackermann, L. Poésies. Paris, 1874.
42553.3 Ackermann, L. Pensées d'une solitaire. Paris, 1903.

42553.5 - .9 Individual authors, etc. - 1850-1899 - Poetry - Autran - Complete and Selected works

42553.5 Autran, J. Oeuvres complètes. Paris, 1875-78. 7v.

42553.10 - .18 Individual authors, etc. - 1850-1899 - Poetry - Autran - Individual works

42553.13 Autran, J. Le poème des Beaux Jours. Paris, 1862.
42553.15 Autran, J. La fille d'Eschyle. Paris, 1848.
42553.17 Autran, J. La légende des Paladins. Paris, 1875.

42553.20 - .33 Individual authors, etc. - 1850-1899 - Poetry - Amiel - Writings

42553.20 Amiel, Henri F. L'escalade de 1602. Genève, 1876.
42553.21 Amiel, Henri F. Les étrangères poésies. Paris, 1878.
42553.24 Amiel, Henri F. Grains de mil. Paris, 1854.
42553.26 Amiel, Henri F. Jour à jour. Paris, 1880.
42553.27 Amiel, Henri F. Amiel's journal. N.Y., 190-?
42553.28 Amiel, Henri F. La part du Rêve. Genève, 1863.
42553.29 Amiel, Henri F. Il pensoroso. Genève, 1858.
42553.32 Amiel, Henri F. Fragments d'un journal intime. Genève, 1884. 2v.
42553.32.2 Amiel, Henri F. Fragments d'un journal intime. Genève, 1885. 2v.
42553.32.5A Amiel, Henri F. Fragments d'un journal intime. Genève, 1887. 2v.
42553.32.5B Amiel, Henri F. Fragments d'un journal intime. Genève, 1887. 2v.
42553.32.7 Amiel, Henri F. Fragments d'un journal intime. Paris, 1927. 2v.
42553.32.10 Amiel, Henri F. Fragments d'un journal intime. Paris, 1931.
42553.32.25 Amiel, Henri F. Fragments d'un journal intime. Genève, 1922. 3v.
42553.32.50 Amiel, Henri F. Daily maxims from Amiel's journal. N.Y., 1902.
42553.32.75 Amiel, Henri F. Amiel's journal. London, 1885.
42553.32.85 Amiel, Henri F. Journal intime de l'année 1866. 5e éd. Paris, 1959.
42553.32.90 Amiel, Henri F. Journal intime, années 1839 à 1848. Genève, 1948. 2v.
42553.32.92 Amiel, Henri F. Journal intime. Paris, 1965.
42553.33 Amiel, Henri F. Amiel's journal. London, 1889.
42553.33.1 Amiel, Henri F. Gems from Amiel's journal. N.Y., 1891.
42553.33.2 Amiel, Henri F. Amiel's journal. N.Y., 1893. 2v.
42553.33.2.2 Amiel, Henri F. Amiel's journal. N.Y., 1906. 2v.
42553.33.3 Amiel, Henri F. The private journal of Henri F. Amiel. N.Y., 1935.
42553.33.5 Amiel, Henri F. En drömmares dagbok. Stockholm, 1925.
42553.33.9 Amiel, Henri F. Philine, fragments inédits du journal intime. Paris, 1927.
42553.33.11 Amiel, Henri F. Philine, from the unpublished journals. Boston, 1930.
42553.33.15 Amiel, Henri F. Essais critiques. Paris, 1932.
42553.33.65 Amiel, Henri F. La jeunesse d'Henri Frédéric Amiel. Paris, 1935.

42553.34 - .35 Individual authors, etc. - 1850-1899 - Poetry - Amiel - Works about

42553.34 Vadier, Berthe. Henri Frédéric Amiel. Paris, 1886.
42553.34.5 Bopp, Leon. Henri Frédéric Amiel. Thèse. Paris, 1925.
42553.34.10 Bouvier, B. Henri Frédéric Amiel. Stockholm, 1925.
42553.34.15 Matthews, John. Amiel et la solitude. Thèse. Annemasse, 1932.
42553.34.20 Thibaudet, A. Henri Frédéric Amiel; ou, La part du rêve. Paris, 1929.
42553.34.25 Maranón, Gregorio. Amiel. 7. ed. Madrid, 1950.
42553.34.30 Weck, René de. Amiel ou La noix creuse. Lausanne, 1931.
42553.35 Pamphlet box. Henri Frédéric Amiel.
42553.35.5 Halda, Bernard. Amiel et les femmes. Lyon, 1964.
42553.35.10 Pfister, Susanne. Expansion et concentration dans la pensées d'Amiel. Berne, 1971.

42553.39 - .47 Individual authors, etc. - 1850-1899 - Poetry - Angellier - Writings

42553.39 Angellier, A. Dans la lumière antique. Les scènes. Paris, 1911.
42553.40 Angellier, A. Les dialogues d'amour. Paris, 1905. 2v.
42553.42 Angellier, A. Les episodes. Paris, 1908-09. 2v.
42553.43 Angellier, A. A l'amie perdue. Paris, 1903.
42553.44 Angellier, A. Le chemin des saisons. Paris, 1903.
42553.47 Angellier, A. Oeuvres posthumes. Paris, 1912.
42553.47.5 Angellier, A. Pages choisies de Auguste Angellier. Oxford, 1908.

42553.48 - .49 Individual authors, etc. - 1850-1899 - Poetry - Angellier - Works about

42553.48.10 Angellier, A. Auguste Angellier. Paris, 1938.
42553.49 Delattre, Floris. La personnalité d'Auguste Angellier. Paris, 1939-44. 2v.
42553.49.5 Clement, Louis. Auguste Angellier, son oeuvre poétique. Lille, 1912.

42553.52 Individual authors, etc. - 1850-1899 - Poetry - Angelés

42553.52 Anglés, Augustin. Les écloses. Paris, 1898.

42553.53 Individual authors, etc. - 1850-1899 - Poetry - Arnaud

42553.53.100 Arnaud, Robert. Les dires de celui qui passe. Alger, 1899.

42553.55 Individual authors, etc. - 1850-1899 - Poetry - Ansaldi

42553.55 Ansaldi, J. Essais poétiques. Toulon, 1854.

42553.60 Individual authors, etc. - 1850-1899 - Poetry - Amanieux

42553.60 Amanieux, M. La révolution. Paris, 1889.

42553.62 Individual authors, etc. - 1850-1899 - Poetry - Amoric

42553.62.30 Amoric, Amédée. Les vibrations. Paris, 1892.

42553.68 Individual authors, etc. - 1850-1899 - Poetry - Baillet

42553.68 Baillet, Eugène. Chansons et petits poèmes. Paris, 1885.

42553.72 Individual authors, etc. - 1850-1899 - Poetry - Baldenne

42553.72 Baldenne, F. En marge de la vie. Paris, 1901.

42554.1 - .10 Individual authors, etc. - 1850-1899 - Poetry - Banville - Writings

42554.1 Banville, Théodore de. Les cariatides. Paris, 1879.
42554.1.05A Banville, Théodore de. Les cariatides. Paris, 1864.
42554.1.05B Banville, Théodore de. Les cariatides. Paris, 1864.
42554.1.07 Banville, Théodore de. Les cariatides. Paris, 1889.
42554.1.2 Banville, Théodore de. Le forgeron. Paris, 1887.
42554.1.25 Banville, Théodore de. Oeuvres. Paris, 1889.
42554.2 Banville, Théodore de. Odes funambulesques. Paris, 1883.
42554.2.2 Banville, Théodore de. Odes funambulesques. Paris, 1892.
42554.2.5 Banville, Théodore de. Trente-six ballades joyeuses. Paris, 1873.
42554.3 Banville, Théodore de. Nous tous. Paris, 1884.
42554.3.2 Banville, Théodore de. Sonnailles et clochettes. Photoreproduction. Paris, 1890.
42554.3.3.5 Banville, Théodore de. Gringoire; comédie en un acte. Paris, 1875.
42554.3.5 Banville, Théodore de. Esope; comédie en trois actes. Paris, 1893.
42554.4 Banville, Théodore de. Comédies. Paris, 1879.
42554.4.2 Banville, Théodore de. Les belles poupées. Paris, 1888.
42554.4.5 Banville, Théodore de. Camées parisiens. 3e sér. Paris, 1873.
42554.4.10 Banville, Théodore de. La comédie française. Paris, 1863.
42554.5 Banville, Théodore de. Enquisses parisiennes. Paris, 1876.
42554.5.2 Banville, Théodore de. Contes bourgeois. Paris, 1885.
42554.5.10 Banville, Théodore de. Charming Léandre; a comedy in one act. N.Y., 1915.
42554.6 Banville, Théodore de. Contes pour les femmes. Paris, 1881.
42554.6.2 Banville, Théodore de. L'âme de Paris. Paris, 1890.
42554.6.3 Banville, Théodore de. Marcelle Rabe. Paris, 1891.
42554.6.4 Banville, Théodore de. Le baiser. Paris, 1906.
42554.6.5 Banville, Théodore de. Socrate et sa femme. Paris, 1897.
42554.6.5.3 Banville, Théodore de. Socrate et sa femme. 3d ed. Paris, 1886.
42554.6.5.5 Banville, Théodore de. Socrates and his wife. 1st ed. N.Y, 1889.
42554.6.6 Banville, Théodore de. Dans la fournaise. Paris, 1892.
42554.6.7 Banville, Théodore de. Idylles Prussiennes. Paris, 1871.
42554.6.9A Banville, Théodore de. Les exilés. Paris, 1867.
42554.6.9B Banville, Théodore de. Les exilés. Paris, 1867.
42554.7 Banville, Théodore de. Contes féeriques. Paris, 1882.
42554.8 Banville, Théodore de. Contes héroiques. Paris, 1884.
42554.8.2 Banville, Théodore de. Lettres chimeriques. Paris, 1885.
42554.8.5 Banville, Théodore de. Gringoire. 5th ed. London, 1903.
42554.8.6 Banville, Théodore de. Gringoire. 2e éd. Berlin, 1881.
42554.8.7.15 Banville, Théodore de. Gringoire; comédie en un acte en prose. London, 1882.
42554.8.8 Banville, Théodore de. Gringoire; comédie en un acte en prose. London, 1888.
42554.8.8.5 Banville, Théodore de. Gringoire; comédie en un acte en prose. Paris, 1890.
42554.8.9 Banville, Théodore de. Gringoire. N.Y., 1921.
42554.8.10 Banville, Théodore de. Gringoire. Paris, 1924?
42554.8.15 Banville, Théodore de. Le sang de la coupe. Paris, 1890.
42554.9 Banville, Théodore de. Mes souvenirs. Paris, 1883.
42554.9.2 Banville, Théodore de. Madame Robert. Paris, 1887.
42554.10 Banville, Théodore de. Paris vécu. Paris, 1883.
42554.10.5 Banville, Théodore de. Les stalactites de Théodore de Banville. Thèse. Paris, 1942.

42554.11 Individual authors, etc. - 1850-1899 - Poetry - Banville - Works about

42554.11.2 Laporte, A. Théodore de Banville. Paris, 1884.
42554.11.5 Grein, Heinrich. Studien über den Reim bei Théodore de Banville. Kiel, 1903.
42554.11.6 Fuchs, Max. Théodore de Banville. Paris, n.d.
42554.11.9 Siciliano, Italo. Dal romanticismo al simbolismo. Torino, 1927.
42554.11.15 Charpentier, John. Théodore de Banville. Paris, 1925.

42554.12 Individual authors, etc. - 1850-1899 - Poetry - Barbier, A.

42554.12 Barbier, Auguste. Iambes et poèmes. 33e éd. Paris, 1883.
42554.12.4 Barbier, Auguste. Iambes et poèmes. 35e éd. Paris, 1888.
42554.12.20 Barbier, Auguste. Iambes et poèmes. Oxford, 1907.
42554.12.35 Barbier, Auguste. Satires et poèmes. Bruxelles, 1840.
42554.12.40 Barbier, Auguste. Souvenirs personnels et silhouettes contemporaines. Paris, 1883.

42554.13 Individual authors, etc. - 1850-1899 - Poetry - Beaufort; Bellot des Minières; Bergerat; etc.

42554.13.25 Beaufort d'Auberval, A.A. Contes erotico-philosophiques. Bruxelles, 1882.
42554.13.30 Poésies de M. Bellot des Minières. Paris, 1882.
42554.13.35 Bergerat, Émile. Le maître d'école. Paris, 1870.
42554.13.36 Bergerat, Émile. Les cuirassiers de Reichshoffen. Paris, 1870.
42554.13.150 Bengoechea, Alfred de. L'orgueilleuse. Paris, 1910.
42554.13.250 Berrichon, Paterne. Le vin maudit; petits poèmes. Paris, 1896.
42554.13.1100 Bengy-Puyvallée, A. de. Emaux sur or. Paris, 1899.

42554.14 Individual authors, etc. - 1850-1899 - Poetry - Barracand; Bocquet; Boissière; etc.

42554.14 Barracand, L. Lamartine et la muse. Paris, 1883.
42554.14.50 Blanchon, Pierre. Solitude; poésies. Paris, 1904.
42554.14.100 Barrucand, V. Une partie d'échecs. Paris, 1889.
42554.14.200 Bocquet, Léon. Les cygnes noirs; poèmes 1899-1903. Paris, 1906.
42554.14.210 Bocquet, Léon. La lumière d'Hellas. Paris, 1936.

42554.14 Individual authors, etc. - 1850-1899 - Poetry - Barracand; Bocquet; Boissière; etc. - cont.

42554.14.325 Tuong Nguyen Manh. Jules Boissière 1863-1897. Thèse. Montpellier, 1932.

42554.15 Individual authors, etc. - 1850-1899 - Poetry - Bonnard; Bouchaud; Botrel; etc.

42554.15 Bonnard, Abel. Les familiers. Paris, 1906.
42554.15.2 Bonnard, Abel. Les histoires: La sous préfête; Le prince persan. Paris, 1908.
42554.15.3 Bonnard, Abel. Les royautés; poèmes. Paris, 1908.
42554.15.4 Bonnard, Abel. Savoir aimer. Paris, 1937.
42554.15.9 Bouchaud, P. de. Rythmes et nombres. Paris, 1895.
42554.15.35 Botrel, Théodore. Songs of Brittany. Boston, 1915.
42554.15.35.5 Botrel, Théodore. Folk songs of Brittany. New Haven, 1918.
42554.15.150 Boulmier, Joseph. Villanelles suivies de poésies en langage. Paris, 1878.

42554.16 Individual authors, etc. - 1850-1899 - Poetry - Le Braz, A.; Boutelleau; Breton, J.; etc.

42554.16 Le Braz, A. La chanson de la Bretagne. Rennes, 1892.
42554.16.4 Le Braz, A. Pâques d'Islande. Paris, 1897.
42554.16.5 Le Braz, A. Pâques d'Islande. Paris, 1898.
42554.16.6.5 Le Braz, A. Au pays des pardons. Paris, 1900?
42554.16.7 Le Braz, A. Du soleil et de la brume. Paris, n.d.
42554.16.8 Le Braz, A. Du soleil et de la brume. 5e éd. Paris, 1919.
42554.16.9 Le Braz, A. Ames d'occident. 3e éd. Paris, n.d.
42554.16.10 Le Braz, A. Le sang de la Sirène. Paris, n.d.
42554.16.10.5 Le Braz, A. Le sang de la Sirène. Paris, 1901.
42554.16.12 Le Braz, A. Le gardien du feu. Paris, 1900.
42554.16.12.5 Le Braz, A. Le gardien du feu. Paris, 1947.
42554.16.13 Le Braz, A. La terre du passé. 2e éd. Paris, 1901?
42554.16.14 Le Braz, A. La terre du passé. 5e éd. Paris, 19- ?
42554.16.18 Schienemann, W. Anatole Le Braz und die Bretonen. Inaug. Diss. Königsberg, 1933.
42554.16.20 Boutelleau, Georges. Le banc de Pierre. Paris, 1905.
42554.16.100 Breton, Jules. Les champs et la mer. Paris, 1875.

42554.17 Individual authors, etc. - 1850-1899 - Poetry - Caillaux; Carné; Carrère; Cantacuzène; etc.

42554.17.25 Caillaux, Charles. La plaine et la mer. Chartres, 1838.
42554.17.35 Carné, Adrien. L'arvor. Paris, 1882.
42554.17.40 Carrère, Jean. Ce qui renait toujours. Vanves, 1891.
42554.17.50 Cantacuzène, C.A. Considerations lyriques. Paris, 19- .
42554.17.55 Cantacuzène, C.A. Les automnes complémentaires; anamorphoses. Paris, 1928.
42554.17.60 Cantacuzène, C.A. Cinglons les souvenirs et cinglons vers les rêves. Paris, 1900.

42554.18 Individual authors, etc. - 1850-1899 - Poetry - Cazales (Lahor); Chambrun; Chavanne; Chatillon; Clément, J.B.; etc.

42554.18 Cazalis, Henry. L'illusion par Jean Lahor. Paris, 1893. 2v.
42554.18.2 Cazalies, Henry. Les quatrains d'Al Ghazali. Paris, 1896.
42554.18.3 Cazalis, Henry. Oeuvres choisies, précédées d'une biographie. Paris, 1909.
42554.18.5 Crouzet-Benaben, J. Jean Lahor. Paris, 1908.
42554.18.7 Masbrenier, J.L. L'oeuvre de Jean Lahor. n.p., 1912.
42554.18.8 Petitbon, René. L'influence de la pensée religieuse indienne dans le romantisme et la parnasse; Jean Lahor. Thèse. Paris, 1962.
42554.18.9 Chambrun, Marie Jean de. La comtesse de Chambrun, ses poésies. Paris, 1893.
42554.18.12 Champon, C. Chansons nouvelles. Paris, 1894.
42554.18.15 Chavanne, A. Murmures. Paris, 1895.
42554.18.25 Chastan, Auguste. Chansons, satires. Valréas, 1858.
42554.18.30 Chatillon, Auguste de. A la grand' pinte. Paris, 1860.
42554.18.32 Chatillon, Auguste de. La grand' pinte. Paris, 1891.
42554.18.50 Clément, Jean B. Cent chansons nouvelles. Paris, 1898?
42554.18.55 Clément, Jean B. La chanson populaire. Paris, 1900.
42554.18.65 Cohendy, Claude. Visions d'Hellas. Paris, 1905.
42554.18.90 Clarens, J.P. L'éternelle douleur. Paris, 1895.

42554.19 - .26.24 Individual authors, etc. - 1850-1899 - Poetry - Coppée, F. - Writings

42554.19 Coppée, François. Pour la Couronne. Drame en cinq actes, en vers. Paris, 1895.
42554.19.2 Coppée, François. Le pater. Boston, 1896.
42554.19.3 Coppée, François. Le pater. Paris, 1889?
42554.19.4 Coppée, François. Le pater. Boston, 1897.
42554.20 Coppée, François. Ten tales. N.Y., 1891.
42554.20.5 Coppée, François. Ten tales. N.Y., 1890.
42554.20.7 Coppée, François. Ten tales. N.Y., 1890.
42554.21 Coppée, François. Vingt contes nouveaux. Paris, 1883.
42554.21.12 Coppée, François. Tales for Christmas. Boston, 1900.
42554.21.17 Coppée, François. Les vrais riches. Paris, 1892.
42554.22 Coppée, François. Contes en vers et poésies diverses. Paris, 1880.
42554.22.2 Coppée, François. Poésies 1864-69. Paris, n.d.
42554.22.4A Coppée, François. Poésies. Paris, 1907. 6v.
42554.22.4B Coppée, François. Poésies. Paris, 1907.
42554.22.5 Coppée, François. Premières poésies. Paris, n.d.
42554.22.6 Coppée, François. Poèmes modernes. Paris, 1870.
42554.22.7 Coppée, François. Oliver, poème. Paris, 1876.
42554.22.25A Coppée, François. Poésies. Paris, 1876. 2v.
42554.22.25B Coppée, François. Poésies. Paris, 1876.
42554.22.30 Coppée, François. Poésies, 1886-1890. Paris, 1891.
42554.22.35 Coppée, François. Poésies choisies de François Coppée. Oxford, 1907.
42554.22.40 Coppée, François. Henriette. Paris, 1889.
42554.23.2 Coppée, François. Le naufragé. Paris, n.d.
42554.23.5 Coppée, François. La maison de Molière; poésie. Paris, 1884.
42554.23.6 Coppée, François. Arrière Saison. Paris, 1887.
42554.23.6.5 Coppée, François. Avant la grande guerre. Paris, 1918.
42554.23.7 Coppée, François. Disillusion. N.Y., 1890.
42554.23.8 Coppée, François. La grève des forgerons; poème. 25e éd. N.Y., 1897.
42554.23.9 Coppée, François. Deux douleurs; drame en un acte en vers. 12e éd. N.Y., 1870.
42554.23.10 Coppée, François. Fais ce que dois; episode dramatique. 19e ed. Paris, 1871.
42554.23.11 Coppée, François. Le Luthier. Paris, 1876.
42554.23.12 Coppée, François. Der Strike der Schmiede. Wien, 1874.
42554.23.13 Coppée, François. Les récits et les élégies. Paris, 1878.
42554.23.14A Coppée, François. On rend l'argent. N.Y., 1896.
42554.23.14B Coppée, François. On rend l'argent. N.Y., 1896.

Classified Listing

42554.19 - .26.24 Individual authors, etc. - 1850-1899 - Poetry - Coppée, F. - Writings - cont.
42554.23.15 Coppée, François. Severo Torelli. N.Y., 189-?
42554.23.16 Coppée, François. La bonne souffrance. N.Y., 1898.
42554.23.17 Coppée, François. La bonne souffrance. N.Y., 1907.
42554.23.19 Coppée, François. Contes rapides. Henriette. Paris, 19- ?
42554.23.20 Coppée, François. Le trésor. 7. ed. Paris, 188-?
42554.23.21 Coppée, François. Une idylle pendant le siège. Paris, 19-?
42554.23.23 Coppée, François. Longues et prèves. Paris, 19- ?
42554.23.25 Coppée, François. Toute une jeunesse. Paris, 19- ?
42554.23.26 Coppée, François. Toute une jeunesse. 12e éd. Paris, 1890.
42554.23.27 Coppée, François. Le passant. Paris, 1869?
42554.23.29 Coppée, François. The wanderer. N.Y., 1890.
42554.23.33 Coppée, François. Le coupable. Paris, 1896.
42554.23.35 Coppée, François. Le coupable. Paris, 1897.
42554.24 Coppée, François. Théâtre 1869-72. Paris, n.d.
42554.24.5 Coppée, François. Théâtre 1869-72. Paris, 18- .
42554.25 Coppée, François. Théâtre 1873-78. Paris, 1882.
42554.25.2 Coppée, François. Théâtre 1873-78. Paris, 1879.
42554.25.3 Coppée, François. Théâtre 1872-78. Paris, 18- .
42554.26 Coppée, François. Théâtre 1879-81. Paris, 1882.
42554.26.1 Coppée, François. Théâtre 1879-81. Paris, 1891?
42554.26.2 Coppée, François. Théâtre 1881-85. Paris, 1886.
42554.26.3A Coppée, François. Théâtre 1885-95. Paris, 1898.
42554.26.3B Coppée, François. Théâtre 1885-95. Paris, 1898.
42554.26.24 Coppée, François. Lettres à sa mère et sa soeur 1862-1908. 6e éd. Paris, 1914.

42554.26.25 - .26.29 Individual authors, etc. - 1850-1899 - Poetry - Coppée, F. - Works about
42554.26.25 Gaubert, E. François Coppée. Paris, 1906.
42554.26.27 Le Meur, Léon. La vie et l'oeuvre de François Coppée. Thèse. Paris, 1932.

42554.26.33 Individual authors, etc. - 1850-1899 - Poetry - Circello
42554.26.33 Circello, marquis de. Entretiens poétiques. Firenze, 1884.

42554.26.35 Individual authors, etc. - 1850-1899 - Poetry - Cremieux
42554.26.35 Crémieux, G. Oeuvres posthumes. Paris, 1879.

42554.26.80 - .26.109 Individual authors, etc. - 1850-1899 - Poetry - Cros
42554.26.80 Cros, Charles. Oeuvres complètes. Paris, 1954.
42554.26.85 Cros, Charles. Oeuvres complètes. Paris, 1964.
42554.26.90 Cros, Charles. Oeuvres complètes. Paris, 1970.
42554.26.95 Cros, Charles. L'homme propre. Paris, 1883.
42554.26.100 Cros, Charles. Le coffret de santal. 4e éd. Paris, 1922.
42554.26.105 Forestier, Louis. Charles Cros, l'homme et l'oeuvre. Paris, 1969.

42554.26.110 - Individual authors, etc. - 1850-1899 - Poetry - Corbière, T.
42554.26.110 Corbière, Tristan. Poèmes, choisis et présentés. Paris, 1949.
42554.26.120 Corbière, Tristan. Poems. N.Y., 1947.
42554.26.130 Corbière, Tristan. Les amours jaunes. Paris, 1947.
42554.26.132 Corbière, Tristan. Les amours jaunes. Paris, 1950.
42554.26.133 Corbière, Tristan. Les amours jaunes. Paris, 1953.
42554.26.135 Corbière, Tristan. Selections from Les amours jaunes. Berkeley, 1954.
42554.26.140 Corbière, Tristan. Litanie du sommeil et autres poèmes. Paris, 1949.
42554.26.150 Corbière, Tristan. A picture of Tristan. London, 1965.
42554.26.700 Corbière, Tristan. Corbière. Poems. Santa Barbara, 1967.
42554.26.800 Trigon, Jean de. Tristan Corbière. Paris, 1950.
42554.26.810 Martineau, René. Tristan Corbière. Paris, 1925.
42554.26.820 Geslin, Olivier. Tristan Corbière, 1845-75. Bordeaux, 1958.
42554.26.830 Sonnenfeld, Albert. L'oeuvre poétique de Tristan Corbière. Paris, 1960.
42554.26.835 Angelet, C. La poétique de Tristan Corbière. Bruxelles, 1961.
42554.26.840 Giovine, Esther. Bibliographie de Corbière, Lautredmont et Laforque en Italie. Firenze, 1962.
42554.26.845 Newman, Pauline. Corbière, Laforgue, Apollinaire, ou le Rire en pleurs. Paris, 1964.
42554.26.850 Jannini, Pasquale Aniel. Introduzione alla lettura de Les amours jaunes di Tristan Corbière. Roma, 1969.
42554.26.855 Burch, Francis F. Tristan Corbière: l'originalité des Amours jaunes et leur influence sur T.S. Eliot. Paris, 1970.

42554.27 Individual authors, etc. - 1850-1899 - Poetry - Dogue
42554.27 Dougue, C.O. Homo. Paris, 1872.

42554.28 Individual authors, etc. - 1850-1899 - Poetry - Dorchain
42554.28 Dorchain, Auguste. La jeunesse pensive. Paris, 1881.
42554.28.5 Dorchain, Auguste. Conte d'April. Paris, n.d.
42554.28.7 Dorchain, Auguste. Oeuvres. Paris, 1881.
42554.28.10 Dorchain, Auguste. Hymne aux cloches de pâques 1915. Paris, 1915.
42554.28.15 Sorel, A.E. Auguste Dorchain. Paris, 1908.
42554.28.50 Dhôtel, André. La vie de Rimbaud; variétés. Paris, 1965.

42554.29 Individual authors, etc. - 1850-1899 - Poetry - Debans; Déroulède; DeGuerois; Dujardin; Dupuy; etc.
42554.29 Debans, Camille. Sous clef. Paris, 1862.
42554.29.2 Deniker, N. Poèmes. Paris, 1907.
42554.29.3 Depont, L. Sérénites. Paris, 1897.
42554.29.4 Déroulède, Paul. Chants du soldat. 62e éd. Paris, 1881.
42554.29.4.5 Déroulède, Paul. Refrains militaires. Paris, 1889.
42554.29.4.10 Déroulède, Paul. Chants du paysan. Paris, 1894.
42554.29.4.110 Da Guerrois, C. Dans le monde des fantomes. Paris, 1930.
42554.29.4.120 Da Guerrois, C. Fleur d'abime. Paris, 1930.
42554.29.4.130 Da Guerrois, C. Musique de rêve. Paris, 1931.
42554.29.5 Despax, E. La maison des Glycines. Paris, 1905.
42554.29.6 Destrée, O.G. Poèmes sans rimes. London, 1894.
42554.29.8 Druilhet, Georges. Les haltes sereines. Paris, 1905.
42554.29.8.10 Druilhet, Georges. Au temps des lilas. Paris, 1897.
42554.29.10 Dubreil, L.A. Poésies. Paris, 1857.
42554.29.100 Ducoté, E. La prairie en fleurs, 1895-1902. Paris, 1904.
42554.29.150 Dujardin, É. Le délassement du guerrier. Paris, 1904.
42554.29.155 Dujardin, É. Les lauriers sont coupés. Paris, 1924.
42554.29.155.5 Dujardin, É. Les lauriers sant coupés. Saint Amand, 1968.
42554.29.160 Dujardin, É. Poésies. Paris, 1913.

42554.29 Individual authors, etc. - 1850-1899 - Poetry - Debans; Déroulède; DeGuerois; Dujardin; Dupuy; etc. - cont.
42554.29.165 Dujardin, É. De Stephane Mallarmé au prophete Ezéchiel. Paris, 1919.
42554.29.170A Dujardin, É. We'll to the woods no more. Norfolk, 1938.
42554.29.170B Dujardin, É. We'll to the woods no more. Norfolk, 1938.
42554.29.172 Dujardin, É. We'll to the woods no more. N.Y., 1957.
42554.29.175 Dujardin, É. De l'ancêtre mythique au chef moderne. London, 1943.
42554.29.200 Dupuy, E. Poèmes. Paris, 1908.
42554.29.200.5 Dupuy, E. Les parques. Paris, 1884.
42554.29.300 Duflot, Claude. Aux enfants morts. Paris, 1872.
42554.29.630 Désaugiers, Eugène. Les épaves. Paris, 1872.
42554.29.730 Desnoyers, Fernani. Le vin. Paris, 1869.

42554.30 Individual authors, etc. - 1850-1899 - Poetry - Elskamp
Htn 42554.30* Elskamp, Max. Salutations. Bruxelles, 1893.
Htn 42554.30.1* Elskamp, M. Enluminures; paysages, heures, vies, chansons, grotesques. Bruxelles, 1898.
42554.30.3 Elskamp, M. Le louange de la vie. 2e éd. Paris, 1898.
42554.30.4 Elskamp, M. L'amitié de Max Elskamp et d'Albert Mockel. Bruxelles, 1955.
42554.30.7 Brussels. Bibliothèque Royale. Exposition Max Elskamp 1862-1931. Bruxelles, 1932.
42554.30.8 Elskamp, M. Correspondance. Bruxelles, 1963.
42554.30.9 Errera, Léo. Recueil d'oeuvres. v.3. Bruxelles, 1908.
42554.30.11 Elskamp, M. Oeuvres complètes. Avant pros de Bernard Delvaille. Paris, 1967.
42554.30.15 Berg, Christian. Max Elskamp et le bouddhisme. Nancy, 1969.

42554.31 Individual authors, etc. - 1850-1899 - Poetry - Eggis; Eichthal; Errera; etc.
42554.31.20 Eggis, Étienne. Poésies. Neuchâtel, 1886.
42554.31.100 Eichthal, Eugène d'. A la musique; sonnets. Chartres, 1894.

42554.32 Individual authors, etc. - 1850-1899 - Poetry - Fabie; Fabre des Essarts; Ferrières; etc.
42554.32 Fabie, François. La poésie des bêtes. Paris, 1886.
42554.32.5 Fabie, François. Vers la maison. Paris, 1899.
42554.32.7 Fabie, François. Oeuvres. Poésies, 1905-18. Paris, 1921.
42554.32.10 Fabre Des Essarts, L.E.J. Humanité. Paris, 1885.
42554.32.15 Ferrières, G. La belle matinée. Paris, 1904.

42554.33 Individual authors, etc. - 1850-1899 - Poetry - Fischer; Fontaines; etc.
42554.33 Fischer, H. Les fugitives. n.p., n.d.
42554.33.10 Battier, A.F. Sous les bambous. Paris, 1881.
42554.33.19 Fontainas, A. Crépuscules. Paris, 1891.
42554.33.41 Fontainas, A. Confession d'un poète. Paris, 1936.

42554.34 Individual authors, etc. - 1850-1899 - Poetry - Fontaubert
42554.34 Fontaubert, Émile de. Chants et chansons de Pourcedugnac II. Paris, 1869.

42554.35 Individual authors, etc. - 1850-1899 - Poetry - Floupette; Fertrault; etc.
42554.35 Floupette, A. Les déliquescences. Paris, 1911.
42554.35.5 Fertraul, Marie. Bonheur révé. Paris, 1880?

42554.36 Individual authors, etc. - 1850-1899 - Poetry - Fontenay, H.
42554.36 Fontenay, Henri de. Boutades d'un promeneur dans Paris. Paris, 1867.

42554.37 Individual authors, etc. - 1850-1899 - Poetry - Fontenelle; Fret; etc.
42554.37 Fontenelle, F. La chanson du cidre. Rennes, 1901.
42554.37.50 Fret, L.J. Le pape de Mortagne. 2e éd. La Chapelle-Montligeon, 1897.

42554.38 Individual authors, etc. - 1850-1899 - Poetry - Le Guyader
42554.38 Le Guyader, Frédéric. L'ére bretonne. Paris, 1896.
42554.38.10 Le Guyader, Frédéric. L'ére bretonne. 3. éd. Quimper, 1935.

42554.39 Individual authors, etc. - 1850-1899 - Poetry - Gérard
42554.39 Gérard, Albert. Poésies, rêves, regrets, hommages, foyers et récits. Paris, 1886.

42554.40 Individual authors, etc. - 1850-1899 - Poetry - Gendry; Gauthiez; etc.
42554.40 Gendry, Eugène. Fleurs d'arvor. St. Servan, 1912.
42554.40.50 Gauthiez, Pierre. Les voix errantes. Paris, 1886.
42554.40.55 Gauthiez, Pierre. Deux poèmes. Paris, 1894.

42554.41 Individual authors, etc. - 1850-1899 - Poetry - Gelu
42554.41 Risson, Paul. La vie et l'oeuvre de Gelu. Avignon, 1901.

42554.44 - .45 Individual authors, etc. - 1850-1899 - Poetry - Ghil
42554.44.9 Ghil, René. Oeuvre. Paris, 1906. 4v.
42554.44.12 Ghil, René. Oeuvres complètes. Paris, 1938. 3v.
42554.44.15 Ghil, René. Choix de poèmes. Paris, 1928.
42554.44.20 Ghil, René. Legendes de rêve et de sang. Paris, 1887.
42554.45 Ghil, René. Légende d'âmes et de sangs. Paris, 1885.
42554.45.10 Ghil, René. Le pantoun des pantoun; poème javanais. Paris, 1902.
42554.45.80 Theile, Wolfgang. René Ghil. Tübingen, 1965.

42554.46 Individual authors, etc. - 1850-1899 - Poetry - Gielkens
42554.46.3 Gielkens, Émile. Au roi. Bruxelles, 1897.
42554.46.5 Gielkens, Émile. Camille. Bruxelles, 1899.
42554.46.6 Gielkens, Émile. Camille. Bruxelles, 1900.
42554.46.7 Gielkens, Émile. David. Bruxelles, 1909.
42554.46.9 Gielkens, Émile. Le progrès; poèmes. Bruxelles, 1903.

42554.47 Individual authors, etc. - 1850-1899 - Poetry - Gnafron
42554.47 Gnafron fils (pseud.). Théâtre. Lyon, 1886.

42554.48 Individual authors, etc. - 1850-1899 - Poetry - Grandmougin
42554.48 Grandmougin, C. Rimes de combat. Paris, 1886.

42554.49 Individual authors, etc. - 1850-1899 - Poetry - Gregh; Guaita; etc.
42554.49 Gregh, F. La beauté de vivre. Paris, 1900.
42554.49.3 Gregh, F. Les clartés humaines. Paris, 1904.
42554.49.5 Gregh, F. La maison de l'enfance. Paris, n.d.
42554.49.7 Gregh, F. L'or des minutes. Paris, 1905.

42554.49 Individual authors, etc. - 1850-1899 - Poetry - Gregh; Guaita; etc. - cont.
42554.49.8 Gregh, F. La gloire du coeur, poèmes. Paris, 1932.
42554.49.10 Gregh, F. Couleur de la vie. Paris, 1923.
42554.49.15 Gregh, F. L'âge d'or. Paris, 1947.
42554.49.17 Gregh, F. L'age d'Airain; souvenirs 1905-25. Paris, 1951.
42554.49.20 Gregh, F. La couronne perdue et retrouvée. Paris, 1945.
42554.49.25 Gregh, F. L'age de fer; souvenirs 1925-1955. Paris, 1956.
42554.49.50 Guaita, Stanislas de. Oiseaux de passage. Paris, 1881.
42554.49.55 Guaita, Stanislas de. Lettres inédites de Stanislas de Guaita. Neuchâtel, 1952.
42554.49.1100 Bouvier, Jean Bernard. L'oeuvre de Jules Gross. Genève, 1960.

42554.50 Individual authors, etc. - 1850-1899 - Poetry - Guérin, C.; Guillemet; etc.
42554.50 Bersancourt, A. de. Charles Guérin. Paris, 1912.
42554.50.4 Guérin, C. Oeuvres. Paris, 1926-30. 3v.
42554.50.9 Guérin, C. Le coeur solitaire. 5e éd. Paris, 1912.
42554.50.9.40 Guérin, C. L'homme intérieur. 3e ed. Paris, 1909.
42554.50.10 Guérin, C. L'homme intérieur 1901-05. 4e éd. Paris, 1912.
42554.50.11 Guérin, C. La semeur de cendres 1898-1900. 6e éd. Paris, 1911.
42554.50.12 Guérin, C. Premiers et derniers vers. Paris, 1923.
42554.50.15 Hanson, J.B. Le poète Charles Guérin. Thèse. Paris, 1935.
42554.50.16A Baldersperger, F. Charles Guérin et son oeuvre lyrique. n.p., 19- .
42554.50.16B Baldersperger, F. Charles Guérin et son oeuvre lyrique. n.p., 19- .
42554.50.17 Quinche, Philippe. Les thèmes principaux de l'oeuvre poétique de C. Guérin. Thèse. Zofingue, 1945.
42554.50.19 Guillemet, A. Le centenaire. Paris, 1869.

42554.51 Individual authors, etc. - 1850-1899 - Poetry - Harel, P.
42554.51 Harel, Paul. Aux champs. Paris, 1886.

42554.52 Individual authors, etc. - 1850-1899 - Poetry - Harel, R.
42554.52 Harel, Rose. Poésies. Lisieux, 1863.

42554.53 Individual authors, etc. - 1850-1899 - Poetry - Héré
42554.53 Héré, J. Fables et poésies. St. Quentin, 1860.

42554.54 Individual authors, etc. - 1850-1899 - Poetry - Heredia - Complete and Selected works
42554.54.10 Heredia, J.M. de. Poésies complètes. Paris, 1924.

42554.55 - .61 Individual authors, etc. - 1850-1899 - Poetry - Heredia - Individual works
NEDL 42554.55 Heredia, J.M. de. Les trophées. Paris, 1893.
Htn 42554.55.2* Heredia, J.M. de. Les trophées. Paris, 1895.
42554.55.5 Heredia, J.M. de. Les trophées. Paris, 189-.
42554.55.8 Heredia, J.M. de. Les trophées. Cambridge, Eng., 1942.
42554.55.9 Heredia, J.M. de. The trophies, sonnets. Boston, 1900.
42554.55.10 Heredia, J.M. de. Les trophées. Paris, 19- .
42554.55.12 Heredia, J.M. de. The trophies. N.Y., 1929.
42554.55.15 Heredia, J.M. de. The trophies. London, 1962.
42554.55.25 Heredia, J.M. de. Los trofeos. Madrid, 1908.
42554.55.30 Heredia, J.M. de. Salut à l'empereur. Paris, 1896.
42554.56 Heredia, J.M. de. Sonnets. San Francisco, 1898.
NEDL 42554.57 Heredia, J.M. de. The trophies. London, 1902.
42554.57.5 Heredia, J.M. de. Les trophées. Paris, 1901?
42554.58 Heredia, J.M. de. Les trophées. 5. éd. Paris, 1913.
42554.59 Heredia, J.M. de. Les trophées. Paris, 1926.
42554.60 Heredia, J.M. de. Translations from José Maria de Heredia. N.Y., 1927.

42554.62 - .63 Individual authors, etc. - 1850-1899 - Poetry - Heredia - Biography and criticism
42554.62 Fromm, Heinrich. Les Trophées von José Maria de Heredia. Inaug. Diss. Greifswald, 1913.
42554.63 Ibrovac, Miodrag. José Maria de Heredia, sa vie, son oeuvre. Paris, 1923.
42554.63.2 Ibrovac, Miodrag. José Maria de Heredia, sa vie, son oeuvre. Thèse. Paris, 1923.
42554.63.6 Ibrovac, Miodrag. Les sources des "Trophées". Thèse. Paris, 1923.

42554.64 Individual authors, etc. - 1850-1899 - Poetry - Herold; Hilbey; etc.
42554.64.31 Herold, A.F. Images tendres et merveilleuses. Paris, 1897.
42554.64.35 Herold, A.F. Guillaume le petit. Paris, 1919.
42554.64.40 Herold, A.F. La route fleurie. Paris, 1911.
42554.64.45 Herold, A.F. Au hasard des chemins, poèmes. Paris, 1900.
42554.64.50 Herold, A.F. Savitri. Paris, 1899.
42554.64.100 Hilbey, C. La révolution. Genève, 1869.
42554.64.801 Danilin, Iurii I. Zabytyi pamfletist. Moskva, 1971.

42554.65 Individual authors, etc. - 1850-1899 - Poetry - Hugues; Ibels; Joncières; etc.
42554.65.5 Hugues, Clovis. Le mauvais larron. Paris, 1895.
42554.65.7 Hugues, Clovis. Les jours de combat; poésies. Paris, 1883.
42554.65.130 Ibels, André. Talentiers; ballades libres. Paris, 1899.
42554.65.231 Joncières, L. de. Tanagra. Paris, 1900.

42554.66 Individual authors, etc. - 1850-1899 - Poetry - Jouy; John Pantaléon; etc.
42554.66 Jouy, Jules. La muse à bébé. Paris, 1892.
42554.66.100 John, Pantaléon. Les secrets du coeur, poésies diverses. Toulouse, 1899.

42554.68 Individual authors, etc. - 1850-1899 - Poetry - Kahn, G.
NEDL 42554.68 Kahn, Gustave. Le livre d'images. Paris, 1897.
42554.68.10 Kahn, Gustave. Contes juifs. Paris, 1926.
42554.68.15 Kahn, Gustave. Images bibliques; poèmes. Paris, 1929.
42554.68.22 Kahn, Gustave. Premiers poèmes. 2e éd. Paris, 1897.
42554.68.800 Ireson, J.C. L'oeuvre poétique de Gustave Kahn. Paris, 1962.

42554.70 Individual authors, etc. - 1850-1899 - Poetry - Kerdaniel
42554.70.65 Fuster, Charles. La prose et les vers de Jean Plémeur. Paris, 1904.

42554.71 Individual authors, etc. - 1850-1899 - Poetry - Kerhalvé
42554.71 Kerhalvé, Sylvane de. Branches d'épines. Nantes, 1896.

42554.75 Individual authors, etc. - 1850-1899 - Poetry - Kerviler
42554.75.80 Fuster, Charles. Par les chemins de Bretagne et les routes de France. St. Etienne, 1902.

42555.1 - .2 Individual authors, etc. - 1850-1899 - Poetry - Laforgue
42555.1 Laforgue, Jules. Oeuvres complètes. 4. éd. v.1 lost 1947. Paris, 1909. 5v.
42555.1.2 Laforgue, Jules. Poésies complètes. Paris, 1970.
42555.1.3 Laforgue, Jules. Poésies complètes. v.3. 6. éd. Paris, 1919.
42555.1.6 Laforgue, Jules. Oeuvres complètes, mélanges posthumes. 8. éd. Paris, 1923.
42555.1.8 Laforgue, Jules. Oeuvres complètes. Paris, 1947. 2v.
42555.1.9A Laforgue, Jules. Dragées, Charles Beaudelaire, Tristan Corbiere. Paris, 1921.
42555.1.9B Laforgue, Jules. Dragées, Charles Beaudelaire, Tristan Corbiere. Paris, 1921.
42555.1.10 Laforgue, Jules. Exil, poésie, spleen. Paris, 1921.
42555.1.20 Laforgue, Jules. Chroniques parisiennes. Paris, 1920.
42555.1.30 Laforgue, Jules. Stéphane Vassiliew. Vésenaz près Genève, 1946.
42555.1.35 Laforgue, Jules. Moralités légendaires. Paris, 1921.
42555.1.55 Laforgue, Jules. Six moral tales. Photoreproduction. N.Y., 1928.
42555.1.60 Laforgue, Jules. Selected writings. N.Y. 1956.
42555.1.65 Laforgue, Jules. Poems. Berkeley, 1958.
42555.1.80A Ramsey, Warren. Jules Laforgue and the ironic inheritage. N.Y., 1953.
42555.1.80B Ramsey, Warren. Jules Laforgue and the ironic inheritage. N.Y., 1953.
42555.1.83 Collie, M. Laforgue. Edinburgh, 1963.
42555.1.85 Reboul, Pierre. Laforgue. Paris, 1960.
42555.1.90 Cuisinier, Jeanne. Jules Laforgue. Paris, 1925.
42555.1.95 Brunfaut, Marie. Jules Laforgue, les Ysaye et leur temps. Bruxelles, 1961.
42555.1.100 Ramsey, Warren. Jules Laforgue. Carbondale, 1969.
42555.2 Mauclair, C. Jules Laforgue. Paris, 1896.
42555.2.10 Ruchon, François. Jules Laforgue, 1860-1887. Genève, 1924.
42555.2.20A Guichard, L. Jules Laforgue et ses poésies. Paris, 1950.
42555.2.20B Guichard, L. Jules Laforgue et ses poésies. Paris, 1950.

42555.3 Individual authors, etc. - 1850-1899 - Poetry - La Grasserie
42555.3 La Grasserie, R. de. La nature. Poésies. Paris, 1896.

42555.4 Individual authors, etc. - 1850-1899 - Poetry - Laroche
42555.4 Laroche, Abel. Fables. San Francisco, 1869.

42555.6 Individual authors, etc. - 1850-1899 - Poetry - Lacaussade
42555.6.80 Barquissau, R. Le poète Lacaussade et l'exotisme tropical. Paris, 1952.

42555.8 Individual authors, etc. - 1850-1899 - Poetry - Laforest
42555.8.33 Laforest, Edmond. Sonnets. Paris, 1910.

42555.9 Individual authors, etc. - 1850-1899 - Poetry - Lalot
42555.9 Lalot, Émile. Poésies. Paris, 1898.

42555.11 Individual authors, etc. - 1850-1899 - Poetry - La Landelle
42555.11 La Landelle, G. de. Poèmes et chants marins. Paris, 1861.
42555.11.10 La Landelle, G. de. Pauvres et mendiants. 2e éd. Paris, 1877.

42555.12 Individual authors, etc. - 1850-1899 - Poetry - Laluyé; La Morvonnais; etc.
42555.12.9 La Morvannais, H. de. La Thébaïde des grèves. Paris, 1864.
42555.12.25 Fleury, E. Hippolyte de La Morvonnais. Paris, 1911.

42555.13 Individual authors, etc. - 1850-1899 - Poetry - Laprade - Biography and criticism
42555.13 Biré, E. Victor de Laprade. Paris, n.d.
42555.13.10 Séchaud, Pierre. Victor de Laprade: l'homme, son oeuvre poétique. Thèse. Paris, 1934.
42555.13.15 Strasser, R. Victor de Laprade, ein Dichter des Lyonnais. Inaug. Diss. Würzburg, 1938.

42555.14 Individual authors, etc. - 1850-1899 - Poetry - Laprade - Complete and Selected works
42555.14 Laprade, Victor de. Oeuvres poétiques. Paris, 1881.

42555.15 - .32 Individual authors, etc. - 1850-1899 - Poetry - Laprade - Individual works
42555.16 Laprade, Victor de. Le sentiment de la nature avant le christianisme. Paris, 1866.
42555.17 Laprade, Victor de. Le sentiment de la nature chez les modernes. Paris, 1868.
42555.19 Laprade, Victor de. Harmodins. Paris, 1870.
42555.20 Laprade, Victor de. Essais de critique idéaliste. Paris, 1882.
42555.22 Laprade, Victor de. Pernette. Paris, 1872.
42555.23 Laprade, Victor de. Poèmes évangéliques. Paris, 1852.
42555.24 Laprade, Victor de. Poèmes évangéliques. 3e éd. Paris, 1860.
42555.26 Laprade, Victor de. Psyché. Paris, 1860.
42555.26.5 Laprade, Victor de. Psyché. Thèse. Paris, 1940.
42555.29 Laprade, Victor de. Les symphonies. Paris, 1862.
42555.31 Laprade, Victor de. Les voix du silence. Paris, 1865.
42555.32.5 Laprade, Victor de. Lettres inédites de Victor de Laprade à Charles Alexandre, 1852-1871. Thèse. Lyon, 1934.
42555.32.30 Laprade, Victor de. Odes et poèmes. Paris, 1843.

42555.33 Individual authors, etc. - 1850-1899 - Poetry - Langel; Laurent; Levey; etc.
42555.33 Langel, A. Flammes et cendres. Paris, 1912.
42555.33.25 Laurent, Charles Marie. France et Bretagne; poésies. Paris, 1863.
42555.33.50 Leconte, Léon. La sorciere de Baincthum. St. Omer, 1884.
42555.33.100 Levey, Henry J.M. Le pavillon. Paris, 1897.

42555.34 - .35 Individual authors, etc. - 1850-1899 - Poetry - Leconte de Lisle - Collected and Selected works

42555.34 Leconte de Lisle, C.M.R. Oeuvres. Poèmes antiques. Paris, 1881.
42555.34.3A Leconte de Lisle, C.M.R. Poèmes barbares. Paris, 1881.
42555.34.3B Leconte de Lisle, C.M.R. Poèmes barbares. Paris, 1881.
42555.34.3C Leconte de Lisle, C.M.R. Poèmes barbares. Paris, 1881.
42555.34.4 Leconte de Lisle, C.M.R. Poèmes antiques. Paris, 19- .
42555.34.5 Leconte de Lisle, C.M.R. Poèmes barbares. Paris, 1872.
42555.34.15 Leconte de Lisle, C.M.R. Poèmes barbares. Paris, 1929?
42555.35.15 Leconte de Lisle, C.M.R. Premières poésies et lettres intimes. Paris, 1902.
42555.35.30 Leconte de Lisle, C.M.R. Leconte de Lisle, un tableau synoptique. Paris, 1967.
42555.35.40A Leconte de Lisle, C.M.R. Poèmes antiques. Paris, 188-.
42555.35.40B Leconte de Lisle, C.M.R. Poèmes antiques. Paris, 188-.
42555.35.50 Leconte de Lisle, C.M.R. Poèmes antiques. Paris, 192-.
42555.35.75 Leconte de Lisle, C.M.R. Poèmes tragiques. Paris, 192-.

42555.36 Individual authors, etc. - 1850-1899 - Poetry - Leconte de Lisle - Individual works

42555.36 Leconte de Lisle, C.M.R. Derniers poèmes. Paris, 1895.
42555.36.5A Leconte de Lisle, C.M.R. Oeuvres. Paris, 1886.
42555.36.5B Leconte de Lisle, C.M.R. Oeuvres. Paris, 1886.
42555.36.7 Leconte de Lisle, C.M.R. Poésies complètes. Paris, 1858.
Htn 42555.36.10* Leconte de Lisle, C.M.R. Poèmes et poésies. Paris, 1855.
Htn 42555.36.11* Leconte de Lisle, C.M.R. Le sacre de Paris. Paris, 1871.
Htn 42555.36.12* Leconte de Lisle, C.M.R. Le soir d'une bataille. Paris, 1871.
42555.36.13 Leconte de Lisle, C.M.R. Les erinnyes. Paris, 1920.
42555.36.14 Leconte de Lisle, C.M.R. Poèmes choisis. Manchester, 1943.
42555.36.15 Leconte de Lisle, C.M.R. Contes en prose. Paris, 1925.
42555.36.20 Leconte de Lisle, C.M.R. Kain. V Praze, 1880.
42555.36.22 Leconte de Lisle, C.M.R. La dernière illusion de Laconte de Lisle. Genève, 1968.
42555.36.30 Leconte de Lisle, C.M.R. Leconte de Lisle: articles, préfaces, discours. Paris, 1971.
42555.36.790 Leconte de Lisle, C.M.R. Erinii. St. Petersburg, 1922.

42555.37 Individual authors, etc. - 1850-1899 - Poetry - Leconte de Lisle - Biography and criticism

42555.37 Lebloud, M.A. Leconte de Lisle. Paris, 1906.
42555.37.01 Pamphlet box. Leconte de Lisle.
42555.37.3 Keiser, Gustav A. Stilstudien zu Leconte de Lisle. Halle, 1917.
42555.37.4 Calmettes, F. Un demi siècle littéraire. Leconte de Lisle et ses amis. Paris, 1902.
42555.37.5 Maurer, Chlothilde. Das persönliche Element in den Werken Leconte de Lisles. Inaug. Diss. Heidelberg, 1917.
42555.37.5.5 Vianey, Joseph. Les sources de Leconte de Lisle. Montpellier, 1907.
42555.37.5.6 Vianey, Joseph. Les poèmes barbares de Leconte de Lisle. Paris, 1955.
42555.37.6 Dornis, J. Essai sur Leconte de Lisle. 2e éd. Paris, 1909.
42555.37.6.10 Falshaw, Gladys. Leconte de Lisle et l'Inde. Thèse. Paris, 1923.
42555.37.6.12 Flottes, Pierre. Le poète Leconte de Lisle. Paris, 1929.
42555.37.6.15 Flottes, Pierre. L'influence d'Alfred de Vigny sur Leconte de Lisle. Thèse. Paris, 1926.
42555.37.6.20 Brown, Irwing. Leconte de Lisle. N.Y., 1929.
42555.37.6.25 Flottes, Pierre. Leconte de Lisle. Paris, 1954.
42555.37.7 Ducros, Jean. Le retour de la poésie française. Paris, 1918.
42555.37.10 Empeirikos, A. Leconte de Lisle. Thonon-les-Bains, 1941.
42555.37.20 Fairlie, Alison. Leconte de Lisle's poems on the Barbarian races. Cambridge, Eng., 1947.
42555.37.25 Carloni Valentini, Renata. Un poète présque oublié. Vimodrone? 1958.
42555.37.30 Lelleik, Lore. Der "Parnassier". Bonn, 1961.

42555.38 Individual authors, etc. - 1850-1899 - Poetry - Lefèvre; Letolle; etc.

42555.38.5 Lefèvre, André. La flute de Pan. Paris, 1861.
42555.38.100 Letalle, Abel. La revanche des fleurs. Paris, 1895.
42555.38.110 Letalle, Abel. La poésie de l'enfance. Paris, 1895.

42555.39 Individual authors, etc. - 1850-1899 - Poetry - Lemoyne; Lerberghe; etc.

42555.39 Lemoyne, André. Poésies. 1855-96. Paris, 1871- 4v.
42555.39.10 Lemoyne, André. Légendes des bois et chansons marines. Paris, 1881.
42555.39.30 Lemoyne, André. Une idylle normande. Paris, 1874.
42555.39.35 Lemoyne, André. La mare aut chevreuils. Paris, 1900.
42555.39.1100 Lerberghe, C. van. La chanson d'Eve. Paris, 1952.
42555.39.1110 Lerberghe, C. van. Lettres à une jeune fille. Bruxelles, 1954.
42555.39.1120 Lerberghe, C. van. Entrevisions suivi des poèmes posthumes. Paris, 1923.
42555.39.1180 Guillaume, Jean. Essai sur la valeur exégétique du substantif dans les Entrevisions. Bruxelles, 1956.
42555.39.1190 Guillaume, Jean. Le mot-thème dans l'exégèse de van Lerberghe. Bruxelles, 1959.
42555.39.1192 Guillaume, Jean. Le mot-thème dans l'exégèse. Namur, 1959.
42555.39.1195 Davignon, Henri. Charles van Lerberghe et ses amis. Bruxelles, 1952.
42555.39.1800 Guillaume, Jean. La poésie de van Lerberghe. Bruxelles, 1962.
42555.39.1802 Guillaume, Jean. La poésie de van Lerberghe. Namur, 1962.

42555.40 Individual authors, etc. - 1850-1899 - Poetry - Le Roy, G.; Le Vavasseur; Lonley; etc.

42555.40.9 Le Roy, G. La chanson du pauvre. Paris, 1907.
42555.40.52 Contades, G. Gustave Le Vavasseur, bibliographie de ses oeuvres (1840-1896). Alençon, 1898.
42555.40.53 Contades, G. Gustave Le Vavasseur; débuts litteraires. Alençon, 1898.
42555.40.55 Le Vavasseur, G. Inauguration du buste de Gustave Le Vavasseur. Alençon, 1899.
42555.40.75 Leygues, Georges. Le coffret brisé. Paris, 1882.
42555.40.110 Lonlay, E. Le livre d'or des enfants. Paris, 1874.
42555.40.230 Liégeard, Stéphen. Les abeilles d'or; chants impériaux. Paris, 1859.
42555.40.2103 Liber, Jules V.F. Les pantagruéliques. 3. éd. Turin, 1871.

42555.41 Individual authors, etc. - 1850-1899 - Poetry - Loridan; etc.

42555.41 Loridan, Henri. Recueil de chansons en patois de Roubaix. Roubaix, 1882.

42555.42 Individual authors, etc. - 1850-1899 - Poetry - Lutel; Lys; Magnant; Mahul; etc.

42555.42 Lutel, Paul. La légende de Campagne. Paris, 1891.
42555.42.25 Lys, Georges de. Les tubereuses. Paris, 1885.
42555.42.75 Magnant, E. Angela ou l'Alsace enchainée. Paris, 1881.
42555.42.100 Mahul, E. Poésies politiques sur les événements d'Italie. Turin, 1862.
42555.42.1100 Mac-Nab, Maurice. Poèmes mobiles, monlogues. Paris, 1886.

42555.43 Individual authors, etc. - 1850-1899 - Poetry - Mallarmé - Writings

42555.43 Mallarmé, Stéphane. Vers et prose. Paris, 1893.
42555.43.1 Mallarmé, Stéphane. Oeuvres complètes. Paris, 1945.
42555.43.2 Mallarmé, Stéphane. Vers et prose. Paris, 1910.
42555.43.3.1 Mallarmé, Stéphane. Poésies. 126. éd. Paris, 1945.
X Cg 42555.43.3.2 Mallarmé, Stéphane. Poésies. 108. éd. Paris, 1949.
42555.43.3.3 Mallarmé, Stéphane. Poésies. Paris, 1924?
42555.43.3.5 Mallarmé, Stéphane. Stéphane Mallarmé: poésies choisies. Londres, 1943.
42555.43.4 Mallarmé, Stéphane. Poésies: poésies, choix de vers de circonstances. Paris, 1966.
42555.43.5 Mallarmé, Stéphane. Oxford, Cambridge. La musique et les lettres. Paris, 1895.
42555.43.6 Mallarmé, Stéphane. Vers de circonstance. 6. éd. Paris, 1920.
42555.43.7 Mallarmé, Stéphane. Oeuvres complètes. Paris, 1961.
42555.43.8 Mallarmé, Stéphane. Opere. Milano, 1963.
42555.43.9 Mallarmé, Stéphane. Divagations. Paris, 1917.
42555.43.10A Mallarmé, Stéphane. La dernière mode. N.Y., 1933.
42555.43.10B Mallarmé, Stéphane. La dernière mode. N.Y., 1933.
42555.43.15 Mallarmé, Stéphane. L'art pour tous. Aurora, N.Y., 1942.
42555.43.17 Mallarmé, Stéphane. Mallarmé, par lui-même. Paris, 1964.
42555.43.20 Mallarmé, Stéphane. Selected prose, poems, essays, and letters. Baltimore, 1956.
42555.43.27 Mallarmé, Stéphane. Poems. N.Y., 1951.
42555.43.28 Mallarmé, Stéphane. Dix poèmes. Lille, 1948.
42555.43.30 Mallarmé, Stéphane. Herodias. Prairie City, Ill., 1940.
42555.43.31 Mallarmé, Stéphane. Herodias. N.Y., 1957.
42555.43.32 Mallarmé, Stéphane. Les noces d'Herodiade, mystère. Paris, 1959.
42555.43.35 Mallarmé, Stéphane. Propos sur la poésie. Monaco, 1946.
42555.43.37 Mallarmé, Stéphane. Propos sur la poésie. Monacoville, 1953.
42555.43.40 Mallarmé, Stéphane. Igitur ou La folie d'Elbehnon. 7. éd. Paris, 1952.
42555.43.45 Mallarmé, Stéphane. Igitur, ou La folie d'Elbehnon. Paris, 1925.
42555.43.50 Mallarmé, Stéphane. Les gossips de Mallarmé. Paris, 1962.
42555.43.70 Mallarmé, Stéphane. Gedichte. Zweisprachige Ausg. Freiburg, 1947.
42555.43.75A Mallarmé, Stéphane. Élucidation du poème Un coup de dés jamais. Neuchâtel, 1943.
42555.43.75B Mallarmé, Stéphane. Élucidation du poème Un coup de dés jamais. Neuchâtel, 1943.
42555.43.80 Mallarmé, Stéphane. Pages. Bruxelles, 1891.
42555.43.85 Mallarmé, Stéphane. Pour un tombeau d'Anatole. Paris, 1961.
42555.43.86 Mallarmé, Stéphane. Mallarmé et son fils Anatole. Paris, 1961.
42555.43.90 Mallarmé, Stéphane. Posie. Praha, 1931.
42555.43.95 Mallarmé, Stéphane. Vingt poèmes. Genève, 1967.

42555.44 Individual authors, etc. - 1850-1899 - Poetry - Mallarmé - Works about; Letters

42555.44.2 Mallarmé, Stéphane. Correspondance inédite de Stéphane Mallarmé et Henry Roujon. Genève, 1949.
42555.44.4 Mallarmé, Stéphane. Ein Würfelwurf. Olten, 1966.
42555.44.5 Mallarmé, Stéphane. Correspondance, 1862-1871. Paris, 1959. 3v.
42555.44.6 Mallarmé, Stéphane. Correspondance Mallarmé-Whistler. Paris, 1964.
42555.44.7 Mallarmé, Stéphane. Lettres de Mallarmé à Aubanel et Mistral. Saint-Felicien-en-Vivarais, 1924.
42555.44.8 Mallarmé, Stéphane. Les lettres; poésie, philosophie. Paris, 1948.
42555.44.9 Thibaudet, A. Poésie de Stéphane Mallarmé. Paris, n.d.
42555.44.10 Mallarmé, Stéphane. Recueil de nursery rhymes. Paris, 1964.
42555.44.11 Soula, Camille. La poésie et la pensée de Stéphane Mallarmé, essai sur l'hermétisme Mallarmé. Paris, 1919.
42555.44.12 Soula, Camille. La poésie et la pensée de Stéphane Mallarmé. Paris, 1931.
42555.44.13A Soula, Camille. La poésie et la pensée de Stéphane Mallarmé. Paris, 1926.
42555.44.13B Soula, Camille. La poésie et la pensée de Stéphane Mallarmé. Paris, 1926.
42555.44.14 Soula, Camille. Gloses sur Mallarmé. Paris, 1945.
42555.44.15A Royère, Jean. Mallarmé. Paris, 1927.
42555.44.15B Royère, Jean. Mallarmé. Paris, 1927.
42555.44.20 Cooperman, H. The aesthetics of Stéphane Mallarmé. Photoreproduction. N.Y., 1933.
42555.44.25 Winkel, Joseph. Mallarmé-Wagner-Wagnerismus. Inaug. Diss. Bückeburg, 1935.
42555.44.30 Dujardin, E. Mallarmé par un des siens. Paris, 1936.
42555.44.35 Naumann, W. Der Sprachgebrauch Mallarmé's. Inaug. Diss. Marburg, 1936.
42555.44.40A Wais, K.K.T. Mallarmé. München, 1938.
42555.44.40B Wais, K.K.T. Mallarmé. München, 1938.
42555.44.42 Aish, D.A.K. La métaphore dans l'oeuvre de S. Mallarmé. Thèse. Paris, 1938.
42555.44.43A Aish, D.A.K. La métaphore dans l'oeuvre de S. Mallarmé. Paris, 1938.
42555.44.43B Aish, D.A.K. La métaphore dans l'oeuvre de S. Mallarmé. Paris, 1938.
42555.44.50 Pamphlet box. Collection of pamphlets relating to Mallarmé.
42555.44.55 Faure, Gabriel. Mallarmé à Tournon. Grenoble, 1941.
42555.44.56 Faure, Gabriel. Mallarmé à Tournon. Paris, 1946.
42555.44.63 Mondor, Henri. Vie de Mallarmé. 3e éd. Paris, 1941.
42555.44.65 Mondor, Henri. Autres précisions sur Mallarmé et inédits. Paris, 1961.
42555.44.66 Mondor, Henri. Mallarmé, documents iconographiques. Genève, 1947.
42555.44.68 Mondor, Henri. Histoire d'un faune. 9. éd. Paris, 1948.
42555.44.70 Mondor, Henri. Vie de Mallarmé. 10. éd. Paris? 1943.

42555.44 Individual authors, etc. - 1850-1899 - Poetry - Mallarmé - Works about; Letters - cont.

42555.44.73 Mondor, Henri. Vie de Mallarmé. 19. éd. Paris, 1946.
42555.44.75A Woolley, Grange. Stéphane Mallarmé, 1842-1898. Madison, 1942.
42555.44.75B Woolley, Grange. Stéphane Mallarmé, 1842-1898. Madison, 1942.
42555.44.78A Scherer, Jacques. L'expression littéraire dans l'oeuvre de Mallarmé. Paris, 1947.
42555.44.78B Scherer, Jacques. L'expression littéraire dans l'oeuvre de Mallarmé. Paris, 1947.
42555.44.80 Mallarmé, Stéphane. Le "live" de Mallarmé. Paris, 1957.
42555.44.82 Chassé, Charles. Lueurs sur Mallarmé. Paris, 1947.
42555.44.82.5 Chassé, Charles. Les clés de Mallarmé. Paris, 1954.
42555.44.84 Miomandre, F. de. Mallarmé. Mulhouse, 1948.
42555.44.86 Cohn, Robert G. Mallarmé's un coup de dés. New Haven, 1949.
42555.44.86.2 Cohn, Robert G. L'oeuvre de Mallarmé. Paris, 1951.
42555.44.88A Noulet, E. L'oeuvre poétique de Stéphane Mallarmé. Paris, 1950.
42555.44.88B Noulet, E. L'oeuvre poétique de Stéphane Mallarmé. Paris, 1950.
42555.44.89 Davies, Gardner. Vers une explication rationnelle du coup de dés. Paris, 1953.
42555.44.90 Davies, Gardner. Les "Tombeaux" de Mallarmé. Paris, 1950.
42555.44.91A Davies, Gardner. Les poèmes commémoratifs de Mallarmé. Thèse. Paris, 1950.
42555.44.91B Davies, Gardner. Les poèmes commémoratifs de Mallarmé. Thèse. Paris, 1950.
42555.44.92 Gengoux, J. Le symbolisme de Mallarmé. Thèse. Paris, 1950.
42555.44.92.5 Gengoux, J. Le symbolisme de Mallarmé. Paris, 1950.
42555.44.92.10 Delfel, Guy. L'esthétique de Stéphane Mallarmé. Paris, 1951.
42555.44.92.15 Wais, K.K.T. Mallarmé. 2. Aufl. München, 1952.
42555.44.94 Roulet, Claude. Nouveaux éléments de poétique mallarméenne. Neuchâtel, 1950.
42555.44.95 Roulet, Claude. Traité de poétique superieure. Neuchâtel, 1956.
42555.44.96 Fowlie, Wallace. Mallarmé. Chicago, 1953.
42555.44.96.5 Fowlie, Wallace. Mallarmé as Hamlet. Yonkers, N.Y., 1949.
42555.44.98 Valéry, P. Écrits divers sur Stéphane Mallarmé. Paris, 1950.
42555.44.100 Bo, Carlo. Mallarmé. Milano, 1945.
42555.44.105 Mauron, Charles. Introduction à la psychanalyse de Mallarmé. Neuchâtel, 1950.
42555.44.105.2 Mauron, Charles. Introdution à la psychanalyse de Mallarmé. 2e éd. Neuchâtel, 1968.
42555.44.110A Michaud, Guy. Mallarmé. Paris, 1953.
42555.44.110B Michaud, Guy. Mallarmé. Paris, 1953.
42555.44.113 Michaud, Guy. Mallarmé. N.Y., 1965.
42555.44.115 Mondor, Henri. Mallarmé lycéen. Paris, 1954.
42555.44.120 Sauriau, M. Le mystère de Mallarmé. Lille, 1955.
42555.44.125 Goffin, Robert. Mallarmé vivant. Paris, 1956.
42555.44.130 Ayda, Adile. Le drame interieur de Mallarmé. Istanbul, 1955.
42555.44.135 Chiari, Joseph. Symbolisme from Poe to Mallarmé. London, 1956.
42555.44.140 Ragusa, Olga. Mallarmé in Italy. N.Y., 1957.
42555.44.145 Nardis, Luigi de. Impressionismo di Mallarmé. Roma, 1957.
42555.44.147 Nardis, Luigi de. Mallarmé in Italia. Milano, 1957.
42555.44.149 Nardis, Luigi de. L'ironia di Mallarmé. Roma, 1962.
42555.44.150 Chisholm, A.R. Mallarmé's L'après-midi d'un faune. Carlton, 1958.
42555.44.150.2 Chisholm, A.R. Mallarmé's L'après-midi d'un faune. Carlton, 1958.
42555.44.151 Chisholm, A.R. Mallarmé's Grand oeuvre. Manchester, 1962.
42555.44.152 Davies, Gardner. Mallarmé et le drame solaire. Paris, 1959.
42555.44.155 Reyes, Alfonso. Mallarmé entre nosotros. México, 1955.
42555.44.158 Bernard, Suzanne. Mallarmé et la musique. 2. éd. Paris, 1959.
42555.44.160 Cellier, Léon. Mallarmé et la morte qui parle. Paris, 1959.
42555.44.162 Boulay, Daniel. L'obscurité esthétique de Mallarmé. Paris, 1960.
42555.44.164 Mauron, Charles. Mallarmé l'obscur. Paris, 1941.
42555.44.166 Girolamo, Nicola di. Stéphane Mallarmé, Ouverture ancienne d'Herodiade. Siena, 1959.
42555.44.168 Fraenrel, Ernest. Les dessins trans-conscients de Stéphane Mallarmé. Paris, 1960.
42555.44.170 Mauron, Charles. Introduction to the psychoanalysis of Mallarmé. Berkeley, 1963.
42555.44.172 Chadwick, Charles. Mallarmé. Paris, 1962.
42555.44.174 Richard, Jean Pierre. L'univers imaginaire de Mallarmé. Paris, 1961.
42555.44.178 Steland, Dieter. Dialektische Gedanken in Stéphane Mallarmés Diragations. München, 1965.
42555.44.180 Block, H. Mallarmé and the symbolist drama. Detroit, 1963.
42555.44.185 Nicolas, H. Mallarmé et le symbolisme. Paris, 1963.
42555.44.190 Fontainas, André. De Stéphane Mallarmé à Paul Valery. Paris, 1928.
42555.44.195 Kansas. University. Museum of Art. Les mardis. Lawrence, 1966.
42555.44.200 Beausire, Pierre. Mallarmé. Lausanne, 1949.
42555.44.205 Cohn, Robert Greer. Mallarmé's masterwork. The Hague, 1966[1967]
42555.44.210 Park Ynhui. L'idée chez Mallarmé. Paris, 1966.
42555.44.215 St. Aubyn, Frederic Chase. Stéphane Mallarmé. N.Y., 1969.
42555.44.220 Paxton, Norman. The development of Mallarmé's prose style. Genève, 1968.
42555.44.225 Cirolamo, Nicola di. Cultura e coscienza critica nell'Hérodiade di Mallarmé. Bologna, 1969.
42555.44.230 Documents Stéphane Mallarmé. Paris. 1,1968 2v.
42555.44.235 Williams, Thomas Andrew. Mallarmé and the language of mysticism. Athens, 1970.
42555.44.240 Agosti, Stefano. Il cigno di Mallarmé. Roma, 1969.
42555.44.245 Haas, Doris. Flucht aus der Wirklichkeit. Bonn, 1970.
42555.44.250 Cohn, Robert Greer. Toward the poems of Mallarmé. Berkeley, 1965.

42555.45 Individual authors, etc. - 1850-1899 - Poetry - Marmier, X.

42555.45 Poitevin, Prosper. Les contes tourangeaux. Paris, 1878.
42555.45.30 Marmier, Xavier. Journal, 1848-1890. Genève, 1968. 2v.
42555.45.75 Menard, Jean. Xavier Marmier et le Canada avec des documents inédits. Québec, 1967.

42555.45 Individual authors, etc. - 1850-1899 - Poetry - Marmier, X. - cont.

42555.45.100 Aymonier, Camille. Xavier marmier, sa vie. Besançon, 1928.
42555.45.105 Lloyd, Wildon. Xavier Marmier: poet and traveler. Washington, 1933.

42555.46 - .49.5 Individual authors, etc. - 1850-1899 - Poetry - Manuel, E.

42555.46 Manuel, Eugène. Poèmes populaires. Paris, 1881.
42555.47 Manuel, Eugène. Pendant la gueurre poésies. Washington, 1933.
42555.48 Manuel, Eugène. Pages intimes, poésies. Washington, 1883.
42555.49 Manuel, Eugène. En voyage, poésies. Washington, 1882.
42555.49.2 Manuel, Eugène. A nos hôtes. Paris, 1878.
42555.49.3 Manuel, Eugène. Poésies du foyer et de l'école. Paris, 1895.

42555.49.7 - .49.99 Individual authors, etc. - 1850-1899 - Poetry - Marc; Mariéton; Martin; Merrill; etc.

42555.49.7 Marc, G. Sonnets parisiens. Paris, 1875.
42555.49.9 Marés, Roland de. Ariettes douloureuses. Paris, 1893.
42555.49.11 Mariéton, Paul. Paul Mariéton d'après sa correspondance. Paris, 1920. 3v.
42555.49.12 Mariéton, Paul. La viole d'amour. Paris, 1886.
42555.49.13 Mariéton, Paul. Le livre de mélancolie. Paris, 1896.
42555.49.14 Mariéton, Paul. Hippolyta. Paris, 1902.
42555.49.19 Mariéton, Paul. Hellas. Paris, 1889.
42555.49.20 Marteau, A. Espoirs et souvenirs. Poèmes. Paris, 1867.
42555.49.21 Martin, Gabriel. Les cantiques impies. Paris, 1888.
42555.49.22 Martin, Gabriel. Les poésies fantaisistes. Paris, 1894.
Htn 42555.49.23* Martin, Gabriel. Les poésies fantaisistes. Paris, 1904.
42555.49.25 Merrill, S. Les quatre saisons. 2. éd. Paris, 1900.
42555.49.27 Merrill, S Les gammes. Paris, 1887.
42555.49.50 Henry, M.L. Stuart Merrill. Thèse. Paris, 1927.
42555.49.150 Marth, Frédéric. Poésies de F. Marth. Paris, 1884.
42555.49.250 Martin, Nicolas. Voyage poétique et pittoresque. Lille, 1869.

42555.50 - .56 Individual authors, etc. - 1850-1899 - Poetry - Monnier, M. - Writings

42555.50 Monnier, Marc. Les Aieux de Figaro. Paris, 1868.
42555.51 Monnier, Marc. Le charmeur. Paris, 1882. 10v.
42555.52 Monnier, Marc. Novelle napoletane. 2. ed. Milano, 1884.
42555.52.10 Monnier, Marc. La renaissance, de Dante à Luther. Paris, 1884.
42555.53 Monnier, Marc. Théâtre de marionettes. Genève, 1871.
42555.53.10 Monnier, Marc. Le réforme, de Luther à Shakespeare. Paris, 1885.
42555.54.80 Lloyd, W. Xavier Marmier. Diss. Washington, 1933.
42555.55 Monnier, Marc. Poésies. Genève, 1872.

42555.58 Individual authors, etc. - 1850-1899 - Poetry - Mendès, C.; Merat; etc.

NEDL 42555.58 Mendès, Catulle. Poésies. Photoreproduction. Paris, 1892. 3v.
42555.58.2 Mendès, Catulle. Les contes du rouet. 6e éd. Paris, 1885.
42555.58.4 Mendès, Catulle. Contes choisis. Paris, 1886.
X Cg 42555.58.4.5 Mendès, Catulle. Contes choisis. Paris, 1897.
42555.58.5 Mendès, Catulle. Médée; tragédie. Paris, 1898.
42555.58.7 Mendès, Catulle. Le carnaval fleuri. Paris, 1904.
42555.58.9 Mendès, Catulle. Scarron; comédie tragique. Paris, 1905.
NEDL 42555.58.10 Mendès, Catulle. Théâtre en prose. Paris, 1908.
42555.58.12 Mendès, Catulle. L'homme tout nu. Paris, 1887.
42555.58.15 Mendès, Catulle. Grande Maguet. Paris, 1888.
42555.58.19A Mendès, Catulle. L'Impératrice. Paris, 1909.
42555.58.19B Mendès, Catulle. L'Impératrice. Paris, 1909.
42555.58.20 Mendès, Catulle. La vierge d'Avila. Paris, 1906.
42555.58.21 Mendès, Catulle. Scarron. Paris, 1905.
42555.58.22 Mendès, Catulle. Glatigny. Paris, 1906.
42555.58.22.5 Mendès, Catulle. Glatigny. Paris, 1906.
42555.58.23 Mendès, Catulle. La première maîtresse; roman contemporain. Paris, 1887.
X Cg 42555.58.24 Mendès, Catulle. Les braises du cendrier. Paris, 1900.
42555.58.25 Mendès, Catulle. La vie et la mort d'un clown. L'argent de Papiol. Paris, 1890.
X Cg 42555.58.26 Mendès, Catulle. Le joyeuses commères de Paris. Paris, 1892.
42555.58.27 Mendès, Catulle. St. Thérése. Paris, 1906.
42555.58.28 Mendès, Catulle. Le cruel berceau. Paris, 1889.
42555.58.29 Mendès, Catulle. Zo'har; roman contemporain. Paris, 1910.
42555.58.31 Mendès, Catulle. Méphistophéla. Paris, 1903.
42555.58.34 Mendès, Catulle. Les poésies. v.1-7. Paris, 1885.
42555.58.35 Mendès, Catulle. Le roman rouge. Paris, 188-?
42555.58.38 Mendès, Catulle. Pierre la Veridique. Paris, n.d.
42555.58.40 Pamphlet box. Mendès, Catulle.
42555.58.45 Mendès, Catulle. L'en vers des feuilles. 6. éd. Paris, 1888.
42555.58.75 Bertrand, A. Catulle Mendès. Paris, 1908.
42555.58.80 Herlihy, J.F. Catulle Mendès: critique dramatique et musical. Thèse. Paris, 1936.
42555.58.85 Losito, Luigo. L'esordio letterario di Catulle Mendès. Bari, 1965.
42555.58.280 Minassian, Jean. Un poète. Paris, 1930.
42555.58.1100 Mérat, Albert. Les trente-six quatrains à madame. Paris, 1903.
42555.58.1110 Mérat, Albert. Vers oubliés. Paris, 1902.
42555.58.1120 Mérat, Albert. Vers le soir. Paris, 1900.
42555.58.1130 Mérat, Albert. Triolets des parisiennes de Paris. Paris, 1900.
42555.58.1140 Mérat, Albert. Les joies de l'heure. Paris, 1902.
42555.58.1150 Mérat, Albert. L'idole. Paris, 1869.
42555.58.1160 Mérat, Albert. Les trente-six dédicaces pour Les trente-six quatrains à madame. Paris, 1903.
42555.58.1170 Mérat, Albert. Les souvenirs. Paris, 1872.
42555.58.1180 Mérat, Albert. La rance et la mer. Paris, 1903.
42555.58.1190 Mérat, Albert. Quelques pages avant le livre. Paris, 1904.
42555.58.1200 Mérat, Albert. Poèmes de Paris. Paris, 1880.
42555.58.1210 Mérat, Albert. Chansons et madrigaux. Paris, 1902.
42555.58.1220 Mérat, Albert. L'Adieu. Paris, 1873.

42555.59 Individual authors, etc. - 1850-1899 - Poetry - Michu; Millet; Mithouard; etc.

42555.59.20 Michu, Claude. Les chants de l'industrie. Paris, 1862.
42555.59.25 Féret, C.T. Les cendres d'Ernest Millet. Alençon, 1904. 2 pam.
42555.59.100 Gerding, A. Adrien Mithouard. Inaug. Diss. n.p., 1931.
42555.59.110 Mithouard,A. Le tourment de l'unité. Paris, 1901.

Classified Listing

42555.59 Individual authors, etc. - 1850-1899 - Poetry - Michu; Millet; Mithouard; etc. - cont.
42555.59.150 Moccaud, L.T. Le devil de la patrie. Annecy, 1870?

42555.60 Individual authors, etc. - 1850-1899 - Poetry - Montesquiou-Ferenzac; Montoya; etc.
42555.60 Montesquiou-Fezensac, Robert de. Le parcours du rêve au souvenir. Paris, 1895.
42555.60.2 Montesquiou-Fezensac, Robert de. Les pas effacés. Mémoires. v.1-3. Paris, 1920.
42555.60.3 Montesquiou-Fezensac, Robert de. Les délices de capharnaüm. Paris, 1921.
42555.60.4 Montesquiou-Fezensac, Robert de. Majeurs et mineurs. Paris, 1917.
42555.60.6 Montesquiou-Fezensac, Robert de. Le mort remontant. Paris, 1922.
42555.60.7 Montesquiou-Fezensac, Robert de. Un moment du pleur éternel. Paris, 1919.
Htn 42555.60.8* Montesquiou-Fezensac, Robert de. Diptyque de Flandre. Triptyque de France. Paris, 1921.
42555.60.9 Montesquiou-Fezensac, Robert de. Assemblée de notables. Paris, 1908.
42555.60.10 Montesquiou-Fezensac, Robert de. Élus et appelés. Paris, 1921.
42555.60.12 Montesquiou-Fezensac, Robert de. Les paons. Paris, 1908.
42555.60.13 Montesquiou-Fezensac, Robert de. La trépidation. Paris, 1922.
42555.60.80 Jullian, Philippe. Robert de Montesquiou, un prince 1900. Paris, 1965.
42555.60.81 Jullian, Philippe. Prince of aesthetes: Count Robert de Montesquiou, 1855-1921. N.Y., 1968.
42555.60.130 Montgomery, Lucy Ditte de. Rondels-sonnets; poésies philosophiques. 3e éd. Paris, 1896.
42555.60.330 Montoya, Gabriel. Chansons naïves et pérverses. 2. éd. Paris, 1896.

42555.61 Individual authors, etc. - 1850-1899 - Poetry - Moréas - Writings
42555.61 Moréas, Jean. Les cantilènes. Paris, 1886.
42555.61.5 Moréas, Jean. Les cantilènes. Paris, 1897.
42555.61.7 Moréas, Jean. Iphigénie. 5e éd. N.Y., 1912.
42555.61.8 Moréas, Jean. Premières poésies 1883-86. 3e éd. N.Y., 1907.
42555.61.9 Moréas, Jean. Poèmes et sylves 1886-96. N.Y., 1907.
42555.61.10 Moréas, Jean. Oeuvres. Paris, 1923-26. 2v.
42555.61.15 Moréas, Jean. Autant en emporte le vent. Paris, 1893.
42555.61.20 Moréas, Jean. Feuillets. Paris, 1902.
42555.61.25 Moréas, Jean. Oeuvres en prose. Paris, 1927.
42555.61.30 Moréas, Jean. Les stances. Paris, 1905.
42555.61.31 Moréas, Jean. Les stances. 6e éd. Paris, 1910.
42555.61.35 Moréas, Jean. Le voyage de Grèce. Paris, 1902.
42555.61.37 Moréas, Jean. Le septième livre des stances. Paris, 1920.
42555.61.39 Moréas, Jean. Trois nouveaux contes de la vielle France. Paris, 1906.
42555.61.42 Moréas, Jean. Paysages et sentiments. Paris, 1906.
42555.61.45 Moréas, Jean. Variations sur la vie et les livres. Paris, 1910.
42555.61.52 Moréas, Jean. L'histoire de Jean de Paris, Roi de France. 2. éd. Paris, 1879.

42555.62 Individual authors, etc. - 1850-1899 - Poetry - Moréas - Works about
42555.62 Moréas, Jean. Le pélerin passionné. Paris, 1891.
42555.62.9 Barrès, M. Adieu à Moréas. Paris, 1910.
42555.62.25 Gourmont, J. de. Jean Moréas. Paris, 1905.
42555.62.30 Kroll, Heinrich. Studien über den Versaufbau in "Les stances" von Jean Moréas. Inaug. Diss. Swinemünde, 1928.
42555.62.35 Weber, Julia. Jean Moréas und die französische Tradition. Inaug. Diss. Nürnberg, 1934.
42555.62.40 Niklaus, R. Jean Moréas, poète lyrique. Paris, 1936.
42555.62.45 Thomas, Louis. Souvenirs sur Moréas. Paris, 1941.
42555.62.50 Empeirikos, A. Les étapes de Jean Moréas. Lausanne, 1948.
42555.62.55 Butler, John Davis. Jean Moréas; a critique of his poetry and philosophy. The Hague, 1967.
42555.62.60 Jouanny, Robert A. Jean Moréas, écrivain français. Paris, 1969.

42555.63 Individual authors, etc. - 1850-1899 - Poetry - Nadaud; Nibor; etc.
42555.63 Nadaud, G. Contes, proverbes, scènes, et récits en vers. Paris, 1870.
42555.63.3 Nadaud, G. Contes, scènes et récits. Paris, 1886.
42555.63.130 Nibor, Yann. Chansons et récits de mer. Paris, 1893?
42555.63.135 Nibor, Yann. La chanson des cols bleus; chants populaires de la flotte française. Paris, 1896.

42555.64 Individual authors, etc. - 1850-1899 - Poetry - Nizet
42555.64 Nizet, Marie. Romania (Chants de la Roumanie). Paris, 1878.

42555.65 Individual authors, etc. - 1850-1899 - Poetry - Michard
42555.65 Michard, d'Humias L. Le roi Grallon. Paris, 1903.

42555.66 - .67 Individual authors, etc. - 1850-1899 - Poetry - Nolhac
Htn 42555.66* Nolhac, Pierre de. Les sonnets. Paris, n.d.
42555.66.5 Nolhac, Pierre de. Poèmes de France et d'Italie. Paris, 1925.
42555.66.25 Nolhac, Pierre de. Le testament d'un Latin. Paris, 1929.
42555.66.30 Nolhac, Pierre de. Laus Florentiae. Fano, 1932.
42555.66.40 Nolhac, Pierre de. Le rameau d'or. Paris, 1933.
42555.66.50 Nolhac, Pierre de. Contes philosophiques. Paris, 1932.
42555.66.55 Nolhac, Pierre de. Paysage de France et d'Italie. Paris, 1894.
42555.67 Nolhac, Pierre de. Ausonia Victrix. Abbeville, 1922.
42555.67.80 Levaillant, M. Pierre de Nolhac. Paris, 1928.
42555.67.90 Karraker, I.O. Pierre de Nolhac: poet, historian and scholar. Urbana, 1940.

42555.68 Individual authors, etc. - 1850-1899 - Poetry - Olivaint; Paban; Paté; etc.
42555.68 Paté, Lucien. Les souffles libres. Paris, 1904.
42555.68.130 Olivaint, Maurice. Fleurs du Mé-kong; poésies. Paris, 1894.
42555.68.330 Paban, Adolphe. Les roses de Kerné. Paris, 1899.

42555.69 Individual authors, etc. - 1850-1899 - Poetry - Paul, J.
42555.69.15 Paul, Jules. Les sept errants de Lan-Illtud. Paris, 1914.

42555.70 Individual authors, etc. - 1850-1899 - Poetry - Pollet; Pierron; etc.
42555.70.100 Pollet, Augustin. Brises basséenes. La Bassée, 1876.
42555.70.1100 Pierron, Ernest. Le barbeau heraldique de Pont-à-Mousson, légende du XVII siècle. Pont-à-Mousson, 1879.

42555.72 Individual authors, etc. - 1850-1899 - Poetry - Pons; Pomairols; etc.
42555.72 Pons, Gaspard de. Adieux poétiques. Paris, 1860. 3v.
42555.72.9 Pomairols, Charles de. Rêves et pensées. Paris, 1880.
42555.72.10 Pomairols, Charles de. Ascension. Paris, n.d.
42555.72.130 Pomairols, Charles de. Poèmes choisis. Paris, 1913.

42555.73 Individual authors, etc. - 1850-1899 - Poetry - Popelin
42555.73.100F Popelin, Claudius. Un livre de sonnets. Paris, 1888.

42556.1 - .2 Individual authors, etc. - 1850-1899 - Poetry - Prarond
42556.1.9 Prarond, Ernest. De Montréal à Jérusalem. Paris, 1869.
42556.2 Prarond, Ernest. Les impressions et pensées d'Albert. Paris, 1854.

42556.4 Individual authors, etc. - 1850-1899 - Poetry - Quillard
42556.4 Quillard, Pierre. La gloire du verbe 1885-90. Paris, 1890.
42556.4.15 Quillard, Pierre. La lyre. 29. éd. Paris, 1897.

42556.6 - .10 Individual authors, etc. - 1850-1899 - Poetry - Reboul - Writings
42556.6 Reboul, Jean. Lettres. Paris, 1865.
42556.7 Reboul, Jean. Poésies. Paris, 1840.
42556.8 Reboul, Jean. Poésies. Paris, 1842.
42556.9 Reboul, Jean. Poésies nouvelles. Paris, 1846.
42556.10 Reboul, Jean. Le dernier jour. Poème en dix chants. Paris, 1839.

42556.11 Individual authors, etc. - 1850-1899 - Poetry - Reboul - Works about
42556.11 Duret, U. Jean Reboul. n.p., n.d.
42556.11.3 Poutmartin, A. de. Jean Reboul. Paris, 1864.
42556.11.4 Besson, M. Oraison funèbre de Jean Reboul. Nimes, 1876.
42556.11.5 Tivier, M. Étude sur Reboul. n.p., 1864.
42556.11.7 Brujère, M. Jean Reboul de Nimes 1796-1864; sa vie et ses oeuvres. Thèse. Paris, 1925.

42556.12 Individual authors, etc. - 1850-1899 - Poetry - Poutgebaud
42556.12 Pontgibaud. Normandies, ou Le décaméron Normand. Caen, 1884.

42556.14 Individual authors, etc. - 1850-1899 - Poetry - Pradels
42556.14 Pradels, O. Chansons. Paris, 1886.

42556.15 Individual authors, etc. - 1850-1899 - Poetry - Prior
42556.15 Prior, Jules. Les veilles d'un artisan. Paris, 1865.

42556.16 - .17 Individual authors, etc. - 1850-1899 - Poetry - Sully-Prudhomme - Biography and criticism
42556.16 Brangsch, W. Philosophie und Dichtung bei Sully-Prudhomme. Berlin, 1911.
42556.16.3 Billigheimer, S. Das religiöse Leben Sully-Prudhommes. Freiburg, 1911.
42556.17 Fons, Pierre. Sully-Prudhomme. Paris, 1907.
42556.17.3 Morice, Henri. La poésie de Sully-Prudhomme. Paris, 1920.
42556.17.3.2 Morice, Henri. La poésie de Sully-Prudhomme. Thèse. Paris, 1920.
42556.17.5 Morice, Henri. L'esthétique de Sully-Prudhomme. Thèse. Vannes, 1920.
42556.17.7 Rebière, Gratien. Conference sur Sully-Prudhomme. Bergerac, 1883.
42556.17.9 Zyromski, Ernest. Sully-Prudhomme. Paris, 1907.
42556.17.11 Estéve, Edmund. Sully-Prudhomme. Paris, 1925.
42556.17.50 Pamphlet box. Sully-Prudhomme.

42556.18 - .19 Individual authors, etc. - 1850-1899 - Poetry - Sully-Prudhomme - Complete and Selected works
42556.18 Sully-Prudhomme, R.F.A. Oeuvres. Paris, 1904.
42556.18.3A Sully-Prudhomme, R.F.A. Oeuvres. Paris, 188-.
42556.18.3B Sully-Prudhomme, R.F.A. Oeuvres. Paris, 188-.
42556.18.5A Sully-Prudhomme, R.F.A. Oeuvres. Paris, n.d.
42556.18.5B Sully-Prudhomme, R.F.A. Oeuvres. Paris, n.d.
42556.19 Sully-Prudhomme, R.F.A. Poésies. Paris, 1877. 4v.
42556.19.2A Sully-Prudhomme, R.F.A. Oeuvres. Paris, n.d.
42556.19.2B Sully-Prudhomme, R.F.A. Oeuvres. Paris, n.d.
42556.19.2C Sully-Prudhomme, R.F.A. Oeuvres. Paris, n.d.
42556.19.5 Sully-Prudhomme, R.F.A. Poésies. Paris, 1882.
42556.19.7 Sully-Prudhomme, R.F.A. Stances et poèmes. Paris, 1865.
42556.19.9A Sully-Prudhomme, R.F.A. Poésies 1865-1866. Paris, 189-?
42556.19.9B Sully-Prudhomme, R.F.A. Poésies 1865-1866. Paris, 189-?
42556.19.11 Sully-Prudhomme, R.F.A. Poésies. Épaves. Paris, 190-?
42556.19.13 Sully-Prudhomme, R.F.A. Poésies. Paris, 190-?

42556.20 Individual authors, etc. - 1850-1899 - Poetry - Sully-Prudhomme - Individual works
42556.20 Sully-Prudhomme, R.F.A. La nymphie des bois de Versailles. Paris, 1896.
42556.20.20 Sully-Prudhomme, R.F.A. La révolte des fleurs. Paris, 1874.

42556.21 Individual authors, etc. - 1850-1899 - Poetry - Raynaud; Reboux; etc.
42556.21 Raynaud, Ernest. Les cornes du Faune. Paris, 1890.
42556.21.2 Raynaud, Ernest. La couronne des jours. Paris, 1905.
42556.21.3 Raynaud, Ernest. Souvenirs de police. Paris, 1923. 3v.
42556.21.4 Raynaud, Ernest. Les deux Allemagne. Paris, 1914.
42556.21.5 Reboux, P. Les matinales. Paris, 1897.
42556.21.6 Reboux, P. Les iris noirs. Paris, 1898.
42556.21.100 Duchesne, J. Un heritier de Brizeux. Rennes, 1886.
42556.21.280 Tacconi, Ilde Brando. Un poeta dei paria. Zara, 1923.
42556.21.2100 Reynold, Berthe. Jardins suspendus. Paris, 1898.

42556.22 Individual authors, etc. - 1850-1899 - Poetry - Richepin

	42556.22.3	Richepin, Jean. Théâtre en vers. Paris, 1919-21. 3v.
	42556.22.5	Richepin, Jean. Le pavé. Paris, 1883.
	42556.22.8	Richepin, Jean. Nana-Sahib. Paris, 1884.
	42556.22.10F	Richepin, Jean. Les blasphèmes. Paris, 1884.
	42556.22.12	Richepin, Jean. Les blasphèmes. 28e éd. Paris, 1885.
	42556.22.15	Richepin, Jean. La mer. Paris, 1886.
	42556.22.17	Richepin, Jean. La mer. Paris, 1890.
Htn	42556.22.20*	Richepin, Jean. Miarka, la fille à l'ourse. Paris, 1888.
	42556.22.22	Richepin, Jean. Miarka, la fille à l'ourse. Paris, 1910.
	42556.22.25	Richepin, Jean. Le cadet. Paris, 1890.
	42556.22.30	Richepin, Jean. Les morts bizarres. Paris, 1890.
	42556.22.32	Richepin, Jean. Choix de poésie. Paris, 1964.
	42556.22.35	Richepin, Jean. Le mage; opera en cinq actes. Paris, 1891.
	42556.22.40	Richepin, Jean. Truandailles. Paris, 1891.
	42556.22.45	Richepin, Jean. Par la glaive; drame. Paris, 1892.
	42556.22.47	Richepin, Jean. Par la glaive. Paris, 1902.
	42556.22.50	Richepin, Jean. Vers la joie; conte bleu. Paris, 1894.
Htn	42556.22.55*	Richepin, Jean. Les étapes d'un réfractaire. Paris, 1896.
	42556.22.60	Richepin, Jean. La martyre. Paris, 1898.
	42556.22.65	Richepin, Jean. Les truands. Paris, 1899.
	42556.22.70	Richepin, Jean. Don Quichotte. Paris, 1905.
	42556.22.71	Richepin, Jean. Don Quichotte. Paris, 1905.
	42556.22.75	Richepin, Jean. L'aimé. Paris, 1906.
	42556.22.80	Richepin, Jean. La chanson des gueux. Paris, 1906.
	42556.22.82	Richepin, Jean. La belle au bois dormant. Paris, 1908.
	42556.22.85A	Richepin, Jean. La route d'émerande. Paris, 1909.
	42556.22.85B	Richepin, Jean. La route d'émerande. Paris, 1909.
	42556.22.90	Richepin, Jean. Le chemineau. Paris, 1907.
	42556.22.95	Richepin, Jean. Braves gens. Paris, 1909.
	42556.22.100	Richepin, Jean. La glu. Paris, 1910.
	42556.22.105	Richepin, Jean. Proses de guerre. Paris, 1915.
	42556.22.110A	Richepin, Jean. Poèmes durant la guerre, 1914-18. Paris, 1919.
	42556.22.110B	Richepin, Jean. Poèmes durant la guerre, 1914-18. Paris, 1919.
	42556.22.115	Richepin, Jean. Le coin des fous. Paris, 1921.
	42556.22.120	Benelli, Sem. La beffa. Paris, 1910.
	42556.22.130	Richepin, Jean. Les glas. Paris, 1922.
	42556.22.140	Richepin, Jean. Interludes. Paris, 1923.
Htn	42556.22.150*	Richepin, Jean. Les débuts de César Borgia. Paris, 1890.
	42556.22.162	Richepin, Jean. Les caresses. Paris, 189-?
	42556.22.800	Stutton, Howard. The life and work of Jean Richepin. Genève, 1961.

42556.23 Individual authors, etc. - 1850-1899 - Poetry - Read

	42556.23	Read, Henri Charles. Poésies. Paris, 1895.
	42556.23.2	Read, Henri Charles. Poésies. 4. éd. Paris, 1897.
	42556.23.5	Read, Henri Charles. Poésies posthumes 1874-1876. Paris, 1879.

42556.24 - .27.33 Individual authors, etc. - 1850-1899 - Poetry - Regnier

	42556.24	Régnier, Henri de. Episodes. Paris, 1891.
	42556.24.5	Régnier, Henri de. Contes à soi-même. Paris, 1894.
	42556.25	Régnier, Henri de. Premiers poèmes. Paris, 1899.
	42556.25.5	Régnier, Henri de. Premiers poèmes. 10e éd. Paris, 1899?
NEDL	42556.26	Régnier, Henri de. Poèmes (1887-1892). Paris, 1895.
	42556.26.3	Régnier, Henri de. Poèmes (1887-1892). Paris, 1897.
	42556.26.6	Régnier, Henri de. Poèmes, 1887-1892. 6. éd. Paris, 1907-1925.
	42556.26.18	Régnier, Henri de. Le bon plaisir. 2e éd. Paris, 1902.
	42556.26.19.5	Régnier, Henri de. Le bon plaisir. Les vacances d'un jeune homme sage. v.1-2. Paris, 1928.
	42556.26.20	Régnier, Henri de. La cité des eaux. Paris, 1911.
	42556.26.21	Régnier, Henri de. Figures et caractères. 3. éd. Paris, 1901.
	42556.26.22	Régnier, Henri de. Le mariage de minuit. Paris, 1910.
	42556.26.22.89	Régnier, Henri de. Le miroir des heures. 7e éd. Paris, 1911.
	42556.26.23	Régnier, Henri de. Le miroir des heures. 8. éd. Paris, 1911.
	42556.26.24	Régnier, Henri de. La peur de l'amour. 6. éd. Paris, 1908.
	42556.26.24.5	Régnier, Henri de. La peur de l'amour. 18. éd. Paris, 191-.
	42556.26.25	Régnier, Henri de. Les rencontres de M. de Bréot. Paris, 1904.
X Cg	42556.26.25.2	Régnier, Henri de. Les rencontres de M. de Bréot. Paris, 1915.
	42556.26.26	Régnier, Henri de. Les scrupules de Sganarelle. 5. éd. Paris, 1908.
	42556.26.27	Régnier, Henri de. Sujets et paysages. 4. éd. Paris, 1906.
	42556.26.28	Régnier, Henri de. Les vacances d'un jeune homme sage. 9. éd. Paris, 1903.
	42556.26.29	Régnier, Henri de. Les amants singuliers. 7. éd. Paris, 1909.
	42556.26.29.15	Régnier, Henri de. La double maîtresse; roman. 13. éd. Paris, 1900.
	42556.26.30	Régnier, Henri de. La double maîtresse. Paris, 1912.
	42556.26.30.2	Régnier, Henri de. La double maîtresse. 26e éd. Paris, 1914.
	42556.26.31	Régnier, Henri de. L'Amphisbène. 2e éd. Paris, 1912.
	42556.26.32	Régnier, Henri de. Romaine Mirmault. Paris, 1914.
	42556.26.33	Régnier, Henri de. Pour les mois d'hiver. Paris, 1912.
	42556.26.34	Régnier, Henri de. Scènes mythologiques. Paris, 1924.
	42556.26.35A	Régnier, Henri de. Histoires incertaines. 9e éd. Paris, 1919.
	42556.26.35B	Régnier, Henri de. Histoires incertaines. 9e éd. Paris, 1919.
	42556.26.39	Régnier, Henri de. La pécheresse. 7e éd. Paris, 1920.
	42556.26.40	Régnier, Henri de. La pécheresse. 15e éd. Paris, 1920.
	42556.26.43	Régnier, Henri de. Le plateau de laque. Paris, 1913.
	42556.27.1	Régnier, Henri de. Les jeux rustiques et divins. 8. éd. Paris, 1911.
	42556.27.2	Régnier, Henri de. 1914-1916. Poésies. 2. éd. Paris, 1918.
	42556.27.3	Régnier, Henri de. Le pavillon fermé. Paris, 1927.
	42556.27.5	Régnier, Henri de. La canne de Jaspe. Paris, 1897.
	42556.27.6.8	Régnier, Henri de. Les médailles d'Argile. 8e éd. Paris, 1911.
	42556.27.7	Régnier, Henri de. Le passé vivant. Paris, 1905.
	42556.27.7.2	Régnier, Henri de. Le passé vivant. Paris, 1911.
	42556.27.8	Régnier, Henri de. Le tréfle blanc. Paris, 1899.

42556.24 - .27.33 Individual authors, etc. - 1850-1899 - Poetry - Regnier - cont.

	42556.27.9	Régnier, Henri de. La sandale ailée 1903-1905. Paris, 1906.
	42556.27.9.7	Régnier, Henri de. La sandale ailée 1903-1905. 7e éd. Paris, 1911.
	42556.27.10	Régnier, Henri de. Couleur du temps. Paris, 1909.
	42556.27.11	Régnier, Henri de. La flambée. Paris, 1909.
	42556.27.12	Regnier, Henri de. Le trèfle noir. Paris, 1895.
	42556.27.13	Régnier, Henri de. Aréthuse. Paris, 1895.
	42556.27.15	Régnier, Henri de. L'escapade; roman. 10e éd. Paris, 1926.
	42556.27.18	Régnier, Henri de. Contes pour chacun de nous. Paris, 1926.
	42556.27.20	Régnier, Henri de. Portraits et souvenirs. 5e éd. Paris, 1921.
	42556.27.25	Régnier, Henri de. Sept médailles amoureuses. Paris, 1928.
	42556.27.30	Régnier, Henri de. Vestigia flammae. Paris, 1921.
	42556.27.30.5	Régnier, Henri de. Flamma tenax, 1922-1928. 3e éd. Paris, 1928.
	42556.27.30.25	Régnier, Henri de. De mon temps. 3e éd. Paris, 1933.
	42556.27.30.45	Régnier, Henri de. Proses datées. 8e éd. Paris, 1925.
	42556.27.30.65	Régnier, Henri de. Nos rencontres. 3. éd. Paris, 1931.
	42556.27.30.75	Régnier, Henri de. Choix de poèmes. Paris, 1932.
	42556.27.30.85	Régnier, Henri de. Le voyage d'amour ou L'initiation venitienne. 2e éd. Paris, 1930.
	42556.27.32	Régnier, Henri de. Poems from The winged sandal. Boston, 1933.
	42556.27.33.800	Leautaud, P. Henri de Régnier. Paris, 1904.
	42556.27.33.805	Hounert, Robert. Henri de Régnier. Paris, 1923.
	42556.27.33.810	Lacretelle, Jacques de. Discours de réception de M. Jacques de Lacretelle à l'Academie Francaise. Paris, 1938.
	42556.27.33.812	Lacretelle, Jacques de. Centenaire de Henri de Régnier. Paris, 1965.
	42556.27.33.815	Jaloux, Edmond. Souvenirs sur Henri de Régnier. Lausanne, 1941.
	42556.27.33.820	Buenzod, Emmanuel. Henri de Régnier; essai. Avignon, 1966.

42556.27.35 - .27.999 Individual authors, etc. - 1850-1899 - Poetry - Renaud; Retté; Riffard; etc.

	42556.27.35	Renaud, A. Drames du peuple. Paris, 1885.
	42556.27.50	Replat, J. Feuilles d'album. Annecy, 1897.
	42556.27.65	Retté, Adolphe. Du diable à dieu. Paris, 1907.
	42556.27.66	Retté, Adolphe. Oeuvres complètes. Paris, 1898.
	42556.27.67	Retté, Adolphe. Similitudes. Paris, 1895.
	42556.27.68	Retté, Adolphe. Quand l'ésprit souffle. 3e éd. Paris, 1914.
	42556.27.70	Retté, Adolphe. L'archipel en fleurs. Paris, 1895.
	42556.27.74	Rette, Adolphe. Campagne première. Paris, 1897.
	42556.27.75	Retté, Adolphe. Trois dialogues nocturnes. Paris, 1895.
	42556.27.76	Retté, Adolphe. La forêt bruissante. Paris, 1896.
	42556.27.78	Retté, Adolphe. Mémoires de Diogène. Paris, 1903.
	42556.27.80	Retté, Adolphe. Poésies, 1892-1906. Paris, 1906.
	42556.27.82	Retté, Adolphe. Promenades subversives. Paris, 1896.
	42556.27.84	Retté, Adolphe. Le régne de la bête. Paris, 1908.
	42556.27.86	Retté, Adolphe. XIII idylles diaboliques. Paris, 1898.
	42556.27.88	Retté, Adolphe. Lumières tranquilles. Paris, 1901.
	42556.27.89	Retté, Adolphe. La seule nuit. Paris, 1899.
	42556.27.90	Retté, Adolphe. Thulé des brumes. Paris, 1891.
	42556.27.92	Retté, Adolphe. La basse-cour d'Apollon. Paris, 1924.
	42556.27.92.800	Cornell, W.K. Adolphe Retté, 1863-1930. New Haven, 1942.
	42556.27.92.810	Nuyens, A.J. De heilige van het symbolisme. Antwerpen, 1955.
	42556.27.100	Renimal, Paul. Chansons. Paris, 1900.
	42556.27.120	Reynier, Paul. Oeuvres choisies. Marseille, 1856.
	42556.27.150	Riffard, Léon. Pièces et morceaux. Paris, 1893.

42556.28 Individual authors, etc. - 1850-1899 - Poetry - Rimbaud

	42556.28.10	Rimbaud, Jean Arthur. Oeuvres complètes. Paris, 1922. 3v.
	42556.28.14	Rimbaud, Jean Arthur. Oeuvres. Paris, 1937.
Htn	42556.28.15F*	Rimbaud, Jean Arthur. Poésies. Paris, 1919.
	42556.28.17	Rimbaud, Jean Arthur. Poésies. 4e éd. Paris, 1939.
	42556.28.19	Rimbaud, Jean Arthur. Poésies. Paris, 1947.
	42556.28.19.10	Rimbaud, Jean Arthur. Poésies. Paris, 1952.
	42556.28.25	Rimbaud, Jean Arthur. Oeuvres complètes. Lausanne, 1948. 2v.
	42556.28.30	Rimbaud, Jean Arthur. À Douai et à Charleville. Paris, 1927.
	42556.28.35	Rimbaud, Jean Arthur. Ébauches. 2e éd Paris, 1937.
	42556.28.40	Rimbaud, Jean Arthur. Une saison en enfer. Montréal, 1946.
	42556.28.43	Rimbaud, Jean Arthur. A season in hell; une saison en enfer. Norfolk, Conn., 1939.
	42556.28.43.10	Rimbaud, Jean Arthur. A season in hell. Norfolk, Conn., 1945.
	42556.28.43.25	Rimbaud, Jean Arthur. A season in hell and The drunken boat. Norfolk, Conn., 1945.
	42556.28.45A	Rimbaud, Jean Arthur. Oeuvres complètes. Buenos Aires, 1943.
	42556.28.45B	Rimbaud, Jean Arthur. Oeuvres complètes. Buenos Aires, 1943.
	42556.28.47	Rimbaud, Jean Arthur. Oeuvres complètes. Paris, 1945.
	42556.28.48	Rimbaud, Jean Arthur. Oeuvres. Paris, 1945.
	42556.28.50	Rimbaud, Jean Arthur. Oeuvres complètes. Paris, 1946.
	42556.28.51	Rimbaud, Jean Arthur. Complete works. Chicago, 1966.
	42556.28.52	Rimbaud, Jean Arthur. Oeuvres complètes. Paris, 1954.
	42556.28.53	Rimbaud, Jean Arthur. Sämtliche Gedichte. Heidelberg, 1946.
	42556.28.54	Rimbaud, Jean Arthur. Oeuvres. Paris, 1957.
	42556.28.55	Rimbaud, Jean Arthur. Lettre du baron de Petdechevré à son secretaire au château de Saint-Magloire. Genève, 1949.
	42556.28.56	Rimbaud, Jean Arthur. Oeuvres. Strasbourg, 1957.
	42556.28.57	Rimbaud, Jean Arthur. Rimbaud par lui-même. Paris, 1961.
	42556.28.58	Rimbaud, Jean Arthur. Oeuvres. Paris, 1958.
	42556.28.65	Rimbaud, Jean Arthur. Lettre du voyant. Paris, 1950.
	42556.28.67	Rimbaud, Jean Arthur. Rimbaud with plain prose translations of each poem. Harmondsworth, Middlesex, 1962.
	42556.28.68	Rimbaud, Jean Arthur. Correspondance, 1881-1891. Paris, 1965.
	42556.28.69	Rimbaud, Jean Arthur. Oeuvres. Paris, 1961.
	42556.28.70A	Rimbaud, Jean Arthur. Prose poems from Les illuminations. London, 1932.
	42556.28.70B	Rimbaud, Jean Arthur. Prose poems from Les illuminations. London, 1932.

42556.28 Individual authors, etc. - 1850-1899 - Poetry - Rimbaud - cont.

42556.28.72	Rimbaud, Jean Arthur. Prose poems from the Illuminations. N.Y., 1946.
42556.28.73.5	Rimbaud, Jean Arthur. Illuminations. Genève, 1967.
42556.28.74	Rimbaud, Jean Arthur. Gesammelte Werk. Leipzig, 1927.
42556.28.75	Rimbaud, Jean Arthur. Leben und Dichtung. 2. Aufl. Leipzig, 1921.
42556.28.77	Rimbaud, Jean Arthur. Leben, Werk, Briefe. Berlin, 1930.
42556.28.78	Rimbaud, Jean Arthur. Bateau ivre. Das trunkene Schiff. Wiesbaden, 1958.
42556.28.80	Rimbaud, Jean Arthur. Some poems of Rimbaud. N.Y., 1939.
42556.28.82	Rimbaud, Jean Arthur. Selected verse poems. London, 1942.
42556.28.83	Rimbaud, Jean Arthur. Four poems. Denver, 1947.
42556.28.84	Rimbaud, Jean Arthur. The drunken boat. London, 1952.
42556.28.85	Rimbaud, Jean Arthur. Opilý korab. 2. vyd. Praha, 1964.
42556.28.86	Rimbaud, Jean Arthur. Pages choisies. Paris, 1955.
42556.28.87	Rimbaud, Jean Arthur. Dílo. Praha, 1930.
42556.28.88	Rimbaud, Jean Arthur. Verše. Praha, 1956.
42556.28.89	Rimbaud, Jean Arthur. Vybor. Praha, 1959.
42556.28.90	Rimbaud, Jean Arthur. Poésies. Paris, 1958.
V42556.28.91	Rimbaud, Jean Arthur. Poezje wybrane. wyd. 1. Warszawa, 1969.
42556.28.98	Centre culturel Arthur Rimbaud. Cahier. Charleville-Mézières. 1,1969+
42556.28.99	Études rimbaudiennes. Paris. 1,1968+
42556.28.100	Berrichon, P. La vie de Jean Arthur Rimbaud. Photoreproduction. Paris, 1897.
42556.28.102	Méléra, M. (Mme.). Rimbaud. 6e éd. Paris, 1930.
42556.28.104	Méléra, M. (Mme.). Resonances autour de Rimbaud. Paris, 1946.
42556.28.105	Ruchon, François. Jean Arthur Rimbaud; sa vie, son oeuvre, son influence. Paris, 1929.
42556.28.110	Carré, Jean Marie. La vie aventureuse de Jean Arthur Rimbaud. Paris, 1926.
42556.28.111	Carré, Jean Marie. Les deux Rimbaud. Paris, 1928.
42556.28.115	Coulon, Marcel. Le problème de Rimbaud, poéte maudit. Nîmes, 1923.
42556.28.118	Coulon, Marcel. La vie de Rimbaud et de son oeuvre. Paris, 1929.
42556.28.120	Delahaye, Ernest. Rimbaud, l'artiste et l'être moral. Paris, 1923.
42556.28.123	Verlaine, Paul. Rimbaud. 4e éd. Paris, 1934.
42556.28.125	Rimbaud, Isabelle. Reliques. 3e éd. Paris, 1921.
42556.28.130	Delattre, Jean Luc. Le déséquilibre mental d'Arthur Rimbaud, 1854-1891. Paris, 1928.
42556.28.135	Krollman, Clara. Arthur Rimbaud; ein Deutungsversuch. Inaug. Diss. Bonn, 1928.
42556.28.145	Étiemble, René. Rimbaud. Paris, 1936.
42556.28.145.5	Étiemble, René. Rimbaud. Paris, 1950.
42556.28.145.6	Étiemble, René. Rimbaud. Paris, 1966.
42556.28.145.8	Étiemble, René. Le mythe de Rimbaud. v.1,2,5. 2e éd. Paris, 1952. 3v.
42556.28.145.10	Étiemble, René. Le mythe de Rimbaud. Paris, 1953. 2v.
42556.28.145.12	Étiemble, René. Le mythe de Rimbaud. v.2. 4e éd. Paris, 1954.
42556.28.145.20	Étiemble, René. Nouveaux aspects du mythe de Rimbaud. Paris, 1965. 2v.
42556.28.145.30	Étiemble, René. Le sonnet des voyelles de Rimbaud. Paris, 1968.
42556.28.147	Izambard, Georges. Rimbaud tel que je l'ai connu. Paris, 1963.
42556.28.150	Godchot, S. Arthur Rimbaud, ne varietur. Nice, 1936-37. 2v.
42556.28.157A	Starkie, Enid. Athur Rimbaud. Oxford, 1954.
42556.28.157B	Starkie, Enid. Athur Rimbaud. Oxford, 1954.
42556.28.160	Starkie, Enid. Rimbaud en Abyssinie. Paris, 1938.
42556.28.165	Reitz, H. Impressionistische und expressionistische Stilmittel bei A. Rimbaud. Inaug. Diss. München, 1937.
42556.28.167	Hackett, Cecil A. Autour de Rimbaud. Paris, 1967.
42556.28.169	Hackett, Cecil A. Le lyrisme de Rimbaud. Thèse. Paris, 1938.
42556.28.171	Hackett, Cecil A. Rimbaud l'enfant. Paris, 1948.
42556.28.172	Hackett, Cecil A. Rimbaud. London, 1957.
42556.28.173	Starkie, Enid. Arthur Rimbaud. N.Y., 1939.
42556.28.178.3	Starkie, Enid. Arthur Rimbaud. N.Y., 1947.
42556.28.178.5	Starkie, Enid. Arthur Rimbaud. London, 1961.
42556.28.178.10	Starkie, Enid. Arthur Rimbaud. N.Y., 1962.
42556.28.179	Starkie, Enid. Das trunkene Schiff. Hamburg, 1948.
42556.28.180	Fowlie, Wallace. Rimbaud. N.Y., 1946.
42556.28.182	Fowlie, Wallace. Rimbaud. London, 1946.
42556.28.183	Fowlie, Wallace. Rimbaud's Illuminations. London, 1953.
42556.28.184	Fowlie, Wallace. Rimbaud. Chicago, 1965.
42556.28.185	Castelnau, Jacques. Rimbaud. Paris, 1944.
42556.28.187	Ruchon, F. Rimbaud. Vésenaz-Genève, 1946.
42556.28.189	Silvain, R. Rimbaud, le précurseur. Paris, 1945.
42556.28.192	Gengoux, Jacques. La symbolique de Rimbaud. Paris, 1947.
42556.28.195	Paillou, Paul. Arthur Rimbaud. Paris, 1947.
42556.28.197	Izambard, Georges. Rimbaud tel que je l'ai connu. Paris, 1946.
42556.28.199	Debray, Pierre. Rimbaud, le magicien désabusé. Paris, 1949.
42556.28.201	Küchler, Walter. Arthur Rimbaud. Heidelberg, 1948.
42556.28.201.5	Küchler, Walter. Trunkene und gläubige Dichtung. Iserlohn, 1948.
42556.28.203	Bouillane de Lacoste, Henry de. Rimbaud et le problème des illuminations. Paris, 1949.
42556.28.204	Bouillane de Lacoste, Henry de. Rimbaud et le problème des illuminations. Paris, 1949.
42556.28.205	Petitfills, P. L'oeuvre et visage d'Arthur Rimbaud. Paris, 1949.
42556.28.206	Rickword, Edgell. Rimbaud, the boy and the poet. London, 1963.
42556.28.207	Rickword, Edgell. Rimbaud. London, 1924.
42556.28.208	Rickword, Edgell. Rimbaud; the boy and the poet. N.Y., 1924.
42556.28.209	Graaf, Daniel. Arthur Rimbaud. Assen, 1948.
42556.28.209.5	Graaf, Daniel. Arthur Rimbaud. Assen, 1960.
42556.28.210	Daniel-Rops, Henry. Rimbaud. Paris, 1936.
42556.28.211	Breton, André. Flagrant délit. Paris, 1949.
42556.28.211.5	Breton, André. Flagrant délit. Paris, 1964.
42556.28.213	Gengoux, Jacques. La pensée poétique de Rimbaud. Paris, 1950.
42556.28.213.5	Gengoux, Jacques. La pensée poétique de Rimbaud. Thèse. Paris, 1950.
42556.28.215	Chisholm, A.R. The art of Arthur Rimbaud. Melbourne, 1930.
42556.28.217	Fusero, C. Vita e poesia di Rimbaud, Milano, 1951.

42556.28 Individual authors, etc. - 1850-1899 - Poetry - Rimbaud - cont.

42556.28.220	Arnoult, Pierre. Rimbaud. Paris, 1943.
42556.28.222	Arnoult, Pierre. Rimbaud. Paris, 1955.
42556.28.225	Dhôtel, A. Rimbaud. 5. éd. Paris, 1952.
42556.28.225.2	Dhôtel, A. Rimbaud et la révolte moderne. 2. éd. Paris, 1952.
42556.28.230	Noulet, E. Le premier visage de Rimbaud. Bruxelles, 1953.
42556.28.235	Paris. Bibliothèque nationale. Arthur Rimbaud. Paris, 1954.
42556.28.240	Mondor, Henri. Rimbaud. 2. éd. Paris, 1955.
42556.28.245	Decaunes, Luc. Arthur Rimbaud. Paris, 1954.
42556.28.250	Miller, Henry. The time of the assassins. Norfolk, 1956.
42556.28.251	Miller, Henry. Rimbaud. Lausanne, 1952.
42556.28.255A	Morrissette, Bruce A. The great Rimbaud forgery. St. Louis, 1956.
42556.28.255B	Morrissette, Bruce A. The great Rimbaud forgery. St. Louis, 1956.
42556.28.256	Morrissette, Bruce A. La bataille Rimbaud. Paris, 1959.
42556.28.260	Eaubonne, F. d'. La vie passionnee d'Arthur Rimbaud. Paris, 1956.
42556.28.265	Goffin, Robert. Rimbaud et Verlaine vivants. Paris, 1948?
42556.28.270	Briet, Suzanne. Rimbaud, notre prochain. Paris, 1956.
42556.28.275	Hanson, Elisabeth M. My poor Arthur. London, 1959.
42556.28.280	Chadwick, Charles. Études sur Rimbaud. Paris, 1960.
42556.28.285	Char, René. Le dernier couac. Paris, 1958.
42556.28.290	Zech, Paul. Jean Arthur Rimbaud. Berlin, 1947.
42556.28.295	Fontaine, A. Génie de Rimbaud. Paris, 1934.
42556.28.300	Vaillant, J. Rimbaud. Paris, 1930.
42556.28.305	Le Hardouir, Maria. Rimbaud, le transfuge. Lyon, 1962.
42556.28.310	Rolland de Reneville, A. Rimbaud le voyant. Paris, 1929.
42556.28.315A	Frohock, Wilbur M. Rimbaud's poetic practice. Cambridge, 1963.
42556.28.315B	Frohock, Wilbur M. Rimbaud's poetic practice. Cambridge, 1963.
42556.28.320	Matarasso, Henri. Vie d'Arthur Rimbaud. Paris, 1962.
42556.28.325	Houston, J.P. The design of Rimbaud's poetry. New Haven, 1963.
42556.28.330	Bateau ivre; Bulletin de la Société des amis de Rimbaud. Charleville.
42556.28.335	Štyrský, J. Život J.A. Rimbauda. Praha, 1930.
42556.28.340	Clauzel, Raymond. Une saison en enfer et Arthur Rimbaud. Paris, 1931.
42556.28.345	Eigeldinger, Marc. Rimbaud et le mythe solaire. Neuchâtel, 1964.
42556.28.350	Morawska, Ludmiła. L'adjectif qualificatif dans la langue des symbolistes français. Poznan, 1964.
42556.28.355	Bouet, Paul. Fantaisies sur deux ardennais: Arthur Rimbaud, Hippolyte Taine. Paris, 1928.
42556.28.360	Missouri. Southwest Missouri State College. The William J. Jones Rimbaud collection. Springfield, 1965.
42556.28.365	Fumet, Stanislas. Rimbaud; mystique contrarié. Paris, 1966.
42556.28.370	Matarasso, Henri. Album Rimbaud. Paris, 1967.
42556.28.375A	Charleville, France. Arthur Rimbaud dans les collections municipales de la bibliothèque et du musée. Charleville, 1966.
42556.28.375B	Charleville, France. Arthur Rimbaud dans les collections municipales de la bibliothèque et du musée. Charleville, 1966.
42556.28.375.1	Charleville, France. Arthur Rimbaud dans les collections municipales de la bibliothèque et du musée. Supplément. Charleville, 1969-
42556.28.380	Plessen, Jacques. Promenade et poésie. Proefschrift. La Haye, 1967.
42556.28.385	Rivière, Jacques. Rimbaud. Paris, 1930.
42556.28.390	Rimbaud. Paris, 1968.
42556.28.395	Nicoletti, Gianni. Rimbaud; una poesia del canto chiuso. Torino, 1965.
42556.28.397	Nicoletti, Gianni. Rimbaud; una poesia del canto chiuso. 2. ed. Bari, 1968.
42556.28.400	Ruff, Marcel A. Rimbaud. Paris, 1968.
42556.28.405	Caddau, Pierre. Dans le sillage du capitaine Cook ou Arthur Rimbaud le Tahitien. Paris, 1968.
42556.28.412	Locker, Malka. Rimbaud; le poéte qui s'enfuit. 2. éd. Paris, 1965.
42556.28.417	Gascar, Pierre. Rimbaud et la commune. Paris, 1971.
42556.28.420	Kloepfer, Rolf. Sprachliche Konstituenten moderner Dichtung. Bad Homburg, 1970.

42556.29 Individual authors, etc. - 1850-1899 - Poetry - Rocca de Vergalo; Romberg; Samain; etc.

	42556.29	Soto, Rafael Arcangel. Un olvidado precursor del modernismo francés. N.Y., 1928.
	42556.29.5	Romberg, E. Au Louvre. Paris, 1897.
	42556.29.6	Samain, Albert. Albert Samain et Francis James. Paris, 1946.
	42556.29.11	Samain, Albert. Le chariot d'or. Paris, 1901.
	42556.29.12	Samain, Albert. Le chariot d'or. Paris, 1905.
	42556.29.15	Samain, Albert. Aux flancs du vase. Paris, 1905.
	42556.29.16	Samain, Albert. Aux flancs du vase. Paris, 1919.
NEDL	42556.29.17	Samain, Albert. Au jardin de l'infante. 7. éd. Paris, 1903.
	42556.29.18	Samain, Albert. Au jardin de l'infante. Paris, 1905.
	42556.29.19	Samain, Albert. Oeuvres. Paris, 1921- 3v.
	42556.29.20	Samain, Albert. La petite princesse Gélide. Paris, 1947.
	42556.29.21	Samain, Albert. Oeuvres choisies. Paris, 1928.
	42556.29.25	Samain, Albert. Polypheme; deux actes en vers. 11. éd. Paris, 1919.
	42556.29.27	Gobin, Ferdinand. L'oeuvre poétique de Albert Samain. Paris, 1919.
	42556.29.28	Bonneau, G. Albert Samain, poète symboliste. Thèse. Paris, 1925. 2 pam.
	42556.29.29	Russell, F. L'art d'Albert Samain. Thèse. Toulouse, 1929.
	42556.29.30	Bocquet, Léon. Albert Samain; sa vie, son oeuvre. Paris, 1905.
	42556.29.32	Bersaucourt, A. de. Albert Samain; son oeuvre. Paris, 1925.
	42556.29.33	Temborius, H. Albert Samains Leben, Persönlichkeit und Stil. Inaug. Diss. Oberlahnstein, 1926.
	42556.29.34	Bocquet, Léon. Autour d'Albert Samain. Paris, 1933.
Htn	42556.29.35*	Saulière, Auguste. Les leçons conjugales, contes lestes. 4. éd. Paris, 1882.
	42556.29.36	Bocquet, Léon. Albert Samain. 6. éd. Paris, 1921.

42556.30 Individual authors, etc. - 1850-1899 - Poetry - Schuré

42556.30 Schuré, Edouard. Les chants de la Montagne. Paris, 1876.
42556.30.3 Schuré, Edouard. Femmes inspiratrices et poètes annonciateurs. Paris, 1908.
42556.30.5 Schuré, Edouard. Le double. 4. éd. Paris, 1921.
42556.30.35 Merlin. (Romance). French. 1924. Schuré. Merlin l'énchanteur, légende dramatique, trilogie. Paris, 1924.
42556.30.40 Schuré, Edouard. Le théâtre de l'ame. Paris, 1900.
42556.30.42 Schuré, Edouard. Le théâtre de l'ame. 2. série. Paris, 1902.
42556.30.43 Schuré, Edouard. Le théâtre de l'ame. 3. série. Paris, 1905.
42556.30.45 Schuré, Edouard. Précurseurs et révoltés. Paris, 1904.
42556.30.81 Beer, G. (Mme.). Un celte d'Alsace; la vie...d'Edouard Schuré. Paris, 1923.
42556.30.85 Romeuf, L. de. Edouard Schuré. Paris, 1908.
42556.30.90 Roux, A. In memoriam Edouard Schuré. Paris, 1931.

42556.31 Individual authors, etc. - 1850-1899 - Poetry - Roussel

42556.31 Roussel, August. Les gauloises; chants patriotiques et populaires. Paris, 1876.
42556.31.9 Roussel, August. Gros-Jean et son curé. Bruxelles, 1865.
42556.31.21 Rollinat, Maurice. Oeuvres. Paris, 1971-

42556.32 Individual authors, etc. - 1850-1899 - Poetry - Rollinat

42556.32.35 Rollinat, Maurice. La nature; poésies. Paris, 1892.
42556.32.40 Rollinat, Maurice. Ruminations; proses d'un solitaire. Paris, 1904.
42556.32.45 Rollinat, Maurice. L'abime; poésies. Paris, 1886.
42556.32.50 Rollinat, Maurice. Paysages et paysans. Paris, 1899.
42556.32.55 Rollinat, Maurice. En errant. Paris, 1903.
42556.32.60 Rollinat, Maurice. Les bêtes. Paris, 1911.
42556.32.65 Rollinat, Maurice. Dans les brandes. Paris, 1883.
42556.32.70 Rollinat, Maurice. Fin d'oeuvre. Paris, 1919.
42556.32.81 Lapaire, Hugues. Rollinat, poète et musicien. Paris, 1930.
42556.32.85 Zevaès, A.B. Maurice Rollinat, son oeuvre. Paris, 1933.
42556.32.90 Vinchon, Émile. Maurice Rollinat. Paris, 1921.

42556.33 Individual authors, etc. - 1850-1899 - Poetry - Severin

42556.33 Severin, F. Poèmes. Paris, 1908.
42556.33.10 Severin, F. Poèmes. Paris, 1951.

42556.35 Individual authors, etc. - 1850-1899 - Poetry - Tellier, J.

42556.35 Tellier, Jules. Ses oeuvres publiées par Raymond de la Tailhède. Paris, 1923. 2v.
42556.35.30 Tellier, Jules. Les deux paradis d'Abd-er-Rhaman. Paris, 1921.
42556.35.50 Aubry, Georges Jean. Essai sur Jules Tellier. Paris, 1904.

42556.36 Individual authors, etc. - 1850-1899 - Poetry - Potez

42556.36.30 Potez, Henri. Jours d'autre fois. Paris, 1895.

42556.37 Individual authors, etc. - 1850-1899 - Poetry - Pagnerre

42556.37.30 Pagnerre, Edmond. Poésies. Fécamp, 1894?

42556.38 Individual authors, etc. - 1850-1899 - Poetry - Sirvey

42556.38 Sirvey, Gaston de. Martyre et délivrance. Lille, 1878.

42557.3 - .4 Individual authors, etc. - 1850-1899 - Poetry - Soulary

42557.3 Soulary, Joséphin. Oeuvres poétiques. Paris, 1872. 3v.
42557.4 Soulary, Joséphin. Sonnets humoristiques. Lyon, 1859.
42557.4.30 Soulary, Joséphin. La lune rousse. Paris, 1879.
42557.4.35 Soulary, Joséphin. La chasse aux mouches d'or. Lyon, 1876.
42557.4.50 Mariéton, Paul. Joséphin Soulary et la pléiade lyonnaise: Victor de Laprade. Paris, 1884.

42557.5 Individual authors, etc. - 1850-1899 - Poetry - Tailhade; Thiebault; Turquety; etc.

42557.5.9 Tailhade, Laurent. Poèmes aristophanesques. 3. éd. Paris, 1910.
42557.5.10 Tailhade, Laurent. Poèmes élégiaques. Paris, 1907.
42557.5.12A Tailhade, Laurent. Lettres à sa mère, 1874-1891. Paris, 1926.
42557.5.12B Tailhade, Laurent. Lettres à sa mère, 1874-1891. Paris, 1926.
42557.5.15 Tailhade, Laurent. Laurent Tailhade intime. 2. éd. Paris, 1924.
42557.5.22 Tailhade, Laurent. Poésies posthumes. Paris, 1925.
42557.5.30 Tailhade, Laurent. La médaille qui s'efface. Paris, 1924.
42557.5.35 Tailhade, Laurent. Discours civiques. Paris, 1902.
42557.5.40 Tailhade, Laurent. Les reflets de Paris, 1918-19. Paris, 1921.
42557.5.45 Tailhade, Laurent. La corne et l'épée. Paris, 1908.
42557.5.50 Tailhade, Laurent. Les commerages de Tybalt. Paris, 1914.
42557.5.55 Tailhade, Laurent. Petits memoires de la vie. Paris, 1922.
42557.5.57 Tailhade, Laurent. La forêt. Paris, 1910.
42557.5.80 Kolney, Fernand. Laurent Tailhade. Paris, 1922.
42557.5.85 Cazals, F.A. Laurent Tailhade. Paris, 1894.
42557.5.250 Thiebault, Henry. Chants d'un français; patrie. Alger, 1886.
42557.5.255 Thiebault, Henry. Nouveaux chants d'un français. Alger, 1899.
42557.5.1100 Turquety, Edouard. Oeuvres de Édouard Turquety: Amour et foi, poésie catholique, hymnes sacrées. 5. éd. Paris, 1857.

42557.6 Individual authors, etc. - 1850-1899 - Poetry - Tiercelin

42557.6 Tiercelin, Louis. Les anniversaires. Poèmes. Paris, 1887.
42557.6.5 Tiercelin, Louis. Trois drames en vers. Paris, 1894.
42557.6.10 Tiercelin, Louis. Sur la harpe, poésies, 1886-1896. Paris, 1897.

42557.7 Individual authors, etc. - 1850-1899 - Poetry - Tisseur

42557.7 Tisseur, Clair. Pauca Paucis. Lyon, 1894.

42557.8 Individual authors, etc. - 1850-1899 - Poetry - Treffier

42557.8 Truffier, J.C. L'échéance. Paris, 1926.

42557.9 Individual authors, etc. - 1850-1899 - Poetry - Valade

42557.9 Valade, Léon. Nocturnes. Paris, 1880.

42557.10 Individual authors, etc. - 1850-1899 - Poetry - Valabrèque; Vannespennes; Vard; etc.

42557.10 Valabrèque, Antony. La chanson de l'hiver. Paris, 1890.
42557.10.5 Vannespennes, J. Au pape, poème lyrique. Belgique, 1863.
42557.10.9 Vard, A. Heures noires et nuits blanches. Paris, 1886.

42557.11 Individual authors, etc. - 1850-1899 - Poetry - Verhaeren - Writings

42557.11 Verhaeren, Émile. Poèmes. Paris, 1906. 3v.
42557.11.1 Verhaeren, Émile. Poèmes. v.1-3. Paris, 1896-1904.
42557.11.2 Verhaeren, Émile. Poems. Photoreproduction. London, 1899.
42557.11.2.15 Verhaeren, Émile. Poems. London, 1915.
42557.11.2.17 Verhaeren, Émile. Poèmes. 7. éd. Paris, 1911.
42557.11.3.5 Verhaeren, Émile. Ausgewählte Gedichte. Leipzig, 1910.
42557.11.4 Verhaeren, Émile. Choix de poèmes. 39. éd. Paris, 1935.
42557.11.4.5 Verhaeren, Émile. Choix de poèmes. 6. éd. Paris, 1917.
42557.11.4.10 Verhaeren, Émile. Choix de poèmes. 13. éd. Paris, 1917.
42557.11.4.15 Verhaeren, Émile. Les blés mouvants; poèmes. 11. éd. Paris, 1918.
42557.11.4.20 Verhaeren, Émile. Les blés mouvants; poèmes. Paris, 1913.
42557.11.4.50 Verhaeren, Émile. The plays of Émile Verhaeren. Boston, 1916.
42557.11.5 Verhaeren, Émile. Les forces tumulteuses. Paris, 1908.
42557.11.6 Verhaeren, Émile. Les villes tentaculaires. Paris, 1908.
42557.11.7 Verhaeren, Émile. Le cloitre. 2. éd. Bruxelles, 1900.
42557.11.8 Verhaeren, Émile. Deux drames: Le cloitre, Philippe II. 3. éd. Paris, 1909.
42557.11.9 Verhaeren, Émile. Deux drames: Le cloitre, Philippe II. Paris, 1909.
42557.11.10 Verhaeren, Émile. Philippe II; drame. Paris, 1901.
42557.11.13 Verhaeren, Émile. Cloister. Boston, 1915.
42557.11.13.2 Verhaeren, Émile. The cloister. London, 1915.
42557.11.13.10 Verhaeren, Émile. Cloister. Boston, 1919.
42557.11.14 Verhaeren, Émile. Poèmes legendaires de Flandre. Paris, 1916.
42557.11.15 Verhaeren, Émile. Deux drames: Le cloitre, Philippe II. 7. éd. Paris, 1915.
42557.11.16 Verhaeren, Émile. Les ailes rouges de la guerre. Poèmes. 19. éd. Paris, 1919.
42557.11.17 Verhaeren, Émile. Toute la Flandre. Paris, 1920. 3v.
42557.11.18 Verhaeren, Émile. Hélène de Sparte. 4. éd. Paris, 1920.
42557.11.19 Verhaeren, Émile. Quinze poèmes. Paris, 1917.
42557.11.20 Verhaeren, Émile. Les flammes hautes. 9. éd. Paris, 1917.
42557.11.23 Verhaeren, Émile. Les visages de la vie. Bruxelles, 1899.
42557.11.25 Verhaeren, Émile. Les heures du soir. 7. éd. Paris, 1921.
42557.11.26 Verhaeren, Émile. Les heures claires. Paris, 1945.
42557.11.27 Verhaeren, Émile. Hymnen an das Leben. Leipzig, 19- .
42557.11.35 Verhaeren, Émile. A la vie qui s'éloigne. 9. éd. Paris, 1924.
42557.11.38 Verhaeren, Émile. Drei Dramen. 2. Aufl. Leipzig, 1914.
42557.11.39 Verhaeren, Émile. Helenas Heimkehr; Drama in vier Akten. Leipzig, 191-.
42557.11.40 Verhaeren, Émile. Impressions. Paris, 1926. 3v.
42557.11.45 Verhaeren, Émile. Five tales. N.Y., 1924.
42557.11.50 Verhaeren, Émile. La multiple splendeur; poèmes. 21. éd. Paris, 1922.
42557.11.55 Verhaeren, Émile. The sunlit hours. N.Y., 1917.
42557.11.60 Verhaeren, Émile. Afternoon. N.Y., 1917.
42557.11.65 Verhaeren, Émile. Gedichten. Lier, 1966.
42557.11.70 Verhaeren, Émile. Poèmes chrétiens de Verhaeren. Gembloux, 1968.
42557.11.160 Verhaeren, Émile. A Marthe Verhaeren; 219 lettres. 2. éd. Paris, 1937.
42557.11.165 Bibliothèque nationale, Paris. Émile Verhaeren. Paris, 1955.
42557.11.170 Mabille de Poncheville, André. Gedichte. Stuttgart, 1909.
42557.11.171 Mabille de Poncheville, André. Fünf Erzählungen. Leipzig, 1922.
42557.11.175 Mabille de Poncheville, André. Deux maisons du poète. Gand, 1922?

42557.12 Individual authors, etc. - 1850-1899 - Poetry - Verhaeren - Works about

42557.12 Mockel, Albert. Émile Verhaeren avec une note biographique. Paris, 1895.
42557.12.01 Pamphlet box. Émile Verhaeren. Miscellaneous pamphlets.
Htn 42557.12.2* Culot, Jean-Marie. Bibliographie de Émile Verhaeren. Bruxelles, 1954.
42557.12.3 Simonson, Raoul. Oeuvres de Émile Verhaeren. Bruxelles, 1959.
42557.12.5 Bazalgette, S. Émile Verhaeren. Paris, 1907.
42557.12.7 Bouglé, C. Les grandes figures de l'entente Verhaeren. Paris, n.d.
42557.12.8 Zweig, Stefan. Émile Verhaeren. 2. Aufl. Leipzig, 1913.
42557.12.9 Zweig, Stefan. Émile Verhaeren. London, 1914.
42557.12.10 Zweig, Stefan. Émile Verhaeren. London, 1915.
42557.12.11 Zweig, Stefan. Erinnerungen an Émile Verhaeren. Leipzig, 1927.
42557.12.15 Baudouin, C. Psychoanalysis and aesthetics. (A study of symbolism in works of Verhaeren). N.Y., 1924.
42557.12.20 Bersaucourt, A. de. Émile Verhaeren, son oeuvre. Paris, 1924.
42557.12.25 Starkie, Enid. Les sources du lyrisme dans la poésie d'Émile Verhaeren. Thèse. Paris, 1927.
42557.12.30 Schlaf, J. Émile Verhaeren. Berlin, 1905.
42557.12.35 Mockel, Albert. Émile Verhaeren. Paris, 1933.
42557.12.40 Mockel, Albert. Un poète de l'énergie. Paris, 1917.
42557.12.45 Fontaine, André. Verhaeren et son oeuvre. Paris, 1929.
42557.12.50 Hoersch, Anton. Der Stil Émile Verhaerens. Inaug. Diss. Dillingen, 1930.
42557.12.55 Commémoration d'Émile Verhaeren à Saint Cloud 4 juillet 1931. Paris, 1931.
42557.12.60 Doutrepont, G. Les débuts littéraires d'Émile Verhaeren à Louvain. Bruxelles, 1914.
42557.12.64 Frets, Huberta. L'élément germanique dans l'oeuvre d'Émile Verhaeren. Thèse. Paris, 1935.
42557.12.65 Frets, Huberta. L'élément germanique dans l'oeuvre d'Émile Verhaeren. Paris, 1935.
42557.12.70 Regoyos, Dario de. La españa negra de Verhaeren. Madrid, 1924.
42557.12.75 Estève, Edmond. Un grand poète de la vie moderne, Émile Verhaeren. Paris, 1928.
42557.12.80 Rosenbaum, Ruth. Die Natur in der Lyrik Verhaerens. Inaug. Diss. Borna, 1935.
42557.12.84 Sussex, R.T. L'idée d'humanité chez Émile Verhaeren. Thèse. Paris, 1938.

42557.12 Individual authors, etc. - 1850-1899 - Poetry - Verhaeren - Works about - cont.

42557.12.85 Sussex, R.T. L'idée d'humanité chez Émile Verhaeren. Paris, 1938.
42557.12.90A Zweig, Stefan. Émile Verhaeren. Boston, 1914.
42557.12.90B Zweig, Stefan. Émile Verhaeren. Boston, 1914.
42557.12.95 Vermeulen, G. Les débuts d'Émile Verhaeren. Bruxelles, 1948.
42557.12.100 Olivero, F. Il contrasto nella lirica di Émile Verhaeren. Torino, 1943.
42557.12.105 Christophe, L. Émile Verhaeren. Paris, 1955.
42557.12.110 Jones, Percy M. Verhaeren. London, 1957.
42557.12.115 Académie...Brussels. Académie royale de langue et de littérature françaises, Brussels. Le centenaire d'Émile Verhaeren, 1855-1955. Bruxelles, 1956.
42557.12.120 Černý, V. Emile Verhaeren a jeho místo v dějinách volného verse. Praha, 1955.
42557.12.125 Borges, F. Émile Verhaeren. Antwerpen, 1962?
42557.12.130 Carneiro Leão, A. O culto da Ação em Verhaeren. Rio de Janeiro, 1959.
42557.12.135 Poortere, Carlo de. Bibliotheque Carlo de Poortere. Courtrai, 1963.
42557.12.140 Kunel, Maurice. Verlaine et Rimbaud en Belgique. Liège, 1945.
42557.12.145 Kalinowska, Zofia I. Les motifs décadents dans les poèmes d'Émile Verhaeren. Wrocław, 1967.
42557.12.150 Bodart, Roger. Émile Verhaeren hier et aujourd'hui. Tournai, 1966.

42557.14 Individual authors, etc. - 1850-1899 - Poetry - Verlaine - Biography and criticism [Discontinued]

42557.14 Martrin-Donos, Charles. Verlaine intime. Paris, 1898.
Htn 42557.14.3* Montel, François. Bibliographie de Paul Verlaine. Paris, 1924.
Htn 42557.14.4* Bever, A. van. Bibliographie et iconographie de Paul Verlaine. Paris, 1926.
42557.14.5 Lepelletier, E. Paul Verlaine. Paris, 1907.
42557.14.5.1 Lepelletier, E. Paul Verlaine; sa vie, son oeuvre. 2. éd. Paris, 1907.
42557.14.5.5 Lepelletier, E. Paul Verlaine. 7. éd. Paris, 1923.
42557.14.6 Lepelletier, E. Paul Verlaine et ses contemporains. Paris, 1897.
42557.14.7 Hommage à Verlaine. Paris, 1910.
42557.14.8 Cazals, F.A. Paul Verlaine. v.1-2. Paris, 1896.
42557.14.9 Cazals, F.A. Les derniers jours de Paul Verlaine. Paris, 1911.
42557.14.10 Tournoux, G.A. Bibliographie verlainienne. Leipzig, 1912.
42557.14.11 Aressy, Lucien. La dernière bohème, Verlaine et son milieu. Paris, 1923.
42557.14.11.9 Aressy, Lucien. Verlaine et la dernière bohème. 9. éd. Paris, 1947.
42557.14.12 Delahaye, Ernest. Documents relatifs à Paul Verlaine. Paris, 1919.
42557.14.14 Delahaye, Ernest. Verlaine. Paris, 1930.
42557.14.16 Martino, P. Verlaine. Paris, 1930.
42557.14.25 Fontains, André. Verlaine-Rimbaud. Paris, 1931.
42557.14.35 Gedeon, Jolán. La fortune intellectuelle de Verlaine. Szeged, 1933.
42557.14.40 Dugas, Marcel. Verlaine; ensayo. La Habana, 1935.
42557.14.42 Dugas, Marcel. Verlaine; essai. Paris, 1928.
42557.14.45 Furtado, Diogo. Verlaine. Lisboa, 1947.
42557.14.55 Pamphlet box. Verlaine, Paul.
42557.14.60 Linhardt, A. Dichtêr und Vagabund. Wien, 1949.
42557.14.65 Bruneau, C. Verlaine. Paris, 1952.
42557.14.70 Underwood, V.P. Verlaine et l'Angleterre. Paris, 1956.
42557.14.75 Hanson, Lawrence. Verlaine. N.Y., 1957.
42557.14.77 Eaubonne, Françoise. La vie passionnée de Verlaine. Paris, 1960.
42557.14.78 Eaubanne, Françoise. Verlaine et Rimbaud. Paris, 1960.
42557.14.80 Sieper, Bernhard. Paul Verlaine. Herne, 1957.
42557.14.85 Fongaro, Antoine. Bibliographie de Verlaine en Italie. Florence, 1957.
42557.14.90 Binet, Léon R. Verlaine à Aix-les-Bains. Paris, 1958.
42557.14.95 Morice, L. Verlaine. Paris, 1946.
42557.14.100 Knauth, Karl. Die poetische Bedeutung der Farbe in Verlaines Lyrik. Bonn, 1966.

42557.15 - .18 Individual authors, etc. - 1850-1899 - Poetry - Verlaine - Complete and Selected works

X Cg 42557.15.5 Verlaine, P. Choix de poésies. Paris, 1904.
42557.15.8 Verlaine, Paul. Choix de poésies. Paris, 1908.
42557.15.10 Verlaine, Paul. Choix de poésies. Paris, 1912.
42557.16 Verlaine, Paul. Poems. London, 1904.
42557.17 Verlaine, Paul. Selected poems. Berkeley, 1948.
42557.18 Verlaine, Paul. Oeuvres complètes. Paris, 1902. 5v.
42557.18.3 Verlaine, Paul. Oeuvres complètes. Paris, 1930. 5v.
X Cg 42557.18.4 Verlaine, Paul. Oeuvres complètes. Paris, 1899- 2v.
42557.18.5 Verlaine, Paul. Poésies complètes. Paris, 1923-26. 7v.
42557.18.9 Verlaine, Paul. Oeuvres poétiques complètes. Paris, 1962.
42557.18.9.2 Verlaine, Paul. Oeuvres poétiques complètes. Paris, 1965.
42557.18.9.4 Verlaine, Paul. Oeuvres poétiques. Paris, 1969.
42557.18.9.5 Verlaine, Paul. Selected poems. London, 1965.
42557.18.10 Verlaine, Paul. Gesammelte Werke in zwei Bänden. Leipzig, 1922. 2v.
42557.18.15 Verlaine, Paul. Poésies religieuses. Paris, 1904.
42557.18.20 Verlaine, Paul. Poèmes saturniens. Paris, 1921.
42557.18.21 Verlaine, Paul. Poèmes saturniens. Paris, 1939.
42557.18.22 Verlaine, Paul. Poèmes saturniens. Paris, 1946.
42557.18.23 Verlaine, Paul. Poèmes saturniens. London, 1946.
42557.18.24 Verlaine, Paul. Poèmes saturniens. Paris, 1958.
42557.18.24.5 Verlaine, Paul. Les poèmes saturniens. Paris, 1967.
42557.18.25 Verlaine, Paul. Gedichte. Berlin, 1902.
42557.18.30 Verlaine, Paul. Ausgewählte Gedichte. Leipzig, 1906.
42557.18.35 Verlaine, Paul. Paralelamente a Paul Verlaine. São Paulo, 1944.
42557.18.40 Verlaine, Paul. Parallèlement. Paris, 1939.
42557.18.45 Verlaine, Paul. Oeuvres complètes. Paris, 1948-53. 5v.
42557.18.50 Verlaine, Paul. Poésies et proses. Paris, 1957.
42557.18.52 Verlaine, Paul. Vers. 3. éd. Munich, 1923.
42557.18.55 Verlaine, Paul. Poèmes. Paris, 1960.
42557.18.705 Verlaine, Paul. Gedichte. Heidelberg, 1959.
42557.18.710 Verlaine, Paul. Poésies choisies. 2. éd. Roma, 1959.
42557.18.800A Le Rouge, Gustave. Verlainiens et décadents. Paris, 1928.
42557.18.800B Le Rouge, Gustave. Verlainiens et décadents. Paris, 1928.
42557.18.805 Nadal, Octave. Paul Verlaine. Paris, 1961.

42557.19 Individual authors, etc. - 1850-1899 - Poetry - Verlaine - Individual works

42557.19 Verlaine, Paul. Oeuvres posthumes. Paris, 1903.
42557.19.5 Verlaine, Paul. Oeuvres posthumes. Paris, 1929. 3v.
42557.19.10 Verlaine, Paul. Jadis et naguère. Paris, 1903.
42557.19.12 Verlaine, Paul. Jadis et naguère. Paris, 1946.
42557.19.15 Verlaine, Paul. Bonheur. Paris, 1923.
42557.19.18 Verlaine, Paul. Bonheur. Paris, 1949.
42557.19.19 Verlaine, Paul. Bonheur. Thèse. Paris, 1949.
Htn 42557.19.20* Verlaine, Paul. Dans les limbes. Paris, 1894.
42557.19.21 Verlaine, Paul. Poèmes choisis. Paris, 1946.
Htn 42557.19.25* Verlaine, Paul. Dédicaces. Paris, 1894.
Htn 42557.19.30* Verlaine, Paul. Odes en son honneur. Paris, 1893.
42557.19.32 Verlaine, Paul. Odes en son honneur. Paris, 1942.
Htn 42557.19.35* Verlaine, Paul. Invectives. Paris, 1896.
42557.19.40 Verlaine, Paul. Mes hopitaux. Paris, 1891.
Htn 42557.19.45* Verlaine, Paul. Mes prisons. Paris, 1893.
42557.19.50 Verlaine, Paul. Sagesse. Paris, 1924.
42557.19.51 Verlaine, Paul. Sagesse. Paris, 1939.
42557.19.52 Verlaine, Paul. Sagesse. Paris, 1946.
42557.19.54 Verlaine, Paul. Sagesse. Paris, 1948.
42557.19.55 Verlaine, Paul. Les uns et les autres. Paris, 1891.
42557.19.56 Verlaine, Paul. Sagesse. Liturgies intimes. Paris, 1958.
Htn 42557.19.65* Verlaine, Paul. Les amies, scène d'amour sapphique. Ségovie, 1870.
42557.19.67 Verlaine, Paul. Verlaine, par lui-même. Paris, 1966.
Htn 42557.19.70* Verlaine, Paul. Élégies. Paris, 1893.
Htn 42557.19.80* Verlaine, Paul. Hombres (hommes). Paris, 1904.
Htn 42557.19.90* Verlaine, Paul. Parallèlement. Paris, 1889.
42557.19.95 Verlaine, Paul. Parallèlement. Paris, 1946.
Htn 42557.19.100* Verlaine, Paul. Romances sans paroles. Harlaam, 1913.
42557.19.110 Verlaine, Paul. La bonne chanson. Paris, 1891.
42557.19.113 Verlaine, Paul. La bonne chanson. Paris, 1940.
42557.19.115 Verlaine, Paul. La bonne chanson. Paris, 1946.
42557.19.117 Verlaine, Paul. Romances sans paroles. Paris, 1940.
42557.19.120 Verlaine, Paul. Romances sans paroles. Paris, 1946.
42557.19.122 Verlaine, Paul. Romances sans paroles. Paris, 1947.
42557.19.130 Verlaine, Paul. Louise Leclercq. Söcking, 1948.
42557.19.140 Verlaine, Paul. The sky above the roof. London, 1957.
42557.19.150F Verwey, Albert. Twee portretten van Paul Verlaine. Amsterdam, 1951.

42557.20 Individual authors, etc. - 1850-1899 - Poetry - Verlaine - Correspondence; Works about

42557.20 Verlaine, Paul. Epigrammes. Paris, 1894.
42557.20.5 Verlaine, Paul. Fêtes galantes. Paris, 1920.
42557.20.5.2 Verlaine, Paul. Fêtes galantes. Paris, 1939.
42557.20.5.3 Verlaine, Paul. Fêtes galantes; La bonne chanson. Manchester, 1942.
42557.20.5.7 Verlaine, Paul. Fêtes galantes. Paris, 1946.
42557.20.6 Verlaine, Paul. Lettres inédites à Charles Morice. Genève, 1964.
42557.20.7 Verlaine, Paul. Correspondance. Paris, 1922-29. 3v.
42557.20.7.5 Verlaine, Paul. Lettres inédites de Verlaine à Cazals. Genève, 1957.
42557.20.8 Verlaine, Paul. Verlaine. Basel, 1944.
Htn 42557.20.9*A Verlaine, Paul. Confessions, notes autobiographiques. Paris, 1895.
Htn 42557.20.9*B Verlaine, Paul. Confessions, notes autobiographiques. Paris, 1895.
42557.20.10 Verlaine, Paul. Confessions. Paris, 1946.
Htn 42557.20.15* Verlaine, Paul. Paul Verlaine; correspondance et documents inédits relatifs à son livre "Quinze jours en Hollande". La Haye, 1897.
42557.20.20A Verlaine, Paul. Confessions of a poet. London, 1950.
42557.20.20B Verlaine, Paul. Confessions of a poet. London, 1950.
42557.20.25 Verlaine, Paul. Il dramma dell'uomo moderno nella poesia cristiana di Paul Verlaine [di] Attilio Galli. Ascoli Piceno, 1960.
42557.20.75 Verlaine, Paul. Frauen. Hannover, 1919.
42557.20.145 Zweig, Stefan. Verlaine. Berlin, 19- .
42557.20.150 Zweig, Stefan. Paul Verlaine. Boston, 1913.
42557.20.155 Bouhier, Jean. Verlaine et l'amour. Bruxelles, 1946.
42557.20.160 Benéteau, André. Étude sur l'inspiration et l'influence de P. Verlaine. Diss. Washington, 1930.
42557.20.170 Adam, Antoine. Le vrai Verlaine; essai psychanalytique. Paris, 1936.
42557.20.172 Adam, Antoine. Le vrai Verlaine; essai psychanalytique. Thèse. Paris, 1936.
42557.20.180 Porché, F. Verlaine. Paris, 1933.
42557.20.190 Fontaine, A. Verlaine, homme de lettres. Paris, 1937.
42557.20.210 Morotini, C. Das Lebensgefühl Paul Verlaines in Sagesse. Lengerich, 1938.
42557.20.215 Ruchon, Francois. Verlaine; documents iconographiques. Vésenaz, 1947.
42557.20.220 Coulon, Marcel. Au coeur de Verlaine et de Rimbaud. Paris, 1925.
42557.20.225 Coulon, Marcel. Verlaine, poète saturnien. Paris, 1929.
42557.20.230 Haessler, E. Paul Verlaine. Finsterwalde, 1908.
42557.20.240 Carco, François. Verlaine. Paris, 1939.
42557.20.241 Carco, François. Verlaine. Paris, 1944.
42557.20.245 Carco, François. Verlaine, poète maudit. Paris, 1948.
42557.20.250 Mondor, Henri. L'amitié de Verlaine et Mallarmé. 8. éd. Paris, 1940.
42557.20.255 Lepelletier, Edmond. Paul Verlaine. London, 1909?
42557.20.256 Lepelletier, Edmond. Paul Verlaine, his life, his work. 1. American ed. N.Y., 1970.
42557.20.260A Barnecque, J.H. Études verlainiennes. Paris, 1952. 2v.
42557.20.260B Barnecque, J.H. Études verlainiennes. v.2. Paris, 1952.
42557.20.265 Adam, Antoine. Verlaine. Paris, 1953.
42557.20.268 Adam, Antoine. Verlaine. Paris, 1955.
42557.20.269 Adam, Antoine. The art of Paul Verlaine. N.Y., 1963.
42557.20.270 Les cahiers Paul Verlaine; revue litteraire des verlainiens. Paris. 1-74,1953-1960
42557.20.275 Micha, Alexandre. Verlaine et les poètes symbolistes. Paris, 1943.
42557.20.280 Raynaud, Ernest. L'assomption de Paul Verlaine. Paris, 1912.
42557.20.285 Seguin, Marc. Ce pauvre bonheur, la "dernière passion humaine" de Paul Verlaine. Paris, 1958.
42557.20.290 Bersancourt, Albert de. Paul Verlaine. Paris, 1909.
42557.20.295 Paris. Bibliothèque Ste. Geneviève. Collection Doncet. Catalogue de l'exposition Paul Verlaine. Paris, 1946.
42557.20.298 Zayed, Georges. La formation litteraire de Verlaine. Genève, 1961.
42557.20.300 Verlaine, Paul. Paul Verlaine a Arthur Rimbaud v překladech F. Hrubina. Praha, 1961.

42557.20 Individual authors, etc. - 1850-1899 - Poetry - Verlaine - Correspondence; Works about - cont.

42557.20.305 Cuénot, C. Le style de Paul Verlaine. Paris, 1963.
42557.20.310 Braun, Thomas. Paul Verlaine en Ardennes. Paris, 1909.
42557.20.315 Moroy, Elie. La guirlande de Verlaine. Genève, 1926.
42557.20.320 Dugas, Marcel. Feux de Bengale à Verlaine glorieux. Montreal, 1915.
42557.20.325 Verlaine, Paul. Prokletí básníci. V Praze, 1966.
42557.20.330 Zimmermann, Éléonore M. Magies de Verlaine, étude de l'évolution poétique de Paul Verlaine. Paris, 1967.
42557.20.335 Carter, Alfred Edward. Verlaine; a study in parallels. Toronto, 1969.
42557.20.336 Carter, Alfred Edward. Paul Verlaine. N.Y., 1971.
42557.20.340 Bollery, Joseph. Un séjour ignoré de Verlaine en Belgique. La Rochelle, 1938.
42557.20.345 Richardson, Joanna. Verlaine. London, 1971.

42557.21 - .25 Individual authors, etc. - 1850-1899 - Poetry - Vielé-Griffin

42557.21 Vielé-Griffin, F. Poèmes et poésies. Paris, 1895.
42557.21.4 Vielé-Griffin, F. Poèmes et poésies. 4. éd. Paris, 1907.
42557.21.14 Vielé-Griffin, F. Choix de poèmes. Paris, 1923.
42557.21.20 Vielé-Griffin, F. Oeuvres. Paris, 1924-30. 4v.
42557.22 Vielé-Griffin, F. La chevauchée d'Yeldis et autres poèmes (1892). Paris, 1893.
42557.22.10 Vielé-Griffin, F. Le domaine royal; discours lyriques. Paris, 1923.
42557.22.20 Vielé-Griffin, F. Les cygnes. Alean-Levy, 1886.
42557.23 Vielé-Griffin, F. Plus loin. Paris, 1906.
42557.24 Vielé-Griffin, F. La clarté de vie. Paris, 1897.
42557.25 Vielé-Griffin, F. La lumière de grèce. Paris, 1912.
42557.25.100 Vielé-Griffin, F. Phocas le jardinier. Paris, 1898.
42557.25.110 Vielé-Griffin, F. Couronne offerte a la muse romaine. Paris, 1922.
42557.25.120 Vielé-Griffin, F. Voix d'Ionie. 2. éd. Paris, 1914.
42557.25.130 Vielé-Griffin, F. La rose au flot, légende du Paitou. Paris, 1922.
42557.25.140 Vielé-Griffin, F. La sagesse d'Ulysse, orné d'une composition de K.-X. Roussel. Paris, 1925.
42557.25.150 Vielé-Griffin, F. La légende ailée de Wieland le forgeron. Paris, 1900.
42557.25.180 Cours, Jean de. Francis Vielé-Griffin. Paris, 1930.
42557.25.800 Kuhn, Reinhard. The return to reality. Genève, 1962.

42557.26 Individual authors, etc. - 1850-1899 - Poetry - Vermersch

42557.26 Vermersch, Eugene. Florilège. Paris, 1929.
42557.26.5 Vermersch, Eugene. Les binettes rimées. Paris, 1868.

42557.27 - .29 Individual authors, etc. - 1850-1899 - Poetry - Vicaire

42557.27 Corbel, H. Un poéte, Gabriel Vicaire (1848-1900). Paris, 1922.
42557.27.5 Vicaire, Jean. Bibliographie de Gabriel Vicaire d'après les notes recueilles par G. Vicaire. Paris, 1925.
42557.28 Vicaire, Gabriel. Le miracle de St. Nicolas. Paris, 1888.
42557.29 Vicaire, Gabriel. L'heure enchantée. Paris, 1890.
42557.29.5 Vicaire, Gabriel. Livingstone. Paris, 1904.

42557.30 Individual authors, etc. - 1850-1899 - Poetry - Vibert

42557.30 Vibert, Théodore. Les Girondins. Paris, 1910.
42557.30.80 Vibert, Paul Théodore. Le cinquantenaire des Girondins, 1860-1910. Paris, 1913.

42558.1 - .14 Individual authors, etc. - 1850-1899 - Poetry - Miscellany [Discontinued]

Htn 42558.7* Le Parnasse contemporain, 1866, 1869 et 1876. Paris, 1866- 3v.
42558.9 Le parnassiculet contemporain. Paris, 1872.
42558.11 Bader, Clarisse. La comtesse Jeanne. Paris, 1887.

42558.15 Individual authors, etc. - 1850-1899 - Poetry - Villemer

42558.15 Villemer-Delormel. Les chansons d'Alsace-Lorraine. Paris, 1885.

42558.30 Individual authors, etc. - 1850-1899 - Poetry - Rouquette

42558.30 Rouquette, Dominique. Fleurs d'Amerique. New Orleans, 1856.

42558.40 - .42 Individual authors, etc. - 1850-1899 - Poetry - Ronchaud

42558.40 Ronchaud, Louis de. Poèmes dramatiques. Paris, 1883.
42558.42 Ronchaud, Louis de. Les heures. Paris, 1844.
42558.42.30 Ronchaud, Louis de. Le filleul de la mort. Paris, 1880.
Htn 42558.50* Noël, fait en manière de dialogue. Orléans, 1897.

42558.60 Individual authors, etc. - 1850-1899 - Poetry - Weil

42558.60 Weil, Alfred. Une douzaine de sonnets. Paris, 1878.

42558.80 Individual authors, etc. - 1850-1899 - Poetry - Walzer

42558.80 Walzer, Pierre Olivier. La révolution des sept: Lautréamont, Mallarmé, Rimbaud, Corbière, Cros, Nouveau, Laforgue. Neuchâtel, 1970.

42558.100 - Individual authors, etc. - 1850-1899 - Poetry - Anonymous poems

42558.100 Les amours des anges. Paris, 1892.

42559 Individual authors, etc. - 1850-1899 - Poetry - Satirical and epigrammatic poems; Cabaret songs

42559.7 Bonie, F. Chansons. 2. éd. Bruxelles, 1864.
NEDL 42559.9 Bruant, A. Chansons et monologues. Paris, 1896-97.
42559.12 Champsaur, F. La chanson du Moulin à Vent. Paris, 189-.
42559.13 Couyba, Charles Maurice. Chansons rouges. Paris, 1896.
42559.13.5 Couyba, Charles Maurice. Nouvelles chansons, rêves, joies, regrets. Paris, 1895.
42559.14 Couyba, Charles Maurice. Stances à Manon. Paris, 19- .
42559.49 Lemercier, Eugène. Autor du Moulin chansons de la batte. Paris, 1898.
42559.50 Les rois de France. Paris, 1874.
42559.53 Masson, A. Pour les quais. Paris, 1905.
42559.54.5 Meusy, Victor. Chansons d'hier et d'aujourd'hui. Paris, 1891.
42559.54.10 Mensy, Victor. Chansons modernes. Paris, 1891.
42559.84 Taravel, Antoine. La chanson sentimentale. Paris, 1906.
42559.84.5 Taravel, Antoine. L'amour chante. Paris, 1904.
42559.97 Xanrof, Léon. Chansons d'étudiants. Paris, 189-.
42559.97.5 Xanrof, Léon. Chansons sans-gène. Paris, 1890.
42559.97.10 Xanrof, Léon. Chansons à rire. Paris, 1891.

42559 Individual authors, etc. - 1850-1899 - Poetry - Satirical and epigrammatic poems; Cabaret songs - cont.

42559.97.15 Xanrof, Léon. L'amour et la vie. Paris, 1894.

42561.1 - .23 Individual authors, etc. - 1850-1899 - Fiction - Folios [Discontinued]

42561.2 L'echo des feuilletons. v.1-6,25. Paris, 1842. 7v.
42561.5 About, Edmond. Le fellah. Paris, 1869.
42561.5.5 About, Edmond. The fellah. London, n.d.
42561.7 About, Edmond. La vielle roche. Paris, 1865-66.
42561.8 Augustin, Marie. Le macandal. Nouvelle Orleans, 1892.
42561.9 Arréat, Lucien. Journal d'un philosophe. Paris, 1887.
NEDL 42561.9.9 Barrès, M. Les bastions de l'est. Au service de l'Allemagne. Paris, n.d.
42561.9.10 Barrès, M. Une journée parlementaire. Paris, 1894.
42561.10 Biart, Lucien. La frontière indienne. Paris, n.d.
42561.12 Berthoud, S. Henry. L'homme depuis cinq mille ans. Paris, n.d.
42561.13 Cahun, Léon. Adventures of Captain Mago. N.Y., 1889.
42561.13.2 Cahun, Léon. Hassan le Janissaire. Paris, n.d.
42561.13.10 Craven, Pauline. Anne Séverin. 11e éd. Paris, 1872.
42561.13.15 Craven, Pauline. Eliane. N.Y., 1882.
42561.13.17 Craven, Pauline. Jettatrice, or The veil withdrawn. Boston, 1875.
42561.13.20 Craven, Pauline. A sister's story. N.Y., 1870.
42561.13.25 Craven, Pauline. Le travail d'une ame. 4e éd. Paris, 1884.
42561.14 Daudet, Alphonse. Histoire d'un enfant. Paris, n.d.
42561.14.5 Daudet, Alphonse. Les Cigognes. Paris, n.d.
Htn 42561.14.7* Daudet, Alphonse. Contes et recits. Paris, n.d.
Htn 42561.15* Daudet, Alphonse. Fromont jeune et Risler ainé. Paris, 1885. 2v.
42561.16 Daudet, Ernest. Robert Darnetal. Paris, 1880.
42561.18 Descaves, Lucien. Sous-offs. Paris, 1892.
42561.22 Fleury, Jules. Les souffrances du professeur Delteil. Paris, 1870.
42561.23 Fleury, Jules. The faience violin. N.Y., 1893.

42561.24 - .38 Individual authors, etc. - 1850-1899 - Fiction - Chandeneux - Writings

42561.24 Chandeneux, Claire de. L'automne d'une femme. Paris, 1880.
42561.25 Chandeneux, Claire de. La croix de Monguerre. Paris, 1879.
42561.26 Chandeneux, Claire de. Une faiblesse de Minerve. Paris, 1877.
42561.27 Chandeneux, Claire de. Une fille Liade. Paris, 1878.
42561.28 Chandeneux, Claire de. Les Giboulées de la vie. Paris, 1878.
42561.29 Chandeneux, Claire de. Le lieutenant de Rancy. Paris, 1877.
42561.30 Chandeneux, Claire de. Les mariages de Garnison. Paris, 1880.
42561.31 Chandeneux, Claire de. Les ménages militaires. Paris, 1880. 4v.
42561.32 Chandeneux, Claire de. Secondes noces. Paris, 1881.
42561.32.15 Chandeneux, Claire de. Souvenirs de Bérénice. Paris, 1882.
42561.33 Chandeneux, Claire de. Vaisseaux brulés. Paris, 1877.
42561.34 Chandeneux, Claire de. Val-Regis la grande. Paris, n.d.

42562.1 - .35 Individual authors, etc. - 1850-1899 - Fiction - About, E. - Writings

42562.2 About, Edmond. A.B.C. Travailleur. Paris, 1868.
42562.3 About, Edmond. A.B.C. Travailleur. Paris, 1869.
42562.4 About, Edmond. Causeries. Paris, 1865.
42562.5 About, Edmond. Le buste. N.Y., 1886.
42562.5.1 About, Edmond. Le buste. N.Y., 1888.
42562.5.2 About, Edmond. Le buste. N.Y., 1891.
42562.5.5 About, Edmond. Le cas de M. Guérin. Paris, 1862.
42562.5.9 About, Edmond. La fille du Chanoine. N.Y., n.d.
42562.5.12 About, Edmond. La fille du Chanoine. London, n.d.
42562.6 About, Edmond. Germaine. Paris, 1872.
42562.6.10 About, Edmond. Germaine. 12e éd. Paris, 1878.
42562.6.20 About, Edmond. Germaine. 3e séries. Paris, 1884.
42562.7 About, Edmond. La Grèce contemporaine. Paris, 1872.
42562.7.5 About, Edmond. La Grèce contemporaine. Paris, 1890.
42562.8 About, Edmond. L'homme a l'oreille cassée. 6e éd. Paris, 1871.
42562.8.2 About, Edmond. L'homme a l'oreille cassée. 2e éd. Paris, 1862.
42562.8.3 About, Edmond. L'homme a l'oreille cassée. 5. éd. Paris, 1868.
42562.8.25 About, Edmond. L'infâme. Paris, 1867.
42562.9 About, Edmond. Lettres d'un bon jeune homme à sa cousine Madeleine. Paris, 1861.
42562.9.5 About, Edmond. Lettres d'un bon jeune homme à sa cousine Madeleine. Paris, 1885.
42562.9.7 About, Edmond. Dernières lettres d'un bon jeune homme à sa cousine Madeleine. Paris, 1872.
42562.10 About, Edmond. Madelon. Paris, 1872.
42562.11 About, Edmond. Maitre Pièrre. Paris, 1870.
42562.11.8 About, Edmond. Le mari imprévu. 2e éd. Paris, 1867.
42562.11.9 About, Edmond. Le mari imprévu. 3e éd. Paris, 1873.
42562.12 About, Edmond. Les mariages de Paris. Paris, 1864.
42562.12.2A About, Edmond. Les mariages de Paris. Paris, 1888.
42562.12.2B About, Edmond. Les mariages de Paris. Paris, 1888.
42562.12.50 About, Edmond. Les mariages de province. 3e éd. Paris, 1869.
42562.13 About, Edmond. Les mariages de province. Paris, 1872.
42562.13.3 About, Edmond. La mère de la marquise. N.Y., 1885.
42562.13.4 About, Edmond. La mère de la marquise. N.Y., 1888.
42562.13.5 About, Edmond. La mère de la marquise. N.Y., 1892.
42562.14 About, Edmond. De Pontoise à Stamboul. Paris, 1884.
42562.15 About, Edmond. Le progrès. Paris, 1867.
42562.16 About, Edmond. Le roman d'un brave homme. Paris, 1881.
42562.16.5A About, Edmond. Le roman d'un brave homme. Paris, 1880.
42562.16.5B About, Edmond. Le roman d'un brave homme. Paris, 1880.
42562.16.9 About, Edmond. Le roi des Montagnes. 4e éd. Paris, 1860.
42562.16.13 About, Edmond. Le roi des Montagnes. Paris, 1886.
42562.16.14 About, Edmond. Le roi des Montagnes. 2e éd. N.Y., 1886.
42562.16.20 About, Edmond. Le roi des Montagnes. 9e éd. Paris, 1871.
42562.17 About, Edmond. Le roi des Montagnes. Paris, 1872.
42562.17.2 About, Edmond. Le roi des Montagnes. N.Y., 1892.
42562.17.3 About, Edmond. Le roi des Montagnes. Paris, 1860.
42562.17.4 About, Edmond. Le roi des Montagnes. Paris, n.d.
42562.17.6 About, Edmond. Le roi des Montagnes. Paris, 1887.
42562.18 About, Edmond. Théâtre impossible. N.Y., 1864.

Classified Listing

42562.1 - .35 Individual authors, etc. - 1850-1899 - Fiction - About, E. - Writings - cont.

42562.19 About, Edmond. Tolla. N.Y., 1872.
42562.19.3 About, Edmond. Tolla. 7e éd. Paris, 1860. 2v.
42562.20 About, Edmond. Trente et quarante. N.Y., 1872.
42562.22 About, Edmond. Le turco. N.Y., 1870.
42562.23 About, Edmond. Chez tante Claire. Paris, 1882.
42562.24 About, Edmond. Le dix-neuvième siéle. Paris, 1892.
42562.26 About, Edmond. Germaine. Boston, 1860.
42562.27 About, Edmond. Germaine. Paris, 1857.
42562.27.5 About, Edmond. Germaine. Le roi des Montagnes. 2. éd. Paris, 1857.
42562.28 About, Edmond. Les mariages de Paris. Boston, 1856.
42562.29 About, Edmond. Les mariages de Paris. Boston, 1858.
42562.29.2 About, Edmond. Les mariages de Paris. Paris, 1911.
42562.29.3 About, Edmond. Trente et quarante. Les mariages de Paris. v.1-2. 3e series. Paris, 1859.
42562.30 About, Edmond. Un mariage de Paris. Boston, 1861.
42562.31 About, Edmond. Le nez d'un notaire. 13. éd. Boston, 1885.
42562.31.1 About, Edmond. Le nez d'un notaire. 14. éd. Boston, 1885.
42562.31.2 About, Edmond. Le nez d'un notaire. 3. éd. Boston, 1862.
42562.31.50 About, Edmond. Le nez d'un notaire. Paris, 1913.
42562.32 About, Edmond. The nose of a notary. Boston, 1863.
42562.33A About, Edmond. The king of the mountains. Boston, 1861.
42562.33B About, Edmond. The king of the mountains. Boston, 1861.
42562.33.2 About, Edmond. The king of the mountains. N.Y., 1902.
42562.33.15 About, Edmond. The man with the broken ear. N.Y., 1872.
42562.33.25 About, Edmond. Salon de 1866. Paris, 1867.
42562.33.30 About, Edmond. Gaëtana. Paris, 1862.
42562.34 About, Edmond. Tolla. Edinburgh, 1856.
42562.35 About, Edmond. Selections. London, 1884.
42562.35.5 About, Edmond. Le capitaine Bitterlin. Paris, 1878.
42562.35.10 About, Edmond. The twins. London, 19- .

42562.36 Individual authors, etc. - 1850-1899 - Fiction - About, E. - Works about

42562.36.5 Thiebaut, Marcel. Edmond About. 9e éd. Paris, 1936.

42562.37 Individual authors, etc. - 1850-1899 - Fiction - Achard; Achkinasi; etc.

42562.37 Achard, Amédée E. Clos pommier et prissonniers du Caucase. Boston, 1865.
42562.37.2 Achard, Amédée E. Clos pommier et prissonniers du Caucase. Boston, 1869.
42562.37.5 Achard, Amédée E. Mademoiselle d'Esparo. Paris, 1888.
42562.37.6 Achard, Amédée E. Les petits fils de Lovelace. Paris, 1858.
42562.37.7 Achard, Amédée E. Le clos pommier et prisonniers du Caucase. 5. éd. Boston, 1870.
42562.37.8 Achard, Amédée E. L'invalide, comédie. Paris, 1872.
42562.37.9 Achard, Amédée E. Les chevauchées de M. de la Guerche. Paris, 1956.
42562.37.210 Achkinasi, M. La chasse aux juifs, histoire d'hier et d'aujourd'hui. 2e éd. Paris, 1887.

42562.38 - .38.1 Individual authors, etc. - 1850-1899 - Fiction - Adam - Works about

42562.38 Batilliat, Marcel. Paul Adam. Paris, 1903.
42562.38.1 Mauclair, C. Paul Adam, 1862-1920. Paris, 1921.
42562.38.1.10 Heinen, F.H. Das Frankreichbild im Werke Paul Adams, 1862-1920. Inaug. Diss. Bochum-Langendreer, 1932.
42562.38.1.20 Fogelberg, T. La langue et le style de Paul Adam. Thèse. Paris, 1939.

42562.38.2 - .38.14 Individual authors, etc. - 1850-1899 - Fiction - Adam - Writings

42562.38.2 Adam, Paul. En décor. Paris, 1891.
42562.38.3 Adam, Paul. L'essence de soleil. Paris, 1890.
42562.38.4 Adam, Paul. La force. Paris, 1899.
42562.38.4.7 Adam, Paul. La force. Paris, 1921. 2v.
42562.38.5 Adam, Paul. Combats. Paris, 1905.
42562.38.6 Adam, Paul. Les lions. Paris, 1906.
42562.38.7 Adam, Paul. Les monettes. Paris, 1907.
42562.38.8 Adam, Paul. Basile et Sophia. Paris, 1900.
42562.38.9 Adam, Paul. Les mouettes. Paris, 1906.
42562.38.10 Adam, Paul. Stéphanie. Paris, 1913.
42562.38.11 Adam, Paul. Les coeur untiles. Paris, 1907.
42562.38.12 Adam, Paul. Le mystère des foules. 4e éd. Paris, 1907. 2v.
42562.38.13 Adam, Paul. Au soleil de juillet, 1829-30. 13e éd. Paris, 1903.
42562.38.14 Adam, Paul. La terre qui tonne; France, Italie. 5e éd. Paris, 1917.
42562.38.14.5 Adam, Paul. La ville inconnue. 3. éd. Paris, 1911.
42562.38.14.8 Adam, Paul. Le vice filial. Paris, 1897.
42562.38.14.9 Adam, Paul. L'année de Clarisse. Paris, 1902.
42562.38.14.10 Adam, Paul. La bataille d'Uhde. 6e éd. Paris, 1903.
42562.38.14.11 Adam, Paul. Les coeurs nouveaux. 5e éd. Paris, 1907.
42562.38.14.13 Adam, Paul. L'infant d'Austerlitz. Paris, 1902.
42562.38.14.14 Adam, Paul. La force du mal. Paris, 1896.
42562.38.14.19 Adam, Paul. Les images sentimentales. 4e éd. Paris, 1907.
42562.38.14.20 Adam, Paul. Irène et les eunugues. 16e éd. Paris, 1907.
42562.38.14.21 Adam, Paul. Jeunesse et amours de M. Henricourt. Paris, 1913.
42562.38.14.22 Adam, Paul. Lettres de Malaisie; roman. Paris, 1898.
42562.38.14.27 Adam, Paul. La parade amoureuse. 4e éd. Paris, 1906.
42562.38.14.29 Adam, Paul. Robes rouges. Paris, 1901.
42562.38.14.30 Adam, Paul. La ruse, 1827-1828. Paris, 1903.
42562.38.14.31 Adam, Paul. Le serpent noir. 17e éd. Paris, 1905.
42562.38.14.32 Adam, Paul. Soir. 3e éd. Paris, 1906.
42562.38.14.35 Adam, Paul. Les tentatives passionnées. 5e éd. Paris, 1898.
42562.38.14.36 Adam, Paul. Le triomphe des médiocres. 4e éd. Paris, 1898?
42562.38.14.37 Adam, Paul. Le tropeau de Clarisse. 12e éd. Paris, 1904.
42562.38.14.38 Adam, Paul. Dans l'air qui tremble. Paris, 1916.
42562.38.14.39 Adam, Paul. Le cuivre. Paris, 1896.
42562.38.14.46 Adam, Paul. Le trust. 6e éd. Paris, 1912.
42562.38.14.50 Adam, Paul. L'automne. Paris, 1893.
42562.38.14.55 Adam, Paul. Le temps et la vie: Le lion d'Arras. Paris, 1920.
42562.38.14.60 Adam, Paul. Chair molle; roman naturaliste. Bruxelles, 1885.

42562.38.15 - .38.17 Individual authors, etc. - 1850-1899 - Fiction - Ardel

42562.38.15 Ardel, H. Coeur de sceptique. Paris, 1893.
42562.38.15.25 Ardel, H. Un conte bleu. 29e éd. Paris, 1922.
42562.38.16 Ardel, H. L'été de Guillemette. 6e éd. Paris, 1908.
42562.38.17 Ardel, H. Près du bonheur. N.Y., 1893.

42562.38.19 Individual authors, etc. - 1850-1899 - Fiction - Asselines

42562.38.19 Asselineau, L. La double vie. Paris, 1858.

42562.38.21 Individual authors, etc. - 1850-1899 - Fiction - Aunet

42562.38.21 Aunet, Léonie d'. Un marriage en province. v.1-2. Paris, 1856.

42562.38.35 - .38.51 Individual authors, etc. - 1850-1899 - Fiction - Aimard, G. - Writings

42562.38.39 Aimard, Gustave. L'Araugan. 2d éd. Paris, n.d.
42562.38.40 Aimard, Gustave. Indian chief. London, 1862.
42562.38.41 Aimard, Gustave. The freebooters. London, 1862.
42562.38.41.5 Aimard, Gustave. The white scalper. Philadelphia, 187-.
42562.38.42 Aimard, Gustave. The pirates of the prairies. London, 1861.
42562.38.43 Aimard, Gustave. Les outlaws du Missouri. Paris, n.d.
42562.38.45 Aimard, Gustave. The prairie flower. Philadelphia, 187-?
42562.38.47.4 Aimard, Gustave. L'éclaireur. 4. éd. Paris, 1860.
42562.38.48 Aimard, Gustave. The Indian scout. London, 1910.
42562.38.49 Aimard, Gustave. The red tracks. Philadelphia, 187-?
42562.38.51 Aimard, Gustave. Last of the Incas. London, 18- ?

42562.38.54 Individual authors, etc. - 1850-1899 - Fiction - Arnold

42562.38.54.5 Arnould, Arthur. La revancha de Clodión. Madrid, 1888.

42562.38.55 Individual authors, etc. - 1850-1899 - Fiction - Aubert

42562.38.55 Aubert, Charles. La marieuse. Paris, n.d.

42562.38.80 Individual authors, etc. - 1850-1899 - Fiction - Aubier

42562.38.80 Aubier, F. C'est Venus tout entière. Paris, 1924.

42562.38.90 Individual authors, etc. - 1850-1899 - Fiction - Aulnay

42562.38.90 Aulnay, Louise d'. Le petit bonhomme. Paris, 1882.
42562.38.90.5 Aulnay, Louise d'. Lettres de deux poupées. Paris, 1864.

42562.38.100 Individual authors, etc. - 1850-1899 - Fiction - Auschitzky

42562.38.100 Auschitsky, Daniel. Dans les couloirs du Vatican. Paris, 1897.
42562.38.100.5 Auschitsky, Daniel. L'épiscopat sous le joug. Paris, 1894.

42562.39 Individual authors, etc. - 1850-1899 - Fiction - Cauvain

42562.39 Cauvain, Henry. Les amours bizarres. Paris, 1879.

42562.41 - .50 Individual authors, etc. - 1850-1899 - Fiction - Celières

42562.41 Celières, Paul. Chef-d'oeuvre de Papa Schmeltz. Paris, 1881.
42562.43 Celières, Paul. Une heure à lire. Paris, 1881.
42562.45 Celières, Paul. Quand il pleut. Paris, n.d.
42562.50 Celières, Paul. The startling exploits of Dr. J.B. Luiès. N.Y., 1887.

42562.55 Individual authors, etc. - 1850-1899 - Fiction - Auriol

42562.55 Auriol, G. Histoire de rire. Paris, 1893?

42562.60 Individual authors, etc. - 1850-1899 - Fiction - Allais, A.

42562.60 Allais, Alphonse. Littéralement. Paris, 1952.
42562.60.3 Allais, Alphonse. Oeuvres complètes. Paris, 1964-1970. 11v.
42562.60.5 Allais, Alphonse. Les zèbres. n.p., 1954.
42562.60.6 Allais, Alphonse. A dire et à lire. Paris, 1956.
42562.60.7 Allais, Alphonse. Cinquante cinq contes d'Alphonse Allais. Paris, 1954.
42562.60.8 Allais, Alphonse. La barbe et autres contes. Paris, 1963.
42562.60.15 Allais, Alphonse. Vive la vie! Paris, 1963.
42562.60.20 Allais, Alphonse. Le parapluie de l'escouade. Paris, 1964.
42562.60.25 Allais, Alphonse. Contes. Paris, 1970.
42562.60.80 Jakovsky, Anatole. Alphonse Allais, le tueur à gags. Paris, 1955.

42562.62 Individual authors, etc. - 1850-1899 - Fiction - Alméras

42562.62 Almeras, Henri d'. Le citoyen Machavoine. Paris, 1903.

42562.65 Individual authors, etc. - 1850-1899 - Fiction - Aubanel

42562.65 Aubanel, Henry. Camarguaises. Paris, 1960.
42562.65.5 Aubanel, Henry. Historiettes. Paris, 1895.

42563.5 Individual authors, etc. - 1850-1899 - Fiction - Beaubourg

42563.5.100 Beaubourg, Maurice. Contes pour les assassins. Paris, 1890.
42563.5.110 Beaubourg, Maurice. Les joueurs de boules de Saint-Mandé. Paris, 1899.
42563.5.120 Beaubourg, Maurice. La saison au Bois de Boulogne. Paris, 1896.

42563.8 Individual authors, etc. - 1850-1899 - Fiction - Bac

42563.8 Bac, Ferdinand. La volupté romaine. Paris, 1922.

42563.13 Individual authors, etc. - 1850-1899 - Fiction - Barbé; Babut; etc.

42563.13 Barbé, Benjamin. La desconsolado. 2. ed. Barcelona, 1882.
42563.13.50 Babut, Jules. Félix Batel. v.1-2. La Haye, 1869.

42563.14 Individual authors, etc. - 1850-1899 - Fiction - Barrès, M. - Bibliographies, etc.

42563.14 Pamphlet box. Barrès, Maurice. Writings.
42563.14.5 Barrès, Maurice. Barrès. Paris, 1954.

42563.15 - .18.74 Individual authors, etc. - 1850-1899 - Fiction - Barrès, M. - Writings

42563.15 Barrès, Maurice. Maurice Barrès, recueil de morceaux chosis. Paris, 1914?
42563.15.5 Barrès, Maurice. En regardant au fond descrevasses. Paris, 1917.
42563.15.7A Barrès, Maurice. Le Quartier Latin, ces messieurs, ces dames. Paris, 1888.
42563.15.7B Barrès, Maurice. Le Quartier Latin, ces messieurs, ces dames. Paris, 1888.
42563.16 Barrès, Maurice. La Vierge assassinée. Paris, 1904.

42563.15 - .18.74 Individual authors, etc. - 1850-1899 - Fiction - Barrès, M. - Writings - cont.

42563.16.3 Barrès, Maurice. Oeuvre. v.1-20. Paris, 1965. 10v.
42563.16.4 Bibliothèque Nationale, Paris. Maurice Barrès, 1862-1923. Paris, 1962.
42563.16.5 Barrès, Maurice. Les amitiés françaises. Paris, n.d.
42563.16.6 Barrès, Maurice. Amori et dolori sacrum. Paris, n.d.
42563.16.6.2 Barrès, Maurice. Amori et dolori sacrum. Paris, 1921.
42563.16.7 Barrès, Maurice. Leurs figures. Paris, 1917.
42563.16.7.2 Barrès, Maurice. Leurs figures. Paris, n.d.
42563.16.8 Barrès, Maurice. Du sang, de la volupté et de la mort. Paris, 1910.
42563.16.9 Barrès, Maurice. Un amateur d'âmes. Paris, 1899.
42563.16.10 Barrès, Maurice. L'ennemi des lois. Paris, 1893.
42563.16.11 Barrès, Maurice. L'ennemi des lois. Paris, 1910.
42563.16.12 Barrès, Maurice. Toute licence saufe, contre l'amour. Paris, 1892.
42563.16.13 Barrès, Maurice. La colline inspirée. Paris, 1913.
42563.16.13.5 Mangenot, Eugène. La colline inspirée. Paris, 1913.
42563.16.13.20 Barrès, Maurice. La colline inspirée. Paris, 1922.
42563.16.13.25 Barrès, Maurice. La colline inspirée. Paris, 1922.
42563.16.13.30 Barrès, Maurice. La colline inspirée. Nancy, 1962.
42563.16.13.35 Barrès, Maurice. La colline inspirée. Paris, 1938.
NEDL 42563.16.14 Barrès, Maurice. L'appel au soldat. Paris, 1900.
42563.16.15 Barrès, Maurice. L'appel au soldat. Paris, 1900.
42563.16.20 Barrès, Maurice. Dante, Pascal et Renan. Paris, 1923.
42563.16.25 Barrès, Maurice. Du sang, de la volupté et de la mort. Paris, 1948.
42563.16.32 Barrès, Maurice. Quelques cadences. 2. éd. Paris, 1904.
42563.17 Barrès, Maurice. Colette Baudoche. Paris, n.d.
42563.17.2 Barrès, Maurice. Colette Baudoche. Paris, 1913.
42563.17.12 Barrès, Maurice. Les deracinés. Paris, 1937. 2v.
Htn 42563.17.15* Barrès, Maurice. Comprendre des américains, c'est les aimer et les honorer. n.p., 191-?
Htn 42563.17.16* Barrès, Maurice. Le secteur américain de la bataille. n.p., 191-.
42563.17.20 Barrès, Maurice. Le depart pour la vie. Paris, 1961.
42563.18.7 Barrès, Maurice. Sous l'oeil des barbares. Paris, 1925.
42563.18.10 Barrès, Maurice. Le culte du moi. Examen de trois idéologies. Paris, 1892.
42563.18.23 Barrès, Maurice. The faith of France. Boston, 1918.
42563.18.25 Barrès, Maurice. The sacred hill. N.Y., 1929.
42563.18.30 Barrès, Maurice. N'importe où hors du monde. Paris, 1958.
42563.18.70 Barrès, Maurice. Mes cahiers. Paris, 1929-57. 14v.
42563.18.72 Barrès, Maurice. Mes cahiers, 1896-1923. Paris, 1963.

42563.18.75 - .18.999 Individual authors, etc. - 1850-1899 - Fiction - Barrès, M. - Works about

42563.18.75 Barrès, Maurice. Vingt-cinq années de vie littéraire. Paris, 1908.
42563.18.80 Gillouin, René. Maurice Barrès. Paris, 1907.
42563.18.85 Jacquet, René. Notre maître Maurice Barrès. Paris, 1900.
42563.18.90 Giraud, Victor. Les maîtres de l'heure: Maurice Barrès. Paris, 1922.
42563.18.95 Duhourcau, F. La voix interieure de Maurice Barrès d'après ses cahiers. Paris, 1929.
42563.18.100 Engeraud, R. Aux fontaines de Barrès. Paris, 1929.
42563.18.105 Jary, Jacques. Essai sur l'art et la psychologie de Maurice Barrès. 2. éd. Paris, 1912.
42563.18.109 King, S.M. Maurice Barrès; la pensée allemande et le problème du Rhin. Thèse. Paris, 1933.
42563.18.110 King, S.M. Maurice Barrès; la pensée allemande et le problème du Rhin. Thèse. Paris, 1933.
42563.18.115 Faure-Biguet, Jacques N. Maurice Barrès, son oeuvre, portrait et autographe. Paris, 1924.
42563.18.120 Lesourd, Paul. La terre et les morts de Maurice Barrès. Paris, 1925.
42563.18.125A Bordeaux, Henry. Le retour de Barrès à sa terre. Paris, 1924.
42563.18.125B Bordeaux, Henry. Le retour de Barrès à sa terre. Paris, 1924.
42563.18.126 Bordeaux, Henry. L'appel du divin ou Maurice Barrès en Orient. Paris, 1925.
42563.18.127 Bordeaux, Henry. Maurice Barrès à Pau, 11 décembre 1926. Pau, 1928.
42563.18.130 Bremond, H. Maurice Barrès. Paris, 1924.
42563.18.135 Empaytaz, F. Reconnaissance à Barrès. Paris, 1925.
42563.18.140 Blanc-Péridier, A. La route ascendante de Maurice Barrès. Paris, 1925.
42563.18.145 Cheydleur, F.D. Maurice Barrès. v.1-2. n.p., 1926.
42563.18.150 Curtius, F.R. Maurice Barrès und die geistigen Grundlagen des französischen Nationalismus. Bonn, 1921.
42563.18.160 Thibaudet, A. Les princes lorrains. 12. éd. Paris, 1924.
42563.18.170 Tharaud, Jérôme. Mes années chez Barrès. Paris, 1928.
42563.18.175 Tharaud, Jérôme. Le roman d'Aïssé. Paris, 1946.
42563.18.180 Thieville, H.L. La pensée de Maurice Barrès. Paris, 1934.
42563.18.190 Cohen, G. Le dernier projet littéraire de Maurice Barrès. Abbéville, 1929.
42563.18.205 Mercanton, Jacques. Poésie et religion dans l'oeuvre de Maurice Barrès Lausanne, 1940.
42563.18.210 Garreau, Albert. Barrès, défenseur de la civilization. Paris, 1945.
42563.18.215 Bley, Liselotte. Auffassung und Gestaltung des Problems der Entwurzlung in Maurice Barrès. Heidelberg, 1938.
42563.18.220 Moreau, Pierre. Maurice Barrès. Paris, 1946.
42563.18.225 Blanc-Péridier, A. Maurice Barrès. Paris, 1929.
42563.18.230 Lalou, René. Maurice Barrès. Paris, 1950.
42563.18.235 Frandon, I.M. L'orient de Maurice Barrès. Genève, 1952.
42563.18.236 Frandon, I.M. L'orient de Maurice Barrès. Paris, 1952.
42563.18.238 Frandon, I.M. Assassins et danseurs mystiques. Genève, 1954.
42563.18.239 Frandon, I.M. Assassins et danseurs mystiques. Thèse. Abbéville, 1954.
42563.18.240.2 Boisdeffre, Pierre de. Barrès parmi nous. Paris, 1969.
42563.18.242 Boisdeffre, Pierre de. Maurice Barrès. Paris, 1962.
42563.18.245 Busse, Curt-Ulrich. Das regionalistische Programm bei Maurice Barrès dargestellt nach den Werken seiner Période de l'énergic nacionale. Inaug. Diss. Bochum, 1936.
42563.18.250 Barbier, Joseph. Les sources de La colline inspirée de Maurice Barrès. Nancy, 1957.
42563.18.255 Bauer, Bernhard. Versuch über Inhalt. Stassburg, 1937.
42563.18.260 Gouhier, H. Notre ami Maurice Barrès. Paris, 1928.
42563.18.270 Godfrin, J. Barrès mystique. Neuchâtel, 1962.
42563.18.275 Tharaud, Jérôme. Un grand maître n'est plus. Liège, 1927.
42563.18.276 Suarès, André. Barrès. Paris, 1899.
42563.18.280 Pastourel, Léonce. Egotisme et acceptation. Paris, 1909.
42563.18.285 Massis, Henri. La pensée de Maurice Barrès. Paris, 1909.

42563.18.75 - .18.999 Individual authors, etc. - 1850-1899 - Fiction - Barrès, M. - Works about - cont.

42563.18.290 Bonnefon, Jean de. M. Auguste Maurice Barrès. Paris, 1908.
42563.18.295 Massis, Henri. Barrès et nous. Paris, 1962.
42563.18.300 Zarach, Alphonse, Bibliographie barrésienne, 1881-1948. Paris, 1951.
42563.18.305 Clouard, Henri. La cocarde de Barrès. Paris, 1910.
42563.18.310 Bancquart, Marie Claire. Les écrivains et l'histoire d'après Maurice Barrès. Paris, 1966.
42563.18.315 Mondor, Henri. Maurice Barrès avant le Quartier Latin. Paris, 1956.
42563.18.320 Pilon, Edmond. Maurice barrès, souvenirs, notes et fragments de lettres inédites. Saint-Félicion, 1926.

42563.19 - .20 Individual authors, etc. - 1850-1899 - Fiction - Barrès, M. - Miscellany [Discontinued]

42563.19.5 Barrès, Maurice. Un homme libre. Paris, 1922.
42563.19.15 Barrès, Maurice. Le mystère en pleine lumière. Paris, 1926.
42563.20 Barrès, Maurice. Le jardin de Bérénice. Paris, 1891.
42563.20.5 Barrès, Maurice. Le jardin de Bérénice. Paris, 1927.
42563.20.7 Barrès, Maurice. Le jardin de Bérénice. Paris, 1938.
42563.20.15 Barrès, Maurice. Un jardin sur l'Oronte. 28. éd. Paris, 1922.
42563.20.18 Barrès, Maurice. Pour nos églises. Paris, 1912.
42563.20.25 Barrès, Maurice. Quelques lettres politiques inédites. Paris, 1924.
42563.20.30 Barrès, Maurice. Une enquête aux pays du levant. Paris, 1924. 2v.
42563.20.40 Barrès, Maurice. Pages choisies. Paris, 1915.

42563.21 Individual authors, etc. - 1850-1899 - Fiction - Bazin

42563.21.27 Bazin, René. Etapes de ma vie. Paris, 1936.
42563.21.30 Bazin, René. La terre qui meurt. Paris, 1900.
42563.21.33 Bazin, René. Contes de bonne Perrette. Paris, 1903.
42563.21.34 Bazin, René. Contes de bonne Perrette. Tours, 1951.
42563.21.35 Bazin, René. Redemption. N.Y., 1908.
42563.21.36.25 Bazin, René. De toute son âme. Paris, 1932.
42563.21.39 Bazin, René. Les Noellet. 9. éd. Paris, 1903?
42563.21.40 Bazin, René. This, my son. N.Y., 1909.
42563.21.42 Bazin, René. Donatienne. 31. éd. Paris, 1904.
42563.21.42.5 Bazin, René. Donatienne. Paris, 1907.
42563.21.42.7 Bazin, René. Donatienne. Paris, 1912.
42563.21.45 Bazin, René. Pages choisies. Paris, 1904.
42563.21.46.5 Bazin, René. Pierre and Joseph. N.Y., 1920.
42563.21.47 Bazin, René. Madame Corentine. Paris, 19- .
42563.21.48 Bazin, René. Récits de la plaine et de la montagne. 14. éd. Paris, 1904.
42563.21.49 Bazin, René. Davidée Birot. Paris, 1929.
42563.21.50 Bazin, René. Une tache d'encre. Paris, 1903.
42563.21.51 Bazin, René. Une tache d'encre. 34. éd. Paris, 1904?
42563.21.52 Bazin, René. A blot of ink. London, 1892.
42563.21.53 Bazin, René. Magnificat. Paris, 1931.
42563.21.54 Bazin, René. L'isolée. 29. éd. Paris, 1905.
42563.21.55 Bazin, René. The nun. N.Y., 1908.
42563.21.58 Bazin, René. Le blé qui lève. Paris, 1911?
42563.21.60 Bazin, René. Le mariage de Mademoiselle Gimel. Paris, 1908.
42563.21.61 Bazin, René. Le guide de l'empereur. Paris, 1903.
42563.21.63 Bazin, René. Mémoires d'une veille fille. 18. éd. Paris, 1908.
42563.21.66 Bazin, René. Gingolphe l'abandonné. 11. éd. Paris, 1914.
42563.21.69A Bazin, René. Récits du temps de la guerre. 19. éd. Paris, 1915.
42563.21.69B Bazin, René. Récits du temps de la guerre. 19. éd. Paris, 1915.
42563.21.70 Bazin, René. Stéphanette. 21. éd. Paris, 1923.
42563.21.70.5 Bazin, René. Stéphanette. N.Y., 1936.
42563.21.71 Bazin, René. The barrier. N.Y., 1910.
42563.21.71.5A Bazin, René. La barrière. Paris, 1909.
42563.21.71.5B Bazin, René. La barrière. Paris, 1909.
42563.21.72 Bazin, René. Aujourd'hui et demain. Paris, 1916.
42563.21.73 Bazin, René. La closerie de champdolent. 9. éd. Paris, 1917.
42563.21.74 Bazin, René. Les oberlé. 289. éd. Paris, 1921.
42563.21.74.5 Bazin, René. Les oberlé. Paris, 1901.
42563.21.75 Bazin, René. Les nouveaux oberlé. 15. éd. Paris, 1919.
42563.21.75.5 Bazin, René. Les nouveaux oberlé. 104. éd. Paris, 1919.
42563.21.76A Bazin, René. Il était quatre petits enfants. 14. éd. Paris, 1923.
42563.21.76B Bazin, René. Il était quatre petits enfants. 14. éd. Paris, 1923.
42563.21.76.5 Bazin, René. Il était quatre petits enfants. 54. éd. Paris, 1923.
42563.21.77 Bazin, René. Le roi des archers. Paris, 1929.
42563.21.79 Bazin, René. Baltus le lorrain. Paris, 1926.
42563.21.80 Bersaucourt, A. de. René Bazin. Paris, 1910.
42563.21.82 Mauriac, F. René Bazin. Paris, 1931.
42563.21.84 Hafner, H.K. René Bazin peintre de la vie rurale. Thèse. Paris, 1935.
42563.21.87 Wood, John S. Un aspect du mouvement traditionaliste et social dans la littérature française contemporaine. Thése. Paris, 1934.
42563.21.88 Wood, John S. Un aspect du mouvement traditionaliste et social dans la littérature française contemporaine. Paris, 1934.
42563.21.93 Ruppe, Fritz. Das Problem der Landflucht im heutigen Frankreich und seine Aktualität im Werke René Bazins. Inaug. Diss. Jena, 1936.
42563.21.95 Moreau, Abel. René Bazin et son oeuvre romanesque. Thèse. Auxerre, 1934.
42563.21.97 Moreau, Abel. René Bazin et son oeuvre romanesque. Auxerre, 1934.
42563.21.100 Catta, Tony. Un romancier de vraie France, René Bazin. Paris, 1936.
42563.21.103 Gelson, Mary Aline. An analysis of the realistic elements in the novels of René Bazin. Thesis. Washington, 1942.
42563.21.105 Leighton, J.H. René Bazin et l'Alsace. Strasbourg, 1953.
42563.21.105.2 Leighton, J.H. René Bazin et l'Alsace. Thèse. Strasbourg, 1953.
42563.21.107 Antoine, Louis. Un témoin de l'église: René Bazin. Paris, 1959.
42563.21.115 Galarneau, Joffre. René Bazin et le problème social. Paris, 1966.

Classified Listing

42563.22 Individual authors, etc. - 1850-1899 - Fiction - Bassanville; Beaume; Beaumont; Belot; etc.

42563.22 Bassanville, Anaïs Lebrun. Les deux familles. Tours, 1866.
42563.22.3 Beaume, G. La bourrasque. Paris, 1906.
42563.22.5 Beaumont, André de. Une histoire de cirque. Tours, n.d.
42563.22.9 Le Beaumont, Maurice. Gringalette. Paris, 1904.
42563.22.10 Belot, Adolphe. L'article 47; or Breaking the ban. N.Y., 1872.
42563.22.11 Belot, Adolphe. Folies de jeunesse. Paris, 1890.
42563.22.12 Belot, Adolphe. Mademoiselle Giraud. 32. éd. Paris, 1872.
42563.22.13 Belot, Adolphe. Hélène et Mathildé. Paris, 1874.
42563.22.13.5 Belot, Adolphe. Dacolard et Lubin, suite du parricide. Paris, 1873.
42563.22.14 Belot, Adolphe. Le drame de la rue de la paix. Paris, 1869.
42563.22.14.3 Belot, Adolphe. Le drame de la rue de la paix. 2. éd. Paris, 1872.
42563.22.14.9 Belot, Adolphe. Le parricide. Paris, 1873.
42563.22.14.19 Belot, Adolphe. El secreto terrible. Madrid, 1907.
42563.22.14.24 Belot, Adolphe. Le testament de César Girodot. 12. éd. Paris, 1883.
42563.22.14.25 Belot, Adolphe. Le testament de César Girodot. N.Y., 1884.
42563.22.14.30 Belot, Adolphe. Le testament de César Girodot. N.Y., 1888.
42563.22.75 Beer, Guillaume (Mme.). La voie douloureuse. Paris, 1894.

42563.23 Individual authors, etc. - 1850-1899 - Fiction - Bérenger; Bernard; Berthet; Bertrand, L.; Bloy, L.; etc.

42563.23 Bérenger, Henry. L'effort. Tours, n.d.
42563.23.4 Le Berre, Léon. Fleurs de Basse-Bretagne. Rennes, 1901.
42563.23.6 Bernard, T. Paris secret. Paris, 1933.
42563.23.7.50 Berthet, E.B. La bella tendera. Matanzas, 1843.
42563.23.7.60 Berthet, E.B. The catacombs of Paris. Westminster, 1900.
42563.23.8.5 Bertrand, Louis. La cina. 3. éd. Paris, 1901.
42563.23.8.15 Bertrand, Louis. Le rival de Don Juan. 6. éd. Paris, 1903.
42563.23.8.20 Bertrand, Louis. L'invasion. Paris, 1907.
42563.23.8.25 Bertrand, Louis. Les bains de Phalère. Paris, 1910.
42563.23.8.30 Bertrand, Louis. Mademoiselle de Jessincourt. Paris, 1917.
42563.23.8.35 Bertrand, Louis. Le sang des races. 8. éd. Paris, 1914.
42563.23.8.40 Bertrand, Louis. Pépète et Balthasar. 4. éd. Paris, 1920.
42563.23.8.45 Bertrand, Louis. Pépète et Balthasar. 7. éd. Paris, 1920.
42563.23.8.50 Bertrand, Louis. Jean Perbal, roman. 20. éd. Paris, 1925.
42563.23.8.55 Bertrand, Louis. La nouvelle éducation sentimentale. 13. éd. Paris, 1928.
42563.23.8.60 Bertrand, Louis. Hippolyte porte-couronnes. 2. éd. Paris, 1932.
42563.23.8.65 Bertrand, Louis. Sur la route du sud. 8. éd. Paris, 1936.
42563.23.8.70 Bertrand, Louis. Mes années d'apprentissage. 5. éd. Paris, 1938.
42563.23.8.72 Bertrand, Louis. Mes ambassades. Paris, 1954.
42563.23.8.75 Bertrand, Louis. Jérusalem. 4. éd. Paris, 1939.
42563.23.8.77 Bertrand, Louis. The art of suffering. N.Y., 1936.
42563.23.8.80 Cabeen, David C. The African novels of Louis Bertrand. Thesis. Philadelphia, 1922.
42563.23.8.88 Husson, Odile. Lorraine et Afrique dans l'oeuvre de Louis Bertrand. Nancy, 1966.
42563.23.9 Blanc, Thérèse. Tchelovek. Paris, 1900.
42563.23.10 Blanc, Thérèse. Yette, histoire d'une jeune créole. Paris, 1880.
42563.23.12 Blanquet, Albert. Le parc aux cerfs. Paris, 1876?
42563.23.15 Blondel, Auguste. The revenge of Lucas Helm. Philadelphia, 1898.
42563.23.16.1 Bloy, Léon. Je m'accuse. Paris, 1947.
42563.23.16.2 Bloy, Léon. Le salut par les Juifs. Paris, 1947.
42563.23.16.3 Bloy, Léon. Histoires désobligeantes. Paris, 1947.
42563.23.16.4 Bloy, Léon. Lettres aux Montchal inédites. v. 1-3. Paris, 1947-48.
42563.23.16.5 Bloy, Léon. Le désespéré. v. 1-2. Paris, 1948.
42563.23.16.6 Bloy, Léon. La chevalière de la mort. Paris, 1948.
42563.23.16.7 Bloy, Léon. Le mendiant ingrat. v.1-12. Paris, 1948-49. 6v.
42563.23.16.8 Bloy, Léon. La femme pauvre. v. 1-2. Paris, 1949.
42563.23.16.9 Bloy, Léon. Celle qui pleure. Paris, 1950.
42563.23.16.10 Bloy, Léon. Le pal. part 1. Paris, 1950.
42563.23.17 Bloy, Léon. Pages. Paris, 1951.
42563.23.18 Bloy, Léon. Belluaires et Porchers. Paris, 1905.
42563.23.18.5 Bloy, Léon. Belluaires et Porchers, 1884-1894. Paris, 1965.
42563.23.19 Bloy, Léon. Le mendiant ingrat. Bruxelles, 1898.
42563.23.20 Bloy, Léon. Quatre ans de captivité à Cochons-sur-Marne. 4. éd. Paris, 1921. 2v.
42563.23.20.2 Bloy, Léon. Quatre ans de captivité à Cochons-sur-Marne. 7. éd. v. 1-2. Paris, 1935.
42563.23.20.5 Bloy, Léon. L'invendable. 4. éd. Paris, 1919.
42563.23.20.7 Bloy, Léon. L'invendable. 5. éd. Paris, 1919.
42563.23.21 Bloy, Léon. Le vieux de la montagne. 4. éd. Paris, 1919.
42563.23.21.2 Bloy, Léon. Le vieux de la montagne. 5. éd. Paris, 1919.
42563.23.21.5 Bloy, Léon. Le pèlerin de l'absolu. 4. éd. Paris, 1919.
42563.23.21.10 Bloy, Léon. Propos d'un entrepreneur de démolitions. Paris, 1884.
42563.23.22 Bloy, Léon. Au seuil de l'apocalypse. 5. éd. Paris, 1921.
42563.23.23 Bloy, Léon. La porte des humbles. 4. éd. Paris, 1920.
42563.23.24 Bloy, Léon. Celle qui pleure. Paris, 1908.
42563.23.25 Bloy, Léon. Lettres à sa fiancée. Paris, 1922.
42563.23.26 Bloy, Léon. Lettres à Véronique. Paris, 1933.
42563.23.27 Bloy, Léon. Correspondance. Paris, 1947.
42563.23.28 Bloy, Léon. Lettres intimes. Paris, 1952.
42563.23.29 Bloy, Léon. Lettres à René Martineau. Paris, 1933.
Htn 42563.23.30* Bloy, Léon. Le fils de Louis XVII. 3. éd. Paris, 1900.
42563.23.31 Bloy, Léon. Oeuvres. Paris, 1964. 10v.
42563.23.32 Bloy, Léon. Dans les ténèbres. 2. éd. Paris, 1918.
42563.23.33 Bloy, Léon. Histoires désobligeantes. Monaco, 1947.
42563.23.34 Bloy, Léon. Le symbolisme de l'apparition, 1879-1880. Paris, 1925.
42563.23.35 Bloy, Léon. Un brelan d'excommuniés. Paris, 1889.
42563.23.36 Bloy, Léon. Exégèse des lieux commus. v.1-2. Paris, 1902..
42563.23.37 Bloy, Léon. Le pal. Paris, 1925.
42563.23.40 Bloy, Léon. Mon journal. Paris, 1924. 2v.
42563.23.43 Bloy, Léon. Le désespéré. Paris, 1946.
42563.23.44 Bloy, Léon. Léon Bloy. Paris, 1946.
42563.23.45 Bloy, Léon. Les dernières colonnes de l'église. 3. éd. Paris, 1903.
42563.23.50 Bloy, Léon. La femme pauvre. 31. éd. Paris, 1939.

42563.23 Individual authors, etc. - 1850-1899 - Fiction - Bérenger; Bernard; Berthet; Bertrand, L.; Bloy, L.; etc. - cont.

42563.23.55 Bloy, Léon. Inédits de Léon Bloy. Montréal, 1945.
42563.23.60 Bloy, Léon. Journal. Paris, 1956. 4v.
42563.23.70A Bloy, Léon. Pilgrim of the absolute. N.Y., 1947.
42563.23.70B Bloy, Léon. Pilgrim of the absolute. N.Y., 1947.
42563.23.75 Bloy, Léon. The woman who was poor. N.Y., 1947.
42563.23.76 Bloy, Léon. Sueur de sang, 1870-1871. Paris, 1893.
42563.23.80 Calleye, Hubert. L'âme de Léon Bloy. Paris, 1930.
42563.23.82 Termier, Pierre. Introduction á Léon Bloy. Paris, 1930.
42563.23.85 Carton, Paul. Un héro de Dieu, Léon Bloy. Paris, 1936.
42563.23.87 Seillière, Ernest, Léon Bloy. Paris, 1936.
42563.23.90 Dillinger, W. Das Frankreichbild im Werke Léon Bloys, 1846-1917. Inaug. Diss. Düsseldorf, 1937.
42563.23.92A Béguin, Albert. Léon Bloy l'impatient. Fribourg, 1944.
42563.23.92B Béguin, Albert. Léon Bloy l'impatient. Fribourg, 1944.
42563.23.93 Béguin, Albert. Léon Bloy; a study in impatience. N.Y., 1947.
42563.23.94 Béguin, Albert. Léon Bloy, mystique de la douleur. Paris, 1948.
42563.23.95 Léon Bloy. Neuchâtel, 1944.
42563.23.97 Polimeni, E. Léon Bloy, the pauper prophet. London, 1947.
42563.23.100 Léon Bloy, études. Toulouse, 1944.
42563.23.102 Lefèbvre, Louis. Léon Bloy. Paris, 1946.
42563.23.104 Bollery, Joseph. Léon Bloy. Paris, 1947-53. 3v.
42563.23.106 Langlois, G. Un mendiant de la souffrance, Léon Bloy. Ottawa, 1948.
42563.23.108 Dubois, E.T. Portrait of Léon Bloy. London, 1950.
42563.23.110 Brady, M.R. Thought and style in the works of Léon Bloy. Thesis. Washington, 1945.
42563.23.112 Heppenstall, Rayner. Léon Bloy. Cambridge, 1953.
42563.23.112.2 Heppenstall, Rayner. Léon Bloy. Cambridge, 1954.
42563.23.114 Lory, M.J. La pensée religieuse de Léon Bloy. Thèse. Bruges, 1951.
42563.23.114.5 Lory, M.J. Léon Bloy et son époque. Paris, 1944.
42563.23.116 Martineau, René. Autour de Léon Bloy. Paris, 1926.
42563.23.117 Martineau, René. Un vivant et deux morts. Villiers de l'isle-Adam, 1901.
42563.23.120A Cattaui, G. Léon Bloy. Paris, 1954.
42563.23.120B Cattaui, G. Léon Bloy. Paris, 1954.
42563.23.122 Steinmann, Jean. Léon Bloy. Paris, 1956.
42563.23.123 Soulon, H. Léon Bloy. n.p., n.d. 2 pam.
42563.23.124 Barbeau, Raymond. Un prophète luciferien. Paris, 1957.
42563.23.126 Juin, Hubert. Léon Bloy. Paris, 1957.
42563.23.128 Laquerrière, A. Biblio-iconographie de Léon Bloy. Paris, 1935.
42563.23.130 Pijls, Pieter J.H. La satire littéraire dans l'oeuvre de Léon Bloy. Leiden, 1959.
42563.23.130.2 Pijls, Pieter J.H. La satire littéraire dans l'oeuvre de Léon Bloy. Leiden, 1959.
42563.23.132 Marie Saint-Louis de Gonzague, sister. Léon Bloy face à la critique. Bibliographie critique. Nashua, 1959.
42563.23.135 Martineau, René. Léon Bloy. Paris, 1924.
42563.23.138 Cahiers Léon Bloy. La Rochelle. 1-15,1924-1939 5v.
42563.23.139 Bros, A.M. Léon Bloy à Logny-sur-Marne. Meaux, 1959.
42563.23.140 Meer de Walcheren, P.B.A. van der. Alles is liefde. Brugge, 1960.
42563.23.143 Marches de Provence. Fascicule spécial consacré à Léon Bloy. Marseille, 1912.
42563.23.150 Meer de Walcheren, P.B.A. van der. Rencontres. Bruges, 1961.
42563.23.160 Arrou, Pierre. Les logis de Léon Bloy. Paris, 1931.
42563.23.165 Fumet, Stanislas. Mission de Léon Bloy. Paris, 1935.
42563.23.170 Bohet, Jeanine. Léon Bloy. Paris, 1961.
42563.23.175 Debran, Isabelle. A mon oncle Léon Bloy. La Rochelle, 1934. 2v.
42563.23.180 Mas, Edouard. Léon Bloy, son oeuvre, portrait et autographe. Paris, 1937.
42563.23.185 Petit, Jacques. Léon Bloy. Paris, 1966.
42563.23.190 Fumet, Stanislas. Léon Bloy, captif de l'absolu. Paris, 1967.
42563.23.195 Hager, Ruth E. Léon Bloy et l'évolution du conte cruel. Paris, 1967.
42563.23.200 Bibliothèque Nationale. Léon Bloy. Paris, 1968.
42563.23.205 Loveilhe, Jacques. Léon Bloy, son oeuvre, sa mission. La Rochelle, 1939.
42563.23.210 Dotoli, Giovanni. Situation des études bloyennes. Paris, 1970.

42563.24 Individual authors, etc. - 1850-1899 - Fiction - Boisson

42563.24 Boisson, Firmin. Jean de la lune. Paris, 1887.

42563.26 Individual authors, etc. - 1850-1899 - Fiction - Blocqueville; Bauer; Boissie; etc.

42563.26 Blocqueville, Louise Adélaïde d'Eckmühl. Chrétienne et musulman. Paris, 1861.
42563.26.2 Blocqueville, Louise Adélaïde d'Eckmûhl. Perdita. Paris, 1859.
42563.26.3 Blocqueville, Louise Adélaïde d'Eckmûhl. Les soirées de la villa des jasmins. Paris, 1874. 4v.
42563.26.5 Achille, A. d'. Discorso. Roma, 1864.
Htn 42563.26.10* Bauer, Henry. Une comédienne; scènes de la vie de théâtre. Paris, 1889.
42563.26.10.5 Bauer, Henry. Une comédienne. Paris, 1889.
42563.26.11 Bauer, Henry. Mémoires d'un jeune homme. Paris, 1895.
42563.26.15 Boissie, A. Dragona y escarcela; novela francesa. Habana, 1889.
42563.26.75 Boisonnas, B. (Mme.). Une famille pendant la guerre. Paris, 1877.

42563.27 Individual authors, etc. - 1850-1899 - Fiction - Bosc

42563.27 Bosc, Jean. Le vice marin. Paris, 1897.

42563.28 Individual authors, etc. - 1850-1899 - Fiction - Biart

42563.28 Biart, Lucien. La terre chaude. Paris, n.d.
42563.28.9 Biart, Lucien. Le fleuve d'or. Paris, 1885.
42563.28.11 Biart, Lucien. La terre tempérée. Paris, 1866.
42563.28.13 Biart, Lucien. Le pensativo. Paris, 1884.
42563.28.15 Biart, Lucien. Entre deux océans. Paris, 1883.
42563.28.17 Biart, Lucien. An involuntary voyage. N.Y., 1880.
42563.28.19 Biart, Lucien. Monsieur Pinson. Paris, n.d.
42563.28.21 Biart, Lucien. Aventures d'un jeune naturaliste. Paris, n.d.
42563.28.23 Biart, Lucien. Unac, der Indianer. Reutlingen, n.d.
42563.28.25 Biart, Lucien. Le bizco. Paris, 1867.
42563.28.27 Biart, Lucien. La capitana. Paris, 1880.
42563.28.29 Biart, Lucien. Les clientes. Paris, 1873.
42563.28.31 Biart, Lucien. Entre frères. Paris, n.d.

42563.28 Individual authors, etc. - 1850-1899 - Fiction - Biart - cont.
42563.28.33 Biart, Lucien. Pile et face. 3. éd. Paris, 1870.
42563.28.37 Biart, Lucien. Le secret de José. Paris, 1883.
42563.28.41 Biart, Lucien. Le roi des prairies. Paris, 1884.

42563.30 Individual authors, etc. - 1850-1899 - Fiction - Blandy
42563.30.31 Blandy, Stella. Le petit roi. Paris, 1877.

42563.32 Individual authors, etc. - 1850-1899 - Fiction - Blouet
42563.32.700 Blouët, Paul. Woman and artist. N.Y., 1900.

42563.33 Individual authors, etc. - 1850-1899 - Fiction - Borden
42563.33.100 Bordeu, Charles de. Le dernier maître. Pau, 1970.

42563.34 Individual authors, etc. - 1850-1899 - Fiction - Boissière
42563.34.100 Boissière, A. Clara Bill, danseuse. Paris, 1906.

42563.36 Individual authors, etc. - 1850-1899 - Fiction - Bordeaux
42563.36.20 Bordeaux, Henry. Une doctrine de vie; extraits de l'oeuvre de Henry Bordeaux. Paris, 1920.
42563.36.30 Bordeaux, Henry. La petite mademoiselle. Paris, 1905.
42563.36.32 Bordeaux, Henry. Die kleine Mamsell. N.Y., 1911.
42563.36.35 Bordeaux, Henry. Les Roquevillard. Paris, 1906.
42563.36.37 Bordeaux, Henry. The will to live. N.Y., 1915.
42563.36.40 Bordeaux, Henry. Paysages romanesques. 5. éd. Paris, 1906.
42563.36.46 Bordeaux, Henry. Les yeux qui s'ouvrent. Paris, 1948?
42563.36.48 Bordeaux, Henry. Les yeux qui s'ouvrent. Paris, 1931.
42563.36.49 Bordeaux, Henry. The awakening. N.Y., 1914.
42563.36.50 Bordeaux, Henry. Portraits de femmes et d'enfants. Paris, 1909.
42563.36.55 Bordeaux, Henry. La croisée des chemins. 49. éd. Paris, 1909.
42563.36.59 Bordeaux, Henry. La peur de vivre. Paris, 1961.
42563.36.60.2 Bordeaux, Henry. La peur de vivre. 100. éd. Paris, 1913.
42563.36.60.3 Bordeaux, Henry. La peur de vivre. N.Y., 1926.
X Cg 42563.36.60.5 Bordeaux, Henry. La peur de vivre. Paris, 1931.
42563.36.61 Bordeaux, Henry. The fear of living. N.Y., 1915.
42563.36.65A Bordeaux, Henry. La robe de laine. 59. éd. Paris, 1910.
42563.36.65B Bordeaux, Henry. La robe de laine. Paris, 1910.
42563.36.65.10 Bordeaux, Henry. La robe de laine. Paris, 1910.
42563.36.65.20 Bordeaux, Henry. La robe de laine. Paris, 1947.
42563.36.65.22 Bordeaux, Henry. La robe de laine. Paris, 1957.
42563.36.70A Bordeaux, Henry. La neige sur les pas. Paris, 1912.
42563.36.70B Bordeaux, Henry. La neige sur les pas. Paris, 1912.
42563.36.70.2 Bordeaux, Henry. Nieve sobre las huellas. Paris, 1912.
42563.36.73 Bordeaux, Henry. La neige sur les pas. Paris, 1927.
42563.36.74 Bordeaux, Henry. La neige sur les pas. Paris, 1940.
42563.36.75 Bordeaux, Henry. La nouvelle croisade des enfants. Paris, 1913.
42563.36.80 Bordeaux, Henry. La vie recommence, la résurrection de la chair. Paris, 1920.
42563.36.80.3 Bordeaux, Henry. La vie recommence, la résurrection de la chair. Paris, 1920.
42563.36.80.5 Bordeaux, Henry. La vie recommence, la résurrection de la chair. Paris, 1920.
42563.36.85 Bordeaux, Henry. La vie recommence. La chair et l'esprit. Paris, 1921.
42563.36.85.5 Bordeaux, Henry. La vie recommence. La chair et l'esprit. Paris, 1921.
42563.36.90 Bordeaux, Henry. Ménages d'après guerre. Paris, 1921.
42563.36.94 Bordeaux, Henry. La maison morte. Paris, 1913.
42563.36.95 Bordeaux, Henry. La maison morte. Paris, 1922.
42563.36.96 Bordeaux, Henry. The house that died. N.Y., 1922.
42563.36.100 Bordeaux, Henry. Le fantôme de la rue Michel-Ange. Paris, 1922.
42563.36.105 Bordeaux, Henry. Le lac noir, ou Le sorcier de Myans. Paris, 1922.
42563.36.107 Bordeaux, Henry. Le lac noir, ou Le sorcier de Myans. Paris, 1924.
42563.36.110 Bordeaux, Henry. Yamilé sous les cèdres. Paris, 1923.
42563.36.115 Bordeaux, Henry. Les jeux dangereux. Paris, 1925-26.
42563.36.120 Bordeaux, Henry. Les jeux dangereux. Paris, 1926.
42563.36.125 Bordeaux, Henry. La chartreuse du reposoir. Paris, 1924.
42563.36.125.5 Bordeaux, Henry. La chartreuse du reposoir. Paris, 1924.
42563.36.140 Bordeaux, Henry. Reflets de la montagne. Paris, 1960.
42563.36.150 Bordeaux, Henry. The gardens of Omar. N.Y., 1924.
42563.36.160 Bordeaux, Henry. Andromède et le monstre. Paris, 1928.
42563.36.170 Bordeaux, Henry. Le calvaire de Cimiez. Paris, 1928.
42563.36.180 Bordeaux, Henry. Tuilette. Paris, 1930.
42563.36.190 Bordeaux, Henry. Visages français. Paris, 1930.
42563.36.202 Bordeaux, Henry. La fée de Port-Cross ou La voie sans retour. Paris, 1927.
42563.36.210 Bordeaux, Henry. Ginette. Paris, 1933.
42563.36.220 Bordeaux, Henry. L'amour et le bonheur. Paris, 1925.
42563.36.230 Bordeaux, Henry. Episodes de la vie littéraire. Paris, 1934.
42563.36.240 Bordeaux, Henry. Le maître de l'amour. Paris, 1937.
42563.36.245 Bordeaux, Henry. Le chêne et les roseaux. Paris, 1934.
42563.36.250 Bordeaux, Henry. La cendre chaude. v.1-3. Paris, 1939.
42563.36.255 Bordeaux, Henry. Mémoires secrets du chevalier de Rosaz. Paris, 1958.
42563.36.257 Bordeaux, Henry. Le pays sans ombre. Paris, 1935.
42563.36.260 Bordeaux, Henry. Sous les pins aroles. Paris, 1929.
42563.36.279 Bordeaux, Henry. Le pays natal. 9. éd. Paris, 190-?
42563.36.286 Bordeaux, Henry. La sonate au clair de lune. Paris, 1941.
42563.36.290 Bordeaux, Henry. Amitiées étrangères. Paris, 1933.
42563.36.300 Bordeaux, Henry. Appolline. Paris, 1946.
42563.36.310 Bordeaux, Henry. Cas de conscience. Paris, 1946.
42563.36.315 Bordeaux, Henry. L'amour de la terre et de la maison. Paris, 1960.
42563.36.320 Bordeaux, Henry. Le jeu de massacre. Paris, 1947.
42563.36.330 Bordeaux, Henry. La lumière au bout du chemin. Paris, 1948.
42563.36.340 Bordeaux, Henry. Le parrain. Paris, 1937.
42563.36.350 Bordeaux, Henry. Histoire d'une vie. Paris, 1951. 12v.
42563.36.550 Britsch, Amédée. Henry Bordeaux. Paris, 1906.
42563.36.555 Benoit, Pierre. Henry Bordeaux. Paris, 1931.

42563.37 Individual authors, etc. - 1850-1899 - Fiction - Bourget
42563.37.2.5 Bourget, Paul. Mensonges. Paris, 1890.
42563.37.3 Bourget, Paul. Mensonges. Paris, 1887.
42563.37.4 Bourget, Paul. Mensonges. Paris, 1914.
42563.37.5A Bourget, Paul. Cruelle énigme. Paris, 1885.
42563.37.5B Bourget, Paul. Cruelle énigme. Paris, 1885.
42563.37.6 Bourget, Paul. Un coeur de femme. Paris, 1893.
42563.37.6.10 Bourget, Paul. Un coeur de femme. Paris, 1921.

42563.37 Individual authors, etc. - 1850-1899 - Fiction - Bourget - cont.
42563.37.7 Bourget, Paul. Un crime d'amour. Paris, 1886.
42563.37.7.8 Bourget, Paul. A love crime. Paris, 1935.
42563.37.8.5 Bourget, Paul. Le disciple. Paris, 1901.
42563.37.8.7A Bourget, Paul. Le disciple. Paris, 1911.
42563.37.8.7B Bourget, Paul. Le disciple. Paris, 1911.
42563.37.8.7C Bourget, Paul. Le disciple. Paris, 1911.
42563.37.8.20 Bourget, Paul. The disciple. N.Y., 1901.
42563.37.9 Bourget, Paul. Pastels. Paris, n.d.
42563.37.9.5 Bourget, Paul. Pastels of men. Boston, 1891.
42563.37.9.10 Bourget, Paul. Pastels of men. Boston, 1892.
42563.37.10 Bourget, Paul. Nouveaux pastels. Paris, 1891.
42563.37.11 Bourget, Paul. Physiologie de l'amour moderne. Paris, 1891.
42563.37.11.4 Bourget, Paul. Physiologie de l'amour moderne. Paris, 192-?
42563.37.11.5 Bourget, Paul. Physiologie de l'amour moderne. Paris, 1929.
42563.37.12 Bourget, Paul. La terre promise. Paris, 1892.
42563.37.12.25 Bourget, Paul. The land of promise. N.Y., 1895.
42563.37.13 Bourget, Paul. Poésie 1872-1876, 1876-1882. Paris, n.d. 2v.
42563.37.14A Bourget, Paul. Un scrupule. Paris, 1893.
42563.37.14B Bourget, Paul. Un scrupule. Paris, 1893.
42563.37.15 Bourget, Paul. Etudes et portraits. Paris, 1889. 3v.
42563.37.15.5 Bourget, Paul. Extraits choisis des oeuvres. Boston, 1894.
42563.37.16A Bourget, Paul. Cosmopolis. Paris, 1894.
42563.37.16B Bourget, Paul. Cosmopolis. Paris, 1894.
42563.37.16.2 Bourget, Paul. Cosmopolis. Paris, 1892.
42563.37.16.4 Bourget, Paul. Cosmopolis. N.Y., 1893.
42563.37.16.8 Bourget, Paul. Cosmopolis. Paris, 1905.
Htn 42563.37.17* Bourget, Paul. Un saint. Paris, 1894.
42563.37.17.5 Bourget, Paul. A saint. Boston, 1895.
Htn 42563.37.18* Bourget, Paul. Steeple-chase. Paris, 1894.
42563.37.19 Bourget, Paul. Une idylle tragique. Paris, 1896.
42563.37.20 Bourget, Paul. Voyageuses. Paris, 1897.
42563.37.21 Bourget, Paul. Complications sentimentales. Paris, 1898.
42563.37.21.25 Bourget, Paul. The screen. N.Y., 1901.
42563.37.22 Bourget, Paul. Sa duchesse bleue. Paris, 1898.
42563.37.23 Bourget, Paul. Domestic dramas. N.Y., 1900.
42563.37.24 Bourget, Paul. Le fantôme. Paris, n.d.
42563.37.25 Bourget, Paul. Un homme d'affaires. Paris, n.d.
42563.37.28 Bourget, Paul. Un divorce. Paris, n.d.
42563.37.28.5 Bourget, Paul. Un divorce. Paris, 1904.
42563.37.29A Bourget, Paul. L'émigré. Paris, 1908.
42563.37.29B Bourget, Paul. L'émigré. Paris, 1908.
42563.37.30 Bourget, Paul. Le tribun. Paris, 1911.
42563.37.31 Bourget, Paul. A tragic idyl. N.Y., 1896.
42563.37.32 Bourget, Paul. L'envers du décor. Paris, 1911.
42563.37.33 Bourget, Paul. Recommencements. Paris, 1897.
42563.37.34 Bourget, Paul. Le démon du midi. Paris, 1914. 2v.
42563.37.34.2F Bourget, Paul. Le démon de midi. pts. 1-6. Paris, 1914. 6v.
42563.37.34.7 Bourget, Paul. Le démon de midi. tom.2. Paris, 1929.
42563.37.34.8 Bourget, Paul. Le démon de midi. Paris, 1929.
42563.37.34.15 Bourget, Paul. Le démon de midi. Paris, 1946.
42563.37.35A Bourget, Paul. L'émigré. Paris, 1907.
42563.37.35B Bourget, Paul. L'émigré. Paris, 1907.
42563.37.36A Bourget, Paul. Le sens de la mort. Paris, 1915.
42563.37.36B Bourget, Paul. Le sens de la mort. Paris, 1915.
42563.37.37 Bourget, Paul. Le sens de la mort. Paris, 1916.
42563.37.37.5 Bourget, Paul. The night cometh. N.Y., 1916.
42563.37.38 Bourget, Paul. Lazarine. Paris, 1917.
42563.37.39 Bourget, Paul. Némésis. Paris, 1918.
42563.37.39.5 Bourget, Paul. Némésis. Paris, 1924.
42563.37.40 Bourget, Paul. L'irréparable. 3. éd. Paris, 1885.
42563.37.41 Bourget, Paul. André Cornélis. Paris, 1887.
42563.37.41.5 Bourget, Paul. André Cornélis. Paris, 1903.
42563.37.42 Bourget, Paul. La barricade chronique de 1910. Paris, 1910.
42563.37.43 Bourget, Paul. Anomalies. Paris, 1920.
42563.37.44 Bourget, Paul. Le justicier. Paris, 1919.
42563.37.45 Bourget, Paul. La dame qui a perdu son peintre. Paris, 1910.
42563.37.46 Bourget, Paul. The weight of the name. Boston, 1908.
42563.37.47 Bourget, Paul. Un drame dans le monde. Paris, 1921.
42563.37.48 Bourget, Paul. Laurence Albani. Paris, 1919.
42563.37.50 Bourget, Paul. L'écuyère. Paris, 1921.
42563.37.51 Bourget, Paul. Au service de l'ordre. Paris, 1929.
42563.37.51.2 Bourget, Paul. Au service de l'ordre. ser. 2. Paris, 1933.
42563.37.53 Bourget, Paul. Nouvelles pages de critique et de doctrine. Paris, 1922. 2v.
42563.37.55 Bourget, Paul. La geôle. Paris, 1923.
42563.37.57 Bourget, Paul. L'eau profonde. Les pas dans les pas. Paris, 1902.
42563.37.59 Bourget, Paul. Nos actes nous suivent. pt.1-6. Paris, 1926-27.
42563.37.59.4 Bourget, Paul. Nos actes nous suivent. v.2. Paris, 1927.
42563.37.60 Bourget, Paul. The goal. N.Y., 1924.
42563.37.63 Bourget, Paul. Conflits intimes. Paris, 1925.
42563.37.65 Bourget, Paul. Le danseur mondain. Paris, 1926.
42563.37.68 Bourget, Paul. L'honneur du nom. Paris, 1933.
42563.37.73 Bourget, Paul. On ne voit pas les coeurs. Le soupçon. La vérité délivre. Paris, 1929.
42563.37.75 Bourget, Paul. La vengeance de la vie. Paris, 1930.
42563.37.76 Bourget, Paul. La crise. Paris, 1912.
42563.37.77.15 Bourget, Paul. L'étape. Paris, 1946.
42563.37.78 Bourget, Paul. Coeur pensif ne sait où il va. Paris, 1924.
42563.37.79 Bourget, Paul. Le roman des quatres. Paris, 1923.
42563.37.80 Reggio, A. L'oeuvre de M. Paul Bourget. Paris, 1902.
42563.37.81 Bernonille, G. Paul Bourget. Paris, 1936.
42563.37.83 Grappe, G. Paul Bourget. Paris, 1904.
42563.37.84 Marsan, Eugène. Les cannes de Paul Bourget. Niort, 1909.
42563.37.85 Pamphlet box. Bourget, Paul.
42563.37.86 Autin, Albert. Le disciple de Paul Bourget. Paris, 1930.
42563.37.87 Bowman, E.M. The early novels of Paul Bourget. N.Y., 1925.
42563.37.88 Maurray, C. Triptyque de Paul Bourget, 1895-1900-1923. Paris, 1931.
42563.37.90 Mannoni, Paul. Les idées sociales dans l'oeuvre de Paul Bourget. Thèse. Oran, 1930.
42563.37.92 Börner, M. Die "Conversion" Bourgets. Inaug. Diss. Stettin, 1932.
42563.37.94 Carco, F. Paul Bourget, suivi de pages inédites et de l'histoire du XXXIII fauteuil. Paris, 1932.

42563.37 Individual authors, etc. - 1850-1899 - Fiction - Bourget - cont.

42563.37.96 Rivasso, R. de. L'unité d'une pensée. Paris, 1914.
42563.37.98 Lardeur, F.J. La vérité psychologique et morale dans les romans de M. Paul Bourget. Paris, 1912.
42563.37.100 Selring, Anna L. La pensée de M. Paul Bourget. L'exotisme, 1852-1902. Grenoble, 1933.
42563.37.102 Feuillerat, A. Paul Bourget. Paris, 1937.
42563.37.105 Raffetto, R. L'évolution du roman de Paul Bourget. Thèse. Toulouse, 1938.
42563.37.110 Pelletier, Séverin. La nature et la grâce chez Paul Bourget. Montréal, 1940.
42563.37.112 Correa Pastene, M. Los caminos de Roma. Santiago, 1944.
42563.37.114 Austin, L.J. Paul Bourget, sa vie et son oeuvre jusqu'en 1889. Thèse. Paris, 1940.
42563.37.115 Austin, L.J. Paul Bourget, sa vie et son oeuvre jusqu'en 1889. Paris, 1940.
42563.37.120A Dimnet, E. Paul Bourget. London, 1913.
42563.37.120B Dimnet, E. Paul Bourget. London, 1913.
42563.37.122 Secor, Walter. Paul Bourget and the nouvelle. N.Y., 1948.
42563.37.125 Mansuy, Michel. Un moderne. Besançon, 1961.
42563.37.130 Maurras, Charles. Un jubilé. Liège, 1926.

42563.38 Individual authors, etc. - 1850-1899 - Fiction - Bouvier; Bovet; etc.

42563.38 Bouvier, Alexis. Etienne Marcel. Paris, 1883.
42563.38.2 Bouvier, Alexis. Chansons du peuple. Paris, n.d.
42563.38.5 Bouvier, Alexis. Les créanciers de l'échafaud. 3. éd. Paris, n.d.
42563.38.9 Bouvier, Alexis. Les petites blanchisseuses. Paris, n.d.
42563.38.10 Bouvier, Alexis. La belle grêlée. Paris, 1879.
42563.38.11 Bouvier, Alexis. La grande Iza. Paris, 1878.
42563.38.12 Bouvier, Alexis. Mademoiselle Olympe. Paris, 1880.
42563.38.503 Bovet, M.A. Partie du pied gauche. 5. éd. Paris, 1897.
42563.38.508 Bovet, M.A. Petites rosseries. 5. éd. Paris, 1898.
42563.38.510 Bovet, M.A. A l'assault de la vie. Paris, 1904.
42563.38.517 Bovet, M.A. Noces blanches. 3. éd. Paris, 1936.
42563.38.520 Bovet, M.A. Autour de l'étendard. Paris, 1904.
42563.38.525 Bovet, M.A. Ballons rouges. Paris, 1903.

42563.39 Individual authors, etc. - 1850-1899 - Fiction - Boylesve; Brown; Buet; Carnoy; Carol; Codet; etc.

42563.39.05 Revon, M. René Boylesve. Paris, 1921.
42563.39.07 Corporon-Bédard, Y. La vie provinciale dans l'oeuvre de René Boylesve. Thèse. Toulouse, 1935.
42563.39.09 Hermant, Abel. Discours de la réception à l'académie française. Paris, 1928.
42563.39.015 Le souvenir de René Boylesve. Paris. 1-5,1931-1932 5v.
42563.39.025 Gérard-Gailly, Emile. Notes sur René Boylesve. Paris, 1937.
42563.39.028 Boylesve, René. Varia. Paris, 1936.
42563.39.030 Ménard, Jean. L'oeuvre de Boylesve avec des documents inédits. Paris, 1956.
42563.39.035 Bourgeois, André. La vie de René Boylesve. Genève, 1958.
42563.39.040 Bourgeois, André. René Boylesve et le problème de l'amour. Lille, 1950.
Htn 42563.39.4* Boylesve, René. Discours prononcés. Paris, 1919.
42563.39.5 Boylesve, René. Mlle Cloque. Paris, 1899.
42563.39.10 Boylesve, René. La becquée. Paris, 1901.
42563.39.12 Boylesve, René. La becquée. N.Y., 1925.
42563.39.15 Boylesve, René. Le bel avenir. 3. éd. Paris, 1905.
42563.39.20 Boylesve, René. Mon amour. 8. éd. Paris, 1908.
42563.39.25 Boylesve, René. Le parfum des îles Borromées. Paris, 1908.
42563.39.30 Boylesve, René. Le meilleur ami. Paris, 1909.
42563.39.35 Boylesve, René. Madeleine, jeune femme. 26. éd. Paris, 1912.
42563.39.40 Boylesve, René. La marchande de petits pains. 10. éd. Paris, 1913.
42563.39.45 Boylesve, René. Tu n'es plus rien. Paris, 1917.
42563.39.46 Boylesve, René. You no longer count. N.Y., 1918.
42563.39.50 Boylesve, René. Le bonheur à cinq sous. Paris, 1917.
42563.39.50.6 Boylesve, René. Le bonheur à cinq sous. 6. éd. Paris, 1917.
42563.39.55 Boylesve, René. Le médecin des dames de Néans. Paris, 1919.
42563.39.60 Boylesve, René. Sainte Marie des fleurs. 14. éd. Paris, 1919.
42563.39.65 Boylesve, René. Nyphes dansant avec des satyres. 9. éd. Paris, 1920.
42563.39.67 Boylesve, René. Nyphes dansant avec des satyres. 13. éd. Paris, 1920.
42563.39.70 Boylesve, René. La leçon d'amour dans un parc. 8. éd. Paris, 1920.
42563.39.72 Boylesve, René. Les nouvelles leçons d'amour dans un parc. Paris, 1926.
42563.39.75 Boylesve, René. Alcindor, ou suite à la leçon d'amour. Paris, 1920.
42563.39.80 Boylesve, René. Le dangereux jeune homme. 5. éd. Paris, 1921.
42563.39.85 Boylesve, René. Le carrosse aux deux lézards verts. Paris, 1921.
42563.39.90 Boylesve, René. Elise. 12. éd. Paris, 1921.
42563.39.95 Boylesve, René. La jeune fille bien élevée. 11. éd. Paris, 1921.
42563.39.100 Boylesve, René. L'enfant à la balustrade. Paris, 192-.
42563.39.105 Boylesve, René. Les deux romanciers. Paris, 1926.
42563.39.110 Boylesve, René. Feuilles tombées. Paris, 1927.
42563.39.115 Boylesve, René. Je vous ai désirée un soir. Paris, 192-.
42563.39.130 Boylesve, René. A gentlewoman of France. N.Y., 1916.
42563.39.140 Boylesve, René. Profils littéraires; romanciers et poètes. Paris, 1962.
42563.39.200 Buet, C. Légendes du pays de Savoie. Limoges, 1880.
42563.39.310 Brown, Alphonse. La station aérienne. Paris, 1893.
42563.39.500 Carnoy, E. Henry. La nuit de Noël. Paris, n.d.
42563.39.600 Carol, Jean. Honneur est sauf. Paris, 1892.
42563.39.700 Cénac-Moncaut, J.E. Aquitaine et Languedoc. Paris, 1844. 2v.
42563.39.800 Codet, Louis. Poèmes et chansons. 2. éd. Paris, 1926.
42563.39.805 Codet, Louis. La fortune de Bécot. Paris, 1921.
42563.39.810 Codet, Louis. The fortunes of Bécot. London, 1954.
42563.39.820 Codet, Louis. Louis l'Indulgent. Paris, 1925.
42563.39.830 Codet, Louis. La petite chiquette. 3. éd. Paris, 1925.
42563.39.840 Codet, Louis. César Capéran ou La tradition. Paris, 1918.

42563.40 - .64 Individual authors, etc. - 1850-1899 - Fiction - Greville, Henri (Mme. Durand) - Writings

42563.40 Durand, Alice M.C.F. L'amie. Paris, 1879.
42563.40.5 Durand, Alice M.C.F. A friend. Philadelphia, 1878.
42563.41 Durand, Alice M.C.F. Ariadne. Paris, 1881.
42563.42 Durand, Alice M.C.F. A travers champs. Paris, 1879.
42563.43 Durand, Alice M.C.F. Bonne-Marie. Paris, 1879.
42563.44 Durand, Alice M.C.F. Cité Ménard. Paris, 1880.
42563.44.3 Durand, Alice M.C.F. Un crime. Paris, 1884.
42563.44.4 Durand, Alice M.C.F. Un crime. 12. éd. Paris, 1885.
42563.44.5 Durand, Alice M.C.F. Clairefontaine. 2. éd. Paris, 1886.
Htn 42563.44.5.10* Durand, Alice M.C.F. Clairefontaine. 12. éd. Paris, 189-.
42563.44.6 Durand, Alice M.C.F. Count Xavier. Boston, 1887.
42563.45 Durand, Alice M.C.F. Dosia. Paris, 1880.
42563.45.2 Durand, Alice M.C.F. Dosia. Paris, 1879.
42563.45.2.5 Durand, Alice M.C.F. Dosia. 44. éd. Paris, 1883.
42563.45.3A Durand, Alice M.C.F. Dosia. N.Y., 1890.
42563.45.3B Durand, Alice M.C.F. Dosia. N.Y., 1890.
42563.45.4 Durand, Alice M.C.F. Dosia. 42. éd. Paris, 1883.
42563.45.5 Durand, Alice M.C.F. Dosia. 4. éd. N.Y., 1885.
42563.45.6 Durand, Alice M.C.F. Dosia. Boston, 1881.
42563.46 Durand, Alice M.C.F. Les épreuves de Raïssa. Paris, 1881.
42563.47 Durand, Alice M.C.F. L'expiation de Savéli. Paris, 1879.
42563.47.1 Durand, Alice M.C.F. Saveli's expiation. Philadelphia, 1878.
42563.47.2 Durand, Alice M.C.F. Frankley. Paris, n.d.
42563.48 Durand, Alice M.C.F. L'héritage de Xénie. Paris, 1880.
42563.48.10 Durand, Alice M.C.F. Idylles. Paris, 1885.
42563.48.15 Durand, Alice M.C.F. Idylles. N.Y., 1885.
42563.49 Durand, Alice M.C.F. Les Koumiassine. Paris, 1879.
42563.49.5 Durand, Alice M.C.F. Louis Breuil. Histoire d'un pautouflard. Paris, 1883.
42563.50 Durand, Alice M.C.F. Lucie Rodey. Paris, 1880.
42563.50.2 Durand, Alice M.C.F. La maison de Maureze. Paris, 1879.
42563.51.2 Durand, Alice M.C.F. Madame de Dreux. Paris, 1882.
42563.52 Durand, Alice M.C.F. Marier sa fille. Paris, 1880.
42563.53 Durand, Alice M.C.F. Le moulin frappier. Paris, 1881. 2v.
42563.54 Durand, Alice M.C.F. Le Niania. Paris, 1879.
42563.54.25 Durand, Alice M.C.F. Nouvelles russes. Paris, 1878.
42563.55 Durand, Alice M.C.F. Nouvelles russes. Paris, 1880.
42563.55.2 Durand, Alice M.C.F. Perdue. Paris, 1881.
42563.55.3 Durand, Alice M.C.F. Perdue. Paris, 1882.
42563.55.4 Durand, Alice M.C.F. Perdue. N.Y., 1888.
42563.55.4.5 Durand, Alice M.C.F. Perdue. N.Y., 1891.
42563.55.5 Durand, Alice M.C.F. Le passé. Paris, 1890.
42563.55.10 Durand, Alice M.C.F. L'ingénue. 6. éd. Paris, 1884.
42563.55.15 Durand, Alice M.C.F. Les degrés de l'échelle. 8. éd. Paris, 1881.
42563.55.90 Durand, Alice M.C.F. La princesse Oghérof. 4. éd. Paris, 1878.
42563.56 Durand, Alice M.C.F. La princesse Oghérof. Paris, 1880.
42563.56.15 Durand, Alice M.C.F. La seconde mère. Paris, n.d.
42563.57 Durand, Alice M.C.F. Sonia. Paris, 1881.
42563.58 Durand, Alice M.C.F. Suzanne Normis. Paris, 1880.
42563.59 Durand, Alice M.C.F. Un violon russe. Paris, 1880. 2v.
42563.60 Durand, Alice M.C.F. Mon chien Bop et ses amis. Paris, 1911.
42563.61 Durand, Alice M.C.F. Un mystère. 6. éd. Paris, n.d.
42563.62 Durand, Alice M.C.F. Cleopatra. Boston, 1886.
42563.63 Durand, Alice M.C.F. Dosia's daughter. Boston, 1886.
42563.63.3 Baudin, Pierre. Le siège de Rhodes. Constantinople, 1873.
42563.63.5 Durand, Alice M.C.F. La fille de Dosia. 27. éd. Paris, 1887.
42563.64 Durand, Alice M.C.F. Le voeu de Nadia. Paris, 1883.

42563.66 Individual authors, etc. - 1850-1899 - Fiction - Cantacuzène; Candeze; etc.

42563.66 Catacuzène-Altiéri, Olga. Croquis russes. Paris, 1897.
42563.66.100 Candèze, Ernest. L'aventures d'un grillon. Paris, n.d.

42563.67 Individual authors, etc. - 1850-1899 - Fiction - Chablas

42563.67.50 Chablas, F. Deux nouvelles neuchâteloises. Le Locle, 1876.

42563.68 Individual authors, etc. - 1850-1899 - Fiction - Chabot

42563.68 Cabot, Adrien. Le marquis de Saint-Etienne. Paris, 1892.

42563.70 Individual authors, etc. - 1850-1899 - Fiction - Chabrillan

42563.70 Chabrillan, Celeste. Mémoires de Célèste Mogador. Paris, 1858.
42563.70.5 Chabrillan, Celeste. Daughter of Paris. London, 1961.

42563.71 Individual authors, etc. - 1850-1899 - Fiction - Challamel

42563.71 Challamel, August. Souvenirs d'un hugolâtre; la génération de 1830. Paris, 1885.

42563.72 Individual authors, etc. - 1850-1899 - Fiction - Champceix

42563.72 Champceix, Léodile Béra de. Aline-Ali. Paris, 1869.
42563.72.5 Champceix, Léodile Béra de. Une veille fille. Paris, 1864.
42563.72.9 Champceix, Léodile Béra de. L'idéal au village par André Léo. Paris, 1865.
42563.72.15 Champceix, Léodile Béra de. Jacques Galéron. Paris, 1865.
42563.72.20 Champceix, Léodile Béra de. Les deux filles de monsieur Plichon. Paris, 1865.
42563.72.31 Champceix, Léodile Béra de. Un divorce. Paris, 1869.

42563.80 Individual authors, etc. - 1850-1899 - Fiction - Champsaur

42563.80 Champsaur, Félicien. Le semeur d'amour, roman hindou. Paris, 1902.
42563.80.100 Champsaur, Félicien. Dinah Samuel. Paris, 1905.
42563.80.110 Champsaur, Félicien. Pierrot et sa conscience. Paris, 1896.
42563.80.120 Champsaur, Félicien. Les éreintés de la vie. Paris, 1888.

42563.89 Individual authors, etc. - 1850-1899 - Fiction - Bourges, E.

42563.89.30 Bourges, Elémir. Le crépuscule des dieux. Paris, 1950.
42563.89.33 Bourges, Elémir. La nef. Paris, 1940.
42563.89.36 Bourges, Elémir. Elémir Bourges. Paris, 1962.
42563.89.40 Bourges, Elémir. Sous la hache. Paris, 1929.
42563.89.45 Bourges, Elémir. Les oiseaux s'envolent et les fleurs tombent. Paris, 1964.
42563.89.80 Lebois, André. Les tendences du symbolisme à travers l'oeuvre d'Elémir Bourges. Thèse. Paris, 1952.
42563.89.85 Schwab, Raymond. La vie d'Elémir Bourges. Paris, 1948.

42564.1 Individual authors, etc. - 1850-1899 - Fiction - Capus
42564.1.9 Capus, Alfred. Qui perd gagne. Paris, 1900.

42564.3 - .54 Individual authors, etc. - 1850-1899 - Fiction - Champfleury (J. Fleury) - Writings
42564.3 Fleury, Jules. Les amoureux. Paris, 1862.
42564.5 Fleury, Jules. Les aventures de mademoiselle Mariette. Paris, 1863.
42564.6 Fleury, Jules. La belle Paule. Paris, 1867.
42564.7 Fleury, Jules. Les bourgeois de Molinchart. Paris, 1878.
42564.8 Fleury, Jules. Les chats. Paris, 1870.
42564.9 Fleury, Jules. Chien-caillou. Paris, 1860.
42564.11 Fleury, Jules. Les demoiselles Tourangeau. Paris, 1864.
42564.13 Fleury, Jules. Les enfants. Paris, 1872.
42564.13.25 Fleury, Jules. Gazette de Champfleury. v.1-2. Paris, 1856.
42564.18 Fleury, Jules. Histoire de l'imagerie populaire. Paris, 1869.
42564.20 Fleury, Jules. L'hôtel des commissaires-priseurs. Paris, 1867.
42564.23 Fleury, Jules. La mascarade de la vie parisienne. Paris, 1861.
42564.25 Fleury, Jules. Monsieur de Boisdhyver. Paris, 1864.
42564.27 Fleury, Jules. Les premiers beaux jours. Paris, 1858.
Htn 42564.28* Fleury, Jules. Le réalisme. Paris, 1857.
42564.30 Fleury, Jules. Les sensations de Josquin. Paris, 1859.
42564.31 Fleury, Jules. Souvenirs des funambules. Paris, 1859.
42564.32 Fleury, Jules. La succession de Camus. Paris, 1864.
42564.34 Fleury, Jules. L'usurier Blaizot. Paris, 1858.
42564.35 Fleury, Jules. Le violon de faience. Paris, n.d.
42564.39 Fleury, Jules. Les aventures de mademoiselle Mariette. Paris, 1859.
42564.40 Fleury, Jules. La petite rose. Paris, 1877.
42564.41 Fleury, Jules. Les bourgeois de Molinchart. Paris, 1856.
42564.44 Fleury, Jules. Les excentriques. Paris, n.d.
42564.47 Fleury, Jules. Madame Eugenio. Paris, 1874.
42564.50 Fleury, Jules. Le secret de M. Ladureau. Paris, 1875.
42564.52 Fleury, Jules. Grandeur et décadence d'une serinette. Paris, 1857.
42564.54 Fleury, Jules. Souvenirs et portraits de jeunesse. Paris, 1872.

42564.55 Individual authors, etc. - 1850-1899 - Fiction - Champfleury (J. Fleury) - Works about
42564.55.9 Fleury, Jules. Un coin de littérature sous le second empire, Sainte-Beuve et Champfleury. Paris, 1908.
42564.55.15 Händel, H. Champfleury, sein Leben und Werk. Inaug. Diss. Borna, 1935

42564.56 Individual authors, etc. - 1850-1899 - Fiction - Chapuis
42564.56 Chapuis, Ernest. Récits et légendes de Franche-Comté. Paris, 1885.

42565.1 - .47 Individual authors, etc. - 1850-1899 - Fiction - Cherbuliez - Writings
42565.1 Pamphlet box. Cherbuliez, Victor.
42565.4 Cherbuliez, Victor. L'aventure de Ladislas Bolski. Paris, 1870.
42565.4.5 Cherbuliez, Victor. L'aventure de Ladislas Bolski. 5. éd. Paris, 1879.
42565.4.7 Cherbuliez, Victor. L'aventure de Ladislas Bolski. 7. éd. Paris, 1883.
42565.5 Cherbuliez, Victor. Amours fragiles. Paris, 1880.
42565.6 Cherbuliez, Victor. Après fortune faite. Paris, 1896.
42565.7A Cherbuliez, Victor. Un cheval de Phidias. Paris, 1864.
42565.7B Cherbuliez, Victor. Un cheval de Phidias. Paris, 1864.
42565.8 Cherbuliez, Victor. La bête. Paris, 1907.
42565.8.15 Cherbuliez, Victor. La bête. Paris, 1929.
42565.9 Cherbuliez, Victor. Le comte Kostia. Paris, 1872.
42565.9.3 Cherbuliez, Victor. Le comte Kostia. Paris, 1863.
42565.9.4 Cherbuliez, Victor. Le comte Kostia. 10. éd. Paris, 1883.
42565.9.5A Cherbuliez, Victor. Le comte Kostia. Paris, 1910.
42565.9.5B Cherbuliez, Victor. Le comte Kostia. Paris, 1910.
42565.9.20 Cherbuliez, Victor. La vocation du comte Ghislain. Paris, 1888.
42565.10 Cherbuliez, Victor. La vocation du comte Ghislain. 8. éd. Paris, 1906.
42565.12 Cherbuliez, Victor. Etudes de littéture et d'art. Paris, 1873.
42565.13 Cherbuliez, Victor. La ferme du Choquard. Paris, 1883.
42565.13.2 Cherbuliez, Victor. La ferme du choquard. Paris, 1883.
42565.14 Cherbuliez, Victor. La fiancé de mademoiselle Saint-Maur. Paris, 1876.
42565.14.3 Cherbuliez, Victor. Le fiancé de mademoiselle Saint-Maur. 3. éd. Paris, 1876.
42565.16 Cherbuliez, Victor. Le grand oeuvre. Paris, 1867.
42565.17 Cherbuliez, Victor. L'idée de Jean Têterol. Paris, 1880.
42565.17.1 Cherbuliez, Victor. L'idée de Jean Têterol. 3. éd. Paris, 1878.
42565.17.3 Cherbuliez, Victor. L'idée de Jean Têterol. 7. éd. Paris, 1890.
42565.17.5 Cherbuliez, Victor. Jacquine Vanesse. Paris, 1898.
42565.18 Cherbuliez, Victor. Hommes et choses du temps présent. Paris, 1883.
42565.19A Cherbuliez, Victor. Meta Holdenis. Paris, 1873.
42565.19B Cherbuliez, Victor. Meta Holdenis. Paris, 1873.
42565.19.3 Cherbuliez, Victor. Meta Holdenis. N.Y., 1877.
42565.21A Cherbuliez, Victor. Miss Rovel. Paris, 1877.
42565.21B Cherbuliez, Victor. Miss Rovel. Paris, 1877.
42565.21.3 Cherbuliez, Victor. Miss Rovel. Boston, 1875.
42565.21.20 Cherbuliez, Victor. Noirs et rouges. Paris, 1881.
42565.22 Cherbuliez, Victor. Noirs et rouges. 5. éd. Paris, 1881.
42565.22.3 Cherbuliez, Victor. Noirs et rouges. 6. éd. Paris, 1882.
42565.22.4 Cherbuliez, Victor. Saints and sinners. N.Y., 1882.
42565.22.5 Cherbuliez, Victor. Oliver Maugant. 9. éd. Paris, 1910.
42565.22.9 Cherbuliez, Victor. Paule Méré. N.Y., 1864.
42565.23 Cherbuliez, Victor. Prosper Randoce. Paris, 1868.
42565.24 Cherbuliez, Victor. Paule Méré. Paris, 1865.
42565.26 Cherbuliez, Victor. La revanche de Joseph Noirel. Paris, 1872.
42565.26.5 Cherbuliez, Victor. La revanche de Joseph Noirel. 4. éd. Paris, 1882.
42565.26.8 Cherbuliez, Victor. La revanche de Joseph Noirel. Paris, 1928.
42565.26.10 Cherbuliez, Victor. Joseph Noirel's revenge. N.Y., 1872.
42565.27 Cherbuliez, Victor. Une gageure. Paris, 1890.
42565.27.5 Cherbuliez, Victor. Une gageure. 6. éd. Paris, 1890.

42565.1 - .47 Individual authors, etc. - 1850-1899 - Fiction - Cherbuliez - Writings - cont.
42565.28 Cherbuliez, Victor. Le roman d'une honnête femme. Paris, 1868.
42565.28.3 Cherbuliez, Victor. Le roman d'une honnête femme. Paris, 1866.
42565.28.15 Cherbuliez, Victor. Le roman d'une honnête femme. Paris, 1929.
42565.31 Cherbuliez, Victor. Samuel Brohl et Cie. Paris, 1880.
42565.31.2 Cherbuliez, Victor. Samuel Brohl et Cie. Paris, 1877.
42565.31.5 Cherbuliez, Victor. Samuel Brohl and company. N.Y., 1877.
42565.31.7 Cherbuliez, Victor. Samuel Brohl and company. N.Y., 1902. 2v.
42565.31.8 Cherbuliez, Victor. Samuel Brohl et Cie. 9. éd. Paris, 1907.
42565.32 Cherbuliez, Victor. Le secret du précepteur. Paris, 1893.
42565.40 Cherbuliez, Victor. Count Kostia. N.Y., 1873.
42565.43 Cherbuliez, Victor. Le prince Vitale. Paris, 1864.
42565.45 Cherbuliez, Victor. Prosper. N.Y., 1874.
42565.47 Cherbuliez, Victor. Romance of an honest woman. Boston, 1874.
42565.47.35 Cherbuliez, Victor. The wish of his life; a novel. London, 1878. 2v.

42565.48 Individual authors, etc. - 1850-1899 - Fiction - Cherbuliez - Works about
42565.48.11 Istrati, Marie Anne. Victor Cherbuliez et le cosmopolitisme. Paris, 1937.
42565.48.12 Celières, A. Victor Cherbuliez::romancier, publiciste, philosophe. Thèse. Paris, 1936.

42565.50 Individual authors, etc. - 1850-1899 - Fiction - Chéri, M.
42565.50 Chéri-Marian. Les maléfices du diable. Paris, 1867.

42565.53 Individual authors, etc. - 1850-1899 - Fiction - Chevalet
42565.53 Chevalet, E. Mil huit cent quarante-huit. Paris, 1878.

42565.54 Individual authors, etc. - 1850-1899 - Fiction - Cladel, L. - Works about
42565.54.225 Ingersoll, J.D. Les romans régionalistes de Léon Cladel. Thèse. Toulouse, 1931.
42565.54.250 Pamphlet box. Léon Cladel.
42565.54.265 Cladel, Judith. La vie de Léon Cladel. Paris, 1905.

42565.55 Individual authors, etc. - 1850-1899 - Fiction - Cladel, L. - Writings
42565.55.5 Cladel, Léon. L'ancien. Paris, 1889.
42565.55.10 Cladel, Léon. Mes paysans. Le bouscassié. Paris, 1869.
42565.55.15 Cladel, Léon. Les va-nu-pieds. Paris, 1881.
42565.55.20 Cladel, Léon. Kerkader garde-barrière. Paris, 1884.
42565.55.25 Cladel, Léon. La fête votive de Saint-Bartholomée Porte-Glaive. Paris, 1882.
42565.55.30 Cladel, Léon. Titi Föyssac IV dit la république et la chrétienté. Paris, 1886.
42565.55.35 Cladel, Léon. N'a-qu'un-oeil. Paris, 1887.
42565.55.40 Cladel, Léon. Urbains et ruraux. Paris, 1890.
42565.55.45 Cladel, Léon. Ompdrailles le tombeau-des-lutteurs. Paris, 1891.
42565.55.50 Cladel, Léon. Bonshommes. Paris, 1879.
42565.55.54 Cladel, Léon. Crête-rouge. Paris, 1880.
42565.55.60 Cladel, Léon. Par devant notaire. Bruxelles, 1880.
42565.55.64 Cladel, Léon. L'amour romantique. Paris, 1882.
42565.55.70 Cladel, Léon. Pierre patient. Paris, 1883.
42565.55.75 Cladel, Léon. Léon Cladel et sa kyrielle de chiens. Paris, 1885.
42565.55.80 Cladel, Léon. Celui de la croix-aux-boeufs. Paris, 1875.
42565.55.84 Cladel, Léon. Mi-diable. Paris, 1886.
42565.55.90 Cladel, Léon. Gueux de marque. 2. éd. Paris, 1887.
42565.55.94 Cladel, Léon. Effigies d'inconnus. Paris, 1888.
42565.55.100 Cladel, Léon. Raca. Paris, 1888.
42565.55.105 Cladel, Léon. Juive-errante. Paris, 1897.
42565.55.109 Cladel, Léon. Seize morceaux de litterature. Paris, 1889.
42565.55.115 Cladel, Léon. Les martyrs ridicules. Paris, 1862.
42565.55.120 Cladel, Léon. Petits cahiers. Paris, 1885.
42565.55.125 Cladel, Léon. Le deuxième mystère de l'incarnation. 4. éd. Paris, 1883.

42565.56 - .57 Individual authors, etc. - 1850-1899 - Fiction - Constant, A. - Writings
42565.56 Constant, A. La dernière incarnation. Paris, 1846.
42565.57 Constant, A. The last incarnation. Gospel legends. Boston, 1848.
42565.57.5 Constant, A. The last incarnation. Gospel legends. N.Y., 1848.
42565.57.20 Constant, A. Eliphas Lévi. 1. éd. Paris, 1969.
42565.57.50 Constant, A. Les trois malfaiteurs. Paris, 1847.
42565.57.53 Constant, A. La mère de Dieu. Paris, 1844.

42565.59 Individual authors, etc. - 1850-1899 - Fiction - Comminges, M.A.
42565.59 Commings, Marie Aimery. Le voluptueux voyage. Paris, 1906.

42565.62 - .64 Individual authors, etc. - 1850-1899 - Fiction - Corday, M. - Writings
42565.62 Corday, Michel. Mariage de demain. Paris, 1908.
42565.63 Corday, Michel. Un remous, nouvelle. Paris, 1914.
42565.64 Corday, Michel. En libre grâce; nouvelle. Paris, 1921.
42565.64.15 Corday, Michel. Des histoires. Paris, 1925.

42565.70 - .75 Individual authors, etc. - 1850-1899 - Fiction - Favre de Coulevain - Writings
42565.70 Favre de Coulevain, Hélène. Eve victorieuse. Paris, 1904.
42565.70.3 Favre de Coulevain, Hélène. Eve victorieuse. Paris, 1900.
42565.70.5 Favre de Coulevain, Hélène. Eve victorieuse. Paris, 19- ?
42565.70.6 Favre de Coulevain, Hélène. Eve triumphant. N.Y., 1902.
42565.70.8 Favre de Coulevain, Hélène. Eve triumphant. N.Y., 1912.
42565.71 Favre de Coulevain, Hélène. L'île inconnue. Paris, 1906.
42565.71.10 Favre de Coulevain, Hélène. L'île inconnue. 174. éd. Paris, 1920.
42565.71.50 Favre de Coulevain, Hélène. The unknown isle. London, 1911.
42565.72 Favre de Coulevain, Hélène. Noblesse américaine. Paris, 1906.
42565.72.2 Favre de Coulevain, Hélène. Noblesse américaine. 61. éd. Paris, 1911?
42565.72.3 Favre de Coulevain, Hélène. Noblesse américaine. 66. éd. Paris, 1912.

Classified Listing

42565.70 - .75 Individual authors, etc. - 1850-1899 - Fiction - Favre de Coulevain - Writings - cont.

42565.72.4 Favre de Coulevain, Hélène. American nobility. N.Y., 1897.
42565.72.5A Favre de Coulevain, Hélène. American nobility. N.Y., 1913.
42565.72.5B Favre de Coulevain, Hélène. American nobility. N.Y., 1913.
42565.72.6 Favre de Coulevain, Hélène. Nobleza americana. Paris, 1920.
42565.72.33 Favre de Coulevain, Hélène. Sur la branche. 126. éd. Paris, 1903.
42565.72.35 Favre de Coulevain, Hélène. Sur la branche. 145. éd. Paris, 1903.
42565.73 Favre de Coulevain, Hélène. Sur la branche. Paris, n.d.
42565.73.5A Favre de Coulevain, Hélène. On the branch. N.Y., 1910.
42565.73.5B Favre de Coulevain, Hélène. On the branch. N.Y., 1910.
42565.74A Favre de Coulevain, Hélène. Au coeur de la vie. 69. éd. Paris, 1908.
42565.74B Favre de Coulevain, Hélène. Au coeur de la vie. 69. éd. Paris, 1908.
42565.74.5 Favre de Coulevain, Hélène. The heart of life. N.Y., 1912.
42565.75 Favre de Coulevain, Hélène. Le roman merveilleux. Paris, n.d.
42565.75.10 Favre de Coulevain, Hélène. The wonderful romance. N.Y., 1914.

42565.100 Individual authors, etc. - 1850-1899 - Fiction - Courtois

42565.100 Courtois, Edgar. Cancans de plage. Paris, 1886.

42566.3 - .13 Individual authors, etc. - 1850-1899 - Fiction - Craven, P. - Writings

42566.3 Craven, Pauline. Adélaide Capece minutolo. Paris, 1870.
42566.3.5 Craven, Pauline. Adélaide Capece minutolo. 9. éd. Paris, 1882.
42566.5 Craven, Pauline. Anne Séverin. Paris, 1868.
42566.6.2 Craven, Pauline. Le mot de l'énigme. 2. éd. Paris, 1874.
42566.7 Craven, Pauline. Eliane. Paris, 1882.
42566.8 Craven, Pauline. Eliane. v.1-2. Paris, 1882.
42566.10 Craven, Pauline. Récit d'une soeur. Paris, 1872. 2v.
42566.10.3 Craven, Pauline. Récit d'une soeur. 26. éd. Paris, 1873. 2v.
42566.13 Craven, Pauline. Fleurange. N.Y., 1873.
42566.13.5 Craven, Pauline. Fleurange. tom. 1-2. 10. éd. Paris, 1873.

42566.14 Individual authors, etc. - 1850-1899 - Fiction - Craven, P. - Works about

42566.14 Pamphlet box. Craven, Pauline.
42566.14.5 Bishop, Maria Catherine. Madame Craven née La Ferronays. Paris, 1897.

42566.15 Individual authors, etc. - 1850-1899 - Fiction - Danville; Darzens; etc.

42566.15 Danville, Gaston. Les infinis de la chair. Paris, 1892.
42566.15.5 Darzens, Rodolphe. L'amante du Christ. Paris, 1888.
42566.15.9 Darzens, Rodolphe. Le roman d'un clown. Paris, 1898.
42566.15.100 Dallard, Charles. Le batard du roi. Paris, 186-?

42566.16 Individual authors, etc. - 1850-1899 - Fiction - Daudet, A. - Biography and criticism

42566.16 Gerstmann, A. Alphonse Daudet. Berlin, 1883.
42566.16.4 Sherard, R.H. Alphonse Daudet. London, 1894.
42566.16.9 Burns, Mary. La langue d'Alphonse Daudet. Thèse. Paris, 1916.
42566.16.10 Albalat, A. L'amour chez Alphonse Daudet. 3. éd. Paris, 1884.
42566.16.12 Bonnet, B. Le "baile" Alphonse Daudet. Paris, 1912.
42566.16.14 Saylor, G.R. Alphonse Daudet as a dramatist. Diss. Philadelphia, 1940.
42566.16.15 Mülbrecht, K. Die Dramatisierungen der daudetschen Romane. Inaug. Diss. Königsburg, 1916.
42566.16.17 Wenzel, D. Der literarische Impressionismus dargestellt an der Prosa Alphonse Daudets. Inaug. Diss. München, 1928.
42566.16.25 Le Roux, H. Notre patron, Alphonse Daudet. Paris, 1888.
42566.16.30 Lancier, E. Kind und junger Mensch in den Werken Alphonse Daudets. Inaug. Diss. Bochum, 1935.
42566.16.35 A. Daudet, 1840-1897. Paris, 1908?
42566.16.40 Kroff, Alexander. Alphonse Daudet et la Provence. Thèse. Paris, 1936.
42566.16.45 Fricker, E. Alphonse Daudet et la société au second empire. Paris, 1937.
42566.16.50 Ashlemann, L.A. La société française d'après l'oeuvre d'Alphonse Daudet. Thèse. Paris, 1910.
42566.16.55 Martinet, Y. Alphonse Daudet (1840-1897). Gap, 1940.
42566.16.75A Daudet, Léon. Quand vivait mon père; souvenirs inédits sur Alphonse Daudet. 11. éd. Paris, 1940.
42566.16.75B Daudet, Léon. Quand vivait mon père; souvenirs inédits sur Alphonse Daudet. 11. éd. Paris, 1940.
42566.16.85 Daudet, Lucien. Vie d'Alphonse Daudet. 17. éd. Gallinard, 1944.
42566.16.90 Clogenson, Y.E. Alphonse Daudet. Paris, 1946.
42566.16.95 Benoit-Guyod, G. Alphonse Daudet. Paris, 1947.
42566.16.100 Daudet, Léon. Alphonse Daudet. To which is added the Daudet family. Boston, 1898.
42566.16.105 Auriant (pseud.). Quatre héros d'Alphonse Daudet. Paris, 1948.
42566.16.110 Dobie, G. Alphonse Daudet. London, 1949.
42566.16.115A Bornecque, J.H. Les années d'apprentissage d'Alphonse Daudet. Paris, 1951.
42566.16.115B Bornecque, J.H. Les années d'apprentissage d'Alphonse Daudet. Paris, 1951.
42566.16.120 Jolly, Maria. Die Stilmittel Alphonse Daudets in der Schilderung der Provence. Wertheim am Main, 1931.
42566.16.125 Dambska-Prokop, W. Le style indirect libre dans la prose narrative d'Alphonse Daudet. Krakow, 1960.
42566.16.130 Beaume, Georges. Les lettres de mon moulin d'Alphonse Daudet. Paris, 1929.
42566.16.140 Michel, L. Le langage méridinal dans l'oeuvre d'Alphonse Daudet. Paris, 1961.
42566.16.145 Die Pseudogenres bei Alphonse Daudet. Inaug. Diss. Borna, 1906.
42566.16.150 Sachs, Murray. The career of Alphonse Daudet. Cambridge, 1965.
42566.16.155 Lestienne, Pierre. Un regard sur Alphonse Daudet. Roubaix, 1902.

42566.16 Individual authors, etc. - 1850-1899 - Fiction - Daudet, A. - Biography and criticism - cont.

42566.16.160 Degoumois, Léon. L'Algérie d'Alphonse Daudet. Genève, 1922.

42566.17 Individual authors, etc. - 1850-1899 - Fiction - Daudet, A. - Complete and Selected works

42566.17 Brivois, Jules. Essai de bibliographie des oeuvres de Daudet. Paris, 1895.
42566.17.5 Pamphlet box. Daudet, Alphonse.
42566.17.9 Daudet, Alphonse. Pages choisies des grands écrivains. 6. éd. Paris, 1913.
42566.17.40A Daudet, Alphonse. The works of Alphonse Daudet. Boston, 1898-1900. 24v.
42566.17.40B Daudet, Alphonse. The works of Alphonse Daudet. Boston, 1898-1900. 24v.
42566.17.45A Daudet, Alphonse. Works. N.Y., 1929.
42566.17.45B Daudet, Alphonse. Works. N.Y., 1929.
42566.17.48A Daudet, Alphonse. Alphonse Daudet. N.Y., 1903.
42566.17.48B Daudet, Alphonse. Alphonse Daudet. N.Y., 1903.
42566.17.50A Daudet, Alphonse. Alphonse Daudet. N.Y., 1903.
42566.17.50B Daudet, Alphonse. Alphonse Daudet. N.Y., 1903.
42566.17.100A Daudet, Alphonse. Morceaux choisis d'Alphonse Daudet. Boston, 1894.
42566.17.100B Daudet, Alphonse. Morceaux choisis d'Alphonse Daudet. Boston, 1894.
42566.17.250 Daudet, Alphonse. Memories of a man of letters. Boston, 1900.
42566.17.255 Daudet, Alphonse. Memories of a man of letters. N.Y., 1900.

42566.18 - .999 Individual authors, etc. - 1850-1899 - Fiction - Daudet, A. - Individual works

42566.18 Daudet, Alphonse. Les amoureuses. Paris, 1876.
42566.18.5 Daudet, Alphonse. Les amoureuses. Paris, 189-?
42566.19.5 Daudet, Alphonse. Aventures prodigieuses de Tartarin. Paris, 1886.
42566.19.7 Daudet, Alphonse. Tartarin de Tarascon. Paris, 1887.
42566.19.7.10 Daudet, Alphonse. Tartarin de Tarascon. Paris, 1887.
42566.19.7.50 Daudet, Alphonse. Tartarin de Tarascon. n.p., 1887.
42566.19.8A Daudet, Alphonse. Tartarin of Tarascon. London, 1887.
42566.19.8B Daudet, Alphonse. Tartarin of Tarascon. London, 1887.
42566.19.8.25 Daudet, Alphonse. Tartarin de Tarascon. Boston, 1911.
42566.19.8.65 Daudet, Alphonse. Tartarin de Tarascon. London, 1906.
42566.19.8.70 Daudet, Alphonse. Tartarin de Tarascon. Paris, 1914.
42566.19.8.74A Daudet, Alphonse. Tartarin de Tarascon. Boston, 1928.
42566.19.8.74B Daudet, Alphonse. Tartarin de Tarascon. Boston, 1928.
42566.19.8.76 Daudet, Alphonse. Tartarin de Tarascon. London, 1927.
42566.19.8.77B Daudet, Alphonse. Tartarin de Tarascon. Boston, 1911.
42566.19.8.78 Daudet, Alphonse. Tartarin de Tarascon. Paris, 1891.
42566.19.8.79 Daudet, Alphonse. Tartarin de Tarascon. N.Y., 1895.
42566.19.8.80 Daudet, Alphonse. Tartarin de Tarascon. 1st ed. N.Y., 1914.
42566.19.8.85 Daudet, Alphonse. Tartarin de Tarascon. Boston, 1918.
42566.19.8.90 Daudet, Alphonse. The prodigious adventures of Tartarin of Tarascon. Boston, 1880.
42566.19.8.95 Daudet, Alphonse. Tartarin of Tarascon. Boston, 1900.
42566.19.8.97 Daudet, Alphonse. Tartarin of Tarascon. N.Y., 1900.
42566.19.8.100 Daudet, Alphonse. Tartarin of Tarascon. London, 1968.
42566.19.15 Daudet, Alphonse. Difesa di Tarascona. 2. ed. Napoli, 1888.
42566.20 Daudet, Alphonse. Contes choisis. Paris, 1884.
42566.20.1 Daudet, Alphonse. Contes choisis. La fantaisie et l'histoire. Paris, 1886.
42566.20.2 Daudet, Alphonse. Contes choisis. La fantaisie et l'histoire. Paris, 1892.
42566.20.5A Daudet, Alphonse. Contes de Daudet including "La Belle-Nivernaise".2. éd. N.Y., 1893.
42566.20.5B Daudet, Alphonse. Contes de Daudet including "La Belle-Nivernaise".2. éd. N.Y., 1893.
42566.20.10 Daudet, Alphonse. Neuf contes choisis. N.Y., 1911.
42566.20.13 Daudet, Alphonse. Le siège de Berlin. N.Y., 1885.
42566.20.13.5 Daudet, Alphonse. Le siège de Berlin. N.Y., 1887.
42566.20.14 Daudet, Alphonse. Le siège de Berlin. N.Y., 1890.
42566.20.15 Daudet, Alphonse. Le siège de Berlin. N.Y., 1892.
42566.21 Daudet, Alphonse. Contes du lundi. Paris, 1877.
42566.21.5 Daudet, Alphonse. Contes du lundi. Paris, 1881.
42566.21.7 Daudet, Alphonse. Contes du lundi. Paris, 1884.
42566.21.9 Daudet, Alphonse. Contes du lundi. Paris, 1910.
42566.21.20 Daudet, Alphonse. Monday tales. N.Y., 1908.
42566.21.25 Daudet, Alphonse. Monday tales. Boston, 1901.
42566.22 Daudet, Alphonse. L'évangéliste; roman parisien. Paris, 1883.
42566.22.5 Daudet, Alphonse. L'évangéliste; roman parisien. 38. éd. Paris, 1883.
42566.22.7 Daudet, Alphonse. L'évangéliste; roman parisien. Paris, 1892.
42566.22.10 Daudet, Alphonse. L'évangéliste; roman parisien. Paris, 1906?
42566.23 Daudet, Alphonse. Les femmes d'artistes. Paris, 1876.
42566.23.3 Daudet, Alphonse. Les femmes d'artistes. Paris, 1889.
42566.23.4A Daudet, Alphonse. Artists' wives. London, 1890.
42566.23.4B Daudet, Alphonse. Artists' wives. London, 1890.
42566.23.5 Daudet, Alphonse. Artists' wives. London, 1892.
42566.24.5 Daudet, Alphonse. Fromont jeune et Risler ainé. 58. éd. Paris, 1880.
42566.24.8 Daudet, Alphonse. Fromont jeune et Risler ainé. Paris, 1884.
42566.24.15 Daudet, Alphonse. Fromont, Jr., and Risler, Sr. Chicago, 189-?
42566.24.17 Daudet, Alphonse. Fromont jeune et Risler ainé. Paris, 1894.
42566.24.18 Daudet, Alphonse. Fromont and Risler. N.Y., 1898.
42566.24.25 Daudet, Alphonse. Kings in exile. Boston, 1880.
42566.24.26 Daudet, Alphonse. Kings in exile. London, 1890.
42566.24.27 Daudet, Alphonse. Kings in exile. London, 1893.
42566.24.28 Daudet, Alphonse. Kings in exile. N.Y., 1899.
42566.25.5 Daudet, Alphonse. Montagsgeschichten. Berlin, 18- ?
42566.26 Daudet, Alphonse. Jack. v.2, photoreproduction. Paris, 1877. 2v.
42566.26.2A Daudet, Alphonse. Jack. Boston, 1877.
42566.26.2B Daudet, Alphonse. Jack. Boston, 1877.
42566.26.2.5 Daudet, Alphonse. Jack. London, 1890.
42566.26.2.10 Daudet, Alphonse. Jack. Paris, 1889.
42566.26.2.15 Daudet, Alphonse. Jack. Boston, 1900. 2v.
42566.26.2.17 Daudet, Alphonse. Jack. Boston, 1900. 2v.
42566.26.2.18 Daudet, Alphonse. Jack. N.Y., 1900. 2v.
42566.26.3 Daudet, Alphonse. Jack. Boston, 1902.

42566.18 - .999 Individual authors, etc. - 1850-1899 - Fiction - Daudet, A. - Individual works - cont.

42566.26.4 Daudet, Alphonse. Jack; costumi contemporanei. 2. ed. Milano, 1877. 2v.
42566.26.5 Daudet, Alphonse. Lettres à un absent. Paris, 1871.
42566.27.4 Daudet, Alphonse. Lettres de mon moulin. Paris, 189-?
42566.27.5 Daudet, Alphonse. Lettres de mon moulin. 20. éd. Paris, 18- ?
42566.27.8A Daudet, Alphonse. Lettres de mon moulin. Paris, 1930.
42566.27.8B Daudet, Alphonse. Lettres de mon moulin. Paris, 1930.
42566.27.9 Daudet, Alphonse. Lettres de mon moulin. Paris, 1931.
42566.27.10 Daudet, Alphonse. Lettres de mon moulin. Paris, 19- ?
42566.27.12 Daudet, Alphonse. Letters from my mill. Boston, 1901.
42566.27.13 Daudet, Alphonse. Letters from my mill. N.Y., 1893.
42566.27.14 Daudet, Alphonse. Letters from my mill. Boston, 1900.
42566.27.15F Daudet, Alphonse. The struggle for life. n.p., 1889.
42566.28A Daudet, Alphonse. Port-Tarascon. Paris, n.d.
42566.28B Daudet, Alphonse. Port-Tarascon. Paris, n.d.
42566.28.1A Daudet, Alphonse. Port-Tarascon. Paris, 1890.
42566.28.1B Daudet, Alphonse. Port-Tarascon. Paris, 1890.
42566.28.1C Daudet, Alphonse. Port-Tarascon. Paris, 1890.
42566.28.2 Daudet, Alphonse. Port-Tarascon. London, 1891.
42566.28.4 Daudet, Alphonse. Port-Tarascon. N.Y., 1891.
42566.28.6 Daudet, Alphonse. Port-Tarascon. N.Y., 1900.
42566.29 Daudet, Alphonse. Le Nabab. Paris, 1877.
42566.29.5B Daudet, Alphonse. The Nabob. Boston, 1878.
42566.29.7 Daudet, Alphonse. The Nabob. N.Y., 1898. 2v.
42566.29.15 Daudet, Alphonse. Le Nabab. Paris, 1881.
42566.29.21 Daudet, Alphonse. Le Nabab. Paris, 1926.
42566.29.23A Daudet, Alphonse. The Nabob. N.Y., 1902.
42566.29.23B Daudet, Alphonse. The Nabob. N.Y., 1902.
42566.29.25 Daudet, Alphonse. The Nabob. London, 19- .
42566.30 Daudet, Alphonse. Numa Roumestan. Paris, 1881.
42566.30.5 Daudet, Alphonse. Numa Roumestan. Boston, 1882.
42566.30.7A Daudet, Alphonse. Numa Roumestan. 17. éd. Paris, 1881.
42566.30.7B Daudet, Alphonse. Numa Roumestan. 50. éd. Paris, 1881.
42566.30.8 Daudet, Alphonse. Numa Roumestan. Paris, 1884.
42566.30.10 Daudet, Alphonse. Numa Roumestan. 1. éd. Paris, 19- .
42566.30.12 Daudet, Alphonse. Numa Roumestan. N.Y., 1900.
42566.30.15 Daudet, Alphonse. Numa Roumestan. Boston, 1900.
42566.31 Daudet, Alphonse. Le petit chose. Paris, n.d.
42566.31.4 Daudet, Alphonse. Le petit chose. Paris, 1897.
42566.31.10 Daudet, Alphonse. Le petit chose. N.Y., 1894.
42566.31.12 Daudet, Alphonse. Le petit chose. N.Y., 1901.
42566.31.15 Daudet, Alphonse. Le petit chose. Paris, 1909?
42566.31.22 Daudet, Alphonse. Le petit chose. Paris, 1947.
42566.31.25 Daudet, Alphonse. Little what's his name. Boston, 1900.
42566.31.27 Daudet, Alphonse. Little what's his name. N.Y., 1900.
42566.32 Daudet, Alphonse. Robert Helmont, journal d'un solitaire. Paris, 1874.
42566.32.10 Daudet, Alphonse. Robert Helmont, journal d'un solitaire. Paris, 1888.
42566.32.15 Daudet, Alphonse. Robert Helmont, journal d'un solitaire. Paris, 189-?
42566.32.25 Daudet, Alphonse. Robert Helmont, diary of a recluse. London, 1892.
42566.32.26 Daudet, Alphonse. Robert Helmont, diary of a recluse. London, 1892.
Htn 42566.32.50* Daudet, Alphonse. Le roman du Chaperon Rouge. Paris, 1862.
42566.33 Daudet, Alphonse. Les rois en exil. Paris, 1879.
42566.33.4 Daudet, Alphonse. Les rois en exile. 4. éd. Paris, 1879.
42566.33.4.2 Daudet, Alphonse. Les rois en exil. 37. éd. Paris, 1879.
42566.33.5 Daudet, Alphonse. Les rois en exil. Paris, 189-?
42566.33.6A Daudet, Alphonse. Les rois en exil. Paris, 1890.
42566.33.6B Daudet, Alphonse. Les rois en exil. Paris, 1890.
42566.33.7 Daudet, Alphonse. Les rois en exil. Paris, n.d.
42566.33.9 Daudet, Alphonse. Les rois en exil. Paris, 1926.
42566.34 Daudet, Alphonse. Sapho. Paris, 1884.
42566.34.2.5 Daudet, Alphonse. Sapho. Paris, 1887.
42566.34.2.10 Daudet, Alphonse. Sappho. Paris, 1887.
42566.34.3A Daudet, Alphonse. Sapho. Paris, 1888.
42566.34.3B Daudet, Alphonse. Sapho. Paris, 1888.
42566.34.5 Daudet, Alphonse. Sapho. Paris, 1893.
42566.34.6 Daudet, Alphonse. Sapho. N.Y., 1895.
42566.34.10 Daudet, Alphonse. Sapho. Paris, 19- .
42566.34.11 Daudet, Alphonse. Sapho. Paris, 19- .
42566.34.12 Daudet, Alphonse. Sapho. Paris, 19- . 3v.
42566.34.15A Daudet, Alphonse. Sappho and Manon Lescaut. N.Y., 1919.
42566.34.15B Daudet, Alphonse. Sappho and Manon Lescaut. N.Y., 1919.
42566.34.30 Daudet, Alphonse. Sappho. N.Y., 1932.
42566.35A Daudet, Alphonse. Sidonie. Boston, 1877.
42566.35B Daudet, Alphonse. Sidonie. Boston, 1877.
Htn 42566.35.3* Daudet, Alphonse. Tartarin sur les Alpes. Paris, 1886.
42566.35.3.5 Daudet, Alphonse. Tartarin sur les Alpes. Paris, 1886.
42566.35.4A Daudet, Alphonse. Tartarin sur les Alpes. Paris, 1886.
42566.35.4B Daudet, Alphonse. Tartarin sur les Alpes. Paris, 1886.
42566.35.4.5 Daudet, Alphonse. Tartarin sur les Alpes. Paris, 1888.
42566.35.6 Daudet, Alphonse. Tartarin sur les Alpes. Paris, 1927.
42566.35.8 Daudet, Alphonse. Tartarin sur les Alpes. Paris, 19- .
42566.35.10 Daudet, Alphonse. Tartarin sur les Alpes. London, 1910.
42566.35.22 Daudet, Alphonse. Tartarin on the Alps. London, 1887.
42566.35.23A Daudet, Alphonse. Tartarin on the Alps. London, 1887.
42566.35.23B Daudet, Alphonse. Tartarin on the Alps. London, 1887.
42566.35.24 Daudet, Alphonse. Tartarin on the Alps. London, 1902.
42566.35.25 Daudet, Alphonse. Tartarin on the Alps. N.Y., 1894.
42566.35.27 Daudet, Alphonse. Tartarin on the Alps. Philadelphia, 189-?
42566.35.28 Daudet, Alphonse. Tartarin on the Alps. London, 1896.
42566.36 Daudet, Alphonse. Théâtre. Paris, 1880.
42566.36.15 Daudet, Alphonse. Théâtre. 3e série. Paris, 1911.
42566.37 Daudet, Alphonse. L'Arlésienne. Paris, n.d.
Htn 42566.38* Daudet, Alphonse. L'Obstacle. Paris, 1891.
42566.39 Daudet, Alphonse. Choix de contes. Boston, 1888.
42566.39.25 Daudet, Alphonse. Short stories. N.Y., 1909.
42566.40 Daudet, Alphonse. Trente ans de Paris. Paris, 1889.
42566.40.2 Daudet, Alphonse. Trente ans de Paris à travers ma vie et mes livres. Paris, 1889.
42566.40.5A Daudet, Alphonse. Trente ans de Paris à travers ma vie et mes livres. Paris, 1888.
Htn 42566.40.5*B Daudet, Alphonse. Trente ans de Paris à travers ma vie et mes livres. Paris, 1888.
42566.41 Daudet, Alphonse. Trois contes choisis. Boston, 1892.
42566.42 Daudet, Alphonse. Trois souvenirs. Paris, n.d.
42566.43 Daudet, Alphonse. L'enterrement d'une étoile. Paris, 1896.
42566.44 Daudet, Alphonse. Contes d'hiver. Paris, n.d.
42566.45 Daudet, Alphonse. Le trésor d'Arlatan. Paris, 1897.

42566.18 - .999 Individual authors, etc. - 1850-1899 - Fiction - Daudet, A. - Individual works - cont.

42566.46 Daudet, Alphonse. Rose et Ninette. Paris, n.d.
42566.46.2A Daudet, Alphonse. Rose et Ninette. Paris, 1892.
42566.46.2B Daudet, Alphonse. Rose et Ninette. Paris, 1892.
42566.47 Daudet, Alphonse. La fédor; pages de la vie. Paris, n.d.
NEDL 42566.48 Daudet, Alphonse. La lutte pour la vie. Paris, 1890.
NEDL 42566.48.2 Daudet, Alphonse. La lutte pour la vie. Paris, 1890.
42566.49 Soutien de la famille, moeurs contemporaines. Paris, 1898.
42566.49.4 Daudet, Alphonse. The head of the family. N.Y., 1898.
42566.49.10 Daudet, Alphonse. The support of the family. Boston, 1900.
42566.49.12 Daudet, Alphonse. The support of the family. N.Y., 1900.
42566.50 Daudet, Alphonse. La menteuse. Paris, n.d.
42566.51 Daudet, Alphonse. La Belle-Nivernaise. Paris, n.d.
42566.51.2A Daudet, Alphonse. La Belle-Nivernaise; story of an old boat. London, 1887.
42566.51.2B Daudet, Alphonse. La Belle-Nivernaise; story of an old boat. London, 1887.
42566.51.5 Daudet, Alphonse. La Belle-Nivernaise; story of an old boat. N.Y., 1887
42566.51.6 Daudet, Alphonse. La Belle-Nivernaise; story of an old boat. Boston, 1896.
42566.51.10 Daudet, Alphonse. La Belle-Nivernaise; story of an old boat. Philadelphia, 1899.
42566.52 Daudet, Alphonse. L'immortel; moeurs parisiennes. Paris, 1888.
42566.52.5 Daudet, Alphonse. L'immortel; moeurs parisiennes. Paris, 1890.
42566.52.20 Daudet, Alphonse. One of the "forty". N.Y., 1888.
42566.52.25 Daudet, Alphonse. The immortal. N.Y., 1889.
42566.52.27 Daudet, Alphonse. The immortal or One of the forty. Chicago, 1884.
42566.53A Daudet, Alphonse. La petite paroisse. Moeurs conjugales. Paris, 1895.
42566.53B Daudet, Alphonse. La petite paroisse. Moeurs conjugales. Paris, 1895.
42566.53.5 Daudet, Alphonse. The little parish church. N.Y., 1899.
Htn 42566.54*A Daudet, Alphonse. Souvenirs d'un homme de lettres. Paris, 1888.
Htn 42566.54*B Daudet, Alphonse. Souvenirs d'un homme de lettres. Paris, 1888.
42566.55 Daudet, Alphonse. Entre les frises et la rampe. Paris, 1894.
42566.56 Daudet, Alphonse. Notes sur la vie. Paris, 1899.
42566.57 Daudet, Alphonse. Premier voyage, premier mensonge. Paris, n.d.
42566.58A Daudet, Alphonse. In the midst of Paris. N.Y., 1896.
42566.58B Daudet, Alphonse. In the midst of Paris. N.Y., 1896.
Htn 42566.59* Daudet, Alphonse. Pages inconnues. Paris, 1930.
42566.60 Daudet, Alphonse. La doulou; la vie; extraits des carnets inédits. Paris, 1931.
42566.61.25 Daudet, Alphonse. Father Gaucher's elixir. Ormond Beach, Fla., 1937.
42566.62 Daudet, Alphonse. Thirty years of Paris and my literary life. London, 1893.
42566.62.2 Daudet, Alphonse. Thirty years of Paris and my literary life. London, 1888.
42566.62.5 Daudet, Alphonse. Thirty years of Paris and my literary life. London, 1896.
42566.63 Daudet, Alphonse. Recollections from a literary man. London, 1892.
42566.63.2 Daudet, Alphonse. Recollections of a literary man. London, 1889.
42566.63.5 Daudet, Alphonse. Recollections of a literary man. London, 1896.
42566.64 Daudet, Alphonse. Oeuvres complètes illustrées. Paris, 1929-1931. 20v.
42566.64.5 Daudet, Alphonse. Les amoureuses. Paris, 1887.
42566.65 Daudet, Julia R.C. Fragments d'un livre inèdit. Paris, 19- ?
42566.66 Bruyère, Marcel. La jeunesse d'Alphonse Daudet. Paris, 1955.
42566.66.19.8.25 Daudet, Alphonse. Tartarin de Tarascon. Boston, 1911.
42566.67 Daudet, Alphonse. Les femmes d'artistes. Paris, 1878.

42567.20 - .48 Individual authors, etc. - 1850-1899 - Fiction - Daudet, E. - Individual works

42567.21 Daudet, Ernest. Les aventures de Raymond Rocheray. Paris, 1875. 2v.
42567.23 Daudet, Ernest. Le crime de Jean Malory. Paris, 1877.
42567.23.5 Daudet, Ernest. L'espionne. Paris, 1905.
42567.24 Daudet, Ernest. Fleur de peéché. Paris, 1875.
42567.26 Daudet, Ernest. Henriette. Paris, 1877.
42567.27 Daudet, Ernest. Jean le Gueux. Paris, 1871.
42567.28 Daudet, Ernest. Mon frère et moi. Paris, 1882.
42567.28.5 Daudet, Ernest. Souvenirs de mon temps. Paris, 1921.
42567.29 Daudet, Ernest. Le prince Pogoutzine. Paris, 1869.
42567.30 Daudet, Ernest. Le roman de Delphine. Paris, 1873.
42567.30.5 Daudet, Ernest. Le roman de Delphine. Paris, 1885.
42567.31 Daudet, Ernest. Le roman d'une jeune fille. Paris, 1876.
42567.32 Daudet, Ernest. La succession Chavanet. Paris, 1867. 2v.
42567.35 Daudet, Ernest. Une femme du monde. Paris, 1877.
42567.37 Daudet, Ernest. De la terreur au consulat. Paris, 1914.
42567.38 Daudet, Ernest. Poussière du passé. Paris, 1896.
42567.39 Daudet, Ernest. Apostate. N.Y., 1889.

42567.100 - .118 Individual authors, etc. - 1850-1899 - Fiction - Delattre, L. - Writings

42567.100 Delattre, Louis. Marionnettes rustiques montrant les bonnes petites gens à leurs métiers. Liège, 1899.
42567.110 Delattre, Louis. Du côté de l'ombre. Bruxelles, 1925.

42568.1 Individual authors, etc. - 1850-1899 - Fiction - Derennes

42568.1 Derennes, Gustave. Le drapeau du Canada. Paris, n.d.

42568.2 Individual authors, etc. - 1850-1899 - Fiction - Deslys; Deschard; Didier; Double; etc.

42568.2 Deslys, Charles. La jarretière rose. v.1-2. Bruxelles, 1855.
42568.2.5 Deschard, Marie. La prima lucia. Madrid, 1912.
42568.2.25 Desnoiresterres, Gustave. Les talons rouges. Paris, 1854.
42568.2.30 Deulin, Charles. Histoires de petite ville. 2. éd. Paris, 1875.
42568.2.35A Didier, Charles. The romance of l'Aiglon. N.Y., 1901.
42568.2.35B Didier, Charles. The romance of l'Aiglon. N.Y., 1901.
42568.2.36 Didier, Charles. The romance of l'Aiglon. N.Y., 1900.

Classified Listing

42568.2 Individual authors, etc. - 1850-1899 - Fiction - Deslys; Deschard; Didier; Double; etc. - cont.

42568.2.37 Didier, Charles. The romance of l'Aiglon. N.Y., 1901.
42568.2.38 Didier, Charles. The romance of l'Aiglon. N.Y., 1900.
42568.2.44 Sellards, John. Dans le sillage du romantisme: Charles Didier. 1805-1864. Thèse. Paris, 1932.
42568.2.46 Sellards, John. Dans le sillage du romantisme: Charles Didier. 1805-1864. Thèse. Paris, 1933.
42568.2.50 Diguet, C. Secret d'alcove. Paris, 1800.
42568.2.75 Double, A.M.A. Carnet d'un mondain, gazette parisienne. Paris, 1881-1882. 2v.

42568.3 - .14 Individual authors, etc. - 1850-1899 - Fiction - Droz - Writings

42568.3 Droz, Gustave. Autour d'une source. Paris, 1872. 3v.
42568.3.5 Droz, Gustave. Autour d'une source. 24. éd. Paris, 1882.
42568.4 Droz, Gustave. Babolain. Paris, 1873.
42568.4.2 Droz, Gustave. Babolain. N.Y., 1873.
42568.5 Droz, Gustave. Le cahier bleu. Paris, 1872.
42568.5.4 Droz, Gustave. Le cahier bleu. Paris, n.d.
42568.7 Droz, Gustave. Entre nous. Paris, 1872.
42568.7.2 Droz, Gustave. Entre nous. 22. éd. Paris, 187-?
42568.8 Droz, Gustave. Les étangs. Paris, 1876.
42568.9 Droz, Gustave. Une femme gênante. Paris, 1880.
42568.9.5 Droz, Gustave. Une femme gênante. 26. éd. Paris, 1884.
42568.11 Droz, Gustave. Monsieur, madame et bébé. Paris, 1887.
42568.11.2 Droz, Gustave. Monsieur, madame et bébé. 126. éd. Paris, 1884.
42568.11.5 Droz, Gustave. Monsieur, madame et bébé. 149. éd. Paris, 1890.
42568.12 Droz, Gustave. Un paquet de lettres. Paris, 1880.
42568.13A Droz, Gustave. Tristesses et sourires. Paris, 1884.
42568.13B Droz, Gustave. Tristesses et sourires. Paris, 1884.
42568.14 Droz, Gustave. The registered letter. Boston, 1901.

42568.16 Individual authors, etc. - 1850-1899 - Fiction - Dinet

42568.16 Dinet, E. Khadra la danseuse des Ouled Naïl. Paris, n.d.

42568.18 - .19.20 Individual authors, etc. - 1850-1899 - Fiction - Du Boisgobey - Writings

42568.18 Du Boisgobey, Fortuné. Rubis sur l'ongle. Paris, 1886.
42568.18.5 Du Boisgobey, Fortuné. Le crime de l'opéra. v.1-2. Paris, 1880.
42568.18.9 Du Boisgobey, Fortuné. Le secret de Berthe. v.1-2. Paris, 1884.
42568.19.3 Du Boisgobey, Fortuné. Le collier d'acier. 2. éd. Paris, 1883.
42568.19.4 Du Boisgobey, Fortuné. Le collier d'acier. 3. éd. Paris, 1883.
42568.19.5 Du Boisgobey, Fortuné. La tresse blonde. 4. éd. Paris, 1879.
42568.19.8 Du Boisgobey, Fortuné. The high roller. N.Y., 1891.
42568.19.9 Du Boisgobey, Fortuné. Collets noirs. Paris, 1874. 2v.
42568.19.10 Du Boisgobey, Fortuné. L'as de coeur. Paris, 1875. 2v.
42568.19.11 Du Boisgobey, Fortuné. L'omnibus du diable. Paris, 1876.
42568.19.12 Du Boisgobey, Fortuné. The lost casket. Paris, 1881.
42568.19.13 Du Boisgobey, Fortuné. Les gredins. Paris, 1872.
42568.19.14 Du Boisgobey, Fortuné. Le chevalier casse-cou. v.1-2. Paris, 1873-1874.
42568.19.14.10 Du Boisgobey, Fortuné. The chevalier casse-cou. N.Y., 1875.
42568.19.15.3 Du Boisgobey, Fortuné. La voilette bleue. 3. éd. Paris, 1886.
42568.19.16 Du Boisgobey, Fortuné. El caballero rompe y rasga. v.1-2. N.Y., 19- ?
42568.19.17 Du Boisgobey, Fortuné. Porte close. Paris, 1886.
42568.19.18.2 Du Boisgobey, Fortuné. Le cochon d'or. 2. éd. Paris, 1882. 2v.
42568.19.19 Du Boisgobey, Fortuné. Doctor Villagos. N.Y., 1889.

42568.19.21 Individual authors, etc. - 1850-1899 - Fiction - Ducasse, I. (Lautréamont) - Writings

42568.19.21 Ducasse, I.L. Oeuvres complètes du Comte de Lautréamont. Paris, 1927.
42568.19.21.5 Ducasse, I.L. Oeuvres complètes. Paris, 1938.
42568.19.21.6 Ducasse, I.L. Oeuvres complètes; les chants de Maldoror. Paris, 1956.
42568.19.21.10 Ducasse, I.L. Oeuvres complètes; les chants de Maldoror. Paris, 1938.
42568.19.21.12 Ducasse, I.L. Oeuvres complètes. Paris, 1946.
42568.19.21.13 Ducasse, I.L. Oeuvres complètes; les chants de Maldoror. Paris, 1969.
42568.19.21.14 Ducasse, I.L. Oeuvres complètes. Paris, 1950.
42568.19.21.15 Ducasse, I.L. Maldoror. (Les chants de Maldoror). n.p., 1943?
42568.19.21.16 Ducasse, I.L. Oeuvres complètes. Paris, 1953.
42568.19.21.17 Ducasse, I.L. Poésies. 1. éd. Paris, 1960.
42568.19.21.18 Ducasse, I.L. Oeuvres complètes de Lautréamont et Germain Nouveau. Paris, 1970.
42568.19.21.20 Ducasse, I.L. Oeuvres complètes. Paris, 1971.

42568.19.22 - .19.999 Individual authors, etc. - 1850-1899 - Fiction - Ducasse, I. (Lautréamont) - Works about

42568.19.22 Bachelard, G. Lautréamont. Paris, 1939.
42568.19.23 Pierre, Q.L. Le comte de Lautréamont. Marseille, 1929.
42568.19.24 Linder, Hans R. Lautréamont, sein Werk und sein Weltbild. Affaltern am Albis, 1947.
42568.19.24.12 Blanchat, M. Lautréamont et Sade. Paris, 1963.
42568.19.25 Duchemin, Léon. Mémoires d'un décavé. Paris, 1874.
42568.19.26 Soulier, Jean-Pierre. Lautréamont. Genève, 1964.
42568.19.27 Pleynet, Marcelin. Lautréamont par lui-même. Paris, 1967.
42568.19.35 Peyrouzet, Edouard. Vie de Lautréamont. Paris, 1970.
42568.19.40 Caradac, François. Isidore Lucien Ducasse. Paris, 1970.
42568.19.45 Nesselroth, P.W. Lautréamont's imagery. A stylistic approach. Genève, 1969.

42568.20 Individual authors, etc. - 1850-1899 - Fiction - Dudevant, M.; Dufresne; etc.

42568.20.5 Dufresne, Abel. Stories of Henry and Henrietta. Boston, 1860.

42568.21 Individual authors, etc. - 1850-1899 - Fiction - Durandal; Duranty; etc.

42568.21 Durandal, Pierre. Le vengeur de Montcalm. Paris, 1887.
42568.21.5 Duranty, Louis E.E. La cause de beau Guillaume. Paris, 1920.
42568.21.7 Duranty, Louis E.E. La cause de beau Guillaume. Paris, 1862?
42568.21.80 Crouzet, Marcel. Un inconnu du réalisme: Duranty, 1833-1880. Paris, 1964.

42568.22 Individual authors, etc. - 1850-1899 - Fiction - Durny

42568.22 Durny, Georges. Andrée. Paris, 1884.
42568.22.5 Durny, Georges. Fin de rêve. Paris, 1890.

42568.23 Individual authors, etc. - 1850-1899 - Fiction - Duval, P.; Eekhoud

42568.23 Duval, Paul. Sonyeuse. Paris, 1891.
42568.23.5 Duval, Paul. Le sang des dieux. Paris, 1882.
42568.23.6 Duval, Paul. Coins de Bysance. Le vice errant. 13. éd. Paris, 1902.
42568.23.7 Duval, Paul. M. de Bougrelon. Paris, 1896.
42568.23.8 Duval, Paul. Une femme par jour. Paris, 1896.
42568.23.9 Duval, Paul. L'ombre ardente; poésies. Paris, 1897.
42568.23.10 Duval, Paul. La maison Philibert. Paris, 192-.
42568.23.12 Duval, Paul. Prométhée. Paris, 1925.
42568.23.13 Duval, Paul. Portraits littéraires et mondains. Paris, 1926.
42568.23.14 Duval, Paul. Un second oratoire. Dijon, 1933.
42568.23.14.10 Duval, Paul. La ville empoisonnée. Paris, 1936.
42568.23.14.30 Duval, Paul. Très russe. Paris, 1886.
42568.23.14.35 Duval, Paul. Yanthis. Paris, 1894.
42568.23.14.42 Duval, Paul. Modernités. Paris, 1885.
42568.23.14.45 Duval, Paul. Princesse d'Italie. Paris, 1898.
42568.23.14.47 Duval, Paul. Loreley. Paris, 1897.
42568.23.14.49 Duval, Paul. Deux heures du matin. Paris, 1904.
42568.23.14.52 Duval, Paul. Les griseries. Paris, 1887.
42568.23.15 Gaubert, E. Jean Lorrain. (Paul Duval). Paris, 1905.
42568.23.16 Normandy, G. Jean Lorrain. (Paul Duval). Paris, 1907.
42568.23.18 Normandy, G. Jean Lorrain. (Paul Duval). Paris, 1927.
42568.23.20 Léon-Gauthier, P. Jean Lorrain. (Paul Duval). Thèse. Paris, 1935.
42568.23.23 Fleischmann, Hector. Le massacre d'une amazone. Paris, 1904.
42568.23.100 Eekhoud, Georges. Kees doorik. Bruxelles, 1883.
42568.23.105 Eekhoud, Georges. La faneuse d'amour. Paris, 1926.
42568.23.110 Eekhoud, Georges. Les pittoresques. Paris, 1879.
42568.23.115 Eekhoud, Georges. The new Carthage. N.Y., 1917.
42568.23.120 Eekhoud, Georges. Burch mitsu. Bruxelles, 1896.
42568.23.150 Black, G.W. Bibliographie de Georges Eekhoud. Boston, 1931.
42568.23.800 Puymbrouck, H. von. Georges Eekhoud en zijn werk. Antwerpen, 1914.

42568.24 - .31 Individual authors, etc. - 1850-1899 - Fiction - Enault, L. - Writings

42568.24 Enault, Louis. Alba. Paris, 1872.
42568.24.5 Enault, Louis. Alba. 3. éd. Paris, 1863.
42568.25 Enault, Louis. Un amour en Lorponie. Paris, 1861.
42568.25.5 Enault, Louis. Carine. N.Y., 1886.
42568.26 Enault, Louis. Le chien du capitaine. N.Y., 1890.
42568.28 Enault, Louis. La pupille de la Légion d'Honneur. N.Y., 1869. 2v.
42568.29 Enault, Louis. La rose blanche. 2. éd. Paris, 1859.
42568.30 Enault, Louis. Tragiques amours. Paris, 1891.
42568.30.800 Enault, Louis. Carine. Boston, 1891.
42568.30.810 Enault, Louis. Christine. N.Y., 1883.
42568.31 Enault, Louis. Le roman d'une Altesse. Paris, 1866.

42568.50 Individual authors, etc. - 1850-1899 - Fiction - Dollivet

42568.50.100 Dollivet, Louis. Sale juif. Paris, 1897.

42568.56 Individual authors, etc. - 1850-1899 - Fiction - Demolder

42568.56.100 Demolder, Eugène. L'arche de Monsieur Cheunus. Paris, 1904.
42568.56.110 Demolder, Eugène. Quatuor. Paris, 1897.

42571.1 - .21 Individual authors, etc. - 1850-1899 - Fiction - Folios [Discontinued]

42571.4 Erckmann, Emile. Contes vosgiens. Paris, 1878.
42571.4.5 Erckmann, Emile. Cuentos de los Vosgos. Valencia, 187-?
42571.10 Blaze de Bury, Y. Anatole France. n.p., 1896.
42571.11 Le Brun, R. Anatole France. Paris, 1904.
42571.11.3 Le Brun, R. Anatole France. Paris, 1904.
42571.11.7 Suffel, Jacques. Anatole France. Paris, 1946.
42571.14 France, Anatole. Nos enfants; scènes de la ville et des champs. Paris, 1887.
42571.15F France, Anatole. Nos enfants; scènes de la ville et des champs. Paris, 1900.
42571.18 Feuillet, Octave. Quelques années de ma vie. Paris, 1894.
42571.20 Feuillet, Octave. The story of Sibylle. Boston, 1872.

42571.22 - .34 Individual authors, etc. - 1850-1899 - Fiction - Gaboriau, E. - Writings

42571.22.11 Gaboriau, Emile. L'affaire Lerouge. 18. éd. Paris, 1877.
42571.23 Gaboriau, Emile. L'affaire Lerouge. Paris, 1887.
42571.23.2 Gaboriau, Emile. The Lerouge case. N.Y., 19- ?
42571.23.3 Gaboriau, Emile. The widow Lerouge. N.Y., 1901.
42571.23.4 Gaboriau, Emile. The widow Lerouge. N.Y., 1910.
42571.23.5 Gaboriau, Emile. El proceso Lerouge. 2a ed. Madrid, 191-.
42571.24 Gaboriau, Emile. L'argent des autres. Paris, 1884. 2v.
42571.24.5 Gaboriau, Emile. Other people's money. Chicago, 18- ?
42571.24.6 Gaboriau, Emile. Other people's money. N.Y., 1900.
42571.24.7 Gaboriau, Emile. Other people's money. N.Y., 1901.
42571.24.12 Gaboriau, Emile. Other people's money. N.Y., 1910.
42571.24.25 Gaboriau, Emile. I danari degli altri. v. 1-2. Milano, 1874.
42571.25 Gaboriau, Emile. La corde au cou. Paris, 1884.
42571.26 Gaboriau, Emile. La clique dorée. Paris, 1886.
42571.27 Gaboriau, Emile. La dégringolade. Paris, 1882. 2v.
42571.28 Gaboriau, Emile. Le crime d'Orcival. Paris, 1885.
42571.28.3 Gaboriau, Emile. The mystery of Orcival. N.Y., 1900.
42571.28.4 Gaboriau, Emile. The mystery of Orcival. N.Y., 1901.
42571.28.5 Gaboriau, Emile. The mystery of Orcival. N.Y., 1904.
42571.28.6 Gaboriau, Emile. The mystery of Orcival. N.Y., 1902.
42571.28.10 Gaboriau, Emile. The mystery of Orcival. N.Y., 1909.
42571.30 Gaboriau, Emile. Le dossier numéro 113. Paris, 1887.
42571.30.7 Gaboriau, Emile. File no. 113. N.Y., 1900.

42571.22 - .34 Individual authors, etc. - 1850-1899 - Fiction - Gaboriau, E. - Writings - cont.

42571.30.9 Gaboriau, Emile. File no. 113. N.Y., 1901.
42571.31 Gaboriau, Emile. Les esclaves de Paris. Paris, 1885. 2v.
42571.32.2 Gaboriau, Emile. Monsieur Lecoq. N.Y., 1901.
42571.32.3 Gaboriau, Emile. Monsieur Lecoq. N.Y., 1904.
42571.32.4 Gaboriau, Emile. Monsieur Lecoq. Paris, 1881-1882. 2v.
42571.32.5 Gaboriau, Emile. Monsieur Lecoq. N.Y., 1908.
42571.32.7 Gaboriau, Emile. Monsieur Lecoq. N.Y., 1910.
42571.32.10 Gaboriau, Emile. The honor of the name. N.Y., 1901.
42571.32.14 Gaboriau, Emile. The honor of the name. N.Y., 1904.
42571.33A Gaboriau, Emile. La vie infernale. 4. éd. Paris, 1870-1872. 2v.
42571.33B Gaboriau, Emile. La vie infernale. v.2. Paris, 1870-1872.
42571.34 Gaboriau, Emile. La vie infernale. 9. éd. Paris, 1890. 2v.
42571.34.5 Gaboriau, Emile. File no. 113. N.Y., 1903.
42571.34.7 Gaboriau, Emile. File no. 113. N.Y., 1908.
42571.34.8 Gaboriau, Emile. File no. 113. London, 1953.
42571.34.12 Gaboriau, Emile. The count's millions. N.Y., 1913.
42571.34.16 Gaboriau, Emile. Baron Trigault's vengeance, sequel to The count's millions. N.Y., 1913.
42571.34.18 Gaboriau, Emile. Within an inch of his life. N.Y., 1913.
42571.34.22 Gaboriau, Emile. Caught in the net. N.Y., 1913.
42571.34.24 Gaboriau, Emile. The clique of gold. N.Y., 1913.
42571.34.26 Gaboriau, Emile. La dégringolade. Paris, 1872. 2v.

42571.36 - .47 Individual authors, etc. - 1850-1899 - Fiction - Miscellany [Discontinued]

42571.37 Hervieu, Paul. Le réveil. 13. éd. Paris, 1906.
42571.37.2 Hervieu, Paul. Le réveil, L'énigme. 6. éd. Paris, 1906.
42571.37.90 Hervieu, Paul. La course du flambeau. 9. éd. Paris, 1901.
42571.38 Hervieu, Paul. La course du flambeau. Boston, 1922.
42571.41 Grousset, P. Une année de collège à Paris. Paris, n.d.
42571.41.5 Grousset, P. Mémoires d'un collégien. N.Y., 1907.
42571.41.10 Grousset, P. Schoolboy days in Japan. Boston, 1895.
42571.41.12 Grousset, P. Schoolboy days in France. Boston, 1896.
42571.43 L'Epine, E. Legend of Croquemitaine. London, n.d.
Htn 42571.47F* Maupassant, Guy de. Pierre et Jean. Paris, 1888. 2v.

42572.1 - .79 Individual authors, etc. - 1850-1899 - Fiction - Erckmann, E. - Writings

42572.1 Erckmann, Emile. Alsace! Paris, n.d.
42572.1.15 Erckmann, Emile. L'Art et les grands idéalistes. Paris, n.d.
42572.2 Erckmann, Emile. L'ami Fritz. Paris, 1867.
42572.2.2 Erckmann, Emile. Le banni. Paris, n.d.
42572.2.15 Erckmann, Emile. L'ami Fritz. Paris, 1927.
42572.3 Erckmann, Emile. Le blocus. Paris, n.d.
42572.3.5 Erckmann, Emile. Le blocus. Paris, n.d.
42572.3.7 Erckmann, Emile. Le blocus. N.Y., 1886.
42572.3.8 Erckmann, Emile. Le blocus. Paris, 1935.
42572.3.9 Erckmann, Emile. The bells. N.Y., 1873.
42572.4 Erckmann, Emile. Une campagne en Kabylie. Paris, n.d.
42572.5 Erckmann, Emile. Confidences d'un joueur de clarinette. Paris, n.d.
42572.6 Erckmann, Emile. Contes des bords du Rhin. Paris, n.d.
42572.6.5 Erckmann, Emile. Stories of the Rhine. London, 1875.
42572.7 Erckmann, Emile. Contes fatastiques. Paris, 1868.
42572.7.5 Erckmann, Emile. Contes de la montagne. Paris, n.d.
42572.7.7 Erckmann, Emile. Contes de la montagne. Paris, 1860.
42572.7.10 Erckmann, Emile. Contes et romans nationaux et populaires. Paris, 1962. 14v.
42572.8 Erckmann, Emile. Contes populaires. Paris, n.d.
42572.8.10 Erckmann, Emile. The count of Nideck. Boston, 1897.
42572.9 Erckmann, Emile. Les deux frères. Paris, 1873.
42572.10 Erckmann, Emile. Le grand-père Lebigre. Paris, n.d.
42572.10.15 Erckmann, Emile. La guerre. Cambridge, 1883.
42572.10.17 Erckmann, Emile. La guerre. Cambridge, 1888.
42572.11.1 Erckmann, Emile. Histoire d'un conscrit de 1813. Boston, 1867.
42572.11.2 Erckmann, Emile. Histoire d'un conscrit de 1813. Boston, 1868.
42572.11.3 Erckmann, Emile. Histoire d'un conscrit de 1813. 3. éd. N.Y., 1867.
42572.11.5 Erckmann, Emile. Histoire d'un conscrit de 1813. 5. éd. Paris, n.d.
42572.11.15 Erckmann, Emile. Histoire d'un conscrit de 1813. Paris, 1931.
42572.11.20 Erckmann, Emile. The conscript; a story of the French war of 1813. N.Y., 1869.
42572.11.22 Erckmann, Emile. The conscript; a story of the French war of 1813. N.Y., 1898.
42572.11.23 Erckmann, Emile. The conscript; a story of the French war of 1813. N.Y., 1899.
42572.11.25 Erckmann, Emile. The history of a conscript of 1813 and Waterloo. London, 1911.
42572.11.30 Erckmann, Emile. The conscript; a story of the French war of 1813. N.Y., 1902.
42572.12 Erckmann, Emile. Histoire d'un homme du peuple. Paris, n.d.
42572.13.10 Erckmann, Emile. Histoire d'un paysan, 1789. 9. éd. Paris, 1868.
NEDL 42572.13.15 Erckmann, Emile. Histoire d'un paysan. 14. éd. Paris, 1869.
42572.14 Erckmann, Emile. Histoire d'un paysan. Paris, 1870-1871. 4v.
42572.14.3 Erckmann, Emile. Histoire d'un paysan. Paris, 1873. 2v.
42572.14.4 Erckmann, Emile. Histoire d'un paysan. Paris, 1933. 3v.
42572.14.5 Erckmann, Emile. Histoire d'un paysan. Paris, 187-? 4v.
42572.14.25 Erckmann, Emile. The outbreak of the great French revolution. London, 1871. 3v.
42572.16 Erckmann, Emile. Histoire du plébiscite. 12. éd. Paris, 1872.
42572.16.5 Erckmann, Emile. Histoire du plébiscite. 13. éd. Paris, 1872.
42572.17 Erckmann, Emile. Histoire d'un sous-maître. Paris, 1872.
42572.19 Erckmann, Emile. L'illustre Docteur Mathéus. Paris, 1859.
42572.19.5 Erckmann, Emile. L'illustre Docteur Mathéus. 3. éd. Paris, n.d.
42572.20 Erckmann, Emile. L'invasion ou Le fou Yégoff. Paris, n.d.
42572.20.5 Erckmann, Emile. L'invasion ou Le fou Yégoff. 3. éd. Paris, 18- ?

42572.1 - .79 Individual authors, etc. - 1850-1899 - Fiction - Erckmann, E. - Writings - cont.

42572.20.15 Erckmann, Emile. L'invasion ou Le fou Yégoff. Paris, 1932.
42572.21 Erckmann, Emile. Le juif polonais. N.Y., 1888.
42572.22 Erckmann, Emile. Le juif polonais. Paris, 18- ?
42572.22.5 Erckmann, Emile. Le juif polonais. 6. éd. Paris, 188-?
42572.22.10 Erckmann, Emile. Le juif polonais. Paris, 1907.
42572.22.50 Erckmann, Emile. Loïs, histoire d'une petite bohémienne. Paris, 1934.
42572.23 Erckmann, Emile. Madame Thérèse. Paris, n.d.
42572.23.8 Erckmann, Emile. Madame Thérèse. 8. éd. Paris, 1863.
42572.23.15 Erckmann, Emile. Madame Thérèse. 23. éd. Paris, 1873.
42572.23.20 Erckmann, Emile. Madame Thérèse. 37. éd. Paris, 188-.
42572.24 Erckmann, Emile. Madame Thérèse. N.Y., 1886.
42572.24.2 Erckmann, Emile. Madame Thérèse. N.Y., 1887.
42572.24.3 Erckmann, Emile. Madame Thérèse. Boston, 1891.
42572.24.5 Erckmann, Emile. Madame Thérèse. Boston, 1897.
42572.24.7 Erckmann, Emile. Madame Thérèse. N.Y., 1898.
42572.24.15 Erckmann, Emile. Madame Thérèse. Paris, 1925.
42572.25 Erckmann, Emile. La maison forestière. Paris, n.d.
42572.26 Erckmann, Emile. Maître Daniel Rock. Paris, n.d.
42572.26.2 Erckmann, Emile. Maître Daniel Rock. Bruxelles, 1861.
42572.27 Erckmann, Emile. Maître Gaspard Fix. Paris, n.d.
42572.27.10 Erckmann, Emile. Maître Gaspard Fix. Paris, 1936.
42572.31 Erckmann, Emile. Les vieux de la vieille. Paris, n.d.
42572.32 Erckmann, Emile. Waterloo. Paris, n.d.
42572.32.5 Erckmann, Emile. Waterloo. N.Y., 1869.
42572.32.8 Erckmann, Emile. Waterloo. N.Y., 1898.
42572.32.10 Erckmann, Emile. Waterloo. N.Y., 1902.
42572.35F Erckmann, Emile. Romans nationaux. Le conscrit de 1813. Waterloo. Paris, 1867.
42572.40 Erckmann, Emile. Hugues le loup et autres contes fantastiques. Verviers, 1966.

42572.85 - .999 Individual authors, etc. - 1850-1899 - Fiction - Erckmann, E. - Works about

42572.85 Hinzelin, E. Erckmann-Chatrian. Paris, 1922.
42572.86 Shoumacker, L. Erckmann-Chatrian. Paris, 1933.
42572.86.5 Schoumacker, L. Erckmann-Chatrian. Thèse. Strasbourg, 1933.

42573.1 - .39 Individual authors, etc. - 1850-1899 - Fiction - Erckmann, E. - Writings [Discontinued]

42573.13 Erckmann, Emile. L'ami Fritz. N.Y., 1888.
42573.16 Erckmann, Emile. Histoire d'un paysan. v.2-3. Paris, 1869.
42573.20 Erckmann, Emile. Invasion of France in 1814. London, 1871.
42573.20.5 Erckmann, Emile. Invasion of France in 1814. N.Y., 1894.
42573.20.7 Erckmann, Emile. Invasion of France in 1814. N.Y., 1898.
42573.20.10 Erckmann, Emile. Invasion of France in 1814. N.Y., 1900.
42573.20.15 Erckmann, Emile. Invasion of France in 1814. N.Y., 1900.
42573.23 Erckmann, Emile. Madame Thérèse. N.Y., 1869.
42573.25 Erckmann, Emile. A miller's story of the war. N.Y., 1872.
42573.25.4 Erckmann, Emile. The plebiscite or A miller's story of the war. N.Y., 1894.
42573.25.4.5 Erckmann, Emile. The plebiscite. N.Y., 1898.
42573.25.5 Erckmann, Emile. The plebiscite or A miller's story of the war. N.Y., 1900.
42573.25.10 Erckmann, Emile. The plebiscite or A miller's story of the war. N.Y., 190-?
42573.25.15 Erckmann, Emile. The plebiscite. N.Y., 1903.
42573.27 Erckmann, Emile. The forest house and Catherine's lovers. Boston, 1871.
42573.27.50 Erckmann, Emile. The blockade of Phalsburg. N.Y., 1898.
42573.28 Erckmann, Emile. The blockade of Phalsburg. N.Y., 1901.
42573.30 Erckmann, Emile. L'Alsace en 1814. Strasbourg, 1850.
42573.35 Erckmann, Emile. Erckmann et Chatrian par Erckmann seul. Thèse. Metz, 1932.

42573.60 Individual authors, etc. - 1850-1899 - Fiction - Eyma

42573.60 Eyma, Louis Xavier. Le roi des Tropiques. Paris, 1860.

42574.5 Individual authors, etc. - 1850-1899 - Fiction - Fabre, A.

42574.5.31 Fabre, Aristide. La pipe de Philibert. Paris, 1899.

42574.14 - .36 Individual authors, etc. - 1850-1899 - Fiction - Fabre, F. - Writings

42574.14 Fabre, Ferdinand. L'abbé Tigrane. Paris, 1873.
42574.14.2 Fabre, Ferdinand. L'abbé Tigrane. Paris, 1890.
42574.14.3 Fabre, Ferdinand. L'abbé Tigrane. Paris, 1886.
42574.14.50 Fabre, Ferdinand. L'abbé Tigrane. N.Y., 1875.
42574.15 Fabre, Ferdinand. Barnabé. Paris, 1875.
42574.15.3 Fabre, Ferdinand. Barnabé. Paris, 1885.
42574.15.9 Fabre, Ferdinand. Les Courbezon. Paris, 1862.
42574.16 Fabre, Ferdinand. Les Courbezon. Paris, 1875.
42574.17 Fabre, Ferdinand. Un illuminé. Paris, 1890.
42574.18 Fabre, Ferdinand. Julien Savignac. Paris, 1863.
42574.19 Fabre, Ferdinand. Lucifer. Paris, 1885.
42574.20 Fabre, Ferdinand. Le marquis de Pierrerue. Paris, 1874. 2v.
42574.21 Fabre, Ferdinand. La petite mère. Paris, 1877. 4v.
42574.22 Fabre, Ferdinand. Mon oncle Célestin. Paris, 1881.
42574.25 Fabre, Ferdinand. Sylviane. Paris, 1892.
42574.28 Fabre, Ferdinand. Le chevrier. Paris, 1867.
42574.31 Fabre, Ferdinand. Madame Fuster. Paris, 1887.
42574.36 Fabre, Ferdinand. Ma jeunesse. Paris, 1903.

42574.37 - .39 Individual authors, etc. - 1850-1899 - Fiction - Fabre, F. - Works about

42574.37 Bowen, Ray Preston. The novels of Ferdinand Fabre. Thesis. Boston, 1918.
42574.38 Duviard, Ferdinand. Ferdinand Fabre, 1827-1898. Thèse. Cahors, 1926.

42575.3 Individual authors, etc. - 1850-1899 - Fiction - Fage, E.

42575.3 Fage, Emile. Causeries limousines. Paris, 1889.

42575.5 - .12 Individual authors, etc. - 1850-1899 - Fiction - Ferry de Bellemare - Writings

42575.5.2 Bellemare, Louis de. Costal l'indien. Paris, 1855.
42575.5.5 Bellemare, Louis de. Le coureur des bois. tom.2. 4. éd. Paris, 1856.
42575.6 Bellemare, Louis de. Le coureur des bois. 6. éd. Paris, 1865. 2v.
42575.8 Bellemare, Louis de. Le coureur des bois. 16. éd. Paris, 1910. 2v.

42575.5 - .12 Individual authors, etc. - 1850-1899 - Fiction - Ferry de Bellemare - Writings - cont.

42575.10 Bellemare, Louis de. Scènes de la vie sauvage. Paris, 1868.
42575.11 Bellemare, Louis de. Scènes de la vie mexicaine. Paris, 1856.
42575.11.2 Bellemare, Louis de. Scènes de la vie militaire au Mexique. Paris, 1858.
42575.11.3 Bellemare, Louis de. Escenas de la vida militar en Mexico. Mexico, 1863.

42575.21 Individual authors, etc. - 1850-1899 - Fiction - Feydeau, E.

42575.21 Feydeau, Ernest. Fanny. Paris, 1877.
42575.21.2 Feydeau, Ernest. Fanny. 2. éd. Paris, 1948.
42575.21.5 Feydeau, Ernest. Le secret du bonheur. N.Y., 1864.
42575.21.6 Feydeau, Ernest. The secret of happiness. Edinburgh, 1867. 2v.
42575.21.7 Feydeau, Ernest. Sylvie. Paris, 1861.
42575.21.9 Feydeau, Ernest. Un coup de bourse; étude dramatique. 2. éd. Paris, 1868.
42575.21.15 Feydeau, Ernest. Mémoires d'une jeune fille de bonne famille. Paris, 1951.

42575.23 - .24 Individual authors, etc. - 1850-1899 - Fiction - Feuillet, O. - Complete and Selected works

42575.23 Feuillet, Octave. Théâtre complet. Paris, 1900. 5v.
42575.23.10 Feuillet, Octave. Le village. Paris, 1874. 6 pam.
42575.23.15 Feuillet, Octave. Le roman d'un jeune homme pauvre. Paris, n.d. 5 pam.

42575.25 - .52 Individual authors, etc. - 1850-1899 - Fiction - Feuillet, O. - Individual works

42575.25 Feuillet, Octave. L'acrobate. Paris, 1873.
42575.25.8 Feuillet, Octave. Les amours de Philippe. 4. éd. Paris, 1877.
42575.26 Feuillet, Octave. Les amours de Philippe. Paris, 1879.
42575.26.2 Feuillet, Octave. The amours of Philippe. Philadelphia, 1877.
42575.27 Feuillet, Octave. Bellah. Paris, 1872.
42575.27.2 Feuillet, Octave. Dalila. Paris, 1857.
42575.27.3 Feuillet, Octave. Le cheveu blanc. Paris, 1860.
42575.27.4 Feuillet, Octave. Circé; scène parisienne. n.p., n.d.
42575.27.5 Feuillet, Octave. Le divorce de Juliette. Paris, 1889.
42575.27.10 Feuillet, Octave. Le sphinx. N.Y., 1880.
42575.27.12 Feuillet, Octave. Le sphinx. 2. éd. Paris, 1874.
42575.28 Feuillet, Octave. La fée. N.Y., 1883.
42575.29 Feuillet, Octave. Histoire d'une parisienne. Paris, 1881.
42575.29.2 Feuillet, Octave. Histoire d'une parisienne. 12. éd. Paris, 1881.
42575.30 Feuillet, Octave. Histoire de Sibylle. Paris, 1871.
42575.30.2 Feuillet, Octave. Histoire de Sibylle. 4. éd. Paris, 1863.
42575.30.3 Feuillet, Octave. Histoire de Sibylle. Paris, 1876.
42575.30.5 Feuillet, Octave. Honneur d'artiste. Paris, 1890.
42575.30.10 Feuillet, Octave. An artist's honor. Chicago, 1890.
42575.31 Feuillet, Octave. Le journal d'une femme. Paris, 1880.
42575.31.5 Feuillet, Octave. Le journal d'une femme. Paris, 1878.
42575.32 Feuillet, Octave. Julia de Trécoeur. Paris, 1872.
42575.32.5 Feuillet, Octave. Julia de Trécoeur. 11. éd. Paris, 1876.
42575.35 Feuillet, Octave. Un mariage dans le monde. Paris, 1877.
42575.35.5 Feuillet, Octave. Un mariage dans le monde. Paris, 19- ?
42575.35.8 Feuillet, Octave. A marriage in high life. Philadelphia, 1876.
42575.36 Feuillet, Octave. Monsieur de Camors. 7. éd. Paris, 1867.
42575.36.4 Feuillet, Octave. Monsieur de Camors. 9. éd. Paris, 1868.
42575.36.5 Feuillet, Octave. Monsieur de Camors. 10. éd. Paris, 1869.
42575.37 Feuillet, Octave. Monsieur de Camors. Paris, 1872.
42575.38 Feuillet, Octave. Monsieur de Camors. 21. éd. Paris, 1877.
42575.38.5 Feuillet, Octave. Monsieur de Camors. 25. éd. Paris, 1880.
42575.38.8 Feuillet, Octave. La morte. 13. éd. Paris, 1886.
42575.38.9 Feuillet, Octave. La morte. 98. éd. Paris, 1886.
42575.38.10 Feuillet, Octave. Aliette. (La morte). N.Y., 1886.
42575.39 Feuillet, Octave. La novela de la vida. Madrid, 1859.
42575.39.40 Feuillet, Octave. Un roman parisien. 3. éd. Paris, 1883.
42575.39.50 Feuillet, Octave. A Parisian romance. N.Y., 1893.
42575.40 Feuillet, Octave. La petite comtesse. Paris, 1871.
42575.40.2 Feuillet, Octave. La petite comtesse. Paris, 1879.
42575.40.5 Feuillet, Octave. La petite comtesse. Paris, 1874.
42575.40.10 Feuillet, Octave. Led astray, or La petite comtesse. N.Y., 1875.
42575.41 Feuillet, Octave. Péril en la demeure. 3. éd. Paris, 1859.
42575.41.5 Feuillet, Octave. Péril en la demeure. Paris, 1873. 3 pam.
42575.43 Feuillet, Octave. Scènes et comédies. Paris, 1870.
42575.43.3 Feuillet, Octave. Scènes et comédies. Paris, 1876.
42575.44 Feuillet, Octave. Scènes et proverbes. Paris, 1872.
42575.45 Feuillet, Octave. Scènes et proverbes. Paris, 1860.
42575.45.5 Feuillet, Octave. Scènes et proverbes. Paris, 1861.
42575.45.10 Feuillet, Octave. Scènes et proverbes. Paris, 1869. 2 pam.
42575.45.15 Feuillet, Octave. Scènes et proverbes. Paris, 1877.
42575.47 Feuillet, Octave. Redemption. Paris, 1861.
42575.47.2 Feuillet, Octave. Le roman d'un jeune homme pauvre. 2. éd. Paris, 1859.
42575.47.5 Feuillet, Octave. Le roman d'un jeune homme pauvre. 3. éd. Paris, 1859.
42575.47.9 Feuillet, Octave. Le roman d'un jeune homme pauvre. 9. éd. Paris, 1859.
42575.47.12 Feuillet, Octave. Le roman d'un jeune homme pauvre. 14. éd. Paris, 1859.
42575.49 Feuillet, Octave. Le roman d'un jeune homme pauvre. Boston, 1865.
42575.49.3 Feuillet, Octave. Le roman d'un jeune homme pauvre. N.Y., 1866.
42575.49.4 Feuillet, Octave. Le roman d'un jeune homme pauvre. N.Y., 1866.
42575.49.5 Feuillet, Octave. Le roman d'un jeune homme pauvre. Boston, 1867.
42575.49.7 Feuillet, Octave. Le roman d'un jeune homme pauvre. 7. éd. N.Y., 1871?
Htn 42575.49.15* Feuillet, Octave. Le roman d'un jeune homme pauvre. Paris, 1887.

42575.25 - .52 Individual authors, etc. - 1850-1899 - Fiction - Feuillet, O. - Individual works - cont.

42575.50A Feuillet, Octave. The romance of a poor young man. N.Y., 1859.
42575.50B Feuillet, Octave. The romance of a poor young man. N.Y., 1859.
42575.50.2 Feuillet, Octave. The romance of a poor young man. N.Y., 1864.
42575.50.3 Feuillet, Octave. Il romanzo di un giovane povero. N.Y., 1873.
42575.50.4A Feuillet, Octave. The romance of a poor young man. N.Y., 1902.
42575.50.4B Feuillet, Octave. The romance of a poor young man. N.Y., 1902.
42575.50.5 Feuillet, Octave. The sphinx. N.Y., 188-?
42575.50.9 Feuillet, Octave. La tentation. 2. éd. Paris, 1860.
42575.51 Feuillet, Octave. La veuve. Le voyageur. 30. éd. Paris, 1884.
42575.51.2 Feuillet, Octave. La veuve. Le voyageur. 16. éd. Paris, 1884.
42575.51.3 Feuillet, Octave. La veuve. Le voyageur. 30. éd. Paris, 1884.
42575.51.4 Feuillet, Octave. La veuve. Le voyageur. 24. éd. Paris, 1884.
42575.51.5 Feuillet, Octave. Le village. Boston, 1864.
42575.51.10 Feuillet, Octave. Le village. Paris, 1874.
42575.51.20 Feuillet, Octave. Vie de Polichinelle et ses nombreuses aventures. Paris, 1846.
42575.51.25 Feuillet, Octave. Vie de Polichinelle et ses nombreuses aventures. Paris, 1890.
42575.52 Feuillet, Octave. Quelques années de ma vie. 4. éd. Paris, 1894.
42575.52.2 Feuillet, Octave. Quelques années de ma vie. Paris, 1894.
42575.52.10 Feuillet, Octave. Souvenirs et correspondances. 3. éd. Paris, 1896.

42575.53 - .53.27 Individual authors, etc. - 1850-1899 - Fiction - Feuillet, O. - Biography and criticism

42575.53 Deries, Léon. Octave Feuillet. Saint-Lô, 1901.
42575.53.5 Pamphlet box. Octave Feuillet.
42575.53.7 Bordeaux, A. La jeunesse d'Octave Feuillet, 1821-1890. 9. éd. Paris, 1922.
42575.53.10 Barresen, A. Le théâtre d'Octave Feuillet, 1821-1890. Thèse. Paris, 1929.

42575.53.28 Individual authors, etc. - 1850-1899 - Fiction - Flammarion

42575.53.28 Flammarion, Camille. Urania. Boston, 1890.
42575.53.28.5 Flammarion, Camille. Uranie. N.Y., 1890.
42575.53.28.10 Flammarion, Camille. Uraine. Paris, 1889.

42575.53.29 Individual authors, etc. - 1850-1899 - Fiction - Formont

42575.53.29 Formont, M. La grande amoureuse. 5. éd. Paris, 1904.

42575.53.35 - .53.99 Individual authors, etc. - 1850-1899 - Fiction - Fould, W.J.S.

42575.53.35A Fould, W. de (Mme.). Le bleuet. 17. éd. Paris, 1882.
42575.53.35B Fould, W. de (Mme.). Le bleuet. 17. éd. Paris, 1882.
42575.53.40 Fould, W. de (Mme.). Renée and Franz. N.Y., 1878.
42575.53.48 Fould, W. de (Mme.). Le sphinx aux perles. Paris, 1884.
42575.53.55 Fould, W. de (Mme.). Vertu. 7. éd. Paris, 1877.

42575.54 Individual authors, etc. - 1850-1899 - Fiction - Goncourt, E. and J. - Complete and Selected works

42575.54 Goncourt, Edmond de. Pages choisies des auteurs contemporains. Paris, 1896.
42575.54.5 Goncourt, Edmond de. Selections from Edmond and Jules de Goncourt. N.Y., 1898.

42575.55 - .79 Individual authors, etc. - 1850-1899 - Fiction - Goncourt, E. and J. - Individual works

42575.55 Goncourt, Edmond de. Charles Demailly. Paris, 1891.
42575.56.5 Goncourt, Edmond de. Chérie. Paris, 1921.
42575.57 Goncourt, Edmond de. En 18... Paris, 1885.
42575.58 Goncourt, Edmond de. Les frères Zemganno. Paris, 1879.
NEDL 42575.59 Goncourt, Edmond de. Madame Gervaisais. Paris, 1889.
42575.59.10 Goncourt, Edmond de. Madame Gervaisais. Paris, 1919.
42575.59.15 Goncourt, Edmond de. Madame Gervaisais. Paris, 1923?
42575.60 Goncourt, Edmond de. Quelques créatures. Paris, 1878.
42575.61 Goncourt, Edmond de. Renée Mauperin. Paris, 1891.
42575.61.5 Goncourt, Edmond de. Renée Mauperin. Paris, 1879.
42575.61.15 Goncourt, Edmond de. Renée Mauperin. N.Y., 1902.
42575.61.25 Goncourt, Edmond de. Renée Mauperin. N.Y., 1919?
42575.62 Goncourt, Edmond de. Soeur Philomène. Paris, 1891.
42575.62.10 Goncourt, Edmond de. Soeur Philomène. Paris, 1877.
42575.62.12 Goncourt, Edmond de. Soeur Philomène. Paris, 1890.
42575.63 Goncourt, Edmond de. Idées et sensations. Paris, 1887.
42575.64 Goncourt, Edmond de. Pages retrouvées. Paris, 1886.
42575.64.50 Goncourt, Edmond de. Préfaces et manifestes littéraires. Paris, 1888.
42575.65 Goncourt, Edmond de. Préfaces et manifestes. Paris, 1888.
42575.67 Goncourt, Jules de. Lettres. Paris, 1885.
NEDL 42575.68 Goncourt, Edmond de. Journal des Goncourt. v.2-9. Paris, 1891. 8v.
42575.68.1 Goncourt, Edmond de. Journal des Goncourt. Paris, 1888-1917. 9v.
42575.68.5 Goncourt, Edmond de. Pages from the Goncourt journal. London, 1962.
42575.68.10 Goncourt, Edmond de. Correspondance inédite, 1876-1896 d'Edmond de Goncourt et Henry Céard. Paris, 1965.
42575.69 Fuchs, Max. Lexique du Journal des Goncourt. Paris, n.d.
42575.69.25 Goncourt, Edmond de. The Goncourt journals, 1851-1870. Garden City, 1937.
42575.69.30 Goncourt, Edmond de. Journal. Monaco, 1956. 22v.
42575.69.35 Goncourt, Edmond de. Journal. Paris, 1959. 4v.
42575.70 Goncourt, Edmond de. Théâtre. Paris, 1879.
42575.71 Goncourt, Edmond de. Germinie Lacerteux. Paris, 1865.
NEDL 42575.71.25 Goncourt, Edmond de. Germinie Lacerteux. Paris, 1913.
42575.71.30 Goncourt, Edmond de. Germinie Lacerteux. N.Y., 1955.
42575.71.35 Goncourt, Edmond de. Germinie Lacerteux. Paris, 1930.
Htn 42575.72.3* Goncourt, Edmond de. Germinie Lacerteux. Paris, 1888.
42575.73.10 Goncourt, Edmond de. La Faustin. Paris, 1882.
42575.75A Goncourt, Edmond de. La fille Elisa. 4. éd. Paris, 1877.
42575.75B Goncourt, Edmond de. La fille Elisa. 4. éd. Paris, 1877.
42575.75.2 Goncourt, Edmond de. La fille Elisa. Paris, 1956.
42575.75.5 Ricatte, Robert. La genèse de "La fille Elisa". Paris, 1960.
42575.76 Goncourt, Edmond de. Première amoureuse. Paris, 1896.
42575.78 Goncourt, Edmond de. Manette Salomon. Paris, 1929?

42575.55 - .79 Individual authors, etc. - 1850-1899 - Fiction - Goncourt, E. and J. - Individual works - cont.
42575.78.5 Goncourt, Edmond de. Manette Salomon. Paris, 1877.

42575.80 - .999 Individual authors, etc. - 1850-1899 - Fiction - Goncourt, E. and J. - Biography and criticism
42575.80A Lowndes, Marie A. (Belloc). Edmond and Jules de Goncourt. London, 1895.
42575.80B Lowndes, Marie A. (Belloc). Edmond and Jules de Goncourt. London, 1895.
42575.81 Lowndes, Marie A. (Belloc). Edmond and Jules de Goncourt. N.Y., 1895. 2v.
42575.82 Koehler, Erich. Edmond und Jules de Goncourt. Leipzig, 1912.
42575.83A Sabatier, Pierre. L'esthétique des Goncourt. Paris, 1920.
42575.83B Sabatier, Pierre. L'esthétique des Goncourt. Paris, 1920.
42575.85 Pamphlet box. Goncourt brothers.
42575.87 Sabatier, Pierre. L'esthétique des Goncourt. Thèse. Paris, 1920.
42575.89 Delzant, A. Les Goncourt. Paris, 1889.
42575.90 Traz, Georges de. Edmond et Jules de Goncourt. Paris, 1941.
42575.91 Loesch, Georg. Die impressionistische Syntax der Goncourt. Inaug. Diss. Nürnberg, 1919.
42575.93 Goncourt, Edmond de. Livres modernes, ouvrages. Paris, 1897.
42575.95 Goncourt, Edmond de. Bibliothèque des Goncourt. 18ème siècle. Paris, 1897.
42575.98 Seillière, E. Les Goncourt moralistes. 2. éd. Paris, 1927.
42575.99 Immergluck, M. La question sociale dans l'oeuvre des Goncourt. Thèse. Strasbourg, 1930.
42575.100 Immergluck, M. La question sociale dans l'oeuvre des Goncourt. Paris, 1930.
42575.105 Jarman, L.M. The Goncourt brothers::modernists in abnormal psychology. Albuquerque, 1939.
42575.107 Goncourt, Edmond de. Hommage à Edmond et Jules de Goncourt à l'occasion du 50ème anniversaire de la mort de Edmond de Goncourt. Paris, 1946.
42575.109A Ricatte, Robert. La création romanesque chez les Goncourt. Paris, 1953.
42575.109B Ricatte, Robert. La création romanesque chez les Goncourt. Thèse. Paris, 1953.
42575.112 Billy, André. Les frères Goncourt. Paris, 1954.
42575.112.5 Billy, André. Vie des frères Goncourt. Monaco, 1956. 3v.
42575.112.10A Billy, André. The Goncourt brothers. 1st American ed. N.Y., 1960.
42575.112.10B Billy, André. The Goncourt brothers. 1st American ed. N.Y., 1960.
42575.113 Caramachi, Enzo. Le réalisme romanesque des Goncourt. Pisa, 1964.
42575.114 Deffoux, Léon. L'immortalité littéraire selon M. de Goncourt. Paris, 1918.
42575.115 Sauvage, Marcel. Jules et Edmond de Goncourt, précurseurs. Paris, 1970.
42575.116 Baldick, Robert. The Goncourts. London, 1960.
42575.118 Grant, Richard Babson. The Goncourt brothers. N.Y., 1972.

42576.3 Individual authors, etc. - 1850-1899 - Fiction - Flore
42576.3.5 Viaud, Julien. Le roman d'un enfant. Paris, 1924.
42576.3.30F Flore, Jeanne. Histoire de la belle Rosemonde et du preux chevalier Andro. Paris, 1888.

42576.4 Individual authors, etc. - 1850-1899 - Fiction - Gevin-Cassal
42576.4 Gevin-Cassal. Souvenirs du Sundgau. Paris, 1892.

42576.5 Individual authors, etc. - 1850-1899 - Fiction - Gebhart
42576.5 Gebhart, Emile. Autour d'une tiare, 1075-1085. Paris, 1894.
42576.5.5 Gebhart, Emile. Petits mémoires. Paris, 1912.
42576.5.7 Gebhart, Emile. D'Ulysse à Panurge. 4. éd. Paris, 1913.
42576.5.11 Gebhart, Emile. Au son des cloches, contes et légendes. 2. éd. Paris, 1898.

42576.6 Individual authors, etc. - 1850-1899 - Fiction - Ginisty
42576.6 Ginisty, Paul. Les Rastaquonères. Paris, n.d.
42576.6.5 Ginisty, Paul. Louis XVII. Paris, 1895.
42576.6.6 Ginisty, Paul. Crime et châtiment. Paris, 1888. 4 pam.
42576.6.7 Ginisty, Paul. Deux tourtereaux. Paris, 1890.
42576.6.9 Ginisty, Paul. La chartreuse de Parme. Paris, 1918.
42576.6.11 Ginisty, Paul. L'histoire singulière de Mlle Leblanc. Paris, 1920.
42576.6.15 Ginisty, Paul. Souvenirs de journalisme et de théâtre. Paris, 1930.
42576.6.17 Ginisty, Paul. Lendemains d'amour. Paris, 1902.
42576.6.20 Ginisty, Paul. Lettres galantes du chevalier de Faques. Paris, 1931.

42576.8 Individual authors, etc. - 1850-1899 - Fiction - Gleizes
42576.8.13 Gleizes, J.A. Salena, ou La famille Samanéenne. Paris, 1838.
42576.8.50 Demarquette, J. J.A. Gleizes et son influence sur le mouvement naturaliste. Thèse. Paris, 1928.

42576.9 Individual authors, etc. - 1850-1899 - Fiction - Godefroy
42576.9 Godefroy, Louis. Récits Champenois et Briards. Paris, 1880.

42576.10 Individual authors, etc. - 1850-1899 - Fiction - Guezenec
42576.10 Guezenec, Alfred de. Les amoureux de vingt ans. Paris, 1870.

42576.11 Individual authors, etc. - 1850-1899 - Fiction - Guillemot
42576.11 Guillemot, Jules. Florimond. Paris, 1891.
42576.11.20 Guillemot, Maurice. Lettres d'un amant. Paris, 1889.

42576.12 Individual authors, etc. - 1850-1899 - Fiction - Cherbonnel, A.
42576.12 Cherbonnel, Alice. Mon oncle et mon curé. N.Y., n.d.
42576.12.5 Cherbonnel, Alice. Mon oncle et mon curé. 27. éd. Paris, n.d.
42576.12.10 Cherbonnel, Alice. Mon oncle et mon curé. 140. éd. Paris, 19- .
42576.12.12 Cherbonnel, Alice. Mon oncle et mon curé. Paris, 19- ?
42576.12.20 Cherbonnel, Alice. My uncle and my curé. N.Y., 1892.
42576.12.30 Cherbonnel, Alice. Un obstacle. 5. éd. Paris, 1912.
42576.12.35 Cherbonnel, Alice. Les deux sommets. Paris, 1920.

42576.12 Individual authors, etc. - 1850-1899 - Fiction - Cherbonnel, A. - cont.
42576.12.40 Cherbonnel, Alice. My uncle and the curé. London, 1957.
42576.12.100 Ducharme, Réjean. La fille de Christophe Colomb. Paris, 1969.

42576.13 Individual authors, etc. - 1850-1899 - Fiction - Garcia, M.
42576.13.30 Garcia, Marie. La confession d'Antonine. Paris, 1864.

42576.14 Individual authors, etc. - 1850-1899 - Fiction - Houssaye, A.
42576.14.9 Houssaye, Arsène. Romans parisiens. Mlle Mariani. v.1-2. Paris, 1859.
42576.14.9.15 Houssaye, Arsène. Mademoiselle Cléopâtre. 7. éd. Paris, 1864.
42576.14.10 Houssaye, Arsène. Contes pour les femmes. v.1-2,5. Paris, 1885-1886.
42576.14.11 Houssaye, Arsène. Les aventures galantes de Margot. Paris, 1866.
42576.14.12 Houssaye, Arsène. Tragique aventure de bal masqué. 2. éd. Paris, 187-?
42576.14.13 Houssaye, Arsène. Voyages humoristiques. Paris, 1856.
42576.14.32 Houssaye, Arsène. La virtu di Rosina. Firenze, 1869.
42576.14.35 Houssaye, Arsène. Les mille et une nuits parisiennes. Paris, 1875. 4v.
42576.14.40 Houssaye, Arsène. Sous la régence et sous la terreur. Paris, 1853.
42576.14.45 Houssaye, Arsène. Les femmes comme elles sont. 2. éd. Paris, 1857.
42576.14.55 Houssaye, Arsène. Les confessions. 1830-1880. Paris, 1885-1891. 6v.
42576.14.58 Houssaye, Arsène. Les confessions. 1830-1880. Paris, 1891. 6v.
42576.14.65 Houssaye, Arsène. Souvenirs de jeunesse. Paris, 1896. 2v.
42576.14.73 Houssaye, Arsène. Philosophers and actresses. N.Y., 1852. 2v.
42576.14.75 Houssaye, Arsène. Philosophers and actresses. N.Y., 1886. 2v.
42576.14.85 Houssaye, Arsène. Les femmes démasquées. 5. éd. Paris, n.d. 2v.
42576.14.95 Houssaye, Arsène. Les grandes dames. Paris, 1868. 4v.
42576.14.96 Houssaye, Arsène. Les courtisanes du monde. Paris, 1870. 2v.
42576.14.105 Houssaye, Arsène. Histoires romanesques. Paris, 1891.
42576.14.110 Houssaye, Arsène. Life in Paris. N.Y., 1879.
42576.14.800 Lemaitre, Ernest. Arsène Houssaye. Reims, 1897.

42576.15 Individual authors, etc. - 1850-1899 - Fiction - Flaubert - Biography and criticism
42576.15.5 Pamphlet vol. Flaubert, Gustave. Criticism, 1863-99.
42576.15.6 Pamphlet vol. Flaubert, Gustave. Criticism, 1900-22.
42576.15.7 Pamphlet box Gustave Flaubert.
42576.15.8 Dumesnil, René. Bibliographie de Gustave Flaubert. Paris, 1937.
42576.15.9 Commauville, Carol. Souvenirs sur Gustave Flaubert. Paris, 1895.
42576.15.10 Tarver, J.C. Gustave Flaubert as seen in his works and correspondence. N.Y., 1895.
X Cg 42576.15.11 Faguet, Emile. Flaubert. Paris, 1899.
42576.15.11.5 Faguet, Emile. Flaubert. Boston, 1914.
42576.15.12 Dumesnil, René. Flaubert. Paris, 1905.
42576.15.12.5 Dumesnil, René. Le grand amour de Flaubert. Genève, 1945.
42576.15.13 Gould, G.M. A biographic clinic on Gustave Flaubert. Philadelphia, 1906.
42576.15.14 Fischer, E.W. Etudes sur Flaubert inédit. Leipzig, 1908.
42576.15.15 Lehmann, R. Die Formelemente des Stils von Flaubert. Marburg, 1911.
42576.15.16 Bertrand, L. Gustave Flaubert. 3. éd. Paris, 1912.
42576.15.17 Elliott monographs. v.1-4. Flaubert. Baltimore, 1914.
42576.15.19 Hamilton, Arthur. Sources of the religious element in Flaubert's Salambô. Diss. Baltimore, 1918.
42576.15.20 Benedetto, Luigi F. Le origini di Salammbô. Firenze, 1920.
42576.15.21 Riddell, Agnes R. Flaubert and Maupassant. Thesis. Chicago, 1920.
42576.15.22 Riddell, Agnes R. Flaubert and Maupassant. Chicago, 1920.
42576.15.25 Seillière, Ernest. Le romantisme des réalistes. Paris, 1914.
42576.15.27 Fusco, Antonio. La filosofia dell'arte in Gustavo Flaubert. Messina, 1907.
42576.15.30 Descharmes, René. Flaubert. Paris, 1909.
42576.15.34 Descharmes, René. Autour de Flaubert. Photoreproduction. Paris, 1912. 2v.
42576.15.35 Ferrère, E.L. L'esthétique de Gustave Flaubert. Thèse. Paris, 1913.
Htn 42576.15.37* Bourget, Paul. Gustave Flaubert. Discours. Paris, 1922.
NEDL 42576.15.40 Thibaudet, A. Gustave Flaubert. Paris, 1922.
42576.15.41A Thibaudet, A. Gustave Flaubert. 6. éd. Paris, 1935.
42576.15.41B Thibaudet, A. Gustave Flaubert. 6. éd. Paris, 1935.
42576.15.41.2 Thibaudet, A. Gustave Flaubert. Paris, 1963.
42576.15.42 Moore, Thomas S. Art and life. (Flaubert and Blake). London, 1910.
42576.15.45 Maynial, E. Flaubert et son milieu. Paris, 1927.
42576.15.48 Maynial, E. La jeunesse de Flaubert. Paris, 1913.
42576.15.49 Maynial, E. Flaubert. Paris, 1943.
42576.15.50 Shanks, Lewis P. Flaubert's youth, 1821-1845. Baltimore, 1927.
42576.15.52 Dumesnil, René. La vocation de Gustave Flaubert. Paris, 1961.
42576.15.53 Dumesnil, René. "L'éducation sentimentale" de Gustave Flaubert. Paris, 1936.
42576.15.54 Dumesnil, René. La publication de "Madame Bovary". Amiens, 1928.
42576.15.55 Dumesnil, René. La publication de "Madame Bovary". 3. éd. Amiens, 1928.
42576.15.56 Dumesnil, René. Madame Bovary de Gustave Flaubert. Paris, 1946.
42576.15.57 Dumesnil, René. En marge de Flaubert. Paris, 1928.
42576.15.58 Herval, René. Les véritables origine de "Madame Bovary". Paris, 1951.
42576.15.59 Dumesnil, René. Gustave Flaubert, l'homme et l'oeuvre. Paris, 1932.
42576.15.60 Doublet, G. La composition de Salambô. Toulouse, 1894.
42576.15.64 Demorest, D.L. L'expression figurée et symbolique dans l'oeuvre de Gustave Flaubert. Thèse. v.1. Paris, 1931. 2v.
42576.15.66 Demorest, D.L. A travers les plans, manuscrits et dossiers de Bouvard et Pécuchet. Thèse. Paris, 1931.

42576.15 Individual authors, etc. - 1850-1899 - Fiction - Flaubert - Biography and criticism - cont.

42576.15.70 Gérard-Gailly, Émile. Flaubert et "Les fantômes de Trouville". Paris, 1930.
42576.15.72 Gérard-Gailly, Émile. L'unique passion de Flaubert:"Madame Arnoux". Paris, 1932.
42576.15.75 Haas, Eugen. Flaubert und die Politik. Inaug. Diss. Biella, 1931.
42576.15.80 Frejlich, Hélène. Flaubert d'après sa correspondance. Thèse. Paris, 1933.
42576.15.83 Frejlich, Hélène. Les amants de Mantes, Flaubert et Louise Calet. Paris, 1936.
42576.15.85 Merezhkovskii, D.S. The life-work of Flaubert. London, 1908.
42576.15.90 Melang, Walter. Flaubert als Begründer des literarischen Impressionismus in Frankreich. Inaug. Diss. Emsdetten, 1933.
42576.15.95A Albalat, A. Gustave Flaubert et ses amis. Paris, 1927.
42576.15.95B Albalat, A. Gustave Flaubert et ses amis. Paris, 1927.
42576.15.100 Wassermann, J.S. Flaubert; ein Selbstporträt nach seinen Briefen. Berlin, 1907.
42576.15.105 Anweiler, J. Die stilistische Funktion der medizinischen und naturwissenschaftlichen Fachausdrücke in Flauberts "Madame Bovary". Inaug. Diss. Heidelberg, 1935?
42576.15.110 Pantke, A. Gustave Flauberts Tentation de Saint-Antoine. Inaug. Diss. Engelsdorf, 1936.
42576.15.115 Lombard, A. Flaubert et Saint-Antoine. Paris, 1934.
42576.15.120 Seznec, Jean. Les sources de l'épisode des dieux dans "La tentation de Saint-Antoine". Paris, 1940.
42576.15.125 Servais, T.H. Gustave Flauberts Urteile über die französische Literatur in seiner "Correspondance". Inaug. Diss. Münster, 1936.
42576.15.130 Schollmeyer, V. Gustave Flaubert in seinem Verhältnis zu Michel de Montaigne. Griefswald, 1934.
42576.15.135A Steegmüller, F. Flaubert and Madame Bovary. N.Y., 1939.
42576.15.135B Steegmüller, F. Flaubert and Madame Bovary. N.Y., 1939.
42576.15.135.2 Steegmüller, F. Flaubert and Madame Bovary. N.Y., 1968.
42576.15.140 Freienmuth von Helms, E.E. German criticism of Gustave Flaubert,1857-1930. N.Y., 1939.
42576.15.145 Muoni, Guido. Gustavo Flaubert. Roma, 1920.
42576.15.150 Degoumois, L. Flaubert à l'école de Goethe. Genève, 1924.
42576.15.155 Guillemin, Henri. Flaubert devant la vie et devant Dieu. Paris, 1939.
42576.15.157 Guillemin, Henri. Flaubert devant la vie et devant Dieu. Paris, 1963.
42576.15.165 Auriant (pseud.). Koutchauk-hauem, l'almée de Flaubert. 4. éd. Paris, 1943.
42576.15.170 Digeon, Claude. Le dernier visage de Flaubert. Paris, 1946.
42576.15.175 Canu, Jean. Flaubert, auteur dramatique. Paris, 1946.
42576.15.181 Seznec, Jean. Nouvelles études sur "La tentation de Saint-Antoine". London, 1949.
42576.15.185 Schöne, Maurice. La langue de Flaubert. Paris, 1946?
42576.15.190 Bertrand, G.E. Les jours de Flaubert. Paris, 1947.
42576.15.195 Merker, Emil. Flaubert. Urack, 1948.
42576.15.200 Durry, M. Flaubert et ses projets inédits. Paris, 1950.
42576.15.205A Bonwit, M. Gustave Flaubert et le principe d'impossibilité. Berkeley, 1950.
42576.15.205B Bonwit, M. Gustave Flaubert et le principe d'impossibilité. Berkeley, 1950.
42576.15.210 Spencer, P. Flaubert. London, 1952.
42576.15.215 Seznec, Jean. Flaubert à l'exposition de 1851. Oxford, 1951.
42576.15.220 Bopp, Léon. Commentaire sur Madame Bovary. Neuchâtel, 1951.
42576.15.225 Laumet, Lucien. La sensibilité de Flaubert. Alençon, 1951.
42576.15.230 Amis de Flaubert. Bulletin. Rouen. 14,1959+ 3v.
42576.15.235 Christensen, Hjalmar. Gustave Flaubert. Kjøbenhavn, 1902.
42576.15.240 Thorlby, Anthony. Gustave Flaubert and the art of realism. London, 1956.
42576.15.250 Bart, Benjamin F. Flaubert's landscape descriptions. Ann Arbor, 1957.
42576.15.251 Bart, Benjamin F. Flaubert. Syracuse, 1967.
42576.15.260 Stein, H.A. Die Legenstandswelt im Werke Flauberts. Bleicherode am Harz, 1938.
42576.15.270 Alboreto, Luciano. Il rapporto vita poesia in Flaubert. Venezia, 1958.
42576.15.275 Vérard, René. Epilogue de "L'affaire Bovary". Rouen, 1959.
42576.15.280 Castex, Pierre. Flaubert, "L'education sentimentale". Paris, 1961.
42576.15.285 Fairlie, Alison. Flaubert. London, 1962.
42576.15.290 Mason, G.M. Les écrits de jeunesse de Flaubert. Paris, 1961.
42576.15.295 Commanville, C. Succession de Mme Franklin Grout-Flaubert. Paris, 1931.
42576.15.300 Bruneau, J. Les débuts littéraires de Gustave Flaubert, 1831-1845. Paris, 1962.
42576.15.305 Colling, Alfred. Gustave Flaubert. Paris, 1947.
42576.15.310A Naaman, A.Y. Les débuts de Gustave Flaubert. Paris, 1962.
42576.15.310B Naaman, A.Y. Les débuts de Gustave Flaubert. Paris, 1962.
42576.15.311 Naaman, A.Y. Les débuts de Gustave Flaubert. Thèse. Paris, 1962.
42576.15.315 Dumesnil, René. Flaubert. Vésenaz, 1948.
42576.15.320 Giraud, R. Flaubert. Englewood Cliffs, 1964.
42576.15.325 Bollème, Geneviève. La leçon de Flaubert. Paris, 1964.
42576.15.330 Lapierre, Charles. Esquisse sur Flaubert intime. Evreux, 1898.
42576.15.335 Buck, Stratton. Gustave Flaubert. N.Y., 1966.
42576.15.340 Bart, Benjamin F. Madame Bovary and the critics. N.Y., 1966.
42576.15.345 Gothot-Mersch, Claudine. La genèse de Madame Bovary. Paris, 1966.
42576.15.350A Brombert, Victor H. The novels of Flaubert. Princeton, 1966.
42576.15.350B Brombert, Victor H. The novels of Flaubert. Princeton, 1966.
42576.15.355 Jackson, Ernest. The critical reception of G. Flaubert in the United States, 1860-1960. The Hague, 1966.
42576.15.360 Neale, Mary. Flaubert en Angleterre, étude sur les lecteurs anglais de Flaubert. Bordeaux, 1966.
42576.15.365 Cortland, Peter. The sentimental adventure. The Hague, 1967.
42576.15.370 Starkie, Enid. Flaubert::the making of the master. London, 1967.
42576.15.375 Fletcher, John. A critical commentary on Flaubert's "Trois contes". London, 1968.

42576.15 Individual authors, etc. - 1850-1899 - Fiction - Flaubert - Biography and criticism - cont.

42576.15.380 Wetherill, Peter M. Flaubert et la création littéraire. Paris, 1964.
42576.15.385 Zimmermann, Inge. Farbsymbolik und Handlungsstruktur im Romanwerk Flauberts. Bonn, 1968.
42576.15.390 Nadeau, Maurice. Gustave Flaubert. Paris, 1969.
42576.15.390.5 Nadeau, Maurice. The greatness of Flaubert. N.Y., 1972.
42576.15.395 Cento, Alberto. Il realismo documentario nell'Education sentimentale. Napoli, 1967.
42576.15.400 Asper-Bruggisser, Kathrin. Genèse du déterminisme de Gustave Flaubert. Zurich, 1968.
42576.15.405 Hardt, Manfred. Flauberts Spätwerk. Frankfurt, 1970.
42576.15.410 Sherrington, R. Three novels by Flaubert; a study of techniques. Oxford, 1970.
42576.15.415 Digeon, Claude. Flaubert. Paris, 1970.
42576.15.420 Sartre, Jean Paul. L'idiot de la famille; Gustave Flaubert. Paris, 1971. 3v.
42576.15.425 Kenner, Hugh. Flaubert, Joyce and Beckett::The stoic comedians. Boston, 1962.
42576.15.430 Maranini, Lorenza. Il 48 [i.e. quarantotto] nella struttura della "Education sentimentale" e altri studi francesi. Pisa, 1963.
42576.15.435 Wiesner, Gerlind. Untersuchungen zum Wortschatz von Gustave Flaubert. Inaug. Diss. Heidelberg? 1965?
42576.15.440 Suffel, Jacques. Gustave Flaubert. Paris, 1958.
42576.15.445 Thorlby, Anthony. Gustave Flaubert and the art of realism. New Haven, 1957.
42576.15.450 Tillett, Margaret G. On reading Flaubert. London, 1961.
42576.15.455 Bibliothèque nationale, Paris. Gustave Flaubert et Madame Bovary. Paris, 1957.
42576.15.460 Frey, G.W. Die ästhetische Begriffswelt Flauberts. München, 1972.

42576.16 - .17 Individual authors, etc. - 1850-1899 - Fiction - Flaubert - Complete and Selected works

42576.16 Flaubert, Gustave. Oeuvres complètes. Paris, 1885. 8v.
42576.16.15 Flaubert, Gustave. Oeuvres de jeunesse inédites. Paris, 1910. 3v.
42576.16.26 Flaubert, Gustave. Complete works. N.Y., 1904.
42576.16.27 Flaubert, Gustave. Best known works. N.Y., 1904.
42576.16.30 Flaubert, Gustave. Flaubert. Paris, 1955.
42576.16.50 Flaubert, Gustave. Gustave Flaubert. N.Y., 1903.
42576.16.52 Flaubert, Gustave. Works. N.Y., 1904.
42576.16.60 Flaubert, Gustave. L'oeuvre de Flaubert. Paris, 1952.
42576.16.62 Flaubert, Gustave. Oeuvres. Paris, 1952. 2v.
42576.16.64 Flaubert, Gustave. Oeuvres. Lausanne, 1964. 18v.
42576.16.66 Flaubert, Gustave. Oeuvres complètes. Paris, 1964. 2v.
42576.16.67 Flaubert, Gustave. Oeuvres complètes. Paris, 1971. 3v.
42576.16.80 Cento, Alberto. La dotterina di Flaubert. Napoli, 1962.
42576.16.85 Cento, Alberto. La dottrina di Flaubert. 2. ed. Napoli, 1964.
42576.17 Flaubert, Gustave. Notes de voyages. Paris, 1910. 2v.
42576.17.5 Flaubert, Gustave. Pages choisies. Paris, 1895.
42576.17.25 Flaubert, Gustave. Correspondance. Paris, 1928. 3v.
42576.17.26 Flaubert, Gustave. Bouvard et Pécuchet. Paris, 1923.
42576.17.27 Flaubert, Gustave. Madame Bovary. Paris, 1921.
42576.17.28 Flaubert, Gustave. Salammbô. Paris, 1922.
42576.17.29 Flaubert, Gustave. La tentation de Saint-Antoine. Paris, 1922.
42576.17.30 Flaubert, Gustave. Trois contes. Paris, 1929.
42576.17.31 Flaubert, Gustave. L'éducation sentimentale. Paris, 1922.

42576.18 - .35 Individual authors, etc. - 1850-1899 - Fiction - Flaubert - Individual works

42576.18A Flaubert, Gustave. Bouvard et Pécuchet. Paris, 1881.
42576.18B Flaubert, Gustave. Bouvard et Pécuchet. Paris, 1881.
42576.19 Flaubert, Gustave. Un coeur simple. Paris, 1894.
42576.19.5 Flaubert, Gustave. Un coeur simple. Paris, 1909.
42576.19.15 Flaubert, Gustave. Un coeur simple. Monaco, 1946.
42576.20.2 Flaubert, Gustave. L'éducation sentimentale. 2. éd. v. 2. Paris, 1870.
X Cg 42576.20.5 Flaubert, Gustave. L'education sentimentale. Paris, 1896.
42576.20.19 Flaubert, Gustave. L'éducation sentimentale. Paris, 1923.
42576.20.20 Flaubert, Gustave. L'éducation sentimentale. v. 1-2. Paris, 1947.
42576.20.23 Flaubert, Gustave. L'éducation sentimentale. Paris, 1957.
42576.20.30 Flaubert, Gustave. La première Éducation sentimentale. Paris, 1963.
42576.20.35 Flaubert, Gustave. The first sentimental education. Berkeley, 1972.
42576.21 Flaubert, Gustave. Dictionnaire des idées reçues. Paris, 1913.
42576.21.5 Flaubert, Gustave. Dictionary of accepted ideas. Norfolk, 1954.
42576.21.10 Flaubert, Gustave. A dictionary of platitudes. London, 1954.
42576.21.15 Flaubert, Gustave. Dictionnaire des idées reçues. Napoli, 1966.
Htn 42576.22* Flaubert, Gustave. Hérodias. Paris, 1892.
Htn 42576.22.2* Flaubert, Gustave. Hérodias. Paris, 1892.
Htn 42576.23* Flaubert, Gustave. La tentation de Saint-Antoine. Paris, 1874.
42576.23.3 Flaubert, Gustave. La tentation de Saint-Antoine. Paris, 1882.
42576.23.4 Flaubert, Gustave. La première tentation de Saint-Antoine. Paris, 1908.
42576.23.5 Flaubert, Gustave. La tentation de Saint-Antoine. Paris, 1924.
42576.23.6.5 Flaubert, Gustave. La tentation de Saint-Antoine. Paris, 1940.
42576.23.6.10 Flaubert, Gustave. La tentation de Saint-Antoine. Paris, 1968.
42576.23.7 Flaubert, Gustave. The temptation of St. Anthony. N.Y., 1911.
42576.23.7.5 Flaubert, Gustave. The temptation of St. Anthony. N.Y., 193-?
42576.23.8 Flaubert, Gustave. The temptation of St. Anthony. N.Y., 1910.
42576.23.9 Flaubert, Gustave. De serzoeking san den H. Antonius. Amsterdam, 1896.
42576.23.15 Seznec, Jean. Saint-Antoine et les monstres. N.Y., 1943.
42576.24.5 Flaubert, Gustave. The candidate. v. 8. Chicago, 1904.
42576.25 Flaubert, Gustave. Two tales of Flaubert. N.Y., 1938.
42576.26 Flaubert, Gustave. Souvenirs. Paris, 1965.

42576.18 - .35 Individual authors, etc. - 1850-1899 - Fiction - Flaubert - Individual works - cont.

42576.26.5 Flaubert, Gustave. Intimate notebook, 1840-1841. 1st ed. Garden City, 1967.
42576.28.1.3 Flaubert, Gustave. Madame Bovary. Paris, 1917.
42576.28.5 Flaubert, Gustave. Madame Bovary. Paris, 1921.
42576.28.6 Flaubert, Gustave. Madame Bovary. Philadelphia, 1896. 2v.
42576.28.12 Flaubert, Gustave. Madame Bovary. N.Y., 1902.
42576.28.14 Flaubert, Gustave. Madame Bovary. Paris, 1905.
42576.28.30 Flaubert, Gustave. Madame Bovary. N.Y., 1930.
42576.28.35 Flaubert, Gustave. Madame Bovary. N.Y., 193-.
42576.28.38 Flaubert, Gustave. Madame Bovary. Paris, 1885.
42576.28.39 Flaubert, Gustave. Madame Bovary. Paris, 1885.
42576.28.50 Flaubert, Gustave. Madame Bovary. Paris, 1936. 2v.
42576.28.55A Flaubert, Gustave. Madame Bovary. London, 1939.
42576.28.55B Flaubert, Gustave. Madame Bovary. London, 1939.
42576.28.55C Flaubert, Gustave. Madame Bovary. London, 1939.
42576.28.60 Flaubert, Gustave. Madame Bovary. Paris, 1945. 2v.
42576.28.65 Flaubert, Gustave. Madame Bovary. Monaco, 1946.
42576.28.70 Flaubert, Gustave. Madame Bovary. Paris, 1946.
42576.28.75 Flaubert, Gustave. Madame Bovary. 1. ed. Philadelphia, 1949.
42576.28.80 Flaubert, Gustave. Madame Bovary. Paris, 1949.
42576.28.85 Flaubert, Gustave. Madame Bovary. Harmondsworth, 1950.
42576.28.90 Flaubert, Gustave. Madame Bovary. N.Y., 1957.
42576.28.92 Flaubert, Gustave. Madame Bovary. N.Y., 1957.
42576.28.95 Flaubert, Gustave. Madame Bovary. Paris, 1957.
42576.28.97 Flaubert, Gustave. Madame Bovary. Paris, 1957.
42576.28.98 Flaubert, Gustave. Madame Bovary. Paris, 1930.
42576.28.100 Flaubert, Gustave. Madame Bovary. 1. ed. N.Y., 1965.
42576.28.102 Flaubert, Gustave. Madame Bovary. Paris, 1968.
42576.29 Flaubert, Gustave. Poésies de jeunesse inédites. Columbia, S.C., 1968.
42576.30.6 Flaubert, Gustave. Salambô. N.Y., 1927.
42576.31 Flaubert, Gustave. Salammbô. Paris, 1888.
42576.31.7 Flaubert, Gustave. Salammbô. N.Y., 1919.
42576.31.9 Flaubert, Gustave. Salammbô. Paris, 1921.
42576.31.15 Flaubert, Gustave. Salammbô. N.Y., 1929.
42576.31.20 Flaubert, Gustave. Salammbô. London, 1944.
42576.31.25 Flaubert, Gustave. Salammbô. Paris, 1944. 2v.
42576.31.30 Flaubert, Gustave. Salammbô. Paris, 1927.
42576.31.35 Flaubert, Gustave. Salammbô. London, 1956.
42576.31.40 Flaubert, Gustave. Salammbô. Paris, 1960.
42576.32.5 Flaubert, Gustave. Die Sage von Sankt Julian dem Gastfreien. Potsdam, 1919.
42576.33 Flaubert, Gustave. Trois contes. Paris, 1877.
42576.33.2 Flaubert, Gustave. Trois contes. 7. éd. Paris, 1885.
42576.33.5A Flaubert, Gustave. Trois contes. Paris, 19- ?
42576.33.5B Flaubert, Gustave. Trois contes. Paris, 19- ?
42576.33.6 Flaubert, Gustave. Trois contes. Paris, 1899.
42576.33.7 Flaubert, Gustave. Trois contes. Paris, 1921.
42576.33.8 Flaubert, Gustave. Trois contes. Paris, 1936.
42576.33.8.3 Flaubert, Gustave. Trois contes. Paris, 1936.
42576.33.8.5 Flaubert, Gustave. Trois contes. Montréal, 1944.
42576.33.8.7 Flaubert, Gustave. Trois contes. Paris, 1930.
42576.33.9.3 Flaubert, Gustave. Bouvard und Pécuchet. Minden, 1909.
42576.33.9.5 Flaubert, Gustave. Bouvard and Pécuchet. London, 1896.
42576.33.9.8 Neuenschwander-Naef, Claudia. Vorstellungswelt und Realität in Flauberts "Bouvard et Pécuchet". Winterthur, 1959.
42576.33.10.7 Flaubert, Gustave. Bouvard et Pécuchet. Napoli, 1964-
42576.33.10.8 Flaubert, Gustave. Le second volume de Bouvard et Pécuchet. Paris, 1966.
42576.33.10.10 Flaubert, Gustave. Bouvard et Pécuchet. Paris, 1966.
42576.33.11 Flaubert, Gustave. The legend of Saint Julian. London, 192-?
42576.33.12 Pamphlet vol. Flaubert, Gustave. French periodicals.
42576.33.15 Flaubert, Gustave. Sentimental education. London, 1961.
42576.33.75 Flaubert, Gustave. Par les champs et par les grèves. Paris, 1886.
42576.33.105A Flaubert, Gustave. Three tales. Norfolk, 1947.
42576.33.105B Flaubert, Gustave. Three tales. Norfolk, 1947.
42576.34 Flaubert, Gustave. Par les champs et par les grèves. Paris, 1927.
42576.34.5 Flaubert, Gustave. Théâtre. Paris, 1927.
42576.34.10 Flaubert, Gustave. Bibliomania. Evanston, 1929.
42576.34.12 Flaubert, Gustave. Der Büchernarr. Hannover, 1910.
42576.34.15 Flaubert, Gustave. Voyages. Paris, 1948. 2v.
42576.34.30F Flaubert, Gustave. La queue de la poire et de la boule de Monseigneur. Paris, 1958.
42576.34.35 Flaubert, Gustave. November. N.Y., 1967.
42576.35 Flaubert, Gustave. Correspondance. Paris, 1887-1892. 4v.
NEDL 42576.35.2 Flaubert, Gustave. Correspondance. Paris, 1894-1905.
42576.35.3 Flaubert, Gustave. Correspondance. Paris, 1922-1925. 4v.
42576.35.4 Miller, L.G. Index de la correspondance de G. Flaubert. Strasbourg, 1934.
42576.35.8A Flaubert, Gustave. Lettres à George Sand précédées d'une étude par Guy de Maupassant. Paris, 1884.
42576.35.8B Flaubert, Gustave. Lettres à George Sand précédées d'une étude par Guy de Maupassant. Paris, 1884.
42576.35.10 Nesselstrauss, B. Flauberts Briefe, 1871-1880. Halle, 1921.
42576.35.12 Flaubert, Gustave. Les lettres d'Egypte de Gustave Flaubert d'après les manuscrits autographes. Paris, 1965.
42576.35.15 Flaubert, Gustave. Lettres inédites à Tourgueneff. Monaco, 1946.
42576.35.20 Flaubert, Gustave. Lettres choisies. Paris, 1947.
42576.35.25 Flaubert, Gustave. Lettres inédites à Maxime du Camp. Sceaux, 1948.
42576.35.28 Flaubert, Gustave. Extraits de la correspondance. Paris, 1963.
42576.35.30 Flaubert, Gustave. Lettres de Grèce. Paris, 1948.
42576.35.32 Flaubert, Gustave. Les plus belles lettres de G. Flaubert. Paris, 1962.
42576.35.33 Flaubert, Gustave. Lettres inédites de G. Flaubert à son éditeur Michel Levy. Paris, 1965.
42576.35.35 Flaubert, Gustave. Letters. London, 1950.
42576.35.38 Flaubert, Gustave. La correspondance de Flaubert. Columbus, 1968.
42576.35.40 Flaubert, Gustave. Lettres inédites à Raoul Duval. Paris, 1950.
42576.35.45 Flaubert, Gustave. Selected letters. N.Y., 1953.
42576.35.48 Flaubert, Gustave. Lettres à sa nièce Caroline. Paris, 1906.

42576.18 - .35 Individual authors, etc. - 1850-1899 - Fiction - Flaubert - Individual works - cont.

42576.35.50A Flaubert, Gustave. Correspondance. Paris, 1926-1935. 9v.
42576.35.50B Flaubert, Gustave. Correspondance. Paris, 1926-1935. 9v.
42576.35.50.1A Flaubert, Gustave. Correspondance. Supplément. Paris, 1954. 4v.
42576.35.50.1B Flaubert, Gustave. Correspondance. Supplément. Paris, 1954. 4v.
42576.35.91 Kenner, Hugh. Flaubert, Joyce and Beckett. London, 1964.

42576.36 Individual authors, etc. - 1850-1899 - Fiction - Fleuriot; Gay; Geffroy; etc.

Htn 42576.36* Flaubert, Gustave. Lettres à George Sand. Paris, 1884.
42576.36.10 Fleuriot, Zenaide Marie A. Nuestos enemigos intimos. Habana, 1876.
42576.36.11 Fleuriot, Zenaide Marie A. Z.M.A. Fleuriot. Paris, 1899.
42576.36.11.15 Fleuriot, Zenaide Marie A. Loyauté. 5. éd. Paris, 1908.
42576.36.12 Fleuriot, Zenaide Marie A. Armelle Traher. 6. éd. Paris, 1888.
42576.36.15 Gay, Ernest. Fille de comtesses. Paris, 1897?
42576.36.19 Gay, Sophie. La duchesse de Châteauroux. Paris, 1873.
42576.36.20 Gay, Sophie. Marie de Mancini. Paris, 1864.
42576.36.21 Gay, Sophie. Physiologie du ridicule. Paris, 1864.
42576.36.23 Gay, Sophie. Souvenirs d'une vieille femme. Paris, 1875.
42576.36.25 Allmendinger, J.F. Die Romanschriftstellerin Sophie Gay. Rottenburg, 1913.
42576.36.50 Geffroy, G. Cécile Pommier. pt. 1-2. Paris, 1923. 2v.
42576.36.180 Dénommé, R.T. The naturalism of Gustave Geffroy. Genève, 1963.

42576.37 Individual authors, etc. - 1850-1899 - Fiction - Gorose; Grave; Grosclaud; etc.

42576.37 Gheusi, P.B. L'opéra romanesque. Paris, 1909.
42576.37.35 Gorsse, H. de. Cinq semaines en aéroplane. Paris, 1911.
42576.37.37 Gorsse, H. de. La jeunesse de Cyrano de Bergerac. N.Y., 1941.
42576.37.40 Grave, Jean. Terre libre. Paris, 1908.
42576.37.50 Grosclaude, E. Les joies du plein air. Paris, 1889.

42576.38 Individual authors, etc. - 1850-1899 - Fiction - Guéroult; Guillemain; Galland; etc.

42576.38.25 Guéroult, Constant. Les exploits de Fifi Vollard. Paris, 1876.
42576.38.26 Guéroult, Constant. Le juif de Gand. v.1-4. Paris, 1857. 2v.
42576.38.1100 Guillemain, E. Autour de la trahison. Paris, 1898.
42576.38.2100 Galland, C. De Mazas à Jérusalem. Paris, 1895.

42576.39 - .40.199 Individual authors, etc. - 1850-1899 - Fiction - Guiches

42576.39 Guiches, Gustave. Céleste Prudhomat. Paris, 1887.
42576.40 Guiches, Gustave. L'ennemi. Paris, 1887.
42576.40.5 Guiches, Gustave. Snob. Paris, 1897.
42576.40.9 Guiches, Gustave. Le nuage. Paris, 1902.
42576.40.13 Guiches, Gustave. Chacun sa vie. Paris, 1907.
42576.40.15 Guiches, Gustave. Chacun sa vie. Paris, 1907.
42576.40.16 Guiches, Gustave. Chacun sa vie. Paris, 1907.
42576.40.17 Guiches, Gustave. Vouloir. Paris, 1913.
Htn 42576.40.79* Guillemot, Maurice. Entr'actes de pierres. Paris, 1899.

42576.40.200 - Individual authors, etc. - 1850-1899 - Fiction - Halevy, L.

42576.40.271 Halévy, Ludovic. Carnets. Paris, 1935- 2v.
42576.40.290 Halévy, Ludovic. Morceaux choisis de Ludovic Halévy. N.Y., 1914.
42576.40.302 Halévy, Ludovic. L'abbé Constantin. 54. éd. Paris, 1883.
42576.40.305 Halévy, Ludovic. L'abbé Constantin. 62. éd. Paris, 1884.
42576.40.306 Halévy, Ludovic. L'abbé Constantin. N.Y., 1886.
42576.40.308F Halévy, Ludovic. L'abbé Constantin. Paris, 1887.
42576.40.312 Halévy, Ludovic. L'abbé Constantin. N.Y., 1889.
42576.40.325 Halévy, Ludovic. The abbé Constantin. N.Y., 18-
42576.40.328 Halévy, Ludovic. L'abbé Constantin. Paris, 1888.
42576.40.330F Halévy, Ludovic. The abbé Constantin. London, 1888.
42576.40.333 Halévy, Ludovic. The abbé Constantin. Chicago, 189-.
42576.40.334 Halévy, Ludovic. The abbé Constantin. N.Y., 189-.
42576.40.338 Halévy, Ludovic. L'abbé Constantin. Boston, 1899.
42576.40.340 Halévy, Ludovic. The abbé Constantin. N.Y., 1895.
42576.40.341 Halévy, Ludovic. The abbé Constantin. N.Y., 1895.
42576.40.342 Halévy, Ludovic. The abbé Constantin. N.Y., 1895.
42576.40.343 Halévy, Ludovic. Abbé Constantin and Le marriage for love. N.Y., 1902.
42576.40.344 Halévy, Ludovic. The abbé Constantin. N.Y., 1898.
42576.40.345 Halévy, Ludovic. The abbé Constantin. N.Y., 1910.
42576.40.346 Halévy, Ludovic. L'abbé Constantin. 219. éd. Paris, 1902.
42576.40.347 Halévy, Ludovic. L'abbé Constantin. Philadelphia, 19- ?
42576.40.348A Halévy, Ludovic. L'abbé Constantin. Boston, 1916.
42576.40.348B Halévy, Ludovic. L'abbé Constantin. Boston, 1916.
42576.40.355 Halévy, Ludovic. Deux mariages. Paris, 1883.
42576.40.365 Halévy, Ludovic. Madame et Monsieur Cardinal. 27. éd. Paris, 1882.
42576.40.366 Halévy, Ludovic. Madame et Monsieur Cardinal. Paris, 1872.
42576.40.368 Halévy, Ludovic. La famille Cardinal. Paris, 1883.
42576.40.371 Halévy, Ludovic. La famille Cardinal. Paris, 1893.
42576.40.375 Halévy, Ludovic. Karikari. 11. éd. Paris, 1892.
42576.40.380 Halévy, Ludovic. Un mariage d'amour. Paris, 1881.
42576.40.382 Halévy, Ludovic. A marriage for love. N.Y., 1893.
42576.40.385 Halévy, Ludovic. Les petites Cardinal. 49. éd. Paris, 1894.
NEDL 42576.40.400A Halévy, Ludovic. Criquette. 23. éd. Paris, 1883.
42576.40.400B Halévy, Ludovic. Criquette. 25. éd. Paris, 1883.
42576.40.400C Halévy, Ludovic. Criquette. 55. éd. Paris, 1883.
42576.40.400D Halévy, Ludovic. Criquette. 56. éd. Paris, 1884.
42576.40.410 Halévy, Ludovic. Mariette. Paris, 1893.
42576.40.415 Halévy, Ludovic. Princesse. Paris, 1887.
42576.40.425 Halévy, Ludovic. Parisian point of view. N.Y., 1894.
42576.40.426 Halévy, Ludovic. Parisian point of view. N.Y., 1894.
42576.40.428A Halévy, Ludovic. Parisian point of view. N.Y., 1894.
42576.40.428B Halévy, Ludovic. Parisian point of view. N.Y., 1894.
42576.40.429 Halévy, Ludovic. Parisian point of view. N.Y., 1894.

Classified Listing

42576.41 Individual authors, etc. - 1850-1899 - Fiction - La Bedollière; Le Blanc, M.; etc.

42576.41 La Bédollièrre, E.G. de. Histoire de la mère Michel et de son chat. N.Y., 1866.
42576.41.4 La Bédollièrre, E.G. de. Histoire de la mère Michel et de son chat. Boston, 1907.
42576.41.5 La Bédollièrre, E.G. de. Storia di un Gatto. Firenze, 1897.
42576.41.10 Lantoine, Albert. Elisçuah. Paris, 1896.
42576.41.20 Le Blanc, Maurice. La frontière. Paris, 1911.
42576.41.20.5 Le Blanc, Maurice. The frontier. N.Y., 1912.
42576.41.20.10 Le Blanc, Maurice. The frontier. London, 19- .
42576.41.21 Le Blanc, Maurice. Le bouchon de cristal. Paris, 1912.
42576.41.21.4 Le Blanc, Maurice. The blonde lady. N.Y., 1910.
42576.41.21.8A Le Blanc, Maurice. The crystal stopper. Garden City, 1913.
42576.41.21.8B Le Blanc, Maurice. The crystal stopper. Garden City, 1913.
42576.41.23 Le Blanc, Maurice. 813. Garden City, 1911.
42576.41.23.5A Le Blanc, Maurice. 813. Paris, 1910.
42576.41.23.5B Le Blanc, Maurice. 813. Paris, 1910.
42576.41.23.10 Le Blanc, Maurice. 813. 4. éd. Paris, 1914.
NEDL 42576.41.24 Le Blanc, Maurice. Le triangle d'or. Paris, 1918.
42576.41.25 Le Blanc, Maurice. The eight strokes of the clock. N.Y., 1922.
42576.41.26 Le Blanc, Maurice. L'éclat d'obus. Paris, 1916.
42576.41.30 Le Blanc, Maurice. The three eyes. N.Y., 1921.
42576.41.35 Le Blanc, Maurice. The tremendous event. N.Y., 1922.
42576.41.40 Le Blanc, Maurice. La comtesse de Cagliostro. Paris, 1924.
42576.41.45 Le Blanc, Maurice. Man of miracles. N.Y., 1931.
42576.41.55 Le Blanc, Maurice. La vie extravagante de Balthazar. Paris, 1925.
42576.41.60 Le Blanc, Maurice. Confessions of Arsène Lupin. N.Y., 1913.
42576.41.62 Le Blanc, Maurice. Confessions of Arsène Lupin. Garden City, 1913.
42576.41.65 Le Blanc, Maurice. Wanton Venus. N.Y., 1935.
42576.41.70 Le Blanc, Maurice. The teeth of the tiger. N.Y., 1914.
42576.41.75A Le Blanc, Maurice. The golden triangle. N.Y., 1917.
42576.41.75B Le Blanc, Maurice. The golden triangle. N.Y., 1917.
42576.41.85 Le Blanc, Maurice. Arsène Lupin, gentleman-cambrioleur. Boston, 1938.

42576.42 Individual authors, etc. - 1850-1899 - Fiction - Labusquière; Le Barillier; Lermina; etc.

42576.42 Labusquière, John. L'autrefois; récits de Gascogne et d'ailleurs. Paris, 1899.
42576.42.9 Le Barillier, Berthe. Le mime Barthylle. Paris, 1894.
42576.42.10 Le Barillier, Berthe. Les vièrges de Syracuse. Paris, 1902.
42576.42.11 Le Barillier, Berthe. Le journal de Marguerite Plantin. Paris, 1908.
Htn 42576.42.12* Le Barillier, Berthe. La danseuse de Pompei. Paris, 1903.
42576.42.14 Le Barillier, Berthe. La couronne d'épines. Paris, 1914.
42576.42.15 Le Barillier, Berthe. Les délices de Mantoue. Paris, 1906.
42576.42.20 Le Barillier, Berthe. La passion d'Héloïse et d'Abélard. Paris, 1910.
42576.42.25 Lermina, Jules. Les mariages maudits. Paris, 1880.
42576.42.50 Lemonnier, A. Les femmes de théâtre. Paris, 1865.

42576.43 Individual authors, etc. - 1850-1899 - Fiction - Lemonnier, C.

42576.43.30 Lemonnier, Camille. La comédie des jouets. Paris, 1888.
42576.43.35 Lemonnier, Camille. Un mâle. Paris, 1926.
42576.43.50 Kiepert, Alexander. Camille Lemonnier und seine Romane. Inaug. Diss. Greifswald, 1924.
42576.43.55A Pope, F.R. Nature in the work of Camille Lemonnier. N.Y., 1933.
42576.43.55B Pope, F.R. Nature in the work of Camille Lemonnier. N.Y., 1933.
42576.43.57 Gilles, Maurice. Camille Lemonnier. Bruxelles, 1943.
42576.43.60 Vanwelkenhuyzen, Gustave. Histoire d'un livre: "Un mâle" de C. Lemonnier. Bruxelles, 1961.
42576.43.65 Bazalgette, Léon. Camille Lemonnier. Paris, 1904.

42576.44 - .45 Individual authors, etc. - 1850-1899 - Fiction - Le Roux, H.

42576.44 Le Roux, H. Ô mon passé. Mémoires d'un enfant. Paris, 1896.
42576.44.2 Le Roux, H. Ô mon passé. Mémoires d'un enfant. Paris, n.d.
42576.44.3 Le Roux, H. Au champ d'honneur. Paris, 1916.
42576.44.4 Le Roux, H. On the field of honor. Boston, 1918.
42576.45 Le Roux, H. Le festéjadon. Récits du sud. Paris, 1895.
42576.45.2 Le Roux, H. Le fils à papa. Paris, n.d.
42576.45.3 Le Roux, H. Gens de poudre. Paris, 1899.
42576.45.4 Le Roux, H. Le maître de l'heure. Paris, 1897.
42576.45.5 Le Roux, H. Marins et soldats. Paris, 1892.
42576.45.6 Le Roux, H. Ménélik et nous. Paris, 1900.
42576.45.7 Le Roux, H. Business and love. N.Y., 1903.
42576.45.10 Pamphlet box. Le Roux, H.
42576.45.12 Le Roux, H. Les fleurs à Paris. Paris, 1890.

42576.46 - .46.49 Individual authors, etc. - 1850-1899 - Fiction - Le Roy; Lesueur; Létang

42576.46 Le Roy, Eugène. Jacquou le croquant. Paris, 1900.
42576.46.2 Le Roy, Eugène. Jacquou the rebel. N.Y., 1919.
42576.46.3 Le Roy, Eugène. Jacquou le croquant. 37. éd. Paris, 1927.
NEDL 42576.46.5 Le Roy, Eugène. Au pays des pierres. Paris, 1906.
42576.46.6 Le Roy, Eugène. L'ennemi de la mort. Paris, n.d.
42576.46.7 Le Roy, Eugène. Le moulin du Frau. Paris, 1905.
42576.46.7.2 Le Roy, Eugène. Le moulin du Frau. Paris, 1969.
42576.46.8 Le Roy, Eugène. La damnation de Saint Guynefort. Périgueux, 1966.
42576.46.9 Le Roy, Eugène. Au pays des pierres. Périgueux, 1967.
42576.46.9.10 Le Roy, Eugène. Carnet de notes d'une excursion de quinze jours en Périgord. Paris, 1970.
42576.46.9.20 Le Roy, Eugène. Mademoiselle de la Ralphie. Paris, 1970.
42576.46.9.30 Le Roy, Eugène. Nicette et Milou. Périgueux, 1965.
42576.46.10 Guillaumie, G. Eugène Le Roy, 1836-1907. Bordeaux, 1929.
42576.46.11 Ratoret, P. Le paysan et le paysage dans l'oeuvre de Eugène Le Roy. Thèse. Sadiac, 1940.
42576.46.12 Rau, Erich. Das Périgord und seine Bewohner in den Romanen Eugène Le Roys. Inaug. Diss. Emsdetten, 1936.
42576.46.13 Shaw, Marjorie. L'histoire du Périgord dans l'oeuvre d'Eugène Le Roy. Thèse. Dijon, 1946.
42576.46.14 Ballot, Marc. Eugène Le Roy. Bordeaux, 1946.

42576.46 - .46.49 Individual authors, etc. - 1850-1899 - Fiction - Le Roy; Lesueur; Létang - cont.

42576.46.14.10 Newman, Pauline. Un romancier périgourdin. Paris, 1957.
42576.46.15 Lapauze, Jeanne L. La force du passé. Paris, 1905.
42576.46.16 Lapauze, Jeanne L. Passion slave. Paris, n.d.
42576.46.17 Lapauze, Jeanne L. Comédienne. Paris, 1898.
42576.46.18 Lapauze, Jeanne L. L'honneur d'une femme. Paris, n.d.
42576.46.19 Lapauze, Jeanne L. Invincible charme. Paris, n.d.
42576.46.20 Lapauze, Jeanne L. Au tournant des jours. Paris, 1912.
Htn 42576.46.21* Lapauze, Jeanne L. La masque d'amour. Paris, 1905.
42576.46.22 Lapauze, Jeanne L. Madame l'ambassadrice. 10. éd. Paris, 1907.
42576.46.23 Lapauze, Jeanne L. Du sang dans les ténèbres. Paris, 1910.
42576.46.24 Lapauze, Jeanne L. Fiancée d'outre-mer. Péril d'amour. Justice mondaine. Une mère. 7. éd. Paris, 1901.
42576.46.28 Lespès, Napoléon. Les matinées de Timothée Trimm. 5. éd. Paris, 1865.
42576.46.30 Létang, Louis. Le lieutenant Philippe. Les deux frères. Paris, 1895.
42576.46.31 Létang, Louis. Le supplice d'un père. Les deux frères. Paris, 1895.
42576.46.35 Le Tersec, M.J.E.M. Âmes de soldats. Paris, 1907.

42576.46.50 - .46.999 Individual authors, etc. - 1850-1899 - Fiction - Viaud, J. (Loti) - Biography and criticism [Discontinued]

42576.46.50 Mariel, Jean. Pierre Loti. Paris, 1909.
42576.46.53 Bargone, C. Pierre Loti. Paris, 1930.
42576.46.60 Serban, Nicolas. Pierre Loti. Paris, 1924.
42576.46.70 Schweickert, E. Pierre Loti und André Gide, zwei Arten von Exotisten. Inaug. Diss. München, 1932.
42576.46.75 Scribner, H.M. Pierre Loti. Thèse. Poitiers, 1932.
42576.46.80 Friderich, Emmy. Baskenland und Basken bei Pierre Loti. Inaug. Diss. Würzburg, 1934.
42576.46.85 Flottes, P. Le drame intérieur de Pierre Loti. Paris, 1937.
42576.46.90 Rafter, B.B. La femme dans l'oeuvre de Pierre Loti. Thèse. Paris, 1938.
42576.46.97 Du Coglay, M. Le vrai Loti. 2. éd. Tunis, 1941.
42576.46.99 Lefèvre, R. Les désenchantées de Pierre Loti. Paris, 1939.
42576.46.105 Traz, Robert de. Pierre Loti. Paris, 1948.

42576.47 - .47.24 Individual authors, etc. - 1850-1899 - Fiction - Viaud, J. (Loti) - Complete and Selected works

42576.47 Viaud, Julien. Pages choisies. Paris, 1896.
42576.47.5 Viaud, Julien. Selections from Pierre Loti. N.Y., 1897.

42576.47.25 - .57.74 Individual authors, etc. - 1850-1899 - Fiction - Viaud, J. (Loti) - Individual works

Htn 42576.47.25* Viaud, Julien. Aziyadé. Paris, 1879.
42576.47.30 Viaud, Julien. Aziyadé. 22. éd. Paris, 1893.
42576.47.40 Viaud, Julien. Aziyadé. Paris, 1913?
42576.48.25 Viaud, Julien. Constantinople. N.Y., 1928?
42576.49 Viaud, Julien. Fleurs d'ennui. Paris, 1886.
42576.50 Viaud, Julien. Le mariage de Loti. Paris, 1886.
Htn 42576.50.5* Viaud, Julien. Barahu or The marriage of Loti. N.Y. 1890.
42576.51 Viaud, Julien. Fantôme d'Orient. Paris, 1892.
42576.51.3 Viaud, Julien. Fantôme d'Orient. Paris, 1911?
42576.51.5 Viaud, Julien. Quelques aspects du vertige mondial. Paris, 1917.
42576.52.2 Viaud, Julien. Pêcheur d'Islande. 6. éd. Paris, 1886.
42576.52.4.2 Viaud, Julien. Pêcheur d'Islande. Paris, 1910? 2v.
42576.52.4.3 Viaud, Julien. Pêcheur d'Islande. Paris, 1919?
42576.52.4.5 Viaud, Julien. Pêcheur d'Islande. N.Y., 1920.
42576.52.4.10 Viaud, Julien. Pêcheur d'Islande. N.Y. 1931.
42576.52.4.15 Viaud, Julien. Pêcheur d'Islande. N.Y., 1920.
42576.52.4.20 Viaud, Julien. Pêcheur d'Islande. Bielefeld, 1901.
42576.52.4.25 Viaud, Julien. Pêcheur d'Islande. Boston, 1922.
42576.52.5 Viaud, Julien. Islandski Ribari. Zagreb, 1891.
X Cg 42576.52.9 Viaud, Julien. An Iceland fisherman. N.Y., 1894.
42576.52.10 Viaud, Julien. An Iceland fisherman. 159. ed. N.Y., 1896.
42576.52.11 Viaud, Julien. An Iceland fisherman. N.Y., 1896.
42576.52.15 Viaud, Julien. An Iceland fisherman. N.Y., 1901.
42576.52.15 Viaud, Julien. An Iceland fisherman. N.Y., 1901.
42576.52.20 Viaud, Julien. An Iceland fisherman. N.Y., 1902.
42576.53 Viaud, Julien. Le roman d'un Spahi. Paris, 1886.
42576.53.10 Viaud, Julien. The romance of a Spahi. N.Y., 19- .
42576.54 Viaud, Julien. Le roman d'un enfant. 33. éd. Paris, 1890.
42576.54.3A Viaud, Julien. Le roman d'un enfant. Paris, 1915.
42576.54.3B Viaud, Julien. Le roman d'un enfant. Paris, 1915.
42576.54.3.5 Viaud, Julien. Le roman d'un enfant. Paris, 1924.
42576.54.4 Viaud, Julien. Pêcheur d'Islande. 107. éd. Paris, 1892.
42576.54.5A Viaud, Julien. The story of a child. Boston, 1901.
42576.54.5B Viaud, Julien. The story of a child. Boston, 1901.
42576.54.20 Viaud, Julien. Les trois dames de la Kasbah. Paris, 1897.
42576.55 Viaud, Julien. Le livre de la pitié. Paris, 1891.
42576.55.4 Viaud, Julien. Madame Chrysanthème. London, 1888.
Htn 42576.55.5* Viaud, Julien. Madame Chrysanthème. Paris, 1888.
42576.55.6 Viaud, Julien. Madame Chrysanthème. Paris, 1888.
42576.56 Viaud, Julien. Madame Chrysanthème. 15. éd. Paris, 1893.
42576.56.3 Viaud, Julien. Madame Chrysanthème. London, 1897.
42576.56.4 Viaud, Julien. Madame Chrysanthème. 82. éd. Paris, 1906?
X Cg 42576.56.5 Viaud, Julien. Madame Chrysanthème. 97. éd. Paris, 1909?
42576.56.5.5 Viaud, Julien. Madame Chrysanthème. N.Y., 1910.
42576.56.6 Viaud, Julien. Madame Chrysanthème. 187. éd. Paris, 1920.
42576.56.6.5 Viaud, Julien. Japan (Madame Chrysanthème). N.Y., 1920.
42576.56.7 Viaud, Julien. Madame Chrysanthème. Paris, 1925.
42576.56.7.5 Viaud, Julien. Madame Chrysanthème. Paris, 1927?
42576.56.8 Viaud, Julien. Madame Prune. N.Y., 1919.
42576.56.9 Viaud, Julien. The daughter of heaven. N.Y., 1912..
42576.56.15 Viaud, Julien. From lands of exile. N.Y., 1888.
42576.56.30 Viaud, Julien. Le désert. 45. éd. Paris, 1896.
42576.57 Viaud, Julien. L'exilée. Paris, 1893.
42576.57.1A Viaud, Julien. Mon frère Yves. Paris, 1883.
42576.57.1B Viaud, Julien. Mon frère Yves. Paris, 1883.
42576.57.2 Viaud, Julien. Mon frère Yves. Paris, 1884.
42576.57.2.3 Viaud, Julien. Mon frère Yves. Paris, 1925.
42576.57.2.9 Viaud, Julien. A tale of Brittany. N.Y., 1924.
42576.57.3 Viaud, Julien. Ramuntcho. Paris, 1897.
42576.57.3.1 Viaud, Julien. Ramuntcho. Paris, 19- .
42576.57.3.2 Viaud, Julien. Ramuntcho. N.Y., 1897.
42576.57.3.5 Viaud, Julien. Pincelados vascas. Buenos Aires, 1942.
42576.57.3.10 Viaud, Julien. Ramuntcho. Boston, 1939.
42576.57.3.20 Viaud, Julien. A tale of the Pyrenees (Ramuntcho). N.Y., 1929?
42576.57.4 Viaud, Julien. Matelot. Paris, 1898.
42576.57.4.2 Viaud, Julien. Matelot. Paris, 1893.

42576.47.25 - .57.74 Individual authors, etc. - 1850-1899 - Fiction - Viaud, J. (Loti) - Individual works - cont.

42576.57.4.3 Viaud, Julien. Matelot. Paris, 1911?
42576.57.4.5 Viaud, Julien. Matelot. Paris, 1914.
42576.57.5 Viaud, Julien. Figures et choses qui passaient. Paris, 1898.
42576.57.6 Viaud, Julien. Reflets sur la sombre route. 10. éd. Paris, 1899.
42576.57.7.2A Viaud, Julien. Les désenchantées. Paris, 1906.
42576.57.7.2B Viaud, Julien. Les désenchantées. Paris, 1906.
42576.57.7.2C Viaud, Julien. Les désenchantées. Paris, 1906.
42576.57.7.5A Viaud, Julien. Les désenchantées. 67. éd. Paris, 1906.
42576.57.7.5B Viaud, Julien. Les désenchantées. 67. éd. Paris, 1906.
42576.57.7.10 Viaud, Julien. Disenchanted. N.Y., 1913.
42576.57.7.15 Viaud, Julien. Disenchanted. N.Y., 1906.
42576.57.7.20 Viaud, Julien. Disenchanted. N.Y., 1910.
42576.57.8 Viaud, Julien. Ramuntcho. Paris, 1908.
42576.57.9.5 Viaud, Julien. Egypt. N.Y., 1910.
42576.57.9.15 Viaud, Julien. La mort de Philae. 55. éd. Paris, 1926.
42576.57.10 Viaud, Julien. Le chateau de la Belle-au-Bois-Dormant. Paris, n.d.
42576.57.10.9 Viaud, Julien. Le chateau de la Belle-au-Bois-Dormant. Paris, 1910.
42576.57.10.20 Viaud, Julien. La hyéne enragée. Paris, 1916.
42576.57.11 Viaud, Julien. Un pélerin d'Angkor. Paris, n.d.
42576.57.12 Viaud, Julien. Carmen Sylva. N.Y., 1912.
42576.57.13 Viaud, Julien. Prime jeunesse. Paris, 1919.
42576.57.15 Viaud, Julien. Un jeune officier pauvre. pt. 1-4. Paris, 1923.
42576.57.17 Viaud, Julien. Un jeune officier pauvre. Paris, 1923.
42576.57.18 Viaud, Julien. The book of pity and of death. N.Y., 1892.
42576.57.19 Viaud, Julien. Le livre de la pitié et de la mort. Paris, 1925.
42576.57.20 Viaud, Julien. Lettres de Pierre Loti. Paris, 1924.
42576.57.22 Viaud, Julien. Lettres de Pierre Loti à madame Juliette Adam 1880-1922. Paris, 1924.
42576.57.25 Viaud, Julien. Correspondance inédite, 1865-1904. Paris, 1929.
42576.57.30 Viaud, Julien. Journal intime par Pierre Loti. v.2. Paris, 1925-29.
Htn 42576.57.35* Viaud, Julien. Journal intime. Paris, 1924.
42576.57.36 Viaud, Julien. Journal intime. v. 1-3. Paris, 1928.
42576.57.40 Viaud, Julien. Pierre Loti; quelques fragments du journal intime. Paris, 1947.
42576.57.45 Viaud, Julien. Pierre Loti; notes of my youth. Garden City, N.Y., 1924.
42576.57.50 Viaud, Julien. Lives of two cats. Boston, 1902.
42576.57.55 Pamphlet box. Pierre Loti.

42576.57.75 - .57.999 Individual authors, etc. - 1850-1899 - Fiction - Viaud, J. (Loti) - Biography and criticism

42576.57.75 Hisar, Abdülhah Sinasi. Istanbul ve Pierre Loti. Istanbul, 1958.
42576.57.80 Broden, Pierre. Loti. Montréal, 1945.
42576.57.83 Hublard, M.J.C. L'attitude religieuse de Pierre Loti. Thèse. Fribourg, 1945.
42576.57.85 Paris, Bibliothèque nationale. Pierre Loti. Paris, 1950.
42576.57.88 Millvard, K.G. L'oeuvre de Pierre Loti et l'esprit "Fin de siécle". Paris, 1955.
42576.57.90 Marchand, Henri. En relisant Loti. Alger, 1953.
42576.57.95 Hirschmann-Guenzel, Gustav. Der Todesgedanke bei Pierre Loti. Hamburg, 1930.
42576.57.100 Krueger, C.O. Symbolic contrasts in the works of Pierre Loti. Missouls, 1957.
42576.57.105 Mallet, Frédéric. Pierre Loti; son oeuvre. Paris, 1923.
42576.57.110 Atabinen, Resit Saffet. Pierre Loti. Istanbul, 1950.
42576.57.115 Cario, Louis. Pierre Loti aux armées. Paris, 1923.
42576.57.120 Ekstroem, Per G. Evasions et désespérances de Pierre Loti. Thèse. Göteborg, 1953.

42576.58 - .59 Individual authors, etc. - 1850-1899 - Fiction - Foa, E.

42576.58 Foa, Eugénie. Le petit Robinson de Paris. Boston, 1864.
42576.59 Foa, Eugénie. Le petit Robinson de Paris. Boston, n.d.
42576.59.5 Foa, Eugénie. Le petit Robinson de Paris. N.Y., 1864.
42576.59.10 Foa, Eugénie. Contes biographiques. N.Y., 1865.

42576.60 Individual authors, etc. - 1850-1899 - Fiction - Fonsegrive; Forbin; etc.

42576.60.500 Fonsegrive, G.L. Le journal d'un évêque. Paris, 1897. 2v.
42576.60.510 Fonsegrive, G.L. Lettres d'un curé de canton. Paris, 1895.
42576.60.1100 Forbin, Victor. Mes aventures sous les tropiques. Paris, 1930?

42576.61 Individual authors, etc. - 1850-1899 - Fiction - Franay; Frémine; Frescaly; etc.

42576.61 Franay, Gabriel. Mon chevalier. Paris, 1893.
42576.61.5 Franay, Gabriel. Comme dans un conte. Paris, 1905.
42576.61.6 Franay, Gabriel. Comme dans un conte. Paris, 1906.
42576.61.50 Frémine, Charles. La chanson du pays; récits normands. Paris, 1893.
42576.61.55 Frémine, Charles. Vieux airs et jeunes chansons. Paris, 1884.
42576.61.100 Frescaly, Marcel. Nouvelles algériennes. Paris, 1888.
42576.61.200 Frisson d'Aulnoy, A. Le proscrit. 2. éd. Bruxelles, 1879.

42576.62 - .63.23 Individual authors, etc. - 1850-1899 - Fiction - France, A. - Writings

42576.62A France, Anatole. Oeuvres complètes. Paris, 1925-1935. 25v.
42576.62B France, Anatole. Oeuvres complètes. v. 1-7,10,12,23. Paris, 1925-1935. 10v.
42576.62.2.3 France, Anatole. Balthasar. Paris, 1903.
42576.62.2.5 France, Anatole. Balthasar. 61. éd. Paris, 1921.
42576.62.2.6 France, Anatole. Balthasar. N.Y., 1924.
42576.62.2.7 France, Anatole. Balthasar. Thaïs. L'étude de nacre. Levallois-Perret, 1968.
42576.62.3.5 France, Anatole. Thaïs. Paris, 1906.
42576.62.3.7 France, Anatole. Thaïs. 109. éd. Paris, 1912?
42576.62.3.15 France, Anatole. Thaïs. 314. éd. Paris, 1924.
42576.62.3.20 France, Anatole. Thaïs. Paris, 1923.
42576.62.3.25 France, Anatole. Thaïs. N.Y., 1925?
42576.62.3.26 France, Anatole. Thaïs. N.Y., 1926.
42576.62.3.30 France, Anatole. Thaïs. N.Y., 1929.
42576.62.3.35 France, Anatole. Thaïs. N.Y., 1932?
42576.62.4 France, Anatole. Jocaste. Paris, 1879.

42576.62 - .63.23 Individual authors, etc. - 1850-1899 - Fiction - France, A. - Writings - cont.

42576.62.4.2 France, Anatole. Jocaste et Le chat maigre. Paris, 191-?
42576.62.4.3 France, Anatole. Jocaste et Le chat maigre. Levallois-Perret, 1969.
42576.62.4.6 France, Anatole. Jocaste et Le chat maigre. Paris, 191-?
42576.62.5 France, Anatole. Le livre de mon ami. Paris, 1892.
42576.62.5.10 France, Anatole. Le livre de mon ami. 16. éd. Paris, 1892.
42576.62.5.30 France, Anatole. Le livre de mon ami. 116. éd. Paris, 1912?
42576.62.5.40 France, Anatole. Le livre de mon ami. N.Y., 1925.
42576.62.5.42 France, Anatole. Le livre de mon ami. N.Y., 1927.
42576.62.5.90 France, Anatole. La rôtisserie de la reine Pédauque. Paris, 1893.
42576.62.6.2 France, Anatole. La rôtisserie de la reine Pédauque. Paris, 1912.
42576.62.6.3 France, Anatole. La rôtisserie de la reine Pédauque. 381. éd. Paris, 1921.
42576.62.6.5 France, Anatole. La rôtisserie de la reine Pédauque. 118. éd. Paris, 1919.
42576.62.6.6 France, Anatole. La rôtisserie de la reine Pédauque. 296. éd. Paris, 1924.
42576.62.6.8 France, Anatole. The queen Pédauque. N.Y., 1923.
42576.62.6.10 France, Anatole. At the sign of the reine Pédauque. N.Y., 1931.
42576.62.6.15 France, Anatole. La rôtisserie de la reine Pédauque. Levallois-Perret, 1968.
42576.62.6.25 France, Anatole. The romance of the queen Pédauque. N.Y., 1931.
42576.62.6.30 France, Anatole. At the sign of the reine Pédauque. London, 1922.
42576.62.7 France, Anatole. Les opinions de M. Jérôme Coignard. Paris, 1895.
42576.62.7.3 France, Anatole. Les opinions de M. Jérôme Coignard. Paris, 1893.
42576.62.7.7 France, Anatole. Les opinions de M. Jérôme Coignard. 56. éd. Paris, 1913.
42576.62.8 France, Anatole. L'orme du mail. Paris, 1898.
42576.62.8.1 France, Anatole. L'orme du mail. 57. éd. Paris, 1897.
42576.62.8.5 France, Anatole. L'orme du mail. Paris, 1912?
42576.62.8.7 France, Anatole. L'orme du mail. Levallois-Perret, 1969.
42576.62.9 France, Anatole. Pages choisies. Paris, 1898.
42576.62.9.10 France, Anatole. Chez Anatole France. Paris, 1907.
42576.62.10 France, Anatole. Le lys rouge. Paris, 1897.
42576.62.10.2 France, Anatole. Le lys rouge. 2. éd. Paris, 1894.
42576.62.10.2.5 France, Anatole. Le lys rouge. 24. éd. Paris, 1894.
42576.62.10.2.8 France, Anatole. Le lys rouge. 36. éd. Paris, 1896.
42576.62.10.2.10 France, Anatole. Le lys rouge. 156. éd. Paris, 191-?
42576.62.10.3 France, Anatole. Le lys rouge. 209. éd. Paris, 1918.
42576.62.10.4 France, Anatole. Le lys rouge. 426. éd. Paris, 1924.
42576.62.10.7 France, Anatole. Le lys rouge. Paris, 1925.
42576.62.10.8 France, Anatole. Le lys rouge. Paris, 1928?
42576.62.10.9 France, Anatole. Le lys rouge. Le jardin d'épicure. Levallois-Perret, 1968.
42576.62.10.15 France, Anatole. The red lily. N.Y., 1917.
42576.62.10.16A France, Anatole. The red lily. N.Y., 1917.
42576.62.10.16B France, Anatole. The red lily. N.Y., 1917.
NEDL 42576.62.11 France, Anatole. Le mannequin d'osier. Paris, 1897.
42576.62.11.2 France, Anatole. Le mannequin d'osier. 44. éd. Paris, 1898.
42576.62.11.5 France, Anatole. Le mannequin d'osier. 46. éd. Paris, 1899.
42576.62.11.10 France, Anatole. Le mannequin d'osier. Paris, 1919?
42576.62.11.20 France, Anatole. Alfred de Vigny; étude. Poésies. Levallois-Perret, 1970.
42576.62.11.25 France, Anatole. Pages d'histoire et de littérature. Levallois-Perret, 1970.
42576.62.12 France, Anatole. Le puits de Sainte Claire. Paris, 1895.
42576.62.12.2 France, Anatole. Le puits de Sainte Claire. Levallois-Perret, 1968.
42576.62.13 France, Anatole. Le jardin d'Epicure. Paris, 1897.
42576.62.13.2 France, Anatole. Le jardin d'Epicure. Paris, 1895.
42576.62.13.5 France, Anatole. Le jardin d'Epicure. 41. éd. Paris, 1908?
42576.62.13.7 France, Anatole. Le jardin d'Epicure. 54. éd. Paris, 1911?
42576.62.13.10 France, Anatole. Le jardin d'Epicure. 93. éd. Paris, 1920.
42576.62.13.15 France, Anatole. The garden of Epicurus. N.Y., 1923.
42576.62.14A France, Anatole. L'anneau d'améthyste. Paris, 1899.
42576.62.14B France, Anatole. L'anneau d'améthyste. Paris, 1899.
42576.62.14C France, Anatole. L'anneau d'améthyste. Paris, 1899.
42576.62.14.2 France, Anatole. L'anneau d'améthyste. Paris, n.d.
42576.62.14.3 France, Anatole. L'anneau d'améthyste. Levallois-Perret, 1969.
42576.62.15 France, Anatole. Pierre Nozière. Paris, 1899.
42576.62.15.2 France, Anatole. Pierre Nozière. 36. éd. Paris, 1899.
42576.62.15.5 France, Anatole. Pierre Nozière. 29. éd. Paris, 1899.
42576.62.15.10 France, Anatole. Pierre Nozière. 87. éd. Paris, 1921.
42576.62.15.75 France, Anatole. Pierre Nozière. London, 1923.
Htn 42576.62.16* France, Anatole. Clio. Paris, 1900.
42576.62.17A France, Anatole. Monsieur Bergeret à Paris. Paris, 1901.
42576.62.17B France, Anatole. Monsieur Bergeret à Paris. Paris, 1901.
42576.62.17.5A France, Anatole. Monsieur Bergeret à Paris. 84. éd. Paris, n.d.
42576.62.17.5B France, Anatole. Monsieur Bergeret à Paris. 84. éd. Paris, n.d.
42576.62.17.10A France, Anatole. Monsieur Bergeret in Paris. London, 1921.
42576.62.17.10B France, Anatole. Monsieur Bergeret in Paris. London, 1921.
42576.62.18 France, Anatole. Crainquebille. Putois. Riquet. Paris, 1904.
42576.62.18.10 France, Anatole. Crainquebille. Putois. Riquet. 64. éd. Paris, 191-?
42576.62.18.12 France, Anatole. Crainquebille. Putois. Riquet. Levallois-Perret, 1969.
42576.62.19A France, Anatole. Histoire comique. Paris, n.d.
42576.62.19B France, Anatole. Histoire comique. Paris, n.d.
42576.62.19C France, Anatole. Histoire comique. Paris, n.d.
42576.62.19D France, Anatole. Histoire comique. Paris, n.d.
42576.62.20 France, Anatole. Sur la pierre blanche. 41. éd. Paris, 1903. 2v.
42576.62.20.5 France, Anatole. Sur la pierre blanche. 43. éd. Paris, 1905. 2v.
42576.62.20.6 France, Anatole. Sur la pierre blanche. Levallois-Perret, 1969.

576.62 - .63.23 Individual authors, etc. - 1850-1899 - Fiction - France, A. - Writings - cont.

42576.62.20.10 France, Anatole. Allocution prononcée. London, 1914?
42576.62.21.5A France, Anatole. L'île des pingouins. Paris, 1908.
42576.62.21.5B France, Anatole. L'île des pingouins. Paris, 1908.
42576.62.21.5C France, Anatole. L'île des pingouins. Paris, 1908.
42576.62.21.7 France, Anatole. L'île des pingouins. 107. éd. Paris, 1911.
42576.62.21.8 France, Anatole. L'île des pingouins. Paris, 1908.
42576.62.21.15 France, Anatole. L'île des pingouins. 175. éd. Paris, 1920.
42576.62.21.20 France, Anatole. Penguin island. London, 1925.
42576.62.21.22 France, Anatole. Penguin island. 11. éd. N.Y., 1929.
42576.62.21.25 France, Anatole. Penguin island. N.Y., 1933.
42576.62.21.31 France, Anatole. L'île des pingouins. Paris, 1947.
42576.62.21.32 France, Anatole. L'île des pingouins. Levallois-Perret, 1969.
42576.62.21.40 France, Anatole. The six greatest novels of Anatole France. 1. ed. Garden City, N.Y., 1918.
42576.62.22A France, Anatole. Les dieux ont soif. Paris, 1912.
42576.62.22B France, Anatole. Les dieux ont soif. Paris, 1912.
42576.62.22.5 France, Anatole. Les dieux ont soif. Paris, 1912. 3v.
42576.62.22.8 France, Anatole. Les dieux ont soif. London, 1967.
42576.62.22.9 France, Anatole. Les dieux ont soif. Levallois-Perret, 1969.
42576.62.22.29 France, Anatole. The gods are athirst. N.Y., 1928.
42576.62.22.35 France, Anatole. The gods are athirst. London, 1933.
42576.62.22.40 France, Anatole. The gods are athirst. London, 1951. 2v.
42576.62.22.42 France, Anatole. The gods are athirst. N.Y., 1957.
tn 42576.62.23* France, Anatole. Crainquebille. Paris, 1905.
tn 42576.62.24* France, Anatole. Au petit bonheur. Paris, 1906. 2 pam.
42576.62.25.3 France, Anatole. La révolte des anges. 15. éd. Paris, 1914.
42576.62.25.5A France, Anatole. La révolte des anges. Paris, 1914.
42576.62.25.5B France, Anatole. La révolte des anges. Paris, 1914.
42576.62.25.5C France, Anatole. La révolte des anges. Paris, 1914.
42576.62.25.7 France, Anatole. La révolte des anges. 72. éd. Paris, 1914.
42576.62.25.9 France, Anatole. La révolte des anges. Evreaux, 1969.
42576.62.25.10 France, Anatole. The revolt of the angels. London, 1924.
42576.62.26 France, Anatole. Filles et garçons. Paris, 1900?
42576.62.27.5 France, Anatole. L'étui de nacre. 2. éd. Paris, 1892.
42576.62.27.8 France, Anatole. L'étui de nacre. Paris, 190-?
42576.62.27.10 France, Anatole. L'étui de nacre. Paris, 1905.
42576.62.28 France, Anatole. L'étui de nacre. 107. éd. Paris, 1921.
42576.62.28.5 France, Anatole. L'étui de nacre. Paris, 1923.
42576.62.28.7 France, Anatole. L'étui de nacre. Paris, 1923.
42576.62.28.10 France, Anatole. Tales from a mother of pearl casket. N.Y., 1890.
42576.62.29 France, Anatole. Les opinions de M. Jérôme Coignard. 114e éd. Paris, 1920.
42576.62.29.5 France, Anatole. Les opinions de M. Jérôme Coignard. 129. éd. Paris, 1920.
42576.62.29.10 France, Anatole. Les opinions de M. Jérôme Coignard recueillies. Paris, 1920.
42576.62.30 France, Anatole. Les désirs de Jean Servien. 60. éd. Paris, 1921.
42576.62.30.5 France, Anatole. Les désirs de Jean Servien. Paris, 1907.
42576.62.30.7 France, Anatole. Les désirs de Jean Servien. Levallois-Perret, 1968.
42576.62.31 France, Anatole. Opinion sociales. Paris, 1916. 2 pam.
42576.62.32.5A France, Anatole. Dernières pages inédites. 12. éd. Paris, 1925.
42576.62.32.5B France, Anatole. Dernières pages inédites. Paris, 1925.
42576.62.34 France, Anatole. Paita. Hämeenlinna, 1953.
42576.62.35 France, Anatole. Le livre de mom ami. 309. éd. Paris, 1925.
42576.62.38 France, Anatole. My friend's book. N.Y., 1924.
42576.62.38.5 France, Anatole. My friend's book. London, 1924.
42576.62.40A France, Anatole. Representative stories. Boston, 1924.
42576.62.40B France, Anatole. Representative stories. Boston, 1924.
42576.62.45A France, Anatole. Golden tales of Anatole France. N.Y., 1926.
42576.62.45B France, Anatole. Golden tales of Anatole France. N.Y., 1926.
42576.62.47 France, Anatole. Amycus et Célestin. N.Y., 1916.
42576.62.50 France, Anatole. Madame de Luzy. Paris, 1902.
Htn 42576.62.50* France, Anatole. Madame de Luzy. Paris, 1902.
Htn 42576.62.60* France, Anatole. Sainte Euphrosine. Paris, 1906.
Htn 42576.62.65* France, Anatole. La leçon bien apprise. Paris, 1898.
Htn 42576.62.70* France, Anatole. Histoire de Dona Maria d'Avalos. Paris, 1902.
Htn 42576.62.75* France, Anatole. Jean Gutenberg. Paris, 1900.
Htn 42576.62.80* France, Anatole. Les poèmes dorés. Paris, 1873.
Htn 42576.62.85* France, Anatole. Les noces corinthiènnes. Paris, 1876.
42576.62.88 France, Anatole. Les noces corinthiènnes. Paris, 1922.
42576.62.90 France, Anatole. Anatole France par lui-même. Paris, 1954.
42576.62.95 France, Anatole. Anatole France himself. London, 1925.
42576.62.96 France, Anatole. Anatole France himself. N.Y., 1925.
42576.62.97 France, Anatole. Franciana. Bruxelles, 1925.
42576.62.100 France, Anatole. The opinions of Anatole France. N.Y., 1922.
42576.62.100.5 France, Anatole. Pensées d'Anatole France. Paris, 1925.
42576.62.105 France, Anatole. Honey-bee. London, 1911.
42576.62.105.2 France, Anatole. Honey-bee. 2. ed. London, 1912.
42576.62.107 France, Anatole. On life and letters. 1st series. London, 1910.
42576.62.110 France, Anatole. On life and letters. 2d series. London, 1914.
42576.62.112 France, Anatole. On life and letters. 3d series. London, 1922.
42576.62.113 France, Anatole. On life and letters. 4th series. London, 1924.
42576.62.114 France, Anatole. Lettres inédites d'Anatole France à Jacques Lion. Paris, 1965.
42576.62.115 France, Anatole. Under the rose. London, 1920.
42576.62.118 France, Anatole. Lettres inédites d'Anatole France à Paul-Louis Couchoud et à sa femme. Paris, 1968.
42576.62.120 France, Anatole. Anatole France à la béchellerie. Paris, 1924.
42576.62.125 France, Anatole. Anatole France à la béchellerie. Paris, 1947.
42576.62.130 France, Anatole. Anatole France at home. N.Y., 1926.

42576.62 - .63.23 Individual authors, etc. - 1850-1899 - Fiction - France, A. - Writings - cont.

42576.62.135A France, Anatole. La vie littéraire. Paris, 1904. 4v.
42576.62.135B France, Anatole. La vie littéraire. v. 1,4. Paris, 1904. 2v.
42576.62.135.3 France, Anatole. La vie littéraire. v. 3. Paris, 1904?
42576.62.135.5 France, Anatole. La vie littéraire. 2. série. Paris, 1919?
42576.62.135.8 France, Anatole. La vie littéraire. Evreux, 1969- 3v.
42576.62.135.10 France, Anatole. La vie littéraire. 3. éd. 5. série. Paris, 1949.
42576.62.140 France, Anatole. Sur la voie glorieuse. 15. éd. Paris, 1915.
42576.62.145 France, Anatole. Mother of pearl. N.Y., 1925.
42576.62.150 France, Anatole. The human tragedy. London, 1917.
42576.62.160 France, Anatole. Discours de réception. Paris, 1897.
42576.62.170 France, Anatole. Théâtre. Evreux, 1970.
42576.62.180A France, Anatole. Les contes de Jacques Tournebroche. Paris, 1921.
42576.62.180B France, Anatole. Les contes de Jacques Tournebroche. Paris, 1921.
42576.62.820 Virtanen, Reino. Anatole France. N.Y., 1968.
42576.63.5 France, Anatole. Le crime de Sylvestre Bonnard. N.Y., 1904.
42576.63.7 France, Anatole. Le crime de Sylvestre Bonnard. Paris, 1881.
42576.63.7.1 France, Anatole. Le crime de Sylvestre Bonnard. Paris, 1889.
42576.63.7.3 France, Anatole. Le crime de Sylvestre Bonnard. N.Y., 1904.
42576.63.7.7 France, Anatole. Le crime de Sylvestre Bonnard. Paris, 1907.
42576.63.7.10 France, Anatole. Le crime de Sylvestre Bonnard. Paris, 1913?
42576.63.7.20 France, Anatole. Le crime de Sylvestre Bonnard. 141. éd. Boston, 1920.
42576.63.7.25 France, Anatole. Le crime de Sylvestre Bonnard. 314. éd. Paris, 1926.
42576.63.7.26 France, Anatole. Le crime de Sylvestre Bonnard. 317. éd. Paris, 1926.
42576.63.7.30 France, Anatole. Le crime de Sylvestre Bonnard. N.Y., 1930.
42576.63.7.35 France, Anatole. The crime of Sylvestre Bonnard. N.Y., 1890.
42576.63.7.38A France, Anatole. The crime of Sylvestre Bonnard. N.Y., 19- ?
42576.63.7.38B France, Anatole. The crime of Sylvestre Bonnard. N.Y., 19- ?
42576.63.7.45 France, Anatole. The crime of Sylvestre Bonnard. London, 1909.
42576.63.7.55 France, Anatole. The crime of Sylvestre Bonnard. N.Y., 1926.
42576.63.7.65 France, Anatole. Sylvestre Bonnard's forbrydelse. Kristiana, 1891.
42576.63.7.100 France, Anatole. Aux étudiants. Paris, 1910.
42576.63.7.103 France, Anatole. Aux étudiants. 3. éd. Paris, 1910.
42576.63.8.20 France, Anatole. The Latin genius. London, 1924.
42576.63.9 France, Anatole. Le petit soldat de plomb. Paris, 1919.
42576.63.10 France, Anatole. Le miracle de la pie. Paris, 1921.
Htn 42576.63.11* France, Anatole. Mémoires d'un volontaire. Paris, 1902.
Htn 42576.63.12* France, Anatole. Le jonglevr de Notre-Dame. Paris, 1906.
42576.63.13 France, Anatole. A la lumière. Paris, 1905.
42576.63.15 France, Anatole. Poésies. Paris, 1896.
42576.63.15.90 France, Anatole. La comédie de celui qui épousa une femme muette. Paris, 1913.
42576.63.16 France, Anatole. La comédie de celui qui épousa une femme muette. 18. éd. Paris, 1913.
42576.63.17A France, Anatole. The man who married a dumb wife. N.Y., 1915.
42576.63.17B France, Anatole. The man who married a dumb wife. N.Y., 1915.
42576.63.17.3 France, Anatole. The man who married a dumb wife. N.Y., 1922.
42576.63.17.5 France, Anatole. The man who married a dumb wife. N.Y., 1924.
42576.63.17.10 France, Anatole. The man who married a dumb wife. N.Y., 1926.
42576.63.18 France, Anatole. Les sept femmes de la Barbe-Bleue. Paris, 1909.
42576.63.18.5 France, Anatole. The seven wives of Bluebeard. London, 1920.
42576.63.18.7F France, Anatole. Il miracolo del grande S. Nicola. Torino, 1944.
42576.63.19 France, Anatole. Les matinées de la villa Saïd. 91. éd. Paris, 1922.
42576.63.20 France, Anatole. Vers les temps meilleurs. v.1-3. Paris, 1906.
42576.63.20.8 France, Anatole. Vers les temps meilleurs. Paris, 1949- 3v.
42576.63.20.10 France, Anatole. Vers les temps meilleurs: trente ans de vie sociale. Evreux, 1971. 4v.
42576.63.21 France, Anatole. La vie en fleur. Paris, 1922.
42576.63.21.6 France, Anatole. La vie en fleur. 53. éd. Paris, 1922.
42576.63.22A France, Anatole. Le petit Pierre. Paris, 1919.
42576.63.22B France, Anatole. Le petit Pierre. Paris, 1919.
42576.63.22.4 France, Anatole. Le petit Pierre. 102. éd. Paris, 1918.
42576.63.22.5 France, Anatole. Le petit Pierre. 197. éd. Paris, 1924.
42576.63.22.10 France, Anatole. Le petit Pierre. Evreux, 1969.
42576.63.23 France, Anatole. La liberté par l'étude. Paris, 1902.

42576.63.24 Individual authors, etc. - 1850-1899 - Fiction - France, A. - Bibliographies

42576.63.24.30 France, Anatole. Anatole France, très rare collection des oeuvres. Paris, 1932.
42576.63.24.35 France, Anatole. The merrie tales of Jacques Tournebroche. N.Y., 1924.
42576.63.24.100 Desvanges, A. Livres, manuscrits dessins...manuscrits d'Anatole France. Paris, 1932.
42576.63.24.110 Lion, J. Anatole France à l'exposition internationale de 1937. Paris, 1937.
42576.63.24.115 Premsela, Martin Jacob. Anatole France en Hollande. La Haye, 1947.

42576.63.25 - .63.999 Individual authors, etc. - 1850-1899 - Fiction - France, A. - Biography and criticism

42576.63.25 Brandes, G. Anatole France. Berlin, n.d.
42576.63.25.10A Brandes, G. Anatole France. N.Y., 1908.
42576.63.25.10B Brandes, G. Anatole France. N.Y., 1908.
42576.63.26 Raphaël, Cor. M. Anatole France et la pensée contemporaine. Paris, 1909.
42576.63.27 Michaut, G. Anatole France. 4. éd. Paris, n.d.
42576.63.28 George, W.L. Anatole France. London, 1915.
42576.63.29 Garrison, F.W. The democracy of Anatole France. N.Y., 1917.
42576.63.32 Gaffiot, M. Les théories sociales d'Anatole France. Alger, 1923.
42576.63.32.2 Gaffiot, M. Les théories sociales d'Anatole France. Thèse. Alger, 1923.
42576.63.33 Masson, G.A. Anatole France, son oeuvre. Paris, 1923.
42576.63.35 Thomas, André. Les conceptions sociales d'Anatole France. Thèse. Paris, 1927.
42576.63.37 Evelpidi, C. Anatole France, critique social. Paris, 1932.
42576.63.40A Brousson, Jean J. Anatole France himself. Philadelphia, 1925.
42576.63.40B Brousson, Jean J. Anatole France himself. Philadelphia, 1925.
42576.63.40C Brousson, Jean J. Anatole France himself. Philadelphia, 1925.
42576.63.41 Brousson, Jean J. Anatole France en pantoufles. 89. éd. Paris, 1924.
42576.63.41.5A Brousson, Jean J. Anatole France en pantoufles. 15. éd. Paris, 1924.
42576.63.41.5B Brousson, Jean J. Anatole France en pantoufles. 15. éd. Paris, 1924.
42576.63.42 Brousson, Jean J. Anatole France en pantoufles. Paris, 1926.
42576.63.43 Brousson, Jean J. Les vêpres de l'avenue Hoche. Paris, 1932.
42576.63.45 Shanks, Lewis Piaget. Anatole France. Chicago, 1919.
42576.63.48A Stewart, H.L. Anatole France, the Parisian. N.Y., 1927.
42576.63.48B Stewart, H.L. Anatole France, the Parisian. N.Y., 1927.
42576.63.50 Gagneur, L. (Mme.). Pour être aimée. Paris, 1886.
42576.63.55 Huard, George. Anatole France et le quai Malaquais. Paris, 1926.
42576.63.60 Des Hons, Gabriel. Anatole France et Racine. Paris, 1925.
42576.63.61 Des Hons, Gabriel. Anatole France et Racine. Paris, 1927.
42576.63.65A Cerf, Barry. Anatole France, the degeneration of a great artist. N.Y., 1926.
42576.63.65B Cerf, Barry. Anatole France, the degeneration of a great artist. N.Y., 1926.
42576.63.70 Pouquet, J.M. (Mme.). Le salon de madame Arman de Caillavet. Couloummiers, 1926.
42576.63.71 Pouquet, J.M. (Mme.). Le salon de madame Arman de Caillavet. Paris, 1926.
42576.63.75 Bédé, Albert. Anatole France vu par la critique d'aujourd'hui. Paris, 1925.
42576.63.80 Smith, Helen B. The skepticism of Anatole France. Paris, 1927.
42576.63.83 Corday, Michel. Anatole France après ses confidences. Paris, 1927.
42576.63.86 Bölöni, I.M.J. (Mme.). Rambles with Anatole France. Philadelphia, 1926.
42576.63.87 Bölöni, I.M.J. (Mme.). Promenades d'Anatole France. Paris, 1927.
42576.63.88 Girard, Georges. La jeunesse d'Anatole France, 1844-1876. Paris, 1925.
42576.63.95 Ajzensztejn, Max. La femme et l'amour dans l'oeuvre d'Anatole France. Thèse. Toulouse, 1928.
42576.63.98 Ahlstrom, A. Le Moyen Age dans l'oeuvre d'Anatole France. Thèse. Paris, 1930
42576.63.100 Ahlstrom, A. Le Moyen Age dans l'oeuvre d'Anatole France. Paris, 1930.
42576.63.105 Guillaume, Louis. Le cerveau d'Anatole France. Tours, 1928.
42576.63.110A Carias, Léon. Anatole France. Paris, 1931.
42576.63.110B Carias, Léon. Anatole France. Paris, 1931.
42576.63.112 Carias, Léon. Les carnets intimes d'Anatole France. Paris, 1946.
42576.63.115 Antoniu, A. Anatole France, critique littéraire. Thèse. Nancy, 1929.
42576.63.120A George, W.L. Anatole France. N.Y., 1915.
42576.63.120B George, W.L. Anatole France. N.Y., 1915.
42576.63.120C George, W.L. Anatole France. N.Y., 1915.
42576.63.125A Chevalier, H.M. The ironic temper; Anatole France. N.Y., 1932.
42576.63.125B Chevalier, H.M. The ironic temper; Anatole France. N.Y., 1932.
42576.63.130 Boillot, Félix. L'humour d'Anatole France. Paris, 1933.
42576.63.135 Seillière, Ernest. La jeunesse d'Anatole France. Paris, 1934.
42576.63.140 Seillière, Ernest. Anatole France, critique de son temps. Paris, 1934.
42576.63.145A Maurras, Charles. Anatole France, politique et poète. Paris, 1924.
42576.63.145B Maurras, Charles. Anatole France, politique et poète. Paris, 1924.
42576.63.150 Truc, G. Anatole France, l'artiste et le penseur. Paris, 1924.
42576.63.155 Johannet, René. Anatole France, est-il grand écrivain? Paris, 1925.
42576.63.158 Walton, L. Anatole France. Durham, 1950.
42576.63.160 Roujon, Jacques. La vie et les opinions d'Anatole France. Paris, 1925.
42576.63.165 Lahy-Hollebecque, M. Anatole France et la femme. Paris, 1924.
42576.63.170 Ségur, N. Conversations avec Anatole France ou Les mélancolies de l'intelligence. Paris, 1925.
42576.63.175 Braidant, Charles. Du Boulangisme au Panama. Paris, 1935.
42576.63.185 Dargan, E.P. Anatole France, 1844-1896. N.Y., 1937.
42576.63.190A Giraud, V. Anatole France. Paris, 1935.
42576.63.190B Giraud, V. Anatole France. Paris, 1935.
42576.63.195 Roberts, E.C. The educational ideals of Anatole France. Urbana, 1940.
42576.63.200A Axelrad, J. Anatole France. N.Y., 1944.
42576.63.200B Axelrad, J. Anatole France. N.Y., 1944.
42576.63.205 Reissig, L. Anatole France. Buenos Aires, 1944.
42576.63.210 Vandegans, A. Anatole France. Paris, 1954.
42576.63.215 Sareil, Jean. Anatole France et Voltaire. Genève, 1961.
42576.63.220 Jusselin, M. Aïeux et parents beaucerons d'Anatole France. Chartres, 1944.

42576.63.25 - .63.999 Individual authors, etc. - 1850-1899 - Fiction - France, A. - Biography and criticism - cont.

42576.63.230 Calmettes, Pierre. La grande passion d'Anatole France. Paris, 1929.
42576.63.410 Kahn, Maurice. Le père d'Anatole France. Paris, 1925.
42576.63.415 Kahn, Maurice. Anatole France et Emile Zola. Paris, 1927.
42576.63.650 France, H. Sous le bournous. Paris, 1898.
42576.63.710 Sherman, Stuart Puth. Anatole France. N.Y., 1924?
42576.63.715 Florian, L. Anatole France. Budapest, 1954.
42576.63.720 Kovaleva, I.S. Tvorchestvo Anatolia Fransa v gody pereloma. Leningrad, 1957.
42576.63.725 Likhodzievskii, S.I. Anatol' Frans. Tashkent, 1962.
42576.63.730 Lacretelle, Jacques de. A la rencontre de France. Paris, 1930.
42576.63.735 Marvaud, Jean. Anatole France. Paris, 1962.
42576.63.740 Bancquart, M C. Anatole France, polémiste. Paris, 1962.
42576.63.745 Delaporte, Louis. Anatole France. Tours, 1901.
42576.63.750 Tylden-Wright, David. Anatole France. London, 1967.
42576.63.755 Schlumbohm, Dietrich. Der Aufstand der Engel. Hamburg, 1966.
42576.63.780 Bresky, Dusham. The art of Anatole France. The Hague, 1969.
42576.63.785 Levaillant, Jean. Essai sur l'évolution intellectuelle d'Anatole France. Paris, 1965.
42576.63.790 May, James Lewis. Anatole France, the man and his work. London, 1924.
42576.63.795 Rumeau, Jacques. Anatole France et Sully-Prudhomme. Bordeaux, 1910.
42576.63.800 Jefferson, Carter. Anatole France; the politics of skepticism. New Brunswick, N.J., 1965.

42576.64 Individual authors, etc. - 1850-1899 - Fiction - Giron; Goron; Grin; Gramont; etc.

42576.64 Giron, Alfred. Histoire d'une ferme. Paris, 1880.
42576.64.2 Goron, Marie F. The truth about the case. Philadelphia, 1907.
42576.64.3 Goron, Marie F. El ahorcado de Passy. Madrid, 1903.
42576.64.4 Grin, Henri L. Incroyables aventures de L. de Rougemont. Paris, 1901.
42576.64.4.5 Clune, Frank. The greatest liar on earth. Melbourne, 1945.
42576.64.5 Grousset, P. Le capitaine Trafalgar. Paris, 1886.
42576.64.7 Gramont, Ferdinand de. Sextines. Paris, 1872.
42576.64.8 Gramont, Ferdinand de. Olim. Paris, 1882.
42576.64.9 Gramont, Ferdinand de. Chant du passé. Paris, 1854.
42576.64.10 Gramont, Louis de. Simone. Paris, 1892.
42576.64.105 Gallet, Louis. The adventures of Cyrano de Bergerac. N.Y., 1898.

42576.65 - .65.12 Individual authors, etc. - 1850-1899 - Fiction - Glouvet (Quesnay de Beaurepaire); Harry; etc.

42576.65 Glouvet, Jules de. Histoires du vieux temps. Paris, 1889.
42576.65.2 Glouvet, Jules de. Le berger. Paris, 1882.
42576.65.2.80 Quesnay de Beaurepaire, Jules. Marie Fougère. 18. éd. Paris, 1889.
42576.65.3 Harden-Hickey, J. Lettres d'un Yankee. 2. éd. Paris, 1879.
42576.65.4 Hardÿ de Périni, Edouard. Contes de garnison. Paris, 1887.
42576.65.5 Harry, Myriam (pseud.). La conquête de Jérusalem. Paris, n.d.
V42576.65.5.5 Harry, Myriam (pseud.). Jeruzsálem meghóditasa. Budapest, 1908. 2v.
42576.65.6 Harry, Myriam (pseud.). Petites epouses. Paris, n.d.
42576.65.7.5 Harry, Myriam (pseud.). Siona à Berlin. Paris, 1928.
42576.65.8F Harry, Myriam (pseud.). La petite fille de Jérusalem. v. 1-4. Paris, 1914.
V42576.65.8.5 Harry, Myriam (pseud.). Den lille pige fra Jerusalem. Kjobenhavn, 1924.
42576.65.9 Harry, Myriam (pseud.). Les amants de Sion. 12. éd. Paris, 1923.
42576.65.9.5 Harry, Myriam (pseud.). L'île de volupté. Paris, 1908?
42576.65.10 Harry, Myriam (pseud.). Le petit prince de Syrie. Paris, 1928.
42576.65.10.15 Harry, Myriam (pseud.). La divine chanson. Paris, 1932.
Htn 42576.65.11* Heusy, Paul. Un coin de la vie de misère. Paris, 1883.
42576.65.12 Houx-Marc, Eugène. Mémorables fredaines d'un singe. Paris, n.d.
42576.65.12.250 Poligny, J.H. Le prêtre marié. Paris, 1863.

42576.65.13 Individual authors, etc. - 1850-1899 - Fiction - Huysmans - Works about

42576.65.13 Bricaud, Joanny. Huysmans occultiste et magicien. Paris, 1913.
42576.65.13.2 Blandin, H. J.K. Huysmans. Paris, 1912.
42576.65.13.4 Besse, Jean M. Joris Karl Huysmans. Paris, 1917.
42576.65.13.5 Lavalée, G. Essai sur la pyschologie morbide de Huysmans. Thèse. Paris, 1917.
42576.65.13.7 Jørgensen, Johannes. J.K. Huysmans. Mainz, 1908.
42576.65.13.9 Pamphlet box. Huysmans, J.K.
42576.65.13.15 Poinsot, Maffei C. Les logis de Huysmans. Paris, 1919.
42576.65.13.19 Bachelin, H. J.K. Huysmans du naturalisme littéraire. Paris, 1926.
42576.65.13.21 Deffoux, Léon. J.K. Huysmans sous divers aspects. Paris, 1927.
42576.65.13.22 Deffoux, Léon. Inconographie de J.K. Huysmans. n.p., n.d.
42576.65.13.23 Grolleau, C. Un logis de J.K. Huysmans. Paris, 1928.
42576.65.13.27A Lefèvre, F. Entretiens sur J.K. Huysmans. Paris, 1931.
42576.65.13.27B Lefèvre, F. Entretiens sur J.K. Huysmans. Paris, 1931.
42576.65.13.31A Seillière, Ernest. J.K. Huysmans. Paris, 1931.
42576.65.13.31B Seillière, Ernest. J.K. Huysmans. Paris, 1931.
42576.65.13.35 Weise, C. J.K. Huysmans Beziehungen zur Malerei. Inaug. Diss. Bochum-Langendreer, 1934.
42576.65.13.40 Coquiot, G. La vrai J.K. Huysmans. Paris, 1912.
42576.65.13.45 Trudgian, Helen. L'évolution des idées esthétiques de J.K. Huysmans. Thèse. Paris, 1934.
42576.65.13.47 Trudgian, Helen. L'esthétique de J.K. Huysmans. Paris, 1934.
42576.65.13.50 Brennan, Donal. La conversion de J.K. Huysmans et son oeuvre religieuse. Thèse. Montpellier, 1933.
42576.65.13.55 Belleville, F. La conversion de M. Huysmans. Bourges, 193-?
42576.65.13.60 Bron, L. Huysmans d'après des documents inédits. Paris, 1937.
42576.65.13.65 Thérive, André. J.K. Huysmans, son oeuvre. Paris, 1924.
42576.65.13.70 Aubault de la Haulte Chambre, G. J.K. Huysmans. 2. éd. Paris, 1924.

Classified Listing

42576.65.13 Individual authors, etc. - 1850-1899 - Fiction - Huysmans - Works about - cont.

42576.65.13.74 Cressot, M. La phrase et le vocabulaire de J.K. Huysmans. Thèse. Paris, 1938.
42576.65.13.75 Cressot, M. La phrase et le vocabulaire de J.K. Huysmans. Paris, 1938.
42576.65.13.80 Garcon, Maurice. Huysmans inconnu. Paris, 1941.
42576.65.13.89 Descaves, Lucien. Les dernières années. 4. éd. Paris, 1941.
42576.65.13.91 Descaves, Lucien. Deux amis, J.K. Huysmans et l'abbé Mugnier. Paris, 1947.
42576.65.13.95 Letters, Francis J.H. Joris Karl Huysmans, a study. Westmead, 1945?
42576.65.13.98 Pirard, Pierre. Huysmans. Paris, 1946.
42576.65.13.100 Martineau, René. Autour de J.K. Huysmans. Bruges, 1946.
42576.65.13.102 Langé, Gabriel U. En la fête de J.K. Huysmans. Fécamp, 1947.
42576.65.13.104 Garreau, Albert. J.K. Huysmans. Tournai, 1947.
42576.65.13.106 Tupigny, J.P. Le sentiment heraldique dans l'oeuvre de J.K. Huysmans. Paris, 1946.
42576.65.13.108 Daoust, J. Les débuts bénédictins. Paris, 1950.
42576.65.13.109 Daoust, J. J.K. Huysmans, directeur de conscience. Fécamp, 1953.
42576.65.13.112 Grassl, M. Die Musik in den Werken des J.K. Huysmans. München, 1938.
42576.65.13.114 Laner, James. The first decadent. London, 1954.
42576.65.13.116 Huysmans et l'abbé Mugnier à Saint-Thomas d'Aquin. Coulommiers? 1952.
42576.65.13.118 Cogny, Pierre. J.K. Huysmans à la recherche de l'unité. Thèse. Paris, 1953.
42576.65.13.119A Cogny, Pierre. Le Huysmans intime de Henry Ceard et Jean de Caldain. Paris, 1957.
42576.65.13.119B Cogny, Pierre. Le Huysmans intime de Henry Ceard et Jean de Caldain. Paris, 1957.
42576.65.13.120 Baldick, Robert. The life of J.K. Huysmans. Oxford, 1955.
42576.65.13.122 Chastel, Guy. J.K. Huysmans et ses amis. Paris, 1957.
42576.65.13.124 Aimery, Christiane. Joris-Karl Huysmans. Paris, 1956.
42576.65.13.126 Guillemain, Charles. J.K. Huysmans et Lyon. Lyon, 1958.
42576.65.13.128 Lobet, Marcel. J.K. Huysmans. Lyon, 1960.
42576.65.13.130 Brandreth, H.R.T. Huysmans. London, 1963.
42576.65.13.135 Société J.K. Huysmans. Bulletin. Paris. 1,1928+ 8v.
42576.65.13.140 Mugnier, Arthur. J.K. Huysmans à la trappe. Paris, 1927.
42576.65.13.145 Du Bourg, Antoine. Huysmans intime. Paris, 1908.
42576.65.13.150 Ridge, George R. Joris-Karl Huysmans. N.Y., 1968.
42576.65.13.157 Bossier, Herman. Geschiedenis van een romanfiguur. 2. uitg. Hasselt, 1965.
42576.65.13.160 Issacharoff, Michael. J.K. Huysmans devant la critique en France (1874-1960). Paris, 1970.
42576.65.13.165 Belval, Maurice M. Des ténèbres à la lumière. Thèse. Paris, 1968.
42576.65.13.170 Bossier, Herman. Un personage de roman. Bruxelles, 1943.
42576.65.13.175 Brunner, Henriette. En marge d'Arebours de J.K. Huysmans. Paris, 1932.
42576.65.13.180 Valéry, Paul. Huysmans, eau-forte de C. Jovas. Paris, 1927.
42576.65.13.185 Cevasco, George A. J.K. Huysmans in England and America. Charlottesville, 196-.

42576.65.14 - .66.4 Individual authors, etc. - 1850-1899 - Fiction - Huysmans - Writings

42576.65.14 Huysmans, Joris Karl. En route. Paris, 1910.
42576.65.16 Huysmans, Joris Karl. En route. N.Y., 1920.
42576.65.17 Huysmans, Joris Karl. En route. Paris, 1928.
42576.65.18 Huysmans, Joris Karl. Oeuvres complètes de J.K. Huysmans. v.1-18. Paris, 1928-34. 23v.
42576.65.19 Huysmans, Joris Karl. Croquis parisiens. Paris, 1908.
42576.65.20.5 Huysmans, Joris Karl. The oblate. London, 1924.
42576.65.21 Huysmans, Joris Karl. Sainte Lydwine de Schiedam. Paris, 1909.
42576.65.22 Huysmans, Joris Karl. De tout. Paris, 1908.
42576.65.23 Huysmans, Joris Karl. Trois eglises et trois primitifs. Paris, 1908.
42576.65.24 Huysmans, Joris Karl. Pages catholiques. Paris, 1899.
42576.65.25.7 Huysmans, Joris Karl. La cathédrale. Paris, 1945.
42576.65.26 Huysmans, Joris Karl. En ménage. Paris, 1908.
42576.65.27 Huysmans, Joris Karl. La Bièvre et Saint-Séverin. Paris, 1898.
42576.65.28.2 Huysmans, Joris Karl. Là-bas. Paris, 1908.
42576.65.28.5 Huysmans, Joris Karl. Down there. N.Y., 1924.
42576.65.28.7 Huysmans, Joris Karl. Down there. Evanston, 1958.
42576.65.29 Huysmans, Joris Karl. Les soeurs Vatard. Paris, 1907.
42576.65.29.5 Huysmans, Joris Karl. Les soeurs Vatard. Paris, 1912?
Htn 42576.65.30* Huysmans, Joris Karl. Prières et pensées chrétiennes. Lyon, 1910.
42576.65.31 Huysmans, Joris Karl. Esquisse biographique sur Don Bosco. n.p., 1902.
42576.65.40 Huysmans, Joris Karl. Croquis parisiens à Vau-l'Eau. Paris, 1929.
42576.65.45 Huysmans, Joris Karl. Là-haut, ou Notre-Dame de la Salette. Tournai, 1965.
42576.65.80.3 Huysmans, Joris Karl. The cathedral. London, 1925.
42576.65.80.10 Huysmans, Joris Karl. Le drageoir aux épices. Paris, 1916.
42576.65.80.15 Huysmans, Joris Karl. La cathédrale, chartres. London, 1936.
42576.65.80.21 Huysmans, Joris Karl. Marthe; histoire d'une fille. Paris, 1914.
42576.65.80.22 Huysmans, Joris Karl. Marthe; histoire d'une fille. Paris, 1955.
42576.65.80.25 Huysmans, Joris Karl. Un dilemme. Paris, 1887.
42576.65.80.30 Huysmans, Joris Karl. La retraite de Monsieur Bougran. Paris, 1964.
42576.65.80.40 Huysmans, Joris Karl. Lettres inédites à Jules Destrée. Genève, 1967.
42576.65.80.50A Huysmans, Joris Karl. Lettres inédites à Emile Zola. Genève, 1953.
42576.65.80.50B Huysmans, Joris Karl. Lettres inédites à Emile Zola. Genève, 1953.
42576.65.80.55 Huysmans, Joris Karl. Lettres inédites à Edmond de Toncourt. Paris, 1956.
42576.65.80.60 Huysmans, Joris Karl. Lettres inédites à Camille Lemonnier. Genève, 1957.
42576.66.2.5 Huysmans, Joris Karl. A rebours. Paris, 1947.
42576.66.2.7 Huysmans, Joris Karl. Against nature. Harmondsworth, 1959.
X Cg 42576.66.3 Huysmans, Joris Karl. Against the grain. N.Y., 1930.
42576.66.3.5 Huysmans, Joris Karl. Against the grain. N.Y., 1931.

42576.65.14 - .66.4 Individual authors, etc. - 1850-1899 - Fiction - Huysmans - Writings - cont.

42576.66.3.10 Huysmans, Joris Karl. Against the grain. Paris, 1926.
42576.66.3.15 Huysmans, Joris Karl. Against the grain. N.Y., 1969.
42576.66.4 Huysmans, Joris Karl. Certains. Photoreproduction. Paris, 1889.
42576.66.4.30 Huysmans, Joris Karl. Les foules de Lourdes. Paris, 1947.

42576.66.5 - .66.20 Individual authors, etc. - 1850-1899 - Fiction - Hericault

42576.66.5 D'Hericault, C. Aventures de deux parisiennes. Paris, 1881.
42576.66.6 D'Hericault, C. En 1792. Le premier amour de Lord St. Albans. Paris, 1879.
42576.66.7 D'Hericault, C. En 1792. Le dernier amour de Lord St. Albans. Paris, 1879.
42576.66.8 D'Hericault, C. La fille de Notre-Dame. Paris, 1882.

42576.67 - .67.39 Individual authors, etc. - 1850-1899 - Fiction - Hervieu, P.

42576.67 Hervieu, Paul. L'alpe homicide. Paris, 1880.
42576.67.2 Hervieu, Paul. La bêtise parisienne. Paris, 1884.
42576.67.3 Hervieu, Paul. Deux plaisanteries. Paris, 1888.
42576.67.4 Hervieu, Paul. L'exorcisée. Paris, 1891.
42576.67.5 Hervieu, Paul. Flirt. Paris, 1892.
42576.67.5.10 Hervieu, Paul. Flirt. Paris, 1890.
42576.67.5.12 Hervieu, Paul. Flirt. N.Y., 1890.
42576.67.6 Hervieu, Paul. L'inconnu. Paris, 1887.
42576.67.7 Hervieu, Paul. Peints par eux-mêmes. Paris, 1893.
42576.67.8 Hervieu, Paul. Les yeux verts. Paris, 1886.
42576.67.9 Hervieu, Paul. Les paroles restent. Paris, 1893.
42576.67.10 Hervieu, Paul. Les tenailles. Paris, n.d.
42576.67.10.5 Hervieu, Paul. Les tenailles. Paris, 191-.
42576.67.11 Hervieu, Paul. Théroigne de Méricourt. Paris, 1902.
42576.67.12 Hervieu, Paul. L'armature. Paris, n.d.
42576.67.12.15 Hervieu, Paul. L'armature. Paris, 1895.
Htn 42576.67.13* Hervieu, Paul. Bagatelle. Paris, 1913.
42576.67.14 Hervieu, Paul. Diogène le chien. 3. éd. Paris, 1882.
42576.67.15 Hervieu, Paul. Le destin est maître. Paris, 1919.
42576.67.18 Hervieu, Paul. Oeuvres::théâtre. v.1,3-4. Paris, 1900?-09. 3v.
42576.67.18.5 Hervieu, Paul. Théâtre complet. Paris, 19- . 4v.
42576.67.25 Malherbe, H. Paul Hervieu. Paris, 1912.
42576.67.30 Estéve, Edmond. Paul Hervieu; conteur, moraliste. Paris, 1917.
42576.67.35 Fahmy, Sabri. Paul Hervieu, sa vie et son oeuvre. Thèse. Marseille, 1942.

42576.67.46 Individual authors, etc. - 1850-1899 - Fiction - Jicé

42576.67.46 Jicé, Michel. Fleurs d'Israël. Photoreproduction. Paris, 1895.

42576.67.50 Individual authors, etc. - 1850-1899 - Fiction - Judices de Mirandol

42576.67.50 Judices de Mirandol, L. Mémoires d'un enfant de troupe. Paris, 1873.

42576.67.100 Individual authors, etc. - 1850-1899 - Fiction - Karélis

42576.67.100 Karélis, André. Mémoires d'un fou. Paris, 1898.

42576.68 - .68.19 Individual authors, etc. - 1850-1899 - Fiction - Lamothe, A.

42576.68 Lamothe, Alexandre. Mémoires d'un déporté. Paris, 1880.

42576.68.25 Individual authors, etc. - 1850-1899 - Fiction - La Vaudère

Htn 42576.68.25* La Vaudère, Jane de. Les prêtresses de Mylitta. Paris, 1907.

42576.68.40 Individual authors, etc. - 1850-1899 - Fiction - Le Corbeiller

42576.68.40 Le Corbeiller, Maurice. Les fourches caudines. Paris, 1891.

42576.68.100 - Individual authors, etc. - 1850-1899 - Fiction - Lecomte du Nouÿ

42576.68.150 Lecomte du Nouÿ, H.O. (Mme.). Amitié amoureuse. Paris, 1890.
42576.68.155 Lecomte du Nouÿ, H.O. (Mme.). Incertidumbre por H.L.N. Buenos Aires, 1902.
42576.68.160 Lecomte du Nouÿ, H.O. (Mme.). L'amour est mon péché. Paris, 1901?

42576.69 Individual authors, etc. - 1850-1899 - Fiction - Legay

42576.69 Legay, Henri. Mémoires d'une pendule. Paris, 1872.

42576.70 Individual authors, etc. - 1850-1899 - Fiction - Lespinasse; Lescure; etc.

42576.70.300 Lepsinasse, L. de. Toute à l'amour. Paris, 189-?
42576.70.432 Lescure, M.F.A. de. Eux et elles. Paris, 1860.

42576.71 Individual authors, etc. - 1850-1899 - Fiction - Lythe

42576.71 Lythe, Marcel. Mais laquelle? Paris, 1882.

42576.72 Individual authors, etc. - 1850-1899 - Fiction - Lombard

42576.72 Lombard, Jean. Byzance. Paris, 1902.
42576.72.3 Lombard, Jean. L'agonie. Paris, 1888.

42576.73 Individual authors, etc. - 1850-1899 - Fiction - Lescot; Lucas; Lurine; Luzarche; etc.

42576.73 Lescot, Marie Meusy. Un peu, beaucoup, passionnement. St. Henri, n.d.
42576.73.3 Lucas, Louis. Le roman alchimique. Paris, 1857.
42576.73.5 Lurine, Louis. Le treizième arrondissement de Paris. Paris, 1850.
42576.73.9 Luzarche, Robert. Le nouveau spectre rouge. Paris, 1870.

42576.74 Individual authors, etc. - 1850-1899 - Fiction - Macé; Mahon; etc.

42576.74 Macé, Jean. L'arithmétique du Grand-papa. 5. éd. Paris, n.d.
42576.74.9 Macé, Jean. Théâtre du petit château. 4. éd. Paris, n.d.
42576.74.100 Mahon, Patrice. Monsieur Pierre. Paris, 1916-17.
Htn 42576.75* Marchal, C. Physiologie de l'anglais à Paris. Paris, n.d.

42576.76 Individual authors, etc. - 1850-1899 - Fiction - Marguerittte, P.

42576.76.4 Margueritte, Paul. Souvenirs de jeunesse. Paris, 1908.
42576.76.10 Margueritte, Paul. Le cuirassier blanc. Paris, 1892.
42576.76.11 Margueritte, Paul. Amants. Paris, 1890.
42576.76.12 Margueritte, Paul. La confession posthume. Paris, 1886.
42576.76.13 Margueritte, Paul. Pascal Géfosse. Paris, 1887.
42576.76.13.10 Margueritte, Paul. Pascal Géfosse. Paris, 1911.
42576.76.14 Margueritte, Paul. Tous quatre. Paris, 1885.
42576.76.15 Margueritte, Paul. La force des choses. Paris, 1891.
42576.76.16 Margueritte, Paul. Jours d'épreuve. Paris, 1889.
42576.76.16.2 Margueritte, Paul. Jours d'épreuve. 7. éd. Paris, 189-?
42576.76.17 Margueritte, Paul. Ma grande. Paris, 1892.
42576.76.18 Margueritte, Paul. Maison ouverte. Paris, 1887.
42576.76.19 Margueritte, Paul. Sur le retour. Paris, 1892.
42576.76.20 Margueritte, Paul. Le jardin du passé. Paris, 1896.
42576.76.21 Margueritte, Paul. Le tourmenté. Paris, 1893.
42576.76.22 Margueritte, Paul. Ame d'enfant. Paris, 1894.
42576.76.23 Margueritte, Paul. L'eau qui dort. Paris, 1896.
42576.76.24 Margueritte, Paul. Fors l'honneur. Paris, 1895.
42576.76.25 Margueritte, Paul. La mouche. Paris, 1893.
42576.76.26 Margueritte, Paul. Simple histoire. Paris, 1895.
42576.76.27 Margueritte, Paul. L'avril. Paris, 1894.
42576.76.27.5A Margueritte, Paul. L'avril. N.Y., 1895.
42576.76.27.5B Margueritte, Paul. L'avril. N.Y., 1895.
42576.76.28 Margueritte, Paul. L'essor. Paris, 1896?
42576.76.29 Margueritte, Paul. La pariétaire. Paris, 1896.
42576.76.30 Margueritte, Paul. Le carnaval de Nice. Paris, 1897.
42576.76.31 Margueritte, Paul. Poum; aventures d'un petit garçon. Paris, 1897.
42576.76.32 Margueritte, Paul. Le désastre. Paris, 1898.
42576.76.32.2 Margueritte, Paul. Les tronçons du glaive. Paris, 1900.
42576.76.32.4 Margueritte, Paul. Les braves gens. Paris, 190-?
42576.76.32.6 Margueritte, Paul. La commune. Paris, 1904.
42576.76.33 Margueritte, Paul. La poste des neiges. Barcelone, 1899.
42576.76.34 Margueritte, Paul. Femmes nouvelles. Paris, 1899.
42576.76.35 Margueritte, Paul. L'eau souterraine. Paris, 1903.
42576.76.36 Margueritte, Paul. Le prisme. Paris, 1905.
42576.76.37 Margueritte, Paul. Sur le vif. Paris, 1906.
42576.76.38 Margueritte, Paul. L'autre. Paris, 1908.
42576.76.39 Margueritte, Paul. Nos tréteaux. Paris, 1910.
42576.76.40 Margueritte, Paul. L'embusqué. Paris, 1916.
42576.76.41 Margueritte, Paul. Quelques idées. Paris, 1905.
42576.76.43F Margueritte, Paul. La flamme. Paris, 1909.
42576.76.44.5 Margueritte, Paul. Le jardin du roi. 9. éd. Paris, 1902?
42576.76.45 Margueritte, Paul. La cité des fauves. Paris, 1928.
42576.76.80 Pilon, Edmond. Paul et Victor Margueritte. Paris, 1905.

42576.77 Individual authors, etc. - 1850-1899 - Fiction - Margueritte, V.

42576.77.10 Margueritte, Victor. Leilah. Paris, 1921.
42576.77.11 Margueritte, Victor. La garconne. Paris, 1922.
42576.77.15 Margueritte, Victor. The bachelor girl. N.Y., 1924.
42576.77.21 Margueritte, Victor. Au fil de l'heure, poésies. Paris, 1929.
42576.77.31 Margueritte, Victor. Le compagnon. Paris, 1923.
42576.77.35 Margueritte, Victor. Le couple. Paris, 1924.
42576.77.39 Margueritte, Victor. Le bétail humain. Paris, 1928.
42576.77.43 Margueritte, Victor. Ton corps est à toi. Paris, 1927.
42576.77.45 Margueritte, Victor. Le chant du berger. Paris, 1930.
42576.77.80 Quesada, Ernesto. Victor Margueritte. Paris, 1927.
42576.77.85 Charton, Jean C. Victor Margueritte. Paris, 1927.

42576.78 Individual authors, etc. - 1850-1899 - Fiction - Jourdan

42576.78.30 Jourdan, Prosper. Rosine et Rosette. Paris, 1862.

42576.79 Individual authors, etc. - 1850-1899 - Fiction - Geruzez

42576.79.30 Geruzez, Paul. A pied, à cheval, en voiture. Paris, 1895.

42577.1 Individual authors, etc. - 1850-1899 - Fiction - Maupassant - Complete and Selected works

42577.1.05 Maupassant, Guy de. Contes de la bécasse. 6. éd. Paris, 1894.
42577.1.1A Maupassant, Guy de. Contes de la bécasse. Paris, 1906.
42577.1.1B Maupassant, Guy de. Contes de la bécasse. Paris, 1906.
42577.1.1.5 Maupassant, Guy de. Contes de la bécasse. Paris, 19- .
42577.1.2 Maupassant, Guy de. Works. N.Y., 1923. 10v.
42577.1.3 Maupassant, Guy de. Works. N.Y., 1909. 10v.
42577.1.4 Maupassant, Guy de. Oeuvres complètes. Paris, 1922-1932. 29v.
42577.1.8 Maupassant, Guy de. Oeuvres complètes illustrées. Lausanne, 1961-1962. 16v.
42577.1.10 Maupassant, Guy de. Huit contes choisis. Boston, 1900.
42577.1.12 Maupassant, Guy de. Huit contes choisis. Boston, 1900.
42577.1.14 Maupassant, Guy de. Huit contes choisis. Halle, 1955.
42577.1.20 Maupassant, Guy de. Contes choisis. Paris, 190-?
42577.1.22 Maupassant, Guy de. Contes choisis. Angers, 1946.
42577.1.23 Maupassant, Guy de. The complete short stories. N.Y., n.d.
42577.1.24 Maupassant, Guy de. The complete short stories. n.p., 1903.
42577.1.25 Maupassant, Guy de. The complete short stories. N.Y., 1941.
42577.1.26 Maupassant, Guy de. The complete short stories. 1. ed. Garden City, 1955.
42577.1.30 Maupassant, Guy de. Short stories of the tragedy and comedy of life. N.Y., 1903.
42577.1.32 Maupassant, Guy de. Selected short stories. N.Y., 1918.
42577.1.36 Maupassant, Guy de. Short stories. N.Y., 1941.
42577.1.38 Maupassant, Guy de. Short stories. London, 1959.
42577.1.40 Maupassant, Guy de. The complete short stories. London, 1970. 3v.
42577.1.50 Maupassant, Guy de. Saint Anthony, and other stories. N.Y., 1924.
42577.1.60 Maupassant, Guy de. Guy de Maupassant, an introduction by Arthur Symone. N.Y., 1903.
42577.1.70 Maupassant, Guy de. Chroniques, études. Paris, 1938.

42577.2 - .4.30 Individual authors, etc. - 1850-1899 - Fiction - Maupassant - Individual works

42577.2.2 Maupassant, Guy de. La maison Tellier. Paris, 1889.
42577.2.3 Maupassant, Guy de. Miss Harriet. Paris, 1884.
42577.2.3.5 Maupassant, Guy de. Miss Harriet. Paris, 1889.
42577.2.4 Maupassant, Guy de. The window, and short stories. N.Y., 1910.
42577.2.4.3 Maupassant, Guy de. Mad, and short stories. N.Y., 1920.
42577.2.4.5 Maupassant, Guy de. Mad, and other stories. N.Y., 1917.
42577.2.5 Maupassant, Guy de. La maison Tellier. Paris, 1893.
42577.2.5.10 Maupassant, Guy de. Madame Tellier's establishment, and stories. N.Y., 1910.

42577.2 - .4.30 Individual authors, etc. - 1850-1899 - Fiction - Maupassant - Individual works - cont.

42577.2.5.15 Maupassant, Guy de. Madame Tellier's establishment and family, and other stories. N.Y., 1917.
42577.2.5.20 Maupassant, Guy de. La maison Tellier. Urbiro?, 1956.
42577.2.6 Maupassant, Guy de. Love, and other stories. N.Y., 1919.
42577.2.8 Maupassant, Guy de. Boule de suif. Paris, 1930.
42577.2.10 Maupassant, Guy de. Boule de suif, and other stories. Harmondsworth, 1946.
42577.2.25 Maupassant, Guy de. Mlle Fifi. Paris, 1883.
42577.2.30 Maupassant, Guy de. Mlle Fifi. Paris, 1907.
42577.2.35 Maupassant, Guy de. Mlle Fifi, and other stories. N.Y., 1917.
42577.2.40 Maupassant, Guy de. Mlle Fifi. Boston, 1919.
Htn 42577.3.10* Maupassant, Guy de. Au soleil. Paris, 1884.
42577.3.25 Maupassant, Guy de. Au soleil or African wanderings. N.Y., 1903.
42577.3.50 Maupassant, Guy de. Contes normands. Paris, 1920.
42577.4 Maupassant, Guy de. Une vie. Paris, 1884.
42577.4.1 Maupassant, Guy de. Les soeurs Rondoli. Paris, 1884.
42577.4.1.3 Maupassant, Guy de. Les soeurs Rondoli. Paris, 1927?
42577.4.2 Maupassant, Guy de. Bel-ami. Paris, 1885.
42577.4.2.5 Maupassant, Guy de. Bel-ami. Paris, 1959.
42577.4.2.15 Maupassant, Guy de. Bel-ami. N.Y., 1890.
42577.4.2.16 Maupassant, Guy de. Bel-ami. London, 1955.
42577.4.2.30 Maupassant, Guy de. Bel-ami. Cleveland, 1947.
42577.4.3 Maupassant, Guy de. Monsieur Parent. Paris, 1885.
42577.4.3.5 Maupassant, Guy de. Monsieur Parent. London, 1911.
42577.4.3.6 Maupassant, Guy de. Monsieur Parent and short stories. N.Y., 1910.
42577.4.4 Maupassant, Guy de. Sur l'eau. Paris, n.d.
42577.4.4.2 Maupassant, Guy de. Sur l'eau. Paris, 189-?
42577.4.4.15 Maupassant, Guy de. Sur l'eau and other tales. N.Y., 1903.
42577.4.4.20 Maupassant, Guy de. Fin de siècle. Paris, 1957.
42577.4.5 Maupassant, Guy de. Contes du jour. Paris, n.d.
42577.4.5.2 Maupassant, Guy de. Contes du jour et de la nuit. Paris, 1885.
42577.4.5.10 Maupassant, Guy de. Contes des beaux jours. Rouen, 1946.
42577.4.6 Shippee, L.B. Stories from French realists. N.Y., 1907.
42577.4.7 Maupassant, Guy de. Mouche. Paris, 19- ?
42577.4.7.15 Maupassant, Guy de. Caresses. London, 1946.
42577.4.8 Maupassant, Guy de. Who knows? n.p., n.d.
42577.4.8.15 Maupassant, Guy de. The Horla, Miss Harriet, Little Louise Roque and other stories. London, 1911.
42577.4.9 Maupassant, Guy de. Musotte. Paris, 1891.
42577.4.10A Maupassant, Guy de. Fort comme la mort. Paris, 1889.
42577.4.10B Maupassant, Guy de. Fort comme la mort. Paris, 1889.
42577.4.10.5 Maupassant, Guy de. Fort comme la mort. Paris, 1892.
42577.4.10.7 Maupassant, Guy de. Fort comme la mort. Paris, 1906.
42577.4.10.8 Maupassant, Guy de. Strong as death and other stories. London, 1911.
42577.4.10.12 Maupassant, Guy de. Fort comme la mort and other tales. N.Y., 1903.
42577.4.11 Maupassant, Guy de. Notre coeur. Paris, 1890.
42577.4.11.5 Maupassant, Guy de. Notre coeur. 69. éd. Paris, 1894.
42577.4.11.25 Maupassant, Guy de. Notre coeur, Yvette, a selection from the writings of G. de Maupassant. N.Y., 1903.
42577.4.12 Maupassant, Guy de. Le père Milon, contes inédits. Paris, 1899.
42577.4.14 Maupassant, Guy de. Les dimanches d'un bourgeois de Paris. Paris, 1901.
42577.4.15 Maupassant, Guy de. Clair de lune. Paris, 1888.
42577.4.17.5 Maupassant, Guy de. Pierre et Jean. Paris, 1888.
42577.4.17.6 Maupassant, Guy de. Pierre et Jean. 7. éd. Paris, 1888.
42577.4.17.10 Maupassant, Guy de. Pierre et Jean and other tales. N.Y., 1903.
42577.4.17.15 Maupassant, Guy de. Pierre and Jean, Father and son, Boitelle and other stories. London, 1911.
42577.4.19.2A Maupassant, Guy de. The odd number. N.Y., 1889.
42577.4.19.2B Maupassant, Guy de. The odd number. N.Y., 1889.
42577.4.19.5 Maupassant, Guy de. The odd number. N.Y., 1889.
42577.4.19.8 Maupassant, Guy de. The odd number, thirteen tales. N.Y., 1903.
42577.4.19.25 Maupassant, Guy de. The second odd number. N.Y., 1917.
42577.4.20 Maupassant, Guy de. L'inutile beauté. Paris, 1890.
42577.4.20.10 Maupassant, Guy de. L'inutile beauté. 26. éd. Paris, 1894.
42577.4.21 Maupassant, Guy de. La main gauche. Paris, 1889.
42577.4.22 Maupassant, Guy de. Toine. Paris, n.d.
42577.4.23 Maupassant, Guy de. L'héritage. Paris, n.d.
42577.4.23.10 Maupassant, Guy de. The inheritance. N.Y., 1920.
NEDL 42577.4.24 Maupassant, Guy de. Le rosier de Madame Husson. Paris, 1888.
42577.4.24.5 Maupassant, Guy de. Le rosier de Madame Husson. Paris, 1888.
NEDL 42577.4.24.7 Maupassant, Guy de. Le rosier de Madame Husson. Paris, 189-?
42577.4.25 Maupassant, Guy de. Histoire d'une fille de ferme. Paris, 1889.
42577.4.25.5 Maupassant, Guy de. Maalaispiika ja perhetyttö. Helsinki, 1945.
42577.4.26A Maupassant, Guy de. Contes et nouvelles. Paris, 1887.
42577.4.26B Maupassant, Guy de. Contes et nouvelles. Paris, 1887.
42577.4.26.2 Maupassant, Guy de. Contes et nouvelles. Paris, 1893.
42577.4.26.5 Maupassant, Guy de. Contes et nouvelles. N.Y., 19- ?
42577.4.27 Maupassant, Guy de. Yvette. Paris, 1889.
42577.4.27.5 Maupassant, Guy de. Yvette. 18. éd. Paris, 1893.
42577.4.28 Maupassant, Guy de. La petite roque. Paris, 1886.
42577.4.28.25 Maupassant, Guy de. Little roque and other stories. N.Y., 1924.
42577.4.28.27 Maupassant, Guy de. Notre coeur. Paris, 1962.
42577.4.28.51 Maupassant, Guy de. Lettres de Guy de Maupassant à G. Flaubert par Pierre Borel. Avignon, 1940.
42577.4.28.55 Maupassant, Guy de. Correspondance inédite. Paris, 1951.
42577.4.29 Maupassant, Guy de. La paix du ménage. Paris, 1893.
42577.4.29.4 Maupassant, Guy de. The necklace. N.Y., n.d.
42577.4.29.5 Maupassant, Guy de. Sur l'eau. Paris, 1888.
42577.4.29.5.3 Maupassant, Guy de. Afloat. London, 1889.
42577.4.29.5.5 Maupassant, Guy de. Sur l'eau. Paris, 1907.
42577.4.29.6 Maupassant, Guy de. Mont Oriol. Paris, 191-.
42577.4.29.6.5 Maupassant, Guy de. Mont Oriol. Paris, 1925?
42577.4.29.7 Maupassant, Guy de. Une vie. (L'humble vérite). 19. éd. Paris, 1883.
42577.4.29.8A Maupassant, Guy de. Une vie. Paris, 1901.
42577.4.29.8B Maupassant, Guy de. Une vie. Paris, 1901.
42577.4.29.9A Maupassant, Guy de. Une vie. N.Y., 1920?
42577.4.29.9B Maupassant, Guy de. Une vie. N.Y., 1920?

Classified Listing

577.2 - .4.30 Individual authors, etc. - 1850-1899 - Fiction - Maupassant - Individual works - cont.

42577.4.29.9.5 Maupassant, Guy de. Naiskohtalo. Helsinki, 1945.
42577.4.29.10A Maupassant, Guy de. Francesca and Carlotta Rondoli. N.Y., 1910.
42577.4.29.10B Maupassant, Guy de. Francesca and Carlotta Rondoli. N.Y., 1910.
42577.4.29.20 Maupassant, Guy de. La vie errante. Paris, n.d.
42577.4.29.30 Maupassant, Guy de. Pierre et Jean. Paris, 1959.
42577.4.29.35 Maupassant, Guy de. Mademoiselle Perle, and other stories. London, 19- ?
42577.4.29.50 Maupassant, Guy de. The life of Maupassant. London, 1903. 17v.
42577.4.29.60A Maupassant, Guy de. Maupassant, journaliste et chroniqueur. Paris, 1956.
42577.4.29.60B Maupassant, Guy de. Maupassant, journaliste et chroniqueur. Paris, 1956.
42577.4.29.70 Schniedt, A.M. Maupassant, par lui-même. Paris, 1962.
42577.4.30 Maupassant, Guy de. La maison Tellier. Paris, 1891.
tn 42577.4.30.1* Maupassant, Guy de. The life work of Maupassant. London, 1903. 17v.
tn 42577.4.30.2* Maupassant, Guy de. The works of Maupassant. v.2-4,6,7,9,10. N.Y., 1909. 7v.
42577.4.30.3 Maynial, E. Maupassant. Berlin, 1907.
42577.4.30.4 Maupassant, Guy de. The works of Guy de Maupassant. v.1,3-10. N.Y., 1909. 9v.

2577.4.31 - .4.999 Individual authors, etc. - 1850-1899 - Fiction - Maupassant - Biography and criticism

42577.4.31.5 Normandy, G. Guy de Maupassant. Paris, 1926.
42577.4.31.10 Fodéré, René. Maupassant, est-il mort fau? Paris, 1947.
42577.4.31.15 Thoraval, J. L'art de Maupassant. Paris, 1950.
42577.4.31.16 Thoraval, J. L'art de Maupassant. Thèse. Paris, 1950.
42577.4.31.20 Urtel, H. Guy de Maupassant. München, 1926.
42577.4.31.25 Los Angeles Public Library. Index to the stories of Guy de Maupassant. Boston, 1960.
42577.4.31.30 Morand, Paul. Vie de Guy de Maupassant. Paris, 1942.
42577.4.31.35 Maynial, Édouard. La vie et l'oeuvre de Guy de Maupassant. 4. éd. Paris, 1907.
42577.4.31.40 Maynial, Édouard. Maupassant. Berlin, 1907.
42577.4.32 Lumbroso, A. Souvenirs sur Maupassant. Rome, 1905.
42577.4.32.5 Lacaze-Duthiers, Gerard de. Guy de Maupassant, son oeuvre. Paris, 1926.
42577.4.32.20 Lacassagne, J. Guy de Maupassant et son Mal. Lyon, 1951.
42577.4.33 Bosson, O. Guy de Maupassant. London, 1907.
42577.4.33.10 Sullivan, E.D. Maupassant the novelist. Princeton, 1954.
42577.4.34 Defoux, Léon. Guy de Maupassant. Paris, 1918.
42577.4.35 Reuel, Fritz. Maupassant als Physiognomiker. Inaug. Diss. Marburg, 1916.
42577.4.35.3 Borel, Pierre. Le destin tragique de Guy de Maupassant d'après des documents originaux. Paris, 1927.
42577.4.35.4 Borel, Pierre. Le vrai Maupassant. Genève, 1951.
42577.4.35.5 Borel, Pierre. Maupassant et l'androgyne. Paris, 1944.
42577.4.36 Pamphlet box. Guy de Maupassant.
42577.4.37 Rolland, J. Guy de Maupassant. Paris, 1924.
42577.4.38 Steegmüller, F. Maupassant, a lion in the path. N.Y., 1949.
42577.4.39 Spaziani, Marcelo. Bibliographie de Maupassant en Italie. Florence, 1957.
42577.4.40 Gelzer, Heinrich. Guy de Maupassant. Heidelberg, 1926.
42577.4.42 Tassart, François. Souvenir sur Guy de Maupassant. Paris, 1911.
42577.4.43 Tassart, François. Recollections of Guy de Maupassant. London, 1912.
42577.4.43.10 Tassart, François. Nouveaux souvenirs intimes sur Guy de Maupassant. Paris, 1962.
42577.4.44 Voivenel, Paul. Sous le signe de la P.G. Paris, 1929.
42577.4.45 Janssen, Carl Luplan. Le décor chez Guy de Maupassant. Copenhagen, 1960-
42577.4.46 Dumesnil, René. Guy de Maupassant. Paris, 1933.
42577.4.48 Jackson, Samuel. Guy de Maupassant. London, 1938.
42577.4.49.110 Gaudefroy-Demomlynes, L. La femme dans l'oeuvre de Maupassant. Thèse. Paris, 1943.
42577.4.49.115 Artinian, Artine. Maupassant criticism in France, 1880-1940. N.Y., 1941.
42577.4.49.116 Artinian, Artine. Pour et contre Maupassant. Paris, 1955.
42577.4.49.125 Togeby, K. L'oeuvre de Maupassant. Copenhague, 1954.
42577.4.49.130 Vial, André. La genèse d'"Une vie". Paris, 1954.
42577.4.49.131 Vial, André. La genèse d'"Une vie". Thèse. Paris, 1954.
42577.4.49.135 Vial, André. Guy de Maupassant et l'art du roman. Thèse. Paris, 1954.
42577.4.49.140 Kirkbride, R. de Levington. The private life of Guy de Maupassant. N.Y., 1947.
42577.4.49.145 Hartoy, Maurice d'. Guy de Maupassant inconnu. Paris, 1957.
42577.4.49.150 Sullivan, Edward. Maupassant. London, 1962.
42577.4.49.155 Butler, A. Les parlers dirlectaux et populaires dans l'oeuvre de Guy de Maupassant. Genève, 1962.
42577.4.49.160 Ignotus, Pal. The paradox of Maupassant. London, 1967.
42577.4.49.165 Lanoux, Armand. Maupassant le "Bel-ami". Paris, 1967.
42577.4.70 Lemoine, F. Guy de Maupassant. Paris, 1957.
42577.4.80 Cogny, Pierre. Maupassant, l'homme sans Dieu. Bruxelles, 1968.
42577.4.85 Danilin, Iurii I. Zhizn' i tvorchestvo Mopassana. Izd. 2. Moskva, 1968.
42577.4.90 Kessler, Helmut. Maupassants Novellen. Braunschweig, 1966.

42577.5 - .11 Individual authors, etc. - 1850-1899 - Fiction - Malot

42577.5 Malot, Hector. Une bonne affaire. Paris, 1870.
42577.5.3 Malot, Hector. Cara. Paris, n.d.
42577.5.5 Malot, Hector. En famille. Paris, n.d. 2v.
42577.5.7 Malot, Hector. La fille de la comédienne. Paris, 1876.
42577.6 Malot, Hector. Folie d'amour. Paris, 1888.
42577.7 Malot, Hector. Justice. Paris, n.d.
42577.8 Malot, Hector. Madame Obernin. Paris, 1872.
42577.8.10 Malot, Hector. Une belle-mère. Paris, 1874.
42577.9 Malot, Hector. Marié par les prêtres. Paris, 1877.
42577.9.2 Malot, Hector. Marié par les prêtres. Paris, n.d.
42577.10 Malot, Hector. Mondaine. Paris, n.d.
42577.10.9 Malot, Hector. Pompon. 9. éd. Paris, 1882.
42577.10.75 Malot, Hector. Romain Kalbris. 7. éd. Paris, 1882.
42577.10.76 Malot, Hector. Romain Kalbris. Philadelphia, 1873.
42577.11 Malot, Hector. Romain Kalbris. Paris, 1869.
42577.11.1 Malot, Hector. Capi et sa troupe. London, 1897.
42577.11.2 Malot, Hector. Episodes from Sans famille. London, 1889.
42577.11.2.5 Malot, Hector. Episodes from Sans famille. London, 1898.
42577.11.2.10 Malot, Hector. Episodes from Sans famille. Boston, 1899.

42577.5 - .11 Individual authors, etc. - 1850-1899 - Fiction - Malot - cont.

42577.11.3 Malot, Hector. Sans famille. Paris, 1881. 2v.
42577.11.5 Malot, Hector. Sans famille. Paris, 1882.
42577.11.6 Malot, Hector. Sans famille. v.2. 40. éd. Paris, 1883.
42577.11.7 Malot, Hector. Sans famille. 2. ed. N.Y., 1913.
42577.11.9 Malot, Hector. La belle madame Donis. 8. éd. Paris, 1878.
42577.11.12 Malot, Hector. Séduction. Paris, n.d.
42577.11.14 Malot, Hector. La marquise de Lucillière. 7. éd. Paris, 1879.
42577.11.16 Malot, Hector. Ida et Carmelita. 6. éd. Paris, 1877.
42577.11.25 Malot, Hector. Pages choisies. Paris, 1898.
42577.11.75 Malot, Hector. The little sister. N.Y., 1928.

42577.12 Individual authors, etc. - 1850-1899 - Fiction - Marsonnière; Martin; Maygrier; etc.

42577.12 Marsonnière, J.L. de la. Un drama au Logis de la Lycorne. London, 1883.
42577.12.5 Marenches, E. Hermine. 2. éd. Paris, 1892.
42577.12.9 Martin, Victor. Sous la terreur. Paris, 1906.
42577.12.19 Mary-Lafon. Silvio ou Le boudoir. Paris, 1835.
42577.12.21 Mary-Lafon. Cinquante ans de vie littéraire. London, 1882.
42577.12.75 Maygrier, Raymond. Les mystères du magnétisme. Paris, 18- ?
42577.12.78 Maygrier, Raymond. Le dernier Faust. Paris, 1916.

42577.13 Individual authors, etc. - 1850-1899 - Fiction - Maynard; Mercier; Montepin; Mouton; etc.

42577.13 Maynard, Félix. Souvenirs d'un Zouave devant Sebastopol. Paris, 1856.
42577.13.9 Mercier, Alfred. L'habitation Saint-Ybars ou Maitres et esclaves en Louisiane. New Orleans, 1881.
42577.13.12 Mérel, Emmanuel. Nouvelles bretonnes. Paris, 1881.
42577.13.15 Montal, Marie. L'idéal de Germaine. Paris, 1891.
42577.13.22 Montépin, X. de. Deux amours; Hermine. Paris, 1885.
42577.13.24 Montépin, X. de. Krvava ruka. Zagreb, n.d.
42577.13.25 Montépin, X. de. Le secret de la comtesse. Paris, 1876. 2v.
42577.13.29 Montépin, X. de. Les viveurs de Paris. Paris, 1857. 4v.
42577.13.35 Morlent, J. Les Robinsons français. Tours, 1867.
Htn 42577.13.40* Morvan, L. The secret of Fougereuse. Boston, 1898.
42577.13.45F Mouton, Eugène. Histoire de l'invalide à la tête de bois. Paris, 1886.

42577.14 - .32 Individual authors, etc. - 1850-1899 - Fiction - Murger, H.

42577.14 Murger, Henry. Les buveurs d'eau. Paris, 1872.
42577.14.9 Murger, Henry. Le bonhomme jadis. Paris, 1872.
42577.14.40 Murger, Henry. Le bonhomme jadis. Paris, 1908.
42577.15 Murger, Henry. Le bonhomme jadis. Paris, 1852.
42577.15.2 Murger, Henry. Le bonhomme jadis. Paris, 1914?
42577.16 Murger, Henry. Dona Sirène. Paris, 1876.
42577.20 Murger, Henry. Madame Olympe. Le dernier rendez-vous. Paris, 1872.
42577.22 Murger, Henry. Les nuits d'hiver. Paris, 1868.
42577.23 Murger, Henry. Le pays latin. Paris, 1878.
42577.23.10 Murger, Henry. Le pays latin. Paris, 1909.
42577.24 Murger, Henry. Le roman de toutes les femmes. Le pays latin. Paris, 1870.
42577.25 Murger, Henry. Propos de ville et propos de théatre. Paris, 1853.
42577.25.2 Murger, Henry. Propos de ville et propos de théatre. Bruxelles, 1854.
42577.26 Murger, Henry. Propos de ville et propos de théâtre. Les vacances de Camille. Paris, 1870.
42577.27 Murger, Henry. Les roueries. Paris, 1876.
42577.28 Murger, Henry. Le serment d'Horace. Paris, 1864.
42577.29 Murger, Henry. Scènes de la vie de jeunesse. Le sabot rouge. Paris, 1872.
42577.29.50 Murger, Henry. Scènes de campagne. Paris, 1856.
42577.30 Murger, Henry. Scènes de campagne. Paris, 1870.
42577.30.9 Murger, Henry. Scènes de la vie de Bohème. v.1-2. Paris, 1859.
42577.31 Murger, Henry. Scènes de la vie de Bohème. Paris, 1866.
42577.32 Murger, Henry. Scènes de la vie de Bohème. Paris, 1871.
Htn 42577.32.5* Murger, Henry. Scènes de la vie de Bohème. Paris, 1879.
42577.32.10 Murger, Henry. Scènes de la vie de Bohème. Paris, 1910.
42577.32.20 Murger, Henry. Scènes de la vie de Bohème. Paris, 1946.
42577.32.22 Murger, Henry. Scènes de la vie de Bohème. Grenoble, 1968. 2v.
42577.32.25 Murger, Henry. The Latin quarter. N.Y., 192-.
42577.32.28 Murger, Henry. Scenes from the life of Bohemia. Indianapolis, 1888?
42577.32.30 Moss, Arthur. The legend of the Latin quarter. N.Y., 1946.
42577.32.40 Murger, Henry. Vie de Bohème. London, 1960.
42577.32.50 Montorgueil, George. Henry Murger, romancier de la Bohème. Paris, 1929.
42577.32.60 Brauns, Walter. Die Lyrik Henry Murgers. Inaug. Diss. Coburg, 1932.
42577.32.65 Baldich, Robert. The first Bohemian. London, 1961.

42577.33 Individual authors, etc. - 1850-1899 - Fiction - Maurel

42577.33 Maurel, André. Candeur. Paris, 1890.

42577.34 Individual authors, etc. - 1850-1899 - Fiction - Masson-Forestier; Mattais; etc.

42577.34 Masson-Forestier, A. Pour une signature. Paris, 1892.
42577.34.5 Masson-Forestier, A. Remords d'Avocat. Paris, 1896.
42577.34.6 Masson-Forestier, A. La jambe coupée. Paris, 1894.
42577.34.7 Masson-Forestier, A. Angoisses de Juge. Paris, 1898.
42577.34.18 Ehmke, W. Masson-Forestier, sein Leben und sein Werk. Inaug. Diss. Altdöbern, 1930.
42577.34.20 Mettais, Hippolyte. L'an 5865, ou Paris dans quatre mille ans. Paris, 1865.
42577.34.21 Mettais, Hippolyte. Paris, avant le déluge. Paris, 1866.

42577.35 Individual authors, etc. - 1850-1899 - Fiction - Michon; Mirecourt; etc.

42577.35 Michon, Jean H. Le jésuite. v.1-5. Paris, 1865.
42577.35.8 Michon, Jean H. Le maudit. 3. éd. Paris, 1864.
42577.35.9 Michon, Jean H. Les mystiques. Paris, 1869.
42577.35.11 Michon, Jean H. Le curé de campagne. v.2. Paris, 1867.
42577.35.15 Michon, Jean H. El fraile. 3. ed. Barcelona, 18- .
42577.35.20 Michon, Jean H. El maldito. v.1-4. Barcelona, 1869. 2v.

42577.35 Individual authors, etc. - 1850-1899 - Fiction - Michon; Mirecourt; etc. - cont.

42577.35.50 Mirecourt, Eugène de. Le fils de Gibaugier; comédie. Paris, 1863.
42577.35.55 Mirecourt, Eugène de. Le petit fils de Pigault-Lebrun. Paris, 1863.

42577.36 Individual authors, etc. - 1850-1899 - Fiction - Monteil

42577.36 Monteil, E. La grande Babylone. Paris, 1887.

42577.37 Individual authors, etc. - 1850-1899 - Fiction - Marmier, X. [Discontinued]

42577.37 Marmier, Xavier. Les fiancés du Spitzberg. Oxford, 1907.

42577.38 Individual authors, etc. - 1850-1899 - Fiction - Morin, L.

42577.38.100 Morin, Louis. Histories d'autrefois. v.2,3. Paris, 1885- 2v.

42577.39 Individual authors, etc. - 1850-1899 - Fiction - Mossé

42577.39.100 Mossé, Armand. Un dieu sur la terre? Paris, 1931.

42577.40 Individual authors, etc. - 1850-1899 - Fiction - Muller, E.

42577.40.100 Muller, Eugène. La mionette. Paris, 1885.

42577.42 Individual authors, etc. - 1850-1899 - Fiction - Meunier, Mme.

42577.42 Meunier, Levallois (Mme.). Le roman du Mont Saint Michel, 1364. Paris, 1891.

42578.5 Individual authors, etc. - 1850-1899 - Fiction - Noir

42578.5.30 Noir, Louis Salmon. La banque juive. Paris, 1888.

42578.7 Individual authors, etc. - 1850-1899 - Fiction - Rendade

42578.7 Rendade, J. Alma Mater. Paris, n.d.

42578.10 - .16 Individual authors, etc. - 1850-1899 - Fiction - Narrey, C. - Writings

42578.10 Narrey, Charles. Le bal du diable. Paris, 1874.
42578.11 Narrey, Charles. Le quatrième larron. Paris, 1861.
42578.12 Narrey, Charles. Ce que l'on dit pendant une contredanse. Paris, 1873.
42578.14 Narrey, Charles. Les derniers jeunes gens. Paris, 1868.
42578.16 Narrey, Charles. Voyage autour du dictionnaire. Paris, 1892.

42578.17 Individual authors, etc. - 1850-1899 - Fiction - Naurroye; Niboget; Neveux; etc.

42578.17.25 Naurouze, Jacques. A travers la tourmente. Paris, 1896.
42578.17.200 Niboyet, Paulin. La vièrge de Belem. Paris, 1884.
42578.17.208 Niboyet, Paulin. L'Américaine. Paris, 1875.
42578.17.400 Neveux, P. Louis. Golo. 10. éd. Paris, 1925.

42578.18 Individual authors, etc. - 1850-1899 - Fiction - Quillot; Rabusson; Racot; Rameau; Richebourg; etc.

42578.18 Quillot, Maurice. L'entrainé. Paris, 1892.
42578.18.3 Rabusson, Henry. Sans entraves. Paris, 1893.
42578.18.3.5 Rabusson, Henry. Gogo et cie, une famille de la bourgeoisie. Paris, 1914.
42578.18.3.10 Rabusson, Henry. Hallali! 5. éd. Paris, 1891.
42578.18.4 Racot, A. Le capitaine Muet. Paris, 1887.
42578.18.5 Rameau, Jean. La rose de Grenade. Paris, 1894.
42578.18.6 Rameau, Jean. La chevelure de Madeleine. Paris, 1895.
42578.18.7 Rameau, Jean. La jungle de Paris. Paris, 1904.
42578.18.8 Rameau, Jean. La bonne étoile. Paris, 1906.
42578.18.9 Rameau, Jean. Zarette. Paris, 1904.
42578.18.10 Rameau, Jean. Le dernier bateau. Paris, 1900.
42578.18.11 Rameau, Jean. Ame fleurie. Paris, 1902.
42578.18.12 Rameau, Jean. Mademoiselle Azur. Paris, 1894.
42578.18.13 Rameau, Jean. Brimborion. Paris, 1905.
42578.18.14 Rameau, Jean. La route bleue. Paris, 1912.
42578.18.15 Rameau, Jean. Les mains blanches. 4. éd. Paris, 1919.
42578.18.16 Rameau, Jean. Flore. Paris, 1932.
42578.18.50 Richebourg, Emile. Deux mères. Paris, 1879. 2v.
42578.18.56 Richebourg, Emile. La fille maudite. Paris, 1876-77. 2v.

42578.19 Individual authors, etc. - 1850-1899 - Fiction - Rod, E.

42578.19 Rod, Edouard. Le sens de la vie. Paris, 1891.
42578.19.1.5A Rod, Edouard. Le sens de la vie. 13. éd. Paris, 1897.
42578.19.1.5B Rod, Edouard. Le sens de la vie. 13. éd. Paris, 1897.
42578.19.1.5C Rod, Edouard. Le sens de la vie. 13. éd. Paris, 1897.
42578.19.2 Rod, Edouard. La course à la mort. 4. éd. Paris, 1891.
42578.19.2.4 Rod, Edouard. La course à la mort. 5. éd. Paris, 1891.
42578.19.2.5 Rod, Edouard. La course à la mort. 6. éd. Paris, 1899.
42578.19.3 Rod, Edouard. Nouvelles romandes. Paris, 1891.
42578.19.4 Rod, Edouard. La sacrifiée. Paris, 1892.
42578.19.5 Rod, Edouard. Scènes de la vie cosmopolite. Paris, 1890.
42578.19.5.3 Rod, Edouard. Scènes de la vie cosmopolite. 2. éd. Paris, 1890.
42578.19.6 Rod, Edouard. Trois coeurs. Paris, 1890.
42578.19.6.3 Rod, Edouard. Les trois coeurs. 3. éd. Paris, 1890.
42578.19.7 Rod, Edouard. La vie privée de Michel Teissier. Paris, 1893.
42578.19.7.3A Rod, Edouard. La vie privée de Michel Teissier. 10. éd. Paris, 1896.
42578.19.7.3B Rod, Edouard. La vie privée de Michel Teissier. 10. éd. Paris, 1896.
42578.19.7.5 Rod, Edouard. La vie privée de Michel Teissier. Paris, 1897.
42578.19.7.9 Rod, Edouard. La vie privée de Michel Teissier. Paris, 1907.
42578.19.8 Rod, Edouard. Giacome Leopardi. Études sur le 19. siècle. Paris, 1888.
42578.19.8.1 Rod, Edouard. Giacome Leopardi. Études sur le 19. siècle. Lausanne, 1888.
42578.19.8.2 Rod, Edouard. Nouvelles études sur le 19. siècle. Paris, 1899.
42578.19.8.10A Rod, Edouard. Études sur le 19. siècle. 2. éd. Paris, 1894.
42578.19.8.10B Rod, Edouard. Études sur le 19. siècle. 2. éd. Paris, 1894.
42578.19.9 Rod, Edouard. Le silence. Paris, 1894.
42578.19.9.5 Rod, Edouard. Le silence. 12. éd. Paris, 1894.
42578.19.10 Rod, Edouard. La seconde vie de Michel Teissier. Paris, 1894.
42578.19.10.5A Rod, Edouard. La seconde vie de Michel Teissier. Paris, 1894.
42578.19.10.5B Rod, Edouard. La seconde vie de Michel Teissier. Paris, 1894.

42578.19 Individual authors, etc. - 1850-1899 - Fiction - Rod, E. - cont.

42578.19.11 Rod, Edouard. Les roches blanches. Paris, 1895.
42578.19.11.3A Rod, Edouard. Les roches blanches. 21. éd. Paris, 1895.
42578.19.11.3B Rod, Edouard. Les roches blanches. 21. éd. Paris, 1895.
42578.19.12 Rod, Edouard. Là-haut. Paris, 1897.
42578.19.12.3 Rod, Edouard. Là-haut. 14. éd. Paris, 1897.
42578.19.13 Rod, Edouard. Dernier refuge. Paris, 1896.
42578.19.13.3 Rod, Edouard. Dernier refuge. 6. éd. Paris, 1896.
42578.19.13.6 Rod, Edouard. Dernier refuge. 12. éd. Paris, 1896.
42578.19.14 Rod, Edouard. La femme d'Henri Vauneau. Paris, 1884.
42578.19.15 Rod, Edouard. L'innocente. Paris, 1897.
42578.19.16 Rod, Edouard. Le ménage du pasteur Naudié. Paris, 1898.
42578.19.16.3 Rod, Edouard. Le ménage du pasteur Naudié. Paris, 1898.
42578.19.16.10 Rod, Edouard. Pastor Naudie's young wife. Boston, 1899.
42578.19.17 Rod, Edouard. Mademoiselle Annette. Paris, 1901.
42578.19.18 Rod, Edouard. L'inutile effort. Paris, 1903.
42578.19.19 Rod, Edouard. Un vainqueur. Paris, 1904.
42578.19.20 Rod, Edouard. L'indocile. Paris, 1905.
42578.19.21 Rod, Edouard. L'incendie. Paris, 1907.
42578.19.22.10 Rod, Edouard. L'ombre s'étend sur la montagne. 1. éd. Paris, 1916.
42578.19.23 Rod, Edouard. Le réformateur. Paris, 1906.
42578.19.24 Rod, Edouard. Aloÿse Valérien. Paris, 1908.
42578.19.25A Rod, Edouard. Les unis. Paris, 1909.
42578.19.25B Rod, Edouard. Les unis. Paris, 1909.
42578.19.26 Rod, Edouard. Le glaive et le bandeau. Paris, 1910.
42578.19.29 Rod, Edouard. Les idées morales du temps présent. Paris, 1897.
42578.19.33A Rod, Edouard. Michel Teissier. Paris, 1894.
42578.19.33B Rod, Edouard. Michel Teissier. Paris, 1894.
42578.19.40 Pamphlet box. Rod, Edouard.
42578.19.45 Roz, F. Edouard Rod. Paris, 1906.
42578.19.48 Beuchat, Charles. Edouard Rod et le cosmopolitisme. Thèse. Paris, 1930.
42578.19.50 Beuchat, Charles. Edouard Rod et le cosmopolitisme. Paris, 1930.
42578.19.55 Delhorbe, C. Edouard Rod d'après des documents inédits. Neuchatel, 1939.

42578.20 - .22 Individual authors, etc. - 1850-1899 - Fiction - Rosny, J.H.

42578.20 Rosny, J.H. Daniel Valgraive. Paris, 1891.
42578.20.2 Rosny, J.H. Les audacieux. Paris, 1910.
42578.20.5 Rosny, J.H. Les corneilles. Paris, 1888.
42578.21 Rosny, J.H. Le termite. Paris, 1890.
42578.22 Rosny, J.H. Le bilatéral. Paris, 1887.
42578.22.2 Rosny, J.H. Marc Fane. Paris, 1888.
42578.22.5 Rosny, J.H. Sous le fardeau. Paris, n.d.
-42578.22.7 Rosny, J.H. Le fauve. Paris, n.d.
X Cg 42578.22.7.12 Rosny, J.H. Les deux femmes. 5. éd. Paris, 1902.
42578.22.8.7 Rosny, J.H. Hellhorn de l'armée du salut. Paris, 189-?
42578.22.8.10 Rosny, J.H. Nornai. Paris, 1897.
42578.22.8.11 Rosny, J.H. La silencieuse. Paris, 1898.
42578.22.8.12 Rosny, J.H. Nouvel amour. Paris, 1897.
42578.22.8.13 Rosny, J.H. La tentatrice. Paris, 1897.
42578.22.8.14 Rosny, J.H. Elem d'Asie. Paris, 1896.
42578.22.8.16 Rosny, J.H. Renouveau. Paris, 1894.
42578.22.8.18 Rosny, J.H. La fille d'affaires. Paris, 1925.
42578.22.8.25 Rosny, J.H. Eyrimah. Paris, 1934.
42578.22.10 Rosny, J.H. Le félin géant. 5. éd. Paris, 1920.
42578.22.10.20 Rosny, J.H. Les plus belles pages de J.H. Rosny. Paris, 1936.
42578.22.10.25 Rosny, J.H. Sabine et son père. Paris, 1932.
42578.22.10.30 Rosny, J.H. La courtisane triomphante. Paris, 1925.
42578.22.10.35 Rosny, J.H. Une jeune fille à la page. Paris, 1926.
42578.22.10.40 Rosny, J.H. Amour étrusque. Paris, 1898.
42578.22.10.45 Rosny, J.H. La flûte de Pan. Paris, 1897.
42578.22.10.50 Rosny, J.H. Dans la nuit des coeurs. Paris, 1922.
42578.22.10.55 Rosny, J.H. Marthe Baraquin. 8. éd. Paris, 1909.
42578.22.10.60 Rosny, J.H. Le vampire de Bethnal Green. Paris, 1935.
42578.22.10.65 Rosny, J.H. Les pures et les impures. v.1-2. Paris, 1921.
42578.22.10.70 Rosny, J.H. L'amour d'abord. Paris, 1924.
42578.22.10.80 Rosny, J.H. Un banquier. Paris, 1937.
42578.22.10.90 Rosny, J.H. Les destins contraires. Paris, 1932.
42578.22.10.100 Rosny, J.H. La vague rouge. Paris, 1910.
42578.22.15 Rosny, J.H. Perdus? Paris, 1916.
42578.22.20 Rosny, J.H. Les femmes des autres. Paris, 1932.
42578.22.25 Rosny, J.H. La force mystérieuse. Paris, 1914.
42578.22.27 Rosny, J.H. Les rafales. Paris, n.d.
42578.22.30 Rosny, J.H. L'assassin surnaturel. Paris, 1924.
42578.22.35 Rosny, J.H. Torches et lumignons. Paris, 1921.
42578.22.40 Rosny, J.H. L'appel du bonheur. Paris, 1919.
42578.22.45 Rosny, J.H. Et l'amour ensuite. Paris, 1919.
42578.22.50 Rosny, J.H. L'énigme de Givreuse. Paris, 1917.
42578.22.55 Rosny, J.H. Un voleur. pt. 1-2. Paris, 1932.
42578.22.60 Rosny, J.H. La guerre du feu. Paris, 1928.
42578.22.70 Rosny, J.H. L'initiation de Diane. Paris, 1934.
42578.22.75 Rosny, J.H. Le destin de Marin Lafaille. Paris, 1945.
42578.22.90 Rosny, J.H. Passion et bonheur. Paris, 1932.
42578.22.95 Rosny, J.H. L'amoureuse aventure. Paris, 1920.
42578.22.100 Rosny, J.H. Dans le calme et dans la tempête. Paris, 1936.
42578.22.105 Rosny, J.H. La vengeance. Paris, 1935.
42578.22.110 Rosny, J.H. La sauvage aventure. Paris, 1935.
42578.22.115 Rosny, J.H. Les instincts. Paris, 1939.
42578.22.120 Rosny, J.H. La mort de la terre. Paris, 1912.
42578.22.130 Rosny, J.H. Les compagnons de l'univers. 9. éd. Paris, 1934.
42578.22.140 Rosny, J.H. Les xipéhuz. Paris, 1910.
42578.22.150 Rosny, J.H. Les beaux yeux de Paris. Paris, 1926.
42578.22.155 Rosny, J.H. Les amours tragiques de la première princesse de Lamballe. Paris, 1930.
42578.22.155.5 Rosny, J.H. La cité infernale. Paris, 1933.
42578.22.160 Rosny, J.H. L'aiguille d'or. 2. éd. Paris, 1899.
42578.22.165 Rosny, J.H. Les arrivistes. Paris, 1934.
42578.22.170 Rosny, J.H. L'impérieuse bonté. Paris, 1894.
42578.22.180 Rosny, J.H. La fille des rocs. Paris, 1928.
42578.22.190 Rosny, J.H. Vamireh. Paris, 192-?
42578.22.200 Rosny, J.H. Les autres vies et les autres mondes. Paris, 1924.
42578.22.210 Rosny, J.H. Les plaisirs passionnés. Paris, 1929.
42578.22.800 Casella, Georges. J.H. Rosny. Paris, 1907.

42578.23 - .27 Individual authors, etc. - 1850-1899 - Fiction - Noriac, J. (Cairon) - Writings

42578.23 Noriac, Jules. La bêtise humaine. Paris, 1870.
42578.23.5 Noriac, Jules. La vie en détail. Paris, 1870.
42578.23.10 Noriac, Jules. Human follies. N.Y., 1863.
42578.24 Noriac, Jules. Le grain de sable. Paris, 1872.
42578.25 Noriac, Jules. La comtesse de Bruges. Paris, 1879.
42578.26 Chevalier, Adrian. Paul Ravenel. Paris, 1903?
42578.27 Noriac, Jules. Paris tel qu'il est. Paris, 1884.

42578.29 - .30.38 Individual authors, etc. - 1850-1899 - Fiction - Ohnet, G. - Writings

42578.29.2 Ohnet, Georges. Dr. Rameau. Philadelphia, 1889.
42578.29.3 Ohnet, Georges. Dr. Rameau. N.Y., 1889.
42578.29.4 Ohnet, Georges. Prince Serge Panine. N.Y., n.d.
42578.29.5 Ohnet, Georges. Lise Fleuron. Paris, 1884.
42578.29.6 Ohnet, Georges. Les dames de croix-mort. Paris, 1886.
42578.29.7 Ohnet, Georges. Noir et rose. Paris, 1887.
42578.29.8 Ohnet, Georges. La dixième muse. Paris, 1907.
42578.29.9 Ohnet, Georges. La serre de l'aigle. Paris, 1912.
42578.29.10 Ohnet, Georges. The eagle's talon. N.Y., 1913.
42578.29.11 Ohnet, Georges. La conquérante. Paris, 1905.
42578.29.11.5 Ohnet, Georges. La conquérante. 3. éd. Paris, 1905.
42578.29.12 Ohnet, Georges. La grande marnière. 38. éd. Paris, 1885.
42578.29.13 Ohnet, Georges. La comtesse Sarah. 21. éd. Paris, 1883.
42578.29.15 Ohnet, Georges. La comtesse Sarah. 45. éd. Paris, 1883.
42578.29.50 Ohnet, Georges. Dernier amour. 68. éd. Paris, 1889.
42578.29.60 Ohnet, Georges. Le brasseur d'affaires. Paris, 1901.
42578.29.70 Ohnet, Georges. Le crépuscule. 17. éd. Paris, 1902.
42578.29.80 Ohnet, Georges. Gens de la noce. Paris, 1900.
42578.29.90 Ohnet, Georges. Marchand de poison. Paris, 1903.
42578.29.100 Ohnet, Georges. Le curé de Favières. 3. éd. Paris, 1897.
42578.29.110 Ohnet, Georges. La dame en gris. 67. éd. Paris, 1895.
42578.29.120 Ohnet, Georges. Dette de haine. Paris, 1891.
42578.30 Ohnet, Georges. Le maître de forges. Paris, 1884.
42578.30.2 Ohnet, Georges. Le maître de forges. Paris, 1907?
42578.30.3 Ohnet, Georges. Le maître de forges. 57. éd. Paris, 1882.
42578.30.5 Ohnet, Georges. Aux avant-postes. n.p., 18- ?
42578.30.10 Ohnet, Georges. Serge Panine. Paris, 1884.
42578.30.12 Ohnet, Georges. Serge Panine. 71. éd. Paris, 1882.
42578.30.13 Ohnet, Georges. Serge Panine. Paris, 1890.
42578.30.15 Ohnet, Georges. La fille du député. N.Y., 1898.
42578.30.20 Ohnet, Georges. Der Hüttenbesitzer. v.1-2. Stuttgart, 1884.
42578.30.25 Ohnet, Georges. La ténébreuse. Paris, 1901.
42578.30.30 Ohnet, Georges. Felipe Derblay. Buenos Aires, 19- .
42578.30.35 Ohnet, Georges. Volonté. Paris, 1888.

42578.30.40 - .30.99 Individual authors, etc. - 1850-1899 - Fiction - Péladan, J.

42578.30.45 Peladan, J. La décadence latine. v. 2-4, 6-10, 12-19. Paris, 1886-1926. 16v.
42578.30.46 Peladan, J. Istar. v.1-2. Paris, 1888.
42578.30.47 Peladan, J. Etudes passionnelles de décadence. 2. éd. Paris, 1884.
42578.30.50 Peladan, J. La queste du Graal. Paris, 1892?
42578.30.52 Peladan, J. Comment on devient artiste; ésthétique. Paris, 1894.
42578.30.53 Peladan, J. Oedipe et le sphinx. 4. éd. Paris, 1903.
42578.30.55 Peladan, J. Le prince de Byzance. Paris, 1896.
42578.30.58 Peladan, J. Les fils des étoiles. Beauvais, 1895.
42578.30.63 Peladan, J. Sémiramis. Paris, 1905.
42578.30.65 Peladan, J. Le livre secret. Paris, 1920.
42578.30.67 Peladan, J. Modestie et vanité. Paris, 1926.
42578.30.70 Peladan, J. Le livre spectre politique. Paris, 1895.
42578.30.72 Peladan, J. Das allmächtige Gold. München, 1911.
42578.30.73 Peladan, J. Das unbekannte Schicksal. München, 1914.
42578.30.74 Peladan, J. St. Francis of Assisi. London, 1913.
42578.30.75 Petitcolin, André. Arvor. Paris, 1898.
42578.30.78 Peladan, J. De l'humanisme. Paris, n.d.
42578.30.80 Aeschylus. Sâr Peladan. Paris, 1895.
42578.30.85 Bertholet, E. La pensée et les secrets du Sâr Joséphin Peladan. Neuchatel, 1952. 4v.
42578.30.90.2 Aubrun, René Georges. Peladan. 2. éd. Paris, 1904.

42578.30.150 Individual authors, etc. - 1850-1899 - Fiction - Pilou

42578.30.150 Pilon, E. Portraits de sentiments. Paris, 1913.

42578.31 - .31.19 Individual authors, etc. - 1850-1899 - Fiction - Pouvillon; Pradels; etc.

42578.31 Pouvillon, E. Césette. Paris, 1882.
42578.31.2 Pouvillon, E. Nouvelles réalistes. Paris, 1878.
42578.31.5 Pouvillon, E. Jep. Paris, 1904.
42578.31.7 Pouvillon, E. Mademoiselle Clémence. Paris, 1896.
42578.31.15 Pradels, O. Les desserts gaulois. Paris, 1891.

42578.31.20 - .31.69 Individual authors, etc. - 1850-1899 - Fiction - Prévost, M. - Writings

42578.31.25 Prévost, Marcel. Lettres de femmes. 20. éd. Paris, 1892.
42578.31.25.2 Prévost, Marcel. Lettres de femmes. 21. éd. Paris, 1892.
42578.31.25.5 Prévost, Marcel. Lettres de femmes. Paris, 1895?
42578.31.25.20 Prévost, Marcel. Letters of women. N.Y., 1897.
42578.31.26 Prévost, Marcel. Nouvelles lettres de femmes. 11. éd. Paris, 1894.
42578.31.26.5 Prévost, Marcel. Nouvelles lettres de femmes. 22. éd. Paris, 1894.
42578.31.26.10 Prévost, Marcel. Dernières lettres de femmes. Paris, 1897.
42578.31.27 Prévost, Marcel. L'automne d'une femme. Paris, 1893?
42578.31.27.5 Prévost, Marcel. L'automne d'une femme. 53. éd. Paris, 189-.
42578.31.28 Prévost, Marcel. Les demi-vièrges. 60. éd. Paris, 1894.
42578.31.28.2 Prévost, Marcel. Les demi-vièrges. 45. éd. Paris, 1894.
42578.31.28.6 Prévost, Marcel. Les demi-vièrges. Paris, 1901.
42578.31.30 Prévost, Marcel. Notre compagne. Paris, 1895.
42578.31.30.2 Prévost, Marcel. Notre compagne. Paris, 1895.
42578.31.32 Prévost, Marcel. Le jardin secret. 32. éd. Paris, 1897.
42578.31.32.5 Prévost, Marcel. Le jardin secret. 53. éd. Paris, 1897.
42578.31.34 Prévost, Marcel. Trois nouvelles. 23. éd. Paris, 1898.
42578.31.34.5 Prévost, Marcel. Trois nouvelles. 36. éd. Paris, 1898.
42578.31.36 Prévost, Marcel. Frédérique. Paris, 1900.
42578.31.37 Prévost, Marcel. Féminités. Paris, 1910.
42578.31.38 Prévost, Marcel. Léa. Paris, 1900.
42578.31.40 Prévost, Marcel. L'heureux ménage. 55. éd. Paris, 1901.
42578.31.43 Prévost, Marcel. Lettres à Françoise. 39. éd. Paris, 1902?
42578.31.44 Prévost, Marcel. Lettres à Françoise mariée. 44. éd. Paris, 1908.

42578.31.20 - .31.69 Individual authors, etc. - 1850-1899 - Fiction - Prévost, M. - Writings - cont.

42578.31.46 Prévost, Marcel. Cousine Laura. Paris, 1903.
42578.31.48 Prévost, Marcel. La plus faible. 5. éd. Paris, 1904.
42578.31.48.90 Prévost, Marcel. Pierre et Thérèse. 23. éd. Paris, 1909.
42578.31.49 Prévost, Marcel. Pierre et Thérèse. Paris, 1912.
42578.31.50 Prévost, Marcel. L'accordeur aveugle. Paris, 1905.
42578.31.52 Prévost, Marcel. Monsieur et Madame Moloch. 58. éd. Paris, 1906.
42578.31.52.5A Prévost, Marcel. Monsieur et Madame Moloch. Paris, 1906.
42578.31.52.5B Prévost, Marcel. Monsieur et Madame Moloch. Paris, 1906.
42578.31.54 Prévost, Marcel. Histoire de la dame potelée. Paris, 1908.
42578.31.55 Prévost, Marcel. Voici ton maître. Paris, 1930.
42578.31.56 Prévost, Marcel. Les anges gardiens. Paris, 1913.
42578.31.56.5 Prévost, Marcel. Les anges gardiens. Paris, 1913.
42578.31.57A Prévost, Marcel. Le domino jaune. Paris, 1901.
42578.31.57B Prévost, Marcel. Le domino jaune. Paris, 1901.
42578.31.58A Prévost, Marcel. L'adjudant Benoît. Paris, 1916.
42578.31.58B Prévost, Marcel. L'adjudant Benoît. Paris, 1916.
42578.31.59 Prévost, Marcel. La fausse bourgeoise. Paris, 1908.
42578.31.60 Prévost, Marcel. Mon cher Tommy. Paris, 1920.
42578.31.61 Prévost, Marcel. Chonchette. Paris, 1901.
42578.31.62 Prévost, Marcel. La nuit finira. 30. éd. Paris, 1920. 2v.
42578.31.63 Prévost, Marcel. La confession d'un amant. Paris, 1891.
42578.31.64 Prévost, Marcel. Les Don Juanes. 53. éd. Paris, 1922.
42578.31.64.5 Prévost, Marcel. The Don Juanes. N.Y., 1924.
42578.31.65 Prévost, Marcel. Mademoiselle Jaufre. Paris, 1889.
42578.31.66 Prévost, Marcel. Sa maitresse et moi. Paris, 1925.
42578.31.66.5 Prévost, Marcel. His mistress and I. N.Y., 1927.
42578.31.67 Prévost, Marcel. L'homme vierge. Paris, 1929.
42578.31.68 Prévost, Marcel. Her master. N.Y., 1931.
42578.31.69 Prévost, Marcel. Le mariage de Julienne. Paris, 1896.

42578.31.70 - .31.75 Individual authors, etc. - 1850-1899 - Fiction - Prévost, M. - Works about

42578.31.70 Jansen, Gretl. Frauenpsychologie und Frauenpädagogik bei Marcel Proust. Würzburg, 1927.
42578.31.74 Mannes, Elisabeth. Marcel Prévosts Ansicht über die Frauen. Inaug. Diss. Bonn, 1914.

42578.31.76 - Individual authors, etc. - 1850-1899 - Fiction - Psichari; Richet; Puaux; Pierret; Reschal; Radet; Reul; Robida; Samopaloff; etc.

42578.31.78 Psichari, Jean. Typesses. Paris, 1923.
42578.31.80 Psichari, Jean. Fioretti per Francesca. Paris, 1925.
42578.31.83 Psichari, Jean. Le crime de Lazarina. Paris, 1926.
42578.31.85 Richet, C. A la recherche de la gloire. Paris, 1892.
42578.31.86 Richet, C. Possessions. Paris, 1887.
42578.31.88 Hommage à Jean Psichari. Paris, 1950.
42578.31.90 Puaux, N.A.E. L'abbaye de la vallée d'Arc. 2. éd. Paris, 1885.
42578.31.95 Pierret, Emile. Les crimes passionnels. Paris, 1896.
42578.31.100 Rude, Maxime. Le cousin infâme. 4. éd. Paris, n.d.
42578.31.105 Reschal, A. Les derniers exploits de Maud. Paris, 1910.
42578.31.110 Radet, L. Le siège de Montargis, 1427. Montargis, 1888.
42578.31.115 Reul, X. de. Le roman d'un géologue. Bruxelles, 1958.
42578.31.120 Revillon, T. La bourgeoise pervertie. Paris, 1884.
42578.31.122 Robida, A. Le trésor de Carcassonne. Paris, 1923?
42578.31.125 Saint-Juirs. J'ai tué ma femme. 4. éd. Paris, 1880.
42578.31.130 Saint-Pol Roux. La dame à la faulx. 2. éd. Paris, 1899.
42578.31.140 Roux, Paul. Le trésor de l'homme. Limoges, 1970.
42578.31.230 Salières, A. Les soirées fantastiques de l'artilleur Baruch. Paris, 1876.
42578.31.330 Samopaloff, Andrée. Le nihiliste. Cleveland, 196-.
42578.31.1100 Ruyters, André. La correspondance du Mauvais-Riche. Bruxelles, 1889.
42578.31.2100 Rennes, Gaston. La roulotte. Paris, 1896.
42578.31.3100 Roujon, Henry. Miremonde. Paris, 1895.
42578.31.4100 Renkin, Jean-François. Ecrits wallons. Liège, 1906?

42578.32 - .35.14 Individual authors, etc. - 1850-1899 - Fiction - Sarcey, F. - Writings

42578.33 Sarcey, Francisque. Etienne Moret. Paris, 1876.
42578.34 Sarcey, Francisque. Souvenirs de jeunesse. Paris, 1885.
42578.34.2 Sarcey, Francisque. Souvenirs d'age mûr. Paris, 1892.
42578.34.5 Sarcey, Francisque. Journal de jeunesse. Paris, 1903.
42578.35 Sarcey, Francisque. Misères d'un fonctionnaire chinois. Paris, 1882.
42578.35.5 Sarcey, Francisque. Recollections of middle life. London, 1893.
42578.35.6 Sarcey, Francisque. Recollections of middle life. N.Y., 1893.

42578.35.15 - .35.99 Individual authors, etc. - 1850-1899 - Fiction - Sarcey, F. - Works about

42578.35.15 Pamphlet box. Sarcey, Francisque.
42578.35.17 Anna, Luigi de. Francisque Sarcey. Florence, 1919.
42578.35.20 Behrens, H. Francisque Sarceys Theaterkritik. Greifswald, 1911.

42578.35.100 - Individual authors, etc. - 1850-1899 - Fiction - Sarton, G.

42578.35.100 Sarton, Georges. Une vie de poète. Gand, 1905.
42578.35.105 Sarton, Georges. La chaîne d'or. Mons, 1909.

42578.36 Individual authors, etc. - 1850-1899 - Fiction - Schultz, J.

42578.36 Schultz, Jeanne. Cinq minutes d'arrêt. Paris, n.d.
42578.36.2 Schultz, Jeanne. Jean de Kerdren. N.Y., 1892.
42578.36.4 Schultz, Jeanne. La neuvaine de Colette. Paris, 1888.
42578.36.5 Schultz, Jeanne. La neuvaine de Colette. 143. éd. Paris, 1920.
42578.36.10A Schultz, Jeanne. La neuvaine de Colette. N.Y., 1899.
42578.36.10B Schultz, Jeanne. La neuvaine de Colette. N.Y., 1899.
42578.36.15 Schultz, Jeanne. La neuvaine de Colette. N.Y., 1905.
42578.36.16 Schultz, Jeanne. Colette. N.Y., 1898.
42578.36.17 Schultz, Jeanne. The story of Colette. N.Y., 1893.
42578.36.30 Schultz, Jeanne. Was der heilige Joseph vermag. Stuttgart, 1888.

42578.40 Individual authors, etc. - 1850-1899 - Fiction - Second, A.

42578.40 Second, Albéric. Jeunesse dorée. Paris, 1879.

42578.48 Individual authors, etc. - 1850-1899 - Fiction - Thiaudière

42578.48 Thiaudière, Edmond. Le roman d'un bossu. Paris, 1880.

42578.49 Individual authors, etc. - 1850-1899 - Fiction - Tinan

42578.49.80 Lebey, André. Jean de Tinan, souvenirs et correspondance. Paris, 1922.

42578.50 Individual authors, etc. - 1850-1899 - Fiction - Töpffer, R.

42578.50.5 Töpffer, Rodolphe. La bibliothèque de mon oncle. N.Y., 1898.

42578.51 Individual authors, etc. - 1850-1899 - Fiction - Tinayre, M.

42578.51.01 Pamphlet box. Tinayre, Marcelle.
42578.51.5 Tinayre, Marcelle. La vie amoureuse de François Barbazauges. 15. éd. Paris, 1908?
42578.51.10 Tinayre, Marcelle. Avant l'amour. 13. éd. Paris, 1909?
42578.51.10.2 Tinayre, Marcelle. Avant l'amour. Paris, 1908.
42578.51.15 Tinayre, Marcelle. Hellé. 9. éd. Paris, 1908?
42578.51.20A Tinayre, Marcelle. La maison du péché. 40. éd. Paris, 1906.
42578.51.20B Tinayre, Marcelle. La maison du péché. 40. éd. Paris, 1906.
42578.51.21 Tinayre, Marcelle. La maison du péché. Paris, 1903.
42578.51.25 Tinayre, Marcelle. L'oiseau d'orage. 3. éd. Paris, 1908?
42578.51.30 Tinayre, Marcelle. La rançon. Paris, 1903.
42578.51.35 Tinayre, Marcelle. La rebelle. 39. éd. Paris, 1909?
42578.51.35.10 Tinayre, Marcelle. La rebelle. Paris, 1921.
42578.51.37 Tinayre, Marcelle. Douceur de vivre. Paris, 1911.
42578.51.40 Tinayre, Marcelle. La douceur de vivre. 27. éd. Paris, 1911.
42578.51.45 Tinayre, Marcelle. La veillée des armes. Le départ:août 1914. Paris, 1915.
42578.51.50 Tinayre, Marcelle. Le bouclier d'Alexandre. Paris, 1922. 2 pam.
42578.51.54 Tinayre, Marcelle. Perséphone. Paris, 1920.
42578.51.55 Tinayre, Marcelle. Perséphone. 13. éd. Paris, 1920.
42578.51.60 Tinayre, Marcelle. Les lampes voilées, Laurence-Valentine. 19. éd. Paris, 1921.
42578.51.65 Tinayre, Marcelle. La légende de Duccio et d'Orsette. Paris, 1923.
42578.51.67 Tinayre, Marcelle. Priscille Séverac. 8. éd. Paris, 1922.
42578.51.70 Tinayre, Marcelle. Priscille Séverac. 11. éd. Paris, 1922.
42578.51.72 Tinayre, Marcelle. Saint Jean, libérateur. Paris, 1926.
42578.51.75 Tinayre, Marcelle. Figures dans la nuit. Paris, 1926.
42578.51.85 Tinayre, Marcelle. L'ennemie intime. Paris, 1931.
42578.51.90 Tinayre, Marcelle. Chateau en limousin. v.1-3. Paris, 1934.
42578.51.100 Tinayre, Marcelle. Sainte Marie du feu. Paris, 1936.
42578.51.250 Martin-Mamy, Eugène. Marcelle Tinayre. Paris, 1909.

42578.52 Individual authors, etc. - 1850-1899 - Fiction - Tinseau, L.

42578.52.5 Tinseau, Léon de. L'attelage de la marquise. N.Y., 1889.
42578.52.10 Tinseau, Léon de. L'attelage de la marquise, le secret de l'abbé Césaire. Paris, 1890.
42578.52.15 Tinseau, Léon de. Faut-il aimer? 11. éd. Paris, 1892.
42578.52.20 Tinseau, Léon de. Mon oncle Alcide. 6. éd. Paris, 1892.
42578.52.23 Tinseau, Léon de. Ma cousine Pot-au-feu et, Le mariage au gant. 6. éd. Paris, 1888.
42578.52.25 Tinseau, Léon de. Ma cousine Pot-au-feu et, Le mariage au gant. 16. éd. Paris, 1893.
42578.52.30 Tinseau, Léon de. Maître Gratien. 4. éd. Paris, 1893.
42578.52.35 Tinseau, Léon de. Le chemin de Damas. Paris, 1894.
42578.52.40 Tinseau, Léon de. La valise diplomatique. Paris, 1904.
42578.52.45A Tinseau, Léon de. Le secrétaire de Madame la duchesse. Paris, 1904.
42578.52.45B Tinseau, Léon de. Le secrétaire de Madame la duchesse. Paris, 1904.
42578.52.50 Tinseau, Léon de. La princesse errante. Montréal, 1904.
42578.52.55 Tinseau, Léon de. Les étourderies de la chanoinesse. Paris, 1906.
42578.52.60 Tinseau, Léon de. Le port d'attache. 6. éd. Paris, 1908.
42578.52.65 Tinseau, Léon de. Le finale de la symphonie. Paris, 1911.
42578.52.70 Tinseau, Léon de. Le duc Rollon. Paris, 1913.
42578.52.72 Tinseau, Léon de. Le duc Rollon. London, 1913.
42578.52.75 Tinseau, Léon de. Thérèse de Guilliane. N.Y., 1892.
42578.52.77 Tinseau, Léon de. Sur les deux rives. 13. éd. Paris, 1909?
42578.52.78 Tinseau, Léon de. Alain de Kerisel. 4. éd. Paris, 1889.
42578.52.79.8 Tinseau, Léon de. Strass et diamants. 8. éd. Paris, 1890.

42578.56 Individual authors, etc. - 1850-1899 - Fiction - Toretain, P.

42578.56.5 Toutain, Paul. Chez nos ancêtres. Paris, 1888.
42578.56.10 Toutain, Paul. Testament d'un moderne. Paris, 1889.
42578.56.15 Toutain, Paul. La fin d'une âme. Paris, 1891.
42578.56.20 Toutain, Paul. Dialogues des vivants. Paris, 1892.
42578.56.25 Toutain, Paul. Ascension. Paris, 1893.
42578.56.30 Toutain, Paul. Multiple vie. Paris, 1894.
42578.56.35 Toutain, Paul. Rustres. Paris, 1898.
42578.56.40 Toutain, Paul. Contes normands. Paris, 1901.
42578.56.45 Toutain, Paul. Les hôtes de l'estuaire. Paris, 1904.
42578.56.50 Toutain, Paul. Terriens. Paris, 1906.

42578.58 Individual authors, etc. - 1850-1899 - Fiction - Uchard, M.

42578.58 Uchard, Mario. Inès Parker. Paris, 1880.
42578.58.5 Uchard, Mario. My uncle Barbassou. London, 1888.

42578.62 - .64 Individual authors, etc. - 1850-1899 - Fiction - Vast, R.

NEDL 42578.62 Vast, Raoul. Pour ces dames! Paris, 18- .
42578.63 Vast, Raoul. Séraphin et cie. Paris, 1880.
42578.64 Vast, Raoul. La vieille garde. 2. éd. Paris, 1881.

42578.65 Individual authors, etc. - 1850-1899 - Fiction - Temple, G.

42578.65.30 Temple, Georges. L'auberge. Lyon, 1867.

42578.66 Individual authors, etc. - 1850-1899 - Fiction - Rouslane, V.

42578.66.30 Rouslane, V. (pseud.). Le juif de Sofievka. Paris, 1883.

42581.1 - .31 Individual authors, etc. - 1850-1899 - Fiction - Verne [Discontinued]

Htn 42581.2* Verne, Jules. Un billet de loterie. Paris, 1886.
42581.2.2 Verne, Jules. Un billet de loterie. Paris, 1886.
42581.3 Verne, Jules. Voyages du capitaine Hatteras. Paris, n.d.
Htn 42581.3.2* Verne, Jules. César Cascabel. Paris, n.d.
42581.4 Verne, Jules. Le chemin de France. Paris, n.d.
Htn 42581.5* Verne, Jules. Le chancellor. Paris, n.d.
Htn 42581.5.2* Verne, Jules. Deux ans de vacances. Paris, n.d.

42581.1 - .31 Individual authors, etc. - 1850-1899 - Fiction - Verne [Discontinued] - cont.

X Cg 42581.6 Verne, Jules. L'étoile du Sud. L'archipel en feu. Paris, n.d.
42581.7 Verne, Jules. L'école des Robinsons. Paris, n.d.
Htn 42581.8* Verne, Jules. Les enfants du capitaine Grant. Paris, n.d.
42581.8.2 Verne, Jules. Famille-sans-nom. Paris, n.d.
Htn 42581.9* Verne, Jules. Les Indes noires. Paris, n.d.
42581.9.5 Verne, Jules. L'île mystérieuse. Paris, 1875.
Htn 42581.9.7* Verne, Jules. L'île mystérieuse. v. 1,3. Paris, 1874. 2v.
42581.9.9 Verne, Jules. L'île mystérieuse. Paris, n.d. 3v.
Htn 42581.10* Verne, Jules. L'île mystérieuse. Paris, n.d.
42581.10.5 Verne, Jules. L'île mystèrieuse. Paris, 1894.
42581.10.7 Verne, Jules. La Jangada. Paris, n.d.
Htn 42581.11*A Verne, Jules. Michel Strogoff. Paris, n.d.
Htn 42581.11*B Verne, Jules. Michel Strogoff. Paris, n.d.
Htn 42581.11.2* Verne, Jules. Mathias Sandorf. Paris, 1885.
Htn 42581.12* Verne, Jules. Pays de fourrures. Paris, n.d.
42581.12.2 Verne, Jules. Nord contre sud. Paris, n.d.
42581.13.9 Verne, Jules. De la terre à la lune. 8. éd. Paris, n.d.
Htn 42581.14* Verne, Jules. De la terre à la lune. Autour de la lune. Paris, n.d.
Htn 42581.14.3* Verne, Jules. De la terre à la lune. Autour de la lune. Paris, n.d.
42581.15 Verne, Jules. Mistress Branican. Paris, n.d.
42581.16 Verne, Jules. Tour du monde. Docteur Ox. Paris, n.d.
42581.16.3 Verne, Jules. Le tour du monde en quatre-vingt jours. Paris, n.d.
42581.16.5 Verne, Jules. Le tour du monde en quatre-vingt jours. N.Y., n.d.
42581.16.10 Verne, Jules. Le tour du monde en quatre-vingt jours. N.Y., 1889.
42581.17 Verne, Jules. Magnifiques aventures de maître Antifer. Paris, n.d.
Htn 42581.17.2* Verne, Jules. Claudias Bembarnae. Paris, n.d.
42581.17.3 Verne, Jules. L'île à hélice. Paris, n.d.
Htn 42581.17.4* Verne, Jules. Clovis Dardentor. Paris, n.d.
42581.17.5 Verne, Jules. Face au drapeau. Paris, n.d.
42581.17.6 Verne, Jules. Le sphinx des glaces. Paris, n.d.
42581.17.7 Verne, Jules. Le testament d'un excentrique. Paris, n.d.
Htn 42581.18* Verne, Jules. Une ville flottante. Paris, n.d.
42581.19 Verne, Jules. Cinq semaines en ballon. Paris, n.d.
42581.19.5 Verne, Jules. Cinq semaines en ballon. 68. éd. Paris, 18-?
42581.19.10 Verne, Jules. Cinq semaines en ballon. Paris, 186-?
42581.20 Verne, Jules. Voyage au centre de la terre. Paris, 1872.
42581.20.5 Verne, Jules. Voyage au centre de la terre. Paris, n.d.
Htn 42581.20.10* Verne, Jules. Voyage au centre de la terre. Paris, 18- ?
42581.20.15 Verne, Jules. Voyage au centre de la terre. London, 1913.
Htn 42581.22* Verne, Jules. Robur le conquérant. Paris, 1886.
42581.23 Verne, Jules. Petit bonhomme. Paris, n.d.
Htn 42581.24* Verne, Jules. Découverte de la terre. Paris, n.d.
Htn 42581.25* Verne, Jules. Les grands navigateurs du 18e siècle. Paris, n.d.
42581.26 Verne, Jules. Les voyageurs du 19. siècle. Paris, n.d.
42581.31.5 Camp, Maxime du. Souvenirs littéraires. Paris, 1962.

42581.33 Individual authors, etc. - 1850-1899 - Fiction - Vallès, J.

Htn 42581.33* Vallès, Jules. Jacques Vingtras. L'enfant. Paris, 1884.
42581.33.5 Vallès, Jules. L'enfant. Paris, 1885.
42581.33.5.5 Vallès, Jules. L'enfant. Lausanne, 1966.
42581.33.7 Vallès, Jules. Jacques Vingtras. L'enfant. Paris, 1937.
42581.33.8 Vallès, Jules. Jacques Vingtras. L'enfant. Paris, 1958.
42581.33.9 Vallès, Jules. Le roman de Jacques Vingtras. Verviers, 1962. 3v.
42581.33.10 Vallès, Jules. Jacques Vingtras, le bachelier. Paris, 1932.
42581.33.15 Vallès, Jules. Jacques Vingtras, l'insurgé, 1871. Paris, 1935.
42581.33.18 Vallès, Jules. Oeuvres complètes. Paris, 1969. 4v.
42581.33.25 Vallès, Jules. Souvenirs d'un étudiant pauvre. 6. éd. Paris, 1930.
42581.33.30 Vallès, Jules. Les réfractaires. Paris, 1935.
42581.33.31 Vallès, Jules. Les réfractaires. Paris, 1955.
42581.33.32 Vallès, Jules. Les franc-parleurs. Paris, 1965.
42581.33.35 Vallès, Jules. La rue à Londres. Paris, 1951.
42581.33.40 Vallès, Jules. Le tableau de Paris. Paris, 1964.
42581.33.42 Vallès, Jules. Un gentilhomme. Paris, 1957.
42581.33.45 Vallès, Jules. La Commune de Paris. Paris, 1970.
42581.33.50 Vallès, Jules. The insurrectionist. Englewood Cliffs, N.J., 1971.
42581.33.81 Flink, G. Jules Vallès. Inaug. Diss. Berlin, 1931.
42581.33.83 Séché, Léon. Portraits à l'encre:Jules Vallès. Paris, 1886.
42581.33.85 Zévaès, A.B. Jules Vallès, son oeuvre. Paris, 1932.
42581.33.87 Gilles, Gaston. Jules Vallès, 1832-1885. Paris, 1941.
42581.33.90 Rouchon, Ulysse. La vie bruyante de Jules Vallès. St. Etienne, 1935-37. 2v.
42581.33.95 Gilles, Gaston. Jules Vallès. v.1-2. Paris, 1941.
42581.33.115 Bancquart, Marie-Claire. Jules Vallès. Paris, 1971.
42581.33.120 Delfau, Gérard. Jules Vallès, l'exil à Londres (1871-1880). Paris, 1971.
42581.33.125 Chazelet, André. Jules Vallès ou l'Enfant révolté. Riom, 1968.

42581.34 Individual authors, etc. - 1850-1899 - Fiction - Vaux

42581.34 Vaux, Ludovic de. Légende de Montford-la-Cane. Paris, 1886.

42581.35 Individual authors, etc. - 1850-1899 - Fiction - Vogüé, E.M.

Htn 42581.35* Vogué, E.M. Le portrait du Louvre. Paris, 1889.

42581.36 Individual authors, etc. - 1850-1899 - Fiction - Viard, J.

42581.36.30 Viard, Jules. Les petites joies de la vie humaine. Paris, 1858.

42581.37 - .44 Individual authors, etc. - 1850-1899 - Fiction - Folios [Discontinued]

42581.38 Rambaud, A. L'anneau de César. Paris, n.d.
Htn 42581.40* Robida, A. Le voyage de M. Dumollet. Paris, 1883.
Htn 42581.44* Zola, Emile. Le rêve. Paris, n.d.

42582.1 Individual authors, etc. - 1850-1899 - Fiction - Verne, J. - Pamphlet volumes

- 42582.1 Pamphlet box. Verne, Jules.

42582.2 Individual authors, etc. - 1850-1899 - Fiction - Verne, J. - Biography and criticism

- 42582.2 Bachmann, Hans. Das englishe Sprachgut in den Romanen Jules Vernes. Greifswald, 1916. 2v.
- 42582.2.3 Moscow. Vsesoiuznaia gosudarstvennaia biblioteka. Inostrannoi literatury. Zhiul' Vern. Moskva, 1955.
- 42582.2.4 Moscow. Vsesoiuznaia gosudarstvennaia biblioteka. Inostrannoi literatury. Zhiul' Vern. Moskva, 1959.
- 42582.2.5 Allotte de la Fuÿe, Marguerite. Jules Verne, sa vie, son oeuvre. 4. éd. Paris, 1928.
- 42582.2.8 Allotte de la Fuÿe, Marguerite. Jules Verne. 6. éd. Paris, 1928.
- 42582.2.9 Allotte de la Fuÿe, Marguerite. Jules Verne, sa vie, son oeuvre. Paris, 1953.
- 42582.2.9.2 Allotte de la Fuÿe, Marguerite. Jules Verne, sa vie, son oeuvre. Paris, 1953.
- 42582.2.9.5 Allotte de la Fuÿe, Marguerite. Jules Verne. 1st American ed. N.Y., 1956.
- 42582.2.10 Allott, Kenneth. Jules Verne. London, 1940?
- 42582.2.15 Schmökel, Gerda. Die Belebheit des Stils in der Darstellung des Jules Verne. Breslau, 1933.
- 42582.2.30 Frank, Bernard. Jules Verne et ses voyages, d'après l'ouvrage biographique Marguerite Allotte de la Fuÿe. Paris, 1941.
- 42582.2.35A Waltz, G.H. Jules Verne. N.Y., 1943.
- 42582.2.35B Waltz, G.H. Jules Verne. N.Y., 1943.
- 42582.2.40 Escarch, R. Voyage à travers le monde vernien. Bruxelles, 1951.
- V42582.2.45 Andreev, Kirill K. Tri zhizni Zhiulia Verna. Moskva, 1957.
- 42582.2.47 Andreev, Kirill K. Na poroge novoi ery. Moskva, 1971.
- 42582.2.50 Deesbach, Ghislain de. Le tour de Jules Verne en quatre-vingt livres. Paris, 1969.
- 42582.2.55 Chesneaux, Jean. Une lecture politique de Jules Verne. Paris, 1971.
- 42582.2.60 Franquinet, Edmond. Jules Verne en zijn wonderreizen. Zeist, 1964.
- 42582.2.65 Métral, Maurice. Sur les pas de Jules Verne. Neuchâtel, 1963.
- 42582.2.70 Berenguer, Carisomo Arturo. Julio Verne. Buenos-Aires, 1930.
- 42582.2.75 Moré, Marcel. Nouvelles explorations de Jules Verne. Paris, 1963.
- 42582.2.80 Moré, Marcel. Le très curieux Jules Verne. Paris, 1960.
- 42582.2.85 Freedman, Russell. Jules Verne, portrait of a prophet. N.Y., 1965.
- 42582.2.90 Evans, I. Oliver. Jules Verne and his work. London, 1965.
- 42582.2.95 Marcucci, Edmondo. Les illustrations des voyages extraordinaires de Jules Verne. Paris, 1956.

42582.3 - .4 Individual authors, etc. - 1850-1899 - Fiction - Verne, J. - Complete and Selected works

- 42582.3 Verne, Jules. Jules Verne. N.Y., 1956.
- 42582.4 Verne, Jules. Works. N.Y., 1911. 15v.

42582.5 - .99 Individual authors, etc. - 1850-1899 - Fiction - Verne, J. - Individual works

- 42582.7.2 Verne, Jules. Journey to the centre of the earth. N.Y., 1874.
- 42582.8.15 Verne, Jules. A voyage round the world. In search of the castaways. Philadelphia, 1873.
- 42582.9.2 Moré, Marcel. Nouvelles explorations de Jules Verne. Boston, 1874. 2v.
- 42582.9.2A Verne, Jules. From the clouds to the mountains. Boston, 1874.
- 42582.9.2B Verne, Jules. From the clouds to the mountains. Boston, 1874.
- 42582.9.4 Verne, Jules. A journey to the center of the earth. N.Y., 1905.
- 42582.9.10 Verne, Jules. A journey to the center of the earth. Westport, 1961.
- 42582.9.20 Verne, Jules. Dick Sands. N.Y., 1879.
- Htn 42582.10* Verne, Jules. Docteur Ox. 8. éd. Paris, n.d.
- 42582.11 Verne, Jules. Doctor Ox and other stories. Boston, 1874.
- 42582.11.2 Verne, Jules. Dr. Ox's experiment. Boston, 1875.
- 42582.12 Verne, Jules. Desert of ice, or Further adventures of Captain Hatteras. Philadelphia, 1874.
- 42582.12.20 Verne, Jules. The English at the North Pole. London, 1879.
- 42582.12.50 Verne, Jules. The floating city. N.Y., 1874.
- 42582.13 Verne, Jules. From the earth to the moon. N.Y., 1874.
- 42582.13.5 Verne, Jules. From the earth to the moon. N.Y., 1877.
- 42582.13.8 Verne, Jules. From the earth to the moon. N.Y., 1889.
- 42582.13.10 Verne, Jules. From the earth to the moon. N.Y., 1905.
- 42582.15 Verne, Jules. Five weeks in a balloon. Boston, 1873.
- Htn 42582.15.5* Verne, Jules. Five weeks in a balloon. N.Y., 1869.
- 42582.17A Verne, Jules. The fur country. Boston, 1874.
- 42582.17B Verne, Jules. The fur country. Boston, 1874.
- 42582.18 Verne, Jules. The giant raft. N.Y., 1882. 2v.
- 42582.19 Verne, Jules. Adventures in the land of Behemoth. Boston, 1874.
- 42582.20 Verne, Jules. Meridiana. London, 1873.
- 42582.21 Verne, Jules. Mistress Branican. N.Y., 1891.
- 42582.22 Verne, Jules. Michael Strogoff. N.Y., 1877.
- 42582.22.4 Verne, Jules. Michael Strogoff. N.Y., 19- ?
- 42582.22.7 Verne, Jules. Michael Strogoff. N.Y., 1905.
- Htn 42582.22.9* Verne, Jules. The mysterious island abandoned. N.Y., 1875.
- 42582.22.10 Verne, Jules. The mysterious island abandoned. Chicago, 188-?
- 42582.22.14 Verne, Jules. The mysterious island. N.Y., 1876.
- 42582.22.14.25 Verne, Jules. The mysterious island. N.Y., 1927.
- 42582.23 Verne, Jules. North against South. London, 1888.
- 42582.24 Verne, Jules. The tour of the world in eighty days. Boston, 1873.
- 42582.24.2 Verne, Jules. The tour of the world in eighty days. Boston, 1874.
- 42582.24.5 Verne, Jules. The tour of the world in eighty days. Chicago, 187-?
- 42582.24.9 Verne, Jules. The tour of the world in eighty days. Chicago, 1885.
- 42582.25 Verne, Jules. The tour of the world in eighty days. Chicago, 1892.

42582.5 - .99 Individual authors, etc. - 1850-1899 - Fiction - Verne, J. - Individual works - cont.

- 42582.25.3 Verne, Jules. The tour of the world in eighty days. N.Y., 1892.
- 42582.25.4 Verne, Jules. The tour of the world in eighty days. N.Y., 1892.
- 42582.25.6 Verne, Jules. The tour of the world in eighty days. N.Y., 18- ?
- 42582.25.10 Verne, Jules. Around the world in eighty days. N.Y., 190-?
- 42582.25.12 Verne, Jules. The tour of the world in eighty days. N.Y., 19- ?
- 42582.25.50 Verne, Jules. Le tour du monde en quatre-vingts jours. Paris, 1959.
- 42582.25.75 Verne, Jules. Il giro del mondo in ottanta giorni. Milano, 1914.
- 42582.25.100 Verne, Jules. The tribulations of a Chinaman in China. Boston, 1880.
- 42582.26.10 Verne, Jules. Twenty thousand leagues under the sea. N.Y., 18- ?
- 42582.27 Verne, Jules. Twenty thousand leagues under the sea. Boston, 1873.
- 42582.27.10 Verne, Jules. Twenty thousand leagues under the sea. N.Y., 1880?
- 42582.28.10 Verne, Jules. Twenty thousand leagues under the sea. N.Y., 1916.
- 42582.28.25 Verne, Jules. Twenty thousand leagues under the sea. N.Y., 1933.
- 42582.30 Verne, Jules. Underground city. Philadelphia, 1887.
- 42582.30.2 Verne, Jules. Underground city. Philadelphia? 188-?
- 42582.32 Verne, Jules. Die Familie ohne Namen. v.1-2. Wien, 1893.
- 42582.35.15 Verne, Jules. The wreck of the chancellor. Boston, 1875.
- 42582.35.18 Verne, Jules. The wreck of the chancellor. Philadelphia, 188-?
- 42582.40 Verne, Jules. Julio Verne y America. Buenos-Aires, 1944.
- 42582.42 Verne, Jules. Hier et demain. Paris, 1910?
- 42582.44 Verne, Jules. The vanished diamond. London, 1885.

42583.1 - .15 Individual authors, etc. - 1850-1899 - Fiction - Verne, J. - Individual works [Discontinued]

- Htn 42583.2* Verne, Jules. Onze jours de siège. Paris, 1861.
- 42583.5 Verne, Jules. Un capitaine de quinze ans. Paris, n.d. 2v.
- 42583.7 Verne, Jules. Cinq cent millions. Paris, n.d.
- 42583.9 Verne, Jules. De la terre à la lune. Paris, n.d.
- Htn 42583.10* Verne, Jules. Hector Servadac. Paris, n.d. 2v.
- 42583.11 Verne, Jules. Hector Servadac. N.Y., n.d.
- 42583.11.5 Verne, Jules. Hector Servadac. London, 1878.
- 42583.11.7 Verne, Jules. Hector Servadac. N.Y., 1935.
- 42583.12 Verne, Jules. La maison à vapeur. N.Y., n.d. 2v.
- 42583.13 Verne, Jules. Vingt mille lieues sous les mers. Paris, 18- ? 2v.
- 42583.14 Verne, Jules. Vingt mille lieues sous les mers. N.Y., n.d.
- 42583.15 Verne, Jules. Les tribulations d'un chinoisen Chine. N.Y., n.d.

42583.16 Individual authors, etc. - 1850-1899 - Fiction - Villars

- 42583.16 Villars, Emile. Le roman de la parisienne. Paris, 1866.

42583.17 - .33 Individual authors, etc. - 1850-1899 - Fiction - Theuriot, A.

- 42583.17.7 Theuriet, André. Pages choisies. Paris, 1898.
- 42583.17.9 Theuriet, André. Le journal de Tristan. Paris, 1883.
- 42583.18 Theuriet, André. Le fils Maugars. Paris, 1880.
- 42583.18.5 Theuriet, André. The godson of a marquis. N.Y., 1878.
- 42583.19 Theuriet, André. Le filleul d'un marquis. Paris, 1879.
- 42583.20 Theuriet, André. Bigarreau. Paris, 1886.
- 42583.21 Theuriet, André. Madame Heurteloup. (La bête noire). Paris, 1882.
- 42583.22 Theuriet, André. Mademoiselle Guignon. Paris, 1874.
- 42583.23 Theuriet, André. La chanoinesse. Paris, n.d.
- 42583.23.2 Theuriet, André. La chanoinesse. Paris, 19- ?
- 42583.24 Theuriet, André. La maison des deux barbeaux. Paris, 1879.
- 42583.25 Theuriet, André. Le mariage de Gérard. Paris, 1878.
- 42583.25.1 Theuriet, André. Gerard's marriage. N.Y., 1877.
- 42583.25.3 Theuriet, André. Les mauvais ménages. Paris, 1882.
- 42583.26 Theuriet, André. Nouvelles intimes. Paris, 1870.
- 42583.26.15 Theuriet, André. Péché mortel. Paris, 1885.
- 42583.27 Theuriet, André. Raymonde. Paris, 1877.
- 42583.28 Theuriet, André. Sauvageonne. Paris, 1882.
- 42583.29 Theuriet, André. Sous-bois. Paris, 1880.
- 42583.29.3 Theuriet, André. Sous-bois. Paris, 1883.
- 42583.30 Theuriet, André. Toute seule. Paris, 1880.
- 42583.31 Theuriet, André. Tante Aurélie. Paris, 1884.
- 42583.32 Theuriet, André. La chanson du jardinier. Boston, n.d.
- 42583.32.2 Theuriet, André. La chanson du jardinier. Boston, 187-?
- 42583.33 Theuriet, André. Michel Verneuil. Paris, 1883.
- 42583.33.3 Theuriet, André. Chemin des bois. Paris, 1876.
- 42583.33.5 Theuriet, André. Contes de la Marjolaine. Paris, 1902.
- 42583.33.10 Theuriet, André. Fleur de Nice. Paris, 1896.
- 42583.33.15 Theuriet, André. Souvenirs des vertes saisons. Paris, 1904.
- 42583.33.16 Theuriet, André. Colette. 12. éd. Paris, 1908.
- 42583.33.17 Theuriet, André. Jean-Marie. Paris, n.d.
- 42583.33.17.5 Theuriet, André. Jean-Marie. Antwerpen, 1909.
- 42583.33.18 Theuriet, André. L'abbé Daniel. N.Y., 1919.
- 42583.33.21 Theuriet, André. Paternité. Paris, 1894.
- 42583.33.22 Theuriet, André. Contes de la forêt. Paris, 1888.
- 42583.33.25 Theuriet, André. Josette. Paris, 1896.
- 42583.33.28 Theuriet, André. Le refuge. Paris, 1898.
- 42583.33.30 Theuriet, André. Charme dangereux. Paris, 1891.
- 42583.33.32 Theuriet, André. L'oncle Scipion. Paris, 1925. 3 pam.
- 42583.33.81 Weiss, Karl. Die Landschaftschilderung bei André Theuriet. Inaug. Diss. Rostock, 1933.

42583.34 - .35 Individual authors, etc. - 1850-1899 - Fiction - Tardieu, J.R.

- 42583.34 Tardieu, J.R. Mignon. Paris, 1860.
- 42583.34.2 Tardieu, J.R. Mignon. Paris, 1871.
- 42583.34.9 Tardieu, J.R. Pour une épingle. 3. éd. Paris, 1857.
- 42583.34.15 Tardieu, J.R. Pour une épingle. 19. éd. N.Y., 1866.
- 42583.35 Tardieu, J.R. Pour une épingle. N.Y., 1867.
- 42583.35.10 Tardieu, J.R. Pour une épingle. London, 1887.

42583.36 - .37 Individual authors, etc. - 1850-1899 - Fiction - Saint-Germain

42583.36 Saint-Germain, J. de. Les extrêmes légendes. Paris, 1866.
42583.37.2 Saint-Germain, J. de. L'art d'être malheureux. 2. éd. Paris, 1857.

42583.50 Individual authors, etc. - 1850-1899 - Fiction - Véron, P.

42583.50 Véron, Pierre. Les phénomènes vivants. Paris, 1868.
42583.50.30 Véron, Pierre. La mascarade de l'histoire. Paris, 1882.

42584.1 Individual authors, etc. - 1850-1899 - Fiction - Zola, E. - Complete and Selected works

42584.1.5 Zola, Emile. Les oeuvres completes. Paris, 1927-1929. 49v.
42584.1.6 Zola, Emile. Oeuvres completes. v.1-12,15. Paris, 1966- 13v.
42584.1.8 Zola, Emile. Pages choisies des auteurs contemporains. Paris, 1897.
42584.1.9 Zola, Emile. Pages choisies des auteurs contemporains. Paris, 1907.
42584.1.15 Zola, Emile. Selections from Emile Zola. N.Y., 1905.
42584.1.20 Zola, Emile. Romans. Lausanne, 1960. 24v.
42584.1.25 Zola, Emile. The experimental novel. N.Y., 1893.
42584.1.30 Zola, Emile. Chefs-d'oeuvre. Paris, 1957.
42584.1.32 Zola, Emile. Autres chefs-d'oeuvre. Paris, 1958.

42584.2 Individual authors, etc. - 1850-1899 - Fiction - Zola, E. - Letters

42584.2 Zola, Emile. Correspondance. Lettres de jeunesse. Paris, 1907.
42584.2.5 Zola, Emile. Lettres inédites à Henry Céard. Providence, Rhode Island, 1959.
42584.2.10 Zola, Emile. Correspondance. Paris, 1907. 2v.
42584.2.15 Zola, Emile. Lettres de Paris. Genève, 1963.
42584.2.20 Zola, Emile. L'atelier de Zola. Genève, 1963.

42584.3 - .23 Individual authors, etc. - 1850-1899 - Fiction - Zola, E. - Individual works

42584.3 Zola, Emile. L'assommoir. Paris, 1877.
42584.3.2 Zola, Emile. L'assommoir. 60. éd. Paris, 1879.
42584.3.3 Zola, Emile. L'assommoir. 74. éd. Paris, 1879.
42584.3.5 Zola, Emile. L'assommoir. 95. éd. Paris, 1881.
42584.3.7 Zola, Emile. L'assommoir. Photoreproduction. Philadelphia, 1882.
42584.3.8 Zola, Emile. L'assommoir. Paris, 1884.
42584.3.9 Zola, Emile. L'assommoir. Paris, 1886.
42584.3.10 Zola, Emile. L'assommoir. Paris, 1896.
42584.3.12 Zola, Emile. L'assommoir. v.2. Philadelphia, 189-?
42584.3.15 Zola, Emile. Gervaise. N.Y., 1879.
42584.3.20 Zola, Emile. The best known works of Emile Zola. N.Y., 1941.
42584.4 Zola, Emile. Au bonheur des dames. Paris, 1883.
42584.4.3 Zola, Emile. Au bonheur des dames. Paris, 1891.
42584.4.3.10 Zola, Emile. Au bonheur des dames. Paris, 1962.
42584.4.4 Zola, Emile. Ladies' delight. London, 1957.
X Cg 42584.4.5 Zola, Emile. Soirées de Medan. Paris, 1886.
42584.4.9 Zola, Emile. Le capitaine Burle. Paris, 1885.
42584.5 Zola, Emile. La confession de Claude. Paris, 1866.
42584.7 Zola, Emile. Contres à Ninon. Paris, n.d.
42584.7.2 Zola, Emile. Nouveaux contes à Ninon. Paris, 1889.
42584.7.9 Zola, Emile. La conquête de Plassans. 2. éd. Paris, 1874.
42584.8 Zola, Emile. La conquête de Plassans. Paris, 1880.
42584.8.9 Zola, Emile. La conquête de Plassans. Paris, 1894.
42584.9 Zola, Emile. La faute de l'abbé Mouret. Paris, 1879.
42584.9.5 Zola, Emile. La faute de l'abbé Mouret. Paris, 1890.
42584.9.8 Zola, Emile. La faute de l'abbé Mouret. Paris, 1918.
42584.9.10 Zola, Emile. The sin of the abbé Mouret. London, 1907.
42584.9.15 Zola, Emile. Albine, or The abbe's temptation. Philadelphia, 1882.
42584.9.20 Zola, Emile. The abbé Mouret's sin. London, 1957.
42584.10 Zola, Emile. Son excellence Eugène Rougon. Paris, 1879.
42584.10.2 Zola, Emile. Clorinda, or The rise of Eugène Rougon. Philadelphia, 1880.
42584.10.3 Zola, Emile. His Excellency. N.Y., 1897.
42584.10.4 Zola, Emile. His Excellency. London, 1958.
X Cg 42584.10.6 Ramond, F.C. Les personnages des Rougon-Macquart. Paris, 1901.
42584.10.20 Zola, Emile. The girl in scarlet. London, 1888.
42584.10.25 Zola, Emile. Savage Paris. London, 1955.
42584.11 Zola, Emile. La débâcle. Paris, 1892.
42584.11.5 Zola, Emile. La débâcle. Paris, 1893.
42584.11.7 Zola, Emile. La débâcle. Boston, 1899.
42584.11.8 Urien, Carlos M. La débâcle. Buenos Aires, 1892.
42584.11.8.50 Zola, Emile. The downfall. N.Y., 1925.
42584.11.9 Zola, Emile. Jacques Damour. Paris, 1888.
42584.11.13 Zola, Emile. Jacques Damour. Boston, 1895.
42584.11.25 Zola, Emile. Slom. [La débâcle]. Beograd, 1893.
42584.12 Zola, Emile. L'argent. Paris, 1891.
42584.12.5 Zola, Emile. Das Geld. v.1-2. 2. Aufl. Stuttgart, 1891.
42584.12.7 Zola, Emile. Madeleine Férat. Paris, 1886.
X Cg 42584.12.13 Zola, Emile. Mystères de Marseille. Paris, 1885.
42584.12.17 Zola, Emile. Nais Micoulin. Paris, 1884.
42584.12.22 Zola, Emile. Nana. 28. éd. Paris, 1880.
42584.12.22.2 Zola, Emile. Nana. 100. éd. Paris, 1881.
42584.12.22.8 Zola, Emile. Nana. 129. éd. Paris, 1885.
42584.12.25 Zola, Emile. Nana. Philadelphia, 189-? 2v.
42584.12.32 Zola, Emile. Nana. N.Y., 1957.
42584.12.33 Zola, Emile. Nana. Paris, 1955.
42584.12.34 Zola, Emile. Les quatre évangiles, fécondité. Paris, 1899.
42584.12.36 Zola, Emile. Nana. Paris, 1955.
42584.12.50 Zola, Emile. Les quatre évangiles, fécondité. Paris, 1900.
42584.13 Zola, Emile. Une campagne. 1880-81. Paris, 1888.
42584.13.2 Zola, Emile. Le docteur Pascal. Paris, 1893.
42584.13.5 Zola, Emile. Le docteur Pascal. Paris, 1893.
42584.13.25 Zola, Emile. Doctor Pascal. N.Y., 1901.
42584.13.30 Zola, Emile. Doctor Pascal. London, 1957.
42584.13.50 Zola, Emile. Mes haines. Paris, 1879.
42584.13.95 Zola, Emile. Mes voyages: Lourdes, Rome. Paris, 1958.
42584.13.100 Zola, Emile. Lourdes. Paris, 1894.
42584.13.105 Zola, Emile. Lourdes. Paris, 1894.
42584.13.115 Zola, Emile. Lourdes. v. 1-2. N.Y., 1897.
42584.14.2 Zola, Emile. Rome. Paris, 1896.
42584.14.3A Zola, Emile. Rome. N.Y., 1896. 2v.
42584.14.3B Zola, Emile. Rome. N.Y., 1896. 2v.
42584.14.5 Zola, Emile. Rome. N.Y., 1898. 2v.
42584.14.6 Zola, Emile. Rome. London, 1899.

42584.3 - .23 Individual authors, etc. - 1850-1899 - Fiction - Zola, E. - Individual works - cont.

42584.14.12 Zola, Emile. Rome. v.1-2. Paris, 1930.
42584.15 Zola, Emile. Nos auteurs dramatiques. Paris, 1881.
42584.16 Zola, Emile. Le naturalisme au théâtre. Paris, 1881.
42584.16.2 Zola, Emile. Le naturalisme au théâtre. 2. éd. Paris, 1881.
X Cg 42584.17.3 Zola, Emile. Le roman expérimental. Paris, 1893.
42584.18 Zola, Emile. Les romanciers naturalistes. 2. éd. Paris, 1881.
42584.18.2 Zola, Emile. Les romanciers naturalistes. Paris, 1881.
42584.19 Zola, Emile. Le rêve. Paris, 1890.
42584.19.2 Zola, Emile. Le rêve. Paris, 1898.
42584.19.3 Zola, Emile. Le rêve. Paris, 1910.
42584.19.4 Zola, Emile. Le rêve. Paris, 1916.
42584.19.4.10 Zola, Emile. Le rêve. Paris, 1935.
42584.19.4.50 Zola, Emile. Le rêve. Philadelphia, 1888.
42584.19.5.2 Zola, Emile. La terre. Paris, 1887.
42584.19.7 Zola, Emile. La terre. Chicago, 1888.
42584.19.13 Zola, Emile. Teresa Raquin. Torino, 1958.
42584.19.14 Zola, Emile. Thérèse Raquin. London, 1969.
X Cg 42584.19.15 Zola, Emile. Le voeu d'une morte. Paris, 1890.
42584.19.60 Zola, Emile. Pot-Bouille. Paris, 1969.
42584.19.75 Zola, Emile. Pot-Bouille. Paris, 1926-28. 2v.
42584.20 Zola, Emile. Pot-Bouille. Philadelphia, 1882.
42584.20.5 Zola, Emile. Pot-Bouille. Philadelphia, 189-? 2v.
42584.20.10 Zola, Emile. Restless house. N.Y., 1953.
42584.21 Zola, Emile. Théâtre. Paris, 1880.
42584.21.20 Zola, Emile. Théâtre. Paris, 1923.
42584.21.25 Zola, Emile. Théâtre. Paris, 1906.
42584.22 Zola, Emile. Documents littéraires. Paris, 1882.
42584.23 Zola, Emile. Une page d'amour. 64. éd. Paris, 1878.
42584.23.2 Zola, Emile. Une page d'amour. Paris, 1898.
42584.23.2.5 Zola, Emile. A love affair. London, 1957.
42584.23.3 Zola, Emile. La bête humaine. Paris, 1890.
NEDL 42584.23.3.2 Zola, Emile. La bête humaine. Paris, 1890.
42584.23.4 Zola, Emile. La curée. Paris, 1879.
42584.23.4.2 Zola, Emile. La curée. Paris, 1906.
42584.23.4.25 Zola, Emile. The rush for the spoil. Paris, 189-?
42584.23.6 Zola, Emile. La joie de vivre. Paris, 1884.
42584.23.6.5 Zola, Emile. La joie de vivre. Paris, 1884.
42584.23.6.25 Zola, Emile. How jolly life is! Paris, 189-?
42584.23.7 Zola, Emile. L'oeuvre. Paris, 1886.
42584.23.7.2 Zola, Emile. L'oeuvre. Paris, 1886.
42584.23.9 Zola, Emile. Germinal. Paris, 1888.
42584.23.9.2 Zola, Emile. Germinal. Paris, 1885.
42584.23.9.25 Zola, Emile. Germinal. N.Y., 1937.
42584:23.9.27 Zola, Emile. Germinal. v.1-2. Paris, 1946.
42584.23.9.30 Zola, Emile. Germinal. Philadelphia, 189-? 2v.
42584.23.9.35 Zola, Emile. Germinal. Paris, 1964.
42584.23.10 Zola, Emile. Paris. Paris, 1898.
42584.23.10.2 Zola, Emile. Paris. Paris, 1898.
42584.23.10.4 Zola, Emile. Paris. Paris, 1898.
42584.23.10.5 Zola, Emile. Paris. London, 1905.
42584.23.10.7 Zola, Emile. Paris. N.Y., 1898. 2v.
42584.23.11A Zola, Emile. Fruitfullness. N.Y., 1900.
42584.23.11B Zola, Emile. Fruitfullness. N.Y., 1900.
42584.23.11.25 Zola, Emile. Fruitfullness. Garden City, 1923.
42584.23.12 Johannis, A.J. de. A proposito del libro di Emile Zola "Fecondita". Firenze, 1900.
42584.23.13 Zola, Emile. Labor. N.Y., 1901.
42584.23.16 Zola, Emile. Truth. N.Y., 1903.
42584.23.17 Zola, Emile. Igazsag. v.1-2. Budapest, n.d.
42584.23.19 Zola, Emile. Salons. Genève, 1959.
42584.23.19.5 Zola, Emile. Madame Neigeon. Paris, 1901.
42584.23.20 Zola, Emile. Pour une nuit d'amour. n.p., n.d.
42584.23.22 Zola, Emile. Les Rougon-Macquart. Paris, 1960- 5v.
42584.23.25 Zola, Emile. La république en marche. Paris, 1956. 2v.
42584.23.27 Zola, Emile. J'accuse, ou La vérité en marche. Paris, 1965.
42584.23.28 Zola, Emile. Le ventre de Paris. Paris, 1969.
42584.23.30 Zola, Emile. Zest for life. Bloomington, 1956.
42584.23.35 Zola, Emile. Poèmes lyriques. Paris, 1921.
42584.23.37 Zola, Emile. Rome. v.1-2. N.Y., 1901.
42584.23.39 Zola, Emile. Rome. N.Y., 1907.
42584.23.45A Zola, Emile. Truth. 2d ed. N.Y., 1903.
42584.23.45B Zola, Emile. Truth. 2d ed. N.Y., 1903.
Htn 42584.23.50* Zola, Emile. Renée, pièce en cinq actes. Paris, 1887.
42584.23.57 Zola, Emile. For a night. The maid of the dawber. Philadelphia, 1911.
42584.23.60 Zola, Emile. Two novelettes: Shell-fish and For a night of love. N.Y., 1926.
42584.23.65 Zola, Emile. Vingt messages inédits de Zola à Céard. Providence, 1961.
42584.23.70 Zola, Emile. The mysteries of the court of Louis Napoléon. Philadelphia, 1882.
42584.23.75 Zola, Emile. A page of love. Philadelphia, 1897. 2v.
42584.23.77 Zola, Emile. A love episode. Paris, 1905?
42584.23.78 Zola, Emile. Three faces of love. N.Y., 1968.
42584.23.79 Zola, Emile. Love's chase. N.Y., 1911.
42584.23.83 Zola, Emile. The masterpiece. N.Y., 1946.
42584.23.83.2 Zola, Emile. The masterpiece. N.Y., 1957.
42584.23.85 Zola, Emile. Piping hot. N.Y., 1951.
42584.23.90 Zola, Emile. The kill. N.Y., 1954.
42584.23.300 Zola, Emile. Das Glück der Familie Rougon. München, 1922.
42584.23.305 Zola, Emile. Die Jagdbeute. München, 1923.
42584.23.310 Zola, Emile. Der Bauch von Paris. München, 1923.
42584.23.315 Zola, Emile. Die Froberung von Plassans. München, 1923.
42584.23.320 Zola, Emile. Die Sünde des Abbé Mouret. München, 1922.
42584.23.325 Zola, Emile. Seine Excellenz Eugen Rougon. München, 1923.
42584.23.330 Zola, Emile. Der Totschläger. München, 1923.
42584.23.335 Zola, Emile. Ein Blatt der Liebe. München, 1923.
42584.23.340 Zola, Emile. Nana. München, 1922.
42584.23.345 Zola, Emile. Am häuslichen Herd. München, 1923.
42584.23.350 Zola, Emile. Das Paradies der Damen. München, 1923.
42584.23.355 Zola, Emile. Die Lebensfreude. München, 1923.
42584.23.360 Zola, Emile. Germinal. München, 1923.
42584.23.365 Zola, Emile. Das Werk. München, 1924.
42584.23.370 Zola, Emile. Mutter Erde. München, 1923.
42584.23.375 Zola, Emile. Der Traum. München, 1924.
42584.23.380 Zola, Emile. Die Bestie im Menschen. München, 1924.
42584.23.385 Zola, Emile. Das Geld. München, 1924.
42584.23.390 Zola, Emile. Der Zusammenbruch. München, 1923.
42584.23.395 Zola, Emile. Doktor Pascal. München, 1924.
42584.23.400 Zola, Emile. Lazarc, suivi de Soeur des Pauvres. Neuchâtel, 1962.
42584.23.410 Zola, Emile. The debacle. London, 1968.

42584.3 - .23 Individual authors, etc. - 1850-1899 - Fiction - Zola, E. - Individual works - cont.

42584.23.413 Zola, Emile. La fortune des Rougon. 3. éd. Paris, 1872.
42584.23.415 Zola, Emile. La fortune des Rougon. Paris, 1955.

42584.24 - .25 Individual authors, etc. - 1850-1899 - Fiction - Zola, E. - Biography and criticism

42584.24 Alexis, Paul. Emile Zola. Paris, 1882.
42584.24.5 Macdonald, A. Emile Zola. Study of his personality. Washington, 1899.
Htn 42584.24.6* Vizetelly, E.A. With Zola in England. London, 1899.
42584.24.6.5 Vizetelly, E.A. Emile Zola. London, 1904.
Htn 42584.24.6.10* Vizetelly, E.A. Extracts principally from English classics. London, 1888.
42584.24.7 L'Aurore. 6 Oct. 1902. Funeral of Emile Zola. Paris, 1902.
42584.24.8 Oehlert, Richard. E. Zola als Theatherdichter. Berlin, 1920.
42584.24.9 Baeza, R. Centenario de Emile Zola, 1840-1902. Buenos-Aires, 1942.
42584.25 Ten Brink, Jan. Emile Zola und seine Werke. Braunschweig, 1887.
42584.25.5 Moncoq. Tribunal du bon sens public. Réponse à Rome de Zola. Caen, 1896.
42584.25.5.5 Moncoq. Réponse complète au Lourdes de Emile Zola. Caen, 1894.
42584.25.6 Martineau, H. Le roman scientifique d'Emile Zola. Paris, 1907.
42584.25.7 Lemm, S. Zur Entstehungsgeschichte von Emile Zolas Rougon-Macquart. Halle, 1913.
42584.25.8 Franke, Carl. Emile Zola als romantischer Dichter. Marburg, 1914.
42584.25.8.2 Franke, Carl. Emile Zola als romantischer Dichter. Marburg, 1914.
42584.25.9 Lepelletier, E. Emile Zola. Paris, 1908.
42584.25.10 Laporte, A. Naturalisme ou l'immortalité littéraire. Paris, 1891.
42584.25.12 Boissarie, P.G. Zola. Paris, 1895.
42584.25.15A Patterson, J.G. A Zola dictionary, the characters of the Rougon-Macquart novels of Emile Zola. N.Y., 1912.
42584.25.15B Patterson, J.G. A Zola dictionary, the characters of the Rougon-Macquart novels of Emile Zola. N.Y., 1912.
42584.25.20 Seillière, Ernest. Emile Zola. Paris, 1923.
42584.25.21 Doucet, Fernand. L'esthétique d'Emile Zola et son application à la critique. Den Haag, 1923.
Htn 42584.25.23* Vouvier, Bernard. L'oeuvre de Zola. Genève, 1903.
42584.25.30 Brown, Sidney B. La peinture des métiers et des moeurs professionnelles dans les romans de Zola. Thèse. Montpellier, 1928.
Htn 42584.25.35* Mallarmé, Stéphane. Dix-neuf lettres de Stéphane Mallarmé à Emile Zola. Paris, 1929.
42584.25.43 Laborde, A. Trente-huit années près de Zola. Paris, 1963.
42584.25.45 Rost, W.H. German criticism of Zola, 1875-1893. N.Y., 1931.
42584.25.50 Batilliat, M. Emile Zola. Paris, 1931.
42584.25.53 Barbusse, H. Zola. 1. ed. N.Y., 1933.
42584.25.55 Barbusse, H. Zola. 9. éd. Paris, 1932.
42584.25.60 Bruneau, Alfred. A l'ombre d'un grand coeur. Paris, 1932.
42584.25.65 Baer, Elisabeth. Das Weltbild Zolas in den Quatre Evangiles. Inaug. Diss. München, 1933.
42584.25.70 Rauch, Franz. Das Verhältnis der Evangelien E. Zolas zu dessen früheren Werken. Inaug. Diss. Nürnberg, 1933.
42584.25.75 Vibe, J. Nogle bemaerkninger i anledning af naturalismen. Kristiania, 1884.
42584.25.80A Josephson, M. Zola and his time. N.Y., 1928.
42584.25.80B Josephson, M. Zola and his time. N.Y., 1928.
42584.25.80C Josephson, M. Zola and his time. N.Y., 1928.
42584.25.80D Josephson, M. Zola and his time. N.Y., 1928.
42584.25.81A Josephson, M. Zola and his time. Garden City, 1928.
42584.25.81B Josephson, M. Zola and his time. Garden City, 1928.
42584.25.85 Baillot, Alex. Emile Zola. Paris, 1924.
42584.25.90 Kneer, G. Das Familienproblem in Emile Zola's Rougon-Macquart. Inaug. Diss. Wertheim, 1934.
42584.25.91 Kneer, G. Das Familienproblem in Emile Zola's Rougon-Macquart. Bechstein, 1934.
42584.25.100 Toulouse, E. Enquête médico-psychologique, Emile Zola. Paris, 1896.
42584.25.105 Romains, J. Zola et son exemple. Paris, 1935.
42584.25.110 Le Blond, Maurice. La publication de La Terre. Paris, 1937.
42584.25.115 Jouvenel, B. de. Vie de Zola. Paris, 1931.
42584.25.120 Schildbach, W. Die Dramatisierung des naturalistischen Romans bei Emile Zola. Inaug. Diss. Halle, 1937.
42584.25.130 Sondel, B.S. Zola's naturalistic theory with particular reference to the drama. Chicago, 1939.
42584.25.135 Le Blond-Zola, Denise. Emile Zola raconté. Paris, 1931.
42584.25.140 Runge, E. Emile Zola. Schlawe, 1903.
42584.25.145 Castaneda, P. Emilio Zola. Guatemala, 1906.
42584.25.147 Castelnau, Jacques. Zola. Paris, 1946.
42584.25.150 Salvan, A.J. Zola aux Etats-Unis. Providence, 1943.
42584.25.152 Luquet, A. Vida e obras de Zola. Porto, 1943.
42584.25.155 Auriant (pseud.). La véritable histoire de "Nana". Paris, 1942.
42584.25.160 Rufener, Helen L. Biography of a war novel: Zola's "La débacle". Morningside Heights, 1946.
42584.25.165 Zévaès, A.B. Zola. Paris, 1946.
42584.25.170 Burrows, H. Zola. London, 1899.
42584.25.175 Wilson, Angus. Emile Zola. London, 1952.
42584.25.180 Nowakowski, Jan. Spór o Zolę zu Polsce. Wrocław, 1951.
42584.25.185 Freville, J. Zola, semeur d'orages. Paris, 1952.
42584.25.190 Hemmings, F.W.J. Emile Zola. Oxford, 1953.
42584.25.191 Hemmings, F.W.J. Emile Zola. 2. ed. Oxford, 1966.
42584.25.195A Zola, Emile. Zola par lui-même. Paris, 1952.
42584.25.195B Zola, Emile. Zola par lui-même. Paris, 1952.
42584.25.200 Lanoux, A. Bonjour, Monsieur Zola. Paris, 1954.
42584.25.202 Lanoux, A. Bonjour, Monsieur Zola. Paris, 1962.
42584.25.210 Lanoux, A. Zola. London, 1955.
42584.25.215 Frandon, Ida Marie. Autour de Germinal. Genève, 1955.
42584.25.216 Frandon, Ida Marie. La pensée politique d'Emile Zola. Paris, 1959.
42584.25.220 Jagmetti, Antoinette. La bête humaine d'Emile Zola. Genève, 1955.
42584.25.225 Bibliothèque Nationale, Paris. Emile Zola. Paris, 1952.
42584.25.230 Présence de Zola. Paris, 1953.
42584.25.235 Matthews, J.H. Les deux Zola. Genève, 1957.
42584.25.240 Lugones, Leopoldo. Emilio Zola. Buenos-Aires, 1920.
42584.25.245 Grant, Richard B. Zola's Son excellence Eugène Rougon. Durham, 1960.

42584.24 - .25 Individual authors, etc. - 1850-1899 - Fiction - Zola, E. - Biography and criticism - cont.

42584.25.250 Brown, Calvin S. Repetition in Zola's novels. Athens, Georgia, 1952.
42584.25.255 Deffoux, Léon. La publication de L'assommoir. Paris, 1931.
42584.25.260 Guillemin, Henri. Zola. Paris, 1960.
42584.25.265 Walter, Gerhard. Emile Zola. München, 1959.
42584.25.270 Menichelli, Gian Carlo. Bibliographie de Zola en Italie. Florence, 1960.
42584.25.275 Puzikov, A.I. Emil' Zolia. Moskva, 1961.
42584.25.280 Les cahiers naturalistes. Paris. 1,1955+ 4v.
42584.25.285 Grant, Elliott M. Notes on Germinal. Lyme, 1962?
42584.25.286 Grant, Elliott M. Zola's Germinal. Leicester, 1962.
42584.25.287 Grant, Elliott M. Zola's Germinal. Leicester, 1970.
42584.25.290 Untersteiner, Gabriella. L'oeuvre di Emile Zola e i suoi rapporti con Cézanne. Milano, 1957.
42584.25.295 Mitterand, H. Zola, journaliste de l'affaire Manet à l'affaire Dreyfus. Paris, 1962.
42584.25.300 Brulat, P. Histoire populaire de Emile Zola. Paris, 1936.
42584.25.305 Carter, L.A. Zola and the theater. 1. ed. New Haven, 1963.
42584.25.310 Ternois, René. Zola et son temps. Dijon, 1961.
42584.25.315 Lapp, J.C. Zola before the Rougon-Macquart. Toronto, 1964.
42584.25.320 Cantoni, Edda. Appunti sull'ideologia di Zola. Torino, 1962.
42584.25.325 Guillemin, Henri. Présentation des Rougon-Macquart. Paris, 1964.
42584.25.330 Psichari, H. Anatomie d'un chef-d'oeuvre. Paris, 1964.
42584.25.335 Mitterand, Henri. Album Zola. Paris, 1963.
42584.25.340 Eikhengol'ts, M. Tvorcheskaia laboratoriia Zolia. Moskva, 1940.
42584.25.345 Herriot, Edouard. Emile Zola et son oeuvre. Paris, 1927.
42584.25.350 Le Blond, Maurice. Les projets littéraires d'Emile Zola au moment de sa mort. Paris, 1927.
42584.25.355 Emel'ianikov, Sergei P. Rugon-Makkary E. Zolia. Moskva, 1965.
42584.25.360 Grant, Elliott M. Emile Zola. N.Y., 1966.
42584.25.365 Kleman, Mikhail K. Emil' Zola. Leningrad, 1934.
42584.25.370 Euvard, Michel. Emile Zola. Paris, 1967.
42584.25.375 Proulx, Alfred C. Aspects épiques des Rougon-Macquart de Zola. The Hague, 1966.
42584.25.380 Brady, Patrick. L'oeuvre de Emile Zola. Roman sur les arts, manifeste, autobiographie, roman à clef. Genève, 1967.
42584.25.385 Niess, Robert. Zola, Cézanne and Manet. Ann Arbor, 1968.
42584.25.390 Kranowski, Nathan. Paris dans les romans d'Emile Zola. Paris, 1968.
42584.25.395 Zola. Paris, 1969.
42584.25.400 Max, Stefan. Les métamorphoses de la grande ville dans les Rougon-Macquart. Paris, 1966.
42584.25.405 Iakimovich, Tat'iana K. Molodoi Zolia. Kiev, 1971.
42584.25.410 Franzen, Nils Olof. Zola et la joie de vivre. Stockholm, 1958.
42584.25.415 Robert, Guy. La terre d'Emile Zola. Paris, 1952.
42584.25.416 Robert, Guy. La terre d'Emile Zola. Thèse. Paris, 1952.
42584.25.420 Robert, Guy. Emile Zola. Paris, 1952.
42584.25.425 Wiegler, Hans. Geschichte und Kritik der Theorie des Milieus bei Emile Zola. Inaug. Diss. Rostock, 1905.

42584.26 - .31 Individual authors, etc. - 1850-1899 - Fiction - Stahl, P.J. (Hetzel) - Writings

42584.26 Hetzel, P.J. Les bonnes fortunes parisiennes; les amours d'un Pierrot. 6. éd. Paris, 1868.
42584.27 Hetzel, P.J. Les bonnes fortunes parisiennes; les amours d'un notaire. 8. éd. Paris, 187-?
42584.28 Hetzel, P.J. Les méfaits de Palichinelle. Paris, 1880.
42584.29 Hetzel, P.J. L'esprit des femmes et les femmes d'esprit. 5. éd. Paris, 1856.
42584.29.5 Hetzel, P.J. Gribouille chez son oncle Jeannot. Paris, n.d.
42584.29.15 Hetzel, P.J. Histoire d'un lièvre. Cambridge, 18- .
42584.30 Hetzel, P.J. Histoire d'un prince et d'une princesse. Paris, 1876.
42584.31 Hetzel, P.J. Maroussia. 11. éd. Paris, 1886.
42584.31.2 Hetzel, P.J. Maroussia. 10. éd. Paris, 1878?
42584.31.25 Hetzel, P.J. Voyage d'un étudiant et ses suites variées. 11. éd. Paris, 1875.

42584.32 Individual authors, etc. - 1850-1899 - Fiction - Stahl, P.J. (Hetzel) - Works about

42584.32.5 Bibliothèque Nationale, Paris. P.J. Hetzel, Paris, 1966. Paris, 1966.
42584.32.7 Bibliothèque Nationale, Paris. P.J. Hetzel, un grande editore del XIX secolo. Milano, 1967.

42584.37 Individual authors, etc. - 1850-1899 - Fiction - Simon, J.

42584.37 Simon, Jules. Les derniers mémoires des autres. Paris, n.d.
42584.37.30 Simon, Jules. Nouveaux mémoires des autres. Paris, 1891.
42584.37.35 Simon, Jules. La peine de mort. Paris, 1869.

42584.47 Individual authors, etc. - 1850-1899 - Fiction - Ulbach, L.

42584.47 Ulbach, Louis. La confession d'un abbé. Paris, 1882.
42584.47.5 Ulbach, Louis. La jardin du chanoine. Paris, 1866.
42584.47.10 Ulbach, Louis. La ronde de nuit. Paris, 1874.
42584.47.15 Ulbach, Louis. Le roman de la bourgeoisie. Paris, 1874.
42584.47.20 Ulbach, Louis. Les parents coupables. Paris, 1874.
42584.47.25 Ulbach, Louis. La csardas. 2. éd. Paris, 1888.

42584.49 Individual authors, etc. - 1850-1899 - Fiction - Vallon, G.

42584.49 Vallon, G. du. Vingt ans plus tard. Paris, n.d.

42584.50 Individual authors, etc. - 1850-1899 - Fiction - Vernet

42584.50 Vernet, Nancy. Dix ans de coulisses. Paris, 1908.

42584.52 Individual authors, etc. - 1850-1899 - Fiction - Vincent

42584.52 Vincent, Jacques. Ce que femme veut. Paris, 1888.

42584.56 Individual authors, etc. - 1850-1899 - Fiction - Walsh, J.A.

42584.56 Walsh, J.A. Le fratricide. Quebec, 1866.

42585 Individual authors, etc. - 1850-1899 - Fiction - Folios [Discontinued]

42585.28 Figuier, L. (Mme.). Soeurs de lait. Paris, 1861.
42585.36 Kock, Henry de. Histoire des farceurs célèbres. Paris, 1872.
42585.41 Pauline, L. Livre d'une mère. Paris, 1875.

42585 Individual authors, etc. - 1850-1899 - Fiction - Folios [Discontinued] - cont.
42585.43 Lavergne, A. Le cadet de famille. N.Y., 1857.
42585.70 Quesada, G. de. Patriotismo; cuentos de guerra. N.Y., 1893.

42586.2 - .3 Individual authors, etc. - 1850-1899 - Fiction - About, E. [Discontinued]
42586.2 About, E. En petit comité. Paris, 1880.
42586.3A About, E. Contes de toutes les couleurs. Paris, 1879.
42586.3B About, E. Contes de toutes les couleurs. Paris, 1879.

42586.4 - .6 Individual authors, etc. - 1850-1899 - Fiction - Achard, A.
42586.4 Achard, Amédée. L'eau qui dort. Paris, 1860.
42586.4.5 Achard, Amédée. Les campagnes d'un roué. Paris, 1886.
42586.5 Achard, Amédée. Madame Rose. Pierre de villerglé. Paris, 1864.
42586.6 Achard, Amédée. L'ombre de Ludovic. Paris, 1860.
42586.6.5 Achard, Amédée. Brunes de blondes. Paris, 1884.
42586.6.10 Achard, Amédée. The golden fleece. Boston, 1901.
42586.6.12 Achard, Amédée. The golden fleece. Boston, 1901.

42586.7 Individual authors, etc. - 1850-1899 - Fiction - Aicard
42586.7.15 Aicard, Jean. Benjamine. Paris, n.d.
42586.7.16 Aicard, Jean. Maurin des Maures. Paris, n.d.
42586.7.16.5 Aicard, Jean. Maurin des Maures. Paris, 1917?
42586.7.17 Aicard, Jean. L'illustre maurin. Paris, n.d.
42586.7.17.5 Aicard, Jean. L'illustre maurin. Paris, 1920.
42586.7.18 Aicard, Jean. Le père Lebonnard. Paris, n.d.
42586.7.19 Aicard, Jean. Théâtre. Paris, n.d. 2v.
NEDL 42586.7.20 Aicard, Jean. L'âme d'un enfant. Paris, 1912?
42586.7.21 Aicard, Jean. King of Carveargue. Philadelphia, 1901.
42586.7.25 Aicard, Jean. Notre-dame-d'amour. Paris, 1896.

42586.8 - .9 Individual authors, etc. - 1850-1899 - Fiction - Arène, P.
42586.8 Arène, Paul. Oeuvres. Paris, 1884.
42586.9 Arène, Paul. La chèvre d'or. Paris, 1893.
42586.9.5 Arène, Paul. La gueuse parfumée. Paris, 1907.
42586.9.10 Arène, Paul. Poémes provenceaux. London, 1956.
42586.9.11 Pamphlet box. Arène, Paul.
42586.9.12 Arène, Paul. Provenzalische Novellen. Halle, 1956.
42586.9.12.10 Arène, Paul. Contes et nouvelles de Provence. Paris, 1961.
42586.9.15 Petry, L. Paul Arène, ein Dichter der Provence. Halle, 1911.
42586.9.20 Duche, Rene. La carque et le style de Paul Arène. Paris, 1949.

42586.10 - .12 Individual authors, etc. - 1850-1899 - Fiction - Assollant, A.
42586.10 Assollant, A. Histoire fantastique du célèbre Pierrot. Paris, 1860.
42586.10.5 Assollant, A. The fantastic history of...Pierrot. London, 1875.
42586.11 Assollant, A. Aventures de Capitaine Corcoran. Paris, 1881. 2v.
42586.11.15 Assollant, A. Récits de la vieille France. Boston, 1893.
42586.12 Assollant, A. Scènes de la vie des États-Unis. Paris, 1859.

42586.13 Individual authors, etc. - 1850-1899 - Fiction - Auriac
42586.13 D'Auriac, J.B. Guerre noire. Paris, 1862.

42586.14 - .14.8 Individual authors, etc. - 1850-1899 - Fiction - Audoux
42586.14 Audoux, M. Marie-Claire. Paris, 1910.
42586.14.3 Audoux, M. Marie-Claire. Paris, 1911.
42586.14.5 Audoux, M. Marie-Claire. N.Y., 1911.
42586.14.6 Audoux, M. Marie-Claire. N.Y., 1911.
42586.14.6.10 Audoux, M. Marie-Claire. Paris, 192-.
42586.14.6.15 Audoux, M. Le chaland de la reine. Nevers, 1910.
42586.14.6.20 Audoux, M. Marie Claire's workshop. N.Y., 1920.
42586.14.6.50 Seybold, Betty. Leben und Werke von Marguerite Audoux. Inaug. Diss. Würzburg, 1935.
42586.14.6.55 Lanoizelée, Louis. Marguerite Audoux. Paris, 1954.
42586.14.7 Audoux, M. Marie-Claire. Paris, 1937.
42586.14.8 Audoux, M. Valserine. N.Y., 1912.

42586.14.9 Individual authors, etc. - 1850-1899 - Fiction - Badin
42586.14.9 Badin, Adolphe. Minine et Pojarski. Paris, 1893.
42586.14.9.5 Badin, Adolphe. Un parisien chez les russes. Paris, 1883.

42586.14.40 Individual authors, etc. - 1850-1899 - Fiction - Bascle de Lagrèze
42586.14.40.5 Bascle de Lagrèze, Gaston. Zurückgekehrt. Einsiedeln, 1910.
42586.14.40.10 Bascle de Lagrèze, Gaston. La lune rousse. Tours, 1903.

42586.14.55 Individual authors, etc. - 1850-1899 - Fiction - Baudry, J.
42586.14.55 Baudry, J. (Mme.). Devant l'obstacle. Paris, 1907.

42586.14.75 Individual authors, etc. - 1850-1899 - Fiction - Baudry, E.
42586.14.75 Baudry, Etienne. Le camp des bourgeois. Paris, 1868.

42586.18 Individual authors, etc. - 1850-1899 - Fiction - Beauvoir
42586.18 Beauvoir, E.R. de. Confidences de Mlle. Mars. Paris, 1855.

42586.19 Individual authors, etc. - 1850-1899 - Fiction - Baudoux
42586.19 Baudoux, F. Bigarrures par F. Baudoux. Bruxelles, 1884.

42586.20 Individual authors, etc. - 1850-1899 - Fiction - Bégon
42586.20 Bégon, F. House on wheels. Boston, 1871.

42586.21 Individual authors, etc. - 1850-1899 - Fiction - Bernard, P.; Blaze de Bury; Bigot; Boissieu; etc.
42586.21 Bernard, Pierre. L'A.B.C. de l'esprit. Paris, 1861.
42586.21.29 Bigot, Charles (Mme.). La tâche du petit Pierre. N.Y., 1896.
42586.21.100 Boissieu, Arthur de. Lettres d'un passant. Paris, 1868-1875. 4v.
42586.21.102 Boissieu, Arthur de. De chute en chute. Paris, 1872.

42586.23 Individual authors, etc. - 1850-1899 - Fiction - Bounières
42586.23 Bounières, R. de. Lord Hyland. Histoire véritable. Paris, 1895.

42586.24 Individual authors, etc. - 1850-1899 - Fiction - Boubée; Bravard; etc.
42586.24 Boubée, Simon. La jeunesse de Tartufé. Paris, 1897. 2v.
42586.24.100 Bravard, Raoul. Une petite ville. Paris, 1859.

42586.25 - .27 Individual authors, etc. - 1850-1899 - Fiction - Bungener
42586.25.9 Bungener, Félix. Trois sermons sous Louis XV. 3. éd. Paris, 1854. 3v.
42586.25.14 Bungener, Félix. The priest and the Huguenot. Boston, 1856. 2v.
42586.25.15 Bungener, Félix. The priest and the Huguenot. Boston, 1856. 2v.
42586.25.16 Bungener, Félix. The priest and the Huguenot. Boston, 1853-1854. 2v.
42586.26 Bungener, Félix. Trois sermons sous Louis XV. Paris, 1861. 3v.
42586.26.90 Bungener, Félix. Un sermon sous Louis XIV. 4. éd. Paris, 1853.
42586.27 Bungener, Félix. Un sermon sous Louis XIV. Paris, 1873.
42586.27.13 Bungener, Félix. The preacher and the king. 12. ed. Boston, 1853.
42586.27.14 Bungener, Félix, The preacher and the king. 12. ed. Boston, 1854.
42586.27.15 Bungener, Félix. The preacher and the king or Bourdaloue in the court of Louis XIV. Boston, 1855.
42586.27.30 Cherot, Henri. Bourdaloue. Paris, 1899.

42586.28 Individual authors, etc. - 1850-1899 - Fiction - Caro; Casale; etc.
42586.28 Caro, E. Amour de jeune fille. Paris, 1892.
42586.28.5 Casale, F. Chanteclair. Paris, 1902.
42586.28.15 Casale, F. La rose du Bocagne. Paris, n.d.

42586.29 Individual authors, etc. - 1850-1899 - Fiction - Castille; Caragual; Causse; Chabrier; etc.
42586.29 Castille, C.H. Gli Uccelli da Preda. Firenze, 1846. 2v.
42586.29.3 Caraguel, J. Le Boul' Mich'. 2. éd. Paris, 1884.
42586.29.4 Caraguel, J. Les Barthozouls. Paris, 1887.
42586.29.9 Maël, Pierre (pseud.). Mademoiselle Pompon. Tours, 1903.
42586.29.10 Maël, Pierre (pseud.). César Borgia. Paris, 1909.
42586.29.100 Chabrier, Jean. Aller et retour. Paris, 1893.
42586.29.110 Chabrier, Jean. La gamelle. Paris, 1890.

42586.30 Individual authors, etc. - 1850-1899 - Fiction - Chazel; Chevalier, E.; Claudin; Coni; etc.
42586.30 Chazel, Prosper. Le chalet des Spains. Paris, n.d.
42586.30.5 Chazel, Prosper. Histoire d'un forestier. Paris, 1881.
42586.30.9 Chevalier, E. Les derniers Iroquois. Paris, 1867.
42586.30.50 Claudin, G. Point et Virgule. Paris, 1860.
42586.30.52 Claudin, G. Mes souvenirs, les boulevards de 1840-1870. 2. éd. Paris, 1884.
42586.30.100 Pagés Larraya, Antonio. Gabriela de Coni y sus ficciones precursoras. Buenos Aires, 1965.

42586.31 Individual authors, etc. - 1850-1899 - Fiction - Claretié
42586.31 Claretié, J. Candidat. Paris, 1887.
42586.31.2 Claretié, J. Les amours d'un interne. Paris, 1881.
42586.31.3 Claretié, J. Le troisième dessous. Paris, 1879.
42586.31.5 Claretié, J. L'Américaine. Paris, 1892.
42586.31.6 Claretié, J. La mausard. Paris, n.d.
42586.31.9 Claretié, J. Brichanteau. Boston, 1897.
42586.31.9.5 Claretié, J. Brichanteau. Paris, 1913.
42586.31.10 Claretié, J. Voyages d'un&Parisien. Paris, 1865.
42586.31.11F Claretié, J. Le drapeau. Paris, 1879.
42586.31.12 Claretié, J. Mademoiselle Cachemire. Paris, 1879.
42586.31.13 Claretié, J. La divette. Paris, 1896.
42586.31.14 Claretié, J. La frontière. Paris, 1894.
42586.31.15 Claretié, J. Preuse Zilah. N.Y., 1910.
42586.31.20 Claretié, J. La canne de M. Michelet. Paris, 1886.
42586.31.25 Grappe, G. Jules Claretié. Paris, 1906
42586.31.30 Claretié, J. Monsieur le ministre. 3. éd. Paris, 1883.
42586.31.31 Claretié, J. Monsieur le ministre. 15. éd. Paris, 1881.
42586.31.72 Claretié, J. Souvenirs du diner Bixio. Paris, 1924.

42586.32 - .32.5 Individual authors, etc. - 1850-1899 - Fiction - Coquelin
42586.32.5 Coquelin, Ernest. Le rire. 5. éd. Paris, 1887.
42586.32.5.2 Coquelin, Ernest. Le rire. Paris, 1887.
42586.32.5.3 Coquelin, Ernest. Le rire. 6. éd. Paris, 1887.
42586.32.5.15 Coquelin, Ernest. Pirouettes. Paris, 1888.

42586.32.7 - .32.699 Individual authors, etc. - 1850-1899 - Fiction - Coster, C.
42586.32.7 Coster, Charles de. Briefe an Elisa. Leipzig, 1919.
42586.32.8 Coster, Charles de. Die Hochzeitsreise, Zoulets Heirat. Berlin, 1920.
42586.32.9 Coster, Charles de. Légendes flamandes. Paris, 1858.
42586.32.11 Coster, Charles de. Flemish legends. London, 1920.
42586.32.15 Coster, Charles de. La legende d'Ulenspiegel. Paris, 1868.
42586.32.20 Coster, Charles de. La legende d'Ulenspiegel. Bruxelles, 1893.
42586.32.30 Coster, Charles de. La legende et les aventures héroiques. Bruxelles, 1928.
42586.32.40 Coster, Charles de. Légendes flamandes. Bruxelles, 1930?
42586.32.45 Coster, Charles de. The glorious adventures of Tyl Ulenspiegel. N.Y., 1943.
42586.32.50 Coster, Charles de. Die Geschichte von Ulenspiegel und Lamme Goedzak und ihren heldenmässigen, fröhlichen und glorreichen Abenteuern. München, 1926. 2v.
42586.32.60 Coster, Charles de. La legende et les aventures héroiques. Bruxelles, 1959.
42586.32.65 Coster, Charles de. Tyll Ulenspiegel. München, 1920.
42586.32.70 Coster, Charles de. La legende d'Ulenspiegel. Paris, 1962.
42586.32.75 Coster, Charles de. La leggenda di Thyl Ulenspiegel. Milano, 196-?
42586.32.100 Coster, Charles de. The legend of Ulenspiegel and Lamme Gaedzak. Garden City, N.Y., 1922. 2v.
42586.32.110 Coster, Charles de. The legend of Ulenspiegel in the land of Flanders and elsewhere. London, 1928.

Classified Listing

42586.32.7 - .32.699 Individual authors, etc. - 1850-1899 - Fiction - Coster, C. - cont.

42586.32.200 Coster, Charles de. De legende en de heldhaftige, vroolijke en roemrijke daden van Uilenspiegel. Amsterdam, 1914.
42586.32.210 Coster, Charles de. Tyll Ulenspiegel und Lamm Goedzak. 2. Aufl. Jena, 1910.
42586.32.215 Coster, Charles de. Charles de Coster, journaliste. Bruxelles, 1959.
42586.32.500 Hanse, Joseph. Charles de Coster. Louvain, 1928.
42586.32.505 Liebrecht, Henri. La vie et le rêve de Charles de Coster. Bruxelles, 1927.
42586.32.510 Voorde, Urbain van de. Charles de Coster's Ulenspiegel. Nijmegen, 1948.
42586.32.515 Gulo, Aloïs. Charles de Coster en Vlaanderen. Antwerpen, 1959.
42586.32.520 Mitskevich, B.P. Sharl' de Koster stanovlenie realizma v bel'giiskoi literature. Minsk, 1960.
42586.32.525 Brussels. Bibliotheque royale. Charles de Coster. Bruxelles, 1960.
42586.32.530 Moscow. Vsesoiznaia Gosudarstvennaia Biblioteka Inostrannoi Literatury. Sharl' de Koster; bibliograficheskii ukazatel'. Moskva, 1964.
42586.32.535 Gheyselinck, Roger. De dood van taai geroddel. Antwerpen, 1969.

42586.32.710 Individual authors, etc. - 1850-1899 - Fiction - Cournier

42586.32.710 Cournier, Jean. Lettres de l'inconnue. Paris, 1874.

42586.32.910 Individual authors, etc. - 1850-1899 - Fiction - Dabadie

42586.32.910 Dabadie, F. Récits et types américains. Paris, 1860.

42586.33 Individual authors, etc. - 1850-1899 - Fiction - Darien, G.

Htn 42586.33* Delaclos, C. Les liaisons dangereuses. Bruxelles, 1869. 2v.
NEDL 42586.33 Delaclos, C. Les liaisons dangereuses. Bruxelles, 1869. 2v.
42586.33.100 Darien, Georges. Le voleur. Sceaux, 1955.
42586.33.112 Darien, Georges. Bas les coeurs; 1870-1871. 2. éd. Paris, 1957.
42586.33.120 Darien, Georges. La Belle France. Paris, 1965.
42586.33.130 Darien, Georges. L'epaulette. Paris, 1971.
42586.33.800 Auriand (pseud.). Darien et l'inhumane comédie. Bruxelles, 1966?

42586.34 Individual authors, etc. - 1850-1899 - Fiction - Deltuf

42586.34 Deltuf, Paul. Aventures&parisiennes. Paris, 1859.

42586.35 Individual authors, etc. - 1850-1899 - Fiction - Delpit

42586.35 Delpit, Albert. Le fils de Coralie. Paris, 1880.
42586.35.5 Delpit, Albert. Toutes les deux. Paris, 1890.
42586.35.7.3 Delpit, Albert. Belle-Madame. 5. éd. Paris, 1892.

42586.36 Individual authors, etc. - 1850-1899 - Fiction - Debrit; Demond; Dewailly; Divat; etc.

42586.36 Debrit, Marc. Laura où l'Italie contemporaine. Paris, 1862.
42586.36.3 Demond, G. Jean de Précour. Une page d'histoire. Paris, 1906.
42586.36.5 Dewailly, A. Le petit monde. Paris, n.d.
42586.36.9 Divat, Joseph. Les dieux d'or. Paris, 1902.

42586.37 - .38 Individual authors, etc. - 1850-1899 - Fiction - DuCamp, M.

42586.37 DuCamp, M. Chevalier du coeur saignant. Paris, 1862.
42586.38 DuCamp, M. Le crépuscule. Paris, 1893.
42586.38.5 DuCamp, M. Mémoires d'un suicidé. Paris, 1890.
42586.38.10 DuCamp, M. Souvenirs littéraires. Paris, 1882-1883. 2v.
42586.38.15 DuCamp, M. Souvenirs littéraires. Paris, 1883. 2v.
42586.38.20 DuCamp, M. Literary recollections. London, 1893. 2v.

42586.39 Individual authors, etc. - 1850-1899 - Fiction - Durantin

42586.39 Durantin, Armand. Légende de l'homme éternel. Paris, 1863.

42586.40 Individual authors, etc. - 1850-1899 - Fiction - Dépret; Deschamps; etc.

42586.40 Dépret, L. Eucharis. Paris, 1870.
42586.40.5 Deschamps, G. Chemin fleuri. 3. éd. Paris, 1896.
42586.40.7 Deschamps, G. Chemin fleuri. Paris, 1896.

42586.41 Individual authors, etc. - 1850-1899 - Fiction - Desjardin

42586.41 Desjardin, P.A. Les mystères de Constantinople. Paris, 1897.
42586.41.5 Desjardin, P.A. Les secrets d'Yildiz. Paris, 1897.

42586.42 Individual authors, etc. - 1850-1899 - Fiction - Desprez, L.; Eprey; etc.

42586.42.4 Desprez, Louis. Lettres inédites de Louis Desprez à Emile Zola. Thèse. Paris, 1950?
42586.42.9 Epry, C. L'ecume. Paris, 1902.

42586.43 Individual authors, etc. - 1850-1899 - Fiction - Erckmann, J.

42586.43 Erckman, Jules. Les veillées alsaciennes. Paris, 1874.

42586.46 - .48 Individual authors, etc. - 1850-1899 - Fiction - Feval

42586.46 Feval, Paul H. Amours de Paris. Bruxelles, 1845. 2v.
42586.46.10 Feval, Paul H. Le bossu ou Le petit parisien. 27. éd. Paris, 1872. 2v.
42586.46.15 Feval, Paul H. Le champ de Bataille. Bruxelles, 1854. 2v.
42586.47 Feval, Paul H. Les contes de nos pères. Paris, n.d.
42586.48 Feval, Paul H. Le fils du diable. Paris, 1877. 4v.
42586.48.5 Feval, Paul H. Contes de Bretagne. Limoges, 1894.
42586.48.7 Feval, Paul H. Contes de Bretagne. Paris, 1928.
42586.48.15 Feval, Paul H. O corcunda ou Um drama da regencia. Rio de Janeiro, 19- . 2v.
42586.48.20 Feval, Paul H. Le vicomte Paul. Paris, 1872.
42586.48.25 Feval, Paul H. La fée des grèves. Boston, 1906.
42586.48.30 Féval, Paul H. Les mystères de Londres. Genève, 1970? 4v.
42586.48.75 Feval, Paul H. Ar pesk aour. Roazhon, 1942.

42586.49 Individual authors, etc. - 1850-1899 - Fiction - Filon, A.

42586.49 Filon, Augustin. Garrick's pupil. Chicago, 1898.

42586.51 Individual authors, etc. - 1850-1899 - Fiction - Fistié

42586.51 Fistié, Camille. L'amour au village. Paris, 1880.

42586.52 Individual authors, etc. - 1850-1899 - Fiction - Foley; Fonville; Fortia de Piles (Caillot-Duval); etc.

42586.52 Foley, Charles. La soif rouge Madame de Lamballe. Paris, 1903.
42586.52.5A Fouvielle, Wilfred de. L'espion aérien. Paris, 1884.
42586.52.5B Fouvielle, Wilfred de. L'espion aérien. Paris, 1884.
Htn 42586.52.7* Caillot-Duval (pseud.). Les mystifications de Caillot-Duval. Paris, 1864.
42586.52.9 Caillot-Duval (pseud.). Les mystifications de Caillot-Duval. Paris, 1901.
42586.52.12 Caillot-Duval (pseud.). Correspondance philosophique de Caillot-Duval. Nancy, 1895.

42586.53 Individual authors, etc. - 1850-1899 - Fiction - Foudras; Fouillée; etc.

42586.53 Foudras, Marquis de. Lord Algernon. Paris, 1863.
42586.53.25 Fouillée, A. (Mme.). Les enfants patriots. Boston, 1893.

42586.54 Individual authors, etc. - 1850-1899 - Fiction - Foulon de Vaulx; Fouquier; François; etc.

42586.54 Foulon de Vaulx, A. Madame de Lauraguais. Paris, 1900.
42586.54.1 Foulon de Vaulx, A. La vie eteinte. Paris, 1897.
42586.54.2 Foulon de Vaulx, A. Les floraisons fanées. Paris, 1895.
42586.54.2.5 Foulon de Vaulx, A. Les vaines romances. Paris, 1896.
42586.54.3 Fouquier, Henry. Le roman d'une conspiration. Paris, 1890.
42586.54.4 Fouquier, Henry. La sagesse parisienne. Paris, 1885.
42586.54.5 Fournier, Charles A. Une volée de merles. 2. éd. Paris, 1863.
42586.54.6 Fournier, Charles A. Le roman de la chair. Paris, 1866.
42586.54.9 Francois (pseud.). Historiettes choisies une mère et ses enfants. Dresden, 1868.

42586.55 Individual authors, etc. - 1850-1899 - Fiction - Frappié

42586.55.4 Frapié, L. L'écolière. Paris, n.d.
42586.55.5 Frapié, L. La maternelle. Paris, 1904.
42586.55.9 Frapié, L. La maternelle. Paris, 1910.
42586.55.12 Frapié, L. La vedette à l'école. Paris, 1946.
42586.55.15 Frapié, L. Gamins de Paris. Paris, 1925.

42586.56 Individual authors, etc. - 1850-1899 - Fiction - Fromentin, E. - Writings

42586.56 Fromentin, Eugène. Dominique. Paris, 1863.
42586.56.10 Fromentin, Eugène. Dominique. Paris, 1937.
42586.56.15 Fromentin, Eugène. Dominique. N.Y., 1930.
42586.56.20 Fromentin, Eugène. Dominique. Paris, 1916.
42586.56.25 Fromentin, Eugène. Dominique. Montréal? 19- .
42586.56.27 Fromentin, Eugène. Dominique. Paris, 1966. 2v.

42586.57 Individual authors, etc. - 1850-1899 - Fiction - Fromentin, E. - Works about

42586.57 Fromentin, Eugène. Dominik. Leipzig, 1907.
42586.57.79 Martino, P. Fromentin. Alger, 1914.
42586.57.81 Suire, Louis. Le paysage charentais. La Rochelle, 1946.
42586.57.85 Lagrange, André. L'art de Fromentin. Paris, 1952.
42586.57.90 Evans, Arthur R. The literary art of Eugène Fromentin. Baltimore, 1946.
42586.57.95 Eckstein, Marie Anne. Le rôle du souvenir dans l'oeuvre d'Eugène Fromentin. Zurich, 1970.

42586.59 - .61 Individual authors, etc. - 1850-1899 - Fiction - Gandon, A.

42586.59 Gandon, Antoine. Les trente-deux duels de J. Gigon. Paris, 1860.
42586.60 Gandon, Antoine. Les 32 duels de Jean Gigon. Paris, 1861.
42586.61 Gandon, Antoine. Le grand Godard. Paris, 1861.

42586.62 Individual authors, etc. - 1850-1899 - Fiction - Gauthier, H.; Gauthier-Villars; etc.

42586.62 Gauthier-Villars, Henry. L'année fantaisiste. Paris, 1892.
42586.62.9 Albert, Henri. Willy. Paris, 1904.
42586.62.15 Solenière, Eugène de. Willy. 2. éd. Paris, 1903.
42586.62.20 Gauthier-Villars, Henry. Souvenirs littéraires et autres. Paris, 1925.
42586.62.25 Gauthier-Villars, Henry. Contes sans feuilles de vigne. Paris, 1928.
42586.62.30 Gauthier-Villars, Henry. L'implaquable Siska. Paris, 1912?

42586.63 Individual authors, etc. - 1850-1899 - Fiction - Gobineau, A. - Works about

42586.63 Kretzer, E. Joseph Arthur, Graf von Gobineau. Leipzig, 1902.
42586.63.2 Cartellieri, A. Gobineau. Strassburg, 1917.
42586.63.3 Schemann, Ludwig. Die Gobineau-Sammlung zu Strassburg. Strassburg, 1907.
42586.63.3.5 Schemann, Ludwig. Neues aus der Welt Gobineaus. Hildburghausen, 1912.
42586.63.4 Gobineau Vereinigung. Bericht. 1-11
42586.63.4.2 Gobineau Vereinigung. Verzeichnis der Mitglieder, Gönner und Förderer. Freiburg. 1908-1914 2v.
42586.63.4.3 Gobineau Vereinigung. Kassenbericht. 1909-1914 2v.
42586.63.4.5 Schemann, Ludwig. Fünfundzwanzig Jahre Gobineau. Strassburg, 1919.
42586.63.6 Schemann, Ludwig. Graf Arthur Gobineau. Stuttgart, 1907.
42586.63.6.5 Schemann, Ludwig. Gobineau. Strassburg, 1913. 2v.
42586.63.6.6 Schemann, Ludwig. Quellen und Untersuchungen zum Leben Gobineaus. Strassburg, 1914-1919. 2v.
42586.63.7 Eulenburg-Hertefeld, P. Graf Arthur Gobineau. Strassburg, 1906.
42586.63.8 Eulenburg-Hertefeld, P. Gobineau und die deutsche Kultur. Leipzig, 1910.
42586.63.9 Pamphlet box. Gobineau, Arthur de.
42586.63.12 Kaufmann, Josef. Gobineau und die Kultur des Abendlandes. Inaug. Diss. Duisburg, 1929.
42586.63.14 Faure-Biguet, J.N. Gobineau. Paris, 1930.
42586.63.16 Spring, G.M. The vitalism of Count de Gobineau. N.Y., 1932.
42586.63.20 Streidl, R. Gobineau in der französischen Kritik. Inaug. Diss. Würzburg, 1935.

42586.63 Individual authors, etc. - 1850-1899 - Fiction - Gobineau, A. - Works about - cont.

42586.63.24 Combris, A. La philosophie des races du comte de Gobineau. Thèse. Paris, 1937.
42586.63.25 Combris, A. La philosophie des races du comte de Gobineau. Paris, 1937.
42586.63.28 Thomas, Louis. Arthur de Gobineau, inventeur du racisme, 1816-1882. Paris, 1941.
42586.63.30 Rifaterre, Michael. Le style des Pléiades de Gobineau. Genève, 1957.
42586.63.35 Theren, R. L'Amadis de Gobineau. Montpellier, 1960.
42586.63.36 Etudes gobiniennes. Paris. 1,1966+ 4v.
42586.63.38 Buenzod, Janine. La formation de la pensée de Gobineau et l'essai sur l'inégalité des races humaines. Paris, 1967.
42586.63.40 Falk, Reinhold. Die weltanschauliche Problematik bei Gobineau. Inaug. Diss. Rostock, 1936.
42586.63.45 Gaulmier, Jean. Spectre de Gobineau. Paris, 1965.
42586.63.50 Biddiss, Michael D. Father of racist ideology. London, 1970.
42586.63.55 Young, E.J. Gobineau und der Rassismus. Meisenheim-an-Glan, 1968.
42586.63.60 Rowbothan, Arnold H. The literary works of Count de Gobineau. Paris, 1929.
42586.63.65 Strasbourg. Bibliotheque national et universaire. Exposition à l'occasion du cinquantième anniversaire de la mort d'Arthur de Gobineau (10-30 nov. 1932.). Paris, 1933.
42586.63.70A Lange, Maurice. Le comte Arthur de Gobineau. London, 1924.
42586.63.70B Lange, Maurice. Le comte Arthur de Gobineau. London, 1924.

42586.64 - .68 Individual authors, etc. - 1850-1899 - Fiction - Gobineau, A. - Writings

42586.64 Gobineau, Arthur de. Les Pléiades. Paris, 1874.
42586.64.5 Gobineau, Arthur de. Les Pléiades. Monaco, 1946.
42586.64.6 Gobineau, Arthur de. Sons of kings. London, 1966.
42586.64.10 Gobineau, Arthur de. Lettres persanes. Paris, 1957.
42586.64.15 Gobineau, Arthur de. Les depeches diplomatiques du comte de Gobineau e Perse. Genève, 1959.
42586.64.20 Gobineau, Arthur de. Lettres bresiliennes. Paris, 1969.
42586.65 Gobineau, Arthur de. La renaisssance. Paris, 1877.
42586.65.3 Gobineau, Arthur de. La renaissance. Paris, 1903.
42586.65.4A Gobineau, Arthur de. La renaissance. Paris, 1934. 2v.
42586.65.4B Gobineau, Arthur de. La renaissance. Paris, 1935. 2v.
42586.65.5 Gobineau, Arthur de. Die Rénaissance. Strassburg, 1908.
42586.65.5.1 Gobineau, Arthur de. Die Rénaissance. Leipzig, 1912.
42586.65.5.2 Gobineau, Arthur de. Die Rénaissance. Leipzig, 1904.
42586.65.5.3 Gobineau, Arthur de. Die Rénaissance. Strassburg, 1913.
42586.65.5.4 Gobineau, Arthur de. Die Rénaissance. Berlin, 1913.
42586.65.5.6A Gobineau, Arthur de. The renaissance. N.Y., 1913.
42586.65.5.6B Gobineau, Arthur de. The renaissance. N.Y., 1913.
42586.65.5.6C Gobineau, Arthur de. The renaissance. N.Y., 1913.
42586.65.6 Gobineau, Arthur de. Michelangelo. Strassburg, 1909.
42586.65.10 Gobineau, Arthur de. Les conseils de Rabelais. Paris, 1962.
42586.66 Gobineau, Arthur de. Typhaines Abbey. Philadelphia, 1869.
42586.66.9 Gobineau, Arthur de. Nouvelles asiatiques. Paris, 1876.
42586.66.9.5 Gobineau, Arthur de. Nouvelles asiatiques. Paris, 1963.
42586.66.9.7 Gobineau, Arthur de. Nouvelles asiatiques. Paris, 1965.
42586.66.10 Gobineau, Arthur de. Romances of the east. N.Y., 1878.
42586.66.12 Gobineau, Arthur de. Souvenirs de voyage. Paris, 1872.
42586.66.20 Gobineau, Arthur de. Nouvelles. Paris, 1956. 2v.
42586.66.25 Gobineau, Arthur de. The dancing girl of Shamokha. N.Y., 1926.
Htn 42586.66.30* Gobineau, Arthur de. La chronique rimée Jean Chouan et de ses compagnons. Paris, 1846.
42586.67 Gobineau, Arthur de. Asiatische Novellen. Leipzig, n.d.
42586.67.5 Gobineau, Arthur de. Five oriental tales. N.Y., 1925.
42586.67.10 Gobineau, Arthur de. Mademoiselle Irnois. Paris, 1961.
42586.67.20 Gobineau, Arthur de. Le prisonnier chanceux. Paris, 1924.
42586.68 Gobineau, Arthur de. Amadis. Paris, 1876.
42586.68.2 Gobineau, Arthur de. Nachgelassene Schriften. Briefe. 2. Aufl. Strassburg, 1911.
42586.68.2.5 Gobineau, Arthur de. Nachgelassene Schriften. Alexandre le Macédonien. 2. Aufl. Strassburg, 1902.
42586.68.3 Gobineau, Arthur de. Kleinere anthropologisch-historische und politische Schriften. Strassburg, 1918.
42586.68.5 Gobineau, Arthur de. Pages choisies, précédées d'une étude. 2. éd. Paris, 1905.
42586.68.9 Gobineau, Arthur de. Alexander. 3. Aufl. Strassburg, 1911.
42586.68.10 Gobineau, Arthur de. Alexander in Weimar. Bayreuth, 1903.
42586.68.15 Gobineau, Arthur de. Études critiques, 1844-1848. Paris, 1927.
Htn 42586.68.20* Gobineau, Arthur de. Ternove. Bruxelles, 1848. 3v.
42586.68.25 Gobineau, Arthur de. Les races et la République, introduction à une lecture de l'Essai sur l'inégalité des races humaines. Paris, 1967.
42586.68.63 Gobineau, Arthur de. Correspondance entre Gobineau et le comte de Prakesch-Osten (1854-1876). 4. éd. Paris, 1933.
42586.68.66 Gobineau, Arthur de. Lettres à deux athéniennes, 1868-1881. Athènes, 1936.
42586.68.68 Gobineau, Arthur de. Correspondance, 1872-1882. Paris, 1958. 2v.
42586.68.70 Gobineau, Arthur de. Gobineau: selected political writings. London, 1970.

42586.69 - .70 Individual authors, etc. - 1850-1899 - Fiction - Gourdon

42586.69 Gourdon de Genouillac, Henri. Le crime de 1804. Paris, 1873.
42586.70 Gobineau, Arthur de. Une vie d'Enfer. Paris, 1877.

42586.71 Individual authors, etc. - 1850-1899 - Fiction - Grandfort

42586.71 Grandfort, M. de. L'autre monde et la rose noire. N.Y., 1855.

42586.76 - .78 Individual authors, etc. - 1850-1899 - Fiction - Guillaumin, E. - Writings

42586.76 Guillaumin, Emile. La vie d'un simple. Paris, 1904.
42586.76.9 Guillaumin, Emile. The life of a simple man. N.Y., 1919.
42586.76.15 Guillaumin, Emile. Ispoved'. Moskva, 1923.
42586.76.20 Guillaumin, Emile. La vie d'un simple. Moulins, 1939.
42586.76.61 Guillaumin, Emile. Cent dix-neuf lettres d'Emile Guillaumin. Paris, 1969.
42586.77 Guillaumin, Emile. Près du sol. Paris, n.d.
42586.78 Guillaumin, Emile. Albert Manceau Adjudant. Paris, 1906.

42586.79 Individual authors, etc. - 1850-1899 - Fiction - Guillaumin, E. - Works about

42586.79.5 Mathé, Roger. Emile Guillaumin. Thèse. Paris, 1966.

42586.90 Individual authors, etc. - 1850-1899 - Fiction - Habeneck

42586.90 Habeneck, Charles. Nouvelles espagnoles. Paris, 1860.

42587.1 Individual authors, etc. - 1850-1899 - Fiction - Heard; Hermant; etc.

42587.1 Heard, John. Esquisses mexicaines. Paris, 1896.
42587.1.15 Hermant, A. Le cavalier Miserey. Paris, 1887.
42587.1.17 Hermant, A. Le cavalier Miserey. Paris, 19- .
42587.1.20 Hermant, A. Amour de tête. Paris, 1929.
42587.2 Hetzel, Pierre Jules. Les bijoux parlants. Paris, 1857.

42587.4 Individual authors, etc. - 1850-1899 - Fiction - Hudry-Menos

42587.4.81 Hudry-Menos, un patriote Savoisien. Genève, 1874.
42587.4.105 Hudry-Menos, J. (Mme.). Ames cévenoles. Paris, 1906.

42587.5 Individual authors, etc. - 1850-1899 - Fiction - Hugo, C.

42587.5 Hugo, Charles. La bohême dorée. Paris, 1859.
42587.5.2 Hugo, Charles. La bohême dorée. Paris, 1859. 4 pam.

42587.6 Individual authors, etc. - 1850-1899 - Fiction - Hugo, F.V.

42587.6 Guille, F.V. François-Victor Hugo et son oeuvre. Paris, 1950.

42587.7 Individual authors, etc. - 1850-1899 - Fiction - Issaurat

42587.7 Issaurat, Cyprien. Moments perdus de Pierre-Jean. Paris, 1868.

42587.8 Individual authors, etc. - 1850-1899 - Fiction - Jeannin

42587.8 Jeannin, J. Contes des champs et des rues. Paris, 1897.

42587.9 Individual authors, etc. - 1850-1899 - Fiction - Jobey

42587.9 Jobey, Charles. L'amour d'un nègre. Paris, 1860.

42587.10 Individual authors, etc. - 1850-1899 - Fiction - Julliot, F.

42587.10 Julliot, François de. La contre-allée. Paris, n.d.
42587.10.5 Julliot, François de. Mademoiselle Solange. N.Y., 1889.

42587.11 Individual authors, etc. - 1850-1899 - Fiction - Kock, H.

42587.11 Kock, Henry de. Les mystères du village. Paris, 1863. 2v.

42587.12 Individual authors, etc. - 1850-1899 - Fiction - Lapauze

42587.12.25 Lapauze, Jeanne. Le mariage de Gabrielle. N.Y., 1886.

42587.13 Individual authors, etc. - 1850-1899 - Fiction - Lebrun, C.

42587.13.7 Lebrun, Camille. Les récréations. Rouen, 1859.

42587.14 Individual authors, etc. - 1850-1899 - Fiction - Lepic, A.

42587.14.20 Lepic, Adèle. L'ombra. N.Y., 1887.
42587.14.21 Lepic, Adèle. Pour l'honneur! Paris, 1892.
42587.14.22 Lepic, Adèle. Marchand d'allumettes. Paris, 1889?

42587.15 Individual authors, etc. - 1850-1899 - Fiction - Lubomirski

42587.15 Lubomirski, Jozef. Safar-Hadgi, or Russ and Turcoman. N.Y., 1878.
42587.15.5 Lubomirski, Jozef. Tatiana, or The conspiracy. London, 1877. 3v.
42587.15.10 Lubomirski, Jozef. Tzar, archiduchesse et Burgraves. Paris, 1886.

42587.16 Individual authors, etc. - 1850-1899 - Fiction - Maindron; Maizeroy; Marrast; etc.

42587.16.10 Maindron, M. Monsieur de Clérambon. Paris, 1904.
42587.16.11 Maindron, M. La gardienne de l'idole noire. Paris, 1910.
NEDL 42587.16.11 Maindron, M. Saint-Cendre. Paris, 1912.
42587.16.12 Maindron, M. Le tournoi de Vanplassane. Paris, n.d.
42587.16.13 Maindron, M. Blancador l'avantageux. Paris, 1901.
42587.16.14 Maindron, M. Dariolette. Paris, 1912.
42587.16.14.5 Maindron, M. Ce bon M. de Véragues. Paris, 1911.
42587.16.15 Maizeroy, Rene. La dernière croisade. Paris, n.d.
42587.16.16 Toussaint, R.J. Mademoiselle. 4. éd. Paris, 1911.
42587.16.20 Marrast, Augustin. Esquisses Byzantines. Paris, 1874.

42587.19 Individual authors, etc. - 1850-1899 - Fiction - Martel; Massabuan; Medina; etc.

42587.19.35 Martel, T. La main aux dames. Paris, n.d.
42587.19.36 Marx, Adrien. Les romans du wagon. 2. éd. Paris, 1867.
42587.19.38 Massabuan, J. Nos maitres. Paris, n.d.
42587.19.75 Médins, F. L'arnice qui souffre. Paris, 1908.

42587.22 Individual authors, etc. - 1850-1899 - Fiction - Menard, L.

42587.22.5 Ménard, Louis. Lettres inédites. Paris, 1932.
42587.22.8 Ménard, Louis. Poèmes et rêveries d'un paien mystique. Paris, 1895.
42587.22.10 Ménard, Louis. Histoire des Israélites d'après l'exégèse biblique. Paris, 1883.
42587.22.11 Ménard, Louis. Abandoné. Paris, 1962?
42587.22.12 Champion, E. Le tombeau de Louis Ménard. Paris, 1902.
42587.22.13 Berthelot, Philippe. Louis Ménard et son oeuvre. Paris, 1902.
42587.22.15 Peyre, Henri. Louis Ménard, 1822-1901. New Haven, 1932.
42587.22.17 Peyre, Henri. Louis Ménard (1822-1901). Thèse. New Haven, 1932.

42587.23 - .25 Individual authors, etc. - 1850-1899 - Fiction - Méry, J. [Discontinued]

42587.23 Mérey, Joseph. Marseille et les marseillais. Paris, n.d.
42587.23.5 Méry, Joseph. Les matinées du Louvre. Paradoxes et rêveries. Paris, 1856.
42587.24 Méry, Joseph. Vénus d'Arles. Paris, 1866.
42587.24.5 Méry, Joseph. Les noches españolas. Valencia, 1877.
42587.25 Méry, Joseph. Une nuit du midi. Paris, 1855.
42587.25.21 Méry, Joseph. La juive au Vatican. Paris, 1859.

42587.26 Individual authors, etc. - 1850-1899 - Fiction - Meyer, A.

42587.26 Méry, Joseph. Through thick and thin. N.Y., 1874.
42587.26.603 Meyer, A. Ce qu'il faut taire. 3. éd. Paris, 1914.

42587.27 Individual authors, etc. - 1850-1899 - Fiction - Michel, A.; Michel, L.
42587.27 Michel, Adolphe. Les missionnaires bottés. Paris, 1872.
42587.27.10 Michel, Adolphe. Le roman d'un vieux garçon. 3. éd. Paris, 1883.
42587.27.15 Michel, Louise. Les microbes humains. Paris, 1886.
42587.27.79 Michel, Louise. Mémoires, écrits par elle-même. Paris, 1886.
42587.27.80 Day, Hem. Bibliographie de Louise Michel, 1830-1905. Bruxelles, 1959.
42587.27.85 Malato, Charles. Luisa Michel; la vita, le oper e l'azione rivoluzionaria. Roma, 1904.
42587.27.90 Day, Hem. Louise Michel, Jules Verne. Bruxelles, 1959.
42587.27.95 Thomas, Edith. Louise Michel, ou La Vélleda de l'anarchie. Paris, 1971.

42587.28 Individual authors, etc. - 1850-1899 - Fiction - Michelet
42587.28 Michelet, Victor Emile. Contes aventureux. Paris, n.d.
42587.28.80 Knowles, R.E. Victor-Emile Michelet. Thèse. Paris, 1954.
42587.29 Mie D'Aghonne, J. L'écluse des cadavres. Paris, 1875.

42587.30 - .33 Individual authors, etc. - 1850-1899 - Fiction - Molènes, P.
42587.30 Molènes, Paul de. L'amant et l'enfant. Paris, 1861.
42587.33 Molènes, Paul de. Caractères et récits du temps. Paris, 1858.

42587.35 Individual authors, etc. - 1850-1899 - Fiction - Moland
42587.35 Moland, Louis. Les méprises comédies. Paris, 1869.

42587.36 Individual authors, etc. - 1850-1899 - Fiction - Moreau; Morgan; Moselly; etc.
42587.36 Moreau, H.C. L'un ou l'autre. Paris, 1901
42587.36.5 Morgan, Jean. Thérèse Heurtot. Paris, 1901.
42587.36.15 Chenin, Emile. Le rouet d'ivoire; enfances lorrains. Paris, 1908?
42587.36.19 Chenin, Emile. Terres lorraines. Paris, n.d.
42587.36.23 Chenin, Emile. Les etudiants. 2. éd. Paris, 1914.

42587.37 Individual authors, etc. - 1850-1899 - Fiction - Musset, P.; Mystère; Nefftzer; Nesmy; Noisey; Noussanne; etc.
42587.37 Musset, Paul de. Lui et elle. Paris, 1859.
42587.37.01 Musset, Paul de. Lui et elle. 2. éd. Paris, 1859.
42587.37.08 Musset, Paul de. Lui et elle. Paris, 1883.
42587.37.09 Musset, Paul de. Lui et elle. 10. éd. Paris, 1877.
42587.37.020 Musset, Paul de. Le dernier duc de Guise. Bruxelles, 1839.
42587.37.1 Mystere, J.E.B. Histoire scandaleuse de la famille d'Orléans. Paris, 1883?
42587.37.4.10 Martin, René. La vie d'un grand journaliste Auguste Nefftzer. Besançon, 1948-1953. 2v.
42587.37.5 Nesmy, Jean. Les égarés. Paris, n.d.
42587.37.6 Noisey, C.B. La fille de l'aveugle. Rouen, 1856.
42587.37.7 Noussanne, H. de. Jasmin Robba. Paris, n.d.
42587.37.8 Noussanne, H. de. Un foyer, un pays, un ciel. Paris, 1921.
42587.37.9 Nion, François de. Les derniers Trianons. Paris, 1900.
42587.37.10 Nion, François de. Bellefleur. Paris, 1903.

42587.38 Individual authors, etc. - 1850-1899 - Fiction - Olivier, U.
42587.38 Olivier, Urbain. Récits du village. Lausanne, 1861.

42587.39 Individual authors, etc. - 1850-1899 - Fiction - Olga Cantacuzène-Altieri
42587.39 Cantacuzène-Altieri, Olga. Poverina. Paris, 1880.
42587.39.5 Cantacuzène-Altieri, Olga. Fleur de Neige. Paris, 1885.

42587.40 Individual authors, etc. - 1850-1899 - Fiction - Paul, V.
Htn 42587.40.9* Paul, Viteau. Sornettes. Paris, 1907.
42587.40.10 Paul, Viteau. Notre premiere école. Paris, 1900.

42587.41 - .42 Individual authors, etc. - 1850-1899 - Fiction - Pelletan, E.
42587.41 Pelletan, Eugène. Le grand Frédéric. Paris, 1878.
42587.42 Pelletan, Eugène. Jarousseau. Le Pasteur du Désart. Paris, 1877.
42587.42.5 Pelletan, Eugène. Les uns et les autres. Paris, 1873.
42587.42.9 Pelletan, Eugène. Heures de travail. Paris, 1854. 2v.
42587.42.20 Pelletan, Eugène. Nouvelles heures de travail. Paris, 1870.

42587.43 Individual authors, etc. - 1850-1899 - Fiction - Pène
42587.43 Pène, Henry de. Trop belle. Paris, 1887.

42587.44 - .45 Individual authors, etc. - 1850-1899 - Fiction - Perret, P.
42587.44 Perret, Paul. La Parisienne. Paris, 1868.
42587.45 Perret, Paul. Les bonnes filles d'Eve. Paris, 1874.

42587.46 Individual authors, etc. - 1850-1899 - Fiction - Peyrebrune; Piazzi; etc.
42587.46 Peyrebrune, G. de. Les frères Colombe. N.Y., 1888.
42587.46.2 Peyrebrune, G. de. Une séparation. Paris, 1884.
42587.46.7 Piazzi, Adriana. Un drame à Constantinople. Paris, 1879.

42587.47 - .48 Individual authors, etc. - 1850-1899 - Fiction - Plouvier, E.
42587.47 Plouvier, Édouard. Contes pour les jours de Pluie. Paris, 1853.
42587.48 Hericourt, Charles. Édouard Plouvier. Arras, 1879.

42587.49 Individual authors, etc. - 1850-1899 - Fiction - Poictevin; Pommerol; etc.
42587.49 Poictevin, Francis. Tout bas. Paris, 1893.
42587.49.19 Pommerol, Jean. Le cas du Lieutenant Sigmarie. Paris, n.d.
42587.49.20 Pommerol, Jean. Un fruit et puis un autre fruit. Paris, n.d.

42587.50 Individual authors, etc. - 1850-1899 - Fiction - Pressensé; Quellien, N.; Rambaud; Rattazzi; Rebell, H.; Renard, G.; etc.
42587.50 Pressensé, E.F.L. de P.G. de. Rosa, or The Parisian girl. N.Y., 1860.
42587.50.01 Pressensé, E.F.L. de P.G. de. Rosa. N.Y., 1869.
42587.50.1 Pressensé, E.F.L. de P.G. de. La maison blanche. 5. éd. Paris, 1870.

42587.50 Individual authors, etc. - 1850-1899 - Fiction - Pressensé; Quellien, N.; Rambaud; Rattazzi; Rebell, H.; Renard, G.; etc. - cont.
42587.50.1.5 Pressensé, E.F.L. de P.G. de. Sabine; Gertrude de Chanzane: deux nouvelles. Paris, 1872.
42587.50.10 Quellien, N. Contes et nouvelles du Pays-de-Tréguier. Paris, 1898.
42587.50.10.5 Quellien, N. Loin de Bretagne. Paris, 1886.
42587.50.15 Rambaud, Alfred. L'anneau de César. 7. éd. Paris, n.d. 2v.
42587.50.16 Rambaud, Alfred. L'anneau de César. pt.1. Paris, 18- .
42587.50.25 Rambaud, Alfred. L'empereur de Carthage. Paris, n.d.
42587.50.45 Rattazzi, Marie Bonaparte-Wyse. O reverso da medalha. Porto, 1880.
42587.50.50 Rattazzi, Marie Bonaparte-Wyse. Si j'étais reine. Paris, 1869.
42587.50.51 Rattazzi, Marie Bonaparte-Wyse. Louise de Kelner. Le dernier rêve d'une ambitieuse. 2. sér. Paris, 18- ?
42587.50.58 Monteiro Ramalho. As ratices da Rattazi; o pello nacional. Porto, 1880.
42587.50.58.10 Broglio, V. Cenni sulla vita e sugli scritti della principessa Maria Wyse-Solms-Bonaparte. Milano, 1857.
42587.50.60 Rebell, Hugues. Baisers d'ennemis. Paris, 1892.
42587.50.65 Rebell, Hugues. Les Méprisants. Paris, 1886.
42587.50.68 Rebell, Hugues. L'espionne impériale. Paris, 1899.
42587.50.70 Rebell, Hugues. La Nichina. Paris, 1897.
42587.50.75 Rebell, Hugues. La femme qui a connu l'Empereur. Paris, 1898.
42587.50.80 Rebell, Hugues. La camorra. Paris, 1900.
42587.50.85 Rebell, Hugues. Union des trois aristocraties. Paris, 1894.
42587.50.90 Rebell, Hugues. Gringalette. Paris, 1905.
42587.50.125 Brückmann, J. Hugues Rebell, ein Vorkämpfer des französischen Nationalismus. Inaug. Diss. Bonn, 1937.
42587.50.130 Auriant (pseud.). Exposition Hugues Rebell, 1867-1967. Nantes, 1967.
42587.50.1203 Renard, Georges. Un exilé. 3. éd. Paris, 1893.

42587.51 - .52 Individual authors, etc. - 1850-1899 - Fiction - Renard, J.
42587.51.5 Renard, Jules. Journal inédit, 1887-1910. Paris, 1925-1927. 5v.
42587.51.7 Renard, Jules. Debuts littéraires, 1883-1890. Paris, 1925.
42587.51.9 Renard, Jules. L'écornifleur suivi de la lanterne sourde. Paris, 1926.
42587.51.11 Renard, Jules. Les Clopartes. II. Chroniques, 1885-1893. Paris, 1926.
42587.51.13 Renard, Jules. Coquecigrues suivies de buceliques. Paris, 1926.
42587.51.15 Renard, Jules. Poil de Carotte, le roman et la pièce suivi des histoires naturelles. Paris, 1926.
42587.51.17 Renard, Jules. Ragotte, suivi de La maîtresse. Paris, 1926.
42587.51.19 Renard, Jules. Comédies. Paris, 1927. 2v.
42587.51.21 Renard, Jules. Le Vigneron dans sa vigne suivi de propos littéraires et mots d'écrit. Paris, 1927.
42587.51.23 Renard, Jules. Correspondance inédite. Paris, 1927. 2v.
42587.51.25 Renard, Jules. L'oeil Clair suivi de chroniques théâtrales et divers inédits. Paris, 1921.
42587.51.27 Renard, Jules. Nos frères farouches. 2. éd. Paris, 1921.
42587.51.30 Renard, Jules. Correspondance. Paris, 1953.
42587.51.32 Renard, Jules. Lettres inédites. 4. éd. Paris, 1957.
42587.51.35 Renard, Jules. Monsieur Vernet; comédie en deux actes. Paris, 1933.
42587.51.40 Renard, Jules. The sponger. London, 1957.
42587.51.45 Renard, Jules. Jules Renard par lui-même. Paris, 1956.
42587.51.50A Renard, Jules. Théatre complet. Paris, 1957.
42587.51.50B Renard, Jules. Théatre complet. Paris, 1957.
42587.51.50.2 Renard, Jules. Théatre complet. Paris, 1959.
42587.51.55 Renard, Jules. La maîtresse. Paris, 1896.
42587.51.60 Renard, Jules. Dans la vigne de Jules Renard. Paris, 1966.
42587.51.65 Renard, Jules. Oeuvres. Paris, 1970- 2v.
42587.52.2 Renard, Jules. Sourires pincés. Paris, 1892.
42587.52.5 Renard, Jules. Carrots. London, 1904.
42587.52.6 Renard, Jules. Carrots. London, 1904.
42587.52.8 Renard, Jules. Carrots. London, 1946.
42587.52.9 Renard, Jules. La lanterne sourde. Paris, 1906.
42587.52.15 Renard, Jules. L'écornifleur. Paris, 1904.
42587.52.19 Renard, Jules. Comédies. Paris, 1904.
Htn 42587.52.20* Renard, Jules. Histoires naturelles. Paris, n.d.
42587.52.23 Renard, Jules. Le plaisir de rompre. Paris, 1898.
42587.52.25 Renard, Jules. Journal. Paris, 1927. 4v.
42587.52.27 Renard, Jules. Journal, 1887-1910. Paris, 1960.
42587.52.28 Renard, Jules. Journal, 1887-1910. Paris, 1965.
42587.52.29 Renard, Jules. Journal. N.Y., 1964.
42587.52.32 Renard, Jules. La demande. Paris, 1896.
42587.52.35 Renard, Jules. Bucoliques. Paris, 1905.
42587.52.40 Renard, Jules. La Bigote. Paris, 1910.
42587.52.42 Renard, Jules. Une femme qui bégaie. Paris, 1872.
42587.52.70 Renard, Jules. Hunting with the Fox. Oxford, 1948.
42587.52.73 Guichard, Léon. L'interprétation graphique. Thèse. Paris, 1936.
42587.52.75 Guichard, Léon. L'interpretation graphique cinématographique et musicale des oeuvres de Jules Renard. Paris, 1936.
42587.52.79 Guichard, Léon. L'ouevre et l'ame de Jules Renard. Thèse. Paris, 1935.
42587.52.80 Guichard, Léon. L'oeuvre et l'ame de Jules Renard. Paris, 1935.
42587.52.85 Mardin, Pierre. La langue et le style de Jules Renard. Thèse. Paris, 1942.
42587.52.90 Knodel, A.J. Jules Renard as critic. Berkeley, 1951.
42587.52.95 Pollitzer, Marcel. Jules Renard. Paris, 1956.
42587.52.100 Kowzan, Tadeusz. Jules Renard i jego teatr. Wroclaw, 1966.

42587.53 Individual authors, etc. - 1850-1899 - Fiction - Regnier, M.S.
42587.53 Regnier, Marie S. Une aventure d'hier. Paris, 1885.

42587.55 Individual authors, etc. - 1850-1899 - Fiction - Rivière, H.; Rivoire, A.; etc.
42587.55.5 Rivière, Henri. La jeunesse d'un désespère. Paris, 1882.
42587.55.9 Rivoire, André. Berthe aux grands pieds. Paris, 1899.
42587.55.10 Rivoire, André. Le chemin de l'oubli. Paris, 1904.
42587.55.11 Rivoire, André. Le bon roi Dagobert. Paris, 1908.
42587.55.12 Rivoire, André. Roger Bontemps. Paris, 1920.

42587.55 Individual authors, etc. - 1850-1899 - Fiction - Rivière, H.; Rivoire, A.; etc. - cont.

42587.55.14 Rivoire, André. Juliette et Roméo. Paris, 1920.
42587.55.20 Rivoire, André. Le songe de l'amour. Paris, 1906.
42587.55.24 Rivoire, André. Le désir et l'amour. Paris, 1929.
42587.55.27 Rivoire, André. Fleurs de cendre. Paris, 1921.
42587.55.30 Rivoire, André. L'humble offrande. Paris, 1916.
42587.55.34 Rivoire, André. Oeuvres. Poèmes d'amour. Paris, 192-.
42587.55.39 Rivoire, André. La cousine Emile. Abbeville, 1924.
42587.55.42 Rivoire, André. Il était une bergère. Paris, 1905.
42587.55.45 Rivoire, André. La peur de souffrir. Paris, 1900.

42587.56 Individual authors, etc. - 1850-1899 - Fiction - Rochefort, H.; Rostaing; Saillens; etc.

42587.56 Rochefort, Henry. L'évadé. 2. éd. Paris, 1880.
42587.56.15 Rostaing, Jules. Petit-bonhomme vit encore. Paris, 1852.
42587.56.16 Rostaing, Jules. Voyage dans les deux Ameriques. Paris, 1854.
42587.56.100 Saint-Aulaire, Auguste. Gilda. Paris, 1892.
42587.56.105 Saint-Aulaire, Auguste. Un prosélyte de l'amour. Paris, 1908.
42587.56.602 Saillens, R. Récits et allégories. 2. éd. Neuchatel, 1896.

42587.57 Individual authors, etc. - 1850-1899 - Fiction - Schwob, M.

42587.57.4 Schwob, Marcel. Oeuvres. Paris, 1921. 2v.
42587.57.4.5 Schwob, Marcel. Oeuvres completes de Marcel Schwob. Paris, 1928.
42587.57.5 Schwob, Marcel. The children's crusade. Boston, 1898.
42587.57.6 Schwob, Marcel. Spicilège. 2. éd. Paris, 1896.
42587.57.7 Schwob, Marcel. Spicilège. Paris, 1896.
42587.57.8 Schwob, Marcel. Spicilège. Paris, 1960.
42587.57.30 Schwob, Marcel. La lampe de Psyché. 9. éd. Paris, 1925.
42587.57.34 Schwob, Marcel. Le livre de Monelle. Paris, 1894.
42587.57.35 Schwob, Marcel. Le livre de Monelle. Paris, 1923.
42587.57.38 Schwob, Marcel. Coeur double. Paris, 1925.
42587.57.75 Schwob, Marcel. Imaginary lives. N.Y., 1924.
42587.57.82 Champion, Pierre. Marcel Schwob. Paris, 1926.
42587.57.85 Trembley, George. Marcel Schwob, faussaire de la nature. Thèse. Genève, 1969.

42587.58 Individual authors, etc. - 1850-1899 - Fiction - Ségur, S.

42587.58 Ségur, Sophie. La soeur de Gribonille. Paris, 1880.
42587.58.5 Ségur, Sophie. Les petites filles modèles. Paris, 1875.
42587.58.6 Ségur, Sophie. Les vacances. Paris, 1869.
42587.58.6.2 Ségur, Sophie. Les vacances. Paris, 1964.
42587.58.7 Ségur, Sophie. Pauvre blaise. Paris, 1892.
42587.58.8.5 Ségur, Sophie. Les malheurs de Sophie. 14. éd. Paris, 1882.
42587.58.8.10 Ségur, Sophie. Les malheurs de Sophie. Paris, 1899.
42587.58.8.15 Ségur, Sophie. Les malheurs de Sophie. Paris, 1911.
42587.58.8.20 Ségur, Sophie. Les malheurs de Sophie. Paris, 1964.
42587.58.9 Ségur, Sophie. Le Général Dourakine. Paris, 1882.
42587.58.10 Ségur, Sophie. Comédies et proverbes. Paris, 1881.
42587.58.12 Ségur, Sophie. Un bon petit diable. Paris, 1888.
42587.58.13 Ségur, Sophie. Un bon petit diable. Paris, 1964.
42587.58.14 Ségur, Sophie. Fairy tales. Philadelphia, 1869.
42587.58.30 Ségur, Sophie. La fortune de Gaspard. Paris, 1964.
42587.58.35 Ségur, Sophie. Nouveaux contes de fées pour les petits enfants. Paris, 1964.
42587.58.40 Ségur, Sophie. L'auberge de l'ange-gardien. Paris, 1964.
42587.58.80 Hedouville, M. de. La comtesse de Ségur et les siens. Paris, 1953.
42587.58.85 Guérande, P. Le petit monde de la comtesse de Ségur. Paris, 1964.
42587.58.90 Gobillot, René. La comtesse de Ségur. Allençon, 1924.

42587.59 Individual authors, etc. - 1850-1899 - Fiction - Sainte-Croix; Soyez; Stapleaux

42587.59 Sainte-Croix, C. de. Contempler. Paris, 1887.
42587.59.8 Soyez-Le Roy, Lettice. Coeur fier. Lille, 1906.
42587.59.9 Soyez-Le Roy, Lettice. Infelice. Paris, 1903.
42587.59.10 Soyez-Le Roy, Lettice. Amour et vaillance. Lille, 1912.
42587.59.18.2 Stapleaux, Leopold. Un dernier amour. 2. éd. Paris, 1874.
42587.59.19 Stapleaux, Leopold. Les viveuses de Paris. Paris, 1880.
42587.59.20 Stapleaux, Leopold. Histoire d'une nuit. 4. éd. Paris, 1880.
42587.59.21 Stapleaux, Leopold. Histoire d'une nuit. Paris? 1873?

42587.60 Individual authors, etc. - 1850-1899 - Fiction - Sternon

42587.60 Sternon, P. Les moines et les sorcières d'Ancy. Nancy, 1886.

42587.61 Individual authors, etc. - 1850-1899 - Fiction - Summer

42587.61 Summer, Mary. La jeunesse de 1830. Paris, 1885.

42587.63 Individual authors, etc. - 1850-1899 - Fiction - Torquet; Toudouze; Testard; etc.

42587.63.50 Torquet, A. Au seuil de l'espoir. Paris, 1897.
42587.63.55 Torquet, A. Force ennemie. 7. éd. Paris, 1904.
42587.63.60 Torquet, A. Hiers bleus. Paris, 1904.
42587.63.65 Torquet, A. Poèmes triviaux et mystiques. Paris, 1924.
42587.63.100 Toudouze, Gustave. Madame Lambelle. N.Y., 1899.
42587.63.300 Testard, Maurice. Juliette à Sylvie. Paris, 1959.

42587.64 Individual authors, etc. - 1850-1899 - Fiction - Uzès, A.; Uzanne; etc.

42587.64.75 Uzès, A. de R. Souvenirs. Paris, 1939.
42587.64.3100 Uzanne, Octave. Contes de la vingtième année. Paris, 1896.

42587.65 Individual authors, etc. - 1850-1899 - Fiction - Vaugny; Vachette; etc.

42587.65 Vaugny, C. de. Ella Wilson-Parley Pratt-Kiana. Paris, 1878.
42587.65.5 Vachette, Eugène. Defunt Brichet. 2. éd. Paris, 1874. 2v.
42587.65.9 Vachette, Eugène. Lilie, Tutue, Bebeth. Paris, 1888.
42587.65.11 Vachette, Eugène. Les petites comédies du vice. Paris, 1879.
42587.65.12 Vachette, Eugène. Les petites comédies du vice. Paris, 1882.
42587.65.12.5 Vachette, Eugène. Les petites comédies du vice. Paris, 1919?
42587.65.13 Vachette, Eugène. Les petits drames de la vertu. Paris, 1919.
42587.65.15 Vachette, Eugène. Le rémouleur. Paris, 1874.

42587.66 Individual authors, etc. - 1850-1899 - Fiction - Valbezen; Vedel; Vigné; Villain; Verly; etc.

42587.66.7 Valbezen, E. de. La malle de l'Inde. Paris, 1861.
42587.66.9 Vedel, Emile. L'Ile d'Epouvante. Paris, 1904.
42587.66.15 Vien, Charles. Madame Frainex. Paris, 1868.
42587.66.19 Vigné d'Octon, P. Les angoisses du Docteur Combalas. Paris, 1893.
42587.66.23 Villain, Henri. Histoire d'un grain de sel. Paris, 1869.
42587.66.25 Villecrose, Julien. Les lamentations du peuple. Paris, 1898.
42587.66.50 Verly, Hippolyte. Les socialistes au pouvoir. Paris, 1897.

42587.67 Individual authors, etc. - 1850-1899 - Fiction - Villedeuil

42587.67 Villedeuil, Charles. Paris a l'envers. Paris, 1853.

42587.69 Individual authors, etc. - 1850-1899 - Fiction - Villemessant; Viollet; Wagner; Walras; etc.

42587.69 Villemessant, H. de. Les cancans, petit almanach de la chronique de Paris. Paris, 1852.
42587.69.2 Villemessant, H. de. Memoires d'un journaliste. Paris, 1878-1884. 6v.
42587.69.9 Viollet, Alphonse. La grande nuit. Paris, 1853.
42587.69.50 Wagner, Charles. Trois contes et deux histoires pour amuser les petits et faire penser les grands. Paris, 1916.
42587.69.70 Walras, Léon. Francis Sauveur. Paris, 1858.

42587.70 Individual authors, etc. - 1850-1899 - Fiction - Weill, A.

42587.70.3 Weill, Alexandre. Blasphèmes; poésies. Paris, 1878.
42587.70.4 Weill, Alexandre. Epitres cinglantes à M. Drumont. Paris, 1888.
42587.70.5 Weill, Alexandre. L'esprit de l'esprit. Paris, 1888.
42587.70.7 Weill, Alexandre. Epapée alsacienne. Paris, 1895.
42587.70.8 Weill, Alexandre. Histoires de village. Paris, 1860.
42587.70.9 Weill, Alexandre. Julie Verrier, une arrière-petite soeur de Jeanne d'Arc. Paris, 1890.
42587.70.12 Weill, Alexandre. Mes contemporains. Paris, 1890.
42587.70.14 Weill, Alexandre. Introduction à mes mémoires. Paris, 1890.
42587.70.16 Weill, Alexandre. Mes poésies d'amour de jeunesse. Paris, 1889.
42587.70.17 Weill, Alexandre. Dix fables oubliées de La Fontaine. Paris, 1892.'
42587.70.18 Weill, Alexandre. Le nouvel Isaïe. Paris, 1892.
42587.70.19 Weill, Alexandre. La nouvelle Phèdre. Paris, 1889.
42587.70.21 Weill, Alexandre. Paris mensonge. Paris, 1887-1888.
42587.70.23 Weill, Alexandre. Le parole nouvelle. 5. éd. Paris, 1892.
42587.70.26 Weill, Alexandre. Robbin et Nonne. Paris, 1895.
42587.70.31 Weill, Alexandre. Sittengemälde aus dem eisässischen Volksleben. 2. Aufl. Stuttgart, 1847.
42587.70.33 Weill, Alexandre. Couronne; histoire juive. Paris, 1857.
42587.70.50 Dreyfus, Robert. Alexandre Weill. Paris, 1908.

42587.71 - .74 Individual authors, etc. - 1850-1899 - Fiction - Witt, H.

42587.71 Witt, Henriette Guizot de. Marie Dierville. Philadelphia, 1873.
42587.72 Witt, Henriette Guizot de. Par monts et par vaux. Paris, 1882.
42587.73 Witt, Henriette Guizot de. Les bourgeois de Calais. Paris, 1890.
42587.73.5 Bouton, Victor. Lettre à Madame de Witt. Paris, 1885.
42587.74 Witt, Henriette Guizot de. Dames of high estate. N.Y., 1872.

42587.84 Individual authors, etc. - 1850-1899 - Fiction - Zaccone

42587.84.31 Zaccone, Pierre. Un duel à mort. Paris, 1883.
42587.84.36 Zaccone, Pierre. L'inconnu de Belleville. Paris, 1885.
42587.84.41 Zaccone, Pierre. La dame d'Auteuil. Paris, 1887.

42588 Individual authors, etc. - 1850-1899 - Fiction - Anonymous fiction

V42588.2 Cinquante et deux anecdotes sur la vie des animaux. Paris, 18- ?
42588.4 Dilettantes. Paris, 1894.
42588.6 Trois nouvelles. Philadelphia, 1862.
42588.8 Le roman de Violette. Lisbonne, 1870.
42588.9 Amours secrétes d'une fille de plaisirs. Genève, 1880.
42588.10 Isidore Baurel. Paris, 1884.
42588.12 Mémoires de Bilboquet recueillis par un bourgeois de Paris. Paris, 1854.

43500 Individual authors, etc. - 1900- - Bizot-Briant collection

V43500.1 Le beau navire; revue de la poesie. Paris. 1-9,1934-1939 9v.
V43500.3 Le bel espoir. Toulouse. 1-3 3v.
V43500.5 Dits et contre-dits d'un homme d'aujourd'hui. Bordeaux. 1-6,1932-1933 12v.
V43500.6 Les facettes; anthologie de la poesie contemporaine. Toulon. 7-17,1921-1928
V43500.6.2 Les facettes; anthologie de la poesie contemporaine. Paris. 1946
V43500.7 Aeschimann, Paul. Feux d'automne. Dizains précédés d'un Choix de poèmes, 1918-1944. Paris, 1946.
V43500.9 Albert-Birot, P. Poèmes à l'autre moi. Paris, 1954.
V43500.11 Allem, Maurice (pseud.). La poésie de l'amour; anthologie poetique du moyen âge à nos jours. Paris, 1932.
V43500.13 Arnold, Jacques. Sonate de la Marne. Paris, 1954.
V43500.15 Arrou, Pierre. Les logis de Leon Bloy. Paris, 1931.
V43500.17 Audiberti, Jacques. L'empire et la trappe; poems. Paris, 1930.
V43500.18 Bénal, Henri. Le chemin du mirage; poèmes. Bordeaux, 1925.
V43500.19 Bérimont, Luc. Malisette; roman. Paris, 1942.
V43500.21 Bérimont, Luc. Sur la terre, qui est au ciel. Preuilly-sur-Claise, 1947.
V43500.23 Bluteau, Jeanne. Chansons de la Baie d'Audierne. Paris, 1954.
V43500.25 Bollery, Joseph. Biblio-iconographie de Villiers de l'Isle-Adam. Paris, 1939.
V43500.27 Bollery, Joseph. Un grand ecrivain français mal connu: Léon Bloy. La Rochelle, 1934.
V43500.29 Bollery, Joseph. Un grand ecrivain français méconnu: Leon Bloy. La Rochelle, 1929.
V43500.31 Bolsée, Berthe. Rosée d'octobre. Dison, 1957.
V43500.33 Bouchaud, Pierre de. Les fêtes de la victoire; 14 juillet 1919. Nior, 1919.
V43500.35 Bouchor, Maurice. Confession de foi; poème. Paris, 1928.
V43500.37 Bouhier, Jean. Calcaire, 1942-1944. n.p., 1944?

43500 **Individual authors, etc. - 1900- - Bizot-Briant collection - cont.**

V43500.39	Bouhier, Jean. De mille endroits. Paris, 1952.
V43500.41	Bouhier, Jean. Dompter le fleuve. Niort, 1942.
V43500.43	Bouhier, Jean. Pour l'amour de Colette. Nantes, 1950.
V43500.45	Bourquin, Francis. Paysages du coeur. Bienne, 1956.
V43500.47	Boyé, Maurice Pierre. Chevreuse et ses environs. Paris, 1939.
V43500.49	Boyé, Maurice Pierre. Nuées; poèmes. Paris, 1938.
V43500.51	Briant, Theophile. Sabatrion. Paramé, 1938.
V43500.53	Carco, Francis. La légende et la vie d'Utrillo. Paris, 1928.
V43500.55	Cazin, Paul. L'hôtellerie du Bacchus sans tête. Paris, 1925.
V43500.57	Cazin, Paul. Lubies. Paris, 1927.
V43500.59	Chabaneix, Philippe. Au souvenir de Federico Garcia Lorca. n.p., 1941.
V43500.61	Chabaneix, Philippe. Comme des songes. Paris, 1928.
V43500.63	Chabaneix, Philippe. Le désir et les ombres. Paris, 1937.
V43500.65	Chabaneix, Philippe. D'un coeur sombre et secret; poèmes. Saint-Félicien-en-Vivarais, 1936.
V43500.67	Chabaneix, Philippe. Les nocturnes. Lyon, 1950.
V43500.71	Coppieters de Gibson, Henri. Les mains de Pygmalion. Bruxelles, 1959.
V43500.77	Cussat Blanc, Jean. Offert aux hommes. Blainville-sur-Mer, n.d.
V43500.81	Delétang-Tardif, Yanette. L'éclair et le temps. Limoges, 1951?
V43500.83	Delétang-Tardif, Yanette. Edellina, ou Les pouvoirs de la musique. Niort, 1943.
V43500.85	Eon, Francis. Suite à Perséphone. Paris, 1933.
V43500.87	Estang, Luc. Au delà de moi-même. Paris, 1938.
V43500.89	Faillet, Georges. Vers et prose. Blainville-sur-Mer, 1946.
V43500.91	Fargue, Leon Paul. Le piéton de Paris. Paris, 1939.
V43500.93	Féret, Charles Theophile. Poèmes normands. Saint-Vaast-la-Houge, 1947.
V43500.95	Flers, Robert de. Discours de reception à l'Academie française le 16 juin 1921. Paris, 1921.
V43500.97	Flers, Robert de. Le roi. L'ange du foyer. Paris, 1924?
V43500.99	Fombeure, Maurice. Chansons de la grande hune. Paris, 1942.
V43500.101	Fombeure, Maurice. D'amour et d'aventure. Paris, 1942.
V43500.103	Forges, Lucien. Limbes; poesies; suivies de poèmes en prose. Paris, 1924.
V43500.105	Forot, Charles. Charmes des jours; poèmes. Saint-Félicien-en-Vivarais, 1934.
V43500.107	Forot, Charles. Dix sonnets. Paris, 1945.
V43500.109	Forot, Charles. Epigrammes; quatrains, 1920-1930. Valence-sur-Rhône, 1937.
V43500.111	Fort, Paul. Ballades françaises. v. 9-13. Paris, 1946-1949. 5v.
V43500.113	Fort, Paul. Livre d'espérance. Paris, n.d.
V43500.115	Fourcade, Claude. De flamme et d'ombre. Paris, 1936.
V43500.117	Fourcade, Claude. Du côté de l'aurore. Paris, 1952.
V43500.119	Fourcade, Claude. Les fugitives. Paris, 1929.
V43500.121	Fourcade, Claude. Magie de septembre. Paris, 1951.
V43500.123	Frenaud, André. Les rois-mages; poèmes. Villeneuve-les-Avignon, 1943.
V43500.125	Fuster, Charles. Guerre, deuil, France. Strasbourg, n.d.
V43500.127	Gali, Christian. Hectares de Paris. Paris, 1955.
V43500.129	Garnier, Georges Louis. Le songe dépouillé. Paris, 1931.
V43500.131	Guégan, Jane. Trace invisible de tes pas. Ixelles, 1960.
V43500.133	Hommage à Max Jacob, avec des inedits de Max Jacob, et la collaboration de Jean Cassou. Bordeaux, 1951.
V43500.135	Houdelot, Robert. Sept poèmes de guerre. Paris, 1945.
V43500.137	Houdelot, Robert. Le temps perdu. Paris, 1937.
V43500.139	Joseph, Roger. Chants alternés pour deux déesses; poèmes. Orléans, 1954.
V43500.141	Julien. De la même forme que l'eau. Paris, 1954.
V43500.143	Klingsor, Tristan (pseud.). Florilège poétique. Blainville-sur-Mer, 1955.
V43500.145	Klingsor, Tristan (pseud.). Second florilège. Blainville-sur-Mer, 1964.
V43500.147	Labour, Magdeleine. Sabliers; poèmes. Nantes, 1960.
V43500.149	La Croix, Robert de. Migrations; poèmes. Nantes, 1948.
V43500.151	Lamireau, Gilbert. La clef de voûte. Paris, 1952.
V43500.153	Lamireau, Gilbert. Traduit du sang. Limoges, 1951?
V43500.155	La Tour du Pin, Patrice de. L'enfer; poème avec la fac-similé d'un feuillet manuscrit. Tunis, 1935.
V43500.157	Lavaud, Guy. Marseillaise reviens! 25 juin 1940 - 25 août 1944. Paris, 1945.
V43500.159	Lebesgue, Philéas. Florilège de poésie rustique. Blainville-sur-Mer, 1943?
V43500.161	Lebois, André. Partage des eaux. Fougères, 1945.
V43500.163	Lebrau, Jean. Alphabet du bestiaire. Preuilly-sur-Claise, 1941.
V43500.167	Lebrau, Jean. Le ciel sur la garrigue. Paris, 1924.
V43500.169	Lebrau, Jean. Couleur de cèpe et de colchique. Bruxelles, 1954.
V43500.171	Le Cunff, Louis. Aux cent routes du Ponant. Paris, 1950.
V43500.173	Le Cunff, Louis. La ville exsangue. Paramé, 1948.
V43500.175	Le Dantec, Yves Gérard. L'Eden futur. Paris, 1950.
V43500.179	Lefèvre, Raymonde. Poèmes pour une ombre. Paris? 1953.
V43500.181	Lepaul, Jacquelyne. Le rhume des foins; poèmes. Paris, 1957.
V43500.183	Le Rossignol, Edouard. Contes normandes et gaulois. Saint-Vaast-la-Hougue, 1948.
V43500.185	Le Sidaner, Louis. La condition de l'écrivain; essai. Paris, 1937.
V43500.187	Magallon, Xavier de. L'ombre. Paris, 1921.
V43500.189	Manoll, Michel. Louisfert-en-poesie. Vitry-sur-Seine, 1952.
V43500.191	Marca, René. Capitales. Paris, 1935.
V43500.193	Martinet, Marcel. Florilège poétique. Blainville-sur-Mer, 1946.
V43500.195	Menanteau, Pierre. Le cheval de l'aube. Paris, 1952.
V43500.197	Messiaen, Alain. Bestiaire mystique. Preuilly-sur-Claise, 1948.
V43500.199	Messiaen, Alain. C'était toi, le démon! Paris, 1936.
V43500.201	Messiaen, Alain. Le miroir vivant; proses. Paris, 1937.
V43500.203	Messiaen, Alian. Orages; poèmes romantiques. Paris, 1937.
V43500.205	Messiaen, Alain. Les rues s'allongent comme des plaintes. Paris, 1935.
V43500.207	Monod, François. Exercices preliminaires. Lyon, 1954.
V43500.209	Muselli, Vincent. Léon Bloy, ou Celui qui exagère. La Rochelle, 1931.
V43500.211	Nollet, Genevieve. Discontinu. Dinard, 1939.
V43500.213	Norge, Géo. Joie aux âmes. Bruxelles, 1941.

43500 **Individual authors, etc. - 1900- - Bizot-Briant collection - cont.**

V43500.215	Olivier, Pascale. Le chant perdu dans le silence. Abbeville, 1937.
V43500.217	Olivier, Pascale. Proses. Frontispice et bandeau de Charles Bernard. Albi, 1946.
V43500.219	Ormoy, Marcel. Le bonheur est dans une île. Lille? 1929.
V43500.221	Ormoy, Marcel. Carrefours. Paris, 1927.
V43500.223	Ormoy, Marcel. Elegies secrètes et marines. Sainte Marguerite de la Mer, 1929.
V43500.225	Ormoy, Marcel. Mon plus tendre climat. Lourmarin de Provence, 1930.
V43500.227	Ormoy, Marcel. Poèmes pour des fantômes. Saint-Félicien-en-Vivarais, 1928.
V43500.229	Ormoy, Marcel. Le visage retrouvé. Paris, 1927.
V43500.231	Parrot, Louis. Cornemuse de l'orage; poèmes. Tours, 1927.
V43500.233	Parrot, Louis. Misery farm, poèmes. n.p., 1934.
V43500.235	Paysan, Catherine. Écrit pour l'âme des cavaliers. Paris, 1956.
V43500.237	Pédoja, Marcel. Flamme rouge. Blainville-sur-Mer, 1951.
V43500.239	Peyre, Sully-André. Escriveto e la roso. Aigues-Vives, 1962.
V43500.241	Peyre, Sully-André. Le grand-père que j'ai en songe. Genève, 1946.
V43500.243	Pic, Marcel. A la merci du feu. Paris, 1957.
V43500.245	Picabia, Francis. Pensées sans langage; poème. 4. ed. Paris, 1919.
V43500.247	Prévost, Ernest. Le livre de l'immortelle amie. Paris, 1924.
V43500.249	Privat, Bernard. Au pied du mur, récit. Paris, 1959.
V43500.251	Renard, Jean Claude. Juan. Toulouse, 1945.
V43500.253	Rieder, Violette. Ex-voto. Rodez? 1953.
V43500.255	Rieder, Violette. Limonaire; douze airs pour orgue de barbarie. Saint-Félicien, 1954.
V43500.257	Rolland de Renéville, André. La nuit, l'esprit. Paris, 1946.
V43500.259	Rousselot, Jean. Deux poèmes. Bruxelles, 1950.
V43500.261	Rousselot, Jean. Homme, c'est ta grandeur. n.p., 1953.
V43500.263	Rousselot, Jean. L'homme en proie. Paris, 1949.
V43500.265	Rousselot, Jean. La mansarde; poèmes en prose. Millau? 1946.
V43500.267	Rousselot, Jean. Les moyens d'existence; poèmes. Limoges, 1950.
V43500.269	Rousselot, Jean. Odes à quelques-uns: Supervielle, Van Gogh, Eluard, Max Jacob, Modigliani, Apollinaire, Holderlin, Voronca, Lorca. Paris, 1948.
V43500.271	Rousselot, Jean. Le pain se fait la nuit. Oran, 1954.
V43500.273	Rousselot, Jean. Refaire la nuit; poèmes. Niort, 1943.
V43500.275	Royère, Jean. La poésie de Mallarmé. Paris, 1919?
V43500.277	Ruet, Noël. L'anneau de feu. Mézières, 1934.
V43500.279	Ruet, Noël. L'Escarpolette fleurie; poèmes. Bruxelles, 1925.
V43500.281	Ruet, Noël. Musique de chambre. Sainte Marguerite de la Mer, 1930.
V43500.283	Ruet, Noël. L'ombre et le soleil. Bruxelles, 1923.
V43500.285	Ruet, Noël. L'urne penchée. 2. ed. Seraing, n.d.
V43500.287	Saint-Clair, Georges. L'absence et les miroirs; poèmes. Paris, 1957.
V43500.289	Salonne, Marie Paule. L'ossuaire charnel. Saint-Brieuc, 1935.
V43500.291	Samain, Albert. Poèmes pour la grande amie. 10. ed. Paris, 1943.
V43500.293	Sandelion, Jeanne. D'un amour tué. Paramé, 1939.
V43500.295	Sandelion, Jeanne. D'un amour vivant. Paramé, 1939.
V43500.297	Schaettel, Marcel. Pierres de lune. Bourges, 1956.
V43500.299	Sentenac, Paul. Gaspard Maillol. Paris, 1932?
V43500.301	Thomas, Charles. Sixième heure; un cri dans le désert. Mouscron, 1958.
V43500.303	Thomé, Jules René. Images. Paramé, 1939.
V43500.305	Thomé, Jules René. Le poème de la Meuse. Charleville, 1949.
V43500.307	Thomin, René. Les chrysalides. Paris, 1959.
V43500.309	Tortel, Jean. Jalons; esthétique. Paris, 1934.
V43500.311	Trente poèmes de Philippe Chabaneix. Paris, 1935.
V43500.313	Trolliet, Gilbert. La colline. Paris, 1955.
V43500.315	Trolliet, Gilbert. L'inespéré. Genève, 1949.
V43500.317	Vérane, Léon. Bars; poèmes. Toulon, 19- ?
V43500.319	Vérane, Léon. Les étoiles noires; poèmes. Toulon, 19- ?
V43500.321	Vérane, Léon. La fête s'loigne. Paris, 1945.
V43500.323	Voisard, Alexandre. Écrit sur un mur. Porrentruy, 1954.

43511 - 43873 Individual authors, etc. - 1900- - Known authors (363 scheme plus 10)

43511.67.100	About, Pierre Edmond. L'ombre verte. N.Y., 1947.
43511.76.100	Abril, M. L'homme abandonné. v. 1-2. Paris, 1938.
43512.2	Abadie, C.A. La nouveaux riches. Paris, 1921.
43512.12.100	Abellio, R. Les yeux d'Ezéchiel sont ouverts. 12. ed. Paris, 1950.
43512.12.800	Brosses, Marie Thérèse de. Entretiens avec Raymond Abellio. Paris, 1966.
43512.13.100	Abirachid, R. L'Emerveillié. Paris, 1963.
43512.23.100	Wielander, Angelus. Ein Tiroler Christenspiegel des 14. Affaltern am Albis, 1959.
43512.41.100	Abirached, Noukad. L'eclaircie; roman. Beyrouth, 1965.
43512.74.100	Abrassart, Lucy. La quête de lumière. Malines en Belgique, 1954.
43512.75.100	Achard, Marcel. Voulez-vous jouer avec moâ? Trois actes. 4. ed. Paris, 1924.
43512.75.110	Achard, Marcel. Je ne vous aime pas. 4. ed. Paris, 1926.
43512.75.120	Achard, Marcel. Jean de la hune. Paris, 1929.
43512.75.130	Achard, Marcel. La belle marineere. Paris, 1930.
43512.75.140	Achard, Marcel. Domino; comedie en trois actes. Paris, 1932.
43512.75.150	Achard, Marcel. La femme en blanc. Paris, 1933.
43512.75.160	Achard, Marcel. Petrus. Paris, 1934.
43512.75.170	Achard, Marcel. Noix de coco. Paris, 1936.
43512.75.180	Achard, Marcel. "Le corsaire". Paris, 1938.
43512.75.195	Achard, Marcel. Histoires d'amour. 2. ed. Paris, 1949.
43512.75.200	Achard, Marcel. Le moulin de la galette. Paris, 1952.
43512.75.210	Achard, Marcel. Le mal d'amour. Paris, 1956.
43512.75.220	Achard, Marcel. Potate. Paris, 1957.
43512.75.230	Achard, Marcel. L'amour est difficile. Paris, 1960.
43512.75.240	Achard, Marcel. L'amour ne paie pas. Paris, 1962.
43512.75.250	Achard, Marcel. Gugusse. Paris, 1968.
43513.1.30F	Acker, Paul. La victoire. pt.1-3. Paris, 1913. 3 pam.
43513.1.31	Acker, Paul. Les Demoiselles Bertram. Paris, 1914.
43513.1.32	Acker, Paul. L'oislau vainquer; roman. Paris, 1917.
43513.1.35	Acker, Paul. Les exilés. Paris, 192-.
43513.1.37	Acker, Paul. Dispensé de l'article 23. Paris, 1898.

43511 - 43873 Individual authors, etc. - 1900- - Known authors (363 scheme plus 10) - cont.

43513.75.100	Acremant, Germaine (Paulain). La hutte d'acajou. Paris, 1924.
43513.75.114	Acremant, Germaine (Paulain). Ces dames aux chapeaux verts. Paris, 1939.
43513.75.120	Acremant, Germaine (Paulain). La route mouvante. Paris, 1939.
43513.75.130	Acremant, Germaine (Paulain). Chapeaux gris, chapeaux verts; roman. Paris, 1970.
43514.3.100	Adam, George. A l'appel de la liberté. Paris, 1945.
43514.4.100	Adam, Juliette. L'auteur à son heroine. n.p., n.d.
43514.4.110	Adam, Juliette. Les olivieres triampheront; roman. Paris, 1927.
43514.5.100	Adam, Juliette. La chanson des nouveaux épout. Paris, 1923.
43514.6.100	Adamov, Arthur. La parodie. Paris, 1950.
43514.6.110	Adamov, Arthur. Théâtre. v.1, 4. éd.; v.2, 3. éd. Paris, 1955. 4v.
43514.6.120	Adamov, Arthur. Paolo Paoli. 3. éd. Paris, 1957.
43514.6.130	Adamov, Arthur. Les âmes mortes. Paris, 1960.
43514.6.140	Adamov, Arthur. Le printemps II. Paris, 1961.
43514.6.150	Adamov, Arthur. Ici et maintenant. Paris, 1964.
43514.6.160	Adamov, Arthur. Off limits. Play in French. Paris, 1969.
43514.6.170	Adamov, Arthur. Si l'été revenait. Paris, 1970.
43514.6.700	Adamov, Arthur. Two plays. London, 1962.
43514.6.800	Gaudy, René. Arthur Adamov. Paris, 1971.
43514.23.100	Adenis, Henri. Les viviers du cri. Paris, 1956.
43514.24.100	Ades, Michèle. J'ai vecu là-bas. Paris, 1961.
43514.24.1100	Adès, Albert. Le livre de Goha le simple. Paris, 1919.
43514.24.2100	Aderca Bouton, Juliette. Ce rire a traversé le bois. Malines, 1955.
43514.25.110	Aderer, A. Comme ils sont tous. Paris, 1910.
43514.25.210	Aderer, A. l'inévitable amour. Paris, 1904.
43514.32.100	Aegerter, E. Poèmes d'Europe. Paris, 1929.
43514.41.100	Adine, France. La cité sur l'Arno. Bruxelles, 1931.
43515.79.100	Aeschimann, Paul. La terre et l'ange; poèmes. Paris, 1945.
43517.1.30	Aguétant, P. La vieille terre. Belley, 1911.
43517.2.100	Agadjanian, G. La vallee des ombres. N.Y., 1946.
43517.2.110	Agadjanian, G. Le froid de l'enfer. Paris, 1960.
43517.3.35	Aguilar, Paul Jean. Poèmes simples. Paris, 1956.
43517.23.100	Agenor, Guy. Rubis, saphirs et topazes, poésies. Paris, 1966.
43518.56.100	Armont, Paul. L'amoureuse aventure. Paris, 1929.
43519.11.100	Aicard, Jean. La poesie. Paris, 1909.
43519.53.100	Aima, Aymé. Thérèse Violette, roman. Besançon, 1969.
43520.54.695	Aimery de Pierrebourg, M.J.G. Cleopatra. Garden City, 1924.
43520.54.700	Aimery de Pierrebourg, M.J.G. Cleopatra. Garden City, 1926.
43520.54.704	Aimery de Pierrebourg, M.J.G. The life and death of Cleopatra. 1st ed. Garden City, 1924.
43520.54.1100	Aimé, Henri. Le bandeau sur le front. Paris, 1917.
43522.4.100	Alanic, Mathilde. En treinte du passe. Paris, 1926.
43522.4.110	Alanic, Mathilde. Bal blanc. Paris, 1910.
43522.6.100	Alba, Joseph. Ce chant qui nous entoure. Paris, 1964.
43522.7.100	Aberny, Jean. Poemás honnis. 1. ed. Cannes, 1957.
43522.7.1100	Alberti, Henri. Les racines tordues. Paris, 1959.
43522.7.2021	Albert-Birot, Pierre. Poésie, 1916-1924. Paris, 1967.
43522.7.2100	Albert-Birot, Pierre. Giabinoulor, épopée. Paris, 1964.
43522.7.2800	Pons, Max. Connaissance de Pierre Albert-Birot, témoignages, hommages, études, notes. Saint-Fronf-sur-Lémance, 1968.
43522.8.100	Albitre, Gilbert. L'ennui d'aimer; roman. Paris, 1959.
43522.15.100	Alcune, Roger. Lilial; ou, L'amandier, poésies. Paris, 1959.
43522.17.100	Aldelbert, M. Les iles désertes. Paris, 1957.
43522.25.100	Alexandre, Maxime. Echoes intimes; poèmes. Paris, 1946.
43522.25.110	Alexandre, Maxime. Mémoires d'un surréaliste. Paris, 1968.
43522.25.1102	Alexis, Jacques Stephen. Les arbres musiciens. 2. ed. Paris, 1957.
43522.25.1110	Alexis, Jacques Stephen. Romancero aux etoiles. Paris, 1960.
43522.25.1120	Alexis, Jacques Stephen. L'espace d'un cillement; roman. Paris, 1959.
43522.25.2100	Alexandnan, Lucien. L'homme des lointains. Paris, 1960.
43522.25.3700	Alexandre, Philippe. The president is dead. London, 1967.
43522.25.4100	Alexandre, Marcel. Souvenirs du passé d'un enfant du Havre, de 1862 à 1960. Paris, 1967.
43522.31.100	Algan, Lauzence. Rue de la Roquette. Paris, 1938.
43522.36.100	Alhau, Max. Atteinte du songe. Goudargues, 1965.
43522.41.100	Alibert, François Paul. Les plus beaux poèmes. Carcassonne, 1929.
43522.41.110	Alibert, François Paul. Le devil des muses. Carcassonne, 1921.
43522.41.120	Alibert, François Paul. Odes. Paris, 1922.
43522.41.130	Alibert, François Paul. Eglogues. Paris, 1923.
43522.41.140	Alibert, François Paul. Le cantique sur la calline. Paris, 1924.
43522.41.150	Alibert, François Paul. La guirlande lyrique. Paris, 1925.
43522.41.160	Alibert, François Paul. La prairie aux narcisses. Marseille, 1927.
43522.41.170	Alibert, François Paul. Le chemin sur la mer. Paris, 1926.
43522.41.180	Alibert, François Paul. Le plainte de Calypas. Paris, 1931.
43522.41.190	Alibert, François Paul. Epigrammes. Paris, 1932.
43522.41.200	Alibert, François Paul. L'arbue qui saigne. Carcassonne, 1907.
43522.41.210	Alibert, François Paul. Elégies romaines. Paris, 1923.
43522.41.220	Alibert, François Paul. Le buisson ardent. Paris, 1912.
43522.47.100	Allard L'Olivier, Audal. Les luminaires. Monte Carlo, 1956.
43522.48.100	Allard, Roger. Poésies légéres, 1911-1927. 2. ed. Paris, 1929.
43522.48.110	Allard, Roger. La divine aventure. Lille, 1905.
43522.48.1100	Allain-Cornic, Pierre. Fugues. Paris, 1954.
43522.49.100	Alleman, Jeanne. L'áréne brûlante. Paris, 1929.
43522.49.110	Alleman, Jeanne. Le goéland. 14. ed. Paris, 1926.
43522.50.100	Allen, Suzanne. L'êle du dedans. Paris, 1960.
43522.51.100	Alloo, Gustave. A poignardé ma vie. Malines, 1954.
43522.90.100	Alvés, Michel. Entre les barricades. Paris, 1962.
43522.90.110	Alvés, Michel. Le pêcheur. Paris, 1962.
43522.98.100A	Alyn, Marc. Le temps des autres. Paris, 1957.
43522.98.100B	Alyn, Marc. Le temps des autres. Paris, 1957.

43511 - 43873 Individual authors, etc. - 1900- - Known authors (363 scheme plus 10) - cont.

43522.98.110	Alyn, Marc. Cruels divertissements. Paris, 1957.
43522.98.120	Alyn, Marc. Délébiles. Neuchâtel, 1962.
43522.98.130	Alyn, Marc. Nuit majeure. Paris, 1968.
43522.98.1100	Alzin, Josse. Ce rein miraculeux. Malines, 1955.
43522.98.2100	Alzon, Claude. Le Pionicat. Ol Marlieux, 1970.
43523.4.100	Amar, Gaston. Deux ans sur les mines. Paris, 1957.
43523.4.3100	Amariu, Constantin. Le pauvre d'esprit, roman. Paris, 1958.
43523.5.100	Amat, J.C. Malespine. pt. 1-2. Paris, 1937.
43523.5.105	Amat, J.C. Malespine; roman. Montréal, 1945.
43523.5.2100	Amat, Robert. L'orgue solaire. Paris, 1958.
43523.5.2110	Amat, Robert. L'horizan s'affirme. Paris, 1958.
43523.6.100	Amavis. L'éternel Paris. Paris, 1957.
43523.21.100	Amédée, Louis. Journal d'un jeune homme triste, ou l'Espoir retrauvé; roman. Paris, 1970.
43523.29.100	Amfreville, Henri d'. Fragments solaires. Neuchâtel, 1963.
43523.41.100	Amiel, Denys. La souriante Madame Beudet. Paris, 1921.
43523.41.103	Amiel, Denys. La souriante Madame Beudet. Paris, 1922.
43523.41.110	Amiel, Denys. Le voyageur. Paris, 1923.
43523.41.120	Amiel, Denys. Décalage. Paris, 1931.
43523.41.130	Amiel, Denys. L'âge du fer. Paris, 1932.
43523.41.140	Amiel, Denys. Trois et une. Paris, 1933.
43523.41.150	Amiel, Denys. La femme en fleur. Paris, 1936.
43523.41.160	Amiel, Denys. Ma liberte! Paris, 1937.
43523.41.180	Amiel, Denys. La carcasse. Paris, 1926.
43523.41.181	Amiel, Denys. Théâtre: Le voyageur. v.1. Paris, 1925.
43523.41.182	Amiel, Denys. Théâtre: L'engrenage. v. 2. Paris, 1928.
43523.41.183	Amiel, Denys. Théâtre: L'image. v. 3. Paris, 1930.
43523.41.184	Amiel, Denys. Théâtre: L'age du fer. v. 4. Paris, 1933.
43523.41.185	Amiel, Denys. Théâtre: Trois et une. v. 5. Paris, 1935.
43523.41.200	Amiel, Denys. Famille. Paris, 1938.
43523.41.210	Amiel, Denys. La maison monestier. Paris, 1939.
43523.41.775	Amiel, Denys. La sorridente signora Beudet. Milano, 1922.
43523.41.2100	Amila, John. Le 9 de pique. Paris, 1956.
43523.66.100	Amoroso, Henri. Les sept péchés capitaux vus par un psychiatre. Paris, 1965.
43523.67.100	Amouroux, Henri. Le Ghetto de la victoire. Paris, 1969.
43524.1	Anthelme, P. L'honneur japonais. Paris, 1912.
43524.3.100	Analis. Le prince des lys. Paris, 1958.
43524.15.100	Andard, Louis. En roulotte a travers l'inde catholique. Paris, 1924.
43524.18.100	Andreau, Marianne. Le pilote aux yeux tristes. n.p., n.d.
43524.18.110	Andreau, Marianne. Carillon du temps perdu. Paris, 1968.
43524.19.100	André, Louis. La mysterieuse Baronne de Feuchères. Paris, 1925.
43524.19.110	André, Paul. Aurore et crepuscule. Paris, 1928.
43524.19.1100	Andrieu, Jean Marie. Rien qu'un prêtre. Bruxelles, 1968.
43524.19.2100	Andry, Marc. A quoi ça rime? Paris, 1963.
43524.19.3100	André, Estelle. Herbier sentimental. Milano, 1962.
43524.20.100	André, Alix. Ordre du prince. Paris, 1954.
43524.21.100	Andro, J.C. Les vacances interdites. Paris, 1959.
43524.22.100	André-May, Pierre. Le matin. Paris, 1945.
43524.22.2100	André, Robert. Un combat opiniâtre. Paris, 1960.
43524.22.2110	André, Robert. L'amour et la vie d'une femme. Paris, 1969.
43524.22.3100	Andries, A. De ci, de là et d'ailleurs. Bruxelles, 1960.
43524.33.100	Anglade, Jean. Des chiens vivants. Paris, 1967.
43524.33.110	Anglade, Jean. Le point de suspension. Paris, 1969.
43524.33.120	Anglade, Jean. Un front de marbre; roman. Paris, 1971.
43524.34.100	Angot, E. Dames du grand siècle. Paris, 1919.
43524.36.100	Angreville, M. d'. Les lilas refleuriront. N.Y., 1944.
43524.67.22	Anouilh, Jean. Nouvelles pièces noires. Paris, 1946.
43524.67.23	Anouilh, Jean. Nouvelles pièces noires. Paris, 1961.
43524.67.26	Anouilh, Jean. Nouvelles pièces grinçantes. Paris, 1970.
43524.67.100	Anouilh, Jean. Y'avait un prisonnier. Paris, 1935.
43524.67.105	Anouilh, Jean. Ardèle. Paris, 1949.
43524.67.110	Anouilh, Jean. Le voyageur sans bagage. Paris, 1937.
43524.67.115	Anouilh, Jean. La valse des toréadors. Paris, 1952.
43524.67.118A	Anouilh, Jean. L'alouette. Paris, 1953.
43524.67.118B	Anouilh, Jean. L'alouette. Paris, 1953.
43524.67.120	Anouilh, Jean. Pièces roses. 29. éd. Paris, 1945.
43524.67.122	Anouilh, Jean. Pièces roses. Paris, 1958.
43524.67.123	Anouilh, Jean. Pièces roses. Paris, 1961.
43524.67.125	Anouilh, Jean. L'hurluberlu, ou Le reactionnaire amoureux. Paris, 1959.
43524.67.130A	Anouilh, Jean. Pièces noires. 36. éd. Paris, 1945.
43524.67.130B	Anouilh, Jean. Pièces noires. Paris, 1945.
43524.67.133	Anouilh, Jean. Pièces noires. Paris, 1963.
43524.67.140	Anouilh, Jean. Le bal des voleurs. Grenoble, 1945.
43524.67.142	Anouilh, Jean. Le bal des voleurs. Paris, 1954.
43524.67.152	Anouilh, Jean. Antigone. Paris, 1954.
43524.67.155	Anouilh, Jean. Antigone. Paris, 1957.
43524.67.160	Anouilh, Jean. La répétition; ou, L'amour puni. Genève, 1950.
43524.67.161	Anouilh, Jean. La répétition; ou, L'amour puni. Paris, 1970.
43524.67.170	Anouilh, Jean. Medée. Paris, 1953.
43524.67.180	Anouilh, Jean. Cécile, ou L'école des pères. Paris, 1954.
43524.67.190	Anouilh, Jean. Ornifle. Paris, 1956.
43524.67.203	Anouilh, Jean. Pièces grinçantes. Paris, 1961.
43524.67.210	Anouilh, Jean. Pièces brillantes. Paris, 1956.
43524.67.213	Anouilh, Jean. Pièces brillantes. Paris, 1962.
43524.67.220	Anouilh, Jean. Pauvres Bitos. Paris, 1958.
43524.67.230	Anouilh, Jean. Becket, ou L'honneur de Dieu. Paris, 1960.
43524.67.235	Anouilh, Jean. Becket; or, The honor of God. N.Y., 1960.
43524.67.240	Anouilh, Jean. Pièces costumées. Paris, 1960.
43524.67.243	Anouilh, Jean. Pièces costumées. Paris, 1962.
43524.67.250	Anouilh, Jean. Léocadia. London, 1961.
43524.67.255	Anouilh, Jean. La grotte. Paris, 1961.
43524.67.260	Anouilh, Jean. Les rendez-vous de Senlis. Paris, 1962.
43524.67.270	Anouilh, Jean. La foire d'empoigne. Paris, 1962.
43524.67.280	Anouilh, Jean. L'invitation au château. Paris, 1951.
43524.67.290	Anouilh, Jean. Tables. Paris, 1962.
43524.67.300	Anouilh, Jean. Deux pièces roses. Paris, 1963.
43524.67.310	Anouilh, Jean. Eurydice, avec une notice...une analyse méthodique des textes choisis. Paris, 1968.
43524.67.320	Anouilh, Jean. Cher Antoine; ou L'amour roté. Paris, 1969.
43524.67.330	Anouilh, Jean. Les poissons rouges; ou, Mon père, a héros. Paris, 1970.
43524.67.340	Anouilh, Jean. Ne réveillez pas madame. Paris, 1970.
43524.67.611	Anouilh, Jean. The collected plays. London, 1966- 2v.
43524.67.690	Anouilh, Jean. The lark. N.Y., 1956.
43524.67.700	Anouilh, Jean. Antigone. N.Y., 1946.
43524.67.710	Anouilh, Jean. Ring-round the moon. London, 1950.

43511 - 43873 Individual authors, etc. - 1900- - Known authors (363 scheme plus 10) - cont.

43524.67.720 Anouilh, Jean. Ardèle. London, 1951.
43524.67.730 Anouilh, Jean. Antigone and Eurydice. London, 1951.
43524.67.740 Anouilh, Jean. Legend of lovers. N.Y., 1952.
43524.67.750 Anouilh, Jean. Colombe. London, 1952.
43524.67.755 Anouilh, Jean. Ornifle. 1st ed. N.Y., 1970.
43524.67.760 Anouilh, Jean. Thieves carnival. London, 1952.
43524.67.765 Anouilh, Jean. The rehearsal. N.Y., 1962.
43524.67.770A Anouilh, Jean. Mademoiselle Colombe. N.Y., 1954.
43524.67.770B Anouilh, Jean. Mademoiselle Colombe. N.Y., 1954.
43524.67.775 Anouilh, Jean. The fighting cock. N.Y., 1960.
43524.67.776 Anouilh, Jean. The fighting cock. London, 1967.
43524.67.780 Anouilh, Jean. Pièces brillantes. Paris, 1953.
43524.67.785 Anouilh, Jean. Time remembered. 1st American ed. N.Y., 1958.
43524.67.790 Anouilh, Jean. The lark. N.Y., 1956.
43524.67.792 Anouilh, Jean. Traveller without luggage. London, 1959.
43524.67.795 Anouilh, Jean. The waltz of the toreadors. 1st American ed. N.Y., 1957.
43524.67.796 Anouilh, Jean. Poor Bitos. London, 1964.
43524.67.797 Anouilh, Jean. Restless heart. London, 1957.
43524.67.798 Anouilh, Jean. Five plays. N.Y., 1958.
43524.67.799 Anouilh, Jean. Dinner with the family. London, 1958.
43524.67.800 Gignoux, H. Jean Anouilh. Paris, 1946.
43524.67.803 Didier, J. A la rencontier de Jean Anouilh. Liege, 1946.
43524.67.805 Radine, S. Anouilh, Lenormand, Salacrou. Genève, 1951.
43524.67.807 Marsh, E.J. Jean Anouilh. London, 1953.
43524.67.809 Hoogland, C. Den briljante Anouilh. Stockholm, 1952.
43524.67.815 Lassalle, J. Jean Anouilh. Rodez, 1958.
43524.67.820 Pronko, L.C. The world of Jean Anouilh. Berkeley, 1961.
43524.67.825 Luppé, Robert de. Jean Anouilh. Paris, 1959.
43524.67.830 Xans, Joseph Anna Guillaume. Toneel en leven; enkle beschouwingen over Anouilh. Groningen, 1962.
43524.67.835 Harvey, John. Anouilh; a study in theatrics. New Haven, 1964.
43524.67.840 Jolivet, P. Le théâtre de J. Anouilh. Paris, 1963.
43524.67.845 Vandromme, Pol. Au auteur et ses personnages. Paris, 1965.
43524.67.850 Borgal, Clement. Anouilh, la peine de vivre. Paris, 1966.
43524.67.855 Thody, Philip. Anouilh. Edinburgh, 1968.
43524.67.860 Canaris, Volker. Jean Anouilh. 1. Aufl. Velber, 1968.
43524.67.865 Della Fazia, Alba Marie. Jean Anouilh. N.Y., 1969.
43524.67.870 Ginestier, Paul. Jean Anouilh. Paris, 1969.
43524.79.100 Ans, Geneviève d'. Lui. Paris, 1954?
43524.85.100 Antelme, J. Soldats de France, simples esquisses. 3. ed. Paris, 1915.
43524.85.103 Anouilh, Jean. Colombe. 2. ed. Paris, 1915.
43524.86.100 Antier, Jean Jacques. La meute silencieuse; roman. Paris, 1969.
43524.87.100 Antoine, André. L'ennemie. Paris, 1929.
43526.24.100 Apesteguy, Pierre. Au nom du Père. Paris, 1960.
43526.65.11 Apollinaire, Guillaume. Oeuvres complètes. v.1-6. Paris, 1965. 8v.
43526.65.61 Apollinaire, Guillaume. Lettres à Lou. Paris, 1969.
43526.65.75 Le Flaneive des deux rives; bulletin d'etudes Apollinariennes. Paris. 1-8,1954-1955
43526.65.100A Apollinaire, Guillaume. Calligrammes. Paris, 1925.
43526.65.100B Apollinaire, Guillaume. Calligrammes. 6. ed. Paris, 1925.
43526.65.101 Apollinaire, Guillaume. Calligrammes. Paris, 1955.
43526.65.102 Apollinaire, Guillaume. Calligrammes. Paris, 1966.
43526.65.103 Apollinaire, Guillaume. Lettres à sa marraine, 1915-1918. Paris, 1951.
43526.65.105 Apollinaire, Guillaume. Selected writings. N.Y., 1950.
43526.65.108 Apollinaire, Guillaume. Les onze mille verges. En Hallander, 1948.
43526.65.110 Apollinaire, Guillaume. La flaneur des deux rives. 5. ed. Paris, 1928.
43526.65.115 Apollinaire, Guillaume. Alcools. Paris, 1950.
43526.65.116 Apollinaire, Guillaume. Alcools. Paris, 1953.
43526.65.117 Apollinaire, Guillaume. Le dossier d'Alcools. Geneve, 1960.
43526.65.120 Apollinaire, Guillaume. Il y a. Paris, 1925.
43526.65.125 Apollinaire, Guillaume. Il y a. n.p., 1941.
43526.65.135 Apollinaire, Guillaume. La fin de Babylone. Paris, 1922.
43526.65.145 Apollinaire, Guillaume. L'enchanteur pourrissant. Paris, 1921.
Htn 43526.65.150* Apollinaire, Guillaume. Les mamelles des Tirésias. 1st ed. Paris, 1946.
43526.65.155 Apollinaire, Guillaume. Le guetteur melancolique. Paris, 1952.
43526.65.160 Apollinaire, Guillaume. Estudio preliminar y paginas. Buenos Aires, 1946.
43526.65.170 Apollinaire, Guillaume. Le poète assassine. Paris, 1947.
43526.65.170.2 Apollinaire, Guillaume. Le poète assassine. Paris, 1959.
43526.65.180 Apollinaire, Guillaume. Couleur du temps. Paris, 1949.
43526.65.190 Apollinaire, Guillaume. Poésies libres. Amsterdam, 1948.
43526.65.200 Apollinaire, Guillaume. Ombre de mon amour. 3. ed. Genève, 1948.
43526.65.202 Apollinaire, Guillaume. Ombre de mon amour. Lausanne, 1957.
43526.65.210 Apollinaire, Guillaume. La femme assise. 11. ed. Paris, 1949.
43526.65.220 Apollinaire, Guillaume. Casanova. Paris, 1952.
43526.65.230 Apollinaire, Guillaume. Textes inédits. Genève, 1952.
43526.65.240 Apollinaire, Guillaume. Anecdotiques. 5. ed. Paris, 1955.
43526.65.242 Apollinaire, Guillaume. Anecdotiques. Paris, 1826.
43526.65.250 Apollinaire, Guillaume. Tendre comme le souvenir. Paris, 1952.
43526.65.260 Apollinaire, Guillaume. Que faire? Paris, 1950.
43526.65.270 Apollinaire, Guillaume. Oeuvres poetiques. Paris, 1956.
43526.65.280 Apollinaire, Guillaume. La Roma des Borgia. Paris, 1913.
43526.65.290 Apollinaire, Guillaume. Les trois Don Juan. Paris, 1914.
43526.65.300 Apollinaire, Guillaume. Chroniques d'art. Paris, 1960.
43526.65.310 Apollinaire, Guillaume. Zwierzyniec albo Świta Orfeusza. Kraków, 1963.
43526.65.320 Apollinaire, Guillaume. Les diables amoureux. Paris, 1964.
43526.65.330 Apollinaire, Guillaume. The poet assassinated. 1st ed. N.Y., 1968.
43526.65.340 Apollinaire, Guillaume. Poèmes à Lou. Paris, 1969.
43526.65.350 Apollinaire, Guillaume. Les exploits d'un jeune Don Juan. Paris, 1970.
43526.65.700 Apollinaire, Guillaume. Alcools: poems, 1898-1913. 1st ed. Garden City, 1964.
43526.65.702 Apollinaire, Guillaume. Alcools. Berkeley, 1965.
43526.65.705 Apollinaire, Guillaume. Selected poems. Harmondsworth, 1965.

43511 - 43873 Individual authors, etc. - 1900- - Known authors (363 scheme plus 10) - cont.

43526.65.710 Apollinaire, Guillaume. The heresiarck and co. 1st ed. Garden City, N.Y., 1965.
43526.65.715 Apollinaire, Guillaume. The wandering Jew, and other stories. London, 1967.
V43526.65.790 Apollinaire, Guillaume. Poezje wybrane. Wyd. 2. Warszawa, 1968.
43526.65.792 Apollinaire, Guillaume. Prsytireswvy. Praha, 1926.
43526.65.793 Apollinaire, Guillaume. Kacir e spoie. Praha, 1926.
43526.65.794 Apollinaire, Guillaume. Pasmo. Praha, 1919.
43526.65.794.5 Apollinaire, Guillaume. Pásmo. Praha, 1963.
43526.65.795 Apollinaire, Guillaume. Básně. Praha, 1935.
43526.65.796 Apollinaire, Guillaume. Alkoholy života. Praha, 1965.
43526.65.797 Apollinaire, Guillaume. Básně-obrazy. Praha, 1965.
43526.65.798 Apollinaire, Guillaume. Stikhi. Moskva, 1967.
43526.65.800 Apollinaire, Guillaume. Apollinaire par lui-même. Paris, 1954.
43526.65.801 Apollinaire, Guillaume. Apollinaire par lui-même. Paris, 1962.
43526.65.805 Fabureau, H. Guillaume Apollinaire, sa oeuvre. Paris, 1932.
43526.65.810 Fettweks, C. Apollinaire en Ardenne. Bruxelles, 1934.
43526.65.815 Soupault, P. Guillaume Apollinaire. Marseille, 1927.
43526.65.820 Wolf, E. Guillaume Apollinaire und das Rhineland. Inaug. Diss. Bonn, 1937.
43526.65.825 Giedion-Welcher, C. Die neue Realität bei Guillaume Apollinaire. Bern, 1945.
43526.65.830 Aegerter, E. Guillaume Apollinaire. Paris, 1943.
43526.65.835 Faure-Favier, Louise. Souvenirs sur Guillaume Apollinaire. Paris, 1945. 2v.
43526.65.840 Bourgois, A. Rene Borflesve. 4th ed. Paris, 1945.
43526.65.845 Cadeau, R.G. Guillaume Apollinaire. Nantes, 1948.
43526.65.850 Cadou, René G. Testament d'Apollinaire temoignage. Paris, 1945.
43526.65.855 Rimes et Raisons. Guilleaume Apollinaire. Abbi, 1946.
43526.65.860 Adéma, Marcel. Guilleaume Apollinaire le mal-aime. Paris, 1952.
43526.65.860.5 Adéma, Marcel. Apollinaire. London, 1954.
43526.65.865 Luca, A.T. Guillaume Apollinaire. Monaco, 1954.
43526.65.865.5 Adéma, Marcel. Guillaume Apollinaire. Paris, 1968.
43526.65.870 Precchioni, P. Le thème du Rhin dans l'inspiration de Guillaume Apollinaire. Paris, 1956.
43526.65.875 Warnier, R. Un conte slave d'Apollinaire. Zagreb, 1962.
43526.65.890 Rouseyne, A.L.M. Amour et poesie d'Apollinaire. Paris, 1955.
43526.65.900 Montfort, Eugene. Apollinaire travesti. Paris, 1948.
43526.65.910A Durry, M.J. Guillaume Apollinaire. Paris, 1956.
43526.65.910B Durry, M.J. Guillaume Apollinaire. v. 2,3. Paris, 1956. 2v.
43526.65.915 Billy, André. Apollinaire vivauf. Paris, 1923.
43526.65.920 Jannine, Pasquale. La fortuna di Apollina+re in Italia. Milano, 1959.
43526.65.925 Tangionge, G. I maggio ad Apollinaire. Roma, 1960.
43526.65.930 Warres, R. Apollinaire. Lisbon, 1960.
43526.65.935 Mackworth, Cecily. Guillaume Apollinaire and the Cubist age. London, 1961.
43526.65.936 Mackworth, Cecily. Guillaume Apollinaire and the Cubist age. 1st American ed. N.Y., 1963.
43526.65.940 Hartwig, J. Apollinaire. Warszawa, 1961.
43526.65.945 Steegmueller, F. Apollinaire. N.Y., 1963.
43526.65.950 Davies, M. Apollinaire. Edinburgh, 1964.
43526.65.955 Grabska, Elżbieta. Apollinaire i teoretycy kubizmu w latach, 1908-1918. Warszawa, 1966.
43526.65.960 Bates, Soctt. Guillaume Apollinaire. N.Y., 1967.
43526.65.965 Couffignal, Robert. L'inspiration biblique dans l'oeuvre de Guillaume Apollinaire. Paris, 1966.
43526.65.970 Billy, André. Avec Apollinaire, souvenirs inédits. Paris, 1966.
43526.65.975 Simonis, Ferdinand. Die Lyrik Guillaume Apollinaires. Bonn, 1967.
43526.65.980 Fonteyne, André. Apollinaire prosateur. Paris, 1964.
43526.65.985 Diviš, Vladimir. Apollinaire; chronique d'une vie. Paris, 196-.
43526.65.990 Breunig, Leroy C. Guillaume Apollinaire. N.Y., 1969.
43526.65.995 Renaud, Philippe. Lecture d'Apollinaire. Lausanne, 1969.
43526.65.1000 Bibliotheque Nationale. Apollinaire, Paris, 1969. Paris, 1969.
43526.65.1005 Chevalier, Jean Claude. Alcools d'Apollinaire. Paris, 1970.
43526.65.1010 Journées Apollinaire, Stavelot, Belgium. Du monde européan à l'univers des mythes. Paris, 1970.
43526.65.1015 Morhange-Bégué, Claude. "La chanson du mal-aimé" d'Apollinaire. Paris, 1970.
43526.65.1020 Themerson, Stefan. Apollinaire's lyrical ideograms. London, 1968.
43527.3.21 Aragon, Louis. Aragon, une étude par Claude Roy. Paris, 1945.
43527.3.41 Aragon, Louis. Chroniques du belcants. Genève, 1947.
43527.3.45 Aragon, Louis. Je n'ai jamais appris à écrire, ou Les incipit. Genève, 1969.
43527.3.100 Aragon, Louis. The red front. Chapel Hill, 1933.
43527.3.110 Aragon, Louis. Hourra l'Oural. Paris, 1934.
43527.3.120 Aragon, Louis. Feu de foie. Paris, 1920.
43527.3.130 Aragon, Louis. Les beaux quartiers. 9th ed. Paris, 1936.
43527.3.132 Aragon, Louis. Les beaux quartiers. Paris, 1970.
43527.3.140 Aragon, Louis. Les cloches de Bâle. Paris, 1934.
43527.3.150 Aragon, Louis. Le crève-coeur. London, 1942.
43527.3.152 Aragon, Louis. Le crève-coeur. N.Y., 1942?
43527.3.155 Aragon, Louis. Le crève-coeur. Paris, 1944.
43527.3.157 Aragon, Louis. Le nouveau crève-coeur, poèmes. 13. éd. Paris, 1948.
43527.3.160A Aragon, Louis. Servitude et grandeur des Français scénes des années terribles. Paris, 1945.
43527.3.160B Aragon, Louis. Servitude et grandeur des Français scénes des années terribles. Paris, 1945.
43527.3.170 Aragon, Louis. Le paysan de Paris. 11. éd. Paris, 1945.
43527.3.180 Aragon, Louis. Brocéliande; poème. Neuchâtel, 1942.
43527.3.190 Aragon, Louis. Les yeux d'Elsa. Neuchâtel, 1945.
43527.3.195 Aragon, Louis. Le fou d'Elsa. Paris, 1964.
43527.3.200 Aragon, Louis. La diare française. Paris, 1946.
43527.3.210 Aragon, Louis. Les yeux d'Elsa. Paris, 1945.
43527.3.210.5 Aragon, Louis. Les yeux d'Elsa. Paris, 1942.
43527.3.215 Aragon, Louis. Elsa. Paris, 1959.
43527.3.220 Aragon, Louis. Aurelien, roman. 31. ed. Paris, 1944.
43527.3.230 Aragon, Louis. Les voyageurs de l'impériale. Paris, 1947.
43527.3.240 Aragon, Louis. En étrange pays dans mon pays lui-même. Paris, 1947.

43511 - 43873 Individual authors, etc. - 1900- - Known authors (363 scheme plus 10) - cont.

43527.3.242 Aragon, Louis. En étrange pays dans mon pays lui-même. Monaco, 1945.
43527.3.250 Aragon, Louis. Anciet, ou Le panorama. 8. éd. Paris, 1936.
43527.3.260 Aragon, Louis. Le musée Grévin. Paris, 1946.
43527.3.261 Aragon, Louis. Le musée Grévin. Paris, 1943.
43527.3.270 Aragon, Louis. Le crime contre l'esprit. Paris, 1944.
43527.3.280 Aragon, Louis. Le libertinage. 7. éd. Paris, 1924.
43527.3.290 Aragon, Louis. Les communistes. Paris, 1949-1951. 5v.
43527.3.300 Aragon, Louis. Pour un réalisme socialiste. Paris, 1935.
43527.3.310 Aragon, Louis. La grande gaîté. Paris, 1929.
43527.3.320 Aragon, Louis. Cantique a Elsa. Alger, 1942.
43527.3.330 Aragon, Louis. Le neveu de M. Duval. Paris, 1953.
43527.3.340 Aragon, Louis. Les yeux et la mémoire. 7. éd. Paris, 1954.
43527.3.350 Aragon, Louis. Le roman inachevé. Paris, 1956.
43527.3.360 Aragon, Louis. La semaine sainte. Paris, 1958.
43527.3.370 Aragon, Louis. J'abats mon jeu. Paris, 1959.
43527.3.380A Aragon, Louis. Les poetes. Paris, 1960.
43527.3.380B Aragon, Louis. Les poetes. Paris, 1960.
43527.3.390 Aragon, Louis. Le mouvement perpétuel. Paris, 1926.
43527.3.391 Aragon, Louis. Le mouvement perpétuel. Paris, 1970.
43527.3.400 Aragon, Louis. Il ne m'est Paris que d'Elsa. Paris, 1964.
43527.3.405 Aragon, Louis. Le voyage de Hollande. Paris, 1964.
43527.3.406 Aragon, Louis. Le voyage de Hollande. 6. éd. Paris, 1965.
43527.3.410 Aragon, Louis. Entretiens avec Francis Cremieux. Paris, 1964.
43527.3.420 Aragon, Louis. Elegie à Pablo Neruda. Paris, 1966.
43527.3.430 Aragon, Louis. Blanche ou l'oubli. Paris, 1967.
43527.3.705 Aragon, Louis. The bells of Basel. N.Y., 1936.
43527.3.710 Aragon, Louis. Residential quartier. N.Y., 1938.
43527.3.715 Aragon, Louis. The century was young. N.Y., 1941.
43527.3.720 Aragon, Louis. Aragon, poet of the French resistance. N.Y., 1945.
43527.3.722 Aragon, Louis. Aragon, poet of resurgent France. London, 1946.
43527.3.725 Aragon, Louis. Passengers of destiny. London, 1947.
43527.3.727 Aragon, Louis. Deux poètes d'aujourd'hui. Paris, 1947.
43527.3.730 Aragon, Louis. L'un ne va pas sans l'autre. Lyon, 1959.
43527.3.735 Aragon, Louis. Holy week, a novel. N.Y., 1961.
43527.3.737 Aragon, Louis. Paris peasant. London, 1971.
43527.3.780 Aragon, Louis. Vstrechi; rasskazy. Moskva, 1946.
43527.3.785 Aragon, Louis. Zu Lieben bis Vernunft verbrennt. Berlin, 1968.
43527.3.800 Breton, André. Misère de la poésie. Paris, 1932.
43527.3.805 Moscow. Vsesoiuznaia gosudarstvennaia biblioteka inostrannykh literatur. Lui Aragon; bio-bibliograficheskii ukazatel'. Moskva, 1956.
43527.3.810 Gavillet, André. La littérature au défi: Aragon surréaliste. Neuchâtel, 1957.
43527.3.815 Lescure, P. de. Aragon. Paris, 1960.
43527.3.820 Juin, Hubert. Aragon. Paris, 1960.
43527.3.825 Garandy, Roger. L'intineraire d'Aragon. Paris, 1961.
43527.3.830 Isbakh, Al. Abr. Lui Aragon; zhizn' i tvorchestvo. Moskva, 1962.
43527.3.835 Raillard, G. Aragon. Paris, 1964.
43527.3.840 Balashova, T.V. Tvorchestvo Aragona. Moskva, 1964.
43527.3.845 Gindine, Yvette. Aragon, prosateur surréaliste. Genève, 1966.
43527.3.850 Haroche, Charles. L'idée de l'amour dans Le fou d'Elsa et l'oeuvre d'Aragon. Paris, 1966.
43527.3.855 Sur, Jean. Aragon, le réalisme de l'amour. Paris, 1966.
43527.3.860 Andrievskaia, Aleksandra A. Nesobstvenno-priamaia rech' v Khudozhestvennoi proze Lui Aragona. Kiev, 1967.
43527.3.865 Arban, Dominique. Aragon parle avec Dominique Arban. Paris, 1968.
43527.3.870 Becker, Lucille. Louis Aragon. N.Y., 1971.
43527.3.875 Huraut, Alain. Louis Aragon, prisonnier politique. Paris, 1970.
43528.1.30F Arnyvèlde, G. La courtisane. Paris, 1906.
43528.2.30F Arquillière. La grand famille. Paris, 1905.
43528.2.130 Aragon, Louis. La mise à mort. Paris, 1965.
43528.3.30 Arnaud, Simone. Myrdhin; opèra-légende. Paris, 1912.
43528.3.1100 Arnaud, Georges. L'enfer des humiliés. Paris, 1959.
43528.7.100 Arbellot, Simon. Journaliste! Paris, 1954.
43528.12.100 Archimede. Poésies d'amour. Rome, 1958.
43528.14.100 Arcos, René. Das Gemeinsame. Leipzig, 1920.
43528.17.100 Ardene, Claude. Longue est la nuit! Paris, 1969.
43528.22.100 Aréga, Leon. Pseudonymes. 2. éd. Paris, 1957.
43528.32.100 Arger, Hubert. De cinabre et d'ombre. Paris, 1955.
43528.35.100 Argyll, Claude. Escale aux Mascareignes. Paris, 1935.
43528.48.100 Arland, Marcel. Étienne. Paris, 1924.
43528.48.105 Arland, Marcel. Le grand pardon. Paris, 1965.
43528.48.110 Arland, Marcel. L'ordre. 28e éd. Paris, 1929. 3v.
43528.48.120 Arland, Marcel. Les plus beaux de nos jours. 2e éd. Paris, 1937.
43528.48.125 Arland, Marcel. La consolation du voyageur. Paris, 1952.
43528.48.130 Arland, Marcel. Les vivants. 7e éd. Paris, 1934.
43528.48.142 Arland, Marcel. La route obscure. 4. éd. Paris, 1930.
43528.48.153 Arland, Marcel. Les âmes en peine. Paris, 1927.
43528.48.175 Arland, Marcel. Nonique. Paris, 1926.
43528.48.183 Arland, Marcel. Ou le coeur se partage. Paris, 1930.
43528.48.195 Arland, Marcel. La vigie. Paris, 1935.
43528.48.200 Arland, Marcel. Heimaterde. Dessau, 1942.
43528.48.205 Arland, Marcel. Essais et nouveaux essais critique. Paris, 1952.
43528.48.210 Arland, Marcel. Nouvelles lettres de France. Paris, 1954.
43528.48.215 Arland, Marcel. Je vaus écris. Paris, 1960.
43528.48.218 Arland, Marcel. La nuit et les sources: Je vous écris. Paris, 1968.
43528.48.220 Arland, Marcel. A perdre haleine. Paris, 1960.
43528.48.230 Arland, Marcel. Carnets de Gilbert. Paris, 1966.
43528.48.240 Arland, Marcel. Faire le point. Paris, 1948.
43528.48.250 Arland, Marcel. La musique des anges. Paris, 1967.
43528.48.260 Arland, Marcel. Lettres de France. Paris, 1951.
43528.48.270 Arland, Marcel. Attendez l'aube. Paris, 1970.
43528.53.100 Armandy, A. L'arc-en-ciel de lume. Paris, 1936.
43528.53.110 Armandy, A. Le padrão; roman. Paris, 1937.
43528.53.113 Armandy, A. Le padrão. Paris, 1939.
43528.53.120 La cité profonde. Paris, 1938.
43528.53.132 Rapa-nui. 8e éd. Paris, 1923.
43528.53.140 Rapa-nui; novela. Madrid, 192-?
43528.53.150 Les réprouvés. Paris, 1930.
43528.53.160 Le demon bleu. Paris, 1931. 2v.
43528.53.1100 Armagnac, M.M. d'. La carrière Bolcheviste d'Alexis Jourouskine. Paris, 1926.

43511 - 43873 Individual authors, etc. - 1900- - Known authors (363 scheme plus 10) - cont.

43528.56.100 Armont, Paul. L'école des cocottes. Paris, 1923.
43528.56.110 Armant, Paul. Ces messieurs de la Santé. Paris, 1931.
43528.56.120 Armont, Paul. Le valet-maitre. Paris, 1938.
43528.57.100 Arnaud, Michel. Manière de Blanc. Paris, 1938.
43528.58.100 Arnal, Émilie. L'Hôte Divin. Paris, 1928.
43528.58.1100 Arnaud, G. Le salaire de la peur. Paris, 1953.
43528.58.2100 Arnac, Marcel. 83 centiméntres d'ovenhure. Paris, 1925.
43528.58.2110 Arnac, Marcel. Saint-Lettres. Paris, 1926.
43528.58.2120 Arnac, Marcel. Le brelan de joie. 205e éd. Paris, 1924.
43528.58.3100 Arnaud, Claude. Véronique. Paris, 1960.
43528.58.4100 Arnaud, Michel. Zoneilles. Paris, 1962.
43528.59.100 Arnaud, René. Trois pages d'histoire. Paris, 1931.
43528.60.100 Arnauld, C. Anthologie Celine Arnauld. Bruxelles, 1936.
43528.60.110 Arnauld, C. Heures intactes. Bruxelles, 1936.
43528.60.120 Arnauld, C. Rien qu'une étoile. Paris, 1948.
43528.61.110 Arnoux, Alexandre. Poésie du hasard. Paris, 1934.
43528.61.120 Arnoux, Alexandre. Abisag. Paris, 1918.
43528.61.127 Arnoux, Alexandre. Carnet de route du Juif errant. 11. éd. Paris, 1931.
43528.61.140 Arnoux, Alexandre. Rhône, mon fleuve. Paris, 1944.
43528.61.150 Arnoux, Alexandre. Les crimes innocents. Paris, 1952.
43528.61.160 Arnoux, Alexandre. Royaume des ombres. Paris, 1954.
43528.61.170 Arnoux, Alexandre. Le seigneur de l'heure, recit. Paris, 1955.
43528.61.175 Arnoux, Alexandre. Le rossignol napolitain. Paris, 1956.
43528.61.180 Arnoux, Alexandre. L'amour des trois oranges. Paris, 1947.
43528.61.190 Arnoux, Alexandre. Marges du temps. Paris, 1959.
43528.61.200 Arnoux, Alexandre. Zulma l'infidelle. Paris, 1960.
43528.61.210 Arnoux, Alexandre. La nuit de Saint Barnabé. Paris, 1921.
43528.61.220 Arnoux, Alexandre. L'allée des mortes; poèmes. Paris, 1906.
43528.61.230 Arnoux, Alexandre. La double Hélène. Paris, 1967.
43528.61.2100 Arnold, Paul. Les dévayés, roman. Paris, 1958.
43528.67.100 Arout, Gabriel. La dame de Tréfle. Paris, 1953.
43528.68.150 Arp, Hans. Le blanc aux pieds de nègre. Paris, 1945.
43528.73.100 Arrabal, Fernando. Théâtre. v.1,3-6,7,8. Paris, 1958. 7v.
43528.73.110 Arrabal, Fernando. Baal Babylone; roman. Paris, 1959.
43528.73.120 Arrabal, Fernando. Arrabal celebrando la ceremonia de la confusion. Madrid, 1966.
43528.73.130 Arrabal, Fernando. L'enterrement de la sardine. Paris, 1970.
43528.73.700 Arrabal, Fernando. The automobile graveyard. N.Y., 1960.
43528.73.705 Arrabal, Fernando. Plays. London, 1962. 2v.
43528.73.710 Arrabal, Fernando. Baal Babylon; a novel. N.Y., 1961.
43528.74.100 Arrault, Albert. Eugénie Grandet. Paris, 1937.
43528.76.100 Arribat, Chantal. Noir et blanc. Paris, 1969.
43528.80.100 Arschat, P. La nuit sur Mytilene. Paris, 1935.
43528.86.11 Artaud, Antonin. Collected works. London, 1968- 3v.
43528.86.13 Artaud, Antonin. Oeuvres complètes. Paris, 1956- 8v.
43528.86.14 Artaud, Antonin. Oeuvres complètes. Paris, 1970- 3v.
43528.86.14.5 Artaud, Antonin. Oeuvres complètes. Supplement. Paris, 1970.
43528.86.57 Artaud, Antonin. Antonin Artaud anthology. San Francisco, 1965.
43528.86.61 Artaud, Antonin. Lettres de Rodez. Paris, 1946.
43528.86.63 Artaud, Antonin. Supplement aux Lettres de Rodez. Paris, 1949.
43528.86.65A Artaud, Antonin. Les nouvelles revelations de l'être. Paris, 1937.
43528.86.65B Artaud, Antonin. Les nouvelles revelations de l'être. Paris, 1937.
43528.86.67 Artaud, Antonin. Correspondance avec Jacques Riviere. Paris, 1927.
43528.86.69 Artaud, Antonin. Lettres d'Antonin Artaud à Jean-Louis. Paris, 1952.
43528.86.70 Artaud, Antonin. L'ombilic des limbes. Paris, 1925.
43528.86.72 Artaud, Antonin. Lettres à Génica Athanasiou. Paris, 1964.
43528.86.100 Artaud, Antonin. Vie et mort de satan le feu. Paris, 1953.
43528.86.110A Artaud, Antonin. Pour en finir avec le jugement de dieu. Paris, 1948.
43528.86.110B Artaud, Antonin. Pour en finir avec le jugement de dieu. Paris, 1948.
43528.86.110C Artaud, Antonin. Pour en finir avec le jugement de dieu. Paris, 1948.
43528.86.700 Artaud, Antonin. The Cenci. London, 1969.
43528.86.800 Hort, Jean. Antonin Artaud. Genève, 1960.
43528.86.805 Sellin, Eric. The dramatic concepts of Antonin Artaud. Chicago, 1968.
43528.86.810 Bonneton, André. Le naufrage prophétique d'Antonin Artaud. Paris, 1961.
43528.86.815 Knapp, Bettina (Liebowitz). Antonin Artaud; man of vision. N.Y., 1969.
43528.86.820 Hahn, Otto. Portrait d'Antonin Artaud. Paris, 1968.
43528.86.825 Virmaux, Alain. Antonin Artaud et le théâtre. Paris, 1970.
43528.86.830 Greene, Naomi. Antonin Artaud. N.Y., 1971.
43528.88.100 Artus, Louis. Mon mal et moi; roman. Paris, 1936.
43528.88.110 Artus, Louis. La maison ou Fou. Paris, 1918.
43528.88.120 Artus, Louis. Le vin de ta vigne. Paris, 1922.
43528.89.100 Arnothy, Christine. God is late. 1st ed. N.Y., 1957.
43528.89.110 Arnothy, Christine. Pique-nique en Sologne. Paris, 1960.
43528.89.120 Arnothy, Christine. Le jardin noir; roman. Paris, 1966.
43528.89.130 Arnothy, Christine. Aviva; roman. Paris, 1968.
43528.89.1100 Arudy, France. Solderon. Paris, 1957.
43528.98.100 Arya. Le placard aux grenouilles. Paris, 1957.
43528.99.775 Arlet, Suzanne. Cisza i wołanie. Warszawa, 1966.
43529.3 Aulnoye, P. de. Le Lieutenant de Trémazan. Paris, 1908.
43529.4.30 Audigier, Camille. La terre qui renaît. Paris, 1917.
43529.5.30 Audoux, Marguerite. L'atelier de Marie-Claire. Paris, 1920.
43529.5.30.5 Audoux, Marguerite. L'atelier de Marie-Claire. Paris, 1920.
43529.6.30 Astier de la Vigerie, E. L'été n'en finit pas. Paris, 1954.
43529.7.30 Astorg, Bertrand d'. D'amour et d'amitié. Paris, 1953.
43529.7.35 Astorg, Bertrand d'. La jeune fille et l'astronaute. Paris, 1966.
43529.8.30 Aspel, Pauline. Goût d'une autre terre. Paris, 1954.
43529.8.35 Aspel, Pauline. Traversées. Crossings. Urbana, Ill., 1966.

Classified Listing

43511 - 43873 Individual authors, etc. - 1900- - Known authors (363 scheme plus 10) - cont.

43529.80.100 Asselineau, Roger. Poésies incomplètes. Paris, 1959.
43530.5 Attal, J.P. Il y avait trois clowns. Paris, 1951.
43530.37.100 Atheros, Dominique. Le poète et l'amour. Monte-Carlo, 1963.
43530.84.100 Attal, Raoul. Le pain de la nuit. Boundary, 1966.
43531.7.33 Aubert, Octave Louis. Contes d'un Breton adoptif. St. Brieuc, 1918?
43531.7.33.10 Aubert, Octave Louis. Le baléer-brô. St. Brieuc, 19- .
43531.7.2100 Aubier, D. La nourriture du feu. Paris, 1954.
43531.7.3100 Aubert, Claude. Terres de cendres. Genève, 1957.
43531.7.3110 Aubert, Claude. Persiennes. [Poèmes]. Boudry, 1953.
43531.7.3120 Aubert, Claude. L'unique belladone. [Poèmes]. Lausanne, 1968.
43531.7.4100 Aubert, Denise. Les année heureuses. 2. éd. Paris, 1921.
43531.8.4110 Aubray, T. Ouvrir des yeux. 3. éd. Paris, 1943.
43531.8.4120 Aubray, T. Un seul chemin. Paris, 1951.
43531.8.6100 Aubret, M. Les jeux de minuit. Paris, 1938.
43531.9 Audiberti, Jacques. L'effet Glapion. Paris, 1959.
43531.9.100 Aubrun, Jacques. Le lys brisé et poèmes divers. 2e éd. Paris, 1929.
43531.9.110 Aubrun, Jacques. La guerre; poème. Paris, 193-?
43531.10.100 Aubry, Octave. Le lit du roi. Paris, 1926.
43531.10.110 Aubry, Octave. Le roi perdu (Louis XVIII retrouvé). Paris, 1924.
43531.10.120 Aubry, Octave. Le roman de Napoléon. Paris, 1927.
43531.10.700 Aubry, Octave. The emperor falls in love. N.Y., 1928.
43531.14.100 Auclair, Marcelle. Changer d'etoile. Paris, 1926.
43531.17.100 Audet, Elaine. Soleil noir, poèmes. Paris, 1958.
43531.18.100 Audiat, Pierre. Les ravages; roman. Paris, 1948.
43531.18.1100 Audiberti, Jacques. Les jardins et les fleures. 7. éd. Paris, 1954.
43531.18.1110 Audiberti, Jacques. Marie Dubois. 2. éd. Paris, 1952.
43531.18.1120 Audiberti, Jacques. L'Abhumanisme. 2. éd. Paris, 1955.
43531.18.1130 Audiberti, Jacques. La beauté de l'amour. Paris, 1955.
43531.18.1140 Audiberti, Jacques. Théâtre. v.3, 3. éd. Paris, 1948. 5v.
43531.18.1150 Audiberti, Jacques. La pluie sur les boulevards. Angers, 1950.
43531.18.1160 Audiberti, Jacques. La pouplé. Paris, 1956.
43531.18.1170 Audiberti, Jacques. Le megére apprivoisee. 4. éd. Paris, 1957.
43531.18.1180 Audiberti, Jacques. L'effet Glapion; parapsychocomedie. Paris, 1959.
43531.18.1184 Audiberti, Jacques. Le cavalier seul. Paris, 1955.
43531.18.1190 Audiberti, Jacques. Infanticide préconisé. Paris, 1958.
43531.18.1200 Audiberti, Jacques. Race des hommes. Paris, 1937.
43531.18.1210 Audiberti, Jacques. Entretiéns avec Georges Charbonnier. Paris, 1965.
43531.18.1220 Audiberti, Jacques. Dimanche m'attend. Paris, 1965.
43531.18.1230 Audiberti, Jacques. Les tombeaux ferment mal. Paris, 1963.
43531.18.1240 Audiberti, Jacques. La nouvelle origine. 4. éd. Paris, 1942.
43531.18.1250 La Nouvelle Revue Française. Hommage à Jacques Audiberti, 1899-1965. Paris, 1965.
43531.18.1800 Giroud, Michel. Jacques Audiberti. Paris, 1967.
43531.18.2100 Audisio, Gabriel. Danger de vie. Limoges, 1953.
43531.18.2110 Audisio, Gabriel. A n'y pas coire, récits et portraits. Paris, 1966.
43531.18.3100 Audibert, Jean Marie. La dame de Beyrouth. Paris, 1958.
43531.19.110 Audry, Colette. On jour perdant. 3. éd. Paris, 1946.
43531.19.120 Audry, Colette. Soledad. Paris, 1956.
43531.19.130 Audry, Colette. Derrière la baignoire. Paris, 1962.
43531.19.1100 Audra, A. Le lendemain des jours. Roder, 1959.
43531.19.2100 Audouard, Yvan. Les secrets de leur réussite. Paris, 1967.
43531.19.2110 Audouard, Yvan. Cocagne. Paris, 1959.
43531.29.100 Aufrèrc, Gaston Henry. Fleurs de guerre et d'exil; poèmes. Paris, 1949.
43531.33.100 Augiu, Gladys. Son juif; roman. Paris, 1930.
43531.42.100 Aujard, Dominique. Le chant interrompu. Paris, 1939.
43531.48.100 Aulagnier, Pierre. Maré, Thécel, Pharès. 2. éd. Valence-sur-Rhône, 1962.
43531.76.23 Aurient (pseud.). Fragments. Bruxelles, 1942.
43531.77.100 Auroire, Georges. Nocturne. Paris, 1962.
43531.78.100 Aury, Dominique. Literary landfalls. London, 1960.
43532.1.30 Avril, R. d'. L'Arbu des Fées. Paris, 1912.
43532.2.30 Avèze, André. Immoralité du Christianisme. Paris, 1908.
43532.23.100 Aveline, Claude. Le prisonnier. Paris, 1936.
43532.23.110 Aveline, Claude. Les devoirs de l'esprit. 3e éd. Paris, 1945.
43532.23.120 Aveline, Claude. Le temps mort. Paris, 1945.
43532.23.121 Aveline, Claude. Le temps mort. Paris, 1944.
43532.23.122 Aveline, Claude. Le temps mort, suisi d'autres récits et de quelques. Paris, 1962.
43532.23.130 Aveline, Claude. Dans Paris retrouvé. Paris, 1945.
43532.23.140 Aveline, Claude. Pegomancie. Paris, 1948.
43532.23.150 Aveline, Claude. Le poids du feu. Paris, 1959.
43532.23.160 Aveline, Claude. Le bestiaire inattendu. Paris, 1959.
43532.23.170 Aveline, Claude. C'est vrai, mais il ne faut pas le croire. Paris, 1960.
43532.23.180 Aveline, Claude. Les reflexions de Monsieur F.A.T. Paris, 1963.
43532.23.190 Aveline, Claude. La vie de Philippe Denis. v. 1-2. Paris, 1930.
43532.23.200 Aveline, Claude. Trois histoires de la nuit. Paris, 1931.
43532.23.210 Aveline, Claude. De. Paris, 1967.
43532.23.700 Aveline, Claude. Prisoner barn. London, 1950.
43532.23.800 Mouret, Florentin. Les ouvrages de Claude Aveline. Paris, 1961.
43532.23.805 Hommage à Claude Aveline. Paris, 1970.
43532.41.100 Avilla, Francis d'. Chansons tristes. Paris, 1928.
43532.41.1100 Avicenne, Paul. Feuilles des hommes. Maliness, 1955.
43535.35.21 Ayguesparse, Albert. Le vin noir de Cahors. Paris, 1957.
43535.35.100 Ayguesparse, Albert. Selon toute vraisemblance. Bruxelles, 1962.
43535.35.800 Rousselot, Jean. Albert Ayguesparse. Bruxelles, 1965.
43535.53.100 Aymard, C.E. Les précurseurs. Paris, 1930.
43535.54.21 Aymé, Marcel. Contes et novelles. Paris, 1953.
43535.54.100 Aymé, Marcel. Le Table-aux-Crevés. 39e éd. Paris, 1930.
43535.54.102 Aymé, Marcel. La Table-aux-Crevés. Paris, 1970.
43535.54.105 Aymé, Marcel. La jument verte. 80e éd. Paris, 1933.
43535.54.110 Aymé, Marcel. Le moulin de la sourdine. 35e éd. Paris, 1936.
43535.54.115 Aymé, Marcel. Le nain. 28e éd. Paris, 1934.
43535.54.120 Aymé, Marcel. Silhouette du scandale. Paris, 1938.

43511 - 43873 Individual authors, etc. - 1900- - Known authors (363 scheme plus 10) - cont.

43535.54.125 Aymé, Marcel. Le boeuf clandestin; roman. 24e éd. Paris, 1939.
43535.54.130 Aymé, Marcel. Gustalin; roman. 14e éd. Paris, 1937.
43535.54.135.15 Aymé, Marcel. Le vin de Paris. 29e éd. Paris, 1947.
43535.54.149 Aymé, Marcel. La rue sans nom. 19e éd. Paris, 1930.
43535.54.160 Aymé, Marcel. Maison basse. 2e éd. Paris, 1935.
43535.54.170 Aymé, Marcel. Vogue la galère. Paris, 1944.
43535.54.180 Aymé, Marcel. Uranus, roman. Paris, 1948.
43535.54.181 Aymé, Marcel. Uranus. Paris, 1948.
43535.54.182 Aymé, Marcel. Romans parisiéns. Paris, 1959.
43535.54.190 Aymé, Marcel. Lucienne et le boucher. 5e éd. Paris, 1947.
43535.54.210 Aymé, Marcel. La belle image. 58e éd. Paris, 1949.
43535.54.220 Aymé, Marcel. Le passe-muraille. 190e éd. Paris, 1943.
43535.54.230 Aymé, Marcel. Travelingue. 90e éd. Paris, 1948.
43535.54.240 Aymé, Marcel. Clérambard. Paris, 1950.
43535.54.250 Aymé, Marcel. La tête des autres. Paris, 1952.
43535.54.260 Aymé, Marcel. Le confort intellectual. Paris, 1949.
43535.54.270 Aymé, Marcel. Le vaurien. 20e éd. Paris, 1948.
43535.54.280 Aymé, Marcel. Les quatre vérités. Paris, 1954.
43535.54.290 Aymé, Marcel. La mouche bleue. 6e éd. Paris, 1957.
43535.54.300 Aymé, Marcel. La jument verte. Paris, 1957.
43535.54.310 Aymé, Marcel. Le puits aux images. 22e éd. Paris, 1957.
43535.54.320 Aymé, Marcel. La Youirve. Paris, 1951.
43535.54.330 Aymé, Marcel. Les tiroirs de l'inconnu. Paris, 1960.
43535.54.340 Aymé, Marcel. Les Maxibules. Paris, 1962.
43535.54.350 Aymé, Marcel. Louisiane; pièce en quatre actes. Paris, 1961.
43535.54.360 Aymé, Marcel. Autres contes de chat perché. Paris, 1954.
43535.54.370 Aymé, Marcel. Le Minotaure. Paris, 1967.
43535.54.380 Aymé, Marcel. Enjambées. Paris, 1967.
43535.54.700 Aymé, Marcel. The transient hour. London, 1948.
43535.54.705 Aymé, Marcel. The fable and the flesh. London, 1949.
43535.54.710 Aymé, Marcel. The miraculous barber. London, 1949.
43535.54.715 Aymé, Marcel. The barkeep of Blemont. 1st ed. N.Y., 1950.
43535.54.720 Aymé, Marcel. The green mare. London, 1938.
43535.54.725 Aymé, Marcel. The second face. London, 1951.
43535.54.730 Aymé, Marcel. The house of men. London, 1952.
43535.54.735 Aymé, Marcel. Clérambard. London, 1952.
43535.54.740 Aymé, Marcel. The wonderful farm. London, 1952.
43535.54.745 Aymé, Marcel. The secret stream. London, 1953.
43535.54.750 Aymé, Marcel. Across Paris. N.Y., 1958?
43535.54.755 Aymé, Marcel. The proverb and other stories. London, 1961.
43535.54.760 Aymé, Marcel. The conscience of love. London, 1962.
43535.54.800 Cathelin, Jean. Marcel Aymé. Paris, 1958.
43535.54.805 Scriabine, H. Les faux dieux. v. 1-2. Paris, 1963.
43535.54.810 Brodin, Dorothy R. Marcel Aymé. N.Y., 1968.
43535.54.816 Dumont, Jean Louis. Marcel Aymé et le merveilleux. Paris, 1970.
43535.58.100F Aynard, R. Traversées. Paris, 1960.
43536.1.30 Azaïs, Marcel. La Chevauchée Nocturne. 2e éd. Paris, 1912.
43536.5.100 Azaïs, Marcel. Le chemin des gardies. Paris, 1926.
43536.74.1100 Azra, Georges. L'ame sous le sexe. Malines, 1955.
43537.1.30 Bailly, F. Rimes galantes. Paris, 1912.
43537.1.1030 Bailby, Léon. Souvenirs. Paris, 1951-
43537.1.2030 Baissette, Gaston. Ces grappes de ma vigne. Paris, 1956.
43537.1.2035 Baissette, Gaston. Isabelle de la garrigue; roman. Paris, 1968.
43537.2.30 Bataille, F. Les trois Foyers. Paris, n.d.
43537.2.1030 Bauër, G. Il faut parler le premier. Ahbenitle, 1924.
43537.3.30 Baye, B. de. Le Temple du Rêve. Paris, 1912.
43537.4.6 Bataille, Henry. Théâtre complet. Paris, 1922-30. 12v.
43537.4.30 Bataille, Henry. Ion Sang précédé de La Lépreuse. 2. éd. Paris, 1898.
43537.4.31 Bataille, Henry. Théâtre - Le Masque - La Marche nuptiale. Paris, 1908.
43537.4.32F Bataille, Henry. Le Phalène. Paris, 1913.
43537.4.33F Bataille, Henry. Le Songe d'un Soir d'Amour. Paris, 1910.
43537.4.34F Bataille, Henry. La femme nue. Paris, n.d.
43537.4.35F Bataille, Henry. Les flambeaux. Paris, 1913.
43537.4.36 Bataille, Henry. La divine tragédie. Paris, 1916.
43537.4.37 Bataille, Henry. Beau voyage, poésies. Paris, 1916.
43537.4.38 Bataille, Henry. L'Amazone: Les flambeaux. Paris, 1917.
43537.4.39 Bataille, Henry. L'animateur. Paris, 1920.
43537.4.40 Bataille, Henry. Les soeurs d'amour. Paris, 1919.
43537.4.41 Bataille, Henry. L'homme à la rose. Paris, 1921.
43537.4.42 Bataille, Henry. La tendresse; pièce. Paris, 1921.
43537.4.42.5 Bataille, Henry. La tendresse. L'homme à la rose. Paris, 1922.
43537.4.43 Bataille, Henry. La quadrature de l'amour. Paris, 1920.
43537.4.44 Bataille, Henry. La possession. Paris, 1922.
43537.4.45 Bataille, Henry. La chair humaine. Paris, 1922.
43537.4.47 Bataille, Henry. Notre image. Paris, 1922.
43537.4.55 Bataille, Henry. L'enchantement. Paris, 1904.
43537.4.60 Bataille, Henry. Vers préférés. Paris, 1923.
43537.4.65 Bataille, Henry. La vierge folle. Paris, 1910.
43537.4.70 Bataille, Henry. La marche nuptiale. Paris, 1905.
43537.4.75 Bataille, Henry. Le scandale. Paris, 1909.
43537.4.80A Bataille, Henry. Ecrits sur le théâtre. 2e éd. Paris, 1917.
43537.4.80B Bataille, Henry. Ecrits sur le théâtre. 6e éd. Paris, 1917.
43537.4.85 Amiel, Denys. Henry Bataille. Paris, 1909.
43537.4.87 Cogo, Guido. L'amore nei drammi di Henry Bataille. Palermo, 1928.
43537.4.90 Catalogne, Gerard de. Henry Bataille. Paris, 1925.
43537.4.875 Besançon, Jacques B. Essai sur le théâtre d'Henry Bataille. Groninque, 1928.
43537.5.30 Barrière, M. L'art des passions. Paris, 1904.
43537.5.31 Barrière, M. Le nouveau Don Juan. Paris, 1900. 3v.
43537.5.35 Barrière, M. Le sang d'Asmodée. Paris, 1924.
43537.6.29 Barbusse, Henri. Le feu (journal d'une escouade). Paris, 1916.
43537.6.29.10 Barbusse, Henri. Le feu. Paris, 1918.
43537.6.29.15 Barbusse, Henri. Le feu; journal d'une escouade, roman. Paris, 1965.
43537.6.30.2 Barbusse, Henri. Under fire. N.Y., 1917.
43537.6.30.5A Barbusse, Henri. Under fire. N.Y., 1918.
43537.6.30.5B Barbusse, Henri. Under fire. N.Y., 1918.
43537.6.30.5C Barbusse, Henri. Under fire. N.Y., 1918.
43537.6.31A Barbusse, Henri. Nous autres. v.1-3. Paris, 1918.
43537.6.31B Barbusse, Henri. Nous autres. v.1-3. Paris, 1918.
43537.6.32 Barbusse, Henri. Les suppliants. Paris, 1903.

43511 - 43873 Individual authors, etc. - 1900- - Known authors (363 scheme plus 10) - cont.

43537.6.33 Barbusse, Henri. Pleureuses. Paris, 1895.
43537.6.34 Barbusse, Henri. Clarté; roman. Paris, 1920.
43537.6.35 Barbusse, Henri. Quelques coins du coeur. Genève, 1921.
43537.6.37 Barbusse, Henri. Les enchainements. v.2. Paris, 1925.
X Cg 43537.6.37 Barbusse, Henri. Les enchainements. v.1. Paris, 1925.
43537.6.39A Barbusse, Henri. Light. N.Y., 1919.
43537.6.39B Barbusse, Henri. Light. N.Y., 1919.
43537.6.45A Barbusse, Henri. I saw it myself. N.Y., 1929.
43537.6.45B Barbusse, Henri. I saw it myself. N.Y., 1929.
43537.6.46 Barbusse, Henri. Tatsachen. Berlin, 1929.
43537.6.50 Barbusse, Henri. We others. N.Y., 1918.
43537.6.56 Barbusse, Henri. The inferno. N.Y., 1918.
43537.6.58 Barbusse, Henri. L'enfer. Paris, 191-?
43537.6.60 Barbusse, Henri. Le couteau entre les clents. Paris, 1921.
43537.6.80 Hertz, Henri. Henri Barbusse. Paris, 1919.
43537.6.85 Duclos, Jacques. Henri Barbusse. Paris, 1946.
43537.6.87 Nikolaev, V.N. Anri Barbius. Moskva, 1953.
43537.6.90 Vidal, A. Henri Barbusse. Paris, 1953.
43537.6.95 Verbyts'kyi, P.P. Polum"ianyi propahandyst velykoho zhovtnia. Kharkiv, 1950.
43537.6.97 Guro, Irina R. Anri Barbius. Moskva, 1962.
43537.6.100 Brett, Vladimir. Henri Barbusse, sa marche vers la clasté. Prague, 1963.
43537.6.105 Brett, Vladimir. Henri Barbusse a oblas jeho díla a činnosti u nás. Praha, 1955.
43537.8.30 Barranx, Serge. Notre France! Paris, 1917.
43537.9.30 Ballieu, A.J. Jean Linquiet. Paris, 1900.
43537.10.31 Baby, Yvonne. Qui, l'espoir. Paris, 1967.
43537.11.30 Barraute du Plessio. Les 13 cauchemars. n.p., 190-?
43537.11.3100 Baccouçhe, Hachime. Ma foi demeure; roman. Paris, 1958.
43537.12.30 Basly, Émile. Le martyre de Lens. Paris, 1918.
43537.12.100 Bach-Sesley, J. L'humble et merveilleux évangile de la pucelle. Brignais, 1928.
43537.12.1100 Bachelard, René. Noirs, mes amis. Paris, 1963.
43537.13.30 Bachelin, H. Le serviteur. Paris, 1918.
43537.13.35 Bachelin, H. La cornemuse de Saulieu. Paris, 1925.
43537.13.1100 Baccio, Jean. Frelons et abeilles. Paris, 1961.
43537.13.1110 Baccio, Jean. Essaims. Rodez, 1968.
43537.14.100 Backer, A.M. de. Les étoiles de novembre. Paris, 1956.
43537.14.110 Backer, A.M. de. L'herbe et le feu. Paris, 1958.
43537.14.1100 Bacri, Roland. Poèmes: colère du temps. Paris, 1971.
43537.18.100 Badin, Charles. Tetus Pallade, le muletier; roman. v. 1-2. Paris, 1928.
43537.18.1100 Badiou, Alain. Trajectoire inverse. Paris, 1964- 2v.
43537.34.100 Bugnet, Charles. Le collier de pierres de lune. Paris, 1922.
43537.41.100 Bailly, A. Néron. Paris, 1930.
43537.41.1100 Baiocchi, A. Acquetinte. Sarzana, 1955.
43537.42.41 Bainville, Jacques. Journal. Paris, 1948-49. 3v.
43537.42.42 Bainville, Jacques. Journal inédit (1914). Paris, 1953.
43537.42.100 Bainville, Jacques. Jaco et Tori; roman. Paris, 1929.
43537.42.110 Bainville, Jacques. Chroniques. Paris, 1938.
43537.42.120 Bainville, Jacques. Le jardin des lettres. Paris, 1929. 2v.
43537.42.130 Bainville, Jacques. Nouveau dialogue dans le salon d'Alienor. Paris, 1926.
43537.42.140 Bainville, Jacques. Tyrrhenus. Saint-Pélicien-en-Vivarais, 1925.
43537.42.150 Bainville, Jacques. Polioute. Liège, 1926.
43537.48.100 Balain, Blanche. Temps loinlain. Paris, 1946.
43537.49.100 Baldassera, P. Recois mon coeur. Paris, 1929.
43537.50.5 Baldensperger, F. Publications. Paris, 1930.
43537.50.41 Baldensperger, F. Une vie parmi d'autres. Paris, 1940.
43537.50.100 Baldensperger, F. Contes et récits vosgiens. Paris, 1913.
43537.50.110 Baldensperger, F. La croisée des routes; poesies, 1901-1914. Paris, 1923.
43537.50.115 Baldensperger, F. Rimes d'exil et d'espoir. Paris, 1950.
43537.50.120 Baldensperger, F. Cassandre. Los Angeles, 1940.
43537.50.130 Baldensperger, F. Mezza voie. Paris, 1895.
43537.51.100 Ballot-Léna, Bernard. Saisons; poèmes. Paris, 1954.
43537.51.110 Ballot-Léna, Bernard. Poèmes, 1948-1956. Paris, 1963.
43537.60.100 Ballet, René. Échec et mat. Paris, 1960.
43537.70.100 Barbier, René. Marie Pietrot. Paris, 1945.
43537.72.100 Baranger, Léon. A la terrasse. Paris, 1922.
43537.73.100 Barbarin, George. Jesusa de Guipuzcoa. pt. 1-2. Paris, 1936.
43537.73.102 Barbarin, George. Jesusa de Guipuzcoa. Paris, 1936.
43537.74.100 Barde, André. Pépé: comédie. Paris, 1924.
43537.74.1100 Barbier, Jean Joël. Irradiante. Paris, 1954.
43537.74.2100 Barraud, Jean. Chants de mer. Paris, 1961.
43537.74.3100 Barbier, Elisabeth. Ni le jour, ni l'heure; roman. Paris, 1969.
43537.76.100 Le Bargy, C.G.A. Une danseuse est morte. Paris, 1922. 2 pam.
43537.76.1100 Barjavel, René. Four de feu. Paris, 1957.
43537.76.1110 Barjavel, René. Le diable l'emporte. Paris, 1959.
43537.77.100 Barle, F. Le coeur passionne. Paris, 1935.
43537.77.1100 Baron, Jacques. Le noir de l'azur. Paris, 1946.
43537.77.1110 Baron, Jacques. L'an I du surréalisme. Suivi de l'an dernier. Paris, 1969.
43537.77.2106A Baroncelli, J. de. Vingt-six hommes, récit. 6e éd. Paris, 1941.
43537.77.2106B Baroncelli, J. de. Vingt-six hommes, récit. 34e éd. Paris, 1941.
43537.77.3100 Barthes, Roland. Mythologies. Paris, 1957.
43537.77.3110 Barthes, Roland. Essais critiques. Paris, 1964.
43537.77.3120 Barthes, Roland. Critique et verité. Paris, 1966.
43537.77.4021 Barre, André. Symptomes; poèmes, 1943-1958. Rodez, 1965.
43537.77.5100 Baroche, Jacques. Au bois cruel. Paris, 1955.
43537.77.5110 Baroche, Jacques. Chants d'amour. Paris, 1952.
43537.77.5120 Baroche, Jacques. Le sang des vierges. Dijon, 1960.
43537.77.6100 Barrault, Jean Louis. Rabelais. Paris, 1968.
43537.77.6110 Barrault, Jean Louis. Jarry sur la Butte. Paris, 1970.
43537.77.6700 Barrault, Jean Louis. Rabelais. 1st American ed. N.Y., 1971.
43537.78.103 Barry, Léon. Au delà du Bonheur. 3e éd. Paris, 1912?
43537.80.100 Baschet, Jacques. Le refuge. pt. 1. Paris, 1922.
43537.81.100 Basile, André. Le fil d'Ariane; poèmes. Paris, 1966.
43537.82.100 Bassan, Jean. Juliette. Paris, 1938.
43537.82.110 Bassan, Jean. Nuls ve s'évadé. Paris, 1957.
43537.82.2100 Basson, Pierre. Chemin d'homme. Paris, 1955.
43537.82.2110 Basson, Pierre. La Tête. Paris, 1969.
43537.82.3100 Bastide, François Régis. Les adieux. N.Y., 1958.
43537.82.3110 Bastide, François Régis. La vie rêvee. Paris, 1962.
43537.82.3120 Bastide, François Régis. La Palme. n.p., n.d.

43511 - 43873 Individual authors, etc. - 1900- - Known authors (363 scheme plus 10) - cont.

43537.82.3130 Bastide, François Régis. La Forêt noire et le Troisième concerto. Paris, 1968.
43537.82.4100 Bastid, Paul. Ailleurs, poèmes. Paris, 1970.
43537.83.100 Bastien, André P. Domaines. Paris, 1958.
43537.84.100 Bataille, Michel. Le chapeau de velours. 2e éd. Paris, 1918.
43537.84.110 Bataille, Michel. La ville des fous; roman. Paris, 1966.
43537.84.120 Bataille, Michel. L'Arbre de Noël. Paris, 1967.
43537.84.140 Bataille, Michel. Une colere balanche; roman. Paris, 1969.
43537.84.1011 Bataille, Georges. Oeuvres complètes. Paris, 1970- 4v.
43537.84.1100 Bataille, Georges. Le bleu du ciel. Paris, 1957.
43537.84.1110 Bataille, Georges. Le coupable. Paris, 1961.
43537.84.1120 Bataille, Georges. L'Archangélique et autres poèmes. Paris, 1967.
43537.84.2100 Bataille, Alfred. Arabesques. Paris, 1959?
43537.84.3100 Bataille, Roger. Les mains de l'éte. Alger, 1953.
43537.88.5 Cahiers Gaston Baty. Paris. 1,1963+
43537.88.100 Baty, Gaston. Crime et chatiment. Paris, 1933.
43537.88.110 Baty, Gaston. Madame Bovary; vingt tableaux adaptés. Paris, 1936.
43537.88.120 Baty, Gaston. Dulcinée; tragi-comédie en deux parties et huit tableaux. Paris, 1939.
43537.88.1100 Bauchau, Henry. Geólogie. Paris, 1958.
43537.88.1110 Bauchau, Henry. La Déchirure. Paris, 1966.
43537.88.1120 Bauchau, Henry. La pierre sans chagrin. Lausanne, 1966.
43537.88.2100 Baudy, Nicolas. Le piano d'Arlequin. Paris, 1946.
43537.88.3100 Baudry, Édouard. Rue principale. Montréal, 194-?
43537.88.4100 Baudouy, Michel Aimé. La quadrelle Sarda. Paris, 1957.
43537.89.100A Baudouin, C. Contemporary studies. N.Y., 1925.
43537.89.100B Baudouin, C. Contemporary studies. N.Y., 1925.
43537.89.110 Baudouin, C. The myth of modernity. London, 1950.
43537.89.1200 Bauër, Gérard. Les billets de guermantes. Paris, 1937. 2v.
43537.89.1210 Bauër, Gérard. Chroniques, 1934-1953. Paris, 1964. 3v.
43537.89.2100 Baumann, Émile. Job le prédestiné. Paris, 1922.
43537.89.2110 Baumann, Émile. L'excommunié. Paris, 1939.
43537.89.2120 Baumann, Émile. Abel et Cain. Paris, 1930.
43537.89.2130 Baumann, Émile. L'immolé. Paris, 1925.
43537.89.2140 Baumann, Émile. Le signe sur les mains. 7. éd. Paris, 1926.
43537.89.2150 Baumann, Émile. La symphonie du désir. Paris, 1933.
43537.89.2160 Baumann, Émile. Le baptême de Pauline Ardel. Paris, 1913.
43537.89.2805 Holthoff, R. Émile Baumann und seine Bedeutung für die heuitige Zeit. Diss. Jena, 1935.
43537.89.3100 Bauer, Anne M. La vigie aveugle. Paris, 1957.
43537.89.4100 Baudin, Suzanne. Le ciel frôla la terre. Paris, 1958.
43537.89.5100 Baudot, Jean A. La machine à écrire mise en marche et programmée. Montréal, 1964.
43537.89.6100 Baudouin, Georges. Traduit de la mer. Bruxelles, 1964.
43537.89.7100 Baudu, Antoinette. Sirocco en kabylie. Paris, 1969.
43537.89.8100 Baud-Bovy, Daniel. L'homme à la femme de bois. Genève, 1970.
43537.90.100 Bausil, Albert. Poèmes d'amour et d'autonne. Paris, 1929.
43537.97.100 Bay, Paul. Miss Gorilla; roman. Spa, 1957.
43537.97.110 Bay, Paul. De la terre au ciel; poésies. Bruxelles, 1963.
43537.98.805 Eicke, W.A. Léon Bazalgette, 1873-1929. Inaug. Diss. Bonn, 1937.
43537.98.809 Eicke, W.A. Léon Bazalgette, 1873-1929 und seine Anschaunungen über Latinität udn Germanentum. Bonn, 1937.
43537.98.2100 Bay, André. La carte du tendre. Paris, 1959.
43537.98.3100 Bayvet, Henri. Dimanche matin. Paris, 1937.
43537.98.4100 Bazin, Jean. Tristie, poèmes. Paris, 1956.
43537.98.5100 Bayo, Gérard. Nostalgies pour paradis; poèmes. Paris, 1956.
43537.99.100 Bazin, Hervé. Vipère au poing, roman. Paris, 1948.
43537.99.110 Bazin, Hervé. La tête contre les murs. 51e éd. Paris, 1949.
43537.99.120 Bazin, Hervé. Lève-toi et marche. Paris, 1952.
43537.99.130 Bazin, Hervé. Humeurs. Paris, 1953.
43537.99.140 Bazin, Hervé. L'huile sur le feu. Paris, 1954.
43537.99.150 Bazin, Hervé. Qui j'ose aimer. Paris, 1956.
43537.99.160 Bazin, Hervé. Anom du fils. Paris, 1960.
43537.99.170 Bazin, Hervé. Plumons l'oiseau. Paris, 1966.
43537.99.180 Bazin, Hervé. Le matrimoine; roman. Paris, 1967.
43537.99.190 Bazin, Hervé. Les bienheureux de la Désolation. Paris, 1970.
43537.99.700 Bazin, Hervé. A tribe of women. N.Y., 1958.
43537.99.710 Bazin, Hervé. In the name of the son. London, 1962.
43537.99.800 Anglade, Jean. Hervé Bazin. Paris, 1962.
43538.1.30 Beauduin, Nicolas. La divine folie. Paris, 1910.
43538.1.31 Beauduin, Nicolas. L'offrande héroïque; poèmes. Neuilly, 1915?
43538.1.33 Beauduin, Nicolas. Les deux regnes. Paris, 1911.
43538.1.200.5 Béalu, Marcel. Marcel Béalu. Rodez, 1956.
43538.1.200.10 Béalu, Marcel. L'air de vie. Paris, 1958.
43538.1.205 Béalu, Marcel. Les messagers clandestins. Paris, 1956.
43538.1.210 Béalu, Marcel. La pérégrination fantasque. Paris, 1951.
43538.1.215 Béalu, Marcel. La rivièra. Aulnay-sous-Bois, 1955?
43538.1.220 Béalu, Marcel. Coeur vivant. Paris, 1941.
43538.1.225 Béalu, Marcel. Ocarina. Paris, 1952.
43538.1.230 Béalu, Marcel. Contes du demi-sommeil. Perigueux, 1960.
43538.1.235 Goldschmidt, Georges-Arthur. Un cas de flagrant délit; les contes de Marcel Béalu. Paris, 1967.
43538.1.335 Béarn, Pierre. Mains sur la mère. Paris, 1941.
43538.1.340 Béarn, Pierre. Dialogues de mon amour. v.1-4. Paris, 1956.
43538.1.430 Gennari, Geneviève. Simone de Beauvoir. Paris, 1959.
43538.1.430.2 Gennari, Geneviève. Simone de Beauvoir. Paris, 1963.
43538.1.435 Beauvoir, Simone de. Les bouches inutiles; pièce en deux actes et huit tableaux. 5. éd. Paris, 1945.
43538.1.440 Beauvoir, Simone de. Tous les hommes sont mortels, roman. Paris, 1946.
43538.1.442 Beauvoir, Simone de. All men are mortal. 1. ed. Cleveland, 1955.
43538.1.445 Beauvoir, Simone de. L'invitée. 29. éd. Paris, 1943.
43538.1.450 Beauvoir, Simone de. L'Amérique au jour le jour. Paris, 1948.
43538.1.452 Beauvoir, Simone de. L'Amérique au jour le jour. Paris, 1954.
43538.1.455 Beauvoir, Simone de. Le Mandarins. 248. éd. Paris, 1954.
43538.1.457 La Vouldie. Mme. Simone de Beauvoir et ses "Mandarins". Paris, 1955.

43511 - 43873 Individual authors, etc. - 1900- - Known authors (363 scheme plus 10) - cont.

	43538.1.460	Beauvoir, Simone de. Le sang des autres; roman. Paris, 1946.
	43538.1.465	Beauvoir, Simone de. Pyrrhus et Cinéas. Paris, 1944.
	43538.1.470	Beauvoir, Simone de. She came to stay. London, 1949.
	43538.1.480	Beauvoir, Simone de. America day by day. London, 1952.
	43538.1.490A	Beauvoir, Simone de. The Mandarins. Cleveland, 1956.
	43538.1.490B	Beauvoir, Simone de. The Mandarins. Cleveland, 1956.
	43538.1.500	Beauvoir, Simone de. Privilèges. 9. éd. Paris, 1955.
	43538.1.510	Beauvoir, Simone de. La longue marche. 30. éd. Paris, 1957.
	43538.1.515	Beauvoir, Simone de. The long march. 1. ed. Cleveland, 1958.
	43538.1.520	Beauvoir, Simone de. Mémoires d'une jeune fille rangée. Paris, 1958.
	43538.1.522	Beauvoir, Simone de. Memoirs of a dutiful daughter. 1. ed. Cleveland, 1959.
	43538.1.524A	Beauvoir, Simone de. La force de l'âge. Paris, 1960.
	43538.1.524B	Beauvoir, Simone de. La force de l'âge. Paris, 1960.
	43538.1.526	Beauvoir, Simone de. The prime of life. Cleveland, 1962.
	43538.1.530	Beauvoir, Simone de. La force des choses. Paris, 1963.
	43538.1.535	Beauvoir, Simone de. Une mort très douce. Paris, 1964.
	43538.1.540	Beauvoir, Simone de. Les belles images. Paris, 1966.
	43538.1.550	Beauvoir, Simone de. La femme rompue. L'age de discrétion. Paris, 1968.
	43538.1.555	Beauvoir, Simone de. The woman destroyed. 1. American ed. N.Y., 1969.
	43538.1.700	Beauvoir, Simone de. Force of circumstance. N.Y., 1965.
	43538.1.705	Beauvoir, Simone de. A very easy death. London, 1966.
	43538.1.800	Henry, A.M. Simone de Beauvoir, ou L'échec d'une chretienté. Paris, 1961.
	43538.1.810	Wasmund, Dagny. Der "Skandal" der Simone Beauvoir. München, 1963.
	43538.1.815	Hourdin, G. Simone de Beauvoir et la liberté. Paris, 1962.
	43538.1.820	Béalu, Marcel. L'araignée d'eau et autres récits fantastiques. Paris, 1964.
	43538.1.825	Jeanson, Francis. Simone de Beauvoir ou l'entreprise. Paris, 1966.
	43538.1.830	Julienne-Caffié, Serge. Simone de Beauvoir. Paris, 1966.
	43538.1.835	Berghe, Christian Louis van den. Dictionnaire des idées dans l'oeuvre de Simone de Beauvoir. The Hague, 1966.
	43538.1.840	Jaccard, Annie Claire. Simone de Beauvoir. Zurich, 1968.
	43538.1.845	Saetre, Solveig. Kvinnen-det annet kjønn? Oslo, 1969.
	43538.1.850	Lasocki, Anne-Marie. Simone de Beauvoir. La Haye, 1971.
	43538.2.30	Benoit, F. Foire aux paysages. Paris, 1911.
	43538.2.1100	Benoit, Pierre André. Oreilles gardées. Paris, 1962.
	43538.2.1110	Benoit, Pierre André. Le chemin resserré. Veilhes, 1966.
	43538.3.30	Bernède, A. Sous l'Epaulette. Paris, 1906.
	43538.3.35	Benoit, Pierre André. Les guerres d'enfer et l'avenir de l'intelligence. Félicien-en-Vivarais, 1925.
	43538.4.30	Bernardin, N.M. L'Abbé Frifillis. Paris, 1911.
	43538.5.35	Benda, Julien. La fin de l'éternel. 4. éd. Paris, 1928.
	43538.5.40	Benda, Julien. Délice d'éleuthère. 4. éd. Paris, 1935.
	43538.5.45A	Benda, Julien. Précision. (1930-1937). 4. éd. Paris, 1937.
	43538.5.45B	Benda, Julien. Précision. (1930-1937). 4. éd. Paris, 1937.
	43538.5.50	Benda, Julien. Prosperee, au Les amants. Paris, 1928.
	43538.5.70	Benda, Julien. La jeunesse d'un clerc. 8. éd. Paris, 1937.
	43538.5.75	Benda, Julien. Un régulier dans le siècle. Paris, 1937.
	43538.5.85	Benda, Julien. Exercise d'un enterré vif (juin 1940 - août 1944). 4. éd. Genève, 1945.
	43538.5.90	Benda, Julien. Les cahiers d'un clerc. 3. éd. Paris, 1950.
	43538.5.100	Benda, Julien. Mémoires d'infra-tombe. Paris, 1952.
	43538.5.800	Niess, R.J. Julien Benda. Ann Arbor, 1956.
	43538.5.805	Doisy, M. Belphégor et le clerc. Paris, 1960?
	43538.5.810	Sarocchi, Jean. Julien Benda, portrait d'un intellectuel. Paris, 1968.
	43538.5.3100	Fonson, Geneviève B. Babillage; poems. Paris, 1958.
	43538.5.4100	Beauvais, Robert. Quand les Chinois. Paris, 1966.
	43538.6.30	Berger, Marcel. Le miracle du feu; roman. Paris, 1917.
	43538.6.32	Berger, Marcel. Jean Darboise auxiliaire. Paris, 1917.
	43538.6.130	Berger, Yves. Le sud. Paris, 1962.
	43538.6.700	Berger, Marcel. The ordeal by fire. N.Y., 1917.
	43538.6.710	Berger, Marcel. The secret of the Maine, how Sergeant Aritsch saved France. N.Y., 1918.
	43538.6.720	Berger, Yves. The garden. N.Y., 1963.
	43538.7.30	Benjamin, René. Le Major Pipe et son père. 8. éd. Paris, 1918.
	43538.7.32	Benjamin, René. La guerre sous le ciel de France. Paris, 1916.
	43538.7.33	Benjamin, René. Les soldats de la guerre. Paris, 1915.
Htn	43538.7.33.5*	Benjamin, René. Les soldats de la guerre. Paris, 1917.
	43538.7.34	Benjamin, René. Les plaisirs du hasard. Paris, 1922.
	43538.7.35	Benjamin, René. Les plaisirs du hasard. Paris, 1922.
	43538.7.37	Benjamin, René. Amadou, bolcheviste. Paris, 1920.
	43538.7.39	Benjamin, René. Chronique d'un temps troublé. Paris, 1938.
	43538.7.40	Benjamin, René. Le soliloque de Maurice Barrès. Paris, 1924.
	43538.7.49	Benjamin, René. Le printemps tragique. Paris, 1941.
	43538.7.52	Benjamin, René. Le vin, lumière du coeur. Paris, 1948.
	43538.7.60	Benjamin, René. La force de la Sorbonne. Paris, 1927.
	43538.7.65	Benjamin, René. Antoine enchaîné. Paris, 1928.
	43538.8.30	Bertrand, Adrien. L'appel du sol. Paris, 1916.
	43538.8.35	Bertrand, Adrien. L'orage sur le jardin de candide. Paris, 1917.
	43538.8.37	Bertrand, Adrien. Le verger de Cypris. Paris, 1917.
	43538.9.30	Berthaut, Léon. Soldats de Jeanne d'Arc. Paris, 1919.
	43538.9.35	Berthaut, Léon. Lueurs dans l'infini. St. Brienc, 1927.
	43538.9.40	Berthaut, Léon. Les amants de Tereul. Paris, 1923.
	43538.9.50	Berthaut, Léon. Rose-Blanche. Havre, 1898.
	43538.10.30	Bernard, Jean J. Le feu qui reprend mal; pièce. Paris, 1921.
	43538.10.31	Bernard, Jean J. Le feu qui reprend mal; pièce en trois actes. Paris, 1922.
	43538.10.35	Bernard, Jean J. Martine; pièce. Paris, 1922.
	43538.10.38	Bernard, Jean J. Martine; play. London, 1932.
	43538.10.45	Bernard, Jean J. Le printemps des autres. Paris, 1924.
	43538.10.50	Bernard, Jean J. Théâtre. Paris, 1925.
	43538.10.53	Bernard, Jean J. Théâtre. Paris, 1946.
	43538.10.54	Bernard, Jean J. Mon ami le théâtre. Paris, 1958.
	43538.10.55	Bernard, Jean J. Nationale 6. Paris, 1935.
	43538.10.65	Bernard, Jean J. Le pain rouge. Paris, 1947.
	43538.10.705	Bernard, Jean J. The sulky five, five plays. London, 1948.
	43538.10.8100	Bernard-Massenat. Le masque creux. Paris, 1957.
	43538.11.33	Beaunier, André. L'amour et les secret. Paris, 1920.
	43538.11.35	Beaunier, André. Figures d'autrefois. Paris, 1917.
	43538.11.40	Beaunier, André. Les souvenirs d'un peintre. Paris, 1906.
	43538.11.50	Beaunier, André. Discours adressé aux élèves du collège Stanislas le 24 décembre 1911. Bruges, 1912.
	43538.11.60	Beaunier, André. La revolté. Paris, 1914.
	43538.12.100	Béchu, Jean Louis. L'Acier, la rose, poèmes. Paris, 1966.
	43538.13.100	Beaumont, G. La longue nuit. Paris, 1936.
	43538.13.2100	Becker, Yves. Puisque voici la joie. Paris, 1947.
	43538.13.3100	Beckers, Alain. Sonnets. Bruxelles, 1949.
	43538.13.3110	Beckers, Alain. Les chorals spirituels. Paris, 1968.
	43538.14.48	Beckett, Samuel. Le Roi Tobol. Paris, 1905.
	43538.14.50	Beckett, Samuel. A Samuel Beckett reader. London, 1967.
	43538.14.100	Beckett, Samuel. L'innommable. Paris, 1953.
	43538.14.110	Beckett, Samuel. Molloy. Paris, 1953.
	43538.14.111	Beckett, Samuel. Molloy l'expulsé. Paris, 1962?
	43538.14.120	Beckett, Samuel. En attendant Godot. Paris, 1952.
	43538.14.125	Beckett, Samuel. En attendant Godot: pièce en deux actes. London, 1966.
	43538.14.130	Beckett, Samuel. Nouvelles et textes pour rien. Paris, 1955.
	43538.14.140	Beckett, Samuel. Melone meurt. Paris, 1951.
	43538.14.150	Beckett, Samuel. Fin de partie. Paris, 1957.
	43538.14.160	Beckett, Samuel. Tous ceux qui tombent. Paris, 1957.
	43538.14.170	Beckett, Samuel. Comment c'est. Paris, 1961.
	43538.14.180	Beckett, Samuel. La derniere bande. Paris, 1960.
	43538.14.190	Beckett, Samuel. Oh les beaux jours. Paris, 1963.
	43538.14.200	Beckett, Samuel. Dramatische Dicktungen. Frankfurt, 1963. 2v.
	43538.14.210	Beckett, Samuel. Imagination morte, imaginez. Paris, 1965.
	43538.14.220	Beckett, Samuel. Comédie et actes divers. Paris, 1966.
	43538.14.230	Beckett, Samuel. Assez. Paris, 1966.
	43538.14.240	Beckett, Samuel. Têtes-mortes. Paris, 1967.
	43538.14.250	Beckett, Samuel. Poèmes. Paris, 1968.
	43538.14.260	Beckett, Samuel. Mercier et Camier. Paris, 1970.
	43538.14.270	Beckett, Samuel. Premier amour. Paris, 1970.
	43538.14.280	Beckett, Samuel. Le dépeupleur. Paris, 1970.
	43538.14.621	Beckett, Samuel. Play, and two short pieces for radio. London, 1964.
	43538.14.702	Beckett, Samuel. Waiting for Godot, tragicomedy in 2 acts. N.Y., 1970.
Htn	43538.14.720*	Beckett, Samuel. Murphy. London, 1938.
	43538.14.721	Beckett, Samuel. Murphy. N.Y., 1957.
	43538.14.730A	Beckett, Samuel. Watt. 1. ed. Paris? 1953.
	43538.14.730B	Beckett, Samuel. Watt. 1. ed. Paris? 1953.
	43538.14.735A	Beckett, Samuel. From an abandoned work. London, 1958.
	43538.14.735B	Beckett, Samuel. From an abandoned work. London, 1958.
	43538.14.738	Beckett, Samuel. Eh, Joe. London, 1967.
	43538.14.740	Beckett, Samuel. More pricks than kicks. London, 1934.
	43538.14.740.2	Beckett, Samuel. More pricks than kicks. 2. ed. London, 1966.
	43538.14.745A	Beckett, Samuel. Poems in English. London, 1961.
	43538.14.745B	Beckett, Samuel. Poems in English. London, 1961.
	43538.14.746	Beckett, Samuel. Poems in English. N.Y., 1963.
	43538.14.747.2	Beckett, Samuel. Poesie in inglese. 2. ed. Torino, 1964.
	43538.14.750	Beckett, Samuel. Molloy. Paris, 1955.
	43538.14.752	Beckett, Samuel. No's knife. London, 1967.
	43538.14.755	Beckett, Samuel. Molloy. London, 1959.
	43538.14.757	Beckett, Samuel. Residua; Prosadichtungen in drei Sprachen. 1. Aufl. Frankfurt, 1970.
	43538.14.760	Beckett, Samuel. Malone dies. N.Y., 1956.
	43538.14.765	Beckett, Samuel. Imagination dead imagine. London, 1966.
	43538.14.770	Beckett, Samuel. All that fall. London, 1957.
	43538.14.775A	Beckett, Samuel. Krapp's last tape. London, 1959.
	43538.14.775B	Beckett, Samuel. Krapp's last tape. London, 1959.
	43538.14.780	Beckett, Samuel. Endgame. N.Y., 1958.
	43538.14.782A	Beckett, Samuel. Endgame. N.Y., 1958.
	43538.14.782B	Beckett, Samuel. Endgame. N.Y., 1958.
	43538.14.785	Beckett, Samuel. Happy days. N.Y., 1961.
	43538.14.788	Beckett, Samuel. Glückliche Tage und andere Stücke. Frankfurt, 1963.
	43538.14.790	Beckett, Samuel. How it is. N.Y., 1964.
	43538.14.791	Beckett, Samuel. Cascando, and other short dramatic pieces. N.Y., 1968?
	43538.14.792	Beckett, Samuel. How it is. London, 1964.
	43538.14.794	Beckett, Samuel. Bing. Paris, 1966.
	43538.14.795	Beckett, Samuel. Wie es ist. Frankfurt, 1963.
	43538.14.796	Beckett, Samuel. Film. N.Y., 1969.
	43538.14.798	Beckett, Samuel. Pronst. London, 1965.
	43538.14.799	Beckett, Samuel. Come and go; dramaticule. London, 1967.
	43538.14.800	Gessner, Niklaus. Die Unzulänglichkeit der Sprache. Zürich, 1957.
	43538.14.805	Hoffman, F.J. Samuel Beckett: the language of self. Carbondale, 1962.
	43538.14.810	Kenner, Hugh. Samuel Beckett. N.Y., 1961.
	43538.14.810.5	Kenner, Hugh. Samuel Beckett, a critical study. Berkeley, 1968.
	43538.14.815	Cohn, Ruby. Samuel Beckett: the comic gamut. New Brunswick, 1962.
	43538.14.820	Marissel, A. Samuel Beckett. Paris, 1963.
	43538.14.825	Jacobsen, J. The testament of Samuel Beckett. 1. ed. N.Y., 1964.
	43538.14.830	Seipel, H. Untersuchungen zum experimentellen Theater von Beckett und Ionesco. Bonn, 1963.
	43538.14.835	Maciel, L.C. Samuel Beckett e a solidão humana. Porto Alegre, n.d.
	43538.14.840	Fletcher, John. The novels of Samuel Beckett. London, 1964.
	43538.14.842	Fletcher, John. The novels of Samuel Beckett. 2. ed. London, 1970.
	43538.14.845	Coe, Richard N. Beckett. Edinburgh, 1964.
	43538.14.850	Scott, Nathan Alexander. Samuel Beckett. London, 1965.
	43538.14.851	Scott, Nathan Alexander. Samuel Beckett. London, 1969.
	43538.14.855	Tindall, William York. Samuel Beckett. N.Y., 1964.
	43538.14.860	Esslin, Martin. Samuel Beckett: a collection of critical essays. Englewood Cliffs, N.J., 1965.
	43538.14.865	Federman, Raymond. Journey to chaos. Berkeley, 1965.
	43538.14.870	Friedman, Melvin J. Samuel Beckett. Paris, 1964.
	43538.14.875	Janvier, Ludovic. Pour Samuel Beckett. Paris, 1966.
	43538.14.876	Janvier, Ludovic. Samuel Beckett par lui-même. Paris, 1969.
	43538.14.880	Mélèse, Pierre. Samuel Beckett. Paris, 1966.

43511 - 43873 Individual authors, etc. - 1900- - Known authors (363 scheme plus 10) - cont.

43538.14.885 Backett at 60: a festschrift. London, 1967.

43538.14.890 Fletcher, John. Samuel Beckett's art. London, 1967.

43538.14.895 Hayman, Ronald. Samuel Beckett. London, 1968.

43538.14.905 Harrison, Robert. Samuel Beckett's Murphy: a critical excursion. Athens, 1968.

43538.14.910 Onimus, Jean. Beckett. Paris, 1967.

43538.14.915 Reid, Alec. All I can manage, more than I could. Dublin, 1968.

43538.14.920 Tagliaferri, Aldo. Beckett e l'iperdeterminazione letteraria. 1. ed. Milano, 1967.

43538.14.925 Ohio State Unviersity, Columbus. Library. Nelson Algren and Samuel Beckett. Columbus, 1966?

43538.14.930 Hensel, Georg. Samuel Beckett. 1. Aufl. Velber, 1968.

43538.14.935 Schoell, Konrad. Das Theater Samuel Becketts. München, 1967.

43538.14.940 Büttner, Gottfried. Absurdes Theater und Bewusstseinswandel. Berlin, 1968.

43538.14.945 Robinson, Michael. The long sonata of the dead. London, 1969.

43538.14.950 Cattanei, Giovanni. Beckett. Firenze, 1967.

43538.14.955 Bernal, Olga. Langage et fiction dans le roman de Beckett. Paris, 1969.

43538.14.960 Perche, Louis. Beckett, l'enfer à notre portée. Paris, 1969.

43538.14.965 Harvey, Lawrence Elliot. Samuel Beckett, poet and critic. Princeton, 1970.

43538.14.970 Barnard, Guy Christian. Samuel Beckett: a new approach. London, 1970.

43538.14.975 Samuel Beckett now. Chicago, 1970.

43538.14.980 Webb, Eugene. Samuel Beckett: a study of his novels. Seattle, 1970.

43538.14.985 Dreysse, Ursula. Realität als Aufgabe. Berlin, 1970.

43538.14.990 Federman, Raymond. Samuel Beckett: his works and critics. Berkeley, 1970.

43538.14.995 O'Hara, James Donald. Twentieth century interpretations of Molloy, Malone dies, The unnamable. Englewood Cliffs, N.J., 1970.

43538.14.1000 Smuda, Manfred. Becketts Prosa als Metasprache. München, 1970.

43538.14.1005 Materialien zu Becketts "Endspiel". Frankfurt, 1968.

43538.14.1010 Hesla, David H. The shape of chaos. Minneapolis, 1971.

43538.14.2100 Beck, Béatrix. Barmy. Paris, 1948.

43538.14.2110 Beck, Béatrix. Le muet. Paris, 1963.

43538.14.2120 Beck, Béatrix. Cou coupé court toujours. Paris, 1967.

43538.14.2700 Beck, Béatrix. The priest. London, 1953.

43538.14.2710 Beck, Béatrix. The passionate heart. N.Y., 1953.

43538.14.2720 Beck, Béatrix. Des accommodements avec le ciel. Paris, 1954-55.

43538.14.3100 Bechtel, Guy. En sortir au pas. Paris, 1960.

43538.17.100A Bedel, Maurice. Jerome, 60 latitude nord. 26. éd. Paris, 1927.

43538.17.100B Bedel, Maurice. Jerome, 60 latitude nord. 107. éd. Paris, 1927.

43538.17.110 Bedel, Maurice. Molinoff, Indre-et-Loire. Paris, 1928.

43538.17.120 Bedel, Maurice. Philippine. 23. éd. Paris, 1930.

43538.17.125A Bedel, Maurice. Zulfu. 58. éd. Paris, 1932.

43538.17.125B Bedel, Maurice. Zulfu. 26. éd. Paris, 1932.

43538.17.130 Bedel, Maurice. Le mariage des couleurs. 4. éd. Paris, 1951.

43538.17.140 Bedel, Maurice. L'alouette aux nuages. Paris, 1935.

43538.17.700 Bedel, Maurice. Molinoff; or, The count in the kitchen. N.Y., 1929.

43538.17.710 Bedel, Maurice. Jerome; or, The latitude of Cove. N.Y., 1928.

43538.18.100 Bédier, Joseph. Tristan et Iseut. Paris, 1929.

43538.18.110 Bédier, Joseph. Chevalerie. Tours, 1931.

43538.18.805 Lot, F. Joseph Bédier, 1864-1938. Paris, 1939.

43538.18.810 Vinaver, E. Hommage a Bédier. Manchester, 1942.

43538.24.100 Beerblock, Maurice. La troisième fois et autres histoires. Bruxelles, 1961.

43538.25.100 Beer, Jean de. Tombeau de Jean Giraudoux. Paris, 1946.

43538.35.100 Albert Béguin. Neuchâtel, 1957.

43538.35.800 Franck, Dorothée Juliane. La quête spirituelle d'Albert Béguin. Neuchâtel, 1965.

43538.35.1100 Beguin, Guy. Monsieur Faust, Madame et l'autre. Ixelles, 1964.

43538.35.1110 Beguin, Guy. Anamorphose. Bruxelles, 1964.

43538.35.1800 Despert, Jehan. Guy Beguin, ou Le théâtre en liberte. Ixelles, 1964.

43538.36.105 Béhaine, René. Histoire d'une société. Paris, 1928. 16v.

43538.36.110 Béhaine, René. Pièces à conviction. Paris, 1960.

43538.36.705 Béhaine, René. The survivors. N.Y., 1938.

43538.36.710 Béhaine, René. Day of glory. London, 1949.

43538.36.715 Béhaine, René. The conquest of life. London, 1939.

43538.48.100 Bellanger, Henri. Les noces de pierre. Fontenoy-en-Puisaye, 1965.

43538.49.100 Belen (pseud.). La géométrie dans les spasmes. Paris, 1959.

43538.49.110 Belen (pseud.). La reine des sabbats. Paris, 1960.

43538.49.120 Belen (pseud.). Et délivrez nous du mâle. Paris, 1960.

43538.49.130 Belen (pseud.). Le réservoir des sens. Paris, 1966.

43538.50.21 Bengoechea, Hernando de. Hernando de Bengoechea, ou L'âme d'un poète. Paris, 1948.

43538.51.100 Belloni, Georges. La porte d'ivoire. Paris, 1934.

43538.51.110 Belloni, Georges. Les chemins de gloire. Paris, 1959.

43538.51.120 Belloni, Georges. Sous le signe du Bélier. Paris, 1954.

43538.51.1100 Belmont, Georges. Un homme au crépuscule; roman. Paris, 1966.

43538.51.2100 Belleval, Guy de. Jean des autres; roman. Paris, 1959.

43538.59.100 Benda, Julien. Billets de Sirius. Paris, 1925.

43538.59.110 Benda, Julien. Le bouquet de Glycère. Paris, 1918.

43538.59.1100 Bénézet, M. Biographies. A novel. Paris, 1970.

43538.59.2100 Benedetto, André. Le petit train de Monsieur Kamodé. Honfleur, 1969.

43538.59.2110 Benedetto, André. Zone rouge, feux interdits. Honfleur, 1969.

43538.59.2120 Benedetto, André. Napalm. Honfleur, 1968.

43538.59.2130 Benedetto, André. Emballage, Le Havre 1970. Théâtre. Paris, 1970.

43538.59.2140 Benedetto, André. Rosa Lux, théâtre. Honfleur, 1970.

43538.60.100 Benjamin, René. L'hôtel des ventes. Paris, 1919.

43538.60.1100 Bénichoo, Aimé. Les Marranes. Paris, 1968.

43538.61.20 Benoît, Pierre. Oeuvres romanesques. Givors, 1957-59. 6v.

NEDL 43538.61.30 Benoît, Pierre. L'Atlantide. Paris, 1919.

43511 - 43873 Individual authors, etc. - 1900- - Known authors (363 scheme plus 10) - cont.

43538.61.33 Benoît, Pierre. L'Atlantide; roman. Paris, 1920.

43538.61.35 Benoît, Pierre. L'Atlantide. Paris, 1928.

43538.61.39A Benoît, Pierre. L'Atlantida. (L'Atlantide). N.Y., 1920.

43538.61.39B Benoît, Pierre. L'Atlantida. (L'Atlantide). N.Y., 1920.

43538.61.40 Benoît, Pierre. Le lac salé. Paris, 1921.

43538.61.50 Benoît, Pierre. Pour Don Carlos. Paris, 1920.

43538.61.56 Benoît, Pierre. De Koenigsmark à Montsalvat. Paris, 1958.

43538.61.59 Benoît, Pierre. Koenigsmark. 55. éd. Paris, 1920.

43538.61.62 Benoît, Pierre. Koenigsmark. 221. éd. Paris, 1923.

43538.61.63 Benoît, Pierre. Koenigsmark. 268. éd. Paris, 1924.

43538.61.65 Benoît, Pierre. Le puits de Jacob. Paris, 1925.

43538.61.66 Benoît, Pierre. Le puits de Jacob. Paris, 1925.

43538.61.70A Benoît, Pierre. Alberte. Paris, 1926.

43538.61.70B Benoît, Pierre. Alberte. Paris, 1926.

43538.61.75 Benoît, Pierre. Le soleil de minuit; roman. pt.1-4. Paris, 1930.

43538.61.75.2 Benoît, Pierre. Le soleil de minuit. Paris, 1930.

43538.61.80 Benoît, Pierre. Saint Jean d'Arce. Paris, 1936.

43538.61.81 Benoît, Pierre. Le prêtre Jean. Paris, 1952.

43538.61.85 Benoît, Pierre. Fort-de-France. Paris, 1933.

43538.61.90 Benoît, Pierre. Le désert de Gobi, roman. Paris, 1941.

43538.61.108 Benoît, Pierre. Le Roi lepreux. Paris, 1927.

43538.61.110 Benoît, Pierre. Notre-Dame de Tortose, roman. Paris, 1939.

43538.61.115 Benoît, Pierre. Les environs d'Aden. Paris, 1940.

43538.61.120 Benoît, Pierre. Seigneur, j'ai tout prevu...roman. Paris, 1943.

43538.61.130 Benoît, Pierre. Martine Juillet. Montréal, 1945.

43538.61.140 Benoît, Pierre. Erromango. Paris, 1929.

43538.61.142 Benoît, Pierre. Erromango. Paris, 1957.

43538.61.150 Benoît, Pierre. Montsalvat. Paris, 1957.

43538.61.160 Benoît, Pierre. Le sentier couvert. Montréal, 1945.

43538.61.170 Benoît, Pierre. La sainte vehme. Paris, 1958.

43538.61.180 Benoît, Pierre. Flamarens, roman. Paris, 1959.

43538.61.190 Benoît, Pierre. Le casino de Barbazon. Montréal, 1949.

43538.61.200 Benoît, Pierre. Le commandeur. Paris, 1960.

43538.61.800 Nicolle, R. Pierre Benoît et Marcelle-Pierre Benoît. Paris, 1963.

43538.61.805 Thiery, Hermann. Pierre Benoît ou l'eloge du Roman romanesque. Paris, 1960.

43538.61.1100 Benoît, Pierre. Trébin du patoès. Auxerre, 1962.

43538.61.3100 Benoit-Guyod, Jeanne. Le chant des pierres. Paris, 1956.

43538.61.4100 Benoit, Raymond. Les voix en chaine. Paris, 1957.

43538.62.100 Benoit-Guyod, Georges. Histoires de gendarmes. 6. éd. Paris, 1937.

43538.62.4100 Bens, Jacques. Chanson recue. Paris, 1958.

43538.62.4110 Bens, Jacques. Valentin. Paris, 1958.

43538.62.4120 Bens, Jacques. La plume et l'angre. 5. éd. Paris, 1959.

43538.62.4130 Bens, Jacques. Adieu Sidonie. Paris, 1969.

43538.74.100A Béraud, Henri. Martyre de l'obèse. Paris, 1922.

43538.74.100B Béraud, Henri. Martyre de l'obèse. Paris, 1922.

43538.74.102 Béraud, Henri. Le martyre de l'obèse; roman. Paris, 1933.

43538.74.110 Béraud, Henri. Le vitriol de lune; roman. Paris, 1921.

43538.74.110.2 Béraud, Henri. Le vitriol de lune; roman. Paris, 1921.

43538.74.115 Béraud, Henri. Le bois du templier pendu. Paris, 1926.

43538.74.116 Béraud, Henri. The wood of the hanging templar. N.Y., 1930.

43538.74.120 Béraud, Henri. Qu'as-tu fait de ta jeunesse? Paris, 1943.

43538.74.130 Béraud, Henri. Les derniers beau jours. Paris, 1953.

43538.74.140 Béraud, Henri. Quinze jours avec la mort. Paris, 1951.

43538.74.150 Béraud, Henri. Au Capucin Gourmand. Paris, 1925.

43538.74.160 Béraud, Henri. Les Lurons de Sabolas. Paris, 1932.

43538.74.170 Béraud, Henri. Sans hoine et sans crainte. Paris, 1942.

43538.74.180 Béraud, Henri. Lazare; roman. Paris, 1924.

43538.74.190 Béraud, Henri. La gerbe d'or. Paris, 1928.

43538.74.200 Béraud, Henri. Ciel du serie. Paris, 1933.

43538.74.210 Béraud, Henri. La flaneur salarié. Paris, 1927.

43538.74.220 Béraud, Henri. La croisade des langues figures. Paris, 1924.

43538.74.230 Béraud, Henri. Les raisons d'un silence. Paris, 1944.

43538.74.240 Béraud, Henri. Pavés rouges. Paris, 1934.

43538.74.250 Béraud, Henri. Trois ans de colère. Paris, 1936.

43538.74.6100 Barbey, Bernard. Lt coeur gros. Paris, 1924.

43538.74.7100 Bergère, André. Sonatines et scherzos pour pulette à cordes. Paris, 1957.

43538.74.8100 Bordonove, G. L'enterrement du comte d'Orgaz. Paris, 1959.

43538.75.100 Bergmans, Simone. Le collier d'épines. Gand, 1948.

43538.75.110 Bergmans, Simone. Le patrémoine secret. Bruxelles, 1947.

43538.75.120 Bergmans, Simone. Faligan. Bruxelles, 1950.

43538.75.130 Bergmans, Simone. Sébastien. Bruxelles, 1959.

43538.75.1100 Berri, Claude. The two of us. N.Y., 1968.

43538.75.2100 Bernard, Jean-Marc. Subtegmine fagi; amours, bergeries et jeux. Paris, 1913.

43538.75.3100 Bergonzo, Jean Louis. Les murs du havre. Paris, 1969.

43538.75.9100 Bernanos, Michel. La Montagne morte de la vie. Paris, 1967.

43538.75.9110 Bernanos, Michel. The other side of the mountain. Boston, 1968.

43538.76.11 Bernanos, Georges. Oeuvres. Paris, 1947. 6v.

43538.76.41A Bernanos, Georges. Bernanos par lui-même. Paris, 1954.

43538.76.41B Bernanos, Georges. Bernanos par lui-même. Paris, 1954.

43538.76.61 Bernanos, Georges. Correspondance. Paris, 1971-

43538.76.100A Bernanos, Georges. Sous le soleil de Satan. Paris, 1926.

43538.76.100B Bernanos, Georges. Sous le soleil de Satan. Paris, 1957.

43538.76.100C Bernanos, Georges. Sous le soleil de Satan. Paris, 1926.

43538.76.102 Bernanos, Georges. Sous le soleil de Satan. Paris, 1926.

43538.76.103 Bernanos, Georges. Sous le soleil de Satan. Paris, 1957.

43538.76.105A Bernanos, Georges. Journal d'un curé de campagne. Paris, 1936.

43538.76.105B Bernanos, Georges. Journal d'un curé de campagne. Paris, 1936.

43538.76.110 Bernanos, Georges. Journal d'un curé de campagne. Paris, 1936.

43538.76.120A Bernanos, Georges. Les grands cimetieres sous la lune. Paris, 1938.

43538.76.120B Bernanos, Georges. Les grands cimetieres sous la lune. Paris, 1938.

43538.76.120C Bernanos, Georges. Les grands cimetieres sous la lune. Paris, 1938.

43538.76.131 Bernanos, Georges. Nouvelle histoire de Mouchette. Paris, 1969.

43538.76.140 Bernanos, Georges. Scandale de la vérité. 4. éd. Paris, 1939.

43538.76.150 Bernanos, Georges. Monsieur Ouine. Rio de Janeiro, 1943.

43538.76.151 Bernanos, Georges. Monsieur Ouine. Paris, 1946.

Classified Listing

43511 - 43873 Individual authors, etc. - 1900- - Known authors (363 scheme plus 10) - cont.

43538.76.151.3 Bernanos, Georges. Monsieur Ouine. 1. éd. Paris? 1955.
43538.76.151.5 Bernanos, Georges. Monsieur Ouine. Paris, 1969.
43538.76.152 Bernanos, Georges. Le chemin de la Croix-des-Ames. "Les cahiers de la victoire II". Rio de Janeiro, 1943.
43538.76.154 Bernanos, Georges. Le chemin de la Croix-des-Ames (1941-1942). "Les cahiers de la victoire IV". Rio de Janeiro, 1944.
43538.76.160 Bernanos, Georges. Dialogues des carmélites. Neuchâtel, 1949.
43538.76.170 Bernanos, Georges. Les enfants humiliés. 16. éd. Paris, 1949.
43538.76.180 Bernanos, Georges. Un mauvais rêne. Paris, 1951.
43538.76.190 Bernanos, Georges. Dialogue d'ombres. Paris, 1955.
43538.76.200 Bernanos, Georges. Le joie. Paris, 1929.
43538.76.210 Bernanos, Georges. Français, si vous saviez. Paris, 1961.
43538.76.220 Bernanos, Georges. La France contre los robots. Paris, 1955.
43538.76.230 Bernanos, Georges. Madame Dargent. Paris, 1928.
43538.76.235 Bernanos, Georges. Une nuit. Paris, 1928.
43538.76.240 Bernanos, Georges. Le lendemain, c'est vous! Paris, 1969.
43538.76.257 Bernanos, Georges. Le crépuscule des vieux. 7. éd. Paris, 1956.
43538.76.712 Bernanos, Georges. The diary of a country priest. N.Y., 1937.
43538.76.712.5 Bernanos, Georges. The diary of a country priest. N.Y., 1954.
43538.76.715 Bernanos, Georges. Star of Satan. London, 1940.
43538.76.720 Bernanos, Georges. Plea for liberty. N.Y., 1944.
43538.76.730 Bernanos, Georges. The open mind. London, 1945.
43538.76.735 Bernanos, Georges. Joy. N.Y., 1946.
43538.76.740 Bernanos, Georges. Reflexions sur le cas de conscience français. Alger, 1943?
43538.76.750 Bernanos, Georges. Tradition of freedom. London, 1950.
43538.76.751 Bernanos, Georges. Tradition of freedom. N.Y., 1950.
43538.76.755 Bernanos, Georges. The crime. London, 1946.
43538.76.760 Bernanos, Georges. The fearless heart. London, 1952.
43538.76.765 Bernanos, Georges. Night is darkest. London, 1953.
43538.76.775 Bernanos, Georges. Oeuvres romanesques, suivis de dialogues des carmélities. Paris, 1961.
43538.76.780 Bernanos, Georges. Georges Bernanos. Roma, 1965.
43538.76.785 Bernanos, Georges. Ultimi scritti politici. Brescia, 1964.
43538.76.800 Estang, Luc. Présence de Bernanos. Paris, 1947.
43538.76.805 Aaraas, Hans. Georges Bernanos. Oslo, 1959.
43538.76.810 Béguin, Albert. Georges Bernanos. Neuchâtel, 1949.
43538.76.815 Jurt, Joseph. Les attitudes politiques de Georges Bernanos jusqu'en 1931. Fribourg, 1968.
43538.76.820 Picon, G. Georges Bernanos. Paris, 1948.
43538.76.830 Nostitz, I. von. Georges Bernanos. Speyer, 1951.
43538.76.840 Chaigne, L. Georges Bernanos. Paris, 1954.
43538.76.850 Balthasar, H.U. von. Bernanos. Köln, 1954.
43538.76.860 Scheidegger, Jean. George Bernanos romancier. Neuchâtel, 1956.
43538.76.870 Gaucher, Guy. Le thème de la mort dans les romans de Georges Bernanos. Paris, 1955.
43538.76.875A Manbrey, Pierre. L'expression de la passion intérieure dans le style de Bernanos Romancier. Washington, 1959.
43538.76.875B Manbrey, Pierre. L'expression de la passion intérieure dans le style de Bernanos Romancier. Washington, 1959.
43538.76.880 Estève, Michel. Le seus de l'amour dans les romans de Bernanos. Paris, 1959.
43538.76.885 Molnar, Thomas. Bernanos. N.Y., 1960.
43538.76.888 Mueggler, Rose M. Die menschlichen Beziehungen in Werke. Winterthur, 1960.
43538.76.895 Gillespie, Jessie Lynn. Le tragique dans l'oeuvre de Georges Bernanos. Genève, 1960.
43538.76.897 Jamet, Henry. Un autre Bernanos. Lyon, 1959.
43538.76.899 Hallen, Oskar. Georges Bernanos. Brugge, 1960.
43538.76.900 Baly, Joseph. Georges Bernanos. Paris, 1960.
43538.76.905 Gaucher, Guy. Georges Bernanos, ou L'invincible espérance. Paris, 1962.
43538.76.910 Bush, William. Souffrance et expiation dans la pensée de Bernanos. Paris, 1962.
43538.76.915 Georges Bernanos. Paris, 1961.
43538.76.920 Marie-Celeste, Sister. Le sens de l'agonie dans l'oeuvre de Georges Bernanos. Paris, 1962.
43538.76.925 Zamarriego, T. Tipología sacerdotal en la novela contemporánea: Bernanos, Maurlac, Geronella. Madrid, 1959.
43538.76.930 Chaigne, Louis. Georges Bernanos. 3. ed. Paris, 1960.
43538.76.935 Faij, Bernard. L'école de l'imprécation. Lyon, 1961.
43538.76.940 Société des amis de Georges Bernanos. Bulletin. Paris. 22,1955+
43538.76.941 Moch, Léa. La sainteté dans les romans de Georges Bernanos. Paris, 1962.
43538.76.945 Fraguière, M.A. Bernanos, fidèle à l'enfant. Fribourg, 1963.
43538.76.950 Murray, S.M. La genèse de Dialogues des Carmélites. Paris, 1963.
43538.76.955 Hebblethwaite, P. Bernanos; an introduction. London, 1965.
43538.76.960 Fabrègues, J. de. Bernanos tel qu'il était. Tours, 1963.
43538.76.963 Burkhard, Willy. La genése de l'idée du mal dans l'oeuvre romanesque de G. Bernanos. Thèse. Zurich, 1967.
43538.76.965 Blumenthal, Gerda. The poetic imagination of George Bernanos. Baltimore, 1965.
43538.76.970 Debluë, Henri. Les Romans de Georges Bernanos. Neuchâtel, 1965.
43538.76.975 Halda, Bernard. Bernanos, le scandale de croire. Paris, 1965.
43538.76.980 Estéve, Michel. Bernanos. Paris, 1965.
43538.76.982 Fitch, Brian T. Dimensions et structures chez Bernanos. Paris, 1969.
43538.76.985 Bridel, Yves. L'esprit d'enfance dans l'oeuvre romanesque de Georges Bernanos. Paris, 1966.
43538.76.990 Grégor, Paul. La conscience du temps chez Georges Bernanos. Zürich, 1966.
43538.76.992 Nettelbeck, Colin W. Les personnages de Bernanos romancier. Paris, 1970.
43538.76.995 Bush, William. L'angoisse du mystère, essai sur Bernanos et Monsieur Ouine. Paris, 1966.
43538.76.1000 Milner, Max. Georges Bernanos. Paris, 1967.
43538.76.1005 Flower, John Ernest. Georges Bernanos: Journal d'un curé de campagne. London, 1970.
43538.76.1010 Baude, Francine. Essai critique sur le roman de G. Bernanos, sous le Soleil de Satan. Diss. Lille? 1968?

43538.76.1100 Bernard, Marc. Une journée tout simple. 5. éd. Paris, 1950.
43538.76.1110 Bernard, Marc. Vacanes. Paris, 1953.
43538.76.1120 Bernard, Marc. Salut. 8. éd. Paris, 1955.
43538.76.1130 Bernard, Marc. La bonne humeur. 3. éd. Paris, 1957.
43538.76.1140 Bernard, Jean-Marc. Haut-Vivarais d'hiver. Saint-Félicen-en-Vivarais, 1921.
V43538.76.1145 Dobraczynski, Jan. Bernanos pouriciopisatz. Lublin, 1937.
43538.76.1150 Sarrazin, Hubert. Bernanos no Brasil. Petrópolis, 1968.
43538.76.1155 Bush, William. Georges Bernanos. N.Y., 1969.
43538.76.2100 Bernard, O. Quand l'amour voyage. Paris, 1911.
43538.76.2110 Bernard, O. A la visite. Paris, 1918.
43538.76.2120 Bernard, O. Le petit Don Juan. Paris, 1918.
43538.76.2130 Bernard, O. Les comédiens ambulants. Paris, 1935.
43538.76.2140 Bernard, O. La petite pharmacienne. Paris, 1935.
43538.76.3105 Bernadi, François. Le vin de lune. 5. éd. Paris, 1957.
43538.76.4100 Bernardine, T. Le chef-d'oeuvre de Claude Harmel. Paris, 1946.
43538.76.5100 Bernard, Michel. Histoire de Martin et de Leannie. Paris, 1957.
43538.76.5110 Bernard, Michel. La plage. Paris, 1960.
43538.76.5120 Bernard, Michel. Brouage. Lausanne, 1967.
43538.76.5130 Bernard, Michel. Les courtisanes. Paris, 1968.
43538.76.5140 Bernard, Michel. La négresse muette. Paris, 1968.
43538.76.5150 Bernard, Michel. La plage. Paris, 1970.
43538.76.6100 Berl, Emmanuel. Meditation sur un amour défunt. Paris, 1925.
43538.76.6110 Berl, Emmanuel. A contretemps. Paris, 1969.
43538.76.7100 Bernouard, F. Franchise militaire. 2. éd. Paris, 1936.
43538.76.7110 Bernouard, F. La berlue rayonnante. Paris, 192-.
43538.76.8100 Bernard-Luc, Jean. Les amants novices. Paris, 1956.
43538.76.9100 Bérénice (pseud.). Le jardin de Marrès. Paris, 1916.
43538.77.100 Berthet, Guy. L'amour s'en vient. Paris, 1958.
43538.77.1100 Berton, Henry. Le coeur effeuillé. Paris, 1921.
43538.77.1110 Berton, Henry. L'humaine rumeur. Paris, 1932.
43538.77.2100 Bertin, Charles. Christoffel Columbus. Brussel, 1958.
43538.77.2103 Bertin, Charles. Christophe Colomb; piece en trois actes. Bruxelles, 1961.
43538.77.2105 Bertin, Charles. Christophe Colomb. Bruxelles, 1966.
43538.77.2110 Bertin, Charles. Journal d'un crime. Paris, 1961.
43538.77.2120 Bertin, Charles. Don Juan. Bruxelles, 1964.
43538.77.3100 Berthault, François. Vaisseaux solaires. Paris, 1936.
43538.77.4100 Bertrand, Mirou. Le chevalet féerique. Paris, 1962.
43538.77.5100 Berry, Gaston. Le lys de sora. Paris, 1958.
43538.77.6100 Berry, André. Lais de Gascogne. Paris, 1933.
43538.77.6102 Berry, André. Chante fable de Murielle et d'Alain. Paris, 1930.
43538.77.6103 Berry, André. La corheille de Ghislaine. Paris, 1933.
43538.77.6105 Berry, André. Sonnets surréels. Limoges, 1957.
43538.77.6800 Rabiniaux, Roger. André Berry. Limoges, 1956.
43538.77.7100 Berson, Simone. Les rencontres imaginaires. Paris, 1952.
43538.77.7110 Berson, Simone. Pour le neilleur et pour le pire. Bruxelles, 1961.
43538.77.7120 Berson, Simone. Le livre de Deborah. Bruxelles, 1966.
43538.77.8100 Berthet, Jean. Les vacances d'Apollon. Paris, 1939.
43538.77.8110 Berthet, Jean. Paroles sans romances, 1950-56. Paris, 1957.
43538.77.9100 Bertoye, Achille. Deux existence tourmentees. Paris, 1960.
43538.78.100 Berton, René. Le precurseur. Paris, 1925.
43538.78.110 Berton, René. La lumière dans le tombeau (Gott mit uns!). Paris, 1929.
43538.78.120 Berton, René. Le roi du cuir. Paris, 1929.
43538.78.2100 Bertin, Célia. La dernière innocence. Paris, 1953.
43538.78.2110 Bertin, Célia. Contre-champ. Paris, 1954.
43538.78.3100 Berton, Henry. Horizons proches. Paris, 1930.
43538.78.3110 Berton, Henry. Sur l'autre rive. Paris, 1930.
43538.78.4100 Bertrand, Mirou. Fériale. Paris, 1960.
43538.78.5100 Berry, Andrée Gabrielle. Le tombeau de Micheline; poèmes. Paris, 1960.
43538.78.6100 Bert, Claude Andrée. Les Kibboutzniks, roman. Paris, 1967.
43538.79.100 Bergot, Erwan. Mourir au Laos. Paris, 1965.
43538.81.100 Beslou, Jaime de. Idéologues. Paris, 1923.
43538.81.110 Beslière, Jean. Le page mutilé. Paris, 1923.
43538.81.120 Beslou, Jaime de. Les cloches de Saint-Amarain. Paris, 1922.
43538.81.1100 Beslière, Jean. Marguerite Fauquenoy. Paris, 1924.
43538.82.100 Besnard, Lucien. Je veux revoir ma Normandie; pièce. Paris, 1924.
43538.82.110 Besnard, Lucien. L'homme qui n'est pas plus de ce monde. Paris, 1924.
43538.82.120 Besnard, Lucien. Le coeur portage. Paris, 1927.
43538.82.130 Besnard, Lucien. Dans l'ombre du harem. Paris, 1927.
43538.82.3100 Bessette, Hélène. La Lour; roman. 2. éd. Paris, 1959.
43538.82.3110 Bessette, Hélène. La route bleue. Paris, 1960.
43538.82.3120 Bessette, Hélène. Les petites Lilshart. Paris, 1967.
43538.82.3130 Bessette, Hélène. Le divorce interrompu. Paris, 1968.
43538.83.100 Bésus, Roger. Cet homme qui vous aimait, roman. Paris, 1954.
43538.83.110 Bésus, Roger. Pour l'amour. Paris, 1966.
43538.83.120 Bésus, Roger. Le Maître, roman. Paris, 1968?
43538.84.100 Bessy, Maurice. Voici le temps des assassins. Paris, 1956.
43538.84.110 Bessy, Maurice. Car c'est Dieu qu'on enterre. Paris, 1960.
43538.85.100 Bessonnet-Favre, C. Poèmes de la terre et des hommes de Francis Andé. Bruxelles, 1959.
43538.88.100 Betz, Maurice. L'incertain; roman. Paris, 1925.
43538.88.120 Betz, Maurice. Dialogues des prisonniers, 1940. Paris, 1940.
43538.88.130 Betz, Maurice. Le démon impur; roman. Paris, 1926.
43538.88.140 Betz, Maurice. Rossignol du Japon. Paris, 1931.
43538.88.150 Betz, Maurice. Le ressac. Paris, 1932.
43538.88.160 Betz, Maurice. La fille qui chante. Paris, 1927.
43538.89.100 Beucler, André. La fleur qui chante; roman. Paris, 1939.
43538.89.110 Beucler, André. Le carnet de vengeance. Paris, 1954.
43538.90.100 Berl, Emmanuel. Sylvia. 13. éd. Paris, 1952.
43538.90.110 Berl, Emmanuel. Présence des morts. Paris, 1956.
43538.90.120 Berl, Emmanuel. La France irréalle. Paris, 1957.
43538.91.100 Bérimont, Luc. Les mots germent la nuit. Paris, 1951.
43538.91.110 Berimont, Luc. L'herbe à Tonnerre. Paris, 1958.
43538.91.120 Bérimont, Luc. Le bruit des amours et des guerres. Paris, 1966.
43538.91.130 Bérimont, Luc. Un feu vivant. Paris, 1968.
43538.92.100 Beckert, A. L'art du poème. Bruxelles, 1963.

43511 - 43873 Individual authors, etc. - 1900- - Known authors (363 scheme plus 10) - cont.

43538.93.100 Berrin, Lucien. Taille-douce. Paris, 1956.
43538.93.110 Berrin, Lucien. Le tisonnier des rêves. Paris, 1958.
43538.97.100 Bergin-le-Plan, Louis. Le rendez-vous de François Villon avec les poètes maudets. Paris, 1957.
43538.98.100 Bengono, Jacques. La Perdrix blanche, trois contes moraux. Yaoundé, 1966.
43538.99.21 Trois poètes. Paris, 1957.
43538.100.100 Beer, Hélène. Holyland tours. Bruxelles, 1968.
43538.101.100 Benacher, Elie. Suite judaïque. Paris, 1968.
43540.1.30 Billaud, V. Jeune amour. Paris, 1901.
43540.2.30 Biollay, Maurice. L'affranchie. Paris, 1908.
43540.3.30 Billy, André. Scènes de la vie littéraire à Paris. Paris, 1918.
43540.3.35 Billy, André. Pudeur. Paris, 1951.
43540.3.40 Billy, André. Le double assassinat de la maison du Boeuf. Genève, 1941.
43540.3.45 Billy, André. Le narthex. Paris, 1950.
43540.3.50 Billy, André. Route cavalière de la solitude. Paris, 1928.
43540.3.55 Billy, André. Les beaux jours de Barbezon. Paris, 1947.
43540.3.67 Billy, André. La terrasse du Luxembourg. Paris, 1945.
43540.3.69 Billy, André. Le balcon au bord de l'eau. Paris, 1949.
43540.3.80 Billy, André. Mort prochaine. Paris, 1946.
43540.3.85 Billy, André. Malvina. Paris, 1949.
43540.3.90 Billy, André. Le badaud de Paris et d'ailleurs. Paris, 1959.
43540.3.95 Billy, André. L'allegretto de septième. Paris, 1960.
43540.3.100 Billy, André. Du noir sur du blanc. Paris, 1963.
43540.3.105 Billy, André. Propos du samedi. Paris, 1969.
43540.3.800 Decreus, Juliette. Le prêtre dans l'oeuvre de André Billy. Paris, 1964.
43540.7.100 Bibescu, M.L. Isvor, le pays des saules. 5. éd. v.1-2. Paris, 1923.
43540.7.105 Bibescu, M.L. La vie d'une amitié. Paris, 1952. 3v.
43540.7.110A Bibescu, M.L. Catherine-Parish. N.Y., 1928.
43540.7.110B Bibescu, M.L. Catherine-Parish. N.Y., 1928.
43540.7.112 Bibescu, M.L. Catherine-Paris. Genève, 1952.
43540.7.120 Bibescu, M.L. Egalité. pt.1-3. Paris, 1935.
43540.7.130 Bibescu, M.L. Images d'Epinal. Paris, 1945.
43540.7.140 Bibescu, M.L. Feuilles de calendrier. Paris, 1939.
43540.7.150 Bibescu, M.L. Prince Imperial. London, 1949.
43540.7.160 Bibescu, M.L. La nymphe Europe. Paris, 1960.
43540.7.700 Bibescu, M.L. Isvor. N.Y., 1924.
43540.7.712 Bibescu, M.L. Katia. N.Y., 1939.
43540.7.720 Bibescu, M.L. The sphinx of Bagatelle. London, 1951.
43540.8.100 Bibes, Jacques. Crier le jour. Paris, 1950.
43540.9.100 Billetdoux, F. Brouillon d'un bourgeois. Paris, 1961.
43540.9.700 Billetdoux, F. A man and his master. London, 1963.
43540.9.705 Billetdoux, F. Chin-chin. London, 1963.
43540.9.710 Billetdoux, F. Chez Torpe. London, 1963.
43540.24.100 Biette, E. Aux mille mers, j'ai navigué. Paris, 1939.
43540.34.102 Bigot, Muguette. Les voix de mon village. 2. éd. Huisseau-sur-Cosson, 1969.
43540.50.100 Billot, F. Mensonges. Paris, 1937.
43540.50.1100 Billetdoux, François. Théâtre. Paris, 1961. 2v.
43540.60.100 Benet-Valmer, Gustave. Le desir, roman. Paris, 1931.
43540.60.110 Binet-Valmer, Gustave. Quand ils furent nus. Paris, 1925.
43540.60.120 Binet-Valmer, Gustave. Lucien. Paris, 1910.
43540.74.100 Birabeau, André. Un jour de folie. Paris, 1923.
43540.74.110 Birabeau, André. La fleur d'oranger; comédie. Paris, 1924.
43540.74.120 Birabeau, André. Chiffarton; comédie. Paris, 1925.
43540.74.125 Birabeau, André. Le chemin des écoliers. Paris, 1927.
43540.74.130 Birabeau, André. Dejeuner d'amoureux. Paris, 1929. 3 pam.
43540.74.140 Birabeau, André. Promesse des fleurs; histoires d'enfants. Paris, 1930.
43540.74.150 Birabeau, André. Côte d'Azur. Paris, 1931.
43540.74.160 Birabeau, André. Baisers perdus. Paris, 1932.
43540.74.170 Birabeau, André. Ma soeur de luxe. Paris, 1933.
43540.74.180 Birabeau, André. Fiston; comédie en quatre actes. Paris, 1936.
43540.74.190 Birabeau, André. Pamplemousse. Paris, 1937.
43540.74.200 Birabeau, André. Chaleur du sein. Paris, 1938.
43540.74.210 Birabeau, André. Le nid. Paris, 1939.
43540.74.220 Birabeau, André. Le jardin aux vingt-cinq allées. Paris, 1928.
43540.74.805A Birabeau, André. Revelation. N.Y., 1930.
43540.74.805B Birabeau, André. Revelation. N.Y., 1930.
43540.74.815 Birabeau, Andre. Dame nature. N.Y., 1939.
43540.82.100 Bisson, Jean Pierre. Le matin rouge. Hanfleur, 1969.
43540.83.100 Bisson, André. Le rosaire; piece en trois actes et quatre tableaux. Paris, 1926.
43540.83.110 Bisson, André. Le chatelaine de Shenstone. Paris, 1927.
43540.83.120 Bisson, André. Le pur de gloire. Paris, 1937.
43540.84.100 Bitard-Viaud, M. De mon coeur à ton coeur. Paris, 1935.
43540.99.21 Bizet, René. Choix de poèmes. Paris, 1957.
43540.99.100 Bizet, René. L'aventure aux quitares. Paris, 1920.
43543.1.30 Blois, Louis A. Contes pour lire au crepuscule. Paris, 1917.
43543.1.31 Blois, Louis A. La vocation. Roman. 7. éd. Paris, 1916.
43543.1.35 Blois, Louis A. Au soleil d'or. Paris, 1926.
43543.1.4105 Blanc, Julien. Seule, la vie. v.1-2. Paris, 1946-47.
43543.2.30 Blancard, Jules César. La carmagnole. St. Paul, 1917.
43543.3.100 Blanchi, J.P. Naissance et mort de la comédie. Paris, 1941.
43543.3.1100 Blanc, Louis. Feuillets épars, poèmes. Paris, 1954.
43543.3.2100 Blancpain, Marc. Le plus long amour. Paris, 1971.
43543.3.3100 Blanchard, Max. Rimes en short. Monte Carlo, 1958.
43543.4.100 Blanchet, Alfred. L'homme de la jungle; roman colonial. Paris, 1929.
43543.4.2100 Blanchet, Louis. Le feu est dans la ville. Magné, 1956.
43543.4.2110 Blanchet, Louis. Le revé des bagnards. Magné, 1956.
43543.4.3100 Blanchard, Maurice. Le pain, la lumière. Paris, 1955.
43543.5.100 Blanche, Jacques Émile. Aymeris. Paris, 1930.
43543.5.110 Blanche, Jacques Emile. Cahiers d'un artiste. v.1,3,5-6. Paris, 1915. 4v.
43543.6.100 Blanchard, André. Capitale. Paris, 1945.
43543.6.110 Blanchard, André. Petit bestiaire moral et fabuleux. Paris, 1951.
43543.8.100 Blanchot, Maurice. L'arrêt de mort. 6. éd. Paris, 1948.
43543.8.110 Blanchot, Maurice. Faux pas. Paris, 1943.
43543.8.120 Blanchot, Maurice. La part du feu. 6. éd. Paris, 1949.
43543.8.130 Blanchot, Maurice. Thomas l'obscur. 5. éd. Paris, 1950.
43543.8.140 Blanchot, Maurice. Le Très-Haut. 5. éd. Paris, 1948.

43511 - 43873 Individual authors, etc. - 1900- - Known authors (363 scheme plus 10) - cont.

43543.8.150 Blanchot, Maurice. Au moment voulu. Paris, 1951.
43543.8.160 Blanchot, Maurice. Le dernier homme. Paris, 1957.
43543.8.170 Blanchot, Maurice. Celui qui ne m'accompagnait pas. Paris, 1953.
43543.8.180 Blanchot, Maurice. Le livre à venir. Paris, 1959.
43543.8.190 Blanchot, Maurice. L'attente. Paris, 1962.
43543.8.200 Blanchot, Maurice. L'entretien infini. Paris, 1969.
43543.8.1100 Blancpain, Marc. Le solitaire. Paris, 1947.
43543.8.1110 Blancpain, Marc. Ulla des antipodes. Paris, 1967.
43543.8.2100 Blanquernon, Claude. Pierres du Hoggar. Paris, 1957.
43543.8.3100 Blancotte, B. Cette lucarne qui mene au fond. Paris, 1957.
43543.9.100 Blanzat, Jean. La Gartempe. Paris, 1957.
43543.9.110 Blanzat, Jean. L'iguane. Paris, 1966.
43543.13.100 Bloch, J.R. Dernier empereur. Paris, 1927.
43543.13.102 Bloch, J.R. Dernier empereur. 3. éd. Paris, 1926.
43543.13.110 Bloch, J.R. Offrande à la musique. Paris, 1930.
43543.13.120 Bloch, J.R. La nuit kurde. Paris, 1933.
43543.13.130 Bloch, J.R. Levy. 5. éd. Paris, 1925.
43543.13.140 Bloch, J.R. Et compagnie. 6. éd. Paris, 1937.
43543.13.145 Bloch, J.R. Et cie. 4. éd. Paris, 1918.
43543.13.156 Bloch, J.R. Destin du siècle. 6. éd. Paris, 1931.
43543.13.160 Bloch, J.R. Toulon. Moscou, 1944.
43543.13.170 Bloch, J.R. Sybilla. 8. éd. Paris, 1932.
43543.13.180 Bloch, J.R. Toulon et autres pièces. Paris, 1948.
43543.13.190 Bloch, J.R. Les chasses de Renaut. 9. éd. Paris, 1927.
43543.13.200 Bloch, J.R. Carnaval est mort. Paris, 1920.
43543.13.210 Bloch, J.R. Offrande à la politique. 9. éd. Paris, 1933.
43543.13.220 Bloch, J.R. Forces monde. Paris, 1927.
43543.13.230 Bloch, J.R. Naissance d'une culture. 7. éd. Paris, 1936.
43543.13.705 Bloch, J.R. A night in Kurdistan. N.Y., 1931.
43543.13.715 Bloch, J.R. "- + Co.". N.Y., 1929.
43543.13.785 Bloch, J.R. Vom Sinn unseres Jahrhunderts. Berlin, 1932.
43543.14.100 Bloch-Michel, J. La fuite en Egypte. 7. éd. Paris, 1952.
43543.14.113 Bloch-Michel, J. Journal du Désordre. 4. éd. Paris, 1955.
43543.14.120 Bloch-Michel, J. Frosinia. Paris, 1966.
43543.14.700 Bloch-Michel, J. The witness. N.Y., 1949.
43543.14.710 Bloch-Michel, J. The flight into Egypt. N.Y., 1955.
43543.41.100 Blin, Louis. Le père Simard. Avignon, 1941.
43543.59.100 Blond, Georges. Les naufragés de Paris. Paris, 1959.
43543.59.700 Blond, Georges. The plunderers. N.Y., 1951.
43543.59.710 Blond, Georges. Goddess Island. London, 1952.
43543.63.100 Bloch, Pierre J. Rêve éveillé; poèmes. Rodez, 1963.
43543.66.100 Blondel. La peau l'aurochs. Paris, 1954.
43543.67.100 Blondin, Antoine. L'humeur vagabonde. Paris, 1955.
43543.67.110 Blondin, Antoine. Un singer en hiver. Paris, 1959.
43543.67.120 Blondin, Antoine. Monsieur Jadis. Paris, 1970.
43543.68.100 Blot, Jean. Les enfants de New York. 2. éd. Paris, 1959.
43543.88.100 Blum, Léon. En listant. Paris, 1906.
43543.88.110 Blum, Léon. Nouvelles conversations de Goethe avec Eckermann, 1887-1900. Paris, 1909.
43543.88.116 Blum, Léon. Nouvelles conversations de Goethe avec Eckermann. 6. éd. Paris, 1937.
43543.89.100 Blum, René. Les amours du poête. Paris, 1932.
43543.89.1100 Blum, Suzanne. Ne savoir rien. Paris, 1970.
43544.1.30 Bonchamps, G. de. Vieux miroirs. Paris, 1908.
43544.2.30 Bouret, G. Les Broussailles. Paris, 1883.
43544.3.30 Bouillon, V. Autour d'une vieille église. Paris, 1914.
43544.4.30 Botrel, Théodore. Les chants du bivouac. Paris, 1915.
43544.4.31 Botrel, Théodore. Chansons de route. Paris, 1915.
43544.4.32 Botrel, Théodore. Chansons de chez nous. Paris, 1918.
43544.4.32.2 Botrel, Théodore. Chansons de chez nous. Paris, 1905.
43544.4.33 Botrel, Théodore. Les alouettes. Paris, 1912.
43544.4.35 Botrel, Théodore. Le fils de la veuve. 5. éd. Paris, 1914?
43544.4.37 Botrel, Théodore. Chansons de chez nous. Paris, 1923.
43544.4.39 Botrel, Théodore. Chansons de clochers-à-jour. Paris, 1912.
43544.4.41 Botrel, Théodore. Chansons en sabots. Paris, 1923.
43544.4.45 Botrel, Théodore. Contes du Lit-Clos. Paris, 1900.
43544.4.47 Botrel, Théodore. Souvenirs d'un barde errant. Paris, 1946.
43544.4.71 Botrel, Théodore. Les mémoires d'un barde Breton. Paris, 1933.
43544.5.30 Boulenger, Marcel. Mes relations. Paris, n.d.
43544.5.31 Boulenger, Marcel. Opinions choisies. Paris, 1902.
43544.5.32 Boulenger, Marcel. Nos élégances. Paris, 1908.
43544.5.33 Boulenger, Marcel. Le marché aux fleurs. Paris, 1912.
43544.5.35 Boulenger, Marcel. Marguerite. Paris, 1921.
43544.5.40 Boulenger, Marcel. Sur un tambour. Paris, 1916.
43544.5.43 Boulenger, Marcel. Les trois graces. Paris, 1919.
43544.6.30 Boulenger, Jacques. Ondine Valmore. Paris, 1909.
43544.6.35 Boulenger, Jacques. Mais l'art est difficite! v.1-2. Paris, 1921.
43544.7.30 Bout de Charlemont, H. Cigale. Monographie. 2. éd. Avignon, 1900.
43544.8.30 Bousquet, Joe. Le meneur de lune. 4. éd. Paris, 1946.
43544.9.30 Boussus, M. L'armoire de citronnier; almanach 1919. Paris, 1919.
43544.10.30 Bourgeois, E. Mariage d'argent. 2. ed. Paris, 1906.
43544.12.100 Bochot, Pierre. Chez eux. Paris, 1946.
43544.13.100 Bock, Paul Aloise. Les chemins de Rome. Paris, 1961.
43544.14.100 Bouquet, L. Crucifixiones. Paris, 1929.
43544.14.110 Bocquet, L. Les branches Lourdes, poèmes, 1903-1910. 3. éd. Paris, 1929.
43544.14.800 Secret, M.N. Léon Bocquet. Paris, 1933.
43544.17.100 Bodart, Roger. Le nègre de Chicago. Paris, 1958.
43544.17.110 Bodart, Roger. Le tour. Paris, 1968.
43544.18.100 Bodin, Jean. L'immortelle. 1. éd. Paris, 1943.
43544.18.110A Bodin, Jean. Théâtre. Paris, 1940- 2v.
43544.18.110B Bodin, Jean. Théâtre. Paris, 1940- 2v.
43544.18.120 Bodin, Jean. Armel. Paris, 1946.
43544.18.130 Bodin, Jean. Reconstitution de la Mêlée. Chambéry, 1955.
43544.18.140 Bodin, Jean. Louis le Grand. Paris, 1962.
43544.18.141 Bodin, Jean. Louis-le-Grand. Paris, 1963.
43544.19.100 Boden, Paul. Les amants du Theil. Paris, 1952.
43544.19.700 Bodin, Paul. A young woman. N.Y., 1969.
43544.21.100 Boecop-Malye, M. Jardin 26. Montréal, 1942.
43544.41.100 Baisdeffre, Pierre de. Les fins dernieres. Paris, 1952.
43544.41.110 Baisdeffre, Pierre de. Des vivants et des morts. Paris, 1954.
43544.41.120 Baisdeffre, Pierre de. L'amour et l'ennui. Paris, 1959.
43544.41.1100 Boissonnas, Edith. L'embellie. Paris, 1966.
43544.48.100 Boldoduc, Michel. Les remontoirs. Paris, 1970.
43544.50.100 Bolloré, Gwenäel. Propos interrompus. Paris, 1958.
43544.50.110 Bolloré, Gwenäel. Moira, la naufrageuse. Paris, 1958.

43511 - 43873 Individual authors, etc. - 1900- - Known authors (363 scheme plus 10) - cont.

43544.51.100 Bollaert, A.A.J. Le porlu de l'etoile (meditations). N.Y., 1923.
43544.51.1100 Boltanski, Luc. Le fusil. Paris, 1957.
43544.53.100 Bolsee, B. Cardiogramme. Belgique, 1963.
43544.55.100 Bommart, Jean. Blanc et rouge. Paris, 1936.
43544.57.100 Bompard, J. L'étrangère. Paris, 1921.
43544.58.100 Bonaparte, Marie. A la memoire des disparus. London, 1952.
43544.59.21 Bonheur, Gaston. Chemin privé; oeuvres poétiques (1930-1970). Paris, 1970.
43544.59.100 La cavalcade héroique. Paris, 1940.
43544.60.100 Bonnamy, George. L'état-major s'en va-t-en guerre. 2. éd. Paris, 1941.
43544.60.110 Bonnamy, George. Souvenirs d'un pseudo vaincu. Paris, 1945.
43544.60.120 Bonnamy, George. Resistantialisme. Paris, 1948.
43544.60.1100 Bonmariage, Sylvein. L'amour songé. Paris, 1948.
43544.60.2100 Bonnefoy, Yves. Du mouvement et de l'immobilité de Douve. Paris, 1954.
43544.60.2101 Bonnefoy, Yves. Du mouvement et de l'immobilité de Douve. Paris, 1970.
43544.60.2110 Bonnefoy, Yves. Hier regnant désent. Paris, 1958.
43544.60.2120 Bonnefoy, Yves. Traité du pianiste. Paris, 1946.
43544.60.2130A Bonnefoy, Yves. L'improbable. Paris, 1959.
43544.60.2130B Bonnefoy, Yves. L'improbable. Paris, 1959.
43544.60.2140 Bonnefoy, Yves. La seconde simplicité. Paris, 1961.
43544.60.2150 Bonnefoy, Yves. Pierre écrite. Paris, 1965.
43544.60.2160 Bonnefoy, Yves. Un Reve fait à Mantoue. Paris, 1967.
43544.60.2700 Bonnefoy, Yves. On the motion and immobility of Douve. Athens, 1968.
43544.60.2800 Arndt, Béatrice. La quête poétique d'Yves Bonnefoy. Thèse. Zürich, 1970.
43544.60.3100 Bonnet, M.R. Enfance, limousine. Paris, 1954.
43544.60.4100 Boni, Nazi. Crépuscale des temps anciens. Paris, 1962.
43544.60.5100 Bonjean, François Joseph. El Azhar. 6. éd. Paris, 1927.
43544.60.5110 Bonjean, François Joseph. Mansour. 13. éd. Paris, 1924.
43544.61.21 Bonneton, André. Echo. Poems. Rodez, 1966.
43544.61.2100 Bonnard, Julien. Le fil d'Ariàne. Rodez, 1966.
43544.62.100 Bontemps, Elisabeth. Lil. Paris, 1957.
43544.65.100 Blondin, Germaine. Le cahier d'Arlequin; poèmes. Paris, 1959.
43544.66.100 Boos, Renée. Les aventures de Boule-de-Gomme. Lausanne, 1967.
43544.71.100 Bopp, Leon. Jean Darien. Paris, 1924.
43544.71.110 Bopp, Leon. Liassons du monde. Paris, 1938.
43544.71.120 Duckworth, C. A study of Leon Bopp. Genève, 1955.
43544.71.130 Kieffler, Rosemarie. Alchimie et toute-puissance. Génève, 1959.
43544.73.100 Bordeaux, Henry. Un crime sous le directoire. Paris, 1946.
43544.74.100 Bordeaux, P.H. Sur la route de Pabmyre. Paris, 1923.
43544.74.112 Bordeaux, P.H. Antaram de Trébizonde. Paris, 1930.
43544.74.2100 Bordonove, Georges. Les lentations. Paris, 1960.
43544.74.2110 Bordonove, Georges. Les Atlantes; roman. Paris, 1965.
43544.74.2120 Bordonove, Georges. Le chevalier Du Landreau. Paris, 1970.
43544.74.3100 Bordier, Roger. Les blés; roman. Paris, 1961.
43544.74.3110 Bordier, Roger. Le tour de ville. Paris, 1969.
43544.74.3120 Bordier, Roger. Un age d'or. Paris, 1967.
43544.74.3130 Bordier, Roger. Les éventails; roman. Paris, 1971.
43544.74.3700 Bordier, Roger. The golden plain. Boston, 1963.
43544.74.3710 Bordier, Roger. The golden plain. London, 1963.
43544.74.4100 Borderie, Roger. Les moineaux de pluie. Paris, 1960.
43544.74.5100 Bordry, Paul. Étude et hypothèse sur la véritable fin dernière de "l'Histoire d'O". Paris, 1970.
43544.75.100 Borel, Marguerite Appeli. Ruth. pt.1-2. Paris, 1933.
43544.75.110 Borel, Marguerite Appeli. Les lettres. Paris, 1959.
43544.75.120 Borel, Marguerite Appeli. A travers deux siècles, souvenirs et rencontres (1883-1967). Paris, 1967.
43544.75.705 Borel, Marguerite Appeli. The man who survived. N.Y., 1918.
43544.75.1100 Borel, Raymond C. L'Affaire Gregory, livre blanc, présenté et annoté. Paris, 1969.
43544.75.3100 Borgeaud, Georges. La vaiselles des évéques. Paris, 1959.
43544.75.4100 Borel-Rosny, Robert. La rouguine au tapis. Paris, 1958.
43544.75.5100 Borel, Jacques. L'adoration; roman. Paris, 1965.
43544.75.5110 Borel, Jacques. Tata ou de l'Education, pièce moral et didactique en 2 actes et 3 tableaux. Paris, 1967.
43544.75.6100 Borel, Pierre Louis. De Péguy à Sartre. Neuchâtel, 1964.
43544.76.100 Borel, Pierre Louis. Les idees. Paris, 1957.
43544.80.785 Borrély, Maria. Das Letze feuer. Zürich, 1939.
43544.80.786 Borrély, Maria. Das Dorf ohne Sonne. Zürich, 1940.
43544.80.787 Borrély, Maria. Mistral. Zürich, 1939.
43544.81.100 Bory, Jean Louis. Mon village à l'heure allemandi; roman. N.Y., 1945.
43544.81.110 Bory, Jean Louis. Fragile. London, 1951.
43544.81.120 Bory, Jean Louis. Un Noël à la Tyrolienne. Paris, 1952.
43544.81.130 Bory, Jean Louis. Une vie de château. Paris, 1954.
43544.81.140 Bory, Jean Louis. Clio dans les blés. Paris, 1955.
43544.81.150 Bory, Jean Louis. Usé par la mer. Paris, 1959.
43544.81.160 Bory, Jean Louis. Musique. Paris, 1960.
43544.81.170 Bory, Jean Louis. L'ordeur de l'herbe. Paris, 1962.
43544.81.180 Bory, Jean Louis. Va dire au lac de patienter. Paris, 1969.
43544.81.2105 Bosco, Henri. L'âne Culotte; roman. 21. éd. Paris, 1946.
43544.81.2110 Bosco, Henri. Malicroix; roman. 25. éd. Paris, 1948.
43544.81.2115 Bosco, Henri. Le roseau et la source. Paris, 1949.
43544.81.2120 Bosco, Henri. Le mas théotime. Paris, 1947.
43544.81.2122 Bosco, Henri. Le mas théotime. Paris, 1957.
43544.81.2125 Bosco, Henri. Antonin. 31. éd. Paris, 1952.
43544.81.2130 Bosco, Henri. La fattoria. Milano, 1947.
43544.81.2135 Bosco, Henri. Hyacinthe. 19. éd. Paris, 1951.
43544.81.2140 Bosco, Henri. L'antiquaire. 21. éd. Paris, 1954.
43544.81.2150 Bosco, Henri. Les Balesta. 5. éd. Paris, 1955.
43544.81.2160 Bosco, Henri. L'Ane Culotte. Tours, 1956.
43544.81.2170 Bosco, Henri. Sabinus. Paris, 1957.
43544.81.2180 Bosco, Henri. Barbache. 17. éd. Paris, 1957.
43544.81.2185 Bosco, Henri. Bargabot. 3. éd. Paris, 1958.
43544.81.2190 Bosco, Henri. Un rameau de la nuit. Paris, 1950.
43544.81.2200 Bosco, Henri. Le renard dans l'île. Paris, 1956.
43544.81.2210 Bosco, Henri. L'enfant et la rivière. Paris, 1953.
43544.81.2220 Bosco, Henri. Pierre Lampédouze. Paris, 1959.
43544.81.2230 Bosco, Henri. Un oubli moins profond. Paris, 1961.
43544.81.2240 Bosco, Henri. L'Epervier. Paris, 1963.
43544.81.2250 Bosco, Henri. Sylvius. Paris, 1948.
43544.81.2260 Bosco, Henri. Irénée; roman. Paris, 1950.

43511 - 43873 Individual authors, etc. - 1900- - Known authors (363 scheme plus 10) - cont.

43544.81.2270 Bosco, Henri. Le jardin des Trintaires. Paris, 1966.
43544.81.2280 Bosco, Henri. Mon compagnon de songes. Paris, 1967.
43544.81.2700 Bosco, Henri. The farm theotime. London, 1946.
43544.81.2710 Bosco, Henri. The dark bough. London, 1955.
43544.81.2720 Bosco, Henri. Barbache. London, 1959.
43544.81.2800 Lambert, Jean. Un voyageur des deux mondes. Paris, 1951.
43544.81.2805 Susini, Jean. Henri Bosco. Alès, 1959.
43544.81.2810 Sussex, Ronald Thomas. Henri Bosco, poet-novelist. Christchurch, 1966.
43544.81.2815 Godin, Jean. Henri Bosco. Montréal, 1968.
43544.81.2820 Poitras, Lionel. Henri Bosco et la participation au monde. Fribourg, 1971.
43544.82.61 Bosschère, Jean de. Lettres de La Châtre à André Lebois. (1939-1953). Paris, 1969.
43544.82.100 Bosschère, Jean de. Satan l'obscur, roman. Paris, 1933.
43544.82.110 Bosschère, Jean de. Peacocks and other mysteries. N.Y., 1941.
43544.82.120 Bosschère, Jean de. Heritiers de l'abêne. Paris, 1950.
43544.82.130 Bosschère, Jean de. Contes de la neige et de la nuit. Blainville-sur-Mer, 1954.
43544.82.800 Jean de Boschère. Paris, 1952.
43544.82.805 Ennetières, Elisabeth d'. Nous et les autres, souvenirs d'un tiers de siècle avec Jean de Boschère. Aurillac, 1967.
43544.83.100 Bost, Pierre. Hercule et mademoiselle. 4. éd. Paris, 1924.
43544.83.120 Bost, Pierre. Monsieur L'admiral va bientôt mourir. 9. éd. Paris, 1945.
43544.83.130A Bost, Pierre. La haute fourche. Paris, 1945.
43544.83.130B Bost, Pierre. La haute fourche. Paris, 1945.
43544.83.140 Bost, Pierre. Voyage de l'esclave. Paris, 1926.
43544.86.100 Bouchéret, Roland. Hibernales. Paris, 1958.
43544.87.100 Bodet, Lucien. Fantasques. Paris, 1929.
43544.87.2100 Boulestin, X.M. Le frequentations de Maurice. Paris, 1912.
43544.87.2700 Boulestin, X.M. Ease and endurance. London, 1948.
43544.87.3100 Bourbon Busset, Jacques de. Memoires d'un lion. Paris, 1960.
43544.87.3110 Bourbon Busset, Jacques de. La grande conference. Paris, 1963.
43544.87.3120 Bourbon Busset, Jacques de. La nuit salernes. Paris, 1965.
43544.87.3130 Bourbon Busset, Jacques de. Journal. Paris, 1966. 4v.
43544.87.3146 Bourbon Busset, Jacques de. Fugue à deux voix; recit. 6. éd. Paris, 1958.
43544.87.4100 Bourdeillette, Jean. Reliques des songes. Paris, 1958.
43544.87.5100 Bourdet, E. Margot. Paris, 1936.
43544.87.5110 Bourdet, E. Fric-frac; pièce en cinq actes. Paris, 1937.
43544.88.100 Boussac de Saint-Marc, A. Le loup de Gubbio. Paris, 1922.
43544.88.101 Boussac de Saint-Marc, A. Le loup de Gubbio. Paris, 1922.
43544.88.110 Boussac de Saint-Marc, A. Cinq pièces. Paris, 1962.
43544.88.2100 Boulanger, Daniel. Le gouverneur Polygame. Paris, 1960.
43544.88.2110 Boulanger, Daniel. Les portes. Paris, 1966.
43544.88.2120 Boulanger, Daniel. La nacelle, roman. Paris, 1967.
43544.88.2130 Boulanger, Daniel. La rose et le reflet. Paris, 1968.
43544.88.2140 Boulanger, Daniel. Tchadiennes. Paris, 1969.
43544.88.2150 Boulanger, Daniel. Retouches. Paris, 1969.
43544.88.2160 Boulanger, Daniel. Mémoire de la ville. Paris, 1970.
43544.88.3100 Bourcier, E. La guerre du Tonkin. Paris, 1931.
43544.88.4100 Boutron, Pierre Noël. Les colliers du nêve. Paris, 1959.
43544.88.5100 Boule de Gomme (pseud.). Vitamines d'estaminet. Poems. Paris, 1960.
43544.88.7100A Bourgeois, A. Ballades louisianaises. Houston, 1938.
43544.88.7100B Bourgeois, A. Ballades louisianaises. Houston, 1938.
43544.89.61 Bousquet, Joë. Correspondance. Paris, 1969.
43544.89.65 Bousquet, Joë. Lettres à Jean Cassou. Limoges, 1970.
43544.89.100 Bousquet, Joë. Comédienne. Paris, 1922.
43544.89.110 Bousquet, Joë. La tisane de Sarments. Paris, 1936.
43544.89.120 Bousquet, Joë. Lumière infranchissable pourriture. Lavaur, 1964.
43544.89.125 Bousquet, Joë. Lettres à Poisson d'Or. Paris, 1967.
43544.89.140 Bousquet, Joë. Le semé chemins. Limoges, 1968.
43544.89.1100 Boutet, Frédéric. Victor et ses amis. Paris, 1916.
43544.89.1110 Boutet, Frédéric. Je jeune homme du rez-de-chaussée. Paris, 1928.
43544.89.2021 Bosquet, Alain. Trois poètes. Paris, 1956.
43544.89.2100 Bosquet, Alain. Langue morte. Paris, 1951.
43544.89.2112 Bosquet, Alain. La grande éclipse. 7. éd. Paris, 1952.
43544.89.2120 Bosquet, Alain. Ni singe. Paris, 1953.
43544.89.2130 Bosquet, Alain. Quel royaume oublié? Paris, 1955.
43544.89.2140A Bosquet, Alain. Premier testament. Paris, 1957.
43544.89.2140B Bosquet, Alain. Premier testament. Paris, 1957.
43544.89.2142 Bosquet, Alain. Premier testament. 4. éd. Paris, 1957.
43544.89.2150 Bosquet, Alain. Deuxième testament. Paris, 1959.
43544.89.2160 Bosquet, Alain. Le mécréant; roman. Paris, 1960.
43544.89.2170 Bosquet, Alain. Maître objet. Paris, 1962.
43544.89.2180 Bosquet, Alain. Un besoin de malheur; roman. Paris, 1963.
43544.89.2190 Bosquet, Alain. Les petites éternités. Paris, 1964.
43544.89.2200 Bosquet, Alain. La confession mexicaine; roman. Paris, 1965.
43544.89.2210 Bosquet, Alain. Quatre testaments et autres poèmes. Paris, 1967.
43544.89.2220 Bosquet, Alain. Les tigres de papier. Paris, 1968.
43544.89.2230 Bosquet, Alain. Syncopes. Paris, 1951.
43544.89.3100 Bourniquel, Camille. Le blé sauvage. Paris, 1955.
43544.89.3110 Bourniquel, Camille. Les abois. Paris, 1957.
43544.89.3120 Bourniquel, Camille. L'ete des solitudes. Paris, 1960.
43544.89.3130 Bourniquel, Camille. Le lac; roman. Paris, 1964.
43544.89.4100 Boucharlat, René. De dessous les eaux. Paris, 1956.
43544.89.5100 Bounoure, Gabriel. Marelles sur le parvis. Paris, 1958.
43544.89.6100 Bouju, Paul M. Vers anciens et nouveaux. Paris, 1930.
43544.89.7100 Bouchet, Paul. Hu Gadam. Paris, 1956.
43544.89.8100 Bourdeillette, Jean. La pierre et l'anémone. Paris, 1964.
43544.89.9100 Boudry, Robert. Le valet de coeur. Paris, 1926.
43544.89.9110 Boudry, Robert. Toussaint Vezzani. Paris, 1929.
43544.90.100 Bouvelet, Jehan. Barbe-blonde. Paris, 1922.
43544.90.110 Bouvelet, Jehan. Au clair de la lune. Paris, 1929.
43544.90.1100 Boujut, Pierre. Sang libre; poèmes. Paris, 1969.
43544.90.2100 Bourricaud, Jean. Coordonnées 44-54. Paris, 1954.
43544.90.3100 Bourgeon, Roger. L'archevêgue des favelles. Paris, 1968.
43544.90.4100 Bouzekri, Marcelle. La codorniz. Paris, 1969.
43544.90.5100 Bourhis, Andrée. La fleur enchantée. Paris, 1946.
43544.90.6100 Baurrec, Jean Roger. La brûlure. Paris, 1970.
43544.90.7100 Bouvier, André. Le collier. Lausanne, 1931.
43544.94.100 Bove, Emmanuel. Mes amis; roman. Paris, 1932.

43511 - 43873 Individual authors, etc. - 1900- - Known authors (363 scheme plus 10) - cont.

43544.94.110 Bove, Emmanuel. Le meurtre de Suzy Pommier; roman. 21. éd. Paris, 1933.
43544.94.120 Bove, Emmanuel. Le piège. Paris, 1945.
43544.94.130 Bove, Emmanuel. Journal écrit en hiver. Paris, 1931.
43544.94.132 Bove, Emmanuel. Journal écrit en hiver. Lausanne, 1965.
43544.94.140 Bove, Emmanuel. L'amour de Pierre Neuhart. Paris, 1929.
43544.94.150 Bove, Emmanuel. La coalition. Paris, 1928.
43544.94.160 Bove, Emmanuel. Coeurs et visages. Paris, 1928.
43544.94.170 Bove, Emmanuel. Armand. Paris, 1927.
43544.94.180 Bove, Emmanuel. Henri Duchemin et ses ombres. Paris, 1928.
43544.97.800 Durieux, Adèle. Robert Boxus, écrivain Wallon. Gilly, 1967.
43544.98.101 Boyer, Lucien. La chanson des poilus. Paris, 1918.
43544.99.100 Bourgeois, André. René Boylesve. Paris, 1945.
43544.101.100 Borne, Alain. L'eau fine. Paris, 1947.
43544.101.110 Borne, Alain. Poèmes à Lislei. Paris, 1946.
43544.101.120 Borne, Alain. La nuit me parle de toi. Limoges, 1964.
43544.101.130 Borne, Alain. Les fêtes sont fanées. Suivi de la dernière ligne. Genève, 1965.
43544.103.100 Bolle, Louis. La faucille et la Carandie. Paris, 1949.
43544.105.100 Boyer, François. The secret game. London, 1950.
43544.105.110 Boyer, François. La gare du ciel. Paris, 1954.
43544.105.120 Boyer, François. Jeux interdits. Paris, 1968.
43544.106.100 Boutelleau, G. Ventriloques, roman. Paris, 1950.
43544.106.110 Boutelleau, G. Les fétiches. Paris, 1955.
43544.106.120 Boutelleau, G. Le grand ensemble. Paris, 1962.
43544.107.100 Boutron, Michel. Hans. London, 1952.
43544.107.110 Boutron, Michel. Les liens; roman. Paris, 1963.
43544.108.100 Boulle, Pierre. Le pont de la rivière Kwai. Paris, 1952.
43544.108.110 Boulle, Pierre. E mc2 récits. Paris, 1957.
43544.108.115 Boulle, Pierre. Contes de l'absurde. Paris, 1963.
43544.108.120 Boulle, Pierre. Un métier de seigneur. Paris, 1960.
43544.108.130 Boulle, Pierre. William Conrad. Paris, 1962.
43544.108.140 Boulle, Pierre. Histoires charitables. Paris, 1964.
43544.108.160 Boulle, Pierre. Aux sources de la rivière Kwai. Paris, 1966.
43544.108.170 Boulle, Pierre. La planète des singes; roman. Paris, 1963.
43544.108.180 Boulle, Pierre. Le photographe. Paris, 1967.
43544.108.700 Boulle, Pierre. The bridge over the River Kwai. N.Y., 1954.
43544.108.705 Boulle, Pierre. Face of a hero. N.Y., 1956.
43544.108.710 Boulle, Pierre. Not the glory. N.Y., 1955.
43544.108.715 Boulle, Pierre. The test. N.Y., 1957.
43544.108.720 Boulle, Pierre. The other side of the coin. N.Y., 1958.
43544.108.725 Boulle, Pierre. Sacrilege in Malaya. London, 1959.
43544.108.730 Boulle, Pierre. A noble profession. N.Y., 1960.
43544.108.735 Boulle, Pierre. For a noble cause. London, 1961.
43544.108.740 Boulle, Pierre. The Chinese executioner. London, 1962.
43544.108.745 Boulle, Pierre. Planet of the apes. N.Y., 1963.
43544.108.750 Boulle, Pierre. My own River Kwai. N.Y., 1967.
43544.108.800 Roy, Paulette. Pierre Boulle et son oeuvre. Paris, 1970.
43544.109.41 Bouchardon, Pierre. Souvenirs. Paris, 1953.
43544.109.100 Bouchardon, Pierre. Le mystère du chateau de Chamblas. Paris, 1922.
43544.111.100 Boucher, Maurice. Quand l'âme est absente. Paris, 1956.
43544.112.100 Boileau, Pierre. Les magiciennes. Paris, 1957.
43544.112.110 Boileau, Pierre. The evil eye. London, 1959.
43544.112.120 Boileau, Pierre. D'entre les morts. Genève, 1971.
43544.112.700 Boileau, Pierre. The tube. London, 1960.
43544.113.100 Boussinot, Roger. L'eau du bain. Paris, 1958.
43544.113.110 Boussinot, Roger. Le sixième sens. Paris, 1959.
43544.114.100 Bourget-Pailleron, Robert. La demoiselle de la Closerie. Paris, 1965.
43545.1.1100 Bradley, J. Frenchie. Paris, 1953.
43545.1.2100 Brachetto, Roland. Ce silence dans mai. Génève, 1962.
43545.1.2110 Brachetto, Roland. Poèmes tunisiens. Paris, 1966.
43545.2.100 Braibant, Charles. Irène Soubeyran. Paris, 1946.
43545.2.110 Braibant, Charles. Un bourgeois sous trois républiques. Paris, 1961.
43545.2.1100 Braekman, Hélène. Pierre à Briguet. Bruxelles, 1964.
43545.3.100 Brandenburg, A.J. Un jeune légionnaire. N.Y., 1923.
43545.3.110 Brandenburg, A.J. Niobé. Paris, 1921.
43545.3.120 Brandenburg, A.J. Le poème royal. Paris, 1922.
43545.3.130 Brandenburg, A.J. L'immortelle bien-aimée. Paris, 1923.
43545.3.1100 Brame, Hector. Illusion et vérité. Poissy, 19- .
43545.4.100 Branson, K.A. La petite illustration. Paris, 1923.
43545.4.2100 Bramson, Fru Karen A. Nous, les barbares. Paris, 1929.
43545.4.4011 Brasillach, Robert. Oeuvres complètes. Paris, 1963. 12v.
43545.4.4100 Brasillach, Robert. Comme le temps passe. Paris, 1937.
43545.4.4110 Brasillach, Robert. Les sept couleurs. Paris, 1939.
43545.4.4110.5 Brasillach, Robert. Les sept couleurs. Paris, 1961.
43545.4.4115 Brasillach, Robert. Le voleur d'étincelles. Paris, 1968.
43545.4.4120 Brasillach, Robert. Poèmes de Fresnes. Louvain, 1946.
43545.4.4130 Brasillach, Robert. Les quatre jeudis. Paris, 1951.
43545.4.4140 Brasillach, Robert. Six heures à perdre. Paris, 1953.
43545.4.4150 Brasillach, Robert. Lettres écrites en prison. Paris, 1952.
43545.4.4160 Brasillach, Robert. Journal d'un homme occupé. Paris, 1955.
43545.4.4170 Brasillach, Robert. Berenice. Paris, 1954.
43545.4.4180 Brasillach, Robert. Le procès de Jeanne d'Arc. 5. éd. Paris, 1941.
43545.4.4190 Brasillach, Robert. Notre avant-guerre. Paris, 1958.
43545.4.4195 Brasillach, Robert. Notre avant-guerre. Paris, 1941.
43545.4.4200 Brasillach, Robert. La reine de Césarée. Paris, 1957.
43545.4.4210 Brasillach, Robert. Presence de Virgile. Paris, 1960.
43545.4.4220 Brasillach, Robert. Poètes oubliés. Lyon, 1961.
43545.4.4230 Brasillach, Robert. Le marchand d'oiseaux. Paris, 1936.
43545.4.4800 Isorni, J. Le procès Robert Brasillach. Paris, 1946.
43545.4.4805 Vandromme, P. Robert Brasillach. Paris, 1956.
43545.4.4810 Madiran, Jean. Brasillach. Paris? 1958.
43545.4.4815 Amis de Robert Brasillach. Cahiers. Lausanne. 5,1955+ 2v.
43545.4.4820 Pellegrin, Réné. Un écrivain nommé Brasillach. Montsecret, 1965.
43545.4.4825 George, Bernard. Robert Brasillach. Paris, 1968.
43545.4.7100 Braunschwig, M. Regards interieurs. Paris, 1937.
43545.5.100 Brauquier, L. Eau douce pour naveres. Paris, 1930.
43545.5.110 Breitman, M. Le pilote, avec deux dessins d'Etienne Bouchaud. Tunis, 1935.
43545.5.1100 Brassens, Georges. La Mauvaise reputation. Paris, 1954.
43545.5.1110 Brassens, Georges. Georges Brassens. Paris, 1965.
43545.22.800 Hogarth, H. Henri Bremond. London, 1950.

43511 - 43873 Individual authors, etc. - 1900- - Known authors (363 scheme plus 10) - cont.

43545.22.805 Moisan, Clément. Henri Bremond et la poésie pure. Paris, 1967.
43545.22.1100 Brémond d'Ars, Ivonne de. Journal d'une antiquaire. Paris, 1962-64. 15v.
43545.22.2100 Brégé, Louis. Sonnets marins. Paris, 1928?
43545.23.100 Brenner, J. La minute heureuse. Paris, 1947.
43545.23.110 Brenner, J. La fête au village. Paris, 1963.
43545.23.2100 Breitman, Michel. Le mal de Dieu. Paris, 1957.
43545.23.2110 Breitman, Michel. D'exil en exil. Paris, 1970.
43545.23.3100 Bremond, Charles. Le train de plaisir. Paris, 1926.
43545.23.3110 Bremond, Charles. Le compartiment des chasseurs. Paris, 1930.
43545.23.4011 Bremond d'Ars, Eusèbe. Oeuvre poétique, 1888-1958. Paris, 1966.
43545.24.100 Breton, André. Arcane 17. N.Y., 1945.
43545.24.100.5 Breton, André. Arcane 17 entré d'ajours. Paris, 1947.
43545.24.100.6 Breton, André. Arcane 17 enté d'ajours. Paris, 1965.
43545.24.110 Breton, André. Le revolver à cheveux blancs. Paris, 1932.
43545.24.120 Breton, André. Martinique, charmeuse de serpents. Paris, 1948.
43545.24.130 Breton, André. Le pas perdus. 6. ed. Paris, 1933.
43545.24.131 Breton, André. Les pas perdus. Paris, 1969.
43545.24.140 Breton, André. Point der jour. 3. éd. Paris, 1934.
43545.24.142 Breton, André. Point du jour. Paris, 1970.
43545.24.150A Breton, André. Nadja. 10. éd. Paris, 1945.
43545.24.155 Breton, André. Nadja. N.Y., 1960.
43545.24.157 Breton, André. Nadja. Paris, 1963.
43545.24.160 Breton, André. L'amour Lou. Paris, 1945.
43545.24.170 Breton, André. Poèmes. 8. éd. Paris, 1948.
43545.24.180 Breton, André. Ode à Charles Fourier. Paris, 1953.
43545.24.182 Breton, André. Ode à Charles Fourier. Paris, 1961.
43545.24.190 Breton, André. La clé des champs. Paris, 1953.
43545.24.200 Breton, André. Les vases communicants. Paris, 1955.
43545.24.210 Breton, André. Entretiens 1913-1952. 7. éd. Paris, 1952.
43545.24.220 Breton, André. La lampe dans l'horloge. Paris, 1948.
43545.24.230 Breton, André. L'immaculée conception. Paris, 1930.
43545.24.240 Breton, André. Les champs magnétiques, Suivis de Vous m'aublierez et s'il vous plaît. Paris, 1967.
43545.24.621 Breton, André. Selected poems. London, 1969.
43545.24.775 Breton, André. Nadja. Neske, 1960.
43545.24.800 Maureac, P. André Breton. Paris, 1949.
43545.24.810 Carrouges, M. André Breton. 5. éd. Paris, 1950.
43545.24.820 Gracq, J. André Breton. Paris, 1948.
43545.24.830 Eigeldinger, Marc. André Breton. Neuchâtel, 1950.
43545.24.831 Eigeldinger, Marc. André Breton. Neuchâtel, 1970.
43545.24.840 Chastre, V. André Breton. n.p., 1952.
43545.24.850 Isou, Isidore. Réflexiions sur André Breton. Paris, 1948.
43545.24.855 André Breton et le mouvement surréaliste. Paris, 1967.
43545.24.860 Matthews, J.H. André Breton. N.Y., 1967.
43545.24.865 Browder, Clifford. André Breton, arbiter of surrealism. Génève, 1967.
43545.24.890 Massot, Pierre de. André Breton ou le Septembriseur. Paris, 1967.
43545.24.895 Caws, Mary Ann. André Breton. N.Y., 1971.
43545.24.900 Audoin, Philippe. Breton. Paris, 1970.
43545.24.905 Balakian, Anna Elizabeth. André Breton. N.Y., 1971.
43545.24.1100 Breton, Jean. Dire non. Dijon, 1964.
43545.24.2100 Brest, Simon. Les yeux mangés. Rodez, 1960.
43545.30.100 Breugnot, A.L. La faire d'embrouille. Alger, 1943.
43545.39.100 Briand, C. Aliaga; roman. Paris, 1932.
43545.39.2000 Briacq, Nicole. La Lande; récit. Paris, 1962.
43545.41.200 Brillaud de Laujardière, C. Péril jaune. Paris, 1906.
43545.41.500 Brival-Gaillard, C. Les sept aventures de Madame Lafarge. Brive, 1913.
43545.41.1021 Brière, Marie Christine. Liesses; poèmes. Rodez, 1965.
43545.41.3100 Brencoutt, A. Le vert paradis. Paris, 1950.
43545.41.4100 Briey, Martin de. Que la paix soit avec nous! Paris, 1964.
43545.41.5100 Brion, Marcel. Le théâtre des esprits. Fribourg, 1941.
43545.41.5110 Brion, Marcel. L'enchanteur. Paris, 1965.
43545.41.5120 Brion, Marcel. Les escales de la haute nuit. Paris, 1965.
43545.41.5130 Brion, Marcel. La musique et l'amour. Paris, 1967.
43545.41.5140 Brion, Marcel. Les miroirs et les gouffres. Paris, 1968.
43545.41.6100 Brillant, Maurice. L'amour sur les treteaux. Paris, 1924. 2v.
43545.41.7100 Brimont, Renée. Les fileuses. Paris, 1937.
43545.41.7110 Brimont, Renée. L'arche. Paris, 1927.
43545.41.8100 Brideron, Jacques. Deux ans sous les hombes. Fontenay-le-Comte, 1968.
43545.41.9100 Brindeau, Serge. Où va la jour. Paris, 1968.
43545.41.9110 Brindeau, Serge. Poèmes pour quelque temps. Paris, 1968.
43545.42.100A Brisson, P. Du meilleur av pire. Paris, 1937.
43545.42.100B Brisson, P. Du meilleur av pire. Paris, 1937.
43545.42.110 Brisson, P. Autre temps. Paris, 1949.
43545.42.120 Brisson, P. Propos de théâtre. 6. éd. Paris, 1957.
43545.42.130 Brisson, P. Vingt ans de Figaro. 5. éd. Paris, 1959.
43545.42.800 Lang, André. Pierre Brisson, le journaliste, l'écrivain, l'homme (1896-1964). Paris, 1967.
43545.42.3100 Brisville, Jean Claude. La présence réelle. Paris, 1954.
43545.42.3110 Brisville, Jean Claude. La fuite au Danemark. Paris, 1962.
43545.42.3120 Brisville, Jean Claude. Le rôdeur. Nora. Le récital. Paris, 1970.
43545.63.100 Brochon, Pierre. Le canare ne chante plus. Paris, 1959.
43545.63.1700 Brock, Mida. Poèmes. Paris, 1963.
43545.66.100 Brosse, Jacques. La chemise rouge. Paris, 1959.
43545.66.110 Brosse, Jacques. L'éphémère. Paris, 1960.
43545.66.120 Brosse, Jacques. Cinq méditations sur le corps. Paris, 1967.
43545.66.2100 Bronne, Carlo. Le bonheur d'Orphée; nouvelles. Bruxelles, 1965.
43545.66.2110 Bronne, Carlo. Bleu d'Ardenne. Bruxelles, 1969.
43545.67.100 Brousset, François. Flirt. Dijon, 1961.
43545.67.1100 Broussard, Yves. Bestiaire des solitudes; poème. Bram, 1970.
43545.89.100 Braunt, A. Dans la rue. Paris, 1899?
43545.89.800 Carco, F. La belle epoque au temps de Braunt. Paris, 1954.
43545.89.2100 Brudieux, André Roland. Le magasén aux accessoires. Bordeaux, 1962.
43545.89.3100 Bruckberger, R.M. The stork and the jewels. N.Y., 1951.
43545.89.3110 Bruckberger, R.M. One sky to share. N.Y., 1952.
43545.89.3120 Bruckberger, R.M. Madeleine et Judas. Chambéry, 1956.
43545.89.3130 Bruckberger, R.M. Golden goat. N.Y., 1952.
43545.89.4100 Brune, Jean. Cette haine qui ressemble a l'amour. Paris, 1961.

Classified Listing

43511 - 43873 Individual authors, etc. - 1900- - Known authors (363 scheme plus 10) - cont.

43545.89.4110 Brune, Jean. Journal d'exil. Paris, 1963.
43545.89.5100 Brucher, Roger. Chair de l'hiver. Bruxelles, 1966?
43545.89.6100 Brunet, Romain. Violet, indigo, bleu. Paris, 1937.
43545.89.7100 Brunoy, Clément. Salyne, Roman. Paris, 1969.
43545.90.100 Brunet, Berthelot. Le mariage blanc d'Armandine. Montréal, 1943.
43545.90.105 Brunet, Berthelot. Chacun sa vie. Montréal, 1942.
43545.90.800 Toupin, Paul. Les paradoxes d'une vie et d'une oeuvre. Montréal, 1965.
43545.91.100 Brunet, G. Ombres vivantes. Paris, 1936.
43545.91.110 Brunet, G. Evocation littéraires. Paris, 1930.
43545.92.100 Brutsch, Jean T. Madame Briboine et autres personnages. Genève, 1964.
43546.37.30 Buhet, Gil. The bouey siege. London, 1953.
43546.37.35 Buhet, Gil. The story-teller. London, 1955.
43546.41.100 Buin, Yves. Les alephs. Paris, 1965.
43546.75.100 Bureau, Jacques. Trois pierres chaudes en Espagne. Paris, 1959.
43546.76.100 Burniaux, Constant. L'autocar. Bruxelles, 1955?
43546.76.110 Burniaux, Constant. Poésie, 1922-1963. Paris, 1965.
43546.76.120 Burniaux, Constant. L'odeur du matin. Bruxelles, 1967.
43546.76.130 Burniaux, Constant. D'humour et d'amour (journal d'un homme sensible. Paris, 1968.
X Cg 43546.82.100 Bustros, Eveline. La main d'Allah. 11. éd. Paris, 1926.
43546.87.30 Butor, Michel. Passage de Mitar. Paris, 1954.
43546.87.32 Butor, Michel. Illustrations. Paris, 1964. 2v.
43546.87.35 Butor, Michel. La modification. Paris, 1957.
43546.87.36 Butor, Michel. La modification. Paris, 1963.
43546.87.38 Butor, Michel. Portrait de l'artiste en jeune singe. Paris, 1967.
43546.87.40 Butor, Michel. Le genie dulieu. Paris, 1958.
43546.87.45 Butor, Michel. Second thoughts. London, 1958.
43546.87.50 Butor, Michel. A change of heart. N.Y., 1959.
43546.87.55 Butor, Michel. L'emploi du temps. Paris, 1958.
43546.87.60 Butor, Michel. Repertoire. Paris, 1960. 2v.
43546.87.62 Butor, Michel. Sobre literatura. Barcelona, 1960.
43546.87.65 Butor, Michel. Degrés. Paris, 1960.
43546.87.68 Butor, Michel. Mobile, étude pour une representation des Etats-Unis. Paris, 1962.
43546.87.69 Butor, Michel. 6810000 litres d'eau par seconde. Paris, 1965.
43546.87.70 Butor, Michel. Passing time. N.Y., 1960.
43546.87.72 Butor, Michel. Degrees. N.Y., 1963.
43546.87.74 Butor, Michel. Mobile, study for a representation of the United States. N.Y., 1961.
43546.87.76 Butor, Michel. Description de San Marco. Paris, 1963.
43546.87.78 Butor, Michel. Essais sur le roman. Paris, 1969.
43546.87.80 Marill, René. Michel Butor. Paris, 1964.
43546.87.82 Roudiez, Léon. Michel Butor. N.Y., 1965.
43546.87.85 Roudaut, Jean. Michel Butor. Paris, 1964.
43546.87.90 Charbonnier, Georges. Entretiens avec Michel Butor. Paris, 1967.
43546.87.95 Raillard, Georges. Butor. Paris, 1968.
43546.87.100 Wolfzettel, Friedrich. Michel Butor und der Kollektivroman. Heidelberg, 1969.
43547.1.30 Buisson, Benjamin. Les Helléniques de Landor et autre poèmes. Paris, 1916.
43547.1.31 Buisson, Benjamin. Teutoniana. Paris, 1917.
43547.12.700 Buchet, E.E. Children of wrath. London, 1947.
43547.13.100 Bucline, Jean. Lili bat. Paris, 1946.
43547.34.100 Bugnet, Georges. La forêt. Montréal, 1953.
43547.34.110 Bugnet, Georges. Voix de la solitude. Montréal, 1938.
43547.34.120 Bugnet, Georges. Siraj, étranges relations. Montréal, 1934.
43547.50.100 Bulliard, Paul. La chanson simple; poèmes. Paris, 1946.
43547.75.100 Burgei, Maurice. En parte-a-faux. Paris, 1959.
43547.76.100 Burnet, Etienne. Soin de icônes. Paris, 1923.
43547.76.110 Burnet, Etienne. Essences: Paul Valéry et l'unité de l'esprit. Paris, 1929.
43547.77.100 Burnat-Provins, Marguerite. Le livre pour toi. 7. éd. Paris, 19- ?
43547.77.110 Burnat-Provins, Marguerite. Poèmes de la Boule de Verre. Paris, 1917.
43547.77.120 Burnat-Provins, Marguerite. Nouveaux poèmes de la Boule de Verre. Paris, 1918.
43547.77.130 Burnat-Provins, Marguerite. Contes en vingt lignes. Saint-Raphaël, 1922.
43547.77.140 Burnat-Provins, Marguerite. Heures d'hiver. Paris, 1920.
43547.77.800 Malo, Henri. Marguerite Burnat-Provins. Paris, 1920.
43547.77.1100 Burnat, Jean. D'comme Dupont. Paris, 1959.
43547.77.2100 Buron, Nicole de. Los pies sobre el escritorio. Santiago de Chile, 1959.
43547.82.100 Busselen, Roland. Dénnis que je sois. Paris, 1964.
43547.82.110 Busselen, Roland. Un quelqu'un. Paris, 1968.
43547.85.100 Byrch, Rita. Amor, in memoriam. Paris, 1935.
43550.1.20 Carco, Francis. Poèmes retrouvés, 1904-1923. Paris, 1927.
43550.1.22 Carco, Francis. Poésies complètes. Paris, 1955.
43550.1.23 Carco, Francis. Poèmes en prose. Paris, 1958.
Htn 43550.1.30* Carco, Francis. La Bohème et mon coeur. n.p., 1912.
43550.1.31 Carco, Francis. La Bohème et mon coeur. 5. éd. Paris, 1929.
43550.1.31.2 Carco, Francis. La Bohème et mon coeur. Paris, 1939.
43550.1.31.10 Carco, Francis. Pour faire suite a la Bohème et mon coeur. Paris, 1933.
43550.1.31.20 Carco, Francis. Bohème d'artiste. Paris, 1940.
43550.1.32 Carco, Francis. L'homme traqué. Paris, 1922.
43550.1.33 Carco, Francis. L'homme traqué. Saverne, 1952.
43550.1.35A Carco, Francis. Le roman de François Villon. Paris, 1926.
43550.1.35B Carco, Francis. Le roman de François Villon. Paris, 1926.
43550.1.40 Carco, Francis. Perversite; roman. Paris, 1925.
43550.1.44 Carco, Francis. Images cachées. Paris, 1928.
43550.1.45 Carco, Francis. Images cachées. Paris, 1929.
43550.1.50 Carco, Francis. Petits airs. Paris, 1920.
43550.1.55 Carco, Francis. L'ombre, roman. Paris, 1933.
43550.1.60 Carco, Francis. Mémoires d'une autre vie. Paris, 1934.
43550.1.65 Carco, Francis. A voix basse. Paris, 1938.
43550.1.70 Carco, Francis. Montmartre à vingt-ans. Paris, 1938.
43550.1.75 Carco, Francis. Les vrais de vrai. Paris, 1928.
43550.1.76 Carco, Francis. Heures d'Egypte. 6. éd. Avignon, 1940.
43550.1.80 Carco, Francis. Nostalgie de Paris. Genève, 1941.
43550.1.100 Carco, Francis. La lumière noire; roman. Paris, 1934.
43550.1.110 Carco, Francis. Palace Egypte; roman. Paris, 1933.
43550.1.120 Carco, Francis. Les innocents. Paris, 1938.
43550.1.125 Carco, Francis. Rue Pigalle. Paris, 1949.
43550.1.127 Carco, Francis. Rue Pigalle. Paris, 1928.
43550.1.130 Carco, Francis. L'homme de minuit. Paris, 1938.

43511 - 43873 Individual authors, etc. - 1900- - Known authors (363 scheme plus 10) - cont.

43550.1.135 Carco, Francis. Jésus-la-Caille. Paris, 1932.
43550.1.140 Carco, Francis. L'ami des peintres, souvenirs. Genève, 1944.
43550.1.150 Carco, Francis. Jésus-la-Caille, roman. Paris, 1945.
43550.1.160 Carco, Francis. Mortefontaine. Paris, 1949.
43550.1.170 Carco, Francis. Morsure; roman. 11. éd. Paris, 1949.
43550.1.180 Carco, Francis. Morsure. 12. éd. Paris, 1949.
43550.1.188 Carco, Francis. De Montmartre au Quartier Latin. Paris, 1927.
43550.1.190 Carco, Francis. De Montmartre au Quartier Latin. Paris, 1949.
43550.1.200 Carco, Francis. Rendez-vous avec moi-même. Paris, 1957.
43550.1.210 Carco, Francis. Rieu qu'une femme. Paris, 1923.
43550.1.220 Carco, Francis. Huit jours à Seville. Paris, 1929.
43550.1.230 Carco, Francis. Amitie avec Joulet. Paris, 1934.
43550.1.240 Carco, Francis. Au coin des rues. Dessins en couleurs d'Henri Mirande. Paris, 1930.
43550.1.700 Carco, Francis. Perversity. Chicago, 1928.
43550.1.800A Champion, E. La poésie de Carco. Paris, 1934.
43550.1.800B Champion, E. La poésie de Carco. Paris, 1934.
43550.1.810 Weiner, S.S. Francis Carco. N.Y., 1952.
43550.2.30 Cartairade, F. Du coeur aux Lévres. Paris, 1874.
43550.2.31 Cartairade, F. Le jour et la nuit. Paris, 1874.
43550.3.30 Castanier, Prosper. El loto del Ganges. Paris, 1909.
43550.6.100 Cabanis, José. Les mariages de raison; roman. 8. éd. Paris, 1958.
43550.6.110 Cabanis, José. Le bonheur du jour. Paris, 1960.
43550.6.120 Cabanis, José. Les cartes du temps. Paris, 1962.
43550.6.130 Cabanis, José. Juliette Bonviolle. Paris, 1954.
43550.6.140 Cabanis, José. L'auberge fameuse, roman. Paris, 1953.
43550.6.150 Cabanis, José. Plaisir et lectures. Paris, 1964. 2v.
43550.6.160 Cabanis, José. Le fils; roman. Paris, 1956.
43550.6.170 Cabanis, José. Les jeux de la nuit. Paris, 1964.
43550.6.180 Cabanis, José. L'age ingrant. Paris, 1966.
43550.6.190 Cabanis, José. La bataille de Toulouse; roman. Paris, 1966.
43550.6.200 Cabanis, José. Des jardins en Espagne. Paris, 1969.
43550.10.100 Cabriès, Jean. Jacob. London, 1957.
V43550.10.105 Cabriès, Jean. Saint Jacob. Les Hautes Plaines de Mane, 1968.
43550.12.1100 Cachera, André. Le porcelet de Delphes. Poems. Paris, 1956?
43550.19.100 Cadou, René Guy. Hélène, ou Le règne végétal. Paris, 1952-53. 2v.
43550.19.105 Cadou, René Guy. Hélène, ou Le règne végétal, 1944-1951. Paris, 1960.
43550.19.110 Cadou, René Guy. Les biens de ce monde. Paris, 1951.
43550.19.120 Cadou, René Guy. Poésie la vie entière. Fay-aux-Loges, 1961.
43550.19.130 Cadou, René Guy. Florilège politique. Paris, 1961.
43550.19.140 Cadou, René Guy. Le coeur définitif. Paris, 1961.
43550.20.100 Cadou, Hélène. Le bonheur du jour. Paris, 1956.
43550.20.110 Cadou, Hélène. Cantate des nuits interieures. Paris, 1958.
43550.39.100 Cahour, Michel. L'amour à froid. Paris, 1967.
43550.40.100 Cahuet, Albéric. Le missel d'amour. pt.1-3. Paris, 1923.
43550.40.105 Cahuet, Albéric. Mademoiselle de Milly; roman. v.1-2. Paris, 1928.
43550.40.110 Cahuet, Albéric. Régime Romani. Paris, 1925.
43550.40.120 Cahuet, Albéric. Les amants du lac; roman. v.1-4. Paris, 1927.
43550.40.130 Cahuet, Albéric. Irène, femme inconnue; roman. v.1-3. Paris, 1930.
43550.40.140 Cahuet, Albéric. Saint Hélène petite ile. v.1-4. Paris, 1932.
43550.40.150 Cahuet, Albéric. La nuit espagnole. v.1-3. Paris, 1934.
43550.40.160 Cahuet, Albéric. La femme aux images. pt.1-3. Paris, 1937.
43550.40.170 Cahuet, Albéric. Pontcarral. Paris, 1937.
43550.41.100 Caillois, Roger. Ponce Pilate. Paris, 1961.
43550.41.110 Caillois, Roger. Obligues. Montpellier, 1967.
43550.41.120 Caillois, Roger. Cases d'un échiquier. Paris, 1970.
43550.41.1100 Caizergues, Jacques. Ritournelles pour traversée. Paris, 1954.
43550.42.100 Cailloux, René. L'eternelle Phèdre. Cavaillon, 1954.
43550.44.100 Calef, Noel. Ascenseur pour l'echafaud. Paris, 1965.
43550.48.100 Calet, Henri. Trente à quarante. Paris, 1947.
43550.48.110 Calet, Henri. Les deux bouts. 2. éd. Paris, 1954.
43550.48.120 Calet, Henri. Peau d'ours pour un roman. Paris, 1958.
43550.48.700 Calet, Henri. Monsieur Paul. 1. ed. N.Y., 1953.
43550.48.710 Calet, Henri. Young man of Paris. 1. ed. N.Y., 1950.
43550.48.1100 Caland, Laurence. Si peu d'amour. Paris, 1946.
43550.49.100 Calendale, François. Demeure aux mews. Paris, 1961.
43550.50.100 Callias, S. de. Jeanne d'Arc répond. Paris, 1929.
43550.50.1100 Caillier, Guy. Tant que tournera la terre, poèmes. Paris, 1957.
43550.51.100 Cali, F. Monsieur Thomas la Brévine. Paris, 1963.
43550.52.41 Calvet, Jean. Memoires de Mgr. Jean Calvet. Lyon, 1967.
43550.52.100 Calvet, Jean. Témoins de la conscience française. Paris, 1943.
43550.53.100 Camara, Sikhé. Poèmes de combat et de vérité. Honfleur, 1967.
43550.55.100 Cami, Henri. Les exploits galants du baron de Crac. Paris, 1925.
43550.55.110 Cami, Henri. L'home à la tête d'epingle. Paris, 1914.
43550.55.115 Cami, Henri. Le poilu aux mille trucs. Paris, 1915.
43550.55.120 Cami, Henri. Christophe Colomb. Paris, 1931.
43550.55.130 Cami, Henri. Pssitt et Pchutt. Paris, 1932.
43550.56.100 Cammaerts, E. Messines and other poems. N.Y., 1918.
43550.56.105 Cammaerts, E. A ma patrie enchainée; poèmes. Bruxelles, 1918.
43550.56.110 Cammaerts, E. Belgian poèms, chants patriotiques et autres poèmes. London, 1915.
43550.56.112A Cammaerts, E. Belgian poèms, chants patriotiques et autres poèmes. London, 1915.
43550.56.112B Cammaerts, E. Belgian poèms, chants patriotiques et autres poèmes. London, 1915.
43550.56.700 Cammaerts, E. Upon this rock. N.Y., 1943.
43550.56.705 Cammaerts, E. The flower of grass. London, 1944.
43550.56.710 Cammaerts, E. The devil takes the chair. London, 1949.
43550.56.800 Lindley, Jeanne. Seeking and finding. London, 1962.
43550.57.100 Camp, Jean. Vin nouveau. 7. éd. Paris, 1929.
43550.57.110 Camp, Jean. Le cid est revenu. Paris, 1931.
43550.58.11 Camus, Albert. Oeuvres complète. Paris, 1962. 6v.
43550.58.21 Camus, Albert. Collected fiction. London, 1960.

43511 - 43873 Individual authors, etc. - 1900- - Known authors (363 scheme plus 10) - cont.

43550.58.22 Camus, Albert. Théâtre récits nouvelles. Paris, 1962.
43550.58.23 Camus, Albert. Essais. Paris, 1965.
43550.58.24 Camus, Albert. Collected plays. London, 1965.
43550.58.25 Camus, Albert. Lyrical and critical essays. London, 1967.
43550.58.26 Camus, Albert. Lyrical and critical essays. N.Y., 1969.
43550.58.63 Camus, Albert. Lettres à un ami allemand. Paris, 1945.
43550.58.100A Camus, Albert. L'étranger. N.Y., 1946.
43550.58.100B Camus, Albert. L'étranger. N.Y., 1946.
43550.58.110 Camus, Albert. Noces. Paris, 1939.
43550.58.112 Camus, Albert. Noces. 11. éd. Paris, 1945.
43550.58.115 Camus, Albert. Noces. Photoreproduction. Paris, 1947.
43550.58.120 Camus, Albert. La peste. 81. éd. Paris, 1947.
43550.58.130A Camus, Albert. Le malentendu. 32. éd. Paris, 1948.
43550.58.130B Camus, Albert. Le malentendu. 46. éd. Paris, 1948.
43550.58.140 Camus, Albert. Les justes. Paris, 1950.
43550.58.150 Camus, Albert. Le minotaure. Paris, 1950.
43550.58.160A Camus, Albert. Actuelles. Paris, 1950-58. 2v.
43550.58.160B Camus, Albert. Actuelles. Paris, 1950-58. 3v.
43550.58.171 Camus, Albert. Le mythe de Sisyphe. Paris, 1964.
43550.58.173 Camus, Albert. Le mythe de Sisyphe. Paris, 1942.
43550.58.180 Camus, Albert. L'été. Paris, 1954.
43550.58.190 Camus, Albert. Le malentendu. 59. éd. Paris, 1954.
43550.58.192 Camus, Albert. Le malentendu. Paris, 1958.
43550.58.200 Camus, Albert. L'état de siege. 23. éd. Paris, 1948.
43550.58.210 Camus, Albert. La chute, récit. 64. éd. Paris, 1956.
43550.58.220 Camus, Albert. L'exil et le royaume. 69. éd. Paris, 1957.
43550.58.230 Camus, Albert. Discours de Suède. 14. éd. Paris, 1958.
43550.58.240 Bonnier, Henry. Albert Camus. Lyon, 1959.
43550.58.250 Nouvelle revue française. Hommage à Albert Camus. Paris, 1960.
43550.58.260 Hourdin, Georges. Camus le Juste. 2. éd. Paris, 1960.
43550.58.270 Camus, Albert. Carnets. Paris, 1962- 2v.
43550.58.272 Camus, Albert. Carnets; mai 1935 - mars 1951. Paris, 1965.
43550.58.280 Camus, Albert. Albert Camus par lui-même. Paris, 1963.
43550.58.290 Cahiers Albert Camus. Paris. 1,1971+
43550.58.700 Camus, Albert. The stranger. 1. American ed. N.Y., 1946.
43550.58.700.5 Camus, Albert. The stranger. N.Y., 1951.
43550.58.700.6 Camus, Albert. The stranger. n.p., n.d.
43550.58.702 Camus, Albert. Notebooks, 1935-1942. N.Y., 1963. 2v.
43550.58.705 Camus, Albert. The outsider. London, 1946.
43550.58.715A Camus, Albert. Caligula. London, 1947.
43550.58.715B Camus, Albert. Caligula. London, 1947.
43550.58.716 Camus, Albert. Caligula and three other plays. 1. American ed. N.Y., 1958.
43550.58.718 Camus, Albert. Caligula and three other plays. N.Y., 1960.
43550.58.720 Camus, Albert. The plague. N.Y., 1948.
43550.58.721 Camus, Albert. The plague. N.Y., 1950.
43550.58.722 Camus, Albert. The plague. N.Y., 1957.
43550.58.723 Camus, Albert. The plague. N.Y., 1958.
43550.58.724 Camus, Albert. The plague. N.Y., 1948.
43550.58.725 Camus, Albert. The rebel. London, 1953.
43550.58.726.5 Camus, Albert. The rebel. N.Y., 1959.
43550.58.726.10 Camus, Albert. The rebel. N.Y., 1962.
43550.58.726.15 Camus, Albert. The rebel; an essay on man in revolt. N.Y., 1961.
43550.58.730A Camus, Albert. The fall. 1. American ed. N.Y., 1957.
43550.58.730B Camus, Albert. The fall. 1. American ed. N.Y., 1957.
43550.58.730C Camus, Albert. The fall. 1. American ed. N.Y., 1957.
43550.58.730D Camus, Albert. The fall. 1. American ed. N.Y., 1957.
43550.58.735 Camus, Albert. The myth of Sisyphus. 1. American ed. N.Y., 1955. 2v.
43550.58.735.5 Camus, Albert. The myth of Sisyphus, and other essays. N.Y., 1955.
43550.58.741 Camus, Albert. Exile and the kingdom. N.Y., 1963.
43550.58.745 Camus, Albert. Speech of acceptance upon the award of the Nobel prize for literature. 1. ed. N.Y., 1958.
43550.58.750 Camus, Albert. L'envers et l'endroit. Paris, 1958.
43550.58.755 Camus, Albert. Récits et théâtre. Gallimard, 1958.
43550.58.757 Camus, Albert. Carnets, 1935-1951. London, 1963-66. 2v.
43550.58.760 Camus, Albert. The possessed. N.Y., 1960.
43550.58.764 Camus, Albert. Resistance, rebellion, and death. N.Y., 1960.
43550.58.765 Camus, Albert. Resistance, rebellion, and death. 1. American ed. N.Y., 1961.
43550.58.770 Camus, Albert Sivulliner. Helsingissa, 1947.
V43550.58.780 Camus, Albert. Neznakomets. Paris, 196-?
43550.58.805 Sartre, J.P. Explication de L'étranger. n.p., 1946.
43550.58.806 Sartre, J.P. Literary and philosophical essays. London, 1955.
43550.58.810 Guido, B. Los dos Albertos en la novela contempóranea. Rosario, 1950.
43550.58.815 Luppé, Robert de. Albert Camus. Paris, 1952.
43550.58.815.5 Luppé, Robert de. Albert Camus. 1. American ed. N.Y., 1968.
43550.58.820 Quilliot, Roger. La mer et les prisons. Paris, 1956.
43550.58.825 Maquet, Albert. Albert Camus. Paris, 1956.
43550.58.827 Maquet, Albert. Albert Camus. N.Y., 1958.
43550.58.830 Thody, Philip. Albert Camus. London, 1957.
43550.58.831 Thody, Philip. Albert Camus, 1913-1960. London, 1961.
43550.58.832A Hanna, Thomas. The thought and art of Albert Camus. Chicago, 1958.
43550.58.832B Hanna, Thomas. The thought and art of Albert Camus. Chicago, 1958.
43550.58.840 Bjurström, C.G. Albert Camus. Stockholm, 1957.
43550.58.842 Bollinger, Renate. Albert Camus. Köln, 1957.
43550.58.845 Cruickshank, John. Albert Camus and the literature of revolt. London, 1959.
43550.58.847 Brisville, Jean A. Camus. 3. éd. Paris, 1959.
43550.58.849 Lanfranchi, Geneviève. La secrète issue. Monte-Carlo, 1958.
43550.58.855 Brée, Germaine. Camus. New Brunswick, 1959.
43550.58.856 Brée, Germaine. Camus. Englewood, 1962.
43550.58.860 Champigny, Robert. Sur un héros paien. Paris, 1959.
43550.58.861 Champigny, Robert. A pagan hero. Philadelphia, 1969.
43550.58.865 Girolamo, N. de. Albert Camus. Siena, 1959.
43550.58.870 Brée, Germaine. Camus. New Brunswick, N.J., 1961.
43550.58.872 Brée, Germaine. Camus. N.Y., 1964.
43550.58.875 Pinnoy, M.B. Albert Camus. Brugge, 1961.
43550.58.880 France. Embassy. United States. Albert Camus, 1913-1960. N.Y., 1960?
43550.58.885 Simon, Pierre Henri. Présence de Camus. Bruxelles, 1961.
43550.58.890 Durand, Anne. Le cas Albert Camus. Paris, 1961.

43511 - 43873 Individual authors, etc. - 1900- - Known authors (363 scheme plus 10) - cont.

43550.58.895 Vestre, Bernt. Albert Camus og menneskets revolte. Oslo, 1960.
43550.58.900 Haggis, Donald. Albert Camus. London, 1962.
43550.58.905 Scott, Nathan. Albert Camus. London, 1962.
43550.58.910 Gennep, Frederik. Albert Camus. Amsterdam, 1962.
43550.58.915 Nguyen-Van-Huy, P. La métaphysique du bonheur chez A. Camus. Neuchâtel, 1962.
43550.58.920 A Albert Camus, ses amis du livre. Paris, 1962.
43550.58.925 Barrier, M.G. L'art du récit dans l'étranger d'A. Camus. Paris, 1962.
43550.58.930 Revue des lettres modernes. Albert Camus. Paris, 1961. 2v.
43550.58.935 Gudenschwager, E. Auffassung und Darstellung des Menschen in Albert Camus' Roman, La Peste. Mainz, 1962.
43550.58.940 Gadourek, C. Les innocents et les coupables. The Hague, 1963.
43550.58.942 Gadourek, C. Les innocents et les coupables. The Hague, 1963.
43550.58.945 La table ronde. Albert Camus. Paris, 1960.
43550.58.950 King, A. Camus. Edinburgh, 1964.
43550.58.955 Gelinas, G.P. La liberté dans la pensée d'Albert Camus. Fribourg, 1965.
43550.58.960 Rizobello, A. Albert Camus. Napoli, 1963.
43550.58.965 Carruth, Hayden. After the stranger. N.Y., 1964?
43550.58.970A Camus. Paris, 1964.
43550.58.970B Camus. Paris, 1964.
43550.58.975 Brée, Germaine. Albert Camus. N.Y., 1964.
43550.58.980 Parker, Emmett. Albert Camus, the artist in the arena. Madison, 1965.
43550.58.990 Leite, Antonio Roberto de Paula. Albert Camus; notas e estudo crítico. São Paulo, 1963.
43550.58.995 Fitch, Brian T. Albert Camus. v.1, pt.1-2. Paris, 1965. 2v.
43550.58.1000 Passeri Pignoni, Vera. Albert Camus. Bologna, 1965.
43550.58.1010 Ginestier, Paul. La pensée de Camus. Paris, 1964.
43550.58.1015 Majault, Joseph. Camus. Paris, 1965.
43550.58.1020 Brogan, Geoffrey. Albert Camus die Kunst in der Geschichte. Mainz, 1965.
43550.58.1025 Bakker, Reinout. Albert Camus. Baarn, 1966.
43550.58.1030 Quilliot, Roger. L'univers théâtral et romanesque de'Albert Camus. Rodez, 1964.
43550.58.1035 Papamalamis, Dimitris. Albert Camus et la pensée grecque. Nancy, 1965.
43550.58.1040 Jenne, Józef. Próba oceny Krytycznej Camusa. Londyn, 1966.
43550.58.1045 Castex, Pierre Georges. Albert Camus et "l'Étranger". Paris, 1965.
43550.58.1050 Nicolas, André. Albert Camus ou le Vrai Prométhée. Paris, 1966.
43550.58.1057 Onimus, Jean. Camus. 2. éd. Paris, 1965.
43550.58.1058 Onimus, Jean. Albert Camus and Christianity. University, 1970.
43550.58.1060 Nicolas, André. Une philosophie de l'existence: Albert Camus. Paris, 1964.
43550.58.1065 Gay-Crosier, Raymond. Les envers d'un échec. Paris, 1967.
43550.58.1070 Degenaar, Johannes. Die wêreld van Albert Camus. Johannesburg, 1966.
43550.58.1075 Lazzari, Francesco. Camus e il cristianesimo. Napoli, 1965.
43550.58.1080 Willhoite, Fred H. Beyond nihilism. Baton Rouge, 1968.
43550.58.1085 Hoy, Peter. Camus in English. Wymondham, 1968.
V43550.58.1090 Kowalska, Amela. Dzuma Alberto Camusa. 1. wyd. Warszawa, 1968.
43550.58.1095 Grenier, Jean. Albert Camus, souvenirs. Paris, 1969.
43550.58.1100 Les critiques de notre temps et Camus. Paris, 1970.
43550.58.1105 Livi, François. Camus. Firenze, 1971.
43550.58.1110 Kampits, Peter. Der Mythos vom Menschen. Salzburg, 1968.
43550.58.1115 Barretto, Vicente. Camus; vida e obra. Rio de Janeiro, 1971.
43550.58.2000 Roeming, Robert F. Camus; a bibliography. Madison, 1968.
43550.58.2005 Hommage à Albert Camus. Paris, 1967.
43550.58.2010 Fetzer, Peter. Themen naturhaften Daseins im Werk von Albert Camus. Tübingen, 1966.
43550.58.2015 Rhein, Phillip H. Albert Camus. N.Y., 1969.
43550.58.2020 Melchinger, Christa. Albert Camus. 1. Aufl. Velbert, 1969.
43550.58.2025 Jonesco, Tony. Un homme, Camus et le destin. Paris, 1968.
43550.58.2030 Bazin de Bezons, Jean de. Index du vocabulaire de "l'Étranger" d'Albert Camus.Paris, 1969.
43550.58.2037 Fitch, Brian T. Narrateur et narration dans L'étranger d'Albert Camus. 2. éd. Paris, 1968.
43550.58.2040 O'Brien, Conor Cruise. Camus. London, 1970.
43550.58.2045 Lambert, B. L'epreuve littéraire aux concours des grandes écoles scientifiques; programme, 1970-1971. Villemomble, 1969.
43550.58.2050 Coombs, Ilona. Camus, homme de théâtre. Paris, 1968.
43550.58.2055 Goedert, Georges. Albert Camus et la question du bonheur. Luxemburg, 1969.
43550.58.2060 Schaub, Karin. Albert Camus und der Tod. Zürich, 1968.
43550.58.2065 Quilliot, Roger. The sea and prisons; a commentary on the life and thought of Albert Camus. University, 1970.
43550.58.2070 Palomares, Alfonso. Albert Camus. Madrid, 1970.
43550.58.2075 Camus 1970. Sherbrooke, 1970.
43550.61.100 Cantraine, R. Une raison de mourir. Bruxelles, 1964.
43550.65.102 Capy, M. L'amour roi. Paris, 1925.
43550.70.100 Caplain, Jean Marie. L'ombre et la lumière, roman. Paris, 1967.
43550.70.1100 Capieu, Henri. Demeures. Paris, 1963.
43550.70.2100 Caplandres, Pierre Arnaud. Ici repose...(un cemetière imaginaire). 1. éd. Paris, 1955.
43550.71.100 Capri, Agnès. Music-hall poésie. Paris, 1957.
43550.74.100 Carco, Francis. Visite à Saint-Lazare. Paris, 1925.
43550.74.1100 Cardon, Roger. Prométhée, ou Le mal du siècle. Paris, 1966.
43550.74.2100 Caraco, Albert. Le mystère d'Eusèbe. Buenos Aires, 1942.
43550.74.2110 Caraco, Albert. Post mortem. Lausanne, 1968.
43550.75.100 Carême, Maurice. La grange bleue. Paris, 1962.
43550.75.110 Carême, Maurice. Pomme de Reinette. Paris, 1962.
43550.75.120 Carême, Maurice. La passagère invisible. Paris, 1966.
43550.75.2100 Cardinal, Marie. Cet été-la. Deux ou trois choses que je sais d'elle. Paris, 1967.
43550.75.3100 Carrez, Michel. Arsenal du jour, poèmes. Paris, 1955.
43550.76.100 Cariguel, Claude. L'insolence. Paris, 1967.
43550.76.1100 Carion, Daniel. L'homme cassé. Paris, 1949.
43550.77.100 Carrouges, M. Les portes Dauphines. Paris, 1954.
43550.77.1700 Carrington, Leonora. La dama oval. México, 1965.

Classified Listing

43511 - 43873 Individual authors, etc. - 1900- - Known authors (363 scheme plus 10) - cont.

43550.77.2100 Caroutch, Yvonne. Lieux probables; poèmes. Paris, 1968.
43550.77.2110 Caroutch, Yvonne. Les veilleurs endormis. Paris, 1955.
43550.77.3100 Carrot, Antoine. Premiers matins; poèmes. Lyon, 19- .
43550.78.100 Cartonde Wiart, H. Souvenirs littéraires. Paris, 1939.
43550.79.100 Cassagnau, Paul. Un nom pour t'appeler. Foutenoy-en-Puisaye, 1963.
43550.79.1100 Casazza, Jean. Virginité. Paris, 1955.
43550.82.105 Cassou, Jean. Les massacres de Paris. 12. éd. Paris, 1936.
43550.82.112 Cassou, Jean. Légion; roman. 9. éd. Paris, 1939.
43550.82.120 Cassou, Jean. Le centre du monde. Paris, 1945.
43550.82.130 Cassou, Jean. Les enfants sans âge. Paris, 1946.
43550.82.140 Cassou, Jean. Trente-trois sonnets composés au secret. Paris, 1944.
43550.82.145 Cassou, Jean. Trente-trois sonnets. Paris, 1962.
43550.82.150 Cassou, Jean. Recueil. Rodg, 1953.
43550.82.160 Cassou, Jean. Suite. Paris, 1951.
43550.82.170 Cassou, Jean. La rose et la vin. Paris, 1952.
43550.82.180 Cassou, Jean. Le livre de Lazare. Paris, 1955.
43550.82.190 Cassou, Jean. Le Janus. Paris, 1957.
43550.82.200 Cassou, Jean. Le temps d'aimer. Paris, 1959.
43550.82.210 Cassou, Jean. Dernières pensées d'un amoureux. Paris, 1962.
43550.82.220 Cassou, Jean. Parti pris. Paris, 1964.
43550.82.230 Cassou, Jean. La clef des songes. Lausanne, 1964.
43550.82.240 Cassou, Jean. Entretiens avec Jean Rousselot. Paris, 1965.
43550.82.250 Cassou, Jean. Comme une grande image. Paris, 1931.
43550.82.260 Cassou, Jean. Eloge de la folie. Paris, 1925.
43550.82.270 Cassou, Jean. Le pays qui n'est à personne. Paris, 1928.
43550.82.280 Cassou, Jean. Le voisinage des cavernes. Paris, 1971.
43550.82.1100 Cassius de Linval, Paule. Reminiscences. Paris, 1959.
43550.82.2100 Castro, Germaine. Passage. Paris, 1932.
43550.83.100 Castiaux, P. Joie vagabonde. Paris, 1909.
43550.83.110 Castiaux, P. Lumières du monde. Paris, 1913.
43550.83.1100 Castillou, Henry. La légion d'Oumrah. Paris, 1960.
43550.83.1110 Castillou, Henry. Frontière sans retour, roman. Paris, 1967.
43550.83.1120 Castillou, Henry. La victorieuse, roman. Paris, 1968.
43550.83.3100 Castex, Pierre. Lagardère, d'après Paul Féval père et fils. Paris, 1967.
43550.84.100 Castier, Jules. Rother like...some endeavours to assume the mantles of the great. London, 1920.
43550.85.100 Cathala, S. Meurtre d'un serin. 3. éd. Paris, 1957.
43550.86.100 Castelane, J. Le léopard. Paris, 1959.
43550.87.100 Cattiaux, Louis. Poèmes: Alchimiques, Tristes, Zen, D'avant, De la resonance, De la connaissance. n.p., n.d.
43550.89.100 Cau, Jean. Un testament de Staline. Paris, 1958.
43550.89.110 Cau, Jean. Les paroissiens. Paris, 1958.
43550.89.120 Cau, Jean. Mon village contés. Paris, 1958.
43550.89.130 Cau, Jean. La pitié de Dieu. Paris, 1961.
43550.89.140 Cau, Jean. Les parachutistes, precéde de Le amaître du monde. Paris, 1963.
43550.89.150 Cau, Jean. Le meurtre d'un enfant. Paris, 1965.
43550.89.160 Cau, Jean. Le spectre de l'amour. Paris, 1968.
43550.89.170 Cau, Jean. Les yeux crevés. Paris, 1968.
43550.89.180 Cau, Jean. Le pape est mort. Paris, 1968.
43550.89.700 Cau, Jean. The mercy of God. 1. ed. N.Y., 1963.
43550.90.100 Cavens, A. Perspectives. Malines, 1955.
43550.98.100 Cayrol, Jean. Poèmes de la nuit et du brouillard. Paris, 1946.
43550.98.105 Cayrol, Jean. La goffe, récit. Paris, 1957.
43550.98.110 Cayrol, Jean. Passe temps de l'homme et des oiseaux. Neuchâtel, 1947.
43550.98.120 Cayrol, Jean. Je vivrai l'amour des autres. v.1-2,3. Neuchâtel, 1947. 2v.
43550.98.130 Cayrol, Jean. L'espace d'une nuit. Neuchâtel, 1954.
43550.98.140 Cayrol, Jean. Pour tous les temps. Paris, 1955.
43550.98.150 Cayrol, Jean. Le deménagement. Paris, 1956.
43550.98.160 Cayrol, Jean. Le vent de la memoire, roman. Neuchâtel, 1952.
43550.98.170 Cayrol, Jean. Les corps etrangers. Paris, 1959.
43550.98.172 Cayrol, Jean. Les corps etrangers. Paris, 1964.
43550.98.180 Cayrol, Jean. Les pleurs et les déliés. Paris, 1960.
43550.98.190 Cayrol, Jean. Le froid du soleil; roman. Paris, 1963.
43550.98.200 Cayrol, Jean. Midi, minuit; roman. Paris, 1966.
43550.98.210 Cayrol, Jean. Les mots sont aussi des demeures. Neuchâtel, 1952.
43550.98.220 Cayrol, Jean. Le coup de grâce. Paris, 1965.
43550.98.230 Cayrol, Jean. Je l'entends encore, roman. Paris, 1967.
43550.98.240 Cayrol, Jean. Poésie-journal. Paris, 1969.
43550.98.250 Cayrol, Jean. N'oubliez pas que nous nous aimons. Paris, 1971.
43550.98.700 Cayrol, Jean. Foreign bodies, a novel. N.Y., 1960.
43550.98.705 Cayrol, Jean. Mittag Mitternacht. (Roman. Uebersetzung aus dem Französischen). Olten, 1968.
43550.98.800 Oster, Daniel. Jean Cayrol et son oeuvre. Paris, 1968.
43550.98.1100 Cazelles, Raymond. Vingt parapoèmes en forme de sonnetes. Paris, 1962?
43550.98.2100 Cazalis, Marc. La marche au cercueil. Paris, 1955.
43550.98.4100 Cazenave, Georges. A l'ombre de mon pin. Paris, 1969.
43551.1.100 Céa, Claire. Épreuves. Paris, 1958.
43551.41.700 Ceillier, Philippe. To see the White Cliffs. London, 1966.
43551.48.100 Celarié, H. Petite "novia" une Française en Espagne. Paris, 1913.
43551.50.100 Celly, R. Un ami pour rien. Paris, 1946.
43551.52.100 Celly, Jean Jacques. Fanfare. Paris, 1956.
43551.59.11 Cendrars, Blaise. Oeuvres, édition complète. v. 2-7,8. Paris, 1960- 7v.
43551.59.13 Cendrars, Blaise. Oeuvres complètes. Paris, 1968-1971. 15v.
43551.59.21 Cendrars, Blaise. À l'aventure. Paris, 1958.
43551.59.22 Cendrars, Blaise. Selected writings. N.Y., 1966.
43551.59.39 Cendrars, Blaise. Petits contes nègres. Paris, 1928.
43551.59.100 Cendrars, Blaise. Du monde entier. Paris, 1919.
43551.59.102 Cendrars, Blaise. Du monde entier au coeur du monde. Paris, 1957.
43551.59.104 Cendrars, Blaise. Du monde entier. Paris, 1963.
43551.59.105 Cendrars, Blaise. Poésies complètes. Paris, 1947.
43551.59.106 Cendrars, Blaise. Poésies complètes, 1912-1924. Paris, 1967.
43551.59.110 Cendrars, Blaise. Dix-neuf poèmes élastiques. Paris, 1919.
43551.59.120 Cendrars, Blaise. Rhum. 24e éd. Paris, 1930.
43551.59.130 Cendrars, Blaise. Histoires vraies. Paris, 1938.

43511 - 43873 Individual authors, etc. - 1900- - Known authors (363 scheme plus 10) - cont.

43551.59.135 Cendrars, Blaise. L'ABC du cinéma. Paris, 1926.
43551.59.140 Cendrars, Blaise. Les confessions de Dan Yack. Paris, 1929.
43551.59.156 Cendrars, Blaise. La vie dangereuse. 6e éd. Paris, 1938.
43551.59.160 Cendrars, Blaise. Le plan de l'Aiguille. 49e éd. Paris, 1927.
43551.59.165 Cendrars, Blaise. D'oultremer à l'indigo. Paris, 1940.
43551.59.170 Cendrars, Blaise. Dan-Yacks: le plan de l'Aiguille. Paris, 1946.
43551.59.180 Cendrars, Blaise. Bourlinguer. Paris, 1948.
43551.59.190 Cendrars, Blaise. Moravagine; roman. Paris, 1947.
43551.59.200 Cendrars, Blaise. La fin du monde. Paris, 1949.
43551.59.210 Cendrars, Blaise. L'homme foudroyé. Paris, 1949.
43551.59.220 Cendrars, Blaise. Blaise Cendrars vous parle. Paris, 1952.
43551.59.230 Cendrars, Blaise. La fin du monde. Paris, 1956.
43551.59.240 Cendrars, Blaise. Emmène-moi au bout du monde; roman. Paris, 1956.
43551.59.250 Cendrars, Blaise. Trop c'est trop. Paris, 1957.
43551.59.253 Cendrars, Blaise. Saint Joseph de Cupertino. Paris, 1960.
43551.59.255 Cendrars, Blaise. Le Transsibérien. Paris, 1957.
43551.59.260 Cendrars, Blaise. Profond aujourd'hui. Paris, 1926.
43551.59.265 Cendrars, Blaise. Noel aux quatre coins du monde. Paris, 1953.
43551.59.270 Cendrars, Blaise. Films sans images. Paris, 1959.
43551.59.280 Cendrars, Blaise. L'eubage aux antipodes de l'unite. Paris, 1926.
43551.59.290 Cendrars, Blaise. Eloge de la vie dangereuse. Paris, 1926.
43551.59.300 Cendrars, Blaise. Amours. Paris, 1961.
43551.59.310 Cendrars, Blaise. La main coupée. Paris, 1946.
43551.59.320 Cendrars, Blaise. Kodak. 5e éd. Paris, 1924.
43551.59.330 Cendrars, Blaise. La banlieue de Paris. Paris, 1966.
43551.59.340 Cendrars, Blaise. Inédits secrets. Paris, 1969.
43551.59.350 Cendrars, Blaise. Dites-nous, Monsieur Blaise Cendrars. Lausanne, 1969.
43551.59.705 Cendrars, Blaise. Panama, or The adventure of my seven uncles. N.Y, 1931.
43551.59.715 Cendrars, Blaise. Rum; a aventura de Jean Galmot. Lisboa, 1966.
43551.59.720 Cendrars, Blaise. Moravagine; a novel. London, 1968.
43551.59.725 Cendrars, Blaise. The astonished man. London, 1970.
43551.59.800 Cendrars, Blaise. Blaise Cendrars. Paris, 1947.
43551.59.810 Rousselot, J. Blaise Cendrars. Paris, 1955.
43551.59.815 Buhler, J. Blaise Cendrars. Bienne, 1960.
43551.59.820 Lovey, Jean Claude. Situation de Blaise Cendrars. Neuchâtel, 1965.
43551.59.825 Amaral, Aracy A. Blaise Cendras no Brasil e os modernistas. São Paulo, 1970.
43551.61.100 Centa, Fuly di. Le manoir de la recontre. Paris, 1968.
43551.77.100 Certigny, H. Le bal masqué de Montparnasse. Paris, 1957.
43551.79.105 Césaire, Aimé. Les armes miraculeuses. 2e éd. Paris, 1946.
43551.79.110 Césaire, Aimé. Et les chiens se taisaient. Paris, 1956.
43551.79.120 Césaire, Aimé. Cahier d'un retour au pays natal. Paris, 1956.
43551.79.130 Césaire, Aimé. Ferrements. Paris, 1960.
43551.79.140 Césaire, Aimé. Cahier d'un retour au pays natal. N.Y., 1947.
43551.79.140.5 Césaire, Aimé. Return to my native land. Paris, 1968.
43551.79.150 Césaire, Aimé. Cadastre; poèmes. Paris, 1961.
43551.79.160 Césaire, Aimé. La tragedie du Roi Christophe. Paris, 1963.
43551.79.170 Césaire, Aimé. Une saison au Congo; théâtre. Paris, 1966.
43551.79.180 Césaire, Aimé. Une tempête. Paris, 1969.
43551.79.190 Césaire, Aimé. Soleil cou-coupé. Nendeln, 1970.
43551.79.700 Césaire, Aimé. Im Kongo; ein Stück über Patrice Lumumba. Berlin, 1966.
43551.79.705 Césaire, Aimé. Return to my native land. Harmondsworth, 1969.
43551.79.775 Césaire, Aimé. Ein Sturm. Berlin, 1970.
43551.79.800 Juin, Hubert. Aimé Cesairé. Paris, 1956.
43551.79.805 Trouillot, Hénock. L'intinéraire d'Aimé Césaire. Port-au-Prince, 1968.
43551.80.21 Cesbron, Gilbert. Oeuvres romanesques. Lausanne, 1947. 12v.
43551.80.100 Cesbron, Gilbert. Les saints vont en enfer. Paris, 1952.
43551.80.110 Cesbron, Gilbert. Chiens perdus sans callier. Paris, 1954.
43551.80.120 Cesbron, Gilbert. Vous verrez le ciel ouvert. Paris, 1956.
43551.80.130 Cesbron, Gilbert. Il est plus tard que tu ne penses. Paris, 1958.
43551.80.140 Cesbron, Gilbert. Notre prison est un royaume. Paris, 1959.
43551.80.150 Cesbron, Gilbert. Avoir été. Paris, 1960.
43551.80.160 Cesbron, Gilbert. Journal sans date. Paris, 1963. 2v.
43551.80.170 Cesbron, Gilbert. Entre chiens et loups. Paris, 1965.
43551.80.180 Cesbron, Gilbert. C'est Mozart qu'on assassine; roman. Paris, 1966.
43551.80.190 Cesbron, Gilbert. Les innocents de Paris. Paris, 1944.
43551.80.200 Cesbron, Gilbert. Des enfants aux cheveux gris. Paris, 1968.
43551.80.210 Cesbron, Gilbert. Lettre ouverte à une jeune fille morte. Paris, 1968.
43551.80.220 Cesbron, Gilbert. Des leçons d'abîme. Paris, 1971.
43551.80.700 Cesbron, Gilbert. No plaster saint. London, 1948.
43551.80.710 Cesbron, Gilbert. Saints in hell. London, 1953.
43551.80.800 Barlow, Michel. Gilbert Cesbron. Paris, 1965.
43552.1.21 Chabaneix, Philippe. Poèmes choisis. Paris, 1947.
43552.1.100 Chabaneix, Philippe. Le bouquet d'Ophélie. Paris, 1929.
43552.1.110 Chabaneix, Philippe. Musiques du temps perdu. Paris, 1960.
43552.1.115 Chabaneix, Philippe. Les tendres amies. Paris, 1922.
43552.1.120 Chabaneix, Philippe. Recuerdos. La Rochelle, 1926.
43552.1.130 Chabaneix, Philippe. Pour une morte. Gap, 1951.
43552.1.1100 Chaamba, Abdallah (pseud.). Le voyage des morts. Paris, 1959.
43552.1.1110 Chaamba, Abdallah (pseud.). Le vieillard et l'enfant de 1958. Périgueux, 1960?
43552.1.1120 Chaamba, Abdallah (pseud.). Une adolescence au temps du Maréchal et de multiples aventures. Paris, 1968.
43552.1.1130 Chaamba, Abdallah (pseud.). Un voyage au Mont Athos. Paris, 1970.
43552.1.2100 Chabannes, Jacques. Mon coeur au Canada. Paris, 1967.
43552.1.2110 Chabannes, Jacques. Printemps rouge; roman. Paris, 1971.

43511 - 43873 Individual authors, etc. - 1900- - Known authors (363 scheme plus 10) - cont.

43552.1.3100 Chabrièr, Agnès. La part des ténèbres; roman. Paris, 1970.
43552.1.4100 Chabrun, Jean François. Les chantiers chimériques. Paris, 1970.
43552.2.100 Chadourne, Louis. Accords, suivi d'autres poèmes. 4e éd. Paris, 1922.
43552.2.110 Chadourne, Louis. L'inquiète adolescence. Paris, 1920.
43552.2.120 Chadourne, Louis. Terre de chanaan. Paris, 1938.
43552.2.1100 Chadourne, Marc. Vasco. N.Y., 1928.
43552.2.1102 Chadourne, Marc. Vasco. N.Y., 1928.
43552.2.1110 Chadourne, Marc. Vasco. Paris, 1927.
43552.2.1120 Chadourne, Marc. Cécile de La Folie. Paris, 1930.
43552.2.1130 Chadourne, Marc. Dieu créa d'abord Lilith. Paris, 1937.
43552.2.1140 Chadourne, Marc. Le mal de Colleen. Paris, 1955.
43552.2.2100 Chabrol, Jean-Pierre. Fleur d'épine. 5e éd. Paris, 1957.
43552.2.2110 Chabrol, Jean-Pierre. Les innocents de Mars. Paris, 1959.
43552.2.2120 Chabrol, Jean-Pierre. Un homme de trop. Paris, 1958.
43552.2.2130 Chabrol, Jean-Pierre. Les rebelles. Paris, 1965. 3v.
43552.2.2140 Chabrol, Jean-Pierre. L'illustre fauteuil et autres récits. Paris, 1967.
43552.2.2150 Chabrol, Jean-Pierre. Les Fous de Dieu. Paris, 1967.
43552.2.2160 Chabrol, Jean-Pierre. Je t'aimerai sans vergogne. Paris, 1967.
43552.2.2170 Chabrol, Jean-Pierre. Ma Déchirure, conte dramatique en seize tableaux. Paris, 1968.
43552.2.2180 Chabrol, Jean-Pierre. Le Canon Fraternité. Paris, 1970.
43552.2.3100 Chaffrol-Debillemont, Fernard. Suicides et misères romantiques. Paris, 1957.
43552.2.4100 Chapuis-Pampagnin, Daisy. Les résistants de l'ombre. Saint-Christol-les-Alés, 1968.
43552.2.7100 Chasle, Raymond. Le corailleur des limbes. Honfleur, 1970.
43552.2.8100 Chambon, Jean. La sentinelle; roman. Paris, 1970.
43552.2.8110 Chambon, Jean. Funeste; roman. Paris, 1965.
43552.2.9100 Chaland, Paul. Le Chat-ours. Paris, 1966.
43552.3.100 Chaine, Pierre. L'étrange aventure de M. Martin-Péquet. Paris, 1920.
43552.3.110 Chaine, Pierre. L'heure H...; comédie en trois actes. Paris, 1936.
43552.3.120 Chaine, Pierre. Ray Blas 38. Paris, 1938.
43552.3.130 Chaine, Pierre. Le Duc Assassin. Paris, 1955.
43552.3.140 Chaine, Pierre. Les commentaires de Ferdinand. Paris, 1919.
43552.3.1100 Chaigne, Louis. Reconnaissance à la lumière. Tours, 1965.
43552.3.1110 Chaigne, Louis. Itinéraires d'une espérance. Paris, 1970.
43552.3.2700 Chambe, René. Still a woman. N.Y., 1931.
43552.3.3100 Charpentier, O. Les vierges de Mai. Paris, 1920.
43552.3.4100 Charpentier, Henry. Signes. Saint-Felicien-en-Vivarais, 1928.
43552.3.4110 Charpentier, Henry. Odes et poèmes. Paris, 1932.
43552.3.4120 Charpentier, Henry. Le poème d'Armageddon. Paris, 1920.
43552.3.4130F Charpentier, Henry. Océan pacifique; poème. Paris, 1925.
43552.3.5100 Charpent, John. Les grands Templiers. Paris, 1935.
43552.3.6100 Charpentier, Léon. L'épopée de la vieille Ecosse. Paris, 1922.
43552.3.7100 Champion, Pierre. Françoise au Calvaire. 18e éd. Paris, 1924.
43552.3.8100 Champigny, Robert. Dépôt. Paris, 1952.
43552.3.8110 Champigny, Robert. L'intermonde. Paris, 1953.
43552.3.8120 Champigny, Robert. Brûler. Paris, 1955.
43552.3.9100 Chamson, André. Les hommes de la route. 27e éd. Paris, 1927.
43552.3.9105 Chamson, André. L'homme qui marchait devant moi, roman. Paris, 1948.
43552.3.9110 Chamson, André. Barren harvest. London, 1935.
43552.3.9120 Chamson, André. Le puits des miracles, roman. 50e éd. Paris, 1945.
43552.3.9130 Chamson, André. Roux the bandit. N.Y., 1929.
43552.3.9135 Chamson, André. Roux le bandit. Paris, 1925.
43552.3.9137 Chamson, André. Suite cévenole, romans. Paris, 1968.
43552.3.9140 Chamson, André. The crime of the just. N.Y., 1930.
43552.3.9147 Chamson, André. Le crime des justes. 32. éd. Paris, 1949.
43552.3.9153 Chamson, André. L'année des vaincus. 9. éd. Paris, 1934.
43552.3.9164 Chamson, André. Héritages; roman. 10e éd. Paris, 1932.
43552.3.9175 Chamson, André. L'auberge de l'abîme; roman. 18e éd. Paris, 1933.
43552.3.9178 Chamson, André. The Mountain Tavern. N.Y., 1933.
43552.3.9184 Chamson, André. Les quatre éléments. 10e éd. Paris, 1935.
43552.3.9190 Chamson, André. The road. N.Y., 1929.
43552.3.9200 Chamson, André. La galève. Paris, 1939.
43552.3.9210 Chamson, André. Si la parole a quelque pouvoir. Genève, 1948.
43552.3.9220 Chamson, André. Histoires de Tabusse. Paris, 1948.
43552.3.9230 Chamson, André. On ne voit pas les coeurs. 6e éd. Paris, 1952.
43552.3.9240 Chamson, André. Le chiffre de nos jours. 24e éd. Paris, 1954.
43552.3.9250 Chamson, André. Adeline Venician. Paris, 1956.
43552.3.9260 Chamson, André. L'auberge de l'abime. 5e éd. Paris, 1957.
43552.3.9270 Chamson, André. Nos ancêtres les Gaulois. Paris, 1958.
43552.3.9280 Chamson, André. Devenir ce qu'on est. Namur, 1959.
43552.3.9290 Chamson, André. Comme une pierre qui tombe. Paris, 1964.
43552.3.9300 Chamson, André. La petite odyssée. Paris, 1965.
43552.3.9310 Chamson, André. La superbe; roman. Paris, 1967.
43552.3.9320 Chamson, André. La tour de Constance; roman. Paris, 1970.
43552.3.9700 Chamson, André. A time to keep. London, 1957.
43552.4.30 Chantal, S. Dieu ne dort pas; roman. N.Y., 1944.
43552.4.30.5 Chantal, S. Dieu ne dort pas. Paris, 1946.
43552.4.100 Chantel, L. Le silence. Paris, 1926.
43552.4.1010 Chaponnière, P. Pensées et arrière-pensées. Boudry, 1945.
43552.4.2021 Char, René. Poèmes et prose choisis. 3e éd. Paris, 1957.
43552.4.2023 Char, René. Anthologie. Paris, 1960.
43552.4.2025 Char, René. René Char. Paris, 1961.
43552.4.2061 Char, René. Lettera amorosa. Paris, 1953.
43552.4.2105 Char, René. Feuillets d'Hypnos. 3e éd. Paris, 1946.
43552.4.2110 Char, René. Seuls demeurent. Paris, 1945.
43552.4.2115 Char, René. Claire, théâtre de verdure. Paris, 1949.
43552.4.2120 Char, René. Dehors la nuit est gouvernée. Paris, 1949.
43552.4.2125 Char, René. Les matinaux. Paris, 1950.
43552.4.2128 Char, René. Les matinaux, suivi de la Parole en archipel. Paris, 1969.
43552.4.2130 Char, René. Fete des arbres et du Chasseur. Paris, 1948.
43552.4.2140 Char, René. Le marteau sans maitre. Paris, 1945.
43552.4.2140.5 Char, René. Le marteau sans maitre. Paris, 1963.
43552.4.2150 Char, René. Le soleil des eaux. Paris, 1951.
43552.4.2160 Char, René. A une serenité crispée. Paris, 1951.

43511 - 43873 Individual authors, etc. - 1900- - Known authors (363 scheme plus 10) - cont.

43552.4.2170 Char, René. A la santé du serpent. Paris, 1954.
43552.4.2180 Char, René. Recherche de la base et du sommet. Paris, 1955.
43552.4.2182 Char, René. Recherche de la base et du sommet. Paris, 1965.
43552.4.2190 Char, René. Poèmes des deux années, 1953-1954. Paris, 1955.
43552.4.2200 Char, René. La paroi et la prairie. Paris, 1952.
43552.4.2210 Char, René. En trente-trois morceaux. Paris, 1956.
43552.4.2220 Char, René. Sur la poésie. Paris, 1958.
43552.4.2221 Char, René. Sur la poésie. Paris, 1967.
43552.4.2230 Char, René. La bibliotheque est en feu. Paris, 1957.
43552.4.2240 Char, René. Fureur et mystère. 3. éd. Paris, 1948.
43552.4.2250 Char, René. La parole en archipel. Paris, 1962.
43552.4.2270 Char, René. Retour amont. Paris, 1966.
43552.4.2280 Char, René. L'âge cassant. Paris, 1965.
43552.4.2661 Char, René. Leaves of Hypnos (extracts) and Lettera amorosa. Roma, 1954.
43552.4.2700 Char, René. Poems. Roma, 1952.
43552.4.2705 Char, René. Impressions anciennes. Paris, 1964.
43552.4.2710 Char, René. Hypnos waking. N.Y., 1956.
43552.4.2780 Char, René. Poésies. Frankfurt, 1959.
43552.4.2790 Char, René. Fureur et mystère. 9e éd. Paris, 1962.
43552.4.2795 Char, René. Commune présence. Paris, 1964.
43552.4.2800 Mounin, G. Avez-vous lu Char? 2e éd. Paris, 1946.
43552.4.2805A René Char's poetry. Roma, 1956.
43552.4.2805B René Char's poetry. Roma, 1956.
43552.4.2810 Rau, Greta. René Char. Paris, 1957.
43552.4.2815 Blanchot, Maurice. La bête de Lascaux. Paris, 1958.
43552.4.2820 Benoit, Pierre André. Bibliographie des oeuvres de René Char de 1928 à 1963. Paris, 1964.
43552.4.3100 Charrier, René Albert. Sommeils. Avignon, 1958.
43552.4.4100 Charasson, H. En chemin de fer; piece en un acte. Paris, 1933.
43552.4.4110 Charasson, H. Attente, 1914-1917. Paris, 1919.
43552.4.5100 Charbonneau, Robert. Ils possideront la terre. Montreal, 1941.
43552.4.5110 Charbonneau, Robert. Fontile; roman. Montreal, 1945.
43552.4.5120 Charbonneau, Robert. Les désirs et les jours. Montreal, 1948.
43552.4.5130 Charbonneau, Robert. Chronique de l'âge a mer. Montreal, 1967.
43552.4.6100 Chardonnal, U.B. Au village. Le Puy-en-Velaz, 1954.
43552.4.7100 Chapron, Marcel. Un chouan fulgurant. Paris, 1945.
43552.4.8100 Charpier, Jacques. Mythologie du vent. Paris, 1955.
43552.4.8110 Charpier, Jacques. Le fer et le Laurier. Paris, 1956.
43552.4.8120 Charpier, Jacques. Paysage du salut. Paris, 1946.
43552.4.9100 Chapuis, Michel. Bâtons rompus. 2e éd. Paris, 1958.
43552.5.100 Chardonne, Jacques. L'épithalame. Paris, 1922. 2v.
43552.5.103 Chardonne, Jacques. L'épithalame. Paris, 1922. 2v.
43552.5.105 Chardonne, Jacques. L'épithalame. v. 1-2. Paris, 1922.
43552.5.106 Chardonne, Jacques. Oeuvres complètes. Paris, 1951- 6v.
43552.5.107 Chardonne, Jacques. Les Varais, roman. Paris, 1929.
43552.5.109 Chardonne, Jacques. Eva, ou Le journal interrompu. 10e éd. Paris, 1930.
43552.5.110 Chardonne, Jacques. L'amour du prochain. Paris, 1932.
43552.5.115 Chardonne, Jacques. Le chant du bienheureux. Paris, 1927.
43552.5.120 Chardonne, Jacques. Romanesques; roman. Paris, 1937.
43552.5.122 Chardonne, Jacques. Romanesques. Paris, 1937.
43552.5.125 Chardonne, Jacques. L'amour c'est beaucoup plus que l'amour. Paris, 1944.
43552.5.130 Chardonne, Jacques. Claire; roman. Paris, 1931.
43552.5.135 Chardonne, Jacques. Attachements (chronique privée). 19e éd. Paris, 1943.
43552.5.140 Chardonne, Jacques. Le bonheur de Barbezieux. Paris, 1938.
43552.5.145 Chardonne, Jacques. Les destinées sentimentales, roman. Paris, 1934.
43552.5.150 Chardonne, Jacques. La femme de Jean Barnery. Paris, 1934.
43552.5.152 Chardonne, Jacques. Pauline, roman. Paris, 1934.
43552.5.160 Chardonne, Jacques. Chronique privée. Paris, 1940.
43552.5.165 Chardonne, Jacques. Voir la figure. Paris, 1941.
43552.5.170 Chardonne, Jacques. Chimériques. Monaco, 1948.
43552.5.170.5 Chardonne, Jacques. Chimériques. Monaco, 1948.
43552.5.180 Chardonne, Jacques. Porcelaine de Limoges. Paris, 1936.
43552.5.190 Chardonne, Jacques. Lettres à Roger Niumier. 6e éd. Paris, 1954.
43552.5.200 Chardonne, Jacques. Matinales. Paris, 1956.
43552.5.210 Chardonne, Jacques. Le ciel dans la fenêtre. Paris, 1959.
43552.5.215 Chardonne, Jacques. Demi-jour. Suite et fin du "Ciel dans la fenêtre". Paris, 1964.
43552.5.220 Chardonne, Jacques. Femmes. Paris, 1961.
43552.5.230 Chardonne, Jacques. Détachements. Paris, 1962?
43552.5.240 Chardonne, Jacques. Propos comme ça. Paris, 1966.
43552.5.250 Chardonne, Jacques. Catherine; roman. Paris, 1964.
43552.5.260 Chardonne, Jacques. Ce que je voulais vous dire aujourd'hui. Paris, 1970.
43552.5.805 Guitard-Auviste, G. La vie de J. Chardonne. Paris, 1953.
43552.5.810 Vandromme, Pol. Jacques Chardonne: c'est beaucoup plus que Chardonne. Lyon, 1962.
43552.5.1020 Chartier, Emile. Vingt et une scenes de comedie. Paris, 1955.
43552.5.1025 Chartier, Émile. Philosophie. Paris, 1954. 2v.
43552.5.1030 Chartier, Émile. Morceaux choisis. Paris, 1960.
43552.5.1045 Chartier, Émile. Les saisons de l'esprit. Paris, 1937.
43552.5.1061 Chartier, Émile. Correspondance avec Elie et Florence Halevy. Paris, 1958.
43552.5.1100 Chartier, Émile. Propos de littérature. Paris, 1934.
43552.5.1102 Chartier, Émile. Propos de littérature. 7e éd. Paris, 1939.
43552.5.1110A Chartier, Émile. Les idées et les âges. Paris, 1927. 2v.
43552.5.1110B Chartier, Émile. Les idées et les âges. Paris, 1928. 2v.
43552.5.1120 Chartier, Émile. Histoire de mes pensées. 7e éd. Paris, 1936.
43552.5.1120.5 Chartier, Émile. Histoire de mes pensées. 3e éd. Paris, 1936.
43552.5.1125 Chartier, Émile. Definitions. 6e éd. Paris, 1954?
43552.5.1130A Chartier, Émile. Portraits de famille. Paris, 1961.
43552.5.1130B Chartier, Émile. Portraits de famille. Paris, 1961.
43552.5.1135 Chartier, Émile. Esquisses de l'homme. 8e éd. Paris, 1938.
43552.5.1140 Chartier, Émile. Humanites. Paris, 1947.

Classified Listing

43511 - 43873 Individual authors, etc. - 1900- - Known authors (363 scheme plus 10) - cont.

43552.5.1145 Chartier, Émile. Alain au lycée d'Alençon. Alençon, 1958.
43552.5.1150 Chartier, Émile. Les aventures du coeur. Paris, 1945.
43552.5.1155 Chartier, Émile. Le roi Pot. Paris, 1959.
43552.5.1165 Chartier, Émile. Entretiens au bord de la mar. 5. éd. Paris, 1949.
43552.5.1170 Chartier, Émile. Souvenirs de guerre. Paris, 1937.
43552.5.1175 Chartier, Émile. Propos d'un Normand. Paris, 1952. 5v.
43552.5.1177 Chartier, Émile. Propos. Paris, 1956. 2v.
43552.5.1180 Chartier, Émile. Les arts et les dieux. Paris, 1958.
43552.5.1185 Chartier, Émile. Les passions et la sagesse. Paris, 1960.
43552.5.1190 Chartier, Émile. Esquisses d'Alain (pseud.). Paris, 1963. 4v.
43552.5.1200 Chartier, Émile. Cahiers de Lorient. Paris, 1963-1964. 2v.
43552.5.1210 Chartier, Émile. Les marchands de sommeil. Paris, 1919.
43552.5.1220 Chartier, Émile. L'autre. Audin, 1965.
43552.5.1230 Chartier, Émile. Salut et fraternité. Paris, 1968.
43552.5.1800A Nouvelle Revue Française. Hommage a Alain. Paris, 1952.
43552.5.1800B Nouvelle Revue Française. Hommage a Alain. Paris, 1952.
43552.5.1805 Association des Amis d'Alain. Bulletin. Le Vesinet, France. 1-16 3v.
43552.5.1807 Association des Amis d'Alain. Annuaire. Le Vesinet, France. 1966+
43552.5.1810 Foulquie, P. Alain. Paris, 1952.
43552.5.1815 Bénézé, G. Généraux Alain. Paris, 1962.
43552.5.1820 Robinson, Judith. Alain. Paris, 1958.
43552.5.1822 Robinson, Judith. Alain. Thèse. Paris, 1958.
43552.5.1825 Carbonara, C. L'arte e le arti secondo Alain. Napoli, 1959.
43552.5.1830 Cahier Alain. La Vesinet. 1-2
43552.5.1835 Gontier, Georges. Alain à la guerre. Paris, 1963.
43552.5.1840 Halda, Bernard. Alain. Paris, 1965.
43552.5.1845 Bridoux, Andre. Alain, sa vie, son oeuvre. Paris, 1964.
43552.5.1850 Pascal, Georges. Alain éducateur. Paris, 1964.
43552.5.1850.5 Pascal, Georges. L'idée de philosophie chez Alain. Paris, 1970.
43552.5.1855 Bibliothèque Nationale, Paris. Alain. Exposition de manuscrits, de livres et de divers souvenirs. Paris, 1955.
43552.5.1860 Reboul, Olivier. L'homme et ses passions d'après Alain. Thèse. Paris, 1968.
43552.5.1865 Giraud, Henri. La morale d'Alain. Toulouse, 1970.
43552.5.2100 Charles-Étienne. Les épices libertines. Paris, 1926.
43552.5.2110 Charles-Étienne. Léon dit Léonie. Paris, 1922.
43552.5.2120 Charles-Étienne. Les désexués. Paris, 1928?
43552.5.2130 Charles-Étienne. La nuit perverse. Paris, 1928.
43552.5.2140 Charles-Étienne. Manon l'ortie; roman. Paris, 1929.
43552.5.2150 Charles-Étienne. Notre-Dame de Lesbos. Paris, 1924.
43552.5.3100 Chassé, Charles. Les contes de la Lande. Paris, 1944.
43552.5.4021 Chauffin, Yvonne. Les Ramboult. v. 1-4. Paris, 1954-1956. 2v.
43552.5.4100 Chauffin, Yvonne. Le séminariste. Paris, 1967.
43552.5.5100 Charpentreau, J. Les Jeux de l'espair. Paris, 1957?
43552.5.6100 Charton, J.C. Le signe féminin, roman. Paris, 1960.
43552.5.7100 Chausse, C. La citadelle et la puissance de l'invention. Paris, 1961.
43552.5.8100 Chaumeix, André. Le fauteuil de Clemenceau. Paris, 1931.
43552.5.9100 Charles, Gilbert. Les signes de la nuit, 1920-1932. Paris, 1934.
43552.6.45 Chateaubriant, Alphonse de. Fragments d'une confession. Paris, 1953.
43552.6.100 Chateaubriant, Alphonse de. Monsieur des Lourdinés. Paris, 1912.
43552.6.103 Chateaubriant, Alphonse de. Monsieur des Lourdinés. Paris, 1924.
43552.6.105 Chateaubriant, Alphonse de. Monsieur des Lourdinés. Paris, 1962.
43552.6.108 Chateaubriant, Alphonse de. La brière. 277e éd. Paris, 1923.
43552.6.110 Chateaubriant, Alphonse de. La brière; roman. 309e éd. Paris, 1923.
43552.6.115 Chateaubriant, Alphonse de. Lettres à la chrétienté mourante. Paris, 1951.
43552.6.120A Chateaubriant, Alphonse de. La réponse du Seigneur. 58e éd. Paris, 1933.
43552.6.120B Chateaubriant, Alphonse de. La réponse du Seigneur. 36e éd. Paris, 1933.
43552.6.125 Chateaubriant, Alphonse de. Les pas ont chanté. 4e éd. Paris, 1938.
43552.6.130 Chateaubriant, Alphonse de. Écrits de l'autre rive. Paris, 1950.
43552.6.135 Chateaubriant, Alphonse de. Cahiers, 1906-1951. 2e éd. Paris, 1955.
43552.6.140 Chateaubriant, Alphonse de. Le baron du Puydreau. Paris, 1926.
43552.6.705 Chateaubriant, Alphonse de. The peat-cutters. N.Y., 1927.
43552.6.715 Chateaubriant, Alphonse de. Gehalte Kraft. Karlsruhe, 1938.
43552.6.1100 Chargan, Maria. La lutte éternelle. Paris, 1963.
43552.6.2100 Charreyre, Eugene. Fatima. Paris, 1960.
43552.6.3100A Charles-Roux, Edmonde. Oublier Palerme; roman. Paris, 1966.
43552.6.3100B Charles-Roux, Edmonde. Oublier Palerme; roman. Paris, 1966.
43552.6.3110 Charles-Roux, Edmonde. Elle, Adrienne. Paris, 1971.
43552.6.3700 Charles-Roux, Edmonde. To forget Palermo. N.Y., 1968.
43552.6.4100 Charles, Jacques. Le journal d'une figurante, roman de moeurs du music hall. Paris, 1933.
43552.6.5100 Charlier, Gustave. De Ronsard à Victor Hugo. Bruxelles, 1931.
43552.6.6100 Charmont, Paul. Les Autrefois. Genève, 1967.
43552.6.7100 Chazai, Louis. Petit florilège. Paris, 1967.
43552.6.8100 Chaude, Antonin. La bouquetière de Saint-Jean. Toulon, 1939.
43552.6.9100 Chateauneu, Roger. Les Myrtes. Paris, 1968.
43552.7.100 Chauviré, R. Mademoiselle de Boisdauphin. pt. 1-3. Paris, 1932.
43552.7.1100 Chauveau, Jacqueline. Charette et l'epopée vendéenne. Paris, 1964.
43552.7.2100 Chazal, Malcolm de. Sens magique. Tananarive? 1957.
43552.7.2112 Chazal, Malcolm de. Sens-plastique. 2e éd. Paris, 1948.
43552.7.2126 Chazal, Malcolm de. La vie filtrée. 6e éd. Paris, 1949.
43552.7.2130 Chazal, Malcolm de. Poèmes. Paris, 1968.
43552.7.3100 Chavée, Achille. L'agenda d'emeraude. La Louvière, 1967?
43552.7.4100 Chastel, Lou. Lumières. Paris, 1955.
43552.7.5100 Château, René. Cantiques sans Dieu. Paris, 1957.

43511 - 43873 Individual authors, etc. - 1900- - Known authors (363 scheme plus 10) - cont.

43552.7.6100 Chapuis, Lucien. La gerbe enrubannée. Paris, 1921.
43552.7.7100 Chappuis, Pierre. Le soleil couronne et diamant. Paris, 1957.
43552.9.100 Chatelain, U.V. Le double destin. Paris, 1912.
43552.12.100 Chavance, L. Le corbeau. Paris, 1948.
43552.13.100 Chaulot, Paul. Comme un vivant. Paris, 1950.
43552.13.110 Chaulot, Paul. L'herbe de chaque escale. Paris, 1956.
43552.13.120 Chaulot, Paul. Soudaine écorce. Paris, 1967.
43552.14.100 Du Chazand, Henri. Printemps. Paris, 1960.
43552.15.100 Chazot, Jacques. Sophie Ripaille. Paris, 1960.
43552.16.100 Chavannes, Éduard. Fables chinoises du IIIe au VIIIe siècle. Paris, 1921.
43552.18.100 Chédid, Andrée. Le sommeil délivré. 8e éd. Paris, 1952.
43552.18.110 Chédid, Andrée. Terre et poésie. Paris, 1956.
43552.18.120 Chédid, Andrée. Le sixième jour. Paris, 1960.
43552.18.130 Chédid, Andrée. Textes pour la terre aimée. Paris, 1955.
43552.18.140 Chédid, Andrée. Jonathan, roman. Paris, 1955.
43552.18.150 Chédid, Andrée. Textes pour le vivant. Paris, 1953.
43552.18.160 Chédid, Andrée. Double-pays. Paris, 1965.
43552.18.170 Chédid, Andrée. Contre-chant. Paris, 1968.
43552.18.180 Chédid, Andrée. L'autre. Paris, 1969.
43552.23.100 Chemin, Émile. Jean des Brebis. Paris, 1907.
43552.23.1100 Chenorg, Léon. Sable et cendres, poèmes. Paris, 1956.
43552.23.2100 Chenevière, Jacques. Daphné, ou l'Ecole des sentiments. Lausanne, 1969.
43552.23.5100 Chenal, A. La cité des ombres. Paris, 1939.
43552.24.100 Chérau, Gaston. La maison de Patrice Perrier; roman. v. 1-4. Paris, 1924.
43552.24.110 Chérau, Gaston. Valentine Pacquault. Paris, 1920.
43552.24.113 Chérau, Gaston. Valentine Pacquault. Paris, 1937. 2v.
43552.24.120 Chérau, Gaston. L'enfant du pays; roman. pt. 1-4. Paris, 1932.
43552.24.130 Chérau, Gaston. Sa destinée. v. 1-2. Paris, 1934.
43552.24.140 Chérau, Gaston. Séverin Dunastier. pt. 1-3. Paris, 1937.
43552.24.150 Chérau, Gaston. Le mulet de Phidias. Paris, 1935.
43552.24.162 Chérau, Gaston. Le petit Dagrello. Paris, 1936.
43552.24.170 Chérau, Gaston. Toi. Paris, 1931.
43552.24.180 Chérau, Gaston. Le monstre. Paris, 1932.
43552.24.190 Chérau, Gaston. Le vent du destin. Paris, 1926.
43552.24.200 Chérau, Gaston. Monseigneur voyage. 5e éd. Paris, 1903.
43552.24.1100 Chérade, R. Possebleu. 4e éd. Paris, 1925.
43552.24.2100 Chessin, S. de. La valse aux enfers. pt. 1-2. Paris, 1932.
43552.24.3100 Cherry, Dominique. Sixieme sens. Paris, 1955.
43552.24.4100 Chessex, Jacques. Le jeûne de huit nuits. Lausanne, 1966.
43552.24.5100 Chesneau, Marc. Fragment du Journal poétique d'une âme, 1948-1965. Stockholm, 1964.
43552.24.5110 Chesneau, Marc. Second fragment du "Journal poétique d'une âme, 1948-1967. Paris, 1967.
43552.25.100 Chevalier, Claude R. Destin, roman. Saint-Etienne, 1941.
43552.25.1100 Chevalier, Toussaint. Parisiens aux États-Unis. Cincinnati? 1901.
43552.25.2100 Chevallier, Gabriel. Clochemerle. 280e éd. Paris, 1936.
43552.25.2102 Chevallier, Gabriel. Clochemerle. 305e éd. Paris, 1937.
43552.25.2103 Chevallier, Gabriel. The scandals of Clochemerle. N.Y., 1937.
43552.25.2104 Chevallier, Gabriel. Clochemerle-Babylon. London, 1955.
43552.25.2105 Chevallier, Gabriel. Clochemerle. 452e éd. Paris, 1942.
43552.25.2106 Chevallier, Gabriel. Clochemerle-Babylone. 170e éd. Paris, 1957.
43552.25.2107 Chevallier, Gabriel. L'envers de "Clochemerle". Paris, 1966.
43552.25.2110 Chevallier, Gabriel. Sainte-Colline. 192e éd. Paris, 1939.
43552.25.2115 Chevallier, Gabriel. Sainte-Colline. 262e éd. Paris, 1941.
43552.25.2120 Chevallier, Gabriel. Ma petite amie Pomme. 170e éd. Paris, 1941.
43552.25.2130 Chevallier, Gabriel. Les filles sont libres. Paris, 1960.
43552.25.2140 Chevallier, Gabriel. Clochemerle les Bains; roman. Paris, 1963.
43552.25.2700 Chevallier, Gabriel. The Euffe inheritance. London, 1948.
43552.25.2710 Chevallier, Gabriel. Mascarade. London, 1950.
43552.25.3100 Chevrier, M. Les trois premiers livres des chants. Paris, 1929.
43552.25.4100 Chevalier, Adrien. Avant et après l'orage. Paris, 1919.
43552.25.4110 Chevalier, Adrien. Paroles pendant l'orage. Paris, 191-?
43552.25.4120 Chevalier, Adrien. Sur le seuil. Paris, 1905.
43552.25.4130 Chevalier, Adrien. Au gré de l'heure. Paris, 1908.
43552.25.4140 Chevalier, Adrien. La mésaventure de M. de Chanqueyras. Paris, 1906.
43552.25.4150 Chevalier, Adrien. Sur l'autre versant. Paris, 1924.
43552.25.5100 Charpentier, Leon. Les transmigrations de Yo-Tcheon. Paris, 1920.
43552.26.105 Chevrillon, André. Études anglaises. 2e éd. Paris, 1901.
43552.26.110 Chevrillon, André. Études anglaises. 4e éd. Paris, 1920.
43552.26.115 Chevrillon, André. Nouvelles études anglaises. 2e éd. Paris, 1918.
43552.26.800 Achard, M. Discours prononcés dans la séance publique tenue par l'Académie francaise. Paris, 1959.
43552.40.22 Chiha, Michel. La maison des champs. 2e éd. Beyrouth, 1965.
43552.40.100 Chiha, Michel. Essais. v. 1-2. Beyrouth, 1950-
43552.41.100 Chivas-Baron, C. Three women of Annam. N.Y., 1925.
43552.41.110 Chivas-Baron, C. Folie exotique (en brousse sedang), roman. Paris, 1924.
43552.41.1700 Chirico, Giorgio de. Hebdomeras: a novel. London, 1968.
43552.63.100 Chobanian, Arshag. La vie et la rève. Paris, 1913.
43552.65.100 Choisy, Maryse. Le serpent. Paris, 1957.
43552.65.110 Choisy, Maryse. Tes yeux m'ont vu. Paris, 1957.
43552.65.120 Choisy, Maryse. Les iles s'enfuirent. Paris? 1959.
43552.66.100 Chollet, Louis. La flamme errante. Paris, 1927.
43552.66.1100 Chonez, Claudine. Ils furent rois tout un matin. Paris, 1967.
43552.67.100 Chottès, Lucien. Premières étreintes. Paris, 1935.
43552.67.1100 Chouard, Claude Henri. L'étude intérieure. Paris, 1957.
43552.68.100 Charpentier, Gabriel. Les amitiés errantes. Paris, 1951.
43552.69.100 Chraibi, Driss. Le passé simple: roman. Paris, 1954.
43552.69.110 Chraibi, Driss. De tous les horizons. Paris, 1958.
43552.69.120 Chraibi, Driss. Un ami viendra vous voir. Paris, 1966.
43552.70.100 Chauviré, Jacques. Partage de la soif. Paris, 1958.
43552.76.100 Christian Yve, Guy. Les tentatives. Paris, 1959.
43552.80.21 Christophe, Lucien. Poèmes, 1913-1963. Paris, 1963.
43552.80.100 Christophe, Lucien. Les cahiers publiés au front. León, 1962.

43511 - 43873 Individual authors, etc. - 1900- - Known authors (363 scheme plus 10) - cont.

43552.93.100 Chweitzer, Lydia. La belle étoffe. Paris, 1959.
43553.3 Cingria, Charles Albert. Charles Albert Cingria. Genève, 1955.
43553.3.11 Cingria, Charles Albert. Oeuvres complètes. Lausanne, 1967? 8v.
43553.3.100 Cingria, Charles Albert. Xénia et le diamant. Lyon, 1955.
43553.3.110 Cingria, Charles Albert. Vingt-cinq lettres à Adrien Bovy, 1902-1908. Lausanne, 1967.
43553.53.100 Cim, Albert. Cesarin. Paris, 1897.
43553.54.100 Ciméze, Jean. Le coeur ébouillanté, suivi de Seconde lecture. Paris, 1958.
43553.71.21 Cipriani, Roland. Premiers poèmes. Paris, 1966.
43553.97.100 Cixous, Hélène. Dedans. Paris, 1969.
43554.1.30 Claude, Catherine. Le magot de Josepha. Paris, 1960.
NEDL 43554.2 Claudel, Paul. Théâtre. Serie 1. Paris, 1911. 4v.
43554.2.11 Claudel, Paul. Oeuvres complètes. Paris, 1952-53. 26v.
43554.2.23 Claudel, Paul. Gedichte. Basel, 1942.
43554.2.25 Claudel, Paul. Pages de prose. 23e éd. Paris, 1944.
43554.2.26 Claudel, Paul. Paul Claudel, par lui-même. Paris, 1963.
43554.2.27 Claudel, Paul. Oeuvres en prose. Paris, 1965.
43554.2.30 Claudel, Paul. L'annonce faite à Marie. 9e éd. Paris, 1914.
43554.2.31 Claudel, Paul. Connaissance de l'est. 4e éd. Paris, 1913.
43554.2.31.5 Claudel, Paul. The East I know. New Haven, 1914.
X Cg 43554.2.32 Claudel, Paul. Cinq grandes odes. Paris, 1913.
43554.2.32.10 Claudel, Paul. Cinq grandes odes. 43e éd. Paris, 1948.
43554.2.32.12 Claudel, Paul. Cinq grandes odes. Paris, 1966.
43554.2.32.15 Claudel, Paul. Five great odes. London, 1967.
43554.2.33 Claudel, Paul. Corona benignitatis anni Dei. 4e éd. Paris, 1915.
43554.2.34 Claudel, Paul. Deux poèmes d'été. 3e éd. Paris, 1914.
43554.2.36A Claudel, Paul. La nuit de Noël 1914. Paris, 1915.
43554.2.36B Claudel, Paul. La nuit de Noël 1914. Paris, 1915.
43554.2.37 Claudel, Paul. Art poetique. 3e éd. Paris, 1915.
43554.2.37.15 Claudel, Paul. Arte poetica. Milano, 1913.
43554.2.37.25A Claudel, Paul. Commentaire à l'Art poétique. Paris, 1949.
43554.2.37.25B Claudel, Paul. Commentaire à l'Art poétique. Paris, 1949.
43554.2.38 Claudel, Paul. Trois poemes de guerre. 7e éd. Paris, 1915.
43554.2.39 Claudel, Paul. Autres poëmes. 2e éd. Paris, 1916.
43554.2.40 Claudel, Paul. The city. New Haven, 1920.
43554.2.41 Claudel, Paul. La messe la-bas. 7e éd. Paris, 1919.
43554.2.42 Claudel, Paul. Oeuvre poétique. Paris, 1957.
43554.2.43 Claudel, Paul. Le pain dur. 6e éd. Paris, 1918.
43554.2.45 Claudel, Paul. Oeuvre poétique. Paris, 1962.
43554.2.49 Claudel, Paul. L'otage; drama. 8e éd. Paris, 1919.
43554.2.50 Claudel, Paul. L'otage. Paris, 1923.
43554.2.55 Claudel, Paul. L'ours et la lune. 4e éd. Paris, 1919.
43554.2.60 Claudel, Paul. Protée. Paris, 1920.
43554.2.63 Claudel, Paul. Le père humiliè. 5e éd. Paris, 1920.
43554.2.63.5 Claudel, Paul. Le père humiliè. 10e éd. Paris, 1945.
43554.2.64 Claudel, Paul. Poèmes et paroles durant la guerre de trente ans. Paris, 1945.
43554.2.65 Claudel, Paul. Poëmes de guerre, 1914-1916. Paris, 1922.
43554.2.66 Claudel, Paul. Three poems of the war. New Haven, 1919.
Htn 43554.2.69* Claudel, Paul. Le chemin de la croix. Anvers, 1914.
Htn 43554.2.71* Claudel, Paul. Sainte Cecile. Paris, 1918.
43554.2.75A Claudel, Paul. Lettres inedites de mon parrain Paul Claudel. Paris, 1959.
43554.2.75B Claudel, Paul. Lettres inedites de mon parrain Paul Claudel. Paris, 1959.
43554.2.78 Claudel, Paul. La jeune fille Violaine. Paris, 1926.
43554.2.83 Claudel, Paul. Morceaux choisis. Paris, 1925.
43554.2.89A Claudel, Paul. Positions et propositions. 4e éd. Paris, 1928-1934. 2v.
43554.2.89B Claudel, Paul. Positions et propositions. v.2. Paris, 1928-1934.
43554.2.89.5 Claudel, Paul. Positions et propositions. Paris, 1946-1948. 2v.
43554.2.93 Claudel, Paul. Ode jubilaire pour le six-centième anniversaire de la mort de Dante. Paris, 1921.
43554.2.98 Claudel, Paul. L'oiseau noir dans la soleil levant. 4e éd. Paris, 1929.
43554.2.105 Claudel, Paul. La cantate à trois voix. Paris, 1931.
43554.2.115 Claudel, Paul. Ecoute, ma fille. 29e éd. Paris, 1934.
43554.2.119 Claudel, Paul. Ecoute, ma fille. Fribourg, 1946.
43554.2.125 Claudel, Paul. Le livre de Christophe Colomb. 16e éd. Paris, 1935.
43554.2.130 Claudel, Paul. Paul Claudel interroge le Cantique des Cantiques. Paris, 1948.
43554.2.140 Claudel, Paul. Ways and crossways. N.Y., 1933.
43554.2.145 Claudel, Paul. Feuilles de saints. 13e éd. Paris, 1930.
43554.2.155 Claudel, Paul. Figures et paraboles. 8e éd. Paris, 1936.
43554.2.165 Claudel, Paul. Le soulier de satin. 21e éd. Paris, 1929. 2v.
43554.2.168 Claudel, Paul. Le soulier de satin. Paris, 1949.
43554.2.170 Claudel, Paul. Un poète regarde la croix. 18e éd. Paris, 1938.
43554.2.180 Claudel, Paul. Presence et prophetie. Fribourg, 1942.
43554.2.190 Claudel, Paul. Jeanne d'Arc au bûcher. Paris, 1939.
43554.2.200 Claudel, Paul. Partage de midi. Lausanne, 1946.
43554.2.200.5 Claudel, Paul. Partage de midi. 12e éd. Paris, 1949.
43554.2.200.10 Claudel, Paul. Two dramas. Chicago, 1960.
43554.2.210 Claudel, Paul. Le livre de Job. Paris, 1946.
43554.2.220 Claudel, Paul. La rose et le rosaire. Paris, 1947.
43554.2.223 Claudel, Paul. La rose et le rosaire. Paris, 1947.
43554.2.226 Claudel, Paul. Toi, qui es-tu? 55e éd. Paris, 1941.
43554.2.230 Claudel, Paul. Toi, qui es-tu? Paris, 1947.
43554.2.231 Claudel, Paul. Toi, qui es-tu? Paris, 1936.
43554.2.240 Claudel, Paul. Cent phrases pour éventails. Paris, 1942.
43554.2.245 Claudel, Paul. L'oeil éconte. Paris, 1946.
43554.2.250 Claudel, Paul. La perle noire. Paris, 1947.
43554.2.260 Claudel, Paul. L'endormie. Neuchâtel, 1947.
43554.2.270 Claudel, Paul. Visages radieux. 7e éd. Paris, 1947.
43554.2.280F Claudel, Paul. La mystique des pierres precieuses. Paris, 1939.
43554.2.290 Claudel, Paul. Sous le signe du dragon. Paris, 1948.
43554.2.300 Claudel, Paul. Contacts et circonstances. 17e éd. Paris, 1947.
43554.2.305 Claudel, Paul. The satin slipper. New Haven, 1931.
43554.2.310 Claudel, Paul. Les aventures de Sophie. Paris, 1937.
43554.2.320 Claudel, Paul. Conversations dans le Loir et Cher. Paris, 1935.

43511 - 43873 Individual authors, etc. - 1900- - Known authors (363 scheme plus 10) - cont.

43554.2.330 Claudel, Paul. Discours et remerciements. 2e éd. Paris, 1947.
43554.2.340 Claudel, Paul. Le chemin de la croix. Paris, 1946.
43554.2.350 Claudel, Paul. L'épée et le miroir. 15e éd. Paris, 1939.
43554.2.360 Claudel, Paul. L'histoire de Tobie et de Sara. Paris, 1942.
43554.2.370 Claudel, Paul. Théâtre. Paris, 1947-1948. 2v.
43554.2.370.5 Claudel, Paul. Théâtre. Paris, 1956.
43554.2.370.10 Claudel, Paul. Théâtre. 3e éd. Paris, 1914.
43554.2.370.15 Claudel, Paul. Théâtre. Paris, 1967.
43554.2.375 Claudel, Paul. Le bestiaire spirituel. Lausanne, 1949.
43554.2.380 Claudel, Paul. Deux farces lyriques. 10e éd. Paris, 1945.
43554.2.390 Claudel, Paul. Accompagnements. 3e éd. Paris, 1949.
43554.2.400 Claudel, Paul. La legende de Prakriti. Paris, 1934.
43554.2.405 Claudel, Paul. Letters from Paul Claudel, my godfather. Westminster, 1964.
43554.2.410 Claudel, Paul. Correspondance, 1899-1926. Paris, 1949.
43554.2.412 Claudel, Paul. The correspondence, 1899-1926 between Paul Claudel and André Gide. N.Y., 1952.
43554.2.430 Claudel, Paul. Une voix sur Israel. Paris, 1950.
43554.2.435 Claudel, Paul. La ravissement de Scapin. n.p., 1952.
43554.2.440 Claudel, Paul. Mémoires improvisés. 6e éd. Paris, 1954.
43554.2.445 Claudel, Paul. Trois figures saintes pour le temps actuel. Paris, 1953.
43554.2.450 Claudel, Paul. L'échange. Paris, 1954.
43554.2.452 Claudel, Paul. L'échange. Paris, 1964.
43554.2.455 Claudel, Paul. Lettres sur la Bible au R.P.R. Paroissin. Paris, 1955.
43554.2.460 Claudel, Paul. La ville. Paris, 1956.
43554.2.462 Claudel, Paul. La ville. Thèse. Paris, 1967.
43554.2.465 Claudel, Paul. L'aime la Bible. Paris, 1955.
43554.2.470 Claudel, Paul. Connaissance de l'Est! Paris, 1960.
43554.2.480 Claudel, Paul. Réflexions sur la poésie. Paris, 1963.
43554.2.490 Claudel, Paul. Au milieu des vitraux de l'Apocalypse. Paris, 1966.
43554.2.500 Claudel, Paul. Journal. Paris, 1968- 2v.
43554.2.510 Claudel, Paul. Qui ne souffre pas. Paris, 1958.
43554.2.705 Claudel, Paul. The tidings brought to Mary. New Haven, 1916.
43554.2.706 Claudel, Paul. The tidings brought to Mary. Chicago, 1960.
43554.2.710 Claudel, Paul. Three plays; The hostage, Trusts, The humiliation of father. Boston, 1945.
43554.2.714 Claudel, Paul. Lord, teach us to pray. London, 1947.
43554.2.720 Claudel, Paul. Poetic art. N.Y., 1948.
43554.2.725 Claudel, Paul. The eye listens. N.Y., 1950.
43554.2.730 Claudel, Paul. A poet before the cross. Chicago, 1958.
43554.2.735 Claudel, Paul. The essence of the Bible. N.Y., 1957.
43554.2.785 Claudel, Paul. Der Bürge. Hellerau, 1926.
43554.2.790 Claudel, Paul. Die Musen. Leipzig, 1917.
43554.2.795 Claudel, Paul. Der Gnadenkranz. Einsiedeln, 1957.
43554.2.796 Claudel, Paul. Images saintes de Bohême. V Rimě, 1958.
43554.2.800 Benoist-Méchin, Jacques. Bibliographie des oeuvres de Paul Claudel. Paris, 1931.
43554.2.805 Paris. Bibliothèque Sainte-Genevieve. Collection Doucet. Paul Claudel; premières oeuvres, 1886-1901. Paris, 1965.
43554.2.810 Casnati, F. Paul Claudel e i suoi drammi. Como, 1919.
43554.2.813 Madaule, Jacques. Le drame de Paul Claudel. 2e éd. Paris, 1936.
43554.2.814 Madaule, Jacques. Le drame de Paul Claudel. 3e éd. Paris, 1947.
43554.2.814.5 Madaule, Jacques. Paul Claudel. Paris, 1956.
43554.2.815 Ste. Marie Perrin, E. Introduction à l'oeuvre de Paul Claudel. Paris, 1926.
43554.2.816A Madaule, Jacques. Le génie de Paul Claudel. 2e éd. Paris, 1933.
43554.2.816B Madaule, Jacques. Le génie de Paul Claudel. 2e éd. Paris, 1933.
43554.2.820 Lefévre, Frédéric. Les sources de Paul Claudel. Paris, 1927.
43554.2.825 Truc, Gonzague. Paul Claudel, portrait et autographe. Paris, 1925.
43554.2.830 Duhamel, Georges. Paul Claudel, le philosophe, le poête. Paris, 1913.
43554.2.835 Angenendt, Paul. Eine syntaktisch-stilistiche Untersuchung der Werke P. Claudels. Inaug. Diss. Bonn, 1932.
43554.2.840 Hirschberger, T. Der drei Fassungen von Claudels "Annonce faite à Marie". Diss. Breslau, 1933.
43554.2.845 Bindel, Victor. Claudel. Paris, 1934.
43554.2.847 Bindel, Victor. Claudel et nous. Tournai, 1947.
43554.2.850 Paul Claudel; l'homme, le chrétien, l'oeuvre. Juvisy, 1935.
43554.2.855 Gillet, Louis. Claudel présent. Fribourg, 1942.
43554.2.860 Jouve, Raymond. Comment lire Paul Claudel. Paris, 1946.
43554.2.865 Perche, Louis. Claudel et les cinq grandes odes. Périgueux, 1945.
43554.2.870 Gillet, Louis. Claudel, Peguy. Paris, 1946.
43554.2.875 Molitor, André. Aspects de Paul Claudel. Paris, 1945.
43554.2.880 Chonez, Claudine. Introduction à Paul Claudel. Paris, 1947.
43554.2.885 Francia, Ennio. Paul Claudel. Brescia, 1947.
43554.2.890 Maurer, Lily Elsa. Gestalt und Bedeutung der Frau im Werke Paul Claudel's "Abhandlung". Zürich, 1947.
43554.2.895 Samson, J. Paul Claudel. Genève, 1947.
43554.2.900 Rywalski, P. La Bible, dans l'oeuvre littéraire de Paul Claudel. Thèse. Porrentruy, 1948.
43554.2.903 Rywalski, P. Claudel et la Bible. Porrentruy, 1948.
43554.2.905 O'Flaherty, K.M.J. Paul Claudel and "The tidings". Cork, 1949.
43554.2.910 Thomas, J. Paul Claudel der Mensch und Dichter. Trier, 1947.
43554.2.915 Ryan, Mary. Introduction to Paul Claudel. Dublin, 1951.
43554.2.920 Dessaintes, M. Paul Claudel et L'annonce faite à Marie. Bruxelles, 1951.
43554.2.925A Barjon, Louis. Paul Claudel. Paris, 1953.
43554.2.925B Barjon, Louis. Paul Claudel. Paris, 1953.
43554.2.930 Chiari, J. The poetic drama of Paul Claudel. London, 1954.
43554.2.935 Dieckmann, H. Die Kunstanschauung Paul Claudel's. München, 1931.
43554.2.940 Beaumont, Ernest. The theme of Beatrice in the plays of Claudel. London, 1954.
43554.2.942 Beaumont, Ernest. Les sens de l'amour dans le théâtre de Claudel. Paris, 1958.
43554.2.945 Guillemin, H. Claudel et son art d'ecrire. 2e éd. Paris, 1955.

Classified Listing

43511 - 43873 Individual authors, etc. - 1900- - Known authors (363 scheme plus 10) - cont.

43554.2.950 Andrieu, J. La foi dans l'oeuvre de Paul Claudel. Paris, 1955.
43554.2.955 Lindemann, R. Kreuz und Eros. Paul Claudels. Frankfurt, 1955.
43554.2.960 Maurocordato, A. L'ode de Paul Claudel. Genève, 1955?
43554.2.963 Maurocordato, A. Anglo-American influences in Paul Claudel. Génève, 1964.
43554.2.965 Lerch, Emil. Versuchung und Gnade. Wien, 1956.
43554.2.970 Fowlie, Wallace. Paul Claudel. London, 1957.
43554.2.972 Fowlie, Wallace. Paul Claudel. N.Y., 1957.
43554.2.975 Ormesson, W. Paul Claudel et son fauteuil. Paris, 1957.
43554.2.980 Bastien, Jacques. L'oeuvre dramatique de Paul Claudel. Reims, 1957.
43554.2.985 Berton, J.C. Shakespeare et Claudel. Génève, 1958.
43554.2.990 Hoorn, H. Poésie et mystique. Genève, 1957.
43554.2.995 Roberto, Eugène. Visions de Claudel. Marseille, 1958.
43554.2.1000 Daniel-Rops, Henry. Claudel tel que je l'ai connu. Strasbourg, 1957.
43554.2.1010 Roy, Paul-Émile. Claudel. Montréal, 1957.
43554.2.1020 Halter, Raymond. La vierge Maire dans la vie et l'oeuvre de Paul Claudel. Tours, 1958.
43554.2.1035 Wahl, Jean André. Defense et elargissement de la philosophie. Paris, 1958.
Htn 43554.2.1040* Académie...Paris. Discours prononcés dans la séance publique tenue. Paris, 1957.
43554.2.1045 Cahiers Paul Claudel. Paris. 1,1959+ 8v.
43554.2.1050 Mondor, Henri. Claudel plus intime. Paris, 1960.
43554.2.1060 Farabel, René. Le jeu de l'acteur. Paris, 1960.
43554.2.1065 Blanc, André. Claudel. Paris, 1965.
43554.2.1070 Babilas, W. Das Frankreichbild in Paul Claudels Personnalité de la France. Münster, 1958.
43554.2.1075 Coenen- Mennemeier, Brigitta. Der aggressive Claudel. Münster, 1957.
43554.2.1080 Antoine, Gérald. Les cinq grandes odes de Claudel. Paris, 1959.
43554.2.1085 Chaigne, Louis. Vie de Paul Claudel et genése de son oeuvre. Tours, 1961.
43554.2.1090 Société Paul Claudel. Bulletin. Paris. 8,1961+ 3v.
43554.2.1090.5 Cahier canadien Claudel. Ottawa. 5,1967+ 4v.
43554.2.1095 Chaigne, Louis. Paul Claudel. N.Y., 1961.
43554.2.1100 Barrault, Jean Z. Adieu à Claudel. Viernheim, 1956.
43554.2.1105 Dendooven, Lucien. Paul Claudel. Brugge, 1961.
43554.2.1110 Paul Claudel devant Tête d'Or. Paris, 1960.
43554.2.1115 Barbier, Joseph. Claudel, poète de la prière. Tours, 1962.
43554.2.1120 Oswald, W. Entwicklung und Funktion der Metaphorik in Claudels Tête d'Or. München, 1962.
43554.2.1125 Czaschke, A. Der Cantique de Mesa. Münster, 1964.
43554.2.1130 Guyard, M.F. Recherches claudeliennes autour des cinq grandes odes. Paris, 1963.
43554.2.1135 Willems, W. Paul Claudel. Bruxelles, 1964.
43554.2.1140 Avré, Barna M. L'otage de Paul Claudel. Québec, 1961.
43554.2.1145 Brunel, Pierre. Le soulier de satin devant la critique. Paris, 1964.
43554.2.1150 Jahier, Piero. Con Claudel, 1913-1955. Milano, 1964.
43554.2.1155 Matheson, William Howard. Claudel and Aeschylus. Ann Arbor, 1965.
43554.2.1160 Marcel, Gabriel. Regards sur le théâtre de Claudel. Paris, 1964.
43554.2.1165 Berchan, Richard. The inner stage. East Lansing, 1966.
43554.2.1170 Vachon, André. Le temps et l'espace dans l'oeuvre de Paul Claudel. Paris, 1965.
43554.2.1175 Landau, Edwin Maria. Paul Claudel. Velber, 1966.
43554.2.1180 Gillet-Maudot, Marie Jeanne. Paul Claudel. Paris, 1966.
43554.2.1185 Donnard, Jean Hervé. Trois écrivains devant Dieu. Paris, 1966.
43554.2.1190 Ganne, Pierre. Claudel, humour, joie et liberté. Paris, 1966.
43554.2.1195 Tricaud, Marie Louise. Le baroque dans le théâtre de Paul Claudel. Genève, 1967.
43554.2.1200 Mueller, Klaus. Die Frühdramen Paul Claudels: l'Endormie, Fragment d'un drame, Tête d'Or, La Ville. Stuttgart, 1965.
43554.2.1205 Claudel newsletter. Kingston, Rhode Island. 1,1968+
43554.2.1210 Espiau de la Maëstre, André. Das göttliche Abenteuer. Salzburg, 1968.
43554.2.1215 Hubert, Marie Clotilde. Paul Claudel 1868-1955. Paris, 1968.
43554.2.1220 Varillon, François. Claudel. Paris, 1967.
43554.2.1225 Griffiths, Richard. Claudel. London, 1968.
43554.2.1230 Cattaui, Georges. Claudel, le cycle des Coûfontaine et le mystère d'Israël. Paris, 1968.
43554.2.1235 Paul Claudel, 1868-1968. Paris, 1968.
43554.2.1240 Mercier-Campiche, Marianne. Le Théâtre de Claudel, ou la Puissance du grief et de la passion. Paris, 1968.
43554.2.1245 Bouchard, Isabelle. L'expérience apostolique de Paul Claudel d'après sa correspondance. Montréal, 1969.
43554.2.1250 Entretiens sur Paul Claudel, Cerisy-La Salle. Entretiens sur Paul Claudel. Paris, 1969.
43554.2.1255 Colliard, Lauro Aimé. Nouvelles recherches historiques sur Paul Claudel. Milano, 1968.
43554.2.1260 Zinke, Ludger. Paul Claudel. Würzburg, 1968.
43554.2.1265 Madaule, Jacques. Claudel et le langage. Bruges, 1968.
43554.2.1270 Tissier, André. "Tête d'Or" de Paul Claudel. Paris, 1968.
43554.2.1275 Waters, Harold A. Paul Claudel. N.Y., 1970.
43554.2.1280 Taviani, Ferdinando. La parabola teatrale. Firenze, 1969.
43554.2.1285 Plourde, Michel. Paul Claudel; une musique du silence. Montréal, 1970.
43554.2.1290 La pensée religieuse de Claudel. Paris, 1969.
43554.2.1295 Guillemin, Henri. Le "Converti" Paul Claudel. Paris, 1968.
43554.2.1300 Harry, Ruth Naomi. Paul Claudel and Saint-John Perse. Chapel Hill, 1971.
43554.2.1305 Brodeur, Léo A. Le corps-sphère, clef de la symbolique Claudélienne. Montréal, 1970.
43554.2.1310 Paul Claudel zu seinem hundertsten Geburtstag. Stuttgart, 1970.
43554.2.1315 Petit, Jacques. Claudel et l'usurpateur. Paris, 1971.
43554.2.1320 Boly, Joseph. L'annonce faite à Marie [par] P. Claudel; étude et analyse. Paris, 1957.
43554.2.1325 Les critiques de notre temps et Claudel. Paris, 1970.
43554.3.30 Clerc, C. Les oasis. London, 1912.
43554.3.100 Clairal, V. Zone dangereuses. Paris, 1953.
43554.3.1100 Clairvaux, Henry. Oeil de mouche. Paris, 1957.
43554.4.30 Clermont, Emile. Amour promis. 2e éd. Paris, n.d.
43554.4.31 Clermont, Emile. Laure. Paris, 1913.

43511 - 43873 Individual authors, etc. - 1900- - Known authors (363 scheme plus 10) - cont.

43554.4.35 Clermont, Emile. Histoire d'Isabelle. Paris, 1917.
43554.4.81 Spiegel, E. Emile Clermont (1880-1916). Inaug. Diss. Würzburg, 1932.
43554.4.81.2 Spiegel, E. Emile Clermont, 1880-1916. Wertheim, 1932.
43554.4.83 Giraudoux, J. Marche vers Clermont avec un portrait de l'auteur par Alereuff. Paris, 1928.
43554.4.85 Études et souvenirs sur Émile Clermont. Paris, 1927.
43554.4.2100 Clappier, L. Festung Königsberg. Köln, 1952.
43554.4.3100 Charasson, Henriette. Jules Tellier. Paris, 1922.
43554.5.30 Claretie, L. Sourires litteraires. Paris, 1909.
43554.5.80 Durel, P. Leo Claretie. Paris, 1906.
43554.5.1021 Clavel, Maurice. Saint Euloge de Cordoue. Paris, 1965.
43554.5.1030 Clavel, Maurice. La Pourpre de Judée, ou Les délices du genre humain. Paris, 1967.
43554.5.1040 Clavel, Maurice. Combat de franc-tireur pour une libération. Paris, 1968.
43554.5.2100 Clavel, Bernard. Le voyage du père; roman. Paris, 1965.
43554.5.2110 Clavel, Bernard. La grande patience. Paris, 1968. 4v.
43554.5.2120 Clavel, Bernard. Qui m'emporte. Paris, 1965.
43554.5.2130 Clavel, Bernard. L'hercule sur la place. Paris, 1966.
43554.5.2140 Clavel, Bernard. L'Espagnol. Paris, 1968.
43554.5.2150 Clavel, Bernard. Malataverne. Paris, 1968.
43554.5.2160 Clavel, Bernard. Le tambour du Bief. Paris, 1970.
43554.6.30 Clément-Janin, Noël. Judith vaincue. Paris, 1914.
43554.7.20 Clemenceau, Georges. Lettres à une amie; 1923-1929. Paris, 1970.
43554.7.30 Clemenceau, Georges. Les plus forts, roman contemporain. Paris, 1919.
43554.7.30.2 Clemenceau, Georges. The strongest. N.Y., 1919.
43554.7.31 Clemenceau, Georges. Aux embuscades de la vie. Paris, 1919.
43554.7.32 Clemenceau, Georges. Au fil des jours. Paris, 1900.
43554.7.33 Clemenceau, Georges. Le voile du bonheur. Paris, 1918.
43554.7.38 Clemenceau, Georges. Figures de Vendée. Paris, 1930.
43554.7.38.5 Clemenceau, Georges. Figures de Vendée. Halle, 1955.
43554.7.40 Clemenceau, Georges. Au pied du Sinaï. Paris, 1898.
43554.7.42 Clemenceau, Georges. Au pied du Sinaï. Paris, 1920.
43554.7.45 Clemenceau, Georges. At the foot of Sinai. N.Y., 1922.
43554.7.50 Clemenceau, Georges. Au soir de la pensée. Paris, 1927.
43554.7.55 Clemenceau, Georges. The surprises of life. Garden City, 1920.
43554.7.80 Ratinaud, Jean. Clemenceau. Paris, 1958.
43554.7.85 Applebaum, Samuel. Clemenceau. N.Y., 1948.
43554.8.30 Clancier, Georges Emmanuel. Terres de memoire. Paris, 1965.
43554.8.35 Clancier, Georges Emmanuel. Les incertains. Paris, 1965.
43554.8.40 Clancier, Georges Emmanuel. Le pain noir. Paris, 1968.
43554.8.100 Clauzel, R. La maison au soleil. pts. 1-2. Paris, 1922.
43554.9.30 Marcenac, J. La beauté du Diable racontée. Paris, 1950.
43554.21.100 Clébert, Jean Paul. The blockhouse. 1st American ed. N.Y., 1958.
43554.21.110 Clébert, Jean Paul. Le silence, l'exil et la ruse. Paris, 1968.
43554.23.100 Clément, Colette Grunbaum. Éblouissement; pièce en trois actes et quatre tableaux. Paris, 1937.
43554.23.1100 Clément, Michel. Confidences d'une prune. Montréal, 1970.
43554.23.3100 Clement-Dechamp, Emile. Au gré du veul. Paris, 1958.
43554.24.100 Clerc, Henri. L'epreuve du bonheur; pièce. Paris, 1924.
43554.24.110 Clerc, Henri. Le beau metier. Paris, 1930.
43554.24.120 Clerc, Henri. La femme de César. Paris, 1938.
43554.26.100 Cros, Charles. L'homme propre. Paris, 1883.
43554.63.100 Clo, Jean. Les frères perdus. Nancy, 1937.
43554.66.100 Clostermann, Pierre. Appui-feu sur l'oued Hallaïl. Paris, 1960.
43554.66.1100 Clot, René Jean. Le ramoneur de neige. Paris, 1962.
43554.67.100 Clos-Jouve, H. Le prétoire dans la boutique. Lyon, 1941.
43554.67.1100 Cloup, François. Sur le chemin de Crête. Paris, 194-.
43554.67.1110 Cloup, François. L'ame prit la parole. Paris, 1957.
43554.89.100 Bosquet, A. Syncopes. Paris, 1951.
43554.89.1100 Cluzel, M.E. Le droit de vivre. Paris, 1958.
43554.89.2100 Cluny, Claude Michel. Un jeune homme de Venise. Paris, 1966.
43556.1.12 Cocteau, Jean. Oeuvres complètes. Lausanne, 1946-1957. 11v.
43556.1.21 Cocteau, Jean. Leben und Werk. Wien, 1961. 2v.
43556.1.30 Cocteau, Jean. Le Prince Frivole. Paris, 1910.
43556.1.31 Cocteau, Jean. La Dance de Sophocles. Paris, 1912.
43556.1.32 Cocteau, Jean. Le bel indifférent. Paris, 1953.
43556.1.33A Cocteau, Jean. Le grand écart. 7e éd. Paris, 1923.
43556.1.33B Cocteau, Jean. Le grand écart. 5e éd. Paris, 1923.
43556.1.35A Cocteau, Jean. Discours de réception. 8e éd. Paris, 1955.
43556.1.35B Cocteau, Jean. Discours de réception. 10e éd. Paris, 1955.
43556.1.37A Cocteau, Jean. Lettre à Jacques Maritain. Paris, 1926.
43556.1.37B Cocteau, Jean. Lettre à Jacques Maritain. Paris, 1926.
43556.1.41A Maritain, Jacques. Réponse à Jean Cocteau. Paris, 1926.
43556.1.41B Maritain, Jacques. Réponse à Jean Cocteau. 17e éd. Paris, 1926.
43556.1.46 Cocteau, Jean. Vocabulaire, poèmes. Paris, 1922.
43556.1.50A Cocteau, Jean. Poésie, 1916-1923. Paris, 1925.
43556.1.50B Cocteau, Jean. Poésie, 1916-1923. Paris, 1925.
43556.1.60 Cocteau, Jean. Opéra, oeuvres poétiques, 1925-1927. Paris, 1927.
43556.1.61 Cocteau, Jean. Opéra. Paris, 1959.
43556.1.62 Cocteau, Jean. Opéra. Paris, 1952.
43556.1.65 Cocteau, Jean. Poèmes. Lausanne, 1945.
43556.1.65.5 Cocteau, Jean. Poèmes. Paris, 1948.
43556.1.65.10 Cocteau, Jean. Poèmes. 5e éd. Paris, 1956.
43556.1.70 Cocteau, Jean. Orphée. Paris, 1927.
43556.1.71 Cocteau, Jean. Orphée. London, 1933.
43556.1.72 Cocteau, Jean. Orphée. Paris, 1951.
43556.1.80 Cocteau, Jean. Antigone. Les mariés de la Tour Eiffel. Paris, 1948.
43556.1.82 Cocteau, Jean. Lettres à André Gide. Paris, 1970.
43556.1.88 Cocteau, Jean. Soixante dessins pour les enfants terribles. 6e éd. Paris, 1935.
43556.1.89 Cocteau, Jean. Les enfants terribles. 65e éd. Paris, 1927.
43556.1.92 Cocteau, Jean. Les enfants terribles. Paris, 1931.
43556.1.97 Cocteau, Jean. Les enfants terribles. 18e éd. Paris, 1939.
43556.1.100 Cocteau, Jean. Oedipe-roi. Paris, 1928.
43556.1.105 Cocteau, Jean. Clair-obscur. Monaco, 1954.
43556.1.110 Cocteau, Jean. Morceaux choisis, poèmes. Paris, 1932.
Htn 43556.1.120* Cocteau, Jean. La lampe d'Aladin. Paris, 1909.
43556.1.132 Cocteau, Jean. Thomas, l'imposteur. Paris, 1965?

43511 - 43873 Individual authors, etc. - 1900- - Known authors (363 scheme plus 10) - cont.

Htn 43556.1.140* Cocteau, Jean. Opium, journal d'une desintoxication. Paris, 1931.
43556.1.141 Cocteau, Jean. Opium. Paris, 1930.
43556.1.150 Cocteau, Jean. Essai de critique indirecte. Paris, 1932.
43556.1.160 Cocteau, Jean. Mon premier voyage. 18e éd. Paris, 1937.
43556.1.170 Cocteau, Jean. Les chevaliers de la table ronde. 13e éd. Paris, 1937.
43556.1.175 Cocteau, Jean. Dessins en marge du texte des Chevaliers de la table ronde. Paris, 1941.
43556.1.180 Cocteau, Jean. Portraits - souvenir, 1900-1914. 6e éd. Paris, 1935.
43556.1.190 Cocteau, Jean. La machine infernale. 7e éd. Paris, 1934.
43556.1.192 Cocteau, Jean. La machine infernale. Paris, 1961.
43556.1.195 Cocteau, Jean. Les monstres sacrés. Paris, 1940.
43556.1.200 Cocteau, Jean. Poésie critique. Paris, 1945.
43556.1.202 Cocteau, Jean. Poésie critique. Paris, 1960. 2v.
43556.1.205 Cocteau, Jean. Leone. Paris, 1945.
43556.1.217 Cocteau, Jean. La belle et la bête. 37e éd. Paris, 1946.
43556.1.230 Cocteau, Jean. La crucifixion, poème. Paris, 1946.
43556.1.245 Cocteau, Jean. Le foyer des artistes. Paris, 1947.
43556.1.250 Cocteau, Jean. La voix humaine, piece en un acte. 7e éd. Paris, 1930.
43556.1.260A Cocteau, Jean. Allégories. Paris, 1941.
43556.1.260B Cocteau, Jean. Allégories. Paris, 1941.
43556.1.270 Cocteau, Jean. Théâtre. Paris, 1948- 2v.
43556.1.275 Cocteau, Jean. Théâtre de poche. Paris, 1949.
43556.1.280 Cocteau, Jean. Le coq et l'arlequin. Paris, 1918.
43556.1.290 Cocteau, Jean. La difficulté d'être. Paris, 1947.
43556.1.300 Cocteau, Jean. L'aigle à deux têtes, trois actes. Paris, 1947.
43556.1.310 Cocteau, Jean. Renaud et Armide. 9e éd. Paris, 1943.
43556.1.320 Cocteau, Jean. Lettre aux Américains. Paris, 1949.
43556.1.330 Cocteau, Jean. Carte blanche. Paris, 1920.
43556.1.340 Cocteau, Jean. Le rappel à l'ordre. Paris, 1948.
43556.1.350 Cocteau, Jean. Maalesh. 16e éd. Paris, 1949.
43556.1.360 Cocteau, Jean. Les mariés de la Tour Eiffel. Paris, 1924.
43556.1.370 Cocteau, Jean. Le sang d'un poète. Paris, 1948.
43556.1.372 Cocteau, Jean. Le sang d'un poète. Monaco, 1957.
43556.1.380.5 Cocteau, Jean. Bacchus; pièce en trois actes. 14e éd. Paris, 1952.
43556.1.390 Cocteau, Jean. Le chiffre sept. Paris, 1952.
43556.1.395 Cocteau, Jean. Journal d'un inconnu. Paris, 1953.
43556.1.400 Cocteau, Jean. Maalesh. London, 1956.
43556.1.405 Cocteau, Jean. Le discours d'Oxford. Paris, 1956.
43556.1.410 Cocteau, Jean. Jean Cocteau. Paris, 1955.
43556.1.412 Cocteau, Jean. Jean Cocteau. Paris, 1960.
43556.1.415 Cocteau, Jean. Le discours de Strasbourg. Metz, 1956.
43556.1.420 Cocteau, Jean. La corrida du premier mai. Paris, 1957.
43556.1.425 Cocteau, Jean. La chapelle Saint Pierre. Monaco, 1957.
43556.1.430 Cocteau, Jean. La Salle des mariages. Monaco, 1958.
43556.1.435 Cocteau, Jean. La difficulté d'être. Monaco, 1957.
43556.1.440 Cocteau, Jean. Le grand écart. Paris, 1957.
43556.1.445 Cocteau, Jean. Cérémonial Espagnol du phénix. Paris, 1961.
43556.1.450 Cocteau, Jean. Guide à l'usage des visiteurs de la Chapelle Saint Blaise des Simples. Monaco, 1960.
43556.1.460 Cocteau, Jean. Le cordon ombilical. Paris, 1962.
43556.1.470 Cocteau, Jean. Le requiem. Paris, 1962.
43556.1.475 Cocteau, Jean. Faire-part. Paris, 1968.
43556.1.621 Cocteau, Jean. Four plays. London, 1962.
43556.1.641 Cocteau, Jean. Professional secrets; an autobiography. N.Y., 1970.
43556.1.703 Cocteau, Jean. The typewriter. London, 1947.
43556.1.710 Cocteau, Jean. The infernal machine. London, 1936.
43556.1.712 Cocteau, Jean. The infernal machine. Norfolk, Conn., 1964.
43556.1.715 Cocteau, Jean. The eagle has two heads. London, 1948.
43556.1.718 Cocteau, Jean. Two screenplays; The blood of a poet, The testament of Orpheus. London, 1970.
43556.1.720 Cocteau, Jean. Diary of a film. N.Y., 1950.
43556.1.725 Cocteau, Jean. The human voice. London, 1951.
43556.1.735 Cocteau, Jean. My contemporaries. London, 1967.
43556.1.740 Cocteau, Jean. Journals. 1st ed. N.Y., 1956.
43556.1.745 Cocteau, Jean. The hand of a stranger. London, 1956.
43556.1.750 Cocteau, Jean. La machine à écrire. Paris, 1956.
43556.1.755 Cocteau, Jean. Paris album, 1900-1914. London, 1956.
43556.1.760 Cocteau, Jean. The holy terrors. N.Y., 1957.
43556.1.765 Cocteau, Jean. The imposter. N.Y., 1957.
43556.1.770 Cocteau, Jean. Opium. N.Y., 1958.
43556.1.775 Cocteau, Jean. The miscreant. London, 1958.
43556.1.780 Cocteau, Jean. My journey round the world. London, 1958.
43556.1.785 Cocteau, Jean. Cock and harlequin. London, 1921.
43556.1.788 Cocteau, Jean. The difficulty of being. London, 1966.
43556.1.790 Cocteau, Jean. Paraprosodies précédées de sept dialogues. Monaco, 1958.
43556.1.795 Cocteau, Jean. A call to order. N.Y., 1923.
43556.1.800 Mauriac, C. Jean Cocteau. Paris, 1945.
43556.1.803A Boni, Gianni. Cocteau e la poetica del film. Roma, 1944.
43556.1.803B Boni, Gianni. Cocteau e la poetica del film. Roma, 1944.
43556.1.806 Cocteau, Jean. Jean Cocteau. Bruxelles, 1950.
43556.1.810 Millecam, J.P. L'étaile de Jean Cocteau. Monaco, 1952.
43556.1.815 Cocteau, Jean. Démarche d'un poète. München, 1953.
43556.1.820 Dubourg, P. Dramaturgie de Jean Cocteau. Paris, 1954.
43556.1.830 Crosland, M. Jean Cocteau. London, 1955.
43556.1.840 Dauven, Jean. Jean Cocteau chez les sirenes. Monaco, 1956.
43556.1.850 Hagen, Friedrich. Zwischen Stern und Spiegel. München, 1956.
43556.1.860 Hugo, V.M. Ruy Blas. Paris, 1948.
43556.1.870A Oxenhandler, N. Scandal and parade. New Brunswick, N.J., 1957.
43556.1.870B Oxenhandler, N. Scandal and parade. New Brunswick, N.J., 1957.
43556.1.880A Galerie Matarasso, Nice. Images de Jean Cocteau. Nice, 1957.
43556.1.880B Galerie Matarasso, Nice. Images de Jean Cocteau. Nice, 1957.
43556.1.890 Fraigneau, André. Cocteau par lui-même. Paris, 1957.
43556.1.900 Simon, Karl. Jean Cocteau. Berlin, 1958.
43556.1.905 Kihm, Jean Jacques. Cocteau. Paris, 1960.
43556.1.910 Meunier, Micheline. Méditerranée. Paris, 1959.
43556.1.915 Pillaudin, R. Jean Cocteau tourne son dernier film. Paris, 1960.
43556.1.920 Hommage à Jean Cocteau. Paris? 1961.
43556.1.925 Massis, Henri. De Radigue à Maritain; hommage à Cocteau. Liège, 1963.

43511 - 43873 Individual authors, etc. - 1900- - Known authors (363 scheme plus 10) - cont.

43556.1.930 Hellens, F. Adieu au poète Jean Cocteau. Liège, 1963.
43556.1.935 Mourgue, Gérard. Jean Cocteau. Paris, 1965.
43556.1.940 Clair, René. Inauguration du buste Jean Cocteau à Milly-la-Forêt (Chapelle Saint-Blaise des Simples) le vendredi 16 octobre 1964; discours. Paris, 1964.
43556.1.945 Fowlie, Wallace. Jean Cocteau. Bloomington, 1966.
43556.1.950 Société des Amis du Musée des Beaux-Arts de Nantes. Hommage à Jean Cocteau...Nantes, 21 mai au 15 juin 1964. Nantes, 1964.
43556.1.955 Paris. Musée Jacques Mart-André. Jean Cocteau et son temps, 1889-1963. Paris, 1965.
43556.1.960 Sprigge, Elizabeth. Jean Cocteau: the man and the mirror. London, 1968.
43556.1.961 Sprigge, Elizabeth. Jean Cocteau, l'homme et les miroirs. Paris, 1968.
43556.1.965 Brown, Frederick. An impersonation of angels; a biography of Jean Cocteau. N.Y., 1968.
43556.1.970 Magnam, Jean Marie. Cocteau. Paris, 1968.
43556.1.975 Borgal, Clément. Cocteau, Dieu, La mort, La poésie. Paris, 1968.
43556.1.980 Brown, Frederick. An impersonation of angels. London, 1969.
43556.1.985 Knapp, Bettina (Liebowitz). Jean Cocteau. N.Y., 1970.
43556.1.990 Steegmuller, Francis. Cocteau, a biography. 1st ed. Boston, 1970.
43556.1.995 Brosse, Jacques. Cocteau. Paris, 1970.
43556.1.997 Cahiers Jean Cocteau. Paris. 1,1969+
43556.1.999 Chanel, Pierre. Album Cocteau. Paris, 1970.
43556.1.1000 Mauriac, Claude. Une amitié contrariée. Paris, 1970.
43556.2.30 Colomb, F. L'Âme éparse. Paris, 1912.
43556.2.31 Colomb, F. L'Écrin. Paris, 1910.
43556.3.100 Coanet, Georges. De bas en haut. Paris? 1958.
43556.13.100 Cochet, Marie A. Le sommeil du solipsiste. Bruxelles, 1926.
43556.15.100 Coculesco, Pius S. Introduction à une manière d'être. Paris, 1932.
43556.15.110 Coculesco, Pius S. Orient, suivi de Leeds Servien. Montreal, 1942.
43556.15.120 Coculesco, Pius S. Sagesse et poésie. Paris, 1947.
43556.37.104 Cohen, Albert. Mangeclous. 7e éd. Paris, 1938.
43556.37.105 Cohen, Albert. Mangeclous. 8e éd. Paris, 1938.
43556.37.110 Cohen, Albert. Solal. Paris, 1930.
43556.37.120 Cohen, Albert. Belle du Seigneur. Paris, 1968.
43556.37.130 Cohen, Albert. Les valeureux. Paris, 1969.
43556.48.100 Colas, Michel. La croix et le glaive. Paris, 1963.
43556.49.11 Colette, Sidonie Gabrielle. Oeuvres complètes. Paris, 1948-1950. 15v.
43556.49.21 Colette, Sidonie Gabrielle. Textes choisis de Colette. Paris, 1936.
43556.49.25 Colette, Sidonie Gabrielle. Colette. Paris, 1954.
43556.49.27 Colette, Sidonie Gabrielle. Contes des mille et un matius. Paris, 1970.
43556.49.41 Colette, Sidonie Gabrielle. Mes cahiers. Paris, 1941.
43556.49.61 Colette, Sidonie Gabrielle. Une amitié inattendue. Paris, 1945.
43556.49.65 Colette, Sidonie Gabrielle. Lettres à Hélène Picard. Paris, 1958.
43556.49.70 Colette, Sidonie Gabrielle. Lettres a Marguerite Moreno. Paris, 1959.
43556.49.110 Colette, Sidonie Gabrielle. L'entrave. Paris, 19- .
43556.49.112 Colette, Sidonie Gabrielle. L'entrave. Paris, 1933.
43556.49.120 Colette, Sidonie Gabrielle. L'éther consolateur. Paris, 19- .
43556.49.130 Colette, Sidonie Gabrielle. Ledos, tapissier. Paris, 19-
43556.49.140 Collette, Sidonie Gabrielle. Les vrilles de la vigne. 19e éd. Paris, 19- .
43556.49.145 Colette, Sidonie Gabrielle. Les vrilles de la vigne. Paris, 1923.
43556.49.150 Colette, Sidonie Gabrielle. La vagabonde. 5e éd. Paris, 1910.
43556.49.154 Colette, Sidonie Gabrielle. La vagabonde. Paris, 1923.
43556.49.155 Colette, Sidonie Gabrielle. La vagabonde. Paris, 1936.
43556.49.156 Colette, Sidonie Gabrielle. La vagabonde. Paris, 1946.
43556.49.160 Colette, Sidonie Gabrielle. Chéri, roman. 85e éd. Paris, 1920.
43556.49.161 Colette, Sidonie Gabrielle. Chéri. Paris, 1922.
Htn 43556.49.163* Colette, Sidonie Gabrielle. Chéri. Paris, 1929.
43556.49.165 Colette, Sidonie Gabrielle. Chéri. Paris, 1931.
43556.49.167 Colette, Sidonie Gabrielle. Chéri; roman. 2e éd. Rio de Janeiro, 1940.
43556.49.168 Colette, Sidonie Gabrielle. Chéri. Genève, 1947.
43556.49.170 Colette, Sidonie Gabrielle. La fin de Chéri. Paris, 1926.
43556.49.173 Colette, Sidonie Gabrielle. La fin de Chéri. Paris, 1930.
43556.49.180 Colette, Sidonie Gabrielle. La maison de Claudine. Paris, 1922.
43556.49.182 Colette, Sidonie Gabrielle. La maison de Claudine. Paris, 1923.
43556.49.185 Colette, Sidonie Gabrielle. Claudine s'en va. 20e éd. Paris, 1903.
43556.49.185.5A Colette, Sidonie Gabrielle. Claudine s'en va. Paris, 1931.
43556.49.185.5B Colette, Sidonie Gabrielle. Claudine s'en va. Paris, 1931.
43556.49.186 Colette, Sidonie Gabrielle. Claudine en ménage. 112e éd. Paris, 1903.
43556.49.186.10 Colette, Sidonie Gabrielle. Claudine en ménage. Paris, 1945.
43556.49.187 Colette, Sidonie Gabrielle. Claudine à Paris. 92e éd. Paris, 1903.
43556.49.188 Colette, Sidonie Gabrielle. Claudine à Paris. Paris, 1925.
43556.49.188.1 Colette, Sidonie Gabrielle. Claudine à Paris. Paris, 1925.
43556.49.189 Colette, Sidonie Gabrielle. Claudine a l'école. Paris, 1929.
43556.49.190 Colette, Sidonie Gabrielle. Ces plaisirs. Paris, 1932.
43556.49.200 Colette, Sidonie Gabrielle. Le blé en herbe. Paris, 1923.
43556.49.210 Colette, Sidonie Gabrielle. La femme cachée. Paris, 1924.
43556.49.220A Colette, Sidonie Gabrielle. Bella-vista. Paris, 1937.
43556.49.220B Colette, Sidonie Gabrielle. Bella-vista. Paris, 1937.
43556.49.229 Colette, Sidonie Gabrielle. La retraite sentimentale. Paris, 1926.
43556.49.235 Colette, Sidonie Gabrielle. Dialogues de bêtes. Paris, 1904.

Classified Listing

3511 - 43873 Individual authors, etc. - 1900- - Known authors (363 scheme plus 10) - cont.

43556.49.240 Colette, Sidonie Gabrielle. Dialogues de bêtes. Paris, 1925.
43556.49.245 Colette, Sidonie Gabrielle. Sept dialogues de bêtes. 71e éd. Paris, 1943.
43556.49.250 Colette, Sidonie Gabrielle. Chambre d'hôtel. Paris, 1940.
43556.49.260 Colette, Sidonie Gabrielle. La seconde; roman. Paris, 1929.
43556.49.270 Colette, Sidonie Gabrielle. Julie de Carneilhan. 24e éd. Paris, 1941.
43556.49.278 Colette, Sidonie Gabrielle. Duo. Paris, 1934.
43556.49.280 Colette, Sidonie Gabrielle. Duo. Paris, 1938.
43556.49.290 Colette, Sidonie Gabrielle. La naissance du jour. Paris, 1931.
43556.49.295 Colette, Sidonie Gabrielle. Le képi. Paris, 1943.
43556.49.298 Colette, Sidonie Gabrielle. Le képi. Paris, 1947.
tn 43556.49.305* Colette, Sidonie Gabrielle. La jumelle noire. Paris, 1934.
43556.49.310 Colette, Sidonie Gabrielle. Gigi. Lausanne, 1944.
43556.49.315 Colette, Sidonie Gabrielle. Gigi. Paris, 1945.
43556.49.320 Colette, Sidonie Gabrielle. Gigi. N.Y., 1952.
43556.49.330 Colette, Sidonie Gabrielle. Paris de ma fenêtre. Genève, 1944.
43556.49.340 Colette, Sidonie Gabrielle. L'ingénue libertine. Lausanne, 1947.
43556.49.350 Colette, Sidonie Gabrielle. Journal à rebours. Paris, 1941.
43556.49.360 Colette, Sidonie Gabrielle. Chambre d'hôtel. Paris, 1946.
43556.49.370 Colette, Sidonie Gabrielle. L'étoile vesper. Genève, 1946.
43556.49.380 Colette, Sidonie Gabrielle. Trois...six...neuf. Paris, 1946.
43556.49.390 Colette, Sidonie Gabrielle. Le toutounier. 100e éd. Paris, 1947.
43556.49.400 Colette, Sidonie Gabrielle. L'envers du music-hall. Rio de Janeiro, Brasil, 1938.
43556.49.410 Colette, Sidonie Gabrielle. Le tendron; nouvelle. Paris, 1946.
43556.49.420 Colette, Sidonie Gabrielle. Les heures lonques, 1914-1917. Paris, 1917.
43556.49.430 Colette, Sidonie Gabrielle. La chatte; roman. 123e éd. Paris, 1944.
43556.49.440 Colette, Sidonie Gabrielle. Prisons et paradis. Paris, 1935.
43556.49.450 Colette, Sidonie Gabrielle. Morceaux choisis. Paris, 1936.
43556.49.460 Colette, Sidonie Gabrielle. Le voyage égoïste. Paris, 1928.
43556.49.470 Colette, Sidonie Gabrielle. De ma fenêtre. Paris, 1942.
43556.49.480 Colette, Sidonie Gabrielle. Le pur et l'impur. Paris, 1941.
43556.49.490 Colette, Sidonie Gabrielle. Mitsou, ou Comment l'esprit vient aux filles. Paris, 1948.
43556.49.500 Colette, Sidonie Gabrielle. Le fanal bleu. Paris, 1949.
43556.49.505 Colette, Sidonie Gabrielle. La fleur de l'âge. Lausanne, 1960.
43556.49.510 Colette, Sidonie Gabrielle. Aventures quotidiennes. Paris, 1924.
43556.49.520 Colette, Sidonie Gabrielle. Chats [de Colette]. Paris, 1950.
43556.49.530 Colette, Sidonie Gabrielle. Journal intermittent. Paris, 1949.
43556.49.540 Colette, Sidonie Gabrielle. Belles saisons. Paris, 1955.
43556.49.550 Colette, Sidonie Gabrielle. La treille muscate. Lausanne, 1956.
43556.49.560 Colette, Sidonie Gabrielle. Chiens. Paris, 1957.
43556.49.565 Colette, Sidonie Gabrielle. La paix chez les bêtes. Paris, 1916.
43556.49.570 Colette, Sidonie Gabrielle. Bêtes libres et prisonnières. Paris, 1958.
43556.49.575 Colette, Sidonie Gabrielle. Notes marocaines. Lausanne, 1958.
43556.49.580 Colette, Sidonie Gabrielle. Sido. Paris, 1935.
43556.49.585 Colette, Sidonie Gabrielle. Lettres au petit corsaire. Paris, 1963.
43556.49.705A Colette, Sidonie Gabrielle. Mitsou, or How girls grow wise. N.Y., 1930.
43556.49.705B Colette, Sidonie Gabrielle. Mitsou, or How girls grow wise. N.Y., 1930.
43556.49.707 Colette, Sidonie Gabrielle. Break of day. London, 1961.
43556.49.708 Colette, Sidonie Gabrielle. Earthly paradise; an autobiography. N.Y., 1966.
43556.49.709 Colette, Sidonie Gabrielle. Autobiographie tirée des oeuvres de Colette. Paris, 1966.
43556.49.710 Colette, Sidonie Gabrielle. The gentle libertine. N.Y., 1931.
43556.49.712 Colette, Sidonie Gabrielle. The pure and the impure. N.Y., 1967.
43556.49.715 Colette, Sidonie Gabrielle. Young lady of Paris. N.Y., 1931.
43556.49.718 Colette, Sidonie Gabrielle. The tender shoot. N.Y., 1959.
43556.49.722 Colette, Sidonie Gabrielle. The ripening seed. N.Y., 1956.
43556.49.723 Colette, Sidonie Gabrielle. The blue lantern. London, 1963.
43556.49.725 Colette, Sidonie Gabrielle. Chéri. N.Y., 1930.
43556.49.725.5 Colette, Sidonie Gabrielle. Cheri, and The last of Chéri. London, 1951.
43556.49.725.10 Colette, Sidonie Gabrielle. Chéri. London, 1963.
43556.49.727 Colette, Sidonie Gabrielle. The twilight of the gods. Hanley, 194-.
43556.49.730 Colette, Sidonie Gabrielle. Renée la vagabonde. 1st ed. Garden City, N.Y., 1931.
43556.49.732 Colette, Sidonie Gabrielle. The vagabond. N.Y., 1955.
43556.49.735 Colette, Sidonie Gabrielle. Short novels. N.Y., 1951.
43556.49.737 Colette, Sidonie Gabrielle. Six novels. N.Y., 1960?
43556.49.740 Colette, Sidonie Gabrielle. Creatures great and small. London, 1951.
43556.49.745 Colette, Sidonie Gabrielle. Julie de Carneilhan. London, 1952.
43556.49.750 Crottet, R. Stranded in heaven. London, 1952.
43556.49.755 Colette, Sidonie Gabrielle. My mother's house and Sido. London, 1953.
43556.49.760 Colette, Sidonie Gabrielle. Claudine at school. London, 1956.
43556.49.765 Colette, Sidonie Gabrielle. My apprenticeships. London, 1957.

43511 - 43873 Individual authors, etc. - 1900- - Known authors (363 scheme plus 10) - cont.

43556.49.770 Colette, Sidonie Gabrielle. Claudine in Paris. N.Y., 1958.
43556.49.775 Colette, Sidonie Gabrielle. Cats, dogs and I. N.Y., 1927.
43556.49.780 Colette, Sidonie Gabrielle. Places, by Colette. London, 1970.
43556.49.800 Koberle, M. Moderne Tendenzen in Colette's Sprache. Inaug. Diss. München, 1930.
43556.49.805A Chauvière, Claude. Colette. Paris, 1931.
43556.49.805B Chauvière, Claude. Colette. Paris, 1931.
43556.49.810 Voigt, W. Colette, Leben und Werk. Inaug. Diss. Jena, 1935.
43556.49.815 Trahard, P. L'art de Colette. Paris, 1941.
43556.49.820A Loos, Anita. Gigi. N.Y., 1952.
43556.49.820B Loos, Anita. Gigi. N.Y., 1952.
43556.49.825 Crosland, M. Madame Colette. London, 1953.
43556.49.826 Crosland, M. Colette. 1st American ed. N.Y., 1954.
43556.49.830 Maulnier, Thierry. Introduction à Colette. Paris, 1954.
43556.49.835 Bonmariage, Sylvain. Willy, Colette et moi. n.p., 1954.
43556.49.840 Cocteau, Jean. Colette. Paris, 1955.
43556.49.845 LeHardouin, M. Colette. Paris, 1956.
43556.49.850 Goudeket, Maurice. Close to Colette. N.Y., 1957.
43556.49.851 Goudeket, Maurice. Près de Colette. Paris, 1956.
43556.49.855 Houssa, Nicole. Le souci de l'expression chez Colette. Bruxelles, 1958.
43556.49.860 Reboux, Paul. Colette, ou Le génie du style. Paris, 1925.
43556.49.870 Fillon, Amélie. Colette. Paris, 1933.
43556.49.875 Truc, Gonzague. Madame Colette. Paris, 1941.
43556.49.880 Larnac, Jean. Colette. Paris, 1927.
43556.49.885 Marks, Elaine. Colette. New Brunswick, 1960.
43556.49.890 Davies, M. Colette. Edinburgh, 1961.
43556.49.895 Boncompain, Claude. Colette. Lyon, 1945?
43556.49.900 Ketchum, Anne A. Colette; ou La naissance du jour. Paris, 1968.
43556.49.905 Raaphorst-Rousseau, Madeleine. Colette, sa vie et son art. Paris, 1964.
43556.49.910 Pavlovic, M.B. Sidonie Gabrielle Colette. Beograd, 1970.
43556.49.2100 Coléno, Alica. Le quai des Indes; roman. Paris, 1946.
43556.50.100 Colling, Alfred. Demain, relâche. Paris, 1939.
43556.50.110 Colling, Alfred. L'iroguois; roman. Paris, 1926.
43556.50.1100 Collin, Sullian. La mort des fleurs. Paris, 1904.
43556.50.2100 Collin, Isi. La valée heureuse. Paris, 1903.
43556.50.3100 Collin, Bernard. Les milliers, les millions et le simple. Seine-et-Marne, 1965.
43556.50.4100 Colin, Gerty. Un tour au purgatoire. Paris, 1967.
43556.50.4110 Colin, Gerty. Un si grand amour. Verviers, 1969.
43556.50.5100 Collin, Robert. Les Bassignots. Chaumont, 1969.
43556.50.6100 Colin, Paul. Les jeux sauvages, roman. Paris, 1950.
43556.51.100 Colombat, Armand. Poèmes. Paris, 1957.
43556.51.1800 Caradec, François. Christophe Colomb. Paris, 1956.
43556.53.1100 Combette, Bernard. Des hommes. Paris, 1912.
43556.53.2100 Combet, Fernand. Schrumm Schrumm. Paris, 1966.
43556.54.100 Comert, Marguerit. Poèmes de retour eternal. Paris, 1936.
43556.55.100 Comiti, Jean Baptiste. Éclos la nuit. Paris, 1963.
43556.56.100 Compére, Gaston. Le signe infortuné. Bruxelles, 1964.
43556.58.100 Conchon, Georges. Les grandes lessives. Paris, 1953.
43556.58.110 Conchon, Georges. Tous comptes faits. Paris, 1957.
43556.58.120 Conchon, Georges. La lorriola de la Vicfaire. Paris, 1960.
43556.58.130 Conchon, Georges. L'état sauvage; roman. Paris, 1964.
43556.58.140 Conchon, Georges. L'apprenti gaucher. Paris, 1967.
43556.58.150 Conchon, Georges. Les honneurs de la guerre. Paris? 1970.
43556.58.700 Conchon, Georges. The measure of victory. N.Y., 1961.
43556.58.705 Conchon, Georges. The savage state. 1st ed. N.Y., 1965.
43556.61.100 Constantineau, Gilles. Simples poèmes et ballades. Montréal, 1960.
43556.61.1100 Conrad, Florence. Camarades de Combat. N.Y., 1942.
43556.61.2100 Conte, Arthur. Les oiseaux n'y savent pas chanter. Paris, 1954.
43556.74.100 Cordés, C. Les feux sur le Léban. Paris, 1924.
43556.74.1100 Cordonnié, Paul. Heurtoirs; poèmes. Paris, 1947.
43556.76.100 Cornélus, Henri. Bakonji, les chefs. Aalter, 1954.
43556.76.110 Cornélus, Henri. De sel et de terre. Bruxelles, 1967.
43556.77.41 Corpechot, Lucien. Souvenirs d'un journaliste. Paris, 1936-1937. 3v.
43556.77.2102 Corm, Charles. La montagne inspirée. 2e éd. Beyrouth, 1964.
43556.77.3100 Cornuz, Jean Louis. Parce que c'etait toi...(roman). Neuchâtel, 1966.
43556.82.700 Cossery, Albert. Men God forgot - a circle edition. Berkeley, 1946.
43556.82.705 Cossery, Albert. The house of certain death. London, 1947.
43556.82.705.5A Cossery, Albert. The house of certain death. N.Y., 1949.
43556.82.705.5B Cossery, Albert. The house of certain death. N.Y., 1949.
43556.82.710 Cossery, Albert. The lazy ones. N.Y., 1952.
43556.82.712 Cossery, Albert. The lazy one. London, 1952.
43556.82.715 Cossery, Albert. Mendiants et orgueilleux. Paris, 1955.
43556.82.720 Cossery, Albert. If all men were beggars. London, 1957.
43556.82.1100 Costantini, Pierre D. Aimons, Chantons, Sauvons la Corse. Bastia, 1967.
43556.82.2100 Coste, Didier. Journal exemplaire d'une enquête en province. Paris, 1969.
43556.87.100 Cottereau, Roger. Manège. Paris, 1957.
43556.87.2100 Cotte, Jean Louis. Le sang des taureaux. Paris, 1960.
43556.87.2110 Cotte, Jean Louis. Histoire d'eau, roman. Paris, 1968.
43556.87.2120 Cotte, Jean Louis. Occis soient-ils, roman. Paris, 1968.
43556.89.100 Coullet-Tessier, Antonine. Marthe. Paris, 1929.
43556.89.110 Coullet-Tessier, Antonine. Poésies d'une enfant. Paris, 1903.
43556.89.1100 Cousin, Gabriel. L'ordinaire amour. 2e éd. Paris, 1958.
43556.89.2100 Couffin, André. Le bouge humain. Paris, 1958.
43556.89.3100 Cousseau, Jacques. Les singes. Paris, 1960.
43556.89.4100 Couteaux, André. Un homme, aujourd'hui; roman. Paris, 1969.
43556.89.5100 Coulonges, Georges. Le grand Guignol. Paris, 1970.
43556.89.6100 Courtir, Charles. Sonnets pour Orphée. Paris, 1955.
43556.89.7100 Coupry, François. Les autocoincés. Paris, 1971.
43556.98.775 Coyné, André. Las vacaciones. Xalapa, 1962.
43556.185.5A Colette, Sidonie Gabrielle. Claudine s'en va. Paris, 1931.
43557.2.100 Crabos, Pierre G. La forêt des Cippes. Paris, 1918. 2v.
43557.4.100 Crance, Gerard. Symphonie circuloire. Paris, 1958.
43557.5.100 Craran, Arthur. Maintenant. Paris, 1957.
43557.24.100 Cremieux, Benjamin. XXe siècle. Paris, 1924.
43557.24.1100 Cressot, Marcel. Musique pour deux saisons. Rodez, 1957.

43511 - 43873 Individual authors, etc. - 1900- - Known authors (363 scheme plus 10) - cont.

43557.25.105 Crevel, René. La mort difficile. 2e éd. Paris, 1926.
43557.25.110 Crevel, René. Êtes-vous fous? Paris, 1929.
43557.25.115 Crevel, René. L'esprit contre la raison. Marseille, 1927.
43557.25.116 Crevel, René. L'esprit contre la raison. Paris, 1969.
43557.25.120 Crevel, René. Babylone. Paris, 1927.
43557.25.130 Crevel, René. Le clavecin de Diderot, 1932. Paris, 1966.
43557.25.1100 Crevel, Bernard. Parce que...poesies. Paris, 1964.
43557.61.106 Constantin-Weyer, Maurice. Un homme se penche sur son passé. 214e éd. Paris, 1928.
43557.61.106.2 Constantin-Weyer, Maurice. Un homme se penche sur son passé. 211e éd. Paris, 1928.
43557.61.110 Constantin-Weyer, Maurice. Cavelier de La Salle. 5e éd. Paris, 1927.
43557.61.120 Constantin-Weyer, Maurice. Les compagnons de la boule. Paris, 1946.
43557.61.130 Constantin-Weyer, Maurice. Le bar de San Miguel. Paris, 1946.
43557.61.140 Constantin-Weyer, Maurice. Pronunciamiento. Paris, 1948.
43557.61.150 Constantin-Weyer, Maurice. Un sourir dans la tempête. Paris, 1934.
43557.64.100 Cressanges, Jeanne. La feuille de betel. Paris, 1962.
43557.64.110 Cressanges, Jeanne. La chambre interdite; roman. Paris, 1969.
43557.65.100 Croht-Legras, Rine. Les champs incultes. Paris, 1964.
43557.66.100 Crommelynck, Fernand. Le cocu magnifique. Paris, 1921.
43557.66.102 Crommelynck, Fernand. Le cocu magnifique. Milano, 1924.
43557.66.110 Crommelynck, Fernand. Théâtre complet. Paris, 1956-
43557.66.120 Crommelynck, Fernand. Les amants puerits. 2e éd. Paris, 1921.
43557.66.130 Crommelynck, Fernand. Une femme qu'a le coeur trop petit. Paris, 1934.
43557.66.150 Crommelynck, Fernand. Théâtre. Paris, 1967- 3v.
43557.66.1100 Cros, Guy-Charles. Mon soleil nouveau, serivi de Soleils anciens. Paris, 1946.
43560.78.100 Curtis, Jean Louis. Les jeunes hommes. Paris, 1946.
43560.78.110 Curtis, Jean Louis. Haute ecole. Paris, 1950.
43560.78.120 Curtis, Jean Louis. Les justes causes. Paris, 1954.
43560.78.130 Curtis, Jean Louis. Les forêts de la nuit. Paris, 1951.
43560.78.140 Curtis, Jean Louis. L'échelle de soie. Paris, 1956.
43560.78.150 Curtis, Jean Louis. Siegfried. Paris, 1946.
43560.78.160 Curtis, Jean Louis. Un saint au néon. Paris, 1956.
43560.78.170 Curtis, Jean Louis. A la recherche du temps posthume. Paris, 1957.
43560.78.180 Curtis, Jean Louis. La parade. Paris, 1960.
43560.78.190 Curtis, Jean Louis. Cygne sauvage. Paris, 1962.
43560.78.200 Curtis, Jean Louis. La quarantine. Paris, 1966.
43560.78.210 Curtis, Jean Louis. Un jeune couple. Paris, 1967.
43560.78.220 Curtis, Jean Louis. Le roseau pensant. Paris, 1971.
43560.78.700 Curtis, Jean Louis. Lucifer's dream. London, 1952.
43560.78.710 Curtis, Jean Louis. The forests of the night. N.Y., 1951.
43560.78.715 Curtis, Jean Louis. The side of the angels. N.Y., 1956.
43560.78.1100 Cury, Maurice. Vert-quatre. Paris, 1955.
43560.78.1110 Cury, Maurice. Mine d'or, suivi de Petits poèmes pour un enfant triste. Paris, 1956.
43560.78.2100 Curvers, Alexis Théophille. Tempo di Roma. Paris, 1957.
43560.78.2102 Curvers, Alexis Théophille. Tempo di Roma. 1st ed. N.Y., 1959.
43560.81.100 Cusin, Pierre. Remords. Paris, 1956.
43560.82.700 Custot, Pierre. Sturly. Boston, 1925.
43560.87.100 Cuttat, Jean. Frère lai. Lausanne, 1968.
43560.87.110 Cuttat, Jean. Les couplets de l'oiseleur. [Poèmes]. Lausanne, 1967.
43560.90.100 Cuvelier, F. Dieu n'habite pas au 74. Malines, 1953.
43560.90.110 Cuvelier, F. Psycalè. Bruxelles, 1952.
43565.1.30 Daireaux, M. Ses pénitents noirs. Paris, 1906.
43565.2.30 Dampierre, J. de. La couronne de Sierre. Paris, 1907.
43565.2.3110 Darbon, Jean F. Les suspects. 3e éd. Paris, 1946.
43565.3.30 Darmet, L. Prés du Piano Fermé, 1909-11. Paris, 1912.
43565.4.30 Dargel, Henri. Trois farces antiques d'après Plaute. Paris, 1913.
43565.5.25 Daudet, Léon A. Memoirs. London, 1926.
43565.5.27 Daudet, Léon A. Memoirs. N.Y., 1925.
43565.5.30 Daudet, Léon A. La vermine du monde de l'éspionnage allemand. Paris, 1916.
43565.5.32 Daudet, Léon A. La vermine du monde de l'éspionnage allemand. Paris, 1916.
43565.5.35 Daudet, Léon A. Les primaires. Paris, 1906.
43565.5.40 Daudet, Léon A. Dans la lumière. Paris, 1919.
43565.5.45 Daudet, Léon A. Le voyage de Shakespeare. 5e éd. Paris, 1929.
43565.5.50 Daudet, Léon A. Flammes. Paris, 1930.
43565.5.56 Daudet, Léon A. Paris vécu. Paris, 1929-30. 2v.
43565.5.58 Daudet, Léon A. Paris, vécu. Paris, 1969.
43565.5.60 Daudet, Léon A. Vingt-neuf mois d'exil. Paris, 1896.
NEDL 43565.5.65 Daudet, Léon A. Les idées en marche. Paris, 1896.
43565.5.70 Daudet, Léon A. Tièvres de Camargue. 17e éd. Paris, 1938.
43565.5.80 Daudet, Léon A. Les oeuvres dans les hommes. Paris, 1922.
43565.5.90 Daudet, Léon A. Le voyage de Shakespeare. Paris, 1896.
43565.5.100 Daudet, Léon A. Le drame des Jardies, 1877-1882. 13. éd. Paris, 1924.
43565.5.120 Daudet, Léon A. Les Lys sanglants. Paris, 1938.
43565.5.130A Daudet, Léon A. Mes idées esthétiques. 6. éd. Paris, 1939.
43565.5.130B Daudet, Léon A. Mes idées esthétiques. 10. éd. Paris, 1939.
43565.5.140 Daudet, Léon A. Mélancholie. Paris, 1928.
43565.5.145 Daudet, Léon A. Le róman et les nouveaux écrivains. Paris, 1925.
43565.5.150 Daudet, Léon A. L'heure qui tourne. Paris, 1945.
43565.5.155 Daudet, Léon A. Souvenirs de milleux littéraires. Paris, 1920.
43565.5.160 Daudet, Léon A. Les dicts et pronostiquations d'Alcofribas deuxième. Paris, 1922.
43565.5.165 Daudet, Léon A. Bréviaire de journalisme. Paris, 1936.
43565.5.170 Daudet, Léon A. La police politique. Paris, 1934.
43565.5.175 Daudet, Léon A. La France en Darme. Paris, 1904.
43565.5.250 Daudet, Léon A. Léon Daudet. Paris, 1926.
43565.5.255 Daudet, Léon A. Oeuvre philosophique: l'hérédo. Paris, 1925.
43565.5.800 Clavière, M. Léon Daudet, ou Le contre-courant d'une décadence. Paris, 1943.
43565.5.805 Dresse, Paul. Léon Daudet. Paris, 1947.
43565.5.810 Breval, René. Philippe Daudet à bel. Paris, 1959.
43565.5.815 Lucchini, P. Léon Daudet. Paris, 1964.
43565.5.820 Fournier, Paul. L'entrevue de Léon Daudet. Paris, 1925.

43511 - 43873 Individual authors, etc. - 1900- - Known authors (363 scheme plus 10) - cont.

43565.5.825 Groh, Hans. Der publizistische Stil des Léon Daudet. Inaug. Diss. Bottrop, 1935.
43565.6.30 Dautrin, E. L'envolée (roman). 11. éd. Paris, 1917.
43565.7.100 Dabadie, Jean. Les dieux du foyer. Paris, 1959.
43565.8.102 Dabit, E. Journal intime, 1928-1936. 2. ed. Paris, 1939.
43565.17.30 Dadelsen, Jean Paul de. Jonas. Paris, 1962.
43565.17.70 Dadelsen, Jean Paul de. Tonah: selected poems. London, 1967.
43565.33.100 Dagneaux, P. Terrain vogue. Paris, 1957.
43565.41.65 Daix, Pierre. Réflexions sur la méthode de Roger Martin du Gard. Paris, 1957.
43565.41.100 Daix, Pierre. Un tueur roman. Paris, 1954.
43565.41.110 Daix, Pierre. La dernière forteresse. Paris, 1954.
43565.41.120 Daix, Pierre. Les embarras de Paris. Paris, 1956.
43565.41.130 Daix, Pierre. L'accident. Paris, 1965.
43565.41.140 Daix, Pierre. La rivière profonde. Paris, 1959.
43565.41.2100 Dainville, Blanche. Au fil des jours. Paris, 1928?
43565.50.100 Dalize, René (pseud.). Au Zanzi des coeurs. Paris, 1931.
43565.53.100 Dambacourt, Georges. Les vespérales. Paris, 1961.
43565.53.1100 Damase, Jean. La comédie héroique. Paris, 1941.
43565.58.100 Danan, Alexis. Graffiti; poèmes. Blainville-sur-Mer, 1965.
43565.60.100 Daniel-Rops, Henry. Notre inquietude, essais. 3. ed. Paris, 1927.
43565.60.110 Daniel-Rops, Henry. La maladie des sentiments. Paris, 1938. 2v.
43565.60.120 Daniel-Rops, Henry. Mort, où est ta victoire? Roman. Paris, 1934.
43565.60.130 Daniel-Rops, Henry. L'ame obscure. Paris, 1938.
43565.60.145 Daniel-Rops, Henry. L'épee de feu; roman. Paris, 1940.
43565.60.150 Daniel-Rops, Henry. Where angels pass. London, 1950.
43565.60.160 Daniel-Rops, Henry. Nocturnes. Paris, 1956.
43565.60.170 Daniel-Rops, Henry. Quêtes de Dieu. Paris, 1946.
43565.60.700 Daniel-Rops, Henry. Death, where is the victory? London, 1946.
43565.60.800 Dournes, P. Daniel-Rops. Paris, 1949.
43565.60.805 Simon, Pierre Henri. Discours de remerciements et de reception à l'académie française...(Dainel-Rops). Paris, 1968.
43565.60.810 Lobet, Marcel. À la rencontre de Daniel-Rops. n.p., 1946.
43565.60.1100 Daninos, Pierre. Les carnets du Major W. Marmaduke Thompson. Paris, 1954.
43565.60.1110A Daninos, Pierre. The notebooks of Major Thompson. 1st American ed. N.Y., 1955.
43565.60.1110B Daninos, Pierre. The notebooks of Major Thompson. 1st American ed. N.Y., 1955.
43565.60.1120 Daninos, Pierre. The secret of Major Thompson. N.Y., 1957.
43565.60.1130 Daninos, Pierre. Un certain Monsieur Blot. Paris, 1960.
43565.60.1140 Daninos, Pierre. Le jacassin. Paris, 1962.
43565.60.1141 Daninos, Pierre. Le jacassin. Lausanne, 1968.
43565.60.1150 Daninos, Pierre. Sonia, ou Le dictionnaire dse maux coulants. Paris, 1963.
43565.60.1160 Daninos, Pierre. Snobissimo ou Le désir de paraître. Paris, 1964.
43565.60.1170 Daninos, Pierre. Daninoscope. Paris, 1963.
43565.60.1180 Daninos, Pierre. Les carnets du bon Dieu. Paris, 1958.
43565.60.1190 Daninos, Pierre. Le secret du Major Thompson. Paris, 1956.
43565.60.1200 Daninos, Pierre. Passeport pour la nuit; ou, Le roi-sommeil. Paris, 1956.
43565.60.1210 Daninos, Pierre. Ludovic Morateur, ou, Le plus que parfait. Paris, 1970.
43565.60.1705 Daninos, Pierre. Sonia, je t'adore. N.Y., 1959.
43565.60.1710 Daninos, Pierre. A certain Monsieur Blot. N.Y., 1962.
43565.60.2100 Danilov, Joel. Les ondes du silence. Paris, 1958.
43565.61.100 Danoën, Émile. Le conseiller hippique. 4e ed. Paris, 1958.
43565.61.1100 Dansart, Olivier. Mouvements, poèmes. Paris, 1955.
43565.74.100 Dard, Michel. Les années profondes, roman. Paris, 1968.
43565.76.100 Dariel, Jean-Loup. Les cahiers d'Olivier. Paris, 1955.
43565.76.700 Dariel, Jean Loup. Oliver kept a diary. London, 1956.
43565.76.2100 Darmangeat, Pierre. Le temps de le Raison Ardente. Paris, 1957.
43565.76.2110 Darmangeat, Pierre. Je crois en l'homme. Paris, 1963.
43565.77.100 Darribehaude, Jacques. Semelles de vent. Paris, 1959.
43565.77.1100 Dartois, Yves. La mosaïque de Balsams, roman. Paris, 1967.
43565.81.100 Dasnoy, Albert. La longueur de temps. Bruxelles, 1968.
43565.88.100 Datz, Philippe P. Jours fériés. Paris, 1923.
43565.89.61 Daumal, René. Lettres à ses amis. Paris, 1958.
43565.89.100 Daumal, René. Le mont analogue. 2. éd. Paris? 1952.
43565.89.105 Daumal, René. Essais et notes. v.1- Paris, 1953-
43565.89.110 Daumal, René. Poésie noire, poésie blanche; poèmes. Paris, 1954.
43565.89.115 Daumal, René. Petit théâtre de René Daumal. Paris, 1957.
43565.89.120 Daumal, René. La grande beuverie. Paris, 1954.
43565.89.130 Daumal, René. Tu t'es toujours trompé. Paris, 1970.
43565.89.140 Daumal, René. Le Lyon rouge. Paris, 196-?
43565.89.700 Daumal, René. Mount Analogues. London, 1959.
43565.89.1100 Dauberoille, H. L'eternel paradoxe. Paris, 1956.
43565.89.5100 Dauguet, Marie. Par l'amour. Paris, 1904.
43565.89.6100 Davzat, Albert. Poèmes de la douleur et du souvenir. Paris, 1936.
43565.89.7100 Dauphin, Marcel. Boisrond Tonnerre. Port-au-Prince, 1954.
43565.89.7110 Dauphin, Marcel. Pierre Sully. Port-au-Prince, 1960.
43565.90.110 Davignon, Henri. Un penitent de Furnes. Paris, 1950.
43565.90.120 Davignon, Henri. Souvenirs d'un écrivain belge, 1879-1945. Paris, 1954.
43565.90.130 Davignon, Henri. De la Princesse de Clères à Thérèse Desqueyroux. Bruxelles, 1963.
43565.90.800 Inial, M.F. Henri Davignon. Washington, 1948.
43565.90.1100 Davallon, A. Le train par la tête. Paris, 1956.
43565.90.3100 David, Jean. Les survivants. Paris, 1958.
43565.90.3110 David, Jean. Assassin. Paris, 1965.
43565.90.4100 David, Marie Laure. L'echappée. Paris, 1967.
43565.90.5100 Daveau, René Raoul. Le mendiant d'eau pure. Paris, 1955.
43565.91.100 Davet, Michel. Le prince qui m'aimait. Paris, 1930.
43565.91.110 Davet, Michel. Une lampe sur la marche. Paris, 1932.
43565.91.120 Davet, Michel. Éclatantes ténères. Paris, 1960.
43565.91.130 Davet, Michel. Biche et le roi de Naples. Paris, 1960.
43565.91.1100 Davy, Marie Magdeleine. Le berger du soleil. Paris, 1965.
43565.91.1110 Davy, Marie Magdeleine. La terre face au soleil. Neuchâtel, 1965.
43565.92.100 David, A. Le roman du plaisir. Paris, 1923.
43565.92.105 David, A. Amour charnel de la patrie. N.Y., 1944.

43511 - 43873 Individual authors, etc. - 1900- - Known authors (363 scheme plus 10) - cont.

43565.92.7000 Davray, Jean. L'eau trouble. Paris, 1939.
43565.92.7100 Davray, Jean. Les complaintes. Paris, 1945.
43565.92.7110 Davray, Jean. Théâtre sans bornes. Paris, 1958.
43565.92.7120 Davray, Jean. Le bruit de la vie. Paris, 1959. 4v.
43565.92.7130 Davray, Jean. La fin du premier acte. Paris, 1946.
43565.92.7140 Davray, Jean. Fraicheur; roman. Paris, 1936.
43565.92.7150 Davray, Jean. Le désert, roman. Paris, 1968.
43565.93.100 Darnal, J.C. Ce soir on joue guignol. Paris, 1956.
43565.97.100 Dax, Claire. Au long du jour. Paris, 1955.
43565.98.100 Day, G. Rapsodies en mauve. Paris, 1927.
43566.2.30 Deberly, Henri. L'ennemi des siens. Paris, 1925.
43566.2.35 Deberly, Henri. Supplice de Phédre. Paris, 1926.
43566.2.36 Deberly, Henri. Le supplice de Phédre. 13e éd. Paris, 1926.
43566.2.37 Deberly, Henri. Le supplice de Phédre. 60. éd. Paris, 1926.
43566.2.38 Deberly, Henri. Le supplice de Phédre. 90. éd. Paris, 1926.
43566.3.30 Delaquys, Georges. Le beau couchant. Paris, 1913.
43566.3.40 Delaquys, Georges. Le marchand de lunettes. Paris, 1927.
43566.3.50 Delaquys, Georges. Saint Barbe-Bleue. pt. 1-2. Paris, 1936.
43566.3.60 Delaquys, Georges. La grande mademoiselle. Paris, 1939.
43566.4.30 Delvert, Charles Laurent. Quelques héros. Paris, 1918.
43566.5.30 Détanger, Émile. Le chemin de la victoire. Paris, n.d.
43566.5.31 Détanger, Émile. Hiên le maboul. 4e éd. Paris, 1915.
43566.5.35 Détanger, Émile. La barque annamite. Paris, 1910.
43566.6.30 Delly, M. (pseud.). Le mystère de Ker-Even. Paris, 1918.
43566.6.35 Delly, M. (pseud.). La petite chanoinesse. Paris, 1919.
43566.6.40 Delly, M. (pseud.). Une misère dorée, roman. Paris, 1929.
43566.6.45 Delly, M. (pseud.). Esclave...ou reine? Paris, 1943.
43566.6.50 Delly, M. (pseud.). Le maître de silence. Paris, 1930-32. 2v.
43566.6.2100 Debotte, Jacqueline. Plus long temps que l'oubli. Rodez, 1966.
43566.6.3021 Debray, Régis. La frontière. Suivi d'un jeune homme à la page. Paris, 1967.
43566.6.3700 Debray, Régis. The frontier and A with-it young man. London, 1968.
43566.7.30 Deval, Jacques. Une faible femme. Paris, 1920.
43566.7.35 Deval, Jacques. Le bien-aimé; pièce. Paris, 1924.
43566.7.40 Deval, Jacques. La rose de septembre. Paris, 1926.
43566.7.45 Deval, Jacques. Ventöse. Paris, 1928.
43566.7.50 Deval, Jacques. Une tant belle fille. Paris, 1929.
43566.7.55 Deval, Jacques. Etienne; pièce en trois actes. Paris, 1930.
43566.7.60 Deval, Jacques. Signor Bracoli. Paris, 1932.
43566.7.65 Deval, Jacques. Prière pour les vivants. Paris, 1934.
43566.8.100 Debille, Léon. La légende du roi d'un jour. Paris, 1927.
43566.9.100 Debout, J. Les voix de Jeanne d'Arc. Paris, 1920.
43566.9.1100 Deblue, Henri. L'alter ego, pièce en trois actes. Lausanne, 1967.
43566.10.100 Debû-Bredel, Jacques. Sous la cendre. Paris, 1951.
43566.13.100 Declercq, A. L'envers vaut l'endroit. Paris, 1933.
43566.14.100 Decour, Jacques. Comme je vous en donne l'exemple. Paris, 1945.
43566.17.100 Dédéyan, Christian. Quatuor pour le temps des ténèbres. Tournai, 1957.
43566.17.1100 Dedet, Christian. Le plus grand des taureaux. Paris, 1960.
43566.17.2100 Dedet, Jean Marie. Polymnie prostituée. Paris, 1963.
43566.27.100 Deffes, Louis. Epevas poétiques et dramatiques. 1. ser. 1. éd. Tarbes, 1920.
43566.28.100 Daffoux, L. Pipe-en-Boise, témoin de la commune. Paris, 1932.
43566.29.100 Defosse, Marcel. Les masques du destin. Paris, 1955.
43566.29.110 Defosse, Marcel. Le juge de Malte. Bruxelles, 1960.
43566.29.1100 Defos, Bertrand. Simon le superbe. 7. éd. Paris, 1957.
43566.31.1100 Dega, Jean Pierre. Muguet du bois joli; poème romantique. Paris, 1957.
43566.32.700 Degée, Olivier. Jean Clarambaux; a novel by Jean Tousseul (pseud.). Philadelphia, 1939.
43566.32.800 Denuit, Désiré. Jean Tousseul. Bruxelles, 1945.
43566.34.100 Degracia. Mariage mixte. Paris, 1968.
43566.35.100 Degny, Adeleine. Les condamnés. Paris, 1966.
43566.35.1021 Deguy, Michel. Oui dire. Paris, 1966.
43566.35.1100 Deguy, Michel. Fragment du cadastre. Paris, 1960.
43566.35.1110 Deguy, Michel. Figurations; poèmes, propositions, études. Paris, 1969.
43566.35.2100 Deguillaume, Jacques. Hippolyte le Grand. Rodez, 1965.
43566.36.110 Deharme, Lise. Cette année-la. 3e éd. Paris, 1945.
43566.36.120 Deharme, Lise. Le poids d'un oiseau. Paris, 1955.
43566.36.130 Deharme, Lise. Laissez-moi tranquille. Paris, 1959.
43566.36.140 Deharme, Lise. Le années perdues. Paris, 1961.
43566.42.100 Dejean, Georges. La confession d'un légionnaire. Paris, 1919.
43566.42.790 Dejean, Georges. Las garras del maligno. México, 1959.
43566.42.1100 Dejacques, Claude. A toi l'angoisse, à moi la rage, mai 68, les fresques de Nanterre. Paris, 1968.
43566.42.2100 Déjean, Jean Luc. La feuille à l'envers. Paris, 1970.
43566.43.42 Dekobra, Maurice. La perruche bleue; journal d'une courtisane sous la terreur nazie. N.Y., 1945.
43566.43.100 Dekobra, Maurice. Sammy, volontaire américain. Paris, 1918.
43566.43.110 Dekobra, Maurice. Venus on wheels. N.Y., 1930.
43566.43.115 Dekobra, Maurice. A Paris, tous les deux. Journal d'un Yankee entre deux guerres. N.Y., 1945.
43566.43.120 Dekobra, Maurice. Le geste de Phryné; amours exotiques. 43. éd. Paris, 1930.
43566.43.140 Dekobra, Maurice. La volupté éclairant le monde, roman. Paris, 1932.
43566.43.150 Dekobra, Maurice. Mon coeur au ralenti. Paris, 1924.
43566.43.160 Dekobra, Maurice. Sérénade au bourreau. Paris, 1928.
43566.43.178 Dekobra, Maurice. Emigrés de luxe, roman. 8e éd. N.Y., 1941.
43566.43.180 Dekobra, Maurice. Le roman d'un lâche; roman. N.Y., 1942.
43566.43.190 Dekobra, Maurice. La madone à Hollywood. N.Y., 1943.
43566.43.200 Dekobra, Maurice. Lune de miel à Shanghaï. N.Y., 1943.
43566.43.210 Dekobra, Maurice. Les lèvres que mentent. Montréal, 1944.
X Cg 43566.43.705 Dekobra, Maurice. Bedroom eyes. N.Y., 1935.
43566.43.715 Dekobra, Maurice. Wings of desire. N.Y., 1925.
43566.43.720 Dekobra, Maurice. The sphinx has spoken. N.Y., 1930.
43566.43.730 Dekobra, Maurice. Paradise in Montparnasse. N.Y., 1946.
43566.43.735 Dekobra, Maurice. The golden-eyed Venus. London, 1963.
43566.45.100 Delacour, André. Les oasis. Paris, 1907.
43566.45.110 Delacour, André. Le rayonnement. Paris, 1910.

43511 - 43873 Individual authors, etc. - 1900- - Known authors (363 scheme plus 10) - cont.

43566.45.120 Delacour, André. Le voyage à l'étoile. Paris, 1928.
43566.45.1100 Delaet, Jean. La petit herboriste. Bruxelles, 1968.
43566.46.100 Delance, Georges. Bluff; comédie en trois actes. Paris, 1932.
43566.46.1100 Delanglade, Frédéric. A Lys et 12. Paris, 1963.
43566.47.100 Delaporte, M. Sonnets. Paris, 1928.
43566.47.5100 Delaquys, Georges. La naissance de Tristan. Paris, 1937.
43566.47.6100 Delarozière, Marie Françoise. Désert, ma citadelle. Paris, 1969.
43566.47.7100 Delamotte, Jean Paul. Sans hâte, cette nuit. Paris, 1967.
43566.47.7110 Delamotte, Jean Paul. La communauté. Paris, 1962.
43566.48.100 Delarue-Mardrus, Lucie. Graine au vent. Paris, 1925.
43566.48.110 Delarue-Mardrus, Lucie. Amaint; roman. pt.1-3. Paris, 1929.
43566.48.120 Delarue-Mardrus, Lucie. Le batard; vie de Guillaume le conquerant. Paris, 1931.
43566.48.130 Delarue-Mardrus, Lucie. Hortensia dégénéré, roman. Paris, 1929.
43566.48.140 Delarue-Mardrus, Lucie. L'amour attend. v. 1-3. Paris, 1936.
43566.48.150 Delarue-Mardrus, Lucie. Ferveur. Paris, 1902.
43566.48.160 Delarue-Mardrus, Lucie. La figure de proue. Paris, 1908.
43566.48.170 Delarue-Mardrus, Lucie. L'enfant au coq. Paris, 1934.
43566.48.180 Delarue-Mardrus, Lucie. Les sept douleurs d'octobre. Paris, 1930.
43566.48.190 Delarue-Mardrus, Lucie. Fleurette. pt. 1-3. Paris, 1938.
43566.48.200 Delarue-Mardrus, Lucie. Le roi des reflets. Paris, 1945.
43566.48.210 Delarue-Mardrus, Lucie. L'ex-voto. Paris, 1922.
43566.48.220 Delarue-Mardrus, Lucie. Marie, fille-mère; roman. Paris, 1923.
43566.48.230 Delarue-Mardrus, Lucie. La mère et le fils. Paris, 1924.
43566.48.400 Delarue-Mardrus, Lucie. Mes mémoires. Paris, 1938.
43566.48.800 Villers, Emilie de. Lucie Delarue-Mardrus. Paris, 1923.
43566.48.1100 Delafosse, B. Le songe du poète. Paris, 1946.
43566.48.2100 Delarge, Léon. Reflets d'une âme. Liège, 1953.
43566.48.3100 Delcarte, Françoise. Sables. Paris, 1969.
43566.48.4021 Delbousquet, Germaine Emmanuel. Coeur; poèmes. Rodez, 1965.
43566.48.4800 Delbousquet, Germaine Emmanuel. Germaine Emmanuel Delbousquet, 1874-1909. Agen, 1959.
43566.48.5100 Delcassan, R. Fables pour illustrer les temps actuels. Paris, 1935.
43566.48.6100 Del Castillo, Michel. Tanguy. Paris, 1957.
43566.48.6110 Del Castillo, Michel. Le colleur d'offiches. Paris, 1958.
43566.48.6120 Del Castillo, Michel. La guitarra. Barcelona, 1960.
43566.48.6130 Del Castillo, Michel. Les aveux interdits. Paris, 1965. 2v.
43566.48.6700 Del Castillo, Michel. Child of our time. 1st American ed. N.Y., 1958.
43566.48.6710 Del Castillo, Michel. The guitar. London, 1959.
43566.48.6715 Del Castillo, Michel. Through the hoop. N.Y., 1963.
43566.48.6720 Del Castillo, Michel. The disinherited. N.Y., 1960.
43566.48.7100 Del Corte, Daniela. Des mystères du rosaire. Fontenay-le-Comte, 1959.
43566.48.7110 Del Corte, Daniela. Vers les cimes. v.1-4. Paris, 1957- 3v.
43566.48.8100 Delamare, G. Vingt années sans guerre, 1919-1939. Paris, 1956.
43566.48.9100 Delahaye, Gilbert. Les racines du coeurs. Tournai, 1961.
43566.48.9110 Delahaye, Gilbert. Les enfants de minuit. Tournai, 1958.
43566.49.100 Delétang-Tardif, Y. Eclats; poèmes. Paris, 1929.
43566.49.110 Delétang-Tardif, Y. La nuit des temps. Paris, 1951.
43566.49.2100 Del Dongo, Fabrice. Amitiés, mes belles etoiles! Monte-Carlo, 1949.
43566.49.3100 Delève, Ernst. Pura seta. Bruxelles, 1959.
43566.49.3110 Delève, Ernst. Je vous salue chéries. Bruxelles, 1961.
43566.49.7100 Delhaye de Marnyhac, Thérèse. La maison sans ame. Paris, 1957.
43566.49.7110 Delhaye de Marnyhac, Thérèse. Savoir aimer. Paris, 1958.
43566.50.100 Delétang, Marie. Nocturnales. Paris, 1929.
43566.50.1100 Dell'Aid. Présence. Paris, 1956.
43566.50.2100 Debisle, Gérard. Rhapsodie caraïbe. Paris, 1960.
43566.50.3100 Delly, M. (pseud.). Entre deux âmes. Paris, 1930.
43566.50.4100 Della Faille, Pierre. Autopsie de sodome. Paris, 1964.
43566.50.4112 Della Faille, Pierre. L'homme inhabitable. 2. éd. Paris, 1961.
43566.50.4120 Della Faille, Pierre. Le grand alléluia. Millau, 1966.
43566.50.4130 Della Faille, Pierre. Mise à feu, 04 le Jas du Revest Saint-Martin. Morel, 1968.
43566.50.5100 Dellac, Louis. La princesse qui ne sourit plus. Paris, 1918.
43566.50.6100 Delmelle, Joseph. Vingt ans. Bruxelles, 1941.
43566.51.100 Delorme, Hugues. Zoo (vers). Paris, 1930.
43566.51.300 Delteil, Joseph. Choléra par Joseph Delteil. Paris, 1923.
43566.51.302 Delteil, Joseph. Les cinq sens, roman. Paris, 1924.
43566.51.310 Delteil, Joseph. Don Juan. Paris, 1930.
43566.51.320 Delteil, Joseph. The Poilus. N.Y., 1927.
43566.51.380 Choisy, Maryse. Delteil tout nu. Paris, 1930.
43566.51.390 Delteil, Joseph. De J.J. Rousseau à Mistral. Paris, 1928.
43566.51.2100 Delvaille, A. Charlas intimas de "Trebla". San José, 1945.
43566.51.3100 Delpy, Jacqueline. La legende de l'homme. Paris, 1958.
43566.51.5100 Delperier, Michelle. Les enfants crucifiés. Paris, 1959.
43566.51.6100 Delvolvé, Laure. Quand les carnassiers n'y sont pas; récit. Paris, 1960.
43566.52.100 Demaison, André. Le livre des bêtes qu'on appelle sauvages. Paris, 1929.
43566.52.110 Demaison, André. Les hommes sur le wharf. Paris, 1933.
43566.52.120 Demaison, André. La comédie animale. 16e éd. Paris, 1930.
43566.52.130 Demaison, André. Trois histoires de Bêtes. Avignon, 1941.
43566.52.140 Demaison, André. Le pacha de Tombouctou. Paris, 1927.
43566.52.160 Demaison, André. Les lions du Kalahari. Paris, 1956.
43566.52.170 Demaison, André. L'étoile de Dakar. Paris, 1963.
43566.52.1100 Delvaille, Bernard. Enfance, mon amour. Rodez, 1957.
43566.53.100 Demasy, Paul. Jésus de Nazareth. Paris, 1924.
43566.53.110 Demasy, Paul. La cavalière Elsa. Paris, 1925.
43566.53.120 Demasy, Paul. Dalilah. Paris, 1926.
43566.53.130 Demasy, Paul. La tragédie d'Alexandre. Paris, 1931.
43566.53.2100 Demange, Charles. Lettres d'italie. Paris, 1913.
43566.53.3100 Demdy, Henri. L'espoir ulcéré. Rodez, 1966.
43566.53.6100 Demêtre, Marie E. Histoire simples de gens simples pour gens simples. Paris, 1945.
43566.54.107 Demians d'Archimbaud, M. À travers la tourmente. Une vie intime. Paris, 1917.
43566.54.110 Demians d'Archimbaud, M. La vie continue. Paris, 1921.

43511 - 43873 Individual authors, etc. - 1900- - Known authors (363 scheme plus 10) - cont.

	43566.54.1100	Demez, Marie Antoinette. L'Adieu d'une larme, ou L'amour scaphandrire. Bruxelles, 1964.
	43566.54.2100	Demélier, Jean. Gens de la rue. Paris, 1971.
	43566.56.100	Demonts, L. Superbea vitae. Paris, 1935.
	43566.57.100	Demorest, J.J. Les passionnés ont vécu. Paris, 1956.
	43566.58.100	Dénes, Tibor. Oiseaux et mortels. Genève, 1962.
	43566.59.100	Deneveure, J. The last supper of nations. N.Y., 1945.
	43566.60.1100	Denis, Henri Pierre. Quelques nouvelles de Jessica. Paris, 1969.
	43566.62.100	Déon, Michel. Les trompeuses espérances. Paris, 1956.
	43566.62.105	Déon, Michel. Tout l'amour du monde. Paris, 1955-
	43566.62.110A	Déon, Michel. Les gens de la nuit; roman. Paris, 1958.
	43566.62.110B	Déon, Michel. Les gens de la nuit; roman. Paris, 1958.
	43566.62.115	Déon, Michel. La carotte et le bâton. Paris, 1960.
	43566.62.120	Déon, Michel. Mégalonose, supplément aux "voyages de Gulliver". Paris, 1967.
	43566.62.125	Déon, Michel. Un parfum de jasmin. Paris, 1967.
	43566.62.5100	Denuzière, Maurice. Les trois dés. Paris, 1959.
	43566.62.5110	Denuzière, Maurice. Une tombe en Toscane. Paris, 1960.
	43566.71.100	Deprat, Jacques. Le capitaine du Fai-Tsi-Long. Paris, 1935.
	43566.71.110	Deprat, Jacques. Le conquérant, roman, présenté par Claude Farrère. Paris, 1925.
	43566.75.100	Derème, Tristan. Le ballet des muses. Paris, 1928.
	43566.75.110	Derème, Tristan. Le zodiaque ou Les étoiles sur Paris. Paris, 1927.
	43566.75.120	Derème, Tristan. La verdure dorée. 11. éd. Paris, 1925.
	43566.75.130	Derème, Tristan. Le quatorze juillet, ou Petit art de rimer. Paris, 192-.
	43566.75.140	Derème, Tristan. La flûte fleurie. Paris, 1913.
	43566.75.150	Derème, Tristan. Patachou, petit garçon. 28. ed. Paris, 1929.
	43566.75.160	Derème, Tristan. Le violon des muses. 5e ed. Paris, 1935.
	43566.75.161	Derème, Tristan. Le violon des muses. Paris, 1935.
	43566.75.170	Derème, Tristan. L'escargot bleu. Paris, 1936.
	43566.75.180	Derème, Tristan. Le poème des griffons. 7. éd. Paris, 1938.
	43566.75.190	Derème, Tristan. Le paisson rouge. 4. ed. Paris, 1934.
	43566.75.200	Derème, Tristan. La bride et le cheval. Tarbes, 1925.
	43566.75.210	Derème, Tristan. L'étoile de poche. Maestricht, 1929.
	43566.75.220	Derème, Tristan. L'enfant perdu, poème. Paris, 1928.
	43566.75.230	Derème, Tristan. Les compliments en vers de Patachou. Paris, 1931.
	43566.75.240	Derème, Tristan. Le livre de Clymène; élégies. Paris, 1927.
	43566.75.250	Derème, Tristan. Poèmes des Colombes. Paris, 1929.
	43566.75.260	Derème, Tristan. Toulouse. Paris, 1927.
	43566.75.800	Ruet, Noël. Derèmiana, ou Jeux, impromptus et divertissements de Tristan Derème. Seraing, 1925.
	43566.75.1100	Dereux, Philippe. Petit traité des épluchures. Paris, 1966.
	43566.76.100	Derennes, Charles. Le noces sur la banquise. Paris, 1928.
	43566.76.110	Derennes, Charles. La matinée du faune, 1906-1926. Paris, 1926.
	43566.76.125	Derennes, Charles. Premières poésies. Paris, 1925. 2v.
	43566.76.130	Derennes, Charles. La fontaine jouvence. Paris, 1923.
	43566.76.3100	Dermèze, Yves. Le mess ager du roi Henri. Paris, 1955.
	43566.76.4100	Deriex, Suzanne. L'enfant et la mort. Roman. Lausanne, 1968.
	43566.77.100	Desaulnier, G. Les lois qui chantent. Montreal, 1930.
	43566.77.2100	Des Baux, C. Les bacchantes; tragédie. Alexandrie, 1944.
	43566.77.3100	Deroisin, Sophie. Les jardins intérieurs; essai. Bruxelles, 1965.
	43566.78.100	Lind, M. Un parnassien universitaire...Emmanuel Des Essarts. Thèse. Paris, 1928.
	43566.78.110	Des Essart, Emmanuel. Poesies. Parisiennes. Paris, 1862.
	43566.78.1100	Des Forêts, Louis R. La chambre des enfants. Paris, 1960.
	43566.78.1110	Des Forêts, Louis R. Le bavard. Paris, 1963.
	43566.78.1700	Des Forêts, Louis R. The children's room. London, 1963.
	43566.79.100	Des Gachons, J. "Huit heures" de M. Colbert. Paris, 1925.
	43566.79.110	Des Gachons, J. Nicolas Poussin: Triptyque. Paris, 1925.
	43566.79.115	Des Gachons, J. M. de Buffon sur les terrasses. Paris, 1927.
	43566.79.130	Des Gachons, J. La grande fable de J. de la Fontaine. Paris, 1936.
	43566.79.2100	Descarmes, Alain. Histoire satirique de la femme à travers les âges. LeMans, 1965?
	43566.79.3100	Descrières, Yves. La glane en gerbe; rimailleries. Paris, 1959.
	43566.80.100	Des Cars, Guy. L'officier sans nom. Cannes, 1941.
	43566.80.110	Des Cars, Guy. La chateau de la juive. Paris, 1958.
	43566.80.120	Des Cars, Guy. De cape et de plume. Paris, 1965.
	43566.80.1100	Deslandes, André. l'escalier. Paris, 1958.
	43566.80.1110	Deslandes, André. Le hasard abolit le hasard. Paris, 1960.
	43566.80.2100	Deslandes, Pierre. Harmonies. Lausanne, 1929.
	43566.81.100	Desjardins, J. Iokonoshi, conte japonais. Paris, 1918.
	43566.81.1100	Des Ligneris, F. Fort Frédérick, roman. Paris, 1957.
	43566.81.1110	Des Ligneris, F. Psyché 58. Paris, 1958.
	43566.81.1120	Des Ligneris, F. Bijoux, roman. Paris, 1960.
	43566.81.2100	Desmarest, M.A. Douce-amère. Paris, 1957.
	43566.81.2110	Desmarest, M.A. Dis moi qui tu aimes. Paris, 1958.
	43566.81.2120	Desmarest, M.A. Le fils Jan. Paris, 1957.
	43566.81.2130	Desmarest, M.A. La maison des Movettes. Paris, 1958.
	43566.81.2140	Desmarest, M.A. A la recherche de l'amour. Paris, 1960.
	43566.81.2150	Desmarest, M.A. Les remparts de Saint-Paul. Paris, 1959.
	43566.81.4100	Desnos, Robert. Choix de poèmes. Paris, 1946.
	43566.81.4110	Desnos, Robert. Domaine public. Paris, 1953.
	43566.81.4112	Desnos, Robert. Domaine public. Paris, 1962.
	43566.81.4120	Desnos, Robert. De l'érotisme. Paris, 1953?
	43566.81.4130	Desnos, Robert. Chantefables et Chantefleurs. Paris, 1955.
	43566.81.4140	Desnos, Robert. Corps et biens. Paris, 1930.
	43566.81.4142	Desnos, Robert. Corps et biens. Paris, 1968.
	43566.81.4150	Desnos, Robert. Colixto, suivi de Coutrée. Paris, 1962.
	43566.81.4160	Desnos, Robert. La liberté ou l'amour! Paris, 1962.
	43566.81.4170	Desnos, Robert. Fortunes. Paris, 1969.
	43566.81.4800	Buchole, Rosa. L'évolution poétique de Robert T. Desnos. Bruxelles, 1956.
	43566.81.5110	Desnos, Youki. Les confidences des Youki. Paris, 1957.
	43566.81.6100	Desnos, L. La fraîche. Paris, 1958.
	43566.81.7100	Desmeuzes, Jean. Les marches de la brume. Paris, 1955.
	43566.81.7110	Desmeuzes, Jean. Les roses vertes. Paris, 1956.
	43566.81.7120	Desmeuzes, Jean. La mort dans l'ame, poèmes. Paris, 1961.
	43566.82.100	Des Rieux, L. Héculie. Paris, 1906.

43511 - 43873 Individual authors, etc. - 1900- - Known authors (363 scheme plus 10) - cont.

	43566.82.1100	Desportes, Georges. Sous l'oeil fixe du soleil, poèmes masqués. Paris, 1961.
	43566.82.3100	Detouches, C. La passion de Marie d'Agoult. Paris, 1959.
	43566.82.3800	Hayman, David. Louis-Ferdinand Céline. N.Y., 1965.
	43566.82.4110	Desternes, J. Clarière de la vie. 3. éd. Paris, 1946.
	43566.82.7011	Destouches, Louis Ferdinand. Oeuvres de Louis Ferdinand Céline. Paris, 1966- 5v.
	43566.82.7100	Destouches, Louis Ferdinand. Mort à crédit. Paris, 1936.
	43566.82.7110	Destouches, Louis Ferdinand. Voyage au tout de la nuit; roman. Paris, 1934.
X Cg	43566.82.7110	Destouches, Louis Ferdinand. Voyage au tout de la nuit; roman. Paris, 1934.
	43566.82.7112	Destouches, Louis Ferdinand. Voyage au tout de la nuit. 3. éd. Paris, 1952.
	43566.82.7115	Destouches, Louis Ferdinand. Nord, roman. Paris, 1960.
	43566.82.7125	Destouches, Louis Ferdinand. Scandale aux Abysses. Paris, 1950.
Htn	43566.82.7130*	Destouches, Louis Ferdinand. L'école des cadavres. 48e éd. Paris, 1938.
	43566.82.7140	Destouches, Louis Ferdinand. Guignol's band; roman. Paris? 1944.
	43566.82.7145	Destouches, Louis Pierre. Guignol's band; roman. Paris, 1944- 2v.
	43566.82.7150	Destouches, Louis Pierre. Les beaux draps. Paris, 1941.
	43566.82.7160	Destouches, Louis Ferdinand. Casse-pipe. Paris, 1949.
	43566.82.7170	Destouches, Louis Ferdinand. Entretiens avec le professeur Y. Paris, 1955.
	43566.82.7180	Destouches, Louis Ferdinand. D'un château à l'autre. Paris, 1957.
	43566.82.7190	Destouches, Louis Ferdinand. Voyage au bout de la nuit. Paris, 1962.
	43566.82.7200	Destouches, Louis Ferdinand. Balleto sans musique. Paris, 1959.
	43566.82.7705	Destouches, Louis Ferdinand. Death on the installment plan. Paris, 1938.
	43566.82.7707A	Destouches, Louis Ferdinand. Death on the installment plan. N.Y.? 1947.
	43566.82.7707B	Destouches, Louis Ferdinand. Death on the installment plan. N.Y.? 1947.
	43566.82.7712	Destouches, Louis Ferdinand. Journey to the end of the night. N.Y., 1949?
	43566.82.7714A	Destouches, Louis Ferdinand. Journey to the end of the night. Boston, 1934.
	43566.82.7714B	Destouches, Louis Ferdinand. Journey to the end of the night. Boston, 1934.
	43566.82.7715A	Destouches, Louis Ferdinand. Journey to the end of the night. N.Y., 1960.
	43566.82.7715B	Destouches, Louis Ferdinand. Journey to the end of the night. N.Y., 1960.
	43566.82.7720	Destouches, Louis Ferdinand. Mea culpa and the life works of Semmelweis. Boston, 1937.
	43566.82.7720.5	Destouches, Louis Ferdinand. Mea culpa...Semmelweis. 20. éd. Paris, 1957.
	43566.82.7725	Destouches, Louis Ferdinand. Vive l'amnistie monsieur. Liège, 1963.
	43566.82.7730	Destouches, Louis Ferdinand. L'église. Paris, 1933.
	43566.82.7740	Destouches, Louis Ferdinand. Guignol's band. Hartford, Conn., 1954.
	43566.82.7745	Destouches, Louis Ferdinand. Castle to castle. N.Y., 1968.
	43566.82.7750	Haurez, M. Céline. Paris, 1961.
	43566.82.7755	Destouches, Louis Ferdinand. Rigodon par Louis-Ferdinand Céline. Paris, 1969.
	43566.82.7760	Destouches, Louis Ferdinand. North. N.Y., 1972.
	43566.82.7800	Hindus, M. Crippled giant. N.Y., 1950.
	43566.82.7810	Poulet, R. Entretiens familiers avec Louis Ferdinand Céline. Paris, 1958.
	43566.82.7815	Debrie, D. Louis-Ferdinand Céline. Paris, 1961.
	43566.82.7820	Keminski, H.E. Céline en chemise brune. Paris, 1938.
	43566.82.7825	Vandromme, P. Louis-Ferdinand Céline. Paris, 1963.
	43566.82.7830	Roux, Dominiques de. La mort de Louis Ferdinand Céline; essai. Paris, 1966.
	43566.82.7835	Ostrovsky, Erika. Céline and his vision. N.Y., 1967.
	43566.82.7840	Denoël, Robert. Apologie de mort à crédit. Paris, 1936.
	43566.82.8100	Desse, G. Et sur cette pierre. Paris, 1960.
	43566.83.100	Des Vallières, Jean. Les hommes sans nom, roman. Paris, 1933.
	43566.83.110	Des Vallières, Jean. Le chevalier de la Camargue. Paris, 1956.
	43566.83.120	Des Vallières, Jean. Essais sur le théâtre. v. 1-2. Paris, 1923-25.
	43566.87.100	Delbrel, Jean-Émile. Gine. Paris, 1923.
	43566.89.61	Deubel, Léon. Lettres de Léon Deubel (1897-1912). Paris, 1930.
	43566.89.100A	Deubel, Léon. Oeuvres. Paris, 1929.
	43566.89.100B	Deubel, Léon. Oeuvres. Paris, 1929.
	43566.89.110	Deubel, Léon. Régner. Paris, 1913.
	43566.89.805	Maunty, G. Léon Deubel (1879-1913) sein Leben und sein Dichten. Inaug. Diss. Velbert, 1932.
	43566.90.100	Deval, Jacques. Marie galante, roman. Paris, 1931.
	43566.90.110	Deval, Jacques. Mademoiselle. Paris, 1932.
	43566.90.120	Deval, Jacques. Lundi huit heures. Paris, 1933.
	43566.90.130	Deval, Jacques. Tovaritch. Paris, 1934.
	43566.90.140	Deval, Jacques. L'âge de Juliette. Paris, 1935.
	43566.90.150	Deval, Jacques. Les voyageurs; roman. Paris, 1964.
	43566.90.1100	Devaré, U. Zariné. N.Y., 1954.
	43566.90.2100	Devilliers, C. Lieutenant Katia. Paris, 1962.
	43566.91.100	Devoncaux, Marie. Le jardin symbolique. Macon, 1910.
	43566.93.100	Devaulx, N. Le pressoir mystique. Neuchâtel, 1948.
	43566.93.700	Devaulx, N. The tailor's cake. London, 1946.
	43566.93.705	Devaulx, N. Sainte Barbegrise. 5. éd. Paris, 1952.
	43566.94.100	Devaux, P. La lanque verte, suivie des propos de l'affranchi. Paris, 1936.
	43567.25.100	Dheur, G. Vrai et usage de vrai. Paris, 1957.
	43567.79.100	Dhôtel, André. Bernard le paresseux. 5. ed. Paris, 1952.
	43567.79.110	Dhôtel, André. Le maître de pension. Paris, 1954.
	43567.79.120	Dhôtel, André. Mémoires de Sebastien. Paris, 1955.
	43567.79.130	Dhôtel, André. Le pays, ou L'on n'arrive jamais. Paris, 1955.
	43567.79.140	Dhôtel, André. La chronique fabuleuse. Paris, 1955.
	43567.79.150	Dhôtel, André. L'île aux oiseaux de fer. Paris, 1956.
	43567.79.160	Dhôtel, André. Faraway. N.Y., 1957.
	43567.79.170	Dhôtel, André. Le neveu de Pareucloud. Paris, 1960.
	43567.79.180	Dhôtel, André. Ma chère âme. Paris, 1961.
	43567.79.190	Dhôtel, André. La tribu Bécaille. Paris, 1963.
	43567.79.200	Dhôtel, André. Lumineux rentre chez lui. Paris, 1967.

43511 - 43873 Individual authors, etc. - 1900- - Known authors (363 scheme plus 10) - cont.

43567.79.210 Dhôtel, André. La maison du bout du monde. Paris, 1970.
43567.89.100 Dhumez, H. Ma cigalière. Cannes, 1940.
43568.4.100 Diamant-Berger, M. Baignoire "B"; pièce en deux actes. Paris, 1939.
43568.4.110 Diamant-Berger, M. Poèmes d'Everlor. Paris, 1951.
43568.6.100 Dib, Mohammed. Un été africain; roman. Paris, 1959.
43568.6.110 Dib, Mohammed. Ombre gardienne. Paris, 1963.
43568.6.120 Dib, Mohammed. Algérie. Paris, 1954-61. 3v.
43568.6.130 Dib, Mohammed. Le talisman, nouvelles. Paris, 1966.
43568.6.140 Dib, Mohammed. La danse du roi, roman. Paris, 1968.
43568.17.100 Didelot, R.F. Au soleil de la Brousse. Paris, 1946.
43568.17.110 Didelot, R.F. Dernier Malin. Paris, 1959.
43568.17.120 Didelot, R.F. L'insolite. Paris, 1959.
43568.23.100 Diego, C. Un homme sans l'occident. Paris, 1946.
43568.23.1100 Dieguez, M. de. Dieu est-il américain? Paris, 1957.
43568.24.700 Diesbach, Ghislain de. The toys of princes. N.Y., 1962.
43568.24.1100 Dieryck, Yves. Promenade en marge. Evreux, 1970.
43568.25.100 Dietrich, L. Le bonheur des tristes. Paris, 1962.
43568.65.100 Dion-Lévesques, Rosaire. En égrenant le chapelet des jours. Montréal, 1928.
43568.66.100 Diop, D. Coups de pilons. Paris, 1956.
43568.67.100 Diolé, Philippe. L'eau profonde; roman. Paris, 1959.
43568.67.110 Diolé, Philippe. L'Okapi. Paris, 1963.
43568.85 Dieulefit, J. Contes celtiques. Paris, 1894.
43568.91.100 Divoire, F. Marathon. Paris, 1924.
43568.91.110 Divoire, F. Marathon. Paris, 1918.
43568.91.120 Divoire, F. Itinéraire. Paris, 1928.
43568.91.130 Divoire, F. L'amoureux. Paris, 1912.
43568.91.140 Divoire, F. Orphée. Paris, 1922.
43568.91.156 Divoire, F. Stratégie littéraire. Paris, 1924.
43568.91.158 Divoire, F. Stratégie littéraire. Evreux, 1928.
43569.21.100 Djebar, Assia. The mischief. N.Y., 1958.
43569.21.110 Djebar, Assia. La soif. Paris, 1957.
43569.21.120 Djebar, Assia. Les alouettes naïves, roman. Paris, 1967.
43573.14.50 Docquois, G. La rôtisserie de la reine Pédauque. Paris, 1920.
43573.14.55 Docquois, G. Bêtes et gens de lettres. Paris, 1895.
43573.16.100 Dodat, François. Etrusques. Paris, 1956.
43573.37.100 Dohet, Adelin Pierre. Tous dieux éteints. Bruxelles, 1960.
43573.74.100 Dorcino, Jean. Pas de dragées pour le baptême. Paris, 1957.
43573.75.100 Doreau, François-Marie. Une de mes vies. Paris, 1921.
43573.76.35 Dorgelès, Roland. Les croix de bois. Paris, 1919.
43573.76.36 Dorgelès, Roland. Les croix de bois. Paris, 1925.
43573.76.37 Dorgelès, Roland. Les croix de bois. Paris, 1964.
43573.76.38 Dorgelès, Roland. Tout est à vendre, roman. Paris, 1956.
43573.76.39 Dorgelès, Roland. Partir. Paris, 1926.
43573.76.40 Dorgelès, Roland. Portraits sans retouche. Paris, 1952.
43573.76.43 Dorgelès, Roland. Le château des brouillards, roman. Paris, 1932.
43573.76.45 Dorgelès, Roland. Montmartre. Paris, 1925.
43573.76.50 Dorgelès, Roland. Le cabaret de la Belle Femme. Paris, 1919.
43573.76.55 Dorgelès, Roland. Wooden crosses. N.Y., 1921.
43573.76.60 Dorgelès, Roland. Si c'était vrai. Paris, 1934.
43573.76.70 Dorgelès, Roland. Route des tropiques. Paris, 1944.
43573.76.72 Dorgelès, Roland. Souvenir sur les croix de bois. Paris, 1929.
43573.76.75 Dorgelès, Roland. Sous le casque blanc. Paris, 1960.
43573.76.100 Dorgelès, Roland. A bas l'argent! Paris, 1965.
43573.76.110 Dorgelès, Roland. Au beau temps de la Butte. Paris, 1963.
43573.76.120 Dorgelès, Roland. Lettre ouverte à un milliardaire. Paris, 1967.
43573.76.800 Dubeux, Albert. Roland Dorgelès. Paris, 1930.
43573.76.1100 Dorian, Jean Pierre. Coups de griffes, suivi d'une lettre au Général de Gaulle. Paris, 1965.
43573.77.100 Dorly, P.A. Amis; pièce en un acte. pt.1-2. Paris, 1935.
43573.77.1700 Dorp, J. van. The sable lion. N.Y., 1954.
43573.78.100 Dorsinville, Roger. Barrières; pièce en trois actes. Haïti, 1946.
43573.89.100 Doucet, Jacques. Lustrales. Porrentruy, 1946.
43573.89.110 Doucet, Jacques. La vue seconde. Paris, 1950.
43573.89.2100 Douassot, Jean. Sens inverse. Paris, 1960.
43573.89.3100 Doubrovsky, Serge. Le jour S, suivi de chronique américaine. Paris, 1963.
43573.89.3110 Doubrovsky, Serge. La dispersion, roman. Paris, 1969.
43573.89.4100 Doublet, Catherine. La courte paille. Paris, 1965.
43573.89.5100 Douce, Paul. Nous serons un seul corps. Paris, 1954.
43573.89.6100 Doucet, R. D'ici et d'ailleurs. Paris, 1963.
43573.98.41 Doyon, René L. Mémoire d'homme. Paris, 1952.
43573.98.100 Doyon, René L. Eloge du maquereau. Paris, 1949.
43573.98.1100 Doysié, Abel. Heures de France et d'exil. Paris, 1912.
43573.110 Dorgelès, Roland. An beau temps de la Butte. Paris, 1963.
43574.1.30 Drouot, Paul. Sous le vocable du chien. (Poèmes). Paris, 1910.
43574.1.31 Drouet, Marcel. L'ombre qui tourne; poèmes. Paris, 1912.
43574.1.35 Drouot, Paul. Eurydice, deux fois perdue. Paris, 1930.
43574.1.40 Drouot, Paul. L'oeillet rouge. Alençon, 19- .
43574.1.45 Drouot, Paul. Les derniers vers de Paul Drouot. Paris, 1920.
43574.1.81 Regnier, Paul. Paul Drouot. Paris, 1923.
43574.41.100 Drieu La Rochelle, Pierre. Plainte contre inconnu. Paris, 1924.
43574.41.110A Drieu La Rochelle, Pierre. Interrogation. Poèmes. Paris, 1917.
43574.41.110B Drieu La Rochelle, Pierre. Interrogation. Poèmes. Paris, 1917.
43574.41.120A Drieu La Rochelle, Pierre. Une femme a sa fenêtre. 14. éd. Paris, 1929.
43574.41.120B Drieu La Rochelle, Pierre. Une femme a sa fenêtre. 14. éd. Paris, 1929.
43574.41.130 Drieu La Rochelle, Pierre. Fond de cantine. 4. éd. Paris, 1920.
43574.41.140 Drieu La Rochelle, Pierre. Beloukia, roman. Paris, 1936.
43574.41.150 Drieu La Rochelle, Pierre. Rêveuse bourgeoisie. 13. éd. Paris, 1937.
43574.41.160 Drieu La Rochelle, Pierre. La comédie de Charleroi. 7. éd. Paris, 1934.
43574.41.170 Drieu La Rochelle, Pierre. Les chiens de paille. Paris, 1964.
43574.41.173 Drieu La Rochelle, Pierre. Gilles; roman. 10. éd. Paris, 1939.
43574.41.180 Drieu La Rochelle, Pierre. Récit secrèt. n.p., 1951.
43574.41.190 Drieu La Rochelle, Pierre. État civil. Paris, 1921.

43511 - 43873 Individual authors, etc. - 1900- - Known authors (363 scheme plus 10) - cont.

43574.41.200 Drieu La Rochelle, Pierre. Sur les écrivains. Paris, 1964.
43574.41.210 Drieu La Rochelle, Pierre. Le feu follet. Paris, 1964.
43574.41.220 Drieu La Rochelle, Pierre. Mémoirs de Dirk Raspe. Paris, 1966.
43574.41.235 Drieu La Rochelle, Pierre. L'homme à cheval, roman. 26. éd. Paris, 1943.
43574.41.700 Drieu La Rochelle, Pierre. The fire within. 1. American ed. N.Y., 1965.
43574.41.805 Grover, Fréderic J. Drieu La Rochelle and fiction of testimony. Berkeley, 1958.
43574.41.806 Grover, Fréderic, J. Drieu La Rochelle. Paris, 1962.
43574.41.810 Vandromme, P. Pierre Drieu La Rochelle. Paris, 1958.
43574.41.815 Mabire, J. Drieu parmi nous. Paris, 1963.
43574.41.1100 Driessche, Andrée Model van den. De tes deux mains offertes. Bruxelles, 1964.
43574.65.100 Droin, Alfred. A l'ombre de Saint-Odile. Paris, 1922.
43574.65.110 Droin, Alfred. La triple symphonie. Paris, 1929.
Htn 43574.65.120* Droin, Alfred. Du sang sur la masquée, poésies. Paris, 1914.
43574.65.1100 Droit, Michel. L'écorché. Paris, 1968.
43574.68.100 Drouin, Henri. Les plus belles années. 22. éd. Paris, 1946.
43574.70.100 Drouet, Minou. First poems. London, 1956.
43574.70.110 Drouet, Minou. Du brouillard dans les yeux. Paris, 1966.
V43574.70.120 Drouet, Minou. La patte bleue. Paris, 1966.
V43574.70.130 Drouet, Minou. La flamme rousse. Paris, 1968.
43574.70.800 Parinaud, A. L'affaire Minou Drouet. Paris, 1956.
43574.70.805 Corot-Gélas, Georgette. Minou Drouet. Paris, 1958.
43574.75.21 Druon, Maurice. Théâtre. v.1. Paris, 1962.
43574.75.100 Druon, Maurice. Mégarée. Paris, 1949.
43574.75.110 Druon, Maurice. Alexandre le Grand. Paris, 1958.
43574.75.112 Druon, Maurice. Alexander. London, 1960.
43574.75.120 Druon, Maurice. Les grandes familles. Paris, 1959.
43574.75.135 Druon, Maurice. Le bonheur des uns, nouvelles et récits. Paris, 1967.
43574.75.140 Druon, Maurice. La fin des hommes. Lausanne, 1968-69. 3v.
43574.75.710 Druon, Maurice. The rise of Simon Lachaume. 1. ed. N.Y., 1952.
43574.75.715 Druon, Maurice. The glass coffin, and other stories. N.Y., 1963.
43574.75.720 Druon, Maurice. The iron king. London, 1956.
43574.75.725 Druon, Maurice. The royal succession. London, 1958.
43574.75.730 Druon, Maurice. The strangled queen. London, 1956.
43574.75.735 Druon, Maurice. The poisoned crown. N.Y., 1957.
43574.75.740 Druon, Maurice. Tistou of the green thumbs. N.Y., 1958.
43574.75.745 Druon, Maurice. The curtain falls. London, 1959.
43574.75.750 Druon, Maurice. Les rois maudits. Paris, 1956. 6v.
43574.75.755 Druon, Maurice. The She-Wolf of France. N.Y., 1961.
43574.75.760 Druon, Maurice. The lily and the lion. London, 1961.
43574.75.765 Druon, Maurice. The memoirs of Zeus. N.Y., 1964.
43574.89.800 Lebois, André. Druelle. Rodez, 1959.
43576.1 Dumas, André. Esther, Princesse d'Israël. Paris, 1912.
43576.1.31 Dumas, André. Le premier couple. Paris, 1920.
43576.1.35 Dumas, André. Paysages. Paris, 1901.
43576.1.38 Dumas, André. A propos. Paris, 1927.
43576.1.42 Dumas, André. La galante surprise. Paris, 1896.
43576.1.45 Dumas, André. Ma petite Yvette. Paris, 1922.
43576.2.30F Dusserre, A. Jean et Louise. pt. 1-3. Paris, 1913.
43576.3.30F Duquesnel, F. La fille. Paris, 1911.
43576.3.31 Duquesnel, F. A la flamme de Paris. Paris, 1910.
43576.4.30 Du Bois-Melly, Charles. "Ceux de Genève." 2. éd. Genève, 1900.
43576.4.31 Du Bois-Meilly, Charles. Eve de la Pasle; épisode de la guerre. 2. éd. Genève, 1909.
43576.4.32 Du Bois-Melly, Charles. The history of Nicolas Muss. N.Y., 1888.
43576.5.30F Dupond, J. Légendes et histoires Trivoltiennes. Trevoux, 1901.
43576.5.100 Dubech, Lucien. Poèmes. Paris, 1928.
43576.5.110 Dubech, Lucien. Poèmes pour Aricil. Paris, 1920.
43576.5.120 Dubech, Lucien. La douceur de vivre. Saint-Félicien, 1925.
43576.6.21 Duhamel, Georges. Textes choisis de Georges Duhamel. Paris, 1937.
43576.6.30 Duhamel, Georges. Lapointe et Ropiteau. Genève, 1919.
43576.6.31 Duhamel, Georges. Civilisation, 1914-1917. 28. éd. Paris, 1919.
43576.6.31.5 Duhamel, Georges. Civilisation française. Paris, 1944.
43576.6.31.10 Duhamel, Georges. Civilisation, 1914-1917. 79. éd. Paris, 1932.
43576.6.32 Duhamel, Georges. Compagnons. 4. éd. Paris, 1918.
43576.6.35 Duhamel, Georges. L'oeuvres des athlètes. 5. éd. Paris, 1920.
43576.6.46 Duhamel, Georges. Deux hommes. Paris, 1944.
43576.6.50 Duhamel, Georges. La Pierre d'Horeb. 5. éd. Paris, 1926.
43576.6.55 Duhamel, Georges. La Pierre d'Horeb. 31. éd. Paris, 1947.
43576.6.60 Duhamel, Georges. Le Prince Jaffar. 20. éd. Paris, 1924.
43576.6.65 Duhamel, Georges. Confession de minuit. 35. éd. Paris, 1927.
43576.6.67 Duhamel, Georges. Confession de minuit. N.Y., 1933.
43576.6.70 Duhamel, Georges. La Belle-Etoile. Paris, 1925.
43576.6.78 Duhamel, Georges. Elégies. 5. éd. Paris, 1920.
43576.6.88 Duhamel, Georges. Lettres au Patagon. 11. éd. Paris, 1926.
43576.6.95 Duhamel, Georges. La journée des aveux. Paris, 1924.
43576.6.100 Duhamel, Georges. La passion de Joseph Pasquier. Paris, 1949.
43576.6.102 Duhamel, Georges. Chronique des Pasquier. Paris, 1964. 2v.
43576.6.105 Duhamel, Georges. La lumière: pièce en quatre actes. 2. éd. Paris, 1919.
43576.6.112 Duhamel, Georges. Journal de Salavin; roman. Paris, 1944.
43576.6.115 Duhamel, Georges. Le dernier. Paris, 1925.
43576.6.120 Duhamel, Georges. Dans l'ombre des statues. 4. éd. Paris, 1920.
43576.6.125 Duhamel, Georges. Ballades. Paris, 1926.
43576.6.128 Duhamel, Georges. Défense des lettres. 22. éd. Paris, 1937.
43576.6.130 Duhamel, Georges. Lettres d'Auspasie. Paris, 1922.
43576.6.135 Duhamel, Georges. Les plaisirs et les jeux. v.1-2. Paris, 1926. 3v.
43576.6.138 Duhamel, Georges. Les plaisirs et les jeux. Paris, 1947.
Htn 43576.6.140* Duhamel, Georges. Suite Hollandaise. Paris, 1925.

43511 - 43873 Individual authors, etc. - 1900- - Known authors (363 scheme plus 10) - cont.

43576.6.145 Duhamel, Georges. Entretien sur l'esprit européen. Paris, 1928.
43576.6.150 Duhamel, Georges. Les sept dernières plaies. Paris, 1928.
X Cg 43576.6.160 Duhamel, Georges. Le club des Lyonnais; roman. 34. éd. Paris, 1929.
43576.6.170 Duhamel, Georges. Pages de mon carnet. Paris, 1931.
43576.6.180 Duhamel, Georges. Le combat. 4. éd. Paris, 1922.
43576.6.190 Duhamel, Georges. Çarré et Lerondeau. Paris, 1922.
43576.6.200 Duhamel, Georges. Élévation et mort d'Armand Branche. Paris, 1919.
43576.6.210 Duhamel, Georges. Scènes de la vie future. 45. éd. Paris, 1930.
NEDL 43576.6.215 Duhamel, Georges. Tel qu'en lui-même...roman. Paris, 1932.
43576.6.217A Duhamel, Georges. Chronique des saisons amères, 1940-1943. 13. éd. Paris, 1944.
43576.6.217B Duhamel, Georges. Chronique des saisons amères, 1940-1943. 13. éd. Paris, 1944.
43576.6.217C Duhamel, Georges. Chronique des saisons amères, 1940-1943. 13. éd. Paris, 1944.
43576.6.219 Duhamel, Georges. Tribulations de l'éspérance. Paris, 1947.
43576.6.220A Duhamel, Georges. Le notaire du Havre. 51. éd. Paris, 1933.
43576.6.220B Duhamel, Georges. Le notaire du Havre. 40. éd. Paris, 1933.
43576.6.222A Duhamel, Georges. Le jardin des bêtes sauvages. 11. éd. Paris, 1934.
43576.6.222B Duhamel, Georges. Le jardin des bêtes sauvages. 23. éd. Paris, 1934.
43576.6.224 Duhamel, Georges. Vue de la Terre Promise. 4. éd. Paris, 1934.
43576.6.224.3 Duhamel, Georges. Vue de la Terre Promise. 11. éd. Paris, 1934.
43576.6.225 Duhamel, Georges. Vue de la Terre Promise. Paris, 1937.
43576.6.226 Duhamel, Georges. La nuit de la Saint-Jean. 37. éd. Paris, 1935.
43576.6.226.10 Duhamel, Georges. La nuit de la Saint-Jean. Paris, 1935.
43576.6.228 Duhamel, Georges. Le désert de Bièvres. 26. éd. Paris, 1937.
43576.6.228.5 Duhamel, Georges. Le désert de Bièvres. 13. éd. Paris, 1937.
43576.6.229 Duhamel, Georges. Le désert de Bièvres. Paris, 1939.
43576.6.230 Duhamel, Georges. Les maîtres. 26. éd. Paris, 1937.
43576.6.238 Duhamel, Georges. Cécile parmi nous. 21. éd. Paris, 1938.
43576.6.238.6 Duhamel, Georges. Cécile parmi nous. 15. éd. Paris, 1938.
43576.6.243 Duhamel, Georges. Le notaire du Havre. Paris, 1936.
43576.6.248 Duhamel, Georges. Travail, ô mon seul repos. Paris, 1959.
43576.6.250 Duhamel, Georges. Selon ma loi. Paris, 1910.
43576.6.255 Duhamel, Georges. Querelles de famille. 13. éd. Paris, 1932.
43576.6.260 Duhamel, Georges. Mémorial de Cauchois. Paris, 1927.
43576.6.270 Duhamel, Georges. Deux patrons, suivi de vie et mort d'un héros de roman. Paris, 1937.
43576.6.275 Duhamel, Georges. La nuit d'orage. Paris, 1947.
43576.6.285 Duhamel, Georges. Semailles au vent. Monaco, 1947.
43576.6.287 Duhamel, Georges. Semailles au vent. Montréal, 1947.
43576.6.290 Duhamel, Georges. Le dernier voyage de Candide suivi d'un choix de nouvelles. Paris, 1938.
43576.6.295 Duhamel, Georges. L'humaniste et l'automate. Paris, 1933.
43576.6.300A Duhamel, Georges. Le combat contre les ombres. 30. éd. Paris, 1939.
43576.6.300B Duhamel, Georges. Le combat contre les ombres. 19. éd. Paris, 1939.
43576.6.305 Duhamel, Georges. Le combat contre les ombres. Paris, 1946.
43576.6.310 Duhamel, Georges. Remarques sur les mémoires imaginaires. 5. éd. Paris, 1934.
43576.6.315 Duhamel, Georges. Delibérations. Paris, 1925.
43576.6.320 Duhamel, Georges. Les confessions sans pénitence. Paris, 1941.
43576.6.325 Duhamel, Georges. La pesée des âmes. Paris, 1949.
43576.6.330 Duhamel, Georges. Suzanne et les jeunes hommes. Paris, 1940.
43576.6.335 Duhamel, Georges. Cri des profondeurs. Paris, 1951.
43576.6.340 Duhamel, Georges. Discours aux nuages. 19. éd. Paris, 1934.
43576.6.345 Duhamel, Georges. Geographie cordiale de l'Europe. 82. éd. Paris, 1931.
43576.6.350A Duhamel, Georges. Les jumeaux de Vallangoujard. Boston, 1940.
43576.6.350B Duhamel, Georges. Les jumeaux de Vallangoujard. Boston, 1940.
43576.6.354 Duhamel, Georges. Biographie de mes fantômes. Paris, 1944.
43576.6.355 Duhamel, Georges. Biographie de mes fantômes, 1901-1906. Paris, 1945.
43576.6.360 Duhamel, Georges. Inventaire de l'abîme, 1884-1901. Paris, 1945.
43576.6.365 Duhamel, Georges. Lieu d'asile. 32. éd. Paris, 1945.
43576.6.370 Duhamel, Georges. Lieu d'asile. Paris, 1945.
43576.6.375 Duhamel, Georges. Georges Duhamel dans ses plus beaux textes. Montréal, 1945.
43576.6.380 Duhamel, Georges. Tables de mon jardin. Paris, 1936.
43576.6.381 Duhamel, Georges. Tables de mon jardin. Paris, 1961.
43576.6.390 Duhamel, Georges. Souvenirs de la vie du paradis. Lausanne, 1946.
43576.6.395 Duhamel, Georges. Souvenirs de la vie du paradis. Paris, 1946.
43576.6.400 Duhamel, Georges. Consultation aux pays d'Islam. Paris, 1947.
43576.6.405 Duhamel, Georges. Le temps de la recherche. Paris, 1947.
43576.6.413 Duhamel, Georges. La musique consolatrice. Monaco, 1947.
43576.6.420 Duhamel, Georges. Discours de réception de M. Georges Duhamel. Paris, 1936.
43576.6.425 Duhamel, Georges. Les espoirs et les épreuves. Paris, 1953.
43576.6.430 Duhamel, Georges. L'Alsace entrevue. Strasbourg, 1931.
43576.6.435 Duhamel, Georges. Problèmes de l'heure. Paris, 1957.
43576.6.440 Duhamel, Georges. Le complexe de Théophile. Paris, 1958.
43576.6.450 Duhamel, Georges. Problèmes de civilisation. Paris, 1962.
43576.6.460 Duhamel, Georges. Vie et aventures de Salavin. Paris, 1955. 5v.
43576.6.710 Duhamel, Georges. The Pasquier chronicles. N.Y., 1938.
43576.6.720A Duhamel, Georges. In defence of letters. N.Y., 1939.
43576.6.720B Duhamel, Georges. In defence of letters. N.Y., 1939.

43511 - 43873 Individual authors, etc. - 1900- - Known authors (363 scheme plus 10) - cont.

43576.6.720C Duhamel, Georges. In defence of letters. N.Y., 1939.
43576.6.725 Duhamel, Georges. Patrice Periot. London, 1952.
43576.6.730 Duhamel, Georges. Cécile Pasquier. N.Y., 1940.
43576.6.740 Duhamel, Georges. Suzanne and Joseph Pasquier. London, 1946.
43576.6.745 Duhamel, Georges. Suzanne; Joseph. N.Y., 1949.
43576.6.750 Duhamel, Georges. Light on my days; an autobiography. London, 1948.
43576.6.755 Duhamel, Georges. Cry out of the depths. London, 1953.
43576.6.756 Duhamel, Georges. Cry out of the depths. Boston, 1954.
43576.6.760 Duhamel, Georges. Refuges de la lecture. Paris, 1954.
43576.6.765 Duhamel, Georges. L'archange de l'aventure. Paris, 1955.
43576.6.770 Duhamel, Georges. Les compagnons de l'Apocalypse. Paris, 1956.
43576.6.775 Duhamel, Georges. Nouvelles du sombre empire. Paris, 1960.
43576.6.800 Durtain, Luc. Georges Duhamel. Paris, 1920.
43576.6.802 Durtain, Luc. Georges Duhamel. Paris, 1927.
43576.6.805 Aveline, Claude. Les ouvrages de Georges Duhamel. Paris, 1925.
43576.6.810 Zehrer, Hanns. George Duhamel. Inaug. Diss. Oettingen, 1928.
43576.6.815 Humbourg, P. Georges Duhamel. Paris, 1929.
43576.6.820 Linsenmaier, W. Die Darstellung des Menschen in Georges Duhamels Roman "Deux Hommes". Inaug. Diss. Würzburg, 19
43576.6.820.5 Keating, Louis Clark. Critic of civilization. Lexington, 1965.
43576.6.825 Mondor, H. Lettre et images pour Georges Duhamel. Paris, 1937.
43576.6.830 Duhamel et nous. Paris, 1937.
43576.6.835 Simon, Pierre-Henri. Georges Duhamel. Paris, 1947.
43576.6.840 Falls, W.F. Le message humain de Georges Duhamel. Paris? 1948.
43576.6.845 Santelli, C. Georges Duhamel. Paris, 1947.
43576.6.850 Héron de Villefosse, A. Chronique de Paris. Paris, 1951.
43576.6.855 Broe, Axel. Georges Duhamel. København, 1938.
43576.6.860 Georges Duhamel (1884-1966). Paris, 1967.
43576.6.865 Zephir, Jacques J. Psychologie de Salavin de Georges Duhamel. Paris, 1970.
43576.6.870 Comeau, Yvan. Georges Duhamel et la possession du monde jusqu'à la chronique des Pasquier. Thèse. Montréal, 1970.
43576.7.30 Du Bois, Albert. L'herodienne. Paris, 1919.
43576.7.35 Du Bois, Albert. Le secret de la ville des 3 Cypres. pt. 1-2. Paris, 1925.
43576.7.40 Du Bois, Albert. Hélène et Penelope (Homère). Paris, 1913.
43576.7.45 Du Bois, Albert. Gazelle de l'Aurore! (David). Paris, 1914.
43576.7.50 Du Bois, Albert. L'Aphrodite et le Khéroub (Ézékiel). Paris, 1914.
43576.7.55 Du Bois, Albert. Le casque de la déesse (Démosthènes). Paris, 1919.
43576.7.60 Du Bois, Albert. La conquête d'Athènes (l'apôtre Paul). Paris, 1913.
43576.7.70 Du Bois, Albert. Bérénice l'hérodienne (Juvenal). Paris, 1919.
43576.7.75 Du Bois, Albert. Rabelais; poème comique en trois actes. Paris, 1913.
43576.7.80 Du Bois, Albert. La dernière dulcinée (Cervantès). Paris, 1913.
43576.7.85 Du Bois, Albert. Betty Hatton; pièce. Paphnuce Smith; comédie (Shakespeare). Paris, 1914.
43576.7.90 Du Bois, Albert. Si Dieu n'éxistait pas...! (Voltaire). Paris, 1919.
43576.7.95 Du Bois, Albert. Lord Byron (l'aristocrate). Paris, 1913.
43576.7.100 Du Bois, Albert. Victor Hugo; poème scénique en trois actes. Paris, 1919.
43576.7.105 Du Bois, Albert. Le dernier vol de l'alouette. Paris, 1928. 2 pam.
43576.7.115 Du Bois, Albert. Corsica. Paris, 1932.
43576.7.125 Du Bois, Albert. Le sourire du roi des juifs. Paris, 1935.
43576.7.130 Du Bois, Albert. Notre déesse. Paris, 1936.
43576.7.1100 Dubé, Théodore. Pétales effeuillés de ma pensée. Etampes, 1928.
43576.8.30 Dubois La Chartre, André. Journal intime d'Hercule. 6. éd. Paris, 1957.
43576.8.35 Dubois La Chartre, André. Les amants de Schoenfelds. Paris, 1960.
43576.8.1100 Dubillard, Roland. Naives hirondelles. Paris, 1962.
43576.8.1110 Dubillard, Roland. Je dirai que je suis tombé; poèmes. Paris, 1966.
43576.8.1120 Dubillard, Roland. La maison d'os. Paris, 1966.
43576.8.1130 Dubillard, Roland. Le jardin aux betteraves. Paris, 1969.
43576.9.42 Du Bos, Charles. Journal. Paris, 1946-59. 9v.
43576.9.43 Du Bos, Charles. Extraits d'un journal, 1908-1928. Paris, 1928.
43576.9.61 Du Bos, Charles. Lettres de Charles Du Bos et réponses de André Gide. Paris, 1950.
43576.9.96 Du Bos, Charles. Approximations. 2. série. Paris, 1927.
43576.9.97 Du Bos, Charles. Approximations. 3. série. Paris? 1929.
43576.9.100 Du Bos, Charles. Approximations. 5. série. Paris, 1932.
43576.9.102 Du Bos, Charles. Approximations. 7. série. Paris, 1937.
43576.9.110 Du Bos, Charles. Approximations. Paris, 1965.
43576.9.120 Du Bos, Charles. Choix de textes. Paris, 1959.
43576.9.800 Bertocci, A.P. Charles Du Bos and English literature. N.Y., 1949.
43576.9.805 Mouton, J. Charles Du Bos. Paris, 1954.
43576.9.810 Charles Du Bos. Toulouse, 1946?
43576.9.815 Gouhier, Marie Anne. Charles Du Bos. Paris, 1951.
43576.9.820 Cahiers Charles du Bos. Paris.
43576.9.825 Mertens, Cornelis Joseph. Émotion et critique chez Charles Du Bos. Proefschrift. Nijmegen, 1967.
43576.9.830 Bossière, Jacques. Perception critique et sentiment de vivre chez Charles Du Bos. Paris, 1969.
43576.9.835 Dédéyan, Charles. Le cosmopolitisme littéraire de Charles du Bos. v.1-3. Paris, 1965. 6v.
43576.9.2100 Du Bouchet, André. Air. Paris, 1951.
43576.9.2110 Du Bouchet, André. Sans couvercle. Paris, 1953.
43576.9.2120 Du Bouchet, André. Le moteur lbanc. Paris, 1956.
43576.9.2130 Du Bouchet, André. Où le soleil. Paris, 1968.
43576.9.3100 Dubreuil, Aline. Ulysse et les sirènes. Paris, 1960.
43576.9.4100 Du Bois, H. Scandale pour une sirène. Lyon, 1962.
43576.9.5100 Dubois, Frédèric. La part du feu. Paris, 1955.
43576.10.100 Dubus, Cyrille. Le poème du chaume. v.3. Paris, 1957.
43576.11.100 Dubrau, Louis. La belle et la bête. Bruxelles, 1961.

43511 - 43873 Individual authors, etc. - 1900- - Known authors (363 scheme plus 10) - cont.

43576.11.110 Dubrau, Louis. A la poursuite de Sandra. Paris, 1963.
43576.11.120 Dubrau, Louis. Les témoins. Bruxelles, 1969.
43576.12.100 Duc, R. Eux et nous. Paris, 1923.
43576.12.1100 Ducharme, Réjean. L'avalée des avalés. Paris, 1966.
43576.12.1110 Ducharme, Réjean. L'océantume. Paris, 1968.
43576.12.1120 Ducharme, Réjean. La fille de Christophe Colomb. Paris, 1969.
43576.13.100 Duchêne, Ferdinand. Kamir; roman d'une femme Arabe. Paris, 1926.
43576.13.2106 Duchemin, J. Le chemin de Poitiers. 6. éd. Paris, 1957.
43576.13.2110 Duchemin, J. Rendez-vous sous l'horloge. Paris, 1960.
43576.14.100 Ducros, C. Inès de Castro. Paris, 1949.
43576.14.2100 Ducros, Emmanuel. Paris. Paris, 1893.
43576.14.2110 Ducros, Emmanuel. Poèmes du midi. Paris, 1896.
43576.14.3100 Du Coffre, Marguerite. Ich suche. Köln, 1958.
43576.15.100 Ducreux, Louis. Les clefs du ciel. Paris, 1946.
43576.15.110 Ducreux, Louis. La folie. n.p., n.d.
43576.15.1100 Ducrocq, Georges. La belle Libanaise. Le journal de Soleiman. Paris, 1930.
43576.24.100 Duesberg, R. Les grenouilles. Paris, 1962.
43576.29.100 Dufour, Liliane. Étape vers l'inconnu. Paris, 1959.
43576.36.1100 Duhamelet, Geneviève. Encore un peu de temps, poèmes. Paris, 1967.
43576.39.100 Duhourcau, F. L'enfant de la victoire. N.Y., 1933.
43576.50.100 Dulière, William L. Notes d'archéologie future. Louvain, 1968.
43576.53.100 Dumas, Roger. Hélène. Paris, 1908.
43576.53.1100 Dumas, Hubert. Passeport pour l'unique frontière. Paris, 1955.
43576.53.2100 Dumay, Raymond. Fannie en Orient. Paris, 1954.
43576.53.2110 Dumay, Raymond. Vanina. 2. éd. Paris, 1957.
43576.53.3100 Dumas, Lucien Henri. Amour, mélancolie. Paris, 1958.
43576.54.100 Dumaine, Philippe. Ame. Paris, 1951.
43576.54.110 Dumaine, Philippe. Arpents secrets. Villeneuve, 1951.
43576.54.120 Dumaine, Philippe. Cortèges. Paris, 1945.
43576.54.2100 Dumesnil, R. Le rideau à l'Italienne. Paris, 1959.
43576.56.100 Dumont-Wilden, L. Les soucis des derniers soirs. Bruxelles, 1906.
43576.57.100 Dumur, Louis. Nach Paris! Paris, 1920.
43576.57.110 Dumur, Louis. Les défaitistes, roman. Paris, 1923.
43576.57.120 Dumur, Louis. Pauline. Paris, 1896.
43576.57.130 Dumur, Louis. Les loups rouges. Paris, 1932.
43576.57.140 Dumur, Louis. Les trois demoiselles du père Marie. Paris, 1909.
43576.57.1100 Dumur, Guy. Le matin de leurs jours. Paris, 1954.
43576.58.115 Dunan, Renée. Pope Joan. London, 1930.
43576.58.120 Dunan, Renée. Les amantes du diable. Paris, 1929.
43576.68.100 Dupays, Paul. Au-dessus de la vie. Paris, 1934.
43576.68.110 Dupays, Paul. L'hiver. 3. éd. Paris, 1934.
43576.68.120 Dupays, Paul. Qualités et tendances. Paris, 1934.
43576.68.130 Dupays, Paul. Heureuses dispositions et déviations de principes. Londres, 1935.
43576.68.140 Dupays, Paul. La paix mondiale. Londres, 1935.
43576.68.150 Dupays, Paul. Vers la paix par le travail. Londres, 1935.
43576.68.160 Dupays, Paul. Efforts. Londres, 1936.
43576.68.170 Dupays, Paul. La femme. n.p., 1936.
43576.68.180 Dupays, Paul. Le printemps. Paris, 1936.
43576.68.190 Dupays, Paul. L'été. Paris, 1936.
43576.68.200 Dupays, Paul. L'automne. Paris, 1937.
43576.68.1100 Dupé, Gilbert. Les mal mariés célèbres. Paris, 1958.
43576.68.3100 Dupé, Gilbert. Le bateau à soupe. 29. éd. Paris, 1945.
43576.69.100 Dupin, Jules. Journal, 1905-1915. Montbrison, 1917.
43576.69.1100 Dupin, Jacques. Cendrier du voyage. Paris, 1950.
43576.69.1110 Dupin, Jacques. Les brisants. Paris, 1958.
43576.69.2100 Dupin d'Aniane, Charlotte R. La route de la joie. Clermont-Ferrand, 1964.
43576.70.100 Du Plessys, M. Le feu sacré. Paris, 1924.
43576.70.110 Du Plessys, M. Odes olympiques. Paris, 1923.
43576.71.100 Dupony, A. L'homme de la palud. Paris, 1931.
43576.71.110 Dupony, A. Roulez, tambours! Paris, 1959.
43576.71.1100 Dupont, Denis. Premiers essais. Paris, 1959.
43576.71.2100 Dupré, Guy. Les fiancées sont froides. Paris, 1953.
43576.71.3100 Duplouy, Fernand. L'homme de quarante ans. Paris, 1960.
43576.71.4100 Dupont-Fromageot, Yves. Entrelacs. Paris, 1958.
43576.71.4110 Dupont-Fromageot, Yves. Bergeries. Bruxelles, 1964.
43576.72.100 Dupuy, Michel. La source et le feu. Montréal, 1954.
43576.72.1100 Dupuy, Jacqueline. Dure est ma joie. Paris, 1967.
43576.72.1110 Dupuy, Jacqueline. Dialogue dans l'infini. Bruges, 1967.
43576.74.100 Duran, Michel. Liberté provisoire. Paris, 1934.
43576.74.110 Duran, Michel. Trois...six...neuf...; comédie en trois actes. Paris, 1936.
43576.74.120 Duran, Michel. Barbara. Paris, 1938.
43576.74.1700 Durafour, Michel. Bettina. London, 1953.
43576.74.2100 Duras, Marguerite. The seawall. N.Y., 1952.
43576.74.2110 Duras, Marguerite. The square. N.Y., 1959.
43576.74.2112 Duras, Marguerite. Le square. Paris, 1956.
43576.74.2115 Duras, Marguerite. Four novels. N.Y., 1965.
43576.74.2120 Duras, Marguerite. Des journées entières. Paris, 1954.
43576.74.2130 Duras, Marguerite. Les petits chevaux de Trequinia. Paris, 1953.
43576.74.2140 Duras, Marguerite. Le marin de Gibraltar. Paris, 1952.
43576.74.2150 Duras, Marguerite. Moderato cantabile. Paris, 1958.
43576.74.2153 Duras, Marguerite. Moderato cantabile. Paris, 1962.
43576.74.2160 Duras, Marguerite. Les viaducs de la Seine-et-Oise. Paris, 1960.
43576.74.2170 Duras, Marguerite. Dix heures et demie du soir en été. Paris, 1960.
43576.74.2180 Duras, Marguerite. Hiroshima mon amour. Paris, 1960.
43576.74.2190 Duras, Marguerite. L'après-midi de Monsieur Unsiesmus. Paris, 1962.
43576.74.2200 Duras, Marguerite. La ravissement de Lol V. Stein, roman. Paris, 1964.
43576.74.2210 Duras, Marguerite. Théâtre. Paris, 1965. 2v.
43576.74.2215 Duras, Marguerite. Le vice-consul. Paris, 1966.
43576.74.2220 Duras, Marguerite. L'amante anglaise. Paris, 1967.
43576.74.2230 Duras, Marguerite. Détruire, dit-elle. Paris, 1969.
43576.74.2240 Duras, Marguerite. Abahn, Sabana, David. Paris, 1970.
43576.74.2700 Duras, Marguerite. Moderato cantabile. N.Y., 1960.
43576.74.2701 Duras, Marguerite. Moderato cantabile. London, 1966.
43576.74.2705 Duras, Marguerite. Ten-thirty on a summer night. N.Y., 1963.
43576.74.2710 Duras, Marguerite. The sailor from Gibraltar. London, 1966.
43576.74.2800 Cismaru, Alfred. Marguerite Duras. N.Y., 1971.
43576.74.3100 Durand, C. Le bord de la mer. Paris, 1960.
43576.74.4100 Durand, Pierre. Vingt ans. Paris, 1965.

43511 - 43873 Individual authors, etc. - 1900- - Known authors (363 scheme plus 10) - cont.

43576.75.100 Duret, Roger-Léon. Demain. Ambilly-Annemane, 1941.
43576.75.1800 Hommage à Georges Duret, 1887-1943. Poitiers, 1965.
43576.76.100 Durry, Marie-Jeanne. La cloison courbe. Paris, 1949.
43576.76.110 Durry, Marie-Jeanne. Mon ombre. Paris, 1962.
43576.76.120 Durry, Marie-Jeanne. Eden; cinq actes. Paris, 1970.
43576.77.100A Durtain, Luc. Quarantième étage. 8. éd. Paris, 1927.
43576.77.100B Durtain, Luc. Quarantième étage. 22. éd. Paris, 1928.
43576.77.110 Durtain, Luc. Captain O.K.; roman. Paris, 1931.
43576.77.120 Durtain, Luc. Le mari singulier. Paris, 1937.
43576.77.130 Durtain, Luc. Dieux blancs, hommes jaunes. Paris, 1930.
43576.77.140 Durtain, Luc. L'étape nécessaire. Paris, 1938.
43576.77.155 Durtain, Luc. Suite brasileira. São Paulo, 1936.
43576.77.165 Durtain, Luc. Le retour des hommes. 2. éd. Paris, 1920.
43576.77.175 Durtain, Luc. Douze cent mille. 5. éd. Paris, 1922.
43576.77.183 Durtain, Luc. La source rouge. 3. éd. Paris, 1924.
43576.77.190 Durtain, Luc. La guerre n'éxiste pas...roman de 1914-1916. Paris, 1939.
43576.77.200 Durtain, Luc. Face à face. Paris, 1921.
43576.77.210 Durtain, Luc. Perspectives. Paris, 1924.
43576.77.810 Harpe, J. L'influence des inventions scientifiques modernes sur le renouvellement des images dans les romans de Luc Durtain. San Francisco, 1929.
43576.77.812 Wessely, Trude. Ein Europäer, Luc Durtain. Brünn, 1933.
43576.77.1100 Durtal, Jean. Les coulisses de la politique: une femme temoigne 1932-1942. Paris, 1966.
43576.78.100 Durussel, André. Le poids léger des jours, poèmes pour trois temps. Genève, 1967.
43576.82.105 Dussap, J.V. (Mme). Ma conscience en robe rose. 16. éd. Paris, 1910.
43576.86.100 Dutheil, Marcel. Gretel Wiesbach; roman. v.1-3. Paris, 1935.
43576.86.110 Dutheil, Marcel. La passion de Puisjoli. v.1-2. Paris, 1937.
43576.87.100 Dutourd, Jean. Une tête de chien. Paris, 1950.
43576.87.110 Dutourd, Jean. Au bon beurre. Paris, 1952.
43576.87.130 Dutourd, Jean. Doucin. 18. éd. Paris, 1955.
43576.87.140 Dutourd, Jean. Le petit Don Juan. Paris, 1955.
43576.87.150 Dutourd, Jean. Les taxis de la Marne. 6. éd. Paris, 1956.
43576.87.160 Dutourd, Jean. Le fond et la forme. v.1-3. Paris, 1958.
43576.87.170 Dutourd, Jean. Le déjeuner du lundi. Paris, 1961.
43576.87.180 Dutourd, Jean. Le demi-solde. Paris, 1965.
43576.87.190 Dutourd, Jean. Pluche ou l'Amour de l'art. Paris, 1967.
43576.87.200 Dutourd, Jean. Petit journal, 1965-1966. Paris, 1969.
43576.87.700 Dutourd, Jean. A dog's head. London, 1951.
43576.87.705 Dutourd, Jean. The best butter. N.Y., 1955.
43576.87.710A Dutourd, Jean. Five a.m. N.Y., 1956.
43576.87.710B Dutourd, Jean. Five a.m. N.Y., 1956.
43576.87.2100 Dubit, Ernest. Domaines, les idées et les mots. Fribourg, 1960.
43576.88.100 Dutreil, Nicole. Le miel acide. 5. éd. Paris, 1955.
43576.89.100 Duvant, Albert. Nida et chansons. Paris, 1936.
43576.90.100 Duverne, René. Victime expiatoire. Paris, 1926.
43576.90.1100 Duvignaud, Jean. Le piège. 2. éd. Paris, 1954.
43576.90.1110 Duvignaud, Jean. L'or de la République. 3. éd. Paris, 1957.
43576.90.1120 Duvignaud, Jean. La chasse à l'aigle. Paris, 1960.
43576.90.2100 Duvert, Tony. Interdit de séjour. Paris, 1969.
43576.90.2110 Duvert, Tony. Le voyageur. Paris, 1970.
43576.91.35F Duvernois, Henri. Morte la bête. Paris, 1921.
43576.91.35.2F Duvernois, Henri. Morte la bête. Paris, 1922. 2 pam.
43576.91.40 Duvernois, Henri. La dame de bronze et le monsieur de cristal. Paris, 1922.
43576.91.42 Duvernois, Henri. Seule. Paris, 1923. 2 pam.
43576.91.44 Duvernois, Henri. Le club des canards mandarins; comédie. Paris, 1924.
43576.91.46 Duvernois, Henri. La guitare et le jazz-band. Paris, 1924.
43576.91.48 Duvernois, Henri. L'élève Chocotte. Paris, 1925.
43576.91.50 Duvernois, Henri. Edgar. Paris, 1925.
43576.91.52 Duvernois, Henri. L'invité. Paris, 1928.
43576.91.53 Duvernois, Henri. L'invité. Paris, 1939.
43576.91.54 Duvernois, Henri. Beauté. Paris, 1931.
43576.91.58 Duvernois, Henri. Le professor. Paris, 1928.
43576.91.65 Duvernois, Henri. Comédies en un acte. Paris, 1927.
43576.91.67 Duvernois, Henri. Comédies en un acte. 3. éd. Paris, 1946.
43576.91.68 Duvernois, Henri. La fugue. Paris, 1929.
43576.91.70 Duvernois, Henri. Crapotte. Paris, 1936.
43576.91.70.5 Pamphlet vol. Duvernois, Henri. 2 pam.
43576.91.72 Duvernois, Henri. Jeanne. Paris, 1933.
43576.91.74 Duvernois, Henri. Maxime. Paris, 1927.
43576.91.76 Duvernois, Henri. Rouge! Paris, 1935.
43576.91.80 Duvernois, Henri. La maison Camille. Paris, 1937.
43576.91.82 Duvernois, Henri. A l'ombre d'une femme. Paris, 1933.
43576.91.84 Duvernois, Henri. La maison des confidences. Paris, 1914.
43576.91.86 Duvernois, Henri. Les soeurs Hortensias; roman. Paris, 1931.
43576.91.90 Duvernois, Henri. Apprentissages. Paris, 1930.
43576.91.150 Duvernois, Henri. The holidays; a book of gay stories. London, 1921.
43576.91.800 Taffel, Abram. The prose fiction and dramatic works of Henri Duvernois. N.Y., 1951.
43576.93.110 Duwez, Maurice. Arsène et Chrysostome. Bruxelles, 1931.
43576.93.120 Duwez, Maurice. La boue des Flandres. Paris, 1965.
43576.95.100 Dumas, Charles. L'Eau souterraine. Paris, 1903.
43576.95.110 Dumas, Charles. Stellus. Paris, 1916.
43576.95.120 Dumas, Charles. L'ombre et les proies. Paris, 1906.
43579.82.100 Dyssord, Jacques. On frappe à la porte. Paris, 1928.
43581.89.100 Eaubonne, Françoise d'. Les tricheurs, roman. Paris, 1959.
43581.89.110 Eaubonne, Françoise d'. Fort des femmes. Paris, 1958.
43581.89.115 Eaubonne, Françoise d'. Le sous-marin de l'espace. Paris, 1959.
43581.89.120 Eaubonne, Françoise d'. Je m'appelle Vristine. Paris, 1959.
43581.89.130 Eaubonne, Françoise d'. Le temps d'apprendre à vivre. Paris, 1960.
43581.89.140 Eaubonne, Françoise d'. L'échiquier du temps. Paris, 1962.
43581.89.150 Eaubonne, Françoise d'. Rêve de feu. Paris, 1964.
43584.92.100 Edwards, Émile. Journal d'un habitant de Constantinople (1914-1915). Paris, 1915.
43585.53.100 Eeman, Jacques. Sillages et pistes. Bruxelles, 1961.
43586.86.100 Eftimiu, Victor. Le nain du théâtre français. Paris, 1931.

43511 - 43873 Individual authors, etc. - 1900- - Known authors (363 scheme plus 10) - cont.

43587.1.100	Ega, Françoise. Le temps des madras. Paris, 1966.
43589.32.100	Eigeldinger, Marc. Les voix de la forêt. Neuchatel, 1964.
43590.50.100	Ekman, Pierre A. Les enfants des collines. Paris, 1959.
43590.50.110	Ekman, Pierre A. Maria des quatre vents. Paris, 1960.
43591.59.251	Éluard, Paul. Les animaux et leurs hommes, les hommes et leurs animaux. Paris, 1937.
43591.66.100	Élot, Maryse. Symphonie des Antilles. Malines, 1953.
43591.89.21	Éluard, Paul. Premiers poèmes. Lausanne, 1948.
43591.89.22	Éluard, Paul. Selected writings. London, 1952.
43591.89.24	Éluard, Paul. Chanson complète. Paris, 1939.
43591.89.61	Éluard, Paul. Lettres de jeunesse. Paris, 1962.
43591.89.100	Éluard, Paul. L'amour, la poesie. 5. éd. Paris, 1929.
43591.89.110A	Éluard, Paul. Capitale de la douleur. Paris, 1926.
43591.89.110B	Éluard, Paul. Capitale de la douleur. Paris, 1926.
43591.89.113	Éluard, Paul. Capitale de la douleur. Paris, 1966.
43591.89.120	Éluard, Paul. La rose publique. Paris, 1934.
43591.89.130	Éluard, Paul. Comme deux gouttes d'eau. Paris, 1933.
43591.89.140	Éluard, Paul. Cours naturel. Paris, 1938.
43591.89.150	Éluard, Paul. Les malheurs des immortels. Paris, 1945.
43591.89.160	Éluard, Paul. Le lit, la table. Genève, 1946.
43591.89.165	Éluard, Paul. Poésie ininterrompue. Paris, 1946. 2v.
43591.89.166	Éluard, Paul. Poésie ininterrompue. Paris, 1969.
43591.89.170F	Éluard, Paul. Souvenirs de la maison des fous. Paris, 1945.
43591.89.180	Éluard, Paul. Poésie et vérité. Bruxelles, 1945.
43591.89.185	Éluard, Paul. Les sentiers et les routes de la poésie. 5. éd. Paris, 1954.
43591.89.195	Éluard, Paul. Choix de poèmes. Paris, 1946.
43591.89.196	Éluard, Paul. Choix de poèmes. Paris, 1951.
43591.89.198	Éluard, Paul. Poèmes pour tous. Paris, 1952.
43591.89.199	Éluard, Paul. Poésies. Paris, 1959.
43591.89.200	Éluard, Paul. Doubles d'ombre. Paris, 1945.
43591.89.210	Éluard, Paul. Quelques-uns des mots qui jusqu'ici m'étaient mysterieusement interdits. Paris, 1937.
43591.89.220	Éluard, Paul. Liberté. Paris, 1946.
43591.89.235	Éluard, Paul. Poèmes politiques. 15. éd. Paris, 1948.
43591.89.240	Éluard, Paul. Le livre ouvert (1938-1944). Paris, 1947.
43591.89.251	Éluard, Paul. Les animaux et leurs hommes, les hommes et leurs animaux. Paris, 1937.
43591.89.260	Éluard, Paul. Une leçon de morale, poèmes. 4. éd. Paris, 1949.
43591.89.270	Éluard, Paul. Paul Éluard. 2. éd. Clichy, 1946.
43591.89.280	Éluard, Paul. Corps mémorable. Paris, 1948.
43591.89.290	Éluard, Paul. Les nécessités de la vie. Paris, 1946.
43591.89.301	Éluard, Paul. Le dur désir de durer. Philadelphia, 1950.
43591.89.302	Éluard, Paul. Le dur désir de durer. Paris, 1950.
43591.89.310	Éluard, Paul. Tout dire. Paris, 1950.
43591.89.315	Éluard, Paul. Le phénix. Paris, 1952.
43591.89.320	Éluard, Paul. La jarre peut-elle être plus belle que l'eau? Paris, 1951.
43591.89.325	Éluard, Paul. Léda. 2. éd. Lausanne, 1956.
43591.89.330	Éluard, Paul. Une longue réfléxion amoureuse. Neuchâtel, 1945.
43591.89.340	Éluard, Paul. Choix de poèmes. Paris, 1963.
43591.89.350	Éluard, Paul. Éluard en die surrealisme. Kaapstad, 1962.
43591.89.621	Éluard, Paul. Selected writings. Norfolk, Conn., 195-.
43591.89.705	Éluard, Paul. Thorns of thunder. London, 1936.
43591.89.800	Gaffé, René. Paul Éluard. Paris, 1945.
43591.89.810	Emmanuel, P. Le Je universel chez Paul Éluard. Paris, 1948.
43591.89.815	Schmitz, K.H. Die Sprach der Farben in der Lyrik Paul Eluards. Erlangen, 1961.
43591.89.820	Perche, Louis. Paul Éluard. Paris, 1963.
43591.89.825	Eglin, Heinrich. Liebe und Inspiration im Werke von Paul Éluard. Bern, 1965.
43591.89.830	Decaunes, Luc. Paul Éluard, biographie. Rodez, 1965.
43591.89.835	Arcangeli Marenzi, Maria Laura. Linguaggio e poesia: Paul Éluard, Simone Weil, Antoine de Saint-Exupéry. Venezia, 1966.
43591.89.840	Velikovskii, Samarii I. K gorizontu vsekh liudei. Moskva, 1968.
43591.89.845	Jean, Raymond. Paul Éluard par lui-même. Paris, 1968.
43591.89.850	Ségalat, Roger Jean. Album Éluard. Paris, 1968.
43591.89.855	Saint Denis, France. Musée Municipal d'Art et Histoire. Paul Éluard, 1895-1952. Saint-Denis, 1963.
43591.89.860	Kittang, Atle. D'amour de poésie. Paris, 1969.
43591.89.1100	Éluard, Paul. Derniers poèmes d'amour. n.p., n.d.
43591.89.1110	Éluard, Paul. Le poète et son ombre. Paris, 1963.
43591.89.1800	Jucker-Wehrli, Ursula. La poésie de Paul Éluard et le thème de la pureté. Zürich, 1965.
43591.89.1805	Meurand, Maryvonne. L'image végétale dans la poésie d'Éluard. Paris, 1966.
43592.41.100	Émié, Louis. Romancero du profil perdu. Paris, 1951.
43592.41.110	Émié, Louis. Présenté par A. Loranquin. Rodez, 1958.
43592.41.120	Émié, Louis. Le volubilis. Villeneuve-sur-Lot, 1960.
43592.41.130	Émié, Louis. Invention de l'amour. Villeneuve-sur-Lot, 1961.
43592.53.41	Emmanuel, Pierre. Autobiographies. Paris, 1970.
43592.53.100	Emmanuel, Pierre. Sodome. Fribourg, 1944.
43592.53.110	Emmanuel, Pierre. Jour de colère. Alger, 1945.
43592.53.125	Emmanuel, Pierre. La colombe. Fribourg, 1943.
43592.53.130	Emmanuel, Pierre. La poète et son Christ 1938. Neuchâtel, 1946.
43592.53.135	Emmanuel, Pierre. Tristesse o ma patrie. Paris, 1946.
43592.53.140	Emmanuel, Pierre. La liberté guide nos pas. Paris, 1947.
43592.53.150	Emmanuel, Pierre. Cantos. Neuchâtel, 1944.
43592.53.155	Emmanuel, Pierre. Tombeau d'Orphée. Fribourg, 1944.
43592.53.155.5	Emmanuel, Pierre. Tombeau d'Orphée. Paris, 1946.
43592.53.160	Emmanuel, Pierre. Chansons du dé à coude. Paris, 1947.
43592.53.170	Emmanuel, Pierre. Poésie raison ardente. 3. éd. Paris, 1948.
43592.53.180	Emmanuel, Pierre. Qui est cet homme. 3. éd. Paris, 1947.
43592.53.185	Emmanuel, Pierre. L'ouvrier de la onzième heure. Paris, 1953.
43592.53.190	Emmanuel, Pierre. Élégies. Paris, 1940.
43592.53.200	Emmanuel, Pierre. Combats avec tes défenseurs. Paris, 1945.
43592.53.210	Emmanuel, Pierre. Orphiques. Paris, 1942.
43592.53.220F	Emmanuel, Pierre. Le poète fou. Monaco, 1944.
43592.53.230	Emmanuel, Pierre. Car enfin je vous aime. Neuchâtel, 1950.
43592.53.240	Emmanuel, Pierre. Le poète fou suivi de élégies. Boudry, 1948.
43592.53.250	Emmanuel, Pierre. Prière d'Abraham. Neuchâtel, 1943.
43592.53.260	Emmanuel, Pierre. Babel. Paris, 1951.

43511 - 43873 Individual authors, etc. - 1900- - Known authors (363 scheme plus 10) - cont.

43592.53.270	Emmanuel, Pierre. Visage nuage. Paris, 1955.
43592.53.280	Emmanuel, Pierre. Versant de l'Âge. Paris, 1958.
43592.53.290	Emmanuel, Pierre. Evangeliaire. Paris, 1961.
43592.53.310	Emmanuel, Pierre. Le Gout de l'un. Paris, 1963.
43592.53.320	Emmanuel, Pierre. La nouvelle naissance. Paris, 1963.
43592.53.330	Emmanuel, Pierre. La face humaine. Paris, 1965.
43592.53.340	Emmanuel, Pierre. Ligne de faite. Paris, 1966.
43592.53.350	Emmanuel, Pierre. Le monde est intérieur, essais. Paris, 1967.
43592.53.360	Emmanuel, Pierre. Choses dites. Paris, 1970.
43592.53.705	Emmanuel, Pierre. The universal singular. London, 1950.
43592.53.710	Emmanuel, Pierre. The mad poet. Baltimore, 1956.
43592.69.100	Empeirikos, Alexandros. Poèmes inutiles. Genève, 1951.
43592.69.110	Empeirikos, Alexandros. Physionomies. Paris, 1934.
43593.29.100	Enfoux, Janine. Cantique de l'amour. Paris, 1959.
43593.30.100	Enfrey, L.M. Le livre des harems. Paris, 1920.
43593.32.100	Engelmann, Jacques. Les amphigourdiers. Paris, 1957.
43593.32.1100	Engelbach, Gérard. Poèmes. Paris, 1967.
43593.33.700	Englebert, O. The wisdom of Father Pecquet. London, 1953.
43593.88.100	Entrevaux, V. d'. La vie secrète de Geraldine Deguith. pt. 1-3. Paris, 1934.
43593.88.110	Entrevaux, V. d'. Compagnons de chaine. pt. 1-3. Paris, 1936.
43593.91.100	Envin, Guy. Du fond de l'ombre. Paris? 1918.
43595.89.100	Epuy, M. Initiation méridionale. La Chaux-de-Fonds, 1941.
43597.55.100	Ermin, France. Les beaux départs. Paris, 1956.
43597.59.105	Ernest-Charles, J. Les samedis litteraires. Paris, 1903-05. 5v.
43597.61.100	Ernout, I. Jeux d'ombres. Paris, 1957.
43597.79.100	Ersam, Roger. L'éspoir et les ombres. Paris, 1953.
43598.11.100	Escande, Jean. Du flouze. Paris, 1958.
43598.12.200A	Eschasseriaux, Bernard. Les dimanches de Ville-d'Avray; roman. Paris, 1963.
43598.12.200B	Eschasseriaux, Bernard. Les dimanches de Ville-d'Avray; roman. Paris, 1963.
43598.13.100	Escholier, R. Cantegril. Paris, 1921.
43598.13.102	Escholier, R. Dansons la trompeuse. 4. éd. Paris, 1919.
43598.13.102.5	Escholier, R. Dansons la trompeuse. Paris, 1926.
43598.13.110	Escholier, R. L'herbe d'amour; roman. Paris, 1931.
43598.13.120	Escholier, R. La nuit; roman. Paris, 1923.
43598.13.135	Escholier, R. Quand on conspire; roman. 39. éd. Paris, 1925.
43598.14.100	Escoula, Yvonne. Six chevaux bleus. Paris, 1967.
43598.54.100	Esménard, Jean d'. Le soleil d'Ethiopie. Paris, 1929.
43598.54.115	Esménard, Jean d'. Thi-Bâ, fille d'Annam. Paris, 1920.
43598.54.120	Esménard, Jean d'. Les chercheurs de amondes. Paris, 1960.
43598.54.700	Esménard, Jean d'. The red gods. N.Y., 1924.
43598.66.100	Esor. Un homme nouveau dans un monde nouveau. Anvers, 1964.
43598.68.90	Espardés, Georges. Les demi solde. Paris, 1910.
43598.68.100	Espardés, Georges. Rocroy, Victoire du Cid. Paris, 1934.
43598.82.100	Estang, Luc. Invitation a la poésie. Marseille, 1943.
43598.82.118	Estang, Luc. Le passage du seigneur. 12. éd. Paris, 1946.
43598.82.130	Estang, Luc. Le mystère apprivoisé. Marseille, 1943.
43598.82.140	Estang, Luc. Cherchant qui devores. Paris, 1951.
43598.82.150	Estang, Luc. Les fontaines du grand abime. Paris, 1954.
43598.82.160	Estang, Luc. Les béatitudes. Paris, 1945.
43598.82.170	Estang, Luc. Les stigmates. Paris, 1954.
43598.82.180	Estang, Luc. L'interrogatoire. Paris, 1957.
43598.82.190	Estang, Luc. L'horloger du cherche-midi. Paris, 1959.
43598.82.200	Estang, Luc. Le bonheur et le salut. Paris, 1961.
43598.82.210	Estang, Luc. D'une nuit noire et blanche. Paris, 1962.
43598.82.220	Estang, Luc. Le jour de Caïn. Paris, 1967.
43598.82.230	Estang, Luc. L'apostat. Paris, 1968.
43598.82.2100	Escarpit, Robert. Les dieux du Patamba. Paris, 1958.
43598.82.2110	Escarpit, Robert. Le litteratron. Paris, 1964.
43598.82.2120	Escarpit, Robert. Paramémoires d'un gaulois. Paris, 1968.
43598.82.2130	Escarpit, Robert. Le fabricant de nuages, nouvelles. Paris, 1969.
43598.82.2700	Escarpit, Robert. The novel computer. London, 1966.
43598.84.100	Estaunié, Édouard. L'infirme aux mains de lumière. Paris, 1923.
43598.84.108	Estaunié, Édouard. L'appel de la route. Paris, 1922.
43598.84.116	Estaunié, Édouard. L'ascension de M. Baslévre. Paris, 1920.
43598.84.120	Estaunié, Édouard. L'ascension de M. Baslévre. Paris, 1928.
43598.84.130	Estaunié, Édouard. "Bonne dame". Paris, 1922.
43598.84.140	Estaunié, Édouard. Le ferment. Paris, 1899.
43598.84.150	Estaunié, Édouard. L'empreinte. Paris, 1909.
43598.84.160	Estaunié, Édouard. La vie secrète. Paris, 1909.
43598.84.170	Estaunié, Édouard. Les choses voient; roman. Paris, 1914.
43598.84.180	Estaunié, Édouard. Solitudes; roman. Paris, 1917.
43598.84.183	Estaunié, Édouard. Solitudes; roman. Paris, 1925.
43598.84.190	Estaunié, Édouard. Le labyrinthe. Paris, 1926.
43598.84.192	Estaunié, Édouard. Le labyrinthe. Paris, 1924.
43598.84.200	Estaunié, Édouard. Un simple. Paris, 1924.
43598.84.208	Estaunié, Édouard. Tels qu'ils furent; roman. Paris, 1927.
43598.84.210	Estaunié, Édouard. Tels qu'ils furent; roman. 40. éd. Paris, 1927.
43598.84.220	Estaunié, Édouard. Le silence dans la campagne. 20. éd. Paris, 1926.
43598.84.230	Estaunié, Édouard. L'épave. Paris, 1902.
43598.84.240	Estaunié, Édouard. Madame Clapain. Paris, 1932.
43598.84.250	Estaunié, Édouard. La vie secrète. Évreux, 1970.
43598.84.700	Estaunié, Édouard. Call of the road. N.Y., 1923.
43598.84.800	Daniel Rops, Henry. Édouard Estaunié. Paris, 1931.
43598.84.805	Hok, Ruth E. Édouard Estaunié. Thesis. N.Y., 1949.
43598.84.810	Zapf, Hasso. Syntaktische Eigentümlichkeiten in den Werken Edouard Estaunié's. Inaug. Diss. Borna, 1933.
43598.84.815	Vallery-Radot, Pasteur. Discours de réception de M. Pasteur Vallery-Radot à l'Académie Française. Paris, 1946.
43598.86.621	Estivals, G. A gap in the wall. N.Y., 1963.
43599.13.100	Etcherelli, Claire. Elise, ou la vraie vie; roman. Paris, 1967.
43599.13.1100	Etchart, Salvat. Le monde tel qu'il est. Paris, 1967.
43599.13.1110	Etchart, Salvat. Les nègres servent d'exemple; roman. Paris, 1964.
43599.38.100	Éthier-Blais, Jean. Mater Europa. Paris, 1968.
43599.41.100	Étiemble, René. Six essais sur trois tyrannies. Paris, 1947.
43599.41.110	Étiemble, René. Hygiène des lettres. Paris, 1952-55. 4v.
43599.41.120	Étiemble, René. L'ennemie publique. Paris, 1957.

Classified Listing

43511 - 43873 Individual authors, etc. - 1900- - Known authors (363 scheme plus 10) - cont.

43599.41.130 Étiemble, René. Le péché vraiment capital. Paris, 1957.
43599.41.147 Étiemble, René. L'enfant de choeur. 7. éd. Paris, 1947.
43599.41.150 Étiemble, René. Blason d'un corps. Paris, 1961.
43600.25.100 Chevalier, Adrien. Sous le ciel changeant. Paris, 1912.
43600.25.110 Chevalier, Adrien. Mémoires d'outre-tombe d'Hannibal Châtaignier. Paris, 1914.
43600.25.120 Chevalier, Adrien. La retraite de M. de Pluviane. Paris, 1920.
43601.23.100 Eveno, Lucien. Frissons et scintillements. Paris, 1957.
43601.41.100 Evian, Jeanne. Chants de Tahiti. Lyon, 1958.
43604.19.100 Eydoux, Emmanuel. Abraham l'hébreu et Samuel le voyant. Neuchâtel, 1946.
43604.19.110 Eydoux, Emmanuel. Eliezer ben Yehouda. Basel, 1966.
43604.19.120 Eydoux, Emmanuel. Capitaine Alfred Dreyfus. Basel, 1967.
43604.19.130 Eydoux, Emmanuel. Pogrom; théâtre. Basel, 1963.
43604.19.140 Eydoux, Emmanuel. La mort d'un poète. Paris, 1968.
43604.19.150 Eydoux, Emmanuel. Le dernier Pourimspiel des orphelins du docteur Janusz Korczak. Basel, 1967.
43604.19.160 Eydoux, Emmanuel. Anéantir Israël. Théâtre. Basel, 1969.
43604.73.100 Eyquem, Marie T. Jeunes filles au soleil. Paris, 1945.
43606.1.30 Falk, H. Poèmes brefs, idylles et comédies. Paris, 1911.
43606.2.30 Faure, A. Justin Pinard. 2. éd. Paris, 1913.
43606.8.100 Fabre, Lucien. Rabevel, ou le mal des ardents. Paris, 1923. 3v.
43606.8.110 Fabre, Lucien. Dieu est innocent. Paris, 1946.
43606.8.120 Fabre, Lucien. Bassesse de Venise. Paris, 1924.
43606.9.100 Fabrici, Delphi. Das Gespenst. Berlin, 1921.
43606.9.2100 Fabre-Luce de Gruson, Françoise. La clôture. Paris, 1969.
43606.9.5100 Fabre, Dominique. Charmants garçons. Paris, 1957.
43606.10.41 Fabre-Luce, Alfred. Journal 1951. Paris, 1952.
43606.10.100 Fabre-Luce, Alfred. Hors d'atteinte. Paris, 1946.
43606.10.110 Fabre-Luce, Alfred. Une minute; roman. Paris, 1957.
43606.10.120 Fabre-Luc, Alfred. Vingt-cinq années de liberté. Paris, 1962-63. 3v.
43606.10.130 Fabre-Luce, Alfred. Haute cour. Lausanne, 1963.
43606.10.140 Fabre-Luce, Alfred. Le procès de Haute Cour. Paris, 1964.
43606.10.150 Fabre-Luce, Alfred. La bombe. Paris, 1964.
43606.10.160 Fabre-Luce, Alfred. Le général en Sorbonne. Paris, 1968.
43606.10.170 Fabre-Luce, Alfred. L'homme journal, 1966-1967. Paris, 1967.
43606.10.700 Fabre-Luce, Alfred. The trial of Charles de Gaulle. N.Y., 1963.
43606.15.100 Fardoulis-Lagrange, Michel. Le texte inconnu. Paris, 1948.
43606.15.110 Fardoulis-Lagrange, Michel. Au temps de Benani. Paris, 1958.
43606.41.100 Faillet, Georges. La prière des quarante heures ou les XIV stations sous l'horloge du destin. Paris, 1920.
43606.41.110 Faillet, Georges. Ixion; poème. Paris, 1903.
43606.48.100 Falaise, Élisabeth. La source des rêves. Paris, 1957.
43606.49.100 Falerne, J. Monsieur Duran de la Tour antiquaire. Paris, 1963.
43606.50.100 Fallet, René. Les vieux de la vieille. Paris, 1958.
43606.50.110 Fallet, René. Une poignée de mains. Paris, 1959.
43606.50.120 Fallet, René. Charleston, roman. Paris, 1967.
43606.58.100 Fanchette, Jean. Identité provisoire; poèmes. Paris, 1965.
43606.74.100 Farge, Yves. L'escalier. Paris, 1948.
43606.75.800 Morgan, Claude. Yves Farge. Paris, 1954.
43606.75.1100 Farell, Dominique. Ellipse. Paris, 195-?
43606.75.3100 Farges, Marcel. Nuit sans passeport, poèmes. Paris, 1958.
43606.76.61 Fargue, Léon P. Correspondance, 1910-1946. Paris, 1971.
43606.76.100A Fargue, Léon P. Espaces. 5. éd. Paris, 1929.
43606.76.100B Fargue, Léon P. Espaces. 7. éd. Paris, 1929.
43606.76.102 Fargue, Léon P. Épaisseurs. Paris, 1928.
43606.76.110A Fargue, Léon P. Sous la lamp. 4. éd. Paris, 1929.
43606.76.110B Fargue, Léon P. Sous la lamp. 3. éd. Paris, 1929.
43606.76.120 Fargue, Léon P. Poèmes suivis de Pour la musique. 4. éd. Paris, 1919.
43606.76.120.10 Fargue, Léon P. Poèmes. 11. éd. Paris, 1947.
43606.76.130 Fargue, Léon P. Meandres. Genève, 1946.
43606.76.140 Fargue, Léon P. Trois poèmes. Paris, 1942.
43606.76.150 Fargue, Léon P. Portrait de famille. Paris, 1947.
43606.76.160 Fargue, Léon P. Etc. Genève, 1949.
43606.76.170 Fargue, Léon P. Refuges. Paris, 1942.
43606.76.180 Fargue, Léon P. Haute solitude. Paris, 1941.
43606.76.190 Fargue, Léon P. Pour la peinture. Paris, 1955.
43606.76.200 Fargue, Léon P. Banalité. Paris, 1928.
43606.76.210 Fargue, Léon P. Poésies. Paris, 1963.
43606.76.800 Beucler, André. Dimanche avec Léon-Paul Fargue. Paris, 1947.
43606.76.810 Beucler, André. The last of the Bohemians. N.Y., 1954.
43606.76.820 Beucler, André. Poet of Paris. London, 1955.
43606.76.830 La Rochefoucauld, Edmée. Léon-Paul Fargue. Paris, 1959.
43606.76.835 Hommage à Léon-Paul Fargue. Paris, 1927.
43606.76.3100 Farlane, Gilbert. Tous pour un. Paris, 1957.
43606.78.100 Farrère, Claude. La bataille. Paris, 1909.
43606.78.100.5 Farrère, Claude. La bataille. 8. éd. Paris, 1911.
43606.78.110 Farrère, Claude. Bêtes et gens qui s'aimèrent. Paris, 1920.
43606.78.110.5 Farrère, Claude. Bêtes et gens qui s'aimèrent. Paris, 1920.
43606.78.120 Farrère, Claude. Les civilisés. 25. éd. Paris, 1906.
43606.78.130 Farrère, Claude. Les condamnés à mort. Paris, 1920.
43606.78.140 Farrère, Claude. Le dernier dieu. Paris, 1926.
43606.78.150 Farrère, Claude. La dernière déesse. Paris, 1920.
43606.78.160 Farrère, Claude. Fumée d'opium. 16. éd. Paris, 191-?
43606.78.170 Farrère, Claude. L'homme qui assassina. 71. éd. Paris, 191-?
43606.78.173 Farrère, Claude. L'homme qui assassina. N.Y., 1930.
43606.78.180 Farrère, Claude. Mademoiselle Dax jeune fille. 34. éd. Paris, 191-?
43606.78.190 Farrère, Claude. La maison des hommes vivants. 27. éd. Paris, 1911.
43606.78.195 Farrère, Claude. La onzième heure; roman. Paris, 1940.
43606.78.200 Farrère, Claude. Les petites alliées. 42. éd. Paris, 191-?
43606.78.210 Farrère, Claude. Quatorze histoires de soldats. Paris, 1916.
43606.78.210.5 Farrère, Claude. Quatorze histoires de soldats. Paris, 1924.
43606.78.220 Farrère, Claude. Thomas l'Agnelet. 2. éd. Paris, 1913.
43606.78.222 Farrère, Claude. Thomas l'Agnelet. 19. éd. Paris, 1913.
43606.78.230 Farrère, Claude. Trois promenades. Paris, 1922.
43606.78.240 Farrère, Claude. La veille d'armes. Paris, 1917.
43606.78.250 Farrère, Claude. La vieille histoire. Paris, 1920.

43511 - 43873 Individual authors, etc. - 1900- - Known authors (363 scheme plus 10) - cont.

43606.78.260 Farrère, Claude. La seconde porte. Paris, 1945.
43606.78.270 Farrère, Claude. Jab, siècle XX; roman. Paris, 1949.
43606.78.280 Farrère, Claude. Roxelane. Paris, 1920.
43606.78.705 Farrère, Claude. The house of the secret. N.Y., 1923.
43606.78.710 Farrère, Claude. Black opium. N.Y., 1931.
43606.78.720 Farrère, Claude. Thomas the Lambkin. N.Y., 1924.
43606.78.800 Troyat, Henri. Discours de reception a l'Académie Française. Paris, 1960.
43606.78.810 Revon, Maxime. Claude Farrère, son oeuvre. Paris, 1924.
43606.82.100 Fasquelle, Solange. L'air de Venise. Paris, 1966.
43606.87.110 Fauchois, René. Prenez garde à la peinture. Paris, 1932.
43606.87.113 Fauchois, René. Prenez garde à la peinture. N.Y., 1937.
43606.87.120 Fauchois, René. La dame aux gants verts. Paris, 1934.
43606.87.130 Fauchois, René. Le chirurgien de Jauvence. Paris, 1938.
43606.87.140 Fauchois, René. Vitrail, un acte. Paris, 1944.
43606.87.150 Fauchois, René. Délices des mourants. Paris, 1953.
43606.87.160 Fauchois, René. L'Augusta. Paris, 1916.
43606.87.170 Fauchois, René. Le miracle. Paris, 1914.
43606.87.180 Fauchois, René. Nocturne. Paris, 1914.
43606.87.190 Fauchois, René. La paix des familles. Paris, 1926.
43606.87.531 Fauconnier, G.A.M. Claude, roman. 99. éd. Paris, 1933.
43606.87.1110 Fauconnier, G.A.M. Les étangs de la double. Paris, 1935.
43606.88.100A Fauconnier, H. Malaisie. N.Y., 1931.
43606.88.100B Fauconnier, H. Malaisie. N.Y., 1931.
43606.88.103 Fauconnier, H. Malaisie. Paris, 1933.
43606.88.110 Fauconnier, H. Visions. Paris, 1938.
43606.89.4 Faure, Gabriel. Oeuvres. Saint-Félicien-en-Vivarais, 1937. 8v.
43606.89.35 Faure, Gabriel. Paysages littéraires. Série 1-2. Paris, 1917-1918. 2v.
43606.89.40 Faure, Gabriel. Les amants enchainées. Paris, 1920.
43606.89.45 Faure, Gabriel. Heures romanesques. Paris, 1928.
43606.89.50 Faure, Gabriel. Paysages passionnés. Paris, 1909.
43606.89.55 Faure, Gabriel. Berthe de Provence. Paris, 1898.
43606.89.60 Faure, Gabriel. Amours romantiques. Paris, 1927.
43606.89.63 Faure, Gabriel. Pages lyriques. Saint-Félicien-en-Vivarais, 1925.
43606.89.65 Faure, Gabriel. Printemps. Paris, 1922.
43606.89.67 Faure, Gabriel. Fleurs rouges. Paris, 1899.
43606.89.70 Faure, Gabriel. Mon lycée. Saint-Félicien-en-Vivarais, 1921.
43606.89.72 Faure, Gabriel. Pages choisies. Vienne, 1938.
43606.89.75 Faure, Gabriel. Pages choisies de Gabriel Faure. Paris, 1934.
43606.89.81 Dujet, A. Gabriel Faure. Paris, 1921.
43606.89.82 Aurenche, Louis. L'oeuvre de Gabriel Faure. Paris, 1926.
43606.89.84F Mey, Ursula. Die Stellung von Gabriel Faure. Erlangen? 1961.
43606.89.86 Conrazier, Joseph. Gabriel Faure. Paris, 1933.
43606.89.88 Chevalier, Adrien. L'Italie de Gabriel Faure. Saint-Félicien-en-Vivarais, 1922.
43606.89.100 Fauré-Fremiet, P. Le souffle du désordre. Paris, 1922.
43606.89.102 Fauré-Fremiet, P. Le souffle du désordre. Paris, 1923.
43606.89.1700 Faux, Claude. The young dogs. N.Y., 1961.
43606.89.2100 Faucher, Jean. Alger la maudite. Paris? 1962.
43606.89.3100 Faure-Favier, Louise. Six contes et deux rêves. Paris, 1918.
43606.89.4100 Fauquez, Arthur. Ambrosio tue l'heure. Malèves Ste-Marie, 1965.
43606.91.100 Favre, André. L'acier victorieux. Avignon, 1955.
43606.97.100 Fay, Bernard. Faites vos jeux. 7. éd. Paris, 1927.
43606.97.102 Fay, Bernard. Faites vos jeux. Paris, 1927.
43606.98.105 Fayard, Jean. Mal d'amour; roman. 7. éd. Paris, 1932.
43606.98.108 Fayard, Jean. Mal d'amour; roman. 15. éd. Paris, 1931.
43606.98.120 Fayard, Jean. Mes maîtresses. Paris, 1931.
43606.98.130 Fayard, Jean. Oxford et Margaret. Paris, 1928.
43606.99.100 Faye, Jean-Pierre. L'écluse; roman. Paris, 1964.
43606.99.110 Faye, Jean-Pierre. Couleurs pliées. Paris, 1965.
43606.99.120 Faye, Jean-Pierre. Le récit hunique, essai. Paris, 1967.
43607.2.30 Fèvre, Henry. En detresse. Paris, 1890.
43607.2.31 Fèvre, Henry. L'honneur; roman. Paris, 19- .
43607.27.700 Feval, P. The mysterious cavalier. N.Y., 1928.
43607.27.705 Feval, P. Martyr to the queen. N.Y., 1928.
43607.27.1100 Feldstein, Jean. Notes de voyage à travers l'Europe du XVe et du XVIe siècle. Paris, 1966.
43607.30.105 Fels, Andrée. Mademoiselle Colifichet, modes. 4. éd. Paris, 193-.
43607.74.100 Ferchaud, Suzanne. Le vent qui lève; poèmes. Paris, 1957.
43607.74.1100 Feraudy, Jacqueline de Gourcy. Marguerites, herbes fleuries; poèmes. Paris, 1945.
43607.74.1110 Feraudy, Jacqueline de Gourcy. Chrysanthèmes. Paris, 1943.
43607.75.100 Ferdinand, Roger. Chatard et Cie. Paris, 1928.
43607.75.110 Ferdinand, Roger. Trois pour cent. Paris, 1933.
43607.75.120 Ferdinand, Roger. Le Président Haudecoeur. Paris, 1938.
43607.75.130 Ferdinand, Roger. Les derniers seigneurs. Paris, 1946.
43607.75.140 Ferdinand, Roger. Théâtre. Genève, 1962. 3v.
43607.75.150 Ferdinand, Roger. Théâtre. Paris, 1946. 2v.
43607.76.100 Féret, Charles Théophile. La Normandie exaltée. 2. éd. Paris, 1928.
43607.76.110 Féret, Charles Théophile. L'arc d'Ulysse. Paris, 1919.
43607.76.120 Féret, Charles Théophile. Les couronnes. Paris, 1922.
43607.76.130 Féret, Charles Théophile. Le verger des muses et des satyres bouquins. Paris, 1924.
43607.76.2100 Fernand. Saint-Pierre. Fort-de-France, 1905.
43607.76.4100 Fernandez, Ramon. Le pari. Paris, 1932.
43607.76.4110 Fernandez, Ramon. L'homme est-il humain? Paris, 1936.
43607.76.6100 Ferniot, Jean. L'ombre portée. Paris, 1961.
43607.76.7100 Fernandez, Dominique. L'écorce. Paris, 1959.
43607.77.100 Ferret, Gilles. La sarabande ensorcelée; poèmes. Paris, 1929.
43607.77.2110 Ferron, Jacques. Contes. Montréal, 1968.
43607.77.3021 Ferrare, Henri. Henry Ferrare, un ami de Max Jacob. Genève, 1968.
43607.77.4100 Ferrière, Anette. Le squelette de Kazan. Paris, 1970.
43607.78.100 Ferré, Léo. Poète. Paris, 1956.
43607.80.100 Fessy, A. L'ange de la patrie. Paris, 1930.
43609.1.30 Fiel, Marthe. Sur le sol d'Alsace. Paris, 1911.
43609.24.100 Fieschi, P. Fête foraine. Paris, 1945.
43609.35.100 Figuéras, André. Poèmes patriotiques. Rodez, 1958.
43609.50.100 Filiatrault, Jean. Chaînes. Montréal, 1955.
43609.50.110 Filiatrault, Jean. Terres stériles; roman. Québec, 1953.
43609.50.1100 Filippi, Louise. Pierres dures. Paris, 1957.
43609.58.100 Finas, Lucette. L'échec; roman. Paris, 1958.
43609.58.700 Finas, Lucette. The faithful shepherd. N.Y., 1963.
43609.58.1100 Firaud, Georges. Herma. Paris, 1925.

43511 - 43873 Individual authors, etc. - 1900- - Known authors (363 scheme plus 10) - cont.

43609.79.100 Fischer, Max. Dans l'ascenseur. Paris, 1920.
43609.79.110 Fischer, Max. Estelle. London, 1923.
43609.79.1100 Fischer, Pierre. Paroles simples. Paris, 1956.
43609.83.100 Fisson, Pierre. Les automobiles. Paris, 1967.
43609.83.700 Fisson, Pierre. No memorial. London, 1952.
43609.83.710 Fisson, Pierre. Fever in Mexico. London, 1954.
43609.88.100 Fitz-George, France. Chansons pour rien. Lausanne, 1948.
43610.1.30F Fleg, Edmond. Le trouble-fête. Paris, 1913.
43610.1.35F Fleg, Edmond. La maison du bon Dieu. Paris, 1920.
43610.4.100 Flament, A. L'enchanteresse errante, la Malibran. Paris, 1937.
43610.4.110 Flament, A. Le bal Pré-Catelan. 5. éd. Paris, 1946.
43610.22.100 Fleg, Edmond. Le marchand de Paris. Paris, 1929.
43610.22.110 Fleg, Edmond. Le mur des pleurs; poème. Paris, 1919.
43610.22.120 Fleg, Edmond. Le Psaume de la terre promise. Genève, 1919.
43610.22.140 Fleg, Edmond. Ecoute, Israël. Paris, 1955.
Htn 43610.22.700* Fleg, Edmond. The wall of weeping. London, 1929.
43610.22.1100 Fleg, Daniel. Journal. Buchet, Chastel, 1959.
43610.23.100 Fleischman, Théo. Le peuple aux yeux clairs. Bruxelles, 1959.
43610.24.100 Flers, Robert de. Les nouveaux messieurs. Paris, 1926.
43610.24.5100 Fleurange, Claude. Mon frère Jack, R.A.F.; roman. Paris, 1940.
43610.25.100 Fleuret, Fernand. Les derniers plaisirs, histoire espagnole. Paris, 1924.
43610.25.102 Fleuret, Fernand. Les derniers plaisirs. Paris, 1924.
43610.25.110 Fleuret, Fernand. Falourdin. Paris, 1927.
43610.25.120 Fleuret, Fernand. Jim Click où La merveilleuse invention. 4. éd. Paris, 1930.
43610.25.130 Fleuret, Fernand. De Ronsard à Baudelaire. Paris, 1935.
43610.25.140 Fleuret, Fernand. Soeur Félicité. Paris, 1926.
43610.25.800 Saint-Jorre, Jean de. Fernand Fleuret et ses amis. Coutances, 1958.
43610.25.1100 Fleury, René-Albert. Quelques musiques encore. Limoges, 1929.
43610.25.2100 Fleury, Hector. Les echos. Paris, 1861.
43610.25.3100 Fleury, Edmond. Ils luttérent jusqu'à l'aube. Paris, 1967.
43610.25.4100 Fleury, François. Jours d'Arés; poèmes. Paris, 1957.
43610.28.100 Flad, Albert. Le feu dérobé. Paris, 1930.
43610.66.100 Floris, A.C. Le mystère. N.Y., 1914.
43610.66.2100 Florenne, Yves. Antigone. Paris, 1954.
43610.66.2110 Florenne, Yves. Le cavalier d'or. 4. éd. Paris, 1958.
43610.68.700 Florez, C. de. Put a log on the fire. N.Y., 1941.
43611.1.21 Fort, Paul. Choix de ballades françaises. Paris, 1913.
43611.1.25 Fort, Paul. Ballades françaises. 1. série. I. Paris, 1914.
43611.1.25.2 Fort, Paul. Montagne, forêt. 2. éd. II. Paris, 1898.
43611.1.25.3 Fort, Paul. Roman de Louis XI. 2. éd. III. Paris, 1898.
43611.1.25.4 Fort, Paul. Les idylles antiques et les hymnes. 2. éd. IV. Paris, 1900.
43611.1.25.5 Fort, Paul. L'amour marin. V. Paris, 1900.
43611.1.25.6 Fort, Paul. Paris sentimental. 2. éd. VI. Paris, 1902.
43611.1.25.7 Fort, Paul. Les hymnes de feu. VII. Paris, 1903.
43611.1.25.8 Fort, Paul. Coxcomb, ou l'Homme tout nu tombé. VIII. Paris, 1906.
43611.1.25.9 Fort, Paul. Ballades françaises. Ile-de-France. IX. Paris, 1908.
43611.1.25.10 Fort, Paul. Mort cerf. X. Paris, 1909.
43611.1.25.11 Fort, Paul. Tristesse de l'homme. XI. Paris, 1910.
43611.1.25.12 Fort, Paul. L'aventure éternelle. Livre I. XII. Paris, 1911.
43611.1.25.13 Fort, Paul. Montlhéry-la-bataille. 3. éd. Livre II. XIII. Paris, 1912.
43611.1.25.14 Fort, Paul. Vivre en Dieu. 2. éd. Livre III. XIV. Paris, 1912.
43611.1.25.15 Fort, Paul. Chansons. 2. éd. XV. Paris, 1913.
43611.1.25.16 Fort, Paul. Les nocturnes. XVI. Paris, 1914.
43611.1.25.17 Fort, Paul. Si peau d'âne m'était conté. 3. éd. XVII. Paris, 1917.
43611.1.25.18 Fort, Paul. Deux chaumières au pays de l'Yveline. XVIII. Paris, 1916.
43611.1.25.19 Fort, Paul. Poèmes de France. 1. série. XIX. Lausanne, 1916.
43611.1.25.21 Fort, Paul. L'alouette. 3. éd. XXI. Paris, 1917.
43611.1.25.22 Fort, Paul. La lanterne de priollet. XXII. Paris, 1918.
43611.1.25.23 Fort, Paul. Les enchanteurs. XXIII. Paris, 1919.
43611.1.25.25 Fort, Paul. Chansons à la Gauloise sur la vie, le rêve, et l'amour. XXV. Paris, 1919.
43611.1.25.26 Fort, Paul. Hélène en fleur. 4. éd. XXVI. Paris, 1921.
43611.1.25.29 Fort, Paul. L'arbre à poèmes. XXIX. Paris, 1922.
43611.1.25.34 Fort, Paul. Le camp du drap d'or. XXXIV. Paris, 1926.
43611.1.25.36 Fort, Paul. La conquête de l'Angleterre. Paris, 1933.
43611.1.25.40 Fort, Paul. Que j'ai de plaisir d'être français. Paris, 1917.
43611.1.25.43 Fort, Paul. Barbe-Bleue, Jeanne d'Arc et mes amours. Paris, 1919.
43611.1.25.48 Fort, Paul. Aux pays des Moulins. Paris, 1921.
43611.1.25.53 Fort, Paul. Louis XI, curieux homme. Paris, 1922.
43611.1.25.58 Fort, Paul. Les compères du Roi Louis. Paris, 1923.
43611.1.25.63A Fort, Paul. Fantômes de chaque jour. Paris, 1925.
43611.1.25.63B Fort, Paul. Fantômes de chaque jour. Paris, 1925.
43611.1.25.68 Fort, Paul. L'or. Paris, 1927.
43611.1.25.73 Fort, Paul. Ballades françaises. 1. série. 8. éd. Paris, 1920.
43611.1.25.76 Fort, Paul. Selected poems and ballads. N.Y., 1921.
43611.1.27 Fort, Paul. Joies désolées et tristesses consolées. Paris, 1937.
43611.1.30 Fort, Paul. La petite Bête; comédie en une route. Paris, 1891.
43611.1.32.2 Fort, Paul. Si peau d'âne m'était. 4. éd. Paris, 1917.
43611.1.35 Fort, Paul. Ysabeau. Paris, 1924.
43611.1.39A Fort, Paul. L'arlequin de plomb. Paris, 1936.
43611.1.39B Fort, Paul. L'arlequin de plomb. Paris, 1936.
43611.1.45 Fort, Paul. Anthologie des ballades françaises, 1897-1920. Paris, 1925.
43611.1.45.2 Fort, Paul. Anthologie des ballades françaises. Paris, 1946.
43611.1.47 Fort, Paul. Ballades françaises. v.1-5, 7-15. Paris, 1922-53. 14v.
43611.1.50 Fort, Paul. Florilège des Ballades françaises. Paris, 1922.
43611.1.55 Fort, Paul. Poèmes de France; bulletin lyrique de la guerre. Paris. 1914-1915

43511 - 43873 Individual authors, etc. - 1900- - Known authors (363 scheme plus 10) - cont.

43611.1.58 Fort, Paul. Expo 37, suivi de Raymonde aux yeux verts. Paris, 1938.
43611.1.80 Fort, Paul. Mes mémoires. Paris, 1944.
43611.1.100 Masson, Georges A. Paul Fort. Paris, 1922.
43611.1.120 Donnay, M.T. Le Paul Fort que j'ai connu. Paris, 1961.
43611.2.30 Fouquier, Henry. Philosophie parisienne. Paris, 1901.
43611.3.30 Fonson, Jean J. La kommandantur. Paris, 1917.
43611.3.31 Fonson, Jean F. La demoiselle de magasin. Paris, 1917.
43611.4.30 Foley, Charles. La guerre vécue. Paris, 1915.
43611.4.35 Foley, Charles. Fleur d'ombre. Paris, 1921.
43611.4.40 Foley, Charles. Pernette en escapade. Paris, 1920.
43611.4.45 Foley, Charles. Femmes aimantes, femmes aimées. Paris, 1926.
43611.4.50 Foley, Charles. Sylvette et son blessé. Paris, 1917.
43611.4.91 Fouchet, Max Pol. Simples sans vertu. Alger, 1937.
43611.4.100 Fouchet, Max Pol. Demeure le secret. Paris, 1961.
43611.4.110 Fouchet, Max Pol. Les Appels. Paris, 1967.
43611.4.120 Fouchet, Max Pol. Un jour, je m'en souviens; mémoire parlée. Paris, 1969.
43611.5.28 Fournier, Alain. Le grand meaulnes. Paris, 1936.
43611.5.30 Fournier, Alain. Le grand meaulnes. Londres, 1920.
43611.5.32 Fournier, Alain. Le grand meaulnes. Paris, 1926.
43611.5.34 Fournier, Alain. Le grand meaulnes. Londres, 1944.
43611.5.40 Fournier, Alain. The wanderer. N.Y., 1928.
43611.5.44 Fournier, Alain. The wanderer (Le grand meaulnes). N.Y., 1928.
43611.5.48 Fournier, Alain. The lost domain. London, 1959.
43611.5.50 Fournier, Alain. Miracles. Paris, 1924.
43611.5.60 Valloton, Henri. Lettres d'Alain-Fournier à sa famille. Paris, 1930.
43611.5.70 Fournier, Alain. Lettres au petit B. Paris, 1930.
43611.5.80 Fombeure, Maurice. Homage à Alain-Fournier. Paris, 1930.
43611.5.81 Jöhr, Walter. Alain-Fournier, le paysage d'une âme. Thèse. Neuchâtel, 1945.
43611.5.83 Ahting, Georg. Henri Alain-Fournier, 1886-1914. Inaug. Diss. Barssel, 1932.
43611.5.87 Rivière, I.F. (Mme.). Images d'Alain-Fournier par sa soeur Isabelle. Paris, 1938.
43611.5.89 Becker, Aimé. Itinèraire spirituel d'Alain-Fournier. Paris, 1946.
43611.5.92 Dedeyan, Christian. Alain-Fournier et la réalité secrète. Paris, 1948.
43611.5.95 Gillet, Henri. Alain-Fournier. Paris, 1948.
43611.5.100 Gibson, Robert. The quest of Alain-Fournier. London, 1953.
43611.5.102 Gibson, Robert. The quest of Alain-Fournier. New Haven, 1954.
43611.5.104 Suire, Pierre. Les raisons du Grand Meaulnes. Riort, 1952.
43611.5.105 Borgal, Clément. Alain-Fournier. Paris, 1955.
43611.5.110 Lampo, Hubert. De roman van een roman. Antwerpen, 1953.
43611.5.115 Delettrez, J.M. Alain-Fournier et le grand meaulnes. Paris, 1954.
43611.5.120A Valloton, Henri. Alain-Fournier. Paris, 1957.
43611.5.120B Valloton, Henri. Alain-Fournier. Paris, 1957.
43611.5.125 Wall, Eva von der. Alain-Fournier. Hamburg, 1932.
43611.5.145 Vandamme, Jan. Alain-Fournier. Brugge, 1960.
43611.5.150 Pilon, Edmond. Alain-Fournier. Abbeville, 1920.
43611.5.155 Rivière, I. Vie et passion d'Alain-Fournier. Monaco, 1963.
43611.5.160 Guiomar, M. Inconscient et imaginaire dans le Grand Meaulnes. Paris, 1964.
43611.5.165 Desonay, F. Le grand Meaulnes d'Alain-Fournier. Paris, 1963.
43611.5.170 Massis, Henri. Alain-Fournier sans Goncourt. Liège, 1963.
43611.5.180 Bastaire, J. Alain-Fournier. Paris, 1964.
43611.5.185 Genuist, Paul. Alain-Fournier face à l'angoisse. Paris, 1965.
43611.5.190 Sonet, Antoine. Le rêve d'Alain-Fournier. Gembloux, 1965.
43611.5.195 Loize, Jean. Alain-Fournier, sa vie et le grand meaulnes. Paris, 1968.
43611.5.200 Suffran, Michel. Alain-Fournier ou le mystère limpide, essai. Paris, 1969.
43611.50.100 Follain, Jean. Tout instant. 2. éd. Paris, 1957.
43611.50.110 Follain, Jean. Des heures. Paris, 1960.
43611.50.120 Follain, Jean. D'après tout. Paris, 1969.
43611.50.130 Follain, Jean. Exister. Paris, 1969.
43611.50.140 Follain, Jean. Appareil de la terre. Paris, 1964.
43611.50.700 Follain, Jean. Transparence of the world: poems. N.Y., 1969.
43611.53.100 Fombeure, Maurice. Pendant que vous dormez. Paris, 1953.
43611.53.110 Fombeure, Maurice. Les patron-minet. Paris, 1952.
43611.53.120 Fombeure, Maurice. Une forêt de charme. Paris, 1955.
43611.53.130 Fombeure, Maurice. J'apprivoise par jeu. Paris, 1947.
43611.53.140 Fombeure, Maurice. Les étoiles brûlées. 4. éd. Paris, 1950.
43611.53.150 Fombeure, Maurice. Les godillots sont lourds. 17. éd. Paris, 1948.
43611.53.160 Fombeure, Maurice. Sous les tambours du ciel. Paris, 1959.
43611.53.170 Fombeure, Maurice. Manille coinchée. Issy-les-Moulineaux, 1943.
43611.53.180 Fombeure, Maurice. Sortilèges vus de près. Paris, 1947.
43611.53.190 Fombeure, Maurice. A chat petit, 1965. Paris, 1967.
43611.59.100 Fondmarin, H. Nos précieuses ridicules. Paris, 1926.
43611.60.100 Fongy, L. de. Réalités. Nyon, 1963.
43611.61.100 Fontanet, Jean C. Qui perd gagne; roman. Neuchâtel, 1959.
43611.62.100 Fons, Pierre. La divinité quotidienne; poèmes. Paris, 1908.
43611.63.100 Fontaine, Anne. Prismes. Fribourg, 1947.
43611.63.110 Fontaine, Anne. Nausicaa, avec une rose de Henri Mondor. Fribourg, 1948.
43611.63.120 Fontaine, Anne. Le premier jour. Paris, 1950.
43611.63.130 Fontaine, Anne. Par-dessus la haie. Paris, 1952.
43611.63.140 Fontaine, Anne. Le cerf-volant. Paris, 1953.
43611.63.150 Fontaine, Anne. Henri Mondor. Paris, 1960.
43611.64.100 Fondane, Benjamin. L'éxode super flumina Babylonis. Veilhes, Tarn, 1965.
43611.75.110 Forestier (pseud.). Les langes. 8. éd. Paris, 1946.
43611.75.1105 Forestier, Marie. Le détour. 5. éd. Paris, 1957.
43611.75.1110 Forestier, Marie. L'écran de fumée. Paris, 1958.
43611.75.2100 Forge, Henry de. Le fils de joie. Paris, 1928.
43611.76.100 Forton, Jean. Cantemerle. Paris, 1957.
43611.76.110 Forton, Jean. Le grand mal. Paris, 1959.
43611.76.120 Forton, Jean. L'épingle du jeu. Paris, 1960.
43611.76.130 Forton, Jean. Les sables mouvants. Paris, 1966.

Classified Listing

43511 - 43873 Individual authors, etc. - 1900- - Known authors (363 scheme plus 10) - cont.

43611.76.1100 Forneret, Xavier. Le diamant de l'herbe. Paris, 1955.
43611.77.100 Fortin, Charles. Primitivité cosmique. Paris, 1960.
43611.88.100 Fougère, Jean. Un don comme l'amour. Paris, 1945.
43611.88.110 Fougère, Jean. Flo. Paris, 1946.
43611.88.120 Fougère, Jean. Un cadeau utile. Paris, 1953.
43611.88.130 Fougère, Jean. Les nouveaux bovidés. Paris, 1966.
43611.89.100 Foulon, Pierre. Angkor dans la forêt. Hanoi, 1931.
43611.89.1100 Fourest, G. Le géranium ovipare. Paris, 1935.
43611.89.1110 Fourest, G. La nègresse blonde. 7. éd. Paris, 1934.
43611.90.100 Fourré, Maurice. Tête-de-Nègre. Paris, 1960.
43611.94.100 Fowlie, W.A. Mausolée de choses mortes. Paris, 1932.
43611.94.110 Fowlie, W.A. Matines et vers, 1933-1935. Paris, 1936.
43611.94.120 Fowlie, W.A. Intervalles. Paris, 1939.
43611.95.100 Fowlie, W.A. La pureté dans l'art. Montréal, 194-.
43612.2.30 Fraudet, René. Le crime de Sylvestre Bonnard. Paris, 1918.
43612.2.31 Fraudet, René. La maison cernée. Paris, 1920.
43612.2.32 Fraudet, René. Montmartre. Paris, 1910.
43612.2.33 Fraudet, René. L'homme qui assassina. Paris, 1913.
43612.2.34 Fraudet, René. Blanche Câline. Paris, 1913.
43612.2.35 Fraudet, René. Colette Baudoche. Paris, 1920.
43612.2.36 Fraudet, René. La bataille. Paris, 1921.
43612.2.37 Fraudet, René. Le reflet. Paris, 1922.
43612.2.39 Fraudet, René. L'insoumise. Paris, 1922.
43612.2.41 Fraudet, René. La gardienne; pièce en 4 actes. Paris, 1923.
43612.2.43 Fraudet, René. L'appassionate. Paris, 1920.
43612.2.45 Fraudet, René. L'homme qui assassina. 4. éd. Paris, 1913.
43612.2.47 Fraudet, René. L'homme a l'hispano. Roman 1-5. Paris, 1925.
43612.2.50 Fraudet, René. L'eau du Nil; roman. Paris, 1926.
43612.2.55 Fraudet, René. Les amants de Paris. Paris, 1928.
43612.2.60 Fraudet, René. Deux fois vingt ans, roman. 102. éd. Paris, 1928.
43612.2.65 Fraudet, René. Prelude aux poèmes du coq. Paris, 1916.
43612.3.30 Frappa, Jean José. L'idée; roman. Paris, 1919.
43612.3.35 Frappa, Jean José. Molière. Paris, 1922.
43612.3.40 Frappa, Jean José. A Paris. Paris, 1927.
43612.3.1100 Fraigneau, André. Les étonnements de Guillaume Francoeur. Paris, 1960.
43612.3.1110 Fraigneau, André. Le livre de raison d'un roi fou. Paris, 1968.
43612.3.2100 Frank, Nino. Mémoire brisée. Paris, 1968. 2v.
43612.4.100 France, Claire. Les enfants qui s'aiment. Paris, 1957.
43612.4.102 France, Claire. Les enfants qui s'aiment; roman. Montréal, 1956.
43612.4.110 France, Claire. Et le septième jour; roman. Montréal, 1958.
43612.4.112 France, Claire. Et le septième jour; roman. Paris, 1958.
43612.4.120 France, Claire. Autour de toi Tristran. Paris, 1962.
43612.4.1100 Francillon, Clarisse. Béatrice et les insectes. Paris, 1936.
43612.4.1110 Francillon, Clarisse. Le carnet à lucarnes; roman. Paris, 1968.
43612.4.1120 Francillon, Clarisse. Vingt-neuf contes. Honfleur, 1968.
43612.4.2100 Francolin, Claude. About de souffle. Paris, 1960.
43612.4.3100 Frank, Jean M. Journal d'un autre. Paris, 1960.
43612.4.4100 Francescat, Pierre. Le bonheur est sur l'autre rive; roman. Paris, 1959.
43612.5.100 Fraudet, René. La menace; pièce en quatre actes. Paris, 1925.
43612.5.110 Fraudet, René. Aphrodite. Paris, 1914.
43612.5.120 Fraudet, René. Auprès de ma blonde. 167. éd. Paris, 1929.
43612.5.130 Fraudet, René. Le voleur de femmes. Paris, 1931.
43612.5.140 Fraudet, René. La côte des dieux. Paris, 1929.
43612.5.150 Fraudet, René. Le lieutenant de Gibraltar. Paris, 1936.
43612.5.160 Fraudet, René. Zigoël. Paris, 1932.
43612.5.170 Fraudet, René. La nuit sur le Rhin. Paris, 1919.
43612.22.110 Frédérique, André. Histoires blanches. 2. éd. Paris? 1945.
43612.23.100 Frenaud, André. Passage de la visitation. Paris, 1956.
43612.23.110 Frénaud, André. Poemas de dessaus le plancher. Paris, 1949.
43612.23.120 Frénaud, André. Il n'y a pas de paradis; poèmes. Paris, 1962.
43612.23.121 Frénaud, André. Il n'y a pas de paradis; poèmes, 1943-1960. Paris, 1967.
43612.23.130 Frénaud, André. André Frénaud. Milano, 1964.
43612.23.140 Frénaud, André. La sainte face; poèmes. Paris, 1968.
43612.23.1100 Frénouville, Anne. Thalassa; poèmes. Paris, 1956.
43612.24.100 Frère, Maud. L'herbe à moi. 3. éd. Paris, 1957.
43612.24.110 Frère, Maud. Les jumeaux millénaires; roman. Paris, 1963.
43612.24.120 Frère, Maud. La delice. Paris, 1961.
43612.24.130 Frère, Maud. Guido. Paris, 1965.
43612.24.140 Frère, Maud. Le temps d'une carte portale. Paris, 1967.
43612.24.150 Frère, Maud. L'ange avengle. Paris, 1970.
43612.24.1100 Frère, André. Nouvelles comédies à une voix. Paris, 1967.
43612.25.100 Freustié, Jean. Les collines de l'Est, nouvelles. Paris, 1967.
43612.25.110 Freustié, Jean. Le droit d'aînesse. Paris, 1968.
43612.30.100 Franco, Guy. Pas de visa pour Abidjan, récit. Toulouse? 1967.
43612.35.100 Frédérix, P. On ne vit qu'une fois; roman. Paris, 1949.
43612.41.100 Frick, Louis de Gonzague. Statures lyriques. Paris, 1955.
43612.41.110 Frick, Louis de Gonzague. Abrupta nubes. Paris, 1955.
43612.41.120 Frick, Louis de Gonzague. Vibones. Paris, 1932.
43612.42.100 Frié, Jacqueline Frédéric. Si peu de temps. Paris, 1957.
43612.58.100 Franche, Paul. Le legende dovée des Bêtes. Paris, 1907.
43612.58.1100 France, Naira. Exil. London, 1944.
43612.58.6100 Francis, Louis. La neige de Galatie. 7. éd. Paris, 1936.
43612.59.103 Francis, Robert (pseud.). La grange aux trois belles. 14. éd. Paris, 1933.
43612.59.110 Francis, Robert (pseud.). Le bateau-refuge. 41. éd. Paris, 1934.
43612.59.112 Francis, Robert (pseud.). Les mariés de Paris. 11. éd. Paris, 1935.
43612.59.120 Francis, Robert (pseud.). La maison de vivre. 21. éd. Paris, 1934.
43612.59.705 Francis, Robert (pseud.). The wolf at the door. Boston, 1925.
43612.60.100 Francisci, Carlo. Fantasies littéraires. Perugia, 1909.
43612.61.100 Franck, Henri. La danse devant l'Arche. 4. éd. Paris, 1917.
43612.61.110 Franck, Henri. Lettres à quelques amis. Paris, 1926.
43612.61.800 Discours prononcé sur la tombe de Henri Franck. n.p., 1912?

43511 - 43873 Individual authors, etc. - 1900- - Known authors (363 scheme plus 10) - cont.

43612.63.100 Franzoni, F. Le printemps tragique; poems. Paris, 1928.
43612.63.4100 Fréminville, Claude de. Des vies exemplaires; roman. Paris, 1946.
43612.63.6100 Freminville, René Marie de la Poix de. Rien que la mer. Paris, 1946.
43612.63.6110 Freminville, René Marie de la Poix de. Cet étrange Christophe Colomb. Paris, 1968.
43612.63.6120 Freminville, René Marie de la Poix de. Marines, nouvelles. N.Y., 1941.
43612.63.6130 Freminville, René Marie de la Poix de. Abandons de postes. Paris, 1939.
43612.63.6140 Freminville, René Marie de la Poix de. Nuit et lumière de la mer; roman. Paris, 1968.
43612.64.100 Frémont, Jean. L'ascension et d'autres poèmes. Oxford, 1944.
43612.65.41 Frank, Bernard. Un siècle d'ebordé. Paris, 1970.
43612.65.100 Frank, Bernard. L'illusion comique. Paris, 1955.
43613.25.100 Fresnay, Pierre. L'écurie Watson. Paris, 1937.
43613.45.100 Frison-Roche, Roger. Retour à la montagne. Paris, 1917.
43613.45.110 Frison-Roche, Roger. Lumière de l'Arctique. Paris, 1962- 2v.
43613.45.700 Frison-Roche, Roger. First on the rope. London, 1949.
43613.45.701 Frison-Roche, Roger. First on the rope. 1. American ed. N.Y., 1950.
43613.45.710 Frison-Roche, Roger. The grand crevasse. 1. American ed. N.Y., 1951.
43613.45.720 Frison-Roche, Roger. The lost crevasse. London, 1952.
43613.45.735 Frison-Roche, Roger. The raid. 1. ed. N.Y., 1964.
43613.45.740 Frison-Roche, Roger. The lost trail of the Sahara. 1. American ed. N.Y., 1952.
43613.64.100 Froment, Jeanne. Au fil de la vie. Paris, 1957.
43613.65.100 Fromentin, A. Paroles volées à l'écoute. Paris, 1938.
43614.1.100 Fua, Albert. Le triomphe de satan. Paris, 1926.
43614.12.100 Fuchs, Janine. Fibres de vie. Paris, 1963.
43615.1.330 Gadala, Marie-Therese. Tels que je les vois. Paris, 1926.
43616.1.30 Ganay, E. de. Le fleures du silence. Paris, 1911.
43616.1.8100 Gautier, Jean Jacques. L'oreille. Paris, 1945.
43616.1.8110 Gautier, Jean Jacques. Une femme prisonnière. Paris, 1968.
43616.1.8120 Gautier, Jean Jacques. La chambre du fond. Paris, 1970.
43616.1.8700 Gautier, Jean Jacques. The bridge of asses. London, 1953.
43616.2.30 Gautier, Judith. Le collier des jours: le second rang du collier. Paris, 1909.
43616.2.30.5 Gautier, Judith. Le collier des jours: le troisième rang du collier. 5. éd. Paris, 1909.
43616.2.33 Gautier, Judith. La marchande de sourires. Paris, 1888.
43616.2.34 Gautier, Judith. Le vieux de la montagne. Paris, 1893.
43616.2.35 Gautier, Judith. Les princesses d'amour. Paris, 1900.
43616.2.36F Gautier, Judith. Poèmes de la libellule. Paris, 1885.
43616.2.37 Gautier, Judith. Fleurs d'Orient. Paris, 1893.
43616.2.38 Gautier, Judith. Khou-n-Atonou; fragments d'un papyrus. Paris, 1898.
43616.2.39 Gautier, Judith. Mémoires d'un éléphant blanc. 7. éd. Paris, 1923.
43616.2.42 Gautier, Judith. Iskender, histoire persane. Paris, 1894.
43616.2.45 Gautier, Judith. La fille du ciel. 10. éd. Paris, 1911.
43616.2.50 Gautier, Judith. L'usurpateur. Paris, n.d. 2v.
43616.2.80A Gourmont, R. de. Judith Gautier. Paris, 1904.
43616.2.80B Gourmont, R. de. Judith Gautier. Paris, 1904.
43616.2.85 Camacho, M. Judith Gautier, sa vie et son oeuvres. Thèse. Paris, 1939.
43616.3.30 Gaubert, E. L'amour Marié. Paris, 1913.
43616.4.30 Gayet, A. Le Roman de Claude D'Antioche. Paris, 1914.
43616.7.30 Gaberel, Henri. Tombeau pour un amour médiéval. Porrentruy, 1944.
43616.9.21 Gabory, Georges. Coeurs à prendre. Poèmes. Paris, 1920.
43616.9.100 Gabriel, Pierre. L'amour de toi. Veilhes, 1967.
43616.12.100 Gachon, Lucien. Maria. Clermont-Ferrand, 1969.
43616.17.100 Gadenne, Paul. L'invitation chez les Stirl. 6. éd. Paris, 1955.
43616.17.110 Gadenne, Paul. Le vent noir. Paris, 1947.
43616.31.21 Gag, Francis. Théâtre niçois. Nice, 1970.
43616.33.100 Gagliolo, F. Drigo. Paris, 1957.
43616.33.1100 Gagnon, Alain. Le pour et le contre; nouvelles. Montréal, 1970.
43616.41.100 Gaillard de Champris, Henry. Sur quelques idéalistes. Paris, 1908.
43616.41.110 Gaillard de Champris, Henry. Anniversaires et pèlerinages. Québec, 1921.
43616.41.120 Gaillard de Champris, Henry. Les heroiques et les tristes. Québec, 1924.
43616.41.1100 Gaillard, André. Le fond du coeur. Marseille, 1927.
43616.41.1110 Gaillard, André. Oeuvres complètes. Marseille, 1941.
43616.41.2100 Gaillard, Robert. Louisiane; roman. Paris, 1949.
43616.41.2110 Gaillard, Robert. Images du neilleur des mondes. Givors, 1955.
43616.41.2120 Gaillard, Robert. Le miel de la haine. Paris, 1958.
43616.41.2130 Gaillard, Robert. Rayaume de la nuit. Paris, 1959.
43616.41.2140 Gaillard, Robert. Les mariés de l'exil. Paris, 1959.
43616.41.2150 Gaillard, Robert. Marie des Isles. Paris, 1960- 7v.
43616.41.2160 Gaillard, Robert. Le sang du tigre. Paris, 1969.
43616.41.2170 Gaillard, Robert. La sultane de Jolo. Paris, 1970.
43616.41.3100 Gaillard, J.C. Croix de bois. Paris, 1959.
43616.41.4021 Gaillard, Yann. Collection particulière. Paris, 1966.
43616.50.5100 Galls, Max Louis. L'age d'homme. Paris, 1957.
43616.50.6100 Galunaud, G. El-l'Ben. La Courneuve, 1958.
43616.50.7100 Gallez, Jean-Paul. Féminaires. Paris, 1967.
43616.50.8100 Galil (pseud.). Les mains coupeuses de mémoire. Paris, 1961.
43616.51.100 Galopin, Arnould. Le bacille. Paris, 1928.
43616.51.102 Galopin, Arnould. Les poilus de la 9e. Paris, 1916?
43616.51.1100 Galtier-Boissière, Jean. Memoires d'un Parisien. Paris, 1960- 3v.
43616.51.1110 Galtier-Boissière, Jean. Loin de la rifflette. Paris, 1921.
43616.52.100 Galzy, Jeanne. Les allonges. 56. éd. Paris, 1923.
43616.52.100.5 Galzy, Jeanne. Les allonges. 35. éd. Paris, 1923.
43616.52.110 Galzy, Jeanne. Le retour dans la vie. Paris, 1929.
43616.52.120 Galzy, Jeanne. Celle qui vient d'ailleurs. Paris, 1958.
43616.52.130 Galzy, Jeanne. La surprise de vivre. Paris, 1969.
43616.53.21 Gambier, Gerard. Rocailles; nouvelles. Bruxelles, 1965.
43616.53.1100 Gamarra, Pierre. La maison de feu. Evreux, 1970.
43616.53.1110 Gamarra, Pierre. Pauchkine. Bram, 1970.
43616.53.1120 Gamarra, Pierre. L'or et le sang. Paris, 1970.
43616.56.100 Gamo, Jean. Héresmédan. London, 1958.
43616.58.100 Gandon, Yves. Ginèvre. Levallois-Perret, 1969.

43511 - 43873 Individual authors, etc. - 1900- - Known authors (363 scheme plus 10) - cont.

43616.58.110 Gandon, Yves. Petite suite d'été. Limoges, 1957.
43616.58.120 Gandon, Yves. Pour un Bourbon Collins. Paris, 1967.
43616.58.130 Gandon, Yves. Monsieur Miracle; roman. Paris, 1968.
43616.58.140 Gandon, Yves. Ginèvre. Levallois-Perret, 1969.
43616.58.150 Gandon, Yves. La ville invisible. Paris, 1953.
43616.59.100 Gandéra, Felix. Atout...coeur. Paris, 1922.
43616.59.2775 Gangateau, Alfredo. Poesía. Quito, 1956.
43616.60.100 Ganne, Gilbert. La panache blanc. Paris, 1960.
43616.60.110 Ganne, Gilbert. Les hauts cris; roman. Paris, 1965.
43616.60.120 Ganne, Gilbert. Interviews impubliables. Paris, 1952.
43616.60.130 Ganne, Gilbert. Un fils unique; roman. Paris, 1968.
43616.62.100 Gantillon, Simon. Cyclone, pièce en deux actes. Paris, 1923.
43616.62.110 Gantillon, Simon. Maya. Paris, 1924.
43616.62.112 Gantillon, Simon. Maya. Paris, 1949.
43616.62.700 Gantillon, Simon. Vessel of wrath. N.Y., 1947.
43616.62.705 Gantillon, Simon. Maya; a play. N.Y., 1928.
43616.62.706 Gantillon, Simon. Maya. N.Y., 1928.
43616.63.21 Ganzo, Robert. Poèmes. Paris, 1942.
43616.63.23 Ganzo, Robert. L'oeuvre poétique. Paris, 1956.
43616.63.100 Ganzo, Robert. Langage, poèmes. Paris, 1947.
43616.64.100 Garnier, Christine. White people smile at me. London, 1952.
43616.64.110 Garnier, Christine. L'essuie-glace; roman. Paris, 1967.
43616.74.100 Gardilanne, Paule de. Le dernier rêve du duc d'Enghien. Paris, 1905.
43616.74.1100 Garçon, Maurice. Plaidoyers chimériques. Paris, 1954.
43616.74.2100 Gardye, Philippe. Matraque. Dessins de Lonchamp. Paris, 1963.
43616.75.100 Garenne, A. La forêt tra. Paris, 1918.
43616.75.110 Garenne, A. L'amour vainqueur. Paris, 1957.
43616.76.100 Garo, Joseph. Pages d'évadé. Paris, 1945.
43616.76.1100 Garnier, Pierre. Perpetuum mobile. Paris, 1968.
43616.77.104 Garr, Max. Le chant de Weyla; la voix. N.Y., 1942.
43616.77.110 Garr, Max. Histoire d'un chien d'émigrées et autres histoires. N.Y., 1943.
43616.77.1100 Garrabé, Michel. Le Déséquilibre. Honfleur, 1969.
43616.77.2100 Garreau, Albert. Inquisitions. Paris, 1970-
43616.78.41 Gary, Romain. Chien blanc. Paris, 1970.
43616.78.110 Gary, Romain. Education européenne. Paris, 1945.
43616.78.112 Gary, Romain. Education européenne. Paris, 1961.
43616.78.120 Gary, Romain. Frère Océan. Paris, 1965. 3v.
43616.78.130 Gary, Romain. Tulipe. 2. éd. Paris, 1946.
43616.78.132 Gary, Romain. Tulipe. Paris, 1970.
43616.78.140 Gary, Romain. Les couleurs du jours. 7. éd. Paris, 1952.
43616.78.150 Gary, Romain. Les racines du ciel, roman. 271. éd. Paris, 1956.
43616.78.160 Gary, Romain. Lady L. N.Y., 1959.
43616.78.170 Gary, Romain. Le grand vestiaire. Paris, 1949.
43616.78.180 Gary, Romain. Johnnie Colier. Paris, 1961.
43616.78.190 Gary, Romain. Gloire à nos illustres pionniers. Paris, 1962.
43616.78.200 Gary, Romain. La promesse de l'aube. Paris, 1960.
43616.78.210 Gary, Romain. Les mangeurs d'étoiles. Paris, 1966.
43616.78.220 Gary, Romain. Adieu Gary Cooper. Paris, 1969.
43616.78.705 Gary, Romain. A European education. N.Y., 1960.
43616.78.715 Gary, Romain. Promise at dawn. 1. American ed. N.Y., 1961.
43616.78.720 Gary, Romain. Nothing important ever dies. London, 1960.
43616.78.730 Gary, Romain. The talent scout. 1. ed. N.Y., 1961.
43616.78.735 Gary, Romain. Hissing tales. 1. ed. N.Y., 1964.
43616.78.740 Gary, Romain. Forest of anger. London, 1944.
43616.78.745 Gary, Romain. The ski bum. N.Y., 1965.
43616.78.750 Gary, Romain. The dance of Genghis Cohn. N.Y., 1968.
43616.78.1100 Garzarolli, Richard. Le grand nocturne. Lausanne, 1967.
43616.79.100 Gascar, Pierre. Les bêtes. Paris, 1953.
43616.79.110 Gascar, Pierre. Le visage clos. Paris, 1951.
43616.79.120 Gascar, Pierre. La graine. 17. éd. Paris, 1955.
43616.79.130 Gascar, Pierre. L'herbe des rues. 16. éd. Paris, 1957.
43616.79.140 Gascar, Pierre. Les pas perdue. 5. éd. Paris, 1958.
43616.79.150 Gascar, Pierre. La barre de corail. 6. éd. Paris, 1958.
43616.79.160 Gascar, Pierre. Soleils. Paris, 1960.
43616.79.170 Gascar, Pierre. Vertiges du présent. Paris, 1962.
43616.79.180 Gascar, Pierre. Les moutons du feu. Paris, 1963.
43616.79.190 Gascar, Pierre. Les charmes. Paris, 1965.
43616.79.200 Gascar, Pierre. Le fugitif; roman. Paris, 1961.
43616.79.210 Gascar, Pierre. Le meilleur de la vie. Paris, 1964.
43616.79.220 Gascar, Pierre. Les femmes. Paris, 1955.
43616.79.230 Gascar, Pierre. Auto. Paris, 1967.
43616.79.700 Gascar, Pierre. Beasts and men. 1. ed. Boston, 1956.
43616.79.705 Gascar, Pierre. Beasts and men. N.Y., 1960.
43616.79.710 Gascar, Pierre. The seed. London, 1959.
43616.79.715 Gascar, Pierre. Women and the sun. Boston, 1964.
43616.79.720 Gascar, Pierre. The fugitive. Boston, 1964.
43616.79.725 Gascar, Pierre. Lambs of fire. N.Y., 1965?
43616.79.730 Gascar, Pierre. The best years. N.Y., 1967.
43616.79.1100 Gascht, André. Le Royaume de Danemark. Bruxelles, 1966.
43616.81.100 Gaspar, Élisabeth. L'amour fantôme. Paris, 1958.
43616.81.110 Gaspar, Élisabeth. Les grilles du parc. Paris, 1960.
43616.82.100 Gasquet, Marie Girard. Une enfance provençale. Paris, 1967.
43616.82.1100 Gastines, Marie de. Miroitements. Paris, 1962.
43616.82.1110 Gastines, Marie de. Conquecigrues. Goudargues, 1964.
43616.83.100 Gasquet, Joachim. Il y a une volupté dans la douleur. Paris, 1921.
43616.83.110 Gasquet, Joachim. Dionysos. Paris, 1905.
43616.83.115 Gasquet, Joachim. Des chants de l'amour et des hymnes. Paris, 1928.
43616.83.120 Gasquet, Joachim. Les printemps; poèmes. Paris, 1909.
43616.83.130 Gasquet, Joachim. Le paradis retrauvé. Paris, 1911.
43616.83.2100 Gastine, Louis. Plaisirs féodaux. Paris, 1935.
43616.83.2110 Gastine, Louis. Souveraines et princesses d'amour. Paris, 1935.
43616.83.2120 Gastine, Louis. Orgies gauloises. Paris, 1935?
43616.83.2130 Gastine, Louis. Voluptés Gallo-Romaines. Paris, 1935.
43616.83.2140 Gastine, Louis. Les nuits galantes du Régent. Paris, 1935.
43616.83.2150 Gastine, Louis. Le roi - soleil s'amus. Paris, 1924.
43616.83.3100 Gasztold, Carmen Bernos de. Prayers from the Ark. London, 1963.
43616.83.3110 Gasztold, Carmen Bernos de. Prayers from the Ark. N.Y., 1962.
43616.87.100 Gattefossé, René M. Paradis; société anonyme. Lyon, 1941.
43616.87.110 Gattefossé, René M. Le roman de Marthe, la salyenne. Lyon, 1942.
43616.88.100 Gatti, Armand. Le poisson noir. Paris, 1958.

43511 - 43873 Individual authors, etc. - 1900- - Known authors (363 scheme plus 10) - cont.

43616.88.110 Gatti, Armand. V comme Vietnam. Paris, 1967.
43616.88.120 Gatti, Armand. La naissance. Paris, 1968.
43616.88.130 Gatti, Armand. La passion du général Franco. Paris, 1968.
43616.89.100 Gaubert, Léo. Amnésie. Paris, 1946.
43616.89.1103 Gauthier, Marie Joséphine. Orages désirés. 3. éd. Paris, 1957.
43616.89.1110 Gauthier, Marie Joséphine. La patte et la main. Paris, 1959.
43616.89.2100 Gautier-Vignal, Louis. Lyncée. Paris, 1950.
43616.89.3100 Gaud, Auguste. Au pays natal. Niort, 1893.
43616.89.4100 Gautier, Yvonne. Mon enfance et elle, souvenirs. Paris, 1965.
43616.89.5100 Gaulis, Louis. Capitaine Karagheuz. Lausanne, 1967.
43616.89.5110 Gaulis, Louis. Le serviteur absolu. Lausanne, 1967.
43616.89.6100 Gaultier, Yvette. Mes vérités. Paris, 1954.
43616.89.7100 Gauzelin, Alain. L'île mouvante. Paris, 1970.
43616.90.100 Gaucheron, Jacques H. La grande épitaphe - misère. Paris, 1946.
43616.90.110 Gaucheron, Jacques H. Les canuts. Paris, 1965.
43616.90.120 Gaucheron, Jacques H. Cahier grec, hommage à Ritsos. Paris, 1968.
43616.98.100 Gazave, Jean. Romain Apuech; roman. Lyon, 1941.
43616.98.1100 Gay-Lussac, Bruno. La mort d'un prêtre. Paris, 1953.
43616.98.1110 Gay-Lussac, Bruno. La robe. Paris, 1966.
43616.98.1120 Gay-Lussac, Bruno. L'ami. Paris, 1968.
43616.98.1130 Gay-Lussac, Bruno. Introduction à la vie profane. Paris, 1970.
43616.98.2100 Gayet Tancrède, Paul. Contes à pic. Paris, 1965.
43616.98.3100 Gazel, Louis. Pro patria. Hanoi, 1907.
43617.1.30 Gérard, Rosemonde. Un bon petit diable. Paris, 1912.
43617.1.31 Gérard, Rosemonde. La marchande d'allumettes. Paris, 1914.
43617.1.35 Gérard, Rosemonde. La robe d'un soir. Paris, 1925.
43617.1.40 Gérard, Rosemonde. Les papillotes. Paris, 1931.
43617.2 Gerbidon, M.M. Une affaire d'or. Paris, 1912.
43617.2.3100 Genet, Louis. Les signets du missel. Paris, 1940.
43617.3.30 Genty, R. Les âmes légères. Paris, 1911.
43617.4.30 Géraldy, Paul. Les petites ames. Paris, 1908.
43617.4.31 Géraldy, Paul. Toi et moi. 30. éd. Paris, 1917.
43617.4.31.10 Géraldy, Paul. Toi et moi. Paris, 1923.
43617.4.32 Géraldy, Paul. La guerre, Madame. 47. éd. Paris, 1917.
43617.4.32.5 Géraldy, Paul. La guerre, Madame. 34. éd. Paris, 1917.
43617.4.32.10 Géraldy, Paul. The war Madame. N.Y., 1917.
43617.4.33 Géraldy, Paul. Les noces d'argent. Paris, 1917.
43617.4.34 Géraldy, Paul. Les noces d'argent. Paris, 1928.
43617.4.35F Géraldy, Paul. Aimer. Paris, 1921.
43617.4.36 Géraldy, Paul. Aimer. Paris, 1922.
43617.4.38 Géraldy, Paul. Carnet d'un auteur dramatique. Paris, 1922.
43617.4.40 Géraldy, Paul. Si je voulais. Paris, 1924.
43617.4.43 Géraldy, Paul. Robert et Marianne. 17. éd. Paris, 1925.
43617.4.45 Géraldy, Paul. Robert et Marianne. Paris, 1926.
43617.4.47 Géraldy, Paul. Le grand-père. Paris, 1915.
43617.4.48 Géraldy, Paul. La fantaisie. Paris, 1908.
43617.4.50 Géraldy, Paul. Son mari. Paris, 1927.
43617.4.55 Géraldy, Paul. Theater. v.2. Berlin, 1928.
43617.4.57 Géraldy, Paul. Le prélude. Paris, 1923.
43617.4.60 Géraldy, Paul. Christine; pièce en quatre actes. Paris, 1932.
43617.4.62 Géraldy, Paul. La comédie des familles. Paris, 1908.
43617.4.65 Géraldy, Paul. Do, mi, sol, do! Paris, 1935.
43617.4.75 Géraldy, Paul. L'amour; or, The art of love. N.Y., 1930.
43617.4.85 Géraldy, Paul. Duo; pièce en trois actes d'après le roman de Colette. Paris, 1939.
43617.4.90 Géraldy, Paul. Ihr Mann (Son Mari). Berlin, 1927.
43617.5.30 Géniaux, Charles. La passion d'Armelle Louanais. Paris, 1918.
43617.5.31 Géniaux, Charles. Le cyprès; a novel. Paris, 1918.
43617.5.32 Géniaux, Charles. Le voueur. Paris, 1909.
43617.5.33 Géniaux, Charles. La victoire du bled; nouvelles. n.p., 1920.
43617.5.34 Géniaux, Charles. La résurrection d'Aphrodite; roman. Paris, 1923.
43617.5.39 Géniaux, Charles. Les feux s'eteigneut. Paris, 1926.
43617.5.45 Géniaux, Charles. Le choc des races. Paris, 1934.
43617.6.30 Germain, André. Renée Vivien. Paris, 1917.
43617.6.1100 Gabalda, Jean. Mortes avant l'été, poèmes. Paris, 1956.
43617.7.30 Génin, Auguste. Poèmes aztèques...1884-1889. Paris, 1890.
43617.7.31 Génin, Auguste. Poèmes aztèques. 2. éd. México, 1907.
43617.7.35 Génin, Auguste. Vers pour la France. México, 1918.
43617.7.40 Génin, Auguste. Legendes et recits du Mexique ancien. Paris, 1923?
43617.24.100 Geeraert, Robert Lucien. La corde à danser. Tournai, 1960.
43617.24.110 Geeraert, Robert Lucien. Les printemps morts. Tournai, 1961.
43617.31.100 Gegauff, Paul. Une partie de plaisir. Paris, 1958.
43617.40.100 Gehri, Alfred. Sixième etage. Paris, 1937.
43617.59.100 Genevoix, Maurice. Raboliot. 89. éd. Paris, 1925.
43617.59.110 Genevoix, Maurice. Roû, roman. Paris, 1931.
43617.59.120 Genevoix, Maurice. Cyrille. Paris, 1949.
43617.59.130 Genevoix, Maurice. L'aventure est en nous. Paris, 1952.
43617.59.140 Genevoix, Maurice. Fatou cissé, roman. Paris, 1954.
43617.59.150 Genevoix, Maurice. Routes de l'aventure. Paris, 1959.
43617.59.160 Genevoix, Maurice. La framboise et bellehumeur. Paris, 1959.
43617.59.170 Genevoix, Maurice. Au cadran de mon clocher. Paris, 1960.
43617.59.180 Genevoix, Maurice. La dernière harde. Paris, 1960.
43617.59.190 Genevoix, Maurice. Vaincre à Olympie. Paris, 1960.
43617.59.200 Genevoix, Maurice. Ceux de 14. Paris, 1962.
43617.59.210 Genevoix, Maurice. Derrière les collines. Paris, 1963.
43617.59.220 Genevoix, Maurice. Rémi des rauches. Paris, 1922.
43617.59.230 Genevoix, Maurice. Beau-françois. Paris, 1965.
43617.59.240 Genevoix, Maurice. La forêt perdue, roman. Paris, 1967.
43617.59.250 Genevoix, Maurice. Jardins sans murs, roman. Paris, 1968.
43617.59.260 Genevoix, Maurice. Tendre bestiaire. Paris, 1969.
43617.59.270 Genevoix, Maurice. Bestiaire sans oubli. Paris, 1971.
43617.59.800 Timbaldi Abruzzese, Eva. Il romanzo rurale di Maurice Genevoix. Torino, 1956.
43617.59.2021 Genette, Gérard. Figures; essais. Paris, 1966. 2v.
43617.66.100 George, Nancy. La chalegane. Paris, 1929.
43617.66.110 George, Nancy. Jeux d'été; nouvelle. Paris, 1931.
43617.66.120 George, Nancy. Une aventure de Don Juan. Paris, 1935.
43617.66.130 George, Nancy. Cinq a sept. Paris, 1937.
43617.66.1100 Georges-Michel, Michel. Left bank. N.Y., 1931.

43511 - 43873 Individual authors, etc. - 1900- - Known authors (363 scheme plus 10) - cont.

43617.67.100 Georges-Michel, Michel. Nulle part dans le monde. N.Y., 1941- 2v.
43617.67.110 Georges-Michel, Michel. Star...roman d'une demoiselle de cinéma. N.Y., 1941.
43617.67.115 Georges-Michel, Michel. Les Montparnos. Paris, 1929.
43617.67.120 Georges-Michel, Michel. Autres personnalités que j'ai connues. N.Y., 1943.
43617.67.130 Georges-Michel, Michel. Bohème a New York. N.Y., 1944.
43617.67.135 Georges-Michel, Michel. Dames éstranges. Montréal, 1944.
43617.72.100 Géraldy, Paul. L'homme de jolie. Paris, 1929.
43617.74.100 Gérard, Rosemonde. Les pipeaux. Paris, 1923.
43617.74.1100 Gerardin, François. Vingt trois. Paris, 1964.
43617.74.2100 Gérard, Jean. Poèmes déchirés. Paris, 1956.
43617.76.100 Germain, Philippe. Trois époques, roman (novembre 1940). Lyon, 1941.
43617.77.100 Germain, André. Famille! Paris, 1894.
43617.77.110 Germain, Andre. La bourgeosée qui brûle. Paris, 1951.
43617.77.120 Germain, André. Pèlerinages européens. 6. éd. Paris, 1924.
43617.77.2100 Germain, Gabriel. La lampe de Sala. Paris, 1958.
43617.78.12A Genêt, Jean. Oeuvres complètes. Paris, 1952. 4v.
43617.78.12B Genêt, Jean. Oeuvres complètes. v.1. Paris, 1952.
43617.78.61 Genêt, Jean. Lettres à Roger Blin. Paris, 1966.
43617.78.100 Genêt, Jean. Haute surveillance. 6. éd. Paris, 1949.
43617.78.102 Genêt, Jean. Haute surveillance. Paris, 1965.
43617.78.110 Genêt, Jean. Journal au voleur. 12. éd. Paris, 1949.
43617.78.120 Genêt, Jean. Le balcon. Décines, 1956.
43617.78.121 Genêt, Jean. Le balcon. Décines, 1962.
43617.78.122 Genêt, Jean. Le balcon. 2. éd. Décines, 1960.
43617.78.130 Genêt, Jean. Miracle de la rose. 2. éd. Décines, 1956.
43617.78.140 Genêt, Jean. Poèmes. Lyon, 1948.
43617.78.142 Genêt, Jean. Poèmes. 2. éd. Barbezat, 1962.
43617.78.150 Genêt, Jean. Les bonnes. Sceaux, 1954.
43617.78.155 Genêt, Jean. The blacks. London, 1960.
43617.78.160A Genêt, Jean. Les nègres. Décines, 1958.
43617.78.160B Genêt, Jean. Les nègres. Décines, 1958.
43617.78.162 Genêt, Jean. Les nègres. 2. éd. Décines, 1960.
43617.78.170 Genêt, Jean. L'atelier d'Alberto Giacometti. Décines, 1958.
43617.78.180 Genêt, Jean. Les parauents. Décines, 1961.
43617.78.190 Genêt, Jean. L'enfant criminel et Adame Miroir. Paris, 1949.
43617.78.200 Genêt, Jean. Funeral rites. N.Y., 1969.
43617.78.700 Genêt, Jean. The maids. N.Y., 1954.
43617.78.702 Genêt, Jean. The maids and Death Watch. N.Y., 1962.
43617.78.710 Genêt, Jean. The balcony. N.Y., 1958.
43617.78.712 Genêt, Jean. The balcony. N.Y., 1960.
43617.78.715 Genêt, Jean. The balcony. N.Y., 1960.
43617.78.718 Genêt, Jean. The balcony. London, 1966.
43617.78.720A Genêt, Jean. The screens. N.Y., 1962.
43617.78.720B Genêt, Jean. The screens. N.Y., 1962.
43617.78.725 Genêt, Jean. Querelle of Brest. London, 1966.
43617.78.730 Genêt, Jean. Miracle of the rose. London, 1965.
43617.78.735 Genêt, Jean. Letters to Roger Blin; reflections on the theater. N.Y., 1969.
43617.78.775 Genêt, Jean. Der zum Tode Verurteilte. 1. Aufl. Hamburg, 1969.
43617.78.800 Konkel, M.H. Sister René Fernantat. Washington, 1952.
43617.78.805 McMahon, J.H. The imagination of Jean Genêt. New Haven, 1963.
43617.78.810 Sartre, J.P. Saint Genêt. London, 1964.
43617.78.815 Bonnefoy, Claude. Jean Genêt. Paris, 1965.
43617.78.820 Driver, Tom Faw. Jean Genêt. N.Y., 1966.
43617.78.825A Coe, Richard Nelson. The vision of Jean Genêt. London, 1968.
43617.78.825B Coe, Richard Nelson. The vision of Jean Genêt. London, 1968.
43617.78.826 Coe, Richard Nelson. The vision of Jean Genêt. N.Y., 1968.
43617.78.830 Thody, Philip. Jean Genêt; a study of his novels and plays. London, 1968.
43617.78.840 Knapp, Bettina. Jean Genêt. N.Y., 1968.
43617.78.845 Kliess, Werner. Genêt. Velber, 1967.
43617.78.1011 Gervais, Maurice. Oeuvres complètes. Paris, 1954-
43617.78.2100 Gervais, Albert. Une fille de H'an. Paris, 1928.
43617.80.100 Gengenbach, E. Judas. Paris, 1949.
43617.82.100 Gennari, Genevieve. Journal d'une bourgeoise. Paris, 1959.
43617.82.700 Gennari, Genevieve. The other woman I am. N.Y., 1961.
43617.82.705 Gennari, Genevieve. Nostalgia. 1. American ed. N.Y., 1964.
43617.85.100 Getten, Gilbert. La lyre ardente. Paris, 1934.
43617.86.100 Gers, José. Thalassa; poèmes. Bruxelles, 1964.
43617.90.100 Gével, Claude. Cher les hommes. Paris, 1929.
43618.90.100 Gevers, Marie. La comtesse des Dignes; roman. pt.1-3. Paris, 1931.
43618.90.110 Gevers, Marie. Madame Orpha, ou La sérénade de mai. pt. 1-2. Paris, 1933.
43618.90.120 Gevers, Marie. Le voyage de frère Jean. Paris, 1935.
43618.90.130 Gevers, Marie. Paravérités. Bruxelles, 1968.
43618.90.800 Goris, Jan Albert. Marie Gevers. Utrecht, 1969.
43619.23.21 Ghelderode, Michel de. Théâtre. 5. éd. Paris, 1950. 5v.
43619.23.25 Ghelderode, Michel de. Seven plays. London, 1961.
43619.23.27 Ghelderode, Michel de. Seven plays. N.Y., 1967.
43619.23.30 Ghelderode, Michel de. Sortilèges et autres contes crépusculaires. Verviers, 1962.
43619.23.31 Ghelderode, Michel de. Sortilèges et autres contes crépusculaires. Verviers, 1962.
43619.23.35 Ghelderode, Michel de. La flandre est un songe. Bruxelles, 1953.
43619.23.800 Lepage, Albert. Michel de Ghelderode. Paris, 1960?
43619.23.805 Vandromme, P. Michel de Ghelderode. Paris, 1963.
43619.23.810 Deberdt-Malaquais, Elisabeth. La quête de l'identité dans le théâtre de Ghelderode. Paris, 1967.
43619.23.815 Francis, Jean. L'eternal aujourd'hui de Michel de Ghelderode. Bruxelles, 1968.
43619.23.820 Decock, Jean. Le théâtre de Michel de Ghelderode. Paris, 1969.
43619.23.825 Beyen, Roland. Michel de Ghelderode. Bruxelles, 1971.
43619.24.100 Ghéon, Henri. La farce du pendu dépendu. Paris, 1920.
43619.24.110 Ghéon, Henri. Le débat de Nicolazia entre Sainte Anne et le recteur. Paris, 1922.
43619.24.120 Ghéon, Henri. L'homme né de la guerre. 3. éd. Paris, 1919.
43619.24.130 Ghéon, Henri. Le miroir de Jésus. Paris, 1920.

43511 - 43873 Individual authors, etc. - 1900- - Known authors (363 scheme plus 10) - cont.

43619.24.140 Ghéon, Henri. Les propos interrompus. Paris, 1926.
43619.24.150 Ghéon, Henri. Le jeux de l'enfer et du ciel, roman. Paris, 1929. 3v.
43619.24.160 Ghéon, Henri. Le comédien et la grâce. Paris, 1925.
43619.24.170 Ghéon, Henri. Les campagnes simples la solitude de l'été. Paris, 1897.
43619.24.180 Ghéon, Henri. Le pauvre sous l'escalier. 25. éd. Paris, 1936.
43619.24.200 Ghéon, Henri. Chants de la vie et la foi, 1897-1934. Paris, 1936.
43619.24.205 Ghéon, Henri. The secret of the curé d'Ars. N.Y., 1929.
43619.24.210 Ghéon, Henri. The secret of the curé d'Ars. London, 1936.
43619.24.220 Ghéon, Henri. La jambe noire, roman. Paris, 1941.
43619.24.230 Ghéon, Henri. Oedipe. Paris, 1952.
43619.24.700 Ghéon, Henri. St. Anne and the gouty rector. 1. ed. N.Y., 1950.
43619.24.710 Ghéon, Henri. The comedian. London, 1952.
43619.24.720 Ghéon, Henri. The marvellous history of St. Bernard. London, 1952.
43619.24.730 Ghéon, Henri. The marriage of St. Francis. London, 1952.
43619.24.800 Deléglise, M. Le théâtre d'Henri Ghéon. Sion, 1947.
43619.24.810 Brochet, Henri. Henri Ghéon. Paris, 1946.
43619.24.820 Reynaud, J. Henri Ghéon, 1875-1944; étude de bibliographie. Paris, 1960.
43619.25.100 Gheorghiu, Georges. Livre du nouveau Job. Paris, 1951.
43619.25.110 Gheorghiu, Georges. Homo Glacticus; roman. Paris, 1961.
43620.1.30 Gilbert, Oscar P. Lumière entrevue. Paris, 1918.
43620.1.35 Gilbert, Oscar P. L'humble bonheur. Paris, 1919.
43620.1.40 Gilbert, Oscar P. Le triomphe de la haine. Florence, 1920.
43620.1.58 Gilbert, Oscar P. Mollenard. 8. éd. Paris, 1936.
43620.1.60 Gilbert, Oscar P. Courrier d'Asie. 5. éd. Paris, 1937.
43620.2.2 Doré, R. Les livres d'André Gide. Abbeville, 1923.
43620.2.4 Uzès. Musée Municipal. André Gide: exposition du centenaire. Uzès, 1969.
43620.2.5 Gide, André. Oeuvres complètes. Paris, 1932-39. 15v.
43620.2.6 O'Brien, J. Index détaillé des quinze volumes. Asnières, 1954.
43620.2.10 Gide, André. André Gide - Paul Valéry. 14. éd. Paris, 1955.
43620.2.11 Gide, André. Self-portraits: The Gide/Valery letters. Chicago, 1966.
43620.2.21 Gide, André. Morceaux choisis. 27. éd. Paris, 1921.
43620.2.30.3 Gide, André. Isabelle. N.Y., 1947.
43620.2.30.4 Gide, André. Isabelle. N.Y., 1947.
43620.2.31 Gide, André. La porte étroite. 7. éd. Paris, 1949.
43620.2.31.5 Gide, André. La porte étroite. Paris, 1934.
X Cg 43620.2.32 Gide, André. L'immoraliste. 4. éd. Paris, 1911.
43620.2.32.15 Gide, André. The immoralist. N.Y., 1948.
43620.2.32.20 Gide, André. L'immoraliste. Paris, 1960.
43620.2.32.25 Gide, André. The immoralist. N.Y., 1970.
43620.2.33 Gide, André. Le roi Candaule. Paris, 1901.
43620.2.33.10 Gide, André. Le roi Candaule. 13. éd. Paris, 1930.
43620.2.34.5 Gide, André. Nouveaux prétextes. 4. éd. Paris, 1918.
43620.2.35.20 Gide, André. La symphonie pastorale. Paris, 1968.
43620.2.35.21 Gide, André. La symphonie pastorale. Paris, 1970.
43620.2.35.50 Gide, André. Two symphonies. N.Y., 1949.
43620.2.35.52 Gide, André. Two symphonies. N.Y., 1960.
43620.2.35.60 Gide, André. La symphonie pastorale and Isabelle. Harmondsworth, 1963.
43620.2.36.5 Gide, André. Strait is the gate (la porte étroite). N.Y., 1924.
43620.2.37.3 Gide, André. Lafcadio's adventures. (Les caves du Vatican . N.Y., 1943.
43620.2.37.4 Gide, André. Lafcadio's adventures. N.Y., 1951.
43620.2.37.5 Gide, André. The Vatican swindle. N.Y., 1925.
43620.2.37.6 Gide, André. The Vatican cellars. London, 1952.
43620.2.37.7 Gide, André. Les caves de Vatican. Paris, 1950.
43620.2.38.12 Gide, André. Corydon. 88. éd. Paris, 1947.
43620.2.38.13 Gide, André. Corydon. Paris, 1924.
43620.2.38.20 Gide, André. Corydon. 1. English ed. N.Y., 1950.
43620.2.38.25 Gide, André. Corydon. London, 1952.
43620.2.39A Gide, André. Prétextes. Paris, 1947.
43620.2.39B Gide, André. Prétextes. Paris, 1947.
43620.2.41 Gide, André. Prétextes. 18. éd. Paris, 1919.
43620.2.41.5 Gide, André. Pretexts. N.Y., 1959.
43620.2.43 Gide, André. Si le grain ne meurt. 48. éd. Paris, 1929.
43620.2.44 Gide, André. Le voyage d'Urien suivi de Paludes. Paris, 1929.
43620.2.44.5 Gide, André. Urien's voyage. London, 1964.
43620.2.45.5A Gide, André. Interviews imaginaires. N.Y., 1943.
43620.2.45.5B Gide, André. Interviews imaginaires. N.Y., 1943.
43620.2.45.15 Gide, André. Imaginary interviews. 1. American ed. N.Y., 1944.
43620.2.45.20 Gide, André. Entrevistas imaginarias. Bogotá, 1944.
43620.2.45.30 Gide, André. Deux interviews imaginaires. Paris, 1946.
43620.2.46 Gide, André. Les nourritures terrestres. 32. éd. Paris, 1921.
43620.2.47 Gide, André. Les nourritures terrestres. 49. éd. Paris, 1930.
43620.2.47.5 Gide, André. Fruits of the earth. London, 1949.
43620.2.47.10 Gide, André. Les nourritures terrestres et les nouvelles nourritures. Paris, 1951.
43620.2.48 Gide, André. Incidences. 11. éd. Paris, 1924.
43620.2.49 Gide, André. Numquid et tu? Paris, 1926.
43620.2.50 Gide, André. Thésée. 1. ed. N.Y., 1946.
43620.2.50.5 Gide, André. Thésée. Paris, 1946.
43620.2.50.10 Gide, André. Theseus. London, 1948.
43620.2.51.5 Gide, André. Journal des faux-monnayeurs. 44. éd. Paris, 1948.
43620.2.52 Gide, André. Journal. Paris, 1946.
43620.2.52.10 Gide, André. Journal, 1942-1949. 57. éd. Paris, 1950.
43620.2.53 Gide, André. Les faux-monnayeurs. Paris, 1925.
43620.2.53.8 Gide, André. Les faux-monnayeurs; roman. Paris, 1963.
43620.2.55.40 Gide, André. The counterfeiters. N.Y., 1959.
43620.2.55.45 Gide, André. The coiners. 3. ed. London, 1958.
43620.2.56A Gide, André. Divers. Paris, 1931.
43620.2.56B Gide, André. Divers. Paris, 1931.
43620.2.58 Gide, André. Les nouvelles nourritures. 15. éd. Paris, 1935.
43620.2.59.5 Gide, André. Le procès, pièce tirée du roman de Kafka. 17. éd. Paris, 1947.
43620.2.60 Gide, André. Saül. Paris, 1922.
43620.2.60.2 Gide, André. Saül; drame en 5 actes, 1896. Paris, 1969.

Classified Listing

43511 - 43873 Individual authors, etc. - 1900- - Known authors (363 scheme plus 10) - cont.

43620.2.64 Gide, André. Die Rückkehr des verlorenen Sohnes. Leipzig, 1914.
43620.2.65 Gide, André. Le retour de l'enfant prodigue. 6. éd. Paris, 1924.
43620.2.65.2 Gide, André. Le retour de l'enfant prodigue. 25. éd. Paris, 1932.
43620.2.66 Gide, André. Le retour. Paris, 1946.
43620.2.67 Gide, André. André Walter. Paris, 1930.
43620.2.68 Gide, André. Pages de journal (1929-1932). Paris, 1934.
43620.2.68.2 Gide, André. Pages de journal (1929-1932). 12. éd. Paris, 1934.
43620.2.68.10 Gide, André. Pages de journal. Alger, 1944.
43620.2.69 Gide, André. Nouvelles pages de journal, 1932-35. Paris, 1936.
43620.2.69.5 Gide, André. Journal, 1889-1939. Paris, 1939.
43620.2.69.15 Gide, André. Journal. Paris, 1948.
43620.2.69.20A Gide, André. Journals. N.Y., 1947-48. 4v.
43620.2.69.20B Gide, André. Journals. v.1,3-4. N.Y., 1947-48. 3v.
43620.2.69.21 Gide, André. Journals. London, 1947. 4v.
43620.2.69.22 Gide, André. The journals of André Gide. 1. ed. N.Y., 1956. 2v.
43620.2.69.23 Gide, André. Journals. N.Y., 1949. 4v.
43620.2.69.40 Gide, André. André Gide. Paris, 1963.
NEDL 43620.2.70 Gide, André. Le prométhée mal enchainé. Paris, 1925.
43620.2.71 Gide, André. Lettres à un sculpteur. Paris, 1952.
43620.2.72 Gide, André. Genevieve. 31. éd. Paris, 1936.
43620.2.73 Gide, André. Paludes. 16. éd. Paris, 1929.
43620.2.75 Gide, André. L'école des femmes. 44. éd. Paris, 1929.
43620.2.76.5 Gide, André. L'école des femmes. Paris, 1965.
43620.2.77A Gide, André. The school for wives. 1. ed. N.Y., 1950.
43620.2.77B Gide, André. The school for wives. 1. ed. N.Y., 1950.
43620.2.78 Gide, André. Robert. Supplement à L'école des femmes. Paris, 1929.
43620.2.79A Gide, André. Si le grain ne meurt. 68. éd. Paris, 1935.
43620.2.79B Gide, André. Si le grain ne meurt. 69. éd. Paris, 1935.
43620.2.79.2 Gide, André. Si le grain ne meurt. Paris, 1931.
43620.2.79.10 Gide, André. If it die. N.Y., 1935.
43620.2.79.15 Gide, André. Amyntas. Paris, 1937.
43620.2.79.17 Gide, André. Amyntas. London, 1958.
43620.2.79.25 Gide, André. L'evolution du théâtre. Manchester, 1939.
43620.2.79.30 Gide, André. Attendu que. Alger, 1943.
43620.2.79.35 Gide, André. Théâtre. Paris, 1948.
43620.2.79.40 Gide, André. L'affaire Redureau. Paris, 1930.
43620.2.79.45 Gide, André. Récits, roman, soties. Paris, 1948. 2v.
43620.2.79.50 Gide, André. Feuillets d'automne. Paris, 1949.
43620.2.79.55 Gide, André. Le traité du Narcisse. Lausanne, 1946.
43620.2.79.60 Gide, André. Souvenirs littéraires et problèmes actuels. Beyrouth, 1946.
43620.2.79.65 Gide, André. Théâtre complete. v.1-8. Neuchâtel, 1947-49. 4v.
43620.2.79.70 Gide, André. Perséphone. Paris, 1934.
43620.2.79.72 Gide, André. Le retour du Tchad. 29. éd. Paris, 1928.
43620.2.79.75 Gide, André. Rencontres. Neuchâtel, 1948.
43620.2.79.77 Gide, André. Et nunc manet in te. Neuchâtel, 1951.
43620.2.79.80 Gide, André. Jeunesse. Neuchâtel, 1945.
43620.2.79.85 Gide, André. Un esprit non prévenu. Paris, 1929.
43620.2.79.90 Gide, André. Two legends: Oedipus and Theseus. N.Y., 1950.
43620.2.79.95 Gide, André. If it die. London, 1950.
43620.2.79.105 Gide, André. The counterfeiters. 1. ed. N.Y., 1951.
43620.2.79.110 Gide, André. Littérature engagée. Paris, 1950.
43620.2.79.115 Gide, André. The immoralist. N.Y., 1951.
43620.2.79.120A Gide, André. My theater. 1. American ed. N.Y., 1952.
43620.2.79.120B Gide, André. My theater. 1. American ed. N.Y., 1952.
43620.2.79.125 Gide, André. Souvenirs de la cour d'assises. 14. éd. Paris, 1950.
43620.2.79.130 Gide, André. The secret drama of my life. Paris, 1951.
43620.2.79.135.5 Gide, André. Ainsi soit-il, ou Les jeux sont faits. 31. éd. Paris, 1952.
43620.2.79.140 Gide, André. Madeleine. N.Y., 1952.
43620.2.79.143 Gide, André. Le Prométhée mal enchainé. Paris, 1959.
43620.2.79.145A Gide, André. Marshlands and Prometheus Misbound. London, 1953.
43620.2.79.145B Gide, André. Marshlands and Prometheus Misbound. London, 1953.
43620.2.79.146 Gide, André. Marshlands and Prometheus Misbound. N.Y., 1953.
43620.2.79.150 Gide, André. Et nunc manet in te and Intimate journal. London, 1952.
43620.2.79.155 Gide, André. Logbook of the coiners. London, 1952.
43620.2.79.160 Gide, André. Caractères. Paris, 1925.
43620.2.79.165 Gide, André. The return of the prodigal. London, 1953.
43620.2.79.167 Gide, André. The return of the prodigal son. Logan, 1960.
43620.2.79.170 Gide, André. So be it. 1. American ed. N.Y., 1959.
43620.2.79.175 Gide, André. Romans. Paris, 1958.
43620.2.79.179 Gide, André. Correspondance André Gide - François Mauriac, 1912-1950. Paris, 1971.
43620.2.79.180A Gide, André. The correspondence of André Gide and Edmund Gosse. N.Y., 1959.
43620.2.79.180B Gide, André. The correspondence of André Gide and Edmund Gosse. N.Y., 1959.
43620.2.79.181 Gide, André. Correspondance André Gide - Arnold Bennett. Genève, 1964.
43620.2.79.182 Gide, André. Correspondance, 1908-1920. Paris, 1963.
43620.2.79.183 Gide, André. Correspondance: André Gide. Paris, 1958.
43620.2.79.184 Gide, André. Correspondance, 1909-1951. Paris, 1967.
43620.2.79.185 Breachfeld, Georges I. André Gide and the Communist temptation. Geneve, 1959.
43620.2.79.190 Gide, André. Voyage au Congo. 23. éd. Paris, 1927.
43620.2.79.194 André Gide et notre temps. Paris, 1935.
43620.2.79.195 Gide, André. The trial. N.Y., 1964.
43620.2.79.197 Gide, André. Travels in the Congo. 2. ed. Berkeley, 1962.
43620.2.79.200 Gide, André. The white notebook. N.Y., 1964.
43620.2.79.205 Gide, André. Correspondance. Paris, 1968. 2v.
43620.2.79.210 Gide, André. The notebooks of André Walter. N.Y., 1968.
43620.2.80 Braak, Sybrandi. André Gide et l'âme moderne. Amsterdam, 1922?
43620.2.81 Schulz, Wilhelm. Der Stil André Gides (Teildruck). Inaug. Diss. Marburg, 1929.
43620.2.83A Sonday, Paul. André Gide. 2. éd. Paris, 1927.
43620.2.83B Sonday, Paul. André Gide. 12. éd. Paris, 1927.
43620.2.88 Laloro, René. André Gide. Strassbourg, 1928.
43620.2.90 Poucel, Victor. L'esprit d'André Gide. Paris, 1929.
43620.2.95 Yang, T.L. L'attitude d'André Gide. Thèse. Lyon, 1930.

43511 - 43873 Individual authors, etc. - 1900- - Known authors (363 scheme plus 10) - cont.

43620.2.98 Schreiber, Lotte. Leben und Denken im Werk von André Gide. Inaug. Diss. Berlin, 1933.
43620.2.100 Schreiber, Lotte. Leben und Denken im Werk von André Gide. Berlin, 1933.
43620.2.105 Pierre-Quint, L. André Gide: sa vie. Paris, 1933.
43620.2.105.5 Pierre-Quint, L. André Gide. 15. éd. Paris, 1952.
43620.2.110 Rauch, Erich. Zur Freundschaftsproblem im Leben und Werk André Gides. Inaug. Diss. Jena, 1933.
43620.2.115 Hofmann, M. Der Moralist André Gide. Inaug. Diss. Würzburg, 1934.
43620.2.120 Klippstein, P. Die Begriffswelt von André Gide. Inaug. Diss. Berlin, 1935.
43620.2.125 Sachs, Maurice. André Gide. Paris, 1936.
43620.2.130 Pell, E.E. André Gide; l'evolution de sa pensée religieuse. Thèse. Grenoble, 1935.
43620.2.140 Iseler, P. Les débuts d'André Gide. Paris, 1937.
43620.2.150 Wittrock, W. Der Gottesbegriff im Werk André Gides. Inaug. Diss. Marburg, 1936.
43620.2.155 Hytier, Jean. André Gide. 3. éd. Alger, 1938.
43620.2.156 Hytier, Jean. André Gide. 1. ed. N.Y., 1962.
Htn 43620.2.160* Naville, Arnold. Notes bibliographiques sur l'oeuvre de André Gide. Paris, 1930.
43620.2.162 Naville, Arnold. Bibliographie des écrits de André Gide. Paris, 1949.
43620.2.163 Naville, Arnold. Bibliographie des écrits de André Gide, jusqu'en 1952. Paris, 1949.
43620.2.165 André Gide. Paris, 1928.
43620.2.170A Mann, Klaus. André Gide and the crisis of modern thought. N.Y., 1943.
43620.2.170B Mann, Klaus. André Gide and the crisis of modern thought. N.Y., 1943.
43620.2.171 Mann, Klaus. André Gide and the crisis of modern thought. London, 1948.
43620.2.171.2 Mann, Klaus. André Gide und die Krise des modernen Denkens. München, 1966.
43620.2.172 Mann, Klaus. André Gide. Zürich, 1948.
43620.2.175 Schäppi, Max. Wesen und Formen der Selbstdarstellung im Jugendwerk André Gides. Luzern, 1941.
43620.2.180 Fayer, M. Harry. Gide, freedom and Dostoevsky. Burlington, 1946.
43620.2.184 Kaas-Albarda, Maria. André Gide et son journal. Arnhem, 1942.
43620.2.185 Kaas-Albarda, Maria. André Gide et son journal. Arnhem, 1942.
43620.2.190 Lepoutre, Raymond. André Gide. Paris, 1946.
43620.2.195 Ames, Van Meter. André Gide. Norfolk, 1947.
43620.2.200 Archambault, Paul. Humanité d'André Gide. Paris, 1946.
43620.2.225 Aubry, G.J. André Gide et la musique. Paris, 1945.
43620.2.230 Lafille, Pierre. Rencontre avec André Gide. Gap, 1947.
43620.2.245 Massis, Henri. D'André Gide à Marcel Proust. 8. éd. Lyon, 1948.
43620.2.250 Mondor, H. Les premiers temps d'une amitié; Andre Gide et Paul Valéry. Monaco, 1947.
43620.2.258 Davet, Yvonne. Autour des Nourritures terrestres. Paris, 1948.
43620.2.260 Schildt, G. Gide och människan, en studie. Stockholm, 1946.
43620.2.261 Schildt, G. Gide et l'homme. Paris, 1949.
43620.2.262 Lang, Renée. André Gide et la pensée allemande. Paris, 1949.
43620.2.264 Uhlig, Helmut. André Gide. Berlin, 1948.
43620.2.266A Thomas, L. André Gide. London, 1950.
43620.2.266B Thomas, L. André Gide. London, 1950.
43620.2.266C Thomas, L. André Gide. London, 1950.
43620.2.268A Gouiran, É. André Gide. Paris, 1934.
43620.2.268B Gouiran, É. André Gide. Paris, 1934.
43620.2.270 Painter, G.D. André Gide. London, 1951.
43620.2.270.5 Painter, G.D. André Gide. London, 1968.
43620.2.272 Guerard, Albert Joseph. André Gide. Cambridge, 1951.
43620.2.273A Guerard, Albert Joseph. André Gide. 2. ed. Cambridge, 1969.
43620.2.273B Guerard, Albert Joseph. André Gide. 2. ed. Cambridge, 1969.
43620.2.274 Derais, F. L'envers du journal de Gide. Paris, 1951.
43620.2.276A March, H. Gide and the Hound of Heaven. Philadelphia, 1952.
43620.2.276B March, H. Gide and the Hound of Heaven. Philadelphia, 1952.
43620.2.278 Mauriac, Claude. Conversations avec André Gide. Paris, 1951.
43620.2.279 Mauriac, Claude. Conversations with Andre Gide. N.Y., 1965.
43620.2.280 Herbart, P. A la recherche d'André Gide. 13. éd. Paris, 1952.
43620.2.282 Combelle, L. Je dois à André Gide. Paris, 1951.
43620.2.284 Nouvelle Revue Française. Hommage à André Gide. Paris, 1951.
43620.2.286 Martin du Gard, Roger. Notes sur André Gide. Paris, 1951.
43620.2.286.2 Martin du Gard, Roger. Notes on André Gide. London, 1953.
43620.2.286.20 Martin du Gard, Roger. Recollections of André Gide. N.Y., 1953.
43620.2.288 Marill, R. L'odyssée d'André Gide. Paris, 1951.
43620.2.290 Vila Selma, José. André Gide y Paul Claudel. Madrid, 1952.
43620.2.292 Planche, H. Le problème de Gide. Paris, 1952.
43620.2.294 Lime, M. Gide. Paris, 1952.
43620.2.296 McLaren, J.C. The theatre of André Gide. Baltimore, 1953.
43620.2.298 O'Brien, J. Portrait of André Gide. 1. ed. N.Y., 1953.
43620.2.300 Prétexte. Cahier André Gide. Bruxelles, 1952.
43620.2.302A Starkie, Enid. André Gide. Cambridge, Eng., 1953.
43620.2.302B Starkie, Enid. André Gide. Cambridge, Eng., 1953.
43620.2.303 Starkie, Enid. André Gide. New Haven, 1954.
43620.2.304 Bongs, Rolf. Das Antlitz André Gides. Düsseldorf, 1953.
43620.2.306 Dubourg, M. Eugène Dabit et André Gide. Paris, 1953.
43620.2.310 Lafille, P. André Gide, romancier. Paris, 1954.
43620.2.315 Theis, Raimund. Untersuchungen über "Poesie" und "Kunst" bei André Gide. Köln, 1954.
43620.2.320 Marchand, Max. Le complexe pedagogique et didactique d'André Gide. Oran, 1954.
43620.2.321 Marchand, Max. Du Marquis de Sade à André Gide. Oran, 1956.
43620.2.325 Beigbeder, M. André Gide. Paris, 1954.
43620.2.330 Delmas-Marsalet, M. Jean Yves. La culpabilité morbile d'André Gide. Bordeaux, 1954.
43620.2.335 Mahias, C.J. La vie d'André Gide. Paris, 1955.

Classified Listing

43511 - 43873 Individual authors, etc. - 1900- - Known authors (363 scheme plus 10) - cont.

43620.2.340 Delmas-Marsalet, M. Jean Yves. André Gide l'enchainé. Bordeaux, 1955.

43620.2.345 Schlumberger, Jean. Madeleine et André Gide. 14. éd. Paris, 1956.

43620.2.350 Delay, J.P.L. La jeunesse d'André Gide. Paris, 1956. 2v.

43620.2.350.5 Delay, J.P.L. The youth of André Gide. Chicago, 1963.

43620.2.355 Tanchot, Jacques. André Gide et la Cour d'Assises. Rouen, 1957.

43620.2.360 Teuler, Gabriel. Apres Gide. Paris, 1959.

43620.2.365 Lamsfuss, G. Der Asthetizismus André Gides. Münster, 1959.

43620.2.370 Eckhoff, Lorentz. André Gide. Oslo, 1947.

43620.2.375 Lambert, Jean. Gide familier. Paris, 1958.

43620.2.380 Krebber, G. Untersuchungen zur Ästhetik und Kritik André Gides. Geneve, 1959.

43620.2.385 Dauvigny, Alain. André Gide au l'impossible morale. Bordeaux, 1954.

43620.2.390 Murdock, Eleanor E. The critical reception of André Gide in Sweden. Cambridge, 1960.

43620.2.395 Teppe, Julien. Sur le purisme d'André Gide. Paris, 1949?

43620.2.400 Michaud, Gabriel. Gide et l'Afrique. Paris, 1961.

43620.2.405 Gagnebin, Laurent. André Gide nous interroge. Lausanne, 1961.

43620.2.410 Davies, John C. A distinguished modern humanist. Armidale, 1960?

43620.2.411 Davies, John C. Gide: l'immoraliste and la porte etroit. London, 1968.

43620.2.415 Du Bos, Charles. Le dialogue avec André Gide. Paris, 1947.

43620.2.420 Thieny, Jean J. Gide. Paris, 1962.

43620.2.425 Ireland, George Wilhelm. Gide. Edinburgh, 1963.

43620.2.425.5 Ireland, George William. André Gide: a study of his creative writings. Oxford, 1970.

43620.2.430 Gabory, G. André Gide, son oeuvre. Paris, 1924.

43620.2.435 Savage, C.H. André Gide. Paris, 1962.

43620.2.440 Schoeler, C. von. Der mittelmeerische Geist André Gides. Tübingen, 1963.

43620.2.445 Got, Maurice. André Gide. Paris, 1962.

43620.2.450 Perault, P.J. A propos d'Isabelle. Blairville-sur-Mer, 1964.

43620.2.455 Fowlie, W. André Gide: his life and art. N.Y., 1965.

43620.2.460 Jahhan, Razmond. André Gide et l'Orient. Paris, 1963.

43620.2.465 Schwob, René. Le vrai drame d'André Gide. Paris, 1932.

43620.2.470 Brée, Germaine. Gide. New Brunswick, 1963.

43620.2.475 Vitanović, Slobodan. Andre Žid i francusko klasično pozorište. Beograd, 1963.

43620.2.476 Vitanović, Slobodan. Andre Žid i francuski klasicizam. Beograd, 1967.

43620.2.780 Last, J. Mijn vriend, André Gide. Amsterdam, 1966.

43620.2.785 Arland, Marcel. Entretiens sur André Gide [du 6 au 14 septembre 1964]. Paris, 1967.

43620.2.790 Falk, Eugene. Types of thematic structure. Chicago, 1967.

43620.2.795 Rossi, Vinio. André Gide; the evolution of an aesthetic. New Brunswick, 1967.

43620.2.800 Bertalot, Enrico Umberto. André Gide et l'attente de Dieu. Paris, 1967.

43620.2.805 Watson-Williams, Helen. André Gide and the Greek myth. Oxford, 1967.

43620.2.810 Labuda, Alberta. Les thèmes de l'adolescence dans l'oeuvre d'André Gide. Poznán, 1968-69. 2v.

43620.2.815 Rossi, Vinio. André Gide. N.Y., 1968.

43620.2.820 Holdheim, William Wolfgang. Theory and practice of the novel. A study on André Gide. Genève, 1968.

43620.2.825 Nersoyan, Hagop J. André Gide; the theism of an atheist. 1. ed. Syracuse, N.Y., 1969.

43620.2.830 Stoltzfus, Ben Frank. Gide's eagles. Carbondale, 1969.

43620.2.835 Trahard, Pierre. "La porte étroite" d'André Gide. Paris, 1968.

43620.2.840 Cordle, Thomas. André Gide. N.Y., 1969.

43620.2.845 Maucuer, Maurice. Gide, l'indécision passionnée. Paris, 1969.

43620.2.850 Chadourne, Jacqueline M. André Gide et l'Afrique. Paris, 1968.

43620.2.855 Les débuts littéraires d'André Walter à l'immoraliste. (André Gide). Paris, 1969.

43620.2.860 Perry, Kenneth I. The religious symbolism of André Gide. The Hague, 1969.

43620.2.865 Petersen, Carol. André Gide. Berlin, 1969.

43620.2.870 Archives et musée de la littérature. Présence d'André Gide. Bruxelles, 1970.

43620.2.875 Moutote, Daniel. Le "Journal" de Gide et les problèmes du moi, 1889-1925. Paris, 1968.

43620.2.876 Moutote, Daniel. Les images végétales dans l'oeuvre d'André Gide. 1. éd. Paris, 1970.

43620.2.880 Littlejohn, David. Gide. Englewood Cliffs, 1970.

43620.2.885 Bibliothèque nationale, Paris. André Gide. Paris, 1970.

43620.2.890 Boisdeffre, Pierre de. Vie d'André Gide, 1869-1951. Paris, 1970-

43620.3.30 Gilbert, M. Celle qui s'en va. v.1-4. Paris, 1921.

43620.3.34 Gilbert, M. Le silence de Cambridge. v.1-2. Paris, 1927.

43620.3.36 Gilbert, M. Camille eu Le reflet de Rome; roman. pt.1-3. Paris, 1931.

43620.3.40 Gilbert, M. Trois jours et trois nuits. v.1-3. Paris, 1935.

43620.3.55 Gilbert, M. Le joug, roman. Paris, 1925.

43620.7.100 Gibert, Charles. Poèmes vagabonds. Paris, 1935. 2v.

43620.7.1100 Gibelin, Colette. Appel. Paris, 1956.

43620.33.100 Gignoux, Régis. La castiglione. Paris, 1929.

43620.33.110 Gignoux, Régis. Le prof' d'anglais. Paris, 1930.

43620.35.100 Gilbert de Voisins, Auguste. L'absence et le retour. Paris, 1929.

43620.35.110 Gilbert de Voisins, Auguste. L'enfant qui prit peur. Paris, 192-.

43620.35.120 Gilbert de Voisins, Auguste. Les miens. Paris, 1926.

43620.39.100 Gillès, Daniel. L'état de grâce; roman. Paris, 1958.

43620.39.110 Gillès, Daniel. La termitiere. Paris, 1960.

43620.39.700 Gillès, Daniels. The Anthill. N.Y., 1962.

43620.40.11 Gilliard, Edmond. Oeuvres complètes. Genève, 1965.

43620.40.100 Gilliard, Edmond. Journal, 1930-1945. Lausanne, 1945. 2v.

43620.40.110 Gilliard, Edmond. Outre journal. Lausanne, 1953.

43620.40.120 Gilliard, Edmond. Hymne terrestre, suivi de dialecte de l'architecte. Paris, 1958.

43620.40.130 Gilliard, Edmond. La chasse de Pan. Genève, 1965.

43511 - 43873 Individual authors, etc. - 1900- - Known authors (363 scheme plus 10) - cont.

43620.48.61 Gilbert-Lecomte, Roger. Correspondance; lettres. Paris, 1971.

43620.48.100 Gilbert-Lecomte, Roger. Testament. Paris, 1955.

43620.49.1100 Gillet, Louis. Amitiés littéraires. Paris, 1928.

43620.49.2100 Gillet, Victor. Le jardin des regrets. Dijon, 1959.

43620.49.3100 Gille, Jules. Feux de fares; poèmes. Bruxelles, 1961.

43620.49.3110 Gille, Jules. Panier de pommes; poèmes. Bruxelles, 1961.

43620.49.3120 Gille, Jules. Simplicité; poèmes. Bruxelles, 1961.

43620.50.805 Dopagne, G. Maurice Gauchez. Bruxelles, 1937.

43620.50.1100 Gillaux, Max. Les violettes acides. Paris, 1959.

43620.51.40 Gillouin, René. Idées et figures d'aujourd'hui. Paris, 1919.

43620.51.50 Gillouin, René. Essais de critique litteraire et philosophique. Paris, 1913.

43620.55.100 Gilson, Paul. Ballades pour fantômés. Paris, 1950.

43620.55.110 Gilson, Paul. Poèmes. Paris, 1951.

43620.55.120 Gilson, Paul. Ce qui me chante. Paris, 1956.

43620.59.100 Ginet, Albert. Aux confins du silence et de la parole. Bruxelles, 1964.

43620.66.100A Giono, Jean. Un de Baumugnes. Paris, 1929.

43620.66.100B Giono, Jean. Un de Baumugnes. Paris, 1929.

43620.66.102 Giono, Jean. Un de Baumugnes. Paris, 1947.

43620.66.110 Giono, Jean. Refus d'obeissances. 30. éd. Paris, 1937.

43620.66.120 Giono, Jean. Colline. 29 éd. Paris, 1929.

43620.66.122 Giono, Jean. Colline. 32. éd. Paris, 1938.

43620.66.130 Giono, Jean. Solitude de la pitié. 20. éd. Paris, 1932.

43620.66.131 Giono, Jean. Solitude de la pitié. Lausanne, 1962.

43620.66.140 Giono, Jean. Le chant du monde. 39. éd. Paris, 1936.

43620.66.150 Giono, Jean. Que ma joie demeure; roman. Paris, 1936.

43620.66.155 Giono, Jean. Que ma joie demeure; roman. Paris, 1949.

43620.66.160 Giono, Jean. Jean Le Bleu. 27. éd. Paris, 1935.

43620.66.165 Giono, Jean. Jean Le Bleu. Paris, 1956.

43620.66.170 Giono, Jean. Le grand troupeau. 24. éd. Paris, 1931.

43620.66.172 Giono, Jean. Le grand troupeau. 25. éd. Paris, 1935.

43620.66.180 Giono, Jean. Regain. 37. éd. Paris, 1937.

43620.66.185 Giono, Jean. Regain. Paris, 1956.

43620.66.190 Giono, Jean. Les vraies richesses. Paris, 1936.

43620.66.200 Giono, Jean. Naissance de l'Odyssée. Paris, 1938.

43620.66.205 Giono, Jean. Naissance de l'Odyssée. Paris, 1959.

43620.66.210 Giono, Jean. Le poids du ciel. Paris, 1938.

43620.66.220 Giono, Jean. Precisions. 18. éd. Paris, 1939.

43620.66.230 Giono, Jean. Théâtre de Jean Giono. Paris, 1943.

43620.66.240 Giono, Jean. Un roi sans divertissement. Paris, 1947.

43620.66.250 Giono, Jean. Pondeur des jous. Alger, 194-.

43620.66.260 Giono, Jean. Noe; chroniques. Paris, 1947.

43620.66.270 Giono, Jean. Le voyage en calèche. Monaco, 1947.

43620.66.280 Giono, Jean. L'eau vine, contes. 23. éd. Paris, 1943.

43620.66.285 Giono, Jean. Hortense, au Leau vive. Paris, 1958.

43620.66.290 Giono, Jean. Le serpent d'étoiles. 30. éd. Paris, 1949.

43620.66.300 Giono, Jean. Batailles dans la montagne; roman. 73. éd. Paris, 1948.

43620.66.302 Giono, Jean. Batailles dans la montagne. Paris, 1937.

43620.66.310 Giono, Jean. Triomphe de la vie. 28. éd. Paris, 1942.

43620.66.320 Giono, Jean. Mort d'un personnage. Paris, 1949.

43620.66.330 Giono, Jean. Manosque-des-Plateaux. Paris, 1930.

43620.66.340 Giono, Jean. Les âmes fortes. Paris, 1949.

43620.66.350 Giono, Jean. Présentation de pan. Paris, 1930.

43620.66.355 Giono, Jean. Le hussard sur le toit. 32. éd. Paris, 1951.

43620.66.360.5 Giono, Jean. Les grands chemins. 23. éd. Paris, 1951.

43620.66.370 Giono, Jean. Accompagnés de la flute. Perigneux, 1951.

43620.66.380 Giono, Jean. Le Moulin de Pologne. Paris, 1952.

43620.66.390 Giono, Jean. Le chant du mode. Paris, 1934.

43620.66.400 Giono, Jean. Voyage en Italie. 38. éd. Paris, 1954.

43620.66.410 Giono, Jean. Notes sur l'affaire Dominici. 3. éd. Paris, 1955.

43620.66.420 Giono, Jean. Giono par lui-même. Paris, 1956.

43620.66.430 Giono, Jean. La bonheur fou. 61. éd. Paris, 1957.

43620.66.440 Giono, Jean. Angelo. Paris, 1958.

43620.66.450 Giono, Jean. Domitien, suivi de Joseph à Dothan. Paris, 1959.

43620.66.460 Giono, Jean. Crésus. Manosque, 1961.

43620.66.470 Giono, Jean. Chroniques romanesques. Paris, 1962.

43620.66.480 Giono, Jean. Deux cavaliers de l'orage. Paris, 1965.

43620.66.490 Giono, Jean. Ennemonde et autres caractères. Paris, 1968.

43620.66.500 Giono, Jean. Une histoire d'amour. Manosque, 1969.

43620.66.510 Giono, Jean. L'Iris de Suse. Paris, 1970.

43620.66.520 Giono, Jean. Préface à "l'Iliade". Paris, 1967.

43620.66.700 Giono, Jean. Joy or man's desiring. N.Y., 1940.

43620.66.705 Giono, Jean. Hill of destiny. N.Y., 1929.

43620.66.710 Giono, Jean. The song of the world. N.Y., 1937.

43620.66.720 Giono, Jean. Harvest. N.Y., 1939.

43620.66.730 Giono, Jean. Blue boy. N.Y., 1946.

43620.66.740 Giono, Jean. The horseman on the roof. 1. American ed. N.Y., 1954.

43620.66.750 Giono, Jean. The malediction. N.Y., 1955.

43620.66.760A Giono, Jean. The Dominici affair. London, 1956.

43620.66.760B Giono, Jean. The Dominici affair. London, 1956.

43620.66.765 Giono, Jean. The straw man. 1. American ed. N.Y., 1959.

43620.66.775 Giono, Jean. Bergschlacht. Stockholm, 1939.

43620.66.805 Michelfelder, C. Jean Giono et les religions de la terre. 5. éd. Photoreproduction. Paris, 1938.

43620.66.810 Josiponici, J. Lettre à Jean Giono. Paris, 1939.

43620.66.815 Bady, René. Le problème de la jaie. Fribourg, 1943.

43620.66.820 Clarke, Katherine A. Le lyrisme dans l'oeuvre de Jean Giono. Thèse. Grenoble, 1938.

43620.66.825 Pugnet, Jacques. Jean Giono. Paris, 1955.

43620.66.826 Pugnet, Jacques. Jean Giono. Paris, 1966.

43620.66.830 Villeneuve, R. de. Jean Giono. Avignon, 1955.

43620.66.840 Ciossek, Heinz Hermann. Jean Giono. Bottrop, 1934.

43620.66.845 Boisdeffre, Pierre de. Giono. Paris, 1965.

43620.66.850 Smith, Maxwell Austin. Jean Giono. N.Y., 1966.

43620.66.855 Redfern, W.D. The private world of Jean Giono. Durham, 1967.

43620.67.700 Giovanni, José. The bread. London, 1960.

43620.73.100 Girard, Georges. Les vainqueurs. 3. éd. Paris, 1924.

43620.73.1100 Girard, Pierre. Lord Algernon. Paris, 1925.

43620.74.21 Giraudoux, Jean. Théâtre. Paris, 1954. 2v.

43620.74.26 Giraudoux, Jean. Théâtre. Paris, 1958. 4v.

43620.74.30 Giraudoux, Jean. Théâtre complet. Neuchâtel, 1945-53. 16v.

43620.74.42.2 Giraudoux, Jean. Giraudoux par lui-même. Paris, 1968.

43620.74.100 Giraudoux, Jean. Bella. Paris, 1926.

43620.74.101 Giraudoux, Jean. Bella. N.Y., 1927.

43620.74.103 Giraudoux, Jean. Bella. Paris, 1954.

43620.74.106 Giraudoux, Jean. Siegfried et le limousin. 17. éd. Paris, 1922.

43511 - 43873 Individual authors, etc. - 1900- - Known authors (363 scheme plus 10) - cont.

	43620.74.107	Giraudoux, Jean. Siegfried. 16. éd. Paris, 1928.
	43620.74.108	Giraudoux, Jean. Siegfried. Paris, 1928.
	43620.74.110	Giraudoux, Jean. Fin de Siegfried. Paris, 1934.
	43620.74.115	Giraudoux, Jean. Amphitryon 38. Photoreproduction. Paris, 1929.
	43620.74.125	Giraudoux, Jean. Elpénor. 34. éd. Paris, 1926.
	43620.74.135	Giraudoux, Jean. Adorable Clio. Paris, 1920.
	43620.74.145	Giraudoux, Jean. Provinciales. Paris, 1909.
	43620.74.145.8	Giraudoux, Jean. Provinciales. 8. éd. Paris, 1922.
Htn	43620.74.155*	Giraudoux, Jean. Adieu à la guerre. Paris, 1919.
	43620.74.165	Giraudoux, Jean. L'école des indifférents. Paris, 1911.
	43620.74.167	Giraudoux, Jean. L'école des indifférents. Paris, 1934.
	43620.74.187	Giraudoux, Jean. Judith, tragédie en trois actes. Paris, 1946.
	43620.74.195	Giraudoux, Jean. Intermezzo; comédie en trois actes. Paris, 1933.
	43620.74.195.2	Giraudoux, Jean. Intermezzo. Neuchâtel, 1946.
	43620.74.196	Giraudoux, Jean. The enchanted. N.Y., 1950.
	43620.74.200	Giraudoux, Jean. La guerre de Troie n'aura pas lieu. Paris, 1935.
	43620.74.202	Giraudoux, Jean. La guerre de Troie n'aura pas lieu. Paris, 1935.
	43620.74.210	Giraudoux, Jean. Electre; pièce en deux actes. Paris, 1937.
	43620.74.212	Giraudoux, Jean. Electre. Paris, 1937.
	43620.74.214	Giraudoux, Jean. Electre; pièce en deux actes. Paris, 1963.
	43620.74.220	Giraudoux, Jean. L'impromptu de Paris. 4. éd. Paris, 1937.
	43620.74.230	Giraudoux, Jean. Simon le pathétique. 30. éd. Paris, 1926.
	43620.74.240	Giraudoux, Jean. Combat avec l'ange. 13. éd. Paris, 1934.
	43620.74.250	Giraudoux, Jean. Cantique des cantiques. Paris, 1938.
	43620.74.250.7	Giraudoux, Jean. Cantique des cantiques. 7. éd. Paris, 1939.
	43620.74.260	Giraudoux, Jean. Ondine; pièce en trois actes. Paris, 1939.
	43620.74.260.2	Giraudoux, Jean. Ondine. Paris, 1939.
	43620.74.270	Giraudoux, Jean. Visite chez le prince. Paris, 1924.
	43620.74.280	Giraudoux, Jean. Choix des éleves. Paris, 1939.
	43620.74.290	Giraudoux, Jean. La prière sur la tour Eiffel. Paris, 1923.
	43620.74.295	Giraudoux, Jean. Sodome et Gomorrhe; pièce en deux actes. Paris? 194-.
	43620.74.310	Giraudoux, Jean. Eglantine. 43. éd. Paris, 1927.
	43620.74.325	Giraudoux, Jean. Littérature. Paris, 1944.
	43620.74.330	Giraudoux, Jean. La folle de Chaillot. Paris, 1946.
	43620.74.331	Giraudoux, Jean. La folle de Chaillot. Cambridge, Eng., 1963.
	43620.74.340	Giraudoux, Jean. La film de la duchesse de Langlois. Montreal, 1946.
	43620.74.350	Giraudoux, Jean. Armistice à Bordeaux. Monaco, 1945.
	43620.74.360	Giraudoux, Jean. Le film de Béthanie. Paris, 1944.
	43620.74.370	Giraudoux, Jean. L'Apollon de Bellac. Paris, 1947.
	43620.74.380	Giraudoux, Jean. Portrait de la Renaissance. Paris, 1946.
	43620.74.390	Giraudoux, Jean. Le sport. Paris, 1928.
	43620.74.400	Giraudoux, Jean. Aventures de Jérôme Bardim, roman. Paris, 1946.
	43620.74.410	Giraudoux, Jean. La France sentimentale. 18. éd. Paris, 1945.
	43620.74.420	Giraudoux, Jean. Juliette au pays des hommes. Paris, 1924.
	43620.74.420.25	Giraudoux, Jean. Juliette au pays des hommes. Paris, 1946.
	43620.74.430	Giraudoux, Jean. Mirage de Bessines. Paris, 1931.
	43620.74.440A	Giraudoux, Jean. Pour ce onze novembre. Paris, 1938.
	43620.74.440B	Giraudoux, Jean. Pour ce onze novembre. Paris, 1938.
	43620.74.450	Giraudoux, Jean. Pour une politique urbaine. Paris, 1947.
	43620.74.460	Giraudoux, Jean. Supplément au voyage de Cook. Paris, 1937.
	43620.74.470	Giraudoux, Jean. La française et la France. Paris, 1951.
	43620.74.480.5	Giraudoux, Jean. Les contes d'un matin. 4. éd. Paris, 1952.
	43620.74.490	Giraudoux, Jean. Visitations. Paris, 1952.
	43620.74.500	Giraudoux, Jean. Pour Lucrèce. Paris, 1953.
	43620.74.510	Giraudoux, Jean. D'exil. Paris, 1945.
	43620.74.520	Giraudoux, Jean. La menteuse. Paris, 1958.
	43620.74.525	Giraudoux, Jean. Un roi. Paris, 1958.
	43620.74.530	Giraudoux, Jean. Portugal. Paris, 1958.
	43620.74.540	Giraudoux, Jean. Choix des études. Paris, 1939.
	43620.74.550	Giraudoux, Jean. Siegfried. London, 1967.
	43620.74.555	Giraoudoux, Jean. Or dans la nuit. Paris, 1969.
	43620.74.621	Giraudoux, Jean. Three plays. 1. ed. N.Y., 1964.
	43620.74.623	Giraudoux, Jean. Judith. N.Y., 1963.
	43620.74.702	Giraudoux, Jean. Four plays. N.Y., 1958.
	43620.74.705	Giraudoux, Jean. Amphitryon 38. N.Y., 1938.
	43620.74.710A	Giraudoux, Jean. Siegfried; a play in four acts. N.Y., 1930.
	43620.74.710B	Giraudoux, Jean. Siegfried; a play in four acts. N.Y., 1930.
	43620.74.720	Giraudoux, Jean. My friend from Limousin. N.Y., 1923.
	43620.74.730	Giraudoux, Jean. Suzanne and the Pacific. N.Y., 1923.
	43620.74.740	Giraudoux, Jean. The madwoman of Chaillot. N.Y., 1947.
	43620.74.750	Giraudoux, Jean. Ondine. N.Y., 1954.
	43620.74.765	Giraudoux, Jean. Tiger at the gates. N.Y., 1956.
	43620.74.775	Giraudoux, Jean. Duel of angels. London, 1958.
	43620.74.780	Giraudoux, Jean. Elpénor. N.Y., 1958.
	43620.74.785	Giraudoux, Jean. Plays. N.Y., 1963- 2v.
	43620.74.790	Giraudoux, Jean. Plays. N.Y., 1967.
X Cg	43620.74.800	Bourdet, M. Jean Giraudoux, son oeuvre. Paris, 1928.
	43620.74.805	Cohen, Robert Carl. Giraudoux. Chicago, 1968.
	43620.74.810	Escande de Messières, R. Le role de l'ironie dans l'oeuvre de Giraudoux. N.Y.? 1938.
	43620.74.820	Tavernier, René. Hommage à Giraudoux. Paris? 1944?
	43620.74.830	Du Genêt, Gabriel. Jean Giraudoux. Paris, 1945.
	43620.74.835	Domec, Pierre. En pensée avec Giraudoux...les cahiers de Claudies. Genève, 1947.
	43620.74.840	Honlet, Jacques. Le théâtre de Jean Giraudoux. Paris, 1945.
	43620.74.845	Morand, Paul. Adieu à Giraudoux. Porrentruy, 1944.
	43620.74.850	Fink, Werner M. Jean Giraudoux; Glück und Tragik. Inaug. Diss. Basel, 1947.
	43620.74.855	Morand, Paul. Giraudoux. Genève, 1948.
	43620.74.860	Beucler, A. Les instants de Giraudoux. Genève, 1948.
	43620.74.865	Meister, G. Gesalt und Bedeutung. Diss. Rorschoch, 1951.
	43620.74.870	Tonssaint, F. Jean Giraudoux. Paris, 1953.

43511 - 43873 Individual authors, etc. - 1900- - Known authors (363 scheme plus 10) - cont.

	43620.74.875	Mercier-Campiche, M. Le théâtre de Giraudoux. Paris, 1954.
	43620.74.880	Debidour, V.H. Jean Giraudoux. Paris, 1955.
	43620.74.885	Bidal, M.L. Giraudoux tel qu'en lui-même. Paris, 1956.
	43620.74.890	Inskip, Donald. Jean Giraudoux. London, 1958.
	43620.74.895	Marrill, René. Esthétique et morale chez Jean Giraudoux. Paris, 1957.
	43620.74.900	LeSage, Laurent. Jean Giraudoux, his life and works. University Park, 1959.
	43620.74.905	Durry, Marie J. L'univers de Giraudoux. Paris, 1961.
	43620.74.910	Marrill, René. La Genèse du Siegfried de Jean Giraudoux. Paris, 1963.
	43620.74.915	Raymond, Agnes G. Giraudoux devant la victoire et la défaite. Paris, 1963.
	43620.74.916	Raymond, Agnes G. Jean Giraudoux: the theatre of victory and defeat. Amherst, 1966.
	43620.74.920	Best, Otto Ferdinand. Der Dualismus im Welt- und Menschenbild Jean Giraudoux das Verhältnis von Mann und Frau. München, 1963.
	43620.74.925	David, Aurel. Vie et mort de Jean Giraudoux. Paris, 1966.
	43620.74.930	Louw, Gilbert. La tragédie grecque dans les théâtre de Giraudoux. Nancy, 1967.
	43620.74.935	Hoest, Gunvar. L'oeuvre de Jean Giraudoux. Oslo, 1942.
	43620.74.940	Lemaître, Georges Edouard. Jean Giraudoux. N.Y., 1971.
	43620.74.945	Lewis, Roy. Giraudoux: La guerre de Troie n'aura pas lieu. London, 1971.
	43620.74.950	Mander, Gertrud. Jean Giraudoux. 1. Aufl. Velber, 1969.
	43620.74.1100	Giraudoux, Jean Pierre. Débuts au théâtre. Paris, 1954.
	43620.74.1110	Giraudoux, Jean Pierre. Ce n'est pas Angeline. Paris, 1955.
	43620.74.1120	Giraudoux, Jean Pierre. Le mauvais charme. 6. éd. Paris, 1957.
	43620.74.1130	Giraudoux, Jean Pierre. Pas assez de silence. Paris, 1948.
	43620.74.1140	Giraudoux, Jean Pierre. Le pays sans chemins. Paris, 1959.
	43620.74.1150	Giraudoux, Jean Pierre. Poeme ingénue. Paris, 1959.
	43620.74.1160	Giraudoux, Jean Pierre. Le fils. Paris, 1967.
	43620.74.1170	Giraudoux, Jean Pierre. Théâtre d'arrière-garde. Belle. Paris, 1968.
	43620.74.3100	Girard, H. Le salaire de la peur. Paris, 1953.
	43620.74.4100	Giraud, V. Portraits d'ames. Paris, 1929.
	43620.74.5100	Girard, Henri G. Mon procès. Paris, 1961.
	43620.74.6100	Giraud, Pierre. L'enfant perdu, et autres contes. Paris, 1969.
	43620.75.100	Girou, Jean. Trencavel et la louve de cennantier. Paris, 1956.
	43620.75.1100	Giroux, Roger. L'arbre le temps. Paris, 1964.
	43620.77.100	Girod, André. L'Ivrogne, poèmes. Paris, 1969.
	43622.1.30	Gleize, Lucien. Le veau d'or, comédie satirique. Paris, 1914.
	43622.23.100	Glejser, Herbert. La rencontre à l'aube. Malines, 1955.
	43622.24.30	Glesener, Edmond. Histoire de M. Aristide Truffaut. Paris, 1898.
	43622.41.100	Glissant, Edouard. Soleil de la conscience. Paris, 1956.
	43622.41.110	Glissant, Edouard. Un champ d'iles. Paris, 1953.
	43622.41.120	Glissant, Edouard. La terre inquiète. Paris, 1955.
	43622.41.130	Glissant, Edouard. Les Indes. Paris, 1956.
	43622.41.140	Glissant, Edouard. La lézarde. Paris, 1958.
	43622.41.150	Glissant, Edouard. Le sel noir. Paris, 1960.
	43622.41.160	Glissant, Edouard. Monsieur Toussaint, théâtre. Paris, 1961.
	43622.41.170	Glissant, Edouard. Le quatrième siècle. Paris, 1964.
	43622.41.180	Glissant, Edouard. L'intention poétique. Paris, 1969.
	43622.41.700	Glissant, Edouard. The ripening. N.Y., 1957.
	43622.66.100	Glotz, René. A mon gré. Paris, 1928.
	43625.1.30	Gojon, E. Les cendres de l'urne, 1904-07. n.p., n.d.
	43625.2.30	Gorsse, Henry. Le procureur Hallers: quatre actes. Paris, 1914.
	43625.3.01	Pamphlet box. Gourmont, Rémy de.
Htn	43625.3.25*	Gourmont, Rémy de. Selected writings. Ann Arbor, 1966.
	43625.3.30	Gourmont, Rémy de. Le chemin de velours. 5e ed. Paris, 1911.
	43625.3.30.5	Gourmont, Rémy de. Le chemin de velours. 60e éd. Paris, 1911.
	43625.3.31	Gourmont, Rémy de. Les chevaux de Diomède. 5e éd. Paris, 1897.
NEDL	43625.3.31	Gourmont, Rémy de. Les chevaux de Diomède. 3e éd. Paris, 1897.
	43625.3.32	Gourmont, Rémy de. Un coeur virginal. 5e ed. Paris, 1914.
	43625.3.33	Gourmont, Rémy de. La culture des idées. 7e ed. Paris, 1916.
	43625.3.33.2	Gourmont, Rémy de. La culture des idées. Paris, 1964.
	43625.3.34	Gourmont, Rémy de. Divertissement. 2e ed. Paris, 1914.
	43625.3.35	Gourmont, Rémy de. Epilogues; reflect sur la vie, 1895-1912. 3e éd. Paris, 1907-16. 6v.
	43625.3.36	Gourmont, Rémy de. Histoires magiques. 4. éd. Paris, 1916.
	43625.3.37	Gourmont, Rémy de. Lilith, suivi de Théodat. 2. éd. Paris, 1906.
	43625.3.37.2	Gourmont, Rémy de. Lilith. Paris, 1925.
	43625.3.38	Gourmont, Rémy de. Rémy de Gourmont; selections. N.Y., 1929.
Htn	43625.3.39*	Gourmont, Rémy de. Merlette. Paris, 1886.
	43625.3.41	Gourmont, Rémy de. Nuit au Luxembourg. 4e ed. Paris, 1912.
	43625.3.41.15	Gourmont, Rémy de. A night in the Luxembourg. Boston, 1912.
	43625.3.41.20	Gourmont, Rémy de. A night in the Luxembourg. N.Y., 1926.
	43625.3.42	Gourmont, Rémy de. D'un pays Lointain. 2e ed. Paris, 1898.
	43625.3.43	Gourmont, Rémy de. Pèlerin du silence. 5e ed. Paris, 1911.
	43625.3.44	Gourmont, Rémy de. Sixtine. 4e ed. Paris, 1915.
	43625.3.45	Gourmont, Rémy de. Songe d'une femme. 5e ed. Paris, 1916.
Htn	43625.3.46*	Gourmont, Rémy de. Phocas; (collection de l'Ymagier). Paris, 1895.
	43625.3.47	Gourmont, Rémy de. Physique de l'amour. Paris, 1917.
	43625.3.48	Gourmont, Rémy de. Le puits de la vérité. Paris, 1922.
	43625.3.49	Gourmont, Rémy de. Pendant l'orage. Paris, 1916.
	43625.3.49.3	Gourmont, Rémy de. Pendant l'orage. Paris, 1915.
	43625.3.50	Gourmont, Rémy de. Dans la tourmente. Paris, 1916.
	43625.3.51	Gourmont, Rémy de. Les pas sur le sable. Paris, 1919.
	43625.3.52	Gourmont, Rémy de. Lettres d'un satyre. 7e éd. Paris, 1919.
	43625.3.53	Gourmont, Rémy de. Le joujou patriotisme. Paris, 1967.

Classified Listing

43511 - 43873 Individual authors, etc. - 1900- - Known authors (363 scheme plus 10) - cont.

NEDL 43625.3.55 Gourmont, Rémy de. Lettres à l'Amazone. 11e éd. Paris, 1921.
43625.3.57 Gourmont, Rémy de. Lettres à Sixtine. 4e éd. Paris, 1921.
43625.3.58 Gourmont, Rémy de. Petits crayons. Paris, 1921.
Htn 43625.3.59* Gourmont, Rémy de. Le vieux roi. Paris, 1897.
43625.3.62 Gourmont, Rémy de. La fin de l'art. Paris, 1925.
43625.3.63 Gourmont, Rémy de. Couleurs. Paris, 1908.
43625.3.64 Gourmont, Rémy de. Fin de promenade et trois autres contes. Paris, 1925.
43625.3.65 Gourmont, Rémy de. L'ombre d'une femme; pièce. Paris, 1923.
43625.3.67 Gourmont, Rémy de. Théodat. Paris, 1893.
43625.3.69 Gourmont, Rémy de. M. Croquant. Paris, 1918.
43625.3.71 Gourmont, Rémy de. Le fantome. Paris, 1893.
43625.3.72 Gourmont, Rémy de. Les nouvelles dissociations. Paris, 1925.
43625.3.73 Gourmont, Rémy de. La petite ville; paysages. Paris, 1913.
43625.3.75 Gourmont, Rémy de. 1874-1880. Journal intime et inédit. Paris, 1923.
Htn 43625.3.76* Gourmont, Rémy de. Ici commence le poème des St. du Paradis. Paris, 1899.
Htn 43625.3.77* Gourmont, Rémy de. La patience de Griseledis. Paris, 1920.
43625.3.78 Gourmont, Rémy de. Pensées inédites. Paris, 1924.
43625.3.79 Gourmont, Rémy de. Dernières pensées inédites. Paris, 1924.
43625.3.79.15A Gourmont, Rémy de. Decadence and other essays on the culture of ideas. N.Y., 1921.
43625.3.79.15B Gourmont, Rémy de. Decadence and other essays on the culture of ideas. N.Y., 1921.
43625.3.79.20 Gourmont, Rémy de. A virgin heart. N.Y., 1925.
43625.3.79.25 Gourmont, Rémy de. Very woman. N.Y., 1922.
43625.3.80 Querlon, Pierre de. Rémy de Gourmont. Paris, 1903.
43625.3.85 Legrand, André. Rémy de Gourmont son oeuvre. Paris, 1925.
43625.3.88 Bencze, Eugène. La doctrine esthétique de Rémy de Gourmont. Thèse. Toulouse, 1928.
43625.3.88.5 Bencze, Eugène. La doctrine esthétique de Rémy de Gourmont. Toulouse, 1928.
43625.3.90 Jacob, P.E. Rémy de Gourmont. Thesis. Urbana, 1931.
43625.3.94 Goedecke, Renate. Der philosophische Gehalt in Rémy de Gourmonts Gesamtwerk. Inaug. Diss. Dresden, 1933.
43625.3.96 Rouveyre, A.L.M. Le reclus et le retors; Gourmont et Gide. Paris, 1927.
43625.3.100 Coalon, Marcel. L'enseignement de Rémy de Gourmont. Paris, 1925.
Htn 43625.3.250* Gourmont, Jean de. Bibliographie des oeuvres de Rémy de Gourmont. Paris, 1922.
43625.3.255 Burne, G. St. Rémy de Gourmont. Carbondale, 1963.
43625.3.260 Imprimerie Gourmontienne. Paris. 1-10,1920-1925
43625.3.270 Uitti, Karl D. La passion littéraire de Remy de Gourmont. Princeton, 1962.
43625.4.80 Henzey, Juliette. Lucie Felix-Faure Goyan. Paris, 1916.
43625.6.30 Gosselin, L.L.T. Les grognards; comédie. Paris, 1921.
43625.6.33 Gosselin, L.L.T. Légendes de Noël. Paris, 19- ?
43625.7.100 Godefroy, Serge. Les loques; roman. Paris 1964.
43625.17.100 Godel, Vahé. Homme parmi les hommes. Paris, 1958.
43625.17.110 Godel, Vahé. Entre l'Arve et le Rhône. Genève, 1960.
43625.17.120 Godel, Vahé. Quatre poèmes géométriques. Genève, 1962.
43625.17.1100 Godeau, Georges L. Rictus. Paris, 1954.
43625.19.100 Godoy, Armand. Le carnaval de Schumann. Paris, 1928.
43625.19.101 Godoy, Armand. Le carnaval de Schumann. Paris, 1927.
43625.19.105 Godoy, Armand. Triste et tendre. Paris, 1927.
43625.19.107 Godoy, Armand. Triste et tendre. 2e éd. Paris, 1935.
43625.19.110 Godoy, Armand. Hosanna sur le sistre. Paris, 1928.
43625.19.115 Godoy, Armand. Bréviaire. Paris, 1954.
43625.19.120 Godoy, Armand. Monologue de la tristesse et colloque de la joie. 5e éd. Paris, 1928.
43625.19.130 Godoy, Armand. Le drame de la passion. 2e éd. Paris, 1929.
43625.19.133 Godoy, Armand. Le drame de la passion. Paris, 1935.
43625.19.140 Godoy, Armand. Foch. Paris, 1929.
43625.19.150 Godoy, Armand. Les litanies de la vierge. Paris, 1930.
43625.19.153A Godoy, Armand. Les litanies de la vierge. Avec une lithographie de M. Lydis. Paris, 1934.
43625.19.153B Godoy, Armand. Les litanies de la vierge. Avec une lithographie de M. Lydis. Paris, 1934.
43625.19.160 Godoy, Armand. Le brasier mystique. Paris, 1930.
43625.19.163 Godoy, Armand. Le brasier mystique. 3e éd. Paris, 1937.
43625.19.170 Godoy, Armand. Quatre nocturnes. Paris, 1929.
43625.19.180 Godoy, Armand. Le poème de l'Atlantique. Paris, 1931.
43625.19.182 Godoy, Armand. Le poème de l'Atlantique. Paris, 1938.
43625.19.190 Godoy, Armand. Marcel; poème dramatique. Paris, 1932.
43625.19.200 Godoy, Armand. Ite, missa est. 5e éd. Paris, 1933.
43625.19.202 Godoy, Armand. Ite, missa est. 9e éd. Paris, 1933.
43625.19.210 Godoy, Armand. Du cantique des cantiques au chemin de la Croix. Paris, 1934.
43625.19.220 Godoy, Armand. Le chemin de la Croix. Paris, 1935.
43625.19.222 Godoy, Armand. Le chemin de la Croix. 3. éd. Paris, 1935.
43625.19.230 Godoy, Armand. Rome. Paris, 1936.
43625.19.240 Godoy, Armand. Trois poèmes de Saint Jean de la Croix. Paris, 1937.
43625.19.250 Godoy, Armand. À Milosz. Lausanne, 1939.
43625.19.260 Godoy, Armand. De vêpres à matines. Fribourg, 1944.
43625.19.270 Godoy, Armand. Mon fils! Mon fils! Fribourg, 1946.
43625.19.275 Godoy, Armand. Colloque de la joie. 3e éd. Paris, 1951.
43625.19.280 Godoy, Armand. Rossignol. Paris, 1949.
43625.19.290 Godoy, Armand. Sonnets pour l'aube. Paris, 1949.
43625.19.300 Godoy, Armand. Les sept jours de la rose. Paris, 1951.
43625.19.310 Godoy, Armand. Monologue de la Tristesse. Paris, 1955.
43625.19.320 Godoy, Armand. Sonnets pour Don Juan. Paris, 1956.
43625.19.330 Godoy, Armand. Dulcinée. Paris, 1957.
43625.19.340 Godoy, Armand. Stéle pour Charles Baudelaire. Paris, 1926.
43625.19.705 Godoy, Armand. Dal contico dei cantici alla via della croce. Milano, 1935.
43625.19.710A Godoy, Armand. The drama of the passion. London, 1935.
43625.19.710B Godoy, Armand. The drama of the passion. London, 1935.
43625.19.800 Mediterranea. 3e année, no. 27, mars 1929. Nice, n.d.
43625.19.810 Devaux, André. Armand Godoy. Paris, 1933.
43625.19.813 Devaux, André. Armand Godoy. Paris, 1936.
43625.19.817 Fontaine, Anne. L'Herbier d'Armand Godoy. Fribourg, 1949.
43625.19.818 Fontaine, Anne. Armand Godoy. Paris, 1959.
43625.19.820 Pasquali, P.S. Armand Godoy. Paris, 1933.
43625.19.825 Deambrosis Martins, Carlos. Armando Godoy, poeta Francés. Santiago, 1935.

43511 - 43873 Individual authors, etc. - 1900- - Known authors (363 scheme plus 10) - cont.

43625.19.830 Mousel, Paul. Armand Godoy. Luxembourg, 1959.
43625.27.100 Goffin, Robert. Le fusillé de Dunkerque. N.Y., 1941.
43625.27.110 Goffin, Robert. Le chat sans tête, roman. N.Y., 1941.
43625.27.120 Goffin, Robert. Le nouveau sphinx, roman. N.Y., 1941.
43625.27.130 Goffin, Robert. La colombe de la Gestapo. N.Y., 1943.
43625.27.135 Goffin, Robert. Sabotages dans le ciel, roman. N.Y., 1942.
43625.27.140 Goffin, Robert. Passeports pour l'au-delá. N.Y., 1944.
43625.27.145 Goffin, Robert. Les cavaliers de la deroute, roman. 9. éd. N.Y., 1941.
43625.27.150 Goffin, Robert. Patrie de la poèsie. Montréal, 1945.
43625.27.155 Goffin, Robert. Oeuvres poetiques. Paris, 1958.
43625.27.160 Goffin, Robert. Corps combustible. Paris, 1964.
43625.27.170 Goffin, Robert. Sablier pour une cosmogonie; poèmes. Bruxelles, 1965.
43625.27.180 Goffin, Robert. Le versant noir. Paris, 1967.
43625.27.190 Goffin, Robert. Faits divers. Paris, 1969.
43625.38.100 Gohier, Gerald. Otto John. Paris, 1958.
43625.45.100 Goldorp V. Un prince franc-maçon, le duc d'Orleans; roman historique. Paris, 1941.
43625.45.2100 Golon, S. (pseud.). Indomptable Angélique. Paris, 1960.
43625.46.100 Gos, C. Song of the high hills. London, 1949.
43625.48.30 Golay, Marthe. Lumière; poèmes. Paris, 1958.
43625.48.2100 Golay, Jean. Les poèmes florentins. Marin, 1959.
43625.48.3100 Goldstein, E. Madame E. Bourgmestre. Bruxelles, 1964.
43625.49.100 Goll, Claire. Le tombeau des amants inconnus. N.Y., 1941.
43625.49.110 Goll, Claire. Éducation barbare. N.Y., 1941.
43625.49.130 Goll, Claire. Une perle, roman. 21e éd. Paris, 1929.
43625.49.140 Goll, Claire. Les larmes pétrifiées. Paris, 1951.
43625.49.150 Goll, Claire. Chants peaux-rouges. Paris, 1958.
43625.49.155 Goll, Claire. Das Tätowierte Herz. Wiesbaden, 1957.
43625.49.160 Goll, Claire. Der Neger Jupider raubt Europa. Basel, 1926.
43625.49.170 Goll, Claire. Un amour au quartier Latin. Paris, 1959.
43625.49.180 Goll, Claire. Neue Blümlein des heiligen Franziskus. Darmstadt, 1957.
43625.49.190 Goll, Claire. Klage um Ivan. Wiesbaden, 1960.
43625.49.700 Goll, Claire. My sentimental zoo. Mt. Vernon, 1942.
43625.49.710F Goll, Claire. Diary of a horse. Brooklyn, 1946.
43625.49.720 Goll, Claire. Diary of a horse. N.Y., 1956.
43625.51.100 Gogon, S. Angélique. Philadelphia, 1958.
43625.76.100 Gorka, Stani. Les cavaliers de Guernica. Paris, 1970.
43625.78.100 Gorz, A. Le traître. Paris, 1958.
43625.78.700 Gorz, A. The traitor. N.Y., 1959.
43625.82.100 Gosset, René Pierre. Du Glizzard sur les magnolias. Paris, 1968.
43625.89.100 Gourfinkel, N. Naissance d'un monde. Paris, 1953.
43625.89.110 Gourfinkel, N. L'autre patrie. Paris, 1953.
43625.89.1100 Goustille-Reinhart, Hélène. Fleurs solitaires. Rodez, 1958.
43625.89.2100 Goudal, J. De mer et d'amour. 7. éd. Paris, 1957.
43625.89.3100 Goudeau, Émile. Dix ans de Bonème. Paris, 1888.
43625.89.4100 Goudeket, Maurice. La douceur de vieillir. Paris, 1965.
43625.89.4700 Goudeket, Maurice. The delights of growing old. N.Y., 1966.
43625.89.5100 Goustine, Luc de. Dix mai 1968, manifestation théâtrale en trois points et un schéma. Paris, 1968.
43625.90.100 Gourbeyre, L. Contes et légendes d'Uzège. Uzès, 1930.
43625.91.100 Govy, G. Le moissonneur d'Epines. Paris, 1955.
43625.92.800 Rees, G. Rémy de Gourmont. Thèse. Paris, 1940.
43626.1.30F Grillet, G. Rachel. Paris, 1914.
43626.1.1100 Grad, Jean. L'anneau pervers. Bruxelles, 1964.
43626.2.30 Grivet, A. Néron. Paris, 1919.
43626.2.1030 Grandmougin, J. Noenoeil, homme d'état. Paris, 1960.
43626.3.100 Grangié, E. Gracieuse au béret bleu. Paris, 1925.
43626.3.1100 Grandmont, Dominique. Histoire de dire, poèmes. Jarnac, 1964.
43626.3.2100 Gramont, Sanche de. Antérôs. Paris, 1913.
43626.3.3100 Grandjean, Jehanne. Shiragiku. Beppu, 1966.
43626.4.100 Granvilliers, J. de. Le prix de l'homme. Paris, 1919-1920.
43626.4.1100 Grasset, P. L'échauffourée du métro. Paris, 1928.
43626.4.2021F Granoff, Katia. Cendres et reflets. Paris, 1965.
43626.5.100 Grasset, B. La chose littéraire. 13. éd. Paris, 1929.
43626.5.110 Grasset, B. Une rencontre. Paris, 1940.
43626.5.120 Grasset, B. Textes choisis. Paris, 1953.
43626.5.130 Grasset, B. Evangile de l'édition selon Péguy. Paris, 1955.
43626.5.140 Grasset, B. Commentaires. Paris, 1936.
43626.5.4100 Grave, J. Malfaiteurs. Paris, 1903.
43626.5.5100 Gratiunt, Gilbert. Une fille majeure. Paris, 1961.
43626.5.6100 Graveraux, Hubert. Devenir; ou, La destinée de l'homme. Paris, 1954?
43626.22.1 Hoy, Peter C. Julien Green. Paris, 1970.
43626.22.2 Hoy, Peter C. Julien Green, 1900-; manuscrits, éditions originales, photographies, documents. Bibliographie. Oxford? 1970?
43626.22.11A Green, Julien. Oeuvres complètes. Paris, 1954. 10v.
43626.22.11B Green, Julien. Oeuvres complètes. v.9. Paris, 1954.
43626.22.43A Green, Julien. Journal. v.7. Paris, 1938.
43626.22.43B Green, Julien. Journal. v.1-8. Paris, 1938. 8v.
43626.22.45 Green, Julien. Diary, 1928-1957. 1st American ed. N.Y., 1964.
43626.22.50 Green, Julien. Personal record, 1928-1939. N.Y., 1939.
43626.22.55 Green, Julien. Julien Green. Paris, 1967.
43626.22.102 Green, Julien. Mont-Cinère. Paris, 1928.
43626.22.103 Green, Julien. Mont-Cinère. N.Y., 1937.
43626.22.105 Green, Julien. The strange river. N.Y., 1932.
43626.22.110 Green, Julien. Adrienne Mesurat. Paris, 1927.
43626.22.120 Green, Julien. Adrienne Mesurat. Paris, 1927.
43626.22.123 Green, Julien. Adrienne Mesurat. Paris, 1927.
43626.22.130 Green, Julien. Léviathan, roman. Paris, 1929.
43626.22.140 Green, Julien. Le voyageur sur la terre. Paris, 1930.
43626.22.150 Green, Julien. L'autre sommeil. Paris, 1931.
43626.22.155 Green, Julien. The dark journey. N.Y., 1929.
43626.22.160 Green, Julien. Miniat. Paris, 1936.
43626.22.170 Green, Julien. Le visionnaire. Paris, 1934.
43626.22.180 Green, Julien. Varouma. N.Y., 1941.
43626.22.190 Green, Julien. L'ennem. Paris, 1954.
43626.22.200 Green, Julien. Épaves. Paris, 1932.
43626.22.210 Green, Julien. Si j'étais vous. Paris, 1947.
43626.22.220 Green, Julien. Moïra. Paris, 1950.
43626.22.230 Green, Julien. Sud, pièce en trois actes. Paris, 1953.
43626.22.240 Gorkine, M. Julien Green. Paris, 1956.
43626.22.250 Green, Julien. Le malfaiteur. Paris, 1956.
43626.22.260 Green, Julien. The transgressor. N.Y., 1957.

43511 - 43873 Individual authors, etc. - 1900- - Known authors (363 scheme plus 10) - cont.

43626.22.270	Green, Julien. Chaque homme dans sa nuit. Paris, 1960.
43626.22.280	Green, Julien. Pamphlet contre les catholiques de France. Paris, 1963.
43626.22.290	Green, Julien. Partir avant le jour. Paris, 1963.
43626.22.300	Green, Julien. Milles chemins ouverts. Paris, 1964.
43626.22.310	Green, Julien. Terre lointaine. Paris, 1966.
43626.22.320	Green, Julien. L'Autre. Paris, 1971.
43626.22.705	Green, Julien. Avarice house. n.p., 1927.
43626.22.710	Green, Julien. Dreamer. N.Y., 1934.
43626.22.715	Green, Julien. Memories of happy days. N.Y., 1942.
43626.22.717	Green, Julien. Memories of happy days. London, 1944.
43626.22.722A	Green, Julien. The closed garden. N.Y., 1928.
43626.22.722B	Green, Julien. The closed garden. N.Y., 1928.
43626.22.725	Green, Julien. If I were you. 1st ed. N.Y., 1949.
43626.22.730	Green, Julien. Moïra. London, 1951.
43626.22.735	Green, Julien. Each in his darkness. London, 1961.
43626.22.740	Green, Julien. Christine, suivi de Léviathan. Paris, 1928.
43626.22.745	Green, Julien. To leave before dawn. 1st ed. N.Y., 1967.
43626.22.800	Eigeldinger, Marc. Julien Green et la lentation de l'irréel. Paris, 1947.
43626.22.810	Stokes, S.E. Julien Green and the thorn of Puritanism. N.Y., 1955.
43626.22.820A	Brodin, Pierre. Julien Green. Paris, 1957.
43626.22.820B	Brodin, Pierre. Julien Green. Paris, 1957.
43626.22.825	Fangara, A. L'existence dans les romans de Julien Green. Roma, 1954.
43626.22.828	Brodin, Pierre. Julien Green. Paris, 1963.
43626.22.830	Prévort, J.L. Julien Green, ou l'âme engagée. Lyon, 1960.
43626.22.835	Cook, M.G. Hallucination and death as motifs of escape in the novels of Julien Green. Washington, 1960.
43626.22.840	Ott, Lydia. Das Erlebnis des Todes in den Erzählungen Julien Greens. Erlangen? 1959?
43626.22.845	Varga von Kibéd, Edmund. Die Welt- und Lebenserfahrung im Werk. München, 1961.
43626.22.850	Kerscher, R. Charaktere und Charakterzeichnung in den Romanen von Julien Green. München, 1962.
43626.22.855	Benoot, Edgar. Julien Green. Brugge, 1963.
43626.22.860	Semolue, Jean. Julien Green, ou l'obsession du mal. Paris, 1964.
43626.22.865	Rousseau, Guy Noël. Sur le chemin de Julien Green. Neuchâtel, 1965.
43626.22.870	Carrel, Janine. L'expérience du seuil dans l'oeuvre de Julien Green. Diss. Zürich, 1967.
43626.22.875	Fitch, Brian T. Julien Green. Paris, 1966.
43626.22.880	Uijterwaal, J. Julien Green, personnalité et création romanesque. Assen, 1968.
43626.22.885	Hoesli, Silvia. Zum Problem der Angst im Werk von Julien Green. Schopfheim, 1958.
43626.22.890	Petit, Jacques. Julien Green. Paris, 1969.
43626.22.895	Rose, Marilyn Gaddis. Julian Green, Gallic-American novelist. Berne, 1971.
43626.22.1100	Gregoire, Jean Albert. Twenty-four hours at Le Mans. 1st ed. N.Y., 1958.
43626.22.1700	Gregoire, Jean Albert. The money masters. London, 1958.
43626.23.100	Grellet-Dumazeau, Albert. Vieux bourbonnais. Moulins, 1938.
43626.23.1108	Grenier, Jean. Les grèves. 8e éd. Paris, 1957.
43626.23.1110	Grenier, Jean. Sur la mort d'un chien. Paris, 1957.
43626.23.1120	Grenier, Jean. Les îles. Paris, 1933.
43626.23.1123	Grenier, Jean. Les îles. Paris, 1959.
43626.23.1130	Grenier, Jean. Lexique. Paris, 1955.
43626.23.1140	Grenier, Jean. La vie quotietienne. Paris, 1968.
43626.23.2100	Grenier, Roger. Years in ambush. 1st American ed. N.Y., 1965.
43626.23.2110	Grenier, Roger. La voie romaine. Paris, 1960.
43626.23.4100	Grendel, Frédéric. Le traité de paix. Paris, 1960.
43626.25.100	Grente, Georges. Ecrits et paroles. Paris, 1937.
43626.41.21	Grimard, Luc. Sur ma flûte de bambou; poèmes. Paris, 1926.
43626.41.100	Grimard, Luc. Ritournelles; poèmes. Paris, 1927.
43626.41.1100	Grilhe, Gillette. Ombres; poèmes. Paris, 1962.
43626.64.100	Grojnowski, Daniel. L'accord parfait. Paris, 1958.
43626.66.100	Groodt-Adant, J. de. Les fruits du combat. Anvers, 194-?
43626.66.1100	Grosjean, Jean. Fils de l'homme. 2e éd. Paris, 1953.
43626.66.1110	Grosjean, Jean. Majestés et passants. Paris, 1956.
43626.66.1120	Grosjean, Jean. Terre du temps. Paris, 1946.
43626.66.1132	Grosjean, Jean. Hypostases. 2e éd. Paris, 1950.
43626.66.1140	Bible. O.T. Prophets. Les prophètes. Paris, 1955.
43626.66.1150	Grosjean, Jean. Le livre du juste. Paris, 1952.
43626.66.1160	Grosjean, Jean. Elégies. Paris, 1967.
43626.66.3100	Gros, Brigitte. Véronique dans l'appareil. Paris, 1960.
43626.66.4100	Groote, Christian de. Adolescences. Paris, 1960.
43626.66.5100	Grosclaude, Pierre. Vers quel rendez-vous? Paris, 1954.
43626.66.5110	Grosclaude, Pierre. Ces autres qui viendront. Paris, 1958.
43626.66.5120	Grosclaude, Pierre. L'éternelle escorte; poèmes. Paris, 1947.
43626.67.100	Groslier, G. Monsieur de la garde, roi. pt.1-2. Paris, 1934.
43626.67.700	Groult, Benoîte. Feminine plural. London, 1968.
43626.68.100	Grout, Marius. Passage de l'homme; roman. Paris, 1944.
43626.70.100	Gracq, Julien. A dark stranger. N.Y., 1950?
43626.70.110	Gracq, Julien. Le roi pêcheur. Paris, 1948.
43626.70.120	Gracq, Julien. Le rivage des syrtes. Paris, 1951.
43626.70.130	Gracq, Julien. La littérature à l'estomac. Paris, 1951.
43626.70.132	Gracq, Julien. La littérature à l'estomac. Paris, 1964.
43626.70.140	Gracq, Julien. Liberté grande. 2e éd. Paris, 1958.
43626.70.150	Gracq, Julien. The castle of Argol. Norfolk, Conn., 1957.
43626.70.160	Gracq, Julien. Un balcon en forêt. Paris, 1958.
43626.70.170	Gracq, Julien. Préférences. Paris, 1961.
43626.70.700	Gracq, Julien. Balcony in the forest. N.Y., 1959.
43626.70.800	Boie, Bernhild. Haupt Motive im Werke...Gracqs. München, 1966.
43626.70.805	Leutrat, Jean Louis. Julien Gracq. Paris, 1967.
43626.72.100	Greeff, E. La nuit est ma lumière. Paris, 1949.
43626.74.100	Groussard, Serge. La femme sans passé. 83e éd. Paris, 1950.
43626.74.110	Groussard, Serge. Talya. 4e éd. Paris, 1951.
43626.74.120.2	Groussard, Serge. La belle espérance. 2. éd. Paris, 1958.
43626.74.130	Groussard, Serge. Quartier chinois. Paris, 1958.
43626.74.140	Groussard, Serge. Jeunesses sauvages. Paris, 1960.
43626.74.150	Groussard, Serge. Taxi de nuit. Paris, 1971.
43627.23.100	Gsell, P. Les gosses dans les ruines. Paris, 1919.
43628.1.23	Guitry, Sacha. Théâtre. Paris, 1934-35. 2v.
43628.1.25	Guitry, Sacha. Théâtre. Paris, 1959-60. 15v.

43511 - 43873 Individual authors, etc. - 1900- - Known authors (363 scheme plus 10) - cont.

43628.1.30	Guitry, Sacha. Un beau mariage. Paris, 1912.
43628.1.31	Guitry, Sacha. La prise de Berg-op-Zoom. Paris, 1913.
43628.1.32	Guitry, Sacha. Deburau; comédie. Paris, 1918.
43628.1.33F	Guitry, Sacha. Mon père avait raison. Paris, 1920.
43628.1.34F	Guitry, Sacha. Le scandale de Monte-Carlo. Paris, 1908.
43628.1.35F	Guitry, Sacha. Jean III. Paris, 1912.
43628.1.36	Guitry, Sacha. Béranger. Paris, 1920.
43628.1.37	Guitry, Sacha. Béranger. Paris, 1920.
43628.1.38	Guitry, Sacha. Pasteur. Paris, 1919.
43628.1.40	Guitry, Sacha. Un sujet de roman. Paris, 1923.
43628.1.42	Guitry, Sacha. L'amour masqué. Paris, 1922.
43628.1.44	Guitry, Sacha. Je t'aime. Paris, 1921.
43628.1.46	Guitry, Sacha. Une étoile nouvelle. Paris, 1925.
43628.1.48	Guitry, Sacha. Mozart; comédie en trois actes. Paris, 1926.
43628.1.49	Guitry, Sacha. Deburau. N.Y., 1921.
43628.1.50	Guitry, Sacha. Deburau. Paris, 1926.
43628.1.53	Guitry, Sacha. Un miracle. Paris, 1928.
43628.1.55	Guitry, Sacha. L'esprit. Paris, 1962.
43628.1.60	Guitry, Sacha. Jean de la Fontaine. Paris, 1928.
43628.1.65	Guitry, Sacha. Mariette ou Comment on écrit l'histoire. Paris, 1929.
43628.1.70	Guitry, Sacha. Histoires de France. Paris, 1929.
43628.1.75	Guitry, Sacha. Frans Hals ou "L'Admiration". Paris, 1931.
43628.1.78	Guitry, Sacha. Quatre ans d'occupations. Paris, 1947.
43628.1.80	Guitry, Sacha. Faisons un rêve. Paris, 1934.
43628.1.85	Guitry, Sacha. Le comédien. Paris, 1921.
43628.1.90	Guitry, Sacha. La jalousie. Paris, 1934.
43628.1.95	Guitry, Sacha. Un tour au paradis (le renard et la grenouille). Paris, 1935.
43628.1.100	Guitry, Sacha. Quand jouons-nous la comédie! Paris, 1936.
43628.1.105	Guitry, Sacha. Souvenirs. Paris, 1934.
43628.1.110	Guitry, Sacha. Toutes reflexions faites. Paris, 1947.
43628.1.115	Guitry, Sacha. Napoléon. Paris, 1955.
43628.1.120	Guitry, Sacha. Et Versailles vous est conté. Paris, 1954.
43628.1.125	Guitry, Sacha. Si Versailles m'était conté. Paris, 1954.
43628.1.130	Guitry, Sacha. Soixante jours de prison. Paris, 1964.
43628.1.140	Guitry, Sacha. Et puis voici des vers. Paris, 1964.
43628.1.405A	Guitry, Sacha. If memory serves. Garden City, 1935.
43628.1.405B	Guitry, Sacha. If memory serves. Garden City, 1935.
43628.1.406	Guitry, Sacha. If memory serves. Garden City, 1936.
43628.1.407	Guitry, Sacha. Si j'ai bonne mémoire. Paris, 1962.
43628.1.500	Sacha Guitry. Paris, 1926.
43628.1.510	Benjamin, R. Sacha Guitry, roi du théâtre. Paris, 1933.
43628.1.515	Sereville, G. del. Sacha Guitry mon mari. Paris, 1959.
43628.1.520	Prince, Stéphane. Sacha Guitry hors sa légende. Paris, 1959.
43628.1.525	Lauwick, Hervé. Le merveilleux humour de Lucien et Sacha Guitry. Paris, 1959.
43628.1.530	Lauwick, Hervé. Sacha Guitry et les femmes. Paris, 1965.
43628.1.535	Harding, James. Sacha Guitry: the last boulevardier. London, 1968.
43628.2.5	Guastalla, P.R. Journal, 1940-44. Paris, 1951.
43628.2.30	Gurval, A. Evit ar vreiziz! Pour les bretons! Dinard? 1914.
43628.4.100	Guarini, Ferida. Le miroir sans tain. Neuchâtel, 1964.
43628.5.100	Gustalla, P. Gérar. Paris, 1925.
43628.22.100	Guénenno, Annie. L'épreure; récit. Paris, 1969.
43628.23.100	Guéhenno, Jean. Conversion à l'humain. Paris, 1931.
43628.23.110	Guéhenno, Jean. Caliban parle. 10e éd. Paris, 1928.
43628.23.112	Guéhenno, Jean. Caliban parle. Paris, 1962.
43628.23.125	Guéhenno, Jean. Journal d'un homme de 40 ans. Paris, 1937.
43628.23.135	Guéhenno, Jean. Dans la prison. Paris, 1944.
43628.23.140	Guéhenno, Jean. Aventures de l'esprit. 19. éd. Paris, 1954.
43628.23.145	Guéhenno, Jean. Voyages. Paris, 1952.
43628.23.150	Guéhenno, Jean. La foi difficile. Paris, 1957.
43628.23.160	Guéhenno, Jean. Sur le chemin des hommes. Paris, 1959.
43628.23.170	Guéhenno, Jean. Changer la vie. Paris, 1961.
43628.23.180	Guéhenno, Jean. Ce que je crois. Paris, 1964.
43628.23.190	Guéhenno, Jean. Notes. Paris, 1963.
43628.23.200	Guéhenno, Jean. La mort des autres. Paris, 1968.
43628.24.100	Guérin, R. Les poupées. 2. éd. Paris, 1953.
43628.24.1100	Guérin, Daniel. Vautrin. Paris, 1962.
43628.24.1110	Guérin, Daniel. Un jeune homme excentrique. Paris, 1965.
43628.24.2100	Guérande, Paul. Lamentable Clio. Paris, 1957.
43628.24.2110	Guérande, Paul. O.A.S. Métro. Paris, 1964.
43628.24.3100	Guéridon, Roland. Rien que la vie. Paris, 1954.
43628.25.100	Guerdan, L. Des minarets aux gratte-ciel. N.Y., 1943.
43628.25.2100	Guersant, M. Jean-Paul. Paris, 1953.
43628.39.100	Guilbeaux, H. Du champs des horreurs. Genève, 1917.
43628.41.100	Guillet, L. Films narquois. 50 fables. Paris, 1927.
43628.41.1100	Guinle, A. Un prête rendu. N.Y., 1914.
43628.41.2100	Guiraud, G. Henri de. Aux frontières de l'enfer. Paris, 1956.
43628.41.2110	Guiraud, G. Henri de. Helène des marais. Paris, 1958.
43628.41.3021	Guillevic, Eugène. Avec; poèmes. Paris, 1966.
43628.41.3100	Guillevic, Eugène. Fractures. Paris, 1946.
43628.41.3110	Guillevic, Eugène. Les chansons d'Antonin Blond. Paris, 1949.
43628.41.3120	Guillevic, Eugène. Trente et un sonnets. Paris, 1954.
43628.41.3130	Guillevic, Eugène. Le arnac, poème. Paris, 1961.
43628.41.3140	Guillevic, Eugène. Terre à bonheur. Paris, 1952.
43628.41.3150	Guillevic, Eugène. Sphior. Paris, 1963.
43628.41.3160	Guillevic, Eugène. Poesias. Lisboa, 1965.
43628.41.3170	Guillevic, Eugène. Euclidiennes. Paris, 1967.
43628.41.3180	Guillevic, Eugène. Paroi. Paris, 1970.
43628.41.3621	Guillevic, Eugène. Selected poems. N.Y., 1969.
43628.41.3700	Guillevic, Eugène. Guillevic. Poems. Santa Barbara, 1968.
43628.41.5100	Guillot, René. Contes de la Brousse fauve. Grenoble, 1945.
43628.41.5110	Guillot, René. Tom-Toms in Kotokio. N.Y., 1957.
43628.41.5700	Guillot, René. The children of the wind. London, 1964.
43628.41.6100	Guinle, Alexandre. Visage de la France. Paris, 1936.
43628.41.6110	Guinle, Alexandre. La lyre couronnée. Paris, 1924.
43628.41.6120	Guinle, Alexandre. Atalante. Orphée. Paris, 1932.
43628.41.6130	Guinle, Alexandre. Pour Béatrice. Paris, 1956.
43628.41.7021	Guiette, Robert. Poésie, 1922-1967. Paris, 1969.
43628.41.7100	Guiette, Robert. Seuils de la nuit. Paris, 1961.
43628.41.7110	Guiette, Robert. Ombres vives. Bruxelles, 1969.
43628.41.8021	Guichet, Robert. Partage d'aimer; poems. Rodez, 1965.
43628.41.9100	Guimard, Paul. Les choses de la vie, roman. Paris, 1967.
43628.42.100	Guilloux, Louis. Histoires de brigands. Paris, 1936.
43628.42.112	Guillevic, Eugène. Le sang noir. 31e éd. Paris, 1936.
43628.42.120	Guilloux, Louis. Le jeu de patience. Paris, 1949.

Classified Listing

43511 - 43873 Individual authors, etc. - 1900- - Known authors (363 scheme plus 10) - cont.

43628.42.130 Guilloux, Louis. Absent de Paris. 7. éd. Paris, 1952.
43628.42.140 Guilloux, Louis. Parpagnacco. 7. éd. Paris, 1954.
43628.42.150 Guilloux, Louis. Les batailles perdues. Paris, 1960.
43628.42.160 Guilloux, Louis. Dossier confidentiel. Paris, 1930.
43628.42.170 Guilloux, Louis. Le pain des rèves; roman. 28. éd. Paris, 1942.
43628.42.180 Guilloux, Louis. La maison du peuple, suivi de Compagnons. Paris, 1953.
43628.42.190 Guilloux, Louis. La confrontation. Paris, 1967.
43628.42.200 Guilloux, Louis. Cripure. Paris, 1967.
43628.42.1100 Guillaume, Bernard. Vingt-quatre préludes, poèmes. Rodez, 1959.
43628.42.3100 Guillaume, Louis. Hans ou Les songes vécus. Rodez, 1958.
43628.42.3110 Guillaume, Louis. L'ancre de lumière. Rodez, 1958.
43628.42.4100 Guillao, Raymond. Prisons nègres pour l'Africain. Honfleur, 1968.
43628.43.100 Guigues, Louis Paul. Lisbeth. Paris, 1953.
43628.43.110 Guigues, Louis Paul. La dernière chambre. Paris, 1958.
43628.44.100 Guislain, J.M. Pan et syrinx. Toulouse, 1928.
43628.75.100 Gurgand, Jean Noël. Israéliennes. Paris, 1966.
43628.85.61 Guth, Paul. Lettre ouverte aux idoles. Paris, 1968.
43628.85.100 Guth, Paul. Le naïf sous les drapeaux. Paris, 1954.
43628.85.110 Guth, Paul. Le naïf aux quarante enfants. Paris, 1955.
43628.85.120 Guth, Paul. Jeanne la mince. Paris, 1960.
43628.85.130 Guth, Paul. Jeanne la mince et l'amour. Paris, 1962.
43628.85.140 Guth, Paul. Quarante contre un. Paris, 1947.
43628.85.700 Guth, Paul. The innocent tenant. London, 1957.
43628.98.100 Guyon-Cesbron, J. Désaxés; roman. Paris, 1931.
43628.98.1100 Guyotat, Pierre. Éden, Éden, Éden. Paris, 1966.
43628.99.100 Guyot, C. La légende de la ville d'Ys, d'après les anciens textes. Paris, 1936.
43628.99.100.5F Guyot, C. La toison d'or. Paris, 1921.
43628.99.105 Huzard, A. de B. (Mme.). Rose, madame, roman inédit. Paris, 1928.
43630.6.100 Gybal, André. Luxure. Paris, 1925.
43631.03.100 Haedens, Kléber. Une jeune serpente; roman. 4. éd. Paris, 1940.
43631.03.110 Haedens, Kléber. Adieu â la rose. 5. éd. Paris, 1955.
43631.03.120 Haedens, Kléber. Salut au Kentucky. Paris, 1960.
43631.03.130 Haedens, Kléber. L'été finit sous les tilleuls. Paris, 1966.
43631.1.30 Halary, P. Du vallon au sommet. Paris, 1908.
43631.2.30 Hamp, Pierre. La peine des hommes; le rail. 4. éd. Paris, 1914.
43631.2.32 Hamp, Pierre. La peine des hommes; marée fraiche vin de champagne. 3. éd. Paris, 1918.
43631.2.34 Hamp, Pierre. La peine des hommes; l'enquête. 6. éd. Paris, 1920.
43631.2.36A Hamp, Pierre. La peine des hommes; travail invincible. 10. éd. Paris, 1918.
43631.2.36B Hamp, Pierre. La peine des hommes; travail invincible. 10. éd. Paris, 1918.
43631.2.36C Hamp, Pierre. La peine des hommes; travail invincible. 10. éd. Paris, 1918.
43631.2.38 Hamp, Pierre. La peine des hommes; les métiers blessés. 2. éd. Paris, 1919.
43631.2.40 Hamp, Pierre. La peine des hommes; la victoire mécanniciene. 6. éd. Paris, 1920.
43631.2.42 Hamp, Pierre. La peine des hommes; les chercheurs d'or. 8. éd. Paris, 1920.
43631.2.44 Hamp, Pierre. La peine des hommes; le cantique des cantiques. 3. éd. Paris, 1922. 2v.
43631.2.46 Hamp, Pierre. La peine des hommes; un nouvel honneur. 4. éd. Paris, 1922.
43631.2.48 Hamp, Pierre. La peine des hommes; mes métiers. 8. éd. Paris, 1929.
43631.2.50 Hamp, Pierre. Marée fraiche. 5. éd. Paris, 1936.
43631.2.51 Hamp, Pierre. Vieille histoire. 4. éd. Paris, 1921.
43631.2.52 Hamp, Pierre. La peine des hommes. 10. éd. Paris, 1937.
43631.2.55 Hamp, Pierre. La peine des hommes. Paris, 1924.
43631.2.57 Hamp, Pierre. La peine des hommes. Paris, 1959-
43631.2.60 Hamp, Pierre. L'art et le travail. Paris, 1923.
43631.2.62 Hamp, Pierre. Gens. 5. éd. Paris, 1917.
43631.2.63 Hamp, Pierre. Gens. Paris, 1923.
43631.2.63.10 Hamp, Pierre. Gens. Paris, 1928.
43631.2.63.25 Hamp, Pierre. People. N.Y., 1921.
43631.2.64 Hamp, Pierre. La maison avant tout pièce. Paris, 1923.
43631.2.68 Hamp, Pierre. La maison. 3. éd. Paris, 1927.
43631.2.70 Hamp, Pierre. Monsieur l'administrateur. 3. éd. Paris, 1928.
43631.2.75 Hamp, Pierre. Et avec ça, Madame? Paris, 1946.
43631.2.77 Hamp, Pierre. Enquêtes Guevles noires. Paris, 1938.
43631.2.79.5 Hamp, Pierre. La victoire de la France sur les Français. 6. éd. Paris, 1915.
43631.16.100 Haddad, Malek. L'élève et la leçon. Paris, 1960.
43631.21.100 Haedrich, Marcel. Les évangiles de la vie. Paris, 1953.
43631.21.110 Haedrich, Marcel. Drame dans un miroir. Paris, 1958.
43631.21.120 Haedrich, Marcel. Le patron; roman. Paris, 1964.
43631.21.130 Haedrich, Marcel. L'entre-deux dieux. Paris, 1967.
43631.22.100 Haeffely, Claude. Le sommeil et la neige. Montréal, 1956.
43631.41.100 Hain, Georges. Le cyprès sur l'Azur. Paris, 1928.
43631.41.2100 Haïk, Farjallah. Jaumana. Paris, 1957.
43631.41.2110 Haïk, Farjallah. De chair et d'ésprit. Paris, 1968.
43631.45.100 Halsdorf, Denyse. Poèmes d'adolescence. Paris, 1955.
43631.49.100 Halla, Bernard. Maximes. Paris, 193-.
43631.49.110 Halla, Bernard. L'inconnue du lac. v.1-2. Paris, 1937.
43631.49.2100 Haldas, Georges. Gens qui soupirent. Neuchâtel, 1963.
43631.49.2110 Haldas, Georges. Boulevard des Philosophes, chronique. Lausanne, 1966.
43631.49.2120 Haldas, Georges. Sans feu ni lieu. Lausanne, 1968.
43631.49.2130 Haldas, Georges. Jardin des éspérances. Lausanne, 1969.
43631.49.3100 Halévy, Dominique. Celine ou la multiplication; histoire. Paris, 1964.
43631.49.4100 Halet, Pierre. La butte de Satory. Paris, 1967.
43631.50.100 Hân, Françoise. Cité des hommes (1951-1955). Paris, 1956.
43631.50.1100 Hallier, Jean-Edern. Le grand écrivain, roman. Paris, 1967.
43631.51.100 Haunaert, Louis. Journal d'une femme. Bruxelles, 1935.
43631.54.100 Hamesse, P.P. La mesaventure. Bruxelles, 1964.
43631.58.100 Handache, Gilbert. L'oeil de Cao Daï, roman. Paris, 1968.
43631.75.100 Harel, Paul. Poèmes à la gloire du Christ. Paris, 1928.
43631.75.111 Harel, Paul. Sous les pommiers. 2. éd. Paris, 1888.
43631.76.100 Hardy, René. La route des cygnes. Paris, 1967.
43631.76.700 Hardy, René. The sword by God. London, 1954.
43631.76.705 Hardy, René. Bitter victory. London, 1956.
43631.76.1100F Harispe, Pierre. La divine tragédie. Paris, 1916.

43511 - 43873 Individual authors, etc. - 1900- - Known authors (363 scheme plus 10) - cont.

43631.76.2100 Harley, Jean. La paix des collines. Bordeaux, 1946.
43631.77.100 Harlaire, André. En croix. Paris, 1928.
43631.78.705 Hart, R.E. The poet of the Indian Ocean. Portland, 1937.
43631.79.100 Hasard, M. Ça et lá. Monte Carlo, 1960.
43631.85.100 Hatem, Amouar. Bétyles. Bienne, 1968.
43631.89.100 Haurigot, Paul. Alphonsine. Paris, 1923.
43631.89.110 Haurigot, Paul. Théâtre. v.2. Paris, 1943-
43631.89.120 Haurigot, Paul. Napoléon noir. Paris, 1946.
43631.89.1100 Haulot, Arthur. Espaces. Bruxelles, 1967.
43631.90.100 Hautier, Raoul. Réconciliation. La Louvière, 1933.
43631.90.110 Hautier, Raoul. L'oiseau phénix. La Louvière, 1932.
43631.98.705 Hazard, Paul. A souvenir of Chicago. Paris, 1930?
43631.98.800 Hommage à Paul Hazard. Paris, 1947?
43631.98.1100 Hazoumé, Roger Aralamon. Fleurs africaines, poèmes. Paris, 1967.
43632.1.30 Hennequin, M. Mon bébé! Paris, 1914.
43632.1.32 Hennequin, M. La sonnette d'alarme. Paris, 1923.
43632.2.30.5 Hellem, Charles. Sabotage; a play. Easton, 1914.
43632.3.27 Hémon, Louis. Lettres à sa famille. Montréal, 1968.
Htn 43632.3.30* Hémon, Louis. Maria Chapdelaine. Montréal, 1916.
43632.3.30.5 Hémon, Louis. Maria Chapdelaine. Paris, 1921.
43632.3.30.8 Hémon, Louis. Maria Chapdelaine. Paris, 1921.
43632.3.30.15 Hémon, Louis. Maria Chapdelaine. 297. éd. Paris, 1921.
43632.3.30.20 Hémon, Louis. Maria Chapdelaine. 509. éd. Paris, 1921.
43632.3.30.25 Hémon, Louis. Maria Chapdelaine. 688. éd. Paris, 1921.
43632.3.31 Hémon, Louis. Maria Chapdelaine. N.Y., 1921.
43632.3.31.5A Hémon, Louis. Maria Chapdelaine. N.Y., 1921.
43632.3.31.5B Hémon, Louis. Maria Chapdelaine. N.Y., 1921.
43632.3.31.6 Hémon, Louis. Maria Chapdelaine. Toronto, 1921.
43632.3.32A Hémon, Louis. Maria Chapdelaine. N.Y., 1921.
43632.3.32B Hémon, Louis. Maria Chapdelaine. N.Y., 1921.
43632.3.33 Hémon, Louis. Maria Chapdelaine. N.Y., 1921.
43632.3.35 Hémon, Louis. Maria Chapdelaine. N.Y., 1921.
43632.3.40A Hémon, Louis. Maria Chapdelaine. N.Y., 1921.
43632.3.40B Hémon, Louis. Maria Chapdelaine. N.Y., 1921.
43632.3.42 Hémon, Louis. Maria Chapdelaine. N.Y., 1927.
43632.3.42.2 Hémon, Louis. Maria Chapdelaine. N.Y., 1924.
43632.3.43 Hémon, Louis. Colin-Maillard. 17. éd. Paris, 1924.
43632.3.45 Hémon, Louis. Colin-Maillard. 64. éd. Paris, 1924.
43632.3.47 Hémon, Louis. Blind man's buff. N.Y., 1925.
43632.3.50 Hémon, Louis. My fair lady. N.Y., 1923.
43632.3.65 Hémon, Louis. La belle que voilà. Paris, 1923.
43632.3.70 Hémon, Louis. The journal of Louis Hémon. N.Y., 1924.
43632.3.75 Hémon, Louis. Monsieur Repois et la Némésis. Paris, 1953.
43632.3.80 Pamphlet box. Hémon, Louis.
43632.3.85 McAndrew, A. Louis Hémon: sa vie et son oeuvre. Thèse. Paris, 1936.
43632.3.87 Montigny, L.T. de. La revanche de Maria Chapdelaine. Montréal, 1937.
43632.3.89 Potuin, Damase. Le roman d'un roman. Québec, 1950.
43632.6.100 Henriot, Émile. Valenti. Paris, 1918.
43632.6.110 Henriot, Émile. Éloge de la curiosité. Paris, 1927.
43632.6.120 Henriot, Émile. Aricie Brun, ou Les vertus bourgeoises. Paris, 1924.
43632.6.122 Henriot, Émile. Aricie Brun, ou Les vertus bourgeoises. Paris, 1924.
43632.6.130 Henriot, Émile. Poésies. Paris, 1928.
43632.6.140 Henriot, Émile. La flamme et les cendres. Paris, 1914.
43632.6.150 Henriot, Émile. Le livre de mon père. Paris, 1939.
43632.6.160 Henriot, Émile. Livres et portraits. Paris, 1923.
43632.6.165 Henriot, Émile. Livres et portraits. 2. éd. Paris, 1925.
43632.6.167 Henriot, Émile. L'enfant perdu. Paris, 1926.
43632.6.170 Henriot, Émile. Livres et portraits. 4. éd. Paris, 1927.
43632.6.180A Henriot, Émile. Tout va finir. Paris, 1936.
43632.6.180B Henriot, Émile. Tout va finir. Paris, 1936.
43632.6.190 Henriot, Émile. Au bord du temps. Paris, 1958.
43632.6.200 Henriot, Émile. On n'est pas perdu sur la terre. Paris, 1960.
43632.6.210 Henriot, Émile. Histoires morales. Paris, 1925.
43632.6.220 Henriot, Émile. Le pénitent de Psalmodi. Paris, 1933.
43632.6.230 Henriot, Émile. Les temps innocents. Paris, 1921.
43632.6.240 Henriot, Émile. Aquarelles. Paris, 1922.
43632.6.250 Henriot, Émile. Vignettes et allégories. Paris, 1925.
43632.6.260 Henriot, Émile. Esquisses d'X. Paris, 1928.
43632.6.270 Henriot, Émile. Le diable à l'hôtel. Paris, 1919.
43632.6.280 Henriot, Émile. Omphale. n.p., 1920.
43632.6.290 Henriot, Émile. L'instant et le souvenir. Paris, 1924.
43632.6.300 Henriot, Émile. Bellica. Paris, 1915.
43632.6.800 Émile Henriot de l'Académie Française, 1889-1961. Paris, 1962?
43632.6.805 Dulière, A. Émile Henriot, sa vie, son oeuvre. Paris, 1963.
43632.7.100 Herbert, Huberte. Elle en est, ma chère. Paris, 1929.
43632.14.100 Hecquet, Stephen. Anne. Paris, 1956.
43632.14.110 Hecquet, Stephen. Les collégiens, roman. Paris, 1960.
43632.20.100 Héduy, Philippe. Au lieutenant des Taglaïts. Paris, 1960.
43632.41.102 Heitz, Robert Marie Charles. Souvenirs de jadis et de naguère. 2. éd. n.p., 1964.
43632.50.19 Hellens, Franz. Poésie complète (1905-1959). Paris, 1959.
43632.50.21 Hellens, Franz. Choix de poèmes. v.1-2. Paris, 1956.
43632.50.22 Hellens, Franz. Florilège poétique. Blainville-sur-Mer, 1963.
43632.50.23 Hellens, Franz. Arrière-saisons (1960-1967). Paris, 1967.
43632.50.41 Hellens, Franz. Documents secrèts, 1905-1956. Paris, 1958.
43632.50.100 Hellens, Franz. La femme partages. Paris, 1929.
43632.50.110 Hellens, Franz. Mélusine. Paris, 1952.
43632.50.120 Hellens, Franz. Una. Paris, 1952.
43632.50.130 Hellens, Franz. Testament. Paris, 1950.
43632.50.140 Hellens, Franz. Mémoires d'Elseneur. Paris, 1954.
43632.50.150 Hellens, Franz. Style et caractère. Bruxelles, 1956.
43632.50.162 Hellens, Franz. Fantômes vivants. 2. éd. Paris, 1955.
43632.50.170 Hellens, Franz. Oeil-de-Dieu. Paris, 1959.
43632.50.180 Hellens, Franz. Comme le raisin promis pour la vendange. Lyon, 1954.
43632.50.190 Hellens, Franz. Entre toutes les femmes. Paris, 1960.
43632.50.200 Hellens, Franz. Petit théâtre aux chandelles. Paris, 1959?
43632.50.210 Hellens, Franz. L'âge dur, 1957-1960. Paris, 1961.
43632.50.220 Hellens, Franz. Objets. Paris, 1966.
43632.50.230 Hellens, Franz. Les hors-le-vent. Liège, 1965.
43632.50.240 Hellens, Franz. Poétique des éléments et des mythes. Paris, 1966.
43632.50.250 Hellens, Franz. Le dernier jour du monde, nouvelles fantastiques. Paris, 1967.

43511 - 43873 Individual authors, etc. - 1900- - Known authors (363 scheme plus 10) - cont.

43632.50.260 Hellens, Franz. Essais de critique intuitive. Bruxelles, 1968.

43632.50.270 Hellens, Franz. Célébration de la pomme. Le Jas du Revest-Saint-Martin, 1967.

43632.50.280 Hellens, Franz. Cet âge qu'on dit grand. Bruxelles, 1970.

43632.50.800 Hommage à Franz Hellens. Hommage à Franz Hellens. Paris, 1957.

43632.50.810 Bosschère, J. de. Franz Hellens. Lyon, 1956.

43632.51.100 Heller, Maximilienne. La mer rouge; roman. Paris, 1923.

43632.59.100 Hennebois, C. La loi de vivre. Clérmont-Ferrand, 1912.

43632.59.1100 Henein, Georges. Le seuil interdit. Paris, 1956.

43632.60.100 Hennart, Marcel. La voix de l'herbe. Paris, 1961.

43632.61.100 Henry, André. D'une voix chuchotée. Paris, 1957.

43632.61.1100 Henry, Jean Marcel. Girondenes, poésies. Bordeaux, 1947.

43632.61.2100 Henry, Fernand. Passages des oiseaux. Paris, 1950.

43632.74.100 Hercourt, Jean. Matière friable. Lausanne, 1968.

43632.75.100 Herbart, Pierre. Souvenirs imaginaires, suivis de la nuit. Paris, 1968.

43632.75.700 Herbart, Pierre. Halcyon. London, 1948.

43632.75.1800 Hommage des poétes à Jacques Hébertot. Paris, 1957.

43632.76.105 Hériat, Philippe. La foire aux garçons. 3. éd. Paris, 1934.

43632.76.110 Hériat, Philippe. La main tendue. Paris, 1933.

43632.76.125 Hériat, Philippe. Les enfants gâtés. 148. éd. Paris, 1939.

43632.76.135 Hériat, Philippe. L'araignée du matin. Paris, 1933.

43632.76.145 Hériat, Philippe. L'innocent. 31. éd. Paris, 1931.

43632.76.150 Hériat, Philippe. Les Boussarde. Paris, 1957-68. 4v.

43632.76.700 Hériat, Philippe. The spoiled children. N.Y., 1956.

43632.76.3100 Hermies, Michel. La mauvaise grâce. Paris, 1958.

43632.76.4100 Hardy, René. Le bois des amants. Paris, 1960.

43632.77.100 Hervieu, Louise. Sangs; roman. Paris, 19- .

43632.77.1100 Herta, Simon. Méditations au Golgotha. Paris, 1957.

43632.77.2100 Hermant, A. La vie littéraire. Paris, 1923-28. 2v.

43632.77.3100 Hermann, Claudine. L'étoile de David. Paris, 1959.

43632.77.3110 Hermann, Claudine. Le cavalier des steppes. Paris, 1963.

43632.77.4100 Herment, Georges. Seuil de terre. Ottigniés, 1963.

43632.77.4110 Herment, Georges. Le poème enseveli. Veilhes, 1967.

43632.77.5100 Herpe, François. Aux tentures du temps. Saint-Brieuc, 1968.

43632.78.100 Hervilliez, G. d'. A louer meublé. Paris, 1935.

43632.78.110 Hervilliez, G. d'. Mouvement judiciaire. Pt. 1-3. Paris, 1938.

43632.78.120 Hervilliez, G. d'. La donation. Paris, 1939.

43632.79.100 Hertz, Henri. Tragédie des temps volages. Paris, 1955.

43632.82.100 Hesse, Raymond. Riquet à la houppe et ses compagnons. Paris, 1923.

43632.89.800 Savoret, André. Simples propos sur l'oeuvre de Jacques Heugel. Montrouge, 1957.

43632.89.1100 Heurtebize, Vital. Le bouffon triste, poèmes. Bordeaux, 1959.

43632.89.1110 Heurtebize, Vital. À fleur de ciel. Paris, 1962.

43632.89.2100 Heurté, Yves. La ruche en feu. Paris, 1970.

43632.98.100 Heyrand, Charles. Le coeur gagne. Paris, 1926.

43633.1.35 Hirsch, Charles H. La danseuse rouge. 6. éd. Paris, 1922.

43633.1.40 Hirsch, Charles H. L'homme aux sangliers. Paris, 1936.

43633.1.50 Hirsch, Charles H. La marieuse. Paris, 1925.

43633.1.80 Carco, Francis. Charles-Henry Hirsch; biographie critique. Paris, n.d.

43633.28.100 Hoffmann, Georges. J'ai régné cette nuit, comédie en trois actes. Genève, 1967.

43636.50.100 Hollier-Larousse, Jules. Les sentiers du destin. Paris, 1957.

43636.55.800 Drion du Chapois, Ferdinand. Luc Hommel. Paris, 1966.

43636.55.1100 L'homme du fonds des camps. Le raisin de Tokay. Malines, 1954.

43636.61.100 Honnert, Robert. Les désirs. 6. éd. Paris, 1930.

43636.64.100 Hoog, Armand. Le dernier tonnerre. Paris, 1958.

43636.64.110 Hoog, Armand. L'accident. Paris, 1948.

43636.64.120 Hoog, Armand. Les deux côtes de la mer. Paris, 1967.

43636.89.100 Hougron, Jean. Reap the whirlwind. N.Y., 1953.

43636.89.110 Hougron, Jean. Mort en fraude. 100. éd. Paris, 1953.

43636.89.120 Hougron, Jean. Les portes de l'aventure. Paris, 1954.

43636.89.130 Hougron, Jean. Blaze of the sun. London, 1954.

43636.89.140 Hougron, Jean. La gueule pleine de dents. Paris, 1970.

43636.89.150 Hougron, Jean. Les Asiates; roman. Paris, 1971.

43636.90.100 Hoveyda, Fereydoun. Le Losange. Paris, 1968.

43636.94.100 Howlett, J. Un temps pour rien. Paris, 1953.

43638.2.100 Huant, Ernest. Voyage en Assurs-Socyalie. Paris, 1965.

43638.2.110 Huant, Ernest. Le troisième triumvirat, fragments des mémoires de Gordien le Cybernétique. Paris, 1967.

43638.7.705 Hubermont, P. Thirteen men in the mine. N.Y., 1931.

43638.7.800 Hubert, R.R. Asymptotes. Paris, 1954.

43638.7.810 Hubert, R.R. La cité borgne. Paris, 1953.

43638.8.100 Hubin, Christian. Le chant décapité la nuit. Bruxelles, 1968.

43638.31.100 Hugard, Jane. Ces demoiselles de l'opéra. Paris, 1923.

43638.34.100 Hugues, Clovis. La chanson de Jehanne Darc. Paris, 1900.

43638.34.1100 Hugot, Noëlle. Symphonie sur le seuil. Honfleur, 1969.

43638.35.100 Huguet, Auguste. La caresse des soirs. Paris, 1927.

43638.35.1041 Huguenin, Jean-René. Journal. Paris, 1964.

43638.35.1100 Huguenin, Jean-René. La côte sauvage. Paris, 1960.

43638.35.1110 Huguenin, Jean-René. Une autre jeunesse. Paris, 1965.

43638.35.1700 Huguenin, Jean-René. The other side of the summer. N.Y., 1961.

43638.51.100 Hulton, Nika. The witch. London, 1960.

43638.53.100 Humbourg, Pierre. Le miroir sans tain. Paris, 1947.

43638.53.110 Humbourg, Pierre. Mort de vieillesse. Paris, 1956.

43638.53.120 Humbourg, Pierre. Par une nuit sans lune. Paris, 1960.

43638.53.130 Humbourg, Pierre. Les sentiers de l'automne. Paris, 1959.

43638.55.100 Humeau, E. L'épreuve au soleil. Paris, 1951.

43638.55.800 Puel, Gaston. Edmond Humeau. Rodez, 1959.

43638.76.100 Huriet, Michel. La fête de la dédicacé. Paris, 1969.

43638.82.100 Husson, Jean H. Le cheval d'Herbeleau. Paris, 1965.

43638.83.100 Huszar, Étienne. La raison d'être. Malines, 1955.

43638.83.110 Huszar, Étienne. J'ai éteint le soleil. Malines, 1955.

43638.92.100 Huwart, Louis. L'odeur de notre amour. Malines, 1954.

43638.99.100 Huzard, A. de B. (Mme.). Comment s'en vont les reines. Paris, 1905.

43638.99.105 Huzard, A. de B. (Mme.). Princesses de science. 26. éd. Paris, 1908.

43638.99.107 Huzard, A. de B. (Mme.). Princesses de science. 47. éd. Paris, 191- ?

43638.99.110 Huzard, A. de B. (Mme.). Les dames du palais. Paris, 1909.

43511 - 43873 Individual authors, etc. - 1900- - Known authors (363 scheme plus 10) - cont.

43638.99.112 Huzard, A. de B. (Mme.). Les dames du palais. 20. éd. Paris, 1910.

43638.99.115 Huzard, A. de B. (Mme.). Le métier de roi. Paris, 1911.

43638.99.120 Huzard, A. de B. (Mme.). Mirabelle de pampelune. Paris, 1917.

43638.99.125 Huzard, A. de B. (Mme.). Les sables mouvants. Paris, 1913.

43638.99.130 Huzard, A. de B. (Mme.). Aujourd'hui. Paris, 1926.

43638.99.140 Huzard, A. de B. (Mme.). Grand mère. Paris, 1945.

43638.99.150 Huzard, A. de B. (Mme.). Cher coeur humain! Paris, 1932.

43643.23.103 Ibals, A. La maison de l'enfer. Paris, 1926.

43643.23.2100 Ibels, J.C. Le péril de vivre. Paris, 1951.

43643.23.2110 Ibels, J.C. Le sang de l'ange. Paris, 1957.

43644.4.100 Icard, Renaud. Le livre d'amour. Lyon, 1922.

43648.32.100 Igé, Jean. Jour le jour; poèmes. Paris, 1954.

43652.46.100 Ikor, Roger. Les fils d'Avrom. Paris, 1955.

43652.46.110 Ikor, Roger. Mise au nef. Paris, 1957.

43652.46.120 Ikor, Roger. Ciel ouvert. Paris, 1959.

43652.46.140 Ikor, Roger. Si le temps. Paris, 1961. 4v.

43652.46.150 Ikor, Roger. A travers nos déserts. Paris, 1950.

43652.46.160 Ikor, Roger. Gloucq. Paris, 1965.

43654.7.100 Imbert, D. La Marie des sept péchés. Paris, 1957.

43655.4.100 Inard d'Argence, Robert. Adalta, poèmes. Paris, 1961.

43655.13.100 Inchakoff, B. Poèmes du long hiver et printemps fidèle. Paris, 1959.

43656.59.50 Ionesco, Eugène. Journal en miettes. Paris, 1967.

43656.59.61 Bonnefoy, Claude. Entretiens avec Eugène Ionesco. Paris, 1966.

43656.59.100 Ionesco, Eugène. Théâtre. Paris, 1953.

43656.59.105 Ionesco, Eugène. Théâtre. 2. éd. Paris, 1954- 4v.

43656.59.106 Ionesco, Eugène. Théâtre. v.2. Paris, 1958-

43656.59.110 Ionesco, Eugène. Four plays. N.Y., 1958.

43656.59.120 Ionesco, Eugène. Le rhinocéros. 1. éd. Paris, 1959.

43656.59.130 Ionesco, Eugène. Rhinocéros. N.Y., 1960.

43656.59.140 Ionesco, Eugène. La photo du Colonel. Paris, 1962.

43656.59.150 Ionesco, Eugène. Notes et contre notes. Paris, 1962.

43656.59.160 Ionesco, Eugène. Le roi se meurt. Paris, 1963.

43656.59.170 Ionesco, Eugène. La cantatrice chauve. Paris, 1964.

43656.59.180 Ionesco, Eugène. Délire à deux, essai de calligraphie sonore. Paris, 1966.

43656.59.190 Ionesco, Eugène. Présent passé, passé présent. Paris, 1968.

43656.59.200 Ionesco, Eugène. Découvertes. Genève, 1969.

43656.59.210 Ionesco, Eugène. Jeux de massacre. Paris, 1970.

43656.59.621 Ionesco, Eugène. Plays. London, 1958-63. 8v.

43656.59.625 Ionesco, Eugène. The chairs, a play. London, 1958.

43656.59.630 Ionesco, Eugène. Amédée. The new tenant. N.Y., 1958.

43656.59.635 Ionesco, Eugène. The killer, and other plays. N.Y., 1960.

43656.59.641 Ionesco, Eugène. Fragments of a journal. N.Y., 1968.

43656.59.661 Bonnefoy, Claude. Conversations with Eugène Ionesco. London, 1970.

43656.59.700 Ionesco, Eugène. Notes and counter notes. N.Y., 1964.

43656.59.705 Ionesco, Eugène. The bald soprano. N.Y., 1965.

43656.59.710F Ionesco, Eugène. The bald prima donna. London, 1966.

43656.59.715 Ionesco, Eugène. Exit the King. N.Y., 1963.

43656.59.720 Ionesco, Eugène. A stroll in the air. N.Y., 1968.

43656.59.725 Ionesco, Eugène. Hunger and thirst, and other plays. N.Y., 1969.

43656.59.800 Coe, Richard Nelson. Ionesco. Edinburgh, 1961.

43656.59.801 Coe, Richard Nelson. Ionesco. London, 1971.

43656.59.805 Pronko, Leonard C. Eugène Ionesco. N.Y., 1965.

43656.59.806 Pronko, Leonard C. Eugène Ionesco. N.Y., 1968.

43656.59.810 Sénart, Phillipe. Ionesco. Paris, 1964.

43656.59.815 Donnard, Jean Hervé. Ionesco dramaturge. Paris, 1966.

43656.59.820 Benmussa, Simone. Eugène Ionesco. Paris, 1966.

43656.59.825 Glukman, Marta. Eugène Ionesco y su teatro. Santiago de Chile, 1965.

43656.59.830 Ronge, Peter. Polemik, Parodie und Satire bei Ionesco. Bad Homburg, 1967.

43656.59.835 Bradesco, Faust. Le monde étrange de Ionesco. Paris, 1967.

43656.59.840 Jacobsen, Josephine. Ionesco and Genêt. 1. ed. N.Y., 1968.

43656.59.845 Mikheeva, Agnessa N. Kogda po stsene khodiat nosorogi. Moskva, 1967.

43656.59.850 Wendt, Ernst. Eugène Ionesco. 1. Aufl. Velber, 1967.

43656.59.855 Vos, Nelvin. Eugène Ionesco and Edward Albee. Grand Rapids, 1968.

43656.59.860 Tarrab, Gilbert. Ionesco à coeur ouvert. Montréal, 1970.

43656.59.1100 Ionesco, Joana. Mes années de lumière, roman vécu. Paris, 1969.

43659.1.100 Isaac, J. Les joyeuses histoires juives. Paris, 1938.

43659.65.100 Isolle, Jacques. Chronique de Saint-Macé. Angers, 1945.

43659.67.31 Isou, Isidore (pseud.). Oeuvres de spectacles. Paris, 1964.

43659.67.100 Isou, Isidore (pseud.). Précisions sur ma poésie et moi. Paris, 1950.

43659.67.110 Isou, Isidore (pseud.). Les journeaux des dieux. Paris, 1950.

43659.67.120 Isou, Isidore (pseud.). Je vous apprendrai l'amour. Paris, 1957.

43659.67.130 Isou, Isidore (pseud.). Les champs de force. Paris, 1964.

43659.67.800 Lemaître, M. Isidore Isou. Paris, 1954.

43659.88.100 Istrati, Panait. Oncle Anghel. 24. éd. Paris, 1924.

43659.88.110 Istrati, Panait. Famille Perlmutter. Paris, 1927.

43659.88.120 Istrati, Panait. Méditerranée lever du soleil. 12. éd. Paris, 1934.

43659.88.130 Istrati, Panait. Présentation des Haïdouce. Paris, 1934.

43659.88.140 Istrati, Panait. Le pêcheur d'éponges. Paris, 1930.

43659.88.150 Istrati, Panait. Le bureau de placement. Paris, 1936.

43659.88.160 Istrati, Panait. La maison Thüringer. Paris, 1935.

43659.88.170 Istrati, Panait. Les chardons du Baragan. Paris, 1928.

43659.88.180 Istrati, Panait. Opere alese. Bucuresti, 1966.

43659.88.700 Istrati, Panait. The bitter orange tree. N.Y., 1931.

43659.88.710 Istrati, Panait. Kyra kyralina. N.Y., 1926.

43659.88.715 Istrati, Panait. Kyra kyralina. Paris, 1958.

43659.88.800 Raydon, Edouard. Panaït Istrati, vagabond de genie. Paris, 1968.

43659.88.805 Jutrin-Klener, Monique. Panaït Istrati: un chardon déraciné, écrivain français, conteur roumain. Paris, 1970.

43666.5 Izoard, Jacques. Aveuglement, Orphée. Bruxelles, 1967.

43667.1.21 Jammes, Francis. Oeuvres inédites. n.p., n.d.

43667.1.25 Jammes, Francis. Mémoires. Paris, 1921-23. 3v.

43667.1.30 Jammes, Francis. Les géorgiques chrétiennes. 4. éd. Paris, 1912.

43511 - 43873 Individual authors, etc. - 1900- - Known authors (363 scheme plus 10) - cont.

43667.1.31 Jammes, Francis. Les géorgiques chrétiennes. Paris, 1911.

43667.1.32 Jammes, Francis. Le deuil des primevères 1898-1900. 5. éd. Paris, 1903.

43667.1.33 Jammes, Francis. Le triomphe de la vie 1900-1901. 3. éd. Paris, 1911.

43667.1.34 Jammes, Francis. De l'angelus de l'aube à l'angelus du soir 1888-1897. 5. éd. Paris, 1911.

43667.1.35 Jammes, Francis. Clairières dans le ciel 1902-1906. 3. éd. Paris, 1910.

43667.1.36 Jammes, Francis. Feuilles dans le vent. Paris, 1913.

43667.1.37 Jammes, Francis. Le roman de lièvre. 11. éd. Paris, 1917.

43667.1.38 Jammes, Francis. Le rosaire au soleil. 9. éd. Paris, 1916.

43667.1.39 Jammes, Francis. Cinq prières pour le temps de la guerre. Paris, 1916.

43667.1.40 Jammes, Francis. Monsieur le curé d'Ozeron. 11. éd. Paris, 1918.

43667.1.41 Jammes, Francis. La vierge. Paris, 1919.

43667.1.42 Jammes, Francis. Une vierge. Paris, 1919.

43667.1.43 Jammes, Francis. La rose. Paris, 1919.

43667.1.44 Jammes, Francis. La noël de mes enfants. Paris, 1919.

43667.1.45 Jammes, Francis. Le poète rustique. 5. éd. Paris, 1920.

43667.1.45.5 Jammes, Francis. Le poète rustique. Paris, 1943.

43667.1.46 Jammes, Francis. Le livre de Saint Joseph. Paris, 1921.

43667.1.48 Jammes, Francis. Le poète et l'inspiration. Neines, 1922.

43667.1.49A Jammes, Francis. Cloches pour deux mariages, le mariage basque, le mariage de raison. 12. éd. Paris, 1923.

43667.1.49B Jammes, Francis. Cloches pour deux mariages, le mariage basque, le mariage de raison. 7. éd. Paris, 1923.

43667.1.50 Jammes, Francis. Rayons de miel. Paris, 1918.

43667.1.55 Jammes, Francis. Le bon Dieu chez les enfants. Paris, 1920.

43667.1.60 Jammes, Francis. Trente-six femmes. 6. éd. Paris, 1926.

43667.1.65 Jammes, Francis. Oeuvres. v.5. Paris, 1926.

43667.1.69 Jammes, Francis. Jeunes filles. Paris, 1964.

43667.1.70 Jammes, Francis. Diane. Paris, 1928.

43667.1.78 Jammes, Francis. Choix de poésies chrétiennes. Paris, 1946.

43667.1.80 Jammes, Francis. Le premier livre des quatrains. Paris, 1923.

43667.1.85 Jammes, Francis. Le deuxième livre des quatrains. Paris, 1923.

43667.1.90 Jammes, Francis. Le troisième livre des quatrains. Paris, 1924.

43667.1.95 Jammes, Francis. Le quatrième livre des quatrains. Paris, 1925.

43667.1.105 Jammes, Francis. Le tombeau de Jean de la Fontaine suivi de poèmes mésurés. 3. éd. Paris, 1921.

43667.1.115 Jammes, Francis. Ma france poétique. 4. éd. Paris, 1926.

43667.1.125 Jammes, Francis. La divine douleur. Paris, 1929.

43667.1.135 Jammes, Francis. Champêteries et méditations. Paris, 1930.

43667.1.145 Jammes, Francis. L'arc en ciel des amours. Paris, 1931.

43667.1.155 Jammes, Francis. De tout temps à jamais. 3. éd. Paris, 1935.

43667.1.165 Jammes, Francis. Leçons poétiques. 3. éd. Paris, 1930.

43667.1.170 Jammes, Francis. Le pélerin de Lourdes. 9. éd. Paris, 1936.

43667.1.175 Jammes, Francis. Dieu, l'âme et le sentiment. 13. éd. Paris, 1936.

43667.1.185 Jammes, Francis. Sources. Paris, 1936.

43667.1.196 Jammes, Francis. L'école buissonnière. 2. éd. Paris, 1931.

43667.1.206 Jammes, Francis. L'antigyde, ou Élie de Nacre. 5. éd. Paris, 1932.

43667.1.216 Jammes, Francis. Pipe, chien. 5. éd. Paris, 1933.

43667.1.226 Jammes, Francis. Janot-poète. 8. éd. Paris, 1928.

43667.1.230 Jammes, Francis. La légende de l'aile, ou Marie-Élisabeth. Uzes, 1938.

43667.1.247 Jammes, Francis. Les Robinsons basques. 11. éd. Paris, 1925.

43667.1.250 Jammes, Francis. Clara d'Ellebeuse. Lausanne, 1947.

43667.1.260 Jammes, Francis. Élegies et autres vers. Lausanne, 1946.

43667.1.270 Jammes, Francis. Poèmes choisis. Paris, 1946.

43667.1.280 Jammes, Francis. Heures chrétiennes. Paris, 1947.

43667.1.290 Jammes, Francis. Les nuits qui me chantent. Paris, 1929.

43667.1.300.25 Jammes, Francis. Le roman du lièvre. 54. éd. Paris, 1946.

43667.1.310 Jammes, Francis. Lettres inédites. Paris, 1947.

43667.1.315 Jammes, Francis. Correspondance de Francis Jammes et de Francis Vielé-Griffin (1893-1937). Genève, 1966.

43667.1.320 Jammes, Francis. Correspondance, 1893-1938 de Francis Jammes et André Gide. 8. éd. Paris, 1948.

43667.1.325 Jammes, Francis. Correspondance, 1898-1930. Paris, 1959.

43667.1.330 Jammes, Francis. Le poème d'ivonie et d'amour. Paris, 1950.

43667.1.335 Jammes, Francis. Le crucifix du poète. Paris, 1934.

43667.1.700 Jammes, Francis. Jammes. Poems. Santa Barbara, 1967.

43667.1.805 Schilla, Alfred. Francis Jammes. Inaug. Diss. Saalfeld, 1929.

43667.1.810 Guidetti, A. Francis Jammes. Torino, 1931.

43667.1.815 Gutheil, Werner. Francis Jammes als Symbolist und Katholik. Inaug. Diss. Marburg, 1932.

43667.1.820 Gauss, H. Francis Jammes in sienem Verhältnis zur Antike. Inaug. Diss. Quakenbrück, 1935.

43667.1.825 Irsch, Anni. Die Themen der Lyrik von Francis Jammes. Inaug. Diss. Bochum, 1935.

43667.1.830 Burckhardt, H. Natur und Heimat bei Francis Jammes. Inaug Diss. Würtzburg, 1937.

43667.1.835 Pilon, Edmond. Francis Jammes et le sentiment de la nature. Paris, 1908.

43667.1.840A Inda, J.P. Francis Jammes du faune au patriache. Thèse. Lyon, 1952.

43667.1.840B Inda, J.P. Francis Jammes du faune au patriache. Thèse. Lyon, 1952.

43667.1.842 Inda, J.P. Francis Jammes. Lyon, 1952.

43667.1.843 Inda, J.P. Francis Jammes. Thèse. Lyon, 1952.

43667.1.845 Dyson, Rose M. Les sensations et la sensibilité chez Francis Jammes. Genève, 1954.

43667.1.850 La Phalange. Francis Jammes. Paris, 1939.

43667.1.855 Parent, Monique. Rythme et versification dans la poésie de Francis Jammes. Paris, 1957.

43667.1.856 Parent, Monique. Francis Jammes. Paris, 1957.

43667.1.860 Bibliothèque Nationale, Paris. Francis Jammes. Paris, 1958.

43511 - 43873 Individual authors, etc. - 1900- - Known authors (363 scheme plus 10) - cont.

43667.1.865 Marie Margarita, Sister. La métrique de Francis Jammes vue dans le cadre de celle de ses contemporains et de ses prédécesseurs imédiats. Boston, 1959.

43667.1.870 Mallet, Robert. Francis Jammes. Paris, 1961.

43667.1.875 Mallet, Robert. Francis Jammes. Paris, 1961.

43667.1.880 Burght, Raymond van der. Francis Jammes. Bruxelles, 1961.

43667.1.885 Mallet, Robert. Francis Jammes. Paris, 1961.

43667.7.100 Jarlot, Gérard. Un chat qui aboie. Paris, 1963.

43667.7.1100 Jabès, Edmond. Elya. Paris, 1969.

43667.11.21 Jaccottet, Philippe. Airs, poèmes, 1961-1964. Paris, 1967. 2v.

43667.11.100 Jaccottet, Philippe. L'effrail et autres poésies. Paris, 1953.

43667.11.112 Jaccottet, Philippe. L'ignorant. Paris, 1958.

43667.11.120 Jaccottet, Philippe. Paysages avec figures absentes. Paris, 1970.

43667.13.100 Jack, Muriel. Kalitka. Paris, 1959.

43667.14.21 Jacob, Max. Morceaux choisis. Paris, 1936.

43667.14.25 Jacob, Max. Max Jacob, mystique et martyr. Paris, 1944.

43667.14.61A Jacob, Max. Choix de lettres de Max Jacob à Jean Cocteau. Paris, 1949.

43667.14.61B Jacob, Max. Choix de lettres de Max Jacob à Jean Cocteau. Paris, 1949.

43667.14.62 Jacob, Max. Lettres à Marcel Béalu. Lyon, 1959.

43667.14.63 Jacob, Max. Correspondance. Paris, 1953. 2v.

43667.14.64 Jacob, Max. Lettres à un ami; correspondance 1922-1937. Paris, 1951.

43667.14.65 Jacob, Max. Les cahiers Max Jacob. v.1-5. Paris? 1951-

43667.14.66 Jacob, Max. Lettres, 1920-1941. Oxford, 1966.

43667.14.100 Jacob, Max. La défense de Tartufe. Paris, 1919.

43667.14.102 Jacob, Max. La défense de Tartufe. Paris, 1964.

43667.14.110 Jacob, Max. Le phanerogame. Paris, 1918.

43667.14.120 Jacob, Max. Cinématoma. 2. éd. Paris, 1929.

43667.14.130 Jacob, Max. Art poétique. Paris, 1922.

43667.14.140 Jacob, Max. Le laboratoire central; poésies. Paris, 1921.

43667.14.145 Jacob, Max. Le laboratoire central. Paris, 1960.

43667.14.150 Jacob, Max. Le cornet à Dés. Paris, 1916.

43667.14.150.2 Jacob, Max. Le cornet à Dés. 2. éd. Paris, 1916.

43667.14.160 Jacob, Max. L'homme de chair et l'homme reflet. 2. éd. Paris, 1924.

43667.14.170 Jacob, Max. Le cabinet noir. 4. éd. Paris, 1928.

43667.14.180 Jacob, Max. Le roi de Béotie. 4. éd. Paris, 1921.

43667.14.190 Jacob, Max. Conseils à un jeune poète. 2. éd. Paris, 1945.

43667.14.200 Jacob, Max. Filibuth; ou La montre en or. Paris, 1923.

43667.14.210 Jacob, Max. Derniers poèmes en vers et en prose. Paris, 1945.

43667.14.215 Jacob, Max. Derniers poèmes en vers et en prose. Paris, 1961.

43667.14.220 Jacob, Max. Saint Matorel. 3. éd. Paris, 1936.

43667.14.230 Jacob, Max. Max Jacob. Lyon, 1946.

43667.14.240 Jacob, Max. Poèmes de morven le Gaëlique. Paris, 1953.

43667.14.250 Jacob, Max. Ballades. Paris, 1954.

43667.14.260 Jacob, Max. Lettres à Bernard Esdras. Gosse. Paris, 1953.

43667.14.270 Jacob, Max. Esthétique de Max Jacob. Paris, 1956.

43667.14.280 Jacob, Max. Lettres aux Salacron. Paris, 1957.

43667.14.290 Jacob, Max. Méditations religieuses. Paris, 1947.

43667.14.300F Jacob, Max. Méditation sur ma mort. Berne, 1959.

43667.14.310 Jacob, Max. Quatre problèmes à résoudre. Liège, 1962.

43667.14.320 Jacob, Max. Le terrain Bouchable. Paris, 1964.

43667.14.330 Jacob, Max. Le nom. Paris, 1926.

43667.14.340 Jacob, Max. L'homme de cristal. Paris, 1967.

43667.14.790 Jacob, Max. Wybór poezji. Warszawa, 1965.

43667.14.800F Salmon, André. Max Jacob, poète, peintre, mystique et homme de qualité. Paris, 1927.

43667.14.805 Belaval, Yvon. La rencontre avec Max Jacob. Paris, 1946.

43667.14.807 Rousselot, Jean. Max Jacob. 6. éd. Paris, 1946.

43667.14.810 Emié, Louis. Dialogues avec Max Jacob. Paris, 1954.

43667.14.815 Andreu, Pierre. Max Jacob. Paris, 1962.

43667.14.820 Wyss, Tobias. Dialog und Stille. Zürich, 1969.

43667.14.825 Kamber, Gerald. Max Jacob and the poetics of cubism. Baltimore, 1971.

43667.14.1100 Jacqueneaux, Edith. Feu de sable. Le Mans, 1959.

43667.15.100 Jacquemaine, M. Monime reine de pont, roman 1870-1885. Paris, 1935.

43667.15.2100 Jacquemard, Simonne. Planant sur les airs. Paris, 1960.

43667.15.2110 Jacquemard, Simonne. Le veilleur de nuit; roman. Paris, 1962.

43667.15.2120 Jacquemard, Simonne. Exploration d'un corps. Paris, 1966.

43667.15.2130 Jacquemard, Simonne. Navigation vers les iles, nouvelles. Paris, 1967.

43667.15.2140 Jacquemard, Simonne. L'Éruption des Krakatoa, ou Des chambres inconnues dans la maison. Paris, 1969.

43667.15.2150 Jacquemard, Simonne. A l'état sauvage, récits. Paris, 1967.

43667.48.100 Jalabert, Pierre. La coupe d'Ambroisie, poèmes. Paris, 1930.

43667.50.100 Jallade, E.J. A vol d'oiseau. N.Y., 1909.

43667.51.21 Jaloux, Edmond. Les saisons littéraires. Fribourg, 1942. 2v.

43667.51.40 Jaloux, Edmond. Fumées dans la campagne. Paris, 1918.

43667.51.50 Jaloux, Edmond. L'incertaine. Paris, 1918.

43667.51.60 Jaloux, Edmond. La fin d'un beau jour. Paris, 1921.

43667.51.70 Jaloux, Edmond. L'ésprit des livres. 1. série. Paris, 1923.

43667.51.80 Jaloux, Edmond. Le jeune homme au masque. Paris, 1905.

43667.51.87 Jaloux, Edmond. La grenade mordue. Paris, 1933.

43667.51.90 Jaloux, Edmond. L'agonie de l'amour. Paris, 1899.

43667.51.100 Jaloux, Edmond. Les amours perdues. Paris, 1919.

43667.51.105 Jaloux, Edmond. Les amours perdues. 20. éd. Paris, 1923.

43667.51.110 Jaloux, Edmond. Au-dessus de la ville. Paris, 1920.

43667.51.120 Jaloux, Edmond. Le reste est silence. Paris, 1909.

43667.51.130 Jaloux, Edmond. L'ennemi des femmes. Paris, 1921.

43667.51.140 Jaloux, Edmond. L'éscalier d'or. Paris, 1922.

43667.51.170 Jaloux, Edmond. L'école des mariages. Paris, 1906.

43667.51.180 Jaloux, Edmond. L'alcyone. 24. éd. Paris, 1925.

43667.51.190 Jaloux, Edmond. L'ami des jeunes filles. Paris, 1926.

43667.51.200 Jaloux, Edmond. L'âge d'or. Paris, 1926.

43667.51.210 Jaloux, Edmond. Le coin des cyprès. Paris, 1925.

43667.51.220 Jaloux, Edmond. Les sangsues. 2. éd. Paris, 1904.

43667.51.230 Jaloux, Edmond. Les profondeurs de la mer. 24. éd. Paris, 1922.

43667.51.240 Jaloux, Edmond. O toi que j'eusse aimée. 23. éd. Paris, 1926.

43667.51.245 Jaloux, Edmond. Essences. Paris, 1952.

43667.51.250 Jaloux, Edmond. L'éventail de crêpe. Paris, 1920.

43511 - 43873 Individual authors, etc. - 1900- - Known authors (363 scheme plus 10) - cont.

43667.51.260 Jaloux, Édmond. Le rayon dans le brouillard. Paris, 1924.
43667.51.280 Jaloux, Édmond. Le boudoir de Proserpine. Paris, 190-?
43667.51.290 Jaloux, Édmond. Déssins aux trois crayons. Paris, 1934.
43667.51.300 Jaloux, Édmond. La chute d'Icare. Paris, 1936.
43667.51.310 Jaloux, Édmond. Le vent souffle sur la flamme. Fribourg, 1941.
43667.51.320 Jaloux, Édmond. La balance faussée. Paris, 1932.
43667.51.330 Jaloux, Édmond. Le demon de la vie. Paris, 1933.
43667.51.340 Jaloux, Édmond. L'amour de Cécile Fougères. Paris, 1923.
43667.51.356 Jaloux, Édmond. L'oiseau-lyre; roman. 6. éd. Paris, 1938.
43667.51.360 Jaloux, Édmond. La capricieuse. Le pèlerin, La surprise. 6. éd. Paris, 1939.
43667.51.370 Jaloux, Édmond. La constellation. Genève, 1950.
43667.51.375 Jaloux, Édmond. Visage français. Paris, 1954.
43667.51.380 Jaloux, Edmond. Le triomphe de la frivolité. Paris, 1903.
43667.51.800 Kolbert, Jack. Edmond Jaloux et sa critique littéraire. Genève, 1962.
43667.51.805 Vaudoyer, Jean Louis. Discours de réception à l'Académie Française. Paris, 1950.
43667.52.105 Janon, René. Les salopards, roman. 5. éd. Alger, 1941.
43667.53.100 Janot, Paul. Le théâtre chrétien. Paris, 1911.
43667.53.1100 Jamati, Georges. La conquête de soi. Paris, 1961.
43667.60.100 Janier, Raymond. Nos yeux s'étaient dit, poèmes. Paris, 1958.
43667.61.21 Jans, Adrien. Poésie 1924-1967. 1. éd. Paris, 1969.
43667.61.100 Jans, Adrien. La tunique de Dieu. Bruxelles, 1964.
43667.61.110 Jans, Adrien. Ivoiriennes. Paris, 1968.
43667.62.100 Janvier, Ludovic. La Balgneuse. Paris, 1968.
43667.75.100 Jardin, Renée. Nostalgie. St. Raphael, 1925.
43667.75.110 Jardin, Renée. Appareillage. Paris, 1928.
43667.76.100 Jarlot, Gérard. Les armes blanches. 8. éd. Paris, 1946.
43667.78.13 Jarry, Alfred. Oeuvres complètes. Monte-Carlo, 1948. 8v.
43667.78.22 Jarry, Alfred. Tout Ubu. Paris, 1962.
43667.78.100 Jarry, Alfred. Ubu roi. Paris, 1921.
43667.78.110 Jarry, Alfred. Ubu sur la butte. Paris, 1906.
43667.78.120 Jarry, Alfred. La revanche de la nuit. Paris, 1949.
43667.78.130 Jarry, Alfred. L'objet aimé. Paris, 1953.
43667.78.140 Jarry, Alfred. L'amour absolu. Paris, 1952.
43667.78.140.5 Jarry, Alfred. L'amour absolu. Paris, 1964.
43667.78.160 Jarry, Alfred. Le surmale. Paris, 1953.
43667.78.170 Jarry, Alfred. Gestes et opinions du docteur Faustroll. Paris, 1911.
43667.78.180 Jarry, Alfred. Saint-Brieuc de choux. Paris, 1964.
43667.78.191 Jarry, Alfred. Les antliaclastes. Paris, 1965?
43667.78.621 Jarry, Alfred. Selected works of Alfred Jarry. N.Y., 1965.
43667.78.700 Jarry, Alfred. Ubu roi. London, 1951.
43667.78.702A Jarry, Alfred. Ubu roi. Norfolk, 1961.
43667.78.702B Jarry, Alfred. Ubu roi. Norfolk, 1961.
43667.78.705 Jarry, Alfred. The Ubu plays. London, 1968.
43667.78.800 Lebois, André. Alfred Jarry l'irremplaçable. Paris, 1950.
43667.78.805 Giedion-Welcker, C. Alfred Jarry. Zürich, 1960.
43667.78.810 Vallette, M.E. Alfred Jarry. Paris, 1928.
43667.78.815 Chauveau, Paul. Alfred Jarry. Paris, 1932.
43667.78.820 Perche, Louis. Alfred Jarry. Paris, 1965.
43667.78.900 Chassé, C. Sous le masque d'Alfred Jarry. Paris, 1921.
43667.78.910 Chassé, C. Dans les coulisses de la gloire. Paris, 1947.
43667.79.100 Jarry, P. Étudiants et grisettes romantiques. Paris, 1927.
43667.98.100 Jay, Marcel. Sur les voies romaines; poésies. Reims, 1928.
43667.98.2100 Jayat, Sandra. Moudravi, ou Va l'amitié. Paris, 1966.
43668.3.100 Jeanne, Paul. Brume de soleil, poésies. Paris, 19- .
43668.4.41 Jeanson, Henri. Soixante-dix ans d'adolescence. Paris, 1972.
43668.4.100 Jeanson, Henri. Toi que j'ai tant aimée. Paris, 1929.
43668.4.110 Jeanson, Henri. Entrée des artistes. Paris, 1946.
43668.4.120 Jeanson, Henri. En verve. Paris, 1971.
43668.4.1100 Jean, Yves. Tourmentes. Avignon, 1941.
43668.4.2100 Jean, Raymond. Les ruines de New York. Paris, 1959.
43668.4.2110 Jean, Raymond. La littérature et la réel de Diderot au "nouveau roman". Paris, 1965.
43668.4.2120 Jean, Raymond. La vive. Paris, 1968.
43668.4.3100 Jean-Charles, J. Les plumes du corbeau. Paris, 1962.
43668.4.4100 Jean, Marie Louis. Au temps du Tonkin paisible. Paris, 1967.
43668.36.100 Jehan, Auguste. Nouvelles méditation versaillaises. Paris, 1929.
43668.50.100 Jelinek, Henriette. Portrait d'un séducteur. Paris, 1965.
43668.50.110 Jelinek, Henriette. La marche du fou. Paris, 1967.
43668.60.100 Jenny, Laurent. Off; roman. Paris, 1971.
43670.1.30 Jouglet, René. Les roses sur la vie. Paris, 1912.
43670.1.35 Jouglet, René. Colombe. Paris, 1928.
43670.1.40 Jouglet, René. Tulipe. Paris, 1933.
43670.1.50 Jouglet, René. Soleil-levant. v.1-3. Paris, 1935.
43670.1.60 Jouglet, René. La nuit magique; nouvelle. Paris, 1939.
43670.1.70 Jouglet, René. Les paysans. Paris, 1951.
43670.1.1100 Joachim, Paulin. Anti-Grâce. Paris, 1967.
43670.24.100 Joel, Yves. Femme, mon ami. Paris, 1958.
43670.38.100 Johnson, Robert. Concentricités. Paris, 1962.
43670.40.100 Joignet, M. La rivière d'argent. Blois, 1926.
43670.50.100 Joliat, Yvette. Un évêché pour une danseuse. Delémont, 1965.
43670.59.100 Jones, Philippe. Amour et autres visages. Paris, 1956.
43670.59.110 Jones, Philippe. Grand largue. Bruxelles, 1949.
43670.79.100 Josa, Solange Claude. Soleil de cendres. Paris, 1955.
43670.80.100 Joseph-Renaud, J. Le clavecin hanté. Paris, 1920.
43670.83.100 Josset, André. Elizabeth, la femme sans homme. Paris, 1936.
43670.83.104 Josset, André. Élizabeth, la femme sans homme. Paris, 1936.
43670.89.51 Jouhandeau, M. Journaliers; 1957-1964. Paris, 1961-63. 16v.
43670.89.61 Jouhandeau, M. Correspondance avec André Gide. Paris, 1958.
43670.89.100 Jouhandeau, M. La jeunesse de Théophile. 4. éd. Paris, 1921.
43670.89.110 Jouhandeau, M. Les Pincengrain. Paris, 1924.
43670.89.120 Jouhandeau, M. L'amateur d'imprudence. Paris, 1932.
43670.89.130 Jouhandeau, M. Essai sur moi-même. Paris, 1947.
43670.89.140 Jouhandeau, M. Véronicana. Paris, 1933.
43670.89.150 Jouhandeau, M. Ménagerie domestique. 6. éd. Paris, 1948.
43670.89.160 Jouhandeau, M. Nouvelles chroniques maritales. Paris, 1943.
43670.89.170 Jouhandeau, M. L'oncle Henri. Paris, 1943.

43670.89.180 Jouhandeau, M. Opales. 5. éd. Paris, 1928.
43670.89.190 Jouhandeau, M. Le saladier. 2. éd. Paris, 1936.
43670.89.200 Jouhandeau, M. Monsieur Godeau intime. Paris, 1943.
43670.89.210 Jouhandeau, M. Monsieur Godeau marié. 2. éd. Paris, 1933.
43670.89.220 Jouhandeau, M. Élise. Paris, 1933.
43670.89.230 Jouhandeau, M. Mémorial. Paris, 1948. 6v.
43670.89.240 Jouhandeau, M. Algèbre des valeurs morales. Paris, 1935.
43670.89.250 Jouhandeau, M. Astaroth. 4. éd. Paris, 1929.
43670.89.260 Jouhandeau, M. Binche-ana. 6. éd. Paris, 1933.
43670.89.270 Jouhandeau, M. Images de Paris. 6. éd. Paris, 1934.
43670.89.290 Jouhandeau, M. Le jardin de Cordoue. 3. éd. Paris, 1938.
43670.89.300 Jouhandeau, M. Le journal du coiffeur. 2. éd. Paris, 1931.
43670.89.310 Jouhandeau, M. Tite-le-Long. 6. éd. Paris, 1932.
43670.89.320 Jouhandeau, M. Chamin adour. Paris, 1934-41. 3v.
43670.89.320.5 Jouhandeau, M. Chamin adour. Paris, 1967.
43670.89.330 Jouhandeau, M. Prudence Hautechaumee. 3. éd. Paris, 1927.
43670.89.340 Jouhandeau, M. La faute plutôt que le scandale. Paris, 1948.
43670.89.350 Jouhandeau, M. L'imposteur. Paris, 1950.
43670.89.360 Jouhandeau, M. Un monde. 4. éd. Paris, 1950.
43670.89.370 Jouhandeau, M. La ferme en folie. Paris, 1950.
43670.89.380 Jouhandeau, M. Nouveau bestiaire. 2. éd. Paris, 1952.
43670.89.390 Jouhandeau, M. Éloge de la volupté. Paris, 1951.
43670.89.400 Jouhandeau, M. Don Juan. Paris, 1948.
43670.89.410 Jouhandeau, M. Carnet du professeur. Paris, 1953.
43670.89.420 Jouhandeau, M. Galande. Paris, 1953.
43670.89.430 Jouhandeau, M. Portraits de famille. Paris, 1951.
43670.89.440 Jouhandeau, M. Dernières années et mort de Véronique. Paris, 1953.
43670.89.450 Jouhandeau, M. Ana de Madame Apremont. 6. éd. Paris, 1954.
43670.89.460 Jouhandeau, M. De l'abjection. Paris, 1951.
43670.89.470 Jouhandeau, M. Contes d'enfer. 4. éd. Paris, 1955.
43670.89.480 Jouhandeau, M. Jaunisse. Paris, 1956.
43670.89.490 Jouhandeau, M. Réflexions sur la vieillesse et la mort. Paris, 1957.
43670.89.500 Jouhandeau, M. Carnets de l'écrivain. Paris, 1957.
43670.89.510 Jouhandeau, M. Chroniques maritales. Paris, 1944.
43670.89.511 Jouhandeau, M. Chroniques maritales. Paris, 1962.
43670.89.520 Jouhandeau, M. Théâtre sans spéctacle. Paris, 1957.
43670.89.530 Jouhandeau, M. L'éternel procès. 2. éd. Paris, 1959.
43670.89.540 Jouhandeau, M. Réflexions sur la vie et le bonheur. 7. éd. Paris, 1958.
43670.89.545 Jouhandeau, M. Les Argonautes. Paris, 1959.
43670.89.550 Jouhandeau, M. Cocu, perdu et content. Paris, 1960.
43670.89.555 Jouhandeau, M. Animaleries. Paris, 1961.
43670.89.560 Jouhandeau, M. Notes sur la magie et le vol. Paris, 1953.
43670.89.565 Jouhandeau, M. Chronique d'une passion. Paris, 1964.
43670.89.570 Jouhandeau, M. Divertissements. Paris, 1965.
43670.89.575 Jouhandeau, M. Riposte à Roger Perfide. Liège, 1966.
43670.89.580 Jouhandeau, M. L'école des filles. Paris, 1961.
43670.89.590 Jouhandeau, M. Léonora; ou Dangers de la vertu. Paris, 1951.
43670.89.600 Jouhandeau, M. Nouvelles images de Paris, suivies de remarques sur les visages. 3. éd. Paris, 1956.
43670.89.610 Jouhandeau, M. Confidences. Paris, 1954.
43670.89.620 Jouhandeau, M. Olympias, suivi de Antistia et de tout ou rien. Paris, 1970.
43670.89.700 Jouhandeau, M. Marcel and Élise. N.Y., 1953.
43670.89.800 Rocle, Henri. Marcel Jouhandeau et ses personnages. Paris, 1950.
43670.89.805 Gaulmier, Jean. L'univers de Marcel Jouhandeau. Paris, 1959.
43670.89.810 Cabanis, José. Jouhandeau. 3. éd. Paris, 1959.
43670.89.815 Jouhandeau, Élise. Le bien de ronces. Paris, 1964.
43670.89.820 Danon, Jacques. Entretiens avec Élise et Marcel Jouhandeau. Paris, 1966.
43670.89.1100 Jouffroy, Alain. La fin des alternances. Paris, 1970.
43670.91.100 Joubert, Marcel P. Mazarinades. Paris, 1929.
43670.92.100 Jouffroy, Alain. A toi. 2. éd. Paris, 1958.
43670.92.110 Jouffroy, Alain. Trajectoire, récit recitatif. Paris, 1968.
43670.92.120 Jouffroy, Alain. Aube à l'antipode. Paris, 1966.
43670.93.100 Jourdan. Midi à mes portes. Paris, 1951.
43670.94.21 Jouve, Pierre Jean. Poésie. Milano, 1963.
43670.94.22 Jouve, Pierre Jean. Poésie: les noces. Paris, 1964. 4v.
43670.94.100 Jouve, Pierre Jean. Heures livre de la grâce. Genève, 1920.
43670.94.110 Jouve, Pierre Jean. Prière. Paris, 1924.
43670.94.115 Jouve, Pierre Jean. Diadème. Paris, 1949.
43670.94.120 Jouve, Pierre Jean. Le monde désert. 3. éd. Paris, 1927.
43670.94.125 Jouve, Pierre Jean. Génie. Paris, 1948.
43670.94.130 Jouve, Pierre Jean. Noces. Paris, 1928.
43670.94.135 Jouve, Pierre Jean. Ode. Paris, 1950.
43670.94.140 Jouve, Pierre Jean. Les mystérieuses noces. Paris, 1925.
43670.94.150 Jouve, Pierre Jean. Le paradis perdu. Paris, 1929.
43670.94.160 Jouve, Pierre Jean. Les ordres qui changent. Paris, 1911.
43670.94.170 Jouve, Pierre Jean. Les muses romaines et florentines. Paris, 1910.
43670.94.180 Jouve, Pierre Jean. Sueur de sang. Paris, 1935.
43670.94.190 Jouve, Pierre Jean. Parler. 2. série. Paris, 1913.
43670.94.200 Jouve, Pierre Jean. Toscanes. Genève, 1921.
43670.94.205 Jouve, Pierre Jean. Danse des morts. 2. éd. La Chaux de Fonds, 1918.
43670.94.210 Jouve, Pierre Jean. Vous êtes des hommes, 1915. Paris, 1915.
43670.94.220 Jouve, Pierre Jean. Présences. Paris, 1912.
43670.94.230 Jouve, Pierre Jean. Les aéroplanes. Paris, 1911.
43670.94.249 Jouve, Pierre Jean. Paulina, 1880. 9. éd. Paris, 1925.
43670.94.260 Jouve, Pierre Jean. Vers majeurs. Fribourg, 1943.
43670.94.270 Jouve, Pierre Jean. La vierge de Paris. Fribourg, 1944.
43670.94.280 Jouve, Pierre Jean. Gloire, 1940. Fribourg, 1944.
43670.94.290 Jouve, Pierre Jean. Défense et illustration. Paris, 1946.
43670.94.300 Jouve, Pierre Jean. Aventure de Catherine Crachat. Paris, 1947.
43670.94.310 Jouve, Pierre Jean. Histoires sanglantes. Paris, 1948.
43670.94.320 Jouve, Pierre Jean. Langue. Paris, 1954.
43670.94.330 Jouve, Pierre Jean. En miroir. Paris, 1954.
43670.94.340 Jouve, Pierre Jean. Lyrique. Paris, 1956.
43670.94.350 Jouve, Pierre Jean. Mélodrame. Paris, 1957.
43670.94.360 Jouve, Pierre Jean. Tombreau de Baudelaire. Paris, 1958.
43670.94.370 Jouve, Pierre Jean. Proses. Paris, 1960.
43670.94.380 Jouve, Pierre Jean. La scène capitale. 3. éd. Paris, 1962.

43511 - 43873 Individual authors, etc. - 1900- - Known authors (363 scheme plus 10) - cont.

43670.94.390 Jouve, Pierre Jean. Moires. Paris, 1965.
43670.94.400 Jouve, Pierre Jean. Ténèbre. Paris, 1935.
43670.94.410 Jouve, Pierre Jean. Nouvelles noces. Paris, 1926.
43670.94.621 Jouve, Pierre Jean. An idiom of night: poems. London, 1968.
43670.94.800 Jouve, Pierre Jean. Pierre Jean Jouve. Paris, 1956.
43670.94.805 Callander, Margaret. The poetry of P.J. Jouve. Manchester, 1965.
43670.94.810 Schneider, Ursula. La quête du Nada dans l'oeuvre de Pierre Jean Jouve. Thèse. Zürich, 1968.
43670.94.2100 Jouvenel, Renard de. Commune mésure; chroniques. Paris, 1938.
43670.94.2110 Jouvenel, Renard de. Il n'y a pas d'oubli. Paris, 1956.
43670.95.100 Jouvet, Louis. Réflexions du comédien. Paris, 1938.
43670.95.110A Jouvet, Louis. Préstiges et perspectives du théâtre, français, quatre ans de tournée en Amérique latine, 1941-1945. 5. éd. Paris, 1945.
43670.95.110B Jouvet, Louis. Préstiges et perspectives du théâtre, français, quatre ans de tournée en Amérique latine, 1941-1945. 5. éd. Paris, 1945.
43670.95.120 Jouvet, Louis. Témoignages sur le théâtre. Paris, 1952. 2v.
43670.95.130 Jouvet, Louis. Le comédien désincarné. Paris, 1954.
43670.95.800 Bibliothèque Nationale, Paris. Louis Jouvet. Paris, 1961.
43670.95.805 Kerien, W. Louis Jouvet, notre patron. Paris, 1963.
43670.98.100 Joyau-Dormoy, Alice. Chart des isles. Paris, 1953.
43670.98.110 Joyau-Dormoy, Alice. La saison éternelle. Fort-de-France, 1957.
43670.99.100 Jozercan, K. Le voeu. Poitier, 1921.
43670.99.110 Jozercan, K. Le champ de bataille. Poitier, 1913.
43671.20.41 Judrin, Roger. Journal d'une monade, du 13 avril au 9 septembre 1968. Paris, 1969.
43671.20.100 Judrin Roger. Boa-Boa. Paris, 1957.
43671.20.110 Judrin, Roger. Lampes de prison. Paris, 1960.
43671.41.100 Juin, Hubert. Chroniques sentimentales. Paris, 1962.
43671.41.110 Juin, Hubert. Le repas chez Marguerite. Paris, 1966.
43671.41.120 Juin, Hubert. Un soleil rouge. Poèmes. Paris, 1967.
43671.41.130 Juin, Hubert. Les trois cousines, roman. Paris, 1968.
43671.50.100 Jullien, J. Casanova a Nîmes. Uzés, 1930.
43671.51.100 Jullian, Philippe. Gilberte regained. London, 1957.
43671.51.110 Jullian, Philippe. Chateau-Bonheur. Paris, 1960.
43671.51.120 Jullian, Philippe. La fuite en Egypte. Paris, 1968.
43671.51.700 Jullian, Philippe. Flight into Egypt; a fantasy. N.Y., 1970.
43671.51.2100 Julian, E. Poèmes et chansons. Avignon, 1955.
43671.59.100 Gung, E. La vie européenne au Tonkin. Paris, 1901.
43671.61.100 Juniac, L. de. Impressions. Paris, 1941.
43671.61.1100 Junod, Roger Louis. Une ombre éblouissante; roman. Lausanne, 1968.
43672.39.100 Kahn, G. La pépinière du Luxembourg. Paris, 1923.
43672.40.100 Karagueuz, Effendi. Le chah du Mahboulistan. Paris, 1923.
43672.58.100 Kanapa, Jean. Les Choucas ou quelques aspects de la vie de Fred Hopper dans l'hiver 1961-1962. Paris, 1967.
43672.58.1100 Kancer, Serge. Les enfants de la colère. (Les loups dans la ville). Paris, 1968.
43672.59.100 Kane, Hamidou. L'ouverture ambiguë. Paris, 1961.
43672.59.700 Kane, Hamidou. Ambiguous adventure. N.Y., 1963.
V43672.74.100 Kar, Catherine. Tatiane. Auxerre, 1961.
43672.84.100 Katcha, Vahé. Galia, roman. Paris, 1967.
43672.84.110 Katcha, Vahé. Un nègre sur la statue de Lincoln. Paris, 1970.
43672.84.700 Katcha, Vahé. The hook. N.Y., 1958.
43672.85.100 Katherine, M. Suite persane. Paris, 1958.
43673.19.100 Kédros, André. Le lit de procuste. Paris, 1957.
43673.19.110 Kédros, André. Même un tigre. Paris, 1967.
43673.32.100 Kegels, Anne Marie. Haute vigne; poèmes. Bruxelles, 1962.
43673.32.110 Kegels, Anne Marie. Les doigts verts. Bruxelles, 1967.
43673.56.100 Kemp, R. Au jour le jour. Paris, 1958.
43673.56.110 Kemp, R. Discours de réception de Robert Kemp à l'Academie. Paris, 1958.
43673.56.800 Huyghe, R. Discours de réception. Paris, 1962.
43673.75.1100 Kerhoas, Émilienne. Saint Cadov. Paris, 1957.
43673.75.2100 Kerest, Franck. Les canons du ciel. Paris, 1960.
43673.76.100 Kerdyk, René. Sentiments. Paris, 1928.
43673.76.1100 Kermoal, Jacques. Le retour du général. Paris, 1969.
43673.76.2100 Kern, Alfred. Le clown. 11. éd. Paris, 1957.
43673.76.2105 Kern, Alfred. The clown. N.Y., 1960.
43673.76.2110 Kern, Alfred. L'amour profane. Paris, 1959.
43673.77.100 Kerpenhir, Jean de. Anna Calvé. Paris, 1928.
43673.77.1100 Kermen, de (Mme.). Clairvoyante. N.Y., 1914.
43673.77.2100 Kerraoul, Bernard de. Le poids des âmes, roman. Paris, 1963.
43673.77.2110 Kerraoul, Bernard de. Une grande conscience. Paris, 1966.
43673.77.2120 Kerraoul, Bernard de. La carapace. Paris, 1968.
43673.77.2130 Kerraoul, Bernard de. La réconciliation; roman. Paris, 1971.
43673.78.100 Kerchove, Arnold de. N. poèmes. Paris, 1951.
43673.78.110 Kerchove, Arnold de. La fureur et la grâce, poèmes. Paris, 1958.
43673.78.120 Kerchove, Arnold de. Sensualité. Bruxelles, 1967.
43673.78.130 Kerchove, Arnold de. La racine et l'oiseau. Paris, 1960.
43673.78.1100 Kervyn de Marcke ten Driessche, Roger. Journal de bord. Bruxelles, 1969.
43673.78.2100 Kervan, Paul. Le bocal aux amulettes. Bruxelles, 1961.
43673.82.100 Kessel, Jacques. Le triplace. Paris, 1926.
43673.83.100 Kessel, Joseph. Les coeurs purs. 6. éd. Paris, 1927.
43673.83.110 Kessel, Joseph. La rage au ventre. Paris, 1930.
43673.83.120 Kessel, Joseph. Une balle perdue. 33. éd. Paris, 1935.
43673.83.130 Kessel, Joseph. L'équipage. 159. éd. Paris, 1929.
43673.83.140 Kessel, Joseph. Le repos de l'équipage. 5. éd. Paris, 1935.
43673.83.155 Kessel, Joseph. La rose de Java. 28. éd. Paris, 1937.
43673.83.158A Kessel, Joseph. Army of shadows. N.Y., 1944.
43673.83.158B Kessel, Joseph. Army of shadows. N.Y., 1944.
43673.83.160 Kessel, Joseph. L'armée des ombres. N.Y., 1944.
43673.83.162 Kessel, Joseph. L'armée des ombres. Alger, 1943.
43673.83.165 Kessel, Joseph. Dames de Californie. Paris, 1929.
43673.83.167 Kessel, Joseph. Le temps de l'espérance. 100. éd. Paris, 1956. 6v.
43673.83.169 Kessel, Joseph. Le lion. Paris, 1958.
43673.83.170 Kessel, Joseph. The lion. N.Y., 1959.
43673.83.175 Kessel, Joseph. Fortune carrée. Paris, 1932.
43673.83.180 Kessel, Joseph. Nouveaux contes. Paris, 1928.
43673.83.190 Kessel, Joseph. Le coup de grâce. Paris, 1931.
43673.83.200 Kessel, Joseph. Wagon-lit. 7. éd. Paris, 1932.
43673.83.210 Kessel, Joseph. Nuits de Montmartre. Paris, 1932.

43511 - 43873 Individual authors, etc. - 1900- - Known authors (363 scheme plus 10) - cont.

43673.83.220 Kessel, Joseph. Bas-fonds. Paris, 1932.
43673.83.230 Kessel, Joseph. La passante du sans-souci. Paris, 1936.
43673.83.240 Kessel, Joseph. La femme de maison. Paris, 1928.
43673.83.250 Kessel, Joseph. Vent de sable. Paris, 1929.
43673.83.252 Kessel, Joseph. Vent de sable. Paris, 1966.
43673.83.260 Kessel, Joseph. Discours de réception de M.J. Kessel. Paris, 1964.
43673.83.270 Kessel, Joseph. The Bernan affair, a novel. N.Y., 1965.
43673.83.280 Kessel, Joseph. Le tour du malheur. Paris, 1950. 4v.
43673.83.290 Kessel, Joseph. Les cavaliers. Paris, 1967.
43673.83.295 Kessel, Joseph. Les amants du tage; roman. Paris, 1968.
43673.83.735 Kessel, Joseph. They weren't all angels. N.Y., 1965.
43673.83.740 Kessel, Joseph. The horsemen. N.Y., 1968.
43673.84.100 Kateha, Vahé. La mort d'un juif. Paris, 1968.
43673.98.100 Keyser, Eugénie de. Le chien. Paris, 1964.
43673.98.110 Keyser, Eugénie de. La surface de l'eau. Paris, 1966.
43674.4.100 Khatchadourian, Alice. Le concert de la nuit. Paris, 1957.
43674.4.110 Khatchadourian, Alice. Hémicycle. Paris, 1962.
43674.5.100 Khayr al-Din, Muhammad. Agadir. Paris, 1967.
43674.5.110 Khayr al-Din, Muhammad. Soleil arachnide; poèmes. Paris, 1969.
43674.5.120 Khayr al-Din, Muhammad. Corps négatif, suivi de: Histoire d'un bon Dieu. Paris, 1968.
43674.23.100 Khaïry, M. Les batailles intérieures. Paris, 1923.
43674.24.100 Kher, Amy. Mes soeurs. Le Caire, 1942.
43674.24.110 Kher, Amy. Salma et son village. Paris, 1933.
43674.67.100 Khoury, Venus. Terres stagnantes. Paris, 1968.
43675.22.100 Kieffer, Jane. Cette sauvage lumière. Paris, 1961.
43675.24.100 Kihm, Jean Jacques. Eloge de l'ombre. Paris, 1956.
43675.39.100 Kihm, Jean Jacques. Soixante-cinq poèmes d'amour. Paris, 1966.
43675.58.100 Kinds, Edmond. Les ornières de l'été. Paris, 1957.
43675.58.110 Kinds, Edmond. Le temps des apôtres. Bruxelles, 1967.
43677.5.100 Klat, Hector. Du cèdre aux lys; poèmes. Beyrouth, 1964.
43677.5.110 Klat, Hector. Ma seule joie, poèmes. Beyrouth, 1966.
43677.23.100 Klein, Guy. Les Culs bénis, ou Un trop fol amour. Montbard, 1965.
43677.66.100 Klossowski, Pierre. Roberte ce coir. Paris, 1953.
43677.66.110 Klossowski, Pierre. Le Baphomet. Paris, 1965.
43677.66.120 Klossowski, Pierre. La vocation suspendue; roman. Paris, 1950.
43677.66.130 Klossowski, Pierre. Les lois de l'hospitalité. Paris, 1965.
43680.12.100 Kochnitzky, Leon. Les éphémérides. Aalter, Belgium, 1960.
43680.12.110 Kochnitzky, Leon. Appogiatures. Bruxelles, 1966.
43680.22.100 Koechlin, L. L'agende. Paris, 1962.
43680.48.100 Kolar, Jean M. La nouveau venu. Paris, 1961.
43680.59.100 Koné, Maurice. Au seuil du crépuscule. Rodez, 1965.
43680.81.100 Kosmann, Claude. Itinéraire. Itinerary. Itinerario. Paris, 1962.
43680.87.100 Kottelanne, Claude. Comment dire ce peu. Veilhes, 1967.
43680.92.100 Kowalski, Roger. Le Ban. Paris, 1964.
43680.92.105 Kowalski, Roger. Augurales. Montpellier, 1964.
43680.92.120 Kowalski, Roger. Sommeils. Paris, 1968.
43681.2.100 Kraemer, Jacques. Splendeur et misère de Minette la bonne Lorraine. Paris, 1970.
43681.3.100 Krakowsky, Georges. Le passenger, roman. Malines, 1954.
43681.21.100 Kréa, Henri. La révolution et la poésie. Paris, 1960.
43681.21.110 Kréa, Henri. Poèmes en forme de vertige. Paris, 1967.
43681.65.100 Krôn, Marianne. Saisons. Paris, 1961.
43683.5.30 Kues, Maurice. Le dire et le penser. Genève, 1954.
43683.62.100 Kunstler, Charles. Les amours de François Villon. Paris, 1934.
43687.2.30 Lafon, André. L'elève Gilles. Récit. 26e éd. Paris, 1912.
43687.2.32A Lafon, André. L'elève Gilles. Récit. 17e éd. Paris, 1912.
43687.2.32B Lafon, André. L'elève Gilles. Récit. 17e éd. Paris, 1912.
43687.2.35 Lafon, André. Poèmes provinciaux. Roubaix, 1908.
43687.3.30 Lafagette, R. d'E. Symphonies pyrénéennes. Paris, 1897.
43687.4.30F Lagros de Langeron, G. Un roman de théâtre. pts.1-4. Paris, 1913.
43687.5.30 Laudet, F. La vie qui passe. Paris, 1914.
43687.6.80 Harlor. Leopold Lacour, biographie critique. Paris, 1914?
43687.6.2100 Labagne, Henri. Lettre à un anecdotique. Ivry-sur-Seine, 1965.
43687.7.30 Lambert, M. de. Debout les morts! n.p., 1915.
43687.7.100 Labeur, F. Jean Klein, légionnaire. Paris, 1912.
43687.8.100 Labbe, Jean. Croisières. Paris, 1946.
43687.8.110 Labin-Bénichow, Gina. Ne pas laisser mourir. Paris, 1964.
43687.9.100 Laborde, Lucien. Partage de la nuit. Paris, 1962.
43687.9.1100 Labruyère, Edith. L'anneau de Saturne. Paris, 1957.
43687.9.2100 Laborde, Jean. L'héritage de violence. Paris, 1969.
43687.9.3100 Labrderie-Roaldés, Guy. L'echelle enfouie. Paris, 1957.
43687.11.100 Lacaze, Raymond. Qu'on me pardonne d'en parler. Rodez, 1958.
43687.11.110 Lacaze, Raymond. Poulido. Rodez, 1959.
43687.12.100 Lachaumeric, Lila. La robe de lumière. Paris, 1960.
43687.13.100 Lacher, W. Le regard de Saturne. Lausanne, 1961.
43687.13.110 Lacher, W. Rueyres. Genève, 1961.
43687.14.100 Lacour, José André. Confession interdite. Paris, 1955.
43687.14.110 Lacour, José André. La mort en ce jardin. Paris, 1956.
43687.14.115 Lacour, José André. Notre peau, mélodrame en 3 actes. Paris, 1950.
43687.15.25 Lacretelle, Jacques de. Morceaux choisis. 5e éd. Paris, 1938.
43687.15.61 Lacretelle, Jacques de. Letters espagnoles. Paris, 1927.
43687.15.100 Lacretelle, Jacques de. Amour nuptial. 25e éd. Paris, 1929.
43687.15.110 Lacretelle, Jacques de. La Bonifas. 29e éd. Paris, 1925.
43687.15.120 Lacretelle, Jacques de. Silbermann. 79e éd. Photoreproduction. Paris, 1923.
43687.15.125 Lacretelle, Jacques de. Silbermann. 105e éd. Paris, 1929.
43687.15.130 Lacretelle, Jacques de. L'écrivain public. 14e éd. Paris, 1936.
43687.15.140 Lacretelle, Jacques de. Sabine. 6e éd. Paris, 1932.
43687.15.145 Lacretelle, Jacques de. Les fiançailles. 24e éd. Paris, 1933.
43687.15.146 Lacretelle, Jacques de. Les fiançailles. 11e éd. Paris, 1933.
43687.15.150 Lacretelle, Jacques de. Années d'espérance. 14e éd. Paris, 1935.
43687.15.153 Lacretelle, Jacques de. Les aveux étudiés. Paris, 1934.
43687.15.155 Lacretelle, Jacques de. La monnaie de plomb. 2e éd. Paris, 1935.
43687.15.170 Lacretelle, Jacques de. Le retour de Silbermann. 10e éd. Paris, 1930.

Classified Listing

43511 - 43873 Individual authors, etc. - 1900- - Known authors (363 scheme plus 10) - cont.

43687.15.172 Lacretelle, Jacques de. Le retour de Silbermann. 24e éd. Paris, 1930.
43687.15.180 Lacretelle, Jacques de. L'heure qui change. Genève, 1941.
43687.15.190 Lacretelle, Jacques de. Aparté: Colère - Jour de colère - Dix jours à Ermenonville. 14e éd. Paris, 1927.
43687.15.200 Lacretelle, Jacques de. La vie inquiète de Jean Hermelin. 15e éd. Paris, 1920.
43687.15.210 Lacretelle, Jacques de. Le demie-dieu on le voyage de Grèce. Paris, 1936.
43687.15.220 Lacretelle, Jacques de. Histoire de Paolo Ferrani. Paris, 1929.
43687.15.230 Lacretelle, Jacques de. Ideés dans un chapeau. Monaco, 1946.
43687.15.240 Lacretelle, Jacques de. La belle journée. Paris, 1925.
43687.15.250 Lacretelle, Jacques de. Le pour et le contre, roman. Genève, 1946. 2v.
43687.15.260 Lacretelle, Jacques de. Deux coeurs simples. Paris, 1953.
43687.15.270 Lacretelle, Jacques de. Etudes. Paris, 1928.
43687.15.280 Lacretelle, Jacques de. Le cachemire écarlate. Paris, 1927.
43687.15.285 Lacretelle, Jacques de. Trebuchet. Liège, 1926.
43687.15.703 Lacretelle, Jacques de. Marie Bonifas. N.Y., 1929.
43687.15.712 Lacretelle, Jacques de. Silbermann. N.Y., 1923.
43687.15.800 Alden, D.W. Jacques de Lacretelle. New Brunswick, 1958.
43687.15.1021 Lacroix, Georgette. Mortes saisons; poèmes. n.p., 1967.
43687.15.2100 Lacrosil, Michèle. Cajou. Paris, 1961.
43687.15.2110 Lacrosil, Michèle. Sapotille et le serin d'argile; roman. Paris, 1960.
43687.16.100 Lacuzon, A. Eternité. Paris, 1902. 2v.
43687.20.100 Lannes, Roger. La peine capitale. Paris, 1942.
43687.20.104 Lannes, Roger. Argelés. Paris, 1943.
43687.24.100 Lafaye, Raymond. Pour monia. Paris, 1957. 3 pam.
43687.25.100 Lafforest, Roger de. Les figurants de la mort, roman. Paris, 1939.
43687.26.100 Lafargue, Marc. Les plaisirs et les regrets. Paris, 1928.
43687.26.110 Lafargue, Marc. L'age d'or. 2e éd. Paris, 1903.
43687.26.120 Lafargue, Marc. Ode aux jeunes filles de Vendôme pour qu'elles aillent récitant Ronsard aux Bords du Loir. Paris, 1924.
43687.26.1100 Laffay, Claire. Imaginaires. Paris, 1966.
43687.26.2100 Laffont, G. De Dunkerque à Hambourg. Marseille, 1945.
43687.26.5100 Lafond, Madeleine. Au tonkin. Lezay, 1955.
43687.27.100 La Forest-Divonne, P. de. La cité des lampes. Paris, 1912.
43687.27.110A La Forest-Divonne, P. de. Bénediction. 53e éd. Paris, 1935.
43687.27.110B La Forest-Divonne, P. de. Bénediction. 53e éd. Paris, 1935.
43687.27.705 La Forest-Divonne, P. de. Benediction. N.Y., 1936.
43687.28.705 De La Fouchardière, Georges de. Poor sap. N.Y., 1930.
43687.29.100 Lafourcode, Georges. Édéa et autres poèmes. La Cailor, 1929.
43687.29.800 Pesquidoux, J.D. Le duc de La Force. Paris, 1931.
43687.30.100 Lafue, P. Fumées sur la ville. Paris, 1947.
43687.32.100 Lagesse, Marcelle. La diligence s'eloigne à l'aube. Paris, 1959.
43687.35.100 Lahayé, Simone. Les rachetées, portraits et récits de bagne. Paris, 1963.
43687.35.1100 La Haye, Marcel. La clef sous la porte; poèmes. Jarnac, 1964.
43687.37.1000 Laheffe, Pierre M. La mesure et l'imaginaire. Paris, 1960.
43687.38.100 Lahille, J. Lettres d'un autre temps. Paris, 1958?
43687.38.1100 La Hire, Jean de. La prisonnière du Dragon Rouge. Paris, 1931?
43687.41.100 Laigret, Christian. Le métis; roman. Paris, 1960.
43687.41.1100 Lainé, Pascal. L'irrévolution. Paris, 1971.
43687.50.100 Lallier, Roger. Pages d'amitiés. Paris, 1937.
Htn 43687.50.110* Lallier, Roger. Tante Elastine. Paris, 1930.
Htn 43687.50.120* Lallier, Roger. L'ami Géo. Niort, 1931.
43687.50.130 Lallier, Roger. Promenons-nous par les airs. Paris, 1932.
43687.50.1100 Lallement, Marcel. Une Famille Lorraine. Paris, 1968.
43687.51.100 Laloy, Louis. Trois drames de l'Asie. Neuchâtel, 1943.
43687.51.1100 Lalou, René. Le clavecin non tempéré. Paris, 1933.
43687.51.1110 Lalou, René. Le chef. Paris, 1923.
43687.53.100 Lamandé, André. Les leviers de commande. 9e éd. Paris, 1930.
43687.53.110 Lamandé, André. L'affaire Soulacroux. Paris, 1931.
43687.53.120 Lamandé, André. Les jeux du mensonge. Paris, 1933.
43687.53.130 Lamandé, André. Sous le clair regard d'Athéné. Paris, 1920.
43687.53.1110 Lambert, Jean. Tobiolo. Paris, 1956.
43687.53.1120 Lambert, Jean. Le Plaisir de voir. Paris, 1969.
43687.53.2100 Lamarre, Lise. Precocités. Paris, 1959.
43687.53.3100 Lambert, Claude. Le moins du monde. Liège, 1962.
43687.53.4100 La Marque, B. Paris brûlera, récit des années, 1965 à 1975. Paris, 1967.
43687.54.800 Synthèses; revue mensuelle internationale, Bruxelles. Maurice Lambilliotte. Bruxelles, 1954?
43687.55.100 Lamoureux, Robert. La brune que voilà. Paris, 1958.
43687.56.100A La Mure, P. Moulin Rouge. N.Y., 1950.
43687.56.100B La Mure, P. Moulin Rouge. N.Y., 1950.
43687.56.1100 Lamouche, André. L'aurore de l'amour. Paris, 1961.
43687.56.2100 Lamoureux, Tristan. L'enfant livré aux hommes. Paris, 1933.
43687.57.100 Lamy, Jacques. Fragments du temple entrevu. Paris, 1957.
43687.58.2100 Landry, Charles François. La légende de St. Nitouche. Uzès, 1935.
43687.58.2120 Landry, Charles François. La merle de novembre. 7e éd. Paris, 1946.
43687.58.2130F Landry, Charles François. Pour un peu plus d'humanité. Lausanne, 1959.
43687.58.2140 Landry, Charles François. Baragne. Lausanne, 1969.
43687.58.2150 Landry, Charles François. Nouvelles méridionales. Lausanne, 1970.
43687.58.2160 Landry, Charles François. Bord du monde. Lausanne, 1970.
43687.58.3100 Landa, Michel L. Les cloches de plomb. Paris, 1959.
43687.58.4100 Landais, Puisné. Durandeau de Shanghai et quelques autres, roman. Paris, 1932.
43687.59.100 Landry, Eugène. Oeuvres choisies. Macon, 1921.
43687.59.1100 Langlade, Emile. A travers la Haine, poèmes dramatiques. Paris, 1904.
43687.59.1110 Langlade, Emile. Le livre des tristesses et des drames. Paris, 193-?
43687.59.2100 Langhade, Jane. Reflets. Beyrouth, 1937.
43687.60.100 Lang, André. Fragile. Paris, 1929.

43511 - 43873 Individual authors, etc. - 1900- - Known authors (363 scheme plus 10) - cont.

43687.60.105 Lang, André. Bagage à la consigne. Paris, 1960.
43687.60.110 Lang, André. Les trois Henry. Paris, 1930.
43687.60.2100 Lange, Monique. Les plantanes. Paris, 1960.
43687.60.2110 Lange, Monique. Cannibales en Sicile. Paris, 1967.
43687.60.3100 Langfus, Anna. Le sel et le soufre. Paris, 1960.
43687.60.3110 Langfus, Anna. Les bagages de sable. Paris, 1962.
43687.60.3120 Langfus, Anna. Saute, Barbara. Paris, 1965.
43687.60.3700 Langfus, Anna. The whole land brimstone. N.Y., 1962.
43687.60.3710 Langfus, Anna. The lost shore. London, 1963.
43687.60.4100 Laniez, Gabriel. Désert, suivi de cinq élégies. Paris, 1949.
43687.61.21 L'Anselme, Jean. The ring around the world: selected poems. London, 1967.
43687.61.100 L'Anselme, Jean. Cahier d'histoires naturelles. Paris, 1950.
43687.61.1100 Lanoux, Armand. Yododo. Paris, 1957.
43687.61.1110 Lanoux, Armand. Le Commandant Watrin. Paris, 1956.
43687.61.1120 Lanoux, Armand. Le photographe délirant. Paris, 1956.
43687.61.1125 Lanoux, Armand. La licorne. Paris, 1954.
43687.61.1130 Lanoux, Armand. A quoi jouent les enfants du bourreau? Paris, 1959.
43687.61.1135 Lanoux, Armand. La tulipe orageuse. Paris, 1959.
43687.61.1140 Lanoux, Armand. Quand la mer se retire. Paris, 1963.
43687.61.2100 Lanoë-Herpe, Jules. Sermur. Paris, 1957.
43687.62.800 Morize, André. Reconnaissance à Gustave Lanson. Cambridge, Mass.? 193-?
43687.62.2100 Lanteuil, H. de. Trois poèmes. Rio de Janeiro, 1940.
43687.62.2780 Lanteuil, H. de. Logaritmos IX poemas. Rio de Janeiro, 1941.
43687.62.3100 Lanzmann, Jacques. Les passagers du Sidi-Brahim. Paris, 1958.
43687.62.3110 Lanzmann, Jacques. Qui vive. Paris, 1965.
43687.62.3120 Lanzmann, Jacques. O rato da América. Lisboa, 1966.
43687.62.3130 Lanzmann, Jacques. Les vangauguin, roman. Paris, 1968.
43687.63.100 Langevin, André. Crade de la nuit. Montreal, 1951.
43687.63.110 Langevin, André. Poussière sur la ville. Montreal, 1953.
43687.63.122 Langevin, André. Le temps des hommes; roman. 2. éd. Montreal, 1956.
43687.65.100 Lanza del Vasto, Joseph Jean. Principes et préceptes du retour à l'évidence. Paris, 1945.
43687.65.101 Lanza del Vasto, Joseph Jean. Principes et préceptes du retour à l'évidence. Paris, 1956.
43687.65.110 Lanza del Vasto, Joseph Jean. Conquiste di vento. Firenze, 1927.
43687.65.115 Lanza del Vasto, Joseph Jean. Approches de la vie intérieure. Paris, 1962.
43687.65.120 Lanza del Vasto, Joseph Jean. Noé. Paris, 1965.
43687.65.130 Lanza del Vasto, Joseph Jean. Judas. Paris, 1968.
43687.65.140 Lanza del Vasto, Joseph Jean. L'homme libre et les ânes sauvages. Paris, 1969.
43687.65.150 Lanza del Vasto, Joseph Jean. Viatique et Enfances d'une pensée. v.1-2. Paris, 1970.
43687.68.100 Lapaire, Hugues. La treille en fleur. 2e éd. Paris, 1923.
43687.68.800 Drouillet, Jean. Hugues Lapaire, maître-poète de la terre de France. Avallon, 1969.
43687.69.100 Lapaquellerie, Yvon. La princesse Tarakanov. Paris, 1928.
43687.69.110 Lapaquellerie, Yvon. Eté indieu; roman. pt.1-2. Paris, 1932.
43687.70.100 Laparcerie-Richepin, Cora. La vraie Carmen. Paris, 1935.
43687.70.110 Riollet, M. La bête; pièce en un acte. Paris, 1939. 3 pam.
43687.71.100 Laporte, René. La tête haute. Paris, 1954.
43687.71.110 Laporte, René. Le gant de fer et le gant de velours. Paris, 1951.
43687.71.120 Laporte, René. Le somnambule. Paris, 1933.
43687.71.130 Laporte, René. Le dîner chez Olga. Paris, 1927.
43687.71.2100 Laporte, Geneviève. Sous le manteau de feu. Paris, 1956.
43687.73.100 Laquiere, Maurice. Fortunée, la juive, roman. Paris, 1941.
43687.74.11 Larbaud, Valéry. Oeuvres complètes. Paris, 1950-9v.
43687.74.15 Larbaud, Valéry. Oeuvres. Paris, 1957.
43687.74.17 Larbaud, Valéry. Oeuvres. Paris, 1961.
43687.74.100 Larbaud, Valéry. Enfantines. 9e éd. Paris, 1918.
43687.74.105 Larbaud, Valéry. A.O. Barnabooth. 22e éd. Paris, 1928.
43687.74.113 Larbaud, Valéry. Amants, heureux amants. 12e éd. Paris, 1924.
43687.74.115 Larbaud, Valéry. Amants, heureux amants. 17e éd. Paris, 1924.
43687.74.125 Larbaud, Valéry. Fermina Márquez. 8e éd. Paris, 1926.
43687.74.130 Larbaud, Valéry. Le gouverneur de Kerguelen. Abbeville, 1933.
43687.74.135 Larbaud, Valéry. Jaune, bleu, blanc. Paris, 1927.
43687.74.145 Larbaud, Valéry. Les poésies de A.O. Barnabooth. 18e éd. Paris, 1923.
43687.74.150 Larbaud, Valéry. Allen. Paris, 1929.
43687.74.155 Larbaud, Valéry. Crayons de couleurs. Liège, 1927.
43687.74.170 Larbaud, Valéry. Caderno. Paris, 1927.
43687.74.180 Larbaud, Valéry. Ce vice impuni. 9e éd. Paris, 1948.
43687.74.190 Larbaud, Valéry. Enfantines. 27e éd. Paris, 1948.
43687.74.200 Larbaud, Valéry. Gaston d'Ercoule. Paris, 1952.
43687.74.210 Larbaud, Valéry. Journal, 1912-1935. 2e éd. Paris, 1955.
43687.74.220 Larbaud, Valéry. Deux artistes lyriques. Paris, 1929.
43687.74.230 Larbaud, Valéry. Beauté, mon beau souci. Paris, 1968.
43687.74.700 Larbaud, Valéry. Poems of a multimillionaire. N.Y.? 1955.
43687.74.800 Aubry, G.J. Valéry Larbaud. Monaco, 1949.
43687.74.805 Association Internationale des Amis de Valéry Larbaud. Valéry Larbaud, notre ami. Moulins, 1961.
43687.74.807 Association Internationale des Amis de Valéry Larbaud. Cahiers des Amis de Valéry Larbaud. Vichy. 1,1967+
43687.74.810 Ruggiero, Ortensia. Valéry Larbaud et l'Italie. Paris, 1963.
43687.74.815 Weissman, Frida. L'éxotisme de Valéry Larbaud. Paris, 1966.
43687.74.820 Segonds, Jean P. L'Enfance bourbonnaise de Valéry Larbaud. Moulins, 1967.
43687.74.1100 Lardanchet, Armand. Le mauvais ange. Paris, 1929.
43687.75.100 Larguier, Léo. L'après-midi chez l'antiquaire. Paris, 1922.
43687.75.110 Larguier, Léo. Sabine. pt.1-2. Paris, 1926.
43687.75.115 Larguier, Léo. Les gardiens; nouvelle. Paris, 1928.
43687.75.120 Larguier, Léo. Les Bonaparte. n.p., 1928.
43687.75.125 Larguier, Léo. Avant le déluge, souvenirs. 10e éd. Paris, 1928.
43687.75.135 Larguier, Léo. Les trésors de Palmyre. Paris, 1938.
43687.75.145 Larguier, Léo. Mes vingt ans et moi. Paris, 1944.

Classified Listing

43511 - 43873 Individual authors, etc. - 1900- - Known authors (363 scheme plus 10) - cont.

43687.75.155 Larguier, Léo. La curiosité. Paris, 1946.
43687.75.160 Larguier, Léo. Petites histories pour bibliophiles. Paris, 1944.
43687.75.170 Larguier, Léo. Roses de papier. Paris, 1934.
43687.75.180 Larguier, Léo. Le père Corot. 4e éd. Paris, 1931.
43687.75.190 Larguier, Léo. Orchestres. Paris, 1914.
43687.75.200 Larguier, Léo. Les heures déchirées; notes du front. Paris, 1918.
43687.77.100 Larronde, Olivier. Les barricades mystérieuses. Paris? 1946.
43687.77.1100 Larrouy, Maurice. Les nostalgiques. Paris, 1929.
43687.77.1110 Larrouy, Maurice. Le révolté. Paris, 1924.
43687.77.1120 Larrouy, Maurice. Rafaël Gatouna, Français d'occasion; roman. Paris, 1921.
43687.77.1130 Larrouy, Maurice. Sirènes et Tritons, le roman du sous-marin. Paris, 1927.
43687.77.2100 Larrive, Georges. L'autre face. Paris, 1958.
43687.77.3100 La Rochefoucauld, Edmée (de Fels). Nombres. Paris, 1926.
43687.77.3110 La Rochefoucauld, Edmée (de Fels). La vie humaine par Gilbert Mauge (pseud.). Paris, 1928.
43687.77.3120 La Rochefoucauld, Edmée (de Fels). Choix de poèmes. Paris, 1955.
43687.78.6021 Lassaigne, Assia. L'Idiote du village. Paris, 1945.
43687.79.100 La Salle, B. de. La pierre philosophale. Paris, 1935.
43687.79.110 La Salle, B. de. Les forces cachées. Paris, 1937.
43687.80.700 Larthomas, P.H. Meeting. London, 1950.
43687.80.710 Larthomas, P.H. Solitaire. Boston, 1951.
43687.80.2100 Lartéguy, Jean. Les prétoriens. Paris, 1961.
43687.80.2120 Lartéguy, Jean. Le mal jaune. Paris, 1963.
43687.80.2130 Lartéguy, Jean. Les baladins de la Margeride. Paris, 1962.
43687.80.2140 Lartéguy, Jean. Les tambours de bronze. Paris, 1965.
43687.80.2150 Lartéguy, Jean. Sauveterre, roman. Paris, 1966.
43687.80.2160 Lartéguy, Jean. Les centurions. Paris, 1967.
43687.80.2700 Lartéguy, Jean. The centurions. 1st ed. N.Y., 1962.
43687.80.2705 Lartéguy, Jean. The bronze drums. 1st American ed. N.Y., 1967.
43687.80.2710 Lartéguy, Jean. The praetorians. 1st American ed. N.Y., 1963.
43687.80.2720 Lartéguy, Jean. Yellow fever. London, 1965.
43687.80.2725 Lartéguy, Jean. The hounds of hell. 1st ed. N.Y., 1966.
43687.82.100 Lassalle, Jean Pierre. Le grand patagon; poèmes. Villefranche-de-Rouergue, 1963.
43687.82.1100 Lasseaux, Marcel. A s'y tromper. Paris, 1970.
43687.83.100 Lasserre, Pierre. Les chapelles litteraires. Paris, 1920.
43687.83.110 Lasserre, Pierre. La promenade insolite. 11e éd. Paris, 1922.
43687.83.115 Lasserre, Pierre. Le secret d'Abélard. Paris, 1926.
43687.83.120 Lasserre, Pierre. Portraits et discussions. Paris, 1921?
43687.83.125 Lasserre, Pierre. Le romantisme français. Paris, 1919.
43687.83.130 Lasserre, Pierre. Henri de Sauvelade, roman. Paris, 1920?
43687.83.135 Lasserre, Pierre. Trente années de vie littéraire. Paris, 1929.
43687.83.140 Lasserre, Pierre. Mise au point. 2e éd. Paris, 1931.
43687.83.145 Lasserre, Pierre. Faust en France. Paris, 1929.
43687.83.805 Gasgtowtt, A.M. Pierre Lasserre, 1867-1930. Paris, 1931.
43687.83.810 Frohock, W.M. Pierre Lasserre. Thesis. Ann Arbor, 1937.
43687.83.1100 Las Vergnas, Raymond. Rendez-vous a Piccadilly. Paris, 1961.
43687.83.1110 Las Vergnas, Raymond. Cavalerie lourde. Paris, 1962.
43687.83.1120 Las Vergnas, Raymond. Le corbillard portugais; roman. Paris, 1963.
43687.83.1130 Las Vergnas, Raymond. Cavalerie céleste; roman. Paris, 1964.
43687.83.1140 Las Vergnas, Raymond. Meurtres à Quiberon, roman. Paris, 1967.
43687.84.100 La Tailhède, Raymond de. Poésies. Paris, 1938.
43687.84.110 La Tailhède, Raymond de. Hymne pour la France. Paris, 1917.
43687.84.120 La Tailhède, Raymond de. Ode à Jean Moréas. Moissac, 1891.
43687.84.2100 Lataillade, Louis. Le groupe sud. Paris, 1959.
43687.85.100 Thibauderie, Ivan de la. Langrottes et margouillats. Coutances, 1956.
43687.85.1100 Lathis. L'organiste athée. Paris, 1964.
43687.87.102A La Tour du Pin, Patrice de. La quête de joie. Paris, 1939.
43687.87.102B La Tour du Pin, Patrice de. La quête de joie. Paris, 1939.
43687.87.110 La Tour du Pin, Patrice de. La contemplation errante. Paris, 1948.
43687.87.120 La Tour du Pin, Patrice de. Une somme de poésie. Paris, 1947. 3v.
43687.87.130 La Tour du Pin, Patrice de. Pepiniere de sapins de Noel. Paris, 1957.
43687.87.140 La Tour du Pin, Patrice de. La vie recluse en poésie. Paris, 1952.
43687.87.700 La Tour du Pin, Patrice de. The dedicated life in poetry. London, 1948.
43687.87.800 Biéville-Nayant. Patrice de La Tour du Pin. Paris, 1948.
43687.88.100 Laubiès, Charles. Musique de danse; poèmes. Grenoble, 1930.
43687.88.110 Laubiès, Charles. Symphonie pastorale; poèmes. Grenoble, 1931.
43687.88.2705 Laubreaux, Alin. Mulatto Johnny. N.Y., 1931.
43687.88.3100 Lavaud, Guy. Sur un vieux livre de marine. Paris, 1918.
43687.88.3110 Lavaud, Guy. Imageries des mers. Paris, 1919.
43687.89.100 Launay, Louis de. La voie sacrée. Paris, 1927.
43687.89.170 Laurent, Jacques. Caroline Chérie. London, 1959.
43687.89.1100 Laurent, Jacques. Neuf perles de culture. 19e éd. Paris, 1952.
43687.89.1110 Laurent, Jacques. Lucrezia Borgia. 2d ed. Milano, 1953.
43687.89.1120 Laurent, Jacques. Le petit canard. Paris, 1954.
43687.89.1130 Laurent, Jacques. Ici Clotilde. Paris, 1958.
43687.89.1140 Laurent, Jacques. L'Espagne et Juan. Paris, 1958.
43687.89.1150 Laurent, Jacques. Napoléon et Juan. Paris, 1958.
43687.89.1160 Laurent, Jacques. Les caprices de Caroline. Paris, 1959.
43687.89.1170 Laurent, Jacques. Au contraire. Paris, 1967.
43687.89.1180 Laurent, Jacques. Les passagers pour Alger. Paris, 1960.
43687.89.1190 Laurent, Jacques. Une affaire est une affaire. Paris, 1960.
43687.89.1200 Laurent, Jacques. La fin de Lamiel. Paris, 1966.
43687.89.1210 Laurent, Jacques. Hortense 14-18. Paris, 1963-67. 5v.
43687.89.1220 Laurent, Jacques. La Communarde; roman. Paris, 1970.
43687.89.1700 Laurent, Jacques. Goribon's folly. London, 1951.
43687.89.1710 Laurent, Jacques. Clotilde. N.Y., 1959.

43511 - 43873 Individual authors, etc. - 1900- - Known authors (363 scheme plus 10) - cont.

43687.89.2100 La Varende, Jean de. Pays d'Ouche, 1740-1933. Paris, 1936.
43687.89.2110 La Varende, Jean de. Nez-de-Auir, gentilhomme d'amour. Paris, 1937.
43687.89.2120 La Varende, Jean de. Man d'Arc. Paris, 1940.
43687.89.2130 La Varende, Jean de. Les manants du roi. Paris, 1938.
43687.89.2140 La Varende, Jean de. Le centaure de Dieu. Paris, 1938.
43687.89.2150 La Varende, Jean de. Le miracle de Janvier. Paris, 1949.
43687.89.2160 La Varende, Jean de. M. le Duc. Paris, 1959.
43687.89.2170 La Varende, Jean de. L'amour sacré et l'amour profane. Paris, 1959.
43687.89.2180 La Varende, Jean de. Jean-Marie. Paris, 1961.
43687.89.2190 La Varende, Jean de. Le demi-solde. Paris, 1962.
43687.89.2200 La Varende, Jean de. L'objet aimé. Paris, 1966.
43687.89.2210 La Varende, Jean de. La Varende, l'ami. Coutances, 1966.
43687.89.2220 La Varende, Jean de. Dans le goût espagnol, suite romanesque. Paris, 1968.
43687.89.2230 La Varende, Jean de. Coeur pensif. Paris, 1964.
43687.89.2800 Brunetière, Philippe. La Varende. Paris, 1959.
43687.89.2805 Lelièvre, R. La Varende. Coutances, 1963.
43687.89.2810 Herbert, Michel. Biographie de l'oeuvre de Jean de La Varende accompagnée de nombreaux documents inédits. Paris, 1964. 3v.
43687.89.3100 Lavaud, Guy. Poétique du ciel. Paris, 1930.
43687.89.3110 Lavaud, Guy. Des fleurs, pourquoi. Paris, 1910.
43687.89.3120 Lavaud, Guy. Sous le signe de l'eau. Paris, 1927.
43687.89.4100 Laugier, Jean. L'espace muet. Paris, 1956.
43687.89.5025 Laurentie, Henri. Choix de poèmes. Paris, 1957.
43687.89.5100 Laurencin, Marie. Le carnet des nuits. Genève, 1956.
43687.89.6100 Laureillard, Rémi. Hiclem. Paris, 1960.
43687.89.7100 Lauran, Annie. La machine a fait "Tilt". Paris, 1960.
43687.89.8100 Lauzanne, Stéphane. La table qui parle. Paris, 1925.
43687.89.9100 Lautrec, Gabriel de. Souvenirs des jours sans souci. Paris, 1938.
43687.89.9110 Lautrec, Gabriel de. Poèmes en prose. Paris, 1898.
43687.90.100 Laude, Jean. Entre deux morts. Paris, 1948.
43687.90.110 Laude, Jean. Les plages de Thulé. Paris, 1964.
43687.90.1100 Launay, Pierre Jean. Aux portes de Trézène, roman. Paris, 1966.
43687.90.2100 Lavacourt, André. Les Français de la décadence. Paris, 1960.
43687.90.3100 Lavclanet, François. Corinne, moeurs haïtiennes. Port-au-Prince, 1907.
43687.91.100 La Ville de Mirmont, Jean de. L'horizon chimérique. Paris, 1929.
43687.91.110 La Ville de Mirmont, Jean de. Les dimanches de Jean Dézert. Paris, 1914.
43687.92.100 Lautère, Adrienne. Madame d'Aulnoy et sa mère; roman. Paris, 1946.
43687.100.100 Lacrosil, Michéle. Demain Jab-Herma. Paris, 1967.
43688.1.20 Leroux, Gaston. Romans fantastiques. v.2. Évreux, 1970-
43688.1.21 Leroux, Gaston. Romans d'aventures. Évreux, 1970- 3v.
43688.1.22 Leroux, Gaston. Chéri-Bibi. Évreux, 1969. 4v.
43688.1.25 Leroux, Gaston. Mister Flou. Paris, 1927.
43688.1.30F Leroux, Gaston. Le mystère de la chambre jaune. Paris, 1912.
X Cg 43688.1.30.3 Leroux, Gaston. Le mystère de la chambre jaune. Paris, 1910.
43688.1.30.5 Leroux, Gaston. The mystery of the yellow room. N.Y., 1908.
43688.1.30.6 Leroux, Gaston. The mystery of the yellow room. N.Y., 1908.
43688.1.30.15 Leroux, Gaston. The mystery of the yellow room. N.Y., 1929.
43688.1.31F Leroux, Gaston. Alsace. Paris, 1913.
X Cg 43688.1.32 Leroux, Gaston. Le parfum de la dame en noir. Paris, n.d.
43688.1.32.5 Leroux, Gaston. The perfume of the lady in black. N.Y., 1909.
43688.1.33 Leroux, Gaston. Le fantôme de l'opéra. 15e éd. Paris, n.d.
43688.1.33.10 Leroux, Gaston. The phantom of the opera. N.Y., 1911.
43688.1.33.11 Leroux, Gaston. The phantom of the opera. N.Y., 1911.
43688.1.34 Leroux, Gaston. Bride of the sun. N.Y., 1915.
43688.1.35 Leroux, Gaston. Les étranges noces de Rouletabille. Paris, 1916.
43688.1.35.10 Leroux, Gaston. The secret of the night. N.Y., 1914.
43688.1.36 Leroux, Gaston. Rouletabille. Levallois-Perret, 1969- 7v.
43688.1.37 Leroux, Gaston. Le fantôme de l'opéra. Paris, 1910.
43688.1.38 Leroux, Gaston. Le capitaine Hyx. Paris, 1920.
43688.1.39 Leroux, Gaston. The double life. N.Y., 1909.
43688.1.42 Leroux, Gaston. Chéri-Bibi and Cecily. London, 1923.
43688.1.44 Leroux, Gaston. Missing men. N.Y., 1923.
43688.1.3700 Leclerc, Marc. "Honorably discharged". Boston, 1933.
43688.2.30 Le Cardonnel, Louis. Poèmes. 4e éd. Paris, 1912.
43688.2.35 Le Cardonnel, Louis. Oeuvres. Paris, 1928-1929. 2v.
43688.2.45 Le Cardonnel, Louis. Carmina sacra. 11e éd. Paris, 1925.
43688.2.50 Le Cardonnel, Louis. Louis Le Cardonnel à San Remo. Grenoble, 1943.
43688.2.55 Le Cardonnel, Louis. De l'une à l'autre aurore, poèmes. Paris, 1924.
43688.2.57 Le Cardonnel, Louis. À Sainte Térèse de Jésus. Saint-Félicien-en-Vivarais, 1921.
43688.2.81 Coulon, Marcel. Louis Le Cardonnel, poète et prêtre. Uzès, 1937.
43688.2.83 Richard, Noël. Louis Le Cardonnel et les revues symbolistes. Paris, 1946.
43688.2.85 Christofour, R. Louis Le Cardonnel. Paris, 1938.
43688.2.90 Barrelle, Georges. Le pelerin lyrique, Entretiens avec Louis Le Cardonnel au Palias du Roure. Paris, 1937.
43688.2.95 Belloni, Georges. La grande âme de Louis Le Cardonnel. Paris, 196-?
43688.2.231 Le Franc, M. Le poste sur la dune. Paris, 1930.
43688.2.240 Le Franc, M. Hélier, fèls des bois; roman. Paris, 1935.
43688.3.30 Lestrange, R. Le miroir enchanté. Paris, 1911.
43688.4.30 Levaillant, M. Le miroir d'Étain. Paris, 1906.
43688.4.31 Levaillant, M. Pierres saintes::Versailles. Paris, 1913.
43688.4.33 Levaillant, M. La porte secrète. Paris, 1921.
43688.4.40 Levaillant, M. Le temple interieur. Paris, 1910.
43688.4.45 Levaillant, M. Des vers d'amour. Paris, 1921.
43688.5.30 Lemaitre, C. Eiou qu'y va le trachi. Caen, 1912.
43688.5.5021 Léautaud, Paul. Poésies. Paris, 1963.
43688.5.5061 Léautaud, Paul. Lettres à Marie Dormoy. Paris, 1966.
43688.5.5065 Léautaud, Paul. Correspondance, 1912-1955. Paris, 1968.

43511 - 43873 Individual authors, etc. - 1900- - Known authors (363 scheme plus 10) - cont.

43688.5.5100 Léautaud, Paul. Choix de pages de Paul Léautaud. Paris, 1946.
43688.5.5110 Léautaud, Paul. Marly-le-Roy et environs. Paris, 1945.
43688.5.5120 Léautaud, Paul. Propos d'un jour. Paris, 1947.
43688.5.5130 Léautaud, Paul. Passe-temps. 8e éd. Paris, 1929.
43688.5.5132 Léautaud, Paul. Passe-temps. Paris, 1964.
43688.5.5140 Léautaud, Paul. Entretiens avec Robert Mallet. 18e éd. Paris, 1951.
43688.5.5150 Léautaud, Paul. Journal littéraire. Paris, 1954-1956. 19v.
43688.5.5155 Léautaud, Paul. Journal of a man of letters. London, 1960.
43688.5.5160 Léautaud, Paul. Le petit ami. Paris, 1956.
43688.5.5170 Léautaud, Paul. Lettres à ma mère. Paris, 1956.
43688.5.5180 Léautaud, Paul. Bestiaire. Paris, 1959.
43688.5.5190 Léautaud, Paul. Le petit ouvrage inachevé. Paris, 1964.
43688.5.5700 Léautaud, Paul. The child of Montmartre. London, 1959.
43688.5.5800 Dormoy, Marie. Léataud. Paris, 1958.
43688.5.5805 Faillet, G. Lettres à Paul Léautaud. Paris, 1928.
43688.5.5810 Auriant (pseud.). Une vipère lubrique; Paul Leautaud. Bruxelles, 1965.
43688.5.5815 Uribe Arce, Armando. Léautaud y el otro. Santiago de Chile, 1966.
43688.6.100 Lebert, E.M. Le masque de la vie. N.Y., 1928.
43688.7.11 Lebesque, Philéas. Oeuvres poetiques. Méru, 1950-52. 3v.
43688.7.11.1 Oeuvres poétiques. Méru, 1952?
43688.7.100 Lebesgue, P. Les servitudes. Paris, 1913.
43688.7.805 Striegler, H. Philéas Lebesgue, ein Dichter der Pikardie. Inaug. Diss. Engelsdorf, 1935.
43688.7.810 Camus, André. Le centenaire de Philéas Lebesque. Grandvilliers, 1969.
43688.7.930 Lebey, André. Sur la route sociale. Paris, 1913. 2v.
43688.7.935 Lebey, André. Disques et pellicules. Paris, 1929.
43688.7.940 Lebey, André. Les blasons du plaisir. Paris, 19- .
43688.7.945 Lebey, André. Chansons grises. Paris, 1896.
43688.7.2100 Lebesque, M. Chroniques du Canard. Paris, 1960.
43688.8.15 Le Goffic, Charles. Poésies complètes. Paris, 1913.
43688.8.18 Le Goffic, Charles. Poésies complètes. Paris, 1921.
43688.8.21 Le Goffic, Charles. Poésies complètes. Paris, 1931-32. 2v.
43688.8.30 Le Goffic, Charles. Le crucifié de Keraliès. Paris, 1917.
43688.8.31 Le Goffic, Charles. Passions celtes. Paris, 1919?
43688.8.32 Le Goffic, Charles. L'abbesse du Guérande. Paris, 1921.
43688.8.35 Le Goffic, Charles. Les pierres-vertes. Paris, 1931.
43688.8.40 Le Goffic, Charles. La double confession. 18e éd. Paris, 1930.
43688.8.50 Le Goffic, Charles. La payse, roman. Paris, 1930.
43688.8.60 Le Goffic, Charles. Amour breton. Paris, 1889.
43688.8.65 Le Goffic, Charles. Sans nouvelles. Paris, 1917.
43688.8.1100 Lebel, Roland. La porte d'or. Paris, 1946.
43688.9.100 Lebrau, Jean. La rumeur des pins. Paris, 1926.
43688.9.110 Lebrau, Jean. Couleur de Vigne et d'Olivier. Paris, 1929.
43688.9.120 Lebrau, Jean. Impasse du romarin. Paris, 1953.
43688.9.130 Lebrau, Jean. Jean Lebrau. Rodez, 1960.
43688.9.1021 Lebois, André. Poèmes. Avignon, 1964.
43688.10.100 Lebrau, Jean. Témoignage. St. Félicien-en-Vivarais, 1925.
43688.11.100 Le Breton, Alain. Car pour Rome. Paris, 1956.
43688.11.1100 Lecache, B. Jacob. Paris, 1925.
43688.13.100 Leclerq, Léna. Pomme endormie. Décines, 1958.
43688.13.110 Leclerq, Léna. Notre coeur est un malfaiteur. Paris, n.d.
43688.13.2021 Leclercq, François J. Du poème à la chansonnette. Niort, 1966. 3v.
43688.13.3100 Le Clec'h, Guy. L'aube sur les remparts, roman. Paris, 1967.
43688.13.3110 Le Clec'h, Guy. Les jours de notre vie. Paris, 1968-
43688.13.4100 Le Clercq, Pierre. En percevant. Paris, 1957.
43688.13.5100 Leclère, Paul. Ecce vita. Paris, 1954?
43688.14.100 Leclerc, Marc. The passion of our brother, the poilu. Berkeley, Calif.? 1918?
43688.14.115 Leclerc, Marc. La passion de notre frère le poilu. Paris, 1916.
43688.14.120 Leclerc, Marc. Les souvenirs de tranchées d'un poilu. Paris, 1917.
43688.14.800 Bruel, André. Marc Leclerc, 1874-1946. Angers, 1947.
43688.14.1021 Lecocq, Albert. Oeuvre poétique, suivie de poemes, de lettres et d'un texte inedits. Bruxelles, 1966.
43688.14.2100 Le Cog, Gabriel. Le Pastour au dur vitrail. Saint-Brieuc, 1968.
43688.14.3100 Leclèrc, Tristan. Schéhérazade. Amiens, 1926.
43688.14.3110 Leclèrc, Tristan. Humoresques. Amiens, 1921.
43688.14.3120 Leclèrc, Tristan. L'éscarbille d'or. Paris, 1921.
43688.14.3130 Leclèrc, Tristan. Le valet de coeur. Paris, 1908.
43688.14.3140 Leclèrc, Tristan. Le livre d'esquisses. Paris, 1902.
43688.14.3150 Leclèrc, Tristan. Le tambour voilé. Paris, 1960.
43688.14.3800 Pronger, Lester J. La poésie de Tristan Klimgsor, 1890-1960. Paris, 1965.
43688.14.4100 Le Clézio, Jean Marie Gustave. Le procès-verbal. Paris, 1963.
43688.14.4110 Le Clézio, Jean Marie Gustave. La fièvre. Paris, 1965.
43688.14.4120 Le Clézio, Jean Marie Gustave. Le déluge, roman. Paris, 1966.
43688.14.4130 Le Clézio, Jean Marie Gustave. Terra amata. Paris, 1967.
43688.14.4140 Le Clézio, Jean Marie Gustave. L'extase matérielle. Paris, 1967.
43688.14.4150 Le Clézio, Jean Marie Gustave. Le livre des fuites, roman. Paris, 1969.
43688.14.4160 Le Clézio, Jean Marie Gustave. La guerre. Paris, 1970.
43688.14.4700A Le Clézio, Jean Marie Gustave. The interrogation. N.Y., 1964.
43688.14.4705 Le Clézio, Jean Marie Gustave. The flood. 1st American ed. N.Y., 1968.
43688.14.4710 Le Clézio, Jean Marie Gustave. Terra amata. London, 1969.
43688.14.5100 Lecoq, Paul. Les yeux nus. Paris, 1957.
43688.15.100 Leconte, S.C. L'esprit qui passe. 3e éd. Paris, 1910.
43688.15.110 Leconte, S.C. Le masque de fer. Paris, 1911.
43688.15.120 Leconte, S.C. Le tentation de l'homme. Paris, 1903.
43688.15.2100 Leconte, Henri. Le Musulman blanc. Paris, 1930.
43688.15.2110 Leconte, Henri. La vie des spectres. Paris, 1930.
43688.15.2120 Leconte, Henri. Dieux et Dieu, poèmes. Paris, 1929.
43688.15.5705 Le Corbeau, A. The forest giant. Garden City, 1936.
43688.16.100 Lecoeur, Yves. L'escalier de J.P. Sartre. 3e éd. Paris, 1956.
43688.17.100 Lécuyer, A.H. (Mme.). Soledad; roman. pt.1-3. Paris, 1931.

43511 - 43873 Individual authors, etc. - 1900- - Known authors (363 scheme plus 10) - cont.

43688.17.110 Lécuyer, A.H. (Mme.). Le printemps sous l'orage; roman. pts.1-3. Paris, 1934.
43688.17.120 Lécuyer, A.H. (Mme.). Cris dans le ciel. Paris, 1939.
43688.17.139 Lécuyer, A.H. (Mme.). Lettres anonymes. 19e éd. Paris, 1946.
43688.19.100 Lédoux, Ph. La poudre aux moineaux. Paris, 1957.
43688.20.100 Leduc, Violette. Trésors à prendre. Paris, 1960.
43688.20.110 Leduc, Violette. La bâtarde. Paris, 1964.
43688.20.120 Leduc, Violette. La bâtarde. N.Y., 1965.
43688.20.130 Leduc, Violette. L'affamée. Paris, 1965.
43688.20.140 Leduc, Violette. Thérèse et Isabelle. Paris, 1968.
43688.20.150 Leduc, Violette. La folie en tête. Paria, 1970.
43688.20.700 Leduc, Violette. Thérèse and Isabelle. N.Y., 1967.
43688.20.705 Leduc, Violette. In the prison of her skin. London, 1970.
43688.21.100 Lec, Emma. Le chant du grillon; poèmes, 1954-1959. Paris, 1959.
43688.27.100 Lefebvre, L. La prière d'un homme. Paris, 1921.
43688.27.110 Lefebvre, L. Prières. Paris, 1928.
43688.27.120 Lefebvre, L. Rectificatione. Paris, 1932.
43688.27.1100 Leféhure, Nadine. Les sources de la mer. 3e éd. Paris, 1957.
43688.27.3100 Lefévre, Raymonde. Le plus secret tombeau. Paris, 1956.
43688.27.4100 Lefeuvre, Jean. Une petite espérance. Paris, 195-.
43688.28.100 Lévrier, Léonce. À bâtons, rompus. Paris, 1913.
43688.29.100 Lefèvre, Fréderic. Monsieur Maubenoît. Avignon, 1941.
43688.29.110 Lefèvre, Fréderic. Ce vagabond. Paris, 1946.
43688.30.100 Le Franc, Marie. Pecheurs de Gaspésie. Paris, 1938.
43688.30.110 Le Franc, Marie. The whisper of a name. Indianapolis, 1928.
43688.31.100 Le Gac, Pierre-Marie. La victoire sans ailes. Paris, 1941.
43688.33.50 Legrand, Ignace. Deux nouvelles du passé. London, 1944.
43688.33.100 Legrand, Ignace. La patrie interieure. Paris, 1928.
43688.33.110 Legrand, Ignace. A sa lumière. Paris, 1934.
43688.33.120 Legrand, Ignace. Renaissance. Paris, 1931.
43688.33.121 Legrand, Ignace. Renaissance. Paris, 1932.
43688.33.700 Legrand, Ignace. The embassy train. London, 1945.
43688.34.110 Legrand, Jean. Journal de Jacques. 5e éd. Paris, 1946.
43688.34.1021 Legrand, Maurice. Poèmes amorphes. Paris, 1969.
43688.34.2100 Le Guen, Jean. Le griot et l'echo. Paris, 1957.
43688.34.3100 Le Gouic, Gérard. À la fonte des Blés. Paris, 1960.
43688.34.3110 Le Gouic, Gérard. Dieu-le-douze. Paris, 1961.
43688.34.4100 Legray, Jacques. Le roman de la vie de Goethe. Paris, 1965.
43688.35.100 Le Grand, Maurice. Les avis de l'oncle Bertrand. Paris, 1920.
43688.35.105 Le Grand, Maurice. Fables. Paris, 1931.
43688.35.110 Le Grand, Maurice. Fables nouvelles. Paris, 192-.
43688.35.120 Le Grand, Maurice. Le chapeau chinois. Paris, 1930.
43688.35.130 Le Grand, Maurice. La nouvelle cuisinière bourgeoise. Paris, 1900.
43688.35.140 Le Grand, Maurice. Le jardin des bêtes et des plantes. Paris, 1923.
43688.35.150 Le Grand, Maurice. Le kiosque à musique. Paris, 1927.
43688.35.160 Le Grand, Maurice. Dites-nous quelque chose de Franc-Nohain (pseud.). Paris, 1930.
43688.35.170 Le Grand, Maurice. L'art de vivre. Paris, 1943.
43688.35.180 Le Grand, Maurice. L'honorable Conque. Paris, 1902?
43688.35.1100 Legueb, Marcel. Hélène, tu perdris Troie. Paris, 1959.
43688.42.100 Le Jeloux, Anne. La harpe du sentier. Paris, 1958.
43688.42.1100 Lejeune, Claire. La ganque et le feu. Paris, 196-.
43688.49.100 Le Leu, Louis. Récits d'un siècle. Paris, 1911.
43688.49.110 Le Leu, Louis. La semence sanglante. Paris, 1922.
43688.49.1100 Lely, Gilbert. Ma civilisation. Paris, 1954.
43688.49.1110 Lely, Gilbert. Ma civilisation, poèmes. Paris, 1967.
43688.52.100F Lemarchand, Jacques. L'odyssée d'Ulysse. Paris, 1954.
43688.52.700 Lemarchand, Jacques. Parenthesis. 1st American ed. N.Y., 1947.
43688.52.705 Lemarchand, Jacques. Genevieve. London, 1947?
43688.53.100 Le Marchand, A. Raoul de Fougères. Rennes, 1923.
43688.53.1100 Lemaitre, Maurice. Carnets d'un fanatique. Paris, 1960.
43688.53.1110 Lemaitre, Maurice. Qu'est-ce que le lettrisme? Paris, 1954.
43688.53.1120 Lemaitre, Maurice. Le temps des assis. Paris, 1963.
43688.53.2021 Le Marois, Jean. La couronne d'Apollon. Poèmes. Genève, 1967.
43688.53.2100 Le Marois, Jean. La dernière nuit d'André Chémier. Genève, 1968.
43688.53.3100 Lemaitre, Gaston. Des vers. Postface d'André Gressier. Paris, 1949.
43688.54.100 LeMercier d'Erm, C. Les exiles; poèmes. Paris, 1909.
43688.54.110 LeMercier d'Erm, C. Léda. 3e éd. Dinard, 192-.
43688.54.120 LeMercier d'Erm, C. Le poème de Paris nocturne. Paris, 1919.
43688.54.130 LeMercier d'Erm, C. La guerre? Paris, 1919.
43688.57.50 Lemonnier, L. Le baiser de Satan. Paris, 1930.
43688.57.55 Lemonnier, L. L'amour intredit. Paris, 1925.
43688.58.100 Menanteau, Pierre. L'arbre et la maison. Preuilly-sur-Claise, 1939.
43688.59.45 Lenéru, Marie. Journal of Marie Lenéru. Paris, 1922. 2v.
43688.59.50 Lenéru, Marie. Journal. 9e éd. v.1-2. Paris, 1922.
43688.59.55 Lenéru, Marie. Journal de Marie Lenéru. Paris, 1939.
43688.59.58 Lenéru, Marie. Journal. 7e éd. Paris, 1945.
43688.59.100 Lenéru, Marie. La paix. Paris, 1922.
43688.59.110A Lenéru, Marie. Les affranchis. Paris, 1926.
43688.59.110B Lenéru, Marie. Les affranchis. Paris, 1926.
43688.59.112 Lenéru, Marie. Les affranchis. Paris, 1927.
43688.59.120 Lenéru, Marie. La maison sur le roc. Paris, 1927.
43688.59.130 Lenéru, Marie. Le bonheur des autres. Paris, 1925.
43688.59.805 Lavaud, S. Marie Lenéru. Thèse. Paris, 1932.
43688.59.810 Dissen, Maria. Marie Lenéru. Inaug. Diss. Gelsenkirchen, 1932.
43688.60.21 Leiris, Michel. Brisées. Paris, 1966.
43688.60.100 Leiris, Michel. Haut mal. Paris, 1943.
43688.60.102 Leiris, Michel. Haut mal, suivi de autres lancers. Paris, 1969.
43688.60.110 Leiris, Michel. Aurora, roman. Paris, 1946.
43688.60.120 Leiris, Michel. L'âge d'homme. 7e éd. Paris, 1946.
43688.60.130 Leiris, Michel. Le point cardinal. Paris, 1927.
43688.60.140 Leiris, Michel. Bagatelles végétales. Paris, 1956.
43688.60.150 Leiris, Michel. Nuits sans nuit et quelques jours sans jour. Paris, 1961.
43688.60.160 Leiris, Michel. La règle du jeu. Paris, 1948- 3v.
43688.60.700 Leiris, Michel. Manhood: a journey from childhood into the fierce order of virility. N.Y., 1963.

43511 - 43873 Individual authors, etc. - 1900- - Known authors (363 scheme plus 10) - cont.

43688.60.800 Nadeau, M. Michel Leiris et la quadrature du cercle. Paris, 1963.
43688.61.100 Lenormand, Henri René. Le simoun. Paris, 1921.
43688.61.110 Lenormand, Henri René. Théâtre complet. Paris, 1921-1938. 9v.
43688.61.125 Lenormand, Henri René. Failures. N.Y., 1923.
43688.61.130 Lenormand, Henri René. Crépuscule du théâtre. Paris, 1935.
43688.61.140 Lenormand, Henri René. Le réveil de l'instinct. Paris, 1908.
43688.61.150 Lenormand, Henri René. À l'ombre du mal. Paris, 1924.
43688.61.160 Lenormand, Henri René. Le lâche. Paris, 1926.
43688.61.170 Lenormand, Henri René. L'armée secrète suivi de fidélité et du juge intérieur. 6e éd. Paris, 1925.
43688.61.180 Lenormand, Henri René. Les confessions d'un auteur dramatique. Paris, 1949-1953. 2v.
43688.61.190 Lenormand, Henri René. Les coeurs anxieux. Paris, 1947.
43688.61.200 Lenormand, Henri René. L'enfant des sables. Paris, 1949.
43688.61.210 Lenormand, Henri René. Renée. N.Y., 1951.
43688.61.220 Lenormand, Henri René. Troubles. Paris, 1951.
43688.61.230 Lenormand, Henri René. Les Pitoëff. Paris, 1943.
43688.61.240 Lenormand, Henri René. Les ratés. Paris, 1936?
43688.61.700 Lenormand, Henri René. Three plays: The dream doctor, Man and his phantoms, The coward. London, 1928.
43688.61.702 Lenormand, Henri René. Three plays. N.Y., 19- ?
43688.61.710 Lenormand, Henri René. Failures. N.Y., 1923.
43688.61.720 Lenormand, Henri René. The rising. London, 1952.
43688.61.787 Lenormand, Henri René. Stimmen aus dem Dunkel. Berlin, 1925.
43688.61.795 Lenormand, Henri René. El hombre y sus fantasmas. 2e éd. Buenos Aires, 1945.
43688.61.800 Rops, Daniel. Sur le théâtre de Henri René Lenormand. Paris, 1926.
43688.61.810 Oria, José A. El teatro de Lenormand. Buenos Aires, 1935.
43688.61.812 Oria, José A. El teatro de Lenormand. Buenos Aires, 1936.
43688.61.820 Blanchart, Paul. Le théâtre de Henri René Lenormand. Paris, 1947.
43688.65.100 Léon-Martin, L. L'ascension d'Élise amour. Paris, 1928.
43688.65.1100 Léonard, Raymond. Les heures algériennes; extraits. Ivry-sur-Seine, 1958-1960. 2v.
43688.65.2100 Léonard. Demain. Neuchâtel, 1963.
43688.68.100 LeNormand, Michelle. La maison aux phlox. N.Y., 1941.
43688.68.110 LeNormand, Michelle. Enthousiasme. Montréal, 1947.
43688.69.800 Roc, Gil. A l'éconte des poètes wagneriens du siècle. Paris, 1964.
43688.70.1100 L'Eplattenier, Gérald. La Colére d'Achille; poèmes. Genève, 1968.
43688.71.100 LePorrier, Herbert. La Demoiselle de Chartres. Paris, 1968.
43688.76.100 Le Roy, Florian. Bonne soeur des chemins. Paris, 1927.
43688.77.100 Leroy-Allais, J. Marie-Rose au couvent. Paris, 1909.
43688.77.1100 Léro, Yva. Doucherie. Martirique, 1958.
43688.77.2100 Leroux, S. Le roi bafoué. Paris, 1953.
43688.77.3100 LeMarquet, Jacques. L'ile des pommes; (théâtre). Paris, 1970.
43688.79.100 Lescure, Pierre de. La saison des consciences. Paris, 1959.
43688.79.110 Lescure, Pierre de. Tendresse inhumaine. Paris, 1936.
43688.79.1100 Lescure, Jean. Treize poèmes. Paris, 1960.
43688.79.2110 Lescure, Jean. Images d'images. Paris, 1964.
43688.79.3110 LeSage, Roger. Go! Paris, 1959.
43688.82.100 Lesort, Paul André. The searcher of hearts. London, 1950.
43688.82.110 Lesort, Paul André. G.B.K. Paris, 1960.
43688.82.120 Lesort, Paul André. Les reins et les coeurs, roman. Paris, 1964.
43688.82.130 Lesort, Paul André. Vie de Guillaume Périer. Paris, 1966.
43688.83.100 Le Stanc, Yves. Chansons de mon village. Paris, 1925.
43688.83.110 Le Stanc, Yves. Chansons du flot le long des grèves. Paris, 1926.
43688.83.1100 Lésu, B.J. Amoureuses confidences. Paris, 1904.
43688.87.100 Leopold, E. Poèmes. Paris, 1949.
43688.88.100 Létraz, Jean de. Bichon. Paris, 1935.
43688.88.110 Létraz, Jean de. Descendez! On vous demande. Paris, 1946.
43688.88.120 Létraz, Jean de. La fessei. Paris, 1948.
43688.88.130 Létraz, Jean de. On demande un ménage. Paris, 1957.
43688.89.105 Leuba, J. L'aile de feu, roman. Paris, 1920.
43688.89.1100 Leuck, René Georges. La nuit en cause. Paris, 1955.
43688.90.100 Levaux, Léopold. Quand Dieu parle. Bruxelles, 1945.
43688.91.100 Level, Maurice. Tales of mystery and horror. N.Y., 1920.
43688.91.104 Level, Maurice. Crises; tales of mystery and horror. 3rd ed. London, 1921.
43688.91.110 Level, Maurice. The grip of fear. N.Y., 1911.
43688.91.1100 Levy, Jacob. Juifs d'aujourd'hui, les Pollaks. Paris, 1925.
43688.92.100 Lévy, Sarah. Henri und Sarah; Roman. Berlin, 1931.
43688.93.100 Levy, Jacques. Journal et correspondance. Grenoble, 1955.
43688.94.100 Lequenne, F. Les pères naturel. Paris, 1956.
43688.95.100 Levy, Paul. Ici tombe la nuit. Paris, 1956.
43688.96.100 Lévy, Edmond. La fin du premier jour. 5e éd. Paris, 1956.
43688.97.100 Lépidis, Clément. La rose de Büyükada; roman. Paris, 1963.
43688.98.100 LeQuintrec, Charles. Les noces de la terre. Paris, 1957.
43688.98.110 LeQuintrec, Charles. Les chemins de Kergrist. Paris, 1959.
43688.98.120 LeQuintrec, Charles. Le mur d'en face; roman. Paris, 1965.
43688.98.130 LeQuintrec, Charles. Stances du verbe amour, poèmes. Paris, 1966.
43688.98.140 LeQuintrec, Charles. Le chemin noir, roman. Paris, 1968.
43688.98.150 LeQuintrec, Charles. La marche des arbres. Paris, 1970.
43689.4.100 Lhande, Pierre. Les mouettes. 9e éd. Paris, 1920.
43689.24.100 Lherm, Gussy. Le secret de Roncevaux, roman historique. Brive, 1970.
43689.25.100 Lhermier, Pierre. Le couvent dans la montagne, roman. Paris, 1939.
43689.66.100 Lhôte, Jean Marie. Sédiment, poème. Paris, 1960.
43689.89.100 L'Huillier, Georges. Mars! Drame lyrique en vers. N.Y., 1943.
43689.2810 Herbert, Michel. Bibliographie de l'oeuvre de Jean de La Varende accompagnée de nombreaux documents inédits. Paris, 1964. 3v.
43690.1.30 Lichtenberger, A. La folle aventure. 6. éd. Paris, n.d.
43690.1.31 Lichtenberger, A. Le sang nouveau. Paris, n.d.
43690.1.33 Lichtenberger, A. Contes heroïques 1789-1795. Paris, n.d.
43690.1.34 Lichtenberger, A. Des enfants dans un jardin; nouvelle. Paris, 1927.

43511 - 43873 Individual authors, etc. - 1900- - Known authors (363 scheme plus 10) - cont.

43690.1.40 Lichtenberger, A. Juste Lobel. Paris, n.d.
43690.1.45 Lichtenberger, A. Léila si blanche. Paris, 1928.
43690.1.50 Lichtenberger, A. Mon petit Trott. Paris, 1898.
43690.1.50.20 Lichtenberger, A. Trott. N.Y., 1941.
43690.1.63 Lichtenberger, A. Le petit roi. Paris, 1920.
43690.1.70 Lichtenberger, A. La petite soeur de Trott. Paris, 1920.
43690.1.80 Lichtenberger, A. Notre Minnie. 30e éd. Paris, 1922.
43690.1.85 Lichtenberger, A. Le coeur est le même. Paris, 1919.
43690.1.800 Lichtenberger, M. Le message de André Lichtenberger. 2. éd. Paris, 1946.
43690.9.21 Libbrecht, Géo. Poésie, 1937-1962. Paris, 1963.
43690.9.23 Libbrecht, Géo. Livres cachés; oeuvres complètes. v.1-6. Bruxelles, 1964-66. 5v.
43690.9.100 Libbrecht, Géo. Géo Libbrecht. Bruxelles, 1969?
43690.24.100 Lienard, Albert. A l'ombre du portique. Paris, 1900.
43690.24.110 Lienard, Albert. Les voiles blanches. Paris, 1905.
43690.24.120 Lienard, Albert. Le collier des heures. Paris, 1913.
43690.24.130 Lienard, Albert. Les esclaves. Paris, 1911.
43690.24.140 Lienard, Albert. Cléopâtre. Paris, 1914.
43690.25.110 Lièvre, Pierre. La vie et le roman. Paris, 1939.
43690.25.120 Lièvre, Pierre. Ouvrages galants et moraux. Paris, 1929.
43690.33.100 Ligi, Isaac. Dans la peau d'un juif, récit. Aulnay-sous Bois, 1968.
43690.48.100 Lilar, Suzanne. Le divertissement portugais. Paris, 1960.
43690.54.100 Limbosch, R. Sisyphe. v.1-3. Bruxelles, 1953.
43690.54.110 Limbosch, R. Il disait. Bruxelles, 1954.
43690.54.800 Coster, Sylvain de. De l'existentialisme...poète R. Limbosch. Bruxelles, 1942.
43690.55.100 Limbour, Georges. La chasse au mérou. Paris, 1963.
43690.55.110 Limbour, Georges. Les vanilliers. Lausanne, 1965.
43690.59.100 Lindon, Raymond. Quand la justice s'en mêle. Paris, 1965.
43690.61.100 Linze, Jacques Gérard. Par le sable et par le feu. Roman, 1962.
43690.61.120 Linze, Jacques Gérard. La conquête de Prague. Paris, 1965.
43690.61.130 Linze, Jacques Gérard. Le fruit de cendre. Paris, 1966.
43690.61.140 Linze, Jacques Gérard. La fabulation. Paris, 1968.
43690.61.150 Linze, Jacques Gérard. L'etang-coeur. Paris, 1967.
43690.62.100 Linze, Georges. Manifestes poétiques, 1951-1961. Paris, 196-.
43690.65.100 Lionel, Frédéric. L'affrontement. Neuchâtel, 1967.
43690.65.110 Lionel, Frédéric. L'étreinte des masques. Neuchâtel, 1969.
43690.68.100 Lip, F. Poèmes dans la nuit. Paris, 1960.
43690.88.100 Litschfousse, V. Alain, ou Les vertus guerrières. Paris, 1924.
43690.90.100 Livio, Robin. La terre est un gateau. Paris, 1957.
43690.90.2100 Lévis Mano, Guy. Il n'y a pas plus solitaire que la nuit. Paris, 1951.
43692.63.100 Lloansi, Cyprien. Lumière d'Olivier. Paris, 1957.
43693.1.30 Loison, F. Les reflets. Paris, 1902.
43693.2.30 Lorquise, C. Les invectives. Paris, 1906.
43693.3.30 Loumaye, Marcel. L'ombre de la guerre; poème. Bruxelles, 1920.
43693.6.100 Loba, Aké. Kocoumbo, l'etudiant noir. Paris, 1960.
43693.6.110 Loba, Aké. Les fils de Kouretcha. Paris, 1970.
43693.7.100 Lobet, M. Les croisés belges à Constantinople. Bruxelles, 1953?
43693.12.100 Lo Celso, André. Eclats dans les nuages. Paris, 1960.
43693.13.100 Lochac, Emmanuel. Le promenoir des élégies. Paris, 1929.
43693.18.700 Lodi, Maria. Charlotte Morel. London, 1968- 3v.
43693.20.30 Lo Duca, G. Journal secret de Napolean Bonaparte 1769-1869. Paris, 1962.
43693.41.100 Loiselel, Pierre. Echantillons. Paris, 1957.
43693.41.1100 Academie...Bordeaux. Academie nationale des sciences, belles-lettres, et arts de Bordeaux. Réception de M. Jean Loiseau a l'Academie. Bordeaux, 1954.
43693.48.100 L'Olagne, Jean. La collina ronde. Paris, 1927.
43693.53.100 Lombard-Maurog, G. Le temps revient. Paris, 1956.
43693.53.1100 Lombard, Ariane. Destinations. Paris, 1960.
43693.53.2100 Lombard, J.C. Ta place. Paris, 1963.
43693.58.110 Looten, Emmanuel. Exil inférieur. Paris, 1966.
43693.58.800 Spilleben, Willy. Emmanuel Looten, de Franse Vlaming. Lier, 1963.
43693.59.100 Londres, A. Au bagne. Paris, 1923.
43693.60.100 Longhy, Claude S. Le goût des sources. Paris, 1959.
43693.74.41 Lorbais, Jean. Les cicatrices. Paris, 1970.
43693.74.100 Lorbais, Jean. Sans armure. Paris, 1970.
43693.75.100 Lorenz, Paul. Notre-Dame de thermidor. Paris, 1946.
43693.75.110 Lorenz, Paul. Le tombeau de Paul Valéry. Paris, 1946.
43693.75.120 Lorenz, Paul. Les monstres innocents. Paris, 1949.
43693.75.1100 Lorho, Robert. Les métamorphoses du biographe. Paris, 1971.
43693.76.100 Lariot de la Salle, C. Coeur transparent. Paris, 1930.
43693.82.100 Lossier, Jean Georges. Du plus loin. Neuchâtel, 1966.
43693.88.805 Grosse, Karl B. Emile Joseph Lotte. Inaug. Diss. Jena, 1932.
43693.89.100 Louwyck, J.H. Retour de flamme. Paris, 1929.
43693.89.110 Louwyck, J.H. Danse pour ton ombre! Paris, 1939. 3 pam.
43693.89.1110 Louwe, Pierre. Les instants d'une vie. Paris, 1956.
43693.89.2100 Loubet, Guillaume. L'Hydre. Paris, 1959.
43693.89.3021 Louis, Fernand. Oeuvres poetiques. Vierzon, 1914.
43693.89.4021 Louis, Edner A. La porte s'ouvre; mes confidences à Marie-Jo. Port-au-Prince, 1965.
43693.89.5100 Louis, Gabriel. Portie civile contre la société. Paris, 1965.
43693.89.6100 Louve, Annie. Route barrée, poèmes. Paris, 1955.
43693.89.7100 Loudet, Louis. Soleils broyés. Paris, 1954.
43693.89.8100 Loumaye, Georges. Cent treize poèmes atroces. Bruxelles, 1962.
43693.98.100 Lozère, T. Nous n'irons plus au bois. Paris, 1953.
43694.1.30 Lugné-Poe, A. Les cinq messieurs de Francfort. Paris, 1914.
43694.8.100 Lubin, Armen. Sainte patience. 4. éd. Paris, 1951.
43694.8.110 Lubin, Armen. Les hautes terrasses. Paris, 1957.
43694.8.120 Lubin, Armen. Transfert nocturne. 4. éd. Paris, 1955.
43694.11.100 Lucchini, Pierre. Colère sur Paris. Paris, 1938.
43694.11.110 Lucchini, Pierre. Weltuntergang. München, 1928.
43694.11.120 Lucchini, Pierre. Notre-Dame de la sagesse. 24. éd. Paris, 1924.
43694.11.2100 Lucas, Wilfrid Louis Eugène. Les cavaliers de Dieu. Paris, 1935.
43694.11.2110 Lucas, Wilfrid Louis Eugène. La couronne de jois. Paris, 1958.

Classified Listing

43511 - 43873 Individual authors, etc. - 1900- - Known authors (363 scheme plus 10) - cont.

43694.11.2120 Lucas, Wilfrid Louis Eugène. Mémoires, impressions, souvenirs, pensées et réflexions. Paris, 1967.
43694.11.2800 Rodenboch, A. Wilfrid Lucas et son grand evangile d'amour chretien. Paris, 1961.
43694.11.2805 Poilvet Le Guenn, J. La grande oeuvre architectural d'un poète inspiré. Paris, 1961.
43694.11.2810 Mex, Alphonse. Dans la splendeur d'un chant de France. Caen, 1966.
43694.11.2815 Canivet, Louis. Un chant de France a l'heure du coeur. Rodez, 1969.
43694.11.2820 Douenel, Henri. Les grandes orgues de Dieu. Paris, 1970.
43694.11.3100 Lucain, Pierre Clotaire. Veillées guadeloupéennes. Paris, 1967.
43694.11.4100 Lucasserie, Louis de. Le soleil et la mort, poèmes. Paris, 1958.
43694.11.4110 Lucasserie, Louis de. Broutilles; poèmes. Paris, 1956.
43694.13.100 Luchaire, J. Altitude 3,200. Paris, 1937.
43694.13.1100 Lucciani, Jean Pierre. Contes à dormir debout. Paris, 1960.
43694.13.2100 Lucien, Henri. Le roman de Saint Savin. Paris, 1957.
43694.14.100 Lucièe, C. La guerre des cerveaux. Paris, 1931.
43694.18.100 Ludin, Elohim. Ceux de Bizerte. Paris, 1967.
43694.41.100 Luissel, Jean. Via poussiere. Lavaur, 1963.
43694.59.101 Lunel, Armand. Nicolo-Peccair. Paris, 1926.
43694.59.110 Lunel, Armand. Jérusalem a Carpentras. 5e éd. Paris, 1937.
43694.59.120 Lunel, Armand. Les amandes d'Aix. Paris, 1949.
43694.82.100 Lusreyran, Jacques. Et la lumière fût. Paris, 1954.
43694.88.100 Lutz, Emile. Poèmes errants. Paris, 1928.
43694.97.100 Luxereau, François. Milieu du gué, suivi de Poèmes pour le Viet Nam. Honfleur, 1968.
43697.1.30 Margrot, Jean H. Paris en l'an 3000. Paris, 1919?
43697.2.30 Mallarmé, C. Le Ressac. Paris, 1912.
43697.2.31 Mallarmé, C. Eome fa l'onda. Milano, 1914.
43697.2.200 Mallet-Joris, Françoise (pseud.). La maison de papier. Paris, 1970.
43697.2.1100 Mallet-Joris, Françoise (pseud.). Le rempart des beguines. Paris, 1957.
43697.2.1110 Mallet-Joris, Françoise (pseud.). L'empire céleste. Paris, 1959.
43697.2.1115 Mallet-Joris, Françoise (pseud.). L'empire céleste. Paris, 1968.
43697.2.1120 Mallet-Joris, Françoise (pseud.). Les mensonges. Paris, 1956.
43697.2.1130 Mallet-Joris, Françoise (pseud.). La chambre rouge. Paris, 1959.
43697.2.1140 Mallet-Joris, Françoise (pseud.). Cordélia. Paris, 1956.
43697.2.1142 Mallet-Joris, Françoise (pseud.). Cordélia and other stories. N.Y., 1965.
43697.2.1150 Mallet-Joris, Françoise (pseud.). Les personages. Paris, 1961.
43697.2.1170 Mallet-Joris, Françoise (pseud.). Lettre à moi-même. Paris, 1963.
43697.2.1180 Mallet-Joris, Françoise (pseud.). Les signes et les prodiges; roman. Paris, 1966.
43697.2.1190 Mallet-Joris, Françoise (pseud.). Trois âges de la nuit. Paris, 1968.
43697.2.1700 Mallet-Joris, Françoise (pseud.). The illusionists. N.Y., 1952.
43697.2.1710 Mallet-Joris, Françoise (pseud.). Into the labyrinth. Paris, 1953.
43697.2.1720 Mallet-Joris, Françoise (pseud.). The red room. N.Y., 1956.
43697.2.1725 Mallet-Joris, Françoise (pseud.). A letter to myself. N.Y., 1964.
43697.2.1730 Mallet-Joris, Françoise (pseud.). Capé Céleste. N.Y., 1959.
43697.2.1735 Mallet-Joris, Françoise (pseud.). House of lies. N.Y., 1957.
43697.2.1740 Mallet-Joris, Françoise (pseud.). Signs and wonders. N.Y., 1967.
43697.2.1745 Mallet-Joris, Françoise (pseud.). The favourite. N.Y., 1962.
43697.2.2100 Mallet, Robert. Amour mot de passe. Paris, 1952.
43697.2.2110 Mallet, Robert. Une mort ambiguë. 7. éd. Paris, 1955.
43697.2.2120 Mallet, Robert. Lapidé lapidaire. 4e ed. Paris, 1957.
43697.2.2140 Mallet, Robert. L'equipage au complet. 4e ed. Paris, 1958.
43697.3.30 Mandelstamm, V. L'amoral. Paris, 1907.
43697.3.35 Mandelstamm, V. New York. pt.1-4. Paris, 1922.
43697.4.30 Mariotti, Jean. Au fil des jours. Paris, 1929.
43697.4.33.5 Mauriac, François. Young man in chains. N.Y., 1963.
43697.4.35.5 Mauriac, François. Thérèse Desqueyroux. Photoreproduction. Paris, 1927.
43697.4.40 Mauriac, François. La province. Paris? 1926.
43697.4.45 Mauriac, François. Genitrix. 66e éd. Paris, 1936.
43697.4.50 Mauriac, François. Le baiser au lépreux. Paris, 1937.
43697.4.55 Mauriac, François. Les mal aimes. Paris, 1945.
43697.6.30 Machard, Alfred. Le massacre des innocents. Paris, 1918.
43697.6.33 Machard, Alfred. Wolf man. N.Y., 1925.
43697.6.40 Machard, Alfred. La guerre des mômes. Paris, 1916.
43697.6.45 Machard, Alfred. Kunder unter sich. Rudolstadt, 1929.
43697.6.50 Machard, Alfred. Titine, histoire d'un viol. Paris, 1922.
43697.6.52 Machard, Alfred. Bout-de-bibi. Paris, 1917.
43697.6.55 Machard, Alfred. Titine. Paris, 1913.
43697.6.58 Machard, Alfred. Popaul et Virginie. Paris, 1918.
43697.6.61 Machard, Alfred. Les cent gosses. Paris, 1912.
43697.6.65 Machard, Alfred. Bout-de-bibi. Paris, 1918.
43697.8.32 Masart, René. Échec au fisc. Paris, 1958.
43697.8.1100 Mabit, Jacqueline. Couleur banlieue. Malines, 1954.
43697.11.100 MacDann, Pierre. Fragments. Auxerre, 1948.
43697.12.100 Machet, Marie Madeleine. Les fêtes du monde. Paris, 1957.
43697.12.1102 Machin, Paul René. Arc-en-ciel. 2e éd. Lure, 1969.
43697.13.100 Mackay, Helen E. Patte-Blanche. Paris, 1929.
43697.13.1100 Macle, Guy. Gaillardes et passagères. Saint-Ouen, 1965.
43697.14.11 MacOrlan, Pierre. Oeuvres poétiques complètes. Paris, 1929.
43697.14.12 MacOrlan, Pierre. Le chant de l'équipage. La bandera. Genève, 1969.
43697.14.13 MacOrlan, Pierre. L'ancre de miséricorde. Le quai des brumes. Genève, 1969.
43697.14.14 MacOrlan, Pierre. Montmartre, Les bandes, suivi de Parades abolies. Genève, 1969.
43697.14.15 MacOrlan, Pierre. Sous la lumiére froide: La pension Mary Stuart. Genève, 1970.
43697.14.16 MacOrlan, Pierre. Le nègre Léonard et maître Jean Mullin. Genève, 1969.
43697.14.17 MacOrlan, Pierre. La cavalière Elsa. La Vénus internationale. Frontispice de Jim. Genève, 1969.
43697.14.21 MacOrlan, Pierre. Mémoires en chansons. Paris, 1965.
43697.14.100 MacOrlan, Pierre. La bandera. 4e ed. Paris, 1931.
43697.14.110 MacOrlan, Pierre. La cavalière Elsa. 29. ed. Paris, 1931.
43697.14.115 MacOrlan, Pierre. Le gros rouge. Monte-Carlo, 1957.
43697.14.120 MacOrlan, Pierre. Le quai des brumes. 2e ed. Paris, 1927.
43697.14.130 MacOrlan, Pierre. La Vénus internationale. 13e ed. Paris, 1923.
43697.14.131 MacOrlan, Pierre. La Vénus internationale. 6e ed. Paris, 1923.
43697.14.135 MacOrlan, Pierre. La Vénus internationale. Paris, 1966.
43697.14.140 MacOrlan, Pierre. A bord de l'Étoile-Matutine. 3e ed. Paris, 1934.
43697.14.142 MacOrlan, Pierre. A bord de l'Étoile-Matutine. Genève, 1970.
43697.14.145 MacOrlan, Pierre. Le bal du pont du Nord. 9. ed. Paris, 1950.
43697.14.150 MacOrlan, Pierre. Le nègre Léonard et maître Jean Mullin. 4. ed. Paris, 1920.
43697.14.160 MacOrlan, Pierre. Le chant de l'equipage. 2e ed. Paris, 1929.
43697.14.179 MacOrlan, Pierre. Les pirates de l'avenue du Rhum. 9e ed. Paris, 1925.
43697.14.190 MacOrlan, Pierre. Marquerite de la nuit. Paris, 1935.
43697.14.192 MacOrlan, Pierre. Marguerite de la nuit. 1. ed. Genève, 1969.
43697.14.200 MacOrlan, Pierre. Dinah Miami. Paris, 1948.
43697.14.210 MacOrlan, Pierre. Chansons pour accordéon. Paris, 1953.
43697.14.220 MacOrlan, Pierre. Chanson de charme pour Faux-Nez. Paris, 1950.
43697.14.230 MacOrlan, Pierre. Poésies documentaires complètes. Paris, 1954.
43697.14.232 MacOrlan, Pierre. Poésies documentaires complètes. 1. ed. Genève, 1969.
43697.14.240 MacOrlan, Pierre. La trádition de minuit. 2e ed. Paris, 1955.
43697.14.250 MacOrlan, Pierre. Malice. 5. ed. Paris, 1956.
43697.14.260 MacOrlan, Pierre. La lanterne sourde. 6e ed. Paris, 1953.
43697.14.270 MacOrlan, Pierre. Babet de Picardie. Paris, 1958.
43697.14.280 MacOrlan, Pierre. Selections sur ondes courtes. Paris, 1929.
43697.14.290 MacOrlan, Pierre. Les jeux du demi-jour. 4e ed. Paris, 1927.
43697.14.300 MacOrlan, Pierre. Le rire jaune, suivi de la bête conquérante. Paris, 1960.
43697.14.310 MacOrlan, Pierre. Picardie; roman. Paris, 1952.
43697.14.320 MacOrlan, Pierre. L'ancre de miséricorde. Paris, 1961.
43697.14.330 MacOrlan, Pierre. Sous la lumière froide. Paris, 1961.
43697.14.340 MacOrlan, Pierre. Petit manuel du parfait aventurier. Paris, 1920.
43697.14.350 MacOrlan, Pierre. Bob, bataillonnaire. Paris, 1919.
43697.14.352 MacOrlan, Pierre. Le bataillonnaire. Genève, 1970.
43697.14.360 MacOrlan, Pierre. Rue Saint-Vincent. Paris, 1928.
43697.14.370 MacOrlan, Pierre. Chronique des jours désespérés. Paris, 1927.
43697.14.380 MacOrlan, Pierre. Masques sur mesure. Paris, 1965.
43697.14.382 MacOrlan, Pierre. Masques sur mesure. 1 ed. Genève, 1970.
43697.14.390 MacOrlan, Pierre. La danse macabre. Paris, 1927.
43697.14.400 MacOrlan, Pierre. Quartier réservé. 13. ed. Paris, 1932.
43697.14.410 MacOrlan, Pierre. Contes de la pipe en terre. Paris, 1930?
43697.14.420 MacOrlan, Pierre. Nuits aux bouges. Paris, 1929.
43697.14.425 MacOrlan, Pierre. Rues secrètes. Nuits aux bouges. Genève, 1970?
43697.14.430 MacOrlan, Pierre. Les pattes en l'air. 1 ed. Genève, 1969.
43697.14.440 MacOrlan, Pierre. Propos d'infanterie: Les poissons morts, La fin, Devant la meuse. 1. éd. Genève, 1970.
43697.14.450 MacOrlan, Pierre. La maison du retour écoeurant; roman. Dinah miami; roman d'aventure. Le tueur no 2, roman policier. 1. éd. Genève, 1970.
43697.14.460 MacOrlan, Pierre. Le bataillon de la mauvaise chance. Le camp domineau. Genève, 1970.
43697.14.800 Barltaud, Bernard. Pierre MacOrlan. Paris, 1971.
43697.14.1100 Macover, Alice. Signes, poèmes. Paris, 1958.
43697.14.1110 Macover, Alice. L'amazone. Paris, 1959.
43697.14.1120 Macover, Alice. Pulsations. Monte-Carlo, 1958.
43697.14.2100 Macouba, Auguste (pseud.). Eïa! Man-maille là! Honfleur, 1968.
43697.18.100 Maud'huit, R. Les poèmes d'Orlando de la Folie. Paris, 1956-
43697.31.100 Magali (pseud.). L'enveloppe aux cachets bleus. Montréal, 1946.
43697.31.1100 Magali, Andrée. Les Fiancés du petit lac. Paris, 1969.
43697.32.100 Magermans, Rémy. La maladie dans la tour. Bruxelles, 1941.
43697.33.100 Magne, Emile. Naissance de l'Academie Française. Paris, 1935.
43697.33.110F Magne, Émile. La princesse Adélaïde ou L'amoureuse contrariée. Paris, 1936.
43697.33.1100 Magnusson, André. Chansons d'écorces. Bruxelles, 1947.
43697.33.2100 Magnan, Jean Marie. La nuit d'Arles. Paris, 1957.
43697.34.100 Magre, Maurice. Comediante. Paris, 1912.
43697.34.110 Magre, Maurice. La mort enchaînée. Paris, 1920.
43697.34.120A Magre, Maurice. La vie amoreuse de Messaline. Paris, 1925.
43697.34.120B Magre, Maurice. La vie amoreuse de Messaline. Paris, 1925.
43697.34.130 Magre, Maurice. Sin, féerie chinoise. Paris, 1921.
43697.34.140 Magre, Maurice. Arlequin. Paris, 1927.
43697.34.150A Magre, Maurice. Confessions sur les femmes, l'amour. Paris, 1930.
43697.34.150B Magre, Maurice. Confessions sur les femmes, l'amour. Paris, 1930.
43697.34.160 Magre, Maurice. Le poème de la jeunesse. Paris, 1901.
43697.34.170 Magre, Maurice. Les belles de nuit. Paris, 1913.
43697.34.180 Magre, Maurice. Les livres et le secret. Paris, 1906.
43697.34.190 Magre, Maurice. La montée aux enfers. Paris, 1918.
43697.34.200 Magre, Maurice. La porte du mystère. Paris, 1924.
43697.34.210 Magre, Maurice. Le trésor des Albigeois. Paris, 1938.
43697.34.220 Magre, Maurice. Le sang de Toulouse. Paris, 1931.
43697.34.230 Magre, Maurice. La tendre camarade. Roman. Paris, 1925?

43511 - 43873 Individual authors, etc. - 1900- - Known authors (363 scheme plus 10) - cont.

	43697.34.240	Magre, Maurice. Priscilla d'Alexandrie; roman. Paris, 1925.
	43697.34.250	Magre, Maurice. La luxure de Grenade; roman. Paris, 1926.
	43697.34.260	Magre, Maurice. Le mystére du tigre. Paris, 1927.
	43697.34.270	Magre, Maurice. Le retour. Toulouse, 1896.
	43697.34.280	Magre, Maurice. Le roman de Confucius. Paris, 1927.
Htn	43697.34.700*	Magre, Maurice. Messalina. N.Y., 1929.
	43697.34.710A	Magre, Maurice. The kingdon of Lu. N.Y., 1929.
	43697.34.710B	Magre, Maurice. The kingdon of Lu. N.Y., 1929.
	43697.34.800	Magre, Maurice. L'oeuvre amoureuse et sentimentale de Maurice Magre. Paris, 1922.
	43697.37.100	Mahé, Henri. La Bringuebale avec Céline. Paris, 1969.
	43697.37.1100	Mahélin, Yves. Grandissante origine. Paris, 1959.
	43697.37.1110	Mahélin, Yves. Six voyages sur une corde tendue. Paris, 1950.
	43697.41.100	Maindron, M. Monsieur de Puymonteil. Paris, 1938.
	43697.41.2021	Maisonneuve, Pierre. Poèmes d'un barbare; choix de poèmes écrits entre 1915 et 1964. Paris, 1966.
	43697.41.3100	Maisongrande, H.G. Le cycle des Héretiers; poèmes. Paris, 1959.
	43697.42.100	Majault, Joseph. Les enfants du soir. Paris, 1962.
	43697.42.110	Majault, Joseph. La conférence de Genève; roman. Paris, 1967.
	43697.45.700	Makhali-Phal. The young concubine. N.Y., 1942.
	43697.48.100	Malan, Jean. Vingt poèmes de la nuit. Marseille, 1927.
	43697.48.1100	Malan, Pierre. La queue du paon. Paris, 1958.
	43697.48.2100	Malaurie, Albert. La femme de Judas. Paris, 1924.
	43697.48.3110	Malaquais, Jean. Les javanais. Paris, 1939.
	43697.48.3112	Malaquais, Jean. Les javanais. Paris, 1954.
	43697.48.3120	Malaquais, Jean. Coups de barre. N.Y., 1944.
	43697.48.3700	Malaquais, Jean. Men from nowhere. N.Y., 1943.
	43697.48.3710	Malaquais, Jean. The joker. Garden City, 1954.
	43697.48.3720	Malaquais, Jean. Le gaffeur. Buchet, 1953.
	43697.48.3730	Malaquais, Jean. World without visa. London, 1949.
	43697.49.100	Malèque, J. Augustin, ou Le maître est lá. v.1-2. Paris, 1935.
	43697.49.800	Varin, G. Foi perdue et retrouvée. Fribourg, 1953.
	43697.49.810	Michaël, Elizabeth. Joseph Malègue. Paris, 1957.
	43697.49.820	Emery, L. Joseph Malègue, romancier inactuel. Lyon, 1962.
	43697.49.825	Lebrec, Jean. Joseph Malègue, romancier et penseur. Thèse. Paris, 1969.
	43697.50.100	Mallat, Robert J. Poémes de la mort juive. Honfleur, 1965.
	43697.50.110	Mallat, Robert J. Saint-Dominque oú je meurs. Honfleur, 1969.
	43697.51.100	Malori, Jacques. Une traversée gratuite. Paris, 1960.
	43697.51.1100	Maloire, Albert. Ecrits dans le soleil. Paris, 1960.
	43697.51.2100	Molle, Louis. Vie privee. Paris, 1962.
	43697.51.3100	Malrieu, Jean. Vesper. Paris, 1962.
	43697.52.30	Malraux miscellany. Lexington, Ky. 1,1969+
	43697.52.42	Malraux, André. Malraux par lui-même. Paris, 1953.
	43697.52.44	Malraux, André. Antimémoires. Paris, 1967.
	43697.52.45	Malraux, André. Anti-memoirs. N.Y., 1968.
	43697.52.100	Malraux, André. Les conquérants. Paris, 1929.
	43697.52.102	Malraux, André. Les conquérants. Paris, 1959.
	43697.52.105	Malraux, André. Les conquérants. Paris, 1967?
	43697.52.110	Malraux, André. La condition humaine. Paris, 1933.
	43697.52.112	Malraux, André. La condition humaine. Paris, 1955.
	43697.52.120	Malraux, André. Scènes choisies. Paris, 1946.
	43697.52.130	Malraux, André. Le temps du mépris. 5e ed. Paris, 1935.
	43697.52.140	Malraux, André. La voie royale. 50e ed. Paris, 1930.
	43697.52.145	Malraux, André. La voie royale. Paris, 1952.
	43697.52.160	Malraux, André. La tentation de l'Occident. 12 éd. Paris, 1926.
	43697.52.170	Malraux, André. Romans. Paris, 1947.
	43697.52.180	Malraux, André. Les noyers de l'Altenburg. Paris, 1948.
	43697.52.200	Malraux, André. Discours prononcé. Paris, 1962.
	43697.52.210	Malraux, André. Les voix du silence. Paris, 1956.
	43697.52.220	Malraux, André. Romans: Les conquérants, La condition humaine, L'espoir. Paris, 1969.
	43697.52.705	Malraux, André. Man's fate. N.Y., 1934.
	43697.52.708	Malraux, André. Man's fate. N.Y., 1936.
	43697.52.710A	Malraux, André. The royal way. N.Y., 1935.
	43697.52.710B	Malraux, André. The royal way. N.Y., 1935.
	43697.52.715	Malraux, André. Days of wrath. N.Y., 1936.
	43697.52.718	Malraux, André. The temptation of the West. N.Y., 1961.
	43697.52.720	Malraux, André. The walnut trees of Altenburg. London, 1952.
	43697.52.725	Malraux, André. Man's hope. N.Y., 1938.
	43697.52.730	Malraux, André. Days of hope. London, 1938.
	43697.52.735	Malraux, André. A second Griselda. London, 1947.
	43697.52.740	Malraux, André. The conquerors. N.Y., 1929.
	43697.52.741	Malraux, André. The conquerors. Boston, 1956.
	43697.52.745	Malraux, André. La lutte avec l'ange. Genève, 1945.
	43697.52.785	Malraux, André. La esperanza. Santiago de Chile, 1938.
	43697.52.790	Malraux, André. Lockung des Okzidents. Berlin, 1966.
	43697.52.800	Malraux, André. André Malraux. Paris, 1962.
	43697.52.805	Levin, Harry. Tragedy and revolution. n.p., 1937.
	43697.52.807	Mauriac, Claude. Malraux. Paris, 1946.
	43697.52.810A	Frohock, W.M. André Malraux and the tragic imagination. Stanford, 1952.
	43697.52.810B	Frohock, W.M. André Malraux and the tragic imagination. Stanford, 1952.
	43697.52.815A	Boisdeffre, O. de. André Malraux. Paris, 1952.
	43697.52.815B	Boisdeffre, O. de. André Malraux. Paris, 1952.
	43697.52.820	Mounier, E. L'espoir des desespérés. Paris, 1953.
	43697.52.825	Delhomme, Jeanne. Temps et destin. 2. éd. Paris, 1955.
	43697.52.830	Gannon, E. The honor of being a man. Chicago, 1957.
	43697.52.835	Kerudter, Fritz. André Malraux, die Suche nach einem neuen Menschenbild. München, 1958.
	43697.52.840A	Hartman, Geoffrey H. André Malraux. London, 1960.
	43697.52.840B	Hartman, Geoffrey H. André Malraux. London, 1960.
	43697.52.854	Boisdeffre, Pierre. André Malraux. 4. éd. Paris, 1957.
	43697.52.855	Boisdeffre, Pierre. André Malraux. 5. éd. Paris, 1960.
	43697.52.860	Blumenthal, Gerda. André Malraux. Baltimore, 1960.
	43697.52.865A	Picon, Gaëlan. André Malraux. 13. éd. Paris, 1946.
	43697.52.865B	Picon, Gaëlan. André Malraux. Paris, 1945.
	43697.52.870	Ferreira, V. André Malraux. Lisboa, 1963.
	43697.52.875	Hoffmann, J. L'humanisme de Malraux. Paris, 1963.
	43697.52.880	Lewis, R.W. Malraux. Englewood Cliffs, N.J., 1964.
	43697.52.885	Blend, C.D. André Malraux, tragic humanist. Columbus, 1963.
	43697.52.890	Righter, W. The rhetorical hero. London, 1964.
	43697.52.900	Vandegans, A. La jeunesse litteraire de André Malraux. Paris, 1964.

43511 - 43873 Individual authors, etc. - 1900- - Known authors (363 scheme plus 10) - cont.

43697.52.905	Langlois, Walter G. André Malraux: the Indochina adventure. N.Y., 1966.
43697.52.910	Wilkinson, David Ormond. Malraux; and essay in political criticism. Cambridge, 1967.
43697.52.915	Brincourt, André. André Malraux ou le Temps du silence. Paris, 1966.
43697.52.920	Boak, Denis. André Malraux. Oxford, 1968.
43697.52.925	Juilland, Ileana. Dictionnaire des idées dans l'oeuvre de André Malraux. The Hague, 1968.
43697.52.930	Balmas, Enea Henri. Le opere giovanili di André Malraux. Milano, 1965?
43697.52.935	Eggart, Dietmer. Das Problem der Einsamkeit und ihrer Überwindung im Romanwerk von André Malraux. Bamberg, 19
43697.52.940	Horvath, Violet M. André Malraux; the human adventure. N.Y., 1969.
43697.52.945	Carduner, Jean René. La Création romanesque chez Malraux. Paris, 1968.
43697.52.950	Dorenlot, F.E. Malraux; ou, L'unité de pensée. Paris, 1970.
43697.52.955	Payne, Robert. A portrait of André Malraux. Englewood Cliffs, N.J., 1970.
43697.52.961	Galante, Pierre. Malraux. 1. ed. N.Y., 1971.
43697.52.2100	Savane, Marcel. André Malraux. Paris, 1946.
43697.52.2110	Malraux, Clara. Par de plus longs chemins. Paris, 1953.
43697.52.2120	Malraux, Clara. La lutte isségale, roman. Paris, 1958.
43697.52.2130	Malraux, Clara. Le bruit de nos pas. Paris, 1963. 3v.
43697.52.2140	Malraux, Clara. Portrait de Grisélidis. Paris, 1945.
43697.52.2700	Malraux, Clara. A second Griselda. London, 1947.
43697.52.2705	Malraux, Clara. Memoirs. N.Y., 1967.
43697.52.3100	Malteste, Louis. Lucile et Ginette ou Les vierges folles. Paris, 1925?
43697.53.705	Malvil, A. The seven stars. N.Y., 1932.
43697.53.1100	Mambrino, Jean. Le veilleur aveugle. Paris, 1965.
43697.54.100	Mammeri, M. The sleep of the just. London, 1956.
43697.54.1100	Mamet, Magda. A l'écoute du temps. Paris, 1965.
43697.54.1110	Mamet, Magda. L'automne à mes semailles. Paris, 1961.
43697.58.100	Manchon, Fernand. Variétés sur la rebellion algerienne. Constantine, 1959.
43697.58.1100	Manceaux, M. Un beau mariage. Paris, 1962.
43697.58.2100	Manan, J. Les mémoires de Bidasse d'après les célèbres chroniques. Paris, 1963.
43697.59.100	Mandin, L. Ariel esclave. Paris, 1912.
43697.59.110	Mandin, L. Les saisons ferventes. Paris, 1914.
43697.59.120	Mandin, L. Les sommeils. Paris, 1904.
43697.59.130	Mandin, L. Ombres voluptueuses. Paris, 1907.
43697.59.1100	Maneil, Adrian van. Essais sur notre monde. Paris, 1939.
43697.60.100	Manier, B. Histoires d'ailleurs et de mille part. Bruxelles, 1961.
43697.61.100	Manoir, Georges. Monsier de Falindor. Paris, 1945.
43697.61.1100	Manot, Léon. Ce verbe et ce silence. Paris, 1946.
43697.61.2100	Mansour, Joyce. Cris. Paris, 1954.
43697.61.2110	Mansour, Joyce. Déchirures. Paris, 1955.
43697.61.2120	Mansour, Joyce. Jules César. Paris, 1956.
43697.61.2130	Mansour, Joyce. Les gisants satisfaits. Paris, 1958.
43697.61.2140	Monsour, Joyce. Rapaces. Paris, 1960.
43697.61.2150	Mansour, Joyce. Carré blanc. Paris, 1965.
43697.61.3100	Mantraud, F. Sa espera. Paris, 1959.
43697.61.3110	Mantrand, F. Les fievres de mars. Paris, 1958.
43697.61.4100	Manoury, Paul. Feuilles au vent et branches mortes. Évreux? 1954-
43697.61.5100	Montéguès, J. Méditations d'un médecin. Paris, 1960.
43697.61.6100	Manoll, Michel. Thérèse; ou La solitude dans la ville. Paris, 1953.
43697.61.6110	Manoll, Michel. Le vent des abimes. Nantes? 1958?
43697.62.100	Manuel, José. Des cris des ombres. Paris, 1958.
43697.62.700	Marchal, L. The Mesh. N.Y., 1949.
43697.63.100	Marcotte, Gilles. Le poids de Dieu. Paris, 1962.
43697.63.110	Marcotte, Gilles. Retour à Coolbrook. Paris, 1965.
43697.74.100	Maran, René. Batouala. Paris, 1921.
43697.74.101	Maran, René. Batouala. Paris, 1921.
43697.74.101.5	Maran, René. Batouala. Paris, 1921.
43697.74.102	Maran, René. Batouala. Paris, 1921.
43697.74.103	Maran, René. Batouala. Paris, 1921.
43697.74.104	Maran, René. Batouala. N.Y., 1922.
43697.74.106	Maran, René. Batouala. Bonibooks. N.Y., 1930.
43697.74.110	Maran, René. Le livre de la brousse. Paris, 1937.
43697.74.120	Maran, René. Bertrand du Gueschin. Paris, 1960.
43697.74.800	Hommage à René Maran. Paris, 1965.
43697.74.2100	Marguerittc, Lucie Paul. A jolie fille, joli garçon. Paris, 1922.
43697.74.3100	Marceau, Félicien. Capri. 9. ed. Paris, 1951.
43697.74.3110	Marceau, Félicien. L'homme du roi. 4. ed. Paris, 1952.
43697.74.3120	Marceau, Félicien. Les élans du coeur. 94. ed. Paris, 1955.
43697.74.3130	Marceau, Félicien. Bergère légère, roman. 8. ed. Paris, 1953.
43697.74.3140	Marceau, Félicien. Les belles natures. 17. ed. Paris, 1957.
43697.74.3150	Marceau, Félicien. L'oeuf, pièce en deux actes. Paris, 1957.
43697.74.3162	Marceau, Félicien. Chair et cuir. 2. ed. Paris, 1951.
43697.74.3170	Marceau, Félicien. La bonne soupe. 5. ed. Paris, 1958.
43697.74.3172	Marceau, Félicien. Théâtre. Paris, 1964.
43697.74.3180	Marceau, Félicien. Les cailloux. Paris, 1962.
43697.74.3185	Marceau, Félicien. Un jour, j'ai rencontré la vérité. Paris, 1967.
43697.74.3190	Marceau, Félicien. Les Années courtes. Paris, 1968.
43697.74.3200	Marceau, Félicien. Le babour, pièce en deux parties. Paris, 1969.
43697.74.3210	Marceau, Félicien. Creezy. Paris, 1969.
43697.74.3700	Marceau, Félicien. The King's man. London, 1954.
43697.74.3705	Marceau, Félicien. The egg. London, 1958.
43697.74.4100	Martel, François. La colère noire; roman. Paris, 1960.
43697.74.5100	Marceau, Alain. A la pointe des yeux. Montreal, 1958.
43697.74.6100	Marchou, Gaston. Les temps imagines. Paris, 1960.
43697.74.7100	Marie-Josèphe (pseud.). Arthurine. Paris, 1960.
43697.74.8100	Marill, Francine. Un temps pour souffrir; roman. Paris, 1964.
43697.74.8110	Marill, Francine. L'été finit en Israël, roman. Paris, 1968.
43697.74.9100	Madrus, Joseph Charles. L'oiseau des hauteurs. Paris, 1933.
43697.74.9110	Madrus, Joseph Charles. La reine de Saba. Paris, 1918.
43697.74.9120	Histoire charmante de l'adolescent sucre d'amour. Paris, 1927.
43697.75.100	Marcel, Gabriel. Le coeur des autres. Paris, 1921.

43511 - 43873 Individual authors, etc. - 1900- - Known authors (363 scheme plus 10) - cont.

43697.75.110 Marcel, Gabriel. La chapelle ardente. Paris, 1925.

43697.75.115A Marcel, Gabriel. Théâtre comique. Paris, 1947.

43697.75.115B Marcel, Gabriel. Théâtre comique. Paris, 1947.

X Cg 43697.75.120 Marcel, Gabriel. L'iconoclaste. Paris, 1923.

43697.75.125 Marcel, Gabriel. Rome n'est plus dans Rome. Paris, 1951.

43697.75.130 Bagot, Jean Pierre. La soif (pièce en trois actes) précédée de Théâtre et mystère par Gaston Fessard. Paris, 1958.

43697.75.135A Marcel, Gabriel. Mon temps n'est pas le vôtre. Paris, 1955.

43697.75.135B Marcel, Gabriel. Mon temps n'est pas le vôtre. Paris, 1955.

43697.75.140 Marcel, Gabriel. La quatuor en fa dièse. Paris, 1925.

43697.75.145 Marcel, Gabriel. Croissez et multipliez. Paris, 1955.

43697.75.150 Marcel, Gabriel. Le dard; pièce en trois actes. Paris, 1938.

43697.75.155 Marcel, Gabriel. L'homme problematique. Paris, 1955.

43697.75.160 Marcel, Gabriel. Les coeurs avides. Paris, 1952.

43697.75.165 Marcel, Gabriel. L'horizon. Paris, 1945.

43697.75.170 Marcel, Gabriel. Présence et immortalité. Paris, 1959.

43697.75.180A Marcel, Gabriel. Théâtre et religion. Lyon, 1959.

43697.75.180B Marcel, Gabriel. Théâtre et religion. Lyon, 1959.

43697.75.190 Marcel, Gabriel. La dimension Florestan. Paris, 1958.

43697.75.200 Marcel, Gabriel. Paix sur la terre. Paris, 1965.

43697.75.210 Marcel, Gabriel. Le secret est dans les îles. Paris, 1967.

43697.75.700 Marcel, Gabriel. A man of God. London, 1952.

43697.75.705 Marcel, Gabriel. Presence and immortality. Pittsburgh, 1967.

43697.75.710 Marcel, Gabriel. Three plays. 1st American ed. N.Y., 1958.

43697.75.800A Existentialisme chrétien: Gabriel Marcel. Paris, 1948.

43697.75.800B Existentialisme chrétien: Gabriel Marcel. Paris, 1947.

43697.75.810 Chenn, Joseph. Le théâtre de Gabriel Marcel. Paris, 1948.

43697.75.820 Prini, Pietro. Gabriel Marcel et la méthodologie de l'invérifiable. Paris, 1953.

43697.75.822 Prini, Pietro. Gabriel Marcel e la metodologia dell'inverificabile. Roma, 1968.

43697.75.830 Stiftung, F.V.S. zu Hamburg. Gedenkschrift zur Verleihung des Hansischen Goethe-Preises 1955. Hamburg, 1956.

43697.75.840 Wolff, Gertrud. Der Todesgedanke im Drama Gabriel Marcel's. Erlangen, 1957.

43697.75.845 Benoat, E. Gabriel Marcel. Brugge, 1961.

43697.75.850 Bagot, Jean Pierre. Connaissance et amour. Paris, 1958.

43697.75.855 Ralston, Z.T. Gabriel Marcel's paradoxical expression of mystery. Washington, 1961.

43697.75.858 Maetze, W. Der Auffassung des Sozialen in Existenzphilosophie und Kultursoziologie. Berlin, 1961.

43697.75.860 Davy, Marie. Un philosophe itinérant. Paris, 1959.

43697.75.865 Wolf, Bernhard. Das ontologische Mysterium. München, 1959.

43697.75.870 Gallagher, Kenneth. The philosophy of Gabriel Marcel. N.Y., 1962.

43697.75.880 Börsenverein des Deutschen Buchhandels. Gabriel Marcel. Frankfurt, 1964.

43697.75.885 Ewijk, Thomas J.M. van. Gabriel Marcel, an introduction. N.Y., 1965.

43697.75.890 Blázquez Carmona, Feliciano. Gabriel Marcel. Madrid, 1970.

43697.75.1100 Margyl, George. Dessus-Dessous. Paris, 1910.

X Cg 43697.75.2000 Marcenac, Jean. Le cavalier de Coupe. Paris, 1945.

43697.75.2021 Marcenac, Jean. L'amour du plus lointain; poèmes 1960-1970. Paris, 1970.

43697.75.2100 Marcenac, Jean. A merveille. Paris, 1945.

43697.75.2110 Marcenac, Jean. La patience des botocudos. Paris, 1970.

43697.75.3000 Marchand, L. Nous ne sommes plus des enfants. Paris, 1927.

43697.75.3010 Marchand, L. Mon gosse de père. Paris, 1926.

43697.75.3020 Marchand, L. J'ai tué. Paris, 1928.

43697.75.3030 Marchand, L. Durand, bijoutier. Paris, 1930.

43697.75.3040 Marchand, L. La vie est si courte. Paris, 1936.

43697.75.3050 Marchand, L. Trois valses. Paris, 1937.

43697.75.4000 Marchon, Albert. Le bachelier sans vergogne. 13e ed. Paris, 1925.

43697.75.4110 Marchon, Albert. Trésor en Espagne. 6. éd. Paris, 1935.

43697.75.4120 Marchon, Albert. L'impasse. Paris, 1928.

43697.75.4130 Marchon, Albert. Sous le signe de la vierge. Paris, 1922.

43697.75.5700 Marchal, L. The sage of Canudos. London, 1954.

43697.75.6100 Mardelle, M. Pierruche au soleil. Paris, 1935.

43697.75.6400 Margat, Yves. La légende de Saint-Cornély. n.p., n.d.

43697.75.7100 Margurette, L.P. (Mme.). Nous attendons l'imperatrice. Paris, 1938.

43697.75.7500 Marnière, Jeanne. Le livre d'une amoureuse. Paris, 1904.

43697.75.7510 Marnière, Jeanne. L'aile. Paris, 1902.

43697.75.8100 Marois, P. Rowena. Paris, 1938.

43697.75.9100 Margerit, Robert. La terre aux loups. Paris, 1958.

43697.75.9110 Margerit, Robert. La révolution, roman. Paris, 1963- 4v.

43697.76.5 Mariel, Anne. Lola Montés. Paris, 1955.

43697.76.100 Marquet, Jean. Nestor, patron pêcheur. Paris, 1923.

43697.76.110 Marquet, Jean. Master Lou Po To. Avignon, 1941.

43697.76.1108 Mars, Antony. Les deux pigeons. 8. éd. Paris, 1925.

43697.76.2100 Marill, René. Les hommes traqués. Paris, 1953.

43697.76.2110 Marill, René. Manuscrit enterré dans le jardin d'Éden. Bienne, 1967.

43697.76.2700 Martel, D. de. Silhouettes of Peking. Peking, 1926.

43697.76.3110 Martet, Jean. Dolorès, roman. Paris, 1929. 3 pam.

43697.76.3120 Martet, Jean. Les portes du desert. v.1-3. Paris, 1932.

43697.76.3130 Martet, Jean. La partie de boules. v.1-4. Paris, 1935.

43697.76.3140 Martet, Jean. La mort du tigre. Paris, 1930.

43697.76.4100 Mars, Claire. Dans l'ombre fraîche. Paris, 1946.

43697.76.5100 Mari, Jeanne. Le sens de la terre. Gap, 1940.

43697.76.6021 Maritain, Raïssa. Poèmes et essais. Paris, 1968.

43697.76.6100 Maritain, Raïssa. Les grandes amitiés. N.Y., 1941-1944. 2v.

43697.76.6110 Maritain, Raïssa. We have been friends together. N.Y., 1942-45. 2v.

43697.76.6120 Maritain, Raïssa. Au creux du rocher. Paris, 1954.

43697.76.6130 Maritain, Raïssa. Notes sur le Pater. Paris, 1962.

43697.76.6142 Maritain, Raïssa. Le prince de ce monde. 2. ed. Bruges, 1963.

43697.76.6150 Maritain, Raïssa. Journal de Raïssa. Paris, 1963.

43697.76.6621 Maritain, Raïssa. Patriarch tree: thirty poems. Worcester, 1965.

43697.76.7100 Marker, C. Le coeur net. Paris, 1949.

43697.76.7110 Marker, C. The forthright spirit. London, 1951.

43511 - 43873 Individual authors, etc. - 1900- - Known authors (363 scheme plus 10) - cont.

43697.76.8021 Marissel, André. Choix de poèmes 1957-1968. Paris, 1969.

43697.76.8100 Marissel, André. L'homme et l'abime. Paris, 1957.

43697.76.9100 Martin du Gard, Maurice. Harmonies critiques. Paris, 1936.

43697.76.9110 Martin du Gard, Maurice. Caractères et confidences. Paris, 1936.

43697.76.9120 Martin du Gard, Maurice. Feux tournants; nouveaux portraits contemporains. Paris, 1925.

43697.76.9130 Martin du Gard, Maurice. Climat tempéré: maximes, caractères et confidences, 1933-1963. Paris, 1964.

43697.76.9140 Martin du Gard, Maurice. Impertinences; portraits contemporains. Paris, 1924.

43697.76.9150 Martin du Gard, Maurice. Vérités du moment. Paris, 1928.

43697.77.61 Martin du Gard, Roger. Lettres de Roger Martin du Gard à un jeune écrivain, 1953-1958. Paris, 1969.

43697.77.100 Martin du Gard, Roger. Les Thibault. v.1-8. Paris, 1923-40. 10v.

43697.77.111 Martin du Gard, Roger. Les Thibault. v.1-8. Montréal, 1944. 9v.

43697.77.120 Martin du Gard, Roger. Vieille France. 15e éd. Paris, 1933.

43697.77.130 Martin du Gard, Roger. La gonfle. Paris, 1928.

43697.77.140 Martin du Gard, Roger. Devenir! 3e éd. Paris, 1930.

43697.77.150 Martin du Gard, Roger. Confidence africaine. Paris, 1931.

43697.77.160 Martin du Gard, Roger. Un taciturne. 6e ed. Paris, 1932.

43697.77.180 Martin du Gard, Roger. Le testament du Père Leleu. Paris, 1920.

43697.77.190 Martin du Gard, Roger. L'une de nous. Paris, 1910.

43697.77.220 Martin du Gard, Roger. Oeuvres complétes. Paris, 1955. 2v.

43697.77.240 Martin du Gard, Roger. Noizemont-les-Vierges. Liège, 1928.

43697.77.705 Martin du Gard, Roger. The Thibaults. N.Y., 1926- 2v.

43697.77.708 Martin du Gard, Roger. The Thibaults. London, 1933-34. 2v.

43697.77.710 Martin du Gard, Roger. The Thibaults. N.Y., 1939.

43697.77.720 Martin du Gard, Roger. Jean Barois. N.Y., 1949.

43697.77.730 Martin du Gard, Roger. Summer 1914. N.Y., 1941.

43697.77.740 Martin du Gard, Roger. The postman. London, 1954.

43697.77.815 Lalon, René. Roger Martin du Gard. 5e éd. Paris, 1937.

43697.77.825 Rice, H.C. Roger Martin du Gard and the world of the Thibaults. N.Y., 1941. 2v.

43697.77.830 Borgal, Clément. Roger Martin du Gard. Paris, 1957.

43697.77.835 Moscow. Vsesoiuznaia gosudarst-vennaia biblioteka inostrannoi literatury. Rozhe Marten diu Gar. Moskva, 1958.

43697.77.840 Borgal, Clément. Roger Martin du Gard. Paris, 1958.

43697.77.845 Brenner, J. Martin du Gard. Paris, 1961.

43697.77.850 Gibson, Robert. Roger Martin du Gard. London, 1961.

43697.77.855 Boak, Denis. Roger Martin du Gard. Oxford, 1963.

43697.77.860 Narkir'er, F.S. Rozhe Marten diu Gar. Moskva, 1963.

43697.77.865 Robidoux, Réjean. Roger Martin du Gard et la religion. Paris, 1964.

43697.77.870 Schlobach, Jochen. Geschichte und Fiktion in "l'été 1914" von Roger Martin du Gard. München, 1965.

43697.77.875 Schalk, David Louis. Roger Martin du Gard. Ithaca, 1967.

43697.77.880 Descloux, Armand. Le Docteur Antoine Thibault. Thèse. Paris, 1965.

43697.77.885 Savage, Catherine. Roger Martin du Gard. N.Y., 1968.

43697.77.890 Filipowska, Irena. Le tragique de l'individu dans les romans de Roger Martin du Gard. Poznan, 1968.

43697.77.895 Roza, Robert. Roger Martin du Gard et la banalité retrouvée. Paris, 1970.

43697.77.900 Gallant, Melvin. Le thème de la mort chez Roger Martin du Gard. Paris, 1971.

43697.77.1100 Mariotti, Jean. Au fil des jours. Paris, 1929.

43697.77.2100 Martel, A. Le mirivis des naturgies. Paris, 1963.

43697.77.3100 Marmouset. Au lion tranquille. Paris, 1922.

43697.77.4100 Martin, Marietta. Cahiers. v.1-2. Paris, 1956.

43697.77.4110 Martin, Marietta. Adieu temps. Neuchâtel, 1947.

43697.77.4800 Adam-Rosé, L. La vie de Marietta Martin. Paris, 1955.

43697.77.5100 Marty, Peské. Le bal des angoisses. Paris, 1957.

43697.77.6100 Martirerie, Andrée. Les autres jours; roman. Paris, 1961.

43697.77.6700 Martinerie, Andrée. Second spring. Chicago, 1964.

43697.77.7100 Martin-Chauffuv, Louis. L'écrivain et la liberté. Neuchâtel, 1958.

43697.77.8100 Martin, Maurice. Le Triptyque. Bordeaux, 1934.

43697.77.9105 Martin, François. L'ange de la mort. 5. éd. Paris, 1945.

43697.78.110 Martinet, Marcel. Les temps Maudits. 3d ed. Paris, 1919.

43697.78.120 Martinet, Marcel. La nuit. Paris, 1921.

43697.78.130 Martinet, Marcel. Chants du passages. Paris, 1934.

43697.78.140 Martinet, Marcel. Eux et moi. Monte-Carlo, 1954.

43697.78.1100 Martin-Chauffier, Simone. La première personne. Paris, 1955.

43697.78.2100 Martine, Claude. La vie de palace. 4. ed. Paris, 1955.

43697.78.3100 Eugène Marsan par Charles Maurras. Lyon, 1925.

43697.78.3110 Marsan, Eugène. Le nouvel amour. Paris, 1925.

43697.78.3120 Marsan, Eugène. Passantes. Paris, 1923.

43697.78.3130 Marsan, Eugène. Amazones. Abbeville, 1921.

43697.78.3140 Marsan, Eugène. Notre costume. Liège, 1926.

43697.78.4100 Marsaux, Lucien. Le carnaval des Vendanges. Paris, 1929.

43697.78.5021 Martin Saint-René (pseud.). Le livre des odes et autres formes de stances. Paris, 1970.

43697.78.5100 Martin Saint-René (pseud.). Les années maudites. Paris, 1944.

43697.78.5110 Martin Saint-René (pseud.). Une lyre tendue à tous les vents du ciel! Paris, 1956.

43697.78.5120 Martin Saint-René (pseud.). La veillée aux étoiles. Paris, 1953.

43697.78.5130 Martin Saint-René (pseud.). Le sang des dieux. Paris, 1954.

43697.78.5140 Martin Saint-René (pseud.). Céruléennes. Paris, 1957.

43697.78.5150 Martin Saint-René (pseud.). Bleu, blanc, rouge. Paris, 1955.

43697.78.5160 Martin Saint-René (pseud.). Précis de poésie, pour servir à la composition rationnelle. Paris, 1953. 2 pam.

43697.78.5170 Martin Saint-René (pseud.). Vitriks et Génowinn. Paris, 1969.

43697.78.5180 Martin Saint-René (pseud.). Le livre des guatrains. Paris, 1970.

43697.78.5200 Martin Saint-René (pseud.). Immortelle. Paris, 1958.

43697.78.6100 Martin, Suzanne. Rue des vivants. Paris, 1959.

43697.78.7100 Marsolle, Edouard. Au clair de mon âme. Paris, 1960.

43697.78.8100 Martinon, R. Messages secrets de la nature. Chauny, 1956.

43697.78.9100 Martin, Vio. Visages de la flame. Neuchâtel, 1963.

Classified Listing

43511 - 43873 Individual authors, etc. - 1900- - Known authors (363 scheme plus 10) - cont.

43697.79.100 Mary, André. Poèmes (1903-1928). Paris, 1928.
43697.79.110 Mary, André. Forêteries. Paris, 1950.
43697.79.120 Mary, André. Symphonies pastorales. Pithiviers, 1903.
43697.79.130 Mary, André. Les sentiers du paradis. Paris, 1906.
43697.79.140 Mary, André. Le cantique de la Seine. Paris, 1911.
43697.79.150 Mary, André. Les profondeurs de la forêt. Paris, 1907.
43697.79.160 Mary, André. Le livre nocturne. Paris, 1935.
43697.79.170 Mary, André. Rimes et bacchanales. Paris, 1942.
43697.79.180 Mary, André. Les rondeaux. Mesnil, 1924.
43697.79.190 Mary, André. Le livre des idylles et passe-temps. Paris, 1922.
43697.79.1100 Martinez-Pagan, Antonio. Sous la poussière des étoiles; roman. Paris, 1966.
43697.79.2100 Martenne, Thérèse de. La chaîne des douleurs, poèmes. Paris, 1958.
43697.79.3100 Mariabère, Jean. Sténogrammes, le troisième livre des poèmes. Casablanca, 1955.
43697.79.4100 Marnat, Jean. Primates, poèmes. Paris, 1960.
43697.79.5100 Marty, Jean. La chanson des vingt ans; poèmes. Paris, 19-
43697.79.6100 Martin, Jean Marie. Chansons pour une marionnette. Paris, 1957.
43697.79.7100 Martin, Jean Claude. Moods. Monte Carlo, 1969.
43697.79.8100 Marvaud, Jean. Printemps charentais. Versailles, 1967.
43697.79.9100 Marie-Jeanne (pseud.). Le labyrinthe. Paris, 1969.
43697.80.1100 Maschino, Blanche. La chaine des temps. Paris, 1936.
43697.80.1110 Maschino, Blanche. Eros: la science et le rêve. Paris, 1936.
43697.80.1120 Maschino, Blanche. Le fléau divin: Némésis, poèmes. Paris, 1936.
43697.80.1130 Maschino, Blanche. Ephémère; poèmes. Paris, 1937.
43697.80.1140 Maschino, Blanche. Rhéa. Paris, 1937.
43697.80.2100 Marti, Sandra. Le choix, roman. Paris, 1968.
43697.81.100 Massip, Renée. Les déesses, roman. Paris, 1958.
43697.81.110 Massip, Renée. La bête quaternaire; roman. Paris, 1963.
43697.81.120 Massip, Renée. Le rire de Sara. Paris, 1967.
43697.81.1100 Masset, G. Le jardin du Scarabée. Paris, 19- .
43697.82.100 Massis, Henri. Evocations; souvenirs, 1905-1911. Paris, 1931.
43697.82.102 Massis, Henri. Evocations; souvenirs. Paris, 1931-
43697.82.110 Massis, Henri. L'honneur de servir. Paris, 1937.
43697.82.127 Massis, Henri. Les idées restent. Lyon, 1941.
43697.82.130 Massis, Henri. Visages des idées. Paris, 1958.
43697.82.140 Massis, Henri. De l'homme à Dieu. Paris, 1959.
43697.82.150 Massis, Henri. Discours de réception de Henri Massis à l'Académie française. Paris, 1961.
43697.82.160 Massis, Henri. Impressions de guerre. Paris, 1916.
43697.82.800 Leitolf, Otto. Die Gedankenwelt von Henri Massis. Berlin, 1940.
43697.82.2100 Massot, Pierre de. De Mallarmé à 391. Saint-Raphaël, 1922.
43697.83.100 Masson, Emile. Le livre des hommes et leurs paroles inouies. 2e éd. Paris, 1919?
43697.83.110 Masson, Emile. Lettre d'un répétiteur en congé. Paris, 190-.
43697.83.120 Masson, Emile. Les rebelles. Paris, 1909.
43697.84.100 Masson, R. Oranges vertes. Paris, 1951.
43697.84.700 Masson, R. Green oranges. 1st American ed. N.Y., 1953.
43697.85.100 Masson, G.A. Ou le parfait plagiaire. Paris, 1924.
43697.85.110 Masson, G.A. A la façon de Jean Anouilh. Paris, 1949.
43697.85.1100 Masson, G.A. L'hostellerie du Foyau. Bruxelles, 1963.
43697.86.110 Masson, Loÿs. Le requis civil, roman. 8. éd. Paris, 1945.
43697.86.120 Masson, Loÿs. La lumière nait le mercredi. Paris, 1945?
43697.86.130 Masson, Loÿs. Icare; ou, Le voyage. Paris, 1950.
43697.86.140 Masson, Loÿs. Les tortues. Paris, 1956.
43697.86.150 Masson, Loÿs. Le notaire des noirs. Paris, 1962.
43697.86.160 Masson, Loÿs. Le feu d'Espagne; roman. Paris, 1965.
43697.86.700 Masson, Loÿs. The shattered sexes, a novel. Great Neck, 1961.
43697.86.705 Masson, Loÿs. The overseer. 1st American ed. N.Y., 1964.
43697.86.2100 Maulnier, Thierry. La course des rois. Paris, 1947.
43697.86.2110 Maulnier, Thierry. La maison de la nuit. Paris, 1954.
43697.86.2120 Maulnier, Thierry. Esquisses littéraires. Paris? 1948.
43697.86.2130 Maulnier, Thierry. La Défaite d'Annibal, suivi de la Ville au fond de la mer. Paris, 1968.
43697.86.3100 Mathieu, Jean. Deux chômeurs, roman. Bruxelles, 1957.
43697.87.100 Maurette, Marcelle. Madame Capet. Paris, 1938.
43697.87.110 Mauretti, Marcelle. Le roi Christine. Paris, 1945.
43697.87.2100 Matthey, P.L. Poésies, 1910-1942. Lausanne, 1943.
43697.87.3100 Matveev, Michel. Ailleurs autrefois; roman. Paris, 1959.
43697.87.4100 Mattéi, G.M. Disponibles. Paris, 1961.
43697.88.12 Mauriac, François. Oeuvres complètes. Paris, 1951- 12v.
43697.88.14 Mauriac, François. Oeuvres romanesques. Paris, 1970. 2v.
43697.88.41A Mauriac, François. Journal. Paris, 1947.
43697.88.41B Mauriac, François. Journal. Paris, 1947.
43697.88.42 Mauriac, François. Pages de journal. Monaco, 1945.
43697.88.45 Mauriac, François. Mauriac par lui-même. Paris, 1953.
43697.88.50 Mauriac, François. Le pain vivant. Paris, 1955.
43697.88.55 Mauriac, François. The stumbling block. London, 1956.
43697.88.60 Mauriac, François. Lettres ouvertes. Monaco, 1952.
43697.88.65 Mauriac, François. Mémoires intérieurs. Paris, 1959.
43697.88.70 Mauriac, François. Mémoires politiques. Paris, 1967.
43697.88.100 Mauriac, François. Le désert de l'amour. Paris, 1925.
43697.88.110 Mauriac, François. Trois récits. 33. éd. Paris, 1929.
43697.88.120 Mauriac, François. Ce qui était perdu, roman. Paris, 1930.
43697.88.130 Mauriac, François. Pèlerins. Paris, 1932.
43697.88.140A Mauriac, François. Le noeud de vipères; roman. Paris, 1932.
43697.88.140B Mauriac, François. Le noeud de vipères; roman. Paris, 1932.
43697.88.150 Mauriac, François. La chair et le sang; roman. Paris, 1928.
43697.88.160 Mauriac, François. Dieu et Mammon. Paris, 1929.
43697.88.160.1 Mauriac, François. Dieu et Mammon. Paris, 1933.
43697.88.160.2 Mauriac, François. Dieu et Mammon. Paris, 1958.
43697.88.162 Mauriac, François. Le romancier et ses personnages. Paris, 1933.
43697.88.165 Mauriac, François. Le jeune homme. Paris, 1947.
43697.88.172A Mauriac, François. Plongées. Paris, 1938.
43697.88.172B Mauriac, François. Plongées. Paris, 1938.
43697.88.180 Mauriac, François. Commencements d'une vie. Paris, 1932.
43697.88.190A Mauriac, François. Journal. Paris, 1934-1953. 5v.
43697.88.190B Mauriac, François. Journal. v.3. Paris, 1934-53.

43511 - 43873 Individual authors, etc. - 1900- - Known authors (363 scheme plus 10) - cont.

43697.88.200 Mauriac, François. La pharisienne. Paris, 1941.
43697.88.210 Mauriac, François. Les péloueyne: le baiser au lépreux. Paris, 1923.
43697.88.215A Mauriac, François. Le cahier noir. Paris, 1943.
43697.88.215B Mauriac, François. Le cahier noir. Paris, 1943.
43697.88.216 Mauriac, François. Le cahier noir. Paris, 1943[1944]
43697.88.218 Mauriac, François. Le cahier noir. Paris, 1947.
43697.88.230 Mauriac, François. Les anges noirs. Paris, 1944.
43697.88.240 Mauriac, François. Le mystère frontenac. 88. ed. Paris, 1933.
43697.88.250 Mauriac, François. La rencontre avec Barrès. Vanves, 1945.
43697.88.260 Mauriac, François. Les chemins de la mer. Paris, 1946.
43697.88.270 Mauriac, François. Trois grands hommes devant Dieu. Paris, 1947.
43697.88.280 Mauriac, François. Réponse à Paul Claudel. Vanves, 1947.
43697.88.292 Mauriac, François. Passage du Malin. Paris, 1948.
43697.88.300 Mauriac, François. Petits essais de psychologie religieuse. 6. ed. Paris, 1933.
43697.88.310 Mauriac, François. Discours de réception à l'Académie française et Réponse de M. André Chaumeix. Paris, 1934.
43697.88.320 Mauriac, François. La robe prétexte. Paris, 1919?
43697.88.323 Mauriac, François. La robe prétexte. Paris, 1930.
43697.88.325 Mauriac, François. La robe prétexte. Paris, 1945.
43697.88.330 Mauriac, François. Asmodée. Paris, 1945.
43697.88.331 Mauriac, François. Asmodée. Paris, 1938.
43697.88.340 Mauriac, François. Les maisons fugitives. Paris, 1939.
43697.88.350 Mauriac, François. L'education des filles. Paris, 1936.
43697.88.360 Mauriac, François. Orages. Paris, 1949.
43697.88.370 Mauriac, François. Mes plus lointains souvenirs. Paris, 1929.
43697.88.380 Mauriac, François. Préséances. Paris, 1928.
43697.88.382 Mauriac, François. Préséances. Paris, 1962.
43697.88.390 Mauriac, François. Ne pas se renier. Alger, 1944.
43697.88.400 Mauriac, François. Le sagouin. Paris, 1951.
43697.88.410 Mauriac, François. La nuit du bourreau de soi-même. Paris, 1929.
43697.88.420A Mauriac, François. Le mal. Paris, 1935.
43697.88.420B Mauriac, François. Le mal. Paris, 1935.
43697.88.430 Mauriac, François. Galigaï. Paris, 1952.
43697.88.440 Mauriac, François. Le feu sur la terre. Paris, 1951.
43697.88.450 Mauriac, François. Écrits intimes. Genève, 1953.
43697.88.460 Mauriac, François. L'agneau. Paris, 1954.
43697.88.470 Mauriac, François. La fin de la nuit. Paris, 1935.
43697.88.480 Mauriac, François. Bloc-notes. Paris, 1958. 5v.
43697.88.490 Mauriac, François. Le fils de l'homme. Paris, 1959.
43697.88.500 Mauriac, François. Le désert de l'amour; roman. Paris, 1927.
43697.88.510 Mauriac, François. Dieu et Mammon. Paris, 1958.
43697.88.520 Mauriac, François. Genitrix. Paris, 1923.
43697.88.530 Mauriac, François. Le fleuve de feu. Paris, 1923[1939]
43697.88.540 Mauriac, François. Le drôle. Paris, 1961.
43697.88.550 Mauriac, François. Ce que je crois. Paris, 1962.
43697.88.560 Mauriac, François. La pierre d'achoppement. Monaco, 1958.
43697.88.570 Mauriac, François. Le mystère frontenac. Paris, 1961.
43697.88.580 Mauriac, François. L'enfant chargé de chaînes. Paris, 1929.
43697.88.590 Mauriac, François. What I believe. N.Y., 1963.
43697.88.600 Mauriac, François. L'adieu à l'adolescence. Paris, 1911.
43697.88.610 Mauriac, François. Fabien. Paris, 1926.
43697.88.620 Mauriac, François. Nouveaux memoires intérieurs. Paris, 1965.
43697.88.630 Mauriac, François. Un adolescent d'autrefois, roman. Paris, 1969.
43697.88.700 Mauriac, François. The lamb. N.Y., 1955.
43697.88.710 Mauriac, François. Vipers' tangle. London, 1933.
43697.88.715 Mauriac, François. Vipers' tangle. N.Y., 1947.
43697.88.718 Mauriac, François. Second thoughts. Cleveland, 1961.
NEDL 43697.88.722 Mauriac, François. Thérèse. N.Y., 1928.
43697.88.724 Mauriac, François. Thérèse; a portrait in four parts. N.Y., 1965.
43697.88.725 Mauriac, François. God and Mammon. London, 1946.
43697.88.726 Mauriac, François. A woman of the Pharisies. London, 1946.
43697.88.730 Mauriac, François. Memoires intérieurs. N.Y., 1961.
43697.88.730.5 Mauriac, François. The inner presence. Indianapolis, 1968.
43697.88.732 Mauriac, François. Destinies. N.Y., 1929.
43697.88.732.5 Mauriac, François. Lines of life. London, 1957.
43697.88.735 Mauriac, François. The unknown sea. N.Y., 1948.
43697.88.740 Mauriac, François. The desert of love. London, 1949.
43697.88.745 Mauriac, François. A kiss for the leper. London, 1950.
43697.88.748 Mauriac, François. Cain, where is your brother? N.Y., 1962.
43697.88.750 Mauriac, François. That which was lost. London, 1951.
43697.88.755 Mauriac, François. The weakling and the enemy. N.Y., 1952.
43697.88.757 Mauriac, François. The Frontenacs. N.Y., 1961.
43697.88.760 Mauriac, François. The little misery. London, 1952.
43697.88.765 Mauriac, François. The knot of vipers. London, 1952.
43697.88.767 Mauriac, François. Five novels. London, 1968[1969]
43697.88.770A Mauriac, François. The loved and the unloved. N.Y., 1952.
43697.88.770B Mauriac, François. The loved and the unloved. N.Y., 1952.
43697.88.775 Mauriac, François. The mask of innocence. N.Y., 1953.
43697.88.780 Mauriac, François. Letters on art and literature. N.Y., 1953.
43697.88.785 Mauriac, François. The river of fire. London, 1954.
43697.88.790 Mauriac, François. Flesh and blood. N.Y., 1955.
43697.88.795 Mauriac, François. Paroles catholiques. Paris, 1954.
43697.88.797 Mauriac, François. Questions of precedence. London, 1958.
43697.88.798 Mauriac, François. The stuff of youth. London, 1960.
43697.88.805 Fillon, Amédie. François Mauriac. Paris, 1936.
43697.88.810 DuBas, C. François Mauriac et la problème du romancier catholjque. Paris, 1933.
43697.88.815 Rideau, Emile. Comment lire François Mauriac. Paris, 1947.
43697.88.817 Palonte, Alain. Mauriac, le roman et la vie. Paris, 1946.
43697.88.819 Pell, Elsie. François Mauriac in search of the infinite. N.Y., 1947.
43697.88.821 Majault, J. Mauriac et l'art du roman. Paris, 1946.
43697.88.825 Hourdin, Georges. Mauriac, romancier chrétien. 2. éd. Photoreproduction. Paris, 1945.
43697.88.827 North, R.L. Le catholicisme dans l'oeuvre de François Mauriac. Paris, 1950.
43697.88.830 Cormeau, Nelly. L'art de François Mauriac. Paris, 1951.
43697.88.832 Robichon, J. François Mauriac. Paris, 1953.

43511 - 43873 Individual authors, etc. - 1900- - Known authors (363 scheme plus 10) - cont.

43697.88.834 Jarrett-Kerr, M. François Mauriac. Cambridge, England, 1954.
43697.88.834.2 Jarrett-Kerr, M. François Mauriac. New Haven, 1954.
43697.88.836 De Bordeaux à Stockholm. Bordeaux, 1953.
43697.88.840 Mauriac, François. De quelques coeurs inquiets. Paris, 1920.
43697.88.842 Landry, Anne G. Represented discourse in the novels of F. Mauriac. Washington, 1953.
43697.88.845 Vandromme, Pol. La politique litteraire de François Mauriac. Paris, 1957.
43697.88.850 Apfelbeck, Senta. François Mauriacs Einstellung zu Sünde. München, 1958.
43697.88.855 Biltrau de Heredia, B. François Mauriac. Madrid, 1959.
43697.88.860 Grall, Xavier. François Mauriac, journaliste. Paris, 1960.
43697.88.865 Czinczoll, J. Die christliche Tendenz in F. Mauriacs Roman "l'agneau". München, 1962.
43697.88.870 Jensen, B. Diktning eller psykologi? Oslo, 1963.
43697.88.875 Laurent, Jacques. Mauriac sous De Gaulle. Paris, 1965.
43697.88.880 Jenkins, Cecil. Mauriac. Edinburgh, 1965.
43697.88.885 Roussel, Bernard. Mauriac. Paris, 1964.
43697.88.890 Goesch, Keith. François Mauriac, essai de bibliographie chronologique, 1908-1960. Paris, 1965.
43697.88.895 Caspary, Anita-Marie. François Mauriac. St. Louis, 1968.
43697.88.900 Chapon, François. François Mauriac, manuscrits. Paris, 1968.
43697.88.905 Flower, John Ernest. Intention and achievement: an essay on the novels of François Mauriac. Oxford, 1969.
43697.88.910 Smith, Maxwell, Austin. François Mauriac. N.Y., 1970.
43697.88.915 Flower, John, Ernest. A critical commentary on Mauriac's Le noeud de vipères. London, 1969.
43697.88.920 Le chrétien Mauriac. Paris, 1971.
43697.88.2100 Maurel, Christian. Pont de l'étoile. Paris, 1950.
43697.88.3041 Mauriac, Claude. Un autre De Gaulle; journal 1944-1954. Paris, 1971.
43697.88.3100 Mauriac, Claude. Le dîner en ville. Paris, 1959.
43697.88.3110 Mauriac, Claude. La marquise sortit. Paris, 1961.
43697.88.3120 Mauriac, Claude. L'agrandissement; roman. Paris, 1963.
43697.88.3130 Mauriac, Claude. L'oubli; roman. Paris, 1966.
43697.88.3150 Mauriac, Claude. Théâtre: La Conversation. Ici, maintenant. Le Cirque. Les Parisiens du dimanche. Le Hun. Paris, 1968.
43697.88.3160 Mauriac, Claude. La conversation. Paris, 1964.
43697.88.3705 Mauriac, Claude. The dinner party. N.Y., 1960.
43697.88.3710 Mauriac, Claude. The marquise went out at five. N.Y., 1962.
43697.88.3715 Mauriac, Claude. All women are fatal. N.Y., 1964.
43697.88.4100 Maurice, Martin. Die Revolution der Reichen. Berlin, 1932.
43697.88.4110 Maurice, Martin. Heureux ceux qui ont faim. Paris, 1931.
43697.88.5100 Matznett, Gabriel. La Caracole, chroniques polémiques, 1863-1968. Paris, 1969.
43697.88.6100 Maurice, Margot. Les routes de la vie; poèmes. Paris, 1959.
43697.89.11 Maurois, André. Oeuvres complètes. Paris, 1951. 16v.
43697.89.12 Maurois, André. Oeuvres. Paris, 1965. 5v.
43697.89.25 Maurois, André. Textes choisis. Paris, 1936.
43697.89.27 Maurois, André. D'Aragon à Montherlant. Paris, 1967.
43697.89.41A Maurois, André. Memoires. N.Y., 1942. 2v.
43697.89.41B Maurois, André. Memoires. N.Y., 1942. 2v.
43697.89.42 Maurois, André. Journal. (États-Unis, 1946). Paris, 1946.
43697.89.45 Maurois, André. Journal d'un tour en Amerique latine. Paris, 1948.
43697.89.47 Maurois, André. Memoires. Paris, 1948-
43697.89.49 Maurois, André. Soixante ans de ma vie littéraire. Périqueux, 1966.
43697.89.61 Maurois, André. Lettres à l'inconnue. Paris, 1953.
43697.89.63 Maurois, André. Lettre ouverte à un jeune homme sur la conduite de la vie. Paris, 1966.
43697.89.100 Maurois, André. Les silences du Colonel Bramble. Paris, 1918.
43697.89.102 Maurois, André. Les silences du Colonel Bramble. Paris, 1920.
43697.89.103 Maurois, André. Le Général Bramble. Paris, 1920.
43697.89.104 Maurois, André. Les silences du Colonel Bramble. Paris, 1921.
43697.89.104.9 Maurois, André. Les silences du Colonel Bramble. Paris, 1926.
43697.89.104.10 Maurois, André. Les silences du Colonel Bramble. Paris, 1926.
43697.89.105 Maurois, André. Bernard Quesnay. Paris, 1926.
43697.89.110 Maurois, André. Dialogues sur le commandement. Paris, 1925.
43697.89.115 Maurois, André. Meïpe; ou La délivrance. Paris, 1926.
43697.89.115.10 Maurois, André. Meïpe; ou La délivrance. 9. éd. Paris, 1926.
43697.89.117 Maurois, André. Meïpe; ou La délivrance. 44. éd. Paris, 1926.
43697.89.120 Maurois, André. Contact. Maestricht, 1928.
43697.89.130 Maurois, André. Climats. 229. éd. Paris, 1928.
43697.89.133 Maurois, André. Climats. Paris, 1928.
43697.89.135 Maurois, André. Climats. Paris, 1958.
43697.89.140A Maurois, André. Fragment d'un journal (aout-septembre 1930) relativisme suite par André Maurois. Paris, 1931.
43697.89.140B Maurois, André. Fragment d'un journal (aout-septembre 1930) relativisme suite par André Maurois. Paris, 1931.
43697.89.145A Maurois, André. Le côté de Chelsea. 14. éd. Paris, 1932.
43697.89.145B Maurois, André. Le côté de Chelsea. 11. éd. Paris, 1932.
43697.89.148 Maurois, André. Le cercle de famille; roman. 174. éd. Paris, 1932.
43697.89.150 Maurois, André. Le cercle de famille; roman. 193. éd. Paris, 1932.
43697.89.151 Maurois, André. Le cercle de famille; roman. Paris, 1933.
43697.89.152 Maurois, André. Le cercle de famille. Paris, 1932.
43697.89.153 Maurois, André. Le cercle de famille. Le livre moderne illustré. Paris, 1939.
43697.89.156 Maurois, André. The family circle. N.Y., 1932.
43697.89.160 Maurois, André. Bernard Quesnay. 31. éd. Paris, 1926.
43697.89.176 Maurois, André. Le livre moderne illustré. Paris, 1936.
43697.89.180 Maurois, André. Le peseur d'âmes. 75. éd. Paris, 1931.
43697.89.190 Maurois, André. Victoria Regina. Paris, 1937.
43697.89.195A Maurois, André. Petite histoire de l'espèce humaine. Paris, 1927.
43697.89.195B Maurois, André. Petite histoire de l'espèce humaine. Paris, 1927.

43511 - 43873 Individual authors, etc. - 1900- - Known authors (363 scheme plus 10) - cont.

43697.89.200 Maurois, André. Mes songes que voici. 46. éd. Paris, 1932.
43697.89.210A Ni ange, ni bête. N.Y., 1932.
43697.89.210B Ni ange, ni bête. N.Y., 1932.
43697.89.220 Maurois, André. La machine à lire les pensées. 46. éd. Paris, 1937.
43697.89.221 Maurois, André. La machine à lire les pensées. N.Y., 1944.
43697.89.230 Maurois, André. Discours de réception à l'Académie française. Paris, 1939.
43697.89.240 Maurois, André. Cinq visages de l'amour. N.Y., 1942.
43697.89.250 Maurois, André. Espoirs et souvenirs. N.Y., 1943.
43697.89.260 Maurois, André. Terre promise, roman. N.Y., 1945.
43697.89.270 Maurois, André. Études américaines. N.Y., 1945.
43697.89.280 Maurois, André. Retour en France. N.Y., 1947.
43697.89.290 Maurois, André. Toujours l'inattendu arrive. Paris, 1946.
43697.89.300 Maurois, André. Eisenhower. Paris, 1945.
43697.89.310 Maurois, André. Franklin. Paris, 1945.
43697.89.320 Maurois, André. Les mondes imaginaires. Paris, 1929.
43697.89.325 Maurois, André. Sept visages de l'amour. 2. éd. Paris, 1947.
43697.89.330A Maurois, André. Les mondes impossibles. Paris, 1947.
43697.89.330B Maurois, André. Les mondes impossibles. Paris, 1947.
43697.89.340 Maurois, André. L'instinct du bonheur. 18. éd. Paris, 1934.
43697.89.350 Maurois, André. Premiers contes. Rouen, 1947.
43697.89.360 Maurois, André. L'Anglaise et d'autres femmes. Paris, 1932.
43697.89.370 Maurois, André. Relativisme. Paris, 1930.
43697.89.380 Maurois, André. La conversation. Paris, 1927.
43697.89.390 Maurois, André. Les anglais. Paris, 1927.
43697.89.400 Maurois, André. Le pays des trente-six mille volontés. Paris, 1928.
43697.89.410 Maurois, André. Les discours du Docteur O'Grady. Paris, 1922.
43697.89.430 Maurois, André. Ce que je crois. Paris, 1951.
43697.89.432 Maurois, André. Ce que je crois. Paris, 1952.
43697.89.440 Maurois, André. A private universe. N.Y., 1932.
43697.89.450 Maurois, André. Captains and kings. N.Y., 1925.
43697.89.460 Maurois, André. Les roses de septembre. Paris, 1956.
43697.89.470 Maurois, André. Dialogues des vivants. Paris, 1959.
43697.89.480 Maurois, André. Portrait d'un ami qui s'appelait moi. Namur, 1959.
43697.89.490 Maurois, André. Pour piano seul. Paris, 1960.
43697.89.500 Maurois, André. L'Amérique inattendue. Paris, 1931.
43697.89.510 Maurois, André. Patapoufs and Filifers. Boston, 1948.
43697.89.520 Maurois, André. Fragments d'un journal de vacances. Paris, 1929.
43697.89.540 Maurois, André. De La Bruyère à Proust. Paris, 1964.
43697.89.550 Maurois, André. Arabesques. Paris, 1925.
43697.89.560 Maurois, André. Les bourgeois de Witzheim. Paris, 1920.
43697.89.570 Maurois, André. Nouvelles directions de la littérature française. Oxford, 1967.
43697.89.580 Maurois, André. Les illusions. Paris, 1968.
43697.89.641 Maurois, André. Memoirs, 1885-1967. London, 1970.
43697.89.705A Maurois, André. Mape; the world of illusion. N.Y., 1926.
43697.89.705B Maurois, André. Mape; the world of illusion. N.Y., 1926.
43697.89.707 Maurois, André. Robert et Elizabeth Browning. Paris, 1955.
43697.89.709 Maurois, André. Illusions. N.Y., 1968.
43697.89.710 Maurois, André. General Bramble. N.Y., 1922.
43697.89.712 Maurois, André. The weigher of souls. N.Y., 1931.
43697.89.713 Maurois, André. The weigher of souls. N.Y., 1963.
43697.89.715 Maurois, André. The silence of Colonel Bramble. N.Y., 1941.
43697.89.718 Maurois, André. Seven faces of Love. N.Y., 1944.
43697.89.720 Maurois, André. A time for silence. N.Y., 1942.
43697.89.722 Maurois, André. I remember, I remember. N.Y., 1942.
43697.89.723 Maurois, André. Call no man happy. London, 1943.
43697.89.725 Maurois, André. The Chelsea way or, Marcel in England: A proustian parody. London, 1966.
43697.89.727A Maurois, André. From my journal. 1st ed. N.Y., 1948.
43697.89.727B Maurois, André. From my journal. 1st ed. N.Y., 1948.
43697.89.730A Maurois, André. Toujours l'inattendu arrive. N.Y., 1943.
43697.89.730B Maurois, André. Toujours l'inattendu arrive. N.Y., 1943.
43697.89.730C Maurois, André. Toujours l'inattendu arrive. N.Y., 1943.
43697.89.735 Maurois, André. The return of doctor O'Grady. London, 1951.
43697.89.742 Maurois, André. Bernard Quesnay. N.Y., 1927.
43697.89.743 Maurois, André. Bernard Quesnay. Paris, 1928.
43697.89.750 Maurois, André. The family circle. London, 1932.
43697.89.755 Maurois, André. The art of writing. London, 1960.
43697.89.762A Maurois, André. Atmosphere of love. N.Y., 1929.
43697.89.762B Maurois, André. Atmosphere of love. N.Y., 1929.
43697.89.765 Maurois, André. Ricochets. N.Y., 1935.
43697.89.772 Maurois, André. Conversation. N.Y., 1930.
43697.89.775 Maurois, André. Woman without love. 1. éd. N.Y., 1945.
43697.89.780 Maurois, André. A voyage to the island of the Articoles. N.Y., 1929.
43697.89.785 Maurois, André. My Latin-American diary. London, 1953.
43697.89.790 Maurois, André. The next chapter. 1. éd. N.Y., 1928.
43697.89.793 Maurois, André. The collected stories of André Maurois. N.Y., 1967.
43697.89.795 Maurois, André. To an unknown lady. 1. éd. N.Y., 1957.
43697.89.796 Maurois, André. September roses. London, 1958.
43697.89.805 Larg, David G. André Maurois. London, 1931.
43697.89.810 Roya, Maurice. André Maurois. Paris, 1934.
43697.89.815 Fillon, A.F. André Maurois. Paris, 1937.
43697.89.820 Bakeless, John. André Maurois. N.Y., 193-.
43697.89.830 Lemâitre, George Édouard. André Maurois. Stanford, 1939.
43697.89.831 Lemâitre, George Édouard. Maurois, the writer and his work. N.Y., 1968.
43697.89.840 Auriant (pseud.). Un écrivain original. Paris, 1941.
43697.89.845 Guiry, S. La pensée d'André Maurois. Paris, 1951.
43697.89.850 Droit, Michel. André Maurois. Paris, 1953.
43697.89.855 Adelhaefer, Inge. Die Interpretation englischen und amerikanischen Geistes in André Maurois' Werk. Berlin? 1961.
43697.89.860 Académie Bordeaux. Réception de M. André Maurois de l'Académie française à l'Académie nationale des sciences, belles lettres et arts de Bordeaux, 18 mai 1953. Bordeaux, 1954.
43697.89.865 Suffel, J. André Maurois. Paris, 1963.
43697.89.870 Keating, Louis Clark. André Maurois. N.Y., 1969.

Classified Listing

43511 - 43873 Individual authors, etc. - 1900- - Known authors (363 scheme plus 10) - cont.

43697.89.875 Arland, Marcel. Discours de réception de Marcel Arland à l'Académie française et réponse de Jean Mistler. Paris, 1969.
43697.89.1000 Mauron, Marie. Le quartier Mortisson. 1. éd. Paris, 1938.
43697.89.1110F Mauron, Marie. Féerie des bois. Genève, 1966.
43697.89.2100 Maurienne (pseud.). Le deserteur. Paris, 1960.
43697.89.2800 Editions de minuit provocation à la desobéissance. Paris, 1960.
43697.89.3100 Maulvault, Lucien. El requête. Paris, 1937.
43697.89.3110 Maulvault, Lucien. Les saintes colères. Paris, 1945.
43697.89.4100 Maurois, Michelle. Les arapèdes. Paris, 1957.
43697.89.4110 Maurois, Michelle. The sweetbread. N.Y., 1959.
43697.89.4120 Maurois, Michelle. L'oeil neuf. Paris, 1963.
43697.89.5100 Mauroc, Daniel. Les jardins suffisent. Paris, 1958.
43697.89.6100 Mauduit, Hyacinthe. L'héritier du ciel. Paris, 1959.
43697.89.7100 Mauget, I. Avec les gloires de mon temps. La Celle-Saint-Cloud, 1963.
43697.89.8100 Maurel, Gérard. La route ardente. Paris, 1924.
43697.89.9100 Maurey, Max. Asile de nuit. Paris, 1905.
43697.90.100 Mavel, Jean. De lys et d'ivoire. Rodez, 1957.
43697.97.700 Maximoff, Mateo. The Ursitory. London, 1949.
43697.97.1100 Maxime, Jean. La fête encercleé. Paris, 1970.
43697.98.35 Mayran, Camille (pseud.). Histoire de Gotton Connixloo. 10. éd. Paris, 1919.
43697.98.40 Mayran, Camille (pseud.). L'épreuve du fils. Paris, 1920.
43697.98.50 Mayran, Camille (pseud.). Larmes et lumière à Oradour. Paris, 1952.
43697.98.55 Mayran, Camille (pseud.). Hiver. Paris, 1926.
43697.98.702 Mayran, Camille (pseud.). The story of Gotton Connixloo. N.Y., 1920.
43697.98.1100 Mayeur, Pierre Xavier. La forêt du symbole, poèmes. Paris, 1969.
43697.98.3100 May, Janine. La jeune fille au masque; roman. Paris, 1932.
43697.98.4100 Mazéas, Gaulven. Kosmanomothéos. Paris, 1946.
43697.99.100 Mazade, Fernand. Les poèmes de Sainte-Marthe. Paris, 1926.
43697.99.110 Mazade, Fernand. De sable et d'or; poèmes. Paris, 1921.
43697.99.120 Mazade, Fernand. Féerie. Uzès, 1931.
43697.99.130 Mazade, Fernand. La rose. Paris, 1945.
43697.99.2100 Mazaud, Émile. La folle journée; comédie en un acte. Paris, 1920.
43697.100 Mazeline, Guy. Le panier flottant; roman. 10. éd. Paris, 1938.
43697.100.20 Mazeline, Guy. Le roman des Jobourg. Paris, 1950-5v.
43697.100.110 Mazeline, Guy. L'amour soi-même; roman. 40. éd. Paris, 1939.
43697.100.120 Mazeline, Guy. Les coups. Paris, 1932.
43697.100.135 Mazeline, Guy. Bêtafeu, roman. 13. éd. Paris, 1937.
43697.100.148 Mazeline, Guy. Le souffle de l'été. Paris, 1946.
43697.100.150 Mazeline, Guy. Les îles du matin. Paris, 1936.
43697.100.700 Mazeline, Guy. The wolves. N.Y., 1934.
43698.1.30 Mendès, Jane C. La ville Merveilleuse, Rio de Janeiro, poèmes. Paris, 191-.
43698.2.30 Meyer, Robert. Quelques mots...avant le spectacle. Paris, n.d.
43698.16.100 Medda, François. Le Molengui, roman. Paris, 1967.
43698.25.100 Meersch, M. van der. L'élu, roman. Paris, 1937.
43698.25.110 Meersch, M. van der. Quand les sirènes se Tausint. Paris, 1933.
43698.25.120 Meersch, M. van der. Pêcheurs d'hommes. Paris, 1940.
43698.25.130 Meersch, M. van der. L'empreinte du Dieu. Paris, 1936.
43698.25.135 Meersch, M. van der. Invasion 14; roman. Paris, 1935.
43698.25.140 Meersch, M. van der. Le coeur pur. Paris, 1948.
43698.25.150 Meersch, M. van der. La maison dans la dune. Paris, 1932.
43698.25.160 Meersch, M. van der. Corps et ames. Paris, 1951.
43698.25.170 Meersch, M. van der. Masque de chair. Paris, 1958.
43698.25.180 Meersch, M. van der. La compagne. Paris, 1957.
43698.25.705 Meersch, M. van der. When the looms are silent. N.Y., 1934.
43698.25.712 Meersch, M. van der. Invasion. N.Y., 1937.
43698.25.715 Meersch, M. van der. Bodies and souls. N.Y., 1948.
43698.25.720 Meersch, M. van der. The poor girl. London, 1949.
43698.25.725 Meersch, M. van der. The bellringer's wife. London, 1951.
43698.25.730 Meersch, M. van der. The dynamite factory. London, 1953.
43698.25.735 Meersch, M. van der. Mash of flesh. London, 1960.
43698.25.775 Meersch, M. van der. Drama um Direktor Bramburger. Luzern, 1949.
43698.25.800 Jans, Adrien. A la rencontre de Maxence van der Meersch. n.p., 1946.
43698.25.810 Reus, Robert. Portrait morpho-psychologique de Maxence van der Meersch. Aurillac, 1952.
43698.25.820 Bordes, Elis. Le drame spirituel dans l'oeuvre de Maxence van der Meersch. 3. éd. Tourcoing, 1944.
43698.25.1100 Mex, Alphonse. L'idéal humain...et autres poèmes. Rodez, 1958.
43698.35.100 Mégret, C. Les anthropophages. 7. ed. Paris, 1937.
43698.35.110 Mégret, C. Les fausses compagnies. Paris, 1939.
43698.35.120 Mégret, C. L'absent. Paris, 1946.
43698.35.130 Mégret, C. Le carrefour des solitudes. Paris, 1957.
43698.41.100 Meiss, H. Choses d'Alsace. Nice, 1920.
43698.41.1100 Meillant, Henry. Poèmes à vivre. Toul, 1961.
43698.51.100 Melon, Joseph. L'archange remember. Paris, 1929.
43698.52.21 Mélot du Dy, Robert. Trois recits. Bruxelles, 1960.
43698.52.100 Mélot du Dy, Robert. A l'amie dormante. Paris, 1931.
43698.52.110 Mélot du Dy, Robert. Choix de poésies, 1919-1956. Paris, 1960.
43698.53.100 Membré, Henri. Petit-Bourgeois. Monaco, 1945.
43698.55.100 Memmi, Albert. The pillar of salt. N.Y., 1955.
43698.55.110 Memmi, Albert. Agar. Paris, 1955.
43698.55.120 Memmi, Albert. La statue de sel. Paris, 1966.
43698.55.130 Memmi, Albert. Le scorpion; ou, La confession imaginaire. Paris, 1969.
43698.58.100 Mendiri, Jacques de. Pensées pour l'actuel. Paris, 1957.
43698.58.3100 Menanteau, Pierre. Bestiaire pour un infant poète. Paris, 1958.
43698.58.3110 Menanteau, Pierre. De chair et de feuilles, poèmes. Paris, 1966.
43698.58.3120 Menanteau, Pierre. L'arbre et la maison. Preuilly-sur-Claise, 1939.
43698.58.4100 Ménard, René. Hymnes à la présence solitaire. Paris, 1950.
43698.58.4110 Ménard, René. L'arbre et l'horizon. Paris, 1949.
43698.58.4120 Ménard, René. La terre tourne. Paris, 1952.
43698.58.5100 Ménard, J. Les myrtes. Montréal, 1963.

43511 - 43873 Individual authors, etc. - 1900- - Known authors (363 scheme plus 10) - cont.

43698.58.5110 Ménard, J. Plages. Beauchemin, 1962.
43698.60.100 Ménez, F. L'envoûté. Paris, 1923.
43698.61.100 Ménot, Alfred. Charmes du souvenir. Paris, 1931.
43698.62.100 Menuau, Georges. Choc en retour. Paris, 1935.
43698.74.100 Mercier, Louis. Lazare le ressucité suivi de Ponce Pilate. Paris, 1924.
43698.74.110 Mercier, Louis. Les cinq mystères joyeux. Saint-Félicien, 1924.
43698.74.112 Mercier, Louis. Verginis corona. 2. éd. Paris, 1928.
43698.74.800 Rambach, Elisabeth. Die Mariendichtungen von Louis Mercier. Münster, 1959.
43698.74.1100 Mer, Jacques. Poème pour la mort de Federico Garcia Lorca. Saint-Front-sur-Lémance, 1969.
43698.74.2100 Mercier, Max. Conscience. Paris, 1935.
43698.74.3100 Mercier, André Charles. Le coeur et les sens. Paris, 1928.
43698.74.4100 Mercatrix. Poèmes gaulois. Paris, 1966.
43698.75.100F Méré, Charles. La flamme. Paris, 1922.
43698.75.102 Méré, Charles. Le vertige. Paris, 1923.
43698.75.110 Méré, Charles. Le prince Jean; pièce en 4 actes. Paris, 1924.
43698.75.120 Méré, Charles. Les conquérants. Paris, 1920.
43698.75.130 Méré, Charles. La danse de minuit. Paris, 1924.
43698.75.140 Méré, Charles. La tentation. Paris, 1925.
43698.75.150 Méré, Charles. Le lit nuptial. Paris, 1926.
43698.75.160 Méré, Charles. Berlioz. Paris, 1927.
43698.75.170 Méré, Charles. Le carnaval de l'amour. Paris, 1928.
43698.75.180 Méré, Charles. Par la farce. Paris, 1925.
43698.75.190 Méré, Charles. Un homme du nord. Paris, 1933.
43698.75.2105 Merglen, Albert. Mission spéciale en France. 3. éd. Grenoble, 1945.
43698.75.3105 Merglen, Albert. Groupe franc. 5. éd. Paris, 1943.
43698.75.7100 Merle, Robert. Flamines. 2. éd. Paris, 1950.
43698.75.7110 Merle, Robert. La mort est mon métier. Paris, 1953.
43698.75.7120 Merle, Robert. L'ile. Paris, 1962.
43698.75.7130 Merle, Robert. Un animal doué de raison. Paris, 1967.
43698.75.7700 Merle, Robert. Death is my trade. London, 1954.
43698.75.7710 Merle, Robert. The day of the dolphin, a novel. N.Y., 1969.
43698.75.8100 Mérens, Louis. Les français, fous, fous, fous. Paris, 1965.
43698.76.100A Merrill, Stuart. Prose et vers; oeuvres posthumes. Paris, 1925.
43698.76.100B Merrill, Stuart. Prose et vers; oeuvres posthumes. Paris, 1925.
43698.76.110 Merrill, Stuart. Petits poèmes d'automne. Paris, 1895.
Htn 43698.76.120* Merrill, Stuart. Les fastes. Paris, 1891.
43698.76.130 Merrill, Stuart. Une voix dans la foule. Paris, 1909.
43698.76.140 Merrill, Stuart. Poèmes, 1887-1897. Paris, 1897.
43698.77.100 Mertens, Pierre. L'Inde ou l'Amérique. Paris, 1969.
43698.78.100 Mery, Andrée. Weekend. Adaptée de l'anglais. Paris, 1928.
43698.78.110 Mery, Andrée. Cinq à sept. Paris, 1933.
43698.78.120 Mery, Andrée. Les jeux sont faits. Paris, 1934.
43698.78.805 Henry, M.L. La contribution d'un Américain au symbolisme français. Paris, 1927.
43698.78.1100 Merville, Patrik. L'ennui. Paris, 1958.
43698.78.2100 Merys, J.A. Solitude. Paris, 1904.
43698.80.21 Mesers, Edward L.J. Poèmes, 1923-1958. Paris, 1959.
43698.82.100 Messiaen, Alain. Cortège d'Euxerge. v.4-5. Paris, 1961-
43698.82.1100 Mestre, Philippe. Quand flambait le bocage. Paris, 1970.
43698.83.100 Mestrallet, Jean Marie. Rythmes épars. Paris, 1930.
43698.83.2100 Mestre, Jean B. Jehanne chez ses bons amis de Compiègne. Compiègne, 1945.
43698.86.100 Métirrer, Pierre. Réalité; poèmes vivants. Paris, 1957.
43698.89.100 Meunier, Lucien. De sable et d'azur. Paris, 1970.
43698.90.100 Mevel, Jean. Existence. Bordeaux, 1959.
43698.98.700 Meynier, Yvonne. The school with a difference. London, 1965.
43698.200.19 Michaux, Henri. Henri Michaux, un étude. Paris, 1946.
43698.200.21 Michaux, Henri. Henri Michaux. Paris, 1948.
43698.200.105 Michaux, Henri. La nuit remue. 2. éd. Paris, 1935.
43698.200.110 Michaux, Henri. Nous deux encore, 1948. Paris, 1948.
43698.200.115 Michaux, Henri. Épreuves. Paris, 1945.
43698.200.120 Michaux, Henri. Au pays de la magie. London, 1946.
43698.200.125 Michaux, Henri. Ailleurs. Paris, 1948.
43698.200.130 Michaux, Henri. L'espace du dedans. Paris, 1944.
43698.200.130.5 Michaux, Henri. L'espace du dedans, pages choisies, 1927-1959. Paris, 1966.
43698.200.135 Michaux, Henri. Un barbare en Asie. 9. éd. Paris, 1945.
43698.200.140 Michaux, Henri. Voyage en Grande Garabagne. Paris, 1936.
43698.200.150 Michaux, Henri. Passages, 1937-1950. Paris, 1950.
43698.200.152 Michaux, Henri. Passages, 1937-1963. Paris, 1963.
43698.200.160 Michaux, Henri. La vie dans les plis. 4. ed. Paris, 1949.
43698.200.162 Michaux, Henri. La vie dans les plis, poèmes. Paris, 1965.
43698.200.170 Michaux, Henri. Nouvelles de l'étranger. Paris, 1952.
43698.200.180 Michaux, Henri. Face aux verrous. Paris, 1954.
43698.200.190 Michaux, Henri. Misérable miracle. Monaco, 1956.
43698.200.200F Michaux, Henri. Mouvements. Paris, 1951.
43698.200.210 Michaux, Henri. L'infini turbulent. Paris, 1957.
43698.200.211 Michaux, Henri. L'infini turbulent. Paris, 1964.
43698.200.220 Michaux, Henri. Vents et poussières, 1955-1962. Paris, 1962.
43698.200.230 Michaux, Henri. Wind und Staub. Olten, 1965.
43698.200.240 Michaux, Henri. Les grandes épreuves de l'esprit et les innombrables petites. Paris, 1966.
43698.200.250 Michaux, Henri. Paix dans les brisements. Paris, 1959.
43698.200.260 Michaux, Henri. La nuit remue. Paris, 1967.
43698.200.270 Michaux, Henri. Poteaux d'angle. Paris, 1971.
43698.200.700 Michaux, Henri. A barbarian in Asia. N.Y., 1949.
43698.200.710A Michaux, Henri. Selected writings. N.Y., 1950.
43698.200.710B Michaux, Henri. Selected writings. N.Y., 1950.
43698.200.711 Michaux, Henri. Selected writings; the space within. N.Y., 1968?
43698.200.720 Michaux, Henri. Light through darkness. N.Y., 1963.
43698.200.725 Michaux, Henri. Michaux (poems). Santa Barbara, 1967.
43698.200.800 Gide, Andre P.G. Decouvrons Henri Michaux. Gallimard, 1941.
43698.200.805 Brechou, Robert. Michaux. 8. éd. Paris, 1959.
43698.200.810 Caulon, P. de. Henri Michaux. Neuchâtel, 1949.
43698.200.815 Badoux, L. La pensée de Henri Michaux. Zürich, 1963.
43698.200.820 Bellour, Raymond. Henri Michaux. Paris, 1965.
43698.200.825 Michaux, Henri. Dichtungen, Schriften. Frankfurt, 1966.
43698.200.830 Engler, Winfried. Henri Michaux; das Michaux Bild, 1922-1959. Inaug. Diss. Tübingen, 1964.
43698.200.835 Murat, Napoléon. Henri Michaux. Paris, 1967.

Classified Listing

43511 - 43873 Individual authors, etc. - 1900- - Known authors (363 scheme plus 10) - cont.

43698.200.840 Michaux, Henri. Plume, précédé de Lointain intérieur. Paris, 1967.
43698.200.845 Place, Georges. Henri Michaux. Paris, 1969.
43698.203.100 Michelet, M. Marraine de guerre. N.Y., 1922.
43698.205.100 Michelin, M. Les riches heures. N.Y., 1944.
43699.1.30 Millet, P. Jenny s'en va-t-en-querre. Paris, 1913.
43699.2.30 Mitchell, Georges. La maison: pièce en trois actes. Paris, 1901.
43699.3.29 Mille, Pierre. Louise et Barnavaux. Paris, 1912.
43699.3.30 Mille, Pierre. Barnavaux et quelques femmes. 8. éd. Paris, 1908.
43699.3.31 Mille, Pierre. Caillon et Tili. 9. éd. Paris, 1914.
43699.3.32 Mille, Pierre. Le monarque. 8. éd. Paris, 1914.
43699.3.33 Mille, Pierre. Sous leur dictée. 5. éd. Paris, 1916.
43699.3.34 Mille, Pierre. Sur la vaste terre. 6. éd. Paris, 1912.
43699.3.35 Mille, Pierre. Histoires exotiques et merveilleuses. Paris, 1920.
43699.3.40 Mille, Pierre. Memoires d'un dada besogneux. 7. éd. Paris, 1921.
43699.3.42 Mille, Pierre. Myrrhine, courtisane et martyre. Paris, 1922.
43699.3.45 Mille, Pierre. En croupe de Bellone. Paris, 1916.
43699.3.48 Mille, Pierre. Trois femmes. Paris, 1920.
43699.3.58 Mille, Pierre. L'illustre partonneau. Paris, 1924.
43699.3.70 Mille, Pierre. Les aventuriers. 9. éd. Paris, 1937.
43699.3.705 Mille, Pierre. Barnavaux. London, 1915.
43699.3.710 Mille, Pierre. Barnavaux et quelques femmes. Paris, 1946.
43699.3.715 Mille, Pierre. Louise and Barnavaux. London, 1916.
43699.3.725 Mille, Pierre. Under the tricolour. London, 1915.
43699.3.735 Mille, Pierre. Two little Parisians. London, 1913.
43699.3.745 Mille, Pierre. Joffre chaps and some others. London, 1915.
43699.3.805 Brendel, Hans. Pierre Mille und die koloniale Frage in Frankreich. Inaug. Diss. Jena, 1935.
43699.4.100 Miatlev, Adrian. Le sacrament du divorce. Paris, 1960.
43699.12.100 Michel, André. Le clavecin mal tempéré suivi de la jungle du livre. Montpellier, 1929.
43699.12.110 Michel, André. Amants bissextils, suivi de soupir au demeurant des pauses. Montpellier, 1953.
43699.12.1100 Michelet, Claude. La Grande muraille, roman. Paris, 1969.
43699.12.1110 Michelet, Claude. Une fois sept. Paris, 1970.
43699.12.2100 Michel, Simonne. Poèmes. Paris, 1950.
43699.13.100 Michel, Georges. Les timides aventures d'un laveur de carreaux. Paris, 1966.
43699.13.110 Michel, Georges. La promenade du dimanche. Paris, 1967.
43699.13.120 Michel, Georges. Les brevos. Paris, 1968.
43699.13.130 Michel, Georges. L'agression. Paris, 1968.
43699.35.100 Miquet, Jacques. Vibrante jeunesse; poèmes. Paris, 1960.
43699.49.100 Millet, Marcel. Cote coeur; prix des poètes, 1929. Paris, 1929.
43699.50.21 Millien, Achille. Anthologie du poète nivernais. Fortin, 1924.
43699.51.11 Les amis de Milosz. Cahiers. Paris. 1,1967+ 4v.
43699.51.13 Milosz, Oscar Vladislas. Oeuvres complètes. v.1-5, 8. Fribourg, 1944-1946. 5v.
43699.51.17 Milosz, Oscar Vladislas. Oeuvres complètes. v.3-5. Paris, 1946- 3v.
43699.51.19 Milosz, Oscar Vladislas. L'amoureuse initiation. v.1-2,5,7,9-11. Paris, 1958- 7v.
43699.51.24 Milosz, Oscar Vladislas. Wybór poezji. Poznań, 1919.
43699.51.25 Milosz, Oscar Vladislas. Poèmes. Paris, 1956.
43699.51.30 Milosz, Oscar Vladislas. Milosz. Choix de textes présenté par Jacques Buge. Paris, 1965.
43699.51.61 Milosz, Oscar Vladislas. Textes inédits de O.V. de L. Milosz. Paris, 1959.
43699.51.63 Milosz, Oscar Vladislas. Soixante-quinze lettres inédites et sept documents originaux. Paris, 1969.
43699.51.100 Milosz, Oscar Vladislas. Ars magna. Paris, 1924.
43699.51.110 Milosz, Oscar Vladislas. Dix-sept poèmes de Milosz. Tunis, 1937.
43699.51.120 Milosz, Oscar Vladislas. La clef de l'apocalypse. Paris, 1938.
43699.51.800 Godoy, Armand. Milosz. Fribourg, 1944.
43699.51.802 Godoy, Armand. Milosz. Paris, 1960.
43699.51.805 Zidonis, G.I. Oscar Vladislas de L. Milosz. Paris, 1951.
43699.51.810 Lebois, A. L'oeuvre de Milosz. Paris, 1960.
43699.51.815 Buge, J. Milosz en quête du divin. Paris, 1963.
43699.51.820 Richter, Anne. Milosz. Paris, 1965.
43699.51.1100 Milon-Capitan, Jeanne. Si je suis, si je fus. Paris, 1963.
43699.61.100 Minne, Jules. Sève bantoue. Bruxelles, 1952.
43699.65.100 Miomandre, Francis de. La jeune fille au jardin. Paris, 1924.
43699.65.105 Miomandre, Francis de. La saison des dupes. Paris, 1917.
43699.65.110 Miomandre, Francis de. Voyages d'un sedentaire. Paris, 1918.
43699.65.115 Miomandre, Francis de. Caprices, nouvelles. Paris, 1960.
43699.65.120 Miomandre, Francis de. La vie amoureuse de Vénus, déesse de l'amour. Paris, 1929.
43699.65.130 Miomandre, Francis de. Ces petits messieurs. 7. éd. Paris, 1922.
43699.65.140 Miomandre, Francis de. Écrit sur l'eau. Paris, 1923.
43699.65.145 Miomandre, Francis de. Écrit sur de l'eau. Paris, 1937.
43699.65.150 Miomandre, Francis de. Le fil d'Ariane. Avignon, 1941.
43699.65.160 Miomandre, Francis de. Olympe et ses amis; roman. Paris, 1937.
43699.65.170 Miomandre, Francis de. La naufragée; roman. Paris, 1928.
43699.65.180A Miomandre, Francis de. Oriental l'aventure de Therese Beauchamps. N.Y., 1929.
43699.65.180B Miomandre, Francis de. Oriental l'aventure de Therese Beauchamps. N.Y., 1929.
43699.65.190 Miomandre, Francis de. Rencontres dans la nuit. Bienne, 1954.
43699.65.200 Miomandre, Francis de. Contes des cloches de cristal. Paris, 1925.
43699.65.210 Miomandre, Francis de. La cabane d'amour. Paris, 1919.
43699.65.220 Miomandre, Francis de. Les taupes. Paris, 1922.
43699.65.230 Miomandre, Francis de. Le jeune homme des palaces. Paris, 1929.
43699.73.100 Miguel, P. Le philatéliste. Toulouse, 1920.
43699.74.100 Mirat, Paul. Le chanson des épées. Paris, 1917.
43699.75.100 Miracle, Anne. Poèmes et leurs dessina. Paris, 1951.
43699.75.1100 Mirande, Raymond. L'apparence et le feu. Bordeaux, 1961.
43699.76.100 Mitaud, J. Hate de vivre. Paris, 1949.
43699.77.100 Miroir, Jean. Pas d'amour pour elle. Paris, 1958.
43699.82.100 Mistler, Jean. La maison du Docteur Clifton. Paris, 1932.

43511 - 43873 Individual authors, etc. - 1900- - Known authors (363 scheme plus 10) - cont.

43699.82.800 Académie française. Académie...Paris. Discours de réception à l'Académie française par Jean Mistler. Paris, 1967.
43699.87.100 Mittet, Émile. Joies et rancoeurs. Paris, 1957.
43699.87.110 Mittet, Émile. Faisceau tournant. Paris, 1958.
43699.98.100 Mizrahi, Rachel. Harry. Paris, 1969.
43701.1.30 Molaine, Pierre. Les orgues de l'enfer. Paris, 1950.
43701.1.30.5 Molaine, Pierre. Strange laughter. N.Y., 1953.
43701.1.35 Molaine, Pierre. Satan. Paris, 1955.
43701.1.40 Molaine, Pierre. Le sang. Paris, 1967.
43701.2.30 Mounet-Sully, J. La vieillesse de Don Juan. Paris, 1906.
43701.2.32PF Mounet-Sully, J. The modern cupid. Boston, 1945.
43701.2.80 Mounet-Sully, J. Souvenirs d'un tragédien. Paris, 1917.
43701.2.82 Cocteau, Jean. Portrait de Mounet-Sully. Paris, 1945.
43701.3.30 Morel, J. Feuilles mortes. Paris, n.d.
43701.4.30 Morice, Charles. Il est ressuscité! 3e éd. Paris, 1911.
43701.4.37 Morice, Charles. The re-appearing. N.Y., 1911.
43701.4.80 Delsemme, Paul. Un théoricien du symbolisme, Charles Morice. Paris, 1958.
43701.5.30 Monnerot Dumaine, M. Le baronne d'Armilly. Paris, 1905.
43701.6.35 Monnerot, Jules. On meurt les yeux ouverts. 8. éd. Paris, 1945.
43701.18.100 Modiano, Patrick. La place de l'étoilé. Paris, 1968.
43701.33.100 Mogin, Georges. La langue verte. Paris, 1954.
43701.33.1100 Mogin, Jean. A chacun selon sa faim. Bruxelles, 1970.
43701.39.100 Mohrt, Michel. Le serviteur fidèle. Paris, 1953.
43701.39.110 Mohrt, Michel. Mon royaume pour un cheval. Paris, 1949.
43701.39.120 Mohrt, Michel. La prison maritime. Paris, 1962.
43701.39.130 Mohrt, Michel. Un jeu d'enfer. Paris, 1970.
43701.39.140 Mohrt, Michel. La campagne d'Italie. Paris, 1965.
43701.39.150 Mohrt, Michel. L'ours des Adirondacks. Paris, 1969.
43701.41.700 Moinot, Pierre. The royal hunt. N.Y., 1955.
43701.41.705 Moinot, Pierre. An ancient enemy. Garden City, 1965.
43701.41.1100 Moirant, René. Parure de pauvre homme. n.p., 1953.
43701.41.2104 Moitier, Suzanne. Le dragon du lac. 4. éd. Paris, 1957.
43701.41.3100 Moinet, Bernard. Opium rouge. Paris, 1965?
43701.48.100 Moll-Collet, Simone. Cris et silences. Paris, 1969.
43701.50.100 Molinard, Barbara. Viens, nouvelles, précédées d'une preface de Marguerite Duras et suivies d'un récit improvisé. Paris, 1969.
43701.58.100 Monod, S. Pastiches. Paris, 1963.
43701.58.1100 Moncelet, Christien. Après le feu. Jarnac, 1964.
43701.59.100 Monfreid, Henri de. Le roi des abeilles. 23. éd. Paris, 1937.
43701.59.110 Monfreid, Henri de. Le serpent rouge. Paris, 1953.
43701.59.120 Monfreid, Henri de. Wahauga. Paris, 1955.
43701.59.130 Monfreid, Henri de. Pilleurs d'épaves. Paris, 1955.
43701.59.140 Monfreid, Henri de. L'envers de l'aventure. Paris, 1960.
43701.59.150 Monfreid, Henri de. Abdi. Paris, 1937.
43701.59.160 Monfreid, Henri de. Les lionnes d'or d'Ethiopie. Paris, 1967.
43701.59.170 Monfreid, Henri de. Abdi, enfant sauvage. Paris, 1968.
43701.59.800 Poisson, Georges M. Henry de Monfreid, le passionné de l'aventure. Paris, 1966.
43701.59.1100 Monestier, Marianne. Kanaïok. Paris, 1957.
43701.59.2100 Monési, Irène. Une tragédie superflue, roman. Paris, 1968.
43701.60.100 Monnier, Mathilde. Dispersion, poèmes. N.Y., 1942.
43701.60.110 Monnier, Mathilde. Instants. Lausanne, 1957.
43701.60.1100 Monnier, Philippe. Mon village. Lausanne, 1968.
43701.60.2021 Monnier, Adrienne. Dernières gazettes et écrits divers. Paris, 1961.
43701.60.2100 Monnier, Adrienne. Les gazettes d'Adrienne Monnier. Paris, 1953.
43701.60.2110 Monnier, Adrienne. Rue de l'Odéon. Paris, 1960.
43701.60.2115 Monnier, Adrienne. Fableaux. Paris, 1960.
43701.60.2120 Monnier, Adrienne. Souvenirs du Londres. Paris, 1957.
43701.60.2130 Monnier, Adrienne. Les poesies. Paris, 1962.
43701.60.3100 Monnier, Jean Pierre. Les algues du fond. Paris, 1960.
43701.60.4100 Monieux, Marie. Le voyageur de janvier. Bruxelles, 1962.
43701.61.100 Monnier, Thyde. Le pain des pauvres; roman. Paris, 1938.
43701.61.110 Monnier, Thyde. J'ai joué le jeu. Paris, 1963.
43701.61.120 Monnier, Thyde. Les Desmichels. Paris, 1945-57. 7v.
43701.61.1100 Montier, Edward. Les mois. n.p., 19- ?
43701.61.2100 Montupet, Janiere. La rose amère. Paris, 1965.
43701.61.3100 Montargis, Jean. De tout et de rien. Paris, 1959.
43701.61.3110 Montargis, Jean. Voyage autour de mon ombre. Paris, 1960.
43701.61.3120 Montargis, Jean. Nous deux. Paris, 1961.
43701.62.100 Montfort, Eugène. La belle-enfant. Paris, 1915?
43701.62.115 Montfort, Eugène. L'oubli des morts, roman. 9. éd. Paris, 1923.
43701.62.120 Montfort, Eugène. Un coeur vierge, roman. Paris, 1920.
43701.62.130 Montfort, Eugène. Ceasar Casteldor. Paris, 1927.
43701.62.140 Montfort, Eugène. La maîtresse américaine. Paris, 1925.
43701.62.150 Montfort, Eugène. Sylvie, ou Les émois passiones. Paris, 1896.
43701.62.160 Montfort, Eugène. Choix de proses. Paris, 1932.
43701.62.170 Montfort, Eugène. La soirée perdue. Abbeville, 1921.
43701.62.2041 Montguerre, Jean-Marc. Journées, 1954-1955. Paris, 1955.
43701.63.10 Montherlant, Henry de. Le théâtre complet. v.1-6. Neuchâtel, 1950-51. 3v.
43701.63.22 Montherlant, Henry de. Théâtre. Paris? 1955.
43701.63.41A Montherlant, Henry de. Montherlant par lui-même. Paris, 1953.
43701.63.41B Montherlant, Henry de. Montherlant par lui-même. Paris, 1953.
43701.63.50 Montherlant, Henry de. Selected essays. London, 1960.
43701.63.100 Montherlant, Henry de. Les bestiaires. Paris, 1929.
43701.63.103 Montherlant, Henry de. Les bestiaires. Monaco, 1947.
43701.63.110 Montherlant, Henry de. Le songe. Paris, 1929.
43701.63.120 Montherlant, Henry de. Les jeunes filles, roman. Paris, 1936.
43701.63.120.5 Montherlant, Henry de. Les jeunes filles, roman. 3e éd. Paris, 1936.
43701.63.120.10 Montherlant, Henry de. Les jeunes filles, roman. 39e éd. Paris, 1936.
43701.63.120.15 Montherlant, Henry de. Les jeunes filles, roman. Paris, 1946.
43701.63.120.70 Montherlant, Henry de. The girls. London, 1968. 2v.
43701.63.121 Montherlant, Henry de. Pitié pour les femmes. Paris, 1936.
43701.63.121.5 Montherlant, Henry de. Pitié pour les femmes. 96e éd. Paris, 1937.
43701.63.121.10 Montherlant, Henry de. Pitié pour les femmes. Paris, 1947.
43701.63.122 Montherlant, Henry de. Le démon du vien. Paris, 1937.

43511 - 43873 Individual authors, etc. - 1900- - Known authors (363 scheme plus 10) - cont.

43701.63.122.10 Montherlant, Henry de. Le démon du vien. Paris, 1947.
43701.63.123.7 Montherlant, Henry de. Les lepreuses. Paris, 1947.
43701.63.126 Montherlant, Henry de. Les Olympiques. 65e éd. Paris, 1938.
43701.63.130 Montherlant, Henry de. Les onze devant le porte darée. 24e éd. Paris, 1924.
43701.63.130.5 Montherlant, Henry de. Les onze devant la porte dorée. Paris, 1924.
43701.63.135 Montherlant, Henry de. Aux fontaines du désir. Paris, 1946.
43701.63.140 Montherlant, Henry de. La relève du matin. Paris, 1933.
43701.63.145 Montherlant, Henry de. Le petite infante de Castille. Paris, 1946.
43701.63.145.10 Montherlant, Henry de. Le petite infante de Castille, historiette. 40e éd. Paris, 1949.
43701.63.150 Montherlant, Henry de. Service inutile. 9e éd. Paris, 1935.
43701.63.160 Montherlant, Henry de. Les célibataires; roman. 63e éd. Paris, 1934.
43701.63.163 Montherlant, Henry de. Les celibataires. 90e éd. Paris, 1934.
43701.63.170 Montherlant, Henry de. Les morts perdues. Abbeville, 1933.
43701.63.180A Montherlant, Henry de. L'équinoxe de septembre. 21e éd. Photoreproduction. Paris, 1938.
43701.63.180B Montherlant, Henry de. L'équinoxe de septembre. Paris, 1938.
43701.63.185 Montherlant, Henry de. Malatesta. Lausanne, 1946.
43701.63.190 Montherlant, Henry de. Fils de personne, fils des autres, un incompris. Bruxelles, 1944.
43701.63.195 Montherlant, Henry de. Fils de personne. 33. éd. Paris, 1944.
43701.63.200 Montherlant, Henry de. Paysage des olympiques. Paris, 1940.
43701.63.210 Montherlant, Henry de. L'exil, pièces en trois actes. Paris, 1946.
43701.63.220 Montherlant, Henry de. La reine morte. Paris, 1947.
43701.63.230 Montherlant, Henry de. Carnets XXIX à XXXV. Paris, 1947.
43701.63.230.5 Montherlant, Henry de. Carnets XXII à XXVIII. Paris, 1955.
43701.63.243 Montherlant, Henry de. Pages catholiques. Paris, 1947.
43701.63.250 Montherlant, Henry de. Pasiphaé. Paris, 1938.
43701.63.260 Montherlant, Henry de. Le maître de Santiago. 53e éd. Paris, 1947.
43701.63.270 Montherlant, Henry de. La vie en forme de proue. 24. éd. Paris, 1942.
43701.63.280 Montherlant, Henry de. Le solstice de juin. 36. éd. Paris, 1941.
43701.63.290 Montherlant, Henry de. Encore un instant de bonheur. Paris, 1946.
43701.63.300 Montherlant, Henry de. Demain il fera jour. Pasiphaé. 3. éd. Paris, 1949.
43701.63.310 Montherlant, Henry de. Pages de tendresse. Paris, 1928.
43701.63.320 Montherlant, Henry de. Hispano-moresque. Paris, 1929.
43701.63.330 Montherlant, Henry de. Il y a encore des paradis. Sceaux, 1947.
43701.63.340 Montherlant, Henry de. Le paradis à l'ombre des épées. Paris, 1924.
43701.63.350 Montherlant, Henry de. Un incompris. Paris, 1944.
43701.63.360 Montherlant, Henry de. Chant funèbre pour les morts de verdun. 11. éd. Paris, 1925.
43701.63.370 Montherlant, Henry de. Les îles de la felicité. Paris, 1929.
43701.63.380 Montherlant, Henry de. Notes sur mon théâtre. Paris, 1950.
43701.63.390 Montherlant, Henry de. L'art et la vie. Paris, 1947.
43701.63.400 Montherlant, Henry de. Celles qu'on prend dans ses bras. 28e éd. Paris, 1950.
43701.63.410 Montherlant, Henry de. La ville dont le prince est un enfant. 37. éd. Paris, 1951.
43701.63.415 Montherlant, Henry de. Le ville dont le prince est un enfant; trois actes. Paris, 1963.
43701.63.420 Montherlant, Henry de. L'histoire d'amour de la Rose de Sable. Paris, 1954.
43701.63.430 Montherlant, Henry de. Sur les femmes. Sceaux, 1946.
43701.63.440 Montherlant, Henry de. Le fichier parisien. Paris, 1952.
43701.63.450 Montherlant, Henry de. Port-Royal. 73. éd. Paris, 1954.
43701.63.460 Montherlant, Henry de. Un voyageur solitaire est un diable. Monaco, 1955.
43701.63.470 Montherlant, Henry de. Brocéliande. 10. éd. Paris, 1956.
43701.63.480 Montherlant, Henry de. Carnets XIX à XXI. Paris, 1956.
43701.63.490 Montherlant, Henry de. Les auligny. Paris, 1956.
43701.63.500 Montherlant, Henry de. Carnets. 16. éd. Paris, 1957.
43701.63.502 Montherlant, Henry de. Carnets, XLII et XLIII. Paris, 1948.
43701.63.510 Montherlant, Henry de. Don Juan. Paris, 1958.
43701.63.520A Montherlant, Henry de. Romans et oeuvres de fiction non théâtrales. Paris, 1959.
43701.63.520B Montherlant, Henry de. Romans et oeuvres de fiction non théâtrales. Paris, 1962.
43701.63.530 Montherlant, Henry de. Le cardinal d'Éspagne. Paris, 1960.
43701.63.540 Montherlant, Henry de. Fléche du sud. Paris, 1937.
43701.63.550 Montherlant, Henry de. Lettre sur le serviteur châtié. Paris, 1927.
43701.63.560 Montherlant, Henry de. Le chaos et la nuit. Paris, 1963.
43701.63.565 Montherlant, Henry de. Discours de réception de M. Henry de Montherlant à l'académie française et réponse de M. le duc de Léuis Mirepoix. Paris, 1963.
43701.63.570A Montherlant, Henry de. Essais. Paris, 1963.
43701.63.570B Montherlant, Henry de. Essais. Paris, 1963.
43701.63.580 Montherlant, Henry de. La guerre civile, pièce en trois actes. Paris, 1965.
43701.63.590 Montherlant, Henry de. Au petit mutilé. Paris, 1930.
43701.63.600 Montherlant, Henry de. Va jover avec cette poussière. Paris, 1966.
43701.63.610 Montherlant, Henry de. Les garçons. Paris, 1969.
43701.63.620 Montherlant, Henry de. Le cardinal d'Espagne. Boston, 1972.
43701.63.705 Montherlant, Henry de. The dream. London, 1962.
43701.63.710 Montherlant, Henry de. Pity for women. N.Y., 1938.
43701.63.720 Montherlant, Henry de. Perish in their pride. N.Y., 1936.
43701.63.732 Montherlant, Henry de. Les lepreuses, roman. Paris, 1934.
43701.63.735 Montherlant, Henry de Costals and the Hippogniff. N.Y., 1940.
43701.63.740A Montherlant, Henry de. The bullfighters. N.Y., 1927.

43511 - 43873 Individual authors, etc. - 1900- - Known authors (363 scheme plus 10) - cont.

43701.63.740B Montherlant, Henry de. The bullfighters. N.Y., 1927.
43701.63.745 Montherlant, Henry de. The master of Santiago. 1st American ed. N.Y., 1951.
43701.63.750 Montherlant, Henry de. Desert love. London, 1957.
43701.63.755 Montherlant, Henry de. The matador. London, 1957.
43701.63.760 Montherlant, Henry de. Chaos and night. London, 1964.
43701.63.800 Saint-Pierre, M. Montherlant. Paris, 1949.
43701.63.810 Sandelion, J. Montherlant et les femmes. Paris, 1950.
43701.63.820 Castay, Marcel. Les heritiers de la couronne. Paris, 1952.
43701.63.830 Henry de Montherlant et son oeuvre. Paris, 1954?
43701.63.840 Empaytaz, F. Essai sur Montherlant. n.p., 1928.
43701.63.850 Bordonove, G. Henry de Montherlant. Paris, 1954.
43701.63.860 Datain, Jean. Montherlant et le mystère malalesta. Alencon, 1954.
43701.63.865 Datain, Jean. Montherlant et l'héritage. Paris, 1956.
43701.63.870 Simon, P.H. Procés du héros. Paris, 1950.
43701.63.875 Laprade, Jacques de. Le théâtre de Montherlant. Paris, 1950.
43701.63.880 Thierry, Jean Jacques. Montherlant vu par des jeunes de 17 à 27 ans. Paris, 1959.
43701.63.885 Perruchot, Henri. Montherlant. Paris, 1959.
43701.63.890 Debrie-Panej, Nicole. Montherlant. Lyon, 1960.
43701.63.895 Champion, Edouard. Montherlant vivant. Paris, 1934.
43701.63.900 Chevalley, Sylvie. Henry de Montherlant, homme de théâtre. Paris, 1961.
43701.63.905 Mohrt, Michel. Montherlant, homme libre. 16. éd. Paris, 1943.
43701.63.910 Beer, J. de. Montherlant, ou L'homme encombré de Dieu. Paris, 1963.
43701.63.915 Mondini, B. Montherlant du coté de Port-Royal. Paris, 1962.
43701.63.920 Cruickshank, J. Montherlant. Edinbde urgh, 1964.
43701.63.925 Rapke, Rudolf. Die Dramen Montherlants. Köln, 1964.
43701.63.930 Johnson, Robert Brown. Henry de Montherlant. N.Y., 1968.
43701.63.935 Batchelor, John W. Existence and imagination; the theatre of Henry de Montherlant. St. Lucia, 1967.
43701.63.940 Blanc, André. Montherlant, un pessimisme heureux. Paris, 1968.
43701.63.945 Saint Robert, Philippe de. Montherlant le séparé. Paris, 1969.
43701.63.950 Becker, Lucille. Henry de Montherlant; a critical biography. Carbondale, 1970.
43701.63.955 Neville, Daniel E. Henry de Montherlant; une revue de la critique de ses oeuvres. v.1-2. Lawrence, 1966-67.
43701.67.100 Moury, Alain. L'affaire d'une nuit. Paris, 1960.
43701.73.100 Mois, André. Neptune - Paris. Paris, 1929.
43701.74.100 Morand, Paul. Lewis et Irène. Paris, 192-.
43701.74.105 Morand, Paul. Champions du monde. Paris, 1930.
43701.74.110A Morand, Paul. Poèmes, 1914-1924. 3e éd. Paris, 1924.
43701.74.110B Morand, Paul. Poèmes, 1914-1924. Paris, 1924.
43701.74.120 Morand, Paul. Lampes à arc. Paris, 1927.
43701.74.125 Morand, Paul. Le Rhône en hydroglisseur. Paris, 1929.
43701.74.132 Morand, Paul. Ouvert la nuit. 2. éd. Paris, 1957.
43701.74.135 Morand, Paul. Bug O'Shea. Dessins de Louis Icart. Paris, 1936.
43701.74.140 Morand, Paul. Fermé la nuit. 140e éd. Paris, 1930.
43701.74.145 Morand, Paul. L'art de mourer. Paris, 1932.
43701.74.150 Morand, Paul. Le voyageur et l'amour. Paris, 1932.
43701.74.155 Morand, Paul. Le voyage. Paris, 1927.
43701.74.160 Morand, Paul. Flèche d'Orient. 35e éd. Paris, 1932.
43701.74.162 Morand, Paul. Flèche d'Orient. 5e éd. Paris, 1932.
43701.74.170 Morand, Paul. L'Europe gallante. 82e éd. Paris, 1925.
43701.74.180A Morand, Paul. Les extravagants. 13e éd. Paris, 1936.
43701.74.180B Morand, Paul. Les extravagants. 13e éd. Paris, 1936.
43701.74.193 Morand, Paul. Réflexes et réflexions. 6. éd. Paris, 1939.
43701.74.200 Morand, Paul. Papiers d'identité. Paris, 1931.
43701.74.204A Morand, Paul. L'heure qu'il est. 4e éd. Paris, 1938.
43701.74.204B Morand, Paul. L'heure qu'il est. Paris, 1938.
43701.74.210 Morand, Paul. Isabeau de Bavière, femme de Charles VI. Paris, 1938.
43701.74.228 Morand, Paul. Le réveille matin. 8e éd. Paris, 1937.
43701.74.240 Morand, Paul. Rococo. 5e éd. Paris, 1933.
43701.74.255 Morand, Paul. Rond-point des Champs-Elysées. 10e éd. Paris, 1935.
43701.74.265 Morand, Paul. Chroniques de l'homme maigre, suivies de propos d'hier. 15. éd. Paris, 1941.
43701.74.270 Morand, Paul. France la doulce. Paris, 1934.
43701.74.280 Morand, Paul. Petit théâtre. Paris, 1942.
43701.74.290 Morland, Paul. Bouddha vivant. Paris, 1927.
43701.74.300 Morand, Paul. Feu m. le duc. Genève, 1942.
43701.74.310 Morand, Paul. Montociel. Genève, 1947.
43701.74.320 Morand, Paul. Propos des 52 semaines. Genève, 1943.
43701.74.330 Morand, Paul. Fin de siècle. Paris, 1957.
43701.74.340 Morand, Paul. Le prisonnier de Cintra. Paris, 1958.
43701.74.350 Morand, Paul. Le lion écarlate. Paris, 1959.
43701.74.360 Morand, Paul. Excelsior, U.S.A. Liège, 1928.
43701.74.370 Morand, Paul. Les amis nouveaux. Paris, 1924.
43701.74.380 Morand, Paul. Mes débuts. Paris, 1933.
43701.74.390 Morand, Paul. La fleur double. Paris, 1924.
43701.74.400 Morand, Paul. Syracusse, U.S.A. Paris, 1928.
43701.74.410 Morand, Paul. Tais-toi. Paris, 1965.
43701.74.429 Morand, Paul. L'eau sous les ponts. 9. éd. Paris, 1954.
43701.74.430 Morand, Paul. A la fregate. Paris, 1930.
43701.74.440 Morand, Paul. Mon plaisir. Paris, 1967.
43701.74.450 Morand, Paul. Nouvelles d'une vie. Paris, 1965. 2v.
43701.74.460 Morand, Paul. Discours de réception de Paul Morand à l'académie française et réponse de Jacques Chastenet. Paris, 1969.
43701.74.470 Morand, Paul. Venises. Paris, 1971.
43701.74.705 Morand, Paul. Closed all night. 2nd ed. London, 1925.
43701.74.715 Morand, Paul. Open all night. N.Y., 1923.
43701.74.718 Morand, Paul. Open all nignt. N.Y., 1930.
43701.74.725 Morand, Paul. Europe at love. N.Y., 1927.
43701.74.735 Morand, Paul. Green shoots. N.Y., 1924.
43701.74.740 Morand, Paul. The flagellant of Seville. London, 1953.
43701.74.805 Sarkany, Stéphane. Paul Morand et le cosmopolitisme littéraire. Paris, 1968.
43701.74.1100 Morane, P. Sybie. Paris, 1931.
43701.74.1110 Morane, P. Poèmes imparfaits. Paris, 1937.
43701.74.2100 Mordreuc, Jean. An distro. Paris, 1956.
43701.74.2110 Mordreuc, Jean. Le charoguard. Paris, 1957.
43701.74.4100 Morax, R. Le théâtre du Jorat et René Morax. Lausanne, 1963.
43701.74.4110 Morax, R. Tell. Lausanne, 1914.
43701.74.5100 Morchan, Frédéric. L'archivolte. Paris, 1958.

43511 - 43873 Individual authors, etc. - 1900- - Known authors (363 scheme plus 10) - cont.

43701.75.100 Moreno, M. La statue de sel et le bonhomme de neige. Paris, 1926.
43701.75.105 Moreno, M. Souvenirs de ma vie. Paris, 1948.
43701.75.1100 Moreau, Serge. La clé des nuits. Paris, 1957.
43701.75.3100 Moreau, Martial. Arc en ciel. Paris, 1956.
43701.75.6102 Morgan, C. La marque de l'homme. Paris, 1944.
43701.75.7101 Moreau, Marcel J. Quintes. Paris, 1962.
43701.75.7110 Moreau, Marcel J. Le chant des paroxismes, suivi de la Nukai. Paris, 1967.
43701.75.7700 Moreau, Marcel J. The selves of Quinte. N.Y., 1965.
43701.75.8100 Morhange, Pierre. Poèmes brefs. n.p., 1965.
43701.76.100 Morienval, H. Sorciere de Montepilloy. Paris, 1925.
43701.76.110 Morienval, H. Dans la lande de Kermar. Paris, 1926.
43701.76.1100 Morand, Germaine. La douloureuse enfance. Paris, 1931.
43701.76.2100 Morand, Pierre. Patria vietrix. Paris, 1918.
43701.76.4100 Morin, Marcelle. Images d'Algérie. Rodez, 1963.
43701.76.6100 Morisseau-Leroy, F. Récolte. Port-au-Prince, 1946.
43701.77.2100 Mortier, Alfred. Le souffleur de bulles. Paris, 1929.
43701.77.2110 Mortier, Alfred. Le temple sans idoles. Paris, 1909.
43701.77.3100 Clouard, Henri. Aurel. Paris, 1922.
43701.77.4100 Mortes, Claude. Ciels et brouillards. Paris, 1959.
43701.79.100 Moussy, Marcel. Les mauvais sentiments. Paris, 1955.
43701.79.110 Moussy, Marcel. Si c'était vous. Paris, 1958.
43701.79.120 Moussy, Marcel. Les 400 coups. Paris, 1959.
43701.80.100 Mogin, Jean. Pâtures du silence. Paris, 1956.
43701.80.1100 Montforez, Georges. Les enfants du Marais. Paris, 1958.
43701.80.1110 Montforez, Georges. La presqu'île Martin. Paris, 1960.
43701.82.100 Mossé, Armand. L'hôtesse du Panthéon. Paris, 1926.
43701.82.110 Mossé, Armand. Les reliefs. Paris, 1924.
43701.82.120 Mossé, Armand. Monsieur Homais. Paris, 1931.
43701.86.100 Moulin, Jeanine. Feux sans joie. Paris, 1957.
43701.86.110 Moulin, Jeanine. Rue chair et pain. Paris, 1961.
43701.87.100 Mottart, Hubert. Le septre et l'anneau. n.p., 1957.
43701.87.110 Mottart, Hubert. Le luth noir. Bruxelles, 1964.
43701.87.1100 Mottier, Christian. Ville pour guitare. Paris, 1956.
43701.88.100 Monchet, Charles. Debus. Genève, 1958.
43701.89.100 Mourgue, Gerard. Chateau-fer. Paris, 1956.
43701.89.1100 Mouloudji, Marcel. Chansons pour ma mélancolie. L'Arbalete, 1958.
43701.89.1110 Mouloudji, Marcel. La guerre buissonnière; roman. Paris, 1959.
43701.89.1120 Mouloudji, Marcel. Le petit vaincu. Paris, 1963.
43701.89.2100 Moustiers, Pierre. La paroi. Paris, 1969.
43701.89.3100 Moureau, Maurice. Touches et notes de poésie. Rodez, 1957.
43701.89.3110 Moureau, Maurice. Les morts-vivants. Honfleur, 1970.
43701.89.4100 Mourthé, Claude. La caméra. Paris, 1970.
43701.90.100 Morucci, P.F. Charts tithonievs. Paris, 1930.
43701.99.100 Mozer, Hélène. Battement. Veilhes, 1966.
43701.99.1100 Moré, Marcel. Accords et dissonances, 1932-1944. Paris, 1967.
43701.99.1110 Moré, Marcel. La foudre de Dieu. Paris, 1969.
43702.88.100 Mounet, L.R. L'ombre sur l'avenir. Paris, 1938.
43702.89.100 Mourguet, M. Amitié; pièce en trois actes et quatre tableaux. Paris, 1932.
43702.89.2100 Mouézy-Eon, A. Les nuits du Hampton-Club. Paris, 1907.
43702.89.3100 Mouquin, F. Dans la mêlée. Paris, 1963.
43703.50.21 Muller, Louis. Echos de mon pays. Porrentruy, 1967.
43703.54.100 Mun, R. de. La mort d'un enfant. Paris, 1959.
43703.61.100 Muno, Jean. L'homme qui s'efface. Bruxelles, 1963.
43703.61.110 Muno, Jean. L'île des pas perdus. Bruxelles, 1967.
43703.73.100 Murat, A. Le livre de poésie. Paris, 1912.
43703.73.110 Murat, A. Vivre encore. Uzès, 1937.
43703.73.2100 Murat, Stéphane. La porte du sud. Paris, 1959.
43703.73.3110 Muray, Jean. La déesse. Paris, 1946.
43703.73.3120 Muray, Jean. Le marchand de Venise. Paris, 1957.
43703.74.100 Muraz, Gaston. Sous le grand soleil, chez les primitifs. Coulommiers, 1923.
43703.75.105 Murciaux, Christian. La fontaine de vie. 2. éd. Paris, 1945.
43703.75.110 Murciaux, Christian. Notre-Dame des désemparés. Paris, 1960.
43703.75.120 Murciaux, Christian. Pedro de Luna; roman. Paris, 1963.
43703.75.700 Murciaux, Christian. The unforsaken. London, 1963.
43703.77.100 Muro, A.L.B. de Baumarchais de. Legends of France and Spain. Stanford, 1937.
43703.80.100 Muselli, Vincent. Les masques; sonnets heroi-comiques. Paris, 1919.
43703.80.110 Muselli, Vincent. Les sonnets à Philis. Paris, 1930.
Htn 43703.80.120* Muselli, Vincent. Les sonnets moraux. Autun, 1934.
Htn 43703.80.130* Muselli, Vincent. L'étrange interview. Argenteuil, 1931.
43703.80.140 Muselli, Vincent. Les travaux et les jeux. Paris, 1914.
43703.80.150 Muselli, Vincent. Les strophes de contre-fortune. Paris, 1931.
43703.80.160 Muselli, Vincent. Les convives. Paris, 1947.
43703.80.170 Muselli, Vincent. Oeuvre poétique. Paris, 1957.
43703.80.180 Muselli, Vincent. La barque allait. Paris, 1954.
43703.80.190 Muselli, Vincent. Les douze pas des muses. Paris, 1952.
43703.80.800 Hommage à Vincent Muselli. Hommage à Vincent Muselli. Paris, 1952.
43703.80.805 Muselli, Vincent. Vincent Muselli. Paris, 1961.
43704.8.35 Nabert, Jeanne. Le cavalier de le mer. Paris, 1932.
43705.1.30 Nadaud, Marcel. Les derniers mousquetaires. Paris, 1917.
43705.1.30.5 Nadaud, Marcel. The flying poilu. London, 1918.
43705.1.31 Nadaud, Marcel. Ma p'tite femme. Paris, 1917.
43705.1.32 Nadaud, Marcel. La guerre aérienne; chignole. Paris, 1917.
43705.1.34 Nadaud, Marcel. Frangipane. Paris, 1919.
43705.1.55 Nadaud, Marcel. Birds of a feather. Garden City, 1919.
43705.2.35 Naudeau, Ludovic. Plaisir du Japon. pts. 1-2. Paris, 1922.
43705.9.100 Nabonne, Bernard. La meunière de Javel. Paris, 1946.
43705.22.100 Naegelen, Marcel-Edmond. Avant que meure le dernier. Paris, 1958.
43705.41.100 Nailly, Charles. Péristyle (de la sincérité). Nogent-le-Rotrou, 1968.
43705.83.100 Natanson, J. Je t'attendais. Paris, 1929.
43705.83.110 Natanson, J. L'été; comédie en 3 actes. Paris, 1935.
43705.83.120 Natanson, J. L'enfant truque. Paris, 1922.
43705.83.130 Natanson, J. L'âge heureux. Paris, 1925.
43705.83.140 Natanson, J. Manigances. Paris, 1946.
43705.84.100 Natanson, L.A. Vieille renommée. Paris, 1926.
43705.86.100 Nathiu, Marcel. Carnet. Paris, 1957.
43705.89.100 Naudin, Pierre. Les dernières foulées. Lausanne, 1968.
43705.91.100 Navel, Georges. Chacun son royaume. Paris, 1960.
43705.91.700 Navel, Georges. Man at work. London, 1949.

43511 - 43873 Individual authors, etc. - 1900- - Known authors (363 scheme plus 10) - cont.

43705.95.100 Newsom, J.D. Garde à vous! A novel. Garden City, N.Y., 1928.
43706.34.100 Négrié, Joseph. Contes et récits de le terre occitane. Paris, 1964.
43706.50.100 Nelli, René. Point de langage. Paris, 1963.
43706.52.100 Nelly, Luce. Chansons de douceur et d'automne. Paris, 1946.
43706.55.105 Némirovsky, Irène. Le bal. 22e éd. Paris, 1930.
43706.55.116 Némirovsky, Irène. Jézabel, roman. Paris, 1936.
43706.55.124 Némirovsky, Irène. Le vin de solitude; roman. Paris, 1935.
43706.55.138 Némirovsky, Irène. La proie, roman. Paris, 1938.
43706.55.140 Némirovsky, Irène. Deux, roman. Paris, 1939.
43706.55.700 Némirovsky, Irène. David Golden. N.Y., 1930.
43706.74.100 Ner, Henri. Jeanne d'Arc et sa mère. Paris, 1950.
43706.74.105 Ner, Henri. J'ai nom Eliacin. Paris, 1956.
43706.74.110 Ner, Henri. Le sillage parfume. Paris, 1958.
43706.87.100 Nette (pseud?). Chansons de mon coeur. Paris, 1962.
43706.90.100 Neveu, Charlotte. Dona Quichotte. Paris, 1957.
43706.90.1100 Neveu, Gerald. Un poète dans la ville. Grenoble, 1961.
43706.97.100 Neveux, Georges. Théâtre. Paris, 1943-
43706.97.1100 Amis de Han Rynes. Cahiers. Les Pavillons-sous-Bois. 1,1946+ 4v.
43706.98.100 Neyrac, Pierre. L'indifférence perdue. Paris, 1933.
43706.105.100 Nguyen-Tien-Lang. Les chemins de la révolte. Paris, 1953.
43707.2.30 Nils, A. La terre de la beauté. Paris, 1902.
43707.3.100 Nimier, Roger. Amour et néant. 2e éd. Paris, 1951.
43707.3.110 Nimier, Roger. Histoire d'un amour. 13e éd. Paris, 1953.
43707.3.120 Nimier, Roger. Le hussard bleu. 30e éd. Paris, 1950.
43707.3.130 Nimier, Roger. Le grand d'Espagne. Paris, 1962.
43707.3.140 Nimier, Roger. D'Artagnan amoureux. Paris, 1962.
43707.3.150 Nimier, Roger. L'étrangère. Paris, 1968.
43707.3.700 Nimier, Roger. The blue Hussar. London, 1952.
43707.3.702 Nimier, Roger. The blue Hussar. N.Y., 1953.
43707.3.710 Nimier, Roger. Children of circumstance. London, 1954.
43707.14.100 Nicolas, André. Je ne suis pas si vilaine. Fontenay-le-Comte, 1956.
43707.14.1100 Nicolet, Arthur. Poèmes. Delémont, 1962.
43707.17.100 Niderst, Alain. Le soleil et la mort. Paris, 1957.
43707.58.100 Ninck, Roger. Les couteaux du destin. Paris, 1956.
43707.81.100 Nisin, Arthur. Un journal de Russie. Lausanne, 1959.
43707.91.100 Nivoix, Paul. Eve toute nue. Paris, 1927.
43707.91.110 Nivoix, Paul. Amours. Paris, 1929.
43707.98.100 Nizan, Paul. La conspiration. Paris, 1938.
43707.98.110 Nizan, Paul. Paul Nizan, intellectuel communiste, 1926-1940. Paris, 1967.
43707.98.705 Nizan, Paul. Trojan horse. London, 1937.
43707.98.710 Ginsbourg, Ariel. Paul Nizan. Paris, 1966.
43707.98.800 Leiner, Jacqueline. Le destin littéraire de Paul Nizan et ses étapes successives. Paris, 1970.
Htn 43709.3.23* Noailles, Anna, E. Poésies. Paris, 19- .
43709.3.42 Noailles, Anna E. Le livre de ma vie. Paris, 1932.
43709.3.100 Noailles, Anna E. La coeur innombrable. Paris, 1901?
43709.3.113 Noailles, Anna E. Le visage émerveillé. 31e éd. Paris, 1927.
43709.3.120 Noailles, Anna E. La domination. 14e éd. Paris, 1905?
43709.3.130 Noailles, Anna E. Les éblouissements. Paris, 1907.
43709.3.134 Noailles, Anna E. Les éblouissements. 34e éd. Paris, 1921.
43709.3.140 Noailles, Anna E. De la rive d'Europe à la rive d'Asie. Paris, 1913.
43709.3.150 Noailles, Anna E. Les forces éternelles. Paris, 1920.
43709.3.170 Noailles, Anna E. Les vivants et les morts. Paris, 1913.
43709.3.180 Noailles, Anna E. L'ombre des jours. Paris, 192-.
43709.3.190 Noailles, Anna E. Poème de l'amour. Paris, 1924.
43709.3.200 Noailles, Anna E. Choix de poésies. Paris, 1930.
43709.3.210 Noailles, Anna E. Exactitudes. Paris, 1930.
43709.3.220 Noailles, Anna E. Les innocentes. Paris, 1923.
43709.3.230 Noailles, Anna E. Dernièrs vers et poèmes d'enfance. 9e éd. Paris, 1934.
43709.3.240 Noailles, Anna E. Poèmes d'enfance. Paris, 1928.
43709.3.250 Noailles, Anna E. La nouvelle espérance. Paris, 1928.
43709.3.260 Noailles, Anna E. L'honneur de souffrir. 23e éd. Paris, 1927.
Htn 43709.3.800* Gillouin, René. La Comtesse Mathieu de Noailles. Paris, 1908.
43709.3.805 Benjamin, René. Au soleil de la poésie. Paris, 1928.
43709.3.815 Masson, G.A. La Comtesse de Noailles, son oeuvre. Paris, 1922.
43709.3.820 Larnac, Jean. Comtesse de Noailles. Paris, 1931.
43709.3.825 Kirseck, Ilse. Anna Elisabeth, comtesse de Noailles. Inaug. Diss. Jena, 1939.
43709.3.830 Du Bos, C. La comtesse de Noailles et le climat du génie. Paris, 1949.
43709.3.835 La Rochefoucauld, E. Anna de Noailles. Paris, 1956.
43709.3.840 Cocteau, J. La comtesse de Noailles - oui et non. Paris, 1963.
43709.3.845 Bibliothèque Nationale, Paris. Anna de Noailles; exposition de manuscripts, livres et documents. Paris, 1953.
43709.14.30 Noctuel. Dictionnaire français-rosse. Paris, 1965.
43709.21.100 Noé, Yvan. Teddy and partner, pièce en trois actes. Paris, 1933.
43709.21.110 Noé, Yvan. "Christian"; pièce en trois actes. Paris, 1937.
43709.23.21 Noël, Marie. L'oeuvre poétique. Paris, 1956.
43709.23.25 Noël, Marie. Chants et psaumes d'automne. Paris, 1947.
43709.23.100 Noël, Marie. Les chansons et les heures. Paris, 1928.
43709.23.112 Noël, Marie. Le rosaire des joies. Paris, 1958.
43709.23.120 Noël, Marie. L'âme en peine. Paris, 1954.
43709.23.125 Noël, Marie. Le judgement de Don Juan. Paris, 1955.
43709.23.130 Noël, Marie. Petit jour et souvenirs du beau mai. Paris, 1964.
43709.23.800 Hommage à Marie Noël. Paris, 1954.
43709.23.810 Escholier, Raymond. La neige qui brûle. Paris, 1957.
43709.23.820 Manoll, Michael. Marie Noël. Paris, 1952.
43709.23.826 Noël, Marie. Marie Noël; une étude de André Blanchet. Paris, 1970.
43709.23.1100 Noël, Dominique. Symphonee en blanc. Paris, 1958.
43709.23.2100 Noël, Sean François. Théâtre. Paris, 1957.
43709.23.3100 Noël, Denise. Pour un nouvel été. Paris, 1968.
43709.23.3110 Noël, Denise. La lettre aux sortilèges. Paris, 1970.
43709.23.4100 Noël, Bernard. La face de silence. Paris, 1967.
43709.41.100 Noir, Jacques. Les maledictions. Paris, 1919.
43709.75.100 Nogelet, Francis. Fresques du souvenir. Paris, 1923.
43709.75.1100 Norge, G. Les cerveaux brûlés. Paris, 1969.

43511 - 43873 Individual authors, etc. - 1900- - Known authors (363 scheme plus 10) - cont.

43709.75.1110 Norge, G. Le vin profond. Paris, 1968.
43709.77.103 Normand, S. Cinq femmes sur un gatere. 6e éd. Paris, 1927.
43709.77.1100 Normand, Gilles. Les barbacoles; moeurs scolaires et provinciales. Paris, 1907?
43709.80.100 Nourissier, François. Les orphelins d'Auteuil. Paris, 1956.
43709.80.110 Nourissier, François. Une histoire française. Paris, 1965.
43709.80.120 Nourissier, François. Bleu comme la nuit. Paris, 1958.
43709.80.130 Nourissier, François. Le corps de Diane. Paris, 1957.
43709.80.140 Nourissier, François. Portait d'un indifférent. Paris, 1958.
43709.80.150 Nourissier, François. Un petit bourgeois. Paris, 1963.
43709.80.160 Nourissier, François. Le maître de maison. Paris, 1968.
43709.80.170 Nourissier, François. La vie parfaite. Paris, 1952.
43709.80.180 Nourissier, François. La crève. Paris, 1970.
43709.85.100 Nothomb, Pierre. Aus de grâce. Paris, 1958.
43709.85.110 Nothomb, Pierre. Le chant du prince. Bruxelles, 1960.
43709.85.130 Nothomb, Pierre. Les miracles, nouvelles. Bruxelles, 1962.
43709.85.140 Nothomb, Pierre. Le buisson ardent; poèmes, 1957-1965. Paris, 1966.
43709.85.800 Bodart, Marie Thérèse. L'impromptu du Pont d'Oye avec Pierre Nothomb. Vieux-Virton, 1965.
43709.85.805 Au pays de Nothomb. Vieux-Virton, 1964.
43709.85.810 Clémeur, Marcel. L'esprit créateur de Pierre Nothomb. Vieux-Virton, 1964.
43709.85.815 Mergeai, Jean. Pierre Nothomb; ou, Les paradis perdus. Vieux-Virton, 1965.
43709.89.25 Nouveau, Germain. Oeuvres poétiques. 5e éd. Paris, 1953. 2v.
43709.89.30 Nouveau, Germain. Valentines et autres vers. Paris, 1921.
43709.89.32 Nouveau, Germain. Le calepin du mendiant. Précédé d'autres poèmes, vers inédits. Paris, 1949.
43709.89.800 Genevieve. Collection Doucet. Catalogue de l'exposition Germain, nouveau, 1851-1951. Paris, 1951.
43709.89.805 Verane, Léon. Humilis. Paris, 1929.
43709.89.810 Sozzi, Giorgio P. Germain Nouveau. Urbino, 1969.
43709.89.2100 Nougé, Paul. L'expérience continue. Bruxelles, 1966.
43712.80.100 Nyssen, Hubert. Préhistoire des estuaires. Bruxelles, 1967.
43712.84.100 Nyanai. La nuit de ma vie (1951) poèmes. Paris, 1961.
43714.5.100 Obaldia, René de. Tamerlan des coeurs. Paris, 1955.
43714.5.110 Obaldia, René de. Le centenaire, roman. Paris, 1959.
43714.5.120 Obaldia, René de. Théâtre. v. 2-4. Paris, 1966- 2v.
43714.5.132 Obaldia, René de. Les richesses naturelles. Paris, 1971.
43714.8.100 Obey, André. Théâtre. v.1- 2e éd. Paris, 1948-
43714.8.110 Obey, André. Le joueur de triangle. Paris, 1954.
43714.8.120A Obey, André. Noe. Boston, 1955.
43714.8.120B Obey, André. Noe. Boston, 1955.
43714.8.700 Obey, André. Lucrece. N.Y., 1933.
43714.8.710 Obey, André. Noah. London, 1949.
43714.75.41 Obret, Muriel. Fragments d'un journal. Port-Louis, 1967.
43714.75.44 Obret, Muriel. D'une enfance. Port-Louis, 1968.
43715.39.100 Ochse, J. D'île en île. Paris, 1912.
43718.27.100 Offel, H. Le retour aux lumières. Paris, 1912.
43723.18.100 Oldenbourg, Zoé. La pierre angulaire. 188. éd. Paris, 1954.
43723.18.110 Oldenbourg, Zoé. Les irreductibles. Paris, 1958.
43723.18.120 Oldenbourg, Zoé. Les brûlés. Paris, 1960.
43723.18.130 Oldenbourg, Zoé. Les cites charnelles. Paris, 1961.
43723.18.141 Oldenbourg, Zoé. Argile et cendres. Paris, 1968.
43723.18.150 Oldenbourg, Zoé. La joie des pauvres. Paris, 1970.
43723.18.703A Oldenbourg, Zoé. The world is not enough. N.Y., 1948.
43723.18.703B Oldenbourg, Zoé. The world is not enough. N.Y., 1948.
43723.18.710 Oldenbourg, Zoé. The corner stone. London, 1954.
43723.18.720 Oldenbourg, Zoé. The awakened. N.Y., 1957.
43723.18.730 Oldenbourg, Zoé. The chains of love. London, 1959.
43723.18.735 Oldenbourg, Zoé. Destiny of fire. London, 1961.
43723.18.740 Oldenbourg, Zoé. Cities of the flesh. London, 1963.
43723.41.100 Olivier, Claude. Chimères et tourments. Angers, 1966.
43723.41.1100 Olivier-Lacamp, Max. Les feux de la colère. Paris, 1969.
43723.50.100 Ollier, Claude. La mise en scene. Paris, 1958.
43723.50.110 Ollier, Claude. Eté indien. Paris, 1963.
43723.50.120 Ollier, Claude. L'Echec de Nolan. Paris, 1967.
43723.50.130 Ollier, Claude. Navettes. Paris, 1967.
43723.51.100 Ollone, Charles. Theâtre en prose. Paris, 1910.
43723.51.110 Ollone, Charles. Heures chantantes. Paris, 1908. 2v.
43723.51.120 Ollone, Charles. Nouvelles heures chantantes. Paris, 1913.
43723.51.125 Ollone, Charles. Dernières heures chantantes. Paris, 1919.
43723.51.130 Ollone, Charles. Soeur Marie-Odile. 2nd éd. Paris, 1909.
43723.51.140 Ollone, Charles. La victoire aileé. Paris, 1911.
43723.88.100 Oltramare, G. L'escalier de service. Paris, 1929.
43725.41.100 Onimus, Jean. Face au monde actuel. Paris, 1962.
43725.41.110 Onimus, Jean. Interrogations autour de l'essentiel. Bruges? 1967.
43728.3.100 Orain, André. Les égarés, roman. Paris, 1939.
43728.18.100 Ordioni, Pierre. Le chant des ténèbres. Paris, 1965.
43728.25.710 Orieux, J. Fontagre. London, 1949.
43728.50.100 Orliac, J. Le deuxième mari de Lady Chatterly. Paris, 1934.
43728.54.100 Ormesson, Jean d'. Les illusions de la mer. Paris, 1968.
43728.54.110 Ormesson, Jean d'. L'amour est un plaisir, roman. Paris, 1956.
43728.56.100 Ormoy, Marcel. Le coeur lourd suivi de sept élégies. Paris, 1926.
43728.56.110 Ormoy, Marcel. La terrasse sur la mer; poèmes. Paris, 1937.
43729.85.100 Oster, Pierre. Le champ de mai. Paris, 1955.
43729.85.110 Oster, Pierre. Solitude de la lumière. 4e éd. Paris, 1957.
43729.85.120 Oster, Pierre. Un nom toujours nouveau; poèmes. Paris, 1960.
43730.85.100 Otte, Guy. Fleurs d'oubli, fleurs des champs, fleurs d'amour, fleurs fanées. Louhans, 1921.
43731.1.30 Oudinot, C. Chaîne anglaise. Paris, 1906.
43731.16.100 Oudard, G. Prosze Pana. Paris, 1933.
43731.16.110 Sokol Slobodskoë (pseud.). La conquête du pôle nord. Paris, 1937.
43731.18.100 Oudiane, S. Chants de la Caravane. Paris, 1926.
43731.50.100 Oulmont, Charles. Message personnel. Lisboa, 1944.

43511 - 43873 Individual authors, etc. - 1900- - Known authors (363 scheme plus 10) - cont.

43731.83.100 Osson-Essui, Denis. Vers de nouveaux horizons; roman. Paris, 1965.
43731.85.100 Out-el-Kouloub. Ramza. Paris, 1958.
43731.85.110 Out-el-Kouloub. Harem. Paris, 1955.
43731.85.120 Out-el-Kouloub. La nuit de la destinée. Paris, 1954.
43736.24.100 Ozeray, Jean Jacques. La tourmente du sentiment, poèmes. Paris, 1967.
43737.12.2100 Pache, Jean. Poèmes de l'autre. Paris, 1960.
43737.12.2110 Pache, Jean. Analogies, poèmes 1958-1961. Neuchâtel, 1966.
43737.14.100 Pacora, Madou. Le pain du jour. Paris, 1969.
43737.34.11 Pagnol, Marcel. Oeuvres complètes. Paris, 1970- 12v.
43737.34.100 Pagnol, Marcel. Les marchands de gloire. Paris, 1926.
43737.34.110 Pagnol, Marcel. Jazz. Paris, 1927.
43737.34.120 Pagnol, Marcel. Topaze; pièce en quatre actes. Paris, 1930.
43737.34.130 Pagnol, Marcel. Marius; pièce en quatre actes. Paris, 1931.
43737.34.132 Pagnol, Marcel. Marius. Monte-Carlo, 1969.
43737.34.140 Pagnol, Marcel. Fanny. Paris, 1934.
43737.34.141 Pagnol, Marcel. Fanny. Paris, 1970.
43737.34.150 Pagnol, Marcel. Merlusse. Paris, 1935.
43737.34.160 Pagnol, Marcel. Notes sur le rire. Paris, 1947.
43737.34.170 Pagnol, Marcel. Discours de récéption à l'Académie française le 27 mars 1947. Paris, 1947.
43737.34.180 Pagnol, Marcel. Critique des critiques. Paris, 1949.
43737.34.190 Pagnol, Marcel. Angèle. Paris, 1953.
43737.34.200 Pagnol, Marcel. Judas. Paris, 1956.
43737.34.210 Pagnol, Marcel. La fille du puisatier. Lyon, 1947.
43737.34.220 Pagnol, Marcel. Souvenirs d'enfance. Monte Carlo, 1957. 3v.
43737.34.222 Pagnol, Marcel. La gloire de mon père. Paris, 1960.
43737.34.230 Pagnol, Marcel. The days were too short. 1st ed. Garden City, 1960.
43737.34.240 Pagnol, Marcel. L'eau des collines. Paris, 1963. 2v.
43737.34.250 Pagnol, Marcel. Le masque de fer. Paris, 1965.
43737.34.260 Pagnol, Marcel. César. Monte-Carlo, 1970.
43737.36.100 Paulhan, Jean. L'aveuglette. Paris, 1952.
43737.36.800 Lefebve, M.J. Jean Paulhan. Paris, 1949.
43737.36.810 Toesca, M. Jean Paulhan. Paris, 1948.
43737.41.100 Paillot, F. Les trois maitresses de M. de Frivolac. Paris, 1920.
43737.46.100 Pakrowan, Emich. La quatrième génération. Paris, 1959.
43737.49.100 Palgen, Paul. Oratorio pour la mort d'un poète. Paris, 1957.
43737.52.100 Paluel-Marmont, A.P.H.J. Sud. Paris, 1934.
43737.56.100 Pampelonne, Roger de. Carnet lyrique. Saint-Félicien-en-Vivarais, 1925.
43737.58.100 Panafieu, Bruno. L'homme à l'odeur de poireau. Paris, 1960.
43737.59.100 Panneel, Henry. Contes et légendes du pays de Flandre. Paris, 1946.
43737.59.110 Panneel, Henry. Les Fioretti du curé d'Ars. Paris, 1957.
43737.60.100 Pange, P.L.M. Comment j'ai vu 1900. Paris, 1962. 3v.
43737.60.110 Pange, P.L.M. Le beau jardin. Paris, 1923.
43737.65.100 Panet, Edmond. Le poète Edmond Panet. Pierrefitte, 1946.
43737.65.110 Panet, Edmond. Les roses galactiques, vision et prophétisme. Paris, 1966.
43737.71.100 Papon, René. Le volcan. Paris, 1957.
43737.72.100 Papy-Sturm, Janine. Vibrer c'est déjà mourir. Paris, 1970.
43737.74.100 Paraf, P. Quand Israël aima. 8e éd. Paris, 1929.
43737.74.1100 Paradis, Louis. Sentence le 21. Montréal, 1958.
43737.74.2100 Paraz, Albert. Le menuet du haricot. Genève, 1958.
43737.74.3100 Parain, Brice. La mort de Jean Modec. Paris, 1945.
43737.74.3110 Parain, Brice. La mort de Socrate. Paris, 1950.
43737.74.3120 Parain, Brice. Sur la dialectique. Paris, 1953.
43737.74.3130 Parain, Brice. Joseph. Paris, 1964.
43737.75.100 Paret, T. Dans la mêlée. Paris, 1932.
43737.75.1100 Parenteau Dencel, Jacques. Les saisons de l'enfance, poèmes. Paris, 1969.
43737.76.100 Paris, Jean. La maison de mon enfance. Paris, 1964.
43737.77.100 Parmelin, Hélène. Le voyage à Lucerne. Paris, 1965.
43737.77.110 Parmelin, Hélène. Le complexe de Filacciano. Paris, 1960.
43737.77.120 Parmelin, Hélène. La gadgeture. Paris, 1967.
43737.77.130 Parmelin, Hélène. La femme-crocodile. Paris, 1968.
43737.77.140 Parmelin, Hélène. Le diplodocus. Paris, 1968.
43737.77.150 Parmelin, Hélène. La manière noire. Paris, 1970.
43737.77.1100 Paron, Charles Louis. Les vagues peuvent mourir. Paris, 1967.
43737.79.100 Pascarel, Charles. Massacre du printemps. Paris, 1966.
43737.80.100 Parrot, Louis. Oeil de fumée. Niort, 1953.
43737.80.110 Parrot, Louis. Paille noire des étables. Paris, 1945.
43737.82.100 Passeur, Delia. Aux jeunes et aux vieux. Limoges, 1954.
43737.82.1100 Pasguier, Claude. Le jour du saigneur. Monte Carlo, 1967.
43737.83.100 Passeur, Steve. Suzanne. Paris, 1929.
43737.83.110 Passeur, Steve. L'acheteuse. Paris, 1930.
43737.83.112 Passeur, Steve. L'acheteuse. 3e éd. Paris, 1930.
43737.83.120 Passeur, Steve. Pas encore; la traversée de Paris à la Nage. 4e éd. Paris, 1927.
43737.83.130 Passeur, Steve. 107'. Paris, 1948.
43737.83.140 Passeur, Steve. La maison ouverte. Paris, 1925.
43737.83.800 Ratiu, Basile. L'oeuvre dramatique de Steve Passeur. Paris, 1964.
43737.83.1100 Pastre, J.L.G. La neuvième croisade. 8e éd. Paris, 1926.
43737.86.100 Patient, Serge. Le mal du pays. Monte Carlo, 1967.
43737.87.800 De la transparence en poésie. Lugano, 1964.
43737.89.100 Pauwels, Louis. Les voies de petite communication. Paris, 1949.
43737.89.110 Pauwels, Louis. L'homme éternel. Paris, 1970.
43737.89.700 Pauwels, Louis. Not into clean hands. London, 1948.
43737.89.1011 Paulhan, Jean. Oeuvres complètes. Paris, 1966. 5v.
43737.89.1100 Paulhan, Jean. Les causes célèbres. Paris, 1951.
43737.89.1110 Paulhan, Jean. Un bruit de guêpe. Paris, 1957.
43737.89.1120 Paulhan, Jean. La métromanie. Paris, 1946.
43737.89.1130 Paulhan, Jean. Le pont traversé. Paris, 1921.
43737.89.1140 Paulhan, Jean. Le guerrier appliqué. Lausanne, 1930.
43737.89.1150 Paulhan, Jean. Les incertitudes du language. Paris, 1970.
43737.89.1800 Judrin, Roger. La vocation transparente de Jean Paulhan. Paris, 1961.
43737.89.2100 Pauphilet, Albert. Arc-en-ciel. Paris, 1936.
43737.89.2110 Pauphilet, Albert. Suite romanesque. Paris, 1930.
43737.89.3100 Pauline, Julia. Poèmes pour vous. Paris, 1947.

43511 - 43873 Individual authors, etc. - 1900- - Known authors (363 scheme plus 10) - cont.

43737.89.4100 Paulus, Jean Olivier. Eläinih. 1. ed. Schlossberg, Belgium, 1968.
43737.94.100 Pawlowski, Gaston William Adam de. Signaux à l'ennemi. Paris, 1918.
43737.94.110 Pawlowski, Gaston William Adam de. On se moque de nous. Paris, 1898.
43737.98.100 Paz, M.L. (Mme.). Femme. Paris, 1919.
43737.98.110 Paz, M.L. (Mme.). Woman. N.Y., 1920.
43737.98.1100 Paysan, Catherine. La Pacifique. Paris, 1957.
43737.98.1110 Paysan, Catherine. Nous autres, les Sanchez; roman. Paris, 1961.
43737.98.1120 Paysan, Catherine. Les feux de la chandeleur, roman. Paris, 1966.
43737.98.1130 Paysan, Catherine. La musique du feu. Paris, 1967.
43737.98.1140 Paysan, Catherine. Histoire d'une salamandre. Levallois, 1967.
43737.98.1150 Paysan, Catherine. Le nègre de Sables, roman. Paris, 1968.
43737.98.2100 Payen, Émile. Sarcasmes. Paris, 1958.
43738.1.2 Fossier, Andrée. Tables analytiques des oeuvres de Péguy. Paris, 1947.
43738.1.3 Péguy, Charles. Lettre à Franklin Bouillon. Paris, 1948.
43738.1.5 Péguy, Charles. Oeuvres complètes. v.1-16. Paris, 1916-52. 15v.
43738.1.19 Péguy, Charles. Pages choisies. Paris, 1952.
43738.1.20 Péguy, Charles. Oeuvres choisies 1900-1910. 3e éd. Paris, n.d.
43738.1.22 Péguy, Charles. Oeuvres en prose. Paris, 1957-59. 2v.
43738.1.25 Péguy, Charles. Morceaux choisies. 30e éd. Paris, 1937.
43738.1.27 Péguy, Charles. La France. Paris, 1939.
43738.1.30 Péguy, Charles. Ève. Paris, 1914.
43738.1.30.10 Péguy, Charles. Les tapisseries Ève. Paris, 1946.
43738.1.32 Péguy, Charles. God speaks. N.Y., 1957.
43738.1.45 Péguy, Charles. Lettres et entretiens. Paris, 1954.
43738.1.46 Péguy, Charles. Souvenirs. 12e éd. Paris, 1938.
43738.1.47 Péguy, Charles. Souvenirs. Paris, 1942.
43738.1.50A Péguy, Charles. Basic verities. N.Y., 1943.
43738.1.50B Péguy, Charles. Basic verities. N.Y., 1943.
43738.1.50C Péguy, Charles. Basic verities. 2nd ed. N.Y., 1943.
43738.1.50D Péguy, Charles. Basic verities. 3rd ed. N.Y., 1943.
43738.1.50.5 Péguy, Charles. Basic verities. 4th ed. N.Y., 1945.
43738.1.52 Charles Péguy. Angouleme, 1941.
43738.1.54 Péguy, Charles. Par ce demi-clair matin. Paris, 1952.
43738.1.56 Péguy, Charles. Men and saints. N.Y., 1944.
43738.1.57 Péguy, Charles. De Jean Coste. Paris, 1937.
43738.1.58 Péguy, Charles. Un poète l'a dit. 10e éd. Paris, 1953.
43738.1.59 Péguy, Charles. Clio. Paris, 1946.
43738.1.60 Péguy, Charles. Deux voix françaises. Paris, 1944.
43738.1.60.2 Péguy, Charles. Deux voix françaises. Paris, 1944.
43738.1.61 Péguy, Charles. Situations. Paris, 1948.
43738.1.62 Péguy, Charles. Notre seigneur. Paris, 1943.
43738.1.63 Péguy, Charles. Oeuvres poétiques complètes. Paris, 1948.
43738.1.64 Péguy, Charles. Pensées. 100. éd. Paris, 1942.
43738.1.66.15 Péguy, Charles. Notre Dame. 17e éd. Paris, 1941.
43738.1.68.20 Péguy, Charles. Saints de France. 40e éd. Paris, 1941.
43738.1.68.25 Péguy, Charles. Jeanne d'Arc. Paris, 1952.
43738.1.70.5 Péguy, Charles. Prières. 2nd éd. Paris, 1934.
43738.1.73 Péguy, Charles. Deuxième élégie XXX. 4e éd. Paris, 1955.
43738.1.75 Péguy, Charles. The mystery of the charity of Joan of Arc. N.Y., 1950.
43738.1.76 Péguy, Charles. The mystery of the holy innocents. N.Y., 1956.
43738.1.77 Péguy, Charles. L'esprit de système. Paris, 1953.
43738.1.78 Péguy, Charles. Temporal and eternal. London, 1958.
43738.1.79A Péguy, Charles. Une amitié française. Paris, 1955.
43738.1.79B Péguy, Charles. Une amitié française. Paris, 1955.
43738.1.80 Halévy, D. Charles Péguy et les Cahiers de la Quinzaine. Paris, 1918.
43738.1.81 Péguy, Charles. Péguy et les Cahiers. Paris, 1947.
43738.1.82 Halévy, D. Charles Péguy et les Cahiers de la Quinzaine. Paris, 1919.
43738.1.82.10 Halévy, D. Péguy and les Cahiers de la Quinzaine. London, 1946.
43738.1.82.12 Halévy, D. Péguy and les Cahiers de la Quinzaine. 1st ed. N.Y., 1947.
43738.1.83 Johannet, René. Les Lettres. Péguy et ses Cahiers. Paris, 1914.
43738.1.85 Johannet, René. Itinéraires d'intellectuels. Paris, 1921.
43738.1.87 Roussel, J. Mesure de Péguy. Paris, 1946.
43738.1.87.5 Roussel, J. Charles Péguy. Paris, 1953.
43738.1.91 Tharaud, J. Pour les fidèles de Péguy. Paris, 1949.
43738.1.93 Amitié Charles Péguy. Cahiers. Paris. 1,1947+ 15v.
43738.1.94 Courrier d'Orléans. Orléans. 2,1961+
43738.1.95 Hommage à Charles Péguy. 2nd éd. Paris, 1929.
43738.1.100 Mounier, E. La pensée de Charles Péguy. pts.1-2. Paris, 1931.
43738.1.105 Quoniam, Théodore. De la sainteté de Péguy. Paris, 1929.
43738.1.109 Le journal vrai. Paris. 1,1929
43738.1.110 Le journal vrai. Paris. 1-6 2v.
43738.1.115 Margenburg, E. Charles Péguy; ein Beitrag zur Geschichts-Philosophie. Berlin, 1937.
43738.1.120 Krakowski, E. Deux poètes de l'heroïsme: Charles Péguy et Stanislaw Wyspiański. Paris, 1937.
43738.1.130 Archambault, P. Charles Péguy; images d'une vie héroïque. St. Amand, 1939.
43738.1.132 Archambault, P. Péguy: la patrie charnelle et la cité du Dieu. Paris, 1940.
43738.1.140 Secrétain, R. Péguy. N.Y., 1941.
43738.1.152 Péguy, M. Le destin de Charles Péguy. 2e éd. Paris, 1941.
43738.1.152.5 Péguy, M. Le destin de Charles Péguy. 12e éd. Paris, 1946.
43738.1.152.10 Péguy, M. La decheance de l'or. Paris, 1933?
43738.1.160 Péguy, Pierre. Pour connaître la pensée de Péguy. Paris? 1940.
43738.1.165 Rousseaux, A. Le prophete Péguy. pts.2,4-5. Neuchatel, 1944-1945. 2v.
43738.1.170 Rolland, R. Péguy. Paris, 1945. 2v.
43738.1.175 Béguin, A. La prière de Péguy. Neuchatel, 1944.
43738.1.180 David, M. Initiation à Charles Péguy. Paris, 1945.
43738.1.185 Dubois-Dumée, J.P. Solitude de Péguy. Paris, 1946.
43738.1.190 Mabille de Poncheville, A. Jeunesse de Péguy. Paris, 1944.
43738.1.200 Chabanon, A. La poétique de Charles Péguy. Paris, 1947.
43738.1.201 Gremminger, E. Charles Péguy. Olten, 1949.

43511 - 43873 Individual authors, etc. - 1900- - Known authors (363 scheme plus 10) - cont.

43738.1.205 Ageorges, Joseph. La sublime folie de Charles Péguy. Paris, 1946.
43738.1.210 Amitié Charles Péguy. Feuillets d'informations. Paris. 25,1952+ 5v.
43738.1.215 Péguy, M. Pourquoi Péguy fonda les "Cahiers". Paris, 1950.
43738.1.220 Reclus, M. Le Péguy que j'ai connu. Paris, 1951.
43738.1.225 Anice, Robert. Péguy. Bruges, 1947?
43738.1.230 Servais, Y. Charles Péguy. Cork, 1953.
43738.1.235 Challaye, F. Péguy socialiste. Paris, 1954.
43738.1.240 Onimus, Jean. L'image dans Ève. Thèse. Paris, 1950.
43738.1.242 Onimus, Jean. La route de Charles Péguy. Paris, 1962.
43738.1.245 Marie-Louis, Mère. Culte marial de Charles Péguy. Nicolet, Quebec, 1955.
43738.1.250 Dru, Alexander. Péguy. London, 1956.
43738.1.260 Barbier, Joseph. Le vocabulaire. Paris, 1957.
43738.1.261 Barbier, Joseph. Le vocabulaire. Thèse principale. Paris, 1957.
43738.1.270 Barbier, Joseph. La prière chrétienne...de Péguy. Paris, 1959.
43738.1.800 Goldie, R. Vers un héroïsme intégral dans la lignée de Péguy. Paris, 1951.
43738.1.805 Dupuy, Jean R. Un utopiste du passé. Aix-en-Provence, 1957.
43738.1.810 Herriot, Edouard. Charles Péguy conférence donnée au théâtre municipal de Chartres. Angers, 1957.
43738.1.815 Suire, Pierre. Le tourment de Péguy. Paris, 1956.
43738.1.820 Brussels. Bibliotheque Royale. Charles Péguy. Bruxelles, 1958.
43738.1.825 Delaporte, Jean. Connaissance de Péguy. Paris, 1959. 2v.
43738.1.830 Guyon, Bernard. Péguy. Paris, 1960.
43738.1.835 Brunet, Frantz. La morale de Charles Péguy. Moulins, 1962?
43738.1.840 Barbier, Joseph. L'Ève de Charles Péguy. Paris, 1963.
43738.1.850 Emmerich, H. Nominalsuffixe im Sprachgebrauch Charles Péguys. Marburg, 1960.
43738.1.855 Christophe, Lucien. Le jeune homme Péguy. Brussels, 1964.
43738.1.860 Tharaud, J. Notre cher Péguy. Paris, 1926. 2v.
43738.1.865 Vandamme, Jan. Charles Péguy. Brugge, 1963.
43738.1.870 Cattaui, Georges. Péguy, témoin du temporel chrétien. Paris, 1964.
43738.1.875 Christophe, Lucien. Les grandes heures de Charles Péguy. Bruxelles, 1964.
43738.1.880 Mueller, Helmut. Charles Péguy und Corneille. München, 1961.
43738.1.890 Duployé, Pie. La religion de Péguy. Paris, 1965.
43738.1.895 Jassem-Wilson, Nelly. Charles Péguy. London, 1965.
43738.1.900 Villiers, Marjorie Howard. Charles Péguy. London, 1965.
43738.1.905 Roberty, Jules Émile. Charles Péguy. Paris, 1916.
43738.1.910 Seippel, Paul. Un poète français tombé au champ d'honneur: Charles Péguy. Paris, 1915.
43738.1.915 Suarès, André. Péguy. Paris, 1915.
43738.1.920 Mabille de Poncheville, André. Charles Péguy et sa mère. Paris, 1918.
43738.1.925 Cimon, Paul. Péguy et le temps présent. Montréal, 1964.
43738.1.930 Schmitt, Hans Adolf. Charles Péguy; the decline of an idealist. Baton Rouge, 1967.
43738.1.935 Delaporte, Jean. Péguy dans son temps et dans le nôtre. Paris, 1967.
43738.1.940 Quoniam, Théodore. La pensée de Péguy. Paris, 1967.
43738.1.945 Vigneault, Robert. L'univers féminin dans l'oeuvre de Charles Péguy. Bruges, 1967.
43738.1.950 Viard, Jacques. Philosophie de l'art littéraire et socialisme selon Péguy et selon Balzac. Paris, 1969.
43738.1.955 Prajs, Lazare. Péguy et Israël. Paris, 1970.
43738.2.30 Perrier, Martial. Aux jardins d'Aspasie. Paris, 1916.
43738.2.35 Perrier, Martial. Ma version de la maison cernée. Paris, 1924.
43738.3.30 Pelsener, A. Dans le vent des hélices. Grand, 1911.
43738.12.100 Peches, Jean Marie. La rose des heures. Bruxelles, 1964.
43738.35.100 Pégue-Vérane, Gabrielle. Racines profondes. Lausanne, 1965.
43738.41.100 Peisson, Edouard. Hans le marin. Paris, 1929.
43738.41.110 Peisson, Edouard. Le pilate, roman. Paris, 1937.
43738.41.120 Peisson, Edouard. Le courrier de la mer blanche. Paris, 1929.
43738.41.130 Peisson, Edouard. Le chalutier 304. Paris, 1935.
43738.41.140 Peisson, Edouard. Parti de Liverpool. 37e éd. Paris, 1932.
43738.41.150 Peisson, Edouard. Gens de mer. Paris, 1936.
43738.41.160 Peisson, Edouard. Une femme. Paris, 1934.
43738.41.170 Peisson, Edouard. Mer baltique, roman. Paris, 1940.
43738.41.171 Peisson, Edouard. Mer baltique, roman. Paris, 1936.
43738.41.175 Peisson, Edouard. La carte marine. 4e éd. Paris, 1939.
43738.41.180 Peisson, Edouard. Dieu te juge! Paris, 1955.
43738.41.185 Peisson, Edouard. Thomas et l'ange. Paris, 1959.
43738.41.190 Peisson, Edouard. Le quart de nuit. Paris, 1960.
43738.41.200 Peisson, Edouard. Mer baltique. Paris, 1936.
43738.41.210 Peisson, Edouard. L'aigle de mer. Paris, 1941.
43738.41.220 Peisson, Edouard. Capitaines de la route de New York. Paris, 1953.
43738.41.1100 Peignot, Jérôme. Jérômiades. Paris, 1957- 3v.
43738.41.1110 Peignot, Jérôme. Grandeur et misères d'un employé de bureau. Paris, 1965.
43738.41.1120 Peignot, Jérôme. L'amour a ses princes. Paris, 1967.
43738.48.100 Pellerin, Pierre. La possession de l'équateur. Paris, 1957.
43738.49.100 Pellerin, Jean. Le bouquet inutile. 8e éd. Paris, 1923.
43738.49.102 Pellerin, Jean. Le bouquet inutile. Paris, 1954.
43738.49.110 Pellerin, Jean. La romance du retour. Paris, 1921.
43738.49.120 Pellerin, Jean. Cécile et ses amours; roman. Paris, 1923?
43738.49.1100 Pelegri, Jean. Les oliviers de la justice. Paris, 1959.
43738.49.1110 Pelegri, Jean. Les monuments du déluge. Paris, 1967.
43738.49.2100 Pelletier Doisy, Jacqueline. L'étang de la breure. Paris, 1967.
43738.49.2110 Pelletier Doisy, Jacqueline. Le domaine de hautefrâgne. Paris, 1967.
43738.50.100 Pellerin, J.V. 32 décembre suivi de quelques mirlitons antérieurs. Paris, 1922.
43738.50.120 Pellerin, J.V. Têtes de rechange. Intimité. Paris, 193-?
43738.50.130 Pellerin, J.V. Choix de poèmes. Paris, 1960.
43738.50.3100 Pelletier, René. Besançon, ville gauloise à la manière de Victor Hugo. Besançon, 1958.
43738.51.100 Pelliot, Marianne. La chevelur de Bérénice. Paris, 1955.
43738.58.100 Pencalet, Marcel. Nos rives sont d'armor. Paris, 1960.

43511 - 43873 Individual authors, etc. - 1900- - Known authors (363 scheme plus 10) - cont.

43738.59.100 Penent, Jacques Arnaud. Les temps morts. Paris, 1965.
43738.60.100 Pemjian, L. Cyrano de Bergerac. Paris, 1921.
43738.62.100 Penzo, Berthe. Cerveau à la broche. Paris, 1959.
43738.74.105 Perdriel-Vaissière, Jeanne. La complainte des jeunes filles qui ne seront pas épousées. 5e éd. Paris, 1919.
43738.75.100 Perec, Georges. Les choses. Paris, 1965.
43738.75.110 Perec, Georges. Un homme qui dort. Paris, 1967.
43738.75.1100 Péret, Benjamin. Oeuvres complètes. Paris, 1969.
43738.75.1110 Péret, Benjamin. Le déshonneur des poètes. Paris, 1965.
43738.75.1800 Courtot, Claude. Introduction à la lecture de Benjamin Péret. Paris, 1965.
43738.76.100 Pergaud, Louis. Poèmes. Paris, 1928.
43738.76.110 Pergaud, Louis. De Goupil à Margot. 42e éd. Paris, 1929.
43738.76.112 Pergaud, Louis. De Goupil à Margot. 60e éd. Paris, 1937.
43738.76.130 Pergaud, Louis. La guerre des boutons. 41e éd. Paris, 1937.
43738.76.140 Pergaud, Louis. Oeuvres. Paris, 1954.
43738.76.150 Pergaud, Louis. Correspondance. Paris, 1955.
43738.76.160 Pergaud, Louis. La revanche du corbeau. Paris, 1911.
43738.76.170 Pergaud, Louis. Les rustiques. Paris, 1921.
43738.76.800 Louis Pergaud. Besançon, 1952?
43738.76.2024 Périer, Odilon Jean. Poèmes. 4e éd. Paris, 1952.
43738.76.2800 Defrenne, M. Odilon-Jean Périer. Bruxelles, 1957.
43738.76.3100 Pericard, Jacques. J'ai huit enfants. Paris, 1926.
43738.76.4100 Périer, Delphine. La sonate écossaise. Paris, 1960.
43738.76.5100 Périn, Cécile. Dicté par une ombre. Paris, 1934.
43738.77.90 Pérochon, Ernest. Nêne. Paris, 1920.
43738.77.100 Pérochon, Ernest. Nêne. Paris, 1921?
43738.77.104 Pérochon, Ernest. Nêne. Paris, 1920.
43738.77.110 Pérochon, Ernest. Le crime étrange de Lise Balzan. Paris, 1929.
43738.77.120 Pérochon, Ernest. Huit gouttes d'opium. Paris, 1925.
43738.77.130 Pérochon, Ernest. Les endiablés. Paris, 1934.
43738.77.140 Pérochon, Ernest. Les gardiennes. Paris, 1924.
43738.77.150 Pérochon, Ernest. Milon. Paris, 1936.
43738.77.160 Pérochon, Ernest. Babette et ses frères. Paris, 1939.
43738.77.700 Pérochon, Ernest. Nêne. N.Y., 1922.
43738.77.1100 Pérol, Jean. Le coeur véhément. Paris, 1968.
43738.77.1110 Pérol, Jean. Ruptures. Paris, 1970.
43738.77.2100 Perrier, A. Gravitation. Paris, 1936.
43738.77.3100 Perrein, Michèle. Barbastre. Paris, 1960.
43738.77.4100 Perry, Jacques. Vie d'un païen; roman. Paris, 1967. 3v.
43738.77.5100 Perrelet, Olivier. Crise de rêves. Genève, 1964.
43738.77.6700 Perrault, Gilles. Dossier 51; an entertainment. London, 1971.
43738.77.7621 Perret, Christopher. Christopher Perret. Memorial volume. Genève, 1967.
43738.78.21A Perse, Saint-John. Oeuvre poétique. Paris, 1953. 2v.
43738.78.21B Perse, Saint-John. Oeuvre poétique. v.2. Paris, 1953.
43738.78.22 Perse, Saint-John. Oeuvre poétique. Paris, 1961-62. 2v.
43738.78.23 Perse, Saint-John. Opere poetiche. Milano, 1960.
43738.78.24 Perse, Saint-John. Saint-John Perse. Paris, 1967.
43738.78.100 Perse, Saint-John. Anabasis; a poem. London, 1930.
43738.78.120 Léger, Alexis S.-L. Poésie. Paris, 1961.
43738.78.130 Perse, Saint-John. Exil. Paris, 1945.
43738.78.140 Perse, Saint-John. Exil. Paris, 1946.
43738.78.150 Perse, Saint-John. Éloges. Paris, 1948.
43738.78.155 Perse, Saint-John. Éloges. N.Y., 1956.
43738.78.160 Perse, Saint-John. Anabase. Paris, 1947.
43738.78.170 Perse, Saint-John. Amers. Paris, 1957.
43738.78.180 Perse, Saint-John. Chronique. Paris, 1960.
43738.78.182 Perse, Saint-John. Chronique. Stockholm, 1960.
43738.78.184 Perse, Saint-John. Chronique. N.Y., 1961.
43738.78.190F Perse, Saint-John. Vents. Paris, 1946.
43738.78.200 Perse, Saint-John. Poème à l'étrangère. n.p., 1942?
43738.78.700F Léger, Alexis S.-L. Seamarks. N.Y., 1958.
43738.78.710A Léger, Alexis S.-L. Anabasis. London, 1959.
43738.78.710B Léger, Alexis S.-L. Anabasis. London, 1959.
43738.78.720 Léger, Alexis S.-L. On poetry. N.Y., 1961.
43738.78.721 Perse, Saint-John. Two addresses. N.Y., 1966.
43738.78.740F Perse, Saint-John. Winds. N.Y, 1953.
43738.78.750 Perse, Saint-John. Birds. Durham, 1967.
43738.78.777 Perse, Saint-John. Exile and other poems. 2d ed. N.Y., 1962.
43738.78.788 Perse, Saint-John. Destierro. Santander, 1960.
43738.78.790 Perse, Saint-John. Jord vindar hav. Stockholm, 1960.
43738.78.800 Little, Roger. Word index of the complete poetry and prose of Saint-John Perse. n.p., 1965.
43738.78.811 Caillois, Roger. Poétique de Saint-John Perse. Paris, 1962.
43738.78.815 Saillet, Maurice. Saint-John Perse. Paris, 1952.
43738.78.820 Charpier, Jean. Saint-John Perse. Paris, 1962.
43738.78.825 Henry, A. Amers de Saint-John Perse. Neuchatel, 1963.
43738.78.830 Loranquin, A. Saint-John Perse. Paris, 1963.
43738.78.835 Knodel, Arthur. Saint-John Perse. Edinburgh, 1966.
43738.78.840 Honneur à Saint-John Perse. Paris, 1965.
43738.78.845 Murciaux, Christian. Saint-John Perse. Paris, 1961.
43738.78.850 Emmanuel, Pierre. Saint-John Perse: praise and presence. Washington, 1971.
43738.78.3100 Perruchot, Henri. Patrice. Paris? 1947.
43738.79.100 Perrier, F. La garde montante. N.Y., 1944.
43738.79.2100 Perrin, André. Mario. Paris, 1955.
43738.80.100 Perron-Louis, G. Lettres du prisonnier. Paris, 1942.
43738.81.21 Perret, Jacques. Histoires sous le vent. Paris, 1957.
43738.81.100 Perret, Jacques. Objets perdus. 10e éd. Paris, 1949.
43738.81.110 Perret, Jacques. Bande à part. Paris, 1951.
43738.81.123 Perret, Jacques. Salades de saison. 3e éd. Paris, 1957.
43738.81.130 Perret, Jacques. Rôle de plaisance. 23e éd. Paris, 1957.
43738.81.140 Perret, Jacques. Le caporal epinglé. Paris, 1957.
43738.81.150 Perret, Jacques. Un homme perdu. Paris, 1950.
43738.81.160 Perret, Jacques. Nouvelles. Paris, 1961.
43738.81.170 Perret, Jacques. La compagnie des eaux. Paris, 1969.
43738.81.180 Perret, Jacques. Ernest le rebelle; roman. Paris, 1949.
43738.81.700 Perret, Jacques. The wind in the sails. London, 1954.
43738.81.1100 Perret, Vivette. Les absents, roman. Paris, 1958.
43738.81.2100 Petibon, Andrée. Sur le chemin du rêve. Paris, 1934.
43738.83.43 Pesquidoux, J.D. La harde. Paris, 1936.
43738.83.100 Pesquidoux, J.D. Sur la glèbe. Paris, 1922.
43738.83.110 Pesquidoux, J.D. Le livre de raison. 27e éd. Paris, 1937.
43738.83.112 Pesquidoux, J.D. Le livre de raison. 18e éd. Paris, 1925.
43738.83.115 Pesquidoux, J.D. Le livre de raison. 16e éd. Paris, 1928.
43738.83.120 Pesquidoux, J.D. Le livre de raison. 12e éd. Paris, 1932.

43511 - 43873 Individual authors, etc. - 1900- - Known authors (363 scheme plus 10) - cont.

43738.83.800 Genevoix, Maurice. Discours de réception de Maurice Genevoix à l'Académie française. Paris, 1948.
43738.85.100 Peter, René. Pouche, comedie en trois actes. Paris, 1924.
43738.85.1100 Petit, Henri. Les justes solitudes. Paris, 1965.
43738.85.1110 Petit, Henri. La route des hommes. Paris, 1968.
43738.90.100 Pevel, Henri. On a crevé le paravent. Paris, 1957.
43738.97.103 Peyre, Joseph. Matterhorn. Paris, 1939.
43738.97.110 Peyre, Joseph. Sang et lumières. Paris, 1935.
43738.97.120 Peyre, Joseph. L'homme de choc. 19e éd. Paris, 1936.
43738.97.130 Peyre, Joseph. Roc-Gibraltar. 10e éd. Paris, 1937.
43738.97.140 Peyre, Joseph. Coups durs. 11e éd. Paris, 1935.
43738.97.150 Peyre, Joseph. Souvenirs d'un enfant. Paris, 1958.
43738.97.153 Peyre, Joseph. Tema. Paris, 1936.
43738.97.160 Peyre, Joseph. Guadalquivir. Paris, 1952.
43738.97.170 Peyre, Joseph. Le plan du soleil, roman. Paris, 1960.
43738.97.180 Peyre, Joseph. Feu et sang de juillet. Paris, 1964.
43738.97.1100 Peyrefitte, Roger. L'oracle. Paris, 1948.
43738.97.1110 Peyrefitte, Roger. Les ambassades. Paris, 1951.
43738.97.1120 Peyrefitte, Roger. La fin des ambassades. Paris, 1953.
43738.97.1130 Peyrefitte, Roger. Les clés de Saint-Pierre. Paris, 1955.
43738.97.1140 Peyrefitte, Roger. Les amitiés particulières. Paris, 1956.
43738.97.1150 Peyrefitte, Roger. Jeunes proies. Paris, 1956.
43738.97.1160 Peyrefitte, Roger. Chevaliers de Malte. Paris, 1957.
43738.97.1170 Peyrefitte, Roger. Les fils de la lumière. Paris, 1962.
43738.97.1180 Peyrefitte, Roger. Du Vésuve à l'Etna. Paris, 1960.
43738.97.1190 Peyrefitte, Roger. Le spectateur nocturne. Paris, 1960.
43738.97.1200 Peyrefitte, Roger. Le prince des Neiges, drame. Paris, 1961.
43738.97.1210 Peyrefitte, Roger. Notre amour. Paris, 1967.
43738.97.1220 Peyrefitte, Roger. Les américains, roman. Paris, 1968.
43738.97.1230 Peyrefitte, Roger. Des français; roman. Paris, 1970.
43738.97.1240 Peyrefitte, Roger. Mademoiselle de Murville. Paris, 1947.
43738.97.1700 Peyrefitte, Roger. Diplomatic conclusions. Paris, 1951.
43738.97.1710 Peyrefitte, Roger. Diplomatic diversions. 2nd ed. London, 1954.
43738.97.1720 Peyrefitte, Roger. South from Naples. London, 1954.
43738.97.1725 Peyrefitte, Roger. Special friendships. N.Y., 1950.
43738.97.1730 Peyrefitte, Roger. The keys of St. Peter. N.Y., 1957.
43738.97.1735 Peyrefitte, Roger. Special friendships. London, 1958.
43738.97.1740 Peyrefitte, Roger. Knights of Malta. N.Y., 1959.
43738.97.1745 Peyrefitte, Roger. Cavalieri di Malta. 2. ed. Firenze, 1958.
43738.97.1750 Peyrefitte, Roger. The Prince's person. London, 1964.
43738.97.1755 Peyrefitte, Roger. Les juifs. Paris, 1965.
43738.97.1760 Peyrefitte, Roger. The Jews. Indianapolis, 1967.
43738.98.100 Peyret-Chappuis, Charles de. "Frenesie"; pièce en trois actes. Paris, 1938.
43738.98.110 Peyret-Chappuis, Charles de. Feu Monsieur Pic. Paris, 1939.
43738.98.1100 Peyre, Christiane. Une société anonyme. Paris, 1962.
43738.98.2100 Peyramaure, Michel. Les Colosses de Carthage, roman. Paris, 1967.
43738.99.100 Pezet, Jacques. Symphonie héroïque; roman. Paris, 1946.
43738.99.2100 Pezeril, D. Rue Notre Dame. N.Y., 1953.
43739.23.100 Pfeiffer, Jean. Traité de l'aventure. Paris, 1946.
43740.1.30 Philippe, Charles Louis. La mère et l'enfant. 5e éd. Paris, n.d.
43740.1.30.5 Philippe, Charles Louis. La mère et l'enfant. 14e éd. Paris, 1923.
43740.1.31 Philippe, Charles Louis. Charles Blanchard. Paris, 1913.
43740.1.32 Philippe, Charles Louis. Lettres de jeunesse à Henri Vandeputte. Paris, 1911.
43740.1.33 Philippe, Charles Louis. Croquignole. Leipzig, 1913?
43740.1.34 Philippe, Charles Louis. Croquignole. Paris, 1906.
43740.1.35 Philippe, Charles Louis. Bubu de Montparnasse. Paris, 1927.
43740.1.35.5 Philippe, Charles Louis. Bubu de Montparnasse. Monte Carlo, 1946.
43740.1.36 Philippe, Charles Louis. Bübü, roman. Berlin, 1913.
43740.1.38 Philippe, Charles Louis. Faits divers. Nevers, 1911.
43740.1.40 Philippe, Charles Louis. Die gute Madeleine und die arme Marie. München, 1923.
43740.1.43 Philippe, Charles Louis. Mutter und Kind. Berlin, 1912.
43740.1.45 Philippe, Charles Louis. Der alte Perdrix. München, 1923.
43740.1.47 Philippe, Charles Louis. Le Père Perdrix. Paris, 1921.
43740.1.50 Philippe, Charles Louis. Marie Donadieu. London, 1949.
43740.1.55 Philippe, Charles Louis. Bubu of Montparnasse. N.Y., 1951.
43740.1.60 Philippe, Charles Louis. Quatre histoires de pauvre amour. Paris, 1897.
43740.1.62 Philippe, Charles Louis. Lettres à sa mère. Paris, 1928.
43740.1.65 Philippe, Charles Louis. Contes du matin. Paris, 1916.
43740.1.81 Kerber, Karl. Charles Louis Philippe. Inaug. Diss. Leipzig, 1931.
43740.1.83 Fourchambault, Jacques de. Charles Louis Philippe. Paris, 1943.
43740.1.85 Kellermann, W. Studien zu Charles Louis Philippe. Wertheim am Main, 1931.
43740.1.87 Bachelin, Henri. Charles Louis Philippe, 1874-1909. Paris, 1929.
43740.1.89 Lanoizelée, L. Charles Louis Philippe, l'homme, l'écrivain. Paris, 1953.
43740.3.100 Pham-Van-Ky. Les contemporains. Paris, 1959.
43740.3.110 Pham-Van-Ky. Perdre la demeure. Paris, 1961.
43740.41.100 Philippe, A. L'acier; roman. Paris, 1937.
43740.41.1100 Philip, Maurice. Maillons. Coutances, 1957.
43740.41.2100 Philipe, Anne. Le temps d'un soupir. Paris, 1963.
43740.41.2110 Philipe, Anne. Les rendez-vous de la colline. Paris, 1966.
43740.64.100 Pholien, Georges. En lisant. Paris, 1959.
43740.66.100 Photiades, Vassily. Marylénè. Paris, 1936.
43741.1.30 Pierrelle, C. Les Pierres qui vivent. Paris, 1914.
43741.2.100 Piachaird, R.L. La tragédie de Coriolan. Paris, 1934.
43741.2.800 Halaenwang, G. Avec René-Louis Piachaud. Genéve, 1958.
43741.4.100 Piat, P. Inquiétudes. Paris, 1929.
43741.10.100 Picard, G. Pour lire entre les lignes. Paris, 1947.
43741.11.100 Pic, M. La Féerie interieure; poèmes. Paris, 1935.
43741.11.1011 Piccard, Eulalie. Collection des oeuvres complètes. v.1,2-3,4-5,6,10,16. Neuchâtel, 1963. 6v.
43741.11.1012 Piccard, Eulalie. Collection des oeuvres complètes. Neuchâtel, 1967-68. 10v.
43741.11.1100 Piccard, Eulalie. Pages choisies des Episodes de la grande tragédie russe. Neuchâtel, 1960.
43741.11.3100 Picabia, Francis. Choix de poèmes. Paris, 1947.

43511 - 43873 Individual authors, etc. - 1900- - Known authors (363 scheme plus 10) - cont.

43741.11.3110 Picabia, Francis. Revue publiée de 1917 à 1924. Paris, 1960. 2v.
43741.11.3120 Picabia, Francis. Dits. Paris, 1960.
43741.11.3800 Benoit, P.A. A propos des poèmes de la fille née sans mère. Alès, 1957.
43741.11.4100 Picard, Étienne. Dans les sentiers. Orleans, 1960.
43741.12.100 Picasso, Pablo. Le désir attrapé par la queue. Paris, 1945.
43741.12.110 Picasso, Pablo. Trozo de piel, poema. Málaga, 1961.
43741.12.120 Picasso, Pablo. Les quatre petites filles, pièce en 6 actes. Paris, 1968.
43741.12.700 Picasso, Pablo. Desire. N.Y., 1948.
43741.12.705 Picasso, Pablo. Desire caught by the tail; a play. N.Y., 1962.
43741.12.710 Picasso, Pablo. Wie man Wünsche beim Schwanz packt. Zürich, 1964.
43741.12.715 Picasso, Pablo. The four little girls. London, 1970.
43741.12.800 Garaudy, R. D'un réalisme sans rivages. Paris, 1963.
43741.13.100 Pichette, Henri. Apoèmes. Paris, 1947.
43741.13.110 Pichette, Henri. Lettres arc-en-ciel. Paris, 1950.
43741.13.120 Pichette, Henri. Rond-point. Paris, 1950.
43741.13.130 Pichette, Henri. Le point vélique. Paris, 1950.
43741.13.140 Pichette, Henri. Nucléa. Paris, 1952.
43741.13.150 Pichette, Henri. Les Epiphanies. Paris, 1948.
43741.13.160 Pichette, Henri. Odes à chacun. Paris, 1961.
43741.13.170 Pichette, Henri. Tombeau de G. Philipe. Paris, 1961.
43741.13.180 Pichette, Henri. Dents de lait, dents de loup. Paris, 1962.
43741.14.100 Picon, Gaëtan. L'usage de la lecture. Paris, 1960. 3v.
43741.14.110 Picon, Gaëtan. Un champ de solitude. Paris, 1968.
43741.14.120 Picon, Gaëtan. L'oeil double. Paris, 1970.
43741.19.100 Pidoux, Edmond. Africaines. Neuchâtel, 1967.
43741.19.110 Pidoux, Edmond. Passage de la ligne. Roisel, 1967.
43741.21.100 Piéchaud, M. Mademoiselle Pascal. Paris, 1922.
43741.21.110 Piéchaud, M. Le sommeil des amants. Paris, 1923.
43741.21.120 Piéchaud, M. Le favori. Paris, 1933.
43741.23.100 Pierhal, A. Jeunes morts chéris des dieux. Paris, 1938.
43741.24.100 Pierron, S. Le bateau Démâté suivi de l'auberge Délaissée. Bruxelles, 1926.
43741.24.1100 Pierre-Quint, Léon. Décheances aimables. Paris, 1924.
43741.24.2100 Pierson-Piérard, Marianne. Plages. Bruxelles, 1964.
43741.24.2110 Pierson-Piérard, Marianne. Entre hier et demain, roman. Paris, 1967.
43741.24.3100 Pierre, Henri. Les carnets blancs. Poèmes. Genéve, 1952-67. 3v.
43741.25.100 Pieyre de Mandiargues, André. Le lis de mer. Paris, 1956.
43741.25.110 Pieyre de Mandiargues, André. Le musée noir. Paris, 1957.
43741.25.120 Pieyre de Mandiargues, André. Le cadran lunaire. Paris, 1958.
43741.25.130 Pieyre de Mandiargues, André. Marbre. Paris, 1953.
43741.25.140 Pieyre de Mandiargues, André. Feu de braise. Paris, 1959.
43741.25.150 Pieyre de Mandiargues, André. Astyanax. Viry-Chatillon, 1957.
43741.25.160 Pieyre de Mandiargues, André. Cahier de poésie. v.1,3-4,5. Paris, 1961. 4v.
43741.25.170 Pieyre de Mandiargues, André. Deuxième Belvedère. Paris, 1962.
43741.25.180 Pieyre de Mandiargues, André. Cartolines et dédicaces. Paris, 1960.
43741.25.190 Pieyre de Mandiargues, André. La motocyclette. Paris, 1963.
43741.25.200 Pieyre de Mandiargues, André. Le musée noir. Paris, 1963.
43741.25.210 Pieyre de Mandiargues, André. Porte devergondée. Paris, 1965.
43741.25.220 Pieyre de Mandiargues, André. Sabine. Paris, 1963.
43741.25.230 Pieyre de Mandiargues, André. Dans les années sordides. Monaco, 1943.
43741.25.240 Pieyre de Mandiargues, André. Le Belvédére. Paris, 1958.
43741.25.250 Pieyre de Mandiargues, André. La marge. Paris, 1967.
43741.25.260 Pieyre de Mandiargues, André. Soleil des loups. Paris, 1966.
43741.25.270 Pieyre de Mandiargues, André. Le marronnier. Paris, 1968.
43741.25.700 Pieyre de Mandiargues, André. The girl beneath the lion. N.Y., 1958.
43741.25.705 Pieyre de Mandiargues, André. The motorcycle. N.Y., 1965.
43741.26.100 Pierre-Lambert, René. Ti et mi. Paris, 1957.
43741.48.100 Pillendin, Roger. La belle jeunesse. Paris, 1957.
43741.49.100 Pillement, Georges. Les femmes ont le coeur sur la main. Paris, 1947.
43741.49.110 Pillement, Georges. Autres pièces cyniques. Paris, 1970.
43741.49.2100 Pilhes, René-Victor. La rhubarbe; roman. Paris, 1965.
43741.50.100A Pillionnel, J.H. Poèmes d'Amérique. Paris, 1928.
43741.50.100B Pillionnel, J.H. Poèmes d'Amérique. Paris, 1928.
43741.50.110 Pillionnel, J.H. Les graminées; poèmes. Paris, 1932.
43741.50.120 Pillionnel, J.H. Les tragiques de l'après-guerre (1918-21). Paris, 1935.
43741.50.130 Pillionnel, J.H. Le puits et autres poésies, 1932-1960. Paris, 1962.
43741.50.1100 Pillet, Roger. Les oraisons amoureuses de Jeanne Aurélie Grivolin. Paris, 1922.
43741.50.2100 Piller, Pedro R. El prófugo. Valencia, 1935. 2 pam.
43741.51.100 Pilon, Edmond. Sites et personnages. Paris, 1912.
43741.51.110 Pilon, Edmond. Dans le buisson des lettres. Paris, 1934.
43741.51.800 Gahisto, Manoel. Edmond Pilon. Paris, 1921.
43741.59.100 Pingaud, Bernard. Le prisonnier. Paris, 1958.
43741.59.110 Pingaud, Bernard. L'amour triste. Paris, 1965.
43741.59.120 Pingaud, Bernard. La scène primitive. Paris, 1965.
43741.59.130 Pingaud, Bernard. Inventaire. Paris, 1965-
43741.59.800 Parain, Brice. Entretiens avec Bernard Pingaud. Paris, 1966.
43741.59.2100 Pineau, Christian. Mon cher député. Paris, 1960.
43741.59.2110 Pineau, Christian. La simple vérité, 1940-1945. Paris, 1961.
43741.59.3021 Pinget, Robert. Plays. London, 1963- 2v.
43741.59.3100 Pinget, Robert. Le fiston. Paris, 1959.
43741.59.3110 Pinget, Robert. Monsieur Levert. N.Y., 1961.
43741.59.3120A Pinget, Robert. La manivelle. Paris, 1960.
43741.59.3120B Pinget, Robert. La manivelle. Paris, 1960.
43741.59.3130 Pinget, Robert. Clope au dossier. Paris, 1961.
43741.59.3140 Pinget, Robert. Ici ou ailleurs, suivi de architruc. Paris, 1961.
43741.59.3150 Pinget, Robert. Graal flibuste. Paris, 1956.
43741.59.3151 Pinget, Robert. Graal flibuste. Paris, 1966.
43741.59.3160 Pinget, Robert. Baga. Paris, 1958.

43511 - 43873 Individual authors, etc. - 1900- - Known authors (363 scheme plus 10) - cont.

43741.59.3170 Pinget, Robert. L'inquisitoire. Paris, 1962.
43741.59.3180 Pinget, Robert. Mahu. Paris, 1952.
43741.59.3190 Pinget, Robert. Autour de Mortin. Paris, 1965.
43741.59.3200 Pinget, Robert. Quelqu'un. Paris, 1965.
43741.59.3700 Pinget, Robert. Three plays. 1st American ed. N.Y., 1966.
43741.59.3705 Pinget, Robert. The inquisitory. London, 1966.
43741.59.3710 Pinget, Robert. Baga. London, 1967.
43741.59.4100 Pinguet, Auguste. Le cantique de la mer. Angers, 1928.
43741.59.4110 Pinguet, Auguste. Le jardin des quatrains. Angers, 1931.
43741.59.4120 Pinguet, Auguste. Nouveaux poèmes de l'Anjou. Angers, 1910.
43741.59.4130 Pinguet, Auguste. La chanson de l'Anjou. Paris, 1923.
43741.59.4140 Pinguet, Auguste. Le poème, 1918. Angers, 1920.
43741.59.4150 Pinguet, Auguste. Oeuvres; poèmes 1910-1930. Angers, 1930.
43741.64.100 Pioch, Georges. La paix inconnue et dolente. Paris, 1929.
43741.66.100 Piot, André. Mémoires poétiques. Paris, 1963.
43741.75.100 Pirey Saint-Alby. A première vue. 9e éd. Paris, 1929.
43741.77.100 Piroué, Georges. Une si grande faiblesse. Paris, 1965.
43741.88.100 Pittard, Hélène (Mme.). Le nouveau déluge. pts.1-5. Paris, 1922.
43741.88.102 Pittard, Hélène (Mme.). Le nouveau déluge. Paris, 1922.
43741.88.105 Pittard, Hélène (Mme.). Le nouvel Adam. pts.1-5. Paris, 1924.
43741.88.110 Pittard, Hélène (Mme.). Celui qui voit; roman. pts.1-4. Paris, 1926.
43741.88.115 Pinget, Robert. Les amours de Corinne. Paris, 1930.
43741.88.120 Pinget, Robert. Le chercheur d'ondes; roman. pts.1-2. Paris, 1931.
43741.88.130 Pittard, Hélène (Mme.). Jean-Jacques ou Le promeneur solitaire. Paris, 1933.
43741.88.140 Pittard, Hélène (Mme.). Le nouveau Lazare. pts.1-3. Paris, 1935.
43741.88.150 Pittard, Hélène (Mme.). La vallée perdue; roman. pts.1-3. Paris, 1939.
43741.89.100 Piroué, Georges. Chansons à dire. Paris, 1956.
43741.89.110 Piroué, Georges. Murir. Paris, 1958.
43741.89.120 Piroué, Georges. Les limbes. Paris, 1959.
43741.89.130 Piroué, Georges. Ces eaux qui ne vont nulle part. Lausanne, 1966.
43741.89.140 Piroué, Georges. La surface des choses. Lausanne, 1970.
43741.91.100 Pivot, Bernard. L'amour en vogue; roman. Paris, 1959.
43741.98.100 Pize, Louis. Chansons du pigeonnier. Paris, 1928.
43741.98.110 Pize, Louis. Les muses champêtres. Paris, 1925.
43741.98.120 Pize, Louis. Les feux de septembre. Paris, 1931.
43742.3.105 Planchon, Michel. Compagnons de silence. 5e éd. Paris, 1957.
43742.3.112 Planchon, Michel. Lumière noire. 2e éd. Paris, 1958.
43742.3.1100 Plaissy, Lucien. Chemins vers l'aube. Paris, 1960.
43742.3.2100 Planté, Louis. Le destin de Marie Baradat. Pau, 1970.
43742.5.100 Plateau, J. Poésie. Hasselt, Belgique, 1937.
43742.25.100 Pleynet, Marcelin. Comme; poésie. Paris, 1965.
43742.41.100 Plisnier, Charles. Faux passeports. Paris, 1937.
43742.41.103 Plisnier, Charles. Faux passeports. 133e éd. Paris, 1937.
43742.41.110 Plisnier, Charles. Mariages. Paris, 1936.
43742.41.115 Plisnier, Charles. Mariages, roman. Paris, 1946-48. 2v.
43742.41.120 Plisnier, Charles. Meurtres. v.1,2,4,5. Paris, 1939. 4v.
43742.41.130 Plisnier, Charles. Sacre. Paris, 1938.
43742.41.140 Plisnier, Charles. Une voix d'or. Freibourg en Swisse, 1944.
43742.41.150 Plisnier, Charles. Ave genitrix. Fribourg, 1943.
43742.41.155 Plisnier, Charles. Ave genitrix. Paris, 1943.
43742.41.160 Plisnier, Charles. Héloise. Paris, 1945.
43742.41.170 Plisnier, Charles. Hospitalité. Fribourg, 1943.
43742.41.180 Plisnier, Charles. Nicole Arnaud. Paris, 1948.
43742.41.190 Plisnier, Charles. Vertu du désordre. Paris, 1949.
43742.41.200 Plisnier, Charles. Bruler vif. Paris, 1957.
43742.41.210 Plisnier, Charles. L'homme et les hommes. Paris, 1953.
43742.41.220 Plisnier, Charles. Mes bien-aimés. Paris, 1946.
43742.41.800 Bodart, R. Charles Plisnier. Paris, 1953.
43742.41.810 Roussel, Jean. La vie et l'oeuvre ferventes de Charles Plisnier. Rodez, 1957.
43742.89.100 Plumyène, Jean. Le complexe de gauche. Paris, 1967.
43743.1.30 Porché, François. A chaque jour. Paris, 1907.
43743.1.31 Porché, François. Humus et Poussière. Poèmes. Paris, 1911.
43743.1.32 Porché, François. Au loin, peut-être. Poèmes. Paris, 1909.
43743.1.33 Porché, François. L'arrêt sur la marne. Paris, 1916.
43743.1.34 Porché, François. La jeune fille. Paris, 1919.
43743.1.35 Porché, François. La jeune fille. Paris, 1919.
43743.1.39 Porché, François. La Dauphine; comédie. Paris, 1921.
43743.1.41 Porché, François. Le chevalier de Colomb. Paris, 1922.
43743.1.43 Porché, François. La vierge au grand coeur. Paris, 1925.
43743.1.45 Porché, François. Le dessous du masque. Paris, 1914.
43743.1.47 Porché, François. Nous poèmes choisis. Paris, 1916.
43743.1.49 Porché, François. La race errante. Paris, 1932.
43743.1.55 Porché, François. Le poème de la delivrance. Paris, 1919.
43743.1.60 Porché, François. Vers, 1928-1933. Paris, 1934.
43743.2.30F Poizat, A. Sophonisbe. Paris, 1913.
43743.2.31 Poizat, A. Classicisme et Catholicisme. Paris, 1911.
43743.2.35 Poizat, A. Çircé. Paris, 1922.
43743.2.40 Poizat, A. Electre. Paris, 1923.
43743.2.45 Poizat, A. Saül; Antigone. Paris, 1910.
43743.2.50 Poizat, A. Méléagre et Atalante. Paris, 1911.
43743.2.55 Poizat, A. Le cyclope. Paris, 1906.
43743.2.81 Just, Otto. Alfred Poizat. Inaug. Diss. Borna, 1936.
43743.3.30 Porré, Emmanuel. Fantaisus. Paris, 190-?
43743.37.100 Polhes, Alban de. Le parfum de l'Amphore. Paris, 1901.
43743.37.110 Polhes, Alban de. Le petit. Paris, 1905.
43743.37.120 Polhes, Alban de. L'enfant du Temple. Paris, 1907.
43743.41.100 Poirier, Jean M. Le prix du souvenir. Ottawa, 1957.
43743.41.3100 Poirot-Delpech, Bertrand. Le grand dadais. Paris, 1958.
43743.41.3110 Poirot-Delpech, Bertrand. Finie la comédie. Paris, 1969.
43743.41.3120 Poirot-Delpech, Bertrand. La grasse matinée. Paris, 1960.
43743.41.3130 Poirot-Delpech, Bertrand. La folle de Lituanie. Paris, 1970.
43743.41.3700 Poirot-Delpech, Bertrand. Fool's paradise. London, 1959.
43743.41.4100 Poilvet Le Guenn, Jean. Galons. Paris, 1959.
43743.41.4110 Poilvet Le Guenn, Jean. Séquences pour une saga. Paris, 1962.
43743.41.5100 Poiteau, Émile. Aux jardins des muses. Paris, 1960.
43743.41.6100 Poitou, Jean. D'un sexe à l'autre. Paris, 1971.
43743.48.100 Poli, François. Gentlemen convicts. London, 1960.

43511 - 43873 Individual authors, etc. - 1900- - Known authors (363 scheme plus 10) - cont.

43743.48.1100	Poldès, Leo. L'éternel ghetto. Paris, 1928.
43743.48.1800	Goublet, Juliette. Léo Poldès: Le Faubourg. Aurillac, 1965.
43743.50.100	Pomier, Jean. Creations en litterature. Paris, 1955.
43743.50.2100	Poliza, Elena. Croisée. Buenos Aires, 1955.
43743.55.100	Pommier, Jean. Le spectacle intérieur. Paris, 1970.
43743.57.100	Poncins, G. de M. Jean Menadieu. N.Y.? 1944.
43743.57.700A	Poncins, G. de M. Home is the hunter. N.Y., 1943.
43743.57.700B	Poncins, G. de M. Home is the hunter. N.Y., 1943.
43743.59.100	Ponchon, Raoul. La muse au carbaret. Paris, 1921.
43743.59.800	Coulon, Marcel. Raoul Ponchon. Paris, 1927.
43743.59.1100	Ponet, Marthe Bordeaux. Un drame d'enfant. Paris, 1925.
43743.60.21	Ponge, Francis. Tome premier. Paris, 1965.
43743.60.100	Ponge, Francis. Le carnet du bois de pins. Lausanne, 1947.
43743.60.110	Ponge, Francis. Le parti pris des choses. Paris, 1942.
43743.60.110.5	Ponge, Francis. Le parti pris des choses. Paris, 1967.
43743.60.120	Ponge, Francis. Poèmes. Paris, 1948.
43743.60.130	Ponge, Francis. L'Araignée. Paris, 1952.
43743.60.140	Ponge, Francis. La rage de l'expression. Lausanne, 1952.
43743.60.150	Ponge, Francis. Le grand recueil. Paris, 1961. 3v.
43743.60.160	Ponge, Francis. Le Savon. Paris, 1967.
43743.60.170	Ponge, Francis. Nouveau recueil. Paris, 1967.
43743.60.180	Ponge, Francis. La fabrique du pré. Genève, 1971.
43743.60.700	Ponge, Francis. Die literarische Praxis. Olten, 1964.
43743.60.800	Paris. Bibliothèque Sainte Géneviève. Collection Doucet. Francis Ponge. Paris, 1960?
43743.60.810	Walther, E. Francis Ponge: analytische Monographie. Stuttgart, 1961?
43743.60.815	Sartre, Jean-Paul. L'homme et les choses. Paris, 1947.
43743.61.100	Potier, André. Un français à l'école americaine. Paris, 1952.
43743.61.1100	Ponthier, François. Le phenix. Paris, 1958.
43743.61.1110	Ponthier, François. Poigne-en-croce. Paris, 1968-69. 3v.
43743.61.2100	Pontremoli, Pascal. Lapidaire. Paris, 1965.
43743.61.2110	Pontremoli, Pascal. Le jonet der fer-blanc. Paris, 1967.
43743.61.3100	Ponty, Bernard. Le séquestre. Paris, 1970.
43743.62.110	Pons, Justin. Jours et nuits de Paris. Paris, 1930.
43743.62.1100	Pons, R. L'après-midi; suivi du déménagement, de journées et de l'enterrement. Paris, 1962.
43743.62.2100	Pons, Maurice. Viriginales nouvelles. Paris, 1955.
43743.62.2110	Pons, Maurice. Le passager de la nuit. Paris, 1960.
43743.62.2120	Pons, Maurice. Rosa. Chronique fidèle des événements sur venus au siècle dernier dans la principauté de Wasquelham. Paris, 1967.
43743.62.2130	Pons, Maurice. La passion de Sébastien N. Paris, 1968.
43743.75.100	Porché, François. Le poème de la tranchée. Paris, 1916.
43743.75.110	Porché, François. Les commandiments du destin. Paris, 1921.
43743.75.120	Porché, François. Les butors et la finette. 8. éd. Paris, 1925.
43743.75.130	Porché, François. Un roi, deux dames et un valet. Paris, 1935.
43743.75.140	Porché, Simone Benda. Sous de nouveaux soleils. Paris, 1957.
43743.75.1100	Poreaux, Denise. Cette année de la Montagne. n.p., 1969.
43743.77.100	Portejoie, Pierre. J'appelle les hommes. Paris, 1956.
43743.77.1100	Portal, Georges. Un protestant. Paris, 1936.
43743.77.2100	Porquerol, Elizabeth. Les voix. Paris, 1965.
43743.77.3100	Porquet, André. Le ciel dans les poches. Paris, 1946.
43743.83.100	Postel-Vinay, G. Refrains d'Espagne traduits. Paris, 1923.
43743.89.100	Pouget, P. L'autre bataille. Paris, 1924.
43743.89.1100	Poulet, Robert. La lanterne magique. Paris, 1956.
43743.89.1110	Poulet, Robert. Les ténèbres. Paris, 1958.
43743.89.1120	Poulet, Robert. Les sources de la vie. Paris, 1967.
43743.89.2100	Poulaille, H. Ames neuves. Paris, 1925.
43743.89.3100	Poupeney, Norbert. Au vent des souvenirs. Paris, 1958.
43743.90.100	Pourrat, Henri. La ligne vente. 4. éd. Paris, 1929.
43743.90.110	Pourrat, Henri. Gaspard des Montagnes. Paris, 1922.
43743.90.115	Pourrat, Henri. Les vaillances. Paris, 1930.
43743.90.120	Pourrat, Henri. La veillée de novembre. Uzès, 1937.
43743.90.130	Ringelmann, A. Henri Pourrat, geb. 1887. Inaug. Diss. Würzburg, 1936.
43743.90.140	Pourrat, Henri. Toucher terre. Uzès, 1936.
43743.90.150	Pourrat, Henri. Le mauvais garçon. 10. éd. Paris, 1926.
43743.90.160	Pourrat, Henri. Vent du Mars. Paris, 1943.
43743.90.170	Pourrat, Henri. L'école buissonnière. Paris, 1949.
43743.90.180	Pourrat, Henri. Le trésor des contes. v.1-13. Paris, 1948-53. 11v.
43743.90.190	Pourrat, Henri. L'homme à la peau de loup. Neuchâtel, 1950.
43743.90.200	Pourrat, Henri. Le chasseur de la nuit. Paris, 1951.
43743.90.210	Pourrat, Henri. A la belle Bergère. Paris, 1925.
43743.90.2100	Pourrat, Henri. Georges. Paris? 1941.
43743.90.2110	Pourrat, Henri. Dans l'herbe des trois vallees. Paris, 1927.
43743.90.2120	Pourrat, Henri. La combe délaissée. Saint-Félicien-en-Vivarais, 1925.
43743.90.4100	Pourtal de Ladevèze, Jean. D'un mirage secret. Paris, 1937.
43743.90.4110	Pourtal de Ladevèze, Jean. Desseins. Paris, 1928.
43743.90.4120	Pourtal de Ladevèze, Jean. Fragments. Paris, 1927.
43743.91.100	Pourtalès, Guy de. La pêche miraculeuse. 47. éd. Paris, 1937.
43743.91.108	Pourtalès, Guy de. La pêche miraculeuse; roman. 58. éd. Paris, 1937.
43743.91.110	Pourtalès, Guy de. Saints de Pierre. Fribourg, 1941.
43743.91.120	Pourtalès, Guy de. Les contes du milieu du monde. Fribourg, 1941.
43743.91.130	Pourtalès, Guy de. A mes amis suisses. Paris, 1916.
43743.92.100	Pouvourville, Albert de. Le mal d'argent, les livres de la brousse. Paris, 1926.
43743.92.110	Pouvourville, Albert de. L'Annam sanglant. Paris, 1912.
43743.92.120	Pouvourville, Albert de. A vingt-neuf agent secret. Paris, 1932.
43743.98.100	Poydenot, H. Impasse de l'avenir. Paris, 1938.
43743.98.430	Pozner, Vladimir. Les gens du pays. N.Y., 1943.
43743.98.440	Pozner, Vladimir. Qui a tuè H.O. Burrell? Paris, 1952.
43743.98.450	Pozner, Vladimir. Deuil en 24 heures. Paris, 1956.
43743.98.460	Pozner, Vladimir. Le mors aux dents. Lausanne, 1965.
43743.98.530A	Pozner, Vladimir. The edge of the sword. N.Y., 1942.
43743.98.530B	Pozner, Vladimir. The edge of the sword. N.Y., 1942.
43743.98.531A	Pozner, Vladimir. First harvest. N.Y., 1943.
43743.98.531B	Pozner, Vladimir. First harvest. N.Y., 1943.

43511 - 43873 Individual authors, etc. - 1900- - Known authors (363 scheme plus 10) - cont.

43743.98.1100	Pozzi, C. Peau d'âme. Paris, 1935.
43744.1.100	Praag, Siegfried Emanuel van. Fille de France. Londres, 1944.
43744.1.1100	Pradelle, François. Le dit du grant pin. Paris, 1937.
43744.2.100	Prado, Jacques. Balises. Paris, 1927.
43744.3.100	Praillet, Arthur. La flute d'herbe. Basse-Yutz, 1967.
43744.5.100	Prassinos, Gisèle. Le rêve. Paris, 1947.
43744.5.110	Prassinos, Gisèle. Le feu maniaque. Paris, 1944.
43744.5.120	Prassinos, Gisèle. Le temps n'est rien. Paris, 1958.
43744.5.130	Prassinos, Gisèle. La voyageuse. Paris, 1959.
43744.5.140	Prassinos, Gisèle. Les mots endormis. Paris, 1967.
43744.5.1100	Praz, Narcisse R. Peau de Moine. Neuchâtel, 1966.
43744.24.21	Prévert, Jacques. Histoires. Paris, 1946.
43744.24.22	Prévert, Jacques. Histoires d'autres histoires. Paris, 1963.
43744.24.23	Prévert, Jacques. Paroles. Paris, 1947.
43744.24.23.7	Prévert, Jacques. Paroles. Paris, 1950.
43744.24.23.8A	Prévert, Jacques. Paroles. Paris, 1957.
43744.24.23.8B	Prévert, Jacques. Paroles. Paris, 1957.
43744.24.23.9	Prévert, Jacques. Selections from "Paroles". Harmondsworth, 1965.
43744.24.25	Jacques Prévert parmi nous. Labastide-Rouairoux, 1953?
43744.24.30	Prévert, Jacques. Lumières d'homme. Paris, 1955.
43744.24.35	Prévert, Jacques. La pluie et le beau temps. 42. éd. Paris, 1955.
43744.24.40	Prévert, Jacques. Guignal. Lausanne, 1952.
43744.24.45	Prévert, Jacques. L'opera de la lune. Lausanne, 1953.
43744.24.50	Prévert, Jacques. Grand bal du printemps. Lausanne, 1951.
43744.24.55	Prévert, Jacques. Lettre des Iles Baladar. Paris, 1952.
43744.24.60	Prévert, Jacques. Fatras. Paris, 1966.
43744.24.65	Prévert, Jacques. Spectacle. 46. éd. Paris, 1951.
43744.24.80	Quéval, Jean. Jacques Prévert. Paris, 1955.
43744.24.85	Lapsley, Mary. Jacques Prévert. N.Y., 1950.
43744.24.90	Baker, William E. Jacques Prévert. N.Y., 1967.
43744.24.95	Bergens, Andrée. Jacques Prévert. Paris, 1969.
43744.25.100	Prévost, Jean. Les frères Bouquinquant. 16. éd. Paris, 1930.
43744.25.102	Prévost, Jean. Les frères Bouquinquant. Paris, 1930.
43744.25.110	Prévost, Jean. Dix-huitième année. 4. éd. Paris, 1929.
43744.25.120	Prévost, Jean. Nous marchons sur la mer. 5. éd. Paris, 1931.
43744.25.130	Prévost, Jean. La chasse du matin. 6. éd. Paris, 1937.
43744.25.140	Prévost, Jean. Polymnie. Paris, 1929.
43744.25.2800	Henriot, Emila. Le fautenial de Marcel Prévost. Paris, 1946.
43744.25.3800	Lenglin, Jeanne. Le poète de la tendresse, Ernest Prévost, sa vie, son oeuvre. Paris, 1947.
43744.25.4100	Prévost, Alain. Bonne chance quand même. Paris, 1958.
43744.25.4110	Prévost, Alain. Le chalutier Minium. Paris, 1959.
43744.25.4120	Prévost, Alain. Les amoureux d'Euville. Paris, 1962.
43744.25.4130	Prévost, Alain. Le pont des absents. Paris, 1967.
43744.25.5021	Prévot, Gérard. Théâtre: La nouvelle Eurydice, La mise à mort, Guillaume Fischer. Paris, 1964.
43744.25.5100	Prévot, Gérard. Un prix Nobel. Paris, 1962.
43744.25.5110	Prévot, Gérard. La Haute note jaune, récit. Bruxelles, 1967.
43744.25.6100	Praviel, Armand. The murder of Monsieur Fualdes. N.Y., 1924.
43744.25.7100	Prévot-Leygonie, Augustin. Mademoiselle de la Talheyrie. Paris, 1968.
43744.41.775	Privat, Maurice. L'avventuriera dagli occhi verdi. Firenze, 1923.
43744.41.2100	Prin, Armand de. La vierge au sourire. Paris, 1925.
43744.41.3100	Privat, Bernard. Une nuit sans sommeil; roman. Paris, 1966.
43744.41.4100	Priou, J.N. Jeux de massacre. Paris, 1950.
43744.64.100	Prody, Alfred. La légende du Bois de la Fage. Aurillac, 1920.
43744.64.110	Prody, Alfred. Par les sentes; poèmes. Brive, 1925.
43744.64.120	Prody, Alfred. Les reflets; poèmes. Brive, 1919.
43744.67.5	Proust Research Association. Newsletter. Lawrence, Kansas. 1,1969+
43744.67.20	Proust, Marcel. Marcel Proust; a selection. London, 1948.
43744.67.21	Proust, Marcel. Marcel Proust. Paris, 1954.
43744.67.30	Les cahiers Marcel Proust. Paris. 1-8,1927-1935 8v.
43744.67.31	Les cahiers Marcel Proust. Nouvelle serie. Paris. 1,1970+ 3v.
43744.67.32	Bulletin Marcel Proust. Paris. 1,1930
43744.67.34	Hindus, M. A reader's guide to Marcel Proust. N.Y., 1962.
43744.67.36	Proust, Marcel. Textes retrouvés. Urbana, 1968.
43744.67.38.5	Proust, Marcel. Du coté de chez Swann. Paris, 1929. 2v.
43744.67.38.10	Proust, Marcel. Du coté de chez Swann. 156. éd. Paris, 1936. 2v.
X Cg 43744.67.38.15	Proust, Marcel. A la recherche du temps perdu. v.1-8. Paris, 1934-39. 16v.
43744.67.38.16	Proust, Marcel. A la recherche du temps perdu. Paris, 1954- 3v.
43744.67.38.20	Proust, Marcel. A la recherche du temps perdu. v.3-5, pt.1-3. Paris, 1933-35. 3v.
43744.67.39	Proust, Marcel. Cities of the plain. N.Y., 1927. 2v.
43744.67.39.5	Proust, Marcel. Cities of the plain. London, 1936. 2v.
43744.67.39.10A	Proust, Marcel. Cities of the plain. 1. ed. N.Y., 1938.
43744.67.39.10B	Proust, Marcel. Cities of the plain. 1. ed. N.Y., 1938.
43744.67.40.15A	Proust, Marcel. Swann's way. N.Y., 1956.
43744.67.40.15B	Proust, Marcel. Swann's way. N.Y., 1956.
43744.67.40.15C	Proust, Marcel. Swann's way. N.Y., 1956.
43744.67.40.15D	Proust, Marcel. Swann's way. N.Y., 1956.
43744.67.41	Proust, Marcel. Within a budding grove. N.Y., 1924.
43744.67.41.5	Proust, Marcel. Within a budding grove. N.Y., 1930.
43744.67.41.15	Proust, Marcel. The Guermantes way. N.Y., 1933.
43744.67.41.20	Proust, Marcel. The Guermantes way. N.Y., 1925.
43744.67.42	Proust, Marcel. The captive. 2. ed. N.Y., 1929.
43744.67.43	Proust, Marcel. Time regained. London, 1931.
43744.67.44	Proust, Marcel. Remembrance of things past. v.2-4. N.Y., 1934. 3v.
43744.67.44.5	Proust, Marcel. Remembrance of things past. v.3. N.Y., 1933.
43744.67.44.10	Proust, Marcel. Pages choisies. Paris, 1954.
43744.67.45	Proust, Marcel. Pastiches et mélanges. 28. éd. Paris, 1919.
43744.67.46	Proust, Marcel. Retratos de pintores y de músicos. Madrid, 194-.
43744.67.47.5	Proust, Marcel. Remembrance of things past. N.Y., 1960? 2v.

43511 - 43873 Individual authors, etc. - 1900- - Known authors (363 scheme plus 10) - cont.

43744.67.47.10 Proust, Marcel. Time regained. London, 1970.
43744.67.48 Proust, Marcel. Jean Santeuil. 19. éd. Paris, 1952. 3v.
43744.67.50 Proust, Marcel. Chroniques. 12. éd. Paris, 1927.
43744.67.51 Proust, Marcel. Contre Sainte-Beuve. 15. éd. Paris, 1954.
43744.67.51.2 Proust, Marcel. Marcel Proust on art and literature, 1896-1919. N.Y., 1958.
43744.67.51.3 Proust, Marcel. By way of Saint Beuve. London, 1958.
43744.67.52 Proust, Marcel. Sus mejores páginas. Santiago, 1933.
43744.67.53 Proust, Marcel. Marcel Proust et Jacques Rivière. Paris, 1955.
Htn 43744.67.54* Proust, Marcel. Le Balzac de Monsieur de Guermantes. Neuchâtel, 1950.
43744.67.56 Proust, Marcel. Pleasures and regrets. N.Y., 1948.
43744.67.57 Proust, Marcel. Maxims. N.Y., 1948.
43744.67.58 Proust, Marcel. Letters. London, 1950.
43744.67.58.5 Proust, Marcel. Lettres retrouvées. Paris, 1966.
43744.67.59 Raphael, N.P. Introduction à la correspondance de M. Proust. Leiden, 1938.
43744.67.60A Raphael, N.P. Introduction à la correspondance de Marcel Proust. Paris, 1938.
43744.67.60B Raphael, N.P. Introduction à la correspondance de Marcel Proust. Paris, 1938.
43744.67.61 Proust, Marcel. Comment parut "Du Côte de chez Swann". Paris, 1930.
43744.67.62 Proust, Marcel. Quelques lettres de M. Proust à Jeanne. Paris, 1929.
43744.67.62.5 Proust, Marcel. Quelques lettres de Marcel Proust à Jeanne. Paris, 1928.
43744.67.63 Proust, Marcel. Lettres à Robert de Montesquiou, 1893-1921. Paris, 1930.
43744.67.64 Proust, Marcel. Lettres à une amie. Manchester, 1942.
43744.67.65 Proust, Marcel. Quelques lettres de Marcel Proust. Paris, 1928.
43744.67.66 Proust, Marcel. Lettres à la comtesse de Noailles, 1901-1919. Paris, 1931.
43744.67.67 Proust, Marcel. Letters. N.Y., 1949.
43744.67.68 Proust, Marcel. Lettres de Marcel Proust à Bibesco. Lausanne, 1949.
43744.67.68.2 Proust, Marcel. Letters to Antoine Bibesco. London, 1953.
43744.67.68.5 Proust, Marcel. Letters to his mother. London, 1956.
43744.67.69A Proust, Marcel. Lettres à Monsieur et Madame Sydney Schiff. Paris, 1932.
43744.67.69B Proust, Marcel. Lettres à Monsieur et Madame Sydney Schiff. Paris, 1932.
43744.67.70 Bibescu, M.L.L. Le voyageur voilé: Marcel Proust. Lettres au duc de Guiche. Genève, 1947.
43744.67.71 Bibescu, M.L.L. The veiled wanderer, Marcel Proust. London, 1949.
43744.67.72A Proust, Marcel. Lettres à P. Lanallée. Paris, 1933.
43744.67.72B Proust, Marcel. Lettres à P. Lanallée. Paris, 1933.
43744.67.73 Proust, Marcel. Lettres à André Gide. Neuchâtel, 1949.
43744.67.74 Proust, Marcel. Lettres à Madame C. Paris, 1946.
43744.67.74.5 Proust, Marcel. Lettres à Reynaldo, Halm. 5. éd. Paris, 1956.
43744.67.74.10 Proust, Marcel. Choix de lettres. Paris, 1965.
43744.67.75A Proust, Marcel. Lettres à Walter Berry. Paris, 1935.
43744.67.75B Proust, Marcel. Lettres à Walter Berry. Paris, 1935.
43744.67.76 Proust, Marcel. Lettres à Madame et Monsieur Émile Straus. Paris, 1936.
Htn 43744.67.77* Proust, Marcel. 47 lettres inédites...à Walter Berry. Paris, 1930.
43744.67.78 Proust, Marcel. Quatre lettres de Marcel Proust à ses concierges. Genève, 1945.
43744.67.79 Proust, Marcel. Comment débuta Marcel Proust; lettres inédites. Paris, 1925.
43744.67.79.2 Proust, Marcel. Comment débuta Marcel Proust; lettres inédites. Paris, 1969.
43744.67.79.20 Proust, Marcel. Correspondance avec sa mère. Paris, 1953.
43744.67.79.30 Proust, Marcel. Correspondance. Paris, 1970.
43744.67.80 Proust, Marcel. Letters to a friend. London, 1949.
43744.67.80.2 Proust, Marcel. A un ami. Paris, 1948.
43744.67.80.5 Scott-Moncrieff, Charles Kenneth. Marcel Proust; an English tribute. Photoreproduction. N.Y., 1923.
43744.67.81 Pierre-Quint, Léon. Marcel Proust. Paris, 1925.
43744.67.82A Pierre-Quint, Léon. Marcel Proust, sa vie, son oeuvre. 7. éd. Paris, 1925.
43744.67.82B Pierre-Quint, Léon. Marcel Proust, sa vie, son oeuvre. 12. éd. Paris, 1925.
43744.67.83 Pierre-Quint, Léon. Marcel Proust. Paris, 1946.
43744.67.85 Sonday, Paul. Marcel Proust. Paris, 1927.
43744.67.87 Bret, Jacques. Marcel Proust. Genève, 1946.
43744.67.90A Bonnet, Henri. Deux etudes sur Marcel Proust. Arras, 1928.
43744.67.90B Bonnet, Henri. Deux etudes sur Marcel Proust. Arras, 1928.
43744.67.95 Mouton, Jean. Le style de Marcel Proust. Paris, 1948.
43744.67.105 Maurois, André. A la recherche de Marcel Proust. 60. éd. Paris, 1949.
43744.67.106 Maurois, André. The quest for Proust. London, 1950.
43744.67.107A Maurois, André. Proust. 1. ed. N.Y., 1950.
43744.67.107B Maurois, André. Proust. 1. ed. N.Y., 1950.
43744.67.109 Autret, Jean. L'influence de Ruskin sur la vie. Genève, 1955.
43744.67.110 Proust. Paris, 1965.
43744.67.800A Marcel Proust. Paris, 1926.
43744.67.800B Marcel Proust. Paris, 1926.
43744.67.805 Cabeen, D.C. A selected bibliography of works on Proust for a small library. N.Y., 1938?
43744.67.810A Gabory, Georges. Essai sur Marcel Proust. Paris, 1926.
43744.67.810B Gabory, Georges. Essai sur Marcel Proust. Paris, 1926.
43744.67.815 Dreyfus, R. Souvenirs sur Marcel Proust. Paris, 1926.
43744.67.818A Dreyfus, R. Marcel Proust a dix-sept ans. Paris, 1926.
43744.67.818B Dreyfus, R. Marcel Proust a dix-sept ans. Paris, 1926.
43744.67.820A Pierre-Quint, Léon. Comment travaillait Proust. Paris, 1928.
43744.67.820B Pierre-Quint, Léon. Comment travaillait Proust. Paris, 1928.
43744.67.824 Pierre-Quint, Léon. Le comique et le mystère chez Proust. Paris, 1928.
43744.67.826 Pierre-Quint, Léon. Marcel Proust. Paris, 1935.
43744.67.828 Pierre-Quint, Léon. Le combat de Marcel Proust. Paris, 1955.
43744.67.830 Bonnet, Henri. Marcel Proust de 1907 à 1914. Paris, 1959.
X Cg 43744.67.830 Bandieu, Arnaud. Marcel Proust. Paris, 1930.

43511 - 43873 Individual authors, etc. - 1900- - Known authors (363 scheme plus 10) - cont.

43744.67.835 Abraham, P. Proust; recherches sur la création intellectuelle. Paris, 1930.
43744.67.837 Aressy, Lucien. A la recherche de Marcel Proust. Paris, 1930.
Htn 43744.67.850* Proust, Marcel. Lettres à Madame Scheikévitch. Paris, 1928.
43744.67.860 Seillière, E. Marcel Proust. Paris, 1931.
43744.67.870A Blondel, Charles. La psychographie de Marcel Proust. Paris, 1932.
43744.67.870B Blondel, Charles. La psychographie de Marcel Proust. Paris, 1932.
43744.67.875A Capasso, Aldo. Marcel Proust. Milano, 1935.
43744.67.875B Capasso, Aldo. Marcel Proust. Milano, 1935.
43744.67.880A Hier, Florence. La musique dans l'oeuvre de Marcel Proust. N.Y., 1933.
43744.67.880B Hier, Florence. La musique dans l'oeuvre de Marcel Proust. N.Y., 1933.
43744.67.885 Feuillerat, A. Comment Marcel Proust a composé son roman. New Haven, 1934.
43744.67.890 Wolters, Klaus. Marcel Proust im literarischen Urteil seiner Zeit. Inaug. Diss. München, 1932.
43744.67.895 Souza, S. de. L'influence de Ruskin sur Proust. Thèse. Montpellier, 1932.
43744.67.900 Spagnoli, J.J. The social attitude of Marcel Proust. N.Y., 1936.
43744.67.910 Beckett, Samuel. Proust. London, 1931.
43744.67.920 Massis, H. Le drame de Marcel Proust. Paris, 1937.
43744.67.930A Bell, Clive. Proust. N.Y., 1929.
43744.67.930B Bell, Clive. Proust. N.Y., 1929.
43744.67.940 Monkhouse, E. La révélation de Marcel Proust. Thèse. Paris, 1936.
43744.67.950 Clermont-Tonnerre, E. de G. Robert de Montesquiou et Marcel Proust. Paris, 1925.
43744.67.955 Clermont-Tonnerre, E. de G. Marcel Proust. Paris, 1948.
43744.67.960A Fiser, Emeric. L'esthétique de Marcel Proust. Paris, 1933.
43744.67.960B Fiser, Emeric. L'esthétique de Marcel Proust. Paris, 1933.
43744.67.962 Fiser, Emeric. La théorie du symbole littéraire et Marcel Proust. Paris, 1941.
43744.67.965 Curtius, E.R. Marcel Proust. Paris, 1928.
43744.67.966 Curtius, E.R. Marcel Proust. Berlin, 1952.
43744.67.970A Crémieux, Benjamin. Du côte de Marcel Proust. Paris, 1929.
43744.67.970B Crémieux, Benjamin. Du côte de Marcel Proust. Paris, 1929.
43744.67.980A Billy, Robert de. Marcel Proust; lettres et conversations. Paris, 1930.
43744.67.980B Billy, Robert de. Marcel Proust; lettres et conversations. Paris, 1930.
43744.67.992 Mauriac, F. Du coté de chez Proust. Paris, 1947.
43744.67.993 Mauriac, F. Proust. Paris, 1926.
43744.67.994 Mauriac, F. Proust's way. N.Y., 1950.
43744.67.995 Green, Frederick C. The mind of Proust. Cambridge, Eng., 1949.
43744.67.996 Le Bidois, Robert. L'inversion du sujet dans la prose contemporaine. Paris, 1952.
43744.67.996.2 Le Bidois, Robert. L'inversion du sujet dans la prose contemporaine. Thèse. Paris, 1952.
43744.67.997 Jaloux, Edmond. Avec Marcel Proust, suivi de dix-sept lettres inedites de Proust. Paris, 1953.
43744.67.998 Bersani, Leo. Marcel Proust; the fictions of life and of art. N.Y., 1965.
43744.67.999 Proust, Marcel. Marcel Proust par lui-même. Paris, 1953.
43744.67.1000 Milon, F.J. Proust, Valéry et le plaisir de la lecture. Paris, 1938.
43744.67.1010A Zaeske, Käthe. Der Stil Marcel Prousts. Emsdetten, 1937.
43744.67.1010B Zaeske, Käthe. Der Stil Marcel Prousts. Emsdetten, 1937.
43744.67.1020 Abatangel, L. Marcel Proust et la musique. Paris, 1937.
43744.67.1030 Souza, S. La philosophie de Marcel Proust. Paris, 1939.
X Cg 43744.67.1030B Souza, S. La philosophie de Marcel Proust. Paris, 1939.
43744.67.1040 Ames, Van Meter. Proust and Santayana; the aesthetic way of life. Chicago, 1937.
43744.67.1050 Pommier, J.J.M. La mystique de Marcel Proust. Paris, 1939.
43744.67.1051A Alden, D.W. Marcel Proust and his French critics. Los Angeles, 1940.
43744.67.1051B Alden, D.W. Marcel Proust and his French critics. Los Angeles, 1940.
43744.67.1051C Alden, D.W. Marcel Proust and his French critics. Los Angeles, 1940.
43744.67.1052 Casnati, Francesco. Proust. Brescia, 1933.
43744.67.1054 Kinds, Edmond. Etude sur Marcel Proust. Paris, 1933.
43744.67.1056 Cremonte, Lelio. Proust. Firenze, 1938.
43744.67.1058 Maranini, Lorenzo. Proust, arte e conoscenza. Firenze, 1933.
43744.67.1060 Lima, Jorge de. Dois en saios. Maceio, 1929.
43744.67.1062 Laget, Auguste. Le roman d'une vocation; Marcel Proust. Marseille, 1925.
43744.67.1064 Wegener, Alfons. Impressionismus und Klassizismus im Werke Marcel Prousts. Frankfurt, 1930.
43744.67.1066A Jacob, Jean. Marcel Proust, son oeuvre. Paris, 1929.
43744.67.1066B Jacob, Jean. Marcel Proust, son oeuvre. Paris, 1929.
43744.67.1068 Benoist-Mechin, J.G.P.M. La musique et l'immortalite dans l'oeuvre de Marcel Proust. Paris, 1926.
43744.67.1070 Ruskin, John. La Bible d'Amiens. 9e éd. Paris, 1926.
43744.67.1072 Coelho, Ruy. Proust e introducão ao método crítico. São Paulo, 1944.
43744.67.1080 Leon, D. Introduction to Proust. London, 1940.
43744.67.1090 Luidner, D. Marcel Proust. Stanford, 1942.
43744.67.1100 Chernowitz, M.E. Proust and painting. N.Y., 1945.
43744.67.1110 Ferré, André. Geographie de Marcel Proust. Paris, 1939.
43744.67.1115 Ferré, André. Géographie de Marcel Proust avec index des noms de lieux et des termes géographiques. Thèse. Paris, 1939.
43744.67.1120 Boylesve, René. Quelques échanges et témoignages. Paris, 1931.
43744.67.1125 Larcher, P.L. Le parfum de Combray. Paris, 1945.
43744.67.1130 Polanšcak, Antun. La peinture du décor et de la nature chez Marcel Proust. Thèse. Paris, 1941.
43744.67.1135 Rivane, Georges. Influence de l'asthme sur l'oeuvre de Marcel Proust. Paris, 1945.
43744.67.1137 Fardwell, F.V. Landscape in the works of Marcel Proust. Washington, 1948.
43744.67.1140 Buchet, E.E. Écrivains intelligents du XXe siècle. Paris, 1945.

43511 - 43873 Individual authors, etc. - 1900- - Known authors (363 scheme plus 10) - cont.

43744.67.1145A March, Harold. The two worlds of Marcel Proust. Philadelphia, 1948.
43744.67.1145B March, Harold. The two worlds of Marcel Proust. Philadelphia, 1948.
43744.67.1150 Bonnet, Henri. Le progrès spirituel dans l'oeuvre de Marcel Proust. v.1-2. Paris, 1946-
43744.67.1155 Martin-Deslias, N. Idealisme de Marcel Proust. Montpellier, 1947.
43744.67.1160 Kinds, Edmond. Marcel Proust. Paris, 1947.
43744.67.1165 Tauman, L. Marcel Proust. Paris, 1949.
43744.67.1166 Tauman, L. Marcel Proust. Thèse. Paris, 1949.
43744.67.1170 Blackert, H. Der Aufbau der Kunstwirklichkeit. Berlin, 1935.
43744.67.1175 Holdane, C.F. Marcel Proust. London, 1951.
43744.67.1180 Briand, C. Le secret de Marcel Proust. Paris, 1950.
43744.67.1185A Spalding, P.A. A reader's handbook. London, 1952.
43744.67.1185B Spalding, P.A. A reader's handbook. London, 1952.
43744.67.1190 Monnin-Hornung, J. Proust et la peinture. Genève, 1951.
43744.67.1195 Adér-Winkler, E. Marcel Proust: Op zaek naar het volmaakte. 's-Graveland, 1950.
43744.67.1200 Castro, C. Marcel Proust. Madrid, 1952.
43744.67.1205 Cattaui, Georges. Marcel Proust. Paris, 1952.
43744.67.1207 Cattaui, Georges. Proust perdu et retrouvé. Paris, 1963.
43744.67.1210 Le Disque Vert. Hommage à Marcel Proust. Bruxelles, 1952.
43744.67.1215 Newman, Pauline. Marcel Proust et l'existentialisme. Thèse. Paris, 1953.
43744.67.1220 Hindus, M. The Proustian vision. N.Y., 1954.
43744.67.1225 Remacle, M. L'élément poétique dans A la Recherche du temps perdu de Marcel Proust. Bruxelles, 1954.
43744.67.1230 Pierre-Quint, Léon. Proust et la stratégie littéraire. Paris, 1954.
43744.67.1235A Brée, Germaine. Marcel Proust and deliverance from time. New Brunswick, N.J., 1955.
43744.67.1235B Brée, Germaine. Marcel Proust and deliverance from time. New Brunswick, N.J., 1955.
43744.67.1235.2 Brée, Germaine. Marcel Proust and deliverance from time. 2. ed. New Brunswick, 1969.
43744.67.1236 Brée, Germaine. The world of Marcel Proust. Boston, 1966.
43744.67.1240 France. Direction genérale des relations culturelles. Marcel Proust and his time. London, 1955.
43744.67.1245 Piroué, Georges. Par les chemins de Marcel Proust. Neuchâtel, 1955.
43744.67.1246 Piroué, Georges. Proust's way. London, 1957.
43744.67.1247 Piroué, Georges. Proust et la musique du devenir. Paris, 1960.
43744.67.1250 Jauss, Hans R. Zeit und Erinnerung in Marcel Prousts A la recherche du temps perdu. Heidelberg, 1955.
43744.67.1255 François, S. Le dandysme et Marcel Proust. Bruxelles, 1956.
43744.67.1260A Cocking, J.M. Proust. London, 1956.
43744.67.1260B Cocking, J.M. Proust. London, 1956.
43744.67.1270 Donze, Roland. Le comique dans l'oeuvre de Marcel Proust. Neuchâtel, 1955.
43744.67.1275A Miller, M.L. Nostalgia. Boston, 1956.
43744.67.1275B Miller, M.L. Nostalgia. Boston, 1956.
43744.67.1280 Adan, Antoine. Marcel Proust. Paris, 1955.
43744.67.1285A Strauss, W.A. Proust and literature. Cambridge, 1957.
43744.67.1285B Strauss, W.A. Proust and literature. Cambridge, 1957.
43744.67.1290 Trahard, P. L'art de Marcel Proust. Paris, 1953.
43744.67.1295 Louria, Yvette. La convergence stylistique chez Proust. Genève, 1957.
43744.67.1300 Société des amis de Marcel Proust et des amis de Combray. Bulletin. Illiers. 1-11,1950-1961 3v.
43744.67.1305 Guichard, Léon. Introduction à la lecture de Proust. Paris, 1956.
43744.67.1310 Czoniczer, E. Quelques antécedénts de A la recherche du temps perdu. Genève, 1957.
43744.67.1315 Benoist-Méchin, Jacque Gabriel Paul Michael. Retour à Marcel Proust. Paris, 1957.
43744.67.1320 Johnson, P.H. Six Proust reconstructions. London, 1958.
43744.67.1322 Johnson, P.H. Proust recaptured. Chicago, 1958.
43744.67.1325 Germain, André. Les clés de Proust. Paris, 1953.
43744.67.1330 Le Sage, Laurent. Marcel Proust and his literary friends. Urbana, 1958.
43744.67.1335 Gregh, Fernand. Mon amitié avec Marcel Proust. Paris, 1958.
43744.67.1340 Goron, Lucien. Le Combray de Marcel Proust et son horizon. Toulouse, 1956?
43744.67.1345 Barker, R.H. Marcel Proust. N.Y., 1958.
43744.67.1350 Cattaui, Georges. Marcel Proust. Genève, 1956-
43744.67.1355 Painter, George Duncan. Proust; the early years. Boston, 1959-65. 2v.
43744.67.1360 Painter, George Duncan. Marcel Proust. London, 1959. 2v.
43744.67.1361 Painter, George Duncan. Marcel Proust. London, 1965. 2v.
43744.67.1365 Koehler, Erich. Marcel Proust. Göttingen, 1958.
43744.67.1370 Adam, international review. Marcel Proust. London, 1957.
43744.67.1375 Hansen, H.P.E. Syntesen af Marcel Prousts vaerk. København, 1929.
43744.67.1380 Vallée, Claude. La féerie de Marcel Proust. Paris, 1958.
43744.67.1385 Revel, J.F. Sur Proust. Paris, 1960.
43744.67.1390A Ferré, André. Les années de collège de Marcel Proust. Paris, 1959.
43744.67.1390B Ferré, André. Les années de collège de Marcel Proust. Paris, 1959.
43744.67.1395 Allamand, Jules. Ce que Proust n'a pas dit. Paris, 1961.
43744.67.1400 Maurois, André. Le monde de Marcel Proust. Paris, 1960.
43744.67.1405 Zéphir, J.J. La personalité humaine. Paris, 1959.
43744.67.1410 Girard, R. Proust. Englewood Cliffs, N.J., 1962.
43744.67.1415 Mein, Margaret. Proust's challenge to time. Manchester, 1962.
43744.67.1420 Le Point; revue artistique et litteraire. Universe de Proust. Souillac, 1959.
43744.67.1425 Bell, William S. Proust's nocturnal muse. N.Y., 1962.
43744.67.1430 Moss, Howard. The magic lantern of Marcel Proust. N.Y., 1962.
43744.67.1435 Shattuck, Roger. Proust's binoculars. N.Y., 1963.
43744.67.1440 Daniel, G. Temps et mystification dans "A la recherche du temps perdu". Paris, 1963.
43744.67.1445 Poulet, G. L'espace proustien. Paris, 1963.
43744.67.1450 Fowlie, Wallace. A reading of Proust. 1. ed. N.Y., 1964.
43744.67.1455 Lowery, B. Marcel Proust et Henry James. Paris, 1964.
43744.67.1460 Butor, M. Les oeuvres d'art imaginaires chez Proust. London, 1964.
43744.67.1465 Deleuze, Gilles. Marcel Proust et les signes. Paris, 1964.
43744.67.1470 Pasquali, Costanza. Proust, Primoli, la moda. Roma, 1961.
43744.67.1475 Błonski, Jan. Widzieć jasno w zachwyceniu. Warszawa, 1965.
43744.67.1480 Vial, André. Proust; structures d'une conscience et naissance d'une esthétique. Paris, 1963.
43744.67.1485 Bibliothèque Nationale, Paris. Marcel Proust. Paris, 1965.
43744.67.1490 Riva, Raymond T. Marcel Proust. 1. ed. N.Y., 1965.
43744.67.1500 Papers on Proust. Hollins, Va., 1966.
43744.67.1505 Nathan, Jacques. La morale de Proust. Paris, 1953.
43744.67.1505.5 Nathan, Jacques. Catations, références et allusions de Marcel Proust dans A la recherche du temps perdu. Paris, 1969.
43744.67.1510A Linn, John G. The theatre in the fiction of M. Proust. Columbus, 1966.
43744.67.1510B Linn, John G. The theatre in the fiction of M. Proust. Columbus, 1966.
43744.67.1515 Waeber, Gottfried. Marcel Proust. München, 1965.
43744.67.1520 Rogers, Brian G. Proust's narrative techniques. Genève, 1965.
43744.67.1525 Clarac, Pierre. Album Proust. Paris, 1965.
43744.67.1530 De Ley, Herbert. Marcel Proust et le duc de Saint-Simon. Urbana, 1966.
43744.67.1535 Muller, Marcel. Les voix narratives dans la "Recherche du temps perdu". Genève, 1965.
43744.67.1540 Graham, Victor Ernest. The imagery of Proust. Oxford, 1966.
43744.67.1545 Plantevignes, Marcel. Avec Marcel Proust; causeries, souvenirs sur Cabourg. Paris, 1966.
43744.67.1550 Torres Bodet, Jaime. Tiempo y memoria en la obra de Proust. 1. ed. México, 1967.
43744.67.1555A Entretiens sur Marcel Proust, sous la direction de Georges Cattaui et Philip Kolb. Paris, 1966.
43744.67.1555B Entretiens sur Marcel Proust, sous la direction de Georges Cattaui et Philip Kolb. Paris, 1966.
43744.67.1560 Jackson, Elizabeth R. L'evolution de la mémoire involontaire dans l'oeuvre de Marcel Proust. Paris, 1966.
43744.67.1565 Bolle, Louis. Marcel Proust, ou Le complex d'Argus. Paris, 1966.
43744.67.1570 Truffaut, Louis. Introduction à Marcel Proust. München, 1967.
43744.67.1575 King, Adele. Proust. Edinburgh, 1968.
43744.67.1580 Soupault, Robert. Marcel Proust, du côté de la médecine. Paris, 1967.
43744.67.1585 Cattaui, Georges. Marcel Proust. London, 1967.
43744.67.1590 Andreev, Leonid G. Marsel' Prust. Moskva, 1968.
43744.67.1595 Newman, Pauline. Dictionnaire des idees dans l'oeuvre de Marcel Proust. The Hague, 1968.
43744.67.1600 Magnani, Loigi. La musica, il tempo, l'eterno nella "Recherche" di Proust. Milano, 1967.
43744.67.1605 Tarizzo, Domenico. Proust. Firenze, 1968.
43744.67.1610 Mouton, Jean. Proust. Paris, 1968.
43744.67.1615 Mendelson, David. Le verre et les objets de verre dans l'univers imaginaire de Marcel Proust. Paris, 1968.
43744.67.1620 Peyre, Henri. Marcel Proust. N.Y., 1970.
43744.67.1625 Bucknall, Barbara J. The religion of art in Proust. Urbana, 1969.
43744.67.1630 Lins, Alvaro. A tecnica do romance em Marcel Proust. 3. ed. Rio de Janeiro, 1968.
43744.67.1635 Chantal, René de. Marcel Proust, critique littéraire. Montréal, 1967. 2v.
43744.67.1640 Rivas, Marta. Un mito proustiano. Santiago de Chile, 1968.
43744.67.1645 Milly, Jean. Les pastiches de Proust. Paris, 1970.
43744.67.1645.5 Milly, Jean. Proust et le style. Paris, 1970.
43744.67.1650.2 Deleuze, Gilles. Proust et le signes. 2. éd. Paris, 1970.
43744.67.1655 Marcel Proust, 1871-1922. N.Y., 1971.
43744.67.1660 Vizcaíno, José Antonio. Marcel Proust. Madrid, 1969.
43744.67.1665 Bardèche, Maurice. Marcel Proust, romancier. Paris, 1971.
43744.67.1670 Kopp, Richard L. Marcel Proust as a social critic. Rutherford, 1971.
43744.67.1675 Eggs, Ekkehard. Möglichkeiten und Grenzen einer wissenschaftlichen Semantik. Bern, 1971.
43744.67.1680 Florival, Ghislaine. Le désir chez Proust. Paris, 1971.
43744.67.4100 Prou, Suzanne. L'été jaune, roman. Paris, 1968.
43744.67.5100 Prous-Guillaumis, Jeanne. Puisque enfin je suis moi. Paris, 1958.
43744.69.100 Proust, Pierre Henry. La maison aux mille fenêtres; poems. Paris, 1925.
43744.77.1100 Péret, Benjamin. Vingt poèmes. Paris, 1965.
43745.1.28 Psichari, Ernest. Lettres du Centurion. Paris, 1947.
43745.1.30 Psichari, Ernest. L'Appel des Armes. 18. éd. Paris, 191-.
43745.1.31 Psichari, Ernest. Le voyage du centurion. Paris, 1916.
43745.1.33 Psichari, Ernest. Le voyage du centurion. Paris, 1947.
43745.1.34 Psichari, Lucien. Le chien et la pierre. Paris, 1956.
43745.1.80 Goichon, A.M. (Mlle.). Ernest Psichari d'après des documents inédits. 9. éd. Paris, 1921.
43745.1.82 Goichon, A.M. (Mlle.). Ernest Psichari d'après des documents inédits. Paris, 1925.
43745.1.85 Becherer, Walter. Ernest Psichari in seiner psychologischen Entwicklung. Inaug. Diss. Leipzig, 1933.
43745.1.87 Peyrade, J. Psichari. Paris, 1948.
43745.1.90 Psichari, H. Ernest Psichari, mon frere. Paris, 1933.
43745.1.100 Massis, Henri. Notre ami Psichari. Paris, 1936.
43745.1.101 Massis, Henri. Notre ami Psichari. Paris, 1944.
43745.1.105A Fowlie, Wallace. Ernest Psichari. N.Y., 1939.
43745.1.105B Fowlie, Wallace. Ernest Psichari. N.Y., 1939.
43745.1.110 Chevalier, I. La vocation de Psichari. Le Sarte, 1937.
43745.1.112 Pacheco, M.J. Ernest Psichari, um neto de Renan. Lisboa, 1948.
43745.1.120 Barres, Maurice. Le tombeau d'Ernest Psichari au seuil de la forêt des Ardennes. Paris, 1920.
43745.1.125 Massis, Henri. La vie d'Ernest Psichari. Paris, 1916.
43747.23.100 Puel, Gaston. Le cinquième chateau. Lavaur, 1965.
43747.23.110 Puel, Gaston. Ce chant entre deux astres. 2. éd. Paris, 1962.
43747.23.120 Puel, Gaston. La lumière du jour. Paris, 1967.
43747.32.100 Puget, C.A. La ligne de coeur. Paris, 1932.
43747.32.130 Puget, C.A. Théâtre. Paris, 1943-46. 3v.
43747.41.100 Puig, André. L'inachevé. Paris, 1970.
43747.50.100 Puliga, H.C.S. La maison de la peur. Paris, 1930.
43747.50.110 Puliga, H.C.S. Retour du flat. Paris, 1913.
43747.50.120 Puliga, H.C.S. Leurs excellences. Paris, 1878.
43747.53.100 Pulsifer, S.F.N. Fighting French ballads. N.Y., 1943.

Classified Listing

43511 - 43873 Individual authors, etc. - 1900- - Known authors (363 scheme plus 10) - cont.

43747.53.102 Pulsifer, S.F.N. L'esprit de la France. N.Y., 1944.
43747.60.100 Punj, Alain. Lettres d'un Samoyède. Thonon-Les-Bains, 1940?
43747.90.100 Puvis de Chavannes, Henri. Le ciel dans mon coeur. Paris, 1955.
43748.3.100 Py, Albert. L'homme rouge et son ombre cheval. [Poèmes]. Neuchâtel, 1966.
43748.19.100 Ordonneau, Maurice. Le jockey malgré lui. Paris, 1903.
43750.2.100 Quaedvlieg, Phillippe. La chose qui vient de la mer. Liège, 1964.
43750.20.100 Queffélec, Henri. Le bout du monde. Paris, 1949.
43750.20.110 Queffélec, Henri. Un homme d'Ouessant. Paris, 1954.
43750.20.120 Queffélec, Henri. Un feu s'allume sur la mer. Paris, 1956.
43750.20.130 Queffélec, Henri. Combat contre l'invisible. Paris, 1958.
43750.20.140 Queffélec, Henri. Frères de la brume. Paris, 1960.
43750.20.150 Queffélec, Henri. Tempête sur la ville d'Ys. Paris, 1962.
43750.20.160 Queffélec, Henri. Sous un ciel noir; récits. Paris, 1962.
43750.20.170 Queffélec, Henri. La voile tendue. Paris, 1967.
43750.20.700 Queffélec, Henri. Island priest. 1. ed. N.Y., 1952.
43750.23.100 Queillé, Yvonne. Au vent qui me pousse. Paris, 1958.
43750.23.110 Queillé, Yvonne. Sur un air sempiternel; poèmes. Paris, 1959.
43750.23.120 Queillé, Yvonne. Le printemps ça m'eblouit. Paris, 1961.
43750.23.130 Queillé, Yvonne. Au rythme du vent de mer. Paris, 1960.
43750.23.140 Queillé, Yvonne. Sur mon coeur en bleu marine. Paris, 1962.
43750.23.1100 Quentin-Maurer, Nicole. Portrait de Raphaël. Paris, 1970.
43750.24.104 Queneau, Raymond. Un rude hiver. 4. éd. Paris, 1939.
43750.24.106 Queneau, Raymond. Exercises in style. London, 1958.
43750.24.110 Queneau, Raymond. Exercices de style. 3. éd. Paris, 1947.
43750.24.120 Queneau, Raymond. Saint Glinglin. 10. éd. Paris, 1948.
43750.24.130 Queneau, Raymond. Pierrot mon ami. 24. éd. Paris, 1943.
43750.24.140 Queneau, Raymond. Odile. Paris, 1937.
43750.24.150 Queneau, Raymond. Loin de Rueil. Paris, 1944.
43750.24.160 Queneau, Raymond. Gueule de Pierre. 3. éd. Paris, 1934.
43750.24.170 Queneau, Raymond. Les temps mêles. 10. éd. Paris, 1941.
43750.24.180 Queneau, Raymond. Chêne et chien. Paris, 1937.
43750.24.182 Queneau, Raymond. Chêne et chien. Paris, 1969.
43750.24.190 Queneau, Raymond. Les ziaux. Paris, 1948.
43750.24.200 Queneau, Raymond. Batons. Paris, 1950.
43750.24.201 Queneau, Raymond. Batons, chiffres et lettres. Paris, 1965.
43750.24.210 Queneau, Raymond. Le dimanche de la vie. 13. éd. Paris, 1951.
43750.24.220 Queneau, Raymond. Si tu t'imagines. 13. éd. Paris, 1952.
43750.24.230 Queneau, Raymond. Les enfants du Limon. 7. éd. Paris, 1938.
43750.24.240 Queneau, Raymond. L'instant fatal. 4. éd. Paris, 1948.
43750.24.241 Queneau, Raymond. L'instant fatal. Précédé de Les Ziaux. Paris, 1966.
43750.24.250 Queneau, Raymond. Zazzie dans le métro. 114. éd. Paris, 1959.
43750.24.251 Queneau, Raymond. Zazie dans le métro. Paris, 1966.
43750.24.260 Queneau, Raymond. Les oeuvres complètes de Sally Mava. Paris, 1962.
43750.24.270 Queneau, Raymond. Entretiens avec Georges Charbonnier. Paris, 1962.
43750.24.280 Queneau, Raymond. Bords: mathématiciens. Paris, 1963.
43750.24.290 Queneau, Raymond. Les fleurs bleues. Paris, 1965.
43750.24.300 Queneau, Raymond. Le chien à la mandoline. Paris, 1965.
43750.24.310 Queneau, Raymond. Une histoire modèle. Paris, 1966.
43750.24.320 Queneau, Raymond. Les derniers jours. Lausanne, 1965.
43750.24.330 Queneau, Raymond. Courir les rues. Paris, 1967.
43750.24.340 Queneau, Raymond. Battre la campagne. Paris, 1968.
43750.24.350 Queneau, Raymond. Le Vol d'Icare. Paris, 1968.
43750.24.360 Queneau, Raymond. On est toujours trop bon avec les femmes. Paris, 1971.
43750.24.700 Queneau, Raymond. A hard winter. London, 1948.
43750.24.710 Queneau, Raymond. Pierrot. London, 1950.
43750.24.720 Queneau, Raymond. The skin of dreams. N.Y., 1948.
43750.24.725 Queneau, Raymond. Zazie. 1. ed. N.Y., 1960.
43750.24.726 Queneau, Raymond. Zazie. London, 1960.
43750.24.730 Queneau, Raymond. Between blue and blue: a sort of novel. London, 1967.
43750.24.735 Queneau, Raymond. Icaro involato. Torino, 1969.
43750.24.800 Simonnet, Claude. Queneau déchiffré. Paris, 1962.
43750.24.805 Bens, Jacques. Queneau. Paris, 1962.
43750.24.810 Bergens, A. Raymond Queneau. Genève, 1963.
43750.24.815 Gayot, Paul. Raymond Queneau. Paris, 1967.
43750.24.820 Guicharnaud, Jacques. Raymond Queneau. N.Y., 1965.
43750.24.1100 Querlin, Marise. Condamné a vivre; roman. Paris, 1959.
43750.24.1110 Querlin, Marise. Le plaisir des hommes; roman. Paris, 1958.
43750.25.1100 Quey, Georges. Bar-Tabac. Villencuve-les-Avignon, 1942.
43750.25.2100 Quéval, Jean. En somme. Poèmes. Paris, 1970.
43750.26.105 Quesnel, Joseph. Tirelire. Paris, 1945.
43750.27.100 Queneau, J. Adieu chansons. Paris, 1951.
43750.41.100 Quillateau, C. Flaques de sel. Paris, 1961.
43750.41.1100 Quinton, René. Maximes sur la guerre. Paris, 1930.
43752.1.30F Rageot, G. La voix qui q'est tué. pt.1-4. Paris, 1913.
43752.1.36 Rageot, G. Tels que nous sommes. Paris, 1933.
43752.1.40 Rageot, G. Pleine eau. v.1-2. Paris, 1936.
43752.1.45 Rageot, G. Anne-Jeanne; roman. v.1-3. Paris, 1938.
43752.1.46 Rageot, G. Prise de vues. 3. éd. Paris, 1928.
43752.1.47 Rageot, G. Sens unique. Paris, 1926.
43752.2.30 Rateau, Jules. Noël Breton. Paris, 1912.
43752.3.30 Rabier, Benjamin A. La tranquillité des parents. Paris, 190-?
43752.8.100 Reboue, Edmond. Si toubib. Paris, 1959.
43752.8.1100 Rabiniaux, Roger. Le soleil des dortoirs. Paris, 1965.
43752.11.100 Raucat, Thomas. L'honorable partie de campagne. Paris, 1924.
43752.11.102 Raucat, Thomas. L'honorable partie de campagne. 2. éd. Paris, 1924.
43752.11.110 Raucat, Thomas. L'honorable partie de campagne. 8. éd. Paris, 1924.
43752.11.120 Raucat, Thomas. The honorable picnic. N.Y., 1927.
43752.11.124 Raucat, Thomas. The honorable picnic. London, 1931.
43752.12.100 Rache, André. Les feux de la roue. Paris, 1960.
43752.18.12A Radiguet, Raymond. Oeuvres complètes. Paris, 1952.
43752.18.12F Radiguet, Raymond. Oeuvres complètes. Paris, 1952.
43752.18.15 Radiguet, Raymond. Oeuvres complètes. Paris, 1959. 2v.
43752.18.110 Radiguet, Raymond. Le diable au corps, roman. 122. éd. Paris, 1923.

43511 - 43873 Individual authors, etc. - 1900- - Known authors (363 scheme plus 10) - cont.

43752.18.120 Radiguet, Raymond. Règle du jeu. Monaco, 1957.
43752.18.700 Radiguet, Raymond. The devil in the flesh. London, 1949.
43752.18.710 Radiguet, Raymond. Count d'Orgel. N.Y., 1953.
43752.18.800 Goesch, Keith. Raymond Radiguet. Paris, 1955.
43752.18.805 Massis, Henri. Raymond Radiguet. Paris, 1927.
43752.21.100 Raeders, Georges. La découverte du nouveau monde. Rio de Janeiro, 1944.
43752.34.100 Ragon, Michel. Drôles de métiers. Paris, 1953.
43752.34.110 Ragon, Michel. Les Americains. Paris, 1959.
43752.38.100 Rohblenbeck, G. L'année glorieuse, 1914; roman. Bruxelles, 1920.
43752.38.1100 Rahnéma, Férydoun. Poèmes anciens. Paris, 1959.
43752.38.1110 Rahnéma, Férydoun. Chant de délivrance. Honfleur, 1968.
43752.41.100 Raimond, Fernande de. La fin des seigneurs blancs. Paris, 1956.
43752.51.100 Ramel-Cals, Jeanne. La ronde. Paris, 1920.
43752.51.110 Ramel-Cals, Jeanne. La grande aventure. Paris, 1920.
43752.54.100 Rameau-Renevey, Camille. Juvéniles et magistrale présences. Chagny-en-Bourgogue, 1954.
43752.56.100 Ramounet, René. La rivage. Ales, 1957.
43752.57.11 Ramuz, Charles Ferdinand. Oeuvres complètes. Lausanne, 1940-41. 23v.
43752.57.13 Ramuz, Charles Ferdinand. Oeuvres complètes. Lausanne, 1967- 20v.
43752.57.41 Ramuz, Charles Ferdinand. Journal, 1896-1942. Paris, 1945.
43752.57.61A Ramuz, Charles Ferdinand. Lettres, 1900-1918. Lausanne, 1956. 2v.
43752.57.61B Ramuz, Charles Ferdinand. Lettres, 1900-1918. Lausanne, 1956.
43752.57.62 Ramuz, Charles Ferdinand. Lettres, 1919-1947. Paris, 1959.
43752.57.63 Ramuz, Charles Ferdinand. C.F. Ramuz, ses amis et son temps (Lettres de et à Ramuz). Lausanne, 1967- 6v.
43752.57.100 Ramuz, Charles Ferdinand. Salutation paysanne et autres morceaux. Genève, 1921.
43752.57.110 Ramuz, Charles Ferdinand. L'amour du monde. Paris, 1925.
43752.57.120 Ramuz, Charles Ferdinand. Pour ou contre. Paris, 1926.
43752.57.130 Ramuz, Charles Ferdinand. La guérison des maladies. 13. éd. Paris, 1924.
43752.57.132 Ramuz, Charles Ferdinand. La guérison des maladies. Lausanne, 1951.
43752.57.140 Ramuz, Charles Ferdinand. Joie dans le ciel. 23. éd. Paris, 1935.
43752.57.143 Ramuz, Charles Ferdinand. Joie dans le ciel. Paris, 1925.
43752.57.150 Ramuz, Charles Ferdinand. Derborence. 18. éd. Paris, 1936.
43752.57.160 Ramuz, Charles Ferdinand. La grande peur dans la montagne. Paris, 1926.
43752.57.170 Ramuz, Charles Ferdinand. La séparation des races. Paris, 1923.
43752.57.180 Ramuz, Charles Ferdinand. Si le soleil ne revenait pas; roman. Lausanne, 1940.
43752.57.190 Ramuz, Charles Ferdinand. Vie de Samuel Belet. Paris, 1944.
43752.57.200 Ramuz, Charles Ferdinand. Nouvelles. Paris, 1947.
43752.57.210 Ramuz, Charles Ferdinand. Les servants et autres nouvelles. Lausanne, 1946.
43752.57.220 Ramuz, Charles Ferdinand. Adieu à beaucoup de personnages et autres nouveaux. Lausanne, 1947.
43752.57.230 Ramuz, Charles Ferdinand. Passage du poète. Lausanne, 1947.
43752.57.245 Ramuz, Charles Ferdinand. Taille de l'homme. 13. éd. Paris, 1945.
43752.57.250 Ramuz, Charles Ferdinand. Farinet, ou La fausse monnaie. Paris, 1948.
43752.57.251 Ramuz, Charles Ferdinand. Farinet. Paris, 1932.
43752.57.255 Ramuz, Charles Ferdinand. Présence de la mort. Lausanne, 1947.
43752.57.260 Ramuz, Charles Ferdinand. Le régne de l'esprit malin. Lausanne, 1946.
43752.57.265 Ramuz, Charles Ferdinand. Vers. Lausanne, 1945.
43752.57.270 Ramuz, Charles Ferdinand. Chant de notre Rhône. Lausanne, 1951.
43752.57.275 Ramuz, Charles Ferdinand. Histoire du soldat. Lausanne, 1944.
43752.57.280 Ramuz, Charles Ferdinand. La guerre dans le Haut-Pays. Lausanne, 1944.
43752.57.285 Ramuz, Charles Ferdinand. Besoin de grandeur. Lausanne, 1951.
43752.57.295 Ramuz, Charles Ferdinand. La faneuse dans son pre. Paris, 1927.
43752.57.300 Ramuz, Charles Ferdinand. Le cirque. Lausanne, 1936.
43752.57.310 Ramuz, Charles Ferdinand. Jean-Luc persécuté. Lausanne, 1966.
43752.57.700 Ramuz, Charles Ferdinand. The triumph of death. Paris, 1946.
43752.57.705 Ramuz, Charles Ferdinand. When the mountain fell. N.Y., 1947.
43752.57.708 Ramuz, Charles Ferdinand. What is man. N.Y., 1948.
43752.57.710 Ramuz, Charles Ferdinand. The end of all men. N.Y., 1944.
43752.57.715 Ramuz, Charles Ferdinand. Terror on the mountain. 1. ed. N.Y., 1968.
43752.57.775 Ramuz, Charles Ferdinand. Die Sühne in feuer Gedichte und Novellen. Basel, 1921.
43752.57.780 Ramuz, Charles Ferdinand. Es geschehen Zeichen; roman. Basel, 1921.
43752.57.785 Ramuz, Charles Ferdinand. Das Regiment des Bösen; roman. Zürich, 1925.
43752.57.787 Ramuz, Charles Ferdinand. Die Geschichte vom Soldaten. Zürich, 1951.
43752.57.795 Ramuz, Charles Ferdinand. Das grosse Grauen in den Bergen. Stuttgart, 1927.
43752.57.797 Ramuz, Charles Ferdinand. Der bergsturz. München, 1936.
43752.57.805 Hartmann, A. C.F. Ramuz, Mensch, Werk und Landschaft. Inaug. Diss. Dresden, 1937.
43752.57.810 Brandner, G. C.F. Ramuz, der Dichter des Waadtlandes. Inaug. Diss. Würzberg, 1938.
43752.57.815 Bringolf, I. Bibliographie de l'oeuvre de C.F. Ramuz. Lausanne, 1942.
43752.57.820 Tissot, André. C.F. Ramuz. Neuchâtel, 1948.
43752.57.825 Guyot, Charly. Comment lire C.F. Ramuz. Paris, 1946.
43752.57.830 Dichamp, Marius. Ramuz. Paris, 1948.
43752.57.835A Claudel, P. Du côté de chez Ramuz. Neuchâtel, 1947.
43752.57.835B Claudel, P. Du côté de chez Ramuz. Neuchâtel, 1947.

Classified Listing

43511 - 43873 Individual authors, etc. - 1900- - Known authors (363 scheme plus 10) - cont.

43752.57.840 Voyenne, B. C.F. Ramuz et la sainteté de la terre. Paris, 1948.
43752.57.845 Marclay, R. C.F. Ramuz et le Valais. Lausanne, 1950.
43752.57.850 Mermod, H.L. Album C.F. Ramuz. Lausanne, 1950.
43752.57.855 Présence de Ramuz. Haute-Savoie, 1951.
43752.57.860 Beaujon, E. La vision du peintre chez Ramuz. Bondy, 1954.
43752.57.865 Guenther, W. C.F. Ramuz. Bern, 1948.
43752.57.870 Cingria, Hélène. Ramuz. Bienne, 1956.
43752.57.875 Zermatten, Maurice. C.F. Ramuz. Neuchâtel, 1948.
43752.57.875.5 Zermatten, Maurice. Ramuz à Lens. Bienne, 1967.
43752.57.880 Guisan, Gilbert. C.F. Ramuz. Genève, 1958.
43752.57.885 Rapin, S. Hommage à Ramuz. Neuchâtel, 1960.
43752.57.890 Schaefer, W. Die Satzverknüpfung bei C.F. Ramuz. Marburg, 1961.
43752.57.895 Parsons, Clarence R. Vision plastique de C.F. Ramuz. Québec, 1964.
43752.57.900 Guers-Villate, Yvonne. Charles Ferdinand Ramuz; l'authenticité éthique et esthétique de l'oeuvre ramuzienne. Paris, 1966.
43752.57.905 Roud, Gustave. Avec Ramuz. Lausanne, 1967.
43752.57.910 Kohler, Pierre. L'art de Ramuz. Genève, 1929.
43752.57.920 Nicod, Marguerite. Du realisme a la réalité. Genève, 1966.
43752.57.930 Haggis, Donald R. C.F. Ramuz, ouvrier du langage. Paris, 1968.
43752.59.100 Randon, G. Les soliloques du pauvre. 5. éd. Paris, 1903.
43752.59.110 Randon, G. Le coeur populaire. Paris, 1949.
43752.59.120 Randon, G. Les soliloques du pauvre. 6. éd. Paris, 1897.
43752.59.122 Randon, G. Les soliloques du pauvre. Paris, 1913.
43752.59.130 Landre, Jeanne. Loin des balles. Paris, 1918.
43752.59.140 Landre, Jeanne. Bob et Bobette. Paris, 1919.
43752.59.800 Landre, Jeanne. Les soliloques du pauvre de Jehran-Rictus. Paris, 1930.
43752.59.810 Doyon, René Louis. Jehan Rictus devant lui-même. Paris, 1943.
X Cg 43752.70.100 Rapin, Simone. L'année de l'amour. Bienne, 1957.
43752.70.110 Rapin, Simone. Une jeune fille juive. Monte-Carlo, 1955.
43752.70.130 Rapin, Simone. La trêve de Dieu. Genève, 1954?
43752.82.100 Raspail, Jean. Welcome honorable visitors. N.Y., 1960.
43752.82.110 Raspail, Jean. Le vent des pins. Paris, 1958.
43752.82.1105 Rassinier, Paul. Le mensonge d'Ulysse. 5. éd. Paris, 1961.
43752.85.100 Ratel, Simonne. Trois parmi les autres. Paris, 1929.
43752.85.110 Ratel, Simonne. Le raison vert. Paris, 1935.
43752.85.702 Ratel, Simonne. The house in the hills. N.Y., 1934.
43752.85.712 Ratel, Simonne. Love's not enough. N.Y., 1930.
43752.90.100 Raveton, Roland. La vie exilée. Paris, 1956.
43752.90.1100 Ravard, Claude. Émaux d'amour. Paris, 1962.
43752.94.700 Rawicz, P. Blood from the sky, a novel. 1. American ed. N.Y., 1964.
43752.98.100 Raynal, Paul. Le tombeau sous l'Arc de Triomphe; tragédie. Paris, 1924.
43752.98.110 Raynal, Paul. Le tombeau sous l'Arc de Triomphe. Paris, 1945.
43752.98.120 Raynal, Paul. Le maître de son coeur. Paris, 1920.
43752.98.130 Raynal, Paul. Au soleil de l'instinct. Paris, 1932.
43752.98.140 Raynal, Paul. Napoléan unique. Paris, 1937.
43752.98.150 Raynal, Paul. A souffert sous Ponce Pilate. 7. éd. Paris, 1946.
43752.98.700 Raynal, Paul. The unknown warrior. N.Y., 1928.
43753.1.30 Reinach, J. Récits et portraits contemporains. Paris, 1915.
43753.2.30 Régnier, M.L.A. de. Jeune fille. Paris, 1916.
43753.2.31 Régnier, M.L.A. de. Le séducteur. 13. éd. Paris, 1914.
43753.2.31.10 Régnier, M.L.A. de. Le séducteur. Paris, 1923.
43753.2.32 Régnier, M.L.A. de. Esclave. Paris, 1905.
43753.2.36 Régnier, M.L.A. de. La vie amoureuse de la belle Hélène. Paris, 1928.
43753.2.40 Régnier, M.L.A. de. Le temps d'aimer. 29. éd. Paris, 1926.
43753.2.45 Régnier, M.L.A. de. Les poésies de Gérard d'Hauville [pseud.]. Paris, 1931.
43753.2.50 Régnier, M.L.A. de. L'inconatante. Paris, 1927.
43753.2.55 Régnier, M.L.A. de. Le chou. Paris, 1924.
43753.2.60 Régnier, M.L.A. de. Paris et les voyages. Paris, 1925.
43753.3.32 Régnier, P. L'abbaye d'Evolayne. Paris, 1934.
43753.3.35 Régnier, P. Fêtes et nuages. 6. éd. Paris, 1956.
43753.4.100 Régnier, Yves. Les ombres. Paris, 1963.
43753.4.110 Régnier, Yves. Les voyages, roman. Paris, 1959.
43753.4.120 Régnier, Yves. Un monde aveugle. Paris, 1967.
43753.9.100 Reboux, Paul. Madame se meurt! Madame est morte! Paris, 1932.
43753.9.110 Reboux, Paul. Liszt, ou Les amours romantiques. Paris, 1940.
43753.9.123 Reboux, Paul. A la manière de Octave Mirbeau. Paris, 1910.
43753.9.125 Reboux, Paul. A la manière de Octave Mirbeau. 2. serie et 1. serie. Paris, 1912.
43753.9.127 Reboux, Paul. A la manière de Racine. 3. serie. Paris, 1913.
43753.9.128 Reboux, Paul. A la manière de Baudelaire. Paris, 1964.
43753.9.130 Reboux, Paul. Les iris noirs. Paris, 1898.
43753.9.140 Reboux, Paul. Chonchon. Paris, 1920.
43753.9.150 Reboux, Paul. Les Matinoles. Paris, 1897.
43753.9.160 Reboux, Paul. Mes mémoires. Paris, 1956.
43753.9.170 Reboux, Paul. Bamboulina. Paris, 1929.
43753.9.180 Reboux, Paul. Colin, ou Les voluptés tropicales. Paris, 1931.
43753.12.100 Recamier, E. L'enfant blond. Avignon, 1941.
43753.17.100 Réda, Jacques. Amen. Paris, 1968.
43753.17.110 Réda, Jacques. Récitatif. Paris, 1970.
43753.18.100 Redier, A. Le capitaine. Lyon, 1941.
43753.30.102 Regis, L. Bastos le hardi. Paris, 1923.
43753.33.100 Régnier, Pierre. Colombine ou La grande semaine. Paris, 1929.
43753.33.1100 Regismanset, Charles. La vaine chanson. Paris, 1912.
43753.41.100 Reiner, S. Le caporal marche nu-tête. 5. éd. Paris, 1957.
43753.57.100 Remy, J. La grande lutte. Paris, 1937.
43753.58.100 Renard, M. Celui qui n'a pas tue. Paris, 1927.
43753.58.110 Renard, M. La jeune fille du yacht. pt.1-3. Paris, 1930.
43753.58.120 Renard, M. Le professeur Krantz. Paris, 1932.
43753.58.130 Renard, M. L'invitation à la peur. Paris, 1958.
Htn 43753.58.702* New bodies for old. N.Y., 1923.
43753.58.1100 Renaitour, Jean Michel. L'enfant chaste. Paris, 1923.
Htn 43753.58.1110* Renaitour, Jean Michel. Robert Le Pieux. Paris, 1952.

43511 - 43873 Individual authors, etc. - 1900- - Known authors (363 scheme plus 10) - cont.

43753.58.1120 Renaitour, Jean Michel. Le tombeau de Tibulle. Paris, 1953.
43753.58.1130 Renaitour, Jean Michel. Poésie de l'histoire. Paris, 194-.
43753.58.1800 Le Mercier d'Erm, Camille. Jean-Michel Renaitour. Paris, 1918.
43753.58.2100 Renard, J.C. Haute-mer. Paris, 1950.
43753.58.2110 Renard, J.C. En une seule vigne. Paris, 1959.
43753.58.2800 Decreus, J. Poesie et transcendance. Paris, 1957.
43753.58.3100 Renauld-Krantz. La grâce. Paris, 1960.
43753.59.100 Rendinger, C.M. Eutretiens de Chevremont. Paris, 1951.
43753.59.1100 René, Claude. La nuit logique. Paris, 1958.
43753.59.2100 René, Commandant (pseud.). Le soleil et le lion. Paris, 1960.
43753.59.2110 René, Commandant (pseud.). Mission confidentielle en Guinée. Paris, 1961.
43753.59.3100 Renglet, Jean Claude. Le dialogue solitude à Monique S. Paris, 1956.
43753.60.100 Rennie, M. L'aigle d'argent. Paris, 1956.
43753.60.1100 Renault-Roulier, Gilbert. De sang et de chair. Paris, 1960.
43753.61.100 Renoux, Alfred. Le grand test secret de Jules Verne. Paris, 1962.
43753.61.110 Renoux, Alfred. Jules Verne. Paris, 1964.
43753.61.1100 Renoux, Isaïe. Feuilles de flammes, poèmes. Paris, 1955.
43753.75.30 Rerfer du Noble-Val, Helmic. Cocktail. Rodez, 1966.
43753.88.100 Retté, M. Les fils de Mammon. N.Y.? 1939.
43753.90.100 Reverdy, P. Les jockeys camoufle's; trois poèmes. Paris, 1918.
43753.90.110 Reverdy, P. La balle au bond. Marseille, 1918.
43753.90.120 Reverdy, P. Le gaut de crin. Paris, 1927.
Htn 43753.90.130* Reverdy, P. Les épaves du ciel. Paris, 1924.
43753.90.140 Reverdy, P. Flaques de verre. 4. éd. Paris, 1929.
43753.90.150 Reverdy, P. Cravates de Chanvre Illustré d'eauxfortes. Paris, 1922.
43753.90.160 Reverdy, P. Antologia poética. Tokio, 1940.
43753.90.170 Reverdy, P. Le livre de mon bord. Paris, 1948.
43753.90.180 Reverdy, P. Main d'oeuvre. Paris, 1949.
43753.90.190 Reverdy, P. Plupart du temps. 5. éd. Paris, 1945.
43753.90.201 Reverdy, P. La peau de l'homme. Paris, 1968.
43753.90.621 Reverdy, P. Selected poems. N.Y., 1969.
43753.90.800 Pierre Reverdy, 1889-1940. Paris, 1962.
43753.90.805 Rizzuto, Anthony. Style und theme in Reverdy's Les ardoises du toit. University, 1971.
43753.90.810 Brunner, Peter. Pierre Reverdy. De la solitude au mystère. Zürich, 1966.
43753.90.820 Guiney, Mortimer. La poésie de Pierre Reverdy. Genève, 1966.
43753.90.2100 Réval, Gabrielle. La chaîne des dames. Paris, 1924.
43753.90.2110 Réval, Gabrielle. Le royaume du printemps. Paris, 1963.
43753.90.3100 Revel, Jean François. Contrecensures: politique, religion, culture en masse. Paris, 1966.
43753.98.100 Rey, E. Ce que femme veut. Paris, 1924.
43753.98.2100 Reynie, Charles. Les flammes mortes. Paris, 1960.
43753.98.3100 Rey, Henri François. Les pianos mécaniques; roman. Paris, 1962.
43753.98.3110 Rey, Henri François. Les chevaux masqués. Paris, 1965.
43753.99.100 Reymond, M.L. Le miracle. Neuchâtel, 1936.
43753.99.1100 Rebatet, L. Les deux étendards. 18. éd. Paris, 1951. 2v.
43753.99.2100 Reynaud, J. Delpheca. St. Félicien, 1935.
43753.99.2110 Reynaud, J. Polymnie. St. Félicien, 1921.
43753.99.4100 Reynaud, J.C. Une etoile qui nait; roman. Paris, 1945.
43753.99.5700 Reynolds, P. When and if. N.Y., 1952.
43753.99.6100 Reynold, Gonzague de. Le chant d'une vie. Fribourg, 1957.
43753.99.6110 Reynold, Gonzague de. Mes memoires. Genève, 1960. 3v.
43753.99.7100 Rezvani, Serge. Les années-lumière, roman. Paris, 1967.
43753.99.7110 Rezvani, Serge. Théâtre. Paris, 1970.
43755.3.100 Rhaïs, Elissa. Le Café-Chontant, Kerkeb, Noblesse arabe. 2. éd. Paris, 1920.
43755.3.110 Rhaïs, Elissa. Les juifs. Paris, 1921.
43755.3.120 Rhaïs, Elissa. Par la voix de la musique. 16. éd. Paris, 1927.
43755.3.130 Rhaïs, Elissa. Le sein blanc. Paris, 1928.
43756.1.30 Riche, D. Le Prétexte. Paris, 1906.
43756.2.30 Rivollet, G. Alkestis. Paris, 1901.
43756.2.31 Rivollet, G. Bénédicte. Paris, 1913.
43756.2.32 Rivollet, G. Jerusalem! Paris, 1913.
43756.2.35 Rivollet, G. Les trois grâces. n.p., 1925.
43756.2.40 Rivollet, G. Les Phéniciennes. Paris, 1922.
43756.3.30 Richepin, Jacques. La reine de Tyr. Paris, 1900.
43756.3.31 Richepin, Jacques. La guerre et l'amour. Paris, 1918.
43756.3.35 Richepin, Jacques. La grève des femmes. Paris, 1919.
43756.3.45 Richepin, Jacques. Mon coeur. Paris, 1924.
43756.3.55 Richepin, Jacques. Falstaff. Paris, 1904.
43756.3.60 Richepin, Jacques. L'image obstinée. Paris, 1946.
43756.3.65 Richepin, Jacques. Cadet Roussel comédie en trois actés en vers. Paris, 1903.
43756.3.75 Richepin, Jacques. Le minaret. Paris, 1914.
43756.3.85F Richepin, Jacques. L'affaire Dreyfus. Paris, 1931.
43756.3.87 Richepin, Jacques. L'affaire Dreyfus. Paris, 1931.
43756.6.100 Ribaud, A. La cour (chronique du royaume). Paris, 1963.
43756.6.110 Ribaud, A. Le roi; chronique de la cour. Paris, 1962.
43756.7.100 Ribemont-Dessaignes, Georges. Le bar du lendemain. Paris, 1927.
43756.7.110 Ribemont-Dessaignes, Georges. Adolescence. Paris, 1930.
43756.7.120 Ribemont-Dessaignes, Georges. Théâtre: L'empereur de Chine, Le serin muet, Le bourreau du Pérou. Paris, 1966.
43756.11.100 Richer, Charline. L'éventail. Paris, 1957.
43756.11.1100 Ricardou, Jan. Révolutions minuscules. Paris, 1971.
43756.12.100 Richard, Marius. La Rapee. Paris, 1944.
43756.12.110 Richard, Marius. Mon ami Broque. Paris, 1959.
43756.12.1100 Richaud, André de. La Douleur. Saint Martin, 1968.
43756.12.2100 Richter, Anne. Les locataires. Paris, 1967.
43756.12.2700 Richter, Anne. The blue dog, and other fables for the French. Boston, 1956.
43756.12.3100 Richard, Lucien. Sketches et monologues fantaisistes. Avignon, 1947.
43756.12.3110 Richard, Lucien. Fables humoristiques. Avignon, 1947.
43756.12.4100 Richard, Gaston Charles. La maison des trois marches noires. Paris, 1929.
43756.13.100 Richer, C. Le dernier voyage du "Pembroke". Paris, 1941.
43756.13.110 Richer, C. Ti-Coyo and his shark. London, 1951.
43756.13.115 Richer, C. Son of Ti-Coyo. 1. American ed. N.Y., 1954.
43756.14.100 Ricquebourg, F. Hai-Kaï d'Indochine. Paris, 1952.

43511 - 43873 Individual authors, etc. - 1900- - Known authors (363 scheme plus 10) - cont.

43756.24.100 Rienzi, Raymond. Le gamin passionné. Paris, 1928.
43756.27.100 Riffaud, Madelenie. De votre envoyee speciale. Paris, 1964.
43756.31.100 Rigaut, Jacques. Écrits. Paris, 1970.
43756.35.100 Riguillaume. Les fleurs du soleil. Paris, 1969.
43756.55.1100 Rimière, Edmond. Conte crépusculaire. Paris, 1946.
43756.58.100 Rinaldi, Angelo. La maison des Atlantes; roman. Paris, 1971.
43756.62.100 Rinval, Claude. Jusqu'à la limite de la chair. Paris, 1963.
43756.66.100 Riotor, Léon. Le parabolain. Paris, 1894.
43756.69.100 Ripert, Émile. La terre des lauriers. Paris, 1912.
43756.69.110 Ripert, Émile. Le train bleu, poèmes. Paris, 1929.
43756.69.120 Ripert, Émile. Le poème d'Assise. 2. éd. Paris, 1926.
43756.69.130A Ripert, Émile. Poèmes d'Amerique. Abbeville, 1926.
43756.69.130B Ripert, Émile. Poèmes d'Amerique. Abbeville, 1926.
43756.69.805 Elliott, B. Émile Ripert, poète et humaniste de Provence. Avignon, 1938.
43756.86.100 Rivière, Bertrande de. Chrysis. Paris, 1957.
43756.87.100 Rivière, Isabelle. Le bouquet de roses rouges. 8. éd. Paris, 1935.
43756.90.100 Rivière, Jacques. Jacques Rivière et Alain Fournier: correspondance, 1905-1914. 5. éd. Paris, 1926- 2v.
43756.90.103 Rivière, Jacques. Jacques Rivière et Alain Fournier: correspondance, 1905-1914. Paris, 1937. 4v.
43756.90.104 Rivière, Jacques. Correspondance, 1905-1914. Paris, 1948. 2v.
43756.90.110 Rivière, Jacques. Correspondance, 1907-1914. Paris, 1926.
43756.90.111 Rivière, Jacques. Correspondance, 1907-1914. Paris, 1963.
43756.90.120 Rivière, Jacques. Aimée. 15. éd. Paris, 1922.
43756.90.130 Rivière, Jacques. A la trace de Dieu. 28. éd. Paris, 1937.
43756.90.148 Rivière, Jacques. Nouvelles études. 9. éd. Paris, 1947.
43756.90.150 Rivière, Jacques. The ideal reader. N.Y., 1960.
43756.90.803 Hommage à Jacques Rivière, 1886-1925. Paris, 1925.
43756.90.805 Roos, E.G. de. Het essayistisch werk van Jacques Rivière. Amsterdam, 1931.
43756.90.815 Jans, A. La pensée de Jacques Rivière. Bruxelles, 1938.
43756.90.820 Gisi, Martha. Die Entwicklung des Moralbegriffs bei Jacques Rivière. Freiburg, 1948.
43756.90.825 Turnell, M. Jacques Rivière. Cambridge, Eng., 1953.
43756.90.830 Beaulieu, Paul. Jacques Rivière. Paris, 1956.
43756.90.835 Cook, Bradford. Jacques Rivière. Oxford, 1958.
43756.90.840 Coquoz, F.M. L'évolution religieuse de Jacques Rivière. Fribourg, 1963.
43756.90.850 Chauvet, Alice. Essai sur Jacques Rivière et Alain-Fournier. Mont-de-Marsan, 1929.
43756.90.855 Mauriac, François. Le tourment de Jacques Rivière. Strasbourg, 1926.
43756.90.860 Naughton, Helen Thomas. Jacques Rivière; the development of a man and a creed. The Hague, 1966.
43756.90.865 Suffran, Michel. Jacques Rivière, ou La conversion à la clarité. Paris, 1967.
43756.90.1100 Riverain, Achille. Le manteau de plomb. Bruxelles, 1964.
43756.90.1110 Riverain, Achille. Aux couleurs de ma mélancolie. Bruxelles, 1964.
43756.91.100 Rivière, P.L. La route. Paris, 1927.
43756.91.2100 Rivet, R. Lueurs aux vitres. Limoges, 1958.
43756.91.3100 Rivoyre, Christine de. Les sultans. Paris, 1964.
43756.91.3110 Rivoyre, Christine de. Le petit matin, noman. Paris, 1968.
43756.91.3700 Rivoyre, Christine de. The wreathed head. London, 1962.
43756.91.3705 Rivoyre, Christine de. The sultans; a novel. London, 1967.
43757.2 Roux, M.X. L'enjôleuse. Paris, 1912.
43757.3.25 Romains, Jules. Morceaux choisis. N.Y., 1941.
43757.3.30 Romains, Jules. Un être en marche. Paris, 1910.
43757.3.31 Romains, Jules. Odes et prières. Paris, 1913.
43757.3.32 Romains, Jules. Mort de quelqu'un; roman. Paris, 1911.
43757.3.33 Romains, Jules. Europe. 2e éd. Paris, 1919.
43757.3.35 Romains, Jules. Cromedeyre-le-Vieil. 3e éd. Paris, 1920.
43757.3.37 Romains, Jules. Lucienne. 14e éd. Paris, 1922.
43757.3.37.5 Romains, Jules. Lucienne. N.Y., 1925.
43757.3.38 Romains, Jules. Knock, ou Le triomphe de la médicine. Paris, 1924.
43757.3.40 Romains, Jules. Knock, ou Le triomphe de la médicine. 2e éd. Paris, 1924.
43757.3.40.2 Romains, Jules. Knock, ou Le triomphe de la médicine. 24e éd. Paris, 1924.
43757.3.40.5A Romains, Jules. Knock, ou Le triomphe de la médicine. N.Y., 1927.
43757.3.40.5B Romains, Jules. Knock, ou Le triomphe de la médicine. N.Y., 1927.
43757.3.40.8 Romains, Jules. Knock, ou Le triomphe de la médicine. 33e éd. Paris, 1928.
43757.3.41 Romains, Jules. Monsieur le Trouhadec saisi, par la débauche. Paris, 1924.
43757.3.44 Romains, Jules. Le mariage de le Trouhadec. Paris, 1925.
43757.3.46 Romains, Jules. La vie unanime. Paris, 1913.
43757.3.48 Romains, Jules. Dictateur. Paris, 1926.
43757.3.48.2 Romains, Jules. Le dictateur. Demetrios. 2. éd. Paris, 1926.
43757.3.48.5 Romains, Jules. Le dictateur. Quatre actes. 5. éd. Paris, 1959.
43757.3.50 Romains, Jules. Jean le Maufranc. Paris, 1927.
43757.3.53 Romains, Jules. Europe. Paris, 1928.
43757.3.55 Romains, Jules. Donogoo; un prologue. Paris, 1930.
43757.3.57 Romains, Jules. Le moulin et l'hospice. Paris, 1949.
43757.3.58 Romains, Jules. Le moulin et l'hospice. Paris, 1949.
43757.3.60 Romains, Jules. Chants des dix années (1914-1924). 3e éd. Paris, 1928.
43757.3.65 Romains, Jules. Pièces en un acte. 3. éd. Paris, 1930.
43757.3.70 Romains, Jules. Volpone, en collaboration avec Stefan Zweig d'après Ben Jonson. 2e éd. Paris, 1929.
43757.3.72 Romains, Jules. Choix de poèmes. 7. éd. Paris, 1948.
43757.3.75 Romains, Jules. Lucienne. 68e éd. Paris, 1929.
43757.3.77 Romains, Jules. Le dieu des corps. 81e éd. Paris, 1929.
43757.3.78 Romains, Jules. Le dieu de corps. 125e éd. Paris, 1947.
43757.3.79 Romains, Jules. Quand le navire. 47e éd. Paris, 1922.
43757.3.80 Romains, Jules. Quand le navire. 81e éd. Paris, 1946.
43757.3.82 Romains, Jules. Boën, ou La possession des biens. Paris, 1929.
43757.3.83 Romains, Jules. Boën, ou La possession des biens. Paris, 1959.
43757.3.85A Romains, Jules. Les hommes de bonne volonté. Paris, 1932-44. 27v.

43511 - 43873 Individual authors, etc. - 1900- - Known authors (363 scheme plus 10) - cont.

43757.3.85B Romains, Jules. Hommes de bonne volonté. v. 1-10,16-20,23. Paris, 1932-43. 16v.
43757.3.85C Romains, Jules. Hommes de bonne volonté. v. 1,2,16,18. Paris, 1932-41. 4v.
43757.3.86 Romains, Jules. Bertrand de ganges. N.Y., 1944.
43757.3.90 Romains, Jules. Ode génoise. Paris, 1925.
43757.3.95 Romains, Jules. Morceaux choisis. 2e éd. Paris, 1931.
43757.3.100 Romains, Jules. Manuel de déification. Paris, 1910.
43757.3.105 Romains, Jules. Pour l'esprit et la liberté. 11e éd. Paris, 1937.
43757.3.110 Romains, Jules. Puissances de Paris. 7. éd. Paris, 1932.
43757.3.115 Romains, Jules. Une vue des choses. N.Y., 1941.
43757.3.120A Romains, Jules. Pierres levées. Paris, 1957.
43757.3.120B Romains, Jules. Pierres levées. Paris, 1957.
43757.3.130A Romains, Jules. Men of good will. N.Y., 1933-46. 14v.
43757.3.130B Romains, Jules. Men of good will. v. 1,4,6,8. N.Y., 1933-46. 4v.
43757.3.130C Romains, Jules. Men of good will. v. 1,8. N.Y., 1933-46. 2v.
43757.3.130D Romains, Jules. Men of good will. v. 1,8. N.Y., 1933-46. 2v.
43757.3.130E Romains, Jules. Men of good will. v. 8. N.Y., 1933-46.
43757.3.135 Romains, Jules. The aftermath. London, 1940.
43757.3.140 Romains, Jules. Le vin blanc de la villette. 13e éd. Paris, 1935.
43757.3.150 Romains, Jules. Les copains. 71e éd. Paris, 1937.
43757.3.160A Romains, Jules. Grace encore pour la terre! N.Y., 1941.
43757.3.160B Romains, Jules. Grace encore pour la terre! N.Y., 1941.
43757.3.165 Romains, Jules. Grace encore pour la terre. Paris, 1947.
43757.3.180 Israël, M. Jules Romains. 3e éd. Paris, 1931.
43757.3.185 Romains, Jules. Le problème numéro un. Paris, 1947.
43757.3.190 Romains, Jules. The death of a nobody. N.Y., 1914.
43757.3.195 Romains, Jules. Une femme singulière. Paris, 1957.
43757.3.196 Romains, Jules. The adventuress. London, 1958.
43757.3.200 Romains, Jules. The boys in the back room. N.Y., 1937.
43757.3.205A Romains, Jules. Problèmes d'aujourd'hui. Paris, 1931.
43757.3.205B Romains, Jules. Problèmes d'aujourd'hui. Paris, 1931.
43757.3.210 Romains, Jules. Problèmes européens. Paris, 1933.
43757.3.215 Romains, Jules. La douceur de la vie lithographie originale de Heuze. Paris, 1951.
43757.3.225 Romains, Jules. The body's rapture. N.Y., 1937.
43757.3.230 Romains, Jules. Les hauts et les bas de la liberté. Paris, 1960.
43757.3.235 Romains, Jules. Salsette discovers America. N.Y., 1942.
43757.3.236 Romains, Jules. Salsette decouvre l'Amerique. N.Y., 1942.
43757.3.240 Romains, Jules. Retrouver la foi. N.Y., 1944.
43757.3.245 Romains, Jules. Retrouver la foi. Paris, 1945.
43757.3.250 Romains, Jules. Le colloque de novembre. Paris, 1946.
43757.3.255 L'amitié, par Charles Vildrac, André Cuisenier, Pierre Labracherie. Paris, 1948.
43757.3.260 Romains, Jules. La vision extra-rétinienne et le sens paroptique. 3. éd. Paris, 1932.
43757.3.263 Romains, Jules. Pour raison garder. Paris, 1961. 2v.
43757.3.265 Romains, Jules. Paris des Hommes de bonne volonté. Paris, 1949.
43757.3.267 Romains, Jules. Amitiés et rencontres. Paris, 1970.
43757.3.270A Romains, Jules. L'homme blanc. Paris, 1937.
43757.3.270B Romains, Jules. L'homme blanc. Paris, 1937.
43757.3.270C Romains, Jules. L'homme blanc. Paris, 1937.
43757.3.275 Romains, Jules. Musse. 8. éd. Paris, 1931.
43757.3.276 Romains, Jules. Musse. Paris, 1959.
43757.3.277 Romains, Jules. As it is on earth. N.Y., 1962.
43757.3.280 Romains, Jules. Tussles with time. London, 1952.
43757.3.282 Romains, Jules. Le voyage des amants. 3. éd. Paris, 1920.
43757.3.285 Romains, Jules. L'armée dans la ville. Paris, 1911.
43757.3.286 Romains, Jules. Passagers de cette planète. Paris, 1955.
43757.3.288 Romains, Jules. Mémoires de Madame Chauvirel. Paris, 1959-60. 2v.
43757.3.290 Romains, Jules. Examen de conscience des Français. Paris, 1954.
43757.3.294 Romains, Jules. Un grand honnete homme. Paris, 1961.
43757.3.295 Romains, Jules. Maisons. Paris, 1953.
43757.3.296 Romains, Jules. A Frenchman examines his conscience. London, 1955.
43757.3.297 Romains, Jules. Le fils de Jerphanion. Paris, 1956.
43757.3.298 Romains, Jules. Réception de M. Jules Romains. Paris, 1946.
43757.3.299 Romains, Jules. Jules Romains. Paris, 1952.
43757.3.300 Vasse, P. Jules Romains et les médicins. Paris, 1936.
43757.3.305 Pfeiffer, Rudolf. Les hommes de bonne volonté von Jules Romains. Winterthur, 1958.
43757.3.310 Glässer, E. Denkform und Gemeinschaft bei Jules Romains. Berlin, 1938.
43757.3.315 Romains, Jules. Lettres à un ami. Paris, 1964. 2v.
43757.3.325 Cuisenier, André. Jules Romains et l'unanimisme. Paris, 1935-48. 2v.
43757.3.330 Ehrenfels, Walter. Das unanimistische Bewusstsein im Werke Jules Romains'. Berlin, 1940.
43757.3.335 Hommage à Jules Romains pour son soixantième anniversaire. Paris, 1945.
43757.3.338 Widdem, Werner. Weltbejahung und Weltflucht im Werke Jules Romains'. Genève, 1960.
43757.3.340 Berry, Madeleine. Jules Romains. Paris, 1953.
43757.3.342 Berry, Madeleine. Jules Romains. Paris, 1959.
43757.3.345 Norrish, Peter John. Drama of the group. Cambridge, Eng., 1958.
43757.3.350 Bourin, André. Connaissance de Jules Romains. Paris, 1960.
43757.3.360 Romains, Jules. Ai-je fait ce que j'ai voulu? Paris, 1964.
43757.3.365 Romains, Gabrielle. Mes voyages avec Jules Romains. Paris, 1967-
43757.3.5100 Roud, Gustave. Air de la solitude. Lausanne, 1945.
43757.4.30 Rougé, P. de. Épaves. Paris, 1913.
43757.4.1100 Robert, Louis de. La servante sans gages. Paris, 1934.
43757.5.30 Robert, Louis de. Le roman du malade. Paris, 1911.
43757.5.100 Robert, Louis de. De Loti à Proust. Paris, 1928.
43757.5.110 Robert, Louis de. La première femme. Paris, 1898.
43757.6.100 Robbe-Grillet, Alain. Les gommes. Paris, 1953.
43757.6.105 Robbe-Grillet, Alain. Les gommes. St. Amand, 1962.
43757.6.110 Robbe-Grillet, Alain. Le voyeur. Paris, 1955.
43757.6.120 Robbe-Grillet, Alain. La jalousie. Roma, 1957.
43757.6.125 Robbe-Grillet, Alain. Jealousy. London, 1959.
43757.6.130 Robbe-Grillet, Alain. Dans le labyrinthe. Paris, 1957.

Classified Listing

43511 - 43873 Individual authors, etc. - 1900- - Known authors (363 scheme plus 10) - cont.

43757.6.140 Robbe-Grillet, Alain. L'année dernière à Marienbad. Paris, 1961.
43757.6.150 Robbe-Grillet, Alain. Instantanes. Paris, 1962.
43757.6.160 Robbe-Grillet, Alain. L'immortelle. Paris, 1963.
43757.6.170 Robbe-Grillet, Alain. Pour un nouveau roman. Paris, 1963.
43757.6.180 Robbe-Grillet, Alain. La maison de rendez-vous. Paris, 1965.
43757.6.190 Robbe-Grillet, Alain. Projet pour une révolution à New York. Paris, 1970.
43757.6.700 Robbe-Grillet, Alain. The voyeur. London, 1959.
43757.6.705 Robbe-Grillet, Alain. Jealousy. N.Y., 1959.
43757.6.710 Robbe-Grillet, Alain. Last year at Marienbad. London, 1962.
43757.6.715 Robbe-Grillet, Alain. The erasers. N.Y., 1964.
43757.6.720 Robbe-Grillet, Alain. Two novels. N.Y., 1965.
43757.6.725 Robbe-Grillet, Alain. For a new novel. N.Y., 1966.
43757.6.730 Robbe-Grillet, Alain. Snapshots, and, Towards a new novel. London, 1965.
43757.6.735 Robbe-Grillet, Alain. La maison de rendez-vous. N.Y., 1966.
43757.6.740 Robbe-Grillet, Alain. The house of assignation. London, 1970.
43757.6.800 Morrissette, Bruce A. Les romans de Robbe-Grillet. Paris, 1963.
43757.6.805 Stoltzfus, B.F. Alain Robbe-Grillet and the new French novel. Carbondale, 1964.
43757.6.810 Morrissette, Bruce A. Alain Robbe-Grillet. N.Y., 1965.
43757.6.815 Bernal, Olga. Alain Robbe-Grillet. Paris, 1964.
43757.6.820 Miesch, Jean. Robbe-Grillet. Paris, 1965.
43757.6.825 Alter, Jean. La vision du monde d'Alain Robbe-Grillet. Genève, 1966.
43757.6.830 Sabato, Ernesto R. Tres aproximaciones a la literatura de nuestro tiempo: Robbe-Grillet, Borges, Sartre. Santiago de Chile, 1968.
43757.7.100 Robert, V.A. Mes dieux sont morts. Paris, 1929.
43757.7.3061 Robert, Louis de. Lettres à Paul Faure (1898-1937). Paris, 1943.
43757.7.3100 Robert, Louis de. De l'amour a la sagesse, suivi de réflexions sur M. Proust. Paris, 1930.
43757.7.5100 Robert-Dumas, Charles. Ceux du S.R. Deuxieme bureau. Paris, 1934.
43757.7.6100 Academie...Bordeaux. Academie nationale des sciences, belles-lettres et arts de Bordeaux. Réception de M. Paul de Robert à l'academie. Bordeaux, 1954.
43757.7.7100 Robert, Jacques. Le dangereux été, roman. Paris, 1968.
43757.7.7110 Robert, Jacques. Si ma mémoire est bonne. Paris, 1969.
43757.7.7120 Robert, Jacques. La dragée haute; roman. Paris, 1970.
43757.8.100 Robinet, Auguste. Cagayous, ses meilleures histoires. Paris, 1931.
43757.8.1100 Robinet, André. Méditaire digest antifilouzofique. La Houssaye-en-Brie, 1970.
43757.8.2100 Robin, Armand. Poésie non traduite. 3. éd. Paris, 1953. 20v.
43757.8.3100 Robin, E. Accuse, live-for. Paris, 1929.
43757.8.4100 Robin, Gilbert. La prison de soie. Paris, 1927.
43757.8.5100 Robin, Liliane. Le sortilège des Antille. Paris, 1963.
43757.8.5110 Robin, Liliane. Le piège. Paris, 1969.
43757.9.30 Roüpnel, Gaston. Nono. Paris, 1910.
43757.9.110 Roüpnel, Gaston. Le vieux garain. Paris, 1939.
43757.9.805 Bernhardt, M. Gaston Roüpnel und Burg. Inaug. Diss. Würzburg, 1934.
43757.10.10 Robida, Michael. Botemry. Paris, 1945.
43757.10.100 Robida, Michael. Les trenandour; roman. Paris, 1939.
43757.10.120 Robida, Michael. Le temps de la longue patiense. Paris, 1946.
43757.11.100 Rogissart, Jean. Mervale; roman. Paris, 1937.
43757.11.110 Rogissart, Jean. Le fer et la forêt. Paris, 1940.
43757.12.100 Roblès, Emmanuel. Travail d'homme. Alger, 1944.
43757.12.110 Roblès, Emmanuel. Frederica. Paris, 1954.
43757.12.120 Roblès, Emmanuel. L'horloge suivi de porferio. Paris, 1958.
43757.12.130 Roblès, Emmanuel. L'homme d'avrile. Paris, 1959.
43757.12.140 Roblès, Emmanuel. Plaidoyer pour un rebelle. Paris, 1965.
43757.12.150 Roblès, Emmanuel. La vérité est morte. Paris, 1952.
43757.12.160 Roblès, Emmanuel. Montserrat. Paris, 1954.
43757.12.170 Roblès, Emmanuel. La croisière, roman. Paris, 1968.
43757.12.180 Roblès, Emmanuel. Un printemps d'Italie; roman. Paris, 1970.
43757.12.800 Depierris, Jean Louis. Entretiens avec Emmanuel Roblès. Paris, 1967.
43757.12.805 Landi-Bénos, Fanny. Emmanuel Roblès ou, Les raisons de vivre. Honfleur, 1969.
43757.12.1100 Roché, Louis. Si proche et lointaine. Paris, 1946.
43757.12.2100 Roché, Henri Pierre. Jules et Jim. Paris, 1953.
43757.12.2110 Roché, Henri Pierre. Les deux anglaises et le continent. Paris, 1971.
43757.13.100 Rachebrune, A. Le calvaire de Islam. Paris, 1913.
43757.13.1100 Rochefort, Christiane. Le repos deu guerrier. Paris, 1958.
43757.13.1110 Rochefort, Christiane. Les stances à Sophie. Paris, 1963.
43757.13.1120 Rochefort, Christiane. Une rose pour Morrison. Paris, 1966.
43757.13.1200 Rochefort, Christiane. Les petits enfants du siecle. Paris, 1961.
43757.13.2100 Roche, Paul. Les chevaux de la nuit. Paris, 1958.
43757.13.3100F Roche, Juliette. Demi cercle. Paris, 1920.
43757.13.4100 Roche, Denis. Les idées centésimales de Miss Elanize. Paris, 1964.
43757.13.4110 Roche, Denis. Éros énergumène suivi du poème du 29 avril 62. Paris, 1968.
43757.17.100 Rodet, Françoise. L'envers de feuilles; poèmes. Paris, 1962.
43757.32.100 Roger-Marx, Claude. Simili. Paris, 1925.
43757.32.110 Roger-Marx, Claude. Dimanche; comédie en un acte. Paris, 1933.
43757.32.1100 Roger, René. Le diapason de l'orage. Paris, 1945.
43757.33.100 Rougier, Paul. La victoire. Paris, 1921.
43757.39.100 Rohou, Guy. Le bateau des îles. Paris, 1971.
43757.48.100 Roland, Claude. L'aiguilleur. Paris, 1900.
43757.48.2100 Roland, Danielle. Rue des Canettes; roman. Tournai, 1966.
43757.49.100 Rolin, Dominique. Les enfants pérdus. Paris, 1951.
43757.49.110 Rolin, Dominique. L'epouvantail. 6. éd. Paris, 1957.
43757.49.120 Rolin, Dominique. Le lit. Paris, 1960.
43757.49.130 Rolin, Dominique. Maintenant. Paris, 1967.
43757.49.140 Rolin, Dominique. Les éclairs, roman. Paris, 1971.
43757.49.1100 Rolin, Gabrielle. Le secret des autres. Paris, 1960.

43511 - 43873 Individual authors, etc. - 1900- - Known authors (363 scheme plus 10) - cont.

43757.50.3F Pamphlet box. Periodical articles by and about Rolland.
43757.50.4 Moscow. Vsesoiuznaia Gosudarstvennaia Biblioteka Inostrannykh Literatur. Romen Rollan; bio-bibliograficheskii ukazatel'. Moskva, 1959.
43757.50.5 Starr, W.T. A critical bibliography of published writings of Romain Rolland. Evanston, Ill., 1950.
43757.50.10 Starr, W.T. Romain Rolland and a world at war. Evanston, Ill., 1956.
43757.50.21 Rolland, Romain. Pages choisis. v. 2, 2. éd. Paris, 1921. 2v.
43757.50.22 Rolland, Romain. Textes politiques, sociaux, et philosophiques choisis. Paris, 1970.
43757.50.30 Rolland, Romain. Richard Strauss et Romain Rolland. Paris, 1951.
43757.50.41A Rolland, Romain. Le cloître de la rue d'Ulm. Paris, 1952.
43757.50.41B Rolland, Romain. Le cloître de la rue d'Ulm. Paris, 1952.
43757.50.43 Rolland, Romain. Inde. Paris, 1951.
43757.50.46 Rolland, Romain. Mémoires et fragments du journal. Paris, 1956.
43757.50.48 Rolland, Romain. Histoire d'une amitie. Paris, 1962.
43757.50.60 Gillet, Louis. Correspondance entre Louis Gillet et Romain Rolland. Paris, 1949. 2v.
43757.50.61 Rolland, Romain. Lettres à un combattant de la resistance. Paris, 1947.
43757.50.62 Rolland, Romain. Printemps romain. Paris, 1954.
43757.50.64 Seché, Alphonse. Ces jours lointains. Paris, 1962.
43757.50.65A Rolland, Romain. Choix de lettres. Paris, 1948.
43757.50.65B Rolland, Romain. Choix de lettres. Paris, 1948.
43757.50.67 Rolland, Romain. Retour au palais Farnèse; choix de lettres. Paris, 1956.
43757.50.70 Rolland, Romain. Correspondance, 1894-1901. Paris, 1957.
43757.50.72 Rolland, Romain. Thèse complementaire - Univ. de Paris. Paris, 1957.
43757.50.74 Rolland, Romain. Un beau visage à tous sens, choix de lettres de Romain Rolland. Paris, 1967.
43757.50.76 Rolland, Romain. Gandhi et Romain Rolland: correspondance. Paris, 1969.
43757.50.105 Rolland, Romain. Jean-Christophe. Paris, 192-? 4v.
43757.50.110 Rolland, Romain. Jean-Christophe. Paris, 1925-1927. 10v.
43757.50.115A Rolland, Romain. Jean Christophe. Paris, 1931-32. 4v.
43757.50.115B Rolland, Romain. Jean Christophe. v. 2. Paris, 1931-32.
43757.50.131 Rolland, Romain. Jean Christophe. Photoreproduction. Paris, 1906-07. 4v.
43757.50.133 Rolland, Romain. Jean Christophe. Paris, n.d. 4v.
43757.50.193 Rolland, Romain. Jean-Christophe à Paris; La foire sur la place. 4e éd. Paris, 1908.
43757.50.203 Rolland, Romain. Jean-Christophe à Paris: Antoinette. 3. éd. Paris, 1908.
43757.50.213 Rolland, Romain. Jean-Christophe à Paris: Dans la maison. 10e éd. Paris, 1909.
43757.50.233 Rolland, Romain. Jean-Christophe - la fin du voyage. Les amies. 7e éd. Paris, 1910.
43757.50.235 Rolland, Romain. Jean-Christophe - la fin du voyage. Les amies. 14e éd. Paris, n.d.
43757.50.243 Rolland, Romain. Jean-Christophe - la fin du voyage. Le buisson ardent. 4e éd. Paris, 1911?
43757.50.245 Rolland, Romain. Jean-Christophe - la fin du voyage. Le buisson ardent. 11e éd. Paris, 1911?
43757.50.251 Rolland, Romain. Jean-Christophe - la fin du voyage. La nouvelle journée. 2e éd. Paris, 1912?
43757.50.253 Rolland, Romain. Jean-Christophe - la fin du voyage. La nouvelle journée. 5e éd. Paris, 1912.
43757.50.254 Rolland, Romain. Jean-Christophe - la fin du voyage. La nouvelle journée. 6. éd. Paris, 1912.
43757.50.270 Rolland, Romain. Jean-Christophe et Armel. Lyon, 1955.
43757.50.280 Rolland, Romain. Fräulein Elsa. Paris, 1964.
43757.50.300 Rolland, Romain. Les vaincus; drame. Anvers, 1922.
43757.50.310 Rolland, Romain. Les tragédies de la foi. 9e éd. Paris, 1925.
43757.50.312 Rolland, Romain. Les tragédies de la foi. 12e éd. Paris, 1926.
43757.50.333 Rolland, Romain. Aërt, drame. Paris, 1926?
43757.50.343 Rolland, Romain. Le triomphe de la raison; drame. Paris, 1899.
43757.50.352 Rolland, Romain. Théâtre de la révolution: 14 juillet - Danton - Les loups. 5e éd. Paris, 1923?
43757.50.354A Rolland, Romain. Théâtre de la révolution. 9e éd. Paris, 1926.
43757.50.354B Rolland, Romain. Théâtre de la révolution. 9e éd. Paris, 1926.
43757.50.359 Rolland, Romain. Le 14 juillet. Paris, 1902.
43757.50.360 Rolland, Romain. Le 14 juillet. Paris, 1909.
43757.50.392 Rolland, Romain. Colas Breugnon. 39e éd. Paris, 1919.
43757.50.394A Rolland, Romain. Colas Breugnon. 78e éd. Paris, 1926.
43757.50.394B Rolland, Romain. Colas Breugnon. 70e éd. Paris, 1925.
43757.50.402 Rolland, Romain. Pierre et Luce. 11e éd. Paris, 1921.
43757.50.402.5A Rolland, Romain. Pierre et Luce. Paris, 192-.
43757.50.402.5B Rolland, Romain. Pierre et Luce. Paris, 192-.
43757.50.403 Rolland, Romain. Pierre et Luce. 40e éd. Paris, 1928.
43757.50.412 Rolland, Romain. Liluli. 2e éd. Paris, 192-.
43757.50.413.5 Rolland, Romain. Liluli. Frankfurt, 1924.
43757.50.413.10 Rolland, Romain. Palmsonntag. Frankfurt, 1929.
43757.50.414 Rolland, Romain. Liluli. 39e éd. Paris, 1926.
43757.50.422A Rolland, Romain. Clerambault, histoire d'une conscience libre pendant la guerre. 18e éd. Paris, 1920.
43757.50.422B Rolland, Romain. Clerambault, histoire d'une conscience libre pendant la guerre. 26e éd. Paris, 1920.
43757.50.425 Rolland, Romain. Aux peuples assasinés. Paris, 1920?
43757.50.431A Rolland, Romain. L'âme enchantée. v. 1-2; v. 3, pt. 1-2; v. 4, pt. 1-3. Paris, 1922-33. 7v.
43757.50.431B Rolland, Romain. L'âme enchantée. v. 1; v.3, pt. 1-2; v. 4, pt. 1-3. Paris, 1933. 6v.
43757.50.431C Rolland, Romain. L'âme enchantée. v. 4, pt. 1. Paris, 1933.
43757.50.440 Rolland, Romain. Le jeu de l'amour et de la mort. Paris, 1925.
43757.50.442 Rolland, Romain. Le jeu de l'amour et de la mort. Paris, 1925.
43757.50.444 Rolland, Romain. Le jeu de l'amour et de la mort. Paris, 1925.
43757.50.450 Rolland, Romain. L'humble vie héroique. Paris, 1912.
43757.50.460 Rolland, Romain. Compagnons de route. Paris, 1936.
Htn 43757.50.470* Rolland, Romain. Pâques fleuries. Paris, 1926.
43757.50.472 Rolland, Romain. Pâques fleuries. Paris, 1926.

Classified Listing

43511 - 43873 Individual authors, etc. - 1900- - Known authors (363 scheme plus 10) - cont.

43757.50.480 Rolland, Romain. Les léonides. Paris, 1928.
43757.50.482 Rolland, Romain. Les léonides. Paris, 1928.
43757.50.490 Rolland, Romain. La montespan. Paris, 1904.
43757.50.500 Gandhi, M.K. Vie de M.-K. Gandhi écrite par lui-même. 7e éd. Paris, 1931.
Htn 43757.50.510* Rolland, Romain. Mahatma Gandhi. Paris, 1924.
43757.50.512A Rolland, Romain. Mahatma Gandhi. 53e éd. Paris, 1926.
43757.50.512B Rolland, Romain. Mahatma Gandhi. 65e éd. Paris, 1930.
43757.50.520A Rolland, Romain. Essai sur la mystique et l'action de l'Inde viviante. v. 1-2. pt. 1-2. Paris, 1929-30. 2v.
43757.50.520B Rolland, Romain. Essai sur la mystique et l'action de l'Inde viviante. v. 1-2. pt. 1-2. Paris, 1929-30. 2v.
43757.50.525 Rolland, Romain. La vie de Vivekananda et l'évangile universel. v. 1-2. Paris, 1948.
43757.50.530 Rolland, Romain. Musiciens d'autrefois. 9e éd. Paris, 1924.
43757.50.532 Rolland, Romain. Voyage musical au pays du passé. Paris, 1920.
43757.50.533 Rolland, Romain. Voyage musical aux pays du passé. Paris, 1919.
43757.50.534 Rolland, Romain. Musiciens d'aujourd'hui. 12e éd. Paris, 1927.
43757.50.536 Rolland, Romain. Les origines du théâtre lyrique moderne. Paris, 1931.
43757.50.537 Rolland, Romain. Goethe und Beethoven. Zürich, 1928.
43757.50.538 Rolland, Romain. Vie de Beethoven. 15e éd. Paris, 1928.
43757.50.539 Rolland, Romain. Zivot Beethovenuv. Praha, 1930.
43757.50.540 Peshkov, A.M. Eux et nous. Paris, 1939.
43757.50.542 Rolland, Romain. Gefährten meines Weges. Zürich, 1937.
43757.50.550 Rolland, Romain. Vie de Tolstoi. Paris, 1929.
43757.50.555 Rolland, Romain. La vie de Tolstoi. Paris, 1928.
43757.50.558 Rolland, Romain. Les precurseurs. Paris, 1919.
43757.50.560 Rolland, Romain. Les precurseurs. Paris, 1920.
43757.50.565 Rolland, Romain. Le voyage interieur. Paris, 1959.
43757.50.570 Rolland, Romain. Le temps viendra. Paris, 1903?
43757.50.580 Rolland, Romain. Le théâtre du peuple. Paris, 1926.
43757.50.590 Rolland, Romain. Vie de Michel-Ange. 11e éd. Paris, 1927.
Htn 43757.50.595* Rolland, Romain. Paroles de Renan à un adolescent. n.p., 1930.
43757.50.597 Rolland, Romain. Le seuil. Genève, 1945.
43757.50.599 Rolland, Romain. Souvenirs de jeunesse (1866-1900). Lausanne, 1947.
43757.50.602 Rolland, Romain. La révolte des machines. Paris, 1947.
43757.50.605 Rolland, Romain. Le périple. Paris, 1946.
43757.50.665 Rolland, Romain. Romain Rolland Malwida von Meyseukug. Stuttgart, 1932.
43757.50.670 Rolland, Romain. Par la révolution. Paris, 1935.
43757.50.675 Rolland, Romain. Romain Rolland et la Belgique. Bruxelles, 1950.
43757.50.680 Rolland, Romain. Journal des anneés de guerre. Paris, 1952.
43757.50.685 Rolland, Romain. Romain Rolland. Paris, 1955.
43757.50.690 Rolland, Romain. Chère Sofia. Paris, 1959. 2v.
43757.50.702A Rolland, Romain. Pierre and Luce. N.Y., 1922.
43757.50.702B Rolland, Romain. Pierre and Luce. N.Y., 1922.
43757.50.710 Rolland, Romain. Jean-Christophe: Dawn, morning, youth, revolt. N.Y., 1910.
43757.50.710.2 Rolland, Romain. Jean-Christophe: Dawn, morning, youth, revolt. N.Y., 1910.
43757.50.711A Rolland, Romain. Jean-Christophe: Dawn, morning, youth, revolt. N.Y., 1911.
43757.50.711B Rolland, Romain. Jean-Christophe: Dawn, morning, youth, revolt. N.Y., 1911.
43757.50.712 Rolland, Romain. Jean-Christophe: Dawn, morning, youth, revolt. N.Y., 1915.
43757.50.713 Rolland, Romain. Jean-Christophe: Dawn, morning, youth, revolt. N.Y., 1913.
43757.50.720 Rolland, Romain. Jean-Christophe in Paris. The market place, Antoinette,The house. N.Y., 1911.
43757.50.721A Rolland, Romain. Jean-Christophe in Paris. The market place, Antoinette,The house. N.Y., 1911.
43757.50.721B Rolland, Romain. Jean-Christophe in Paris. The market place, Antoinette,The house. N.Y., 1911.
43757.50.721C Rolland, Romain. Jean-Christophe in Paris. The market place, Antoinette,The house. N.Y., 1911.
43757.50.722 Rolland, Romain. Jean-Christophe in Paris. The market-place, Antoinette, The house. N.Y., 1912.
43757.50.723A Rolland, Romain. Jean-Christophe in Paris: The market-place, Antoinette, The house. N.Y., 1915.
43757.50.723B Rolland, Romain. Jean-Christophe in Paris: The market-place, Antoinette, The house. N.Y., 1915.
43757.50.725 Rolland, Romain. Jean-Christophe in Paris. N.Y., 1926.
43757.50.730A Rolland, Romain. Jean-Christophe - Journey's end: Love and friendship, The burning bush, The new dawn. N.Y., 1913.
43757.50.730B Rolland, Romain. Jean-Christophe - Journey's end: Love and friendship, The burning bush, The new dawn. N.Y., 1913.
43757.50.731 Rolland, Romain. Jean Christophe: Journey's end, Love and friendship, The burning bush, The new dawn. N.Y., 1913.
43757.50.732A Rolland, Romain. Jean-Christophe: Journey's end, Love and frienship, The burning bush, The new dawn. N.Y., 1915.
43757.50.732B Rolland, Romain. Jean-Christophe: Journey's end, Love and frienship, The burning bush, The new dawn. N.Y., 1915.
43757.50.732.5 Rolland, Romain. Journey within. N.Y., 1947.
43757.50.732.10A Rolland, Romain. Jean-Christophe. N.Y., 1938.
43757.50.732.10B Rolland, Romain. Jean-Christophe. N.Y., 1938.
43757.50.733 Rolland, Romain. De Jean Christophe à Colas Breugnon; pages de journale de Romain Rolland. Paris, 1946.
43757.50.740A Rolland, Romain. The revolt of the machines: or, Invention run wild; a motion picture fantasy. Ithaca, 1932.
43757.50.740B Rolland, Romain. The revolt of the machines: or, Invention run wild; a motion picture fantasy. Ithaca, 1932.
43757.50.750A Rolland, Romain. Annette and Sylvie. v.1. N.Y., 1925.
43757.50.750B Rolland, Romain. Annette and Sylvie. v.1. N.Y., 1925.
43757.50.752A Rolland, Romain. Summer. v.2. N.Y., 1925.
43757.50.752B Rolland, Romain. Summer. v.2. N.Y., 1925.
43757.50.753 Rolland, Romain. Mother and son. v.3. N.Y., 1927.
43757.50.754 Rolland, Romain. The death of a world. v.4. N.Y., 1933.
43757.50.755 Rolland, Romain. A world in birth. v.5. N.Y., 1934.
43757.50.760 Rolland, Romain. The people's theater. N.Y., 1918.
43757.50.762 Rolland, Romain. Above the battlefield. Cambridge, 1914.
43757.50.763 Rolland, Romain. The montespan. N.Y., 1923.
43757.50.765 Rolland, Romain. Les leonides. N.Y., 1929.
43757.50.766 Rolland, Romain. The wolves. N.Y., 1937.
43757.50.766.2 Rolland, Romain. Les loups. Paris, 1925.
43757.50.767 Rolland, Romain. Clerambault; the story of an independent spirit during the war. N.Y., 1921.

43511 - 43873 Individual authors, etc. - 1900- - Known authors (363 scheme plus 10) - cont.

43757.50.768 Rolland, Romain. Mahatma Gandhi. N.Y., 1924.
43757.50.769 Rolland, Romain. The game of love and death. N.Y., 1926.
43757.50.770 Rolland, Romain. Roland and Tagore. Calcutta, 1945.
43757.50.771 Rolland, Romain. Rabindranath Tagore et Romain Rolland. Paris, 1961.
43757.50.775 Rolland, Romain. Menschen auf der Strasse. Stuttgart, 1931.
43757.50.776 Rolland, Romain. Ein Spiel von Tod und Liebe. Erlenbach, 1925.
43757.50.777 Rolland, Romain. Die Leoniden. Frankfurt, 1929.
43757.50.778 Rolland, Romain. Peter und Lutz. München, 1923.
43757.50.785 Rolland, Romain. Vidas ejemplares: Beethoven - Miguel Angel - Tolstoi. México, 1923.
43757.50.800 Zweig, Stefan. Romain Rolland. Frankfurt, 1921.
43757.50.802 Zweig, Stefan. Romain Rolland. Frankfurt, 1929.
43757.50.804 Zweig, Stefan. Romain Rolland. Paris, 1929.
43757.50.806 Zweig, Stefan. Romain Rolland élete. Budapest, 193-?
43757.50.810A Jouve, Pierre J. Romain Rolland vivant, 1914-1919. Paris, 1920.
43757.50.810B Jouve, Pierre J. Romain Rolland vivant, 1914-1919. Paris, 1920.
43757.50.820 Bonnerot, Jean. Romain Rolland; sa vie, son oeuvre. Paris, 1921.
43757.50.830 Maxe, Jean. Le bolchevisme littéraire. Paris, 1922.
43757.50.840 Küchler, W. Romain Rolland. 2. Aufl. Würzburg, 1920.
43757.50.845 Küchler, W. Romain Rolland. 3. Aufl. Frankfurt, 1949.
43757.50.850 Seippel, Paul. Romain Rolland, l'homme et l'oeuvre. Paris, 1913.
43757.50.860 Key, Ellen. Själarnas neutralitet. Stockholm, 1916.
43757.50.870 Schüler, G. Studien zur Romain Rollands "Colas Breugnon". Inaug. Diss. Erlangen, 1927.
43757.50.880 Gotzfried, J.L. Der heroische Idealismus bei Romain Rolland. Inaug. Diss. Freudenstadt, 1929.
43757.50.890 Kaempffer, A. Romain Rolland's Frauengestalten. Inaug. Diss. Charlottenburg, 1931.
43757.50.900 Vogt, W. A propos du moins Romain der Rollands furieux. Paris, 1916.
43757.50.910 Krakowski, B. La psychologie des peuples allemand et juif dans les romans de Romain Rolland. Thèse. Toulouse, 1931.
43757.50.920 Grautoff, Otto. Romain Rolland. Frankfurt, 1914.
43757.50.930 Dvorak, Robert. Das ethische und das asthetische bei Romain Rolland. Inaug. Diss. Boltrop, 1933.
43757.50.940 Fest, Otto. Stilistische Untersuchungen zu Romain Rolland's "Pierre et Luce". Inaug. Diss. Borna, 1935.
43757.50.950 Altamira, D.R. La nueva literatura pacifista el "Clerambault" de Romain Rolland. Madrid, 1921.
43757.50.960A Wilson, R.A. The pre-war biographies of Romain Rolland and their place in his work and the period. London, 1939.
43757.50.960B Wilson, R.A. The pre-war biographies of Romain Rolland and their place in his work and the period. London, 1939.
43757.50.970 Aguirre, M. Palabras en Juan Cristobal. La Habana, 1940.
43757.50.980 Hochstaelter, M. Essai sur l'oeuvre de Romain Rolland. Paris, 1914.
43757.50.990 Der Romain Rolland Almanach. Frankfurt, 1926.
43757.50.1000A Liber amicorum Romain Rolland. Zürich, 1926.
43757.50.1000B Liber amicorum Romain Rolland. Zürich, 1926.
43757.50.1004 Mühlestein, H. Geist und Politik, Romain Rolland's politische Sendung. Zürich, 1945.
43757.50.1006A Hommage à Romain Rolland. Genève, 1945.
43757.50.1006B Hommage à Romain Rolland. Genève, 1945.
43757.50.1008 Rolland, Romain. Das Romain Rolland Buch. Zürich, 1946.
43757.50.1010 Levy, Arthur R. L'idéalisme de Romain Rolland. Thèse. Paris, 1946.
43757.50.1020 Rolano-Holst, Henriëtte. Romain Rolland. Amsterdam, 1946.
43757.50.1025 Doisy, Marcel. Romain Rolland, 1866-1944. Bruxelles, 1945.
43757.50.1030 Association des Amis de Romain Rolland. Bulletin. Paris. 1,1946+ 3v.
43757.50.1035 Descotes, M. Romain Rolland. Paris, 1948.
43757.50.1040 Weiss, H. Romain Rolland. Berlin, 1948.
43757.50.1045 Connes, G. The tragedy of Romain Rolland. Buffalo, 1948.
43757.50.1048 Ilberg, Werner. Der schwere Weg. Schwerin, 1955.
43757.50.1050 Ilbert, Werner. Traum und Tat. Halle, 1950.
43757.50.1055 Arcos, René. Romain Rolland. Paris, 1950.
43757.50.1060 Hellwig, Hans. Romain Rolland. Lübeck, 1947.
43757.50.1070A Grappin, P. Le bund neues Naterland. Lyon, 1952.
43757.50.1070B Grappin, P. Le bund neues Naterland. Lyon, 1952.
43757.50.1080 Europe. Revue Mensuelle. Romain Rolland. Paris, 1955.
43757.50.1090 Rolland, Romain. Colas Breugnon. N.Y., 1919.
43757.50.1100 Gugenheim, S. Romain Rolland e l'Italia. Milano, 1955.
43757.50.1105 Motyleva, Tamara L. Romen Rollan. Moskva, 1969.
43757.50.1110 Krampf, Miriam. La conception de la vie héroique dans l'oeuvre de Romain Rolland. Paris, 1966.
43757.50.1115 Pichler, R. Romain Rolland. Leipzig, 1957.
43757.50.1120 Greshoff, Jan. Sans famille. 1. druk. Amsterdam, 1947.
43757.50.1125 Relgis, Eugen. El hombre libre frente a la barbarie totalitaria. Montevideo, 1954.
43757.50.1167 Relgis, Eugen. Romain Rolland. Montevideo, 1951.
43757.50.1170 Vanovskaia, T.V. Romen Rollan, 1866-1944. Leningrad, 1957.
43757.50.1175 Scanno, Teresa di. Romain Rolland. Parma, 1957.
43757.50.1180 Motyleva, Tamara L. Tvorchestvo Romena Rollana. Moskva, 1959.
43757.50.1185 Hulia, O.P. Romen Rollan. Chernivtsi, 1960.
43757.50.1190 Robichez, Jacques. Romain Rolland. Paris, 1961.
43757.50.1195 Kaplan, M.S. Stilisticheskoe upotreblenie antonimov v romane Romena Rollana ocharovannaia chesha. Kazan, 1960.
43757.50.1200 Kempf, Marcelle. Romain Rolland et l'Allemagne. Paris, 1962.
43757.50.1205 Karczewska-Markiewicz, Zofia. Struktura Jana Kruzysztofa. Wrocław, 1963.
43757.50.1210 Cheval, René. Romain Rolland. Paris, 1963.
43757.50.1211 Cheval, René. Romain Rolland's Begegnungen mit Österreich. Innsbruck, 1968.
43757.50.1215 Bloch, J.R. Deux hommes se rencontvent. Paris, 1964.
43757.50.1220 Karczewska-Markiewicz, Zofia. Romain Rolland. Warszawa, 1964.
43757.50.1225 Balakhonov, Viktor E. Romen Rollan v 1914-1924 gody. Leningrad, 1958.
43757.50.1230 Guilbeaux, Henri. Pour Romain Rolland. Genève, 1915.
43757.50.1235 Diushen, Igor' B. Zhan-kristof Romena Rollana. Moskva, 1966.
43757.50.1240 Josimović, Radoslav. Književni pogledi Romena Rolana. Beograd, 1966.
43757.50.1245 Gil'dina, Z.M. Romen Rollan i mirovaia kul'tura. Riga, 1966.

43511 - 43873 Individual authors, etc. - 1900- - Known authors (363 scheme plus 10) - cont.

43757.50.1250 Rolland, Romain. Romain Rolland et le mouvement Florentin de La Voce. Paris, 1966.
43757.50.1255 Barrère, Jean Bertrand. Romain Rolland: l'âme et l'art. Paris, 1966.
43757.50.1260 Boissevain, W. Romain Rolland. Den Haag, 1966.
43757.50.1265 Kobi, Emil Erich. Die Erziehung zum Einzelnen. Frauenfeld, 1966.
43757.50.1270 France. Archives Nationales. Romain Rolland, sa vie, son oeuvre, 1866-1944. Paris, 1966.
43757.50.1275 Balakhonov, Viktor E. Romen Rollan i ego vremir. Leningrad, 1968.
43757.50.1280 Romen Rollan. 1866-1966. Moskva, 1968.
43757.50.1285 Pesis, Boris A. Ot XIX k XX veka. Moskva, 1968.
43757.50.1290 Pérus, Jean. Romain Rolland et Maxime Gorki. Paris, 1968.
43757.50.1295 Sices, David. Music and the musician in Jean-Christophe: the harmony of contrasts. New Haven, 1968.
43757.50.1300 Mentel, Marianne. Romain Rolland und die bildende Kunst. Salzburg, 1966.
43757.50.1305 Reinhardt, Hans. Romain Rolland's unveräffentlichte Dramen. München, 1967.
43757.50.1310 Duchatelet, B. La question du mariage dans Jean-Christophe de Romain Rolland. Groningen, 1965.
43757.50.1315 Gersbach-Bäschlin, Annette. Reflektorischer Stil und Erzählstruktur. Bern, 1970.
43757.50.1320 Nedeljković, Dragoljub. Romain Rolland et Stefan Zweig. Thèse. Paris, 1970.
43757.50.1325 Romain Rolland (Hommage). Neuchâtel, 1969.
43757.53.100 Román, José. Mes souvenirs de Chasseur de chez Maxim's. Paris, 1939.
43757.53.1100 Romains, Gabrielle. Dix-neuf cent quatorze - dix-neuf cent dix-huit. Paris, 1969.
43757.55.100 Romilly, Édouard. Théâtre. 3e éd. Paris, 1926.
43757.55.110 Romilly, Édouard. Vers l'effort. Paris, 1909.
43757.57.100 Romus, André. Voix dans le labyrinthe. Paris, 1954.
43757.58.21 Rondeau-Luzeau, Lucie. Le livre du souvenir: Témoignage, 1914-1918. Paris, 1950?
43757.58.100 Rondeau-Luzeau, Lucie. Les voix du mystère. Paris, 1959.
43757.68.800 Djemil, Enyn. J. Guy Ropartz, ou La recherche d'une vocation. Le Mans, 1967.
43757.73.100 Roques, Jeanne. La vie sentimentale de George Sand. Paris, 1946.
43757.73.2100 Roques, René. Ici on est heureux. Paris, 1950.
43757.75.100 Rouré, Jacques. Tutti frutti. Paris, 1958.
43757.79.100 Rosciszewska, Rita de. L'aventure; poèmes. Paris, 1957.
43757.82.700 Rossi, J.B. The false start. London, 1951.
43757.82.1100 Rossi, Pierre. Un soir à pise. Paris, 1971.
43757.83.30 Rostand, Maurice. La messe de cinq heures. Paris, 1921.
43757.83.33 Rostand, Maurice. La gloire. Paris, 1921.
43757.83.34A Rostand, Maurice. La gloire. Paris, 1922.
43757.83.34B Rostand, Maurice. La gloire. Paris, 1922.
43757.83.35 Rostand, Maurice. La mort de Molière. Paris, 1922. 3 pam.
43757.83.37 Rostand, Maurice. Le phénix. Paris, 1923.
43757.83.40 Rostand, Maurice. Le masque de fer; pièce...en vers. Paris, 1923.
43757.83.45 Rostand, Maurice. Le secret du sphinx; pièce en vers. Paris, 1924.
43757.83.47 Rostand, Maurice. L'archange. Paris, 1925.
43757.83.49 Rostand, Maurice. Deserteuse. Paris, 1926.
43757.83.53 Rostand, Maurice. Napoléon IV. Paris, 1928.
43757.83.55 Rostand, Maurice. Napoléon IV. Paris, 1928.
43757.83.56 Rostand, Maurice. Napoléon IV. Paris, 1928.
43757.83.60 Rostand, Maurice. L'homme que j'ai tué. Paris, 1925.
43757.83.61 Rostand, Maurice. L'homme que j'ai tué. Paris, 1930.
43757.83.63 Rostand, Maurice. Les insomnies. Paris, 1923.
43757.83.65 Rostand, Maurice. La lettre à Dieu. Paris, 1952.
43757.83.70 Rostand, Maurice. Conversation avec la gloire. Paris, 1910.
43757.83.73 Rostand, Maurice. Poèmes. Paris, 1911.
43757.83.80 Rostand, Maurice. Page de la vie. Paris, 1913.
43757.83.90 Rostand, Maurice. Morbidezza. Paris, 1928.
43757.83.100 Rostand, Maurice. La nuit des amants. Paris, 1925.
43757.83.105 Rostand, Maurice. Le dernier tzar...en vers. Paris, 1929.
43757.83.110 Rostand, Maurice. Le général Boulanger. Paris, 1931.
43757.83.120 Rostand, Maurice. Une jeune fille espagnole. Paris, 1932.
43757.83.130 Rostand, Maurice. L'homme que j'ai fait naitre; roman. Paris, 1934.
43757.83.140 Rostand, Maurice. Confession d'un demi-siècle. Paris, 1948.
43757.83.2100 Rostand, Jean. Page d'un moraliste. Paris, 1952.
43757.83.2110 Rostand, Jean. La vie. Paris, 1953.
43757.83.2120 Rostand, Jean. Ce que je crois. Paris, 1956.
43757.83.2130 Rostand, Jean. Discours de réception de Jean Rostand. Paris, 1960.
43757.83.2800 Delaunay, Albert. Jean Rostand. Paris, 1956.
43757.88.100 Rouff, Marcel. La vie de fête sans le second empire. Paris, 1931.
43757.88.1100 Rouffanche, J. Dans la foule de gui. Paris, 1962.
43757.88.3100 Rougemont, Denis de. Journal d'un intellectuel. Paris, 1937.
43757.88.3110 Rougemont, Denis de. Les personnes du drame. Paris, 1947.
43757.88.3120 Rougemont, Denis de. Comme toi-même. Paris, 1961.
43757.88.3125 Rougemont, Denis de. The myths of love. London, 1964.
43757.88.3700 Rougemont, Denis de. Love declared. N.Y., 1963.
43757.88.3710 Rougemont, Denis de. Dramatic personnages. N.Y., 1964.
43757.89.100 Roukhomousky, Suzanne. Le temple d'argile. Paris, 1929.
43757.89.1100 Rousset, Jean Paul. Poaimes. Paris, 1957.
43757.89.2100 Rougier, Henry. L'or et la paille. Paris, 1960.
43757.89.3100 Rouart, Eugène. La victime. Paris, 1902.
43757.89.4100 Rouff, Marcel. Les étranglés. Paris, 1927.
43757.89.4110 Rouff, Marcel. Sur le quai Wilson. Paris, 1926.
43757.89.4120 Rouff, Marcel. L'homme et la montagne. Paris, 1925.
43757.89.4130 Rouff, Marcel. Jubabau. Paris, 1928.
43757.89.5100 Rouvres, Alain. Un coeur de pierre. Paris, 1966.
43757.89.6100 Roux, Dominique de. L'ouverture de la chasse. Lausanne, 1968.
43757.89.7100 Roubaud, Jacques. E. Paris, 1967.
43757.89.8100 Roussel, Romain. La vallée sans printemps. Paris, 1937.
43757.89.8101 Roussel, Romain. Le vallée sans printemps. Paris, 1937.
43757.89.8112 Roussel, Romain. Papa, tu me fais rire. 2. éd. Paris, 1969.
43757.90.1100 Rouger, Henri. La retraite fleuril. Paris, 1906.
43757.91.100 Rouquette, Louis-Frédéric. La chanson du pays. Paris, 1927.
43757.91.110 Rouquette, Louis-Frédéric. La bête bleue. Paris, 1928.
43757.91.2100 Rouquette, Yves. L'escriveire public. Toulouse, 1958.

43511 - 43873 Individual authors, etc. - 1900- - Known authors (363 scheme plus 10) - cont.

43757.91.2700 Rouquette, Yves. Lo poëta es una vaca; racònte. Lavit, 1967.
43757.91.4100 Rousseau, B. Quatre contes. Bruxelles, 1938.
43757.92.113 Roussel, Raymond. L'étoile au front. 3. éd. Paris, 1925.
43757.92.114 Roussel, Raymond. L'étoile au front; pièce en trois actes, en prose. Paris, 1963.
43757.92.120 Roussel, Raymond. Comment j'ai écrit certains de mes livres. Paris, 1935.
43757.92.122 Roussel, Raymond. Comment j'ai écrit certains de mes livres. Paris, 1963.
43757.92.130 Roussel, Raymond. La poussière de soleils. Paris, 1926.
43757.92.132 Roussel, Raymond. La poussière de soleils; pièce en cinq actes et vingt-quatre tableaux. Paris, 1964.
43757.92.143 Roussel, Raymond. Nouvelles impressions d'Afrique suivies de l'ame de Victon Hugo. 3. éd. Paris, 1932.
43757.92.144 Roussel, Raymond. Nouvelles impressions d'Afrique. Paris, 1963.
43757.92.150 Roussel, Raymond. La vue. Paris, 1904.
43757.92.152 Roussel, Raymond. La vue. Paris, 1963.
43757.92.160 Roussel, Raymond. Chiquenaude. Paris, 1900.
43757.92.175 Roussel, Raymond. La doublure. 2. éd. Paris, 1897.
43757.92.176 Roussel, Raymond. La doublure. Paris, 1963.
43757.92.180 Roussel, Raymond. Locus solus. Lausanne, 1963.
43757.92.182 Roussel, Raymond. Locus solus. Paris, 1965.
43757.92.190 Roussel, Raymond. Impressions d'Afrique. Paris, 1932.
43757.92.192 Roussel, Raymond. Impressions d'Afrique. Paris, 1963.
43757.92.700 Roussel, Raymond. Impressions of Africa. London, 1966.
43757.92.800 Ferry, Jean. Une étude sur Raymond Roussel. Paris, 1953.
43757.92.805 Foucault, Michel. Raymond Roussel. Paris, 1963.
43757.92.810 Ferry, Jean. Une autre étude sur Raymond Roussel. Paris, 1964.
43757.92.815 Heppenstall, Rayner. Raymond Roussel: a critical guide. London, 1966.
43757.92.820 Ferry, Jean. L'Afrique des impressions. Paris, 1967.
43757.92.2100 Rousselot, Jean. Poèmes choises. Paris, 1953.
43757.92.2110 Rousselot, Jean. Le coeur bronzé. Paris, 1950.
43757.92.2120 Rousselot, Jean. Une fleur de sang. Paris, 1954.
43757.92.2130 Rousselot, Jean. Il n'y a pas d'exil. Paris, 1954.
43757.92.2140 Rousselot, Jean. Les papiers. Paris, 1951.
43757.92.2150 Rousselot, Jean. Les heureux de la terre. Paris, 1957.
43757.92.2160 Rousselot, Jean. Une certaine Diane. Paris, 1956.
43757.92.2170 Rousselot, Jean. Agrégation du temps. Paris, 1957.
43757.92.2180 Rousselot, Jean. Présences contemporaines: rencontres sur les chemins. Paris, 1958.
43757.92.2190 Rousselot, Jean. Route du silence. Goudargues, 1965.
43757.92.2800 Marissel, André. Jean Rousselot. Rodez, 1956.
43757.93.100 Roussin, André. Comédies conjugales. Paris, 1961.
43757.93.110 Roussin, André. Les glorieuses. Monaco, 1961.
43757.93.120 Roussin, André. Comédies de fantaisie. Paris, 1960.
43757.93.130 Roussin, André. Comédies d'amour. Paris, 1959.
43757.93.140 Roussin, André. Comédies de famille. Paris, 1960.
43757.93.150 Roussin, André. Comédies de la scène et de la ville. Paris, 1962.
43757.93.700 Roussin, André. The little hut. London, 1951.
43757.93.710 Roussin, André. Le mari. Monaco, 1955.
43757.93.1100 Rouveret, René. Si les fleuves parlaient. Paris, 1959.
43757.94.105 Roux, F. de. Brune; roman. 23e éd. Paris, 1938.
43757.94.1100 Roux, Paul. Anciennetés...réposoirs de procession. n.p., 1946.
43757.94.1110 Roux, Paul. L'ancienne à la coiffe innombrable. Nantes, 1946.
43757.94.1120 Roux, Paul. L'âme noire du prieur blanc. Paris, 1893.
43757.94.1800 Aragon, Louis. Saint Paul Roux, ou L'espoir. Paris, 1945.
43757.96.20 Roy, Claude. Somme toute. Paris, 1969.
43757.96.100 Roy, Claude. La mer à boire. Paris, 1944.
43757.96.116 Roy, Claude. Çlefs pour l'Amerique. 6. éd. Paris, 1949.
43757.96.120 Roy, Claude. A toit ou à raison. 7. éd. Paris, 1955.
43757.96.130 Roy, Claude. Le soleil sur la terre. Paris, 1956.
43757.96.140 Roy, Claude. Le parfait amour. Paris, 1952.
43757.96.150F Roy, Claude. Farandoles et fariboles. Lausanne, 1957.
43757.96.160 Roy, Claude. Le malheur d'aimer. Paris, 1958.
43757.96.170 Roy, Claude. Léone, et les siens. Paris, 1963.
43757.96.180 Roy, Claude. La nuit est le manteau des pauvres. Paris, 1968.
43757.96.190 Roy, Claude. La dérobée. Paris, 1968.
43757.96.200 Roy, Claude. Le verbe aimer et autres essais. Paris, 1969.
43757.96.210 Roy, Claude. Un seul poème. 6. éd. Paris, 1954.
43757.96.220 Roy, Claude. Poésies. Paris, 1970.
43757.96.4103 Roy, Jules. Le navigateur. 47. éd. Paris, 1954.
43757.96.4110 Roy, Jules. Beau sang. Paris, 1952.
43757.96.4116 Roy, Jules. Retour de l'enfer. Paris, 1963.
43757.96.4125 Roy, Jules. L'homme à l'épée. 5. éd. Paris, 1957.
43757.96.4130 Roy, Jules. Les belles croisades. Paris, 1959.
43757.96.4140 Roy, Jules. Sept poèmes de ténèbres. n.p., 1957.
43757.96.4150 Roy, Jules. Les chevaux du soleil. Paris, 1967- 4v.
43757.96.4152 Roy, Jules. Les chevaux du soleil. Paris, 1969.
43757.96.4160 Roy, Jules. Le fleuve rouge. Paris, 1957.
43757.96.4170 Roy, Jules. La femme infidèle. Paris, 1955.
43757.96.4700 Roy, Jules. The navigator. 1st American ed. N.Y., 1955.
43757.96.4707 Roy, Jules. Return from hell. 2d ed. London, 1954.
43757.96.4710 Roy, Jules. The unfaithful wife. N.Y., 1956.
43757.97.102 Royer, L.C. La maitresse noire. Paris, 1928.
43757.98.100 Royère, Jean. Exil daré; poésies. Paris, 1898.
43757.98.110 Royère, Jean. Eurythmies. Paris, 1904.
43757.98.120 Royère, Jean. Par la lumière peints. Paris, 1919.
43757.98.130 Royère, Jean. Quiétude. Paris, 1923.
43757.98.140 Royère, Jean. Soeur de narcisse nue. Paris, 1907.
43757.98.150 Royère, Jean. Poésies. Amiens, 1924.
43757.98.160 Royère, Jean. Clartes sur la poésie. Paris, 1925.
43757.98.170 Royère, Jean. Frantans. 1e série. Paris, 1932.
43757.98.1100 Roy, Francis Joachim. Les chiens; roman. Paris, 1961.
43758.9.100 Rubsel, Raoul S. Messages de l'enfer. Paris, 1958.
43758.17.100 Rudel, Yves M. Johnny de Roscoff. Paris, 1945.
43758.17.110 Rudel, Yves M. Telle était notre race. Paris, 1960.
43758.17.120 Rudel, Yves M. Mon curé à l'heure du concile. Paris, 1970.
43758.18.100 Rudigoz, Roger. Armande ou le roman. Paris, 1970.
43758.24.100 Ruet, Noël. Les sources dans le coeur. Paris, 1963.
43758.24.110 Ruet, Noël. Le bouquet du sang. Loiret, 1958.
43758.24.120 Ruet, Noël. Cercle magique. Paris, 1931.
43758.24.130 Ruet, Noël. Chants pour l'amour et la mort. Bruxelles, 1966.
43758.24.140 Ruet, Noël. Le musicien du coeur. Liège, 1928.
43758.27.100 Ruffin, Alfred. Poésies variees et nouvaux chats. Paris, 1890.

Classified Listing

43511 - 43873 Individual authors, etc. - 1900- - Known authors (363 scheme plus 10) - cont.

43758.70.100 Rupied, J. Élysée, 1928-34. Paris, 1952.
43758.82.100 Russo, Antoine. Réflexions, sentiments, souvenirs de jeunesse (1956-1966). Paris, 1967.
43758.87.100 Ruttgers, Paul. Silences en moi. Paris, 1954.
43761.1.100 Sandoz, Maurice Yves. Le labyrinthe. Paris, 1957.
43761.1.700 Sandoz, Maurice Yves. Fantastic memories. Garden City, N.Y., 1944.
43761.1.701 Sandoz, Maurice Yves. Fantastic memories. London, 193-.
43761.1.710 Sandoz, Maurice Yves. The maze. 1st ed. Garden City, 1945.
43761.3.30 Savignon, André. Filles de la pluie. Paris, 1912.
43761.3.35 Savignon, André. Le secret des laux. v.1-3. Paris, 1923.
43761.3.40 Savignon, André. Une femme dans chaque port. Paris, 1936.
43761.3.45 Savignon, André. Dans ma prison Le Londres. 2. éd. Bruxelles, 1962.
43761.3.1030 Sabliaux, V. de. Le pied fourchu. Paris, 1956.
43761.4.30 Saulnay, S. de. Ombres colorées. Paris, 1906.
43761.5.30 Savoir, Alfred. La huitième femme de Barbe-bleue. Paris, 1921.
43761.5.32 Savoir, Alfred. Bauco! Paris, 1922.
43761.5.34 Savoir, Alfred. La couturière de Lunéville; comédie. Paris, 1923.
43761.5.36 Savoir, Alfred. La nouvelle Héloise; comédie. Paris, 1923.
43761.5.38 Savoir, Alfred. La grande-duchesse et le garçon d'étage. Paris, 1924.
43761.5.40 Savoir, Alfred. La fuite en avant. 3. éd. Paris, 1930.
43761.5.3100 Sabatier, P. "Tu crois avoir airué". Paris, 1938.
43761.5.4100 Sabatier, Robert. Le marchand de sable. Paris, 1954.
43761.5.4110 Sabatier, Robert. Alain et le nègre. Paris, 1953.
43761.5.4120 Sabatier, Robert. Boulevard. Paris, 1956.
43761.5.4122 Sabatier, Robert. Boulevard. N.Y., 1958.
43761.5.4130 Sabatier, Robert. Les fêtes solaires. Paris, 1955.
43761.5.4140 Sabatier, Robert. Le grût de la cendre. Paris, 1955.
43761.5.4150 Sabatier, Robert. Canard au sang. Paris, 1958.
43761.5.4160 Sabatier, Robert. La sainte force. Paris, 1960.
43761.5.4170 Sabatier, Robert. Le chinois d'Afrique. Paris, 1966.
43761.5.4700 Sabatier, Robert. The little barrier. London, 1955.
43761.5.4705 Sabatier, Robert. The safety matches. 1st ed. N.Y., 1972.
43761.6.15 Sarment, Jean. Le mariage d'Hamlet. 4e éd. Paris, 1923.
43761.6.16 Sarment, Jean. Je suis trop grand pour moi. Paris, 1924.
43761.6.17 Sarment, Jean. Madelon. Paris, 1926.
43761.6.18 Sarment, Jean. Les plus beaux yeux du monde. Paris, 1926.
43761.6.19 Sarment, Jean. Le pêcheur d'ombres. Paris, 1926.
43761.6.20 Sarment, Jean. La couronne de carton. Paris, 1926.
43761.6.25 Sarment, Jean. Poèmes. Paris, 1964.
43761.6.30 Sarment, Jean. Le pêcheur d'hombres; comédie. Paris, 1921.
43761.6.32 Sarment, Jean. Le mariage d'Hamlet. Paris, 1922.
43761.6.35 Sarment, Jean. Je suis trop grand pour moi; pièce. Paris, 1924.
43761.6.38 Sarment, Jean. Les six grimaces de Don Juan. Paris, 1923.
43761.6.40 Sarment, Jean. Madelon. Paris, 1925.
43761.6.45 Sarment, Jean. Les plus beaux yeux du monde. Paris, 1926.
43761.6.50 Sarment, Jean. As tu du coeur. Paris, 1926.
43761.6.65 Sarment, Jean. Leopold le bien-aimé. Paris, 1927.
43761.6.70 Sarment, Jean. Sur mon beau navire. Paris, 1929.
43761.6.75 Sarment, Jean. Bobard. Paris, 1930.
43761.6.80 Sarment, Jean. Le plancher der vaches. Paris, 1932.
43761.6.90 Sarment, Jean. Peau d'Espagne. Paris, 1933.
43761.6.100 Sarment, Jean. La couronne de carton. Paris, 1934.
43761.6.110 Sarment, Jean. Le discours des prix; pièce en 3 actes. Paris, 1934.
43761.6.120 Sarment, Jean. Madame Quinze. Paris, 1935.
43761.6.130 Sarment, Jean. L'impromptu de Paris. Paris, 1935.
43761.6.140F Sarment, Jean. Le voyage a Biarritz. Paris, 1936.
43761.6.150 Sarment, Jean. Othello. Paris, 1938.
43761.7.30 Samain, Alfred. Contes. 22e éd. Paris, 1916.
43761.7.40 Samain, Albert. Le chariot d'or. Paris, 1947.
43761.9.100 Sabouraud, R. Sur les pas de Montaigne. Paris, 1937.
43761.13.100 Sachs, Maurice. Abracadalera. 7. éd. Paris, 1952.
43761.13.110 Sachs, Maurice. Derriere cinq barreaux. 6. éd. Paris, 1952.
43761.13.120 Sachs, Maurice. Histoire de John Cooper d'Albany. 6. éd. Paris, 1955.
43761.13.130 Sachs, Maurice. Le voile de Veronique. Paris, 1959.
43761.13.641 Sachs, Maurice. Day of wrath. London, 1953.
43761.13.642 Sachs, Maurice. Witches' sabbath. N.Y., 1964.
43761.31.100 Sagan, Françoise. Boujour tristesse. Paris, 1954.
43761.31.110 Sagan, Françoise. Un certain sourire. Paris, 1956.
43761.31.120 Sagan, Françoise. Dans un mois. Paris, 1957.
43761.31.130 Sagan, Françoise. Aimez-vous Brahms. 1st American ed. N.Y., 1960.
43761.31.140 Sagan, Françoise. Aimez-vous Brahms. Paris, 1959.
43761.31.150 Sagan, Françoise. Château en Suede. Paris, 1960.
43761.31.160 Sagan, Françoise. Les violons parfois. Paris, 1962.
43761.31.170 Sagan, Françoise. La robe mauve de Valentine. Paris, 1963.
43761.31.180 Sagan, Françoise. Landru. Paris, 1963.
43761.31.190F Sagan, Françoise. Joxique Bernard Buffet. Paris, 1964.
43761.31.200 Sagan, Françoise. La chamade; roman. Paris, 1965.
43761.31.210 Sagan, Françoise. Le cheval évanoui, suivi de l'écharde. Paris, 1966.
43761.31.220 Sagan, Françoise. Le garde du coeur, roman. Paris, 1968.
43761.31.230 Sagan, Françoise. Un peu de soleil dans l'eau froide. Paris, 1969.
43761.31.240 Sagan, Françoise. Un piano dans l'herbe. Paris, 1970.
43761.31.700A Sagan, Françoise. Bonjour tristesse. N.Y., 1955.
43761.31.700B Sagan, Françoise. Bonjour tristesse. N.Y., 1955.
43761.31.705 Sagan, Françoise. A certain smile. 1st ed. N.Y., 1956.
43761.31.710 Sagan, Françoise. Those without shadows. 1st ed. N.Y., 1957.
43761.31.715 Sagan, Françoise. Wonderful clouds, a novel. London, 1961.
43761.31.720 Sagan, Françoise. The heart-keeper. London, 1968.
43761.31.725 Sagan, Françoise. Sunlight on cold water. London, 1971.
43761.31.800 Hourdin, Georges. Le cas Françoise Sagan. Paris, 1958.
43761.31.805 Mourgue, Gerard. Françoise Sagan. Paris, 1959.
43761.31.810 Lignieré, Jean. Françoise Sagan et le success. Paris, 1957.
43761.32.100 Sage, Kay. Faut dire ce qui est. Paris, 1959.
43761.39.106 St. Exupéry, A. de. Terre des hommes. 527. éd. Paris, 1956.
X Cg 43761.39.115 St. Exupéry, A. de. Vol de nuit. Paris, 1939.
43761.39.117 St. Exupéry, A. de. Vol de nuit. N.Y., 1939.
43761.39.130 St. Exupéry, A. de. Le petit prince. N.Y., 1943.

43511 - 43873 Individual authors, etc. - 1900- - Known authors (363 scheme plus 10) - cont.

43761.39.140 St. Exupéry, A. de. Lettre à un otage. Paris, 1953.
43761.39.140.5 St. Exupéry, A. de. Lettre à un otage. 26. éd. Paris, 1944.
43761.39.141 St. Exupéry A. de. Lettres de jeunesse. 55. éd. Paris, 1953.
43761.39.142 St. Exupéry, A. de. Lettres à l'âmie inventée. Paris, 1953.
43761.39.145 St. Exupéry, A. de. Lettres à sa mère. 2. éd. Paris, 1955.
43761.39.150 St. Exupéry, A. de. Carnets. 18. éd. Paris, 1953.
43761.39.152A St. Exupéry, A. de. Citadelle. 71. éd. Paris, 1948.
43761.39.152B St. Exupéry, A. de. Citadelle. 71. éd. Paris, 1948.
43761.39.160 St. Exupéry, A. de. St. Exupéry par lui même. Paris, 1956.
43761.39.170 St. Exupéry, A. de. Courrier sud. Paris, 1958.
43761.39.180 St. Exupéry, A. de. Courrier sud. Vol de nuit. Terre des hommes. Paris, 1966.
43761.39.705A St. Exupéry, A. de. Night flight. N.Y., 1932.
43761.39.705B St. Exupéry, A. de. Night flight. N.Y., 1932.
43761.39.710A St. Exupéry, A. de. Flight to Arras. N.Y., 1942.
43761.39.710B St. Exupéry, A. de. Flight to Arras. N.Y., 1942.
43761.39.713A St. Exupéry, A. de. The little prince. N.Y., 1943.
43761.39.713B St. Exupéry, A. de. The little prince. N.Y., 1943.
43761.39.713.2 St. Exupéry, A. de. The little prince. N.Y., 1943.
43761.39.715A St. Exupéry, A. de. Wind, sand and stars. N.Y., 1939.
43761.39.715B St. Exupéry, A. de. Wind, sand and stars. N.Y., 1939.
43761.39.717 St. Exupéry, A. de. Wind, sand and stars. N.Y., 1940.
43761.39.721 St. Exupéry, A. de. The wild garden. 1st ed. N.Y., 1939.
43761.39.725 St. Exupéry, A. de. The wisdom of the sands. N.Y., 1950.
43761.39.730 St. Exupéry, A. de. Un sens à la vie. 37. éd. Paris, 1956.
43761.39.775 St. Exupéry, A. de. Regulus vel pueri soli sapiunt qui liber le petit prince inscribitur ab Augusto Haury. Latatiae, 1961.
43761.39.800 Marill, René. St. Exupéry. Paris, 1946.
43761.39.802 Marill, René. St. Exupéry. Paris, 1961.
43761.39.805 Anet, Daniel. Antoine de St. Exupéry. Paris, 1946.
43761.39.810 Crisnoy, Maria de. Antoine de St. Exupéry. Paris, 1948.
43761.39.815 Gascht, André. L'humanisme cosmique d'Antoine de St. Exupéry. Bruges, 1947.
43761.39.820 Zeller, Renée C.T. La vie secrète d'Antoine. Paris, 1948.
43761.39.822 Zeller, Renée C.T. La grande quête d'Antoine. Paris, 1961.
43761.39.825 Chevrier, Pierre A. Antoine de St. Exupéry. 13. éd. Paris, 1949.
43761.39.826 Chevrier, Pierre A. St. Exupéry. 4. éd. Paris, 1958.
43761.39.830 Pellissier, G. Les cinq visages de St. Exupéry. Paris, 1951.
43761.39.835 Roy, Jules. Passion de St. Exupéry. Paris, 1951.
43761.39.837 Roy, Jules. Passion et mort de St. Exupéry. Paris, 1964.
43761.39.840 Rauch, Karl. Antoine de St. Exupéry. 2. Aufl. Esslinger, 1951.
43761.39.845 Ibert, J.C. Antoine de St. Exupéry. Paris, 1953.
43761.39.855 Kessel, Patrick. La vie de St. Exupéry. Paris, 1954.
43761.39.860 Le Hir, Y. Fantasie et mystique dans Le petit prince de St. Exupéry. Paris, 1954.
43761.39.865 Racky, E.A. Die Auffassung vom Menschen. Weisbaden, 1954.
43761.39.870 François, Carlo Roger. L'ésthétique d'Antoine de St. Exupéry. Neuchâtel, 1957.
43761.39.880 Huguet, Jean. St. Exupéry; ou, L'ensignement du désert. Paris, 1956.
43761.39.885 Eitzenberger, Helmut. Antoine de St. Exupéry. München, 1958.
43761.39.890 Smith, Maxwell A. Knight of the air. London, 1959.
43761.39.895 Migeo, Marcel. St. Exupéry. Paris, 1958.
43761.39.896 Migeo, Marcel. St. Exupéry. N.Y., 1960.
43761.39.900 Angelet, Christian. Antoine de St. Exupéry. Brugge, 1959.
43761.39.905 Borgal, Clément. St. Exupéry. Paris, 1964.
43761.39.910 Pagé, Pierre. St. Exupéry et le monde de l'enfance. Montréal, 1963.
43761.39.915 Devaux, André A. St. Exupéry. Paris, 1965.
43761.39.920 Quesnel, Michel. St. Exupéry. Paris, 1965.
43761.39.925 Benedetto, Domenicantonio di. L'humanisme di A. de St. Exupéry. Sulmona, 1965.
V43761.39.930 Bukowska, Anna. St. Exupéry czyi parakodsy humanizmu. Warszawa, 1968.
43761.39.933 Kwiatkowski, Władysław. Humanizm St. Exupéry'ego. Wyd. 1. Warszawa, 1969.
43761.39.935 Tavernier, René. St. Exupéry en procés. Paris, 1967.
43761.39.940 Young, Michael Tomas. St. Exupéry; Vol de nuit. London, 1971.
43761.39.945 France. Cour d'appel (Bastia). Audience solennelle d'installation de M. le PremierPrésident Marcel Armand. Melun, 1964.
43761.39.950 Major, Jean Louis. Saint-Exupéry, l'écriture et la pensée. Ottawa, 1968.
43761.39.955 Cate, Curtis. Antoine de St. Exupéry. N.Y., 1970.
43761.39.960 Breaux, Adèle. St. Exupéry in America, 1942-1943; a memoir. Rutherford, N.J., 1971.
43761.39.965 Ouellet, Réal. Les relations humaines dans l'oeuvre de St. Exupéry. Paris, 1971.
43761.40.100 St. Gal de Prus, H. Galilée, carrefour du temps. Paris, 1962.
43761.40.4100 St. Ange (pseud.). Les cavaliers de mai. Paris, 1969.
43761.41.100 St. Georges de Bouhelier. O Edipe, roi de Thébes. Paris, 1919.
43761.41.110 St. Georges de Bouhelier. La vie d'une femme. Paris, 1919.
43761.41.120 St. Georges de Bouhelier. Carnaval des enfants. Paris, 1911.
43761.41.130 St. Georges de Bouhelier. La romance de l'homme. Paris, 1912.
43761.41.140 St. Georges de Bouhelier. Les chants de la vie ardente. Paris, 1902.
43761.41.150 St. Georges de Bouhelier. Le sang de Danton. Paris, 1931.
43761.41.160 St. Georges de Bouhelier. Napoléon. Paris, 1933.
43761.41.170 St. Georges de Bouhelier. Jeanne d'Arc. Paris, 1934.
43761.41.180 St. Georges de Bouhelier. Le roi sans couronne. Paris, 1906.
43761.41.190 St. Georges de Bouhelier. La tragédie de Tristan et Iseult. Paris, 1923.
43761.41.200 St. Georges de Bouhelier. Le roi soleil. Paris, 1938.
43761.41.800 Blanchart, Paul. St. Georges de Bouhelier, son oeuvre. Paris, 1920.
43761.41.1100 St. Gil, Philippe. Dialogues à une voix. Paris, 1967.
43761.41.2100 St. Marcoux, Jeanne. La guitare andalouse. Paris, 1959.

Classified Listing

43511 - 43873 Individual authors, etc. - 1900- - Known authors (363 scheme plus 10) - cont.

43761.41.2110	St. Marcoux, Jeanne. Le voleur de lumière. Paris, 1970.
43761.41.3100	St. Pierre, Michel de. Les écrivains. Paris, 1957.
43761.41.3110	St. Pierre, Michel de. Les nouveaux prêtres. Paris, 1965.
43761.41.4100	Saintouge, Jacques A. Natales. Bruxelles, 1961.
43761.41.5100	St. Sorny. Bicchii. Paris, 1922.
43761.41.5110	St. Sorny. Palaces. Paris, 1925.
43761.41.6100	St. René, Martin. La carnyx d'Airain. Paris, 1927.
43761.41.7100	St. Phalle, Thérèse de. Le tournesol. Paris, 1969.
43761.41.7110	St. Phalle, Thérèse de. Le souverain. Paris, 1970.
43761.41.8100	St. Clair, Georges. L'automne et les courlis. Paris, 1959.
43761.41.9100	St. Agrève, Marc. Le puits. Paris, 1957.
43761.42.100	St. Helièr, Monique. Bois-mort. 13e éd. Paris, 1934.
43761.42.800	Hommage à Monique St. Helièr. Neuchâtel, 1960.
43761.42.3100	St. Prix, J. de. Lettres. Paris, 1924.
43761.43.105	St. René Taillandier, M.M.L. Ce monde disparu. Paris, 1947-
43761.44.100	St. Soline, Claire. Et l'enfant que je fus. Paris, 1944.
43761.44.110	St. Soline, Claire. D'une haleine. Paris, 1935.
43761.44.120	St. Soline, Claire. Les années fraiches. Paris, 1966.
43761.44.2100	Salmon, André. Le monocle a deux coups, roman. Paris, 1968.
43761.45.100	Saintillac, Hector. L'ensorceleuse. Paris, 1956.
43761.47.100	Sales, Henri. Almanach. Paris, 1946.
43761.48.100	Salacrou, Armand. "Atlas-hotel" (version défintive). Pièce en trois actes. Paris, 1937.
43761.48.110	Salacrou, Armand. Théâtre. v.1-7. Paris, 1943-47. 5v.
43761.48.120	Salacrou, Armand. Poof. Paris, 1950.
43761.48.125	Salacrou, Armand. Boulevard durand. Paris, 1960.
43761.48.130	Salacrou, Armand. Les invités du Bon Dieu. Paris, 1953.
43761.48.140	Salacrou, Armand. L'inconnue d'Arras. Paris, 1936.
43761.48.150	Salacrou, Armand. Une femme, trop honnête. 3. éd. Paris, 1956.
43761.48.160	Salacrou, Armand. Les idées de la nuit. Paris, 1960.
43761.48.170	Salacrou, Armand. Comme les chardons; pièce sans entracte. Paris, 1964.
43761.48.800	Mignon, Paul L. Salacrou. Paris, 1960.
43761.48.805	Silenieks, Juris. Themes and dramatic forms in the plays of Armand Salacrou. Lincoln, 1967.
43761.48.810	Di Franco, Fiorenza. Le théâtre de Salacrou. Paris, 1970.
43761.49.110	Salmon, André. Peindre. Paris, 1921.
43761.49.120	Salmon, André. Venus dans la balance. Paris, 1926.
43761.49.133	Salmon, André. Créances, 1905-1910: Les clés ardentes - Féeries - Le calumet. 3e éd. Paris, 1926.
43761.49.144	Salmon, André. Carreaux, 1918-1921. 4e éd. Paris, 1928.
43761.49.150	Salmon, André. Les féeries. Paris, 1907.
43761.49.160	Salmon, André. Poèmes. Paris, 1905.
43761.49.170	Salmon, André. Le calumet; poèmes. Paris, 1910.
43761.49.180	Salmon, André. Ventes d'amour. Paris, 1921.
43761.49.190A	Salmon, André. Une orgil à Saint-Petersbourg. Paris, 1925.
43761.49.190B	Salmon, André. Une orgil à Saint-Petersbourg. Paris, 1925.
43761.49.200	Salmon, André. Les étoiles dans l'encrier. Paris, 1952.
43761.49.210	Salmon, André. Sylvére. Paris, 1956.
43761.49.220	Salmon, André. Vocalises. Paris, 1957.
43761.49.230	Salmon, André. Prikaz. Paris, 1956.
43761.49.240	Salmon, André. L'amant des Amazones. Paris, 1921.
43761.49.250	Salmon, André. La négresse du sacré-coeur. Paris, 1968.
43761.49.2100	Salgas, Simone. Folles saisons. Paris, 1959.
43761.49.2110	Salgas, Simone. Atalaya del sol. Paris, 1960.
43761.49.2120	Salgas, Simone. La toupie. Paris, 1970.
43761.49.2130	Salgas, Simone. Le goupil. Lausanne, 1969.
43761.49.3100	Sallèles, Louis A. Boulevards et états d'âme (1912-1956). Paris, 1956.
43761.50.100	Salis, J.R. de. Im Lauf der Jahre. Zürich, 1962.
43761.51.100	Salomon, Michel. Portraits et paysages. Paris, 1920.
43761.51.2100	Salomon, Xavier. Un homme à la porte. Paris, 1960.
43761.53.100	Samboo, Gopaljee. Un Indien à Paris. Paris, 1966.
43761.55.100	Samson, Jean Paul. Journals de l'an quarante. Montreux, 1967.
43761.56.21	Sandoz, Maurice Yves. Choix de poèmes. Monaco, 1957.
43761.56.100	Sandoz, Maurice Yves. On the verge. 1st ed. Garden City, 1950.
43761.56.110	Sandoz, Maurice Yves. The house without windows. London, 1950.
43761.56.120	Sandoz, Maurice Yves. Imitation des Sonnets from the Portuguese. Genève, 1955.
43761.58.100	Sandre, Thierry. Le chèvre feuille. Paris, 1924.
43761.58.105	Sandre, Thierry. Le chèvre feuille. 26e éd. Paris, 1924.
43761.58.110	Sandre, Thierry. Mousseline. Paris, 1926.
43761.58.1100	Sandier, Gilles. L'an n'aura plas d'hiver. Paris, 1960.
43761.59.100	Sandy, Isabelle. Andorra, ou Les hommes d'Airain. v.1-4. Paris, 1923.
43761.59.103	Sandy, Isabelle. Andorra, ou Les hommes d'Airain. Paris, 1923.
43761.59.105	Sandy, Isabelle. Les soutanes vertes. Paris, 1927.
43761.59.110	Sandy, Isabelle. Le dieu noir, roman. pt.1-3. Paris, 1929.
43761.59.120F	Sandy, Isabelle. Quand les loups ont faim. Paris, 1936.
43761.59.125	Sandy, Isabelle. Nuits Andorranes. Paris, 1938.
43761.59.2100	Sandra, C. Mortvigne. Paris, 1957.
43761.71.100	Saporta, Marc. Les invités; roman. Paris, 1964.
43761.77.100	Sarraute, Nathalie. Portrait d'un inconnu, roman. Paris, 1956.
43761.77.113	Sarraute, Nathalie. Martereau. 3. éd. Paris, 1953.
43761.77.120	Sarraute, Nathalie. Tropismes. Paris, 1957.
43761.77.149	Sarraute, Nathalie. Le planétarium. Paris, 1959.
43761.77.160	Sarraute, Nathalie. Les fruits d'or. Paris, 1963.
43761.77.170	Sarraute, Nathalie. Le silence, suivi de la mensonge. Paris, 1967.
43761.77.180	Sarraute, Nathalie. Entre lavie et la mort. Paris, 1968.
43761.77.190	Sarraute, Nathalie. Isma; ou, Ce qui s'appelle rien. Paris, 1970.
43761.77.700	Sarraute, Nathalie. Portrait of a man unknown. N.Y., 1958.
43761.77.705	Sarraute, Nathalie. Martereau. N.Y., 1959.
43761.77.710	Sarraute, Nathalie. The age of suspicion. N.Y., 1963.
43761.77.715	Sarraute, Nathalie. The planetarium. N.Y., 1960.
43761.77.720A	Sarraute, Nathalie. The golden fruits. N.Y., 1964.
43761.77.720B	Sarraute, Nathalie. The golden fruits. N.Y., 1964.
43761.77.725	Sarraute, Nathalie. Between life and death. N.Y., 1969.
43761.77.800	Kranakė, Mimika. Nathalie Sarraute. Paris, 1965.
43761.77.805	Micha, René. Nathalie Sarraute. Paris, 1966.
43761.77.810	Temple, Ruth Zabriskie. Nathalie Sarraute. N.Y., 1968.

43511 - 43873 Individual authors, etc. - 1900- - Known authors (363 scheme plus 10) - cont.

43761.77.815	Jaccard, Jean-Luc. Nathalie Sarraute. Zürich, 1967.
43761.77.820	Wonderli-Müller, Christine B. Le thème du masque et les banalités dans l'oeuvre de Nathalie Sarraute. Thèse. Zürich, 1970.
43761.77.1100	Sarrazin, Albertine. L'astragale; roman. Paris, 1965.
43761.77.2101	Sartin, Pierrette. Une femme à part entière; roman. Paris, 1968.
43761.77.3100	Sarte, Sylvie. Variations urbaines. Paris, 1969.
43761.78.41A	Sartre, Jean Paul. Sartre. Paris, 1955.
43761.78.41B	Sartre, Jean Paul. Sartre. Paris, 1955.
43761.78.103A	Sartre, Jean Paul. La nausée. 13e éd. Paris, 1938.
43761.78.103B	Sartre, Jean Paul. La nausée. 4. éd. Paris, 1938.
43761.78.110	Sartre, Jean Paul. La putain respectueuse. 12. éd. Paris, 1946.
43761.78.120	Sartre, Jean Paul. Morts sans sepulture. Lausanne, 1946.
43761.78.130A	Sartre, Jean Paul. Théâtre. 35. éd. Paris, 1947-
43761.78.130B	Sartre, Jean Paul. Théâtre. 116. éd. Paris, 1947-
43761.78.140	Sartre, Jean Paul. Théâtre. Paris, 1960-
43761.78.145	Sartre, Jean Paul. Théâtre. Paris, 1962.
43761.78.160	Sartre, Jean Paul. Les mains sales. 50e éd. Paris, 1948.
43761.78.170	Sartre, Jean Paul. L'engrenage. 2. éd. Paris, 1948.
43761.78.180A	Sartre, Jean Paul. Le sursis, roman. v.2. Paris, 1945.
43761.78.180B	Sartre, Jean Paul. Le sursis, roman. v.2. Paris, 1945.
43761.78.180C	Sartre, Jean Paul. Le sursis, roman. v.2. Paris, 1945.
43761.78.190A	Sartre, Jean Paul. Situations. Paris, 1949- 7v.
43761.78.190B	Sartre, Jean Paul. Situations. v.4, 6. Paris, 1949- 2v.
43761.78.203	Sartre, Jean Paul. Les jeux sont faits. Paris, 1955.
43761.78.210A	Sartre, Jean Paul. L'âge de raison, roman. Paris, 1945.
43761.78.210B	Sartre, Jean Paul. L'âge de raison, roman. Paris, 1945.
43761.78.210C	Sartre, Jean Paul. L'âge de raison, roman. Paris, 1945.
43761.78.230	Sartre, Jean Paul. Visages. Paris, 1948.
43761.78.240	Sartre, Jean Paul. La mort dans l'âme, roman. Paris, 1949.
43761.78.260	Sartre, Jean Paul. Le diable et le bon dieu. Paris, 1952.
43761.78.265	Sartre, Jean Paul. Le diable et le bon dieu. Paris, 1968.
43761.78.270	Sartre, Jean Paul. Nekrassov. 15. éd. Paris, 1956.
43761.78.280	Sartre, Jean Paul. Le mur. Paris, 1954.
43761.78.285	Sartre, Jean Paul. Les séquestrés d'Altona. Paris, 1960.
43761.78.290	Sartre, Jean Paul. Les mots. Paris, 1964.
43761.78.300	Sartre, Jean Paul. Qu'est-ce que la littérature? Paris, 1964.
43761.78.310	Sartre, Jean Paul. Les mouches, drame en trois actes. N.Y., 1963.
43761.78.322	Sartre, Jean Paul. Bariona. 2e éd. Paris, 1967.
43761.78.330	Sartre, Jean Paul. Les communistes ont peru de la révolution. Paris, 1969.
43761.78.622.5	Sartre, Jean Paul. No exit (Huis clos). N.Y., 1952.
43761.78.622.10	Sartre, Jean Paul. No exit (Huis clos) a play in one act. N.Y., 1954.
43761.78.622.11	Sartre, Jean Paul. No exit (Huis clos) a play in one act and The flies (Les mouches) a play in three acts. N.Y., 1970.
43761.78.622.15	Sartre, Jean Paul. Huis clos, suivi de Les mouches. Paris, 1969.
43761.78.624	Sartre, Jean Paul. Three plays. 1st American ed. N.Y., 1949.
43761.78.625	Sartre, Jean Paul. The respectable prostitute - Lucifer and the Lord. Harmondsworth, Eng., 1965.
43761.78.630	Sartre, Jean Paul. Literary and philosophical essays. London, 1955.
43761.78.631	Sartre, Jean Paul. Literary and philosophical essays. N.Y., 1962.
43761.78.641A	Sartre, Jean Paul. The words. N.Y., 1964.
43761.78.641B	Sartre, Jean Paul. The words. N.Y., 1964.
43761.78.641C	Sartre, Jean Paul. The words. N.Y., 1964.
43761.78.703	Sartre, Jean Paul. The age of reason. N.Y., 1966.
43761.78.705	Sartre, Jean Paul. The flies (Les mouches) and In camera (Huis clos). London, 1946.
43761.78.707	Sartre, Jean Paul. Loser wins. London, 1960.
43761.78.710A	Sartre, Jean Paul. Portrait of the anti-semite. N.Y., 1946.
43761.78.710B	Sartre, Jean Paul. Portrait of the anti-semite. N.Y., 1946.
43761.78.712A	Sartre, Jean Paul. Anti-semite and Jew. N.Y., 1948.
43761.78.712B	Sartre, Jean Paul. Anti-semite and Jew. N.Y., 1948.
43761.78.715A	Sartre, Jean Paul. The reprieve. 1st American ed. N.Y., 1947.
43761.78.715B	Sartre, Jean Paul. The reprieve. 1st American ed. N.Y., 1947.
43761.78.716	Sartre, Jean Paul. The reprieve. Harmondsworth, 1963.
43761.78.720	Sartre, Jean Paul. The chips are down. N.Y., 1948.
43761.78.725	Sartre, Jean Paul. What is literature? N.Y., 1949.
43761.78.726	Sartre, Jean Paul. What is literature? N.Y., 1965.
43761.78.730	Sartre, Jean Paul. The diary of Antoine Roquentin. London, 1949.
43761.78.735A	Sartre, Jean Paul. Nausea. Norfolk, 1949.
43761.78.735B	Sartre, Jean Paul. Nausea. Norfolk, 1949.
43761.78.735C	Sartre, Jean Paul. Nausea. Norfolk, 1949.
43761.78.735.5	Sartre, Jean Paul. Nausea. Norfolk, 1959.
43761.78.740	Sartre, Jean Paul. Three plays. London, 1949.
43761.78.745.2	Sartre, Jean Paul. Intimacy, and other stories. N.Y., 1948.
43761.78.745.5	Sartre, Jean Paul. Intimacy. London, 1956.
43761.78.750	Sartre, Jean Paul. Iron in the soul. London, 1950.
43761.78.755	Sartre, Jean Paul. Troubled sleep. 1st American ed. N.Y., 1951.
43761.78.758	Sartre, Jean Paul. Nekrassov. London, 1956.
43761.78.760	Sartre, Jean Paul. Lucifer and the Lord. London, 1952.
43761.78.765	Sartre, Jean Paul. In the mesh. London, 1954.
43761.78.770	Sartre, Jean Paul. The wall. N.Y., 1948.
43761.78.775	Sartre, Jean Paul. The devil and the good Lord. N.Y., 1960.
43761.78.780	Sartre, Jean Paul. The condemned of Altona. 1st American ed. N.Y., 1961.
43761.78.785	Sartre, Jean Paul. Sartre visita a Cuba. 2. ed. La Habana, 1961.
43761.78.790	Sartre, Jean Paul. Situations. N.Y., 1965.
43761.78.800	Varet, Gilbert. L'ontologie de Sartre. 1. éd. Paris, 1948.
43761.78.810	Murdoch, Iris. Sartre. New Haven, 1953.
43761.78.812	Murdoch, Iris. Sartre. Cambridge, Eng., 1953.
43761.78.820A	Marill, René. Jean-Paul Sartre. Paris, 1953.
43761.78.820B	Marill, René. Jean-Paul Sartre. Paris, 1953.
43761.78.823	Marill, René. Jean-Paul Sartre. 5. éd. Paris, 1960.
43761.78.824	Marill, René. Jean-Paul Sartre. N.Y., 1961.

43511 - 43873 Individual authors, etc. - 1900- - Known authors (363 scheme plus 10) - cont.

43761.78.825 Rooks, A.G. Jean-Paul Sartre's concepts of freedom and value. Natal, 1959.
43761.78.830 Manno, Ambrogio. L'esistenzialismo di Jean Paul Sartre. Napoli, 1958.
43761.78.835 Dellevaux, Raymond. L'existentialisme et le théâtre de Jean Paul Sartre. 3. éd. Bruxelles, 1959.
43761.78.840 Dumas, Alexandre. Kean. London, 1954.
43761.78.845 Arntz, Joseph. Die liefde in de ontologie van Jean Paul Sartre. Nijmegen, 1960.
43761.78.850A Thody, Philip. Jean Paul Sartre. London, 1960.
43761.78.850B Thody, Philip. Jean Paul Sartre. London, 1960.
43761.78.855 Zuidema, S.U. Sartre. Philadelphia, 1960.
43761.78.860 Kummer, Bernhard. Fehlentscheidung des deutschen Theaters. Lienau, 1960.
43761.78.865 Cranston, M.W. Sartre. Edinburgh, 1962.
43761.78.870 Kern, Edith. Sartre; a collection of critical essays. Englewood Cliffs, 1962.
43761.78.875 Schlisske, G. Die Ontologie Jean-Paul Sartres als subjektiver Idealismus. München, 1961.
43761.78.880 Verhoeff, J.P. Sartre als toueelschrijver. Groningen, 1962.
43761.78.885 Bauters, Paul. Jean-Paul Sartre. Brugge, 1964.
43761.78.890 Warnock, Mary. The philosophy of Sartre. London, 1965.
43761.78.895 Zehm, Günter Albrecht. Jean Paul Sartre. Velber, 1965.
43761.78.900A Jameson, F. Sartre. New Haven, 1961.
43761.78.900B Jameson, F. Sartre. New Haven, 1961.
43761.78.905 Lilar, Suzanne. A propos de Sartre et de l'amour. Paris, 1967.
43761.78.910 Haug, Wolfgang Fritz. Jean-Paul Sartre und die Konstruktion des Absurden. Frankfurt, 1966.
43761.78.915 Pollmann, Leo. Sartre und Camus; Literature der Existenz. Stuttgart, 1967.
43761.78.916 Pollmann, Leo. Sartre and Camus; literature of existence. N.Y., 1970.
43761.78.920 Biemel, Walter. Jean-Paul Sartre in Selbstzeugnissen und Bilddokumenten. Reinbek, 1967.
43761.78.923 Biemel, Walter. Jean-Paul Sartre in Selbstzeugnissen und Bilddokumenten. Reinbek, 1967.
43761.78.925 Peyre, Henri. Jean-Paul Sartre. N.Y., 1968.
43761.78.930 Prince, Gérald Joseph. Métaphysique et technique dans l'oeuvre romanesque de Sartre. Genève, 1968.
43761.78.935 Boros, Marie Denise. Un séquestré, l'homme sartrien. Paris, 1968.
43761.78.940 McCall, Dorothy. The theatre of Jean-Paul Sartre. N.Y., 1969.
43761.78.945 Gore, Keith. Sartre: La nausée and Les mouches. London, 1970.
43761.78.950 Presseault, Jacques. L'être-pour-autrui dans la philosophie de Jean-Paul Sartre. Bruxelles, 1970.
43761.79.100 Desan, W. The marxism of Jean-Paul Sartre. Garden City, 1965.
43761.89.100 Saunier, R. Deux hommes, une femme. Paris, 1924.
43761.89.5100 Saurat, Denis. Tendances. Paris, 1928.
43761.89.5105 Saurat, Denis. Tendances ideas françaises. Paris, 1946.
43761.89.5110 Saurat, Denis. Encaminament catar. Tolosa, 1955.
43761.89.5700 Saurat, Denis. The end of fear. London, 1938.
43761.89.5710 Saurat, Denis. Death and the dreamer. London, 1946.
43761.90.25 Sauvage, C. Oeuvres. Paris, 1929.
43761.90.2021 Sauvage, Tristan. Choix de poèmes (1949-1956). Paris, 1956.
43761.90.3100F Save, Michel. Made in Magony. Lyon, 1961.
43761.90.3110F Save, Michel. Icebergs de la mémoire. Dijon, 1961.
43761.91.100 Savoy, Bernard. La fuite; roman. Paris, 1965.
43761.92.100 Savarion, A. Visages et paysages du Marias Poitevin. Paris, 1944.
43763.1 Schwob, M. Bagatelle. Paris, 1910.
43763.2.21 Schopfer, Jean. Théâtre: Mademoiselle Bourrat. Paris, 1924.
43763.2.30 Schopfer, Jean. Quand la terre trembla; roman. v.1-4. Paris, 1921.
43763.2.35 Schopfer, Jean. Ariane. Paris, 1920[1921]
43763.2.37 Schopfer, Jean. Ariane. N.Y., 1927.
43763.2.38 Schopfer, Jean. Ariane. London, 192-.
43763.2.39 Schopfer, Jean. Ariane, jeune fille russe. Paris, 1930.
43763.2.40 Schopfer, Jean. Mademoiselle Bourrat. Paris, 1923.
43763.2.45 Schopfer, Jean. Petite ville. Paris, 1921.
43763.2.50 Schopfer, Jean. L'amour en Russie. Paris, 1930.
43763.2.50.5 Schopfer, Jean. Mayerling, the love and tragedy of a crown prince. London, 193-.
43763.2.52 Schopfer, Jean. Mayerling. Paris, 1944.
43763.2.52.2 Schopfer, Jean. Mayerling. London, 1968.
43763.2.54 Schopfer, Jean. La fin d'un monde. Paris, 1925.
43763.2.1100 Schaettel, Marcel. Sonnets du no man's land. Paris, 1956.
43763.3.30 Schneider, Édouard. Le dieu d'Argile. Paris, 1921.
43763.3.32 Schneider, Édouard. Le dieu d'Argile. Paris, 1923.
43763.3.38 Schneider, Édouard. L'exaltation. Paris, 1928.
43763.4.100 Schaltin, Raymond. Poèmes essentiels. Rodez, 1956-57. 4v.
43763.4.110 Schaltin, Raymond. Quinzains et troisneufs, formes poétiques et modernes. Paris, 1957.
43763.36.100 Scheler, Lucien. La lampe tempête. Paris, 1946.
43763.36.2100 Schehadé, Georges. Monsieur Bob'le. 4. éd. Paris, 1951.
43763.36.2106 Schehadé, Georges. Les poésies. 6. éd. Paris, 1952.
43763.36.2110 Schehadé, Georges. La soirée des proverbes. Paris, 1954.
43763.36.2122 Schehadé, Georges. Histoire de Vasco. 2. éd. Paris, 1956.
43763.36.2140 Schehadé, Georges. Le voyage. Paris, 1961.
43763.36.2150 Schehadé, Georges. L'émigré de Brisbane. Paris, 1965.
43763.36.3100 Schakovskoy, Zinaïda. Lumières et ombres. Paris, 1964.
43763.36.3110 Schakovskoy, Zinaïda. Une manière de vivre. Paris, 1965.
43763.37.100 Scheinert, David. L'homme qui allait à Gotterwald; théâtre. Paris, 1970.
43763.37.110 Scheinert, David. Le mal du docteur Laureys. Bruxelles, 1962.
43763.37.1100 Schewaebel, Joseph. La pentecôte à Arras, 1915. Paris, 1916.
43763.37.2100 Schehadé, Laurice. La fille royale et blanche. Paris, 1953.
43763.37.2110 Schehadé, Laurice. Portés disparues. Paris, 1956.
43763.38.12 Schlumberger, Jean. Oeuvres. Paris, 1958. 7v.
43763.38.100 Schlumberger, Jean. Saint-Saturnin. Paris, 1931.
43763.38.110 Schlumberger, Jean. Un homme heureux. 11. éd. Paris, 1924.
43763.38.120 Schlumberger, Jean. Les yeux de dix-huit ans. 3. éd. Paris, 1928.
43763.38.123 Schlumberger, Jean. Les yeux de dix-huit ans. 8. éd. Paris, 1945.

43511 - 43873 Individual authors, etc. - 1900- - Known authors (363 scheme plus 10) - cont.

43763.38.130 Schlumberger, Jean. Sur les frontiers religieuses. Paris, 1934.
43763.38.140 Schlumberger, Jean. Histoire de quatre potiers. Paris, 1935.
43763.38.150 Schlumberger, Jean. L'enfant qui s'accuse. Paris, 1927.
43763.38.160 Schlumberger, Jean. Césaire ou La puissance de l'ésprit. Paris, 1927.
43763.38.170 Schlumberger, Jean. Nouveaux jalons. Marseille, 1943.
43763.38.185 Schlumberger, Jean. Théâtre. 3. éd. Paris, 1943.
43763.38.190 Schlumberger, Jean. Stéphane le Glorieux. 14. éd. Paris, 1948.
43763.38.201 Schlumberger, Jean. L'inquiète paternité. Paris, 1933.
43763.38.216 Schlumberger, Jean. Le camarade infidèle. 21. éd. Paris, 1922.
43763.38.223 Schlumberger, Jean. Essais et dialogues. 6. éd. Paris, 1937.
43763.38.230 Schlumberger, Jean. Dialogues avec le corps endormi. Paris, 1927.
43763.38.240 Schlumberger, Jean. Ţalons. Montréal, 1941.
43763.38.250 Schlumberger, Jean. Éveils. Paris, 1950.
43763.38.260 Schlumberger, Jean. Passion. Paris, 1956.
43763.38.700 Schlumberger, Jean. Saint Saturnin. N.Y., 1932.
43763.38.800 Hosbach, J.D. Jean Schlumberger. Genève, 1962.
43763.38.805 Delcourt, Marie. Jean Schlumberger. 2. éd. Paris, 1945.
43763.38.1100 Schneeberger, P.F. Emmanuelle ou Le doute. Paris, 1958.
43763.38.2100 Schmidt, Claude. À travers la haie. Genève, 1968.
43763.38.3011 Schlunegger, Jean Pierre. Oeuvres. Lausanne, 1968.
43763.38.4021 Schmidt, Albert Marie. Chroniques de réforme, 1945-1966. Lausanne, 1970.
43763.39.110 Schneider, Pierre. Les cinq saisons. Paris, 1955.
43763.39.1100 Schneider, Marcel. L'escurial et l'amour, roman. Paris, 1958.
43763.39.1110 Schneider, Marcel. La sibylle de Cumes. Paris, 1966.
43763.39.1120 Schneider, Marcel. La nuit de longtemps. Paris, 1968.
43763.39.1130 Schneider, Marcel. Entre deux vanités. Paris, 1967.
43763.39.1200 Schneider, Marcel. Le jeu de l'oie. Paris, 1960.
43763.39.2100 Schreiber, Boris. Le droit d'asile. Paris, 1957.
43763.39.2110 Schreiber, Boris. Les heures qui restent. Paris, 1958.
43763.39.3100 Schmidt, William. L'affaire. Paris, 1960.
43763.39.4100 Schritta, Alain Gérard. Chant dans la nuit. Paris, 1966.
43763.39.5100 Schreiber, Isabelle G. Nouvelles petites fables. Villefranche-de-Rouergue, 1933.
43763.40.100 Schwaeblé, René. Chez Satan pages à l'index possession. Paris, 1913.
43763.40.3100 Schwob, René. Cinq mystères en forme de rétable. Montréal, 1941.
43763.40.3110 Schwob, René. Mistère de Jeanne d'Arc. Paris, 1946.
43763.40.3120 Schwab, Raymond. La conquête de la joie. Paris, 1922.
43763.41.100 Schultz, Yvonne. La flamme sur le rampart. v.1-4. Paris, 1926.
43763.41.105 Schultz, Yvonne. L'idylle passionnée. v.1-2. Paris, 1928.
43763.41.107 Schultz, Yvonne. Les nuits de fer. Roman. Paris, 1923.
43763.41.110 Schultz, Yvonne. Le sampanier de la Baie d'Along. Paris, 1930.
43763.41.120 Schultz, Yvonne. Au fond d'un temple Hindou. v.1-2. Paris, 1937.
43763.41.130 Schultz, Yvonne. La divine inconnue. pts.1-2. Paris, 1939.
43763.41.2100 Schwaller de Lubicz, Isha. Her-Bak, disciple de la sagesse egyptienne. Paris, 1956.
43763.41.3100 Scialom, Marc. Journal d'été. Paris, 1955.
43763.41.6110 Scipion, Robert. Prête-moi ta plume. 7. éd. Paris, 1945.
43763.42.100 Scize, Pierre. Vingt dieux de république. Lyon, 1945.
43763.45.100 Schwarz-Bart, André. Le dernier des justes. Paris, 1959.
43763.45.102 Schwarz-Bart, André. The last of the just. 1. American ed. N.Y., 1960.
43763.45.110 Schwarz-Bart, Simone. La mulâtresse solitude. Paris, 1967.
43763.55.100 Schmitz, André. A voix double et jointe. Bruxelles, 1965.
43763.63.100 Schoendoerffer, Pierre. L'adieu au roi. Paris, 1969.
43763.63.700 Schoendoerffer, Pierre. Farewell to the king. London, 1970.
43765.6.100 Sébastien, R. La chapelle des Saints-Anges, roman. Paris, 1928.
43765.13.800 Jean-Desthieux, F. Alphonse Séché. Paris, 1923.
43765.17.100 Sedeyn, Émile. Nihilia; nouvelle. Paris, 1931.
43765.21.30 Sée, Edmond. Un ami de jeunesse. Paris, 1921. 2 pam.
43765.21.32 Sée, Edmond. Le bel amour. Paris, 1925.
43765.21.35 Sée, Edmond. Les miettes. Paris, 1899.
43765.21.37 Sée, Edmond. Les miettes. Paris, 1930.
43765.21.40 Sée, Edmond. La Brebis. Paris, 1912.
43765.21.43 Sée, Edmond. La dépositaire. Paris, 1924.
43765.21.47 Sée, Edmond. Le métier d'amant. Paris, 1928. 2 pam.
43765.21.51 Sée, Edmond. L'indiscret; comédie en trois actes. Paris, 1923.
43765.22.100 Seers, E. Un manuscrit retrouvé à Kor-el-Fantin. Eleutheropolis, 1963.
43765.31.100 Ségalen, Victor. Équipée, voyage au pays du réel. Paris, 1929.
43765.31.110 Ségalen, Victor. Équipée, de Pékin aux marches Thibétaines. Paris, 1929.
43765.31.120 Ségalen, Victor. Les immemoriaux. Paris, 1921.
43765.31.130 Ségalen, Victor. René Leys. Paris, 1950.
43765.31.140 Ségalen, Victor. Stèles. Paris, 1955.
43765.31.150 Ségalen, Victor. Peintures. Paris, 1916.
43765.31.800 Bouillier, H. Victor Ségalen. Paris, 1961.
43765.32.21 Seghers, Pierre. Poèmes choisis, 1939-52. Paris, 1952.
43765.32.100 Seghers, Pierre. Le futur anterieur. Paris, 1947.
43765.32.110 Seghers, Pierre. Le chien de pique. Neuchâtel, 1943.
43765.32.120 Seghers, Pierre. Le domaine public. Paris, 1945.
43765.32.130 Seghers, Pierre. Racines. Paris, 1956.
43765.32.140 Seghers, Pierre. Les pierres. Paris, 1958.
43765.32.150 Seghers, Pierre. Piranese. Neuchâtel, 1960.
43765.32.160 Seghers, Pierre. Nouvelles chansons et complaintes. Paris, 1964.
43765.32.170 Seghers, Pierre. Dialogue. Avec 2 photos par Fina Gomez. Paris, 1965.
43765.34.100 Segonzac, R. La légende de Flarinda. 4. éd. Paris, 1928.
43765.35.100 Seguin, Hélène. Le miroir de Clélie. Paris, 1928.
43765.41.100 Seidner, Mireille. Les nouveaux lotophages. Tunis, 1968.
43765.41.3100 Seignolle, Claude. L'événement. Paris, 1960.
43765.41.3800 Rousseaux, André. Terroirs et diableries de Claude Seignolle. Paris, 1960?

Classified Listing

43511 - 43873 Individual authors, etc. - 1900- - Known authors (363 scheme plus 10) - cont.

43765.41.3805 Plangue, Bernard. Un aventurier de l'insolite: Claude Seignolle. Perigueux, 1960.
43765.41.3810 Doyon, René Louis. A la recherche du vrai à travers l'oeuvre de Claude Seignolle. Paris, 1959.
43765.56.100 Semprum, Jorge. La deuxième mort de Ramon Mercader. Paris, 1969.
43765.58.100 Senard, Pierre. Le regne de Venus. Paris, 1957.
43765.59.100 Sénéchal, Georges. Droit de cité. Vitry-sur-Seine, 1957.
43765.75.100 Sernet, Claude. Étapes. Paris, 1956.
43765.76.100 Sernin, André. L'apprenti philosophe. Paris, 1954.
43765.76.110 Sernin, André. Icare, ou Comment on tue un écrivain. Paris, 1956.
43765.76.2100 Serge, Jean. Elena et les hommes. Paris, 1956.
43765.76.3100 Serguine, Jacques. Le petit Lussard. Paris, 1960.
43765.76.3110 Serguine, Jacques. La mort confuse. Paris, 1970.
43765.76.4100 Sermaise, Robert. Prélude charnel; roman. Paris, 1970.
43765.77.100 Serreau, Geneviève. Le fondateur. Paris, 1959.
43765.77.1100 Sertillanges, Antonin Gilbert. Prière de la femme française pendant la guerre. Paris, 1916.
43765.77.1110 Sertillanges, Antonin Gilbert. Aux morts de la guerre. Paris, 1916.
43765.77.2100 Serstevens, Albert t'. Petites trilogies. Paris, 1921.
43765.78.100 Servais, Jean. Itinéraires; roman. Bruxelles, 1966.
43765.78.1100 Servain, Élisabeth. Cendres chaudes, chants de vie et de mort. Paris, 1958.
43765.80.100 Serge, Victor (pseud.). Les derniers temps. Montréal, 1946. 2v.
43765.80.110 Serge, Victor (pseud.). L'affaire Toulaév. Paris, 1949.
43765.80.120 Serge, Victor (pseud.). Mémoires d'un révolutionnaire, 1901-1941. Paris, 1951.
43765.80.130 Serge, Victor (pseud.). Carnets. Paris, 1952.
43765.80.140 Serge, Victor (pseud.). Les révolutionnaires, romans. Paris, 1967.
43765.80.700 Serge, Victor (pseud.). The case of Comrade Tulayer. 1. éd. Garden City, 1950.
43765.80.705 Serge, Victor (pseud.). Memoirs of a revolutionary, 1901-1941. London, 1963.
43765.80.706 Serge, Victor (pseud.). Memoirs of a revolutionary, 1901-1941. London, 1967.
43765.89.100 Seuphor, Michel. Les évasions d'Olivier Trickmanshoh. Paris, 1939.
43765.89.110 Seuphor, Michel. Le monde est plein d'oiseaux. Lausanne, 1968.
43765.89.120 Seuphor, Michel. Paraboliques. Lausanne, 1968.
43765.90.100 Sénac, Jean. Poèmes. 3. éd. Paris, 1954.
43765.90.110 Sénac, Jean. Avant-corps. Paris, 1968.
43765.90.120 Sénac, Jean. Citoyens de beauté, poèmes. Rodez, 1967.
43765.90.2100 Séveyrat, Aimé. Finie l'ére des chrysalides. Gap, 1956.
43765.90.3100 Séverin, Charles. L'agonie sans mort. Paris, 1960.
43765.90.4100 Sevac, H. Poèmes parisiens. Paris, 1957.
43768.21.100 Shedrow, A. Berceau sans promesses. Paris, 1956.
43769.11.100 Sicaud, Sabine. Poèmes. Paris, 1958.
43769.11.1100 Sicard, Maurice Ivan. Aurélia; scènes de la vie fantastique. Paris, 1957.
43769.11.1110 Sicard, Maurice Ivan. Les maudits; scènes de la vie révolutionnaire. Paris, 1958. 2v.
43769.27.100 Signoret, E. Chants vers la berge. Paris, 1949.
43769.48.100 Silva, Edouard. La vie et la mort. Paris, 1930.
43769.49.100 Silvain, Pierre. La part de l'ombre. Paris, 1960.
43769.49.110 Silvain, Pierre. La dame d'Elché. Paris, 1965.
43769.50.100 Silvester, Charles. Le vent du Gauffre. Paris, 1928.
43769.50.110 Silvester, Charles. Mère et fils. Paris, 1938.
43769.51.100 Sils, Marie. Saint Georges et le dragon. Paris, 1960.
43769.52.100 Silvy, René. Le chemin de nuage. Toulouse, 1928.
43769.54.11 Simenon, Georges. Oeuvres complètes. Lausanne, 1967. 38v.
43769.54.12 Simenon, Georges. Oeuvres complètes. Lausanne, 1967. 25v.
43769.54.41 Simenon, Georges. Quand j'étais vieux. Paris, 1970.
43769.54.100 Simenon, Georges. Un crime en Hollande. Paris, 1931.
43769.54.110A Simenon, Georges. Un crime en Hollande. Paris, 1931.
43769.54.110B Simenon, Georges. Un crime en Hollande. Paris, 1931.
43769.54.120A Simenon, Georges. La tête d'un homme. Paris, 1931.
43769.54.120B Simenon, Georges. La tête d'un homme. Paris, 1931.
43769.54.130 Simenon, Georges. L'écluse. Paris, 1933.
43769.54.140 Simenon, Georges. Les gens d'en face. Paris, 1933.
43769.54.155A Simenon, Georges. Les soeurs Lacroix. 22. éd. Paris, 1938.
43769.54.155B Simenon, Georges. Les soeurs Lacroix. 22. éd. Paris, 1938.
43769.54.160 Simenon, Georges. Le coup de lune. Paris, 1933.
43769.54.170 Simenon, Georges. L'homme de Londres. Paris, 1934.
43769.54.185 Simenon, Georges. Les suicidés. 72. éd. Paris, 1934.
43769.54.196 Simenon, Georges. Les rescapés du Télémaque. 16. éd. Paris, 1938.
43769.54.205 Simenon, Georges. L'assassin. 22. éd. Paris, 1937.
43769.54.210 Simenon, Georges. Pietr-le-Letton. Paris, 1936.
43769.54.220 Simenon, Georges. Les Pitard. 38. éd. Paris, 1935.
43769.54.235 Simenon, Georges. Touriste de bananes, ou Les dimanches de Tahiti. 18. éd. Paris, 1938.
43769.54.240 Simenon, Georges. M. Gallet décédé. Paris, 1933.
43769.54.250 Simenon, Georges. Les trois crimes de mes amis. Paris, 1938.
43769.54.260 Simenon, Georges. Les 13 énigmes. Paris, 1932.
43769.54.275 Simenon, Georges. Le blanc à lunettes. 24. éd. Paris, 1937.
43769.54.280 Simenon, Georges. Le passager du Palarlys. Paris, 1932.
43769.54.290 Simenon, Georges. Au rendez-vous des terre-neuves. Paris, 1938.
43769.54.305 Simenon, Georges. Le suspect. 19. éd. Paris, 1938.
43769.54.315 Simenon, Georges. Le charretier de la providence. Paris, 1936.
43769.54.325 Simenon, Georges. Le testament Donadien. 18. éd. Paris, 1937.
43769.54.335 Simenon, Georges. Le Marie du port. 22. éd. Paris, 1938.
43769.54.345 Simenon, Georges. La danseuse du Gai-Moulin. Paris, 1938.
43769.54.350 Simenon, Georges. La nuit du carrefour. Paris, 1932.
43769.54.365 Simenon, Georges. Quartier nègre. 39 éd. Paris, 1935.
43769.54.368 Simenon, Georges. Quartier nègre. Paris, 1966.
43769.54.375 Simenon, Georges. Le bourgemestre. 5. éd. Paris, 1939.
43769.54.380 Simenon, Georges. Les fiancailles de Mr. Hire. Paris, 1933.
43769.54.385 Simenon, Georges. La fuite de M. Monde, roman. Paris, 1945.
43769.54.390 Simenon, Georges. Au bout du rouleau. Paris, 1947.
43769.54.395 Simenon, Georges. Tante Jeanne. Paris, 1952.

43511 - 43873 Individual authors, etc. - 1900- - Known authors (363 scheme plus 10) - cont.

43769.54.400 Simenon, Georges. Le petit homme d'Arkhaugelsk. Paris, 1956.
43769.54.405 Simenon, Georges. Le voyageur de la Toussaint. Paris, 1958.
43769.54.410 Simenon, Georges. Une confidence de Maigret. Paris, 1959.
43769.54.415 Simenon, Georges. Quarante-cinq degrés à l'ombre. Paris, 1951.
43769.54.420 Simenon, Georges. Le fils Cardinaud. Paris, 1960.
43769.54.425 Simenon, Georges. Les noces de Poitiers. Paris, 1960.
43769.54.430 Simenon, Georges. L'homme qui regardait passer les trains. Paris, 1938.
43769.54.440 Simenon, Georges. Le roman de l'homme. Paris, 1959.
43769.54.450 Simenon, Georges. Signe Picpus. Paris, 1964.
43769.54.455 Simenon, Georges. L'escalier de fer. Paris, 1967.
43769.54.460 Simenon, Georges. Les nouvelles enquêtes de Maigret. Paris, 1964.
43769.54.470 Simenon, Georges. Maigret revient. Paris, 1964.
43769.54.480 Simenon, Georges. Les dossiers de l'agence "O". Paris, 1964.
43769.54.490 Simenon, Georges. Les petit docteur. Paris, 1964.
43769.54.500 Simenon, Georges. Le petit Saint. Paris, 1965.
43769.54.510 Simenon, Georges. Le train de Venise. Paris, 1966.
43769.54.520 Simenon, Georges. La patience de Maigret. Paris, 1965.
43769.54.530 Simenon, Georges. Le passage de la ligne. Paris, 1965.
43769.54.535 Simenon, Georges. Maigret et le voleur paresseux. Paris, 1967.
43769.54.540 Simenon, Georges. L'ours en peluche. Paris, 1965.
43769.54.545 Simenon, Georges. Le président. Paris, 1970.
43769.54.550 Simenon, Georges. Dimanche. Paris, 1965.
43769.54.555 Simenon, Georges. La folle de Maigret. Paris, 1970.
43769.54.560 Simenon, Georges. Trois chambres à Manhattan. Paris, 1965.
43769.54.565 Simenon, Georges. Le train. Paris, 1970.
43769.54.570 Simenon, Georges. Les volets verts. Paris, 1965.
43769.54.575 Simenon, Georges. En cas de malheur. Paris, 1965.
43769.54.580 Simenon, Georges. Le confessional; roman. Paris, 1966.
43769.54.585 Simenon, Georges. Le coup de vague. Paris, 1960.
43769.54.590 Simenon, Georges. L'horloger d'Everton. Paris, 1966.
43769.54.595 Simenon, Georges. Maigret et le marchand de vin; roman. Paris, 1970.
43769.54.600 Simenon, Georges. Les temoins. Paris, 1965.
43769.54.606 Simenon, Georges. Betty. Paris, 1970.
43769.54.610 Simenon, Georges. La boule noire, roman. Paris, 1965.
43769.54.616 Simenon, Georges. Le veuf. Paris, 1970.
43769.54.620 Simenon, Georges. Lettre à mon juge, roman. Paris, 1967.
43769.54.625 Simenon, Georges. Strip-tease. Paris, 1965.
43769.54.630 Simenon, Georges. L'Outlaw. Paris, 1967.
43769.54.635 Simenon, Georges. Le chat. Paris, 1967.
43769.54.637 Simenon, Georges. Maigret triumphant. London, 1969.
43769.54.640 Simenon, Georges. Le riche homme; roman. Paris, 1970.
43769.54.641 Simenon, Georges. When I was old. 1. ed. N.Y., 1971.
43769.54.642 Simenon, Georges. Le passager clandestin. Paris, 1970.
43769.54.645 Simenon, Georges. Les complices. Paris, 1970?
43769.54.648 Simenon, Georges. La porte. Paris, 1970.
43769.54.650 Simenon, Georges. Feux rouges, roman. Paris, 1970.
43769.54.652 Simenon, Georges. Maigret et le fantôme, suivi de Maigret hésite. Paris, 1970.
43769.54.654 Simenon, Georges. La mort de Belle. Paris, 1971.
43769.54.656 Simenon, Georges. Maigret chez le coronet; roman. Paris, 1970.
43769.54.658.1 Simenon, Georges. Le grand Bob. Paris, 1970.
43769.54.660 Simenon, Georges. Je me souviens. Paris, 1970.
43769.54.662 Simenon, Georges. Maigret et la vieille dame. Paris, 1970.
43769.54.664 Simenon, Georges. Les autres. Paris, 1970.
43769.54.666 Simenon, Georges. Les mémoires de Maigret. Paris, 1970.
43769.54.668 Simenon, Georges. La vieille. Paris, 1959.
43769.54.670 Simenon, Georges. La prison, roman. Paris, 1968.
43769.54.700 Simenon, Georges. The iron staircase. London, 1963.
43769.54.703 Simenon, Georges. A Simenon omnibus. London, 1965.
43769.54.705 Simenon, Georges. The death of Monsieur Gallet. N.Y., 1932.
43769.54.707 Simenon, Georges. A wife of sea. London, 1949.
43769.54.708 Simenon, Georges. Strange inheritance. London, 1950.
43769.54.710 Simenon, Georges. Maigret to the rescue. London, 1940.
43769.54.710.5 Simenon, Georges. Maigret to the rescue. N.Y., 1941.
43769.54.713 Simenon, Georges. Affairs of destiny. London, 1947.
43769.54.714 Simenon, Georges. Maigret's pickpocket. London, 1968.
43769.54.715 Simenon, Georges. Escape in vain. N.Y., 1944.
43769.54.717 Simenon, Georges. Poisoned relation. London, 1950.
43769.54.720 Simenon, Georges. The shadow falls. London, 1945.
43769.54.722 Simenon, Georges. Tidal wave. Garden City, 1954.
43769.54.723 Simenon, Georges. The snow was black. 1. ed. N.Y., 1950.
43769.54.725 Semenon, Georges. Lost moorings. London, 1946.
43769.54.728 Simenon, Georges. Maigret's special murder. London, 1964.
43769.54.730 Simenon, Georges. Magnet of doom. London, 1948.
43769.54.732 Simenon, Georges. Maigret has doubts. London, 1968.
43769.54.733 Simenon, Georges. Black rain. N.Y., 1947.
43769.54.735 Simenon, Georges. Black rain. London, 1949.
43769.54.738 Simenon, Georges. The Burgomaster of Furnes. London, 1952.
43769.54.740 Simenon, Georges. The first-born. N.Y., 1947.
43769.54.742 Simenon, Georges. The little saint. 1. ed. N.Y., 1965.
43769.54.743 Simenon, Georges. Pedigree. N.Y., 1963.
43769.54.745 Simenon, Georges. The heart of a man. 1. American ed. N.Y., 1951. 2v.
43769.54.748 Simenon, Georges. Maigret keeps a rendez-vous. N.Y., 1941.
43769.54.750 Simenon, Georges. Maigret on holiday. London, 1950.
43769.54.752 Simenon, Georges. The patience of Maigret. N.Y., 1940.
43769.54.754 Simenon, Georges. The confessional. London, 1967.
43769.54.755 Simenon, Georges. The stain on the snow. London, 1953.
43769.54.756 Simenon, Georges. The old men dies. 1. ed. N.Y., 1967.
43769.54.762 Simenon, Georges. November. London, 1970.
43769.54.765 Simenon, Georges. Across the street. London, 1954.
43769.54.768 Simenon, Georges. Maigret and the headless corpse. London, 1967.
43769.54.770 Simenon, Georges. Inspector Maigret and the strangled stripper. 1. ed. Garden City, 1954.
43769.54.771 Simenon, Georges. Maigret goes home. Harmondsworth, 1967.
43769.54.773 Simenon, Georges. No vacation for Maigret. Roslyn, 1953.
43769.54.775 Simenon, Georges. The strangers in the house. London, 1951.
43769.54.778 Simenon, Georges. The move. 1. American ed. N.Y., 1968.
43769.54.778.5 Simenon, Georges. The neighbours. London, 1968.

Classified Listing

43511 - 43873 Individual authors, etc. - 1900- - Known authors (363 scheme plus 10) - cont.

43769.54.780 Simenon, Georges. The girl in the past. 1. American ed. N.Y., 1952.
43769.54.782 Simenon, Georges. The prison. 1. ed. N.Y., 1969.
43769.54.783 Simenon, Georges. The blue room. 1. ed. N.Y., 1964.
43769.54.785 Simenon, Georges. Maigret and the burglar's wife. London, 1955.
43769.54.786 Simenon, Georges. Maigret takes the waters. London, 1969.
43769.54.788 Simenon, Georges. Five times Maigret. N.Y., 1964.
43769.54.790 Simenon, Georges. My friend Maigret. London, 1956.
43769.54.791 Simenon, Georges. The novel of man. N.Y., 1964.
43769.54.792 Simenon, Georges. Maigret's boyhood friend. London, 1970.
43769.54.793 Simenon, Georges. The premier. London, 1961.
43769.54.794 Simenon, Georges. The premier. 1. American ed. N.Y., 1966.
43769.54.795 Simenon, Georges. Teddy bear. London, 1971.
43769.54.796 Simenon, Georges. Maigret and the lazy burglar. London, 1963.
43769.54.797 Simenon, Georges. An American omnibus. 1. ed. N.Y., 1967.
43769.54.798 Simenon, Georges. The stowaway. London, 1957.
43769.54.799 Simenon, Georges. Maigret cinq: Maigret and the young girl. 1. American ed. N.Y., 1965.
43769.54.800 Narcejac, T. The art of Simenon. London, 1952.
43769.54.805 Parinaud, André. Connaissance de Georges Simenon. Paris, 1957.
43769.54.810 Hart, Willem A. De psychologie van Maigret. Utrecht, 1962.
43769.54.815 Raymond, John. Simenon in court. London, 1968.
43769.55.100 Simoncelly, Hermine. Le grand collège. Paris, 1950.
43769.55.110 Simoncelly, Hermine. Trinité pour deux. Paris, 1957.
43769.56.100 Simon, Pierre Henri. Les raisins verts. Paris, 1957.
43769.56.110 Simon, Pierre Henri. Les hommes ne veulent pas mourir. Paris, 1956.
43769.56.120 Simon, Pierre Henri. Le somnambule. Paris, 1960.
43769.56.130 Simon, Pierre Henri. Portrait d'un officier. Paris, 1959.
43769.56.140 Simon, Pierre Henri. Le jardin et la ville. Paris, 1962.
43769.56.150 Simon, Pierre Henri. Histoire d'un bonheur; roman. Paris, 1965.
43769.56.160 Simon, Pierre Henri. Le ballet de modène, suivi de entre confrères. Paris, 1968.
43769.56.170 Simon, Pierre Henri. La sagesse du soir. Paris, 1971.
43769.56.700 Simon, Pierre Henri. An end to glory. 1. American ed. N.Y., 1961.
43769.56.2100 Simon, Claude. L'herbe. Paris, 1958.
43769.56.2110 Simon, Claude. Le sacré du printemps, roman. Paris, 1954.
43769.56.2120 Simon, Claude. Le vent. Roman. Paris, 1958.
43769.56.2130 Simon, Claude. Gulliver, roman. Paris, 1952.
43769.56.2140 Simon, Claude. La route des Flandres, roman. Paris, 1960.
43769.56.2150 Simon, Claude. Le palace, roman. Paris, 1962.
43769.56.2160 Simon, Claude. Histoire. Paris, 1967.
43769.56.2170 Simon, Claude. Les corps conducteurs. Paris, 1971.
43769.56.2700 Simon, Claude. The wind. N.Y., 1959.
43769.56.2705 Simon, Claude. The grass. N.Y., 1958.
43769.56.2710 Simon, Claude. The Flanders road. London, 1962.
43769.56.2715 Simon, Claude. The palace. N.Y., 1963.
43769.56.2800 Sturrock, John. The French novel: Claude Simon, Michel Bulor, Alain Robbe-Grillet. London, 1969.
43769.56.3100 Simon, Jean Pierre. Terre de violence, roman. Paris, 1959.
43769.56.4100 Simonin, A. Touchez pas au grisbi. Paris, 1959.
43769.56.5100 Simonne, Jean Philippe. Les lois de l'été. Paris, 1970.
43769.59.100 Sindral, J. Mars cover. 5. éd. Paris, 1926.
43769.64.100 Sjöberg, Henri. Hors paison à Vichy. Paris, 1945.
43769.65.100 Sion, Georges. La malle de Pamela. Bruxelles, 1956.
43769.65.110 Sion, Georges. La princesse de Chine. Bruxelles, 1962.
43769.90.800 Canard, J. Daniel Sivet. Roanne, 196-?
43769.92.100 Sikorska, Andrée. Musique dans le noir, roman. Paris, 1968.
43775.1.30 Sorel, Albert E. L'écueil. 4. éd. Paris, 1911.
43775.1.35 Sorel, Albert. E. Regine et nous, roman. pt.1-3. Paris, 1929.
43775.2.30 Souvestre, Pierre. La fiacre de nuit. Paris, 19- .
43775.2.35 Souvestre, Pierre. Fantômes P. Souvestre et M. Allain. Paris, 1961. 11v.
43775.14.100 Socorri, C. (Mme.). Fabienne; pièce en trois actes. Paris, 1939.
43775.49.100 Soleillant, M. À la claire fontaine. Uzès, 1937.
43775.50.100 Sollers, Philippe. Une curieuse solitude. Paris, 1958.
43775.50.110 Sollers, Philippe. Le défi. Abbeville, 1957.
43775.50.120 Sollers, Philippe. Le parc; roman. Paris, 1961.
43775.50.125 Sollers, Philippe. Drame; roman. Paris, 1965.
43775.50.130 Sollers, Philippe. Nombres; roman. Paris, 1968.
43775.50.141 Sollers, Philiipe. L'écriture et l'expérience des limites. Paris, 1971.
43775.50.700 Sollers, Philippe. A strange solitude. N.Y., 1961.
43775.50.701 Sollers, Philippe. A strange solitude. London, 1961.
43775.50.705 Sollers, Philippe. The park. London, 1968.
43775.52.100 Soleymieu, Jacques (pseud.). Dimanche. N.Y., 1945.
43775.61.100 Sonkin, F. La dame. Paris, 1964.
43775.61.110 Sonkin, F. Admirable. Paris, 1965.
43775.74.100 Sorbets, G. L'embrassement. Paris, 1923.
43775.74.110 Sorbets, G. La colombe poignardie. Paris, 1932.
43775.74.120 Sorbets, G. La maison verte. Paris, 1932.
43775.75.100 Sorel, G. Propos de Georges Sorel. Paris, 1935.
43775.75.800 Wanner, J. Georges Sorel et la décadence. Lausanne, 1943.
43775.76.100 Soriana, M. L'enclume ou Le marteau. Paris, 1952.
43775.89.100 Souchon, Paul. Le Dieu nouveau. Paris, 1906.
43775.89.110 Souchon, Paul. La beauté de Paris, poèmes. Paris, 1904.
43775.89.1100 Soulat, Robert. Un nommé songe. Paris, 1958.
43775.89.2100 Soubiran, André. Les hommes en blanc. Paris, 1949-51. 3v.
43775.89.2700 Soubiran, André. The doctors. N.Y., 1953.
43775.89.2710A Soubiran, André. The healing oath. N.Y., 1954.
43775.89.2710B Soubiran, André. The healing oath. N.Y., 1954.
43775.89.3100 Sounac, Denis. L'Hagion-Oros. Marseille, 1940.
43775.89.4100 Soulages, Gabriel. L'idylle vénitienne. Paris, 1913.
43775.89.4110 Soulages, Gabriel. Ce bougre d'original. n.p., 1912?
43775.90.100 Souday, Paul. Les livres du temps. 2. éd. Paris, 1913.
43775.90.105 Souday, Paul. Les livres du temps. 2. série. Paris, 1914.
43775.90.110 Souday, Paul. Les livres du temps. 3. série. Paris, 1930.
43775.90.120 Souday, Paul. Les livres du temps. Paris, 1929.
Htn 43775.90.7100* Soupault, Philippe. Rose des vents. Paris, 1920.
43775.90.7110 Soupault, Philippe. Poésies complètes 1917-1937. Paris, 1937.
43775.90.7120 Soupault, Philippe. Le grand homme. 2. éd. Paris, 1929.
43775.90.7125 Soupault, Philippe. Le grand homme, roman. Paris, 1947.

43511 - 43873 Individual authors, etc. - 1900- - Known authors (363 scheme plus 10) - cont.

43775.90.7134 Soupault, Philippe. Les dernières nuits de Paris. 4. éd. Paris, 1928.
43775.90.7152 Soupault, Philippe. Le coeur d'or. 12. éd. Paris, 1927.
43775.90.7165 Soupault, Philippe. Les frères Durandeau, roman. 10. éd. Paris, 1924.
43775.90.7170 Soupault, Philippe. En joue, roman. Paris, 1925.
43775.90.7175 Soupault, Philippe. Tous ensemble au bout du monde. Algers, 1944.
43775.90.7180 Soupault, Philippe. Les moribonds. 7. éd. Paris, 1934.
43775.90.7190 Soupault, Philippe. Chansons. Rolle, 1949.
43775.90.7200 Soupault, Philippe. Sans phrases. Paris, 1953.
43775.90.7210 Soupault, Philippe. Carte postale. Paris, 1926.
43775.90.7220 Soupault, Philippe. L'amitié. Paris, 1965.
43775.90.7230 Soupault, Philippe. Terpsichore. Paris, 1928.
43775.90.7240 Soupault, Philippe. Histoire d'un blanc. Paris, 1927.
43775.90.7702 Soupault, Philippe. Last nights of Paris. N.Y., 1929.
43775.90.7710 Soupault, Philippe. Ode to bombed London. Algiers, 1944.
43775.90.8100 Sourgens, J.M. Le feu sous la neige. Paris, 1956.
43775.91.100 Souza, R. de. Sources vers la fleure. Paris, 1897.
43775.95.100 Solore, C.G. Comme une odeur de nuit. 4. éd. Paris, 1957.
43775.96.100 Sorel, Claude. Le comédien de plume. Paris, 1957.
43775.96.110 Sorel, Claude. Poésie et publicité. Paris, 1958.
43775.96.120 Sorel, Claude. Europole. Paris, 1960.
43775.97.100 Soréil, Arséne. Raisons vives. Bruxelles, 1965.
43775.97.800 Au pays de dure ardenne: Arsène Soreil. Vieux-Virton, 1968.
43775.98.100 Sodenkamp, Andrée. Femmes des longs matins. n.p., 1965.
43775.98.110 Sodenkamp, Andrée. Arivederci Italia; impressions d'Italie. Bruxelles, 1965.
43776.1.100 Spade, Henri. Les enfants de la guerre. Paris, 1968- 2v.
43776.1.110 Spade, Henri. La Polonaise. Paris, 1969.
43776.1.1100 Spaak, Claude. L'ordre et le désordre. Paris, 1971.
43776.25.100 Sperling, Janine. La longue soirée. Paris, 1960.
43776.41.100 Spire, André. Le secret. Paris, 1919.
43776.41.110 Spire, André. Tentations. Paris, 1920.
43776.41.120 Spire, André. Poèmes juifs. Genève, 1919.
43776.41.125 Spire, André. Poèmes juifs. Paris, 1959.
43776.41.130 Spire, André. Poèmes de Laire. Paris, 1929.
43776.41.140 Spire, André. Fourisseur. Paris, 1923.
43776.41.150 Spire, André. Refuges. Paris, 1926.
43776.41.160 Spire, André. Versets et vous riez. Poèmes juifs. 2. éd. Paris, 1908.
43776.41.170 Spire, André. J'ai trois robes distinguées. Paris, 1910.
43776.41.180 Spire, André. Vers les routes absurdes. Paris, 1911.
43776.41.190 Spire, André. Lacité présente, poèmes 1892-1902. Paris, 1903.
43776.41.200 Spire, André. Poèmes d'ici et de là-bas. N.Y., 1944.
43776.41.210 Spire, André. Poèmes d'hier et d'aujourd'hui. Paris, 1953.
43776.41.810 Barnshaw, Stanley. André Spire and his poetry. Philadelphia, 1933.
43776.41.820 Hommage à André Spire. Paris, 1939.
43776.42.705 Spitz, J. Sever the earth. London, 1936.
43776.43.100 Spens, Willy de. Éléonore d'Aquitaine et ses troubadours. Paris, 1957.
43776.64.100 Spoerri, Daniel. An anecdoted topography of chance. N.Y., 1966.
43779.1.30 Stradiot, J. A la Venvole. Paris, 1912.
43779.3.100 Stalla-Bourdillon, Jules. Au foyer de la comédie-française. Marseille, 1931.
43779.4.100 Staines, Charles R. Constance. Paris, 1960.
43779.4.1100 Starobinski, Jean. L'oeil vivant, essai. Paris, 1961-70. 2v.
43779.15.100 Steiman, S.A. L'assassin habite au 21. Paris, 1939.
43779.23.100 Steiner, Jean François. Les Métègues. Paris, 1970.
43779.23.1100 Sten, Oliven. Le passant démesuré. Paris, 1954.
43779.24.100 Stéphane, R. Portrait de l'aventurier. Paris, 1950.
43779.24.110 Stéphane, R. Une singulière affinité, roman. Paris, 1959.
43779.24.2103 Stéphane, Nelly. Les chercheurs. 6. éd. Paris, 1957.
43779.24.3100 Stéphane, Marc. Aphorismes, boutades et cris de révolte. Paris, 1904.
43779.24.3110 Stéphane, Marc. Savants devis et joyeux rythmes d'un buveur de soleil. Paris, 1894.
43779.24.4100 Steppe, André. Camarade Zolobine. Paris, 1963.
43779.24.5100 Stéphant-Beudeff, Joseph. De tribord à babord. Rodez, 1966.
43779.25.100 Sternberg, Jacques. La géométrie dans la terreur. Paris, 1956.
43779.25.110 Sternberg, Jacques. L'employé. Paris, 1958.
43779.25.120 Sternberg, Jacques. L'architecte. Illustrations de Topor. Paris, 1960.
43779.25.130 Sternberg, Jacques. C'est la guerre, Monsieur Gruber. Paris, 1968.
43779.25.3100 Steuer, Raphaëla. David Rex; drame. Paris, 1959.
43779.41.104 Stiebel, G. Décadence et grandeur. Alger, 1941.
43779.41.1100 Stiénon du Pré, Jean André. Alterable délice. Saint-Félicien-en-Vivarais, 1935.
43779.52.100 St. Lys, Odette. L'auberge. Londres, 1916.
43779.67.100 Stoumon, M. Dans l'Alpille d'Or. Bruxelles, 1959.
43779.68.100 Stor, K. Les nouvelles histoires Marseillaises de Marius. Paris, 1937?
43779.77.105 Strouski, Fortunat. Les libérateurs. Rio de Janeiro, 1943.
43779.77.1100 Stroheim, Erich von. Les feux de la Saint-Jean. v.1-2. Paris, 1967. 4v.
43780.5.61 Suarès, André. Correspondance. 2. éd. Paris, 1951.
43780.5.63 Suarès, André. Cette âme ardente. Paris, 1938.
43780.5.65 Suarès, André. Correspondance. Paris, 1961.
43780.5.67 Suarès, André. Correspondance. Paris, 1961.
43780.5.100 Suarès, André. Trois grands vivants. Paris, 1938.
43780.5.110 Suarès, André. Trois hommes. Paris, 1935.
43780.5.120 Suarès, André. Voici l'homme. Paris, 1948.
43780.5.130 Suarès, André. Hélène chez Archimèdes. Paris, 1949.
43780.5.140 Suarès, André. Minos et Pasiphoé. Paris, 1950.
43780.5.150 Suarès, André. Valeurs. 9. éd. Paris, 1936.
43780.5.160 Suarès, André. Ignorées du destinataire. Paris, 1955.
43780.5.170 Suarès, André. Sur la mort de mon frère. Paris, 1917.
43780.5.190 Suarès, André. Lais et cônes. Paris, 1909.
43780.5.200 Suarès, André. Polyxène. Paris, 1925.
43780.5.210 Suarès, André. Variables. Paris, 1929.
43780.5.220 Suarès, André. Haï Kaï d'Occident. Paris, 1926.
43780.5.230 Saurès, André. Remarques. v.1-12. Paris, 1917-18. 2v.
43780.5.240 Suarès, André. Essais. Paris, 1913.
43780.5.250 Suarès, André. Sur la vie. Paris, 1925. 2v.

43511 - 43873 Individual authors, etc. - 1900- - Known authors (363 scheme plus 10) - cont.

43780.5.260 Suarès, André. Sur la vie. v.3. Paris, 1912.
43780.5.270 Suarès, André. Idées et visions. Paris, 1913.
43780.5.280 Suarès, André. Bouclier du Zodiaque. Paris, 1907.
43780.5.290 Suarès, André. Italie, Italie. Paris, 1915.
43780.5.300 Suarès, André. Angleterre. Paris, 1916.
43780.5.310 Suarès, André. Ceux de Verdun. Paris, 1916.
43780.5.320 Suarès, André. Airs; 5 livres de poèmes. Paris, 1900.
43780.5.330 Suarès, André. Cressida. Paris, 1913.
43780.5.340 Suarès, André. Saint Juin de la Primevère. Nimes, 1926.
43780.5.350 Suarès, André. Portraits. Paris, 1913.
43780.5.805 Helmke, Bruno. André Suarès als Denker und Künster. inaug. -Diss. Coburg, 1933.
43780.5.810 Savet, Gabrielle. André Suarès. Paris, 1959.
43780.5.815 Dommartin, Henry. Suarès. Paris, 1913.
43780.5.820 Marseilles. Exposition. André Suarès. Catalogue de l'exposition André Suarès. Saint-Maur, 1950.
43780.5.825 Busi, Fréderick. L'ésthétique d'André Suarès. Wetteren, 1969.
43780.5.830 Paris. Musée Bourdelle. André Suarès, 1868-1948, 2 nov. - 2 dec., 1968. Paris, 1968.
43780.7.100 Suberville, Jean. Deux pièces jouées au front. 2. éd. Paris, 1913.
43780.7.110 Suberville, Jean. Le Dieu inconnu. 2. éd. Paris, 1921?
43780.9.100 Subra, Marie France. Lettres anciennes. Paris, 1962.
43780.50.100 Sulivan, Jean. Le voyage intérieur. Paris, 1958.
43780.50.110 Sulivan, Jean. Provocation. Paris, 1959.
43780.50.120 Sulivan, Jean. Bonheur des rebelles. Paris, 1959.
43780.50.130 Sulivan, Jean. L'obsession de Delphes. Paris, 1967.
43780.50.140 Sulivan, Jean. Bonheur des rebelles. Paris, 1968.
43780.50.150 Sulivan, Jean. Consolation de la nuit, roman. Paris, 1968.
43780.69.15 Paris. Bibliothèque Sainte-Geneviève. Collection Doucet. Jules Supervielle. Paris, 1958.
43780.69.21 Supervielle, Jules. A poesia de Jules Supervielle; estudo. Lisboa, 194-.
43780.69.25 Supervielle, Jules. Poèmes choisis. Montevideo, 1959.
43780.69.61 Supervielle, Jules. Correspondance, 1936-1959. Paris, 1969.
43780.69.100 Supervielle, Jules. Gravitations. 3. éd. Paris, 1925.
43780.69.109 Supervielle, Jules. Gravitations, poèmes. 13. éd. Paris, 1949.
43780.69.110 Supervielle, Jules. Les amis inconnus. 3. éd. Paris, 1934.
43780.69.120 Supervielle, Jules. Saisir. Paris, 1928.
43780.69.130 Supervielle, Jules. Le voleur d'enfants. 5. éd. Paris, 1926.
43780.69.130.10 Supervielle, Jules. Le voleur d'enfants. 8. éd. Paris, 1949.
43780.69.135 Supervielle, Jules. The colonel's children. London, 1950.
43780.69.140 Supervielle, Jules. Bolivar. 5. éd. Paris, 1936.
43780.69.152 Supervielle, Jules. La belle au bois. 2. éd. Paris, 1932.
43780.69.162 Supervielle, Jules. La fable du monde. 3. éd. Paris, 1938.
43780.69.173 Supervielle, Jules. L'homme de la pampa. 8. éd. Paris, 1938.
43780.69.183 Supervielle, Jules. Le forçat innocent. 4. éd. Paris, 1937.
43780.69.193 Supervielle, Jules. L'enfant de la haute mer. 8. éd. Paris, 1933.
43780.69.203 Supervielle, Jules. L'arche de Noé. 6. éd. Paris, 1938.
43780.69.213 Supervielle, Jules. Le survivant. 5. éd. Paris, 1938.
43780.69.220 Supervielle, Jules. Le petit bois. México, 1942.
43780.69.230 Supervielle, Jules. Choix de poèmes. Buenos Aires, 1944.
43780.69.240 Supervielle, Jules. Choix de poèmes. Paris, 1947.
43780.69.250 Supervielle, Jules. A la nuit. Neuchâtel, 1947.
43780.69.260 Supervielle, Jules. Contes et poèmes. Edinburgh, 1950.
43780.69.270 Supervielle, Jules. Oublieuse mémoire. Paris, 1949.
43780.69.280 Supervielle, Jules. Robinson. Paris, 1948.
43780.69.290 Supervielle, Jules. Premiers pas de l'univers. Paris, 1950.
43780.69.300 Supervielle, Jules. Shéhérazade. 3. éd. Paris, 1949.
43780.69.310 Supervielle, Jules. Naissances. Paris, 1951.
43780.69.320 Supervielle, Jules. Boire à la source. Paris, 1951.
43780.69.330 Supervielle, Jules. Le jeune homme du dimanche et des autres jours. 3. éd. Paris, 1955.
43780.69.335 Supervielle, Jules. Les suites d'une course. Paris, 1959.
43780.69.340 Supervielle, Jules. Bolivar. 2. éd. Paris, 1955.
43780.69.345 Supervielle, Jules. Léscalier. Paris, 1956.
43780.69.350 Supervielle, Jules. Poèmes de la France malheureuse. Neuchâtel, 1942.
43780.69.710 Supervielle, Jules. The survivor. London, 1951.
43780.69.715 Supervielle, Jules. Selected writings. N.Y., 1967.
43780.69.720 Supervielle, Jules. Supervielle, Poèmes. Santa Barbara, 1967.
43780.69.780 Supervielle, Jules. Gedichte. Deutsch von Paul Celan. Frankfurt, 1968.
43780.69.785 Supervielle, Jules. La desconocida del Sena. Buenos Aires, 1941.
43780.69.790 Supervielle, Jules. In viaggio con Supervielle. Milano, 1956.
43780.69.795 Supervielle, Jules. Bosque sin horas. Montévideo, 1937.
43780.69.800 Greene, Tatiana W. Jules Supervielle. Genève, 1958.
43780.69.805 Etiemble, René. Supervielle. Paris, 1960.
43780.69.810 Hiddleston, James A. L'univers de Jules Supervielle. Paris, 1965.
43780.69.815 Kwiatkowski, Jerzy. Poezje bez granic. Kraków, 1967.
43780.69.1100 Supervielle, Anne M. La guinta. Paris, 1960.
43780.75.100 Surdez, Raymond. Jeunesse, aller et retour. Genève, 1967.
43780.81.100 Susini Holden, (Mme.). Chienne de journée. Paris, 1957.
43780.81.1100 Susini, Marie. Le premier regard. Paris, 1960.
43780.82.100 Sussan, René. Les conflents. Paris, 1960.
43783.19.100 Sydol, Francis. Qui donc est mon prochain? Paris, 1966.
43783.52.2100 Sylvain, Claude. Un dimanche à la campagne. Paris, 1960.
43783.85.100 Syte, Raymond. Mots a personne; litanies parisiennes. Paris, 1949.
43785.2.20 Taravel, Antoine. La douce chanson. Paris, 1913.
43785.9.705 Taboureau, Jean. Bourru, soldier of France. N.Y., 1929.
43785.12.100 Tôche, Pierre-Alain. Ventre des fontaines. Lausanne, 1967.
43785.53.100 Tamboise, Pierre Louis. Arnaout roi. Paris, 1968.
43785.75.100 Tardieu, Jean. Jours pétrifés, 1942-1944. Paris, 1948.
43785.75.105 Tardieu, Jean. L'éspace et la flûte. Paris, 1958.
43785.75.110 Tardieu, Jean. Monsieur. Paris, 1951.
43785.75.120 Tardieu, Jean. Théâtre de chambre. Paris, 1955.
43785.75.130 Tardieu, Jean. Une voix sans personne. Paris, 1954.

43511 - 43873 Individual authors, etc. - 1900- - Known authors (363 scheme plus 10) - cont.

43785.75.140 Tardieu, Jean. La première personne du singulier. Paris, 1952.
43785.75.150 Tardieu, Jean. Poèmes à jouer. Paris, 1960.
43785.75.155 Tardieu, Jean. Poèmes à jouer. Paris, 1969.
43785.75.160 Tardieu, Jean. Le fleuve caché, poésies, 1938-1961. Paris, 1968.
43785.75.170 Tardieu, Jean. Conversation-sinfonietta. Paris, 1966.
43785.75.700 Tardieu, Jean. The underground lovers, and other experimental plays. London, 1968.
43785.76.100 Taricat, Jacques. Médailles; poèmes. Paris, 1954.
43785.77.100 Tarpiniau, Armen. Le chant et l'ombre. Paris, 1953.
43785.89.100 Taupin, René. Quatre essais indifferents pour une esthétique de l'inspiration. Paris, 1932.
43785.89.3100 Tauziac, Etienne. Poésies de chez nous, Périgord. Montauban, 1958.
43785.98.100 Jay, Henri. Collinades; contes de Provence. Marseille, 1965.
43786.25 Fchecaja u Tam'pi, Gerald Félix. Feu le Brousse. Paris, 1957.
43787.1.30 Tendron, Marcel. Le peuple de la mer. Paris, 1914.
43787.1.35 Tendron, Marcel. La belle Eugénie, roman. Paris, 1931.
43787.1.40 Tendron, Marcel. La maison du pas périlleux, roman. Paris, 1933.
43787.1.45 Tendron, Marcel. Deux essais. Paris, 1914.
43787.2.30 Teramond, Guy de. Mystery of Lucien Delorme. N.Y., 1915.
43787.2.100 Téramond, Edmond Gautier. Les joies de la possession. Paris, 1896.
43787.7.100 Tebelen, A. Mennan. L'inconscience du destin. Genève, 1968.
43787.29.100 Tefri (pseud.). Nouvelles. Lausanne, 1958. 2v.
43787.29.110 Tefri (pseud.). Cent réponses. Lausanne? 1957.
43787.29.120A Tefri (pseud.). Les succès du docteur Olfa. Lausanne, 1956.
43787.29.120B Tefri (pseud.). Les succès du docteur Olfa. Lausanne, 1956.
43787.29.130 Tefri (pseud.). Au gravitor. Lausanne, 1960.
43787.29.140 Tefri (pseud.). Au Piladre. Paris, 1963.
43787.50.100 Tellier, Marcel. Traduit du coeur. Rodez, 1957.
43787.55.100 Temkine Raymonde. Paul et Isabelle. Paris, 1960.
43787.71.100 Teppe, Julien. La vie blette. Paris, 1964.
43787.77.100 Terre, J. Echos de Chine. Shanghai, 1900.
43787.77.1100 Terna, Marieve. Au jardin de mon coeur. Paris, 1966.
43787.78.200 Téry, Simone. Où l'aube se lève. N.Y., 1945.
43787.78.1100 Brienne, Maxine. Gustave Téry et son oeuvre. Paris, 1919.
43788.3.100 Thaly, Daniel. Chants de l'Atlantique. Paris, 1928.
43788.5.100 Tharaud, Jérôme. Dingley, l'illustre écrivain. Paris, 1906.
43788.5.103 Tharaud, Jérôme. Un drame de l'automne. Paris, 1923.
43788.5.105 Tharaud, Jérôme. La chronique des frères ennemis. Paris, 1929.
43788.5.108 Tharaud, Jérôme. La fête arabe. Paris, 1912.
43788.5.110 Tharaud, Jérôme. La fête arabe. 4e éd. Paris, 1912.
43788.5.115 Tharaud, Jérôme. Les bien aimées. Paris, 1932.
43788.5.117 Tharaud, Jérôme. La lumière. Paris, 1900.
43788.5.120 Tharaud, Jérôme. Une relève. Paris, 1919.
43788.5.122 Tharaud, Jérôme. Une relève. 30e éd. Paris, 1924.
43788.5.125 Tharaud, Jérôme. La double confidence. Paris, 1951.
43788.5.130 Tharaud, Jérôme. Un royaume de Dieu. 24e éd. Paris, 1920.
43788.5.140 Tharaud, Jérôme. La ville et les champs, 1870-71. 8e éd. Paris, 1907.
43788.5.150 Tharaud, Jérôme. L'ombre de la croix. Paris, 1920.
43788.5.160F Tharaud, Jérôme. La Rose de Sâron. Paris, 1927.
43788.5.162 Tharaud, Jérôme. La Rose de Sâron. Paris, 1927.
43788.5.170A Tharaud, Jérôme. Tragédie de Ravaillac. Paris, 1922.
43788.5.170B Tharaud, Jérôme. Tragédie de Ravaillac. Paris, 1922.
43788.5.175 Tharaud, Jérôme. La vie et la mort de Déroudèda. 34e éd. Paris, 1925.
43788.5.180 Tharaud, Jérôme. L'oiseau d'or. Paris, 1931.
43788.5.190 Tharaud, Jérôme. La randonnée de Samba Diouf. Paris, 1922.
43788.5.195 Tharaud, Jérôme. The long walk of Samba Diouf. N.Y., 1924.
43788.5.198 Tharaud, Jérôme. En Bretagne; essais ornés de compositions originales. Paris, 1927.
43788.5.200 Tharaud, Jérôme. Discours de réception de Jérôme Tharaud à l'Académie française. Paris, 1940.
43788.5.205 Tharaud, Jérôme. Vers d'almanach. Paris, 1946.
43788.5.210 Tharaud, Jérôme. Les contes de la Vierge. Paris, 1960.
43788.5.220 Tharaud, Jérôme. Contes de Notre Dame. Paris, 1959.
43788.5.230 Tharaud, Jérôme. Les contes de la Vierge. Paris, 1944.
43788.5.240 Tharaud, Jérôme. Le coltineur débile. Paris, 1898.
43788.5.250 Tharaud, Jérôme. La maison des Mirabeau. Félicien-en-Vivarais, 1923.
43788.5.700 Tharaud, Jérôme. The shadow of the cross. N.Y., 1924.
43788.5.800 Halevy, D. Eloge de Jérôme Tharaud. Paris, 1954.
43788.22.100 Thémer. Coccinelle. Paris, 1907.
43788.23.100 Thénon, Georges. La revue du vaudeville. Paris, 1923.
43788.24.100 Thérive, André. La charbon ardent. 9e éd. Paris, 1929.
43788.24.110 Thérive, André. Noir et or. Paris, 1931.
43788.24.120 Thérive, André. Anna. Paris, 1932.
43788.24.130 Thérive, André. Fils du jour, roman. Paris, 1936.
43788.24.140 Thérive, André. Sans âme. Paris, 1928.
43788.24.158 Thérive, André. Les souffrances perdues. 12e éd. Paris, 1927.
43788.24.165 Thérive, André. La revanche; roman. Paris, 1930.
43788.24.170 Thérive, André. Le retour d'Amazan ou Une histoire de la littérature française. 3e éd. Paris, 1926.
43788.24.180 Thérive, André. La foire littéraire. Paris, 1963.
43788.24.1100 Théron, Germaine. Le secret merveilleux. 7e éd. Paris, 1957.
43788.24.1110 Théron, Germaine. L'arbre et l'écorce. Paris, 1959.
43788.24.3100 Therame, Victoria. Morbidezza. Paris, 1960.
43788.25.100 Thévenin, Léon. La robe sans couture. Paris, 1925.
43788.25.110 Thoorens, L. La vie passionne de Honoré de Balzac. Paris, 1959.
43788.41.100 Thibaudet, Albert. Trente ans de vie française. Paris, 1920-23. 4v.
43788.41.110A Thibaudet, Albert. Réflexions sur le roman. 6e éd. Paris, 1938.
43788.41.110B Thibaudet, Albert. Réflexions sur le roman. 6e éd. Paris, 1938.
43788.41.800 Glauser, A. Albert Thibaudet et la critique créatrice. Paris, 1952.
43788.41.810 Davies, J.C. L'oeuvre critique d'Albert Thibaudet. Genève, 1955.
43788.41.815 Devaud, Marcel. Albert Thibaudet. Fribourg, 1967.

43511 - 43873 Individual authors, etc. - 1900- - Known authors (363 scheme plus 10) - cont.

43788.41.1100 Thiery, Herman. Les dentelles de Montmirail. Bruxelles, 1966.
43788.41.2100 Thiry, Marcel. Poésie, 1924-1957. Paris, 1958.
43788.41.2110 Thiry, Marcel. Échec au temps. Bruxelles, 1962.
43788.41.2120 Thiery, Michel. La tentation d'Adam. 4e éd. Paris, 1958.
þ3788.41.2130 1 f Thiry, Marcel. Le festin d'attente. Bruxelles, 1963.
43788.41.2130 Thiry, Marcel. Le festin d'attente. Bruxelles? 1963.
43788.41.2140 Thiry, Marcel. Simul et autres cas. Bruxelles, 1963.
43788.41.2150 Thiry, Marcel. Nondum jam non. Bruxelles, 1966.
43788.41.2160 Thiry, Marcel. Saison cinq, et quatre proses. Bruxelles, 1969.
43788.41.2170 Thiry, Marcel. Le jardin fixe. Lausanne, 1969.
43788.41.2800 Clémeur, Marcel. L'oeuvre poétique de Marcel Thiry, du symbolisme à l'école du regard. Vieux-Virton, 1960.
43788.41.3100 Thierry, J.J. La tentation du cardinal. Paris, 1960.
43788.41.4100 Thibaudeau, Jean. Une cérémonie royale. Paris, 1960.
43788.41.4110 Thibaudeau, Jean. Ouverture. Paris, 1966- 2v.
43788.41.4120 Thibaudeau, Jean. Mai dix-neuf cent soixante-huit en France. Drama. Paris, 1970.
43788.41.5100 Thibon, Gustave. Vous serez comme des dieux. Paris, 1959.
43788.41.6100 Thinès, Georges. L'aporie. Bruxelles, 1968.
43788.55.100 Tharaud, Jérôme. La maîtresse servante. Paris, 1911.
43788.65.110 Thomas, E. Le champ libre; roman. Paris, 1945.
43788.65.120 Thomas, E. Contes d'Auxois. Paris, 1943.
43788.65.130 Thomas, Henri. John Perkins. Paris, 1960.
43788.65.1021 Thomas, Henri. Poésies: Travaux d'aveugle, Signe de vie. Paris, 1970.
43788.65.1100 Thomas, Henri. La dernière année. Paris, 1960.
43788.65.1110 Thomas, Henri. Histoire de Pierrot. Paris, 1960.
43788.65.1120 Thomas, Henri. La chasse aux trésors. Paris, 1961.
43788.65.1130 Thomas, Henri. Le promontori. Paris, 1961.
43788.65.1140 Thomas, Henri. Sous le lien de temps. Paris, 1963.
43788.65.1150 Thomas, Henri. Le parjure, roman. Paris, 1964.
43788.65.2800 Llona, Victor. Notes sur Louis Thomas. Paris, 1924.
43788.65.2805 Martineau, Henri. Louis Thomas. Niort, 1909.
43788.65.3100 Thomas, Charles. Alouettes. Coutances, 1965.
43788.67.100 Thouy, Louis. Au diapason de la raison pure. Aurillac, 1948?
43789.3.100 Tian, André. Nouveaux poèmes. Lyon, 1919.
43789.22.100 Tieghem, Olivier van. Les chats sauvages. Paris, 1960.
43789.48.100 Tillac, Charles. Essai de joie. Paris, 1929.
43789.49.100 Tillard, Paul. On se bat dans la ville. Paris, 1946.
43789.49.110 Tillard, Paul. La racon des purs. Paris, 1960.
43789.82.100 Tissier, Jacques. Le gachis. Paris, 1960.
43789.98.100 Tizé, Bertrand de. Sansonnets. Photoreproduction. Rennes, 1903.
43792.1.30 Marchandeau, Marcel. La pâque des roses, 1900-1908. Paris, 1909.
43792.1.40 Marchandeau, Marcel. Touny-Lérys. Paris, 1960.
43792.16.100 Todd, O. La traversée de la Manche, roman. Paris, 1960.
43792.19.100 Todrani, Jean. Je parle de l'obscur. Paris, 1963.
43792.24.100 Toetenel, Albert. Florilège. Paris, 1948.
43792.40.41 Toesca, Maurice. Trois semaines chaque année. Paris, 1960.
43792.40.100 Toesca, Maurice. Deux contes. Paris? 1949.
43792.40.110 Toesca, Maurice. L'expérience amoureuse. Paris, 1954.
43792.40.120 Toesca, Maurice. Le dernier cri d'un homme, roman. Paris, 1954.
43792.40.130 Toesca, Maurice. Le fantassin à cheval. Paris, 1953.
43792.40.140 Toesca, Maurice. A la grâce de Dieu. Paris, 1955.
43792.40.150 Toesca, Maurice. L'esprit du coeur. Paris, 1946.
43792.40.160 Toesca, Maurice. Le réquisitoire; roman. Paris, 1968.
43792.40.410 Toesca, Maurice. A la grace de Dieu. Paris, 1955.
43792.50.100 Tollet, Marcel. Des blancs, des noirs. Bruxelles, 1956.
43792.51.100 Tolstoi, Catherine. Ce que savait la rose. Paris, 1965.
43792.70.100 Topliceano, Roxane. Bagatelles et autres. Paris, 1946.
43792.74.100 Tordeur, Jean. Conservateur des charges. Paris, 1964.
43792.74.1100 Torday, Sandor. Les miroirs se mirent. Paris, 1957.
43792.75.110 Torres, Henry. Édition speciale. Paris, 1932.
43792.75.2700 Torres, Tereska. Not yet. London, 1959.
43792.75.2705 Torres, Tereska. The converts. London, 1970.
43792.76.100 Torma, J. Porte battante. Paris, 1963.
43792.77.100 Torreilles, Pierre. Corps dispersé d'Orphée. Neuchâtel, 1963.
43792.89.100 Toudouze, G.G. Parmi les loups. Paris, 1926.
43792.89.1700 Tourville, A. de. Wedding dance. N.Y., 1953.
43792.89.2100 Toucas-Massillon, Edmond. Saturnin. Paris, 1911.
43792.89.3100 Touroude, Georges. Les pavés de la haine. Paris, 1970.
43792.90.61 Toulet, Paul Jean. Lettres à Madame Bulteau. Paris, 1924.
43792.90.105 Toulet, Paul Jean. Les contrerimes. Paris, 1921.
43792.90.110 Toulet, Paul Jean. Vers inedits. Paris, 1936.
43792.90.115 Toulet, Paul Jean. Journal et voyages. Paris, 1955.
43792.90.120 Toulet, Paul Jean. Lettres de P.J. Toulet et d'Émile Henriot. Paris, 1959.
43792.90.130 Toulet, Paul Jean. Comme une fantaisie. Coutonges-sur-l'Autize, 1918.
43792.90.140 Perdicras (pseud.). Le metier d'Amant, roman. Paris, 1900.
43792.90.150 Toulet, Paul Jean. Les contes de Béhanzigue. Paris, 1920.
43792.90.160 Toulet, Paul Jean. Les tendres ménages, roman. Paris, 1923.
43792.90.170 Toulet, Paul Jean. Quatre contes. Paris, 1925.
43792.90.180 Toulet, Paul Jean. Les demoiselles la mortagne. Paris, 1923.
43792.90.190 Toulet, Paul Jean. Notes de littérature. Paris, 1926.
43792.90.805 Dyssord, J. L'aventure de Paul Jean Toulet. 4e éd. Paris, 1928.
43792.90.810 Waezer, P.A. Paul Jean Toulet. Paris, 1949.
43792.90.815 Martineau, Henri. P.J. Toulet et Arthur Machen. Paris, 1957.
43792.90.820 Martineau, Henri. P.J. Toulet, collaborateur de Tilly. Paris, 1957.
43792.90.825 Martineau, Henri. Le séjour de P.J. Toulet à Alger. Paris, 1959.
43792.91.105 Toussaint, Franz. Sentiments distingués. 16e éd. Paris, 1945.
43792.91.110 Toussaint, Franz. Le tapis de Jasmins. Paris, 1918.
43792.91.120 Toussaint, Franz. Lénine inconnu. Paris, 1952.
43792.92.100 Toulouse, Gilbert. Un été au Mexique. Paris, 1964.
43792.93.100 Toursky, Alexandre. Christine. Paris, 1950.
43792.94.100 Tournier, Michel. Vendredi ou les Limbes du Pacifique. Paris, 1967.
43792.94.110 Tournier, Michel. Le roi des Aulnes. Paris, 1970.
43792.99.100 Torreilles, Pierre. Corps dispersé d'Orphée. Neuchâtel, 1963.

43511 - 43873 Individual authors, etc. - 1900- - Known authors (363 scheme plus 10) - cont.

43793.3.100 Tranchepain, Jacques. Vie. Paris, 1960.
43793.3.2100 Trahard, Pierre. Césarion; satire. Paris, 1965.
43793.5.100 Traz, R. de. La puritaine et l'amour. Paris, 1928.
43793.23.1100 Trenet, Charles. Un noir eblouissant. Paris, 1965.
43793.24.100 Trezel, Germain. Les feux du prisme. Paris, 1929.
43793.41.105 Trintziers, René. La grande peur. Grenoble, 1946.
43793.41.110 Trintziers, René. Fin et commencement. Paris, 1932.
43793.42.21 Triolet, Elsa. Oeuvres romanesques croisées d'Elsa Triolet et Aragon. Paris, 1964-65. 38v.
43793.42.100 Triolet, Elsa. Le premier accroc coûte deux francs. Paris, 1945.
43793.42.110 Triolet, Elsa. Personne ne m'aime. Paris, 1946.
43793.42.120 Triolet, Elsa. Six entre autres. Lausanne, 1945.
43793.42.130 Triolet, Elsa. Les amants d'Avignon. Paris, 1947.
43793.42.135 Triolet, Elsa. Les amants d'Avignon. Paris, 1943[1945]
43793.42.140 Triolet, Elsa. Les amants d'Avignon. Paris, 1945.
43793.42.150 Triolet, Elsa. Les fantômes armés; roman. Paris, 1947.
43793.42.160 Triolet, Elsa. L'inspecteur de ruines; roman. Paris, 1948.
43793.42.170 Triolet, Elsa. Le mythe de la baronne Mélanie. Neuchâtel, 1945.
43793.42.180 Triolet, Elsa. Le cheval blanc; roman. Paris, 1943.
43793.42.190 Triolet, Elsa. Dessins animés. Paris, 1947.
43793.42.200 Triolet, Elsa. Mille regrets. Paris, 1943.
43793.42.210 Triolet, Elsa. Le rendez-vous des étrangers. Paris, 1956.
43793.42.220 Triolet, Elsa. Le monument. 7e éd. Paris, 1957.
43793.42.230 Triolet, Elsa. Elsa Triolet choisie par Aragon. Paris, 1960.
43793.42.240 Triolet, Elsa. L'âge de nylon. Paris, 1959. 3v.
43793.42.250 Triolet, Elsa. Écoutez-voir. Paris, 1968.
43793.42.700 Triolet, Elsa. A fine of 200 francs. N.Y., 1947.
43793.42.710 Triolet, Elsa. The inspector of ruins. London, 1952.
43793.42.715 Triolet, Elsa. The white horse. London, 1951.
43793.42.2100 Triolaire, I. Poèmes. Gap, 1959.
43793.43.100 Tristan, Frédérick. Le Dieu des mouches. Paris, 1959.
43793.64.100 Trofimoff, André. Au jardin des muses françaises. Paris, 1947.
43793.65.100 Trolliet, Gilbert. Avec la rose. Genève, 1967.
43793.65.110 Trolliet, Gilbert. Laconiques. Paris, 1966.
43793.65.120 Trolliet, Gilbert. Le fleuve et l'être; choix de poèmes. Neuchâtel, 1968.
43793.66.100 Trooz, Charles de. Le concert dans la bibliothèque. Bruxelles, 1959.
43793.67.100 Troyat, Henri. L'araigne. Paris, 1938.
43793.67.110 Troyat, Henri. La clef de voûte. Paris, 1937.
43793.67.128 Troyat, Henri. Le jugement de Dieu. 14e éd. Paris, 1941.
43793.67.130 Troyat, Henri. Faux jour. 41 bois originaux d'Irène Kolsky. Paris, 1938.
43793.67.140 Troyat, Henri. Grandeur nature. Paris, 1936.
43793.67.145 Troyat, Henri. La fosse commune. Paris, 1939.
43793.67.150 Troyat, Henri. Le vivier. Paris, 1935.
43793.67.160 Troyat, Henri. Judith Madrier. Paris, 1940.
43793.67.170 Troyat, Henri. La case de l'Oncle Sam. Paris, 1948.
43793.67.180 Troyat, Henri. Les vivants, pièce en trois actes. Paris, 1947.
43793.67.190 Troyat, Henri. Le sac et la cendre; roman. Paris, 1948.
43793.67.200 Troyat, Henri. Étrangers sur la terre. Paris, 1950.
43793.67.210 Troyat, Henri. La tête sur les épaules. Paris, 1951.
43793.67.220 Troyat, Henri. La neige en deuil. Paris, 1952.
43793.67.230 Troyat, Henri. Les semailles et les moissons. Paris, 1954.
43793.67.240 Troyat, Henri. Les compagnons du coquelicot. Paris, 1959.
43793.67.250 Troyat, Henri. La Barynia; roman. Paris, 1960.
43793.67.260 Troyat, Henri. Les dames de Sibéria. Paris, 1962.
43793.67.270 Troyat, Henri. Une extrême amitie. Paris, 1963.
43793.67.280 Troyat, Henri. Le geste d'Ève. Paris, 1964.
43793.67.282 Troyat, Henri. Le geste d'Ève. Paris, 1969.
43793.67.290 Troyat, Henri. Les Eygletière. Paris, 1965.
43793.67.300 Troyat, Henri. Les Eygletière: La faim des lionceax; roman. v.2. Paris, 1966.
43793.67.310 Troyat, Henri. Les Eygletière: La malandre; roman. Paris, 1967.
43793.67.320 Troyat, Henri. Tant que la terre durera; roman. Paris, 1968.
43793.67.330 Troyat, Henri. Les héritiers de l'avenir, roman. Paris, 1968- 3v.
43793.67.340 Troyat, Henri. Sophie, ou La fin des combats; roman. Paris, 1963.
43793.67.350 Troyat, Henri. La grive. Paris, 1969.
43793.67.700A Troyat, Henri. My father's house. N.Y., 1951.
43793.67.700B Troyat, Henri. My father's house. N.Y., 1951.
43793.67.700.2 Troyat, Henri. My father's house. London, 1952.
43793.67.710 Troyat, Henri. The mountain. London, 1953.
43793.67.715 Troyat, Henri. Amelie and Pierre. N.Y., 1957.
43793.67.720 Troyat, Henri. Amelie in love. N.Y., 1956.
43793.67.730 Troyat, Henri. Strangers in the land. 1st ed. London, 1958.
43793.67.735 Troyat, Henri. Strangers on earth. N.Y., 1958.
43793.67.740 Troyat, Henri. The red and the white. N.Y., 1956.
43793.67.745 Troyat, Henri. Elizabeth. N.Y., 1959.
43793.67.750 Troyat, Henri. The brotherhood of the Red Poppy. N.Y., 1961.
43793.67.755 Troyat, Henri. The baroness. N.Y., 1961.
43793.67.760 Troyat, Henri. The encounter. N.Y., 1962.
43793.67.765 Troyat, Henri. An extreme friendship. 1st ed. N.Y., 1968.
43793.89.100 Truck, Robert Paul. Heures folles. Lille, 1938.
43793.89.1100 Truchot, Robert. Ephemeres et noctuelles. Rouen, 1948?
43795.51.100 Tuloup, A. Aphrodite moderne; roman. Rennes, 1936.
43795.77.100 Turon, Jean. C'était un adoloscent; roman. Paris, 1960.
43795.77.1100 Turpin, René. Willy Jones apprenti. Paris, 1912.
43795.78.100 Turquet-Milnes, G. From Pascal to Proust. N.Y., 1926.
43795.82.100 Tustes, Albert. Les sirènéennes. Paris, 1928.
43799.5.100 Tzara, Tristan. De nos oiseaux. Paris, 1929?
Htn 43799.5.110* Tzara, Tristan. Sept manifestes Dada. Paris, 192-.
43799.5.120A Tzara, Tristan. Terre sur terre. Genève, 1946.
43799.5.120B Tzara, Tristan. Terre sur terre. Genève, 1946.
43799.5.130 Tzara, Tristan. Morceaux choisis. Paris, 1947.
43799.5.140 Tzara, Tristan. Vingt-cinq-et-un poèmes. Paris, 1946.
43799.5.150 Tzara, Tristan. Le surréalisme et l'après-guerre. 3e éd. Paris, 1947.
43799.5.160 Tzara, Tristan. Phases. Paris, 1949.
43799.5.170 Tzara, Tristan. Parler seul. Paris, 1955.
43799.5.180 Tzara, Tristan. La face intérieure. Paris, 1953.
43799.5.190 Tzara, Tristan. Où boivent les loups. Paris, 1932.
43799.5.200 Tzara, Tristan. Lampjsteries. Paris, 1963.
43799.5.205 Tzara, Tristan. Pamět člověka. Praha, 1966.

Classified Listing

43511 - 43873 Individual authors, etc. - 1900- - Known authors (363 scheme plus 10) - cont.

43799.5.210 Tzara, Tristan. Les premiers poèmes. Paris, 1965.
43799.5.800 Peterson, Elmer. Tristan Tzara: dada and surrational theorist. New Brunswick, 1971.
43811.1.30 Ulmes, T. de. Pension de famille. Paris, 1912.
43812.89.100 Vaunois, L. Le roman de Louis XIII. Paris, 1932.
43816.1.30 Urville, G. d'. Spectacles et rêves. Paris, 1907.
43816.53.100 Urmatt, F. Les possédés du Saint-Esprit. Paris, 1938.
43816.53.110 Urmatt, F. La damnation de Georges Bruckner. Paris, 1936.
43822.1.30 Valentin, A. Je dirae sur la route. Paris, 1911.
43822.2.30 Vallery-Radot, Robert. Les grains de myrrhe, 1904-06. Paris, 1907.
43822.2.31 Vallery-Radot, Robert. Homme de désir. Paris, 1913.
43822.2.32 Vallery-Radot, Robert. Le réveil de l'esprit. Paris, 1917.
43822.3.30 Vandelbourg, R.H. de. La châine des heures. Paris, 1903.
43822.3.31 Vandelbourg, R.H. de. L'Algerie contemporaine sur les Hauts Plateaux. Paris, n.d.
43822.4.30 Variot, Jean. Les hasards de la guerre. 5e éd. Paris, 1914.
43822.4.35 Variot, Jean. La belle de Haguenau; comédie. Paris, 1922.
43822.4.40 Variot, Jean. Petits écrits de 1915. Paris, 1915.
43822.5.30 Vanzype, Gustave. Mother nature. Progress. 2 Belgian plays. Boston, 1917.
43822.6 Vallotton, Benjamin. Nous sommes fort. Quel est ton pays. v.1. Paris, 1929.
43822.6.5 Vallotton, Benjamin. Suspects. Quel est ton pays. v.2. Paris, 1930.
43822.6.10 Vallotton, Benjamin. Et voici la France. Quel est ton pays. v.3. Paris, 1931.
43822.6.15 Vallotton, Benjamin. Ceux de Barivier. Lausanne, 1920.
43822.6.20 Vallotton, Benjamin. Comme volent les années. v.1,2-3. Lausanne, 1960-62. 2v.
43822.6.30 Vallotton, Benjamin. The heart of Alsace. N.Y., 1918.
43822.8.30 Vaudoyer, Jean L. Le dernier rendez-vous. Paris, 1920.
43822.8.40 Vaudoyer, Jean L. La bien-aimée. Paris, 1927.
43822.8.50 Vaudoyer, Jean L. Italie retrouvée. Paris, 1950.
43822.8.60 Vaudoyer, Jean L. Italiennes. Paris, 1945.
43822.9.30 Vandervelden, Joseph. Les nocturnes. Bruxelles, 1912.
43822.9.40 Vandervelden, Joseph. La rançon de l'âme. Gand, 1907.
43822.10.30 Vaillat, Léandre. Le peintre et l'amant. Paris? 1920.
43822.11.30 Văcărescu, Elena. Amor vincit. Paris, 1909.
43822.11.40 Văcărescu, Elena. La dormeuse éveillée. Paris, 1914.
43822.11.50 Văcărescu, Elena. Le sortilège. 3e éd. Paris, 191-.
43822.11.60 Văcărescu, Elena. Memorial sur le mode mineur. Paris, 1946.
43822.12.100 Vachey, Michel. C'était à Mégara, roman. Paris, 1968.
43822.12.110 Vachey, Michel. Amulettes maigres. Honfleur, 1970.
43822.14.100 Vacquin, Pierre. Flârtes et tambours. Paris, 1956.
43822.35.100 Vaguer, J.P. Les paysages vénéneaux. Paris, 1956.
43822.41.100A Vaillant-Couturier, Paul. The French boy. Philadelphia, 1931.
43822.41.100B Vaillant-Couturier, Paul. The French boy. Philadelphia, 1931.
43822.41.110 Vaillant-Couturier, Paul. Poésie; oeuvres choisies. Paris, 1938.
43822.41.120 Vaillant-Couturier, Paul. Vers des lendemains qui chantent. Paris, 1962.
43822.41.1100 Vaillard, Pierre Jean. Tu parles, Charles. Paris, 1969.
43822.48.1100 Valeri, Diego. Jeux de mots. Paris, 1956.
43822.49.3 Davis, Ronald. Bibliographie des oeuvres de Paul Valéry (1895-1925). Paris, 1926.
43822.49.10A Valéry, Paul. L'ame et la danse, Eupalinos ou l'architecte. Paris, 1931.
43822.49.10B Valéry, Paul. L'ame et la danse, Eupalinos ou l'architecte. Paris, 1931.
43822.49.11A Valéry, Paul. Monsieur Teste. Paris, 1931.
43822.49.11B Valéry, Paul. Monsieur Teste. Paris, 1931.
43822.49.12A Valéry, Paul. Album de vers anciens. Paris, 1933.
43822.49.12B Valéry, Paul. Album de vers anciens. Paris, 1933.
43822.49.13 Valéry, Paul. Variété. Paris, 1934-37. 2v.
43822.49.14A Valéry, Paul. Discours. Paris, 1935.
43822.49.14B Valéry, Paul. Discours. Paris, 1935.
43822.49.15A Valéry, Paul. L'idée fixe. Paris, 1936.
43822.49.15B Valéry, Paul. L'idée fixe. Paris, 1936.
43822.49.16 Valéry, Paul. Pièces sur l'art. Paris, 1931.
43822.49.17A Valéry, Paul. Les divers essais sur Leonard de Vinci. Paris, 1938.
43822.49.17B Valéry, Paul. Les divers essais sur Leonard de Vinci. Paris, 1938.
43822.49.18 Valéry, Paul. Oeuvres. Paris, 1957. 2v.
43822.49.23 Valéry, Paul. Morceaux choisis; prose et poésie. Paris, 1930.
43822.49.25 Valéry, Paul. Conférences. Paris, 1939.
43822.49.50 Got, Maurice. Assomption de l'espace. Paris, 1957.
43822.49.61 Valéry, Paul. Correspondance 1887-1933. 5e éd. Paris, 1957.
43822.49.100 Valéry, Paul. Variété. Paris, 1924.
43822.49.100.5 Valéry, Paul. Variété. 27e éd. Paris, 1926.
43822.49.102 Valéry, Paul. Variété. 29e éd. Paris, 1924.
43822.49.103 Valéry, Paul. Variété II. Paris, 1930.
43822.49.104 Valéry, Paul. Variété II. Paris, 1929.
43822.49.105A Valéry, Paul. Variety. N.Y., 1927.
43822.49.105B Valéry, Paul. Variety. N.Y., 1927.
43822.49.106 Valéry, Paul. Variété III. Paris, 1936.
43822.49.106.2 Valéry, Paul. Variété III. 50e éd. Paris, 1953.
43822.49.106.10 Valéry, Paul. Variété IV. Paris, 1947.
43822.49.107 Valéry, Paul. Variété V. Paris, 1948.
Htn 43822.49.110* Valéry, Paul. Album de vers anciens. Paris, 1927.
43822.49.115 Valéry, Paul. Charmes. Paris, 1920.
43822.49.118 Valéry, Paul. Charmes. 4e éd. Paris, 1952.
43822.49.120 Valéry, Paul. Discours de réception à l'Académie française. Paris, 1927.
43822.49.125 Valéry, Paul. Eupalinos, ou L'architecte, précédé de L'ame et la danse. 29e éd. Paris, 1924.
43822.49.128 Valéry, Paul. Eupalinos, ou L'architecte, précédé de L'ame et la danse. 45e éd. Paris, 1924.
Htn 43822.49.135* Valéry, Paul. Réponses. Saint-Félicien-en-Vivarais, 1928.
43822.49.150 Valéry, Paul. Monsieur Teste. Paris, 1946.
43822.49.152 Valéry, Paul. Monsieur Teste. Paris, 1954.
43822.49.155A Valéry, Paul. Regards sur le monde actuel. Paris, 1931.
43822.49.155B Valéry, Paul. Regards sur le monde actuel. Paris, 1931.
43822.49.155C Valéry, Paul. Regards sur le monde actuel. Paris, 1931.
43822.49.156A Valéry, Paul. Regards sur le monde actuel. Paris, 1938.
43822.49.156B Valéry, Paul. Regards sur le monde actuel. Paris, 1938.
Htn 43822.49.165* Valéry, Paul. Moralités. Paris, 1931.
43822.49.166 Valéry, Paul. Moralités. Paris, 1932.

43511 - 43873 Individual authors, etc. - 1900- - Known authors (363 scheme plus 10) - cont.

43822.49.170 Valéry, Paul. Le serpent. Paris, 1922.
43822.49.171 Valéry, Paul. Poésies. Paris, 1946.
43822.49.172 Valéry, Paul. Poésies. Paris, 1930.
NEDL 43822.49.173 Valéry, Paul. Poésies. 10e éd. Paris, 1931.
43822.49.175 Valéry, Paul. Poésies. 34e éd. Paris, 1935.
43822.49.177 Valéry, Paul. Poésies. 40e éd. Paris, 1936.
43822.49.179 Valéry, Paul. Pièces sur l'art. Paris, 1934.
43822.49.185 Aguettant, Louis. Les dialogues de Paul Valéry. Saint-Félicien-en-Vivarais, 1926.
43822.49.190A Valéry, Paul. La jeune parque. Paris, 1936.
43822.49.190B Valéry, Paul. La jeune parque. Paris, 1936.
43822.49.192 Valéry, Paul. La jeune parque. 2e éd. Paris, 1955.
43822.49.192.2 Valéry, Paul. La jeune parque. Paris, 1957.
43822.49.200 Valéry, Paul. Poésie et pensée abstraite. Oxford, 1939.
43822.49.210A Valéry, Paul. Introduction à la poétique. 11e éd. Paris, 1938.
43822.49.210B Valéry, Paul. Introduction à la poétique. 11e éd. Paris, 1938.
43822.49.220 Valéry, Paul. La politique de l'esprit. Manchester, 1941.
43822.49.228 Valéry, Paul. El cementerio marino. Paris, 1930.
43822.49.229 Valéry, Paul. El cementerio marino. Montevideo, 1932.
43822.49.230 Valéry, Paul. Cementerio marino. Caracas, 1940.
43822.49.232 Valéry, Paul. El cementerio marino. Santiago, 1940.
43822.49.255 Valéry, Paul. Mélange. 11e éd. Montrouge, 1941.
43822.49.256A Valéry, Paul. Mélange. n.p., 1941.
43822.49.256B Valéry, Paul. Mélange. n.p., 1941.
43822.49.267 Valéry, Paul. Tel quel. Paris, 1941-43.
43822.49.275F Valéry, Paul. L'ange. Paris, 1946.
43822.49.280 Valéry, Paul. Mon Faust. Paris, 1946.
43822.49.290 Valéry, Paul. Mauvaises pensées et autres. Marseille, 1941.
43822.49.300 Valéry, Paul. Mauvaises pensées et autres. 30e éd. Paris, 1947.
43822.49.310 Valéry, Paul. Souvenirs poétiques. 2e éd. Paris, 1947.
43822.49.320 Valéry, Paul. Vues. Paris, 1948.
43822.49.330 Valéry, Paul. De la diction des vers. Paris, 1933.
43822.49.340 Valéry, Paul. Rhumbs. Paris, 1926.
43822.49.350 Valéry, Paul. Poesía de Paul Valéry. Mexico, 1943.
43822.49.359 Valéry, Paul. Littérature. Paris, 1929.
43822.49.360 Valéry, Paul. Littérature. Paris, 1930.
43822.49.370F Valéry, Paul. Sémiramis. Paris, 1934.
Htn 43822.49.380* Valéry, Paul. Discours aux chirurgiens. Paris, 1938.
Htn 43822.49.390* Valéry, Paul. La soirée avec M. Teste. Paris, 1919.
43822.49.400 Valéry, Paul. Remarques extérieures. Paris, 1929.
43822.49.405 Valéry, Paul. Histoires brisées. Paris, 1950.
43822.49.410F Valéry, Paul. Le physique du livre. Paris, 1945.
43822.49.415 Valéry, Paul. État de la vertu. Paris, 1935.
43822.49.420 Valéry, Paul. Lettres à quelques-uns. 5e éd. Paris, 1952.
43822.49.425 Valéry, Paul. Choses tues. Paris, 1932.
43822.49.430 Valéry, Paul. Collected works. v.1,3-5,7,9-13. N.Y., 1956- 10v.
43822.49.440 Valéry, Paul. L'idée fixe. Paris, 1933.
43822.49.460 Valéry, Paul. Propos sur l'intelligence. Paris, 1926.
43822.49.470 Valéry, Paul. Les essais de Paul Valéry; poèmes et proses. Paris, 1964.
43822.49.705 Valéry, Paul. The graveyard by the sea. Philadelphia, 1932.
43822.49.710 Valéry, Paul. Monsieur Teste. 1st American ed. N.Y., 1947.
43822.49.710.3 Valéry, Paul. Monsieur Teste. London, 1951.
43822.49.715 Valéry, Paul. Variety. 2nd series. N.Y., 1938.
43822.49.720 Valéry, Paul. Reflections on the world today. N.Y., 1948.
43822.49.722 Valéry, Paul. Reflections on the world today. London, 1951.
43822.49.725 Valéry, Paul. Eupalinos; or The architect. London, 1932.
43822.49.735 Valéry, Paul. Dance and the soul. London, 1951.
43822.49.745 Valéry, Paul. An evening with Mr. Teste. Paris, 1925.
43822.49.750 Valéry, Paul. Cahiers. Paris, 1957-61. 29v.
43822.49.790 Valéry, Paul. Cuatra maestros franceses: Stendhal - Baudelaire - Verlaine - Mallarmé. Bogotá, 1944.
43822.49.795 Valéry, Paul. Anfion. Buenos Aires, 1947.
43822.49.800 Valéry, Paul. Básně. Praha, 1966.
43822.49.900A De l'art pour tous à l'art pour l'art. Valéry ou Boileau? Paris, 1926.
43822.49.900B De l'art pour tous à l'art pour l'art. Valéry ou Boileau? Paris, 1926.
43822.49.905 Fernandat, René. Paul Valéry. Paris, 1927.
43822.49.907 Fernandat, René. Autour de Paul Valéry. Grenoble, 1933.
43822.49.907.5 Fernandat, René. Autour de Paul Valéry. Grenoble, 1944.
43822.49.908 Hanotaux, Gabriel. Réponse au discours de M. Paul Valéry. Paris, 1927.
43822.49.912 Sonday, Paul. Paul Valéry. Paris, 1927.
43822.49.915 Paul Valéry. Paris, 1926.
43822.49.916A Paul Valéry, vivant. Marseille, 1946.
43822.49.916B Paul Valéry, vivant. Marseille, 1946.
43822.49.916C Paul Valéry, vivant. Marseille, 1946.
43822.49.918 Gueguen, P. Paul Valéry. Paris, 1928.
43822.49.920A Fisher, H.A.L. Paul Valéry. Oxford, 1927.
43822.49.920B Fisher, H.A.L. Paul Valéry. Oxford, 1927.
43822.49.924 Larbaud, Valery. Paul Valéry et la Méditerranée. 1. éd. Maestricht, 1926.
43822.49.925A Larbaud, Valery. Paul Valéry. Paris, 1931.
43822.49.925B Larbaud, Valery. Paul Valéry. Paris, 1931.
43822.49.930 Thibaudet, Albert. Paul Valéry. Paris, 1923.
43822.49.935 Maurois, A. Introduction à la méthode de Paul Valéry. Paris, 1933.
43822.49.940 Porché, F. Paul Valéry et la poésie pure. Paris, 1926.
43822.49.945 Gillet, Martin Stanislas. Paul Valéry et la métaphysique. Paris, 1927.
43822.49.946 Gillet, Martin Stanislas. Paul Valéry et la métaphysique. Paris, 1935.
43822.49.950 Cohen, G. Essai d'explication du cimetière marin. Paris, 1933.
43822.49.955 Rauhut, Franz. Paul Valéry, Geist und Mythos. München, 1930.
43822.49.957 Bolle, Louis. Paul Valéry. Fribourg en Swisse, 1944.
43822.49.960 Bosanquet, Theodora. Paul Valéry. London, 1933.
43822.49.965 Droin, Alfred. M. Paul Valéry et la tradition poétique française. Paris, 1923.
43822.49.975 Latour, Jane de. Examen de Valéry. Paris, 1935.
43822.49.980A Bendz, E. Paul Valéry et l'art de la prose. Göteborg, 1936.
43822.49.980B Bendz, E. Paul Valéry et l'art de la prose. Göteborg, 1936.
43822.49.985A Noulet, Emilie. Paul Valéry; études suivi de Fragments des mémoirs d'un poème par P. Valéry. Paris, 1938.

43511 - 43873 Individual authors, etc. - 1900- - Known authors (363 scheme plus 10) - cont.

43822.49.985B Noulet, Emilie. Paul Valéry; études suivi de Fragments des mémoirs d'un poème par P. Valéry. Paris, 1938.
43822.49.986 Noulet, Emilie. Paul Valéry. Bruxelles, 1950.
43822.49.987 Noulet, Emilie. Suite valeryenne. Bruxelles, 1959. 2 pam.
43822.49.988 Noulet, Emilie. Suites; Mallarmé, Rimbaud, Valéry. Paris, 1964.
43822.49.990 Chisholm, A.R. An approach to M. Valéry's Jeune parque. Melbourne, 1938.
43822.49.995 Lefévre, Fréderic. Entretiens avec Paul Valéry. Paris, 1926.
43822.49.1000 Venettis, Jean. Exégèse poétique de l'Ebauche d'un serpent de Paul Valéry. Paris, 1941.
43822.49.1005 Berne-Joffroy, A. Présence de Valéry. Paris, 1945.
43822.49.1010 Sørensen, Hans. La poésie de Paul Valéry. Thesis. Aarhus, 1944.
43822.49.1015A Dresden, Samuel. L'artiste et l'absolu, Paul Valéry et Marcel Proust. Assen, 1941.
43822.49.1015B Dresden, Samuel. L'artiste et l'absolu, Paul Valéry et Marcel Proust. Assen, 1941.
43822.49.1020 Raymond, Marcel. Paul Valéry et la tentation de l'esprit. Neuchâtel, 1946.
43822.49.1025 Eigeldinger, Marc. Paul Valéry. Neuchâtel, 1945.
43822.49.1030 Gide, André. Paul Valéry. Paris, 1947.
43822.49.1035A Mascagni, P. Initation à Paul Valéry. Paris, 1946.
43822.49.1035B Mascagni, P. Initation à Paul Valéry. Paris, 1946.
43822.49.1045 Pommier, Jean. Paul Valéry et la création littéraire. Paris, 1946.
43822.49.1050A Mondor, Henri. Trois discours pour Paul Valéry. 7e éd. Paris, 1948.
43822.49.1050B Mondor, Henri. Trois discours pour Paul Valéry. 7. éd. Paris, 1948.
43822.49.1050.5A Mondor, Henri. Précocité de Valéry. 4e éd. Paris, 1957.
43822.49.1050.5B Mondor, Henri. Précocité de Valéry. 6e éd. Paris, 1957.
43822.49.1055 Monod, Jules P. Regard sur Paul Valéry. Lausanne, 1948.
43822.49.1060A Pelmont, Raoul. Paul Valéry et les beaux-arts. Cambridge, Mass., 1949.
43822.49.1060B Pelmont, Raoul. Paul Valéry et les beaux-arts. Cambridge, Mass., 1949.
43822.49.1065 Lannes, Roger. Appel à Paul Valéry. Paris, 1947.
43822.49.1070 Fargue, L. Rue de Villejust. Paris, 1946.
43822.49.1075 Andouard, Y. Recherche de Paul Valéry. Albi, 1946.
43822.49.1080 La Rochefoucauld, Edmée de Fels. Images de Paul Valéry. Strasbourg, 1949.
43822.49.1081 La Rochefoucauld, Edmée de Fels. En lisant les cahiers de Paul Valéry. Paris, 1964-67. 3v.
43822.49.1082 La Rochefoucauld, Edmée de Fels. Paul Valéry. Paris, 1954.
43822.49.1085 Marcailhou d'Aymeric, A.L.A.C. Paul Valéry. Thèse. Toulouse, 1946.
43822.49.1090 Paul Valéry. Ciudad Trujillo, 1945.
43822.49.1095 Duchesne-Guillemin, J. Essai sur La jeune parque de Paul Valéry. Bruxelles, 1946.
43822.49.1095.10 Duchesne-Guillemin, J. Étude de Charmes de Paul Valéry. Bruxelles, 1947.
43822.49.1100 Eschmann, E.W. Paul Valéry. Herrliberg, 1948.
43822.49.1105 Parize, J.H. Essai sur la pensée et l'art de Paul Valéry. Paris, 1946.
43822.49.1110 Felici, Noël. Regards sur Valéry. Paris, 1953.
43822.49.1120 Paris. Bibliothèque Sainte-Geneviève. Collection Doucet. Catalogue de l'exposition Paul Valéry. Paris, 1946?
43822.49.1130 Sewell, E. Paul Valéry. Cambridge, Eng., 1952.
43822.49.1140 Henry, Albert. Language et poésie chez Paul Valéry. Paris, 1952.
43822.49.1150 Bémol, Maurice. Paul Valéry. Thèse. Clermont-Ferrand, 1949.
43822.49.1152 Bémol, Maurice. Variations sur Valéry. Sarrebruck, 1952. 2v.
43822.49.1154 Bémol, Maurice. La parque et le serpent. Paris, 1955.
43822.49.1155 Bémol, Maurice. La méthode critique de Paul Valéry. Paris, 1960.
43822.49.1160 Romain, W.P. Paul Valéry. Paris, 1951.
43822.49.1170 Doisy, M. Paul Valéry. Paris, 1952.
43822.49.1180 Hytier, Jean. La poétique de Valéry. Paris, 1953.
43822.49.1181 Hytier, Jean. The poetics of Paul Valéry. 1st ed. Garden City, N.Y., 1966.
43822.49.1185 Hytier, Jean. Questions de littérature. Genève, 1967.
43822.49.1190 Soulairol, Jean. Paul Valéry. Paris, 1952.
43822.49.1200A Scarfe, F. The art of Paul Valéry. London, 1954.
43822.49.1200B Scarfe, F. The art of Paul Valéry. London, 1954.
43822.49.1210 Suckling, N. Paul Valéry. London, 1954.
43822.49.1220 Walzer, P.O. La poésie de Valéry. Genève, 1953.
43822.49.1230 Maurer, K. Interpretation zur späteren Lyrik Paul Valérys. München, 1954.
43822.49.1240 Faure, G. Paul Valéry, méditerranéen. Paris, 1954.
43822.49.1250 Michel, Pierre. Valéry. pts.1-2. Paris, 195-.
43822.49.1255 Fehr, A.J.A. Les dialogues antiques de Paul Valéry. Leiden, 1960.
43822.49.1260 Guiraud, P. Langage et versification d'après l'oeuvre de Paul Valéry. Paris, 1953.
43822.49.1260.2 Guiraud, P. Langage et versification d'après l'oeuvre de Paul Valéry. Thèse. Paris, 1953.
43822.49.1265 Mondor, Henri. L'heureuse rencontre de Valéry et Mallarmé. Paris, 1948.
43822.49.1270 Sutcliffe, J.E. La pensée de Paul Valéry. Paris, 1955[1954]
43822.49.1275 Garrigue, F. Goeth et Valéry. Paris, 1955.
43822.49.1280 Poulain, Gaston. Paul Valéry. Montpellier, 1955.
43822.49.1285 Bibliothèque nationale, Paris. Paul Valéry. Paris, 1956.
43822.49.1290 Christensen, Alfred. Paul Valéry. Oslo, 1952.
43822.49.1295 Morawska, L. Studium o jezyku poezji Pawła Valéry. Lublin, 1955.
43822.49.1300 Lanfranchi, Geneviève. Paul Valéry et l'experience du moi pur. Lausanne, 1958.
43822.49.1305 Cain, L. Trois essais sur P. Valéry. Paris, 1958.
43822.49.1310 Bellivier, André. Henri Poincaré et Paul Valéry. Chevreuse, 1958.
43822.49.1315 Lawler, James. Form and meaning in Valéry's Le cimetière marin. Carlton, 1959.
43822.49.1320 Parisier-Plottel, J. Les dialogues de Paul Valéry. Paris, 1960.
43822.49.1325 Laitenberger, Hugo. Der Begriff der "Absence" bei Paul Valéry. Wiesbaden, 1960.
43822.49.1330 Blucher, Karl. Strategie des Geistes. Frankfurt, 1960.
43822.49.1335 Whiting, Charles. Valéry, jeune poète. 1e éd. New Haven, 1960.

43511 - 43873 Individual authors, etc. - 1900- - Known authors (363 scheme plus 10) - cont.

43822.49.1340 Berne-Joffroy, André. Valéry. Paris, 1960.
43822.49.1345 Denat, A. L'art poétique après Valéry. Sydney, 1959.
43822.49.1350 Mondor, Henri. Propos familiers de Paul Valéry. Paris, 1957.
43822.49.1355 Ingrosso, O. Note su Valéry. Bari, 1960.
43822.49.1360 Ince, Walter Newcombe. The poetic theory of Paul Valéry. Leicester, 1961.
43822.49.1362 Ince, Walter Newcombe. The poetic theory of Paul Valéry: inspiration and technique. 2nd ed. Leicester, 1970.
43822.49.1365 Machon, Agnes. The universal self; a study of Paul Valéry. Toronto, 1961.
43822.49.1366 Machon, Agnes. The universal self. London, 1961.
43822.49.1370 Richthofen, Erich von. Commentaire sur mon Faust de Paul Valéry. Paris, 1961.
43822.49.1375 Choux, Jean. Michel-Ange et Paul Valéry. Paris, 1932.
43822.49.1380 Noulet, Emilie. Paul Valéry. Bruxelles, 1927.
43822.49.1385 Robinson, J. L'analyse de l'esprit dans les cahiers de Valéry. Paris, 1963.
43822.49.1390 Lawler, J.R. Lecture de Valéry. Paris, 1963.
43822.49.1395 Roulin, P. Paul Valéry. Neuchâtel, 1964.
43822.49.1400 Ducresne-Guillemine, Jacques. Études pour un Paul Valéry. Neuchâtel, 1964.
43822.49.1405 Thomson, Alastair. Valéry. Edinburgh, 1965.
43822.49.1410 Bourbon Busset, J. de. Paul Valéry. Paris, 1964.
43822.49.1415 Bergeron, Léandre. Le son et le sens dans quelques poèmes de Charmes de Paul Valéry, Gap, 1963.
43822.49.1420 Laurette, Pierre. Le thème de l'arbre chez Paul Valéry et Rainer Maria Rilke. Saarbrücken, 1962.
43822.49.1422 Laurette, Pierre. Le thème de l'arbre chez Paul Valéry et Rainer Maria Rilke. Paris, 1967.
43822.49.1425 Aigrisse, Gilberte. Psychanalyse de Paul Valéry. Paris, 1964.
43822.49.1430 Clauzel, Raymond. Trois introductions à Paul Valéry. La Rochelle, 1927.
43822.49.1435 Pire, Francois. La tentation du sensible chez Paul Valéry. Bruxelles, 1964.
43822.49.1440 Rouart Valéry, Agathe. Paul Valéry. Paris, 1966.
43822.49.1445 Schmitz, Alfred. Valéry et la tentation de l'absolu. Gembloux, 1964.
43822.49.1550 Koehler, Hartmut. Poésie et profondeur sémantique dans La jeune parque. Nancy, 1965.
43822.49.1555 Brunelli, Giuseppe Antonio. Paul Valéry e il canzoniere, 1887-1892. Messina, 1965.
43822.49.1556 Brunelli, Giuseppe Antonio. Introduzione alla poesia di Paul Valéry, da Solitude a Intermède, 1887-1892. v.1-2. Messina, 1964-65.
43822.49.1560 Perche, Louis. Valéry, les limites de l'humain. Paris, 1966.
43822.49.1565 Wais, Karin. Studien zu Rilkes Valéry Übertragungen. Tübingen, 1967.
43822.49.1570 Grubbs, Henry Alexander. Paul Valéry. N.Y., 1968.
43822.49.1575 Entretiens sur Paul Valéry. Paris, 1968.
43822.49.1580 Nadal, André. Abeille spirituelle. Poème. Nîmes, 1968.
43822.49.1585 Arnold, Albert James. Paul Valéry and his critics; a bibliography. Charlottesville, 1970.
43822.49.1590 Tauman, Léon. Paul Valéry ou le Mal de l'art. Paris, 1969.
43822.49.1595 Giaveri, Maria Teresa. L'album de vers anciens di Paul Valéry. Padove, 1969.
43822.49.1600 Charney, Hanna. Le scepticisme de Valéry. Paris, 1969.
43822.49.1605 Maka-de Schepper, Monique. Le thème de La Pythie chez Paul Valéry. Paris, 1969.
43822.49.1610 Cloran, Émile M. Valéry face à ses idoles. Paris, 1970.
43822.49.1615 Parent, Monique. Cohérence et résonance dans le style de Charmes de Paul Valéry. Paris, 1970.
43822.49.1620 Schmidt-Radefeldt, Jürgen. Paul Valéry linguiste dans les Cahiers. Paris, 1970.
43822.49.1625 Les critiques de notre temps et Valéry. Paris, 1971.
43822.49.3100 Valet, Paul. La parole qui me porte. Paris, 1965.
43822.50.100 Vailland, Roger. Drôle de jeu. Paris, 1946.
43822.50.110 Vailland, Roger. Un jeune homme seul. Paris, 1951.
43822.50.120 Vailland, Roger. La loi, roman. Paris, 1958.
43822.50.122 Vailland, Roger. La loi, roman. Paris, 1957.
43822.50.130 Vailland, Roger. Les mauvais coups. Paris, 1959.
43822.50.140 Vailland, Roger. La fête. Paris, 1960.
43822.50.142 Vailland, Roger. Fête. N.Y., 1961.
43822.50.150 Vailland, Roger. La truite. Paris, 1964.
43822.50.160 Vailland, Roger. Oeuvres complètes. Lausanne, 1967. 12v.
43822.50.170 Vailland, Roger. Écrits intimes. Paris, 1969.
43822.50.700 Vailland, Roger. Playing for keeps. Boston, 1948.
43822.50.710 Vailland, Roger. Playing with fire. London, 1948.
43822.50.715 Vailland, Roger. Expérience du drame. Paris, 1953.
43822.50.716 Arlet, Suzanne. Reflections sur la création littéraire. Paris, 1961.
43822.50.720A Vailland, Roger. The law. 1st American ed. N.Y., 1958.
43822.50.720B Vailland, Roger. The law. 1st American ed. N.Y., 1958.
43822.50.725 Vailland, Roger. Monsieur Jean. 4e éd. Paris, 1959.
43822.50.730 Vailland, Roger The sovereigns. London, 1960.
43822.50.735 Vailland, Roger. Turn of the wheel. N.Y., 1962.
43822.50.740 Vailland, Roger. The trout. 1st ed. N.Y., 1965.
43822.50.800 Brochier, Jean Jacques. Roger Vailland, tentative de description. Paris, 1969.
43822.50.805 Bott, François. Les saisons de Roger Vailland. Paris, 1969.
43822.50.810 Recanati, Jean. Vailland. Paris, 1971.
43822.50.1100 Vallerey, G. Les chansons de l'esclave. Bordeaux, 1932.
43822.51.100 Valmy-Baysse, Jean. La vie enchantée; poèmes, 1902-05. Paris, 1906.
43822.51.110 Valmy-Baysse, Jean. Le coeur et les yeux; poèmes. Paris, 1932.
43822.51.2100 Valorbe, François. La vierge aux chimeres. Paris, 1957.
43822.51.3100 Valschaerts, Jean. Points de vue. Louvain, 1929.
43822.51.4100 Valois, Michel. Des souvenirs...que le vent...poèmes. Paris, 1964.
43822.55.100 Valton, André. Le banquet pantagruélique et poétique. Fontenay-le-Comte, 1957.
43822.58.100 Vandal, Linda. A cloche-coeur. Paris, 1958.
43822.58.1100 Vandamme, Robert. Briser te convient. Malines, 1954.
43822.58.2100 Vandycke, Yvon. Les os creux, avec un complément de cinc linogravures. Ixelles, 1960.
43822.60.100 Vannier, Angèle. La nuit ardente, roman. Paris, 1969.
43822.74.100 Varasteh, Khosro. Rapsodie persane, roman. Paris, 1951.
43822.74.1100 Vercel, Simone Roger. La fin du grand hiver. Paris, 1969.
43822.75.100 Varel, André. Musiques dominantes. Paris, 1956.
43822.76.100 Varney, Charles. Igor Youriewitch. Paris, 1931.

43511 - 43873 Individual authors, etc. - 1900- - Known authors (363 scheme plus 10) - cont.

43822.82.100 Vasseur, Pierre. Tunique; poèmes. Paris, 1952.
43822.87.100 Vaucher, N.Z. (Mme.). L'oasis sentimentale; poèmes. Paris, 1929.
43822.88.100 Vaucienne, François. Un rêve du jeune Jean Racine aux portes d'or de la Provence. Paris, 1962.
43822.89.100 Vautel, Clément. Candide; pièce...(d'après le roman de Voltaire). Paris, 1924.
43822.89.110 Vautel, Clément. La réouverture. Paris, 1919.
43822.89.120 Vautel, Clément. Les folies bourgeoises. Paris, 1921.
43822.89.130 Vautel, Clément. Mademoiselle Sans-Gêne. Paris, 1922.
43822.89.140 Vautel, Clément. Mon curé chez les riches. Paris, 1923.
43822.89.142 Vaulet, Clément. Mon curé chez les riches. Paris, 1923.
43822.89.150 Vaulet, Clément. Mon curé chez les pauvres. Paris, 1925.
43822.89.160 Vaulet, Clément. Je suis un affreux bourgeois. Paris, 1926.
43822.89.170 Vaulet, Clément. Madame ne vent pas d'enfant. Paris, 1924.
43822.89.180 Vaulet, Clément. La grande rafle. Paris, 1929.
43822.89.190 Vautel, Clément. "Mon film". Souvenirs d'un journaliste. Paris, 1941.
43822.89.1100 Vaure, Jean Jacques. Sequences. Paris, 1957.
43822.90 Vauthier, Jean. Théâtre. Paris, 1954-
43822.90.100 Vauthier, Jean. Le personage combattent; ou, Fortissimo. Paris, 1955.
43822.90.110 Vauthier, Jean. Les prodiges. Paris, 1958.
43822.90.1100 Vauthier, M. Faon l'héroique. Paris, 1962.
43822.92.100 Vandercammen, Edmond. Poèmes choisis, 1931-1959. Paris, 1961.
43822.92.110 Vandercammen, Edmond. Les sang partagé. Bruxelles, 1963.
43822.92.120 Vandercammen, Edmond. Le jour est provisoire. Bruxelles, 1966.
43823.1.30 Vérola, P. Les nuages de pourpre. Paris, 1907.
43823.2.30 Védrès, Nicole. L'exécuteur. Paris, 1958.
43823.2.35 Védrès, Nicole. Les cordes rouges, roman. Paris, 1953.
43823.2.40 Védrès, Nicole. Paris, le... Paris, 1958.
43823.2.42 Védrès, Nicole. Paris. 6e éd. Paris, 1965.
43823.2.45 Védrès, Nicole. La bête lointaine, roman. Paris, 1960.
43823.2.50 Védrès, Nicole. Suite parisienne. Paris, 1960.
43823.25.100 Veraldi, Gabriele. La machine humaine. 80. éd. Paris, 1954.
43823.48.100 Velan, Yves. Je. Paris, 1959.
43823.50.100 Velleroy, Guy. Le feu grégois. Paris, 1924.
43823.73.100 Véquaud, Yves. Le petit livre avalé; roman. Paris, 1966.
43823.74.100 Vérane, Léon. Le livre des passe-temps. Paris, 1930.
43823.74.110 Vérane, Léon. La calanque au soleil. Paris, 1946.
43823.74.1100 Vercel, Simone Roger. La fin du grand hiver. Paris, 1969.
43823.74.2100 Vercammen, Louky. La volière aux chimères. Bruxelles, 1964.
43823.75.100 Vercel, Roger. Sous le pied de l'archange. Paris, 1937.
43823.75.105 Vercel, Roger. Capitaine Conan. Paris, 1934.
43823.75.110 Vercel, Roger. Léna, roman. Paris, 1936.
43823.75.120 Vercel, Roger. La clandestine. Paris, 1941.
43823.75.125 Vercel, Roger. Jean Villemeur. Paris, 1939.
43823.75.132 Vercel, Roger. La caravane de Paques. Paris, 1948.
43823.75.140 Vercel, Roger. La fosse aux vents. v.2. Paris, 1950.
43823.75.150 Vercel, Roger. Les 4 temps vus par les écrivains du demi-siècle. n.p., 1950.
43823.75.160 Vercel, Roger. Visage perdu. Paris, 1953.
43823.75.170 Vercel, Roger. Au bont du môle. Paris, 1960.
43823.75.180 Vercel, Roger. L'île des revenants, roman. Paris, 1954.
43823.75.190 Vercel, Roger. Vent de terre. Paris, 1961.
43823.75.200 Vercel, Roger. Remorques; roman. Paris, 1935.
43823.75.210 Vercel, Roger. Au large de l'Eden. Paris, 1947.
43823.75.705A Vercel, Roger. Tides of Mont St. Michel. N.Y., 1938.
43823.75.705B Vercel, Roger. Tides of Mont St. Michel. N.Y., 1938.
43823.75.710 Vercel, Roger. Madman's memory. N.Y., 1947.
43823.75.715 Vercel, Roger. Troubled waters, a novel. N.Y., 1940.
43823.75.720 Vercel, Roger. Northern lights. N.Y., 1948.
43823.75.730 Vercel, Roger. In sight of Eden. 1st ed. N.Y., 1934.
43823.75.740 Vercel, Roger. The Easter fleet. N.Y., 1950.
43823.75.750 Vercel, Roger. Ride out the storm. N.Y., 1953.
43823.75.760 Vercel, Roger. La Hourie. Paris, 1952.
43823.75.770 Vercel, Roger. En dérive. Levallois-Perret, 1967?
43823.75.2100 Bruller, Jean. Le songe. Paris, 1945.
43823.75.2110A Bruller, Jean. La marche à l'étoile. Paris, 1943[1945]
43823.75.2110B Bruller, Jean. La marche à l'étoile. Paris, 1943[1945]
43823.75.2120 Bruller, Jean. Les ormes de la nuit. Paris, 1946.
43823.75.2121 Bruller, Jean. Les ormes de la nuit et La puissance du jour. Paris, 1951.
43823.75.2130 Bruller, Jean. Portrait d'une amitié. Paris, 1946.
43823.75.2140A Bruller, Jean. Le songe. Paris, 1949.
43823.75.2140B Bruller, Jean. Le songe. Paris, 1949.
43823.75.2150 Bruller, Jean. Les yeux et la lumière. Paris, 1950.
43823.75.2160 Bruller, Jean. Les animaux dénaturés. Paris, 1952.
43823.75.2163 Bruller, Jean. Les animaux dénaturés. Paris, 1957.
43823.75.2170 Bruller, Jean. Plus ou moins homme. Paris, 1950.
43823.75.2180 Bruller, Jean. Les pas dans la sable. Paris, 1954.
43823.75.2190 Bruller, Jean. Les divagations d'un français en Chine. Paris, 1956.
43823.75.2202 Bruller, Jean. Le silence de la mer. N.Y., 1943.
43823.75.2203 Bruller, Jean. Le silence de la mer. Paris, 1944.
43823.75.2204 Bruller, Jean. Le silence de la mer. Paris, 1964.
43823.75.2205A Bruller, Jean. Le silence de la mer. N.Y., 1951.
43823.75.2205B Bruller, Jean. Le silence de la mer. N.Y., 1951.
43823.75.2206 Bruller, Jean. Colères, roman par Vercors (pseud.). Paris, 1956.
43823.75.2210 Bruller, Jean. P.P.C. Paris, 1957.
43823.75.2220 Bruller, Jean. Sylva. Paris, 1961.
43823.75.2230 Bruller, Jean. Sur ce rivage. Paris, 1958- 3v.
43823.75.2240 Bruller, Jean. Quota. N.Y., 1966.
43823.75.2250 Bruller, Jean. Les chemins de l'être. Paris, 1965.
43823.75.2260 Bruller, Jean. Quota ou Les Pléthoriens, roman. Paris, 1966.
43823.75.2700A Bruller, Jean. The silence of the sea. N.Y., 1944.
43823.75.2700B Bruller, Jean. The silence of the sea. N.Y., 1944.
43823.75.2710 Bruller, Jean. Put out the light. London, 1944.
43823.75.2715 Bruller, Jean. Three short novels. 1st ed. Boston, 1947.
43823.75.2720 Bruller, Jean. Guiding star. London, 1946.
43823.75.2725 Bruller, Jean. You shall know them. 1st ed. Boston, 1953.
43823.75.2730A Bruller, Jean. Borderline. London, 1954.
43823.75.2730B Bruller, Jean. Borderline. London, 1954.
43823.75.2735A Bruller, Jean. The insurgents. 1st ed. N.Y., 1956.
43823.75.2735B Bruller, Jean. The insurgents. 1st ed. N.Y., 1956.
43823.75.2741 Bruller, Jean. Paths of love. N.Y., 1961.
43823.75.2742 Bruller, Jean. Freedom in December. London, 1961.
43823.75.2745 Bruller, Jean. For the time being. London, 1960.

43511 - 43873 Individual authors, etc. - 1900- - Known authors (363 scheme plus 10) - cont.

43823.75.2750 Bruller, Jean. Sylva. N.Y., 1962.
43823.75.2755 Bruller, Jean. La bataille du silence. Paris, 1967.
43823.75.2757 Bruller, Jean. The battle of silence. 1st ed. N.Y., 1968.
43823.75.2762 Bruller, Jean. The raft of the Medusa. 1st American ed. N.Y., 1971.
43823.75.2800 Konstantinović, Radivoje D. Vercors. Paris, 1969.
43823.75.3100 Verdot, Guy. Demain à Pompei. Paris, 1958.
43823.75.4100 Vergez, Raoul. Les tours inachevées. Paris, 1959.
43823.75.5100 Verfrey, Maurice Michel. La chanson des rivages; poèmes. Paris, 1948.
43823.76.110 Verne, Marc. Marie Villarceaux; un roman d'amour. Haiti, 1945.
43823.76.1100 Vergnes, Georges. La vie passionnée de Guillaume Apollinaire. Paris, 1958.
43823.76.2100 Vermorel, Claude. Jeanne avec nous; pièce en quatre actes. Paris, 1942.
43823.76.3100 Verne, Maurice. Musées de voluptés. 78e éd. Paris, 1930.
43823.76.4100 Vernay, Andrée. Dernière terre. Paris, 1962.
43823.76.5100 Vermeil, Jules. Rose des marais; roman. Aire-sur-la-Lys, 1970.
43823.77.11 Verneuil, Louis. Théâtre complet. N.Y., 194-. 4v.
43823.77.100 Verneuil, Louis. La banque Nemo. Paris, 1932.
43823.77.110 Verneuil, Louis. Une femme ravie; pièce en quatre actes. Paris, 1932.
43823.77.120 Verneuil, Louis. L'école des contribuables. Paris, 1934.
43823.77.130 Verneuil, Louis. Pile ou face. Paris, 1934.
43823.77.140 Verneuil, Louis. L'amant de Madame Vidal. Paris, 1935.
43823.77.150 Verneuil, Louis. Dora Nelson, un film de Louis Verneuil. pt.2. Paris, 1935.
43823.77.160 Verneuil, Louis. Vive le roi! pts.1-2. Paris, 1936.
43823.77.170 Verneuil, Louis. La femme de ma vie. Paris, 1939.
43823.77.700 Verneuil, Louis. Affairs of state. N.Y., 1952.
43823.77.1100 Vert, Marie Louise. Refoulement. Paris, 1934.
43823.78.100 Verrier, A. Le croisie train de plaisir. Angers, 1913.
43823.78.1100 Véry, Pierre. Série de sept. 7e éd. Paris, 1938.
43823.78.1110 Véry, Pierre. Un grand patron, le guérisseur. Lausanne, 1969.
43823.78.1120 Véry, Pierre. Les anciens de Saint Loup. Lausanne, 1969.
43823.78.1700 Véry, Pierre. In what strange land? London, 1949.
43823.80.100 Verdet, André. Souvenirs du présent. Paris, 1945.
43823.81.100F Vella, Pierre. Maledicte. Paris, 1958.
43823.82.100 Virt, Marie Louise. Le rayon dans l'ombre; poèmes. Calais, 1919?
43823.83.100 Vuillemin, Jules. Le miroir de Venise. Paris, 1965.
43823.98.100 Veyrin, Emile. L'embarquement pour Cythère. Paris, 1904.
43824.1.30 Vilade, J. de. Sur un thème éternel. Paris, 1908.
43824.2.21 Vivien, Renée. Poésies complètes. Paris, 1934. 2v.
43824.2.30 Vivien, Renée. Etudes et préludes. 2e éd. Paris, 1903.
43824.2.35 Vivien, Renée. Poèmes. Paris, 1923.
43824.2.38 Vivien, Renée. Brumes de Fjords. Paris, 1902.
43824.2.41 Vivien, Renée. La dame à la louve. Paris, 1904.
43824.2.43 Vivien, Renée. Du vert au violet. Paris, 1903.
43824.2.46 Vivien, Renée. Évocations. Paris, 1903.
43824.2.48 Vivien, Renée. Le vent des vaisseaux. Paris, 1910.
43824.2.51 Vivien, Renée. Poèmes en prose. Paris, 1909.
43824.2.54 Vivien, Renée. Vagabondages. Paris, 1919?
43824.2.56 Vivien, Renée. Le Christ, Aphrodite et M. Pépin. Paris, 1907.
43824.2.58 Vivien, Renée. Chansons pour mon ombre. Paris, 1907.
43824.3.30 Villeroy, A. La vierge de Lutée (St. Geneviève). Paris, 1915?
43824.3.35 Villeroy, A. Le lion devenu vieux; comédie. Paris, 1918.
43824.3.40 Villeroy, A. La double passion. Paris, 1930.
43824.3.100 Vialar, Paul. L'âge de caison. Paris, 1924.
43824.3.130 Vialar, Paul. Rose of the sea. N.Y., 1940.
43824.3.135 Vialar, Paul. La rose de la mer. Paris, 1940.
43824.3.140 Vialar, Paul. La mort est un commencement. Paris, 1946. 8v.
43824.3.150 Vialar, Paul. Une ombre. Paris, 1946.
43824.3.160 Vialar, Paul. Le bouc étourdi. Paris, 1949.
43824.3.170 Vialar, Paul. L'éperon d'Argent. Paris, 1951.
43824.3.175 Vialar, Paul. The silver spur. London, 1954.
43824.3.180 Vialar, Paul. La chasse aux hommes! Paris, 1952-1953. 10v.
43824.3.190 Vialar, Paul. Belada. Paris, 1957.
43824.3.200 Vialar, Paul. La grande meute. Paris, 1957.
43824.3.210 Vialar, Paul. Le roman des oiseaux de chasse. Paris, 1958.
43824.3.220 Vialar, Paul. Pas de temps pour mourir. Paris, 1958.
43824.3.230 Vialar, Paul. Pas de pitié pour les cobayes. Paris, 1958.
43824.3.240 Vialar, Paul. Clara et les méchants. Paris, 1958.
43824.3.250 Vialar, Paul. Ligne de vie. Paris, 1960.
43824.3.260 Vialar, Paul. La candinière de l'empereur. Paris, 1959.
43824.3.270 Vialar, Paul. Le roman des bêtes de chasse. Paris, 1959.
43824.3.280 Vialar, Paul. Les quatre Zingari. Paris, 1959.
43824.3.290 Vialar, Paul. La cravache d'or, roman. Paris, 1968.
43824.3.1100 Vian, Boris. L'automne à Pékin. Paris, 1956.
43824.3.1110 Vian, Boris. L'arrache-coeur. Paris, 1962.
43824.3.1120 Vian, Boris. Je voudrais pas crever. Paris, 1962.
43824.3.1130 Vian, Boris. Les batisseurs d'empire. Paris, 1959.
43824.3.1140 Vian, Boris. Théâtre. Paris, 1965.
43824.3.1150 Vian, Boris. L'écume des jours. Paris, 1965.
43824.3.1160 Vian, Boris. L'herbe rouge; roman. Paris, 1965.
43824.3.1170 Vian, Boris. Les fourmis. Couverture d'Alain Tercinet. Paris, 1966.
43824.3.1180 Vian, Boris. Le dernier des métiers; saynète pour patronages. Paris, 1966.
43824.3.1190 Vian, Boris. Trouble dans les Andains, roman inédit. Paris, 1966.
43824.3.1200 Vian, Boris. Elles se rendent pas compte. Paris, 1967.
43824.3.1210 Vian, Boris. Et on tuera tous les affreux. Paris, 1965.
43824.3.1220 Vian, Boris. Théâtre inédit: Tête de Méduse. Paris, 1970.
43824.3.1230 Vian, Boris. Le loup-garou, suivi de douze autres nouvelles. Paris, 1970.
43824.3.1240 Vian, Boris. J'irai cracher sur vos tombes. n.p., 196-?
43824.3.1250 Vian, Boris. Textes et chansons. Paris, 1969.
43824.3.1700 Vian, Boris. Froth on the daydream. London, 1967.
43824.3.1705 Vian, Boris. Die Ameisen; sieben Erzählungen. Berlin, 1967.
43824.3.1710 Vian, Boris. The generals' tea party. N.Y., 1967.
43824.3.1715 Vian, Boris. Heartsnatcher. London, 1968.
43824.3.1720 Vian, Boris. The Kuacker's ABC. N.Y., 1968.
43824.3.1800 Noakes, Warren David. Boris Vian. Paris, 1964.

43511 - 43873 Individual authors, etc. - 1900- - Known authors (363 scheme plus 10) - cont.

43824.3.1805 Baudin, Henri. Boris Vian, la poursuite de la vie totale. Paris, 1966.
43824.3.1810 Vree, Freddy de. Boris Vian, essai. Paris, 1965.
43824.3.1815 Rybalka, Michel. Boris Vian, essai d'interprétation et de documentation. Paris, 1969.
43824.3.1821 Armaud, Noël. Les vies paralleles de Boris Vian. Paris, 1970.
43824.3.2100 Vialatte, A. Badonce et les créatures. Uzès, 1937.
43824.3.2110 Vialatte, A. Fruit of the Congo. London, 1954.
43824.4.30 Villetard, P. Les amoureuses. Paris, 1910.
43824.4.36F Villetard, P. Le château sous les roses; roman. v. 1-4. Paris, 1921.
43824.4.40 Villetard, P. Monsieur Bille dans la tourmente. Paris, 1921.
43824.4.43 Villetard, P. M. et Mme. Bille. Paris, 1921?
43824.4.1100 Viat, Denys. Le coeur en bandoulière. Paris, 1970.
43824.5.30 Vindry, F. Dahut. Lyon, 1920.
43824.6.100 Vigée, Claude. Avent. Paris, 1951.
43824.6.110A Vigée, Claude. Aurore souterraine. Paris, 1952.
43824.6.110B Vigée, Claude. Aurore souterraine. Paris, 1952.
43824.6.120 Vigée, Claude. La corne du grand pardon, poème. Paris, 1954.
43824.6.130 Vigée, Claude. L'été indien. 4e éd. Paris, 1957.
43824.6.140 Vigée, Claude. Les articles de la faim. Paris, 1960.
43824.6.150 Vigée, Claude. La lutte avec l'ange. Paris, 1950.
43824.6.160 Vigée, Claude. Révolte et louanges. Paris, 1962.
43824.6.170 Vigée, Claude. Canaan d'exil. Paris, 1962.
43824.6.180 Vigée, Claude. Le poème du retour. Paris, 1962.
43824.6.190 Vigée, Claude. La lune d'hivers; récèt, journal, essai. Paris, 1970.
43824.7.100 Victor, P.E. Poèmes esquimaux. Paris, 1951.
43824.7.105 Victor, P.E. Poèmes eskimo. Paris, 1958.
43824.16.100 Vidal, B. Fleurs de montagne. n.p., 1920?
43824.16.700 Vidal, Nicole. Ring of jade. London, 1966.
43824.16.1100 Vidalie, Albert. The moonlight jewelers. N.Y., 1958.
43824.16.1110 Vidalie, Albert. La bonne ferte; roman. Paris, 1956.
43824.16.1120 Vidalie, Albert. Le pont des arts. Paris, 1961.
43824.16.1130 Vidalie, Albert. Les Hussards de la Sorque. Paris, 1968.
43824.16.2100 Vidal, Nicole. Emmanuel, ou Le livre de l'homme. Paris, 1960.
43824.16.2110 Vidal, Nicole. Emmanuel; a novel. N.Y., 1965.
43824.16.3100 Vidal, Maurice. La vie qui passe. Paris, 1963.
43824.17.100 Viderot, Toussaint. Pour toi, nègre mon frère. Monte-Carlo, 1960.
43824.17.110 Viderot, Toussaint. Courage! Paris, 1957.
43824.24.30 Viel, R. Notre-Dame de la paix; roman. Paris, 1939.
43824.25.702 Vignaud, J. Venus. N.Y., 1930.
43824.25.1100 Vieu, R. La petite énigme. Paris, 1901.
43824.48.100 Vilallonga, José Luis de. L'homme de sang. Paris, 1959.
43824.48.110 Vilallonga, José Luis de. L'homme de plaisir, roman. Paris, 1961.
43824.48.112 Vilallonga, José Luis de. L'homme de plaisir. Paris, 1962.
43824.48.120 Vilallonga, José Luis de. L'heure dangereuse du petitquotin. Paris, 1957.
43824.48.130 Vilallonga, José Luis de. Allegro barbaro. Paris, 1967.
43824.48.140 Vilallonga, José Luis de. Fiesta. Paris, 1971.
43824.48.705 Vilallonga, José Luis de. The man of blood. N.Y., 1960.
43824.48.1100 Vilar, Jean. Le dossier Oppenheimer. Genève, 1965.
43824.48.1800 Roy, Claude. Jean Vilar. Paris, 1968.
43824.49.41 Vildrac, Charles. Pages de journal, 1922-1966. Paris, 1968.
43824.49.100 Vildrac, Charles. Le paquebot Tenacity. 2e éd. Paris, 1920.
43824.49.110 Vildrac, Charles. Madame Béliard. Paris, 1925.
43824.49.113 Vildrac, Charles. Madame Béliard. Paris, 1928.
43824.49.120 Vildrac, Charles. Le pèlerin; pièce en un acte. Paris, 1926.
43824.49.130 Vildrac, Charles. Chants du désespéré, 1914-1920. Paris, 1920.
43824.49.140 Vildrac, Charles. Poèmes de l'abbaye suivis de esquisse d'un pégase. Paris, 1925.
43824.49.150 Vildrac, Charles. Livre d'amour. 12e éd. Paris, 1928.
43824.49.160 Vildrac, Charles. Images et mirages. Paris, 1908.
43824.49.170 Vildrac, Charles. La brouille. Paris, 1930.
43824.49.180 Vildrac, Charles. Michel Auclair. 18e éd. Paris, 1936.
43824.49.190 Vildrac, Charles. L'air du temps. Paris, 1938.
43824.49.200 Vildrac, Charles. Découvertes. 13e éd. Paris, 1931.
43824.49.210 Vildrac, Charles. Poèmes, 1905. Lille, 1906.
43824.49.220 Vildrac, Charles. Théâtre. 8e éd. Paris, 1946. 2v.
43824.49.230 Vildrac, Charles. Lazare. Paris, 1946.
43824.49.240 Vildrac, Charles. Recits. Paris, 1926.
43824.49.250 Vildrac, Charles. D'après l'écko. Paris, 1949.
43824.49.260 Vildrac, Charles. Vitrines. Paris, 1930.
43824.49.700 Vildrac, Charles. A book of love. N.Y., 1923.
43824.50.100 Villars, M. Les deux Madame Carroll. Paris, 1938.
43824.50.1041 Villard-Gilles, Jean. Mon demi-siècle et demi. [Mémoires]. Lausanne, 1970.
43824.50.1100 Villard-Gilles, Jean. La Venoge, et autres poèmes. Lausanne, 1960.
43824.50.2100 Villanti, Paul Joseph Victor. Amour, bonheur et volupté. Nice, 1968.
43824.50.3100 Vilmain, Anne Marie. Terre et ciel. Paris, 1961.
43824.51.100 Villemain, P. Confessions de Numida. Paris, 1957.
43824.51.1100 Villandry, A. La croisière de psyche. Paris, 1958.
43824.51.1110 Villandry, A. Meridien 40. Paris, 1959.
43824.51.1120 Villandry, A. Eros-protée. Paris, 1960.
43824.52.105 Villèle, A. de. Allemand d'Amérique. 3e éd. Paris, 1918.
43824.53.100 Villevieille, J. Le moulin de Bayard. Paris, 1958.
43824.54.21 Vilmorin, Louise de. Poèmes. Paris, 1970.
43824.54.100 Vilmorin, Louise de. Juilletta. London, 1952.
43824.54.105 Vilmorin, Louise de. Madame de. Paris, 1954.
43824.54.110 Vilmorin, Louise de. L'alphabet des aveux. Paris, 1954.
43824.54.115 Vilmorin, Louise de. Les belles amours, roman. Paris, 1954.
43824.54.120 Vilmorin, Louise de. Histoire d'aimer. 11e éd. Paris, 1955.
43824.54.125 Vilmorin, Louise de. La lettre dans un tapi. Paris, 1958.
43824.54.130 Vilmorin, Louise de. Le violon. Paris, 1960.
43824.54.135 Vilmorin, Louise de. L'Heure maliciôse. Paris, 1967.
43824.54.1021 Vimereu, Paul. Tertres et cratères; recueil de nouvelles et extraits de carnets de guerre, 1914-1918. Abbeville, 1970.
43824.58.100 Vinaver, M. Les Coréens. Paris, 1956.
43824.58.1100 Vinçotte, J.H. Le bouguet dans l'incendie. Paris, 1954.

43511 - 43873 Individual authors, etc. - 1900- - Known authors (363 scheme plus 10) - cont.

43824.58.2100 Vinant, Gaby. Poèmes et paradis. Paris, 1957.
43824.58.3100 Vincent, Edouard. Les Mureddu: la vie d'une famille sarde. Grenoble, 1970.
43824.59.100 Vincent, R. Campagne. Paris, 1937.
43824.59.105 Vincent, R. Campagne. 119e éd. Paris, 1938.
43824.59.110 Vincent, R. Blanche. 2e éd. Paris, 1939.
43824.59.120 Vilmorin, L. de. Histoire d'aimer. 11e éd. Paris, 1935.
43824.59.130 Vincent, R. Seigneur. Paris, 1945.
43824.59.2100 Vincent, J. Livre de l'amour. Paris, 1960.
43824.67.100 Vioux, Marcelle. Les amours d'Héloïse et d'Abélard. Paris, 1929.
43824.67.110 Vioux, Marcelle. La nuit en flammes. pt. 1-2. Paris, 1933.
43824.67.120 Vioux, Marcelle. Le désert victorieux. Paris, 1930.
43824.67.130 Vioux, Marcelle. Anne de Boleyn, la favorite-vierge d'Henri VIII. Paris, 1937.
43824.67.140 Vioux, Marcelle. Jeanne d'arc. Paris, 1942.
43824.67.150 Vioux, Marcelle. Une enlisée. Paris, 1920.
43824.84.100 Vitta, Émile. Le lac des pleurs et quelques autres poésies nouyelles. Paris, 1926.
43824.84.110 Vitta, Émile. La promenade franciscaine. Paris, 1927.
43824.84.120 Vitta, Émile. Vere l'étoile. Paris, 1892.
43824.84.800 Fillon, Amélie. L'oeuvre imprimée et inédite d'Émile Vitta. Paris, 1929?
43824.87.100 Vitrac, Roger. Dès-Lyre, poésies complètes. Paris, 1964.
43824.87.800 Béhar, Henri. Roger Vitrac. Paris, 1966.
43824.90.100 Vivan, M. Village noir. Paris, 1937.
43824.90.1100 Vivier, Robert. Le calendrier du distrait. Bruxelles, 1961.
43824.90.1110 Vivier, Robert. À quoi l'on pense. Bruxelles, 1965.
43824.90.1120 Vivier, Robert. Un cri du hasard. Bruxelles, 1966.
43824.90.1130 Vivier, Robert. Chronos rêve. Bruxelles, 1959.
43824.90.1140 Vivier, Robert. Des nuits et des jours. Paris, 1968.
43826.3.100 Vlaminck, Maurice de. Histoires et poèmes de mon époque. Paris, 1927.
43826.3.110 Vlaminck, Maurice de. Tournant dangereux. Paris, 1929.
43826.3.120 Vlaminck, Maurice de. Le garde-fou. Paris, 1958.
43826.3.130 Vlaminck, Maurice de. D'un lit dans l'autre. Monte-Carlo, 1959.
43826.11.100 Vocance, J. Le livre des Haï-Kaï. Paris, 1937.
43827.41.100 Voidies, Jean Pierre. Irène, poèmes. Paris, 1955.
43827.41.1100 Voillemot, Germaine. Les clés de l'adieu; poèmes. Paris, 1957.
43827.41.1110 Voillemot, Germaine. L'oeil solaire, poèmes. Paris, 1959.
43827.50.100 Vollard, Ambroise. Sainte Monique. Paris, 1927.
43827.89.100 Vaudoyer, J.L. La reine évanouie. Paris, 1923.
43827.89.105 Vaudoyer, J.L. Les permissions de Clément Bellin. Paris, 1918.
43827.89.110 Vaudoyer, J.L. Poésies. Paris, 1913.
43827.89.115 Vaudoyer, J.L. Rayons croisés, Léonardesques, Héliade, A. Thamar Karsavina. Paris, 1928.
43827.89.117 Vaudoyer, J.L. Rayons croisés, Léonardesques, Héliade. Paris, 1928.
43827.89.120 Vaudoyer, J.L. Peau d'ange. Paris, 1924.
43827.89.125 Vaudoyer, J.L. Premières amours. Paris, 1928.
43827.89.130 Vaudoyer, J.L. Raymonde Mangematin. Paris, 1925.
43827.89.135 Vaudoyer, J.L. La maitresse et l'amie. Paris, 1924.
43827.89.140 Vaudoyer, J.L. Les papiers de Cléonthe. Paris, 1919.
43827.89.800 Brion, Marcel. Discours de réception de Marcel Brion à l'Académie française et réponse de René Huyghe. Paris, 1965.
43827.91.100 Voisin, Joseph. Fontaine revient. Moulins, 1945.
43827.91.1100 Voronca, Ilarie. Poèmes choisis. Paris, 1967.
43827.92.100 Voëlin, Henri. Les saints innocents. Porrentruy, 1955.
43828.41.100 Vrigny, Roger. Barbegal, récit. Paris, 1958.
43828.41.110 Vrigny, Roger. La nuit de Mougins. Paris, 1963.
43828.41.120 Vrigny, Roger. Fin de journée. Paris, 1968.
43830.39.100 Wahl, J.A. Poèmes. Montréal, 1945.
43830.39.110 Wahl, J.A. Poésie, pensée, perception. Paris, 1948.
43830.48.100 Walder, Francis. Saint-Germain. 2e éd. Paris, 1958.
43830.48.110 Walder, Francis. The negotiators. N.Y., 1959.
43830.48.120 Walder, Francis. Cendre et or. 7e éd. Paris, 1959.
43830.48.130 Walder, Francis. Une lettre de voiture. Paris, 1962.
43832.33.100 Wagner, Paul. Graine d'ortie. Paris, 1971.
43832.51.100 Wallet, Régina. Le sang de la vigne. Paris, 1958.
43832.52.100 Walter, Georges. Les enfants d'Attila. Paris, 1967.
43832.77.100 Warnod, A. Lina de Montparnasse. Paris, 1928.
43833.1.30 Weyl, Fernand. Prière dans la nuit; drame en un acte. Paris, 1915.
43833.1.31 Weyl, Fernand. L'illustration théatrale. Paris, 1910.
43833.1.32 Weyl, Fernand. Joconde; fantaisie en deux actes. Paris, 1910.
43833.1.33 Weyl, Fernand. Au temps d'Adrien. Paris, 1910.
43833.1.35 Weyl, Fernand. La sonate à Kreutzer. Paris, 1924.
43833.1.40 Weyl, Fernand. La vie amoureuse de Ninon de Lanclos. Paris, 1928.
43833.1.45 Weyl, Fernand. La pure courtisane. Paris, 1924.
43833.1.75 Weyl, Fernand. Three gallant plays: A Byzantine afternoon, Beauty and the beast, The slippers of Aphrodite. N.Y., 1929.
43833.7.100 Weker, Jean Paul. L'Orient extrême. Paris, 1960.
43833.13.42 Weck, René de. Souvenirs littéraires. 2e éd. Paris, 1939.
43833.20.20 Weil, Simone. Cahiers. Paris, 1951- 3v.
43833.20.20.2 Weil, Simone. Cahiers. Paris, 1970.
43833.20.100 Weil, Simone. Le pesânteur et la grâce. Paris, 1949.
43833.20.120 Weil, Simone. Venise sauvée. Paris, 1955.
43833.20.120.2 Weil, Simone. Venise sauvée. Paris, 1965.
43833.20.130 Weil, Simone. Ecrits de Londres et dernières lettres. 10e éd. Paris, 1957.
43833.20.140 Weil, Simone. Leçons de philosophie. Paris, 1959.
43833.20.150 Weil, Simone. Sur la science. Paris, 1966.
43833.20.621 Weil, Simone. Selected essays, 1934-1943. London, 1962.
43833.20.700 Weil, Simone. Gravity and grace. N.Y., 1952.
43833.20.705 Weil, Simone. The Iliad. Wallingford, Pa., 1956.
43833.20.710 Weil, Simone. Seventy letters. London, 1965.
43833.20.715 Weil, Simone. Notebooks. London, 1952-55. 2v.
43833.20.720 Weil, Simone. First and last notebooks. N.Y., 1970.
43833.20.800 Davy, M.M. The mysticism of Simone Weil. London, 1951.
43833.20.810 Perrin, J.M. Simone Weil. Paris, 1952.
43833.20.820 Tomin, E.W.F. Simone Weil. Cambridge, Eng., 1954.
43833.20.830 Davy, M.M. Introduction au message de Simone Weil. Paris, 1954.
43833.20.835 Davy, M.M. Simone Weil. Paris, 1956.
43833.20.835.2 Davy, M.M. Simone Weil. Paris, 1961.
43833.20.840 Dugnion-Secretan, Perle. Simone Weil. Neuchâtel, 1954.

43511 - 43873 Individual authors, etc. - 1900- - Known authors (363 scheme plus 10) - cont.

	43833.20.850	Berger, Herman. De gedachtenwereld van Simone Weil. Antwerpen, 1955.
	43833.20.860	Cabaud, Jacques. L'expérience vécue de Simone Weil. Paris, 1957.
	43833.20.865	Sfamurri, Antonio. L'umanesimo cristiano di Simone Weil. L'Aguila, 1970.
	43833.20.870	Perrin, Joseph Marie. Simone Weil as we knew her. London, 1953.
	43833.20.890	Ottensmeyer, Hilary. Le thème de l'amour dans l'oeuvre de Simone Weil. Paris, 1958.
	43833.20.895	Piccard, Eulalie. Simone Weil. Paris, 1960.
	43833.20.900	Hensen, Robert. Simone Weil. Lochem, 1962.
	43833.20.905	Debidour, V.H. Simone Weil, ou La transparence. Paris, 1963.
	43833.20.910	Malan, I.R. L'énracinement de Simone Weil. Paris, 1961.
	43833.20.915	Cabaud, Jacques. Simone Weil. N.Y., 1965.
	43833.20.920	Halda, Bernard. L'évolution spirituelle de Simone Weil. Paris, 1964.
	43833.20.925	Rees, Richard. Simone Weil; a sketch for a portrait. Carbondale, 1966.
	43833.20.930	Heidsieck, François. Simone Weil. Paris, 1965.
	43833.20.940	Cabaud, Jacques. Simone Weil à New York et à Londres, les quinze derniers mois, 1942-1943. Paris, 1967.
	43833.41.100	Weingarten, Romain. Tomalnaut. Paris, 1956.
	43833.41.110	Weingarten, Romain. Le théâtre de la chrysalide. Paris, 1950.
	43833.41.120	Weingarten, Romain. L'été. Paris, 1967.
	43833.41.130	Weingarten, Romain. Poèmes. Paris, 1968.
	43833.41.800	Wohmann, Gabriele. Theater von Innen. Olten, 1966.
	43833.41.1100	Weiss, Louise. La Marseillaise. Paris, 1945-1947. 2v.
	43833.41.3100	Weité, Pierre. L'adieu à l'Afrique. Paris, 1958.
	43833.41.4100	Weiss, Otto G. La route de Berlin. Paris, 1966.
	43833.41.5100	Weideli, Walter. Un banquier sans visage. Lausanne, 1964.
	43833.77.100	Werth, Léon. La maison blanche. Paris, 1913.
	43833.82.100	Westphal, Eric. La Manifestation. Paris, 1967.
	43833.87.50	Wetterlé, Émile. Au service de l'ennemi. Paris, 1917.
	43833.98.100	Weygand, J. Légionnaire. Paris, 1951.
	43833.98.110	Weygand, J. Goumier de l'Atlas. Paris, 1954.
	43833.98.1100	Weyergans, Franz. Mon amour dans l'île. Paris, 1968.
	43833.98.1110	Weyergans, Franz. L'Operation, roman. Paris, 1968.
	43833.98.1120	Weyergans, Franz. On dira, cet hiver; roman. Paris, 1970.
	43835.23.100	Wiehn, P. Vade-mecum du petit homme d'état. Paris, 1952.
	43835.24.100	Wiesel, Eliezer. L'aube; recits. Paris, 1960.
	43835.24.110	Wiesel, Eliezer. Le chant des morts; nouvelles. Paris, 1966.
	43835.24.120	Wiesel, Eliezer. Le jour; roman. Paris, 1961.
	43835.24.130	Wiesel, Eliezer. Zalmen ou la folie de Dieu. Paris, 1968.
	43835.24.140	Wiesel, Eliezer. Le Mendiant de Jérusalem. Paris, 1968.
	43835.24.150	Wiesel, Eliezer. Entre deux soleils. Paris, 1970.
	43835.24.621	Wiesel, Eliezer. Legends of our time. 1st ed. N.Y., 1968.
	43835.24.700	Wiesel, Eliezer. The town beyond the wall. 1e éd. N.Y., 1964.
	43835.24.705	Wiesel, Eliezer. Dawn. N.Y., 1965.
	43835.24.710	Wiesel, Eliezer. The accident. N.Y., 1962.
	43835.24.715	Wiesel, Eliezer. The gates of the forest. 1st ed. N.Y., 1966.
	43835.24.720	Wiesel, Eliezer. A beggar in Jerusalem. N.Y., 1970.
	43835.37.100	Wilhem, Daniel Cerne. Poèmes. Neuchâtel, 1966.
	43835.50.100	Willame, Georges. Sonnets. Namur, 1960.
	43835.50.1100	Williame, Elie. Reflets de la durée. Bruxelles, 1968.
	43835.80.100	Wise, Conrad. Le massacre des innocents. Paris, 1956.
	43835.80.110	Wise, Conrad. La montagne de Zander. Paris? 1957.
	43835.81.100	Wislenet, Paule. Le dépossédé; roman. Paris, 1957.
	43835.87.100	Wittig, Monique. The Opoponax. London, 1966.
	43837.49.100	Wolf, André. Les fleurs de l'exil. Paris, 1958.
	43837.49.1100	Wolff, Philippe. La flippeuse. Paris, 1970.
	43837.50.100	Wolf, Pierre René. A leur mesure. Paris, 1960.
	43837.76.100	Worms, Jeannine. Un magnolia. Paris, 1960.
	43837.77.25	Wurmser, André. Un homme vient au monde. Paris, 1950. 8v.
	43837.77.100	Wurmser, André. L'enfant enchainé. Paris, 1946.
	43837.89.100	Wouters, Liliane. Le Gel. Paris, 1966.
	43840.9.100	Wybot, Roger. Pourquoi Barabbas? Paris, 1965.
	43841.90.100	Xavier, François. Le sexe et l'argent. Paris, 1960.
	43845.13.100	Yacine, Kateb. Nedjma. Paris, 1956.
	43845.13.120	Yacine, Kateb. Le cercle des représailles, théâtre. Paris, 1959.
	43845.13.130	Yacine, Kateb. Le Polygone étoile. Paris, 1966.
	43848.76.100	Yerlès, Pierre. Peintures de craie. Malines, 1954.
	43848.76.705	Yergath, A. The weaver by the Nile. Portland, 1936.
	43852.89.110	Yourcenar, Marguerite. Le coup de grâce. 8e éd. Paris, 1939.
Htn	43852.89.120*	Yourcenar, Marguerite. Mémoires d'Hadrien. Paris, 1951.
	43852.89.125	Yourcenar, Marguerite. La nouvelle Eurydice. Paris, 1931.
	43852.89.130	Yourcenar, Marguerite. Alexis. Paris, 1952.
	43852.89.140	Yourcenar, Marguerite. Électre, ou La chute des masques. Paris, 1954.
	43852.89.150A	Yourcenar, Marguerite. Feux. Paris, 1957.
	43852.89.150B	Yourcenar, Marguerite. Feux. Paris, 1957.
	43852.89.160	Yourcenar, Marguerite. Les charités d'Alcippe. Liège, 1956.
	43852.89.170	Yourcenar, Marguerite. Denier du rêve. Paris, 1959.
	43852.89.180	Yourcenar, Marguerite. Les songes et les sorts. Paris, 1938.
	43852.89.190	Yourcenar, Marguerite. Sous bénéfice d'inventaire. Paris, 1962.
	43852.89.200	Yourcenar, Marguerite. Le mystère d'Alceste. Paris, 1963.
	43852.89.220	Yourcenar, Marguerite. L'oeuvre au noir. Paris, 1968.
	43852.89.700A	Yourcenar, Marguerite. Memoirs of Hadrian. N.Y., 1954.
	43852.89.700B	Yourcenar, Marguerite. Memoirs of Hadrian. N.Y., 1954.
	43852.89.702	Yourcenar, Marguerite. Memories of Hadrian, and reflections on the composition of memories of Hadrian. N.Y., 1963.
	43856.65.100	Yvon, Monique. Les pèlerins du destin, poèmes. Lyon, 1957.
	43856.89.705	Yourcenar, Marguerite. Coup de grâce. N.Y., 1957.
	43858.1.30	Zamacois, Miguel. Redites-nous quelque chose! 4e éd. Paris, 1907.
	43858.1.31	Zamacois, Miguel. Les bouffons. Paris, 1907.
	43858.1.32	Zamacois, Miguel. La fleur merveilleuse. Paris, 1910.
	43858.1.32.5	Zamacois, Miguel. La fleur merveilleuse. Paris, 1910.
	43858.1.33	Zamacois, Miguel. The jesters. N.Y., 1908.
	43858.1.34	Zamacois, Miguel. Monsieur Césarin. Paris, 1919.
	43858.1.35	Zamacois, Miguel. Monsieur Césarin. Paris, 1919.
	43858.1.37	Zamacois, Miguel. Seigneur Pohchinelle. Paris, 1925.
	43858.1.45	Zamacois, Miguel. Suzanne et les deux vieillards. Paris, 1924.
	43858.1.55	Zamacois, Miguel. L'avant-scène D. Paris, 1918.
	43858.1.59	Zamacois, Miguel. L'ineffacable. La grande guerre. Paris, 1916.
	43858.1.62	Zamacois, Miguel. Bohémos. Paris, 1904.
	43858.1.65	Zamacois, Miguel. L'arche de Noé. Paris, 1911.
	43858.90.100	Zavie, Emile. Les beaux soirs de l'Iran. 4e éd. Paris, 1929.
	43858.90.110	Zavie, Émile. Les dieux de la tribu. 4e éd. Paris, 1929.
	43858.90.120	Zavie, Emile. La course aux rebelles. 5e éd. Paris, 1927.
	43861.2.100	Zeraffa, Michel. Les daublures. Paris, 1958.
	43861.2.700	Zeraffa, Michel. The living and the lost. London, 1952.
	43861.39.100	Zehoval-Bandalin, Iada. Tragédie et espoir d'Israël. Bruxelles, 1964.
	43861.77.102	Zermatten, Maurice. Erzählungen aus dem Walliser Hochland. Einsiedeln, 1940.
	43861.77.113	Zermatten, Maurice. Unnützes Herz; Roman. Einsiedeln, 1939.
	43861.77.122	Zermatten, Maurice. La montagne sans étoiles. 2e éd. Paris, 1956.
	43861.77.130	Zermatten, Maurice. Le lierre et le figuier. Bruges? 1957.
	43861.77.140	Zermatten, Maurice. La louve, pièce en 5 actes. Bienne, 1967.
	43861.77.150	Zermatten, Maurice. Visages. Zürich, 1968.
	43863.50.100	Zilkha, Berthie. La voie et les detours; roman. N.Y., 1946.
	43863.54.100	Zimmer, Bernard. Adaptations du théâtre antique. Paris, 1968-1969. 3v.
	43863.54.110	Zimmer, Bernard. Théâtre. Paris, 1968-
	43863.55.100	Zimmermann, J.P. Cantique de notre terre. Neuchatel, 1942.
	43870.43.621	Zuk, Georges. Georges Zuk; selected verse. San Francisco, 1969.

43874 - 43899 Individual authors, etc. - 1900- - Anonymous works (A-Z by title)

	43874.5	Au bruit du canon; contes véridiques, 1916. Paris, 1916.
	43874.99.30	Les âges de la vie. v. 1-3. Paris, 1925-
	43877.5	De la somme à Verdun et sur le front d'Orient. Paris, 1918.
	43877.10	Dunois, D. (pseud.). A lover returns. N.Y., 1931.
X Cg	43877.15	Dunois, D. (pseud.). Suspicion. N.Y., 1933.
	43877.20	Dunois, D. (pseud.). Georgette Garou. Paris, 1928.
	43877.25	Decalandrier ou, De l'autobus Passy-Bourse à la poesie pure. Paris, 1927.
Htn	43878.5*	Eridan. Paris, 1919.
	43880.87.100	Les trois. L'initiation de reine Dermine. Paris, 1925.
	43885.10	La Vrille. Le journal d'une masseuse. Paris, 1923.
	43885.15	Luc-Cyl (pseud.). Le beau chanteur du Boris's bar. Paris, 1926.
	43885.20	Lettres à Lucilia. Paris, 1932.
	43886.5	Magd-Abril (pseud.). Nos voisins de campagne; nouvelle. Paris, 1932.
	43886.10	Monsier Jalabert. Paris, 1922.
	43886.15	Monsieur X et le mensonge. Paris, 1957.
	43889.77	Les propos d'Alain. 3e éd. Paris, 1920. 2v.
	43891.5	Le roman des quatre par Paul Bourget. v.2. Paris, 1926.
	43892.5A	Sous les obus; contes véridiques, 1914-1916. Paris, 1916.
	43892.5B	Sous les obus; contes véridiques, 1914-1916. Paris, 1916.
	43892.7	Saint Mary Magdalen; a drama. Philadelphia, 1900.
	43892.9	Sijenna. Humble Moisson; poésies. Paris, 1903.
	43892.11	Porche, Simone Benda. Le désordre. Paris, 1930.
	43892.11.5	Porche, Simone Benda. Mon nouveau testament. Paris, 1970.
	43892.13	Sainte Seductre; an inner view of the Boche at Bay. N.Y., 1917.
	43893.2	Le tombeau de Michel Abadie. Nevers, 1924.
Htn	43895.5*	Villiot, Jean de (pseud.). Black lust. N.Y., 1931.

FL 355.1 - .699 French drama and stage - Reference works

Htn	FL 355.5*	Maupoint. Bibliothèque des théâtres. Paris, 1733.
Htn	FL 355.7*	Brenner, C.D. A bibliographical list of plays in the French language, 1700-1789. Berkeley, Calif., 1947.
	FL 355.9	Léris, Antoine de. Dictionnaire portatif des théâtres. Paris, 1754.
	FL 355.9.2	Léris, Antoine de. Dictionnaire portatif des théâtres. Paris, 1763.
	FL 355.15	Parfaict, F. Dictionnaire des théâtres de Paris. Paris, 1767. 7v.
	FL 355.19	Bibliothèque du théâtre François depuis son origine. Dresden, 1768. 3v.
Htn	FL 355.19.2*	Bibliothèque du théâtre François depuis son origine. Dresden, 1768. 3v.
	FL 355.24	Clement, J.M.B. Anecdotes dramatiques. Paris, 1775. 3v.
	FL 355.25	Chamfort, Sébastien R.N. Dictionnaire dramatique. Paris, 1776.
	FL 355.30	Babault. Annales dramatiques. Paris, 1808-12. 9v.
	FL 355.33	Reunion des théâtres. n.p., 1817.
	FL 355.34	Pont de Veyle, A. Bibliothèque dramatique de Pont de Veyle. Paris, 1846.
Htn	FL 355.35*	Lacroix, Paul. Bibiothèque dramatique de M. de Soleinne. v.1-6. Paris, 1843-45. 3v.
	FL 355.35.4	Filippi, Joseph de. Essai d'une bibliographique du théâtre. Paris, 1861.
	FL 355.40	Guiraud, P. Index du vocabulaire du théâtre classique. v.1-4. Paris, 1955- 19v.
	FL 355.40F	Guiraud, P. Index du vocabulaire du théâtre classique. v.5-6. Paris, 1955. 2v.
Htn	FL 355.55*	Brunet, Charles. Tables des pièces de théâtre. Paris, 1914.
	FL 355.65	Bethleem, Louis. Les pièces de théâtre. Paris, 1924.
	FL 355.65.2	Bethleem, Louis. Les pièces de théâtre. Paris, 1910.
	FL 355.73	Ferrari, Luigi. Traduzioni italiane del teatro. Paris, 1925.
	FL 355.73.5	Ferrari, Luigi. Traduzioni italiane del teatro tragico francese nei secoli XVII e XVIII. Paris, 1925.
	FL 355.75	Rolland, Joachim. Le théâtre comique en France avant le XVe siècle. Paris, 1926.
	FL 355.90A	Travers, S. Catalogue of nineteenth century French theatrical parodies. N.Y., 1941.
	FL 355.90B	Travers, S. Catalogue of nineteenth century French theatrical parodies. N.Y., 1941.
	FL 355.90.5	Weingarten, J.A. Modern French dramatists. N.Y., 1941.

FL 355.1 - .699 French drama and stage - Reference works - cont.
FL 355.95 Mongrédien, Georges. Dictionnaire biographique des comédiens français du XVIIe siècle. Paris, 1961.

FL 355.700 - .999 French drama and stage - Exhibition catalogues
FL 355.700 Théâtre d'application, Paris. Cultures et acteurs; catalogue de l'exposition. Paris, 1888. 2 pam.
FL 355.705 Paris. Bibliotheque de l'Arsenal. Art and action. Paris, 195-.
FL 355.710 Bouchot, Henri. Catalogue des dessins relatifs à l'histoire du théâtre. Paris, 1896.
FL 355.715 Institut d'études françaises, Saarbruecken. Catalogue de l'exposition. Le théâtre en France au Moyen-Age. Sarrebruck, 1958.

FL 356 - 359 French drama and stage - General histories (By date)
FL 357.35 Beauchamps, P.F. Recherches sur les théâtres de France. Paris, 1735. 3v.
FL 357.45 Parfaict, F. Histoire du théâtre français. Paris, 1745-49. 15v.
FL 358.19 Geoffroy, J.L. Cours de littérature dramatique. Paris, 1819-20. 5v.
FL 358.19.5 Geoffroy, J.L. Cours de littérature dramatique. Paris, 1825. 6v.
FL 358.45 Foucard, Édouard. Histoire du théâtre en France. Paris, 1845.
FL 358.61 Lucas, Hippolyte. Histoire philosophique et littéraire du théâtre français. Paris, 1843.
FL 358.62 Lucas, Hippolyte. Histoire...de théâtre français. Paris, 1862-63. 3v.
FL 358.63.10 Du Casse, Albert. Histoire anecdotique de l'ancien théâtre en France. Paris, 1862-64. 2v.
FL 358.64 Du Casse, Albert. Histoire anecdotique de l'ancien théâtre en France. Paris, 1864. 2v.
FL 358.84A Hawkins, F. Annals of the French stage. London, 1884. 2v.
FL 358.84B Hawkins, F. Annals of the French stage. London, 1884. 2v.
FL 358.85 Parodi, D.A. Le théâtre en France. Paris, 1885.
FL 358.87 Lacroix, Paul. Le théâtre. Mystères. Paris, 1887.
FL 358.89 Petit de Julleville, L. Le théâtre en France. Paris, n.d.
FL 358.92 Brunetière, F. Conférences de l'Odéon. Les époque du théâtre français (1636-1850). Paris, 1892.
FL 358.93FA Bapst, Germain. Essai sur l'histoire du théâtre. Paris, 1893.
FL 358.93FB Bapst, Germain. Essai sur l'histoire du théâtre. Paris, 1893.
FL 359.04 Lintilhac, E. Histoire générale du théâtre en France. Paris, 1904. 5v.
FL 359.10 Guillemot, J. L'évolution de l'idée dramatique. Paris, 1910.
FL 359.32 Levrault, Léon. Le théâtre des origines à nos jours. Paris, 1932.

FL 360.01 - .099 French drama and stage - General special - Pamphlet volumes
FL 360.01 Pamphlet vol. French drama (from 1500 on). 12 pam.

FL 360.1 - .9 French drama and stage - General special - Congresses
FL 360.4 Société des historiens du théâtre. Bulletin. Paris. 1-7,1933-1939 4v.
FL 360.4.10 Société des historiens du théâtre. Travaux. Paris.
FL 360.4.15 Revue à histoire du théâtre. Paris. 1,1948+ 20v.
FL 360.5 De Lapommeraye, H. Conférences...du théâtre Nationale de l'Odéon. Paris, 1889. 14v.
FL 360.9 Gavault, Paul. Conférence de l'Odéon (1915-1916). Paris, 1916.
FL 360.9.2 Gavault, Paul. Conférence de l'Odéon. 2. sér (1916-17). Paris, 1918.
FL 360.9.3 Gavault, Paul. Conférence de l'Odéon. 3. sér (1917-18). Paris, 1919.
FL 360.9.4 Gavault, Paul. Conférence de l'Odéon. 4. sér. (1918-19). Paris, 1920.

FL 360.10 - .999 French drama and stage - General special - Essays, introductions, etc.
FL 360.12 Samson, J.I. L'art théâtral. Paris, 1912.
FL 360.15 Foucher, Paul. Entre cour et jardin. Études de théâtre. Paris, 1867.
FL 360.17 Tisserant, Hippolyte. Plaidoyer pour ma maison. Paris, 1866.
FL 360.19 Foucher, Paul. Les coulisses du passé. Paris, 1873.
FL 360.21 Avril, A. Le théâtre en France depuis le moyen âge jusqu'à nos jours. Paris, 1877.
FL 360.23 Edwards, H.S. Famous first representations. London, 1886.
FL 360.25 Soubies, Albert. Une première par jour. Paris, 1888.
FL 360.26 Fortia de Piles, A.T.J. Quelques réflexions d'un homme du monde. Paris, 1812.
FL 360.28 Lemaitre, Jules. Impressions de théâtre. Sér. 1-11. Paris, 1888-1920. 11v.
FL 360.28.2 Lemaitre, Jules. Impressions de théâtre. Sér. 1,5. Paris, 1888- 2v.
FL 360.28.10 Lemaitre, Jules. Theatrical impressions. London, 1924.
FL 360.30 Larroumet, G. Études d'histoire et de critique dramatique. Paris, 1892.
FL 360.30.2 Larroumet, G. Nouvelle études d'histoire et de critique dramatique. Paris, 1899.
FL 360.30.3 Larroumet, G. Études de critique dramatique. Paris, 1906. 2v.
FL 360.40 Maillet-Duclairon, A. Essai sur la connoissance des théâtres français. Paris, 1751.
FL 360.45 Parigot, H. Génie et Métier. Paris, 1894.
FL 360.50 Dejob, C. Études sur la tragédie. Paris, n.d.
FL 360.52 Poinsot, Edmond A. Le scandale au théâtre. Paris, 1861.
FL 360.55 Faguet, Émile. Drame ancien, drame modern. Paris, 1898.
FL 360.55.5 Faguet, Émile. Drame ancien, drame modern. Paris, 1903.
FL 360.60 Quet, Édouard. La puissance du théâtre en France. Paris, 1900.
FL 360.60.20 Dreyfus, Abraham. Mellan kulisserna. Visby, 1884.
FL 360.65 Bernardin, N.M. Devant le Rideau. Paris, 1901.
FL 360.65.5 Pergameni, H. Le théâtre politique en France depuis 1789. Bruxelles, 1901.
FL 360.72 Veuillot, François. Les prédicateurs de la scène. Paris, 1904.
FL 360.75 Ginisty, P. Choses et gens de théâtre. Paris, 1892.
FL 360.80 Lintilhac, E. Conférences dramatiques. Paris, 1898.
FL 360.85 Florentino, P.A. Comédies et comédiens. Paris, 1866. 2v.

FL 360.10 - .999 French drama and stage - General special - Essays, introductions, etc. - cont.
FL 360.88 Pottecher, Maurice. Le théâtre du peuple. Paris, 1899.
FL 360.90 Rolland, Romain. Le théâtre du peuple. Paris, 1913.
FL 360.90.3 Rolland, Romain. The people's theater. N.Y., 1918.
FL 360.90.4 Rolland, Romain. The people's theatre. London, 1919.
FL 360.91 Brunetiére, F. Les epoques du théâtre français, 1636-1850. Paris, 1892.
FL 360.92 Mortier, Alfred. Dramaturgie de Paris. Paris, 1917.
FL 360.93 Gheon, Henri. L'art du théâtre. Montréal, 1944.
FL 360.93.5 Gheon, Henri. The art of the theatre. N.Y., 1961.
FL 360.95 Copeau, Jacques. Le théâtre populaire. 2. éd. Paris, 1942.
FL 360.97 Duhamel, G. Essai sur une renaissance dramtique. Paris, 1926.
FL 360.98 Kemp, Robert. La vie du théâtre. Paris, 1956.
FL 360.100 Achard, Marcel. Rions avec eux. Paris, 1957.
FL 360.101 Descotes, Maurice. Le public de théâtre et son histoire. Paris, 1964.
FL 360.102 Coppermann, Émile. Le théâtre populaire, pourquoi? Paris, 1965.
FL 360.105 Berrettini, Célia. Teatro francês. São Paulo, 1970.

FL 361 French drama and stage - Biographies of actors, directors, etc. - Collected - General works
FL 361.9 Houssaye, Arsène. Princesses de comédie. Paris, 1860.
FL 361.11 Sorel, Jacques. Les reines de la rampe. Paris, 1863.
FL 361.12 Gaborian, Émile. Les comédiennes adorées. Paris, 1863.
FL 361.15 Rambaud, Y. Photographies à la plume. Paris, 1866.
FL 361.19 Loire, Louis. Anecdotes de théâtre; comédien-comédiennes. Paris, 1875.
FL 361.25 Lyden, E.F.M. de. Le théâtre d'autrefois et d'aujourd'hui. Paris, 1882.
FL 361.29 La Rounat, C. Études dramatiques. Le théâtre français. Paris, 1884.
FL 361.32 Audebrand, P. Petits mémoirs d'une stalle d'orchestre. Paris, 1885.
FL 361.35.2 Regnier, P. Souvenirs et études de théâtre. 2e ed. Paris, 1887.
FL 361.35.3 Regnier, P. Souvenirs et études de théâtre. 3e ed. Paris, 1887.
FL 361.39 Edwards, Henry S. Idols of the French stage. London, 1889. 2v.
FL 361.40 Edwards, Henry S. Idols of the French stage. 2d ed. London, 1889. 2v.
FL 361.42 Prost, J.C.A. Famille d'artistes: les Thénards. Paris, 1900.
FL 361.45 Williams, H. Noel. Queens of the French stage. London, 1905.
FL 361.45.2 Williams, H. Noel. Later queens of the French stage. London, 1906.
FL 361.45.5 Williams, H. Noel. Queens of the French stage. N.Y., 1905.
FL 361.50 Gribble, F. Romances of the French theatre. London, 1912.
FL 361.60 Lacour, Léo. Les premières actrices françaises. Paris, 1921.
FL 361.65 Péricaud, L. Le panthéon des comédiens. Paris, 1922.
FL 361.70 Poizat, Alfred. Les maitres du théâtre, d'Eschyle à Curel. Paris, 1924. 2v.
FL 361.72 Mongrédien, Georges. Les grands comédiens du XVIIe siècle. Paris, 1927.
FL 361.75 Dussane, B. Reines de théâtre, 1633-1941. Montréal, 1945.
FL 361.77 Marquet, Mary. Les impérissables. Paris, 1958.
FL 361.80 Pollitzer, Marcel. Grandes acteurs: leur vie, leurs amours. Paris, 1958.

FL 362 French drama and stage - Special topics - Special forms of drama
FL 362.2 Barthélemy, C. Histoire de la comédie en France. Paris, 1886.
FL 362.4 Failly. Sur l'art du comédien. Paris, 1852.
FL 362.5 Une tradition théâtrale. Paris, 1945.
FL 362.6 Gaiffe, Felix A. Le rire et la scène française. Paris, 1931.
FL 362.10 Levrault, L. Drame et tragédie. (Évolution du Geure). Paris, n.d.
FL 362.12A Lanson, Gustav. Esquisse d'une histoire de la tragédie française. N.Y., 1920.
FL 362.12B Lanson, Gustav. Esquisse d'une histoire de la tragédie française. N.Y., 1920.
FL 362.15A Ginisty, Paul. Le mélodrame. Paris, n.d.
FL 362.15B Ginisty, Paul. Le mélodrame. Paris, n.d.
FL 362.18 Loukoutch, K. La tragédie religieuse classique en France. Thèse. Paris, 1933.
FL 362.20 Souriau, Maurice. De la convention dans la tragedie classique. Paris, 1885.
FL 362.22 Hainleén, G. Die vorromantischen Angriffe in Frankreich auf die klassische Tragödie. Inaug. Diss. Jena, 1933.
FL 362.23 Jördens, W. Die französischen Odipusdramen. Inaug. Diss. Bochum, 1933.
FL 362.23.10 Marignac, A. de. Les imitations françaises de l'Oedipé Roi de Saphocle. Le Caire, 1946?
FL 362.25 Des Granges, C.M. De scenico soliloquio. Thèse. Paris, 1897.
FL 362.30 Møller, P.L. Det nyere lystspil i Frankrig og Danmark. København, 1858.
FL 362.32 Lewicka, Halina. La lanque et le style du théâtre comique. Warszawa, 1960. 2v.
FL 362.35 Sharon d'Obremer, M.A. Les rôles des femmes dans la comédie française de Moliére à Marivoux. Paris, 1941.
FL 362.40 Germain, F. Une tragédie. v.1-2. Paris, 1952?
FL 362.45 Garapon, Robert. La fantasie verbale et le comique dans le théâtre français du moyen âge. Paris, 1957.
FL 362.50 Morel, Jacques. La tragédie. Paris, 1964.

FL 363 French drama and stage - Special topics - Special characters and literary types
FL 363.5A Celler, Ludovic (pseud.). Études dramatiques. Les types populaires. v.1. Paris, 1870-75.
FL 363.5B Celler, Ludovic (pseud.). Études dramatiques. Les types populaires. v.1. Paris, 1870-75.
FL 363.6 Celler, Ludovic (pseud.). Études dramatiques. Les valets. v.2. Paris, 1870-75.
FL 363.7A Celler, Ludovic (pseud.). Études dramatiques. La galanterie. v.3. Paris, 1870-75.
FL 363.7B Celler, Ludovic (pseud.). Études dramatiques. La galanterie. v.3. Paris, 1870-75.
FL 363.10 Rottenbacher, L. Die französischen Virginia. Dramen. Dessau, 1908.

Classified Listing

FL 363 French drama and stage - Special characters and literary types - cont.

FL 363.12 Peirce, W.T. The bourgeois from Molière to Beaumarchais. Columbus, Ohio, 1907.
FL 363.15 Fest, Otto. Der miles gloriosus in der französischen Komödie. Erlangen, 1897.
FL 363.20 Warland, H. Die literargeschichtliche Entwickelung des französischen Harleken. Inaug. Diss. Köln, 1913.
FL 363.25.01 Pamphlet box. Physician in French drama.
FL 363.28 Garçon, Émile. Du crime...avec l'art dramatique. Paris, 1922.
FL 363.30 Wade, Ira O. "Philosophe" in French drama of 18th century. Princeton, 1926.
FL 363.30.5 Wade, Ira O. "Philosophe" in French drama of 18th century. Princeton, N.J., 1926.
FL 363.33 Cherpack, Clifton. The call of blood in French classical tragedy. Baltimore, 1958.
FL 363.35 Thiel, M.A. Figure de Saül. Amsterdam, 1926.
FL 363.38 Calvet, Jean. Les types universéls dans la littérature française. Paris, 1926.
FL 363.39 Calvet, Jean. Les types universéls dans la littérature française. series 1-2. Paris, 1928. 2v.
FL 363.42 Norman, H.L. Swindlers and rouges in French drama. Chicago, 1928.
FL 363.44 Hill, L.A. The Tudors in French drama. Baltimore, 1932.
FL 363.46 Baudin, Maurice. Les bâtards au théâtre en France de la renaissance à la fin du XVIIIe siècle. Baltimore, 1932.
FL 363.48 Dussane, B. (Mme.). Le comédien sans parodoxe. Paris, 1933.
FL 363.50 Tzoneff, Stoyan. L'homme d'argent au théâtre français jusqu'à la révolution. Thèse. Gap, 1934.
FL 363.52 Turcotte, S.J. Les gens d'affaires sur la scène française de 1870 à 1914. Thèse. Paris, 1936.
FL 363.58 Newton, W. Le thème de phèdre et d'Hippolyte dans la littérature française. Thèse. Paris, 1939.
FL 363.60 Bernard, Rene. Le bègue sur la scène française. Paris, 1945.
FL 363.62 Kadler, Eric H. Literary figures in French drama, 1784-1834. The Hague, 1969.

FL 364.1 - .24 French drama and stage - Special topics - Special kinds of theatricals - Court theatricals

FL 364.10 Leveaux, Alphonse. Le théâtre de la cour à Compiegne. Paris, 1882-85.
FL 364.12 Jullien, Adolphe. Histoire du théâtre du Mme. de Pampadour. Paris, 1874.
FL 364.20 Jullien, Adolphe. La comédie à la cour de Louis XVI. Paris, 1875.

FL 364.25 - .49 French drama and stage - Special topics - Special kinds of theatricals - Society theatricals - General works

FL 364.26 Claretie, L. Histoire des théâtres de société. Paris, 1905.

FL 364.50 - .74 French drama and stage - Special topics - Special kinds of theatricals - Society theatricals - Special topics

FL 364.52 Jullien, Adolphe. Le théâtre des Mlles. Verrières. Paris, 1875.
FL 364.55 Taphanel, A. Le théâtre de Saint-Cyril. Versailles, 1886.
FL 364.60 Jullien, Adolphe. Les grandes nuits de Sceaux. Paris, 1876.

FL 364.75 - .99 French drama and stage - Special topics - Special kinds of theatricals - Jesuit theatricals

FL 364.75 Boysse, E. Le théâtre de Jésuites. Paris, 1880.
FL 364.75.5 Richard, P.J. Montaigne comédien et le théâtre des Jésuites. Valence-sur-Rhone, 1947.

FL 364.100 - .124 French drama and stage - Special topics - Special kinds of theatricals - School and college theatricals

FL 364.100 Dorcy, Jean. The mime. 1st ed. N.Y., 1961.
FL 364.105 Tisserand, L.M. Le théâtre au college...dans les écoles. Sens, 1858.

FL 364.125 - .149 French drama and stage - Special topics - Special kinds of theatricals - Street theater

FL 364.125 Ginisty, Paul. Le théâtre de la rue. Paris, 1925.

FL 365.1 - .49 French drama and stage - Special topics - Actors and actresses in relation to the law, the church, etc.

FL 365.5 Deschanel, Émile. La vie des comédiens. Paris, n.d.
FL 365.14 Hénin de Cuvillers, E.F. Des comédiens et du clergé. Paris, 1825.
FL 365.15 Hénin de Cuvillers, E.F. Encore des comédiens et du clergé. Paris, 1825.
FL 365.17 Maugras, Gaston. Les comédiens hors la loi. Paris, 1887.
FL 365.25 Lelion-Damièms, L. Le bréviare des comédiens. Paris, 1883.

FL 365.50 - .99 French drama and stage - Special topics - Foreign influences

FL 365.50 Attinger, Gustave. L'esprit de la commedia dell'arte dans le théâtre français. Paris, 1950.
FL 365.60 Lacroix, Albert. Histoire de l'influence de Shakespeare sur le théâtre français. Bruxelles, 1856.
FL 365.60.5 Wattendorff, L. Essai sur l'influence que Shakespeare a exercée sur la tragédie. Coblenz, 1888.

FL 365.100 - .499 French drama and stage - Special topics - Stage setting and scenery

FL 365.105 Perrin, Émile. Étude sur la mise en scène. Paris, 1883.
FL 365.110 Drugis, N. Le decor de théâtre en France du Moyen Age, à 1925. Paris, 1953.

FL 366.1 - .24 French drama and stage - Special topics - Censorship

FL 366.4 Hallays-Dabot, V. Histoire de la censure théatrals en France. Paris, 1862.
FL 366.6 Hallays-Dabot, V. La censure dramatique et le théâtre. Paris, 1871.
FL 366.8 La censure dramatique. Paris, 1873.
FL 366.9 Chatillon, Louis. Anastasie et sa besace. Paris, 1892.
FL 366.12 Cahuet, Albéric. La liberté en France et a l'etranger. Paris, 1902.

FL 366.25 - .49 French drama and stage - Special topics - Law

FL 366.25 Constant, Charles. Code des théâtres. Paris, 1876.
FL 366.26 Guichard, A. De la législation du théâtre en France. Paris, 1880.
FL 366.28 Charles le Senne, M. Code du théâtre: lois, règlements. Paris, 1882.
FL 366.32 Sauton, Maurice. L'engagement théâtre. Thèse. Paris, 1901.
FL 366.33 Hesse, André. Code pratique du théâtre. Paris, 1903.
FL 366.35 Lailler, Jean. Le contrat de représentation théatrale. Paris, 1913.
FL 366.36 Lang, Jack. L'état et le théâtre. Paris, 1968.
FL 366.38 Grante, Marcel. Protection legale des oeuvre dramatique. Paris, 1925.
FL 366.40 Bechet, H. Les impots sur les spectacles. Thèse. Paris, 1928.

FL 366.50 - .74 French drama and stage - Special topics - Employees

FL 366.57 Bex, Maurice. Contribution à l'histoire du salaire au théâtre en France de 1658. Paris, 1913.
FL 366.60 Oeuvre française de trente ans de théâtre, 1902-1912. Paris, 1903- 2v.

FL 366.75 - .99 French drama and stage - Special topics - Museums

FL 366.77 Pougin, Arthur. Le théâtre à l'exposition universelle de 1889. Paris, 1890.

FL 367 French drama and stage - Special topics - Special themes in drama

FL 367.5 Christout, Marie Françoise. Le merveilleux et le théâtre du silence en France à partie du XVIIe siècle. La Haye, 1965.
FL 367.10 Forkey, Leo O. The role of money in French comedy during the reign of Louis XIV. Baltimore, 1947.
FL 367.15 Eyriès, Eugène. Les idées médicales dans le théâtre contemporain. Montpellier, 1904.

FL 368 French drama and stage - Special topics - Other special topics

FL 368.5 Carmouche, Pierre F.A. Le théâtre en province. Paris, 1859.
FL 368.10 Goizet, J. Histoire anecdotique de la collaboration au théâtre. Paris, 1867.
FL 368.15 Carré, Ambrosius M. L'église s'est-elle réconciliée avec le théâtre? Paris, 1956.
FL 368.20 Thierry, Edouard. De l'influence du théâtre sur la classe ouvrière. Paris, 1862.

FL 370 French drama and stage - History by periods - Before ca. 1500 - General works

FL 370.01 Pamphlet vol. Old French drama up to 1500. 4 pam.
FL 370.5 Baudrais, Jean. Essais...sur l'art dramatique en France. Paris, 1784-86.
FL 370.8 Leroy, Onésime. Epoques de l'histoire de France en rapport avec le théâtre. Paris, 1843.
FL 370.9 Leroy, Onésime. Histoire comparée théâtre et des Moeurs en France. Paris, 1844.
FL 370.15 La Fons, A. Cérémonies dramatiques. Paris, 1850.
FL 370.16 Boutarel, Maurice. "Mires, fisisciens, navrés" dans notre théâtre...XVIe siècle. Thèse. Caen, 1918.
FL 370.35 Milliet, Paul. De l'origine de théâtre à Paris. Paris, 1870.
FL 370.40 Meyer, A.C.T. Origin of...dramatic art in France. Göttingen, 1872.
NEDL FL 370.45 Tivier, H. Histoire de la littérature dramatique en France. Paris, 1873.
FL 370.50 Pifteau, B. Histoire du théâtre en France (1398-1636). Paris, 1879.
FL 370.55 Petit de Julleville, L. Les comédiens en France au Moyen Age. Paris, 1885.
FL 370.57 Petit de Julleville, L. Répertoire du théâtre comique en France au Moyen Age. Paris, 1886.
FL 370.62 Rigal, E. De l'établissement de la tragédie en France. Paris, 1892.
FL 370.65 Clédat, Léon. Le théâtre en France au Moyen Age. Paris, 1896.
FL 370.67 Mortensen, Johan. Profandramat i Frankrike. Lund, n.d.
FL 370.67.10 Mortensen, Johan. Medeltidsdramit i Frankrike. Göteborg, 1899.
FL 370.75 Sepet, Marius. Origines catholiques de théâtre moderne. Paris, 1901.
NEDL FL 370.77 Roy, Émile. Études sur le théâtre français du XIV et du XV siècle. Paris, 1902.
FL 370.79 Jacobsen, J.P. Det komiske dramas. København, 1903.
FL 370.79.5 Jocobsen, J.P. Essai sur les origines de la comédie en France au Moyen-Age. Paris, 1910.
FL 370.80 Mortensen, Johan. Le théâtre français au Moyen Age. Paris, 1903.
FL 370.82 Mignon, N. Études sur le théâtre français et italien de la renaissance. Paris, 1923.
FL 370.84A Cohen, Gustave. Le théâtre en France au Moyen Age. Paris, 1928-31. 2v.
FL 370.84B Cohen, Gustave. Le théâtre en France au Moyen Age. Paris, 1928-31. 2v.
FL 370.84C Cohen, Gustave. Le théâtre en France au Moyen Age. Paris, 1928-31.
FL 370.84.5 Cohen, Gustave. Le théâtre en France au Moyen-Age. Paris, 1948.
FL 370.84.10 Cohen, Gustave. Études d'histoire du théâtre en France au Moyen Âge et à la renaissance. Paris, 1956.
FL 370.86 Frappier, Jean. Le théâtre comique au Moyen Âge. Paris, 1935.
FL 370.90 Wiedenhofen, A. Beiträge zur Entwicklungsgeschichte der Französischen Farce. Münster, 1913.
FL 370.100 Reyval, Albert. L'église et le théâtre. Paris, 1924.
FL 370.102 Fuchs, Max. France des origines à la periode classique. Paris, 1945.
FL 370.104.5 Thiry, Paul. Le théâtre français au Moyen Age. 2. ed. Bruxelles, 1944.
FL 370.106 Frank, Grace. The medieval French drama. Oxford, 1954.
FL 370.106.2 Frank, Grace. The medieval French drama. Oxford, 1967.
FL 370.108 Frappier, Jean. Le théâtre profane en France. Paris, 1961.

FL 371 French drama and stage - History by periods - Before ca. 1500 - Religious drama

FL 371.5 Leroy, Onésime. Études sur les mystères. Paris, 1837.
FL 371.13 Sepet, Marius. Le drame chrétien au Moyen Age. Paris, 1878.
FL 371.15A Petit de Julleville, L. Les mystères (histoire au théâtre en France). v.1-2. Paris, 1880. 2v.
FL 371.15B Petit de Julleville, L. Les mystères (histoire au théâtre en France. v.2. Paris, 1880.
FL 371.15.3 Petit de Julleville, L. La comédie et les moeurs en France. Paris, 1886.
FL 371.27 Bapst, G. Études sur les mystères au Moyen Age. Paris, 1892.
FL 371.40A Carnahan, D.H. The prologue in the old French and Provencal mystery. New Haven, 1905.
FL 371.40B Carnahan, D.H. The prologue in the old French and Provencal mystery. New Haven, 1905.
FL 371.41 Heinze, Paul. Die Engel auf der mittelalterlichen Mysterienbühne Frankreichs. Inaug. Diss. Griefswald, 1905.
FL 371.58 Petzold, H. Das französische Jesus Christus-Drama nach dem Verfall der mittelalterlichen Misterienspile, 1539-1936. Inaug. Diss. Dresden, 1937.
FL 371.60 Axelson, Angelica. Supernatural beings in the French medieval dramas...miracles of the Virgin. Copenhagen, 1923.
FL 371.70 Jeanroy, A. Le théâtre religieux en France du XIe au XIIe siècles. Paris, 1924.
FL 371.73 Wright, E.A. The dissemination of the liturgical drama in France. Bryn Mawr, Pa., 1936.
FL 371.75 Cohen, Gustave. Le livre de conduite du régisseur. Strasbourg, 1925.
FL 371.75.2 Cohen, Gustave. Le livre de conduite du régisseur. Paris, 1925.
FL 371.77 Lebègue, Raymond. La tragédie religieuse en France; les debuts, 1514-1573. Paris, 1929.
FL 371.77.5 Lebègue, Raymond. La tragédie religieuse en France; les debuts, 1514-1573. Thèse. Paris, 1929.
FL 371.79A Wright, J.G. A study of the themes of the resurrection in the mediaeval French drama. Bryn Mawr, 1935.
FL 371.79B Wright, J.G. A study of the themes of the resurrection in the media eval French drama. Bryn Mawr, 1935.
FL 371.80 Goodman, H.P. Original elements in the French and German Passion plays. Thesis. Bryn Mawr, Pa., 1951.
FL 371.82 McKean, Mary F. The interplay of realistic and flamboyant art elements in the French mystères. Washington, 1959.

FL 372.1 - .26 French drama and stage - History by periods - Before ca. 1500 - Local (A-Z by place)

FL 372.3 Jalibois, E. La diablerie de Chaumont. Chaumont, 1838.
FL 372.13 Piolin, D. Paul. Recherches sur les mystères dans le Maine. Angers, 1853.
FL 372.13.5 Piolin, D. Paul. Le théatre Chrétien dans le Maine. Mamers, 1891.
FL 372.16 Schäfer, Johannes. Das Pariser Reformationsspiel...1524. Inaug. Diss. Halle, 1917.
FL 372.18 Gosselin, E. Recherches sur les origines et l'histoire du théâtre à Rouen avant P. Corneille. Rouen, 1868.
FL 372.18.5 Young, Carl. Contributions to the history of liturgical drama at Rouen. Chicago, 1908.
NEDL FL 372.18.9 Gasté, Armand. Les drames liturgiques de la Cathédrale de Rouen. Evreux, 1893.
FL 372.19 Pas, Justine de. Mystères et jeux scéniques à St. Omer. Lille, 1913.
FL 372.22F Konigson, Elie. La représentation d'un mystère de la passion à Valenciennes en 1547. Paris, 1969.

FL 373 French drama and stage - History by periods - Before ca. 1500 - Stage setting and scenery

FL 373.5 Morice, Émile. Histoire de la mise en scène. Paris, 1836.
FL 373.5.2 Morice, Émile. Essai sur la mise en scène. Paris, 1836.
FL 373.6 Cohen, Gustave. Histoire de la mise en scène dans le théâtre religieux français du Moyen Age. Paris, 1906.
NEDL FL 373.6.5 Cohen, Gustave. Histoire de la mise en scène dans le théâtre religieux français du Moyen Age. Paris, 1926.
FL 373.6.6 Cohen, Gustave. Histoire de la mise en scène dans le théâtre religieux français du Moyen Age. Paris, 1951.
FL 373.6.10 Cohen, Gustave. Geschichte der Inszenierung im geistlichen Schauspiele des Mittelalters in Frankreich. Leipzig, 1907.
FL 373.9 Stuart, D.C. Stage decoration in France in the Middle Ages. N.Y., 1910.
FL 373.10 Cohen, Gustave. L'évolution de la mise en scène dans le théâtre français. Lille, 1910.

FL 374 French drama and stage - History by periods - Before ca. 1500 - Other special topics

FL 374.5 Witkowski, Gustave Joseph. Les médecins au théâtre. Paris, 1905.
FL 374.6 Boutarel, M. La médecine dans notre théâtre comique. Caen, 1918.
FL 374.7 Sletsjoee, Leif. Franske profane middelalderspill. Oslo, 1964.
FL 374.9 Fabre, A. Les clercs du palais. 2e ed. Lyon, 1875.
FL 374.10 Harvey, H.G. The theatre of the Basoche. Cambridge, 1941.
FL 374.11 Brown, Howard. Music in the French secular theater, 1400-1550. Cambridge, 1963.
FL 374.12 Brown, Howard. Theatrical chansons of the fifteenth and early sixteenth centuries. Cambridge, 1963.
FL 374.14 Bowen, B.C. Les caractéristiques essentielles de la farce française. Urbana, 1964.
FL 374.15 Hermann, Tage. Den latinske tradition i det førklassiske franske drama. København, 1941.

FL 375 French drama and stage - History by periods - 16th century

FL 375.5 Ebert, A. Entwicklungs-Geschichte des Französischen Tragödien im 16 Jahrhunderts. Gotha, 1856.
FL 375.12 Chasles, Emile. La comédie en France au seizième siècle. Paris, 1862.
FL 375.20 Cougny, M.E. Des représentations dramatiques. n.p., n.d.
NEDL FL 375.35 Faguet, Émile. La tragédie française au XVI siècle. Paris, 1883.
FL 375.50 Klein, Friedrich. Das Chor in den wichtigsten Tragödien der Französischen Renaissance. Leipzig, 1897.
FL 375.55 Böhm, Karl. Beiträge zur Kenntnis des Einflusses Seneca's...Französischen Tragödien. Erlangen, 1902.
FL 375.56 Roemer, Matthaus. Der Aberglaube bei den Dramatikern des 16. Jahrhunderts. München, 1903.
FL 375.57 Holl, Fritz. Das politische Tendenzdrama des 16 Jahrhunderts in Frankreich. Erlangen, 1903.

FL 375 French drama and stage - History by periods - 16th century - cont.

FL 375.65 Kohler, E. Entwicklung des Biblischen Dramas des XVI Jahrhunderts. Leipzig, 1911.
Htn FL 375.70* Chamard, H. La tragédie de la renaissance. Paris, 1929-30.
FL 375.75 Jonker, G.D. Le protestantisme et le théâtre de langue française au XVIe siècle. Groningen, 1939.
FL 375.80 Lawton, H. Handbook of French Renaissance dramatic theory. Manchester, Eng., 1949.
FL 375.83 Lebègue, Raymond. La tragédie française de la renaissance. Bruxelles, 1944.
FL 375.83.2 Lebègue, Raymond. La tragédie française de la renaissance. 2. éd. Bruxelles, 1954.
FL 375.84 Dabney, Lancaster Eugene. French dramatic literature in the reign of Henri IV. Austin, Texas, 1952.
FL 375.85 Veil, Irene. Einige Personen der französischen Renaissancekomödie. Köln? 1965?

FL 376 French drama and stage - History by periods - 16th and 17th centuries together

FL 376.8 Sakharoff, Micheline. Le héros, sa liberté et son efficacité. Paris, 1967.
FL 376.9 Meier, Konrad. Über die Didotragödien des Jodelle. Zwiçkau, 1891.
FL 376.11 Picot, Émile. Le monologue dramatique dans l'ancien théâtre français. Paris, 1886-88.
FL 376.11.1 Picot, Émile. Le monologue dramatique dans l'ancien théâtre français. Genève, 1970.
FL 376.13 Wiley, William. The early public theatre in France. Cambridge, 1960.
FL 376.15.1 Rigal, Eugène. Le théâtre français avant la période classique. Genève, 1969.
FL 376.18 Reuter, Otto. Der Chor in den Französischen Tragödie. Berlin, 1904.
FL 376.19 Marsan, Jules. La pastorale dramatique en France. Paris, 1905.
FL 376.20 Schaberth, F.W. Das komische Element in der französischen Tragikomödies. Inaug. Diss. Nürnberg, 1930.
FL 376.21 Lancaster, H.C. The French tragi-comedy. Baltimore, 1907.
FL 376.22 Friedrich, Ernst. Die Magie im Französischen Theater 16. und 17. Jahrhunderts. Leipzig, 1908.
FL 376.25 Rigal, E. De Jodelle à Molière. Tragédie. Paris, 1911.
FL 376.26 Loukovitch, Kosta. L'évolution de la tragédie religieuse classique en France. Paris, 1933.
FL 376.28 Roaten, Darnell. Structural forms in the French theater, 1500-1700. Philadelphia, 1960.
FL 376.30 Dietschy, Charlotte. Die "dame d'intrigue". Inaug. Diss. Basel, 1916.
FL 376.32 Forsyth, E. La tragédie française Jodelle à Corneille. Paris, 1962.
FL 376.34 Jeffery, Brian. French Renaissance comedy, 1552-1630. Oxford, 1969.
FL 376.35 Huether, Jochen. Die monarchische Ideologie in den Französischen Römerdramen des 16. und 17. Jahrhunderts. München, 1966.

FL 377 French drama and stage - History by periods - 17th century

FL 377.5 Rambert, Eugene. Corneille, Racine et Molière. Lausanne, 1861.
FL 377.6 Levertin, Oscar. Studier ofver fars och farsörer i frankrike. Upsala, 1888.
FL 377.7 Fournier, Édouard. L'Espagne et ses comédiens en France. Paris, 1864.
FL 377.9 Leclercq, L. Les décors, les costumes et la mise en scène. Paris, 1869.
FL 377.15 Despois, Eugene. Théâtre français sous Louis XIV. Paris, 1874.
FL 377.16 Chappuzeau, S. Le théâtre français. Paris, 1875.
FL 377.17 Chardon, Henri. La troupe du Roman comique Devoilée. Le Mans, 1876.
FL 377.27 Degenhardt, E. Die Metaphor bei den Vorläufern Molière's, 1612-1654. Marburg, 1886.
FL 377.28 Mennechet, E. Théâtre français classique. N.Y., 1887.
FL 377.31 Kenne, C.H. Formulas in the language of the French poet-dramatists of the 17th century. Boston, 1891.
FL 377.33 Fournel, Victor. Le théâtre au XVIIe siècle. Paris, 1892.
FL 377.37 Maatz, Anton. Der Einfluss des heroisch-galanten Romans. Rostock, 1896.
FL 377.41A Martinenche, E. La comédie espagnole en France de Hardy à Racine. Paris, 1900.
FL 377.41B Martinenche, E. La comédie espagnole en France de Hardy à Racine. Paris, 1900.
FL 377.43 Kingler, O. Die Comédie-Italienne in Paris nach der Sammlung von Gherardi. Strassburg, 1902.
FL 377.44 Schwartz, I.A. The commedia dell'arte and its influence on French comedy in the seventeenth century. Paris, 1933.
FL 377.46 Reiss, T.J. Toward dramatic illusion; theatrical technique and meaning from Hardy to Horace. New Haven, 1971.
FL 377.53 Feichtinger, W.M. Die Rolle des Vertrauten in der klassischen Tragödie der Franzözen. Wien, 1912.
FL 377.54A Jourdain, E.F. An introduction to the French classical drama. Oxford, 1912.
FL 377.54B Jourdain, E.F. An introduction to the French classical drama. Oxford, 1912.
FL 377.56 Bernardin, N.M. Les chefs du choeur: Corneille, Molière, Racine, Boileau. Paris, 1914.
FL 377.57 Mongrédien, Georges. La vie quotidienne des comédiens au temps de Molière. Paris, 1966.
FL 377.57.1 Mongrédien, Georges. Daily life in the French theatre at the time of Molière. London, 1969.
FL 377.70 Mersmann, A. Das "Schauspiel im Schauspiel" im französischen Drama des XVII Jahrhunderts. Münster, 1925.
FL 377.75A Lancaster, H.C. History of French dramatic literature in 17th century. v.1-5. Baltimore, 1929-32. 9v.
FL 377.75B Lancaster, H.C. History of French dramatic literature in 17th century. v.4. Baltimore, 1929-32. 2v.
FL 377.75.10 Lancaster, H.C. Sunset, a history of Parisian drama in the last years of Louis XIV, 1701-1715. Baltimore, 1945.
FL 377.78 Pascol, M.E. Les drames religieux du milieu du XVIIe siècle. No. 36-1650. Paris, 1932.
FL 377.79 Macchila, G. La scuola dei sentimenti. Caltanissetta, 1963.
FL 377.80 Deierkauf-Holsboer, Sophie Wilma. L'histoire de la mise en scène dans le théâtre français de 1600 à 1657. Thèse. Paris, 1933.
FL 377.80.5 Deierkauf-Holsboer, Sophie Wilma. L'histoire de la mise en scène dans le théâtre français de 1600 à 1657. Thèse. Paris, 1933.

Classified Listing

FL 377 French drama and stage - History by periods - 17th century - cont.

FL 377.82 Pascoe, M.E. Les drames religieux du milieu du XVIIe siècle 1636-1650. Paris, 1932.
FL 377.83 Geisler, K. Das Nachwirken des Mimus in der satirischen und burlesken Literatur Frankreichs in 17. Jahrhunderts. Inaug. Diss. Würzburg, 1935.
FL 377.84 Turnell, Martin. The classical moment. London, 1947.
FL 377.85 Auerbach, E. Das französische Publikum des 17. Jahrhunderts. München, 1933.
FL 377.86 Schérer, Jacques. La dramaturgie classique en France. Paris, 1950.
FL 377.86.5 Schérer, Jacques. La dramaturgie classique en France. Paris, 1950?
FL 377.90 Deierkauf-Holsboer, Sophie Wilma. L'histoire de la mise en scène dans le théâtre français à Paris de 1600 à 1673. Paris, 1960.
FL 377.95 Moore, Will Grayburn. The classical drama of France. London, 1971.
Htn FL 377.139* Scudery, G. L'apologie du théâtre. Paris, 1639.
Htn FL 377.145* Torelli, G. Explication des decorations du théâtre. Paris, 1645.
FL 377.150 Vedier, Georges. Origine et évolution de la dramaturgie néo-classique. 1. ed. Paris, 1955.
FL 377.174 Le théâtre français divisé en trois livres. Lyon, 1674.
FL 377.180 Lawrenson, T.E. The French stage in the XVIIth century. Manchester, Eng., 1957.
FL 377.182 Lockert, Lacy. Studies in French-classical tragedy. Nashville, 1958.
FL 377.185F Mélèse, Pierre. Le théâtre en France au XVIIe siècle. Paris, 1957.
FL 377.188 Chevalley, Sylvie Bostsarron. Album théâtre classique. Paris, 1970.

FL 378 French drama and stage - History by periods - 17th and 18th centuries together

FL 378.5 Fleischhammer, Alfred. Der Provinziale in der FranzösischenKomödie von 1650 bis 1750. Halle, 1909.
FL 378.10 Dollfus, Paul. Reines de théâtre. Paris, 1914.
FL 378.15 Poctevin, A. Le théâtre de la foire. Paris, 1889.
FL 378.20 Bonnassies, J. Les auteurs dramatiques et les théâtres de province aux XVIIe et XVIIIe siècles. Paris, 1875.
FL 378.22 Borgerhoff, E.B.O. The evolution of liberal theory and practice in the French theater, 1680-1757. Diss. Princeton, 1936.

FL 379 French drama and stage - History by periods - 18th century - General works

Htn FL 379.5* Les souvenirs et les regrets du vieil amateur dramatique. Paris, 1829.
FL 379.10 Mémoires de Mlle Clairon, de Lekain, de Préville, de Dazincourt. Paris, 1846.
FL 379.15 Jullien, Adolphe. Les spectateurs sur le théâtre. Paris, 1875.
FL 379.17A Jullien, Adolphe. La comédie et la galanterie. Paris, 1879.
FL 379.17B Jullien, Adolphe. La comédie et la galanterie. Paris, 1879.
FL 379.18 Fontaine, Léon. Le théâtre et la philosophie au 18e siècle. Paris, 1879.
FL 379.25 Jullien, Adolphe. La comédie à la cour. Paris, n.d.
FL 379.30 Lenient, C. La comédie en France au XVIIIe siècle. Paris, 1888. 2v.
FL 379.30.3 Lanson, G. La comédie au XVIIIe siècle. Paris, 1889.
X Cg FL 379.31 Hawkins, F. The French stage in the 18th century. Photoreproduction. London, 1888. 2v.
Htn FL 379.34* Beyier, Agne. Recueil de plusieurs fragments des premières comédies italiennes. Paris, 1928.
FL 379.41 Dejob, C. Les femmes dans la comédie française et italienne au XVIIIe siècle. Paris, 1899.
FL 379.45 Ginisty, Paul. Mémoires et souvenirs de comédiennes, XVIIIe siècle. Paris, 1914.
X Cg FL 379.51 Capon, Gaston. Les théâtres clandestins. Paris, 1905.
FL 379.52 Alméras, Henri d'. Les théâtres libertins au XVIIIe siècle. Paris, 1905.
FL 379.57 Gaiffe, F. Étude sur le drame en France au XVIIIe siècle. Paris, 1910.
FL 379.65A Kurz, Harry. European characters in French drama. N.Y., 1916.
FL 379.65B Kurz, Harry. European characters in French drama. N.Y., 1916.
FL 379.70 Joudoin, Eleanor Frances. Dramatic theory and practice in France, 1690-1808. N.Y., 1968.
FL 379.75 Ivanov, I.I. Politicheskaia rol' frantsuzskago teatra. Moskva, 1895.
FL 379.82 Grohmann, W. Die pronominalen Anredeformen in Drama des 18. Jahrhunderts. Inaug. Diss. Leipzig, 1926.
FL 379.86 Brenner, Clarence D. L'histoire nationale dans la tragédie française du XVIIIe siècle. Berkeley, Calif., 1929.
FL 379.88 Grannis, V.B. Dramatic parody in eighteenth century France. N.Y., 1931.
FL 379.90 Fredrick, E.C. The plot and its construction in 18th century criticism of French comedy. Diss. Bryn Mawr, 1934.
FL 379.92.15 Fuchs, Max. La vie théâtrale en province au XVIIIe siècle. Paris, 1933-
FL 379.92.20 Fuchs, Max. Lexique des troupes de comédiens au XVIIIe siècle. Paris, 1944.
FL 379.94 Moore, A.P. The Genre Paissard and the French stage of the eighteenth century. N.Y., 1935.
FL 379.97 Petersen, C.E. The doctor in French drama, 1700-1775. N.Y., 1938.
FL 379.139 Scuderi, Georges de. L'apologie du théâtre. Paris, 1639.
Htn FL 379.151* Gaultier, J.B. Critique de ballet moral. n.p., 1751.
Htn FL 379.152* Monhy, C. de F. Tablettes dramatiques contenant l'abrégé de l'histoire du théâtre français. Paris, 1752.
FL 379.162 Vernon. Apologie du théâtre adressée à Mlle. Cl... La Haye, 1762.
FL 379.164 Les baladins. Amsterdam, 1764.
FL 379.168 Causes de la Décadence du gout sur de théâtre. Amsterdam, 1768.
Htn FL 379.170* Restif de la Bretonne. La mimographe. Amsterdam, 1770.
FL 379.174 Desprez de Boissy, Charles. Lettres sur les spectacles. 5e éd. Paris, 1774. 2v.
FL 379.179 Desprez de Boissy, Charles. Lettres sur les spectacles. 7e éd. Paris, 1779. 2v.
FL 379.189 Parises, N.P. Questions importantes sur la comédie de nos jours. Valenciennes, 1789.
FL 379.191 Gaiffe, Félix. Le drame en France au XVIIIe siècle. Paris, 1971.

FL 379 French drama and stage - History by periods - 18th century - General works - cont.

FL 379.250 Lancaster, H.C. French tragedy in the time of Louis XV and Voltaire. Baltimore, 1950.
FL 379.253 Lancaster, H.C. French tragedy in the reign of Louis XVI and the early years of the French revolution. Baltimore, 1953.

FL 380 French drama and stage - History by periods - 18th century - Revolutionary period

FL 380.3 Sur l'état actuel du théâtre de la republique. Paris, n.d.
FL 380.4 Lamarque, F. Opinion sur les théâtres. Paris, 1798.
FL 380.5 Jauffret, Eugène. Le théâtre révolutionnaire. Paris, 1869.
FL 380.9 La Combe, René de. Les hommes et les oeuvres du théâtre révolutionnaire. Paris, 1882.
FL 380.10 Welschinger, Henri. Le théâtre de la révolutionnaire. Paris, 1880.
Htn FL 380.12* Lumiere, Henry. Le théâtre français pendant la révolution. Paris, 1894.
FL 380.15 Lunel, E. Le théâtre et la révolution. Paris, 1909.
FL 380.20 Duchosal, Marie E.G. Journal des théâtres et des fêtes nationales. Paris. 1795
FL 380.30 Hérissay, Jacques. Le monde des théâtres pendant la révolution, 1789-1800. Paris, 1922.
FL 380.40 Quentin, Henri. Le théâtre sous la terreur (théâtre de la peur), 1793-1794. Paris, 1913.
Htn FL 380.45* Lemazurier, P.D. L'opinion du parterre. Paris, 1803.
FL 380.50 Rivoire, J.A. Le patriotisme dans le théâtre serieux de la révolution (1789-1799). Thèse. Paris, 1950.

FL 381 French drama and stage - History by periods - 18th and 19th centuries together

FL 381.3 Ruphy, J.F. Lettres champenoises. Paris, 1809.
FL 381.5 Formentin, C. Essai sur les origines du drame moderne en France. Paris, 1879.
FL 381.10 Huszar, G. L'influence de l'Espagne sur le théâtre. Photoreproduction. Paris, 1912.
FL 381.15 Melcher, Edith. Stage realism in France between Diderot and Antoine. Diss. Bryn Mawr, 1928.
FL 381.17 Kromsigt, A.L.C. Le théâtre biblique à la veille du romantisme (1789-1830). Zutphen, 1931.
FL 381.19 Reizov, B.G. Mezhdu klassitsizmom i romantizmom. Leningrad, 1962.
FL 381.20 Schaefer, Rotraut. Das eindringen schlichter Sprache in das französische Alexandrenerdrama, 1740-1840. Göppingen, 1969.

FL 382 French drama and stage - History by periods - 19th century - General works

FL 382.3 Marteau, Édouard. De la decadence de l'art dramatique. Paris, 1849.
FL 382.5 Gautier, T. Histoire de l'art dramatique en France depuis vingt-cinq ans. Paris, 1858-59. 6v.
FL 382.5.2 Gautier, T. Histoire de l'art dramatique en France depuis vingt-cinq ans. Bruxelles, 1858-59. 6v.
FL 382.10 Wismewski, Jules. Études sur les poetes dramatiques. Paris, 1861.
FL 382.15A Muret, Théodore C. L'histoire par le théâtre. Paris, 1865. 3v.
FL 382.15B Muret, Théodore C. L'histoire par le théâtre. Paris, 1865. 3v.
FL 382.22 Monval, Georges. Les théâtres subventionnes. Paris, 1879.
FL 382.24.10 Matthews, J.B. French dramatists of the 19th century. 2. ed. London, 1882.
FL 382.24.15 Matthews, J.B. French dramatists of the 19th century. N.Y., 1891.
FL 382.24.20 Matthews, J.B. French dramatists of the 19th century. 5. ed. N.Y., 1919.
FL 382.27 Leveaux, Alphonse. Nos théâtres de 1800 à 1880. Pari, 1881-86.
FL 382.30 Bonnassies, J. Le théâtre et le peuple. Paris, 1872.
FL 382.32.4 Mirbeau, Octave. Le comédien. 4e ed. Paris, 1883.
FL 382.32.7 Mirbeau, Octave. Le comédien. 7e ed. Paris, 1883.
FL 382.35 Lenient, C. La comédie en France au XIX siècle. Paris, 1898. 2v.
FL 382.37 L'Homme, François. Études sur le théâtre contemporain. Paris, 1887.
FL 382.40 Lecomte, Louis H. Napoléon et l'empire racontés par le théâtre. Paris, 1900.
FL 382.42 Lencon, Hippolyte. Le théâtre nouveau. Paris, 1896.
FL 382.45 Weiss, Jean Jacques. Le théâtre et les moeurs. 3. ed. Paris, 1889.
FL 382.47 Huret, Jules. Loges et coulisses. Paris, 1901.
FL 382.50 Granges, C.M. La comédie et les moeurs, 1815-1848. Paris, 1904.
FL 382.52 Méré, Charles. La tragédie contemporaine. Paris, 1905.
FL 382.53 Kahn, Armand. Le théâtre social en France de 1870 à nos jours. Paris, 1907.
FL 382.55 Benoist, Antoine. Essais de critique dramatique. Paris, 1898.
FL 382.57 Doumic, René. De scribe à Ibsen. Paris, 1893.
FL 382.57.3 Doumic, René. De scribe à Ibsen. Paris, 1913.
FL 382.57.10 Doumic, René. Essais sur le théâtre contemporain. Paris, 1897.
FL 382.57.15 Doumic, René. Le théâtre nouveau. Paris, 1908.
FL 382.65A Filon, Augustin. De Dumas à Rostand. Paris, 1898.
FL 382.65B Filon, Augustin. De Dumas à Rostand. Paris, 1898.
FL 382.65.3 Filon, Augustin. The modern French drama. London, 1898.
FL 382.70 Trotain, M. Les scènes historiques; étude du théâtre livresque à la veille du drame romantique. Thèse. Paris, 1923.
FL 382.70.5 Trotain, M. Les scènes historiques; étude du théâtre livresque à la veille du drame romantique. Thèse. Paris, 1923.
FL 382.75 Saint-Auban, Émile de. L'idée sociale au théâtre. Paris, 1901.
FL 382.77 Sarcey, Françisque. Quarante ans de théâtre. Paris, 1900-1902. 8v.
Htn FL 382.80* Ginisty, Paul. France d'antan: le théâtre romantique. Paris, 1922.
FL 382.82 Draper, F.W.M. Rise and fall of the French romantic drama. London, 1923.
FL 382.83 Sächer, H. Die Melodramatik und das romantische Drama in Frankreich. Inaug. Diss. Borna, 1936.
FL 382.84A Allard, Louis. La comédie de moeurs en France au XIXe siècle. Cambridge, Mass., 1923.

FL 382 French drama and stage - History by periods - 19th century - General works - cont.

FL 382.84B Allard, Louis. La comédie de moeurs en France au XIXe siècle. Cambridge, Mass., 1923.
FL 382.84C Allard, Louis. La comédie de moeurs en France au XIXe siècle. Cambridge, Mass., 1923.
FL 382.84.5 Allard, Louis. La comédie de moeurs en France au XiXe siècle. v.2. Paris, 1933.
FL 382.86 Smith, Hugh Allison. Main currents of modern French drama. N.Y., 1925.
FL 382.88 Evans, David O. Le drame moderne à l'époque romantique. Paris, 1923.
FL 382.90 Delvau, A. Le théâtre érotique français sous le bas-empire. Paris, 1883.
FL 382.92 Parigot, Hippolyte. Le théâtre d'hier. Paris, 1893.
FL 382.94 Dumas, Alexandre. Souvenirs dramatiques. Paris, 188-. 2v.
FL 382.95 Gottschall, R. vón. Teater och drama under andra kejsardömet. Stockholm, 1869.
FL 382.97 Aderer, Adolph. Hommes et chosis de théâtre. Paris, 1905.
FL 382.100 Clement-Janin, N. Drames et comédies romantiques. Paris, 1928.
FL 382.110 Giesse, Hermann. Die Engländer in der französischen Komödie des 19. Jahrhunderts. Diss. n.p., 1928.
FL 382.115 Wiener, Francis. La vie parisienne au théâtre. 14e éd. Paris, 1929.
FL 382.160 Cecchi, A. Il teatro francese. Milano, 1935.

FL 383 French drama and stage - History by periods - 19th century - Special periods

Htn FL 383.00.2* Pamphlet vol. Henriette Bleville. Paris, 1798. 2 pam.
FL 383.07 Cailhava d'Estendoux, Jean François. Les causes de la décadence du théâtre. Paris, 1807.
FL 383.12 Granges, C.M. de. Geoffroy et la critique dramatique 1800-1814. Paris, 1897.
FL 383.12.10 Molènes, Gaschon de. La critique sous l'empire. Paris, 1841.
FL 383.15 Borgekhoff, J.L. Théâtre anglais à Paris sous le restauration. Paris, n.d.
FL 383.16 Evans, D.O. Les problèmes d'actualité au théâtre, 1827-1850. Thèse. Paris, 1923.
FL 383.17 Le Breton, André. Le théâtre romantique (1829-1843). Paris, 1923?
FL 383.17.15 Treille, Marguerite. Le conflit dramatique en France de 1823 a 1830. Paris, 1929.
FL 383.18.5 Nebout, Pierre. Le drame romantique. Thèse. Photoreproduction. Paris, 1895.
FL 383.19 Welsch, A. De la réédification du théâtre en France. Paris, 1855.
FL 383.20 Guex, Jules. Le théâtre et la société française. Vevey, 1900.
X Cg FL 383.21 Le Roy, Albert. L'aube du théâtre romantique. 3. ed. Paris, 1904.
FL 383.25 Laforet, L.P. Le carillon théâtral. Paris, 1889.
FL 383.33 Duval, M.A. Lettre à M. Victor Hugo. Paris, 1833.
FL 383.34 Crémieux, A. Autographes. Paris, 1885.
FL 383.39 Devrient, E. Dramatische und dramaturgische Schriften. v.4. Leipzig, 1846.
FL 383.45 Claretie, Jules. La vie moderne au théâtre. Paris, 1869-1875. 2v.
FL 383.50 Rutenberg, Adolf. Die dramatischen Schriftsteller. Berlin, 1874.
FL 383.53 Figuier, Louis. Le théâtre scientifique. Paris, 1882.
FL 383.55 Faguet, Émile. Notes sur le théâtre contemporain. ser. 1-3. Paris, 1889-1891. 3v.
FL 383.57 Vitu, Auguste. Le mille et une nuits du théâtre. Paris, 1884-94. 9v.
FL 383.60 Baret, Charles. Le théâtre en province. Paris, 1918.
FL 383.73 Memorial dramatique, ou Almanach théâtre pour 1808. Paris, 1708[1808]
FL 383.75 Indicateur général de spectacles de Paris. Paris, 1821-22.
FL 383.77 Montégat, Emile. Dramaturges et romansiers. Paris, 1890.
FL 383.80 Liste des pièces représentées pour la première fois à Paris...1879-1889. n.p., n.d.
FL 383.85F Mobisson. Costumes of the modern stage. pt.1-5. London, 1889-91.
FL 383.86 Allevy, M.A. La mise en scène en France. Thèse. Paris, 1938.
FL 383.87 Allevy, M.A. La mise en scène en France dans la première moitié du dix-neuvième siècle. Paris, 1934.
FL 383.89 Nostrand, H.L. Le théâtre antique et à l'antique en France de 1840 à 1900. Thèse. Paris, 1934.
FL 383.90A Nostrand, H.L. Le théâtre antique et à l'antique en France de 1840 à 1900. Thèse. Paris, 1934.
FL 383.90B Nostrand, H.L. Le théâtre antique et à l'antique en France de 1840 à 1900. Thèse. Paris, 1934.
FL 383.95 Hsi-Wen, Tsao. La question d'argent dans le théâtre français sous le second empire. Thèse. Paris, 1934.
FL 383.100 Gratacap, M. Le théâtre français comtemporain. Vienne, 1905.
FL 383.115 Clark, B.H. Contemporary French dramatists. Cincinnati, 1915.
FL 383.123 Bissell, Clifford H. Les conventions du théâtre Bourgeois contemporain en France, 1887-1914. Paris, 1930.
FL 383.123.3 Bissell, Clifford H. Les conventions du théâtre Bourgeois contemporain en France, 1887-1914. Paris, 1930.
FL 383.125 Sebille, Henri. Toute la troupe. Paris, 1903.
FL 383.130 Bayet, Jean. La société des auteurs et compositeurs dramatiques. Paris, 1908.
FL 383.132 Borbey d'Aurevilly, Jules. Le théâtre contemporain, 1866-1869. Paris, 1908-1909. 3v.
FL 383.133 Borbey d'Aurevilly, Jules. Théâtre contemporain, 1870-1883. Paris, 1892.
FL 383.150 Ihrig, G.P. Heroines in French drama of the romantic period. N.Y., 1950.
FL 383.160 Descotes, M. Le drame romantique et ses grands createurs, 1827-1839. Paris, 1955.
FL 383.165 Braun, Sidney D. The courtisane in the French theatre from Hugo to Becque. Baltimore, Md., 1947.
FL 383.170 Kovatchévitch, M. Le sort artistes français et russes en 1812 et le décret de Moscou. Clement-Ferrand, 1941.
FL 383.180 Labarthe, Gustave. Le théâtre pendant les jours au siège et de la commune. Paris, 1910.
FL 383.195 Danilin, Iurii Iv. Parizhskaia kommuna i frantsuzskii teatr. Moskva, 1963.
FL 383.215 Danilin, Iurii Iv. Teatral'naia zhizn' v epokhu parizhskoi kommuny. Moskva, 1936.

FL 384 French drama and stage - History by periods - 19th and 20th centuries together - Collected biographies

FL 384.3 Etrennes de Thalie, ou Précis historique sur les acteurs et actrices célèbres. Paris, 1811.
FL 384.5 Alhoy, P.M. Grande biographie dramatique. Paris, 1824.
FL 384.7 Galerie de la presse. Paris, 183-?
FL 384.9 Petite biographie des acteurs et actrices des théâtres de Paris. Paris, 1831-32.
FL 384.12 Géréon, L. de. La rampe et les coulisses. Paris, 1832.
FL 384.18 Masques. Paris. 1-27
FL 384.30 Le Chevalier de Maison-Rouge. n.p., 1847.
FL 384.32 Hervey, C. The theatres of Paris. Paris, 1847.
FL 384.40 Geoffroy, C. Nouvelle galerie des artistes dramatiques vivants. Paris, 1855. 2v.
FL 384.41PF Gallois, N. Théâtre et artistes dramatiques de Paris. Paris, 1855.
FL 384.44 Audibert, Hilanon. Indiscrétions et confidences. Paris, 1858.
FL 384.50 Manne, Edmond D. Galerie historique des comédiens de la troupe de Nicolet. Lyon, 1869.
FL 384.52 Sarcey, F. Comédiens et comédiennes. Paris, 1875-81.
FL 384.53 Manne, Edmond D. Galerie historique des acteurs français. Lyon, 1877.
FL 384.55 Pollock, Walter H. The modern French theatre. Paris, 1878.
FL 384.57 Mayer, M.L. The gayety French plays. London, 1880.
Htn FL 384.58* Liphart, E. de. Les actrices de Paris. Paris, 1882.
FL 384.60 Sarcey, F. Comédiens et comédiennes. Théâtres divers. Paris, 1884.
Htn FL 384.61* Borbey d'Aurevilly, Jules. Les vielles actrices. Paris, 1884.
FL 384.80 Martin, Jules. Nos artistes. Paris, 1895.
FL 384.90 Martin, Jules. Nos auteurs et compositeurs dramatiques. Paris, 1897.
FL 384.95PF Appiello, Leonetto. Nos actrices. 4. ed. Paris, 1899.
FL 384.97 Claretie, Jules. Profils de théâtre. Paris, 1902.
FL 384.100 Berton, Pierre. Souvenirs de la vie de théâtre. Paris, 1914.
FL 384.102 Abraham, E. Les acteurs et les actrices de Paris. Paris, 1861.
FL 384.110 Dubeux, Albert. Acteurs: Julia Bartet, Mounet-Sully. Paris, 1929.
FL 384.115 Delini, J. Nos vedettes. Paris, 1922.
FL 384.125 Mignon, Paul L. Le théâtre d'aujourd'hui de A jusqu'à Z. Paris, 1966.

FL 385 French drama and stage - History by periods - 19th and 20th centuries together - General works (99 scheme, A-Z)

FL 385.3 Alibert, F.P. La renaissance de la tragedie. Carcassonne, 1929?
FL 385.4.25 Ascoli, Alfredo. Il diritto privato nel teatro contemporanço francese ed italiano. Milano, 1914.
FL 385.6 Basch, Victor. Études d'esthétique dramatique. Ser. I. Paris, 1920.
FL 385.6.2 Basch, Victor. Études d'esthétique dramatique. Ser. I. 2e ed. Paris, 1929.
FL 385.7 Benoist, A. Le théâtre d'aujourd'hui. Paris, 1911. 2v.
FL 385.7.15 Bernheim, Adrien. Trente ans de théâtre. Paris, 1903. 5v.
FL 385.8.50 Bloch, J.R. Destin du théâtre. 6e éd. Paris, 1930.
NEDL FL 385.8.100 Blum, Leon. Au théâtre réflexions critiques. Paris, 1906-1911. 4v.
FL 385.9.25 Brisson, A. Le théâtre. Paris, n.d. 9v.
FL 385.11 Capus, Alfred. Le théâtre. Paris, 1913.
Htn FL 385.11.5* Capus, Alfred. Notre époque et le théâtre. Paris, 1906.
FL 385.12.50 Chandler, Frank W. The contemporary drama of France. Boston, 1920.
FL 385.12.51A Chandler, Frank W. The contemporary drama of France. Boston, 1921.
FL 385.12.51B Chandler, Frank W. The contemporary drama of France. Boston, 1921.
FL 385.12.55 Chiari, Joseph. The contemporary French theatre. London, 1958.
FL 385.14 Capeau, Jacques. Études d'art dramatique; critiques d'une autre temps. 2e ed. Paris, 1923.
FL 385.14.5 Capeau, Jacques. Études d'art dramatique; critiques d'une autre temps. Paris, 1923.
FL 385.14.8 Capeau, Jacques. Études d'art dramatique; critiques d'une autre temps. 7e ed. Paris, 1923.
FL 385.16 Daniels, May. The French drama of the unspoken. Edinburgh, 1953.
FL 385.26.5 Faguet, Émile. Propos de théâtre. Series 1-5. Paris, 1906. 5v.
FL 385.28.9 Flat, P. Figures du théâtre contemporain. Paris, 1912. 2v.
FL 385.37 Héros, Eugène. Le théâtre anecdotique. Paris, 1912.
FL 385.38 Hobson, H. The French theatre of to-day. London, 1953.
FL 385.53 Marsan, Jules. Théâtre d'hier et d'aujourd'hui. Paris, 1926.
Htn FL 385.54* Mendes, C. L'art au théâtre. Paris, 1897-1900. 3v.
FL 385.69 Peter, René. Le théâtre et la vie sous la troisième République. Paris, 1945-1947. 2v.
FL 385.80 Séché, Alphonse. L'evolution du théâtre comtemporain. Paris, 1908.
FL 385.80.10 Sée, Edmond. Le mouvement dramatique. 1. ser. Paris, 1930.
FL 385.80.15 Sée, Edmond. Le théâtre français contemporain. Paris, 1928.
FL 385.80.50 Serreau, Geneviève. Histoire du "nouveau théâtre". Paris, 1966.
FL 385.82 Sorel, A.E. Essais de psychologie dramatique. Paris, 1911.
FL 385.88 Turcotte, S.J. Les gens d'affaires sur la scène française de 1870 à 1914. Paris, 1936.
FL 385.90.5A Vilar, Jean. De la tradition théâtrale. Paris, 1955.
FL 385.90.5B Vilar, Jean. De la tradition théâtrale. Paris, 1955.

FL 386.1 - .363 French drama and stage - History by periods - 20th century - General works (363 scheme, A-Z)

FL 386.28 Behar, Henri. Étude sur le théâtre dada et surréaliste. Paris, 1967.
FL 386.46 Colnen-Mennemeier, Brigitta. Einsamkeit und Revolte. Dortmund, 1966.
FL 386.46.5 Corvin, Michel. Le théâtre nouveau en France. Paris, 1963.

Classified Listing

FL 386.1 - .363 French drama and stage - History by periods - 20th century - General works (363 scheme, A-Z) - cont.

FL 386.46.6 Corvin, Michel. Le théâtre nouveau en France. 2e ed. Paris, 1966.
FL 386.63 Dominique, Léon. Le théâtre russe et la scène française. Paris, 1969.
FL 386.101 Fowlie, Wallace. Dionysus in Paris. N.Y., 1960.
FL 386.116 Grossvogel, David I. The self-conscious stage in modern French drama. N.Y., 1958.
FL 386.118A Guicharnaud, Jacques. Modern French theatre from Giraudoux to Beckett. New Haven, 1961.
FL 386.118B Guicharnaud, Jacques. Modern French theatre from Giraudoux to Beckett. New Haven, 1961.
FL 386.160 Jones, Robert Emmet. The alienated hero in modern French drama. Athens, 1962.
FL 386.177 Lalou, René. Le théâtre en France depuis 1900. Paris, 1951.
FL 386.177.3 Lalou, René. Cinquant'anni di teatro francese. Rocca San Casciano, 1960.
FL 386.187 Marcel, Gabriel. L'heure théâtrale de Giraudoux à Jean-Paul Sartre. Paris, 1959.
FL 386.270 Surer, Paul. Le théâtre français contemporain. Paris, 1964.
FL 386.277 Temkine, Raymonde. L'entreprise théâtre. Paris, 1967.
FL 386.278 Le théâtre contemporain. Paris, 1952.
FL 386.313 Versini, Georges. Le théâtre français depuis 1900. 1. éd. Paris, 1970.

FL 386.400 - .499 French drama and stage - History by periods - 20th century - Special periods - 1st half, 1900-1945 in general

FL 386.402 Antonini, Giacomo. Il teatro contemporaneo in Francia. Milano, 1930.
FL 386.403 Knowles, Dorothy. La réaction idéaliste au théâtre depuis 1890. Paris, 1934.
FL 386.405 Doisy, Marcel. Le théâtre français contemporain. Bruxelles, 1947.
FL 386.406 Talmon-Gros, Walter. Das moderne französische Theater. München, 1947.

FL 386.500 - .599 French drama and stage - History by periods - 20th century - Special periods - 1900-1919

FL 386.500 Bidou, Henry. L'année dramatique. Paris, 1930. 2v.
FL 386.501 Guillot de Saix, Léon. Le théâtre de demain. Paris, 1915.
FL 386.502 Bataille, Henry. Le théâtre après la guerre. Paris, 1918.
FL 386.503 Coindreau, Maurice Edgar. La farce est jouée. N.Y., 1942.
FL 386.504 Bordeau, Henry. La vie au théâtre, 1907-1921. Paris, 1910-1921. 5v.

FL 386.600 - .699 French drama and stage - History by periods - 20th century - Special periods - 1920-1945

FL 386.602 Martin du Gard, Maurice. Carte rouge. Paris, 1930.
FL 386.603 Fox, Mary Constantia. The miracle and the mystère in France in the last decade, 1920-30. Urbana, Ill., 1931.
FL 386.604 Mortier, Alfred. Quinze ans de théâtre, 1917-1932. Paris, 1933.
FL 386.605 Aykroyd, Phyllis. The dramatic art of La compagnie des quinze. London, 1935.
FL 386.607 Brisson, Pierre Anatole François. Le théâtre des années folles. Genève, 1943.
FL 386.608 Radine, Serge. Essais sur le théâtre, 1919-1939. Genève-Annemasse, 1944.
FL 386.609A Dubech, Lucien. Le théâtre, 1918-1923. Paris, 1925.
FL 386.609B Dubech, Lucien. Le théâtre, 1918-1923. Paris, 1925.
FL 386.615 Knowles, Dorothy. French drama of the inter-war years, 1918-1939. London, 1967[1968]

FL 386.800 - .899 French drama and stage - History by periods - 20th century - Special periods - 1945-1969

FL 386.802 Ambrière, Francis. La galerie dramatique, 1945-1948. Paris, 1949.
FL 386.805 Dussane, Beatrix. Notes de théâtre, 1940-1950. Lyon, 1951.
FL 386.805.5 Dussane, Beatrix. J'étais dans la salle. Paris, 1963.
FL 386.808 Beigbeder, M. Le théâtre en France depuis la libération. Paris, 1959.
FL 386.812 Pronko, Leonard Cabell. Avant-garde: the experimental theatre in France. Berkeley, 1962.
FL 386.813 Baecque, Andée de. Le théâtre d'aujourd'hui. Paris, 1964.
FL 386.816 Proskurnikovg, T.B. Frantsuzskaia antidrama. Moskva, 1968.
FL 386.817 Iakimovich, Tat'iana Konstantinovna. Dramaturgiia i teatr sovremennoi Frantsii. Kiev, 1968.
FL 386.820 Lee, Vera G. Quest for a public. Cambridge, Mass., 1970.
FL 386.821 Schoell, Konrad. Das französische Drama seit Zweiten Weltkrieg. Göttingen, 1970. 2v.

FL 390 French drama and stage - Local history - Paris - General works

FL 390.5 Brazier, Nicolas. Chroniques des petits théâtres de Paris. v.1-2. Paris, 1837.
FL 390.5.5 Brazier, Nicolas. Histoire des petits théâtres de Paris. Paris, 1838. 2v.
FL 390.5.10 Brazier, Nicolas. Chroniques des petits théâtres de Paris. Paris, 1883. 2v.
FL 390.30F Prestigieux théâtres de France. Paris, 1961.
FL 390.35 Desessarts, N.T.L. Les trois théâtres de Paris. Paris, 1777.
FL 390.40 Hervey, C. The theatres of Paris. Paris, 1846.
FL 390.42 Perrin, Maximilian. Biographie histoire de tous les théâtres de Paris. Paris, 1850.
FL 390.45 Vizentini, Albert. Derrière la toile...théâtres parisiens. Paris, 1868.
FL 390.50 Matthews, Brander. The theatres of Paris. N.Y., 1880.
X Cg FL 390.50 Matthews, Brander. The theatres of Paris. N.Y., 1880.
FL 390.60 Weiss, Jean Jacques. Trois années de théâtre, 1883-1885. Paris, 1892-96. 4v.
FL 390.65 Sarcey, Francisque. Paris vivant; le théâtre. Paris, 1893.
FL 390.70 Pougin, A. Acteurs et actrices d'autrefois. Paris, 1897?
FL 390.70.2 Pougin, A. Acteurs et actrices d'autrefois. Paris, 1896.
FL 390.75 Savard, Felix. Les actrices de Paris. Paris, 1867.
FL 390.80 Cain, Georges. Anciens théâtres de Paris. Paris, 1920.
FL 390.82 Bossuet, Pierre. Histoire des théâtres nationaux. Paris, 1909.
FL 390.84 Jallais, A. de. Sur la scène et dans la salle. Paris, 1854.
FL 390.85 Grönstedt, J. Teaterlitvet i Paris. Stockholm, 1879.
FL 390.90 Lecomte, L.H. Histoire des théâtres de Paris, 1402-1904. v.1. Paris, 1905.

FL 390 French drama and stage - Local history - Paris - General works - cont.

FL 390.91 Lecomte, L.H. Histoire des théâtres de Paris, 1838-1904. v.2. Paris, 1905.
FL 390.92 Lecomte, L.H. Histoire des théâtres de Paris. Le théâtre histoire. v.3. Paris, 1906.
FL 390.93 Lecomte, L.H. Histoire des théâtres de Paris. Le théâtre national, 1793-4. v.4. Paris, 1907.
FL 390.94 Lecomte, L.H. Histoire des théâtres de Paris. Les Nouveautés. v.5. Paris, 1907.
FL 390.95 Lecomte, L.H. Histoire des théâtres de Paris. Les jeux gymniques. v.6. Paris, 1908.
FL 390.96 Lecomte, L.H. Histoire des théâtres de Paris. Les variétés Amus. v.7. Paris, 1908.
FL 390.97 Lecomte, L.H. Histoire des théâtres de Paris. Les folies-nouvelles. v.8. Paris, 1909.
FL 390.98 Lecomte, L.H. Histoire des théâtres de Paris. Théâtre de la cité, 1792-1807. Paris, 1910.
FL 390.99 Lecomte, L.H. Histoire des théâtres de Paris. Les fantaisies-parisiennes. v.9. Paris, 1912.
FL 390.115 Touchard, Pierre Aimé. Grandes heures de théâtre à Paris. Paris, 1965.

FL 391 French drama and stage - Local history - Paris - Special periods

FL 391.7 Mélèse, Pierre. Le théâtre et le public à Paris sous Louis XIV. Paris, 1934.
FL 391.7.2 Mélèse, Pierre. Le théâtre et le public à Paris sous Louis XIV, 1659-1715. Thèse. Paris, 1934.
FL 391.7.8 Mélèse, Pierre. Répertoire analytique des documents contemporains d'information...théâtre à Paris sous Louis XIV. Thèse. Paris, 1934.
FL 391.7.10 Mélèse, Pierre. Répertoire analytique des documents contemporains d'information...théâtre à Paris sous Louis XIV. Paris, 1934.
FL 391.10 Du Tralage, J.N. de. Notes et documents sur l'histoire des théâtres de Paris par Jacob. Paris, 1880.
FL 391.15 Aghion, Max. Le théâtre à Paris au XVIIIe siècle. Paris, 1926.
FL 391.17 Le théâtre à Paris au XVIIIe siècle. Paris, 1930.
FL 391.25 Mémorial dramatique; ou Almanach théâtral, pour l'an. Paris. 1807-1819 4v.
FL 391.25.3 Mémorial dramatique. Paris. 1808
FL 391.30 Le coup de Foulet ou Revue des tous les théâtres. Paris, 1802.
FL 391.40 Chalons D'Argé, A.P. Histoire critique des théâtres de Paris pendant 1821. Paris, 1822.
FL 391.40.2 Chalons D'Argé, A.P. Histoire critique des théâtres de Paris année 1822. Paris, 1823.
FL 391.41 Almanach des Spectacles. Paris. 1-12,1822-1838 12v.
Htn FL 391.43PF* L'entr'acte. Paris.
FL 391.45 Nodler, Thomas. Mémoire, a l'appui de la demande d'un privilège pour l'établissement d'un théâtre dramatique. Paris, 18- .
FL 391.59 Duflot, Joachim. Les secrets des coulisses des théâtres de Paris. Paris, 1865.
FL 391.60 Goncourt, E. Mystères des théâtres, 1852. Paris, 1853.
FL 391.65 Alhoy, Maurice. Paris-actrice. Paris, 1854.
FL 391.70 Veron, Louis. Paris en 1860. Les théâtres de Paris, 1806-1860. Paris, 1860.
FL 391.72 Monselet, C. Les premières représentations célèbres. Paris, 1867.
FL 391.80 Giffard, Pierre. Comédie-française; les Fourchambault. Paris, 1878.
FL 391.81 Giffard, Pierre. Théâtre-lyrique; les amants de Vérone. Paris, 1879.
FL 391.82 Giffard, Pierre. Théâtre de la Porte Saint-Martin. Paris, 1879.
FL 391.90 Saint-Mor, Guy de. Paris sur scène. Saison, 1886-87. 2e ed. Paris, 1888.
FL 391.95 Théâtre fin de siècle 1881-1888. Paris, 1888?
FL 391.100 Lacour, Leopold. Gaulois et parisiens. Paris, 1883.
FL 391.102 Aderer, A. Le théâtre à Côté. Paris, 1894.
FL 391.110 Raphanel, Jean. Histoire anecdotique des théâtres de Paris. Paris, 1896.
FL 391.120 Antoine, André. Le Théâtre. Paris, 1932-1933. 2v.
FL 391.130 Dreyfus, R. Petite histoire de la revue de fin d'année. Paris, 1909.
FL 391.135 Winkler, E.G. Moderne Französische Klassikeraufführungen auf Pariser Bühnen. Inaug. Diss. Stuttgart, 1933.
FL 391.140 McKee, K.N. The rôle of the priest on the Parisian stage during the French revolution. Thesis. Baltimore, 1939.
FL 391.144A Brasillach, Robert. Animateurs de théâtre. Paris, 1936.
FL 391.144B Brasillach, Robert. Animateurs de théâtre. Paris, 1936.
FL 391.145 Brasillach, Robert. Animateurs de théâtre. Paris, 1954.
FL 391.150 Veinstein, André. Du théâtre libre au théâtre Louis Jouvet;...1887-1934. Paris, 1955.
FL 391.155 Schuermann, Joseph L. Secret de coulisses. Paris, 1911.

FL 393 French drama and stage - Local history - Paris - Special topics

FL 393.3 Bizet, René. L'époque du music-hall. Paris, 1927.
Htn FL 393.7* Les spectacles des foires et des boulevards de Paris. Paris, 1766-78. 3v.
FL 393.10 Campardon, E. Les spectacles de la foire. Paris, 1877. 2v.
Htn FL 393.11* Les spectacles de Paris. Paris. 1779-1792 14v.
FL 393.12A Albert, Maurice. Les théâtres de la foire. Paris, 1900.
FL 393.12B Albert, Maurice. Les théâtres de la foire. Paris, 1900.
FL 393.13 Albert, Maurice. Les théâtres des boulevards. Paris, 1902.
FL 393.14 Macaire, S. Les petits théâtres du boulevards. Paris, 1833.
FL 393.15 Bernardin, N.M. La comédie italienne en France et les théâtres de la foire et du boulevard. Paris, 1902.
FL 393.18 Challamel, A. L'ancien boulevard de Temple. Paris, 1873.
FL 393.20 Beaulieu, H. Les théâtres du boulevard du crime. Paris, 1905.
FL 393.25A Cain, G. Anciens théâtres de Paris (Boulevard). Paris, 1906.
FL 393.25B Cain, G. Anciens théâtres de Paris (Boulevard). Paris, 1906.
FL 393.26 Mayeur de Saint Paul, F.M. Le désoeuvré. Londres, 1782.
FL 393.27 Mayeur de Saint Paul, F.M. Le chroniqueur désoeuvre. 2. éd. Londres, 1782. 2v.
FL 393.50 Bercy, Anne de. A Montmartre, le soir; cabarets et chansonniers d'Hier. Paris, 1951.
FL 393.52 Montorgueil, G. Les déshabilles au théâtre. Paris, 1896.
FL 393.55 Laugh, John. Paris theatre audiences in the seventeenth and eighteenth centuries. London, 1957.

Classified Listing

FL 394 French drama and stage - Local history - Paris - Individual theaters - Comédie Française - General works

FL 394.01 Pamphlet box. Comédie Française.
FL 394.1 Almanach de la comédie-française. Paris. 1928
FL 394.5 Etienne, C.G. Histoire du théâtre français. v. 1-4. Paris, 1802. 2v.
FL 394.6 Pamphlet vol. Collection de la comédie française. 7 pam.
FL 394.50 Lemazurier, Pierre D. Galerie historique des acteurs du théâtre français depuis 1600 jusqu'à nos jours. Paris, 1810. 2v.
FL 394.52 Lindsay, Frank W. Dramatic parody by marionettes in 18th century Paris. Thesis. N.Y., 1946.
FL 394.60 Lerebours, P.V. Documens pour sevir à l'histoire du théâtre-français sous la restauration. Paris, 1834.
FL 394.62 Bouilly, J.N. Soixante ans du théâtre-français. Paris, 1842.
FL 394.75 Bonnassies, J. La comédie française. Histoire adminstrative. Paris, 1874.
FL 394.77 Bonnassies, J. Les spectales forains et la comédie française. Paris, 1875.
FL 394.79 Poinsot, E.A. Comédie-française. Paris, 1877. 2v.
FL 394.81A Campardon, E. Les comédiens du roi de la troupe française. Paris, 1879.
FL 394.81B Campardon, E. Les comédiens du roi de la troupe française. Paris, 1879.
FL 394.84PF Houssaye, A. La comédie française, 1680-1880. Paris, 1880.
Htn FL 394.84.2PF* Houssaye, A. La comédie française, 1680-1880. Paris, 1880.
FL 394.85PF Guillaumot, Auguste E. Costumes de la comédie française. Paris, 1885.
FL 394.97 Soubies, A. La comédie française, 1825-1894. Paris, 1895.
FL 394.99PF Figaro Illustré. La comédie française. Paris, 1897.
FL 394.105 Monval, Georges. Liste alphabétique des societaires (de la comédie-française). Paris, 1900.
FL 394.107 Joannidès, A. La comédie-française de 1680-1900. Paris, 1901.
FL 394.108 Gautier, Jean Jacques. La comédie française. Paris, 1964.
FL 394.112 Moeller van den Bruck, A. Das Théâtre français. Berlin, 1905.
FL 394.115 Lollée, F. La maison de Molière. Paris, 1908.
FL 394.115.10 Genest, E. La maison de Molière. Paris, 1922.
FL 394.120 Dussane, B. (Mme.). La comédie-française. Paris, 1921.
FL 394.122 Dussane, B. (Mme.). La comédie-française. Paris, 1960.
FL 394.125 Ricord, Alexandre. Les fastes de la comédie française. Paris, 1821-22. 2v.
FL 394.127 Marcerou, Louis. La comédie française, l'association des comédiens français. Thèse. Paris, 1925.
FL 394.129 Dubech, Lucien. La comédie-française d'aujourd'hui. Paris, 1926.
FL 394.131 Bib (pseud.). La comédie française vue par Bib. Paris, 1931.
FL 394.133 Comédie française, Paris. A collect of magazine articles on the Comédie française. n.p., n.d.
FL 394.134 Siaud, Simon. La comédie française, son statut juridique. Thèse. Lyon, 1935.
FL 394.135 Siaud, Simon. La comédie française, son histoire, son statut. Paris, 1936.
FL 394.137 Valmy-Baysse, J. Naissance et vie de la comédie-française...1402-1945. Paris, 1945.
FL 394.140 France in the United States Monthly. A special issue in honor of the first appearance in the United States of the Comédie française. N.Y., 1955.
FL 394.142 Versailles, France. Musée National. La comédie-française, 1680-1962. Paris, 1962.
FL 394.144 Comédie française; la revue mensuelle de la comédie-française. 1,1971+

FL 395 French drama and stage - Local history - Paris - Individual theaters - Comédie Française - Special periods

FL 395.10A Bonnassies, J. Comédie-française. Notice historique sur les anciens bâtiments. Paris, 1868.
FL 395.10B Bonnassies, J. Comédie-française. Notice historique sur les anciens bâtiments. Paris, 1868.
FL 395.15F La Grange, C.V. Registre (1658-1685). Paris, 1876.
FL 395.15.5 La Grange, C.V. Le registre de La Grange. Paris, 1947. 2v.
FL 395.20 Monval, Georges. Premier registre de La Thorillière (1663-1664). Paris, 1890.
FL 395.30 Lancaster, H.C. The comédie française, 1680-1701. Baltimore, Md., 1941.
FL 395.40 Bonnassies, J. Les auteurs dramatiques et la comédie, 17e et 18e siècles. Paris, 1874.
FL 395.42 Bonnassies, J. Comédie-française et les comédiens de province aux 17e et 18e siècles. Paris, 1875.
FL 395.43F Febvre, F. Album de la comédie française. Paris, 1880.
FL 395.44 Gueullette, C. Acteurs and actrices du temps passé. Paris, 1881.
FL 395.45 Sarcey, F. Comédien des comédiennes. ser. 1. Paris, 1875.
FL 395.55 Manne, E.D. Galerie historique des comédiens françois de la troupe de Voltaire. Lyon, 1877.
FL 395.60 Lamington, A.C.B. The théâtre français in the reign of Louis XV. London, 1879.
FL 395.65 Alasseur, Claude. La comédie française au 18e siècle, étude économique. Paris, 1967.
FL 395.102 Pougin, Arthur. La comédie française et la révolution. Paris, 1902.
FL 395.110 Observations pour les comédiens français, sur petition adressée par les auteurs dramatiques. Paris, 1790.
FL 395.120 Manne, E.D. Galerie historique des comédiens de la troupe de Talma. Lyon, 1866.
FL 395.125 Langier, Eugène. Documents historiques sur la comédie française pendant le régne de S.M. l'Empereur Napoléon I. Paris, 1853.
FL 395.127 Observations pour les comédiens françois, ordinaries du Roi occupant le théâtre de la nation. Paris, 1790.
FL 395.130 Le Petit Homme Noir aux acteurs et actrices de théâtre française. Paris, 1815.
Htn FL 395.132* Costumes des comédiens françaises dans Omasis. n.p., n.d.
FL 395.150 Soubies, A. La comédie-française depuis l'époque romantique, 1825-1894. Paris, 1895.
FL 395.155 Alencon, Edouard d'. Masque i besace. Roma, 1894.
FL 395.160 Langier, Eugène. De la comédie française depuis 1830. Paris, 1844.
FL 395.161 Boisanger, Claude de. Neuf mois à la comédie française. Paris, 1964.

FL 395 French drama and stage - Local history - Paris - Individual theaters - Comédie Française - Special periods - cont.

FL 395.200 D'Heylli, George. Journal intime de la comédie française. Paris, 1879.
FL 395.215 Gueullette, C. Répetoire de la comédie-française, 1883-1891. Paris, 1885-92. 8v.
FL 395.220 Joannidès, A. La comédie française. Paris, 1901-1925. 18v.
FL 395.220.5 Champion, E. La comédie française. Paris, 1927-1937. 5v.
FL 395.222 Gaulot, Paul. Le foyer de la comédie française, 1870-1900. Paris, 1926.
FL 395.240 Poinsot, E.A. La comédie française à Londres, 1871-1879. Paris, 1880.
FL 395.241F Angus, J.K. The comédie française. London, 1879.
FL 395.245 Boucheron, M. La divine comédie française. Paris, 1888.
FL 395.247 Giffard, P. La vie au théâtre. Paris, 1888.
FL 395.250 Truffier, Jules C. La comédie-française, 1902. Paris, 1903.
Htn FL 395.255* Grandval, C. De la comédie-française aux boulevards. Paris, 1906.
FL 395.260 Rouveyre, A.L.M. La comédie-française. Paris, 1906.
FL 395.263 Thierry, E. La comédie-française pendant les deux sièges, 1870-1871. Paris, 1887.
FL 395.265 Noel, Edouard. La comédie-française en 1878-1879. Paris, 1879.
FL 395.270 Truffier, Jules C. Comédie-française, 1914-1918. Paris, 1921.
FL 395.280 Touchard, P.A. Six années de comédie française. Paris, 1953.
FL 395.285 Bretty, Béatrice. La comédie-française à l'envers. Paris, 1957.
FL 395.290 Cardinue-Petit, Robert. Les secrets de la comédie française, 1936-1945. Paris, 1958.

FL 396 French drama and stage - Local history - Paris - Individual theaters - Other Paris theaters (99 scheme, A-Z by theater]

FL 396.4 Buguet, Henry. Foyers et coulisses. Ambigu-comique. Paris, 1880.
FL 396.20 France. Embassy. United States. Theatre national populaire. N.Y., 1958.
FL 396.20.5 Marteo, Gian. Il teatro poplare in Francia. Bologna, 1960.
FL 396.20.10 Lapoint; Revue artistique et littéraire. Le théâtre national populaire. Souillar, 1957.
FL 396.30 Péricaud, L. Le théâtre des funambules. Paris, 1897.
FL 396.32 Buguet, Henry. Foyers et coulisses. Gaîté. v.2. Paris, 1875.
FL 396.38 Notice descriptive du théâtre historique ornée de 32 gravures. Paris, n.d.
FL 396.39 Deierkauf-Holsboer, Sophie Wilma. Le théâtre de l'hôtel de Bourgogne. Paris, 1968-70. 2v.
FL 396.41 Sand, Maurice. Masque et Bouffons. Paris, 1860.
FL 396.41.2 Campardon, E. Les comédiens du roi de la troupe italienne. Paris, 1880. 2v.
Htn FL 396.41.3* Parfaict, F. Histoire de l'ancien théâtre italien depuis son origine en France. Paris, 1753.
FL 396.41.4 Baschet, A. Les comédiens italiens à la cour de France. Paris, 1882.
FL 396.41.5 Desboulmiers, Jean. Histoire anecdotique et raisonée du théâtre italien. Paris, 1769. 7v.
FL 396.41.6 Gueullette, T.S. Notes et souvenirs sur le théâtre-italien au XVIIIe siècle. Thèse. Paris, 1938.
FL 396.41.7 Gueullette, T.S. Notes et souvenirs sur le théâtre-italien au XVIIIe siècle. Paris, 1938.
FL 396.41.8 Du Gérard, N. Tables alphabetiques et chronologiques. Paris, 1750.
FL 396.50 Le théâtre libre. Saisons 1887 à 1890. n.p., n.d.
FL 396.50.2 Thalasso, A. Le théâtre libre. Paris, 1909.
FL 396.50.3 Pruner, Francis. Les luttes d'Antoine. Paris, 1964.
FL 396.50.4 Pruner, Francis. Le théâtre libre d'Antoine. Paris, 1958-
FL 396.50.5 Antoine, André. "Mes souvenirs" sur le théâtre-libre. Paris, 1921.
FL 396.50.8 Antoine, André. Memories of the theatre-libre. Coral Gables, 1964.
FL 396.50.10A Waxman, S.M. Antoine and the théâtre-libre. Cambridge, 1926.
FL 396.50.10B Waxman, S.M. Antoine and the théâtre-libre. Cambridge, 1926.
FL 396.50.15 Prince, Felix. André Antoine et la renouveau du théâtre, 1880-1900. Amsterdam, 1941.
FL 396.52 Soubies, Albert. Histoire du théâtre-lyrique, 1851-70. Paris, 1899.
FL 396.53 Deierkauf-Holsboer, Sophie Wilma. Le théâtre du Marais. Paris, 1954. 2v.
FL 396.54 Boissard, M. Le théâtre de Maurice Boissard, 1907-1923. v.1, 4. ed; v.2, 8. ed. Paris, 1926-45. 2v.
FL 396.54.10 Léautaud, Paul. Le théâtre de Maurice Boissard. 7. ed. Paris, 1958. 2v.
FL 396.56 Artus, M. Le théâtre Montmarte. Paris, 1904.
FL 396.56.9 Thelmier. Histoire du théâtre Montparnasse. Paris, 1886.
FL 396.64 Porel, P. L'Odéon. Paris, 1882. 2v.
FL 396.64.1 Genty, Raymond. Les souterrains de l'Odéon. Paris, 1945.
FL 396.64.2 Du théâtre français...la nouvelle troupe de l'Odéon. Paris, 1819.
FL 396.64.5 Antoine, André. Mes souvenirs sur le théâtre Antoine. 1e ed. Paris, 1928.
FL 396.64.8 Antoine, André. Mes souvenirs sur le théâtre Antoine. 12e ed. Paris, 1928.
FL 396.66 Fischer, Carlos. Les costumes de l'opéra. Paris, 1931.
FL 396.68 Hugot, Eugène. Histoire littéraire, critique et anecdotique du théâtre du Palais-Royal, 1784-1884. Paris, 1886.
FL 396.68.3 Hugot, Eugène. Histoire...du théâtre du Palais-Royal, 1784-1884. Paris, 1886.
FL 396.68.9 Bouget, Henry. Palais-royal. Paris, 1874.
FL 396.69 Lecomte, L.H. Histoire des théâtres. Le panorama dramatique, 1821-23. Paris, 1900.
FL 396.70 Pamphlet vol. La petite scène.
FL 396.80 Derval, Paul. The Folies Bergère. London, 1955.
FL 396.90 Boutet, R. Les variétés, 1850-1870. Paris, 1905.
FL 396.90.2 Buguet, Henry. Foyers et coulisses; histoire anecdotique de tous les théâtres de Paris. Variétés. Paris, 1881.
FL 396.90.9 Buguet, Henry. Foyers et coulisses; histoire anecdotique des théâtres de Paris. Vaudeville. Paris, 1881.
FL 396.90.20F Théâtres des Champs-Elysées, 1913-63. Paris, 1963.
FL 396.90.50 Frank, Waldo. The art of the Vieux Colonibier. Paris, 1918.

FL 396 French drama and stage - Local history - Paris - Individual theaters - Other Paris theaters (99 scheme, A-Z by theater] - cont.

FL 396.90.52 Copeau, J. Souvenirs du Vieux-Colonibier. Paris, 1931.
FL 396.90.52.5 Kurtz, Maurice. Jacques Copeau. Paris, 1950.

FL 397.1 - .99 French drama and stage - Local history - Other French cities, towns, etc. (99 scheme, A-Z by place)

FL 397.3.9 Despierres, G. (Mme.). Le théâtre et les comédiens à Alençon 16 et 17 siècle. Paris, 1892.
FL 397.3.12 Schoen, Henri. Le théâtre Alsacien. Strasbourg, 1903.
FL 397.3.12.5 Schoen, Henri. Le théâtre populaire en Alsace. Paris, 1903.
FL 397.3.15 Prologue pour l'inauguration à Angers le 4 Nov. 1865 du théâtre Auber. Paris, 1865.
FL 397.3.17 Prologue pour l'inauguration du théâtre d'Angers. Angers, 1871.
FL 397.7 Charvet, E. Recherches sur les anciens théâtres de Beauvais. Beauvais, 1881.
FL 397.7.25 Robert, Ulysse. Les origines du théâtre à Besançon. n.p., 1900.
FL 397.7.29 Besançon, France. Laws, statutes, etc. Ordonnance et réglement concernant la police des spectacles de la ville de Besançon. Paris? 1784.
FL 397.8 Durieu, Jules. Les samedis littéraires du théâtre discours d'ouverture. Bordeaux, 1904.
FL 397.8.5 Minier, H. Le théâtre à Bordeaux, étude historique. Bordeaux, 1897.
FL 397.8.9 Detcheverry, A. Histoire des théâtres de Bordeaux. Bordeaux, 1860.
FL 397.8.15 Courteault, P. La révolution et les théâtres à Bordeaux d'après des documents inédits. Paris, 1926.
FL 397.8.20 Boisson, F.A. Les douze colonnes de Louis. Bordeaux, 1964.
FL 397.8.25 Mahelot, L. Le mémoire de Mahelot...de l'hôtel de Bourgogne. Paris, 1920.
FL 397.9 Notice illustré sur le théâtre du peuple de Bussang. Paris, 1897.
FL 397.11 Lavalley, G. La censure théâtrale à Caen en l'an VII. Caen, 1908.
FL 397.34.15 Rousset, Henry. Le théâtre à Grenoble, 1500-1890. Grenoble, 1891.
FL 397.34.25 Delucinge, Edmond. Grenoble et son théâtre, de Molière à nos jours. Grenoble, 1952.
FL 397.52.24 Vingtrinier, E. Le théâtre à Lyon du XVIIIe siècle. Lyon, 1879.
FL 397.52.25 Vermorel, Jean. Quelques petits théâtres Lyonnais des XVIIIe et XIXe siècles. Lyon, 1918.
FL 397.53.5 Deschamps, Robert. Le théâtre au Mans. Maniers, 1900.
FL 397.53.50 Combarnous, V. L'histoire du Grand-théâtre de Marseille, 31 Octobre 1778 - 13 Novembre 1919. Marseille, 1927.
FL 397.56 Declève, Jules. Le théâtre à Mons. Mons, 1892.
FL 397.58 Destranges, E. Le théâtre à Nantes, 1430-1901. Paris, 1902.
FL 397.66.14 Fernand-Michel, P. Le théâtre antique d'Orange. Paris, 1894.
FL 397.66.15 Fernand-Michel, P. Le théâtre antique d'Orange. 2nd ed. Paris, 1894.
FL 397.66.16 Digonnet, F. Le théâtre antique d'Orange. Avignon, 1897.
FL 397.66.17 Boissy, G. La dramaturgie d'Orange. Paris, 1907.
FL 397.70 Lecocq, Georges. Histoire du théâtre en Picardie. Paris, 1880.
FL 397.70.5 Nattiez, Jean. La vie théâtrale des troupes ambulantes en Picardie. Amiens, 1967.
FL 397.71 Clouzot, Henri. L'ancien théâtre en Poitou. Niort, 1901.
FL 397.72 Herelle, Georges. Études sur le théâtre basque. Le répertoire du théâtre tragique. Paris, 1928.
FL 397.72.5 Herelle, Georges. Études sur le théâtre basque. La répresentation des pastorales. Paris, 1923.
FL 397.72.7 Herelle, Georges. Études sur le théâtre basque. Les pastorales à sujets tragediques considérées littéairement. Paris, 1926.
FL 397.75 Paris, Louis. Le théâtre à Reims. Reims, 1885.
FL 397.75.5 Fleary, Edouard. Origines et développements de l'art théâtral dans la province ecclésiastique de Reims. Laon, 1880.
FL 397.77 Bouteiller, Jules E. Histoire complete et methodique des théâtres de Rouen. Rouen, 1860-80. 4v.
Htn FL 397.77.5* Bouteiller, Jules E. Les théâtres de société de Rouen. Rouen, 1877.
FL 397.79 Lecocq, Georges. Histoire du théâtre de St. Quentin. Paris, 1878.
FL 397.79.15 Mugrier, F. Le théâtre en Savoie. Chamberg, 1887.
FL 397.82 Fischbach, Gustave. Le théâtre de Strasbourg et la dotation apffel. Strasbourg, 1884.
FL 397.82.5 Deck, Panteléon. Histoire du théâtre français à Strasbourg. Thèse. Strasbourg, 1948.
FL 397.82.6 Deck, Panteléon. Histoire du théâtre français à Strasbourg. Strasbourg, 1948.
FL 397.87 Cézan, Claude. Le Grenier de Toulouse tel que je l'ai on. Toulouse, 1952.
FL 397.88 Fage, René. Un demi-siècle de théâtre à Tulle, 1800-1850. Brive, 1907.

FL 397.100 French drama and stage - Local history - Other European countries - Belgium - Periodicals

FL 397.100 Bruxelles-théâtres Verviers.
FL 397.100.5 Annuaire dramatique de la Belgique. Bruxelles. 1-9,1839-1847// 5v.

FL 397.110 French drama and stage - Local history - Other European countries - Belgium - General histories

FL 397.110 Faber, Frederic Jules. Histoire du théâtre français en Belgique. Bruxelles, 1878-80. 5v.
FL 397.110.25 Cohen, G. Le théâtre français en Belgique au Moyen Age. Bruxelles, 1953.

FL 397.111 French drama and stage - Local history - Other European countries - Belgium - Special periods

FL 397.111 Le théâtre contemporain de Belgique. Bruxelles, 1969.
FL 397.111.10 Lilar, Suzanne. Soixante ans de théâtre belge. Bruxelles, 1952.
FL 397.111.18 Lilar, Suzanne. The Belgian theater since 1890. 3d ed. N.Y., 1962.

FL 397.114 French drama and stage - Local history - Other European countries - Belgium - Brussels

FL 397.114 Liebrecht, Henri. Histoire du théâtre français à Bruxelles au XVIIe et au XVIIIe siècle. Paris, 1923.
FL 397.114.5 Renieu, Lionel. Histoire des théâtres de Bruxelles. Paris, 1928. 2v.
FL 397.114.100 Isnardon, Jacques. Le théâtre de la monnaie depuis sa fondation jusqu'à nos jours. Bruxelles, 1890.
FL 397.114.105 Gersdorff, Arthur. Théâtre royal de la monnaie 1856-1926. Bruxelles, 1926.

FL 397.115 French drama and stage - Local history - Other European countries - Belgium - Other Belgian cities (99 scheme, A-Z by place)

FL 397.115.31 Neuville, A. Revue historique, chronologique et anecdotique du théâtre de Gand, 1750-1828. Gand, 1828.
FL 397.115.32 Claeys, Prosper. Histoire du théâtre à Gand. Gand, 1892. 3v.
FL 397.115.50 Martiny, Jules. Histoire du théâtre de Liège depuis son origine jusqu'à nos jours. Liège, 1887.
FL 397.115.82 Body, Albin. Le théâtre et la musique à Spa au temps passé et au temps présent. 2. éd. Bruxelles, 1885.

FL 397.161 French drama and stage - Local history - Other European countries - Holland - Special periods

FL 397.161 Fransen, Jan. Les comédiens français en Hollande au XVIIe et au XVIIIe siècles. Paris, 1925.

FL 397.211 French drama and stage - Local history - Other European countries - Switzerland - Special periods

FL 397.211 Vallon, Claude. Le dossier canadien du théâtre romand. Lausanne, 1967.

FL 397.215 French drama and stage - Local history - Other European countries - Switzerland - Individual cities, towns, etc. (99 scheme, A-Z by place)

FL 397.215.32 Duvillard, A. Quelques réflexions sur les moeurs républicaines et sur l'établissement d'un théâtre à Genève. Genève, 1814.
FL 397.215.48.2 Huguenin, Auguste. La belle époque. 2e éd. Lausanne, 1964.

FL 397.261 French drama and stage - Local history - Other European countries - Germany - Special periods

FL 397.261 Steltz, Michael. Geschichte und Spielplan der Französischen Theater an Deutschen Fürstenhöfen in 17. und 18. Jahrhundert. München, 1964[1965]

FL 397.311 French drama and stage - Local history - Other European countries - Rumania - Special periods

FL 397.311 Radulescu, Ion Horia. Le théâtre français dans les pays Roumaine, 1826-1852. Paris, 1965.

FL 398 French drama and stage - Biographies of actors, directors, managers, etc. - Individual (99 scheme, A-Z, by person)

FL 398.3 Laire, Raymond. Mlle. Agar de la comédie-française. Vienne, 1878.
FL 398.3.50 Rochefort, C. Le film de mes souvenirs. Paris, 1943.
FL 398.3.75 Antoine, A.P. Antonine, père et fils. Paris, 1962.
FL 398.4.9 Arnoldianna, ou Sophie Arnould et ses contemporaines. Paris, 1813.
FL 398.4.12 Douglas, R.B. Sophie Arnould. Paris, 1898.
FL 398.4.20 Poinsot, Edmond A. Madame Arnould-Plessy. Paris, 1876.
FL 398.4.25 Billy, André. La vie amoureuse de Sophie Arnould. Paris, 1929.
FL 398.4.30 Goucourt, E. Sophie Arnould. Paris, 1877.
FL 398.6.5 Baret, C. Propos d'un homme que à bien tourné. Dijon, n.d.
FL 398.6.15 Bellanger, J. Les matinées Ballande. Paris, 1901.
FL 398.6.20 Barrault, J.L. Réflexions sur le théâtre. Paris, 1949.
FL 398.6.20.2 Barrault, J.L. Reflections on the theatre. London, 1951.
FL 398.6.20.5 Barrault, J.L. Une troupe et ses auteurs. Paris, 1950.
FL 398.6.20.10 Barrault, J.L. Nouvelles réflexions sur le théâtre. Paris, 1959.
FL 398.6.20.15 Barrault, J.L. Journal de Bord: Japon, Israël, Grèce, Yougoslavie. Paris, 1961.
FL 398.6.20.20 Barrault, J.L. Le phénomène théâtral. Oxford, 1961.
FL 398.6.20.25 Barrault, J.L. The theatre of Jean-Louis Barrault. N.Y., 1961.
FL 398.6.20.80 Poesio, Paolo Emilio. Jean Louis Barrault. Bologna, 1961.
FL 398.6.25 Young, B. Michel Baron. Paris, 1904.
FL 398.6.30 Allainval, Léon J.C.S. d'. Lettre à Mylord...sur Baron. Paris, 1870.
FL 398.6.50F Bonnefont, G. Mademoiselle Bartet. Paris, 1897.
FL 398.6.55 Duleux, Albert. Julia Bartet. Paris, 1938.
FL 398.7 Ginisty, P. Mlle. Gogo, Mlle. Beaumenard, 1730-1799. Paris, 1913.
FL 398.7.7 Becque, Henry. Souvenirs d'un auteur dramatique. Paris, 1895.
FL 398.7.8 Fabre, E. De Tholie à Melpoméne. Paris, 1947.
FL 398.7.15 Bernhardt, Sarah. Memories of my life. N.Y., 1907.
FL 398.7.15.5 Bernhardt, Sarah. Memories of my life. N.Y., 1923.
FL 398.7.15.8 Bernhardt, Sarah. My double life. London, 1907.
FL 398.7.16F Renner, A.L. Sarah Bernhardt: artist and woman. N.Y., n.d.
FL 398.7.17.5 Huret, Jules. Sarah Bernhardt. London, 1899.
FL 398.7.18 Gallus, A. Sarah Bernhardt: her artistic life. N.Y., 1901.
FL 398.7.19A Bernhardt, Sarah. Ma double vie. Mémoires de Sarah Bernhardt. Paris, 1907.
FL 398.7.19B Bernhardt, Sarah. Ma double vie. Mémoires de Sarah Bernhardt. Paris, 1907.
FL 398.7.19C Bernhardt, Sarah. Ma double vie. Mémoires de Sarah Bernhardt. Paris, 1907.
FL 398.7.19.9 Bernhardt, Sarah. Ma double vie; mémoires. Paris, 1923. 2v.
FL 398.7.20 Colombier, Marie. Voyages de Sarah Bernhardt en Amérique. Paris, n.d.
FL 398.7.21 Griffith, F.R. Sarah Bernhardt. n.p., n.d.
FL 398.7.22 London Coleseum. Mme. S. Bernhardt season. Prospectus. London, 1911.
FL 398.7.23 Clament, Clément. Esquisses d'aujourd'hui...Bernhardt. Paris, 1879.
Htn FL 398.7.24F* All about Sarah "Barnum" Bernhardt. London, 188-? 2 pam.
FL 398.7.25 Pamphlet vol. Sarah Bernhardt. 8 pam.
FL 398.7.26F Bernhardt, Sarah. Sarah Bernhardt souvenir. N.Y., 1880.
FL 398.7.27 Colombier, Marie. Les mémoires de Sarah Barnum. Paris, 1884.

FL 398 French drama and stage - Biographies of actors, directors, managers, etc. - Individual (99 scheme, A-Z, by person) - cont.

FL 398.7.28 Colombier, Marie. The memoirs of Sarah Barnum. N.Y., 1884.
FL 398.7.29 Colombier, Marie. Les mémoires de Sarah Barnum. Paris, 1883.
FL 398.7.29.5 Pamphlet vol. Analysis of four plays. 4 pam.
Htn FL 398.7.30* Colombier, Marie. The life...of Sarah Barnum. London, 1883? 2 pam.
FL 398.7.31 Farewell American tour...Sarah Bernhardt...1905-06. N.Y., 19- ?
FL 398.7.33 Arthur, George. Sarah Bernhardt. London, 1923.
FL 398.7.34 Berton, Thérèse M. The real Sarah Bernhardt. N.Y., 1924.
FL 398.7.35 Berton, Thérèse M. The real Sarah Bernhardt. N.Y., 1924.
FL 398.7.35.5 Berton, Thérèse M. The real Sarah Berndardt, as I knew her. London, 1923.
FL 398.7.36 Bron, Ludovic. Sarah Bernhardt. Paris, 1925.
FL 398.7.37 Hahn, Reynaldo. La grande Sarah. Paris, 1930.
FL 398.7.38 Hahn, Reynoldo. Sarah Bernhardt. London, 1932.
FL 398.7.39.6 Geller, G.G. Sarah Bernhardt. 6e éd. Paris, 1931.
FL 398.7.40 Geller, G.G. Sarah Bernhardt. London, 1933.
FL 398.7.41 Brisson, Adolphe. Phèdre et Mme. Sarah Bernhardt. Paris, 19- ?
Htn FL 398.7.42* Baring, Maurice. Sarah Bernhardt. London, 1933.
FL 398.7.44 Binet-Valmer, G. Sarah Bernhardt. Paris, 1936.
FL 398.7.46 Verneuil, Louis. La vie merveilleuse de Sarah Bernhardt. N.Y., 1942.
FL 398.7.48 Jochamowitz, A. Sarah Bernhardt en Lima. Lima, 1943?
FL 398.7.50 Berendt, Rachel. Sarah Bernhardt en mi recuerdo. Buenos Aires, 1945.
FL 398.7.55 Agate, May. Madame Sarah. London, 1945.
FL 398.7.60 Bernhardt, L.S. Sarah Bernhardt. Paris, 1945.
FL 398.7.65 Bernhardt, L.S. Sarah Bernhardt. London, 1949.
FL 398.7.70 Pronier, Ernest. Sarah Bernhardt. Genève, 1942.
FL 398.7.75 Lanco, Ivonne. Sarah Bernhardt. Paris, 1961.
FL 398.7.80 Richardson, Joanna. Sarah Bernhardt. London, 1959.
FL 398.7.85 Colombier, Marie. Voyages de Sarah Bernhardt en Amerique. Paris, 19- ?
FL 398.7.90 Castelol, André. Sarah Bernhardt. Paris, 1961.
FL 398.7.95 Baring, Maurice. Sarah Bernhardt. Westport, 1970.
FL 398.8 Ginisty, Paul. Bocage. Paris, 1926.
FL 398.8.5 Verneuil, Louis. Rideau à neuf heures. N.Y., 1944-
FL 398.8.10 Verneuil, Louis. Rideau à neuf heures. Paris, 1945.
FL 398.9 Bouffé, Marie. Mes souvenirs, 1800-1880. Paris, 1880.
FL 398.9.10A Bourgeois, J. Toute ma vie. v.1-2. Paris, 1954.
FL 398.9.10B Bourgeois, J. Toute ma vie. v.1. Paris, 1954.
FL 398.9.11 Cocteau, Jean. Adieu à Mistinguett. Liège, 1956.
FL 398.9.15F Germain, Auguste. Albert Brasseur. Paris, n.d.
FL 398.9.19 D'Heylli, Georges. Bressant, 1833-1877. Paris, 1877.
FL 398.9.25 D'Heylli, Georges. Brindeau. Paris, 1882.
FL 398.10 Gaulot, Paul. Les trois Brohan. Paris, 1930.
FL 398.11 Capon, G. Les Vestries Vestris family. Paris, 1908.
FL 398.11.5 Castel, Louis. Mémoires d'un claqueur. Paris, 1829.
FL 398.12 Chevalier, Maurice. Ma route et mes chansons. Paris, 1946.
FL 398.12.2 Chevalier, Maurice. Ma route et mes chansons. Paris, 1950-57. 9v.
FL 398.12.5 Chevalier, Maurice. The man in the straw hat. N.Y., 1949.
FL 398.12.10 Chevalier, Maurice. With love. Boston, 1960.
FL 398.12.20 Chevalier, Maurice. Les pensées de Momo. Paris, 1970.
FL 398.12.30 Boyer, William. The romantic life of Maurice Chevalier. London, 1937.
FL 398.13.9A Clairon, Hypolite. Mémoirs. London, 1800. 2v.
FL 398.13.9B Clairon, Hypolite. Mémoirs. London, 1800. 2v.
NEDL FL 398.13.10 Goncourt, E. de. Mademoiselle Clairon. Paris, 1890.
FL 398.13.12 Mémoires de Mlle. Clairon. Paris, 1882.
FL 398.13.12.2 Chevalier, Maurice. With love. Boston, 1960.
Htn FL 398.13.13* Dispute between Mlle. Clairon...and the Fathers of the Church. London, 1768.
FL 398.13.14 Gaillard de la Bataille, Pierre A. Histoire de Mademoiselle Cronel, dite Fretillon. La Haye, 1758.
FL 398.13.15 Gaillard de la Bataille, Pierre A. Histoire de Mademoiselle Cronel, dite Fretillon. La Haye, 1743-52.
FL 398.13.50 Bibliographie des oeuvres de Gustave Cohen. Paris, 1955.
FL 398.14 Gaillet, Eugène. La vie de Marie Pigeonnier (Marie Colombier). Paris, 1884.
FL 398.14.62 Dussane, (Mme.). La célimène de thermidor, Louis Cordat, 1760-1813. Paris, 1929.
FL 398.15 Doisy, Marcel. Jacques Copeau. Paris, 1954.
FL 398.17 Janin, Jules. Deburau. Paris, 1832. 2v.
FL 398.17.3 Janin, Jules. Deburau. Paris, 1881.
FL 398.17.5 Janin, Jules. Deburau. N.Y., 1928.
FL 398.17.8 Duval, Georges. Virgin Déjazet. Paris, 1876.
FL 398.17.9 Jacquot, C.J.B. Déjazet. Paris, 1854.
FL 398.17.10 Duval, Georges. Mademoiselle Déjazet. n.p., 1870.
FL 398.17.11 D'Heylli, Georges. Delaunay. Paris, 1883.
FL 398.17.12 Delaunay, Louis A. Souvenirs. Paris, 1901.
FL 398.17.15 Desclée, Aimée. Lettres. 3e éd. Paris, 1895.
FL 398.17.16 Desclée, Aimée. Lettres de Aimée Desclée à Fanfan. Paris, 1895.
FL 398.17.50 Ronzis, R. de. Aimée Desclée. Roma, 1935.
FL 398.19 Lecomte, L.H. Marie Dorval. Paris, 1900.
FL 398.19.5 Weyl, Fernand. Madame Dorval. Paris, 1926.
FL 398.19.7 Weyl, Fernand. Madame Dorval par Nozière (pseud.). Paris, 1930.
FL 398.19.10 Polletzco, Marcel. Trois reines de théâtre. Paris, 1958.
FL 398.20 Mémoires de Mlle. Dumesnil. Paris, 1823.
FL 398.20.2 Dumesnil, M.J. Mémoires de Mlle. Dumesnil. Paris, 1798.
FL 398.20.7 Olivier, Jean J. (pseud.). Madame Dugazon de la comédie-italienne, 1755-1821. Paris, 1917.
FL 398.20.8 La Roux, Hugues. La Dugazon. Paris, 1926.
FL 398.20.10 Pougin, Arthur. Figures d'opéra-comique. Paris, 1875.
FL 398.20.15 Dullin, Charles. Souvenirs et notes de travail d'un acteur. Paris, 1946.
FL 398.20.16 Dullin, Charles. Ce sont les dieux qu'il nous faut. Paris, 1969.
FL 398.20.30 Chagny, André. Marquise de Parc créatrice du rôle d'Andromaque. Paris, 1961.
FL 398.21.5 Palmstedt, C. Edouard du Puy. Stockholm, 1866.
FL 398.26.7 Bouvet, Charles. Cornélie Falcon. Paris, 1927.
FL 398.27 Febvre, F. Journal d'un comédien. Paris. 1-2,1850-1894 2v.
FL 398.27.5 Frédéric Febvre. Paris, n.d.
FL 398.28.8 Fleury, J.A.B. Mémoires de la comédie française. Paris, 1835-38. 6v.
FL 398.28.9 Lafitte, J.B.P. Mémoires de Fleury de la comédie française. Paris, 1844. 2v.
FL 398.28.12 Bourgogne, Jean de. Un comédien d'autrefois. Paris, 1914.

FL 398 French drama and stage - Biographies of actors, directors, managers, etc. - Individual (99 scheme, A-Z, by person) - cont.

FL 398.29 Flore, C. (Mlle.). Mémoirs de Mlle. Flore. Paris, 1903.
FL 398.29.5 Dumerson, T.M. Mémoires de Mlle. Flore. Paris, 1845. 3v.
FL 398.30.15 Fusil, Louise. Souvenirs d'une actrice. Paris, 1904.
FL 398.30.20 Janin, Jules. Rachel et la tragédie. Paris, 1861.
FL 398.31 Gabel, C.F. Dramatic biography. N.Y., 1868.
FL 398.32 George, Marguerite Joséphine Weimer. Mémoires inédits. Paris, 1908.
FL 398.34 Got, M. Journal de Edmond Got. 2e ed. Paris, 1910. 2v.
FL 398.35 Guilbert, Yvette. Yvette Guilbert. Struggles and victories. London, 1910.
FL 398.35.5 Robert, Louis de. The eternal enigma. Romance in the life of Yvette Guilbert. N.Y., 1897.
FL 398.35.7 Guilbert, Yvette. La passante émerveillée. Paris, 1929.
FL 398.35.9 Guilbert, Yvette. La chanson de ma vie. Paris, 1927.
FL 398.35.10 Guilbert, Yvette. La chanson de ma vie. Paris, 1927.
FL 398.35.11 Guilbert, Yvette. Autres temps, autres chants. 12. éd. Paris, 1946.
FL 398.35.12 Goncourt, Edmond de. La Guimard. Paris, 1893.
FL 398.35.15 Knapp, B.L. That was Yvette. N.Y., 1964.
FL 398.35.20 Houville, Gerard d' (pseud.). Lucien Guitry. Paris, 1924.
FL 398.37 D'Héricault, C. Une reine de théâtre souvenirs de jeunesse. Paris, 1891.
FL 398.39 Houssaye, Arsène. Behind the scenes of comédie française. Philadelphia, 1889.
FL 398.39.2 Houssaye, Arsène. Behind the scenes of comédie française. London, 1889.
FL 398.39.9 Hostein, Hippolyte. Historiettes et souvenirs d'un Homme de théâtre. Paris, 1878.
FL 398.42 Dulomboy, N.F.R.F. Aux manes de Marie-Elisabeth Joly. Paris, n.d.
FL 398.42.2 Tisseau, P. Une comédienne, Marie-Elisabeth Joly. Paris, 1928.
FL 398.42.5 Judith, Julie B. La vie d'une grande comédienne. Paris, 1911.
FL 398.42.9 Cézan, Claude. Louis Jouvet et le théâtre d'aujourd'hui. Paris, 1938.
FL 398.42.10 Knapp, B.L. Louis Jouvet. N.Y., 1957.
FL 398.42.15 Lipnitzky, Haim E.B. Images de Louis Jouvet. Paris, 1952.
FL 398.43 Brisebarre, Jean Bernard. L'acteur Joanny et son journal inédit. Paris, 195-.
FL 398.47 Lassouche, J.P. Mémoires anecdotiques. Paris, 1903.
FL 398.47.50 Raphanel, Jean. Mlle. Marie Leconte, biographie critique. Paris, n.d.
FL 398.47.60 Rivollet, Georges. Adrienne Lecouvreur. Paris, 1925.
FL 398.47.65 Sorel, Cécile. La vie amoureuse d'Adrienne Lecouvreur. Paris, 1925.
FL 398.47.70 Rykova, Nadezhda I. Adrienna Lekuvrer. Leningrad, 1967.
FL 398.47.75 Richtman, Jack. Adrienne Lecouvreur: the actress and the age. Englewood Cliffs, 1971.
FL 398.48 Criticisms of Eugénie Legrand in America. N.Y., 1883?
FL 398.48.50 Jiménez-Placer, Carlos. Ana de La-Grange. Sevilla, 1866.
FL 398.49 Lekain, H.L. Mémoires. Paris, 1801.
FL 398.49.5 Olivier, J.J. Henri-Louis Lekain. Paris, 1907.
FL 398.49.9 Lekain, H.L. Mémoires. Paris, 1825.
FL 398.49.11 Talma, F. Réflexions sur Lekain et sur l'art théâtral. Paris, 1825.
FL 398.49.13 Talma, F. Réflexions de Talma sur Lekain et l'art théâtral. Paris, 1856.
FL 398.49.20 Lekain, H.L. Lekain dans sa jeunesse. Paris, 1816.
FL 398.49.25 Duval, G.F. Lemaitre et son temps. Paris, 1876.
FL 398.49.27 Lecomte, L.H. Frédérick Lemaitre. Paris, 1865.
FL 398.49.29 Lemaitre, Frédérick. Souvenirs de Frédérick Lemaitre. 2d ed. Paris, 1880.
FL 398.49.31 Praag, M.M. De toneelspeler. 's-Gravenhage, 1963.
FL 398.49.33 Silvain, Eugene. Frédérick Lemaitre. Paris, 1926.
FL 398.49.34 Baldick, Robert. The life and times of Frédérick Lamaitre. Fair Lawn, N.J., 1959.
FL 398.49.35 Lemounier, A. Les mille et un souvenirs d'un Homme de théâtre. Paris, 1902.
FL 398.49.40 Finkel'shtein, Elena L. Frederik-Lemetr. Leningrad, 1968.
FL 398.50 Pitoeff, A. Ludmilla. Paris, 1955.
FL 398.50.10 Hort, Jean. La vie héroique des Pitoëff. Genève, 1966.
FL 398.52 Galipaux, Félix. Les Luguet, une dynastie des comédiens. Paris, 1929.
FL 398.52.35 Lugné, P.A. Le sot du tremplin. 3e éd. Paris, 1930.
FL 398.52.37 Lugné, P.A. Acrobaties; tremplin. 3e éd. Paris, 1931.
FL 398.52.39 Lugné, P.A. Sous les étoiles. 6e éd. Paris, 1933.
FL 398.52.45 Lassalle, E. Comédiens et amateurs. Montréal, 1919.
FL 398.52.50 Robichez, Jacques. Le symbolisme au théâtre. Paris, 1957.
FL 398.52.55 Béranger, Jacques. Une vie de théâtre. Bienne, 1964.
FL 398.54 Truffier, J. Mélinque; le comédien, l'Homme. Paris, 1925.
FL 398.56 Mole, François René. Mémoires. Paris, 1825.
FL 398.56.5 Etienne, C.G. Vie de François René Mole, comédien français. Paris, 1803.
FL 398.56.9 Lecomte, L.H. La Montansier. Ses aventures, 1730-1820. Paris, 1904.
FL 398.56.10 Fromagot, P. Le théâtre de Versailles et la Montansier. Versailles, 1905.
FL 398.56.12 Monnet, Jean. Supplement au Roman comique. London, 1772. 2v.
FL 398.56.15 Monnet, Jean. Mémoires de Jean Monnet. Paris, 1884.
FL 398.56.20 Heulhard, A. Jean Monnet. Paris, 1884.
FL 398.56.50 Cottier, E. Le comédien Auvergant, Montdory. Clermont-Ferrand, 1937.
FL 398.63.30 Lecomte, L.H. Odry et ses oeuvres.Paris, 1900.
FL 398.63.31 Odryana, ou La boite au gros sel. Paris, 1825.
FL 398.66 Oswald, Marianne. One small voice. N.Y., 1945.
FL 398.67 Vaudoyer, J.L. Alice Ozy, ou L'asposie moderne. Paris, 1930.
FL 398.68 Paccard, J.E. Mémoires et confessions. Comédien. Paris, 1839.
FL 398.69 Gianndi, Paul. La vie inspirée de Gerald Philipe. Paris, 1960.
Htn FL 398.70PF* Porel, Paul. Souvenirs d'un vieil homme de théâtre. Paris, 1908.
FL 398.70.20 Pitoëff, Georges. Notre théâtre. Paris, 1949.
FL 398.71.9 Cahaisse, H.A. Mémoires de Préville et de Dazincourt. Paris, 1823.
FL 398.72 Nohain, Jean. Le Pétomane, 1857-1945. Paris, 1967.
FL 398.74 Coquatrix, E. Rachel à Rouen. Rouen, 1840.
FL 398.74.5 Rachel et la comédie-française. Bruxelles, 1842.
FL 398.74.15 Maurice-Descombes, C. La vérité-Rachel; examen du talent de la première tragédienne du théâtre-français. Paris, 1850.

FL 398 French drama and stage - Biographies of actors, directors, managers, etc. - Individual (99 scheme, A-Z, by person) - cont.

FL 398.74.17 Chambrun, C.A. Quelques réflexions sur l'art dramatique. Mlle. Rachel; ses succes, ses defants. Paris, 1853.
FL 398.74.20 Darcie, John. The biography of Mdlle. Rachel. N.Y., 1855.
FL 398.74.21 Darcie and Corbyn's edition of Mlle. Rachel's readings. N.Y., 1855.
FL 398.74.22 Beauvallet, Léon. Rachel et le nouveau-monde. Paris, 1856.
FL 398.74.24A Beauvallet, Léon. Rachel and the new world. N.Y., 1856.
FL 398.74.24B Beauvallet, Léon. Rachel and the new world. N.Y., 1856.
Htn FL 398.74.26* Tampier, L.C. Dernières heures de Rachel. Paris, 1858. 2 pam.
FL 398.74.28A B., de Madame. Mémoirs of Rachel. London, 1858. 2v.
FL 398.74.28B B., de Madame. Mémoirs of Rachel. London, 1858.
FL 398.74.29 B., de Madame. Mémoirs of Rachel. London, 1858.
FL 398.74.30 Janin, Jules G. Rachel et la tragédie. Paris, 1859.
FL 398.74.40 Jacquot, C.J.B. Rachel. 3e ed. Paris, 1869.
FL 398.74.53 Poinsot, E.A. Rachel à après sa correspondance. Paris, 1882.
FL 398.74.56 Kennard, Nina H. Rachel. London, 1885.
FL 398.74.57 Kennard, Nina H. Rachel. Boston, 1886.
FL 398.74.60 Kennard, Nina H. Rachel. Boston, 1888.
FL 398.74.62 Kennard, Nina H. Rachel. Boston, 1895.
FL 398.74.66 Kennard, Nina H. Rachel. London, 1894.
FL 398.74.70 Samson, J.I. (Mme.). Rachel et Samson. 3e ed. Paris, 1898.
FL 398.74.76 Agate, James E. Rachel. London, 1928.
FL 398.74.78 Houssaye, A. La comédienne. 8e ed. Paris, 1884.
FL 398.74.82 Faucignyy-Lucinge, A. Rachel et son temps. Paris, 1910.
FL 398.74.83 Fleischmann, H. Rachel intime. Paris, 1910.
FL 398.74.85 Gribble, F. Rachel, her stage life and real life. London, 1911.
NEDL FL 398.74.85 Gribble, F. Rachel, her stage life and real life. London, 1911.
FL 398.74.86 Gribble, F. Rachel, her stage life and real life. N.Y., 1911.
FL 398.74.87 A collection of librettos of plays acted by Mlle. Rachel. N.Y., 1855. 5 pam.
FL 398.74.90 Falk, Bernard. Rachel. London, 1935.
FL 398.74.92 Berthon, Louis. Rachel. Paris, 1926.
FL 398.74.94 Morrison, P. Rachel. London, 1947.
FL 398.74.96 Piechaud, M. La vie privée de Rachel. Paris, 1954.
FL 398.74.98 Richardson, J. Rachel. London, 1956.
FL 398.74.115 Racovita, Elena von Donniges. Princesse et comédienne; souvenirs de ma vie. Paris, 1910.
FL 398.74.300 Notice sur l'interrement de Mlle. Raucourt. Paris, 1821.
FL 398.74.305 Reuilly, Jean de. Le Raucourt et ses amies. Paris, 1909.
FL 398.75 Poinsot, E.A. Regnier. Paris, 1872.
FL 398.75.10 Alexandre, Arsène. Suzanne Reichenberg. Paris, 1898.
FL 398.75.15 Poral, Jacques. Fils de Réjane. v.1-2. Paris, 1851-52.
FL 398.75.35 Pamphlet vol. Portrait and biographical sketch of Mlle. Rhéa. 2 pam.
FL 398.76 Rigolbache, Marguerite (pseud.). Mémoires. 3. ed. Paris, 1860.
FL 398.76.3 Rigolbache, Marguerite (pseud.). Mémoires. 5. ed. Paris, 1860.
FL 398.76.5 Rigolbache, Marguerite (pseud.). Mémoires. 6. ed. Paris, 1861.
FL 398.76.15F La rigolbachomanie. Paris, 18- ?
FL 398.77 Roll, Maximin. Souvenirs d'un Claqueur et d'un Figurant. Paris, 1904.
FL 398.77.100 Roussin, A. Patience et impatience. Genève, 1953.
FL 398.78 Sainval, (Mlle.). Lettres de Madame la contesse de Mal. Paris, 1779.
FL 398.79 Samson, J.I. Mémoires. Paris, 1882.
FL 398.79.5 Veber, Pierre. Samson. Paris, 1925.
FL 398.79.15 Gonzalès, E. Les caravanes de Scaromouche. Paris, 1881.
FL 398.80 Séchan, C. Souvenirs d'un homme de théâtre. Paris, 1893.
FL 398.81 Sorel, Cécile. Les belles heurs de ma vie. Monaco, 1946.
FL 398.81.20 Sorel, Cécile. Cécile Sorel. London, 1953.
FL 398.81.30 Raillard, Jacques. Mes dix années à après de Cécile. Paris, 1969.
FL 398.82 Silvain, Jean. Tel etait Silvain. Paris, 1934.
FL 398.83 Talma, F.J. Lettres d'amour inédits de Talma à la princesse Pauline Bonaparte. Paris, 1911.
FL 398.83.20 Mejanel, A. Mémoires de Talma. Londres, 1817.
FL 398.83.22 Talma, F.J. Mémoires. v.1-2,3-4. Paris, 1849-50. 2v.
FL 398.84.01 Pamphlet box. François Joseph Talma.
FL 398.84.02F Pamphlet box. François Joseph Talma.
FL 398.84.5 Moreau, M. Mémoires...sur F.J. Talma. Paris, 1826.
FL 398.84.8 Copin, Alfred. Talma et l'empire. Paris, 1887.
FL 398.84.9 Copin, Alfred. Études dramatiques; Talma et la révolution. Paris, 1887.
FL 398.84.11 Lecomte, L.H. Talma en paradis. Paris, 1900.
FL 398.84.12 Leport, Charles. Étude critique sur l'opération de Talma comme traitement de l'ascite. Thèse. Paris, 1902.
FL 398.84.13 Regnault-Warin, J.J. Mémoires sur Talma. Paris, 1904.
FL 398.84.14 Regnault-Warin, J.J. Mémories historiques et critiques sur F.J. Talma. Paris, 1827.
FL 398.84.15 Collins, H.F. Talma. London, 1964.
FL 398.84.16 Talma. Paris, 1914.
Htn FL 398.84.18* Lafon, Pierre. Discours...sur la tombe de Talma. Paris, 1826.
Htn FL 398.84.20* Laugier, Adolph. Notice sur Talma. Paris, 1826.
FL 398.84.23 Tissot, Pierre F. Souvenirs historiques sur la vie et la mort de F. Talma. Paris, 1826.
FL 398.84.27 Antoine, André. La vie amoureuse de François Joseph Talma. Paris, 1924.
FL 398.84.30 Talma, F.J. Correspondance avec Mme. de Staäl. Paris, 1928.
FL 398.90.10 Fromentin, A. Elisa Verneuil de la comédie-française. Paris, 1847.
FL 398.91 Lavedan, Henri. Volange, comédien de la Foire, 1756-1808. Paris, 1933.
FL 398.97 X. Ce que mes jolis yeux ont vu. Paris, 1913.

FL 399 French drama and stage - Periodicals (99 scheme, A-Z by title)

FL 399.3.2 Almanach général de tous le spectacles de Paris. Paris. 1791-1792 2v.
Htn FL 399.3.4* Almanach des spectacles. Paris. 1823
FL 399.3.5 Almanach des spectacles. Paris. 1874-1913 42v.
FL 399.3.6 Almanach des spectacles. Table décennale. Paris. 1892-1913 2v.
FL 399.3.7 Almanach des théâtre. Paris. 1922

FL 399 French drama and stage - Periodicals (99 scheme, A-Z by title) - cont.

FL 399.3.9 Noël, E. Les annales du théâtre et de la musique. Paris. 1875-1916 40v.
FL 399.3.10 Annuaire général du spectacle en France. 1942+ 14v.
FL 399.4 Duval, Georges. L'année théâtrale. Paris. 1-3,1873-1876 3v.
FL 399.4.9 L'art dramatique et musical. Paris. 1901-1904 4v.
FL 399.4.15F L'art du théâtre. Paris. 1-3,1901-1903 3v.
FL 399.9F Bref. Paris. 69,1963+
FL 399.11F Camées artistiques. Paris. 1-152,1880-1883
FL 399.11.5 Cahiers de la compagnie Madeleine Renaud - Jean Louis Barrault. Paris. 1,1953+ 15v.
FL 399.14F Comoedia illustré. Paris. 1-8,1908-1921 11v.
FL 399.14.10 Collection le théâtre et les jours. Paris. 5-8 4v.
FL 399.16 Danse, musique, théâtre en Belgique. Bruxelles. 1957-1960 3v.
FL 399.42 Journal des spectacles. Paris. 1793
FL 399.56.15 Le monde dramatique. Paris. 1-8,1835-1839
Htn FL 399.57.5* Le musée des théâtres. Paris. 1823
Htn FL 399.66* L'opinion du parterre. Paris. 1-10,1803-1813 8v.
FL 399.68F Paris qui chante. Paris. 1903-1907 5v.
FL 399.68.5F Paris-théâtre; journal hebdomadaire. Paris. 1873-1879 6v.
FL 399.68.6F Paris-théâtre; journal hebdomadaire. Paris. 1873-1875 4v.
Htn FL 399.68.15F* La parisienne. Paris. 1895
FL 399.71.9 Touché, Raoul. Les premières illustrées. v.1-6. Paris, 1882-87. 3v.
FL 399.74F La rampe. Paris. 1899-1902
FL 399.75 Revue d'art dramatique. Paris. 1886-1909 60v.
FL 399.76F La revue théâtrale. Paris. 1904-1906 6v.
FL 399.82F Sports et théâtres. Paris. 1-21,1894-1895
FL 399.83 Les succès du jour. Paris. 2,1869
FL 399.85F Le théâtre et comédie illustré. Paris. 1898-1926 33v.
FL 399.85.4F Le théâtre libre illustré. Paris. 1868-1870
FL 399.85.6 Le théâtre libre illustré. 1889-1891 2v.
FL 399.85.10F Théâtre contemporain illustré. Paris. 1856-1858
FL 399.86 Théâtre de Belgique. Bruxelles. 1,1954+ 3v.
FL 399.86.10 L'information sur l'théâtre. Paris. 11,1955+ 8v.
FL 399.87 Le tout-théâtre. Paris. 1905-1906 2v.

FL 1010 - 1019 Literature in French dialects - Dialects of Normandy - Norman proper

FL 1018.46.100 Cotis-Capel. Raz-Bannes; poémes en langue normande. Coutances, 1970.
FL 1018.97.21 Ferrand, David. La musse normande de David Ferrand. Rouen, 1891-94. 5v.

FL 1020 - 1029 Literature in French dialects - Dialects of Normandy - Anglo-Norman, Anglo-French

FL 1022.5 Walberg, Emanuel. Quelques aspects de la littérature anglo-normande. Paris, 1936.
FL 1022.10 Legge, Mary Dominica. Anglo-Norman in the cloisters. Edinburgh, 1950.
FL 1022.10.5 Legge, Mary Dominica. Anglo-Norman literature and its background. Oxford, 1963.
FL 1022.15 West, C.B. Courtisie in Anglo-Norman literature. Oxford, 1938.
FL 1026.2 Aspin, Isabel Stewart Tod. Anglo-Norman political songs. Oxford, 1953.
FL 1028.116.100 Gregorius I, the Great, Saint, Pope. Dialogues, translated into Angle-Norman French by Angier. Strassburg, 1901.
FL 1029.4A Anglo-Norman poem on the conquest of Ireland by Henry the II. London, 1837.
FL 1029.4B Anglo-Norman poem on the conquest of Ireland by Henry the II. London, 1837.
FL 1029.66 L'ornement des dames, ornatus mulierum. Bruxelles, 1967.
FL 1029.87 Verkvitz, Wilhelm. Tractate zur Unterweisung in der Anglo-Normannischen Briefschreibkunst. Greifswald, 1898.

FL 1040 - 1049 Literature in French dialects - Dialects of Southwestern France

FL 1048.177.102 Lacuve, Édouard. Fables en patois poitevin. 2. éd. Melle, 1968.
FL 1048.251.100 Saint Long (pseud.). Les amours de Colas. Paris, 1843.

FL 1090 - 1099 Literature in French dialects - Dialect of Picardy

FL 1098.47.101 Crimon, Hector. Satires picarde. Péronne, 1876.
FL 1098.47.800 Debrie, René. Hector Crimon. Grandvilliers, 1970.
FL 1098.55.11 David, Édouard. Oeuvres complétes...Amiens, musée de Picardie. Paris, 1969-

FL 1100 - 1109 Literature in French dialects - Walloon dialect

FL 1101.5 Coppe, Paul. Dictionnaire bio-bibliographique des littérateurs d'expression wallone, 1622 à 1950. Gembloux, 1951.
FL 1102.5.2 Lejeune-Dehousse, Rita. Histoire sommaire de la littérature wallonne. 2. ed. Bruxelles, 1942.
FL 1102.6.2 Piron, Maurice. Les lettres wallonnes contemporaines. 2. ed. Tournai, 1944.
FL 1102.7 Barry, Félicien. Deux cent septante écrivains dialectaux du pays noir. Charleroi? 1958.
FL 1106.5 Maréchal, Lucien. Anthologie des poètes wallons namurois. Namur, 1930.
FL 1106.6 Piron, Maurice. Poètes wallons d'aujourd'hui. Paris, 1961.
FL 1106.8.2 Èn kèrtinéye dè fleûrs. 2. ed. Nivelles, 1961.
FL 1106.10.3 Werotte, Charles. Ch'oix di ch'ansons wallonnes et otres poésies. 3. éd. Namur, 1860. 2 pam.
FL 1108.28.21 Bertrand, Jacques. Les oeuvres wallonnes. Charleroi, 1960.
FL 1108.56.100 Defrecheux, Nicolas. Chansons wallonnes. Liège, 1860.
FL 1108.126.10 Hock, Auguste. Oeuvres complètes. Liège, 1872-74. 4v.
FL 1108.243.100 Renard, Michel. Les aventures de Jean d'Nivelles, el fils dé s'paire. Bruxelles, 1857.
FL 1108.243.105 Renard, Michel. Lès aventures dè Djan d'Nivèle èl fi dè s'pére. Naumur, 1963.
FL 1109.71.10 Poème moral. Le poème moral, traité de vie chretienne ecrit dans la région wallonne vers l'an 1250. Liège, 1929.

FL 1210 - 1219 Literature in French dialects - Franco-Provençal dialects - Dauphinois dialect

FL 1218.33.100F Blanc, François. Poésies en patois du Dauphiné. Grenoble, 1966.

FL 6001 Jean Jacques Rousseau - Complete and Selected works - French editions - Complete works (By date, e.g. .960 for 1960)

Htn FL 6001.769* Rousseau, J.J. Oeuvres. Amsterdam, 1762-69. 11v.
FL 6001.781.2 Rousseau, J.J. Oeuvres posthumes. Genève, 1781. 3v.
FL 6001.782 Rousseau, J.J. Collection complette des oeuvres. v.1-24. Deux-Ponts, 1782. 12v.
FL 6001.782.2 Rousseau, J.J. Supplement à la collection des oeuvres. v.25-30. Deux-Ponts, 1782. 3v.
FL 6001.788 Rousseau, J.J. Oeuvres completes. v.1-38. n.p., 1788-93. 37v.
FL 6001.793 Rousseau, J.J. Oeuvres complettes. Paris, 1793. 37v.
FL 6001.817 Rousseau, J.J. Oeuvres. Paris, 1817. 8v.
FL 6001.817.2 Rousseau, J.J. Oeuvres. Paris, 1817. 18v.
FL 6001.818 Rousseau, J.J. Oeuvres complètes. Paris, 1818-22. 24v.
FL 6001.819 Rousseau, J.J. Oeuvres avec notes historiques. v.1-22. Paris, 1819. 21v.
FL 6001.821 Rousseau, J.J. Oeuvres. Paris, 1821. 21v.
FL 6001.823 Rousseau, J.J. Oeuvres. Paris, 1823-26. 25v.
FL 6001.826 Rousseau, J.J. Oeuvres complètes. Paris, 1826.
FL 6001.826.5 Rousseau, J.J. Oeuvres complètes. Paris, 1826. 25v.
FL 6001.834 Rousseau, J.J. Oeuvres complètes avec notes historiques et critiques. Paris, 1834. 17v.
FL 6001.835 Rousseau, J.J. Oeuvres complètes avec notes historiques. Paris, 1835. 4v.
FL 6001.840 Rousseau, J.J. Oeuvres. Paris, 1798-99. 18v.
FL 6001.883 Rousseau, J.J. Oeuvres complètes. v.1- Paris, 1883-95.
NEDL FL 6001.885 Rousseau, J.J. Oeuvres complètes. v.1-8,11-13. Paris, 1905. 6v.
FL 6001.959 Rousseau, J.J. Oeuvres complètes. Paris, 1959. 4v.

FL 6002 Jean Jacques Rousseau - Complete and Selected works - French editions - Selected works (By date, e.g. .970 for 1970)

Htn FL 6002.760* Rousseau, J.J. Oeuvres diverses. Amsterdam, 1760. 2v.
Htn FL 6002.763* Rousseau, J.J. Les pensées. Amsterdam, 1763.
Htn FL 6002.764.5* Rousseau, J.J. Esprit, maximes, et principes. Neuchâtel, 1764.
Htn FL 6002.764.10* Rousseau, J.J. Oeuvres de Rousseau de Genève. Neuchâtel, 1764. 5v.
Htn FL 6002.764.15* Rousseau, J.J. Esprit, maximes, et principes. Neuchâtel, 1764.
Htn FL 6002.766* Rousseau, J.J. Le pensées. v.1-2. Amsterdam, 1766.
FL 6002.766.5 Rousseau, J.J. Oeuvres choisies. Paris, 1766.
FL 6002.781 Rousseau, J.J. Mélanges. Tome. 2-3. Berne, 1781. 2v.
FL 6002.782 Rousseau, J.J. Pièces diverses. London, 1782. 4v.
X Cg FL 6002.782.3 Rousseau, J.J. Mélanges. London, 1782. 6v.
FL 6002.786 Rousseau, J.J. Pensées de J.J. Rousseau. London, 1786. 2v.
FL 6002.789 Rousseau, J.J. Pensées. Genève, 1789. 2v.
FL 6002.810 Rousseau, J.J. Rousseaua, ou Recueil d'anecdotes. Paris, 1810.
FL 6002.853 Rousseau, J.J. Fragments inédits. Paris, 1853.
FL 6002.861 Rousseau, J.J. Oeuvres et correspondance inédites. Paris, 1861.
FL 6002.878 Comité du Centenaire. Jean Jacques Rousseau et ses oeuvres. Genève, 1878.
FL 6002.878.2 Rousseau, J.J. Jean-Jacques et le pays Romand. Genève, 1878.
FL 6002.878.3 Comité du Centenaire. Sagesse de Jean-Jacques: fragments écrits de Rousseau. Genève, 1878.
FL 6002.884 Rousseau, J.J. Morceaux choisis. Paris, 1884.
FL 6002.891 Rousseau, J.J. Lectures choisies. Paris, 1891.
FL 6002.892 Rousseau, J.J. Extraits en prose. Paris, 1892.
FL 6002.892.2 Rousseau, J.J. Morceaux choisis. Paris, 1892.
FL 6002.896 Rousseau, J.J. Extraits de J.J. Rousseau publiés avec une introduction et des notes par L. Brunel. 3. éd. Paris, 1896.
FL 6002.899 Rousseau, J.J. Petits chefs-d'oeuvres. Paris, 1899.
FL 6002.905 Rousseau, J.J. Pages choisies des grands écrivains. 7. ed. Paris, 1905.
FL 6002.906 Schroeder, V. Jean Jacques Rousseau morceaux choisis. Paris, 1906.
FL 6002.906.2 Guy, J. Jean Jacques Rousseau. Paris, 1906.
FL 6002.908 Simond, C. Jean-Jacques Rousseau. Paris, 1908.
FL 6002.911 Rousseau, J.J. Extraits. Paris, 1911.
FL 6002.914A Rousseau, J.J. Selections from the work of J.J. Rousseau. C. Gauss. Princeton, 1914.
FL 6002.914B Rousseau, J.J. Selections from the work of J.J. Rousseau. C. Gauss. Princeton, 1914.
NEDL FL 6002.915 Rousseau, J.J. Political writings, edited from the original manuscripts...text in French. v.1-2. Cambridge, Eng., 1915. 2v.
NEDL FL 6002.920.4 Rousseau, J.J. Morceaux choisis. 4. ed. Paris, 1920.
FL 6002.921A Rousseau, J.J. Vie et oeuvres de Jean-Jacques Rousseau. Boston, 1921.
FL 6002.921B Rousseau, J.J. Vie et oeuvres de Jean-Jacques Rousseau. Boston, 1921.
X Cg FL 6002.922 Rousseau, J.J. Extraits publiés avec une introduction. L. Brunel. 13. éd. Paris, 1922.
FL 6002.926 Rousseau, J.J. Pages choisies. 15. éd. Paris, 1926.
FL 6002.936 Rousseau, J.J. Extraits, publiés avec une introduction. Paris, 1936.
FL 6002.936.5 Rousseau, J.J. Extraits des oeuvres autobiographiques. Paris, 1936.
FL 6002.962A Rousseau, J.J. Political writings. Oxford, 1962. 2v.
FL 6002.962B Rousseau, J.J. Political writings. Oxford, 1962. 2v.
FL 6002.962.5 Rousseau, J.J. Choix de textes. Paris, 1962.

FL 6003 Jean Jacques Rousseau - Complete and Selected works - French editions - Special selections

FL 6003.2 Rousseau, J.J. Traites sur la musique. Genève, 1781.
FL 6003.3 Rousseau, J.J. Traites sur la musique. Deux-Ponts, 1782.
FL 6003.5 Rousseau, J.J. Écrits autobiographiques. Paris, 1955.
FL 6003.6 Rousseau, J.J. A la rencontre de Jean-Jacques Rousseau. Genève, 1962.

FL 6004 Jean Jacques Rousseau - Complete and Selected works - English editions - Complete works

FL 6004.2 Rousseau, J.J. Miscellaneous works of Jean-Jacques Rousseau. London, 1767. 5v.

FL 6005 Jean Jacques Rousseau - Complete and Selected works - English editions - Selected works

FL 6005.2 The beauties of Rousseau, selected by a lady. London, 1788. 2v.
FL 6005.20 Rousseau, J.J. Minor educational writings of Jean-Jacques Rousseau. London, 1911.
FL 6005.22 Rousseau, J.J. The minor educational writings of Jean-Jacques Rousseau. N.Y., 1962.
FL 6005.30A Rousseau, J.J. The living thoughts of Rousseau. N.Y., 1939.
FL 6005.30B Rousseau, J.J. The living thoughts of Rousseau. N.Y., 1939.
FL 6005.40 Rousseau, J.J. Political writings containing The social contract. Edinburgh, 1953.

FL 6006 Jean Jacques Rousseau - Complete and Selected works - German editions - Complete works

FL 6006.2 Rousseau, J.J. Philosophische Werke. Reval, 1779. 3v.

FL 6007 Jean Jacques Rousseau - Complete and Selected works - German editions - Selected works

FL 6007.5 Rousseau, J.J. Jean-Jacques Rousseau: in seinen Werken. Stuttgart, 1908.

FL 6010 Jean Jacques Rousseau - Complete and Selected works - Editions in other languages

VFL 6010.1 Rousseau, J.J. Traktaty. Moskva, 1969.

FL 6015 Jean Jacques Rousseau - Correspondence - French editions

Htn FL 6015.2* Contestation entre Hume et Rousseau, 1766. London, 1766.
FL 6015.3 Dusaulx, J. De mes rapports avec Jean-Jacques Rousseau. Paris, 1798.
FL 6015.4 Rousseau, J.J. Correspondance - originale et inédite. Paris, 1803. 2v.
FL 6015.6 Rousseau, J.J. Les plus belles lettres de Jean-Jacques Rousseau et de ses correspondants choisies par Jules Baillods. Neuchâtel, 1938.
FL 6015.8 Rousseau, J.J. Lettre inédite à M.M. Rey. Amsterdam, 1858.
FL 6015.9 Streckeisen-Moultu, George. Jean-Jacques Rousseau, ses amis et ses ennemis. v.1-2. Paris, 1865.
FL 6015.10 Rothschild, H. de. Lettres inédites de Jean-Jacques Rousseau. Paris, 1892.
FL 6015.11 Buffenoir, H. Jean-Jacques Rousseau et Henriette. Paris, 1902.
FL 6015.12 Petitpierre, A. Jean-Jacques Rousseau et Isabelle d'Ivernois. Paris, 1878.
FL 6015.13 Rousseau, J.J. Correspondance avec L. Usteri. Zurich, 1910.
FL 6015.14 Rousseau, J.J. Lettres inédites à Mmes. Boy de La Tour. Paris, 1911.
FL 6015.15 Lettre d'un anonime à Mr. Jean -Jacques Rousseau. Paris, 1766.
FL 6015.16 Rousseau, J.J. Matériaux pour la correspondance. Paris, 1923.
FL 6015.17A Rousseau, J.J. Correspondance général de Jean-Jacques Rousseau. Paris, 1924-34. 20v.
FL 6015.17B Rousseau, J.J. Correspondance général de Jean-Jacques Rousseau. v.5-7. Paris, 1924-34. 3v.
FL 6015.18 Plan, P.P. Table de la correspondance général de Jean-Jacques Rousseau. Genève, 1953.
FL 6015.19 Rousseau, J.J. Correspondance complète. Genève, 1965. 14v.

FL 6016 Jean Jacques Rousseau - Correspondence - English editions

FL 6016.5 Rousseau, J.J. Citizens of Geneva. N.Y., 1937.

FL 6017 Jean Jacques Rousseau - Correspondence - Editions in other languages

FL 6017.2 Rousseau, J.J. Ausgewählte Briefe. Hildburghausen, 1872.
FL 6017.3 Rousseau, J.J. Briefe in Answahl. Genf, 1907.

FL 6020 - 6023 Jean Jacques Rousseau - Confessions - French editions - Complete (By date, e.g. 6021.80 for 1880, 6022.60 for 1960)

Htn FL 6020.82* Rousseau, J.J. Les confessions suivies à des rèveries. Genève, 1782. 2v.
FL 6020.82.5 Rousseau, J.J. Les confessions suivies à des rèveries. Genève, 1782-89. 4v.
FL 6020.95 Rousseau, J.J. Confessions. v.3-4. Genève, 1795.
FL 6021.01 Rousseau, J.J. Les confessions. Paris, 1801. 2v.
FL 6021.13 Rousseau, J.J. Les confessions. Paris, 1813. 4v.
FL 6021.13.2 Rousseau, J.J. Les confessions. v.1-2,4. Paris, 1913. 3v.
FL 6021.19 Rousseau, J.J. Les confessions. Paris, 1819. 2v.
FL 6021.22 Rousseau, J.J. Les confessions. Paris, 1822. 4v.
FL 6021.24 Rousseau, J.J. Confessions de Jean-Jacques Rousseau. Paris, 1824. 5v.
FL 6021.36 Rousseau, J.J. Les confessions. v.1-5. Paris, 1836. 2v.
FL 6021.41 Rousseau, J.J. Les confessions. Paris, 1841.
FL 6021.46 Rousseau, J.J. Les confessions. Paris, 1846.
FL 6021.55F Bougy, A. de. Les confessions de Jean-Jacques Rousseau. Paris, 1855.
FL 6021.73 Rousseau, J.J. Les confessions. Paris, 1873.
FL 6021.81A Rousseau, J.J. Les confessions. Paris, 1881.
FL 6021.81B Rousseau, J.J. Les confessions. Paris, 1881.
FL 6021.86 Rousseau, J.J. Les confessions. Paris, 1886.
FL 6022.00 Rousseau, J.J. Les confessions. Paris, 1900.
FL 6022.10 Rousseau, J.J. Confessions. Paris, 1910.
FL 6022.25A Rousseau, J.J. Les confessions. Paris, n.d. 2v.
FL 6022.25B Rousseau, J.J. Les confessions. v.2. Paris, 1924-25.
FL 6022.33 Rousseau, J.J. Les confessions. Argenteuil, 1933.
FL 6022.47 Rousseau, J.J. Les confessions. Paris, 1947.
FL 6022.49 Rousseau, J.J. Les confessions. Paris, 1949. 2v.
FL 6022.62 Rousseau, J.J. Les confessions. Paris, 1962.
FL 6022.64 Rousseau, J.J. Les confessions. Paris, 1964.

FL 6024 Jean Jacques Rousseau - Confessions - French editions - Selections

FL 6024.2 Rousseau, J.J. Fragments inédits des confessions. Neuchâtel, 1850.
FL 6024.5 Rousseau, J.J. N'a jamais eu d'enfants. Nice, 1912.
FL 6024.10 Rousseau, J.J. Jean-Jacques Rousseau en Savoie; Annecy, chambéry, les charmettes. Chambéry, 1922.

Classified Listing

FL 6024 Jean Jacques Rousseau - Confessions - French editions - Selections - cont.
FL 6024.15 Rousseau, J.J. Selections from the confession and rêveries d'un promeneur solitaire. N.Y., 1937.
FL 6024.20 Rousseau, J.J. Introduction à l'étude de Jean-Jacques Rousseau: les confessions, I-IV. Paris, 1963.

FL 6026 Jean Jacques Rousseau - Confessions - English editions
FL 6026.5 Rousseau, J.J. The confessions. London, n.d.
FL 6026.8 Rousseau, J.J. The confessions. London, 1875.
FL 6026.8.5 Rousseau, J.J. The confessions. Philadelphia, 189-. 2v.
FL 6026.8.10 Rousseau, J.J. The confessions of Jean-Jacques Rousseau. London, 1891. 2v.
Htn FL 6026.8.15* Rousseau, J.J. The confessions. n.p., 1896. 2v.
FL 6026.8.16 Rousseau, J.J. The confessions of Jean-Jacques Rousseau. n.p., 1896. 2v.
FL 6026.8.20 Rousseau, J.J. The confessions. v.1,3-4. n.p., 1901. 3v.
FL 6026.8.25 Rousseau, J.J. The confessions of Jean-Jacques Rousseau. N.Y., 19- ?
FL 6026.10A Rousseau, J.J. The confessions. Edinburgh, 1904. 2v.
FL 6026.10B Rousseau, J.J. The confessions. Edinburgh, 1904. 2v.
FL 6026.10.3 Rousseau, J.J. Collection of etchings used in Rousseau's confessions. n.p., n.d.
FL 6026.10.15A Rousseau, J.J. The confessions of Jean-Jacques Rousseau. N.Y., 190-?
FL 6026.10.15B Rousseau, J.J. The confessions of Jean-Jacques Rousseau. N.Y., 190-?
FL 6026.11 Rousseau, J.J. Confessions of Jean-Jacques Rousseau. London, 1931. 2v.
FL 6026.12 Rousseau, J.J. Confessions. N.Y., 1856. 2v.
FL 6026.16 Rousseau, J.J. Confessions. London, 1872.
FL 6026.18 Rousseau, J.J. Confessions. n.p., 1901. 2v.
FL 6026.19 Rousseau, J.J. Confessions. London, 1903.
FL 6026.20 Rousseau, J.J. The confessions. N.Y., 1955.

FL 6027 Jean Jacques Rousseau - Confessions - Editions in other languages
FL 6027.2 Rousseau, J.J. Bekenntnisse. Leipzig, 186-? 2v.
FL 6027.3 Rousseau, J.J. Bekenntnisse. Hildburghausen, 1870. 2v.
FL 6027.4 Rousseau, J.J. Bekenntnisse. Berlin, 1907.

FL 6029 Jean Jacques Rousseau - Confessions - Criticism
FL 6029.2 Estienne, C. Essai sur les confessions de Jean-Jacques Rousseau. Paris, 1856.
FL 6029.3 Ritter, E. Nouvelles recherches; confessions et correspondance de Rousseau. Oppeln, 1880.
FL 6029.4 Sehinz, A. Confessions de Jean-Jacques Rousseau. Paris, 1906.
FL 6029.5 Servan, A.J.M. de. Réflexions sur les Confessions de Jean-Jacques Rousseau. Hambourg, 1783.
FL 6029.6 Chas, F. Jean-Jacques Rousseau justifié ou Réponse à M. Servan. Neuchâtel, 1784.
FL 6029.7 Calemard, J. L'édition originale des Confessions de Jean-Jacques Rousseau. Paris, 1928.
FL 6029.8 Guéhenno, Jean. Jean-Jacques. Paris, 1948-52. 3v.
FL 6029.8.5 Guéhenno, Jean. Jean-Jacques. Paris, 1962. 2v.
FL 6029.8.10 Guéhenno, Jean. Jean-Jacques Rousseau. London, 1966. 2v.
FL 6029.9 Gingnené, Pierre Louis. Lettres sur les confessions de Jean-Jacques Rousseau. Paris, 1791.
FL 6029.10 Saussure, Hermine de. Rousseau et les manuscrits des Confessions. Paris, 1958.
FL 6029.12 Ritzel, Wolfgang. Rousseaus Selbstverständnis in den Confessions. Wilhelmshaven, 1958.
FL 6029.14 Ellis, Madeleine. Rousseau's Venetian story. Baltimore, 1966.

FL 6030 - 6033 Jean Jacques Rousseau - Contrat social - French editions - Complete (By date, e.g. 6031.90 for 1890, 6032.70 for 1970)
Htn FL 6030.62* Rousseau, J.J. Du contrat social. Amsterdam, 1762.
Htn FL 6030.62.2* Rousseau, J.J. Principes du droit politique. Amsterdam, 1762.
Htn FL 6030.62.3* Rousseau, J.J. Du contrat social. Amsterdam, 1762.
Htn FL 6030.62.4* Rousseau, J.J. Du contrat social. Amsterdam, 1762.
FL 6030.65 Rousseau, J.J. Oeuvres. Contrat social. v.8. Neufchâtal, 1765.
FL 6030.82 Rousseau, J.J. Du contrat social ou Principes du droit politique. London, 1782.
FL 6030.91 Rousseau, J.J. Du contrat social ou Principes du droit politique. Paris, 1791.
FL 6031.25 Rousseau, J.J. Du contrat social ou Principes du droit politique. Paris, 1822.
FL 6031.89 Rousseau, J.J. Du contrat social. Paris, 1889.
FL 6031.93 Rousseau, J.J. Contrat social. Paris, 1893.
FL 6031.96 Rousseau, J.J. Contrat social. Paris, 1896.
FL 6032.03 Rousseau, J.J. Du contrat social. Paris, 1903.
FL 6032.18 Rousseau, J.J. Du contrat social. Manchester, 1918.
FL 6032.30 Rousseau, J.J. Du contrat social. 5. ed. Paris, 1930.
FL 6032.43 Rousseau, J.J. Du contrat social. Paris, 1943.
FL 6032.47 Rousseau, J.J. Du contrat social. Genève, 1947.
FL 6032.56 Rousseau, J.J. Du contrat social. Paris, 1956.
FL 6032.66 Rousseau, J.J. Du contrat social. Paris, 1966.

FL 6036 Jean Jacques Rousseau - Contrat social - English editions
FL 6036.5 Rousseau, J.J. An inquiry into the nature of The social contract. London, 1791.
FL 6036.5.5 Rousseau, J.J. An inquiry into the nature of The social contract; or Principles of political right. Dublin, 1791.
FL 6036.5.10 Rousseau, J.J. The social contract. London, n.d.
FL 6036.10 Rousseau, J.J. The social contract. N.Y., 1893.
FL 6036.11.5 Rousseau, J.J. The social contract. London, 1924.
NEDL FL 6036.11.7 Rousseau, J.J. The social contract. 3. ed. London, 1902.
FL 6036.13.15 Rousseau, J.J. The social contract. N.Y., 1947.

FL 6037 Jean Jacques Rousseau - Contrat social - Editions in other languages
FL 6037.15 Rousseau, J.J. El contrato social. Madrid, 1821.
FL 6037.25 Rousseau, J.J. Il contratto sociale. Italia, 1850.
FL 6037.26 Rousseau, J.J. Del contratto sociale. Pinerolo, 1850.
FL 6037.28 Rousseau, J.J. Il contratto sociale. Messina, 1928.

FL 6039 Jean Jacques Rousseau - Contrat social - Criticism
FL 6039.2 Berthier, P.G.F. Observations sur le Contrat social. Paris, 1789.
FL 6039.3 Landes, P. Rousseau, Grundsätze des natürlichen Staatsrechts. Leipzig, 1804.
FL 6039.4 Bertrand, A. Le texte primitif du Contrat social. Paris, 1891.

FL 6039 Jean Jacques Rousseau - Contrat social - Criticism - cont.
FL 6039.5 Rodet, St. Le contrat social...de Jean-Jacques Rousseau. Paris, 1909.
FL 6039.6 Larmartine, A. de. Jean-Jacques Rousseau, son faux. Paris, 1890.
FL 6039.9 Schinz, Albert. La question du "Contrat social". Paris, 1913.
FL 6039.10 Krömer, Emil J. Der Staats-Vertrag. Leipzig, 1874.
FL 6039.11 Rousseau, J.J. Gian Giaco Rousseau all assemblia nazionale o commentario postumo di qusto filosofo sud Contratto sociale. Filadelfia, 1791.
FL 6039.12 Schwarz, Erich. Freiheit und Staatsomnipotenz in Rousseaus "Contrat social". Inaug. Diss. Schramberg, 1936.
FL 6039.13 Lanjuinais, J.D. Examen du 8e chapitre du Contrat social de Jean-Jacques Rousseau. Paris, 1825.
FL 6039.14 Vecchio, G. Su la teoria del Contratto sociale. Bologna, 1906.
FL 6039.15 Lo Gatto Napolitano, M. Il contratto sociale di Gian Giacomo Rousseau. Napoli, 1951.
FL 6039.17 Testa, Aldo. Meditazioni su Rousseau dal Contratto sociale al dialogo sociale. Bologna, 1963.
FL 6039.18 McManners, John. The social contract and Rousseau's revolt against society. London, 1968.
FL 6039.19 Crocker, Lester G. Rousseau's Social contract. Cleveland, 1968.

FL 6040 - 6043 Jean Jacques Rousseau - Émile - French editions - Complete (By date, e.g. 6041.70 for 1870, 6042.50 for 1950)
Htn FL 6040.62* Rousseau, J.J. Émile, ou De l'éducation. Francfort, 1762. 2v.
Htn FL 6040.62.2* Rousseau, J.J. Émile, ou De l'éducation. La Haye, 1762. 4v.
Htn FL 6040.62.3* Rousseau, J.J. Émile ou De l'éducation. Paris, 1762.
FL 6040.77 Rousseau, J.J. Émile ou De l'éducation. Amsterdam, 1777.
FL 6040.80 Rousseau, J.J. Émile ou De l'éducation. Genève, 1780. 4v.
X Cg FL 6040.80.2 Rousseau, J.J. Émile ou De l'éducation. Londres, 1780-81. 4v.
FL 6040.93 Rousseau, J.J. Émile ou De l'éducaton. Paris, 1793. 3v.
FL 6041.17 Rousseau, J.J. Émile ou De l'éducation. Paris, 1817. 3v.
FL 6041.26 Rousseau, J.J. Oeuvres complètes. Paris, 1826. 3v.
FL 6041.44 Rousseau, J.J. Émile ou De l'éducation. Paris, 1844.
FL 6041.54 Rousseau, J.J. Émile ou De l'éducation. Paris, 1854.
FL 6041.60 Rousseau, J.J. Émile ou De l'éducation. Paris, 1860?
FL 6041.84 Rousseau, J.J. Émile ou De l'éducation. Paris, 1884.
FL 6042.00 Rousseau, J.J. Émile ou De l'éducation. Paris, 1900.
FL 6042.05 Rousseau, J.J. Émile ou De l'éducation. Paris, 1900.
FL 6042.06 Rousseau, J.J. Émile ou De l'éducation. Paris, 1906.
FL 6042.13 Rousseau, J.J. Émile. Paris, 1913.
FL 6042.51 Rousseau, J.J. Émile. 16. éd. Paris, 1951.
FL 6042.58 Rousseau, J.J. Émile. Paris, 1958.

FL 6046 Jean Jacques Rousseau - Émile - English editions
Htn FL 6046.2* Rousseau, J.J. Emilius and Sophia. London, 1762-63. 4v.
FL 6046.7 Rousseau, J.J. Emilius or, A treatise of education. Edinburgh, 1773. 3v.
FL 6046.7.5 Rousseau, J.J. Émilius. Edinburgh, 1773. 3v.
FL 6046.10.15 Rousseau, J.J. Émile or Education. London, 1925.
FL 6046.11 Rousseau, J.J. Émile ou De l'éducation. Paris, 1874.
FL 6046.12.10 Rousseau, J.J. Émile ou De l'éducation. Boston, 1883.
FL 6046.12.13 Rousseau, J.J. Emile, or Concerning education. Boston, 1888.
FL 6046.12.20 Rousseau, J.J. Émile. London, 1969.
NEDL FL 6046.13.30 Rousseau, J.J. Emile; or Concerning education. Boston, 1885.
FL 6046.13.35 Rousseau, J.J. Emile for today. London, 1956.
FL 6046.13.40 Rousseau, J.J. The Emile of Jean-Jacques Rousseau. N.Y., 1962.
FL 6046.14.5 Rousseau, J.J. Rousseau's estimate of the manual arts. Paris, 1924.

FL 6047 Jean Jacques Rousseau - Émile - Editions in other languages
FL 6047.1.5 Rousseau, J.J. Emil, oder von der Erziehung. pt.1-4. Berlin, 1762. 2v.
FL 6047.2 Rousseau, J.J. Emil oder über die Erziehung. Leipzig, 1881.
FL 6047.3 Rousseau, J.J. Émil oder über die Erziehung. Wien, 1905.
FL 6047.4 Rousseau, J.J. Emil oder über Erziehung. Langensalza, 1893. 2v.
FL 6047.7 Rousseau, J.J. Emil oder über die Erziehung. Potsdam, 1919.
FL 6047.11 Rousseau, J.J. Jean-Jacques Rousseau. 2. Aufl. v.1-2. Langensalza, 1882-83.
FL 6047.75 Rousseau, J.J. Emil. Přerově, 1907.

FL 6048.1 - .499 Jean Jacques Rousseau - Émile - Special parts - Profession de Foi du Vicaire Savoyard
FL 6048.35.5 Rousseau, J.J. Profession of faith of a Savoyard vicar. N.Y., 1889.
FL 6048.37 Rousseau, J.J. The creed of a priest of Savoy. N.Y., 1956.
FL 6048.49.14 Rousseau, J.J. La "Profession de foi du Vicaire Savoyard". Thèse. Fribourg, 1914.
FL 6048.49.17 Rousseau, J.J. La "Profession de foi du Vicaire Savoyard". Paris, 1914.
FL 6048.49.20 Rousseau, J.J. Profession de foi du Vicaire Savoyard. Paris, 1964.

FL 6049 Jean Jacques Rousseau - Émile - Criticism
FL 6049.2 Marceille, G. Examen de la Profession de foi du Vicaire Savoyard (Jean-Jacques Rousseau. Emile.). Paris, 1828.
FL 6049.3 Peltzer, P. Jean-Jacques Rousseau's Glaubensbekenntniss des Vikars aus Savoyen. Köln, 1885.
FL 6049.4 Censori, V. Dei criteri educativi di J.J. Rousseau. Tivoli, 1895.
FL 6049.5 Viridet, M. Documents officiels sur le condamnation d'Emile. Genève, 1850.
FL 6049.6 Görland, A. Rousseau als Klassiker des Sozialpädagogik. Gotha, 1906.
FL 6049.7 Voltaire, F.M.A. de. Notes inédites sur la Profession de foi du Vicaire Savoyard. n.p., n.d.
FL 6049.10 Gerdil, G.S. L'anti-Emilio. Firenze, 1924.
FL 6049.10.5 Gerdil, G.S. L'anti-Emilo. Firenze, 1826.
FL 6049.10.15 Gerdil, G.S. Reflections on education. Holborn, 1965.

FL 6049 Jean Jacques Rousseau - Émile - Criticism - cont.
- FL 6049.12 Vial, Francisque. La doctrine l'éducation de Jean-Jacques Rousseau. Paris, 1920.
- FL 6049.13 Carrara, Vincenza. Jean-Jacques Rousseau. Firenze, 1926.
- FL 6049.14 Sertz, Edwin. Werte, Wertarten und ihre Rangordung in Jean-Jacques. Diss. Giessen, 1928.
- FL 6049.16 Tieng-yd'n, Liang. L'éducation masculine et l'éducation féminine selon Jean-Jacques Rousseau. Thèse. Dijon, 1931.
- FL 6049.18 Flores d'Arcais, G. Il problema pedagogico nell'Emilio di G.G. Rousseau. Padova, 1951.
- FL 6049.20 Guarnieri, Primo. L'educazione femmile nel pensiero di G.G. Rousseau. Adria, 1955.
- FL 6049.22 Sorge, Giuseppe. Rousseau e la pedagogia sociale contemporanea. Mazara, 1958.
- FL 6049.24 Velde, Isaac Van der. Jean-Jacques Rousseau pedagoog. Amsterdam, 1967.
- FL 6049.26 Tobiassen, Rolf. Nature et nature humaine dans l'Emile de Jean-Jacques Rousseau. Oslo, 1961.
- FL 6049.28 Scarlata, Giuseppe. La struttura del problema pedagogico nell' Emile di Jean Jacques Rousseau. Trapani, 1968.

FL 6050 - 6053 Jean Jacques Rousseau - Nouvelle Héloise - French editions - Complete (By date, e.g. 6051.80 for 1880, 6052.60 for 1960)
- Htn FL 6050.62* Rousseau, J.J. Julie ou La nouvelle Héloise. Amsterdam, 1762. 2v.
- Htn FL 6050.63* Rousseau, J.J. Lettres de deux Amans. 2. ed. Amsterdam, 1763. 3v.
- FL 6050.64 Rousseau, J.J. La nouvelle Héloise. Neuchâtel, 1764. 4v.
- FL 6050.81 Rousseau, J.J. La nouvelle Héloise. v.2-7. London, 1781. 6v.
- FL 6050.91 Rousseau, J.J. Julie ou la nouvelle Héloise. Amsterdam, 1791. 3v.
- FL 6050.92 Rousseau, J.J. La nouvelle Héloise. Paris, 1792. 3v.
- FL 6051.01 Rousseau, J.J. Julie ou la nouvelle Héloise. Leipzig, 1801. 3v.
- FL 6051.06 Rousseau, J.J. La nouvelle Héloise. Paris, 1806. 4v.
- FL 6051.17 Rousseau, J.J. Julie, ou la nouvelle Héloise. Paris, 1817. 4v.
- FL 6051.27 Rousseau, J.J. Julie ou la nouvelle Héloise. Paris, 1827. 6v.
- FL 6051.45 Rousseau, J.J. Julie ou la nouvelle Héloise. Paris, 1845. 2v.
- FL 6051.56 Rousseau, J.J. La nouvelle Héloise. Paris, 1856.
- FL 6051.73 Rousseau, J.J. La nouvelle Héloise. Paris, 1873.
- FL 6051.77 Rousseau, J.J. La nouvelle Héloise. Paris, 1877.
- FL 6051.78 Rousseau, J.J. Julie, ou la nouvelle Héloise. Paris, 1878.
- FL 6052.00 Rousseau, J.J. La nouvelle Héloise. Paris, 1900.
- FL 6052.25 Rousseau, J.J. La nouvelle Héloise. Paris, 1925- 4v.
- FL 6052.60 Rousseau, J.J. Julie. Paris, 1960.

FL 6054 Jean Jacques Rousseau - Nouvelle Héloise - French editions - Selections
- FL 6054.5 Formey, M. L'ésprit de Julie, ou éxtrait de la nouvelle Héloise. Berlin, 1763.

FL 6056 Jean Jacques Rousseau - Nouvelle Héloise - English editions
- FL 6056.4 Rousseau, J.J. Eloisa. 3. ed. London, 1764. 4v.
- X Cg FL 6056.4.5 Rousseau, J.J. Eloisa. London, 1784. 4v.
- FL 6056.5 Rousseau, J.J. Julia: or, The new Eloisa. v.2-3. Edinburgh, 1794. 2v.
- FL 6056.6 Rousseau, J.J. Eloisa. Dublin, 1795. 4v.
- FL 6056.7 Rousseau, J.J. Eloisa. Philadelphia, 1796. 3v.
- FL 6056.12 Rousseau, J.J. La nouvelle Héloise. University Park, 1968.

FL 6057 Jean Jacques Rousseau - Nouvelle Héloise - Editions in other languages
- FL 6057.2 Rousseau, J.J. Die neue Heloise. v.1-2,5-6. Leipzig, 1776.
- FL 6057.3 Rousseau, J.J. Romane. Neue Heloise. Leipzig, 1788. 3v.

FL 6059 Jean Jacques Rousseau - Nouvelle Héloise - Criticism
- FL 6059.2 Brunel, L. La nouvelle Héloise et Mme. d'Houdetot. Paris, 1888.
- FL 6059.3 Vreeland, W.V.D. Rapport litteraire entre Genève et l'Angleterre. Genève, 1901.
- FL 6059.4 François, Alexis. Le premier baiser de l'amour. Genève, 1920.
- FL 6059.5 Blatz, Heinrich. Die Aufnahme der nouvelle Héloise. Heidelberg, 1914.
- FL 6059.10 Schinz, Albert. Date d'achèvement de La nouvelle Héloise. Baltimore, 1926.
- FL 6059.15 Mornet, Daniel. La nouvelle Héloise; étude et analyse. Paris, 1928.
- FL 6059.18 Carzou, Jean M. La conception de la nature humaine dans la nouvelle Héloise. Monte Carlo, 1965?
- FL 6059.20 Ellis, M.B. Julie, ou la nouvelle Héloise. Toronto, 1949.
- FL 6059.21 Geller, Hermann. Die Funktion der Geständnisse in Rousseaus La nouvelle Héloise. Bonn, 1964.
- FL 6059.22 Van Laere, François. Une lecture du temps dans la nouvelle Héloise. Neuchâtel, 1968.

FL 6061 Jean Jacques Rousseau - Minor works - Allegorie
- FL 6061.76 Thomas, L. Allégorie: la dernière phase de la pensée religieuse. Lausanne, 1902.

FL 6062 Jean Jacques Rousseau - Minor works - Botanique
- FL 6062.2 Rousseau, J.J. La botanique. Paris, 1802.
- Htn FL 6062.3PF* Rousseau, J.J. La botanique. Paris, 1805.
- FL 6062.5 Rousseau, J.J. Lettres sur la botanique. Paris, 1962.
- FL 6062.49 Rousseau, J.J. Letters on the elements of botany. Addressed to a lady. 2. ed. London, 1787.
- FL 6062.50 Rousseau, J.J. Letters on the elements of botany. Addressed to a lady. London, 1802.

FL 6063 Jean Jacques Rousseau - Minor works - Considérations sur le gouvernement de Pologne
- FL 6063.2 Rousseau, J.J. Considerations sur le gouvernement de Pologne. London, 1782.

FL 6064 Jean Jacques Rousseau - Minor works - Devin de Village
- Htn FL 6064.3* Rousseau, J.J. Le devin du village, intermede. Genève, 1760.
- Htn FL 6064.4* Rousseau, J.J. Le devin du village. Paris, 1761.
- FL 6064.5 Rousseau, J.J. Le devin du village. Paris, n.d.
- FL 6064.15 Rousseau, J.J. The cunning man. Dublin, 1767.
- FL 6064.16 Rousseau, J.J. The cunning man. London, 1766.

FL 6065 Jean Jacques Rousseau - Minor works - Dictionnaire de musique
- FL 6065.3 Rousseau, J.J. Dictionnaire de musique. Amsterdam, 1768. 2v.
- FL 6065.3.5 Rousseau, J.J. Dictionnaire de musique. Tom. 2. Amsterdam, 1769.
- FL 6065.3.8 Rousseau, J.J. A complete dictionary of music. 2. ed. Dublin, 1779.
- FL 6065.4 Rousseau, J.J. Dictionnaire de musique. 2. éd. London, 1779.
- FL 6065.50 Rousseau, J.J. A dictionary of music. London, n.d.

FL 6067 Jean Jacques Rousseau - Minor works - Discours - L'Établissement des Sciences - Editions and modern criticism
- Htn FL 6067.5* Rousseau, J.J. Discours qui à remporté le prix a l'Académie de Dijon en l'année 1750. Genève, 1750?
- FL 6067.8 Rousseau, J.J. Discours sur les sciences et les arts. Paris, 1945.
- FL 6067.10A Rousseau, J.J. Jean-Jacques Rousseau; discours sur les sciences et les arts. N.Y., 1946.
- FL 6067.10B Rousseau, J.J. Jean-Jacques Rousseau; discours sur les sciences et les arts. N.Y., 1946.
- FL 6067.15A Rousseau, J.J. Über Kunst und Wissenschaft. Hamburg, 1955.
- FL 6067.15B Rousseau, J.J. Über Kunst und Wissenschaft. Hamburg, 1955.
- FL 6067.76 Krueger, G. Fremde Gedanken in J.J. Rousseaus ersten Discours. Braunschweig, 1891.

FL 6070 Jean Jacques Rousseau - Minor works - Discours - Quelle est l'origine de l'inégalité parmi les hommes?
- Htn FL 6070.2* Rousseau, J.J. Discours sur l'origine et les fondements de l'inégalité parmi les hommes. Amsterdam, 1755.
- Htn FL 6070.3* Rousseau, J.J. Discours sur l'origine et les fondements de l'inégalité parmi les hommes. Amsterdam, 1759.
- FL 6070.4 Rousseau, J.J. Discours sur l'origine et les fondements de l'inégalité parmi les hommes. Paris, 1965.
- FL 6070.50 Rousseau, J.J. Discourse on the origin of inequality. London, 1761.
- FL 6070.80 Bosshard, Peter. Die Beziehungen zwischen Rousseaus Zweitem Discours und dem 90. Thesis. Zürich, 1967.

FL 6071 Jean Jacques Rousseau - Minor works - Discours - Sur l'economie politique
- Htn FL 6071.2* Rousseau, J.J. Discours sur l'economie politique. Genève, 1758.
- FL 6071.50A Rousseau, J.J. Dissertation on political economy. Albany, 1797.
- FL 6071.50B Rousseau, J.J. Dissertation on political economy. Albany, 1797.

FL 6072 Jean Jacques Rousseau - Minor works - Discours - Sur les richesses
- FL 6072.2 Rousseau, J.J. Discours sur les richesses. Paris, 1853.

FL 6073 Jean Jacques Rousseau - Minor works - Dissertation sur la musique moderne
- Htn FL 6073.2* Rousseau, J.J. Dissertation sur la musique moderne. Paris, 1743.

FL 6074 Jean Jacques Rousseau - Minor works - Essai sur l'origine des langues
- FL 6074.2 Rousseau, J.J. Essai sur l'origine des langues. Frankfort, 185-.
- FL 6074.2.2 Rousseau, J.J. Essai sur l'origine des langues. Paris, 1967?
- FL 6074.3 Rousseau, J.J. Essai sur l'origine des langues où il est parlé de la mélodie et de l'imitation musicale. Bordeaux, 1968.
- FL 6074.52 Moran, John H. On the origin of language; Jean-Jacques Rousseau, essay on the origin of languages. N.Y., 1967.
- FL 6074.80 Verri, Antonio. Origine delle lingue e civiltà in Rousseau. Ravenna, 1970.

FL 6075 Jean Jacques Rousseau - Minor works - Imitation théâtrale
- Htn FL 6075.5* Rousseau, J.J. De l'imitation théatrale. Amsterdam, 1764.

FL 6076 Jean Jacques Rousseau - Minor works - Institutions chimiques
- FL 6076.77 Dufour, T. Les institutions chimiques de Jean-Jacques Rousseau. Genève, 1905.

FL 6077 Jean Jacques Rousseau - Minor works - Lettres - Lettre à d'Alembert
- Htn FL 6077.3* Rousseau, J.J. Letter to Mr. d'Alembert of Paris. London, 1759.
- FL 6077.5 Rousseau, J.J. Lettre à Mr. d'Alembert sur les spectacles. Paris, 1896.
- FL 6077.8 Rousseau, J.J. Lettre à Mr. d'Alembert sur les spectacles. Lille, 1948.
- FL 6077.9 Rousseau, J.J. Politics and the arts. Glencoe, Ill., 1960.
- Htn FL 6077.10* Rousseau, J.J. A letter from Mr. Rousseau, of Geneva. London, 1759.
- FL 6077.80 Ayres, E.H. Histoire de l'impression et de la publication de la lettre à d'Alembert de Jean-Jacques Rousseau. Menasha, 1922.
- FL 6077.82 Moffat, M.M. La controverse sur la moralité du théatre après la lettre à d'Alembert de Jean-Jacques Rousseau. Thèse. Paris, 1930.

FL 6078 Jean Jacques Rousseau - Minor works - Lettres - Lettre à C. de Baumont
- Htn FL 6078.50* Rousseau, J.J. Lettre à Marie-François Polymathos. n.p., 1770.

FL 6080 Jean Jacques Rousseau - Minor works - Lettres - Lettres à Malesherbes
- FL 6080.7 Rousseau, J.J. Lettres à Mr. de Malesherbes. London, 1928.
- FL 6080.10 Rousseau, J.J. Jean-Jacques Rousseau et Malesherbes. Paris, 1960.

Classified Listing

FL 6081 Jean Jacques Rousseau - Minor works - Lettres - Lettres de la Montagne

Htn FL 6081.2* Rousseau, J.J. Lettres écrites de la montagne. Amsterdam, 1764.
Htn FL 6081.3* Rousseau, J.J. Lettres écrites de la montagne. Amsterdam, 1765.
FL 6081.5 Rousseau, J.J. Lettres écrites de la montagne. Neuchâtel, 1962.
FL 6081.70 Rousseau, J.J. Lettere dalla montagna. Milan, 1905.

FL 6082 Jean Jacques Rousseau - Minor works - Lettres - Lettres sur la musique française

Htn FL 6082.2* Rousseau, J.J. Lettre sur la musique française. n.p., 1753.

FL 6084 Jean Jacques Rousseau - Minor works - Narcisse

Htn FL 6084.5* Rousseau, J.J. Narcisse. Paris? 1753.

FL 6085 Jean Jacques Rousseau - Minor works - Nouveau Dédale

FL 6085.5 Rousseau, J.J. Le nouveau Dédale, 1742. Genève, 1910.
FL 6085.10 Rousseau, J.J. Le nouveau Dédale. 1. ed. Pasadena, Calif., 1950.

FL 6087 Jean Jacques Rousseau - Minor works - Pensées d'un esprit droit

Htn FL 6087.2* Rousseau, J.J. Pensées d'un esprit droit et sentimens. Paris, 1826.

FL 6090 Jean Jacques Rousseau - Minor works - Projet de paix perpétuelle

Htn FL 6090.5* Saint-Pierre, Charles J.C. Extrait du projet de paix perpétuelle de monsieur l'abbé de St. Pierre. n.p., 1761.
FL 6090.25A Rousseau, J.J. L'état de guerre et projet de paix perpetuelle. N.Y., 1920.
FL 6090.25B Rousseau, J.J. L'état de guerre et projet de paix perpetuelle. N.Y., 1920.
FL 6090.50 Rousseau, J.J. A lasting peace through the federation of Europe. London, 1917.

FL 6091 Jean Jacques Rousseau - Minor works - Pygmalion

Htn FL 6091.10* Rousseau, J.J. Pigmalion; monologue. n.p., 1772.
FL 6091.50 Rousseau, J.J. Pygmalion...from the Franch. London, 1779.
FL 6091.55 Rousseau, J.J. Pygmalion and Galathea. Baltimore, 1823.
FL 6091.76.10 Istel, Edgar. Jean-Jacques Rousseau als Komponist seiner lyrischen scene Pygmalion. Leipzig, 1901.

FL 6094 Jean Jacques Rousseau - Minor works - Réveries du promeneur solitaire

FL 6094.5 Rousseau, J.J. Les rêveries du promeneur solitaire. n.p., n.d.
FL 6094.8 Rousseau, J.J. Les rêveries d'un promeneur solitaire. Paris, 1927.
FL 6094.8.5 Rousseau, J.J. Les rêveries du promeneur solitaire. Paris, 1933.
FL 6094.8.10 Rousseau, J.J. Les rêveries d'un promeneur solitaire. Manchester, 1942.
FL 6094.8.15 Rousseau, J.J. Les rêveries du promeneur solitaire. Lille, 1948.
FL 6094.8.20 Rousseau, J.J. Rêveries du promeneur solitaire. Paris, 1955.
FL 6094.8.22 Rousseau, J.J. Les rêveries du promeneur solitaire. Paris, 1958.
FL 6094.8.24 Rousseau, J.J. Les rêveries du promeneur solitaire. Paris, 1960.
FL 6094.8.25 Rousseau, J.J. Les rêveries du promeneur solitaire. Genève, 1948.
FL 6094.8.26 Rousseau, J.J. Les rêveries du promeneur solitaire. Paris, 1964.
FL 6094.10 Rousseau, J.J. Les rêveries du promeneur solitaire. Paris, 1948.
FL 6094.15 Rousseau, J.J. The reveries of a solitary. London, 1927.
Htn FL 6094.20* Rousseau, J.J. Les rêveries du promeneur solitaire. Paris, 1952.
FL 6094.93 Ricattle, Robert. Reflexions sur les rêveries. Paris, 1960.

FL 6095 Jean Jacques Rousseau - Minor works - Rousseau juge de Jean Jacques

Htn FL 6095.2* Rousseau, J.J. Juge de Jean-Jacques. Dialogue. London, 1780.
Htn FL 6095.3* Rousseau, J.J. Juge de Jean-Jacques. Dialogue. Lichfield, 1780.
Htn FL 6095.10* Rousseau, J.J. Rousseau Juge de Jean-Jacques. Dialogues. Paris, 1962.

FL 6096 Jean Jacques Rousseau - Minor works - Testament

Htn FL 6096.1* Rousseau, J.J. Le testament. n.p., 1771.
FL 6096.2 Rousseau, J.J. Un testament littéraire. Paris, 1897.
FL 6096.3 Dufour, T. Le testament de Jean-Jacques Rousseau. Genève, 1907.

FL 6109 Jean Jacques Rousseau - Attributed works

FL 6109.2 Rousseau, J.J. Letters of an Italian nun and an English gentleman. Worcester, 1796.

FL 6111 Jean Jacques Rousseau - Works about Rousseau - Societies

FL 6111.2 Pamphlet box. Société Jean-Jacques Rousseau.
FL 6111.13 Société Jean-Jacques Rousseau. Annales. Genève. 1,1905+ 36v.
FL 6111.13.5 Société Jean-Jacques Rousseau. Annales. Tables. v.1-35, 1905-1962. Genève, n.d.

FL 6112 Jean Jacques Rousseau - Works about Rousseau - Periodicals

FL 6112.2 Amis de la Collection Neuchâteloise des manuscrits de Jean-Jacques Rousseau. Bulletin d'information; études. Neuchâtel.

FL 6113 Jean Jacques Rousseau - Works about Rousseau - Reference works - Bibliographies

FL 6113.2A Asse, E. Jean-Jacques Rousseau. Paris, n.d.
FL 6113.2B Asse, E. Jean-Jacques Rousseau. Paris, 1900.
FL 6113.3 Bachelin, A. Iconographie de J.J. Rousseau. Paris, 1878.
FL 6113.4 Boston. Public Library. Titles of books added 1891. (Rousseau). Boston, 1891.
FL 6113.5 Girardin, Fernand. Iconographie de Jean-Jacques Rousseau. Paris, 1908.
FL 6113.5.2 Girardin, Fernand. Iconographie des oeuvres de Jean-Jacques Rousseau. Paris, 1910.
FL 6113.6 Du Bus, Charles. L'exposition Jean-Jacques Rousseau à la bibliothèque nationale. Paris, 1912.
Htn FL 6113.10* Du Four, Théophile. Recherches bibliographique sur les oeuvres imprimées de Jean-Jacques Rousseau. Paris, 1925. 2v.

FL 6113 Jean Jacques Rousseau - Works about Rousseau - Reference works - Bibliographies - cont.

FL 6113.12 Delestre, M. Catalogue d'une précieuse collection de lettres autographes comprenant une correspondance de Jean-Jacques Rousseau. Paris, 1886.
FL 6113.16 Schinz, Albert. État présent des travaux sur Jean-Jacques Rousseau. N.Y., 1941.
FL 6113.17F François, A. L'exposition iconographique. Genève, 1913.
FL 6113.18 Sénelier, J. Bibliographie générale des oeuvres. Paris, 1950.
FL 6113.19 Barbier, A.A. Notice bibliographique sur les diverses éditions des ouvrages de Jean-Jacques Rousseau. Paris, 1836.
FL 6113.20 Neuchâtel. Catalogue de la correspondance. Neuchâtel, 1963. 2v.

FL 6115 Jean Jacques Rousseau - Works about Rousseau - Pamphlet volumes

FL 6115 Pamphlet box. Works on Rousseau.
FL 6115.2 Pamphlet box. Rousseau.

FL 6117 - 6120 Jean Jacques Rousseau - Works about Rousseau - Biographical material - General works (By date, e.g. 6119.60 for 1960)

FL 6117.89 Barruel-Beauvert, Antoine Joseph. Vie de Jean-Jacques Rousseau. London, 1789.
FL 6118.03 Buman, J.N. Éloge de Jean-Jacques Rousseau. Paris, 1803.
FL 6118.21 Musset, Victor Donatien. Histoire vie et ouvrages de Jean-Jacques Rousseau. Paris, 1821. 2v.
FL 6118.21.2 Musset, Victor Donatien. Histoire vie et ouvrages de Jean-Jacques Rousseau. Paris, 1827.
FL 6118.51 Morin, G.H. Essai vie et caractère de Jean-Jacques Rousseau. Paris, 1851.
FL 6118.63 Brockerhoff, F. Jean-Jacques Rousseau. Leben und Werke. v.1-3. Leipzig, 1863. 2v.
FL 6118.68 Hamel, E. La statue de Jean-Jacques Rousseau. Paris, 1868.
FL 6118.70 Vogt, T. Jean-Jacques Rousseau's Leben. Wien, 1870.
FL 6118.73A Morley, John Morley. Rousseau. London, 1873. 2v.
FL 6118.73B Morley, John Morley. Rousseau. London, 1873. 2v.
X Cg FL 6118.73C Morley, John Morley. Rousseau. London, 1873. 2v.
FL 6118.73.1.5 Morley, John Morley. Rousseau. London, 1878.
FL 6118.73.3 Morley, John Morley. Rousseau. 3. ed. Boston, 1886. 2v.
FL 6118.73.5A Morley, John Morley. Rousseau. London, 1886. 2v.
FL 6118.73.5B Morley, John Morley. Rousseau. London, 1886. 2v.
FL 6118.73.6 Morley, John Morley. Rousseau. v.2. N.Y., 1891.
FL 6118.73.7 Morley, John Morley. Rousseau. London, 1896. 2v.
FL 6118.73.9 Morley, John Morley. Rousseau. London, 1922. 2v.
FL 6118.75 Girardin, S.M. Jean-Jacques Rousseau vie et ouvrages. Paris, 1875. 2v.
FL 6118.77 Craddock, T. Rousseau as described by himself and others. London, 1877.
FL 6118.78 Meylan, A. Jean-Jacques Rousseau. Sa vie et ses oeuvres. Berne, 1878.
FL 6118.78.2 Daret, M. Jean-Jacques Rousseau. Sa vie, ses idées religieuses. Genève, 1878.
FL 6118.82 Graham, H.G. Rousseau. Edinburgh, 1882.
FL 6118.87 Aleksyeef, A.S. Etiudy o J.J. Rousseau, 1741-1762. Moskva, 1887.
FL 6118.88.2 Ducros, L. Jean-Jacques Rousseau. Paris, 1888.
FL 6118.89 Mahrenholtz, R. Jean-Jacques Rousseau. Leben, Geistesentwickelung und Hauptwerke. Leipzig, 1889.
FL 6118.90 Grand-Carteret, J. Jean-Jacques Rousseau jugé par les Français d'aujourd'hui. Paris, 1890.
FL 6118.91 Beaudouin, H. Jean-Jacques Rousseau, la vie et les oeuvres. Paris, 1891. 2v.
FL 6118.93A Chuquet, A. Jean-Jacques Rousseau. Paris, 1893.
FL 6118.93B Chuquet, A. Jean-Jacques Rousseau. Paris, 1893.
FL 6118.93.3 Chuquet, A. Jean-Jacques Rousseau. 3. ed. Paris, 1906.
FL 6119.00 Gehrig, H. Jean-Jacques Rousseau. Leben und Schriften. Leipzig, 1900. 3v.
FL 6119.03A Hudson, H.W. Rousseau and naturalism in life and thought. N.Y., 1903.
FL 6119.03B Hudson, H.W. Rousseau and naturalism in life and thought. N.Y., 1903.
FL 6119.03.2 Nourrisson, J.F. Jean-Jacques Rousseau et le Rousseauisme. Paris, 1903.
FL 6119.05 Feller, L. Jean-Jacques Rousseau de sa vie et de ses oeuvres. Paris, 1905.
FL 6119.06 Belcourt, V. Petite vie du grand Jean-Jacques Rousseau. Paris, 1906.
FL 6119.06.5 MacDonald, F. Jean-Jacques Rousseau, a new criticism. London, 1906. 2v.
FL 6119.06.7 Sommerfelt, V. Jean-Jacques Rousseau. Kristiania, 1906.
FL 6119.06.8 Stoppoloni, A. Gian Giacomo Rousseau. Roma, 1906.
FL 6119.07.3 Lemaitre, J. Jean-Jacques Rousseau. N.Y., 1907.
FL 6119.07.3.5 Lemaitre, J. Jean-Jacques Rousseau. 32. éd. Paris, 1913?
FL 6119.07.4 Lemaitre, J. Jean-Jacques Rousseau. Paris, 1921.
FL 6119.07.5 Saint-Pierre, B. de. Jean-Jacques Rousseau, vie et ouvrages. Paris, 1907.
FL 6119.08.5 Graham, H. Grey. J.J. Rousseau; ego zhin' i...sreda. Moskva, 1908.
FL 6119.09 Buffenoir, H. Le prestige de Jean-Jacques Rousseau. Paris, 1909.
FL 6119.09.5 Lemaitre, J. Jean-Jacques Rousseau. Paris, 1909.
FL 6119.10 Dide, A. Jean-Jacques Rousseau. Le protestantisme et la Révolution française. Paris, 1910.
FL 6119.10.3A Faguet, E. Vie de Rousseau. Paris, 1911.
FL 6119.10.3B Faguet, E. Vie de Rousseau. Paris, 1911.
FL 6119.11 Vallette, G. J.J. Rousseau Génevois. Paris, 1911.
FL 6119.12 Gran, G. Jean-Jacques Rousseau. Edinburgh, 1912.
FL 6119.12.5 Plan, P.P. Jean-Jacques Rousseau. 3. éd. Paris, 1912.
FL 6119.12.7 Bouvier, B. Jean-Jacques Rousseau. Genève, 1912.
FL 6119.12.15 Sahlin, Enar. Jean-Jacques Rousseau; en levnadsteckning. Uppsala, 1912.
FL 6119.14.2 Tarozzi, Guiseppi. Gian Giacomo Rousseau. 2. ed. Roma, 1926.
FL 6119.21 Roland-Holst, Henriette. Jean-Jacques Rousseau. München, 1921.
FL 6119.22 Stark, Georg. Rousseau und das Gefühl. Schwabach, 1922.
FL 6119.23 Fusil, C.A. Rousseau juge de Jean-Jacques. Paris, 1923.
FL 6119.25 Monglond, A. Vies préromantiques. Paris, 1925.
FL 6119.29 Sells, Arthur L. The early life and adventures of Jean-Jacques Rousseau, 1712-1740. Cambridge, 1929.
FL 6119.31 Charpentier, John. Rousseau, the child of nature. N.Y., 1931.
FL 6119.31.3 Charpentier, John. Jean-Jacques Rousseau ou Le démocrate par dépit. Paris, 1931.
FL 6119.31.5 Vulliamy, Colwyn E. Rousseau. London, 1931.

FL 6117 - 6120 Jean Jacques Rousseau - Works about Rousseau - Biographical material - General works (By date, e.g. 6119.60 for 1960) - cont.

FL 6119.31.10A Josephson, M. Jean-Jacques Rousseau. N.Y., 1931.
FL 6119.31.10B Josephson, M. Jean-Jacques Rousseau. N.Y., 1931.
FL 6119.32 Fusil, C.A. La contagion sacrée ou Jean-Jacques Rousseau de 1778 à 1820. Paris, 1932.
FL 6119.36 Guyot, Charly. De Rousseau à Mirabeau. Neuchâtel, 1936.
FL 6119.38 Mowot, R.B. Jean-Jacques Rousseau. Bristol, 1938.
FL 6119.38.5 Trintzius, R. La vie privée de Jean-Jacques Rousseau. Paris, 1938.
FL 6119.40A Cresson, André. Jean-Jacques Rousseau; sa vie, son oeuvre, avec un exposé de sa philosophie. Paris, 1940.
FL 6119.40B Cresson, André. Jean-Jacques Rousseau; sa vie, son oeuvre, avec un exposé de sa philosophie. Paris, 1940.
FL 6119.40.3 Cresson, André. Jean-Jacques Rousseau; sa vie, son oeuvre, avec un exposé de sa philosophie. 3. éd. Paris, 1962.
FL 6119.42.5 Guillemin, Henri. Les philosophes contre Jean-Jacques. 5. éd. Paris, 1942.
FL 6119.43 Guillemin, Henri. Un homme. Genève, 1943.
FL 6119.48 Faure, Gabriel. Essais sur Jean-Jacques Rousseau. Grenoble, 1948.
FL 6119.52 Ziegenfuss, U. Jean-Jacques Rousseau. Erlangen, 1952.
FL 6119.54 Mondolfo, R. Rousseau e la conscienza moderna. 1. ed. Firenze, 1954.
FL 6119.54.5 Atene, Paolo. Gian Giacomo Rousseau. Genova, 1954.
FL 6119.55 Grien, J. Charles. Jean-Jacques Rousseau. Cambridge, 1955.
FL 6119.56 Röehrs, Hermann. Jean-Jacques Rousseau. Heidelberg, 1957.
FL 6119.58 Vertsman, I.E. Zhan-Zhak Russo. Moskva, 1958.
FL 6119.61 Wiuwar, Frances. Jean-Jacques Rousseau. N.Y., 1961.
FL 6119.61.5 Bretonneau, G. Valeurs humaines de Jean-Jacques Rousseau. Paris, 1961.
FL 6119.62A Geneva. Université. Jean-Jacques Rousseau. Neuchâtel, 1962.
FL 6119.62B Geneva. Université. Jean-Jacques Rousseau. Neuchâtel, 1962.
FL 6119.62.5 Dhôtel, André. Le roman de Jean-Jacques. Paris, 1962.
FL 6119.64 Snethlage, Jacob L. Rousseau, stormvogel der revolutie. Den Haag, 1964.
FL 6119.66 Borel, Jacques. Génie et folie de Jean-Jacques Rousseau. Paris, 1966.
FL 6119.67 Einaudi, Mario. The early Rousseau. Ithaca, 1967.
FL 6119.67.5 Blanchard, William H. Rousseau and the spirit of revolt. Ann Arbor, 1967.
FL 6119.68 Grimsley, Ronald. Rousseau and the religious quest. Oxford 1968.
FL 6119.69 Dobinson, Charles Henry. Jean-Jacques Rousseau. London, 1969.
FL 6119.71 Launay, Michel. Jean-Jacques Rousseau, ecrivain politique, 1712-1762. Cannes, 1971.

FL 6127 - 6130 Jean Jacques Rousseau - Works about Rousseau - Biographical material - Special topics (By date, e.g. 6129.70 for 1970)

FL 6127.58 Villaret, Claude. Considératons sur l'art du théâtre. Genève, 1759.
FL 6127.59 Marmontel, J.J. Réponse à Jean-Jacques Rousseau. Genève, 1759.
FL 6127.60 Dancourt, L.H. À Mr. Jean-Jacques Rousseau. Berlin, 1760.
Htn FL 6127.62* André. Refutation de Jean-Jacques Rousseau. Paris, 1762.
FL 6127.62.5 Censure de la faculté...de Paris. Paris, 1762.
Htn FL 6127.63* Formey, J.H.S. Anti-Émile. Berlin, 1763.
FL 6127.63.2 Vernes, J. Lettres sur le christianisme de Jean-Jacques Rousseau. Genève, 1763.
FL 6127.63.3 Geneva, Switzerland. Citizens. Representations des citoyens et bourgeois de Genève, 1763. Genève, 1763.
FL 6127.64 Réponse aux lettres écrites de la campagne 1764. n.p., 1764.
FL 6127.64.5 Roustan, A.J. Offrande aux autels et à la patrie. Amsterdam, 1764.
FL 6127.65 Tronchin, J.R. Lettres populaires. n.p., 1765.
FL 6127.65.2 Réponses aux lettres populaires. n.p., 1765.
FL 6127.65.3 Vernes, J. Examen du christianisme de Jean-Jacques Rousseau. Genève, 1765.
FL 6127.65.4 Claparede, D. Consideration sur les miracles de l'evangile. Genève, 1765.
Htn FL 6127.65.5* Du Peyrou, Pierre Alexandre. Lettre à monsieur...relative à monsieur Jean-Jacques Rousseau. Goa, 1765.
FL 6127.66 Geneva. Représentations et écrits, 1763-1766. Genève, 1766.
FL 6127.66.2 Cajob, J. Plagiats de M.J.J.R. sur l'éducation. La Haye, 1766.
FL 6127.68 Rousseau, J.J. Plaidoyer pour et contre Jean-Jacques Rousseau. London, 1768.
FL 6127.71 Bergier, M. Le déisme réfuté par lui-même. Paris, 1771.
FL 6127.78 Le Begue de Presle, A.G. Relation ou notice des derniers jours de monsieur Jean-Jacques Rousseau. London, 1778.
Htn FL 6127.79* Rousseau, J.J. Ancedotes...suite du supplément. 2. éd. Amsterdam, 1779.
FL 6127.80 Artaud, Giuseppe. Emilio religioso opposto all' Emilio ateo negativo di Gian Giacomo Rousseau. Pesaro, 1780.
FL 6127.87 Réfléxions philosophiques et impartiales sur Rousseau. Genève, 1787.
FL 6127.94 Guillaume, J.M. Éloge de Jean-Jacques Rousseau. Montpellier, 1794.
FL 6127.94.5 Guillaume, J.M. Éloge de Jean-Jacques Rousseau. Montpellier, 1794.
FL 6128.15 Wagner, Sigmund von. L'ile de Saint-Pierre, ou L'ile de Rousseau. Berne, 1815.
FL 6128.15.5 Wagner, Sigmund von. L'ile de Saint-Pierre, ou l'ile de Rousseau...Pierre Kohler. Lausanne, 1926.
FL 6128.24 Girardin, S. Lettre à M. Musset-Pathay. Paris, 1824.
FL 6128.58 Gaberel, M.J. Rousseau et les Genévois. Genève, 1858.
FL 6128.59 Mercier, L.A. Explication de la maladie de Jean-Jacques Rousseau. Paris, 1859.
FL 6128.60 Fochier, L. Séjour de Jean-Jacques Rousseau à Bourgoin. Bourgoin, 1860.
FL 6128.61 Viridet, M. Almanach de Jean-Jacques Rousseau pour 1861. Genève, 1861.
FL 6128.63 Junod, L. Jean-Jacques Rousseau au val-de-travers. Neuchâtel, 1863.
FL 6128.64 Houssaye, A. Les charmettes. Jean-Jacques Rousseau et Mme. de Warens. 2. éd. Paris, 1864.
FL 6128.66 Chereau, A. La vérité sur la mort de Jean-Jacques Rousseau. Paris, 1866.
Htn FL 6128.76* Poulet, Malassis. La querelle des Bouffons. Paris, 1876.
FL 6128.77 Metzger, A. Jean-Jacques Rousseau à l'ile Saint-Pierre. Lyon, 1877. 3 pam.

FL 6127 - 6130 Jean Jacques Rousseau - Works about Rousseau - Biographical material - Special topics (By date, e.g. 6129.70 for 1970) - cont.

FL 6128.78 Vadier, Berthe (pseud.). Pourquoi nous fêtons Rousseau. Genève, 1878.
FL 6128.78.2 Gaberel, J. Condamnation de l'Émile et du Contrat Social de Rousseau. Paris, 1878.
FL 6128.78.3F Jeanneret, G. Un séjour à l'ile de Saint-Pierre. Paris, 1878.
FL 6128.78.4 Dufour-Vernes, L. Recherches sur Jean-Jacques Rousseau et sa parenté. Genève, 1878.
FL 6128.80 Ritter, E. La famille de Jean-Jacques Rousseau. Genève, 1880.
FL 6128.81 Berthoud, F. Jean-Jacques Rousseau au val-de-travers, 1762-1765. Paris, 1881.
FL 6128.82 Jansen, A. Jean-Jacques Rousseau. Fragments inédits. Paris, 1882.
FL 6128.83 Ritter, E. Conseil de Genève jugeant les oeuvres de Rousseau. Genève, 1883.
FL 6128.83.2 Bougeault, A. Étude sur l'état mental de Jean-Jacques Rousseau. Paris, 1883.
FL 6128.84 Jansen, A. Jean-Jacques Rousseau als Musiker. Berlin, 1884.
FL 6128.84.2 Berthoud, F. Jean-Jacques Rousseau et le pasteur de Montmollin. Fleurier, 1884.
FL 6128.85 Ceresole, V. Jean-Jacques Rousseau à Venise, 1743-1744. Genève, 1885.
FL 6128.85.2 Jansen, A. Documents sur Jean-Jacques Rousseau, 1762-1765. Genève, 1885.
FL 6128.85.3 Jansen, A. Jean-Jacques Rousseau als Botaniker. Berlin, 1885.
FL 6128.89 Mörbius, P.J. Jean-Jacques Rousseau's Krankheitsgeschichte. Leipzig, 1889.
FL 6128.89.2 Lebasteur, H. Essai sur le caractère de Jean-Jacques Rousseau. Chambéry, 1889.
FL 6128.89.3 Mentha, F.H. Discours sur le système politique de Rousseau. Neuchâtel, 1889.
NEDL FL 6128.90 Chatelain, D. La folie de Jean-Jacques Rousseau. Neuchâtel, 1890.
FL 6128.90.3 Dufour, L. Les ascendants de Jean-Jacques Rousseau. Genève, 1890.
FL 6128.91 Ritter, E. Isaac Rousseau. Paris, 1891.
FL 6128.94 Buffenois, H. Une journée à Ermenonville. n.p., 1894.
FL 6128.95 MacDonald, F. Studies in the France of Voltaire and Rousseau. London, 1895.
FL 6128.95.2 Buffenois, H. Jean-Jacques Rousseau et ses visiteurs. Paris, 1895.
FL 6128.96 Ritter, E. Famille et jeunesse de Jean-Jacques Rousseau. Paris, 1896.
FL 6128.96.2 Claretie, L. Jean-Jacques Rousseau et ses amies. Paris, 1896.
FL 6128.97 Dubois, A. Jean-Jacques Rousseau au champ du moulin. Neuchâtel, 1897.
FL 6128.98 Dufour, E. Jacob Vernes, 1728-1791. Genève, 1898.
FL 6129.01 Pougin, A. Jean-Jacques Rousseau. Paris, 1901.
FL 6129.01.2 Thomas, L. Grange-canal et Jean-Jacques Rousseau. Genève, 1901.
FL 6129.01.5 Stoppoloni, A. Le donne nella vita di G.G. Rousseau. Roma, 1901.
FL 6129.02.2 Thomas, L. Genève, Rousseau et Voltaire, 1775-1778. Genève, 1902.
FL 6129.02.3 Ritter, E. La parenté de Jean-Jacques Rousseau, 1614. Genève, 1902.
FL 6129.02.4 Buffenois, H. Les charmettes et Jean-Jacques Rousseau. Paris, 1902.
FL 6129.02.5 Buffenois, H. Les charmettes et Jean-Jacques Rousseau. Paris, 1911.
FL 6129.03 Thorolfsson, S. Jean-Jacques Rousseau. Reykjavik, 1903.
FL 6129.04 Buffenois, H. Jean-Jacques Rousseau à Montmorency. Paris, 1904.
FL 6129.04.2 Montaigu, A. Démêlés du comte de Montaigu. Paris, 1904.
FL 6129.05 Gaidau, E. Le lieu de naissance de Jean-Jacques Rousseau. Genève, 1905.
FL 6129.06.2 Perrin, L. Rousseau à Motiers-Travers et sa lapidation. Fleurier, 1906.
FL 6129.06.3 Lenz, K.G. Über Rousseaus Verbindung mit Weibern. Berlin, 1906.
FL 6129.06.4 Rod, E. L'affaire Jean-Jacques Rousseau. Paris, 1906.
FL 6129.08 Buffenois, H. Causeries familial sur Jean-Jacques Rousseau. Paris, 1908.
X Cg FL 6129.08.3 Gribblo, F. Rousseau and the women he loved. N.Y., 1908.
FL 6129.08.6 Dueros, L. Jean-Jacques Rousseau de Genève à l'Hermitage, 1757-1765. Paris, 1917.
FL 6129.08.7 Dueros, L. Jean-Jacques Rousseau de Genève à l'Hermitage, 1765-1778. Paris, 1918.
FL 6129.09 Rey, A. Jean-Jacques Rousseau dans la Vallée de Montmorency. Paris, 1909.
FL 6129.10 Faguet, E. Les amies de Rousseau. Paris, 1910.
FL 6129.11 Künzler, Fritz. Die Ermitage-Zeit als ein Markstein in Rousseaus Leben. Solothurn, 1911.
FL 6129.11.11 Courtois, Louis J. Le séjour de Jean-Jacques Rousseau en Angleterre, 1766-1767. Genève, 1970.
FL 6129.12 Meynier, A. Jean-Jacques Rousseau révolutionnaire. Paris, 1912.
FL 6129.12.5 Martin-Decaen, A. Le Marquis René de Girardin, 1735-1808. Paris, 1912.
FL 6129.13 Buffenois, H. Les portraits de Jean-Jacques Rousseau. Paris, 1913.
FL 6129.15 Cordier, Leopold. Jean-Jacques Rousseau und der Calvinismus. Inaug. Diss. Heidelberg, 1915.
FL 6129.16 Schinz, Albert. Jean-Jacques Rousseau et le libraire. Genève, 1916.
FL 6129.21 Foster, E.A. Le dernière séjour de Rousseau à Paris, 1770-1778. Northampton, 1921.
FL 6129.21.5 Foster, E.A. Le dernière séjour de Rousseau à Paris, 1770-1778. Northampton, 1921.
FL 6129.23 Proal, Louis. La psychologie de Jean-Jacques Rousseau. Paris, 1923.
FL 6129.23.5 Faure, Gabriel. Jean-Jacques Rousseau en Dauphine, 1768-1770. Grenoble, 1923.
FL 6129.25 Larsson, Hans. Rousseau och Pestalozzi. Lund, 1910.
FL 6129.26 De Crue de Stoutz, Francis. L'ami de Rousseau et des Necker. Paul Moultou à Paris en 1778. Paris, 1926.
FL 6129.29 Casotti, Mario. Il moralismo di G.G. Rousseau. Milano, 1929?
FL 6129.29.10 Kehrwald, Max. Jean-Jacques Rousseau's Religionsphilosophie und moralischreligiöse Erziehungsmaxime. Inaug. Diss. München, 1929.

FL 6127 - 6130 Jean Jacques Rousseau - Works about Rousseau - Biographical material - Special topics (By date, e.g. 6129.70 for 1970) - cont.

FL 6129.30 Moffat, M.M. Rousseau et la querelle du théatre au XVIIIe siècle. Paris, 1930.
FL 6129.31 Cornelissen, A.J.M. Calvijn en Rousseau. Nijmengen, 1931.
FL 6129.31.5 Baillods, Jules. L'ile de Saint-Pierre. Neuchâtel, 1931.
FL 6129.33 Grosclaude, Pierre. Jean-Jacques Rousseau à Lyon. Lyon, 1933.
FL 6129.33.5 Grosclaude, Pierre. Jean-Jacques Rousseau à Lyon. Thèse. Lyon, 1933.
FL 6129.34 Aimery de Pierrebough, M.T.G. Jean-Jacques Rousseau et les femmes. 9. éd. Paris, 1934.
FL 6129.41 Speerli, Leonore. Rousseau and Zürich. Brugg, 1941.
FL 6129.45 Labrousse, Roger. Rousseau y su tiempo. La Plata, 1945.
FL 6129.50 Roddier, Henri. Jean-Jacques Rousseau en Angleterre au XVIIIe siècle. Paris, 1950.
FL 6129.50.5 Gilliard, E. De Rousseau à Jean-Jacques. Lausanne, 1950.
FL 6129.50.10 Roddier, Henri. Jean-Jacques Rousseau en Angleterre au XVIIIe siècle. Thèse principale. Paris, 1950.
FL 6129.52 Burgelin, Pierre. La philosophie de l'existence de Jean-Jacques Rousseau. Paris, 1952.
FL 6129.52.2 Burgelin, Pierre. La philosophie de l'existence de Jean-Jacques Rousseau. Thèse. Paris, 1952.
FL 6129.53 Lathion, Lucien. Jean-Jacques Rousseau et le Valais. Lausanne, 1953.
FL 6129.53.5 Carlsen, Olaf. Rousseau og Dannmark. Aarhus, 1953.
FL 6129.54 Wille, Hans J. Die Gefährtin. 2. Aufl. Berlin, 1954.
FL 6129.55 Stutzer, H. Jean-Jacques Rousseau und die Schweiz. Basel, 1950.
FL 6129.57 Healey, F.G. Rousseau et Napoléon. Genève, 1957.
FL 6129.62 Burgelin, Pierre. Jean-Jacques Rousseau et la religion de Genève. Genève, 1962.
FL 6129.62.5 Guyot, Charly. Plaidoyer pour Thérèse Levasseur. Neuchâtel, 1962.
FL 6129.62.10 Jost, François. Rousseau et la Suisse. Neuchâtel, 1962.
FL 6129.64 May, Gita. De Jean-Jacques Rousseau à madame Roland. Genève, 1964.
FL 6129.64.5 Bovier, Gaspard. Journal du séjour à Grenoble de Jean-Jacques Rousseau. Grenoble, 1964.
FL 6129.67 Gionnuzzi, Paolo. J.J. Rousseau e la chimica. Bari, 1967.
FL 6129.68 Crocker, Lester Gilbert. Jean-Jacques Rousseau. N.Y., 1968-
FL 6129.70 Cohler, Anne Meyers. Rousseau and nationalism. N.Y., 1970.

FL 6132 Jean Jacques Rousseau - Works about Rousseau - Biographical material - Madame de Warens - Writings

FL 6132.2 Mémoires de Mme. de Warens suivis de ceux de Claude Anet. Chambery, 1786.
Htn FL 6132.2.2* Mémoires de Mme. de Warens et de Claude Anet. Chambery, 1786.
FL 6132.3 Metzger, A. Les pensées de Mme. de Warens. Lyon, 1888.
FL 6132.4 Vuy, J. Lettres inédites de Madame de Warens. Annecy, 1870.
FL 6132.5 Mugnier, F. Nouvelles lettres de Mme. Warens. Paris, 1900.

FL 6133 Jean Jacques Rousseau - Works about Rousseau - Biographical material - Madame de Warens - Biography and criticism

FL 6133.2 Metzger, A. La conversion de Mme. de Warens. Paris, 1888.
FL 6133.3 Montet, A. de. Madame de Warens et le pays de Vaud. Lausanne, 1891.
FL 6133.4 Serand, J. L'habitation de Mme. de Warens à Annecy. Annecy, 1900.
FL 6133.5 Serand, J. Nouveaux documents sur Mme. de Warens. n.p., 1900.
FL 6133.6 Mugnier, F. Mme. de Warens et Jean-Jacques Rousseau. Paris, 1890.
FL 6133.7 Benedetto, L.F. Madame de Warens, d'après de nouveaux documents. Paris, 1914.
FL 6133.8 Benedetto, L.F. Madame de Warens. Firenze, 1921.

FL 6134 Jean Jacques Rousseau - Works about Rousseau - Biographical material - Other friends and associates

FL 6134.2 Guyot, Charly. Un ami et défenseur de Rousseau. Neuchâtel, 1958.

FL 6135 Jean Jacques Rousseau - Works about Rousseau - Biographical material - Monuments; Anniversaries

FL 6135.1 Guyot, A.J. Epitaphe de Jean-Jacques Rousseau. Paris, 1802.
FL 6135.2 Wuaren, J.F. De l'inauguration de la statue de Jean-Jacques Rousseau. Genève, 1855.
FL 6135.3 Janin, A. Deux mots au sujet de la fête de Rousseau. n.p., 1844.
FL 6135.4 Thomas, L. La réhabilitation publique de Jean-Jacques Rousseau. Genève, 1903.
FL 6135.5 Buffenoir, H. Les tombeaux de Rousseau et de Voltaire. Paris, 1904.
FL 6135.6 Dunant, D. Rousseau n'a-t-il rien fait pour sa patrie? Genève, 1828.
FL 6135.7 Dumur, Louis. Le centenaire de Jean-Jacques. Paris, n.d.
FL 6135.8 Centenaire de J.J. Rousseau. Honneurs publics rendus de Jean-Jacques Rousseau. Genève, 1878.
FL 6135.8.3 Per il IIe centenario di G.G. Rousseau. Genova, 1913.
FL 6135.8.5A Barrés, Maurice. Le bi-centenaire de Jean-Jacques Rousseau. Paris, 1912.
FL 6135.8.5B Barres, Maurice. Le bi-centenaire de Jean-Jacques Rousseau. Paris, 1912.
FL 6135.9 Tauro, Giacomo. A l'occasion du second centenaire de la naissance de Rousseau. Rome, 1912.
FL 6135.10 Castellant, A. Jean-Jacques Rousseau. Paris, 1887.
FL 6135.11 Konferetsiia, posviashchen 252 letiiu sodnia...Odessa, 1962. Tezisy. Konferents. posviashchennoi 250 letiiu sodnia rozhdeniia Zh. Zh. Russo, 1712. Odessa, 1962.
FL 6135.12 Société des études robspierristes. Jean-Jacques Rousseau, 1712-1778. Gap, 1963.
VFL 6135.13 Czestochowa, Poland. Wystawa Zycie i Dzielo Jana Jakuba Rousseau. Katalog wystawy 26.XI do 10.XII. Czestochowa, 1962.

FL 6137 - 6140 Jean Jacques Rousseau - Works about Rousseau - Criticism - General works (By date, e.g. 6139.50 for 1950)

FL 6137.79 Eloge de Mr. Rousseau de Genève. n.p., 1779.
FL 6137.80 Bruny, de. Lettre sur Jean-Jacques Rousseau. Genève, 1780.
FL 6137.85 Le Gros, Charles F. Analyse des ouvrages de Jean-Jacques Rousseau de Genève. Genève, 1785.
FL 6137.86 Le Gros, Charles F. Examen des systèmes de Jean-Jacques Rousseau de Genève. Genève, 1786.
FL 6137.89 Lettres sur les ouvrages et caractère de Jean-Jacques Rousseau. Lausanne, 1789.
FL 6137.89.2 Straël-Holstein, A.L. Lettres sur les ouvrages et le caractère de Rousseau. 2. éd. n.p., 1789.
FL 6137.89.5 Straël-Holstein, A.L. Lettres sur les ouvrages et le caractère de Jean-Jacques Rousseau. n.p., 1789.
FL 6137.91 Mercier, M. De Jean-Jacques Rousseau. Paris, 1791. 2v.
Htn FL 6137.98* Stael, de (Mrs.). Lettres, ouvrages et caractère de Jean-Jacques Rousseau. 2. éd. Lausanne, 1789.
Htn FL 6137.98.1* Stael, de (Mrs.). Lettres, ouvrages et caractère de Jean-Jacques Rousseau. Paris, 1798.
FL 6137.98.2 Muzzarelli, A. G.G. Rousseau, accusator de filosofi. Assisi, 1798.
FL 6138.58 Estienne, C. Essai sur les oeuvres de Jean-Jacques Rousseau. Paris, 1858.
FL 6138.70 Moreau, L. Jean-Jacques Rousseau et le siècle philosophe. Paris, 1870.
FL 6138.75 Koeune, F. Quelques pages sur Jean-Jacques Rousseau. Lausanne, 1875.
FL 6138.78 Gaberel, J. Calvin et Rousseau. Genève, 1878.
FL 6138.78.2 Martin, A.J. Centenaire de Jean-Jacques Rousseau. Genève, 1878.
FL 6138.78.3 Sigogne, E. Eloge de Jean-Jacques Rousseau. Paris, 1878.
FL 6138.78.4 Vuy, J. Origine des idées politiques de Rousseau. Genève, 1878.
FL 6138.78.5 Vuy, J. Origine des idées politiques de Rousseau. Genève, 1889.
FL 6138.79 Braillard, J. Jean-Jacques Rousseau jugé par les Genevois. Genève, 1879.
FL 6138.79.5 Gehrig, H. Jean-Jacques Rousseau; sein Leben und seine pädagogische Bedeutung. Neuwied, 1879.
FL 6138.83 Borgeaud, C. Jean-Jacques Rousseau's Religionsphilosophie. Genève, 1883.
FL 6138.87 Schmidt, Otto. Rousseau und Byron. Greifswald, 1887.
FL 6138.89 Schneider, Karl. Rousseau und Pestalozzi. 4. Aufl. Berlin, 1889.
FL 6138.90 Fester, R. Rousseau und der deutsche Geschichtsphilosophie. Stuttgart, 1890.
FL 6138.91 Buffenoir, H. Jean-Jacques Rousseau et les femmes. Paris, 1891.
FL 6138.92 Spitzer, A. Natur und Naturgemässheit bei Jean-Jacques Rousseau. Leipzig, 1892.
FL 6138.92.2 Salomon, Otto. Förelasningar öfver Jean-Jacques Rousseau. Göteborg, 1892.
FL 6138.94 Izoulet, Jean. De Jean-Jacques Rousseau (Jean-Jacques Rousseau) utrum misopolis fuerit an philopolis. Paris, 1894.
FL 6138.94.5 Bocquillon, E. Jean-Jacques Rousseau, ce méconnu. Paris, 1962.
FL 6138.95A Texte, J. Jean-Jacques Rousseau et...cosmopolitisme littéraire. Paris, 1895.
FL 6138.95B Texte, J. Jean-Jacques Rousseau et...cosmopolitisme littéraire. Paris, 1895.
FL 6138.95.2A Texte, J. Jean-Jacques Rousseau and the cosmopolitan spirit in literature. London, 1899.
FL 6138.95.2B Texte, J. Jean-Jacques Rousseau and the cosmopolitan spirit in literature. London, 1899.
FL 6138.95.4 Texte, J. Jean-Jacques Rousseau et les origines de cosmopolitisme littéraire. 2. éd. Paris, 1909.
FL 6138.95.5 Fleuriaux, J. Jean-Jacques Rousseau; sa vie, ses oeuvres. Bruxelles, 1895.
FL 6138.97 Haymann, F. Begriff der volonté générale. Leipzig, 1897.
FL 6138.97.2 Lincoln, C.H. Rousseau and the French revolution. Philadelphia, 1897.
FL 6138.98A Davidson, T. Rousseau and education according to nature. N.Y., 1898.
Htn FL 6138.98*B Davidson, T. Rousseau and education according to nature. N.Y., 1898.
FL 6138.98.1 Davidson, T. Rousseau and education according to nature. N.Y., 1900.
FL 6138.98.3 Haymann, F. Jean-Jacques Rousseau Sozialphilosophie. Leipzig, 1898.
FL 6138.98.4 Leipmann, M. Die Rechtsphilosophie des Jean-Jacques Rousseau. Berlin, 1898.
FL 6138.99 Fährmann, E. Jean-Jacques Rousseau's Naturanschauung. Plauen, 1899.
FL 6138.99.2 Windenberger, J.L. Système politique étrangère de Jean-Jacques Rousseau. Paris, 1899.
FL 6139.01 Campayré, G. Jean-Jacques Rousseau et l'éducation de la nature. Paris, 1901.
FL 6139.01.3 Campayré, G. Jean-Jacques Rousseau and education from nature. N.Y., 1907.
FL 6139.01.5 Mettrier, Henri. L'impot et la milice dans Jean-Jacques Rousseau et Mably. Thèse. Paris, 1901.
FL 6139.02 Höffding, H. Rousseau und seine Philosophie. Stuttgart, 1902.
FL 6139.02.2 Dalleggio, A. Beiträge zur Psychologie Jean-Jacques Rousseau's. Jena, 1902.
FL 6139.04 Benrubi, J. Jean-Jacques Rousseaus ethisches Ideal. Langensalza, 1904.
FL 6139.04.8 Hartmann, E. Jean-Jacques Rousseaus Einfluss auf J.H. Campe. Inaug.-Diss. Nevenburg, 1904.
FL 6139.06 Lassudrie-Duchêne, G. Jean-Jacques Rousseau et le droit des gens. Paris, 1906.
FL 6139.06.2 Buffenoir, H. Jean-Jacques Rousseau, jugé par Chateaubriand. Genève, 1906.
FL 6139.06.3 Findeisen, Hermann. Die philosophischen Grundgedanken der Pädagogiks Jean-Jacques Rousseaus. Borna, 1906.
FL 6139.06.10A Brédif, L. Du caractère intellectuel et moral de Jean-Jacques Rousseau. Paris, 1906.
FL 6139.06.10B Brédif, L. Du caractère intellectuel et moral de Jean-Jacques Rousseau. Paris, 1906.
FL 6139.07.5 Bonnard, R. Prétendu individualisme de Jean-Jacques Rousseau. Paris, 1907.
FL 6139.07.7 Mensch, E. Jean-Jacques Rousseau der Philosoph das Naturrechts. Berlin, 1907.
FL 6139.07.9 Culcasi, C. Gli Influssi Italiani nell' Opera di G.G. Rousseau. Roma, 1907.

FL 6137 - 6140 Jean Jacques Rousseau - Works about Rousseau - Criticism - General works (By date, e.g. 6139.50 for 1950) - cont.

FL 6139.08 Zabel, E. Die soziale Bedeutung von J.J. Rousseaus Erziehungstheorie. Quedlinburg, 1908.
FL 6139.08.5 Krausbauer, Theodor. Rousseaus Pädogogik und ihre nach, bis auf die Neuzeit. 3. ed. Minden, 1908.
FL 6139.08.10 Puibaraud, L. Le gouvernement direct chez J.J. Rousseau. Poitiers, 1908.
FL 6139.09 Pons, A.A. Jean-Jacques Rousseau et le théâtre. Genève, 1909.
FL 6139.09.3 Schinz, A. Jean-Jacques Rousseau a forerunner of pragmatism. Chicago, 1909.
FL 6139.09.5A Champion, E. Jean-Jacques Rousseau et la révolution Française. Paris, 1909.
FL 6139.09.5B Champion, E. Jean-Jacques Rousseau et la révolution Française. Paris, 1909.
FL 6139.10 Faguet, E. Rousseau artiste. Paris, 1910.
FL 6139.10.5 Faguet, E. Rousseau penseur. Paris, 1910.
Htn FL 6139.11* Boyd, William. The educational theory of Jean-Jacques Rousseau. London, 1911.
FL 6139.11.3 Boyd, William. The educational theory of Jean-Jacques Rousseau. N.Y., 1963.
FL 6139.11.5 Krstitsch, M. Rousseaus pädagogische Ansichten im lichte der Gegenwartigen Erziehungswissenschaft. Zürich, 1911.
FL 6139.12 Tiersot, J. Jean-Jacques Rousseau. Paris, 1912.
FL 6139.12.4 Höffding, H. Jean-Jacques Rousseau og hans filosofi. København, 1912.
FL 6139.12.5 Höffding, H. Jean-Jacques Rousseau et sa philosophie. Paris, 1912.
FL 6139.12.6A Höffding, H. Jean-Jacques Rousseau and his philosophy. New Haven, 1930.
FL 6139.12.6B Höffding, H. Jean-Jacques Rousseau and his philosophy. New Haven, 1930.
FL 6139.12.6C Höffding, H. Jean-Jacques Rousseau and his philosophy. New Haven, 1930.
FL 6139.12.7 Wasmuth, E. Jean-Jacques Rousseau. Leipzig, 1912.
FL 6139.12.8 Jean-Jacques Rousseau. Paris, 1912.
FL 6139.12.9 Mertaut, J. Un entretien inconnu de George Sand et de Flaubert sur Jean-Jacques Rousseau. Montpellier, 1912.
FL 6139.13 Cuendet, W. La philosophie religieuse de Jean-Jacques Rousseau et ses sources. Genève, 1913.
FL 6139.13.3 Sakmann, P. Jean-Jacques Rousseau. Berlin, 1913.
FL 6139.13.3.2 Sakmann, P. Jean-Jacques Rousseau. 2. Aufl. Leipzig, 1923.
FL 6139.14 Bartissol, Carlos. Sources des idées médicales de Rousseau. Paris, 1914.
FL 6139.14.5 Eppensteiner, Friedrick. Rousseaus Einfluss. Inaug. Diss. Tübingen, 1914.
FL 6139.16 Masson, Pierre M. La religion de Jean-Jacques Rousseau. Thèse. Paris, 1916.
FL 6139.16.2 Masson, Pierre M. La religion de Jean-Jacques Rousseau. Paris, 1916. 3v.
FL 6139.16.5 Hofer, Cuno. L'influence de Jean-Jacques Rousseau sur le droit de la guerre. Genève, 1916.
FL 6139.19A Babbitt, Irving. Rousseau and romanticism. Boston, 1919.
FL 6139.19B Babbitt, Irving. Rousseau and romanticism. Boston, 1919.
FL 6139.19C Babbitt, Irving. Rousseau and romanticism. Boston, 1919.
FL 6139.19.2F Draper, John N. The summa of romanticism. N.Y.? 1922?
FL 6139.19.4 Babbitt, Irving. Rousseau and romanticism. Boston, 1924.
FL 6139.19.4.5 Babbitt, Irving. Rousseau and romanticism. Boston, 1968.
FL 6139.19.5 Pons, Jacques. L'éducation en Angleterre entre 1750 et 1800. Paris, 1919.
FL 6139.19.7 Alessiani, Paolina. Rousseau et il metodo Montessori. Fermo, 1919.
FL 6139.21 Seillière, Ernest. Jean-Jacques Rousseau. Paris, 1921.
FL 6139.22 Amiel, Henri F. Jean-Jacques Rousseau. N.Y., 1922.
FL 6139.22.5 Johnson, Mary L. Contemporary opinion of Rousseau in English periodicals. Thesis. Raleigh, N.C., 1922.
FL 6139.24 Haymann, Franz. Weltbürgertum und Vaterlandsliebe in der Staatslehre Rousseau und Fichtes. Berlin, 1924.
FL 6139.25 Rice, R.A. Rousseau and the poetry of nature in eighteenth century France. Northampton, 1925.
FL 6139.26 Boschann, Johannes. Die Spontaneitätsidee bei Jean-Jacques Rousseau. Inaug. Diss. Berlin, 1926?
FL 6139.26.5 Kühl, Erich. Die Natur des Menschen und die Struktur der Erzishung bei Rousseau und Pestalozzi. Inaug. Diss. n.p., 1926.
FL 6139.27A Hubert, René. Rousseau et l'encyclopédie. Paris, 1928.
FL 6139.27B Hubert, René. Rousseau et l'encyclopédie. Paris, 1928.
FL 6139.27.5 Schinz, A. La pensée religieuse de Rousseau et ses récents interprètes. Paris, 1927.
FL 6139.28 Bitsilli, P.M. Jean-Jacque Rousseau et la démocratie. Sofia, 1928.
FL 6139.28.5 Frässdorf, W. Die psychologischen Anschauungen Jean-Jacques Rousseau. Inaug. Diss. Langensalza, 1928.
FL 6139.28.10 Schaad, Herbert. Der Ausbruch der Geisteskrankeit Jean-Jacques Rousseau's und ihre Anzeichen in seinen letzten Werken und Briefen. Inaug. Diss. Erlangen, 1928.
FL 6139.29A Wright, Ernest Hunter. The meaning of Rousseau. London, 1929.
FL 6139.29B Wright, Ernest Hunter. The meaning of Rousseau. London, 1929.
FL 6139.29.3 Wright, Ernest Hunter. The meaning of Rousseau. N.Y., 1963.
FL 6139.29.5 Moreau-Rendu, S. L'idée de Bonté naturelle chez Jean-Jacques Rousseau. Paris, 1929.
FL 6139.29.10 Schinz, A. La pensée de Jean-Jacques Rousseau. Paris, 1929.
FL 6139.30 Marzano, L. L'unità di pensiero nell'opera di Gian-Giacomo Rousseau. Palermo, 1930.
FL 6139.31 Carton, Paul. Le faux naturisme de Jean-Jacques Rousseau. Paris, 1931.
FL 6139.31.5 Nourrisson, Paul. Jean-Jacques Rousseau et Robinson Crusot. Paris, 1931.
FL 6139.31.10 Schreiben, P. Gedanken- und Satzverbindung bei Jean-Jacques Rousseau. Inaug. Diss. Regenslenrg, 1931.
FL 6139.32 Dedeck-Héry, E. Jean-Jacques Rousseau et le projet de constitution pour la corsé. Thèse. Philadelphia, 1932.
FL 6139.34 Cobban, Alfred. Rousseau and the modern state. London, 1934.
FL 6139.34.2 Cobann, Alfred. Rousseau and the modern state. Hamden, 1961.
FL 6139.34.3A Cobban, Alfred. Rousseau and the modern state. 2. ed. Hamden, 1964.
FL 6139.34.3B Cobban, Alfred. Rousseau and the modern state. 2. ed. Hamden, 1964.
FL 6139.34.5A Hendel, C.W. Jean-Jacques Rousseau, moralist. London, 1934. 2v.

FL 6139.34.5B Hendel, C.W. Jean-Jacques Rousseau, moralist. London, 1934. 2v.
FL 6139.34.8 Spink, J.S. Jean-Jacques Rousseau et Genève. Thèse. Paris, 1934.
FL 6139.34.10 Spink, J.S. Jean-Jacques Rousseau et Genève. Paris, 1934.
FL 6139.34.15 Meyer, Hans. Rousseau und Shelley; ein typologischer Vergleich. Inaug. Diss. Würzburg, 1934.
FL 6139.35 Baldanzi, E.R. Il pensiero religioso di Gian Giacomo Rousseau. Firenze, 1935.
FL 6139.35.5 Erdmann, Karl D. Das Verhältnis von Staat und Religion nach der Sozialphilosophie Rousseaus. Berlin, 1935.
FL 6139.36 Hellweg, Martin. Der Begriff des Gewissens bei J.J. Rousseau. Marburg, 1936.
FL 6139.36.5 Brunello, Bruno. Gian Giacomo Rousseau. Modena, 1936.
FL 6139.36.6 Brunello, Bruno. Gian Giacomo Rousseau, filosofo della politica. 2. ed. Bologna, 1961.
FL 6139.36.10 Mühlenkamp, I. Der Begriff der Revolution bei Jean-Jacques Rousseau im Rahmen der Grundbegriffe seines Systems. Inaug. Diss. Leipzig, 1936.
FL 6139.37 Buckner, M.L. A contribution to the study of the descriptive technique of Jean-Jacques Rousseau. Baltimore, 1937.
FL 6139.38 Sciaky, G. Il problema dello stato nel pensiero del Rousseau. Firenze, 1938.
FL 6139.38.5 Spell, J.R. Rousseau in the Spanish world before 1833. Austin, 1938.
FL 6139.39 Pahlmann, Franz. Mensch und Staat bei Rousseau. Berlin, 1939.
FL 6139.39.2 Pahlmann, Franz. Mensch und Staat bei Rousseau. Berlin, 1965.
FL 6139.39.5 Robert, Ella. Rousseau és a zene. Budapest, 1939.
FL 6139.39.10 Grusemann, Hans. Die Natur-Kulturantithese bei Delisle de la Drévetière und J.J. Rousseau. Lengerich, 1939.
FL 6139.40 Osborn, A.M. Rousseau and Burke. London, 1940.
FL 6139.40.2 Osborn, A.M. Rousseau and Burke. N.Y., 1964.
FL 6139.40.5 Bernadiner, B.M. Sotsial' no-politicheskaia Filosofiia Zh.Zh. Russo. Voronezh, 1940.
FL 6139.40.10 Benrubi, Isaak. L'idéal moral chez Rousseau, Mme. de Staël et Amiel. pt.1. Benrubi. Paris, 1940.
FL 6139.44 Sacheli, Calogero. Rousseau. 2. ed. Messina, 1944.
FL 6139.44.2 Sacheli, Calogero. Rousseau. 2. ed. Messina, 1942.
FL 6139.46 Petruzzellis, N. Il pensiero politico e pedagogico. Milano, 1946.
FL 6139.48 Derathé, Robert. Le rationalisme de Jean-Jacques Rousseau. 1. éd. Paris, 1948.
FL 6139.48.2 Derathé, Robert. Le rationalisme de Jean-Jacques Rousseau. Thèse. Paris, 1948.
FL 6139.49 Groethuysen, B. Jean-Jacques Rousseau. 4. éd. Paris, 1949.
FL 6139.49.5A Mornet, Daniel. Rousseau. Paris, 1950.
FL 6139.49.5B Mornet, Daniel. Rousseau. Paris, 1950.
FL 6139.49.6 Mornet, Daniel. Rousseau. 5. éd. Paris, 1963.
FL 6139.49.10 Saloni, Alfredo. Rousseau. Milano, 1949.
FL 6139.50 Derathé, Robert. Jean-Jacques Rousseau et la science politique de son temps. Thèse. Paris, 1950.
FL 6139.50.2 Derathé, Robert. Jean-Jacques Rousseau et la science politique de son temps. 1. éd. Paris, 1950.
FL 6139.52 Lama, E. Rousseau. Milano, 1952.
FL 6139.52.5 Ziegenfuss, W. Jean-Jacques Rousseau. Erlanzen, 1952.
FL 6139.53 Bruno, A. Illuminismo e romanticismo in Rousseau e in Hegel. Bari, 1953.
FL 6139.53.5 Di Napoli, G. Il pensiero di Gian Giacomo Rousseau. Dreocae, 1953.
FL 6139.54 Cassirer, E. The question of Jean-Jacques Rousseau. N.Y., 1954.
FL 6139.54.5 Cassirer, E. The question of Jean-Jacques Rousseau. Bloomington, 1963.
FL 6139.54.10 Testa, Aldo. Sulle orme di Rousseau. Mazara, 1954.
FL 6139.56 Chapman, J.W. Rousseau, totalitarian or liberal? N.Y., 1956.
FL 6139.56.5 Voisine, Jacques. Jean-Jacques Rousseau en Angleterre à l'époque romantique. Paris, 1956.
FL 6139.56.5.2 Voisine, Jacques. Jean-Jacques Rousseau en Angleterre à l'époque romantique. Thèse. Paris, 1956.
FL 6139.56.10 Ravary, Bethe. Une conscience chrétienne devant la pensée religieuse. Paris, 1956.
FL 6139.56.15 Thomas, J.F. Le pélagianisme de Jean-Jacques Rousseau. Paris, 1956.
FL 6139.56.20 Glum, Friedrich. Jean-Jacques Rousseau. Stuttgart, 1956.
FL 6139.56.27 Röhrs, Hermann. Jean-Jacques Rousseau. Vision und Wirklichkeit. 2. Aufl. Heidelberg, 1966.
FL 6139.57 Nemo, Maxime. L'homme nouveau. Paris, 1957.
FL 6139.57.5 Deregibas, Arturo. Il problema morale in Jean-Jacques Rousseau. Torino, 1957.
FL 6139.57.10 Volpe, G. della. Rousseau e Marx e altri saggi di critica materialistica. Roma, 1957.
FL 6139.57.15 Mirabella, Tommaso. Fortuna di Rousseau in Sicilia. Caltanissetta, 1957.
FL 6139.58 Starobinski, Jean. Jean-Jacques Rousseau. Paris, 1958.
FL 6139.58.1 Starobinski, Jean. Jean-Jacques Rousseau. Paris, 1971.
FL 6139.58.5 Krafft, Olivier. La politique de Jean-Jacques Rousseau. Paris, 1958[1957]
FL 6139.58.10 Petruzzellis, N. Il pensiero politico e pedagogico di G.G. Rousseau. 2. ed. Bari, 1958.
FL 6139.58.15 Morando, Dante. Jean-Jacques Rousseau. Brescia, 1958.
FL 6139.58.20 Temmer, M.J. Time in Rousseau and Kant. Genève, 1958.
FL 6139.59 Rang, Martin. Rousseaus Lehre vom Menshen. Göttingen, 1959.
FL 6139.60 Fetscher, Iring. Rousseaus politische Philosophie zur Geschichte des demokratischen Freiheitsbegriffs. Neuwied, 1960.
FL 6139.61 May, G.C. Rousseau par lui-même. Paris, 1961.
FL 6139.61.5 Grimsley, Ronald. Jean-Jacques Rousseau. Cardiff, 1961.
FL 6139.61.7 Grimsley, Ronald. Jean-Jacques Rousseau; a study in self-awareness. 2. ed. Cardiff, 1969.
FL 6139.61.10 Jost, François. Jean-Jacques Rousseau Suisse. Fribourg, 1961. 2v.
FL 6139.61.15 Rota, Ghibaudi, S. La fortuna di Rousseau in Italia, 1750-1815. Torino, 1961.
FL 6139.61.20 Dédéyan, Charles. Rousseau et la sensibilité littéraire. Paris, 1961.
FL 6139.61.25 Roggerone, G.A. Le idee di Gian Giacomo Rousseau. Milano, 1961.
FL 6139.62 Ciampi, Vincenzo. Il problema educativo in Rousseau. Milano, 1962?

Classified Listing

FL 6137 - 6140 Jean Jacques Rousseau - Works about Rousseau - Criticism - General works (By date, e.g. 6139.50 for 1950) - cont.

FL 6139.62.5 Eigeldinger, Marc. Jean-Jacques Rousseau et la réalité. Neuchâtel, 1962.
FL 6139.62.10 Château, Jean. Rousseau, sa philosophie de l'éducation. Paris, 1962.
FL 6139.62.15 Raymond, M. Jean-Jacques Rousseau. Paris, 1962.
FL 6139.62.20 México. Universidad Nacional Coordinación de Humanidades. Presencia de Rousseau a los 250 años de su nacimiento y a los dos siglos de la aparición del Emilio y El contrato social. México, 1962.
FL 6139.62.25 Velde, Isaac van der. De verhouding Rousseau-Locke. Groningen, 1962.
FL 6139.63 Vossler, Otto. Rousseaus Freiheitslehre. Gottingen, 1963.
FL 6139.63.5 Broome, Jack H. Rousseau; a study of his thought. London, 1963.
FL 6139.63.10 Weissel, B. Von wem die Gewalt in der Staaten Herrührt. Berlin, 1963.
FL 6139.63.15 Gobbers, W. Jean-Jacques Rousseau in Holland. Gent, 1963.
FL 6139.63.20 Haegi, Klaus Donat. Die politische Freiheit im Werk von Jean-Jacques. Winterthur, 1963.
FL 6139.64 Jean-Jacques Rousseau et son oeuvre. Paris, 1964.
FL 6139.64.5 Baczko, Bronisław. Rousseau. Warszawa, 1964.
FL 6139.64.10 Orias, Arturo. Ethik und Staatsphilosophie bei Jean-Jacques Rousseau. n.p., 1964.
FL 6139.65 McDonald, Joan. Rousseau and the French revolution, 1762-1791. London, 1965.
FL 6139.65.5 Bruno, Antonino. La formazione del pensiero politico di Rousseau. Catania, 1965.
FL 6139.65.10 Jean-Jacques Rousseau et l'homme moderne. Paris, 1965.
FL 6139.66 Millet, Louis. La pensée de Jean-Jacques Rousseau. Paris, 1966.
FL 6139.68 Masters, Roger Davis. The political philosophy of Rousseau. Princeton, 1968.
FL 6139.69 Spurlin, Paul Merrill. Rousseau in America, 1760-1809. University, 1969.
FL 6139.69.5 Shklar, Judith Nisse. Men and citizens. Cambridge, 1969.
FL 6139.69.10 Lecercle, Jean Louis. Rousseau et l'art du roman. Paris, 1969.
FL 6139.69.15 Launay, Michel. Jean-Jacques Rousseau et son temps. Paris, 1969.
FL 6139.70 Baczko, Bronisław. Rousseau. Wien, 1970.
FL 6139.70.5 Metelli Di Lollo, Carmela. Componenti anarchiche nel pensiero di J.J. Rousseau. Firenze, 1970.
FL 6139.70.10 Gouhier, Henri. Les méditations métaphysiques de Jean-Jacques Rousseau. Paris, 1970.
FL 6139.70.15 Roggerone, Giuseppe Agostino. Studi su Rousseau. Lecce, 1970.

FL 6147 - 6150 Jean Jacques Rousseau - Works about Rousseau - Literary works relating to Rousseau (By date)

FL 6147.69 Épître à Jean-Jacques Rousseau. Paris, 1769.
FL 6148.57 Genoux, C. Les enfants de Jean-Jacques Rousseau. Paris, 1857.
FL 6148.59 Caumont, H. Jean-Jacques Rousseau et l'Isle de Saint-Pierre. Zurich, 1859.
FL 6148.69 Schücking, L. Jean-Jacques Rousseau: zwei Episoden. Leipzig, 1869.

Mol 6 - 9 Complete and Selected works - French editions - Complete works - Folios [Discontinued]

Htn Mol 7.34* Molière, Jean Baptiste Poquelin. Oeuvres. Paris, 1734. 6v.
Htn Mol 7.91* Molière, Jean Baptiste Poquelin. Oeuvres. Paris, 1791-94. 6v.
Mol 8.35 Molière, Jean Baptiste Poquelin. Oeuvres. Paris, 1835-36. 2v.
Mol 8.38 Molière, Jean Baptiste Poquelin. Oeuvres. v.1-2,3-4,5-6,7-8. Paris, 1838. 4v.
Mol 8.45A Molière, Jean Baptiste Poquelin. Oeuvres. 3e éd. Paris, 1845. 6v.
Mol 8.45B Molière, Jean Baptiste Poquelin. Oeuvres. 3e éd. Paris, 1845. 6v.
Mol 8.51F Molière, Jean Baptiste Poquelin. Oeuvres. Paris, 1851?
Mol 8.66F Molière, Jean Baptiste Poquelin. Oeuvres complètes. v.1-2. Paris, 1863?
Htn Mol 8.68* Molière, Jean Baptiste Poquelin. Oeuvres complètes. Paris, 1868.
Mol 8.69F Molière, Jean Baptiste Poquelin. Oeuvres complètes. Paris, 1869?
Mol 8.71 Molière, Jean Baptiste Poquelin. Oeuvres complètes. Paris, 1871.
Mol 8.78F Molière, Jean Baptiste Poquelin. Oeuvres complètes. Paris, 1878. 5v.
Mol 8.78.2 Molière, Jean Baptiste Poquelin. Théâtre choisi. Tours, 1878-79. 2v.
Htn Mol 8.82* Molière, Jean Baptiste Poquelin. Oeuvres. Paris, 1882-96. 32v.
Mol 8.82.5 Molière, Jean Baptiste Poquelin. Chefs-d'oeuvre de Molière. Tom.1-2. Paris, 1882.
Htn Mol 8.88* Molière, Jean Baptiste Poquelin. Oeuvres. Paris, 1888-96. 31v.
Mol 8.88.2 Molière, Jean Baptiste Poquelin. Six plays, with introduction. Paris, 1888.
NEDL Mol 8.91 Molière, Jean Baptiste Poquelin. Oeuvres choisies. Paris, 1891.

Mol 16 - 20 Complete and Selected works - French editions - Complete works - Other (By date)

Htn Mol 16.66* Molière, Jean Baptiste Poquelin. Oeuvres. Paris, 1666. 2v.
Htn Mol 16.74* Molière, Jean Baptiste Poquelin. Oeuvres. Paris, 1674-75. 7v.
Htn Mol 16.75* Molière, Jean Baptiste Poquelin. Oeuvres. Amsterdam, 1675. 5v.
Htn Mol 16.75.2* Molière, Jean Baptiste Poquelin. Oeuvres posthumes. Amsterdam, 1689.
Htn Mol 16.79* Molière, Jean Baptiste Poquelin. Oeuvres posthumes. Amsterdam, 1679. 5v.
Htn Mol 16.81* Molière, Jean Baptiste Poquelin. Oeuvres posthumes. Paris, 1681. 5v.
Htn Mol 16.81.2* Molière, Jean Baptiste Poquelin. Oeuvres posthumes. Paris, 1681. 5v.
Htn Mol 16.82* Molière, Jean Baptiste Poquelin. Oeuvres posthumes. Paris, 1682. 8v.
Htn Mol 16.84* Molière, Jean Baptiste Poquelin. Oeuvres posthumes. Amsterdam, 1684. 6v.

Mol 16 - 20 Complete and Selected works - French editions - Complete works - Other (By date) - cont.

Htn Mol 16.94* Molière, Jean Baptiste Poquelin. Oeuvres. Bruxelles, 1694. 4v.
Htn Mol 16.94.3* Molière, Jean Baptiste Poquelin. Comédies. v.1-3. Nuremberg, 1694.
Mol 16.97 Molière, Jean Baptiste Poquelin. Oeuvres. Paris, 1697. 8v.
Htn Mol 16.98* Molière, Jean Baptiste Poquelin. Oeuvres. Amsterdam, 1698. 4v.
Htn Mol 16.99* Molière, Jean Baptiste Poquelin. Oeuvres. Toulouse, 1697-99. 8v.
Htn Mol 17.03* Molière, Jean Baptiste Poquelin. Oeuvres. Liége, 1703.
Htn Mol 17.10* Molière, Jean Baptiste Poquelin. Oeuvres. Paris, 1710. 8v.
Htn Mol 17.13* Molière, Jean Baptiste Poquelin. Ses oeuvres. Amsterdam, 1713. 4v.
Htn Mol 17.18* Molière, Jean Baptiste Poquelin. Oeuvres. Paris, 1718. 8v.
Htn Mol 17.25* Molière, Jean Baptiste Poquelin. Oeuvres. Amsterdam, 1725. 4v.
Htn Mol 17.30* Molière, Jean Baptiste Poquelin. Oeuvres. Paris, 1730. 8v.
Htn Mol 17.32* Molière, Jean Baptiste Poquelin. Oeuvres. v.1-8. Rotterdam, 1732. 4v.
Htn Mol 17.34* Molière, Jean Baptiste Poquelin. Oeuvres. Amsterdam, 1735. 4v.
Htn Mol 17.35* Molière, Jean Baptiste Poquelin. Oeuvres. Amsterdam, 1735. 4v.
Htn Mol 17.39* Molière, Jean Baptiste Poquelin. Oeuvres. Paris, 1739. 8v.
Htn Mol 17.49* Molière, Jean Baptiste Poquelin. Oeuvres. Paris, 1749. 8v.
Htn Mol 17.53* Molière, Jean Baptiste Poquelin. Oeuvres. Paris, 1753.
Htn Mol 17.53.2* Molière, Jean Baptiste Poquelin. Oeuvres. Paris, 1753. 8v.
Htn Mol 17.60* Molière, Jean Baptiste Poquelin. Oeuvres. Basle, 1760. 4v.
Htn Mol 17.60.5* Molière, Jean Baptiste Poquelin. Oeuvres. Paris, 1760. 8v.
Mol 17.61 Molière, Jean Baptiste Poquelin. Les oeuvres. Jene, 1761. 3v.
Htn Mol 17.65* Molière, Jean Baptiste Poquelin. Oeuvres...vie...par Voltaire. Amsterdam, 1765. 6v.
Htn Mol 17.68* Molière, Jean Baptiste Poquelin. Oeuvres. Paris, 1768. 8v.
Htn Mol 17.73* Molière, Jean Baptiste Poquelin. Oeuvres...remarques...par Bret. Paris, 1773. 6v.
Htn Mol 17.84* Molière, Jean Baptiste Poquelin. Oeuvres. Londres, 1784. 7v.
Htn Mol 17.86* Molière, Jean Baptiste Poquelin. Oeuvres...Bret. v.1-6,8. Paris, 1786. 7v.
Htn Mol 17.86.3* Molière, Jean Baptiste Poquelin. Oeuvres...Bret. Paris, 1786. 8v.
Htn Mol 17.88* Molière, Jean Baptiste Poquelin. Oeuvres...Bret. Paris, 1788. 6v.
Mol 17.88.2 Molière, Jean Baptiste Poquelin. Oeuvres de Molière. Paris, 1788. 6v.
Mol 17.88.3 Molière, Jean Baptiste Poquelin. Oeuvres...vie par Voltaire. Berlin, 1788-91. 6v.
Htn Mol 17.99* Molière, Jean Baptiste Poquelin. Oeuvres. v.6. Paris, 1799.
Mol 18.00 Molière, Jean Baptiste Poquelin. Oeuvres complètes. Tom. 4. Paris, 18- .
Mol 18.04 Molière, Jean Baptiste Poquelin. Oeuvres. v.2. Paris, 1804.
Mol 18.06 Molière, Jean Baptiste Poquelin. Works. Oeuvres. Paris?, 18- . 6v.
Mol 18.09 Molière, Jean Baptiste Poquelin. Oeuvres...Bret. Londres, 1809. 8v.
Mol 18.12 Molière, Jean Baptiste Poquelin. Oeuvres. Paris, 1812. 6v.
Htn Mol 18.13* Molière, Jean Baptiste Poquelin. Oeuvres. Paris, 1813. 8v.
Htn Mol 18.13.2* Molière, Jean Baptiste Poquelin. Oeuvres. v.1-4,8. Paris, 1813. 5v.
Mol 18.13.3A Molière, Jean Baptiste Poquelin. Oeuvres. v.1-2, 3-4, 5-6, 7-8. Paris, 1813. 4v.
Mol 18.13.3B Molière, Jean Baptiste Poquelin. Oeuvres. v.1-2, 3-4, 5-6, 7-8. Paris, 1813. 4v.
Htn Mol 18.15* Molière, Jean Baptiste Poquelin. Oeuvres. v.1-7. Paris, 1815. 4v.
Mol 18.17 Molière, Jean Baptiste Poquelin. Oeuvres. Paris, 1817. 7v.
Mol 18.19 Molière, Jean Baptiste Poquelin. Oeuvres...Auger. Paris, 1819-25. 9v.
Mol 18.19.2 Molière, Jean Baptiste Poquelin. Oeuvres...Auger. Paris, 1819-25. 9v.
Mol 18.20 Molière, Jean Baptiste Poquelin. Oeuvres. Paris, 1820. 6v.
Mol 18.21 Molière, Jean Baptiste Poquelin. Oeuvres...Bret. Paris, 1821. 6v.
Mol 18.22 Molière, Jean Baptiste Poquelin. Oeuvres. Paris, 1822. 8v.
Mol 18.22.3 Molière, Jean Baptiste Poquelin. Oeuvres. Paris, 1822. 8v.
Htn Mol 18.22.5* Molière, Jean Baptiste Poquelin. Oeuvres. Paris, 1822. 6v.
Mol 18.23 Molière, Jean Baptiste Poquelin. Oeuvres complètes. Paris, 1823-24. 8v.
Mol 18.24 Molière, Jean Baptiste Poquelin. Oeuvres...Petitot. Paris, 1824. 6v.
Mol 18.24.2 Molière, Jean Baptiste Poquelin. Oeuvres...L. Aimé-Martin. Paris, 1824-26. 8v.
Mol 18.24.3A Molière, Jean Baptiste Poquelin. Oeuvres...L. Aimé-Martin. Paris, 1824-26. 8v.
Mol 18.24.3B Molière, Jean Baptiste Poquelin. Oeuvres...L. Aimé-Martin. Paris, 1824-26. 8v.
Mol 18.25 Molière, Jean Baptiste Poquelin. Oeuvres complètes...Chamfort. Paris, 1825.
Mol 18.25.2 Molière, Jean Baptiste Poquelin. Oeuvres complètes...Simonnin. Paris, 1825.
Mol 18.25.3 Molière, Jean Baptiste Poquelin. Oeuvres complètes...Picard. Paris, 1825. 6v.
Mol 18.25.4 Molière, Jean Baptiste Poquelin. Oeuvres de J.B. Poquelin de Molière. Paris, 1825. 6v.
Mol 18.26 Molière, Jean Baptiste Poquelin. Oeuvres complètes. Paris, 1826.

Mol 16 - 20 Complete and Selected works - French editions - Complete works - Other (By date) - cont.

Mol 18.27 Molière, Jean Baptiste Poquelin. Oeuvres complètes. Paris, 1827.

Mol 18.28 Molière, Jean Baptiste Poquelin. Oeuvres. v.1-5,8. Paris, 1828. 6v.

Mol 18.29 Molière, Jean Baptiste Poquelin. Oeuvres. v. 1-2, 3-4, 5-6, 7-8. Paris, 1829. 4v.

Mol 18.30 Molière, Jean Baptiste Poquelin. Oeuvres. Paris, 1830. 8v.

Mol 18.32 Molière, Jean Baptiste Poquelin. Oeuvres. Paris, 1832. 6v.

Mol 18.33 Molière, Jean Baptiste Poquelin. Oeuvres. Paris, 1833. 8v.

Mol 18.34 Molière, Jean Baptiste Poquelin. Oeuvres. Paris, 1834. 8v.

Mol 18.36 Molière, Jean Baptiste Poquelin. Oeuvres...Petitot. Paris, 1836. 6v.

Mol 18.38 Molière, Jean Baptiste Poquelin. Oeuvres. Paris, 1838. 2v.

Mol 18.38.5 Molière, Jean Baptiste Poquelin. Oeuvres. Paris, 1838.

Mol 18.40 Molière, Jean Baptiste Poquelin. Oeuvres. v. 1-8. Paris, 1840. 4v.

Mol 18.42 Molière, Jean Baptiste Poquelin. Oeuvres. Paris, 1842. 8v.

Mol 18.43 Molière, Jean Baptiste Poquelin. Oeuvres complètes. Paris, 1843.

Mol 18.44 Molière, Jean Baptiste Poquelin. Oeuvres. Paris, 1844.

Mol 18.45 Molière, Jean Baptiste Poquelin. Oeuvres...Aimé-Martin. 3e éd. Paris, 1845. 6v.

Mol 18.45.2 Molière, Jean Baptiste Poquelin. Oeuvres complètes. Paris, 1845.

Mol 18.45.3 Molière, Jean Baptiste Poquelin. Oeuvres...Aimé-Martin. 4e éd. Paris, 1845. 4v.

Mol 18.45.4 Molière, Jean Baptiste Poquelin. Oeuvres de Molière. Paris, 1845. 2v.

Mol 18.49 Molière, Jean Baptiste Poquelin. Oeuvres. Paris, 1849. 2v.

Mol 18.51.5 Molière, Jean Baptiste Poquelin. Oeuvres. Paris, 1851. 2v.

Mol 18.52 Molière, Jean Baptiste Poquelin. Oeuvres complètes...Louandre. Paris, 1852. 3v.

Mol 18.54A Molière, Jean Baptiste Poquelin. Oeuvres. Paris, 1854. 2v.

Mol 18.55 Molière, Jean Baptiste Poquelin. Oeuvres complètes...Charles. Paris, 1855-56. 5v.

Mol 18.57 Molière, Jean Baptiste Poquelin. Oeuvres complètes...Louandre. Paris, 185-? 3v.

Mol 18.58 Molière, Jean Baptiste Poquelin. Oeuvres complètes...Louandre. Paris, 1858. 3v.

Mol 18.58.9 Molière, Jean Baptiste Poquelin. Oeuvres complètes...Louandre. Paris, 185-. 3v.

Mol 18.58.15 Molière, Jean Baptiste Poquelin. Oeuvres complètes...Louandre. Paris, 185-? 3v.

Mol 18.59 Molière, Jean Baptiste Poquelin. Oeuvres complètes...Lahure. Paris, 1859. 2v.

Mol 18.62 Molière, Jean Baptiste Poquelin. Oeuvres complètes...Lemaistre. Paris, 1862. 3v.

Mol 18.62.2 Molière, Jean Baptiste Poquelin. Oeuvres complètes. Paris, 1862. 8v.

Mol 18.63 Molière, Jean Baptiste Poquelin. Oeuvres complètes...Taschereau. Paris, 1863. 6v.

Mol 18.63.2 Molière, Jean Baptiste Poquelin. Oeuvres complètes...Taschereau. Paris, 1863. 6v.

Mol 18.63.3 Molière, Jean Baptiste Poquelin. Oeuvres complètes...Moland. Paris, 1863-64. 7v.

Mol 18.63.4 Molière, Jean Baptiste Poquelin. Oeuvres complètes...Moland. Paris, 1863-64. 7v.

Mol 18.63.10 Molière, Jean Baptiste Poquelin. Oeuvres. Paris, 1863. 2v.

Htn Mol 18.64* Molière, Jean Baptiste Poquelin. Théâtre...Hillemacher. Lyon, 1864-70. 8v.

Mol 18.67 Molière, Jean Baptiste Poquelin. Oeuvres complètes. Paris, 1867. 3v.

Mol 18.68 Molière, Jean Baptiste Poquelin. Oeuvres complètes. Paris, 1868? 3v.

Mol 18.69 Molière, Jean Baptiste Poquelin. Oeuvres complètes. Paris, 1869. 3v.

Mol 18.69.2 Molière, Jean Baptiste Poquelin. Oeuvres complètes. Paris, 1869. 3v.

Mol 18.71 Molière, Jean Baptiste Poquelin. Oeuvres complètes. Paris, 1871. 3v.

Mol 18.71.10 Molière, Jean Baptiste Poquelin. Oeuvres complètes. Paris, n.d. 2v.

Mol 18.72 Molière, Jean Baptiste Poquelin. Oeuvres...Pauly. Paris, 1872-74. 8v.

Mol 18.72.2 Molière, Jean Baptiste Poquelin. Oeuvres...Pauly. Paris, 1872-74. 8v.

Htn Mol 18.72.3* Molière, Jean Baptiste Poquelin. Oeuvres...Pauly. Paris, 1876.

Mol 18.73 Molière, Jean Baptiste Poquelin. Oeuvres...Despois. v.1-13 and album. Paris, 1873-1900. 14v.

Mol 18.73.2A Molière, Jean Baptiste Poquelin. Oeuvres...Despois. v.1-12 and album. Paris, 1873-1900. 13v.

Mol 18.73.2B Molière, Jean Baptiste Poquelin. Oeuvres...Despois. Album. Paris, 1873-1900.

Mol 18.73.3 Molière, Jean Baptiste Poquelin. Oeuvres. Paris, 1873. 2v.

Mol 18.73.5 Molière, Jean Baptiste Poquelin. Molière...Laun. v.1-14. Berlin, 1873-85. 9v.

Mol 18.73.8A Molière, Jean Baptiste Poquelin. Oeuvres complètes. Paris, 1873. 3v.

Mol 18.73.8B Molière, Jean Baptiste Poquelin. Oeuvres complètes. Paris, 1873. 3v.

Mol 18.75 Molière, Jean Baptiste Poquelin. Oeuvres. v.1-8. Paris, 1875. 4v.

Mol 18.76 Molière, Jean Baptiste Poquelin. Oeuvres...France. Paris, 1876-95. 6v.

Mol 18.76.2 Molière, Jean Baptiste Poquelin. Oeuvres...France. Paris, 1876-95. 7v.

Htn Mol 18.76.3* Molière, Jean Baptiste Poquelin. Théâtre complet...Jouast. Paris, 1876-83. 8v.

Mol 18.80 Molière, Jean Baptiste Poquelin. Oeuvres complètes...Moland. 2e éd. Paris, 1880-85. 12v.

Mol 18.80.2 Molière, Jean Baptiste Poquelin. Oeuvres complètes...Moland. 2e éd. Paris, 1880-85. 12v.

Mol 18.80.5 Molière, Jean Baptiste Poquelin. Oeuvres...Sainte-Beuve. Paris, 1880.

Mol 18.82 Molière, Jean Baptiste Poquelin. Théâtre complet...Monval. Paris, 1882-83. 8v.

Mol 18.82.2 Molière, Jean Baptiste Poquelin. Théâtre complet...Monval. Paris, 1882-83. 8v.

Mol 18.82.3 Molière, Jean Baptiste Poquelin. Oeuvres. Paris, 1882. 2v.

Mol 18.83 Molière, Jean Baptiste Poquelin. Werke...Laun. 2e Aufl. v.1-5. Leipzig, 1883-87.

Mol 18.86 Molière, Jean Baptiste Poquelin. Oeuvres complètes...Louandre. Paris, 1886-87. 8v.

Mol 18.89 Molière, Jean Baptiste Poquelin. Oeuvres complètes...Louandre. Paris, 1889. 3v.

Mol 18.91 Molière, Jean Baptiste Poquelin. Théâtre. v.1-11. Paris, 1891-95. 4v.

Mol 18.92 Molière, Jean Baptiste Poquelin. Théâtre complet. Paris, 1892. 8v.

Mol 18.93A Molière, Jean Baptiste Poquelin. Oeuvres complètes...Fournier. Paris, 1893. 12v.

Mol 18.93B Molière, Jean Baptiste Poquelin. Oeuvres complètes...Fournier. Paris, 1893. 12v.

Mol 18.94 Molière, Jean Baptiste Poquelin. Oeuvres complètes. v.1-3,4-6,7-9,10-12,15-16. Paris, 1894. 5v.

Mol 18.96 Molière, Jean Baptiste Poquelin. Oeuvres...Bon marché. Paris, 1896. 2v.

Mol 19.00 Molière, Jean Baptiste Poquelin. Oeuvres complètes. Oxford, 1900.

Htn Mol 19.00.2* Molière, Jean Baptiste Poquelin. Oeuvres complètes. Oxford, 1900. 4v.

Mol 19.04 Molière, Jean Baptiste Poquelin. Oeuvres complètes. Paris, 1904? 3v.

Mol 19.10 Molière, Jean Baptiste Poquelin. Théâtre complet illustré. v.1-3, 4-7. Paris, n.d. 2v.

Mol 19.13 Molière, Jean Baptiste Poquelin. Oeuvres complètes. v.1,3-6. Paris, 1913? 5v.

Mol 19.25 Molière, Jean Baptiste Poquelin. Oeuvres de Molière illustrées des gravoures anciennes. Paris, 1925-29. 7v.

Mol 19.26 Molière, Jean Baptiste Poquelin. Oeuvres de Molière. Paris, 1926-29. 10v.

Mol 19.29 Molière, Jean Baptiste Poquelin. Oeuvres complètes. Paris, 1929-30. 6v.

Mol 19.30 Molière, Jean Baptiste Poquelin. Molière; sa vie, son oeuvres. Paris, 1930. 6v.

Mol 19.32 Molière, Jean Baptiste Poquelin. Théâtre complet. Paris, 1932. 10v.

Mol 19.35 Molière, Jean Baptiste Poquelin. Théâtre de 1655 à 1660. Paris, 1935.

Mol 19.35.3 Molière, Jean Baptiste Poquelin. Théâtre de 1661 à 1663. Paris, 1939.

Mol 19.35.5 Molière, Jean Baptiste Poquelin. Théâtre 1664-1665. Paris, 1943.

Mol 19.35.7 Molière, Jean Baptiste Poquelin. Théâtre 1666 à 1668. Paris, 1946.

Mol 19.35.9 Molière, Jean Baptiste Poquelin. Théâtre, 1668-1669. Paris, 1947.

Mol 19.35.11 Molière, Jean Baptiste Poquelin. Théâtre, 1669-1670. Paris, 1949.

Mol 19.35.13 Molière, Jean Baptiste Poquelin. Théâtre de l'annee 1671. Paris, 1950.

Mol 19.36 Molière, Jean Baptiste Poquelin. Théâtre. Paris, 1936?

Mol 19.49 Molière, Jean Baptiste Poquelin. Oeuvres complètes. Paris, 1949. 11v.

Mol 19.54 Molière, Jean Baptiste Poquelin. Oeuvres complètes. Paris, 1954-56. 3v.

Mol 19.58 Molière, Jean Baptiste Poquelin. Théâtre. Paris, 1958. 4v.

Mol 19.59 Molière, Jean Baptiste Poquelin. Oeuvres complètes. Paris, 1959. 2v.

Mol 19.61 Molière, Jean Baptiste Poquelin. Théâtre. Paris, 1961-62. 2v.

Mol 19.62 Molière, Jean Baptiste Poquelin. Théâtre complet. Lausanne, 1962. 5v.

Mol 19.64 Molière, Jean Baptiste Poquelin. Oeuvres complètes. Paris, 1964- 4v.

Mol 19.65 Molière, Jean Baptiste Poquelin. Oeuvres complètes. Paris, 1965. 2v.

Mol 19.68 Molière, Jean Baptiste Poquelin. Oeuvres complètes. Paris, 1968- 10v.

Mol 36 - 40 Complete and Selected works - French editions - Selected works (By date)

Mol 37.60 Molière, Jean Baptiste Poquelin. Oeuvres choisies. v.1-5. Paris, 1760-62.

Mol 37.70 Molière, Jean Baptiste Poquelin. Chef-d'oeuvres. Liége, 1770. 2v.

Mol 37.99 Molière, Jean Baptiste Poquelin. Oeuvres choisies...Bret. Oxford, 1799. 2v.

Mol 38.20 Molière, Jean Baptiste Poquelin. Oeuvres choisies. v.1-8. Paris, 1820-67.

Mol 38.36 Molière, Jean Baptiste Poquelin. Le Molière de la jeunesse. v.2. Lyon, 1836.

Mol 38.50 Molière, Jean Baptiste Poquelin. Oeuvres choisies. N.Y., 185-?

Mol 38.57 Molière, Jean Baptiste Poquelin. Oeuvres choisies. N.Y., 1857.

Mol 38.58 Molière, Jean Baptiste Poquelin. Oeuvres choisies. N.Y., 1858.

Mol 38.66 Molière, Jean Baptiste Poquelin. Oeuvres choisies...Hillemacher. Paris, 1866-75. 2v.

Mol 38.68 Molière, Jean Baptiste Poquelin. Comédies...jouées par des jeunes gens. v.1-5. Paris, 1868? 3v.

Mol 38.68.2 Molière, Jean Baptiste Poquelin. Comédies...jouées par des jeunes gens. Paris, 1868?

Mol 38.76 Molière, Jean Baptiste Poquelin. Ausgewählte Lustspiele...Brunnemann. v.1-6. Berlin, 1876-77.

Mol 38.77 Molière, Jean Baptiste Poquelin. Ausgewählte Lustspiele...H. Fritsche. v.1-7. Berlin, 1877-86.

Mol 38.78 Molière, Jean Baptiste Poquelin. Oeuvres choisies. Paris, 1878.

Mol 38.93 Molière, Jean Baptiste Poquelin. Théâtre choisi...Albert. 5e éd. Paris, 1893.

Mol 38.98 Molière, Jean Baptiste Poquelin. Théâtre choisi...Léna. Paris, 1898.

Mol 39.05 Molière, Jean Baptiste Poquelin. Théâtre classique populaire. Paris, 1905.

Mol 39.08 Molière, Jean Baptiste Poquelin. Théâtre choisi. 6e éd. Paris, 1908.

Classified Listing

Mol 36 - 40 Complete and Selected works - French editions - Selected works (By date) - cont.

Mol 39.12 Thirion, E. Théâtre choisi de Molière. Paris, 1912.
Mol 39.20 Molière, Jean Baptiste Poquelin. Théâtre choisi. 5e éd. Paris, 1920.
Mol 39.35A Molière, Jean Baptiste Poquelin. The principal comedies of Molière. N.Y., 1935.
Mol 39.35B Molière, Jean Baptiste Poquelin. The principal comedies of Molière. N.Y., 1935.

Mol 46 - 50 Complete and Selected works - French editions - Selections (By date)

Mol 47.77 Molière, Jean Baptiste Poquelin. L'esprit de Molière. Londres, 1777. 2v.
Mol 47.99 Molière, Jean Baptiste Poquelin. Dialogues français, anglais et italiens. Paris, 1799.
Mol 48.18 Molière, Jean Baptiste Poquelin. Dialoghi francesi, italiani, tedeschi ed inglesi. 11e éd. Milano, 1818.
Mol 48.38 Molière, Jean Baptiste Poquelin. Dictionnaire de morale et de littérature. Paris, 1838.
Mol 48.95 Molière, Jean Baptiste Poquelin. Principales scènes. Paris, 1895?
Mol 48.96 Molière, Jean Baptiste Poquelin. Le misanthrope...fragments...Boitel. Paris, 1896.
Mol 48.96.2 Molière, Jean Baptiste Poquelin. Scènes choisies...Thirion. Paris, 1896.
Mol 48.97 Molière, Jean Baptiste Poquelin. Scènes choisies...Cahen. Paris, 1897.
Mol 48.99 Molière, Jean Baptiste Poquelin. Scènes choisies...Bouchor. Paris, 1899-1900. 2v.
Mol 48.99.2 Molière, Jean Baptiste Poquelin. Scènes choisies...Bouchor. Paris, 1899-1900. 2v.
Mol 49.57 Molière, Jean Baptiste Poquelin. Molière par lui-même. Paris, 1957.
Mol 49.59 Molière, Jean Baptiste Poquelin. Maximes de Molière. La Haye, 1959.

Mol 60 Complete and Selected works - Translations - English

Htn Mol 60.1* Molière, Jean Baptiste Poquelin. Works. London, 1714. 6v.
Mol 60.2 Molière, Jean Baptiste Poquelin. Select comedies. London, 1732. 8v.
Mol 60.3 Molière, Jean Baptiste Poquelin. Works. v.1,3-7,9,10. London, 1739. 8v.
Mol 60.4 Molière, Jean Baptiste Poquelin. Works. London, 1748. 10v.
Mol 60.7 Molière, Jean Baptiste Poquelin. Works. London, 1755. 10v.
Mol 60.10 Molière, Jean Baptiste Poquelin. Works. Berwick, 1771. 6v.
Mol 60.15 Lennard, D.B. Tales from Molière's plays. London, 1859.
Mol 60.20 Molière, Jean Baptiste Poquelin. Dramatic works...van Laun. Edinburgh, 1875-76. 6v.
Mol 60.20.2 Molière, Jean Baptiste Poquelin. Dramatic works...van Laun. Edinburgh, 1875-76. 6v.
Mol 60.20.3A Molière, Jean Baptiste Poquelin. The dramatic works of Molière. Edinburgh, 1875-76. 6v.
NEDL Mol 60.20.3B Molière, Jean Baptiste Poquelin. The dramatic works of Molière. Edinburgh, 1875-76. 6v.
Mol 60.20.4 Molière, Jean Baptiste Poquelin. The dramatic works of Molière. v.2-3. N.Y., 1880. 2v.
Mol 60.21 Molière, Jean Baptiste Poquelin. Dramatic works...C.H. Wall. London, 1876-77. 3v.
Mol 60.21.2 Molière, Jean Baptiste Poquelin. Dramatic works..C.H. Wall. London, 1876-77. 2v.
Mol 60.22 Molière, Jean Baptiste Poquelin. Dramatic works...C.H. Wall. London, 1919. 3v.
Mol 60.22.5 Molière, Jean Baptiste Poquelin. Dramatic works. v.2. London, 1911.
Mol 60.23 Molière, Jean Baptiste Poquelin. Molière in outline...F.C. Brewster. Philadelphia, 1885.
NEDL Mol 60.25 Molière, Jean Baptiste Poquelin. Comedies...Mathew. 3rd ed. London, 1894.
Mol 60.26A Molière, Jean Baptiste Poquelin. Molière...K.P. Wormeley. Boston, 1894-97. 6v.
Mol 60.26B Molière, Jean Baptiste Poquelin. Molière...K.P. Wormeley. Boston, 1894-97. 5v.
Mol 60.27 Molière, Jean Baptiste Poquelin. Molière. Boston, 1912-1919. 6v.
Mol 60.30 Molière, Jean Baptiste Poquelin. Plays in French...A.R. Waller. v.2-4. London, 1902-03. 3v.
Mol 60.31A Molière, Jean Baptiste Poquelin. Plays in French...A.R. Waller. Edinburgh, 1907. 3v.
Mol 60.31B Molière, Jean Baptiste Poquelin. Plays in French...A.R. Waller. Edinburgh, 1907. 3v.
Mol 60.31.5 Molière, Jean Baptiste Poquelin. Plays. N.Y., 1904.
Mol 60.31.12 Molière, Jean Baptiste Poquelin. Plays...A.R. Waller. Edinburgh, 1926. 8v.
Mol 60.31.15 Molière, Jean Baptiste Poquelin. Eight plays. N.Y., 1957.
NEDL Mol 60.32 Molière, Jean Baptiste Poquelin. Molière. N.Y., 1908. 2v.
Mol 60.34 Molière, Jean Baptiste Poquelin. The Kiltartan Molière by Lady Gregory. Dublin, 1911.
Mol 60.38 Molière, Jean Baptiste Poquelin. Comedies. London, 1929. 2v.
Mol 60.42 Molière, Jean Baptiste Poquelin. Four Molière comedies. London, 1931.
Mol 60.44 Molière, Jean Baptiste Poquelin. Six prose comedies. London, 1956.
Mol 60.45 Molière, Jean Baptiste Poquelin. One act comedies of Molière. 1st ed. Cleveland, 1964.
Mol 60.46 Molière, Jean Baptiste Poquelin. Three Molière plays; Tartufe, Scapin the Trickster, The School for wives. London, 1933.
Mol 60.48 Molière, Jean Baptiste Poquelin. The miser and other plays. Harmondsworth, 1962.
Mol 60.50 Molière, Jean Baptiste Poquelin. Tartuffe and other plays. N.Y., 1967.

Mol 62 Complete and Selected works - Translations - German

Htn Mol 62.3* Molière, Jean Baptiste Poquelin. Derer Komödien. Nuremberg, 1694. 3v.
Mol 62.10 Molière, Jean Baptiste Poquelin. Sämmtliche Lustspiele. Hamburg, 1752. 4v.
Mol 62.11 Molière, Jean Baptiste Poquelin. Sämmtliche Lustspiele. 2e Aufl. Hamburg, 1769. 4v.
Mol 62.15 Molière, Jean Baptiste Poquelin. Lustspiele und Possen. Zürich, 1810. 6v.

Mol 62 Complete and Selected works - Translations - German - cont.

Mol 62.19 Molière, Jean Baptiste Poquelin. Dramatische Meisterwerke...Alvensleben. Leipzig, 1837?
Mol 62.20 Molière, Jean Baptiste Poquelin. Sämmtliche Werke...Lax. Aachen, 1838.
Mol 62.23 Molière, Jean Baptiste Poquelin. Charakter-Komödien...Laun. v.1-3. Hildburghausen, 1865.
Mol 62.24 Molière, Jean Baptiste Poquelin. Lustspiele...Baudissin. Leipzig, 1865-67. 4v.
Mol 62.25 Molière, Jean Baptiste Poquelin. Sämtliche Werke...Schröder. Leipzig, 1871? 2v.
Mol 62.28 Molière, Jean Baptiste Poquelin. Ausgewählte Lustspiele...Laun. Leipzig, 1880?
Mol 62.30 Molière, Jean Baptiste Poquelin. Ausgewählte Lustspiele...Bierling. Stuttgart, 1883. 3v.
Mol 62.33 Molière, Jean Baptiste Poquelin. Meisterwerke...Fulda. Stuttgart, 1892.
Mol 62.35 Molière, Jean Baptiste Poquelin. Meisterwerke...Fulda. 2e Aufl. Stuttgart, 1896.
Mol 62.37 Molière, Jean Baptiste Poquelin. Meisterwerke...Fulda. 3e Aufl. Stuttgart, 1901.
Mol 62.39 Molière, Jean Baptiste Poquelin. Meisterwerke...Fulda. 5e Aufl. Stuttgart, 1911.
Mol 62.53 Molière, Jean Baptiste Poquelin. Sämtliche Werke. München, 1921. 6v.
Mol 62.54 Molière, Jean Baptiste Poquelin. In Deutscher Sprache...O. Hauser. Berlin, 1911-12. 2v.
Mol 62.60 Molière, Jean Baptiste Poquelin. Sämtliche Werke...P.A. Becker. v.1-3,4-6. Leipzig, 1912. 2v.

Mol 64 Complete and Selected works - Translations - Italian

Mol 64.1 Molière, Jean Baptiste Poquelin. Opere...Castelli. Lipsia, 1698. 4v.
Mol 64.1.2 Molière, Jean Baptiste Poquelin. Opere...Castelli. v.2-4. Lipsia, 1698. 3v.
Mol 64.5 Molière, Jean Baptiste Poquelin. Repertorio scelto...Barbieri. v.1-5. Milano, 1823-24.
Mol 64.5.2 Molière, Jean Baptiste Poquelin. Repertorio scelto...Barbieri. v.1-6. Milano, n.d.
Mol 64.6 Molière, Jean Baptiste Poquelin. Commedie...in lengua zeneize. v.1-6. Zena, 1830. 2v.
Mol 64.15 Molière, Jean Baptiste Poquelin. Commedie scelte. Milano, 1930.

Mol 68 Complete and Selected works - Translations - Spanish

Mol 68.5 Molière, Jean Baptiste Poquelin. Tartufo, o El impostor; La escuela de los maridos; El burgues gentilhombre. Buenos Aires, 1940.

Mol 95 Complete and Selected works - Translations - Greek

Mol 95.1 Molière, Jean Baptiste Poquelin. Arista erga...Skylissē. Tergestē, 1871.

Mol 115 Complete and Selected works - Translations - Polish

Mol 115.1 Molière, Jean Baptiste Poquelin. Dzieła. Warszawa, 1952. 6v.
Mol 115.1.5 Molière, Jean Baptiste Poquelin. Skąpiec. Wrocław, 1959.

Mol 130 Complete and Selected works - Translations - Russian

Mol 130.3 Molière, Jean Baptiste Poquelin. Sobranie sochinenii. Sankt Peterburg, 1884.

Mol 150 Individual plays - Folios [Discontinued]

Htn Mol 150.3* Lully, J.B. de. L'amour medecin-music. Manuscript. n.p., n.d.
Htn Mol 150.3.5* Lully, J.B. de. Le ballet du Sicilien. Manuscript n.p., n.d.
Htn Mol 150.5* Les plaisirs de l'isle enchantée. Paris, 1673.
Mol 150.15F Molière, Jean Baptiste Paquelin. Psyché...Bocher. Paris, 1880.
Mol 150.25 Molière, Jean Baptiste Paquelin. Le sicilien...Sauzay. Paris, 1881.

Mol 151 Individual plays - Les Amants Magnifiques - French editions

Mol 151.15 Molière, Jean Baptiste Paquelin. Les amants magnifiques...Monval. Paris, 1894.

Mol 155 Individual plays - L'Amour Médecin - French editions

Mol 155.20 Molière, Jean Baptiste Poquelin. L'amour médecin. n.p., n.d.
Mol 155.25 Molière, Jean Baptiste Poquelin. L'amour médecin...Lacour. Paris, 1876.
Mol 155.30 Molière, Jean Baptiste Poquelin. L'amour médecin...Monval. Paris, 1892.
Mol 155.40 Molière, Jean Baptiste Poquelin. L'amour médecin. Strasbourg, 191-?

Mol 157 Individual plays - L'Amour Médecin - Criticism

Mol 157.5 Girard, Joseph. A propos de "L'amour médecin". Paris, 1948.

Mol 161 Individual plays - Amphitryon - French editions

Mol 161.25 Molière, Jean Baptiste Poquelin. Amphitryon...Gombert. London, 1838.
Mol 161.30 Molière, Jean Baptiste Poquelin. Amphitryon...Lacour. Paris, 1876.
Mol 161.35 Molière, Jean Baptiste Poquelin. Amphitryon...Monval. Paris, 1893.
Mol 161.36 Molière, Jean Baptiste Poquelin. Amphitryon; comédie. Paris, 1946.
Mol 161.37 Molière, Jean Baptiste Poquelin. Amphitryon; comédie. Genève, 1950.

Mol 162 Individual plays - Amphitryon - Translations

Mol 162.38.5 Molière, Jean Baptiste Poquelin. Amphitryon...Phragia. Ermoupolis, 1877.
Mol 162.45.5 Molière, Jean Baptiste Poquelin. Jupiter en Amphitryon, of de twee gelyke Sosias. Amsterdam, 1730.
Mol 162.50 Molière, Jean Baptiste Poquelin. Amfitrione; commedia. Lauciano, 1931.

Mol 163 Individual plays - Amphitryon - Criticism

Mol 163.5 Lorin, T. Quelques observations...sur l'amphitryon. Soissons, 1855.
Mol 163.10 Romer, Paul. Molières Amphitryon und sein gesellschaftlicher Hintergrund. Bonn, 1967.

Mol 165 Individual plays - L'Avare - French editions

Mol 165.21 Molière, Jean Baptiste Poquelin. L'avare and The miser. Paris, 1751.
Mol 165.25 Molière, Jean Baptiste Poquelin. L'avare...Schwalb. Essen, 1850.
Mol 165.26 Molière, Jean Baptiste Poquelin. L'avare...Köhler. Altenburg, 1851.
Mol 165.26.2 Molière, Jean Baptiste Poquelin. L'avare...Barbieux. Frankfurt, 1851.
Mol 165.28 Molière, Jean Baptiste Poquelin. L'avare...Fiebig and Leportier. Leipzig, 1856.
Mol 165.30 Molière, Jean Baptiste Poquelin. L'avare...Estienne. Paris, 186-.
Mol 165.31 Molière, Jean Baptiste Poquelin. L'avare...George Dandin. Paris, 1869.
Mol 165.32 Molière, Jean Baptiste Poquelin. L'avare...Lacour. Paris, 1876.
Mol 165.35 Molière, Jean Baptiste Poquelin. L'avare...Lion. Leipzig, 1879.
Mol 165.38 Molière, Jean Baptiste Poquelin. L'avare...Joynes. N.Y., 1882.
Mol 165.39 Molière, Jean Baptiste Poquelin. L'avare...Moriarty. London, 1882.
Mol 165.40 Molière, Jean Baptiste Poquelin. L'avare...Livet. Paris, 1882.
Mol 165.42 Molière, Jean Baptiste Poquelin. L'avare...Marcou. Paris, 1885.
Mol 165.43 Molière, Jean Baptiste Poquelin. L'avare...Cotte. N.Y., 1887.
Mol 165.44 Molière, Jean Baptiste Poquelin. L'avare...Livet. Paris, 1887.
Mol 165.45 Molière, Jean Baptiste Poquelin. L'avare...Pontsevrez. Paris, 1887.
Mol 165.46 Molière, Jean Baptiste Poquelin. L'avare...Boully. Paris, 1887.
Mol 165.46.5 Molière, Jean Baptiste Poquelin. L'avare...de Vere. N.Y., 1888.
Mol 165.47 Molière, Jean Baptiste Poquelin. L'avare...Gasc. London, 1889.
Mol 165.48 Molière, Jean Baptiste Poquelin. L'avare...Humbert. Leipzig, 1889.
Mol 165.48.2 Molière, Jean Baptiste Poquelin. L'avare...Humbert: Anmerkungen. Leipzig, 1889.
Mol 165.49 Molière, Jean Baptiste Poquelin. L'avare...Lavigne. Paris, 1889.
Mol 165.50 Molière, Jean Baptiste Poquelin. L'avare...Masson. 12th ed. London, 1889.
Mol 165.53 Molière, Jean Baptiste Poquelin. L'avare...Gosset. London, 1890.
Mol 165.54 Molière, Jean Baptiste Poquelin. L'avare...Pellisson. 3e éd. Paris, 1886.
Mol 165.55 Molière, Jean Baptiste Poquelin. L'avare...Pellisson. 5e éd. Paris, 1891.
Mol 165.56 Molière, Jean Baptiste Poquelin. L'avare...Marandet. Paris, 1891.
Mol 165.58 Molière, Jean Baptiste Poquelin. L'avare...Friese. Bielefeld, 1893.
Mol 165.59 Molière, Jean Baptiste Poquelin. L'avare...Monval. Paris, 1893.
Mol 165.60 Molière, Jean Baptiste Poquelin. L'avare...Boully. Paris, 1894.
Mol 165.61 Molière, Jean Baptiste Poquelin. L'avare. Boston, 1894.
Mol 165.62 Molière, Jean Baptiste Poquelin. L'avare...Henckels. Boston, 1894.
Mol 165.63 Bué, H. The new conversational French reader. London, 1894.
Mol 165.65 Molière, Jean Baptiste Poquelin. L'avare...Boully. Paris, 1895.
Mol 165.66 Molière, Jean Baptiste Poquelin. L'avare...Braunholtz. Cambridge, 1897.
Mol 165.69 Molière, Jean Baptiste Poquelin. L'avare...M. Levi. Boston, 1900.
Mol 165.70 Molière, Jean Baptiste Poquelin. L'avare...Lanson. Paris, 1901.
Mol 165.71 Molière, Jean Baptiste Poquelin. L'avare. London, 1901.
Mol 165.75 Molière, Jean Baptiste Poquelin. L'avare...M. Levi. Boston, 1904.
Mol 165.80 Molière, Jean Baptiste Poquelin. L'avare. Ann Arbor, 1907.
Mol 165.82 Molière, Jean Baptiste Poquelin. L'avare. Ann Arbor, 1908.
Mol 165.83 Molière, Jean Baptiste Poquelin. L'avare. Strasbourg, 1908?
Mol 165.88 Molière, Jean Baptiste Poquelin. L'avare. N.Y., 1911.
Mol 165.95A Molière, Jean Baptiste Poquelin. L'avare. Manchester, 1918.
Mol 165.95B Molière, Jean Baptiste Poquelin. L'avare. Manchester, 1918.
Mol 165.96 Molière, Jean Baptiste Poquelin. L'avare. Paris, 1931.
Mol 165.109 Molière, Jean Baptiste Poquelin. L'avare...R.A. Wilson. London, 1945.
Mol 165.110 Molière, Jean Baptiste Poquelin. L'avare. Paris, 1946.
Mol 165.112 Molière, Jean Baptiste Poquelin. L'avare. London, 1959.

Mol 166 Individual plays - L'Avare - Translations

Mol 166.1.3 Molière, Jean Baptiste Poquelin. L'avare...mise en vers par A. Rastoul. Avignon, 1836.
Mol 166.1.5 Molière, Jean Baptiste Poquelin. L'avare...mise en vers par A. Malouin. Paris, 1859.
Mol 166.1.8 Molière, Jean Baptiste Poquelin. L'avare...Ostrowski. Paris, 1874.
Mol 166.1.9 Molière, Jean Baptiste Poquelin. L'avare...L.F.A. Paris, 1875.
Mol 166.2.76 Molière, Jean Baptiste Poquelin. L'avare...M.Levi. Boston, 1900.
Mol 166.3 Molière, Jean Baptiste Poquelin. L'avare...C.H. Page. Photoreproduction. N.Y., 1913.
Mol 166.4 Molière, Jean Baptiste Poquelin. The miser. Iowa City, Iowa, 1946.
Mol 166.4.5 Molière, Jean Baptiste Poquelin. The miser, and Coxcombs in petticoats. St. Albans, 1953.
Mol 166.4.10 Molière, Jean Baptiste Poquelin. The miser. N.Y., 1964.
Mol 166.5.4 Molière, Jean Baptiste Poquelin. Der Geizige...F. Dingelstedt. Weimar, 1858.
Mol 166.5.5 Molière, Jean Baptiste Poquelin. Der Geizige...Krais. Stuttgart, 1868.
Mol 166.5.7 Molière, Jean Baptiste Poquelin. Der Geizige...Cornelius. Leipzig, n.d.

Mol 166 Individual plays - L'Avare - Translations - cont.

Mol 166.6 Molière, Jean Baptiste Poquelin. L'avaro...N. Cacudi. Firenze, 1926.
Mol 166.7 Molière, Jean Baptiste Poquelin. L'avaro...Soncini. n.p., n.d.
Mol 166.8.5 Molière, Jean Baptiste Poquelin. O avarento...A.F. de Castilho. Lisboa, 1871.
Mol 166.25 Molière, Jean Baptiste Poquelin. De vrek...T.H. de Beer. 's Gravenhage, 1898.
Mol 166.38 Molière, Jean Baptiste Poquelin. O Philargos. Vienne, 1816.
Mol 166.43 Molière, Jean Baptiste Poquelin. Lakomec. Praha, 1852.
Mol 166.50 Molière, Jean Baptiste Poquelin. Skupoi. Moskva, 1832.

Mol 167 Individual plays - L'Avare - Criticism

Mol 167.4 Saegelken, E. De Molieri fabula avari nomine. Bremae, 1856.
Mol 167.5 Lorin, T. Remarques sur l'avare. Soissons, 1856.
Mol 167.6 Claus, W. De Aulularia Plauti fabula. Sedini, 1862-87.
Mol 167.7 Bromig, J. Vergleichung der Komödien Aulularia des Plautus und l'Avare des Molière. Burgsteinfurt, 1854.
Mol 167.10 Groon. Comparaison entre l'Avare de Molière et l'Aululaire de Plaute. Berden, 1874?
Mol 167.12 Klapp, A. L'avare ancien et moderne. Parchim, 1877.
Mol 167.15 Morin, L. Les ancêtres de "L'avare" de Molière. Troyes, 1939.

Mol 171 Individual plays - Le Bourgeois Gentilhomme - French editions

Mol 171.16 Molière, Jean Baptiste Poquelin. Le bourgeois gentilhomme. Bielefeld, 1861.
Mol 171.22 Molière, Jean Baptiste Poquelin. Le bourgeois gentilhomme. Paris, 1869.
Mol 171.24 Molière, Jean Baptiste Poquelin. Le bourgeois gentilhomme. Boston, 1873.
Mol 171.25 Molière, Jean Baptiste Poquelin. Le bourgeois gentilhomme...Lacour. Paris, 1874.
Mol 171.28 Molière, Jean Baptiste Poquelin. Le bourgeois gentilhomme. London, 1881.
Mol 171.30 Molière, Jean Baptiste Poquelin. Le bourgeois gentilhomme...Figuière. Paris, 1883.
Mol 171.31 Molière, Jean Baptiste Poquelin. Le bourgeois gentilhomme...Pellisson. Paris, 1883.
Mol 171.32 Molière, Jean Baptiste Poquelin. Le bourgeois gentilhomme...Clapin. Cambridge, 1884.
Mol 171.33 Molière, Jean Baptiste Poquelin. Le bourgeois gentilhomme...Moriarty. London, 1884.
Mol 171.33.2 Molière, Jean Baptiste Poquelin. Le bourgeois gentilhomme; comedie. Boston, 1891.
Mol 171.33.3 Molière, Jean Baptiste Poquelin. Le bourgeois gentilhomme...Moriarty. London, 1892.
Mol 171.34 Molière, Jean Baptiste Poquelin. Le bourgeois gentilhomme...Tarver. London, 1886?
Mol 171.35 Molière, Jean Baptiste Poquelin. Le bourgeois gentilhomme...Livet. Paris, 1886.
Mol 171.35.2 Molière, Jean Baptiste Poquelin. Le bourgeois gentilhomme...Livet. Paris, 1886.
Mol 171.36 Molière, Jean Baptiste Poquelin. Le bourgeois gentilhomme...Cotte. N.Y., 1887.
Mol 171.37 Molière, Jean Baptiste Poquelin. Le bourgeois gentilhomme...Gasté. Paris, 1887.
Mol 171.39 Molière, Jean Baptiste Poquelin. Le bourgeois gentilhomme...Schele de Vere. N.Y., 1889.
Mol 171.40 Molière, Jean Baptiste Poquelin. Le bourgeois gentilhomme...Humbert. Leipzig, 1890.
Mol 171.40.2 Molière, Jean Baptiste Poquelin. Le bourgeois gentilhomme...Humbert. Anmerkungen. Leipzig, 1890.
Mol 171.41 Molière, Jean Baptiste Poquelin. Le bourgeois gentilhomme...Gasté. Paris, 1891.
Mol 171.43 Molière, Jean Baptiste Poquelin. Le bourgeois gentilhomme...Gasc. London, 1892.
Mol 171.46 Molière, Jean Baptiste Poquelin. Le bourgeois gentilhomme...Monval. Paris, 1894.
Mol 171.47 Molière, Jean Baptiste Poquelin. Le bourgeois gentilhomme...Fischer. Bielefeld, 1895.
Mol 171.48 Molière, Jean Baptiste Poquelin. Le bourgeois gentilhomme...Delbos. N.Y., 185-?
Mol 171.50 Molière, Jean Baptiste Poquelin. Le bourgeois gentilhomme...Jacquinet. Paris, 1899.
Mol 171.50.2 Molière, Jean Baptiste Poquelin. Le bourgeois gentilhomme...Jacquinet. Paris, 1899.
Mol 171.51 Molière, Jean Baptiste Poquelin. Le bourgeois gentilhomme...Moland. Paris, 1882.
Mol 171.55 Molière, Jean Baptiste Poquelin. Le bourgeois gentilhomme; comédie-ballet. Strasbourg, 19- .
Mol 171.57 Molière, Jean Baptiste Poquelin. Le bourgeois gentilhomme; comédie-ballet. Paris, 1917?
Mol 171.59 Molière, Jean Baptiste Poquelin. Le bourgeois gentilhomme. London, 1906.
Mol 171.62 Molière, Jean Baptiste Poquelin. Le bourgeois gentilhomme. N.Y., 1910.
Mol 171.69 Molière, Jean Baptiste Poquelin. Le bourgeois gentilhomme. Boston, 1914.
Mol 171.69.25 Molière, Jean Baptiste Poquelin. Le bourgeois gentilhomme. Paris, 1937.
Mol 171.70 Molière, Jean Baptiste Poquelin. Le bourgeois gentilhomme. Boston, 1947.
Mol 171.72 Molière, Jean Baptiste Poquelin. Le bourgeois gentilhomme. London, 1966.

Mol 172 Individual plays - Le Bourgeois Gentilhomme - Translations

Mol 172.3 Molière, Jean Baptiste Poquelin. The gentleman cit. London, 1828.
Mol 172.5 Molière, Jean Baptiste Poquelin. Le bourgeois gentilhomme. N.Y., 1912.
Mol 172.5.25 Molière, Jean Baptiste Poquelin. The would-be nobleman (Le bourgeois gentilhomme). London, 1929.
Mol 172.5.35 Molière, Jean Baptiste Poquelin. The would-be gentleman. Chicago, 1946.
Mol 172.5.40 Molière, Jean Baptiste Poquelin. The merchant gentleman (le bourgeois gentilhomme). N.Y., 1915.
Mol 172.7 Molière, Jean Baptiste Poquelin. Il cittadino gentiluomo. n.p., 1756?
Mol 172.9 Molière, Jean Baptiste Poquelin. The burgher in purple. St. Albans, 1952.

Classified Listing

Mol 173 Individual plays - Le Bourgeois Gentilhomme - Criticism
Htn Mol 173.3* Cohen. Molière, l'académicien Cordemoy. Rouen, 1870.
Mol 173.4 Oliver, Thomas E. Notes on the Bourgeois gentilhomme. n.p., 1913.
Mol 173.5 Ayda, Adile. Un diplomate turc auprès du Roi Soleil. Istanbul, 1956.
Mol 173.6 Ganz, Hans U. Zur Quellenfrage des Bourgeois gentilhomme. Firenze, 1964.

Mol 175 Individual plays - La Comtesse d'Escarbagnas - French editions
Mol 175.5 Molière, Jean Baptiste Poquelin. La comtesse d'Escarbagnas...Monval. Paris, 1895.
Htn Mol 175.100* Molière, Jean Baptiste Poquelin. Ballet des ballets. Paris, 1671.

Mol 178 Individual plays - La Critique de l'École des Femmes - French editions
Htn Mol 178.3* Molière, Jean Baptiste Poquelin. La critique de l'École des femmes. Amsterdam, 1663.
Htn Mol 178.6* Molière, Jean Baptiste Poquelin. La critique de l'École des femmes. Amsterdam, 1680.
Mol 178.10 Molière, Jean Baptiste Poquelin. La critique de l'École des femmes...Lacour. Paris, 1873.
Mol 178.15 Molière, Jean Baptiste Poquelin. La critique de l'École des femmes...Vitu. Paris, 1890.

Mol 181 Individual plays - Dépit Amoureux - French editions
Mol 181.10 Molière, Jean Baptiste Poquelin. Dépit amoureux...Lacour. Paris, 1873.
Mol 181.20A Molière, Jean Baptiste Poquelin. Dépit amoureux...Vitu. Paris, 1888.
Mol 181.20B Molière, Jean Baptiste Poquelin. Dépit amoureux...Vitu. Paris, 1888.
Mol 181.30 Molière, Jean Baptiste Poquelin. Dépit amoureux. London, 1908.
Mol 181.40 Molière, Jean Baptiste Poquelin. Dépit amoureux. Cambridge, 1929.

Mol 182 Individual plays - Dépit Amoureux - Translations
Mol 182.1.9 Molière, Jean Baptiste Poquelin. Dépit amoureux...Cailhava. Paris, 1801.
Mol 182.1.10 Molière, Jean Baptiste Poquelin. Dépit amoureux...Valville. Paris, 1822.
Mol 182.1.11 Molière, Jean Baptiste Poquelin. Dépit amoureux en deux actes. n.p., n.d.
Mol 182.5.5 Molière, Jean Baptiste Poquelin. Liebeszwist...Maltzan. Leipzig, n.d.
Mol 182.7.5 Molière, Jean Baptiste Poquelin. I dispetti amorosi...Castelvecchio. Milano, 1877.
Mol 182.9.5 Molière, Jean Baptiste Poquelin. Ta erotika poiēmata. Athēnai, 1912.

Mol 185 Individual plays - Dom Garcia de Navarre, ou Prince Jaloux - French editions
Mol 185.10 Molière, Jean Baptiste Poquelin. Dom Garcie de Navarre...Vitu. Paris, 1889.
Mol 185.15 Molière, Jean Baptiste Poquelin. Dom Garcie de Navarre...Vitu. London, 1909.

Mol 191 Individual plays - Dom Juan, ou Le Festin de Pierre - French editions
Mol 191.10 Molière, Jean Baptiste Poquelin. Dom Juan...Monval. Paris, 1891.
Mol 191.30 Molière, Jean Baptiste Poquelin. Dom Juan. Strasbourg, 1922.
Mol 191.35 Molière, Jean Baptiste Poquelin. Dom Juan. Cambridge, Eng., 1934.
Mol 191.40 Molière, Jean Baptiste Poquelin. Dom Juan. Oxford, 1958.
Mol 191.45 Molière, Jean Baptiste Poquelin. Dom Juan. Paris, 1960.

Mol 192 Individual plays - Dom Juan, ou Le Festin de Pierre - Translations
Htn Mol 192.1* Molière, Jean Baptiste Poquelin. Le Festin de Pierre mise en vers. Paris, 1683.
Mol 192.2 Molière, Jean Baptiste Poquelin. Don Juan. St. Albans, 1954.
Mol 192.4 Molière, Jean Baptiste Poquelin. Don Juan. N.Y., 1964.

Mol 193 Individual plays - Dom Juan, ou Le Festin de Pierre - Criticism
Mol 193.6 Marmier, X. Les Don Juan. Paris, 1834. 2 pam.
Mol 193.9 Burgtorf, C. Etude...sur le Festin de Pierre. Gottingue, 1874.
Mol 193.10 Reissig, A. J.B. Molière's Leben...sein Dom Juan. Leipzig, 1876.
Mol 193.13 Récy, René de. Don Juan, le antenaire et la légende. Paris, 1887. 5 pam.
Mol 193.14 Engel, Karl. Die Don Juan - Sage auf der Bühne. Oldenburg, 1887.
Mol 193.16 Schädel, O. Ein Beitrag zur Don Juan-Litteratur. Bensheim? 1891?
Mol 193.25 Siccardi, V. Les Don Juan célèbres. Asti, 1907.
Mol 193.30 Schröder, Theodor. Die Quellen des "Don Juan" von Molière. Inaug. Diss. Halle, 1911.
Mol 193.35 Maranini, L. Morte e commedia di Don Juan. Bologna, 1937.
Mol 193.40 Arnavon, Jacques. Le Don Juan de Molière. Copenhague, 1947.
Mol 193.40.2 Arnavon, Jacques. Le Don Juan de Molière. Thèse. Copenhague, 1947.
Mol 193.45 Scherer, Jacques. Sur le Dom Juan de Molière. Paris, 1967.

Mol 194 Individual plays - Dom Juan, ou Le Festin de Pierre - Related works
Mol 194.2 Gendarme de Bévotte, Georges. Le Festin de Pierre avant Molière. Paris, 1907.
Mol 194.2.2 Gendarme de Bévotte, Georges. Le Festin de Pierre avant Molière. Thèse. Paris, 1907.
Htn Mol 194.7* Rosimond, Claude La Rose de. Le nouveau Festin de Pierre. Paris, 1660.
Htn Mol 194.10* Villiers, C.D. de. Le Festin de Pierre. Paris, 1660.
Htn Mol 194.15* Cicognini, G.A. Il convitato di Pietra. Bologna, n.d.
Mol 194.18 L'impressario in angustie. Milano, 1789.
Mol 194.21 Mozard. Il Don Giovanni. Don Juan. London, 1821.
Mol 194.22 Mozard. Don Juan, opera en cinq actes. Paris, n.d.
Mol 194.23 Mozard. Don Giovanni; Don Juan. Parigi, n.d.

Mol 195 Individual plays - L'École des Femmes - French editions
Htn Mol 195.8* Molière, Jean Baptiste Poquelin. L'escole des femmes. Amsterdam, 1684.
Mol 195.12 Molière, Jean Baptiste Poquelin. L'école des femmes. Paris, 18- ?

Mol 195 Individual plays - L'École des Femmes - French editions - cont.
Htn Mol 195.18* Molière, Jean Baptiste Poquelin. L'école des femmes...Anger. Paris, 1819.
Mol 195.20 Molière, Jean Baptiste Poquelin. L'école des femmes...Gombert. London, 1848.
Mol 195.25 Molière, Jean Baptiste Poquelin. L'école des femmes...Lacour. Paris, 1873.
Mol 195.26 Molière, Jean Baptiste Poquelin. L'école des femmes...Gasc. London, 1876.
Mol 195.30 Molière, Jean Baptiste Poquelin. L'école des femmes...Scheffler. Bielefeld, 1886.
Mol 195.32 Molière, Jean Baptiste Poquelin. L'école des femmes...Saintsbury. Cambridge, 1888.
Mol 195.34 Molière, Jean Baptiste Poquelin. L'école des femmes...Vitu. Paris, 1890.
Mol 195.45 Molière, Jean Baptiste Poquelin. L'école des femmes. Strasbourg, 1914.
Mol 195.50 Molière, Jean Baptiste Poquelin. L'école des femmes; comédie. Paris, 1935.
Mol 195.55 Molière, Jean Baptiste Poquelin. L'escole des femmes. n.p., n.d.
Mol 195.60 Molière, Jean Baptiste Poquelin. L'école des femmes. Paris, 1964.

Mol 196 Individual plays - L'École des Femmes - Translations
Mol 196.5A Molière, Jean Baptiste Poquelin. The school for wives. Dublin, 1948.
Mol 196.5B Molière, Jean Baptiste Poquelin. The school for wives. Dublin, 1948.
Mol 196.5.5 Molière, Jean Baptiste Poquelin. Die Schule der Frauen...Schröder. Leipzig, n.d.
Mol 196.5.10 Molière, Jean Baptiste Poquelin. The school for wives. London, 1960.
Mol 196.5.15 Molière, Jean Baptiste Poquelin. The school for wives. 1st ed. N.Y., 1971.
Mol 196.7.5 Molière, Jean Baptiste Poquelin. La scuola delle mogli...Castelvecchio. Milano, 1876.
Mol 196.30.3 Molière, Jean Baptiste Poquelin. Het school voor de nouwen...Arendsz. Amsterdam, 1753.

Mol 197 Individual plays - L'École des Femmes - Criticism
Mol 197.5 Féval, P. Le théâtre-femme. Paris, 1873.
Mol 197.7 Willenberg, G. Analyse et examen de l'École des femmes. Gotha, 1880.
Mol 197.8 Coquelin, C. L'arnolphe de Molière. Paris, 1882.
Mol 197.9 Bernardin, N.M. L'école des femmes. Paris, 1904.

Mol 201 Individual plays - L'École des Maris - French editions
Htn Mol 201.10* Molière, Jean Baptiste Poquelin. L'escole des maris. Amsterdam, 1684.
Mol 201.20 Molière, Jean Baptiste Poquelin. L'école des maris...Gombert. London, 1835.
Mol 201.25 Molière, Jean Batiste Poquelin. L'escole des maris...Lacour. Paris, 1873.
Mol 201.27 Molière, Jean Baptiste Poquelin. L'escole des maris...Gasc. London, 1876.
Mol 201.30 Molière, Jean Baptiste Poquelin. L'escole des maris...Schefflr. Bielefeld, 1887.
Mol 201.32A Molière, Jean Baptiste Poquelin. L'escole des maris...Vitu. Paris, 1889.
Mol 201.32B Molière, Jean Baptiste Poquelin. L'escole des maris...Vitu. Paris, 1889.

Mol 202 Individual plays - L'École des Maris - Translations
Mol 202.5.5 Molière, Jean Baptiste Poquelin. Die Schule der Ehemänner...Schröder. Leipzig, n.d.
Mol 202.20 Molière, Jean Baptiste Poquelin. Molière i "L'escola des maritas. Barcelona, 1933.
Mol 202.25.3 Molière, Jean Baptiste Poquelin. Steiloorige Egbert of de twee ongelijke broeders. Amsterdam, 1690.
Mol 202.30.3 Molière, Jean Baptiste Poquelin. Het school van de mannen. 's-Gravenhage, 1716?
Mol 202.30.5 Molière, Jean Baptiste Poquelin. De listige vryster, of De verschalkte voogd. Amsterdam, 1730.
Mol 202.77 Molière, Jean Baptiste Poquelin. La escuela de los maridos...Celenio. Madrid, 1812.

Mol 203 Individual plays - L'École des Maris - Criticism
Mol 203.5 Baguenault de Puchesse, Gustave. Les Adelphes de Térence et l'École des maris. Orleans, 1872.

Mol 205 Individual plays - L'Étourdi, ou Les Contretemps - French editions
Mol 205.15 Molière, Jean Baptiste Poquelin. L'étourdi...Fiebig und Courvoisier. Leipzig, 1868.
Mol 205.17 Molière, Jean Baptiste Poquelin. L'étourdi...Lacour. Paris, 1871.
Mol 205.20 Molière, Jean Baptiste Poquelin. L'étourdi...Vitu. Paris, 1888.
Mol 205.25 Molière, Jean Baptiste Poquelin. L'estourdi, ou Les contretemps. Lille, 1951.
Mol 205.40 Molière, Jean Baptiste Poquelin. L'étourdi. London, 1907.

Mol 207 Individual plays - L'Étourdi, ou Les Contretemps - Criticism
Mol 207.5 Weidler, W. Das Verhältnis von Mrs. Antlivrés. Halle, 1900.

Mol 208 Individual plays - Les Fâcheux - French editions
Mol 208.20 Molière, Jean Baptiste Poquelin. Les facheux...Lacour. Paris, 1874.
Mol 208.25 Molière, Jean Baptiste Poquelin. Les facheux...Vitu. Paris, 1890.

Mol 209 Individual plays - Les Fâcheux - Translations
Mol 209.5.5 Molière, Jean Baptiste Poquelin. Die Plagegeister...Schröder. Leipzig, n.d.
Mol 209.5.6 Molière, Jean Baptiste Poquelin. Die Plagegeister. Oldenburg, 1855.

Mol 210 Individual plays - Les Fâcheux - Criticism
Mol 210.10 Pech, R. Les fâcheux de Molière comparés à son Misanthrope. Königshütte, 1895.

Mol 211 Individual plays - Les Femmes Savantes - French editions
Mol 211.15 Molière, Jean Baptiste Poquelin. Les femmes savantes. n.p., n.d.
Mol 211.17 Molière, Jean Baptiste Poquelin. Les femmes savantes. Toulouse, 1803.

Mol 211 Individual plays - Les Femmes Savantes - French editions - cont.
Mol 211.25 Molière, Jean Baptiste Poquelin. Les femmes savantes...Geruzez. Paris, 1864.
Mol 211.26 Molière, Jean Baptiste Poquelin. Les femmes savantes...Estienne. Paris, 1856?
Mol 211.30 Molière, Jean Baptiste Poquelin. Les femmes savantes...Lion. Leipzig, 1871.
Mol 211.31 Molière, Jean Baptiste Poquelin. Les femmes savantes...Peschier. Dresde, 1872.
Mol 211.32 Molière, Jean Baptiste Poquelin. Les femmes savantes...Roche. London, 1872.
Mol 211.33 Molière, Jean Baptiste Poquelin. Les femmes savantes...Lacour. Paris, 1876.
Mol 211.35 Molière, Jean Baptiste Poquelin. Les femmes savantes...Person. Paris, 1881?
Mol 211.36 Molière, Jean Baptiste Poquelin. Les femmes savantes...Fasnacht. London, 1881.
Mol 211.36.5 Molière, Jean Baptiste Poquelin. Les femmes savantes. London, 1895.
Mol 211.37 Molière, Jean Baptiste Poquelin. Les femmes savantes...Geruzez. Paris, 1881.
Mol 211.38 Molière, Jean Baptiste Poquelin. Les femmes savantes...Vapereau. Paris, 1883.
Mol 211.40 Molière, Jean Baptiste Poquelin. Les femmes savantes...Livet. Paris, 1884.
Mol 211.40.2 Molière, Jean Baptiste Poquelin. Les femmes savantes...Livet. Paris, 1884.
Mol 211.42 Molière, Jean Baptiste Poquelin. Les femmes savantes...Masson. Oxford, 1886.
Mol 211.43 Molière, Jean Baptiste Poquelin. Les femmes savantes...Henry. Paris, 1887.
Mol 211.46 Molière, Jean Baptiste Poquelin. Les femmes savantes...Gasc. London, 1892.
Mol 211.47 Molière, Jean Baptiste Poquelin. Les femmes savantes...Roche. London, 1892.
Mol 211.48 Molière, Jean Baptiste Poquelin. Les femmes savantes...Marandet. Paris, 1892?
Mol 211.50 Molière, Jean Baptiste Poquelin. Les femmes savantes...Figuière. 2e éd. Paris, 1894.
Mol 211.51 Molière, Jean Baptiste Poquelin. Les femmes savantes...Henry. Paris, 1894.
Mol 211.52 Molière, Jean Baptiste Poquelin. Les femmes savantes...Pellisson. 6e éd. Paris, 1894.
Mol 211.53 Molière, Jean Baptiste Poquelin. Les femmes savantes...Scheffler. Bielefeld, 1894.
Mol 211.55 Molière, Jean Baptiste Poquelin. Les femmes savantes...Monval. Paris, 1895.
Mol 211.57 Molière, Jean Baptiste Poquelin. Les femmes savantes...Fortier. Boston, 1896.
Mol 211.59 Molière, Jean Baptiste Poquelin. Les femmes savantes. 8e éd. Paris, 1898.
Mol 211.60 Molière, Jean Baptiste Poquelin. Les femmes savantes...Pille. Paris, 1899.
Mol 211.61 Molière, Jean Baptiste Poquelin. Les femmes savantes...Lanson. Paris, 1900.
Mol 211.61.2 Molière, Jean Baptiste Poquelin. Les femmes savantes...Lanson. Paris, 1900.
Mol 211.72 Molière, Jean Baptiste Poquelin. Les femmes savantes. Strasbourg, 1906.
Mol 211.73 Molière, Jean Baptiste Poquelin. Les femmes savantes. London, 1907.
Mol 211.74 Molière, Jean Baptiste Poquelin. Les femmes savantes. 2e éd. Paris, 1909.
Mol 211.75 Molière, Jean Baptiste Poquelin. Les femmes savantes. Paris, 1910.
Mol 211.77 Molière, Jean Baptiste Poquelin. Les femmes savantes...M.P. Brush. N.Y., 1911.
Mol 211.80A Molière, Jean Baptiste Poquelin. Les femmes savantes...C.H.C. Wright. N.Y., 1920.
Mol 211.80B Molière, Jean Baptiste Poquelin. Les femmes savantes...C.H.C. Wright. N.Y., 1920.
Mol 211.80.9 Molière, Jean Baptiste Poquelin. Les femmes savantes...C.H.C. Wright. N.Y., 1929.
Mol 211.80.12 Molière, Jean Baptiste Poquelin. Les femmes savantes. Paris, 1959.

Mol 212 Individual plays - Les Femmes Savantes - Translations
Mol 212.3 Molière, Jean Baptiste Poquelin. Les femmes savantes. N.Y., 1908.
Mol 212.5.5 Molière, Jean Baptiste Poquelin. Die gelehrten Weiber...Nicolay. Leipzig, 1817.
Mol 212.5.7 Molière, Jean Baptiste Poquelin. Die gelehrten Frauen...Maltzan. Leipzig, n.d.
Mol 212.15.5 Molière, Jean Baptiste Poquelin. Femmes savantes. Leipzig, 1898. 2 pam.
Mol 212.15.75 Molière, Jean Baptiste Poquelin. Le saccenti...Alceste Bisi. Firenze, 1926.
Mol 212.50 Molière, Jean Baptiste Poquelin. As Sabichonas...Castilho. Lisboa, 1872.

Mol 213 Individual plays - Les Femmes Savantes - Criticism
Mol 213.3 Lion, C.T. Einleitung zu Molière's Femmes savantes. Langensalza, 1870.
Mol 213.5 Follioley, L. Les femmes savantes. Tours, 1885.
Mol 213.13 Tendering, T. Molière's Femmes savantes. Hamburg, 1898.
Mol 213.14 Campbell, R.W. Studies in modern languages. Oxford, 1916.
Mol 213.16 Arnavon, Jacques. La mise en scène des femmes savantes. Paris, 1912.
Mol 213.20 Reynier, G. Les femmes savantes de Molière. Paris, 1948.

Mol 215 Individual plays - Les Fourberies de Scapin - French editions
Mol 215.7 Molière, Jean Baptiste Poquelin. Les Fourberies de Scapin. Comédie. Paris, 1671.
Mol 215.16 Molière, Jean Baptiste Poquelin. Les Fourberies de Scapin. Comédie. Paris, 18- ?
Mol 215.17 Molière, Jean Baptiste Poquelin. Les Fourberies de Scapin...Gombert. London, 18- .
Mol 215.20 Molière, Jean Baptiste Poquelin. Les Fourberies de Scapin...Peschier. Dresde, 1872.
Mol 215.22 Molière, Jean Baptiste Poquelin. Les Fourberies de Scapin...Candole. London, 1874.
Mol 215.31 Molière, Jean Baptiste Poquelin. Les Fourberies de Scapin...Scheffler. Bielefeld, 1885.
Mol 215.32 Molière, Jean Baptiste Poquelin. Les Fourberies de Scapin...Gasc. London, 1886.
Mol 215.36 Molière, Jean Baptiste Poquelin. Les Fourberies...de Scapin...Gasc. London, 1894.

Mol 215 Individual plays - Les Fourberies de Scapin - French editions - cont.
Mol 215.37 Molière, Jean Baptiste Poquelin. Les Fourberies de Scapin...Monval. Paris, 1895.
Mol 215.45 Molière, Jean Baptiste Poquelin. Les Fourberies...de Scapin. London, 1901.

Mol 216 Individual plays - Les Fourberies de Scapin - Translations
Mol 216.30.5 Molière, Jean Baptiste Poquelin. De schelmenstreken van Scapin. Amsterdam, 1906.
Mol 216.53.3 Molière, Jean Baptiste Poquelin. Pseudoli follaciae...Münter. Cellis, 1778.
Mol 216.64.5 Molière, Jean Baptiste Poquelin. Le trappolerie de Scapino. Palermo, 1925.

Mol 217 Individual plays - Les Fourberies de Scapin - Criticism
Mol 217.5 Humbert, C.H. Le Phormion de Térence et Les Fourberies de Scapin. Elberfeld, 1859.

Mol 218 Individual plays - George Dandin, ou Le Mari Confondu - French editions
Htn Mol 218.4* Molière, Jean Baptiste Poquelin. George Dandin. Amsterdam, 1669.
Mol 218.15 Molière, Jean Baptiste Poquelin. George Dandin...Lacour. Paris, 1876.
Mol 218.20 Molière, Jean Baptiste Poquelin. George Dandin...Monval. Paris, 1893.

Mol 219 Individual plays - George Dandin, ou Le Mari Confondu - Translations
Mol 219.1.5 Molière, Jean Baptiste Poquelin. George Dandin mise en vers...C.L.B. Esnault. Arras, 1853.
Mol 219.5.5 Molière, Jean Baptiste Poquelin. George Dandin...A. Cornelius. Leipzig, n.d.
Mol 219.6 Molière, Jean Baptiste Poquelin. George Dandin...Karl Vollmöller. Leipzig, 1912.
Mol 219.25 Molière, Jean Baptiste Poquelin. George Dandin. Paris, 1924.

Mol 220 Individual plays - George Dandin, ou Le Mari Confondu - Criticism
Mol 220.5 Molière, Jean Baptiste Poquelin. Un ancêtre italien de George Dandin. n.p., 1926?

Mol 221 Individual plays - L'Impromptu de Versailles - French editions
Mol 221.10 Molière, Jean Baptiste Poquelin. L'impromptu de Versailles. Paris, 1880.
Mol 221.12 Molière, Jean Baptiste Poquelin. L'impromptu de Versailles...Vitu. Paris, 1890.

Mol 225 Individual plays - Jalousie du Barbouillé - French editions
Mol 225.1 Molière, Jean Baptiste Poquelin. La jalousie du Barbouille. Paris, 1819.
Mol 225.89 Molière, Jean Baptiste Poquelin. La jalousie du Barbouille. London, 1907.

Mol 228 Individual plays - Le Malade Imaginaire - French editions
Htn Mol 228.10* Molière, Jean Baptiste Poquelin. Le malade imaginaire. n.p., 1683.
Mol 228.18 Molière, Jean Baptiste Poquelin. Le malade imaginaire. Limoges, n.d.
Mol 228.21 Molière, Jean Baptiste Poquelin. Le malade imaginaire...Gombert. London, n.d.
Mol 228.25 Molière, Jean Baptiste Poquelin. Le malade imaginaire...Ragon. 3e éd. London, 1875.
Mol 228.26 Molière, Jean Baptiste Poquelin. Le malade imaginaire...Lacour. Paris, 1877.
Mol 228.28 Molière, Jean Baptiste Poquelin. Le malade imaginaire...Tarver. London, 1879.
Mol 228.30 Molière, Jean Baptiste Poquelin. Le malade imaginaire...Gasc. London, 1888.
Mol 228.34 Molière, Jean Baptiste Poquelin. Le malade imaginaire...Friese. Bielefeld, 1891.
Mol 228.35 Molière, Jean Baptiste Poquelin. Le malade imaginaire...Humbert. 3e éd. Paris, 1892?
Mol 228.36 Molière, Jean Baptiste Poquelin. Le malade imaginaire...Pellisson. Paris, 1893.
Mol 228.39 Molière, Jean Baptiste Poquelin. Le malade imaginaire...Fasnacht. London, 1895.
Mol 228.40 Molière, Jean Baptiste Poquelin. Le malade imaginaire...Friese. Bielefeld, 1895.
Mol 228.41 Molière, Jean Baptiste Poquelin. Le malade imaginaire...Monval. Paris, 1896.
Mol 228.41.2 Molière, Jean Baptiste Poquelin. Le malade imagimaire...Monval. Paris, 1896.
Mol 228.51 Molière, Jean Baptiste Poquelin. Le malade imaginaire...E.W. Olmsted. Boston, 1905.
Mol 228.60 Molière, Jean Baptiste Poquelin. Le malade imaginaire. Ann Arbor, 1910.
Mol 228.64 Molière, Jean Baptiste Poquelin. Le malade imaginaire...Heitz et Mündel. Strasbourg, 1914.
Mol 228.70 Molière, Jean Baptiste Poquelin. Le malade imaginaire. Paris, 1921?
Mol 228.85 Molière, Jean Baptiste Poquelin. Le malade imaginaire. London, 1946.
Mol 228.86 Molière, Jean Baptiste Poquelin. Le malade imaginaire. London, 1965.

Mol 229 Individual plays - Le Malade Imaginaire - Translations
Mol 229.5.5 Molière, Jean Baptiste Poquelin. Der eingebildete Kranke. Dresden, 1879.
Mol 229.8 Molière, Jean Baptiste Poquelin. De ingebeelde zieke. Kortrijk, 1930.
Mol 229.10 Molière, Jean Baptiste Poquelin. Il malato immaginario. Torino, 1929.
Mol 229.19 Molière, Jean Baptiste Poquelin. O Doente de Scisma. Lisboa, 1878.
Mol 229.20 Molière, Jean Baptiste Poquelin. Dos cartas autógrafas é inéditas de Blanco White y El enfermo de aprehension. Sevilla, 1891.

Mol 230 Individual plays - Le Malade Imaginaire - Criticism
Mol 230.5 Molière, Jean Baptiste Poquelin. Receptio publicus unius juvenis medici. Lugduni, 1870.
Mol 230.7 Thierry, E. Documents sur le Malade imaginaire. Paris, 1880.
Mol 230.9 Molière, Jean Baptiste Poquelin. Receptio publicus unius juvenis medici...Hillemacher. 5e éd. Paris, 1885.
Mol 230.12 Debove, G.M. Le malade imaginaire. Paris, 1900.
Mol 230.14 Arnavon, Jacques. Le malade imaginaire de Molière. Paris, 1938.

Classified Listing

Mol 231 Individual plays - Le Mariage Forcé - French editions
Mol 231.18 Molière, Jean Baptiste Poquelin. Le mariage forcé...Celler. Paris, 1867.
Mol 231.20 Molière, Jean Baptiste Poquelin. Le mariage forcé...Lacour. Paris, 1873.
Mol 231.25 Molière, Jean Baptiste Poquelin. Le mariage forcé...Vitu. Paris, 1891.

Mol 232 Individual plays - Le Mariage Forcé - Translations
Mol 232.5 Molière, Jean Baptiste Poquelin. Married in spite of himself. n.p., 1873.
Mol 232.9 Molière, Jean Baptiste Poquelin. De gedwongen Knecht...J.J.G. Wahlen. Nijmegen, 1898.
Mol 232.12 Molière, Jean Baptiste Poquelin. Het gedwongene huuwelyk. Amsterdam, 1747.

Mol 233 Individual plays - Le Mariage Forcé - Criticism
Mol 233.5 Leveaux, A. Le mariage forcé. Compiegne, 1881.

Mol 235 Individual plays - Le Médecin Malgré Lui - French editions
Mol 235.15 Molière, Jean Baptiste Poquelin. Le médecin malgré lui. Avignon, 1820.
Mol 235.18 Molière, Jean Baptiste Poquelin. Le médecin malgré lui...Gombert. London, n.d.
Mol 235.20 Molière, Jean Baptiste Poquelin. Le médecin malgré lui...Lacour. Paris, 1874.
Mol 235.21 Molière, Jean Baptiste Poquelin. Le médecin malgré lui...Lallemand. London, 1874.
Mol 235.23 Molière, Jean Baptiste Poquelin. Le médecin malgré lui...Gasc. London, 1883.
Mol 235.24 Molière, Jean Baptiste Poquelin. Le médecin malgré lui...Fasnacht. London, 1883.
Mol 235.27 Molière, Jean Baptiste Poquelin. Le médecin malgré lui; Mariage forcé; Le sicilien. Paris, 1887.
Mol 235.28 Molière, Jean Baptiste Poquelin. Le médecin malgré lui...Monval. Paris, 1892.
Mol 235.29 Molière, Jean Baptiste Poquelin. Le médecin malgré lui...Gasc. Boston, 1891.
Mol 235.49A Molière, Jean Baptiste Poquelin. Le médecin malgré lui...R.L. Hawkins. Boston, 1911.
Mol 235.49B Molière, Jean Baptiste Poquelin. Le médecin malgré lui...R.L. Hawkins. Boston, 1911.
Mol 235.50 Molière, Jean Baptiste Poquelin. Le médecin malgré lui. Paris, 192-.
Mol 235.55 Molière, Jean Baptiste Poquelin. Le médecin malgré lui. Boston, 1873?

Mol 236 Individual plays - Le Médecin Malgré Lui - Translations
Mol 236.30 Molière, Jean Baptiste Poquelin. Klaos Pompernikkel. Mastreeg, 1856.
Mol 236.35 Molière, Jean Baptiste Poquelin. El médico a Palos. Habana, 1881.
Mol 236.38.5 Molière, Jean Baptiste Poquelin. O pros bian iatpos. Parisiois, 1875.
Mol 236.50 Molière, Jean Baptiste Poquelin. O medico á força. Lisboa, 1869.
Mol 236.70 Molière, Jean Baptiste Poquelin. Lou medecin maugratéu. Avignon, 1892.
Mol 236.76.5 Molière, Jean Baptiste Poquelin. Nasilu stal sa lekárom...Smetana. Senici, n.d.

Mol 237 Individual plays - Le Médecin Malgré Lui - Criticism
Mol 237.10 Kugel, A. Untersuchungen zu Molière's Médecin malgré lui. Berlin, 1897.

Mol 238 Individual plays - Le Médecin Volant - French editions
Mol 238.5 Molière, Jean Baptiste Poquelin. Le médecin volant...Pagés. Paris, 1866.

Mol 239 Individual plays - Le Médecin Volant - Translations
Mol 239.1.5 Molière, Jean Baptiste Poquelin. Le médecin volant...colvé des jardins. Paris, 1899.

Mol 240 Individual plays - Le Médecin Volant - Criticism
Mol 240.5 Baluffe, A. Le médecin volant de M. à Pézenas. Paris, 1881.

Mol 241 Individual plays - Mélicerte - French editions
Mol 241.5 Molière, Jean Baptiste Poquelin. Mélicerte...Monval. Paris, 1892.

Mol 242 Individual plays - Mélicerte - Translations
Mol 242.1.5 Guérin, Nicolas Armand Martial. Myrtil et Mélicerte. Jacob. Paris, 1882.

Mol 245 Individual plays - Le Misanthrope - French editions
Htn Mol 245.1* Guérin, Nicolas Armand Martial. Le misantrope. Paris, 1667.
Htn Mol 245.5* Guérin, Nicolas Armand Martial. Le misantrope. Paris, 1675.
Mol 245.20 Molière, Jean Baptiste Poquelin. Le misanthrope; comédie. Paris, 18- ?
Mol 245.26 Molière, Jean Baptiste Poquelin. Le misanthrope...Kiszling. Heilbronn, 1846.
Mol 245.29 Molière, Jean Baptiste Poquelin. Le misanthrope. Le mariage forcé. Edinbourg, 185-?
Mol 245.30 Molière, Jean Baptiste Poquelin. Le misanthrope. Ploetz. Berlin, 1851.
Mol 245.33 Molière, Jean Baptiste Poquelin. Le misanthrope. Paris, 1855.
Mol 245.36 Molière, Jean Baptiste Poquelin. Le misanthrope. Schwalb. Essen, 1860.
Mol 245.38 Molière, Jean Baptiste Poquelin. Le misanthrope. Fiebig et Leportier. Leipzig, 1863.
Mol 245.40 Molière, Jean Baptiste Poquelin. Le misanthrope. Dubois. Paris, n.d.
Mol 245.43.2 Molière, Jean Baptiste Poquelin. Le misanthrope. Joynes. N.Y., 1872.
Mol 245.43.5 Molière, Jean Baptiste Poquelin. Le misanthrope. Les femmes savantes. v.2. Boston, 1873.
Mol 245.43.15 Molière, Jean Baptiste Poquelin. Le misanthrope. 7. éd. Bielefeld, 1873.
Mol 245.45 Molière, Jean Baptiste Poquelin. Le misanthrope. Brette. London, 1874.
Mol 245.46 Molière, Jean Baptiste Poquelin. Le misanthrope. Lacour. Paris, 1874.
Mol 245.50 Molière, Jean Baptiste Poquelin. Le misanthrope. Fiebig et Leportier. 2. éd. Dresde, 1877.

Mol 245 Individual plays - Le Misanthrope - French editions - cont.
Mol 245.51 Molière, Jean Baptiste Poquelin. Le misanthrope. Lïon. Leipzig, 1877.
Mol 245.53 Molière, Jean Baptiste Poquelin. Le misanthrope. Fasnacht. London, 1882.
Mol 245.54 Molière, Jean Bpatiste Poquelin. Le misanthrope. Gasc. London, 1882.
Mol 245.54.3 Molière, Jean Baptiste Poquelin. Le misanthrope. Fasnacht. 2. éd. London, 1893.
Mol 245.55 Molière, Jean Baptiste Poquelin. Le misanthrope. Leys. Paris, n.d.
Mol 245.56 Molière, Jean Baptiste Poquelin. Le misanthrope. Livet. Paris, 1883.
Mol 245.57 Molière, Jean Baptiste Poquelin. Le misanthrope. Cambridge, 1886.
Mol 245.58 Molière, Jean Baptiste Poquelin. Le misanthrope. Boully. Paris, 1886.
Mol 245.59 Molière, Jean Baptiste Poquelin. Le misanthrope. Livet. Paris, 1887.
Mol 245.60 Molière, Jean Baptiste Poquelin. Le misanthrope. Pélissier. Paris, 1887.
Mol 245.61 Molière, Jean Baptiste Poquelin. Le misanthrope. Aulard. Paris, 1888.
Mol 245.62 Molière, Jean Baptiste Poquelin. Le misanthrope. Brette. London, 1889.
Mol 245.63 Molière, Jean Baptiste Poquelin. Le misanthrope. Boston, 1891.
Mol 245.64 Molière, Jean Baptiste Poquelin. Le misanthrope. Boully. Paris, 1891.
Mol 245.65 Molière, Jean Baptiste Poquelin. Le misanthrope. Markheim. Oxford, 1891.
Mol 245.66 Molière, Jean Baptiste Poquelin. Le misanthrope. Lavigne. Paris, 1892.
Mol 245.67 Molière, Jean Baptiste Poquelin. Le misanthrope. Monval. Paris, 1892.
Mol 245.68 Molière, Jean Baptiste Poquelin. Le misanthrope. Pellisson. 4. éd. Paris, 1892.
Mol 245.69 Molière, Jean Baptiste Poquelin. Le misanthrope. Scheffler. Bielefeld, 1892.
Mol 245.73 Molière, Jean Baptiste Poquelin. Le misanthrope. Braunholtz. Cambridge, 1894.
Mol 245.74 Molière, Jean Baptiste Poquelin. Le misanthrope. Boully. Paris, 1895.
NEDL Mol 245.75 Molière, Jean Baptiste Poquelin. Le misanthrope. Figuière. 4. éd. Paris, 1896.
Mol 245.80 Molière, Jean Baptiste Poquelin. Le misanthrope. Eggert. Boston, 1899.
Mol 245.81 Molière, Jean Baptiste Poquelin. Le misanthrope. Eggert. Boston, 1899.
Mol 245.90 Molière, Jean Baptiste Poquelin. Le misanthrope. Strasbourg, 1906.
Mol 245.94 Molière, Jean Baptiste Poquelin. Le misanthrope. F. Spencer. London, 1902.
Mol 245.96 Molière, Jean Baptiste Poquelin. Le misanthrope. London, 1908.
Mol 245.98 Molière, Jean Baptiste Poquelin. Le misanthrope. Lausm. 2. éd. Paris, 1910.
Mol 245.103 Molière, Jean Baptiste Poquelin. Le misanthrope. G. Arnavon. Paris, 1914.
Mol 245.103.3 Molière, Jean Baptiste Poquelin. Le misanthrope. Paris, 1923.
Mol 245.103.5 Molière, Jean Baptiste Poquelin. Le misanthrope de Molière. Paris, 1930.
Mol 245.104 Molière, Jean Baptiste Poquelin. Le misanthrope. R.A. Wilson. London, 1945.
Mol 245.105 Molière, Jean Baptiste Poquelin. Le misanthrope. Boston, 1947.
Mol 245.106 Molière, Jean Baptiste Poquelin. Le misanthrope. Oxford, 1947.
Mol 245.107 Molière, Jean Baptiste Poquelin. Le misanthrope. Paris, 1962.
Mol 245.110 Molière, Jean Baptiste Poquelin. Le misanthrope. Paris, 1963.

Mol 246 Individual plays - Le Misanthrope - Translations
Mol 246.3.3 Molière, Jean Baptiste Poquelin. The misanthrope. B.B. Bart. Boulogne, 1879.
X Cg Mol 246.3.5 Molière, Jean-Baptiste Poquelin. The great French triumvirate. Constable. London, 1898.
Mol 246.3.9 Molière, Jean-Baptiste Poquelin. The misanthrope of Molière. Boston, 1928.
Mol 246.4 Molière, Jean Baptiste Poquelin. Le misanthrope. C.H. Page. N.Y., 1913.
Mol 246.5.4 Molière, Jean Baptiste Poquelin. Le misanthrope. Kayser. n.p., 1867?
Mol 246.5.5 Molière, Jean Baptiste Poquelin. Der Menschenfrind. Kayser. Delitzsch, n.d.
Mol 246.5.6 Molière, Jean Baptiste Poquelin. Der Misanthrop. Werther. Essen, 1887.
Mol 246.5.8 Molière, Jean Baptiste Poquelin. Der Menschenfrind. Wien, 1774.
Mol 246.7.5 Molière, Jean Baptiste Poquelin. Il misantropo. Castelvecchio. Milano, 1876.
Mol 246.7.10 Molière, Jean Baptiste Poquelin. Il misantropo. Parma, 1878.
Mol 246.8.5 Molière, Jean Baptiste Poquelin. O misanthropo. Lisboa, 1874.
Mol 246.30.5 Molière, Jean Baptiste Poquelin. De menschenhater. Thijm. Amsterdam, 1885.
Mol 246.40.5 Molière, Jean-Baptiste Poquelin. De menschenhater. W.J. van Zeggelen. Haarlem, 1872.
Mol 246.41.5 Molière, Jean Baptiste Poquelin. Le misanthrope "en" Amphitryon. Antoine Ooms. Deventer, 1880.
Mol 246.42.5 Molière, Jean Baptiste Poquelin. The misanthrope. 1. ed. N.Y., 1955.

Mol 247 Individual plays - Le Misanthrope - Criticism
NEDL Mol 247.5 Frigoult, C. Deux misanthropes. Cherbourg, n.d.
Mol 247.6 Widal, A. Des divers caractères du misanthrope. Paris, 1851.
Mol 247.10 Lavoix, H. La première représentation du Molière. Paris, 1877.
Mol 247.11 Neuss. Sur le misanthrope de Molière. Montabaur, 1877.
Mol 247.12A Du Boulan, Gérard (pseud.). L'énigme d'Alceste. Paris, 1879.
Mol 247.12B Du Boulan, Gérard (pseud.). L'énigme d'Alceste. Paris, 1879.
Mol 247.13A Coquelin, C. Molière et le misanthrope. Paris, 1881.

Mol 247 Individual plays - Le Misanthrope - Criticism - cont.

Mol 247.13B Coquelin, C. Molière et le misanthrope. Paris, 1881.
Mol 247.14 Veselovskii, A. Mizantrop. Moskva, 1881.
Mol 247.15 Chantavoino, S. Le misanthrope. n.p., 1904.
Mol 247.17 Ferchlandt, H. Molière's Misanthrop und seine englischen Nachahmungen. Inaug. Diss. Halle, 1907.
Mol 247.18 Markheim, H.W.G. Molière and the misanthrope. Oxford, 1891.
Mol 247.19 Jasinski, René. Molière et le misanthrope. Paris, 1951.
Mol 247.21 Doumic, René. Le misanthrope de Molière; étude et analyse. Paris, 1930.
Mol 247.22 Fischmann, W. Molière Misanthrope. n.p., n.d.
Mol 247.23 Molière, Jean Baptiste Poquelin. Le misanthrope. 6. éd. Paris, 1920.

Mol 248 Individual plays - Monsieur de Pourceaugnac - French editions

Htn Mol 248.1* Molière, Jean Baptiste Poquelin. M. de Porceaugnac. Paris, 1670.
Mol 248.15 Molière, Jean Baptiste Poquelin. M. de Pourceaugnac. Paris, 18- ?
Mol 248.23 Molière, Jean Baptiste Poquelin. M. de Pourceaugnac. Gombert. London, 1835.
Mol 248.30 Molière, Jean Baptiste Poquelin. M. de Pourceaugnac. Lacour. Paris, 1876.
Mol 248.35 Molière, Jean Baptiste Poquelin. M. de Pourceaugnac. Monval. Paris, 1894.
Mol 248.45 Molière, Jean-Baptiste Poquelin. M. de Pourceaugnac. Strasbourg, 191-?

Mol 249 Individual plays - Monsieur de Pourceaugnac - Translations

Mol 249.3 Molière, Jean Baptiste Poquelin. M. de Pourceaugnac or Squire Trelooby...Ozell. Paris, 1704.
Mol 249.3.5 Molière, Jean Baptiste Poquelin. M. de Pourceaugnac or Squire Trelooby...Ozell. London, 1704.

Mol 250 Individual plays - Monsieur de Pourceaugnac - Criticism

Mol 250.5 Celler, L. Une représentation de M. de Pourceaugnac. Paris, 1868.
Mol 250.5.5 Hodges, J.C. Authorship of Squire Trelooby. London, 1928.
Mol 250.9 Fage, R. Molière et les limousins. Limoges, 1883.
Mol 250.9.2 Fage, R. Molière et les limousins. Limoges, 1883.

Mol 251 Individual plays - Les Précieuses Ridicules - French editions

Mol 251.10 Molière, Jean Baptiste Poquelin. Les précieuses ridicules. n.p., 17- ?
Mol 251.25 Molière, Jean Baptiste Poquelin. Les précieuses ridicules. Lacour. Paris, 1867.
Mol 251.27 Molière, Jean-Baptiste Poquelin. Les précieuses ridicules. Fiebig et Courvoisier. Leipzig, 1868.
Mol 251.28 Molière, Jean Baptiste Poquelin. Les précieuses ridicules. Perréaz. Schaffhouse, 1868.
Mol 251.32 Molière, Jean Baptiste Poquelin. Les précieuses ridicules. Dupuis. London, 1876.
Mol 251.32.5 Molière, Jean Baptiste Poquelin. Les précieuses ridicules. London, 1896.
Mol 251.35 Molière, Jean Baptiste Poquelin. Les précieuses ridicules. Livet. Paris, 1884.
Mol 251.35.2 Molière, Jean Baptiste Poquelin. Les précieuses ridicules. Livet. Paris, 1884.
Mol 251.36 Molière, Jean Baptiste Poquelin. Les précieuses ridicules. Lang. Oxford, 1884.
Mol 251.37 Molière, Jean Baptiste Poquelin. Les précieuses ridicules. Larroumet. Paris, 1884.
Mol 251.40 Molière, Jean Baptiste Poquelin. Les précieuses ridicules. Larroumet. Paris, 1887.
Mol 251.42 Molière, Jean Baptiste Poquelin. Les précieuses ridicules. Reynier. Paris, 1887.
Mol 251.43 Molière, Jean Baptiste Poquelin. Les précieuses ridicules. Scheffler. Bielefeld, 1887.
Mol 251.44 Molière, Jean Baptiste Poquelin. Les précieuses ridicules. Lermina. Paris, n.d.
Mol 251.45 Molière, Jean Baptiste Poquelin. Les précieuses ridicules. Vitu. Paris, 1889.
Mol 251.48 Molière, Jean Baptiste Poquelin. Les précieuses ridicules. Fasnacht. London, 1891.
Mol 251.49 Molière, Jean Baptiste Poquelin. Les précieuses ridicules. Braunholtz. Cambridge, 1891.
Mol 251.50 Molière, Jean Baptiste Poquelin. Les précieuses ridicules. Gasc. London, 1891.
Mol 251.51 Molière, Jean Baptiste Poquelin. Les précieuses ridicules. Dupuis. London, 1891.
Mol 251.52 Molière, Jean Baptiste Poquelin. Les précieuses ridicules. Figuière. Paris, 1892.
Mol 251.54 Molière, Jean Baptiste Poquelin. Les précieuses ridicules. Jacquinet et Boully. Paris, 1893.
Mol 251.55 Molière, Jean Baptiste Poquelin. Les précieuses ridicules. Vapereau. 4. éd. Paris, 1893.
Mol 251.56 Molière, Jean Baptiste Poquelin. Les précieuses ridicules. A. Dupuis. London, 1894.
Mol 251.58A Molière, Jean Baptiste Poquelin. Les précieuses ridicules. Davis. Boston, 1895.
Mol 251.58B Molière, Jean Baptiste Poquelin. Les précieuses ridicules. Davis. Boston, 1895.
Mol 251.60 Molière, Jean Baptiste Poquelin. Les précieuses ridicules. Pellisson. 2. éd. Paris, 1897.
Mol 251.63 Molière, Jean Baptiste Poquelin. Les précieuses ridicules. Toy. Boston, 1899.
Mol 251.63.2 Molière, Jean Baptiste Poquelin. Les précieuses ridicules. Toy. Boston, 1899.
Mol 251.64 Molière, Jean Baptiste Poquelin. Les précieuses ridicules. Lanson. Paris, 1900.
Mol 251.65 Molière, Jean Baptiste Poquelin. Les précieuses ridicules. (The temple Molière). London, 1901.
Mol 251.70 Molière, Jean Baptiste Poquelin. Les précieuses ridicules. Truffier. Paris, 1905.
Mol 251.80 Molière, Jean Baptiste Poquelin. Les précieuses ridicules. Paris, 1910.
Mol 251.90 Molière, Jean Baptiste Poquelin. Les précieuses ridicules. C.H. Page. Paris, 191-?

Mol 252 Individual plays - Les Précieuses Ridicules - Translations

Mol 252.2 Molière, Jean Baptiste Poquelin. The precious ridiculous. N.Y., 1888.
Mol 252.2.1 Molière, Jean Baptiste Poquelin. The precious ridiculous. N.Y., 1888.
Mol 252.3 Molière, Jean Baptiste Poquelin. The precious ridiculous. N.Y., 1912.

Mol 252 Individual plays - Les Précieuses Ridicules - Translations - cont.

Mol 252.3.15 Molière, Jean Baptiste Poquelin. The affected young ladies. N.Y., 1915.
Mol 252.3.25 Molière, Jean Baptiste Poquelin. Les précieuses ridicules. Toronto, 1924.
Mol 252.3.30 Molière, Jean Baptiste Poquelin. Molière's masterpieces, Les précieuses ridicules and Le médecin malgré lui. N.Y., 1930.
Mol 252.3.35 Molière, Jean Baptiste Poquelin. Les précieuses ridicules, Le Tartuffe - Le misanthrope. N.Y., 1929.
Mol 252.5.5 Molière, Jean Baptiste Poquelin. Die Gezierten. Cornélius. Leipzig, n.d.

Mol 253 Individual plays - Les Précieuses Ridicules - Criticism

Mol 253.5 Spoelgen, J. Analyse et critique des Précieuses ridicules. Rostock, 1873.
Mol 253.5.2 Spoelgen, J. Analyse et critique des Précieuses ridicules. Rostock, 1873.
Mol 253.7 Dalimier, H. A propos des Précieuses ridicules. Saint-Lo, 1890.
Mol 253.8 Treloar, Bronnie. Molière: les Précieuses ridicules. London, 1970.

Mol 255 Individual plays - La Princesse d'Elide - French editions

Htn Mol 255.9* Molière, Jean Baptiste Poquelin. La princesse d'Élide. Amsterdam, 1684.
Htn Mol 255.9.2* Molière, Jean Baptiste Poquelin. La princesse d'Élide. Paris, 1684.
Mol 255.13 Molière, Jean Baptiste Poquelin. Les plaisirs de l'isle enchantée (princesse d'Élide). Lacour. Paris, 1880.
Mol 255.15 Molière, Jean Baptiste Poquelin. La princesse d'Élide. Vitu. Paris, 1891.

Mol 258 Individual plays - Psyché - French editions

Mol 258.15 Molière, Jean Baptiste Poquelin. Psyché. Lacour. Paris, 1877.
Mol 258.20 Molière, Jean Baptiste Poquelin. Psyché. Monval. Paris, 1895.

Mol 260 Individual plays - Psyché - Criticism

Mol 260.10 Erdmann, H. Molière's Psyché. Insterburg, 1892.

Mol 261 Individual plays - Sganarelle, ou Le Cocu Imaginaire - French editions

Htn Mol 261.6* Molière, Jean Baptiste Poquelin. Sganarelle. Paris, 1665.
Mol 261.20 Molière, Jean Baptiste Poquelin. Sganarelle. Lacour. Paris, 1872.
Mol 261.25 Molière, Jean Baptiste Poquelin. Sganarelle. Vitu. Paris, 1889.
Mol 261.40 Molière, Jean Baptiste Poquelin. Sganarelle. London, 1908.

Mol 262 Individual plays - Sganarelle, ou Le Cocu Imaginaire - Translations

Mol 262.1.5 Molière, Jean Baptiste Poquelin. Sganarelle...un acte. Gardy. Paris, 1802.
Mol 262.2.5 Molière, Jean Baptiste Poquelin. Esgauarel l'amour Melge. Barcelona, 1909.
Mol 262.5.5 Molière, Jean Baptiste Poquelin. Eifersucht in allen ecken. n.p., 1807.
Mol 262.43.5 Molière, Jean Baptiste Poquelin. Skoromĕl. Praha, 1875.
Mol 262.50.5 Molière, Jean Baptiste Poquelin. De verwarde Jalouzy. Amsteldam, 1730.

Mol 263 Individual plays - Sganarelle, ou Le Cocu Imaginaire - Criticism

Mol 263.5 Friedmann, A. Ein Versuch den Sganarelle des Molière. Wien, 1879.
Mol 263.10 Delécluze, Étienne Jean. Othello et Sganarelle. Paris, 1846.

Mol 265 Individual plays - Le Sicilien, ou L'Amour Peintre - French editions

Mol 265.15 Molière, Jean Baptiste Poquelin. Le sicilien. Lacour. Paris, 1875.
Mol 265.20 Molière, Jean Baptiste Poquelin. Le sicilien. Monval. Paris, 1892.

Mol 266 Individual plays - Le Sicilien, ou L'Amour Peintre - Translations

Mol 266.1.5 Molière, Jean Baptiste Poquelin. Le sicilien. Laval. n.p., 1780.
Mol 266.5 Bourrelly, Marius. Lou Sicilian de Molière. Ais, 1881.
Mol 266.10 Molière, Jean Baptiste Poquelin. El amor pintor. Matanzas, 1856.

Mol 267 Individual plays - Le Sicilien, ou L'Amour Peintre - Criticism

Mol 267.10 Pougin, A. Molière et l'opéra - comique; le Sicilien. Paris, 1882.

Mol 268 Individual plays - Le Tartuffe, ou L'Imposteur - French editions

Mol 268.20 Molière, Jean Baptiste Poquelin. Le Tartuffe. Étienne. Paris, 1817.
Mol 268.25 Molière, Jean Baptiste Poquelin. Le Tartuffe. Étienne. Paris, 1824.
Mol 268.40 Molière, Jean Baptiste Poquelin. Le Tartuffe. J. Oxenford. London, 185-?
Mol 268.43 Molière, Jean Baptiste Poquelin. Le Tartuffe. Fiebig et Leportier. Leipzig, 1856.
Mol 268.45 Molière, Jean Baptiste Poquelin. Le Tartuffe. 3. Aufl. Stuttgart, 1863.
Mol 268.50 Molière, Jean Baptiste Poquelin. Le Tartuffe. Lïon. Leipzig, 1872.
Mol 268.53 Molière, Jean Baptiste Poquelin. Le Tartuffe. Bué. London, 1874.
Mol 268.58 Molière, Jean Baptiste Poquelin. Le Tartuffe. Lacour. Paris, 1876.
Mol 268.60 Molière, Jean Baptiste Poquelin. Le Tartuffe; Le dépit amoureux. Paris, 1879.
Mol 268.63 Molière, Jean Baptiste Poquelin. Le Tartuffe. Livet. Paris, 1882.
Mol 268.65 Molière, Jean Baptiste Poquelin. Le Tartuffe. Moland. 3. éd. Paris, n.d.
Mol 268.67 Molière, Jean Baptiste Poquelin. Le Tartuffe. Boully. Paris, 1885.
Mol 268.69 Molière, Jean Baptiste Poquelin. Le Tartuffe. Livet. n.p., 1887.
Mol 268.70 Molière, Jean Baptiste Poquelin. Le Tartuffe. Gasc et Holmes. London, 1888.
Mol 268.71 Molière, Jean Baptiste Poquelin. Le Tartuffe. Mayer. Paris, 1888.
Mol 268.74 Molière, Jean Baptiste Poquelin. Le Tartuffe. Lavigne. Paris, 1889.

Classified Listing

Mol 268 Individual plays - Le Tartuffe, ou L'Imposteur - French editions - cont.
Mol 268.78 Molière, Jean Baptiste Poquelin. Le Tartuffe. Friese. Bielefeld, 1892.
Mol 268.79 Molière, Jean Baptiste Poquelin. Le Tartuffe. Boully. Paris, 1893.
Mol 268.81 Molière, Jean Baptiste Poquelin. Le Tartuffe. Monval. Paris, 1894.
Mol 268.82 Molière, Jean Baptiste Poquelin. Le Tartuffe. Pellisson. 4. éd. Paris, 1894.
Mol 268.84 Molière, Jean Baptiste Poquelin. Le Tartuffe. Figuière. 2. éd. Paris, 1895.
Mol 268.89 Molière, Jean Baptiste Poquelin. Le Tartuffe des comédiens. Régnier. Paris, 1896.
Mol 268.89.2 Molière, Jean Baptiste Poquelin. Le Tartuffe des comédiens. Régnier. 2. éd. Paris, 1896.
Mol 268.99 Molière, Jean Baptiste Poquelin. Le Tartuffe. Gasc. Boston, 1900.
NEDL Mol 268.116 Molière, Jean Baptiste Poquelin. Le Tartuffe. Paris, 1905.
Mol 268.117A Molière, Jean Baptiste Poquelin. Le Tartuffe. Dreyfus. Brisac. Paris, 1905.
Mol 268.117B Molière, Jean Baptiste Poquelin. Le Tartuffe. Dreyfus. Brisac. Paris, 1905.
Mol 268.120A Molière, Jean Baptiste Poquelin. Le Tartuffe. Wright. Boston, 1906.
Mol 268.120B Molière, Jean Baptiste Poquelin. Le Tartuffe. Wright. Boston, 1906.
Mol 268.120.2A Molière, Jean Baptiste Poquelin. Le Tartuffe. Wright. Boston, 1905.
Mol 268.120.2B Molière, Jean Baptiste Poquelin. Le Tartuffe. Wright. Boston, 1905.
Mol 268.121 Molière, Jean Baptiste Poquelin. Le Tartuffe. Matzke. N.Y., 1906.
Mol 268.126 Molière, Jean Baptiste Poquelin. Le Tartuffe. J. Arnavon. Paris, 1909.
Mol 268.127 Molière, Jean Baptiste Poquelin. Le Tartuffe. Strasbourg, n.d.
Mol 268.128 Molière, Jean Baptiste Poquelin. Tartuffe, or The imposter. N.Y., 1888.
Mol 268.130 Molière, Jean Baptiste Poquelin. Le Tartuffe. N.Y., 1918.
Mol 268.141 Alméras, Henri d'. Le Tartuffe de Molière. Amiens, 1928.
Mol 268.145 Alméras, Henri d'. Le Tartuffe de Molière. Paris, 1946.
Mol 268.150 Alméras, Henri d'. Le Tartuffe, ou L'imposteur. Paris, 1939.
Mol 268.155 Molière, Jean Baptiste Poquelin. Tartuffe (1669) avec une notre biographique. Paris, 1945.
Mol 268.160 Molière, Jean Baptiste Poquelin. Le Tartuffe. H. Ashton. Oxford, 1946.

Mol 269 Individual plays - Le Tartuffe, ou L'Imposteur - Translations
Htn Mol 269.3.4* Molière, Jean Baptiste Poquelin. Tartuffe. Medbourne. London, 1670.
Mol 269.3.5 Molière, Jean Baptiste Poquelin. Tartuffe. Medbourne. London, 1707.
Mol 269.3.15 Molière, Jean Baptiste Poquelin. Tartuffe. N.Y., 1963.
Mol 269.3.25 Molière, Jean Baptiste Poquelin. Tartuffe. C.H. Page. N.Y., 1912.
Mol 269.4A Molière, Jean Baptiste Poquelin. Tartuffe. C.H. Page. N.Y., 1912.
Mol 269.4B Molière, Jean Baptiste Poquelin. Tartuffe. C.H. Page. N.Y., 1912.
Mol 269.4.10F Molière, Jean Baptiste Poquelin. Tartuffe. C.H. Page. Leipzig, 1930.
Htn Mol 269.5* Molière, Jean Baptiste Poquelin. Tartuffo commedia. Firenze, 1850.
Mol 269.5.5 Molière, Jean Baptiste Poquelin. Der Tartüff. Laun. Oldenburg, 1855.
Mol 269.5.8 Molière, Jean Baptiste Poquelin. Tartuffo. Milano, 1958.
Mol 269.5.10 Molière, Jean Baptiste Poquelin. Tartüffe. Schröder. Leipzig, n.d.
Mol 269.5.12 Molière, Jean Baptiste Poquelin. Tartuffe. G. Grunert. Stuttgart, 1863.
Mol 269.15.5 Molière, Jean Baptiste Poquelin. Tartuffe. N. Destanberg. Gent, 1867.
Mol 269.30.3 Molière, Jean Baptiste Poquelin. De Huigchelaar. Tartuffe. Amsterdam, 1789.
Mol 269.30.5 Molière, Jean Baptiste Poquelin. Tartuffe. Zeggelen. Haarlem, 1875.
Mol 269.30.7 Molière, Jean Baptiste Poquelin. Tartuffe. Thijm. Amsterdam, 1879.
Mol 269.38.5 Molière, Jean Baptiste Poquelin. Ho Tartoûphos. Skylisse. Snyrna, 1851.
Mol 269.43.5 Molière, Jean Baptiste Poquelin. Tartufe. Züngel. Praha, 1866.
Mol 269.63.5 Molière, Jean Baptiste Poquelin. Tartufo. Castilho. Lisboa, 1870.
Mol 269.70.5 Molière, Jean Baptiste Poquelin. Tartuf. A. Mascras. Barcelona, 1908.
Mol 269.70.9 Molière, Jean Baptiste Poquelin. El Tartufo. Caracas, 1832.
Mol 269.70.10 Molière, Jean Baptiste Poquelin. Tartufo: comedia refundida. Barcelona, 1916.
Mol 269.70.12 Molière, Jean Baptiste Poquelin. El hipocrita; comédia. Madrid, 1858.

Mol 270 Individual plays - Le Tartuffe, ou L'Imposteur - Criticism
Mol 270.5 Loère-Veimars, F.A. Tartufe et le malade imaginaire. Paris, 1833.
Mol 270.9 Pignot, J.H. Un évêque...G. de Roquette...le Tartuffe. Paris, 1876. 2v.
Mol 270.11.2 Lacour, L. Études sur Molière...le Tartuffe. Paris, 1877.
Mol 270.13 Veselovskii, A. Tartiuff. Moskva, 1879.
Mol 270.15 Norman, H. Klassische Dichterwerke. Stuttgart, 1880.
Mol 270.17 Mangold, W. Molière's Tartuffe. Oppeln, 1881.
Mol 270.19A Coquelin, C. Tartuffe. Paris, 1884.
Mol 270.19B Coquelin, C. Tartuffe. Paris, 1884.
Mol 270.19.5 Mantegazza, P. Il secolo Tartufo. Milano, 1889.
Mol 270.21 Brunetière, F. Tartuffe. Paris, 1891. 4 pam.
Mol 270.24 Socin, A. Zur Metrik emiger ins Arabische übersetzter Dramen Molière's. Lipsiae, 1897?
Mol 270.24.2 Socin, A. Zur Metrik emiger ins Arabische übersetzter Dramen Molière's. Leipzig, 1897?
Mol 270.28 Matić, Tomo. Molière's Tartuffe. Berlin, 1901. 11 pam.
Mol 270.29 Waechter, A. Les sources du Tartuffe de Molière. Erfurt, 1901.
Mol 270.31 Baumal, Francis. La genèse du Tartufe. Paris, 1914.
Mol 270.32 Charlier, Gustave. Le premier "Tartuffe". Paris, 1923.

Mol 270 Individual plays - Le Tartuffe, ou L'Imposteur - Criticism - cont.
Mol 270.33 Baumal, Francis. Tartuffe et ses avatars. Paris, 1925.
Mol 270.34 Hähnel, Oskar. Die Tendenz von Molières Tartuffe in der fronziösischen Kritik. Inaug. Diss. Mannheim, 1911.
Mol 270.35 Hall, H.G. Molière: Tartuffe. London, 1960.
Mol 270.36 Salomon, H.P. Tartuffe devant l'opinion française. Paris, 1962.
Mol 270.37 Brandwajn, Rachmiel. Twarz i maska. Warszawa, 1965.
Mol 270.38 Schérer, Jacques. Structures de "Tartuffe". Paris, 1966.
Mol 270.38.5 Schérer, Jacques. Tartuffe; histoire et structure. Paris, 1965.

Mol 310 Poems - Individual poems in French
Mol 310.5 Mazières, S.P. La vie de P. Mignard: Avec la poème de Molière sur les peintures du Val-de-Grace. Amsterdam, 1731.

Mol 438 Attributed works - Individual works - Le Docteur Amoureux - Editions in French
Mol 438.1 Les incompatibles. Lacroix. Genève, 1868.

Mol 451 Attributed works - Individual works - Joguenet - Editions in French
Mol 451.1 Molière, Jean Baptiste Poquelin. Joguenet. Jacob. Genève, 1868.

Mol 453 Attributed works - Individual works - Joguenet - Criticism
Mol 453.2 Lacroix, Paul. Un manuscrit du souffleur...Molière. Paris, 1865.
Mol 453.5 Galuski, Charles. Réponse à l'auteur d'un article. Saint Germain, 1868.

Mol 464 Attributed works - Individual works - Mélisse - Editions in French
Mol 464.5A Melisse. Jacob. Paris, 1879.
Mol 464.5B Melisse. Jacob. Paris, 1879.

Mol 491 Attributed works - Individual works - Vers Espanols - Editions in French
Mol 491.1 Molière, Jean Baptiste Poquelin. Vers espagnols. Jacob. Paris, 1864.

Mol 494 Attributed works - Individual works - Other poems - Editions in French
Mol 494.5 Molière, Jean Baptiste Poquelin. Poésies diverses recueillies. Jacob. Paris, 1869.

Mol 496 Attributed works - Individual works - Other poems - Criticism
Mol 496.1 Henusse, Theodor. Une pièce de Molière inconnue. Bruxelles, 1954.

Mol 501 - 526 Works about Molière - Periodicals (A-Z)
Mol 513.1 Monval, G. Le Molieriste; revue mensuelle (1879-1889). Paris, 1879-89. 10v.
Mol 513.1.1 Currier, T.F. Index to Le Molieriste. Cambridge, 1906.
Mol 513.1.2 Monval, G. Le Molieriste; revue mensuelle. Paris, 1879-89. 10v.
Mol 513.1.3 Currier, T.F. Index to Le Molieriste. Cambridge, 1906.

Mol 560 Works about Molière - Reference works - Bibliographies
Mol 560.3 Taschereau, J. Bibliographie de Molière. Paris, 1828.
Mol 560.5 Lacroix, P. Bibliographie Molièresque. Turin, 1872.
Mol 560.5.2 Lacroix, P. Bibliographie Molièresque. Turin, 1872.
Htn Mol 560.5.4* Lacroix, P. Bibliographie Molièresque. 2. éd. Paris, 1875.
Mol 560.5.5 Lacroix, P. Bibliographie Molièresque. 2. éd. Paris, 1875.
Mol 560.7 Lacroix, P. La véritable édition originale des oeuvres de Molière, étude bibliographique. Paris, 1874.
Mol 560.11 Poche. Bibliographie Molièresque. Paris, 1878.
Mol 560.12 Dulait, Suzanne. Inventaire raisonné des autographes de Molière. Genève, 1967.
Mol 560.15 Despois, P. Oeuvres de Molière. Paris, 1893.
Mol 560.16 Currier, T.F. Catalogue of the Molière collection. Cambridge, 1906.
Mol 560.18 Wohlfeil, P. Die deutschen Molière Übersetzungen. Frankfurt, 1904.
Mol 560.20 Thuasne, L. Les privilèges des éditions originales de Molière. Paris, 1924.
Mol 560.22 Paris. Bibliothèque Nationale. Catalogue des ouvrages de Molière. Paris, 1933.
Mol 560.25A Saintonge, Paul F. Fifty years of Molière studies. Baltimore, 1942.
Mol 560.25B Saintonge, Paul F. Fifty years of Molière studies. Baltimore, 1942.
Mol 560.28 Guibert, A.J. Bibliographie des oeuvres de Molière publiées au XVIIe siècle. v.1-2. and supplement. Paris, 1961. 3v.

Mol 570 Works about Molière - Reference works - Dictionaries, encyclopedias, etc.
Mol 570.3 Fritsche, H. Molière Studien. Danzig, 1868.
Mol 570.4 Fritsche, H. Molière Studien. 2. Aufl. Berlin, 1887.
Mol 570.5A Genin, F. Lexique confare de la langue de Molière. Paris, 1846.
Mol 570.5B Genin, F. Lexique confare de la langue de Molière. Paris, 1846.
Mol 570.10 Livet, Charles L. Lexique de la langue de Molière. Paris, 1895-97. 3v.
Mol 570.10.2 Livet, Charles L. Lexique de la langue de Molière. Paris, 1895-97. 3v.

Mol 598 Works about Molière - General critical works - Folios [Discontinued]
Mol 598.20F Schneegans, H. Molière als Satiriker. München, 1899.

Mol 600 Works about Molière - General critical works - Pamphlet volumes
Mol 600.3 Pamphlet vol. Braquehay. Les petits-fils de Diafoirus. Abbeville, 1896. 17 pam.
Mol 600.5 Pamphlet vol. Allais. De l'éducation des femmes. Clermont, 1885. 12 pam.
Mol 600.6 Pamphlet vol. B., G. A propos d'une critique. Paris, 1881. 18 pam.
Mol 600.7 Pamphlet vol. Cordellier-Delanoue. Tartufe. Paris, 1840. 12 pam.
Mol 600.8F Pamphlet vol. Houben, H.H. Molière's Tartüffe. Berlin, 1899. 8 pam.
Mol 600.9F Pamphlet vol. Filon, A. Baluffe: Autour de Molière. Paris, 1889. 23 pam.
Mol 600.11F Pamphlet vol. Bôcher, F. Molière et ses prédécesseurs. Paris, 1869. 21 pam.
Mol 600.14 Collection of clippings relating to Molière. n.p., n.d.
Mol 600.15 Pamphlet box. Molière criticism.

Mol 601 - 626 (A-Z) **Works about Molière - General critical works - Monographs**

Mol 601.1F Achkinasi, M. Molière, ses traducteurs en Russie. Paris, 1884.
Mol 601.2 Aderer, A. Les femmes dans les comédies de Molière. St. Cloud, 1865.
NEDL Mol 601.3 Angot, E. Roles et caractères dans les comédies de Molière. Paris, 1922.
Mol 601.5 Arnavon, J. La représentation de la comédie classique. Paris, 1923.
Mol 601.5.10 Arnavon, J. Molière, notre contemporain. Paris, 1929.
Mol 601.5.15 Arnavon, J. Morale de Molière. Paris, 1945.
Mol 601.13 American Academy of Arts and Letters. Proceedings at the commemoration of the 300th anniversary of the birth of Molière. N.Y., 1926.
Mol 601.18 Apollonio, Mario. Molière. 2. ed. Brescia, 1947.
Mol 601.20 Audiberti, J. Molière. Paris, 1954.
Mol 602.1 Baudouin, F.M. Les femmes dans Molière. Rouen, 1865.
Mol 602.2 Becker, Joseph. Die Entwickelung der Dienerrolle bei Molière. Strassburg, 1890.
Mol 602.3 Bennewitz, A. Molière's Einfluss auf Congreve. Leipzig, 1889.
Mol 602.4 Bennewitz, A. Congreve und Molière. Leipzig, 1890.
Mol 602.5 Berg, Peter. Die Syntax des Verbums bei Molière. Kiel, 1886.
Mol 602.6 Bindel, Karl. Zur Geschichte der dramatischen Werke Molière. Hamm, 1875.
Mol 602.8 Bouillier, F. Molière, élève de Gassendi. Lyon, 1852.
Mol 602.9 Berneburg, E. Charakterkomik bei Molière. Marburg, 1912.
Mol 602.9.5 Berneburg, E. Charakterkomik bei Molière. Diss. Marburg, 1912.
Mol 602.10 Bailly, Jean. Éloge de Molière. n.p., 1769.
Mol 602.11 Beekom, W.L. van. De la formation intellectuelle et morale de la femme, d'après Molière. Thèse. Paris, 1922.
Mol 602.12 Besing, Max. Molières Einfluss auf das englische Lustspiel bis 1700. Diss. Borna, 1913.
Mol 602.13 Bruyelle, Roland. Les personnages de la comédie de Molière. Paris, 1946.
Mol 602.14 Bray, René. Molière. Paris, 1954.
Mol 602.15 Billeter, Regula. Les valeurs spectaculaires dans l'oeuvre de Molière. Thèse. Boulogne, 1962.
Mol 603.1 Cailhava d'Estendoux, Jean François. Études sur Molière. Paris, 1802.
Mol 603.1.5 Cailhava d'Estendoux, Jean François. Essai sur la tradition théatrale. Paris, 1798.
Mol 603.2 Canora, Jean. Molière moraliste. Paris, 1901.
Mol 603.4 Clarke, C.C. Molière characters. Edinburgh, 1865.
Mol 603.5 Comte, Charles. Les stances libres dans Molière. Versailles, 1893.
Mol 603.6 Cordier, H. Molière jugé par Stendhal. Paris, 1898.
Mol 603.7 Cormenin, L. de. Comédie sociale: types de Molière. Paris, 1852.
Mol 603.8 Claretie, Jules. Shakspere and Molière. N.Y., 1900.
Mol 603.9 Chaumartin, H. Gens de Molière. Vienne, 1939.
Mol 603.10 Cairncross, John. Molière bourgeois et libertin. Paris, 1963.
Mol 604.1 Danschacher, H. Molière's Monomanen. Fürth, 1901.
Mol 604.2 Degenhardt, E. Die Metapher bei den Vorlaufern Molière's. Marburg, 1888.
Mol 604.3 Despine, P. La science du coeur humain. Paris, 1884.
Mol 604.5 Dumoustier, L. Molière, auteur et comédien. Paris, 1883.
Mol 604.6 Davignon, St. Molière et la vie. Photoreproduction. Paris, 1904.
Mol 604.7 Donnay, M. Molière. Paris, n.d.
Mol 604.8 Descaves, Pierre. Molière en U.R.S.S. Paris, 1954.
Mol 604.9 Daillant, de La Touche. Eloge de Molière. Paris, 1771.
Mol 604.10 Descotes, Maurice. Les grands rôles du théâtre de Molière. Paris, 1960.
Mol 604.10.5 Descotes, Maurice. Molière et sa fortune littéraire. Saint-Médard-en-Jullcs, 1970.
Mol 605.1 Ehrhard, A. Les comédies de Molière en Allemagne. Paris, 1888.
Mol 605.2 Eloesser, A. Die älteste deutsche Übersetzung Molièrescher Lustspiele. Berlin, 1893.
Mol 605.2.2 Eloesser, A. Die älteste deutsche Übersetzung Molièrescher Lustspiele. Berlin, 1893.
Mol 605.3 Epagny, F. d'. Molière et Scribe. Paris, 1865.
Mol 605.4 Espagne, A. Des influences provencales dans la langue de Molière. Paris, 1876.
Mol 605.5 Essai sur Molière. n.p., n.d.
Mol 605.6 Enderlein, Erich. Zur Bedeutungsentwicklung des bestimmten Artikels im Französischen mit besonderer Molières. Marburg, 1908.
Mol 606.1 Fagan, Christophe Barthélemy. Nouvelles observations au sujet des condemnations contre les comédies. Paris, 1751.
Mol 606.2 Fest, O. Der Miles Gloriosus in der französischen Komödie. Erlangen, 1897.
Mol 606.3 Feugère, G. Discours. Toulouse, 1859.
Mol 606.4 Fischer, F. Molière, ein Beitrag. Duisburg, 1864.
Mol 606.5 Fournier, E. Étude sur la vie et les oeuvres de Molière. Paris, 1885.
Mol 606.5.2 Fournier, E. Études sur la vie et les oeuvres de Molière. Paris, 1885.
Mol 606.6 Faguet, E. Rousseau contre Molière. Paris, n.d.
Mol 606.7.5A Faguet, E. En lisant Molière. 5. éd. Paris, 1914.
Mol 606.7.5B Faguet, E. En lisant Molière. 4. éd. Paris, 1914.
Mol 606.9 Fellows, O.E. French opinion of Molière 1800-1850. Diss. Providence, 1937.
Mol 606.10 Fabre, Emile. Notre Molière. Paris, 1951.
Mol 607.1 Gallert, G. Über den Gebrauch des Infinitions bei Molière. Halle, 1886.
Mol 607.7 Gheorghiu, X. Molière: l'école des maris si Regnard. Tassy, n.d.
Mol 607.8 Gillet, J.E. Molière en Angleterre 1660-1670. Paris, 1913.
Mol 607.10 Guicharnaud, J. Molière; a collection of critical essays. Englewood, 1964.
Mol 607.11 Guicharnaud, J. Molière. Paris, 1963.
Mol 607.12 Gulkind, K.S. Molière und das komische Drama. Halle, 1928.
Mol 607.13 Gossman, L. Men and masks: a study of Molière. Baltimore, 1963.
Mol 607.15 Gutwirth, Marcel Marc. Molière ou L'invention comique. Paris, 1966.
Mol 607.16 Glikman, Isaak D. Mol'er. Leningrad, 1966.
Mol 608.1 Haber. Remarques sur la langue de Molière. Culni, 1859.
Mol 608.2 Hagberg, J.T. Om arten af Molières lustspel. Upsala, 1851.

Mol 601 - 626 (A-Z) - cont. **Works about Molière - General critical works - Monographs**

Mol 608.3 Hamel, F.A. Molière-Syntax. Halle, 1895.
Mol 608.4 Hanriot, Charles. Leçon d'ouverture du cours de littérature française. Troyes, 1874.
Htn Mol 608.5* Henning, G.N. Molières doctrine. n.p., 1898.
Mol 608.6 Heydkamp, W. Remarques sur la langue de Molière. Bonn, 1882.
Mol 608.7 Hillebrand, K. Des conditions de la bonne comédie. Paris, 1863.
Mol 608.8 Humbert, C. Deutschlands Urteil über Molière. Oppeln, 1883.
Mol 608.8.2 Humbert, C. Deutschlands Urteil über Molière. Oppeln, 1883.
Mol 608.9 Humbert, C. Englands Urteil über Molière. Leipzig, 1884.
Mol 608.10 Humbert, C. Lustige Puppen Tragödie. Bielefeld, n.d.
Mol 608.11 Humbert, C. Friederich Jacobs über Molière. Bielefeld, 1870.
Mol 608.12 Humbert, C. Molière, Shakspeare und die deutsche Kritik. Leipzig, 1869.
Mol 608.13 Humbert, C. Molière in England. Bielefeld, 1874.
Mol 608.14 Humbert, C. Molière, Vater der deutschen Schauspielkunst. Berlin, 1885.
Mol 608.15 Humbert, C. Zu Molière's Leben und Werken. Bielefeld, 1899.
Mol 608.16 Hartmann, C. Einfluss Molière auf Dryden's...Dichtungen. Leipzig, 1885.
Mol 608.16.10 Hartmann, H. Die literarische Satire bei Molière. Diss. Tübingen, 1910.
Mol 608.17 Huszár, G. Molière et l'Espagne. Paris, 1907.
Mol 608.18 Heller, Kurt. Michel de Montaigne's Einfluss auf die Aerztestücke Molière's. Diss. Jena, 1908.
Mol 608.19 Hubert, Judd. Molière and the comedy of intellect. Berkeley, 1962.
Mol 609.1 Ilutowicz, S. Le peuple dans le théâtre de Molière. Thèse. Toulouse, 1932.
Mol 610.1 Janet, Paul. La philosophie dans les comédies de Molière. n.p., 1872.
Mol 610.2 Jeannel, C.J. La morale de Molière. Paris, 1867.
Mol 610.4 John, A. Les traits conventionnels de domestiques de Molière. Meiningen, 1905-06.
Mol 610.5 Jouvet, Louis. Molière et la comédie classique. Paris, 1965.
Mol 611.1 Kayser, H. Zur Syntax Molières. Kiel, 1885.
Mol 611.2 Klug, Gustav. Molière in seinen Farcen. Strausberg, 1877.
Mol 611.3 Köhler, I. Molières und Fenelons Stellung. Plauen, 1895.
Mol 611.4 Krause, H. Wycherley und seine französischen Quellen. Halle, 1883.
Mol 611.5 Klatt, W. Molières Bezichungen zum Stirtendrama. Berlin, 1908.
Mol 611.5.5 Klatt, W. Molières Bezichungen zum Stirtendrama. Diss. Göttingen, 1908.
Mol 611.6 Kerby, W.M. Molière and the Restoration comedy in England. London, n.d.
Mol 611.8 Kapp, Max. Die Frauengestalten in Molières Werken. Halle, 1925.
Mol 611.9 Küchler, Walther. Molière. Leipzig, 1929.
Mol 611.10 Krauss, W. Molière und das Problem des Verstehens. Düsseldorf, 1953.
Mol 612.1 Lapommeraye, H. de. Molière et Bossuet. Paris, 1877.
Mol 612.2 Laprade, V. de. La morale de Molière. n.p., 1876.
Mol 612.3 Larocque, J. La plume et le pouvoir au XVIIe siècle. Paris, 1888.
Mol 612.4 Larroumet, G. La comédie de Molière. Paris, 1887.
Mol 612.5 Larroumet, G. La comédie de Molière. Paris, 1887.
Mol 612.6 Legouvé, E. Eugène Scribe. Paris, 1874.
Mol 612.7 Legrelle, A. Holberg considéré comme imitateur de Molière. Paris, 1864.
Mol 612.8 Lemaitre, J. La comédie après Molière. Paris, 1882.
Mol 612.9 Leveaux, A. L'enseignement moral dans les comédies de Molière. Compiègne, 1883.
Mol 612.10 Levinstein, K. Christian Weise und Molière. Berlin, 1899.
Mol 612.11 Lindau, P. Molière in Deutschland. Wien, 1867.
Mol 612.12 Linder, F. Henry Fieldings dramatische Werke. Leipzig, 1895.
Mol 612.13 Lucas, H. Le foyer du théâtre-français. Paris, n.d.
Mol 612.14 Luder, H.A. Carlo Goldini in seinem Verhältnis zu Molière. Oppeln, 1883.
Mol 612.15 Lecocq, G. Molière et la comédie en province. Paris, 1880.
Mol 612.16 Lyonnet, H. Les "premières" de Molière. Paris, 1921.
Mol 612.17 Langer, Carl. Molières Ideen über die Frauenerzichung. Inaug. Diss. Berlin, 1908.
Mol 612.18 Leupold, W. Die aristotelische Lehre in Molières Werken. Berlin, 1935.
Mol 612.19 Loiselot, J.L. De quoi vivait Molière. Paris, 1950.
Mol 613.1 Maffre de Bauge, A. Molière et le régionalisme. Paris, 1897.
Mol 613.2 Mangold, W. Archivalische Notizen zur franzosischen Literatur des 17. Jahrhunderts. Berlin, 1893.
Mol 613.3 Meier, D. Vergleich und Metapher in den Lustspielen Molières. Marburg, 1885.
Mol 613.4 Moland, L. Molière et la comédie italienne. Paris, 1867.
Mol 613.5 Moland, L. Molière et le comédie italienne. Paris, 1867.
Mol 613.6 Molière, commenté d'après les observations de nos meilleurs critiques. Paris, 1913. 2v.
Mol 613.7 Martinenche, E. Molière et le théâtre espagnol. Paris, 1906.
Mol 613.8A Miles, D.H. The influence of Molière on restoration comedy. N.Y., 1910.
Mol 613.8B Miles, D.H. The influence of Molière on restoration comedy. N.Y., 1910.
Mol 613.9 Meyier, F. de. Molière en zijn vijanden. n.p., 1914.
Mol 613.10 Moore, W.G. Molière. Oxford, 1949.
Mol 613.11 Mullins, Marjorie. La famille au XVIIe siècle, d'après le théâtre de Molière. Thèse. Toulouse, 1927.
Mol 613.12A Mandach, André. Molière et la comédie de moeurs en Angleterre. Neuchâtel, 1946.
Mol 613.12B Mandach, André. Molière et la comédie de moeurs en Angleterre. Neuchâtel, 1946.
Mol 613.13 Miller, Elizabeth. A collection of pamphlets on Molière. Paris? n.d.? 9 pam.
Mol 613.14 Miller, Elizabeth. Articles on Molière. n.p., n.d. 2 pam.
Mol 613.15 Mander, Gertrud. Jean-Baptiste Molière. 1. Aufl. Velber, 1967.
Htn Mol 614.1* Nash, F.H. The commedia dell'arte. n.p., 1895.
Mol 614.2 Nisard, Désiré. La comédie après Molière. n.p., 1860.

Classified Listing

Mol 601 - 626 (A-Z) - cont. **Works about Molière - General critical works - Monographs**

Mol 614.3 Neri, Nicoletta. Molière e il teatro inglese della Restaurazione. Torino, 1966.
Mol 615.1 Ott, Philipp. Über das Verhältniss Drydens zu Molière. Landshut, n.d.
Mol 615.2 Oettinger, W. Das Komische bei Molière. Strassburg, 1901.
Mol 616.1 Paringault, E. La langue de droit dans le théâtre de Molière. n.p., 1851.
Mol 616.2 Perlet, A. De l'influence des moeurs sur la comédie. Paris, 1848.
Mol 616.3 Pohlisch, B. Patoisformen in Molières Lustspielen. Halle, 1884.
Mol 616.4 Prevost, G. Le peuple dans Molière. n.p., 1890.
Mol 616.5 Pellisson, M. Les comédies-ballets de Molière. Paris, 1914.
Mol 616.6.16 Présence de Molière. Cahiers de la compagnie Madeleine Renaud, Jean Louis Barrault. Paris, 1961.
Mol 618.1 Rambert, E. Corneille, Racine et Molière. Lausanne, 1861.
Mol 618.2 Rossmann, G. Der Aberglaube bei Molière. Burg, 1898.
Mol 618.3 Riccoboni, L. Observations sur la comédie de Molière. Paris, 1736.
Mol 618.4 Rigal, E. Molière. Paris, 1908. 2v.
Mol 618.5 Rudolph, M. Der Aufbau der Komödien bei Molière. Inaug. Diss. Leipzig, 1928.
Mol 618.6 Rummel, W. Die Berücksichtigung der Schauspieler bei Molières Schaffen. Inaug. Diss. Leipzig, 1928.
Mol 618.7A Romano, D. Essai sur le comique de Molière. Berne, 1950.
Mol 618.7B Romano, D. Essai sur le comique de Molière. Berne, 1950.
Mol 619.1 St. Prosper. Essai sur la comédie. Paris, 1812.
Mol 619.2 Schaunsland. Les farces de Molière. Osterode, 1878.
Mol 619.3 Schneegans, H. Groteske Satire bei Molière? Halle, 1899.
Mol 619.4 Schulze, H. Zur Würdigung Molières. Zittau, 1878.
Mol 619.5A Schweitzer, H. Molière und seine Bühne. pt.1-3. Leipzig, 1879.
Mol 619.5B Schweitzer, H. Molière und seine Bühne. pt.1-3. Leipzig, 1879.
Mol 619.6 Souriau, M. La versification de Molière. Paris, 1888.
Mol 619.7 Stapfer, P. Molière et Shakespeare. Paris, 1887.
Mol 619.7.3 Stapfer, P. Molière et Shakespeare. 3. éd. Paris, 1895.
Mol 619.8A Stapfer, P. Petite comédie de la critique littéraire. Paris, 1866.
Mol 619.8B Stapfer, P. Petite comédie de la critique littéraire. Paris, 1866.
Mol 619.9 Stichling, O.W. Molière und kein Ende. Berlin, 1887.
Mol 619.10 Sundermann, A. Aus Molières Dichtung. Berlin, 1891.
Mol 619.11 Schmidt, H. Das Pronomen bei Molière. Kiel, 1885.
Mol 619.12 Sanlaville, F. Molière et le Droit. Paris, 1913.
Mol 619.13 Sous le masque de Molière. Louis XIV et Molière. Paris, 1919.
Mol 619.15 Salzmann, Wolfgang. Molière und die lateinsche Komödie. Heidelberg, 1969.
Mol 620.1F Thierry, Edouard. Le realisme sur le théâtre de Molière. Paris, 1874.
Mol 620.2 Toldo, P. L'oeuvre de Molière. Turin, 1910.
Mol 620.3A Tilley, Arthur. Molière. Cambridge, 1921.
Mol 620.3B Tilley, Arthur. Molière. Cambridge, 1921.
Mol 620.4 Tiersot, Julien. La musique dans la comédie de Molière. Paris, 1921?
Mol 622.2 Veselovskii, A. Etiudy i Kharateristiki. Moskva, 1894.
Mol 622.3 Veuillot, L. Molière et Bourdaloue. Paris, 1877.
Mol 622.4 Vree, T.J. van. Les pamphlets et libelles litteraires contre Molière. Thèse. Paris, 1932?
Mol 622.5 Vedel, Valdemar. Molière. København, 1929.
Mol 623.1 Wasserzieher, E. Die tragischen Zuge bei Molière. Neustadt, 1882.
Mol 623.2 Waschow, J. Molière et ses prédécesseurs. Oppeln, 1883.
Mol 623.3 Weyl, H. Beitrage zu den Molière Studien. Konigsberg, 1870.
Mol 623.4 Wilke, W. Ce que Molière doit aux anciens poètes français. Lauban, 1880.
Mol 623.5 Weiss, J.J. Molière. Paris, 1900.
Mol 623.5.2 Weiss, J.J. Molière. Paris, 1900.
Mol 623.6 Warsitz, Franz V. Erweiterte Barbeitung...nomenatque omen. Inaug. Diss. Breslau, 1928.
Mol 623.7 Wheatley, K.E. Molière and Terence. Austin, 1931.
Mol 623.7.10 Wheatley, K.E. Molière and Terence. Austin, 1931.
Mol 623.8 Wilcox, John. The relation of Molière to restoration comedy. N.Y., 1938.
Mol 623.10 Walker, H. Molière. N.Y., 1971.

Mol 698 **Works about Molière - Biographical works - Folios [Discontinued]**

Htn Mol 698.1* Houssaye, A. Molière, sa femme et sa fille. Paris, 1888.
Htn Mol 698.2* Moland, Louis. Molière, sa vie et ses oeuvres. Paris, 1887.
Mol 698.2.3 Moland, Louis. Molière sa vie et ses oeuvres. Paris, 1887.
Mol 698.3F Jean-Baptiste Pocquelin de Molière. n.p., 1732.
Mol 698.5F Registre de la Grange (1658-1685). Paris, 1876.
Mol 698.6F Leveaux, Eugène. A l'ombre de Molière. Paris, n.d.
Mol 698.7F Massenet, J. Serenade de Molière. Paris, n.d.
Mol 698.8F Guiffrey, J. Les amours de Sombaut et Macée. Paris, 1882.
Mol 698.9F Taschereau, M.J. Histoire de la vie et des ouvrages de Molière. Paris, 1851.
Mol 698.10F St. Amand, D. de. Une visite de Molière chez Fouquet. n.p., 1880.
Mol 698.11 Wechssler, E. Molière als Philosoph. Marburg, 1910.

Mol 700 **Works about Molière - Biographical works - Pamphlet volumes**

Mol 700.1 Pamphlet vol. Taillefer. Molière. Versailles, 1785. 7 pam.
Mol 700.2 Pamphlet vol. Mangold, W. L'illustre théâtre. Berlin, 1886. 9 pam.
Mol 700.3 Pamphlet box. Molière.

Mol 701 - 726 (A-Z) **Works about Molière - Biographical works - General works**

Mol 701.1F Arago, Etienne. Molière (1622-1673). Paris, 1866?
Mol 701.2 Auger, L.S. Vie de Molière. n.p., n.d.
Mol 701.4 Ashton, Harry. A preface to Molière. N.Y., 1927.
Mol 701.4.10 Ashton, Harry. Molière. Photoreproduction. London, 1930.
Mol 702.1 Baluffe, A. Autour de Molière. Paris, 1889.
Mol 702.2 Baluffe, A. Molière inconnu; sa vie. Paris, 1886.
Mol 702.3 Bazin, A. Les dernières années de Molière. Paris, 1848.
Mol 702.4 Bazin, A. Notes historiques sur la vie de Molière. Paris, 1851.
Mol 702.4.2 Bazin, A. Notes historiques sur la vie de Molière. Paris, 1851.

Mol 701 - 726 (A-Z) - cont. **Works about Molière - Biographical works - General works**

Mol 702.5 Bazin, A. Notes historiques sur la vie de Molière. Paris, 1851.
Mol 702.6 Blaz de Bury. Molière and the French classical drama. London, 1846.
Mol 702.7 Beffara, S.F. Dissertation sur J.B.P. Molière. Paris, 1821.
Mol 702.8 Benjamin, R. Molière. 21e éd. Paris, 1936.
Mol 702.9.5 Brisson, P. Molière. Paris, 1942.
Mol 702.10 Bulgakov, Mikhail Afanas'evich. Zhizh' gospodina de Mol'era. Moskva, 1962.
Mol 702.11 Bulgakov, Mikhail Afanas'evich. The life of Monsieur de Molière. N.Y., 1970.
Mol 702.15 Bordonove, Georges. Molière génial et familiar. Paris, 1967.
Mol 703.1A Campardon, E. Documents inédits sur Jean Baptiste Poquelin Molière. Paris, 1871.
Mol 703.1B Campardon, E. Documents inédits sur Jean Baptiste Poquelin Molière. Paris, 1871.
Mol 703.2A Campardon, E. Nouvelles pièces sur Molière. Paris, 1876.
Mol 703.2B Campardon, E. Nouvelles pièces sur Molière. Paris, 1876.
Mol 703.3A Claretie, J. Molière, sa vie et ses oeuvres. Paris, 1873.
Mol 703.3B Claretie, J. Molière, sa vie et ses oeuvres. Paris, 1873.
Mol 703.4 Claretie, J. Molière, sa vie et ses oeuvres. Paris, 1874.
Mol 703.5 Cousin d'Avallon, C.Y. Moliérana. Paris, 1801.
Mol 703.6A Chatfield-Taylor, Herbert C. Molière; a biography. N.Y., 1906.
Mol 703.6B Chatfield-Taylor, Herbert C. Molière; a biography. N.Y., 1906.
Mol 703.6.5A Chatfield-Taylor, Herbert C. Molière, a biography. N.Y., 1906.
Mol 703.6.5B Chatfield-Taylor, Herbert C. Molière, a biography. N.Y., 1906.
Mol 703.6.5C Chatfield-Taylor, Herbert C. Molière, a biography. N.Y., 1906.
Mol 703.7 Cairncross, John. New light on Molière. Genève, 1956.
Mol 704.1A Durand, H. Molière. Paris, 1889.
Mol 704.1B Durand, H. Molière. Paris, 1889.
NEDL Mol 704.2 Des Granges, René. La querelle de Molière et de Boursault. Paris, 1899.
Mol 704.3 The life of Jean Baptiste Poquelin de Molière. London, 18-?
Mol 704.4 Duhamel, R. Le rire et les larmes de Molière. Paris, 1933.
Mol 704.5 Dussame, Béatrix. Un comédien nommé Molière. Paris, 1936.
Mol 705.1 Emery, Léon. Molière. Lyon, 1956.
Mol 706.1 Fulda, Pastor. Molière. n.p., n.d.
Mol 706.2 Fournier, Edouard. Le roman de Molière. Paris, 1863.
Mol 706.2.2 Fournier, Edouard. Le roman de Molière. Paris, 1863.
Mol 706.5 Flutre, F. Molière. Paris, 1925.
Mol 706.8 Fernandez, Ramon. La vie de Molière. 2. éd. Paris, 1929.
Mol 706.8.5 Fernandez, Ramon. Molière. N.Y., 1958.
Mol 706.9 France. Archives Nationales. Cent ans de recherches sur Molière. Paris, 1963.
Htn Mol 707.1* Grimarest, J.L. La vie de Monsieur de Molière. Paris, 1705.
Mol 707.2 Grimarest, J.L. Les oeuvres de Monsieur de Molière. Paris, 1718.
Mol 707.3 Grimarest, J.L. Mémoires sur la vie de Molière. Paris, 1824.
Mol 707.4 Grimarest, J.L. La vie de Monsieur de Molière. Paris, 1877.
Mol 707.5 Grimarest, J.L. La vie de Monsieur de Molière. Paris, 1955.
Mol 707.30 Garcon, Maurice. Sous le masque de Molière. 2. éd. Paris, 1953.
Mol 708.1 Hall, J.N. Molière en zijn vijanden. Amsterdam, 1879.
Mol 708.2 Heiss, Hanns. Molière. Leipzig, 1929.
Mol 710.5 Jasinski, René. Molière. Paris, 1969.
Mol 711.1A Kreiten, W. Molière's Leben und Werke. Freiburg, 1887.
Mol 711.1B Kreiten, W. Molière's Leben und Werke. Freiburg, 1887.
Mol 711.2 Kühns, C. Molière. Lüneberg, 1877.
Mol 712.2 Lacroix, Paul. La jeunesse de Molière. Bruxelles, 1856.
Mol 712.2.2 Lacroix, Paul. La jeunesse de Molière. Bruxelles, 1858.
Mol 712.2.3 Lacroix, Paul. La jeunesse de Molière. Paris, 1859.
Mol 712.3 Lindau, Paul. Molière; eine Ergänzung. Leipzig, 1872.
Mol 712.3.2 Lindau, Paul. Molière, eine Ergänzung. Leipzig, 1872.
Mol 712.4 Loiseleur, J. Molière, nouvelles controverses. Orleans, 1886.
Mol 712.5A Loiseleur, J. Les points obscurs de la vie de Molière. Paris, 1877.
Mol 712.5B Loiseleur, J. Les points obscurs de la vie de Molière. Paris, 1877.
Mol 712.6A Lotheissen, F. Molière: Leben und Werke. Frankfurt, 1880.
Mol 712.6B Lotheissen, F. Molière: Leben und Werke. Frankfurt, 1880.
Mol 712.7 Lafenestre, G. Molière. Paris, 1909.
Mol 712.8 Levi, Cesare. Molière. Roma, 1922.
Mol 712.10 Lewis, Dominic Bevan Wyndham. Molière; the comic mask. London, 1959.
Mol 713.1 Mahrenholtz, R. Molière: Einführung in Leben und Werke. Heilbronn, 1883.
Mol 713.2 Mahrenholtz, R. Molière's Leben und Werke. Heilbronn, 1881.
Mol 713.3 Malassis, A.P. Molière jugé par ses contemporains. Paris, 1877.
Mol 713.3.2 Malassis, A.P. Molière jugé par ses contemporains. Paris, 1877.
Mol 713.4 Mazzoni, G. La vita de Molière. n.p., 1887.
Mol 713.5 Moland, L. Vie de Jean Baptiste Poquelin Molière. Paris, 1892.
Mol 713.6 Monval, G. Chronologie Moliéresque. Paris, 1897.
Mol 713.6.2 Monval, G. Chronologie Moliéresque. Paris, 1897.
Mol 713.7 Monval, G. Lettres au Mercure sur Molière. Paris, 1887.
Mol 713.7.2 Monval, G. Lettres au Mercure sur Molière. Paris, 1887.
Mol 713.8 Morf, H. Zeittafel zu Vorlesungen über Molière. Bern, 1886.
Mol 713.9 Musset, P. de. Le déjeuner de Molière. n.p., n.d.
Mol 713.10 Moulin, H. Molière et les registres de l'état civil. Paris, 1878.
Mol 713.11.5 Mantzius, K. Molière. Paris, 1908.
Mol 713.12 Mémoires sur Molière. Paris, 1822.
Mol 713.12.2 Mémoires sur Molière. Paris, 1822. 2 pam.
Mol 713.13A Marzials, F.J. Molière. London, 1906.
Mol 713.13B Marzials, F.J. Molière. London, 1906.
Mol 713.14A Matthews, B. Molière his life and his works. N.Y., 1910.
Mol 713.14B Matthews, B. Molière his life and his works. N.Y., 1910.
Mol 713.14.5 Matthews, B. Molière his life and his works. N.Y., 1916.

Mol 701 - 726 Works about Molière - Biographical works - General works (A-Z) - cont.

Mol 713.15A Michaut, G. La jeunesse de Molière. Paris, 1922.
Mol 713.15B Michaut, G. La jeunesse de Molière. Paris, 1922.
NEDL Mol 713.15.5A Michaut, G. Les luttes de Molière. Paris, 1925.
NEDL Mol 713.15.5B Michaut, G. Les luttes de Molière. Paris, 1925.
Mol 713.16 Magne, Émile. Une amie inconnue de Molière. 3. éd. Paris, 1922.
Mol 713.17 Mornet, Daniel. Molière. Paris, 1943.
Mol 713.17.5 Mornet, Daniel. Molière. 5. éd. Paris, 1958.
Mol 713.18 Meyer, J. Molière. Paris, 1963.
Mol 713.20 Mongrédien, George. La vie privée de Molière. Paris, 1950.
Mol 713.20.5 Mongrédien, George. Recueil des textes et des documents du XVIIe siècle relatifs à Molière. Paris, 1965. 2v.
Mol 714.1 Noël, Eugène. Molière. Paris, 1852.
Mol 714.2 Noël, Eugène. Molière, son théâtre et son ménage. Paris, 1880.
Mol 715.1 Oliphant, M.O. Molière. London, 1879.
Mol 716.1 Picard, L.B. Notice sur Molière. n.p., n.d.
Mol 716.2 Prescott, W.H. Essais de biographie et de critique. Paris, 1864.
Mol 716.3 Peisert, P. Molière's Leben in Bühnenarbeitungen. Halle, 1905.
Mol 716.4 Picco, Francesco. Molière. Firenze, 1930.
Mol 716.5A Palmer, John. Molière. N.Y., 1930.
Mol 716.5B Palmer, John. Molière. N.Y., 1930.
Mol 718.1 Rondel, Auguste. Commémoration de Molière, Racine, Corneille, Shakespeare et Cervantes à la comédie française. Paris, 1919.
Mol 719.1 Scheffler, Wilhelm. Molière-Studien. n.p., 1878.
Mol 719.2 Schneegans, H. Molière. Berlin, 1902.
Mol 719.3 Soulié, E. Rapport sur des recherches relatives à la vie de Molière. Paris, 1865.
Mol 719.4 Süss, O. Questionnaire sur vie et oeuvres de Molière. Strehlen, 1892.
Mol 719.5 Schweitzer, H. Molière's Tod, vor 200 Jahren. Weisbaden, 1873.
Mol 719.6 Soulié, E. Recherches sur Molière et sur sa famille. Paris, 1863.
Mol 719.7 Szana, Tamás. Molière élete és müvei. Budapest, n.d.
Mol 719.10 Salza, Livia. Molière nel III centenario della sua nascita. Novara, 1922.
Mol 720.1A Taschereau, M.J. Histoire de la vie et des ouvrages de Molière. Paris, 1825.
Mol 720.1B Taschereau, M.J. Histoire de la vie et des ouvrages de Molière. Paris, 1825.
Htn Mol 720.2* Taschereau, M.J. Histoire de la vie et des ouvrages de Molière. Paris, 1828.
Mol 720.2.2 Taschereau, M.J. Histoire de la vie et des ouvrages de Molière. Paris, 1828.
Mol 720.3 Taschereau, M.J. Histoire de la vie et des ouvrages de Molière. Paris, 1844.
Mol 720.5 Thierry, Edouard. Quatre mois du théâtre de Molière. Cherbourgh, 1873.
Mol 720.6 Trollope, H.M. The life of Molière. London, 1905.
Mol 720.7A Thuillier, R. La vie maladive de Molière. Paris, 1932.
Mol 720.7B Thuillier, R. La vie maladive de Molière. Paris, 1932.
Mol 720.8 Toudouze, Georges G. Molière. Paris, 1946.
Mol 720.9 Thoorens, Léon. Le dossier Molière. Verviers, 1964.
Mol 720.10 Thoorens, Léon. La vie passionée de Molière. Paris, 1958.
Htn Mol 722.1* Voltaire, François Marie Arouet. Vie de Molière avec des jugements. Paris, 1739.
Mol 722.2 Voltaire, François Marie Arouet. Leben des Molière. Leipzig, 1754.
Mol 722.3A Vincent, L.H. Molière. Boston, 1902.
Mol 722.3B Vincent, L.H. Molière. Boston, 1902.
Mol 722.3.5 Vincent, L.H. Molière. Boston, 1902.
Mol 722.4 Vitu, Auguste. Molière et les Italiens. Paris, 1879.
Mol 723.1 Warburg, K. Molière; en Lefnadsteckning. Stockholm, 1884.
Mol 723.3 Wolff, Max I. Molière der Dichter und sein Werk. München, 1910.
Mol 723.4 Wechssler, E. Über die Bezichungen von Weltanschauung...Molière und V. Hugo. Marburg, 1911.
Mol 723.5 Weddigen, Eduard. Volkstümliche Rede und Lebensweisheit bei Molière. Inaug. Diss. Marburg, 1918.

Mol 728 Works about Molière - Biographical works - Special topics - Molière in special localities

Mol 728.2 Raymond, E. Histoire des peregrinations de Molière dans le Languedoc (1642-1658). Paris, 1858.
Mol 728.4 Brouchoud, C. Notice sur les origines du théâtre de Lyon. n.p., 1865.
Mol 728.5 Soulié, E. Molière et sa troupe à Lyon. Lyon, 1866.
Mol 728.6 Robert, L. Molière en province. Niort, 1869.
Mol 728.6.2 Gosselin, M.E. Molière à Rouen en 1643. Rouen, 1870.
Mol 728.7 Fillon, B. Recherches sur le séjour de Molière dans l'ouest de la France en 1648. Fontenay-le-Comte, 1871.
Mol 728.8 Magen, A. La troupe de Molière à Agen. Paris, 1877.
Mol 728.9 Constant, C. Molière à Fontainebleau (1661-1664). Meaux, 1873.
Mol 728.10 Brouchoud, C. Les origines du théâtre de Lyon. Lyon, 1865.
Mol 728.11 Bleton, Auguste. Molière à Lyon. Lyon, 1900?
Mol 728.11.5 Farnoux-Reynaud, Lucien. L'aventure comique. Lyon, 1944.
Mol 728.12 Bouquet, F. La troupe de Molière et les deux Corneille a Rouen en 1658. Paris, 1880.
Mol 728.15 Bricauld de Verneuil, E. Molière à Poiteurs en 1648. Paris, 1887.
Mol 728.18A Loquin, A. Molière à Bordeaux vers 1647 et en 1656. Paris, 1898. 2v.
Mol 728.18B Loquin, A. Molière à Bordeaux vers 1647 et en 1656. Paris, 1898. 2v.
Mol 728.20F L'Hérault. L'Hérault-Artiste à Molière. Paris, 1897.

Mol 730 Works about Molière - Biographical works - Special topics - Special aspects

Mol 730.1 Blaze, F.H.C. Molière musicien. Paris, 1852. 2v.
Mol 730.2 Fischmann, P. Molière als Schauspieldirektor. Halle, 1904.
Mol 730.3 Guillard, L. Molière, directeur. Paris, 1871.
Mol 730.4 Lapommeraye, H. de. Les amours de Molière. Paris, 1873.
Mol 730.6 Pifteau, B. Les maitresses de Molière. Paris, 1879.
Mol 730.6.2 Pifteau, B. Les maitresses de Molière. Paris, 1879.
Mol 730.9 Larroumet, G. Molière, l'homme et le comédien. Paris, 1886.

Mol 730 Works about Molière - Biographical works - Special topics - Special aspects - cont.

Mol 730.10 Lacour, L. Les maitresses et la femme de Molière. Paris, 1914.
Mol 730.11 Wechssler, E. Molière als Philosoph. 2e. Aufl. Marburg, 1915.
Mol 730.12 Jurgens, Madeleine. Quelques amis et protégés de Molière. n.p., 1961.
Mol 730.13 Heussler, Otto. Molières religiöse Ueberzeugung. Greifswald, 1917.
Mol 730.15 Baumal, F. Molière, auteur précieux. Paris, 1923.
Mol 730.19 Lacour, L. Molière acteur. Paris, 1928.
Mol 730.20 Poulaille, Henry. Corneille sous le masque de Molière. Paris, 1957.

Mol 735 Works about Molière - Biographical works - Special topics - Iconography

Mol 735.1 Lavoix, H. Les portraits de Molière. Paris, 1872.
Mol 735.1.5 Musée Molière; Catalogue. Paris, 1873.
Mol 735.2 Lenient, Charles. Molière - son portrait physique et moral. Paris, 1874.
Mol 735.2.5 Wismes, Bon de. Un portrait de Molière en Bretagne. Nantes, 1874?
Mol 735.4 Lacroix, Paul. Iconographie Moliéresque. Paris, 1876.
Mol 735.4.2 Lacroix, Paul. Iconographie Moliéresque. Paris, 1876.
Mol 735.6 Perrin, E. Deux portraits de Molière. Paris, 1883.
Mol 735.8 Chapman, P.A. The spirit of Molière; an interpretation. Princeton, 1940.

Mol 740 Works about Molière - Biographical works - Special topics - Habitations

Mol 740.1 Gurgy, B. de. La chambre de Molière. Paris, 1838.
Mol 740.2 Vitu, Auguste. La maison des Poquelins et la maison de Regnard aux piliers des Halles. Paris, 1885.
Mol 740.3 Vitu, Auguste. La maison mortuaire de Molière. Paris, 1880.
Mol 740.3.2 Vitu, Auguste. La maison mortuaire de Molière. Paris, 1880.

Mol 745 Works about Molière - Biographical works - Special topics - Death and Burial

Mol 745.2 Davin, V. La mort de Molière. Paris, 1877.
Mol 745.4 Monval, G. Les tombeaux de Molière et de la Fontaine. Pons, 1882.
Mol 745.5A Monval, G. Recueil sur la mort de Molière. Paris, 1885.
Mol 745.5B Monval, G. Recueil sur la mort de Molière. Paris, 1885.
Mol 745.6 Ubalde. Le secret du masque de fer. Bordeaux, 1883. 3 pam.

Mol 750 Works about Molière - Biographical works - Special topics - Wife of Molière

Mol 750.1 Desjardins, Marie Catherine Hortense. Les aventures ou mémoires de la vie d'Henriette-Sylvie de Molière. Amsterdam, 1732.
Htn Mol 750.1.5* Alègre, d'. The memoires of the life and rare adventures of Henrietta S. Molière. London, 1672.
Mol 750.2 Fortia d'Urban. Sur le mariage de Molière. Paris, 1821.
Mol 750.3 Fortia, d'Urban. Dissertation sur la femme de Molière. Paris, 1824.
Mol 750.4 Taschereau, M.J. Lettre à Monsieur le Marquis de Fortia d'Urban. Paris, 1824.
Mol 750.5 Fortia d'Urban. Supplement aux diverses éditions de Molière. Paris, 18, La Gué
Mol 750.6 La fameuse comédienne, la Guérin. Genève, 1868.
Mol 750.7 Bonnassies, J. La fameuse comédienne, La Guérin. Paris, 1870.
Mol 750.8 Les intrigues de Molière et celles de sa femme, ou La fameuse comédienne, La Guèrin. Paris, 1876.
Mol 750.9 Les intrigues de Molière et celles de sa femme, ou La fameuse comédienne, La Guérin. Paris, 1877.
Mol 750.10 Moulin, H. Armande Béjart, sa fille et ses 2 maris. Paris, 1881.
Mol 750.25 Lyonnet, Henry. Mademoiselle Molière. Paris, 1925.
Mol 750.27 Chabannes, Jacques. Mademoiselle Molière. Paris, 1961.

Mol 755 Works about Molière - Biographical works - Special topics - Genealogy and Heraldry

Mol 755.2 Mathon, M. La famille de Molière était originaire de Beauvais. Paris, 1877.
Mol 755.3F Fillon, B. Le blason de Molière. Paris, 1878.
Mol 755.4 Thoinan, E. Un bisaïeul de Molière. Paris, 1878.
Mol 755.5 Révérend du Mesnil, E. La famille de Molière. Paris, 1879.
Mol 755.6 Depping, G. Trois pièces inédits concernant la famille de Molière. Paris, 1882.
Mol 755.6.5 Baluffe, A. Le père de Molière. n.p., 1887.
Mol 755.7 Angot, A. Les Pocquelin ecclésiastiques. Mamers, 1887.
Mol 755.8 Révérend du Mesnil, E. François de Molière, Anne Picardet. Charolles, 1888.

Mol 765 Works about Molière - Biographical works - Special topics - Monuments

Mol 765.1 Colet, Louise. Le monument de Molière. Paris, 1843.
Mol 765.2 Notice sur le monument de Molière. Paris, 1844.
Mol 765.3 Aimé-Martin, L. Histoire du monument à Molière. Paris, 1845.
Mol 765.4 Marmottan, P. Molière rue Richelieu. Paris, 1886.
Mol 765.5 Saint Martin. La Fontaine Molière. Paris, 1844.

Mol 775 Works about Molière - Biographical works - Special topics - Relics

Mol 775.1 Notice sur le fauteuil de Molière. Pézenas, 1836.
Mol 775.2 Fontaine, P.J. Découverte d'un autographe de Molière. Paris, 1840.
Mol 775.5 Richard-Desaix, W. La relique de Molière du cabinet du baron Vivant Denon. Paris, 1880.

Mol 800 Works about Molière - Miscellaneous topics - Molière's acting troupe - General works

Mol 800.1 Picard, L.B. Histoire de la troupe de Molière. Paris, 182-?
Mol 800.2 Soleirol, H.A. Molière et sa troupe. Paris, 1858.
Mol 800.3 Hillemacher, F. Galerie des portraits des comédiens de la troupe de Molière. Lyon, 1858.
Mol 800.3.3 Hillemacher, F. Galerie des portraits des comédiens de la troupe de Molière. 2. éd. Lyon, 1869.
Mol 800.4 Thierry, Edouard. Charles Varlet de La Grange. Paris, 1876.
Mol 800.5 Houssaye, A. Les comédiennes de Molière. Paris, 1879.
Mol 800.6 Copin, A. Histoire des comédiens de la troupe de Molière. Paris, 1886.

Classified Listing

Mol 800 Works about Molière - Miscellaneous topics - Molière's acting troupe - General works - cont.

Mol 800.7 Copin, A. Histoire des comédiens de la troupe de Molière. Paris, 1886.
Mol 800.8 Monval, G. Premier registre de La Thorillière. Paris, 1890.
Mol 800.15 Michaut, G. Les débuts de Molière à Paris. Paris, 1923.

Mol 803 Works about Molière - Miscellaneous topics - Molière's acting troupe - Individual actors

Mol 803.1 Larroumet, G. Une famille des comédiens au XVIIe siècle, les Béjart. Paris, 1885.
Mol 803.3 Chardon, H. Nouveau documents. v.1. Paris, 1886.
Mol 803.3.2 Chardon, H. Nouveau documents. v.2. Paris, 1905.
Mol 803.4 Monval, G. Un comédien amateur d'art. Michel Baron. Paris, 1893.
Mol 803.5 Tuffet, S. Baron le comédien. Paris, 1837.

Mol 805 Works about Molière - Miscellaneous topics - Molière's theater at Paris

Mol 805.1 Collardeau, P. Le salle de théâtre de Molière au Port St. Paul. Paris, 1876.
Mol 805.2 Vitu, Auguste. Le jeu de paume des Mestayers. Paris, 1883.

Mol 810 Works about Molière - Miscellaneous topics - French theater in the time of Molière

Mol 810.1 Fournier, E. La farce avant Molière. Paris, 1858.
Mol 810.1.5 Bonnassies, J. La musique à la Comédie-Française. Paris, 1874.
Mol 810.2 Chappuzeau, S. Le théâtre français. Bruxelles, 1867.
Mol 810.2.2 Monval, G. Le théâtre français. Paris, 1875.
Mol 810.3 Chardon, H. La troupe du roman comique XVIIe siècle. Le Mans, 1876.
Mol 810.4 Tralage, J.N. du. Notes et documents sur l'histoire des théâtres de Paris au XVIIe siècle. Paris, 1880.
Mol 810.5 Kohler, Pierre. Autour de Molière. L'ésprit classique. Paris, 1925.
Mol 810.6 Leveaux, Alphonse. Les premières de Molière. Compiégne, 1882.
Mol 810.7 Pighi, Lana. Molière e il teatro italiano in Francia. Bologna, 1958.

Mol 815 Works about Molière - Miscellaneous topics - Social conditions in the time of Molière

Mol 815.1 Roederer, P.L. Fragments de divers mémoires pour servir à l'histoire de la société polie en France. Paris, 1834.
Htn Mol 815.2* Roederer, P.L. Mémoire pour servir à l'histoire de la société polie en France. Paris, 1835.
Mol 815.3 Fischer, F.A. Das Hôtel de Rambouillet et die Precieusen. Jena, 1868.
Mol 815.4 Weisser, E. L'Hôtel de Rambouillet. Breslau, 1873.
Mol 815.6 Breitinger, H. Der Salon Rambouillet und seine kulturgeschichtliche Bedeutung (in Programm der Thurgauischen Kantonsschule 1873-1874). Frauenfeld, 1874.
Mol 815.7 Tiburtius, G. Molière und das Precieusentum. Neumark, 1875.
Mol 815.8 Kreutzinger, K. Das Precieusenthum und Molière. Jagendorf, 1881. 2 pam.

Mol 820 Works about Molière - Miscellaneous topics - Contemporaries of Molière

Mol 820.1 Taillandier, St. R. Un poète comique du temps de Molière. Paris, 1878.
Mol 820.2 Bernardin, N.M. Un mari d'actrice au XVIIe siècle. Paris, 1897.
Mol 820.3 Cherot, R.P.H. Le Béarnais professeur de seconde de Molière. Auch, 1897.
Mol 820.4 Monval, G. Le laquais de Molière. Paris, 1887.
Mol 820.5 Schwartz, F. Somaize und seine Précieuses ridicules. Könisberg, 1903.

Mol 825 Works about Molière - Miscellaneous topics - Molière and the doctors

Mol 825.1 Alexandre, M. Molière et les médecins. Amiens, 1854.
Mol 825.2 Fournier, Edouard. Molière et le procès du pain mollet. Paris, 1855.
Mol 825.3 Raynaud, M. Les médecins au temps de Molière. Paris, 1862.
Mol 825.4 Raynaud, M. Les médecins au temps de Molière. Paris, 1863.
Mol 825.4.2 Raynaud, M. Les médecins au temps de Molière. Paris, 1866.
Mol 825.5 Drouineau, G. Molière et les médecins au XVIIe siècle. La Rochelle, 1873.
Mol 825.7 Graaf, R. de. L'instrument de Molière. Paris, 1878.
Mol 825.8 Nivelet, F. Molière et Gui Patin. Paris, 1880.
Mol 825.9 Chereau, A. Le médecin de Molière. Paris, 1881.
Mol 825.9.2 Chereau, A. Le médecin de Molière. Paris, 1881.
Mol 825.10 Saucerotte, C. Les médecins au théâtre depuis Molière. Paris, 1881.
Mol 825.11 Léon-Petit. Les médecins de Molière. Paris, 1890.
Mol 825.12 Folet, H. Molière et la médecine de son temps. Lille, 1895.
NEDL Mol 825.13 Brown, A.M. Molière and his medical associations. London, 1897.
Mol 825.14 Vialard, M.J. Essai médical sur Molière. Bordeaux, 1908.
Mol 825.15 Farez, Paul. Les médecins de Molière. Paris, 1922.
Mol 825.16 Carcassonne, L. Molière et la médecine. Nimes, 1877.

Mol 828 Works about Molière - Miscellaneous topics - Molière and other professions

Mol 828.1 Truinet, Charles. Pourquoi Molière n'a pas joué les avocats. Paris, 1855.
Mol 828.2 Cauvet, Jules. La science du droit dans les comédies de Molière. Caen, 1866.

Mol 840 Works about Molière - Miscellaneous topics - Molière and folklore

Mol 840.1 Sebillot, P. Molière et les traditions populaires. Yannes, 1890.

Mol 845 Works about Molière - Literary works relating to Molière - General collections

Mol 845.1 Collection Molierèsque. Genève, 1867.
Mol 845.1.2 Collection Molierèsque. Genève, 1868.
Mol 845.1.3 Collection Molierèsque. Genève, 1868.
Mol 845.1.4 Collection Molierèsque. Genève, 1868.
Mol 845.1.5 Collection Molierèsque. Turin, 1870.
Mol 845.1.6 Collection Molierèsque. San Remo, 1874.

Mol 850 Works about Molière - Literary works relating to Molière - Contemporaneous works - Poetry

Mol 850.1 Cheron, E.S. La coupe de Val de Grace. Paris, 1880.
Htn Mol 850.2* L'enfer burlesque: le mariage de Belphégor. Cologne, 1577.
Mol 850.3 L'enfer burlesque: le mariage de Belphégor. Genève, 1868.
Mol 850.4 Le songe du rêveur. Genève, 1867.

Mol 853 Works about Molière - Literary works relating to Molière - Contemporaneous works - Prose

Mol 853.1 Un compte-rendu de la comédie des "Précieuses Ridicules" de Molière. Paris, 1877.
Mol 853.1.5A Des Jardins. Recit en prose et en vers de la farce des Précieuses. Paris, 1879.
Mol 853.1.5B Des Jardins. Recit en prose et en vers de la farce des Précieuses. Paris, 1879.
Mol 853.2A Déscente de l'ame de Molière dans les Champs-Élysées. Paris, 1901.
Mol 853.2B Déscente de l'ame de Molière dans les Champs-Élysées. Paris, 1901.
Mol 853.3 Gueret, G. La promenade de Saint-Cloud. Paris, 1888.
Mol 853.4 Roulés, Pierre. Le roy glorieux au monde. Genève, 1867.
Mol 853.5 Cotin. La satyre des satyres. Paris, 1883.
Mol 853.5.2 Cotin. La satyre des satyres. Paris, 1887.
Mol 853.6 Vizé, J.D. de. Oraison funebre de Molière. Paris, 1879.
Mol 853.6.2 Vizé, J.D. de. Oraison funebre de Molière. Paris, 1879.
Mol 853.7 Visé, J.D. de. Lettre sur les affaires du théâtre en 1665. San Remo, 1865.
Mol 853.8 Lettre sur la comédie de l'Imposteur. Turin, 1870.
Mol 853.9 Vizé, J.D. de. Novvelles novvelles. Paris, 1663. 3v.

Mol 855 Works about Molière - Literary works relating to Molière - Contemporaneous works - Plays

Mol 855.1 Fournel, V. Les contemporains de Molière. Paris, 1863.
Mol 855.2 Le Boulanger de Chalussay. Elomire hypocondre. Genève, 1867.
Mol 855.3 Le Boulanger de Chalussay. Elomire hypocondre. Paris, 1878.
Htn Mol 855.4* Boursault, E. Le portrait du peintre. Paris, 1663.
Mol 855.5 Boursault, E. Le portrait du peintre. Paris, 1879.
Mol 855.6 Boursault, E. Le medecin volant. Paris, 1884.
Mol 855.7 Brecourt. L'ombre de Molière. Paris, 1880.
Mol 855.8 Chevalier. Les amours de Calotin. Turin, 1870.
Htn Mol 855.9* La critique de Tartuffe. Paris, 1670.
Mol 855.10 La critique de Tartuffe. Genève, 1868.
Mol 855.11 Doneau, F. La cocue imaginaire. Turin, 1870.
Mol 855.11.3 La folle querelle. Jacob. Paris, 1881.
Mol 855.12 La Croix, Paul de. La guerre comique. Genève, 1868.
Htn Mol 855.12.2* La Croix, Paul de. La guerre comique. Paris, 1664.
Mol 855.12.5 Le livre abominable de 1665. Ménard. Paris, 1883. 2v.
Mol 855.13 Marcel. Le mariage sans mariage. Turin, 1869.
Mol 855.14 Montfleury, A.J. L'impromptu de l'Hostel de Condé. San Remo, 1875.
Mol 855.15 Panégyrique de l'école des femmes. Paris, 1883.
Mol 855.15.2 Panégyrique de l'école des femmes. Paris, 1883.
Mol 855.16 Rochemont, de. Observations sur le Festin de Pierre. Paris, 1869.
Mol 855.17 La vengeance des marquis. Turin, 1869.
Mol 855.18 Les véritables prétieuses. Genève, 1868.
Mol 855.19 La veuve à la mode. Paris, 1881.
Mol 855.20 Zelinde. Genève, 1868.

Mol 860 Works about Molière - Literary works relating to Molière - Later works - Plays

Mol 860.1 Le Noble, E. Molière le critique. Hollande, 1709.
Mol 860.5 Goldini, C. Scelta delle commedie di Goldini. Lipsia, 1781.
Mol 860.6 Goldini, C. Il Molière commedia in cinque atti in versi. n.p., n.d.
Mol 860.7 Briol, Marcel. Molière à Nantes. Nantes, 1863.
Mol 860.11 Mercier, M. Molière drame en cinq actes. Amsterdam, 1776.
Mol 860.12 Mercier, M. Molière drame en cinq actes. La Haye, 1777.
Mol 860.13 Mercier, M. Molière à la nouvelle salle. Paris, 1782.
Mol 860.14 Desbarreaux, P. Molière à Toulouse. Toulouse, 1787.
Mol 860.15 Gouges, Marie Olympe de. Molière chez Ninon. Paris, 1788.
Mol 860.16 Cubières, Michel de. La mort de Molière. Londres, 1788.
Mol 860.17 Mercier, M. La maison de Molière. Paris, 1789.
Mol 860.18 Cadet de Gassicourt, Charles Louis. Le souper de Molière. Paris, 1795.
Mol 860.19 Coupigny, Antoine François de. Hommage du petit vaudeville. Paris, 1798.
Mol 860.20 Creuzé, A. Ninon de Lenclos. Paris, 1800.
Mol 860.21 Rigaud, A.F. Molière avec ses amis. Paris, 1801.
Mol 860.22 Chazet, André R.P.A. de. Molière chez Ninon. Paris, 1802.
Mol 860.22.5 Palmezeaux, C. La mort de Molière. Paris, 1802.
Mol 860.23 Andrieux, F.G.J.B. Molière avec ses amis. Paris, 1804.
Mol 860.24 Desfontaines, Henri Dupin. Le voyage de Chambord. Paris, 1808.
Mol 860.26 Simon, H. Ninon, Molière et Tartuffe. Paris, 1815.
Mol 860.27 Laurent, A. du. Ninon à la campagne. Lyon, 1826.
Mol 860.28 Garnier, F. Le mariage de Molière. Paris, 1828.
Mol 860.28.2 Garnier, F. Le mariage de Molière. Paris, 1828.
Mol 860.30 Un amour de Molière. Paris, 1838.
Mol 860.31 Alphonse, F. Molière et son Tartuffe. Paris, 1839.
Mol 860.34.5 Sand, George. Molière. Paris, 1851.
Mol 860.35 Sand, George. Molière. Paris, 1851.
Mol 860.36 Sand, George. Molière. Bruxelles, 1851.
Mol 860.37 Sand, George. Molière. London, 1868.
Mol 860.37.2 Gutzkow, Karl. Das Urbild des Tartüffe. N.Y., 1851.
Mol 860.37.3 Gutzkow, Karl. Das Urbild des Tartüffe. Jena, 1880.
Mol 860.38 Brucker, R. Le carême du roi. Paris, 1853.
Mol 860.39 Peillon, F. Un poète inçonnu. Paris, 1855.
Mol 860.40 Beaume, Alex. Dialogue des morts. Paris, 1862.
Mol 860.41 Hurtado, A. El collar de Lescot. Madrid, 1868.
Mol 860.42 Bellet, Paul. La maison de Molière. Toulouse, 1872.
Mol 860.43 Pinchon. La mort de Molière. Paris, 1872.
Mol 860.44 Aubryet, X. Le docteur Molière. Paris, 1873.
Mol 860.45 Ponsard, F. Molière a Vienne. n.p., 1876.
Mol 860.47 Barbier, P. Le roi chez Molière. Paris, 1876.
Mol 860.48 Bondroit, E. Molière chez lui. Liège, 1879.
Mol 860.49 Nancey, A. Un souper chez Molière. Troyes, 1879.
Mol 860.51 Billard, E. La vocation de Molière. Paris, 1885.
Mol 860.52 La Motte, M. de. Molière au berceau. Paris, 1887.
Mol 860.52.2 Jouin, Henry. Corneille et Lulli. Paris, 1887.
Mol 860.53 Bernede, A. La vocation de Poquelin. Paris, 1891.
Mol 860.54 Bois, George. Racine à Chevreuse. Paris, 1893.
Mol 860.55 Blémont, E. Molière en bonne fortune. Paris, 1897.
Mol 860.55.5 Griselin, J. Alliance. Paris, 1897.

Mol 860 Works about Molière - Literary works relating to Molière - Later works - Plays - cont.

Mol 860.56 Marsolleau, L. Le dernier madrigal. Paris, 1898.
Mol 860.57 Blémont, E. Théâtre Molièresque et Cornélien. Paris, 1898.
Mol 860.59 Lafenestre, Pierre. La farce du medecin; comédie. Paris, 1905.
Mol 860.60 Yvan, A. Jardin de Molière. Paris, 1909.
Mol 860.61F Donnay, M. Le ménage de Molière. Paris, 1912. 2v.
Mol 860.62 Rovetta, G. Molière e sua moglie. Milano, 1920.

Mol 863 Works about Molière - Literary works relating to Molière - Later works - Poetry

Mol 863.1 Van Effen, J. Le misanthrope. La Haye, 1726. 2v.
Mol 863.1.5 Baar, G.L. de. Epîtres diverses sur des sujets diverses. Londres, 1740.
Mol 863.1.6 Baar, G.L. de. Epîtres diverses sur des sujets diverses. v.1-2. 2e. éd. Londres, 1745.
Mol 863.1.7 Baar, G.L. de. Epîtres diverses sur des sujets diverses. v.1-2. Francfort, 1765.
Mol 863.2 Bailly, J.S. Eloges de Charles V, de Molière. Berlin, 1770.
Mol 863.3 Chamfort, de. Eloge de Molière. Paris, 1769.
Mol 863.4 Chateau-Lyon, A. de. Eloge de Molière. Londres, 1725.
Mol 863.5 Gallois-Mailly, T. Epître à Molière. Paris, 1814. 9 pam.
Mol 863.8 Beuchot, A.J.I. Hommage à MM. les membres de la chambre des députés. Paris, 1838.
Mol 863.12 Colet, Louise. Le monument de Molière. Paris, 1843.
Mol 863.13 Drouin. L'éloge de Molière. Paris, 1843.
Mol 863.17 Minier, H. Les bas-bleus; à Molière. Bordeaux, 1844.
Mol 863.19 Soupé, A.P. L'ombre de Molière. Grenoble, 1857.
Mol 863.19.2 Barré, F. Poésies pour Alceste. Paris, 1869.
Mol 863.20 Truffier, J. Sous les frises. Paris, 1879.
Mol 863.21 Aicard, J. Molière à Shakspeare. Paris, 1879.
Htn Mol 863.21.2* Aicard, J. Molière à Shakspeare. Paris, 1879.
Mol 863.22 Allart, L.F. Ode à Molière. Paris, 1880.
Mol 863.23 Coppée, F. La maison de Molière. Paris, 1880.

Mol 865 Works about Molière - Literary works relating to Molière - Later works - Prose

Mol 865.1 Cailhava d'Estendoux, Jean François. Discours prononcé par Molière. Amsterdam, 1779.
Mol 865.2 Gaillard, L. Eloge de Molière. n.p., 1806.
Mol 865.3 Théolier. L'ésprit français. Paris, n.d.
Mol 865.5 Dussane, B. (Mrs.). An actor named Molière. N.Y., 1937.

Mol 870 Works about Molière - Literary works relating to Molière - Anniversary works - Plays - Birth

Mol 870.1 Moreau, Émile. Scène ajoutée au "Boulevard bonne nouvelle". Paris, 1821.
Mol 870.2 Gensoul, J. Le ménage de Molière. Paris, 1822.
Mol 870.3 Bayard. Molière au théâtre. Paris, 1824.
Mol 870.4 Samson, Joseph Isidore. La fête de Molière. Paris, 1825.
Mol 870.5 Dercy, F. Molière; comédie épisodique. Paris, 1828.
Mol 870.5.5 Dupeuty. La vie de Molière. Paris, 1832.
Mol 870.6 D'Epagny. A propos sur l'anniversaire de la naissance de Molière. n.p., 1842.
Mol 870.7 Desportes, A. Molière à Chambord. Paris, 1843.
Mol 870.7.4 Clairville. Le monument de Molière. Troyes? 1844?
Mol 870.8 Barbier, P.J. L'ombre de Molière. Paris, 1847.
Mol 870.9 Lesguillon. Le protégé de Molière. Paris, 1848.
Mol 870.9.5 Ponsard, F. Le mariage d'Angélique. Paris, 1902.
Mol 870.10 Dumas, A. Trois entr'actes pour l'Amour médecin. Paris, 1874.
Mol 870.11 Vierne, Edouard. Molière enfant. Paris, 1855.
Mol 870.12 Minier, H. Molière à Bordeaux. Bordeaux, 1865.
Mol 870.13 Bornier, H. de. Le quinze janvier. Paris, 1860.
Mol 870.14 Martin, Alexis. La fête de Molière. Paris, 1860.
Mol 870.15 Roche, E. La dernière fourberie de Scapin. n.p., 1863.
Mol 870.16 Fournier, Edouard. La fille de Molière. Paris, 1863.
Mol 870.17 Carcassonne, A. La fête de Molière. Paris, 1863.
Mol 870.18 La valise de Molière. Paris, 1868.
Mol 870.19 Delpit, A. La voix du maître. Paris, 1870.
Mol 870.20 Glatigny, A. Le compliment à Molière. Paris, 1872.
Mol 870.21 Arène, P. Les comédiens errants. Paris, 1873.
Mol 870.22 d'Hervilly, E. Cinq anniversaires de Molière. Paris, 1887.
Mol 870.23 d'Hervilly, E. Le docteur sans pareil. Paris, 1873.
Mol 870.24 Blémont, E. Molière à Auteuil. Paris, 1876.
Mol 870.25 Blémont, E. Molière à Auteuil. Paris, 1876.
Mol 870.26 d'Hervilly, E. Le magister. Paris, 1877.
Mol 870.27 Blémont, E. Le barbier de Pézenas. Paris, 1877.
Htn Mol 870.28* Mussy, P. de. L'amour poète; ou Corneille chez Molière. Rouen, 1878.
Mol 870.29 Roger, A. Le médecin de Molière. Paris, 1878.
Mol 870.30 Hugues, Clovis. Une nuit de Molière. Marseille, 1879.
Mol 870.30.5 Pifteau, B. Molière en province. Paris, 1879.
Mol 870.30.6 Pifteau, B. Molière en province. Paris, 1879.
Mol 870.30.9 Rivet, Gustave. Le cimetière de Saint Joseph. Paris, 1880.
Mol 870.31 Adenis, Eugène. Diogène et Scapin. Paris, 1880.
Mol 870.32 d'Hervilly, E. Poquelin père et fils. Paris, 1881.
Mol 870.33 Fabié, F. Molière et Montespan. Toulon, 1882.
Mol 870.34 Valade, Léon. Les papillotes. Paris, 1883.
Mol 870.35 Bertol-Graivil. Maître et valets. Paris, 1884.
Mol 870.36 Legendre, L. Célimène. Paris, 1885.
Mol 870.37 d'Hervilly, E. Molière en prison. Paris, 1886.
Mol 870.38 Ephraim, A. La première du "Misanthrope". Paris, 1886.
Mol 870.39 Copin, A. Molière chez Conti. Paris, 1886.
Mol 870.40 Moreau, E. Protestation. Paris, 1887.
Mol 870.41 Lambert, A. Une collaboration. Paris, 1888.
Mol 870.42 Tiercelin, L. Le rire de Molière. Paris, 1888.
Mol 870.43 Godin, Eugène. La lyre de Cahors. Paris, 1888.
Mol 870.44 Zidler, G. Le baiser à Molière. Paris, 1889.
Mol 870.45 Bouchinet, A. Le docteur Mascarille. Paris, 1890.
Mol 870.46 Villetard, A. Monsieur Dorine. Paris, 1890.
Mol 870.47 Roger-Milés, L. Alceste converti. Paris, 1891.
Mol 870.48 Augé de Lassus, L. La Saint Jean. Paris, 1893.
Mol 870.48.2 Augé de Lassus, L. Les grands maîtres mis en petites comédies. 2. éd. Paris, 1894.
Mol 870.49 Rengade, J. Novus doctor. Paris, 1894.
Mol 870.50 Lambert, A. Vieux camerades. Paris, 1895.
Mol 870.51 Caristie-Martel. Célimène aux enfers. Paris, 1895.
Mol 870.52 d'Hervilly, E. L'hommage de Flipote. Paris, 1896.
Mol 870.53 Claretie, L. Le prêcheur converti. Paris, 1896.
Mol 870.56 Bertheroy, J. Aristophane et Molière. Paris, 1897.

Mol 870 Works about Molière - Literary works relating to Molière - Anniversary works - Plays - Birth - cont.

Mol 870.57 Croze, J.L. Les bergers de Molière. Paris, 1898.
Mol 870.58 Jubin, G. Molière et Cyrano. Paris, 1899.
Mol 870.59 Des Essarts, E. L'illustre théâtre. Moulins, 1900.
Mol 870.60 Henriquet, S. La voix du rêve. Paris, 1900.
Mol 870.62 Moinaux, G. La conversion d'Alceste. Paris, 1905.
Mol 870.63 Frappa, Jean José. Molière: pièce. Paris, 1922.

Mol 873 Works about Molière - Literary works relating to Molière - Anniversary works - Plays - Death

Mol 873.1 Artaud de Montpellier. Le centenaire de Molière. Paris, 1773.
Mol 873.2 Lebeau de Schosne. L'assemblée comédie. Paris, 1773.
Mol 873.5 Dumersan. La mort de Molière. Paris, 1830.
Mol 873.10 Longhaye, G. Le souper d'Auteuil. Paris, 1864.

Mol 875 Works about Molière - Literary works relating to Molière - Anniversary works - Poetry

Mol 875.1 Rheal, S. La tribune independante. Paris, 1844.
Mol 875.2 Samson, Joseph Isidore. Discours en vers. Paris, 1846.
Mol 875.3F Dingelstedt, F. Zu Molière's Gedachtnissfeier. Wien, 1873.
Mol 875.4 Gondinet, E. A Molière. Paris, 1871.
Mol 875.5 Aicard, J. Mascarille. Paris, 1873.
Mol 875.6 Paté, Lucien. A Molière. Paris, 1876.
Mol 875.7 Joliet, Charles. Molière. Paris, 1879.
Mol 875.8 Cros, Antoine. Ode à Molière. Paris, 1882.
Mol 875.9 Roger-Milés, L. L'Agnès moderne. Paris, 1889.
Mol 875.10 Souza, R. de. Toinette à Molière. Paris, 1890.
Mol 875.11 Bertal, G. Molière. Paris, 1892.
Mol 875.12 Blémont, E. La soubrette de Molière. Paris, 1897.
Mol 875.13 Lefebvre, Henri. La revanche de Thomas Diafoirus. Paris, 1902.

Mol 878 Works about Molière - Literary works relating to Molière - Anniversary works - Prose

Mol 878.1 Geffroy, G. Salut à Molière. Paris, 1899.
Mol 878.3 Academie Française, Paris. Fêtes du tricentenaire de la naissance de Molière. Paris, 1922
Mol 878.5 Modern Languages. Molière tercentenary, special no. v.3. no. 6. London, 1922.
Mol 878.7 Société des Auteurs Dramatiques. Tricentenaire de Molière: recueil des discours. Paris, 1923.
Htn Mol 878.7.3* Société des Auteurs Dramatiques. Tricentenaire de Molière: recueil des discours. Paris, 1923.

Mol 880 Works about Molière - Literary works relating to Molière - Works based on Molière's writings - Plays

Mol 880.1 Dryden, J. Plays from Molière. London, 1883.
Mol 880.1.3 Molière, Jean Baptiste Poquelin. Plays froms Molière, by English dramatists. London, 1889.
Mol 880.1.5 Dryden, J. Plays from Molière. London, 1891.
Htn Mol 880.2* Bordelon, L. La Lotterie de Scapin. Paris, 1838.
Mol 880.3 Cauvet, A. L'ermitage du misanthrope. Paris, 1869.
Mol 880.4 Cénac-Moncaut, J. Avant et pendant. Paris, 1850.
Mol 880.5 Champmesté, C.C. Les fragments de Molière. San Reno, 1874.
Htn Mol 880.5.3* Champmesté, C.C. Les fragments de Molière. Paris, 1682.
Mol 880.6 Chatelain, de. Madame de Tartuffe. London, 1877.
Mol 880.7 Chiari, P. I fanatici. Bologna, 1760.
Mol 880.8 Coluzzi, G. I due Tartufi. Milano, 1855.
Mol 880.9 Calonne, E. de. Le docteur amoureux. Paris, 1862.
Htn Mol 880.11* Corally. M. de Pourceaugnac. Paris, 1826.
Mol 880.13 Cramero, M. Del Molière redivivo. Norimberga, 1723.
Mol 880.14 Daubin. Le Misanthrope travesti. Castres, 1797.
Mol 880.15 Demoustier, C.A. Alceste à la campagne. Paris, 1798.
Mol 880.16 Fabre d'Eglantine, P.F.N. Le Philinte de Molière. Paris, 1802.
Mol 880.17 Scènes du Tartuffe di Gigli. Paris, 1889.
Mol 880.20 Joliet, Charles. Le mariage d'Alceste. Paris, 1874.
Mol 880.21 Jouhaud, A. L'Orgon de Tartuffe. Paris, 1873.
Mol 880.22 Kleist, H. von. Amphitryon. Berlin, n.d.
Mol 880.23 Lubbertze, L. Geadelde Boer. Amsteldam, 1753.
Mol 880.24 Lubbertze, L. De Schynheilige. Amsterdam, 1686.
Mol 880.25 La Boullaye, F. de. Molière au 19e siècle. Paris, 1844.
Mol 880.25.7 Merle. A bas Molière. Paris, 1809.
Mol 880.26 Petit, A. Le Sicilien. Paris, 1827.
Mol 880.27 Querelles, A. de. Le misanthrope politique. Paris, 1846.
Mol 880.28 Richepin, J. Monsieur Scapin. Paris, 1886.
Mol 880.29 Richepin, J. Monsieur Scapin. Paris, 1888.
Mol 880.32 Santini, N. Il conte d'Altamura. Lucca, 1672.
Mol 880.32.5 Smith, Solomon. The hypocrite. N.Y., 18- ?
Mol 880.33 Villars, E. Les précieuses du jour. Paris, 1866.
Mol 880.34 Wood, George. The Irish doctor. London, 1856?
Mol 880.36 Mouton, E. L'affaire Scapin. Paris, 1888.
Mol 880.37 Le Mercier de Neuville. Le sac de Scapin. 3. éd. Paris, 1890.

Mol 882 Works about Molière - Literary works relating to Molière - Works based on Molière's writings - Operas

Mol 882.1 Castil-Blaze. Bernalo, opéra bouffe. Paris, 1856.
Mol 882.2 Castil-Blaze. Don Juan, ou le festin de Pierre. Paris, 1821.
Mol 882.3 Coveliers, F. George Dandin, opéra-comique. Bruxelles, 1877.
Mol 882.4 Monselet, Charles. L'amour médecin. Paris, 1881.
Htn Mol 882.10* Sully. Les festes de l'amour et de Bacchus, Pastorale. Paris, 1682.
Htn Mol 882.15* Rugarli, A. Il figlio de gran Turco. Parma, 1774.
Mol 882.25 Artusi. Teresa vedova. Milano, 1803.

Mol 886 Works about Molière - Literary works relating to Molière - Works based on Molière's writings - Other

Mol 886.1 Coquatrix, E. Alceste. Rouen, 1872.

Mol 900 Works about Molière - Collections - Scrapbooks

Mol 900.1F Molière scrap-book. n.p., n.d.
Mol 900.2F Sarcey et Lanoumet. Chronique théâtrale. Paris, 1879-1902.

Mol 910 Works about Molière - Collections - Programs

Mol 910.1 Pamphlet vol. Cercle français. Molière performances. 10 pam.

Classified Listing

Mol 925 Works about Molière - Collections - Portraits

Htn Mol 925.1PF* Portfolio of Molière portraits. n.p., n.d.
Mol 925.2 Molière en images. n.p., 190-?
Htn Mol 925.7F* French and Co., N.Y. The comedies of Molière; tapestries. N.Y., 1916?

Mon 15 - 20 Complete and Selected works; Essays - French editions - Complete works (By date)

Mon 16.03.5F Montaigne, Michel de. Essays. 1603. Facsimile. Menston, Eng., 1969.
Htn Mon 16.36* Montaigne, Michel de. Essais. Paris, 1636.
Htn Mon 16.40F* Montaigne, Michel de. Essais. Paris, 1640.
Htn Mon 16.52* Montaigne, Michel de. Essais. Paris, 1652.
Mon 16.52.5F Montaigne, Michel de. Essais. Paris, 1652.
Htn Mon 16.57F* Montaigne, Michel de. Essais. Paris, 1657.
Htn Mon 16.57.2F* Montaigne, Michel de. Essais. Paris, 1657.
Htn Mon 16.57.5F* Montaigne, Michel de. Essais. Paris, 1657.
Htn Mon 16.59* Montaigne, Michel de. Essais. Amsterdam, 1659. 3v.
Htn Mon 16.69* Montaigne, Michel de. Essais. Lyon, 1669. 3v.
Htn Mon 16.69.2* Montaigne, Michel de. Essais. v.1-3. Paris, 1669. 6v.
Mon 17.24F Montaigne, Michel de. Essais. Coste. London, 1724. 3v.
Mon 17.25F Montaigne, Michel de. Essais. Coste. Paris, 1725. 3v.
Mon 17.27 Montaigne, Michel de. Essais. Coste. La Haye, 1727. 5v.
Htn Mon 17.39* Montaigne, Michel de. Essais. Coste. 4. ed. London, 1739. 7v.
Mon 17.39.2 Montaigne, Michel de. Essais. Coste. 4. ed. London, 1739. 6v.
Mon 17.54 Montaigne, Michel de. Essais. Coste. London, 1754. 10v.
Mon 17.69 Montaigne, Michel de. Essais. Coste. London, 1769. 10v.
Mon 17.79 Montaigne, Michel de. Essais. Coste. Genève, 1779. 10v.
Htn Mon 17.81* Montaigne, Michel de. Les essais de Michel de Montaigne. Amsterdam, 1781. 3v.
Mon 17.93 Montaigne, Michel de. Essais. Paris, 1793. 3v.
Mon 18.01 Montaigne, Michel de. Essais. Paris, 1801. 16v.
Mon 18.01.5 Montaigne, Michel de. Essais. Paris, 18- . 2v.
Mon 18.02A Montaigne, Michel de. Essais. Naigeon. Paris, 1802. 4v.
Mon 18.02B Montaigne, Michel de. Essais. Naigeon. Paris, 1802. 4v.
Htn Mon 18.02.2* Montaigne, Michel de. Essais. Naigeon. Paris, 1802. 4v.
Mon 18.02.3 Montaigne, Michel de. Essais. Naigeon. Paris, 1802. 5v.
Mon 18.18 Montaigne, Michel de. Essais. Johanneau. Paris, 1818. 5v.
Htn Mon 18.18.2* Montaigne, Michel de. Essais. Johanneau. Paris, 1818. 5v.
Mon 18.18.3 Montaigne, Michel de. Essais. Johanneau. Paris, 1818. 6v.
Mon 18.18.5 Montaigne, Michel de. Essais. Paris, 1818.
Mon 18.19 Montaigne, Michel de. Essais. Paris, 1819. 9v.
Mon 18.20 Montaigne, Michel de. Essais. A. Duval. Paris, 1820-24. 6v.
Mon 18.20.2 Montaigne, Michel de. Essais. A. Duval. Paris, 1820-22. 6v.
Mon 18.20.3 Montaigne, Michel de. Essais. A. Duval. Paris, 1820-22. 5v.
Mon 18.23 Montaigne, Michel de. Essais. Johanneau. Paris, 1823. 5v.
Mon 18.25 Montaigne, Michel de. Essais. Villemain. Paris, 1825. 8v.
Mon 18.26 Montaigne, Michel de. Essais. J.V. Le Clerc. Paris, 1826. 5v.
Mon 18.27 Montaigne, Michel de. Essais. Paris, 1827. 10v.
Mon 18.27.3 Montaigne, Michel de. Essais. A. Duval. Paris, 1827. 6v.
Mon 18.31 Montaigne, Michel de. Essais. Paris, 1831.
Mon 18.36 Montaigne, Michel de. Essais. Paris, 1836.
Mon 18.37 Montaigne, Michel de. Oeuvres. Buchon. Paris, 1837.
Mon 18.43 Montaigne, Michel de. Essais. Paris, 1843.
Mon 18.44 Montaigne, Michel de. Essais. Le Clerc. Paris, 1844. 3v.
Mon 18.54 Montaigne, Michel de. Essais. Louandre. Paris, 1854? 4v.
Mon 18.54.2A Montaigne, Michel de. Essais. Louandre. Paris, 1854. 4v.
Mon 18.54.2B Montaigne, Michel de. Essais. Louandre. Paris, 1854. 4v.
Mon 18.59 Montaigne, Michel de. Essais. Delvau. v.1-2. Paris, 1859.
Mon 18.62 Montaigne, Michel de. Essais. Paris, 1862? 4v.
Mon 18.62.3 Montaigne, Michel de. Essais. Paris, 1862. 4v.
Mon 18.65 Montaigne, Michel de. Essais. Le Clerc. Paris, 1865-66. 4v.
Mon 18.68A Montaigne, Michel de. Essais de Michel de Montaigne. Paris, 1868. 2v.
Mon 18.68B Montaigne, Michel de. Essais de Michel de Montaigne. Paris, 1868. 2v.
Mon 18.70 Montaigne, Michel de. Essais de Michel de Montaigne, Dezeimeris et Barckhausen. Photoreproduction. Bordeaux, 1870-73. 2v.
Mon 18.70.3 Montaigne, Michel de. Essais. Louandre. Paris, 1870-73. 4v.
Mon 18.72A Montaigne, Michel de. Essais. Courbet et Royer. Paris, 1872-1900. 5v.
Mon 18.72B Montaigne, Michel de. Essais. Courbet et Royer. Paris, 1872-1900. 5v.
Mon 18.72.3 Montaigne, Michel de. Essais. v.1-2. Paris, 1872-1900.
Mon 18.73 Montaigne, Michel de. Essais. Motheau et Jouaust. Paris, 1873-75. 4v.
Mon 18.73.2 Montaigne, Michel de. Essais. Motheau et Jouaust. Paris, 1873-75. 4v.
Mon 18.76 Montaigne, Michel de. Essais de Montaigne. Paris, 1876. 4v.
Mon 18.78A Montaigne, Michel de. Essais. Le Clerc. Paris, 1878? 2v.
Mon 18.78B Montaigne, Michel de. Essais. Le Clerc. Paris, 1878? 2v.
Mon 18.78.2 Montaigne, Michel de. Essais. 4. éd. Paris, 187-? 2v.
Mon 18.80.2 Montaigne, Michel de. Essays. 4. ed. London, 1880.
Mon 18.86.2 Montaigne, Michel de. Essais. Motheau et Jouaust. Paris, 1886-89. 7v.

Mon 15 - 20 Complete and Selected works; Essays - French editions - Complete works (By date) - cont.

Mon 18.86.3A Montaigne, Michel de. Essais. Motheau et Jouaust. Paris, 1886-89. 7v.
Mon 18.86.3B Montaigne, Michel de. Essais. Motheau et Jouaust. Paris, 1886-89. 7v.
Mon 18.93 Montaigne, Michel de. Essais, lettres, journal de voyage. 5e éd. Paris, 1893.
Mon 19.06F Montaigne, Michel de. Les essais. Bordeaux, 1906-33. 5v.
Mon 19.06.3F Montaigne, Michel de. Essais. Paris, 1906-31. 3v.
Htn Mon 19.06.5F* Montaigne, Michel de. Essais. v.4. mss. notes. Paris, 1920.
Mon 19.07 Montaigne, Michel de. Essais de Montaigne. Paris, 1907-09. 4v.
Mon 19.22 Montaigne, Michel de. Les essais de Michel de Montaigne. Paris, 1922-23. 3v.
Mon 19.24 Montaigne, Michel de. Essais. Paris, 1924-29. 6v.
Mon 19.28 Montaigne, Michel de. Essais de Messire Michel de Montaigne. Paris, 1927-30. 7v.
Mon 19.28.5 Montaigne, Michel de. Les essais. Paris, 1928? 6v.
Mon 19.30 Montaigne, Michel de. Les essais de Michel de Montaigne. Paris, 1930. 3v.
Mon 19.30.5 Montaigne, Michel de. Essais. Paris, 1930-31. 6v.
Mon 19.31 Montaigne, Michel de. Essais. Livre. Paris, 1931-32. 6v.
Mon 19.31.5 Montaigne, Michel de. Essais. Paris, 1931. 6v.
Mon 19.33 Montaigne, Michel de. Essais. Texte. Argenteuil, 1933.
Mon 19.53 Montaigne, Michel de. Essais. Brie-Comte-Robert, 1953- 3v.
Mon 19.57 Montaigne, Michel de. Essais. Paris, 1957. 5v.
Mon 19.57.5 Montaigne, Michel de. Les essais. Paris, 1957.
Mon 19.60 Montaigne, Michel de. Essais. Paris, 1960.
Mon 19.62 Montaigne, Michel de. Essais. Paris, 1962. 2v.
Mon 19.62.5 Montaigne, Michel de. Oeuvres complètes. Paris, 1962.
Mon 19.62.10 Montaigne, Michel de. Essais. Paris, 1962-63. 5v.
Mon 19.64 Montaigne, Michel de. Essais. v.1; v.2, pt.1-2. Paris, 1964. 3v.
Mon 19.65 Montaigne, Michel de. Les essais. Paris, 1965.
Mon 19.65.5 Montaigne, Michel de. Essais. Paris, 1965. 3v.
Mon 19.69 Montaigne, Michel de. Essais. Paris, 1969. 3v.

Mon 28 Complete and Selected works; Essays - French editions - Selected works

Mon 28.3 Hennet, A.J.U. Pétition à l'Assemblée Nationale. Paris, 1791.
Mon 28.5 Labouderie, J. de. Le Christianisme de Montaigne. Paris, 1819.
Mon 28.9 Catalan, E. Études sur Montaigne. Paris, 1846.
Mon 28.10 Montaigne, Michel de. Essais. Paris, 1847.
Mon 28.14 Montaigne, Michel de. Des vaines subtilitez. Rouen, 1872.
Mon 28.15.5 Montaigne, Michel de. Extraits. Paris, 1883.
Mon 28.16 Réaume, E. Rabelais et Montaigne pédagogues. Paris, 1886.
Mon 28.17 Saucerotte, C. L'esprit de Montaigne. Paris, 1886.
Mon 28.18 Montaigne, Michel de. Extraits. Réaume. Paris, 1888.
Mon 28.18.3 Montaigne, Michel de. Extraits. Réaume. Paris, 1894.
Htn Mon 28.18.5* Montaigne, Michel de. De l'institution des enfants. Cambridge, 18- .
Mon 28.19 Montaigne, Michel de. De l'institution des enfants. Paris, 1889.
Mon 28.20 Montaigne, Michel de. Essais. Paris, 1893.
Mon 28.21 Montaigne, Michel de. Les essais. Paris, 1893.
Mon 28.22 La Brière, L. de. Montaigne chrétien. Paris, 1894.
Mon 28.23 Montaigne, Michel de. Extraits. Klein. Paris, 1895.
Mon 28.24 Montaigne, Michel de. Pages choisies. Thiery. Paris, 1896.
Mon 28.25A Montaigne, Michel de. Selections from Montaigne. Wright. Boston, 1914.
Mon 28.25B Montaigne, Michel de. Selections from Montaigne. Wright. Boston, 1914.
Mon 28.26 Montaigne, Michel de. Oeuvres choisis. Radouant. Paris, 1914.
Mon 28.27A Montaigne, Michel de. Textes choisis. Paris, 1912.
Mon 28.27B Montaigne, Michel de. Textes choisis. Paris, 1912.
Mon 28.30 Montaigne, Michel de. Montaigne. Preface de Anatole France. Paris, 1922.
Mon 28.35 Montaigne, Michel de. De l'institution des enfants. Paris, 1924.
Mon 28.37 Montaigne, Michel de. L'esprit de Montaigne. Londres, 1783. 2v.
Mon 28.38 Montaigne, Michel de. L'esprit de Montaigne. Paris, 1829.
Mon 28.40 Montaigne, Michel de. Les essais de Michel de Montaigne. Paris, 1929.
Mon 28.41 Montaigne, Michel de. L'apologie de Raymond Sebond. Thèse. Paris, 1937.
Mon 28.42 Montaigne, Michel de. L'apologie de Raymond Sebond. Paris, 1937.
Mon 28.45 Montaigne, Michel de. Discours de la servitude volontaire, lettres, éphémérides, notes marginales. Paris, 1939.
Mon 28.48A Montaigne, Michel de. Les pages immortelles de Montaigne. Paris, 1939.
Mon 28.48B Montaigne, Michel de. Les pages immortelles de Montaigne. Paris, 1939.
Mon 28.50 Montaigne, Michel de. Trois essais. Paris, 1947.
Mon 28.50.5 Montaigne, Michel de. Trois essais. Paris, 1951.
Mon 28.52 Montaigne, Michel de. De la vanité; essai. Paris, 1947.
Mon 28.54 Montaigne, Michel de. Annotations sur les annales de Nicole Gills. Paris, 1941.
Mon 28.56 Montaigne, Michel de. Du pedantisme. Paris, 1936.
Mon 28.58 Montaigne, Michel de. Des livres. Paris, 1936.
Mon 28.58.5 Montaigne, Michel de. Om böcker. Stockholm, 1960.
Mon 28.60 Montaigne, Michel de. Montaigne par lui-même. Paris, 1951.
Mon 28.62 Montaigne, Michel de. Selected works. N.Y., 1953.
Mon 28.64 Montaigne, Michel de. Sagesse de Montaigne. Paris, 1957.

Mon 30 Complete and Selected works; Essays - Translations - English - Florio

Htn Mon 30.1* Montaigne, Michel de. Essayes. Florio. London, 1603.
Htn Mon 30.2* Montaigne, Michel de. Essayes. Florio. London, 1613.
Htn Mon 30.3* Montaigne, Michel de. Essayes. Florio. 3. ed. London, 1632.
Mon 30.5 Montaigne, Michel de. Essayes. Florio (Morley). London, 1886.
Htn Mon 30.5.2* Montaigne, Michel de. Essays. Florio (Morley). London, 1886.
Htn Mon 30.6* Montaigne, Michel de. Essayes. McCarthy. London, 1889. 2v.
Mon 30.7 Montaigne, Michel de. The essayes of Michael Lord of Montaigne. Florio. London, 1891.

Mon 30 Complete and Selected works; Essays - Translations - English - Florio - cont.

Mon 30.8A Montaigne, Michel. Essays. Florio (Saintsbury). London, 1892-93. 3v.
Mon 30.8B Montaigne, Michel. Essays. Florio (Saintsbury). London, 1892-93. 3v.
Mon 30.8C Montaigne, Michel. Essays. Florio (Saintsbury). London, 1892-93. 3v.
Mon 30.9 Montaigne, Michel de. Essays. Florio (Chubb). London, 1893.
Mon 30.10A Montaigne, Michel de. Essays. Florio. London, 1897. 5v.
Mon 30.10B Montaigne, Michel de. Essays. Florio. London, 1897. 5v.
Mon 30.10C Montaigne, Michel de. Essays. Florio. v.1,3. London, 1897. 2v.
Mon 30.10.3A Montaigne, Michel de. Essays. Florio. v.2-6. London, 1898. 5v.
Mon 30.10.3B Montaigne, Michel de. Essays. Florio. v.3. London, 1898.
Mon 30.10.15 Montaigne, Michel de. Essays of Montaigne. London, 190-?
Mon 30.11F Montaigne, Michel de. Essays. Florio. Boston, 1902-04. 3v.
Mon 30.12 Montaigne, Michel de. Essayes. Florio. v.1-6. London, 1603-06. 3v.
Mon 30.13 Montaigne, Michel de. Essays. Florio. N.Y., 1907.
Mon 30.14 Montaigne, Michel de. Essays. Florio. London, 1908. 3v.
Mon 30.15 Montaigne, Michel de. Essays. London, 1915.
Mon 30.16A Montaigne, Michel de. Essays. London, 1910. 3v.
Mon 30.16B Montaigne, Michel de. Essays. London, 1910 2v.
Mon 30.16.3 Montaigne, Michel de. Essays. London, 1923. 3v.
Mon 30.16.7 Montaigne, Michel de. Essays of Michael lord of Montaigne. London, 1928. 3v.
Mon 30.28 Montaigne, Michel de. Essays. v.1,3. London, 1928. 2v.
Mon 30.31 Montaigne, Michel de. Essays. Florio. London, 1931. 2v.
Mon 30.33A Montaigne, Michel de. Essayes. N.Y., 1933.
Mon 30.33B Montaigne, Michel de. Essayes. N.Y., 1933.
Mon 30.64 Montaigne, Michel de. Selected essays of Montaigne. Boston, 1964.
Mon 30.80 Dieckow, F. John Florio's Englische Übersetzung Montaignes. Strasburg, 1903.

Mon 31 Complete and Selected works; Essays - Translations - English - Cotton

Htn Mon 31.1* Montaigne, Michel de. Essays. Cotton. London, 1685-86. 3v.
Mon 31.2 Montaigne, Michel de. Essays of Michael seigneur de Montaigne. London, 1685-86.
Htn Mon 31.3* Montaigne, Michel de. Essays. London, 1693. 3v.
Mon 31.6 Montaigne, Michel de. Essays. Cotton. 6. ed. London, 1743. 3v.
Htn Mon 31.7* Montaigne, Mcihel de. Essays. Cotton. 7. ed. London, 1759. 3v.
Mon 31.8 Montaigne, Michel de. Essays. Cotton. 8. ed. London, 1776. 3v.
Mon 31.12 Montaigne, Michel de. Essays. Cotton. 3. ed. London, 1869.
Mon 31.13A Montaigne, Michel de. Essays. Cotton. 3. ed. London, 1870.
Mon 31.13B Montaigne, Michel de. Essays. Cotton. 3. ed. London, 1870.
Mon 31.25 Montaigne, Michel de. Works. Hazlitt. London, 1842.
Mon 31.25.2 Montaigne, Michel de. Works. Hazlitt. 2. ed. London, 1845.
Mon 31.26 Montaigne, Michel de. Works. Hazlitt. London, 1865.
Mon 31.28 Montaigne, Michel de. Works. Philadelphia, 1850.
Mon 31.30 Montaigne, Michel de. Works...essays, letters...journey through Germany and Italy. 4. ed. Philadelphia, 1856.
Mon 31.31 Montaigne, Michel de. Works. Hazlitt (Wight). v.1,3,4. N.Y., 1861. 3v.
Mon 31.32A Montaigne, Michel de. Works. v.1,3,4. Boston, 1862. 3v.
Mon 31.32B Montaigne, Michel de. Works. v.1,3,4. Boston, 1862. 3v.
Mon 31.35 Montaigne, Michel de. Works. Hazlitt (Wight). N.Y., 1866. 4v.
Mon 31.37 Montaigne, Michel de. Works. Boston, 1879-80. 4v.
Mon 31.37.9 Montaigne, Michel de. Works. Wight. Boston, 1887. 4v.
Mon 31.40A Montaigne, Michel de. Essays. Cotton (Hazlitt). London, 1877. 3v.
Mon 31.40B Montaigne, Michel de. Essays. Cotton (Hazlitt). London, 1877. 3v.
Mon 31.40.2 Montaigne, Michel de. Essays. Cotton (Hazlitt). London, 1877. 3v.
Mon 31.42 Montaigne, Michel de. Essays. Hazlitt. v.1-2. N.Y., 1894?
Mon 31.43A Montaigne, Michel de. Essays. Cotton (Hazlitt). London, 1902. 4v.
Mon 31.43B Montaigne, Michel de. Essays. Cotton (Hazlitt). London, 1902. 4v.
Mon 31.43C Montaigne, Michel de. Essays. Cotton (Hazlitt). London, 1902. 4v.
Mon 31.44 Montaigne, Michel de. Selected essays. Cotton. N.Y., 1903.
Mon 31.46 Montaigne, Michel de. Essays. Cotton. London, 1905. 3v.
Mon 31.50 Montaigne, Michel de. Essays. Cotton (Hazlitt). 2. ed. London, 1911. 3v.
Mon 31.50.1 Montaigne, Michel de. Essays. Cotton (Hazlitt). N.Y., 1949.

Mon 32 Complete and Selected works; Essays - Translations - English - Other translators

Mon 32.5.3 Montaigne, Michel de. Essays. 2. ed. London, 1869.
Mon 32.6 Montaigne, Michel de. Education of children. N.Y., 1899.
Mon 32.7 Montaigne, Michel de. Montaigne's essay on friendship. Boston, 1915.
Mon 32.20 Montaigne, Michel de. Love and marriage, being Montaigne's essay "Sur des vers de Virgil". Florence, 192-?
Mon 32.25A Montaigne, Michel de. Essays. Cambridge, 1925. 4v.
Mon 32.25B Montaigne, Michel de. Essays. Cambridge, 1925. 4v.
Htn Mon 32.25.2* Montaigne, Michel de. Essays. Cambridge, 1925. 4v.
Mon 32.34 Montaigne, Michel de. Selected essays. Manchester, 1934.
Mon 32.34.3 Montaigne, Michel de. Selected essays. 2. ed. Manchester, 1948.
Mon 32.34.5 Montaigne, Michel de. Essays. N.Y., 1934-36. 3v.
Mon 32.35A Montaigne, Michel de. The autobiography...selected...by M. Lowenthal. Boston, 1935.

Mon 32 Complete and Selected works; Essays - Translations - English - Other translators - cont.

Mon 32.35B Montaigne, Michel de. The autobiography...selected...by M. Lowenthal. Boston, 1935.
Mon 32.35C Montaigne, Michel de. The autobiography...selected...by M. Lowenthal. Boston, 1935.
Mon 32.37 Montaigne, Michel de. Essays. 9. ed. London, 1811. 3v.
Mon 32.39 Montaigne, Michel de. The living thoughts of Montaigne. 1. ed. N.Y., 1939.
Mon 32.43 Montaigne, Michel de. Selected essays. N.Y., 1943.
Mon 32.46 Montaigne, Michel de. The essays of Montaigne. N.Y., 1946.
Mon 32.47 Montaigne, Michel de. The essays of Michel de Montaigne. N.Y., 1947. 3v.
Mon 32.48 Montaigne, Michel de. Essays. Hillesborough, Calif., 1948.
Mon 32.50 Montaigne, Michel de. Selected essays. N.Y., 1959.
Mon 32.57A Montaigne, Michel de. The complete works of Montaigne. Stanford, 1957.
Mon 32.57B Montaigne, Michel de. The complete works of Montaigne. Stanford, 1957.
Mon 32.58 Montaigne, Michel de. Complete works. London, 1958.
Mon 32.59 Montaigne, Michel de. Essays. Harmondsworth, 1959.
Mon 32.65 Montaigne, Michel de. Complete essays. Stanford, 1965.

Mon 35 Complete and Selected works; Essays - Translations - German

Mon 35.2 Montaigne, Michel de. Gedanken. Berlin, 1793-99. 7v.
Mon 35.5 Montaigne, Michel de. Essays. Breslau, 1896.
Mon 35.5.2 Montaigne, Michel de. Essays. Breslau, 1898.
Mon 35.6 Montaigne, Michel de. Die Essais und das Raisetagebuch. Stuttgart, 1948.
Mon 35.9 Montaigne, Michel de. Versuche. Berlin, 1908.
Mon 35.10 Montaigne, Michel de. Gesammelte Schriften. München, 1908. 8v.

Mon 37 Complete and Selected works; Essays - Translations - Italian

Htn Mon 37.5* Montaigne, Michel de. Discorsi morali politici et militari. Ferrara, 1590.
Htn Mon 37.25* Montaigne, Michel de. Saggi, overo Discorsi. Venetia, 1633.
Mon 37.50 Montaigne, Michel de. Saggi scetti. Torino, 1931.
Mon 37.60 Montaigne, Michel de. Saggi, a cura di Fausta Garavini. Milano, 1966. 2v.

Mon 39 Complete and Selected works; Essays - Translations - Other languages

Mon 39.5 Montaigne, Michel de. Páginas escogidas. Madrid, 1917.
Mon 39.10 Montaigne, Michel de. Ensayos. Buenos Aires, 1941. 4v.
Mon 39.50 Montaigne, Michel de. Opyty. 2. izd. Moskva, 1958. 3v.

Mon 45 Other writings by Montaigne - Journal de Voyage en Italie - Complete editions in French

Mon 45.1F Montaigne, Michel de. Journal du voyage. Rome, 1774.
Mon 45.1.2F Montaigne, Michel de. Journal du voyage. Rome, 1774.
Mon 45.3 Montaigne, Michel de. Journal du voyage. Querlon. Rome, 1774. 3v.
Mon 45.5A Montaigne, Michel de. Journal du voyage. Ancona. Castello, 1889.
Mon 45.5B Montaigne, Michel de. Journal du voyage. Ancona. Castello, 1889.
Mon 45.9 Montaigne, Michel de. Journal du voyage. Laritrey. Paris, 1906.
Mon 45.10 Montaigne, Michel de. L'Italia alla fine del secolo XVI. Lapi, 1895.
Mon 45.15 Montaigne, Michel de. Journal de voyage en Italie par la Suisse et l'Allemagne. Paris, 1932.
Mon 45.20 Montaigne, Michel de. Journal de voyage en Italie. Paris, 1928-29. 2v.
Mon 45.22 Montaigne, Michel de. Journal de voyage en Italie. Paris, 1942.
Mon 45.24 Montaigne, Michel de. Journal de voyage en Italie. Paris, 1946.
Mon 45.25 Montaigne, Michel de. Journal de voyage de Michel Seigneur de Montaigne. Paris, 1931.
Mon 45.26 Montaigne, Michel de. Journal de voyage en Italie par la Suisse et l'Allemagne. Paris, 1948.

Mon 50 Other writings by Montaigne - Journal de Voyage en Italie - Translations - English

Mon 50.1 Montaigne, Michel de. Journal. Waters. London, 1903. 3v.
Mon 50.29 Montaigne, Michel de. The diary of Montaigne's journey to Italy in 1580 and 1581. London, 1929.
Mon 50.30A Montaigne, Michel de. The diary of Montaigne's journey to Italy in 1580 and 1581. N.Y., 1929.
Mon 50.30B Montaigne, Michel de. The diary of Montaigne's journey to Italy in 1580 and 1581. N.Y., 1929.

Mon 55 Other writings by Montaigne - Journal de Voyage en Italie - Translations - Italian

Mon 55.5 Montaigne, Michel de. Giornale del viaggio di Michel de Montaigne in Italia. Firenze, 1958. 3v.

Mon 59 Other writings by Montaigne - Journal de Voyage en Italie - Criticism

Mon 59.7 Dedeyan, Charles. Essai sur le Journal de voyage de Montaigne. Paris, 1944.
Mon 59.10 Buffum, Imbrie. L'influence du voyage de Montaigne sur les essais. Diss. Princeton, 1946.

Mon 68 Other writings by Montaigne - Letters - Selections in French

Mon 68.3 Jubinal, A. Une lettre inédite de Montaigne. Paris, 1850.
Mon 68.3.4 Jubinal, A. Une lettre inedite de Montaigne. 2. éd. Paris, 1850.
Mon 68.3.6 Jubinal, A. Henri IV et Montaigne; lettre. 3. éd. Paris, 1873.
Mon 68.4 Lepelle de Bois-Gallais, Frédéric. Encore une lettre inédite de Montaigne. London, 1850.
Mon 68.6 Feuillet de Conches, F. Réponse...touchant une lettre. v.1-2. Paris, 1851.
Mon 68.6.5 Feuillet de Conches, F. Lettres inédites de Montaigne. Paris, 1863.
Mon 68.8 Du Boys, E. Une nouvelle lettre de Montaigne. Paris, 1886.

Mon 80 Other writings by Montaigne - Montaigne's translation of Raymond de Sebonde - Editions

Htn	Mon 80.1*	Sabunde, Ramón. La theologie naturelle. Paris, 1569.
Htn	Mon 80.2*	Sabunde, Ramón. La theologie naturelle. Paris, 1581.
Htn	Mon 80.50*	Norton, Grace. Lexique to the Theologie naturelle of Raymond Sebond. n.p., n.d. 3v.

Mon 82 Other writings by Montaigne - Montaigne's translation of Raymond de Sebonde - Criticism

	Mon 82.1	Compayre, G. De Ramundo Sebundo. Paris, 1872.
	Mon 82.2	Coppin, Joseph Leon. Montaigne. Thèse. Lille, 1925.
	Mon 82.2.1	Coppin, Joseph Leon. Montaigne. Lille, 1925.

Mon 88 Other writings by Montaigne - Montaigne's edition of Etienne de la Boetie - Criticism

	Mon 88.1	Monthizon, J. Étude sur la vie et l'oeuvre de la Boetie. Paris, 1852- 5 pam.
	Mon 88.2	Feugère, L. Etienne de la Boetie, ami de Montaigne. Paris, 1845.
	Mon 88.3	Payen, J.F. Notice bio-bibliographique sur la Boetie. Paris, 1853.
	Mon 88.3.2	Payen, J.F. Notice bio-bibliographique sur la Boetie. Paris, 1853.
	Mon 88.3.3	Payen, J.F. Notice bio-bibliographique sur la Boetie. Paris, 1853.

Mon 100 Works about Montaigne - Periodicals

	Mon 100.15	Amis de Montaigne. Bulletin. Paris. 1,1937+ 9v.

Mon 105 Works about Montaigne - Reference works - Bibliographies

	Mon 105.1	Pamphlet vol. Bibliography of Montaigne. 7 pam.
	Mon 105.3	Tannenbaum, Samuel A. Michel Eyquem de Montaigne. N.Y., 1942.
Htn	Mon 105.5*	Payen, J.F. Notice bibliographique sur Montaigne. Paris, 1837.
	Mon 105.6	Paris. Bibliothèque National. Inventaire de la collection sur Montaigne. Paris, 1878.
	Mon 105.7F	Ives, G.B. Bibliography of the essays. Boston, 1902-04.
	Mon 105.8	Payen, J.F. Inventaire de la collection sur M. de Montaigne. Bordeaux, 1877.
	Mon 105.10	Armaingand, A. Bibliothèque du Dr. A. Armaingand. Paris, 1927.

Mon 108 Works about Montaigne - Reference works - Dictionaries, encyclopedias, etc.

	Mon 108.3	Spalikowski, E. Dictionnaire medical de Montaigne. Paris, 1897.
Htn	Mon 108.5F*	Norton, Grace. Lexique de la langue de Montaigne. Cambridge, 1912. 5v.
Htn	Mon 108.7F*	Norton, Grace. Lexique de la langue de Montaigne. Cambridge, 1912. 3v.
Htn	Mon 108.8F*	Norton, Grace. Index of the names in Montaigne's essays. Cambridge, 1912.
	Mon 108.9	Marcu, Eva. Répertoire des idées de Montaigne. Genève, 1965.

Mon 110 Works about Montaigne - General critical works - Pamphlet volumes

	Mon 110.1	Villemain, Abel Francois. Eloge de Montaigne. Paris, 1812. 6 pam.
	Mon 110.2	Pamphlet vol. Montaigne. Literary criticism. 6 pam.
	Mon 110.3	Pamphlet vol. Philosophy of Montaigne. 5 pam.
	Mon 110.4	Pamphlet vol. Notices sur Montaigne. 3 pam.
	Mon 110.5F	Pamphlet vol. Montaigne. Miscellanea. 7 pam.
	Mon 110.6	Pamphlet box. Montaigne. Miscellaneous pamphlets.

Mon 111 - 136 Works about Montaigne - General critical works - Monographs (A-Z)

	Mon 111.1	Armaingand, A. Montaigne Pamphlétaire. Paris, 1910.
	Mon 112.1	Bourdic-Viot, H. Eloge de Montaigne. Paris, 1800?
	Mon 112.2	Bigorie de Laschamps, F. Michel de Montaigne. Paris, 1860.
	Mon 112.3	Bimbent, J.E. Essais de Montaigne. Paris, 1863.
	Mon 112.3.3	Bimbent, J.E. Essais de Montaigne. Orleans, 1864.
	Mon 112.4	Bachus, H. Essai sur les "Essais" de Montaigne. Linz, 1870.
	Mon 112.5	Bruns, Ivo. Montaigne und die Alten. Kiel, 1898.
	Mon 112.6	Bailey, W.H. Shakespeare and Montaigne. Manchester, 1895.
Htn	Mon 112.7*	Brunet, G. Les essais de Michel de Montaigne. Paris, 1844.
	Mon 112.7.5	Brunet, G. Les essais de Michel de Montaigne. Paris, 1844.
	Mon 112.8	Bond, R.W. Montaigne. London, 1906.
	Mon 112.9	Bouillier, Victor. La renommée de Montaigne en Allemagne. Paris, 1921.
	Mon 112.9.5	Bouillier, Victor. La fortune de Montaigne en Italie et en Espagne. Paris, 1922.
	Mon 112.10	Belleli, M.L. Modernita di Montaigne. Roma, 1933.
	Mon 112.11	Billeskov Jansen, F.J. Sources vives de la pensée de Montaigne. Copenhague, 1935.
	Mon 112.12	Boase, Alan Martin. The fortunes of Montaigne. London, 1935.
	Mon 112.12.1	Boase, Alan Martin. The fortunes of Montaigne. N.Y., 1970.
	Mon 112.13	Blasberg, H. Die Wortstellung bei Montaigne. Inaug. Diss. Bochum-Langendreer, 1937.
	Mon 112.14	Brunschvicq, L. Descartes et Pascal; lectures de Montaigne. N.Y., 1944.
	Mon 112.16	Brown, F.S. Religious and political conservatism. Geneva, 1963.
	Mon 112.17	Batisse, F. Montaigne et la médicine. Paris, 1962.
	Mon 112.18	Bowman, Frank Paul. Montaigne: Essays. London, 1965.
	Mon 112.19	Brush, Craig B. Montaigne and Bayle. The Hague, 1966.
	Mon 112.20	Buton, Michel. Essais sur "les Essais". Paris, 1968.
	Mon 112.21	Baraz, Michaël. L'etre et la connaissance selon Montaigne. Paris, 1968.
	Mon 112.22	Battista, Anna Maria. Alle origini del pensiero politico libertino: Montaigne e Charron. Milano, 1966.
	Mon 113.2	Champion, E. Introduction aux essais de Montaigne. Paris, 1900.
	Mon 113.3	Compayré, G. Montaigne and education of the judgement. N.Y., 1908.
	Mon 113.4	Cancalon. L'esprit positif et scientifique dans Montaigne. Paris, 1911.
	Mon 113.5	Coppin, Joseph. Étude sur la grammaire et le vocabulaire de Montaigne. Thèse. Lille, 1925.
	Mon 113.5.3	Coppin, Joseph. Étude sur le grammaire et le vocabulaire de Montaigne. Lille, 1925.
	Mon 113.10A	Cresson, Andre. Montaigne. Paris, 1947.

Mon 111 - 136 Works about Montaigne - General critical works - Monographs (A-Z) - cont.

	Mon 113.10B	Cresson, Andre. Montaigne. Paris, 1947.
	Mon 113.15A	Citoleux, Marc. Le vrai Montaigne, théologien et soldat. Paris, 1937.
	Mon 113.15B	Citoleux, Marc. Le vrai Montaigne, théologien et soldat. Paris, 1937.
	Mon 113.18	Château, Jean. Montaigne, psychologie et pédagogue. Paris, 1964.
	Mon 113.20	Conche, Marcel. Montaigne, ou La conscience heureuse. Paris, 1964.
	Mon 114.1	DuRoure, Auguste F.L.S.G. Eloge de Montaigne. Paris, 1812.
	Mon 114.2	Dutens, J. Eloge de Michel de Montaigne. Paris, 1818.
	Mon 114.3	Dumont, L. La morale de Montaigne. Valenciennes, 1866.
	Mon 114.4	Dezeimeris, R. Recherches sur la texte des essais. Bordeaux, 1866.
	Mon 114.5	Dembski, M. Montaigne und Voiture. Greifswald, 1888.
	Mon 114.7.5	Dréano, M. La renommée de Montaigne en France au XVIII siècle. Angers, 1952.
	Mon 114.9	Dow, N. The concept and term "nature" in Montaigne's essays. Philadelphia, 1940.
	Mon 114.10	Dédéyan, C. Montaigne chez ses amis Anglo-Saxons. Paris, 1944? 2v.
	Mon 114.10.2	Dédéyan, C. Montaigne dans le romantisme Anglo-Saxon. Thèse. v.1-2. Paris, 1943.
	Mon 114.12	Dresden, Samuel. Montaigne, de spelende wijsgeer. Leiden, 1952.
	Mon 114.14	Duhamel, Roger. Lecture de Montaigne. Ottawa, 1965.
	Mon 115.1	Espezel, Pierre d'. Presence et actualité de Montaigne. Paris, 1957.
	Mon 116.1	Feis, Jacob. Shakespeare and Montaigne. London, 1884.
	Mon 116.2	Favre, J. (Mrs.). Montaigne, moraliste et pedagogue. Paris, 1887.
	Mon 116.3	Fabre, M.J.J.V. Eloge de Michel de Montaigne. Paris, 1812.
	Mon 116.3.2	Fabre, M.J.J.V. Eloge de Michel de Montaigne. Paris, 1812.
	Mon 116.35	Faure, Élie. Montaigne et ses trois premiers-nés. Paris, 1926.
	Mon 116.40	Frame, Donald Murdoch. Montaigne in France, 1812-1852. N.Y., 1940.
	Mon 116.42	Frame, Donald Murdoch. Montaigne's discovery of man. N.Y., 1955.
	Mon 116.43	Frame, Donald Murdoch. Montaigne's Essais; a study. Englewood Cliffs, N.J., 1969.
	Mon 116.45	Friedrich, Hugo. Montaigne. Bern, 1949.
Htn	Mon 116.45.5*	Friedrich, Hugo. Montaigne. Paris, 1968.
	Mon 116.50	Friedenthal, Richard. Entdecker des Ich. München, 1969.
	Mon 117.1	Grimm, F.M. de. Voyages et essais de Montaigne. Cahors, 1883.
	Mon 117.2	Georgov, Ivan. Montaigne als vertreter des Relativismus. Leipzig, 1889.
	Mon 117.3	Guizot, G. Montaigne, etudes et fragments. Paris, 1899.
	Mon 117.4	Gauthiez, P. Etudes sur le XVIe siècle. Paris, 1893.
	Mon 117.6	Gracey, P. Montaigne et la poésie. Thèse. Paris, 1935.
	Mon 117.7	Gray, Floyd. Le style de Montaigne. Paris, 1958.
	Mon 118.1	Henning, A. Skepticismus Montaignes. Jena, 1879-81. 2 pam.
	Mon 118.2	Herzberg, Curt. Die skeptischen, naturalischen und rigoristischen Elemente in Montaignes ethischen Anschauugen. Inaug. Diss. Leipzig, 1904.
	Mon 120.1	Jay, Antoine. Eloge de Montaigne. Paris, 1812.
NEDL	Mon 120.2	Jeudy, R. De l'education dans Rabelais et dans Montaigne. Paris, 1874-88. 3 pam.
	Mon 120.5	Jenzer, Carlo. Lebensnahe, Lebensferne und Realismus in den pädagogischen Ansichten von Michel de Montaigne. Bern, 1969.
	Mon 121.1	Kühn, Emil. Die Bedeutung Montaignes für unsere Zeit. Strassburg, 1904.
	Mon 122.1	Bricaire de la Dixmerie, Nicolas. Eloge analytique historique de Montaigne. Amsterdam, 1781.
	Mon 122.2	LeClerc, J.V. Eloge de Messire Michel, seigneur de Montaigne. Paris, 1812.
	Mon 122.3	Leveaux, A. Etude sur les essais de Montaigne. Paris, 1870.
	Mon 122.10	LaCharité, Raymond C. The concept of judgment in Montaigne. The Hague, 1968.
	Mon 122.12	Lablénie, Edmond. Essais sur Montaigne. Paris, 1967.
	Mon 123.1	Mazure, F.A.J. Eloge de Montaigne. Angers, 1814.
	Mon 123.2	Moët, E. Des opinions et des jugements litteraires. Auch, 1859.
Htn	Mon 123.2.2*	Moët, E. Des opinions et des jugements litteraires. Auch, 1859.
	Mon 123.4F	Memoires pour servir aux essais. London, 1741.
	Mon 123.5	Michaut, G. Montaigne: De la vanité. Paris, 1938.
	Mon 123.6	Moreau, P. Montaigne; l'homme et l'oeuvre. Paris, 1939.
	Mon 123.7	Micha, Alexandre. Le singulier Montaigne. Paris, 1964.
	Mon 123.8	Metschies, Michael. Zitat und Zitier Kunst in Montaignes Essais. Genève, 1966.
	Mon 123.9	Michel, Pierre. Montaigne. Bourdeaux, 1969[1970]
	Mon 124.1A	Norton, Grace. Early writings of Montaigne. N.Y., 1904.
	Mon 124.1B	Norton, Grace. Early writings of Montaigne. N.Y., 1904.
	Mon 124.1C	Norton, Grace. Early writings of Montaigne. N.Y., 1904.
	Mon 124.1.5A	Norton, Grace. Studies in Montaigne. N.Y., 1904.
	Mon 124.1.5B	Norton, Grace. Studies in Montaigne. N.Y., 1904.
	Mon 124.1.5C	Norton, Grace. Studies in Montaigne. N.Y., 1904.
	Mon 124.1.5D	Norton, Grace. Studies in Montaigne. N.Y., 1904.
	Mon 124.1.6A	Norton, Grace. Le plutarque de Montaigne. Boston, 1906.
	Mon 124.1.6B	Norton, Grace. Le plutarque de Montaigne. Boston, 1906.
	Mon 124.1.6C	Norton, Grace. Le plutarque de Montaigne. Boston, 1906.
	Mon 124.1.7A	Norton, Grace. Montaigne (influence of). Boston, 1908.
	Mon 124.1.7B	Norton, Grace. Montaigne (influence of). Boston, 1908.
	Mon 124.1.7C	Norton, Grace. Montaigne (influence of). Boston, 1908.
	Mon 124.1.8A	Norton, Grace. The spirit of Montaigne. Boston, 1908.
	Mon 124.1.8B	Norton, Grace. The spirit of Montaigne. Boston, 1908.
	Mon 124.1.8C	Norton, Grace. The spirit of Montaigne. Boston, 1908.
	Mon 125.1	Owen, John. Skeptics of the French Renaissance. London, 1893.
	Mon 126.2	Peyre, Albert. Du prestige de la pensée. Paris, 1936.
	Mon 126.5	Papic, Marko. L'expression et la place du sujet dans les Essais de Montaigne. 1. éd. Paris, 1970.
	Mon 126.10	Povilloux, Jean Yves. Lire les essais de Montaigne. Paris, 1969.
	Mon 128.2	Ruel, E. Du sentiment artistique dans la morale de Montaigne. Paris, 1901.
	Mon 128.3	Rey-Pailhade, E. de. Montaigne philosophie-moraliste, étude. Toulouse, 1912.

Mon 111 - 136 (A-Z) - cont. **Works about Montaigne - General critical works - Monographs**

Mon 128.4 Rech, Bruno. Grundbegriffe und Wertbegriffe bei Michel de Montaigne. Inaug. Diss. Berlin, 1931.
Mon 128.4.5 Rech, Bruno. Grundbegriffe und Wertbegriffe bei Michel de Montaigne. Inaug. Diss. Berlin, 1934.
Mon 128.5 Renart, F. Zigzags dans les parterres de Montaigne. Paris, 1951.
Mon 128.6 Revel, Bruno. Verso un saggio di Montaigne. Varese, 1950.
Mon 129.1 Stapfer, P. Montaigne. Paris, 1895.
Mon 129.1.2 Stapfer, P. Montaigne. Paris, 1895.
Mon 129.2 Schwabe, P. Michel de Montaigne als philosophischer Charakter. Hamburg, 1899.
Mon 129.3 Strowski, F. Montaigne. Paris, 1906.
Mon 129.4A Sichel, E. Michel de Montaigne. N.Y., 1911.
Mon 129.4B Sichel, E. Michel de Montaigne. N.Y., 1911.
Mon 129.5 Sclafert, C. L'ame religieuse de Montaigne. Paris, 1951.
Mon 129.6 Schon, Peter M. Vorformen des Essays in Antike und Humanismus. Wiesbaden, 1954.
Mon 130.1 Talbert, François Xavier. Eloge de Michel de Montaigne. Londres, 1775.
Mon 130.2 Thimme, Hermann. Der Skepticismus Montaigne's. Inaug. Diss. Gottingen, 1875.
Mon 130.3 Tauro, Giacomo. Montaigne. Milano, 1928.
Mon 130.4 Tavera, François. L'idée d'humanité dans Montaigne. Paris, 1932.
Mon 130.5.4 Toffanir, Giuseppe. Montaigne e l'idea classica. 2. ed. Bologna, 1942.
Mon 130.6 Traeger, Wolf. Aufban und Gedankenführung in Montaignes Essays. Heidelberg, 1961.
Mon 130.7 Thibandet, A. Montaigne. Paris, 1963.
Mon 132.1 Vernier, T. Notices et observations. Paris, 1810. 2v.
Mon 132.3 Vincens, E. Eloge de Michel de Montaigne. Paris, 1812.
Mon 132.4 Voizard, E. Etude sur la langue de Montaigne. Thèse. Paris, 1885.
Mon 132.4.5 Voizard, E. Etude sur la langue de Montaigne. Photoreproduction. Paris, 1885.
Mon 132.5 Villey, P. Les livres d'histoire moderne utilisés par Montaigne. Thèse. Paris, 1908.
Mon 132.5.2 Villey, P. Les livres d'histoire moderne utilisés par Montaigne. Paris, 1908.
Mon 132.5.5 Villey, P. Les sources et l'évolution des essais de Montaigne. v.1-2. Thèse. Paris, 1908.
NEDL Mon 132.5.6 Villey, P. Les sources et l'évolution des essais de Montaigne. Paris, 1908.
Mon 132.5.7 Villey, P. Montaigne a-t-il en quelque influence sur François Bacon? Paris, 1911-12.
Mon 132.5.9A Villey, P. L'influence de Montaigne...de Locke. Paris, 1911.
Mon 132.5.9B Villey, P. L'influence de Montaigne...de Locke. Paris, 1911.
Mon 132.5.10 Villey, P. Montaigne a-t-il lu le traité de l'education de J. Sadolet? Paris, 1909.
Mon 132.5.11 Villey, P. Encore un livre italien de la bibliothèque de Montaigne. Florence, 1912.
Mon 132.5.15 Vivier, P. Montaigne, auteur scientifique. Paris, 1920?
Mon 132.5.20 Villey, P. Montaigne devant la postérité. Paris, 1935.
NEDL Mon 132.5.25 Villey, P. Les essais de Michel de Montaigne. Paris, 1932.
Mon 133.1 Wendell, H. Etude sur la langue des essais. Stockholm, 1882.
Mon 133.2 Wittkomer, E. Die Form der Essais von Montaigne. Diss. Berlin, 1935.
Mon 133.3 Weiler, M. La pensée de Montaigne. Paris, 1948.
Mon 136.1 Zangroniz, J. de. Montaigne, Amyot et Saliat. Paris, 1906.

Mon 140 **Works about Montaigne - Biographical works - Pamphlet volumes**

Mon 140.1 Pamphlet vol. Montaigne. Biography. 6 pam.
Mon 140.2 Pamphlet vol. Montaigne. Biographical miscellany. 4 pam.

Mon 141 - 166 (A-Z) **Works about Montaigne - Biographical works - General works**

Mon 142.1 Bonnefon, P. Montaigne; l'homme et l'oeuvre. Bordeaux, 1893.
Mon 142.1.5A Bonnefon, P. Montaigne et ses amis. Paris, 1898. 2v.
Mon 142.1.5B Bonnefon, P. Montaigne et ses amis. Paris, 1898. 2v.
Mon 142.2 Barrière, P. Montaigne, gentilhomme français. 2. éd. Bordeaux, 1949.
Mon 142.4 Blinkenberg, Andreas. Montaigne. København, 1970.
Mon 143.1 Collins, W.L. Montaigne. Edinburgh, 1879.
Mon 143.2 Carlyle, T. Montaigne, and other essays. London, 1897.
Mon 143.3 Coquelin, L. Montaigne 1533-1592...la vie, les essais. Paris, n.d.
Mon 144.1 Dowden, E. Michel de Montaigne. London, 1905.
Mon 144.1.1 Dowden, E. Michel de Montaigne. Philadelphia, 1905.
Mon 144.1.3 Dowden, E. Michel de Montaigne. Philadelphia, 1906.
Mon 146.5A Frame, Donald Murdoch. Montaigne: a biography. 1. ed. N.Y., 1965.
Mon 146.5B Frame, Donald Murdoch. Montaigne: a biography. 1. ed. N.Y., 1965.
Mon 148.2 Hallie, Philip Paul. The scar of Montaigne; an essay in personal philosophy. 1. ed. Middleton, Conn., 1966.
Mon 150.1 Jarry, L. Pierre Daniel et les erudits de son temps. Orleans, 1876.
Mon 152.1 Lanusse, M. Montaigne. Paris, 1895.
Mon 152.2A Lowndes, M.E. Michel de Montaigne. Cambridge, 1898.
Mon 152.2B Lowndes, M.E. Michel de Montaigne. Cambridge, 1898.
Mon 152.3 Lugli, Vittorio. Montaigne. Milano, 1935.
Mon 152.4 Lamandé, André. La vie gaillarde et sage de Montaigne. Paris, 1927.
Mon 153.2 Merezhkovskiĭ, Dimitriĭ S. The life-work of Montaigne. London, 1907.
Mon 153.20 Montagnon, F. Trois portraits de Montaigne. Paris, 1928.
Mon 153.22 Mueller, Armand. Montaigne. Bruges? 1965.
Mon 154.1 Neyrac, J. Montaigne. Bergerac, 1904.
Mon 154.2 Nicolai, A. Montaigne intimé. Paris, 1941.
Htn Mon 156.1.2* Payen, J.F. Documents inedits sur Montaigne. Paris, 1847-
Mon 156.1.3 Payen, J.F. Documents inedits sur Montaigne. Paris, 1847.
Mon 156.1.4 Payen, J.F. Documents inedits sur Montaigne. Paris, 1847-56.
Mon 156.2A Plattard, J. Montaigne et son temps. Paris, 1933.
Mon 156.2B Plattard, J. Montaigne et son temps. Paris, 1933.
Mon 156.10 Peursen, C.A. van. Michel de Montaigne. Paris, 1954.
Mon 159.1A St. John, B. Montaigne the essayist. London, 1858. 2v.
Mon 159.1B St. John, B. Montaigne the essayist. London, 1858. 2v.

Mon 141 - 166 (A-Z) - cont. **Works about Montaigne - Biographical works - General works**

Mon 159.2A Sichel, E. Michel de Montaigne. London, 1911.
Mon 159.2B Sichel, E. Michel de Montaigne. London, 1911.
Mon 159.5 Prévost, Jean. La vie de Montaigne. 8. éd. Paris, 1926.
Mon 159.25 Strowski, F. Montaigne. Paris, 1938.
Mon 159.30 Sáenz Hayes, R. Miguel de Montaigne, 1533-1592. Buenos Aires, 1939.
Mon 159.32 Snethlage, J.L. Montaigne. Den Haag, 1963.
Mon 160.1 Truc, Gonzague. Montaigne. Paris, 1945.
Mon 161.5 Villey, P.J. Montaigne. Paris, 1933.
Mon 161.10 Valeri, Diego. Montaigne. Roma, 1925.
Mon 162.15 Willis, Irene C. Montaigne. N.Y., 1927.

Mon 168 **Works about Montaigne - Biographical works - Special topics - Montaigne in special localities**

Mon 168.1 Pamphlet vol. Montaigne in Italy. 5 pam.
Mon 168.2 James, C. Montaigne; ses voyages aux eaux minerales. Paris, 1859.
Mon 168.3 Balmas, E.H. Montaigne e Padova e altri studi. Padova, 1962.

Mon 170 **Works about Montaigne - Biographical works - Special topics - Special aspects**

Mon 170.1 Grün, A. Vie publique de Michel Montaigne. Paris, 1855.
Mon 170.1.5 Grün, A. Montaigne magistrat. Paris, 1854.
Mon 170.2.5 Taylor, J.S. Montaigne and médicine. N.Y., 1922.
Mon 170.3 Fränkel, R. Montaignes Stellung zum Staat und zur Kirche. Leipzig, 1907.
Mon 170.4 Dréano, M. La pensée religieuse de Montaigne. Thèse. Paris, 1936.
Mon 170.5 Jaunssen, H.J.J. Montaigne fideiste. Nijmegen, 1930.
Mon 170.19 Hay, C.H. Montaigne. Thèse. Poitiers, 1938.
Mon 170.20 Hay, C.H. Montaigne. Poitiers, 1938.
Mon 170.23 Riveline, Maurice. Montaigne et l'amitié. Thèse. Paris, 1939.
Mon 170.24 Riveline, Maurice. Montaigne et l'amitié. Paris, 1939.
Mon 170.28 Nicolai, Alexandre. Les belles amies de Montaigne. Paris, 1950.

Mon 172 **Works about Montaigne - Biographical works - Special topics - Iconography**

Mon 172.2 Lafon, Charles. Iconographie de Montaigne. Paris, 1960.

Mon 175 **Works about Montaigne - Biographical works - Special topics - Habitations**

Mon 175.1 Pamphlet vol. Chateau de Montaigne. 5 pam.
Mon 175.2 Marionneau, C. Visite aux ruines du Chateau de Montaigne. Bordeaux, 1885.
Mon 175.3 Malvezin, T. Notes sur la maison d'habitation de Montaigne. Bordeaux, 1889.
Mon 175.4 Courtois. Voyage en Périgord. Paris, 1878.

Mon 178 **Works about Montaigne - Biographical works - Special topics - Family and Heraldry**

Mon 178.1 Malvezin, T. Michel de Montaigne, son origine, sa famille. Bordeaux, 1875.
NEDL Mon 178.1.2 Malvezin, T. Michel de Montaigne, son origine, sa famille. Bordeaux, 1875.
Mon 178.2A Stapfer, P. La famille et les amis de Montaigne. Paris, 1896.
Mon 178.2B Stapfer, P. La famille et les amis de Montaigne. Paris, 1896.
Mon 178.3A Montaigne, Michel de. Le livre de raison de Montaigne. Paris, 1948.
Mon 178.3B Montaigne, Michel de. Le livre de raison de Montaigne. Paris, 1948.
Mon 178.8 Uildriks, Anne. Les idées littéraires de Mlle. de Gournay. Groningen, 1963?
Htn Mon 178.11* Gournay, Marie de Jars de. Le proumenoir de M. de Montaigne. Paris, 1594.
Mon 178.12 Schiff, M. La fille d'alliance de Montaigne et Mario de Gournay. Paris, 1910.
Mon 178.14 Ilsley, M.H. A daughter of the Renaissance. The Hague, 1963.
Mon 178.20 Pinson, P. Un disciple de Montaigne. Paris, 1868.

Mon 180 **Works about Montaigne - Biographical works - Special topics - Death and Burial**

Mon 180.1 Payen, J.F. Recherches sur Montaigne. Paris, 1862.
Mon 180.1.3 Payen, J.F. Recherches sur Montaigne. n.p., n.d.

Mon 182 **Works about Montaigne - Biographical works - Special topics - Tomb**

Mon 182.1 Dezeimeris, R. Recherches sur l'auteur des epitaphes. Paris, 1861. 2 pam.
Mon 182.2 Dosquet. Compte-rendu de la commission des monuments. Paris, 1855.

Mon 190 **Works about Montaigne - Miscellaneous topics - Montaigne and medicine**

Mon 190.1 Rodríguez Portillo, M. La medicina y los médicos vistos por Montaigne. Barcelona, 1932.
Mon 190.2 Delacroix, Raymond. Montaigne, malade et médecin. Lyon, 1907.

Mon 192 **Works about Montaigne - Miscellaneous topics - J.F. Payen as a collector of Montaigne**

Htn Mon 192.1* Le Petit, J. Quelques nots sur le docteur J.F. Payen. Paris, 1873.

Mon 194 **Works about Montaigne - Miscellaneous topics - Montaigne and education**

Mon 194.5 Thiele, Ernst A. Montaigne und Locke. Leipzig, 1920.
Mon 194.10 Porteau, Paul. Montaigne et la vie pédagogique de son temps. Thèse. Paris, 1935.
Mon 194.11 Porteau, Paul. Montaique et la vie pédagogique de son temps. Paris, 1935.

Mon 200 **Works about Montaigne - Literary works relating to Montaigne**

Mon 200.1 Bernard de Ballainvilliers, Simon Charles Sebastien. Montaigne aux Champs-Elysées. Paris, 1823.
Mon 200.2F Faugère, A.P. Du courage civil, ou L'hopital chez Montaigne. Paris, 1836.
Mon 200.3 La Rounat, C. Imitation on de Montaigne. n.p., n.d.
Mon 200.4 Almanach de la petite gazette pour 1869. Bagnères, 1869.

Classified Listing

Mon 210 Works about Montaigne - Anniversary celebrations

Mon 210.15A IVe centenaire de la naissance de Montaigne, 1533-1933. Conferences. Bordeaux, 1933.

Mon 210.15B IVe centenaire de la naissance de Montaigne, 1533-1933. Conferences. Bordeaux, 1933.

Mon 210.25 Paris. Lycée Montaigne. Montaigne en son temps à travers "Les Essais"; le voyage en Halie de 1580. Paris, 1965?

Mon 215 Works about Montaigne - Collections - Scrapbooks

Mon 215.1 Pamphlet vol. Montaigne. Celebrations. Scrapbook.

Mon 220 Works about Montaigne - Collections - Portraits

Mon 220.2 Lafon, Charles. Iconographie de Montaigne. Paris, 1960.

WIDENER LIBRARY SHELFLIST, 47

FRENCH LITERATURE

CHRONOLOGICAL LISTING

Chronological Listing

No date

42561.5.5 About, Edmond. The fellah. London, n.d.
42562.5.12 About, Edmond. La fille du Chanoine. London, n.d.
42562.5.9 About, Edmond. La fille du Chanoine. N.Y., n.d.
42562.17.4 About, Edmond. Le roi des Montagnes. Paris, n.d.
42551.8 Ackermann, L. Oeuvres. Paris, n.d.
43514.4.100 Adam, Juliette. L'auteur à son heroine. n.p., n.d.
41564.47 Aicard, J. Alfred de Vigny. Paris, n.d.
42586.7.15 Aicard, Jean. Benjamine. Paris, n.d.
42586.7.17 Aicard, Jean. L'illustre maurin. Paris, n.d.
42586.7.16 Aicard, Jean. Maurin des Maures. Paris, n.d.
42586.7.18 Aicard, Jean. Le père Lebonnard. Paris, n.d.
42586.7.19 Aicard, Jean. Théâtre. Paris, n.d. 2v.
42562.38.39 Aimard, Gustave. L'Araugan. 2d éd. Paris, n.d.
42562.38.43 Aimard, Gustave. Les outlaws du Missouri. Paris, n.d.
Htn 42548.78* L'ainé. Mss. n.p., n.d.
37556.29 Albalat, A. Le mal d'écrire et le roman contemporain. Paris, n.d.
37543.10.3 Albert, Paul. La littérature française des origines au XVIe siècle. 8. éd. Paris, n.d.
40563.21 Allier, Achille. Illusions et realités. n.p., n.d.
40535.14.15 Almeras, H. de. Fabre d'Eglantine. Paris, n.d.
40529.1 Ana, ou Collection de bons mots. Amsterdam, n.d. 10v.
41583.4.5 Ancelot, Marguerite Louise Virginie (Chardon). Tragédies. Paris, n.d. 4 pam.
43524.18.100 Andreau, Marianne. Le pilote aux yeux tristes. n.p., n.d.
37567.205 Annuaire des lettres, des arts et des théatres du journal "Le Constitutionnel". n.p., n.d.
37573.16 Anthologie des poètes français. Paris, n.d.
37573.17 Anthologie des prosateurs français. Paris, n.d.
39594.18.9A Archambault, P. Montesquieu. Paris, n.d.
37585.27 Armade, F. de. Le théâtre français des origines à nos jours. Paris, n.d.
42515.33.11 Articles de journeaux relatifs à la vie de M. Renan. n.p., n.d.
FL 6113.2A Asse, E. Jean-Jacques Rousseau. Paris, n.d.
37551.52 Asse, Eugène. L'Académie Française. Paris, n.d.
42562.38.55 Aubert, Charles. La marieuse. Paris, n.d.
Mol 701.2 Auger, L.S. Vie de Molière. n.p., n.d.
41577.14.5 B., Th. Lettres à M. de Lamartine. Paris, n.d.
38547.18 Badolle, Maurice. Anne d'Urfé, l'homme, le poète. Paris, n.d.
40597.17 Balzac, Honoré de. L'amour masqué ou imprudence et bonheur. Paris, n.d.
40597.15.101 Balzac, Honoré de. Le cousin Pons. N.Y., n.d.
40597.16.61 Balzac, Honoré de. Don Juan. N.Y., n.d.
40597.22 Balzac, Honoré de. Une fille d'Eve. Paris, n.d.
40597.29.25 Balzac, Honoré de. Petites misères de la vie conjugale. Paris, n.d.
40597.35.65 Balzac, Honoré de. A tragedy by the sea and other stories. N.Y., n.d.
40597.35.61 Balzac, Honoré de. A tragedy by the sea and other stories. N.Y., n.d.
40596.13.120 Balzac, Honoré de. The works. N.Y., n.d. 17v.
38527.76 Le banquet du Boys. Paris, n.d.
41522.1.5 Barbey d'Aurevilly, Jules. Les diaboliques. Paris, n.d.
FL 398.6.5 Baret, C. Propos d'un homme que à bien tourné. Dijon, n.d.
NEDL 42561.9.9 Barrès, M. Les bastions de l'est. Au service de l'Allemagne. Paris, n.d.
42563.16.5 Barrès, Maurice. Les amitiés françaises. Paris, n.d.
42563.16.6 Barrès, Maurice. Amori et dolori sacrum. Paris, n.d.
42563.17 Barrès, Maurice. Colette Baudoche. Paris, n.d.
42563.16.7.2 Barrès, Maurice. Leurs figures. Paris, n.d.
42542.27.26.200 Barrière, Théodore. A collection of reprints on Barrière. n.p., n.d.
42542.27.24 Barrière, Théodore. Le feu au couvent. Paris, n.d.
42542.27.26.5 Barrière, Théodore. The old house on the bridge. London, n.d.
42542.27.25 Barrière, Théodore. La vie de Bohème. Paris, n.d.
43537.82.3120 Bastide, François Régis. La Palme. n.p., n.d.
43537.2.30 Bataille, F. Les trois Foyers. Paris, n.d.
43537.4.34F Bataille, Henry. La femme nue. Paris, n.d.
41522.13.9.10 Baudelaire, Charles. Les fleurs du mal. Leipzig, n.d.
38563.7 Bayle, Pierre. Commentaire philosophique sur ces paroles de Jésus-Christ. n.p., n.d.
40532.7A Beaumarchais, Pierre A.C. de. Le mariage de Figaro. Paris, n.d.
40532.12 Beaumarchais, Pierre A.C. de. Théâtre. Paris, n.d.
42563.22.5 Beaumont, André de. Une histoire de cirque. Tours, n.d.
37564.25 Beaurepaire, Eugène de Robillard de. Histoire de deux sonnets. n.p., n.d.
42542.28.8 Becque, Henri. La parisienne. Paris, n.d.
38557.24.20 Bellon, E. Bossuet directeur de conscience. Paris, n.d.
41522.25 Belot, Adolphe. Le testament de César Girodot. Paris, n.d.
41591.15 Béranger, P.J. de. Correspondance. Paris, n.d. 4v.
41591.12 Béranger, P.J. de. Dernières chansons. Paris, n.d.
41591.13 Béranger, P.J. de. Musique. Paris, n.d.
41592.29 Béranger, P.J. de. Songs. London, n.d.
42563.23 Bérenger, Henry. L'effort. Tours, n.d.
38527.48 Bernage, Siméon. Étude sur Robert Garnier. Paris, n.d.
42542.29.15 Bernard, Tristan. L'anglais tel qu'on le parle. 25. éd. Paris, n.d.
42542.29.39 Bernstein, H. La griffe. La marché. Paris, n.d.
Htn 38528.16.10* Béroalde de Verville. Le moyen de parvenir. Manuscript. n.p., n.d.
40517.17 Berquin, Arnaud. The childrens' friend. Newburyport, n.d. 2v.
37567.100 Bertaut, J. La littérature féminine d'aujourd'hui. Paris, n.d.
41596.66 Berthier, Alfred. Le poète savoyard Jean-Pierre Veyrat, 1810-1844. Thèse. Paris, n.d.
42561.12 Berthoud, S. Henry. L'homme depuis cinq mille ans. Paris, n.d.
37574.28.9 Bever, A. van. Les poètes du terroir du XVe siècle au XXe siècle. Paris, n.d. 4v.
40582.10 Beyle, Henri. Chroniques italiennes. Paris, n.d.
40582.11 Beyle, Henri. Correspondence inédite. Paris, n.d. 2v.
40582.14 Beyle, Henri. Lucien Leuwen. Photoreproduction. Paris, n.d.
40582.18.5 Beyle, Henri. Nouvelles inédites. Paris, n.d.
40582.25.5 Beyle, Henri. Le rouge et le noir. Strassbourg, n.d.
42563.28.21 Biart, Lucien. Aventures d'un jeune naturaliste. Paris, n.d.
42563.28.31 Biart, Lucien. Entre frères. Paris, n.d.

No date - cont.

42561.10 Biart, Lucien. La frontière indienne. Paris, n.d.
42563.28.19 Biart, Lucien. Monsieur Pinson. Paris, n.d.
42563.28 Biart, Lucien. La terre chaude. Paris, n.d.
42563.28.23 Biart, Lucien. Unac, der Indianer. Reutlingen, n.d.
Htn 37575.16* Bibliothèque gothique. v.1-3. n.p. n.d.
Htn 37575.17* Bibliothèque gothique. v.4-6. n.p., n.d.
42545.3.845 Bibliothèque nationale, Paris. Maurice Maeterlinck, 1862-1949. Paris, n.d.
40529.15 Bièvre, François Georges Maréchal. Bièvriana, ou Jeux de mots. Paris, n.d.
42514.4 Bigelow, John. Some recollections of the late Edward Laboulaye. N.Y., n.d.
37542.28 Biré, E. Études et portraits. Lyon, n.d.
42555.13 Biré, E. Victor de Laprade. Paris, n.d.
40587.18 Biro, E. Les dernières années de Chateaubriand. Paris, n.d.
37565.40 Blei, Franz. Die galante Zeit und ihr Ende. Berlin, n.d.
37555.324.3 Bock, Moriz. Vergleich und Gleichnisse. n.p., n.d. 2 pam.
38566.33 Boileau Despréaux, Nicolas. Le Lutrin. Strasbourg, n.d.
37566.18 Bonnefon, D. Les écrivains moderne de la France. Paris, n.d.
37566.18.5 Bonnefon, D. Les écrivains moderne de la France. 7th ed. Paris, n.d.
37567.70.2 Bordeaux, H. Les ecrivains et les moeurs, 1900-1902. 2e éd. Paris, n.d.
37567.116 Bordeaux, H. Vies intimes. 6th ed. Paris, n.d.
FL 383.15 Borgekhoff, J.L. Théâtre anglais à Paris sous le restauration. Paris, n.d.
37572.40 Bornecque, H. Contes et récits en prose...des XVIIe et VIIIe siècles. Paris, n.d.
38557.51.20 Bossuet, J.B. Élevations à Dieu sur tous les mystères de la religion chrétienne. Paris, n.d.
38557.41.38 Bossuet, J.B. Histoire des variations des églises protestantes. n.p., n.d. 2v.
42542.30.7 Bouchor, Maurice. La légende de Sainte Cécile. Paris, n.d.
42542.30.40 Bouchor, Maurice. Mystères bibliques et chrétiens. Paris, n.d.
Htn 40516.65* Bougeant, G.H. Wonderful travels of Prince Fan Feredin. Northhampton, n.d.
42557.12.7 Bouglé, C. Les grandes figures de l'entente Verhaeren. Paris, n.d.
38562.20 Bouillier, F. Éloges de Fontenelle. Paris, n.d.
41566.14.23 Bouilly, Jean N. Causeries d'un vieillard. 2e éd. Paris, n.d.
41566.14.9 Bouilly, Jean N. Mes recapitulations. Paris, n.d. 3v.
43544.5.30 Boulenger, Marcel. Mes relations. Paris, n.d.
41581.5 Bourgeois, A. Théâtre. Paris, n.d. 9 pam.
41583.15.14 Bourgeois, Anicet. The duke's daughter. N.Y., n.d.
42563.37.28 Bourget, Paul. Un divorce. Paris, n.d.
42563.37.24 Bourget, Paul. Le fantôme. Paris, n.d.
42563.37.25 Bourget, Paul. Un homme d'affaires. Paris, n.d.
42563.37.9 Bourget, Paul. Pastels. Paris, n.d.
42563.37.13 Bourget, Paul. Poésie 1872-1876, 1876-1882. Paris, n.d. 2v.
37572.13 Bourgoin, A. Récits de nos elèves. Paris, n.d.
42563.38.2 Bouvier, Alexis. Chansons du peuple. Paris, n.d.
42563.38.5 Bouvier, Alexis. Les créanciers de l'échafaud. 3. éd. Paris, n.d.
42563.38.9 Bouvier, Alexis. Les petites blanchisseuses. Paris, n.d.
37567.129 Bouvier, E. La bataille realiste. Paris, n.d.
41593.9.60 Brad, J.L. L'Italie, poème. Alexandrie, n.d.
42576.63.25 Brandes, G. Anatole France. Berlin, n.d.
42541.7.9 Brieux, Eugène. La petite amie. Paris, n.d.
FL 385.9.25 Brisson, A. Le théâtre. Paris, n.d. 9v.
41593.11 Brizeux, Auguste. Oeuvres. Paris, n.d. 4v.
38576.11 Brueys, D.A. de. L'avocat Pathelin. Paris, n.d.
42524.13.3 Brunetière, F. Art and morality. N.Y., n.d.
37543.58.2 Brunetière, Ferdinand. Histoire de la littérature française classique. Paris, n.d.
37543.58 Brunetière, Ferdinand. Histoire de la littérature française classique. Paris, n.d. 4v.
40546.28 Brunius, Teddy. Alexis de Tocqueville. Uppsala, n.d.
42524.20 Büchner, Alexander. Considérations sur le roman moderne. n.p., n.d.
39527.26 Buffon, George L. de. Fables de La Fontaine. Paris, n.d.
42542.47.60 Burion, A. Une cause célèbre. Paris, n.d.
Htn 39534.3* Bussy-Rabutin. Histoire amoureuse de Gaules. Paris, n.d. 2v.
39534.4 Bussy-Rabutin. Histoire amoureuse de Gaules. Paris, n.d. 2v.
42542.47.70 Cadol, Édouard. La grand maman. Paris, n.d.
42561.13.2 Cahun, Léon. Hassan le Janissaire. Paris, n.d.
43550.58.700.6 Camus, Albert. The stranger. n.p., n.d.
37543.116 Canat, R. Littérature française par les textes. Paris, n.d.
42563.66.100 Candèze, Ernest. L'aventures d'un grillon. Paris, n.d.
Htn 39585.21.5* Caraccioli, L.A. Le livre à la mode. n.p., n.d.
43633.1.80 Carco, Francis. Charles-Henry Hirsch; biographie critique. Paris, n.d.
42563.39.500 Carnoy, E. Henry. La nuit de Noël. Paris, n.d.
42542.48.47 Carré, Michel. Faust and Marguerite. London, n.d.
42542.48.46 Carré, Michel. Faust and Marguerite. London, n.d. 2 pam.
Htn 37530.30* Carron, Pierre Siméon. Notice des livres facetieux...Bibliothèque de l'Arsenal. Manuscript. n.p., n.d.
42586.28.15 Casale, F. La rose du Bocagne. Paris, n.d.
43550.87.100 Cattiaux, Louis. Poèmes: Alchimiques, Tristes, Zen, D'avant, De la resonance, De la connaissance. n.p., n.d.
42562.45 Celières, Paul. Quand il pleut. Paris, n.d.
38527.34.5 Ceriziers, R. de. Het leven van de heylige Susanna ofte Genoveva. Antwerpen, n.d.
42561.34 Chandeneux, Claire de. Val-Regis la grande. Paris, n.d.
37574.3 Chasles, Émile. Histoire abrégé de la littérature française. Paris, n.d. 2v.
37563.2 Chasles, Philarète. Études sur le seizième siècle. Paris, n.d.
40586.5.5 Chateaubriand, F.A.R. Atala. Paris, n.d.
40586.12 Chateaubriand, F.A.R. Atala. Paris, n.d.
40586.14.20 Chateaubriand, F.A.R. Atala et ses critiques. n.p., n.d.
40586.5.15 Chateaubriand, F.A.R. Itinéraire de Paris à Jérusalem. Paris, n.d.
40586.21 Chateaubriand, F.A.R. Moyse. St. Germain, n.d.

Chronological Listing

No date - cont.

	40586.4	Chateaubriand, F.A.R. Oeuvres complètes. Paris, n.d. 12v.
	42586.30	Chazel, Prosper. Le chalet des Spains. Paris, n.d.
	41574.45	Chenay, P. Victor Hugo à Guernesey. Paris, n.d.
	42587.36.19	Chenin, Emile. Terres lorraines. Paris, n.d.
	42576.12	Cherbonnel, Alice. Mon oncle et mon curé. N.Y., n.d.
	42576.12.5	Cherbonnel, Alice. Mon oncle et mon curé. 27. éd. Paris, n.d.
	39594.19.13	Chevalley, E. La théorie de différents ordres de lois. Le Caire, n.d.
Htn	Mol 194.15*	Cicognini, G.A. Il convitato di Pietra. Bologna, n.d.
	42542.52.3	Clairville, Louis François Nicolaïe. Les parisiens à Londres. n.p., n.d.
	42542.52.13	Clairville, Louis François Nicolaïe. Les petites misères de la vie humaine. 3. éd. N.Y., n.d.
	42586.31.6	Claretié, J. La mausard. Paris, n.d.
	37595.66	Les classiques français du Moyen Âge. Paris, n.d. 5v.
	37562.15	Clédat, Léon. La poésie lyrique et satirique en France au moyen âge. Paris, n.d.
	43554.4.30	Clermont, Emile. Amour promis. 2e éd. Paris, n.d.
	37556.61	Clouzet, G. Le roman français. Paris, n.d.
Htn	37575.30*	Collection de poésies, romans, chroniques. v.1-24. n.p., n.d. 5v.
	Mol 600.14	Collection of clippings relating to Molière. n.p., n.d.
	40534.23.301	Collot d'Herbois, J.M. Théâtre. n.p., n.d. 2v.
	FL 398.7.20	Colombier, Marie. Voyages de Sarah Bernhardt en Amérique. Paris, n.d.
	FL 394.133	Comédie française, Paris. A collect of magazine articles on the Comédie française. n.p., n.d.
	40553.7	Constant de Rebecque, Benjamin. Adolphe. Paris, n.d.
	42554.23.2	Coppée, François. Le naufragé. Paris, n.d.
	42554.22.2	Coppée, François. Poésies 1864-69. Paris, n.d.
	42554.22.5	Coppée, François. Premières poésies. Paris, n.d.
	42554.24	Coppée, François. Théâtre 1869-72. Paris, n.d.
	Mon 143.3	Coquelin, L. Montaigne 1533-1592...la vie, les essais. Paris, n.d.
	38575.26	Corneille, Pierre. Le Cid. Paris, n.d.
	38575.29.6	Corneille, Pierre. Le Cid. Strasbourg, n.d.
	38575.32.5	Corneille, Pierre. Horace. Strasbourg, n.d.
	38575.33.13	Corneille, Pierre. Le menteur. Strasbourg, n.d.
	38571.6F	Corneille, Pierre. Oeuvres. Paris, n.d.
	38575.34.8.10	Corneille, Pierre. Polyeucte. Strasbourg, n.d.
	38575.31.6	Corneille, Pierre. Polyeucte. Strasbourg, n.d.
	38574.7A	Corneille, Pierre. Théâtre. Paris, n.d.
	38574.8	Corneille, Pierre. Théâtre. Paris, n.d. 2v.
	38574.5	Corneille, Pierre. Théâtre. Texte de 1682. Paris, n.d. 8v.
Htn	FL 395.132*	Costumes des comédiens françaises dans Omasis. n.p., n.d.
	40588.1	Cottin, Marie R. (Mme.). Elizabeth. London, n.d.
	FL 375.20	Cougny, M.E. Des représentations dramatiques. n.p., n.d.
	40546.5.10	Courier de Méré, Paul Louis. Oeuvres complètes. Paris, n.d.
	42548.69	Courteline, G. Les pièces à succès. Paris, n.d. 2v.
Htn	38526.10.17.25*	Crenne, Helisenne de. Les angoysses douloureuses qui procedent d'amours. n.p., n.d.
	38512.60	Crescini, V. On the Pharsalia of Nicolo da Verona. n.p., n.d.
	V43500.77	Cussat Blanc, Jean. Offert aux hommes. Blainville-sur-Mer, n.d.
	40565.17	Cuvillier-Fleury, A.A. Journal intime. Paris, n.d. 2v.
	38576.12.44	Dancourt, Florent C. Le mari retrouvé; comédie. n.p., n.d.
	37573.70	Daniels, W.M. Poèms et chants de France. Boston, n.d.
	41566.5	D'Arlincourt, Charles V.P. The recluse. n.p., n.d.
	41593.17.9	Daru, P. La Cléopédie. Paris, n.d.
	42566.37	Daudet, Alphonse. L'Arlésienne. Paris, n.d.
	42566.51	Daudet, Alphonse. La Belle-Nivernaise. Paris, n.d.
	42561.14.5	Daudet, Alphonse. Les Cigognes. Paris, n.d.
	42566.44	Daudet, Alphonse. Contes d'hiver. Paris, n.d.
Htn	42561.14.7*	Daudet, Alphonse. Contes et recits. Paris, n.d.
	42566.47	Daudet, Alphonse. La fédor; pages de la vie. Paris, n.d.
	42561.14	Daudet, Alphonse. Histoire d'un enfant. Paris, n.d.
	42566.50	Daudet, Alphonse. La menteuse. Paris, n.d.
	42566.31	Daudet, Alphonse. Le petit chose. Paris, n.d.
	42566.28A	Daudet, Alphonse. Port-Tarascon. Paris, n.d.
	42566.57	Daudet, Alphonse. Premier voyage, premier mensonge. Paris, n.d.
	42566.33.7	Daudet, Alphonse. Les rois en exil. Paris, n.d.
	42566.46	Daudet, Alphonse. Rose et Ninette. Paris, n.d.
	42566.42	Daudet, Alphonse. Trois souvenirs. Paris, n.d.
	42576.65.13.22	Deffoux, Léon. Inconographie de J.K. Huysmans. n.p., n.d.
	FL 360.50	Dejob, C. Études sur la tragédie. Paris, n.d.
	42548.8.5	Delair, Paul. Argument of La mégère apprivoisée. N.Y., n.d.
	41583.28.3	Delavigne, Casimir. Louis XI. N.Y., n.d.
	41583.23	Delavigne, Casimir. Théâtre français. Paris, n.d.
	41583.24	Delavigne, Casimir. Théâtre français. Paris, n.d. 5 pam.
	42524.19.10	Delmont, T. Ferdinand Brunetière. Paris, n.d.
	41583.25	Delvaigne, Casimir. Théâtre français. Paris, n.d. 3 pam.
	40535.2.60	Demonstier, C.A. Le tolérant. Paris, n.d.
	42513.7	Denis, F. Journal (1829-1848) publié avec une introduction et des notes par Pierre Moreau. Fribourg, n.d.
	42545.69.19	Dennery, Adolphe Philippe. Marie-Jeanne. Paris, n.d.
	42545.69.17	Dennery, Adolphe Philippe. The two orphans. N.Y., n.d.
	40515.4.5A	D'Epinay, Louise F. Mémoires. Paris, n.d. 2v.
	40586.20.50	Deplace, Guy M. Examen de la critique des Martyrs, insérée dans le Journal de l'empire. n.p., n.d.
	42568.1	Derennes, Gustave. Le drapeau du Canada. Paris, n.d.
	37567.121.2	Derôme, L. Causeries d'un amie des livres. Paris, n.d. 2v.
	41578.58	Deschanel, E. Lamartine. Paris, n.d. 2v.
	FL 365.5	Deschanel, Émile. La vie des comédiens. Paris, n.d.
Htn	37578.36*	Desciseaux, M. Recueil de contes a rire. Paris, n.d.
Htn	37578.37*	Desciseaux, M. Recueil de contes a rire. Paris, n.d.
	40546.9.25	Desternes, Louis. Paul Louis Courier et les Bourbons. Moulin, n.d.
	43566.5.30	Détanger, Émile. Le chemin de la victoire. Paris, n.d.
	42586.36.5	Dewailly, A. Le petit monde. Paris, n.d.
	39564.7.2	Diderot, Denis. Morceaux choisis. Paris, n.d.
	39564.8.3	Diderot, Denis. Pages choisies des grands ecrivains. Paris, n.d.

No date - cont.

	39564.8.5	Diderot, Denis. Le paradoxe sur le comédien le neveu de Rameau. Strassburg, n.d.
	42568.16	Dinet, E. Khadra la danseuse des Ouled Naïl. Paris, n.d.
	38575.23.60	Doenhardt, Willibaldis S. Lessing und Corneille. n.p., n.d.
	Mol 604.7	Donnay, M. Molière. Paris, n.d.
	42542.65.4	Donnay, Maurice. La bascule. Paris, n.d.
	42554.28.5	Dorchain, Auguste. Conte d'April. Paris, n.d.
	41564.34	Dorison, Léon. Alfred de Vigny. Paris, n.d.
	38585.15	Dreyfus-Brisac, E. Plagiats et réminiscences. Paris, n.d.
	37543.3	Drioux, Claude. Histoire de la littérature française. Paris, n.d.
	42568.5.4	Droz, Gustave. Le cahier bleu. Paris, n.d.
	40556.7.5	Droz, Gustave. Diplomacy. N.Y., n.d.
	38557.21	Druon, H. Bossuet à Meaux. Paris, n.d.
Htn	38526.48.21*	Du Bartas, Guillaume de Salluste. Bartas: his divine weekes and workes. London, n.d.
	37562.327	Dubruck, E. The theme of death in French poetry. The Hague, n.d.
	40535.11.19	Ducis, Jean F. Othello, ossia il moro di Venezia. Firenze, n.d.
	43576.15.110	Ducreux, Louis. La folie. n.p., n.d.
	FL 398.42	Dulomboy, N.F.R.F. Aux manes de Marie-Elisabeth Joly. Paris, n.d.
	42542.69.6	Dumanoir, M. Le gentilhomme pauvre. N.Y., n.d.
	41538.19	Dumas, Alexandre. The bird of fate, a modern Gil Blas. London, n.d.
	41538.69.5	Dumas, Alexandre. Le Chevalier de Maison Rouge. N.Y., n.d.
	42543.17	Dumas, Alexandre. Diana de Lys. n.p., n.d.
	42543.19.35	Dumas, Alexandre. Francillon. 35. éd. n.p., n.d. 2 pam.
	41538.54.2	Dumas, Alexandre. The iron mask. Philadelphia, n.d.
	41538.60	Dumas, Alexandre. Le mari de la veuve. n.p., n.d.
	41538.30	Dumas, Alexandre. Pauline, Pascal Bruno and Boutekoe. London, n.d.
	41538.35	Dumas, Alexandre. Père la ruine. London, n.d.
	41538.72	Dumas, Alexandre. Romans et nouvelles. N.Y., n.d.
	42543.11.2	Dumas, Alexandre. Théâtre complet. v.7. Paris, n.d. 8v.
NEDL	42543.4	Dumas, Alexandre. Théâtre complet. 2. série. n.p., n.d.
NEDL	42543.5	Dumas, Alexandre. Théâtre complet. 3. série. n.p., n.d.
NEDL	42543.6	Dumas, Alexandre. Théâtre complet. 4. série. n.p., n.d.
	FL 6135.7	Dumur, Louis. Le centenaire de Jean-Jacques. Paris, n.d.
	42563.47.2	Durand, Alice M.C.F. Frankley. Paris, n.d.
	42563.61	Durand, Alice M.C.F. Un mystère. 6. éd. Paris, n.d.
	42563.56.15	Durand, Alice M.C.F. La seconde mère. Paris, n.d.
	39533.28	Durand, M. Laurent. Nouvelle édition des Cantiques de l'ame devoti. Lyon, n.d.
	42543.28.15.2	Durantin, Armand. Héloise Paranquet. n.p., n.d.
	42556.11	Duret, U. Jean Reboul. n.p., n.d.
	38539.7.5	Du Vair, Guillaume. De l'éloquence françoise. Paris, n.d.
	37574.33.3	Ebener, Gottfried. Album poétique. n.p., n.d.
	41597.26	Les Échecs. Poëme. n.p., n.d.
	43591.89.1100	Éluard, Paul. Derniers poèmes d'amour. n.p., n.d.
	37555.724.7	Elwert, Wilhelm Theodor. Französische Metrik. 2. Aufl. München, n.d.
	41598.10	L'épicurien normand. Rouen, n.d.
	42572.1	Erckmann, Emile. Alsace! Paris, n.d.
	42572.1.15	Erckmann, Emile. L'Art et les grands idéalistes. Paris, n.d.
	42572.2.2	Erckmann, Emile. Le banni. Paris, n.d.
	42572.3.5	Erckmann, Emile. Le blocus. Paris, n.d.
	42572.3	Erckmann, Emile. Le blocus. Paris, n.d.
	42572.4	Erckmann, Emile. Une campagne en Kabylie. Paris, n.d.
	42572.5	Erckmann, Emile. Confidences d'un joueur de clarinette. Paris, n.d.
	42572.7.5	Erckmann, Emile. Contes de la montagne. Paris, n.d.
	42572.6	Erckmann, Emile. Contes des bords du Rhin. Paris, n.d.
	42572.8	Erckmann, Emile. Contes populaires. Paris, n.d.
	42572.10	Erckmann, Emile. Le grand-père Lebigre. Paris, n.d.
	42572.11.5	Erckmann, Emile. Histoire d'un conscrit de 1813. 5. éd. Paris, n.d.
	42572.12	Erckmann, Emile. Histoire d'un homme du peuple. Paris, n.d.
	42572.19.5	Erckmann, Emile. L'illustre Docteur Mathéus. 3. éd. Paris, n.d.
	42572.20	Erckmann, Emile. L'invasion ou Le fou Yégoff. Paris, n.d.
	42572.23	Erckmann, Emile. Madame Thérèse. Paris, n.d.
	42572.25	Erckmann, Emile. La maison forestière. Paris, n.d.
	42572.26	Erckmann, Emile. Maître Daniel Rock. Paris, n.d.
	42572.27	Erckmann, Emile. Maître Gaspard Fix. Paris, n.d.
	42572.31	Erckmann, Emile. Les vieux de la vieille. Paris, n.d.
	42572.32	Erckmann, Emile. Waterloo. Paris, n.d.
	37555.70	Ernest-Charles, J. Théâtre des poètes 1850-1910. Paris, n.d.
	Mol 605.5	Essai sur Molière. n.p., n.d.
	40586.18.50	Extrait de différens écrits sur le génie du christianisme. n.p., n.d.
	42543.38.29	Fabre, Joseph. Jeanne d'Arc. Paris, n.d.
	37572.51	Faguet, E. Ce que disent les livres. Paris, n.d.
	37572.50	Faguet, E. La prose française. Paris, n.d.
	Mol 606.6	Faguet, E. Rousseau contre Molière. Paris, n.d.
	37544.24	Faguet, Émile. Les dix commandements de la vieillesse. 4. éd. Paris, n.d.
	37544.22.5	Faguet, Émile. Propos littéraires. 5. séries. Paris, n.d.
	42543.40	Faramond, Maurice de. Monsieur Bonnet. Paris, n.d.
	40587.127	Fauré, Gabriel. Chateaubriand en Italie. Roma, n.d.
	40535.15.4.5	Favart, Charles S. Soliman Second; comédie. n.p., n.d.
	42565.75	Favre de Coulevain, Hélène. Le roman merveilleux. Paris, n.d.
	42565.73	Favre de Coulevain, Hélène. Sur la branche. Paris, n.d.
	38553.35	Fénelon, F. de S. de la Mothe. Adventures of Telemachus. N.Y., n.d. 2v.
	38554.1.3	Fénelon, F. de S. de la Mothe. Adventures of Telemachus. Books 1-24. n.p., n.d.
	38553.28	Fénelon, F. de S. de la Mothe. Les aventures de Télémaque. Boston, n.d.
	38553.27.5	Fénelon, F. de S. de la Mothe. Aventures de Télémaque. Philadelphia, n.d.
NEDL	38552.16	Fénelon, F. de S. de la Mothe. Fénelon; pages choisies. Paris, n.d.
Htn	38554.738*	Fénelon, F. de S. de la Mothe. Responsio illustrissimi ac reverenendissimi archiepiscopi Cameracensis. n.p., n.d.

Chronological Listing

No date - cont.

Htn	38554.516*	Fénelon, F. de S. de la Mothe. 1ère-5ème lettre de Monseigneur l'Archévêque Duc de Cambrai à Monseigneur l'Evêque de Meaux. n.p., n.d.
	42575.27.4	Feuillet, Octave. Circé; scène parisienne. n.p., n.d.
	42575.23.15	Feuillet, Octave. Le roman d'un jeune homme pauvre. Paris, n.d. 5 pam.
	42586.47	Feval, Paul H. Les contes de nos pères. Paris, n.d.
	42554.33	Fischer, H. Les fugitives. n.p., n.d.
	Mol 247.22	Fischmann, W. Molière Misanthrope. n.p., n.d.
	38513.67	Fleischer, M. Christi Leben von der Geschichte von der Samariterin bis zur Passion. Greifswald, n.d. 4 pam.
	42564.44	Fleury, Jules. Les excentriques. Paris, n.d.
	42564.35	Fleury, Jules. Le violon de faience. Paris, n.d.
	40515.24	Florian, Jean P.C. de. Fables. Paris, n.d.
	42576.59	Foa, Eugénie. Le petit Robinson de Paris. Boston, n.d.
	40524.15	Fontaines, M.L.C. Oeuvres. Paris, n.d.
	37562.19	Formentin, Charles. Essai sur les fabliaux français du XIIe-XIIIe siècles. n.p., n.d.
	V43500.113	Fort, Paul. Livre d'espérance. Paris, n.d.
	38513.4	Fournier, Eugene. Le mystère de Robert le Diable. Paris, n.d.
	42576.62.14.2	France, Anatole. L'anneau d'améthyste. Paris, n.d.
	42576.62.19A	France, Anatole. Histoire comique. Paris, n.d.
	42576.62.17.5A	France, Anatole. Monsieur Bergeret à Paris. 84. éd. Paris, n.d.
	37551.30	Franke. Quelles sont les différences. n.p., n.d.
	37557.6.2	Franz, Arthur. Das literarische Portrat in Frankreich Beilage. Leipzig, n.d.
	42586.55.4	Frapié, L. L'écolière. Paris, n.d.
	42524.60	Frary, Raoul. Essais de critique. Paris, n.d.
	FL 398.27.5	Frédéric Febvre. Paris, n.d.
	37572.35	French miscellany. n.p., n.d.
	37571.57	French novels. n.p., n.d. 2v.
NEDL	Mol 247.5	Frigoult, C. Deux misanthropes. Cherbourg, n.d.
	42575.69	Fuchs, Max. Lexique du Journal des Goncourt. Paris, n.d.
	42554.11.6	Fuchs, Max. Théodore de Banville. Paris, n.d.
	Mol 706.1	Fulda, Pastor. Molière. n.p., n.d.
	V43500.125	Fuster, Charles. Guerre, deuil, France. Strasbourg, n.d.
	42543.43.25	Galipaux, Felix. Confetti. Paris, n.d.
	39534.45	Gaultier, Garguille. Comédien. Paris, n.d.
	43616.2.50	Gautier, Judith. L'usurpateur. Paris, n.d. 2v.
X Cg	41542.37	Gautier, Théophile. Mademoiselle Dafué. Paris, n.d.
	41567.18	Gay, M.F.S.N. de. L. Anatole. n.p., n.d.
	FL 398.9.15F	Germain, Auguste. Albert Brasseur. Paris, n.d.
	37537.9	Geruzez, Eugène. Essais de littérature française. Paris, n.d. 2v.
	Mol 607.7	Gheorghiu, X. Molière: l'école des maris si Regnard. Tassy, n.d.
	37565.17	Gidel, Charles. Histoire de la littérature française fin du XVIIe siècle - 1815. Paris, n.d.
	40526.26	Gilbert, N.J.L. Oeuvres. Paris, n.d.
	FL 362.15A	Ginisty, Paul. Le mélodrame. Paris, n.d.
	42576.6	Ginisty, Paul. Les Rastaquonères. Paris, n.d.
	41541.10	Girardin, Delphine Gay. Il cappello dell'Orinolojo. Milano, n.d.
	37557.36	Glaser, E. Le mouvement littéraire. 1905-1912. Paris, n.d. 7v.
	42543.49.10	Glatigny, Albert. Le jour de l'an d'un vacabond. Paris, n.d.
	42586.67	Gobineau, Arthur de. Asiatische Novellen. Leipzig, n.d.
	42548.10	Goetsehy, G. Pressé pour le salon. Paris, n.d.
	42543.51	Gohier, Urbain. Spartacus. Paris, n.d.
	43625.1.30	Gojon, E. Les cendres de l'urne, 1904-07. n.p., n.d.
	Mol 860.6	Goldini, C. Il Molière commedia in cinque atti in versi. n.p., n.d.
	37574.24.2	Gouttes de poèsie. Paris, n.d.
	41543.35	Grandville, J.I.I.G. Un autre monde. Paris, n.d.
	42554.49.5	Gregh, F. La maison de l'enfance. Paris, n.d.
	40526.14	Gresset, Jean B. Oeuvres. Paris, n.d.
	40526.15.5	Gresset, Jean B. Les poésies. n.p., n.d. 2v.
	FL 398.7.21	Griffith, F.R. Sarah Bernhardt. n.p., n.d.
	39544.29	Grimm, Hermann. Voltaire und Frankreich. n.p., n.d.
	42571.41	Grousset, P. Une année de collège à Paris. Paris, n.d.
	40516.12.5	Gudin, Paul-Phillippe. Le royaume mis en interdit. n.p., n.d.
	41593.34.5	Guérin, Maurice de. Journal, lettres et poèmes. Strasbourg, n.d.
	41593.35	Guérin, Maurice de. Journal. N.Y., n.d.
	40536.33.5	Guieysse-Frère, E. Sedaine, ses protecteurs et ses amis. Paris, n.d.
	42586.77	Guillaumin, Emile. Près du sol. Paris, n.d.
	38526.21.5	Guymond de la Touche. Iphigénie en Tauride. Paris, n.d.
	42525.9	Hallays, A. En flânant. Paris, n.d.
	39526.2	Hamel, Frank. Jean de la Fontaine. London, n.d.
	39532.7	Hamilton, Anthony. Drei Hübsche, kurzweilige Märlein. n.p., n.d.
	42546.12.19	Hangmard, L. Edmond Rostand. Paris, n.d.
	38539.102.80	Harris, Margaret A. A study of Théodore Valentinen's Amant resucité de la mort d'amour. n.p., n.d.
	42576.65.5	Harry, Myriam (pseud.). La conquête de Jérusalem. Paris, n.d.
	42576.65.6	Harry, Myriam (pseud.). Petites epouses. Paris, n.d.
	40522.16	Heinrich, P. L'Abbé Prévost et la Louisiane. Paris, n.d.
	39576.15	Henrion, Charles. Mémoires philosophiques. Paris, n.d.
	42543.65.5	Hermant, Abel. L'esbroufe. Paris, n.d.
	42541.18.2	Hermant, Abel. Monsieur de Courpière marié. Paris, n.d.
	42541.18	Hermant, Abel. Souvenirs du Vte. de Courpière. Paris, n.d.
	42543.65.20	Hermant, Abel. Trains de luxe. Paris, n.d.
	37543.112A	Herriot, E. Précis de l'histoire des lettres françaises. 2. éd. Paris, n.d.
	42576.67.12	Hervieu, Paul. L'armature. Paris, n.d.
	42543.69.7	Hervieu, Paul. Le dédale. Paris, n.d.
	42576.67.10	Hervieu, Paul. Les tenailles. Paris, n.d.
	42584.29.5	Hetzel, P.J. Gribouille chez son oncle Jeannot. Paris, n.d.
	37594.7	Hippeau, M.C. Sermon du XIIIe siècle. Paris, n.d.
	41567.60	Historiettes et contes à ma petite fille. Paris, n.d.
	41569.12	Historiettes et contes à ma petite fille et à mon petit garçon. Paris, n.d.
	41584.58	Hoffman, F.B. Le brigand. Paris, n.d.
	41522.17A	Holitscher, A. Charles Baudelaire. Berlin, n.d.
	42576.14.85	Houssaye, Arsène. Les femmes démasquées. 5. éd. Paris, n.d. 2v.
	42576.65.12	Houx-Marc, Eugène. Mémorables fredaines d'un singe. Paris, n.d.

No date - cont.

	37594.12	Hublocher, J.V. Hélinand von Froidmont und sein Verhältnis zu J. von Salisbury. Regensburg, n.d.
	41571.21	Hugo, Victor. Les chatiments. Paris, n.d.
	41572.23	Hugo, Victor. Les châtiments. Paris, n.d.
Htn	41573.38*	Hugo, Victor. Le Christ au Vatican. Bruxelles, n.d.
	41573.30.5	Hugo, Victor. Dramas. v.1-4. Boston, n.d. 2v.
	41571.30	Hugo, Victor. Les feuilles d'automne. Paris, n.d.
	41573.36.4	Hugo, Victor. Les feuilles d'automne. Paris, n.d.
	41573.36.5	Hugo, Victor. Les feuilles d'automne. Chants du crépuscule. Paris, n.d.
Htn	41573.32.2*	Hugo, Victor. Hernani. n.p., n.d.
	41572.8.10	Hugo, Victor. Histoire d'un crime. N.Y., n.d.
	41571.6.10	Hugo, Victor. Les misérables. Chicago, n.d. 3v.
	41573.32.52	Hugo, Victor. Lucretia Borgia. New Orleans, n.d.
	41572.18	Hugo, Victor. Napoléon le petit. Paris, n.d.
Htn	41571.29*	Hugo, Victor. Quatre-vingt treize. Paris, n.d.
	41574.16.9	Hugo, Victor. Le roman de Juliette et de Victor Hugo. Paris, n.d.
	41573.23.15	Hugo, Victor. The story of Esmeralda; condensed from the hunchback. N.Y., n.d.
	Mol 608.10	Humbert, C. Lustige Puppen Tragödie. Bielefeld, n.d.
	41588.60	Les Hussietes, ou Le siége de Neurnbourg. n.p., n.d.
	42548.75	L'ingrat, comédie en cinq actes. Mss. n.p., n.d.
	43667.1.21	Jammes, Francis. Oeuvres inédites. n.p., n.d.
	40567.17	Janin, Jules. Contes non estampillés. Paris, n.d.
	40561.22	Janin, Jules. L'été à Paris. Paris, n.d.
	40567.26	Janin, Jules. Les petits bonheurs. n.p., n.d.
	40567.23	Janin, Jules. La semaine des trois jeudis. n.p., n.d.
	37567.29	Jaubert, Caroline. Souvenirs de la vie littéraire. Paris, n.d.
	37558.37.5	Jeanroy-Félix, V. Fauteuils contemporains de l'Académie. Paris, n.d.
	37566.22	Jeanroy-Felix, Victor. Nouvelle histoire de la littérature française pendant la restauration. Paris, n.d.
	37566.23	Jeanroy-Felix, Victor. Nouvelle histoire de la littérature française sous la monarchie de juillet. Paris, n.d.
	38524.842	Jesus Maria, sur le martyre des SS. Innocens. n.p., n.d.
	39576.2.5	Johnston, Elsie. Le marquis d'Argens, sa vie et ses oeuvres. Thèse. Paris, n.d.
	40516.22	Jouin, Nicolas. Remonstrances. n.p., n.d.
	37588.10	Journal singe, par Fiaud. London, n.d.
	37574.31	Joyeux refrains de nos pères. Paris, n.d.
	42546.31.14	Julien, B. De da production indéfinie d'ouvrages dramatiques. n.p., n.d.
	FL 379.25	Jullien, Adolphe. La comédie à la cour. Paris, n.d.
	42587.10	Julliot, François de. La contre-allée. Paris, n.d.
	41544.34	Karr, Alphonse. Voyage autour de mon jardin. Paris, n.d.
	37563.76	Keating, L.C. Studies on the literary salon in France, 1550-1615. n.p., n.d.
	Mol 611.6	Kerby, W.M. Molière and the Restoration comedy in England. London, n.d.
	38516.11	Kervyn de Lettenhove. Le telemaque du XVe siècle. Bruxelles, n.d.
	37567.38	Klein, Félix. Le mouvement Néo-Chrétien. Paris, n.d.
	Mol 880.22	Kleist, H. von. Amphitryon. Berlin, n.d.
	41552.4	Kock, Charles Paul de. L'amant de la lune. Paris, n.d. 3v.
	41552.5	Kock, Charles Paul de. L'amoureux transi. Paris, n.d.
	41552.10	Kock, Charles Paul de. La bouqtière du chateau d'eau. Paris, n.d. 2v.
	41552.11	Kock, Charles Paul de. Carotin. Paris, n.d.
	41552.12	Kock, Charles Paul de. Ce monsieur. Paris, n.d.
	41552.13	Kock, Charles Paul de. Cerisette. Paris, n.d.
	41552.15	Kock, Charles Paul de. Les demoiselles de magasin. Paris, n.d.
	41552.16	Kock, Charles Paul de. Une drôle de maison. Paris, n.d.
	41552.17	Kock, Charles Paul de. Les étuvistes. Paris, n.d.
	41552.19	Kock, Charles Paul de. La femme à trois visages. Paris, n.d.
	41552.20	Kock, Charles Paul de. Les femmes, le jeu et le vin. Paris, n.d.
	41552.21	Kock, Charles Paul de. La fille aux trois jupons. Paris, n.d.
	41552.22	Kock, Charles Paul de. Friquette. Paris, n.d.
	41552.23	Kock, Charles Paul de. Une gaillarde. Paris, n.d.
	41552.24	Kock, Charles Paul de. La grande ville. Paris, n.d.
	41552.25	Kock, Charles Paul de. Une grappe de groseille. Paris, n.d.
	41552.29	Kock, Charles Paul de. Les intrigants. Paris, n.d. 2v.
	41553.5	Kock, Charles Paul de. Un jeune homme mystérieux. Paris, n.d.
	41553.6	Kock, Charles Paul de. La jolie fille du faubourg. Paris, n.d.
	41553.8	Kock, Charles Paul de. Madame de Montflanquin. Paris, n.d.
	41553.9	Kock, Charles Paul de. Madame Pantalon. Paris, n.d.
	41553.10	Kock, Charles Paul de. Madame Papin. Paris, n.d.
	41553.35	Kock, Charles Paul de. Madame Saint Lambert. Paris, n.d.
	41553.14	Kock, Charles Paul de. La mariée de Fontenay-aux-Roses. Paris, n.d.
	41553.15	Kock, Charles Paul de. Mon ami Piffard. Paris, n.d.
	41553.17	Kock, Charles Paul de. Monsieur Choublanc. Paris, n.d.
	41553.19	Kock, Charles Paul de. Papa beau-père. Paris, n.d.
	41553.21	Kock, Charles Paul de. La petite Lise. Paris, n.d.
	41553.22	Kock, Charles Paul de. Les petits ruisseaux. Paris, n.d.
	41553.23	Kock, Charles Paul de. La prairie aux coquelicots. Paris, n.d.
	41553.24	Kock, Charles Paul de. Le professeur Ficheclaque. Paris, n.d.
	41553.25	Kock, Charles Paul de. Sans cravate. Paris, n.d.
	41553.26	Kock, Charles Paul de. Le sentier aux prunes. Paris, n.d.
	41551.3	Kock, Paul de. L'enfant de ma femme. Paris, n.d.
	41551.4	Kock, Paul de. Les femmes, le jeu, le vin. Paris, n.d.
	41551.6	Kock, Paul de. Une fête aux environs de Paris. Paris, n.d.
	41551.5	Kock, Paul de. Mon ami Piffard. Paris, n.d.
	40547.14.80	Kuhn, Hildegard. Michelets Landschaft in La Mer und La Montagne. Wertheim, n.d.
	37597.11.5	Kupka, Paul. Zur Chronologie und Genesis des Roman de la rose. Gardelegen, n.d.
	42548.28.15	Labiche, Eugène. La poudre aux yeux. N.Y., n.d.
	40571.4	Labitte, Charles. Études littéraires. Paris, n.d. 2v.
	42511.13	Laboulaye, Édourd. Abdallah. Nashville., n.d.
	42511.13.5	Laboulaye, Édourd. Abdallah. 9. ed. London, n.d.

No date - cont.

Htn 38564.12* La Bruyère, J. de. Discours sur Théophraste. n.p., n.d.
38564.24 La Bruyère, J. de. Oeuvres. Strasbourg, n.d.
41554.12 Lacroix, Paul. Le bon vieux temps. n.p., n.d.
39524.7 La Fontaine, Jean de. Fables. Paris, n.d.
38576.23 La Fosse d'Aubigny, A. de. Manlius Capitolinus. Paris, n.d.
37574.55A Lamartine, Alfred. Love songs of France, from original of De Musset. N.Y., n.d.
37543.38.1 Lanson, Gustave. Histoire de la littérature française. 4. éd. Paris, n.d.
42576.46.18 Lapauze, Jeanne L. L'honneur d'une femme. Paris, n.d.
42576.46.19 Lapauze, Jeanne L. Invincible charme. Paris, n.d.
42576.46.16 Lapauze, Jeanne L. Passion slave. Paris, n.d.
Mon 200.3 La Rounat, C. Imitation on de Montaigne. n.p., n.d.
42544.24.4 Lavedan, Henri. Catherine. Paris, n.d.
42544.23 Lavedan, Henri. Inconsolables. (Fiction). Paris, n.d.
42544.24.6 Lavedan, Henri. Le marquis de Priola. (Drama). Paris, n.d.
Htn 42544.24.14* Lavedan, Henri. Le nouveau jeu. Paris, n.d.
42544.24.7 Lavedan, Henri. Le prince d'Aurec. Paris, n.d.
42544.24.9 Lavedan, Henri. Le vieux marcheur. Paris, n.d.
42544.24.5 Lavedan, Henri. Viveurs. (Drama). Paris, n.d.
42554.16.9 Le Braz, A. Ames d'occident. 3e éd. Paris, n.d.
42554.16.7 Le Braz, A. Du soleil et de la brume. Paris, n.d.
42554.16.10 Le Braz, A. Le sang de la Sirène. Paris, n.d.
41595.7 Lebrun, Pierre. Oeuvres. Théâtre. Poésies. Discours. Paris, n.d. 4v.
43688.13.110 Leclerq, Léna. Notre coeur est un malfaiteur. Paris, n.d.
42544.19 Legouvé, Gabriel. Conferences parisiennes. Paris, n.d.
39527.29.5 Lemaistre, Felix. Fables de La Fontaine. Paris, n.d.
40587.13A Lemaître, J. Chateaubriand. Paris, n.d.
42544.33.13 Lemaître, Jules. Bertrade. Paris, n.d.
42544.33.9 Lemaître, Jules. La massiere. Paris, n.d.
42544.33.12A Lemaître, Jules. Théâtre. Paris, n.d. 3v.
42544.33.17 Lemaître, Jules. La vieillesse d'Hélène. Paris, n.d.
37530.15 Lemcke, Ernst. Additional list of the classics and belles lettres. Supplement. N.Y., n.d.
42571.43 L'Epine, E. Legend of Croquemitaine. London, n.d.
43688.1.33 Leroux, Gaston. Le fantôme de l'opéra. 15e éd. Paris, n.d.
X Cg 43688.1.32 Leroux, Gaston. Le parfum de la dame en noir. Paris, n.d.
42576.45.2 Le Roux, H. Le fils à papa. Paris, n.d.
42576.44.2 Le Roux, H. Ô mon passé. Mémoires d'un enfant. Paris, n.d.
42576.46.6 Le Roy, Eugène. L'ennemi de la mort. Paris, n.d.
40511.2 LeSage, Alain René. Bibliographical notes upon an unique set of his editions. London, n.d.
41574.47 Lesclide, Richard (Mme.). Victor Hugo intime. Paris, n.d.
42576.73 Lescot, Marie Meusy. Un peu, beaucoup, passionnement. St. Henri, n.d.
FL 396.50 Le théâtre libre. Saisons 1887 à 1890. n.p., n.d.
39533.32 Lettres de....Guy Patin. n.p., n.d.
41592.11 Lettres inédites de Béranger à Dupont de l'Eure. Paris, n.d.
37543.44 Levallois, Jules. Mémoires d'un critique. Paris, n.d.
Mol 698.6F Leveaux, Eugène. A l'ombre de Molière. Paris, n.d.
FL 362.10 Levrault, L. Drame et tragédie. (Évolution du Geure). Paris, n.d.
37556.35 Levrault, Léon. Le roman (Évolution du genre). Paris, n.d.
37564.49 Lezat, A. De la prédication sous Henri IV. Paris, n.d.
43690.1.33 Lichtenberger, A. Contes heroïques 1789-1795. Paris, n.d.
43690.1.30 Lichtenberger, A. La folle aventure. 6. éd. Paris, n.d.
43690.1.40 Lichtenberger, A. Juste Lobel. Paris, n.d.
43690.1.31 Lichtenberger, A. Le sang nouveau. Paris, n.d.
FL 383.80 Liste des pièces représentées pour la première fois à Paris...1879-1889. n.p., n.d.
41586.17 Lombard, V. de Langires. Le meunier de Sans-Souci. Paris, n.d.
Mol 612.13 Lucas, H. Le foyer du théâtre-français. Paris, n.d.
37573.11A Lucas, St. John. The Oxford book of French verse. N.Y., n.d.
Htn Mol 150.3* Lully, J.B. de. L'amour medecin-music. Manuscript. n.p., n.d.
Htn Mol 150.3.5* Lully, J.B. de. Le ballet du Sicilien. Manuscript n.p., n.d.
42576.74 Macé, Jean. L'arithmétique du Grand-papa. 5. éd. Paris, n.d.
42576.74.9 Macé, Jean. Théâtre du petit château. 4. éd. Paris, n.d.
43538.14.835 Maciel, L.C. Samuel Beckett e a solidão humana. Porto Alegre, n.d.
42541.21.17 Maeterlinck, M. Douze chansons. Paris, n.d.
42545.3.43.15 Maeterlinck, Maurice. Der Eindrinqling, die Blinden. Leipzig, n.d.
37581.40.17 Magasin théâtral. Miscellaneous unbound plays. Paris, n.d.
40571.7 Maignien, E.A.N. Études littéraires et philosophiques. Paris, n.d.
42587.16.12 Maindron, M. Le tournoi de Vanplassane. Paris, n.d.
40588.40 Maistre, Xavier. Oeuvres complètes. Boston, n.d.
40588.38 Maistre, Xavier. Oeuvres complètes. Paris, n.d.
42587.16.15 Maizeroy, Rene. La dernière croisade. Paris, n.d.
42577.5.3 Malot, Hector. Cara. Paris, n.d.
42577.5.5 Malot, Hector. En famille. Paris, n.d. 2v.
42577.7 Malot, Hector. Justice. Paris, n.d.
42577.9.2 Malot, Hector. Marié par les prêtres. Paris, n.d.
42577.10 Malot, Hector. Mondaine. Paris, n.d.
42577.11.12 Malot, Hector. Séduction. Paris, n.d.
41554.45 Manceau, A.V.A. (Mme.). Céline. Paris, n.d.
Htn 42545.7* Maquet, A. The double marriage. London, n.d.
Htn 42576.75* Marchal, C. Physiologie de l'anglais à Paris. Paris, n.d.
43697.75.6400 Margat, Yves. La légende de Saint-Cornély. n.p., n.d.
38526.32.17A Marguerite d'Angoulême. The Heptaméron. London, n.d.
40537.58 Le mariage de la princesse du L'anturelu. n.p., n.d.
Htn 40535.29* Marivaux, Pierre Carlet de Chamblain de. Les fausses confidences; comédie. Paris, n.d.
40535.27.5 Marivaux, Pierre Carlet de Chamblain de. Théâtre choisi. Paris, n.d.
40535.30 Marivaux, Pierre Carlet de Chamblain de. La vie de Marianne. Paris, n.d. 2v.
42587.19.35 Martel, T. La main aux dames. Paris, n.d.
42545.9.4 Martel de Janville, S.G. Napoléonette. Paris, n.d.
42587.19.38 Massabuan, J. Nos maitres. Paris, n.d.
Mol 698.7F Massenet, J. Serenade de Molière. Paris, n.d.
37558.60 Masson, Frédéric. L'Académie française 1629-1793. 2. éd. Paris, n.d.

No date - cont.

42577.1.23 Maupassant, Guy de. The complete short stories. N.Y., n.d.
42577.4.5 Maupassant, Guy de. Contes du jour. Paris, n.d.
42577.4.23 Maupassant, Guy de. L'héritage. Paris, n.d.
42577.4.29.4 Maupassant, Guy de. The necklace. N.Y., n.d.
42577.4.4 Maupassant, Guy de. Sur l'eau. Paris, n.d.
42577.4.22 Maupassant, Guy de. Toine. Paris, n.d.
42577.4.29.20 Maupassant, Guy de. La vie errante. Paris, n.d.
42577.4.8 Maupassant, Guy de. Who knows? n.p., n.d.
43625.19.800 Mediterranea. 3e année, no. 27, mars 1929. Nice, n.d.
42545.10.11.8 Meilhac, Henri. Froufrou. London, n.d.
42545.10.25 Meilhac, Henri. Mam'zelle Nitouche. Paris, n.d.
42545.13 Meilhac, Henri. Théâtre. v.2. Paris, n.d.
42545.14 Meilhac, Henri. Théâtre. v.3. n.p., n.d.
42545.15 Meilhac, Henri. Théâtre. v.4. n.p., n.d.
42545.16 Meilhac, Henri. Théâtre. v.5. n.p., n.d.
42545.17 Meilhac, Henri. Théâtre. v.6. n.p., n.d.
42545.18 Meilhac, Henri. Théâtre. v.7. n.p., n.d.
41578.59 Mélanges sur Lamartine. n.p., n.d.
42555.58.38 Mendès, Catulle. Pierre la Veridique. Paris, n.d.
42587.23 Mérey, Joseph. Marseille et les marseillais. Paris, n.d.
41555.23.6 Mérimée, Prosper. Colomba. Paris, n.d.
37574.45 Merlet, Gustave. Extraits de poètes lyriques du XIXe siècle. Paris, n.d.
42548.70 Metenier, O. Les pièces à succès. Paris, n.d. 2v.
42545.21.9 Méténier, Oscar. En famille. Paris, n.d.
42545.23 Meurice, Paul. Benvenuto Cellini. Paris, n.d.
43698.2.30 Meyer, Robert. Quelques mots...avant le spectacle. Paris, n.d.
42576.63.27 Michaut, G. Anatole France. 4. éd. Paris, n.d.
38514.47 Michel, F. Chroniques françaises de Jacques Gondar. Paris, n.d.
40547.14 Michelet, Jules. Pages choisies. Paris, n.d.
42587.28 Michelet, Victor Emile. Contes aventureux. Paris, n.d.
Mol 613.14 Miller, Elizabeth. Articles on Molière. n.p., n.d. 2 pam.
Mol 613.13 Miller, Elizabeth. A collection of pamphlets on Molière. Paris? n.d.? 9 pam.
38513.6 Miracle de mon Seigneur Saint Nicolas. n.p., n.d.
42545.28.7.16 Mirbeau, Octave. La guerre. Bruxelles, n.d.
Htn 38513.2* Le mistère de la Saincte Hostie. Paris, n.d.
39545.5.6 Mohr, L. Les centenaires de Voltaire et Rousseau. n.p., n.d.
42545.28.9 Moinaux, Georges. Boubouroche. Paris, n.d.
X Cg 42545.28.9.5 Moinaux, Georges. La paix chez soi. Paris, n.d. 8 pam.
42545.28.20 Moinaux, Jules. Les deux aveugles. n.p., n.d.
37538.6 Moke, Henry G. Histoire de la littérature française. Brussels, n.d. 2v.
Mol 155.20 Molière, Jean Baptiste Poquelin. L'amour médecin. n.p., n.d.
Mol 166.7 Molière, Jean Baptiste Poquelin. L'avaro...Soncini. n.p., n.d.
Mol 182.1.11 Molière, Jean Baptiste Poquelin. Dépit amoureux en deux actes. n.p., n.d.
Mol 195.55 Molière, Jean Baptiste Poquelin. L'escole des femmes. n.p., n.d.
Mol 211.15 Molière, Jean Baptiste Poquelin. Les femmes savantes. n.p., n.d.
Mol 166.5.7 Molière, Jean Baptiste Poquelin. Der Geizige...Cornelius. Leipzig, n.d.
Mol 212.5.7 Molière, Jean Baptiste Poquelin. Die gelehrten Frauen...Maltzan. Leipzig, n.d.
Mol 219.5.5 Molière, Jean Baptiste Poquelin. George Dandin...A. Cornelius. Leipzig, n.d.
Mol 252.5.5 Molière, Jean Baptiste Poquelin. Die Gezierten. Cornélius. Leipzig, n.d.
Mol 182.5.5 Molière, Jean Baptiste Poquelin. Liebeszwist...Maltzan. Leipzig, n.d.
Mol 228.21 Molière, Jean Baptiste Poquelin. Le malade imaginaire...Gombert. London, n.d.
Mol 228.18 Molière, Jean Baptiste Poquelin. Le malade imaginaire. Limoges, n.d.
Mol 235.18 Molière, Jean Baptiste Poquelin. Le médecin malgré lui...Gombert. London, n.d.
Mol 246.5.5 Molière, Jean Baptiste Poquelin. Der Menschenfrind. Kayser. Delitzsch, n.d.
Mol 245.40 Molière, Jean Baptiste Poquelin. Le misanthrope. Dubois. Paris, n.d.
Mol 245.55 Molière, Jean Baptiste Poquelin. Le misanthrope. Leys. Paris, n.d.
Mol 236.76.5 Molière, Jean Baptiste Poquelin. Nasilu stal sa lekárom...Smetana. Senici, n.d.
Mol 18.71.10 Molière, Jean Baptiste Poquelin. Oeuvres complètes. Paris, n.d. 2v.
Mol 209.5.5 Molière, Jean Baptiste Poquelin. Die Plagegeister...Schröder. Leipzig, n.d.
Mol 251.44 Molière, Jean Baptiste Poquelin. Les précieuses ridicules. Lermina. Paris, n.d.
Mol 64.5.2 Molière, Jean Baptiste Poquelin. Repertorio scelto...Barbieri. v.1-6. Milano, n.d.
Mol 202.5.5 Molière, Jean Baptiste Poquelin. Die Schule der Ehemänner...Schröder. Leipzig, n.d.
Mol 196.5.5 Molière, Jean Baptiste Poquelin. Die Schule der Frauen...Schröder. Leipzig, n.d.
Mol 269.5.10 Molière, Jean Baptiste Poquelin. Tartüffe. Schröder. Leipzig, n.d.
Mol 268.127 Molière, Jean Baptiste Poquelin. Le Tartuffe. Strasbourg, n.d.
Mol 268.65 Molière, Jean Baptiste Poquelin. Le Tartuffe. Moland. 3. éd. Paris, n.d.
Mol 19.10 Molière, Jean Baptiste Poquelin. Théâtre complet illustré. v.1-3, 4-7. Paris, n.d. 2v.
Mol 900.1F Molière scrap-book. n.p., n.d.
41595.31.100 Mollevant, C.L. Ode sur le 18 brumaire. n.p., n.d.
42545.32 Monnier, Henry. La religion des imbeciles. Paris, n.d.
42541.22 Monnier, Henry. Scènes populaires. Paris, n.d.
42577.13.24 Montépin, X. de. Krvava ruka. Zagreb, n.d.
39594.12A Montesquieu, C.L. de S. Lettres persanes. Paris, n.d.
41555.66 Montgolfier, Adelaide. Barnabé, conte vrai. 2. éd. Paris, n.d.
41555.65 Montgolfier, Adelaide. Piccolissima. 2. éd. Paris, n.d.
42545.43 Moreau, Emile. Théâtre. Paris, n.d. 2v.
42545.44.16 Moreau, Eugène. The courier of Lyons. v.1-2. London, n.d.
43701.3.30 Morel, J. Feuilles mortes. Paris, n.d.

Chronological Listing

No date - cont.

FL 370.67 Mortensen, Johan. Profandramat i Frankrike. Lund, n.d.
42533.18 Mortier, Arnold. Les soirées parisiennes. 1874-1884. Paris, n.d. 11v.
42542.64.28 Moselly, E. Lucien Descaves. Paris, n.d.
41586.27.75 Mourier, J.F. Zara, ou La soeur de l'Arabe. Paris, n.d.
Mol 194.23 Mozard. Don Giovanni; Don Juan. Parigi, n.d.
Mol 194.22 Mozard. Don Juan, opera en cinq actes. Paris, n.d.
39566.33 Murobian, A. Les conceptions pédagogiques de Diderot. Paris, n.d.
41596.18.5.5 Musset, Alfred de. Barberine. Lorenzaccio. Strassburg, n.d.
Mol 713.9 Musset, P. de. Le déjeuner de Molière. n.p., n.d.
42587.37.5 Nesmy, Jean. Les égarés. Paris, n.d.
42542.48.26 Noel, C.M. Bourgeoisie française et l'oeuvre de M. A. Capus. n.p., n.d.
40524.17.80 Nogaret, François Félix. Profession de foi. n.p., n.d. 2 pam.
Htn 42555.66* Nolhac, Pierre de. Les sonnets. Paris, n.d.
Htn Mon 80.50* Norton, Grace. Lexique to the Theologie naturelle of Raymond Sebond. n.p., n.d. 3v.
FL 396.38 Notice descriptive du théâtre historique ornée de 32 gravures. Paris, n.d.
42587.37.7 Noussanne, H. de. Jasmin Robba. Paris, n.d.
Htn 38513.36* Nouvelle moralité d'une pauvre fille villageoise. Paris, n.d.
39582.4 Oeuvres complètes de Mably. v.1-24. Paris, n.d. 12v.
39531.7 Oeuvres de Jean Baptiste Rousseau. Brussels, n.d. 3v.
Htn 39531.5* Oeuvres diverses de Jean Baptiste Rousseau. London, n.d. 2v.
42578.29.4 Ohnet, Georges. Prince Serge Panine. N.Y., n.d.
37574.628 Oradour, B. d'. Album poétique illustré. 2. éd. Stuttgart, n.d.
Mol 615.1 Ott, Philipp. Über das Verhältniss Drydens zu Molière. Landshut, n.d.
37574.29.5 Oxenford, John. Book of French songs. London, n.d.
42545.68.5 Pailleron, Edouard. Le monde ou l'on s'amuse. 11e éd. Paris, n.d.
40593.45.5 Pange, P.L.M. de B. Madame de Staël et la découverte de l'Allemagne. n.p., n.d.
37556.24.8 Paris, Gaston. Piétro Toldo. Contributo allo studio della novella francese del XV e XVI secolo. n.p., n.d.
38542.33 Passard, F.L. Bibliothèque épistolaire. Paris, n.d.
38513.22.10 Pathelin. Maistre Pierre Pathelin. Strasbourg, n.d.
39535.55 Pauckoucke, A.J. L'arte de Desoppiler La Rote. n.p., n.d.
Mon 180.1.3 Payen, J.F. Recherches sur Montaigne. n.p., n.d.
43738.1.20 Péguy, Charles. Oeuvres choisies 1900-1910. 3e éd. Paris, n.d.
42578.30.78 Peladan, J. De l'humanisme. Paris, n.d.
37573.29 Pellissier, G. Anthologie des poètes du XIXe siècle. Paris, n.d.
37572.42 Pellissier, G. Le XVIIe siècle par les textes. Paris, n.d.
37543.120A Pellissier, Georges. Précis de l'histoire de la littérature française. Paris, n.d.
41586.27.8 Perin, René. Fitz-Henri, ou maison des fous. n.p., n.d.
37566.38 Perrens, F.T. Histoire sommaire de la littérature française au XIXe siècle. Paris, n.d.
38576.42 Perrin, Pierre. Bacchus et Ariane. n.p., n.d.
37556.21.12 Perrodil, E. de. Un an de journalisme à Lourdes. Paris, n.d.
FL 358.89 Petit de Julleville, L. Le théâtre en France. Paris, n.d.
37572.14 Petit de Julleville, S. Morceaux choisies des auteurs français. Paris, n.d.
38529.9 La petite bourgeoise poème satirique de l'an 1610. Strasbourg, n.d.
37574.12 Les petits poètes du XVIIIe siècle. Paris, n.d.
38513.68 Pfühl, E. Die weitere Fassung der alterfranzösischen Dichtung in achtsilbigen Reimpaaren. Greifswald, n.d. 2 pam.
43740.1.30 Philippe, Charles Louis. La mère et l'enfant. 5e éd. Paris, n.d.
Mol 716.1 Picard, L.B. Notice sur Molière. n.p., n.d.
42545.69.60 Pierron, Eugène. Two can play at that game. v.1-2. N.Y., n.d.
41586.28 Pixerécourt, R.C.G. de. Les petits Auvergnats. Paris, n.d.
42555.72.10 Pomairols, Charles de. Ascension. Paris, n.d.
42587.49.19 Pommerol, Jean. Le cas du Lieutenant Sigmarie. Paris, n.d.
42587.49.20 Pommerol, Jean. Un fruit et puis un autre fruit. Paris, n.d.
41596.50.7 Pommier, A. Poésies. n.p., n.d.
41596.51.2 Porchat, Jacques. Trois mois sous la neige. N.Y., n.d.
Htn Mol 925.1PF* Portfolio of Molière portraits. n.p., n.d.
42541.31.9.5 Pottecher, Maurice. Les spectacles du théâtre du peuple. v.1-4,5-7. n.p., n.d. 2 pam.
42511.21 Poujoulat, M. Variétés littéraires. Lille, n.d.
37530.85 Princeton University. Library. List of French periodicals of the eighteenth and early nineteeth century. n.p., n.d.
Htn 40527.26* Quesnel, Pierre. Almanach du diable. Enfers, n.d.
38588.16.30 Quinault, Philippe. Cadmus et Hermione; tragédie en musique. n.p., n.d.
38526.46.1500 Quinault, Philippe. Persée, tragédie. n.p., n.d.
42515.51 Quinet, Edgar. Ahasvérus. (Oeuvres complètes, 7). Paris, n.d.
42515.68.10 Quinet, Edgar. Ahasvérus. Paris, n.d.
42515.47 Quinet, Edgar. Christianisme et la revolution française. (Oeuvres complètes, 3). Paris, n.d.
42515.68.3 Quinet, Edgar. Le Christianisme et la revolution française. Paris, n.d.
42515.58 Quinet, Edgar. Correspondance. Lettres à sa mere. (Oeuvres complètes, 19, 20). Paris, n.d. 2v.
42515.68.24 Quinet, Edgar. Correspondance. Lettres à sa mère. Paris, n.d. 2v.
42515.59 Quinet, Edgar. La création. (Oeuvres complètes, 21, 22). Paris, n.d. 2v.
42515.68.18 Quinet, Edgar. La création. Paris, n.d. 2v.
42515.54 Quinet, Edgar. L'enseignement du peuple. (Oeuvres complètes, 11). Paris, n.d.
42515.68.13 Quinet, Edgar. L'enseignement du peuple. Paris, n.d.
42515.60 Quinet, Edgar. L'esprit nouveau. (Oeuvres complètes, 23). Paris, n.d.
42515.68.22 Quinet, Edgar. L'esprit nouveau. Paris, n.d.
42515.68 Quinet, Edgar. Le génie des religions. Paris, n.d.
42515.64 Quinet, Edgar. La Grèce moderne. (Oeuvres complètes, 27). Paris, n.d.

No date - cont.

42515.68.8 Quinet, Edgar. La Grèce moderne. Paris, n.d.
42515.56 Quinet, Edgar. Histoire de la campagne de 1815. (Oeuvres complètes, 15). Paris, n.d.
42515.68.17 Quinet, Edgar. Histoire de la campagne de 1815. Paris, n.d.
42515.53 Quinet, Edgar. Histoire de mes idées. (Oeuvres complètes, 10). Paris, n.d.
42515.68.14 Quinet, Edgar. Histoire de mes idées. Paris, n.d.
42515.68.2 Quinet, Edgar. Les Jésuites. Paris, n.d.
42515.46 Quinet, Edgar. Le Jésuits. (Oeuvres complètes, 2). Paris, n.d.
42515.63 Quinet, Edgar. Le livre de l'exilé. (Oeuvres complètes, 26). Paris, n.d.
42515.68.19 Quinet, Edgar. Le livre de l'exilé. Paris, n.d.
42515.49 Quinet, Edgar. Marnix de Sainte-Aldegonde. (Oeuvres complètes, 5). Paris, n.d.
42515.68.5 Quinet, Edgar. Marnix de Sainte-Aldegonde. 6. éd. Paris, n.d.
42515.57 Quinet, Edgar. Merlin l'enchanteur. (Oeuvres complètes, 17, 18). Paris, n.d.
42515.68.15 Quinet, Edgar. Merlin l'enchanteur. Paris, n.d. 2v.
42515.52.5 Quinet, Edgar. Mes vacances en Espagne. (Oeuvres complètes, 9). Paris, n.d.
42515.68.9 Quinet, Edgar. Mes vacances en Espagne. 5. éd. Paris, n.d.
42515.68.7 Quinet, Edgar. Premiers travaux. Paris, n.d.
42515.68.11 Quinet, Edgar. Prométhée. Paris, n.d.
42515.52 Quinet, Edgar. Prométhie, les esclaves. (Oeuvres complètes, 8). Paris, n.d.
42515.62 Quinet, Edgar. La république. (Oeuvres completes, 25). Paris, n.d.
42515.68.21 Quinet, Edgar. La république. Paris, n.d.
42515.55 Quinet, Edgar. La révolution. (Oeuvres complètes, 12-14). Paris, n.d. 3v.
42515.68.16 Quinet, Edgar. La révolution précédée de la critique de la révolution. Paris, n.d. 3v.
42515.48 Quinet, Edgar. Les révolutions d'Italie. (Oeuvres complètes, 4). Paris, n.d.
42515.68.4 Quinet, Edgar. Les révolutions d'Italie. Paris, n.d. 2v.
42515.50 Quinet, Edgar. Les roumains. (Oeuvres complètes, 6). Paris, n.d.
42515.68.6 Quinet, Edgar. Les roumains. Allemagne et Italie. Paris, n.d.
42515.61 Quinet, Edgar. Le siège de Paris. (Oeuvres complètes, 24). Paris, n.d.
42515.68.20 Quinet, Edgar. Le siège de Paris. Paris, n.d.
42515.65 Quinet, Edgar. Vie et mort du genie grec. (Oeuvres complètes, 28). Paris, n.d.
42515.68.23 Quinet, Edgar. Vie et mort du génie grec. Paris, n.d.
38536.24 Rabelais, F. Gargantua et Pantagruel. Paris, n.d.
38536.24.3 Rabelais, F. Gargantua et Pantagruel. Paris, n.d. 3v.
38585.19.7 Racine, Jean. Andromaque. Strasbourg, n.d.
38585.20.10 Racine, Jean. Athalie. Strasbourg, n.d.
38583.4 Racine, Jean. Oeuvres. Paris, n.d. 5v.
38585.42 Racine, Jean. Phèdre. Strasbourg, n.d.
38583.5.5 Racine, Jean. Théâtre complet. Paris, n.d.
38583.6.13 Racine, Jean. Théâtre complet. Paris, n.d.
38583.5.12 Racine, Jean. Théâtre complet. Paris, n.d.
NEDL 38583.5.10 Racine, Jean. Théâtre complet. Paris, n.d.
38583.8 Racine, Jean. Théâtre complet. Paris, n.d.
38583.6.15 Racine, Jean. Théâtre complet. Illustré. v.1-3. Paris, n.d.
42581.38 Rambaud, A. L'anneau de César. Paris, n.d.
42587.50.15 Rambaud, Alfred. L'anneau de César. 7. éd. Paris, n.d. 2v.
42587.50.25 Rambaud, Alfred. L'empereur de Carthage. Paris, n.d.
40516.37 Ramsay, A.M. de. A new cyropaedia. Edinburgh, n.d.
FL 398.47.50 Raphanel, Jean. Mlle. Marie Leconte, biographie critique. Paris, n.d.
42535.19.5 Ratisbonne, Louis. La comédie enfantine. Pt. 1. 91. éd. Paris, n.d.
37574.345 Recueil d'hymnes, odes, etc., relatifs aux fêtes décadaire. n.p., n.d. 3 pam.
38587.9.5A Regnard, Jean François. Théâtre. Paris, n.d.
Htn 42587.52.20* Renard, Jules. Histoires naturelles. Paris, n.d.
42578.7 Rendade, J. Alma Mater. Paris, n.d.
FL 398.7.16F Renner, A.L. Sarah Bernhardt: artist and woman. N.Y., n.d.
40524.29 Restif de la Bretonne, Nicolas E. L'an 2000. Strasbourg, n.d.
Htn 40524.28.5* Restif de la Bretonne, Nicolas E. Les contemporaines mêlées. Paris, n.d.
39586.27.20 Rochery, Paul. Rivarol, sa vie et des écrits. n.p., n.d.
42546.8.9 Rodenbach, G. Bruges-la-Morte. Paris, n.d.
40537.16 Roederer, A.L. Lettre à Adrien Lézay sur Chénier. Paris, n.d.
43757.50.133 Rolland, Romain. Jean Christophe. Paris, n.d. 4v.
43757.50.235 Rolland, Romain. Jean-Christophe - la fin du voyage. Les amies. 14e éd. Paris, n.d.
Htn 38525.17.5* Ronsard, Pierre de. Choix de sonnets. n.p., n.d.
Htn 38525.15* Ronsard, Pierre de. Oeuvres - odes. v.1, 2, 3-5. Strassbourg, n.d. 3v.
38525.18 Ronsard, Pierre de. XI sonnets nouvellement recueillis. Texte de 1552 et 1578. n.p., n.d.
42546.31.8 Roosevelt, B. Victorien Sardou...a personal study. N.Y., n.d.
42578.22.7 Rosny, J.H. Le fauve. Paris, n.d.
42578.22.27 Rosny, J.H. Les rafales. Paris, n.d.
42578.22.5 Rosny, J.H. Sous le fardeau. Paris, n.d.
FL 6026.10.3 Rousseau, J.J. Collection of etchings used in Rousseau's confessions. n.p., n.d.
FL 6026.5 Rousseau, J.J. The confessions. London, n.d.
FL 6022.25A Rousseau, J.J. Les confessions. Paris, n.d. 2v.
FL 6064.5 Rousseau, J.J. Le devin du village. Paris, n.d.
FL 6065.50 Rousseau, J.J. A dictionary of music. London, n.d.
FL 6094.5 Rousseau, J.J. Les rêveries du promeneur solitaire. n.p., n.d.
FL 6036.5.10 Rousseau, J.J. The social contract. London, n.d.
42578.31.100 Rude, Maxime. Le cousin infâme. 4. éd. Paris, n.d.
V43500.285 Ruet, Noël. L'urne penchée. 2. ed. Seraing, n.d.
38542.22 Saint-Evremond, C. de M. de S.D. Oeuvres choisies. Paris, n.d.
39595.22 St. Pierre, J.H.B. de. Paul et Virginie. Strasbourg, n.d.

No date - cont.

	40578.4	Sainte-Beuve, Charles A. Causeries du lundi. Paris, n.d. 16v.
	40577.4	Sainte-Beuve, Charles A. Causeries du lundi. 3. éd. Paris, n.d. 15v.
	40575.45	Sainte-Beuve, Charles A. Sainte-Beuve; textes choisis. Neuchâtel, n.d.
	41557.9.19	Sand, George. Les Beaux Messieurs. Paris, n.d. 2v.
	41557.9.25	Sand, George. The countess of Rudolstadt. Philadelphia, n.d.
	41557.9.40	Sand, George. The last Aldini. A love story. Philadelphia, n.d.
	41557.32	Sand, George. Madame de Sommerville. n.p., n.d.
	41557.26.4	Sandeau, Jules. La Roche aux Mouettes. 25e ed. Paris, n.d.
	41557.27.15	Sandeau, Jules. Tears! Idle tears! n.p., n.d.
	38527.66	Sanlecque, Louis de. Poésies du Père Sanlecque. v.1-2. n.p., n.d.
	42546.30.7.5	Sardou, Victorien. Fédora. Milano, n.d.
	42546.30.7.7	Sardou, Victorien. Fédora. n.p., n.d.
	42546.30.39	Sardou, Victorien. Our boon companions. N.Y., n.d.
	42546.20.2	Sardou, Victorien. Rabagas; comedie en 5 actes, en prose. Paris, n.d.
	42546.27	Sardou, Victorien. La sorcière. 12e éd. Paris, n.d.
	39534.29.5	Scarron, Paul. Le roman comique. v.1-3. Paris, n.d.
	39534.31	Scarron, Paul. Virgile travesti. Paris, n.d.
	42578.36	Schultz, Jeanne. Cinq minutes d'arrêt. Paris, n.d.
	41588.16	Scribe, Augustin E. French plays. Paris, n.d. 7 pam.
	41588.13.15	Scribe, Eugène. La camera verde. n.p., n.d.
	41588.3.15	Scribe, Eugène. Les doigts de fée. Strassburg, n.d.
	41588.13	Scribe, Eugène. Théâtre. n.p., n.d.
	41588.14	Scribe, Eugène. Théâtre. n.p., n.d. 6 pam.
	41588.14.6	Scribe, Eugène. Le verre d'eau. Strasbourg, n.d.
	38521.12	Séché, Léon. Joachim du Bellay et la Bretagne-Angevine. n.p., n.d.
	41578.53	Séché, Léon. Le roman de Lamartine. Paris, n.d.
	40536.31A	Sedaine, Michel Jean. Guillaume Tell drame. Paris, n.d.
	41596.59	Ségur, Anatole de. Fables. Paris, n.d.
	41588.29.5	Séjour, Victor. The outlaw of the Adriatic. London, n.d.
	41592.4	Silbergleit, L.G. Béranger als Bonapartist. n.p., n.d.
	42584.37	Simon, Jules. Les derniers mémoires des autres. Paris, n.d.
	42546.43	Siraudin, Paul. Left the stage. London, n.d.
	38537.25.19	Smith, W.F. Rabelais in his writings. Cambridge, n.d.
	42534.1	Société Amicale Gaston, Paris. Bulletin. Paris, n.d.
	FL 6111.13.5	Société Jean-Jacques Rousseau. Annales. Tables. v.1-35, 1905-1962. Genève, n.d.
	41564.31	Sorrento, Luigi. Correspondance, 1816-1863. Paris, n.d.
	41574.280.10	Souchon, Paul. Claire Pradier et Victor Hugo. n.p., n.d.
	42563.23.123	Soulon, H. Léon Bloy. n.p., n.d. 2 pam.
	40516.7	Le soupe des petits-maitres ouvrage moral. Bruxelles, n.d.
	41558.59	Souvestre, Émile. Le monde tel qu'il sera. Paris, n.d.
	40592.26	Staël Holstein, Anne Louise. Corinne. Paris, n.d.
	40593.12	Staël Holstein, Anne Louise. Pages choisies des grands écrivains. Paris, n.d.
	42546.12.5	Strachey, L. Cyrano de Bergerac. n.p., n.d.
	41562.9	Sue, Eugène. Les enfants de l'amour. Paris, n.d.
	41562.2	Sue, Eugène. Oeuvres choisies. Paris, n.d.
	42556.18.5A	Sully-Prudhomme, R.F.A. Oeuvres. Paris, n.d.
	42556.19.2A	Sully-Prudhomme, R.F.A. Oeuvres. Paris, n.d.
	FL 380.3	Sur l'état actuel du théâtre de la republique. Paris, n.d.
	Mol 719.7	Szana, Tamás. Molière élete és müvei. Budapest, n.d.
	38537.1.05	Table de la revue des études Rabelaisienne. n.p., n.d.
	39527.28.8	Tarver, Francis. Fables de La Fontaine. London, n.d.
	37585.3.5	Théâtre classique. Paris, n.d.
	37584.5	Théâtre pour rire. Paris, n.d.
	Mol 865.3	Théolier. L'ésprit français. Paris, n.d.
	42583.23	Theuriet, André. La chanoinesse. Paris, n.d.
	42583.32	Theuriet, André. La chanson du jardinier. Boston, n.d.
	42583.33.17	Theuriet, André. Jean-Marie. Paris, n.d.
	42555.44.9	Thibaudet, A. Poésie de Stéphane Mallarmé. Paris, n.d.
	41568.26	Tiller, Claude. Mon oncle Benjamin. Strasbourg, n.d.
	41568.26.5	Tillier, Claude. Belle-Plante et Cornélius. Strasbourg, n.d.
Htn	37581.8*	Tournier, Édouard. Théâtre français au XVIe et au XVIIe siècle. Paris, n.d.
	37581.9	Tournier, Édouard. Théâtre français au XVIe et au XVIIe siècle. Paris, n.d. 2v.
	37581.8.2	Tournier, Édouard. Théâtre français au XVIe et au XVIIe siècle. Paris, n.d.
Htn	37581.6*	Tournier, Édouard. Théâtre français avant la Renaissance. Paris, n.d.
	42547.4.19	Tourte, Francis. Almanach du théâtre comique. Paris, n.d.
	42547.5.12	Trarieux, Gabriel. La lanterne de Diogène (notes sur le théâtre.). Paris, n.d.
NEDL	40525.8	Tressan, L.E. Histoire de Huon de Bordeaux. Paris, n.d.
	42547.6	Trézenik, Léo. La ménage rousseau. Paris, n.d.
	38525.35.16	Tristan L'Hermite, F. Amarillis. VIII. Paris, n.d.
	38525.35.12	Tristan L'Hermite, F. La folie du sage. IV. Paris, n.d.
	38525.35.10	Tristan L'Hermite, F. La mariane. II. Paris, n.d.
	38525.36.3	Tristan L'Hermite, F. La mort de Chrispe. Marian. n.p., n.d.
	38525.35.14	Tristan L'Hermite, F. La mort de Chrispe. VI. Paris, n.d.
	38525.35.11	Tristan L'Hermite, F. La mort de Sénèque. III. Paris, n.d.
	38525.35.15	Tristan L'Hermite, F. Osman. VII. Paris, n.d.
	38525.35.13	Tristan L'Hermite, F. Panthée. V. Paris, n.d.
	38525.35.9	Tristan L'Hermite, F. Le parasite. I. Paris, n.d.
	38528.27	Le triumphe de Haulte Folie. Poème du XVIe siècle. Paris, n.d.
	39535.70	Trotti de la Chélardie. Maximes sur la cour. Amsterdam, n.d.
	38547.5	Urfé, Honoré d'. L'Astrée. Paris, n.d. 5v.
	40526.69.110	Vadé, Jean Joseph. Les troqueurs. Paris, n.d. 3 pam.
	37555.37	Valbel, H. Les chansonniers et les cabarets artistiques. Paris, n.d.
	42584.49	Vallon, G. du. Vingt ans plus tard. Paris, n.d.
	43822.3.31	Vandelbourg, R.H. de. L'Algerie contemporaine sur les Hauts Plateaux. Paris, n.d.
	41522.17.11	Van Roosbroek, Gustava. Charles Baudelaire. Haarlem, n.d.
	40586.24.80	Variantes de l'édition de 1797. n.p., n.d.
	42543.1.9	Vattier, F. Réponse à Alexandre Dumas fils à propos de la préface de l'ami des femmes. Paris, n.d.
	42547.11.11	Vaucaire, Maurice. Janne et Blanche. Paris, n.d.
	42547.11.10	Vaucaire, Maurice. Mlle X...souris d'hôtel. Paris, n.d.

No date - cont.

	42547.11.9	Vaucaire, Maurice. La petite madame Bec et ougles. Paris, n.d.
	37558.37	Vedrenne, P. Fauteuils de l'Académie Française. Paris, n.d. 4v.
	42583.5	Verne, Jules. Un capitaine de quinze ans. Paris, n.d. 2v.
Htn	42581.3.2*	Verne, Jules. César Cascabel. Paris, n.d.
Htn	42581.5*	Verne, Jules. Le chancellor. Paris, n.d.
	42581.4	Verne, Jules. Le chemin de France. Paris, n.d.
	42583.7	Verne, Jules. Cinq cent millions. Paris, n.d.
	42581.19	Verne, Jules. Cinq semaines en ballon. Paris, n.d.
Htn	42581.17.2*	Verne, Jules. Claudias Bembarnae. Paris, n.d.
Htn	42581.17.4*	Verne, Jules. Clovis Dardentor. Paris, n.d.
	42583.9	Verne, Jules. De la terre à la lune. Paris, n.d.
Htn	42581.14.3*	Verne, Jules. De la terre à la lune. Autour de la lune. Paris, n.d.
Htn	42581.14*	Verne, Jules. De la terre à la lune. Autour de la lune. Paris, n.d.
	42581.13.9	Verne, Jules. De la terre à la lune. 8. éd. Paris, n.d.
Htn	42581.24*	Verne, Jules. Découverte de la terre. Paris, n.d.
Htn	42581.5.2*	Verne, Jules. Deux ans de vacances. Paris, n.d.
Htn	42582.10*	Verne, Jules. Docteur Ox. 8. éd. Paris, n.d.
	42581.7	Verne, Jules. L'école des Robinsons. Paris, n.d.
Htn	42581.8*	Verne, Jules. Les enfants du capitaine Grant. Paris, n.d.
X Cg	42581.6	Verne, Jules. L'étoile du Sud. L'archipel en feu. Paris, n.d.
	42581.17.5	Verne, Jules. Face au drapeau. Paris, n.d.
	42581.8.2	Verne, Jules. Famille-sans-nom. Paris, n.d.
Htn	42581.25*	Verne, Jules. Les grands navigateurs du 18e siècle. Paris, n.d.
	42583.11	Verne, Jules. Hector Servadac. N.Y., n.d.
Htn	42583.10*	Verne, Jules. Hector Servadac. Paris, n.d. 2v.
	42581.17.3	Verne, Jules. L'île à hélice. Paris, n.d.
	42581.9.9	Verne, Jules. L'île mystérieuse. Paris, n.d. 3v.
Htn	42581.10*	Verne, Jules. L'île mystérieuse. Paris, n.d.
Htn	42581.9*	Verne, Jules. Les Indes noires. Paris, n.d.
	42581.10.7	Verne, Jules. La Jangada. Paris, n.d.
	42581.17	Verne, Jules. Magnifiques aventures de maître Antifer. Paris, n.d.
	42583.12	Verne, Jules. La maison à vapeur. N.Y., n.d. 2v.
Htn	42581.11*A	Verne, Jules. Michel Strogoff. Paris, n.d.
	42581.15	Verne, Jules. Mistress Branican. Paris, n.d.
	42581.12.2	Verne, Jules. Nord contre sud. Paris, n.d.
Htn	42581.12*	Verne, Jules. Pays de fourrures. Paris, n.d.
	42581.23	Verne, Jules. Petit bonhomme. Paris, n.d.
	42581.17.6	Verne, Jules. Le sphinx des glaces. Paris, n.d.
	42581.17.7	Verne, Jules. Le testament d'un excentrique. Paris, n.d.
	42581.16	Verne, Jules. Tour du monde. Docteur Ox. Paris, n.d.
	42581.16.5	Verne, Jules. Le tour du monde en quatre-vingt jours. N.Y., n.d.
	42581.16.3	Verne, Jules. Le tour du monde en quatre-vingt jours. Paris, n.d.
	42583.15	Verne, Jules. Les tribulations d'un chinoisen Chine. N.Y., n.d.
Htn	42581.18*	Verne, Jules. Une ville flottante. Paris, n.d.
	42583.14	Verne, Jules. Vingt mille lieues sous les mers. N.Y., n.d.
	42581.20.5	Verne, Jules. Voyage au centre de la terre. Paris, n.d.
	42581.3	Verne, Jules. Voyages du capitaine Hatteras. Paris, n.d.
	42581.26	Verne, Jules. Les voyageurs du 19. siècle. Paris, n.d.
	42576.57.10	Viaud, Julien. Le chateau de la Belle-au-Bois-Dormant. Paris, n.d.
	42576.57.11	Viaud, Julien. Un pélerin d'Angkor. Paris, n.d.
	41564.15.2	Vigny, Alfred de. Poésies complètes. Paris, n.d.
	42547.21	Villiers de l'Isle Adam, Auguste. Contes cruels. Paris, n.d.
	42547.20	Villiers de l'Isle Adam, Auguste. Histoires insolites. Paris, n.d.
	42547.20.3	Villiers de l'Isle Adam, Auguste. Isis. Paris, n.d.
	38514.20.9A	Villon, François. Oeuvres complètes. Paris, n.d.
	38514.20.10A	Villon, François. Oeuvres de Maître François Villon. Strasbourg, n.d.
	42522.9	Vogüé, E.M. de. Heures d'histoire. Paris, n.d.
	42522.17	Vogüé, E.M. de. Le maitre de la mer. Paris, n.d.
	42522.15	Vogüé, E.M. de. Les morts qui parlent. Paris, n.d.
	42522.12	Vogüé, E.M. de. Souvenirs et vision. Paris, n.d.
	38542.2.5	Voiture, Vincent. Les lettres (and other works). n.p., n.d.
	FL 6049.7	Voltaire, F.M.A. de. Notes inédites sur la Profession de foi du Vicaire Savoyard. n.p., n.d.
Htn	39545.37.8*	Voltaire, François Marie Arouet de. Candide. London, n.d.
	39545.34.9	Voltaire, François Marie Arouet de. La Doncella de Orleans. Madrid, n.d.
	39545.29.4	Voltaire, François Marie Arouet de. A new system of theology. n.p., n.d.
Htn	39545.52*	Voltaire, François Marie Arouet de. La pucelle...d'Orleans. n.p., n.d.
	39545.25.10	Voltaire, François Marie Arouet de. Tancrède. Strassburg, n.d.
	39545.66	Voltaire, François Marie Arouet de. Zayre-Alzire. La Henriade de Voltaire. Breslau, n.d.
	37573.35	Vrignault, P. Anthologie de la chanson française. Paris, n.d.
	37597.26.20	Wace, Maistre. Life of Saint Nicholas. Thesis. Philadelphia, n.d.
	38512.10	Wailly, Natalis de. Notice sur Guillaume Guiart. n.p., n.d.
	40556.38	Wandoul, J. Un homme d'état Italien. Joseph de Maistre. Paris, n.d.
	37562.282	Weeks, R. A collection of works. n.p., n.d.
	37564.4	Weisser, E. L'Hotel de Rambouillet. Breslau, n.d.
	42547.30	Wolff, Pierre. Le béguin. Paris, n.d.
	42547.31	Wolff, Pierre. Le secret de Polichinelle. Paris, n.d.
	38551.126.10	Wunderlich, F.R. Fenelon, ein Lebensbild. Hamburg, n.d.
	40546.32	Zeitlin, Irving M. Liberty, equality and revolution in Alexis de Tocqueville. Boston, n.d.
	42584.7	Zola, Emile. Contres à Ninon. Paris, n.d.
	42584.23.17	Zola, Emile. Igazsag. v.1-2. Budapest, n.d.
	42584.23.20	Zola, Emile. Pour une nuit d'amour. n.p., n.d.
Htn	42581.44*	Zola, Emile. Le rêve. Paris, n.d.

15-

Htn	38528.70*	La mode qui court au temps présent avec le supplement. Rouen, 15- ?

Chronological Listing

1500-1509

Htn	37597.2*	Lorris, Guillaume de. Le rommant de la rose. Paris, 150-.
Htn	37596.2*	Guillaume de Deguilleville. Le romant des trois pelerinages. Paris, 1500.
Htn	37597.2.5*	Lorris, Guillaume de. Cest le romant de la rose. Paris, 1500.

1510-1519

Htn	38526.73*	Ponte, Petrus de. Petru de Pote ceci burgensis incomparanda G. Colophon, 1512.

1520-1529

Htn	38526.48.5*	Sottie à dix personnages. Lyon, 1523.
	38562.32	Bouhours, D. La manière de bien penser dans les ouvrages d'ésprit. Amsterdam, 1525.
Htn	38526.13.225*	Tombeau de feu de...Fremin Douri. Paris, 1528.
	37578.53	Guégan, Bertrand. Le grand kalendrier et compost des bergiers. Troyes, 1529.

1530-1539

Htn	38536.22.10*	Rabelais, F. Les grandes et inestimables croniques...Gargantua. London, 1532.
	38536.22.5	Rabelais, F. Les grandes et inestimables croniques...Gargantua. n.p., 1532.
Htn	38526.27.15*	Lemaire de Belges, Jean. L'epistre du Roy à Hector de Troye. Paris, 1533.
Htn	38514.37.10*	Meschinot, Jean. Les lunettes des princes. Paris, 1534.
Htn	38526.3.5.165*	Bouchet, Jean. Les angoyses et remedes daniouis. Poictiers, 1536. 2 pam.
Htn	38523.12.5*	Marot, Clément. L'adolescence Clementine ou Autrement. Bourgogne, 1536? 3 pam.
Htn	38523.3.25*	Les disciples et amys de Marot. Paris, 1537.
Htn	38514.69.7.40*	Martial de Paris. Aresta amorum. Lugduni, 1538.
Htn	38523.3.20*	Plusieurs traictez du different de Marot, Sagon et La Hueterie. Paris, 1539.

1540-1549

Htn	38527.37*	Dolet, Etienne. La manière de bien traduire. Lyon, 1540.
Htn	38513.19.3*	Le triumphant mystère des actes des apôtres. Paris, 1540. 2v.
Htn	38527.39*	Le second enfer d'Etienne Dolet. Lyon, 1544.
Htn	38526.3.5.150*	Bouchet, Jean. Epistres morales et familières du traverseur. Poictieurs, 1545.
Htn	38526.3.5.155*	Bouchet, Jean. Triumphes de la noble et amoureuse dame. Paris, 1545.
Htn	38514.69.7.50*	Martial de Paris. Aresta amorum. Lugduni, 1546.

1550-1559

Htn	38526.47.23.250*	Rus, Jean. Description poétique de l'histoire du beau Narcissus. Lyon, 1550.
Htn	37578.53.10*	Kalendrier des Bergers. Le grand calendier et compost des bergiers. Colophon, 1551.
Htn	38526.22.20*	La Perrière, G. de. Les considerations des quatre mondes. Lyon, 1552.
Htn	38536.24.11*	Rabelais, F. Le quart livres des faicts et dictz hëroiques du bon Pantagruel. Lyon, 1552.
Htn	38525.15.75*	Ronsard, Pierre de. Les amours de Pierre de Ronsard Vaudomois. Paris, 1553. 2v.
Htn	38525.14.80*	Ronsard, Pierre de. Les cinquieme [!] des odes augmente. Paris, 1553.
Htn	38525.16*	Ronsard, Pierre de. Les odes. n.p., 1553.
Htn	38526.6.25*	Du Bellay, Joachim. L'olive. Paris, 1554.
Htn	38525.14.75*	Ronsard, Pierre de. Les quatres premiers livres des odes. Paris, 1555.
Htn	38528.4*	Bouaistuau, Pierre. Histoire de Chelidonius Tigurinus. Paris, 1556.
Htn	37555.314.25*	Sebillet, T. Art poétique français. Lyon, 1556.
Htn	38523.5.2*	Marot, Clément. Oeuvres. Paris, 1557.
Htn	38526.10.11.100*	Corrozet, Gilles. Les divers et memorables propos des nobles et illustres hommes. Lyon, 1558.
Htn	38526.6.30*	Du Bellay, Joachim. Le premier livre des antiquitez de Rome. Paris, 1558.
Htn	38526.32.100*	Marguerite d'Angoulême. Les Marguerites de la Marguerite. Paris, 1558.
Htn	38536.2.15*	Rabelais, F. Oeuvres. Lyon, 1558.
Htn	38526.6.40*	Du Bellay, Joachim. Entreprise du roy-daulphin pour le tournoy. Paris, 1559.
Htn	38526.6.14*	Du Bellay, Joachim. Les regrets et autres oeuvres. Paris, 1559.

1560-1569

	38526.6.35	Du Bellay, Joachim. Louange de la France et du roy. Paris, 1560.
Htn	38526.70.8*	Viret, Pierre. Satyres chrestienes de la cuisine papale. Genève, 1560.
Htn	38526.6.10*	Du Bellay, Joachim. Recueil de poésie. Paris, 1561.
Htn	38528.90*	La Polymachie des marmitons. Lyon, 1563.
Htn	38526.10.100*	Desiré, Artus. Les batailles et victoires du Chevalier Celeste côtre le Chevalier Terrestre. Paris, 1564.
Htn	38528.6.8*	Estienne, Henri. L'introduction au Traité...ou Traité...à l'Apologie pour Hérodote. Paris, 1566.
Htn	38523.5*	Marot, Clément. Oeuvres. Paris, 1568.
Htn	38525.30.5*	Tahureau, Jacques. Dialogues. Paris, 1568.
Htn	38526.27.5.270*	La Tayssonière, G.C. de. Sourdine royale, sonnant le bouteselle. Paris, 1569.
Htn	Mon 80.1*	Sabunde, Ramón. La theologie naturelle. Paris, 1569.
Htn	38539.33.15*	Saillans, Gaspar de. Premier livre de Gaspar de Saillans. Lyon, 1569.

1570-1579

	42514.5	Laboulaye, Édouard. Discours populaires. Paris, 1570.
Htn	38524.65*	Corrozet, Gilles. Le Parnasse des poetes françois modernes. Paris, 1571.
Htn	38525.12*	Ronsard, Pierre de. Les oeuvres. v.1-2,3-4,5-6. Paris, 1571. 3v.
Htn	38526.14.65*	Du Verdier, Antoine. Les omonimes; satire des moeurs. Lyon, 1572.
Htn	38539.28*	Maisonneuve, Étienne de. Le premier livre de la plaisante et délectable histoire de Gerlon d'Angleterre. Paris, 1572.

1570-1579 - cont.

Htn	38525.12.2*	Ronsard, Pierre de. Les oeuvres. v.1,2,3,4,5-6. Paris, 1572-73. 5v.
Htn	38524.11.25*	Baïf, Jean A. de. Euvres en rime. Paris, 1573.
Htn	37578.22*	Facecies et motz subtilz, en françois et italien. Lyon, 1573.
Htn	38514.61*	La Marche, Olivier de. El cavallero determmado. Salamanca, 1573.
Htn	38523.6*	Marot, Clément. Oeuvres. Lyon, 1573. 2v.
Htn	38525.20.7*	Ronsard, Pierre de. Les quatres premiers livres de la Franciade. Paris, 1573.
Htn	38526.47.73*	Saint-Gelais, Mellin de. Oeuvres poétiques. Lyon, 1574.
Htn	38526.52.15*	Tyard, Pontus. Solitaire premier, ou Dialogue de la fureur poétique. Paris, 1575?
Htn	38526.27.7*	Le Loyer, Pierre. L'erotopegnie. Paris, 1576.
Htn	39532.34*	Bible. O.T. Psalms. French, 1577. Perles d'eslite...François Perrot. Genève, 1577.
Htn	38528.45*	Le danger de mariage. Paris, 1577.
Htn	Mol 850.2*	L'enfer burlesque: le mariage de Belphégor. Cologne, 1577.
Htn	38526.42.10.50*	Paquelin, G. Apologem. Lyon, 1577.
Htn	38526.1.35.15*	Belleau, R. Les oeuvres poétiques. Paris, 1578. 2v.
Htn	38539.3.250*	Des Autels, Guillaume. Mythistoire barragouyne de Fanfreluche et Gandichon. Rouen, 1578.
Htn	38526.27.5.300*	Le Fèvre. Hymnes ecclesiastiques. pts.1-2. Paris, 1578-79.
Htn	38526.29.2*	Navarre, M. de. L'Heptaméron. Lyon, 1578.
Htn	38539.65*	Yver, Jacques. Le printemps. Paris, 1578.
Htn	38526.22.5*	Jamyn, Amadis. Oeuvres poétiques. v.1-2. Paris, 1579-84.
Htn	38526.27.3*	Larivey, P. de. Les six premières comédies. Paris, 1579.
Htn	38523.6.3*	Marot, Clément. Clément Marot [works]. Lyon, 1579.
Htn	38526.48.8*	Sainte-Marthe, S. Oeuvres. Paris, 1579. 2 pam.

1580-1589

Htn	38539.3.10*	Contreras, Jeonimo de. Les etranges avantures. Lyon, 1580.
Htn	38524.11.50*	Baïf, Jean A. de. Les mimes. Paris, 1581.
Htn	37597.34*	Meun, Jehan de. Le plaisant jeu du dodechedIron de fortune. Lyon, 1581.
Htn	37555.5*	Recueil de l'origine de la langue et poésie française. Paris, 1581.
Htn	Mon 80.2*	Sabunde, Ramón. La theologie naturelle. Paris, 1581.
Htn	38526.48.15*	Du Bartas, Guillaume de Salluste. Les oeuvres. n.p., 1582. 2v.
Htn	38526.13.250*	Du Buys, Guillaume. L'oreille du prince. Paris, 1582.
Htn	38527.42*	Garnier, Robert. Les tragédies. Paris, 1582.
Htn	38526.22.24*	La Primaudaye, Pierre de. Cent quatrains consolatoires. Lyon, 1582.
Htn	38528.16.40*	Béroalde de Verville. Les souspirs amoureux. Paris, 1583.
Htn	38526.2.4.200*	Blanchon, Joachim. Les premières oeuvres poétiques. Paris, 1583.
Htn	38526.48.16*	Du Bartas, Guillaume de Salluste. Le sepmaine ou création du monde. Paris, 1583.
Htn	38525.7.5*	Jodelle, d'Estienne. Les oeuvres et meslanges. Paris, 1583.
Htn	38539.1.50*	Beroaede de Verville, F. Apprehensions spirituelles, poems. Paris, 1584.
Htn	38526.10.8.29*	Chevalier, Guillaume. Le decez ov fin dv monde. Paris, 1584.
Htn	38526.48.16.5*	Du Bartas, Guillaume de Salluste. Commentaires et annotations du monde. Paris, 1584.
Htn	38526.6.2*	Du Bellay, Joachim. Les oeuvres françoises. Paris, 1584.
	37530.4	La Croix du Maine, F.G. Premier vol...bibliothèque du Sieur de la Croix du Maine. Paris, 1584.
Htn	38526.9.23*	Birague, Flaminio de. Premières oeuvres poétiques. Paris, 1585.
Htn	38526.21.12*	Habert, Isaac. Les trois livres des meteors avecques autres oeuvres. Paris, 1585.
Htn	38526.56.25*	Tabourot, Étienne. Les bigarrvres du seigneur. Paris, 1585. 3 pam.
Htn	38526.56*	Tabourot, Étienne. Les touches du seigneur des accords. Livre 1-5. Paris, 1585. 2v.
Htn	38539.2.250*	Cholières, Nicolas de. Les neuf matinées. Paris, 1586.
	38539.2.80	Garreau, Albert. Jean-Pierre Camus. Paris, 1586.
	38526.27.5.15	Le Gras, J. Le tombeau de...Richard Le Gras. Paris, 1586. 2 pam.
Htn	38528.80*	Ode sacrée de l'église française. n.p., 1586.
Htn	38526.13.265*	Du Chesne, Joseph. Le grand miroir dv monde. Lyon, 1587.
Htn	38526.39.27*	Montreux, N. de. Le premier livre des bergeries de Juelliette. 2e éd. Paris, 1587.
Htn	38526.39.25*	Montreux, N. de. Les premières oeuvres poétiques chrestiennes. Paris, 1587.
Htn	38526.43.30*	Perrache, J. Vanité du jeu. Paris, 1587.
Htn	38526.66*	Trelon, G. Six chants des vertus. Paris, 1587.
Htn	38526.52.31*	Tyard, Pontus. Les discours philosophiques. Paris, 1587.
Htn	38525.34.5*	Bouchet, Guillaume. Les serees. Poitiers, 1588.
Htn	38526.10.8.25*	Cholières, Nicolas de. Les apres disness du Seigneur de Cholières. Paris, 1588.
Htn	38539.2.270*	Cholières, Nicolas de. Les aprèsdisnees. Paris, 1588.
Htn	38539.2.260*	Cholières, Nicolas de. La guerre des masles contre les femelles. Paris, 1588.
Htn	38526.10.8.27*	Cholières, Nicolas de. La guerre des masles contre les femelles. Paris, 1588.
Htn	38526.6.20*	Du Bellay, Joachim. Ample discours au roy. Paris, 1588.
Htn	38527.42.3*	Garnier, Robert. Tragédies. Tholose, 1588.
Htn	38526.70.125*	Vitel, Jean de. Premiers exercices poétiques. Paris, 1588.
Htn	38526.3.5*	Bosquier, F.P. Tragoedie nouvelle. Mons, 1589.
Htn	38526.37.225*	Mondin, Jean. Deploration et vers lamentables sur la mort de Monseigneur le duc de Guyse. Paris, 1589.
Htn	38526.69.50*	Viel, Marc A. Consolation et reconfort de noble, et illustre dame, Helen d'O. Paris, 1589.
Htn	38539.70*	Yver, Jacques. Le printemps. Lyon, 1589.

1590-1599

Htn	Mon 37.5*	Montaigne, Michel de. Discorsi morali politici et militari. Ferrara, 1590.
Htn	38526.42.14*	Pasquier, Étienne. Les lettres d'Estienne Pasquier. Avignon, 1590.
Htn	38526.48.26*	Du Bartas, Guillaume de Salluste. Hebdomas a Gabriele Lermaeo latinitate donata. Londini, 1591.
Htn	38526.48.16.3*	Du Bartas, Guillaume de Salluste. Le sepmaine ou création du monde. v.1-4. Rouen, 1591.
Htn	38526.39.29*	Montreux, N. de. Second livre des bergeries de Juelliette. Lyon, 1591. 2v.
Htn	38525.12.9*	Ronsard, Pierre de. Les oeuvres. Lyon, 1592. 5v.

Chronological Listing

1590-1599 - cont.

Htn	38524.53*	Alizet, Benoit. La calliope chretienne. Genève, 1593.
Htn	38526.44.3*	Perrot de La Sale, Paul. Gigantomachie. Middleburg, 1593.
Htn	38528.8.19*	Satyre Ménippée de la vertu du catholicon d'Espagne. n.p., 1593.
Htn	38526.16.300*	Godard, Jeane. Oeuvres. v.1-2. Lyon, 1594.
Htn	Mon 178.11*	Gournay, Marie de Jars de. Le proumenoir de M. de Montaigne. Paris, 1594.
Htn	38514.61.20*	La Marche, Olivier de. The resolved gentleman. London, 1594.
Htn	38526.44.5.10*	Perrot de La Sale, Paul. Tableaus sacrey. Francfort, 1594.
Htn	38526.10.8.75*	Coignard, G. Oeuvres chrestiennes. Tournon, 1595.
Htn	38528.38*	Demons, Jean. La sextessence diallactique. Paris, 1595.
	39534.30.9	Scarron, Paul. Le virgile travesty en vers burlesque. Amsterdam, 1595.
Htn	38514.64.25*	Chartier, Alain. Delectable demaundes and pleasant questions. London, 1596.
Htn	38526.27.5.250*	La Roque, Siméon G. Les premières oeuvres de sieur de la Roque de Clermont. Rouen, 1596.
Htn	38523.6.5*	Marot, Clément. Oeuvres. Rouen, 1596.
Htn	38536.2.45*	Rabelais, F. Les oeuvres. Lion, 1596.
Htn	38528.15*	Béroalde de Verville. Le cabinet de Minerve. Rouen, 1597.
Htn	38526.6.3*	Du Bellay, Joachim. Oeuvres. Rouen, 1597. 2v.
Htn	38528.20.3*	Du Fail, Noël. Les contes et discours d'Eutrapel. Rennes, 1597.
Htn	38527.42.3.12*	Garnier, Robert. Tragédies. Lyon, 1597.
Htn	38526.27.4*	Larivey, P. de. Les comédies facecievses de Pierre de Larivey. 2e éd. Lyon, 1597.
Htn	38526.46.500*	Quillian, M. Dernière semaine. Rouen, 1597.
Htn	38525.12.12*	Ronsard, Pierre de. Les oeuvres. v.1-10. Paris, 1597. 5v.
Htn	38528.20.5*	Du Fail, Noël. Les contes et discours d'Eutrapel. Rennes, 1598.
Htn	38526.20.75*	Guyet, Nicolas. Pila palmaria. Aureliae, 1598.
Htn	38529.95*	Montreux, N. de. Les amours de Cleandre et Dorniphille. Paris, 1598.
Htn	38526.11.20*	Despinelle. Muses françoises. Paris, 1599.
Htn	38526.48.17.2*	Du Bartas, Guillaume de Salluste. Commentaires sur la second sepmaine. Rouen, 1599.
Htn	38526.48.17*	Du Bartas, Guillaume de Salluste. Commentaires sur la sepmaine de la création du monde. Rouen, 1599.
Htn	38562.21.3*	Fontenelle, B. Le B. de. Lettres galantes de M. le chevalier d'Her***. Paris, 1599.
Htn	38526.39.35*	Montreux, N. de. Les chastes et delectables jardins d'amour. Paris, 1599.
Htn	38528.34*	Ouville, Antoine. L'élite des contes. Rouen, 1599.
Htn	38526.44.5*	Perrot de La Sale, Paul. Le contr'empire des sciences. Lyon, 1599.
Htn	38526.48.28.50*	Scalion de Virbluneau. Loyales et pudiques amours. Paris, 1599.
Htn	38526.69.25*	Veins, Aymard de. Clorinde; tragedie. Paris, 1599. 2 pam.
Htn	38539.75*	Yver, Jacques. Le printemps. Rouen, 1599.

16-

Htn	38526.10.75*	Desfontaines. Saint Alexis; tragédie. Rouen, 16- ?
Htn	38528.65*	Les fleurs des musés françaises. Rouen, 16- ?
	38576.27.35	Longepierre, M. de. Medée. Paris? 16- ?

1600-1609

Htn	38526.8.75*	Bertaut, Jean. Recueil des oeuvres poétiques de Jean Bertaut. Paris, 1601.
Htn	38545.12*	Regnerye. Les constantes...amours de Lintason. Paris, 1601.
Htn	38526.1.15*	Avity, Pierre de. Les travaux sans travail. Paris, 1602.
	38523.13	Bible. O.T. Psalms. French. Les pseaumes mis en rime françoise. Delf, 1602.
	38527.42.3.20	Garnier, Robert. Tragédies. Saumur, 1602.
Htn	38539.27.75*	Maisonneuve, Étienne de. La plaisante et delectable histoire de Gerilon d'Angleterre. 3. éd. Lyon, 1602.
Htn	38526.12.40*	Bible. O.T. Psalms. French. Paraphras. 1603. Les CL. Pseavmes de David, mis en vers françois, par Philippe Desportes. Paris, 1603.
Htn	38526.10.17.200*	Deimier, P. de. Illustres avantures. Lyon, 1603.
Htn	38528.20.8*	Du Fail, Noël. Les contes et discours d'Eutrapel. Rennes, 1603.
Htn	38529.6*	Goulart, Simon. Histoires admirables et memorables. Paris, 1603.
Htn	38529.5*	Goulart, Simon. Histoires admirables et mémorables. Paris, 1603.
Htn	Mon 30.1*	Montaigne, Michel de. Essayes. Florio. London, 1603.
	Mon 30.12	Montaigne, Michel de. Essayes. Florio. v.1-6. London, 1603-06. 3v.
Htn	38527.42.3.22*	Garnier, Robert. Tragédies. Rouen, 1604.
Htn	38543.28.30*	La Mothe le Vayer, F. de. Quatre dialogues. Francfort, 1604.
Htn	38526.25.140*	Laudun d'Aigaliers, P. de. Franciade. Paris, 1604.
Htn	38526.47.22*	Roland de Richeville, L. Expicedión de Diane. Paris, 1604.
Htn	38526.47.23.200*	Rosset, François de. Les XII beautez de Phyllis. Paris, 1604.
Htn	38526.65*	Trellon, C. La muse guerrière. Rouen, 1604.
Htn	38526.1.20*	Bauter, Charles. La rodomontade, Mort de Roger; tragedies et amours de Catherine. Paris, 1605.
Htn	38526.10.15.20*	Colomby, François. Les plaintes de la captive Caliston. n.p., 1605.
Htn	38539.6.25*	Doré, Pierre. La tourtrelle de viduité; enseignant les vefues comment elles doivent vivre en leur estat. Arras, 1605.
Htn	38526.48.22*	Du Bartas, Guillaume de Salluste. Bartas: his divine weekes and workes. London, 1605-06.
Htn	38526.35.250*	Massac, R. de. Les fontenes de Pougues. Paris, 1605.
Htn	38526.39.55*	Morenne, C. de. Poèmes divers. Paris, 1605. 3 pam.
Htn	38536.2.50*	Rabelais, F. Les oeuvres. Anvers, 1605.
Htn	38526.10.8.65*	Coeffeteau, N. Paraphrase de la prose des morts. Nantes, 1606. 3 pam.
Htn	38526.12.24*	Desportes, Philippe. Les oeuvres. Lyon, 1606.
	38539.5	Du Vair, Guillaume. Recueil des harangues et traictez. Paris, 1606.
Htn	38543.30.2*	La Mothe le Vayer, F. de. Quatres dialogues. Frankfort, 1606.
Htn	38526.42.75*	Passerat, Jean. Recueil des oeuvres poétiques de Ian Passerat. Paris, 1606. 2 pam.
Htn	38526.12.25*	Desportes, Philippe. Les premières oeuvres. Rouen, 1607.

1600-1609 - cont.

Htn	38526.12.75*	Desportes, Philippe. Rodomonths infernall, or The divell conquered. London, 1607.
	38528.6.9	Estienne, Henri. L'introduction au Traité...ou Traité...à l'Apologie pour Hérodote. Hasles, 1607.
Htn	38528.6.3*	Estienne, Henri. A world of wonders. London, 1607.
Htn	38528.6.4*	Estienne, Henri. A world of wonders. London, 1607.
Htn	38526.14.175*	Garel, Hélye. Le triomphe d'Astrée; [poem]. Bordeaux, 1607.
Htn	38527.42.3.25*	Garnier, Robert. Tragédies. Paris, 1607.
Htn	38524.66*	Le parnasse des plus excellens poètes de ce temps. Paris, 1607.
Htn	38525.34.10*	Bouchet, Guillaume. Premier-douzième livres de serées. Paris, 1608.
Htn	38526.12.26*	Desportes, Philippe. Les oeuvres. Lyon, 1608.
Htn	38529.25*	Des Rues, F. Les marguerites françoyses. Rouen, 1608?
Htn	38528.6.5*	Estienne, Henri. A world of wonders. Edinburgh, 1608.
Htn	38526.42.6.25*	Nostredame, C. de. Pièces héroiques. Colonuéz, 1608. 2 pam.
Htn	38536.2.55*	Rabelais, F. Oeuvres. Lyon, 1608.
Htn	38526.57.2*	Tabourot, Étienne. Les bigarrvres. Paris, 1608.
Htn	38526.01.15*	Ambillon, R. Sidere; pastorelle. Paris, 1609.
Htn	38539.21.15*	Intras de Bazas, Jean d'. Le duel de Tithamante; histoire Gascone. Paris, 1609.
Htn	38526.27.5.260*	La Roque, Siméon G. Oeuvres. Paris, 1609.
Htn	37574.205*	Rosset, François de. Nouveau recueil des plus beaux vers de temps. Paris, 1609.

1610-1619

Htn	38528.70.5*	La mode qui court au temps present avec le supplement. Paris, 161-?
Htn	38528.16.8.23*	Béroalde de Verville. L'histoire véritable, ou Le voyage des princes fortunez. Paris, 1610.
Htn	38528.16.45*	Béroalde de Verville. L'histoire véritable, ou Le voyage des princes fortunez. Paris, 1610.
Htn	38528.4.9*	Deslauriers, N. Fantaisies. n.p., 1610?
Htn	38526.14.115*	Ezanville, R. d'. Invention nouvelle des esperviers. Paris, 1610.
Htn	38539.8*	Guyon, Louis. Les diverses leçons de Loys Guyon, Dolois, sieur de la Nanche. 2. éd. Lyon, 1610-25. 3v.
	38526.27.5.10	Le Blanc, J. Neotemachie poétiques. Poèmes. Paris, 1610. 2 pam.
Htn	38526.42.6*	Nancel, P. de. De la soveraineté des roys. Poems. n.p., 1610.
Htn	38526.42.14.3*	Pasquier, Étienne. Jeunesse d'Estienne Pasquier. Paris, 1610.
Htn	38526.42.14.5*	Pasquier, Étienne. La jeunesse d'Estienne Pasquier et sa suite. Paris, 1610.
Htn	38526.47.13*	Rapin, Nicolas. Les oeuvres latines et françoises. Paris, 1610.
Htn	38525.12.19*	Ronsard, Pierre de. Les oeuvres. Paris, 1610. 5v.
Htn	38529.77*	Roulhard, Sibout. La magnifique déxologie du festu. Paris, 1610.
Htn	38528.38.15*	Sonnet, Thomas. Satyre contre les charlatans. Paris, 1610.
Htn	38526.10.15.30*	Colomby, François. Consolation à la royne regente. Paris, 1611.
Htn	38526.27.4.8*	Larivey, P. de. Trois comédies des six dernières de Pierre de Larivey chanpenois. Troyes, 1611.
Htn	38526.10.8.30*	Chrestien, Nicolas. Les amantes. Rouen, 1613.
Htn	Mon 30.2*	Montaigne, Michel de. Essayes. Florio. London, 1613.
	38539.4	Du Vair, Guillaume. Oeuvres. 2. éd. Rouen, 1614. 2v.
Htn	38528.50*	Le Mathois, ou Marchand meslé propre à tout faire. Paris, 1614.
Htn	38525.22.68*	Régnier, Mathurin. Satyres. Paris, 1614.
Htn	38528.4.13*	Deslauriers, N. Les fantaisies de Bruscambille. Paris, 1615.
Htn	38528.4.11*	Deslauriers, N. Les nouvelles et plaisantes imaginations de Bruscambille. Bergerac, 1615.
Htn	38526.14.140*	Gamon, Christophe de. La semaine, ou Création du monde. 2. éd. Niort, 1615.
Htn	38526.44.10*	Pibrac, Guy du Faur. Les quatrains du seigneur de Pybrac. n.p., 1615.
Htn	38526.28.75*	Maillet, M. de. Les poésies de M. de Mailliet. Bourdeaux, 1616.
Htn	38529.75*	Romany, Richard de. Le carabinage et matoiserie soldatesque. Paris, 1616.
Htn	38526.28.50*	Lortique, A. Les poemes divers, ou Il est traicté de guerre. Paris, 1617.
Htn	38528.60*	Le normant sourt, aveugle et muet. Paris, 1617.
Htn	38514.64*	Oeuvres de...Alain-Chartier. Paris, 1617.
Htn	38526.47.18.25*	Remi de Beauvais. La Magdaleine. Tournay, 1617.
Htn	38525.13*	Ronsard, Pierre de. Les oeuvres. v.1-11. Paris, 1617. 5v.
Htn	38525.16.50*	Ronsard, Pierre de. Recueil des sonnets, odes. Paris, 1617.
Htn	38529.80*	Vigoureux. La défense des femmes, contre l'alphabet. Paris, 1617.
Htn	38526.45.100*	Picardet, Anne. Odes spirituelles. Lyon, 1618.
Htn	38526.46.550*	Prevost, J. Tragédies et autres oeuvres. Poictiers, 1618.
Htn	38526.10.15.50*	Colony, J.D. Enseignemens moraux. Coloniae Allgbrogum, 1619. 3 pam.
Htn	38539.6.50*	Duperier, Antoine. Les amours de Lozie. Lyon, 1619. 2 pam.
Htn	38525.22.70*	Régnier, Mathurin. Les satyres de sieur Régnier. Paris, 1619.

1620-1629

Htn	38524.817*	Les delices satyriques. Paris, 1620.
Htn	37578.25*	Favoral. Les plaisantes journées. Paris, 1620.
	38544.8	Sonan. Chrisérionte de Gaulé, histoire...trouvée en la Terre Sainte. Lyon, 1620.
	38542.13	Baudoin, I. Diversitez historiques. Paris, 1621.
Htn	38529.45*	Langlois. The favourites chronicle. London, 1621.
Htn	38529.150*	La grande division arrivée ces derniers iours, entre les femmes et les filles de Montpellier. Paris, 1622.
Htn	38528.38.30*	Sonnet, Thomas. Oeuvres satyriques. 2. éd. Paris, 1622.
Htn	38587.24*	Hardy, Alexandre. Les chastes et loyal amours de Théagène et Cariclée. Paris, 1623.
Htn	38526.46.175*	Poille, Jacques. Oeuvres divisées en onze livres. Paris, 1623.
	38588.11	Poisson, Raymond. Oeuvres. Paris, 1623.
Htn	38528.38.20*	Sonnet, Thomas. Satyre Menippee contre les femmes. Lyon, 1623.

1620-1629 - cont.

Htn 38528.4.75* Du Lorens, J. Satyres, divisees en deux livres. Paris, 1624.
Htn 38526.17.4* Gombauld, J.O. de. Endimion. Paris, 1624.
Htn 38587.22* Hardy, Alexandre. Théâtre. Paris, 1624-28. 5v.
Htn 38539.11* Lannel, Jean de. Le romant satyrique. Paris, 1624.
Htn 38528.55* Le passe par tout des Ponts-Bretons. n.p., 1624.
Htn 38539.29.50* Ravand, Abraham. Les amours d'Endimion et de la lune. Paris, 1624.
Htn 38524.85* Le théâtre françois. Paris, 1624.
Htn 38539.2.18* Camus, Jean P. La pieuse Jullie. Paris, 1625.
Htn 38526.10.11* Colletet, Guillaume. Les amours de Melisse. Paris, 1625.
Htn 38526.14.128* Favereau, J.I. France consolée. Paris, 1625.
Htn 38528.4.15* Deslauriers, N. Les oeuvres de Bruscambille. Rouen, 1626.
38544.6 Du Verdier, Gilbert. Le roman des romans. n.p., 1626-29. 7v.
38526.56.5 Tabourot, Étienne. Les touches du seigneur des accords. Rouen, 1626.
Htn 38526.3* Borce, M. Les princes victorieux. Lyon, 1627.
Htn 38527.31* Montchrétien, Antoine de. Les tragédies. Rouen, 1627.
Htn 38528.31* Croque-Lardon, Josselin. La grande et universelle pronostication de Maistre Josselin Croque-Lardon. Paris, 1628.
38588.20.5 Dufresny, Charles Rivière. Amusements sèrieux et comiques. 6. éd. Amsterdam, 1629[1729]

1630

Htn 38527.17.75* Aubigné, Théodore Agrippa d'. Les avantures du Baron de Foeneste. Dezert, 1630.
Htn 38539.13.5* La Serre, Jean Puget de. Le brevière des courtisans. Paris, 1630.
Htn 38539.16* Montluc, A. de. Deux de l'incognu. Paris, 1630.
Htn 38526.46* Pichou. Les folies de Cardenio. Paris, 1630.
Htn 38526.47.12* Rampalle, M. La belinde. Lyons, 1630.

1631

Htn 38526.48.27* Du Bartas, Guillaume de Salluste. Wilhelms von Saluste, Herren zu Bartas vornemsten Sinn. Leipzig, 1631.
Htn 38526.17.2* Gombauld, J.O. de. L'amaranthe. Paris, 1631.
Htn 38539.15* Le Roux, C. de. La tourterelle gemissante sur Hierusalem. Paris, 1631.
Htn 38529.50* Lescale. Alphabet de l'éccellence...des femmes. Paris, 1631.
Htn 38576.29* Mairet, Jean de. La Sylvie et autres oeuvres poétiques. Paris, 1631.
Htn 38523.22.45* Malherbe, François de. Oeuvres. 2. éd. Paris, 1631.
Htn 38526.35.2* Maréchal, Antoine. La genereuse allemande. Paris, 1631.
Htn 38525.75* Rotrou, Jean de. L'hypocondriaque; ou, le mort amoureux. Paris, 1631.

1632

Htn 38547.7.15* Baro, Balthasar. La conclusion et dernière partie d'Astrée. 3. éd. Paris, 1632.
Htn 38539.9* Du Verdier, G.S. Les chevalier hipocondriaque. Paris, 1632.
Htn 38526.16.50* Frenicle, Nicolas. Palemon, fable bocagère, et pastoralle. Paris, 1632.
Htn 38526.16.250* Gody, Simplicien. Les honestes poësies de Placidas Philemon Gody [pseud.]. Paris, 1632.
Htn 38539.25* Logeas, H.M. de. Le romant héroique. Paris, 1632.
Htn Mon 30.3* Montaigne, Michel de. Essayes. Florio. 3. ed. London, 1632.
Htn 38526.47.15* Rayssiguier, N. Tragicomédie pastorale. Paris, 1632.
Htn 38526.47.19* Richemont. L'esperance glorieuse. Paris, 1632. 2 pam.
Htn 38528.8.25* Satyre Ménippée de la vertu du catholicon d'Espagne. n.p., 1632.
Htn 38526.70* Vievget. Les adventures de policandre. Paris, 1632.

1633

38521.68.5 Audiguier, Vital d'. Histoire trage-comique de nostre temps. Paris, 1633.
Htn 38526.9.5* Bertaut, Jean. Les oeuvres poétiques. Paris, 1633.
Htn 38526.2.11* Boisrobert, F. le M. de. Le pyrandre. Paris, 1633.
Htn 38526.48.18F* Du Bartas, Guillaume de Salluste. Du Bartas - his works. London, 1633.
Htn Mon 37.25* Montaigne, Michel de. Saggi, overo Discorsi. Venetia, 1633.
Htn 38526.48.245* Théophile de Viau. Oeuvres. Avignon, 1633.

1634

Htn 38542.4.9* Balzac, J.L.G. de. Letters. London, 1634.
Htn 38528.1.20* Le cabinet satyrique. Rouen, 1634.
Htn 38539.2.5* Camus, Jean P. Le rabat-joye du triomphe monacal. L'Isle, 1634.
38539.104 DuSoucy, François. Histoire asiatique de Cerinthe, de Calianthe et d'Artenice. Paris, 1634.
Htn 38526.16.51* Frenicle, Nicolas. L'entreien des illustres berges. Paris, 1634.
Htn 38526.20* Gournay, Marie de Jars de. Les advis. Paris, 1634.
Htn 38539.32.5* Rosset, François de. Theatrum tragicum das ist neue Wahrhaftige traurig claeglich und wunderliche Geschichten. Tübingen, 1634.
Htn 38546.22.28* Scudéry, Georges de. Le trompeur puny. Paris, 1634.

1635

Htn 38526.2.13* Boisrobert, F. le M. de. Le Parnasse royal. Paris, 1635.
Htn 38526.22.15* La Pinelière, G. de. Hippolyte. Paris, 1635.
Htn 38576.30* Mairet, Jean de. La Sophonisbe. Paris, 1635.
Htn 38576.29.3* Mairet, Jean de. La Sylvie. Paris, 1635.
Htn 38526.45.25* Pibrac, Guy du Faur. Recueil de plusieurs pieces. Paris, 1635.
Htn 38525.58* Rotrou, Jean de. La bague de l'oubly. Paris, 1635.
Htn 38525.68* Rotrou, Jean de. La Diane. Paris, 1635.
Htn 38525.70* Rotrou, Jean de. La Doristée. Paris, 1635.
Htn 38525.80* Rotrou, Jean de. Les occasions perdues. Paris, 1635.

1636

Htn 38528.14* Auvray, Jean. Le banquet des muses, ou Les divers satires. Rouen, 1636.

1636 - cont.

Htn 39534.6.5* Benserade, Isaac de. La Cleopatra. Paris, 1636-41. 5 pam.
Htn 38526.2* Beys, Charles. Theatre. Paris, 1636-53.
Htn 38526.13.300* Durval, J.G. Agarite. Paris, 1636.
Htn Mon 16.36* Montaigne, Michel de. Essais. Paris, 1636.
Htn 38525.72* Rotrou, Jean de. Hercule mourant. Paris, 1636.
Htn 38525.73* Rotrou, Jean de. L'heureuse Constance. Paris, 1636.
Htn 38525.79* Rotrou, Jean de. Les Ménechmes. Paris, 1636.
Htn 38546.22.24* Scudéry, Georges de. La mort de Caesar. Paris, 1636.
Htn 38546.22.35* Scudéry, Georges de. Le prince d'éguise. Paris, 1636.
Htn 38526.48.250* Théophile de Viau. Les oeuvres de Théophile, en trois parties divisées. Paris, 1636.

1637

Htn 38526.11.7* Desmarets de Saint Sorlin, Jean. Les visionnaires. Paris, 1637.
Htn 38539.18* Faret, Nicolas. L'honeste homme, ou L'art de plaire à la cour. Paris, 1637.
38539.20 Humbert, H. Les amours d'Ircandre et Sophonie. Paris, 1637.
Htn 38526.48.18.5* A learned summarie upon the famous poems of William of Salvst. London, 1637.
Htn 38526.38* Monléon, de. Le Thyeste. Paris, 1637. 3 pam.
Htn 38525.55* Rotrou, Jean de. Agesilan de Colchos. Paris, 1637.
Htn 38525.62* Rotrou, Jean de. La Celiane. Paris, 1637.
Htn 38525.63* Rotrou, Jean de. La Celimene. Paris, 1637.
Htn 38525.71* Rotrou, Jean de. Le filandre. Paris, 1637.
Htn 38525.76* Rotrou, Jean de. L'innocente infidélité. Paris, 1637.
Htn 38525.81* Rotrou, Jean de. La pèlerine amoureuse. Paris, 1637.
Htn 38524.60* Tragédies. Paris, 1637-47.
Htn 38525.36.2* Tristan L'Hermite, F. La Mariane. Paris, 1637.

1638

Htn 38575.28.8* Chapelain, J. Les sentimens de l'Académie français sur la tragi-comédie du Cid. Paris, 1638.
Htn 38526.10.8.5* Chapoton. Coriolan. Paris, 1638.
Htn 38576.11.25* Chevreau, U. Coriolan; tragédie. Paris, 1638.
Htn 38526.14.85* Elis, Charles. Paranymph de la cour. Rouen, 1638.
Htn 38523.22.50* Malherbe, François de. Oeuvres. 3. éd. Paris, 1638.
Htn 38523.22.47* Malherbe, François de. Oeuvres. 3. éd. Troyes, 1638.
Htn 38526.35.6* Maréchal, Antoine. Le railleur. Paris, 1638.
Htn 38525.56* Rotrou, Jean de. Amélie. Paris, 1638.
Htn 38525.74* Rotrou, Jean de. L'heureux naufrage. Paris, 1638.
38525.36.10 Tristan L'Hermite, F. Les amours de Tristan. Paris, 1638.

1639

Htn 38539.2.15* Camus, Jean P. Admirable events. London, 1639.
Htn 38526.17.5* Gombauld, J.O. de. Endimion. London, 1639.
Htn 38526.42.7* Nouvelon, N. Hercule furieux; tragédie. Paris, 1639.
Htn 38526.47.18* Regnault. Marie Stvard. Paris, 1639.
Htn 38525.57* Rotrou, Jean de. Antigone. Paris, 1639.
Htn 38525.60* Rotrou, Jean de. La belle Alphrède. Paris, 1639.
Htn 38525.78* Rotrou, Jean de. Laure persécutée. Paris, 1639.
Htn 38526.48.12* Sallebray. Le jugement de Paris. Paris, 1639.
FL 379.139 Scuderi, Georges de. L'apologie du théâtre. Paris, 1639.
Htn FL 377.139* Scudery, G. L'apologie du théâtre. Paris, 1639.
Htn 38546.22.12* Scudéry, Georges de. L'amour tirannique. Paris, 1639.
Htn 38525.36.6* Tristan L'Hermite, F. Panthée. Paris, 1639.

1640

Htn 38526.2.9* Boisrobert, F. le M. de. Palène. Paris, 1640.
Htn 38526.10.8.50* Claveret, Jean. Le ravissement de Proserpine. Paris, 1640.
Htn 38526.11.6* Desmarets de Saint Sorlin, Jean. Roxane. Paris, 1640. 5 pam.
Htn 38526.48.27.10* Du Bartas, Guillaume de Salluste. Die erste und andere Woche Wilhelms von Saluste. Cöthen, 1640.
Htn 38541.18* Duverdier, Gilbert. Loves...of the Greek Princes. London, 1640.
Htn 38541.19* Duverdier, Gilbert. Loves...of the Greek Princes. London, 1640.
Htn 38526.15.2.5* Gillet de la Tessonerie. La belle Quixaire; tragi-comédie. Paris, 1640.
Htn 38526.24* La Mesnadière, H.J. La poétique. Paris, 1640.
38539.13 La Serre, Jean Puget de. La Clytie, ou le romant de la cour. Paris, 1640.
Htn 38576.28.5* Mairet, Jean de. L'illustre corsaire. Paris, 1640.
Htn 38526.35* Maréchal, Antoine. La cour bergère. Paris, 1640.
Htn 38526.35.8* Maréchal, Antoine. Le veritable Capitan Matamore. Paris, 1640.
Htn Mon 16.40F* Montaigne, Michel de. Essais. Paris, 1640.
Htn 38525.61* Rotrou, Jean de. Les captifs; ou, Les esclaves. Paris, 1640.
Htn 38525.66* Rotrou, Jean de. Crisante. Paris, 1640.
Htn 38546.22.15* Scudéry, Georges de. L'amour tirannique. Paris, 1640.

1641

Htn 38526.11.8* Desmarets de Saint Sorlin, Jean. Ariana in two parts. 2d ed. London, 1641.
Htn 38526.11.5* Desmarets de Saint Sorlin, Jean. Mirame. Paris, 1641.
Htn 38526.48.18.2F* Du Bartas, Guillaume de Salluste. Du Bartas - his works. London, 1641.
Htn 38526.15.23* Gilbert, Gabriel. Marguerite de France. Paris, 1641.
38526.22.8 La Caze. L'inceste suposé, cammane. Paris, 1641. 2 pam.
Htn 38526.22.10* La Croix, C.S. de. L'inconstance punie. Paris, 1641.
Htn 38525.77* Rotrou, Jean de. Iphygénie. Paris, 1641.
Htn 38526.48.14* Sallebray. La troade. Paris, 1641.
Htn 38546.22.18* Scudéry, Georges de. Eudoxe. Paris, 1641.
Htn 38546.22.61* Scudéry, Georges de. Lettres amoureuses de divers auteurs de ce temps. Paris, 1641.
Htn 38525.36* Tristan L'Hermite, F. La lyre, l'Orphée. Paris, 1641.

1642

Htn 38526.10.10* Colletet, Guillaume. Cyminde. Paris, 1642.
Htn 38526.15.31* Gilbert, Gabriel. Téléphonte. Paris, 1642.
38544.2 La Calprenède, G. de. Cassandre. Paris, 1642-45. 10v.
Htn 38576.30.5* Mairet, Jean de. L'Athenais. Paris, 1642.
Htn 38523.22.60* Malherbe, François de. Les oeuvres. Paris, 1642.

1642 - cont.

Htn	38526.35.4*	Maréchal, Antoine. Le mauzolée. Paris, 1642.
Htn	38526.48.10*	Sallebray. L'amante ennemie. Paris, 1642.

1643

Htn	38526.8.30*	Baro, Balthasar. La clarimonde. Paris, 1643.
Htn	38576.12.52*	Desmares. Roxelane; tragédie-comédie. Paris, 1643.
Htn	38526.15.2*	Gillet de la Tessonerie. Policritte. Paris, 1643.
Htn	38525.64*	Rotrou, Jean de. Clarice; ou, L'amour constant. Paris, 1643.
Htn	38546.22.21*	Scudéry, Georges de. Ibrahim. Paris, 1643.
Htn	38546.22.40*	Scudéry, Georges de. L'ombre du grand Armand. Paris, 1643.

1644

Htn	38526.9.22*	Billaut, Adam. Les chevilles de Maître Adam, manuisier de Nevers. Paris, 1644.
	38527.33.9	Ceriziers, R. de. L'innocence reconnuë en la personne de s. Geneviève de Brabant. 5e éd. Tournay, 1644.
Htn	38539.5.15*	Desfontaines. L'inceste innocent; histoire véritable. Paris, 1644.
Htn	38543.28.5*	La Mothe le Vayer, F. de. Opuscules ou petits traictez. Paris, 1644.
Htn	38525.59*	Rotrou, Jean de. Le Belissaire. Paris, 1644.
Htn	38546.21.20*	Scudéry, Madeleine de. Les femmes illustrées. Paris, 1644-54. 2v.

1645

Htn	38526.01.35*	Arnauld d'Andilly, R. Lettres. Paris, 1645.
Htn	38576.10*	Brosse, N. de. Les innocens coupables. Paris, 1645.
	38526.76.5	Du Bois-Hus, Gabriel. Le prince illustre. Paris, 1645.
	39535.29	Garon, L. Le chasse ennuy, ou L'honneste. 4th éd. Paris, 1645.
Htn	38539.23.10*	Le Vayer de Boutigny, R. Le grand Selim. Paris, 1645.
	39531.20	Morisot, C.B. Pervirana. Divion, 1645.
Htn	38526.68.5*	Regnier, Mathurin. Satyres. Paris, 1645.
Htn	38525.22.75*	Régnier, Mathurin. Les satyres du sieur Régnier. Paris, 1645.
Htn	FL 377.145*	Torelli, G. Explication des decorations du théâtre. Paris, 1645.
Htn	38525.36.2.50*	Tristan L'Hermite, F. La mort de Chrispe ou Les maleurs domestiques du grand Constantin. Paris, 1645.
Htn	38525.36.4*	Tristan L'Hermite, F. La mort de Sénèque. Paris, 1645.

1646

Htn	38576.7.76*	Boyer, Claude. La Porcie romaine. Paris, 1646.
Htn	38576.10.2*	Brosse, N. de. Les songes des hommes esveillez. Paris, 1646.
Htn	38526.15.27*	Gilbert, Gabriel. Rodogune. Paris, 1646.
Htn	39527.45*	La Fontaine, Jean de. Les oeuvres postumes. Paris, 1646.
Htn	38526.28.7*	Le Vert. Aricidie, ou Le mariage de Tite. Rouen, 1646.
Htn	38526.37.4*	Maynard, F. de. Oeuvres. Paris, 1646.
Htn	38524.869*	Perselide. Paris, 1646.
Htn	38526.44.19*	Pibrac, Guy du Faur. Les quatrains. Paris, 1646.
Htn	38526.46.205*	Poirier, Hélie. Les soupirs salutaires. Amsterdam, 1646.
Htn	38521.54*	Sorel, Charles. Les berger extravagant. Rouen, 1646.

1647

Htn	38542.4.9.20*	Balzac, J.L.G. de. Lettres choisies. Paris, 1647. 2v.
Htn	38576.7.80*	Boyer, Claude. La soeur généreuse. Paris, 1647.
Htn	38575.50*	Corneille, Pierre. Rodogune. Rouen, 1647.
Htn	38526.15.21*	Gilbert, Gabriel. Hypolite. Paris, 1647.
Htn	38526.15.29*	Gilbert, Gabriel. Sémiramis. Paris, 1647.
	38576.27.28	Magnon, J. de. Josaphat, tragi-comédie. Paris, 1647.
Htn	38526.39*	Montfleury, A. Jacob. La mort d'Asdrubal. Paris, 1647.
Htn	38525.69*	Rotrou, Jean de. Dom Bernard de Cabrère. Paris, 1647.
Htn	38525.82*	Rotrou, Jean de. La soeur. Paris, 1647.
Htn	38525.82.5*	Rotrou, Jean de. La soeur généreuse. Paris, 1647.
Htn	38525.83*	Rotrou, Jean de. Les sosies. Paris, 1647.

1648

	38563.4.5	Audin, Prieur de Termes et de la Fage. Fables héroïques. 1. partie. Paris, 1648.
Htn	38526.1*	Auger, Jacques. La mort de Caton. Paris, 1648.
Htn	38576.7.78*	Boyer, Claude. Porus; ou La generosité d'Alexandre. Paris, 1648.
	38526.10.8.7	Chapoton. La grande iovrnee des machines. Paris, 1648.
Htn	38526.14.20*	Du Ryer, Pierre. Thémistocle. Paris, 1648.
Htn	39532.36*	Gacon, François. Le poète sans fard. Contenant. Libreville, 1648.
Htn	38525.84*	Rotrou, Jean de. Venceslas. Paris, 1648.
Htn	38525.85*	Rotrou, Jean de. Le veritable St.Genest. Paris, 1648.
	38526.48.3	S., I.M. La mort de Roxane. Paris, 1648.
Htn	38524.879*	Le sage jaloux. Paris, 1648.
	38526.48.4	Saint Germain. Le grand Timoléon. Paris, 1648.
Htn	39534.27.10*	Scarron, Paul. Recueil des oeuvres burlesques. Paris, 1648. 6 pam.
Htn	39533.15.30*	Segrais, Jean R. Berenice. Paris, 1648-50. 2v.
	39533.15.35	Segrais, Jean R. Le Toledan. v.1-5. Paris, 1648-55. 10v.
	38526.57.5	Tabourot, Étienne. Les bigarrvres. Rouen, 1648.

1649

Htn	38576.7.52*	Boyer, Claude. Aristodème. Paris, 1649.
Htn	38576.7.82*	Boyer, Claude. Tyridate; tragédie. Paris, 1649.
Htn	39534.17*	Ferrand, David. Les l'armes et complaintes de la reyne d'Angleterre. Paris, 1649.
Htn	38526.22.30*	Le Royer de Prade, Jean. La victime d'estat. Paris, 1649.
Htn	38525.65*	Rotrou, Jean de. Cosroes. Paris, 1649.
Htn	38546.22.31*	Scudéry, Georges de. Poésies diverses. Paris, 1649. 2 pam.
	38526.48.257	Théophile de Viau. Les oeuvres de Théophile, en trois parties divisées. Rouen, 1649.

1650

Htn	38576.7.84*	Boyer, Claude. Ulysse dans l'isle de Circé. Paris, 1650.
Htn	38539.2.10*	Camus, Jean P. The loving enemie. London, 1650.
Htn	38575.26.5*	Corneille, Pierre. Le Cid. London, 1650.
Htn	38575.31.18*	Corneille, Pierre. Don Sanche d'Arragon. Comédie hèroique. Paris, 1650.
Htn	38526.47.39*	Saint-Julien. Le courrier burlesque de la guerre de Paris. Anvers, 1650.
Htn	39534.30.25*	Scarron, Paul. L'heritier ridicule, ou La dame interessée. Paris, 1650.

1651

Htn	38542.5*	Balzac, J.L.G. de. Oeuvres...du Sieur de Balzac. Leide, 1651.
Htn	38544.4.15*	La Calprenède, G. de. Le comte Dessex; tragédie. Paris, 1651.
Htn	38536.1.5*	Rabelais, F. Les épistres...pendant son voyage d'Italie. Paris, 1651.
Htn	38528.38.10*	Saint Julien. L'esclite des bouts rimez de ce temps. pt.1. Paris, 1651.

1652

Htn	39532.29*	Aegidii Menagii miscellanea. Paris, 1652.
Htn	38539.2.25*	Camus, Jean P. Nature's paradox or The innocent impostor. London, 1652.
Htn	38541.24F*	La Calprenede, G. de C. Cassandra, the fam'd romance. 1. ed. pt. 1-5. London, 1652.
Htn	38541.24.20*	La Calprenede, G. de C. La mort des enfans d'Herode, ou Suite a la Marian. Tolose, 1652.
	Mon 16.52.5F	Montaigne, Michel de. Essais. Paris, 1652.
Htn	Mon 16.52*	Montaigne, Michel de. Essais. Paris, 1652.
Htn	38526.68*	Regnier, Mathurin. Les satyres, et autres oeuvres. Leiden, 1652.
Htn	38546.22.25*	Scudéry, Georges de. La mort de Caesar. Tolose, 1652.
Htn	38546.19.2*	Scudéry, Madeleine de. Ibrahim...romance. pt. 1-4. 1. ed. London, 1652.
Htn	38542.01.9*	Voiture, Vincent. Les oeuvres. Paris, 1652.

1653

Htn	38526.2.7*	Boisrobert, F. le M. de. La folle gageure. Paris, 1653.
Htn	38539.2.55*	Godeau, Antoine. Oraison funèbre de Messieur Jean Pierre Camus. Paris, 1653.
Htn	38544.28*	Montauban, Jacques P. de. Zenobie, reyne d'Armenie. v.1-5. Paris, 1653.
Htn	38525.67*	Rotrou, Jean de. Les deux pucelles. Lyon, 1653.

1654

Htn	38526.2.5*	Boisrobert, F. le M. de. Cassandre. Paris, 1654.
Htn	38541.19.75*	La Calprenede, G. de C. Hymen's praeludia, or Love's masterpieces. Pt. 1-12. London, 1654-59. 6v.
Htn	38526.32.7*	Marguerite d'Angoulême. Heptaméron, or The history of the fortunate lovers. London, 1654.
Htn	38526.47.25*	Saint-Amant, Marc Antoine Gérard. Moyse saove. Leyde, 1654.
	38542.2.7	Voiture, Vincent. Les lettres de Mr. de Voiture. Paris, 1654.

1655

Htn	38575.31.20*	Corneille, Pierre. Don Sanche d'Arragon. Comédie hèroique. Paris, 1655.
Htn	38526.14.25*	Du Ryer, Pierre. Anaxandre; tragi-comédie. Paris, 1655.
Htn	39534.18*	Ferrand, David. Inventaire de la Muse Normande. Rouen, 1655.
Htn	38524.83*	Poésies choisies de Messieurs Corneille. Paris, 1655. 2 pam.
Htn	38525.22.80*	Régnier, Mathurin. Les satyres et autres oeuvres. Paris, 1655.
Htn	38539.30*	Renaudot, I. Recueil général des questions traitées. Paris, 1655.
Htn	38539.30.5*	Renaudot, I. Recueil général des questions traitées. Paris, 1655-56. 5v.

1656

Htn	38526.2.21*	Boisrobert, F. le M. de. Les apparences trompeuses. Paris, 1656. 5 pam.
Htn	39534.37*	Brébeuf, Georges de. Lucain Travesty ou Les guerres civiles. Paris, 1656.
Htn	39533.8.10F*	Chapelain, Jean. La Pucelle; ou La France delivrée. Paris, 1656.
Htn	38575.34.40*	Corneille, Pierre. Pertharite roy des Lombards. Tragédie. Paris, 1656.
Htn	38588.16.6*	Quinault, Philippe. Le fantasme amoureux. Paris, 1656.
Htn	38588.12*	Quinault, Philippe. Oeuvres. Paris, 1656.
Htn	38526.48*	Sarasin, Jean F. Oeuvres. Paris, 1656.
Htn	39534.35*	Scarron, Paul. Les nouvelles tragi-comiques. Paris, 1656.
	38546.22.3	Scudéry, Georges de. Alaric, ou Rome vaincue. Bruxelles, 1656.
Htn	38546.10*	Scudéry, Madeleine de. Clélie, histoire romaine. Paris, 1656-61. 16v.
Htn	38546.21*	Scudéry, Madeleine de. Triumphant arch...to the...feminine sexe. London, 1656.

1657

Htn	38526.3.7.150*	Bourneuf, Sieur. L'algouasil burlesque, imité du visions. Paris, 1657.
	39533.8	Chapelain, Jean. La Pucelle ou La France delivrée. Paris, 1657.
Htn	38526.11.8.5*	Desmarets de Saint Sorlin, Jean. Clovis, ou La France chrestienne. Paris, 1657.
Htn	38526.17.3*	Gombauld, J.O. de. Epigrammes. Paris, 1657.
	38544.3	La Calprenède, G. de. Cléopatre. Paris, 1657-58. 24v.
Htn	Mon 16.57F*	Montaigne, Michel de. Essais. Paris, 1657.
Htn	Mon 16.57.5F*	Montaigne, Michel de. Essais. Paris, 1657.
Htn	Mon 16.57.2F*	Montaigne, Michel de. Essais. Paris, 1657.
Htn	37558.30.65*	Pellison-Fontanier, Paul. The history of the French Academy. London, 1657.
Htn	38588.16.7*	Quinault, Philippe. La genereuse ingratitude. Paris, 1657.

Chronological Listing

1658

38542.10.8 Balzac, J.L.G. de. Aristippe. Leide, 1658.
38542.10.9 Balzac, J.L.G. de. Aristippe. Leide, 1658.
Htn 39534.39* Brébeuf, Georges de. Poésies diverses. Paris, 1658.
Htn 39533.20.3* Cyrano de Bergerac. Satyrical characters and handsome descriptions. London, 1658.
Htn 38526.15* Gillet de la Tessonerie. Le desniaise. Paris, 1658.
Htn 38526.17* Gombauld, J.O. de. Les danaides. Paris, 1658.
Htn 38526.48.1* Sarasin, Jean F. Oeuvres. Rouen, 1658.
Htn 38546.10.5* Scudéry, Madeleine de. Clélia; an excellent new romance. v.1-5. London, 1658-60. 2v.
Htn 38528.36* Valcroissant, Pierre de Marmet. Entertainment of the cours. London, 1658.

1659

38526.01.20 Arnauld d'Andilly, R. Oeuvres chrestiennes. 9e éd. Paris, 1659. 2 pam.
Htn 38542.4.15* Balzac, J.L.G. de. Les entretiens. Leide, 1659.
Htn 38542.4* Balzac, J.L.G. de. Lettres de feu M. de Balzac à M. Conrart. Paris, 1659.
38542.4.11 Balzac, J.L.G. de. Les lettres diverses. Paris, 1659.
Htn 38526.2.17* Boisrobert, F. le M. de. Les epistres en vers et autres oeuvres poétiques. Paris, 1659.
Htn 38526.2.19* Boisrobert, F. le M. de. La jalouse d'elle-mesme. Paris, 1659.
Htn 38576.7.56* Boyer, Claude. Clotilde; tragédie. Paris, 1659.
Htn 38575.36* Corneille, Pierre. Oedipe. Paris, 1659.
Htn 38575.55* Corneille, Thomas. Darius, tragédie. Paris, 1659.
Htn 39534.22.15* Furetière, Antoine. Nouvelle allegorique. Paris, 1659.
Htn 38523.22.65* Malherbe, François de. Oeuvres. Paris, 1659. 2 pam.
Htn Mon 16.59* Montaigne, Michel de. Essais. Amsterdam, 1659. 3v.
Htn 39534.27.5* Scarron, Paul. Oeuvres. Rouen, 1659.
Htn 38546.22.6* Scudéry, Georges de. Alaric, ou Rome vaincue. Rouen, 1659.
38546.12 Scudéry, Madeleine de. Artemene, ou Le Grand Cyrus. Paris, 1659. 10v.
Htn 39533.15.20* Segrais, Jean R. Diverses poesies. Paris, 1659.

166-

Htn 39535.64* Berthod, François. La ville de Paris. Paris, 166-?

1660

Htn 38542.4.16* Balzac, J.L.G. de. Les entretiens. Paris, 1660.
Htn 38576.7.58* Boyer, Claude. Fédéric; tragicomédie. Paris, 1660.
Htn 39534.37.40* Brébeuf, Georges de. Entretiens solitaires. Paris, 1660.
38576.8.2 Brécourt, G.M. de. La feinte mort de Jodelet. Paris, 1660.
Htn 38572.7.5* Corneille, Pierre. Le théâtre. Rouen, 1660. 3v.
Htn 38526.15.19* Gilbert, Gabriel. Arie et Petus. Paris, 1660.
Htn 38526.16.350* Godeau, A. Poésies chrestiennes. Paris, 1660.
Htn 38526.27.12* Lesfargus, B. David. Paris, 1660.
Htn 38523.22.90* Malherbe, François de. Les poésies. Paris, 1660.
Htn 38544.30.15* Ortigue, P. de. The grand Scipio. London, 1660.
Htn 38588.16.3* Quinault, Philippe. Les coups de l'amour et de la fortune. Rouen, 1660. 5 pam.
Htn Mol 194.7* Rosimond, Claude La Rose de. Le nouveau Festin de Pierre. Paris, 1660.
Htn 38546.14* Scudéry, Madeleine de. Almahide. Paris, 1660-63. 8v.
Htn Mol 194.10* Villiers, C.D. de. Le Festin de Pierre. Paris, 1660.

1661

38547.33 Ariane, ou Se voit les aventures de Mélinte. v.1-2. Lyon, 1661.
Htn 38542.4.12* Balzac, J.L.G. de. Lettres familières de M. de Balzac à M. Chapelain. Amsterdam, 1661.
NEDL 38576.7.70 Boyer, Claude. La mort de Démétrius, ou Le rétablissement. Paris, 1661.
Htn 39534.60* L'inconstant vaincu. Paris, 1661.
38526.22.13 Jacques, J. Le faut-mourir. v.1-2. Lyon, 1661.
Htn 38541.22.50* La Calprenede, G. de C. Cassandra, the fam'd romance. London, 1661.
Htn 38526.27.2* Lambert. La magie sans magie. Paris, 1661.
Htn 38543.30.8* La Mothe le Vayer, F. de. Prose chagrine. Pt.1-3. Paris, 1661.
Htn 38576.41* Perrin, Pierre. Les oeuvres de poesie. Paris, 1661.
Htn 38528.17.30* Philippot, the Savoyard. Recueil nouveau des chansons du Savoyart. Paris, 1661.
Htn 38588.16.9* Quinault, Philippe. Amalasonte, tragi-comédie. Paris, 1661.
Htn 38546.11* Scudéry, Madeleine de. Célinte; nouvelle. Paris, 1661.
37564.26.90 Somaize, Antoine de. Le grand dictionaire des pretieuses. Paris, 1661. 2v.

1662

Htn 39534.39.5* Brébeuf, Georges de. Poésies diverses. Rouen, 1662.
Htn 38576.12.32* Chappuzeau, Samuel. Le riche mécontent; ou Le noble imaginaire. Paris, 1662.
Htn 38543.30.10* La Mothe le Vayer, F. de. La promenade dialogue entre Tubertus Ocella et Marcus Bibulus. Paris, 1662-64. 4v.
Htn 38526.27.25* Le Petit, Claude. L'heure du berger. Revue. Paris, 1662.
39534.48 Nicole, Claude. Les oeuvres. Paris, 1662.
38529.3 Pithoys, Claude. L'apocalypse de Meliton ou révélation. St. Leger, 1662.
Htn 38525.35.50* Tristan L'Hermite, F. Poésies galantes et heroiques. Paris, 1662.

1663

Htn 38526.2.4.150* Billaut, Adam. Le ville brequin de Me Adam, menvisier de Nevers. Paris, 1663.
Htn 38526.3.7.50* Boüillon. Les oeuvres de feu Monsieur de Boüillon. Paris, 1663.
Htn Mol 855.4* Boursault, E. Le portrait du peintre. Paris, 1663.
Htn 38576.7.72* Boyer, Claude. Oropaste, ou Le faux Tonaxare. Paris, 1663.
Htn 38576.12.30* Chappuzeau, Samuel. L'avare duppé; ou L'homme de paille. Paris, 1663.
Htn 38526.15.17* Gilbert, Gabriel. Les amours d'Ovide. Paris, 1663.
Htn Mol 178.3* Molière, Jean Baptiste Poquelin. La critique de l'École des femmes. Amsterdam, 1663.

1663 - cont.

Htn 38588.16.25* Quinault, Philippe. Agrippa, roy d'Abbe, ou Le faux Tiberinus. Paris, 1663.
Mol 853.9 Vizé, J.D. de. Novvelles novvelles. Paris, 1663. 3v.

1664

38542.11 Balzac, J.L.G. de. Aristippe. Amsterdam, 1664.
Htn 38542.4.5* Balzac, J.L.G. de. Lettres de feu Monsieur de Balzac à Monsieur Conrart. Amsterdam, 1664.
38542.10.5 Balzac, J.L.G. de. Les oeuvres diverses. Paris, 1664.
Htn 38529.20* Barry, René. L'esprit de cour. Bruxelles, 1664.
Htn 38575.34.10* Corneille, Pierre. Pompey the great. London, 1664.
Htn 38574.1* Corneille, Pierre. Le théâtre. Paris, 1664.
Htn 38571.3* Corneille, Pierre. Le théâtre. Paris, 1664. 2v.
Htn 38526.13.200* Descret, L.C. Alizon. 2e éd. Paris, 1664.
Htn 38526.15.15* Gilbert, Gabriel. Les amours d'Angélique et de Médor. Paris, 1664.
38544.4 La Calprenède, G. de. Faramond ou L'histoire de France. Paris, 1664. 12v.
Htn Mol 855.12.2* La Croix, Paul de. La guerre comique. Paris, 1664.
Htn 38543.28.10* La Mothe le Vayer, F. de. Homilies académiques. Paris, 1664.
Htn 39533.12* Le Laboureur, Louis. Charlemagne, poëme heroïque. Paris, 1664.
37555.33 Lorel, Charles. Bibliothèque française. Paris, 1664.
Htn 38528.9* Satyre Ménippée. Ratisbon, 1664.
38526.63 Tausianus, P. Latina interpretatio eximii poematis Gallici à Arnaldo d'Andilly. 2a ed. Paris, 1664.

1665

Htn 38526.10.8.55* Claveret, Jean. Le cuyer. Paris, 1665.
38542.34 Colin, Claude. Eraste, ou Les amours du grand Alcandre. Paris, 1665.
39535.40 Cypriot, O. Almanach d'amour. n.p., 1665.
Htn 38543.28.15* La Mothe le Vayer, F. de. Suite des homiliés académiques. Paris, 1665.
Htn 38543.6.9* La Rochefoucauld, François. Réfléxions ou Sentences et maximes morales. Paris, 1665.
Htn Mol 261.6* Molière, Jean Baptiste Poquelin. Sganarelle. Paris, 1665.
38526.42 Montluc, A. de. La comédie des proverbes. Paris, 1665.
Htn 38524.62* Nouveau recueil de plusieurs et diverses pièces galantes de ce temps. n.p., 1665. 2v.
38541.8 Oeuvres de Monsieur Jean L.G. Balzac. Paris, 1665. 2v.
Htn 38588.16.8* Quinault, Philippe. Astrate. Paris, 1665.
Htn 39534.29.9* Scarron, Paul. Typhon. The Gyant's war with the gods. London, 1665.

1666

Htn 38576.7.50* Boyer, Claude. Les amours de Jupiter et de Sémélé. Paris, 1666.
Htn 38575.24.9* Corneille, Pierre. Agesilas. Paris, 1666.
Htn 38544.27.275* La Fayette, Marie M. The princess of Monpensier. London, 1666.
Htn 38543.28.20* La Mothe le Vayer, F. de. Dernières homiliés académiques. Paris, 1666.
Htn 38543.30.20* La Mothe le Vayer, F. de. Problems sceptiques. Paris, 1666.
Htn 38523.22.80* Malherbe, François de. Poésies avec les observations de M. Menage. Paris, 1666.
Htn Mol 16.66* Molière, Jean Baptiste Poquelin. Oeuvres. Paris, 1666. 2v.
Htn 38576.34.4* Montfleury, Antoine Jacob. L'escole des filles. Paris, 1666.

1667

Htn 39533.35* Carel, Jacques. Les Sarrazins chassez de France; poeme heroïque. Paris, 1667.
Htn Mol 245.1* Guérin, Nicolas Armand Martial. Le misantrope. Paris, 1667.
Htn 38543.30.25* La Mothe le Vayer, F. de. Doubte sceptique. Paris, 1667.
Htn 38545.40* Recueil de quelques pièces. Pt.1-2. Cologne, 1667. 2v.
Htn 38546.19.9* Scudéry, Madeleine de. Mathilde. Paris, 1667.

1668

38547.45.5 Alluis, Jacques. Le accommodement de l'ésprit et du coeur. Paris, 1668.
Htn 38576.12.27* Champmesle, C.C. Délie; pastorale. Paris, 1668.
Htn 38576.21.25* Desjardins, Marie C.H. Le jaloux par force et le bonheur des femmes. Fribourch, 1668.
Htn 38541.20* La Calprenede, G. de C. Hymen's praeludia, or Love's masterpieces. London, 1668.
Htn 38543.30.15* La Mothe le Vayer, F. de. Observations diverses sur la composition. Paris, 1668.
Htn 38576.34.6* Montfleury, Antoine Jacob. L'escole des jaloux. Paris, 1668.
38576.48 Rosimond, C. la R. Le duel fantasque; ou Les valets. Grenoble, 1668.
38545.18 Saint Maurice, A. de. Les fleurs des nouvelles galantes. Paris, 1668.
39534.33.12 Scarron, Paul. Le Jodelet, duelliste. Paris, 1668.
39534.33.7 Scarron, Paul. Le Jodelet, duelliste. Paris, 1668.
39534.26.7 Scarron, Paul. Oeuvres reveues. Paris, 1668. 2v.
Htn 38546.68* Torche, Antoine de. La cassette des bijovx. Paris, 1668.

1669

38547.45 Alluis, Jacques. Le chat d'Espagne. Cologne, 1669.
Htn 38576.7.60* Boyer, Claude. La feste de Venus. Paris, 1669.
Htn 38576.7.64* Boyer, Claude. Le jeune Marius; tragédie. Paris, 1669.
Htn 37564.13* Guéret, G. La parnasse reformé. Paris, 1669.
Htn 39527.33* La Fontaine, Jean de. Les amours de Psyché et de Cupidon. Paris, 1669.
Htn 38543.30.29* La Mothe le Vayer, F. de. Discours pour montrer que les doutes de la philosophie sceptique sont de grand usage. Paris, 1669.
Htn 38543.30.36* La Mothe le Vayer, F. de. Mémorial de quelques conférences. Paris, 1669.
Htn Mol 218.4* Molière, Jean Baptiste Poquelin. George Dandin. Amsterdam, 1669.

1669 - cont.

Htn Mon 16.69* Montaigne, Michel de. Essais. Lyon, 1669. 3v.
Htn Mon 16.69.2* Montaigne, Michel de. Essais. v.1-3. Paris, 1669. 6v.
Htn 38576.34.8* Montfleury, Antoine Jacob. La femme juge et partie. Paris, 1669.
38539.60 La prison sans chagrin; histoire comique du temps. Paris, 1669.
38542.19.5 Saint-Evremond, C. de M. de S.D. Recueil de diverses pièces. La Haye, 1669.
38588.48 Yvernaud. Le martyre de Sainete Valerie. Limoges, 1669.

1670

Htn 38557.31.6* Bossuet, J.B. Oraison funèbre de Henriette d'Angleterre. Paris, 1670.
Htn 38576.7.74* Boyer, Claude. Policrate. Paris, 1670.
38576.12 Cheffault, F. de. Le martyre de Saint Gervais. Paris, 1670.
Htn 37585.7* Comédies françaises. Paris, 1670-85.
Htn Mol 855.9* La critique de Tartuffe. Paris, 1670.
Htn 39533.11.50* Labadie, Jean de. Le chant royal du grand roy Jesus. Amsterdam, 1670.
Htn 38543.30.40* La Mothe le Vayer, F. de. Hexaméron rustique. Paris, 1670.
Htn 38543.28.7* La Mothe le Vayer, F. de. Soliloques sceptiques. Paris, 1670.
Htn Mol 248.1* Molière, Jean Baptiste Poquelin. M. de Porceaugnac. Paris, 1670.
Htn Mol 269.3.4* Molière, Jean Baptiste Poquelin. Tartuffe. Medbourne. London, 1670.
Htn 38542.21* Saint-Evremond, C. de M. de S.D. Jugement sur Seneque, Plutarque et Petrone. Paris, 1670.
39534.32.20 Scarron, Paul. Le marquis ridicule. Paris, 1670. 4 pam.

1671

Htn 38557.52* Bossuet, J.B. Éxposition de la doctrine de l'église catholique sur les matières de controverse. Paris, 1671.
38547.25 Le comte de Dunois. Paris, 1671.
Htn 38575.34.5* Corneille, Pierre. Nicomède. London, 1671.
Htn 39534.21* Furetière, Antoine. Scarron's city romance made English. Savoy, 1671.
Htn 37564.14* Guéret, G. La guerre des auteurs anciens et modernes. Paris, 1671.
Htn 38543.29* La Mothe le Vayer, F. de. Cinq dialogues. Amons, 1671.
Htn Mol 175.100* Molière, Jean Baptiste Poquelin. Ballet des ballets. Paris, 1671.
Mol 215.7 Molière, Jean Baptiste Poquelin. Les Fourberies de Scapin. Comédie. Paris, 1671.
39534.47 Montreüil, M. Les oeuvres. Paris, 1671.
Htn 38539.29.5* Pielat, B. Le secrétaire incogne. Amsterdam, 1671. 2 pam.

1672

Htn Mol 750.1.5* Alègre, d'. The memoires of the life and rare adventures of Henrietta S. Molière. London, 1672.
Htn 38576.7.62* Boyer, Claude. Le fils supposé. Paris, 1672.
Htn 38576.7.68* Boyer, Claude. Lisimène, ou Le jeune bergère. Paris, 1672.
Htn 38542.28* Gaultier, Jacques. Al-man-sir. London, 1672.
Htn 38526.15.25* Gilbert, Gabriel. Opera pastorale héroique. Paris, 1672.
Htn 38576.34.10* Montfleury, Antoine Jacob. La fille capitaine. Paris, 1672.
Mol 880.32 Santini, N. Il conte d'Altamura. Lucca, 1672.

1673

37585.10 Corneille, T. La mort d'Annibal. Tragedie. Paris, 1673. 9 pam.
38576.19 Hauteroche, N. le B. de. Les apparences trompeuses. Paris, 1673.
38576.19.7 Hauteroche, N. le B. de. Le deüil. Paris, 1673.
Htn 38543.27.35* Le Pays, René. The drudge: or The jealous extravagant. London, 1673.
Htn 38576.34.2* Montfleury, Antoine Jacob. L'ambigu comique. Paris, 1673.
Htn Mol 150.5* Les plaisirs de l'isle enchantée. Paris, 1673.

1674

38526.01.45 Arnauld d'Andilly, R. Lettres. Lyon, 1674.
Htn 38527.33.20* Ceriziers, R. de. The innocent lady. 2nd ed. London, 1674.
Htn 38576.19.5* Hauteroche, N. le B. de. Crispin musicien. Paris, 1674.
Htn 38541.21* La Calprenede, G. de C. Hymen's praeludia, or Cleopatra. London, 1674.
Htn Mol 16.74* Molière, Jean Baptiste Poquelin. Oeuvres. Paris, 1674-75. 7v.
Htn 38576.34.16* Montfleury, Antoine Jacob. Trigaudin. Paris, 1674.
38546.19.3 Scudéry, Madeleine de. Ibrahim, or The illustrious Bassa. London, 1674.
FL 377.174 Le théâtre français divisé en trois livres. Lyon, 1674.

1675

Htn 38566.3* Boileau Despréaux, Nicolas. Oeuvres diverses. Paris, 1675.
38542.31 Du Pré, M. Le moine seculaire. Franche, 1675?
Htn Mol 245.5* Guérin, Nicolas Armand Martial. Le misantrope. Paris, 1675.
Htn Mol 16.75* Molière, Jean Baptiste Poquelin. Oeuvres. Amsterdam, 1675. 5v.
39534.26.9 Scarron, Paul. Les nouvelles oeuvres tragi-comiques. Amsterdam, 1675.
39534.30.11 Scarron, Paul. Le virgile travesty en vers burlesque. Paris, 1675. 2v.
Htn 39534.11* Vairasse, Denis. History of the Sevarites. London, 1675.

1676

38557.31.8 Bossuet, J.B. Oraison funèbre de Henriette d'Angleterre. Lyon, 1676.
38557.31.14 Bossuet, J.B. Oraison funèbre de Henriette Marie de France. Lyon, 1676.
Htn 38542.13.7* Brémond, Sébastien. Haltige ou Les amours. Cologne, 1676.
Htn 39533.19.9* Cyrano de Bergerac. Oeuvres. Paris, 1676.

1676 - cont.

Htn 38563.29.15* Perrault, C. Recueil de divers ouvrages en prose et en vers. 2. éd. Paris, 1676.
Htn 38576.49* Rosimond, C. la R. Le volontaire. Paris, 1676.
Htn 38545.20.9* Saint Réal, César V. de. Don Carlos. London, 1676.
Htn 39534.32.50* Scarron, Paul. Comical romance. London, 1676.
Htn 38542.2.30* Voiture, Vincent. Zelinda. London, 1676.

1677

Htn 38539.2.35* Camus, Jean P. A true tragical history of two illustrious families...Alcimus and Vannoza. London, 1677.
Htn 38576.21.45* Desjardins, Marie C.H. The disorders of love. London, 1677.
Htn 38541.22* La Calprenede, G. de C. Pharamond, or The history of France. London, 1677.
Htn 38576.47.5* Pradon, J. Phèdre et Hippolyte. Paris, 1677.
Htn 38541.28F* Scudery, Madeleine de. Almahide, or The captive queen. London, 1677.

1678

38542.4.10 Balzac, J.L.G. de. Lettres choisies. Amsterdam, 1678.
39535.12.5 Callières, François de. Nouvelles amoureuses et galantes. Paris, 1678.
38547.28 Les entretiens de Thémiste et de Lisias. Saumur, 1678.
38576.19.9 Hauteroche, N. le B. de. Les nobles de province. Lyon, 1678.
Htn 38544.44.35* Préchac, L.M. de. Yolande de Sicile. Paris, 1678.
Htn 38544.56* Subligny, A.F.P. de. The mock Clelia. London, 1678.
Htn 38539.55* Villiers, J. de. The gentleman-apothecary. London, 1678.

1679

Htn 38544.27.50.5* La Fayette, Marie M. The Princess of Cleves. London, 1679.
Htn Mol 16.79* Molière, Jean Baptiste Poquelin. Oeuvres posthumes. Amsterdam, 1679. 5v.
39533.45 Morillon, Gatien de. Joseph, ou L'esclave fidele. Turin, 1679.
Htn 38576.47* Pradon, J. Phèdre et Hippolyte; tragédie. Paris, 1679.
38544.40 Préchac, L.M. de. L'illustre parisienne historique, galante et véritable. v.1-2. Paris, 1679.

1680

38557.52.2.3 Bossuet, J.B. Éxposition de la doctrine de l'église catholique sur les matières de controverse. 5. éd. Paris, 1680.
38557.52.2 Bossuet, J.B. Éxposition de la doctrine de l'église catholique sur les matières de controverse. 4. éd. Paris, 1680.
Htn 38557.52.2.10* Bossuet, J.B. Éxposition de la doctrine de l'église catholique sur les matières de controverse. Paris, 1680. 3 pam.
38557.25.195 Bossuet, J.B. Oraisons funèbres. 3. éd. Paris, 1680. 2 pam.
Htn 38547.27* Dom Sébastien. Paris, 1680.
38576.19.3 Hauteroche, N. le B. de. Crispin médecin. Paris, 1680.
Htn 39533.27* Lauvergne, (Mme.) de. Recueil de poesies. Paris, 1680.
Htn Mol 178.6* Molière, Jean Baptiste Poquelin. La critique de l'École des femmes. Amsterdam, 1680.
Htn 38576.34.12* Montfleury, Antoine Jacob. Le mariage de rien. Paris, 1680.
38544.55 Subligny, A.F.P. de. La fausse Clélie. Histoire française galante. Nymegue, 1680.

1681

Htn Mol 16.81* Molière, Jean Baptiste Poquelin. Oeuvres posthumes. Paris, 1681. 5v.
Htn Mol 16.81.2* Molière, Jean Baptiste Poquelin. Oeuvres posthumes. Paris, 1681. 5v.
Htn 37578.16* Recueil curieux de contes à rire. Utopie, 1681.

1682

Htn 38576.3.50* Bernard, Catherine. The female, or Frederick of Sicily. London, 1682.
Htn 38566.34* Boileau Despréaux, Nicolas. Le Lutrin. London, 1682.
Htn 38557.46.25* Bossuet, J.B. Conference avec M. Claude. Paris, 1682.
Htn 38557.59.150* Bossuet, J.B. Sermon presché à l'ouverture de l'assemblée generale du clergé de France. Paris, 1682.
Htn 38557.67* Bossuet, J.B. Traité de la communion sous les deux espèces. Paris, 1682.
Htn Mol 880.5.3* Champmesté, C.C. Les fragments de Molière. Paris, 1682.
38576.16 Genest, C.C. Zelonide. Paris, 1682.
39527.41 La Fontaine, Jean de. Poëme du Quinquina. Paris, 1682.
Htn 38526.28.5* Lestoile, C. de. L'intrigue des filous. Paris, 1682.
Htn Mol 16.82* Molière, Jean Baptiste Poquelin. Oeuvres posthumes. Paris, 1682. 8v.
37574.200 Poésies nouvelles. Paris, 1682.
Htn 38546.8.5.5* Scudéry, Madeleine de. Conversations nouvelles sur divers sujets. Amsterdam, 1682.
Htn Mol 882.10* Sully. Les festes de l'amour et de Bacchus, Pastorale. Paris, 1682.

1683

Htn 38566.27* Boileau Despréaux, Nicolas. The art of poetry. London, 1683.
Htn 38557.46.28* Bossuet, J.B. Conference avec M. Claude. Paris, 1683.
Htn 38557.31.12* Bossuet, J.B. Oraison funèbre de Marie Terese d'Austriche. Paris, 1683.
Htn 38576.7.54* Boyer, Claude. Artaxerce. Paris, 1683.
38576.22 La Chapelle, Jean de. Oeuvres. Paris, 1683.
Htn Mol 192.1* Molière, Jean Baptiste Poquelin. Le Festin de Pierre mise en vers. Paris, 1683.
Htn Mol 228.10* Molière, Jean Baptiste Poquelin. Le malade imaginaire. n.p., 1683.
Htn 38544.44.45* Préchac, L.M. de. The lovely polander. London, 1683.

1684

Htn 38557.31.13* Bossuet, J.B. A sermon preached at the funeral of Mary Terese of Austria. London, 1684.

Chronological Listing

1684 - cont.

Htn 38547.43* Courtilz, G. de. Les conquestes amoureuses du grand Alcandre dans les Pays-Bas. Cologne, 1684.
38542.14.25 Dubosco de la Roberdière. Love victorious. London, 1684.
39534.49 La Suze, Henriette de Coligny. Recueil de pieces galantes en prose et en vers. Paris, 1684. 4v.
Htn 38576.25* Latuillerie, M. Les oeuvres. Paris, 1684.
Htn Mol 195.8* Molière, Jean Baptiste Poquelin. L'escole des femmes. Amsterdam, 1684.
Htn Mol 201.10* Molière, Jean Baptiste Poquelin. L'escole des maris. Amsterdam, 1684.
Htn Mol 16.84* Molière, Jean Baptiste Poquelin. Oeuvres posthumes. Amsterdam, 1684. 6v.
Htn Mol 255.9* Molière, Jean Baptiste Poquelin. La princesse d'Élide. Amsterdam, 1684.
Htn Mol 255.9.2* Molière, Jean Baptiste Poquelin. La princesse d'Élide. Paris, 1684.
Htn 38588.16.20* Quinault, Philippe. Amadis; tragédie en musique. Amsterdam, 1684.

1685

Htn 38557.31.20* Bossuet, J.B. Oraison funèbre de tres haute et tres puissante Princesse Anne de Gonzague de Clèves. Paris, 1685.
38576.19.2 Hauteroche, N. le B. de. Le cocher. Paris, 1685.
Htn 39527.8.3* La Fontaine, Jean de. Contes et nouvelles en vers. Amsterdam, 1685.
Htn 38539.23.5* Le Vayer de Boutigny, R. The famous romance of Taris and Zelie. London, 1685. 2 pam.
Htn Mon 31.1* Montaigne, Michel de. Essays. Cotton. London, 1685-86. 3v.
Mon 31.2 Montaigne, Michel de. Essays of Michael seigneur de Montaigne. London, 1685-86.
Htn 38567.9* Pradon, Jacques. Nouvelles remarques sur tous les ouvrages du sieur D***. La Hague, 1685.
Htn 38544.43* Préchac, L.M. de. The chaste Seraglian. London, 1685.
38544.42 Préchac, L.M. de. L'illustre génoise. Paris, 1685.
38546.22.9 Scudéry, Georges de. Alaric, ou Rome vaincue. La Haye, 1685.
Htn 38546.8.6* Scudéry, Madeleine de. Conversations nouvelles sur divers sujets. Amsterdam, 1685.
Htn 38546.8.5* Scudéry, Madeleine de. Conversations nouvelles sur divers sujets. La Haye, 1685.
38546.20 Scudéry, Madeleine de. Les conversations sur divers sujets. 4. éd. Amsterdam, 1685.
38539.35 Vanel, Charles. Histoire du temps ou Journal. Paris, 1685.

1686

Htn 38576.2.3* Baron, M.B. L'homme à bonne fortune. Paris, 1686.
Htn 38557.52.3* Bossuet, J.B. Exposition de la doctrine de l'église catholique sur les matières de controverse. 6. éd. Paris, 1686.
38557.52.4 Bossuet, J.B. Exposition de la doctrine de l'église catholique sur les matières de controverse. 7. éd. Paris, 1686.
38557.52.4.12 Bossuet, J.B. Exposition de la doctrine de l'église catholique sur les matières de controverse. 12. éd. Paris, 1686.
38557.52.4.5 Bossuet, J.B. Exposition de la doctrine de l'église catholique sur les matières de controverse. 8. éd. Paris, 1686.
38557.52.4.9 Bossuet, J.B. Exposition de la doctrine de l'église catholique sur les matières de controverse. 9. éd. Paris, 1686.
Htn 38557.52.24* Bossuet, J.B. An exposition of the doctrine of the Catholic Church in matters of controversie. London, 1686.
Htn 38557.36.10* Bossuet, J.B. Lettre pastorale de monseigneur l'evesque de Meaux. Paris, 1686.
Htn 38557.31.15* Bossuet, J.B. Oraison funèbre de Michel Le Tellier. Paris, 1686.
Htn 38557.36.12* Bossuet, J.B. A pastoral letter from the Lord Bishop of Meaux to the new Catholics. London, 1686.
Htn 38557.67.5* Bossuet, J.B. Traité de la communion sous les deux espèces. 2. éd. Paris, 1686.
Htn 38542.13.6* Brémond, Sébastien. The happy slave. London, 1686.
38557.67.5* fBossuet, J.B. Traité de la communion sous les deux espèces. 2. éd. Paris, 1686.
Mol 880.24 Lubbertze, L. De Schynheilige. Amsterdam, 1686.
Htn 38544.30.5* Ortigue, P. de. Agiatis, queen of Sparta. London, 1686.
Htn 38546.9* Scudéry, Madeleine de. La morale du monde, ou Conversations. Amsterdam, 1686.

1687

39535.50 Aubignac, F.H. Les conseils d'Ariste à Celimene. La Haye, 1687.
38557.46.31 Bossuet, J.B. Conference avec M. Claude. 2e éd. Paris, 1687.
Htn 38557.31.2* Bossuet, J.B. Oraisons funèbres, Louis de Bourbon. Paris, 1687.
Htn 38557.68* Bossuet, J.B. A treatise of communion under both kinds. London, 1687.
Htn 38562.33* Bouhours, D. La manière de bien penser dans les ouvrages d'ésprit. Paris, 1687.
Htn 38557.44.150* Catholic Church. France. Catechisme du diocese de Meaux. Paris, 1687.
Htn 39533.20.3.25* Cyrano de Bergerac. The comical history of the states and empires of the worlds of the moon and sun. v.1-2. London, 1687.
Htn 38554.350* Fénelon, F. de S. de la Mothe. Éducation des filles. Paris, 1687.
Htn 38588.16.5* Quinault, Philippe. Alceste ou Le triomphe d'Alcide. Paris, 1687.
Htn 38588.16.15* Quinault, Philippe. Thesée; tragédie en musique. Paris, 1687.

1688

Htn 38557.41.15* Bossuet, J.B. Histoire des variations des églises protestantes. Paris, 1688. 2v.
Htn 38544.14* Brilhac, J.B. de. Agnes de Castro. Amsterdam, 1688.
38544.13 Callières, François de. Histoire poétique. Amsterdam, 1688.

1688 - cont.

Htn 38554.846* Fénelon, F. de S. de la Mothe. Traité du ministère des pasteurs. Paris, 1688.
Htn 38564.7* La Bruyère, J. de. Les caractères de Théophraste. Lyon, 1688.
Htn 38576.46* Pradon, J. Oeuvres. Paris, 1688.

1689

Htn 38557.47* Bossuet, J.B. L'apocalypse avec une explication. Paris, 1689.
Htn 38557.41.5* Bossuet, J.B. Avertissement aux protestans sur les lettres du ministère Jurieu. Paris, 1689-91. 2v.
Htn 38557.52.25* Bossuet, J.B. Explication de quelques difficultez sur les prières de la messe. Paris, 1689.
Htn 38557.41.17* Bossuet, J.B. Histoire des variations des églises protestantes. 2e éd. Paris, 1689. 4v.
38557.41 Bossuet, J.B. Premier avertissement aux protestans. Paris, 1689.
Htn 38557.58.25* Bossuet, J.B. Prières écclésiastiques à l'usage de Meaux. Paris, 1689.
Htn 39534.1.13* Bussy-Rabutin. La France galante ou Histoires. Cologne, 1689.
Htn 38564.8* La Bruyère, J. de. Les caractères de Théophraste. 4. éd. Lyon, 1689.
Htn 38564.34* La Bruyère, J. de. The characters. London, 1689.
Htn 38523.29* Malherbe, François de. Poésies. 2. éd. Paris, 1689.
Htn Mol 16.75.2* Molière, Jean Baptiste Poquelin. Oeuvres posthumes. Amsterdam, 1689.
Htn 38585.28* Racine, Jean. Esther. Paris, 1689.

169-

Htn 38554.738.15* Fénelon, F. de S. de la Mothe. Responsio archiepiscopi. n.p., 169-.

1690

38563.4 Audin, Prieur de Termes et de la Fage. Favole Heroiche. Venice, 1690.
Htn 38557.44* Bible. Latin. O.T. Psalms. 1690. Liber psalmorum cum notis Jacobi Benigni Bossueti. Lugduni, 1690.
Htn 38557.47.5* Bossuet, J.B. L'apocalypse avec une explication. Paris, 1690.
Htn 38557.59.10* Bossuet, J.B. Réponse au huitième et dernier moyen decassation. Paris? 1690.
Htn 38544.27.400* La Fayette, Marie M. Zayde: a Spanish history, or romance. 2. ed. London, 1690.
Mol 202.25.3 Molière, Jean Baptiste Poquelin. Steiloorige Egbert of de twee ongelijke broeders. Amsterdam, 1690.
Htn 38546.7*A Scudéry, Madeleine de. Artamenes, or The grand Cyrus. v.1-10. London, 1690-91. 5v.

1691

38576.3 Bernard, Catherine. Brutus: tragédie. Paris, 1691.
Htn 38557.44.6* Bible. Latin. O.T. Psalms. Liber psalmorum cum notis Jacobi Benigni Bossueti. Lugduni, 1691.
Htn 38557.44.5* Bible. Latin. O.T. Psalms. Liber psalmorum cum notis Jacobi Benigni Bossueti. Lugduni, 1691.
38557.46.32 Bossuet, J.B. Conference avec M. Claude. 2e éd. Paris, 1691.
Htn 38557.41.75* Bossuet, J.B. Défense de l'histoire des variations contre la réponse de M. Basnage. Paris, 1691.
Htn 38557.51.75* Bossuet, J.B. Explication des prières de la messe. Paris, 1691.
38557.41.19 Bossuet, J.B. Histoire des variations des églises protestantes. 2e éd. Paris, 1691. 4v.
38562.30 Bouhours, D. Les entretiens d'Ariste et d'Eugène. Paris, 1691.
38576.12.42.30 Corneille, Thomas. Antiochus. Paris, 1691.
38544.24 Ferrand, B. Histoire des amours de Cleante et Bélise. Leyde, 1691.
Htn 38564.9* La Bruyère, J. de. Les caractères de Théophraste. 6. éd. Paris, 1691.
Htn 38576.26* Le Noble, E. Esope. Paris, 1691.
39533.33 Lettres choisies de Guy Patin. Cologne, 1691. 3v.
Htn 38557.59.250* Meaux, France (Diocese). Statuts et ordonnances synodales. Paris, 1691.
Htn 38581.17* Racine, Jean. Athalie. Paris, 1691.

1692

Htn 38566.2* Boileau Despréaux, Nicolas. Oeuvres diverses. Paris, 1692.
Htn 38557.36.5* Bossuet, J.B. Lettre de M. l'evesque de Meaux à frère N. moine de l'abbaye de N. Paris, 1692.
Htn 38564.9.5* La Bruyère, J. de. Les caractères de Théophraste. 7. éd. Paris, 1692.
Htn 38544.44.25* Préchac, L.M. de. L'heroïne mousquetaire. Amsterdam, 1692.
Htn 38524.140* Recueil des plus belles pièces des poètes françois. Paris, 1692.
Htn 38542.19.6* Saint Evremond, C. de M. de S.D. Miscellaneous essays. London, 1692.
Htn 38546.8* Scudéry, Madeleine de. Nouvelles conversations de morale. La Haye, 1692.

1693

Htn 38557.43* Bible. Latin. O.T. Selections. Libri Salomonis. Paris, 1693.
38562.35 Bouhours, D. Pensées ingénieuses des anciens et des modernes. Lyon, 1693.
39535.10 Callières, François de. Recueil des bons contes et de bons mots. Paris, 1693.
38575.40 Corneille, Pierre. De dood van Hannibal; treurspel. Amsterdam, 1693.
Htn Mon 31.3* Montaigne, Michel de. Essays. London, 1693. 3v.
38544.30 Ortigue, P. de. Les galanteries amoureuses de la cour de grêce. Paris, 1693.
Htn 38563.30* Perrault, C. Paralelle des anciens. Amsterdam, 1693.

Chronological Listing

1694

Htn 38557.53.200* Bossuet, J.B. Maximes et réfléxions sur la comédie. Paris, 1694.
Htn 39533.19.10* Chéron, E.S. Essay de pseaumes et cantiques mis en vers. Paris, 1694.
Htn 38542.35* Cotolendi, C. Arliquiniana, ou Les bons mots. Paris, 1694.
38588.18.5 Dufresny, Charles Rivière. Théâtre. Paris, 1694.
Htn 38564.10* La Bruyère, J. de. Les caractères de Théophraste. 8. éd. Paris, 1694.
Htn 38564.10.2* La Bruyère, J. de. Les caractères de Théophraste. 8. éd. Paris, 1694.
Htn Mol 16.94.3* Molière, Jean Baptiste Poquelin. Comédies. v.1-3. Nuremberg, 1694.
Htn Mol 62.3* Molière, Jean Baptiste Poquelin. Derer Komödien. Nuremberg, 1694. 3v.
Htn Mol 16.94* Molière, Jean Baptiste Poquelin. Oeuvres. Bruxelles, 1694. 4v.
38526.48.2 Sarasin, Jean F. Oeuvres de Sarasin. Paris, 1694.
Htn 39535.15* Sorbiere, S. Sorberiana ou Bon mots. Paris, 1694.
Htn 39535.16* Sorbiere, S. Sorberiana sive excerpta. Tolosae, 1694.
Htn 38537.27* Urchard, Thomas. Works of François Rabelais. London, 1694. 4v.
Htn 38563.65* Valois, D.A. Valeseana, ou Les pensées critiques. Paris, 1694.
38563.65.2 Valois, D.A. Valeseana, ou Les pensées critiques. Paris, 1694.

1695

Htn 38566.29* Boileau Despréaux, Nicolas. Ode pindarique...sur la prise de Namur. London, 1695.
Htn 38576.7.66* Boyer, Claude. Judith; tragédie. Paris, 1695.
Htn 38576.14* Donneau de Vizé, Jean. Les dames Vangées. Paris, 1695.
Htn 38576.45* Pradon, J. Le théâtre. Paris, 1695.
Htn 38563.66* Valois, D.A. Valeseana, ou Les pensées critiques. Paris, 1695.
38568.870 Villiers, P. de. Traité de la satire. Paris, 1695.

1696

39535.45 Bernier, J. Reflexions, pensées. Paris, 1696.
Htn 38557.54* Bossuet, J.B. Méditations sur la rémission des pechez. Paris, 1696.
Htn 38576.12.50* Desmares. La dragonne; ou Merlin dragon. La Haye, 1696.
Htn 39534.22.20* Furetière, Antoine. Furetieriana ou Les mots et les remarques d'histoire. Brusselles, 1696.
Htn 39525.2* La Fontaine, Jean de. Oeuvres postumes. Bordeaux, 1696.
Htn 38576.23.6* La Fosse d'Aubigny, A. de. Polixene; tragédie. Paris, 1696.

1697

Htn 39534.6* Benserade, Isaac de. Les oeuvres. Paris, 1697. 2v.
Htn 38557.34.5* Bossuet, J.B. Instruction sur les états d'oraison. Paris, 1697.
38557.34.8 Bossuet, J.B. Instruction sur les états d'oraison. 2. éd. Paris, 1697.
Htn 38576.11.30* Chevreau, U. Cheveraenna. Paris, 1697-1700. 2v.
38539.9.15 Du Verdier, G.S. Don Clarazce de Gontarnos. Amsterdam, 1697.
NEDL 38563.28 F.A.M.D. Le Parnasse assiégé. Lyon, 1697.
Htn 38554.378* Fénelon, F. de S. de la Mothe. Explication des maximes des saints sur la vie intérieure. Paris, 1697.
Htn 38554.378.2* Fénelon, F. de S. de la Mothe. Explication des maximes des saints sur la vie intérieure. Paris, 1697.
Htn 38554.518.50* Fénelon, F. de S. de la Mothe. Lettre de M. de S. Fénelon et duc de Cambrai. Roterdam, 1697.
Htn 38554.737.45* Fénelon, F. de S. de la Mothe. Réponse de Monseigneur l'Archévêque de Cambrai à la déclaration....Explication des maximes des saints. n.p., 1697.
37585.10.5 Gherardi, Evaristo. Suplement du théâtre italien. 1. éd. v.2,3. Bruxelles, 1697. 2v.
38547.47 Histoire curieuse du fameux Francion. Amsterdam, 1697. 2v.
38576.25.17 Le Noble, E. Les avantures provinciales, ou, Le voyage de Falaize. Paris, 1697.
Mol 16.97 Molière, Jean Baptiste Poquelin. Oeuvres. Paris, 1697. 8v.
Htn Mol 16.99* Molière, Jean Baptiste Poquelin. Oeuvres. Toulouse, 1697-99. 8v.
Htn 38557.48.5* Noailles, L.A. Declaratio ecclesiae principium Ludovici Antonii de Noailles. Paris, 1697.
Htn 38582.2* Racine, Jean. Oeuvres. Paris, 1697. 2v.

1698

Htn 38557.49* Bossuet, J.B. De nova quaestione tractatus tres. Paris, 1698.
Htn 38557.48.10* Bossuet, J.B. Divers écrits, ou Mémoires sur...Éxplication des maximes des saints. Paris, 1698.
Htn 38557.55* Bossuet, J.B. Quakerism a-la-mode. London, 1698.
Htn 38557.55.12* Bossuet, J.B. Relation sur le quiétisme. Paris, 1698.
Htn 38557.55.10* Bossuet, J.B. Remarques sur la réponse de M. l'Archévèque de Cambray. Paris, 1698.
Htn 38557.55.80* Bossuet, J.B. Réponse de M. l'Archévèque de Cambray. Paris? 1698?
38554.379.5 Fénelon, F. de S. de la Mothe. Instruction pastorale touchant son livre Des maximes des Saints. A'darn, 1698.
Htn 38554.517* Fénelon, F. de S. de la Mothe. Lettre de Monseigneur l'Archévêque Duc de Cambrai [Fénelon] à Monseigneur l'Évêque de Meaux, sur la charité. n.p., 1698?
Htn 38554.516.50* Fénelon, F. de S. de la Mothe. Première lettre de Monseigneur l'Archévêque Duc de Cambray. v.1-4. n.p., 1698.
Htn 38554.737.35* Fénelon, F. de S. de la Mothe. Réponce de Monseignenr l'Archévêque de Cambrai à l'ecrit de Monseigneur l'Evêque de Meaux. Paris, 1698.
Htn 38554.867* Fénelon, F. de S. de la Mothe. Verae oppositiones inter doctrinam Meldensis episcopi et doctrinam archiepiscopi Cameracensis. n.p., 1698.
38562.18.10 Fontenelle, B. Le B. de. Histoire des Oracles. Paris, 1698.
38547.30 Ismaël, prince de Maroc; nouvelle historique. Paris, 1698.
38576.26.5 Le Noble, E. L'histoire...de la conjuration des Pazzi. v.1-2. Paris, 1698.

1698 - cont.

Htn Mol 16.98* Molière, Jean Baptiste Poquelin. Oeuvres. Amsterdam, 1698. 4v.
Mol 64.1 Molière, Jean Baptiste Poquelin. Opere...Castelli. Lipsia, 1698. 4v.
Mol 64.1.2 Molière, Jean Baptiste Poquelin. Opere...Castelli. v.2-4. Lipsia, 1698. 3v.

1699

38537.25.150 Bernier, Jean. Jugement et observations sur la vie de F. Rabelais. Paris, 1699.
Htn 38557.54.10* Bossuet, J.B. Mandement...pour la publication de la constitution de nostre saint pere le pape Innocent XII. Paris, 1699.
Htn 38557.54.12* Bossuet, J.B. Mandement...pour la publication de la constitution de nostre saint pere le pape Innocent XII. Paris? 1699?
Htn 38557.25.200* Bossuet, J.B. Recueil des oraisons funèbres. Paris, 1699.
Htn 38557.59* Bossuet, J.B. Réponse aux prejugez décisifs pour M. l'Archévèque de Cambray. Paris, 1699.
38576.8.4 Brécourt, G.M. de. Les flateurs trompez...par Mr. B. Caen, 1699.
Htn 38553.16.10* Fénelon, F. de S. de la Mothe. Les avantures de Télémaque. Paris, 1699.
Htn 38553.16.5* Fénelon, F. de S. de la Mothe. Les avantures de Télémaque fils d'Ulysse. Bruxelles, 1699. 2v.
38564.13 La Bruyère, J. de. Les caractères de Théophraste. 10. éd. Paris, 1699.
Htn 38564.35.15* La Bruyère, J. de. Dialogues posthumus. Paris, 1699.
Htn 40526.21* La Grange-Chancel, Joseph de. Recueil des tragédies. Paris, 1699-1700.
39535.57 Pringy, de Marenville de (Mme.). Les differens caractères des femmes du siècle. 2e éd. Paris, 1699.

17-

39576.5.10 Argens, Jean Baptiste de Boyer. La fortune Florentin; ou Le mémoirs du comte della Valle. Amsterdam, 17- ?
40534.10.15 Belloy, Pierre L.B. La Gabriela. Barcelona, 17- .
40527.3 Bernard, Pierre Joseph. Oeuvres complètes. n.p., 17- ?
Mol 251.10 Molière, Jean Baptiste Poquelin. Les précieuses ridicules. n.p., 17- ?
39545.60 Refutation du sermon des cinquante. n.p., 17- ?
38543.1.5 Rochefort, J. de. Le passe temps agréable. Rotterdam, 17- .
37585.3.7 Théâtre classique; ouvrage adopté par l'Université de France. Paris, 17- .

1700

38547.21 Anonimiana, ou Mélanges de poésies d'éloquence. Paris, 1700.
37565.22 Argonne, Bonaventure d'. Melanges d'histoire et de littérature. Rouen, 1700. 2v.
37565.22.2 Argonne, Bonaventure d'. Melanges d'histoire et de littérature. 2nd ed. Paris, 1700. 2v.
40517.86 Bédacier, C.D. La comtesse de Mortane. La Haye, 1700.
40517.88 Bédacier, C.D. Histoire des amours de Gregoire VII. Cologne, 1700.
Htn 38557.56.60* Bossuet, J.B. Instruction pastorale sur les promesses de l'église. Paris, 1700. 2 pam.
Htn 38557.54.50* Bossuet, J.B. Propositiones examinandae. Paris? 1700?
Htn 38542.26.9* Cotolendi, C. Saint-Evremoniana ou dialogues. Paris, 1700.
38576.21.35 Desjardins, Marie C.H. Annales Galantes (Mme. de Villedieu de 1683). La Haye, 1700.
38564.17 La Bruyère, J. de. Les caractères de Théophraste. Paris, 1700.
38563.55 Leclerc, Jean. Parrhasiana; or Thoughts on several subjects. London, 1700.
Htn 38526.29.4* Navarre, M. de. Contes et nouvelles. Amsterdam, 1700. 2v.
Htn 38544.44.5* Préchac, L.M. de. The serasquier bassa: an historical novel of the times. London, 1700?
Htn 38542.27* Saint Dennis, C.M. de. Works. London, 1700. 3v.
Htn 39534.32.7* Scarron, Paul. The whole comical works of Paul Scarron. London, 1700.

1701

NEDL 38564.41 Brillon, J.P. Apologie de Monsieur de La Bruyère. Paris, 1701.
39534.1.9 Bussy-Rabutin. Discours...sur le bon usage des adversitez. Paris, 1701.
Htn 38553.16.40* Fénelon, F. de S. de la Mothe. Avantures de Télémaque. La Haye, 1701.
38544.60 Grandchamp. Le Télémaque moderne. Cologne, 1701. 2 pam.
Htn 38553.15.15* Gueudeville, Nicolas. Critique génerale des aventures. Cologne, 1701.
Htn 38563.46* Leclerc, Jean. Parrhasiana, ou Pensées diverses. Amsterdam, 1701. 2v.
Htn 39535.35* L'enclos, Anne. Portrait ou Le veritable caractere de le Coquette. Paris, 1701.
Htn 39535.6* Naude, G. Naudaeana et Patiniana. Paris, 1701.
Htn 39533.30* Renoult, J.B. Avantures de la Madona. Amsterdam, 1701.

1702

38566.3.25 Boileau Despréaux, Nicolas. Oeuvres diverses. v.1-2. Amsterdam, 1702.
Htn 38557.49.28* Bossuet, J.B. Instructions sur la version du Nouveau Testament. Paris, 1702.
Htn 38576.11.23* Chevreau, U. La suite et le mariage du Cid. Caen, 1702.
38553.11 Fénelon, F. de S. de la Mothe. Lettres de direction. Paris, 1702.
38523.6.9 Marot, Clément. Les oeuvres. La Haye, 1702. 2v.
39535.14 Neretti, Filippo. Dialogues et historiettes diverses. Venise, 1702.
38582.2.5 Racine, Jean. Oeuvres. Paris, 1702. 2v.
38587.10 Regnard, Jean François. Democrite, comédie. Amsterdam, 1702.
Htn 38541.27* Scudery, Madeleine de. Almahide. London, 1702.
Htn 39534.10* Vairasse, Denis. Histoire des Sevarambes. Amsterdam, 1702.

Chronological Listing

1703

Htn 38557.49.30* Bossuet, J.B. Seconde instruction: sur les passages particuliers de la version du Nouveau Testament. Paris, 1703.
Htn 40517.80* Caumont de la Force, Charlotte R. de. Anecdote galante. Nancy, 1703.
38543.29.10 La Mothe le Vayer, F. de. L'ésprit de La Mothe le Vayer. n.p., 1703.
39527.50 Mandeville, Bernard de. Some fables after the easie and familiar method of M. de La Fontaine. London, 1703.
Htn Mol 17.03* Molière, Jean Baptiste Poquelin. Oeuvres. Liége, 1703.
39535.7 Naude, G. Naudaeana et Patiniana ou Singularitez. Amsterdam, 1703.

1704

40517.7.1 Aulnoy, Marie C.J. de B. Histoire de Jean de Bourbon, prince de Carency. La Haye, 1704.
Htn 38557.49.25* Bossuet, J.B. Explication de la prophétie d'Isaie sur l'enfantement de la Sainte Vierge. Paris, 1704.
Htn 38557.5.15* Delarue, Charles. Oraison funèbre de Jacques-Benigne Bossuet. Paris, 1704.
Htn 38554.656* Fénelon, F. de S. de la Mothe. Ordonnance et instruction pastorale de Monseigneur l'Archévêque. Valenciennes, 1704. 2 pam.
39534.19.5 Furetière, Antoine. Roman bourgeois, ouvrage comique. Amsterdam, 1704.
Mol 249.3.5 Molière, Jean Baptiste Poquelin. M. de Pourceaugnac or Squire Trelooby...Ozell. London, 1704.
Mol 249.3 Molière, Jean Baptiste Poquelin. M. de Pourceaugnac or Squire Trelooby...Ozell. Paris, 1704.

1705

Htn 39535.12* Callières, François de. Characters and criticisms upon the ancient orators. London, 1705.
38553.16.45 Fenelon, F. de S. de la Mothe. Avantures de Télémaque. La Haye, 1705-17. 2v.
Htn Mol 707.1* Grimarest, J.L. La vie de Monsieur de Molière. Paris, 1705.
38576.34.20 Montfleury, Antoine Jacob. Les oeuvres de Monsieur Montfleury. Paris, 1705.
Htn 38576.34.14* Montfleury, Antoine Jacob. Trasibule. Paris, 1705.
38588.16.10 Quinault, Philippe. La mère coquette, ou Les amans brouillez. Paris, 1705.
Htn 38542.2.19* Voiture, Vincent. Works. London, 1705.

1706

40517.86.10 Bédacier, C.D. Les avantures galantes du Chevalier de Tre. Lion, 1706.
38557.52.4.15 Bossuet, J.B. Exposition de la doctrine de l'église catholique sur les matières de controverse. 12. éd. Paris, 1706.
Htn 38553.16.50* Fénelon, F. de S. de la Mothe. Les avantures de Télémaque. Bruxelles, 1706. 3v.
40529.81 Graaft, de. Avantures secrettes et plaisantes. Brusselles, 1706.
Htn 38543.16* La Rochefoucauld, François. Moral maxims and reflections. 2. ed. London, 1706.
38545.33 L'Heritier de Villandon, Marie J. La tour ténébreuse et les jours lumineux. Amsterdam, 1706.
37555.7 Mervesin, Joseph. Histoire de la poésie française. Paris, 1706.
39534.28.2 Scarron, Paul. Le romant comique. Paris, 1706.

1707

40525.40 Les amours d'Eumène et de Flora. Cologne, 1707.
38562.36 Bouhours, D. Pensées ingénieuses des anciens et des modernes. Paris, 1707.
39534.24.15 Deshoulières, A. du L. del G. (Mme.). Poésies. v.2. Brusselles, 1707.
Htn 38554.350.223* Fénelon, F. de S. de la Mothe. Instructions for the education of a daughter. London, 1707.
Htn 38562.17.25* Fontenelle, B. Le B. de. Poésies pastorales. London, 1707.
Mol 269.3.5 Molière, Jean Baptiste Poquelin. Tartuffe. Medbourne. London, 1707.
X Cg 37577.38 Recueil de bons mots des anciens et des modernes. Paris, 1707.
Htn 39533.20.20* Russen, David. Iter lunare; or A voyage to the moon. London, 1707.

1708

Htn 38566.30* Boileau Despréaux, Nicolas. The Lutrin. London, 1708.
39534.52 Bruslé de Montpleinchamp, Jean. Le diable bossu. Nancy, 1708.
40512.3.18 LeSage, Alain René. Le diable boiteux. London, 1708.
FL 383.73 Memorial dramatique, ou Almanach théâtre pour 1808. Paris, 1708[1808]
38547.37 Pluton maltotier. Cologne, 1708.
38588.16.11 Quinault, Philippe. Les coups de l'amour et de la fortune. Paris, 1708.
38539.32 Rosset, François de. Les histoires tragiques de nos temps. 2. éd. Lyon, 1708.
37578.26 Vasconiana, ou Recueil des bons mots. Cologne, 1708.

1709

37542.2 Ancillon, Charles. Memoires concernant les vies de plusieurs modernes célèbres. Amsterdam, 1709.
Htn 38557.54.40* Bossuet, J.B. Politique tirée des propres paroles de l'Écriture Sainte. Paris, 1709.
39533.19.12 Cyrano de Bergerac. Oeuvres. Amsterdam, 1709. 2v.
Htn 38564.34.5* La Bruyère, J. de. Characters, or The manners of the age. 5. ed. London, 1709.
Mol 860.1 Le Noble, E. Molière le critique. Hollande, 1709.
39535.67.5 Lettres choisies de messieurs de l'Academie française. Paris, 1709.
Htn 37578.27* Nouveaux contes à rire. Cologne, 1709.
X Cg 40525.37 Les partisans demasquez. Cologne, 1709.
38563.34 Rapin, P. Les oeuvres. Amsterdam, 1709-10. 3v.
Htn 38528.9.5* Satyre Ménippée. Brussels, 1709. 3v.
39534.28.3 Scarron, Paul. Les oeuvres de M. Scarron. v.1-2. Paris, 1709.

1710

39535.58 L'Art plumer la poule sans crier. Cologne, 1710.
38576.1 Barbier, Marie Anne. La mort de Cesar. Paris, 1710.
40517.19 Bossigny, Louise de. Les chevaliers errans et le genie familier. Amsterdam, 1710.
Htn 38557.49.35* Bossuet, J.B. Justification des réfléxions sur le Nouveau Testament. Lille, 1710.
38576.25.15 Le Noble, E. Les aventures provinciales. La Haye, 1710.
Htn Mol 17.10* Molière, Jean Baptiste Poquelin. Oeuvres. Paris, 1710. 8v.
38536.1.6 Rabelais, F. Les lettres...écrites pendant son voyage d'Italie. Bruxelles, 1710.
Htn 38546.70* Tyssot de Patot, Simon. Voyages et avantures de Jacques Massé. Bordeaux, 1710.
37578.26.5 Vasconiana, ou Recueil des bons mots. Paris, 1710.

1711

38576.12.42.35 Corneille, Thomas. La forza dell'ambizione. Bologna, 1711.
40517.20 Drouet de Maupertuis. Les aventures d'Euphormion. Anvers, 1711. 3v.
Htn 38554.515* Fénelon, F. de S. de la Mothe. Lettres de Monseigneur l'Archécêque de Cambrai. n.p., 1711.
40524.41 Garouville, de. L'amant oisif. v.1-3. Bruxelles, 1711.
38576.23.5 La Fosse d'Aubigny, A. de. Manlius Capitolinus. Amsterdam, 1711.
38543.1.15 Le passe temps agréable, ou Nouveaux choix de Bons-Mots. 2. éd. Rotterdam, 1711.
40524.20 Rustaing de Saint-Jory, Louis. Avantures secretes arrivées au siege de Constantinople. Paris, 1711.

1712

40529.17 Bordelon, L. Les coudées franches. Paris, 1712. 2 pam.
38576.21.50 Desjardins, Marie C.H. Les amours des grands hommes. v.1-2. Amsterdam, 1712.
Htn 38554.324.250* Fénelon, F. de S. de la Mothe. Dialogues des morts. Paris, 1712.
39534.19.7 Furetière, Antoine. Roman bourgeois. Nancy, 1712.
38543.6.25 La Rochefoucauld, François. Réfléxions ou Sentences et maximes morales. Amsterdam, 1712.
38576.39 Palaprat, Jean. Oeuvres. Paris, 1712. 2v.
Htn 38585.19.10* Racine, Jean. The distrest mother. London, 1712.
Htn 39532.2.10* Rousseau, J.B. Anti-Rousseau. Rotterdam, 1712.
39532.2.9 Rousseau, J.B. Les oeuvres. Rotterdam, 1712. 2v.
39532.3.5 Rousseau, J.B. Oeuvres diverses. Soleure, 1712.
39534.30.7 Scarron, Paul. Virgile travesty. Amsterdam, 1712. 2v.
Htn 38566.70* The works of Monsieur Boileau. London, 1712. 2v.

1713

39533.13 Blainville, J. de. Oeuvres diverses. Paris, 1713.
38565.2 Boileau Despréaux, Nicolas. Oeuvres. Paris, 1713.
38554.322.102 Fénelon, F. de. S. de la Mothe. Demonstration...existence...God. London, 1713.
38554.320.5 Fénelon, F. de S. de la Mothe. Démonstration de l'existence de Dieu. Amsterdam, 1713.
Htn 38554.320* Fénelon, F. de S. de la Mothe. Démonstration de l'existence de Dieu. Paris, 1713.
Htn 38554.520.5* Fénelon, F. de S. de la Mothe. Lettres sur divers sujets concernant la religion et la métaphysique. Paris, 1713.
Htn 38554.735* Fénelon, F. de S. de la Mothe. Recueil des mandements a l'occasion des jubilés. Paris, 1713.
38558.15 Fléchier, Esprit. Dess Hochwürdigsten in Gott Herzens Spiritus Fleschier. Constanz, 1713.
Htn 39532.5* Hamilton, Anthony. Memoires de la vie du comte de Grammont. Cologne, 1713.
Htn 39532.28* Ménage, Gilles. Menagiana ou Bon mots. 3. éd. Amsterdam, 1713. 4v.
Htn Mol 17.13* Molière, Jean Baptiste Poquelin. Ses oeuvres. Amsterdam, 1713. 4v.
39534.26.15 Scarron, Paul. Les dernières oeuvres. Amsterdam, 1713.

1714

38563.8 Bayle, Pierre. Lettres choises. Rotterdam, 1714. 3v.
38566.31 Boileau Despréaux, Nicolas. The Lutrin. London, 1714.
39534.4.9 Bussy-Rabutin. Lettres, avec les réponses. Paris, 1714. 5v.
Htn 40516.23* Deslandes, A.F.B. Réflexions sur les grands hommes. Rochefort, 1714.
Htn 38554.462.2* Fénelon, F. de S. de la Mothe. Instruction pastorale de Monseigneur l'Archévêque Duc de Cambrai. Cambrai, 1714.
Htn 38554.462* Fénelon, F. de S. de la Mothe. Mandement et instruction pastorale de Monseigneur l'Archévêque Duc de Cambrai. Cambrai, 1714.
39532.12 Hamilton, Anthony. Memoires of the life of Count de Grammont. London, 1714.
Htn Mol 60.1* Molière, Jean Baptiste Poquelin. Works. London, 1714. 6v.
38582.2.9 Racine, Jean. Oeuvres. Amsterdam, 1714. 2v.
38585.24 Racine, Jean. Two tragedies. London, 1714.
37572.1 Recueil en prose. La Haye, 1714. 2v.
39585.6 St. Hyacinthe, H.C. Le chef d'oeuvre d'un inconnu. La Haye, 1714.

1715

38567.50 Des Maizeaux, Pierre. La vie de monsieur Boileau Despréaux. Amsterdam, 1715.
Htn 38554.1* Fénelon, F. de S. de la Mothe. Adventures of Telemachus. v.1-2. London, 1715.
38554.462.10 Fénelon, F. de S. de la Mothe. Instruction pastorale de Monseigneur l'Archévêque Duc de Cambrai. Cambrai, 1715.
38558.16 Fléchier, Esprit. Lettres choisies, avec une relation des fanatiques du vivarez et des réfléxions sur les différens caractères des hommes. Paris, 1715. 2v.
39532.38 Gacon, François. Homere vengé. Paris, 1715.
40529.20 Gayot, F. Heures perdues du chevalier de Rior. Paris, 1715.
38544.3.25 La Calprenède, G. de. La Cléopatra. Venetia, 1715.
38543.27 Le Pays, René. Les nouvelles oeuvres. Amsterdam, 1715.
39532.28.5 Ménage, Gilles. Menagiana ou Les bons mots. Paris, 1715. 4v.

1715 - cont.

	38539.16.5	Montluc, A. de. La comédie des proverbes; pièce comique. 5. éd. Troyes, 1715.
	38526.42.5	Montluc, A. de. La comédie des proverbes. Paris, 1715.
	38543.1	Rochefort, J. de. Le passe temps agréable. Rotterdam, 1715.

1716

Htn	38565.3*	Brossette, C. Oeuvres de...Nicolas Boileau. Geneva, 1716. 2v.
	38563.22.55	La Monnoye, Bernard de. Histoire de Mr. Bayle et de ses ouvrages. Amsterdam, 1716.
Htn	38543.30*	La Mothe le Vayer, F. de. Cincq dialogues. Frankfort, 1716. 2v.
	Mol 202.30.3	Molière, Jean Baptiste Poquelin. Het school van de mannen. 's-Gravenhage, 1716?
	39532.2.11	Rousseau, J.B. Anti-Rousseau Histoire satyrique de la vie...de Rousseau. Paris, 1716.

1717

	40524.42	Lecoq-Madeleine. La fidelité couronnée. Bruxelles, 1717.
	40525.17.10	Moncrif, François A.P. de. Les aventures de Zeloïde et d'Amangarifdine. Paris, 1717.
	39534.28.5	Scarron, Paul. Le romant comique. Amsterdam, 1717.
	37585.10.9	Le théâtre italien de Gherardi. Receuil toutes les comédies et scènes françaises. Paris, 1717. 6v.
	39534.12.5	Vairasse, Denis. A. Roberts Historie der Neu-gefundenen Völcker Severambes. Nürnberg, 1717.

1718

Htn	38565.3.10*	Boileau Despréaux, Nicolas. Oeuvres de Nicolas Boileau. Amsterdam, 1718. 2v.
	38576.4.6	Boursault, Edme. Les apparences trompeuses, ou Ne pas croire ce qu'ou void. Amsterdam, 1718.
Htn	38554.325*	Fénelon, F. de S. de la Mothe. Dialogues des morts anciens et modernes. Paris, 1718. 2v.
Htn	38554.326*	Fénelon, F. de S. de la Mothe. Dialogues sur l'éloquence en général. Paris, 1718.
Htn	38554.520*	Fénelon, F. de S. de la Mothe. Lettres sur divers sujets concernant la religion et la métaphysique. Paris, 1718.
Htn	38554.322*	Fénelon, F. de S. de la Mothe. Oeuvres philosophiques; démonstration de l'existence de Dieu. Paris, 1718.
Htn	38552.12*	Fénelon, F. de S. de la Mothe. Oeuvres spirituelles. Anvers, 1718. 2v.
	38552.9	Fénelon, F. de S. de la Mothe. Sermons choisis. Paris, 1718.
	Mol 707.2	Grimarest, J.L. Les oeuvres de Monsieur de Molière. Paris, 1718.
Htn	Mol 17.18*	Molière, Jean Baptiste Poquelin. Oeuvres. Paris, 1718. 8v.
	38543.1.10	Le passe temps agréable. v. 1-2. Rotterdam, 1718.
	39533.33.15	Patin, Guy. Nouvelle lettres de feu Mr. Gui Patin. v.2. Amsterdam, 1718.

1719

Htn	40517.7.4*	Aulnoy, Marie C.J. de B. The prince of Carency, a novel. London, 1719.
	38544.27.25	La Fayette, Marie M. La Princesse de Clèves. Paris, 1719. 3 pam.
	40535.34.5	La Motte, Antoine Houdar de. Fables nouvelles. Paris, 1719.
	40535.34.7	La Motte, Antoine Houdar de. Fables nouvelles. 3. éd. Paris, 1719.
	40535.34.50	La Motte, Antoine Houdar de. Odes. 5. éd. Amsterdam, 1719. 3v.
	38526.47.75	Saint-Gelais, Mellin de. Oeuvres poétiques de Mellin S.Gelais. Paris, 1719.

1720

	38554.322.105	Fénelon, F. de S. de la Mothe. A demonstration of the existence and attributes of God. London, 1720.

1721

	38562.34	Bouhours, D. Pensées ingénieuses des anciens et des modernes. La Haye, 1721.
	37585.10.12	Gherardi, Evaristo. Le théâtre italien de Gherardi. v.2,4. Amsterdam, 1721. 2v.
Htn	40535.34.15*	La Motte, Antoine Houdar de. One hundred new court fables. London, 1721.
Htn	39594.9.77*	Montesquieu, C.L. de S. Lettres persanes. Amsterdam, 1721.
Htn	39594.9.75*	Montesquieu, C.L. de S. Lettres persanes. v.1-2. Amsterdam, 1721.
	40529.25	Rémond de Saint Mard, J. Lettres galantes et philosophiques. Cologne, 1721.

1722

	38566.10	Boileau Despréaux, Nicolas. Oeuvres de Nicolas Boileau Despréaux. La Haye, 1722. 4v.
Htn	38557.57.6*	Bossuet, J.B. Introduction à la philosophie. Paris, 1722.
	38557.57.5	Bossuet, J.B. Introduction à la philosophie. Paris, 1722.
	38557.57	Bossuet, J.B. Introduction à la philosophie. Paris, 1722.
	40525.31	Cleandre et Caliste ou L'amour veritable. Amsterdam, 1722.
	38576.12.42.2	Corneille, Thomas. Poèmes dramatiques. Paris, 1722. 5v.
Htn	39576.18*	Desnoiresterres, F.H. Sacre bouquet de differentes fleurs d'Hyacinte. Caen, 1722.
	38554.326.10	Fénelon, F. de S. de la Mothe. Dialogues concerning eloquence in general. London, 1722.
Htn	38545.29*	Huet, M.P.D. Heutiana, ou Pensées diverses. Paris, 1722.
	40535.22	Legrand, Marc Antoine. Cartouche, or The robbers. London, 1722.
Htn	37595.1*	Nouveau recueil...lettres d'Abailard et d'Héloise. Anvers, 1722.
Htn	38585.20.15*	Racine, Jean. Athaliah. London, 1722.
Htn	38524.42*	Le seiour des muses ou La cresme des Bons Vers. Lyon, 1722.

1723

	40529.18	Bordelon, L. Les solitaires en belle humeur. Paris, 1723. 2v.
	38574.2	Corneille, Pierre. Le théâtre. Paris, 1723. 5v.
	38574.2.3	Corneille, Pierre. Le théâtre de Pierre Corneille. 9. éd. Amsterdam, 1723. 5v.
	Mol 880.13	Cramero, M. Del Molière redivivo. Norimberga, 1723.
Htn	38526.10.17.65*	Cretin, Guillaume D. Les poésies. Paris, 1723.
Htn	38528.25*	Despériers, Bonaventure. Cymbalum mundi. London, 1723.
	38553.37	Fénelon, F. de S. de la Mothe. Les aventures de Télémaque. Paris, 1723.
Htn	38564.33*	La Bruyère, J. de. The works. London, 1723. 2v.
	38526.42.12F	Pasquier, Etienne. Les oeuvres. Amsterdam, 1723. 2v.
	38585.19.11	Racine, Jean. Andromache eller ett oint Moders-Hierta. Stockholm, 1723.
	38551.104.20	Ramsay, A.M. de. The life of François de Salignac de la Motte Fénelon. London, 1723.
	38546.19.5	Scudéry, Madeleine de. Ibrahim; ou L'illustre Bassa. Paris, 1723. 4v.
NEDL	39533.15	Segrais, Jean R. Oeuvres diverses. Amsterdam, 1723.
	39533.15.2	Segrais, Jean R. Oeuvres diverses. v.1-2. Amsterdam, 1723.
Htn	39545.38.5*	Voltaire, François Marie Arouet de. La ligne, ou Henry le Grande. Genève, 1723.

1724

	40517.7.5	Aulnoy, Marie C.J. de B. The history of John of Bourbon, Prince of Carency. 2. ed. London, 1724.
Htn	39585.24*	Charpentier, F. Carpentariana ou Remarques d'histoire. Paris, 1724.
	38576.27	Le Noble, E. Le gage touché. Histoires galantes et comiques. Amsterdam, 1724.
	Mon 17.24F	Montaigne, Michel de. Essais. Coste. London, 1724. 3v.
	37555.300.10	Mourgues, M. Traité de la poésie française. Paris, 1724.
	38547.46	La princesse de Portien. Paris, 1724.

1725

	37575.784	Académie française, Paris. Recueil de plusieurs pièces d'éloquence et de poésie presentées à l'académie française. Paris, 1725.
	37565.22.5	Argonne, Bonaventure d'. Melanges d'histoire et de littérature. 4th ed. Paris, 1725. 3v.
	39534.4.20	Bussy-Rabutin. The amorous history of the Gauls. London, 1725.
	40517.4	Challes, Robert. Les illustres françoises. Paris, 1725. 4v.
	Mol 863.4	Chateau-Lyon, A. de. Éloge de Molière. Londres, 1725.
	38544.16	Mailly. Les disgrâces des Amans. La Haye, 1725.
Htn	Mol 17.25*	Molière, Jean Baptiste Poquelin. Oeuvres. Amsterdam, 1725. 4v.
	Mon 17.25F	Montaigne, Michel de. Essais. Coste. Paris, 1725. 3v.
Htn	38576.55*	Les privileges du Cocuage. Vicon, 1725.
	39533.15.10	Segrais, Jean R. Five novels. London, 1725.

1726

	38542.13.5	Brémond, Sébastien. L'heureux esclave. Paris, 1726.
	39535.25	Du Cerceau, Jean Antoine. Recueil de poésies diverses. 3e éd. Paris, 1726.
Htn	38554.107*	Fénelon, F. de S. de la Mothe. Abrégé des vies des anciens philosophes. Paris, 1726.
	40526.28.20	Grandval, Nicolas Racot de. Le vice puni, ou Cartouche. Paris, 1726.
	37572.44	Recueil de pièces du regiment de la Calotte. Paris, 1726.
	Mol 863.1	Van Effen, J. Le misanthrope. La Haye, 1726. 2v.

1727

	38561.4F	Bayle, Pierre. Oeuvres. La Haye, 1727-31. 4v.
	38561.6F	Bayle, Pierre. Oeuvres. La Haye, 1727-37. 4v.
	38551.30F	Bayle, Pierre. Oeuvres diverses. La Haye, 1727-31. 4v.
	38557.46.45	Bossuet, J.B. Conference avec M. Claude. 3e éd. Paris, 1727.
	38557.41.77	Bossuet, J.B. Défense de l'histoire des variations contre la réponse de M. Basnage. Paris, 1727.
Htn	38557.50.75*	Bossuet, J.B. Élévations à Dieu sur tous les mystères. 1. éd. Paris, 1727. 2v.
Htn	38557.51*	Bossuet, J.B. Élévations à Dieu sur tous les mystères de la religion chrétienne. Paris, 1727. 2v.
	38557.64	Bossuet, J.B. Traité de la communion sous les deux espèces. Paris, 1727.
	40516.15.7	Coquelet, L. Eloge de la goute. Paris, 1727.
	39586.21.9	Duchannavie neologique. 2. éd. n.p., 1727.
	40538.15	La femme jalouse; comedie. Paris? 1727?
	37572.2	Kerr, Guillaume. Recueil tire des auteurs français tant en prose qu'en vers. Edinburgh, 1727.
	Mon 17.27	Montaigne, Michel de. Essais. Coste. La Haye, 1727. 5v.
Htn	39534.28.6*	Scarron, Paul. Le roman comique. pt.1-3. Roterdam, 1727-30. 2v.
Htn	39545.37.23*	Voltaire, François Marie Arouet de. An essay upon the civil wars of France. London, 1727.

1728

	38557.53.232	Bossuet, J.B. Maximes et réfléxions sur la comédie. Paris, 1728. 3 pam.
	38544.12	Caillière, Jacques de. Courtisan prédestiné. Paris, 1728.
	40524.15.5	Fontaines, M.L.C. Histoire d'Amenophis. Paris, 1728.
Htn	38561.15*	Oeuvres de Fontenelle. La Haye, 1728-29. 3v.
	40516.36	Ramsay, A.M. de. Voyages de Cyrus. Amsterdam, 1728.
	38542.17.12	Saint-Evremond, C. de M. de S.D. Works. London, 1728. 2v.

1729

Htn	40517.65*	Les amours de Sainfroid Jesuite et d'Eulalie. La Haye, 1729.
	38527.18	Aubigné, Théodore Agrippa d'. Avantures du Baron de Foeneste. Cologne, 1729. 2v.
	38563.9	Bayle, Pierre. Lettres. Amsterdam, 1729. 3v.
Htn	40515.18.20*	Bignon, Jean P. The adventures of Abdalla. London, 1729.

Chronological Listing

1729 - cont.

38557.56.65 Bossuet, J.B. Instruction pastorale sur les promesses de Jésus-Christ à son église. Paris, 1729. 2 pam.
40535.15.19 Fuzelier, Louis. Momus turned fabulist. London, 1729.
39525.4 La Fontaine, Jean de. Oeuvres diverses. Paris, 1729. 3v.
39532.28.10 Ménage, Gilles. Menagiana ou Les bons mots. Paris, 1729. 4v.
37558.30.75 Pellison-Fontanier, Paul. Histoire de l'Academie française depuis son établissement jusqu'à 1652. Paris, 1729.

1730

Htn 39576.26* Bernard, J.F. Dialogue critiques et philosophiques. Amsterdam, 1730.
Htn 38557.48* Bossuet, J.B. Defensio declarationis celeberrimae. Chevalier, 1730. 2v.
Htn 38557.48.2* Bossuet, J.B. Defensio declarationis celeberrimae. v.1-2. Chevalier, 1730.
39535.11 Callières, François de. Recueil des bons contes et de bons mots. Utrecht, 1730.
37576.14 Continuation des memoires de littérature et d'histoire. Paris, 1730-31. 11v.
40516.15.5 Coquelet, L. L'eloge de quelque chose dédié à quelqu'un. Paris, 1730. 2 pam.
40516.15 Coquelet, L. Le triumphe de la charlatanerie dédié au Grand T***.Paris, 1730.
Htn 40515.6* Desfontaines, P.F.G. Le nouveau Gulliver. Paris, 1730.
38562.18.20 Fontenelle, B. Le B. de. Dialogues of the dead. London, 1730.
40517.27.25 Gomez, M.A.P. de. Persian anecdotes. London, 1730.
40535.22.19 Le Maingre de Bonciqualt, Louis. Les Amazones revoltées. Rotterdam, 1730.
Mol 162.45.5 Molière, Jean Baptiste Poquelin. Jupiter en Amphitryon, of de twee gelyke Sosias. Amsterdam, 1730.
Mol 202.30.5 Molière, Jean Baptiste Poquelin. De listige vryster, of De verschalkte voogd. Amsterdam, 1730.
Htn Mol 17.30* Molière, Jean Baptiste Poquelin. Oeuvres. Paris, 1730. 8v.
Mol 262.50.5 Molière, Jean Baptiste Poquelin. De verwarde Jalouzy. Amsteldam, 1730.
40516.38.1 Ramsay, A.M. de. Travels of Cyrus. 4th ed. London, 1730.
38545.20.3A Saint Réal, César V. de. Oeuvres. Paris, 1730. 5v.
Htn 39534.26.20* Scarron, Paul. Les dernières oeuvres. v.1-2. La Haye, 1730.
38568.790 Simon, R. Lettres choisies. Amsterdam, 1730. 4v.

1731

38527.19 Aubigné, Théodore Agrippa d'. Avantures du Baron de Foeneste. Amsterdam, 1731. 2v.
Htn 38557.53.250* Bossuet, J.B. Méditations sur l'évangile. Paris, 1731. 4v.
38557.60 Bossuet, J.B. Traitez du libre-arbitre et de la concupiscence. Paris, 1731.
Htn 38526.3.6* Bougeant, G.H. La critique de la femme docteur. London, 1731.
Htn 38526.3.6.10* Bougeant, G.H. La femme docteur ou la theologie tombée en quenouille. Liege, 1731.
38563.12 Des Maizeaux, Pierre. Das Leben des Weltberühmten Peter Bayle. Hamburg, 1731.
39534.15 Drelincourt, Laurent. Sonnets chrétiens. Amsterdam, 1731.
40535.22.2 Legrand, Marc Antoine. Théâtre. Paris, 1731. 4v.
38523.6.12 Marot, Clément. Oeuvres. La Haye, 1731. 6v.
38523.10.15 Marot, Clément. Oeuvres. La Haye, 1731. 4v.
Htn 38514.70* Martial d'Auvergne. Les arrêts d'amour. Amsterdam, 1731.
Mol 310.5 Mazières, S.P. La vie de P. Mignard: Avec la poème de Molière sur les peintures du Val-de-Grace. Amsterdam, 1731.
37585.11.12 Les parodies du nouveau théâtre italien. Paris, 1731. 3v.
39535.22 Roger Bontems, en belle humeur. 4th éd. Cologne, 1731.

1732

40537.71 Academie galante contenant diverses histoires très curieuses. Amsterdam, 1732.
Htn 38526.3.6.3* Bougeant, G.H. Le saint Deniche ou La bauqueroute. La Haye, 1732.
Htn 38526.3.6.8* Bougeant, G.H. Suite de la femme docteur. La Haye, 1732.
Mol 750.1 Desjardins, Marie Catherine Hortense. Les aventures ou mémoires de la vie d'Henriette-Sylvie de Molière. Amsterdam, 1732.
40516.24 Deslandes, A.F.B. Réflexions sur les grands hommes. Amsterdam, 1732.
38528.25.3 Despériers, Bonaventure. Cymbalum mundi. Amsterdam, 1732.
Mol 698.3F Jean-Baptiste Pocquelin de Molière. n.p., 1732.
38544.27.250 La Fayette, Marie M. La Princesse de Monpensier. Paris, 1732.
40516.76 La Vieuville d'Orville, A. Les avantures du Prince Jakaya. Paris, 1732. 2v.
Htn Mol 17.32* Molière, Jean Baptiste Poquelin. Oeuvres. v.1-8. Rotterdam, 1732. 4v.
Mol 60.2 Molière, Jean Baptiste Poquelin. Select comedies. London, 1732. 8v.
40517.58 Pernetti, J. Le repos de Cyrus. Paris, 1732.
Htn 40525.3* Terrasson, Jean. The life of Sathos. London, 1732. 2v.
37551.58 Titon du Tillet, E. Le Parnasse François. Paris, 1732. 2v.

1733

38554.7 Les adieux du Duc de Bourgogne et de l'Abbé de Fénelon. Stockholm, 1733.
40531.2.9 Allainval, L.J.C. de. L'Embarras des richesses. London, 1733.
40517.7 Aulnoy, Marie C.J. de B. Histoire d'Hypolite comte de Duglas. v.1-2. Paris, 1733.
Htn 38557.56.50* Bossuet, J.B. Instruction pastorale au sujet des calomnies avancées dans le Journal de Trévoux. Paris, 1733.
40534.32.5 Crébillon, Claude Prosper Jolyot de. L'ecumoire. Bruxelles, 1733-1884.
40535.2.20 Delaunay. Le paresseux, comédie en vers. Paris, 1733.
40535.3.30 Deschamps, F.M.C. La religion defendue. Rotterdam, 1733.

1733 - cont.

38553.33 Fénelon, F. de S. de la Mothe. Aventuras de Telemaco. Paris, 1733. 2v.
40517.26 Gomez, M.A.P. de. Les cent nouvelles nouvelles. La Haye, 1733. 20v.
40517.35.50 Gueulette, T.S. Les Sultanes de Guzarate, ou Les songes des hommes eveillés. Paris, 1733. 3v.
37531.2 Histoire litteraire de la France. v.1-38. Paris, 1733-1950. 41v.
38526.34.5 Marguerite d'Angoulême. Contes et nouvelles de Marguerite de Valois. La Haye, 1733. 2v.
Htn FL 355.5* Maupoint. Bibliothèque des théâtres. Paris, 1733.
37585.11.8 Le nouveau théâtre italien. Paris, 1733. 8v.
40536.20.4 Piron, Alexis. Gustave. Paris, 1733.
38525.22.82 Régnier, Mathurin. Satyres et autres oeuvres de Régnier. Londres, 1733.
37576.310 Saunier de Beaumont. Lettres philosophiques. Paris, 1733.
38547.6 Urfé, Honoré d'. L'Astrée. Pastorale allégorique. Paris, 1733. 10v.

1734

37556.12 Camusat, D.F. Histoire critique des journaux. Amsterdam, 1734.
40517.32 Gueulette, T.S. Les milles et une heure; contes peruviens. v.1-2. Paris, 1734.
40517.32.9 Gueulette, T.S. Peruvian tales. Dublin, 1734. 2v.
Htn Mol 7.34* Molière, Jean Baptiste Poquelin. Oeuvres. Paris, 1734. 6v.
37555.11 Rémond de St. Mard, Toussaint. Réfléxions sur la poésie. Photoreproduction. La Haye, 1734.

1735

V37551.2 Beauchamps, M. de. Recherches sur les théâtres de France. Paris, 1735.
FL 357.35 Beauchamps, P.F. Recherches sur les théâtres de France. Paris, 1735. 3v.
38576.11.4 Brueys, D.A. de. Les oeuvres de théâtre. Paris, 1735. 3v.
Htn 40534.32* Crébillon, Claude Prosper Jolyot de. Lecumoire. Histoire japonoise. v.1-2. London, 1735.
40534.34.15 Crébillon, Claude Prosper Jolyot de. Letters from Marchioness de M***. London, 1735.
38528.6.12 Estienne, Henri. Apologie pour Hérodote. La Haye, 1735. 3v.
38553.16.75 Fénelon, F. de S. de la Mothe. Les aventures de Télémaque. Paris, 1735.
39535.3 La grande confrairie des saouls d'ouvrer. Rouen, 1735. 4 pam.
40516.85 La Barre de Beaumarchais, A. de. La retraite de la marquise de Gozanne. Amsterdam, 1735.
40535.19.80 La Chaussée, Pierre Claude Nivelle de. La fausse antipathie. Paris, 1735.
37597.9 Lorris, Guillaume de. Le roman de la rose. Amsterdam, 1735. 3v.
40535.25.20 Marivaux, Pierre Carlet de Chamblain de. Le paysan parvenu. London, 1735.
Htn Mol 17.35* Molière, Jean Baptiste Poquelin. Oeuvres. Amsterdam, 1735. 4v.
Htn Mol 17.34* Molière, Jean Baptiste Poquelin. Oeuvres. Amsterdam, 1735. 4v.
37572.44.2 Regiment de la Calotte. Memoires...à l'histoire de la Calotte. pt.1-4. Amsterdam, 1735. 3v.
40524.1.15 Tencin, Claudine A.G. de. Mémoires du Comte de Comminge. La Haye, 1735.
40516.64 Voyage merveilleux du prince Fan Feredin dans la romancie. Paris, 1735.

1736

39576.6 Argens, Jean Baptiste de Boyer. Mémoires de madmoiselle de Mainville. La Haye, 1736.
Htn 38557.65* Bossuet, J.B. Traité de l'amour de Dieu. Paris, 1736.
40517.36 Gueulette, T.S. Mogul tales. London, 1736. 2v.
38576.19.1 Hauteroche, N. le B. de. Les oeuvres de théâtre. Paris, 1736. 2v.
Htn 38543.7* La Rochefoucauld, François. Réfléxions, sentences et maximes morales. Paris, 1736.
40535.29.30 Marivaux, Pierre Carlet de Chamblain de. The life of Marianne. London, 1736.
39532.29.5 Ménage, Gilles. Mescolanza d'Egidio Menagio. Venezia, 1736.
Mol 618.3 Riccoboni, L. Observations sur la comédie de Molière. Paris, 1736.
Htn 39545.35.5* Voltaire, François Marie Arouet de. Alzire, ou Les Americains. Paris, 1736.
Htn 39544.27.18* Voltaire, François Marie Arouet de. Lettres ecrites de Londres sur les Anglois. Amsterdam, 1736.
Htn 39545.47* Voltaire, François Marie Arouet de. La mort de César. Paris, 1736.

1737

39576.9 Argens, Jean Baptiste de Boyer. Lettres cabalistiques. La Haye, 1737. 4v.
39576.12.5 Argens, Jean Baptiste de Boyer. Lettres morales et critiques sur les differens états. Amsterdam, 1737.
39576.5 Argens, Jean Baptiste de Boyer. Mémoirs du comte de Vaxère. Amsterdam, 1737.
38575.34.12 Corneille, Pierre. Pompejus. Amsterdam, 1737.
41540.50.32 Ferrière, Théophile de. Les romans et le mariage. v.2. v.1 lost 1965. Paris, 1737.
40535.72 Guyot de Merville, M. Les mascarades amoureuses. Amsterdam, 1737.
40516.66 Le Givre de Richebourg, Mme. Avantures de Don Ramire de Roxas et de Dona Leonor de Mendoce. pt.1-2. Paris, 1737.
Htn 40512.58* LeSage, Alain René. The bachelor of Salamanca. London, 1737-39. 2v.
40512.55 LeSage, Alain René. The comical history and humorous adventures of Estevanille Gonzalez. 2. ed. London, 1737.
Htn 37584.6* Le Sage, Alain René. Le théâtre de La Foire. Paris, 1737. 10v.
40517.2 Martorell, Joannot. Histoire du vaillant chevalier Tiran le Blanc. London, 1737. 2v.
38537.29.10 Rabelais, F. Works. v.1,3-5. London, 1737. 4v.

Chronological Listing

1738

	40525.28	L'amour magot. Les tisons. London, 1738.
	38561.9	Bayle, Pierre. Dictionnaire historique et critique. 5e éd. Basle, 1738. 4v.
	38576.7.10	Boursault, Edme. Lettres nouvelles. Paris, 1738. 3v.
	39534.5	Bussy-Rabutin. Lettres. Amsterdam, 1738.
	38576.12.42.3	Corneille, Thomas. Poèmes dramatiques. Paris, 1738. 5v.
	40535.74	Du Berry. Les rivaux indiscrets. La Haye, 1738.
	39585.35	Ducatiana ou Remarques de feu M.C. Duchat. Amsterdam, 1738. 2v.
Htn	40515.2.85*	Duperron de Castéra, L. Entretiens litteraires et galans. Amsterdam, 1738. 2v.
	38554.3.14	Fénelon, F. de S. de la Mothe. Die Begebenheiten des Printzen von Ithaca. v.1-3. Berlin, 1738-39.
	38554.19	Fénelon, F. de S. de la Mothe. Dissertation on pure love. 2. ed. London, 1738.
	40525.17	Moncrif, François A.P. de. Les ames rivales. Histoire fabulense. London, 1738.
	37585.11.10	Les parodies du nouveau théâtre italien. Paris, 1738. 4v.
	38537.30	Rabelais, F. Works. Dublin, 1738. 4v.
	39534.12	Vairasse, Denis. The history of the Sevarambians. London, 1738.

1739

	39576.7.15	Argens, Jean Baptiste de Boyer. The Jewish spy. London, 1739. 5v.
Htn	40534.16.7*	Cahusac, Louis de. Grigri. Pt.1-2. Paris? 1739.
	38544.20	Claude, I. Les amours de Madame d'Elbeuf. Amsterdam, 1739.
	38554.20	Fénelon, F. de. S. de la Mothe. A dissertation on pure love. Dublin, 1739.
	38554.322.20	Fénelon, F. de S. de la Mothe. Oeuvres philosophiques. Demonstration de l'existence de Dieu. Paris, 1739.
Htn	38564.18*	La Bruyère, J. de. Les caractères de Théophraste. Amsterdam, 1739. 2v.
	40512.2	LeSage, Alain René. Le diable boiteux. Amsterdam, 1739. 2v.
Htn	40535.28*	Marivaux, Pierre Carlet de Chamblain de. Le petit maître corrigé. Paris, 1739.
	37555.9	Massieu, Guillaume. Histoire de la poésie française. Paris, 1739.
Htn	Mol 17.39*	Molière, Jean Baptiste Poquelin. Oeuvres. Paris, 1739. 8v.
	Mol 60.3	Molière, Jean Baptiste Poquelin. Works. v.1,3-7,9,10. London, 1739. 8v.
Htn	Mon 17.39*	Montaigne, Michel de. Essais. Coste. 4. ed. London, 1739. 7v.
	Mon 17.39.2	Montaigne, Michel de. Essais. Coste. 4. ed. London, 1739. 6v.
	38576.33	Montfleury, Zacherie Jacob. Théâtre de Messieurs de Montfleury. Paris, 1739. 3v.
	38588.13	Quinault, Philippe. Le théâtre. Paris, 1739. 5v.
Htn	Mol 722.1*	Voltaire, François Marie Arouet. Vie de Molière avec des jugements. Paris, 1739.

1740

	40529.45	Amusmens de Beau-Sexe ou Nouvelles histoire et avantures. v.1-2. La Haye, 1740.
	40516.22.10	Annecdotes jesuitiques. La Haye, 1740. 3v.
	Mol 863.1.5	Baar, G.L. de. Epîtres diverses sur des sujets diverses. Londres, 1740.
	38561.10A	Bayle, Pierre. Dictionnaire historique et critique. Amsterdam, 1740. 4v.
	38557.41.22	Bossuet, J.B. Histoire des variations des églises protestantes. Paris, 1740. 4v.
	39585.19.25	Bruhier d'Ablaincourt, J. Caprices d'imagination. Paris, 1740.
	39534.24.20	Deshoulières, A. du L. del G. (Mme.). Poésies de Madame et Mlle. Deshoulières. Bruxelles, 1740.
	38558.6	Fléchier, Esprit. Recueil des oraisons funèbres. Paris, 1740.
	40517.27.15	Gomez, M.A.P. de. Anecdotes, ou histoire secrette de la maison ottomane. Amsterdam, 1740.
	40517.43	Lambert, C.F. Mémoires et avantures. Francfort, 1740. 3v.
	38558.35	La Ruë, Charles de. Oraisons funèbres. Paris, 1740.
	40529.5	Lettres infernales et les tisons. Paris? 1740.
	38558.20	Mascaron, Jules. Recueil des oraisons funèbres. Paris, 1740.
	39535.13.7	Matanasiana, ou Memoires litteraires, historiques, et critiques du...Matanasius. La Haye, 1740.
	38542.17	Saint-Evremond, C. de M. de S.D. Oeuvres. Paris, 1740. 10v.
	38545.20	Saint Réal, César V. de. Oeuvres de l'abbé Saint-Réal. Amsterdam, 1740. 3v.
	40524.2.10	Tencin, Claudine A.G. de. The siege of Calais. London, 1740.
Htn	39545.33.3*	Voltaire, François Marie Arouet de. Recueil de pièces. Fugitives en prose et en vers. Paris, 1740.

1741

	39576.12	Argens, Jean Baptiste de Boyer. Chinese letters. London, 1741.
NEDL	40517.7.2	Aulnoy, Marie C.J. de B. The history of Hypolitus, earl of Douglas. London, 1741.
	38563.6.5	Bayle, Pierre. Verschiedene Gedanken bey Gelegenheit des Cometen, der im Christmonate 1680 erschienen. Hamburg, 1741.
	40529.18.5	Bordelon, L. Les solitaires en belle humeur. Utrecht, 1741. 3v.
Htn	38557.48.15*	Bossuet, J.B. De la connaissance de Dieu et de soi-même. Paris, 1741.
	39585.20	Bruhier d'Ablaincourt, J. Caprices d'imagination. Amsterdam, 1741.
	39576.60	Brusnoy, Pierre. Recueil de divers ouvrages en prose et en vers. Paris, 1741. 3v.
	39585.24.2	Charpentier, F. Carpentariana. Paris, 1741.
	40535.15.7	Favart, Charles S. La chercheuse d'esprit. Paris, 1741.
	38553.18.2	Fénelon, F. de S. de la Mothe. Les aventures de Télémaque. Amsterdam, 1741.
	38554.3.15	Fénelon, F. de S. de la Mothe. Die seltsame Begebenheiten des Telemach. Frankfurt, 1741.

1741 - cont.

	37533.5	Goujet, Claude P. Bibliothèque française, ou Histoire de la littérature. Paris, 1741-56. 18v.
	40517.43.5	Lambert, C.F. Le nouveau Telemaque. La Haye, 1741. 3v.
	41554.35.105	Lambert de Saumery, P. The Devil turn'd hermit, or The adventures of Astaroth banish'd hell. London, 1741.
	39545.126	Le Brun. Remarques historiques, politiques, mythologiques et critiques, sur la Henriade de Mr. de Voltaire. La Haye, 1741. 3 pam.
Htn	38536.4*	Le Duchat. Oeuvres de Rabelais. Amsterdam, 1741. 3v.
Htn	40535.25.3*	Marivaux, Pierre Carlet de Chamblain de. Oeuvres choisies. Le jeu de l'amour. Paris, 1741-73. 3 pam.
	Mon 123.4F	Memoires pour servir aux essais. London, 1741.
	40522.5.20	Prévost, Antoine F. Mémoires pour servir à l'histoire de Malte. pt.1-2. Amsterdam, 1741.
Htn	38582.3*	Racine, Jean. Oeuvres. Paris, 1741. 2v.
	40516.67	St. Quenain, de. Le Hollandois raisonnable; ou Sort digne d'envie. Amsterdam, 1741. 3v.

1742

Htn	38576.12.25*	Champmesle, C.C. Les oeuvres. Paris, 1742. 2v.
	39533.9.3	Chapelle, C.E.L. Voyage de Messieures Chapelle et Bachaumont. La Haye, 1742.
	39576.45	Le cocq ou Mémoires de chevalier de V. Amsterdam, 1742.
Htn	40517.23.10*	Duclos, C.P. Les confessions du Comte de ***. 4. ed. Amsterdam, 1742.
	40535.14.25	Fagan, C.B. La pupile. Paris, 1742.
	40517.2.5	Godard d'Aucour, C. Lettres du Chevalier Danteuil et de mademoiselle de Thelis. n.p., 1742.
	40535.19.77	La Chaussée, Pierre Claude Nivelle de. Diana en Endimion. Amsterdam, 1742.
	37596.42	Levisque, Pierre. Poésies du...Thibaut IV. Paris, 1742. 2v.
Htn	40522.5.5*	Prévost, Antoine F. The Dean of Coleraine. A moral history. London, 1742. 3v.
	40526.42.25	Racine, Louis. La religion, poëme. Paris, 1742.
	39585.45	St. Martin de Chassonville. Les delassemens d'un galant-homme. Amsterdam, 1742.

1743

	40534.24	Crébillon, Prosper Jolyot de. Oeuvres. Paris, 1743. 2v.
	FL 398.13.15	Gaillard de la Bataille, Pierre A. Histoire de Mademoiselle Cronel, dite Fretillon. La Haye, 1743-52.
	40535.19.85	La Chaussée, Pierre Claude Nivelle de. De tover - buryloft, of het huwelyk door tovery. Amsterdam, 1743.
	40536.3	Le Blanc, J.B. Aben-said, empereur des Mogols. 2. éd. Paris, 1743.
	Mon 31.6	Montaigne, Michel de. Essays. Cotton. 6. ed. London, 1743. 3v.
	37583.343	Nouveau recueil choisi et mélé des meilleures pièces du théâtre français et italien. Utrecht, 1743-50. 12v.
	40525.35	Promenades de Mr. de Clairenville. Cologne, 1743.
	38582.3.7	Racine, Jean. Oeuvres. Amsterdam, 1743. 3v.
Htn	FL 6073.2*	Rousseau, J.J. Dissertation sur la musique moderne. Paris, 1743.
	40536.33.100	Tannevot, Alex. Adam et Eve. Amsterdam, 1743.

1744

	39576.7.20	Argens, Jean Baptiste de Boyer. The Jewish spy. 2. ed. London, 1744. 5v.
	40517.23.9	Duclos, C.P. Acajou et Zirphile, conte. Paris, 1744.
	38552.10	Fénelon, F. de S. de la Mothe. Sermons choisis. Paris, 1744.
	40517.27	Gomez, M.A.P. de. The memoires of Baron Du Tan. London, 1744.
	40517.40	Gueuderville, N. Histoire abregée. Amsterdam, 1744.
	39527.34	La Fontaine, Jean de. The loves of cupid and psyche. London, 1744.
	40512.11.6	LeSage, Alain René. Adventures of Gil blas. v.1-2. London, 1744.
	38526.34	Marguerite d'Angoulême. Contes. Londres, 1744. 2v.
Htn	39594.10*	Montesquieu, C.L. de S. Lettres persanes. Cologne, 1744.
	38583.3.7	Racine, Jean. Oeuvres. Amsterdam, 1744. 2v.
	39585.10	St. Hyacinthe, H.C. Le chef d'oeuvre d'un inconnu. La Haye, 1744. 2v.
	39583.20	Trublet, N.C.J. Essais sur divers sujets. v.1,3-4. Paris, 1744-60. 3v.
	40513.14	La vie de Don Alphonse Blas de Lirias, fils de Gil Blas de Santillane. Amsterdam, 1744.

1745

	Mol 863.1.6	Baar, G.L. de. Épîtres diverses sur des sujets diverses. v.1-2. 2e. éd. Londres, 1745.
	38576.1.50	Barbier, Marie Anne. Théâtre de Mademoiselle Barbier. Paris, 1745.
	38557.47.260	Bossuet, J.B. Défense de la déclaration de l'assemblé...1682. Amsterdam, 1745. 3v.
Htn	38557.47.250*	Bossuet, J.B. Defensio declarationis conventus cleri Gallicani an. 1682. Amstelodami, 1745. 2v.
	40526.39	Fougeret de Monbron, Louis Charles. La Henriade travestie. Berlin, 1745.
Htn	40516.19.10*	Fromaget, N. Mirima, Impératrice du Japon. La Haye, 1745.
	40517.27.35	Gomez, M.A.P. de. Select novels. London, 1745.
	40517.38.5	Gueulette, T.S. Chinese tales. 3. ed. London, 1745.
	38576.25.5	Latuillerie, M. Théâtre. Amsterdam, 1745.
	37574.160	Lefert de la Morinière, A.C. Bibliothèque poétique. Paris, 1745. 4v.
Htn	39545.34.15*	Marchand, J.H. Requete du Curé de Fontemy au Roy. n.p., 1745.
	37541.13	Papillon, Philibert. Bibliothèque des auteurs de Bourgogne. Dijon, 1745.
	FL 357.45	Parfaict, F. Histoire du théâtre français. Paris, 1745-49. 15v.
	39533.25	Pecquet, A. Memoires secrets pour servir à l'histoire de Perse. Amsterdam, 1745.
	39533.25.9	Pecquet, A. The secret history of Persia. London, 1745.
	39585.7	St. Hyacinthe, H.C. Le chef d'oeuvre d'un inconnu. 8. éd. La Haye, 1745. 2v.

Chronological Listing

1746

39576.7.25 Argens, Jean Baptiste de Boyer. Jewish letters. Newcastle, 1746. 4v.

Htn 38557.35* Bossuet, J.B. Lettres spirituelles. Paris, 1746.

38576.4 Boursault, Edme. Théâtre. Paris, 1746. 3v.

40525.51 Gaudriole; conte. La Haye, 1746.

40526.76 Guérin, François Nicolas. La victoire de Fontenoy, poëme. Paris, 1746.

40539.22 Joubert de la Rue, J. Lettres d'un Sauvage Depaysé. Amsterdam, 1746. 2v.

40516.8 Menin, Nicolas. Cleodamis et Lelex. La Haye, 1746.

39544.3 Meusnier de Querlon, Anne Gabriel. Testament littéraire de Pierre-François Guyot. La Haye, 1746.

39533.25.5 Pecquet, A. Memoires secrets pour servir à l'histoire de Perse. Amsterdam, 1746.

38525.22.51 Régnier, Mathurin. Oeuvres. London, 1746. 2v.

1747

39576.4 Argens, Jean Baptiste de Boyer. New mémoirs. London, 1747. 2v.

39577.5 Condorcet, Marie Jean Antoine. Oeuvres complètes. Paris, 1747-49. 12v.

38588.18.10 Dufresny, Charles Rivière. Oeuvres. Paris, 1747. 4v.

Htn 38554.327* Fénelon, F. de S. de la Mothe. Directions pour la conscience d'un roi. La Haye, 1747.

Htn 38554.327.2* Fenelon, F. de S. de la Mothe. Directions pour la conscience d'un roi. La Haye, 1747.

Htn 38554.327.5* Fénelon, F. de S. de la Mothe. Examen de conscience pour un roi. Londres, 1747.

Htn 38553.29.100* Fénelon, F. de S. de la Mothe. Telemace. Rome, 1747. 2v.

Mol 232.12 Molière, Jean Baptiste Poquelin. Het gedwongene huuwelyk. Amsterdam, 1747.

40522.5.22 Prévost, Antoine F. Memoirs of a man of honour. v.1-2. London, 1747.

39586.12 Venturi, Franco. Antichità svelata e l'idea del progresso in N.A. Boulanger, 1722-1759. Bari, 1747.

1748

Htn 40529.6* Bazin, Gilles A. Le livre jaune. Bâle, 1748.

Htn 38557.35.5* Bossuet, J.B. Lettres et opuscules. Paris, 1748. 2v.

40534.33.5 Crébillon, Claude Prosper Jolyot de. Les egaremens du coeur et de l'esprit, ou Memoires de Mr. De Meilsour. La Haye, 1748.

Htn 39564.10* Diderot, Denis. Les bijoux indescrets. Paris, 1748. 2v.

39586.21.10 Duchannavie neologique. Amsterdam, 1748.

38554.327.8 Fénelon, F. de S. de la Mothe. Directions pour la conscience d'un roi. La Haye, 1748.

40535.19.9 Graffigny, Françoise d'Issembourg d'Happoncourt de. Letters written by a Peruvian princess. London, 1748.

38516.18 Michault, Pierre. La dance aux aveugles et autres poésies du XVe siècle. Lille, 1748.

Mol 60.4 Molière, Jean Baptiste Poquelin. Works. London, 1748. 10v.

Htn 39591.15* Montesquieu, C.L. de S. De l'esprit des loix. Genève, 1748? 2v.

40517.55 Pajon, H. Histoire des trois fils d'Hal i-Bassa. Constantinople, 1748.

40536.21 Poisson, Philippe. Les ruses d'amour. La Haye, 1748.

37576.320 Saunier de Beaumont. Lettres philosophiques, serieuses. v.1-2. La Haye, 1748.

Htn 39545.62* Voltaire, François Marie Arouet de. Zadig et voyage de St. Cloud. n.p., 1748.

Htn 39545.28* Voltairiana, ou Eloges amphigouriques de M. Arouet. Paris, 1748.

1749

Htn 39576.3* Argens, Jean Baptiste de Boyer. Man, a machine. London, 1749.

37586.30 Artigny, Antoine Gachet d'. Nouveaux mémoires d'histoire, et critique et de littérature. Paris, 1749-56. 7v.

38558.6.5 Fléchier, Esprit. Recueil des oraisons funèbres. Paris, 1749.

37555.11.5 Gailloro, G.H. Poétique française à l'usage des dames. Paris, 1749. 2v.

40517.25 Gomez, M.A.P. de. La belle assemblée. 6. ed. London, 1749. 4v.

39532.11.5 Hamilton, Anthony. Le Belier, conte. n.p., 1749.

39532.11.10 Hamilton, Anthony. Histoire de fleur d'epine. n.p., 1749.

39532.11.15 Hamilton, Anthony. Les quatre Facardins, conte. Paris? 1749.

38516.19 Michault, Pierre. La dance aux aveugles et autres poésies du XVe siècle. Amsterdam, 1749.

Htn Mol 17.49* Molière, Jean Baptiste Poquelin. Oeuvres. Paris, 1749. 8v.

39594.1.10 Montesquieu, C.L. de S. De l'esprit des loix. Amsterdam, 1749.

39594.1 Montesquieu, C.L. de S. De l'esprit des loix. Genève, 1749.

39532.4.9 Rousseau, J.B. Lettres. Genève, 1749. 5v.

39545.29.10 Voltaire, François Marie Arouet de. Voltairiana. Paris, 1749. 2v.

39545.65 Voltaire, François Marie Arouet de. Zadig. London, 1749.

1750

38557.52.4.81 Bossuet, J.B. Éxposition de la doctrine de l'église catholique sur les matières de controverse. Paris, 1750.

38576.12.20 Campistron, J.G. de. Oeuvres. Paris, 1750. 3v.

FL 396.41.8 Du Gérard, N. Tables alphabetiques et chronologiques. Paris, 1750.

38553.25.9 Fénelon, F. de S. de la Mothe. Les aventures de Télémaque. London, 1750.

Htn 38554.25* Fénelon, F. de S. de la Mothe. Dissertation on pure love. London, 1750.

38554.350.225 Fénelon, F. de S. de la Mothe. Instructions for the education of daughters. Glasgow, 1750.

38554.520.10 Fénelon, F. de S. de la Mothe. Letters upon divers subjects. Glasgow, 1750.

40516.19 Fromaget, N. Kara Mustapha et Basch-Savi. Amsterdam, 1750.

1750 - cont.

39576.50 Godard d'Aucour, C. Mémoires turcs ou Histoire galente. Francfort, 1750.

39578.17 Lambert, Anne Thérèse. Oeuvres. Lausanne, 1750.

39594.3.20 La Roche, J.B.L. Critique de l'esprit des loix. Genève, 1750. 2 pam.

38576.27.5 Le Noble, E. Pure love. London, 1750.

39585.8 Lettres d'un inconnu. n.p., 1750.

40535.30.45 Marivaux, Pierre Carlet de Chamblain de. Pharsamond. London, 1750. 2v.

39591.15.5 Montesquieu, C.L. de S. De l'esprit des loix. Genève, 1750. 3v.

39594.3.19 Montesquieu, C.L. de S. Defense de l'esprit des lois. Genève, 1750.

40517.53 Mouhy, Charles de F. Le masque de fer. v.1-5. La Haye, 1750.

39585.38 Puisieux, M. d'A. de. Le caractères. London, 1750.

40526.42.4 Racine, Louis. Oeuvres. 6e éd. Amsterdam, 1750. 6v.

Htn FL 6067.5* Rousseau, J.J. Discours qui à remporté le prix a l'Académie de Dijon en l'année 1750. Genève, 1750?

39584.31 Saint, Foix, G.F.P. de. Lettres turques. Amsterdam, 1750. 2v.

39584.30 Saint Foix, G.F.P. de. Lettres turques. Cologne, 1750.

40517.70 Soliman ou Les aventures de Macanet. Amsterdam, 1750.

Htn 39545.73* Voltaire, François Marie Arouet de. Oreste; tragédie. Paris, 1750.

1751

Htn 40525.32* L'art de Peter. Westphalie, 1751. 2 pam.

39594.3.23 Bonnaire, L. de. L'esprit des lois quintessencié par...lettres. n.p., 1751. 2v.

38557.25.125 Bossuet, J.B. Opuscules. Paris, 1751. 5v.

39576.24 Chicaneau de Neuville, Didier R. Dictionnaire philosophique. Londres, 1751.

40535.2 Danchet, M. Théâtre. Paris, 1751. 4v.

40517.23.30 Duclos, C.P. Considerations sur les moeurs de ce siècle. Paris, 1751.

Mol 606.1 Fagan, Christophe Barthélemy. Nouvelles observations au sujet des condemnations contre les comédies. Paris, 1751.

40537.55 The force of education. London, 1751.

39586.21.3 Fréron, Elie Catharine. Lettres sur quelques écrits de ce temps. London, 1751-54. 13v.

Htn FL 379.151* Gaultier, J.B. Critique de ballet moral. n.p., 1751.

37564.2 Lambert, Claude F. Histoire littéraire du Regne de Louis XIV. Paris, 1751. 3v.

39594.3.25 Laporte, J. de. Obserbations sur l'esprit des loix. 2. ed. Amsterdam, 1751.

FL 360.40 Maillet-Duclairon, A. Essai sur la connoissance des théâtres français. Paris, 1751.

40524.17.50 Mainvilliers, G.S. The beau-philosopher. London, 1751.

40527.30 Mélanges de Poezie. La Haye, 1751- 2v.

Mol 165.21 Molière, Jean Baptiste Poquelin. L'avare and The miser. Paris, 1751.

1752

40529.32 Campan. Le mot et la chose. n.p., 1752.

38554.325.30 Fénelon, F. de S. de la Mothe. Dialogues des morts anciens et modernes. Paris, 1752. 2v.

38552.12.8 Fénelon, F. de S. de la Mothe. Oeuvres spirituelles. n.p., 1752. 4v.

40517.54 La Place, P.A. de. L'orpheline angloise, ou Histoire de Charlotte Summers. London, 1752. 4v.

40529.24 Marchadier. L'isle de France, ou La nouvelle colonie de Venus. Amsterdam, 1752.

Mol 62.10 Molière, Jean Baptiste Poquelin. Sämmtliche Lustspiele. Hamburg, 1752. 4v.

Htn FL 379.152* Monhy, C. de F. Tablettes dramatiques contenant l'abrégé de l'histoire du théâtre français. Paris, 1752.

39594.3.2 Montesquieu, C.L. de S. Spirit of laws. 2. ed. v.2. London, 1752.

38536.4.10 Rabelais, F. La Rabelais moderne, ou Les oeuvres de maitre. v1,3-6. Amsterdam, 1752. 6v.

40526.42.15 Racine, Louis. Die Religion entworfen von Herren Racine. Frankfurt, 1752.

Htn 39545.58* Voltaire, François Marie Arouet de. Rome sauvée. Berlin, 1752.

1753

39574.26.15 Alembert, J. Le Rond d'. Mélanges de littérature. v.2. Berlin, 1753.

40516.75 Bastide, J.F. La trentaine de Cithere. London, 1753.

38557.25.100 Bossuet, J.B. Oeuvres posthumes. Amsterdam, 1753. 3v.

39585.1 Chevrier, F.A. Le Colporteur. London, 1753. 2 pam.

40515.2.80 Duperron de Castéra, L. La pierre philosophale des dames. n.p., 1753.

Mol 880.23 Lubbertze, L. Geadelde Boer. Amsteldam, 1753.

Htn Mol 17.53* Molière, Jean Baptiste Poquelin. Oeuvres. Paris, 1753.

Htn Mol 17.53.2* Molière, Jean Baptiste Poquelin. Oeuvres. Paris, 1753. 8v.

Mol 196.30.3 Molière, Jean Baptiste Poquelin. Het school voor de nouwen...Arendsz. Amsterdam, 1753.

39594.3.13 Montesquieu, C.L. de S. Werk von den Gesetzen. Frankfurt, 1753. 3v.

Htn FL 396.41.3* Parfaict, F. Histoire de l'ancien théâtre italien depuis son origine en France. Paris, 1753.

37585.11.9 Pièces du nouveau théâtre italien. Paris, 1753. 3v.

Htn FL 6082.2* Rousseau, J.J. Lettre sur la musique française. n.p., 1753.

Htn FL 6084.5* Rousseau, J.J. Narcisse. Paris? 1753.

38542.17.2 Saint-Evremond, C. de M. de S.D. Oeuvres. Paris, 1753. 12v.

Htn 39545.35.8* Voltaire, François Marie Arouet de. Amelie, ou Le duc de foix. London, 1753.

Htn 39545.37.15* Voltaire, François Marie Arouet de. Diatribe du Docteur Akakia. Rome, 1753.

Htn 39545.27* Voltaire, François Marie Arouet de. Micromégas. London, 1753.

Chronological Listing

1754

	39576.11	Argens, Jean Baptiste de Boyer. Lettres cabalistiques. La Haye, 1754. 7v.
	39576.10	Argens, Jean Baptiste de Boyer. Lettres cabalistiques. La Haye, 1754-70. 7v.
	40517.6	Baret, Paul. Le grelot. Paris, 1754.
	40529.13	Beausobre, L. de. Le Pirrhonisme du Sage. Berlin, 1754.
Htn	39534.1.15*	Bussy-Rabutin. Histoire amoureuse des Gaules. n.p., 1754.
	40534.24.5	Crébillon, Prosper Jolyot de. Oeuvres. Paris, 1754. 2v.
	39586.21.500	Desfontaines, P.F.G. L'esprit de l'abbé Desfontaines. Londres, 1754-57. 4v.
Htn	39564.10.50*	Diderot, Denis. Pensées sur l'interpretation de la nature. Paris, 1754.
	37547.24	Dreux de Radier, Jean François. Bibliothèque...critique du Poitou. Paris, 1754. 5v.
	37588.7	La France littéraire; ou Almanach des beaux arts. Paris, 1754
	40517.25.2	Gomez, M.A.P. de. La belle assemblée. 6. ed. et 7. ed. London, 1754- 4v.
	40535.33.5	La Motte, Antoine Houdar de. Oeuvres. v.1-10. Paris, 1754. 11v.
	FL 355.9	Léris, Antoine de. Dictionnaire portatif des théâtres. Paris, 1754.
	Mon 17.54	Montaigne, Michel de. Essais. Coste. London, 1754. 10v.
	40529.36	Les sotises du tems, ou Memoires. La Haye, 1754.
	40517.61	Tiphaigne de la Roche, C.F. Amilec, ou La graine d'hommes qui sert a peuple les planetes. 3. ed. pt.1-2. Luneville, 1754?
	Mol 722.2	Voltaire, François Marie Arouet. Leben des Molière. Leipzig, 1754.

1755

	40516.75.10	Bastide, J.F. L'etre pensant. pt. 1-2. Amsterdam, 1755.
	38563.6.20	Bayle, Pierre. Analyse raisonnée de Bayle, ou Abrégé méthodique de ses ouvrages. London, 1755- 8v.
	38566.28.10	Boileau Despréaux, Nicolas. The art of poetry. Glasgow, 1755.
	40535.2.5	Boissy, Louis de. The Frenchman in London. London, 1755.
	39585.43	Dreux du Radier, J.F. Essai...sur les lanternes, leur origin. Dôle, 1755.
	40517.42.7	Hecquet, Mme. Histoire d'une jeune fille sauvage. Paris, 1755.
	40524.17.54	Maubert de Gouvest, J.H. Lettres iroquoises. Irocopolis, 1755.
	Mol 60.7	Molière, Jean Baptiste Poquelin. Works. London, 1755. 10v.
Htn	FL 6070.2*	Rousseau, J.J. Discours sur l'origine et les fondements de l'inégalité parmi les hommes. Amsterdam, 1755.
	39533.15.5	Segrais, Jean R. Oeuvres. Paris, 1755. 2v.
	39583.19	Trublet, N.C.J. Essais. Amsterdam, 1755-60. 4v.
Htn	39545.48.17*	Voltaire, François Marie Arouet de. La pucelle d'Orleans. Louvain, 1755.

1756

Htn	40526.49*	Boccage, Marie Anne F. du. La Colombiade. Paris, 1756.
	40526.50	Boccage, Marie Anne F. du. La Colombiade. Paris, 1756.
	40526.48	Boccage, Marię Anne F. du. La Colombiade. Paris, 1756.
	38557.52.4.75	Bossuet, J.B. Exposition de la doctrine de l'église catholique sur les matières de controverse. Paris, 1756.
	39585.2.15	Clement, Pierre. Les cinq années littéraires, ou Lettres...1748-52. Berlin, 1756. 2v.
	40516.13	Cointreau. L'amant Salamendre. London, 1756.
Htn	39533.20.3.2*	Cyrano de Bergerac. The agreement...dream. n.p., 1756.
	40534.16	Du Boccage, Marie Anne (Le Page) Fiquet (Mme.). Le amazzoni. Tragedia. Venezia, 1756.
	40535.19.3	Graffigny, Françoise d'Issembourg d'Happoncourt de. Lettres d'une peruvienne. Paris, 1756. 2v.
	39586.34.6	Grosley, P.J. Mémoires de l'académie des sciences...satire. Troyes, 1756.
	39586.34.5	Grosley, P.J. Mémoires de l'académie des sciences...satire. 2. ed. v.1-2. Troyes, 1756.
	38543.28.2	La Mothe le Vayer, F. de. Oeuvres. Précédé de L'Abrégé de la vie de M. de la Mothe de la Vayer. v.1-7, (Pt.1-2). Dresde, 1756-59. 14v.
	40516.46	Lassay, A.L. de. Recueil de différentes chose. Lausanne, 1756. 4v.
	40535.29.10	Marivaux, Pierre Carlet de Chamblain de. Le paysan parvenu. v.1-8. Paris, 1756. 4v.
	Mol 172.7	Molière, Jean Baptiste Poquelin. Il cittadino gentiluomo. n.p., 1756?
	38585.30.15	Racine, Jean. Die uneinigen Brüder. Berlin, 1756?
	40526.69.70	Vadé, Jean Joseph. Nicaise. Paris, 1756.
Htn	39545.48.15*	Voltaire, François Marie Arouet de. The orphan of China. Dublin, 1756.
Htn	39545.48.5*	Voltaire, François Marie Arouet de. The orphan of China. London, 1756.
Htn	39545.61*	Voltaire, François Marie Arouet de. Religion naturelle, poeme. Genève, 1756.

1757

	37581.12	Corneille, Pierre. Rodogune. Cologne, 1757-74. 10 pam.
	37533.12	Formey, M. La France littéraire, ou Dictionnaire des auteurs français. Berlin, 1757.
	40517.21	G*** de la Bataille. Jeannette Seconde. Amsterdam, 1757.
	40537.65	Harlequin, vivandier à l'armée françois au Lord de la mer; comédie. London, 1757.
	38523.22.85	Malherbe, François de. Poésies. Paris, 1757.
Htn	39545.37.20F*	Voltaire, François Marie Arouet de. Epistle from M. Voltaire to king of Prussia. London, 1757.

1758

	39576.37	Benouville, de (Mme.). Les pensées errantes. London, 1758.
	FL 398.13.14	Gaillard de la Bataille, Pierre A. Histoire de Mademoiselle Cronel, dite Fretillon. La Haye, 1758.
	40526.9	Gresset, Jean B. Oeuvres. London, 1758. 2v.
	40526.18	La Grange-Chancel, Joseph de. Oeuvres. Paris, 1758. 5v.
	39592.8.20	Montesquieu, C.L. de S. Oeuvres. Amsterdam, 1758. 3v.

1758 - cont.

	39594.3.3	Montesquieu, C.L. de S. The spirit of laws. London, 1758. 2v.
	40527.36	Poëmes sur des sujets pris de l'histoire de notre tems. Liège, 1758. 2v.
Htn	40517.56*	Porée, C.G. Histoire de D. Ranucio d'Aletes. Venise, 1758. 2v.
Htn	FL 6071.2*	Rousseau, J.J. Discours sur l'economie politique. Genève, 1758.

1759

Htn	38576.2*	Baron, M.B. Le théâtre. Paris, 1759. 3v.
	39576.17	Coyer, G.F. Bagatelles morales et dissertations. London, 1759.
	40526.17.3	Gresset, Jean B. Ver-Vert. London, 1759.
	40517.35	Gueulette, T.S. Tartarian tales. London, 1759.
	37595.15.5	Hue de Tabarie. L'ordene de chavalerie. Lausanne, 1759.
	39535.5	Le Roy, A. de. Le Momus François ou Les avantures. Cologne, 1759.
	FL 6127.59	Marmontel, J.J. Réponse à Jean-Jacques Rousseau. Genève, 1759.
Htn	Mon 31.7*	Montaigne, Mcihel de. Essays. Cotton. 7. ed. London, 1759. 3v.
	39592.2	Montesquieu, C.L. de S. Oeuvres. Copenhagen, 1759-61. 6v.
	40536.21.7	Poinsinet de Sivry, M. La berlue. Paris, 1759.
	40524.24	Riccoboni, M.J.L. de (Mme.). Lettres de Milady G. Catesby à H. Campley. Amsterdam, 1759.
Htn	FL 6070.3*	Rousseau, J.J. Discours sur l'origine et les fondements de l'inégalité parmi les hommes. Amsterdam, 1759.
Htn	FL 6077.10*	Rousseau, J.J. A letter from Mr. Rousseau, of Geneva. London, 1759.
Htn	FL 6077.3*	Rousseau, J.J. Letter to Mr. d'Alembert of Paris. London, 1759.
	39534.27.3	Scarron, Paul. The whole comical works of M. Scarron. London, 1759. 2v.
	FL 6127.58	Villaret, Claude. Considératons sur l'art du théâtre. Genève, 1759.
Htn	39545.36.10*	Voltaire, François Marie Arouet de. Candid. 2d ed. London, 1759.
Htn	39545.35.5.48*	Voltaire, François Marie Arouet de. Candide, ou L'optimisme. Genève, 1759.
Htn	39545.35.5.50*	Voltaire, François Marie Arouet de. Candide, ou L'optimisme. n.p., 1759.
Htn	39543.3*	Voltaire, François Marie Arouet de. Histoire de l'empire de Russie. Genèva, 1759-65. 2v.
Htn	39541.5.18*	Voltaire, François Marie Arouet de. Histoire de l'empire de Russie sous Pierre le Grand. n.p., 1759-63. 2v.

176-

Htn	40517.42*	Hecquet, Mme. The history of a slave girl. London, 176-?

1760

Htn	40531.2.20*	Annet, Peter. Saul et David. London, 1760.
	39576.28	Bernard, J.F. The praise of Hell. London, 1760. 2v.
	39576.55	Blondel, J. Des hommes tels qu'ils sont et doivent etre. Hamburg, 1760.
	39585.22.20	Caraccioli, L.A. La conversation aves soi-même. 9. éd. Liège, 1760.
Htn	39585.21*A	Caraccioli, L.A. Le livre de quatre couleurs. Paris, 1760.
	Mol 880.7	Chiari, P. I fanatici. Bologna, 1760.
	38576.12.45	Dancourt, Florent C. Les oeuvres de théâtre. Paris, 1760. 12v.
	FL 6127.60	Dancourt, L.H. À Mr. Jean-Jacques Rousseau. Berlin, 1760.
	38558.7	Fléchier, Esprit. Recueil des oraisons. Paris, 1760.
	39533.2	Hamilton, Anthony. Memoires....de Grammont. n.p., 1760. 2v.
	38543.8	La Rochefoucauld, François. Réfléxions, sentences et maximes morales. Lausanne, 1760.
Htn	Mol 17.60*	Molière, Jean Baptiste Poquelin. Oeuvres. Basle, 1760. 4v.
Htn	Mol 17.60.5*	Molière, Jean Baptiste Poquelin. Oeuvres. Paris, 1760. 8v.
	Mol 37.60	Molière, Jean Baptiste Poquelin. Oeuvres choisies. v.1-5. Paris, 1760-62.
	40522.5.10	Prévost, Antoine F. Le doyen de Killerine, histoire morale. La Haye, 1760. 2v.
	38585.38	Racine, Jean. Mithridate; tragédie. Paris, 1760.
	38585.39	Racine, Jean. Mithridate. Paris, 1760.
	38581.3	Racine, Jean. Oeuvres. Paris, 1760. 3v.
	40526.66.100	Ramier, J.D. La lyre protestante consacrée aux partisans de la bonne cause. 2e éd. n.p., 1760?
	40524.24.5	Riccoboni, M.J.L. de (Mme.). Letters from Juliet Lady Catesby, to her friend, Lady Henrietta Campley. London, 1760.
Htn	FL 6064.3*	Rousseau, J.J. Le devin du village, intermede. Genève, 1760.
Htn	FL 6002.760*	Rousseau, J.J. Oeuvres diverses. Amsterdam, 1760. 2v.
	40536.29.5	Sedaine, Michel Jean. Le diable à quatre. La Haye, 1760.
	40536.28	Sedaine, Michel Jean. Recueil de poesies. 2. éd. London, 1760.
	38546.40	Sévigné, Marie de R.C. Letters from...to her daughter. London, 1760-65. 8v.
Htn	40517.62*	Tiphaigne de la Roche, C.F. Giphantie. Babylone, 1760. 2 pam.
Htn	39545.37.9*	Voltaire, François Marie Arouet de. The coffee house, or Fair fugitive. London, 1760.

1761

	38557.48.35	Bossuet, J.B. De la connaissance de Dieu et de soi-même. Paris, 1761.
	40535.4.5	Destouches, Philippe Néricault. Der poetische Dorfjunker...Ein Lustspiel in 5 Aufzügen. Wien, 1761.
Htn	38553.18.5*	Fénelon, F. de S. de la Mothe. Les aventures de Télémaque. Ulm, 1761.
	39576.31	Friedrich II, der Grosse.al guerra...tratta dal poema francese. In Parigi, 1761.
	39535.5.5	Le Roy, A. de. Le Momus François ou Les avantures. Cologne, 1761.
Htn	39576.23.6*	Mes pensées. Supplement. Berlin, 1761.

Chronological Listing

1761 - cont.

	Mol 17.61	Molière, Jean Baptiste Poquelin. Les oeuvres. Jene, 1761. 3v.
	39594.11	Montesquieu, C.L. de S. Lettres persanes. Amsterdam, 1761.
Htn	FL 6064.4*	Rousseau, J.J. Le devin du village. Paris, 1761.
	FL 6070.50	Rousseau, J.J. Discourse on the origin of inequality. London, 1761.
Htn	FL 6090.5*	Saint-Pierre, Charles J.C. Extrait du projet de paix perpétuelle de monsieur l'abbé de St. Pierre. n.p., 1761.
Htn	40517.62.5*	Tiphaigne de la Roche, C.F. Giphantie. London, 1761. 2 pam.
	40526.69.90	Vadé, Jean Joseph. Le suffisant. Paris, 1761.
	39545.25.7	Voltaire, François Marie Arouet de. Dramatic works. v.1-2, 4. London, 1761-62. 2v.
Htn	39545.25.6*	Voltaire, François Marie Arouet de. Tancréde, tragédie en vers croisés. Genève, 1761.
Htn	39545.25.5*	Voltaire, François Marie Arouet de. Tancréde, tragédie en vers croisés. Paris, 1761.

1762

Htn	FL 6127.62*	André. Refutation de Jean-Jacques Rousseau. Paris, 1762.
	40526.2	Boccage, Marie Anne F. du. Recueil des oeuvres. Lyon, 1762. 3v.
Htn	39586.11.2*	Boulanger, N.A. Dissertation sur Elie et Enoch. n.p., 1762.
	FL 6127.62.5	Censure de la faculté...de Paris. Paris, 1762.
	37586.15	Foote, Samuel. The comic theatre. London, 1762. 5v.
	37581.14	Hauteroche, Noël. Le deuil. Paris, 1762-67. 12 pam.
Htn	39527.8.15*	La Fontaine, Jean de. Contes et nouvelles en vers. Amsterdam, 1762.
	40527.2	L'Attaignant, Gabriel Charles de. Cantiques spirituels. Paris, 1762.
	40535.29.19	Marivaux, Pierre Carlet de Chamblain de. La fause suivante. Paris, 1762.
	38513.20	Pathelin. La farce de Maistre Pierre Pathelin. Paris, 1762.
Htn	FL 6030.62.3*	Rousseau, J.J. Du contrat social. Amsterdam, 1762.
Htn	FL 6030.62.4*	Rousseau, J.J. Du contrat social. Amsterdam, 1762.
Htn	FL 6030.62*	Rousseau, J.J. Du contrat social. Amsterdam, 1762.
	FL 6047.1.5	Rousseau, J.J. Emil, oder von der Erziehung. pt.1-4. Berlin, 1762. 2v.
Htn	FL 6040.62*	Rousseau, J.J. Émile, ou De l'éducation. Francfort, 1762. 2v.
Htn	FL 6040.62.2*	Rousseau, J.J. Émile, ou De l'éducation. La Haye, 1762. 4v.
Htn	FL 6040.62.3*	Rousseau, J.J. Émile ou De l'éducation. Paris, 1762.
Htn	FL 6046.2*	Rousseau, J.J. Emilius and Sophia. London, 1762-63. 4v.
Htn	FL 6050.62*	Rousseau, J.J. Julie ou La nouvelle Héloise. Amsterdam, 1762. 2v.
Htn	FL 6001.769*	Rousseau, J.J. Oeuvres. Amsterdam, 1762-69. 11v.
Htn	FL 6030.62.2*	Rousseau, J.J. Principes du droit politique. Amsterdam, 1762.
	39584.36	Saint Foix, G.F.P. de. Oeuvres de théâtre. Paris, 1762. 4v.
	FL 379.162	Vernon. Apologie du théâtre adressée à Mlle. Cl... La Haye, 1762.

1763

	38557.48.3	Bossuet, J.B. Défense de la tradition et des saints pères. Paris, 1763. 2v.
	39585.21.10	Caraccioli, L.A. L'esprit de monsieur le marquis Caraccioli. Liège, 1763.
	40552.17	Castel, P. Esprit, Saillies et Singularités. Amsterdam, 1763.
	37574.351	Couret de Villeneuve, M. Le trésor du Parnasse. v.1-4. London, 1763-70. 2v.
	40535.1.25	Dampierre de La Salle. Le bienfait rendu, ou Le négociant. Paris, 1763.
	40535.15.12	Favart, Charles S. Théâtre, ou Recueil des comédies, parodies et opera-comiques. Paris, 1763. 8v.
	38553.19	Fénelon, F. de S. de la Mothe. Les aventures de Télémaque. Paris, 1763. 2v.
Htn	FL 6127.63*	Formey, J.H.S. Anti-Émile. Berlin, 1763.
	FL 6054.5	Formey, M. L'ésprit de Julie, ou éxtrait de la nouvelle Héloise. Berlin, 1763.
	FL 6127.63.3	Geneva, Switzerland. Citizens. Representations des citoyens et bourgeois de Genève, 1763. Genève, 1763.
Htn	40534.34.5*	Le hazard du coin du feu, dialogue moral. La Haye, 1763.
	FL 355.9.2	Léris, Antoine de. Dictionnaire portatif des théâtres. Paris, 1763.
	39597.7	Marmontel, J.F. Poetique françoise. Paris, 1763. 2v.
	40536.18	Pannard, Charles François. Théâtre et oeuvres diverses. Paris, 1763. 4v.
	40516.38	Ramsay, A.M. de. Travels of Cyrus. London, 1763.
Htn	FL 6050.63*	Rousseau, J.J. Lettres de deux Amans. 2. ed. Amsterdam, 1763. 3v.
Htn	FL 6002.763*	Rousseau, J.J. Les pensées. Amsterdam, 1763.
	FL 6127.63.2	Vernes, J. Lettres sur le christianisme de Jean-Jacques Rousseau. Genève, 1763.
Htn	39543.4.5*	Voltaire, François Marie Arouet de. Traité sur la tolérance. Genèva, 1763. 3 pam.
	39543.4	Voltaire, François Marie Arouet de. Traité sur la tolérance. Genèva, 1763.

1764

Htn	39574.26*	Alembert, J. Le Rond d'. Mélanges de littérature. Amsterdam, 1764. 4v.
	39576.7	Argens, Jean Baptiste de Boyer. Lettres juives. La Haye, 1764. 8v.
	FL 379.164	Les baladins. Amsterdam, 1764.
Htn	39586.11*	Boulanger, N.A. Dissertation sur Elie et Enoch. n.p., 1764.
	39585.22.10	Caraccioli, L.A. La grandeur d'ame. Paris, 1764.
Htn	38572.7.25*	Corneille, Pierre. Théâtre. Tome III-XII. Genève, 1764. 10v.
	38576.12.42.40	Corneille, Thomas. Ariane. Paris, 1764.
	39534.25	Deschoulières, A. du L. del G. (Mme.). Oeuvres. Paris, 1764. 2v.
	40524.16.5	Elie de Beaumont, A.L. Lettres du Marquis de Roselle. London, 1764.

1764 - cont.

	40515.55.8	Fauques, Marianne Agnès de. Oriental anecdotes, or The history of Haroun Alrachid. London, 1764. 2v.
	38554.326.50	Fénelon, F. de S. de la Mothe. Dialogues sur l'éloquence en général. Paris, 1764.
	38562.14	Fontenelle, B. Le B. de. Oeuvres. Amsterdam, 1764. 12v.
	39576.14	Gondar, Ange. L'espion chinois. Cologne, 1764. 6v.
	40516.22.5	Jouin, Nicolas. Le vrai recueil de Sarcelles. Amsterdam, 1764. 2v.
	40535.19.25	LaHarpe, J.F. de. Le comte de Warwik. Paris, 1764.
	40535.19.805	Landois, Paul. Serena. Photoreproduction. Frankfurt, 1764.
	40535.25.2	Maillet-Duclairon, A. Cromwell; tragédie en cinq actes. Paris, 1764.
	40536.16	Palissot de Montenoy, Charles. La dunciade. Chelsea, 1764.
	FL 6127.64	Réponse aux lettres écrites de la campagne 1764. n.p., 1764.
Htn	FL 6075.5*	Rousseau, J.J. De l'imitation théatrale. Amsterdam, 1764.
	FL 6056.4	Rousseau, J.J. Eloisa. 3. ed. London, 1764. 4v.
Htn	FL 6002.764.15*	Rousseau, J.J. Esprit, maximes, et principes. Neuchâtel, 1764.
Htn	FL 6002.764.5*	Rousseau, J.J. Esprit, maximes, et principes. Neuchâtel, 1764.
Htn	FL 6081.2*	Rousseau, J.J. Lettres écrites de la montagne. Amsterdam, 1764.
	FL 6050.64	Rousseau, J.J. La nouvelle Héloise. Neuchâtel, 1764. 4v.
Htn	FL 6002.764.10*	Rousseau, J.J. Oeuvres de Rousseau de Genève. Neuchâtel, 1764. 5v.
	FL 6127.64.5	Roustan, A.J. Offrande aux autels et à la patrie. Amsterdam, 1764.
	40526.69.50	Vadé, Jean Joseph. Jerosme et Franchonnette. Paris, 1764.
	39543.2	Voltaire, François Marie Arouet de. Collection complette des oeuvres. Genèva, 1764. 21v.

1765

	Mol 863.1.7	Baar, G.L. de. Épîtres diverses sur des sujets diverses. v.1-2. Francfort, 1765.
	40534.10.12	Belloy, Pierre L.B. The siege of Calais. London, 1765.
	FL 6127.65.4	Claparede, D. Consideration sur les miracles de l'evangile. Genève, 1765.
Htn	40526.8.15*	Collé, Charles. Chansons joyeuses, mises au jour. Paris, 1765.
	39545.2.3	Comparet, J.A. La vérité, ode à M. de Voltaire, suivie d'une dissertation sur la gouvernement de Genève. Londres, 1765.
	38572.8	Corneille, Pierre. Théâtre. Paris, 1765. 12v.
Htn	FL 6127.65.5*	Du Peyrou, Pierre Alexandre. Lettre à monsieur...relative à monsieur Jean-Jacques Rousseau. Goa, 1765.
	40524.16.7	Elie de Beaumont, A.L. History of the Marquis de Roselle. London, 1765. 2v.
	40524.16.6	Elie de Beaumont, A.L. Lettres de Sophie et du chevalier de **. Londres, 1765. 2v.
Htn	40535.15.8*	Favart, Charles S. La fée urgele. Paris, 1765.
	39576.13	Gondar, Ange. The Chinese spy. Paris, 1765. 6v.
	39576.14.5	Gondar, Ange. L'espion chinois. v.1-6. Cologne, 1765. 3v.
	40526.9.2	Gresset, Jean B. Oeuvres. Londres, 1765. 2v.
	40535.23.12	Harny de Guerville. Le petit maître en province. Paris, 1765.
	40516.26	Jonval, de. Les erreurs instructives. pt.1-3. London, 1765.
	40517.42.50	Jussy, de. Lettres de Mademoiselle de Jussy. Amsterdam, 1765.
Htn	38561.28*	La Bruyère, J. Les caracteres de Théophraste. Paris, 1765.
	39585.30	La Fargue, de. Oeuvres mélées. Paris, 1765. 2v.
	40536.27.150	La Noue, Jean Sauvé de. Oeuvres de théatre de M. de la Noue. Paris, 1765.
	37578.29.5	Lockman, J. The entertaining instructor. London, 1765.
	40529.50	M***, de. Le carnaval de la Barbarie et le temple d'Yurognes. Barbarie, 1765.
	40535.29.45	Marivaux, Pierre Carlet de Chamblain de. L'Iliade en vers burlesques. Paris, 1765.
Htn	Mol 17.65*	Molière, Jean Baptiste Poquelin. Oeuvres...vie...par Voltaire. Amsterdam, 1765. 6v.
	37575.2	Nouveaux melanges, philosophiques, historiques, critiques. n.p., 1765-76. 19v.
	37574.8	Porte-feuille d'un homme de goute. Amsterdam, 1765. 2v.
	FL 6127.65.2	Réponses aux lettres populaires. n.p., 1765.
Htn	FL 6081.3*	Rousseau, J.J. Lettres écrites de la montagne. Amsterdam, 1765.
	FL 6030.65	Rousseau, J.J. Oeuvres. Contrat social. v.8. Neufchâtal, 1765.
	40527.24.15	Saint-Lambert, Jean F. Sara Th. Paris? 1765?
	40536.27.5	Saurin, Bernard J. L'orpheline lé guée. Paris, 1765. 3 pam.
	FL 6127.65	Tronchin, J.R. Lettres populaires. n.p., 1765.
	FL 6127.65.3	Vernes, J. Examen du christianisme de Jean-Jacques Rousseau. Genève, 1765.
Htn	39543.7*	Voltaire, François Marie Arouet de. Lettres secrettes. Genèva, 1765.
Htn	39543.6*	Voltaire, François Marie Arouet de. La philosophie de l'histoire. Genèva, 1765.

1766

	40531.3.100	Anseaume, Louis. Théâtre de M. Anseaume. Paris, 1766. 3v.
	39576.8	Argens, Jean Baptiste de Boyer. Jewish letters. London, 1766. 5v.
	39576.12.6	Argens, Jean Baptiste de Boyer. Lettres chinoises, ou Correspondance philosophique. La Haye, 1766. 6v.
	38565.5	Boileau Despréaux, Nicolas. Oeuvres. Paris, 1766. 2v.
	40534.16.3	Boissy, Louis de. Oeuvres de théâtre. Paris, 1766. 9v.
	FL 6127.66.2	Cajob, J. Plagiats de M.J.J.R. sur l'éducation. La Haye, 1766.
Htn	FL 6015.2*	Contestation entre Hume et Rousseau, 1766. London, 1766.
	38562.19	Fontenelle, B. Le B. de. Éloges des académiciens. v.2. Paris, 1766.
	FL 6127.66	Geneva. Représentations et écrits, 1763-1766. Genève, 1766.

1766 - cont.

40527.34.5 Guimonde de la Touche, Claude. Les soupirs du cloitre. London, 1766.
FL 6015.15 Lettre d'un anonime à Mr. Jean -Jacques Rousseau. Paris, 1766.
38562.15 Oeuvres de Fontenelle. Paris, 1766. 11v.
37558.3 Raynal, Thomas G.L. Anecdotes littéraires. La Haye, 1766. 3v.
FL 6064.16 Rousseau, J.J. The cunning man. London, 1766.
FL 6002.766.5 Rousseau, J.J. Oeuvres choisies. Paris, 1766.
Htn FL 6002.766* Rousseau, J.J. Le pensées. v.1-2. Amsterdam, 1766.
40529.60 Sélis, Nicolas J. L'inoculation du bon sens. Oxfort, 1766.
Htn FL 393.7* Les spectacles des foires et des boulevards de Paris. Paris, 1766-78. 3v.
40524.2.5 Tencin, Claudine A.G. de. Les malheurs de l'amour. Amsterdam, 1766.
40524.2.8 Tencin, Claudine A.G de. The female adventurers. v.1-2. Dublin, 1766.
39576.40 Verzure, de (Mme.). Réflexions hazardées d'une femme ignorante. Amsterdam, 1766.

1767

Htn 40534.15* Billardon, Louis E. Hirra. Paris, 1767.
40526.1 Blin de Sainmore, A.M.H. Lettre de Biblis à Caunus son frère. 3e éd. Paris, 1767.
39585.22.9 Caraccioli, L.A. Lettres récréatives et morales. Paris, 1767-68. 4v.
39585.22.7 Caraccioli, L.A. Le tableau de la mort. Paris, 1767.
40516.2 Charpentier, L. Nouveaux contes moraux. Amsterdam, 1767. 3 pam.
Htn 39564.20* Diderot, Denis. Dorval; or The test of virtue. London, 1767.
Htn 37581.13* Dominique, P. François. Arlequin Hulla. v.11. Paris, 1767-72.
40526.34.60 Dorat, C.J. Amilka, ou Pierre-le-grand, tragédie. Paris, 1767.
Htn 40526.34.5* Dorat, C.J. Lettres envers et oeuvres mêlées. Paris, 1767. 2v.
39585.40 Dreux du Radier, J.F. Récréations historiques, critiques, morales. Paris, 1767. 2v.
40535.15.11 Favart, Charles S. A cajou. Avignon, 1767.
40526.78 Giraud, Claude Marie. Vision de Silvius Graphalètes. v.2. Londres, 1767.
39576.51 Godard d'Aucour, C. Mémoires turcs ou Histoire galente. Amsterdam, 1767. 2v.
40516.70 Marin, R.P.M.A. La marquise de los Valientes. Avignon, 1767. 2v.
39598.15.6 Marmontel, J.F. Bélisaire. Paris, 1767.
Htn 39598.15* Marmontel, J.F. Belisaire. Paris, 1767.
Htn 39594.9.50* Montesquieu, C.L. de S. Lettres familières. Florence, 1767.
39591.4 Montesquieu, C.L. de S. Oeuvres. London, 1767. 3v.
39544.62 Nonnotte, C.F. Les erreurs de Voltaire. 3e éd. Lyon, 1767. 2v.
FL 355.15 Parfaict, F. Dictionnaire des théâtres de Paris. Paris, 1767. 7v.
FL 6064.15 Rousseau, J.J. The cunning man. Dublin, 1767.
FL 6004.2 Rousseau, J.J. Miscellaneous works of Jean-Jacques Rousseau. London, 1767. 5v.
40536.31.5 Sedaine, Michel Jean. L'huitre et les plaideurs. Paris, 1767.
39583.6 Thomas, Antoine L. Oeuvres diverses. Lyon, 1767-71. 2v.
Htn 39545.46.3* Voltaire, François Marie Arouet de. L'ingénu. Utrecht, 1767.
Htn 39545.46.3.6* Voltaire, François Marie Arouet de. L'ingénu. 1st ed. Paris, 1767.
Htn 39545.78* Voltaire, François Marie Arouet de. Les scythes, tragédie. Paris, 1767.

1768

39582.23 Arnaud, F.T.M. de B. Euphémie. Paris, 1768.
Htn FL 355.19.2* Bibliothèque du théâtre François depuis son origine. Dresden, 1768. 3v.
FL 355.19 Bibliothèque du théâtre François depuis son origine. Dresden, 1768. 3v.
38566.4 Boileau Despréaux, Nicolas. Oeuvres. Paris, 1768. 2v.
39585.22 Caraccioli, L.A. Dictionnaire critique. Lyon, 1768. 3v.
FL 379.168 Causes de la Décadence du gout sur de théâtre. Amsterdam, 1768.
Htn FL 398.13.13* Dispute between Mlle. Clairon...and the Fathers of the Church. London, 1768.
40535.13.12 Falbaire de Quingey, C.G. Fenouillot de. L'honnête criminel. 2. éd. Amsterdam, 1768.
Htn 38554.1.5* Fénelon, F. de S. de la Mothe. The adventures of Telemachus. London, 1768.
Htn 40535.25* Henault, Charles. Cornélie. Vestale. Strawberry-Hill, 1768.
38575.101 Langéac, Eyide Louis Edome Joseph de l'Espenasse. Eloge de Corneille. Paris, 1768.
39598.23 Marmontel, J.F. Bélisarius. London, 1768.
Htn Mol 17.68* Molière, Jean Baptiste Poquelin. Oeuvres. Paris, 1768. 8v.
FL 6065.3 Rousseau, J.J. Dictionnaire de musique. Amsterdam, 1768. 2v.
FL 6127.68 Rousseau, J.J. Plaidoyer pour et contre Jean-Jacques Rousseau. London, 1768.
38546.38 Sévigné, Marie de R.C. Letters from the marchioness de Sévigné to her daughter. v.1-10. Dublin, 1768. 5v.

1769

Mol 602.10 Bailly, Jean. Éloge de Molière. n.p., 1769.
Htn 38557.52.5* Bossuet, J.B. Exposition de la doctrine de l'église catholique. Paris, 1769.
Htn 40525.30* Candide en Dannemarc. Genève, 1769.
39585.22.15 Caraccioli, L.A. Les derniers adieux de la Maréchale de *** à des enfans. Paris, 1769.
Mol 863.3 Chamfort, de. Éloge de Molière. Paris, 1769.
FL 396.41.5 Desboulmiers, Jean. Histoire anecdotique et raisonée du théâtre italien. Paris, 1769. 7v.
FL 6147.69 Épître à Jean-Jacques Rousseau. Paris, 1769.

1769 - cont.

39579.24 An essay on laughter. London, 1769.
38554.1.4 Fénelon, F. de S. de la Mothe. Adventures of Telemachus. Dublin, 1769.
40516.80 Frenais, Joseph Pierre. Histoire d'Agathe de St. Bohaire. v.1-2. Amsterdam, 1769.
39544.57.2 Guénée, Antoine. Lettres de quelques juifs portugais et allemands. 2e éd. Paris, 1769.
37533.21 Hébrail, J. La France littéraire. Paris, 1769. 3v.
39578.17.5 Lambert, Anne Thérèse. The works of the Marchioness de Lambert. London, 1769. 2v.
39598.13.15 Marmontel, J.F. Contos morals. Lisboa, 1769.
39598.34 Marmontel, J.F. Lucile. Besançon, 1769.
40524.17.57 Maubert de Gouvest, J.H. Lettres cherakusiennes. Rome, 1769.
Htn 39585.34* Mirabaud, Jean Baptiste. Réflexions impartiales sur l'évangile. London, 1769.
Mol 62.11 Molière, Jean Baptiste Poquelin. Sämmtliche Lustspiele. 2e Aufl. Hamburg, 1769. 4v.
Mon 17.69 Montaigne, Michel de. Essais. Coste. London, 1769. 10v.
39592.9 Montesquieu, C.L. de S. Oeuvres. Amsterdam, 1769.
39594.1.35 Montesquieu, C.L. de S. Oeuvres. v.2-4. Londres, 1769. 3v.
FL 6065.3.5 Rousseau, J.J. Dictionnaire de musique. Tom. 2. Amsterdam, 1769.
39585.23 Sablier, M. Variétés sérieuses et amusantes. Amsterdam, 1769. 3v.
37533.15 Sablons, M. (pseud.). Les grands hommes vengés. Amsterdam, 1769. 2v.
40536.31.9 Sedaine, Michel Jean. L'anneau perdu et retrouvé. Paris, 1769.
40524.44 Siret, Louis Pierre. L'homme au latin; ou, La destinée des savans. Genève, 1769.
38562.12 Trublet, N.C.J. Mémoires...de Fontenelle. Amsterdam, 1769.
39545.37.21 Voltaire, François Marie Arouet de. Evangile du jour. London, 1769. 4 pam.

1770

39582.15 Arnaud, F.T.M. de B. Oeuvres. Paris, 1770. 12v.
Mol 863.2 Bailly, J.S. Éloges de Charles V, de Molière. Berlin, 1770.
Htn 40529.15.10* Bièvre, François Georges Maréchal. Vercingentarixe, tragedie, oeuvre posthume du sieur de Bois-Flotte. Paris, 1770.
39586.18.15 Chamfort, S.R.N. Le marchand de Smyrne. Paris, 1770.
39585.5 Dulaurens, H.J. Le porte-feuille d'un philosophe. Cologne, 1770. 2v.
40535.13.30 Falbaire de Quingey, C.G. Fenouillot de. Les deux avares. Paris? 1770.
40515.54 Falconet, Ambroise. Le début. London, 1770.
40535.15.13 Favart, M.J.B.D. (Mme.). Annette et Lubin. Paris, 1770.
39544.54 Findlay, Robert. A vindication of the sacred books and of Josephus. Glasgow, 1770.
39576.32 Friedrich II, der Grosse. Examen de l'essai sur les préjugés. London, 1770.
38526.14.200 Garnier, S. La henriade et la loyssée. 2e éd. Paris, 1770.
40527.34 Guimonde de la Touche, Claude. Les soupirs du cloitre. London, 1770.
40535.24 Henault, Charles. Pièces de théâtre. n.p., 1770.
40535.23.7 Le Mierre, A.M. Artaxerce; tragédie. Paris, 1770.
Mol 37.70 Molière, Jean Baptiste Poquelin. Chef-d'oeuvres. Liége, 1770. 2v.
40522.5.25 Prévost, Antoine F. Memoires of a man of quality. London, 1770. 2v.
Htn FL 379.170* Restif de la Bretonne. La mimographe. Amsterdam, 1770.
Htn FL 6078.50* Rousseau, J.J. Lettre à Marie-François Polymathos. n.p., 1770.
40536.29.3 Sedaine, Michel Jean. Le deserteur. 2. éd. Paris, 1770.
39545.21.9 Voltaire, François Marie Arouet de. Théâtre. Amsterdam, 1770. 6v.

1771

40525.24 Adolphus. Histoire des diables modernes. Cleves, 1771.
40517.7.55 Beaurieu, G.G. de. Eleve de la nature. Amsterdam, 1771. 3v.
FL 6127.71 Bergier, M. Le déisme réfuté par lui-même. Paris, 1771.
40526.51 Boccage, Marie Anne F. du. La Colombiade. Milan, 1771.
40527.32 Collection ó Héroïdes. Frankfurt, 1771-76. 12v.
37585.22 Comédies. Paris, 1771-1809. 5 pam.
38575.31.5 Corneille, Pierre. Polyeucte. Paris, 1771.
Mol 604.9 Daillant, de La Touche. Eloge de Molière. Paris, 1771.
40526.40 Fougeret de Monbron, Louis Charles. La Henriade travestie. Amsterdam, 1771.
37565.44 Lambert, Claude F. Relation singulière, ou Le courier des Champs Elisées. Cologne, 1771.
40529.30 Maréchal, Pierre S. Le temple de l'Hymen, de dié à l'amour. Paris, 1771.
Htn 40516.16* Masson, Alexandre F.J. de. Les tableaux. Amsterdam, 1771.
40516.49.50 Mercier, Louis S. L'an deux mille quatre cent quarante. Amsterdam, 1771.
Mol 60.10 Molière, Jean Baptiste Poquelin. Works. Berwick, 1771. 6v.
40536.17 Palissot de Montenoy, Charles. La dunciade. v.1-2. Londres, 1771.
Htn FL 6096.1* Rousseau, J.J. Le testament. n.p., 1771.
39586.29 Rustaut, Christophe. Le nogzag. Amsterdam, 1771.
40536.44 Saint-Chamond, Claire Marie. Les amants sans le sçavoir. Paris, 1771.
37585.35.5 Voisenon, C.H. de G. La coquette fixée; comédie en trois actes et en vers. Copenhague, 1771. 5 pam.

1772

Htn 38566.4.10* Boileau Despréaux, Nicolas. Oeuvres. Amsterdam, 1772. 5v.
38557.41.23 Bossuet, J.B. Histoire des variations des églises protestantes. Paris, 1772. 5v.
40516.1 Carra, J.L. Odazir ou le jeune Syrien. La Haye, 1772.
37565.31.7 Chaumeix, A.J. La petite encyclopédie. Anvers, 1772. 3 pam.

1772 - cont.

40534.24.10 Crébillon, Prosper Jolyot de. Oeuvres. Paris, 1772. 2v.
39563.8 Diderot, Denis. Oeuvres philosophiques et dramatiques. Amsterdam, 1772. 6v.
Htn 40535.11.30* Ducis, Jean F. Romeo et Juliette, tragédie. Paris, 1772.
39544.58 Guénée, Antoine. Lettres de quelques juifs portugais. 3e éd. Paris, 1772. 2v.
Htn 40535.19.32* Imbert, B. Le jugement de Paris. Amsterdam, 1772.
40525.38 Les matinées du Palais royal. Paris, 1772.
40516.50 Mercier, Louis S. L'an deux mille quatre cent quarante. London, 1772.
Htn 40516.53* Mercier, Louis S. L'indigent; drame en quatre actes en prose. La Haye, 1772.
FL 398.56.12 Monnet, Jean. Supplement au Roman comique. London, 1772. 2v.
40524.19 Poinsinette de Sivry, Louis. Le phasma, ou L'apparition. Paris, 1772.
40522.6 Prévost, Antoine F. Mémoires. La Haye, 1772. 2v.
40524.24.10 Riccoboni, M.J.L. de (Mme.). Letters from Elizabeth Sophia de Valiere to her friend Louisa Hortensia de Canteleu. London, 1772. 2v.
Htn 37530.5* Rigoley, J.A. Les bibliothèques françoises de la Croix du Maien. v.1-6. Paris, 1772-73. 3v.
Htn FL 6091.10* Rousseau, J.J. Pigmalion; monologue. n.p., 1772.
37533.17 Sabatier de Castras, A. Les trois siècles de notre littérature. Amsterdam, 1772.
Htn 38565.6* Saint-Marc, Charles H. Oeuvres de Boileau. Paris, 1772. 5v.
Htn 39545.37.13* Voltaire, François Marie Arouet de. Le dépositaire. Genève, 1772.
39541.5 Voltaire, François Marie Arouet de. La Henriade. Neuchâtel, 1772.
39541.5.16 Voltaire, François Marie Arouet de. Histoire de Charles XII. n.p., 1772. 2v.

1773

Mol 873.1 Artaud de Montpellier. Le centenaire de Molière. Paris, 1773.
40526.1.5 Blin de Sainmore, A.M.H. Lettre de la duchesse de La Valliere à Louis XIV. London, 1773.
40526.47.2 Bourgeois, N. Christophe Colombe. Paris, 1773. 2v.
39585.2 Chomel. Aménités littéraires et recueil d'anecdotes. Amsterdam, 1773.
39563.5 Diderot, Denis. Collection...des oeuvres. London, 1773. 5v.
38553.19.2 Fénelon, F. de S. de la Mothe. Les aventures de Télémaque, fils d'Ulysse. Leyde, 1773.
38526.21.7 Guymond de la Touche. Iphigénie en Tauride. Paris, 1773.
40535.19.90 La Chaussée, Pierre Claude Nivelle de. Le préjuge à la mode. Paris, 1773.
Mol 873.2 Lebeau de Schosne. L'assemblée comédie. Paris, 1773.
38557.2.20 Maury. Eloge à l'Allemande. Eleutheropolis, 1773.
40516.50.2 Mercier, Louis S. L'an deux mille quatre cent quarante. London, 1773.
40516.53.5 Mercier, Louis S. Jean Hennuyer, bishop of Lizieux. London, 1773.
Htn Mol 17.73* Molière, Jean Baptiste Poquelin. Oeuvres...remarques...par Bret. Paris, 1773. 6v.
39594.9.55 Montesquieu, C.L. de S. Lettres familières à divers amis d'Italie. Rome, 1773.
39592.3.5 Montesquieu, C.L. de S. Oeuvres. Amsterdam, 1773. 6v.
39594.14 Montesquieu, C.L. de S. Persian letters. 6th ed. Edinburgh, 1773.
Htn 40526.34.9* Régulus, tragédie et la feinte par amour. Paris, 1773.
40536.21.9 Renou, M. Térée et Philomele. Amsterdam, 1773.
FL 6046.7.5 Rousseau, J.J. Emilius. Edinburgh, 1773. 3v.
FL 6046.7 Rousseau, J.J. Emilius or, A treatise of education. Edinburgh, 1773. 3v.
39583.3 Thomas, Antoine L. Oeuvres. Paris, 1773. 4v.
39545.35.8.9 Voltaire, François Marie Arouet de. Astérite, ou Les loix de minos. Genève, 1773.
Htn 39545.36.5* Voltaire, François Marie Arouet de. Candidus, or All for the best. London, 1773.
Htn 39545.37.32* Voltaire, François Marie Arouet de. L'enfant prodigue. Paris, 1773.
39541.5.4 Voltaire, François Marie Arouet de. Essais sur les moeurs et l'esprit des nations. Neuchâtel, 1773. 8v.
Htn 39545.76* Voltaire, François Marie Arouet de. Les loix de Minos. Genève, 1773.
39541.5.12 Voltaire, François Marie Arouet de. Mélanges de poésies. Neuchâtel, 1773.
39541.5.6 Voltaire, François Marie Arouet de. Mélanges philosophiques. Neuchâtel, 1773. 6v.

1774

39586.19.4 Chamfort, S.R.N. La jeune Indienne. Paris, 1774.
38571.5 Corneille, Pierre. Théâtre. Genève, 1774. 8v.
FL 379.174 Desprez de Boissy, Charles. Lettres sur les spectacles. 5e éd. Paris, 1774. 2v.
40526.34.31 Dorat, C.J. The fatal effects of inconstancy. London, 1774. 2v.
40517.23.25 Duclos, C.P. The pleasures of retirement preferable to the joys of dissipation. London, 1774.
Htn 40515.55* Fauques, Marianne Agnès de. The Vizirs. London, 1774. 3v.
40535.15.10 Favart, Charles S. Soliman Second. Avignon, 1774.
40535.19.15 Graffigny, Françoise d'Issembourg d'Happoncourt de. The Peruvian letters. London, 1774.
40536.10 Laujon, Pierre. Silvie. Opera en trois actes. Stockholm, 1774.
40517.46 Le Gouz de Gerland, B. Histoire de Lates. Corinthe, 1774.
40512.11.5 LeSage, Alain René. Adventures of Gil Blas. London, 1774. 2v.
Mol 246.5.8 Molière, Jean Baptiste Poquelin. Der Menschenfrind. Wien, 1774.
Mon 45.1F Montaigne, Michel de. Journal du voyage. Rome, 1774.
Mon 45.1.2F Montaigne, Michel de. Journal du voyage. Rome, 1774.
Mon 45.3 Montaigne, Michel de. Journal du voyage. Querlon. Rome, 1774. 3v.
Htn Mol 882.15* Rugarli, A. Il figlio de gran Turco. Parma, 1774.
Htn 39544.28.35* Voltaire, François Marie Arouet de. Lettre philosophique. Berlin, 1774.

1775

40515.1 Albert, Mlle. d'. Les confidences d'une jolie femme. pt. 1-4. Francfort, 1775.
Htn 40532.4* Beaumarchais, Pierre A.C. de. Le barbier de Séville. n.p., 1775. 3 pam.
37565.31.9 Chaudon, Louis M. Anti-dictionnaire philosophique. 4e éd. Paris, 1775. 2v.
FL 355.24 Clement, J.M.B. Anecdotes dramatiques. Paris, 1775. 3v.
40517.23.15 Duclos, C.P. A course of gallantries. v.1-2. London, 1775.
38554.325.50 Fénelon, F. de S. de la Mothe. Dialogues des morts anciens et modernes. Paris, 1775.
38543.16.5 La Rochefoucauld, François. Maxims and moral reflexions. London, 1775.
40517.31.30 Le Prince de Beaumont, M. The triumph of truth, or Memoirs of Mr. de la Villette. London, 1775. 2v.
39597.9 Marmontel, J.F. Contes moraux. Paris, 1775. 3v.
40516.50.4 Mercier, Louis S. L'an deux mille quatre cent quarante. Londres, 1775.
38576.34 Montfleury, Zacherie Jacob. Théâtre de Messieurs de Montfleury, père et fils. Paris, 1775. 4v.
Htn 40527.22.15* Saint-Lambert, Jean F. Les saisons. 7. éd. Amsterdam, 1775.
Mon 130.1 Talbert, François Xavier. Eloge de Michel de Montaigne. Londres, 1775.
39545.48.19 Voltaire, Franç3is Marie Arouet de. La pucelle d'Orleans. London, 1775.

1776

40517.5.20 Beauharnais, F.M. de C. Mélange de poésies fugitives et de prose sans conséquence. Amsterdam, 1776.
FL 355.25 Chamfort, Sébastien R.N. Dictionnaire dramatique. Paris, 1776.
38574.2.5 Corneille, Pierre. Théâtre. n.p., 1776. 10v.
40516.25 Deslandes, A.F.B. Réflexions sur les grands hommes. Amsterdam, 1776.
40526.34.70 Dorat, C.J. Les malheurs de l'inconstance. Neuchâtel, 1776.
40535.13.25 Falbaire de Quingey, C.G. Fenouillot de. L'école des moeurs. Paris, 1776.
Htn 38554.297* Fénelon, F. de S. de la Mothe. Les commandements de l'honnête homme. Paris, 1776.
40535.16.9 Gobemouche, Leonard. I.K.L. Essai dramatique. Montmartre, 1776.
Htn 39527.31.125* La Fontaine, Jean de. Fables en vers gascouns. Bayoune, 1776.
39535.33 L'enclos, Anne. The memoirs of Anne L'enclos. London, 1776.
39585.32 Lormberg, J.M. de. Mémorial d'un mondain. London, 1776.
38523.23 Malherbe, François de. Poésies de Malherbe. Paris, 1776.
40516.54 Mercier, Louis S. Eloges et discours philosophiques. Amsterdam, 1776.
Mol 860.11 Mercier, M. Molière drame en cinq actes. Amsterdam, 1776.
Mon 31.8 Montaigne, Michel de. Essays. Cotton. 8. ed. London, 1776. 3v.
40536.20 Piron, Alexis. Oeuvres complettes. Paris, 1776. 7v.
Htn 40524.30* Restif de la Bretonne, Nicolas E. La paysan perverti. v.1-4. Amsterdam, 1776. 2v.
FL 6057.2 Rousseau, J.J. Die neue Heloise. v.1-2,5-6. Leipzig, 1776.
40525.5.7 Tressan, L.E. Oeuvres diverses. Amsterdam, 1776.
40516.31 Vernes, Jacob. Confidence philosophique. Genève, 1776.
Htn 39545.71* Voltaire, François Marie Arouet de. Histoire de Jenni, ou Le sage et l'Athée par Sherloc (pseud.). Londres, 1776.
39541.5.14 Voltaire, François Marie Arouet de. Romans. Londres, 1776. 2v.

1777

40534.16.12 Cailleau, A.C. Clef du grand oeuvre, ou Lettres du Sancelrien Tourangeau. Corinte, 1777.
39533.9.4 Chapelle, C.E.L. Voyage de Chapelle et Bachaumont. Genève, 1777.
39532.16.05 Chaulieu, G.A. de. Oeuvres. La Haye, 1777. 2v.
40534.20.25 Collé, Charles. Théâtre de société. Paris, 1777. 3v.
39579.14 Congo, ou Nouvelle histoire politique et morale de la cacomonade. Aux Pays-Bas, 1777.
39585.27 Delacroix, J.V. Peinture des moeurs du siècle. Amsterdam, 1777. 2v.
FL 390.35 Desessarts, N.T.L. Les trois théâtres de Paris. Paris, 1777.
40526.34.20 Dorat, C.J. Poésies. Genève, 1777. 4v.
40535.8 Dorvigny, Louis A. De witte-neger; blyspel. Amsteldam? 1777.
39576.27.2 Éloge de l'enfer. 2. éd. London, 1777.
38553.16.90 Fénelon, F. de S. de la Mothe. Les aventures de Télémaque, fils d'Ulysse. Genève, 1777. 2v.
40535.19.4 Graffigny, Françoise d'Issembourg d'Happoncourt de. Lettres d'une peruvienne. Genève, 1777.
39544.58.35 Guénée, Antoine. Letters of certain Jews to Monsieur de Voltaire. Dublin, 1777. 2v.
40535.19.75 La Chaussée, Pierre Claude Nivelle de. Oeuvres. Paris, 1777. 5v.
39584.4 La Harpe, Jean François de. Oeuvres. Yverdon, 1777. 3v.
37595.2 Lettres...d'Héloise et d'Abeilard. Genève, 1777. 2v.
40526.66 Luchet, Mary de. Recueil de poésies. London, 1777.
38523.23.5 Malherbe, François de. Poésies. Genève, 1777.
Mol 860.12 Mercier, M. Molière drame en cinq actes. La Haye, 1777.
Mol 47.77 Molière, Jean Baptiste Poquelin. L'esprit de Molière. Londres, 1777. 2v.
39592.10 Montesquieu, C.L. de S. Complete works. v.2-4. Dublin, 1777. 3v.
40517.53.4 Mouhy, Charles de F. La paysame parvenue. Amsterdam, 1777. 4v.
37585.24 Pièces de théâtre. Paris, 1777-1808. 13v.
40536.20.07 Piron, Alexis. Oeuvres choisis de Piron. Genève, 1777. 2v.
40522.7 Prévost, Antoine F. P. Angloise ou Histoire de M. Cleveland. London, 1777. 6v.
Htn 38525.22.50* Régnier, Mathurin. Oeuvres. Genève, 1777. 2v.
FL 6040.77 Rousseau, J.J. Emile ou De l'éducation. Amsterdam, 1777.

1777 - cont.

40536.30.5 Sedaine, Michel Jean. Felix, ou L'enfant trouvé. Paris, 1777.
40526.67.5 Vadé, Jean Joseph. Oeuvres complettes. Genève, 1777. 4v.
39545.55.2 Voltaire, François Marie Arouet de. La pucelle d'Orleans. Genève, 1777.
39541.5.8 Voltaire, François Marie Arouet de. Questions sur l'encyclopedie. Neuchâtel, 1777.
39544.367 Zabuesnig, Johann Christoph von. Historische und kritische Nachrichten von dem Leben und den Schriften des Herrn von Voltaire und anderer Neuphilosophen unserer Zeiten. Augsburg, 1777. 2v.

1778

40517.7.3 Aulnoy, Marie C.J. de B. The earl of Douglas. 2. ed. v.1-3. Lyon, 1778.
40517.5.15 Beauharnais, F.M. de C. Lettres de Stéphanie. Paris, 1778. 3v.
40534.16.5 Chamfort, Sebastian. Mustapha et Zéangir. Paris, 1778.
40529.75.10 Clément, Jean Marie B. Satire sur la fausse philosophie. n.p., 1778.
40535.13.10 Falbaire de Quingey, C.G. Fenouillot de. Les Jammabos, ou Les moines japonais. Londres, 1778?
40535.15.4 Favart, Charles S. Les jeunes mariés. Paris, 1778? 3 pam.
39526.29.20 La Fontaine, Jean de. Fables choisies. Paris, 1778.
39584.6 La Harpe, Jean François de. Oeuvres. Paris, 1778. 6v.
FL 6127.78 Le Begue de Presle, A.G. Relation ou notice des derniers jours de monsieur Jean-Jacques Rousseau. London, 1778.
40535.30.15 Marivaux, Pierre Carlet de Chamblain de. La vie de Marianne. London, 1778. 4v.
40516.48 Mercier, Louis S. Théâtre complet. Amsterdam, 1778-1784. 4v.
Mol 216.53.3 Molière, Jean Baptiste Poquelin. Pseudoli follaciae...Münter. Cellis, 1778.
38587.4 Oeuvres de Regnard. Paris, 1778. 4v.
39585.12 Orbessan, Anne Marie d'Aignon. Mélanges historiques...de physique, de littérature et de poésie. v.3. Paris, 1778.
40524.24.15 Riccoboni, M.J.L. de (Mme.). Letters from Lord Rivers to Sir Charles Cardigan. London, 1778. 2v.
40536.22.8 Rosoy, B.F. de. Le réduction de Paris. Paris, 1778.
37533.17.10 Sabatier de Castras, A. Les trois siècles de la littérature. 5. éd. La Haye, 1778. 4v.
39584.35 Saint Foix, G.F.P. de. Oeuvres complètes. Paris, 1778. 6v.
Htn 39545.26* Voltaire, François Marie Arouet de. Miscellanies. Philadelphia, 1778.
39545.69.5 Voltaire, François Marie Arouet de. Zayre. Leipzig? 1778.

1779

40526.32.6 Bernis, François Joachim de Pierre de. Oeuvres complettes. Londres, 1779. 2v.
40534.14 Billard-Dumonceau, Edme. Voltaire apprécié; comédie. n.p., 1779?
40526.82 Boisard, Jean Jacques François Marius. Fables. Paris, 1779.
Mol 865.1 Cailhava d'Estendoux, Jean François. Discours prononcé par Molière. Amsterdam, 1779.
39585.26 Chassaigon, J.M. Cataractes de l'imagination. n.p., 1779. 3v.
40534.19 Colardeau, Charles P. Oeuvres choisies. Paris, 1779. 2v.
Htn 40517.22* Delaunay. Histoire d'un pou françois. 4. ed. Paris, 1779.
Htn 40517.23.5* Delaunay. History of a French louse. London, 1779.
Htn 40517.23.5.2* Delaunay. History of a French louse. 4. ed. London, 1779.
FL 379.179 Desprez de Boissy, Charles. Lettres sur les spectacles. 7e éd. Paris, 1779. 2v.
FL 6137.79 Eloge de Mr. Rousseau de Genève. n.p., 1779.
40517.24 Feutry, M. Choix d'histoires tirées. London, 1779. 2v.
40526.10 Gresset, Jean B. Oeuvres. London, 1779.
40512.2.25 LeSage, Alain René. Le diable boiteux. v.1-2. Paris, 1779.
40512.47 LeSage, Alain René. Gil Blas von Santillana. Berlin, 1779. 6v.
40535.29.9 Marivaux, Pierre Carlet de Chamblain de. Le paysan parvenu. La Haye, 1779.
39597.10 Marmontel, J.F. Contes moraux. Amsterdam, 1779. 3v.
Mon 17.79 Montaigne, Michel de. Essais. Coste. Genève, 1779. 10v.
38527.35.10 Née de La Rochelle. Vie d'Etienne Dolet. Paris, 1779.
40536.14.5 Palissot de Montenoy, Charles. Oeuvres complètes. London, 1779. 7v.
Htn 40524.19.50* Raby. Le viellard abyssin rencontré. Paris, 1779.
38582.4 Racine, Jean. Oeuvres. Paris, 1779. 3v.
40527.21.10 Roucher, Jean Antoine. Les mois; poëme en douze chants. Paris, 1779. 2v.
Htn FL 6127.79* Rousseau, J.J. Ancedotes...suite du supplément. 2. éd. Amsterdam, 1779.
FL 6065.3.8 Rousseau, J.J. A complete dictionary of music. 2. ed. Dublin, 1779.
FL 6065.4 Rousseau, J.J. Dictionnaire de musique. 2. éd. London, 1779.
FL 6006.2 Rousseau, J.J. Philosophische Werke. Reval, 1779. 3v.
FL 6091.50 Rousseau, J.J. Pygmalion...from the Franch. London, 1779.
FL 398.78 Sainval, (Mlle.). Lettres de Madame la contesse de Mal. Paris, 1779.
39544.14.5 Vita del Signor di Voltaire...di lui opere. Londra, 1779.
Htn 39545.45.25* Voltaire, François Marie Arouet de. L'Enriade. Augusta, 1779.
Htn 39545.37.20.5* Voltaire, François Marie Arouet de. Eriphile. Paris, 1779.
39543.15 Voltaire, François Marie Arouet de. Works. London, 1779-80. 5v.

178-

40517.54.10 La Place, P.A. de. Le supplice des cloches. n.p., 178-?

1780

X Cg 37595.2.5 Abailard, P. Lettres et épitres amoureuses d'Héloise et d'Abeilard. Londres, 1780. 2v.
FL 6127.80 Artaud, Giuseppe. Emilio religioso opposto all' Emilio ateo negativo di Gian Giacomo Rousseau. Pesaro, 1780.
39586.2 Bachaumont, Louis Petit de. Mémoires secrets. v.1-36. London, 1780-89. 18v.
40517.5.7 Beauharnais, F.M. de C. L'Abailard supposé, ou sentiment à l'épreuve. Amsterdam, 1780.
38565.6.9 Boileau Despréaux, Nicolas. Oeuvres. Londres, 1780. 2v.
FL 6137.80 Bruny, de. Lettre sur Jean-Jacques Rousseau. Genève, 1780.
40526.34.35 Dorat, C.J. Mélanges de poésies fugitives. Paris, 1780.
40535.19.50 Hele, T. Les événements imprevus. Paris, 1780.
39544.365 La Roche de Maine, Jean Pierre. Histoire littéraire de Monsieur de Voltaire. Cassel, 1780. 3v.
40516.68 Maquin. Je ne sçais quoi. n.p., 1780.
Mol 266.1.5 Molière, Jean Baptiste Poquelin. Le sicilien. Laval. n.p., 1780.
40536.24.5 Ramond de Carbonnierès, L.F.E. La guerre d'Alsace pendant le grand schisme d'occident. Basle, 1780.
X Cg 38525.26.26 Régnier, Mathurin. Oeuvres. 9. éd. Londres, 1780. 2v.
FL 6040.80 Rousseau, J.J. Émile ou De l'éducation. Genève, 1780. 4v.
X Cg FL 6040.80.2 Rousseau, J.J. Émile ou De l'éducation. Londres, 1780-81. 4v.
Htn FL 6095.3* Rousseau, J.J. Juge de Jean-Jacques. Dialogue. Lichfield, 1780.
Htn FL 6095.2* Rousseau, J.J. Juge de Jean-Jacques. Dialogue. London, 1780.
37558.9 Ticknesse, Ann. Sketches of the ladies of France. London, 1780. 3v.
Htn 39541.1* Voltaire, François Marie Arouet de. The maid of Orleans. London, 1780.
39545.24.3 Voltaire, François Marie Arouet de. The works of Voltaire. London, 1780. 10v.

1781

40517.5.35 Beauharnais, F.M. de C. L'aveugle par amour. Paris, 1781.
38566.6 Boileau Despréaux, Nicolas. Poésies. Paris, 1781.
Mon 122.1 Bricaire de la Dixmerie, Nicolas. Eloge analytique historique de Montaigne. Amsterdam, 1781.
Htn 40534.16.9* Cailhava d'Estendoux, J.F. Théâtre. Paris, 1781-82. 2v.
Htn 37578.30* Contes à rire. Paris, 1781. 3v.
Htn 40517.23* Delaunay. Histoire d'un pou françoise. Paris, 1781.
40535.12.180 Dufresnes. Idylles et pièces fugitives. Paris, 1781.
38554.1.9 Fénelon, F. de S. de la Mothe. The adventures of Telemachus. 7th ed. Rouen, 1781.
40516.18 Fromaget, N. Le cousin de Mahomet. Constantin, 1781. 2v.
40588.10 Genlis, S.F.D. de St. Theatre of education. London, 1781. 4v.
Mol 860.5 Goldini, C. Scelta delle commedie di Goldini. Lipsia, 1781.
39527.8.7 La Fontaine, Jean de. Contes et nouvelles en vers. London, 1781.
38543.16.10 La Rochefoucauld, François. Maxims and moral reflexions. London, 1781.
40529.31 Maréchal, Pierre S. Ad majorem gloriam virtutis. Atheopolis, 1781.
40535.25.9 Marivaux, Pierre Carlet de Chamblain de. Oeuvres complettes. Paris, 1781. 12v.
Htn Mon 17.81* Montaigne, Michel de. Les essais de Michel de Montaigne. Amsterdam, 1781. 3v.
40534.4 Opéras-comiques. Paris, 1781-1827.
40522.7.9 Prévost, Antoine F. Histoire de Manon Lescaut et du chevalier des Grieux. Paris, 1781. 2v.
38585.32 Racine, Jean. Ifigenia in Aulis. Amsterdam, 1781.
Htn 40524.28.2* Restif de la Bretonne, Nicolas E. Les contemporaines. v.1-42. Leipzip, 1781-92. 21v.
Htn 40524.29.5* Restif de la Bretonne, Nicolas E. La decouverte australe par un homme volant. Leipzig, 1781. 4v.
40536.21.55 Rochon de Chabannes, Marc Antoine Jacques. La tribu. Strasbourg, 1781.
FL 6002.781 Rousseau, J.J. Mélanges. Tome. 2-3. Berne, 1781. 2v.
FL 6050.81 Rousseau, J.J. La nouvelle Héloise. v.2-7. London, 1781. 6v.
FL 6001.781.2 Rousseau, J.J. Oeuvres posthumes. Genève, 1781. 3v.
FL 6003.2 Rousseau, J.J. Traites sur la musique. Genève, 1781.
40536.27 Saint-Marc, J.P.A. Oeuvres. Paris, 1781. 3v.
40536.35 Villemain d'Abancourt, J.F. Proverbes dramatiques. Berlin, 1781.
Htn 39545.35.7* Voltaire, François Marie Arouet de. Alzire, of de Amerikanen. Amsterdam, 1781.
39545.30.25 Voltaire, François Marie Arouet de. Romans et contes. London, 1781. 4v.

1782

Htn 40517.10* Berquin, Arnaud. L'ami des enfans. London, 1782-83. 12v.
40526.29.5 Boufflers, Stanislas de. Oeuvres. Londres, 1782.
40517.80.10 Caumont de la Force, Charlotte R. de. Histoire secrete de Bourgogne. Paris, 1782. 3v.
Htn 40517.44.3* Choderlos de Laclos, Pierre A.F. Les liaisons dangereuses. pt.1-4. Amsterdam, 1782. 2v.
40515.5.30 D'Epinay, Louise F. Les conversations d'Émilie. Paris, 1782. 2v.
Htn 40529.19* Etrennes gaillades. Lampsaque, 1782.
38558.5 Fléchier, Esprit. Oeuvres. Nimes, 1782. 10v.
40536.4 Le Blanc, J.B. Manco-Capac, premier ynca du Pérou. Paris, 1782.
37575.5 M.P.D.L. Recueil d'épitaphes. Bruxelles, 1782. 3v.
37572.6 Masson, Arthur. Nouveau recueil de pièces. Edinburgh, 1782.
FL 393.27 Mayeur de Saint Paul, F.M. Le chroniqueur désoeuvre. 2. éd. Londres, 1782. 2v.
FL 393.26 Mayeur de Saint Paul, F.M. Le désoeuvré. Londres, 1782.
Mol 860.13 Mercier, M. Molière à la nouvelle salle. Paris, 1782.

1782 - cont.

	40517.53.7	Mouhy, Charles de F. The fortunate country maid. London, 1782.
Htn	40536.10.19*	Noverre, J.G. Historical account of Adela of Ponthieu. London, 1782.
	40536.15	Palissot de Montenoy, Charles. L'écueil des moeurs, comédie. Paris, 1782.
	40536.22.9	Rosoy, B.F. de. Richard III. Paris, 1782.
	FL 6001.782	Rousseau, J.J. Collection complette des oeuvres. v.1-24. Deux-Ponts, 1782. 12v.
Htn	FL 6020.82*	Rousseau, J.J. Les confessions suivies à des rèveries. Genève, 1782. 2v.
	FL 6020.82.5	Rousseau, J.J. Les confessions suivies à des rèveries. Genève, 1782-89. 4v.
	FL 6063.2	Rousseau, J.J. Considerations sur le gouvernement de Pologne. London, 1782.
	FL 6030.82	Rousseau, J.J. Du contrat social ou Principes du droit politique. London, 1782.
X Cg	FL 6002.782.3	Rousseau, J.J. Mélanges. London, 1782. 6v.
	FL 6002.782	Rousseau, J.J. Pièces diverses. London, 1782. 4v.
	FL 6001.782.2	Rousseau, J.J. Supplement à la collection des oeuvres. v.25-30. Deux-Ponts, 1782. 3v.
	FL 6003.3	Rousseau, J.J. Traites sur la musique. Deux-Ponts, 1782.
	40536.30	Sedaine, Michel Jean. Aucassin et Nicolette. Paris, 1782.
	39545.33	Voltaire, François Marie Arouet de. Pièces fugitives de Voltaire. London, 1782.

1783

	39586.3	Bachaumont, Louis Petit de. Mémoires secrets...des lettres en France. London, 1783.
	37583.383	Baudrais, J. Petite bibliothèque des théâtres. v.2-6. Paris, 1783-84. 5v.
	40529.8	Boudouin de Guemadene. L'espion de balisé. London, 1783.
	40526.61	Cerutti, G.A.G. L'aigle et le hibou. Glascow, 1783.
	39545.17.25	Ehrenborg, M. Reponse à la lettre qu'un citoyen. Lund, 1783.
	38553.16.95	Fénelon, F. de S. de la Mothe. Les aventures de Télémaque, fils d'Ulysse. Ulm, 1783.
	40588.11	Genlis, S.F.D. de St. Théâtre à l'usage des jeunes personnes. v.4. Paris, 1783.
	40588.19	Genlis, S.F.D. de St. Théâtre de société. Dublin, 1783.
	39532.5.2	Hamilton, Anthony. Memoires du comte de Grammont. London, 1783.
	38543.29.5	La Mothe le Vayer, F. de. La philosophie de La Mothe le Vayer. Paris, 1783.
	38543.17	La Rochefoucauld, François. Maxims and moral reflexions. Edinburgh, 1783.
	40535.20.9	Leblanc de Guillet, Antoine Blanc. Les druides; tragédie. Saint-Petersbourg, 1783.
	Mon 28.37	Montaigne, Michel de. L'esprit de Montaigne. Londres, 1783. 2v.
Htn	39592.12*	Montesquieu, C.L. de S. Oeuvres posthumes. London, 1783.
Htn	40517.52*	Mouhy, Charles de F. Les mille et une faveurs. London, 1783. 5v.
	40526.41	Le pot-pourri. London, 1783.
	40524.23	Riccoboni, M.J.L. de (Mme.). Histoire de Christine, reine de Suabe; et celle d'Aloise de Livarot. Histoire d'Enguerrand et celle des amours de Gertrude. Paris, 1783.
	FL 6029.5	Servan, A.J.M. de. Réflexions sur les Confessions de Jean-Jacques Rousseau. Hambourg, 1783.
	40516.29	Vasse, C.P.B.W. de. L'art de corriger...les hommes. London, 1783.
	39541.5.10	Voltaire, François Marie Arouet de. Siècle de Louis XIV. Neuchâtel, 1783. 4v.
	39541.5.2	Voltaire, François Marie Arouet de. Théâtre. Neuchâtel, 1783. 8v.

1784

	FL 370.5	Baudrais, Jean. Essais...sur l'art dramatique en France. Paris, 1784-86.
	FL 397.7.29	Besançon, France. Laws, statutes, etc. Ordonnance et réglement concernant la police des spectacles de la ville de Besançon. Paris? 1784.
	37585.12	Bibliothèque des théâtres. v.4,5,10,11,12,29,31,35,36,38,39,40. Paris, 1784- 12v.
	FL 6029.6	Chas, F. Jean-Jacques Rousseau justifié ou Réponse à M. Servan. Neuchâtel, 1784.
	40529.75.20	Clément, Jean Marie B. Le cri d'un citoyen, satire. Paris, 1784.
	40516.33	Confessions d'un courtisane. London, 1784.
	40516.44	Doray de Longrais, Jean Paul. Faustin. Amsterdam, 1784.
	40535.11.5	Ducis, Jean F. Le roi Lear. Paris, 1784.
	40535.13.9.5	Faur, Louis F. L'amour à l'épreuve. Paris, 1784.
X Cg	40515.31.7	Florian, Jean P.C. de. Galatée. Genève, 1784.
Htn	40515.18.50*	Florian, Jean P.C. de. Les six nouvelles de M. de Florian. Paris, 1784.
	40517.29	La Roche du Maint, J.P.L. de. Olinde. n.p., 1784.
NEDL	40517.30.10	La Roche du Maint, J.P.L. de. Le vicomte de Barjac. v.1-2. Paris, 1784.
	37565.22.25	Lycée de Paris, club littéraire. Paris, 1784.
	40535.40	Mayeur de Saint Paul, François Marie. Jeanne Hachette, ou Le siège de Beauvais. Paris, 1784.
	40516.47	Mercier, Louis S. Mon bonnet de nuit. Amsterdam, 1784. 2v.
Htn	Mol 17.84*	Molière, Jean Baptiste Poquelin. Oeuvres. Londres, 1784. 7v.
X Cg	39594.11.20	Montesquieu, C.L. de S. Lettres persanes. London, 1784. 2v.
	39592.13	Montesquieu, C.L. de S. Oeuvres. v.1-8. Deux-Ponts, 1784. 5v.
	38557.25	Oeuvres choisies de Bossuet. Nimes, 1784. 10v.
	40524.18	Perreau, J.A. Le roi voyageur. London, 1784.
	37585.11	Petite bibliothèque des théâtres. Théâtre italien. Paris, 1784- 6v.
	40524.23.15	Riccoboni, M.J.L. de (Mme.). The history of Christina, princess of Swabia. London, 1784. 2v.
X Cg	FL 6056.4.5	Rousseau, J.J. Eloisa. London, 1784. 4v.
	38546.38.5	Sévigné, Marie de R.C. Recueil des lettres...à...sa fille. Rouen, 1784. 10v.
	40524.1	Tencin, Claudine A.G de. Mémoires du Comte de Comminge. London, 1784.
	39544.25.5	Voltaire, François Marie Arouet de. Memoirs of the life of Voltaire. London, 1784.
	39551.3	Voltaire, François Marie Arouet de. Oeuvres complètes. n.p., 1784. 72v.

1785

	37558.72	Alembert, J.L. d'. Histoire des membres de l'Académie française. Paris, 1785-87. 6v.
	40525.26	Aventures singulieres d'un voyageur aérien mises au jour par M. J***. v.1-2. Londres, 1785.
Htn	40532.6.2*	Beaumarchais, Pierre A.C. de. La folle journée, ou Le mariage de Figaro. n.p., 1785.
Htn	40532.6*	Beaumarchais, Pierre A.C. de. La folle journée, ou Le mariage de Figaro. n.p., 1785.
Htn	40532.6.4*	Beaumarchais, Pierre A.C. de. La folle journée, ou Le mariage de Figaro. Paris, 1785.
	37585.13	Comédies françaises. A collection. Paris, 1785-1800. 20v.
Htn	40534.25*	Crébillon, Prosper Jolyot de. Oeuvres complètes. Paris, 1785. 3v.
Htn	38553.19.3F*	Fénelon, F. de S. de la Mothe. Les aventures de Télémaque. Paris, 1785. 2v.
	40526.9.3	Gresset, Jean B. Oeuvres. London, 1785. 2v.
	39576.46	L'hermite philosophe, ou Lettres et réflexions. n.p., 1785.
	40529.40	Junquieres, J.B. de. Caquet-Bonbec, la poule à ma tante. n.p., 1785.
Htn	37575.4*	La Place, Antoine de. Pieces intéressantes. Brussels, 1785-90. 8v.
	FL 6137.85	Le Gros, Charles F. Analyse des ouvrages de Jean-Jacques Rousseau de Genève. Genève, 1785.
	40535.28.5	Marivaux, Pierre Carlet de Chamblain de. La surprise de l'amour français; comédie. Paris, 1785.
	38583.10	Racine, Jean. Letters from Mons. Racine...to his son. London, 1785.
	38546.34	Sévigné, Marie de R.C. Recueil des lettres. Paris, 1785. 8v.
	37542.6	Taillefer, Antoine. Tableau historique de l'ésprit et du caractère des littérateurs français. Versailles, 1785. 4v.
	39551.5	Voltaire, François Marie Arouet de. Oeuvres complètes. n.p., 1785. 92v.
	39543.17	Voltaire, François Marie Arouet de. Oeuvres complètes de Voltaire. v.1-32,34-35,37-46,48-70. Kehl, 1785-89. 67v.

1786

	39582.25	Arnaud, F.T.M. de B. Warbeck. London, 1786. 2v.
	40517.5	Beauharnais, F.M. de C. Le somnambule. Paris, 1786.
Htn	38528.16*	Béroalde de Verville. Le moyen de parvenir. London, 1786. 3v.
	40515.2.4	Bitaubé, P.J. Joseph. 4. éd. Paris, 1786.
	40529.75	Clément, Jean Marie B. Satires. Amsterdam, 1786.
	39586.20	Constant de Rebecque, Samuel. Laure. v.6. Genève, 1786.
	39544.290	Duvernet, T.I. La vie de Voltaire. Genève, 1786.
	40515.21	Florian, Jean P.C. de. Mélanges de poésies et de littérature. Paris, 1786.
	40515.42.5	Florian, Jean P.C. de. Numa Pompelius, second roi de Rome. Paris, 1786. 2v.
	40588.20.5	Genlis, S.F.D. de St. Sacred dramas. London, 1786.
X Cg	40517.50	Lamorlière, J.R. de. Angola. Histoire indienne. London, 1786. 2v.
	40517.30	La Roche du Maint, J.P.L. de. Mémoires de Madame de Baudéon. Strassbourg, 1786.
	FL 6137.86	Le Gros, Charles F. Examen des systèmes de Jean-Jacques Rousseau de Genève. Genève, 1786.
NEDL	40516.17	Mayer, Charles Joseph de. Geneviève de Cournouailles et le damoisel sans nom. London, 1786.
Htn	FL 6132.2.2*	Mémoires de Mme. de Warens et de Claude Anet. Chambery, 1786.
	FL 6132.2	Mémoires de Mme. de Warens suivis de ceux de Claude Anet. Chambery, 1786.
	40516.50.10	Mercier, Louis S. L'an deux mille quatre cent quarante. n.p., 1786. 3v.
Htn	Mol 17.86.3*	Molière, Jean Baptiste Poquelin. Oeuvres...Bret. Paris, 1786. 8v.
Htn	Mol 17.86*	Molière, Jean Baptiste Poquelin. Oeuvres...Bret. v.1-6,8. Paris, 1786. 7v.
	40588.25	Montolieu, I.P. de. Caroline de Lichtfield. Londres, 1786. 2v.
	40525.34	Nouvelles folies sentimentales. Paris, 1786.
	40524.21	Riccoboni, M.J.L. de (Mme.). Oeuvres complettes. v.1-2,4-8. Paris, 1786. 7v.
	40536.21.50	Rochon de Chabannes, Marc Antoine Jacques. Théâtre, suivi de quelques pièces fugitives. Paris, 1786. 2v.
	40536.22	Ronsin, Charles P. Théâtre. Paris, 1786.
	40527.21	Roucher, M. Maximilien-Jules-Leopold Duc de Brunswick-Lunebourg. Paris, 1786.
	FL 6002.786	Rousseau, J.J. Pensées de J.J. Rousseau. London, 1786. 2v.
	39534.27	Scarron, Paul. Oeuvres. Paris, 1786. 7v.
	37548.5	Senebier, Jean. Histoire littéraire de Genève. Genève, 1786. 3v.
	38546.34.2	Sévigné, Marie de R.C. Recueil des lettres. v.1-9. Paris, 1786. 7v.

1787

	40517.5.45	Beauharnais, F.M. de C. Les amans l'autrefois. Paris, 1787. 3v.
	40517.5.55	Beauharnais, F.M. de C. La fausse inconstance, ou Le triomphe de l'honnêteté. Paris, 1787.
	40532.8	Beaumarchais, Pierre A.C. de. Tarare, an opera. London, 1787.
	40534.10	Belloy, Pierre L.B. Oeuvres complètes. Paris, 1787. 6v.
	40534.10.9	Belloy, Pierre L.B. Le siege de Calais. Paris, 1787.
	38576.11.6	Brueys, D.A. de. Choix de pieces de théâtre de Brueys et Palaprat. Londres, 1787.
	39585.22.5	Caraccioli, L.A. Entretiens du Palais-Royal. Utrecht, 1787. 2v.
	40517.1	Caylus, Anne C.P. Oeuvres badines complettes. Amsterdam, 1787.
	39586.19.5	Chamfort, S.R.N. La jeune Indienne. Paris, 1787.
	Mol 860.14	Desbarreaux, P. Molière à Toulouse. Toulouse, 1787.
	40535.8.100	Dubuisson, P.N. Trasime et timagene. Paris, 1787.
	41584.27.16	Dumaniant, A.J. Diamond cut diamond. London, 1787.
	39545.17	Dupanloup, F.A.P. Lettres à les membres du conseil municipal de Paris "centenaire de Voltaire." Paris, 1787.
	40515.21.5	Florian, Jean P.C. de. Mélanges de poésies et de littérature. Genève, 1787.

Chronological Listing

1787 - cont.

Htn 40515.21.3* Florian, Jean P.C. de. Mélanges de poésies et de littérature. Paris, 1787.
40515.18.53 Florian, Jean P.C. de. Les six nouvelles de M. de Florian. 3e éd. Genève, 1787.
40515.48.10 Florian, Jean P.C. de. Théâtre. Genève, 1787. 3v.
40535.15.14 Forgeot, Nicolas. Les dettes; comedie. Paris, 1787.
40588.14 Genlis, S.F.D. de St. Tales of the the castle. 3. ed. London, 1787. 5v.
39586.34 Grosley, P.J. Mémoires de l'académie des sciences...satire. Troyes, 1787.
40526.52 Le Suire, Robert M. Le philosophe parvenu. London, 1787.
40535.23.15 Lougueil. L'orphelin anglais. Toulouse, 1787.
39597.3 Marmontel, J.F. Oeuvres complètes. Paris, 1787. 17v.
40588.24 Montolieu, I.P. de. Caroline de Lichtfield. Londres, 1787. 2v.
38552.2 Oeuvres de Fénelon. Paris, 1787-92. 9v.
FL 6127.87 Réfléxions philosophiques et impartiales sur Rousseau. Genève, 1787.
FL 6062.49 Rousseau, J.J. Letters on the elements of botany. Addressed to a lady. 2. ed. London, 1787.
40516.9 Saint-Clair. Les égaremens d'un philosophe. Genève, 1787. 2v.

1788

FL 6005.2 The beauties of Rousseau, selected by a lady. London, 1788. 2v.
40517.15 Berquin, Arnaud. L'amico de fanciulli. London, 1788-89. 4v.
38566.6.5 Boileau Despréaux, Nicolas. Oeuvres. Paris, 1788. 3v.
37572.5.5 Chef d'oeuvres politiques et littéraires de la fin du 18e siècle. Paris, 1788.
Mol 860.16 Cubières, Michel de. La mort de Molière. Londres, 1788.
40535.13.50 Dénonciation au public à l'occasion quelques écrits anonymes. Paris, 1788.
40535.13.5 Duveyrier, H. La cour pléniére. Paris, 1788.
40535.13.2 Duveyrier, H. La cour pléniére. Paris, 1788.
40535.13 Duveyrier, H. La cour pléniére. Paris, 1788.
40535.13.7 Duveyrier, H. Supplément à la cour pléniére. Baville, 1788.
40515.42 Florian, Jean P.C. de. Look before you leap. London, 1788.
Htn 38562.18* Fontenelle, B. Le B. de. République des philosophes. Geneva, 1788.
39544.1 Gibert, M.E. Obiero sur les écrits de M. de Voltaire. London, 1788. 2v.
40535.16.45 Gorsas, A.J. Le grand-bailliage. Harcourt, 1788.
Mol 860.15 Gouges, Marie Olympe de. Molière chez Ninon. Paris, 1788.
40526.9.5 Gresset, Jean B. Oeuvres. Rouen, 1788. 2v.
38543.18 La Rochefoucauld, François. Maxims and moral reflexions. London, 1788.
39586.10.10 Le Gros, C.F. Analyse et examen de l'antiquité devoilée. Genève, 1788.
40537.48 Le lever de Bâville. Rome, 1788.
39576.20 Maimieux, J. Éloge...de l'impertinence. Abdère, 1788.
40535.30.50 Marivaux, Pierre Carlet de Chamblain de. Le legs. Paris, 1788.
Htn Mol 17.88* Molière, Jean Baptiste Poquelin. Oeuvres...Bret. Paris, 1788. 6v.
Mol 17.88.3 Molière, Jean Baptiste Poquelin. Oeuvres...vie par Voltaire. Berlin, 1788-91. 6v.
Mol 17.88.2 Molière, Jean Baptiste Poquelin. Oeuvres de Molière. Paris, 1788. 6v.
39594.7.5 Montesquieu, C.L. de S. Der Geist des herrn von Montesquieu. Basel, 1788.
40536.14 Palissot de Montenoy, Charles. Oeuvres. Paris, 1788. 4v.
FL 6001.788 Rousseau, J.J. Oeuvres completes. v.1-38. n.p., 1788-93. 37v.
FL 6057.3 Rousseau, J.J. Romane. Neue Heloise. Leipzig, 1788. 3v.
40536.30.6 Sedaine, Michel Jean. A key to the lock. London, 1788.

1789

FL 6117.89 Barruel-Beauvert, Antoine Joseph. Vie de Jean-Jacques Rousseau. London, 1789.
40517.14 Berquin, Arnaud. L'ami de l'adolescence. Paris, 1789.
FL 6039.2 Berthier, P.G.F. Observations sur le Contrat social. Paris, 1789.
40534.17.10.5 Bonnay, François. La prise des annonciades. Paris? 1789?
40534.17.10.7 Bonnay, François. La prise des annonciades. v.1-2. Paris? 1789?
40531.14 Bonneville, N. de. L'année, MDCCLXXIX. Paris, 1789?
40531.15 Boutillier, Maximilien Jean. Le souper d'Henri IV. Paris, 1789.
40531.15.250 Brizard, Gabriel. La destruction de l'Aristocratisme. Chantilly, 1789.
40537.39 La chasse a la grand bête. Mayence, 1789.
41593.26.5 Delille, J. The garden. London, 1789.
40537.60 La disolation des procureurs. Paris, 1789.
40535.8.5 Dorvigny, Louis A. Les noces du pere Duchesne. Paris, 1789.
40515.42.3 Florian, Jean P.C. de. Look before you leap. Dublin, 1789.
Mol 194.18 L'impressario in angustie. Milano, 1789.
40517.30.5 La Roche du Maint, J.P.L. de. Analyse raisonnée de la sagesse de Charron. London, 1789. 2v.
40517.31.8 Le Prince de Beaumont, M. Magasin des adolescentes. v.1-4. Bruxelles, 1789. 2v.
FL 6137.89 Lettres sur les ouvrages et caractère de Jean-Jacques Rousseau. Lausanne, 1789.
39576.21 Maimieux, J. Souvenirs d'un homme du monde. v. 1-2. Leipzig, 1789.
40516.53.15 Mercier, Louis S. Charles II, roi d'Angleterre en certain lieu. Venise, 1789.
Mol 860.17 Mercier, M. La maison de Molière. Paris, 1789.
Mol 269.30.3 Molière, Jean Baptiste Poquelin. De Huigchelaar. Tartuffe. Amsterdam, 1789.
FL 379.189 Parises, N.P. Questions importantes sur la comédie de nos jours. Valenciennes, 1789.
40536.21.5 Poinsinet de Sivry, M. Caton d'utique. Paris, 1789.
38582.5 Racine, Jean. Oeuvres. Paris, 1789. 3v.

1789 - cont.

38587.4.10 Regnard, Jean François. Oeuvres. Paris, 1789-90. 4v.
FL 6002.789 Rousseau, J.J. Pensées. Genève, 1789. 2v.
Htn 39594.32.10* St. Pierre, J.H.B. de. Paul and Mary. Dublin, 1789.
Htn 39596.14* St. Pierre, J.H.B. de. Voeux d'un solitaire, pour servir de suite aux Études de la nature. Paris, 1789.
Htn FL 6137.98* Stael, de (Mrs.). Lettres, ouvrages et caractère de Jean-Jacques Rousseau. 2. éd. Lausanne, 1789.
FL 6137.89.5 Straël-Holstein, A.L. Lettres sur les ouvrages et le caractère de Jean-Jacques Rousseau. n.p., 1789.
FL 6137.89.2 Straël-Holstein, A.L. Lettres sur les ouvrages et le caractère de Rousseau. 2. éd. n.p., 1789.
40524.2.6 Tencin, Claudine A.G. de. Louise de Valrose; ou Mémoires d'une autrichienne. v.1-2. Paris, 1789.
40537.49 Le triomphe du tiers-état. n.p., 1789.

179-

41583.9.15 Barré, Pierre y. La chaste Suzanne. Paris? 179-.
40531.6.28 Barthès de Marmorieres, Antoine. Le martyre de Marie-Antoinette. n.p., 179-?
40534.17.10.9 Bonnay, François. Expedition du général Lamethore. La prise des annonciades. Paris? 179-.
40534.17.10.15 Bonnay, François. La prise des annonciades. 5. éd. Paris? 179-?
40536.4.75 Lebeau de Schosne, A.T.V. L'assemblée. Paris? 179-.
40512.2.40 LeSage, Alain René. The devil upon two sticks. London, 179-.
40538.25 Une matinée du Luxembourg. Paris, 179-.
40537.44 Le Vicomte de Barjolean. n.p., 179-?

1790

40537.38 L'attentat de Versailles. Genève, 1790.
40534.17.10.12 Bonnay, François. La prise des annonciades. 2. éd. Paris? 1790?
38557.52.35 Bossuet, J.B. An exposition of the doctrine of the Catholic Church in matters of controversy. London, 1790.
40531.15.255 Brizard, Gabriel. Les imitateurs de Charles Neuf. Paris, 1790.
40535.15.25 Carbon Flins des Oliviers, C.M.L.E. Le reveil d'épiménide, à Paris. Toulouse, 1790.
40537.11.12 Chénier, Marie Joseph. Charles IX ou L'école des rois. Beaucaire, 1790.
40534.23.265 Collot d'Herbois, J.M. La famille patriote. Paris, 1790.
40534.23.255 Collot d'Herbois, J.M. La famille patriote. Paris, 1790.
40534.23.260 Collot d'Herbois, J.M. Le paysan magistrat. Paris, 1790.
39545.3 Condorcet, Marie Jean A.N.C. Life of Voltaire. v.2. London, 1790.
40537.37 Les confidences aux états généraux. n.p., 1790.
40537.70 Eloisa de Clairville. London, 1790. 2v.
40535.14.9 Fabre d'Eglantine, P.F.N. Théâtre. Le Présomptueux. Paris, 1790. 5 pam.
Htn 38553.19.4* Fénelon, F. de S. de la Mothe. Les aventures de Télémaque. Paris, 1790. 2v.
40515.42.9 Florian, Jean P.C. de. The adventures of Numa Pompelius. Brussels, 1790.
40535.16 Gardel, Pierre Gabriel. Télémaque dans l'Isle de Calipso. Paris, 1790.
40526.28 Guyétand, M. Poésies diverses. Paris, 1790.
40535.19.30 Imbert, B. Marie de Brabant. Paris, 1790.
40537.41 La journée des dupes. n.p., 1790.
40516.77 Laveaux, J.C.T. de. Euseb. Wien, 1790.
40536.2.100 Laya, Jean L. Les dangers de l'opinion. Paris, 1790.
39544.2 Linguet, Simon N.H. Critical analysis...of Voltaire's works. London, 1790.
40529.31.10 Maréchal, Pierre S. Nouvelle légende dorée, ou Dictionnaire des saintes. Rome, 1790. 2v.
40537.43 Naissance de très-haute, très-puissante et très-désirée madame constitution. n.p., 1790.
FL 395.110 Observations pour les comédiens français, sur petition adressée par les auteurs dramatiques. Paris, 1790.
FL 395.127 Observations pour les comédiens françois, ordinaries du Roi occupant le théâtre de la nation. Paris, 1790.
38562.16A Oeuvres de Fontenelle. Paris, 1790-92. 8v.
40531.10 Puységur, Armand Marie Jacques de Chastenet. La journée des dupes. n.p., 1790.
40531.10.5 Puységur, Armand Marie Jacques de Chastenet. La journée des dupes. n.p., 1790.
40537.47 Les quatres préjugés du ministre. n.p., 1790.
37581.42 Théâtre contemporain, 1790-1853. Paris, 1790-1853.
40537.46 Théroigne et populus. London, 1790.

1791

40517.5.9 Beauharnais, F.M. de C. L'Abailard supposé. Lyon, 1791.
41583.12.9 Beffroy De Reigny, L.A. Le club des bonnes-gens. Paris, 1791.
41583.12.7 Beffroy De Reigny, L.A. Nicodème dans la lune. Paris, 1791.
37583.385 Billardon de Sauvigny, L.E. Vashington; ou La liberté du nouveau monde, tragédie en quatré actes. Paris, 1791. 5 pam.
40538.5 La Blanchisseuse de Mousseaux. Paris, 1791.
Htn 40534.16.10* Cailhava d'Estendoux, J.F. Les Menechmes grecs. Paris, 1791.
40535.15.29 Carbon Flins des Oliviers, C.M.L.E. Le mari directeur. Paris, 1791.
40534.23.250 Collot d'Herbois, J.M. Les porte-feuilles comedie. Paris, 1791.
41584.27.20 Dumaniant, A.J. Le soldat Prussien. Paris, 1791.
40535.12.200 Dupuis. L'artiste patriote. Paris, 1791.
40535.14.17 Fabre d'Eglantine, P.F.N. Le collatéral. Paris, 1791.
40535.14.11 Fabre d'Eglantine, P.F.N. Le convalescent de qualité. Paris, 1791.
40588.21 Genlis, S.F.D. de St. Las veladas de la quinta. Madrid, 1791. 3v.
FL 6029.9 Gingnené, Pierre Louis. Lettres sur les confessions de Jean-Jacques Rousseau. Paris, 1791.
38537.2.5 Ginguené, P.L. De l'autorité de Rabelais dans la revues present. Utopie, 1791.
40537.42 Le grand denouement de la constitution. Bruxelles, 1791.
Mon 28.3 Hennet, A.J.U. Pétition à l'Assemblée Nationale. Paris, 1791.
41584.58.9 Hoffman, F.B. Euphrosine. Paris, 1791.

Chronological Listing

1791 - cont.

40535.24.10 Huvier des Fontenelles, Pierre M.F. La targetade, tragédie un peu burlesque. Paris? 1791.
41585.36.10 Lamey, Auguste. Gedichte eines Franken an Rheinstrom. Strassburg, 1791.
40536.2.105 Laya, Jean L. Jean Calas. Paris, 1791.
40535.20.15 Leblanc de Guillet, Antoine Blanc. Le clergé dévoilé. Paris, 1791.
40535.22.50 Le Grand, Jérôme. Louis XIV et le masque der fer. Paris, 1791.
40535.23.5 Le Mierre, A.M. Barnevelt. Paris, 1791.
40516.28.10 Louvet de Couvral, J.B. Émilie de Varmont ou le divorce nécessaire. Paris, 1791. 3v.
40516.28 Louvet de Couvral, J.B. Vie du chevalier de Faublas. Londres, 1791. 7v.
41586.19.9.15 Marsollier des Vivetières, B.J. Camille. Paris, 1791.
40536.21.15 Martelly, Honoré François Richaud de. Les deux Figaro. La Haye, 1791.
39582.10.15 Maury, J.S. Esprit, pensées et maximes de l'abbé Maury. Paris, 1791.
FL 6137.91 Mercier, M. De Jean-Jacques Rousseau. Paris, 1791. 2v.
Htn Mol 7.91* Molière, Jean Baptiste Poquelin. Oeuvres. Paris, 1791-94. 6v.
40536.19.800 Radet, Jean B. La soirée orageuse. Paris, 1791.
40536.22.10 Ronsin, Charles P. La ligne des fanatiques et des tyrans. Paris, 1791.
FL 6030.91 Rousseau, J.J. Du contrat social ou Principes du droit politique. Paris, 1791.
FL 6039.11 Rousseau, J.J. Gian Giaco Rousseau all assemblia nazionale o commentario postumo di qusto filosofo sud Contratto sociale. Filadelfia, 1791.
FL 6036.5.5 Rousseau, J.J. An inquiry into the nature of The social contract; or Principles of political right. Dublin, 1791.
FL 6036.5 Rousseau, J.J. An inquiry into the nature of The social contract. London, 1791.
FL 6050.91 Rousseau, J.J. Julie ou la nouvelle Héloise. Amsterdam, 1791. 3v.
Htn 39596.16* St. Pierre, J.H.B. de. La chaumière indienne. Paris, 1791.
Htn 39594.31* St. Pierre, J.H.B. de. Paolo e Virginia. n.p., 1791.
40536.29 Sedaine, Michel Jean. Le deserteur. Avignon, 1791.
40536.34.40 Le Vendemie; drama giocoso in tre atti. Paris, 1791.
40536.35.5 Villemain d'Abancourt, J.F. La bienfaisance de Voltaire. Paris, 1791.

1792

41583.12.11 Beffroy De Reigny, L.A. Le club des bonnes-gens. Paris, 1792.
40515.2.10 Bitaubé, P.J. José. pt. 1-2. Lisboa, 1792.
39586.10 Boulanger, N.A. Oeuvres. Paris, 1792-93.
40535.15.32 Carbon Flins des Oliviers, C.M.L.E. La jeune hôtesse. Paris, 1792.
39585.3 Dulaurens, H.J. Le compère Mathieu. Paris, 1792. 3v.
40535.15.18 Favières, Edme G.F. de. Les espiègleries de Garnison. Paris, 1792.
38554.1.15 Fénelon, F. de S. de la Mothe. Adventures of Telemachus. London, 1792.
38553.17 Fénelon, F. de S. de la Mothe. Les aventures de Télémaque. London, 1792.
40515.24.5 Florian, Jean P.C. de. Fables. Paris, 1792.
40515.36.2 Florian, Jean P.C. de. Gonsalve de Cordoue. 2e éd. Paris, 1792. 3v.
40515.36.50 Florian, Jean P.C. de. Gonsalve de Cordoue ou Grenade reconquise. 2. éd. Paris, 1792. 3v.
40515.19.5 Florian, Jean P.C. de. Nouvelles nouvelles. Paris, 1792.
40515.19 Florian, Jean P.C. de. Nouvelles nouvelles. Paris, 1792.
40535.16.50 Gouges, M.O. de. (Mme.). Le convent. Paris, 1792.
41584.58.5 Hoffman, F.B. Stratonice. Lyon, 1792.
40535.19.27 LaHarpe, J.F. de. Mélanie. Paris, 1792.
40535.21.50 LeFranc-Ponteuil, N. L'école des frères, ou L'incertitude. Lyon, 1792.
40535.22.53 Le Grand, Jérôme. Louis XIV et le masque de fer. Paris, 1792.
39598.16 Marmontel, J.F. Bélisarius. Brussels, 1792. 2v.
40516.51 Mercier, Louis S. La brouette vinaigrier. Avignon, 1792.
40516.53.30 Mercier, Louis S. Le ci-devant noble. Paris, 1792.
40516.55 Mercier, Louis S. Fictions; morales. Paris, 1792. 3v.
40535.65 Monvel, Jacques Marie Boutet de. Les victimes cloitrées. Bordeaux, 1792.
Htn 38526.29.5* Navarre, M. de. Les nouvelles de Marguerite, reine de Navarre. Berne, 1792. 3v.
41587.6.2 Picard, Louis Benoît. Les visitandines. Paris, 1792.
40536.19.805 Radet, Jean B. Arlequin afficheur. 2. éd. Paris, 1792.
40536.19.900 Raffard-Brienne, Jean S. Le retour du père Gérard a sa ferme. Lille, 1792.
40527.20.10 Robbé de Beauveset, P.H. Les victimes du despotisme episcopal. Paris, 1792.
FL 6050.92 Rousseau, J.J. La nouvelle Héloise. Paris, 1792. 3v.
Htn 39594.20.07* St. Pierre, J.H.B. de. La chaumière indienne. London, 1792.
39596.6 St. Pierre, J.H.B. de. Étude de la nature. Paris, 1792. 5v.
40536.27.15 Saurin, Bernard J. Spartacus. Paris, 1792.
40536.34.75 Vigée, L.J.B.E. La matinée d'une jolie femme, comédie en un acte. n.p., 1792.
39542.30 Voltaire, François Marie Arouet de. Oeuvres complètes. Hamburg, 1792. 18v.
39541.2 Voltaire, François Marie Arouet de. Oeuvres de Voltaire. Paris, 1792. 55v.

1793

40531.2 Aignan, Étienne. La mort de Louis XVI. Paris, 1793.
40531.2.4 Aignan, Étienne. La mort de Louis XVI. Paris, 1793.
39582.23.10 Arnaud, F.T.M. de B. Les amans malheureux. Avignon, 1793.
41583.9.15.2 Barré, Pierre y. La chaste Suzanne. Paris, 1793.
41583.9.15.4 Barré, Pierre y. La chaste Suzanne. Paris, 1793.
41583.9.11 Barré, Pierre y. Favart aux Champs-Élysées. Paris, 1793.
41583.9.5 Barré, Pierre y. L'heureuse décade. 2e éd. Paris, 1793-1794.
41583.12.15 Beffroy De Reigny, L.A. Allons, ça va, ou Le quaker en France. 2e éd. Paris, 1793.

1793 - cont.

40534.16.15 Cammaille-Saint-Aubin, M.C. L'ami du peuple. Paris, 1793.
40534.16.17.5 Candeille, Julie. Catherine. Paris, 1793.
40534.16.17.8 Candeille, Julie. Catherine. Paris, 1793.
40537.11.9 Chénier, Marie Joseph. Cains Gracchus. Paris, 1793.
40537.11.35 Chénier, Marie Joseph. Fénelon...tragédie. Paris, 1793.
40537.11.5 Chénier, Marie Joseph. Jean Calas. Paris, 1793.
40535.2.7 Defauconpret, A.J.B. La papesse Jeanne. Paris, 1793.
40535.2.8.3 Desfontaines, F.G. Fouques. La chaste Suzanne. Paris, 1793.
40535.2.8 Desfontaines, F.G. Fouques. La chaste Suzanne. Paris, 1793.
40535.2.8.7 Desfontaines, F.G. Fouques. Le divorce. Paris, 1793-94.
40526.34.11 Dorat, C.J. Les sacrifices de l'amour. Avignon, 1793. 3v.
40535.8.170 Duchaume. L'hiver, ou Les deux moulins. Paris, 1793.
38553.19.5 Fénelon, F. de S. de la Mothe. Les aventures de Télémaque. Maestricht, 1793. 2v.
40515.36A Florian, Jean P.C. de. Gonzalva of Cordova. Dublin, 1793. 2v.
39532.5.3 Hamilton, Anthony. Memoires du comte de Grammont. London, 1793.
40536.7 La Marteliere, J.H.F. Robert chef de brigands. Paris, 1793.
40536.7.5 La Marteliere, J.H.F. Le tribunal redoutable ou La suite de Robert chef de brigands. Paris, 1793.
40536.2.110 Laya, Jean L. L'ami des loix. Paris, 1793.
40536.2.115 Laya, Jean L. L'ami des loix. Paris, 1793.
40536.2.112 Laya, Jean L. L'ami des loix. Paris, 1793.
40536.10.103 Lebrun-Tossa, J.A. La folie de Georges. Paris, 1793.
40536.10.255 Léger, F.P.A. Le dédit mal gardé. Paris, 1793.
40536.10.250 Léger, F.P.A. La gageure inutile. Paris, 1793.
40536.10.260 Léger, F.P.A. Georges et gros-Jean. Paris, 1793.
40536.10.265 Léger, F.P.A. La papesse Jeanne. Paris, 1793.
40536.10.310 Legouvé, Gabriel. La mort d'Abel. Paris, 1793.
41586.16.20 Loaisel-Tréogate, J.M. La bisarrerie de la fortune. Paris, 1793.
41586.16.23 Loaisel-Tréogate, J.M. Le chateau du diable. Paris, 1793.
40516.28.2 Louvet de Couvral, J.B. Vie du chevalier de Faublas. pt.1-13. Paris, 1793. 6v.
39597.11 Marmontel, J.F. Contes moraux. Deux-Ponts, 1793.
Mon 17.93 Montaigne, Michel de. Essais. Paris, 1793. 3v.
Mon 35.2 Montaigne, Michel de. Gedanken. Berlin, 1793-99. 7v.
40535.80 Orvigny. On fait ce qu'on peut, et non pas ce qu'on veut. Toulouse, 1793.
40517.59 Pagès, François. La France républicaine. 2e éd. Paris, 1793.
41587.7.35 Picard, Louis Benoît. Arlequin friand. Paris, 1793.
41587.7 Picard, Louis Benoît. Le cousin de tout le monde. Paris, 1793.
41587.6.3 Picard, Louis Benoît. Les visitandines. Paris, 1793.
41587.6 Picard, Louis Benoît. Les visitandines. Paris, 1793.
40536.19.105 Piis, Augustin. La saint Deniche, ou La saint Nicolas d'été. Paris, 1793.
40536.33.15 Pujoulx, Jean B. Les montagnards. Paris, 1793-94.
40536.19.810 Radet, Jean B. Encore un curé, fait historique et patriotique. Paris, 1793-94.
40536.19.3002 Rézicourt. Les vrais sans-culottes. Paris, 1793.
40536.22.5 Ronsin, Charles P. Arétaphile. Toulouse, 1793.
FL 6040.93 Rousseau, J.J. Émile ou De l'éducaton. Paris, 1793. 3v.
FL 6001.793 Rousseau, J.J. Oeuvres complettes. Paris, 1793. 37v.
40536.25.75 Saint Firmin. La jeune esclave. Paris, 1793.
40536.26 Saint Romain. Louis XVI. En Allemagne, 1793.
40536.27.60 Saulnier, G. Le siége de Thionville, drame lyrique en deux actes. Paris, 1793?
37585.21 Théâtre. Paris, 1793-1853. 7 pam.
Htn 40536.34.55* Vieillard De Boismartin, A. Blanchard. Saint Lo, 1793.
40536.39 Viller. Cange. Paris, 1793.
41588.48 Villeterque, A.L. de. Enguerrand sire de Rosemont. Paris, 1793.
39545.48.25 Voltaire, François Marie Arouet de. La pucelle d'Orleans. Genève, 1793.

1794

41583.6.5 Andrieux, François G.J.S. L'enfance de Jean-Jacques Rousseau. Paris, 1794.
40531.6.25 Barthès de Marmorieres, Antoine. Le martyre de Marie-Antoinette. Amsterdam, 1794.
41583.12.13 Beffroy De Reigny, L.A. Toute la Grèce. Paris, 1794.
40517.13 Berquin, Arnaud. L'ami des enfans. v.4. Lausanne, 1794.
40534.17.12 Cizos, François. Les peuples et les rois. Paris, 1794.
40535.2.50 Demonstier, C.A. Le conciliateur. Paris, 1794.
40535.2.9 Desforges, Pierre Jean Baptiste. Le sourd, ou L'auberge pleine. Paris, 1794.
40535.3.60 Desorgues, Théodore. Rousseau ou l'enfance. Paris, 1794?
41584.6.5 Desprez, C.A. L'allarmiste, impromptu, républicain. Paris, 1794.
40535.8.9 Dubuisson, M. La parfaite égalité ou Les tu et toi. Paris, 1794.
40535.8.200 Dugazon, J.B.H.G. Le modéré. Paris, 1794.
38554.1.20 Fénelon, F. de S. de la Mothe. The adventures of Telemachus. London, 1794. 2v.
Htn 40535.19.19* Griffet de la Baume, A. La messe de Gnide. Paris, 1794.
FL 6127.94 Guillaume, J.M. Éloge de Jean-Jacques Rousseau. Montpellier, 1794.
FL 6127.94.5 Guillaume, J.M. Éloge de Jean-Jacques Rousseau. Montpellier, 1794.
40535.19.40 Joigny. Le siège de Lille. Paris, 1794.
41585.36.5 Lamey, Auguste. Dekadische Lieder für die Franken am Rheim. Strassburg, 1794-95. 2 pam.
40536.10.30 Laugier, Marie. Les épreuves du républicain. Paris, 1794.
40536.10.50 Laus DeBoissy, L. de. La tete sans cervelle. Paris, 1794.
40536.10.200 Lavallé, J. Manlius Torquatus. Paris, 1794.
40536.2.118 Laya, Jean L. L'amj des loix. Paris, 1794?
40536.10.305 Legouvé, Gabriel. Epicharis et Neron. Paris, 1794.
39581.3 Mably. Collection...des oeuvres de...Mably. Paris, 1794-95. 15v.
39581.20 Mably. Collection...des oeuvres de...Mably. Paris, 1794-95. 15v.
40529.28 Maréchal, Pierre S. Dieu et la prêtres. Paris, 1794?
40529.27 Maréchal, Pierre S. Le jujement dernier des rois. Paris, 1794.
39598.24 Marmontel, J.F. Bélisarius. London, 1794.
39598.29.75 Marmontel, J.F. Les incas. Paris, 1794. 3v.
39598.14 Marmontel, J.F. Nowe powiesci moralne. Warszawie, 1794.

1794 - cont.

41586.19.9.5 Marsollier des Vivetières, B.J. Les détenus. Paris, 1794-95.

40536.7.150 Mathelin, Nicolas B. Marat dans le soutterrain des Cordeliers. Paris, 1794.

40527.55 Mes j'ai vu, ou Les prédictions accomplies dans ces derniers tems. Babylone, 1794.

39594.3.4 Montesquieu, C.L. de S. The spirit of laws. 5. ed. London, 1794. 2v.

41587.7.30 Picard, Louis Benoît. Le conteur, ou Les deux postes. Paris, 1794-1795.

41587.7.25 Picard, Louis Benoît. La moitié du chemin. Paris, 1794.

41587.6.7 Picard, Louis Benoît. Les visitandines. Paris, 1794.

41547.13.5 Pigault-Lebrun, C.A.G.R. de. Les dragons et les bénédictines. Paris, 1794.

41547.13.7 Pigault-Lebrun, C.A.G.R. de. Les dragons et les bénédictines. Paris, 1794.

41547.13.30 Pigault-Lebrun, C.A.G.R. de. L'orphelin. Paris, 1794.

40536.19.100 Piis, Augustin. La nourrice républicaine. Paris, 1794.

40536.19.200 Pillet, Fabien. Wenzel. Paris, 1794.

40536.20.150 Plancher-Valcour, P.A.L.P. Les petits montagnards. Paris, 1794.

41587.19.60 Pompigny, M. de. L'époux républicain. Paris, 1794.

40536.20.500 Prevost-Montfort, P. L'esprit des prêtres. Paris, 1794.

40536.33.9 Pujoulx, Jean B. L'anti-célibataire. Paris, 1794.

Htn 40534.16.100* Puységur, Armand Marie Jacques de Chastenet. L'intérieur d'un ménage republicain. Paris, 1794.

40536.19.815 Radet, Jean B. Le faucon. Paris, 1794.

Htn 40524.28.10* Restif de la Bretonne, Nicolas E. Monsieur Nicolas. Paris, 1794-97. 7v.

FL 6056.5 Rousseau, J.J. Julia: or, The new Eloisa. v.2-3. Edinburgh, 1794. 2v.

41596.58.10 Salm-Rufferscheid-Dyck, C. Sapho. Paris, 1794.

40536.31.12 Sedaine, Michel Jean. Guillame Tell. Paris, 1794.

41569.22 T., A. of Rochefort. Adraste et Nancy V.Y., anecdote américaine. St. Maixent, 1794.

40536.37 Villeneuve, (Mdme.). Les crimes de la noblesse. Paris, 1794-95.

39545.66.75 Voltaire, François Marie Arouet de. Zadig: or, The book of fate. London, 1794?

1795

41583.12.12 Beffroy De Reigny, L.A. Le club des bonnes-gens. Paris, 1795.

40531.15.200 Boyer. Le bienfait récompensé. Paris, 1795.

Mol 860.18 Cadet de Gassicourt, Charles Louis. Le souper de Molière. Paris, 1795.

40534.16.17.11 Candeille, Julie. Le commissionaire. Paris, 1795.

39586.16 Chamfort, S.R.N. Oeuvres, recueillies et publiées par un ami. Paris, 1795. 4v.

40534.16.80 Charlemagne, A. Le souper des Jacobins. Paris, 1795.

40537.11 Chénier, Marie Joseph. Timoléon. Paris, 1795.

40534.22.15 Collin d'Harleville, J.F. Rose et Picara. Paris, 1795.

38576.12.42.45 Corneille, Thomas. The labyrinth. Dublin, 1795.

40535.2.55 Demonstier, C.A. Le divorce. Paris, 1795.

40535.8.14 Dorvigny, Louis A. L'hospitalité. Paris, 1795.

40535.8.55 Dorvo, H. Le faux député. Paris, 1795.

40535.8.50 Dorvo, H. Figaro de retour à Paris. Paris, 1795.

40535.8.155 Ducancel, Charles Pierre. Le hableur. Paris, 1795.

40535.12.150 Duclos, P.G. La prise de Paris. Paris, 1795.

41584.27.25 Dumaniant, A.J. Isaure et gernance. Paris, 1795.

39586.14 Faulcon, Félix. Fruits de la solitude et du malheur. Paris, 1795-96. 3 pam.

40515.48.5 Florian, Jean P.C. de. Estelle. Genève, 1795.

40535.15.50 Fonvielle, B.F.A. Collot dans Lyon. n.p., 1795.

40538.20 Frédegonde et Brunehaut. Paris, 1795.

Htn 39544.58.40* Guénée, Antoine. Letter of certain Jews to Monsieur Voltaire. Philadelphia, 1795.

41584.58.7 Hoffman, F.B. Callais. Paris, 1795.

Htn 39527.8.20* La Fontaine, Jean de. Contes et nouvelles en vers. Paris, 1795.

38543.19 La Rochefoucauld, François. Maxims and moral reflexions. London, 1795.

40536.10.100 Lebrun-Tossa, J.A. Arabelle et vascos. Paris, 1795.

40526.22.5 Malfilâtre, J.C.L. de C. de. Narcisse dans l'Isle de Vénus. Paris, 1795.

39598.9.20 Marmontel, J.F. Moral tales. London, 1795? 2v.

41586.19.9.22 Marsollier des Vivetières, B.J. La pauvre femme. Paris, 1795.

Htn 40516.52* Mercier, Louis S. Memoirs of the year 2500. Philadelphia, 1795.

39592.3 Montesquieu, C.L. de S. Oeuvres. Paris, 1795. 5v.

40588.27 Montolieu, I.P. de. Caroline of Litchfield; a novel. Dublin, 1795. 2v.

40516.35 Pechméja, Jean de. Télèphe. Paris, 1795. 2v.

41587.7.40 Picard, Louis Benoît. Les conjectures. Paris, 1795.

41547.13.25 Pigault-Lebrun, C.A.G.R. de. Les empiriques. Paris, 1795.

41547.13.20 Pigault-Lebrun, C.A.G.R. de. Les moeurs, ou Le divorce. Paris, 1795.

41587.19.54 Pompigny, M. de. Le franc marin. Paris, 1795.

40536.19.820 Radet, Jean B. Le noble roturier. Paris, 1795.

40516.39 Ramsay, A.M. de. Travels of Cyrus. London, 1795.

40536.19.3000 Rézicourt. Les vrais sans-culottes. Avignon, 1795.

40536.21.75 Rolland. Arlequin Perruquier. Paris, 1795.

39532.2.19 Rousseau, J.B. Oeuvres. Paris, 1795. 4v.

FL 6020.95 Rousseau, J.J. Confessions. v.3-4. Genève, 1795.

FL 6056.6 Rousseau, J.J. Eloisa. Dublin, 1795. 4v.

40527.24 Saint-Lambert, Jean F. Oeuvres mêlées. Paris, 1795.

40527.23 Saint-Lambert, Jean F. Les saisons, poëme. Paris, 1795.

39595.30 St. Pierre, J.H.B. de. Paolo e Virginia. Firenze, 1795.

39596.18 St. Pierre, J.H.B. de. Voyages of Amasis. Boston, 1795.

40535.20 Sally-Tolendal, T.A. Le comte de Strafford: tragédie. London, 1795.

40536.27.3 Sanchaman, J.J. Les décemvirs. Paris, 1795.

40537.45 Tactique des cannibales. Paris, 1795.

Htn 39545.36* Voltaire, François Marie Arouet de. Candidus, or All for the best. Berwick, 1795.

1796

40531.2.5 Aignan, Étienne. La mort de Louis XVI. Paris, 1796.

40531.6.30 Barthès de Marmorieres, Antoine. Le martyre de Marie-Antoinette. Paris, 1796.

40532.9 Beaumarchais, Pierre A.C. de. Les deux amis. Paris, 1796.

41583.12.3 Beffroy De Reigny, L.A. La petite Nannette. Paris, 1796.

1796 - cont.

41583.12.14 Beffroy De Reigny, L.A. Testament d'un électeur de Paris. Paris, 1796.

40526.32.5 Bernis, François Joachim de Pierre de. La religion vengée. n.p., 1796.

40531.7 Bizet. Les boites. Paris, 1796.

Htn 40551.19.25* Bonald, L.G.A. de. Théorie du pouvoir politique et religieux. Constance, 1796. 3v.

40534.17.10 Bonnay, François. La prise des annonciades. Hamburg, 1796.

40534.16.75 Charlemagne, A. Le souper des Jacobins. Paris, 1796-97.

41583.19.20 Cuvelier de Trie, J.G.A. L'enfant du malheur. Paris, 1796-97.

40535.2.40 Déniot. Le français a Burgos. Paris? 1796.

Htn 39564.6.17* Diderot, Denis. Jacques le fataliste et son maître. Paris, 1796-97. 2v.

Htn 40516.4.5* Ducray-Duminil, F.G. Alexis: or The cottage in the woods. Boston, 1796.

39585.4 Dulaurens, H.J. Le compère Mathieu. n.p., 1796. 3v.

39585.4.2 Dulaurens, H.J. Le compère Mathieu. Paris, 1796. 3v.

40535.13.9.10 Faur, Louis F. La fête de la cinquantaine. Paris, 1796.

38553.20 Fénelon, F. de S. de la Mothe. Les aventures de Télémaque. London, 1796.

40526.10.2 Gresset, Jean B. Oeuvres choisies. Paris, 1796.

40535.16.100 Gueroult, Jean F. La journée de Marathon. Paris, 1796.

39532.13.20 Hamilton, Anthony. History of May-Flower. 2e ed. Salisbury, 1796.

40527.45 L'immaculée conception de la très-sainte vierge. Rome, 1796.

Htn 39527.11.5* La Fontaine, Jean de. Fables. Paris, 1796. 4v.

38543.19.5 La Rochefoucauld, François. Maxims and moral reflections. Edinburgh, 1796.

40536.10.320 Legouvé, Gabriel. Quintus Fabius. Paris, 1796.

41586.15.2A Lemercier, N.L. Agamemnon, tragédie en 5 actes. Paris, 1796-1797.

39598.25 Marmontel, J.F. Bélisarius. Newburyport, 1796.

41586.19.9.12 Marsollier des Vivetières, B.J. La pauvre femme. 4e éd. Paris, 1796-1777.

40535.65.3 Monvel, Jacques Marie Boutet de. De slacht-offers van kloosterdwang. Amsterdam, 1796.

37574.340 Nougaret, P.B. Hymnes pour toutes les fêtes nationales. Paris, 1796. 2 pam.

40536.11.50 Patrat, Joseph. L'orpheline. Paris, 1796.

Htn 40573.1* Peignot, Gabriel. Opuscules philosophiques et poétiques. Paris, 1796.

41587.17.5 Picard, Louis Benoît. La perruque blonde. Paris, 1796?

41547.13.40 Pigault-Lebrun, C.A.G.R. de. Les sabotiers. Paris, 1796.

40536.20.200 Planterre, Berthelemi Ambroise. La famille indigente, fait historique. Paris, 1796.

41587.19.55 Pompigny, M. de. Le franc marin. Paris, 1796-1797.

40517.56.35 Pougens, Marie C. Julie ou La religieuse de Nismes. Paris, 1796.

Htn 37585.30* Recueil des pièces de théâtre relative à la révolution. 1er part. Paris, 1796?

Htn 41596.53.2* Rouget de Lisle, Joseph. Essais en vers et en prose. Paris, 1796.

FL 6056.7 Rousseau, J.J. Eloisa. Philadelphia, 1796. 3v.

FL 6109.2 Rousseau, J.J. Letters of an Italian nun and an English gentleman. Worcester, 1796.

39594.33 St. Pierre, J.H.B. de. Paul and Virginia. 2. ed. London, 1796.

40543.20 Segur, Alexandre Joseph Pierre. Le parti le plus gai. Paris, 1796.

40543.10 Segur, Alexandre Joseph Pierre. Les vieux fous. Paris, 1796.

40536.33.75 Souriguere de St. Marc, J.M. Cécile. Paris, 1796.

Htn 39545.53.15* Voltaire, François Marie Arouet de. La pucelle: or the maid of Orleans. Dublin, 1796-97. 2v.

1797

41583.14.60 Baudouin, Théodore. Démétrius. Paris, 1797.

40534.16.11 Cailhava d'Estendoux, J.F. Ziste et zeste. Paris, 1797.

40537.40 Charlotte Corday. Caen, 1797.

38572.9A Corneille, Pierre. Théâtre. n.p., 1797. 12v.

Mol 880.14 Daubin. Le Misanthrope travesti. Castres, 1797.

39564.21.10 Diderot, Denis. The nun. Dublin, 1797.

40535.8.150 Ducancel, Charles Pierre. L'interieur des comités révolutionnaires. Paris, 1797.

39585.4.5 Dulaurens, H.J. Le compère Mathieu. v.1-4. Paris, 1797. 2v.

39578.13 Du Marsais, César C. Oeuvres. Paris, 1797. 7v.

41584.29.21 Duval, A. La jeunesse du duc de Richelieu. Paris, 1797.

37533.31 Ersch, J.S. La France littéraire. Hambourg, 1797. 3v.

38553.21 Fénelon, F. de S. de la Mothe. Les aventures de Télémaque. Paris, 1797.

40588.14.25 Genlis, S.F.D. de St. The knights of the swan. Dublin, 1797. 2v.

40588.20 Genlis, S.F.D. de St. Sacred dramas. Fredericksburg, 1797.

40535.16.25 Godard D'Aucour de Saint Just, Claude. L'heureuse nouvelle. Paris, 1797.

41584.58.10 Hoffman, F.B. L'original comédie. Paris, 1797.

38543.9 La Rochefoucauld, François. Maximes et réfléxions morales. Calais, 1797.

40517.31 Le Prince de Beaumont, M. Le magasin de enfans. v.1-4. Paris, 1797. 2v.

40536.10.500 Lessieur. Les déguisemens villageois. Paris, 1797.

40535.25.7 Maillot, A.F.E. Madame Angot. Paris, 1797.

40535.50.3 Mignan. L'enrôlement supposé. Paris, 1797.

39594.8 Montesquieu, C.L. de S. The temple of Gnidus and Arsaces and Ismenia. Londón, 1797.

40535.65.5 Monvel, Jacques Marie Boutet de. Junius. Paris, 1797.

37574.320 Nouveau recueil de cantiques. n.p., 1797.

40536.19.75 Petitot, C.B. Géta. Paris, 1797.

41587.7.15 Picard, Louis Benoît. Médiocre et rampant. Paris, 1797.

41587.18.10 Picard, Louis Benoît. Les suspects. Paris, 1797.

41587.6.10 Picard, Louis Benoît. Les visitandines. Paris, 1797.

40536.33.7 Pipelet, C.D.T. Eloge historique de M.J. Sédaine. n.p., 1797.

40536.33.10 Pujoulx, Jean B. L'école des parvenus. Paris, 1797?

38536.4.20 Rabelais, F. Oeuvres. Paris, 1797-98. 3v.

40536.19.835 Radet, Jean B. Honorine, ou La femme difficile a vivre. Paris, 1797.

Chronological Listing

1797 - cont.

40536.19.830 Radet, Jean B. Pauline. Paris, 1797.
40536.19.825 Radet, Jean B. Pauline. Paris, 1797.
40536.19.2000 Ravrio, A.A. Arlequin journaliste. Paris, 1797.
39586.25.5 Rivarol, Antoine. Discours préliminaire du nouveau dictionnaire de la lanque française. Paris, 1797.
FL 6071.50A Rousseau, J.J. Dissertation on political economy. Albany, 1797.
X Cg 40516.60.20 Sade, D.A.F. de. La nouvelle justine. Hollande, 1797. 4v.
39596.8 St. Pierre, J.H.B. de. Studies of nature. Worcester, 1797. 3v.
39596.7 St. Pierre, J.H.B. de. Studies of nature. Worcester, 1797. 3v.
Htn 40536.34.50* Vieillard De Boismartin, A. Theraméne. Saint Lo, 1797.
39578.10 Voyer, Réné Louis. Essays. Worcester, 1797.

1798

40531.2.12 Amar, A.D. Le double divorce. Paris, 1798.
40531.2.15 Andrews, James P. The inquisitor, tragedy in 5 acts. London, 1798.
41583.12.5 Beffroy De Reigny, L.A. Jean Baptiste. Paris, 1798.
41583.15.150 Boullault, M.J. La mort de Cadet-Roussel. Paris, 1798.
Mol 603.1.5 Cailhava d'Estendoux, Jean François. Essai sur la tradition théatrale. Paris, 1798.
Htn 38528.1.5* Caron, P.S. Collection de différens ouvrages anciens. Paris, 1798-1806. 4v.
41583.18.53.5 Chazet, André René P.A. Les français à Cythère. Paris, 1798.
39572.3 Condillac, E.B. de. Oeuvres. Paris, 1798. 16v.
39571.25 Condillac, E.B. de. Oeuvres. Paris, 1798. 7v.
Mol 860.19 Coupigny, Antoine François de. Hommage du petit vaudeville. Paris, 1798.
40534.29.12 Crébillon, Prosper Jolyot de. Radamisto e Zenobia. Paris, 1798.
41583.19.15 Cuvelier de Trie, J.G.A. Le petit poucet. Paris, 1798.
40535.2.65 Demonstier, C.A. Alceste à la campagne. Paris, 1798.
Mol 880.15 Demoustier, C.A. Alceste à la campagne. Paris, 1798.
40535.73 Desaudras. Minuit, comédie en un acte. Bordeaux, 1798.
Htn 40535.2.15* Desforges, Pierre Jean Baptiste. Le poéte. Hambourg, 1798. 4v.
Htn 39562.2* Diderot, Denis. Oeuvres. Paris, 1798. 15v.
FL 398.20.2 Dumesnil, M.J. Mémoires de Mlle. Dumesnil. Paris, 1798.
FL 6015.3 Dusaulx, J. De mes rapports avec Jean-Jacques Rousseau. Paris, 1798.
41584.29.28 Duval, A. Le souper imprévu. Paris, 1798.
40524.17 Fiévée, Joseph. La dot de Suzette...Histoire de Mme. de Senneterre. Paris, 1798.
40515.48.7 Florian, Jean P.C. de. Estelle, pastorale. Paris, 1798.
40515.48.8 Florian, Jean P.C. de. Estelle. v.1-2. London, 1798.
Htn 40515.32* Florian, Jean P.C de. Galatea. Boston, 1798.
40535.16.5 Gardel, Pierre Gabriel. La rociere. n.p., 1798?
40516.45 Guerle, J.N.M. Eloge des Perrugues. Paris, 1798.
FL 380.4 Lamarque, F. Opinion sur les théâtres. Paris, 1798.
40536.7.15 La Marteliere, J.H.F. Le testament, ou Les mysteres d'Udolphe. Paris, 1798.
40536.7.10 La Marteliere, J.H.F. Les trois espiègles. Paris, 1798.
40536.2 Larnac, François. Thémistocle. Paris, 1798.
41586.13.5 Lemercier, N.L. Ophis. Paris, 1798-1799.
37597.3.5A Lorris, Guillaume de. Le roman de la rose. Paris, 1798-99. 5v.
39592.4 Montesquieu, C.L. de S. Oeuvres. Paris, 1798. 5v.
FL 6137.98.2 Muzzarelli, A. G.G. Rousseau, accusator de filosofi. Assisi, 1798.
37574.315 Parent, F.N. Recueil d'hymnes philosophiques, civiques, et moraux. Paris, 1798-99.
40536.11.30 Patissier de la Foretille. La culte du vrai Dieu rétable. Berne, 1798.
41547.13.50 Pigault-Lebrun, C.A.G.R. de. Le cordonnier de Damas. Paris, 1798.
40536.20.505 Prevost-Montfort, P. Ténais et zeliska. Paris, 1798.
40536.20.600 Privat, Jean F. Demonville. Perpignan, 1798.
37574.330 Rallier, Louis Antoine Esprit. Recueil de chants moraux et patriotiques. Paris, 1798-99.
37572.5 Recueil des chefs d'oeuvre des plus celebres kauy-esprits françois. Edinbourg, 1798.
Htn 37574.310* Roucalli, C. Epigrammi francesi, tradotti i versi italiano. Parma, 1798.
FL 6001.840 Rousseau, J.J. Oeuvres. Paris, 1798-99. 18v.
Htn FL 6137.98.1* Stael, de (Mrs.). Lettres, ouvrages et caractère de Jean-Jacques Rousseau. Paris, 1798.
40526.67 Vadé, Jean Joseph. Oeuvres complettes. Troyes, 1798. 6v.
40537.53 Le Vatican...tragédie. Paris, 1798.

1799

39574.20 Alembert, J. Le Rond d'. Oeuvres posthumes. Berlin, 1799. 2v.
39574.21 Alembert, J. Le Rond d'. Oeuvres posthumes. Paris, 1799.
39582.27 Arnaud, F.T.M. de B. Les matinées, nouvelles anecdotes par d'Arnaud. Paris, 1799. 3v.
40532.9.10 Beaumarchais, Pierre A.C. de. L'autre tartuffe. Avignon, 1799.
39577.8 Condorcet, Marie Jean Antoine. Éloges des academiciens. Brunswick, 1799. 5v.
40526.32.40 Cubières, Michel de. Le calendrier républicain, poëme. Paris, 1799.
37558.28 D'Alembert, Jean le Rond. Select eulogies of members of the French academy. London, 1799. 2v.
39534.25.5A Deshoulières, A. du L. del G. (Mme.). Oeuvres. Paris, 1799. 2v.
40537.12.5 Dialogue entre l'ex-pape Pie VI et le roi très-chrétien, Louis XVIII. n.p., 1799?
40526.34.10 Dorat, C.J. La feinte par amour. Troyes, 1799?
40535.14.10 Fabre d'Eglantine, P.F.N. Les précepteurs. Paris, 1799-1800.
40515.16.50 Florian, Jean P.C. de. Oeuvres posthumes. Paris, 1799?
40537.52 La foi couronée...poëme en cinq chants. Londres, 1799.
40526.61.100 Gallet, Pierre. Dieu; poëme épique en huit chants. Paris? 1799.
41584.51.12 Gardy, J.A. Celestine, ou La fille alcade. Paris, 1799.
40588.21.90 Genlis, S.F.D. de St. Rash vows. Dublin, 1799. 2v.
39527.11 La Fontaine, Jean de. Fables. Paris, 1799. 2v.
39527.11.2 La Fontaine, Jean de. Fables. Paris, 1799.

1799 - cont.

37531.3 Laharpe, Jean F de. Lycée, ou Cours de littérature. v.1-16. Paris, 1799-1805. 19v.
40536.10.267 Léger, F.P.A. Il faut un état. Paris, 1799.
40536.10.270 Léger, F.P.A. Il faut un état. Paris, 1799.
37561.29 Legrand d'Aussy, C. Notices sur des Mss. français. Paris, 1799.
40511.24 LeSage, Alain René. Aventuras de Gil Blas de Santillana. Madrid, 1799. 5v.
39598.9.15 Marmontel, J.F. Tales, selected. London, 1799.
Mol 47.99 Molière, Jean Baptiste Poquelin. Dialogues français, anglais et italiens. Paris, 1799.
Htn Mol 17.99* Molière, Jean Baptiste Poquelin. Oeuvres. v.6. Paris, 1799.
Mol 37.99 Molière, Jean Baptiste Poquelin. Oeuvres choisies...Bret. Oxford, 1799. 2v.
39592.15 Montesquieu, C.L. de S. Oeuvres complètes. Basle, 1799. 8v.
40535.68 Morel. L'intérieur d'un comité révolutionnaire. Paris, 1799-1800.
40536.11 Pain, M.J. L'appartement à louer. Paris, 1799.
37574.336 Parent, F.N. Recueil de chants philosophiques, civiques et moraux...fêtes nationales. Paris, 1799.
37574.335 Parent, F.N. Recueil de chants philosophiques, civiques et moraux...fêtes nationales. Paris, 1799.
Htn 41596.46.2* Parny, Évariste. La guerre des dieux. Paris, 1799.
41596.46.10 Parny, Évariste. La guerre des dieux. Paris, 1799.
41596.46.5 Parny, Évariste. La guerre des dieux anciens et modernes. 2. éd. Paris, 1799.
40536.18.105A Pelletier-Volméranges, B. Le mariage du Capucin. Marseille, 1799.
40536.18.100 Pelletier-Volméranges, B. Le mariage du Capucin. Paris, 1799.
40536.19.76 Petitot, C.B. Laurent de Médicis. Paris, 1799.
41587.7.20 Picard, Louis Benoît. Les comédies ambulans. Paris, 1799.
41587.7.85 Picard, Louis Benoît. Les voisins. Paris, 1799?
40536.20.165 Plancher-Valcour, P.A.L.P. Le consistoire; poème. Paris, 1799.
40536.20.160 Plancher-Valcour, P.A.L.P. La république; poème. n.p., 1799.
38582.6 Racine, Jean. Oeuvres. v.1-2,4-5. Paris, 1799. 4v.
40536.21.19 Roger, Jean François. La dupe de soi-même. Paris, 1799.
41557.8.10 Rome, Marne de Morville de (Mme.). Eulalie. Paris, 1799.
Htn 39578.34* Saint-Martin, Louis Claude. Le crocodile, ou La guerre du bien et du mal. Paris, 1799.
39596.18.5 St. Pierre, J.H.B. de. Amasis. London, 1799.
39596.9 St. Pierre, J.H.B. de. Beauties of the studies of nature. London, 1799.
41588.17 Scribe, Eugène. French drama. Paris, 1799-1850. 3 pam.
40536.33.50 Sequier, A.L.M. Le Marechal Ferrant de la ville d'Anvers. Paris, 1799.
Htn 37573.425* Théâtre de l'hermitage de Catherine II. Paris, 1799. 2v.
39576.65 Valentin. Instruction tirée des saintes ecritures sur l'ordre social. Venise, 1799.

18-

42562.38.51 Aimard, Gustave. Last of the Incas. London, 18- ?
41598.3 Album drôlatique. Paris, 18- ?
41597.20 Appoloniana, ou Recueil de pieces fugitives en vers. Lille, 18- ?
42542.1.75 Audouard, O. (Mme.). Il n'y a pas d'amour sans jalousie et de jalousie sans amour. Paris, 18- ?
39544.245 Auger, L.S. Notice sur la vie et les ouvrages de Voltaire. Paris? 18- .
42542.21.9 Augier, Émile. Good for evil. London, 18- ?
40597.34.5 Balzac, Honoré de. Ursule Mirouet. Paris, 18- .
41583.11.3 Basté, Eugène Pierre. Les frères corses. London, 18- ?
42542.27.55 Bayard, J.F.A. Le gamin de Paris. Paris? 18- .
42548.5.10 Bayard, J.F.A. La niaise de Saint Flour. N.Y., 18- ?
41592.11.10 Béranger, P.J. de. Le Béranger des familles. Paris, 18- .
41591.6 Béranger, P.J. de. Dernières chansons. Paris, 18- .
41566.14.3 Bouilly, Jean N. Contes offerts aux enfans de France. 1Paris, 18- ? 2v.
41583.15.13 Bourgeois, Anicet. The black doctor. London, 18- ?
41583.15.14.5 Bourgeois, Anicet. The duke's daughter. N.Y., 18- ?
40551.26 Bourget, Paul. Bonald. Paris, 18- .
38528.14.3 Brantôme, P. de B. de. Vies des dames galantes. Paris, 18- .
41583.16.7 Brazier, Nicholas. Catharine, ou La croix d'or. Paris, 18- ?
39544.165 A brief sketch of the life and writings of M. de Voltaire. London, 18- ?
38528.40 Les Caquets de l'accouchée. Paris, 18- .
41593.15.5 Charron, J. Pocancy, stances à M***. Châlons, 18- .
40586.18.12 Chateaubriand, F.A.R. Génie du Christianisme. Paris, 18- ? 2v.
40586.19.5 Chateaubriand, F.A.R. Les martyrs. Paris, 18- ?
V42588.2 Cinquante et deux anecdotes sur la vie des animaux. Paris, 18- ?
42554.24.5 Coppée, François. Théâtre 1869-72. Paris, 18- .
42554.25.3 Coppée, François. Théâtre 1872-78. Paris, 18- .
38575.32.4 Corneille, Pierre. Horace. Paris, 18- .
38574.8.5 Corneille, Pierre. Oeuvres...théâtre complet. Paris, 18- . 3v.
40588.2.3 Cottin, Marie R. (Mme.). Elizabeth, or The exiles of Siberia. N.Y., 18- .
42566.27.5 Daudet, Alphonse. Lettres de mon moulin. 20. éd. Paris, 18- ?
42566.25.5 Daudet, Alphonse. Montagsgeschichten. Berlin, 18- ?
42545.69.13 Dennery, Adolphe Philippe. A celebrated case. N.Y., 18- ?
42545.69.13.3 Dennery, Adolphe Philippe. A celebrated case. N.Y., 18- .
42545.69.18 Dennery, Adolphe Philippe. Ernestine. N.Y., 18- .
42545.69.19.3 Dennery, Adolphe Philippe. Jocrisse, the juggler. London, 18- ?
42545.69.25 Dennery, Adolphe Philippe. The sea of ice. London, 18- ?
41593.29.25 Deshayes, Valentin. Hymne national, liberté, egalité, fraternité. Paris, 18- ?
41538.77 Dumas, Alexandre. Andree de Javerney, or The downfall of French monarchy. N.Y., 18- .
41538.45 Dumas, Alexandre. Captain Paul Jones. London, 18- .
41538.69 Dumas, Alexandre. The chevalier de Maison Rouge. London, 18- .
41538.10 Dumas, Alexandre. The chevalier d'Harmental. Boston, 18-

18- - cont.

	41538.16.3.10	Dumas, Alexandre. Count of Monte Cristo. N.Y., 18- .
	41538.68	Dumas, Alexandre. The countess de Charny. London, 18- ?
	41538.47	Dumas, Alexandre. Henri III et sa cour. Paris, 18- .
	42543.16.9.2	Dumas, Alexandre. The lady of the camelias; a tragic drama. London, 18- ?
	42543.16.9	Dumas, Alexandre. The lady of the camelias. London, 18- ?
	41538.63.25	Dumas, Alexandre. The queen's necklace. London, 18- .
	41538.48.15	Dumas, Alexandre. The two Dianas. London, 18- .
	38551.50.10	Dumolard, Joseph Vincent. Éloge de Fénelon. Cambrai, 18- ?
	37573.415	Duvert, F.A. Ce que femme veut. Poizzy, 18- . 6 pam.
	41584.32.20	Duveyrier, A.H.J. Le chevalier de St. George. London, 18- ?
	42572.20.5	Erckmann, Emile. L'invasion ou Le fou Yégoff. 3. éd. Paris, 18- ?
	42572.22	Erckmann, Emile. Le juif polonais. Paris, 18- ?
	37572.46	L'étincelle, souvenirs de littérature. Paris, 18- .
	38553.27.22	Fénelon, F. de S. de la Mothe. Les aventures de Télémaque. Philadelphia, 18- .
	38554.4.10	Fénelon, F. de S. de la Mothe. Fables. Cambridge, 18- .
	38554.4.15	Fénelon, F. de S. de la Mothe. Fables. Paris, 18- ?
Htn	41584.41.9*	Flareau. The ocean spectre. n.p., 18- .
	42571.24.5	Gaboriau, Emile. Other people's money. Chicago, 18- ?
	41584.8.5	Gonbaux, Prosper Parfait. Louise de Lignerolles. London, 18- ?
	41542.46F	Gozlan, Léon. Louise de Nanteuil. Paris, 18- .
	42576.40.325	Halévy, Ludovic. The abbé Constantin. N.Y., 18- .
	42543.62.88	Hennique, Léon. Benjamin Royes. Bruxelles, 18- ?
	42584.29.15	Hetzel, P.J. Histoire d'un lièvre. Cambridge, 18- .
	41571.30.5	Hugo, Victor. By order of the king. N.Y., 18- .
	41573.12	Hugo, Victor. Les chants du crépuscule. Paris, 18- .
	41573.36.30	Hugo, Victor. Les enfants. Paris, 18- .
	41572.7.15	Hugo, Victor. Hans of Iceland. N.Y., 18- .
	41573.32.1A	Hugo, Victor. Hernani. Paris, 18- .
	41571.12.4	Hugo, Victor. Les misérables. N.Y., 18- .
	41571.10.4	Hugo, Victor. Les misérables. N.Y., 18- . 2v.
	41573.10.5	Hugo, Victor. Marion de Lorme. Paris, 18- .
	41573.21.5	Hugo, Victor. Notre Dame de Paris. Paris, 18- . 2v.
NEDL	41573.50	Hugo, Victor. The novels of Victor Hugo. N.Y., 18- . 5v.
	41573.35.10	Hugo, Victor. Odes et ballades. Paris, 18- .
	41573.37.9	Hugo, Victor. Poems. The history of a crime. Boston, 18- ? 2 pam.
	41572.50	Hugo, Victor. Les quatre vents de l'esprit. Paris, 18- . 2v.
	41571.32.9	Hugo, Victor. The toilers of the sea. v.1-2. Boston, 18-
	41572.60	Hugo, Victor. Toute la lyre. Paris, 18- . 3v.
	42548.11.5	Labiche, Eugène. La cagnotte. N.Y., 18- ?
	39527.11.10	La Fontaine, Jean de. Fables et epitres. Paris, 18- .
Htn	41578.35.95*	Lamartine, Alphonse. Discours prononcé dans la séance du 15 février 1834 sur les frères des écoles chrétiennes. n.p., 18- .
	41577.15.14	Lamartine, Alphonse de. Les confidences. Boston, 18- . 2v.
	41578.5.11	Lamartine, Alphonse de. Harmonies poétiques et religieuses. Boston, 18- ?
	41578.7.5	Lamartine, Alphonse de. Méditations poétiques. Boston, 18- ?
	42544.7.6	Legouvé, Ernest. Medea. London, 18- ?
	42548.39	Legouvé, Ernest. Théâtre de campagne. Tom. 1-3,5-8. Paris, 18- ? 7v.
	37567.32.15	Lemaître, Jules. Les contemporains. Paris, 18- . 8v.
	40512.31.5	LeSage, Alain René. Histoire de Gil Blas de Santillana. Madrid, 18- .
	Mol 704.3	The life of Jean Baptiste Poquelin de Molière. London, 18- ?
	37544.7.8	Lintilhac, Eugène. Précis historique et critique de la littérature française. 3. éd. Paris, 18- ?
	41588.29.10	Lockroy, Joseph P.S. Good night, Signor Pantaloon. London, 18- ?
	40588.33	Maistre, Xavier. Oeuvres complètes. Paris, 18- .
	38526.32.18A	Marguerite d'Angoulême. The Heptaméron. London, 18- .
	38526.32.19	Marguerite d'Angoulême. The Heptaméron. London, 18- .
	38526.32.11	Marguerite d'Angoulême. The Heptaméron. Philadelphia, 18- .
	38526.32.12	Marguerite d'Angoulême. The Heptaméron. Philadelphia, 18-
	38523.9.15	Marot, Clément. Oeuvres complètes. v.1-4. Paris, 18- ? 2v.
	42577.12.75	Maygrier, Raymond. Les mystères du magnétisme. Paris, 18- ?
	42577.35.15	Michon, Jean H. El fraile. 3. ed. Barcelona, 18- .
	Mol 195.12	Molière, Jean Baptiste Poquelin. L'école des femmes. Paris, 18- ?
	Mol 215.17	Molière, Jean Baptiste Poquelin. Les Fourberies de Scapin...Gombert. London, 18- .
	Mol 215.16	Molière, Jean Baptiste Poquelin. Les Fourberies de Scapin. Comédie. Paris, 18- ?
	Mol 248.15	Molière, Jean Baptiste Poquelin. M. de Pourceaugnac. Paris, 18- ?
	Mol 245.20	Molière, Jean Baptiste Poquelin. Le misanthrope; comédie. Paris, 18- ?
	Mol 18.00	Molière, Jean Baptiste Poquelin. Oeuvres complètes. Tom. 4. Paris, 18- .
	Mol 18.06	Molière, Jean Baptiste Poquelin. Works. Oeuvres. Paris?, 18- . 6v.
Htn	Mon 28.18.5*	Montaigne, Michel de. De l'institution des enfants. Cambridge, 18- .
	Mon 18.01.5	Montaigne, Michel de. Essais. Paris, 18- . 2v.
	41555.67	Montgolfier, Adelaide. Contes devenues histoires. Paris, 18- .
	41596.29.5	Musset, Alfred de. A good little wife, from "Un caprice". London, 18- ?
	41596.30	Musset, Alfred de. A good little wife, from "Un caprice". London, 18- ?
	41596.23A	Musset, Alfred de. Histoire d'un merle blanc. Cambridge, 18- ?
	FL 391.45	Nodler, Thomas. Mémoire, a l'appui de la demande d'un privilége pour l'établissement d'un théâtre dramatique. Paris, 18- .
	42578.30.5	Ohnet, Georges. Aux avant-postes. n.p., 18- ?
	42541.22.5	Pailleron, Edouard. Le monde où l'on s'ennuie. Paris. 18- .
	41588.70	La Passion de N.S. Jésus-Christ. Jerusalem, 18- ?
	37572.1.5	Pensées. Recueil en prose. Genève, 18- .
	38563.32.15	Perrault, C. Les contes des fées de Charles Perrault. Paris, 18- .
	37573.400.30	Le petit moissonneur des théâtres. Paris, 18- .
	42545.69.50	Pierron, Eugène. Book the third, chapter the first, a comedy. London, 18- ?
	41586.28.6.5	Pixerécourt, R.C.G. de. Adelaide. London, 18- ?
	38588.16.13	Quinault, Philippe. Sceaux, poeme en deux chants. Paris? 18- .
	37555.327.2	Quitard, Pierre M. Dictionnaire des rimes. 7. éd. Paris, 18- ?
	38536.18.50A	Rabelais, F. Works. London, 18- .
	38585.19.8	Racine, Jean. Andromaque, tragédie. Paris, 18- .
	38585.22	Racine, Jean. Bajazet. Paris, 18- .
	42587.50.16	Rambaud, Alfred. L'anneau de César. pt.1. Paris, 18- .
	42535.19	Ratisbonne, Louis. La comédie enfantine. Pt. 2. 77. éd. Paris, 18- .
	42587.50.51	Rattazzi, Marie Bonaparte-Wyse. Louise de Kelner. Le dernier rêve d'une ambitieuse. 2. sér. Paris, 18- ?
	42515.30.20	Renan, Ernest. L'abbesse de Jouarre. London, 18- ?
	40524.28.2.5	Restif de la Bretonne, Nicolas E. Les contemporaines du commun. Paris, 18- .
	FL 398.76.15F	La rigolbachomanie. Paris, 18- ?
	41557.3	Ropartz, S. Récits bretons. St. Brieuc, 18- .
	42546.14.4	Rostand, Edmond. Cyrano de Bergerac. N.Y., 18- .
	37583.505	Rotrou, Jean de. Chefs-d'oeuvre tragiques de Rotrou. Paris, 18- .
Htn	39595.25*	St. Pierre, J.H.B. de. Paul et Virginie. Paris, 18- .
Htn	39594.26.4*	St. Pierre, J.H.B. de. Paul et Virginie. Paris, 18- ?
Htn	39594.26.5*	St. Pierre, J.H.B. de. Paul et Virginie. Paris, 18- .
	39595.19	St. Pierre, J.H.B. de. The shipwreck of Paul and Virginia. London, 18- .
	40576.3.10	Sainte-Beuve, Charles A. Causeries du lundi. Paris, 18- . 15v.
	40576.3.7	Sainte-Beuve, Charles A. Causeries du lundi. v.7. 3. éd. Paris, 18- .
	41557.8.79.5	Sand, George. L'homme de neige. Paris, 18- . 2v.
	41557.9.30.5	Sand, George. Little Fadette. A domestic story. London, 18- ?
	41557.9.45.10	Sand, George. La mare au diable. Cambridge, 18- .
	41557.9.80	Sand, George. Marianne. Boston, 18- .
	41588.3.20	Scribe, Eugène. I ciarlatani in Ispagna. n.p., 18- ?
	41587.32	Scribe, Eugène. Le colonel. Paris, 18- ?
	41588.14.9	Scribe, Eugène. Das Glas Wasser. 2. ed. Hamburg, 18- .
	41588.14.35	Scribe, Eugène. L'intérieur d'un bureau. Bruxelles, 18- .
	42548.18.6	Siraudin, P. Les femmes qui pleurent. N.Y., 18- ?
	Mol 880.32.5	Smith, Solomon. The hypocrite. N.Y., 18- ?
	41558.27	Soulié, Frédéric. La claserie des genêts. Paris, 18- .
	41558.81	Souvestre, Emile. Mrs. Willis's will; a comic drama. Boston, 18- .
	41558.85	Souvestre, Emile. A slight mistake, a comedy. Boston, 18-
	41558.72F	Souvestre, Émile. Souvenirs d'un Bas-Breton. Paris, 18- .
	40592.27.2	Staël Holstein, Anne Louise. Corinne, or Italy. N.Y., 18-
	40592.25.5	Staël Holstein, Anne Louise. Corinne, ou l'Italie. Paris, 18- ?
	41563.11.6	Sue, Eugène. Martin the foundling. n.p., 18- .
	37556.13	Texier, E. Biographie des journalistes. Paris, 18- .
NEDL	42578.62	Vast, Raoul. Pour ces dames! Paris, 18- .
	42581.19.5	Verne, Jules. Cinq semaines en ballon. 68. éd. Paris, 18- ?
	42582.25.6	Verne, Jules. The tour of the world in eighty days. N.Y., 18- ?
	42582.26.10	Verne, Jules. Twenty thousand leagues under the sea. N.Y., 18- ?
	42583.13	Verne, Jules. Vingt mille lieues sous les mers. Paris, 18- ? 2v.
Htn	42581.20.10*	Verne, Jules. Voyage au centre de la terre. Paris, 18- ?
	41564.16.5	Vigny, Alfred de. Poèmes antiques et modernes. Les meilleurs auteurs classiques, français et étrangers. Paris, 18- .
	39544.27.3.5	Voltaire, François Marie Arouet de. Lettres choisies. Paris, 18- ? 2v.
	41588.49	Wafflard, A.J.M. Un moment d'imprudence. n.p., 18- ?

18,

	Mol 750.5	Fortia d'Urban. Supplement aux diverses éditions de Molière. Paris, 18, La Gué

180-

	40527.7	Bernard, Pierre Joseph. Oeuvres complètes. Paris, 180-?

1800

	41583.6.10	Andrieux, François G.J.S. Contes et opuscules. Paris, 1800.
	41583.9.8	Barré, Pierre y. Gessner. Paris, 1800.
	40529.15.3	Bièvre, François Georges Maréchal. Bièvriana, ou Jeux de mots. Paris, 1800.
	38566.6.9	Boileau Despréaux, Nicolas. Oeuvres. v.1-2. Paris, 1800.
	41566.14.28	Bouilly, Jean N. L'abbé de l'épée; comédie historique. Paris, 1800.
	Mon 112.1	Bourdic-Viot, H. Eloge de Montaigne. Paris, 1800?
	41522.69.150	Bruno, Louis de. Lioncel, ou l'émigré, nouvelle historique. Paris, 1800.
	41583.18.50	Chaussier, Hector. Maria ou La forête de Limberg. Paris, 1800.
	FL 398.13.9A	Clairon, Hypolite. Mémoirs. London, 1800. 2v.
	40534.22.19	Collin d'Harleville, J.F. Les moeurs du jour. Paris, 1800.
	39535.18	Colnet du Ravel, C.J.A.M. de. Satiriques du 18e siècle. Paris, 1800. 7v.
	37574.370	Contes théologiques et autres poésies. Paris, 1800.
	38576.12.42.20	Corneille, Thomas. Chefs-d'oeuvre de Thomas Corneille. Paris, 1800.
	40534.29.15	Crébillon, Prosper Jolyot de. Rhadamiste et Zenobie. Paris, 1800.
	Mol 860.20	Creuzé, A. Ninon de Lenclos. Paris, 1800.
	41593.21	Delille, J. L'homme des Champs. Basle, 1800.
	40535.2.30	Demautort, J.B. Vadé chez lui. Paris, 1800.
	37541.17	Dessessarts, N.L.N. Les siècles littéraires de la France. Paris, 1800-03. 7v.
	39562.3	Diderot, Denis. Oeuvres. Paris, 1800. 15v.

1800 - cont.

42568.2.50 Diguet, C. Secret d'alcove. Paris, 1800.
40535.11.20 Ducis, Jean F. Othello, ou le more de Venise. Paris, 1800.
40588.21.15 Genlis, S.F.D. de St. La Bruyère the less. London, 1800.
40588.9.8 Genlis, S.F.D. de St. Les mères rivales, ou La calomnie. Berlin, 1800. 3v.
41584.52 Gibert, B. Rozélina. Paris, 1800.
39527.9 La Fontaine, Jean de. Contes et nouvelles en vers. Paris, 1800.
40526.64 Lalanne, Jean B. Le potager. Paris, 1800.
41586.12.3 Le Feure, Pierre. Zuma, a tragedy. London, 1800.
40536.10.273 Léger, F.P.A. La journée de Saint-Cloud. Paris, 1800.
40536.10.304 Legouvé, Gabriel. Epicharis et Néron. Paris, 1800.
40536.10.315 Legouvé, Gabriel. Etéocle. Paris, 1800.
41586.15.2.30 Lemercier, N.L. Agamenon. Madrid, 1800.
41586.15.12 Lemercier, N.L. Pinto, ou La journée d'une conspiration. Paris, 1800.
40512.25.5 LeSage, Alain René. Aventuras de Gil Blas de Santillana. Madrid, 1800. 5v.
40526.56 Le Suire, Robert M. Le nouveau monde. Paris, 1800.
40536.10.600 Ligier, F. Grécourt, ou La dinée de la diligence. Paris, 1800.
40536.10.800 Lourdet de Santerre, J.B. Ziméo. Paris, 1800.
40529.26.4 Maréchal, Nicolas. La renaissance de la religion en France. 4e éd. Blois, 1800.
39598.9.25 Marmontel, J.F. Moral tales. London, 1800.
40535.60.10 Milcent, Jean B.G.M. de. Hécube; tragédie-lyrique en quatre actes. Paris, 1800.
Htn 41597.50* Le mystère du chevalier. Paris, 1800.
41587.7.75 Picard, Louis Benoît. Les trois maris. Paris, 1800.
40536.20.30 Piron, Alexis. Poésies libres et joyeuses. n.p., 1800?
39545.34 Poemes...de Voltaire. Paris, 1800.
40527.50 Poésie sacrée. 2e éd. n.p., 1800. 2 pam.
40536.19.2500 Révéroni St. Cyr, J.A. Le délire. Paris, 1800.
41586.29.75 Revoil, P.H. Sterne à Paris. Paris, 1800.
40536.21.22 Roger, Jean François. Caroline, ou Le tableau. Paris, 1800.
40539.5 Rosny, Joseph de. La rêve d'un philosophe, ou Voici toute mon ambition! Rodez, 1800.
39594.34 St. Pierre, J.H.B. de. Paul and Virginia. London, 1800.
39564.29.10 Salverte, Eugsèbe. Eloge philosophique de Denis Diderot. Paris, 1800-01.
40543.15 Segur, Alexandre Joseph Pierre. La portrait de Fielding. Paris, 1800.
40536.42 Serieys, Antoine. La mort de Robespierre. Paris, 1800-01.
40525.7 Tressan, L.E. Le chevalier Robert, surnommé le Brave. Paris, 1800.
39542.32 Voltaire, François Marie Arouet de. Chef-d'oeuvres dramatique. Paris, 1800? 4v.
39545.34.7 Voltaire, François Marie Arouet de. Epitres, stances et odes. Paris, 1800.
39545.39 Voltaire, François Marie Arouet de. La Henriade. London, 1800.

1801

40517.5.5A Beauharnais, F.M. de C. L'ile de la félicité ou Anaxis et Théoni. Paris, 1801.
41583.12.100 Bignon, E.A. Les chevaliers du soleil. Paris, 1801.
38557.52.10 Bossuet, J.B. Exposition de la doctrine de l'église catholique sur les matières de controverse. St. Brieuc, 1801.
41522.69.5 Breton, Louis Julien. A lala. Au grand Village, 1801. 2 pam.
41522.69 Breton, Louis Julien. A lala. 3. é. Paris, 1801.
41593.27.20 Chaussard, P.J.B. Examen de l'homme des champs. Paris, 1801.
41583.18.50.5 Chaussier, Hector. Les prestiges, ou Amine et Sohi. Paris, 1801.
41583.18.53 Chazet, André René P.A. Philippe le Savoyard, ou L'origine des ponts neufs. Paris, 1801.
41593.16.17 Clemenceau. Le vengeur des rois, poème. Londres, 1801.
40586.14.60 Clément, J.M.B. Roman poétique: Atala. Paris, 1801.
40534.22 Collin d'Harleville, J.F. Le vieux célibataire. Paris, 1801.
38573.2 Corneille, Pierre. Oeuvres. v.1-3, 5-12; v.4, lost. Paris, 1801. 11v.
40588.5 Cottin, Marie R. (Mme.). Malvina. Paris, 1801. 4v.
Htn 37578.32* Cousin, Charles Y. Gasconiana. Paris, 1801.
Mol 703.5 Cousin d'Avallon, C.Y. Moliérana. Paris, 1801.
39545.29.20 Cousin d'Avallon, Charles Ives Cousin. Voltairians. 2. ed. Paris, 1801.
40553.11 Cousin d'Avallon, Charles Yves Cousin. Le nouveau tambour du monde. Paris, 1801.
41593.190.5 Croiszetière, G.J.C. Poésies morales et philosophiques. Paris, 1801.
Htn 41593.24* Delille, J. The rural philosopher. London, 1801.
41584.7 Dieu-La-Foy, J.M.A.M. La revue de l'an huit, suite de la revue de l'an six. Paris, 1801.
38588.20.7 Dufresny, Charles Rivière. Petit voyage dans le grand monde. Paris, 1801.
38553.31A Fénelon, F. de S. de la Mothe. Le aventure di Telemace. London, 1801. 2v.
41584.49 Ferrand of Rouen. Le savetier de Péronne. Rouen, 1801.
41584.51.10 Gardy, J.A. Gilles bon ami. Paris, 1801.
40588.9.12 Genlis, S.F.D. de St. Herbier moral. Paris, 1801.
40588.21.16 Genlis, S.F.D. de St. La Bruyère the less. Dublin, 1801.
41584.58.11 Hoffman, F.B. Le jeune sage et le vieux fou. Paris, 1801-02.
40535.19.63 La Chabeaussière, A.E.T.P. de. Oeuvres diverses. Paris, 1801.
38512.12 La Curne de St. Palaye. Memoirs of Froissart. London, 1801.
39527.12 La Fontaine, Jean de. Fables. Agen, 1801.
Htn 40516.27* Lavallée, Joseph. The negro equalled by few Europeans. Philadelphia, 1801. 2v.
FL 398.49 Lekain, H.L. Mémoires. Paris, 1801.
41569.24 The little mountaineers of Auvergne. London, 1801.
40529.31.5 Maréchal, Pierre S. La femme abbé. Paris, 1801.
Htn 40529.29.2* Maréchal, Pierre S. Projet d'une loi portant defense d'apprendre à lire aux femmes. Paris, 1801.
40529.29.3 Maréchal, Pierre S. Projet d'une loi portant defense d'apprendre à lire aux femmes. Paris, 1801.
Htn 39598.13* Marmontel, J.F. Select translations and imitations from the French. N.Y., 1801.
40536.10.1100 Mazoïer, F. Thesée. Paris, 1801.

1801 - cont.

Mol 182.1.9 Molière, Jean Baptiste Poquelin. Dépit amoureux...Cailhava. Paris, 1801.
Mon 18.01 Montaigne, Michel de. Essais. Paris, 1801. 16v.
40588.27.75 Montolieu, I.P. de. The enchanted plants. 2. ed. London, 1801.
40586.14.50 Morellet, A. Observations critiques sur le roman intitulé Atala. Paris, 1801.
39578.18 Necker, S.C. (Mme.). Nouveaux mélanges extraits des manuscrits. Paris, 1801. 2v.
Htn 40525.36* Oderahi, histoire américaine. Paris, 1801.
41587.8.5 Picard, Louis Benoît. Duhautcours; ou Le contrat d'union. Paris, 1801.
41587.7.60 Picard, Louis Benoît. La petite ville. Paris, 1801.
41547.11 Pigault-Lebrun, C.A.G.R. de. La folie espagnole. Paris, 1801. 4v.
41547.13.45 Pigault-Lebrun, C.A.G.R. de. My uncle Thomas. London, 1801. 4v.
41586.28.65 Pixerécourt, R.C.G. de. Le pélerin blanc. Paris, 1801.
Htn 38582.6.10F* Racine, Jean. Oeuvres. The 56 plates only. Paris, 1801-05.
Mol 860.21 Rigaud, A.F. Molière avec ses amis. Paris, 1801.
Htn 40527.20* Robbé de Beauveset, P.H. Oeuvres badines. London, 1801. 2v.
40536.21.20 Roger, Jean François. Le valet de deux maîtres. 2. éd. Paris, 1801.
FL 6021.01 Rousseau, J.J. Les confessions. Paris, 1801. 2v.
FL 6051.01 Rousseau, J.J. Julie ou la nouvelle Héloise. Leipzig, 1801. 3v.
40536.27.7 Saurin, Bernard J. Spartacus; tragédie. Paris, 1801.
40536.42.1 Serieys, Antoine. La mort de Robespierre. Paris, 1801.
41588.29.8.10 Servières, Joseph. La martingale, ou Le secret de Gagner au jeu. Paris, 1801.
41568.20 Sewrin, C.A. Hilaire et Berthille. Paris, 1801.
41588.47.250 Villemontez, Bidon de. Ovinska, ou Les exilés en Sybérie. Paris, 1801.
39545.34.5 Voltaire, François Marie Arouet de. Contes en vers, satires et poesies melées. Paris, 1801.
39545.38 Voltaire, François Marie Arouet de. La Henriade. Paris, 1801.
39545.49 Voltaire, François Marie Arouet de. La pucelle. Paris, 1801.

1802

X Cg 40515.1.30 Belin de Ballu, J.N. Le prêtre. Paris, 1802.
Htn 40517.8* Berquin, Arnaud. Oeuvres complètes. Paris, 1802. 10v.
41593.13 Berquin-Duvallon. Recueil de poésies d'un colon de St. Domingue. Brest, 1802.
41583.14.22 Bonel, P.G.A. L'auberge de Calais. Paris, 1802.
38557.26 Bossuet, J.B. Oraisons funèbres. Paris, 1802.
41583.15.250 Bouquier, G. La réunion du dix août. Paris, 1802.
41566.19.10 Cadet, Jêsus. (pseud.). Les aventures de Jêsus Cadet, par lui. Paris, 1802.
Mol 603.1 Cailhava d'Estendoux, Jean François. Études sur Molière. Paris, 1802.
40586.9 Chateaubriand, F.A.R. Atala. Boston, 1802.
Htn 40586.18.10* Chateaubriand, F.A.R. Génie du Christianisme. Paris, 1802. 5v.
Mol 860.22 Chazet, André R.P.A. de. Molière chez Ninon. Paris, 1802.
40537.11.39 Chénier, Marie Joseph. Fénelon...tragédie. Paris, 1802.
40537.11.41 Chénier, Marie Joseph. Fénelon...tragédie. 4. éd. Paris, 1802.
40537.10 Chénier, Marie Joseph. Les miracles. 4. éd. Paris, 1802.
40529.52 Contes et épigrammes en vers. 2e éd. Paris, 1802.
FL 391.30 Le coup de Foulet ou Revue des tous les théâtres. Paris, 1802.
40586.18.25 Coup-d'oeil rapide sur le génie du Christianisme. Paris, 1802.
40534.26.2 Crébillon, Prosper Jolyot de. Oeuvres. Paris, 1802.
40534.26 Crébillon, Prosper Jolyot de. Oeuvres. Paris, 1802.
41593.26.50 Delille, J. Dithyrambe sur l'immortalité de l'âme. Paris, 1802.
41593.20.25 Delille, J. Poésies fugitives. Paris, 1802-1805. 8v.
41593.20.27 Delille, J. Poésies fugitives et morceaux choisis. Paris, 1802.
Htn 41591.24.30* Delille, Jacques. L'homme des champs. Strasbourg, 1802.
39545.29.5 Despréaux de la Condamine Simien. Soirées de Ferney, ou Confidences de Voltaire. Paris, 1802.
37533.31.2 Ersch, J.S. La France littéraire. Supplement. Hambourg, 1802. 2v.
FL 394.5 Etienne, C.G. Histoire du théâtre français. v. 1-4. Paris, 1802. 2v.
40535.14.5 Fabre d'Eglantine, P.F.N. Oeuvres mêlées et posthumes. Paris, 1802. 2v.
Mol 880.16 Fabre d'Eglantine, P.F.N. Le Philinte de Molière. Paris, 1802.
40524.17.20 Fiévée, Joseph. Le divorce, Le faux revolutionnaire, et L'héroïsme des femmes. London, 1802.
40524.17.5 Fiévée, Joseph. Suzette's marriage portion; a novel. Dublin, 1802.
40588.9.14 Genlis, S.F.D. de St. La philosophie chrétienne. Paris, 1802.
FL 6135.1 Guyot, A.J. Epitaphe de Jean-Jacques Rousseau. Paris, 1802.
40545.13 Lauraguais, L.B. Lettres à Madame ***. Paris, 1802.
42544.17.4 Legouvé, Gabriel. Il merto delle donne. Paris, 1802.
40524.40 Lentier, E.F. de. Voyages d'Antenor en Grèce et en Asie. 5e éd. Paris, 1802. 3v.
39598.33 Marmontel, J.F. Trial of friendship. Boston, 1802.
41586.19.9.18 Marsollier des Vivetières, B.J. Alexis, ou L'erreur d'un bon père. Paris, 1802.
40516.52.5 Mercier, Louis S. Memoirs of the year 2500. Liverpool, 1802.
Mol 262.1.5 Molière, Jean Baptiste Poquelin. Sganarelle...un acte. Gardy. Paris, 1802.
Mon 18.02A Montaigne, Michel de. Essais. Naigeon. Paris, 1802. 4v.
Htn Mon 18.02.2* Montaigne, Michel de. Essais. Naigeon. Paris, 1802. 4v.
Mon 18.02.3 Montaigne, Michel de. Essais. Naigeon. Paris, 1802. 5v.
39594.3.5 Montesquieu, C.L. de S. The spirit of laws. Philadelphia, 1802. 2v.

1802 - cont.

	39584.20.5	Palissot de Montevoy, C. Étrennes à M. de La Harpe. Paris, 1802.
	Mol 860.22.5	Palmezeaux, C. La mort de Molière. Paris, 1802.
	41586.27.15	Perin, René. La grande ville. Paris, 1802.
	40536.19.50	Pessey, H. Ortalbano. Paris, 1802.
	41586.27.200	Petit, P.A.S. L'Anglais à Berlin. Paris, 1802.
	38526.45	Pibrac, Guy du Faur. Quatrains. Paris, 1802.
	41587.7.5	Picard, Louis Benoît. Encore des menechmes. Paris, 1802.
	41587.7.45	Picard, Louis Benoît. L'entrée dans le monde. 2e éd. Paris, 1802.
	41587.13	Picard, Louis Benoît. Mediocre et rampant. Paris, 1802.
	41587.7.55	Picard, Louis Benoît. Les provinciaux a Paris. Paris, 1802.
	41587.7.65	Picard, Louis Benoît. La Saint-Jean. n.p., 1802.
	41547.7	Pigault-Lebrun, C.A.G.R. de. Les barons de Felsheim. Pts. 1,3,4. Paris, 1802.
	41597.47	Le regard de Dieu sur la France. Paris, 1802.
	38525.84.5	Rotrou, Jean de. Venceslas. Paris, 1802.
	FL 6062.2	Rousseau, J.J. La botanique. Paris, 1802.
	FL 6062.50	Rousseau, J.J. Letters on the elements of botany. Addressed to a lady. London, 1802.
	41568.21	Serwin, C.A. La première nuit des mes noces. Paris, 1802. 2v.
	41568.27	Villiers, Pierre. Souvenirs d'un déporté. Paris, 1802.
Htn	39545.100*	Voltaire, François Marie Arouet de. Pensées, remarques et observations. Paris, 1802.
Htn	39545.31*	Voltaire, François Marie Arouet de. Romans et contes. Paris, 1802. 2v.

1803

	39582.24.5	Arnaud, F.T.M. de B. Lorimon, or Man in every stage of life. London, 1803. 2v.
	Mol 882.25	Artusi. Teresa vedova. Milano, 1803.
	41593.3.10	Baour-Lormian, P.M.L. Recueil de poésies diverses. Bordeaux, 1803.
	41583.11.250	Bazin, Rigomer. Jacqueline d'Olzebourg. Paris, 1803.
	41522.23	Bellin de La Liborlière, L. Voyage de M. Candide fils. Paris, 1803. 2v.
	40527.4.5	Bernard, Pierre Joseph. Oeuvres. Paris, 1803. 2v.
Htn	38557.32*	Bossuet, J.B. Select sermons and funeral orations. Boston, 1803.
	FL 6118.03	Buman, J.N. Éloge de Jean-Jacques Rousseau. Paris, 1803.
	40586.10.2	Chateaubriand, F.A.R. Atala. Valencia, 1803.
Htn	40586.18.30*	Chateaubriand, F.A.R. Défense du génie du Christianisme. Paris, 1803.
	39532.16.02	Chaulieu, G.A. de. Poésies de Chaulieu. Paris, 1803.
	40538.10	Chimère et réalité. Paris, 1803.
	40534.22.5	Collin d'Harleville, J.F. Le vieillard et les jeunes gens. Paris, 1803.
	41593.26	Delille, J. Le malheur et la pitié. London, 1803.
	41593.26.8	Delille, J. La pitié, poème. Paris, 1803.
	41593.26.9	Delille, J. La pitié, poème. Paris, 1803.
	40516.95	Desboulmiers, J.A.J. Kerwald Castle, or Memoirs of the Marquis de Solanges. Maidstone, 1803.
	41584.33.5	Dumolard, Henri François. Le Philinte de Destouches. Paris, 1803.
	41593.27.30	Dupuy des Islets. Examen critique du poème de La Pitié de Jacques Delille. Paris, 1803.
	FL 398.56.5	Etienne, C.G. Vie de François René Mole, comédien français. Paris, 1803.
	38554.107.100	Fénelon, F. de S. de la Mothe. Lives of the ancient philosophers. v.2. Edinburgh, 1803.
	38552.10.10	Fénelon, F. de S. de la Mothe. Sermons choisis. Paris, 1803.
	38558.8	Fléchier, Esprit. Oraisons funèbres. Paris, 1803. 2v.
	40515.31.1	Florian, Jean P.C. de. Éliezer et Nephtaly. Paris, 1803.
NEDL	40515.16.10	Florian, Jean P.C. de. Oeuvres complèttes. v.2,4. Paris, 1803. 2v.
	40586.18.40	Fontanes, Louis. Extraits critiques du génie du Christianisme. Paris, 1803.
	40588.9.16	Genlis, S.F.D. de St. Les petits émigrés. 3. éd. Paris, 1803. 2v.
	39526.3	Guillon, M.N.S. La Fontaine et tous les fabulistes. Paris, 1803. 2v.
	40535.19.45	Jars, Antoine G. Les confidences. Paris, 1803.
	39527.12.5	La Fontaine, Jean de. Fables. Paris, 1803.
Htn	FL 380.45*	Lemazurier, P.D. L'opinion du parterre. Paris, 1803.
	41586.15.6	Lemercier, N.L. Isule et Orovèse; tragédie en 5 actes. Paris, 1803.
	41586.19.12	Martainville, Alphonse Louis Dieudonné. Le suicide de Falaise. Paris, 1803.
	40536.21.16	Martelly, Honoré François Richaud de. L'intrigant dupé par lui-même. Paris, 1803.
	Mol 211.17	Molière, Jean Baptiste Poquelin. Les femmes savantes. Toulouse, 1803.
	39594.3	Montesquieu, C.L. de S. De l'esprit des lois. v.3-5. Paris, 1803. 2v.
	39594.4	Montesquieu, C.L. de S. Lettres persanes. Paris, 1803.
	40588.28A	Montolieu, I.P. de. The enchanted plants. N.Y., 1803.
	40535.65.2	Monvel, Jacques Marie Boutet de. Les victimes cloitrées. Paris, 1803.
	37571.1	Moysant, François. Bibliothèque portative des écrivains françois. 2e éd. Londres, 1803. 3v.
	40586.18.28	Notes critiques...sur le Génie du Christianisme. Paris, 1803.
	40536.17.80	Palissot de Montenoy, Charles. Mémoires pour servir à l'histoire de notre littérature. Paris, 1803. 2v.
	37582.2.50	Petitot, Claude Bernard. Répertoire du théâtre français. Paris, 1803-04. 23v.
	41587.18.30	Picard, Louis Benoît. Le mari ambitieux. Paris, 1803.
	41587.7.80	Picard, Louis Benoît. Le vieux comédien. Paris, 1803.
	41547.8.2	Pigault-Lebrun, C.A.G.R. de. Le citateur. Hamborg, 1803. 2v.
	41547.8	Pigault-Lebrun, C.A.G.R. de. Le citateur. Pt.1-2. Paris, 1803.
	41587.19.150	Prévost, Augustin. La vengeance inattendue. 2e éd. Paris, 1803.
	41586.29.50	Reynery. Les conscrits, ou Le triomphe de la vertu. Lyon, 1803.
	FL 6015.4	Rousseau, J.J. Correspondance - originale et inédite. Paris, 1803. 2v.
	41586.29.100	Saulnier, G. Mahomet II. Paris, 1803.
	41588.29.82	Simmonin, A.J.B. Parlez pour moi. Paris, 1803.

1803 - cont.

	41588.29.90	Simonnin, A.J.B. Lisette toute seule, ou Ils se trompent tous deux. Paris, 1803.
	41588.29.85	Simonnin, A.J.B. Tricotinet, ou Parlez pour mai. Paris, 1803.
Htn	40592.36*	Staël Holstein, Anne Louise. Delphine. Paris, 1803. 3v.
	40593.18	Staël Holstein, Anne Louise. Treatise on...literature. London, 1803. 2v.
Htn	38514.13*	Surville, Joseph Étienne. Poésies de Madame de Surville. Paris, 1803.

1804

	41591.05	Alhoy, Louis. Les hospices; poëme. Paris, 1804.
	Mol 860.23	Andrieux, F.G.J.B. Molière avec ses amis. Paris, 1804.
	39585.25	Arnaud, F. Variétés littéraires. Paris, 1804. 4v.
	41522.23.10	Bellin de La Liborlière, L. Travels of young Candid. v.1-3. London, 1804.
	39576.25.10	Bérenger, L.P. La morale en action et en exemples. Lyon, 1804. 3v.
	40526.32.20	Blandurel, Antoine. La lyre chrétienne. Beauvais, 1804.
	41583.14.19	Bonel, P.G.A. La tour du sud. Paris, 1804.
	40527.40	Les charmes de mon exil. 2e éd. En Allemagne, 1804.
	39577.3	Condorcet, Marie Jean Antoine. Oeuvres complètes. Paris, 1804. 21v.
	40526.32.45	Cubières, Michel de. La mort de Caton, tragédie. Paris, 1804.
Htn	41593.23*	Delille, J. The rural philosopher. Newbern, North Carolina, 1804.
	41584.5	Demoustier, Charles A. Théâtre de C.A. Demoustier. Paris, 1804. 2v.
	37541.17.8	Dessessarts, N.L.N. Nouveau dictionnaire bibliographique portatif. 2. éd. Paris, 1804.
	42542.65.2	Donnay, Maurice. Le retour de Jérusalem. Paris, 1804.
	41584.33	Dumolard, Henri François. Vincent de Paul; drame. Paris, 1804.
	41584.27.12	Dupaty, Emmanuel. La jeune prude. Paris, 1804.
	38553.34	Fénelon, F. de S. de la Mothe. Aventuras de Telemaco. Paris, 1804.
	38554.3.10	Fénelon, F. de S. de la Mothe. Aventuras de Telémaco. Paris, 1804.
	38553.30	Fénelon, F. de S. de la Mothe. Le aventure di Telemace. Paris, 1804. 2v.
	38553.18	Fénelon, F. de S. de la Mothe. Les aventures de Télémaque. Paris, 1804.
Htn	38553.13.5*	Fénelon, F. de S. de la Mothe. Pious reflections for every day of the month. Salem, 1804.
	40515.32.5	Florian, Jean P.C. de. La Galatea de Miguel de Cervantes. Perpignan, 1804.
	40588.9.20	Genlis, S.F.D. de St. Adèle et Théodore. 4. éd. Paris, 1804. 4v.
	40588.9.22	Genlis, S.F.D. de St. Nouveaux contes moraux. Paris, 1804. 3v.
	40588.9.18	Genlis, S.F.D. de St. Le petit La Bruyère. 2. éd. Paris, 1804.
	40588.9.24	Genlis, S.F.D. de St. Les veillées du chateau. v.2,3. Paris, 1804. 2v.
	41584.55	Gougibus, J.T. L'homme d'Airain. Paris, 1804.
	40526.61.200	Henriquez, L.M. Les graces à confesse, poëme. Paris, 1804.
	37572.3	Ideler, L. Handbuch der französischen Sprache und Literatur. Berlin, 1804.
Htn	38553.13.2*	Kendall, John. Extracts from...Fénelon. Philadelphia, 1804.
Htn	38553.13*	Kendall, John. Extracts from the writings of François Fénelon. Philadelphia, 1804.
	38564.14	La Bruyère, J. de. Les caractères de Théophraste. Lyon, 1804.
	39527.54	La Fontaine, Jean de. Théâtre. Paris, 1804.
	40535.19.28	LaHarpe, J.F. de. Mélanie. Paris, 1804.
	39584.10	La Harpe, Jean François de. Correspondance littéraire. Paris, 1804.
	FL 6039.3	Landes, P. Rousseau, Grundsätze des natürlichen Staatsrechts. Leipzig, 1804.
	38543.10.14	La Rochefoucauld, François. Mémoires. Paris, 1804.
	38551.139	The life of Salignac de la Mothe Fénelon. N.Y., 1804.
	41586.16.19	Loaisel-Tréogate, J.M. Le grand chasseur. Paris, 1804.
	40535.25.8.10	Marchant, François. Fénélon; poème. 2. éd. Cambrai, 1804.
	39597.13	Marmontel, J.F. Contes moraux, anciens et nouveaux. Paris, 1804. 8v.
	39597.29	Marmontel, J.F. Oeuvres posthumes. Paris, 1804. 4v.
	39597.23	Marmontel, J.F. Oeuvres posthumes. Paris, 1804. 4v.
	Mol 18.04	Molière, Jean Baptiste Poquelin. Oeuvres. v.2. Paris, 1804.
	41587.7.70	Picard, Louis Benoît. Les tracasseries. Paris, 1804.
	41557.2.25	Picquemard, Jean B. Zoflora. London, 1804. 2v.
	41586.28.6	Pixerécourt, R.C.G. de. Tékéli, ou le siège de Montgatz. Paris, 1804.
	41587.19.100	Pradel, H. Le contrariant, comédie en cinq actes et en vers. Paris, 1804.
	39586.31	Sabatier, Antoine de Castres. Considérations politiques sur les gens d'esprit et de talent, tirées d'un ouvrage inédit de...S. de Castres. Paris, 1804.
	38542.23	Saint-Evremond, C. de M. de S.D. Oeuvres choisies de Saint Evremont. Paris, 1804.
	41565.27	St. Mars, G.A.C. de C. Mémoires des autres. Paris, 1804-72. 6v.
	41588.29.8	Servières, Joseph. Le dansomane de la rue Quincampoix. Paris, 1804.
	41588.29.7	Servières, Joseph. Toujours le même. Paris, 1804.
	39585.17	Suard, J.B.A. Mélanges de littérature. 2. éd., v.1-3; 3. éd., v.4-5. Paris, 1804-06. 5v.
	38514.14	Surville, Joseph Étienne. Poésies de Madame de Surville. Paris, 1804.
	39545.39.5	Voltaire, François Marie Arouet de. La Henriade. Paris, 1804.

1805

	39574.16	Alembert, J. Le Rond d'. Oeuvres. Paris, 1805. 18v.
	40526.32	Bernis, François Joachim de Pierre de. La religion vengée. Paris, 1805.
	41522.69.250	Blaze, Henri Sebastien. Julien, ou le prêtre. pts.1-2. Paris, 1805.
	40534.16.17.9	Candeille, Julie. Catherine. Paris, 1805.

1805 - cont.

Htn 40586.10.5* Chateaubriand, F.A.R. Atala. Paris, 1805.
39584.20.10 Chazet, A.R.P.A. de. Éloge de La Harpe. Paris, 1805.
37581.39 Choix de pièces de théâtres de Paris, 1805-1839. Paris, 1805-39.
41583.19.5 Cuvelier de Trie, J.G.A. La fille hussard, ou Le sergent suédois. Paris, 1805.
39544.85.10 De la philosophie de la Henriade. Paris, 1805.
41584.4 Delaunay, A.J. L'un pour l'autre. Paris, 1805.
41593.22 Delille, J. L'homme des Champs. Paris, 1805.
41593.26.10 Delille, J. La pitié, poème. Paris, 1805.
Htn 39564.16* Diderot, Denis. Rameau's Neffe...Übersetzt von Goethe. Leipzig, 1805.
41584.34 Dubois, Jean B. La fausse marquise. Paris, 1805.
41584.27.150 Duval, George. Ildamor et Tubéma. Paris, 1805.
41588.65.5 Le fantôme de Bérezule. Paris, 1805.
38553.21.5 Fénelon, F. de S. de la Mothe. Les adventures de Télémaque, fils d'Ulysse. N.Y., 1805.
38554.325.65 Fénelon, F. de S. de la Mothe. Dialogues des morts anciens et modernes. Limoges, 1805.
40588.9.9 Genlis, S.F.D. de St. Dwie matki jednego dzieciétcia, czyli Matki rywalki. Warszawie, 1805. 2v.
39578.14 Gerando, J.M. Éloge de Du Marsais. Paris, 1805.
40526.25 Gilbert, N.J.L. Oeuvres complètes. v.2. Paris, 1805.
41593.32.200 Grobert, Joseph. Napoleone al Danubio, canzone. Parigi, 1805.
39532.5.9 Hamilton, Anthony. Oeuvres complètes d'Hamilton. Paris, 1805. 3v.
41584.56.5 Hapdé, J.B. La guerrière des sept Montagnes. Paris, 1805.
41584.56.50 Henrion, Charles. Les persécutions diaboliques. Liège, 1805.
41567.25.25 Hilarion, père. Le triomphe de l'amour conjugal. Paris, 1805.
40526.61.300 Isnard, Maximin. Dithyrambe sur l'immortalité de l'âme. Paris, 1805.
Htn 38544.27.290* La Fayette, Marie M. The princess of Monpensier. London, 1805.
41586.1.5 La Roche, Philippe J. de. Ramire, ou Le fils naturel. 2e éd. Paris, 1805.
37578.95 Le livre des singularites. Paris, 1805.
39597.30 Marmontel, J.F. Mémoires. Paris, 1805. 4v.
39598.3 Marmontel, J.F. Memoirs. London, 1805. 4v.
39597.26 Marmontel, J.F. Regence du duc d'Orléans. Paris, 1805. 2v.
41588.69 Mellinet, Anne François. Le muette de sénès. Paris, 1805.
40588.28.50 Montolieu, I.P. de. Tales. London, 1805. 3v.
41596.43.10 Paillet, Julien. Le panthéon dijonnais. Dijon, 1805.
41596.47 Parny, Évariste. Porte-feuille volé. Paris, 1805.
41586.27.150 Pitt. Les bandoléros. Paris, 1805.
41586.28.15 Pixerécourt, R.C.G. de. Robinson Crusoé. Paris, 1805.
40536.19.2505 Réveroni St. Cyr, J.A. Le vaisseau amiral. Paris, 1805.
Htn FL 6062.3PF* Rousseau, J.J. La botanique. Paris, 1805.
41587.27.150 Sidoni. Cadet Roussel. Paris, 1805.
41588.29.95 Simonnin, A.J.B. Danières à gonesse. Paris, 1805.
39545.43.14 Voltaire, François Marie Arouet de. La Henriade. Paris, 1805.

1806

41583.10 Aumer, Pierre. Jemry, ou Le mariage secret. Paris, 1806.
41583.11.2 Barthelemy-Hadot, M.A. (Mme.). Jules, ou Le toit paternel. Paris, 1806.
40526.1.25 Berchoux, J. de. La danse, ou Les dieux de l'opera, poëme. Paris, 1806.
40582.19 Beyle, Henri. Promenades dans Rome. Paris, 1806. 2v.
41583.14.7 Boirie, E.C. de. La caverne de Sonabe. Paris, 1806.
41583.18.20.9 Caigniez, Louis Charles. La forêt d'Hermanstad. Paris, 1806.
41583.18.25 Charrin, P.J. Le lion parlant. Paris, 1806.
40537.11.27 Chénier, Marie Joseph. Épitre à Voltaire. Paris, 1806.
41591.24.25 Delille, Jacques. L'imagination, poëme. Paris, 1806. 2v.
41593.29.2.3 Désaugiers, M.A. Le mari intrigué. Paris, 1806.
41584.27.90 Dupetit-Méré, F. A Spandau, ou le libelle. Paris, 1806.
40555.3 Dutens, M. Mémoires d'un voyageur qui se repose. Paris, 1806. 3v.
41593.32.12 Esménard, J. La navigation. Poème. Paris, 1806.
38553.22 Fénelon, F. de S. de la Mothe. Les adventures de Télémaque. Philadelphia, 1806-07. 2v.
Mol 865.2 Gaillard, L. Éloge de Molière. n.p., 1806.
40526.61.150 Gence, J.B.M. Dieu, l'être infini. Paris, 1806.
40588.9.26 Genlis, S.F.D. de St. Les annales de la vertu. v.2,5. Paris, 1806. 2v.
40588.9.28 Genlis, S.F.D. de St. La duchesse de la Vallière. 8. éd. Paris, 1806. 2v.
Htn 40588.21.110* Genlis, S.F.D. de St. Madame de Maintenon. London, 1806. 2v.
40516.12 Gudin, Paul-Phillippe. Contes. Paris, 1806. 2v.
41584.56.10 Hapdé, J.B. Le pont du diable. Paris, 1806.
39584.7 La Harpe, Jean François de. Oeuvres choisies et posthumes. Paris, 1806. 4v.
40536.10.300 Legouvé, Gabriel. La mort de Henri quatre, roi de France. Paris, 1806.
40586.18.60 Lettre à M. de Chateaubriand, sur deux chapitres du Génie du Christianisme. Gèneve, 1806.
38546.25 Lettres de Mesdames de Scudéry, de S. de Saliez. Paris, 1806.
37572.35.3 Mélanges sur Charles Nodier, Paillet, Dronineau. Paris, 1806-33.
40537.72 Memoirs of a traveller now in retirement. London, 1806. 5v.
Htn 41556.29* Nodier, Charles. Les tristes. Paris, 1806.
41586.28.20 Pixerécourt, R.C.G. de. Le solitaire de la roche noir. Paris, 1806.
FL 6051.06 Rousseau, J.J. La nouvelle Héloise. Paris, 1806. 4v.
41588.29.6 Servières, Joseph. Alphonsine, ou La tendresse maternelle. Paris, 1806.

1807

41597.31 Annales poétiques. Paris, 1807. 2v.
FL 383.07 Cailhava d'Estendoux, Jean François. Les causes de la décadence du théâtre. Paris, 1807.
42546.31.13 Castelfranco, A. Il teatro francese contemporaneo. Firenze, 1807.

1807 - cont.

41593.170.5 Collet, L. Josué, ou La conquête de la terre promise. Bourg, 1807.
38574.11 Corneille, Pierre. Chefs-d'oeuvres. Paris, 1807. 3v.
Htn 41597.46* Couronne poétique de Napoléon-le-Grand. Paris, 1807.
41593.29.2.5 Désaugiers, M.A. Un diner par victoire. Paris, 1807.
41593.29.2.4 Désaugiers, M.A. Le valet d'emprunt. Paris, 1807.
39585.5.25 Dulaurens, H.J. La chandelle d'Arras; poéme. Paris, 1807.
41584.29.25 Duval, A. Die Jugend Heinrichs. Wien, 1807.
38554.2.5 Fénelon, F. de S. de la Mothe. Telemachus. London, 1807.
41584.49.150 Friedelle, A. Amélie, ou Le protecteur mystérieux. Paris, 1807.
40588.16 Genlis, S.F.D. de St. Juvenile theatre. N.Y., 1807.
38575.11 Geoffrey, M. La revue des Feuilletons du journal de l'empire. Paris, 1807.
41586.12.9 Le Hoc, M. Pyrrhus, ou les Aeacides. Paris, 1807.
40529.82 Le Plat du Temple, Victor Alexandre Chretien. Virgile en France, ou La nouvelle Enéide. Bruxelles, 1807-08. 2v.
41595.19 Lesseps, M. Ode aux français residant a Livourne pour le jour de la fête de St. Napoléon. Livourne, 1807?
38542.3 Lettres...de Voiture et Balzac. Paris, 1807.
41595.20 Luce de Lancival, J.C.J. Achille. Paris, 1807.
40529.31.25 Maréchal, Pierre S. De la vertu. Paris, 1807.
39598.5 Marmontel, J.F. Memoirs. v.1-2. Philadelphia, 1807.
41586.19.12.10 Martainville, Alphonse Louis Dieudonné. Grivoisiana, ou Recueil facétieux. 3. éd. Paris, 1807.
40538.30 Les moeurs de Londres. Paris, 1807.
Mol 262.5.5 Molière, Jean Baptiste Poquelin. Eifersucht in allen ecken. n.p., 1807.
39594.5 Montesquieu, C.L. de S. Oeuvres mélées et posthumes. Paris, 1807. 12v.
41596.46.25 Parny, Évariste. La guerre des dieux. Paris, 1807.
41587.17.10 Picard, Louis Benoît. Le jeune médecin. Paris, 1807.
41587.17.11 Picard, Louis Benoît. Le mariage des grenadiers. Paris, 1807.
40536.20.170 Plancher-Valcour, P.A.L.P. Eginard et Imnia. Paris, 1807.
38582.7 Racine, Jean. Oeuvres. Paris, 1807. 5v.
41597.27 Roman, J.J.T. Les Échecs. Poëme. Paris, 1807.
39594.20 St. Pierre, J.H.B. de. La chaumière indienne. Paris, 1807.
38585.43.10 Schlegel, A.W. Comparaison entre la Phèdre de Racine et celle d'Euripide. Paris, 1807.
41588.29.75 Simonnin, A.J.B. Caroline de Lichtfield. Paris, 1807.
41588.29.80 Simonnin, A.J.B. La jardinière de Vincennes. Paris, 1807.
40592.35.5 Staël Holstein, Anne Louise. Corinna, oder Italien. Berlin, 1807. 4v.
Htn 40592.21* Staël Holstein, Anne Louise. Corinne. Paris, 1807. 3v.

1808

37565.2 Aillaud, P.T. Discours sur cette question: Quels ont été les effets de la décadence des moeurs sur la littérature français? Paris, 1808.
39582.17 Arnaud, F.T.M. de B. Oeuvres. Paris, 1808.
41583.8.40 Aude, Joseph. La veille d'une grande fête. Paris, 1808.
FL 355.30 Babault. Annales dramatiques. Paris, 1808-12. 9v.
38557.2.55 Baudot, Pierre Louis. Lettre à M. C.X. Girault. Dijon, 1808.
39576.25 Bérenger, L.P. Le mentor vertueux. Paris, 1808.
40517.11 Berquin, Arnaud. L'ami des enfans. Paris, 1808. 12v.
41566.14.20 Bouilly, Jean N. Haine aux femmes. Paris, 1808.
41583.18.20.6 Caigniez, Louis Charles. La belle-mère et les deux orphelins. Paris, 1808.
Htn 40588.1.3* Cottin, Marie R. (Mme.). Elizabeth, or Exiles of Siberia. Philadelphia, 1808.
41583.19.6 Cuvelier de Trie, J.G.A. La bataille d'Aboukir. Paris, 1808.
Mol 860.24 Desfontaines, Henri Dupin. Le voyage de Chambord. Paris, 1808.
40535.15.5 Favart, Charles S. Memoires et correspondance littéraires. Paris, 1808. 3v.
40515.36.5 Florian, Jean P.C. de. Gonsalve de Cordoue. London, 1808.
Htn 40588.21.95* Genlis, S.F.D. de St. Belisaire. v.1-2. Paris, 1808.
40588.21.80 Genlis, S.F.D. de St. The Duke of Lauzun. London, 1808. 2v.
40588.17.50 Genlis, S.F.D. de St. The siege of Rochelle. London, 1808. 3v.
41584.51.150 Gibelin, A.E. Epitre aux chretiens de toutes les communions. London, 1808.
38557.2.30 Girault, C.X. Notice historique sur les aïeux de J.B. Bossuet. Dijon, 1808.
37574.325 Lablée, Jacques. Le nouveau parnasse chrétien. 2. éd. Paris, 1808.
41585.36 Lamey, Auguste. Elvérine de Wertheim. Paris, 1808.
41586.1.12 La Roche, Philippe J. de. Clara. Paris, 1808.
40512.14 LeSage, Alain René. Aventuras de Gil Blas. London, 1808. 4v.
39598.18 Marmontel, J.F. Bélisaire. Paris, 1808.
41569.6 Maucheron, Claude Athanase. Omniana. Paris, 1808.
38582.7.5 Racine, Jean. Oeuvres. Paris, 1808. 7v.
40526.42.5 Racine, Louis. Oeuvres. Paris, 1808. 6v.
39586.23.15 Rivoral, Antoine. Esprit de Rivarol. Paris, 1808.
39595.26 St. Pierre, J.H.B. de. Pablo y Virginia. Philadelphia, 1808.
39596.10 St. Pierre, J.H.B. de. Studies of nature. Philadelphia, 1808. 3v.
40592.34 Staël Holstein, Anne Louise. La Corinna. Firenze, 1808. 2v.
40592.27.5 Staël Holstein, Anne Louise. Corinne, or Italy. Philadelphia, 1808.
Htn 40592.27.6* Staël Holstein, Anne Louise. Corinne, or Italy. Philadelphia, 1808. 2v.
Htn 40592.27* Staël Holstein, Anne Louise. Corinne. Boston, 1808. 2v.
37582.2.25 Théâtre des auteurs du sécond ordre...stéréotype d'Herhan. Paris, 1808-10. 40v.
41596.64.30 Treneuil, Joseph. La princesse Amélie, élégie. Paris, 1808.
41596.64.3 Treneuil, Joseph. Les tombeaux de Saint-Denis. Paris, 1808.

1809

41583.9 Barré, Pierre y. Santara. Paris, 1809.

41583.11.2.5 Barthelemy-Hadot, M.A. (Mme.). Cosme de Médicis. Paris, 1809.

40532.3 Beaumarchais, Pierre A.C. de. Oeuvres complètes. Paris, 1809. 7v.

41583.12.35 Bernos, Alexandre. Le siège du clocher. Paris, 1809.

37574.9 Le Chansonnier du bon vieux temps. v.1-2. Paris, 1809-10.

Htn 40586.18.10.7* Chateaubriand, F.A.R. Génie du Christianisme. 2. éd. Paris, 1809. 2v.

Htn 40553.3* Constant de Rebecque, Benjamin. Wallstein. Paris, 1809.

40588.1.2 Cottin, Marie R. (Mme.). Elizabeth. Carlisle, 1809.

40554.15 Cousin, Victor. Gasconiana. Paris, 1809.

39544.355 Cousin d'Avallon, Charles Ives Cousin. Voltairiana. 3. ed. Paris, 1809?

41583.19.12 Cuvelier de Trie, J.G.A. La fille mendiante. Paris, 1809.

41584.3 Delisle de Sales, J.C. Oeuvres dramatiques et littéraires. Paris, 1809. 2v.

41584.27.80 Dupetit-Méré, F. L'isle des mariages. Paris, 1809.

40588.21.100 Genlis, S.F.D. de St. Belisarius; an historical romance. London, 1809. 2v.

Htn 39532.12.15* Hamilton, Anthony. Memoires of the life of Count de Grammont. 2d ed. London, 1809. 3v.

41586.15.9 Lemercier, N.L. Christopher Colomb. Paris, 1809.

40517.31.3 Le Prince de Beaumont, M. Magasin de enfans. v.1-4. Paris, 1809. 2v.

40511.25 LeSage, Alain René. Adventures of Gil Blas. London, 1809. 2v.

40512.32 LeSage, Alain René. Gil Blas di Santillano. London, 1809. 4v.

40512.14.2 LeSage, Alain René. Histoire de Gil Blas de Santillane. London, 1809. 4v.

Htn 40515.7* Lespinasse, J.J.E. de. Lettres, 1773-1776. Paris, 1809. 3v.

39598.31 Marmontel, J.F. Principes d'éloquence de Marmontel. Paris, 1809.

40556.40 Ménégault, A.P.F. Dictionnaire amusant et instructif. Paris, 1809. 2v.

38516.52 Méon, Dominique Martin. Blasons. Paris, 1809.

Mol 880.25.7 Merle. A bas Molière. Paris, 1809.

Mol 18.09 Molière, Jean Baptiste Poquelin. Oeuvres...Bret. Londres, 1809. 8v.

37562.4 Rosny, J. de. Tableau littéraire de la France. Paris, 1809.

FL 381.3 Ruphy, J.F. Lettres champenoises. Paris, 1809.

40536.30.7 Sedaine, Michel Jean. La gageure imprévue; comedie. Paris, 1809.

41587.27.160 Sidony. Jocrisse suicide. 2e éd. Paris, 1809.

38556.10 Tabaraud, M.M. Lettre à M. de Beausset, pour servir de supplement à son histoire de Fénelon. Paris, 1809.

38557.2.50 Tabaraud, M.M. Lettre à M. de Beausset. Paris, 1809. 2 pam.

181-

39545.29 Cousin d'Avallon, Charles Ives Cousin. Voltairiana, ou Recueil...de Voltaire. Paris, 181-.

41567.23.10 Guizot, Elizabeth C.P. de M. Les enfans. pt. 1. 2e éd. Paris, 181-?

1810

37595.8.3 Abailard, Pierre. Correspondencia de Abélardo y Eloisa. Madrid, 1810.

38545.28 Aiken, John. Memoirs of...Pierre Daniel Huet. London, 1810. 2v.

41591.1 Arnassant, M.L. Atala, poëme en six chants. Lyon, 1810.

41583.9.2 Barré, Pierre y. Des deux lions. Paris, 1810.

40531.6.100 Beaunoir, A.L.B.R. de. Les couronnes. Paris, 1810.

39576.25.15 Bérenger, L.P. La morale en action. Paris, 1810.

38566.9 Boileau Despréaux, Nicolas. Oeuvres. Paris, 1810.

38565.8 Boileau Despréaux, Nicolas. Oeuvres à l'usage des lycées. Paris, 1810.

38575.30 Corneille, Pierre. Le Cid...de Pierre Corneille. Paris, 1810.

40588.5.10 Cottin, Marie R. (Mme.). The Saracen, or Matilda and Malek Adhel. N.Y., 1810. 2v.

39534.25.10 Deshoulières, A. du L. del G. (Mme.). Oeuvres. Paris, 1810.

40526.35 Dougados, Jean. Oeuvres. Paris, 1810.

40516.90 Ducas de Bois St. Just, J.L.M. Les sires de Beaujeu. Lyon, 1810. 2v.

40517.23.20 Duclos, C.P. Morceaux choisis ou Recueil de pensées, remarques. Paris, 1810. 2v.

37571.2.3A Faucon, Nicolas. Bibliothèque portative. Boston, 1810.

Htn 37571.2* Faucon, Nicolas. Bibliothèque portative. Boston, 1810.

38554.326.100 Fénelon, F. de S. de la Mothe. Dialogues concerning eloquence in general. 1st American ed. Boston, 1810.

40515.34 Florian, Jean P.C. de. Gonzalve de Cordoue. Paris, 1810. 3v.

40515.37.2 Florian, Jean P.C. de. Guillaume Tell. Paris, 1810.

NEDL 40515.39.8 Florian, Jean P.C. de. William Tell, or Swisserland delivered. Baltimore, 1810.

40526.16 Gresset, Jean B. Le Parrain Magnifique. Paris, 1810.

37565.4 Jay, Antoine. Tableau littéraire de la France pendant le XVIII siècle. Paris, 1810.

39527.33.5 La Fontaine, Jean de. Les amours de psyché et de cupidon. Paris, 1810.

39527.15 La Fontaine, Jean de. Fables choisies de La Fontaine. N.Y., 1810.

FL 394.50 Lemazurier, Pierre D. Galerie historique des acteurs du théâtre français depuis 1600 jusqu'à nos jours. Paris, 1810. 2v.

40535.23 Le Mierre, A.M. Oeuvres. Paris, 1810. 3v.

40517.31.10 Le Prince de Beaumont, M. Le magasin des adolescentes. Paris, 1810.

40512.13 LeSage, Alain René. Adventures of Gil Blas of Santillane. Leominster, 1810.

40511.3 LeSage, Alain René. Oeuvres choisies. Paris, 1810. 16v.

41586.17.150 Luce de Lancival, J.C.J. Hector; a tragedy in five acts. London, 1810.

Mol 62.15 Molière, Jean Baptiste Poquelin. Lustspiele und Possen. Zürich, 1810. 6v.

41597.45 Ode à sa majesté imperiale et royale Napoléon à l'occasion de son mariage. Paris, 1810.

38552.3 Oeuvres de Fénelon. Toulouse, 1810. 19v.

1810 - cont.

40536.20.1 Piron, Alexis. Oeuvres choisies. Paris, 1810. 2v.

41586.28.25 Pixerécourt, R.C.G. de. Les ruines de Babylone. Paris, 1810.

40521.2 Prévost, Antoine F. Oeuvres choisies. Paris, 1810-16. 39v.

38588.14 Quinault, Philippe. Chefs-d'oeuvre de Quinault. Paris, 1810.

38582.8 Racine, Jean. Oeuvres. Paris, 1810. 4v.

38582.9 Racine, Jean. Oeuvres. v.5. Paris, 1810.

38587.6 Regnard, Jean François. Oeuvres. v.4. Paris, 1810.

FL 6002.810 Rousseau, J.J. Rousseaua, ou Recueil d'anecdotes. Paris, 1810.

38546.38.10 Sévigné, Marie de R.C. Lettres choisies de Mones. de Sévigné. Paris, 1810.

41586.31 Soumet, A. L'incrédulité. Paris, 1810.

41586.30.11 Soumet, A. Ode sur les drapeaux. Paris, 1810.

38556.10.15 Tabaraud, M.M. Second lettre à M. de Beausset, pour servir de supplement à histoire de Fénelon. Supplement. Limoges, 1810.

40534.2 Théâtre des auteurs du second ordre. v.37. Paris, 1810.

41588.40.20 Trauvé, Claude Joseph. Pausanias. Carcassonne, 1810.

Htn 41596.64.5* Treneuil, Joseph. Les tombeaux de Saint-Denis. 5. éd. Paris, 1810.

Mon 132.1 Vernier, T. Notices et observations. Paris, 1810. 2v.

39545.23.3 Voltaire, François Marie Arouet de. Chefs-d'oeuvre dramatiques. v.3. Paris, 1810.

39545.41 Voltaire, François Marie Arouet de. La Henriade. Paris, 1810.

1811

40517.5.25 Beauharnais, F.M. de C. La marmote philosophie, ou La philosophie en domino. Paris, 1811. 3v.

40527.5 Bernard, Pierre Joseph. Oeuvres choisies. Paris, 1811.

38551.40.12 Butler, Charles. The life of Fénelon. Baltimore, 1811.

38551.40.10 Butler, Charles. The life of Fénelon. Philadelphia, 1811.

41593.15.3 Chapais de Monval. Cantate à l'occasion de la naissance du roi de Rome. Rouen, 1811?

41583.18.53.10 Chazet, André René P.A. L'officier de quinze ans. Paris, 1811.

40534.18 Colardeau, Charles P. Oeuvres choisies. Paris, 1811.

41593.17.8.50 Cormenin, L.M. de L. Odes, précédées de réflexions sur la poésie lyrique. Paris, 1811.

40537.15A Daunou, Pierre C.F. Notice sur La vie et les ouvrages de M.J. de Chénier. Paris, 1811.

41593.19.200 Delaurel, S. Chant épique sur la naissance du roi de Rome. Rome, 1811?

37556.20.30 Delisle de Sales, J.C.I. Essai sur le journalisme depuis 1735 jusqu'à l'an 1800. Paris, 1811. 2 pam.

41584.6 Desprez, C.A. L'espoir realisé. Paris, 1811.

40535.4 Destouches, Philippe Néricault. Oeuvres dramatiques. Paris, 1811. 6v.

39594.3.30 Destutt de Tracy, A.L.C. Commentary and review... spirit of laws. Philadelphia, 1811.

39578.15 Escherny, F.L. Mélanges de littérature, d'histoire. Paris, 1811. 3v.

FL 384.3 Etrennes de Thalie, ou Précis historique sur les acteurs et actrices célèbres. Paris, 1811.

Htn 38553.13.15* Fénelon, F. de S. de la Mothe. Pious reflections for every day of the month. Salem, 1811.

38558.8.2 Fléchier, Esprit. Oraisons funèbres. Paris, 1811. 2v.

40515.22.5 Florian, Jean P.C. de. Fables. Paris, 1811.

40515.35 Florian, Jean P.C. de. Gonzalo de Cordoba. Perpignan, 1811. 2v.

40526.15 Gresset, Jean B. Oeuvres. Paris, 1811. 2v.

41542.98.102 Guyot-Duvigneul, T. Etrennes aux B ... nois. 2. éd. Paris, 1811.

41593.60.5 Halma, N. La maltéide ou Le siége de Malte. Paris, 1811.

Htn 39527.13* La Fontaine, Jean de. Fables de La Fontaine. Paris, 1811. 2v.

41585.31 La Gleyenhaye, L.T. de. La loi singuliere. Paris, 1811.

41586.1.18 La Roche, Philippe J. de. Amélasis, ou Amour et ambition. Paris, 1811.

40536.10.5 Laujon, Pierre. Oeuvres choisies. Paris, 1811. 4v.

40527.28 Le Brun, Ponce Denis Ecouchard. Oeuvres. Paris, 1811. 4v.

41586.16.12 Le Riche, Mlle. Caroline et Storm. Paris, 1811.

41586.19.50 Marie, Hyppolite. Dialogue mêlé de complets sur la naissance du roi de Rome. Paris, 1811.

Mon 32.37 Montaigne, Michel de. Essays. 9. ed. London, 1811. 3v.

37572.4 Noël et La Place. L'abeille française. N.Y., 1811.

41586.27.9 Perin, René. Itinéraire de Pautin au Mont Clavaire. Paris, 1811.

41547.12 Pigault-Lebrun, C.A.G.R. de. Une macédoine. Paris, 1811. 4v.

38546.42 Sévigné, Marie de R.C. Letters. London, 1811. 9v.

40588.30.35 Sousa Botelho Mourão e Vasconcellos, A.M.E.F. A peep into the Thuilleries, or Parisian manners. London, 1811. 2v.

1812

37565.3 Beuchot, A.J.Q. Nouveau nécrologe français. Paris, 1812.

37574.47 Chansonnier de société. Paris, 1812.

40586.17.6 Chateaubriand, F.A.R. Itinéraire de Paris à Jérusalem. 2. éd. Paris, 1812. 2v.

40586.18.100 Chateaubriand, F.A.R. The martyrs. N.Y., 1812. 3v.

40586.15.9 Chateaubriand, F.A.R. Travels in Greece, Palestine, Egypt. London, 1812. 2v.

37572.7 Chefs-d'oeuvre d'eloquence et de poèsie française. Paris, 1812.

Htn 40588.1.6* Cottin, Marie R. (Mme.). Elizabeth, or Exiles of Siberia. N.Y., 1812.

40534.27A Crébillon, Prosper Jolyot de. Oeuvres. Paris, 1812. 3v.

40587.38 Damaze de Raymond. Réponse aux attaques dirigées contre M. de Chateaubriand. Paris, 1812.

40517.19.110 Daubenton, M. Zelia in the desert. New Haven, 1812.

41593.26.7.5 Delille, J. La conversation, poème. Paris, 1812.

41593.26.7 Delille, J. La conversation, poème. Paris, 1812.

Mon 114.1 DuRoure, Auguste F.L.S.G. Eloge de Montaigne. Paris, 1812.

41584.39 Étienne, Charles Guillaume. Conaxa ou les Gendres Dupés. Paris, 1812.

1812 - cont.

41584.39.8 Étienne, Charles Guillaume. Conaxa ou les Gendres Dupés. Comédie. Paris, 1812. 9 pam.
Mon 116.3.2 Fabre, M.J.J.V. Eloge de Michel de Montaigne. Paris, 1812.
Mon 116.3 Fabre, M.J.J.V. Eloge de Michel de Montaigne. Paris, 1812.
40515.31 Florian, Jean P.C. de. Éliezer. Paris, 1812.
40515.22 Florian, Jean P.C. de. Fables. Paris, 1812.
40515.37 Florian, Jean P.C. de. Gonsalve de Cordoue. v.1-2. Paris, 1812.
40515.37.5 Florian, Jean P.C. de. Guillaume Tell. Paris, 1812.
40515.20 Florian, Jean P.C. de. Nouvelles. Paris, 1812.
40515.43 Florian, Jean P.C. de. Numa Pompelius. Paris, 1812.
FL 360.26 Fortia de Piles, A.T.J. Quelques réflexions d'un homme du monde. Paris, 1812.
39567.3 Grimm, F.M. von. Correspondance. Paris, 1812-14. 17v.
Htn 39567.3.6* Grimm, F.M. von. Correspondance. pt.2. Paris, 1812. 5v.
40587.54 His, Charles. Lettre à M. le Comte de B***. Paris, 1812.
41588.30 Humbert de Superville. Jésus. Leide, 1812.
41597.40.5 L'hymen et la naissance. Paris, 1812.
41597.40 L'hymen et la naissance. Paris, 1812.
Mon 120.1 Jay, Antoine. Eloge de Montaigne. Paris, 1812.
41586.1.14 La Roche, Philippe J. de. Rodolphe, ou La tour de Falkenstein. Paris, 1812.
Mon 122.2 LeClerc, J.V. Eloge de Messire Michel, seigneur de Montaigne. Paris, 1812.
Htn 40517.31.15* Le Prince de Beaumont, M. The farmers, mechanics, and servants' magazine. N.Y., 1812.
40512.25.18 LeSage, Alain René. De Gil Blas de Santillana. Valencia, 1812. 6v.
37572.47 Marottes à vendre or Triboulet tabletier. London, 1812.
Mol 202.77 Molière, Jean Baptiste Poquelin. La escuela de los maridos...Celenio. Madrid, 1812.
Mol 18.12 Molière, Jean Baptiste Poquelin. Oeuvres. Paris, 1812. 6v.
38588.9 Oeuvres de Raimond et Philippe Poisson. Paris, 1812.
41587.17.7 Picard, Louis Benoît. Les prometteurs. Paris, 1812.
41587.16.5 Picard, Louis Benoît. Théâtre. Paris, 1812. 5v.
41547.9 Pigault-Lebrun, C.A.G.R. de. Jérôme. Paris, 1812. 4v.
41586.28.30 Pixerécourt, R.C.G. de. Le fanal de Messive. Paris, 1812.
41586.28.40 Pixerécourt, R.C.G. de. Le petit carillonneur. Paris, 1812.
41587.19.50 Pompigny, M. de. La princesse de Jérusalem. Paris, 1812.
41587.20.100 Rousseau, E. Herminie. Paris, 1812.
Mol 619.1 St. Prosper. Essai sur la comédie. Paris, 1812.
39527.7 Solvet, P.L. Études sur La Fontaine. Paris, 1812.
41588.42.75 Verez, E.F. La fille coupable, repentante. Paris, 1812.
Mon 110.1 Villemain, Abel Francois. Eloge de Montaigne. Paris, 1812. 6 pam.
Mon 132.3 Vincens, E. Éloge de Michel de Montaigne. Paris, 1812.

1813

FL 398.4.9 Arnoldianna, ou Sophie Arnould et ses contemporaines. Paris, 1813.
38566.7 Boileau Despréaux, Nicolas. Oeuvres. Paris, 1813. 2v.
38557.48.8 Bossuet, J.B. Abrégé du célèbre ouvrage de M. Bossuet. Londres, 1813.
40526.29 Boufflers, Stanislas de. Oeuvres. Paris, 1813. 2v.
40586.16 Chateaubriand, F.A.R. Travels in Greece, Palestine, Egypt and Barbary. Philadelphia, 1813.
41593.26.6 Delille, J. Les jardins. Paris, 1813.
40535.3 Desmahis, J.F.E. Oeuvres choisies. Paris, 1813.
41584.27.55 Ducange, Victor. Palmérin. Paris, 1813.
41584.27.9 Dufresny, C. Les deux jaloux. Paris, 1813.
Htn 40588.21.120* Genlis, S.F.D. de St. Sainclair, or the victim of the arts and sciences. N.Y., 1813.
40526.11 Gresset, Jean B. Oeuvres choisies. Paris, 1813.
Htn 39567.3.5* Grimm, F.M. von. Correspondance. pt.1. Paris, 1813. 5v.
Htn 39567.3.7* Grimm, F.M. von. Correspondance. pt.3. v.1-5. Paris, 1813.
41584.56 Hapdé, J.B. La naissance d'Arlequin. Paris, 1813.
38564.18.75 La Bruyère, J. de. Les caractères de La Bruyère. Paris, 1813.
37532.3 Laharpe, Jean F. de. Lycée, ou Cours de littérature. Paris, 1813. 16v.
41586.1.9 La Roche, Philippe J. de. Le faux martinguerre. Paris, 1813.
41586.10.250 Leblanc de Ferrière, A. Archambaud. Paris, 1813.
39598.10 Marmontel, J.F. Moral tales. N.Y., 1813.
41586.22.45 Merle, Jean T. Crispin financier. Paris, 1813.
Htn Mol 18.13* Molière, Jean Baptiste Poquelin. Oeuvres. Paris, 1813. 8v.
Mol 18.13.3A Molière, Jean Baptiste Poquelin. Oeuvres. v.1-2, 3-4, 5-6, 7-8. Paris, 1813. 4v.
Htn Mol 18.13.2* Molière, Jean Baptiste Poquelin. Oeuvres. v.1-4,8. Paris, 1813. 5v.
41586.26.5 Monperlier, J.A.M. Les chevaliers de Malte. Paris, 1813.
40517.48.5 Montjoie, C.F.L. D'Aveyro, or The head in the glass cage. v.1-4. London, 1813. 2v.
41598.12 Le nouvel Angotiana. Lille, 1813.
38557.1.35 Observations sur le prospectus...de la nouvelle édition des oeuvres de Bossuet. Paris, 1813.
37582.1 Répertoire général du théâtre français. v.1-49,51. Paris, 1813. 50v.
FL 6021.13 Rousseau, J.J. Les confessions. Paris, 1813. 4v.
40573.45 Salgues, J.B. De Paris, des moeurs, de la littérature. Paris, 1813.
41587.27 Salverte, E. Phédosie. Tragédie en cinq actes. Paris, 1813.
40536.28.10 Sedaine, Michel Jean. Oeuvres choisies. Paris, 1813. 3v.
40525.2 Sénac de Meilhan, G. Portraits et caractères de personnages distingué de la fin du dix-huitième siècle. Paris, 1813.
40593.21 Staël Holstein, Anne Louise. Influence of literature on society. v.2. Boston, 1813.
39545.24.5 Théâtre de Voltaire. v.1-12. Paris, 1813. 6v.
39545.40 Voltaire, François Marie Arouet de. La Henriade. Paris, 1813.

1814

37565.7 Barante, Amable Guillaume P.B. De la littérature française pendant le dix-huitième siècle. 2. éd. Paris, 1814.
40531.6.35 Barthès de Marmorieres, Antoine. La mort de Marie-Antoinette. Paris, 1814.
38557.4 Bausset, L.F. Histoire de J.B. Bossuet. Versailles, 1814. 4v.
41583.12.17 Belfort. Hommage à Louis XVIII; scène lyrique. Montpellier, 1814.
40526.1.30 Berchoux, J. de. Voltaire ou Le triomphe de la philosophie moderne. Lyon, 1814.
38566.11 Boileau Despréaux, Nicolas. Oeuvres. Paris, 1814.
38565.8.15 Boileau Despréaux, Nicolas. Oeuvres à l'usage des collèges. Lyon, 1814. 2 pam.
41591.20 Bonaparte, Lucien. Charlemagne. Rome, 1814. 2v.
38557.48.9 Bossuet, J.B. Abrégé du célèbre ouvrage de M. Bossuet. Paris, 1814.
38557.26.8 Bossuet, J.B. Oraisons funèbres. Paris, 1814.
39584.20.15 Boulard, A.M.H. Lettre adressée au rédacteur du moniteur. Paris, 1814.
41593.9.12 Boussot, P.L. Le triomphe de la religion catholique. Dithyrambe. Aix-la-Chapelle, 1814.
X Cg 40586.11.5 Chateaubriand, F.A.R. Atala. 2. ed. Boston, 1814.
40586.11.5 Chateaubriand, F.A.R. Atala. 2. ed. Boston, 1814.
40586.24.60 Chateaubriand, F.A.R. Essai historique, politique et moral. v.1-2. Londres, 1814.
40586.16.3 Chateaubriand, F.A.R. Travels in Greece, Palestine, Egypt and Barbary. N.Y., 1814.
40534.16.30 Chateaubrun, Jean B.V. de. Oeuvres choisis de Chateaubrun et de Guimond de la Touche. Paris, 1814.
40588.1.10 Cottin, Marie R. (Mme.). Elizabeth. London, 1814.
40516.4 Ducray-Duminil, F.G. Victor, ou L'enfant de la forêt. Paris, 1814. 4v.
41584.27.21 Dumersan, Théophile Marion. Le tyran peu délicat. 2e éd. Paris, 1814.
41584.29.22 Duval, A. Invloed der gelijkenis of gewaande. Amsterdam, 1814.
FL 397.215.32 Duvillard, A. Quelques réflexions sur les moeurs républicaines et sur l'établissement d'un théâtre à Genève. Genève, 1814.
Htn 41593.32.14* Fantelin. Ode à S.M. Alexander I. Rouen, 1814?
38553.36 Fénelon, F. de S. de la Mothe. Telemachiada. Paris, 1814.
40515.43.2 Florian, Jean P.C. de. Numa Pompelius, second roi de Rome. v.1-2. Paris, 1814.
Mol 863.5 Gallois-Mailly, T. Épître à Molière. Paris, 1814. 9 pam.
40588.17.5 Genlis, S.F.D. de St. Mademoiselle de la Fayette. 1st American ed. v.1-2. Baltimore, 1814.
39532.12.20 Hamilton, Anthony. Memorie del conte di Grammont. Milano, 1814. 2v.
41588.61 L'influence des femmes sur les moeurs. Paris, 1814.
40535.19.60 La Chabeaussière, A.E.T.P. de. Apologues moreaux. Paris, 1814? 2 pam.
39527.31.50 La Fontaine, Jean de. Fabulas escolhidas. v.1-2. Lisboa, 1814-15.
Htn 39527.10.50* La Fontaine, Jean de. La Fontaine's tales. London, 1814. 2v.
39525.5.15 La Fontaine, Jean de. Oeuvres complètes. Paris, 1814. 6v.
40535.19.23 LaHarpe, J.F. de. Le triomphe de la religion. Paris, 1814.
40535.21 Le Blanc de Villeneufve. La fête du petit blé. New Orléans, 1814.
41586.16.14 Leroy, Onésime. Le méfiant. Paris, 1814.
40512.10.5 LeSage, Alain René. Adventures of Gil Blas. v.1-2,3-4. N.Y., 1814. 2v.
37597.3A Lorris, Guillaume de. Le romant de la rose. Paris, 1814. 4v.
Mon 123.1 Mazure, F.A.J. Eloge de Montaigne. Angers, 1814.
41595.23.150 Michaud, Joseph. Le printemps d'un proscrit. 7. éd. Paris, 1814. 2v.
41586.26 Monperlier, J.A.M. Le prince et le soldat. Paris, 1814.
Htn 40593.25* Staël Holstein, Anne Louise. Réflexions sur le suicide. Paris, 1814.
39545.50 Voltaire, François Marie Arouet de. La pucelle. Paris, 1814.

1815

37562.5 Benoiston-de-Chateauneuf, Louis François. Essai sur la poésie...au XIIe, XIIIe et XIVe siècles. Paris, 1815.
38565.9 Boileau Despréaux, Nicolas. Oeuvres. Paris, 1815. 3v.
38566.8 Boileau Despréaux, Nicolas. Oeuvres. Paris, 1815.
41591.20.10 Bonaparte, Lucien. Charlemagne. Paris, 1815. 2v.
38557.25.23 Bossuet, J.B. Oeuvres. Versailles, 1815-19. 43v.
38557.26.3A Bossuet, J.B. Oraisons funèbres. Paris, 1815.
41566.17A Buonaparte, Louis. Maria. Boston, 1815. 2v.
41583.18.20 Caigniez, Louis Charles. The maid and the magpie, or Who is the thief? London, 1815.
41583.18.19 Caigniez, Louis Charles. La pie voleuse. Paris, 1815.
37578.34.5 Capelle, Pierre. Aneries révolutionnaires. Paris, 1815.
40586.63 Chateaubriand, F.A.R. The beauties of Christianity. Philadelphia, 1815.
40586.33 Chateaubriand, F.A.R. Discours de réception à l'Académie Française. Paris, 1815.
40534.17.9 Cizos, François. Adieux à l'univers. Comédies. Toulouse, 1815.
37536.3 Craufurd, Quintin. Essais sur la littérature française. Paris, 1815. 3v.
40534.33 Crébillon, Claude Prosper Jolyot de. Les egaremens. Paris, 1815.
41583.19 Cuvelier de Trie, J.G.A. Bélisaire. Paris, 1815.
40535.12.15 Ducis, Jean F. Hamlet. Paris, 1815.
41584.39.2 Étienne, Charles Guillaume. Conaxa ou les Gendres Dupés. Paris, 1815.
40556.13 Fénélon, C.E. de Salignac. Un mot a tout le monde, ou Gros Jean qui prêche son curé. Paris, 1815.
Htn 38544.27.30* La Fayette, Marie M. La Princesse de Clèves. Paris, 1815. 2v.
38543.10 La Rochefoucauld, François. Maximes et réfléxions. Paris, 1815.
Htn 41554.39* Le Brun, P. The history of Tekeli. Albany, 1815.
40512.15 LeSage, Alain René. Aventuras de Gil Blas. London, 1815. 4v.
40515.8 Lespinasse, J.J.E. de. Lettres. Paris, 1815. 2v.
41567.42 Manesca, J. Historiettes nouvelles. Philadelphia, 1815.

1815 - cont.

	39598.36	Marmontel, J.F. The widow of the village. Hartford, 1815.
	41586.19.12.5	Martainville, Alphonse Louis Dieudonné. Buonabarte, ou L'abus de l'abdication. 2. éd. Paris, 1815.
Htn	Mol 18.15*	Molière, Jean Baptiste Poquelin. Oeuvres. v.1-7. Paris, 1815. 4v.
	40587.60	Montgaillard, Jean G.M.R. de. Esprit, maximes et principes de M. François Auguste de Chateaubriand. Paris, 1815.
	FL 395.130	Le Petit Homme Noir aux acteurs et actrices de théâtre française. Paris, 1815.
	41569.10	Le petit pélerin de Parme et de Plaisance. Parme, 1815.
	41547.6	Pigault-Lebrun, C.A.G.R. de. Adelaide de Meran. Paris, 1815. 4v.
	41586.28.7	Pixerécourt, R.C.G. de. Christophe Colomb. Paris, 1815.
	38585.20.17	Racine, Jean. Athaliah. Edinburgh, 1815.
	38585.47.10	Racine, Jean. Bérénice. N.Y., 1815.
	37562.10	Rocquefort-Flaméricourt, Jean Baptiste B. de. De l'état de la poésie française. Paris, 1815.
	39596.12	St. Pierre, J.H.B. de. Harmonies of nature. Sequel to Studies of nature. London, 1815. 3v.
	Mol 860.26	Simon, H. Ninon, Molière et Tartuffe. Paris, 1815.
	41596.64.20	Treneuil, Joseph. Le martyre de Louis XVI. Paris, 1815.
	39545.46.25	Voltaire, François Marie Arouet de. Merope; tragedia francesa puesta en español par D.M. de B. Madrid, 1815.
	FL 6128.15	Wagner, Sigmund von. L'ile de Saint-Pierre, ou L'ile de Rousseau. Berne, 1815.

1816

	40586.15	Chateaubriand, F.A.R. Recollections of Italy, England and America. Philadelphia, 1816.
	37566.2.5	Chenier, Marie J. Tableau historique de l'etat...de la littérature française. Paris, 1816.
	40537.8	Chénier, Marie Joseph. Oeuvres diverses et inédites. Bruxelles, 1816.
	40588.2	Cottin, Marie R. (Mme.). Elizabeth. Paris, 1816.
	41584.27.60	Ducange, Victor. Adolphe et Sophie. Paris, 1816.
	41584.27.22	Dumersan, Théophile Marion. Jocrisse grand-père, Jocrisse fils, et Jocrisse petit-fils. Paris, 1816.
	38553.13.25	Fénelon, F. de S. de la Mothe. A guide to true peace. 1st Aamerican ed. N.Y., 1816.
	39544.7	Flottes, J.B.M. Introduction aux ouvrages de Voltaire. Montpellier, 1816.
	39533.3	Hamilton, Anthony. Memoires....de Grammont. Paris, 1816. 2v.
	40535.19.35.3	Jacquelin, J.A. L'amour à l'anglaise. 2. éd. Paris, 1816.
	FL 398.49.20	Lekain, H.L. Lekain dans sa jeunesse. Paris, 1816.
	41586.15.8	Lemercier, N.L. Charlemagne; tragédie en 5 actes. Paris, 1816.
	39598.27	Marmontel, J.F. Bélisaire. Paris, 1816.
	39597.18	Marmontel, J.F. Nouveaux contes moraux. Paris, 1816-17. 4v.
	37567.2	Ménégault, A.P.F. Martyrologe littéraire. Paris, 1816.
	Mol 166.38	Molière, Jean Baptiste Poquelin. O Philargos. Vienne, 1816.
	39592.6	Montesquieu, C.L. de S. Oeuvres complètes. Paris, 1816. 6v.
Htn	40587.31*	Senancour, E.P. Observations critiques sur les Génie du christianisme. Paris, 1816.
	39545.45	Voltaire, François Marie Arouet de. La Henriada. Alais, 1816.

1817

	40545.16	Bazin, Rigomer. Le lynx; coup-d'oeil et réflexions libres sur les écrits. Mans, 1817.
	41522.23.20	Bellin de La Liborlière, L. The hero. London, 1817. 2v.
	41583.14	Boirie, E.C. de. La jeunesse du Grand Frédéric. Paris, 1817.
	40551.3	Bonald, L.G.A. de. Essai analytique. Oevres I. Paris, 1817.
	40551.12	Bonald, L.G.A. de. Essai analytique. Oevres I. Paris, 1817.
	40551.4	Bonald, L.G.A. de. Législation primitive. Oevres II-IV. Paris, 1817. 3v.
	40551.13	Bonald, L.G.A. de. Législation primitive. Oevres II-IV. Paris, 1817. 3v.
	40551.15	Bonald, L.G.A. de. Pensées. Oevres VI-VII. Paris, 1817. 2v.
	40551.6	Bonald, L.G.A. de. Pensées. Oevres VI-VII. Paris, 1817. 2v.
	41566.14.12	Bouilly, Jean N. Les encourgaments de la jeunesse. 2. éd. Paris, 1817.
	37597.18	Bröndsted, P.O. Bidrag til den danske historie. Kjobenhavn, 1817.
	40516.5	Cazotte, Jacques. Oeuvres badines et morales, historiques et philosophiques. 1e éd. Paris, 1817. 4v.
	41566.22	Choiseul, Felicite de. Recreations morales et amusantes. Paris, 1817.
	38575.30.3	Corneille, Pierre. Le Cid. Paris, 1817.
	41583.19.30	Cuvelier de Trie, J.G.A. Macbeth, ou les sorcières de la forêt. Paris, 1817.
	39594.3.28	Destutt de Tracy, A.L.C. Commentaire sur l'esprit des lois de Montesquieu. Liège, 1817.
	41584.27.75	Dupetit-Méré, F. Aurengzeb, ou La famille indienne. Paris, 1817.
	41593.27.40	Fayolle. Pour et contre Delille. Paris, 1817.
	40588.15	Genlis, S.F.D. de St. Jane of Paris. v.1-2. Boston, 1817.
	40588.14.5	Genlis, S.F.D. de St. Tales of the castle. London, 1817.
	40535.19	Graffigny, Françoise d'Issembourg d'Happoncourt de. Lettere d'una peruviana. Avignone, 1817.
	40526.12	Gresset, Jean B. Oeuvres choisies. Paris, 1817. 2v.
	40526.17	Gresset, Jean B. Ver-Vert. W. Briné, 1817.
	40517.37	Gueulette, T.S. Chinese tales. London, 1817.
	40517.33	Gueulette, T.S. Peruvian tales. London, 1817.
	38564.19	La Bruyère, J. de. Les caractères de Théophraste. Avignon, 1817. 2v.
	39527.14	La Fontaine, Jean de. Fables de La Fontaine. Paris, 1817.
	37532.5	Laharpe, Jean F. de. Lycée, ou Cours de littérature. Paris, 1817. 16v.
	40588.50.10	Maistre, Xavier. The leper of the city of Aoste. London, 1817.
	38523.24.10	Malherbe, François de. Poésies. Paris, 1817.
	39598.30	Marmontel, J.F. Les Incas. Parris, 1817.
	FL 398.83.20	Mejanel, A. Mémoires de Talma. Londres, 1817.

1817 - cont.

	Mol 212.5.5	Molière, Jean Baptiste Poquelin. Die gelehrten Weiber...Nicolay. Leipzig, 1817.
	Mol 18.17	Molière, Jean Baptiste Poquelin. Oeuvres. Paris, 1817. 7v.
	Mol 268.20	Molière, Jean Baptiste Poquelin. Le Tartuffe. Étienne. Paris, 1817.
	39592.5	Montesquieu, C.L. de S. Oeuvres. Paris, 1817.
	40586.70	Observations critiques sur l'ouvrage intitulé: La Génie du Christianisme. Paris, 1817.
	41569.8	Parafaragaramus, ou Croquiguole et sa famille. Paris, 1817.
	40536.11.60	Patrat, Joseph. L'heureuse erreur. Paris, 1817.
	37582.4	Petitot, Claude Bernard. Répertoire du théâtre français. Drames. v.7. Paris, 1817-18.
	37582.3	Petitot, Claude Bernard. Répertoire du théâtre français. Tragedies. Paris, 1817-18. 6v.
	37582.5	Petitot, Claude Bernard. Répertoire du théâtre français. v.8-25. Paris, 1817-18. 18v.
	40536.20.2	Piron, Alexis. Oeuvres choisies. Paris, 1817.
	41597.65	Recueil de cantiques à l'usage des missions de France. Bordeaux, 1817. 2 pam.
	38587.6.5	Regnard, Jean François. Oeuvres. v.1-5. Paris, 1817-1901. 3v.
	FL 355.33	Reunion des théâtres. n.p., 1817.
	FL 6041.17	Rousseau, J.J. Émile ou De l'éducation. Paris, 1817. 3v.
	FL 6051.17	Rousseau, J.J. Julie, ou la nouvelle Héloise. Paris, 1817. 4v.
	FL 6001.817.2	Rousseau, J.J. Oeuvres. Paris, 1817. 18v.
	FL 6001.817	Rousseau, J.J. Oeuvres. Paris, 1817. 8v.
	41596.58	Salm-Rufferscheid-Dyck, C. Poésies. 2. éd. Paris, 1817.
	41588.24	Sewrin, C.A. Les Anglais pour Rire. 2e éd. Paris, 1817. 2 pam.

1818

	41583.6.15	Andrieux, François G.J.S. Oeuvres de F.G.J.S. Andrieux. Paris, 1818-23. 4v.
	41583.11.50	Bawr, A.S. (Goury de Champgrand). La suite d'un bal masque. Paris, 1818.
	41583.14.9	Boirie, E.C. de. La fille maudite. Paris, 1818.
	40551.5	Bonald, L.G.A. de. Du divorce. Oevres V. Paris, 1818.
	40551.14	Bonald, L.G.A. de. Du divorce. Oevres V. Paris, 1818.
	40551.7	Bonald, L.G.A. de. Recherches philosophiques. Oevres VIII-IX. Paris, 1818. 2v.
	41583.16.6	Brazier, Dumersan. L'école de village. Paris, 1818.
	40586.11	Chateaubriand, F.A.R. Atala. London, 1818.
	37541.17.18	Chénier, M.J. Fragmens du cours de littérature. Paris, 1818.
	37566.2	Chenier, Marie J. Tableau historique de la littérature française. Paris, 1818.
	40537.6.5	Chénier, Marie Joseph. Théâtre de M.J. de Chénier. Paris, 1818. 3v.
	41593.16.11.15	Cherpilloud, J. La nouvelle Helvétie, ou Les regrets et l'espérance. Londres, 1818.
	40534.28	Crébillon, Prosper Jolyot de. Oeuvres. Paris, 1818. 2v.
	40515.3	D'Épinay, Louise F. Mémoires et correspondence. Paris, 1818. 3v.
	40515.4	D'Épinay, Louise F. Mémoires et correspondence. Paris, 1818. 3v.
	41557.8.10.5	De Rome. (Mme.). Pélage. Paris, 1818.
	39563.3A	Diderot, Denis. Oeuvres. Paris, 1818-19. 12v.
	39578.5	Du Châtelet, G.É. Lettres inédites...correspondance de Voltaire. Paris, 1818.
	41584.27.15	Dumaniant, A.J. Le soeur rival. Paris, 1818.
	38585.12	Dupin, Charles. Lettre à mylady Morgan sur Racine et Shakespeare. Paris, 1818.
	40566.8	Dussault, Jean J. Annales littéraires. Paris, 1818-24. 5v.
	Mon 114.2	Dutens, J. Eloge de Michel de Montaigne. Paris, 1818.
	41584.32.36	Duveyrier, A.H.J. Le chateau de Paluzzi. Paris, 1818.
	38554.2	Fénelon, F. de S. de la Mothe. The adventures of Telemachus. N.Y., 1818.
	38553.24	Fénelon, F. de S. de la Mothe. Les aventures de Télémaque. Paris, 1818.
Htn	38553.23*	Fénelon, F. de S. de la Mothe. Le Télémaque. N.Y., 1818.
	38585.9.5	Fontanier, Pierre. Études de la langue française sur Racine. Paris, 1818.
	38585.9.10	Fontanier, Pierre. Études de la langue française sur Racine. v.1-2. Paris, 1818.
	38562.16.2	Fontenelle, B. Le B. de. Oeuvres. Paris, 1818.
	40588.21.5	Genlis, S.F.D. de St. Zuma, or The tree of health. London, 1818.
	41584.54	Gouffe, Armand. Le duel et le Dejeuner. Paris, 1818.
	39568.6.25	Grimm, F.M. von. Esquisses européennes, commencées en 1798, et finies en 1815. Paris, 1818.
	41586.29.5	Guilbert, R.C. Le Belvéder. Paris, 1818.
	38564.20	La Bruyère, J. de. Les caractères de La Bruyère suivis des caractères de Théophraste. Paris, 1818. 2v.
	39527.16	La Fontaine, Jean de. Fables de La Fontaine. Paris, 1818.
	41586.1.100	La Rochefoucauld-Liancourt, F.G. La révolution française et Bonaparte. Paris, 1818.
	40512.4.5	LeSage, Alain René. Histoire de Gil Blas de Santillane. Paris, 1818. 4v.
	39598.27.5	Marmontel, J.F. Bélisaire. London, 1818.
	Mol 48.18	Molière, Jean Baptiste Poquelin. Dialoghi francesi, italiani, tedeschi ed inglesi. 11e ed. Milano, 1818.
	Mon 18.18.5	Montaigne, Michel de. Essais. Paris, 1818.
Htn	Mon 18.18.2*	Montaigne, Michel de. Essais. Johanneau. Paris, 1818. 5v.
	Mon 18.18	Montaigne, Michel de. Essais. Johanneau. Paris, 1818. 5v.
	Mon 18.18.3	Montaigne, Michel de. Essais. Johanneau. Paris, 1818. 6v.
	39582.12	Morellet, André. Mélanges de littérature. Paris, 1818. 4v.
	39526.27	Nodier, Charles. Fables de La Fontaine. Paris, 1818. 2v.
	37582.2	Répertoire général du théâtre français. Paris, 1818. 67v.
	FL 6001.818	Rousseau, J.J. Oeuvres complètes. Paris, 1818-22. 24v.
	38546.44	Sévigné, Marie de R.C. Lettres. Paris, 1818. 10v.

Chronological Listing

1818 - cont.

39586.30 Stael-Holstein, A.L. Memoirs of the private life of my father. London, 1818.
41588.43 Victor, M. Le prince de Norwège. Paris, 1818.
39544.28.20 Voltaire, François Marie Arouet de. Lettre philosophique. Paris, 1818.

1819

38557.4.5 Bausset, L.F. Histoire de J.B. Bossuet. 2. éd. Versailles, 1819. 4v.
37595.9 Berinton, J. History of Abaillard and Héloise. Philadelphia, 1819.
40551.17 Bonald, L.G.A. de. Mélanges littéraires. Oevres X-XI. Paris, 1819. 2v.
40551.8 Bonald, L.G.A. de. Mélanges littéraires. Oevres X-XI. Paris, 1819. 2v.
38557.41.80 Bossuet, J.B. Histoire universelle. Paris, 1819.
41583.19.25 Cuvelier de Trie, J.G.A. La mort de Kléber. Paris, 1819.
41593.26.15 Delille, J. L'imagination, poème. 2. éd. Paris, 1819. 2v.
41593.29.50 Desquiron de Saint-Agnan, Antoine Toussaint. Solyme conquise. Paris, 1819. 2v.
39563.4A Diderot, Denis. Supplément aux oeuvres. Paris, 1819.
FL 396.64.2 Du théâtre français...la nouvelle troupe de l'Odéon. Paris, 1819.
41584.32.25 Duveyrier, A.H.J. Les Mexicains. Paris, 1819.
41597.29 L'écho des bardes. Année 5. Paris, 1819.
40588.21.10 Genlis, S.F.D. de St. The new aera. London, 1819. 4v.
FL 358.19 Geoffroy, J.L. Cours de littérature dramatique. Paris, 1819-20. 5v.
41584.53 Gosse, Etienne. Proverbes dramatiques. Paris, 1819. 2v.
Mon 28.5 Labouderie, J. de. Le Christianisme de Montaigne. Paris, 1819.
38564.21 La Bruyère, J. de. Les caractères de La Bruyère suivis des caractères de Théophraste. Paris, 1819. 2v.
39545.4.2 Lepan, E.M.J. Vie politique. 2d ed. Paris, 1819.
40517.31.5 Le Prince de Beaumont, M. The young misses' magazine. v.1-2. N.Y., 1819.
Htn 40512.10.15* LeSage, Alain René. Aventures de Gil Blas de Santillane. London, 1819. 3v.
40512.3 LeSage, Alain René. Le diable boiteux. Paris, 1819. 2v.
37572.8 Lycée français. Paris, 1819. 5v.
Htn Mol 195.18* Molière, Jean Baptiste Poquelin. L'école des femmes...Anger. Paris, 1819.
Mol 225.1 Molière, Jean Baptiste Poquelin. La jalousie du Barbouille. Paris, 1819.
Mol 18.19.2 Molière, Jean Baptiste Poquelin. Oeuvres...Auger. Paris, 1819-25. 9v.
Mol 18.19 Molière, Jean Baptiste Poquelin. Oeuvres...Auger. Paris, 1819-25. 9v.
Mon 18.19 Montaigne, Michel de. Essais. Paris, 1819. 9v.
41555.62 Montbron, J.C. de. Essais sur la littérature des Hébreux. v.1-3. Paris, 1819. 2v.
41595.60.2 Moussard, P. Les prêtres tels qu'ils devraient être. Paris, 1819.
41556.24 Nodier, Charles. Thérèse Aubert. Paris, 1819.
41586.28.35 Pixerécourt, R.C.G. de. La fille de l'exilé. Paris, 1819.
37582.2.53 Répertoire du théâtre français, 3. ordre; ou, Supplement aux deux editions du répertoire publiées en 1803 et on 1807. Paris, 1819-20. 8v.
FL 6021.19 Rousseau, J.J. Les confessions. Paris, 1819. 2v.
FL 6001.819 Rousseau, J.J. Oeuvres avec notes historiques. v.1-22. Paris, 1819. 21v.
Htn 39594.34.10* St. Pierre, J.H.B. de. Paul and Virginia. London, 1819.
39594.27 St. Pierre, J.H.B. de. Paul et Virginie. Paris, 1819.
38545.20.10 Saint Réal, César V. de. Oeuvres choisies. Paris, 1819.
Htn 41568.18.5* Sénancour, Étienne Pivert de. Libres méditations d'un solitaire inconnu. Paris, 1819.
39583.4 Thomas, Antoine L. Oeuvres. Paris, 1819. 4v.
41596.120 Valori, F. Odes choisies. Paris, 1819.
39545.35.9 Voltaire, François Marie Arouet de. Candide, ou L'optimisme. Azwickau, 1819.

182-

Mol 800.1 Picard, L.B. Histoire de la troupe de Molière. Paris, 182-?

1820

41592.1.50 Allo, Marie. Bretons d'après nature. Paris, 1820.
37574.20 Batteux, Charles. Chefs-d'oeuvres d'éloquence poetique. Toulouse, 1820.
Htn 38557.35.22* Bossuet, J.B. Lettres inédites. Versailles, 1820.
Htn 38557.35.20* Bossuet, J.B. Lettres inédites. Versailles, 1820.
41583.15.300 Boutroux, L.A. de Montargis. La mort de Charles Ier. Paris, 1820.
40586.24.75A Chateaubriand, F.A.R. Essai historique, politique et moral. Londres, 1820.
Htn 41593.16* Chênedollé, C. de. Études poétiques. Paris, 1820.
38512.20 Collin de Plancy, Jacques. Mémoires d'un vilain. Paris, 1820.
41583.19.9 Cuvelier de Trie, J.G.A. Le petit poucet. Paris, 1820.
41593.22.5 Delille, J. L'homme des Champs. Paris, 1820.
41593.26.17 Delille, J. Les jardins, poème. Paris, 1820.
40517.23.7 Duclos, C.P. Oeuvres complètes. Paris, 1820-21. 9v.
38554.350.245 Fénelon, F. de S. de la Mothe. Treatise on the education of daughters. Boston, 1820.
40515.48.9 Florian, Jean P.C. de. Estelle. Paris, 1820.
40515.28 Florian, Jean P.C. de. Fables. Paris, 1820.
40515.32.9 Florian, Jean P.C. de. Gonzalve de Cordoue. v.1-2. Paris, 1820.
40515.32.11 Florian, Jean P.C. de. Gonzalve de Cordoue. v.1-2. Paris, 1820.
40515.37.10 Florian, Jean P.C. de. Guillaume Tell ou La Suisse libre. Paris, 1820.
40515.43.5 Florian, Jean P.C. de. Numa Pompelius. Paris, 1820.
40515.40 Florian, Jean P.C. de. William Tell. Boston, 1820.
41584.50.25 Gain-Montaignac, J.R. Théâtre. Paris, 1820.
40588.21.85 Genlis, S.F.D. de St. Petrarch and Laura. London, 1820.
39568.6.30 Grimm, F.M. von. Freiherr Grimm's und Diderot's Correspondenz, von 1753 bis 1790. Brandenburg, 1820.

1820 - cont.

41584.55.700 Guilleau de Formont. Jean de Bourgogne. Paris, 1820.
38564.23 La Bruyère, J. de. Oeuvres. Paris, 1820. 2 pam.
40524.14 La Fite, M. Entretiens et contes moraux. v.1-2,4. Paris, 1820. 2v.
39527.16.5 La Fontaine, Jean de. Oeuvres complètes. v.3. Paris, 1820.
NEDL 39527.31 La Fontaine, Jean de. Traducção livre das melhores fabulas. Lisboa, 1820.
41595.9 Lebrun, Pierre. Marie Stuart, tragédie en cinq actes. Paris, 1820.
41595.9.2 Lebrun, Pierre. Marie Stuart, tragédie en cinq actes. 2. éd. Paris, 1820.
41586.13 Lemercier, N.L. Clovis, tragédie. Paris, 1820.
41586.15.3 Lemercier, N.L. La démence de Charles VI; tragédie en 5 actes. Paris, 1820.
40512.57 LeSage, Alain René. Le bachelier de Salamanque. Paris, 1820.
40515.10 Lespinasse, J.J.E. de. Nouvelles lettres. Paris, 1820.
39598.28 Marmontel, J.F. Bélisario. 2. ed. Burdeos, 1820.
41586.19.9 Marsollier des Vivetières, B.J. Gulnare, ou L'esclave Persane. Paris, 1820.
Mol 235.15 Molière, Jean Baptiste Poquelin. Le médecin malgré lui. Avignon, 1820.
Mol 18.20 Molière, Jean Baptiste Poquelin. Oeuvres. Paris, 1820. 6v.
Mol 38.20 Molière, Jean Baptiste Poquelin. Oeuvres choisies. v.1-8. Paris, 1820-67.
Mon 18.20.2 Montaigne, Michel de. Essais. A. Duval. Paris, 1820-22. 6v.
Mon 18.20.3 Montaigne, Michel de. Essais. A. Duval. Paris, 1820-22. 5v.
Mon 18.20 Montaigne, Michel de. Essais. A. Duval. Paris, 1820-24. 6v.
41588.67 La mort du duc d'Enguien; tragédie. Paris, 1820.
41596.40 Moyria, G. de. Le malheur, poème. Paris, 1820.
40592.3 Oeuvres complètes de Mme. de Staël. Paris, 1820-21. 17v.
37536.4 Pierrot, Jules. Journal des cours publics. Paris, 1820. 2v.
38536.5 Rabelais, F. Oeuvres. Paris, 1820. 3v.
38587.7 Regnard, Jean François. Oeuvres. Paris, 1820. 6v.
38525.45 Rotrou, Jean de. Oeuvres. Paris, 1820. 5v.
39594.24 St. Pierre, J.H.B. de. La caboña indiana. Madrid, 1820.
39595.11 St. Pierre, J.H.B. de. Oeuvres complètes. Paris, 1820. 2v.
41588.14.30 Scribe, Eugène. Marie Jobard, imitation burlesque, en six actes et en vers. Paris, 1820.
41597.53 Les soupers lyriques. 2. année. v.1-2. Paris, 1820.
40592.35 Staël Holstein, Anne Louise. Corinna, ossia l'Italia. Venezia, 1820. 2v.
41588.65 Le vampire. Paris, 1820.
39545.23.3.5 Voltaire, François Marie Arouet de. Chefs-d'oeuvre dramatiques. v.2-4. Paris, 1820. 4v.
39545.37.14 Voltaire, François Marie Arouet de. Dialogues et entretiens philosophiques. Paris, 1820. 2v.
39545.41.5 Voltaire, François Marie Arouet de. La Henriade. Paris, 1820.
39545.43 Voltaire, François Marie Arouet de. La Henriade. Paris, 1820.
39543.20 Voltaire, François Marie Arouet de. Oeuvres complètes. v.4, 6-7. Paris, 1820-21. 3v.
39545.58.10 Voltaire, François Marie Arouet de. Saul; a drama. London, 1820.

1821

39574.19 Alembert, J. Le Rond d'. Oeuvres. Paris, 1821-22. 5v.
37574.21 Batteux, Charles. Chefs-d'oeuvres d'éloquence poetique. Paris, 1821.
Mol 702.7 Beffara, S.F. Dissertation sur J.B.P. Molière. Paris, 1821.
Htn 41592.13* Béranger, P.J. de. Chansons. Paris, 1821.
38565.10.8A Boileau Despréaux, Nicolas. Oeuvres. Paris, 1821. 4v.
38565.10.5 Boileau Despréaux, Nicolas. Oeuvres complètes, contenant ses poésies, ses écrits en prose. Paris, 1821. 3v.
38557.41.25 Bossuet, J.B. Histoire des variations des églises protestantes. Paris, 1821. 3v.
40534.43.30 Caigniez, Louis. Le mandarin Houng-Pouf. Paris, 1821.
Mol 882.2 Castil-Blaze. Don Juan, ou le festin de Pierre. Paris, 1821.
41583.18.54 Claude Macée, frère. Pastorale sur la naissence de Jesus-Christ. Rennes, 1821.
40588.2.6 Cottin, Marie R. (Mme.). Elisabetta, ossia Gli esiliati nella Siberia. 2a ed. Londra, 1821.
41566.3.9 D'Arlincourt, Charles V.P. Le solitaire. Paris, 1821. 2v.
39564.3 Diderot, Denis. Oeuvres. Paris, 1821. 20v.
39564.4 Diderot, Denis. Oeuvres inédites. Paris, 1821.
38514.34 Du Bois, Louis. Vaux-de-vire d'Olivier Basselin. Paris, 1821.
38553.24.5 Fénelon, F. de S. de la Mothe. Les aventures de Télémague. Philadelphia, 1821.
38554.350.80 Fénelon, F. de S. de la Mothe. De l'éducation des filles. Paris, 1821.
38554.350.250 Fénelon, F. de S. de la Mothe. Treatise on the education of daughters. Boston, 1821.
40515.35.5 Florian, Jean P.C. de. Gonzalo de Cordoba. v.1-2. Madrid, 1821.
40526.59 Fontanes, Louis. Collection complète des discours de M. de Fontanes. Paris, 1821.
Mol 750.2 Fortia d'Urban. Sur le mariage de Molière. Paris, 1821.
40545.8 Genonde, Eugène de. Considérations sur les grecs et les turcs. Paris, 1821.
40535.19.2 Graffigny, Françoise d'Issembourg d'Happoncourt de. Lettere d'una peruviana. Londres, 1821.
40535.17 Graffigny, Françoise d'Issembourg d'Happoncourt de. Oeuvres complètes. Paris, 1821.
FL 383.75 Indicateur général de spectacles de Paris. Paris, 1821-22.
Htn 39527.8.30* La Fontaine, Jean de. La Fontaine en estamps. Paris, 1821.
41586.15 Lemercier, N.L. Louis IX en Egypte. Paris, 1821.
41586.16.13 Leroy, Onésime. Les deux candidats. Paris, 1821.
40512.59 LeSage, Alain René. El bachiller de Salamanca. Madrid, 1821. 2v.

1821 - cont.

Location	Call number	Entry
	40512.49	LeSage, Alain René. Oeuvre. Paris, 1821. 12v.
	40516.28.4	Louvet de Couvral, J.B. Vie du chevalier de Faublas. v.1-8. Paris, 1821-22. 4v.
	40588.42	Maistre, Xavier. Voyage autour de ma chambre. Boston, 1821.
Htn	38512.29*	Malo, Charles. Livre d'amour. Paris, 1821.
	39598.29	Marmontel, J.F. Bélisaire. Paris, 1821.
	Mol 18.21	Molière, Jean Baptiste Poquelin. Oeuvres...Bret. Paris, 1821. 6v.
	Mol 870.1	Moreau, Émile. Scène ajoutée au "Boulevard bonne nouvelle". Paris, 1821.
	41586.26.100	Moreau. La femme du sous-préfélt. 2e éd. Paris, 1821.
	Mol 194.21	Mozard. Il Don Giovanni, Don Juan. London, 1821.
	FL 6118.21	Musset, Victor Donatien. Histoire vie et ouvrages de Jean-Jacques Rousseau. Paris, 1821. 2v.
	39564.5	Naigeon, J.A. Mémoires sur la vie de Diderot. Paris, 1821.
	FL 398.74.300	Notice sur l'interrement de Mlle. Raucourt. Paris, 1821.
	41586.27.11	Perin, René. Isabelle de Levanzo ou La fille écuyer. Paris, 1821.
	41587.18.9	Picard, Louis Benoît. Un jeu de bourse. Paris, 1821.
	41587.5	Picard, Louis Benoît. Oeuvres. Paris, 1821. 10v.
	37574.35	Poésies révolutionnaires. Paris, 1821.
	40526.43	Racine, Louis. Le religion, poëme. Paris, 1821.
	37584.1	Répertoire général du théâtre français. v.39. Paris, 1821.
	FL 394.125	Ricord, Alexandre. Les fastes de la comédie française. Paris, 1821-22. 2v.
	37562.7A	Roquefort, Bonaventure. De l'état de la poésie française. Paris, 1821.
	FL 6037.15	Rousseau, J.J. El contrato social. Madrid, 1821.
	FL 6001.821	Rousseau, J.J. Oeuvres. Paris, 1821. 21v.
	38565.10	Saint-Surin, M. de. Oeuvres de Boileau. v.2-4. Paris, 1821. 3v.
	40588.29	Sousa Botelho Mourão e Vasconcellos, A.M.E.F. Oeuvres complètes. Paris, 1821-22. 12v.
	40593.3	Staël Holstein, Anne Louise. Oeuvres inédites de Mme. de Staël. Paris, 1821. 3v.
	39544.30	Standish, F.H. Life of Voltaire. London, 1821.
	41588.38.5	Théaulon de Lambert, Marie Emmanuel G.M. Jeanne d'Arc. Paris, 1821.
	40545.26.2	Touchard-Lafosse, Georges. Le lutin couleur de feu. 2. éd. Paris, 1821.
	41588.50	Wafflard, A.J.M. Le voyage a Dieppe. Paris, 1821.

1822

Location	Call number	Entry
	38543.13	Aimé-Martin, Louis. Examen critique. Paris, 1822.
	40597.32.30	Balzac, Honoré de. Jean Louis, ou La fille trouvée. v.1-4. Paris, 1822. 2v.
	38542.8	Balzac, J.L.G. de. Oeuvres de Jean Louis de Balzac. Paris, 1822. 2v.
	40552.2	Baudouin, Alexandre. The man of the world's dictionary. London, 1822.
	41583.14.5	Boirie, E.C. de. Le couvrier de Naples. Paris, 1822.
	41566.14.15	Bouilly, Jean N. Aguador de Paris. Valencia, 1822.
	39544.2.15	Boulogne, Étienne Antoine de. Istruzione pastorale sopra la pubblicazione de'cattivi libri. Firenze, 1822.
	41593.9.15	Bouzon de Mairet, E. Le testament du diable. Paris, 1822.
	41583.18.20.3A	Caigniez, Louis Charles. The magpie. Boston, 1822.
	40534.16.19	Carmontelle, L.G. Proverbes dramatiques. Paris, 1822. 4v.
	FL 391.40	Chalons D'Argé, A.P. Histoire critique des théâtres de Paris pendant 1821. Paris, 1822.
Htn	41593.16.3*	Chênedollé, C. de. Études poétiques. 2. éd. Bruxelles, 1822.
Htn	41593.16.2*	Chênedollé, C. de. Études poétiques. 2. éd. Paris, 1822.
	40517.44.20	Choderlos de Laclos, Pierre A.F. Las amistades peligrosas. Madrid, 1822. 3v.
	40588.2.5	Cottin, Marie R. (Mme.). Elizabeth, or Exiles of Siberia. London, 1822.
	40534.28.2	Crébillon, Prosper Jolyot de. Oeuvres. Paris, 1822. 3v.
	41566.4	D'Arlincourt, Charles V.P. The solitary. N.Y., 1822.
	41566.30	Daux, curé de Vauxbuin. Les petits hommes, ou Recueil d'anecdotes sur les hommes de petite stature qui se sont fait un nom par leurs vertus. Paris, 1822. 2v.
	41583.31	Delavigne, Casimir. Trois messéniennes, sur les malheurs de la France. 5e éd. Paris, 1822.
	41593.26.11	Delille, J. La pitié, poème. Paris, 1822.
	39564.11	Diderot, Denis. La religieuse. Paris, 1822.
	41584.28	Duval, A. Oeuvres. Paris, 1822. 9v.
	Mol 870.2	Gensoul, J. Le ménage de Molière. Paris, 1822.
	40535.19.5	Graffigny, Françoise d'Issembourg d'Happoncourt de. Lettres d'une peruvienne. Paris, 1822.
	41584.55.9	Guénard, Elisabeth. La jolie ferme. Paris, 1822.
	41593.45	Guttinguer, Ulric. Nadir, lettres orientales. Paris, 1822.
	41585.16	Jouy, Étienne. Sylla. 2e éd. Paris, 1822. 6 pam.
	39527.16.10	La Fontaine, Jean de. Oeuvres. Paris, 1822.
	38543.10.3	La Rochefoucauld, François. Réfléxions ou Sentences et maximes morales. Paris, 1822.
	37571.6	Lemonnier, A.H. Nouvelles leçons françaises. Paris, 1822. 2v.
	40513.7	Llorente, J.A. Obeservations critiques...Gil Blas de Santillane. Paris, 1822.
	40513.8	Llorente, J.A. Observaciones criticas...Gil Blas de Santillana. Madrid, 1822.
	41554.41.50	Lourdoueix, H. Les seductions politiques. Paris, 1822.
	41595.31.75	Loynes d'Autroche, Claude de. Ode au pape Pie VII. Paris?, 1822?
	40571.20	Maillet-Lacoste, P.L. Oeuvres. Paris, 1822.
	40556.27.100	Maistre, Joseph de. Die Werke des Grafen. v.1-2, 3-5. Frankfurt, 1822-25. 4v.
	38523.25	Malherbe, François de. Poésies de Malherbe. Paris, 1822.
	41567.42.5	Manesca, J. Historiettes nouvelles. N.Y., 1822.
	39597.14	Marmontel, J.F. Contes moraux. v.1-2,3,4. Paris, 1822. 3v.
	Mol 713.12.2	Mémoires sur Molière. Paris, 1822. 2 pam.
	Mol 713.12	Mémoires sur Molière. Paris, 1822.
	41595.24	Millevoye, Charles H. Oeuvres complètes. Paris, 1822. 4v.
	Mol 182.1.10	Molière, Jean Baptiste Poquelin. Dépit amoureux...Valville. Paris, 1822.
Htn	Mol 18.22.5*	Molière, Jean Baptiste Poquelin. Oeuvres. Paris, 1822. 6v.

1822 - cont.

Location	Call number	Entry
	Mol 18.22	Molière, Jean Baptiste Poquelin. Oeuvres. Paris, 1822. 8v.
	Mol 18.22.3	Molière, Jean Baptiste Poquelin. Oeuvres. Paris, 1822. 8v.
Htn	37573.435*	Noël, François J.M. Études et leçons françaises de littérature et de morale. v.4. Gand, 1822.
	41547.5	Pigault-Lebrun, C.A.G.R. de. Oeuvres complètes. Paris, 1822-29. 21v.
	41586.28.45	Pixerécourt, R.C.G. de. Le château de Loch-Leven. Paris, 1822.
	41586.28.60	Pixerécourt, R.C.G. de. Valentine. Paris, 1822.
	39583.12	Portets, Xavier de. Oeuvres choisies de Servan. Paris, 1822. 5v.
	38582.10	Racine, Jean. Oeuvres. Paris, 1822. 4v.
	38583.3.4	Racine, Jean. Oeuvres complètes. 2. éd. Paris, 1822. 6v.
	41587.20	Raimond, M. Bertram, ou le Pirate. Paris, 1822.
	FL 6021.22	Rousseau, J.J. Les confessions. Paris, 1822. 4v.
	FL 6031.25	Rousseau, J.J. Du contrat social ou Principes du droit politique. Paris, 1822.
	39594.31.5	St. Pierre, J.H.B. de. Pablo y Virginia. Paris, 1822.
	39584.20.20	Saint-Surin, P.T. de. Notice sur La Harpe. Paris, 1822.
	41557.9.22.20	Sand, George. Consuelo. Paris, 1822. 3v.
	41557.9.42.15	Sand, George. Correspondance, 1812-1876. Paris, 1822-84. 6v.
	41586.30.3.2	Soumet, A. Clytemnestre, tragédie en 5 actes. 2e éd. Paris, 1822.
	41586.30.3	Soumet, A. Clytemnestre, tragédie en 5 actes. 2e éd. Paris, 1822.
	37582.6	Suite du répertoire général du théâtre français. v.1-71. Paris, 1822-1823. 69v.
	38557.3	Tabaraud, M.M. Supplément aux histoires de Bossuet. Paris, 1822.
	40525.5	Tressan, L.E. Oeuvres. Paris, 1822-23. 10v.
	40525.5.2	Tressan, L.E. Oeuvres. Paris, 1822-23. 10v.
	41563.35	Vanhove, C.C.C. (Mlle.). L'ile des fées. Paris, 1822. 2v.
	39545.23.6	Voltaire, François Marie Arouet de. Chefs-d'oeuvre. Paris, 1822.
	39543.30	Voltaire, François Marie Arouet de. Filosofia. Madrid, 1822.

1823

Location	Call number	Entry
	40531.4.15	Arnault, A.Y. Les loisirs d'un banni. Paris, 1823. 2v.
	40597.35.180	Balzac, Honoré de. La dernière fée. v.1-2. Paris, 1823.
	41583.14.50	Baudouin, Théodore. Les inseparables. Paris, 1823.
	41583.14.55	Baudouin, Théodore. Le pauvre berger. Paris, 1823.
	40527.6	Bernard, Pierre Joseph. Oeuvres. Paris, 1823.
	Mon 200.1	Bernard de Ballainvilliers, Simon Charles Sebastien. Montaigne aux Champs-Élysées. Paris, 1823.
	41583.13	Blache, M. Polichinel vampire. Paris, 1823.
	38565.14	Boileau Despréaux, Nicolas. Oeuvres. Paris, 1823.
	41583.15.5	Bonjour, Casimir. L'education, ou Les deux cousines. Paris, 1823.
	38557.49.15	Bossuet, J.B. Discours sur l'histoire universelle. Paris, 1823. 2v.
	41583.18.12	Brunneaux, Jean. Pyrame et Thisbé. Tragédie. Paris, 1823.
	41583.18.13	Brunneaux, Jean. Ulysse. Tragédie. Paris, 1823.
	37574.305	Buisson, J.B. Souvenirs des muses. Paris, 1823.
	FL 398.71.9	Cahaisse, H.A. Mémoires de Préville et de Dazincourt. Paris, 1823.
	FL 391.40.2	Chalons D'Argé, A.P. Histoire critique des théâtres de Paris année 1822. Paris, 1823.
	38572.6	Corneille, Pierre. Chefs-d'oeuvres. Paris, 1823. 2v.
	38576.12.42.21	Corneille, Thomas. Chefs-d'oeuvre. Paris, 1823.
	40588.6.9	Cottin, Marie R. (Mme.). Mathilde. Paris, 1823. 3v.
	40588.01.4	Cottin, Marie R. (Mme.). Oeuvres complètes. Paris, 1823. 8v.
	41583.18.75	Crosnier, Edmond. Le contrebandier. 2e éd. Paris, 1823.
	41566.3	D'Arlincourt, Charles V.P. Le renégat. Paris, 1823. 2v.
	41583.30.3	Delavigne, Casimir. Messéniennes et poésies diverses. 6e éd. Paris, 1823.
	41593.29.15	De Selves, A. Catou, ou La guerre electorale. Paris, 1823.
	41593.32.13	Fabre, J.R.A. La Calédonie. Poème. Paris, 1823.
	38552.15	Fénelon, F. de S. de la Mothe. Werke, religiösen Inhalte. Hamburg, 1823. 3v.
	40526.23	Gilbert, N.J.L. Oeuvres complètes. Paris, 1823.
	40535.16.40	Godard, Louis. Poesie di Cimante Micenis. Roma, 1823.
	41567.28	Herbster, de (Mme.). The sisters of the cavern. Boston, 1823.
	41585.5	Jouy, Étienne. Oeuvres complètes. Paris, 1823-28. 27v.
	39545.4.5	Lepan, E.M.J. Vie politique littéraire de Voltaire. 3d ed. Paris, 1823.
	41595.22	Magalon, J.D. Souvenirs poétiques de deux prisonniers. Paris, 1823.
	FL 398.20	Mémoires de Mlle. Dumesnil. Paris, 1823.
	40556.40.10	Ménégault, A.P.F. L'impiété. 3. éd. Lyon, 1823.
	41595.25	Millevoye, Charles H. Oeuvres complètes. Bruxelles, 1823. 2v.
	Mol 18.23	Molière, Jean Baptiste Poquelin. Oeuvres complètes. Paris, 1823-24. 8v.
	Mol 64.5	Molière, Jean Baptiste Poquelin. Repertorio scelto...Barbieri. v.1-5. Milano, 1823-24.
	Mon 18.23	Montaigne, Michel de. Essais. Johanneau. Paris, 1823. 5v.
	41587.17.9	Picard, Louis Benoît. L'absence. Paris, 1823.
	41587.19.70	Ponet, Louis. Le pâtre. Paris, 1823.
	38536.6	Rabelais, F. Oeuvres. Paris, 1823. 9v.
	FL 6001.823	Rousseau, J.J. Oeuvres. Paris, 1823-26. 25v.
	FL 6091.55	Rousseau, J.J. Pygmalion and Galathea. Baltimore, 1823.
	41568.10.5	Saintine, Joseph Xavier Boniface. Poèmes, odes, épitres, et poésie diverse. Paris, 1823.
	40556.42.2	Senli, Piérre-Elie. Purgatoire de feu M. le comte Joseph de Maistre. Paris, 1823.
	40556.42	Senli, Piérre-Elie. Purgatoire de feu M. le comte Joseph de Maistre. Paris, 1823.
	38565.13	Viollet-Le-Duc, Emmanuel L.N. Oeuvres de Boileau. Paris, 1823.
	39545.23.4	Voltaire, François Marie Arouet de. Chefs-d'oeuvre dramatiques. Paris, 1823. 3v.

Chronological Listing

1824

FL 384.5 Alhoy, P.M. Grande biographie dramatique. Paris, 1824.
Htn 41584.47* Allarde, M.F.D.T.L.R. L'imprimeur sans caractère. Paris, 1824.
38565.16 Amar, Jean A. Oeuvres de Boileau. Paris, 1824. 4v.
40531.4 Arnault, A.Y. Oeuvres. Paris, 1824-27. 8v.
38512.3 Auguis, Pierre René. Les poets français...jusqu'à Malherbe. Paris, 1824. 6v.
40597.35.8 Balzac, Honoré de. Annette et le criminel. v.1-4. Paris, 1824. 2v.
37565.5 Barante, Amable Guillaume P.B. De la littérature française. 4. éd. Paris, 1824.
Mol 870.3 Bayard. Molière au théâtre. Paris, 1824.
41593.14 Brifant, Charles. Dialogues, contes et autres poésies. Paris, 1824. 2v.
40535.12.10 Campenon, Vincent. Essais de mémoires...de J.F. Ducis. Paris, 1824.
39586.17 Chamfort, S.R.N. Oeuvres. Paris, 1824-25. 5v.
40537.7 Chénier, Marie Joseph. Oeuvres posthumes. Paris, 1824. 3v.
38574.9 Corneille, Pierre. Chefs-d'oeuvre...et de nouvelles remarques par C. Nodier et P. Lepeintre. Paris, 1824-25. 2v.
38573.3 Corneille, Pierre. Oeuvres. Paris, 1824. 12v.
40588.01.2 Cottin, Marie R. (Mme.). Oeuvres complètes. Paris, 1824. 12v.
41593.17.10 Daru, P. Epitre à M. le Duc de la Rochefoucauld. Paris, 1824.
41583.30.10 Delavigne, Casimir. Messénienne sur Lord Byron. 2e éd. Paris, 1824.
41583.30.19 Delavigne, Casimir. Messéniennes et poesies nouvelles. 5. éd. Paris, 1824.
41593.20.8 Delille, J. Oeuvres. Paris, 1824. 16v.
37567.108 Desmarais, C. Essai sur les classiques et les romantiques. Paris, 1824.
41584.27.50 Ducange, Victor. Le diamant. Paris, 1824.
41585.24 Dulong, Jules. La prise de tarifa. Paris, 1824.
41584.27.85 Dupetit-Méré, F. Minuit, ou La révélation. Paris, 1824.
41567.11 Duras, Claire de Durfort. Ourika. Paris, 1824.
41584.38 Étienne, Charles Guillaume. Works. Paris, 1824. 2v.
38553.25.2 Fénelon, F. de S. de la Mothe. Les aventures de Télémaque. Paris, 1824. 2v.
38553.24.7 Fénelon, F. de S. de la Mothe. Les aventures de Télémaque. Philadelphia, 1824.
37582.8 Fin du répertoire du théâtre français. v.1-45. Paris, 1824. 22v.
Mol 750.3 Fortia, d'Urban. Dissertation sur la femme de Molière. Paris, 1824.
FL 6128.24 Girardin, S. Lettre à M. Musset-Pathay. Paris, 1824.
Mol 707.3 Grimarest, J.L. Mémoires sur la vie de Molière. Paris, 1824.
41543.29 Guiraud, Alexandre. Poëmes et chants elegiaques. Paris, 1824.
41593.46 Guttinguer, Ulric. Mélanges poétiques. Paris, 1824.
38526.26.12 Labé, Louise Charly. Oeuvres. Lyon, 1824.
38564.22 La Bruyère, J. de. Les caractères de La Bruyère suivis des caractères de Théophraste. Paris, 1824. 2v.
41586.16.75 Lacoste, A. Le platrier. Paris, 1824.
38523.4 Lacroix, Paul. Oeuvres de Clément Marot. Paris, 1824. 3v.
41585.35 Laloue, Ferdinand. Le commissionnaire. Paris, 1824.
X Cg 38543.10.8 La Rochefoucauld, François. Pensées et maximes. Paris, 1824.
42544.17.2 Legouvé, Gabriel. Le mérite des femmes. Paris, 1824.
41586.15.7 Lemercier, N.L. Richard III et Jeanne Shore; drame historique en vers. Paris, 1824.
40512.4A LeSage, Alain René. Histoire de Gil Blas. Paris, 1824. 3v.
40512.5 LeSage, Alain René. Histoire de Gil Blas. v.2-4. Paris, 1824. 3v.
41554.50 Maydieu, Jean. Histoire de la vertueuse portugaise. Besançon, 1824.
Mol 18.24.2 Molière, Jean Baptiste Poquelin. Oeuvres...L. Aimé-Martin. Paris, 1824-26. 8v.
Mol 18.24.3A Molière, Jean Baptiste Poquelin. Oeuvres...L. Aimé-Martin. Paris, 1824-26. 8v.
Mol 18.24 Molière, Jean Baptiste Poquelin. Oeuvres...Petitot. Paris, 1824. 6v.
Mol 268.25 Molière, Jean Baptiste Poquelin. Le Tartuffe. Étienne. Paris, 1824.
41587.17.13 Picard, Louis Benoît. L'exalté. 3e éd. Bruxelles, 1824. 3v.
41587.13.40 Picard, Louis Benoît. Le Gilblas de la revolution. Paris, 1824.
37597.12.7 Pluquet, Frédéric. Notice sur la vie et les écrits de Robert Wace. Rouen, 1824.
41587.19.75 Ponet, Louis. Les hussards. Paris, 1824.
38588.15 Quinault, Philippe. Oeuvres choisies de Quinault. Paris, 1824. 2v.
38582.11.25 Racine, Jean. Oeuvres dramatiques. London, 1824-34. 3v.
FL 6021.24 Rousseau, J.J. Confessions de Jean-Jacques Rousseau. Paris, 1824. 5v.
39594.27.5 St. Pierre, J.H.B. de. Paul et Virginie. London, 1824.
38528.11 Satyre Ménippée. Paris, 1824. 2v.
40543.3 Ségur, Louis P. de. Oeuvres complètes. Paris, 1824-27. 34v.
39544.85 Tabaraud, M.M. De la philosophie de la Henriade. Paris, 1824.
Mol 750.4 Taschereau, M.J. Lettre à Monsieur le Marquis de Fortia d'Urban. Paris, 1824.
39527.1A Walckenaer, C.A. Histoire de la vie de La Fontaine. Paris, 1824.

1825

40597.35.190 Balzac, Honoré de. Wann-Chlore. v.1-4. Paris, 1825. 2v.
40526.22.12 Bandre, M. de. Discours sur la vie...de Malfilâtre. Caen, 1825.
41593.3.6 Baour-Lormian, P.M.L. Le classique et le romantique. Paris, 1825.
41566.11 Bazot, Étienne F. Historiettes. Paris, 1825.
38566.15 Boileau Despréaux, Nicolas. Oeuvres. Paris, 1825. 4v.

1825 - cont.

37555.300.1 Bonaparte, Louis. Essai sur la versification. v.1-2. Rome, 1825.
40534.16.20 Carmontelle, L.G. Proverbes et comédies posthumes. Paris, 1825. 3v.
39532.16 Chaulieu, G.A. de. Poésies. Paris, 1825.
38516.12 Le débat de deux demoyselles. Paris, 1825.
41593.20.9 Delille, J. Oeuvres. Paris, 1825.
40551.24 Des conséquences funestes des principes philosophiques de M. de Bonald et de M. l'abbé de la Mennais. Paris, 1825.
41567.8 Dinocourt, T. Mozanino. Paris, 1825. 4v.
38554.3 Fénelon, F. de S. de la Mothe. Adventures of Telemachus. v.2. N.Y., 1825.
38554.107.105 Fénelon, F. de S. de la Mothe. Lives of the ancient philosophers. London, 1825.
38554.11 Fénelon, F. de S. de la Mothe. Le livre de prières. 2. éd. Paris, 1825.
38558.10 Fléchier, Esprit. Choix d'oraisons funèbres. Paris, 1825.
FL 358.19.5 Geoffroy, J.L. Cours de littérature dramatique. Paris, 1825. 6v.
39532.6 Hamilton, Anthony. Oeuvres du comte Hamilton. Paris, 1825. 2v.
FL 365.14 Hénin de Cuvillers, E.F. Des comédiens et du clergé. Paris, 1825.
FL 365.15 Hénin de Cuvillers, E.F. Encore des comédiens et du clergé. Paris, 1825.
41585.10 Jouy, Étienne. Bélisaire. 3e éd. Paris, 1825.
41593.125 Jullien, M.A. La France en 1825, ou Mes regrets et mes espérances. Paris, 1825.
38544.27.5 La Fayette, Marie M. Oeuvres complètes. Paris, 1825. 5v.
FL 6039.13 Lanjuinais, J.D. Examen du 8e chapitre du Contrat social de Jean-Jacques Rousseau. Paris, 1825.
41586.1 La Roche, Philippe J. de. Gustave, ou Le Napolitain. Paris, 1825.
41586.4.10 La Ville de Mirmont, Alexandre Jean Joseph. Le roman, comédie en cinq actes. Paris, 1825.
41595.14 Le Fevre-Deumier, J. Le clocher de Saint-Marc. Paris, 1825.
FL 398.49.9 Lekain, H.L. Mémoires. Paris, 1825.
37567.110 Le Prévost, M.A. Sur la poésie romantique. Rouen, 1825.
41586.16.15 Leroy, Onésime. Une première représentation. Paris, 1825.
37572.26.5 Lettres diverses. Paris, 1825.
41584.51 Lurieu, Gabriel de. Jocko, ou Le singe du Brésil. 3e éd. Paris, 1825.
40588.51 Maistre, Xavier. The Leper of Aost. Boston, 1825.
41588.62 Les Marchandes de Modes. Paris, 1825.
41555.27.5 Mérimée, Prosper. Plays of Clara Gazul. London, 1825.
FL 398.56 Mole, François René. Mémoires. Paris, 1825.
Mol 18.25 Molière, Jean Baptiste Poquelin. Oeuvres complètes...Chamfort. Paris, 1825.
Mol 18.25.3 Molière, Jean Baptiste Poquelin. Oeuvres complètes...Picard. Paris, 1825. 6v.
Mol 18.25.2 Molière, Jean Baptiste Poquelin. Oeuvres complètes...Simonnin. Paris, 1825.
Mol 18.25.4 Molière, Jean Baptiste Poquelin. Oeuvres de J.B. Poquelin de Molière. Paris, 1825. 6v.
Mon 18.25 Montaigne, Michel de. Essais. Villemain. Paris, 1825. 8v.
37585.12.5 Nodier, Charles. Bibliothèque dramatique. v.1-4. Paris, 1825-26. 7v.
37583.395 Nouvelle bibliothèque dramatique. v.1-7. Jena, 1825-29. 3v.
FL 398.63.31 Odryana, ou La boite au gros sel. Paris, 1825.
38543.4 Oeuvres de...La Rochefoucauld. Paris, 1825.
41587.13.45 Picard, Louis Benoît. The Gil Blas of the revolution. London, 1825. 3v.
41587.17 Picard, Louis Benoît. L'honnête homme. 2e éd. Paris, 1825. 3v.
38581.7A Racine, Jean. Oeuvres complètes. Paris, 1825. 7v.
38581.8 Racine, Jean. Oeuvres complètes. Paris, 1825-1826. 5v.
39526.4A Robert, A.C.M. Fables inédites der XII, XIII et XIV siècles, et de La Fontaine. Paris, 1825. 2v.
Mol 870.4 Samson, Joseph Isidore. La fête de Molière. Paris, 1825.
41557.34 Sarrazin, Adrien de. Bardouc. Paris, 1825.
41587.30 Scribe, Eugène. Le charlataniseme. 2e éd. Paris, 1825. 11 pam.
41588.3.8 Scribe, Eugène. Le charlatanisme. 2e éd. Paris, 1825.
41586.30.2 Soumet, A. Cléopatre, tragédie. Paris, 1825.
41586.30.8 Soumet, A. Pharamond. Paris, 1825.
FL 398.49.11 Talma, F. Réflexions sur Lekain et sur l'art théâtral. Paris, 1825.
Mol 720.1A Taschereau, M.J. Histoire de la vie et des ouvrages de Molière. Paris, 1825.
39583.5 Thomas, Antoine L. Oeuvres. Paris, 1825. 6v.
41563.34 Trognon, Auguste. Manuscrits de l'ancienne abbaye de Saint Julien, à Brioude. Paris, 1825.
40584.17 Villemain, Abel L. Discours et mélanges littéraires. 3. éd. Paris, 1825.
39545.23 Voltaire, François Marie Arouet de. Chefs-d'oeuvre dramatiques. v.1-4. Paris, 1825. 2v.
39544.27.2 Voltaire, François Marie Arouet de. Correspondance avec P.M. Hennin. Paris, 1825.
39545.34.8 Voltaire, François Marie Arouet de. Cuentos y satiras. N.Y., 1825.
39536.32 Voltaire, François Marie Arouet de. Oeuvres complètes. 2d ed. Paris, 1825-28.

1826

37573.410 Annales romantiques. v.3. Paris, 1826.
43526.65.242 Apollinaire, Guillaume. Anecdotiques. Paris, 1826.
41583.8 Arago, E. C'est demain le treise. Paris, 1826.
41593.3.5 Baour-Lormian, P.M.L. Satire. Paris, 1826.
Htn 41592.13.5* Béranger, P.J. de. Chansons. v.1-4. Paris, 1826. 2v.
40551.16 Bonald, L.G.A. de. Recherches philosophiques. Oevres VIII-IX. Paris, 1826. 2v.
41583.15.16 Bonnechose, Emile. Rosemonde; tragédie. Paris, 1826.
41566.12.5 Bonnellier, Hippolyte. Les vieilles femmes de l'Ile de Sein. v.1-2. Paris, 1826.
38557.40.10 Bossuet, J.B. Betrachtungen über die Zeit des Jubiläum. 3. Aufl. Würzburg, 1826.
41583.16 Brazier, Dumersan. Les filles de Vulcain. Paris, 1826.
40586.27 Chateaubriand, F.A.R. Mémoires d'outre-tombe. Paris, 1826-28. 6v.

1826 - cont.

	40586.6	Chateaubriand, F.A.R. Oeuvres, v. XXI. Atala, René et les Abencérages. Brussels, 1826.
	40585.3	Chateaubriand, F.A.R. Oeuvres complètes. v.1-28. Paris, 1826-31. 31v.
	40526.5	Chénier, André. Oeuvres anciennes. Paris, 1826.
	40526.6	Chénier, André. Oeuvres posthumes. Paris, 1826.
	40537.6	Chénier, Marie Joseph. Oeuvres. Paris, 1826. 5v.
Htn	Mol 880.11*	Corally. M. de Pourceaugnac. Paris, 1826.
	40546.7.5	Courier de Méré, Paul Louis. Collection complète des pamphlets politiques. Bruxelles, 1826.
	41588.19	D'Arlincourt, Victor. La siége de Paris. Paris, 1826.
	41583.20.5	Delavigne, Casimir. Théâtre. Paris, 1826. 4v.
	40535.5	Destouches, Philippe Néricault. Oeuvres choisies. Paris, 1826. 3v.
	40556.8	Droz, Gustave. Oeuvres. Paris, 1826. 3v.
	40535.11	Ducis, Jean F. Hamlet. Paris, 1826.
	40535.9	Ducis, Jean F. Oeuvres. Paris, 1826. 3v.
	40535.10	Ducis, Jean F. Oeuvres. Paris, 1826.
Htn	41538.43*	Dumas, Alexandre. Canaris. Paris, 1826.
	38557.26.4	Dussault, Jean Joseph. Oraisons funèbres de Bossuet, Fléchier, et autres orateurs. Paris, 1826. 4v.
	38552.4	Fénelon, F. de S. de la Mothe. Oeuvres. Paris, 1826. 12v.
	41540.125	Francois de Nantes, Antoine. Recueil de fadaises. Paris, 1826. 2v.
	37558.14	Genlis, Stephanie. De l'influence des femmes sur la littérature française. Paris, 1826. 2v.
	FL 6049.10.5	Gerdil, G.S. L'anti-Emilo. Firenze, 1826.
	41585.17	Jouy, Étienne. Sylla, a tragedy. N.Y., 1826.
	38564.22.5	La Bruyère, J. de. Les caractères de La Bruyère suivis des caractères de Théophraste. Paris, 1826. 2v.
Htn	FL 398.84.18*	Lafon, Pierre. Discours...sur la tombe de Talma. Paris, 1826.
	39525.20	La Fontaine, Jean de. Oeuvres complètes. Paris, 1826.
	39525.6	La Fontaine, Jean de. Oeuvres complètes. Paris, 1826. 6v.
	41578.12	Lamartine, Alphonse de. Auserlesene Gedichte. Stuttgart, 1826.
Htn	FL 398.84.20*	Laugier, Adolph. Notice sur Talma. Paris, 1826.
	Mol 860.27	Laurent, A. du. Ninon à la campagne. Lyon, 1826.
	41586.4	La Ville de Mirmont, Alexandre Jean Joseph. L'intrigue et l'amour. Paris, 1826.
Htn	40512.7*	LeSage, Alain René. The adventures of Gil Blas of Santillane. London, 1826. 2v.
	40512.6	LeSage, Alain René. Histoire de Gil Blas. London, 1826. 2v.
	39536.33	Longchamp, Sebastian G. Mémoires sur Voltaire. Paris, 1826. 2v.
	41595.20.5	Luce de Lancival, J.C.J. Oeuvres. Paris, 1826. 2v.
	39595.17.2	Martin, L.A. Mémoire sur la vie...de J.H. Bernardin de St. Pierre. Paris, 1826.
	41595.23	Massas, Charles. Dithyrambes et poésies diverses. Paris, 1826.
	41586.21.5	Mazères, Edouard Joseph E. La demoiselle de campagnie. Paris, 1826.
	41586.21	Mazères, Edouard Joseph E. Le fin du mois. Paris, 1826.
	37596.14	Meon, D.M. Le roman de Renart. Paris, 1826. 4v.
	41586.22.50	Merle, Jean T. Le monstre et le magicien. Paris, 1826.
	37558.48.10	Méry, Joseph. Biographie des quarante de l'Académie française. Paris, 1826.
	Mol 18.26	Molière, Jean Baptiste Poquelin. Oeuvres complètes. Paris, 1826.
	Mon 18.26	Montaigne, Michel de. Essais. J.V. Le Clerc. Paris, 1826. 5v.
	39591.10	Montesquieu, C.L. de S. Oeuvres. Paris, 1826. 8v.
	FL 398.84.5	Moreau, M. Mémoires...sur F.J. Talma. Paris, 1826.
	41596.42.9	Ourry, E.T.M. Bourbons et la France. Paris, 1826.
	41586.27.6	Outrepont, Chardles d'. La mort de Henri III. Paris, 1826.
	41586.27.7	Outrepont, Charles d'. Le Saint-Barthélemi; drame. Paris, 1826.
	37584.2	Picard, L.B. Répertoire du théâtre français. Paris, 1826. 4v.
	41597.56	Poirié Saint-Aurèle. Les veillées françaises. Paris, 1826.
	40517.56.25	Pougens, Marie C. Abel, ou Les trois frères. Paris, 1826.
	37585.18	Recueil de pièces de théâtre. Paris, 1826- 8 pam.
	38587.8	Regnard, Jean François. Oeuvres complètes de Regnard. Paris, 1826. 6v.
	37596.57	Richelet, Charles J. Fragmens de l'éxplication allégorique du cantique des cantiques. Paris, 1826.
	FL 6041.26	Rousseau, J.J. Oeuvres complètes. Paris, 1826. 3v.
	FL 6001.826	Rousseau, J.J. Oeuvres complètes. Paris, 1826.
	FL 6001.826.5	Rousseau, J.J. Oeuvres complètes. Paris, 1826. 25v.
Htn	FL 6087.2*	Rousseau, J.J. Pensées d'un esprit droit et sentimens. Paris, 1826.
	41587.25	Saint-Just, Antoine. Essais littéraires. Paris, 1826. 2v.
	40527.22	Saint-Lambert, Jean F. Poésies. Paris, 1826.
	39595.17	St. Pierre, J.H.B. de. Correspondance. Paris, 1826. 3v.
	39595.5	St. Pierre, J.H.B. de. Oeuvres. Paris, 1826. 12v.
	39595.27	St. Pierre, J.H.B. de. Pablo y Virginia. Paris, 1826.
	41591.55	Tastu, A. (Mme.). Poésies. Paris, 1826.
	FL 398.84.23	Tissot, Pierre F. Souvenirs historiques sur la vie et la mort de F. Talma. Paris, 1826.
	40527.25	Verny, Pierre. Oeuvres poétiques. Paris, 1826.
	41596.67	Viennet, J.P.G. Epître à empereur Nicolas, en faveur des grecs. Paris, 1826.
	39545.46.5	Voltaire, François Marie Arouet de. Lord Chesterfield's ears. London, 1826.
	41588.52	Wailley, G. de. Amour et intrigue. Paris, 1826.

1827

	41583.8.5	Arago, E. Les quatres artistes. Paris, 1827.
	41593.5.30	Barthélemy, Auguste Marseille. Rome à Paris, poëme. 8. éd. Paris, 1827.
	41593.5.5	Barthélemy, Auguste Marseille. Une soirée chez M. de Peyronnet. Paris, 1827.
	38557.26.2	Bossuet, J.B. Oraisons funèbres. Paris, 1827.
	41566.14.2	Bouilly, Jean N. Contes à mes petites amies. Paris, 1827?
	41583.16.5	Brazier, Dumersan. Tony, ou Cinq années en deux heures. Paris, 1827.

1827 - cont.

	40586.45	Chateaubriand, F.A.R. Las aventuras del ultimo Abencerrage. Paris, 1827.
Htn	37556.20.50*	Chateaubriand, François A.R. Du retablissement de la censure par l'ordnance du 24 juin 1827. Paris, 1827.
	41522.70	Clarke, M.L. Olésia, ou la Pologne. Paris, 1827.
	38511.14.2	Le combat de trente Bretons contre trente Anglois. Paris, 1827.
X Cg	38526.28.15	Contes et nouvelles. v.1-5. Paris, 1827. 3v.
	40588.4	Cottin, Marie R. (Mme.). Isabel. Paris, 1827.
	41583.30.5	Delavigne, Casimir. Sept messéniennes nouvelles. Paris, 1827.
	41593.29	Désaugiers, M.A. Chansons et poésies diverses. Paris, 1827. 4v.
	41584.23	Dittmer, Antoine D.A. Les soirées de Neuilly. Paris, 1827. 2v.
	38557.11.5	Floquet, Amable. Éloge de Bossuet. Paris, 1827.
	40515.31.5	Florian, Jean P.C. de. Eleazar and Naphtaly. London, 1827.
	41543.30	Guiraud, Alexandre. Virginie. Paris, 1827.
	41593.47	Guttinguer, Ulric. Poèmes et poésies nouvelles. Paris, 1827.
	37561.5	Henrion, Mathieu R. Histoire littéraire de la France. Paris, 1827.
	37532.7	Laharpe, Jean F. de. Lycée, ou Cours de littérature. Paris, 1827. 18v.
	41586.15.4	Lemercier, N.L. Les deux filles spectres; mélodrame 3 actes en prose. Paris, 1827.
	39582.10	Maury, J.S. Oeuvres choisies. Paris, 1827. 5v.
	41555.12.5	Mérimée, Prosper. La guzla, ou choix de poésies illyriques. Paris, 1827.
	41586.23.3	Merville, P.F.C. Les deux anglais. Paris, 1827.
	41586.23	Merville, P.F.C. La prèmiere affaire. Paris, 1827.
	41586.23.25	Méry, Joseph. Le congrès des ministres. 8e éd. Paris, 1827.
	41586.23.15	Méry, Joseph. Peyronnéide. Paris, 1827.
	Mol 18.27	Molière, Jean Baptiste Poquelin. Oeuvres complètes. Paris, 1827.
	Mon 18.27	Montaigne, Michel de. Essais. Paris, 1827. 10v.
	Mon 18.27.3	Montaigne, Michel de. Essais. A. Duval. Paris, 1827. 6v.
Htn	38511.6.5*	Moralité de Mundus, Caro, Demonia. Paris, 1827.
	FL 6118.21.2	Musset, Victor Donatien. Histoire vie et ouvrages de Jean-Jacques Rousseau. Paris, 1827.
	41584.55.200	Nézel, Théodore. Cartouche. 2e éd. Paris, 1827.
	41596.48	Parny, Évariste. Oeuvres choisies. Paris, 1827.
	Mol 880.26	Petit, A. Le Sicilien. Paris, 1827.
	41587.18	Picard, Louis Benoît. Les trois quartiers. Paris, 1827.
	41586.28.8	Pixerécourt, R.C.G. Les natchez. Paris, 1827.
	38582.10.5A	Racine, Jean. Oeuvres. Paris, 1827-1828. 5v.
	FL 398.84.14	Regnault-Warin, J.J. Mémories historiques et critiques sur F.J. Talma. Paris, 1827.
Htn	41587.20.80*	Romieu, Auguste. Proverbes romantiques. Paris, 1827.
	FL 6051.27	Rousseau, J.J. Julie ou la nouvelle Héloise. Paris, 1827. 6v.
	41587.33	Scribe, Eugène. La chatte métamorphosée en femme. Paris, 1827. 10 pam.
	38514.14.10	Suryille, Joseph Étienne. Poésies inédites de Marguerite Eleonore Clotilde. Paris, 1827.
	41596.63	Tastu, Amable. Poésies. 4. éd. Paris, 1827.
	41588.41	Vanderburch, Émile. Le barbier de Paris. Paris, 1827.
	39578.8.43	Vauvenargues, L. de C. Oeuvres complètes de Vauvenargues. Paris, 1827.
	39578.8.44	Vauvenargues, L. de C. Oeuvres posthumes de Vauvenargues. Paris, 1827.
	40584.19.3	Villemain, Abel L. Mélanges. Paris, 1827.
	40584.19.5	Villemain, Abel L. Nouveaux mélanges historiques et littéraires. Paris, 1827.

1828

	37597.14.2	Abrahams, L. De Roberti Wacii Carmine quod inecribitur Brutus. Hafinae, 1828.
	41592.14	Béranger, P.J. de. Chansons inédites. Paris, 1828.
	41593.11.20	Brizeux, Auguste. Racine. Paris, 1828.
	40534.23	Collin d'Harleville, J.F. Oeuvres. Paris, 1828. 4v.
	40588.2.5.4	Cottin, Marie R. (Mme.). Elizabeth, or Exiles of Siberia. Boston, 1828.
	40588.2.5.5	Cottin, Marie R. (Mme.). Elizabeth, or The exiles of Siberia. Boston, 1828.
	40534.28.6	Crébillon, Prosper Jolyot de. Oeuvres. Paris, 1828. 2v.
	40534.28.5	Crébillon, Prosper Jolyot de. Oeuvres. Paris, 1828. 2v.
	41583.34	Delavigne, G. La muette de Portici. Paris, 1828.
	Mol 870.5	Dercy, F. Molière; comédie épisodique. Paris, 1828.
	39594.3.29	Destutt de Tracy, A.L.C. Commentaire sur l'esprit des loix de Montesquieu. Paris, 1828.
	FL 6135.6	Dunant, D. Rousseau n'a-t-il rien fait pour sa patrie? Genève, 1828.
	41584.29	Duval, A. Charles II, ou Le Labyrinthe de Woodstock. Paris, 1828.
	40566.9.5	Félitz, C.M. de. Melanges de philosophie. Paris, 1828-30. 6v.
	38553.31.5	Fénelon, F. de S. de la Mothe. Le aventure di Telemace. v.1-2. Livorno, 1828.
	38554.11.3	Fénelon, F. de S. de la Mothe. Le livre de prières de M. de Fénelon. Besancon, 1828.
	40515.35.10	Florian, Jean P.C. de. Gonzalo de Cordoba. Perpignan, 1828.
	40515.33	Florian, Jean P.C. de. Gonzalve de Cordoue. v.1-3. Paris, 1828.
	Mol 860.28	Garnier, F. Le mariage de Molière. Paris, 1828.
	Mol 860.28.2	Garnier, F. Le mariage de Molière. Paris, 1828.
	41584.55.12	Guénard, Elisabeth. Vie et aventures de Marion de Lorme. 3e éd. v.1-2,3-4. Paris, 1828. 2v.
	39532.13	Hamilton, Anthony. Memoires of Count Grammont. London, 1828. 2v.
Htn	41573.35.3*	Hugo, Victor. Odes et ballades. 5e éd. Paris, 1828. 2v.
	39527.17	La Fontaine, Jean de. Fables de La Fontaine. Paris, 1828.
	41578.6	Lamartine, Alphonse de. Méditations poétiques. v.1-2. Stuttgart, 1828.
	41586.14	Lemercier, N.L. Comédies historiques. Paris, 1828.
	41588.23	Loeve-Weimars, A. Scènes contemporaines. Paris, 1828-30. 2v.

Chronological Listing

1828 - cont.

37596.41.13 Lorens, Frère. Volgarizzamento dell'esposizione del paternostro fatto da Zucchero Bencivenni. Firenze, 1828.
38523.26 Malherbe, François de. Poésies, suivies d'un choix de lettres. Paris, 1828.
FL 6049.2 Marceille, G. Examen de la Profession de foi du Vicaire Savoyard (Jean-Jacques Rousseau. Emile.). Paris, 1828.
Mol 172.3 Molière, Jean Baptiste Poquelin. The gentleman cit. London, 1828.
Mol 18.28 Molière, Jean Baptiste Poquelin. Oeuvres. v.1-5,8. Paris, 1828. 6v.
X Cg 39594.5.9 Montesquieu, C.L. de S. Considérations sur...des Romains. Paris, 1828.
FL 397.115.31 Neuville, A. Revue historique, chronologique et anecdotique du théâtre de Gand, 1750-1828. Gand, 1828.
41596.43.5 Paillet, M. Epitres et poésies diverses. Paris, 1828.
40573.2.10 Peignot, Gabriel. Mélanges littéraires. v.1-4. Lyon, 1828.
41596.49.12 Pellet, D'Epinal. Le barde des vosages. Paris, 1828.
41586.28.50 Pixerécourt, R.C.G. de. Guillaume Tell. Paris, 1828.
41586.28.55 Pixerécourt, R.C.G. de. La tête de mort. Paris, 1828.
41587.22 Saint-Hilaire, Amable Villain de. Valentine ou La chute des feuilles. Paris, 1828.
39594.22 St. Pierre, J.H.B. de. La chaumière indienne. Paris, 1828.
39594.27.8 St. Pierre, J.H.B. de. Paul et Virginie. Paris, 1828.
41588.15.1 Scribe, Eugène. Valérie. London, 1828.
41586.30 Soumet, A. Elisabeth de France. Paris, 1828.
Mol 560.3 Taschereau, J. Bibliographie de Molière. Paris, 1828.
Htn Mol 720.2* Taschereau, M.J. Histoire de la vie et des ouvrages de Molière. Paris, 1828.
Mol 720.2.2 Taschereau, M.J. Histoire de la vie et des ouvrages de Molière. Paris, 1828.
41588.41.10 Vanderburch, Emile. Henri IV en famille. Paris, 1828.
39545.23.7 Voltaire, François Marie Arouet de. Chefs-d'oeuvre dramatiques de Voltaire. Paris, 1828. 4v.
Htn 39544.27.15* Voltaire, François Marie Arouet de. Lettres de Voltaire et de J.J. Rousseau à C.J. Panckoucke. Paris, 1828.

1829

41593.3 Baour-Lormian, P.M.L. Légendes, ballades et fabliaux. Paris, 1829.
41593.5.10 Barthélemy, Auguste Marseille. Napoléon en Egypte. Paris, 1829.
41593.6.40 Barthélemy, Auguste Marseille. Waterloo al generale Bourmont. Lugano, 1829.
41583.12.19 Benjamin, A. Le jeune médecin. Paris, 1829.
41592.15 Béranger, P.J. de. Chansons. v.1-4. Paris, 1829-33. 3v.
37557.2 Berger de Xivrey. Recherches sur...la littérature française. Paris, 1829.
Htn 40582.19.3* Beyle, Henri. Promenades dans Rome. Paris, 1829. 2v.
Htn 38557.35.30* Bossuet, J.B. Lettres inédites de Bossuet à Madame de la Maisonfort. Paris, 1829.
41583.15.14.7 Bourgeois, Anicet. Clarisse. Paris, 1829.
FL 398.11.5 Castel, Louis. Mémoires d'un claqueur. Paris, 1829.
40586.5.16 Chateaubriand, F.A.R. Voyages en Amérique, en Italie. Paris, 1829.
40553.8 Constant de Rebecque, Benjamin. Mélanges de littérature et de politique. Bruxelles, 1829.
39568.5A Correspondance inédits de Grimm et Diderot. Paris, 1829.
41583.29 Delavigne, Casimir. Marino Faliero. Paris, 1829.
41593.29.9 Deschamps, E. Etudes françaises et étrangères. Paris, 1829.
41584.27.5 Drichatellier, A. Théâtre historique de la Révolution. v.2. Paris, 1829.
Htn 41538.47.5* Dumas, Alexandre. Henri et sa cour. Paris, 1829.
41567.10 Duras, Claire de Durfort. Ourika. Boston, 1829.
38558.8.5 Fléchier, Esprit. Oraisons funèbres. Paris, 1829.
40515.29 Florian, Jean P.C. de. Fables. 2e éd. Paris, 1829.
41588.25.5 Gallois, Léonard. Le citateur dramatique. 5e éd. Paris, 1829.
41588.25.9 Gallois, Léonard. Trois actes d'un grand drame. Paris, 1829.
41588.25 Gallois, Léonard. Le vingt-mars. Bruxelles, 1829.
41593.32.18 Gaudy-Le Fort, Jean A. Esquisses genevoises. Genève, 1829.
41584.51.25 Germeau. La reforme en 1560, ou Le tumulte d'Amboise. Paris, 1829.
41541.7 Girardin, Delphine Gay. Le dernier jour de Pompei. 2. ed. Paris, 1829.
39568.5.5 Grimm, F.M. von. Correspondance inédite de Grimm et de Diderot. Paris, 1829.
39567.4 Grimm, F.M. von. Correspondance littéraire. Paris, 1829-31. 15v.
41542.85.100 Guillot, Henry. Le cousin germain de Vadé. Paris, 1829.
41584.57 Hoffman, F.B. Oeuvres. Paris, 1829-34. 10v.
Htn 37577.3* Les joyeusetez facecies...et Faceties, raréties et cur. Paris, 1829. 16v.
38564.24.9 La Bruyère, J. de. Les caractères de La Bruyère. Paris, 1829.
39527.17.10 La Fontaine, Jean de. Fables. v.1-2. Paris, 1829.
38543.10.9 La Rochefoucauld, François. Maximes et réfléxions morales. 2. éd. Paris, 1829.
40545.14 Lemontey, P.E. Oeuvres. Paris, 1829. 5v.
40512.8 LeSage, Alain René. Histoire de Gil Blas de Santillane. Paris, 1829. 4v.
40588.45 Maistre, Xavier. Journey round my room. Philadelphia, 1829.
X Cg 40526.22.3 Malfilâtre, J.C.L. de C. de. Oeuvres. Paris, 1829.
41586.19 Marie, M. Paul Morin. Paris, 1829.
41595.22.25 Martin-Maillefer, P.D. Les fiancés de Caracas. Paris, 1829.
40516.56 Mercier, Louis S. Voyage philosophique dans l'Amérique. Paris, 1829.
41593.8.10 Mery, Joseph. Il figlio dell'uomo. Brusselles, 1829.
41593.8.1 Mery, Joseph. Le fils de l'homme. Bruxelles, 1829.
41593.8 Mery, Joseph. Le fils de l'homme. Bruxelles, 1829.
41593.7 Mery, Joseph. Le fils de l'homme. Bruxelles, 1829.
41593.8.2 Mery, Joseph. Le fils de l'homme. Bruxelles, 1829.
Mol 18.29 Molière, Jean Baptiste Poquelin. Oeuvres. v. 1-2, 3-4, 5-6, 7-8. Paris, 1829. 4v.
Mon 28.38 Montaigne, Michel de. L'esprit de Montaigne. Paris, 1829.
41596.49.7 Parseval, F.A. Philippe-Auguste. Poème héroïque. Paris, 1829.
38582.11 Racine, Jean. Oeuvres. Paris, 1829. 5v.

1829 - cont.

37597.20 Raynouard, Franc J. Observations sur le roman de rose. Rouen, 1829.
Htn 38528.1.7* Recueil de livrets singuliers et rares. Paris, 1829-30.
Htn 38528.1.6* Recueil de livrets singuliers et rares. Paris, 1829-30.
41587.20.5 Regmer d'Estourbet, H. Les septembriseurs. 2e éd. Paris, 1829.
41588.1 Scribe, Eugène. Le secrétaire et le cuisinier. Paris, 1829.
38553.14 Selections from the writings of Fénelon. Boston, 1829.
38553.15 Selections from the writings of Fénelon. 2. ed. Boston, 1829.
Htn FL 379.5* Les souvenirs et les regrets du vieil amateur dramatique. Paris, 1829.
40593.905 Staël Holstein, Auguste Louis. Oeuvres diverses. Paris, 1829. 3v.
38575.3 Tachereau, Jules. Histoire de...Pierre Corneille. Paris, 1829.
37542.10 Ventouillac, L.T. The French librarian or literary guide. London, 1829.
40584.19 Villemain, Abel L. Mélanges. Brussels, 1829.
40584.26 Vitet, L. Les états de Blois, ou La mort de Mme. de Guise. Bruxelles, 1829.
40584.24 Vitet, L. La mort de Henri III. Bruxelles, 1829.
39545.37.19 Voltaire, François Marie Arouet de. Le duc d'Alencon. Paris, 1829.

183-

FL 384.7 Galerie de la presse. Paris, 183-?

1830

41583.8.6 Arago, E. 27, 28 et 29 juillet. Paris, 1830.
40563.22 Ballanche, Pierre Simon. Oeuvres. Paris, 1830. 4v.
Htn 40597.32.9* Balzac, Honoré de. Physiologie du mariage. Paris, 1830. 2v.
41593.6.20 Barthélemy, Auguste Marseille. L'insurrection, poème. Bruxelles, 1830.
40551.9 Bonald, L.G.A. de. Démonstration philosophique. Oevres XII. Paris, 1830.
41593.9.7 Boucher de Crèvecoeur de Perthes, Jacques. Romances, ballads et légendes. Paris, 1830.
41583.15.12 Bourgeois, Anicet. Napoleon, pièce historique. Paris, 1830.
41583.18.22 Carmouche, P.F.A. N.i.ni, ou Le danger des Castilles. Paris, 1830.
Htn 40516.6.2* Cazotte, Jacques. The devil in love. Boston, 1830.
40586.18.11.2 Chateaubriand, F.A.R. Génie du Christianisme. v.1-4. Paris, 1830. 2v.
40586.19 Chateaubriand, F.A.R. Les martyrs. Paris, 1830. 2v.
40585.5 Chateaubriand, F.A.R. Oeuvres complètes. Paris, 1830-31. 20v.
38573.4 Corneille, Pierre. Oeuvres. Paris, 1830-31. 12v.
41584.2 Debraux, Paul Emile. Les barricades de 1830. Paris, 1830.
39566.3 Diderot, Denis. Mémoires. Paris, 1830-31. 4v.
41584.27 Druancel, P.C. Esquisses dramatiques du gouvernement Révolutionnaire de France. Paris, 1830.
Htn 41538.49* Dumas, Alexandre. Stockholm. Paris, 1830.
40566.7.9 Du Meril, E. Mélanges archéologiques et littéraires. Paris, 1830.
Mol 873.5 Dumersan. La mort de Molière. Paris, 1830.
38553.24.15 Fénelon, F. de S. de la Mothe. Aventures de Télémaque. Livre III. Paris, 1830.
40515.38 Florian, Jean P.C. de. Guilherme Tell. Paris, 1830.
40515.44 Florian, Jean P.C. de. Numa Pompelius. Paris, 1830.
41593.240.5 Forget. La France nouvelle. Paris, 1830.
41584.44 Fougher, P. Yseult Raimbaud. Paris, 1830.
41593.32.20 Gaudois, G. Les romantiques. Satire. Paris, 1830.
38524.130 Gerard de Neval, G.L. Choix des poésies de Ronsard, Dubellay, Baïf, Belleau. Paris, 1830.
41573.32.3 Hugo, Victor. Hernani. 2e éd. Paris, 1830.
41573.32.3.2 Hugo, Victor. Hernani. 3e éd. Paris, 1830.
40567.36 Janin, Jules. Confession. Paris, 1830.
37567.97 Jay, A. La conversion d'un romantique. Paris, 1830.
38514.53 La Sale, Antoine de. L'histoire...du Jehan de Saintré. Paris, 1830.
41554.38 Lebras, Auguste. Les Armoricaines. Paris, 1830.
41586.11.5 Leclercq, Théodore. Nouveaux proverbes dramatiques. Paris, 1830.
40512.3.5 LeSage, Alain René. Le diable boiteux. v.1-2. Paris, 1830.
40511.22 LeSage, Alain René. Théâtre choisi. Paris, 1830.
39598.6 Marmontel, J.F. Memoirs. London, 1830. 2v.
41555.32.5 Mérimée, Prosper. 1572. N.Y., 1830.
40535.60.9 Milcent, Jean B.G.M. de. Lord Davenant. Valencia, 1830.
Mol 64.6 Molière, Jean Baptiste Poquelin. Commedie...in lengua zeneize. v.1-6. Zena, 1830. 2v.
Mol 18.30 Molière, Jean Baptiste Poquelin. Oeuvres. Paris, 1830. 8v.
39594.6 Montesquieu, C.L. de S. Considérations sur...des Romains. Paris, 1830.
Htn 41556.15* Nodier, Charles. Histoire du roi de Bohême. Paris, 1830.
40592.5 Oeuvres complètes de Mme. de Staël. v.1-17. Bruxelles, 1830. 10v.
37591.31 Perne. Chansons du Châtelain de Coucy. Paris, 1830.
37581.37 Picard, L.B. Une matinée de Henri IV; comédie. N.Y., 1830-63. 8 pam.
41587.18.11 Picard, Louis Benoît. L'album. Paris, 1830.
41587.14 Picard, Louis Benoît. Oeuvres choisies. N.Y., 1830.
41547.13.15 Pigault-Lebrun, C.A.G.R. de. Les dragons en cantonnement. Paris, 1830.
41547.13.17 Pigault-Lebrun, C.A.G.R. de. Les dragons en cantonnement. Paris, 1830.
Htn 38516.4* Poésies des XVe et XVIe siècles. Paris, 1830-32.
38582.11.2 Racine, Jean. Oeuvres. v.4. Paris, 1830.
41587.20.9 St. Esteben. La mort de Coligny ou la nuit de Saint-Barthelemy, 1572. Paris, 1830.
41587.26 Saint-Maurice, C.R.E. Rome, Londres et Paris. Scènes contemporaines. Paris, 1830.
41588.15.8 Scribe, Eugène. Avant, pendant et après. Paris, 1830.
41588.3 Scribe, Eugène. Les grisettes. Paris, 1830.
41588.2 Scribe, Eugène. La lune de miel. Paris, 1830.
37572.11 Soulié, J.B.A. Keepsake français, 1830. Paris, 1830.
41586.30.10 Soumet, A. Une fête de Néron. Paris, 1830.
37536.5 Villemain, A.F. Cours de littérature française. Paris, 1830. 2v.

1830 - cont.

	40584.25	Vitet, L. Les barricades. Scènes historiques. 4. éd. Paris, 1830.

1831

	41565.6	Albitte, Gustave. Une vie d'homme. Paris, 1831.
	41592.1	Alletz, E. La nouvelle messiade. Paris, 1831.
	41593.6.4	Barthélemy, Auguste Marseille. Némésis. Paris, 1831-1832.
	41593.5	Barthélemy, Auguste Marseille. Oeuvres. Paris, 1831. 2v.
	41583.15.40	Bonnais, Henri. Le 9 thermidor, ou La mort de Robespierre. Paris, 1831.
	41566.18.9	Buonaparte, Louis. Poésies. Florence, 1831.
	40532.30	Castil-Blare, F.H.J. Barbier de Séville. Boston, 1831.
	41583.18.23	Cavaignac, Godefroy. Dubois cardinal, proverbe historique. Paris, 1831.
	40586.7	Chateaubriand, F.A.R. Nouvelles. Paris, 1831. 3v.
	40597.2.370	Desnoiresterres, G. M. De Balzac. Paris, 1831.
	41538.46	Dumas, Alexandre. Catharine of Clèves. London, 1831.
	41538.62	Dumas, Alexandre. Napoléon Bonaparte. Paris, 1831.
	38553.15.3A	Fénelon, F. de S. de la Mothe. Selections from the writings. 3. ed. Boston, 1831.
Htn	40515.30.50*	Florian, Jean P.C. de. Fabulas de Florian. Madrid, 1831.
	40515.20.5	Florian, Jean P.C. de. Nouvelles. v.1-2. Paris, 1831.
	41573.10.2	Hugo, Victor. Marion de Lorme. Bruxelles, 1831.
	41573.10	Hugo, Victor. Marion de Lorme. Bruxelles, 1831.
	41573.10.10	Hugo, Victor. Marion de Lorme. 3. éd. Paris, 1831.
	39527.18	La Fontaine, Jean de. Choix de fables de La Fontaine. Paris, 1831.
Htn	41578.35.10*	Lamartine, Alphonse. Sur la politique rationelle. Paris, 1831.
	41586.3	Latouche, Henri de. La reine d'Espagne. Paris, 1831.
	40511.28	LeSage, Alain René. The adventures of Gil Blas. Hartford, 1831.
	37581.40.12	Magasin théâtral, 1831-1851. Miscellaneous plays. Paris, 1831-51.
	40556.41	Maître, Pierre. Le savant de village. Paris, 1831-33. 3v.
	Mon 18.31	Montaigne, Michel de. Essais. Paris, 1831.
Htn	38511.5*	Moralitę des Blasphemateurs de Dieu. Paris, 1831.
Htn	41596.49*	Parny, Evariste. Oeuvres complètes. Paris, 1831. 4v.
	FL 384.9	Petite biographie des acteurs et actrices des théâtres de Paris. Paris, 1831-32.
	41596.49.30	Peyre-Terry, F. Conseils de l'esprit d'un vieillard septuagenaire. Philadelphia, 1831.
Htn	41588.3.14*	Scribe, Eugène. La dame blanche, or The white lady. Baltimore, 1831.
	41588.3.2	Scribe, Eugène. Louise. Paris, 1831.
	41586.30.9	Soumet, A. Norma. Paris, 1831.
	40592.21.3	Staël Holstein, Anne Louise. Corinne. Paris, 1831. 2v.
	41588.38	Théaulon de Lambert, Marie Emmanuel G.M. Le petit chaperon rouge. Baltimore, 1831.
	41588.38.3	Théaulon de Lambert, Marie Emmanuel G.M. Le petit chaperon rouge. Baltimore, 1831.
	37574.23	Ventouillac, L.T. French poetry. London, 1831.

1832

	37565.6	Barante, Amable Guillaume P.B. De la littérature française pendant le XVIIIe siècle. 5. éd. Paris, 1832.
	41566.9	Barginet, A.P. La trente-deuxième demi-brigade. Bruxelles, 1832.
	41593.6	Barthélemy, Auguste Marseille. Douze journées de la révolution. Poèmes. Paris, 1832.
	41522.20.10	Beauvoir, E. Roger de. L'ecolier de Cluny, ou le sophisme, 1315. Paris, 1832.
	41592.16A	Béranger, P.J. de. Chansons. Bruxelles, 1832-1833. 4v.
Htn	41592.16.2*	Béranger, P.J. de. Chansons. v.1. Bruxelles, 1832.
	38565.17	Boileau Despréaux, Nicolas. Oeuvres. Paris, 1832. 3v.
	41593.9.10	Bourlier, Louis. La prêtréxide, poème. Paris, 1832.
	41566.16.50	Bruckar, R. Le puritain de Seine et Marne. Bruxelles, 1832.
	41583.21	Delavigne, Casimir. Oeuvres complètes. v.3. Bruxelles, 1832.
	38511.14	Deschampes, Eustache. Poésies morales. Paris, 1832.
	41595.5.50	Le dix-neuf brumaire. Paris? 1832.
	41522.150	Drouineau, Gustave. Le manuscrit vert. 2. éd. Paris, 1832. 2v.
	Mol 870.5.5	Dupeuty. La vie de Molière. Paris, 1832.
	41584.29.5	Duval, A. Le misantrope du Marais. Paris, 1832.
	38554.107.40	Fénelon, F. de S. de la Mothe. Abrégé des vies des anciens philosophes. Londres, 1832.
	38553.24.20	Fénelon, F. de S. de la Mothe. Les aventures de Télémaque. Paris, 1832.
	38553.24.22	Fénelon, F. de S. de la Mothe. Les aventures de Télémaque. Philadelphia, 1832.
	41540.75.32	Floquet, A. Louis XI et la Normande; anecdote rouennaise du XVe siècle. Rouen, 1832.
	FL 384.12	Géréon, L. de. La rampe et les coulisses. Paris, 1832.
	39533.3.5	Hamilton, Anthony. Memoires du comte de Grammont. Paris, 1832.
	41573.36.6	Hugo, Victor. Les feuilles d'automne. v.1-2. 3. éd. Paris, 1832.
	41572.29.2	Hugo, Victor. Le roi s'amuse; drame. Paris, 1832.
	41572.29	Hugo, Victor. Le roi s'amuse. Paris, 1832.
	FL 398.17	Janin, Jules. Deburau. Paris, 1832. 2v.
	41545.20	Karr, Alphonse. Sous les Tilleuls. Paris, 1832. 2v.
	41554.15	Lacroix, Paul. La danse maccabre. Bruxelles, 1832.
Htn	41577.10*	Lamartine, Alphonse de. Oeuvres. Paris, 1832. 4v.
	41554.36	Lanjiunais, J.D. Oeuvres, avec une notice biographique. Paris, 1832. 4v.
	40535.12.9	Leroy, Onésime. Études morales et litteraires sur...J.F. Ducis. Paris, 1832.
	41588.29.9	Lockroy, Joseph P.S. Un duel sous le Cardinal de Richelieu. Paris, 1832.
	41586.19.19	Martin, Pierre Henri. La vielle Fronde, 1648. Paris, 1832.
	41586.23.9	Méry, Joseph. L'assassinat; scènes méridionales de 1815. Paris, 1832.
	Mol 18.32	Molière, Jean Baptiste Poquelin. Oeuvres. Paris, 1832. 6v.
	Mol 166.50	Molière, Jean Baptiste Poquelin. Skupoi. Moskva, 1832.

1832 - cont.

	Mol 269.70.9	Molière, Jean Baptiste Poquelin. El Tartufo. Caracas, 1832.
	39594.2	Montesquieu, C.L. de S. De l'esprit des lois. Paris, 1832. 3v.
Htn	38513.8*	Le mystère de Griselidis. Paris, 1832.
	41556.6	Nodier, Charles. Oeuvres. v.5,8,9. Paris, 1832. 3v.
	41596.43	Paillet, M. Oromaze. Paris, 1832.
	39532.17	Peignot, Gabriel. Nouvelles recherches sur la vie et les ouvrages de Bernard de La Monnoye. Dijon, 1832.
	41587.15	Picard, Louis Benoît. Théâtre républicain, posthume et inédit. Paris, 1832.
	41586.28.5	Pixerécourt, R.C.G. de. L'abbaye aux Bois. Paris, 1832.
	40522.8	Prévost, Antoine F. Histoire de Manon Lescaut et du chevalier des Grieux. Paris, 1832.
	38536.21	Rabelais, F. Gargantua and Pantagruel. Leipzig, 1832. 3v.
	41587.20.75	Ratier, Victor. Le Te-Deum et le De Profundis. Paris, 1832.
	37596.136.5A	Renauld de Beaujeu. Le lai d'Ignaurès ou lai du prisonnier. Paris, 1832.
Htn	37596.100*	Richelet, Charles J. Du baro mors et vis. Conte du XIIe siècle. Paris, 1832.
	41587.26.9	Sadler, P. Fifty years...an allegorical play. Paris, 1832.
	41587.31	Scribe, Eugène. Dix ans de la vie d'une femme. Paris, 1832. 6 pam.
	41588.3.19	Scribe, Eugène. La grande aventure. Paris, 1832.
	41588.15.8.9	Scribe, Eugène. Toujours, ou L'avenir d'un fils. Paris? 1832?
	41596.60	Servan de Sugny, P.F.J. Satires contemporaines et mélanges. Paris, 1832.
	37585.3.8	Théâtre classique, contenant Esther, Athalie. Tours, 1832.
	41564.9.5	Vigny, Alfred de. Stello. Bruxelles, 1832.
	38514.19.25	Villon, François. Oeuvres. Paris, 1832.
	41565.32	Waldor, Mélanie. L'ecuyer Dauberon. Paris, 1832.

1833

	40563.8	Ampère, Jean J. Litterature et voyages. Paris, 1833.
	40563.22.5	Ballanche, Pierre Simon. Oeuvres. Paris, 1833. 6v.
	41522.1.3.9	Barbey d'Aurevilly, Jules. Amour et haine. Paris, 1833.
NEDL	41592.16.5	Béranger, P.J. de. Chansons nouvelles et dernières. Bruxelles, 1833.
	41565.3	Bibliothèque choisie. Paris, 1833-34. 4v.
	41593.9.8	Boucher de Crèvecoeur de Perthes, Jacques. Satires, contes et chansonnettes. Paris, 1833.
	41593.13.5	Bourlet-Delavallée, E. Derniers chants du soir. Paris, 1833.
	40546.5	Courier de Méré, Paul Louis. Oeuvres complètes. Bruxelles, 1833.
	41566.5.5	D'Arlincourt, Charles V.P. Les écorcheurs ou l'usurpation et la peste. Bruxelles, 1833.
	41583.27	Delavigne, Casimir. Les enfans d'Édouard. Paris, 1833.
	41522.152	Drouineau, Gustave. Résignée. Paris, 1833. 2v.
	42542.68.9	Dumanoir, M. Sous clé; comédie vaudeville. Paris, 1833.
	41584.27.30	Dupin, Jean Henri. Tigresse; mort-aux-rats. Paris, 1833.
	FL 383.33	Duval, M.A. Lettre à M. Victor Hugo. Paris, 1833.
	41584.32.39	Duveyrier, A.H.J. Les vieux péchés. Paris, 1833.
	38553.24.23	Fénelon, F. de S. de la Mothe. Les aventures de Télémaque. Philadelphia, 1833.
	40515.45	Florian, Jean P.C. de. Numa Pompelius. v.1-2. Paris, 1833.
	41584.42	Fontan, Louis Marie. Bergami et la reine d'Angleterre. Paris, 1833.
	41567.23.4	Guizot, Elizabeth C.P. de M. Nouveaux contes. Paris, 1833. 2v.
	37567.11	Huber, Victor A. Neuromantische Poesie in Frankreich. Leipzig, 1833.
	41554.3	Labutte, Augustine. Chronique du jour des morts. Paris, 1833.
Htn	41578.6.10*	Lamartine, Alphonse de. Oeuvres. Méditations. Bruxelles, 1833.
	41554.37	Lassailly, Charles. Les roueries de Trialph. Paris, 1833.
	41586.3.19	Laverpillière, A. L'homme et ses écrits. Paris, 1833.
Htn	41595.16*	Le Fevre-Deumier, J. Confidences. Paris, 1833.
	37564.43	Lodin de Lalaire, T. De la Mission de Pascal de Bossuet et de Fénélon au 17e siècle. Paris, 1833.
	Mol 270.5	Loère-Veimars, F.A. Tartufe et le malade imaginaire. Paris, 1833.
	FL 393.14	Macaire, S. Les petits théâtres du boulevards. Paris, 1833.
	37581.40.5	Magasin théâtral. 2. ed. v.7-27. Paris, 1833-1843. 7v.
	41567.44	Masson, Michel. Thadéus le ressuscité. Bruxelles, 1833.
	41555.32	Mérimée, Prosper. La double méprise. Bruxelles, 1833.
	37572.16	Merlet, P.F. Petit tableau littéraire. London, 1833.
	37595.23.2	Michel, F. Des XXIII manières de vilains (XIIIe siècle). Paris, 1833.
	41555.58	Moke, Henri G. Herman of Natuur en beschaving. v.1-2. Amsterdam, 1833.
	Mol 18.33	Molière, Jean Baptiste Poquelin. Oeuvres. Paris, 1833. 8v.
	39594.11.6	Montesquieu, C.L. de S. Lettres persanes. Paris, 1833.
	37571.4	Noël, François J.M. Leçons françaises de littérature. Brussels, 1833-36.
	38581.10	Racine, Jean. Oeuvres. Paris, 1833.
	37596.72	Salmon, P. Les demandes faites par le roi Charles VI. Paris, 1833.
	41588.13.19	Scribe, Eugęne. Las capas; comedia. Madrid, 1833.
	41568.18	Sénancour, Ętienne Pivert de. Isabelle. Paris, 1833.
	41568.19.5	Sénancour, Étienne Pivert de. Rêveries. 3. éd. Paris, 1833.
	40584.25.3	Vitet, L. Les barricades. Scènes historiques. 4. éd. Bruxelles, 1833.
	39545.68	Voltaire, François Marie Arouet de. Chefs d'oeuvres dramatiques. Paris, 1833-
	39545.43.5	Voltaire, François Marie Arouet de. La Henriade. Paris, 1833.
	39545.30	Voltaire, François Marie Arouet de. Romans de Voltaire. v.3-4. Paris, 1833.

Chronological Listing

1834

Htn 40597.32.11* Balzac, Honoré de. The fatal skin. v.1-2. Paris, 1834.
40517.12 Berquin, Arnaud. Abregé de l'ami des enfans. v.1-4. Paris, 1834. 2v.
38566.35 Boileau Despréaux, Nicolas. A estante do coro. Lisboa, 1834.
37595.21 Boucherie, Anatole. Fragment d'une anthologie picarde. Photoreproduction. Paris, 1834-72.
41593.13.4.10 Boulay-Paty, Évariste. Elie Mariaker. Paris, 1834.
41574.597 Cantú, Cesare. Di Vittore Hugo e del romanticismo in Fríncia. Milano, 1834.
40586.25 Chateaubriand, F.A.R. Études ou Discours historiques. Paris, 1834. 4v.
41583.18.35 Chateauneuf, A. L'infidelité conjugale. Paris, 1834.
41583.18.55 Coquatrix. Italie. Paris, 1834.
41566.27 Craon, princesse de. Thomas Morus. Paris, 1834.
41566.2.10 D'Arlincourt, Charles V.P. El cervecero rey. Barcelona, 1834. 2v.
41566.5.20 D'Arlincourt, Charles V.P. Nagy Károly. Pesten, 1834. 2v.
41584.26.9 Drague, Joseph. Urbain-Grandier. Dijon, 1834.
42542.66.60 Dugué, Ferdinand. La semaine de Pâques. Paris, 1834.
38553.27A Fénelon, F. de S. de la Mothe. Aventures de Télémaque. Philadelphia, 1834.
37573.400.25 Fleurs de poésie moderne; tirées des oeuvres de A. de Lamartine, V. Hugo, De Béranger, C. De Cavigne. Londres, 1834.
41541.1 Flint, Timothy. The bachelor reclaimed. Philadelphia, 1834.
37581.41 La France dramatique au XIXe siècle, 1834-1839. Paris, 1834-39.
37596.23.5 Grant mal fist Adam. Publié par A. Jubinal. Paris, 1834.
37596.51 Guichard de Beaulieu. Le sermon de G. de B. Paris, 1834.
41567.23.5 Guizot, Elizabeth C.P. de M. Nouveaux contes. Paris, 1834. 2v.
41593.48 Guttinguer, Ulric. Arthur. Rouen, 1834.
41573.22 Hugo, Victor. The hunchback of Notre Dame. Philadelphia, 1834.
41572.12 Hugo, Victor. Littérature et philosophie mêlées. Paris, 1834. 2v.
37595.20 Jubinal, Achille. Lettre. Paris, 1834-49.
41548.50 Kermel, A. Une ame en peine. Paris, 1834.
39527.18.3F La Fontaine, Jean de. Fables. v.1-2. Paris, 1834.
Htn 41578.35.15* Lamartine, Alphonse. Discours sur la dette americaine, 1 avril 1834. Paris, 1834.
37562.3 La Rue, Gervais de. Essais historiques sur les bardes anglo-normans. Caen, 1834. 3v.
Htn 40586.31.20* Lectures des Mémoires de m. de Chateaubriand. Paris, 1834.
FL 394.60 Lerebours, P.V. Documens pour sevir à l'histoire du théâtre-français sous la restauration. Paris, 1834.
37581.40.3 Magasin théâtral. v.1-31. Paris, 1834-1842. 29v.
Mol 193.6 Marmier, X. Les Don Juan. Paris, 1834. 2 pam.
41554.54 Mercey, Frédéric. Tiel, le rodeur; romans et tableaux de genre. Paris, 1834. 2v.
37595.24 Michel, F. La riote du monde. Paris, 1834.
Mol 18.34 Molière, Jean Baptiste Poquelin. Oeuvres. Paris, 1834. 8v.
41586.25 Monbrion, M. Le Siége de Grenade. Paris, 1834.
38541.11 Moralistes français. Paris, 1834.
41547.8.25 Pigault-Lebrun, C.A.G.R. de. O citader. Paris, 1834. 2v.
41596.51.60 Puycousin, E. de. Poésies maritimes et fantastiques. Toulon, 1834.
41586.29 Pyat, F. Le brigand et le philosophe. Paris, 1834.
Mol 815.1 Roederer, P.L. Fragments de divers mémoires pour servir à l'histoire de la société polie en France. Paris, 1834.
FL 6001.834 Rousseau, J.J. Oeuvres complètes avec notes historiques et critiques. Paris, 1834. 17v.
39594.34.15 St. Pierre, J.H.B. de. Paul and Virginia. Boston, 1834.
39594.27.12 St. Pierre, J.H.B. de. Paul et Virginie. Paris, 1834.
39594.32 St. Pierre, J.H.B. de. Paulo e Virginia. Paris, 1834.
40575.26 Sainte-Beuve, Charles A. Volupté. Bruxelles, 1834.
41587.29 Scribe, Eugène. Le chanoinesse. Paris, 1834. 9 pam.
41588.7.5 Scribe, Eugène. Théâtre complet. 2e éd. Paris, 1834-42. 24v.
41586.30.5 Soumet, A. La France dramatique au 19 siècle. Paris, 1834.
41563.23 Thibaudeau, Antoine C. La Bohême. Paris, 1834. 2v.
40526.68 Vadé, Jean Joseph. Oeuvres choisies. Paris, 1834.
41564.3.50 Vigny, Alfred de. Cinq-Mars. v.1-2. 8e éd. Bruxelles, 1834.
41564.16 Vigny, Alfred de. Poèmes. Bruxelles, 1834.
39545.44.15 Voltaire, François Marie Arouet de. The Henriade. Mobile, 1834.
39536.34 Voltaire, François Marie Arouet de. Oeuvres. Paris, 1834-39. 74v.
41596.100 Yvaren, Prosper. Cromwel; ode. n.p., 1834.

1835

41583.8.25 Arnoult, S. Proverbes anecdotiques. Paris, 1835.
41566.8 Auger, Hippolyte Nicolas Just. Priesterlist über alles. v.1-2. Leipzig, 1835. 2v.
41593.6.3 Barthélemy, Auguste Marseille. Douze journées de la révolution. Poèmes. Paris, 1835.
38511.31 Beauvau, Louis de. Le pas d'armes de la Bergère. 2e éd. Paris, 1835.
41566.14 Bouilly, Jean N. Contes à ma fille. Bruxelles, 1835.
40587.56 Cantù, Cesare. Chateaubriand; discorso. Milano, 1835.
41566.15 Chabot de Bouin, Jules. Histoire de deux soeurs. Brusselles, 1835.
40586.17.35 Chateaubriand, F.A.R. Travels to Jerusalem and the Holy Land. 3. ed. London, 1835. 2v.
37566.3 Chenier, Marie J. Tableau historique de l'etat...de la littérature française. Paris, 1835.
41566.24 Corbière, Edouard. Les aspirans de marine. Bruxelles, 1835.
41522.77 Cordellier-Delanoue, A. Cronwell; A drama. Paris, 1835.
38512.6 Costello, Louisa S. Specimens of the early poetry of France. London, 1835.
38512.6.2 Costello, Louisa S. Specimens of the early poetry of France. London, 1835.
40588.2.6.50 Cottin, Marie R. (Mme.). Elisabeth. Paris, 1835.
41566.26 Craon, princesse de. Henri Percy. Paris, 1835. 2v.
38512.35 Le dit de ménage, pièce en vers du XIVe siècle. Paris, 1835.

1835 - cont.

41584.26 Drague, Joseph. Que deviendra-t-elle? Paris, 1835.
41593.32.15 Favier, Eulalie. Poésies de l'ame. Paris, 1835.
38553.29 Fénelon, F. de S. de la Mothe. Telemak. Copenhagen, 1835.
FL 398.28.8 Fleury, J.A.B. Mémoires de la comédie française. Paris, 1835-38. 6v.
41543.27.10 Guiraud, Alexandre. Flavien ou De Rome au désert. Paris, 1835. 3v.
41567.22 Guizot, Elizabeth C.P. de M. Caroline. Boston, 1835.
41567.23 Guizot, Elizabeth C.P. de M. Tales in French. Boston, 1835.
41573.24 Hugo, Victor. Cromwell. Bruxelles, 1835.
41585.2 Imbert de Saint-Armand. Le Réveillon dramatique. Paris, 1835.
37596.36 Jubinal, A. La complainte et le jeu. Paris, 1835.
41548.10 Kérardven, L. Guionvach. Études sur la Bretagne. 2e éd. Paris, 1835.
41567.40 La Madelaine, Stephen. La grande-prieure de Malte. Bruxelles, 1835.
38543.19.20 La Rochefoucauld, François. Maxims and moral reflections. N.Y., 1835.
41586.11 Leclercq, Théodore. Proverbs dramatiques. Paris, 1835. 8v.
41586.15.5 Lemercier, N.L. L'héroine de Montpellier; mélodrame en 5 actes. Paris, 1835.
40511.31.2 LeSage, Alain René. Histoire de Gil Blas. Paris, 1835.
40511.31 LeSage, Alain René. Historia de Gil Blas. Paris, 1835.
41567.34.5 Lottin de Laval, René V. Maria von Medicis. Heidelberg, 1835.
41567.34 Lottin de Laval, René V. Robert le magnifique. Bruxelles, 1835.
41586.18 Luchet, A. Ango. Paris, 1835.
42577.12.19 Mary-Lafon. Silvio ou Le boudoir. Paris, 1835.
41567.44.25 Masson, Michel. La lampe de fer de Daniel le lapidaire. Bruxelles, 1835.
40564.8 Mélanges. Brussels, 1835. 3v.
41555.16 Mérimée, Prosper. Notes d'un voyage dans le midi de la France. Bruxelles, 1835.
Mol 201.20 Molière, Jean Baptiste Poquelin. L'école des maris...Gombert. London, 1835.
Mol 248.23 Molière, Jean Baptiste Poquelin. M. de Pourceaugnac. Gombert. London, 1835.
Mol 8.35 Molière, Jean Baptiste Poquelin. Oeuvres. Paris, 1835-36. 2v.
41567.27 Montpezat, Charles de (Mme.). Corisande de Mauléon. Bruxelles, 1835.
Htn 38511.6* Moralité de la Vendition de Joseph. Paris, 1835.
40573.1.5 Peignot, Gabriel. Quelques recherches sur...l'oraison domenicale. Dijon, 1835-39. 4 pam.
40573.3.30 Peignot, Gabriel. Recherches historiques et philosophiques sur la philatesie ou usage de boire à la santé. Dijon, 1835.
41596.49.19 Périn, F.C. Nuits poétiques. Paris, 1835.
41586.28.300 Pourchel, Alfred. Une Chrétienne et Néron. Paris, 1835.
38514.20 Prompsault, Jean H.R. Oeuvres de...Villon. Paris, 1835.
38582.12 Racine, Jean. Oeuvres. v.3-4. Paris, 1835.
38514.71.80 Reiffenbery, F.A.F.T. Mémoire sur Jean Molinet. Cambrai, 1835.
37564.26 Roederer, P.L. Mémoire pour servir a l'histoire de la Société Polie en France. Paris, 1835.
Htn Mol 815.2* Roederer, P.L. Mémoire pour servir à l'histoire de la société polie en France. Paris, 1835.
40536.21.18 Roger, Jean François. Oeuvres. Paris, 1835. 2v.
FL 6001.835 Rousseau, J.J. Oeuvres complètes avec notes historiques. Paris, 1835. 4v.
41568.9 St. Genois, Ludger D.G. Hembyse. Habana, 1835. 2v.
40575.26.4 Sainte-Beuve, Charles A. Volupté. v.1-2. Bruxelles, 1835.
38546.4.5 Scudéry, Madeleine de. Lettres de Mlle. de Scudéry à M. Godeau. Paris, 1835.
41588.37 Tardif, A. Essais dramatiques. Paris, 1835.
41596.63.5 Tastu, Amable. Poésies nouvelles. Paris, 1835.
37596.71 Thibaud de Montmorency, seigneur de Marly. Vers sur la mort. Paris, 1835.
41564.24 Vigny, Alfred de. Chatterton. Brussels, 1835.
39545.43.15 Voltaire, François Marie Arouet de. La Henriade. London, 1835.
39545.24.9 Voltaire, François Marie Arouet de. Oeuvres complètes. Paris, 1835-38. 13v.

1836

41566.1 Abrantes, L. St.M.P.J. L'amirante de Castille. 2e éd. Paris, 1836.
40597.25 Balzac, Honoré de. Le livre mystique. Brussels, 1836.
40597.35.5 Balzac, Honoré de. Le vicaire des Ardennes. Paris, 1836. 2v.
FL 6113.19 Barbier, A.A. Notice bibliographique sur les diverses éditions des ouvrages de Jean-Jacques Rousseau. Paris, 1836.
38557.45 Bossuet, J.B. The Catholic's manual. N.Y., 1836.
38557.41.30 Bossuet, J.B. History of the variations of the protestant churches. 2nd ed. Dublin, 1836. 2v.
40586.17 Chateaubriand, F.A.R. Itinerario da Parigi a Gerusalemme. v. 6. Naples, 1836.
37575.109 Contes et nouvelles butonnes. Rennes, 1836.
38574.11.5 Corneille, Pierre. Chefs-d'oeuvres. v.1-4. Paris, 1836. 2v.
38576.12.42.22 Corneille, Thomas. Chefs-d'oeuvre. v.1-2. Paris, 1836.
40588.4.10 Cottin, Marie R. (Mme.). Amélie Mansfield. v.1-3. Paris, 1836.
40588.2.7 Cottin, Marie R. (Mme.). Élisabeth, ou Les exilés de Siberia. Paris, 1836.
40588.6 Cottin, Marie R. (Mme.). Malvina. v.1-3. Paris, 1836.
41581.7 Delavigne, C. Oeuvres complètes. Paris, 1836.
41583.28 Delavigne, Casimir. Une famille au temps de Luther. Paris, 1836.
42542.66.63 Dugué, Ferdinand. Horizons de la poésie. Paris, 1836.
41593.32.10 Durand, J.B.A. La forêt de Fontainebleau, poème. Paris, 1836.
Mon 200.2F Faugère, A.P. Du courage civil, ou L'hopital chez Montaigne. Paris, 1836.
41540.50 Ferrière, Théophile de. Il vivere par Samuel Bach. Paris, 1836.
40515.33.7 Florian, Jean P.C. de. Gonzalve de Cordoue. v.1-2. Paris, 1836.
40515.33.5 Florian, Jean P.C. de. Gonzalve de Cordoue. v.1-2. Paris, 1836.

Chronological Listing

1836 - cont.

	40515.39	Florian, Jean P.C. de. Guilherme Tell. Greenfield, 1836.
	37555.34	Géruzez, Eugène. Cours d'éloquence française. Paris, 1836.
	41542.48	Gozlan, Léon. Le notaire. Bruxelles, 1836. 2v.
	41573.32.23	Hugo, Victor. Marie Tudor. Angelo. Paris, 1836.
	41571.3.60	Hugo, Victor. Oeuvres. Bruxelles, 1836-37. 2v.
	41545.5	Karr, Alphonse. Le chemin le plus court. Bruxelles, 1836. 2v.
	41553.34	Kock, Charles Paul de. Andrew the Savoyard. Philadelphia, 1836. 2v.
	41554.22	Lacroix, Paul. Pignerol. Bruxelles, 1836. 2v.
	39527.30	La Fontaine, Jean de. Fables choisies de La Fontaine. Morlaix, 1836.
Htn	41578.29.10*	Lamartine, Alphonse. Jocelyn. v.1-2. Paris, 1836.
	41577.11	Lamartine, Alphonse de. Oeuvres. Bruxelles, 1836.
	41577.10.12	Lamartine, Alphonse de. Oeuvres. Paris, 1836.
	40535.12.11	Leroy, Onésime. Études sur la personne et les écrits de J.F. Ducis. 3. éd. Paris, 1836.
	37595.11	Michel, Francisque. Lais inédits des XIIe et XIIIe siècles. Paris, 1836.
	38513.5.2A	Miracle de...Robert de Dyable. Rouen, 1836.
Htn	38513.5*	Miracle de...Robert de Dyable. Rouen, 1836.
	Mol 166.1.3	Molière, Jean Baptiste Poquelin. L'avare...mise en vers par A. Rastoul. Avignon, 1836.
	Mol 38.36	Molière, Jean Baptiste Poquelin. Le Molière de la jeunesse. v.2. Lyon, 1836.
	Mol 18.36	Molière, Jean Baptiste Poquelin. Oeuvres...Petitot. Paris, 1836. 6v.
	Mon 18.36	Montaigne, Michel de. Essais. Paris, 1836.
	FL 373.5.2	Morice, Émile. Essai sur la mise en scène. Paris, 1836.
	FL 373.5	Morice, Émile. Histoire de la mise en scène. Paris, 1836.
	40572.5	Muret, Théodore. Mademoiselle de Montpensier. Brusselles, 1836. 2v.
	38511.16A	Mystère de Saint Crespin. Paris, 1836.
	37571.5	Noël, François J.M. Leçon françaises de littérature. 21e éd. Bruxelles, 1836.
	Mol 775.1	Notice sur le fauteuil de Molière. Pézenas, 1836.
	40573.1.6	Peignot, Gabriel. Moeurs et usage au moyen-âge. Paris, 1836.
	37574.36A	Poésies nationale de la révolution française. Paris, 1836.
	41568.1	Rabbé, Alphonse. Album d'un pessimiste. Paris, 1836.
	38582.12.3	Racine, Jean. Oeuvres. Angers, 1836. 3v.
	37591.30	Reiffenberg. Chronique rimée de Philippe Mousket. Brussels, 1836. 3v.
	FL 6021.36	Rousseau, J.J. Les confessions. v.1-5. Paris, 1836. 2v.
	41588.12.9	Scribe, Eugène. Tu amor, o La muerte! Comedia en un acto. Madrid, 1836.
	41558.63	Souvestre, Émile. Riche et pauvre. Bruxelles, 1836.
	40592.21.4	Staël Holstein, Anne Louise. Corinne, ou l'Italie. Paris, 1836. 2v.
Htn	38527.38*	Taillandier, Alphonse H. Proces d'Etienne Dolet. Paris, 1836.
	41563.23.5	Thibaudeau, Antoine C. Böhmen in den Jahren 1600 bis 1621. Gotha, 1836. 2v.
	39545.46	Voltaire, François Marie Arouet de. La Henriade. Charlestown, 1836.
	39545.43.20	Voltaire, François Marie Arouet de. La Henriade. Paris, 1836.
	37597.15.2	Wace, Maistre. Le roman de Brut. Rouen, 1836.
	37597.15	Wace, Maistre. Roman de Brutus. Rouen, 1836-38. 4v.
	41568.32	Waldor, Mélancé. Pages de la vie intime. Bruxelles, 1836. 2v.

1837

	FL 1029.4A	Anglo-Norman poem on the conquest of Ireland by Henry the II. London, 1837.
	40596.40	Balzac, Honoré de. Le centenaire, ou Les deux Béringheld. Bruxelles, 1837. 2v.
	40596.3	Balzac, Honoré de. Oeuvres. Bruxelles, 1837. 4v.
	41566.13	Bonnellier, Hippolyte. Un malheur domestique. Bruxelles, 1837. 2v.
	41566.12	Bonnellier, Hippolyte. Matinées. Paris, 1837.
	FL 390.5	Brazier, Nicolas. Chroniques des petits théâtres de Paris. v.1-2. Paris, 1837.
	41593.16.19	Clément, René. Albert-love, ou L'enfer. 2. éd. Paris, 1837.
	37541.23	Colomb de Batines, Paul. Mélanges...relatifs à l'histoire littéraire. Paris, 1837.
	41566.28	Creuzé de Lesser, A. 1800 ans. Paris, 1837. 3v.
	41593.28	Delonne, Joseph. Vie, poésies et pensées. Bruxelles, 1837.
	41567.5	Delrieu, Andre. Virginité. Bruxelles, 1837. 2v.
	41583.45	Désnoyer, C. L'ombre de Nicolet. Paris, 1837.
	37595.37A	Dinaux, Arthur. Les trouvères cambrésiens. v.1-4. Photoreproduction. Paris, 1837-1763. 3v.
	37595.40	Dinaux, Arthur. Les trouvères Cambrésiens. 3. éd. Paris, 1837.
	41538.31	Dumas, Alexandre. Pascal Bruno. London, 1837.
	38557.26.10	Dussault, Jean Joseph. Oraisons funèbres de Bossuet, Fléchier, et autres orateurs. Paris, 1837. 3v.
	38553.32F	Fénelon, F. de S. de la Mothe. Télémaque Polyglotte. Paris, 1837.
	38553.15.7	Fénelon, F. de S. de la Mothe. La vraie et solide vertu sacerdotale; recueillie. Paris, 1837.
	40515.17	Florian, Jean P.C. de. Oeuvres posthumes. Paris, 1837. 5v.
	41567.16	Fouinet, E. Roch le corsaire. Bruxelles, 1837. 2v.
	41542.45	Gozlan, Léon. Les Méandres. Bruxelles, 1837. 2v.
	41573.21	Hugo, Victor. Notre Dame de Paris. v.1-4. Paris, 1837. 2v.
	38513.11A	Jubinal, Achille. Mystères inédits. Paris, 1837. 2v.
	41554.9	Lacroix, Jules. La justice des hommes. Bruxelles, 1837.
	37532.8	Laharpe, Jean F. de. Lycée, ou Cours de littérature. Paris, 1837. 2v.
	41578.29.5	Lamartine, Alphonse. Jocelyn. Paris, 1837.
Htn	38513.30*	Leroux de Lincy. Recueil de farces. Paris, 1837. 4v.
	FL 371.5	Leroy, Onésime. Études sur les mystères. Paris, 1837.
	40512.37	LeSage, Alain René. The bachelor of Salamanca. Paris, 1837. 4v.
	40512.50	LeSage, Alain René. Historia d'Estevenho Goncalves. Paris, 1837.
	40513.9	Llorente, J.A. Observaciones criticas sobre el romance de Gil Blas de Santillana. Barcelona, 1837.

1837 - cont.

	37581.40.14	Magasin théâtral, 1837. Miscellaneous plays. Paris, 1837.
	41567.44.15	Masson, Michel. Ne touchez pas à la reine. Bruxelles, 1837.
	Mol 62.19	Molière, Jean Baptiste Poquelin. Dramatische Meisterwerke...Alvensleben. Leipzig, 1837?
	Mon 18.37	Montaigne, Michel de. Oeuvres. Buchon. Paris, 1837.
Htn	Mon 105.5*	Payen, J.F. Notice bibliographique sur Montaigne. Paris, 1837.
	41596.50.9	Pommier, A. Les assassins. Paris, 1837.
	41596.50.10	Pommier, A. La république ou le livre de sang. Paris, 1837.
Htn	37577.4*	Les quinze joies de mariage. Paris, 1837.
	38582.12.5	Racine, Jean. Oeuvres. v.1-4. Paris, 1837. 2v.
	41588.15.8.15	Scribe, Eugène. La somnambule. N.Y., 1837.
	41568.16	Sénancour, Étienne Pivert de. Obermann. Bruxelles, 1837. 2v.
	38514.14.15	Surville, Joseph Étienne. Clotilde von Vallon-Chalys. Berlin, 1837.
	41563.29.30	Toepffer, Rodolphe. L'histoire véritable de Mr. Crépin. n.p., 1837.
	Mol 803.5	Tuffet, S. Baron le comédien. Paris, 1837.

1838

	Mol 860.30	Un amour de Molière. Paris, 1838.
	41522.21	Badon, Edmond. Montbrun, ou Les Huguenots en Dauphiné. Paris, 1838. 2v.
	40597.12	Balzac, Honoré de. Histoire de...César Birotteau. Paris, 1838.
	40588.7.103	Belloc, Louise Swauton. Pierre et Pierrette. 3. éd. Paris, 1838.
	Mol 863.8	Beuchot, A.J.I. Hommage à MM. les membres de la chambre des députés. Paris, 1838.
Htn	Mol 880.2*	Bordelon, L. La Lotterie de Scapin. Paris, 1838.
	FL 390.5.5	Brazier, Nicolas. Histoire des petits théâtres de Paris. Paris, 1838. 2v.
	42554.17.25	Caillaux, Charles. La plaine et la mer. Chartres, 1838.
	40597.2.62	Cantù, C. Di Onorato Balzac e delle sue opere. Milano, 1838.
	41593.15	Chalette. La joinvilleide, poème héroïque. Châlons, 1838.
	40586.21.18	Chateaubriand, F.A.R. Congres de Vérone. Paris, 1838. 2v.
	40586.21.25	Chateaubriand, F.A.R. The Congress of Verona. London, 1838. 2v.
	42524.26.10	Circourt, Adolphe. Le mystère des Alpes. Dijon, 1838.
	40588.2.9	Cottin, Marie R. (Mme.). Elisabeth, ou Les exilés de Sibérie. Paris, 1838.
	40588.01.3	Cottin, Marie R. (Mme.). Oeuvres complètes. v.1-3. Paris, 1838.
	41593.30	Direy, Louis. Les orphelines. Paris, 1838.
	41523.2.10	Dumas, Alexandre. Oeuvres. Bruxelles, 1838-43. 6v.
	41584.40	Eustache, A.J.R. Les filles savantes. Paris, 1838.
	41593.225.5	Flamen, P. Paris, ou Nouvelle mission de Belphégor. Paris, 1838.
	40515.16	Florian, Jean P.C. de. Oeuvres. Paris, 1838. 7v.
	42576.8.13	Gleizes, J.A. Salena, ou La famille Samanéenne. Paris, 1838.
	Mol 740.1	Gurgy, B. de. La chambre de Molière. Paris, 1838.
	37594.18	Henri d'Andeli. La bataille et le mariage des XII arts. Paris, 1838.
	FL 372.3	Jalibois, E. La diablerie de Chaumont. Chaumont, 1838.
	41551.10	Lacroix, Paul. Romans relatifs à l'histoire de France. Paris, 1838.
	39527.20.10	La Fontaine, Jean de. Fables, avec des notes par Francis Sales. Boston, 1838.
	39527.20	La Fontaine, Jean de. Fables. Paris, 1838. 2v.
	41578.4	Lamartine, Alphonse de. Harmonies. Tome 2. Paris, 1838.
	V39527.80	Lent, P. Van. Recueil de fables de La Fontaine. Rotterdam, 1838.
	40511.35	LeSage, Alain René. Histoire de Gil Blas. Paris, 1838.
	40512.25.30	LeSage, Alain René. Historia de Gil Blas de Santillana. Paris, 1838.
	40556.27	Maistre, Joseph de. Oeuvres. Bruxelles, 1838. 7v.
	37542.9	Martin, Charles. Les classiques et les romantiques. Paris, 1838. 2v.
	38527.65	Mermet, Thomas. La vie de l'homme...et la destruction de Jérusalem. Vienne, 1838.
	Mol 161.25	Molière, Jean Baptiste Poquelin. Amphitryon...Gombert. London, 1838.
	Mol 48.38	Molière, Jean Baptiste Poquelin. Dictionnaire de morale et de littérature. Paris, 1838.
	Mol 18.38.5	Molière, Jean Baptiste Poquelin. Oeuvres. Paris, 1838.
	Mol 18.38	Molière, Jean Baptiste Poquelin. Oeuvres. Paris, 1838. 2v.
	Mol 8.38	Molière, Jean Baptiste Poquelin. Oeuvres. v.1-2,3-4,5-6,7-8. Paris, 1838. 4v.
	Mol 62.20	Molière, Jean Baptiste Poquelin. Sämmtliche Werke...Lax. Aachen, 1838.
	39591.7	Montesquieu, C.L. de S. Oeuvres. Paris, 1838.
	38541.12	Moralistes français. Paris, 1838.
Htn	38511.7*	Moralité de Mundus, Caro, Demonia. Paris, 1838.
	41588.28	Quinet, Edgar. Prométhée. Paris, 1838.
Htn	39594.26*	St. Pierre, J.H.B. de. Paul et Virginie. Paris, 1838.
	40575.25	Sainte-Beuve, Charles A. Pensées d'Août. Bruxelles, 1838.
	41581.3	Saintine, X.B. Oeuvres complètes de M. Ancelot. Paris, 1838.
	41557.8.83.2	Sand, George. Indiana. Paris, 1838. 2v.
	41557.9.43	Sand, George. Lettres d'un voyageur. Bruxelles, 1838.
	41557.8.123.2	Sand, George. Simon. Paris, 1838.
	41588.13.5	Scribe, Eugène. Teatro italiano. Montepulciano, 1838. 4 pam.
	41588.14.20	Scribe, Eugène. Tonadillas. Paris, 1838. 2v.
	38512.17.35	Senonnes. Jean Froissart, ne vers l'an 1337; mort vers 1410. Paris? 1838?
	37542.13	Shelley, M.W. Godwin (Mrs.). Lives of the most eminent literary and scientific men of France. London, 1838-39. 2v.
	38514.58	Thomassy, Raimond. Essai sur...Christine de Pisan. Paris, 1838.
	38514.58.1.5	Vanblanc, V.V.H. de. Christine de Pisan, née en 1363. n.p., 1838?

Chronological Listing

1839

Mol 860.31 Alphonse, F. Molière et son Tartuffe. Paris, 1839.
37561.3 Ampère, J.J. Histoire littéraire de la France. Paris, 1839. 3v.
40597.32.15 Balzac, Honoré de. Scenes de la vie de province. 2 series. Paris, 1839. 2v.
41592.23 Béranger, P.J. de . Hundert-drei Lieder. Braunschweig, 1839.
41522.30.2 Bernard, Charles de. Les ailes d'icare. Bruxelles, 1839.
41522.45 Bernard, Charles de. Le paravent. Bruxelles, 1839. 2v.
41593.19 Delasalle, Paul. Fleurs de Pommier. Paris, 1839.
40588.8.5 Des Essars, Eugène. Catherine de Lescun. v.1-2. Paris, 1839.
42542.66.58 Dugué, Ferdinand. Le vol des heures; poésies. Paris, 1839.
41538.38.10 Dumas, Alexandre. Acté. Bruxelles, 1839. 2v.
41538.14 Dumas, Alexandre. Caligula; drama. Madrid, 1839.
41538.45.5 Dumas, Alexandre. Paul Jones. Philadelphia, 1839.
41538.210 Dumas, Alexandre. Quinze jours au Sinai. v.1-2. Bruxelles, 1839.
40515.29.4 Florian, Jean P.C. de. Fables. Paris, 1839.
41593.32.17 Garnier, J.H. Mélancolies et miscellanées. Paris, 1839.
41593.49.5 Guttinguer, Ulric. Jumiéges, prose et vers et poésies diverses. Rouen, 1839.
39594.15 Heemskerk, J. Speciminis inauguralis de Montesquiro pars prior. Amsterdam, 1839.
40567.10 Janin, Jules. Les catacombes. II. Paris, 1839.
37596.8A Jubinal, A. Oeuvres de Rutebeuf. Paris, 1839. 2v.
41567.32 Junot, Laure. La duchesse de Valombrai. Bruxelles, 1839. 2v.
42544.3.5 Lafont, C. Un cas de conscience. Paris, 1839.
Htn 39526.34* La Fontaine, Jean de. Contes et nouvelles. Paris, 1839.
37595.3 Lettres d'Abailard et d'Héloise. Paris, 1839. 2v.
41595.23.3 Maury, François. Le concile de Paris. Clermont-Ferrand, 1839.
41593.28.5 Moll, J.J. de. La liberté en Belgique. Bruxelles, 1839.
37581.2.57 Monmerqué, Louis J.N. Théâtre français au moyen age. Paris, 1839.
37581.2.55 Monmerqué, Louis J.N. Théâtre français au moyen âge. Paris, 1839.
40555.12 Muravef, graf. 4 numeros du livre sans titre. Paris, 1839.
42587.37.020 Musset, Paul de. Le dernier duc de Guise. Bruxelles, 1839.
39545.33.5 Nagel, C. Voltaire et la revolution française, 1789-1830. Paris, 1839.
FL 398.68 Paccard, J.E. Mémoires et confessions. Comédien. Paris, 1839.
42556.10 Reboul, Jean. Le dernier jour. Poème en dix chants. Paris, 1839.
39594.28.5 St. Pierre, J.H.B. de. Paul et Virginie. London, 1839.
41568.11 Saintine, Joseph Xavier Boniface. Picciola. 2d ed. Philadelphia, 1839.
Htn 41557.9.54* Sand, George. Spiridion. Paris, 1839.
41568.14.53 Say, Jean Baptiste. Petit volume contenant quelques aperçus des hommes et de la société. 3. éd. Paris, 1839.
41558.21 Soulié, Frédéric. El proscripto; drama. Madrid, 1839.

184-

40588.7.150 Cronbach, Louise. Jeune fille du peuple. 2. éd. Paris, 184-.
41541.13.12 Girardin, Delphine Gay. The clockmaker's hat. N.Y., 184-.
Htn 41598.6F* Huart, Louis. Les physiologies parisiennes. Paris, 184-?
37575.400 Nouvelles nouvelles, souvenirs de littérature contemporain. Paris, 184-.

1840

41566.7 Arnould, Auguste. La mère-folle. Bruxelles, 1840.
40597.21 Balzac, Honoré de. Revue Parisienne. Paris, 1840.
42554.12.35 Barbier, Auguste. Satires et poèmes. Bruxelles, 1840.
41591.3.2 Béranger, P.J. de. Oeuvres ccomplètes. Paris, 1840.
41522.34 Bernard, Charles de. La chasse aux amants. Bruxelles, 1840.
41522.54 Bernard, Charles de. La peau du lion. Bruxelles, 1840.
40517.16 Berquin, Arnaud. Childrens' fireside book. Philadelphia, 1840.
40551.18 Bonald, L.G.A. de. Démonstration philosophique. Oevres XII. Paris, 1840.
41583.15.9 Bouchardy, Joseph. Cristobal el Señador. Madrid, 1840.
38551.19.5 Caron, Augustin P.P. Recherches bibliographiques sur le Télémaque, les oraisons de Bossuet et le Discours sur l'histoire universelle. 2. éd. Paris, 1840.
41522.72.10 Chevalier, Pierre M.F. Jeanne de Montfort; epoque guerrière: 1342; régne de Philippe de Valois. v.1-2. Paris, 1840.
FL 398.74 Coquatrix, E. Rachel à Rouen. Rouen, 1840.
41593.17.5 Coquerel, Athan. Le calendrier. 2. éd. Paris, 1840.
40588.3 Cottin, Marie R. (Mme.). Elizabeth. Boston, 1840.
41565.8 D'Arlincourt, Victor. Les trois châteaux. Paris, 1840.
41583.30 Delavigne, Casimir. Messéniennes et chants populairs. Paris, 1840.
37584.23 Dumas, Adolphe. El campamento de los cruzados. Habana, 1840.
42543.28.19 Empic, A.S. Théâtre. Paris, 1840. 2v.
41540.4 Fazy, James. Jean d'Yvoire au bras de fer. Paris, 1840.
37567.4 Feletz, Charles Marie de. Jugements historiques et littéraires sur quelques écrivains et...écrits du temps. Paris, 1840.
37596.65 Fitz Warine, Fulk. Histoire de fulques Fitz-Warin. Paris, 1840.
Mol 775.2 Fontaine, P.J. Découverte d'un autographe de Molière. Paris, 1840.
37581.41.2 La France dramatique au XIXe siècle, 1840-1881. Paris, 1840-81.
40526.17.5 Gresset, Jean B. Vert-vert. London, 1840.
41573.19 Hugo, Victor. Notre Dame de Paris. Bruxelles, 1840.
41553.32 Kock, Charles Paul de. La jolie fille du faubourg. Bruxelles, 1840.
40516.61 Kruedener, B.J. Valérie. Paris, 1840.
41578.5 Lamartine, Alphonse de. Harmonies. Paris, 1840. 2v.
41554.58 Laponneraye, A. Stéphanowa; histoire russe. Paris, 1840.
41586.3.12 Laurençot, Charles H.L. Toma y daga, ó Que se queje aquel que pierda, comedia. Madrid, 1840.

1840 - cont.

40512.31 LeSage, Alain René. Histoire de Gil Blas de Santillana. Barcelona, 1840.
40512.30 LeSage, Alain René. Histoire de Gil Blas de Santillana. Barcelona, 1840-41. 2v.
40511.6 LeSage, Alain René. Oeuvres. Paris, 1840.
41567.37 Lorvergne A. de. Le comte de Mansfeldt. Bruxelles, 1840.
41595.22.9 Magu. Poésies. Paris, 1840.
41586.19.20 Martin, Pierre Henri. Les roueries du Marquis de Lansac. Paris, 1840? 2 pam.
Mol 18.40 Molière, Jean Baptiste Poquelin. Oeuvres. v. 1-8. Paris, 1840. 4v.
37596.3.15 Philippe de Remi. Roman de la Marekine. Paris, 1840.
42556.7 Reboul, Jean. Poésies. Paris, 1840.
41568.6 Reybaud, Charles (Mrs.). La pauvre paysanne. Bruxelles, 1840.
41587.20.170 Rousseau, Pierre Joseph. Robert-Macaire, der unsterbliche Betrüger. Berlin, 1840.
41565.30 St. Mars, G.A.C. de C. Madame de la Sablière. Paris, 1840.
40575.10 Sainte-Beuve, Charles A. Poésies complètes. Paris, 1840.
41588.14.7F Scribe, Eugène. Le verre d'eau. Paris, 1840?
37542.13.5 Shelley, M.W. Godwin (Mrs.). Lives of the most eminent French writers. Philadelphia, 1840. 2v.
41558.18 Soulié, Frédéric. La chambière. Paris, 1840.
41563.6 Sue, Eugène. Jean Cavalier, ou Les fanatiques des Cévennes. Bruxelles, 1840.
37536.6 Villemain, A.F. Cours de littérature française. Bruxelles, 1840. 7v.
37573.2 Vinet, Alexander R. Choix de lectures prises dans les auteurs classiques de la littérature française...chrestomathie française. Lausanne, 1840-43. 2v.

1841

37595.10 Abailard, Pierre. Abaelardi et Héloisae Epistolae. Turici, 1841.
41566.6 Arnould, Auguste. Adèle Launay. Bruxelles, 1841.
40584.35 Aufzeichnungen eines nachgeborenen Prinzen. Stuttgart, 1841.
38528.16.5 Béroalde de Verville. Le moyen de parvenir. Paris, 1841.
41583.12.50 Bertrand, Leon. Oliver Cromwell. Paris, 1841.
40551.24.5 Bonald, Henri. Notice sur le vicomte de Bonald. Paris, 1841.
38557.25.30 Bossuet, J.B. Oeuvres. Paris, 1841. 4v.
41583.15.10 Bouchardy, Joseph. El hijo de la tempestad. Madrid, 1841.
37566.17 Chaudes-Aigues, J. Les écrivains modernes. Paris, 1841.
41522.72 Chevalier, Pierre M.F. Michel Columb, le tailleur d'images; epoque des arts et de la décadence: 1490, règnes de Charles VIII et de Louis XII. v.1-2. Paris, 1841.
37581.39.2 Choix de pièces de théâtres de Paris, 1841-1885. Paris, 1841-1885.
40588.3.5 Cottin, Marie R. (Mme.). Élisabeth, ou Les exilés de Sibérie. Paris, 1841?
41598.9.6 Delord, Taxile. Physiologie de la parisienne. Paris, 1841. 4 pam.
42543.28.29 Dennery, A.F. Le grace de Dieu. Paris, 1841.
41593.28.9 Dénoix des Vergnes, F. Guerrières et sentimentales. Poésies. Paris, 1841.
39566.4 Diderot, Denis. Mémoires. Paris, 1841. 2v.
38526.48.19 Du Bartas, Guillaume de Salluste. Judith. Lipsk, 1841.
38553.25.5 Fénelon, F. de S. de la Mothe. Les aventures de Télémaque. Paris, 1841.
38553.15.4 Fénelon, F. de S. de la Mothe. Selections from the writings. 4. ed. Boston, 1841.
41567.19 Geoffroy, J. Louis. Napoléon apocryphe, 1812-1852. Paris, 1841.
41598.9.4 Huart, Louis. Physiologie de l'étudiant. Paris, 1841. 4 pam.
41598.9.3 Huart, Louis. Physiologie du tailleur. Paris, 1841. 4 pam.
40567.12 Janin, Jules. The cross roads. London, 1841.
38511.21 Joret, Jean. La jardrin salutaire. Paris, 1841.
41569.14 Keepsake breton, par A.V.B.O. Paris, 1841.
39527.18.5 La Fontaine, Jean de. Fables, avec des notes...par Francis Sales. 2e éd. Boston, 1841.
39526.30.10 La Fontaine, Jean de. Fables. 2d ed. Boston, 1841.
41577.11.5 Lamartine, Alphonse de. Oeuvres. Bruxelles, 1841.
Htn 40512.3.25* LeSage, Alain René. Asmodeus. London, 1841.
38511.9 Li romans de Bauduin de Seboure (XIVe siècle). Valenciennes, 1841. 2v.
40556.27.3 Maistre, Joseph de. Oeuvres. Paris, 1841.
40529.29 Maréchal, Pierre S. Projet d'une loi portant defense d'apprendre à lire aux femmes. Lille, 1841.
FL 383.12.10 Molènes, Gaschon de. La critique sous l'empire. Paris, 1841.
38541.13 Moralistes français. Paris, 1841.
41596.39 Moyria, G. de. Esquisses poétiques du département de l'Ain. Bourg, 1841.
41598.9 Ourliac, Édouard. Physiologie de l'écolier. Paris, 1841? 4 pam.
40573.2 Peignot, Gabriel. Le livre des singularités. Dijon, 1841.
40573.3 Peignot, Gabriel. Predicatoriana, ou revélations singulières. Dijon, 1841.
41598.9.5 Physiologie de l'homme de loi. Paris, 1841? 4 pam.
37585.8 Pixerécourt, G. de. Théâtre choisi. Paris, 1841- 4v.
Htn 40522.9.50* Prévost, Antoine F. Manon Lescaut. London, 1841.
40573.19 Pyat, Félix. Les deux serruriers. Paris, 1841.
41568.7 Reybaud, Charles (Mrs.). Esther de Chazeuil. Habana, 1841.
38525.18.80 Ronsard, Pierre de. Oeuvres choisies. Paris, 1841.
41596.56 Rouquette, Adrien E. Les savanes. Paris, 1841.
Htn 41596.56.2* Rouquette, Adrien E. Les savanes. Paris, 1841.
FL 6021.41 Rousseau, J.J. Les confessions. Paris, 1841.
41598.7 Rousseau, T.J. Physiologie de la portière. v.1-5. Paris, 1841.
41598.9.2 Saint-Hilaire, E.M.H. Physiologie du troupier. Paris, 1841. 4 pam.
41586.30.6 Soumet, A. Un soirée du théâtre-français, 24 avril 1841. Paris, 1841.
41558.56.5 Souvestre, Émile. Le mari de Madame de Solange suivi de Les préventions. La Haye, 1841.
41588.41.5 Vanderburch, Emile. Théâtre de l'enfance. Paris, 1841. 2v.

1841 - cont.

39526.30 Wright, Elizur. Fables of La Fontaine. Boston, 1841. 2v.

1842

38546.55 Aubenas, J.A. Histoire de Mme. de Sévigné. Paris, 1842.

Htn 40597.23* Balzac, Honoré de. Histoire de l'Empereur. Paris, 1842.

37537.6 Baron, Auguste. Histoire de la littérature française. Paris, 1842.

41592.18.10 Béranger, P.J. de. Dernières chansons de 1834 à 1851. Frankfurt, 1842.

FL 394.62 Bouilly, J.N. Soixante ans du théâtre-français. Paris, 1842.

41522.72.7 Chevalier, Pierre M.F. Aliénor, prieure de Lok Maria; de la ligne: 1594, règne de Henri IV. 2. éd. v.1-2. Paris, 1842.

41593.18 De Foudras. Chants pour Tous. Poésies. Paris, 1842.

Mol 870.6 D'Epagny. A propos sur l'anniversaire de la naissance de Molière. n.p., 1842.

41593.29.3.3 Desbordes-Valmore, Marceline. Poésies. Paris, 1842.

37547.26 Dreux de Radier, Jean François. Bibliothèque...critique du Poitou. Niort, 1842-49. 3v.

38528.20.9 Du Fail, Noël. Propos rustique...contes et discours d'Eutrapel. Paris, 1842.

41538.28 Dumas, Alexandre. Impressions de voyage. Paris, 1842.

41538.190 Dumas, Alexandre. La tour de Nesle. Bruxelles, 1842.

42561.2 L'echo des feuilletons. v.1-6,25. Paris, 1842. 7v.

38553.25.6 Fénelon, F. de S. de la Mothe. Les aventures de Télémaque. Paris, 1842.

40515.32.17 Florian, Jean P.C. de. Gonzalve de Cordoue. v.1-2. Paris, 1842.

40515.45.5 Florian, Jean P.C. de. Numa Pompelius. Paris, 1842.

41541.13.15 Girardin, Delphine Gay. Poésies complètes. Paris, 1842.

41593.32.300 Guérin, Amand. Bretagne. Paris, 1842.

38514.24 Guichard, J. Marie. Poésies de Charles d'Orleans. Paris, 1842.

37561.8A Ideler, Julius Ludwig. Geschichte der altfranzösischen National-Literatur. Berlin, 1842.

40567.6.5 Janin, Jules. L'ane mort. Paris, 1842.

40556.19 Joubert, Joseph. Pensées, essais, et maximes. Paris, 1842. 2v.

41553.30 Kock, Charles Paul de. Gustave ou le mauvais sujet. Paris, 1842.

41553.33.5 Kock, Charles Paul de. Soeur Anne. Paris, 1842.

39526.29.9 La Fontaine, Jean de. Fables. Paris, 1842-43. 2v.

39526.30.20A La Fontaine, Jean de. Fables. 3d ed. Boston, 1842. 2v.

39527.20.15 La Fontaine, Jean de. Fables. 5. ed. v.1-2. Boston, 1842.

41588.29.9.5 Lockroy, Joseph P.S. Un duel sous le Cardinal de Richelieu. Paris, 1842.

40516.28.6 Louvet de Couvral, J.B. Les aventures du chevalier de Faublas. Paris, 1842. 2v.

37547.50 Mandet, F. Histoire poétique et littéraire de l'ancien Velaz. Paris, 1842.

37566.16 Michiels, Alfred. Histoire des idées littéraires. Paris, 1842. 2v.

Mol 18.42 Molière, Jean Baptiste Poquelin. Oeuvres. Paris, 1842. 8v.

37581.3A Monmerqué, Louis J.N. Théâtre français au moyen age. Paris, 1842.

Mon 31.25 Montaigne, Michel de. Works. Hazlitt. London, 1842.

40536.19 Perrin, J.B. Pièces dramatiques. Lons-le-Saunier, 1842.

FL 398.74.5 Rachel et la comédie-française. Bruxelles, 1842.

42556.8 Reboul, Jean. Poésies. Paris, 1842.

41557.9.21 Sand, George. Consuelo. Bruxelles, 1842. 2v.

41557.9.44 Sand, George. Les maîtres mosaistes. Bruxelles, 1842. 2v.

41557.9.41 Sand, George. Oeuvres de George Sand. Paris, 1842.

41588.13.9 Scribe, Eugène. La calumnia. Milano, 1842.

41558.20 Soulié, Frédéric. Marguerite. Bruxelles, 1842. 2v.

41558.42.25 Souvestre, Émile. Claude Rionel; suivi de Une femme célèbre. Bruxelles, 1842.

41558.57 Souvestre, Émile. La goutte d'eau. Bruxelles, 1842. 2v.

37566.4 Véricour, L. Raymond. Modern French literature. Edinburgh, 1842.

39545.34.6 Voltaire, François Marie Arouet de. Contes, satires, epitrus. Paris, 1842.

37597.24 Wace, Maistre. L'etablissement de la fête de la conception. Caen, 1842.

38546.28 Walckenaer, Charles Athanase. Mémoire sur Mme. de Sévigné. Paris, 1842. 4v.

1843

37555.645.2 Ackermann, Paul. Traité de l'accent...Versification. 2. éd. Paris, 1843.

41592.01.9 Agnant, A. Gusman ou l'expiation. Paris, 1843.

42563.23.7.50 Berthet, E.B. La bella tendera. Matanzas, 1843.

40551.19 Bonald, L.G.A. de. Théorie du pouvoir. Oevres XIII-XV. Paris, 1843. 3v.

41522.69.500 Careñou, A. Le sire de Montpegat. Montauban, 1843.

37555.3 Catalogue de...Viollet le duc. Paris, 1843.

38514.24.5A Charles d'Orleans. Les poésies. Paris, 1843.

40585.10 Chateaubriand, F.A.R. Oeuvres complètes. Paris, 1843. 5v.

41593.15.9 Chatelain, J. La première parole du coeur. Epinal, 1843.

Mol 863.12 Colet, Louise. Le monument de Molière. Paris, 1843.

Mol 765.1 Colet, Louise. Le monument de Molière. Paris, 1843.

Htn 40565.75* Collombet, F.Z. Notice sur Guy-Marie Deplace. Lyon, 1843.

40554.11 Cousin, Victor. Fragments littéraires. Paris, 1843.

37596.101 Craon, Pierre de. Chansons. Caen, 1843.

41565.9 D'Arlincourt, Victor. L'étoile polaire. Paris, 1843. 2v.

Mol 870.7 Desportes, A. Molière à Chambord. Paris, 1843.

Mol 863.13 Drouin. L'éloge de Molière. Paris, 1843.

41584.29.19 Duval, A. Shakespeare enamorado; comedia. 2a ed. Madrid, 1843.

40524.16.25 Fiévée, Joseph. Oeuvres. Paris, 1843.

Htn 40515.30* Florian, Jean P.C. de. Fables. Paris, 1843.

40515.40.10 Florian, Jean P.C. de. William Tell. Concord, 1843.

40556.14 Frayssinous, Denis L. Conférences et discours inédits. 2. éd. Paris, 1843.

37564.4.50 Fremy, A. Essai sur les variations du style français au dix-septième siècle. Paris, 1843.

1843 - cont.

40588.18.4 Genlis, S.F.D. de St. Le siège de la Rochelle. Paris, 1843.

41593.32.55 Germigny, Paul. Une lyre a l'atelier. 2. éd. Orléans, 1843.

41541.14 Girardin, Delphine Gay. Judith. Paris, 1843.

42543.68.5 Halévy, Leon. Un mari, s'il vous plait. Paris, 1843.

37546.20 Hauréau, B. Histoire littéraire du Maine. Paris, 1843-52. 4v.

41572.29.3 Hugo, Victor. Le roi s'amuse. London, 1843.

40561.20 Janin, Jules. Un hiver à Paris. Paris, 1843.

41548.25 Kératry, A.H. de. La baronne de Kerléya. v.1-2. Bruxelles, 1843.

41552.26 Kock, Charles Paul de. Un homme à marier. Paris, 1843.

38564.25 La Bruyère, J. de. Caractères. Paris, 1843.

Htn FL 355.35* Lacroix, Paul. Bibiothèque dramatique de M. de Soleinne. v.1-6. Paris, 1843-45. 3v.

42555.32.30 Laprade, Victor de. Odes et poèmes. Paris, 1843.

38514.52 La Sale, Antoine de. L'histoire...du Jehan de Saintré. Paris, 1843.

41595.18 Léon, Louis de. La tragédie du monde. Paris, 1843.

FL 370.8 Leroy, Onésime. Epoques de l'histoire de France en rapport avec le théâtre. Paris, 1843.

FL 358.61 Lucas, Hippolyte. Histoire philosophique et littéraire du théâtre français. Paris, 1843.

40571.9 Magnin, Charles. Causeries et meditations. Paris, 1843. 2v.

38523.27 Malherbe, François de. Oeuvres; oeuvres de J.B. Rousseau. Paris, 1843.

41595.31.85 Mercoeur, Elisa. Oeuvres complètes d'Elisa Mercoeur de Nantes. Paris, 1843. 3v.

Mol 18.43 Molière, Jean Baptiste Poquelin. Oeuvres complètes. Paris, 1843.

Mon 18.43 Montaigne, Michel de. Essais. Paris, 1843.

39594.6.8 Montesquieu, C.L. de S. Grandeur et décadence des Romains. Paris, 1843.

Htn 41596.33* Musset, Alfred de. Voyage ou Il vous plaira. Paris, 1843.

40572.45 Ozenne, Louise. Mélanges critiques et littéraires. Paris, 1843.

42545.83.8 Ponsard, F. Lucrèce. 4e éd. Paris, 1843.

FL 1048.251.100 Saint Long (pseud.). Les amours de Colas. Paris, 1843.

39595.14.3 St. Pierre, J.H.B. de. Oeuvres choisies. Paris, 1843.

37563.23 Sainte-Beuve, C.A. Tableau...historique et critique de la poésie française. Paris, 1843.

37563.23.5 Sainte-Beuve, C.A. Tableau historique et critique. Paris, 1843.

41568.11.2.1 Saintine, Joseph Xavier Boniface. Picciola, the prisoner of Fenestrella. 3. ed. Philadelphia, 1843.

41568.11.2 Saintine, Joseph Xavier Boniface. Picciola. Paris, 1843.

41557.8.69.3 Sand, George. La Derniere Aldini. Paris, 1843.

41557.13.5 Sandeau, Jules. El doctor Herbeau. v.1-2. Habana, 1843.

41562.23 Sue, Eugène. Les mystères de Paris. Paris, 1843-44. 2v.

41563.15 Sue, Eugène. The mysteries of Paris. v.1-2. N.Y., 1843.

41563.28.1.25 Toepffer, Rodolphe. Caricatures. Genève, 1843- 8v.

39545.24.11 Voltaire, François Marie Arouet de. Théâtre. Paris, 1843.

1844

37578.50 Almanach comique. Paris, 1844.

38565.18 Amar, M. Oeuvres de Boileau. Paris, 1844.

40597.16 Balzac, Honoré de. David Séchard. Brussels, 1844.

37558.47 Barbat de Bignicourt, Arthur. Les petits mystères de l'Academie Française. Paris, 1844.

41583.12 Bayard, Jean F.A. El articulo V. Habana, 1844.

40545.5 Bazin, M.A. Etudes d'histoire et de biographie. Paris, 1844.

40532.10A Beaumarchais, Pierre A.C. de. Théâtre. Paris, 1844.

38557.56.75 Bossuet, J.B. Oeuvres philosophiques de Bossuet. Paris, 1844.

41593.13.4 Boulay-Paty, Évariste. Odes. Brest, 1844.

Mon 112.7.5 Brunet, G. Les essais de Michel de Montaigne. Paris, 1844.

Htn Mon 112.7* Brunet, G. Les essais de Michel de Montaigne. Paris, 1844.

40526.17.80 Cayrol, Louis Nicolas Jean Joachim de. Essai historique sur la vie et les ouvrages de Gresset. v.1-2. Amiens, 1844.

42563.39.700 Cénac-Moncaut, J.E. Aquitaine et Languedoc. Paris, 1844. 2v.

Mol 870.7.4 Clairville. Le monument de Molière. Troyes? 1844?

41593.17.2 Colet, Louise. Poésies complètes. Paris, 1844.

42565.57.53 Constant, A. La mère de Dieu. Paris, 1844.

38571.8.5 Corneille, Pierre. Oeuvres de Pierre et Thomas Corneille. Paris, 1844.

41566.2.9 D'Arlincourt, Charles V.P. The brewer king. N.Y., 1844.

40516.4.10 Ducray-Duminil, F.G. Carlos y Fanny, o aventuras de dos niños abandonados em una isla desierta. México, 1844. 2v.

41593.32.3 Dupont, Pierre. Les deux anges. Provins, 1844.

41584.32.45 Duveyrier, A.H.J. Michel Perrin. Paris, 1844.

41567.14 Fouinet, E. Les douze nations. Paris, 1844.

41569.4 Les fous douteux et les fous sublimes. Paris, 1844.

40588.17 Genlis, S.F.D. de St. Mademoiselle de Clermont. Paris, 1844.

40517.34 Gueulette, T.S. Tausend und eine Viertelstunde. Erlangen, 1844. 2v.

41567.23.15 Guizot, Elizabeth C.P. de M. The young student. N.Y., 1844.

41598.9.3.25 Huart, Louis. The student at Paris. N.Y., 1844.

41571.22 Hugo, Victor. Notre Dame de Paris. Paris, 1844.

FL 6135.3 Janin, A. Deux mots au sujet de la fête de Rousseau. n.p., 1844.

37567.12 Julien, Bernard. Histoire de la poésie française à l'époque impériale. Paris, 1844. 2v.

41545.13 Karr, Alphonse. Histoire invraisemblable. v.2. Bruxelles, 1844.

37595.12 Keller, Von Adelbert. Romvart. Mannheim, 1844.

Mol 880.25 La Boullaye, F. de. Molière au 19e siècle. Paris, 1844.

FL 398.28.9 Lafitte, J.B.P. Mémoires de Fleury de la comédie française. Paris, 1844. 2v.

FL 395.160 Langier, Eugène. De la comédie française depuis 1830. Paris, 1844.

41595.4 Lapointe, S. Une voix d'en bas. Poésies. Paris, 1844.

41586.3.6 Latouche, Henri de. Clement XIV et Carlo Bertinazzi, correspondance inédite. Paris, 1844.

41595.12 Le Fevre-Deumier, J. Poésies. Paris, 1844.

Chronological Listing

1844 - cont.

FL 370.9 Leroy, Onésime. Histoire comparée théâtre et des Moeurs en France. Paris, 1844.
40512.29 LeSage, Alain René. Histoire de Gil Blas de Santillana. Paris, 1844.
37572.35.4 Mélanges sur Victor Hugo, De Musset et Charles Nodier. Paris, 1844-1908.
Mol 863.17 Minier, H. Les bas-bleus; à Molière. Bordeaux, 1844.
Mol 18.44 Molière, Jean Baptiste Poquelin. Oeuvres. Paris, 1844.
42545.39.20 Monselet, Charles. Un carreau brisé. Bordeaux, 1844.
Mon 18.44 Montaigne, Michel de. Essais. Le Clerc. Paris, 1844. 3v.
39594.2.2 Montesquieu, C.L. de S. Esprit des lois par Montesquieu. Paris, 1844.
40572.2 Montlaur, Eugène de. Essais littéraires. Paris, 1844.
38557.14.75 Monty, Léopold. De politica Bossuetii doctrina. Thesis. Paris, 1844.
37536.12 Nisard, Désiré. Histoire de la littérature française. Paris, 1844-61. 4v.
41556.25 Nodier, Charles. Trésor des Feves et Fleur des Pois. Paris, 1844. 3 pam.
Mol 765.2 Notice sur le monument de Molière. Paris, 1844.
41586.28.100 Pixerécourt, R.C.F. de. Polder, o El verdugo de Amsterdam. Madrid, 1844.
41596.50.11 Pommier, A. Colères. Paris, 1844.
40537.17 Pyat, Félix. Marie Joseph Chénier et le prince des critiques. Paris, 1844.
38582.18 Racine, Jean. Théâtre complète. Paris, 1844.
41557.5.3 Reybaud, Louis. Jérôme Paturot. 4e éd. Paris, 1844.
Mol 875.1 Rheal, S. La tribune independante. Paris, 1844.
42558.42 Ronchaud, Louis de. Les heures. Paris, 1844.
FL 6041.44 Rousseau, J.J. Émile ou De l'éducation. Paris, 1844.
Mol 765.5 Saint Martin. La Fontaine Molière. Paris, 1844.
41581.25 Scribe, Augustin E. Théâtre. N.Y., 1844-1858.
41588.13.10 Scribe, Eugène. La calumnia; comedia. Madrid, 1844.
41588.13.25 Scribe, Eugène. El diplomático, comedia. Madrid, 1844.
41558.2 Soulié, Frédéric. Au jour le jour. v.1-2. Bruxelles, 1844.
41558.3 Soulié, Frédéric. Beltram el napolitano; drama. Madrid, 1844.
41586.30.7 Soumet, A. Jane Grey, tragédie en 5 actes et en vers. Paris, 1844.
40555.20 Stapfer, M.P.A. Mélanges. Paris, 1844. 2v.
41563.17.5 Sue, Eugène. Das Mährlein von Fletsch und Winzelchen. Frankfurt, 1844.
Htn 41563.11.5* Sue, Eugène. The salamander. N.Y., 1844.
41561.15.10 Sue, Eugène. Wandering Jew. London, 1844-45. 2v.
41561.15.2 Sue, Eugène. Wandering Jew. N.Y., 1844-45.
Mol 720.3 Taschereau, M.J. Histoire de la vie et des ouvrages de Molière. Paris, 1844.
41596.71 Violeau, Hippolyte. Loisirs; poétiques. 2. éd. Paris, 1844.

1845

Mol 765.3 Aimé-Martin, L. Histoire du monument à Molière. Paris, 1845.
41522.2.70.5 Barbey d'Aurevilly, J.A. Du dandysme et de G. Brummell. Caen, 1845.
41593.6.5 Barthélemy, Auguste Marseille. Némésis. Satire hebdomadaire. 7. éd. Paris, 1845.
41593.6.9 Barthélemy, Auguste Marseille. Nouvelle Némésis. Paris, 1845.
41591.3.3 Béranger, P.J. de. Oeuvres complètes. Paris, 1845. 2v.
38566.17 Boileau Despréaux, Nicolas. Oeuvres poétiques. Paris, 1845.
Htn 38512.56* Bonet, Honoré. L'apparition de Jehan de Meun. Paris, 1845.
38557.41.31 Bossuet, J.B. History of the variations of the protestant churches. Paris, 1845. 2v.
38557.33.5 Bossuet, J.B. Sermons choisis. Paris, 1845.
39544.42.5 Brougham, H.B. Voltaire et Rousseau. London, 1845.
X Cg 38585.2.3 Bury, Blaize (Mme.). Racine and the French classical drama. London, 1845.
37572.22 Chapsal, C.P. Leçons de littérature française. N.Y., 1845.
40516.40 Charrière, P.A.C. de. Caliste. Paris, 1845.
38512.24A Chavannes, Félix. Le mireour du monde. Lausanne, 1845.
X Cg 37584.10 Chefs-d'oeuvre des auteurs comiques. 3. Paris, 1845.
37584.11 Chefs-d'oeuvre des auteurs comiques. 4. Paris, 1845.
40553.4 Constant de Rebecque, Benjamin. Adolphe. Paris, 1845.
40546.6 Courier de Méré, Paul Louis. Oeuvres. Paris, 1845.
41538.34 Dumas, Alexandre. Sketches of Naples. Philadelphia, 1845.
FL 398.29.5 Dumerson, T.M. Mémoires de Mlle. Flore. Paris, 1845. 3v.
41593.32.8.15 Dupont, Pierre. Le siècle. Paris, 1845?
Mon 88.2 Feugère, L. Etienne de la Boetie, ami de Montaigne. Paris, 1845.
38527.53 Feugère, Léon. Etienne de La Boëtie. Paris, 1845.
42586.46 Feval, Paul H. Amours de Paris. Bruxelles, 1845. 2v.
FL 358.45 Foucard, Édouard. Histoire du théâtre en France. Paris, 1845.
41542.20 Gautier, Théophile. Nouvelles. Paris, 1845.
39544.58.40 Guénée, Antoine. Letters of certain Jews to Monsieur Voltaire. Paris, 1845.
41543.27 Guiraud, Alexandre. Oeuvres. v.1-2,3. Paris, 1845. 2v.
38561.29 La Bruyère, J. Les caracteres ou les moeurs de ce siècle. Paris, 1845.
41554.13 Lacroix, Paul. Les catacombes de Rome. v.1-2. Bruxelles, 1845.
41551.11 Lacroix, Paul. Les deux fous. Paris, 1845.
38511.1 Les Sires de Gavre. Histoire des seigneurs de Gavres. Bruxelles, 1845.
40556.27.9 Maistre, Joseph de. Oeuvres. Paris, 1845-60. 13v.
40556.28.8 Maistre, Joseph de. Les soirées de Saint Petersbourg. 5. éd. Lyon, 1845. 2v.
40588.46 Maistre, Xavier. Journey round my room. London, 1845.
Mol 18.45 Molière, Jean Baptiste Poquelin. Oeuvres...Aimé-Martin. 3e éd. Paris, 1845. 6v.
Mol 18.45.3 Molière, Jean Baptiste Poquelin. Oeuvres...Aimé-Martin. 4e éd. Paris, 1845. 4v.
Mol 8.45A Molière, Jean Baptiste Poquelin. Oeuvres. 3e éd. Paris, 1845. 6v.

1845 - cont.

Mol 18.45.2 Molière, Jean Baptiste Poquelin. Oeuvres complètes. Paris, 1845.
Mol 18.45.4 Molière, Jean Baptiste Poquelin. Oeuvres de Molière. Paris, 1845. 2v.
Mon 31.25.2 Montaigne, Michel de. Works. Hazlitt. 2. ed. London, 1845.
37556.36.11 Nettement, Alfred. Études critiques sur le feuilleton, roman. Paris, 1845-46. 2v.
Htn 41567.48* Philipon, C. Parodie des ewingen Judens. Frankfurt, 1845.
41567.47 Philipon, C. Parodie du Juif errant. Bruxelles, 1845.
37562.69 Reiffenberg, M. de. Histoire litteraire et politique. Bruxelles, 1845.
38511.2 René I, d'Anjou, King of Naples. Oeuvres complètes. Angers, 1845. 4v.
FL 6051.45 Rousseau, J.J. Julie ou la nouvelle Héloise. Paris, 1845. 2v.
41568.11.5 Saintine, Joseph Xavier Boniface. Picciola. Bruxelles, 1845.
41557.9.24.50 Sand, George. La comtesse de Rudolstadt. v.1-2. Paris, 1845.
41588.8A Scribe, Eugène. Oeuvres choisies. Paris, 1845. 5v.
41563.7 Sue, Eugène. The hotel Lambert. N.Y., 1845.
41561.12 Sue, Eugène. El judio errante. Madrid, 1845. 4v.
41561.8 Sue, Eugène. Le Juif errant. Paris, 1845. 2v.
41563.10 Sue, Eugène. Mathilde. Paris, 1845. 3v.
41563.17 Sue, Eugène. Los misterios de Paris. Madrid, 1845. 4v.
41563.16 Sue, Eugène. The mysteries of Paris. London, 1845-46.
41561.15.5 Sue, Eugène. Wandering Jew. N.Y., 1845.
38587.9 Théâtre de Regnard. Paris, 1845.

1846

41591.2 Astouin, L. Ephemérides ou Loisirs poetiques. Paris, 1846.
37547.22.10 Baratte, L.H. Poètes normands. Paris, 1846.
41593.6.30 Barthélemy, Auguste Marseille. A sa sainteté Pie IX. Paris, 1846.
38557.4.10 Bausset, L.F. Histoire de Bossuet. Besançon, 1846. 3v.
40532.11A Beaumarchais, Pierre A.C. de. Théâtre. Paris, 1846.
41591.3.5 Béranger, P.J. de. Oeuvres complètes. Paris, 1846. 2v.
Mol 702.6 Blaz de Bury. Molière and the French classical drama. London, 1846.
38565.21.20 Boileau Despréaux, Nicolas. Oeuvres complètes. Paris, 1846. 3v.
38547.8 Bonafous, Norbert. Études sur l'Astrée et sur Honoré d'Urfé. Paris, 1846.
41522.69.105 Briffaulk, E. Le secret de Rome au XIXme siècle. Paris, 1846.
42586.29 Castille, C.H. Gli Uccelli da Preda. Firenze, 1846. 2v.
Mon 28.9 Catalan, E. Études sur Montaigne. Paris, 1846.
37584.12 Chefs-d'oeuvre des auteurs comiques. 5. Paris, 1846.
37584.13 Chefs-d'oeuvre des auteurs comiques. 6. Paris, 1846.
37584.14 Chefs-d'oeuvre des auteurs comiques. 7. Paris, 1846.
41593.16.15 Chevremont, Alexander. La destinée du pauvre. Rennes, 1846.
42524.26 Circourt, Adolphe. Histoire des États Unis...par Bancroft. n.p., 1846-64.
41593.17.4.5 Collot, J.P. La chute de Napoléon. Paris, 1846.
42565.56 Constant, A. La dernière incarnation. Paris, 1846.
40553.15 Cousin, Victor. Cours de l'histoire de la philosophie moderne. Paris, 1846. 5v.
Mol 263.10 Delécluze, Étienne Jean. Othello et Sganarelle. Paris, 1846.
FL 383.39 Devrient, E. Dramatische und dramaturgische Schriften. v.4. Leipzig, 1846.
37595.19 Diez, Friedrich. Altromanische Sprachdenkmale. Bonn, 1846.
41538.24.9 Dumas, Alexandre. La hija del regente; comedia. Madrid, 1846.
41538.86 Dumas, Alexandre. Isabel of Bavaria. London, 1846.
41538.29.2 Dumas, Alexandre. Marguerite de Valois. London, 1846.
41538.53.20 Dumas, Alexandre. The three guardsmen. N.Y., 1846. 2 pam.
41528.10.2 Dumas, Alexandre. Trois mousquetaires. Paris, 1846.
41586.22.9 Duveyrier, A.H.J. Mort civilement. Bruxelles, 1846.
41584.37 Étienne, Charles Guillaume. Oeuvres. Paris, 1846. 5v.
42575.51.20 Feuillet, Octave. Vie de Polichinelle et ses nombreuses aventures. Paris, 1846.
40515.30.2A Florian, Jean P.C. de. Fables de Florian. Paris, 1846.
Mol 570.5A Genin, F. Lexique confare de la langue de Molière. Paris, 1846.
41588.26 Geoffrey, M. Théâtre des jeunes étudiants. Paris, 1846.
Htn 42586.66.30* Gobineau, Arthur de. La chronique rimée Jean Chouan et de ses compagnons. Paris, 1846.
41593.32.150 Godard-Lange. La congrégation. Paris, 1846.
41541.25 Gozlan, Léon. Oeuvres. Paris, 1846.
41543.35.25 Grandville, J.I.I.G. Bilder aus dem Staats- und Familienleben der Thière. Leipzig, 1846. 2v.
41593.49 Guttinguer, Ulric. Les deux ages du poétes. 2. éd. Paris, 1846.
39532.13.4A Hamilton, Anthony. Memoires of the court of Charles the second, by Count Grammont. London, 1846.
FL 390.40 Hervey, C. The theatres of Paris. Paris, 1846.
38527.58A La Boëtie, Estienne de. Oeuvres...d'Estienne de La Boëtie. Paris, 1846.
Htn 39526.26* La Fontaine, Jean de. Les bombous. Fort-Royal, 1846.
41586.4.5 La Ville de Mirmont, Alexandre Jean Joseph. Oeuvres dramatiques. Paris, 1846. 4v.
41565.23 Legrand, Alex A. Le philosophe crétien. Paris, 1846.
38512.89 Le ménagier de Paris. Le ménagier de Paris. Paris, 1846. 2v.
37576.7 Matter, Jacques. Lettres et pièces rares. Paris, 1846.
FL 379.10 Mémoires de Mlle Clairon, de Lekain, de Préville, de Dazincourt. Paris, 1846.
Mol 245.26 Molière, Jean Baptiste Poquelin. Le misanthrope...Kiszling. Heilbronn, 1846.
39591.12 Montesquieu, C.L. de S. Oeuvres complètes. Paris, 1846.
NEDL 37536.13 Nisard, Désiré. Histoire de la littérature française. v.1-6. Bruxelles, 1846-62. 3v.
41596.44 Pécontal, Simeon. Ballades et légendes. Paris, 1846.
41596.45 Poncy, Charles. Poésies. Paris, 1846.

Chronological Listing

1846 - cont.

	FL 355.34	Pont de Veyle, A. Bibliothèque dramatique de Pont de Veyle. Paris, 1846.
	Mol 880.27	Querelles, A. de. Le misanthrope politique. Paris, 1846.
	42515.70	Quinet, Edgar. Allemagne et Italie. Paris, 1846. 2v.
	42515.70.5A	Quinet, Edgar. Allemagne et Italie. 2. éd. Paris, 1846. 2v.
	42556.9	Reboul, Jean. Poésies nouvelles. Paris, 1846.
	39532.32	Reveillé-Parise, J.H. Lettres de Guy Patin. Paris, 1846. 3v.
	FL 6021.46	Rousseau, J.J. Les confessions. Paris, 1846.
	39595.14	St. Pierre, J.H.B. de. Oeuvres choisies. Paris, 1846.
	39595.16	St. Pierre, J.H.B. de. Works. London, 1846. 2v.
	40575.31	Sainte-Beuve, Charles A. Portraits contemporains. Paris, 1846-47. 3v.
	41568.11.2.2	Saintine, Joseph Xavier Boniface. Picciola. Boston, 1846.
	Mol 875.2	Samson, Joseph Isidore. Discours en vers. Paris, 1846.
	41557.9.23A	Sand, George. Consuelo. Boston, 1846. 2v.
	41568.14	Saunders, J. Les deux créoles. Tours, 1846.
	39534.28.7	Scarron, Paul. Le roman comique. Paris, 1846.
	41586.30.4	Soumet, A. David, opera en 3 actes. Paris, 1846.
	37555.25	Strobel, Adam W. Französische Volksdichter. Baden, 1846.
	41561.6	Sue, Eugène. Colonel de Surville. N.Y., 1846.
	41561.9	Sue, Eugène. Le Juif errant. Bruxelles, 1846. 3v.
	41563.11	Sue, Eugène. Martin, or The foundling. N.Y., 1846?
	41561.13A	Sue, Eugène. Wandering Jew. N.Y., 1846. 2v.
	41561.15	Sue, Eugène. Wandering Jew. N.Y., 1846.
	41568.24.6	Thenaisie, Charles. Le cornette; chronique de Bretagne, 1588-89. 2. éd. Paris, 1846.
	41568.25.50	Tillier, Claude. Oeuvres. Nevers, 1846. 4v.
	38571.12	Vignier, Adrien. Anecdotes...sur Pierre Corneille. Rouen, 1846.
	40584.18	Villemain, Abel L. Discours et mélanges. Paris, 1846.
	37595.13	Wackernagel, Wilhelm. Altfranzösische Lieder und Leiche. Basel, 1846.

1847

	37576.410	Aird, D.M. The modern novelists of France. London, 1847.
	Mol 870.8	Barbier, P.J. L'ombre de Molière. Paris, 1847.
	41593.6.50	Barthélemy, Auguste Marseille. A Léopold II. Paris, 1847.
	41591.3A	Béranger, P.J. de. Oeuvres complètes. Paris, 1847-52. 2v.
	38566.17.3	Boileau Despréaux, Nicolas. Oeuvres poétiques. 3. éd. Paris, 1847.
Htn	41522.68*	Bouis, A.T. Whip-poor-will. Paris, 1847.
	37555.4	Catalogue de...Viollet, chansons, fabliaux. Paris, 1847.
	FL 384.30	Le Chevalier de Maison-Rouge. n.p., 1847.
	41543.36.5	Cleaveland, Nehemiah. The flowers personified. N.Y., 1847.
	42565.57.50	Constant, A. Les trois malfaiteurs. Paris, 1847.
	38515.3	Coquillart, Guillaume. Oeuvres. Paris, 1847. 2v.
	38514.63.2	Coquillart, Guillaume. Oeuvres. Paris, 1847. 2v.
	41522.75	Cordellier-Delanoue, A. Jacques Coeur. Tours, 1847.
	40553.16	Cousin, Victor. Cours de l'histoire de la philosophie moderne. Paris, 1847. 3v.
	40553.17	Cousin, Victor. Fragments philosophiques. Paris, 1847. 4v.
	41566.33	Delafaye-Brehier, J. Les Portugais d'Amérique. Paris, 1847.
	41583.28.15	Delavigne, Casimir. El paria. Nueva Orleans, 1847.
	39564.7.6	Diderot, Denis. Oeuvres choisies. Paris, 1847. 2v.
	41538.20.5	Dumas, Alexandre. Les deux Diane. Bruxelles, 1847. 3v.
	41538.21.9	Dumas, Alexandre. Edmund Kean. London, 1847.
	38554.3.3	Fénelon, F. de S. de la Mothe. Adventures of Telemachus. N.Y., 1847.
	38521.29	François I. Poésies. Paris, 1847.
	FL 398.90.10	Fromentin, A. Elisa Verneuil de la comédie-française. Paris, 1847.
	40588.18.3	Genlis, S.F.D. de St. Le siège de la Rochelle. Paris, 1847.
	40588.13.5	Genlis, S.F.D. de St. Les veillées du chateau. Paris, 1847. 2v.
	FL 384.32	Hervey, C. The theatres of Paris. Paris, 1847.
	38526.27.5.500	Jolimont, T. de. Notice historique sur la vie et les oeuvres de Jacques Le Lieur. Moulins, 1847.
	37572.21	Ladreyt, Casimir. Chrestomathie de la littérature française. N.Y., 1847.
	40512.11	LeSage, Alain René. Adventures of Gil Blas. Hartford, 1847. 3v.
	40588.35	Maistre, Xavier. Oeuvres complètes. Leipzig, 1847.
	Mon 28.10	Montaigne, Michel de. Essais. Paris, 1847.
	41596.41	Norvins, J.M. de. Napoléon et Pie IX, poème. Paris, 1847.
	41596.42	Olivier, Juste. Les chansons lointaines. Lausanne, 1847.
	Mon 156.1.3	Payen, J.F. Documents inedits sur Montaigne. Paris, 1847.
Htn	Mon 156.1.2*	Payen, J.F. Documents inedits sur Montaigne. Paris, 1847-
	Mon 156.1.4	Payen, J.F. Documents inedits sur Montaigne. Paris, 1847-56.
	37567.3	Pérennès, F. Les noviciats littéraires. Paris, 1847.
	40536.20.20	Piron, Alexis. Voyage à Beaune. Dijon, 1847.
	37538.9	Prat, Henry. Études littéraires. Moyen Âge. Paris, 1847.
	38583.7.10	Racine, Jean. Théâtre complet. Paris, 1847.
	38582.19	Racine, Jean. Théâtre complète. Paris, 1847.
	40573.29	Rémusat, Charles de. Passé et présent, Mélanges. Paris, 1847. 2v.
Htn	41557.9.25.5*	Sand, George. The countess of Rudolstadt. v.1-2. Boston, 1847.
	41557.9.39A	Sand, George. Jacques. N.Y., 1847.
	38539.7.9	Sapey, Charles A. Essai sur la vie et les ouvrages de Guillaume Du Vair. Boston, 1847.
	37537.2	Schnabel, C. Abrégé de l'histoire de la littérature française. Leipzig, 1847.
	41588.14.15	Scribe, Eugène. Maitre Jean, ou la Comédie a la Cour. Bruxelles, 1847.
	41588.14.40	Scribe, Eugène. La protégée sans le savoir. Bruxelles, 1847.
	40592.29	Staël Holstein, Anne Louise. Corinne, or Italy. London, 1847.
	40592.21.5	Staël Holstein, Anne Louise. Corinne, ou l'Italie. Paris, 1847.
	41588.37.25	Tardif, Marc Louis de. Fables et tragédies. Paris, 1847.
	41563.32	Toepffer, Rodolphe. Rosa et Gertrude. Paris, 1847.
	42587.70.31	Weill, Alexandre. Sittengemälde aus dem eisässischen Volksleben. 2. Aufl. Stuttgart, 1847.

1848

	41583.4	Ancelot, Marguerite Louise Virginie (Chardon). Théâtre complet. Paris, 1848.
	42553.15	Autran, J. La fille d'Eschyle. Paris, 1848.
	Mol 702.3	Bazin, A. Les dernières années de Molière. Paris, 1848.
	37596.84.4	Bible. French. (Old). N.T. Revelation. The romaunt version of the Gospel. London, 1848.
	38528.14.5	Brantôme, P. de B. de. Vies des dames galantes. Paris, 1848.
	41583.18.21	Carmouche, P.F.A. Le marquis de Lauzun. Paris, 1848.
Htn	40586.27.10*	Chateaubriand, F.A.R. Mémoires d'outre-tombe. N.Y., 1848-49. 2v.
	40586.30	Chateaubriand, F.A.R. Memorias de ultra-tumba. Madrid, 1848-50. 4v.
	42565.57	Constant, A. The last incarnation. Gospel legends. Boston, 1848.
	42565.57.5	Constant, A. The last incarnation. Gospel legends. N.Y., 1848.
	38575.32	Corneille, Pierre. Horace. Paris, 1848.
	42542.60.701	Decourcelle, Adrien. Les extrêmes se touchent. Paris, 1848.
	40587.39	Duclos, H.L. Éloge funèbre de M. Chateaubriand. Paris, 1848.
	41538.5.10	Dumas, Alexandre. Ascanio. Paris, 1848.
	38553.25	Fénelon, F. de S. de la Mothe. Les aventures de Télémaque. Paris, 1848.
	41542.81.30	Germaine. La petite fille de Robinson. Paris, 1848.
Htn	42586.68.20*	Gobineau, Arthur de. Ternove. Bruxelles, 1848. 3v.
	41591.28	Gonzalle, J.L. L'Enménide. Paris, 1848.
	41567.24	Guizot, Elizabeth C.P. de M. Cecilia. Boston, 1848.
Htn	41578.35.70*	Lamartine, Alphonse. Discours prononcé à l'Assemblée nationale sur le projet de constitution. Paris, 1848.
	41578.35.70.5	Lamartine, Alphonse. Discours prononcé à l'Assemblée nationale sur le projet de constutution. Paris, 1848,
Htn	41578.35.100*	Lamartine, Alphonse. La presidence. Paris, 1848.
X Cg	41578.10	Lamartine, Alphonse de. Poetic meditations. London, 1848.
	Mol 870.9	Lesguillon. Le protégé de Molière. Paris, 1848.
	37596.41.9	Lorens, Frère. Trattato del Ben Vivere. Firenze, 1848.
	Mol 195.20	Molière, Jean Baptiste Poquelin. L'école des femmes...Gombert. London, 1848.
	41596.28	Musset, Alfred de. Un caprice. Paris, 1848.
	Mol 616.2	Perlet, A. De l'influence des moeurs sur la comédie. Paris, 1848.
	40573.10	Planche, Gustave. Portraits littéraires. Paris, 1848. 2v.
	37547.17	Puymaigre, Théodore de. Poètes et romanciers de la Lorraine. Paris, 1848.
	38511.3	René I, d'Anjou, King of Naples. Oeuvres choisies. Angers, 1848. 2v.
	37574.36.5	Les republiaines chansons populaires des révolutions. v.1-3. Paris, 1848.
	41557.5	Reybaud, Louis. Jérôme Paturot. Paris, 1848. 4v.
	41557.5.2	Reybaud, Louis. Jérôme Paturot. v.1-4. Paris, 1848. 2v.
	39595.15	St. Pierre, J.H.B. de. Oeuvres choisies. Paris, 1848.
	41558.63.5	Souvestre, Émile. Riche et pauvre. Paris, 1848.
	38564.47	Speckert, L. De politica et sociali Bruyerii doctrina. Tolosae, 1848.
	41596.65.75	Urbain, Charles. Simples vérités. Bruxelles, 1848.
	37566.6	Véricour, L. Raymond. Modern French literature. Boston, 1848.
	41563.50	Vidocq, Eugène François. Life in Paris. London, 1848.
	40584.20.5	Villemain, Abel L. Études d'histoire moderne. Paris, 1848.
	41596.80	Weustenraad, T. Poésies lyriques. Bruxelles, 1848.

1849

	42541.6.5	Barbier, Paul Jules. Graziella. Paris, 1849.
	41588.20	Barthet, Armand. Le moineau de Lesbie. Paris, 1849.
	41598.8	Blague-en-Main, M. Nouveau catechisme Poissard. Paris, 1849.
	41583.18.5	Brisebarre, Édouard. Adrienne de Carotteville. Paris, 1849.
	41583.18.9	Broban, Augustine S. Compter sans son hote; proverbe. Paris, 1849.
	41593.15.4	Charles, V. La revolution de fevrier, poème. Pt. 1. Paris, 1849.
	40586.11.15	Chateaubriand, F.A.R. Atala. Paris, 1849.
	38515.7	Chrestien de Troyes. Roman du chevalier de la charette. Reims, 1849.
	42542.52.20	Clairville, Louis François Nicolaïe. La propriété c'est le vol. Paris, 1849.
	41593.17.4.10	Collot, J.P. Prédictions de Napoléon. Paris, 1849.
	40553.18	Cousin, Victor. Littérature. Paris, 1849. 3v.
	37584.22	Delepierre, Joseph Octave. Description bibliographique...d'un livre unique. Receuil de 64 pièces dramatique...au XVIe siècle. Bruxelles? 1849.
	41543.36.6	Delord, Taxile. The flowers personified. N.Y., 1849.
	41540.2.10	Dumesnil, Pierre. Alain Blauchart; chronique normande. pt.1-2. Paris, 1849.
	38543.31	Étienne, Louis. Essai sur La Mothe le Vayer. Rennes, 1849.
	40515.39.5	Florian, Jean P.C. de. Guillaume Tell ou La Suisse libre. Boston, 1849.
	38512.115.2	Guillaume de Machaut. Oeuvres. Reims, 1849.
	39532.7.9	Hamilton, Anthony. Fairy tales and romances. London, 1849.
	41595.1.5	Lacan, E. La mort de l'archevêque de Paris. 2. éd. Paris, 1849.
	41554.11	Lacroix, Jules. Le testament de César. Paris, 1849.
	41578.34	Lamartine, Alphonse. Raphael. N.Y., 1849.
	41577.15	Lamartine, Alphonse de. Les confidences. N.Y., 1849.
	41578.18A	Lamartine, Alphonse de. Les confidences. Confidential disclosures. N.Y., 1849.
	41577.22	Lamartine, Alphonse de. Memoirs of my youth. N.Y., 1849.
	40536.5	Leroy, Onésime. L'irresolu. Paris, 1849.
	38526.32.10	Marguerite d'Angoulême. The Heptaméron. London, 1849.
	FL 382.3	Marteau, Édouard. De la decadence de l'art dramatique. Paris, 1849.
	Mol 18.49	Molière, Jean Baptiste Poquelin. Oeuvres. Paris, 1849. 2v.
	38526.6	Montaiglon, Anatole de. Huit sonnets de...Du Bellay. Paris, 1849.
	40587.29	Noailles, M. de. Discours...le 6 décembre 1849. Paris, 1849.

Chronological Listing

1849 - cont.

38515.5 Oeuvres inédites d'Eustache Deschamps. Paris, 1849. 2v.
38537.30.7 Rabelais, F. Works. London, 1849. 2v.
38511.3.2F René I, d'Anjou, King of Naples. Oeuvres choisies. v.1-2. Paris, 1849.
41557.5.5 Reybaud, Louis. Jérôme Paturot. Paris, 1849.
41557.7 Reybaud, Louis. Jérôme Paturot. v.1-4. Paris, 1849. 2v.
37571.60 Les romans populaires. Series 2-7,10,13. Paris, 1849- 3v.
39595.20.15 St. Pierre, J.H.B. de. Paul et Virginie. Paris, 1849.
41568.11.2.3 Saintine, Joseph Xavier Boniface. Picciola, the prisoner of Fenestrella. Philadelphia, 1849.
41588.3.4.5 Scribe, Eugène. Adrienne Lecouvreur. Paris? 1849?
38546.34.25 Sévigné, Marie de R.C. Lettres. Paris, 1849.
FL 398.83.22 Talma, F.J. Mémoires. v.1-2,3-4. Paris, 1849-50. 2v.
38515.4 Tarbé, Prosper. Oeuvres de Guillaume de Machault. Paris, 1849.
38515.6 Tarbé, Prosper. Le roman d'Aubrey le Bourgoing. Reims, 1849.
40584.20 Villemain, Abel L. Études de littérature ancienne et etrangère. Paris, 1849.
40584.28.10 Vitet, L. Les états d'Orléans; scenes historiques. Paris, 1849.
40584.22 Vitet, L. Les états d'Orléans. Paris, 1849.
39545.24.12 Voltaire, François Marie Arouet de. Théâtre. Paris, 1849.
41588.50.3 Wafflard, A.J.M. Le voyage a Dieppe. Liepsic, 1849?
38511.4 Wailly, Natalis de. Mémoire sur Geffroi de Paris. Paris, 1849.

185-

41583.11.4 Basté, Eugène Pierre. The Corsican brothers. N.Y., 185-. 4 pam.
41538.16.16 Dumas, Alexandre. Il conte di Morcerf ed il conte di Monte Cristo. Milano? 185-?
41538.28.5F Dumas, Alexandre. Impressions de voyage. Paris, 185-?
41538.36.8 Dumas, Alexandre. Mademoiselle de belle-isle. Paris, 185-?
38554.3.5 Fénelon, F. de S. de la Mothe. Adventures of Telemachus. n.p., 185-?
X Cg 38554.322.225 Fénelon, F. de S. de la Mothe. On the knowledge and love of God. Worcester, 185-.
42543.30.5 Fournier, Narcisse. Comedy and tragedy. N.Y., 185-?
41572.35F Hugo, Victor. Théâtre complète. Paris, 185-.
Mol 171.48 Molière, Jean Baptiste Poquelin. Le bourgeois gentilhomme...Delbos. N.Y., 185-?
Mol 245.29 Molière, Jean Baptiste Poquelin. Le misanthrope. Le mariage forcé. Edinbourg, 185-?
Mol 38.50 Molière, Jean Baptiste Poquelin. Oeuvres choisies. N.Y., 185-?
Mol 18.58.9 Molière, Jean Baptiste Poquelin. Oeuvres complètes...Louandre. Paris, 185-. 3v.
Mol 18.58.15 Molière, Jean Baptiste Poquelin. Oeuvres complètes...Louandre. Paris, 185-? 3v.
Mol 18.57 Molière, Jean Baptiste Poquelin. Oeuvres complètes...Louandre. Paris, 185-? 3v.
Mol 268.40 Molière, Jean Baptiste Poquelin. Le Tartuffe. J. Oxenford. London, 185-?
FL 6074.2 Rousseau, J.J. Essai sur l'origine des langues. Frankfort, 185-.
42546.15.20.9 Saglier, Louis. Le théâtre en famille. 2e éd. Paris, 185-?
38546.39.5 Sévigné, Marie de R.C. Lettres de...avec les notes de tous les commentateurs. Paris, 185-? 6v.
40592.23.5 Staël Holstein, Anne Louise. Corinne. N.Y., 185-?
37597.26A Wace, Maistre. Saint Nicholas. Bonn, 185-.

1850

41583.2 Adamoli, Luigi. Les deux chaises de poste. Genève, 1850.
Htn 37578.54* Almanach astrologique. Paris, 1850.
42542.25 Augier, Emile. Gabrielle. Paris, 1850.
42542.27.20.15 Barrière, Théodore. Un monsieur qui suit les femmes. Paris, 1850.
41583.11.4.5 Basté, Eugène Pierre. The Corsican brothers. N.Y., 1850?
38556.7 Beausset, Le Card. Histoire de Fénelon. Paris, 1850. 4v.
41592.30.15A Béranger, P.J. de. Béranger, two hundred of his lyrical poems. N.Y., 1850.
41592.30.15.2 Béranger, P.J. de. Béranger, two hundred of his lyrical poems. N.Y., 1850.
38515.10 Bertrand of Bar-sur-Aube. Roman de Girard de Viane. Reims, 1850.
38557.26.5 Bossuet, J.B. Oraisons funèbres. Paris, 1850.
Mol 880.4 Cénac-Moncaut, J. Avant et pendant. Paris, 1850.
40564.29 Chasles, Philarète. Études sur les hommes et les moeurs au XIXe siècle. Paris, 1850.
39532.16.9 Chaulieu, G.A. de. Lettres inédites. Paris, 1850.
38575.34.5.25 Corneille, Pierre. Polyeucte martyr. Paris, 1850.
40553.19 Cousin, Victor. Instruction publique. Paris, 1850. 3v.
37574.24 Coutan, A. (Mme.). Choix de poésies. N.Y., 1850.
41566.5.15 D'Arlincourt, Charles V.P. La rosa di Firenze. Napoli, 1850.
41583.20 Delavigne, Casimir. Oeuvres complètes. Paris, 1850. 6v.
37575.410 Desbordes-Valmone. Confidences poétiques, dédiées à la jeunesse. Paris, 1850.
41593.32 Duchapt, Théophile. Fables. Paris, 1850.
41593.32.9 Ducos, Florentin. Épopée toulousaine, ou Guerre des Albigeois. Toulouse, 1850. 2v.
42542.66.65 Dugué, Ferdinand. L'oasis. Paris, 1850.
41538.54 Dumas, Alexandre. The iron mask. Philadelphia, 1850.
41538.32 Dumas, Alexandre. Quarante-cinq. Paris, 1850.
41538.63.30 Dumas, Alexandre. The queen's necklace. N.Y., 1850. 2 pam.
42573.30 Erckmann, Emile. L'Alsace en 1814. Strasbourg, 1850.
40515.46 Florian, Jean P.C. de. Numa Pompelius. Boston, 1850.
Htn 40566.23* Janin, Jules. La réligieuse de Toulouse. Paris, 1850. 2v.
Mon 68.3 Jubinal, A. Une lettre inédite de Montaigne. Paris, 1850.
Mon 68.3.4 Jubinal, A. Une lettre inedite de Montaigne. 2. éd. Paris, 1850.
FL 370.15 La Fons, A. Cérémonies dramatiques. Paris, 1850.

1850 - cont.

41578.35.125 Lamartine, Alphonse. Lamartine on atheism. Boston, 1850.
41578.35 Lamartine, Alphonse. Toussaint Louverture. Bruxelles, 1850.
41578.105 Lamartine; memorie particolari e segrete. Italia, 1850.
42544.17 Legouvé, Gabriel. Le mérite des femmes. Poëme. Paris, 1850.
Htn 40586.31* Lenormant, Charles. M. de Chateaubriand et les Mémoires d'outre-tombe. Paris, 1850.
Mon 68.4 Lepelle de Bois-Gallais, Frédéric. Encore une lettre inédite de Montaigne. London, 1850.
40512.42 LeSage, Alain René. Histoire de Gil Blas de Santillane. Paris, 1850.
42576.73.5 Lurine, Louis. Le treizième arrondissement de Paris. Paris, 1850.
37581.40.16 Magasin théâtral. 2 plays, 1850, 1861. Paris, 1850-61.
FL 398.74.15 Maurice-Descombes, C. La vérité-Rachel; examen du talent de la première tragédienne du théâtre-français. Paris, 1850.
Mol 165.25 Molière, Jean Baptiste Poquelin. L'avare...Schwalb. Essen, 1850.
Htn Mol 269.5* Molière, Jean Baptiste Poquelin. Tartuffo commedia. Firenze, 1850.
Mon 31.28 Montaigne, Michel de. Works. Philadelphia, 1850.
41596.17.5 Musset, Alfred de. Comédies et proverbes. Paris, 1850.
40542.6.5 Ozanam, Antoine P. Les germains avant le christianisme. Liège, 1850.
FL 390.42 Perrin, Maximilian. Biographie histoire de tous les théâtres de Paris. Paris, 1850.
38511.33.5 Philippe de Vitry. Les oeuvres de Philippe de Vitry. Reims, 1850.
37555.321.2 Quicherat, L. Traité de versification française. 2. éd. Paris, 1850.
FL 6037.25 Rousseau, J.J. Il contratto sociale. Italia, 1850.
FL 6037.26 Rousseau, J.J. Del contratto sociale. Pinerolo, 1850.
FL 6024.2 Rousseau, J.J. Fragments inédits des confessions. Neuchâtel, 1850.
41568.11.4 Saintine, Joseph Xavier Boniface. Picciola. N.Y., 1850.
41568.11.3 Saintine, Joseph Xavier Boniface. Picciola. Philadelphia, 1850.
41557.9.45.25 Sand, George. La mare au diable. Paris, 1850.
41557.27.5 Sandeau, Jules. Money bags and titles. Philadelphia, 1850.
41557.34.2 Sarrazin, Adrien de. Bardouc. Boston, 1850.
41557.35 Sarrazin, Adrien de. La caravanserail. Paris, 1850. 2v.
41557.36 Sarrazin, Adrien de. Contes nouveaux. Paris, 1850. 3v.
37576.3 Société des bibliophiles. Mélanges de littérature et d'histoire. Paris, 1850.
40592.28 Staël Holstein, Anne Louise. Corinne, or Italy. London, 1850.
40592.22 Staël Holstein, Anne Louise. Corinne, ou l'Italie. Paris, 1850.
38515.9 Tarbé, Prosper. Chansonniers de Champagne aux XIIe et XIIIe siècles. Reims, 1850.
38515.8 Tarbé, Prosper. Oeuvres de Philippe de Vitry. Reims, 1850.
40584.18.5 Villemain, Abel L. Discours et mélanges littéraires. Paris, 1850.
FL 6049.5 Viridet, M. Documents officiels sur le condamnation d'Emile. Genève, 1850.

1851

40591.9 Balzac, Honoré de. Oeuvres illustrées. Paris, 1851-54. 3v.
40591.15 Balzac, Honoré de. Paris Marié. Paris, 1851.
Mol 702.4.2 Bazin, A. Notes historiques sur la vie de Molière. Paris, 1851.
Mol 702.4 Bazin, A. Notes historiques sur la vie de Molière. Paris, 1851.
Mol 702.5 Bazin, A. Notes historiques sur la vie de Molière. Paris, 1851.
39566.14 Bersot, Enrest. Études sur Diderot. Paris, 1851.
40582.4.150F Beyle, Henri. Oeuvres complètes de Stendhal. Paris, 1851?
Htn 38512.5* Le bibliophile Troyen. Troyes, 1851.
37563.5 Blignières, Auguste de. Essai sur Amyot. Paris, 1851.
38566.17.5 Boileau Despréaux, Nicolas. Oeuvres. Paris, 1851.
39545.1 Bungener, F. Voltaire et son temps. Paris, 1851. 2v.
38515.11 Chansons de Thibault IV. Reims, 1851.
40586.6.5 Chateaubriand, F.A.R. Atala. Paris, 1851.
37574.410 Choix de cantiques a l'usage des églises indépendantes de Jersey et Guernesey. Jersey, 1851.
37581.17 Collot, A.G. Chefs-d'oeuvres dramatiques. N.Y., 1851.
40553.20 Cousin, Victor. Discours politiques. Paris, 1851.
41538.17.5A Dumas, Alexandre. Countess of Salisbury. N.Y., 1851.
41538.20.9 Dumas, Alexandre. Le drame de quatre-vingt-treize. Bruxelles, 1851.
41538.59 Dumas, Alexandre. Kean o sia genio e sregolatezza. n.p., 1851.
41538.56.10 Dumas, Alexandre. Louise La Vallière. Philadelphia, 1851.
41593.32.6 Dupont, Pierre. Chants et chansons. Paris, 1851-1862. 4v.
Mon 68.6 Feuillet de Conches, F. Réponse...touchant une lettre. v.1-2. Paris, 1851.
40556.14.2 Frayssinous, Denis L. Conférences et discours inédits. Paris, 1851.
40588.18.5 Genlis, S.F.D. de St. Le siège de la Rochelle. N.Y., 1851.
40588.13.2 Genlis, S.F.D. de St. Les veillées du chateau. Paris, 1851.
Mol 860.37.2 Gutzkow, Karl. Das Urbild des Tartüffe. N.Y., 1851.
Mol 608.2 Hagberg, J.T. Om arten af Molières lustspel. Upsala, 1851.
37596.81.10 Huon de Mery. Das tornoiement de l'antechrist. Reims, 1851.
38515.12 Huon de Mery. Tornoiement de l'antichrist. Reims, 1851.
40566.18 Janin, Jules. Les gaités champêtres. Paris, 1851. 2v.
39526.27.15 La Fontaine, Jean de. Fables de La Fontaine. 3e éd. Cambridge, 1851.
41578.35.127 Lamartine, Alphonse. England in 1850. N.Y., 1851.
41578.27 Lamartine, Alphonse de. Geneviève, histoire d'une servante. Paris, 1851.
Htn 41578.25* Lamartine, Alphonse de. Nouveau voyage en Orient. Paris, 1851. 2 pam.

1851 - cont.

38543.19.25 La Rochefoucauld, François. Moral reflections. N.Y., 1851.
Mol 165.26.2 Molière, Jean Baptiste Poquelin. L'avare...Barbieux. Frankfurt, 1851.
Mol 165.26 Molière, Jean Baptiste Poquelin. L'avare...Köhler. Altenburg, 1851.
Mol 245.30 Molière, Jean Baptiste Poquelin. Le misanthrope. Ploetz. Berlin, 1851.
Mol 18.51.5 Molière, Jean Baptiste Poquelin. Oeuvres. Paris, 1851. 2v.
Mol 8.51F Molière, Jean Baptiste Poquelin. Oeuvres. Paris, 1851?
Mol 269.38.5 Molière, Jean Baptiste Poquelin. Ho Tartoûphos. Skylissê. Snyrna, 1851.
39594.6.10 Montesquieu, C.L. de S. Grandeur et décadence des Romains. Paris, 1851.
FL 6118.51 Morin, G.H. Essai vie et caractère de Jean-Jacques Rousseau. Paris, 1851.
Mol 616.1 Paringault, E. La langue de droit dans le théâtre de Molière. n.p., 1851.
42545.71 Piestre, P.E. La goton de Biranger. Paris, 1851.
FL 398.75.15 Poral, Jacques. Fils de Réjane. v.1-2. Paris, 1851-52.
38585.21 Racine, Jean. Esther. Tragôdia. En Hermoupolie, 1851.
38587.9.4 Regnard, Jean François. Théâtre de Regnard, suivi de ses voyages en Laponie. Paris, 1851.
41568.11.9 Saintine, Joseph Xavier Boniface. Picciola. Philadelphia, 1851.
41568.11.8 Saintine, Joseph Xavier Boniface. Picciola. 17. ed. Paris, 1851.
41568.12.5 Saintine, Joseph Xavier Boniface. The solitary of Juan Fernadez. Boston, 1851.
NEDL 39527.19 Sales, F. Fables de La Fontaine. Cambridge, 1851.
41557.9.24 Sand, George. Consuelo. N.Y., 1851.
41557.9.30 Sand, George. Fadette. A domestic story. 2e ed. N.Y., 1851.
41557.9.37 Sand, George. Histoire du véritable Gribonille. Paris, 1851.
Mol 860.36 Sand, George. Molière. Bruxelles, 1851.
Mol 860.35 Sand, George. Molière. Paris, 1851.
Mol 860.34.5 Sand, George. Molière. Paris, 1851.
41588.3.4.10 Scribe, Eugène. Adrienne Lecouvreur. Paris, 1851.
38553.15.2A Selections from the writings of Fénelon. 6th ed. Boston, 1851.
41561.7 Sue, Eugène. Deux histoires: Aventures d'Hercule Hardi, le colonel de Surville. Paris, 1851.
41561.10 Sue, Eugène. Le Juif errant. Paris, 1851.
41563.4 Sue, Eugène. Les sept péchés capitaux. La luxure. La paresse. Paris, 1851.
41563.4.5 Sue, Eugène. Les sept péchés capitaux. L'orgueil. Paris, 1851-82. 2v.
38515.13 Tarbé, Prosper. Poétes de Champagne...proverbes. Reims, 1851.
38515.14 Tarbé, Prosper. Recherches sur...Champagne. Reims, 1851. 2v.
Mol 698.9F Taschereau, M.J. Histoire de la vie et des ouvrages de Molière. Paris, 1851.
41563.26.2 Toepffer, Rodolphe. Nouvelles genevoises. Paris, 1851.
38557.9 Vaillant, V. Études sur les sermons de Bossuet. Paris, 1851.
Mol 247.6 Widal, A. Des divers caractères du misanthrope. Paris, 1851.

1852

42548.60 Barrière, Théodore. Les bourgeois gentilhommes. Paris, 1852-57.
40597.1.95 Baschet, Armand. Honoré de Balzac. Paris, 1852.
40597.2 Baschet, Armand. Honoré de Balzac. 2. éd. Paris, 1852.
Mol 730.1 Blaze, F.H.C. Molière musicien. Paris, 1852. 2v.
Mol 602.8 Bouillier, F. Molière, élève de Gassendi. Lyon, 1852.
41593.13.3 Boulay-Paty, Évariste. Sonnets de la vie humaine. Brest, 1852.
41583.15.15 Bourgeois, Anicet. Marthe et Marie. Paris, 1852.
38537.4A Brunet, Jacques C. Recherches sur...Rabelais. Paris, 1852.
42542.48.30 Caraguel, C. Le bougeoir. Paris, 1852.
41597.28 Le Caveau. Paris, 1852.
40586.18.12.3 Chateaubriand, F.A.R. Le génie du Christianisme. Paris, 1852. 2v.
40586.17.10 Chateaubriand, F.A.R. Itinéraire de Paris à Jérusalem. Paris, 1852. 2v.
Mol 603.7 Cormenin, L. de. Comédie sociale: types de Molière. Paris, 1852.
40588.3.10 Cottin, Marie R. (Mme.). Élizabeth ou Les exilés de Sibérie. Paris, 1852.
42545.69.19.25 Dennery, Adolphe Philippe. Si j'étais roi! ... opéra comique. Paris, 1852.
41538.13 Dumas, Alexandre. Acte of Corinth. N.Y., 1852.
41538.16.11 Dumas, Alexandre. Il conte di Monte Cristo. Milano? 1852.
42543.15 Dumas, Alexandre. La dame aux camélias. 6. éd. Paris, 1852.
41538.20.7F Dumas, Alexandre. La dame de Monsoreau. Paris, 1852.
41538.55 Dumas, Alexandre. Vicomte de Bragelonne. Paris, 1852.
FL 362.4 Failly. Sur l'art du comédien. Paris, 1852.
42543.39 Fallet, C. (Mme.). Théâtre de la jeunesse. Lyon, 1852.
38554.350.260 Fénelon, F. de S. de la Mothe. Treatise on the education of daughters. Baltimore, 1852.
42543.30.15 Fournier, Narcisse. Les nuits de la Seine. Paris, 1852.
Htn 41542.37.15* Gautier, Théophile. Un trio de Romans. Paris, 1852.
40588.13 Genlis, S.F.D. de St. Les veillées du chateau. Paris, 1852. 2v.
38523.20 Gournay, François A. Malherbe; recherches sur sa vie. Caen, 1852.
37596.43 Guillaume le Clerc. Le bestiaire divin. Caen, 1852.
38575.5 Guizot, François. Corneille and his time. N.Y., 1852.
42576.14.73 Houssaye, Arsène. Philosophers and actresses. N.Y., 1852. 2v.
41578.10.5 Lamartine, Alphonse de. Translations from the meditations of Lamartine. N.Y., 1852.
42555.23 Laprade, Victor de. Poèmes évangéliques. Paris, 1852.
42544.16 Legouvé, Ernest. Édith de Falsen. Paris, 1852.
40512.8.7 LeSage, Alain René. Histoire de Gil Blas de Santillane. Paris, 1852.
38523.22 Lettres inédites de Malherbe. Caen, 1852.
38575.16 Lisle, J.A. Essai sur les théories dramatiques de Corneille. Paris, 1852.

1852 - cont.

39526.6 Lorin, Théodore. Vocabulaire pour...La Fontaine. Paris, 1852.
37566.25 Menche de Loisne, Charles. Influence de la littérature française 1830. Paris, 1852.
Mol 166.43 Molière, Jean Baptiste Poquelin. Lakomec. Praha, 1852.
Mol 18.52 Molière, Jean Baptiste Poquelin. Oeuvres complètes...Louandre. Paris, 1852. 3v.
Mon 88.1 Monthizon, J. Étude sur la vie et l'oeuvre de la Boetie. Paris, 1852- 5 pam.
40572.2.20 Montlaur, Eugène de. De l'Italie et de l'Espagne. Paris, 1852.
42577.15 Murger, Henry. Le bonhomme jadis. Paris, 1852.
41543.9 Nerval, Gerard de. Contes et facéties. Paris, 1852.
41556.16 Nodier, Charles. Les sept chateaux. Paris, 1852.
Mol 714.1 Noël, Eugène. Molière. Paris, 1852.
38557.5.1 Nourrisson, J.F. Essai sur la philosophie de Bossuet. Paris, 1852.
40542.7.50 Ozanam, Antoine P. Les poètes franciscains en Italie au treizième siècle. Paris, 1852.
37573.31 Pellissier, Jean B. L'abeille poétique du XIIe siècle. Limoges, 1852.
42545.83.6 Ponsard, F. Études antiques. Paris, 1852.
37567.5 Prarond, Ernest. De quelques écrivains nouveaux. Paris, 1852.
38583.4.20 Racine, Jean. Théâtre complet. Paris, 1852.
42546.9.5 Rosier, Joseph Bernard. El secreto de la reina: Zarzuela en tres actos. Madrid, 1852.
42587.56.15 Rostaing, Jules. Petit-bonhomme vit encore. Paris, 1852.
39595.18 St. Pierre, J.H.B. de. Paul et Virginie. N.Y., 1852.
40575.31.5 Sainte-Beuve, Charles A. Portraits contemporains. Paris, 1852. 3v.
39586.23 Sainte-Beuve. Oeuvres de Rivarol. Paris, 1852.
41557.8.45 Sand, George. Oeuvres illustrées. v.1-9. Paris, 1852-56. 3v.
41557.31 Sandeau, Jules. Mademoiselle de la Seiglière. Paris, 1852.
41587.27.75 Sassernò, A.S. Glorie e sventure. Turin, 1852. 2v.
41588.14.1 Scribe, Eugène. Le verre d'eau. 4e éd. Leipzig, 1852.
41588.29.4 Séjour, Victor. Richard III. 2e éd. Paris, 1852.
42546.43.3 Siraudin, Paul. Left the stage. London, 1852?
41558.50 Souvestre, Émile. Dans la prairie. Paris, 1852.
40592.22.5 Staël Holstein, Anne Louise. Corinne, ou l'Italie. N.Y., 1852.
41563.25 Toepffer, Rodolphe. Mélanges. Paris, 1852.
41563.28.2 Toepffer, Rodolphe. Le Presbytère. Paris, 1852.
41564.1.6.15 Vigny, Alfred de. Stello. 6e éd. Paris, 1852.
42587.69 Villemessant, H. de. Les cancans, petit almanach de la chronique de Paris. Paris, 1852.
Htn 42547.13.75* Villemin, Eugène. Alfred le rimeur. Oréans, 1852.
39545.42 Voltaire, François Marie Arouet de. La Herniade. Boston, 1852.
38546.30 Walckenaer, Charles Athanase. Mémoire sur Mme. de Sévigné. Paris, 1852. 5v.
38546.29 Walckenaer, Charles Athanase. Mémoire sur Mme. de Sévigné. Paris, 1852. 5v.
41568.70 Yvan, Melchior. Les déportés. Bruxelles, 1852.

1853

38528.13.9 Alcripe, Philippe de. La nouvelle fabrique. Paris, 1853.
41583.8.20 Arnault, A. Les Casaques. Paris, 1853.
42542.26 Augier, Émile. Philiberte. 4. éd. Paris, 1853.
42542.26.1 Augier, Émile. Philiberte. 5. éd. Paris, 1853.
Htn 40597.13.5* Balzac, Honoré de. Les fantaisies de Claudine. Paris, 1853.
42542.27.21 Barrière, Théodore. Les filles de Marbre. Paris, 1853.
41583.11.55 Bawr, A.S. (Goury de Champgrand). Mes souvenirs. 2e éd. Paris, 1853.
42548.6 Bayard, J.F.A. Un fils de famille. Paris, 1853.
41522.20.15 Beauvoir, E. Roger de. Les enfers de Paris, cinq actes mêlés de chant. Paris, 1853.
38565.20 Boileau Despréaux, Nicolas. Oeuvres. Paris, 1853.
Mol 860.38 Brucker, R. Le carême du roi. Paris, 1853.
42586.27.13 Bungener, Félix. The preacher and the king. 12. ed. Boston, 1853.
42586.25.16 Bungener, Félix. The priest and the Huguenot. Boston, 1853-1854. 2v.
42586.26.90 Bungener, Félix. Un sermon sous Louis XIV. 4. éd. Paris, 1853.
FL 398.74.17 Chambrun, C.A. Quelques réflexions sur l'art dramatique. Mlle. Rachel; ses succes, ses defants. Paris, 1853.
38585.76 Champseix, P.G. Considération générales sur Phèdre et le théâtre. Lausanne, 1853.
41566.20 Chapus, Eugène. Les chasses princières en France. Paris, 1853.
37596.20 Charsant, Alphonse. La muse Normande. Rouen, 1853.
40564.30 Chasles, Philarète. Notabilities in France and England. N.Y., 1853.
42524.30 Clément de Ris, Louis. Portraits à la plume. Paris, 1853.
39574.23 Condorcet, J.M. de. Oeuvres de d'Alembert. Paris, 1853.
37572.60 Le conteur suisse; recueil des plus interessantes. v.1-2. Berne, 1853.
38574.3.2 Corneille, Pierre. Théâtre. Paris, 1853. 2v.
38574.3 Corneille, Pierre. Théâtre. Paris, 1853.
Htn 37576.510* Critical notices of French literature. Brighton, 1853.
42545.69.19.5 Dennery, Adolphe Philippe. Maria Giovanna, o La famiglia del Beone. Milano, 1853.
42545.69.19.20 Dennery, Adolphe Philippe. Sept merveilles du monde. Paris, 1853.
41538.40 Dumas, Alexandre. L'alchimista, dramma in cinque atti. n.p., 1853.
41538.28.9.5 Dumas, Alexandre. Impressions de voyage. v.1-3. Paris, 1853-54.
38528.5 Estienne, Henri. Conformité du Langagu François avec le Grec. Paris, 1853.
38527.30.3 Feugère, L. Agrippa d'Aubigné. Paris, 1853.
39544.10 Foisset, M.T. Voltaire et le président de Brosses. Paris, 1853.
41584.50.8 Gaillardet, Frédéric. La tour de Nesle. N.Y., 1853?
41584.50.5 Gaillardet, Frédéric. La tour de Nesle. N.Y., 1853.
41541.11 Girardin, Delphine Gay. Lady Tartuffe. Paris, 1853.
FL 391.60 Goncourt, E. Mystères des théâtres, 1852. Paris, 1853.
39532.13.6 Hamilton, Anthony. Memoires of the court of Charles the second by Count Grammont. London, 1853.
37556.17 Hatin, E. Histoire du journal en France. Paris, 1853.

Chronological Listing

1853 - cont.

42576.14.40 Houssaye, Arsène. Sous la régence et sous la terreur. Paris, 1853.
41572.29.4 Hugo, Victor. Le roi s'amuse. Paris, 1853.
41571.6 Hugo, Victor. Han d'Islande. Notre Dame de Paris. Paris, 1853.
Htn 41571.3.75* Hugo, Victor. Oeuvres oratoires. Bruxelles, 1853.
40567.30 Janin, Jules. Histoire de la littérature dramatique. n.p., 1853-58. 6v.
41567.30 Jauffret, Louis F. Travels of Rolando. London, 1853.
41544.7.5 Karr, Alphonse. Les femmes. Paris, 1853.
41544.28 Karr, Alphonse. Lettres écrites de mon jardin. Paris, 1853.
37597.19 Kloppe, Gustav A. Recherches sur le dialecte de Guace (Wace). Magdeburg, 1853.
38564.25.6 La Bruyère, J. de. Les caractères. Paris, 1853.
39526.32 La Fontaine, Jean de. Fables of La Fontaine. London, 1853.
38551.75.10 Lamartine, A. de. Fénelon (1651-1715). Paris, 1853.
Htn 41578.35.110* Lamartine, Alphonse. Heloïse et Abélard. Paris, 1853.
41578.15 Lamartine, Alphonse de. Dos perlas literarias del célebre Adolfo de Lamartine. Madrid, 1853.
FL 395.125 Langier, Eugène. Documents historiques sur la comédie française pendant le régne de S.M. l'Empereur Napoléon I. Paris, 1853.
38514.56 La Sale, Antoine de. Les quinze joyes de mariage. Paris, 1853.
42514.27.15 Lerne, E. de. Socières blondes. Paris, 1853.
37595.15A Mätzner, Eduard. Altfranzösische Lieder. Berlin, 1853.
40556.28 Maistre, Joseph de. Lettres et opuscules inédits. Paris, 1853. 2v.
40588.34 Maistre, Xavier. Oeuvres complètes. Paris, 1853.
42545.20.19 Mazilier, N. Aelia et Mysis. Paris, 1853.
42545.26 Mercier, P. Le roman du village. Paris, 1853.
39533.10 Michel, F. Extrait abrégé de vieux mémoriaux. Paris, 1853-57.
Mol 219.1.5 Molière, Jean Baptiste Poquelin. George Dandin mise en vers...C.L.B. Esnault. Arras, 1853.
42514.27.11 Mondor, Henri. Alain. 9. éd. Paris, 1853.
42577.25 Murger, Henry. Propos de ville et propos de théatre. Paris, 1853.
41596.31 Musset, Alfred de. Mademoiselle Mimi Pinson. Paris, 1853.
37595.7 Neulan, Elizabeth C.P. de. Abailard et Héloise. Paris, 1853.
38545.25 Nisard, Charles. Mémoires de Daniel Huet. Paris, 1853.
41556.26 Nodier, Charles. Trésor des Feves et Fleur des Pois. Paris, 1853.
Mon 88.3.2 Payen, J.F. Notice bio-bibliographique sur la Boetie. Paris, 1853.
Mon 88.3.3 Payen, J.F. Notice bio-bibliographique sur la Boetie. Paris, 1853.
Mon 88.3 Payen, J.F. Notice bio-bibliographique sur la Boetie. Paris, 1853.
38527.50 Payen, Jean François. Notice sur...La Boëtie. Paris, 1853.
FL 372.13 Piolin, D. Paul. Recherches sur les mystères dans le Maine. Angers, 1853.
40536.20.5 Piron, Alexis. La métromanie. Paris, 1853.
40573.9 Planche, Gustave. Portraits d'artistes. Paris, 1853. 2v.
42587.47 Plouvier, Édouard. Contes pour les jours de Pluie. Paris, 1853.
42545.82 Ponsard, F. L'honneur et l'argent. 4. éd. Paris, 1853.
37538.10 Prat, Henry. Études littéraires. XIVe et XVe siècles. Paris, 1853.
37544.3 Rathery, Edme J.B. Influence de l'Italie sur les lettres françaises. Paris, 1853.
38525.22.60 Régnier, Mathurin. Oeuvres complètes. Paris, 1853. 2 pam.
41557.7.9 Reybaud, Louis. Geronimo Paturot. Habana, 1853.
41596.52 Reynaud, Charles. Epitres, contes et pastorales. Paris, 1853.
40541.5 Roederer, Pierre L. Oeuvres. Paris, 1853-59. 8v.
FL 6072.2 Rousseau, J.J. Discours sur les richesses. Paris, 1853.
FL 6002.853 Rousseau, J.J. Fragments inédits. Paris, 1853.
42511.5 Sand, G. Le diable à Paris. Paris et les Parisiens. Paris, 1853.
Htn 41557.9.45* Sand, George. Les maîtres sonneurs. Bruxelles, 1853.
41557.8.108.5 Sand, George. Le meunier d'Angibault. Paris, 1853.
37564.15 Sayous, Pierre André. Histoire de la littérature française. Paris, 1853. 2v.
38546.39 Sévigné, Marie de R.C. Lettres de...avec les notes de tous les commentateurs. Paris, 1853. 6v.
41558.61 Souvestre, Émile. Le mendiant de Saint-Roch. Paris, 1853.
41558.65.1 Souvestre, Émile. Un philosophe sous les toits. 6e éd. Paris, 1853.
40592.23.3 Staël Holstein, Anne Louise. Corinne. N.Y., 1853.
40592.23 Staël Holstein, Anne Louise. Corinne. Paris, 1853.
37581.43 Théâtre contemporain, 1853-1857. Paris, 1853-57.
39545.25 Théâtre de Voltaire. Paris, 1853.
41584.36 Thiesse, Léon. M. Étienne. Paris, 1853.
41563.26 Toepffer, Rodolphe. Nouvelles genevoises. Rosa et Gertrude. Paris, 1853.
42587.67 Villedeuil, Charles. Paris a l'envers. Paris, 1853.
37565.8 Vinet, Alexandre R. Histoire de la littérature française au 18me siècle. Paris, 1853.
42587.69.9 Viollet, Alphonse. La grande nuit. Paris, 1853.
41568.28 Viollet-Le-Duc, E.L.N. Six mois de vie d'un jeune homme. Paris, 1853.
37595.10.10 Wight, O.W. Romance of Abélard and Héloise. N.Y., 1853.

1854

Mol 825.1 Alexandre, M. Molière et les médecins. Amiens, 1854.
FL 391.65 Alhoy, Maurice. Paris-actrice. Paris, 1854.
38557.10 Allou, A. Reconnaissance du tombeau de Bossuet. Meaux, 1854.
42553.24 Amiel, Henri F. Grains de mil. Paris, 1854.
42553.55 Ansaldi, J. Essais poétiques. Toulon, 1854.
42542.9.90 Augier, Émile. Le gendre de M. Poirier. 5. sér. Bielefeld, 1854.
42542.10.6 Augier, Émile. Il genero del signor Poirier. Milano, 1854.
42542.14.5 Augier, Émile. La pietra del Paragone. Milano, 1854.
38542.10 Balzac, J.L.G. de. Oeuvres de Jean Louis de Balzac. Paris, 1854. 2v.
42542.27.23 Barrière, Théodore. La vie en rose. Paris, 1854.

1854 - cont.

41583.11.60 Bawr, A.S. (Goury de Champgrand). Nouvelles. Paris, 1854.
41522.44 Bernard, Charles de. Nouvelles et mélanges. Paris, 1854.
40582.16 Beyle, Henri. Mémoires d'un touriste. Paris, 1854. 2v.
40582.21 Beyle, Henri. Racine et Shakespeare. Paris, 1854.
40582.22 Beyle, Henri. Romans et nouvelles. Paris, 1854.
41566.14.5 Bouilly, Jean N. Pavidky pro magi d ceru. V Praze, 1854.
Mol 167.7 Bromig, J. Vergleichung der Komödien Aulularia des Plautus und l'Avare des Molière. Burgsteinfurt, 1854.
42586.27.14 Bungener, Félix. The preacher and the king. 12. ed. Boston, 1854.
42586.25.9 Bungener, Félix. Trois sermons sous Louis XV. 3. éd. Paris, 1854. 3v.
39533.9 Chapelle, C.E.L. Oeuvres de Chapelle et de Bachaumont. Paris, 1854.
40565.20 Cuvillier-Fleury, A.A. Études historiques et littéraires. Paris, 1854. 2v.
39574.31 Damiron, J.P. Mémoire sur d'Alembert. Paris, 1854.
41566.31 De Fontenay. Star ou de Cassiopée. Paris, 1854.
40588.8.200 Des Essarts, Alfred. La muger del espia. v.1-2. Matanzas, 1854.
37584.19.5 Desmahis, J.F.E. de C. Chefs d'oeuvre des auteur comiques. Paris, 1854. 8v.
42568.2.25 Desnoiresterres, Gustave. Les talons rouges. Paris, 1854.
41538.19.5 Dumas, Alexandre. La conscience, drame en cinq actes en six tableaux. Paris, 1854.
41538.19.9 Dumas, Alexandre. Conscience. London, 1854.
41538.25 Dumas, Alexandre. The foresters. N.Y., 1854.
41538.57 Dumas, Alexandre. Louisa, or the adventures of a French milliner. Cincinnati, 1854.
42543.28.25 Empic, A.S. Les six femmes de Henri VIII. Paris, 1854. 2v.
42586.46.15 Feval, Paul H. Le champ de Bataille. Bruxelles, 1854. 2v.
39534.19.9 Furetière, Antoine. Le Roman bourgeois. Paris, 1854.
38525.22.2 Gandar, E. Ronsard considéré comme imitateur d'Homère et de Pindare. Metz, 1854.
39568.7 Gazette littéraire de Grimm. Paris, 1854.
41541.8 Girardin, Delphine Gay. La joie fait peur, comédie en un acte et en prose. Paris, 1854.
42576.64.9 Gramont, Ferdinand de. Chant du passé. Paris, 1854.
38546.48 Grignan, Françoise M. Extrait de quelques lettres de Mme. la comtesse de Grignan. Troyes, 1854.
Mon 170.1.5 Grün, A. Montaigne magistrat. Paris, 1854.
41567.23.2 Guizot, Elizabeth C.P. de M. Popular tales. Boston, 1854.
41573.32.4 Hugo, Victor. Hernani. Paris, 1854.
FL 398.17.9 Jacquot, C.J.B. Déjazet. Paris, 1854.
FL 390.84 Jallais, A. de. Sur la scène et dans la salle. Paris, 1854.
38564.25.8 La Bruyère, J. de. Les caractères. Paris, 1854.
38512.32 La Tour-Landry, Geoffrey de. Livre. Paris, 1854.
40512.58.9 LeSage, Alain René. The bachelor of Salamanca. Philadelphia, 1854. 2v.
40512.8.9 LeSage, Alain René. Histoire de Gil Blas de Santillane. Paris, 1854.
37596.23A Luzarche, Victor. Adam; drame Anglo-Normand. Tours, 1854.
38526.36 Maucroix, F. de. Oeuvres diverses. Paris, 1854. 2v.
42588.12 Mémoires de Bilboquet recueillis par un bourgeois de Paris. Paris, 1854.
42545.24.5 Meurice, Paul. Louspillac et Beautrubin. Paris, 1854.
42514.34.5 Mignet, F.A.M. Notices et portraits historiques et littéraires. 3. éd. Paris, 1854. 2v.
Mol 18.54A Molière, Jean Baptiste Poquelin. Oeuvres. Paris, 1854. 2v.
42545.38.10 Monnier, Henry. Les bourgeois de Paris. Paris, 1854.
42545.39 Monselet, Charles. Les aveux d'un pamphlétaire. Paris, 1854.
38512.33 Montaiglon, Anatole de. Livre du chevalier de La Tour-Landry. Paris, 1854.
Mon 18.54 Montaigne, Michel de. Essais. Louandre. Paris, 1854? 4v.
Mon 18.54.2A Montaigne, Michel de. Essais. Louandre. Paris, 1854. 4v.
Htn 42545.44.15* Moreau, Eugène. The courier of Lyons. v.1-2. London, 1854?
42577.25.2 Murger, Henry. Propos de ville et propos de théatre. Bruxelles, 1854.
38513.19 Mystère des actes des apôtres. Paris, 1854.
37566.21 Nettement, A.F. Histoire de la littérature française sous le gouvernement de juillet. Paris, 1854. 2v.
37547.20 Nicolas, Michel. Histoire littéraire de Nimes. Nimes, 1854. 3v.
38511.27 Pathelin. Maistre Pierre Patelin. Paris, 1854.
37593.54 Peigné-Delacourt, Achille. Analyse du Roman du Hem du trouvère Sarrazin. Arras, 1854.
42587.42.9 Pelletan, Eugène. Heures de travail. Paris, 1854. 2v.
40573.12 Planche, Gustave. Nouveaux portraits littéraires. Paris, 1854. 2v.
42534.30 Pontmartin, A.F. de. Le fond de la coupe. Paris, 1854.
38527.30 Postansque, M.A. Théodore Agrippa d'Aubigné. Montpellier, 1854.
42556.2 Prarond, Ernest. Les impressions et pensées d'Albert. Paris, 1854.
41547.19 Privat d'Anglemont, A. Paris anecdote. Paris, 1854.
Htn 38531.12.9* Rabelais, F. Oeuvres de...nouvelle. Paris, 1854.
38537.30.9 Rabelais, F. Works. London, 1854-55. 2v.
38585.43.45 Racine, Jean. Les plaideurs. Leipzig, 1854.
38583.4.21 Racine, Jean. Théâtre complet. Paris, 1854.
38527.9.26 Rathery, E.J.B. Vauquelin des Yveteaux. Paris, 1854.
38587.8.5 Regnard, Jean François. Oeuvres complètes avec notice et de nombreuses notes critiques. Paris, 1854. 2v.
42587.56.16 Rostaing, Jules. Voyage dans les deux Ameriques. Paris, 1854.
FL 6041.54 Rousseau, J.J. Émile ou De l'éducation. Paris, 1854.
41557.9.34 Sand, George. Histoire de ma vie. Paris, 1854. 10v.
Htn 41557.18.5* Sandeau, Jules. Mlle. de la Seiglière. 4e éd. Paris, 1854.
37563.27 Sayous, Pierre André. Études littéraires sur...la reformation. Paris, 1854. 2v.
42546.39 Serret, Ernest. Que dira le monde. 2e ed. Paris, 1854.
41578.41 Soullié, P. Études morales et littéraires sur la poésie lyrique en France. Paris, 1854.
41558.67.5 Souvestre, Émile. An attic philosopher in Paris. N.Y., 1854.

1854 - cont.

41558.41 Souvestre, Émile. Causeries historiques littéraires. Genève, 1854. 2v.
41558.62 Souvestre, Émile. Le mémorial de famille. Paris, 1854.
40592.29.5 Staël Holstein, Anne Louise. Corinne, or Italy. Philadelphia, 1854.
40592.23.2 Staël Holstein, Anne Louise. Corinne. N.Y., 1854.
41563.4.10 Sue, Eugène. Les sept péchés capitaux. L'envie - La colère. Paris, 1854-78. 2v.
38527.9.20 Vauquelin des Yveteaux, N. Les oeuvres poétiques de Vauquelin. Paris, 1854.
40584.20.3 Villemain, Abel L. Études de littérature ancienne et etrangère. Paris, 1854.
37565.9 Vinet, Alexandre R. History of French literature in the 18th century. Edinburgh, 1854.
37584.20A Viollet-Le-Duc, E.L.N. Ancien théâtre français. Paris, 1854-57. 20v.
39545.43.9 Voltaire, François Marie Arouet de. La Henriade. Paris, 1854.
42522.37 Weyer, Sylvain van der. Lettres fur les Anglais qui ont écrit en français. London? 1854?
38514.18.13A Ziwes, Armand. Oeuvres. Paris, 1854. 2 pam.

1855

37564.7 Astié, J.F. Louis XIV and the writers of his age. Boston, 1855.
38527.19.5 Aubigné, Théodore Agrippa d'. Avantures du Baron de Foeneste. Paris, 1855.
42542.24 Augier, Émile. Le mariage d'Olympe. Paris, 1855.
40596.4 Balzac, Honoré de. Oeuvres complètes. Paris, 1855. 20v.
41588.20.3 Barthet, Armand. The sparrow of Lesbia. N.Y., 1855.
42542.27.50 Bayard, J.F.A. Théâtre. Paris, 1855-58. 12v.
42586.18 Beauvoir, E.R. de. Confidences de Mlle. Mars. Paris, 1855.
42575.5.2 Bellemare, Louis de. Costal l'indien. Paris, 1855.
41522.27 Bernard, Charles de. Poésies et théâtre. Paris, 1855.
37565.20 Bersot, Ernest. Études sur le XVIIIe siècle. Etudes générale. Paris, 1855. 2v.
40582.30A Beyle, Henri. Chronique et nouvelles. Paris, 1855.
40582.18 Beyle, Henri. Nouvelles inédites. Paris, 1855.
37543.5 Bossange, H. Ma bibliothèque française. Paris, 1855.
FL 6021.55F Bougy, A. de. Les confessions de Jean-Jacques Rousseau. Paris, 1855.
39544.42 Brougham, H.B. Lives of men of letters. Voltaire, Rousseau, etc. London, 1855.
42586.27.15 Bungener, Félix. The preacher and the king or Bourdaloue in the court of Louis XIV. Boston, 1855.
39533.17 Chasles, Émile. Oeuvres choisies de Sénecé. Paris, 1855.
38512.22A Chassant, Alphonse. L'advocacie Notre Dame. Paris, 1855.
41593.17.3 Colet, Louise. Quatre poèmes. Paris, 1855.
FL 398.74.87 A collection of librettos of plays acted by Mlle. Rachel. N.Y., 1855. 5 pam.
38526.10.9 Collerye, Roger de. Oeuvres. Paris, 1855.
Mol 880.8 Coluzzi, G. I due Tartufi. Milano, 1855.
41593.175.5 Corday, Aglaé de. Les fleurs neustriennes. Mortagne, 1855-1857. 2v.
38575.32.9 Corneille, Pierre. Horacio...Original Frances con la traduccion...española. Naveva York, 1855.
40546.6.9 Courier de Méré, Paul Louis. Oeuvres. Paris, 1855.
40565.21 Cuvillier-Fleury, A.A. Nouvelles études historiques et littéraires. Paris, 1855.
FL 398.74.20 Darcie, John. The biography of Mdlle. Rachel. N.Y., 1855.
FL 398.74.21 Darcie and Corbyn's edition of Mlle. Rachel's readings. N.Y., 1855.
41583.22 Delavigne, Casimir. Oeuvres complètes. Paris, 1855. 6v.
38557.5.3 Delondre, Adrien. Doctrine philosophique de Bossuet. Paris, 1855.
42568.2 Deslys, Charles. La jarretière rose. v.1-2. Bruxelles, 1855.
Mon 182.2 Dosquet. Compte-rendu de la commission des monuments. Paris, 1855.
42543.14 Dumas, Alexandre. Le demi-monde. 6. éd. Paris, 1855.
41538.36.5 Dumas, Alexandre. Mademoiselle de belle-isle. N.Y., 1855.
41538.36 Dumas, Alexandre. Mademoiselle de belle-isle. N.Y., 1855.
42543.24.6 Dumas, Alexandre. Le roman d'une femme. Paris, 1855.
42543.25 Dumas, Alexandre. Trois hommes forts. Paris, 1855.
38514.59 Les evangiles des quenouilles. Paris, 1855.
38513.10 Flamang, Guillaume. La vie et passion de Monseigneur Sainct Didier. Paris, 1855.
38557.11 Floquet, Amable. Mémoires...sur Bossuet. Paris, 1855. 3v.
Mol 825.2 Fournier, Edouard. Molière et le procès du pain mollet. Paris, 1855.
37575.22 Fournier, Édouard. Variétés historiques et littéraires. Paris, 1855-63. 10v.
Htn 37575.20* Fournier, Édouard. Variétés historiques et littéraires. Paris, 1855-63. 10v.
42543.32 Fremy, Arnould. Les maitresses parisiennes. Paris, 1855.
FL 384.41PF Gallois, N. Théâtre et artistes dramatiques de Paris. Paris, 1855.
41542.34.10 Gautier, Théophile. Italia. 2. éd. Paris, 1855.
41542.37.3 Gautier, Théophile. Théâtre de poche. Paris, 1855.
FL 384.40 Geoffroy, C. Nouvelle galerie des artistes dramatiques vivants. Paris, 1855. 2v.
41593.32.40 Gerando, Joseph Marie de. Le fabuliste des familles. Strasbourg, 1855.
41541.13 Girardin, Delphine Gay. La croix de Berny. Paris, 1855.
41541.10.5 Girardin, Delphine Gay. La gioia fa paura. Milano, 1855.
41541.11.5 Girardin, Delphine Gay. Lady Tartuffe. N.Y., 1855.
41541.11.10 Girardin, Delphine Gay. Lady Tartuffe. N.Y., 1855.
42586.71 Grandfort, M. de. L'autre monde et la rose noire. N.Y., 1855.
41567.20 Grandfort, Manoël de. L'autre monde. Paris, 1855.
Mon 170.1 Grün, A. Vie publique de Michel Montaigne. Paris, 1855.
37537.4 Haas, F. Tableau historique de la littérature française. Darmstadt, 1855.
41573.32.20 Hugo, Victor. Angelo. N.Y., 1855.
37574.29 Illustrated book of French songs. London, 1855.
40562.19 Jacquot, C.J.B. Les contemporains - Lacordaire. Paris, 1855.
41545.14 Karr, Alphonse. Histoires normandes. Paris, 1855.
41544.36 Karr, Alphonse. A tour round my garden. London, 1855.
41578.27.5 Lamartine, Alphonse de. Geneviève, histoire d'une servante. Paris, 1855.

1855 - cont.

41577.12.55 Lamartine, Alphonse de. Lectures pour tous. 2e éd. Paris, 1855.
41554.36.50 Lanjiunais, Victor. Notice historique sur la vie et les ouvrages du Comte Lanjiunais. 2. éd. Paris, 1855.
38585.9 Larochefoucauld-Liancourt, Frédéric Gaëtan. Études littéraires et morales de Racine. Paris, 1855.
41586.2 Latour, Isidore. Virginie. N.Y., 1855.
41595.9.5 Lebrun, Pierre. Maria Stuardo. N.Y., 1855.
Htn 42555.36.10* Leconte de Lisle, C.M.R. Poèmes et poésies. Paris, 1855.
38563.11 Lenient, C. Étude sur Bayle. Paris, 1855.
40511.32 LeSage, Alain René. Historia de Gil Blas. Paris, 1855.
38512.18A Lescurel, Jehannot de. Chansons, ballades. Paris, 1855.
Mol 163.5 Lorin, T. Quelques observations...sur l'amphitryon. Soissons, 1855.
42526.6 Lucas, Hippolyte. Curiosités dramatiques. Paris, 1855.
38526.32.9 Marguerite d'Angoulême. The Heptaméron of Margaret, queen of Navarre. London, 1855.
38526.32.9.5 Marguerite d'Angoulême. The Heptaméron of Margaret, queen of Navarre. London, 1855.
39534.46 Marolles, Michel de. Le livre des peintres et graveurs. Poetry. Paris, 1855.
41595.23.5.8 Mayer, G. Eugène de Mirecourt. Paris, 1855.
42587.25 Méry, Joseph. Une nuit du midi. Paris, 1855.
42545.22 Meurice, Paul. Paris. Paris, 1855.
41595.23.5 Mirecourt, E. de. Méry. 4. éd. Paris, 1855.
Mol 245.33 Molière, Jean Baptiste Poquelin. Le misanthrope. Paris, 1855.
Mol 18.55 Molière, Jean Baptiste Poquelin. Oeuvres complètes...Charles. Paris, 1855-56. 5v.
Mol 209.5.6 Molière, Jean Baptiste Poquelin. Die Plagegeister. Oldenburg, 1855.
Mol 269.5.5 Molière, Jean Baptiste Poquelin. Der Tartüff. Laun. Oldenburg, 1855.
Htn 38516.3*A Montaiglon, Anatole. Recueil de poésies françaises des XVe et XVIe siècles. n.p., 1855-78. 13v.
39591.6 Montesquieu, C.L. de S. Oeuvres complètes. Paris, 1855.
39544.392A Noël, Eugene. Voltaire. Paris, 1855.
Mol 860.39 Peillon, F. Un poète inconnu. Paris, 1855.
40573.8 Planche, Gustave. Études littéraires. Paris, 1855.
40573.6 Planche, Gustave. Études sur l'école française. Paris, 1855. 2v.
40573.5 Planche, Gustave. Études sur les arts. Paris, 1855.
42541.30.3 Ponsard, François. L'honneur et l'argent. Paris, 1855.
37538.11 Prat, Henry. Études littéraires. XVIe siècle. Paris, 1855.
38585.19.10.5 Racine, Jean. Andrómaca; tragédia en cincos actos. Nueva York, 1855.
38585.18.35 Racine, Jean. Andromaque....with English translation. N.Y., 1855.
38585.23.30 Racine, Jean. Bajazet. Neuva-York, 1855.
38585.42.6 Racine, Jean. Fedra. Neuva-York, 1855.
38582.19.525 Racine, Jean. Oeuvres choisies. N.Y., 1855.
38582.19.15 Racine, Jean. Théâtre complète. Paris, 1855.
42535.15 Ratisbonne, Louis. Impressions littéraires. Paris, 1855.
41557.8.30 Saint-Félix, Jules de. Cléopatre, reine d'Egypte. v.1-2. Bruxelles, 1855.
41565.28 St. Mars, G.A.C. de C. Mademoiselle Robespierre. v.1-2. Paris, 1855.
41557.9.34.5 Sand, George. Histoire de ma vie. Paris, 1855. 4v.
41557.9.43.9 Sand, George. Maître Favilla. Paris, 1855.
41557.8.111 Sand, George. Mont-Revêche. Paris, 1855.
41557.9.55A Sand, George. Teverino; a romance. N.Y., 1855.
41557.16 Sandeau, Jules. Un héritage. Paris, 1855.
41588.3.5.6 Scribe, Eugène. Adriana Lecouvreur. N.Y., 1855.
41588.3.5 Scribe, Eugène. Adrienne Lecouvreur. N.Y., 1855.
41588.15.8.7 Scribe, Eugène. The ladies' battle. Boston, 1855? 2 pam.
41588.15.8.6 Scribe, Eugène. The ladies' battle. N.Y., 1855? 9 pam.
41558.54 Souvestre, Émile. The lake shore. Boston, 1855.
41558.52 Souvestre, Émile. Leaves from a family journal. N.Y., 1855.
41558.65.2 Souvestre, Émile. Un philosophe sous les toits. 8e éd. Paris, 1855.
38575.4 Tachereau, Jules. Histoire de...Pierre Corneille. 2e éd. Paris, 1855.
Mol 828.1 Truinet, Charles. Pourquoi Molière n'a pas joué les avocats. Paris, 1855.
Mol 870.11 Vierne, Edouard. Molière enfant. Paris, 1855.
41564.3.53 Vigny, Alfred de. Cinq-Mars. 11. éd. Paris, 1855.
37573.2.10 Vinet, Alexander R. Chrestomathie française. Littérature de l'adolescence. v.2. 6. éd. Bale, 1855.
37573.1 Vinet, Alexander R. Chrestomathie française. Littérature de l'enfance. Bruxelles, 1855.
38542.2 Voiture, Vincent. Oeuvres. Lettres et poésies. Paris, 1855. 2v.
39543.45 Voltaire, François Marie Arouet de. Esprit de Voltaire. Paris, 1855.
41588.50.5 Wafflard, A.J.M. Théatre français...Le voyage a Dieppe. 5e éd. Bielefeld, 1855.
FL 383.19 Welsch, A. De la réédification du théâtre en France. Paris, 1855.
FL 6135.2 Wuaren, J.F. De l'inauguration de la statue de Jean-Jacques Rousseau. Genève, 1855.

1856

42562.28 About, Edmond. Les mariages de Paris. Boston, 1856.
42562.34 About, Edmond. Tolla. Edinburgh, 1856.
37596.251 Agnès de Navarre. Champagne. Poésies. Paris, 1856.
42542.20 Augier, Émile. Gabrielle. Paris, 1856.
42562.38.21 Aunet, Léonie d'. Un marriage en province. v.1-2. Paris, 1856.
41522.2.33 Barbey d'Aurevilly, Jules. Memorandum. Caen, 1856.
42542.27.21.5 Barrière, Théodore. Les faux bonshommes. Paris, 1856.
38514.120 Baude, Henri. Les vers de maître Henri Baude. Paris, 1856.
FL 398.74.24A Beauvallet, Léon. Rachel and the new world. N.Y., 1856.
FL 398.74.22 Beauvallet, Léon. Rachel et le nouveau-monde. Paris, 1856.
42575.5.5 Bellemare, Louis de. Le coureur des bois. tom.2. 4. éd. Paris, 1856.
42575.11 Bellemare, Louis de. Scènes de la vie mexicaine. Paris, 1856.
41592.11.12 Béranger, P.J. de. Oeuvres complétes de P.J. de Béranger. Paris, 1856. 2v.

Chronological Listing

1856 - cont.

41592.30 Béranger, P.J. de. Songs. London, 1856.

38526.2.4 Bèze, Théodore de. Tragédie Françoise du sacrifice d'Abraham. N.Y., 1856.

X Cg 37573.24 Blocquel, S. Le tresor des bons mots. Paris, 1856.

42542.35 Bouilhet, Louis. Madame de Montarcy. Paris, 1856.

42542.47.45 Bruno, W. Études shakespeariennes. 1. série. Paris, 1856.

42586.25.15 Bungener, Félix. The priest and the Huguenot. Boston, 1856. 2v.

42586.25.14 Bungener, Félix. The priest and the Huguenot. Boston, 1856. 2v.

Mol 882.1 Castil-Blaze. Bernalo, opéra bouffe. Paris, 1856.

38566.25 Castres, G.H.F. de. L'art poétique de Boileau. Leipzig, 1856.

39544.80 Ceballos, F. Juicio final de Voltaire. v.1-2. Sevilla, 1856.

41593.17.50 Debuire du Buc, L. Les lilloises. Lille, 1856-1859. 2 pam.

42542.60.703 Decourcelle, Adrien. Fais ce que dois. Paris, 1856.

42542.61.14 Decourcelle, Adrien. Je dine chez ma mère. Paris, 1856.

41584.27.63 Ducange, Victor. Trente ans. Paris, 1856.

37555.326 Ducondut, J.A. Essai de rhythmique française. Paris, 1856.

42542.68 Dumanoir, M. Les fanfarons de vices. Paris, 1856.

42543.13.7 Dumas, Alexandre. Aventuras de cuatro mugeres y un loro. v.1,4,5. Madrid, 1856-57. 3v.

42543.13 Dumas, Alexandre. Aventures de quatre femmes. Paris, 1856.

42543.15.8 Dumas, Alexandre. Camille; or The fate of a coquette. N.Y., 1856?

42543.18 Dumas, Alexandre. Diane de Lys. Paris, 1856.

41538.26 Dumas, Alexandre. Lièvre de mon grand-père. Paris, 1856.

42543.27 Dumas, Alexandre. La vie à vingt ans. Paris, 1856.

FL 375.5 Ebert, A. Entwicklungs-Geschichte des Französischen Tragödien im 16 Jahrhunderts. Gotha, 1856.

FL 6029.2 Estienne, C. Essai sur les confessions de Jean-Jacques Rousseau. Paris, 1856.

38582.20 Fasquelle, Louis. Chefs d'oeuvre de Jean Racine. N.Y., 1856.

38553.25.7 Fénelon, F. de S. de la Mothe. Les aventures de Télémaque. Paris, 1856.

38558.5.5 Fléchier, Esprit. Oeuvres complètes. Paris, 1856. 2v.

42564.41 Fleury, Jules. Les bourgeois de Molinchart. Paris, 1856.

42564.13.25 Fleury, Jules. Gazette de Champfleury. v.1-2. Paris, 1856.

42543.30.3 Fournier, Narcisse. Les absences de monsieur. Paris, 1856.

42543.32.3 Fremy, Arnould. Les maitresses parisiennes. Paris, 1856.

37548.8 Gaullieur, Eusèbe H. Études...littéraires de la Suisse française. Paris, 1856.

41542.17.5 Gautier, Théophile. Voyage en Espagne. Paris, 1856.

41541.9.5 Girardin, Delphine Gay. Nouvelles. Paris, 1856.

37596.53 Guillaume de Ferrières. Chansons and saluts d'amour. Paris, 1856.

42584.29 Hetzel, P.J. L'esprit des femmes et les femmes d'esprit. 5. éd. Paris, 1856.

37595.17 Heyse, Paul. Romanische Inedita auf Italianischen Bibliotheken. Berlin, 1856.

42576.14.13 Houssaye, Arsène. Voyages humoristiques. Paris, 1856.

41572.24.7 Hugo, Victor. Les contemplations. 2e éd. Paris, 1856.

40575.1.5 Jacquol, Eugene de Mirecourt. Sainte-Beuve. Paris, 1856.

38528.22.2A Lacour, Louis. Oeuvres des Periers. Paris, 1856. 2v.

Htn 38528.22* Lacour, Louis. Oeuvres des Periers. Paris, 1856. 2v.

FL 365.60 Lacroix, Albert. Histoire de l'influence de Shakespeare sur le théâtre français. Bruxelles, 1856.

41554.34 Lacroix, Appoline. Falcone. Bruxelles, 1856.

Mol 712.2 Lacroix, Paul. La jeunesse de Molière. Bruxelles, 1856.

41577.15.10 Lamartine, Alphonse de. Les confidences. Paris, 1856. 2 pam.

41578.2 Lamartine, Alphonse de. Cours familier de littérature. Paris, 1856-69. 28v.

41578.8 Lamartine, Alphonse de. Nouvelles méditations poétiques. v.2. Paris, 1856.

39532.17.5 La Monnoye, Bernard de. Lettres inédites de Bernard de La Monnoye addressées à son fils le R.P. de La Monnoye. Dijon, 1856.

38557.8 Le Dieu, François. Mémoires...sur Bossuet. Paris, 1856-57. 4v.

42544.7.4 Legouvé, Ernest. Médée. Paris, 1856.

42541.20 Legouvé, Ernest. Médée. Paris, 1856.

40583.128 The life and writings of M. de Stendhal (Henri Beyle). London, 1856.

Mol 167.5 Lorin, T. Remarques sur l'avare. Soissons, 1856.

42548.13.9 Madinier, Henry. Amour et typographie. Paris, 1856.

42541.71 Magasin théâtral illustré. Paris, 1856- 3v.

41586.24 Maurice-Descombes, Charles. Histoire anecdotique du théatre de la littérature. Paris, 1856. 2v.

42577.13 Maynard, Félix. Souvenirs d'un Zouave devant Sebastopol. Paris, 1856.

38547.38 Mémoires de Hollande. Paris, 1856.

41586.23.45 Méry, Joseph. André Chénier. Paris. 1856.

42587.23.5 Méry, Joseph. Les matinées du Louvre. Paradoxes et rêveries. Paris, 1856.

39545.16 Meyer, J.B. Voltaire und Rousseau. Berlin, 1856.

41578.68.45 Mirecourt, E. de. Lamartine. 7. éd. Paris, 1856.

41588.15.9 Mirécourt, Eugène de. Scribe. Paris, 1856.

Mol 266.10 Molière, Jean Baptiste Poquelin. El amor pintor. Matanzas, 1856.

Mol 165.28 Molière, Jean Baptiste Poquelin. L'avare...Fiebig and Leportier. Leipzig, 1856.

Mol 211.26 Molière, Jean Baptiste Poquelin. Les femmes savantes...Estienne. Paris, 1856?

Mol 236.30 Molière, Jean Baptiste Poquelin. Klaos Pompernikkel. Mastreeg, 1856.

Mol 268.43 Molière, Jean Baptiste Poquelin. Le Tartuffe. Fiebig et Leportier. Leipzig, 1856.

Mon 31.30 Montaigne, Michel de. Works...essays, letters...journey through Germany and Italy. 4. ed. Philadelphia, 1856.

42577.29.50 Murger, Henry. Scènes de campagne. Paris, 1856.

41596.18 Musset, Alfred de. Comédies et proverbes. Paris, 1856. 2v.

40572.25 Nisard, Désiré. Études d'histoire de la littérature. Paris, 1856.

42587.37.6 Noisey, C.B. La fille de l'aveugle. Rouen, 1856.

41587.18.18 Picard, Louis Benoît. The parasite. Leipzig, 1856.

1856 - cont.

42545.78.30 Plouvier, Édouard. Le sang-mêlé; drame en cinq actes, en prose. Paris, 1856.

38515.15 Poésies d'Agnès...Dame de Foia. Reims, 1856.

42545.83.3 Ponsard, F. La bourse. 2e éd. Paris, 1856.

42534.18 Pontmartin, A.F. de. La fin du procès. Paris, 1856.

42534.27 Pontmartin, A.F. de. Mémoires d'un notaire. Paris, 1856.

37538.12 Prat, Henry. Études littéraires. XVIIe siècle. Paris, 1856-59. 3v.

38514.21.15 Profillet, A. De la vie et des ouvrage de François Villon. Chalans-sur-Maine, 1856.

38582.13 Racine, Jean. Oeuvres complètes. Paris, 1856. 2v.

41568.6.5 Reybaud, Charles (Mrs.). Mademoiselle de Malepeire. Paris, 1856.

41557.4 Reybaud, Louis. Le dernier des commis voyageurs. Paris, 1856.

42556.27.120 Reynier, Paul. Oeuvres choisies. Marseille, 1856.

42558.30 Rouquette, Dominique. Fleurs d'Amerique. New Orleans, 1856.

FL 6026.12 Rousseau, J.J. Confessions. N.Y., 1856. 2v.

FL 6051.56 Rousseau, J.J. La nouvelle Héloise. Paris, 1856.

Mol 167.4 Saegelken, E. De Molieri fabula avari nomine. Bremae, 1856.

41587.21.5 Saint-Georges, J.H.V. de. Fanchonette; opéra comique en trois actes. Paris, 1856.

39594.34.20 St. Pierre, J.H.B. de. Paul and Virginia. Philadelphia, 1856.

41557.8.65 Sand, George. Consuelo. Paris, 1856. 3v.

41557.9.29 Sand, George. Evenor et Leucippe. Paris, 1856.

41557.8.85.5 Sand, George. Jacques. Paris, 1856.

41557.8.93.5 Sand, George. Lucie. Paris, 1856.

41557.8.107.5 Sand, George. Mauprat. Paris, 1856.

41557.27.4 Sandeau, Jules. Sacs et parchemins. Paris, 1856.

41557.27.3 Sandeau, Jules. Sacs et parchemins. Paris, 1856.

41588.11 Scribe, Eugène. Nouvelles. Paris, 1856.

41588.4 Scribe, Eugène. Théâtre. 1e série. Paris, 1856.

41588.5 Scribe, Eugène. Théâtre. 2e série. Paris, 1856.

38546.42.5 Sévigné, Marie de R.C. Letters. N.Y., 1856.

38546.44.2 Sévigné, Marie de R.C. Lettres. Paris, 1856.

37576.4 Société des bibliophiles. Mélanges de littérature et d'histoire. pt.1-2. Paris, 1856-67. 2v.

37564.27A Somaize, Antoine de. Le dictionnaire des precieuses. Paris, 1856. 2v.

41558.6.25 Soulié, Frédéric. La lionne. Oeuvres complètes. Paris, 1856.

41558.67 Souvestre, Émile. An attic philosopher in Paris. N.Y., 1856.

41558.43 Souvestre, Émile. Au coin du feu. Paris, 1856.

41558.48.5 Souvestre, Émile. Les derniers paysans. Paris, 1856. 2 pam.

41563.3 Sue, Eugène. Le fils de famille. Bruxelles, 1856. 7v.

FL 398.49.13 Talma, F. Réflexions de Talma sur Lekain et l'art théâtral. Paris, 1856.

39545.25.3 Théâtre de Voltaire. Paris, 1856.

38526.49 Théophile de Viau. Oeuvres complètes. Paris, 1856. 2v.

41564.10 Vigny, Alfred de. Stello. 7. ed. Paris, 1856.

41593.27.50 Villeneuve, M.T. de. Éloge de Jacques Delille. Toulouse, 1856.

38542.1 Voiture, Vincent. Les oeuvres. Paris, 1856.

Mol 880.34 Wood, George. The Irish doctor. London, 1856?

1857

42562.27 About, Edmond. Germaine. Paris, 1857.

42562.27.5 About, Edmond. Germaine. Le roi des Montagnes. 2. éd. Paris, 1857.

38527.28.2 Aubigné, Théodore Agrippa d'. Les tragiques. Paris, 1857.

42542.7 Augier, Émile. Un homme de bien. Paris, 1857.

42542.15.5 Augier, Émile. Poésies complètes. Paris, 1857.

42542.27.21.9A Barrière, Théodore. Les faux bonshommes. 2. éd. Paris, 1857.

42542.27.21.7 Barrière, Théodore. Les faux bonshommes. 3. éd. Paris, 1857.

41592.18.14A Béranger, P.J. de. Dernières chansons. Paris, 1857.

41591.13.50 Béranger, P.J. de. Ma biographie, ouvrage posthume. Paris, 1857.

41592.31 Béranger, P.J. de. Two hundred lyrical poems. N.Y., 1857.

41522.39.4 Bernard, Charles de. Un homme sérieux. Paris, 1857.

40582.8.5 Beyle, Henri. Chartreuse de Parme. Paris, 1857.

40582.8.3.50 Beyle, Henri. De l'amour. Paris, 1857.

38566.17.8 Boileau Despréaux, Nicolas. Oeuvres poétiques. Paris, 1857.

42542.35.5 Bouilhet, Louis. Melaenis. Paris, 1857.

38527.37.55 Boulmier, J. Etienne Dolet. Paris, 1857.

41566.16 Bourgeois, A. Brins d'herbe et un tour à pied. Morlaux, 1857.

38528.14.7 Brantôme, P. de B. de. Oeuvres. Paris, 1857.

42587.50.58.10 Broglio, V. Cenni sulla vita e sugli scritti della principessa Maria Wyse-Solms-Bonaparte. Milano, 1857.

39534.1.20 Bussy-Rabutin. Histoire amoureuse des Gaules. Paris, 1857. 2v.

39534.2 Bussy-Rabutin. Histoire amoureuse des Gaules. 2. éd. Paris, 1857-58. 2v.

37572.23 Chapsal, C.P. Leçons de littérature française. N.Y., 1857.

37584.8 Chefs-d'oeuvre des auteurs comiques. 1. Paris, 1857.

41592.12 Colet, Louise. Quarante-cinq letters de Béranger. Paris, 1857.

38514.63.3A Coquillart, Guillaume. Oeuvres. Paris, 1857. 2v.

38574.4 Corneille, Pierre. Oeuvres complètes. Paris, 1857. 2v.

40554.8 Cousin, Victor. Fragments et souvenirs. Paris, 1857.

41583.20.10 Delavigne, Casimir. Théâtre. Paris, 1857. 3v.

41595.23.5.9 Deschamps, Théophile. Biographie de Jaquot dit de Mirecourt. 3. éd. Paris, 1857.

42554.29.10 Dubreil, L.A. Poésies. Paris, 1857.

42543.15.11.5 Dumas, Alexandre. The camelia-lady. Philadelphia, 1857.

42543.15.3 Dumas, Alexandre. La dame aux camélias. Paris, 1857.

41538.19.15 Dumas, Alexandre. Dame de volupte. v.1-3. Bruxelles, 1857.

42543.14.2 Dumas, Alexandre. Le demi-monde. 6. éd. Paris, 1857.

42543.22 Dumas, Alexandre. La question d'argent. Paris, 1857.

42543.15.10 Dumas Alexandre. Camille. Cincinnati, 1857.

38575.16.3 Duparay, B. Des principes de Corneille sur l'art dramatique. Lyon, 1857.

1857 - cont.

38554.322.60 Fénelon, F. de S. de la Mothe. De l'existence et des attributs de Dieu. Paris, 1857.
42575.27.2 Feuillet, Octave. Dalila. Paris, 1857.
42564.52 Fleury, Jules. Grandeur et décadence d'une serinette. Paris, 1857.
Htn 42564.28* Fleury, Jules. Le réalisme. Paris, 1857.
40515.30.5 Florian, Jean P.C. de. Fables de Florian. Paris, 1857.
37558.6 Fontaine de Resbecq, Adolphe C.T. Voyages littéraires sur le Quais de Paris. Paris, 1857.
38561.25 Fournier, E. La Bruyère. Paris, 1857.
38537.42A Francon, Marcel. Autour de la lettre de Gargantua à son fils. Rachecorbon, 1857.
39545.2 Gaberel, J. Voltaire et les Genevois. Paris, 1857.
Htn 41542.37.13* Gautier, Théophile. Paul d'Aspremont. Paris, 1857.
40588.18 Genlis, S.F.D. de St. Le siège de la Rochelle. N.Y., 1857.
FL 6148.57 Genoux, C. Les enfants de Jean-Jacques Rousseau. Paris, 1857.
41541.12 Girardin, Delphine Gay. Contes d'une vieille fille à ses neveux. Paris, 1857.
38539.7 Gougny, Edmond. Guillaume Du Vair. Paris, 1857.
41542.83.30 Guérin, Eugène Louis. Le testament d'un gueux. v.1-2. Bruxelles, 1857.
42576.38.26 Guéroult, Constant. Le juif de Gand. v.1-4. Paris, 1857. 2v.
42587.2 Hetzel, Pierre Jules. Les bijoux parlants. Paris, 1857.
42576.14.45 Houssaye, Arsène. Les femmes comme elles sont. 2. éd. Paris, 1857.
37558.35.5 Houssaye, Arsène. Histoire de 41me fauteuil. Paris, 1857.
41544.6.9 Karr, Alphonse. Les femmes. Paris, 1857.
41545.10 Karr, Alphonse. Geneviève. Paris, 1857.
41545.12 Karr, Alphonse. Hortense. Feu Bressier. Paris, 1857.
41544.34.5 Karr, Alphonse. Voyage autour de mon jardin. Paris, 1857.
NEDL 38512.14 Kervyn de Lettenhove. Froissart. Étude littéraire. Brussels, 1857. 2v.
41554.24 Lacroix, Paul. De près et de loin. Bruxelles, 1857. 2v.
41578.16 Lamartine, Alphonse de. Les confidences. Paris, 1857.
38514.56.3 La Sale, Antoine de. Les quinze joyes de mariage. Paris, 1857.
42585.43 Lavergne, A. Le cadet de famille. N.Y., 1857.
41595.6 Lebrèton, T. Heures de repos d'un ouvrier. Rouen, 1857.
41595.13 Le Fevre-Deumier, J. Le couvre-feu. Paris, 1857.
42544.16.5 Legouvé, Ernest. Medea. London, 1857.
42544.7.7 Legouvé, Ernest. Medea. N.Y., 1857.
39545.10 Léouzon le Duc, L. Voltaire et la Police. Paris, 1857.
39532.18 Loret, Jean. Muse historique. Paris, 1857-78. 4v.
42576.73.3 Lucas, Louis. Le roman alchimique. Paris, 1857.
42545.8 Maquet, A. Valéria. Paris, 1857.
41595.23.5.10 Mazerolle, Pierre. Confession d'un biographe. Paris, 1857.
37558.30 Mesnard, Paul. Histoire de l'Académie française. Paris, 1857.
38512.9 Meunier, Francis. Essai sur Nicole Oresme. Paris, 1857.
Mol 38.57 Molière, Jean Baptiste Poquelin. Oeuvres choisies. N.Y., 1857.
42545.34 Monnier, Henry. Mémoires de M. Joseph Prudhomme. Paris, 1857. 2v.
37542.34.25 Monselet, Charles. La lorgnette littéraire. Paris, 1857.
42577.13.29 Montépin, X. de. Les viveurs de Paris. Paris, 1857. 4v.
41596.19.2 Musset, Alfred de. Nouvelles. Paris, 1857.
42545.69.62A Pierron, Eugène. Two can play at that game. Boston, 1857?
42515.66 Quinet, Edgar. Oeuvres complètes de Edgar Quinet. Paris, 1857-70. 11v.
38531.13A Rabelais, F. Oeuvres. Paris, 1857.
38583.4.23 Racine, Jean. Théâtre complet. Paris, 1857.
37577.36 Recueil des Plaisants devis recites par les supposts du Seigneur de la Coquille. Lyon, 1857.
37585.20 Recueils de comédies. Paris, 1857. 6 pam.
37585.19 Recueils de comédies. Paris, 1857-69. 6 pam.
40573.25 Rémusat, Charles de. Critiques et études littéraires. Paris, 1857. 2v.
FL 1108.243.100 Renard, Michel. Les aventures de Jean d'Nivelles, el fils dé s'paire. Bruxelles, 1857.
38525.10 Rochambeau, Vimeur. La famille de Ronsart. Paris, 1857.
38525.14A Ronsard, Pierre de. Oeuvres. Paris, 1857. 8v.
42583.37.2 Saint-Germain, J. de. L'art d'être malheureux. 2. éd. Paris, 1857.
38526.48.6 Saint-Julien. Les courriers de la fronde. Paris, 1857. 2v.
39594.34.23 St. Pierre, J.H.B. de. Paul and Virginia. N.Y., 1857.
40576.3 Sainte-Beuve, Charles A. Causeries du lundi. Paris, 1857-62. 15v.
40576.3.12 Sainte-Beuve, Charles A. Causeries du lundi. 3. éd. Paris, 1857?-83. 15v.
41557.8.62 Sand, George. La comtesse de Rudolstadt. v.1-2. Paris, 1857.
41557.8.85 Sand, George. Jacques. Paris, 1857.
41557.8.94.3 Sand, George. Lucrezia Floriani. Paris, 1857.
39534.28.9 Scarron, Paul. Le roman comique. Paris, 1857. 2v.
41588.5.2 Scribe, Eugène. Théâtre. Paris, 1857.
X Cg 41588.6 Scribe, Eugène. Théâtre. 6e série. Paris, 1857.
41588.7 Scribe, Eugène. Théâtre. 7e série. Paris, 1857.
40545.24 Simonde de Sismondi, Jean Charles Léonard. Fragments de son journal et correspondance. Genève, 1857.
Mol 863.19 Soupé, A.P. L'ombre de Molière. Grenoble, 1857.
41558.40.10 Souvestre, Émile. Brittany and La Vendée. N.Y., 1857.
41558.57.5 Souvestre, Émile. La goutte d'eau. Paris, 1857.
41558.65.3 Souvestre, Émile. Un philosophe sous les toits. Paris, 1857.
40592.24.10 Staël Holstein, Anne Louise. Corinne. Paris, 1857.
41561.16 Sue, Eugène. Les mystères du peuple. Boston, 1857.
42583.34.9 Tardieu, J.R. Pour une épingle. 3. éd. Paris, 1857.
37596.42.2 Thibaut I, King of Navarre. Chansons. Reins, 1857.
42557.5.1100 Turquety, Edouard. Oeuvres de Edouard Turquety: Amour et foi, poésie catholique, hymnes sacrées. 5. éd. Paris, 1857.
42547.8.25 Uchard, Mario. La fiammina. Cienfuegos, 1857.
42547.7.3 Uchard, Mario. La fiammina. Paris, 1857.
42547.7.4 Uchard, Mario. La fiammina. Paris, 1857.
42547.7 Uchard, Mario. La fiammina. 3e éd. Paris, 1857.
41564.7 Vigny, Alfred de. Servitude et grandeur militaires. 7. ed. Paris, 1857.
37536.7 Villemain, A.F. Cours de littérature française. Paris, 1857. 2v.
37566.8 Vinet, Alexandre R. Études sur la littérature française au 19me siècle. Paris, 1857. 3v.
38526.70.9 Viret, Pierre. Satyres chrestienes de la cuisine papale. Genève, 1857.
38514.21.13 Watripon, Antonio. Les génies de la tradition française. François Villon. Paris, 1857.
42587.70.33 Weill, Alexandre. Couronne; histoire juive. Paris, 1857.

1858

42562.29 About, Edmond. Les mariages de Paris. Boston, 1858.
42562.37.6 Achard, Amédée E. Les petits fils de Lovelace. Paris, 1858.
42553.29 Amiel, Henri F. Il pensoroso. Genève, 1858.
42562.38.19 Asselineau, L. La double vie. Paris, 1858.
FL 384.44 Audibert, Hilanon. Indiscrétions et confidences. Paris, 1858.
42542.22 Augier, Émile. Les lionnes pauvres. Paris, 1858.
FL 398.74.29 B., de Madame. Mémoirs of Rachel. London, 1858.
FL 398.74.28A B., de Madame. Mémoirs of Rachel. London, 1858. 2v.
42542.27.21.13 Barrière, Théodore. Les faux bonshommes. Paris, 1858.
42542.27.21.11 Barrière, Théodore. Les faux bonshommes. 4. éd. Paris, 1858.
42575.11.2 Bellemare, Louis de. Scènes de la vie militaire au Mexique. Paris, 1858.
41592.18 Béranger, P.J. de. Chansons, 1815-1834. Paris, 1858.
41592.11.5 Béranger, P.J. de. Memoirs of Béranger. London, 1858.
41592.11.7 Béranger, P.J. de. Memoirs of Béranger. 2nd ed. London, 1858.
41591.3.7A Béranger, P.J. de. Oeuvres complètes. v.2. Paris, 1858.
41592.35 Béranger, P.J. de. Oeuvres posthumes de...dernières chansons. Paris, 1858.
41522.46 Bernard, Charles de. Le paravent. Bruxelles, 1858.
41522.55 Bernard, Charles de. La peau du lion. Paris, 1858.
41592.8.5 Bernard, Joseph. Béranger et ses chansons. Paris, 1858.
40582.19.5 Beyle, Henri. Promenades dans Rome. Paris, 1858. 2v.
Htn 37575.8* Bibliothèque façétieuse. Paris, 1858. 8v.
39578.7 Bore, Léon. Étude sur Vauvenargues. Paris, 1858.
38557.50.30 Bossuet, J.B. Le Bossuet des gens du monde. Paris, 1858.
Htn 37578.42* Bougy, Alfred de. Un million de rimes gauloises. Paris, 1858.
42542.45 Bourgeois, Anicet. Les petites Lachetes. Paris, 1858.
38514.48 Brézé, Jacques de. Le livre de la chasse du grand seneschal. Paris, 1858.
41583.17 Brifaut, Charles. Oeuvres. Paris, 1858. 6v.
39534.5.4 Bussy-Rabutin. Correspondance de Roger de Rabutin. Paris, 1858-59. 6v.
42563.70 Chabrillan, Celeste. Mémoires de Célèste Mogador. Paris, 1858.
42554.18.25 Chastan, Auguste. Chansons, satires. Valréas, 1858.
41593.16.12 Chevigné, L. de. Les contes Rémois. 3. éd. Paris, 1858.
41593.16.13 Chevigné, L. de. Les contes Rémois. 3. éd. Paris, 1858.
42586.32.9 Coster, Charles de. Légendes flamandes. Paris, 1858.
39586.27.40 Curnier, Léonce. Rivarol, sa vie et ses oeuvres. Nîmes, 1858.
39533.20.4A Cyrano de Bergerac. Histoire comique des etats...de la lune et du soleil. Paris, 1858.
38528.23 Despériers, Bonaventure. Cymbalum mundi. Paris, 1858.
38526.12.33 Desportes, Philippe. Oeuvres. Paris, 1858.
41584.17 Doucet, Camille. Le fruit défendu. Paris, 1858.
42542.67 Dumanoir, M. Les femmes terribles. Paris, 1858.
42543.15.5 Dumas, Alexandre. La dame aux camélias. Paris, 1858.
42543.14.5A Dumas, Alexandre. The "Demi-Monde". Philadelphia, 1858.
42543.19.19 Dumas, Alexandre. Le fils naturel. Paris, 1858.
37585.23 Essais dramatiques. Moulins, 1858. 3 pam.
FL 6138.58 Estienne, C. Essai sur les oeuvres de Jean-Jacques Rousseau. Paris, 1858.
42564.27 Fleury, Jules. Les premiers beaux jours. Paris, 1858.
42564.34 Fleury, Jules. L'usurier Blaizot. Paris, 1858.
Mol 810.1 Fournier, E. La farce avant Molière. Paris, 1858.
FL 6128.58 Gaberel, M.J. Rousseau et les Génévois. Genève, 1858.
39534.44A Gaultier, Garguille. Chansons. Paris, 1858.
FL 382.5.2 Gautier, T. Histoire de l'art dramatique en France depuis vingt-cinq ans. Bruxelles, 1858-59. 6v.
FL 382.5 Gautier, T. Histoire de l'art dramatique en France depuis vingt-cinq ans. Paris, 1858-59. 6v.
Htn 41542.8.6* Gautier, Théophile. Émaux et camées. 2. éd. Paris, 1858.
41541.5.30 Girardin, Émile de. La fille du millionnaire. Paris, 1858.
41542.51 Gozlan, Léon. Un petit bout d'oreille; comédie. Paris, 1858.
38526.18 Gringore, Pierre. Oeuvres complètes. Paris, 1858. 2v.
38575.6 Guizot, François. Corneille and his time. Paris, 1858.
42543.68 Halévy, Leon. Ce que fille veut. Paris, 1858.
Mol 800.3 Hillemacher, F. Galerie des portraits des comédiens de la troupe de Molière. Lyon, 1858.
37567.14 Honnegger, J.J. Victor Hugo, Lamartine. Zürich, 1858.
39544.5 Houssaye, Arsène. Le Roi Voltaire. Paris, 1858.
39544.4 Houssaye, Arsène. Le Roi Voltaire. Paris, 1858.
41572.24.8 Hugo, Victor. Les contemplations. 5e ed. Paris, 1858. 2v.
41572.9 Hugo, Victor. Notre-Dame de Paris. Paris, 1858. 2v.
41572.32.10 Hugo, Victor. Théâtre. Paris, 1858. 2 pam.
41572.32.5 Hugo, Victor. Théâtre. Paris, 1858.
41573.27 Hugo, Victor. Théâtre. Paris, 1858.
41572.32 Hugo, Victor. Théâtre. Marie Tudor. Paris, 1858.
40561.24 Janin, Jules. Les symphonies. Paris, 1858.
41544.11.5 Karr, Alphonse. Les guêpes. Paris, 1858. 3v.
42514.23 Laboulaye, Edouard. Souvenirs d'un voyageur. Paris, 1858.
Mol 712.2.2 Lacroix, Paul. La jeunesse de Molière. Bruxelles, 1858.
Htn 39533.20* Lacroix, Paul. Oeuvres...de Cyrano de Bergerac. Paris, 1858.
38514.36 Lacroix, Paul. Vaux-de-vire d'Olivier Basselin. Paris, 1858.
39526.32.5 La Fontaine, Jean de. Fables. Paris, 1858.
40526.20 La Grange-Chancel, Joseph de. Les Philippiques Odes. Paris, 1858.
38543.10.7 La Rochefoucauld, François. Maximes. Pensées...Montesquieu oeuvres...Vauvenagues. Paris, 1858.
Htn 39533.24* Laurent, Émile. Aventures....de D'Assoucy. Paris, 1858.
37558.15 Laurent, Émile. Ruelles, salons, et cabarets. Paris, 1858.
38567.4 Laverdet, Auguste. Correspondence entre Boileau et Brossette. Paris, 1858.

Chronological Listing

1858 - cont.

42513.49 Le Carpentier, P.H.M. Essais lipogrammatiques. Paris, 1858.
42555.36.7 Leconte de Lisle, C.M.R. Poésies complètes. Paris, 1858.
42544.12.2 Legouvé, Ernest. Par droit de conquête. Paris, 1858.
41588.29.15 Lockroy, Joseph P. Pourquoi? 2e éd. Bielefeld, 1858.
42544.35 Lurine, Louis. La boite d'argent. Paris, 1858.
40556.28.4 Maistre, Joseph de. Lettres inédits. St. Petersbourg, 1858.
40588.37 Maistre, Xavier. Oeuvres complètes. Paris, 1858.
41586.20 Mazères, Edouard Joseph E. Comédies et souvenirs. Paris, 1858. 3v.
FL 362.30 Møller, P.L. Det nyere lystspil i Frankrig og Danmark. København, 1858.
42587.33 Molènes, Paul de. Caractères et récits du temps. Paris, 1858.
Mol 166.5.4 Molière, Jean Baptiste Poquelin. Der Geizige...F. Dingelstedt. Weimar, 1858.
Mol 269.70.12 Molière, Jean Baptiste Poquelin. El hipocrita; comédia. Madrid, 1858.
Mol 38.58 Molière, Jean Baptiste Poquelin. Oeuvres choisies. N.Y., 1858.
Mol 18.58 Molière, Jean Baptiste Poquelin. Oeuvres complètes...Louandre. Paris, 1858. 3v.
42545.38 Monnier, Henry. Les Bourgeois aux champs. Paris, 1858.
42545.38.15 Monnier, Henry. Croquis à la plume. Paris, 1858.
42545.38.5 Monnier, Henry. Galerie d'originaux. Paris, 1858.
40524.32.25 Monselet, Charles. Restif de la Bretonne. Paris, 1858.
41596.10.5 Musset, Alfred de. Premières poésies. Paris, 1858.
37566.20 Nettement, A.F. Histoire de la littérature française sous la restauration. Paris, 1858. 2v.
40572.24 Nisard, Désiré. Études de la critique littéraire. Paris, 1858.
Htn 37578.39* Passard, L. Un million de Calembours. Paris, 1858.
37558.31 Pellisson-Fontanier, Paul. Histoire de l'Académie française. Paris, 1858. 2v.
42515.35.211 Plasman, L. Les Strauss français....Littré et Renan. Paris, 1858.
40522.9 Prévost, Antoine F. Histoire de Manon Lescaut. Paris, 1858.
38536.10 Rabelais, F. Oeuvres. v.1-2. Paris, 1858.
40526.44 Racine, Louis. Correspondance littéraire inédite de Louis Racine avec René Chevaye. Paris, 1858.
Mol 728.2 Raymond, E. Histoire des peregrinations de Molière dans le Languedoc (1642-1658). Paris, 1858.
42515.30.380 Renan, Ernest. Études d'histoire religieuse. 4. éd. Paris, 1858.
37564.76 Robiou, Felix. Essai sur l'histoire de la littérature. Paris, 1858.
37538.3 Roche, Antonin. Histoire des principaux écrivains français. Paris, 1858-60. 2v.
FL 6015.8 Rousseau, J.J. Lettre inédite à M.M. Rey. Amsterdam, 1858.
41592.8 Rowland, John Thomas. Lecture on Béranger. Drogheda, 1858.
Mon 159.1A St. John, B. Montaigne the essayist. London, 1858. 2v.
40575.34 Sainte-Beuve, Charles A. Derniers portraits. Paris, 1858.
40575.19.7 Sainte-Beuve, Charles A. Portraits de femmes. Paris, 1858.
41557.31.2 Sandeau, Jules. Mademoiselle de la Seiglière. Bielefeld, 1858.
41557.18.9 Sandeau, Jules. Mademoiselle de la Seiglière. Paris, 1858.
39534.31.3 Scarron, Paul. Virgile travesti. Paris, 1858.
37566.9 Schmidt, Julian. Geschichte der französischen Literatur seit der Revolution 1789. Leipzig, 1858. 2v.
41588.15.3 Scribe, Eugène. Feu Lionel. Paris, 1858.
41588.10 Scribe, Eugène. Historiettes et proverbes. Paris, 1858.
42535.24 Silvestre, Samuel U. Variétés littéraires. Paris, 1858. 2v.
Mol 800.2 Soleirol, H.A. Molière et sa troupe. Paris, 1858.
39533.22 Sorel, Charles. Vraie Histoire....de Francion. Paris, 1858.
41558.11 Soulié, Frédéric. Olivier Duhamel. Paris, 1858.
41558.45 Souvestre, Émile. Les derniers Bretons. v.1-2. Paris, 1858.
41562.8 Sue, Eugène. La coucaratcha. Latréaumont. Paris, 1858.
41562.6 Sue, Eugène. Eugène Sue photographié par lui-même. Genève, 1858.
41562.24 Sue, Eugène. Paula Monti - Commandeur de Malte. Paris, 1858.
40597.1.7 Surville, L. Balzac, sa vie et ses oeuvres. Paris, 1858.
38528.26 Tabarin. Oeuvres complètes. Paris, 1858. 2v.
42536.11.5 Taine, Hippolyte. Essais de critique et d'histoire. Paris, 1858.
Htn FL 398.74.26* Tampier, L.C. Dernières heures de Rachel. Paris, 1858. 2 pam.
37581.44 Théâtre contemporain, 1858-1866. Paris, 1858-66.
42547.4 Thomas, André. Le pamphlétaire. Paris, 1858.
FL 364.105 Tisserand, L.M. Le théâtre au college...dans les écoles. Sens, 1858.
41561.23.2 Toepffer, Rodolphe. Nouveaux voyages en zigzag. 2e éd. Paris, 1858.
42547.8 Uchard, Mario. La fiammina. Paris, 1858.
42581.36.30 Viard, Jules. Les petites joies de la vie humaine. Paris, 1858.
41564.18 Vigny, Alfred de. Théâtre complet. 7. éd. Paris, 1858.
37536.9 Villemain, A.F. Cours de littérature française. Paris, 1858. 4v.
42587.69.70 Walras, Léon. Francis Sauveur. Paris, 1858.

1859

42562.29.3 About, Edmond. Trente et quarante. Les mariages de Paris. v.1-2. 3e series. Paris, 1859.
42586.12 Assollant, A. Scènes de la vie des États-Unis. Paris, 1859.
37564.12 Aubieneau, Léon. Notices littéraire sur le XVIIe siècle. Paris, 1859.
42542.22.3 Augier, Émile. Les lionnes pauvres. 3. éd. Paris, 1859.
40564.5 Barante, A.G.P. de. Études littéraires. Paris, 1859. 2v.
41522.1.3.5 Barbey d'Aurevilly, Jules. L'amour impossible. Paris, 1859.
39532.30.5 Baret, Eugene. Menage, sa vie et ses écrits. Lyon, 1859.

1859 - cont.

40556.25 Barthelémy, Charles. L'esprit du Comte Joseph de Maistre. Paris, 1859.
41592.16.10 Béranger, P.J. de. Chansons. Paris, 1859. 2v.
41592.18.5 Béranger, P.J. de. Dernières chansons, 1834-1851. Paris, 1859. 2 pam.
41591.13.52 Béranger, P.J. de. Ma biographie. 2. éd. Paris, 1859.
41522.43 Bernard, Charles de. Le noeud gordien. Bruxelles, 1859. 2v.
42563.26.2 Blocqueville, Louise Adélaïde d'Eckmûhl. Perdita. Paris, 1859.
40551.21 Bonald, L.G.A. de. Oeuvres complètes. Paris, 1859. 3v.
41566.58.30 Bonnardot, Alfred. Fantaisies multicolores. Paris, 1859.
41566.14.30 Bouilly, Jean N. The abbé de l'épée. Munich, 1859.
38526.64 Boyer, H. Un ménage littéraire en Berry au 16 siècle (Jacques Thiboust et Jeanne de la Font). Bourges, 1859.
42586.24.100 Bravard, Raoul. Une petite ville. Paris, 1859.
38576.11.1 Brueys, D.A. de. L'avocat Pathelin. Paris, 1859.
38514.21.1 Campaux, Antoine. François Villon, sa vie et ses oeuvres. Paris, 1859.
FL 368.5 Carmouche, Pierre F.A. Le théâtre en province. Paris, 1859.
40584.13.10 Castille, H. M. Villemain. Paris, 1859.
FL 6148.59 Caumont, H. Jean-Jacques Rousseau et l'Isle de Saint-Pierre. Zurich, 1859.
42515.39 Chassin, C.L. Edgar Quinet. Paris, 1859.
40586.11.20 Chateaubriand, F.A.R. Atala. Paris, 1859.
40586.19.50 Chateaubriand, F.A.R. The martyrs. N.Y., 1859.
40586.27.5 Chateaubriand, F.A.R. Mémoires d'outre-tombe. Bruxelles, 1859-60. 6v.
38574.10 Corneille, Pierre. Chefs-d'oeuvres; suivies des oeuvres...T. Corneille. Paris, 1859.
40565.22 Cuvillier-Fleury, A.A. Derniers études historiques et littéraires. Paris, 1859. 2v.
38585.3 Deltour, Felix. Les enemis de Racine. Paris, 1859.
42586.34 Deltuf, Paul. Aventures&parisiennes. Paris, 1859.
37564.9 Demogeot, Jacques. Tableau de la littérature française. Paris, 1859.
42543.16.4 Dumas, Alexandre. La dama de las perlas. 2a ed. Barcelona, 1859.
42543.24.5 Dumas, Alexandre. Le roman d'une femme. Paris, 1859.
41593.32.4 Dupont, Pierre. Études littéraires, vers et prose. Paris, 1859.
42568.29 Enault, Louis. La rose blanche. 2. éd. Paris, 1859.
42572.19 Erckmann, Emile. L'illustre Docteur Mathéus. Paris, 1859.
42543.39.5 Fallet, C. (Mme.). Le coffret d'Ebène ou Les diamants de l'aieule. Rouen, 1859.
38553.15.4.10 Fénelon, F. de S. de la Mothe. Selections from the writings. Boston, 1859.
Mol 606.3 Feugère, G. Discours. Toulouse, 1859.
37563.13 Feugère, M. Leon. Charactères et portraits littéraires du XVI siècle. Paris, 1859. 2v.
42575.39 Feuillet, Octave. La novela de la vida. Madrid, 1859.
42575.41 Feuillet, Octave. Péril en la demeure. 3. éd. Paris, 1859.
42575.47.2 Feuillet, Octave. Le roman d'un jeune homme pauvre. 2. éd. Paris, 1859.
42575.47.5 Feuillet, Octave. Le roman d'un jeune homme pauvre. 3. éd. Paris, 1859.
42575.47.9 Feuillet, Octave. Le roman d'un jeune homme pauvre. 9. éd. Paris, 1859.
42575.47.12 Feuillet, Octave. Le roman d'un jeune homme pauvre. 14. éd. Paris, 1859.
42575.50A Feuillet, Octave. The romance of a poor young man. N.Y., 1859.
42564.39 Fleury, Jules. Les aventures de mademoiselle Mariette. Paris, 1859.
42564.30 Fleury, Jules. Les sensations de Josquin. Paris, 1859.
42564.31 Fleury, Jules. Souvenirs des funambules. Paris, 1859.
42543.31.1100 Fournier, Edouard. L'hôtesse de Virgille. Paris, 1859.
37596.30A Garnier de Pont Sainte Maxence. La vie de Saint Thomas. Paris, 1859.
40597.6.2 Gautier, T. Honoré de Balzac. Paris, 1859.
41542.9.11 Gautier, Théophile. Les grotesques. Paris, 1859.
41541.13.5 Girardin, Delphine Gay. Le chapeau d'un horloger. Paris, 1859.
41541.9 Girardin, Delphine Gay. Nouvelles. Paris, 1859.
37537.12 Godefroy, Frédéric. Histoire de la littérature française. Paris, 1859-76. 9v.
Mol 608.1 Haber. Remarques sur la langue de Molière. Culni, 1859.
37556.15 Hatin, Eugène. Histoire...de la presse en France. Paris, 1859-61. 8v.
38524.75 Helbig, H. Fleurs des vieux poètes Liègeois (1550-1650). Liège, 1859.
42515.35.128 Hello, Ernest. M. Renan. Paris, 1859.
42576.14.9 Houssaye, Arsène. Romans parisiens. Mlle Mariani. v.1-2. Paris, 1859.
42587.5 Hugo, Charles. La bohême dorée. Paris, 1859.
42587.5.2 Hugo, Charles. La bohême dorée. Paris, 1859. 4 pam.
Htn 41572.25* Hugo, Victor. La légende des siècles. Paris, 1859. 2v.
41573.33 Hugo, Victor. Les orientales. Paris, 1859.
Mol 217.5 Humbert, C.H. Le Phormion de Térence et Les Fourberies de Scapin. Elberfeld, 1859.
38537.25.20 Jacob, P.L. Rabelais, sa vie et ses ouvrages. Paris, 1859.
Mon 168.2 James, C. Montaigne; ses voyages aux eaux minerales. Paris, 1859.
FL 398.74.30 Janin, Jules G. Rachel et la tragédie. Paris, 1859.
41544.20 Karr, Alphonse. Roses noires et roses bleues. Paris, 1859.
Mol 712.2.3 Lacroix, Paul. La jeunesse de Molière. Paris, 1859.
39532.24 Lacroix, Paul. Paris ridicule et burlesque. Paris, 1859.
Htn 38513.26* Lacroix, Paul. Recueil de farces. Paris, 1859.
38513.26.5 Lacroix, Paul. Recueil de farces. Paris, 1859.
42544.3 Lafont, C. Le passé d'une femme. Paris, 1859.
39526.32.10 La Fontaine, Jean de. Fables et oeuvres diverses. Paris, 1859.
41578.30.3 Lamartine, Alphonse. Raphael. Paris, 1859.
41578.30 Lamartine, Alphonse. The stone-mason of Saint Point. N.Y., 1859.
41578.5.15 Lamartine, Alphonse de. Les harmonies. Paris, 1859.
41578.19 Lamartine, Alphonse de. Les confidences. Confidential disclosures. N.Y., 1859.
42587.13.7 Lebrun, Camille. Les récréations. Rouen, 1859.

1859 - cont.

	42544.31.30	Lecomte, Jules. Le luxe. 2. éd. Paris, 1859.
	37563.33A	Lenient, Charles. La satire en France au moyen âge. Paris, 1859.
	Mol 60.15	Lennard, D.B. Tales from Molière's plays. London, 1859.
	42555.40.230	Liégeard, Stéphen. Les abeilles d'or; chants impériaux. Paris, 1859.
	41561.5F	Louvet, Jean Baptiste. Histoire du chevalier de Faublas. Paris, 1859.
	37556.19	Maillard, F. Histoire...de la presse Parisienne. Paris, 1859.
	40587.47.5	Marcellus, M.L. Chateaubriand et son temps. Paris, 1859.
	37578.87	Marchal, C. Dictionnaire amusant. Paris, 1859.
	38563.27	Marcou, F.L. Étude sur la vie et les oeuvres de Pellisson. Paris, 1859.
	37577.12	Martin, P.J. L'esprit de tout le monde. Paris, 1859.
	42545.12	Meilhac, Henri. Théâtre. v.1. Paris, 1859-80.
	FL 6128.59	Mercier, L.A. Explication de la maladie de Jean-Jacques Rousseau. Paris, 1859.
	42545.21	Méry, J. Herculanum. Paris, 1859.
	42587.25.21	Méry, Joseph. La juive au Vatican. Paris, 1859.
	42514.32	Mignet, F.A.M. Mémoires historiques. Paris, 1859.
	38557.14.50	Moët, E. Bossuetius et Fenelo. Thesis. Paris, 1859.
	Mon 123.2	Moët, E. Des opinions et des jugements litteraires. Auch, 1859.
Htn	Mon 123.2.2*	Moët, E. Des opinions et des jugements litteraires. Auch, 1859.
	Mol 166.1.5	Molière, Jean Baptiste Poquelin. L'avare...mise en vers par A. Malouin. Paris, 1859.
	Mol 18.59	Molière, Jean Baptiste Poquelin. Oeuvres complètes...Lahure. Paris, 1859. 2v.
	40557.85	Monsieur de Montalembert. Paris, 1859.
	Mon 18.59	Montaigne, Michel de. Essais. Delvau. v.1-2. Paris, 1859.
	42577.30.9	Murger, Henry. Scènes de la vie de Bohème. v.1-2. Paris, 1859.
	41596.20.90	Musset, Alfred de. La confession d'un enfant du siècle. Paris, 1859.
	42587.37	Musset, Paul de. Lui et elle. Paris, 1859.
	42587.37.01	Musset, Paul de. Lui et elle. 2. éd. Paris, 1859.
	41556.10.5	Nodier, Charles. Contes. Paris, 1859.
	38537.25.12	Noël, E. Rabelais. Bruxelles, 1859.
	40526.58	Oeuvres de M. de Fontanes. Paris, 1859. 2v.
	40542.15	Ozanam, Antoine F. Oeuvres choisies. Paris, 1859.
	40542.9	Ozanam, Antoine P. Dante. n.p., 1859.
	40542.10	Ozanam, Antoine P. Mélanges. n.p., 1859. 2v.
Htn	37578.40*	Passard, L. Un million de plaisanteries. Paris, 1859.
	41588.33	Passard, L. Petit théâtre bouffon. Paris, 1859.
	38513.24	Pathelin. Maistre Pierre Pathelin. Nouveau Pathelin...Testament de Pathelin. Paris, 1859.
	40536.20.10	Piron, Alexis. Oeuvres inédites. Paris, 1859.
	42534.19	Pontmartin, A.F. de. Causeries du Samedi. Paris, 1859.
	42534.35.15	Pontmartin, A.F. de. Contes et nouvelles. Paris, 1859.
	42534.16	Pontmartin, A.F. de. Nouvelles causeries littéraires. Paris, 1859.
	42534.26	Pontmartin, A.F. de. Or et linquant. Paris, 1859.
	42515.20.9	Prevost-Paradol, L.A.P. de. Essais de politique et de littérature. Paris, 1859.
	42535.17.10	Ratisbonne, Louis. Hero et Léandre. Paris, 1859.
	42515.30.350	Renan, Ernest. Essais de morale et de critique. Paris, 1859.
	40573.34	Rigault, H. Oeuvres. Paris, 1859. 4v.
	38526.47.20	Rivaudeau, André de. Les oeuvres poétiques. Paris, 1859.
	41568.10	Saintine, Joseph Xavier Boniface. Les métamorphoses de la femme. Paris, 1859.
Htn	41557.9.27.9*	Sand, George. Elle et lui. Paris, 1859.
Htn	41557.9.52*	Sand, George. Les sept cordes de la Lyre. Bruxelles, 1859.
	37565.34	Schmidt-Weissenfels, Eduard. Geschichte der französischen Revolutions-Litteratur. Prague, 1859.
	41588.3.9	Scribe, Eugène. Los cuentos de la reina de Navarra. Santiago, 1859.
	42557.4	Soulary, Joséphin. Sonnets humoristiques. Lyon, 1859.
	41558.12	Soulié, Frédéric. Sathaniel. Paris, 1859.
	41558.42	Souvestre, Émile. Chroniques de la mer. Paris, 1859.
	41558.51.5	Souvestre, Émile. Histoires d'autrefois. Paris, 1859.
	41558.64	Souvestre, Émile. Pendant la moisson. Paris, 1859.
	40526.33	Tamisier, F. Étude biographique sur Pierre Dorange. Marseille, 1859.
	41561.23	Toepffer, Rodolphe. Premiers voyages en zigzag. 5e éd. Paris, 1859.
	42547.7.10	Uchard, Mario. La seconde jeunesse. Paris, 1859.
	37564.5	Venet, A.R. Moralistes des 16me et 17me siècles. Paris, 1859.
	42521.11	Veuillot, Louis. Mélanges. 2. série. Paris, 1859-61. 6v.
	41564.3.55	Vigny, Alfred de. Cinq-Mars. 2e éd. Paris, 1859.
	41564.16.9	Vigny, Alfred de. Poèmes antiques et modernes. 7. ed. Paris, 1859.
	41568.29	Wailly, Leon de. Angelica Kauffmann. Paris, 1859.
	40553.12	Wallon, J. Cousin. Paris, 1859.
	40597.1.5	Werdet, E. Portrait intime de Balzac, sa vie, son humeur et son caractère. Paris, 1859.

186-

	40532.14.5A	Beaumarchais, Pierre A.C. de. Théâtre. Paris, 186-.
	41583.15.14.3	Bourgeois, Anicet. The duke's daughter. N.Y., 186-?
	40546.5.5	Courier de Méré, Paul Louis. Oeuvres. Paris, 186-?
	42566.15.100	Dallard, Charles. Le batard du roi. Paris, 186-?
	42542.64.55.80	Durantin, Armand. La moglie di un grand'uomo. n.p., 186-?
	Mol 165.30	Molière, Jean Baptiste Poquelin. L'avare...Estienne. Paris, 186-.
	41596.29.3	Musset, Alfred de. Un caprice. Boston, 186-?
	37597.29	Péan Gatineau. Vie de Saint Martin. Tours, 186-.
	FL 6027.2	Rousseau, J.J. Bekenntnisse. Leipzig, 186-? 2v.
	41557.8.74	Sand, George. La famille de Germandre. 3e éd. Paris, 186-.
	41557.8.86	Sand, George. Jean de la Roche. Paris, 186-.
	41557.8.98	Sand, George. Les maîtres sonneurs. Paris, 186-.
	42581.19.10	Verne, Jules. Cinq semaines en ballon. Paris, 186-?

1860

	42562.26	About, Edmond. Germaine. Boston, 1860.
	42562.17.3	About, Edmond. Le roi des Montagnes. Paris, 1860.
	42562.16.9	About, Edmond. Le roi des Montagnes. 4e éd. Paris, 1860.
	42562.19.3	About, Edmond. Tolla. 7e éd. Paris, 1860. 2v.

1860 - cont.

	42586.4	Achard, Amédée. L'eau qui dort. Paris, 1860.
	42586.6	Achard, Amédée. L'ombre de Ludovic. Paris, 1860.
	42562.38.47.4	Aimard, Gustave. L'éclaireur. 4. éd. Paris, 1860.
Htn	37578.51*	Almanach comique. Paris, 1860-71. 4v.
	37578.56	Almanach prophetique. Paris, 1860.
	40587.2	Ancelot, Jacques A.F.P. Vie de Chateaubriand. Paris, 1860.
	42586.10	Assollant, A. Histoire fantastique du célèbre Pierrot. Paris, 1860.
	42542.21.5	Augier, Émile. Home truths; a domestic drama. London, 1860.
	42524.8	Babou, H. Lettres satiriques et critiques. Paris, 1860.
	40597.14	Balzac, Honoré de. The greatness of César Birotteau. N.Y., 1860.
	40597.28	Balzac, Honoré de. Le lys dans la vallée. Paris, 1860.
	37566.11	Barbey d'Aurevilly, J.A. Les oeuvres et les hommes. Paris, 1860-1878. 7v.
	39544.6	Bavoux, Evariste. Voltaire a Ferney. Sa correspondance. Paris, 1860.
	41592.18.7	Béranger, P.J. de. Dernières chansons de Béranger de 1834-1851. Paris, 1860.
	41591.9	Béranger, P.J. de. Ma biographie. Paris, 1860.
	41522.41	Bernard, Charles de. Le noeud gordien. Paris, 1860.
	42542.29.79	Berton, C.S. (Mme.). La diplomatie du ménage. Paris, 1860.
	37596.125	Bible. O.T. Psalms (French-old). Oxonii, 1860.
	Mon 112.2	Bigorie de Laschamps, F. Michel de Montaigne. Paris, 1860.
	Mol 870.13	Bornier, H. de. Le quinze janvier. Paris, 1860.
	FL 397.77	Bouteiller, Jules E. Histoire complete et methodique des théâtres de Rouen. Rouen, 1860-80. 4v.
	41593.10	Brizeux, Auguste. Oeuvres complètes. Paris, 1860. 2v.
	42512.8	Broglie, Albert de. Questions de religion et d'histoire. Paris, 1860. 2v.
	40586.27.20	Chateaubriand, F.A.R. Mémoires d'outre-tombe. Paris, 1860. 6v.
	40586.5.20	Chateaubriand, F.A.R. Voyages en Amérique, en Italie. Paris, 1860.
	42554.18.30	Chatillon, Auguste de. A la grand' pinte. Paris, 1860.
	37584.9	Chefs-d'oeuvre des auteurs comiques. 2. Paris, 1860.
	37584.15	Chefs-d'oeuvre des auteurs comiques. 8. Paris, 1860.
	42586.30.50	Claudin, G. Point et Virgule. Paris, 1860.
	40587.3	Clergeau, l'abbé. Chateaubriand. Paris, 1860.
	40587.3.2	Clergeau, l'abbé. Chateaubriand. 2. éd. Paris, 1860.
	37556.16.55	Cocheris, H. Histoire du journal des savants. Paris, 1860.
	37581.31	Coussemaker, E. de. Drames liturgiques au moyen age. Rennes, 1860.
	42542.54.10	Crémieux, Hector. Orphée. Paris, 1860.
	42542.54.11	Crémieux, Hector. Théâtre. Paris, 1860-61. 4 pam.
	42586.32.910	Dabadie, F. Récits et types américains. Paris, 1860.
	FL 1108.56.100	Defrecheux, Nicolas. Chansons wallonnes. Liège, 1860.
	37543.18	Deloid, T. Les matinées littéraires. Paris, 1860.
	37538.25	Demogeot, Jacques Claude. Histoire de la littérature française. Paris, 1860.
	FL 397.8.9	Detcheverry, A. Histoire des théâtres de Bordeaux. Bordeaux, 1860.
	41584.16	Doucet, Camille. La consideration. Paris, 1860.
	42568.20.5	Dufresne, Abel. Stories of Henry and Henrietta. Boston, 1860.
	42542.69	Dumanoir, M. Jeanne qui pleure et Jeanne qui rit. Paris, 1860.
	42543.12	Dumas, Alexandre. Antonine. Paris, 1860.
	42543.15.11	Dumas, Alexandre. Camille. Philadelphia, 1860.
	41523.22	Dumas, Alexandre. Canseries. Paris, 1860.
	41525.19	Dumas, Alexandre. Impressions de voyage. L'Arabie heureuse. Paris, 1860. 3v.
	41526.10	Dumas, Alexandre. Jane. Paris, 1860.
	41538.29	Dumas, Alexandre. La maison de glace. Paris, 1860. 2 pam.
	41527.11	Dumas, Alexandre. Le pasteur d'Ashbourn. Paris, 1860.
	41527.14	Dumas, Alexandre. Le Père Gigogne. Paris, 1860.
	42572.7.7	Erckmann, Emile. Contes de la montagne. Paris, 1860.
	42573.60	Eyma, Louis Xavier. Le roi des Tropiques. Paris, 1860.
	37563.14	Feugère, M. Leon. Les femmes poètes au XVIe siècle. Paris, 1860.
	42575.27.3	Feuillet, Octave. Le cheveu blanc. Paris, 1860.
	42575.45	Feuillet, Octave. Scènes et proverbes. Paris, 1860.
	42575.50.9	Feuillet, Octave. La tentation. 2. éd. Paris, 1860.
	42564.9	Fleury, Jules. Chien-caillou. Paris, 1860.
	37556.21.40	Flotte, G. Révues parisiennes. Marseille, 1860-68. 2v.
	FL 6128.60	Fochier, L. Séjour de Jean-Jacques Rousseau à Bourgoin. Bourgoin, 1860.
	37596.50	Fournival, Richard de. Le bestiaire d'amour. Paris, 1860.
	42586.59	Gandon, Antoine. Les trente-deux duels de J. Gigon. Paris, 1860.
	41541.6	Girardin, Delphine Gay. Oeuvres complètes. Paris, 1860.
Htn	38523.14*	Guiffrey, G. Poeme inedit de Jehan Marot. Paris, 1860.
	42586.90	Habeneck, Charles. Nouvelles espagnoles. Paris, 1860.
	42554.53	Héré, J. Fables et poésies. St. Quentin, 1860.
	FL 361.9	Houssaye, Arsène. Princesses de comédie. Paris, 1860.
	39544.5.5	Houssaye, Arsène. Le Roi Voltaire. Paris, 1860.
	40567.6.9	Janin, Jules. L'ane mort. Paris, 1860.
	40567.9	Janin, Jules. Barnave. n.p., 1860.
	37597.33A	Jean de Condé. Gedichte. Stuttgart, 1860.
	38526.53	Jeandet, Jean Pierre A. Pontus de Tyard. Paris, 1860.
	42587.9	Jobey, Charles. L'amour d'un nègre. Paris, 1860.
	41544.16	Karr, Alphonse. La pêche. Les fleurs. Paris, 1860.
	42555.24	Laprade, Victor de. Poèmes évangéliques. 3e éd. Paris, 1860.
	42555.26	Laprade, Victor de. Psyché. Paris, 1860.
	41586.8	Laya, Léon. Le duc job. Paris, 1860.
	38515.16	Leduc, Herbert. Roman de Foulgue de Candie. Reims, 1860.
	37596.166.2	Le Duc de Danmartin, Herbert. Le roman de Foulque de Candie. Reims, 1860.
	42576.70.432	Lescure, M.F.A. de. Eux et elles. Paris, 1860.
	38575.28	Lucas, Hippolyte. Documents relatifs à l'historie du Cid. Paris, 1860.
	42545.5.245	Maiziere, Anot de. Cromwell protecteur de la république anglaise. Paris, 1860-[1861]
	Mol 870.14	Martin, Alexis. La fête de Molière. Paris, 1860.
	Mol 245.36	Molière, Jean Baptiste Poquelin. Le misanthrope. Schwalb. Essen, 1860.

Chronological Listing

1860 - cont.

	40557.5	Montalembert, Charles F.R. Discours. Paris, 1860. 3v.
	40557.6	Montalembert, Charles F.R. Oeuvres polémiques. n.p., 1860. 3v.
	41596.14	Musset, Alfred de. Oeuvres posthumes. Paris, 1860.
	Mol 614.2	Nisard, Désiré. La comédie après Molière. n.p., 1860.
	37572.35.9	Nodier, Charles. Le nouveau magasin des enfants. Paris, 1860.
	42545.65	Pailleron, Edouard. Théâtre. v.1. Paris, 1860.
	38511.19	Paris, Paulin. Nouvelles recherches sur la vie de Froissart. Paris, 1860.
	41587.18.17	Picard, Louis Benoît. Der Parasit. Stuttgart, 1860.
	42545.78.35	Plouvier, Édouard. Toute seule. Paris, 1860.
	42555.72	Pons, Gaspard de. Adieux poétiques. Paris, 1860. 3v.
	42545.83	Ponsard, F. Ce qui plait aux femmes. 2e éd. Paris, 1860.
	42534.20	Pontmartin, A.F. de. Nouvelles causeries du Samedi. Paris, 1860.
	37538.14	Prat, Henry. Études littéraires. XVIIIe siècle. Paris, 1860-61. 2v.
	42587.50	Pressensé, E.F.L. de P.G. de. Rosa, or The Parisian girl. N.Y., 1860.
	40522.9.2	Prévost, Antoine F. Histoire de Manon Lescaut et du chevalier des Grieux. Paris, 1860.
	41547.19.2	Privat d'Anglemont, A. Paris anecdote. Paris, 1860.
	42535.17	Ratisbonne, Louis. Morts et vivants. Paris, 1860.
	42515.30.351A	Renan, Ernest. Essais de morale et de critique. Paris, 1860.
	42515.30.512	Renan, Ernest. Le livre de Job. Paris, 1860.
	FL 398.76	Rigolbache, Marguerite (pseud.). Mémoires. 3. ed. Paris, 1860.
	FL 398.76.3	Rigolbache, Marguerite (pseud.). Mémoires. 5. ed. Paris, 1860.
	FL 6041.60	Rousseau, J.J. Émile ou De l'éducation. Paris, 1860?
	39594.29.5	St. Pierre, J.H.B. de. Paul et Virginie suivi de La chaumière indienne. Paris, 1860.
	41568.12	Saintine, Joseph Xavier Boniface. Un rossignol. Paris, 1860.
	41557.8.64	Sand, George. Constance Verrier. Paris, 1860.
	41557.9.28	Sand, George. Elle et lui. 2d éd. Paris, 1860.
	41557.8.86.5	Sand, George. Jean de la Roche. Paris, 1860.
	41557.9.49	Sand, George. Le marquis de Villemer. Paris, 1860.
	FL 396.41	Sand, Maurice. Masque et Bouffons. Paris, 1860.
	37538.23	Saucié, D. Histoire de la littérature française. Tours, 1860.
	37565.12	Schnitzler, Johann H. Aperçu sommaire de la littérature française. Strasbourg, 1860.
	37595.10.5	Schuster, Gustav. Abälard und Heloise. Hamburg, 1860.
	41588.15.7	Scribe, Eugène. La fille de trente ans. Comédie. Paris, 1860.
	41588.15	Scribe, Eugène. Valérie. Bielefeld, 1860. 8 pam.
	41588.29.2	Séjour, Victor. La tireuse de cartes. Drame. 2. éd. Paris, 1860.
	41562.15	Sue, Eugène. Gilbert et Gilberte. Paris, 1860. 3v.
	42583.34	Tardieu, J.R. Mignon. Paris, 1860.
	41563.26.3	Toepffer, Rodolphe. Nouvelles genevoises. 2. ed. Bielefeld, 1860.
	41563.26.5	Toepffer, Rodolphe. Nouvelles genevoises. 2. éd. Bielefeld, 1860.
	37543.28.9	Vapereau, L.G. L'année littéraire et dramatique. 1858-1868. Paris, 1860. 11v.
	37556.21.10	Vaudin, J.F. Gazetiers et gazettes; histoire critique. Paris, 1860.
	FL 391.70	Veron, Louis. Paris en 1860. Les théâtres de Paris, 1806-1860. Paris, 1860.
	42521.5	Veuillot, Louis. Mélanges. 1. série. Paris, 1860-61. 6v.
NEDL	37573.4	Vinet, Alexander R. Chrestomathie française. Littérature de l'adolescence. v.2. Lausanne, 1860.
	37597.17.9F	Wace, Maistre. The conquest of England from poem of the roman de rou. London, 1860.
	42587.70.8	Weill, Alexandre. Histoires de village. Paris, 1860.
	FL 1106.10.3	Werotte, Charles. Ch'oix di ch'ansons wallonnes et otres poésies. 3. éd. Namur, 1860. 2 pam.

1861

Htn	38511.20*	Abel, Charles. Le mystère de Clement. Metz, 1861.
	42562.33A	About, Edmond. The king of the mountains. Boston, 1861.
	42562.9	About, Edmond. Lettres d'un bon jeune homme à sa cousine Madeleine. Paris, 1861.
	42562.30	About, Edmond. Un mariage de Paris. Boston, 1861.
	FL 384.102	Abraham, E. Les acteurs et les actrices de Paris. Paris, 1861.
	42562.38.42	Aimard, Gustave. The pirates of the prairies. London, 1861.
	40597.33	Balzac, Honoré de. Alchemist. N.Y., 1861.
	40597.30	Balzac, Honoré de. Petty annoyances of married life. N.Y., 1861.
	42542.27.27	Barthet, Armand. Théâtre complète. Paris, 1861.
	38514.27	Beaufils, Constant. Étude sur Charles d'Orleans. Paris, 1861.
	41592.17	Béranger, P.J. de. Chansons. Paris, 1861.
	42586.21	Bernard, Pierre. L'A.B.C. de l'esprit. Paris, 1861.
	42563.26	Blocqueville, Louise Adélaïde d'Eckmûhl. Chrétienne et musulman. Paris, 1861.
	41592.10.35	Boiteau, Paul. Vie de Béranger, 1780-1857. Paris, 1861.
	38557.57.10	Bossuet, J.B. Écrits philosophiques. Paris, 1861.
	38526.10.8.2	Brach, Pierre de. Oeuvres poétiques. Paris, 1861-62. 2v.
	37583.561	Buchheim, C.A. Théâtre français. Modern French plays arranged for schools. pt.1. London, 1861.
	42586.26	Bungener, Félix. Trois sermons sous Louis XV. Paris, 1861. 3v.
	40586.25.30	Chateaubriand, F.A.R. Mélanges politiques. Paris, 1861.
	37581.32	Coussemaker, E. de. Drames liturgiques du moyen age. Paris, 1861.
	37573.10	Crépet, Eugene. Les poètes français. Paris, 1861-62. 4v.
	40515.2.49	Denon, Vivant. Point de lendemain. Strasbourg, 1861.
	40556.4	Deschanel, Émile. Causeries de Quinzaine. Paris, 1861.
	38575.9	Desjardins, Ernest. Le grand Corneille. Paris, 1861.
	Mon 182.1	Dezeimeris, R. Recherches sur l'auteur des epitaphes. Paris, 1861. 2 pam.
	41524.8	Dumas, Alexandre. Conscience l'innocent. Paris, 1861.
	41538.29.15	Dumas, Alexandre. Un mariage sous Louis XV. Paris, 1861.

1861 - cont.

	42568.25	Enault, Louis. Un amour en Lorponie. Paris, 1861.
	42572.26.2	Erckmann, Emile. Maître Daniel Rock. Bruxelles, 1861.
	38582.20.5	Fasquelle, Louis. Chefs d'oeuvre de Jean Racine. N.Y., 1861.
	38554.326.80	Fénelon, F. de S. de la Mothe. Dialogues sur l'éloquence en général et sur celle de la chaire en particulier. Paris, 1861.
	41540.15	Fére, Octave. Les mystères de Rouen. 3. éd. Rouen, 1861.
	42575.47	Feuillet, Octave. Redemption. Paris, 1861.
	42575.45.5	Feuillet, Octave. Scènes et proverbes. Paris, 1861.
	42575.21.7	Feydeau, Ernest. Sylvie. Paris, 1861.
	42585.28	Figuier, L. (Mme.). Soeurs de lait. Paris, 1861.
	FL 355.35.4	Filippi, Joseph de. Essai d'une bibliographique du théâtre. Paris, 1861.
	43610.25.2100	Fleury, Hector. Les echos. Paris, 1861.
	42564.23	Fleury, Jules. La mascarade de la vie parisienne. Paris, 1861.
	42543.30	Fournier, Narcisse. La vie indépendante. Paris, 1861.
	42543.34	Foussier, E. La famille de Pluiméné. Paris, 1861.
	42586.61	Gandon, Antoine. Le grand Godard. Paris, 1861.
	42586.60	Gandon, Antoine. Les 32 duels de Jean Gigon. Paris, 1861.
Htn	37575.10*	Genty, Achille. La Fontaine des amoureux de science. Paris, 1861.
Htn	37575.13*	Genty, Achille. Oeuvres poétiques...de Nicolas Ellain. Paris, 1861.
Htn	37575.12*	Genty, Achille. Rimes inédites en patois Percheron. Paris, 1861.
	37556.21	Germain, A. Martyrologe de la presse 1789-1861. Paris, 1861.
	37537.7	Geruzez, Eugène. Histoire de la littérature française. Paris, 1861. 2v.
	42513.44.5	Haureau, Barthélemy. Singularités historiques et littéraires. Paris, 1861.
	40567.15	Janin, Jules. La confession. n.p., 1861.
	40566.19	Janin, Jules. La fin d'un monde. Paris, 1861.
	FL 398.30.20	Janin, Jules. Rachel et la tragédie. Paris, 1861.
	41544.6.3	Karr, Alphonse. La famille Alain. Paris, 1861.
	38564.25.10	La Bruyère, J. de. Les caractères de Théophraste. Paris, 1861. 2v.
	39526.29.12	La Fontaine, Jean de. Fables. Boston, 1861. 2v.
	42555.11	La Landelle, G. de. Poèmes et chants marins. Paris, 1861.
	41576.9	Lamartine, Alphonse de. La chute d'un ange. (Oeuvres comp.16). Paris, 1861.
	41576.10	Lamartine, Alphonse de. Histoire de la Restauration. (Oeuvres comp.17-22). Paris, 1861-1862. 10v.
	41576.8	Lamartine, Alphonse de. Histoire des Girondins. (Oeuvres comp.9-15). Paris, 1861-1862. 7v.
	41586.7	Laya, Léon. Les jeunes gens. Paris, 1861.
	37546.31	Lecouvet, F.F.I. Tournay littéraire. Gand, 1861.
	42555.38.5	Lefèvre, André. La flute de Pan. Paris, 1861.
	42544.5	Legouvé, Ernest. Beatrix. Paris, 1861.
	42544.11	Legouvé, Ernest. Beatrix. Paris, 1861.
	37555.13	Lespy, V. Notes pour l'histoire de la chanson. Paris, 1861.
	42544.40	Lubac, Jules de. Les Français devant Pékin. Lyon, 1861.
	42545.1	Maeterlinck, Maurice. Les aveugles. Bruxelles, 1861.
	40588.43	Maistre, Xavier. Voyage autour de ma chambre. Boston, 1861.
	37572.24	Masson, Gustave. Class-book of French literature. Edinburgh, 1861.
	40547.16	Michelet, Jules. The sea. N.Y., 1861.
	40573.4.25	Milsand, P. Catalogue par ordre alphabétique des ouvrages imprimés de Gabriel Peignot. Supplement. Paris, 1861.
	42587.30	Molènes, Paul de. L'amant et l'enfant. Paris, 1861.
	Mol 171.16	Molière, Jean Baptiste Poquelin. Le bourgeois gentilhomme. Bielefeld, 1861.
	42545.41	Monselet, Charles. Théâtre de Figaro. Paris, 1861.
	Mon 31.31	Montaigne, Michel de. Works. Hazlitt (Wight). v.1,3,4. N.Y., 1861. 3v.
	40557.8	Montalembert, Charles F.R. Histoire de Sainte Élisabeth de Hongrie. n.p., 1861. 2v.
	40557.7	Montalembert, Charles F.R. Mélanges. n.p., 1861.
	41595.32	Moreau, Hégésippe. Oeuvres complètes. Paris, 1861.
	42545.45	Najac, Émile de. La poule et ses poussins. Paris, 1861.
	42578.11	Narrey, Charles. Le quatrième larron. Paris, 1861.
	42587.38	Olivier, Urbain. Récits du village. Lausanne, 1861.
	40542.7	Ozanam, Antoine P. La civilisation chrétienne. n.p., 1861.
	40542.6	Ozanam, Antoine P. Les germains avant le christianisme. n.p., 1861.
	FL 360.52	Poinsot, Edmond A. Le scandale au théâtre. Paris, 1861.
	42534.22	Pontmartin, A.F. de. Les semaines littéraires. Paris, 1861.
	38536.7.5A	Rabelais, F. Oeuvres. Paris, 1861.
	38536.7	Rabelais, F. Oeuvres. Paris, 1861.
	38583.4.25	Racine, Jean. Théâtre complet. N.Y., 1861.
	Mol 618.1	Rambert, E. Corneille, Racine et Molière. Lausanne, 1861.
	FL 377.5	Rambert, Eugene. Corneille, Racine et Molière. Lausanne, 1861.
	41557.4.20	Reybaud, Louis. César Falempin. Paris, 1861.
	41557.4.30	Reybaud, Louis. Pierre Mouton. Paris, 1861.
	FL 398.76.5	Rigolbache, Marguerite (pseud.). Mémoires. 6. ed. Paris, 1861.
	FL 6002.861	Rousseau, J.J. Oeuvres et correspondance inédites. Paris, 1861.
	40586.22	St. Beuve, C.A. Chateaubriand et son groupe littéraire sous l'Empire. Paris, 1861. 2v.
	41568.9.8	St. Genois, Jules. Le chateau de Wildenborg. 3e éd. Paris, 1861.
	41557.8.61	Sand, George. Le compagnon du tour de France. Paris, 1861. 2v.
	41557.8.74.5	Sand, George. La famille de Germandre. 3e éd. Paris, 1861.
	41557.8.114	Sand, George. Nouvelles. Paris, 1861.
	41557.8.130.2	Sand, George. La ville noire. 2. éd. Paris, 1861.
	42546.30.25A	Sardou, Victorien. Les femmes fortes, comédie. Paris, 1861.
	37565.19	Sayous, André. Le dix-huitième siècle à l'etranger. Paris, 1861. 2v.
	38536.30	Schönermark, W. Beitrage zur Geschichte Rabelais' Werken. Breslau, 1861.
	42546.40.100	Scholl, Aurélien. Jaloux du passé. Paris, 1861.
	39527.4.5	Soullié, P. La Fontaine et ses devanciers ou Histoire de l'Apologue. Paris, 1861.
	41558.44	Souvestre, Émile. Au coin du feu. Paris, 1861.
	41558.49F	Souvestre, Émile. Deux misères. Paris, 1861.

1861 - cont.

41558.58 Souvestre, Émile. L'homme et l'argent. Paris, 1861.
41558.69F Souvestre, Émile. Pierre Landais. Paris, 1861.
40592.24.15 Staël Holstein, Anne Louise. Corinne. Paris, 1861.
41562.5 Sue, Eugène. La bonne aventure. Paris, 1861.
41562.14 Sue, Eugène. Les fils de famille. Paris, 1861.
41563.12 Sue, Eugène. Les mystères du monde. Berlin, 1861.
41562.34 Sue, Eugène. La vigie de Koat-Ven. Paris, 1861.
39527.4.9A Taine, H.A. La Fontaine et ses fables. Paris, 1861.
38515.16.2 Tarbé, Prosper. Le roman des quatres fils aymon. Reims, 1861.
40546.19A Tocqueville, Alexis de. Oeuvres et correspondance inédites. Paris, 1861. 2v.
41592.3 Travers, Julien. Béranger. Paris, 1861.
X Cg 37574.30 Tresor des chansons joyeuses et populaires. Paris, 1861.
42587.66.7 Valbezen, E. de. La malle de l'Inde. Paris, 1861.
37564.6 Venet, A.R. Poètes du siècle de Louis XIV. Paris, 1861.
Htn 42583.2* Verne, Jules. Onze jours de siège. Paris, 1861.
37536.9.5 Villemain, A.F. Cours de littérature française. Paris, 1861. 2v.
FL 6128.61 Viridet, M. Almanach de Jean-Jacques Rousseau pour 1861. Genève, 1861.
38526.70.130 Vitel, Jean de. La prinse du Mont-Saint-Michel de Jan de Vitel. Auranches, 1861.
FL 382.10 Wismewski, Jules. Études sur les poetes dramatiques. Paris, 1861.

1862

42562.5.5 About, Edmond. Le cas de M. Guérin. Paris, 1862.
42562.33.30 About, Edmond. Gaëtana. Paris, 1862.
42562.8.2 About, Edmond. L'homme a l'oreille cassée. 2e éd. Paris, 1862.
42562.31.2 About, Edmond. Le nez d'un notaire. 3. éd. Boston, 1862.
42562.38.41 Aimard, Gustave. The freebooters. London, 1862.
42562.38.40 Aimard, Gustave. Indian chief. London, 1862.
42553.13 Autran, J. Le poème des Beaux Jours. Paris, 1862.
38546.32 Babon, H. Les amoreux de Mme. de Sévigné. Paris, 1862.
38545.26 Barach, Karl Sigmund. Pierre Daniel Huet als Philosoph. Wien, 1862.
41574.590 Barbey d'Aurevilly, Jules. Les misérables de M.V. Hugo. Paris, 1862.
42542.27.20.5 Barrière, Théodore. Une corneille qui abat des noix. Paris, 1862.
Mol 860.40 Beaume, Alex. Dialogue des morts. Paris, 1862.
40562.22 Beslay, François. Lacordaire. Paris, 1862.
37596.94.2 Blondel de Néele. Oeuvres. Reims, 1862.
38557.25.50 Bossuet, J.B. Oeuvres inédites. Paris, 1862.
42542.31 Bouilhet, Louis. Hélène Peyron. Paris, 1862.
42542.32 Bouilhet, Louis. L'oncle million. Paris, 1862.
41583.18 Brisebarre, Édouard. Monsieur de la Raclée. Paris, 1862.
37551.33 Brisson, J. Les grands journaux de France. Paris, 1862.
Mol 880.9 Calonne, E. de. Le docteur amoureux. Paris, 1862.
38576.12.40 Chappuzeau, Samuel. Genève delivrée; comédie. Genève, 1862.
FL 375.12 Chasles, Émile. La comédie en France au seizième siècle. Paris, 1862.
40586.25.50 Chateaubriand, F.A.R. Politique. Paris, 1862.
42565.55.115 Cladel, Léon. Les martyrs ridicules. Paris, 1862.
Mol 167.6 Claus, W. De Aulularia Plauti fabula. Sedini, 1862-87.
42524.31 Clément de Ris, Louis. Critiques d'art et de littérature. Paris, 1862.
Htn 37574.17* Contes et nouvelles en vers. Paris, 1862. 2v.
38575.31.9 Corneille, Pierre. Cinna, ou La Clémence d'Auguste; tragédie. Paris, 1862.
38575.31.9.2 Corneille, Pierre. Cinna, ou La Clémence d'Auguste. 2. éd. Paris, 1862.
38573.5 Corneille, Pierre. Oeuvres. v.1-12 and album. Paris, 1862-68. 13v.
Htn 42566.32.50* Daudet, Alphonse. Le roman du Chaperon Rouge. Paris, 1862.
42586.13 D'Auriac, J.B. Guerre noire. Paris, 1862.
42554.29 Debans, Camille. Sous clef. Paris, 1862.
42586.36 Debrit, Marc. Laura où l'Italie contemporaine. Paris, 1862.
41566.36 Delécluze, E.J. Souvenirs de soixante années. Paris, 1862.
43566.78.110 Des Essart, Emmanuel. Poesies. Parisiennes. Paris, 1862.
39564.13.5 Diderot, Denis. Le neveu de Rameau. Paris, 1862.
39564.7.10 Diderot, Denis. Oeuvres choisies. Paris, 1862. 2v.
42586.37 DuCamp, M. Chevalier du coeur saignant. Paris, 1862.
FL 358.63.10 Du Casse, Albert. Histoire anecdotique de l'ancien théâtre en France. Paris, 1862-64. 2v.
41526.7 Dumas, Alexandre. Italiens et Flamands. Paris, 1862.
42568.21.7 Duranty, Louis E.E. La cause de beau Guillaume. Paris, 1862?
42574.15.9 Fabre, Ferdinand. Les Courbezon. Paris, 1862.
38554.325.80 Fénelon, F. de S. de la Mothe. Dialogues des morts anciens et modernes. Paris, 1862.
42564.3 Fleury, Jules. Les amoureux. Paris, 1862.
37564.38.10 Fournel, Victor. La littérature independante et les écrivains oubliés. Paris, 1862.
42513.35 Gasparin, V.B.C. de. Vesper. Paris, 1862.
42513.38 Gasparin, V.B.C de. Near and heavenly horizons. N.Y., 1862.
Htn 37575.11* Genty, Achille. L'art poetique de Jean Vauquelin. Paris, 1862.
41541.16 Girardin, Delphine Gay. Marguerite. N.Y., 1862.
37563.3 Girardin, Saint-Marc. Tableau de la littérature française. Paris, 1862.
40597.3 Gozlan, Léon. Balzac chez lui. Paris, 1862.
41593.34 Guérin, Maurice de. Journal, lettres et poèmes. Paris, 1862.
40545.10 Guizot, M. François. Discours académiques. Paris, 1862.
FL 366.4 Hallays-Dabot, V. Histoire de la censure théatrals en France. Paris, 1862.
37573.8.10 Herrig, L. La France littéraire. 6. éd. Brunsvic, 1862.
41573.23.9 Hugo, Victor. The hunchback of Notre Dame. N.Y., 1862.
41571.10.3 Hugo, Victor. Les misérables. N.Y., 1862. 2v.
41571.15.10 Hugo, Victor. Les misérables. N.Y., 1862. 2v.
41571.15 Hugo, Victor. Les misérables. N.Y., 1862. 5v.
41571.10 Hugo, Victor. Les misérables. pts.3,4,5. N.Y., 1862. 3v.
41571.17 Hugo, Victor. Les misérables. v.1-5. N.Y., 1862.
41571.10.5 Hugo, Victor. Les misérables. 8. éd. Paris, 1862. 10v.

1862 - cont.

38563.19.5 Jeanmaire, Émile. Essai sur la critique religieuse de Pierre Bayle. Thèse. Strasbourg, 1862.
40556.19.8 Joubert, Joseph. Pensées. 3. éd. Paris, 1862.
42576.78.30 Jourdan, Prosper. Rosine et Rosette. Paris, 1862.
41544.24 Karr, Alphonse. De loin et de près. Paris, 1862.
41544.26 Karr, Alphonse. En fumant. Paris, 1862.
41544.19.2 Karr, Alphonse. Promenades hors de mon jardin. Sous les orangers. Paris, 1862.
37558.10 Kavanagh, Julia. French women of letters. Leipzig, 1862.
38526.26.55 Labé, Louise Charly. Oeuvres de Louize Labé. Lyon, 1862.
42514.9 Laboulaye, Édouard. Études morales et politiques. Paris, 1862.
41576.4 Lamartine, Alphonse de. Harmonies poétiques. (Oeuvres comp.2 + 3). Paris, 1862. 2v.
41576.11 Lamartine, Alphonse de. Histoire de la Turquie. (Oeuvres comp.23-25). Paris, 1862. 3v.
41577.1 Lamartine, Alphonse de. Histoire de la Turquie. v.4-6. (Oeuvres comp.26-28). Paris, 1862. 3v.
41576.5 Lamartine, Alphonse de. Jocelyn. (Oeuvres comp.4). Paris, 1862.
41576.3 Lamartine, Alphonse de. Méditations poétiques. (Oeuvres comp.1). Paris, 1862.
41576.6 Lamartine, Alphonse de. Recueillements poétiques. (Oeuvres comp.5). Paris, 1862.
41576.7 Lamartine, Alphonse de. Voyage en Orient, 1832-1833. (Oeuvres comp.6-8). Paris, 1862. 3v.
42555.29 Laprade, Victor de. Les symphonies. Paris, 1862.
38514.54 La Sale, Antoine de. History...of Little Jehan de Saintré. London, 1862.
42515.36.156 Laurentie, P.S. L'athéisme scientifique. Paris, 1862. 2 pam.
41586.6 Laya, Léon. Un coup de Lansquenet. Paris, 1862.
42544.34.2A Lemercier de Neuville, Louis. Les tourniquets. Paris, 1862.
FL 358.62 Lucas, Hippolyte. Histoire...de théâtre français. Paris, 1862-63. 3v.
42555.42.100 Mahul, E. Poésies politiques sur les événements d'Italie. Turin, 1862.
38523.28A Malherbe, François de. Oeuvres de Malherbe. v.1-5 et album. Paris, 1862-69. 6v.
41555.23 Mérimée, Prosper. Colomba. Paris, 1862.
42555.59.20 Michu, Claude. Les chants de l'industrie. Paris, 1862.
37561.10 Moland, Louis. Origines littéraires de la France. Paris, 1862.
Mol 18.62 Molière, Jean Baptiste Poquelin. Oeuvres complètes...Lemaistre. Paris, 1862. 3v.
Mol 18.62.2 Molière, Jean Baptiste Poquelin. Oeuvres complètes. Paris, 1862. 8v.
Mon 18.62.3 Montaigne, Michel de. Essais. Paris, 1862. 4v.
Mon 18.62 Montaigne, Michel de. Essais. Paris, 1862? 4v.
Mon 31.32A Montaigne, Michel de. Works. v.1,3,4. Boston, 1862. 3v.
40572.8 Muret, Théodore. Souvenirs et causeries d'un journaliste. Paris, 1862. 2v.
37595.32 Mussafia, A. Handschriftliche Studien. Wien, 1862.
37562.68 Mussafia, Adolf. Handschriftliche Studien. Wien, 1862.
41556.14 Nodier, Charles. Romans. Paris, 1862.
41556.17 Nodier, Charles. Souvenirs de jeunesse. Paris, 1862.
38515.17 Oeuvres de Blondel de Nésle. Reims, 1862.
Htn 38541.4* Oeuvres de La Mothe le Vayer. Paris, 1862. 2v.
40542.5 Ozanam, Antoine P. La civilisation au cinquième siècle. Paris, 1862. 2v.
40542.11 Ozanam, Antoine P. Le purgatoire de Dante. n.p., 1862.
Mon 180.1 Payen, J.F. Recherches sur Montaigne. Paris, 1862.
42515.10.5 Pelletan, Eugene. La nouvelle Babylone. Paris, 1862.
41557.2 Perrin, Max. Le secret de Madame. Paris, 1862.
42541.30.5 Ponsard, François. L'honneur et l'argent. Paris, 1862.
42534.15 Pontmartin, A.F. de. Causeries littéraires. Paris, 1862.
42534.17 Pontmartin, A.F. de. Derniers causeries littéraires. Paris, 1862.
37574.52 Quitard, Pierre M. Anthologie de l'amour, extraite des poètes français. Paris, 1862.
38583.9 Racine, Jean. Lettres inédites. Paris, 1862.
38585.46 Racine, Jean. The suitors. Detroit, 1862. 2v.
42542.2.9 Rainneville, J. Lettre d'un gentilhomme à Émile Augier. Paris, 1862.
Mol 825.3 Raynaud, M. Les médecins au temps de Molière. Paris, 1862.
37574.18 La récréation et passetemps des tristes. Paris, 1862.
38525.22.65 Régnier, Mathurin. Oeuvres de Mathurin Régnier. Paris, 1862.
42515.30.120 Renan, Ernest. La chaire d'hébreu au college de France. 4. éd. Paris, 1862.
Htn 42515.30.174* Renan, Ernest. De la part des peuples sémitiques dans l'histoire de la civilisation. Paris, 1862.
42515.30.175 Renan, Ernest. De la part des peuples sémitiques dans l'histoire de la civilisation. 5. éd. Paris, 1862.
42515.30.385 Renan, Ernest. Études d'histoire religieuse. 5. éd. Paris, 1862.
38513.13 Robillard de Beaupaire. Les miracles du Mont Saint Michel - Théâtre arranches. Paris, 1862.
38525.17 Ronsard, Pierre de. Choix de poésies. Paris, 1862. 2v.
39544.23 Saint-René Taillandier, René. La Suisse chrétienne et le dix-huitième siècle. Pages inédites de Voltaire et de Rousseau. Genève, 1862.
40575.20.10 Sainte-Beuve, Charles A. Galerie de femmes célèbres tirée des causeries des lundi. Paris, 1862.
41568.11.5.10 Saintine, Joseph Xavier Boniface. Picciola. N.Y., 1862.
41557.8.130 Sand, George. La ville noire. 3e éd. Paris, 1862.
41557.28.5 Sandeau, Jules. Valcreuse. Paris, 1862.
38546.45A Sévigné, Marie de R.C. Lettres. v.1-14 and album. Paris, 1862. 15v.
38546.36 Sévigné, Marie de R.C. Lettres choisies. Paris, 1862.
38526.49.5 Théophile de Viau. La tragédie de Pasiphaè. Paris, 1862.
FL 368.20 Thierry, Édouard. De l'influence du théâtre sur la classe ouvrière. Paris, 1862.
42588.6 Trois nouvelles. Philadelphia, 1862.
37564.21 Vissac, J.A. De la poésie latine en France. Paris, 1862.
40584.21 Vitet, L. Essais historiques. Paris, 1862.
37530.10 Wolff, Boleslas Maurice. Manuel bibliographique. Catalogue...de la littérature française. St. Petersbourg, 1862.

Chronological Listing

1863

	42562.32	About, Edmond. The nose of a notary. Boston, 1863.
	42553.28	Amiel, Henri F. La part du Rêve. Genève, 1863.
	40563.5	Ampère, Jean J. Heures de poésie. Paris, 1863.
	42542.6.5A	Augier, Émile. Compte-rendu de débats...fils de Giboyer. Toulouse, 1863.
	42554.4.10	Banville, Théodore de. La comédie française. Paris, 1863.
	42542.27.22.5	Barrière, Théodore. Le bout de l'an de l'amour. Paris, 1863.
	42575.11.3	Bellemare, Louis de. Escenas de la vida militar en Mexico. Mexico, 1863.
	Mon 112.3	Bimbent, J.E. Essais de Montaigne. Paris, 1863.
	40563.30	Boissonade, Jean F. Critique littéraire. Paris, 1863. 2v.
	38557.56.80	Bossuet, J.B. Oeuvres philosophiques. Paris, 1863.
	39533.16	Bredif, M. Segrais, sa vie et ses oeuvres. Paris, 1863.
	Mol 860.7	Briol, Marcel. Molière à Nantes. Nantes, 1863.
	FL 6118.63	Brockerhoff, F. Jean-Jacques Rousseau. Leben und Werke. v.1-3. Leipzig, 1863. 2v.
	Mol 870.17	Carcassonne, A. La fête de Molière. Paris, 1863.
	38516.10	Chastellain, Georges. Oeuvres. Bruxelles, 1863-66. 8v.
	42515.36.55	Chauvelot, Barnabé. À M. Ernest Renan. Paris, 1863.
	42565.9.3	Cherbuliez, Victor. Le comte Kostia. Paris, 1863.
	42515.36.56	Cheret. Lettres d'un curé de campagne à M. Renan sur sa Vie de Jésus. Paris, 1863.
	42542.52	Clairville, Louis François Nicolaïe. La corde sensible. Paris, 1863.
	39527.22	Colincamp, Ferdinand. Fables de La Fontaine. Paris, 1863.
	40565.24	Cuvillier-Fleury, A.A. Historiens, poétes et romanciers. Paris, 1863. 2v.
	42515.36.72	Delaunay, F. de F. Le Vme Évangile de M. Renan. Paris, 1863.
	42515.36.73	Deshaires, G. La vie de Jésus, les évangiles et M. Renan. Paris, 1863.
	42542.67.3	Dumanoir, M. Le code des femmes. Boston, 1863.
	42586.39	Durantin, Armand. Légende de l'homme éternel. Paris, 1863.
	42568.24.5	Enault, Louis. Alba. 3. éd. Paris, 1863.
	42572.23.8	Erckmann, Emile. Madame Thérèse. 8. éd. Paris, 1863.
	42574.18	Fabre, Ferdinand. Julien Savignac. Paris, 1863.
	42515.36.96	Felix, C.J. M. Renan et sa Vie de Jésus. 4. éd. Paris, 1863.
	42515.35.168	Félix, Célestin Joseph. M. Renan et sa vie de Jésus. Paris, 1863. 3 pam.
	42575.30.2	Feuillet, Octave. Histoire de Sibylle. 4. éd. Paris, 1863.
	Mon 68.6.5	Feuillet de Conches, F. Lettres inédites de Montaigne. Paris, 1863.
	42548.72	Le fils Gibaugier. Paris, 1863.
	42564.5	Fleury, Jules. Les aventures de mademoiselle Mariette. Paris, 1863.
	42586.53	Foudras, Marquis de. Lord Algernon. Paris, 1863.
	37581.18A	Fournel, V. Les contemporains de Molière, recueil de comédies...de 1650 à 1680. Paris, 1863-75. 3v.
	Mol 855.1	Fournel, V. Les contemporains de Molière. Paris, 1863.
	42586.54.5	Fournier, Charles A. Une volée de merles. 2. éd. Paris, 1863.
	Mol 870.16	Fournier, Edouard. La fille de Molière. Paris, 1863.
	Mol 706.2	Fournier, Edouard. Le roman de Molière. Paris, 1863.
	Mol 706.2.2	Fournier, Edouard. Le roman de Molière. Paris, 1863.
	42515.36.106	Freppel, C.E. Examen critique de la Vie de Jésus de M. Renan. 6. éd. Paris, 1863.
	42586.56	Fromentin, Eugène. Dominique. Paris, 1863.
	FL 361.12	Gaborian, Émile. Les comédiennes adorées. Paris, 1863.
	42513.38.5	Gasparin, V.B.C. de. Near and heavenly horizons. N.Y., 1863.
	41542.36	Gautier, Théophile. The romance of the mummy. N.Y., 1863.
	42515.36.116	Ginoulhiac, Jacques Marie Achille. Lettre de monseigneur l'évêque de Grenoble à l'un de ses vicaires généraux sur la Vie de Jésus. Grenoble, 1863.
	40597.3.2	Gozlan, Léon. Balzac chez lui. Paris, 1863.
	41542.42	Gozlan, Léon. Comédie des comédiens. Paris, 1863.
	41593.34.2	Guérin, Maurice de. Journal, lettres et poèmes. Paris, 1863.
	42513.43.10	Guizot, F.P.G. Un projet de mariage royal. Paris, 1863.
	42554.52	Harel, Rose. Poésies. Lisieux, 1863.
	39545.4	Havard, J.A. Voltaire et Mme. du Chatelet. Paris, 1863.
	Mol 608.7	Hillebrand, K. Des conditions de la bonne comédie. Paris, 1863.
	41571.4A	Hugo, Adèle F. Victor Hugo. N.Y., 1863.
	41571.18.5	Hugo, Victor. Illustrations to Les misérables. N.Y., 1863.
Htn	41571.19*	Hugo, Victor. Les misérables. pt.1,3,4,5. Richmond, 1863-64.
	37564.48	Jacquinet, P. Des predicateurs du XVIIe siècle avant Bosquet. Paris, 1863.
	40567.16	Janin, Jules. Contes fantastiques. n.p., 1863.
	FL 6128.63	Junod, L. Jean-Jacques Rousseau au val-de-travers. Neuchâtel, 1863.
	42587.11	Kock, Henry de. Les mystères du village. Paris, 1863. 2v.
	39525.17	La Fontaine, Jean de. Oeuvres inédites par P. Lacroix. Paris, 1863.
	41577.3	Lamartine, Alphonse de. Histoire de la Russie. (Oeuvres comp.31). Paris, 1863.
	41577.7	Lamartine, Alphonse de. Mémoires politiques. (Oeuvres comp.37-40). Paris, 1863. 4v.
	41577.5	Lamartine, Alphonse de. Nouveau voyage en Orient (1850). (Oeuvres comp.33). Paris, 1863.
	41577.2	Lamartine, Alphonse de. Nouvelles confidences. (Oeuvres comp.29-30). Paris, 1863. 2v.
	41577.4	Lamartine, Alphonse de. Toussaint Louverture. (Oeuvres comp.32). Paris, 1863.
	41577.6	Lamartine, Alphonse de. Vies de quelques hommes illustres. (Oeuvres comp.34-36). Paris, 1863. 3v.
	38543.15	La Rochefoucauld, François. Oeuvres inédites. Paris, 1863.
	42515.36.154	Larroque, Patrice. Opinion des déistes rationalistes sur la Vie de Jésus selon M. Renan. 2. éd. Paris, 1863.
	42515.36.155.4	Lasserre, Henri. L'évangile selon Renan. 5. éd. Paris, 1863.
	42555.33.25	Laurent, Charles Marie. France et Bretagne; poésies. Paris, 1863.
	42513.50	Lemoinne, John. Nouvelles études critiques. Paris, 1863.
	42515.35.157	LeRoy, Ernest. Réponse d'un poète à E. Renan. Paris, 1863.

1863 - cont.

	40571.5	Levallois, Jules. Critique militante. Paris, 1863.
	37572.29	Louandre, Charles. Histoire de la litterature française. Paris, 1863.
	42515.36.161	Loyseau, Jean. Lettres sur la vie d'un nommé Jésus selon M. E. Renan. Paris, 1863.
	42515.36.162	Loyson, Jules T. Une prétendue vie de Jésus ou Ernest Renan. 3. éd. Paris, 1863.
	40535.26	Marivaux, Pierre Carlet de Chamblain de. Théâtre. Paris, 1863.
	42515.35.167	Marriot, Maurice. La vie de Renan suite à la vie de Jésus. 4. éd. Toulouse, 1863.
	42515.36.170	Meignan, G. M. Renan réfuté par les rationalistes allemands. Paris, 1863.
	42545.10.10	Meilhac, Henri. La clé de Metella. 2. éd. Paris, 1863.
	42533.5	Merlet, Gustave. Portraits d'hier et d'aujourd'hui, antiques. Paris, 1863.
	42533.8	Merlet, Gustave. Réalistes et fantaisies. Paris, 1863.
	37566.15	Michiels, Alfred. Histoire des idées littéraires. Paris, 1863. 2v.
	42577.35.50	Mirecourt, Eugène de. Le fils de Gibaugier; comédie. Paris, 1863.
	42577.35.55	Mirecourt, Eugène de. Le petit fils de Pigault-Lebrun. Paris, 1863.
	Mol 245.38	Molière, Jean Baptiste Poquelin. Le misanthrope. Fiebig et Leportier. Leipzig, 1863.
	Mol 18.63.10	Molière, Jean Baptiste Poquelin. Oeuvres. Paris, 1863. 2v.
	Mol 18.63.4	Molière, Jean Baptiste Poquelin. Oeuvres complètes...Moland. Paris, 1863-64. 7v.
	Mol 18.63.3	Molière, Jean Baptiste Poquelin. Oeuvres complètes...Moland. Paris, 1863-64. 7v.
	Mol 18.63.2	Molière, Jean Baptiste Poquelin. Oeuvres complètes...Taschereau. Paris, 1863. 6v.
	Mol 18.63	Molière, Jean Baptiste Poquelin. Oeuvres complètes...Taschereau. Paris, 1863. 6v.
	Mol 8.66F	Molière, Jean Baptiste Poquelin. Oeuvres complètes. v.1-2. Paris, 1863?
	Mol 269.5.12	Molière, Jean Baptiste Poquelin. Tartuffe. G. Grunert. Stuttgart, 1863.
	Mol 268.45	Molière, Jean Baptiste Poquelin. Le Tartuffe. 3. Aufl. Stuttgart, 1863.
NEDL	40561.4	Montalembert, Charles F.R. Memoir of the Abbe Lacordaire. London, 1863.
	37575.405	Nisard, Charles. La Muse pariétaire...ou Les chansons des rues. Paris, 1863.
	42578.23.10	Noriac, Jules. Human follies. N.Y., 1863.
	42545.50.5	Nus, Eugène. Un mari brulé. Boston, 1863.
	42515.36.195	Orth, Jacques. La Vie de Jésus selon M. Renan. Mulhouse, 1863.
	42515.35.208	Pavy, L.C. Conférence contre le livre de M. Renan. 2. éd. Constantine, 1863.
	42515.36.211	Pinard, C. Notes à l'usage des lecteurs du Jésus de M. Renan. Paris, 1863.
	42515.36.213	Plantier, C.H.A. Instruction pastorale de Mgr. Plantier. 2. éd. Paris, 1863.
	42576.65.12.250	Poligny, J.H. Le prêtre marié. Paris, 1863.
	42534.25	Pontmartin, A.F. de. Contes d'un planteur de choux. Paris, 1863.
	42534.23	Pontmartin, A.F. de. Nouvelles semaines littéraires. Paris, 1863.
	42515.36.214	Potrel, Eugène. Vie de N.S. Jésus-Christ. Paris, 1863.
	42515.36.216	Pressense, E. L'école critique et Jésus-Christ à propos de la vie de Jésus de M. Renan. 3. éd. Paris, 1863.
	42515.20.15	Prevost-Paradol, L.A.P. de. Essais de politique et de littérature. 2. éd. 2. ser. Paris, 1863.
	38583.4.30A	Racine, Jean. Théâtre complet. Paris, 1863.
	Mol 825.4	Raynaud, M. Les médecins au temps de Molière. Paris, 1863.
Htn	42515.29.2.5*	Renan, Ernest. Vie de Jésus. Paris, 1863.
	42515.29.2	Renan, Ernest. Vie de Jésus. Paris, 1863.
	42515.29.2.8	Renan, Ernest. Vie de Jésus. 5. éd. Paris, 1863.
	Mol 870.15	Roche, E. La dernière fourberie de Scapin. n.p., 1863.
	38515.18	Romancero de Champagne. Reims, 1863-64. 5v.
	38525.27.8	Rothschild, J. de. Essai sur les satires de Mathurin Régnier, 1573-1613. Paris, 1863.
	41557.8.15.13	Roy, Just J.E. Solange de Chateaubrun. 3. éd. Tours, 1863.
	39594.30.3	St. Pierre, J.H.B. de. Paul et Virginie. Paris, 1863.
	39594.30	St. Pierre, J.H.B. de. Paul et Virginie suivi de La chaumière indienne. Paris, 1863.
	41557.9.33	Sand, George. Fanchon the Cricket. N.Y., 1863.
	41557.8.129	Sand, George. Valvèdre. Paris, 1863.
	41557.12	Sandeau, Jules. Un début dans la magistrature. Paris, 1863.
	42546.25.30	Sardou, Victorien. Les ganaches. N.Y., 1863.
	42535.22.50	Scherer, Edmond. Études critiques sur la littérature contemporaine. Paris, 1863-95. 10v.
	41592.1.75	Schuré, M. Étude sur les sonnets d'Edmond Arnould. Paris, 1863.
	41568.17	Sénancour, Étienne Pivert de. Obermann. Paris, 1863.
	38546.46	Sévigné, Marie de R.C. Lettres. v.1-8. Paris, 1863. 7v.
	40573.4	Simonnet, Jules. Essai sur la vie et les ouvrages de Gabriel Peignot. Paris, 1863.
	37547.2.10	Société archéologique et historique de la Charente, Angoulême. Le trésor des pièces angoumoisines inédites ou rares. Paris, 1863-66. 2v.
	FL 361.11	Sorel, Jacques. Les reines de la rampe. Paris, 1863.
	Mol 719.6	Soulié, E. Recherches sur Molière et sur sa famille. Paris, 1863.
	41558.22	Soulié, Frédéric. Les quatre soeurs. Paris, 1863.
	41563.31	Toepffer, Rodolphe. Rosa et Gertrude. Paris, 1863.
	37543.634	Tricotel, Édouard. Variétés bibliographiques. Paris, 1863.
Htn	38512.27*	Tross, Edwin. Cent cinq rondeaux d'amour. Paris, 1863.
	42557.10.5	Vannespennes, J. Au pape, poème lyrique. Belgique, 1863.
	42521.17	Veuillot, Louis. Le fond de Giboyer. 5. éd. Paris, 1863.
	41596.69	Viennet, J.P.G. Franciade; poëme en dix chants. Paris, 1863.
	37555.302.2	Weigand, G. Traité de versification française. Bromberg, 1863.
	42522.36	Weyer, Sylvain van der. Choix d'opuscules. Bruxelles, 1863. 4v.
	42522.36.2	Weyer, Sylvain van der. Choix d'opuscules. N.Y., 1863.

Chronological Listing

1864

42562.12 About, Edmond. Les mariages de Paris. Paris, 1864.
42562.18 About, Edmond. Théâtre impossible. N.Y., 1864.
42586.5 Achard, Amédée. Madame Rose. Pierre de villerglé. Paris, 1864.
42563.26.5 Achille, A. d'. Discorso. Roma, 1864.
41592.7 Arnould, Arthur. Béranger. Paris, 1864. 2v.
42562.38.90.5 Aulnay, Louise d'. Lettres de deux poupées. Paris, 1864.
41591.2.9 Aveline, Alexandre. Poésies. v.1-2. La Havane, 1864.
40597.35 Balzac, Honoré de. Vendetta. Boston, 1864.
42554.1.05A Banville, Théodore de. Les cariatides. Paris, 1864.
Htn 37558.48* Barbey d'Aurevilly, Jules. Les quarante médaillons de l'académie. Paris, 1864.
42542.27.15 Barbier, Jules. La fille du Maudit. Paris, 1864.
40587.4.2 Benoit, Charles. Éloge de Chateaubriand. Cuttings. n.p., 1864. 2 pam.
41522.37.2 Bernard, Charles de. Le gentilhomme Campagnard. Paris, 1864. 2v.
41522.49 Bernard, Charles de. Le paratonnerre. Paris, 1864.
40582.9.5 Beyle, Henri. Chartreuse de Parme. Paris, 1864.
40582.8.3 Beyle, Henri. De l'amour. Paris, 1864.
40582.27 Beyle, Henri. Vie de Rossini. Paris, 1864.
Mon 112.3.3 Bimbent, J.E. Essais de Montaigne. Orleans, 1864.
37558.50 Biré, Edmond. Les poètes lauréats de l'Académie française. Paris, 1864. 2v.
42559.7 Bonie, F. Chansons. 2. éd. Bruxelles, 1864.
38557.48.50 Bossuet, J.B. Traité de la connaissance de Dieu et de soi-même. Paris, 1864.
42515.36.40 Bourgade, F. Lettre à M.E. Renan à l'occasion de son ouvrage intutulé, Vie de Jésus. Paris, 1864.
42515.36.43 Brunner, Sebastian. Der Atheist Renan und sein Evangelium. Regensburg, 1864.
Htn 42586.52.7* Caillot-Duval (pseud.). Les mystifications de Caillot-Duval. Paris, 1864.
42515.35.51 Castro y Rossi, Adolfo de. Ernesto Renan ante la erudición sagrada y profana. Cadiz, 1864.
42563.72.5 Champceix, Léodile Béra de. Une veille fille. Paris, 1864.
42565.7A Cherbuliez, Victor. Un cheval de Phidias. Paris, 1864.
42565.22.9 Cherbuliez, Victor. Paule Méré. N.Y., 1864.
42565.43 Cherbuliez, Victor. Le prince Vitale. Paris, 1864.
37567.31.10 Claretie, J. Elisa Mercoeur, Hippolyte de la Morvonnais, George Farcy, Charles Doyalle, Alphonse Rabbe. Paris, 1864.
42515.36.62 Colani, T. Examen de La vie de Jésus de M. Renan. 2. éd. Strassburg, 1864.
40534.20 Collé, Charles. Correspondance inédite. Paris, 1864.
42515.36.66 Crelier, H.J. M.E. Renan trahissant le Christ par un roman. 2. ed. Paris, 1864.
40587.50 Danielo, Julien. Les conversations de M. de Chateaubriand. Paris, 1864.
42515.36.70 Daspers, L. Le Christ de l'histoire en face du Christ de M. Renan. Paris, 1864.
42542.63 Délerot, E. Vercingétorix. Paris, 1864.
40556.5 Deschanel, Émile. Physiologie des écrivains. Paris, 1864.
37563.16 Dezeimeris, Reinhold. De la renaissance des lettres à Bordeaux. Bordeaux, 1864.
39564.8.50 Diderot, Denis. Romans et contes. Paris, 1864.
FL 358.64 Du Casse, Albert. Histoire anecdotique de l'ancien théâtre en France. Paris, 1864. 2v.
42542.66.200 DuGuillet, P. Rymes de gentile et vertueuse dame. Lyon, 1864.
41538.63.10 Dumas, Alexandre. Napoléon. N.Y., 1864.
42543.20.5 Dumas, Alexandre. Un paquete de cartas. Habana, 1864.
41538.50 Dumas, Alexandre. Théâtre complet. Paris, 1864.
41593.32.8 Dupont, Pierre. Dix églogues, poèmes bycoliques. Lyon, 1864.
37558.45 Edwards, Edward. Chapters of the biographical history of the French academy. London, 1864.
41593.32.75 Feburel, Edmond. Fleurettes. Strasbourg, 1864. 2 pam.
42575.50.2 Feuillet, Octave. The romance of a poor young man. N.Y., 1864.
42575.51.5 Feuillet, Octave. Le village. Boston, 1864.
42575.21.5 Feydeau, Ernest. Le secret du bonheur. N.Y., 1864.
Mol 606.4 Fischer, F. Molière, ein Beitrag. Duisburg, 1864.
Htn 38516.36* La fleur de poésie françoyse. Paris, 1864.
42564.11 Fleury, Jules. Les demoiselles Tourangeau. Paris, 1864.
42564.25 Fleury, Jules. Monsieur de Boisdhyver. Paris, 1864.
42564.32 Fleury, Jules. La succession de Camus. Paris, 1864.
38557.13 Floquet, Amable. Bossuet, précepteur du Dauphin. Paris, 1864.
42576.58 Foa, Eugénie. Le petit Robinson de Paris. Boston, 1864.
42576.59.5 Foa, Eugénie. Le petit Robinson de Paris. N.Y., 1864.
37564.18 Follioley, Léopold. Histoire de la littérature françoise. Paris, 1864.
37558.7 Fontaine de Resbecq, Adolphe C.T. Voyages littéraires sur le Quaiș de Paris. Paris, 1864.
FL 377.7 Fournier, Édouard. L'Espagne et ses comédiens en France. Paris, 1864.
42515.36.105 Fregier, J.C. Jésus devant le droit. Paris, 1864.
42576.13.30 Garcia, Marie. La confession d'Antonine. Paris, 1864.
42513.39 Gasparin, V.B.C. de. Near and heavenly horizons. N.Y., 1864.
42513.36 Gasparin, V.B.C. de. Les tristesses humaines. Paris, 1864.
41542.6.5 Gautier, Théophile. Le capitaine Fracasse. N.Y., 1864.
42576.36.20 Gay, Sophie. Marie de Mancini. Paris, 1864.
42576.36.21 Gay, Sophie. Physiologie du ridicule. Paris, 1864.
41541.8.5 Girardin, Delphine Gay. La joie fait peur. Boston, 1864.
41541.8.6 Girardin, Delphine Gay. La joie fait peur. 5. éd. N.Y., 1864.
42543.55 Gondinet, Edmond. Sous cloche. Paris, 1864.
41593.34.2.5 Guérin, Maurice de. Journal, lettres et poèmes. 6. éd. Paris, 1864.
42515.35.127 Harrisse, Henry. M. Ernest Renan. Paris, 1864.
FL 6128.64 Houssaye, A. Les charmettes. Jean-Jacques Rousseau et Mme. de Warens. 2. éd. Paris, 1864.
37558.35 Houssaye, Arsène. Histoire de 41e fauteuil. Paris, 1864.
42576.14.9.15 Houssaye, Arsène. Mademoiselle Cléopâtre. 7. éd. Paris, 1864.
41571.18 Hugo, Victor. Les chandeliers. pt.4. N.Y, 1864.
39545.14 Jacquot, C.J.B. La queue de Voltaire. Paris, 1864.
40556.21.10 Joubert, Joseph. Pensées de J. Joubert précédées de sa correspondance. 4. éd. Paris, 1864.
37596.6 Jubinal, A. Études sur...Rutebeuf. Paris, 1864.
41544.7.9 Karr, Alphonse. Las mujeres. Madrid, 1864.
41553.29 Kock, Charles Paul de. Zizine. Paris, 1864.

1864 - cont.

42548.29 Labiche, Eugène. Les petits oiseaux. Boston, 1864.
42548.28 Labiche, Eugène. La poudre aux yeux. Boston, 1864.
38561.30 La Bruyère, J. Les caracteres ou les moeurs de ce siècle. Paris, 1864.
39527.22.5 La Fontaine, Jean de. Fables. Tours, 1864.
41574.80 Lalanne, M. Maxime. Chez Victor Hugo. Paris, 1864.
41578.35.115 Lamartine, Alphonse. Antar. Paris, 1864.
42555.12.9 La Morvannais, H. de. La Thébaïde des grèves. Paris, 1864.
41578.61.5 Lebailly, Armand. Madame de Lamartine. Paris, 1864.
Mol 612.7 Legrelle, A. Holberg considéré comme imitateur de Molière. Paris, 1864.
40512.12 LeSage, Alain René. Adventures of Gil Blas. Boston, 1864. 3v.
40512.33 LeSage, Alain René. Historia de Gil Blas de Santillana. Paris, 1864.
Mol 873.10 Longhaye, G. Le souper d'Auteuil. Paris, 1864.
37597.5A Lorris, Guillaume de. Le roman de la rose. Paris, 1864. 2v.
42548.13 Maltchycé, Marie de. La petite maman. Boston, 1864.
42548.13.2 Maltchycé, Marie de. La petite maman. 4. éd. N.Y., 1864. 2 pam.
41586.23.30 Méry, Joseph. Poésies intimes; mélodies. Paris, 1864.
42577.35.8 Michon, Jean H. Le maudit. 3. éd. Paris, 1864.
42514.29 Mignet, F.A.M. Éloges historiques. Paris, 1864.
42515.36.3 Milsand, P. Bibliographie des publications relatives au livre de M. Renan Vie de Jésus. Paris, 1864.
42515.35.173 Mirville, J.E. Le vrai secret de M. Renan. Paris, 1864.
Mol 211.25 Molière, Jean Baptiste Poquelin. Les femmes savantes...Geruzez. Paris, 1864.
Htn Mol 18.64* Molière, Jean Baptiste Poquelin. Théâtre...Hillemacher. Lyon, 1864-70. 8v.
Mol 491.1 Molière, Jean Baptiste Poquelin. Vers espagnols. Jacob. Paris, 1864.
39586.21.5 Monselet, C. Fréron ou L'illustre critique. Paris, 1864.
38526.39.50 Morenne, C. de. Poésies profanes. Caen, 1864.
42577.28 Murger, Henry. Le serment d'Horace. Paris, 1864.
41596.30.25 Musset, Alfred de. El capricho. Madrid, 1864.
37567.365 Nettement, A. Le roman contemporain. Paris, 1864.
42515.36.184 Nicolas, A. Renan et sa Vie de Jésus sous les rapports moral, légal et littéraire. Paris, 1864.
40572.27 Nisard, Désiré. Nouvelles études d'histoire et de littérature. Paris, 1864.
41593.16.5 Oeuvres complètes de Charles de Chênedollé. Paris, 1864.
37572.27 Oppen, Edward A. French reader. London, 1864.
38511.35 Oresme, N. Traictie de la première invention des monnoies. Paris, 1864.
42515.36.204 Passaglia, Carlo. Étude sur la Vie de Jésus de Ernest Renan. 2. éd. Paris, 1864.
38528.17 Passerat, Jean. Le chien courant. Paris, 1864.
42515.36.213.2 Plantier, C.H.A. La vraie vie de Jésus. 2. éd. Paris, 1864.
41567.50 Ponson du Terrail. Le capitaine Curebourse. N.Y., 1864.
42534.24 Pontmartin, A.F. de. Derniers semaines littéraires. Paris, 1864.
41596.51.5 Porchat, Jacques. Trois mois sous la neige. Philadelphia, 1864.
42556.11.3 Poutmartin, A. de. Jean Reboul. Paris, 1864.
Mol 716.2 Prescott, W.H. Essais de biographie et de critique. Paris, 1864.
38583.3.2 Racine, Jean. Oeuvres. Paris, 1864.
42515.29.3 Renan, Ernest. Jésus. 3. éd. Paris, 1864.
42515.29.7 Renan, Ernest. Jésus. 16. éd. Paris, 1864.
42515.29.100 Renan, Ernest. Life of Jesus. London, 1864.
42515.30.400A Renan, Ernest. Studies of religious history and criticism. N.Y., 1864.
42515.29.5 Renan, Ernest. Vie de Jésus. 7. éd. Paris, 1864.
37563.9 Revillout, M.C. La prose française avant le XVIIe siècle. Montpellier, 1864.
37567.23 Reymond, W. Corneille, Shakspeare et Goethe. Berlin, 1864.
42535.3.5 Romey, Charles. Hommes et choses de divers temps. Paris, 1864.
42546.9 Rosier, Joseph Bernard. Brutus, lâche César comédie en un acte mêleé de chant. Paris, 1864.
41587.20.150F Rousseau, Pierre Joseph. La mort de Bucéphale. Paris, 1864.
41565.31.10 St. Mars, G.A.C. de C. La chambre bleue. Paris, 1864.
40575.33.5A Sainte-Beuve, Charles A. Portraits littéraires. Paris, 1864? 3v.
40536.25 Salles, Jean Baptiste. Charlotte Corday. Paris, 1864.
41557.9.33.2 Sand, George. Fanchon the Cricket. N.Y., 1864.
41557.8.97.5 Sand, George. Les maîtres mosaistes. Paris, 1864.
41557.8.105.15 Sand, George. Le marquis de Villemer. 2. éd. Paris, 1864.
42548.27 Sandeau, Jules. La maison de Penarvan. Boston, 1864.
42515.35.234 Saquet, J. Ernest Renan et ses oeuvres. Rodez, 1864.
42546.19 Sardou, Victorien. Le dégel. Paris, 1864.
42546.19.5 Sardou, Victorien. Le dégel. Paris, 1864.
41588.15.8.4 Scribe, Eugène. La bataille de dames. N.Y., 1864.
41588.15.8.3 Scribe, Eugène. La bataille de dames. 5e éd. N.Y., 1864.
42548.21 Souvestre, Emile. La vieille cousine. Boston, 1864.
42535.27 Spach, Louis. Mélanges d'histoire et de critique littéraire. v.1-2,3-4,5. Strasbourg, 1864-70. 3v.
42556.11.5 Tivier, M. Étude sur Reboul. n.p., 1864.
40546.22 Tocqueville, Alexis de. De la democratie en Amérique. 14. éd. Paris, 1864. 3v.
42515.36.261 Tullock, John. The Christ of the Gospels and the Christ of modern criticism. London, 1864.
41565.34 Vacquerie, Auguste. Profils et grimances. 4. ed. Paris, 1864.
37558.43 Vattier, G. Galerie des Académiciens et 1st et 3d. 2nd Série. Paris, 1864. 3v.
41564.20 Vigny, Alfred de. Théâtre complet. Paris, 1864.
37591.35 Wolf, Ferdinand. Über...Altfranzosische Doctrinen von der Minne. Vienna, 1864.

1865

42562.4 About, Edmond. Causeries. Paris, 1865.
42561.7 About, Edmond. La vielle roche. Paris, 1865-66.
41598.16 Une academie en province, par un étudiant. Paris, 1865.
42562.37 Achard, Amédée E. Clos pommier et prissonniers du Caucase. Boston, 1865.
37597.36A Adenès li rois. Li roumans de Cléomodès. Brussels, 1865.
Mol 601.2 Aderer, A. Les femmes dans les comédies de Molière. St. Cloud, 1865.

1865 - cont.

40563.13	Ampère, Jean J. La science et les lettres en Orient. Paris, 1865.
42542.1.30	Arnault, L. Oeuvres dramatiques. Paris, 1865. 3v.
42542.10.3	Augier, Émile. Le gendre de M. Poirier. 2e éd. Bielefeld, 1865.
42542.8	Augier, Émile. Maître Guérin. Paris, 1865.
42542.8.1	Augier, Émile. Maître Guérin. 2. éd. Paris, 1865.
42542.9	Augier, Émile. Les méprises de l'amour. Paris, 1865-68.
42542.15	Augier, Émile. Poésies complètes. Paris, 1865.
37565.23	Barni, Jules. Histoire des idées morales. Paris, 1865. 2v.
42542.27.22	Barriere, Théodore. Les jocrisses de l'amour. v.1-7. Paris, 1865.
Mol 602.1	Baudouin, F.M. Les femmes dans Molière. Rouen, 1865.
42548.5	Bayard, J.F.A. La niaise de Saint Flour. Boston, 1865.
42575.6	Bellemare, Louis de. Le coureur des bois. 6. éd. Paris, 1865. 2v.
40587.4	Benoit, Charles. Chateaubriand, sa vie et ses oeuvres. Paris, 1865.
41522.40	Bernard, Charles de. Un homme sérieux. Paris, 1865.
40582.23	Beyle, Henri. Rome, Naples, et Florence. Paris, 1865.
Mol 728.4	Brouchoud, C. Notice sur les origines du théâtre de Lyon. n.p., 1865.
Mol 728.10	Brouchoud, C. Les origines du théâtre de Lyon. Lyon, 1865.
37543.9	Brunet, P.G. La France littéraire au XVe siècle. Paris, 1865.
42563.72.20	Champceix, Léodile Béra de. Les deux filles de monsieur Plichon. Paris, 1865.
42563.72.9	Champceix, Léodile Béra de. L'idéal au village par André Léo. Paris, 1865.
42563.72.15	Champceix, Léodile Béra de. Jacques Galéron. Paris, 1865.
40564.24	Chasles, Philarète. Voyages d'un critique. n.p., 1865. 2v.
42565.24	Cherbuliez, Victor. Paule Méré. Paris, 1865.
42542.52.11	Clairville, Louis François Nicolaïe. Les petites misères de la vie humaine. Boston, 1865.
42586.31.10	Claretié, J. Voyages d'un&Parisien. Paris, 1865.
41522.67.90	Claretie, Jules. Pétrus Borel le lycanthrope. Paris, 1865.
Mol 603.4	Clarke, C.C. Molière characters. Edinburgh, 1865.
38571.8	Corneille, Pierre. Oeuvres des deux Corneille (Pierre et Thomas). Paris, 1865. 2v.
38526.10.11.150	Corrozet, Gilles. Les blasons domestiques. Paris, 1865.
40546.7	Courier de Méré, Paul Louis. Oeuvres. Paris, 1865.
40553.21.5	Cousin, Victor. Fragments philosophiques. 5. éd. Paris, 1865-66. 5v.
40565.23	Cuvillier-Fleury, A.A. Études et portraits. Paris, 1865. 2v.
41591.24	Delille, Jacques. Oeuvres complètes. Paris, 1865.
41543.19	Delvan, A. Gerard de Nerval. Paris, 1865.
38514.44.5	Deschamps, Eustache. Le miroir de marriage. Reims, 1865.
41593.29.80	Deshayes, Adrien. Étude historique et littéraire sur Madame de Maintenon. St. Petersbourg, 1865.
42513.10	Despois, Eugene. Les lettres et la liberté. Paris, 1865.
FL 391.59	Duflot, Joachim. Les secrets des coulisses des théâtres de Paris. Paris, 1865.
41525.27	Dumas, Alexandre. Impressions de voyage. En Russie. v.1,2,3-4. Paris, 1865. 3v.
41526.3	Dumas, Alexandre. Impressions de voyage. La villa Palmieri. Paris, 1865.
41525.24	Dumas, Alexandre. Impressions de voyage. Midi de la France. Paris, 1865.
41525.22	Dumas, Alexandre. Impressions de voyage. Voyage au Caucase. Paris, 1865. 3v.
41526.22	Dumas, Alexandre. Mes mémoires. v.1-10. Paris, 1865. 5v.
40524.16	Elie de Beaumont, A.L. Oeuvres. Paris, 1865.
Mol 605.3	Epagny, F. d'. Molière et Scribe. Paris, 1865.
38553.26	Fénelon, F. de S. de la Mothe. Les aventures de Télémaque. Philadelphia, 1865.
38554.6	Fénelon, F. de S. de la Mothe. Fables. 2. éd. Paris, 1865.
42575.49	Feuillet, Octave. Le roman d'un jeune homme pauvre. Boston, 1865.
42576.59.10	Foa, Eugénie. Contes biographiques. N.Y., 1865.
37542.33	Fournier, E. Les écrivains sur le trône. Paris, 1865.
42515.36.110	Furness, W.H. Remarks on Renan's Life of Jésus. Philadelphia, 1865.
42515.44.10	Gaetani-Tamburini, N. Edgardo Quinet; studi. 2. ed. Milano, 1865.
41542.37.4	Gautier, Théophile. Quand on voyage. Paris, 1865.
41541.15	Girardin, Delphine Gay. Marguerite ou deux amours. Paris, 1865.
42548.25	Girardin, Émile de. La joie fait peur. Boston, 1865.
42575.71	Goncourt, Edmond de. Germinie Lacerteux. Paris, 1865.
41542.40	Gozlan, Léon. Balzac en Pantoufles. Paris, 1865.
39544.120	Horn, Georg. Voltaire und die Markgräfin von Baireuth. Berlin, 1865.
41571.10.15	Hugo, Victor. Les misérables. Paris, 1865.
40567.7	Janin, Jules. L'ane mort. n.p., 1865.
40567.33	Janin, Jules. Discours de réceptions a la porte de l'académie française. Paris, 1865.
38527.32	Joly, A. Antoine de Montchrétien. Caen, 1865.
41544.15	Karr, Alphonse. Midi à quatorze heures. Paris, 1865.
41544.32	Karr, Alphonse. Sur la plage. Paris, 1865.
38511.24	Keller, Adelbert von. Miracle de Notre Dame. Tübingen, 1865.
41553.33	Kock, Charles Paul de. Le sentier aux prunes. Paris, 1865.
42548.11	Labiche, Eugène. La cagnotte. Boston, 1865.
38528.10	Labitte, Charles. Satyre Ménippée. Ratisbon, 1865.
42514.6	Laboulaye, Édouard. Études contemporaines sur l'Allemagne. Paris, 1865.
38564.27	La Bruyère, J. de. Oeuvres. v.1-3 and album. Paris, 1865. 4v.
40562.25	Lacordaire, Jean Baptiste Henri. Le Père Lacordaire et son ordre. 2. ed. Paris, 1865.
Mol 453.2	Lacroix, Paul. Un manuscrit du souffleur...Molière. Paris, 1865.
39526.32.25	La Fontaine, Jean de. Fables et oeuvres diverses. Paris, 1865.
42555.31	Laprade, Victor de. Les voix du silence. Paris, 1865.
37561.12A	Le Clerc, V. Histoire littéraire de la France au 14th siècle. Paris, 1865. 2v.
41586.11.8	Leclercq, Théodore. Trois proverbes. Boston, 1865.

1865 - cont.

FL 398.49.27	Lecomte, L.H. Frédérick Lemaitre. Paris, 1865.
42576.42.50	Lemonnier, A. Les femmes de théâtre. Paris, 1865.
41541.20.125	Le Rousseau, Julien. Progrès de la littérature dramatique. Paris, 1865.
40512.26A	LeSage, Alain René. Histoire de Gil Blas. Paris, 1865.
42576.46.28	Lespès, Napoléon. Les matinées de Timothée Trimm. 5. éd. Paris, 1865.
40588.48	Maistre, Xavier. Les prisonniers du Caucase. Boston, 1865.
41567.43	Masson, Michel. La femme du réfractaire. Paris, 1865.
40529.80	Maurepas, J.F.P. Recueil dit de Maurepas. v.1-6. Leyde, 1865. 3v.
41586.24.5	Maurice-Descombes, Charles. Épaves, théâtre, histoire, anecdotes, mots. Paris, 1865.
42548.14	Mazeres, E.J.E. Le collier de perles. Paris, 1865.
38583.3	Mensard, Paul. Oeuvres de Jean Racine. Album et musique. Paris, 1865-73. 10v.
42533.6	Merlet, Gustave. Causeries sur les femmes et les livres. Paris, 1865.
42577.34.20	Mettais, Hippolyte. L'an 5865, ou Paris dans quatre mille ans. Paris, 1865.
42577.35	Michon, Jean H. Le jésuite. v.1-5. Paris, 1865.
Mol 870.12	Minier, H. Molière à Bordeaux. Bordeaux, 1865.
Mol 62.23	Molière, Jean Baptiste Poquelin. Charakter-Komödien...Laun. v.1-3. Hildburghausen, 1865.
Mol 62.24	Molière, Jean Baptiste Poquelin. Lustspiele...Baudissin. Leipzig, 1865-67. 4v.
42551.15	Montaiglon, Anatole de. L'Aubepine et le Marronnier de Sannois. Paris, 1865. 5 pam.
Mon 18.65	Montaigne, Michel de. Essais. Le Clerc. Paris, 1865-66. 4v.
Mon 31.26	Montaigne, Michel de. Works. Hazlitt. London, 1865.
FL 382.15A	Muret, Théodore C. L'histoire par le théâtre. Paris, 1865. 3v.
41596.21	Musset, Alfred de. La confession d'un enfant du siècle. Paris, 1865.
41596.10	Musset, Alfred de. Premières poésies. Paris, 1865.
42545.47	Nuitter de Beaumont, E. La flute enchantée. Paris, 1865.
41587.18.15	Picard, Louis Benoît. L'impostore o L'arte di far Fortuna. Firenze, 1865.
42545.82.3	Ponsard, F. L'honneur et l'argent. 4. éd. Bielefeld, 1865.
42541.29	Ponsard, François. Oeuvres complètes. Paris, 1865. 2v.
42556.15	Prior, Jules. Les veilles d'un artisan. Paris, 1865.
FL 397.3.15	Prologue pour l'inauguration à Angers le 4 Nov. 1865 du théâtre Auber. Paris, 1865.
37574.165	Rabion. Les fleurs de la poésie française. 8. éd. Toura, 1865.
42535.18	Ratisbonne, Louis. Les figures jeunes. Paris, 1865.
42556.6	Reboul, Jean. Lettres. Paris, 1865.
40524.22	Riccoboni, M.J.L. de (Mme.). Oeuvres. Paris, 1865.
42556.31.9	Roussel, August. Gros-Jean et son curé. Bruxelles, 1865.
40576.4.20	Sainte-Beuve, Charles A. Nouvelle gallerie de femmes célèbres tirée des Causeries du lundi. Paris, 1865.
41568.11.6	Saintine, Joseph Xavier Boniface. Picciola. 3. ed. London, 1865.
41557.8.63A	Sand, George. La confession d'une jeune fille. 2. éd. Paris, 1865. 2v.
41557.8.91	Sand, George. Laura. Voyages et impressions. Paris, 1865.
41557.8.106	Sand, George. Le marquis de Villemer. 2. éd. Paris, 1865.
41557.9.30.50	Sand, George. La petite Fadette. N.Y., 1865.
41557.8.132	Sand, George. Théâtre de Nohant. Paris, 1865.
42548.30.2	Sandeau, Jules. Mademoiselle de la Seiglière. N.Y., 1865.
41557.19.4	Sandeau, Jules. Mademoiselle de la Seiglière. 5. ed. N.Y., 1865.
41557.22.5	Sandeau, Jules. La maison de Penarvan. Boston, 1865.
42546.26.10	Sardou, Victorien. Les pommes du voisin. Paris, 1865.
42546.22.5	Sardou, Victorien. Les vieux garçons. Paris, 1865.
42546.22	Sardou, Victorien. Les vieux garçons. 5e éd. Paris, 1865.
42548.26	Scribe, E. La bataille de dames. Boston, 1865.
42548.32	Scribe, E. Les doigts de fée. Boston, 1865.
42548.16	Scribe, E. Valérie. Boston, 1865.
42548.17	Scribe, E. Valérie. N.Y., 1865.
41588.3.17	Scribe, Eugène. Les doigts de fée. N.Y., 1865.
41588.3.16	Scribe, Eugène. Les doigts de fée. N.Y., 1865.
42551.20	Serment, J.H. A Abraham Lincoln. Paris, 1865.
38546.35A	Sévigné, Marie de R.C. Lettres choisies. Paris, 1865.
42548.18	Siraudin, P. Les femmes qui pleurent. Boston, 1865.
42548.18.5	Siraudin, P. Les femmes qui pleurent. N.Y., 1865.
37556.20.60	Sirven, A. Journaux et journalistes. Paris, 1865-66. 4v.
Mol 719.3	Soulié, E. Rapport sur des recherches relatives à la vie de Molière. Paris, 1865.
40588.30	Sousa Botelho Mourão e Vasconcellos, A.M.E.F. Oeuvres complètes. Paris, 1865.
41558.55	Souvestre, Émile. Loterie de Francfort . N.Y., 1865.
42548.20	Souvestre, Émile. Le testament. Boston, 1865.
FL 6015.9	Streckeisen-Moultu, George. Jean-Jacques Rousseau, ses amis et ses ennemis. v.1-2. Paris, 1865.
41562.25	Sue, Eugène. Plik et Plok. Atar Gull. Deux histoires, 1772-1870. Paris, 1865.
41562.28	Sue, Eugène. Les secrets de l'oreiller. Paris, 1865. 3v.
42556.19.7	Sully-Prudhomme, R.F.A. Stances et poèmes. Paris, 1865.
42536.9	Taine, Hippolyte. Nouveaux essais de critique et d'histoire. Paris, 1865.
37555.209	Ten Brink, B. Coniectanea in Historiam. Bonnae, 1865.
40546.17	Tocqueville, Alexis de. Mélanges. Paris, 1865.
41563.26.10	Toepffer, Rodolphe. Nouvelles genevoises. Paris, 1865. 3v.
42547.10.26	Vallon-Colley, H.M. Garibaldis et François II. Lausanne, 1865.
42521.15.5	Veuillot, Louis. Ca et la. v.2. 5. éd. Paris, 1865.
38514.21.10	Villioniana. François Villon; drame historique. Paris, 1865.
Mol 853.7	Visé, J.D. de. Lettre sur les affaires du théâtre en 1665. San Remo, 1865.
37543.26	Weiss, J.J. Essais sur l'histoire de la littérature française. Paris, 1865.

Chronological Listing

1866

	Mol 701.1F	Arago, Etienne. Molière (1622-1673). Paris, 1866?
	37530.25	Asselineau, Charles. Mélanges tirés d'une petite bibliothèque romantique. Paris, 1866.
	42542.21	Augier, Émile. Gabrielle. Paris, 1866.
	39586.2.2	Bachaumont, Louis Petit de. Mémoires secrets. Table. Bruxelles, 1866.
	41522.2.53	Barbey d'Aurevilly, Jules. Une vieille maîtresse. 2. éd. Paris, 1866.
	42542.27.19	Barrière, Théodore. Malheur aux vaincus. Paris, 1866.
	42563.22	Bassanville, Anaïs Lebrun. Les deux familles. Tours, 1866.
	41592.17.5	Béranger, P.J. de. Chansons. Paris, 1866.
	42563.28.11	Biart, Lucien. La terre tempérée. Paris, 1866.
	38575.18.5	Bonieux, B. Critique des tragedies de Corneille et de Racine par Voltaire. Paris, 1866.
	37565.16	Bonnal, Edmond. Étude sur l'histoire de la littérature pendant de la revolution. Toulouse, 1866.
	Mol 828.2	Cauvet, Jules. La science du droit dans les comédies de Molière. Caen, 1866.
	40564.20	Chasles, Philarète. Études contemporaines. Paris, 1866. 2v.
	42565.28.3	Cherbuliez, Victor. Le roman d'une honnête femme. Paris, 1866.
	FL 6128.66	Chereau, A. La vérité sur la mort de Jean-Jacques Rousseau. Paris, 1866.
	40562.14.2	Chocarne, B. Le R.P.H.D. Lacordaire...sa vie intime et religieuse. Paris, 1866. 2v.
	37547.14	Colletet, Guillaume. Vies des poètes gascons. Paris, 1866.
	41522.76	Cordellier-Delanoue, A. Jacques Coeur. Tours, 1866.
	39545.22	Deschanel, E. Le théâtre de Voltaire. Paris, 1866.
	Mon 114.4	Dezeimeris, R. Recherches sur la texte des essais. Bordeaux, 1866.
	38524.34	Du Bellay, Joachim. Oeuvres Françoises. Paris, 1866. 2v.
	41523.5.2	Dumas, Alexandre. Ange Pitou. v.1-2. Bruxelles, 1866.
	41525.10	Dumas, Alexandre. Les grands hommes en robe de Chambre. César. Paris, 1866.
	Mon 114.3	Dumont, L. La morale de Montaigne. Valenciennes, 1866.
	37565.31	Duprat, Pascal. Les encyclopédistes. Paris, 1866.
	42543.28.15	Durantin, Armand. Héloise Paranquet. Paris, 1866.
	42568.31	Enault, Louis. Le roman d'une Altesse. Paris, 1866.
	40587.16	Essai sur Chateaubriand. Paris, 1866.
	38552.7	Fénelon, F. de S. de la Mothe. Oeuvres de Fénelon. Paris, 1866.
	38554.322.68	Fénelon, F. de S. de la Mothe. Triaté de l'existence de Dieu. Paris, 1866.
	42575.49.4	Feuillet, Octave. Le roman d'un jeune homme pauvre. N.Y., 1866.
	42575.49.3	Feuillet, Octave. Le roman d'un jeune homme pauvre. N.Y., 1866.
	FL 360.85	Florentino, P.A. Comédies et comédiens. Paris, 1866. 2v.
	41567.15	Fouinet, E. L'ile des cinq. Tours, 1866.
	42586.54.6	Fournier, Charles A. Le roman de la chair. Paris, 1866.
	42515.37.5	Freppel, C.E. Examen critique des apôtres de M. Renan. Paris, 1866.
	42513.37	Gasparin, V.B.C. de. Au bord de la mer. 2. éd. Paris, 1866.
	38514.39	Gasté, Armand. Étude sur Olivier Basselin. Caen, 1866.
	42546.31.27	Gastineau, B. Victorien Sardon. Paris, 1866.
	41542.37.2	Gautier, Théophile. La peau de Tigre. Paris, 1866.
	42515.35.112	Gerbert, Philippe. La stratégie de M. Renan. 2. éd. Paris, 1866.
	41541.8.10	Girardin, Delphine Gay. La joie fait peur. Boston, 1866.
	37574.38.5	Gouttes de Rosée. Petit trésor poétique des jeunes personnes. N.Y., 1866.
	41593.34.3	Guérin, Maurice de. Journal, lettres et poèmes. 9. éd. Paris, 1866.
Htn	37530.78*	Hatin, Eugène. Bibliographie historique et critique de la presse périodique française. Paris, 1866.
	42576.14.11	Houssaye, Arsène. Les aventures galantes de Margot. Paris, 1866.
	41573.32.25	Hugo, Victor. Angelo. N.Y., 1866.
	41572.4.2	Hugo, Victor. Jargal. N.Y., 1866.
	41571.25	Hugo, Victor. Les travailleurs de la mer. N.Y., 1866.
	41573.16.12	Hugo, Victor. Les travailleurs de la mer. N.Y., 1866.
	41573.16.10	Hugo, Victor. Les travailleurs de la mer. Paris, 1866. 2v.
	41592.9	Janin, Jules. Béranger et son temps. Paris, 1866.
	FL 398.48.50	Jiménez-Placer, Carlos. Ana de La-Grange. Sevilla, 1866.
	41544.6	Karr, Alphonse. La famille Alain. Paris, 1866.
	41544.17	Karr, Alphonse. La pénélope normande. Les Soirées de Sainte-Adresse. Paris, 1866.
	41552.8.15	Kock, Charles Paul de. La baronne Blaguiskof. Paris, 1866.
	41552.27	Kock, Charles Paul de. L'homme de la nature. Paris, 1866.
	41553.27	Kock, Charles Paul de. Un tourlonrou. Paris, 1866.
	42576.41	La Bédollièrre, E.G. de. Histoire de la mère Michel et de son chat. N.Y., 1866.
	42544.28.5	Labiche, Eugène. La poudre aux yeux. 4. éd. Boston, 1866.
	40597.2.345	Lamartine, A. de. Balzac et ses oeuvres. Paris, 1866.
	41577.8	Lamartine, Alphonse de. Fior d'Aliza. (Oeuvres complètes 41). Paris, 1866.
	41578.21	Lamartine, Alphonse de. Milly o La terra natale. Trieste, 1866.
	42555.16	Laprade, Victor de. Le sentiment de la nature avant le christianisme. Paris, 1866.
	42544.7.2	Legouvé, Ernest. Medea. N.Y., 1866.
	37563.34	Lenient, Charles. La satire en France au XVIe siècle. Paris, 1866.
	37596.83	Lindfors, W.E. VII anciens textes français. Lund, 1866.
	FL 395.120	Manne, E.D. Galerie historique des comédiens de la troupe de Talma. Lyon, 1866.
	41586.23.40	Méry, Joseph. Les nuits anglaises. Paris, 1866.
	42587.24	Méry, Joseph. Vénus d'Arles. Paris, 1866.
	42577.34.21	Mettais, Hippolyte. Paris, avant le déluge. Paris, 1866.
Htn	37596.37*	Michelaut, Henri. La clef d'amour. Lyons, 1866.
	Mol 238.5	Molière, Jean Baptiste Poquelin. Le médecin volant...Pagès. Paris, 1866.
	Mol 38.66	Molière, Jean Baptiste Poquelin. Oeuvres choisies...Hillemacher. Paris, 1866-75. 2v.
	Mol 269.43.5	Molière, Jean Baptiste Poquelin. Tartufe. Züngel. Praha, 1866.
Htn	42545.31*	Monnier, Henry. Bas-fonds de la société. Amsterdam, 1866.
	42545.30	Monnier, Henry. Paris et la province. Paris, 1866.

1866 - cont.

	37542.35.5	Monselet, Charles. Portraits après décès. Paris, 1866.
	Mon 31.35	Montaigne, Michel de. Works. Hazlitt (Wight). N.Y., 1866. 4v.
	39594.6.25	Montesquieu, C.L. de S. Grandeur et décadence...politique...dialogue de Sylla et d'Eucrate...et temple de Gnide. Paris, 1866.
	42577.31	Murger, Henry. Scènes de la vie de Bohème. Paris, 1866.
	41596.6.5	Musset, Alfred de. Oeuvres complètes de Alfred de Musset. Paris, 1866. 10v.
	41543.8	Nerval, Gerard de. La bohème galante. Paris, 1866.
Htn	38528.18*	Nicolas de Troyes. Le grand parangon. Brussels, 1866.
Htn	40524.17.65*	Nogaret, François Félix. Le fond du sac. Paris, 1866.
	41586.26.210	Ourliac, Edouard. Théâtre du seigneur croquignole. Paris, 1866.
	FL 398.21.5	Palmstedt, C. Edouard du Puy. Stockholm, 1866.
Htn	42558.7*	Le Parnasse contemporain, 1866, 1869 et 1876. Paris, 1866-3v.
	38526.44	Perrin, François. Les escoliers. Bruxelles, 1866.
	39545.21.2	Pierron, Alexis. Voltaire et ses maitres. Paris, 1866.
	40536.20.11	Piron, Alexis. Complément de ses oeuvres inédites. Paris, 1866.
	42534.21	Pontmartin, A.F. de. Derniers causeries du Samedi. Paris, 1866.
	41596.51.7	Porchat, Jacques. Trois mois sous la neige. N.Y., 1866.
	37574.38	Pylodet, L. Gouttes de Rosée. French lyric poems. N.Y., 1866?
	38585.43.4	Racine, Jean. Phaedre. N.Y., 1866.
	FL 361.15	Rambaud, Y. Photographies à la plume. Paris, 1866.
	40536.22.25	Randon de Malboissière, G.F. Laurette de Malboissière. Lettres d'une jeune fille au temps de Louis XV, 1761-1766. Paris, 1866.
	Mol 825.4.2	Raynaud, M. Les médecins au temps de Molière. Paris, 1866.
	42515.29.250	Renan, Ernest. The apostles. N.Y., 1866.
	42515.29.252	Renan, Ernest. Les apotres. Paris, 1866.
	42515.27.10A	Renan, Ernest. Histoire des origines du christianisme. Paris, 1866-77. 7v.
	42515.29.12	Renan, Ernest. Vie de Jésus. 12. éd. Boston, 1866.
	39566.16A	Rosenkranz, Karl. Diderot's Leben und Werke. v.1-2. Leipzig, 1866.
	42515.36.231	Sabatier, Auguste. Essai sur les sources de la Vie de Jésus. Paris, 1866.
	38542.17.9	Saint-Evremond, C. de M. de S.D. Oeuvres melées. Paris, 1866. 3v.
	42583.36	Saint-Germain, J. de. Les extrêmes légendes. Paris, 1866.
	39595.13	St. Pierre, J.H.B. de. Oeuvres choisies. Paris, 1866.
	40577.6	Sainte-Beuve, Charles A. Nouveau lundis. v.1, 3. éd. v.2-5, 2. éd. Paris, 1866-72. 13v.
	41568.11.12	Saintine, Joseph Xavier Boniface. Picciola. N.Y., 1866.
	41568.11.13	Saintine, Joseph Xavier Boniface. Picciola. N.Y., 1866.
	41557.8.59	Sand, George. Le chateau des Desertes. Paris, 1866.
	41557.8.69	Sand, George. La derniere Aldini. Paris, 1866.
	41557.8.87	Sand, George. Jacques. Paris, 1866.
	41557.8.110	Sand, George. Monsieur Sylvestre. Paris, 1866.
	41557.9.31	Sand, George. La petite Fadette. Boston, 1866.
	41557.8.131	Sand, George. Théâtre complet. Paris, 1866-67. 4v.
	39534.28.12A	Scarron, Paul. Le roman comique de M. Scarron. Paris, 1866.
	41588.3.5.10	Scribe, Eugène. Adriana Lecouvreur. N.Y., 1866.
	42546.34.21	Silvestre, Armand. Rimes, neuves et vieilles. Paris, 1866.
	Mol 728.5	Soulié, E. Molière et sa troupe à Lyon. Lyon, 1866.
	41558.46	Souvestre, Émile. Les derniers Bretons. Paris, 1866. 2v.
	37573.7	Staaff, F.N. Lectures choisies de la littérature française. Paris, 1866.
	Mol 619.8A	Stapfer, P. Petite comédie de la critique littéraire. Paris, 1866.
	41562.3	Sue, Eugène. L'alouette de casque - Adèle Verneuil. Paris, 1866.
	41562.7	Sue, Eugène. Clémence Hervé. Jeanne Darc. Paris, 1866.
	41562.16	Sue, Eugène. Le diable médecin: La grande dame, Henriette Dumesnil. Paris, 1866.
	41562.12	Sue, Eugène. La faucille d'or. La croix d'argent. Le collier de fer. Paris, 1866.
	41562.31	Sue, Eugène. Les sept péchés capitaux, luxure, paresse, avarice, gourmandise. Paris, 1866.
	42536.11.7	Taine, Hippolyte. Essais de critique et d'histoire. 2. éd. Paris, 1866.
	42536.10	Taine, Hippolyte. Nouveaux essais. Paris, 1866.
	42583.34.15	Tardieu, J.R. Pour une épingle. 19. éd. N.Y., 1866.
	FL 360.17	Tisserant, Hippolyte. Plaidoyer pour ma maison. Paris, 1866.
	40546.13	Tocqueville, Alexis de. L'ancien régime et la revolution. Paris, 1866.
	40546.14	Tocqueville, Alexis de. Correspondance et oeuvres posthumes. Paris, 1866.
	40546.18	Tocqueville, Alexis de. Études économiques. Paris, 1866.
	40546.16	Tocqueville, Alexis de. Nouvelle correspondance. Paris, 1866.
	40546.20	Tocqueville, Alexis de. Oeuvres complètes publiées. v.4, 7-8. Paris, 1866- 3v.
	42584.47.5	Ulbach, Louis. La jardin du chanoine. Paris, 1866.
	Mol 880.33	Villars, E. Les précieuses du jour. Paris, 1866.
	42583.16	Villars, Emile. Le roman de la parisienne. Paris, 1866.
Htn	42541.45*	Villiers de l'Isle-Adam, A. Morgane. Saint-Brieuc, 1866.
	38514.18	Villon, François. Les deux Testaments. Paris, 1866.
	39545.30.5	Voltaire, François Marie Arouet de. Romans de Voltaire. Paris, 1866.
	42584.56	Walsh, J.A. Le fratricide. Quebec, 1866.
	42584.5	Zola, Emile. La confession de Claude. Paris, 1866.

1867

	42562.8.25	About, Edmond. L'infâme. Paris, 1867.
	42562.11.8	About, Edmond. Le mari imprévu. 2e éd. Paris, 1867.
	42562.15	About, Edmond. Le progrès. Paris, 1867.
	42562.33.25	About, Edmond. Salon de 1866. Paris, 1867.
	37561.2	Ampère, J.J. Histoire littéraire de la France avant Charlemagne. Paris, 1867-1868. 2v.
	40563.11	Ampère, Jean J. Mélanges d'histoire littéraire. Paris, 1867. 2v.
Htn	40597.14.12*	Balzac, Honoré de. Les contes drolatiques. 7. éd. Paris, 1867.

1867 - cont.

42541.6 Banet-Rivet, L. La mort de Lincoln. Paris, 1867-68. 2v.
42554.6.9A Banville, Théodore de. Les exilés. Paris, 1867.
40513.18 Barao y Clemente, Gerónimo. LeSage y su novéla de costumbres Gil Blas de Santillana. Barcelona, 1867.
39544.8 Beaune, Henri. Voltaire au collége. Paris, 1867.
41591.4 Béranger, P.J. de. Oeuvres. Paris, 1867. 2 pam.
41522.38.2 Bernard, Charles de. Gerfaut. Paris, 1867.
40582.15 Beyle, Henri. Mélanges...de littérature. Paris, 1867.
42563.28.25 Biart, Lucien. Le bizco. Paris, 1867.
38557.32.7 Bossuet, J.B. Choix de sermons. Paris, 1867.
38557.25.35 Bossuet, J.B. Oeuvres complètes. Paris, 1867.
38521.16 Büscher. La versification de Ronsard. Weimar, 1867.
37556.3 Canel, Alfred. Recherches sur les jeux d'esprit. Evreux, 1867. 2v.
Mol 810.2 Chappuzeau, S. Le théâtre français. Bruxelles, 1867.
40564.23 Chasles, Philarète. Questions du temps. n.p., 1867.
42565.16 Cherbuliez, Victor. Le grand oeuvre. Paris, 1867.
42565.50 Chéri-Marian. Les maléfices du diable. Paris, 1867.
42586.30.9 Chevalier, E. Les derniers Iroquois. Paris, 1867.
40562.14.4 Chocarne, B. The inner life of Père Lacordaire. Dublin, 1867.
40562.14 Chocarne, B. Le R.P.H.D. Lacordaire...sa vie intime et religieuse. Paris, 1867. 2v.
39527.24 Closset, A. de. Fables choisies de Jean de La Fontaine. Brussels, 1867.
Mol 845.1 Collection Molierèsque. Genève, 1867.
40553.4.15 Constant de Rebecque, Benjamin. Adolphe. Paris, 1867.
42567.32 Daudet, Ernest. La succession Chavanet. Paris, 1867. 2v.
37543.4 Demogeot, Jacques Claude. Histoire de la littérature française. Paris, 1867.
39544.15 Desnoiresterres, G. Jeunesse de Voltaire. Paris, 1867.
41525.4 Dumas, Alexandre. Les frères corses. Paris, 1867.
42543.13.33 Dumas, Alexandre. Les idées de Mme. Aubray. 3. éd. Paris, 1867.
41525.18 Dumas, Alexandre. Impressions de voyage. Une année à Florence. Paris, 1867.
41526.18 Dumas, Alexandre. La maison de Glace. Paris, 1867.
41526.24 Dumas, Alexandre. Mémoires d'une aveugle. Paris, 1867.
42572.2 Erckmann, Emile. L'ami Fritz. Paris, 1867.
42572.11.1 Erckmann, Emile. Histoire d'un conscrit de 1813. Boston, 1867.
42572.11.3 Erckmann, Emile. Histoire d'un conscrit de 1813. 3. éd. N.Y., 1867.
42572.35F Erckmann, Emile. Romans nationaux. Le conscrit de 1813. Waterloo. Paris, 1867.
41596.2 Étude critique et bibliographique des oeuvres de Alfred de Musset. Paris, 1867.
42574.28 Fabre, Ferdinand. Le chevrier. Paris, 1867.
42575.36 Feuillet, Octave. Monsieur de Camors. 7. éd. Paris, 1867.
42575.49.5 Feuillet, Octave. Le roman d'un jeune homme pauvre. Boston, 1867.
42575.21.6 Feydeau, Ernest. The secret of happiness. Edinburgh, 1867. 2v.
42564.6 Fleury, Jules. La belle Paule. Paris, 1867.
42564.20 Fleury, Jules. L'hôtel des commissaires-priseurs. Paris, 1867.
42554.36 Fontenay, Henri de. Boutades d'un promeneur dans Paris. Paris, 1867.
FL 360.15 Foucher, Paul. Entre cour et jardin. Études de théâtre. Paris, 1867.
42531.20 Gastineau, Benjamin. H. Taine. Paris, 1867.
37595.22 Génac, Mongeaut. Lettre à...Paul Meyer. Paris, 1867-69.
37556.21.3 Giraudeau, F. La presse périodique de 1789 à 1867. Paris, 1867.
42543.49 Glatigny, Albert. Théâtre. v.1-5. Paris, 1867-72.
FL 368.10 Goizet, J. Histoire anecdotique de la collaboration au théâtre. Paris, 1867.
37581.2 Goizet, M.J. Dictionnaire universel du théâtre en France. Paris, 1867.
40562.21 Greenwell, Dora. Lacordaire. Edinburgh, 1867.
41593.35.5 Guérin, Maurice de. Journal. N.Y., 1867.
38523.7 Héricault, C. Oeuvres de Clément Marot. Paris, 1867.
Htn 41573.39* Hugo, Victor. La voix de Guernesey. Bruxelles, 1867.
40567.6 Janin, Jules. Les amours du Chevalier de Fosseuse. Paris, 1867.
40567.24 Janin, Jules. La Sorbonne et les gazetiers. Paris, 1867.
38512.46 Jean d'Arkel. Li ars d'amour. Bruxelles, 1867. 2v.
Mol 610.2 Jeannel, C.J. La morale de Molière. Paris, 1867.
38516.5 Joly, A. La vraye histoire de Triboulet et autres poésies des XVe et XVIe siècles. Lyon, 1867.
40556.20.20 Joubert, Joseph. Some of the "Thoughts". Boston, 1867.
41544.2 Karr, Alphonse. Agathe et Cécile. Clovis Gosselin. Paris, 1867.
41544.11 Karr, Alphonse. Les guêpes. Paris, 1867-69. 6v.
37597.11 Körting, Gustav. Über die Quellen des Roman de rose. Leipzig, 1867.
42544.28.6 Labiche, Eugène. La poudre aux yeux. Boston, 1867.
42514.21.10 Laboulaye, Édouard. Finette; a legend of Brittany. Boston, 1867.
Htn 41578.35.90* Lamartine, Alphonse. Antoniella. Paris, 1867.
Htn 37578.20* Larchey, Lorédoin. Les joueurs de mots. Paris, 1867.
38543.10.10 La Rochefoucauld, François. Réfléxions, sentences. Paris, 1867.
Mol 855.2 Le Boulanger de Chalussay. Elomire hypocondre. Genève, 1867.
42544.7.3 Legouvé, Ernest. Medea. N.Y., 1867.
42544.12 Legouvé, Ernest. Par droit de conquête. Paris, 1867.
37575.415A Leypoldt, F. La littérature française contemporaine. N.Y., 1867.
37543.4.5 Leypoldt, Frédérick. Leçons de littérature française classique. N.Y., 1867.
Mol 612.11 Lindau, P. Molière in Deutschland. Wien, 1867.
38537.18 Loiseau, Arthur. Rapports de la langue de Rabelais. Angers, 1867.
42544.34.7 Lomon, A. Théâtre et poésies diverses. Paris, 1867.
42555.49.20 Marteau, A. Espoirs et souvenirs. Poèmes. Paris, 1867.
42587.19.36 Marx, Adrien. Les romans du wagon. 2. éd. Paris, 1867.
37574.6A Masson, Gustave. French classics. Oxford, 1867-68. 7v.
37574.26.5 Masson, Gustave. La lyre française. London, 1867.
37574.26.6 Masson, Gustave. La lyre française. London, 1867.
37574.26A Masson, Gustave. La lyre française. London, 1867.
42545.10.8.5 Meilhac, Henri. La grande-duchesse de Gérolstein. Paris, 1867.
42545.10.9.5 Meilhac, Henri. Pariser Leben; romische Operette. Berlin, 1867.
42545.10.9.3 Meilhac, Henri. La vie Parisienne. Paris, 1867.
41555.3 Mérimée, Prosper. Les deux héritages. Paris, 1867.
37595.23 Meyer, Paul. Salut d'amour. Paris, 1867.
42577.35.11 Michon, Jean H. Le curé de campagne. v.2. Paris, 1867.
41595.23.5.2 Mirecourt, E. de. Méry. Paris, 1867.
Mol 613.4 Moland, L. Molière et la comédie italienne. Paris, 1867.
Mol 613.5 Moland, L. Molière et le comédie italienne. Paris, 1867.
Mol 231.18 Molière, Jean Baptiste Poquelin. Le mariage forcé...Celler. Paris, 1867.
Mol 246.5.4 Molière, Jean Baptiste Poquelin. Le misanthrope. Kayser. n.p., 1867?
Mol 18.67 Molière, Jean Baptiste Poquelin. Oeuvres complètes. Paris, 1867. 3v.
Mol 251.25 Molière, Jean Baptiste Poquelin. Les précieuses ridicules. Lacour. Paris, 1867.
Mol 269.15.5 Molière, Jean Baptiste Poquelin. Tartuffe. N. Destanberg. Gent, 1867.
FL 391.72 Monselet, C. Les premières représentations célèbres. Paris, 1867.
37578.67 Monselet, Charles. Almanach for 1867. Chaillot, 1867.
42577.13.35 Morlent, J. Les Robinsons français. Tours, 1867.
41596.18.12 Musset, Alfred de. Les chefs-d'oeuvre lyriques. Paris, 1867.
41596.18.5 Musset, Alfred de. Comédies et proverbes. Paris, 1867. 2v.
41596.22 Musset, Alfred de. La confession d'un enfant du siècle. Paris, 1867.
41596.20 Musset, Alfred de. Contes. Paris, 1867.
41596.16 Musset, Alfred de. Mélanges de littérature. Paris, 1867.
41596.19 Musset, Alfred de. Nouvelles. London, 1867.
41596.12.2 Musset, Alfred de. Poésies. Paris, 1867.
41596.12 Musset, Alfred de. Poésies nouvelles. Paris, 1867.
41596.10.7 Musset, Alfred de. Premières poésies. 1829-1835. Paris, 1867.
41556.36 Nodier, M. (Mme.). Charles Nodier. Paris, 1867.
38557.15 Nourrisson, J.F. La politique de Bossuet. Paris, 1867.
42545.69.6.10 Pelletier, Claude. Les hérétiques revolutionnaires-socialistes du XVème siècle. N.Y., 1867.
42545.83.5 Ponsard, F. Galilée. 3e éd. Paris, 1867.
Htn 38514.15* Regnier, Jehan. Les fortunes et adversitez. Genève, 1867.
38514.15.2 Regnier, Jehan. Les fortunes et adversitez. Genève, 1867.
42515.29.15 Renan, Ernest. Vie de Jésus. 13. éd. Paris, 1867.
41596.52.75.3 Richard, C. Le bon Célime; poème anodin. Paris, 1867.
Mol 853.4 Roulés, Pierre. Le roy glorieux au monde. Genève, 1867.
39595.13.5A St. Pierre, J.H.B. de. Oeuvres choisies. Paris, 1867.
41557.8.70 Sand, George. Le dernier amour. Paris, 1867.
41557.8.72 Sand, George. Le diable aux champs. Paris, 1867.
41557.8.80 Sand, George. Un hiver à Majorque. Spiridion. Paris, 1867.
41557.8.88 Sand, George. Jean Zyska. Gabriel. Paris, 1867.
41557.8.89 Sand, George. Jeanne. Paris, 1867.
41557.8.124 Sand, George. Tamaris. 3e éd. Paris, 1867.
41557.22 Sandeau, Jules. La maison de Penarvan. Paris, 1867.
42546.18 Sardou, Victorien. Maison neuve. Paris, 1867.
42546.18.5 Sardou, Victorien. Maison neuve. Paris, 1867.
42546.17 Sardou, Victorien. Nos bons villageois. Paris, 1867.
42546.17.5 Sardou, Victorien. Nos bons villageois. Paris, 1867.
FL 390.75 Savard, Felix. Les actrices de Paris. Paris, 1867.
38512.7 Scheler, Auguste. Notice et extraits de deux manuscrits français. Bruxelles, 1867.
41588.3.6 Scribe, Eugène. Adrienne Lecouvreur. N.Y., 1867.
Mol 850.4 Le songe du rêveur. Genève, 1867.
41558.25 Soulié, Frédéric. Si jeunesse savait, si vieillesse pouvait. Paris, 1867. 2v.
41561.17 Sue, Eugène. Mysteries of the people. N.Y., 1867.
38528.3 Tanizey de Larroque. Essai sur...Florimond de Raymond. Paris, 1867.
42583.35 Tardieu, J.R. Pour une épingle. N.Y., 1867.
42578.65.30 Temple, Georges. L'auberge. Lyon, 1867.
40546.15 Tocqueville, Alexis de. Correspondance. Paris, 1867.
38514.31 Travers, Julien. Olivier Basselin. Caen, 1867.
42547.10.9.5 Vacquerie, Auguste. Jean Baudrey. Boston, 1867.
42521.13 Veuillot, Louis. Les odeurs de Paris. Paris, 1867.
41564.14 Vigny, Alfred de. Journal d'un poète. Paris, 1867.
41564.6 Vigny, Alfred de. Laurette. Paris, 1867.
41564.11 Vigny, Alfred de. La veillée de Vincennes. Paris, 1867.
41564.3 Vigny, Alfred de. La vie du Capitaine Renaud. Paris, 1867.
40584.23 Vitet, L. Étude sur...l'art. Paris, 1867-68. 4v.

1868

42562.2 About, Edmond. A.B.C. Travailleur. Paris, 1868.
42562.8.3 About, Edmond. L'homme a l'oreille cassée. 5. éd. Paris, 1868.
42542.1.2 Abraham, Émile. L'amour d'une ingénue. Paris, 1868.
42513.47.20 Adam, Juliette. Mon village. Paris, 1868.
37596.26.20 Aléxius, Saint. Légend. Aléxis. Pariser Glossar. 3692. München, 1868.
37561.2.2 Ampère, J.J. Histoire littéraire de la France sous Charlemagne. v.3. Paris, 1868.
40532.44 Arneth, A. Ritter von. Beaumarchais und Sonnenfels. Wien, 1868.
42542.5 Augier, Émile. La cigue. Paris, 1868.
42541.4 Augier, Émile. Paul Forestier. Paris, 1868.
40597.19.1.5 Balzac, Honoré de. Eugénie Grandet. Paris, 1868.
42586.14.75 Baudry, Etienne. Le camp des bourgeois. Paris, 1868.
41522.20.30 Beauvoir, E. Roger de. Les soupeurs de mon temps. Paris, 1868.
42575.10 Bellemare, Louis de. Scènes de la vie sauvage. Paris, 1868.
41591.8 Béranger, P.J. de. Ma biographie. Paris, 1868.
41591.14 Béranger, P.J. de. Ma biographie. Paris, 1868.
41591.7 Béranger, P.J. de. Musique. Paris, 1868.
41522.32 Bernard, Charles de. Un beau-père. Bruxelles, 1868. 2v.
38528.16.6 Béroalde de Verville. Le moyen de parvenir. Paris, 1868.
37555.22 Besant, Walter. Studies in early French poetry. London, 1868.
42586.21.100 Boissieu, Arthur de. Lettres d'un passant. Paris, 1868-1875. 4v.
37565.38 Bonhomme, Honoré. Journal et mémoires de Charles Collé (1748-1772). Paris, 1868. 3v.

1868 - cont.

	FL 395.10A	Bonnassies, J. Comédie-française. Notice historique sur les anciens bâtiments. Paris, 1868.
	41522.65.2	Borel, d'Hauterive, Petrus. Rapsodies. Bruxelles, 1868.
	42542.29.140	Bornier, Henri de. Agamemnon. Paris, 1868.
	38557.33.10	Bossuet, J.B. Choix de sermons de la jeunesse de Bossuet. 2. éd. Paris, 1868.
	38557.25.55	Bossuet, J.B. Oeuvres choisies. v.1-3,5. Paris, 1868. 4v.
	40583.5	Bougy, Alfred de. Stendhal, sa vie. Paris, 1868.
	39578.4	Capfigue, M. La marquise du Chatelet. Paris, 1868.
	Mol 250.5	Celler, L. Une représentation de M. de Pourceaugnac. Paris, 1868.
	42565.23	Cherbuliez, Victor. Prosper Randoce. Paris, 1868.
	42565.28	Cherbuliez, Victor. Le roman d'une honnête femme. Paris, 1868.
	42524.27	Circourt, Adolphe. L'abbaye de Westminster. Paris, 1868. 2 pam.
	Mol 845.1.3	Collection Molierèsque. Genève, 1868.
	Mol 845.1.2	Collection Molierèsque. Genève, 1868.
	Mol 845.1.4	Collection Molierèsque. Genève, 1868.
	40583.2	Collignon, Albert. L'art et la vie de Stendhal. Paris, 1868.
	40553.5	Constant de Rebecque, Benjamin. Adolphe. Paris, 1868.
	38575.33.3	Corneille, Pierre. Horace. Paris, 1868.
	42586.32.15	Coster, Charles de. La legende d'Ulenspiegel. Paris, 1868.
	42566.5	Craven, Pauline. Anne Séverin. Paris, 1868.
	Mol 855.10	La critique de Tartuffe. Genève, 1868.
	38512.25A	De Queux de St. Hilaire. Livre des cent ballades. Paris, 1868.
	39544.16	Desnoiresterres, G. Voltaire au Chateau de Cirey. Paris, 1868.
	38527.37.10	Dolet, Etienne. Le second enfer. Paris, 1868.
	39544.75	DuBois-Reymond, E. Voltaire in seiner Beziehung zur Naturwissenschaft. Berlin, 1868.
	38527.10	Du Lorens, J. Satire. Genève, 1868.
	41525.6	Dumas, Alexandre. Les Garibaldiens. Paris, 1868.
	41525.26	Dumas, Alexandre. Impressions de voyage. Quinze jours au Sinai. Paris, 1868.
	41525.28	Dumas, Alexandre. Impressions de voyage. Suisse. Paris, 1868. 3v.
	41527.2	Dumas, Alexandre. Le meneur de loups. Paris, 1868.
	41527.10	Dumas, Alexandre. Parisiens et provinciaux. Paris, 1868.
	42543.10.25	Dumas, Alexandre. Théâtre complet. série 1-4. v.1-2,3-4. Paris, 1868-70. 2v.
	Mol 850.3	L'enfer burlesque: le mariage de Belphégor. Genève, 1868.
	42572.7	Erckmann, Emile. Contes fatastiques. Paris, 1868.
	42572.11.2	Erckmann, Emile. Histoire d'un conscrit de 1813. Boston, 1868.
	42572.13.10	Erckmann, Emile. Histoire d'un paysan, 1789. 9. éd. Paris, 1868.
	Mol 750.6	La fameuse comédienne, la Guérin. Genève, 1868.
Htn	37578.24*	Favoral. Les plaisantes journées. Genève, 1868.
	42513.27	Favre, Jules. Discours de M. Jules Favre prononcé à sa réception à l'academie francaise, le 23 avril 1868. Paris, 1868. 2 pam.
	38554.518.37	Fénelon, F. de S. de la Mothe. Lettre sur les occupations de l'Académie française. Paris, 1868.
	42575.36.4	Feuillet, Octave. Monsieur de Camors. 9. éd. Paris, 1868.
	42575.21.9	Feydeau, Ernest. Un coup de bourse; étude dramatique. 2. éd. Paris, 1868.
	Mol 815.3	Fischer, F.A. Das Hôtel de Rambouillet und die Precieusen. Jena, 1868.
	42586.54.9	Francois (pseud.). Historiettes choisies une mère et ses enfants. Dresden, 1868.
	Mol 570.3	Fritsche, H. Molière Studien. Danzig, 1868.
	FL 398.31	Gabel, C.F. Dramatic biography. N.Y., 1868.
	Mol 453.5	Galuski, Charles. Réponse à l'auteur d'un article. Saint Germain, 1868.
	38557.33.11	Gandar, E. Bossuet orateur. 2. éd. Paris, 1868.
	42513.34	Gasparin, V.B.C. de. Les horizons célestes. Paris, 1868.
	41542.37.5	Gautier, Théophile. La belle Jenny. Paris, 1868.
	37563.3.5	Girardin, Saint-Marc. Tableau de la littérature française. Paris, 1868.
	FL 372.18	Gosselin, E. Recherches sur les origines et l'histoire du théâtre à Rouen avant P. Corneille. Rouen, 1868.
	37541.5	Guigniant, J.D. Progrès études classiques et du Moyen Âge. Paris, 1868. 2 pam.
	42513.43	Guizot, F.P.G. Mélanges biographiques et littéraires. Paris, 1868.
	FL 6118.68	Hamel, E. La statue de Jean-Jacques Rousseau. Paris, 1868.
	37573.9	Herrig, L. La France littéraire. 12. éd. Brunsvic, 1868.
	42584.26	Hetzel, P.J. Les bonnes fortunes parisiennes; les amours d'un Pierrot. 6. éd. Paris, 1868.
	37592.5	Hofmann, C. Altfranzösische lyrische Gedichte. München, 1868.
	42576.14.95	Houssaye, Arsène. Les grandes dames. Paris, 1868. 4v.
	41574.17	Hugo, A.F. (Mme.). Victor Hugo raconté par un temoin de sa vie. Photoreproduction. Paris, 1868. 2v.
	41572.7	Hugo, Victor. Han d'Islande. Paris, 1868. 2v.
	41572.13	Hugo, Victor. Littérature et philosophie mêlées. Paris, 1868. 2v.
	Mol 860.41	Hurtado, A. El collar de Lescot. Madrid, 1868.
	Mol 438.1	Les incompatibles. Lacroix. Genève, 1868.
	42587.7	Issaurat, Cyprien. Moments perdus de Pierre-Jean. Paris, 1868.
	37596.52A	Jacques d'Amiens. L'art d'amours. Leipzig, 1868.
	38525.91	Jarry, J. Essai sur les oeuvres dramatiques de Jean Rotrou. Lille, 1868.
	38524.35	Jodelle, d'Estienne. Les oeuvres et meslanges poétique. Paris, 1868. 2v.
	41553.18	Kock, Charles Paul de. Moustache. Paris, 1868.
	42514.19	Laboulaye, Edouard. Contes et nouvelles. Paris, 1868.
	42514.7	Laboulaye, Edouard. Études contemporaines sur l'Allemagne. 3. éd. Paris, 1868.
	42514.21.5	Laboulaye, Edouard. Laboulaye's fairy book. N.Y., 1868.
	42514.22	Laboulaye, Edouard. Le prince-Caniche. Paris, 1868.
	42511.13.10	Laboulaye, Edourd. Abdallah. London, 1868.
	42511.10	Laboulaye, Edourd. Nouveaux contes bleus. Paris, 1868.
	38564.26	La Bruyère, J. de. Le premier texte de La Bruyère. Paris, 1868.
	37584.25	Lacroix, Paul. Ballets et Mascarades de Cour de Henri III à Louis XIV. Geneva, 1868. 6v.
	Mol 855.12	La Croix, Paul de. La guerre comique. Genève, 1868.

1868 - cont.

	37556.21.35	Laferrière, E. La censure et la régime correctionnel. Paris, 1868.
	41522.17.5	La Fizelière, A. de. Bibliographie de Charles Baudelaire. Paris, 1868.
	39526.33	La Fontaine, Jean de. Fables. Paris, 1868.
	41578.24	Lamartine, Alphonse de. Fior d'Aliza. N.Y., 1868.
	42555.17	Laprade, Victor de. Le sentiment de la nature chez les modernes. Paris, 1868.
	38543.6	La Rochefoucauld, François. Oeuvres de La Rochefoucauld. v.1-3 et album. Paris, 1868-74. 4v.
	38543.11	La Rochefoucauld, François. Réfléxions ou sentences et maximes morales. Paris, 1868.
	41586.8.10	Laya, Léon. Madame Desroches. Paris, 1868.
	37562.25	Lecoy de la Marche, A. La chaire française au moyen âge. Paris, 1868.
	37597.8	Lorris, Guillaume de. Die Rose. Gravenhage, 1868.
	37555.14	Malherbe, Jules. Conférence sur la chanson. Caen, 1868.
	38536.15	Marly-Laveaux, Charles. Les oeuvres de...Rabelais. Paris, 1868-73. 6v.
	39544.11	Maynard, Michel U. Voltaire, sa vie. Paris, 1868. 2v.
	38537.3	Mayrargues, A. Rabelais, étude sur le seizième siècle. Paris, 1868.
	41555.8	Mérimée, Prosper. Mélanges historiques et littéraires. Paris, 1868.
	41586.23.35	Méry, Joseph. Les nuits italiennes. Paris, 1868.
	Mol 38.68.2	Molière, Jean Baptiste Poquelin. Comédies...jouées par des jeunes gens. Paris, 1868?
	Mol 38.68	Molière, Jean Baptiste Poquelin. Comédies...jouées par des jeunes gens. v.1-5. Paris, 1868? 3v.
	Mol 205.15	Molière, Jean Baptiste Poquelin. L'étourdi...Fiebig und Courvoisier. Leipzig, 1868.
	Mol 166.5.5	Molière, Jean Baptiste Poquelin. Der Geizige...Krais. Stuttgart, 1868.
	Mol 451.1	Molière, Jean Baptiste Poquelin. Joguenet. Jacob. Genève, 1868.
Htn	Mol 8.68*	Molière, Jean Baptiste Poquelin. Oeuvres complètes. Paris, 1868.
	Mol 18.68	Molière, Jean Baptiste Poquelin. Oeuvres complètes. Paris, 1868? 3v.
	Mol 251.27	Molière, Jean-Baptiste Poquelin. Les précieuses ridicules. Fiebig et Courvoisier. Leipzig, 1868.
	Mol 251.28	Molière, Jean Baptiste Poquelin. Les précieuses ridicules. Perréaz. Schaffhouse, 1868.
	42555.50	Monnier, Marc. Les Aieux de Figaro. Paris, 1868.
	38536.12	Montaiglon, Anatole. Les quarte livres de...Rabelais. Paris, 1868-70. 3v.
	Mon 18.68A	Montaigne, Michel de. Essais de Michel de Montaigne. Paris, 1868. 2v.
	42577.22	Murger, Henry. Les nuits d'hiver. Paris, 1868.
	42578.14	Narrey, Charles. Les derniers jeunes gens. Paris, 1868.
	41543.4	Nerval, Gerard de. Oeuvres complètes. Paris, 1868-73. 4v.
	40572.29	Nisard, Désiré. Mélanges d'histoire et de littérature. Paris, 1868.
	41586.26.231	Ourliac, Edouard. Proverbes et scènes Bourgeoises. Paris, 1868.
	38563.31	Perrault, C. L'oublieux, petite comédie. Paris, 1868.
	42587.44	Perret, Paul. La Parisienne. Paris, 1868.
	Mon 178.20	Pinson, P. Un disciple de Montaigne. Paris, 1868.
	42534.35.10	Pontmartin, A.F. de. Les corbeaux du Gévaudan. Paris, 1868.
	37538.15	Prat, Henry. Études littéraires. Époque révolutionaire. Paris, 1868.
Htn	38536.22*	Rabelais, F. La chronique de Gargantua. 1. éd. Paris, 1868.
	38536.8	Rabelais, F. Les songes drolatiques. Genve, 1868.
	37596.17	Raoul de Houdenc. Le romans des Eles. Brussels, 1868.
	42515.30.660	Renan, Ernest. Questions contemporaines. Paris, 1868.
	42515.30.662A	Renan, Ernest. Questions contemporaines. 2. éd. Paris, 1868.
	38521.15	Rochambeau, Eugène Achille Lacroix de Vimeur. La famille de Ronsard. Paris, 1868.
	37538.3.10	Roche, Antonin. Histoire des principaux écrivains français depuis l'origine de la littérature jusqu'a nos jours. 4. éd. Paris, 1868. 2v.
	40575.20	Sainte-Beuve, Charles A. Portraits of celebrated women. Boston, 1868.
	41557.8.51	Sand, George. André. Paris, 1868.
	41557.8.55	Sand, George. Beaux messieurs de Bois-Doré. Paris, 1868. 2v.
	41557.8.56	Sand, George. Cadio. Paris, 1868.
	41557.9.110	Sand, George. Mlle. Merguem. N.Y., 1868.
	Mol 860.37	Sand, George. Molière. London, 1868.
	41557.8.121	Sand, George. Le secrétaire intime. Paris, 1868.
	41557.8.125	Sand, George. Teverino. Leone Leoni. Paris, 1868.
	41557.15	Sandeau, Jules. Fernand Vallaince Richard. Paris, 1868.
	41557.20	Sandeau, Jules. Madame de Sommerville. Paris, 1868.
	42546.26.6.1	Sardou, Victorien. Les pattes de mouche. Paris, 1868.
	38512.44	Scheler, Auguste. Dits de Watriquet de Couvin. Bruxelles, 1868.
	41588.14.1.5	Scribe, Eugène. Le verre d'eau. Bielefeld, 1868.
	38526.47.300	Sedege. Le légat de la Vache. Paris, 1868.
	41558.40	Souvestre, Emile. Les anges du foyer. Paris, 1868.
	41558.65.5	Souvestre, Emile. Un philosophe sous les toits. N.Y., 1868.
	41562.11	Sue, Eugène. La famille Jouffroy. Paris, 1868. 3v.
	38514.69.5	Tivier, H. Étude sur le Mystère du siège d'Orléans. Paris, 1868.
	40546.12	Tocqueville, Alexis de. De la démocratie en Amérique. Paris, 1868. 3v.
	41561.24	Toepffer, Rodolphe. Premiers voyages en zigzag. Paris, 1868.
	Mol 870.18	La valise de Molière. Paris, 1868.
	Mol 855.18	Les véritables prétieuses. Genève, 1868.
	42557.26.5	Vermersch, Eugene. Les binettes rimées. Paris, 1868.
	42583.50	Véron, Pierre. Les phénomènes vivants. Paris, 1868.
	42587.66.15	Vien, Charles. Madame Frainex. Paris, 1868.
	FL 390.45	Vizentini, Albert. Derrière la toile...théâtres parisiens. Paris, 1868.
	39542.32.10	Voltaire, François Marie Arouet de. Théâtre de Voltaire. Paris, 1868.
	38514.69.7	Wunder, Curt. Über Jacques Milet's Destruction de Troye la Grant. Leipzig, 1868.
	Mol 855.20	Zelinde. Genève, 1868.

Chronological Listing

1869

	42562.3	About, Edmond. A.B.C. Travailleur. Paris, 1869.
	42561.5	About, Edmond. Le fellah. Paris, 1869.
	42562.12.50	About, Edmond. Les mariages de province. 3e éd. Paris, 1869.
	42562.37.2	Achard, Amédée E. Clos pommier et prissonniers du Caucase. Boston, 1869.
	Mon 200.4	Almanach de la petite gazette pour 1869. Bagnères, 1869.
	41578.60	Alphonse Lamartine. Angers, 1869.
	42563.13.50	Babut, Jules. Félix Batel. v.1-2. La Haye, 1869.
	Mol 863.19.2	Barré, F. Poésies pour Alceste. Paris, 1869.
	42542.27.20	Barrière, Théodore. Une corneille qui abat des noix. 2. éd. Paris, 1869.
	41522.5	Baudelaire, Charles. Les fleurs du mal. Paris, 1869. 4v.
	40532.14	Beaumarchais, Pierre A.C. de. Théâtre complet. Paris, 1869-71. 4v.
	40532.14.2	Beaumarchais, Pierre A.C. de. Théâtre complet. Paris, 1869-71. 4v.
	42563.22.14	Belot, Adolphe. Le drame de la rue de la paix. Paris, 1869.
NEDL	41592.31.2	Béranger, P.J. de. Béranger, two hundred of his lyrical poems. 4. ed. N.Y., 1869.
	41591.11	Béranger, P.J. de. Chansons. Paris, 1869. 2v.
	41522.35	Bernard, Charles de. L'écueil. Paris, 1869.
	40582.9	Beyle, Henri. Chartreuse de Parme. Paris, 1869.
	38565.20.50	Boileau Despréaux, Nicolas. Oeuvres. Paris, 1869.
	37597.21	Broberg, S. Romanen om rosen. Odense, 1869.
	42512.11	Broglie, Albert de. Nouvelles études de littérature. Paris, 1869.
	41522.69.528	Carraud, Z.T. (Mme.). Une servante d'autrefois. 2. éd. Paris, 1869.
	Mol 880.3	Cauvet, A. L'ermitage du misanthrope. Paris, 1869.
	42563.72	Champceix, Léodile Béra de. Aline-Ali. Paris, 1869.
	42563.72.31	Champceix, Léodile Béra de. Un divorce. Paris, 1869.
	40564.21	Chasles, Philarète. Encore sur les contemporaines. Paris, 1869.
	42565.55.10	Cladel, Léon. Mes paysans. Le bouscassié. Paris, 1869.
	42542.52.12	Clairville, Louis François Nicolaïe. Les petites misères de la vie humaine. 3. éd. Boston, 1869.
	FL 383.45	Claretie, Jules. La vie moderne au théâtre. Paris, 1869-1875. 2v.
	41578.56	Combes, A. Mes souvenirs sur Lamartine. Castres, 1869.
	42554.23.27	Coppée, François. Le passant. Paris, 1869?
	38571.6.9	Corneille, Pierre. Oeuvres. Paris, 1869.
	42567.29	Daudet, Ernest. Le prince Pogoutzine. Paris, 1869.
Htn	42586.33*	Delaclos, C. Les liaisons dangereuses. Bruxelles, 1869. 2v.
NEDL	42586.33	Delaclos, C. Les liaisons dangereuses. Bruxelles, 1869. 2v.
	40515.5	D'Épinay, Louise F. Oeuvres. Paris, 1869. 2v.
	39544.17	Desnoiresterres, G. Voltaire a la cour. Paris, 1869.
	42554.29.730	Desnoyers, Fernani. Le vin. Paris, 1869.
	41541.20	D'Heilly, G. Madame E. de Girardin. Paris, 1869.
	38511.13	DuFresne de Beaucourt, G. Les Chartier. Recherches sur Guillaume, Alain et Jean Chartier. Caen, 1869.
	38588.20	Dufresny, Charles Rivière. Entretiens, ou Amusements. Paris, 1869.
	38527.10.5	Du Lorens, J. Satires. Paris, 1869.
	41538.2.5	Dumas, Alexandre. Ange Pitou. v.1-2. Paris, 1869.
	42543.16.2	Dumas, Alexandre. La dame aux perles. Paris, 1869.
	41527.24	Dumas, Alexandre. La route de Varennes. Paris, 1869.
	41528.14	Dumas, Alexandre. La vie au désert. Paris, 1869.
	37557.4A	Egger, Émile. L'Hellénisme en France. Paris, 1869. 2v.
	42568.28	Enault, Louis. La pupille de la Légion d'Honneur. N.Y., 1869. 2v.
	42572.11.20	Erckmann, Emile. The conscript; a story of the French war of 1813. N.Y., 1869.
	42573.16	Erckmann, Emile. Histoire d'un paysan. v.2-3. Paris, 1869.
NEDL	42572.13.15	Erckmann, Emile. Histoire d'un paysan. 14. éd. Paris, 1869.
	42573.23	Erckmann, Emile. Madame Thérèse. N.Y., 1869.
	42572.32.5	Erckmann, Emile. Waterloo. N.Y., 1869.
	42575.36.5	Feuillet, Octave. Monsieur de Camors. 10. éd. Paris, 1869.
	42575.45.10	Feuillet, Octave. Scènes et proverbes. Paris, 1869. 2 pam.
	37564.29	Fialon, Eugene. Leçons d'histoire littéraires. Paris, 1869.
	42564.18	Fleury, Jules. Histoire de l'imagerie populaire. Paris, 1869.
	42554.34	Fontaubert, Émile de. Chants et chansons de Pourcedugnac II. Paris, 1869.
	37583.500	La France dramatique. ser. II, livre 1-4. Leipzig, 1869.
	41541.20.100	Girardin, Francois. Le supplice d'une femme. Paris, 1869.
	42586.66	Gobineau, Arthur de. Typhaines Abbey. Philadelphia, 1869.
	FL 382.95	Gottschall, R. vón. Teater och drama under andra kejsardömet. Stockholm, 1869.
	41543.37	Grandville, J.I.I.G. Les metamorphoses du jour par Grandville. Paris, 1869.
	37596.44.2A	Guillaume le Clerc. Le besant de Dieu. Halle, 1869.
	42554.50.19	Guillemet, A. Le centenaire. Paris, 1869.
	38514.45	Guilloche, Bourdelois. La prophécie du Roy Charles VIII. Paris, 1869.
	42554.64.100	Hilbey, C. La révolution. Genève, 1869.
	Mol 800.3.3	Hillemacher, F. Galerie des portraits des comédiens de la troupe de Molière. 2. éd. Lyon, 1869.
	42576.14.32	Houssaye, Arsène. La virtu di Rosina. Firenze, 1869.
	41572.4.10	Hugo, Victor. Claude Gueux. N.Y., 1869.
	41572.24.5	Hugo, Victor. Les contemplations. Paris, 1869.
	41571.8	Hugo, Victor. L'homme qui rit. N.Y., 1869.
	41572.16	Hugo, Victor. Le Rhin. Paris, 1869. 3v.
	41573.16.20	Hugo, Victor. Les travailleurs de la mer. v.1-2. 17e éd. Paris, 1869.
	41572.30	Hugo, Victor. Les voix interieures. Les rayons et les ombres. Paris, 1869.
	Mol 608.12	Humbert, C. Molière, Shakspeare und die deutsche Kritik. Leipzig, 1869.
	FL 398.74.40	Jacquot, C.J.B. Rachel. 3e ed. Paris, 1869.
	40567.20	Janin, Jules. L'interné. n.p., 1869.
	40567.34	Janin, Jules. Lamartine. Paris, 1869.
	40567.27	Janin, Jules. Petits romans. n.p., 1869.
	FL 380.5	Jauffret, Eugène. Le théâtre révolutionnaire. Paris, 1869.
	40556.20	Joubert, Joseph. Pensées. Paris, 1869. 2v.

1869 - cont.

	41544.4	Karr, Alphonse. Contes et nouvelles. Paris, 1869.
	41544.25	Karr, Alphonse. Les dents du dragon. Paris, 1869.
	41544.13	Karr, Alphonse. Histoire de Rose et de Jean Duchemin-Clotilde. Paris, 1869.
	37596.4	Klint, A.H. Le miracle de Théophile de Rutebeuf. Upsala, 1869.
	41552.6	Kock, Charles Paul de. André le Savoyard. Paris, 1869.
	41553.11	Kock, Charles Paul de. Madeleine. Paris, 1869.
	41553.13	Kock, Charles Paul de. Un mari perdu. Paris, 1869.
	42513.46	Kuhn, Emile. La légende des rues; histoire de mon temps, politique critique et littéraire. Paris, 1869-70. 2v.
	42514.18	Laboulaye, Edouard. Contes bleus. Paris, 1869.
	42514.24	Laboulaye, Edouard. Souvenirs d'un voyageur. Paris, 1869.
	38564.28.2	La Bruyère, J. de. Les caractères des caractères de Théophraste. Paris, 1869.
	39526.33.5	La Fontaine, Jean de. Fables. Paris, 1869.
	37555.660	Landais, Napoléon. Dictionnaire des rimes françaises. Paris, 1869.
	42555.4	Laroche, Abel. Fables. San Francisco, 1869.
	38543.12	La Rochefoucauld, François. Le premier texte de La Rochefoucauld. Paris, 1869.
	39532.3	Latour, Antoine de. Oeuvres de J.B. Rousseau. Paris, 1869.
	42513.60	Laveleye, Émile de. Études et essais. Paris, 1869.
	41586.5	Laya, Léon. Les coeurs d'or. Paris, 1869.
	FL 377.9	Leclercq, L. Les décors, les costumes et la mise en scène. Paris, 1869.
	42544.13	Legouvé, Ernest. À deux de jeu. Paris, 1869.
	42544.6	Legouvé, Ernest. À deux jeu. Paris, 1869.
	38528.19	Mabille, E. Le grand parangon. Paris, 1869.
	42545.5.250	Maiziere, Anot de. Un coup d'etat ou Cromwell, tragédie en cinq actes et en vers. 2e éd. Paris, 1869.
	42577.11	Malot, Hector. Romain Kalbris. Paris, 1869.
	FL 384.50	Manne, Edmond D. Galerie historique des comédiens de la troupe de Nicolet. Lyon, 1869.
	Mol 855.13	Marcel. Le mariage sans mariage. Turin, 1869.
	42555.49.250	Martin, Nicolas. Voyage poétique et pittoresque. Lille, 1869.
Htn	38528.75*	Les médecins au XVIIe siècle. Paris, 1869.
	42545.10.19	Meilhac, Henri. La diva. Paris, 1869.
	42555.58.1150	Mérat, Albert. L'idole. Paris, 1869.
	42533.7	Merlet, Gustave. Hommes et livres. Paris, 1869.
	42577.35.20	Michon, Jean H. El maldito. v.1-4. Barcelona, 1869. 2v.
	42577.35.9	Michon, Jean H. Les mystiques. Paris, 1869.
	41595.23.5.3	Mirecourt, E. de. Méry. 3. éd. Paris, 1869.
	42587.35	Moland, Louis. Les méprises comédies. Paris, 1869.
	Mol 165.31	Molière, Jean Baptiste Poquelin. L'avare...George Dandin. Paris, 1869.
	Mol 171.22	Molière, Jean Baptiste Poquelin. Le bourgeois gentilhomme. Paris, 1869.
	Mol 236.50	Molière, Jean Baptiste Poquelin. O medico á força. Lisboa, 1869.
	Mol 18.69	Molière, Jean Baptiste Poquelin. Oeuvres complètes. Paris, 1869. 3v.
	Mol 8.69F	Molière, Jean Baptiste Poquelin. Oeuvres complètes. Paris, 1869?
	Mol 18.69.2	Molière, Jean Baptiste Poquelin. Oeuvres complètes. Paris, 1869. 3v.
	Mol 494.5	Molière, Jean Baptiste Poquelin. Poésies diverses recueillies. Jacob. Paris, 1869.
	Mon 31.12	Montaigne, Michel de. Essays. Cotton. 3. ed. London, 1869.
	Mon 32.5.3	Montaigne, Michel de. Essays. 2. ed. London, 1869.
	41596.29A	Musset, Alfred de. Un caprice. N.Y., 1869.
	41556.11	Nodier, Charles. Contes fantastiques. Paris, 1869.
	42545.50	Nus, Eugène. Miss Multon. 3d ed. Paris, 1869.
	40595.3	Oeuvres complètes de H. de Balzac. Paris, 1869-76. 24v.
	42545.62.7	Pailleron, Edouard. Les faux menages. Paris, 1869.
	40536.20.3	Piron, Alexis. Oeuvres choisies. Paris, 1869.
	41596.51	Porchat, Jacques. Trois mois sous la neige. N.Y., 1869.
	42556.1.9	Prarond, Ernest. De Montréal à Jérusalem. Paris, 1869.
	42587.50.01	Pressensé, E.F.L. de P.G. de. Rosa. N.Y., 1869.
	37574.39	Pylodet, L. Gouttes de Rosée. N.Y., 1869.
	42515.44.5	Quinet, E. (Mme.). Mémoires d'exil (Bruxelles-Oberland). Paris, 1869.
	38585.25.10	Racine, Jean. Britannicus. 3e éd. Bielefeld, 1869.
	38583.5	Racine, Jean. Théâtre complet. Paris, 1869.
	38554.299	Ramsay, A.M. Fénelon's conversations with M. de Ramsay on the truth of religion. Photoreproduction. n.p., 1869.
	42515.36.220	Ratiolisme étudie dans la vie de Jésus de E. Renan par un catholique. Besançon, 1869.
	42587.50.50	Rattazzi, Marie Bonaparte-Wyse. Si j'étais reine. Paris, 1869.
	38557.15.5	Reaume, A. Histoire de Jacques Bénigne Bossuet. Paris, 1869. 3v.
	37563.8	Réaume, Eugène. Prosateurs français du XVIe siècle. Paris, 1869.
	37563.8.2	Réaume, Eugène. Les prosateurs français du XVIe siècle. 2. éd. Paris, 1869.
	41567.30.80	Reboul, R.M. Louis François Jauffret. Paris, 1869.
Htn	38516.31*	Recueil de vraye poésie françoise. Genève, 1869.
	38525.23.5	Régnier, Mathurin. Oeuvres complètes. Paris, 1869.
	42515.29.255	Renan, Ernest. The apostles. London, 1869.
	42515.29.257	Renan, Ernest. Les apostles. N.Y., 1869.
	42515.29.350	Renan, Ernest. Saint Paul. N.Y., 1869.
	42515.29.345	Renan, Ernest. Saint Paul. Paris, 1869.
	Mol 728.6	Robert, L. Molière en province. Niort, 1869.
	37574.19	Rochè, A. Les poètes français. Recueil de morceaux choisis. Paris, 1869.
	Mol 855.16	Rochemont, de. Observations sur le Festin de Pierre. Paris, 1869.
	39584.32	Saint, Foix, G.F.P. de. Lettres turques. Paris, 1869.
	41565.29	St. Mars, G.A.C. de C. Le soupers de la régence. Paris, 1869.
	39594.30.5	St. Pierre, J.H.B. de. Paul et Virginie et La chaumière indienne. N.Y., 1869.
	41578.68.5	Saint-Victor, P. Lamartine. Paris, 1869.
	37563.22	Sainte-Beuve, C.A. Tableau...de la poésie française. Paris, 1869.
	40575.10.3	Sainte-Beuve, Charles A. Poésies complètes. Paris, 1869.
	40575.19.05	Sainte-Beuve, Charles A. Portraits de femmes. Paris, 1869.
	41568.11.7	Saintine, Joseph Xavier Boniface. Picciola. N.Y., 1869.
	41557.8.68	Sand, George. La Daniella. Paris, 1869. 2v.

1869 - cont.

	41557.8.73	Sand, George. Elle et lui. 6e éd. Paris, 1869.
	41557.9.28.3	Sand, George. Elle et lui. 6e ed. Paris, 1869.
	41557.8.75	Sand, George. La filleule. Paris, 1869.
	41557.8.79	Sand, George. L'homme de neige. Paris, 1869. 3v.
	41557.8.81	Sand, George. Horace. Paris, 1869.
	41557.8.83	Sand, George. Indiana. Paris, 1869.
	41557.8.84	Sand, George. Isidora. Paris, 1869.
	41557.8.92	Sand, George. Lélia. Paris, 1869. 2v.
	41557.8.93.3	Sand, George. Lettres d'un voyageur. Paris, 1869.
	41557.8.93	Sand, George. Lettres d'un voyageur. Paris, 1869.
	41557.8.94	Sand, George. Lucrezia Floriani. Lavinia. Paris, 1869.
	41557.8.100	Sand, George. Les maîtres sonneurs. Paris, 1869. 2v.
	41557.8.102	Sand, George. La mare au diable. Paris, 1869.
	41557.8.104	Sand, George. Le marquis de Villemer. Paris, 1869.
	41557.8.107.3	Sand, George. Mauprat. Paris, 1869.
	41557.8.108	Sand, George. Le meunier d'Angibault. Paris, 1869.
	41557.8.113	Sand, George. Narcisse. Paris, 1869.
	41557.8.117	Sand, George. Le peche de monsieur Antoine. Paris, 1869. 2v.
	41557.8.103.5	Sand, George. La petite Fadette. Paris, 1869.
	41557.9.31.3	Sand, George. La petite Fadette. 5. ed. Boston, 1869.
	41557.8.118	Sand, George. Le Piccinino. Paris, 1869. 2v.
	41557.8.120	Sand, George. Promenades autour d'un village. Paris, 1869.
	41557.8.122	Sand, George. Les sept cordes de la lyre. Paris, 1869.
	41557.8.123	Sand, George. Simon. La marquis. Paris, 1869.
	41557.8.127	Sand, George. L'Uscoque. Paris, 1869.
	41557.8.128	Sand, George. Valentine. Paris, 1869.
	41557.11	Sandeau, Jules. Catherine. Paris, 1869.
	41557.28	Sandeau, Jules. Valcreuse. Paris, 1869.
	42541.32	Sardou, Victorien. Fernande. Patrie. Paris, 1869-70.
	42546.30.29	Sardou, Victorien. Patrie! Paris, 1869.
	42546.29.5	Sardou, Victorien. La perle noire. 2d ed. Paris, 1869.
	42546.21.5	Sardou, Victorien. Séraphine. Paris, 1869.
	42546.21.2	Sardou, Victorien. Séraphine. Paris, 1869.
	FL 6148.69	Schücking, L. Jean-Jacques Rousseau: zwei Episoden. Leipzig, 1869.
	42587.58.14	Ségur, Sophie. Fairy tales. Philadelphia, 1869.
	42587.58.6	Ségur, Sophie. Les vacances. Paris, 1869.
	42584.37.35	Simon, Jules. La peine de mort. Paris, 1869.
	41558.8	Soulié, Frédéric. Les mémoirs du diable. Paris, 1869. 3v.
	41558.15	Soulié, Frédéric. Le vicomte de Bréziers. Paris, 1869.
	41558.65	Souvestre, Émile. Un philosophe sous les toits. Paris, 1869.
	42535.30	Stapfer, Paul. Causeries guernesiaises. Guernesey, 1869.
	41562.4	Sue, Eugène. Arthur. Paris, 1869.
	41562.13	Sue, Eugène. Les fils de famille. Paris, 1869.
	41562.18	Sue, Eugène. Le Juif errant. Paris, 1869. 2v.
	41562.22	Sue, Eugène. Les mystères de Paris. Paris, 1869. 2v.
	40556.30	Sybel, H. von. Graf Joseph de Maistre. München, 1869.
	41563.29	Toepffer, Rodolphe. The Presbytère. Paris, 1869.
	38527.8	Travers, Julien. Les diverses poésies de Jean Vauquelin. Caen, 1869-72. 3v.
Htn	38527.9.5*	Vauquelin de la Fresnaye, Jean. Foresteries. Caen, 1869.
	Mol 855.17	La vengeance des marquis. Turin, 1869.
	42548.53	Verconsin, Eugène. En wagon. Paris, 1869.
Htn	42582.15.5*	Verne, Jules. Five weeks in a balloon. N.Y., 1869.
	37555.16	Veyrières, Louis de. Monographie du sonnet. Paris, 1869. 2v.
	42587.66.23	Villain, Henri. Histoire d'un grain de sel. Paris, 1869.
	41564.3.65A	Vingy, Alfred de. Cinq-Mars. Boston, 1869.

187-

	42562.38.45	Aimard, Gustave. The prairie flower. Philadelphia, 187-?
	42562.38.49	Aimard, Gustave. The red tracks. Philadelphia, 187-?
	42562.38.41.5	Aimard, Gustave. The white scalper. Philadelphia, 187-.
	42542.18.20	Augier, Émile. Haus Fourchambault. 2. Aufl. Leipzig, 187-?
	40597.14.40	Balzac, Honoré de. Droll stories. London, 187-? 2v.
	38557.41.35	Bossuet, J.B. History of the variations of the protestant churches. v.2. N.Y., 187-?
	37574.34	Chansonnier republicain. Paris, 187-.
	42568.7.2	Droz, Gustave. Entre nous. 22. éd. Paris, 187-?
	41538.16.1	Dumas, Alexandre. Count of Monte-Cristo. London, 187-?
	41538.16.2	Dumas, Alexandre. Count of Monte Cristo. N.Y., 187-?
	41538.45.15	Dumas, Alexandre. Paul Jones. London, 187-?
	42571.4.5	Erckmann, Emile. Cuentos de los Vosgos. Valencia, 187-?
	42572.14.5	Erckmann, Emile. Histoire d'un paysan. Paris, 187-? 4v.
	42584.27	Hetzel, P.J. Les bonnes fortunes parisiennes; les amours d'un notaire. 8. éd. Paris, 187-?
	42576.14.12	Houssaye, Arsène. Tragique aventure de bal masqué. 2. éd. Paris, 187-?
	41572.34.10	Hugo, Victor. Théâtre. Paris, 187-.
	42543.16.27.15	Korvin-Krukovskii, P. The Danicheffs. n.p., 187-?
	37577.10	Larousse, P. Fleurs historiques. Paris, 187-?
	Mon 18.78.2	Montaigne, Michel de. Essais. 4. éd. Paris, 187-? 2v.
	39545.5.5	Noël, Eugène. Voltaire et Rousseau. Paris, 187-?
	41557.8.96	Sand, George. Mademoiselle Merquem. 3e éd. Paris, 187-.
	42546.26.5.2	Sardou, Victorien. Flattersucht. Wien, 187-.
	42583.32.2	Theuriet, André. La chanson du jardinier. Boston, 187-?
	42582.24.5	Verne, Jules. The tour of the world in eighty days. Chicago, 187-?

1870

	42562.11	About, Edmond. Maitre Pièrre. Paris, 1870.
	42562.22	About, Edmond. Le turco. N.Y., 1870.
	42562.37.7	Achard, Amédée E. Le clos pommier et prisonniers du Caucase. 5. éd. Boston, 1870.
	FL 398.6.30	Allainval, Léon J.C.S. d'. Lettre à Mylord...sur Baron. Paris, 1870.
	42542.4	Augier, Émile. L'aventurière. Paris, 1870.
	42542.6	Augier, Émile. Le fils de Giboyer. Paris, 1870.
	Mon 112.4	Bachus, H. Essai sur les "Essais" de Montaigne. Linz, 1870.
	41522.2.50	Barbey d'Aurevilly, Jules. A côté de la grande histoire. Paris, 1870.
	41522.2.47	Barbey d'Aurevilly, Jules. Poésies. Bruxelles, 1870.
	37596.39	Bartsch, Karl. Romances et pastourelles françaises. Leipzig, 1870.

1870 - cont.

	42542.27.57	Bayard, J.F.A. La reine de seize ans. 7. éd. Bielefeld, 1870.
	41522.24	Belot, Adolphe. L'article 47. Paris, 1870.
	42554.13.36	Bergerat, Émile. Les cuirassiers de Reichshoffen. Paris, 1870.
	42554.13.35	Bergerat, Émile. Le maître d'école. Paris, 1870.
	41522.38	Bernard, Charles de. Gerfaut. Paris, 1870.
	41522.39	Bernard, Charles de. Un homme sérieux. Paris, 1870.
	41522.47	Bernard, Charles de. Le paravent. Paris, 1870.
	38528.16.7	Béroalde de Verville. Le moyen de parvenir. Paris, 1870-72. 2v.
	40582.24	Beyle, Henri. Le rouge et le noir. Paris, 1870.
	42563.28.33	Biart, Lucien. Pile et face. 3. éd. Paris, 1870.
	38525.30	Blanchemain, Prosper. Poésies de Jacques Tahureau. Paris, 1870. 2v.
	38566.26.4	Boileau Despréaux, Nicolas. Art poétique. Paris, 1870?
	38566.18	Boileau Despréaux, Nicolas. Oeuvres. Paris, 1870-73. 4v.
	Mol 750.7	Bonnassies, J. La fameuse comédienne, La Guérin. Paris, 1870.
	38524.80	Bordier, H.L. Le chansonnier Huguenot du XVIe siècle. Paris, 1870.
	38557.26.50	Bossuet, J.B. Oraisons funèbres. Paris, 1870.
	37547.60	Bouchard, Ernest. Poètes Bourbonnais. Moulins, 1870.
	42542.47.71	Cadol, Édouard. Jaques Cernol. Paris, 1870.
	FL 363.7A	Celler, Ludovic (pseud.). Études dramatiques. La galanterie. v.3. Paris, 1870-75.
	FL 363.5A	Celler, Ludovic (pseud.). Études dramatiques. Les types populaires. v.1. Paris, 1870-75.
	FL 363.6	Celler, Ludovic (pseud.). Études dramatiques. Les valets. v.2. Paris, 1870-75.
	39533.7.5	Chapelain, Jean. De la lecture des vieux romans. Paris, 1870.
	37537.16	Chasles, Emile. Histoire nationale de la littérature française. Paris, 1870.
	40527.15	Chenier, André. Poésies. Paris, 1870.
	42565.4	Cherbuliez, Victor. L'aventure de Ladislas Bolski. Paris, 1870.
	Mol 855.8	Chevalier. Les amours de Calotin. Turin, 1870.
Htn	Mol 173.3*	Cohen. Molière, l'académicien Cordemoy. Rouen, 1870.
	Mol 845.1.5	Collection Molierèsque. Turin, 1870.
	38525.31	Conscience, F. Les dialogues de Jacques Tahureau. Paris, 1870.
	42554.23.9	Coppée, François. Deux douleurs; drame en un acte en vers. 12e éd. N.Y., 1870.
	42554.22.6	Coppée, François. Poèmes modernes. Paris, 1870.
	38575.29.1.5	Corneille, Pierre. Le Cid. 2d éd. N.Y., 1870.
	42566.3	Craven, Pauline. Adélaide Capece minutolo. Paris, 1870.
	42561.13.20	Craven, Pauline. A sister's story. N.Y., 1870.
	Mol 870.19	Delpit, A. La voix du maître. Paris, 1870.
	38557.13.5	Denis, J.F. Critique et controverse ou Richard Simon et Bossuet. Caen, 1870.
	42586.40	Dépret, L. Eucharis. Paris, 1870.
	37563.15	Desjardins, Albert. Moralistes français du XVIXe siècle. Paris, 1870.
	39544.18	Desnoiresterres, G. Voltaire et Frédéric. Paris, 1870.
	Mol 855.11	Doneau, F. La cocue imaginaire. Turin, 1870.
	37564.23	Duchesne, Julien. Histoire des poëmes épiques français. Paris, 1870.
	41523.12	Dumas, Alexandre. Les blancs et les bleus. Paris, 1870. 3v.
	41525.17	Dumas, Alexandre. L'île de feu. Paris, 1870.
	41525.25	Dumas, Alexandre. Impressions de voyage. De Paris à Cadix. Paris, 1870.
	41525.21	Dumas, Alexandre. Impressions de voyage. Le capitaine Aréna. Paris, 1870.
	FL 398.17.10	Duval, Georges. Mademoiselle Déjazet. n.p., 1870.
	42572.14	Erckmann, Émile. Histoire d'un paysan. Paris, 1870-1871. 4v.
	38527.60.25	Faure, H. Antoine de Laval et les écrivains bourbonnais. Moulins, 1870.
	42575.43	Feuillet, Octave. Scènes et comédies. Paris, 1870.
	42576.20.2	Flaubert, Gustave. L'éducation sentimentale. 2. éd. v. 2. Paris, 1870.
	42564.8	Fleury, Jules. Les chats. Paris, 1870.
	42561.22	Fleury, Jules. Les souffrances du professeur Delteil. Paris, 1870.
	40562.34	Foisset, T. Vie du r.p. Lacordaire. Paris, 1870. 2v.
	37574.520	La France a Rome. Lyon, 1870.
NEDL	38511.18A	Froissart, Jean. Oeuvres. v.2-3. Bruxelles, 1870-72. 2v.
	42571.33A	Gaboriau, Emile. La vie infernale. 4. éd. Paris, 1870-1872. 2v.
	37555.17	Gaudin, Paul. Du Rondeau, du Triolet, du Sonnet. Paris, 1870.
	41542.15	Gautier, Théophile. Premières poésies. Paris, 1870.
	42543.49.8	Glatigny, Albert. Le bois. Paris, 1870.
	Mol 728.6.2	Gosselin, M.E. Molière à Rouen en 1643. Rouen, 1870.
	42576.10	Guezenec, Alfred de. Les amoureux de vingt ans. Paris, 1870.
	37546.20.2	Hauréau, B. Histoire littéraire du Maine. Paris, 1870. 10v.
	42576.14.96	Houssaye, Arsène. Les courtisanes du monde. Paris, 1870. 2v.
	41571.30.8	Hugo, Victor. By order of the king. London, 1870. 3v.
	Mol 608.11	Humbert, C. Friederich Jacobs über Molière. Bielefeld, 1870.
	42545.84.10	Inauguration de la statue de F. Ponsard. Vienne, 1870.
	40567.11	Janin, Jules. Le chemin de traverse. n.p., 1870.
	40567.13	Janin, Jules. Un coeur pour deux amours. Paris, 1870.
	40566.30	Janin, Jules. Le livre. Paris, 1870.
	38543.26	Jouanst, D. Maximes de Mme. de Sablé. Paris, 1870.
	41544.27	Karr, Alphonse. Les gaietés romaines. Paris, 1870.
	41544.29	Karr, Alphonse. La maison close. Paris, 1870.
	41553.4	Kock, Charles Paul de. Un jeune homme charmant. Paris, 1870.
	41553.7	Kock, Charles Paul de. La laitière de Montfermeil. Paris, 1870.
	41553.12	Kock, Charles Paul de. La maison blanche. Paris, 1870.
	42548.11.3	Labiche, Eugène. La cagnotte. Boston, 1870.
	42548.29.5	Labiche, Eugène. Les petits oiseaux. 5. éd. Boston, 1870.
	42548.28.9	Labiche, Eugène. La poudre aux yeux. 5. éd. Boston, 1870.
	39527.23	La Fontaine, Jean de. Fables de La Fontaine. Boston, 1870.
	40536.10.9	La Porte, J. de. L'antiquaire; comédie en trois actes (1751). Paris, 1870.

Chronological Listing

1870 - cont.

42555.19 Laprade, Victor de. Harmodins. Paris, 1870.
42544.7 Legouvé, Ernest. Médée. Paris, 1870.
40512.9.15 LeSage, Alain René. Aventures de Gil Blas de Santillane. London, 1870.
40512.28 LeSage, Alain René. Histoire de Gil Blas de Santillana. Leipzig, 1870. 2v.
40512.8.12 LeSage, Alain René. Histoire de Gil Blas de Santillane. Paris, 1870.
Mol 853.8 Lettre sur la comédie de l'Imposteur. Turin, 1870.
Mon 122.3 Leveaux, A. Etude sur les essais de Montaigne. Paris, 1870.
Mol 213.3 Lion, C.T. Einleitung zu Molière's Femmes savantes. Langensalza, 1870.
42576.73.9 Luzarche, Robert. Le nouveau spectre rouge. Paris, 1870.
38514.11 Macé, Antonin. Poésies de Clotilde de Surville. Grenoble, 1870.
40556.27.11 Maistre, Joseph de. Oeuvres inédites. Paris, 1870.
42577.5 Malot, Hector. Une bonne affaire. Paris, 1870.
40535.26.5 Marivaux, Pierre Carlet de Chamblain de. Théâtre. Paris, 1870.
42545.10.10.9 Meilhac, Henri. Froufrou. Paris, 1870.
42545.10.31 Meilhac, Henri. La périchole. London, 1870.
41555.27 Mérimée, Prosper. Théâtre de Clara Gazul. Paris, 1870.
38542.14 Merlet, G. Saint-Evremond, étude historique. Paris, 1870.
FL 370.35 Milliet, Paul. De l'origine de théâtre à Paris. Paris, 1870.
42555.59.150 Moccaud, L.T. Le devil de la patrie. Annecy, 1870?
Mol 230.5 Molière, Jean Baptiste Poquelin. Receptio publicus unius juvenis medici. Lugduni, 1870.
Mol 269.63.5 Molière, Jean Baptiste Poquelin. Tartufo. Castilho. Lisboa, 1870.
37581.3.10 Monmerqué, Louis J.N. Théâtre français au moyen age. Paris, 1870.
37542.35 Monselet, Charles. La lorgnette littéraire dictionnaire de mon temps. Paris, 1870.
37543.2 Montaiglon, Anatole de. Catalogue raisonné de la bibliothèque Elzevirienne, 1853-70. Paris, 1870.
Mon 18.70.3 Montaigne, Michel de. Essais. Louandre. Paris, 1870-73. 4v.
Mon 18.70 Montaigne, Michel de. Essais de Michel de Montaigne, Dezeimeris et Barckhausen. Photoreproduction. Bordeaux, 1870-73. 2v.
Mon 31.13A Montaigne, Michel de. Essays. Cotton. 3. ed. London, 1870.
40562.18 Montalembert, Charles F.R. Le testament du P. Lacordaire. Paris, 1870.
41595.35 Moreau, Hégésippe. Oeuvres. Selections. Paris, 1870.
FL 6138.70 Moreau, L. Jean-Jacques Rousseau et le siècle philosophe. Paris, 1870.
42577.26 Murger, Henry. Propos de ville et propos de théâtre. Les vacances de Camille. Paris, 1870.
42577.24 Murger, Henry. Le roman de toutes les femmes. Le pays latin. Paris, 1870.
42577.30 Murger, Henry. Scènes de campagne. Paris, 1870.
41596.18.5.20 Musset, Alfred de. Selections from the prose and poetry of Alfred de Musset. N.Y., 1870.
42555.63 Nadaud, G. Contes, proverbes, scènes, et récits en vers. Paris, 1870.
38537.6 Noël, Eugène. Rabelais et son oeuvre. Paris, 1870.
38525.27.7 Nordström, T. Observations sur la langue...de Mathurin Régnier. Lund, 1870.
42578.23 Noriac, Jules. La bêtise humaine. Paris, 1870.
42578.23.5 Noriac, Jules. La vie en détail. Paris, 1870.
42587.42.20 Pelletan, Eugène. Nouvelles heures de travail. Paris, 1870.
37561.14 Potvin, Charles. Nos premiers siècles littéraires. Brussels, 1870. 2v.
42587.50.1 Pressensé, E.F.L. de P.G. de. La maison blanche. 5. éd. Paris, 1870.
38511.12.2 Pyne, H. England and France in the 15th century. "The debate between the heralds of France and England." London, 1870.
42515.44.6 Quinet, E. (Mme.). Mémoires d'exil. L'amniste. Suisse orientale. Bords du Leman. 2. éd. Paris, 1870.
38536.18 Rabelais, F. Oeuvres. 2. éd. Paris, 1870-73. 2v.
38583.3.5 Racine, Jean. Oeuvres. Paris, 1870.
38525.26.5 Régnier, Mathurin. Quelques pièces attribuées à Régnier. Paris, 1870?
42515.29.18 Renan, Ernest. Vie de Jésus. Paris, 1870.
42515.29.19 Renan, Ernest. Vie de Jésus. Paris, 1870.
41557.6 Reybaud, Louis. Jérôme Paturot. Paris, 1870.
42588.8 Le roman de Violette. Lisbonne, 1870.
FL 6027.3 Rousseau, J.J. Bekenntnisse. Hildburghausen, 1870. 2v.
41587.21 Saint-Georges, J.H.V. de. L'ombre. Paris, 1870. 4 pam.
40575.22 Sainte-Beuve, Charles A. Madame Desbordes-Valmore. Paris, 1870.
40576.5 Sainte-Beuve, Charles A. Nouveaux lundis. Paris, 1870. 13v.
40575.32 Sainte-Beuve, Charles A. Portraits contemporains. Paris, 1870-71. 5v.
41557.9.90 Sand, George. Antonia. Boston, 1870.
41557.8.54 Sand, George. Le Beau Laurence. 2e éd. Paris, 1870.
41557.8.54.5 Sand, George. Le Beau Lawrence. Paris, 1870.
41557.9.24.7 Sand, George. Consuelo. Philadelphia, 1870.
41557.9.25.10 Sand, George. The countess of Rudolstadt. Philadelphia, 1870.
41557.8.67 Sand, George. Les dames vertes. Paris, 1870.
41557.8.101 Sand, George. Malgrétout. 3e éd. Paris, 1870.
41557.9.95 Sand, George. Mauprat. Boston, 1870.
41557.9.115 Sand, George. Monsieur Sylvestre. Boston, 1870.
41557.8.115 Sand, George. Pauline. Paris, 1870.
41557.8.119 Sand, George. Pierre qui roule. 2e ed. Paris, 1870.
41557.21 Sandeau, Jules. Mademoiselle de Keronare. Paris, 1870.
41557.24 Sandeau, Jules. Nouvelles. Paris, 1870.
41557.27 Sandeau, Jules. Sacs et parchemins. Paris, 1870.
42546.26.6.08 Sardou, Victorien. Les pattes de mouche. Paris, 1870.
41588.15.8.5 Scribe, Eugène. La bataille de dames...notes by F. Bôcher. Boston, 1870.
42546.32.6 Second, Albéric. A mysterious kiss. Boston, 1870.
38546.36.3 Sévigné, Marie de R.C. Lettres choisies. Paris, 1870.
Htn 37573.15* Société des bibliophiles de Belgique. Recueil dr chansons. Bruxelles, 1870-79. 4v.
41558.4 Soulié, Frédéric. Le comte de Toulouse. Paris, 1870.
41558.5 Soulié, Frédéric. Les deux cadavres. Paris, 1870.

1870 - cont.

41565.30.5 St, Mars, G.A.C. de C. La jolie Bohémienne. Paris, 1870.
39544.11.2 Strauss, D.F. Voltaire. Leipzig, 1870.
41562.29 Sue, Eugène. Les sept péchés capitaux, orgueil. Paris, 1870.
39527.5 Taine, Hippolyte. La Fontaine et ses fables. 5e éd. Paris, 1870.
42536.15 Taine, Hippolyte. Vie et opinions de M. Graindorge. Paris, 1870.
37585.3.9 Théâtre classique; contenant Le Cid, Horace. Boston, 1870.
42583.26 Theuriet, André. Nouvelles intimes. Paris, 1870.
37558.38 Tisserand, E. Etude sur la première moitié du XVIIme siècle. Paris, 1870.
41561.25 Toepffer, Rodolphe. Nouveaux voyages en zigzag. Paris, 1870.
42548.55 Verconsin, Eugène. La matrone d'Éphèse. Paris, 1870.
Htn 42557.19.65* Verlaine, Paul. Les amies, scène d'amour sapphique. Ségovie, 1870.
Htn 42547.18.9.2* Villiers de l'Isle Adam, Auguste. La révolte. Paris, 1870.
FL 6118.70 Vogt, T. Jean-Jacques Rousseau's Leben. Wien, 1870.
FL 6132.4 Vuy, J. Lettres inédites de Madame de Warens. Annecy, 1870.
37586.16 Ware, J. Redding. Un soir qu'il neigeat. Opera comique, Oct. 1870. London, 1870?
Mol 623.3 Weyl, H. Beitrage zu den Molière Studien. Konigsberg, 1870.

1871

42562.8 About, Edmond. L'homme a l'oreille cassée. 6e éd. Paris, 1871.
42562.16.20 About, Edmond. Le roi des Montagnes. 9e éd. Paris, 1871.
38575.18.7 Aretz, P. Remarques gramaticales et lexicologiques sur la langue de Corneille. Bonn, 1871.
42554.6.7 Banville, Théodore de. Idylles Prussiennes. Paris, 1871.
42542.27.17 Barbier, Jules. Le franc-tireur; chants de guerre, 1870-1871. Limoges, 1871.
42542.27.23.50 Barrière, Théodore. Les bêtises du coeur. Paris, 1871.
42542.27.56 Bayard, J.F.A. Le mari a la campagne. 6. éd. Bielfeld, 1871.
40532.4.15A Beaumarchais, Pierre A.C. de. Le barbier de Séville. Paris, 1871.
42586.20 Bégon, F. House on wheels. Boston, 1871.
42542.29.14.20 Bergerat, Émile. A Châteaudin. Paris, 1871.
41522.30 Bernard, Charles de. Les ailes d'icare. Paris, 1871.
37543.6 Bonnefon, D. Écrivains célèbres de la France. Alais, 1871.
37567.25 Borcharot, A. Littérature française pendant...1870-1871. Berlin, 1871.
37574.10 Brakelmann, J. Les plus anciens chansonniers française. Paris, 1871-91.
Mol 703.1A Campardon, E. Documents inédits sur Jean Baptiste Poquelin Molière. Paris, 1871.
38512.38 Casola, Nicola da. Il padiglione foresto. Imola, 1871.
40516.6.5 Cazotte, Jacques. Le diable amoureux. Paris, 1871.
40586.18.12.5 Chateaubriand, F.A.R. Le génie du Christianisme. Paris, 1871. 2v.
42554.23.10 Coppée, François. Fais ce que dois; episode dramatique. 19e ed. Paris, 1871.
37573.420 Curwen, Harry. French love songs and other poems. N.Y., 1871.
42566.26.5 Daudet, Alphonse. Lettres à un absent. Paris, 1871.
42567.27 Daudet, Ernest. Jean le Gueux. Paris, 1871.
37555.345 Devel, Félix. Le quatrain. Paris, 1871.
Htn 41593.31.20* Dierx, Léon. Les paroles du vaincu. Paris, 1871.
42542.68.5 Dumanoir, M. Smiles and tears. Boston, 1871.
41523.24 Dumas, Alexandre. Charles le téméraire. Paris, 1871.
41523.30 Dumas, Alexandre. Colomba. Paris, 1871.
41538.16.9 Dumas, Alexandre. Countess of Monte Cristo. Philadelphia, 1871.
41525.13 Dumas, Alexandre. Histoire d'un Casse-Noisette. Paris, 1871.
41526.2 Dumas, Alexandre. Impressions de voyage. Le véloce. Paris, 1871.
38576.15 Dumas. Le cocu en herbe et en gerbe. Turin, 1871.
42573.27 Erckmann, Emile. The forest house and Catherine's lovers. Boston, 1871.
42573.20 Erckmann, Emile. Invasion of France in 1814. London, 1871.
42572.14.25 Erckmann, Emile. The outbreak of the great French revolution. London, 1871. 3v.
38558.3 Fabre, Antonin. De la correspondance de Fléchier avec Mme. Des Houlières et sa fille. Paris, 1871.
42575.30 Feuillet, Octave. Histoire de Sibylle. Paris, 1871.
42575.40 Feuillet, Octave. La petite comtesse. Paris, 1871.
42575.49.7 Feuillet, Octave. Le roman d'un jeune homme pauvre. 7. éd. N.Y., 1871?
Mol 728.7 Fillon, B. Recherches sur le séjour de Molière dans l'ouest de la France en 1648. Fontenay-le-Comte, 1871.
41542.6 Gautier, Théophile. Le capitaine Fracasse. Paris, 1871. 2v.
41542.10 Gautier, Théophile. Les grotesques. Paris, 1871.
Mol 875.4 Gondinet, E. A Molière. Paris, 1871.
Mol 730.3 Guillard, L. Molière, directeur. Paris, 1871.
FL 366.6 Hallays-Dabot, V. La censure dramatique et le théâtre. Paris, 1871.
41572.4 Hugo, Victor. Bug-Jargal. Claude Gueux. Paris, 1871.
41572.26 Hugo, Victor. La légende des siècles. Paris, 1871.
41572.10 Hugo, Victor. Notre-Dame de Paris. Paris, 1871. 2v.
41544.7 Karr, Alphonse. Les femmes. Encore les femmes. Paris, 1871.
41544.12 Karr, Alphonse. Une heure trop tard. Paris, 1871.
41544.18 Karr, Alphonse. Une poignée de vérités. Raoul. Paris, 1871.
41544.31 Karr, Alphonse. La queue d'or. Paris, 1871.
42514.16 Laboulaye, Edouard. Abdallah. Paris, 1871.
42514.8 Laboulaye, Édouard. Études morales. Paris, 1871.
42514.11 Laboulaye, Edouard. Le parti libéral. Paris, 1871.
42514.12 Laboulaye, Edouard. La république - le progrès. Paris, 1871.
38564.28 La Bruyère, J. de. Les caractères. Paris, 1871. 2v.
40562.4 Lacordaire, Jean Baptiste Henri. Vie de Saint Domenique. Paris, 1871.
38513.22.15 Lange, C. Die Farce von Pierre Pathelin. Berlin, 1871.

1871 - cont.

38543.19.30 La Rochefoucauld, François. Reflections, or Sentences and moral maxims. London, 1871.
Htn 42555.36.11* Leconte de Lisle, C.M.R. Le sacre de Paris. Paris, 1871.
Htn 42555.36.12* Leconte de Lisle, C.M.R. Le soir d'une bataille. Paris, 1871.
42555.39 Lemoyne, André. Poésies. 1855-96. Paris, 1871-4v.
42555.40.2103 Liber, Jules V.F. Les pantagruéliques. 3. éd. Turin, 1871.
38527.61.8 Magny, Olivier de. Les gayetez. Paris, 1871.
40588.46.2 Maistre, Xavier. Journey round my room. N.Y., 1871.
37543.8 Marcillac, F. Manuel d'histoire de la littérature française. Lausanne, 1871.
37596.45 Maréchal, Théodore. Sur les chansons de Thibaut. Photoreproduction. Rostock, 1871.
37595.26A Meyer, Paul. Documents manuscrits de l'ancienne littérature de la France. Paris, 1871.
Mol 95.1 Molière, Jean Baptiste Poquelin. Arista erga...Skylíssè. Tergéstè, 1871.
Mol 166.8.5 Molière, Jean Baptiste Poquelin. O avarento...A.F. de Castilho. Lisboa, 1871.
Mol 205.17 Molière, Jean Baptiste Poquelin. L'étourdi...Lacour. Paris, 1871.
Mol 211.30 Molière, Jean Baptiste Poquelin. Les femmes savantes...Lion. Leipzig, 1871.
Mol 18.71 Molière, Jean Baptiste Poquelin. Oeuvres complètes. Paris, 1871. 3v.
Mol 8.71 Molière, Jean Baptiste Poquelin. Oeuvres complètes. Paris, 1871.
Mol 62.25 Molière, Jean Baptiste Poquelin. Sämtliche Werke...Schröder. Leipzig, 1871? 2v.
42555.53 Monnier, Marc. Théâtre de marionettes. Genève, 1871.
42577.32 Murger, Henry. Scènes de la vie de Bohème. Paris, 1871.
41556.13 Nodier, Charles. Nouvelles. Paris, 1871.
38512.66A Ovidius. Altfranzösische Übersetzung des Remedia amoris. Leipzig, 1871.
42545.63.12 Pailleron, Edouard. Prière pour la France. Paris, 1871.
42534.34 Pontmartin, A.F. de. Le radeau de la méduse. Paris, 1871.
FL 397.3.17 Prologue pour l'inauguration du théâtre d'Angers. Angers, 1871.
42515.72 Quinet, Edgar. La creación. Madrid, 1871. 2v.
38585.19.50 Racine, Jean. Athalie. N.Y., 1871.
38585.19.51 Racine, Jean. Athalie. N.Y., 1871.
38585.46.5 Racine, Jean. The suitors. N.Y., 1871.
41565.31 St. Mars, G.A.C. de. C. Une rivale de la Pompadour. Paris, 1871.
41557.8.50 Sand, George. Les amours de l'Age d'or. Paris, 1871.
41557.9.20A Sand, George. Cesarine Dietrich. Boston, 1871.
41557.9.51 Sand, George. Handsome Lawrence. Boston, 1871.
41557.8.90 Sand, George. Journal d'un voyageur pendant la guerre. Paris, 1871.
41557.8.95 Sand, George. Mademoiselle la Quintinie. 5e éd. Paris, 1871.
41557.9.49.2 Sand, George. The marquis de Villemer. Boston, 1871.
41557.9.105 Sand, George. The miller of Angibault. Boston, 1871.
41557.9.50 Sand, George. The rolling stone. Boston, 1871.
41557.9.120 Sand, George. The snow man. Boston, 1871.
41557.23 Sandeau, Jules. Marianna. Paris, 1871.
41558.48 Souvestre, Émile. Les derniers paysans. Paris, 1871.
40592.24.20A Staël Holstein, Anne Louise. Corinne. Paris, 1871.
37596.70 Stengel, F. Codicem manu scriptum Digby 86. Halle, 1871. 2v.
42583.34.2 Tardieu, J.R. Mignon. Paris, 1871.
37581.8.3 Tournier, Edouard. Théâtre français au XVIe et au XVIIe siècle. Paris, 1871.
38526.26 Tross, Edwin. Oeuvres de Louise Labé. Paris, 1871.
42521.12 Veuillot, Louis. Le lendemain de la victoire vision. 2. éd. Paris, 1871.
37573.3 Vinet, Alexander R. Chrestomathie française. Littérature de la jeunesse et de l'âge mur. Lausanne, 1871-70. 3v.
37555.302.3 Weigand, G. Traité de versification française. Bromberg, 1871.

1872

42562.9.7 About, Edmond. Dernières lettres d'un bon jeune homme à sa cousine Madeleine. Paris, 1872.
42562.6 About, Edmond. Germaine. Paris, 1872.
42562.7 About, Edmond. La Grèce contemporaine. Paris, 1872.
42562.10 About, Edmond. Madelon. Paris, 1872.
42562.33.15 About, Edmond. The man with the broken ear. N.Y., 1872.
42562.13 About, Edmond. Les mariages de province. Paris, 1872.
42562.17 About, Edmond. Le roi des Montagnes. Paris, 1872.
42562.19 About, Edmond. Tolla. N.Y., 1872.
42562.20 About, Edmond. Trente et quarante. N.Y., 1872.
42562.37.8 Achard, Amédée E. L'invalide, comédie. Paris, 1872.
37591.39A Adam de la Halle. Oeuvres complètes (Poésies et musique). Paris, 1872.
39545.35 Advielle, M.V. Voltaire. Lettres er poesies. Paris, 1872.
37543.10 Albert, Paul. Littérature française. Paris, 1872.
37596.26.15 Aléxius, Saint. Légend. La vie de Saint Aléxis. Paris, 1872.
38537.8 Arnstadt, F.A. François Rabelais. Leipzig, 1872.
38527.28A Aubigné, Théodore Agrippa d'. Les tragiques. Paris, 1872.
Mol 203.5 Baguenault de Puchesse, Gustave. Les Adelphes de Térence et l'École des maris. Orleans, 1872.
42542.27.17.15 Barbier, Jules. Sous le même loit. Paris, 1872.
40532.7.9 Beaumarchais, Pierre A.C. de. Le mariage de Figaro. Paris, 1872.
Mol 860.42 Bellet, Paul. La maison de Molière. Toulouse, 1872.
42563.22.14.3 Belot, Adolphe. Le drame de la rue de la paix. 2. éd. Paris, 1872.
42563.22.10 Belot, Adolphe. L'article 47; or Breaking the ban. N.Y., 1872.
42563.22.12 Belot, Adolphe. Mademoiselle Giraud. 32. éd. Paris, 1872.
41522.36 Bernard, Charles de. L'écueil. Paris, 1872.
41522.37 Bernard, Charles de. Le gentilhomme Campagnard. Paris, 1872. 2v.
40582.26 Beyle, Henri. Vies de Haydn, de Mozart. Paris, 1872.
38514.90 Bible. Old Testament. Psalms. French (Old). 1872. Les psaumes de David. Paris, 1872.
39598.43 Body, Albin. Annette et Lubin. 2e ed. Bruxelles, 1872.
42586.21.102 Boissieu, Arthur de. De chute en chute. Paris, 1872.
39527.4.70 Boissonade, Gustave. La Fontaine, économiste. Paris, 1872.
FL 382.30 Bonnassies, J. Le théâtre et le peuple. Paris, 1872.

1872 - cont.

41522.64 Borel d'Hauterive, Petrus. Champavert. Bruxelles, 1872.
42542.35.35 Bouilhet, Louis. Dernières chansons. Paris, 1872.
42542.33 Bouilhet, Louis. Mademoiselle Aissé. Paris, 1872.
42542.34 Bouilhet, Louis. Mademoiselle Aissé. v.1-3. Paris, 1872.
42543.23.25 Charnace, Guy. Reponse à l'homme-femme de M. A. Dumas. Paris, 1872.
40586.25.5 Chateaubriand, F.A.R. Études historiques. v.2. Paris, 1872.
40534.5 Chefs-d'oeuvre dramatiques du XVIIIe siècle. Paris, 1872.
40527.14 Chenier, André. Oeuvres en prose. Paris, 1872.
40527.16A Chenier, André. Poésies. 2e éd. Paris, 1872.
42565.9 Cherbuliez, Victor. Le comte Kostia. Paris, 1872.
42565.26.10 Cherbuliez, Victor. Joseph Noirel's revenge. N.Y., 1872.
42565.26 Cherbuliez, Victor. La revanche de Joseph Noirel. Paris, 1872.
38525.2 Chotard, Raoul. Les ecrivains français du XVIe siècle. Tours, 1872.
Mon 82.1 Compayre, G. De Ramundo Sebundo. Paris, 1872.
Mol 886.1 Coquatrix, E. Alceste. Rouen, 1872.
38574.15 Corneille, Pierre. Théâtre. Paris, 1872. 2v.
37596.13.3 Coucy, G.C. Le lai de la dame de Fayel. St. Quentin, 1872.
37542.34 Cournot, A.A. Considérations sur la marche des idées. Paris, 1872. 2v.
NEDL 37542.34 Cournot, A.A. Considérations sur la marche des idées. Paris, 1872. 2v.
39544.26 Courtat, Félix-Titus. Défense de Voltaire. Paris, 1872.
42561.13.10 Craven, Pauline. Anne Séverin. 11e éd. Paris, 1872.
42566.10 Craven, Pauline. Récit d'une soeur. Paris, 1872. 2v.
42554.29.630 Désaugiers, Eugène. Les épaves. Paris, 1872.
41593.29.5 Deschamps, E. Oeuvres complètes. Poésie. Prose. Théâtre. Paris, 1872. 6v.
Htn 38528.30* Despériers, Bonaventure. Contes...Cymbalum mundi. Paris, 1872.
42554.27 Dougue, C.O. Homo. Paris, 1872.
42568.3 Droz, Gustave. Autour d'une source. Paris, 1872. 3v.
42568.5 Droz, Gustave. Le cahier bleu. Paris, 1872.
42568.7 Droz, Gustave. Entre nous. Paris, 1872.
42568.19.13 Du Boisgobey, Fortuné. Les gredins. Paris, 1872.
42554.29.300 Duflot, Claude. Aux enfants morts. Paris, 1872.
41523.8 Dumas, Alexandre. Aventures de John Davys. Paris, 1872.
41523.25 Dumas, Alexandre. Chasseur de sauvagine. Paris, 1872.
41523.28 Dumas, Alexandre. Chevalier de Maison-Rouge. Paris, 1872.
41524.11 Dumas, Alexandre. Dame de Monsoreau. Paris, 1872. 2v.
41525.9 Dumas, Alexandre. Un Gil-Blas in Californie. Paris, 1872.
42543.23 Dumas, Alexandre. L'homme-femme. Paris, 1872.
42543.23.2 Dumas, Alexandre. L'homme-femme. 27e éd. Paris, 1872.
41525.23 Dumas, Alexandre. Impressions de voyage. Le corricolo. Paris, 1872.
41526.6 Dumas, Alexandre. Isabel de Bavière. Paris, 1872.
41526.21 Dumas, Alexandre. Les médicis. Paris, 1872.
41527.8 Dumas, Alexandre. Olympe de Clèves. Paris, 1872.
41528.3 Dumas, Alexandre. Les Stuarts. Paris, 1872.
41528.6 Dumas, Alexandre. La terreur prussienne. Paris, 1872.
NEDL 42543.3 Dumas, Alexandre. Théâtre complet. 1. série. Paris, 1872-70.
41528.12 Dumas, Alexandre. La tulipe noire. Paris, 1872.
41528.13 Dumas, Alexandre. Le vicomte de Bragelonne. v.1-6. Paris, 1872. 3v.
42568.24 Enault, Louis. Alba. Paris, 1872.
42572.16 Erckmann, Emile. Histoire du plébiscite. 12. éd. Paris, 1872.
42572.16.5 Erckmann, Emile. Histoire du plébiscite. 13. éd. Paris, 1872.
42572.17 Erckmann, Emile. Histoire d'un sous-maître. Paris, 1872.
42573.25 Erckmann, Emile. A miller's story of the war. N.Y., 1872.
Htn 40562.24* Falloux, C. de. Correspondance du R.P. Lacordaire et de Mme. Swetchine. Paris, 1872.
38553.27.4 Fénelon, F. de S. de la Mothe. Aventures de Télémaque. Paris, 1872.
42575.27 Feuillet, Octave. Bellah. Paris, 1872.
42575.32 Feuillet, Octave. Julia de Trécoeur. Paris, 1872.
42575.37 Feuillet, Octave. Monsieur de Camors. Paris, 1872.
42575.44 Feuillet, Octave. Scènes et proverbes. Paris, 1872.
42571.20 Feuillet, Octave. The story of Sibylle. Boston, 1872.
42586.46.10 Feval, Paul H. Le bossu ou Le petit parisien. 27. éd. Paris, 1872. 2v.
42586.48.20 Feval, Paul H. Le vicomte Paul. Paris, 1872.
42564.13 Fleury, Jules. Les enfants. Paris, 1872.
42564.54 Fleury, Jules. Souvenirs et portraits de jeunesse. Paris, 1872.
38564.6 Fournier, E. Comédie de...Bruyère. Pairs, 1872. 2v.
37574.570 Frey, Jules. Les chants de guerre de la France en 1870-71. Paris, 1872.
42571.34.26 Gaboriau, Emile. La dégringolade. Paris, 1872. 2v.
42513.33 Gasparin, V.B.C. de. Les horizons prochains. Paris, 1872.
41542.8 Gautier, Théophile. Émaux et camées. Paris, 1872.
Mol 870.20 Glatigny, A. Le compliment à Molière. Paris, 1872.
42586.66.12 Gobineau, Arthur de. Souvenirs de voyage. Paris, 1872.
42576.64.7 Gramont, Ferdinand de. Sextines. Paris, 1872.
42576.40.366 Halévy, Ludovic. Madame et Monsieur Cardinal. Paris, 1872.
FL 1108.126.10 Hock, Auguste. Oeuvres complètes. Liège, 1872-74. 4v.
41572.2 Hugo, Victor. L'année terrible. Paris, 1872.
41572.24 Hugo, Victor. Les contemplations. Paris, 1872. 2v.
41571.20 Hugo, Victor. Gavroche, from "Les misérables". Philadelphia, 1872.
41573.32.4.12 Hugo, Victor. Hernani. 5e éd. Bielefeld, 1872.
41571.11 Hugo, Victor. Les misérables. Paris, 1872.
41572.28 Hugo, Victor. Les orientales. Paris, 1872.
41572.34 Hugo, Victor. Théâtre. Paris, 1872. 4v.
41572.33 Hugo, Victor. Théâtre. v.1,2,4. Paris, 1872. 3v.
41572.36 Hugo, Victor. Théâtre complète. Paris, 1872.
Mol 610.1 Janet, Paul. La philosophie dans les comédies de Molière. n.p., 1872.
42545.84.15 Janin, J.G. F. Ponsard, 1814-67. Paris, 1872.
40567.32 Janin, Jules. Deux discours. Paris, 1872.
41544.8 Karr, Alphonse. Feu Bressier. Menus propos. Paris, 1872.
41544.19 Karr, Alphonse. Promenades hors de mon jardin. Sous les orangers. Paris, 1872.
41552.7 Kock, Charles Paul de. L'ane à M. Martin. Paris, 1872.

Chronological Listing

1872 - cont.

42585.36 Kock, Henry de. Histoire des farceurs célèbres. Paris, 1872.
38527.60 La Boétie, Estienne de. La servitude volontaire. Paris, 1872.
42514.7.2 Laboulaye, Édouard. Études contemporaines sur l'Allemagne. 4. éd. Paris, 1872.
38564.30 La Bruyère, J. de. Les caractères. Paris, 1872-73. 2v.
40562.5 Lacordaire, Jean Baptiste Henri. Conférences de Notre-Dame de Paris. Paris, 1872. 5v.
40562.8 Lacordaire, Jean Baptiste Henri. Mélanges. Paris, 1872.
40562.7 Lacordaire, Jean Baptiste Henri. Notices et panegyriques. Paris, 1872.
40562.26 Lacordaire, Jean Baptiste Henri. Oeuvres du R.P.H.D. Lacordaire. Paris, 1872.
40562.6 Lacordaire, Jean Baptiste Henri. Oeuvres philosophiques. Paris, 1872.
Mol 560.5 Lacroix, P. Bibliographie Molièresque. Turin, 1872.
Mol 560.5.2 Lacroix, P. Bibliographie Molièresque. Turin, 1872.
39524.4F La Fontaine, Jean de. The fables. London, 1872.
41577.12.3 Lamartine, Alphonse de. Recueillements poétiques. Paris, 1872.
42555.22 Laprade, Victor de. Pernette. Paris, 1872.
40575.2 Lavallon, Jules. Sainte-Beuve. Paris, 1872.
Mol 735.1 Lavoix, H. Les portraits de Molière. Paris, 1872.
42555.34.5 Leconte de Lisle, C.M.R. Poèmes barbares. Paris, 1872.
42576.69 Legay, Henri. Mémoires d'une pendule. Paris, 1872.
42515.37.15 Le Nordez, Albert. M. Renan d'après lui-même...La reforme intellectuelle et morale de la France. Coutances, 1872.
Mol 712.3.2 Lindau, Paul. Molière, eine Ergänzung. Leipzig, 1872.
Mol 712.3 Lindau, Paul. Molière; eine Ergänzung. Leipzig, 1872.
Htn 38513.33.5* Mabille, E. Choix de farces soties et moralités de XVe et XVIe siècles. Nice, 1872-75. 2v.
40588.39 Maistre, Xavier. Oeuvres complètes. Paris, 1872.
40588.39.5 Maistre, Xavier. Oeuvres complètes. Paris, 1872.
42577.8 Malot, Hector. Madame Obernin. Paris, 1872.
40535.25.8 Marchant, François. La constitution en vaudevilles, Paris 1792. Paris, 1872.
41578.39 Mazade, Charles de. Lamartine. Paris, 1872.
42545.10.15 Meilhac, Henri. Barbe-bleue. Paris, 1872.
42555.58.1170 Mérat, Albert. Les souvenirs. Paris, 1872.
41555.9 Mérimée, Prosper. Nouvelles. Paris, 1872.
FL 370.40 Meyer, A.C.T. Origin of...dramatic art in France. Göttingen, 1872.
42521.25 Michaud, Eugène. Guignot et la révolution dans l'église romaine. Paris, 1872.
42587.27 Michel, Adolphe. Les missionnaires bottés. Paris, 1872.
39526.23 Moland, Louis. Oeuvres complètes de La Fontaine. Paris, 1872-76. 7v.
Mol 211.31 Molière, Jean Baptiste Poquelin. Les femmes savantes...Peschier. Dresde, 1872.
Mol 211.32 Molière, Jean Baptiste Poquelin. Les femmes savantes...Roche. London, 1872.
Mol 215.20 Molière, Jean Baptiste Poquelin. Les Fourberies de Scapin...Peschier. Dresde, 1872.
Mol 246.40.5 Molière, Jean-Baptiste Poquelin. De menschenhater. W.J. van Zeggelen. Haarlem, 1872.
Mol 245.43.2 Molière, Jean Baptiste Poquelin. Le misanthrope. Joynes. N.Y., 1872.
Mol 18.72 Molière, Jean Baptiste Poquelin. Oeuvres...Pauly. Paris, 1872-74. 8v.
Mol 18.72.2 Molière, Jean Baptiste Poquelin. Oeuvres...Pauly. Paris, 1872-74. 8v.
Mol 212.50 Molière, Jean Baptiste Poquelin. As Sabichonas...Castilho. Lisboa, 1872.
Mol 261.20 Molière, Jean Baptiste Poquelin. Sganarelle. Lacour. Paris, 1872.
Mol 268.50 Molière, Jean Baptiste Poquelin. Le Tartuffe. Lïon. Leipzig, 1872.
42555.55 Monnier, Marc. Poésies. Genève, 1872.
Mon 28.14 Montaigne, Michel de. Des vaines subtilitez. Rouen, 1872.
Mon 18.72A Montaigne, Michel de. Essais. Courbet et Royer. Paris, 1872-1900. 5v.
Mon 18.72.3 Montaigne, Michel de. Essais. v.1-2. Paris, 1872-1900.
39594.2.3 Montesquieu, C.L. de S. Esprit des lois par Montesquieu. Paris, 1872.
40575.5 Morand, François. Les jeunes annees de C.A. Sainte-Beuve. Paris, 1872.
X Cg 39544.32.3 Morley, John. Voltaire. London, 1872.
39544.32.1 Morley, John. Voltaire. N.Y., 1872.
39544.32.4A Morley, John. Voltaire. 2d ed. N.Y., 1872.
42577.14.9 Murger, Henry. Le bonhomme jadis. Paris, 1872.
42577.14 Murger, Henry. Les buveurs d'eau. Paris, 1872.
42577.20 Murger, Henry. Madame Olympe. Le dernier rendez-vous. Paris, 1872.
42577.29 Murger, Henry. Scènes de la vie de jeunesse. Le sabot rouge. Paris, 1872.
41556.12 Nodier, Charles. Contes de la veillée. Paris, 1872.
41556.18 Nodier, Charles. Souvenirs de la révolution. Paris, 1872. 2v.
42578.24 Noriac, Jules. Le grain de sable. Paris, 1872.
37596.54A Paris, Gaston. La vie de Saint Aléxis. Paris, 1872.
42558.9 Le parnassiculet contemporain. Paris, 1872.
38513.22 Pathelin. La farce de Maître Pathelin. Paris, 1872.
42545.69.7 Petit, Georges. La dame d'en face. Paris, 1872.
Mol 860.43 Pinchon. La mort de Molière. Paris, 1872.
FL 398.75 Poinsot, E.A. Regnier. Paris, 1872.
42541.30.7 Ponsard, François. L'honneur et l'argent. Paris, 1872.
42534.29 Pontmartin, A.F. de. La filleul de Beaumarchais. Paris, 1872.
42534.35.25 Pontmartin, A.F. de. Les jeudis de Madame Charbonneau. Paris, 1872.
42534.28 Pontmartin, A.F. de. Nouveaux Samedis. Paris, 1872-80. 20v.
42587.50.1.5 Pressensé, E.F.L. de P.G. de. Sabine; Gertrude de Chanzane: deux nouvelles. Paris, 1872.
38527.33 La puce de Mme. Desroches. Paris, 1872.
37597.6 Püschell, D. Li romanz de la rose. Berlin, 1872.
38536.23 Rabelais, F. La seconde chronique de Gargantua. Paris, 1872.
38536.18.56 Rabelais, F. Works. London, 1872?
38585.44.3 Racine, Jean. Les plaideurs. London, 1872.
38525.26 Régnier, Mathurin. Oeuvres complètes. Paris, 1872.
42515.30.683 Renan, Ernest. La réforme intellectuelle et morale. 3. éd. Paris, 1872.
42587.52.42 Renard, Jules. Une femme qui bégaie. Paris, 1872.

1872 - cont.

39578.7.5 Reyher, Gustave. Essai sur Vauvenargues et sa morale. Neustadt, 1872.
42546.4 Richard, G. Les enfants. 2e ed. Paris, 1872.
37572.34 Roche, Antoine. Les prosateurs français. Paris, 1872.
FL 6017.2 Rousseau, J.J. Ausgewählte Briefe. Hildburghausen, 1872.
FL 6026.16 Rousseau, J.J. Çonfessions. London, 1872.
38585.6 Roy, Just Jean Ést. Histoire de Jean Racine. Tours, 1872.
40586.22.3 St. Beuve, C.A. Chateaubriand et son groupe littéraire sous l'Empire. Paris, 1872. 2v.
40575.9A Sainte-Beuve, Charles A. Souvenirs et indiscrétions. Paris, 1872.
41557.8.57 Sand, George. Cesarine Dietrich. 3e éd. Paris, 1872.
41557.9.32 Sand, George. La famille de Germandre. Paris, 1872.
41557.8.77 Sand, George. Flavie. Les majoliques florentines. Paris, 1872.
41557.8.78 Sand, George. Francia. Un bienfait n'est jamais perdu. 3e éd. Paris, 1872.
41557.9.32.5 Sand, George. La petite Fadette. 5e éd. Paris, 1872.
41557.13 Sandeau, Jules. Le docteur Herbeau. Paris, 1872.
41557.26 Sandeau, Jules. La Roche aux Mouettes. Paris, 1872.
42546.20 Sardou, Victorien. Rabagas. Paris, 1872.
42546.20.8 Sardou, Victorien. Rabagas. 28e éd. Paris, 1872.
42557.3 Soulary, Joséphin. Oeuvres poétiques. Paris, 1872. 3v.
41558.6 Soulié, Férdéric. Le lion amoureux. Paris, 1872.
40593.22 Staël Holstein, Anne Louise. De la littérature considérée dans ses rapports avec les institutions sociales. Paris, 1872.
39544.12 Strauss, D.F. Voltaire. Leipzig, 1872.
37562.30 Strümpell, Gustav. Ersten Bibelübersetzungen der Franzosen. Braunschweig, 1872.
41562.30 Sue, Eugène. Les sept péchés capitaux, l'envie, la colère. Paris, 1872.
41563.27 Toepffer, Rodolphe. Nouvelles genevoises. Paris, 1872.
41563.28 Toepffer, Rodolphe. Nouvelles genevoises. 4. éd. Bielefeld, 1872.
41563.30 Toepffer, Rodolphe. Réflexions et menus proper. Paris, 1872.
38527.4 Travers, Julien. Essai sur...Jean Vauquelin. Caen, 1872.
42581.20 Verne, Jules. Voyage au centre de la terre. Paris, 1872.
41564.8 Vigny, Alfred de. Nevolia i velichie soldata. Paris, 1872.
38512.82 Vital de Blois. Le traicté de Getta et d'Amphitrion. Paris, 1872.
40584.28 Vitet, L. La ligue precédée des États d'Orléans. Paris, 1872. 2v.
42587.74 Witt, Henriette Guizot de. Dames of high estate. N.Y., 1872.
42584.23.413 Zola, Emile. La fortune des Rougon. 3. éd. Paris, 1872.

1873

42562.11.9 About, Edmond. Le mari imprévu. 3e éd. Paris, 1873.
Mol 875.5 Aicard, J. Mascarille. Paris, 1873.
42524.7 Alaux, Jules E. Études esthétiques. Paris, 1873.
37564.44.25 Albert, Paul. La littérature française au dix-septième siècle. Paris, 1873.
41555.51 Allart de Méritens, Hortense. Les nouveaux enchantements. Paris, 1873.
Mol 870.21 Arène, P. Les comédiens errants. Paris, 1873.
38527.23 Aubigné, Théodore Agrippa d'. L'enfer. Satire. Paris, 1873.
38527.16 Aubigné, Théodore Agrippa d'. Oeuvres complètes. Paris, 1873-77. 6v.
Mol 860.44 Aubryet, X. Le docteur Molière. Paris, 1873.
40597.11 Balzac, Honoré de. Beatrix. Contract du mariage. Paris, 1873-74.
Htn 40597.14.53* Balzac, Honoré de. Les contes drolatiques. Paris, 1873.
40597.15.7 Balzac, Honoré de. Le cousin Pons. Paris, 1873.
40597.19 Balzac, Honoré de. Eugénie Grandet. Paris, 1873.
40597.31 Balzac, Honoré de. Memoires de deux jeunes mariées. La femme de 30 ans. London, 1873-75.
40596.4.10 Balzac, Honoré de. Oeuvres complètes. Paris, 1873-79. 24v.
42554.4.5 Banville, Théodore de. Camées parisiens. 3e sér. Paris, 1873.
42554.2.5 Banville, Théodore de. Trente-six ballades joyeuses. Paris, 1873.
37565.24 Barni, Jules. Le moralistes français au 18th siècle. Paris, 1873.
42563.63.3 Baudin, Pierre. Le siège de Rhodes. Constantinople, 1873.
41522.19 Beaumont-Vassy, E.F. Le fils de la polonaise. Paris, 1873.
42563.22.13.5 Belot, Adolphe. Dacolard et Lubin, suite du parricide. Paris, 1873.
42563.22.14.9 Belot, Adolphe. Le parricide. Paris, 1873.
37556.5 Besant, Walter. The French humorists from the 12th to the 19th century. London, 1873.
40582.19.8 Beyle, Henri. Promenades dans Rome. v.1-2. Paris, 1873.
42563.28.29 Biart, Lucien. Les clientes. Paris, 1873.
38525.34A Bouchet, Guillaumę. Les serees. Paris, 1873. 6v.
38542.15 Broglé, Adolphe. Etude sur Saint Evremond. Rostock, 1873.
42586.27 Bungener, Félix. Un sermon sous Louis XIV. Paris, 1873.
FL 366.8 La censure dramatique. Paris, 1873.
FL 393.18 Challamel, A. L'ancien boulevard de Temple. Paris, 1873.
42565.40 Cherbuliez, Victor. Count Kostia. N.Y., 1873.
42565.12 Cherbuliez, Victor. Etudes de littéture et d'art. Paris, 1873.
42565.19A Cherbuliez, Victor. Meta Holdenis. Paris, 1873.
Mol 703.3A Claretie, J. Molière, sa vie et ses oeuvres. Paris, 1873.
37546.4 Colletet, Guillaume. Vies des poètes Bordelais. Paris, 1873.
Mol 728.9 Constant, C. Molière à Fontainebleau (1661-1664). Meaux, 1873.
38575.27 Corneille, Pierre. Le Cid. Horace (chef d'oeuvre). Boston, 1873.
38571.7 Corneille, Pierre. Oeuvres. Paris, 1873.
42546.31.24 Cournier, J.M.J.J.M. Cournier contre Montigny et Sardou. Paris, 1873.
42566.13 Craven, Pauline. Fleurange. N.Y., 1873.
42566.13.5 Craven, Pauline. Fleurange. tom. 1-2. 10. éd. Paris, 1873.
42566.10.3 Craven, Pauline. Récit d'une soeur. 26. éd. Paris, 1873. 2v.
42567.30 Daudet, Ernest. Le roman de Delphine. Paris, 1873.

Chronological Listing

1873 - cont.

37538.26 Demogeot, Jacques Claude. Histoire de la littérature française. Paris, 1873.
39544.19 Desnoiresterres, G. Voltaire aux Délices. Paris, 1873.
38528.24 Despériers, Bonaventure. Cymbalum mundi. Paris, 1873.
Mol 870.23 d'Hervilly, E. Le docteur sans pareil. Paris, 1873.
Mol 875.3F Dingelstedt, F. Zu Molière's Gedachtnissfeier. Wien, 1873.
Mol 825.5 Drouineau, G. Molière et les médecins au XVIIe siècle. La Rochelle, 1873.
42568.4.2 Droz, Gustave. Babolain. N.Y., 1873.
42568.4 Droz, Gustave. Babolain. Paris, 1873.
42568.19.14 Du Boisgobey, Fortuné. Le chevalier casse-cou. v.1-2. Paris, 1873-1874.
42542.66.68 Dugué, Ferdinand. Ismène; comédie en vers. Paris, 1873.
42541.8.5 Dumanior, P.F.P. Don Caesar de Bazan. Paris, 1873.
41523.5 Dumas, Alexandre. Ange Pitou. Paris, 1873.
41523.6.2 Dumas, Alexandre. Aventure d'amour. Paris, 1873.
41523.21 Dumas, Alexandre. Catherine Blum. Paris, 1873.
41523.27 Dumas, Alexandre. Chevalier d'Harmental. Paris, 1873.
41523.29 Dumas, Alexandre. Collier de la reine. Paris, 1873. 3v.
41524.17 Dumas, Alexandre. Drames de la mer. Paris, 1873.
42543.19.10 Dumas, Alexandre. La femme de Claude. Paris, 1873.
41525.1 Dumas, Alexandre. Une fille du régent. Paris, 1873.
41538.48 Dumas, Alexandre. The history of a nutcracker. London, 1873.
41526.1 Dumas, Alexandre. Impressions de voyage. Le speronare. Paris, 1873.
41526.4 Dumas, Alexandre. Ingénue. Paris, 1873.
42543.23.5 Dumas, Alexandre. Man-woman. Philadelphia, 1873.
41527.13 Dumas, Alexandre. Un pays inconnu. Paris, 1873.
42543.24 Dumas, Alexandre. La princesse Georges. 5. éd. Paris, 1873.
41527.20 Dumas, Alexandre. Quarante-Cinq. Paris, 1873. 3v.
41527.22 Dumas, Alexandre. La reine-Margot. Paris, 1873.
41527.26 Dumas, Alexandre. Salvator. v.1-2, 3-5. Paris, 1873. 2v.
41538.53.22 Dumas, Alexandre. The three guardsmen. Philadelphia, 1873.
41528.11 Dumas, Alexandre. Le trou de l'enfer. Paris, 1873.
41584.32.33 Duveyrier, A.H.J. Sullivan. N.Y., 1873.
42572.3.9 Erckmann, Emile. The bells. N.Y., 1873.
42572.9 Erckmann, Emile. Les deux frères. Paris, 1873.
42572.14.3 Erckmann, Emile. Histoire d'un paysan. Paris, 1873. 2v.
42572.23.15 Erckmann, Emile. Madame Thérèse. 23. éd. Paris, 1873.
42574.14 Fabre, Ferdinand. L'abbé Tigrane. Paris, 1873.
42513.29 Favre, Jules. Conferences et discours littéraires. Paris, 1873.
38553.27.6 Fénelon, F. de S. de la Mothe. Aventures de Télémaque. Paris, 1873.
42575.25 Feuillet, Octave. L'acrobate. Paris, 1873.
42575.41.5 Feuillet, Octave. Péril en la demeure. Paris, 1873. 3 pam.
42575.50.3 Feuillet, Octave. Il romanzo di un giovane povero. N.Y., 1873.
Mol 197.5 Féval, P. Le théâtre-femme. Paris, 1873.
41539.3 Fitzgerald, Percy. Alexandre Dumas, life and adventures. London, 1873. 4v.
37541.6 Fleury, Jean. Du charactère speciale de la langue française. St. Petersbourg, 1873.
37596.247.2 Floriant et Florete. Floriant and Florete. Edinburgh, 1873.
FL 360.19 Foucher, Paul. Les coulisses du passé. Paris, 1873.
38565.21 Fournier, E. Oeuvres complètes de Nicolas Boileau. Paris, 1873.
Htn 42576.62.80* France, Anatole. Les poèmes dorés. Paris, 1873.
38526.33 Frank, Félix. Les Marguerites de la Marguerite. Paris, 1873. 4v.
41542.26.9 Gautier, Théophile. Les jeunes-France. Paris, 1873.
41542.10.90 Gautier, Théophile. Mademoiselle de Maupin. Paris, 1873.
Htn 41542.31.10* Gautier, Théophile. Poésies de T. Gautier qui ne figureront pas dans ses oeuvres. n.p., 1873.
41542.17 Gautier, Théophile. Voyage en Espagne. Paris, 1873.
42576.36.19 Gay, Sophie. La duchesse de Châteauroux. Paris, 1873.
37546.24 Geslain, Théodomir. Littérature contemporaine en Provence. Paris, 1873.
41541.13.2 Girardin, Delphine Gay. The cross of Berny. Philadelphia, 1873.
38523.3.3 Glauning, F. Syntaktische Studien zu Marot. Nördlingen, 1873.
42543.54.6 Gondinet, Edmond. La cravate blanche. Paris, 1873.
42543.54.11 Gondinet, Edmond. Le roi l'a dit. Paris, 1873.
42586.69 Gourdon de Genouillac, Henri. Le crime de 1804. Paris, 1873.
39532.7.5 Hamilton, Anthony. Contes d'Hamilton. Paris, 1873. 2v.
41573.21.20 Hugo, Victor. Notre Dame de Paris. Paris, 1873.
Mol 880.21 Jouhaud, A. L'Orgon de Tartuffe. Paris, 1873.
Mon 68.3.6 Jubinal, A. Henri IV et Montaigne; lettre. 3. éd. Paris, 1873.
42576.67.50 Judices de Mirandol, L. Mémoires d'un enfant de troupe. Paris, 1873.
42541.41 Jules, F. Un moment de Toute-Puissance. Paris, 1873.
41553.38.1 Kock, Charles Paul de. Le barbier de Paris. Paris, 1873.
41552.9 Kock, Charles Paul de. Un bon enfant. Paris, 1873.
41552.14 Kock, Charles Paul de. La demoiselle du cinquième. Paris, 1873.
41553.68 Kock, Charles Paul de. Mémoires. Paris, 1873.
37542.5 Kreyssig, Friedrich. Geschichte des französischen Nationalliter. Berlin, 1873.
41578.13 Lamartine, Alphonse de. Poésies inédites de Lamartine. Photoreproduction. Paris, 1873.
Mol 730.4 Lapommeraye, H. de. Les amours de Molière. Paris, 1873.
38543.10.25 La Rochefoucauld, François. Maximes et réfléxions morales. Paris, 1873.
42515.36.155 Lasserre, Henri. Evangelho segundo Renan. 25. éd. Porto, 1873.
38526.23 Laur, E. Louize Labé. Strassburg, 1873.
42544.8 Legouvé, Ernest. Les deux reines de France. Paris, 1873.
Htn 41542.4.15* Lemerre, Alphonse. Le tombeau de Théophile Gautier. Paris, 1873.
Htn Mon 192.1* Le Petit, J. Quelques nots sur le docteur J.F. Payen. Paris, 1873.
40512.33.3 LeSage, Alain René. Historia de Gil Blas de Santillana. Paris, 1873.

1873 - cont.

39527.3 Leveaux, Alphonse. De la poesie dans...La Fontaine. Paris, 1873.
40556.28.3 Maistre, Joseph de. Lettres et opuscules inédits. 6. éd. Paris, 1873. 2v.
42577.10.76 Malot, Hector. Romain Kalbris. Philadelphia, 1873.
42545.5.150 Manuel, Eugène. L'absent. Drame en un acte en vers. 4e éd. Paris, 1873.
38526.35.75 Marion, J. Rondeaulx et vers d'amour. Paris, 1873.
38523.9A Marot, Clément. Oeuvres. Paris, 1873. 4v.
38523.9.3A Marot, Clément. Oeuvres complètes. Paris, 1873. 4v.
42545.10.17 Meilhac, Henri. Le chateau à Toto. Paris, 1873.
42545.10.11 Meilhac, Henri. Froufrou. 7. éd. Paris, 1873.
42555.58.1220 Mérat, Albert. L'Adieu. Paris, 1873.
41555.22 Mérimée, Prosper. Chronique du règne de Charles IX. Paris, 1873.
37567.10 Milliet, Paul. Notes romantiques a propos de Marion Delorme. Paris, 1873.
Mol 171.24 Molière, Jean Baptiste Poquelin. Le bourgeois gentilhomme. Boston, 1873.
Mol 178.10 Molière, Jean Baptiste Poquelin. La critique de l'École des femmes...Lacour. Paris, 1873.
Mol 181.10 Molière, Jean Baptiste Poquelin. Dépit amoureux...Lacour. Paris, 1873.
Mol 195.25 Molière, Jean Baptiste Poquelin. L'école des femmes...Lacour. Paris, 1873.
Mol 231.20 Molière, Jean Baptiste Poquelin. Le mariage forcé...Lacour. Paris, 1873.
Mol 232.5 Molière, Jean Baptiste Poquelin. Married in spite of himself. n.p., 1873.
Mol 235.55 Molière, Jean Baptiste Poquelin. Le médecin malgré lui. Boston, 1873?
Mol 245.43.5 Molière, Jean Baptiste Poquelin. Le misanthrope. Les femmes savantes. v.2. Boston, 1873.
Mol 245.43.15 Molière, Jean Baptiste Poquelin. Le misanthrope. 7. éd. Bielefeld, 1873.
Mol 18.73.5 Molière, Jean Baptiste Poquelin. Molière...Laun. v.1-14. Berlin, 1873-85. 9v.
Mol 18.73.2A Molière, Jean Baptiste Poquelin. Oeuvres...Despois. v.1-12 and album. Paris, 1873-1900. 13v.
Mol 18.73 Molière, Jean Baptiste Poquelin. Oeuvres...Despois. v.1-13 and album. Paris, 1873-1900. 14v.
Mol 18.73.3 Molière, Jean Baptiste Poquelin. Oeuvres. Paris, 1873. 2v.
Mol 18.73.8A Molière, Jean Baptiste Poquelin. Oeuvres complètes. Paris, 1873. 3v.
Mol 201.25 Molière, Jean Batiste Poquelin. L'escole des maris...Lacour. Paris, 1873.
42545.42 Monselet, Charles. Panier fleuri prose et vers. Paris, 1873.
Mon 18.73 Montaigne, Michel de. Essais. Motheau et Jouaust. Paris, 1873-75. 4v.
Mon 18.73.2 Montaigne, Michel de. Essais. Motheau et Jouaust. Paris, 1873-75. 4v.
39594.12.7 Montesquieu, C.L. de S. Lettres persanes. Paris, 1873.
FL 6118.73A Morley, John Morley. Rousseau. London, 1873. 2v.
Mol 735.1.5 Musée Molière; Catalogue. Paris, 1873.
42578.12 Narrey, Charles. Ce que l'on dit pendant une contredanse. Paris, 1873.
41551.15 Nodier, Charles. Le génie bonhomme. Paris, 1873.
37571.3 Noël, François J.M. Leçons françaises de littérature. Paris, 1873.
42541.23 Pailleron, Edouard. Hélène. Drame en trois actes. Paris, 1873.
42545.66 Pailleron, Edouard. Théâtre. v.2. Paris, 1873.
42587.42.5 Pelletan, Eugène. Les uns et les autres. Paris, 1873.
37596.69 Philippe, de Thaon. Li cumpoz. Strassburg, 1873.
42534.35.20 Pontmartin, A.F. de. Le mandarine. Paris, 1873.
42545.88.47 Porto-Riche, G. Le vertige. Paris, 1873.
37544.5.2 Potvin, Charles. De la corruption littéraire en France. 2. éd. Bruxelles, 1873.
38525.22 Prarond, Ernest. Les poëtes historiens, Ronsard et d'Aubigné. Paris, 1873.
38546.58A Puliga, Henriette C.S. Mme. de Sévigné. London, 1873. 2v.
38583.3.16 Racine, Jean. Album. Paris, 1873.
38583.3.17 Racine, Jean. Musique des choeurs. Paris, 1873.
38581.15 Racine, Jean. Oeuvres. Paris, 1873.
38546.4 Rathéry, Edme J.B. Mademoiselle de Scudéry. Paris, 1873.
37577.30 Recueil de pieces rares et facetieuses. v.3. Paris, 1873.
38525.26.3 Régnier, Mathurin. Oeuvres complètes. Paris, 1873.
42515.29.401A Renan, Ernest. L'antéchrist. Paris, 1873.
42546.6.5 Ringal, Gustave. Le vidame. Paris, 1873.
FL 6021.73 Rousseau, J.J. Les confessions. Paris, 1873.
FL 6051.73 Rousseau, J.J. La nouvelle Héloise. Paris, 1873.
37543.11 Sabatier, A. De l'influence des femmes sur la littérature française. Paris, 1873.
38526.47.77 Saint-Gelais, Mellin de. Oeuvres complètes de Melin de Sainct-Gelais. Paris, 1873. 3v.
40575.8 Sainte-Beuve, Charles A. Lettres à la princesse. Paris, 1873.
40575.22.5 Sainte-Beuve, Charles A. Memoirs of Madame Desbordes-Valmore. Boston, 1873.
41557.9.27 Sand, George. Les dames vertes. Paris, 1873.
41557.8.82 Sand, George. Impressions et souvenirs. Paris, 1873.
41557.9.49.5 Sand, George. Nanon. 6e éd. Paris, 1873.
41557.18 Sandeau, Jules. Jean de Thommeray. Paris, 1873.
42546.17.3 Sardou, Victorien. La famille Benoiton. Paris, 1873. 3 pam.
42516.6 Schaeffer, Adolphe. Mélanges d'histoire. Neuchâtel, 1873.
38525.22.45.75 Scheffler, W. Essai sur Ronsard et sa réforme litteraire. Dresde, 1873.
37566.10 Schmidt, Julian. Geschichte der französischen Literatur seit Ludwig XVI. 1774. Leipzig, 1873-1874. 2v.
Mol 719.5 Schweitzer, H. Molière's Tod, vor 200 Jahren. Weisbaden, 1873.
42548.26.2 Scribe, E. La bataille de dames. N.Y., 1873.
40543.6 Ségur, Louis P. de. Mélanges. Paris, 1873.
41586.30.12 Soumet, A. The gladiator...performed by Salvini. N.Y., 1873.
Mol 253.5.2 Spoelgen, J. Analyse et critique des Précieuses ridicules. Rostock, 1873.
Mol 253.5 Spoelgen, J. Analyse et critique des Précieuses ridicules. Rostock, 1873.
40592.24.25 Staël Holstein, Anne Louise. Corinne. N.Y., 1873.
42587.59.21 Stapleaux, Leopold. Histoire d'une nuit. Paris? 1873?

Chronological Listing

1873 - cont.

41563.9 Sue, Eugène. The Marquis of Létorière. Boston, 1873.
41563.16.5 Sue, Eugène. The mysteries of Paris. v.1-3. London, 1873.
41561.15.20 Sue, Eugène. Wandering Jew. London, 1873?
Mol 720.5 Thierry, Edouard. Quatre mois du théâtre de Molière. Cherbourgh, 1873.
NEDL FL 370.45 Tivier, H. Histoire de la littérature dramatique en France. Paris, 1873.
41553.100 Trimm, T. La vie de Charles Paul de Kock. Paris, 1873.
42582.15 Verne, Jules. Five weeks in a balloon. Boston, 1873.
42582.20 Verne, Jules. Meridiana. London, 1873.
42582.24 Verne, Jules. The tour of the world in eighty days. Boston, 1873.
42582.27 Verne, Jules. Twenty thousand leagues under the sea. Boston, 1873.
42582.8.15 Verne, Jules. A voyage round the world. In search of the castaways. Philadelphia, 1873.
38514.21 Villon, François. Oeuvres complètes. Paris, 1873.
38514.23 Vitu, Auguste. Notice sur François Villon. Paris, 1873.
Mol 815.4 Weisser, E. L'Hôtel de Rambouillet. Breslau, 1873.
42587.71 Witt, Henriette Guizot de. Marie Dierville. Philadelphia, 1873.

1874

42553.2 Ackermann, L. Poésies. Paris, 1874.
37565.15 Albert, Paul. Littérature française au XVIII siècle. Paris, 1874.
37567.8 Asselineau, Charles. Bibliographie romantique. Paris, 1874.
42542.10.1 Augier, Émile. Le gendre de M. Poirier. Paris, 1874.
42542.13 Augier, Émile. Jean de Thommeray. 2. éd. Paris, 1874.
39586.6 Bachaumont, Louis Petit de. Mémoires secrets. Paris, 1874.
38526.8A Baif, Jean Antoine de. Poésies choisies. Paris, 1874.
40597.14.55A Balzac, Honoré de. Droll stories. London, 1874.
40597.14.56 Balzac, Honoré de. Droll stories. London, 1874.
X Cg 40597.14.50 Balzac, Honoré de. Droll stories. London, 1874. 2v.
Htn 40597.10* Balzac, Honoré de. Droll stories. London, 1874.
40597.14.58A Balzac, Honoré de. Droll stories. N.Y., 1874.
40597.14.58 Balzac, Honoré de. Droll stories. N.Y., 1874. 2v.
40597.29 Balzac, Honoré de. La maison du chat-qui-pelote. La paix du ménage. London, 1874-75.
40595.5 Balzac, Honoré de. Oeuvres complètes. Paris, 1874. 20v.
42542.27.26 Barrière, Théodore. Aux crochets d'un gendre. Paris, 1874.
42515.35.28 Bauer, Bruno. Philo, Straus und Renan und das Urchristenthum. Berlin, 1874.
40532.3.10 Beaumarchais, Pierre A.C. de. Oeuvres complètes. Paris, 1874.
42563.22.13 Belot, Adolphe. Hélène et Mathildé. Paris, 1874.
42542.29.11 Bergerat, Émile. Séparés de corps. Paris, 1874.
41522.38.5 Bernard, Charles de. Gerfaut. Paris, 1874.
38528.16.7.5 Béroalde de Verville. Contes en vers imités du Moyen de parvenir. Paris, 1874.
37556.6A Besant, Walter. French humorists. Boston, 1874.
38526.2.3A Bèze, Théodore de. Abraham sacrifiant (1550). Genève, 1874.
42563.26.3 Blocqueville, Louise Adélaïde d'Eckmühl. Les soirées de la villa des jasmins. Paris, 1874. 4v.
38551.38 Blörklund, J. Fénélon. Göteborg, 1874.
39586.9 Bodemann, E. Julie von Bondeli und ihr Freundeskreis. Hannover, 1874.
FL 395.40 Bonnassies, J. Les auteurs dramatiques et la comédie, 17e et 18e siècles. Paris, 1874.
FL 394.75 Bonnassies, J. La comédie française. Histoire adminstrative. Paris, 1874.
Mol 810.1.5 Bonnassies, J. La musique à la Comédie-Française. Paris, 1874.
38557.5 Bossuet. London, 1874.
42542.30.5 Bouchor, Maurice. Les chansons joyeuses poesies. Paris, 1874.
FL 396.68.9 Bouget, Henry. Palais-royal. Paris, 1874.
Mol 815.6 Breitinger, H. Der Salon Rambouillet und seine kulturgeschichtliche Bedeutung (in Programm der Thurgauischen Kantonsschule 1873-1874). Frauenfeld, 1874.
Mol 193.9 Burgtorf, C. Étude...sur le Festin de Pierre. Gottingue, 1874.
40587.45 Carne, Louis. Études sur la vie et les ouvrages de M. de Chateaubriand. Paris, 1874.
43550.2.30 Cartairade, F. Du coeur aux Lévres. Paris, 1874.
43550.2.31 Cartairade, F. Le jour et la nuit. Paris, 1874.
40517.1.15 Caylus, Anne C.P. Mémoires et réflexions. Paris, 1874.
Mol 880.5 Champmesté, C.C. Les fragments de Molière. San Reno, 1874.
38514.25 Charles d'Orleans. Poésies complètes. v.1-2. Paris, 1874.
42565.45 Cherbuliez, Victor. Prosper. N.Y., 1874.
42565.47 Cherbuliez, Victor. Romance of an honest woman. Boston, 1874.
Mol 703.4 Claretie, J. Molière, sa vie et ses oeuvres. Paris, 1874.
39526.8 Cocheris, Hippolyte. Premier livre des fables de La Fontaine. Paris, 1874-75.
Mol 845.1.6 Collection Molierèsque. San Remo, 1874.
42554.23.12 Coppée, François. Der Strike der Schmiede. Wien, 1874.
38575.27.2 Corneille, Pierre. Le Cid. 10. éd. Bielefeld, 1874.
38575.33.6 Corneille, Pierre. Horace; tragédie. London, 1874.
42542.54.3 Cottinet, E. Le docteur Bourguibus. Paris, 1874.
37563.7 Cougny, Edouard. François Hotoman-Montesquieu et mad. de Lambert. Vers, 1874-77.
42586.32.710 Cournier, Jean. Lettres de l'inconnue. Paris, 1874.
42566.6.2 Craven, Pauline. Le mot de l'énigme. 2. éd. Paris, 1874.
42566.32 Daudet, Alphonse. Robert Helmont, journal d'un solitaire. Paris, 1874.
42542.63.5 Denayrouze, L. La belle Paule. Paris, 1874.
38512.25.2 De Queux de St. Hilaire. Livre des cent ballades. Paris, 1874.
39544.20 Desnoiresterres, G. Voltaire et J.J. Rousseau. Paris, 1874.
Htn 38528.32* Despériers, Bonaventure. Nouvelles recréations. Paris, 1874. 2v.
FL 377.15 Despois, Eugene. Théâtre français sous Louis XIV. Paris, 1874.
41584.15 Doucet, Camille. Oeuvres complètes. Paris, 1874. 2v.
42568.19.9 Du Boisgobey, Fortuné. Collets noirs. Paris, 1874. 2v.

1874 - cont.

42568.19.25 Duchemin, Léon. Mémoires d'un décavé. Paris, 1874.
38528.20 Du Fail, Noël. Oeuvres facetieuses. Paris, 1874. 2v.
Mol 870.10 Dumas, A. Trois entr'actes pour l'Amour médecin. Paris, 1874.
41523.16 Dumas, Alexandre. Cadet de famille. Paris, 1874.
41538.65 Dumas, Alexandre. The conscript. N.Y., 1874.
41525.5 Dumas, Alexandre. Gabriel Lambert. Paris, 1874.
41526.8 Dumas, Alexandre. Ivanhoe par Walter Scott. v.1-2. Paris, 1874.
41526.12 Dumas, Alexandre. Jehanne la Pucelle. Paris, 1874.
41538.29.5 Dumas, Alexandre. Margarita de Borgona; drama. Madrid, 1874.
41527.4 Dumas, Alexandre. Les mohicans de Paris. v.1-4. Paris, 1874. 2v.
41527.12 Dumas, Alexandre. Pauline et Pascal Bruno. Paris, 1874.
41527.18 Dumas, Alexandre. La princesse de Monaco. Paris, 1874.
41527.23 Dumas, Alexandre. Robin Hood. Le proscrit. v.1-2. Paris, 1874.
41538.51.5 Dumas, Alexandre. Théâtre complet. Paris, 1874. 25v.
41528.15 Dumas, Alexandre. Une vie d'artiste. Paris, 1874.
42586.43 Erckman, Jules. Les veillées alsaciennes. Paris, 1874.
42574.20 Fabre, Ferdinand. Le marquis de Pierrerue. Paris, 1874. 2v.
42513.30 Favre, Jules. Quatre conférences. Paris, 1874.
42575.40.5 Feuillet, Octave. La petite comtesse. Paris, 1874.
42575.27.12 Feuillet, Octave. Le sphinx. 2. éd. Paris, 1874.
42575.51.10 Feuillet, Octave. Le village. Paris, 1874.
42575.23.10 Feuillet, Octave. Le village. Paris, 1874. 6 pam.
41542.3 Feydeau, Ernst. Théophile Gautier. Paris, 1874.
Htn 42576.23* Flaubert, Gustave. La tentation de Saint-Antoine. Paris, 1874.
42564.47 Fleury, Jules. Madame Eugenio. Paris, 1874.
37563.12 Froment, Théodore. Essai sur...l'eloquence judiciare. Paris, 1874.
42571.24.25 Gaboriau, Emile. I danari degli altri. v. 1-2. Milano, 1874.
38514.43 Gasté, Armand. Jean Le Houx et le Vau de vire. Paris, 1874.
41542.12 Gautier, Théophile. Histoire du romantisme. Paris, 1874.
41542.20.5 Gautier, Théophile. Nouvelles. 11. éd. Paris, 1874.
41542.14 Gautier, Theophile. Portraits contemporains. Paris, 1874.
41541.17.5 Girardin, Delphine Gay. Marguerite. Paris, 1874.
42586.64 Gobineau, Arthur de. Les Pléiades. Paris, 1874.
42543.54.7 Gondinet, Edmond. Les grandes demoiselles. Paris, 1874.
Mol 167.10 Groon. Comparaison entre l'Avare de Molière et l'Aulularie de Plaute. Berden, 1874?
39533.4 Hamilton, Anthony. Memoires...de Grammont. v.1-2. Paris, 1874.
Mol 608.4 Hanriot, Charles. Leçon d'ouverture du cours de littérature française. Troyes, 1874.
42541.16 Henneguy, Félix. Panthéia. Paris, 1874.
37565.13 Herrmann, T.A. Resumé de la littérature française au XVIII siècle. Dresden, 1874.
42543.69.14.10 Hervilly, Ernest. Le Harem. Paris, 1874.
42587.4.81 Hudry-Menos, un patriote Savoisien. Genève, 1874.
41573.18.2 Hugo, Victor. Ninety-three. N.Y., 1874.
41573.18A Hugo, Victor. Ninety-three. N.Y., 1874.
41572.20.2 Hugo, Victor. Quatre-vingt-treize. Paris, 1874. 3v.
41572.20 Hugo, Victor. Quatre-vingt-treize. Paris, 1874. 2v.
Mol 608.13 Humbert, C. Molière in England. Bielefeld, 1874.
NEDL Mon 120.2 Jeudy, R. De l'education dans Rabelais et dans Montaigne. Paris, 1874-88. 3 pam.
Mol 880.20 Joliet, Charles. Le mariage d'Alceste. Paris, 1874.
37596.8.3 Jubinal, A. Oeuvres completes de Rutebeuf. Paris, 1874-75. 3v.
FL 364.12 Jullien, Adolphe. Histoire du théâtre du Mme. de Pampadour. Paris, 1874.
41553.20 Kock, Charles Paul de. Le petit bonhomme du coin. Paris, 1874.
FL 6039.10 Krömer, Emil J. Der Staats-Vertrag. Leipzig, 1874.
38564.29 La Bruyère, J. de. Les caractères. Paris, 1874.
41554.5 Lacroix, Jules. Oeuvres. Théâtre. Paris, 1874. 3v.
Mol 560.7 Lacroix, P. La véritable édition originale des oeuvres de Molière, étude bibliographique. Paris, 1874.
39527.23.4 La Fontaine, Jean de. Fables. Paris, 1874.
41578.20 Lamartine, Alphonse de. Prosper Mérimée's letters...with recollections by Lamartine. N.Y., 1874.
37558.20 Laur, E. Zur Geschichte der französischen Litteratur. Mannheim, 1874.
Mol 612.6 Legouvé, E. Eugène Scribe. Paris, 1874.
42544.34.2.30 Lemercier de Neuville, Louis. Le passé. Lyon, 1874.
42555.39.30 Lemoyne, André. Une idylle normande. Paris, 1874.
Mol 735.2 Lenient, Charles. Molière - son portrait physique et moral. Paris, 1874.
40587.6 Lenormant, C. Souvenirs d'enfance et de jeunesse de Chateaubriand. Paris, 1874.
42555.40.110 Lonlay, E. Le livre d'or des enfants. Paris, 1874.
37574.15 Louandre, Charles. Chefs-d'oeuvres des conteurs français, 17e siècle. Paris, 1874.
37574.16 Louandre, Charles. Chefs-d'oeuvres des conteurs français, 18e siècle. Paris, 1874.
37574.14 Louandre, Charles. Chefs-d'oeuvres des conteurs français, 1051-1650. Paris, 1874.
38527.62 Magny, Olivier de. Les souspirs. Paris, 1874.
37542.8 Maillard, A. Histoire de la littérature française. Dresden, 1874.
NEDL 37567.130 Maillard, F. Les derniers bohêmes. Paris, 1874.
38523.30.35 Malherbe, François de. Oeuvres poétiques. Paris, 1874.
42577.8.10 Malot, Hector. Une belle-mère. Paris, 1874.
42587.16.20 Marrast, Augustin. Esquisses Byzantines. Paris, 1874.
42545.10.30 Meilhac, Henri. L'été de la Saint-Martin. 2e éd. Paris, 1874.
42545.10.13 Meilhac, Henri. La petite marquise. Paris, 1874.
41555.23.30 Mérimée, Prosper. Colomba, suivi de la mosaique. Paris, 1874.
41555.10.5 Mérimée, Prosper. Derniers nouvelles. 6. éd. Paris, 1874.
41555.10 Mérimée, Prosper. Derniers nouvelles. 7. éd. Paris, 1874.
41555.7A Mérimée, Prosper. Letters to an incognita. N.Y., 1874.
Htn 41555.5.5* Mérimée, Prosper. Lettres à une inconnue. Paris, 1874. 2v.
41555.6 Mérimée, Prosper. Lettres à une inconnue. 9. éd. Paris, 1874. 2v.

Chronological Listing

1874 - cont.

41555.12 Mérimée, Prosper. Portraits historiques et littéraires. Paris, 1874.
42546.31.22 Les merveilleuses; analyse et notes. Paris, 1874.
42587.26 Méry, Joseph. Through thick and thin. N.Y., 1874.
41586.23.48 Méry, Joseph. Through thick and thin. N.Y., 1874.
37595.28 Meyer, Paul. Recueil d'anciens textes bas-latins, provencaux et français. Paris, 1874. 2v.
41595.27 Millevoye, Charles H. Oeuvres. Paris, 1874.
37574.79 Mixer, A.H. Manual of French poetry. N.Y., 1874.
NEDL 39526.24 Moland, Louis. Oeuvres complètes de La Fontaine. Paris, 1874-75. 2v.
Mol 166.1.8 Molière, Jean Baptiste Poquelin. L'avare...Ostrowski. Paris, 1874.
Mol 171.25 Molière, Jean Baptiste Poquelin. Le bourgeois gentilhomme...Lacour. Paris, 1874.
Mol 208.20 Molière, Jean Baptiste Poquelin. Les facheux...Lacour. Paris, 1874.
Mol 215.22 Molière, Jean Baptiste Poquelin. Les Fourberies de Scapin...Candole. London, 1874.
Mol 235.20 Molière, Jean Baptiste Poquelin. Le médecin malgré lui...Lacour. Paris, 1874.
Mol 235.21 Molière, Jean Baptiste Poquelin. Le médecin malgré lui...Lallemand. London, 1874.
Mol 245.45 Molière, Jean Baptiste Poquelin. Le misanthrope. Brette. London, 1874.
Mol 245.46 Molière, Jean Baptiste Poquelin. Le misanthrope. Lacour. Paris, 1874.
Mol 246.8.5 Molière, Jean Baptiste Poquelin. O misanthropo. Lisboa, 1874.
Mol 268.53 Molière, Jean Baptiste Poquelin. Le Tartuffe. Bué. London, 1874.
37548.6 Monnier, Marc. Genève et ses poètes. Paris, 1874.
42582.9.2 Moré, Marcel. Nouvelles explorations de Jules Verne. Boston, 1874. 2v.
42578.10 Narrey, Charles. Le bal du diable. Paris, 1874.
37566.14 Nescis, J.J. La littérature sous les deux empires. Paris, 1874.
37536.14.5 Nisard, Désiré. Histoire de la littérature française. 5e éd. Paris, 1874. 4v.
37543.13 Noël, Auguste. Histoire de la littérature française. Paris, 1874.
41578.168 Olivier, Émile. Lamartine. Paris, 1874.
Htn 37571.28* Pagès, Alphonse. Les grands poètes français. Paris, 1874.
40583.3 Paton, A.A. Henry Beyle. London, 1874.
42587.45 Perret, Paul. Les bonnes filles d'Eve. Paris, 1874.
38526.45.5 Pibrac, Guy du Faur. Quatrains. Paris, 1874.
38585.19.1 Racine, Jean. Chefs-d'oeuvre de Jean Racine. Andromaque. Les plaideurs. Paris, 1874.
37548.11 Rambert, Eugène. Écrivains nationaux. Geneva, 1874.
38587.8.6 Regnard, Jean François. Le joueur; comédie en cinq actes. Paris, 1874.
38525.23 Régnier, Mathurin. Oeuvres complètes. Paris, 1874.
41557.8 Robert, Clémence. Les mendiants de la mort. Paris, 1874.
42559.50 Les rois de France. Paris, 1874.
FL 6046.11 Rousseau, J.J. Émile ou De l'éducation. Paris, 1874.
FL 383.50 Rutenberg, Adolf. Die dramatischen Schriftsteller Berlin, 1874.
40575.36.2 Sainte-Beuve, Charles A. Premiers lundis. Paris, 1874-75. 3v.
41557.8.58 Sand, George. Contes d'une grand'mere. 3e éd. Paris, 1874.
41557.8.107 Sand, George. Ma soeur Jeanne. Paris, 1874.
41557.9.100A Sand, George. My sister Jeannie. Boston, 1874.
41557.19.18 Sandeau, Jules. Mademoiselle de la Seiglière. Paris, 1874.
42546.26.5 Sardou, Victorien. La papillonne. Paris, 1874.
41587.91 Scribe, Eugène. Oeuvres complètes. Serie I. Paris, 1874. 9v.
41587.95 Scribe, Eugène. Oeuvres complètes. Serie V. Paris, 1874. 8v.
41588.14.3 Scribe, Eugène. Le verre d'eau. Bielefeld, 1874.
38546.42.15 Sévigné, Marie de R.C. Letters. Boston, 1874.
41558.66 Souvestre, Émile. Un philosophe sous les toits. London, 1874.
42587.59.18.2 Stapleaux, Leopold. Un dernier amour. 2. éd. Paris, 1874.
38521.13 Stoetzer, O.G. Étude sur Ronsard et son école. Buetzow, 1874.
41562.20 Sue, Eugène. Mémoires d'un mari. Paris, 1874. 2v.
41562.21 Sue, Eugène. Le morne-au-diable. Paris, 1874.
41562.32 Sue, Eugène. Thérèse Dunoyer. Paris, 1874.
42556.20.20 Sully-Prudhomme, R.F.A. La révolte des fleurs. Paris, 1874.
38525.3.3 Talbot, Eugène. Morceaux choisis...du XVIe siècle. Paris, 1874-75.
42583.22 Theuriet, André. Mademoiselle Guignon. Paris, 1874.
Mol 620.1F Thierry, Edouard. Le realisme sur le théâtre de Molière. Paris, 1874.
42584.47.20 Ulbach, Louis. Les parents coupables. Paris, 1874.
42584.47.15 Ulbach, Louis. Le roman de la bourgeoisie. Paris, 1874.
42584.47.10 Ulbach, Louis. La ronde de nuit. Paris, 1874.
42587.65.5 Vachette, Eugène. Defunt Brichet. 2. éd. Paris, 1874. 2v.
42587.65.15 Vachette, Eugène. Le rémouleur. Paris, 1874.
42582.19 Verne, Jules. Adventures in the land of Behemoth. Boston, 1874.
42582.12 Verne, Jules. Desert of ice, or Further adventures of Captain Hatteras. Philadelphia, 1874.
42582.11 Verne, Jules. Doctor Ox and other stories. Boston, 1874.
42582.12.50 Verne, Jules. The floating city. N.Y., 1874.
42582.9.2A Verne, Jules. From the clouds to the mountains. Boston, 1874.
42582.13 Verne, Jules. From the earth to the moon. N.Y., 1874.
42582.17A Verne, Jules. The fur country. Boston, 1874.
Htn 42581.9.7* Verne, Jules. L'île mystérieuse. v. 1,3. Paris, 1874. 2v.
42582.7.2 Verne, Jules. Journey to the centre of the earth. N.Y., 1874.
42582.24.2 Verne, Jules. The tour of the world in eighty days. Boston, 1874.
39545.44 Voltaire, François Marie Arouet de. La Henriade. Paris, 1874.
Mol 735.2.5 Wismes, Bon de. Un portrait de Molière en Bretagne. Nantes, 1874?
42584.7.9 Zola, Emile. La conquête de Plassans. 2. éd. Paris, 1874.

1875

37595.5.10 Abailard, Pierre. Lettres d'Abélard et Héloïse. 2. éd. Paris, 1875.
37543.10.1A Albert, Paul. Littérature française. 2. éd. Paris, 1875.
37564.44.27 Albert, Paul. La littérature française au dix-septième siècle. 2e éd. Paris, 1875.
42586.10.5 Assollant, A. The fantastic history of...Pierrot. London, 1875.
42553.17 Autran, J. La légende des Paladins. Paris, 1875.
42553.5 Autran, J. Oeuvres complètes. Paris, 1875-78. 7v.
39566.9 Avezac-Lavigne, C. Diderot et Baron d'Holbach. Paris, 1875.
37566.42 Babou, Hippolyte. Les sensations d'un juré. Paris, 1875.
40597.32 Balzac, Honoré de. Les parents. London, 1875.
40597.29.2 Balzac, Honoré de. La maison Nucingen. Paris, 1875.
38527.77 Le banquet du Boys. Paris, 1875.
42554.3.3.5 Banville, Théodore de. Gringoire; comédie en un acte. Paris, 1875.
41583.11.5 Basté, Eugène Pierre. Les domestiques. Paris, 1875.
41522.19.5 Beaumont-Vassy, E.F. Papiers curieux d'un homme de cour, 1770-1870. Paris, 1875.
41522.20.5 Beauvoir, E. Roger de. Le chevalier de Saint-Georges. Paris, 1875.
40527.8 Becq de Fouquières, L. Documents nouveaux sur André Chenier. Paris, 1875.
37561.35 Berblinger, W. Das hotel Rambouillet und seine culturgeschichtliche Bedentung. Berlin, 1875.
41522.33 Bernard, Charles de. Un beau-père. Bruxelles, 1875-85. 2v.
41522.48 Bernard, Charles de. Le paravent. Paris, 1875.
Mol 602.6 Bindel, Karl. Zur Geschichte der dramatischen Werke Molière. Hamm, 1875.
FL 378.20 Bonnassies, J. Les auteurs dramatiques et les théâtres de province aux XVIIe et XVIIIe siècles. Paris, 1875.
FL 395.42 Bonnassies, J. Comédie-française et les comédiens de province aux 17e et 18e siècles. Paris, 1875.
FL 394.77 Bonnassies, J. Les spectales forains et la comédie française. Paris, 1875.
42542.29.136.4 Bornier, Henri de. La fille de Roland. 25. éd. Paris, 1875.
42542.29.136.5 Bornier, Henri de. La fille de Roland. 28. éd. Paris, 1875.
38557.29 Bossuet, J.B. Oraisons funèbres. v.1-2. Paris, 1875.
38525.5 Brachet, Auguste. Morceaux choisis...du XVIe siècle. Paris, 1875.
42554.16.100 Breton, Jules. Les champs et la mer. Paris, 1875.
FL 396.32 Buguet, Henry. Foyers et coulisses. Gaîté. v.2. Paris, 1875.
38516.40 Cent quarante cinq rondeaux d'amour. Paris, 1875.
FL 377.16 Chappuzeau, S. Le théâtre français. Paris, 1875.
42565.21.3 Cherbuliez, Victor. Miss Rovel. Boston, 1875.
42565.55.80 Cladel, Léon. Celui de la croix-aux-boeufs. Paris, 1875.
38575.34.8.12 Corneille, Pierre. Polyeucte. Bielefeld, 1875.
39544.27 Courtat, Félix-Titus. Vraies lettres de Voltaire. Paris, 1875.
42561.13.17 Craven, Pauline. Jettatrice, or The veil withdrawn. Boston, 1875.
42567.21 Daudet, Ernest. Les aventures de Raymond Rocheray. Paris, 1875. 2v.
42567.24 Daudet, Ernest. Fleur de peéché. Paris, 1875.
38528.21 Defrémery, C. Examen de la nouvelle édition de Noël du Fail. Paris, 1875.
42545.69.16 Dennery, Adolphe Philippe. Les deux orphelines. Paris, 1875.
42546.31.18 Deraismes, M. Le théâtre de M. Sardou. Paris, 1875.
39544.21 Desnoiresterres, G. Voltaire et Genève. Paris, 1875.
39544.43 Desnoiresterres, G. Voltaire et J.J. Rousseau. Paris, 1875.
42568.2.30 Deulin, Charles. Histoires de petite ville. 2. éd. Paris, 1875.
39561.20A Diderot, Denis. Oeuvres complètes. Paris, 1875-77. 20v.
37567.141 Dondey, Théophile. Lettre inédite de Philothée O'Neddy. Paris, 1875.
38524.33 Dorat, Jean. Oeuvres poétiques. Paris, 1875.
38551.49.50 Douen, O. L'intolerance de Fénelon; étude historique. Paris, 1875.
42568.19.10 Du Boisgobey, Fortuné. L'as de coeur. Paris, 1875. 2v.
42568.19.14.10 Du Boisgobey, Fortuné. The chevalier casse-cou. N.Y., 1875.
38528.20.12 Du Fail, Noël. Contes et discours d'Eutrapel. Paris, 1875. 2v.
41523.11 Dumas, Alexandre. Black. Paris, 1875.
41524.7 Dumas, Alexandre. Confessions de la marquise. Paris, 1875.
41524.12 Dumas, Alexandre. Dame de Volupté. Paris, 1875.
42543.14.3 Dumas, Alexandre. Le demi-monde. Paris, 1875.
41524.14 Dumas, Alexandre. Deux reines. Paris, 1875.
41524.9 Dumas, Alexandre. Docteur mystérieux. v.1-2. Paris, 1875.
41524.16 Dumas, Alexandre. Drame de quatre-vingt-treize. Paris, 1875.
41524.10 Dumas, Alexandre. La fille du marquis. v.1-2. Paris, 1875.
41525.7 Dumas, Alexandre. Gaule et France. Paris, 1875.
41525.15 Dumas, Alexandre. Les hommes de Fer. Paris, 1875.
41525.16 Dumas, Alexandre. L'horoscope. Paris, 1875.
41526.15 Dumas, Alexandre. Louis XVI et la révolution. Paris, 1875.
41527.15 Dumas, Alexandre. Le Père la Ruine. Paris, 1875.
41593.32.5 Dupont, Pierre. Chants et poésies. Paris, 1875.
41593.32.5.5 Dupont, Pierre. Muse populaire. Chants et poésies. 9. éd. Paris, 1875.
42572.6.5 Erckmann, Emile. Stories of the Rhine. London, 1875.
FL 374.9 Fabre, A. Les clercs du palais. 2e ed. Lyon, 1875.
42574.14.50 Fabre, Ferdinand. L'abbé Tigrane. N.Y., 1875.
42574.15 Fabre, Ferdinand. Barnabé. Paris, 1875.
42574.16 Fabre, Ferdinand. Les Courbezon. Paris, 1875.
38554.2.7 Fénelon, F. de S. de la Mothe. Adventures of Telemachus. N.Y., 1875.
38554.378.10.2 Fénelon, F. de S. de la Mothe. Éxplication des principales vérités de la foi catholique. Tours, 1875.
42543.40.5 Ferrier, Paul. Fabarin. Paris, 1875. 6 pam.
42575.40.10 Feuillet, Octave. Led astray, or La petite comtesse. N.Y., 1875.
40597.4 Fleury, Jules. Documents pour servir à la biographie de Balzac. Paris, 1875-79. 3 pam.

Chronological Listing

1875 - cont.

	42564.50	Fleury, Jules. Le secret de M. Ladureau. Paris, 1875.
	37563.10	Froment, Théodore. L'éloquence et le barreau. Paris, 1875.
	38514.42	Gasté, Armand. Les Vaux-de-vire de Jean Le Houx. Paris, 1875.
	41542.13	Gautier, Theophile. Portraits et souvenirs. Paris, 1875.
	41542.19.5	Gautier, Théophile. Voyage en Russie. Paris, 1875.
	42576.36.23	Gay, Sophie. Souvenirs d'une vieille femme. Paris, 1875.
	37543.15	Gidel, Charles. Histoire de la littérature française. Paris, 1875.
	FL 6118.75	Girardin, S.M. Jean-Jacques Rousseau vie et ouvrages. Paris, 1875. 2v.
	37574.28	Godefroy, Frédéric. Morceaux choisis des poètes et prosateurs français du XVIe siècle. Paris, 1875.
	42543.54.12	Gondinet, Edmond. Gravaut Minard et cie; comédie. Paris, 1875.
	41542.53	Gozlan, Léon. La pluie et le beau temps. Paris, 1875.
	37538.29	Grangier, Louis. Histoire de la littérature française. Leipzig, 1875.
	39535.60	Grécourt, Jean B.J.W. de. Maranzakiniana. Paris, 1875.
	38512.36	La guerre de Metz en 1324. Paris, 1875.
	38512.115.10A	Guillaume de Machaut. Le livre du voir-dit. Paris, 1875.
	42543.61.150	Guillemot, Jules. Une heure en gare; comédie. Paris, 1875.
	39532.8	Hamilton, Anthony. Mémoires du Chevalier de Grammont. Paris, 1875.
	40575.3	Haussonville, Gabriel Paul Othenin de Cléron. E.A. Sainte-Beuve. Paris, 1875.
	42584.31.25	Hetzel, P.J. Voyage d'un étudiant et ses suites variées. 11. éd. Paris, 1875.
	37531.2.2	Histoire litteraire de la France. Table générale. Paris, 1875.
	42576.14.35	Houssaye, Arsène. Les mille et une nuits parisiennes. Paris, 1875. 4v.
	37596.31	Hucher, Eugène. Le Saint-Graal. Paris, 1875. 3v.
	41572.23.5	Hugo, Victor. Les châtiments. Paris, 1875.
	41573.32.50	Hugo, Victor. Lucretia Borgia. N.Y., 1875.
	41573.32.51A	Hugo, Victor. Lucretia Borgia. N.Y., 1875.
	41573.35	Hugo, Victor. Odes et ballades. Les orientales. Paris, 1875. 2v.
Htn	40524.27*	Jacob, P.L. Bibliographie et iconographie...de Restif de la Bretonne. Paris, 1875.
	FL 364.20	Jullien, Adolphe. La comédie à la cour de Louis XVI. Paris, 1875.
	FL 379.15	Jullien, Adolphe. Les spectateurs sur le théâtre. Paris, 1875.
	FL 364.52	Jullien, Adolphe. Le théâtre des Mlles. Verrières. Paris, 1875.
	38514.8	Koenig, Wilhelm. Étude sur...Clotilde de Surville. Halle, 1875.
	FL 6138.75	Koeune, F. Quelques pages sur Jean-Jacques Rousseau. Lausanne, 1875.
	38564.30.3	La Bruyère, J. de. Les caractères ou Les moeurs...Suivis des caractères de Théophraste. Paris, 1875.
	Mol 560.5.5	Lacroix, P. Bibliographie Molièresque. 2. éd. Paris, 1875.
Htn	Mol 560.5.4*	Lacroix, P. Bibliographie Molièresque. 2. éd. Paris, 1875.
	39525.16	La Fontaine, Jean de. Contes et nouvelles en vers. v.1-2. Paris, 1875?
	39527.23.5A	La Fontaine, Jean de. Fables. Paris, 1875.
	39525.13A	La Fontaine, Jean de. Oeuvres. Paris, 1875-79. 7v.
	40526.19	La Grange-Chancel, Joseph de. Les Philippiques Odes. Paris, 1875.
	41578.22	Lamartine, Alphonse de. Voyage en Orient. Paris, 1875. 2v.
	38543.30.42	La Mothe le Vayer, F. de. Hexaméron rustique. 2. éd. Paris, 1875.
	38543.28	La Mothe le Vayer, F. de. Soliloques sceptiques. Paris, 1875.
	37596.10.235	Le Coultre, Jules. De l'ordre des mots dansCrestien de Troyes. Diss. Dresde, 1875.
	38514.42.5	Le Houx, Jean. The Vaux-de vire. London, 1875.
	40512.9	LeSage, Alain René. Aventures de Gil Blas de Santillane. Paris, 1875.
	38525.34.15	Liotard, Charles. Étude sur les serées de Guillaume Bouchet. Nimes, 1875.
	42513.99	Littré, Émile. Littérature et histoire. Paris, 1875.
	38511.10	Le livre des Mestiers. Paris, 1875.
	FL 361.19	Loire, Louis. Anecdotes de théâtre; comédien-comédiennes. Paris, 1875.
	40588.43.5	Maistre, Xavier. Voyage autour de ma chambre. 1. édition américaine. N.Y., 1875?
NEDL	Mon 178.1.2	Malvezin, T. Michel de Montaigne, son origine, sa famille. Bordeaux, 1875.
	Mon 178.1	Malvezin, T. Michel de Montaigne, son origine, sa famille. Bordeaux, 1875.
	42555.49.7	Marc, G. Sonnets parisiens. Paris, 1875.
	42533.2	Mazade, C. de. Portraits d'histoire morale et politique. Paris, 1875.
	42545.10.16	Meilhac, Henri. Les brigands. Paris, 1875.
	41555.20	Mérimée, Prosper. Carmen. 9. éd. Paris, 1875.
	41555.4	Mérimée, Prosper. Lettres à une autre inconnue. Paris, 1875.
	41555.7.5	Mérimée, Prosper. Prosper Mérimée's letters to an incognita. N.Y., 1875.
	41595.23.9	Michaux, Clovis. Poésies posthumes. Paris, 1875.
	42587.29	Mie D'Aghonne, J. L'écluse des cadavres. Paris, 1875.
	38513.14A	Miracle de Nostre Dame. Stockholm, 1875.
	38544.29	Moisant de Brieux, J. Oeuvres choisies. Caen, 1875.
	Mol 166.1.9	Molière, Jean Baptiste Poquelin. L'avare...L.F.A. Paris, 1875.
	Mol 60.20	Molière, Jean Baptiste Poquelin. Dramatic works...van Laun. Edinburgh, 1875-76. 6v.
	Mol 60.20.2	Molière, Jean Baptiste Poquelin. Dramatic works...van Laun. Edinburgh, 1875-76. 6v.
	Mol 60.20.3A	Molière, Jean Baptiste Poquelin. The dramatic works of Molière. Edinburgh, 1875-76. 6v.
	Mol 228.25	Molière, Jean Baptiste Poquelin. Le malade imaginaire...Ragon. 3e éd. London, 1875.
	Mol 236.38.5	Molière, Jean Baptiste Poquelin. O pros bian iatpos. Parisiois, 1875.
	Mol 18.75	Molière, Jean Baptiste Poquelin. Oeuvres. v.1-8. Paris, 1875. 4v.
	Mol 265.15	Molière, Jean Baptiste Poquelin. Le sicilien. Lacour. Paris, 1875.

1875 - cont.

	Mol 262.43.5	Molière, Jean Baptiste Poquelin. Skoromĕl. Praha, 1875.
	Mol 269.30.5	Molière, Jean Baptiste Poquelin. Tartuffe. Zeggelen. Haarlem, 1875.
	39592.7	Montesquieu, C.L. de S. Oeuvres complètes. Paris, 1875-79. 7v.
	Mol 855.14	Montfleury, A.J. L'impromptu de l'Hostel de Condé. San Remo, 1875.
	Mol 810.2.2	Monval, G. Le théâtre français. Paris, 1875.
	41543.12	Nerval, Gerard de. Voyage en Orient. Paris, 1875. 2v.
	42578.17.208	Niboyet, Paulin. L'Américaine. Paris, 1875.
	40572.30	Nisard, Désiré. Portraits et études. Paris, 1875.
	37542.3	Noiré, Louis. Résumé de l'histoire de la littérature française. Mayence, 1875.
	38514.50A	Paris, Gaston. Chansons du XVe siècle. Paris, 1875.
	42585.41	Pauline, L. Livre d'une mère. Paris, 1875.
	42545.69.10	Petitdidier, L.E. Pour les inondés. Paris, 1875.
	41547.10	Pigault-Lebrun, C.A.G.R. de. Le mouchard. Paris, 1875.
	40536.20.5.8	Piron, Alexis. La métromanie. Cambridge, 1875.
	FL 398.20.10	Pougin, Arthur. Figures d'opéra-comique. Paris, 1875.
	42511.20	Poujoulat, M. Souvenirs d'histoire et de littérature. Lille, 1875.
Htn	40522.9.12*	Prévost, Antoine F. Histoire de Manon Lescaut et de chevalier des Grieux. Paris, 1875.
	41547.17	Privat d'Anglemont, A. Paris inconnu. Paris, 1875.
	38536.26.5	Rabelais, F. Le disciple de Pantagruel. Paris, 1875.
	38525.24	Régnier, Mathurin. Oeuvres complètes. Paris, 1875.
Htn	40524.28.3*	Restif de la Bretonne, Nicolas E. Les contemporaines. Paris, 1875? 2v.
	40524.28.6	Restif de la Bretonne, Nicolas E. Les contemporaines. Paris, 1875-76. 3v.
	37541.25	Robert, U. Documents inédits concernant l'histoire littéraire de la France. Paris, 1875.
	37538.3.12A	Roche, Antonin. Histoire des principaux écrivains français. 5. éd. Paris, 1875. 2v.
	38525.20	Ronsard, Pierre de. Poésies choisies. Paris, 1875.
	FL 6026.8	Rousseau, J.J. The confessions. London, 1875.
	40575.16A	Sainte-Beuve, Charles A. English portraits. N.Y., 1875.
	41568.11.15	Saintine, Joseph Xavier Boniface. Picciola. London, 1875.
	41557.8.53	Sand, George. Autour de al table. Paris, 1875.
	41557.8.71	Sand, George. Les deux frères. Paris, 1875.
	41557.8.76	Sand, George. Flamarande. 6e éd. Paris, 1875.
	FL 395.45	Sarcey, F. Comédien des comédiennes. ser. 1. Paris, 1875.
	FL 384.52	Sarcey, F. Comédiens et comédiennes. Paris, 1875-81.
	42546.26	Sardou, Victorien. La haine. Paris, 1875.
	42546.28.5	Sardou, Victorien. L'oncle Sam. Paris, 1875.
	42546.30.35	Sardou, Victorien. Les prés Saint Gervais; opéra bouffe en trois actes. Paris, 1875.
	41587.93	Scribe, Eugène. Oeuvres complètes. Serie III. Paris, 1875. 6v.
	42587.58.5	Ségur, Sophie. Les petites filles modèles. Paris, 1875.
	38511.11.2	Sorel, Alexandre. Notice sur Arnoul et Simon Greban. Compiègne, 1875.
	37573.8	Staaff, F.N. La littérature française. Paris, 1875-77. 3v.
	40592.25	Staël Holstein, Anne Louise. Corinne. Paris, 1875.
	39527.5.6	Taine, Hippolyte. La Fontaine et ses fables. Paris, 1875.
	39527.5.1	Taine, Hippolyte. La Fontaine et ses fables. 6e éd. Paris, 1875.
	42536.17A	Taine, Hippolyte. Notes on Paris. N.Y., 1875.
	38525.3	Talbot, Eugène. Morceaux choisis...du XVIe siècle. 2e éd. Paris, 1875.
	Mon 130.2	Thimme, Hermann. Der Skepticismus Montaigne's. Inaug. Diss. Gottingen, 1875.
	Mol 815.7	Tiburtius, G. Molière und das Precieusentum. Neumark, 1875.
	39534.7	Uzanne, Octave. Poésies de Benserade. Paris, 1875.
	41565.35	Vacquerie, Auguste. Aujourd'hui et demain. 2. éd. Paris, 1875.
	42582.11.2	Verne, Jules. Dr. Ox's experiment. Boston, 1875.
	42581.9.5	Verne, Jules. L'île mystérieuse. Paris, 1875.
Htn	42582.22.9*	Verne, Jules. The mysterious island abandoned. N.Y., 1875.
	42582.35.15	Verne, Jules. The wreck of the chancellor. Boston, 1875.
	37536.9.10	Villemain, A.F. Cours de littérature française. Paris, 1875. 2v.
	40584.30	Vitet, L. Études philosophiques et littéraires. Paris, 1875.
	39533.21	Vitu, Auguste. La mort d'Agrippine. Paris, 1875.

1876

	37596.11.5	Aiol et Mirable und Elie de Saint Gille. Heilbronn, 1876-82.
	42553.20	Amiel, Henri F. L'escalade de 1602. Genève, 1876.
	37578.46	Anthologie satyrique. v.1,8. Luxembourg, 1876-78. 2v.
	37591.32A	Atkinson, Robert. Vie de Seint Auban. London, 1876.
	37561.17	Aubertin, Charles. Histoire de la langue et de la littérature françaises au moyen âge. Paris, 1876-1878.
	42542.11	Augier, Émile. Madame Caverlet. Paris, 1876.
	42542.3A	Augier, Émile. Théâtre complet. Paris, 1876-78. 7v.
	40597.24	Balzac, Honoré de. Histoire des Treize. Paris, 1876.
	40594.23	Balzac, Honoré de. Oeuvres de jeunesse. Dom Gigadas. L'excommunié. Paris, 1876.
	40594.25	Balzac, Honoré de. Oeuvres de jeunesse. Jean Louis. L'Israëlite. Paris, 1876.
	40594.22	Balzac, Honoré de. Oeuvres de jeunesse. La dernière fée. Paris, 1876.
	40597.34A	Balzac, Honoré de. Les rivalités. Paris, 1876.
	42554.5	Banville, Théodore de. Enquisses parisiennes. Paris, 1876.
	Mol 860.47	Barbier, P. Le roi chez Molière. Paris, 1876.
	41591.4.5	Béranger, P.J. de. Oeuvres. Paris, 1876. 2v.
	41522.36.5	Bernard, Charles de. L'écueil. Paris, 1876.
	42556.11.4	Besson, M. Oraison funèbre de Jean Reboul. Nimes, 1876.
	40582.25	Beyle, Henri. Le rouge et le noir. v.1-2. Paris, 1876.
	42563.23.12	Blanquet, Albert. Le parc aux cerfs. Paris, 1876?
	Mol 870.24	Blémont, E. Molière à Auteuil. Paris, 1876.
	Mol 870.25	Blémont, E. Molière à Auteuil. Paris, 1876.
	38542.29	Blessebois, P.C. Alosie ou Les amours de Madame T.P. Paris, 1876.
	38566.21	Boileau Despréaux, Nicolas. Oeuvres poétiques. Paris, 1876-92. 2v.
	41592.5	Brivois, Jules. Bibliographie de l'oeuvre de P.J. de Béranger. Paris, 1876.

Chronological Listing

1876 - cont.

	Mol 703.2A	Campardon, E. Nouvelles pièces sur Molière. Paris, 1876.
	42563.67.50	Chablas, F. Deux nouvelles neuchâteloises. Le Locle, 1876.
	Mol 810.3	Chardon, H. La troupe du roman comique XVIIe siècle. Le Mans, 1876.
	FL 377.17	Chardon, Henri. La troupe du Roman comique Devoilée. Le Mans, 1876.
	38561.22	Chassong, A. Oeuvres complètes de J. de la Bruyère. Paris, 1876. 2v.
	42565.14	Cherbuliez, Victor. La fiancé de mademoiselle Saint-Maur. Paris, 1876.
	42565.14.3	Cherbuliez, Victor. Le fiancé de mademoiselle Saint-Maur. 3. éd. Paris, 1876.
	Mol 805.1	Collardeau, P. Le salle de théâtre de Molière au Port St. Paul. Paris, 1876.
	FL 366.25	Constant, Charles. Code des théâtres. Paris, 1876.
	42554.23.11	Coppée, François. Le Luthier. Paris, 1876.
	42554.22.7	Coppée, François. Oliver, poème. Paris, 1876.
	42554.22.25A	Coppée, François. Poésies. Paris, 1876. 2v.
	38571.10	Corneille, Pierre. Chefs-d'oeuvre. Paris, 1876.
	40597.6A	Correspondance de Honoré de Balzac. Paris, 1876. 2v.
	FL 1098.47.101	Crimon, Hector. Satires picarde. Péronne, 1876.
	37563.17.5	Darmesteter, Arsène. Morceaux choisis des...écrivains du XVIe siècle. Paris, 1876.
	42566.18	Daudet, Alphonse. Les amoureuses. Paris, 1876.
	42566.23	Daudet, Alphonse. Les femmes d'artistes. Paris, 1876.
	42567.31	Daudet, Ernest. Le roman d'une jeune fille. Paris, 1876.
	38514.65	Delaunay, D. Étude sur Alain Chartier. Rennes, 1876.
	39544.22	Desnoiresterres, G. Voltaire, son retour et sa mort. Paris, 1876.
	40566.4	Doudan, Ximénès. Mélanges et lettres. Paris, 1876-77. 4v.
	42568.8	Droz, Gustave. Les étangs. Paris, 1876.
	42568.19.11	Du Boisgobey, Fortuné. L'omnibus du diable. Paris, 1876.
	41523.19	Dumas, Alexandre. Capitaine Rhino. Paris, 1876.
	41523.31	Dumas, Alexandre. Compagnons de Jéhu. Paris, 1876.
	41524.18	Dumas, Alexandre. Drames galants. Paris, 1876.
	41524.19	Dumas, Alexandre. Emma Lyonna. v.1-2,3,4-5. Paris, 1876. 3v.
	41527.9	Dumas, Alexandre. Le page du Duc de Savoie. Paris, 1876.
	41528.1	Dumas, Alexandre. La San-Filia. v.1-4. Paris, 1876. 2v.
	FL 398.49.25	Duval, G.F. Lemaitre et son temps. Paris, 1876.
	FL 398.17.8	Duval, Georges. Virgin Déjazet. Paris, 1876.
	Mol 605.4	Espagne, A. Des influences provencales dans la langue de Molière. Paris, 1876.
	42575.30.3	Feuillet, Octave. Histoire de Sibylle. Paris, 1876.
	42575.32.5	Feuillet, Octave. Julia de Trécoeur. 11. éd. Paris, 1876.
	42575.35.8	Feuillet, Octave. A marriage in high life. Philadelphia, 1876.
	42575.43.3	Feuillet, Octave. Scènes et comédies. Paris, 1876.
	42576.36.10	Fleuriot, Zenaide Marie A. Nuestos enemigos intimos. Habana, 1876.
	37591.25.2	Foerster, Wendelin. Li dialoge Gregoire lo Pape. Halle, 1876.
Htn	42576.62.85*	France, Anatole. Les noces corinthiènnes. Paris, 1876.
	39586.21	Fréron, Elie Catharine. Les confessions de Fréron (1719-1776). Paris, 1876.
	42548.77	Géraldine. 3e ed. London, 1876.
	42586.68	Gobineau, Arthur de. Amadis. Paris, 1876.
	42586.66.9	Gobineau, Arthur de. Nouvelles asiatiques. Paris, 1876.
	38531.19	Gordon, R. F. Rabelais à la faculté de médecine de Montpellier. Montpellier, 1876.
	42576.38.25	Guéroult, Constant. Les exploits de Fifi Vollard. Paris, 1876.
	37595.18	Gullberg, Gotthard. Deux lais du XIIIe siècle. Kalmar, 1876.
	42543.69.14	Hervilly, Ernest. La belle saïnara. Paris, 1876.
	42584.30	Hetzel, P.J. Histoire d'un prince et d'une princesse. Paris, 1876.
	41571.3.85	Hugo, Victor. Oeuvres. Paris, 1876. 4v.
	Mol 750.8	Les intrigues de Molière et celles de sa femme, ou La fameuse comédienne, La Guèrin. Paris, 1876.
	Mon 150.1	Jarry, L. Pierre Daniel et les erudits de son temps. Orleans, 1876.
	38514.68.3	Joret-Desclosières, G. Un écrivain national au XVe siècle Alain Chartier. Thèse. Paris, 1876.
	FL 364.60	Jullien, Adolphe. Les grandes nuits de Sceaux. Paris, 1876.
	41544.35	Karr, Alphonse. Voyage autour de mon jardin. Paris, 1876.
	37551.37	Kerviler, René. Guillaume Bautru. Paris, 1876.
	37551.39	Kerviler, René. J. Ogier de Gombauld 1570-1666. Paris, 1876.
	37551.38	Kerviler, René. J.F.P. Lefebvre de Caumartin. Vannes, 1876.
	37551.41	Kerviler, René. Jean de Silhou. Paris, 1876.
	37551.42	Kerviler, René. Jean de Sirmond 1589-1649. Paris, 1876.
	37551.40	Kerviler, René. Marin le Roy sieur de Gomberville, 1600-1674. Paris, 1876.
	37596.62	Koschwitz, E. Chanson du voyage de Charlemagne à Jérusalem et à Constantinople. Heilbronn, 1876.
	Mol 735.4.2	Lacroix, Paul. Iconographie Moliéresque. Paris, 1876.
	Mol 735.4	Lacroix, Paul. Iconographie Moliéresque. Paris, 1876.
	FL 395.15F	La Grange, C.V. Registre (1658-1685). Paris, 1876.
	Mol 612.2	Laprade, V. de. La morale de Molière. n.p., 1876.
	41578.40	Legouvé, Ernest. Lamartine. Paris, 1876.
	42548.40	Legouvé, Ernest. Théâtre de campagne. ser. 1. Paris, 1876.
	41586.15.4.15	Lemercier, N.L. Frédégonde et Brunehaut. Cambridge, 1876.
Htn	37555.19*	Lemerre, Alphonse. Livre des ballades. Paris, 1876.
	40512.39	LeSage, Alain René. Avventure di Gil Blas di Santillana. Milano, 1876.
	40512.3.7	LeSage, Alain René. Le diable boiteux. Paris, 1876. 2v.
	40515.8.5	Lespinasse, J.J.E. de. Lettres. Paris, 1876.
	38575.12	Levallois, Jules. Corneille inconnu. Paris, 1876.
	37572.29.5	Louandre, Charles. Histoire de la litterature française. v.1-2. Paris, 1876.
	38527.61	Magny, Olivier de. Les odes d'Olivier de Magny. Paris, 1876. 2v.
	42577.5.7	Malot, Hector. La fille de la comédienne. Paris, 1876.
X Cg	38523.10	Marot, Clement. Oeuvres de Clément Marot. v.2. Paris, 1876.
	37543.19.5	Masson, Gustave. Introduction to the history of French literature. 3. ed. Edinburgh, 1876.

1876 - cont.

	37596.30.5	Mebes, A. Über Garnier von Pont Sainte-Maxence. Breslau, 1876.
	42545.10.12	Meilhac, Henri. Loulou. Paris, 1876.
	41555.6.2	Mérimée, Prosper. Lettres à une inconnue. 10. éd. Paris, 1876. 2v.
	37542.18	Merlet, Gustave. Études littéraires...des classiques français. XVII et XVIII siècles. Paris, 1876.
	37564.1	Merlet, Gustave. Études littéraires des classiques français XVII et XVIII siècles. Paris, 1876.
	38513.14.3A	Mielot, Jean. Miracles de Nostre Dame. Paris, 1876-93. 8v.
	Mol 155.25	Molière, Jean Baptiste Poquelin. L'amour médecin...Lacour. Paris, 1876.
	Mol 161.30	Molière, Jean Baptiste Poquelin. Amphitryon...Lacour. Paris, 1876.
	Mol 38.76	Molière, Jean Baptiste Poquelin. Ausgewählte Lustspiele...Brunnemann. v.1-6. Berlin, 1876-77.
	Mol 165.32	Molière, Jean Baptiste Poquelin. L'avare...Lacour. Paris, 1876.
	Mol 60.21	Molière, Jean Baptiste Poquelin. Dramatic works...C.H. Wall. London, 1876-77. 3v.
	Mol 60.21.2	Molière, Jean Baptiste Poquelin. Dramatic works..C.H. Wall. London, 1876-77. 2v.
	Mol 195.26	Molière, Jean Baptiste Poquelin. L'école des femmes...Gasc. London, 1876.
	Mol 201.27	Molière, Jean Baptiste Poquelin. L'escole des maris...Gasc. London, 1876.
	Mol 211.33	Molière, Jean Baptiste Poquelin. Les femmes savantes...Lacour. Paris, 1876.
	Mol 218.15	Molière, Jean Baptiste Poquelin. George Dandin...Lacour. Paris, 1876.
	Mol 248.30	Molière, Jean Baptiste Poquelin. M. de Pourceaugnac. Lacour. Paris, 1876.
	Mol 246.7.5	Molière, Jean Baptiste Poquelin. Il misantropo. Castelvecchio. Milano, 1876.
	Mol 18.76	Molière, Jean Baptiste Poquelin. Oeuvres...France. Paris, 1876-95. 6v.
	Mol 18.76.2	Molière, Jean Baptiste Poquelin. Oeuvres...France. Paris, 1876-95. 7v.
Htn	Mol 18.72.3*	Molière, Jean Baptiste Poquelin. Oeuvres...Pauly. Paris, 1876.
	Mol 251.32	Molière, Jean Baptiste Poquelin. Les précieuses ridicules. Dupuis. London, 1876.
	Mol 196.7.5	Molière, Jean Baptiste Poquelin. La scuola delle mogli...Castelvecchio. Milano, 1876.
	Mol 268.58	Molière, Jean Baptiste Poquelin. Le Tartuffe. Lacour. Paris, 1876.
Htn	Mol 18.76.3*	Molière, Jean Baptiste Poquelin. Théâtre complet...Jouast. Paris, 1876-83. 8v.
	Mon 18.76	Montaigne, Michel de. Essais de Montaigne. Paris, 1876. 4v.
	42577.13.25	Montépin, X. de. Le secret de la comtesse. Paris, 1876. 2v.
	42577.16	Murger, Henry. Dona Sirène. Paris, 1876.
	42577.27	Murger, Henry. Les roueries. Paris, 1876.
	41596.7	Musset, Alfred de. Oeuvres complètes. Paris, 1876. 10v.
	41596.6.9	Musset, Alfred de. Oeuvres complètes de Alfred de Musset. Paris, 1876. 10v.
	38528.35	Ouville, Antoine. L'élite des contes. Paris, 1876.
	42545.69.4.75	Parodi, A. Rome vaincue. 6. éd. Paris, 1876.
	42545.69.4.80	Parodi, A. Rome vaincue. 10. éd. Paris, 1876.
	Mol 875.6	Paté, Lucien. A Molière. Paris, 1876.
	38575.22.3	Picot, Émile. Bibliographie Cornélienne. Paris, 1876.
Htn	38575.22*	Picot, Émile. Bibliographie Cornélienne. Paris, 1876.
	Mol 270.9	Pignot, J.H. Un évêque...G. de Roquette...le Tartuffe. Paris, 1876. 2v.
Htn	38531.18*	Plan, P.P. Les éditions de Rabelais à la faculté de Médecine de Montpellier. Montpellier, 1876.
	FL 398.4.20	Poinsot, Edmond A. Madame Arnould-Plessy. Paris, 1876.
	42555.70.100	Pollet, Augustin. Brises basséenes. La Bassée, 1876.
	Mol 860.45	Ponsard, F. Molière a Vienne. n.p., 1876.
Htn	FL 6128.76*	Poulet, Malassis. La querelle des Bouffons. Paris, 1876.
	42545.101	Prével, Jules. Un mari qui pleure. Paris, 1876.
	Mol 698.5F	Registre de la Grange (1658-1685). Paris, 1876.
	38587.9.6	Regnard, Jean François. Théâtre de Jean François Regnard. Paris, 1876. 2v.
	38525.25.5	Régnier, Mathurin. Oeuvres complètes. Paris, 1876.
	38525.25	Régnier, Mathurin. Oeuvres complètes. Paris, 1876.
	Mol 193.10	Reissig, A. J.B. Molière's Leben...sein Dom Juan. Leipzig, 1876.
	42515.30.190	Renan, Ernest. Dialogues et fragments philosophiques. Paris, 1876.
	42578.18.56	Richebourg, Emile. La fille maudite. Paris, 1876-77. 2v.
	42556.31	Roussel, August. Les gauloises; chants patriotiques et populaires. Paris, 1876.
	37563.23.10	Sainte-Beuve, C.A. Tableau de la poésie française au XVIe siècle. Paris, 1876. 2v.
	40575.11	Sainte-Beuve, Charles A. Les cahiers. Paris, 1876.
	40575.13	Sainte-Beuve, Charles A. Chroniques parisiennes. Paris, 1876.
	40575.19	Sainte-Beuve, Charles A. Portraits de femmes. Paris, 1876.
	40575.33	Sainte-Beuve, Charles A. Portraits littéraires. Paris, 1876-78. 3v.
	42578.31.230	Salières, A. Les soirées fantastiques de l'artilleur Baruch. Paris, 1876.
	41557.8.60	Sand, George. Le Chêne parlant. Paris, 1876.
	41557.8.66	Sand, George. La coupe; Lupo Liverani; Le toast. 2e éd. Paris, 1876.
	41557.19.2	Sandeau, Jules. Mademoiselle de la Seiglière. Paris, 1876.
	42578.33	Sarcey, Francisque. Etienne Moret. Paris, 1876.
X Cg	37595.29	Scheler, M. Auguste. Trouvères belges du XII au XIV siècle. 1st et 2nd séries. Bruxelles, 1876-79.
	42535.22.55	Scherer, Edmond. Études critiques de littérature. Paris, 1876.
	42556.30	Schuré, Edouard. Les chants de la Montagne. Paris, 1876.
	41587.92	Scribe, Eugène. Oeuvres complètes. Serie II. Paris, 1876. 33v.
	38546.47	Sévigné, Marie de R.C. Lettres inédites à Mme. de Grignan. Paris, 1876. 2v.
	38528.38.25	Sonnet, Thomas . Oeuvres poétiques. Paris, 1876.
	42557.4.35	Soulary, Joséphin. La chasse aux mouches d'or. Lyon, 1876.

1876 - cont.

40592.30 Staël Holstein, Anne Louise. Corinne. N.Y., 1876.
40592.26.5 Staël Holstein, Anne Louise. Corinne. Paris, 1876.
39544.13 Strauss, D.F. Voltaire. Six Conférences. Paris, 1876.
37591.32.2A Suchier, Hermann. Über die M. Paris. Vie de Seïnt Auban. Halle, 1876.
41588.39 Théaulon de Lambert, Marie Emmanuel G.M. Un mari dans du Coton. Paris, 1876.
42583.33.3 Theuriet, André. Chemin des bois. Paris, 1876.
Mol 800.4 Thierry, Édouard. Charles Varlet de La Grange. Paris, 1876.
37556.24.10 Topin, Marius. Romanciers contemporains. Paris, 1876.
37542.11.2A Van Laun, Henri. History of French literature. London, 1876-77. 3v.
37542.11 Van Laun, Henri. History of French literature. N.Y., 1876-77. 3v.
37546.34 Vaschalde, Henry. Histoire des poètes du Vivarais. Paris, 1876.
42582.22.14 Verne, Jules. The mysterious island. N.Y., 1876.
37596.40 Vietor, W. Die Handschriften der Geste des Loherains. Halle, 1876.
38514.21.2 Villon, François. Oeuvres complètes. N.Y., 1876.

1877

41555.55.30 Allart de Méritens, Hortense. Les enchantements de Prudence. Paris, 1877.
37597.17 Andersen, Hugo. Maistre Wace's Roman de rou. Heilbronn, 1877-79. 3v.
40515.9.10 Asse, E. Mlle. de L'Espinasse et la marquise du Deffand. Paris, 1877.
FL 360.21 Avril, A. Le théâtre en France depuis le moyen âge jusqu'à nos jours. Paris, 1877.
40596.5 Balzac, Honoré de. Oeuvres complètes. Paris, 1877. 20v.
41542.4.3.9 Bergerat, Émile. Théophile Gautier, peintre. Paris, 1877.
37555.22.5 Besant, Walter. Studies in early French poetry. Boston, 1877.
38576.32 Bizos, G. Étude sur la vie et les oeuvres de Jean de Mairet. Paris, 1877.
42563.30.31 Blandy, Stella. Le petit roi. Paris, 1877.
Mol 870.27 Blémont, E. Le barbier de Pézenas. Paris, 1877.
42563.26.75 Boisonnas, B. (Mme.). Une famille pendant la guerre. Paris, 1877.
Htn FL 397.77.5* Bouteiller, Jules E. Les théâtres de société de Rouen. Rouen, 1877.
FL 393.10 Campardon, E. Les spectacles de la foire. Paris, 1877. 2v.
Mol 825.16 Carcassonne, L. Molière et la médecine. Nimes, 1877.
42561.26 Chandeneux, Claire de. Une faiblesse de Minerve. Paris, 1877.
42561.29 Chandeneux, Claire de. Le lieutenant de Rancy. Paris, 1877.
42561.33 Chandeneux, Claire de. Vaisseaux brulés. Paris, 1877.
40586.18.12.7 Chateaubriand, F.A.R. Le génie du Christianisme. Tours, 1877.
Mol 880.6 Chatelain, de. Madame de Tartuffe. London, 1877.
42565.19.3 Cherbuliez, Victor. Meta Holdenis. N.Y., 1877.
42565.21A Cherbuliez, Victor. Miss Rovel. Paris, 1877.
42565.31.5 Cherbuliez, Victor. Samuel Brohl and company. N.Y., 1877.
42565.31.2 Cherbuliez, Victor. Samuel Brohl et Cie. Paris, 1877.
42542.52.5 Clairville, Louis François Nicolaïe. Les cloches de Corneville. 7. éd. Paris, 1877.
38511.12 Coke, John. Le débat des hérauts d'armes. Paris, 1877.
40534.21 Collin d'Harleville, J.F. Théâtre. Paris, 1877.
Mol 853.1 Un compte-rendu de la comédie des "Précieuses Ridicules" de Molière. Paris, 1877.
40556.18.80 Condamin, J. Essai sur les pensées de J. Joubert. Thèse. Paris, 1877.
38574.6 Corneille, Pierre. Théâtre. Paris, 1877-79. 5v.
41574.78 Courtat, Félix-Titus. Discours de successeur de Victor Hugo. Paris, 1877.
37548.39 Courvoisier, A. Les lettres françaises en Alsace depuis la restauration. Strasbourg, 1877.
Mol 882.3 Coveliers, F. George Dandin, opéra-comique. Bruxelles, 1877.
FL 6118.77 Craddock, T. Rousseau as described by himself and others. London, 1877.
42566.21 Daudet, Alphonse. Contes du lundi. Paris, 1877.
42566.26.4 Daudet, Alphonse. Jack; costumi contemporanei. 2. ed. Milano, 1877. 2v.
42566.26.2A Daudet, Alphonse. Jack. Boston, 1877.
42566.26 Daudet, Alphonse. Jack. v.2, photoreproduction. Paris, 1877. 2v.
42566.29 Daudet, Alphonse. Le Nabab. Paris, 1877.
42566.35A Daudet, Alphonse. Sidonie. Boston, 1877.
42567.23 Daudet, Ernest. Le crime de Jean Malory. Paris, 1877.
42567.35 Daudet, Ernest. Une femme du monde. Paris, 1877.
42567.26 Daudet, Ernest. Henriette. Paris, 1877.
Mol 745.2 Davin, V. La mort de Molière. Paris, 1877.
42542.64.3 Déroulède, Paul. L'hetman. 15. éd. Paris, 1877.
39527.27 Desandré, J. Fables de Jean de La Fontaine. Paris, 1877.
39586.22 Desnoiresterres, G. Grimod de la Reynière et son groupe. Paris, 1877.
Mol 870.26 d'Hervilly, E. Le magister. Paris, 1877.
FL 398.9.19 D'Heylli, Georges. Bressant, 1833-1877. Paris, 1877.
39564.7.15 Diderot, Denis. Oeuvres choisies. Paris, 1877-79. 6v.
41522.100.25 Dondey, T. Poésies posthumes de Philothée O'Neddy. Paris, 1877.
41523.9 Dumas, Alexandre. Les baleiniers. Paris, 1877.
41523.10 Dumas, Alexandre. Le bâtard de Mauléon. Paris, 1877.
41538.16.3.20 Dumas, Alexandre. Le comte de Monte-Cristo. Paris, 1877. 5v.
42543.18.5 Dumas, Alexandre. L'étrangère. Paris, 1877.
41525.11 Dumas, Alexandre. Les grands hommes en robe de Chambre. Henri IV. Paris, 1877.
41526.16 Dumas, Alexandre. Les louves de Machecoul. Paris, 1877. 3v.
41526.20 Dumas, Alexandre. Les mariages du Père Olifus. Paris, 1877.
41527.7 Dumas, Alexandre. Une nuit à Florence. Paris, 1877.
41527.17 Dumas, Alexandre. La princesse Flora. Paris, 1877.
41527.19 Dumas, Alexandre. Propos d'art et de cuisine. Paris, 1877.
41527.25 Dumas, Alexandre. Le salteador. Paris, 1877.
41528.1.2 Dumas, Alexandre. Souvenirs d'Antony. Paris, 1877.

1877 - cont.

41528.2 Dumas, Alexandre. Souvenirs d'une favorite. v.1-4. Paris, 1877. 2v.
41584.30 Duvert, F.A. Théâtre choisi. Paris, 1877-1879. 6v.
42574.21 Fabre, Ferdinand. La petite mère. Paris, 1877. 4v.
38554.526 Fénelon, F. de S. de la Mothe. Spiritual letters: letters to men. London, 1877.
42575.25.8 Feuillet, Octave. Les amours de Philippe. 4. éd. Paris, 1877.
42575.26.2 Feuillet, Octave. The amours of Philippe. Philadelphia, 1877.
42575.35 Feuillet, Octave. Un mariage dans le monde. Paris, 1877.
42575.38 Feuillet, Octave. Monsieur de Camors. 21. éd. Paris, 1877.
42575.45.15 Feuillet, Octave. Scènes et proverbes. Paris, 1877.
42586.48 Feval, Paul H. Le fils du diable. Paris, 1877. 4v.
42575.21 Feydeau, Ernest. Fanny. Paris, 1877.
42576.33 Flaubert, Gustave. Trois contes. Paris, 1877.
38537.5 Fleury, Jean. Rebelais et ses oeuvres. Paris, 1877. 2v.
42564.40 Fleury, Jules. La petite rose. Paris, 1877.
42575.53.55 Fould, W. de (Mme.). Vertu. 7. éd. Paris, 1877.
42571.22.11 Gaboriau, Emile. L'affaire Lerouge. 18. éd. Paris, 1877.
41542.21.5 Gautier, Théophile. Spirite. N.Y., 1877.
41542.21 Gautier, Théophile. Spirite. Paris, 1877.
38537.22.3A Gebhart, Émile. Rabelais. Paris, 1877.
37543.16 Gidel, Charles. Histoire de la littérature française. Paris, 1877.
41541.13.10 Girardin, Delphine Gay. Le chapeau d'un horloger. Paris, 1877.
41541.8.12 Girardin, Delphine Gay. La joie fait peur. Paris, 1877.
42586.65 Gobineau, Arthur de. La renaisssance. Paris, 1877.
42586.70 Gobineau, Arthur de. Une vie d'Enfer. Paris, 1877.
42575.75A Goncourt, Edmond de. La fille Elisa. 4. éd. Paris, 1877.
42575.78.5 Goncourt, Edmond de. Manette Salomon. Paris, 1877.
42575.62.10 Goncourt, Edmond de. Soeur Philomène. Paris, 1877.
FL 398.4.30 Goucourt, E. Sophie Arnould. Paris, 1877.
40526.13.2 Gresset, Jean B. Oeuvres choisies. Paris, 1877.
Mol 707.4 Grimarest, J.L. La vie de Monsieur de Molière. Paris, 1877.
39567.5 Grimm, F.M. von. Correspondance littéraire. Paris, 1877-79. 16v.
38526.18.3 Gringore, Pierre. La vie Monseigneur Saint Louis. Paris, 1877.
40522.10 Harrisse, Henry. Bibliographie de Manon Lescaut. Paris, 1877.
37574.22 Haupt, Moriz. Französische Volkslieder. Leipzig, 1877.
41522.100.81 Havet, Ernest. Notice sur Philothée O'Neddy. Paris, 1877.
41572.8 Hugo, Victor. Histoire d'un crime. Paris, 1877-78. 2v.
41572.7.25 Hugo, Victor. Histoire d'un crime. Paris, 1877-78. 2v.
41572.8.2 Hugo, Victor. Histoire d'un crime. Première journée et deuxième journée. 2e éd. Paris, 1877.
41572.8.3 Hugo, Victor. Histoire d'un crime. v.1. 4e éd. Paris, 1877-78. 2v.
Htn 41573.18.11* Hugo, Victor. La légende des siècles. Paris, 1877. 2v.
41572.29.5 Hugo, Victor. Le roi s'amuse. London, 1877.
Mol 750.9 Les intrigues de Molière et celles de sa femme, ou La fameuse comédienne, La Guérin. Paris, 1877.
42525.22 Jal, A. Souvenirs d'un homme de lettres (1795-1873). Paris, 1877.
39526.10 Joly, Aristide. Histoire de deux fables de La Fontaine. Paris, 1877.
40556.20.15 Joubert, Joseph. Pensées of Joubert. London, 1877.
41544.14 Karr, Alphonse. Notes de voyage d'un casanier. Paris, 1877.
37551.35 Kerviler, René. Abel Servien. Le Mans, 1877. 4 pam.
37558.33 Kerviler, René. Essai d'une bibliographie raisonnée (de l'Académie française). Paris, 1877.
37551.43 Kerviler, René. Marin et Pierre Cureau de la chambre. Le Mans, 1877.
Mol 167.12 Klapp, A. L'avare ancien et moderne. Parchim, 1877.
Mol 611.2 Klug, Gustav. Molière in seinen Farcen. Strausberg, 1877.
41552.28 Kock, Charles Paul de. L'homme aux trois culottes. Paris, 1877.
37596.59 Kölbing, Eugen. La chanson de Roland. Heilbronn, 1877.
Mol 711.2 Kühns, C. Molière. Lüneberg, 1877.
Mol 270.11.2 Lacour, L. Études sur Molière...le Tartuffe. Paris, 1877.
38544.27.32 La Fayette, Marie M. La Princesse de Clèves. Paris, 1877.
39527.27.10 La Fontaine, Jean de. Fables. Tours, 1877.
39525.19.5 La Fontaine, Jean de. Oeuvres: théâtre, fables, poésies. Paris, 1877.
42555.11.10 La Landelle, G. de. Pauvres et mendiants. 2e éd. Paris, 1877.
42545.84.5 Landström, A.R. Om François Ponsard som dramatisk skald. Stockholm, 1877.
38557.14 Lapommeraye, H. de. Molière et Bossuet. Paris, 1877.
Mol 612.1 Lapommeraye, H. de. Molière et Bossuet. Paris, 1877.
Mol 247.10 Lavoix, H. La première représentation du Molière. Paris, 1877.
42548.41A Legouvé, Ernest. Théâtre de campagne. ser. 2. 3. ed. Paris, 1877.
37563.33.5 Lenient, Charles. La satire en France au moyen âge. Paris, 1877.
40511.21 LeSage, Alain René. Théâtre. Paris, 1877.
41596.1 Lindan, Paul. Alfred de Musset. Berlin, 1877.
Mol 712.5A Loiseleur, J. Les points obscurs de la vie de Molière. Paris, 1877.
42544.34.9 Lomon, Charles. Jean Dacier. 2e éd. Paris, 1877.
42544.34.10 Lomon, Charles. Jean Dacier. 3e éd. Paris, 1877.
38514.22.5 Longnon, Auguste. Étude biographique sur François Villon. Paris, 1877.
37564.34 Lotherssen, F. Geschichte der französischen Literatur in XVII Jahrhundert. Vienna, 1877. 2v.
42587.15.5 Lubomirski, Jozef. Tatiana, or The conspiracy. London, 1877. 3v.
37595.31.2 Luchier, H. Mariengebete. Halle, 1877.
37595.31 Luchier, Herman. Mariengebete. Halle, 1877.
Mol 728.8 Magen, A. La troupe de Molière à Agen. Paris, 1877.
Mol 713.3 Malassis, A.P. Molière jugé par ses contemporains. Paris, 1877.
Mol 713.3.2 Malassis, A.P. Molière jugé par ses contemporains. Paris, 1877.

1877 - cont.

	38523.31	Malherbe, François de. Oeuvres poétiques. Paris, 1877.
	38523.31.5A	Malherbe, François de. Oeuvres poétiques de Malherbe réimprimées sur l'édition de 1630. Paris, 1877.
	38516.6	Malmberg, T. Le passe-temps Michault. Upsala, 1877.
	42577.11.16	Malot, Hector. Ida et Carmelita. 6. éd. Paris, 1877.
	42577.9	Malot, Hector. Marié par les prêtres. Paris, 1877.
	FL 395.55	Manne, E.D. Galerie historique des comédiens françois de la troupe de Voltaire. Lyon, 1877.
	FL 384.53	Manne, Edmond D. Galerie historique des acteurs français. Lyon, 1877.
	37543.19	Masson, Gustave. Outlines of French literature. London, 1877.
	Mol 755.2	Mathon, M. La famille de Molière était originaire de Beauvais. Paris, 1877.
	42545.10.14	Meilhac, Henri. Le fandango. Paris, 1877.
	42587.24.5	Méry, Joseph. Les noches españolas. Valencia, 1877.
	FL 6128.77	Metzger, A. Jean-Jacques Rousseau à l'ile Saint-Pierre. Lyon, 1877. 3 pam.
	37595.28.5A	Meyer, Paul. Recueil d'anciens textes bas-latins, provencaux et français. Paris, 1877.
	38537.7	Michel, Louis. Essai sur Rabelais. Paris, 1877.
	42514.33	Mignet, F.A.M. Études historiques. Paris, 1877.
	42514.30	Mignet, F.A.M. Nouveaux éloges historiques. Paris, 1877.
	42514.34	Mignet, F.A.M. Portraits et notices. Paris, 1877. 2v.
	Mol 162.38.5	Molière, Jean Baptiste Poquelin. Amphitryon...Phragia. Ermoupolis, 1877.
	Mol 38.77	Molière, Jean Baptiste Poquelin. Ausgewählte Lustspiele...H. Fritsche. v.1-7. Berlin, 1877-86.
	Mol 182.7.5	Molière, Jean Baptiste Poquelin. I dispetti amorosi...Castelvecchio. Milano, 1877.
	Mol 228.26	Molière, Jean Baptiste Poquelin. Le malade imaginaire...Lacour. Paris, 1877.
	Mol 245.50	Molière, Jean Baptiste Poquelin. Le misanthrope. Fiebig et Leportier. 2. éd. Dresde, 1877.
	Mol 245.51	Molière, Jean Baptiste Poquelin. Le misanthrope. Lion. Leipzig, 1877.
	Mol 258.15	Molière, Jean Baptiste Poquelin. Psyché. Lacour. Paris, 1877.
	42545.42.5	Monselet, Charles. Le revue sans titre...1876. Paris, 1877.
	Mon 31.40.2	Montaigne, Michel de. Essays. Cotton (Hazlitt). London, 1877. 3v.
	Mon 31.40A	Montaigne, Michel de. Essays. Cotton (Hazlitt). London, 1877. 3v.
	38523.2	Morley, Henry. Clément Marot, and other studies. London, 1877. 2v.
	37597.30	Der münchener Brutus. Halle, 1877.
	41596.8	Musset, Alfred de. Oeuvres complètes. Paris, 1877. 10v.
	41596.4.161A	Musset, Paul. The biography of Alfred de Musset. Boston, 1877.
	41596.6	Musset, Paul de. Biographie de Alfred de Musset. Paris, 1877.
	41596.5	Musset, Paul de. Biographie de Alfred de Musset. Paris, 1877.
	42587.37.09	Musset, Paul de. Lui et elle. 10. éd. Paris, 1877.
	38514.22	Nagel, G. François Villon. Berlin, 1877.
	Mol 247.11	Neuss. Sur le misanthrope de Molière. Montabaur, 1877.
	40517.1.7	Nisard, C. Le comte de Caylus. Paris, 1877.
	37596.25	Palustre, Léon. Adam mystère du 12e siècle. Paris, 1877.
	Mon 105.8	Payen, J.F. Inventaire de la collection sur M. de Montaigne. Bordeaux, 1877.
	42587.42	Pelletan, Eugène. Jarousseau. Le Pasteur du Désart. Paris, 1877.
	41587.16	Picard, Louis Benoît. Théâtre. Paris, 1877.
	FL 394.79	Poinsot, E.A. Comédie-française. Paris, 1877. 2v.
	42545.88.52	Porto-Riche, G. Tout n'est pas rose. Paris, 1877.
	38536.16	Rabelais, F. Oeuvres. Paris, 1877.
	40573.26.7	Rémusat, Charles de. Abélard; drame inédit. 2. éd. Paris, 1877.
	40573.26.8	Rémusat, Charles de. Abélard; drame inédit. 3. éd. Paris, 1877.
	42515.29.501A	Renan, Ernest. Les évangiles et la seconde génération. Paris, 1877.
	42515.29.503	Renan, Ernest. Les évangiles et la seconde génération chrétienne. 3. éd. Paris, 1877.
	FL 6051.77	Rousseau, J.J. La nouvelle Héloise. Paris, 1877.
	40575.6A	Sainte-Beuve, Charles A. Correspondance. Paris, 1877. 2v.
	40575.6.5	Sainte-Beuve, Charles A. Correspondance. Paris, 1877-99. 2v.
	40575.29	Sainte-Beuve, Charles A. Monday-chats. Chicago, 1877.
	41557.9.38	Sand, George. Impressions and reminiscences. Boston, 1877.
	41557.8.126	Sand, George. La tour de Percemont. 5e éd. Paris, 1877.
	41557.9.125	Sand, George. The tower of Percemont. N.Y., 1877.
	42546.26.6	Sardou, Victorien. Les pattes de mouche. Paris, 1877.
	38528.12	Satyre Ménippée. Paris, 1877. 2v.
	39527.25	Sauveur, L. Fables de La Fontaine. N.Y., 1877.
	39534.28	Scarron, Paul. Oeuvres. Paris, 1877. 2v.
	37555.300.2	Schnatter, J. Cours de versification française. 2. éd. Berlin, 1877.
	41587.94	Scribe, Eugène. Oeuvres complètes. Serie IV. Paris, 1877. 20v.
	38546.36.7	Sévigné, Marie de R.C. Choix de lettres. v.1-3. Paris, 1877-80.
	37576.5	Société des bibliophiles français. Mélanges de littérature et d'histoire. Paris, 1877.
	41558.70	Souvestre, Emile. Scènes et récits des Alpes. Paris, 1877.
	42556.19	Sully-Prudhomme, R.F.A. Poésies. Paris, 1877. 4v.
	37576.515	Théatre de la révolution, ou Choix de pièces de théâtre qui ont fair sensation pendant la periode révolutionnaire. Paris, 1877.
	37581.50	Le théâtre inédit du XIXe siècle. Paris, 1877.
	42583.25.1	Theuriet, André. Gerard's marriage. N.Y., 1877.
	42583.27	Theuriet, André. Raymonde. Paris, 1877.
Htn	39532.25*	Travers, Emile. Une promenade dans Paris en 1650 avec un poëte burlesque. Caen, 1877.
	37566.176	Vallery-Radot, Vincent Félix. Souvenirs littéraires. Paris, 1877.
	40526.61.175	Vallier, Gustave. Notes sur l'Abbé Guilloud. Vienne, 1877.
	42548.54	Verconsin, Eugène. En wagon. Paris, 1877.
	42582.13.5	Verne, Jules. From the earth to the moon. N.Y., 1877.
	42582.22	Verne, Jules. Michael Strogoff. N.Y., 1877.
	Mol 622.3	Veuillot, L. Molière et Bourdaloue. Paris, 1877.
	41564.3.66	Vigny, Alfred de. Cinq-Mars. Boston, 1877.
	38514.19	Villon, François. Oeuvres. Paris, 1877.
	39551.30A	Voltaire, François Marie Arouet de. Oeuvres complètes. n.p., 1877-85. 52v.
	42584.3	Zola, Emile. L'assommoir. Paris, 1877.

1878

	42562.35.5	About, Edmond. Le capitaine Bitterlin. Paris, 1878.
	42562.6.10	About, Edmond. Germaine. 12e éd. Paris, 1878.
	38583.6	Albert, Paul. Théâtre de J. Racine. Paris, 1878. 2v.
	42553.21	Amiel, Henri F. Les étrangères poésies. Paris, 1878.
	41592.2.31	Arvers, Félix. Mes heures perdues. Paris, 1878.
	39578.6	Asse, Eugène. Lettres de le Marquise de Châtelet. Paris, 1878.
Htn	42541.4.9*	Augier, Émile. Les Fourchambault. N.Y., 1878.
	42542.16.5	Augier, Émile. Les Fourchambault. 8. éd. Paris, 1878.
	42542.16	Augier, Émile. Les Fourchambault. 11. éd. Paris, 1878.
	42542.17	Augier, Émile. Les Fourchambault. 15. éd. Paris, 1878.
	37583.12	Auriac, Eugène d'. Théâtre de la foire. Paris, 1878.
	FL 6113.3	Bachelin, A. Iconographie de J.J. Rousseau. Paris, 1878.
	40597.28.2	Balzac, Honoré de. Le lys dans la vallée. Paris, 1878.
	37561.21	Bancel, François Désiré. Histoire des révolutions de l'esprit français. Paris, 1878.
	38524.32	Belleau, Renny. Oeuvres poétiques. Paris, 1878. 2v.
	37596.8.5	Bida, A. Aucassin et Nicolette. Paris, 1878.
	37543.20	Blaze de Bury, H. Tableaux romantiques de littérature et d'art. Paris, 1878.
	38566.17.10	Boileau Despréaux, Nicolas. Oeuvres poétiques. Paris, 1878.
	42554.15.150	Boulmier, Joseph. Villanelles suivies de poésies en langage. Paris, 1878.
	42563.38.11	Bouvier, Alexis. La grande Iza. Paris, 1878.
	42542.47.50	Burani, P. Le droit du seigneur. Paris, 1878.
	FL 6135.8	Centenaire de J.J. Rousseau. Honneurs publics rendus de Jean-Jacques Rousseau. Genève, 1878.
	42561.27	Chandeneux, Claire de. Une fille Liade. Paris, 1878.
	42561.28	Chandeneux, Claire de. Les Giboulées de la vie. Paris, 1878.
	40586.11.25	Chateaubriand, F.A.R. Atala. Porto, 1878.
	42565.17.1	Cherbuliez, Victor. L'idée de Jean Têterol. 3. éd. Paris, 1878.
	42565.47.35	Cherbuliez, Victor. The wish of his life; a novel. London, 1878. 2v.
	42565.53	Chevalet, E. Mil huit cent quarante-huit. Paris, 1878.
	42542.52.9	Clairville, Louis François Nicolaïe. La fille de madame Angot. Paris, 1878.
	37556.14	Colletet, F. Le journal de Colletet. Paris, 1878.
	FL 6002.878	Comité du Centenaire. Jean Jacques Rousseau et ses oeuvres. Genève, 1878.
	FL 6002.878.3	Comité du Centenaire. Sagesse de Jean-Jacques: fragments écrits de Rousseau. Genève, 1878.
	42554.23.13	Coppée, François. Les récits et les élégies. Paris, 1878.
	38575.33.11	Corneille, Pierre. La suite du menteur. Cambridge, 1878.
	Mon 175.4	Courtois. Voyage en Périgord. Paris, 1878.
	39544.76	Damilaville, Édouard. Voltaire à Paris. Paris, 1878.
	FL 6118.78.2	Daret, M. Jean-Jacques Rousseau. Sa vie, ses idées religieuses. Genève, 1878.
	42566.67	Daudet, Alphonse. Les femmes d'artistes. Paris, 1878.
	38563.19.15	Deschamps, Arsène. La genèse du scepticisme erudit chez Bayle. Liége, 1878.
	38514.44A	Deschamps, Eustache. Oeuvres complètes. Paris, 1878-80. 11v.
	37541.3	Diancourt, A. Atlas littéraire de la France. Paris, 1878.
	41522.100.21	Dondey, T. Oeuvres en prose. Paris, 1878.
	40566.4.5A	Doudan, Ximénès. Mélanges et lettres. Paris, 1878. 4v.
	38521.8	Douen, O. Clement Marot et le Psautier Huguenot. Paris, 1878. 2v.
	FL 6128.78.4	Dufour-Vernes, L. Recherches sur Jean-Jacques Rousseau et sa parenté. Genève, 1878.
	38585.10	Dugit, Ernest. Racine. Paris, 1878.
	41524.6	Dumas, Alexandre. Comtesse de Salisbury. Paris, 1878.
	42543.15.7	Dumas, Alexandre. La dame aux camélias. v.1-2. Paris, 1878.
	42543.16.3	Dumas, Alexandre. La dame aux perles. Paris, 1878. 2 pam.
	42543.12.10	Dumas, Alexandre. Entr'actes. Paris, 1878-79. 3v.
	42543.19	Dumas, Alexandre. L'étrangère. Paris, 1878.
	41525.12	Dumas, Alexandre. La guerre des femmes. Paris, 1878.
	41525.14	Dumas, Alexandre. L'homme aux Contes. Paris, 1878.
	41526.5	Dumas, Alexandre. Isaac Laguedem. v.1-2. Paris, 1878.
	41528.9	Dumas, Alexandre. Trois maitres. Paris, 1878.
	42563.40.5	Durand, Alice M.C.F. A friend. Philadelphia, 1878.
	42563.54.25	Durand, Alice M.C.F. Nouvelles russes. Paris, 1878.
	42563.55.90	Durand, Alice M.C.F. La princesse Oghérof. 4. éd. Paris, 1878.
	42563.47.1	Durand, Alice M.C.F. Saveli's expiation. Philadelphia, 1878.
	42543.28.35	Ennes, Antonie. Un divorce: drame. Paris, 1878.
	42571.4	Erckmann, Emile. Contes vosgiens. Paris, 1878.
	FL 397.110	Faber, Frederic Jules. Histoire du théâtre français en Belgique. Bruxelles, 1878-80. 5v.
	42575.31.5	Feuillet, Octave. Le journal d'une femme. Paris, 1878.
	Mol 755.3F	Fillon, B. Le blason de Molière. Paris, 1878.
	42564.7	Fleury, Jules. Les bourgeois de Molinchart. Paris, 1878.
	42575.53.40	Fould, W. de (Mme.). Renée and Franz. N.Y., 1878.
	38526.5	Frank, Félix. Les comptes du monde adventureux. Paris, 1878. 2v.
	39534.20	Furetière, Antoine. Le Roman bourgeois, ouvrage comique. Paris, 1878.
	FL 6138.78	Gaberel, J. Calvin et Rousseau. Genève, 1878.
	FL 6128.78.2	Gaberel, J. Condamnation de l'Émile et du Contrat Social de Rousseau. Paris, 1878.
	37543.17.3	Gidel, Charles. Histoire de la littérature française. Paris, 1878.
	37543.17.2	Gidel, Charles. Histoire de la littérature française. Paris, 1878.
	FL 391.80	Giffard, Pierre. Comédie-française; les Fourchambault. Paris, 1878.
	42586.66.10	Gobineau, Arthur de. Romances of the east. N.Y., 1878.

Chronological Listing

1878 - cont.

42575.60 Goncourt, Edmond de. Quelques créatures. Paris, 1878.
42543.54 Gondinet, Edmond. La belle madame Donis. Paris, 1878.
42543.54.5 Gondinet, Edmond. Le club. Paris, 1878.
42543.54.8 Gondinet, Edmond. Le homard. Paris, 1878.
41542.54 Gozlan, Léon. La pluie et le beau temps. Paris, 1878.
Mol 825.7 Graaf, R. de. L'instrument de Molière. Paris, 1878.
42543.60.8 Grandmougin, Charles. Prométhée. Paris, 1878.
38511.11 Greban, Arnoul. Le mystère de la Passion. Paris, 1878.
40526.13 Gresset, Jean B. Oeuvres choisies. Paris, 1878.
39545.9 Griswold, G.C. Voltaire als Historiker. Halle, 1878.
38554.13 Griveau, Algar. Étude sur la condamnation du livre des maximes des saints. Paris, 1878. 2v.
38528.6 Grouchy, Ernest Henri. Étude sur Nicolas de Grouchy. Paris, 1878.
37558.11 Guy, Jules. Les femmes de lettres. Paris, 1878.
38524.6 Guy de Tours. Le paradis d'amour. Paris, 1878.
38524.5 Guy de Tours. Premières oeuvres. Paris, 1878.
41557.10.210 Haussonville, Gabriel Paul Othenin de Cléron. George Sand, sa vie et ses oeuvres. Paris, 1878.
42543.68.19 Hennequin, Alfred. Niniche: vaudeville en trois actes. Paris, 1878.
42584.31.2 Hetzel, P.J. Maroussia. 10. éd. Paris, 1878?
FL 398.39.9 Hostein, Hippolyte. Historiettes et souvenirs d'un Homme de théâtre. Paris, 1878.
41573.32.4.9 Hugo, Victor. Hernani. Paris, 1878.
41573.32.4.15 Hugo, Victor. Hernani. 6e éd. Bielefeld, 1878.
41573.36 Hugo, Victor. Odes et ballades. Paris, 1878.
41573.26.2 Hugo, Victor. The prompt book...drama of Ruy Blas. N.Y., 1878.
42543.69.100 Ivry, marquis d'. Les amants de Vérone; drame. Paris, 1878.
37567.9A James, Henry. French poets and novelists. London, 1878.
38524.4 Jamyn, Amadis. Oeuvres poetiques. Paris, 1878. 2v.
40567.9.5 Janin, Jules. Barnave. v.1-2. Paris, 1878.
38524.7 Jean de la Taille. Oeuvres. Paris, 1878. 4v.
FL 6128.78.3F Jeanneret, G. Un séjour à l'ile de Saint-Pierre. Paris, 1878.
37596.60 Julleville, L. La chanson de Roland. Paris, 1878.
40516.61.5 Kruedener, B.J. Valérie. Paris, 1878.
37596.89 Kutschera, Oscarus. Le manuscrit des sermons français de Saint Bernard. Halis, 1878.
41578.37 Lacretelle, Henri de. Lamartine et ses amis. Paris, 1878.
39532.24.5 Lacroix, Paul. Paris ridicule et burlesque. Paris, 1878.
40526.21.5 La Grange-Chancel, Joseph de. Poésies inédites. Paris, 1878.
FL 398.3 Laire, Raymond. Mlle. Agar de la comédie-française. Vienne, 1878.
42544.31.3 Lapointe, A. Les rivalites. Paris, 1878.
Mol 855.3 Le Boulanger de Chalussay. Elomire hypocondre. Paris, 1878.
FL 397.79 Lecocq, Georges. Histoire du théâtre de St. Quentin. Paris, 1878.
42548.42 Legouvé, Ernest. Théâtre de campagne. ser. 3. Paris, 1878.
42548.43 Legouvé, Ernest. Théâtre de campagne. ser. 4. Paris, 1878.
38558.28 Lehanneur, L. Mascaron. La Rochelle, 1878.
40512.12.3 LeSage, Alain René. Adventures of Gil Blas of Santillane. London, 1878?
37597.1 Lorris, Guillaume de. Le rommánt de la rose. Paris, 1878.
42587.15 Lubomirski, Jozef. Safar-Hadgi, or Russ and Turcoman. N.Y., 1878.
38527.61.7 Magny, Olivier de. Les amours. Paris, 1878.
42577.11.9 Malot, Hector. La belle madame Donis. 8. éd. Paris, 1878.
42555.49.2 Manuel, Eugène. A nos hôtes. Paris, 1878.
40531.30 Marivaux, Pierre Carlet de Chamblain de. Oeuvre. Paris, 1878.
39598.7 Marmontel, J.F. Memoirs. Boston, 1878. 2v.
37597.7 Marteau, Pierre. Le roman de la rose. Orléans, 1878. 5v.
FL 6138.78.2 Martin, A.J. Centenaire de Jean-Jacques Rousseau. Genève, 1878.
42545.10 Meilhac, Henri. Le petit duc. Paris, 1878.
37565.35 Merlet, Gustave. Tableau de la littérature française 1800-1815. Paris, 1878. 3v.
FL 6118.78 Meylan, A. Jean-Jacques Rousseau. Sa vie et ses oeuvres. Berne, 1878.
Mol 229.19 Molière, Jean Baptiste Poquelin. O Doente de Scisma. Lisboa, 1878.
Mol 246.7.10 Molière, Jean Baptiste Poquelin. Il misantropo. Parma, 1878.
Mol 38.78 Molière, Jean Baptiste Poquelin. Oeuvres choisies. Paris, 1878.
Mol 8.78F Molière, Jean Baptiste Poquelin. Oeuvres complètes. Paris, 1878. 5v.
Mol 8.78.2 Molière, Jean Baptiste Poquelin. Théâtre choisi. Tours, 1878-79. 2v.
Mon 18.78A Montaigne, Michel de. Essais. Le Clerc. Paris, 1878? 2v.
38585.16.365 Montifaud, Marc de. Racine et la voisin. Paris, 1878.
39566.12.2 Morley, John. Diderot and the encyclopaedists. London, 1878. 2v.
FL 6118.73.1.5 Morley, John Morley. Rousseau. London, 1878.
38527.85 La mort de Silvandre...Poème, 1660. Paris, 1878.
Mol 713.10 Moulin, H. Molière et les registres de l'état civil. Paris, 1878.
42577.23 Murger, Henry. Le pays latin. Paris, 1878.
41596.17.10 Musset, Alfred de. Comédies et proverbes. Paris, 1878. 3v.
Htn Mol 870.28* Mussy, P. de. L'amour poète; ou Corneille chez Molière. Rouen, 1878.
38526.8.9 Nagel, H. Die metrischen Verse Jean Antoine de Baifs. Leipzig, 1878.
42548.50.5 Newport, Rhode Island. Bellevue Drama Club. Plays for private acting. N.Y., 1878.
42548.50 Newport, Rhode Island. Bellevue Drama Club. Plays for private acting. N.Y., 1878.
42555.64 Nizet, Marie. Romania (Chants de la Roumanie). Paris, 1878.
39545.5 Noël, Eugène. Voltaire. Paris, 1878.
Mon 105.6 Paris. Bibliothèque National. Inventaire de la collection sur Montaigne. Paris, 1878.
42587.41 Pelletan, Eugène. Le grand Frédéric. Paris, 1878.
38563.29.10 Perrault, C. Mémoires. Paris, 1878.
FL 6015.12 Petitpierre, A. Jean-Jacques Rousseau et Isabelle d'Ivernois. Paris, 1878.

1878 - cont.

38526.18.14 Picot, Émile. Pierre Gringore et les comédiens italiens. Paris, 1878.
Mol 560.11 Poche. Bibliographie Molièresque. Paris, 1878.
42555.45 Poitevin, Prosper. Les contes tourangeaux. Paris, 1878.
FL 384.55 Pollock, Walter H. The modern French theatre. Paris, 1878.
39544.38 Pompery, E. de. La vie de Voltaire. Paris, 1878.
38585.4 Pons, A.J. Les éditions illustrées de Racine. Paris, 1878.
42578.31.2 Pouvillon, E. Nouvelles réalistes. Paris, 1878.
43747.50.120 Puliga, H.C.S. Leurs excellences. Paris, 1878.
40573.26 Rémusat, Charles de. La Saint-Barthélemy, drame inédit. Paris, 1878.
42515.30.63 Renan, Ernest. Caliban, suite de La tempète. 2. éd. Paris, 1878.
42515.30.61 Renan, Ernest. Caliban. Paris, 1878. 2 pam.
42515.30.60 Renan, Ernest. Caliban. Paris, 1878.
41574.20 Rivet, Gustave. Victor chez lui. Paris, 1878.
40587.9 Roche, A. Chateaubriand et Madame de Staël. Paris, 1878.
Mol 870.29 Roger, A. Le médecin de Molière. Paris, 1878.
38526.47.23.100 Romieu, Marie de. Oeuvres poétiques. Paris, 1878.
38523.3 Rose, Hermann. Der Einfluss Villons auf Marot. Glückstadt, 1878.
38513.12A Rothschild, James de. Le mistère du Viel Testament. Paris, 1878-81. 6v.
FL 6002.878.2 Rousseau, J.J. Jean-Jacques et le pays Romand. Genève, 1878.
FL 6051.78 Rousseau, J.J. Julie, ou la nouvelle Héloise. Paris, 1878.
40516.60 Sade, D.A.F. de. Idée sur les romans. Paris, 1878.
40586.22.7A St. Beuve, C.A. Chateaubriand et son groupe littéraire sous l'Empire. Paris, 1878. 2v.
39595.12 St. Pierre, J.H.B. de. Oeuvres choisies. Paris, 1878.
40575.37 Sainte-Beuve, Charles A. Premiers lundis. Paris, 1878-82. 3v.
41557.8.112 Sand, George. Nanon. Paris, 1878.
41557.8.133 Sand, George. Questions d'art et de littérature. Paris, 1878.
42546.24.9 Sardou, Victorien. Don Quichotte. Paris, 1878.
42546.30.9 Sardou, Victorien. L'heure du spectacle. Paris, 1878. 4 pam.
42546.26.7 Sardou, Victorien. Les pommes du voisin. 3e ed. Paris, 1878.
38514.44.9 Sarradin, A. Étude sur Eustache Deschamps. Versailles, 1878.
42516.6.5 Schaeffer, Adolphe. Roses et épines. Colmar, 1878.
Mol 619.2 Schaunsland. Les farces de Molière. Osterode, 1878.
Mol 719.1 Scheffler, Wilhelm. Molière-Studien. n.p., 1878.
37555.20 Schlüter, Joseph. Die Französische Kriegs- und Revanche-Dichtung. Heilbronn, 1878.
Mol 619.4 Schulze, H. Zur Würdigung Molières. Zittau, 1878.
FL 371.13 Sepet, Marius. Le drame chrétien au Moyen Age. Paris, 1878.
FL 6138.78.3 Sigogne, E. Eloge de Jean-Jacques Rousseau. Paris, 1878.
42556.38 Sirvey, Gaston de. Martyre et délivrance. Lille, 1878.
38585.7 Soullie, P. Études sur les tragédies de Racine. Paris, 1878.
41558.71 Souvestre, Émile. Théâtre de la jeunesse. Paris, 1878.
39544.265 Straeten, E. Voltaire. Paris, 1878.
Mol 820.1 Taillandier, St. R. Un poète comique du temps de Molière. Paris, 1878.
38528.13 Le texte primitif de la satyre Ménippée. Paris, 1878.
42583.18.5 Theuriet, André. The godson of a marquis. N.Y., 1878.
42583.25 Theuriet, André. Le mariage de Gérard. Paris, 1878.
39545.12 Thiérist, A. Voltaire en Prusse. Paris, 1878.
Mol 755.4 Thoinan, E. Un bisaïeul de Molière. Paris, 1878.
41563.28.4 Toepffer, Rodolphe. Le Presbytère. Paris, 1878.
41563.30.2 Toepffer, Rodolphe. Réflexions et menus propos. Paris, 1878.
39544.28.70 Tribolati, F. Sill'epistolario italiano del Voltaire. Pisa, 1878.
42536.48 Troubat, Jules. Plume et pinceau. Paris, 1878.
FL 6128.78 Vadier, Berthe (pseud.). Pourquoi nous fêtons Rousseau. Genève, 1878.
42587.65 Vaugny, C. de. Ella Wilson-Parley Pratt-Kiana. Paris, 1878.
42583.11.5 Verne, Jules. Hector Servadac. London, 1878.
41564.3.67 Vigny, Alfred de. Cinq-Mars. 14e éd. Paris, 1878.
42587.69.2 Villemessant, H. de. Memoires d'un journaliste. Paris, 1878-1884. 6v.
NEDL 40517.63 Voisenon, C.H.F. Contes de l'abbé de Voisenon. Paris, 1878.
39542.31 Voltaire, François Marie Arouet de. Oeuvres choisies. Paris, 1878.
39545.29.3 Voltaire, François Marie Arouet de. Prayers, sermons and religious thoughts. Philadelphia, 1878.
FL 6138.78.4 Vuy, J. Origine des idées politiques de Rousseau. Genève, 1878.
42558.60 Weil, Alfred. Une douzaine de sonnets. Paris, 1878.
42587.70.3 Weill, Alexandre. Blasphèmes; poésies. Paris, 1878.
42584.23 Zola, Emile. Une page d'amour. 64. éd. Paris, 1878.

1879

42586.3A About, E. Contes de toutes les couleurs. Paris, 1879.
Htn Mol 863.21.2* Aicard, J. Molière à Shakspeare. Paris, 1879.
Mol 863.21 Aicard, J. Molière à Shakspeare. Paris, 1879.
42512.3.5 Albert, Paul. Variétés morales et litteraires. Paris, 1879.
Htn 37578.43* Album drolatique. Paris, 1879.
FL 395.241F Angus, J.K. The comédie française. London, 1879.
37585.2 Archer, William. English analyses of the French plays represented at the Gaiety Theatre, London,...by the Comédie française. London, 1879.
42542.18 Augier, Émile. Les Fourchambault. 20. éd. Paris, 1879.
40597.29.1.5 Balzac, Honoré de. The cat and battledore. Chicago, 1879.
42554.1 Banville, Théodore de. Les cariatides. Paris, 1879.
42554.4 Banville, Théodore de. Comédies. Paris, 1879.
38563.10.25 Bayle, Pierre. Sur les obscénités. Bruxelles, 1879.
38527.68A Becq de Fouquières, L. Oeuvres choisies des poètes français du XVIe siècle. Paris, 1879.
37555.319 Becq de Fouquières, L. Traité général de versification française. Paris, 1879.
41542.4.5 Bergerat, Émile. Théophile Gautier. Paris, 1879.
41542.4.4 Bergerat, Émile. Théophile Gautier. 2. éd. Paris, 1879.
38528.16.8.12 Béroalde de Verville. Le moyen de parvenir. Paris, 1879.

1879 - cont.

40528.4 Bertin, Antoine. Poésies. Paris, 1879.
38537.21 Besant, Walter. Rabelais. Edinburgh, 1879.
38537.25.75 Besant, Walter. Rabelais. Philadelphia, 1879.
Mol 860.48 Bondroit, E. Molière chez lui. Liège, 1879.
38557.60.100 Bossuet, J.B. Traité de la concupiscence. Paris, 1879.
37562.25.4 Bourgain, L. La chaire française au XIIe siècle. Paris, 1879.
Mol 855.5 Boursault, E. Le portrait du peintre. Paris, 1879.
38576.6 Boursault, Edme. Le portrait du peintre. Paris, 1879.
41574.79 Bouvenne, Aglaus. Victor Hugo, ses portraits et ses charges. Paris, 1879.
42563.38.10 Bouvier, Alexis. La belle grêlée. Paris, 1879.
FL 6138.79 Braillard, J. Jean-Jacques Rousseau jugé par les Genevois. Genève, 1879.
37542.31 Breitinger, H. Aus neuern Litteraturen. Zürich, 1879.
FL 394.81A Campardon, E. Les comédiens du roi de la troupe française. Paris, 1879.
40587.906 Caud, Lucile (de Chateaubriand) de (Mme.). Ses contes, ses poèmes, ses lettres. Paris, 1879.
42562.39 Cauvain, Henry. Les amours bizarres. Paris, 1879.
42561.25 Chandeneux, Claire de. La croix de Monguerre. Paris, 1879.
41564.32 Charavay, Étienne. Alfred de Vigny et Charles Baudelaire. Paris, 1879.
40564.23.9 Chasles, Philarète. Scènes des camps et des Bivouacs Hongrois. Paris, 1879.
42565.4.5 Cherbuliez, Victor. L'aventure de Ladislas Bolski. 5. éd. Paris, 1879.
38539.2.200 Cholières, Nicolas de. Paris, 1879. 2v.
42565.55.50 Cladel, Léon. Bonshommes. Paris, 1879.
FL 398.7.23 Clement, Clément. Esquisses d'aujourd'hui...Bernhardt. Paris, 1879.
42586.31.11F Claretié, J. Le drapeau. Paris, 1879.
42586.31.12 Claretié, J. Mademoiselle Cachemire. Paris, 1879.
42586.31.3 Claretié, J. Le troisième dessous. Paris, 1879.
Mon 143.1 Collins, W.L. Montaigne. Edinburgh, 1879.
42554.25.2 Coppée, François. Théâtre 1873-78. Paris, 1879.
Htn 38575.28.12* Corneille, Pierre. Le défense du Cid. v.1-2. Rouen, 1879.
38575.33.20 Corneille, Pierre. Le menteur. London, 1879.
42554.26.35 Crémieux, G. Oeuvres posthumes. Paris, 1879.
40565.25 Cuvillier-Fleury, A.A. Posthumes et revenants. Paris, 1879.
42566.33 Daudet, Alphonse. Les rois en exil. Paris, 1879.
42566.33.4.2 Daudet, Alphonse. Les rois en exil. 37. éd. Paris, 1879.
42566.33.4 Daudet, Alphonse. Les rois en exile. 4. éd. Paris, 1879.
40515.2.50 Denon, Vivant. Point de lendemain. Rouen, 1879.
Mol 853.1.5A Des Jardins. Recit en prose et en vers de la farce des Précieuses. Paris, 1879.
39544.78 Desnoiresterres, G. Inconographie voltairienne. Paris, 1879.
37565.29.2 Desnoiresterres, Gustave. Epicuriens et lettres XVIIe et XVIIIe siècle. Paris, 1879.
42576.66.7 D'Hericault, C. En 1792. Le dernier amour de Lord St. Albans. Paris, 1879.
42576.66.6 D'Hericault, C. En 1792. Le premier amour de Lord St. Albans. Paris, 1879.
FL 395.200 D'Heylli, George. Journal intime de la comédie française. Paris, 1879.
39566.120 Diderot; célébration à Langres. Langres, 1879.
40566.4.11 Doudan, Ximénès. Lettres. Paris, 1879. 4v.
40556.7 Droz, Gustave. Betsy's profile. N.Y., 1879.
40566.7 Dubois, P.F. Fragments littéraires. Paris, 1879. 2v.
42568.19.5 Du Boisgobey, Fortuné. La tresse blonde. 4. éd. Paris, 1879.
Mol 247.12A Du Boulan, Gérard (pseud.). L'énigme d'Alceste. Paris, 1879.
41593.12.25 Duchesne, Julien. Étude sur Auguste Brizeux. Rennes, 1879.
40535.12 Ducis, Jean F. Lettres. Paris, 1879.
41523.14 Dumas, Alexandre. La boule de Neige. Paris, 1879.
41523.26 Dumas, Alexandre. Château d'Eppstein. Paris, 1879.
41524.15 Dumas, Alexandre. Dieu dispose. Paris, 1879.
42543.19.21 Dumas, Alexandre. Le fils naturel. London, 1879.
41526.11 Dumas, Alexandre. Jane. Paris, 1879.
41529.107.2.3 Dumas, Alexandre. The memoirs of a physician. London, 1879.
41527.5 Dumas, Alexandre. Les morts vont vite. Paris, 1879.
41528.4 Dumas, Alexandre. Sultanetta. Paris, 1879.
41528.7 Dumas, Alexandre. Le testament de M. Chavelin. Paris, 1879.
42563.42 Durand, Alice M.C.F. A travers champs. Paris, 1879.
42563.40 Durand, Alice M.C.F. L'amie. Paris, 1879.
42563.43 Durand, Alice M.C.F. Bonne-Marie. Paris, 1879.
42563.45.2 Durand, Alice M.C.F. Dosia. Paris, 1879.
42563.47 Durand, Alice M.C.F. L'expiation de Savéli. Paris, 1879.
42563.49 Durand, Alice M.C.F. Les Koumiassine. Paris, 1879.
42563.50.2 Durand, Alice M.C.F. La maison de Maureze. Paris, 1879.
42563.54 Durand, Alice M.C.F. Le Niania. Paris, 1879.
42542.72.7 Duru, A. Madame Favar; opera. Paris, 1879.
37565.30 Duval, Georges. Histoire de la littérature révolutionnaire. Paris, 1879.
42568.23.110 Eekhoud, Georges. Les pittoresques. Paris, 1879.
38528.7A Estienne, Henri. Apologie pour Hérodote. Paris, 1879. 2v.
38554.8 Fénelon, F. de S. de la Mothe. A dialogue between Dionysius, Damon. Lowell, Mass., 1879?
38552.7.20 Fénelon, F. de S. de la Mothe. Oeuvres choisies. Paris, 1879-81. 4v.
38553.15.4.35 Fénelon, F. de S. de la Mothe. Selections from Fénelon. Boston, 1879.
38553.15.4.37 Fénelon, F. de S. de la Mothe. Selections from Fénelon. Boston, 1879.
42575.26 Feuillet, Octave. Les amours de Philippe. Paris, 1879.
42575.40.2 Feuillet, Octave. La petite comtesse. Paris, 1879.
FL 379.18 Fontaine, Léon. Le théâtre et la philosophie au 18e siècle. Paris, 1879.
FL 381.5 Formentin, C. Essai sur les origines du drame moderne en France. Paris, 1879.
37555.307 Foth, K. Die Französische Metrik. Berlin, 1879.
42576.62.4 France, Anatole. Jocaste. Paris, 1879.
Mol 263.5 Friedmann, A. Ein Versuch den Sganarelle des Molière. Wien, 1879.
42576.61.200 Frisson d'Aulnoy, A. Le proscrit. 2. éd. Bruxelles, 1879.
NEDL 37567.7 Gautier, Theophile. Famous French authors. N.Y., 1879.
41542.18.5A Gautier, Théophile. Voyage en Espagne. Paris, 1879.

1879 - cont.

FL 6138.79.5 Gehrig, H. Jean-Jacques Rousseau; sein Leben und seine pädagogische Bedeutung. Neuwied, 1879.
40588.12 Genlis, S.F.D. de St. Souvenirs de Félicie. Paris, 1879.
FL 391.82 Giffard, Pierre. Théâtre de la Porte Saint-Martin. Paris, 1879.
FL 391.81 Giffard, Pierre. Théâtre-lyrique; les amants de Vérone. Paris, 1879.
37537.12.5 Godefroy, Frédéric. Histoire de la littérature française. v.5. 2. éd. Paris, 1879-
42575.58 Goncourt, Edmond de. Les frères Zemganno. Paris, 1879.
42575.61.5 Goncourt, Edmond de. Renée Mauperin. Paris, 1879.
42575.70 Goncourt, Edmond de. Théâtre. Paris, 1879.
42543.54.10 Gondinet, Edmond. Les tapageurs. Paris, 1879.
37574.31.5 Gourdon de Genouillac, H. Les refrains de la rue de 1830 à 1870. Paris, 1879.
FL 390.85 Grönstedt, J. Teaterlitvet i Paris. Stockholm, 1879.
37596.67.5 Haase, G. Untersuchung über die Reime in der Image du monde. Halle, 1879.
Mol 708.1 Hall, J.N. Molière en zijn vijanden. Amsterdam, 1879.
42576.65.3 Harden-Hickey, J. Lettres d'un Yankee. 2. éd. Paris, 1879.
Mon 118.1 Henning, A. Skepticismus Montaignes. Jena, 1879-81. 2 pam.
42587.48 Hericourt, Charles. Édouard Plouvier. Arras, 1879.
42543.69.16.10 Hervilly, Ernest. Bric-a-brac. N.Y., 1879.
42543.69.16 Hervilly, Ernest. Carried by assault. N.Y., 1879.
37596.27 Herz, Joseph. De Saint Aléxis. Frankfurt, 1879.
Mol 800.5 Houssaye, A. Les comédiennes de Molière. Paris, 1879.
42576.14.110 Houssaye, Arsène. Life in Paris. N.Y., 1879.
41573.32.5 Hugo, Victor. Hernani. Paris, 1879.
41573.36.15 Hugo, Victor. La petié suprème. Paris, 1879.
41572.30.6 Hugo, Victor. Les voix interieures. Les rayons et les ombres. Paris, 1879.
Mol 870.30 Hugues, Clovis. Une nuit de Molière. Marseille, 1879.
Mol 875.7 Joliet, Charles. Molière. Paris, 1879.
FL 379.17A Jullien, Adolphe. La comédie et la galanterie. Paris, 1879.
37551.36 Kerviler, René. La Bretagne a l'Academie Française. Paris, 1879.
38543.31.25 Kerviler, René. François de la Mothe le Vayer. Paris, 1879.
37596.63 Koschwitz, E. Karls des grossen Reise nach Jerusalem und Constantin. Heilbronn, 1879.
42544.27.9 Labiche, Eugène. La grammaire. Paris, 1879.
38513.34 Lackner, E. Les 5 moralités publiées dans le IIIe volume de l'ancien théâtre. Bartenstein, 1879.
FL 395.60 Lamington, A.C.B. The théâtre français in the reign of Louis XV. London, 1879.
40517.51 Lamorlière, J.R. de. Contes du chevalier de la Morlière. Paris, 1879.
42544.4 Launay, Alphonse. Le supplice d'une mère. Paris, 1879.
41586.11.10 Leclercq, Théodore. Trois proverbes dramatiques. 2e éd. Bielefeld, 1879.
42544.17.8A Legouvé, Gabriel. Nos filles et nos fils. 6e éd. Paris, 1879.
42548.44 Legouvé. Ernest. Théâtre de campagne. ser. 5. Paris, 1879.
42513.78 Leroy-Beaulieu, A. Un empereur, un roi, un pape. Paris, 1879.
42514.27.250 Lomenie, Louis de. Esquises en historiques et littéraires. Paris, 1879.
37555.309 Lubarsch, E.O. Französische Verslehre. Berlin, 1879.
39544.14.3 Mahrenholtz, R. Voltaire - Studien. Wien, 1879.
42577.11.14 Malot, Hector. La marquise de Lucillière. 7. éd. Paris, 1879.
38537.2 Martin, Henri. De l'autorité de Rabelais dans la revues present. Paris, 1879.
42515.37.10 Meissas, A.F.N. M. Renan, apologiste malgré lui. Paris, 1879.
Mol 464.5A Melisse. Jacob. Paris, 1879.
38514.20.12A Moland, M.L. Oeuvres complètes de François Villon. Paris, 1879.
Mol 165.35 Molière, Jean Baptiste Poquelin. L'avare...Lion. Leipzig, 1879.
Mol 229.5.5 Molière, Jean Baptiste Poquelin. Der eingebildete Kranke. Dresden, 1879.
Mol 228.28 Molière, Jean Baptiste Poquelin. Le malade imaginaire...Tarver. London, 1879.
Mol 246.3.3 Molière, Jean Baptiste Poquelin. The misanthrope. B.B. Bart. Boulogne, 1879.
Mol 268.60 Molière, Jean Baptiste Poquelin. Le Tartuffe; Le dépit amoureux. Paris, 1879.
Mol 269.30.7 Molière, Jean Baptiste Poquelin. Tartuffe. Thijm. Amsterdam, 1879.
42545.39.15 Monselet, Charles. Une troupe de comédiens. Paris, 1879.
Mon 31.37 Montaigne, Michel de. Works. Boston, 1879-80. 4v.
Mol 513.1.2 Monval, G. Le Molieriste; revue mensuelle. Paris, 1879-89. 10v.
Mol 513.1 Monval, G. Le Molieriste; revue mensuelle (1879-1889). Paris, 1879-89. 10v.
FL 382.22 Monval, Georges. Les théâtres subventionnes. Paris, 1879.
42555.61.52 Moréas, Jean. L'histoire de Jean de Paris, Roi de France. 2. éd. Paris, 1879.
40556.26 Moreau, Louis. Joseph de Maistre. Paris, 1879.
39564.33 Morley, John M. Diderot and the encyclopaedists. N.Y., 1879.
Htn 42577.32.5* Murger, Henry. Scènes de la vie de Bohème. Paris, 1879.
Htn 41596.12.3* Musset, Alfred de. Premières poésies. 1829-1835. Paris, 1879.
Mol 860.49 Nancey, A. Un souper chez Molière. Troyes, 1879.
38526.30 Navarre, M. de. Heptaméron. Paris, 1879. 2v.
38526.31 Navarre, M. de. Heptaméron. Paris, 1879. 2v.
38526.29 Navarre, M. de. L'Heptaméron. Paris, 1879. 3v.
38526.30.2 Navarre, M. de. Heptaméron. Paris, 1879. 3v.
FL 395.265 Noel, Edouard. La comédie-française en 1878-1879. Paris, 1879.
40524.17.65.5 Nogaret, François Félix. Le fond du sac. Rouen, 1879. 2v.
42578.25 Noriac, Jules. La comtesse de Bruges. Paris, 1879.
Mol 715.1 Oliphant, M.O. Molière. London, 1879.
42532.10 Paris-Murcie. Paris, 1879.
38567.29 Une parodie curieuse de l'art poétique de Boileau. Rouen, 1879.
42587.46.7 Piazzi, Adriana. Un drame à Constantinople. Paris, 1879.

Chronological Listing

1879 - cont.

38513.19.4 Picot, Emile. Notice sur Jehan Chaponneau, docteur de l'église réformée, metteur en scène du Mistère des actes des apostres...1536. Paris, 1879.
42555.70.1100 Pierron, Ernest. Le barbeau heraldique de Pont-à-Mousson, légende du XVII siècle. Pont-à-Mousson, 1879.
FL 370.50 Pifteau, B. Histoire du théâtre en France (1398-1636). Paris, 1879.
Mol 730.6 Pifteau, B. Les maitresses de Molière. Paris, 1879.
Mol 730.6.2 Pifteau, B. Les maitresses de Molière. Paris, 1879.
Mol 870.30.5 Pifteau, B. Molière en province. Paris, 1879.
Mol 870.30.6 Pifteau, B. Molière en province. Paris, 1879.
40528.3 Piron, Alexis. Poésies choisies. Paris, 1879.
42515.36.212 Plasman, L.C. de. M. Renan, peint par ses oeuvres. Paris, 1879.
40575.5.115 Pons, A.J. Sainte-Beuve et ses inconnues. Paris, 1879.
42534.33 Pontmartin, A.F. de. Souvenirs d'un vieux mélomane. Paris, 1879.
42545.88.57 Porto-Riche, G. Les deux fautes. Paris, 1879.
42545.88.50 Porto-Riche, G. Vanina. Paris, 1879.
42545.89 Potron, Ç. A bad temper. N.Y., 1879?
40528.20A Raunie, Emile. Chansonniers historiques du XVIIIe siècle. Paris, 1879-84. 10v.
42556.23.5 Read, Henri Charles. Poésies posthumes 1874-1876. Paris, 1879.
42515.30.210 Renan, Ernest. Discours. Paris, 1879.
42515.29.601A Renan, Ernest. L'église chrétienne. Paris, 1879.
42515.29.600 Renan, Ernest. L'église chrétienne. 4. éd. Paris, 1879.
42515.34.30 Renan, Ernest. Lettre à un ami d'Allemagne. Paris, 1879.
42515.29.20 Renan, Ernest. Vie de Jésus. 16. éd. Paris, 1879.
Mol 755.5 Révérend du Mesnil, E. La famille de Molière. Paris, 1879.
42578.18.50 Richebourg, Emile. Deux mères. Paris, 1879. 2v.
37546.2 Rolland, Jules. Histoire littéraire de la Ville d'Albi. Toulouse, 1879.
38525.19.5A Ronsard, Pierre de. Oeuvres choisies. Paris, 1879.
Htn 41596.57* Rouquette, Adrien E. La nouvelle Atala. New Orleans, 1879.
37595.8 Sabatini, Francesco. Abelardo ed Eloisa. Roma, 1879.
38542.25.2 Saint Evremond, C. de M. de S.D. Les académiciens. Étude par Robert de Bonnières. Paris, 1879.
38542.25 Saint Evremond, C. de M. de S.D. Les académiciens. Étude par Robert de Bonnières. Paris, 1879.
38523.12A Saint-Marc, B. Oeuvres complètes de Clèment Marot. Paris, 1879. 2v.
41593.17.20 Sainte-Beuve, C.A. M. Daru. Cambridge, 1879.
41557.9.35 Sand, George. Histoire de ma vie. Paris, 1879. 4v.
41557.9.35.5 Sand, George. Histoire de ma vie. Paris, 1879. 4v.
41557.8.109 Sand, George. Le meunier d'Angibault. Paris, 1879.
41557.30.5 Sandeau, Jules. Madeleine. Chicago, 1879.
41557.19.10 Sandeau, Jules. Mademoiselle de la Seiglière. 7. ed. Bielefeld, 1879.
Mol 900.2F Sarcey et Lanoumet. Chronique théâtrale. Paris, 1879-1902.
42546.30.12 Sardou, Victorien. L'heure du spectacle. Paris, 1879.
39534.26.5 Scarron, Paul. Théâtre complet. Paris, 1879.
Mol 619.5A Schweitzer, H. Molière und seine Bühne. pt.1-3. Leipzig, 1879.
42548.26.5 Scribe, E. La bataille de dames. Paris, 1879.
42546.32.5 Second, Albéric. Les demoiselles du Ponçay. 7e éd. Paris, 1879.
42578.40 Second, Albéric. Jeunesse dorée. Paris, 1879.
37562.24 Sepet, Marius. Les etudes relatives à la littérature française du moyen âge depuis 1867. Paris, 1879.
42557.4.30 Soulary, Joséphin. La lune rousse. Paris, 1879.
40597.5.1.2A Spoelberch de Lovenjoul, Charles. Histoire des oeuvres de Honoré de Balzac. Paris, 1879.
42583.19 Theuriet, André. Le filleul d'un marquis. Paris, 1879.
42583.24 Theuriet, André. La maison des deux barbeaux. Paris, 1879.
42543.69.16.25 Too windy for an umbrella. N.Y., 1879.
41555.41 Tourneux, M. Prosper Mérimée. Paris, 1879.
42513.5.80 Trübner, Nikolaus. Joseph Octave Delepierre. Edinburgh, 1879.
Mol 863.20 Truffier, J. Sous les frises. Paris, 1879.
40525.15 Uzanne, Octave. Contes de A.P. de Moncrif. Paris, 1879.
42587.65.11 Vachette, Eugène. Les petites comédies du vice. Paris, 1879.
42547.10.9 Vacquerie, Auguste. Théâtre complet. Paris, 1879. 2v.
40526.69 Vadé, Jean Joseph. La pipe casée. Rouen, 1879.
40528.2 Vadé, Jean Joseph. Poésies. Paris, 1879.
42582.9.20 Verne, Jules. Dick Sands. N.Y., 1879.
42582.12.20 Verne, Jules. The English at the North Pole. London, 1879.
Mol 270.13 Veselovskii, A. Tartiuff. Moskva, 1879.
39591.20 Vian, Louis. Histoire de Montesquieu. Paris, 1879.
Htn 42576.47.25* Viaud, Julien. Aziyadé. Paris, 1879.
38514.20.13 Villon, François. Oeuvres complètes de Villon. Paris, 1879?
FL 397.52.24 Vingtrinier, E. Le théâtre à Lyon du XVIIIe siècle. Lyon, 1879.
Mol 722.4 Vitu, Auguste. Molière et les Italiens. Paris, 1879.
Mol 853.6 Vizé, J.D. de. Oraison funebre de Molière. Paris, 1879.
Mol 853.6.2 Vizé, J.D. de. Oraison funebre de Molière. Paris, 1879.
37567.28 Werdet, Edmond. Souvenirs de la vie littéraire. Paris, 1879.
38513.33.7 Werner, R. Drei Farcen des 15. Jahrhunderts. Berlin, 1879.
42584.3.2 Zola, Emile. L'assommoir. 60. éd. Paris, 1879.
42584.3.3 Zola, Emile. L'assommoir. 74. éd. Paris, 1879.
42584.23.4 Zola, Emile. La curée. Paris, 1879.
42584.9 Zola, Emile. La faute de l'abbé Mouret. Paris, 1879.
42584.3.15 Zola, Emile. Gervaise. N.Y., 1879.
42584.13.50 Zola, Emile. Mes haines. Paris, 1879.
42584.10 Zola, Emile. Son excellence Eugène Rougon. Paris, 1879.

188-

Htn FL 398.7.24F* All about Sarah "Barnum" Bernhardt. London, 188-? 2 pam.
41522.1.5.5 Barbey d'Aurevilly, Jules. Les diaboliques. Paris, 188-?
42554.23.20 Coppée, François. Le trésor. 7. ed. Paris, 188-?
41583.28.5 Delavigne, Casimir. Louis XI. N.Y., 188-.
41538.55.15 Dumas, Alexandre. Bragelonne. N.Y., 188-?
41538.20.25 Dumas, Alexandre. The forty-five guardsmen, a sequel to La dame de Monsoreau. N.Y., 188-?

188- - cont.

41538.54.1 Dumas, Alexandre. Man in the iron mask. N.Y., 188-?
FL 382.94 Dumas, Alexandre. Souvenirs dramatiques. Paris, 188-. 2v.
41538.63.50A Dumas, Alexandre. Taking the Bastile, or Six years later. London, 188-.
41538.53.23 Dumas, Alexandre. The three guardsmen. Philadelphia, 188-?
41538.53.102 Dumas, Alexandre. Twenty years after. N.Y., 188-?
42572.22.5 Erckmann, Emile. Le juif polonais. 6. éd. Paris, 188-?
42572.23.20 Erckmann, Emile. Madame Thérèse. 37. éd. Paris, 188-.
42575.50.5 Feuillet, Octave. The sphinx. N.Y., 188-?
41572.14F Hugo, Victor. L'ârt d'être grand-père. Paris, 188-.
41573.24.5 Hugo, Victor. Cromwell. Paris, 188-?
41572.26.10 Hugo, Victor. La légende des siècles. Paris, 188-?
41572.26.12 Hugo, Victor. La légende des siècles. v.2-3. Paris, 188-? 2v.
41572.29.6 Hugo, Victor. Le roi s'amuse. Paris, 188-?
41573.26.12A Hugo, Victor. Ruy Blas. Paris, 188-.
41553.38 Kock, Charles Paul de. Le barbier de Paris. Paris, 188-.
41553.40 Kock, Charles Paul de. Un bon enfant. Paris, 188-.
41553.42 Kock, Charles Paul de. Le concierge de la rue de Bac. Paris, 188-.
41553.46 Kock, Charles Paul de. La femme, le mari et l'amant. Paris, 188-.
41553.48 Kock, Charles Paul de. Les femmes de jeu et le vin. Paris, 188-.
41553.50 Kock, Charles Paul de. Frère Jacques. Paris, 188-.
41553.52 Kock, Charles Paul de. Georgette. Paris, 188-.
41553.54 Kock, Charles Paul de. Un jeune homme mystérieux. Paris, 188-.
41553.56 Kock, Charles Paul de. Un mari perdu, l'homme à marier. Paris, 188-.
41553.58 Kock, Charles Paul de. Mon voisin Raymond. Paris, 188-.
41553.60 Kock, Charles Paul de. Monsieur Dupont. Paris, 188-.
41553.62 Kock, Charles Paul de. La pucelle de Belleville. Paris, 188-.
42555.35.40A Leconte de Lisle, C.M.R. Poèmes antiques. Paris, 188-.
42545.10.11.3 Meilhac, Henri. Froufrou. N.Y., 188-?
42545.10.11.4 Meilhac, Henri. Froufrou. N.Y., 188-?
42555.58.35 Mendès, Catulle. Le roman rouge. Paris, 188-?
40522.9.19 Prévost, Antoine F. Histoire du chevalier des Grieux et de Manon Lescaut. Paris, 188-?
38536.16.10A Rabelais, F. François Rabelais. Tout ce-qui éxiste de ses oeuvres. Paris, 188-.
38585.43.5 Racine, Jean. Phèdre. N.Y., 188-?
40576.3.11 Sainte-Beuve, Charles A. Causeries du lundi; table générale et analytique. Paris, 188-?
42556.18.3A Sully-Prudhomme, R.F.A. Oeuvres. Paris, 188-.
42582.22.10 Verne, Jules. The mysterious island abandoned. Chicago, 188-?
42582.30.2 Verne, Jules. Underground city. Philadelphia? 188-?
42582.35.18 Verne, Jules. The wreck of the chancellor. Philadelphia, 188-?
39542.31.5 Voltaire, François Marie Arouet de. Oeuvres choisies. Paris, 188-.

1880

42586.2 About, E. En petit comité. Paris, 1880.
42562.16.5A About, Edmond. Le roman d'un brave homme. Paris, 1880.
Mol 870.31 Adenis, Eugène. Diogène et Scapin. Paris, 1880.
38537.25.10 Albenas, G. d'. Les portraits de Rabelais. Montpellier, 1880.
Mol 863.22 Allart, L.F. Ode à Molière. Paris, 1880.
42553.26 Amiel, Henri F. Jour à jour. Paris, 1880.
42588.9 Amours secrétes d'une fille de plaisirs. Genève, 1880.
42542.4.3 Augier, Emile. L'aventurière. Paris, 1880.
42542.22.7 Augier, Émile. Les lionnes pauvres. Paris, 1880.
38524.12 Baïf, Jean A. de. Les mimes. Paris, 1880. 2v.
37567.137 Barbey d'Aurevilly, J. Les prophètes du passé. Paris, 1880.
41574.22 Barbou, Alfred. Victor Hugo. Paris, 1880.
38546.5 Barthélemy, Édouard. Sapho le mage de Sidon. Zenocrate. Paris, 1880.
42542.29.29.5F Bernhardt, S. (Mme.). In the clouds. N.Y., 1880.
FL 398.7.26F Bernhardt, Sarah. Sarah Bernhardt souvenir. N.Y., 1880.
42563.28.27 Biart, Lucien. La capitana. Paris, 1880.
42563.28.17 Biart, Lucien. An involuntary voyage. N.Y., 1880.
42563.23.10 Blanc, Thérèse. Yette, histoire d'une jeune créole. Paris, 1880.
42541.7 Bornier, Henri de. Noces d'Attila. Fille de Roland. Paris, 1880.
42542.29.139 Bornier, Henri de. Les noces d'Attila. 3. ed. Paris, 1880.
37561.15 Boucherie, A. La langue et la littérature françaises au moyen âge. Paris, 1880.
FL 398.9 Bouffé, Marie. Mes souvenirs, 1800-1880. Paris, 1880.
Mol 728.12 Bouquet, F. La troupe de Molière et les deux Corneille a Rouen en 1658. Paris, 1880.
38526.3.7.100 Bourdigné, C. La légende de Pierre Faifeu. Paris, 1880.
42563.38.12 Bouvier, Alexis. Mademoiselle Olympe. Paris, 1880.
FL 364.75 Boysse, E. Le théâtre de Jésuites. Paris, 1880.
38576.8 Brécourt, G.M. de. L'ombre de Molière. Paris, 1880.
Mol 855.7 Brecourt. L'ombre de Molière. Paris, 1880.
37595.30 Bretel, Jean. Les chansons publiées par G. Raynaud. Paris, 1880.
42542.47.30 Brieux, Eugène. Bernard Palissy. Paris, 1880.
37557.14 Brunetière, F. Études critiques sur l'histoire de la littérature française. Paris, 1880.
42563.39.200 Buet, C. Légendes du pays de Savoie. Limoges, 1880.
FL 396.4 Buguet, Henry. Foyers et coulisses. Ambigu-comique. Paris, 1880.
38526.10.8.22 Buttet, M.C. de. Oeuvres poétiques. v.1-2. Paris, 1880.
FL 396.41.2 Campardon, E. Les comédiens du roi de la troupe italienne. Paris, 1880. 2v.
42587.39 Cantacuzène-Altieri, Olga. Poverina. Paris, 1880.
37565.32 Caro, E. La fin du dix-huitième siècle. Paris, 1880. 2v.
40546.8 Caussade, François de. Oeuvres de P.L. Courier. Paris, 1880.
40516.6.1.2 Cazotte, Jacques. Contes de J. Cazotte. Paris, 1880.
40516.6 Cazotte, Jacques. Contes de J. Cazotte. Paris, 1880.
40516.6.6 Cazotte, Jacques. Le diable amoureux. Paris, 1880.
Htn 38527.34* Ceriziers, R. de. The triumphant lady or The crowned innocence. London, 1880.

1880 - cont.

42561.24 Chandeneux, Claire de. L'automne d'une femme. Paris, 1880.
42561.30 Chandeneux, Claire de. Les mariages de Garnison. Paris, 1880.
42561.31 Chandeneux, Claire de. Les ménages militaires. Paris, 1880. 4v.
37566.26 Charpentier, P. Une maladie morale, le mal du siècle. Paris, 1880.
42565.5 Cherbuliez, Victor. Amours fragiles. Paris, 1880.
42565.17 Cherbuliez, Victor. L'idée de Jean Têterol. Paris, 1880.
42565.31 Cherbuliez, Victor. Samuel Brohl et Cie. Paris, 1880.
Mol 850.1 Cheron, E.S. La coupe de Val de Grace. Paris, 1880.
39533.19 Chéron, E.S. La coupe du Val de Grace. Paris, 1880.
42542.50 Chriecki, K.E. Zephyrin Cazavan en Egypte. Paris, 1880.
38527.35 Christie, R.C. Etienne Dolet. London, 1880.
42565.55.54 Cladel, Léon. Crête-rouge. Paris, 1880.
42565.55.60 Cladel, Léon. Par devant notaire. Bruxelles, 1880.
40517.1.20 Cochin, C.N. Mémoires inédits de Charles Nicolas Cochin sur le comte de Caylus. Paris, 1880.
41593.17 Colet, Louise. Lui. Paris, 1880.
40531.4.50 La confession générale d'Audinot. Rouen, 1880.
Mol 863.23 Coppée, F. La maison de Molière. Paris, 1880.
42554.22 Coppée, François. Contes en vers et poésies diverses. Paris, 1880.
40534.34.7 Crébillon, Claude Prosper Jolyot de. Le hazard du coin du feu. Bruxelles, 1880.
42566.24.5 Daudet, Alphonse. Fromont jeune et Risler ainé. 58. éd. Paris, 1880.
42566.24.25 Daudet, Alphonse. Kings in exile. Boston, 1880.
42566.19.8.90 Daudet, Alphonse. The prodigious adventures of Tartarin of Tarascon. Boston, 1880.
42566.36 Daudet, Alphonse. Théâtre. Paris, 1880.
42561.16 Daudet, Ernest. Robert Darnetal. Paris, 1880.
40535.6 Defrémery, Charles. Note bibliographique et littéraire. Destouches Le Philosophe marié, Paris, 1880.
41583.27.20 Delavigne, Casimir. Les enfants d'Édouard. London, 1880?
37555.320 Della Rocca de Vergalo, N.A. La poétique nouvelle. 2. éd. Paris, 1880.
42586.35 Delpit, Albert. Le fils de Coralie. Paris, 1880.
42542.64.1100 Descamps, Frederic. Le billet rose. Mons, 1880.
40528.5 Desforges-Maillard, Paul. Poésies diverses. Paris, 1880.
40566.3 Doudan, Ximénès. Pensées, essais et maximes. Paris, 1880.
42542.66.10 Dreyfus, A. Scènes de la vie de théâtre. Paris, 1880.
42568.9 Droz, Gustave. Une femme gênante. Paris, 1880.
42568.12 Droz, Gustave. Un paquet de lettres. Paris, 1880.
42568.18.5 Du Boisgobey, Fortuné. Le crime de l'opéra. v.1-2. Paris, 1880.
42543.16.10 Dumas, Alexandre. Camille or The fate of a coquette. Philadelphia, 1880.
42543.16.7.2A Dumas, Alexandre. La dame aux camélias. (Camille). N.Y., 1880.
42543.15.12A Dumas, Alexandre. La dame aux camélias. N.Y., 1880.
42543.16.6 Dumas, Alexandre. La dame aux camélias. N.Y., 1880.
42543.16.7A Dumas, Alexandre. La dame aux camélias. N.Y., 1880.
42543.19.2 Dumas, Alexandre. L'étrangère. Paris, 1880.
42543.19.9 Dumas, Alexandre. Les femmes qui tuent et les femmes qui votent. 22. éd. Paris, 1880.
42543.11 Dumas, Alexandre. Théâtre complet. v.3-6. Paris, 1880-85. 4v.
NEDL 42543.7 Dumas, Alexandre. Théâtre complet. 5. série. Paris, 1880.
NEDL 42543.8 Dumas, Alexandre. Théâtre complet. 6. série. Paris, 1880.
42543.27.5 Dumas, Alexandre. La vie à vingt ans. v.1-2. Paris, 1880.
42563.44 Durand, Alice M.C.F. Cité Ménard. Paris, 1880.
42563.45 Durand, Alice M.C.F. Dosia. Paris, 1880.
42563.48 Durand, Alice M.C.F. L'héritage de Xénie. Paris, 1880.
42563.50 Durand, Alice M.C.F. Lucie Rodey. Paris, 1880.
42563.52 Durand, Alice M.C.F. Marier sa fille. Paris, 1880.
42563.55 Durand, Alice M.C.F. Nouvelles russes. Paris, 1880.
42563.56 Durand, Alice M.C.F. La princesse Oghérof. Paris, 1880.
42563.58 Durand, Alice M.C.F. Suzanne Normis. Paris, 1880.
42563.59 Durand, Alice M.C.F. Un violon russe. Paris, 1880. 2v.
42542.72.5 Duru, A. La fille du Tambour major. Paris, 1880.
FL 391.10 Du Tralage, J.N. de. Notes et documents sur l'histoire des théâtres de Paris par Jacob. Paris, 1880.
41584.32.34 Duveyrier, A.H.J. Sullivan. N.Y., 1880.
42513.30.30 Favre, Jules. Henry Belval. Paris, 1880.
FL 395.43F Febvre, F. Album de la comédie française. Paris, 1880.
38525.8 Fehse, Hermann. Estienne Jodelle's Lyrik. Oppeln, 1880.
38544.25 Ferrand, Anne B. Lettres au Baron de Breteuil. Paris, 1880.
42554.35.5 Fertraul, Marie. Bonheur rêvé. Paris, 1880?
42575.31 Feuillet, Octave. Le journal d'une femme. Paris, 1880.
42575.38.5 Feuillet, Octave. Monsieur de Camors. 25. éd. Paris, 1880.
42575.27.10 Feuillet, Octave. Le sphinx. N.Y., 1880.
37578.48.2 Finod, J. de. A thousand flashes of French wit, wisdom. N.Y., 1880.
42586.51 Fistié, Camille. L'amour au village. Paris, 1880.
FL 397.75.5 Fleary, Edouard. Origines et développements de l'art théâtral dans la province ecclésiastique de Reims. Laon, 1880.
37595.35 Foerster, Wendelin. Altfranzösische Bibliothek. Heilbroun, 1880. 13v.
37596.29 Foerster, Wendelin. De Venus la deesse d'amor. Bonn, 1880.
37594.5 Gauthier, Jules. Un poème franc-comtois inédit du XIIIe siècle. Besancon, 1880.
42525.5 Gautier, Leon. Portraits contemporains et questions actuelles. Paris, 1880.
41542.22 Gautier, Théophile. Fusains et eaux-fortes. Paris, 1880.
42576.64 Giron, Alfred. Histoire d'une ferme. Paris, 1880.
37585.4 Godefroy, Frédéric. Théâtre classique. Paris, 1880.
42576.9 Godefroy, Louis. Récits Champenois et Briards. Paris, 1880.
42543.54.13 Gondinet, Edmond. Jean de Nivelle; opéra-comique. Paris, 1880.
42543.54.9 Gondinet, Edmond. Johathan. 2d éd. Paris, 1880.
41542.38 Gozlan, Léon. Aristide Froissart. Paris, 1880.
41542.56 Gozlan, Léon. La pluie et le beau temps. Paris, 1880.
38546.49 Grignan, Françoise M. Lettres. Paris, 1880.
38526.13.4 Groebedinkel, P. Der Versbau bei Philippe Desportes und François de Malherbe. Altenburg, 1880.
40545.20.10 Gubernatis, A. de. Il Manzoni ed il Fauriel. Roma, 1880.
FL 366.26 Guichard, A. De la législation du théâtre en France. Paris, 1880.

1880 - cont.

Mol 860.37.3 Gutzkow, Karl. Das Urbild des Tartüffe. Jena, 1880.
38524.13 Hémard, Le Sieur. Les restes de la Guerre d'Estampes. Paris, 1880.
Htn 42543.62.89* Hennique, Léon. Les hauts faits de M. de Ponthau. Paris, 1880.
37594.17 Henri d'Andeli. Oeuvres. Rouen, 1880.
42576.67 Hervieu, Paul. L'alpe homicide. Paris, 1880.
42584.28 Hetzel, P.J. Les méfaits de Palichinelle. Paris, 1880.
Htn 38537.25.95* Holmes, Oliver. To the honorary secretaries of the Rabelais club. Letter, 21 mr. 1880. n.p., 1880.
37597.11.7 Hormel, H. Untersuchung über die Chronique Ascendante. Inaug. Diss. Marburg, 1880.
Htn FL 394.84.2PF* Houssaye, A. La comédie française, 1680-1880. Paris, 1880.
FL 394.84PF Houssaye, A. La comédie française, 1680-1880. Paris, 1880.
41573.32.26 Hugo, Victor. Angelo. London, 1880.
41573.32.7.10 Hugo, Victor. Hernani. N.Y., 1880.
41573.35.5 Hugo, Victor. Odes et ballades. Paris, 1880.
41573.42 Hugo, Victor. Oeuvres complètes. Paris, 1880. 48v.
41573.41 Hugo, Victor. Oeuvres complètes. v.1-23,25-48. v.24 lost 1963. Paris, 1880. 48v.
41573.24.25 Hugo, Victor. Religions et religion. 12. éd. Paris, 1880.
Htn 38537.25.100* Hugo, Victor. To the members of the Rabelais Club. Letter dated 10 April, 1880. n.p., 1880.
42525.10 Hugues, Edmond. Essais de littérature et d'histoire. Paris, 1880.
39526.29 Jannet, Pierre. Fables de La Fontaine. v.1-2. Paris, 1880.
42526.3 Lacour, Léopold. Trois théâtres. Paris, 1880.
41551.7 Lacroix, Paul. Contes du bibliophile Jacob. Paris, 1880.
39526.29.4 La Fontaine, Jean de. Fables. Paris, 1880.
42576.68 Lamothe, Alexandre. Mémoires d'un déporté. Paris, 1880.
42514.26.5 Lanfrey, P. Les lettres d'Everard. Paris, 1880.
38543.10.27 La Rochefoucauld, François. Maximes et réfléxions morales. Paris, 1880.
38563.25 Larroque, P.T. de. Les correspondants de Peiresc. Marseille, 1880-91. 5v.
Mol 612.15 Lecocq, G. Molière et la comédie en province. Paris, 1880.
FL 397.70 Lecocq, Georges. Histoire du théâtre en Picardie. Paris, 1880.
42555.36.20 Leconte de Lisle, C.M.R. Kain. V Praze, 1880.
42548.45 Legouvé, Ernest. Théâtre de campagne. ser. 6. Paris, 1880.
FL 398.49.29 Lemaitre, Frédérick. Souvenirs de Frédérick Lemaitre. 2d ed. Paris, 1880.
42576.42.25 Lermina, Jules. Les mariages maudits. Paris, 1880.
42544.34.6.50F Leroy, Louis. Les pensionnaires du Louvre. Paris, 1880.
41596.53.55 Le Roy de Sainte Croix, François Noël. Le chant de guerre pour l'armée du Rhin ou la Marseillaise. Strasbourg, 1880.
40512.34.2 LeSage, Alain René. Historia de Gil Blas de Santillana. N.Y., 1880.
38537.9 Ligier, Hermann. La politique de Rabelais. Paris, 1880.
37557.18A Littré, E. Études et Glanures. Paris, 1880.
Mol 712.6A Lotheissen, F. Molière: Leben und Werke. Frankfurt, 1880.
38527.61.5 Magny, Olivier de. Dernières poésies. Paris, 1880.
40531.21 Marchand, J.H. Le vindangeur sensible. L'assommoire du XVIII siècle. Paris, 1880.
X Cg FL 390.50 Matthews, Brander. The theatres of Paris. N.Y., 1880.
FL 390.50 Matthews, Brander. The theatres of Paris. N.Y., 1880.
FL 384.57 Mayer, M.L. The gayety French plays. London, 1880.
42545.10.11.9 Meilhac, Henri. Froufrou. N.Y., 1880.
42545.10.11.5 Meilhac, Henri. Froufrou. N.Y., 1880.
42545.10.11.6 Meilhac, Henri. Froufrou. 8. éd. Paris, 1880.
42555.58.1200 Mérat, Albert. Poèmes de Paris. Paris, 1880.
41555.23.1 Mérimée, Prosper. Colomba. Paris, 1880.
40537.67 Les moines. Rouen, 1880.
Mol 150.15F Molière, Jean Baptiste Paquelin. Psyché...Bocher. Paris, 1880.
Mol 62.28 Molière, Jean Baptiste Poquelin. Ausgewählte Lustspiele...Laun. Leipzig, 1880?
Mol 60.20.4 Molière, Jean Baptiste Poquelin. The dramatic works of Molière. v.2-3. N.Y., 1880. 2v.
Mol 221.10 Molière, Jean Baptiste Poquelin. L'impromptu de Versailles. Paris, 1880.
Mol 246.41.5 Molière, Jean Baptiste Poquelin. Le misanthrope "en" Amphitryon. Antoine Ooms. Deventer, 1880.
Mol 18.80.5 Molière, Jean Baptiste Poquelin. Oeuvres...Sainte-Beuve. Paris, 1880.
Mol 18.80.2 Molière, Jean Baptiste Poquelin. Oeuvres complètes...Moland. 2e éd. Paris, 1880-85. 12v.
Mol 18.80 Molière, Jean Baptiste Poquelin. Oeuvres complètes...Moland. 2e éd. Paris, 1880-85. 12v.
Mol 255.13 Molière, Jean Baptiste Poquelin. Les plaisirs de l'isle enchantée (princesse d'Élide). Lacour. Paris, 1880.
Mon 18.80.2 Montaigne, Michel de. Essays. 4. ed. London, 1880.
42587.50.58 Monteiro Ramalho. As ratices da Rattazi; o pello nacional. Porto, 1880.
39594.13.2 Montesquieu, C.L. de S. Lettres persanes. v.1-2. Paris, 1880-
37591.20 Montille, Léone de. Cronicques de Girart de Roussilou. Paris, 1880.
41596.34.15 Musset, Alfred de. The poet and the muse. London, 1880.
37574.530 Nadaud, G. La chanson depuis Béranger. Paris, 1880.
42545.45.5 Najac, Emile de. Babie; a comedy in three acts. Boston, 1880.
38526.32.2 Navarre, M. de. Heptaméron. Paris, 1880. 3v.
38526.32A Navarre, M. de. Heptaméron. Paris, 1880. 4v.
Mol 825.8 Nivelet, F. Molière et Gui Patin. Paris, 1880.
Mol 714.2 Noël, Eugène. Molière, son théâtre et son ménage. Paris, 1880.
Mol 270.15 Norman, H. Klassische Dichterwerke. Stuttgart, 1880.
FL 371.15A Petit de Julleville, L. Les mystères (histoire au théâtre en France). v.1-2. Paris, 1880. 2v.
38513.33 Picot, Emile. Nouveau recueil de farces françaises des XVe et XVIe siècles. Paris, 1880.
37573.580 Ploetz, K. Manuel de litterature française. 6. éd. Berlin, 1880.
FL 395.240 Poinsot, E.A. La comédie française à Londres, 1871-1879. Paris, 1880.
42555.72.9 Pomairols, Charles de. Rêves et pensées. Paris, 1880.
42534.14.2 Pons, A.J. Coups de plume indépendants. 2. éd. Paris, 1880.
38514.55.9 Les quinze joyes de mariage. Paris, 1880.

1880 - cont.

38537.33.20 Rabelais, F. Rabelais Gargantus und Pantagruel. Leipzig, 1880. 2v.
38585.43.7.5 Racine, Jean. Phaedra. N.Y., 1880.
38585.53 Racine, Jean. Théâtre. Paris, 1880. 3v.
38583.6.5 Racine, Jean. Théâtre. Paris, 1880. 3v.
42587.50.45 Rattazzi, Marie Bonaparte-Wyse. O reverso da medalha. Porto, 1880.
37596.48 Reinbrecht, August. Legends von den sieben Schläfern. Göttingen, 1880.
42515.30.130 Renan, Ernest. Conférences d'Angleterre Rome et le Christianisme Marc-Aurèle. Paris, 1880.
42515.30.132 Renan, Ernest. Conférences d'Angleterre Rome et le Christianisme Marc-Aurèle. 2. éd. Paris, 1880.
42515.30.152A Renan, Ernest. English conferences. Boston, 1880.
42515.30.150A Renan, Ernest. Lectures on the influence of the institutions. London, 1880.
Mol 775.5 Richard-Desaix, W. La relique de Molière du cabinet du baron Vivant Denon. Paris, 1880.
38512.16 Riese, Julius. Recherches sur l'usage syntaxique de Froissart. Halle, 1880.
FL 6128.80 Ritter, E. La famille de Jean-Jacques Rousseau. Genève, 1880.
FL 6029.3 Ritter, E. Nouvelles recherches; confessions et correspondance de Rousseau. Oppeln, 1880.
39586.25 Rivarol, Antoine. Oeuvres choisis de A. Rivarol. Paris, 1880. 2v.
Mol 870.30.9 Rivet, Gustave. Le cimetière de Saint Joseph. Paris, 1880.
42587.56 Rochefort, Henry. L'évadé. 2. éd. Paris, 1880.
42558.42.30 Ronchaud, Louis de. Le filleul de la mort. Paris, 1880.
37596.149 Rose, H. Über die Metrik der Chronik Fantosmès. Bonn, 1880.
Mol 698.10F St. Amand, D. de. Une visite de Molière chez Fouquet. n.p., 1880.
42578.31.125 Saint-Juirs. J'ai tué ma femme. 4. éd. Paris, 1880.
42535.21.2 Saint-Victor, Paul de. Les deux masques. Paris, 1880-84. 3v.
Htn 40575.14* Sainte-Beuve, Charles A. Le clou d'or la pendule. Paris, 1880.
40575.7A Sainte-Beuve, Charles A. Nouvelle correspondance. Paris, 1880.
37556.8 Sainte-Croix, le roy de (pseud.). L'Alsacien qui rit, boit, chante, et danse. Paris, 1880.
37543.21 Saintsbury, George. Primer of French literature. Oxford, 1880.
37543.20.9A Saintsbury, George. Primer of French literature. Oxford, 1880.
41557.9.15 Sand, George. Adriani. Paris, 1880.
41557.8.84.10 Sand, George. Isidora. Paris, 1880.
41557.9.68 Sand, George. Souvenirs de 1848. Paris, 1880.
41578.52 Sanvert, P.A. Notes sur la poésie religieuse de Lamartine. Macon, 1880.
42546.23 Sardou, Victorien. Andrea. Paris, 1880.
42541.34 Sardou, Victorien. Daniel Rochat. Paris, 1880.
42546.23.30 Sardou, Victorien. Daniel Rochat. 4e ed. Paris, 1880.
42541.34.2 Sardou, Victorien. Daniel Rochat. 9. éd. Paris, 1880.
42546.24.4 Sardou, Victorien. Divorçons. N.Y., 1880.
39534.29.6 Scarron, Paul. Le roman comique. Paris, 1880. 3v.
39534.29 Scarron, Paul. Le roman comique. Paris, 1880. 2v.
39566.13A Scherer, E. Diderot. Paris, 1880.
37596.44.9 Schmidt, Adolf. Guillaume, le clerc de Normandie. Bonn, 1880.
37596.154 Schwan, E. Philippe de Rimi...und seine Werke. Bonn, 1880.
41588.3.7 Scribe, Eugène. Adrienne Lecouvreur. N.Y., 1880.
41588.14.8 Scribe, Eugène. Le verre d'eau. Cambridge, 1880.
42587.58 Ségur, Sophie. La soeur de Gribonille. Paris, 1880.
38546.36.20 Sévigné, Marie de R.C. Le premier texte des lettres de Mme. de Sévigné, réimpression de l'édition de 1725. Paris, 1880.
Htn 37576.525* Les soirees de médan. Paris, 1880.
41586.30.12.2 Soumet, A. The gladiator...performed by Salvini. N.Y., 1880.
40597.2.8.10 Spoelberch de Lovenjoul, Charles. Un dernier chapitre de l'histoire des oeuvres de H. de Balzac. Paris, 1880.
42587.59.20 Stapleaux, Leopold. Histoire d'une nuit. 4. éd. Paris, 1880.
42587.59.19 Stapleaux, Leopold. Les viveuses de Paris. Paris, 1880.
42583.18 Theuriet, André. Le fils Maugars. Paris, 1880.
42583.29 Theuriet, André. Sous-bois. Paris, 1880.
42583.30 Theuriet, André. Toute seule. Paris, 1880.
42578.48 Thiaudière, Edmond. Le roman d'un bossu. Paris, 1880.
Mol 230.7 Thierry, É. Documents sur le Malade imaginaire. Paris, 1880.
37555.301 Tobler, A. Vom Französischen Versbau alter und neuer Zeit. Leipzig, 1880.
Mol 810.4 Tralage, J.N. du. Notes et documents sur l'histoire des théâtres de Paris au XVIIe siècle. Paris, 1880.
42578.58 Uchard, Mario. Inès Parker. Paris, 1880.
41565.36 Vacquerie, Auguste. Jean Baudry. Paris, 1880.
42557.9 Valade, Léon. Nocturnes. Paris, 1880.
42578.63 Vast, Raoul. Séraphin et cie. Paris, 1880.
42582.25.100 Verne, Jules. The tribulations of a Chinaman in China. Boston, 1880.
42582.27.10 Verne, Jules. Twenty thousand leagues under the sea. N.Y., 1880?
42546.31.20 Vibert, P. Affaire Sardou. Paris, 1880.
Mol 740.3 Vitu, Auguste. La maison mortuaire de Molière. Paris, 1880.
Mol 740.3.2 Vitu, Auguste. La maison mortuaire de Molière. Paris, 1880.
42522.11 Vogüé, E.M. de. Histoires orientales. Paris, 1880.
37558.2 Voisenon, Claude Henri de. Anecdotes littéraires. Paris, 1880.
39545.70 Voltaire, François Marie Arouet de. Le Sottisier. Paris, 1880.
FL 380.10 Welschinger, Henri. Le théâtre de la révolutionnaire. Paris, 1880.
Mol 623.4 Wilke, W. Ce que Molière doit aux anciens poètes français. Lauban, 1880.
Mol 197.7 Willenberg, G. Analyse et examen de l'École des femmes. Gotha, 1880.
42584.10.2 Zola, Emile. Clorinda, or The rise of Eugène Rougon. Philadelphia, 1880.
42584.8 Zola, Emile. La conquête de Plassans. Paris, 1880.
42584.12.22 Zola, Emile. Nana. 28. éd. Paris, 1880.

1880 - cont.

42584.21 Zola, Emile. Théâtre. Paris, 1880.

1881

42562.16 About, Edmond. Le roman d'un brave homme. Paris, 1881.
42512.3 Albert, Paul. Poètes et poésies. Paris, 1881.
37578.58 Almanach du monde plaisant 1881. Paris, 1881.
37567.131 Amicis, Edmondo de. Ritratti letterari. 2a ed. Milano, 1881.
42586.11 Assollant, A. Aventures de Capitaine Corcoran. Paris, 1881. 2v.
38524.31 Baïf, Jean A. de. Oeuvres en rime. Paris, 1881-5v.
Mol 240.5 Baluffe, A. Le médecin volant de M. à Pézenas. Paris, 1881.
40597.19.2 Balzac, Honoré de. Eugénie Grandet. Paris, 1881.
40597.31.10 Balzac, Honoré de. Modeste Mignon. Paris, 1881.
40597.30.15 Balzac, Honoré de. Petites misères de la vie conjugale. Paris, 1881.
37555.99 Banville, T. de. Petit traité de poésie française. Paris, 1881.
42554.6 Banville, Théodore de. Contes pour les femmes. Paris, 1881.
42554.8.6 Banville, Théodore de. Gringoire. 2e éd. Berlin, 1881.
41522.1 Barbey d'Aurevilly, Jules. Un prêtre marié. Paris, 1881. 2v.
41522.1.1 Barbey d'Aurevilly, Jules. Un prêtre marié. Paris, 1881. 2v.
41574.22.5 Barbou, Alfred. Victor Hugo; his life and works. Chicago, 1881.
41574.22.4 Barbou, Alfred. Victor Hugo et son temps. Paris, 1881.
42554.33.10 Battier, A.F. Sous les bambous. Paris, 1881.
40527.9 Becq de Fouquières, L. Lettres critiques sur la vie, d'André Chenier. Paris, 1881.
37596.11A Berneville, G. La vie de Saint Gilles. Paris, 1881.
FL 6128.81 Berthoud, F. Jean-Jacques Rousseau au val-de-travers, 1762-1765. Paris, 1881.
38527.11 Blanchemain, Prosper. Premières satires de Du Lorens. Paris, 1881.
42542.29.135 Bornier, Henri de. Poésies complètes (1850-1881). Paris, 1881.
38557.53.200.45 Bossuet, J.B. Maximes et réfléxions sur la comédie. Photoreproduction. Paris, 1881.
Mol 266.5 Bourrelly, Marius. Lou Sicilian de Molière. Ais, 1881.
37556.21.7 Breyne-Dubois, G. de. Ce qu'il y a dans une collection de journaux. Bruxelles, 1881.
FL 396.90.2 Buguet, Henry. Foyers et coulisses; histoire anecdotique de tous les théâtres de Paris. Variétés. Paris, 1881.
FL 396.90.9 Buguet, Henry. Foyers et coulisses; histoire anecdotique des théâtres de Paris. Vaudeville. Paris, 1881.
42562.41 Celières, Paul. Chef-d'oeuvre de Papa Schmeltz. Paris, 1881.
42562.43 Celières, Paul. Une heure à lire. Paris, 1881.
42561.32 Chandeneux, Claire de. Secondes noces. Paris, 1881.
FL 397.7 Charvet, E. Recherches sur les anciens théâtres de Beauvais. Beauvais, 1881.
42586.30.5 Chazel, Prosper. Histoire d'un forestier. Paris, 1881.
42565.21.20 Cherbuliez, Victor. Noirs et rouges. Paris, 1881.
42565.22 Cherbuliez, Victor. Noirs et rouges. 5. éd. Paris, 1881.
Mol 825.9.2 Chereau, A. Le médecin de Molière. Paris, 1881.
Mol 825.9 Chereau, A. Le médecin de Molière. Paris, 1881.
42565.55.15 Cladel, Léon. Les va-nu-pieds. Paris, 1881.
42586.31.2 Claretié, J. Les amours d'un interne. Paris, 1881.
42586.31.31 Claretié, J. Monsieur le ministre. 15. éd. Paris, 1881.
Mol 247.13A Coquelin, C. Molière et le misanthrope. Paris, 1881.
38575.35 Corneille, Pierre. Sertorius. Paris, 1881.
38576.12.42.10 Corneille, Thomas. Théâtre complet. Paris, 1881.
40534.33.9 Crébillon, Claude Prosper Jolyot de. Nuit et le moment ou Les matins de Cynthère. Bruxelles, 1881.
40534.34.9 Crébillon, Claude Prosper Jolyot de. Le sopha, conte moral. Bruxelles, 1881.
42542.54.9 Crémieux, Hector. Le petit Faust. Paris, 1881.
42566.21.5 Daudet, Alphonse. Contes du lundi. Paris, 1881.
42566.29.15 Daudet, Alphonse. Le Nabab. Paris, 1881.
42566.30 Daudet, Alphonse. Numa Roumestan. Paris, 1881.
42566.30.7A Daudet, Alphonse. Numa Roumestan. 17. éd. Paris, 1881.
41583.22.15 Delavigne, Casimir. Oeuvres complètes. Paris, 1881. 3v.
42554.29.4 Déroulède, Paul. Chants du soldat. 62e éd. Paris, 1881.
42542.64 Déroulède, Paul. La moabite. Paris, 1881.
42576.66.5 D'Hericault, C. Aventures de deux parisiennes. Paris, 1881.
Mol 870.32 d'Hervilly, E. Poquelin père et fils. Paris, 1881.
39564.7 Diderot, Denis. Morceaux choisis. Paris, 1881.
38576.13 Donneau de Vizé, Jean. La veuve à la mode. Paris, 1881.
42554.28 Dorchain, Auguste. La jeunesse pensive. Paris, 1881.
42554.28.7 Dorchain, Auguste. Oeuvres. Paris, 1881.
42568.2.75 Double, A.M.A. Carnet d'un mondain, gazette parisienne. Paris, 1881-1882. 2v.
40566.3.5 Doudan, Ximénès. Pensées et fragments. Paris, 1881.
42568.19.12 Du Boisgobey, Fortuné. The lost casket. Paris, 1881.
41523.3 Dumas, Alexandre. Acté. Paris, 1881.
41523.6 Dumas, Alexandre. Ascanio. Paris, 1881.
41523.7 Dumas, Alexandre. Aventure d'amour. Paris, 1881.
41523.13 Dumas, Alexandre. La bouillie de la comtesse Berthe. Paris, 1881.
41523.15 Dumas, Alexandre. Bric-a-Brac. Paris, 1881.
41523.17A Dumas, Alexandre. Capitaine Pamphile. Paris, 1881.
41523.18 Dumas, Alexandre. Capitaine Paul. Paris, 1881.
41523.23 Dumas, Alexandre. Cécile. Paris, 1881.
42543.16.5.5 Dumas, Alexandre. La dame aux camélias. Paris, 1881.
41538.21.10 Dumas, Alexandre. Edmund Kean. n.p., 1881.
42543.19.3 Dumas, Alexandre. L'étrangère. N.Y., 1881.
41524.20 Dumas, Alexandre. Femme au Collier de Velours. Paris, 1881.
41524.21 Dumas, Alexandre. Fernande. Paris, 1881.
42543.19.15 Dumas, Alexandre. Filles, Lorettes et Courtisanes. Paris, 1881.
41525.3 Dumas, Alexandre. Le fils du forçat. Paris, 1881.
41525.8 Dumas, Alexandre. Georges. Paris, 1881.
41526.9 Dumas, Alexandre. Jacques Ortis. Paris, 1881.
41526.17 Dumas, Alexandre. Madame de Chamblay. Paris, 1881.
41526.19 Dumas, Alexandre. Le maitre d'Armes. Paris, 1881.
41527.3 Dumas, Alexandre. Les mille et un fontomes. Paris, 1881.
41527.6 Dumas, Alexandre. Napoléon. Paris, 1881.
42543.24.3 Dumas, Alexandre. La princesse Georges. N.Y., 1881.

1881 - cont.

41527.21 Dumas, Alexandre. La régence. Paris, 1881.
41528.5 Dumas, Alexandre. Sylvandire. Paris, 1881.
42543.25.15 Dumas, Alexandre. Une visite de noces. 10e éd. Paris, 1881.
42563.41 Durand, Alice M.C.F. Ariadne. Paris, 1881.
42563.55.15 Durand, Alice M.C.F. Les degrés de l'échelle. 8. éd. Paris, 1881.
42563.45.6 Durand, Alice M.C.F. Dosia. Boston, 1881.
42563.46 Durand, Alice M.C.F. Les épreuves de Raïssa. Paris, 1881.
42563.53 Durand, Alice M.C.F. Le moulin frappier. Paris, 1881. 2v.
42563.55.2 Durand, Alice M.C.F. Perdue. Paris, 1881.
42563.57 Durand, Alice M.C.F. Sonia. Paris, 1881.
42542.72 Duru, A. La mascotte. Paris, 1881.
38512.15 Ebering, Emil. Syntaktische Studien zu Froissart. Halle, 1881.
42574.22 Fabre, Ferdinand. Mon oncle Célestin. Paris, 1881.
38553.27.10 Fénelon, F. de S. de la Mothe. Aventures de Télémaque. N.Y., 1881.
42575.29 Feuillet, Octave. Histoire d'une parisienne. Paris, 1881.
42575.29.2 Feuillet, Octave. Histoire d'une parisienne. 12. éd. Paris, 1881.
37578.48 Finod, J. de. A thousand flashes of French wit, wisdom. N.Y., 1881.
42576.18A Flaubert, Gustave. Bouvard et Pécuchet. Paris, 1881.
40535.32A Fleury, Jean. Marivaux et le Marivaudage. Paris, 1881.
Mol 855.11.3 La folle querelle. Jacob. Paris, 1881.
38587.16 La folle querelle ou La critique d'Andromaque. Paris, 1881.
42543.31 Fournier, Marc. Le monde et la comédie. Paris, 1881.
42576.63.7 France, Anatole. Le crime de Sylvestre Bonnard. Paris, 1881.
42571.32.4 Gaboriau, Emile. Monsieur Lecoq. Paris, 1881-1882. 2v.
42525.6 Gautier, Leon. Portraits littéraires. Paris, 1881.
X Cg 41542.26.12 Gautier, Théophile. Les jeunes-France. Paris, 1881.
41542.23 Gautier, Théophile. Loin de Paris. Paris, 1881.
39586.7 Gay, Jean. Anecdotes piquantes de Bachaumont. Bruxelles, 1881.
37565.97.5 Géruzez, Eugéne. Histoire de la littérature française pendant la révolution. 7. éd. Paris, 1881.
FL 398.79.15 Gonzalès, E. Les caravanes de Scaromouche. Paris, 1881.
40535.31.5 Gossot, Emile. Marivaux moraliste. Paris, 1881.
42554.49.50 Guaita, Stanislas de. Oiseaux de passage. Paris, 1881.
FL 395.44 Gueullette, C. Acteurs and actrices du temps passé. Paris, 1881.
42576.40.380 Halévy, Ludovic. Un mariage d'amour. Paris, 1881.
38514.66 Hannappel, M. Poetik Alain Chartiers. Altenburg, 1881.
42515.42 Heath, Richard. Edgar Quinet. London, 1881.
42543.62.93 Hennique, Léon. Pierrot Sceptique. Paris, 1881.
42524.25 Huber-Saladin, J. Le comte de Circourt. Paris, 1881.
42524.24A Huber-Saladin, J. Le comte de Circourt. Paris, 1881.
41573.32.8 Hugo, Victor. Hernani. N.Y., 1881?
41572.28.11 Hugo, Victor. Les orientales. Les feuilles d'automne. Les chants du crépuscule. Paris, 1881.
Htn 41571.28* Hugo, Victor. Les quatre vents de l'esprit. Paris, 1881. 2v.
40516.62 Jacob, P.L. Madame de Kruedener. Paris, 1881.
FL 398.17.3 Janin, Jules. Deburau. Paris, 1881.
37567.29.2 Jaubert, Caroline. Souvenirs de Madame Caroline Jaubert; lettres et correspondances. Paris, 1881.
37596.19 Jean de Tuim. Li hystore de Julius César. Halle, 1881.
38523.32 Johannesson, Fritz. Die Bestrebungen Malherbes. Halle, 1881.
41544.3 Karr, Alphonse. Les cailloux blancs du Petit Poucet. Paris, 1881.
37558.32 Kerviler, René. Les trois cardinaux de Rohan (de l'Académie Française). Nantes, 1881.
38527.14 Kerviler, René. Valentin Conrart. Paris, 1881.
Mol 815.8 Kreutzinger, K. Das Precieusenthum und Molière. Jagendorf, 1881. 2 pam.
38564.30.5 La Bruyère, J. de. Les caractères. Paris, 1881. 2v.
41577.13 Lamartine, Alphonse de. Correspondance. Paris, 1881.
41577.21 Lamartine, Alphonse de. Mémoires inédits de Lamartine, 1790-1815. Paris, 1881.
42555.14 Laprade, Victor de. Oeuvres poétiques. Paris, 1881.
38543.10.22 La Rochefoucauld, François. Les maximes. Pairs, 1881.
40528.6 L'Attaignant, Gabriel Charles de. Poésies diverses. Paris, 1881.
42555.34 Leconte de Lisle, C.M.R. Oeuvres. Poèmes antiques. Paris, 1881.
42555.34.3A Leconte de Lisle, C.M.R. Poèmes barbares. Paris, 1881.
42548.46 Legouvé, Ernest. Théâtre de campagne. ser. 7. Paris, 1881.
42555.39.10 Lemoyne, André. Légendes des bois et chansons marines. Paris, 1881.
40512.12.1 LeSage, Alain René. Adventures of Gil Blas of Santillane. London, 1881. 3v.
Mol 233.5 Leveaux, A. Le mariage forcé. Compiegne, 1881.
FL 382.27 Leveaux, Alphonse. Nos théâtres de 1800 à 1880. Pari, 1881-86.
41595.50 Lhuillier, T. Hégésippe Moreau et son Diogenè. Paris, 1881.
37597.10 Lorris, Guillaume de. Étude historique et biographique. Photoreproduction. Orléans, 1881.
42555.42.75 Magnant, E. Angela ou l'Alsace enchainée. Paris, 1881.
Mol 713.2 Mahrenholtz, R. Molière's Leben und Werke. Heilbronn, 1881.
42577.11.3 Malot, Hector. Sans famille. Paris, 1881. 2v.
Mol 270.17 Mangold, W. Molière's Tartuffe. Oppeln, 1881.
42555.46 Manuel, Eugène. Poèmes populaires. Paris, 1881.
37543.8.4 Marcillac, F. Manuel d'histoire de la littérature française. 5. éd. Genève, 1881.
40535.27.3 Marivaux, Pierre Carlet de Chamblain de. Théâtre. Paris, 1881. 2v.
38514.71A Martial de Paris. L'amant rendu cordelier. Paris, 1881.
37574.26.8 Masson, Gustave. La lyre française. London, 1881.
42545.10.11.2 Meilhac, Henri. Froufrou. N.Y., 1881.
42545.10.18 Meilhac, Henri. Janot. Paris, 1881.
42577.13.9 Mercier, Alfred. L'habitation Saint-Ybars ou Maitres et esclaves en Louisiane. New Orleans, 1881.
42577.13.12 Mérel, Emmanuel. Nouvelles bretonnes. Paris, 1881.
41555.7.90 Mérimée, Prosper. Lettere di Prospero Mérimée ad Antonio Panizzi. Bolongna, 1881. 2v.

1881 - cont.

41555.7.78 Mérimée, Prosper. Letters of Prosper Mérimée to Panizzi. London, 1881. 2v.
41555.7.74 Mérimée, Prosper. Lettres à M. Panizzi, 1850-1870. 2. éd. Paris, 1881. 2v.
41555.7.70 Mérimée, Prosper. Lettres à M. Panizzi, 1850-1870. 5. éd. Paris, 1881. 2v.
41555.7.72 Mérimée, Prosper. Lettres à M. Panizzi, 1850-1870. 5. éd. Paris, 1881. 2v.
38524.30 Merlet, Gustave. Les grands ecrivains du seizième siècle. Paris, 1881.
42545.28.30 Moinaux, Jules. Les tribunaux comiques. Paris, 1881.
Mol 150.25 Molière, Jean Baptiste Paquelin. Le sicilien...Sauzay. Paris, 1881.
Mol 171.28 Molière, Jean Baptiste Poquelin. Le bourgeois gentilhomme. London, 1881.
Mol 211.36 Molière, Jean Baptiste Poquelin. Les femmes savantes...Fasnacht. London, 1881.
Mol 211.37 Molière, Jean Baptiste Poquelin. Les femmes savantes...Geruzez. Paris, 1881.
Mol 211.35 Molière, Jean Baptiste Poquelin. Les femmes savantes...Person. Paris, 1881?
Mol 236.35 Molière, Jean Baptiste Poquelin. El médico a Palos. Habana, 1881.
Mol 882.4 Monselet, Charles. L'amour médecin. Paris, 1881.
41595.34 Moreau, Hégésippe. Contes. Paris, 1881.
Mol 750.10 Moulin, H. Armande Béjart, sa fille et ses 2 maris. Paris, 1881.
41596.17 Musset, Alfred de. Comédies et proverbes. Paris, 1881. 3v.
41596.6.6 Musset, Alfred de. Oeuvres complètes. Paris, 1881. 9v.
41596.14.3 Musset, Alfred de. Oeuvres posthumes. Paris, 1881.
41596.12.4 Musset, Alfred de. Premières poésies. Paris, 1881.
41596.6.4 Musset, Paul de. Biographie de Alfred de Musset. Paris, 1881.
42541.24.5 Pailleron, Édouard. Le monde où l'on s'ennuie. Paris, 1881.
42545.68 Pailleron, Edouard. Le théâtre chez madame. Paris, 1881.
Htn 42545.68.2* Pailleron, Edouard. Le théâtre chez madame. Paris, 1881.
40597.2.36 Parran, A. Romantique. Paris, 1881.
39544.33A Parton, James. Life of Voltaire. Boston, 1881. 2v.
38527.29.13 Pergameni, H. La satire au XVIe siècle et les tragiques d'Agrippa d'Aubigné. n.p., 1881.
40577.5 Pierrot, Charles. Causeries du lundi...Table générale. Paris, 1881.
38514.57.2 Pisan, Christine de. Le livre du chemin de long estude. Berlin, 1881.
42534.31 Pontmartin, A.F. de. Souvenirs d'un vieux critique. Paris, 1881-82. 10v.
41596.49.100 Popelin, Claudius. Un cent de Strophes à Pailleron. Paris, 1881.
40517.57 Pougens, Marie C. Jocko; précédé d'une notice par Anatole France. Paris, 1881.
40522.9.5 Prévost, Antoine F. Histoire de Manon Lescaut et du chevalier des Grieux. Paris, 1881.
37595.16 Raynaud, G. Recueil de motets français des XII et XIII siècle. Paris, 1881-84. 3v.
38558.32 Revillout, M.C.J. Un maitre de conférences au milieu du XVIIe siècle. Montpellier, 1881.
Htn 38546.56.2* Ritchie, Anne Isabella Thackeray. Mme. de Sévigné. Edinburgh, 1881.
38546.56.4 Ritchie, Anne Isabella Thackeray. Mme. de Sévigné. Philadelphia, 1881.
39532.20 Rothschild, James de. Les continuateurs de Loret. Paris, 1881. 2v.
FL 6021.81A Rousseau, J.J. Les confessions. Paris, 1881.
FL 6047.2 Rousseau, J.J. Emil oder über die Erziehung. Leipzig, 1881.
38542.24 Saint Evremond, C. de M. de S.D. Oeuvres choisies. Paris, 1881.
42535.21 Saint-Victor, Paul de. Les deux masques. Paris, 1881-5. 3v.
40577.10 Sainte-Beuve, Charles A. Portraits contemporains. Paris, 1881-82. 5v.
40575.26.10 Sainte-Beuve, Charles A. Volupté. 10. éd. Paris, 1881.
37543.21.2 Saintsbury, George. Primer of French literature. N.Y., 1881.
37543.21.1 Saintsbury, George. Primer of French literature. 2. ed. Oxford, 1881.
37586.2 Sammlung Französisches Neudrucke. v.1-2. Heilbronn, 1881.
41557.30 Sandeau, Jules. Madeleine: a story of French love. Chicago, 1881.
Mol 825.10 Saucerotte, C. Les médecins au théâtre depuis Molière. Paris, 1881.
37585.15 Saynètes et monologues. Paris, 1881. 8v.
39568.10 Sbornik russkago istoricheskago obshchestva. Sankt Peterburg, 1881.
42587.58.10 Ségur, Sophie. Comédies et proverbes. Paris, 1881.
39527.4.42 Soullié, Prosper. Critique comparative des fables de La Fontaine. Reims, 1881.
39527.4.40 Soullié, Prosper. Études sur les fables de La Fontaine. Reims, 1881.
41586.30.12.3 Soumet, A. The gladiator...performed by Salvini. N.Y., 1881.
42535.31 Stapfer, Paul. Études sur la littérature française. Paris, 1881.
42535.35 Stapfer, Paul. Variétés morales et littéraires. Paris, 1881.
37597.14 Stehlich, F. Messire Thibaut, le romanz de la poire. Halle, 1881.
37596.9 Suchier, H. Aucassin und Nicolite. Paderborn, 1881.
41562.19 Sue, Eugène. Le juif errant. v.1-4. Paris, 1881. 2v.
42536.4 Taillandier, Saint-René. Études littéraires. Paris, 1881.
38575.18 Trollope, H.M. Corneille and Racine. Edinburgh, 1881.
42578.64 Vast, Raoul. La vieille garde. 2. éd. Paris, 1881.
Mol 247.14 Veselovskii, A. Mizantrop. Moskva, 1881.
Mol 855.19 La veuve à la mode. Paris, 1881.
39544.28 Voltaire, François Marie Arouet de. Lettres choisies. Paris, 1881.
37596.35 Weber, Alfred. Athis und Prophilias. Staefa, 1881.
37596.47 Weidner, Georg. Der Prosaroman von Joseph von Arimathia. Oppeln, 1881.
42584.3.5 Zola, Emile. L'assommoir. 95. éd. Paris, 1881.
42584.12.22.2 Zola, Emile. Nana. 100. éd. Paris, 1881.
42584.16 Zola, Emile. Le naturalisme au théâtre. Paris, 1881.

1881 - cont.

42584.16.2 Zola, Emile. Le naturalisme au théâtre. 2. éd. Paris, 1881.

42584.15 Zola, Emile. Nos auteurs dramatiques. Paris, 1881.

42584.18.2 Zola, Emile. Les romanciers naturalistes. Paris, 1881.

42584.18 Zola, Emile. Les romanciers naturalistes. 2. éd. Paris, 1881.

1882

42562.23 About, Edmond. Chez tante Claire. Paris, 1882.

38571.14 Adeline, Jules. Un portrait de Pierre Corneille. Paris, 1882.

37564.44.34 Albert, Paul. La littérature française au dix-septième siècle. 5e éd. Paris, 1882.

42584.24 Alexis, Paul. Emile Zola. Paris, 1882.

41583.6 Andrieux, François G.J.S. Les contes en vers d'Andrieux. Paris, 1882.

37555.35 Aubertin, Charles. L'éloquence politique et parlementaire avant 1789. Paris, 1882.

42562.38.90 Aulnay, Louise d'. Le petit bonhomme. Paris, 1882.

40597.34.3 Balzac, Honore de. Une ténébreuse affaire. Paris, 1882.

40594.13 Balzac, Honoré de. Vie politique. Une ténèbreuse affaire. Paris, 1882.

42554.7 Banville, Théodore de. Contes féeriques. Paris, 1882.

42554.8.7.15 Banville, Théodore de. Gringoire; comédie en un acte en prose. London, 1882.

42563.13 Barbé, Benjamin. La desconsolado. 2. ed. Barcelona, 1882.

41522.1.3 Barbey d'Aurevilly, Jules. Une histoire sans nom. Paris, 1882.

41574.22.6 Barbou, Alfred. Victor Hugo and his time. N.Y., 1882.

38576.12.43 Barthelemy, Charles. La comédie de Dancourt, 1685-1714. Paris, 1882.

FL 396.41.4 Baschet, A. Les comédiens italiens à la cour de France. Paris, 1882.

37556.8.12 Bavardages de mesdames mes cousines. Rioz, 1882.

42554.13.25 Beaufort d'Auberval, A.A. Contes erotico-philosophiques. Bruxelles, 1882.

Htn 39545.20* Bengesco, G. Voltaire. Bibliographie de ses oeuvres. Paris, 1882. 4v.

39543.800 Bengescu, G. Voltaire; bibliographie de ses oeuvres. Paris, 1882-90. 4v.

38514.23.3 Bijvanck, W.G.C. Specimen d'un essai sur François Villon. v.1-2. Leyden, 1882.

38546.33 Briere, L. de la. Madame de Sévigné. Paris, 1882.

37557.15 Brunetière, F. Nouvelles études critiques sur la littérature française. Paris, 1882.

40515.4.9 Campardon, Emile. Les prodigalités d'un fermier général. Paris, 1882.

42554.17.35 Carné, Adrien. L'arvor. Paris, 1882.

40516.6.1 Cazotte, Jacques. Plates. Paris, 1882.

42561.32.15 Chandeneux, Claire de. Souvenirs de Bérénice. Paris, 1882.

39533.7 Chapelain, Jean. Les douze derniers chants du poème de La Pucelle. Orleans, 1882.

FL 366.28 Charles le Senne, M. Code du théâtre: lois, règlements. Paris, 1882.

42565.22.3 Cherbuliez, Victor. Noirs et rouges. 6. éd. Paris, 1882.

42565.26.5 Cherbuliez, Victor. La revanche de Joseph Noirel. 4. éd. Paris, 1882.

42565.22.4 Cherbuliez, Victor. Saints and sinners. N.Y., 1882.

42565.55.64 Cladel, Léon. L'amour romantique. Paris, 1882.

42565.55.25 Cladel, Léon. La fête votive de Saint-Bartholomée Porte-Glaive. Paris, 1882.

39526.5.2 Collins, W. Lucas. La Fontaine and other French fabulists. Edinburgh, 1882.

Htn 40551.30* Constant, B. Lettres à Madame Récamier 1807-1830. Paris, 1882.

40553.9.15 Constant de Rebecque, Benjamin. Lettres de Benjamin Constant à Madame Récamier, 1807-1830. Paris, 1882.

39526.36 Contance, A. La Fontaine et la philosophie naturelle. Paris, 1882.

42554.25 Coppée, François. Théâtre 1873-78. Paris, 1882.

42554.26 Coppée, François. Théâtre 1879-81. Paris, 1882.

Mol 197.8 Coquelin, C. L'arnolphe de Molière. Paris, 1882.

38575.31.2 Corneille, Pierre. Cinna. Paris, 1882.

NEDL 38575.33.1 Corneille, Pierre. Horace. Oxford, 1882.

38575.33.1 Corneille, Pierre. Horace. Oxford, 1882.

42566.3.5 Craven, Pauline. Adélaide Capece minutolo. 9. éd. Paris, 1882.

42561.13.15 Craven, Pauline. Eliane. N.Y., 1882.

42566.7 Craven, Pauline. Eliane. Paris, 1882.

42566.8 Craven, Pauline. Eliane. v.1-2. Paris, 1882.

Mol 875.8 Cros, Antoine. Ode à Molière. Paris, 1882.

42566.30.5 Daudet, Alphonse. Numa Roumestan. Boston, 1882.

41574.27 Daudet, Alphonse. Victor Hugo. N.Y., 1882.

42567.28 Daudet, Ernest. Mon frère et moi. Paris, 1882.

40528.8 De Bernis, C. Poésies diverses. Paris, 1882.

38546.31 Depping, G. Quelques pièces inédites concernant Mme. de Sévigné. Paris, 1882.

Mol 755.6 Depping, G. Trois pièces inédits concernant la famille de Molière. Paris, 1882.

42576.66.8 D'Hericault, C. La fille de Notre-Dame. Paris, 1882.

FL 398.9.25 D'Heylli, Georges. Brindeau. Paris, 1882.

42568.3.5 Droz, Gustave. Autour d'une source. 24. éd. Paris, 1882.

42568.19.18.2 Du Boisgobey, Fortuné. Le cochon d'or. 2. éd. Paris, 1882. 2v.

42586.38.10 DuCamp, M. Souvenirs littéraires. Paris, 1882-1883. 2v.

41523.4 Dumas, Alexandre. Amaury. Paris, 1882.

41523.20 Dumas, Alexandre. Capitaine Richard. Paris, 1882.

41538.14.5 Dumas, Alexandre. Le collier de la reine. Paris, 1882. 2v.

41538.16 Dumas, Alexandre. Comte de Monte-Cristo. v.1-4. Paris, 1882. 2v.

41524.13 Dumas, Alexandre. Les deux Diane. v.1-2,3. Paris, 1882. 2v.

41526.13 Dumas, Alexandre. Louis XIV et son siècle. Paris, 1882. 2v.

41527.16 Dumas, Alexandre. Le prince des voleurs. v.1-2. Paris, 1882.

42543.24.4 Dumas, Alexandre. La princesse Georges. Paris, 1882.

Htn 42543.11.5* Dumas, Alexandre. Théâtre complet. Paris, 1882-93. 7v.

42563.51.2 Durand, Alice M.C.F. Madame de Dreux. Paris, 1882.

42563.55.3 Durand, Alice M.C.F. Perdue. Paris, 1882.

42542.72.3 Duru, A. La mascotte. Paris, 1882.

1882 - cont.

42568.23.5 Duval, Paul. Le sang des dieux. Paris, 1882.

38526.14.50 Du Val, Pierre. Théâtre mystique de Pierre Du Val. Paris, 1882.

37541.27 Engel, Eduard. Geschichte der Französischen Literatur. Leipzig, 1882.

Mol 870.33 Fabié, F. Molière et Montespan. Toulon, 1882.

38514.100 Fabre, Adolphe. Les clercs du palais. Vienne en Dauphiné, 1882.

38558.4 Fabre, Antonin. La jeunesse de Fléchier. Paris, 1882. 2v.

FL 383.53 Figuier, Louis. Le théâtre scientifique. Paris, 1882.

42576.23.3 Flaubert, Gustave. La tentation de Saint-Antoine. Paris, 1882.

37543.23 Fleury, Jean. Histoire élémentaire de la littérature française. Paris, 1882.

42575.53.35A Fould, W. de (Mme.). Le bleuet. 17. éd. Paris, 1882.

42571.27 Gaboriau, Emile. La dégringolade. Paris, 1882. 2v.

41542.37.7 Gautier, Théophile. My household of pets. Boston, 1882.

41542.37.11 Gautier, Théophile. One of Cleopatra's nights. N.Y., 1882.

41542.30.85 Gautier, Théophile. Poésies complètes. Paris, 1882. 2v.

41542.24 Gautier, Théophile. Théâtre, mystère, comédies et ballets. Paris, 1882.

37565.97 Géruzez, Eugéne. Histoire de la littérature française. 5. éd. Paris, 1882. 2v.

40528.7 Gilbert. Poésies diverses. Paris, 1882.

39526.5 Girardin, Saint-Marc. La Fontaine et les fabulistes. Paris, 1882. 2v.

42576.65.2 Glouvet, Jules de. Le berger. Paris, 1882.

42575.73.10 Goncourt, Edmond de. La Faustin. Paris, 1882.

FL 6118.82 Graham, H.G. Rousseau. Edinburgh, 1882.

42576.64.8 Gramont, Ferdinand de. Olim. Paris, 1882.

38543.23.20 Granges de Surgères, Anatole. Les portraits du duc de La Rochefoucauld. Paris, 1882.

41593.34.17 Guérin, Maurice de. Maurice de Guérin; Journal, lettres et poèmes. Paris, 1882.

38576.17 Guerin, N.A.M. Myrtil et Mélicerte. Paris, 1882.

Mol 242.1.5 Guérin, Nicolas Armand Martial. Myrtil et Mélicerte. Jacob. Paris, 1882.

42543.62.23 Guiard, Émile. Mon fils. Paris, 1882.

40516.25.9 Guiard de Servigné, J. Les sonnettes, ou Mémoires de M. le Marquis. Bruxelles, 1882.

Mol 698.8F Guiffrey, J. Les amours de Sombaut et Macée. Paris, 1882.

42576.40.365 Halévy, Ludovic. Madame et Monsieur Cardinal. 27. éd. Paris, 1882.

40515.5.85 Herpin, C.A.L. Une femme du monde au XVIIIe siècle. La jeunesse de Madame d'Épinay. Paris, 1882.

42576.67.14 Hervieu, Paul. Diogène le chien. 3. éd. Paris, 1882.

Mol 608.6 Heydkamp, W. Remarques sur la langue de Molière. Bonn, 1882.

37596.15 Hofmann, K. Amis et amiles du jourdains de Blaivies. Erlangen, 1882.

41573.28 Hugo, Victor. Torquemada drame. 5e éd. Paris, 1882.

41573.28.3 Hugo, Victor. Torquemada drame. 6e éd. Paris, 1882.

37574.50 Janon, Camille de. Recueil de poésies à l'usage de la jeunesse américaine. N.Y., 1882.

FL 6128.82 Jansen, A. Jean-Jacques Rousseau. Fragments inédits. Paris, 1882.

38512.85 Jean de Mote. Li regret Guillaume Comte de Haunaut. Louvain, 1882.

37596.134.30 Jean Renart. Versions inédites de la chanson de Jean Renaud. Paris, 1882.

39526.35 Kulpe, Wilhelm. La Fontaine sein Leben und seine Fabelen. Leipzig, 1882.

38564.35.9 La Bruyère, J. de. Des ouvrages de l'Ésprit. Paris, 1882.

FL 380.9 La Combe, René de. Les hommes et les oeuvres du théâtre révolutionnaire. Paris, 1882.

39526.30.45 La Fontaine, Jean de. Fables. London, 1882.

41578.30.5 Lamartine, Alphonse. Le tailleur de pierre de Saint-Point. Paris, 1882.

42555.20 Laprade, Victor de. Essais de critique idéaliste. Paris, 1882.

40535.31 Larroumet, Gustave. Marivaux, sa vie et ses oeuvres. Paris, 1882.

40562.15 Lear, H.L. Sidney. Henri Dominique Lacordaire. London, 1882.

37571.9 La lecture en famille. Paris, 1882.

42548.47 Legouvé, Ernest. Théâtre de campagne. ser. 8. Paris, 1882.

Mol 612.8 Lemaitre, J. La comédie après Molière. Paris, 1882.

38588.21 Lemaitre, Jules. La comédie après Molière et le théâtre de Dancourt. Paris, 1882.

42544.34 Lemercier de Neuville, Louis. Nouveau théâtre des pupazzi. Paris, 1882.

42547.10.41 Letérrier, E. Le jour et la nuit. Paris, 1882.

Mol 810.6 Leveaux, Alphonse. Les premières de Molière. Compiégne, 1882.

FL 364.10 Leveaux, Alphonse. Le théâtre de la cour à Compiegne. Paris, 1882-85.

42555.40.75 Leygues, Georges. Le coffret brisé. Paris, 1882.

37596.86 Li Miserere, pikardisches Gedicht aus dem XII. Jahrhundert von Reclus de Mollens. Landshut, 1882.

37591.29 Link, Theodor. Über du Sprache der Chronique rimée von Philippe Mousket. Erlangen, 1882.

Htn FL 384.58* Liphart, E. de. Les actrices de Paris. Paris, 1882.

42555.41 Loridan, Henri. Recueil de chansons en patois de Roubaix. Roubaix, 1882.

FL 361.25 Lyden, E.F.M. de. Le théâtre d'autrefois et d'aujourd'hui. Paris, 1882.

42576.71 Lythe, Marcel. Mais laquelle? Paris, 1882.

39544.14 Mahrenholtz, R. Voltaire - Studien. Oppeln, 1882.

40526.3 Maillard, Porges. Oeuvres nouvelles. Nantes, 1882. 2v.

42577.10.9 Malot, Hector. Pompon. 9. éd. Paris, 1882.

42577.10.75 Malot, Hector. Romain Kalbris. 7. éd. Paris, 1882.

42577.11.5 Malot, Hector. Sans famille. Paris, 1882.

42555.49 Manuel, Eugène. En voyage, poésies. Washington, 1882.

40556.29 Margerie, Amédée de. Le Comte Joseph de Maistre. Paris, 1882.

42577.12.21 Mary-Lafon. Cinquante ans de vie littéraire. London, 1882.

FL 382.24.10 Matthews, J.B. French dramatists of the 19th century. 2. ed. London, 1882.

42545.10.23 Meilhac, Henri. Le mari à Babette. Paris, 1882.

42545.10.22.5 Meilhac, Henri. Rip Van Winkle. London, 1882.

1882 - cont.

FL 398.13.12 Mémoires de Mlle. Clairon. Paris, 1882.

37542.19 Merlet, Gustave. Études littéraires sur...Racine, Corneille et Molière, Chanson de Roland. Paris, 1882. 2v.

Mol 165.38 Molière, Jean Baptiste Poquelin. L'avare...Joynes. N.Y., 1882.

Mol 165.40 Molière, Jean Baptiste Poquelin. L'avare...Livet. Paris, 1882.

Mol 165.39 Molière, Jean Baptiste Poquelin. L'avare...Moriarty. London, 1882.

Mol 171.51 Molière, Jean Baptiste Poquelin. Le bourgeois gentilhomme...Moland. Paris, 1882.

Mol 8.82.5 Molière, Jean Baptiste Poquelin. Chefs-d'oeuvre de Molière. Tom.1-2. Paris, 1882.

Mol 245.53 Molière, Jean Baptiste Poquelin. Le misanthrope. Fasnacht. London, 1882.

Mol 18.82.3 Molière, Jean Baptiste Poquelin. Oeuvres. Paris, 1882. 2v.

Htn Mol 8.82* Molière, Jean Baptiste Poquelin. Oeuvres. Paris, 1882-96. 32v.

Mol 268.63 Molière, Jean Baptiste Poquelin. Le Tartuffe. Livet. Paris, 1882.

Mol 18.82 Molière, Jean Baptiste Poquelin. Théâtre complet...Monval. Paris, 1882-83. 8v.

Mol 18.82.2 Molière, Jean Baptiste Poquelin. Théâtre complet...Monval. Paris, 1882-83. 8v.

Mol 245.54 Molière, Jean Bpatiste Poquelin. Le misanthrope. Gasc. London, 1882.

37596.195 Moniot, Jean. Poésies inédites, publiées par Gaston Raynaud. Nogent-le-Rotrou, 1882.

42555.51 Monnier, Marc. Le charmeur. Paris, 1882. 10v.

Mol 745.4 Monval, G. Les tombeaux de Molière et de la Fontaine. Pons, 1882.

42545.44.22 Moreau, Pol. Nos alliées. Paris, 1882.

38525.28 Motin, Pierre. Oeuvres inédites. Paris, 1882.

41596.17.3 Musset, Alfred de. Comédies et proverbes. v.2. Paris, 1882.

41596.12.7 Musset, Alfred de. Poésies nouvelles. 1836-1852. Paris, 1882.

37567.8.5 Nauroy, C. Bibliographie des plaquettes romantiques. Paris, 1882.

42545.48 Nuitter de Beaumont, E. Le coeur et main. Paris, 1882.

42578.30.3 Ohnet, Georges. Le maître de forges. 57. éd. Paris, 1882.

42578.30.12 Ohnet, Georges. Serge Panine. 71. éd. Paris, 1882.

37562.12.22 Orth, F. Ueber Reim und Strophenbau in der altfranzösischen Lyrik. Cassel, 1882.

42545.64 Pailleron, Edouard. Cabotins! La Poupée. Le Narcotique. Paris, 1882-97.

42541.24.6 Pailleron, Edouard. Le monde où l'on s'ennuie. 22e éd. Paris, 1882.

42545.63.3 Pailleron, Edouard. Le monde ou l'on s'ennuie. 24. éd. Paris, 1882.

37595.27 Pannier, L. Les lapidaires français XII-XIV siècles. Paris, 1882.

37562.27 Paris, Gaston. Paulin Paris et la littérature française au moyen âge. Paris, 1882.

37555.556 Pellissier, Georges. De sexti decimi saeculi in Francia artibus poeticis. Paris, 1882.

38525.93 Person, Léonce. Histoire du Venceslas de Rotrou. Paris, 1882.

38525.94 Person, Léonce. Histoire du Véritable Saint-Genest de Rotrou. Paris, 1882.

42554.13.30 Poésies de M. Bellot des Minières. Paris, 1882.

FL 398.74.53 Poinsot, E.A. Rachel à après sa correspondance. Paris, 1882.

FL 396.64 Porel, P. L'Odéon. Paris, 1882. 2v.

Mol 267.10 Pougin, A. Molière et l'opéra - comique; le Sicilien. Paris, 1882.

42578.31 Pouvillon, E. Césette. Paris, 1882.

38588.16 Quinault, Philippe. Théâtre choisi. Paris, 1882.

38585.25.25 Racine, Jean. Britannicus. Paris, 1882.

38581.16 Racine, Jean. Oeuvres. Paris, 1882.

38583.6.9 Racine, Jean. Théâtre complet. Paris, 1882. 4v.

42515.30.310 Renan, Ernest. Ecclésiaste. Paris, 1882.

42515.30.520 Renan, Ernest. Le livre de Job. 4. éd. Paris, 1882.

42515.29.702 Renan, Ernest. Marc-Auréle et la fin du monde antique. 2. éd. Paris, 1882.

42515.29.704 Renan, Ernest. Marc-Aurèle et la fin du monde antique. 4. éd. Paris, 1882.

42515.30.650 Renan, Ernest. Qu'est-ce qu'une nation? Paris, 1882.

42515.29.25 Renan, Ernest. Vie de Jésus. 17. éd. Paris, 1882.

37562.51 Richter, O. Die französische Litteratur am Hofe der Herzöge von Burgund. Halle, 1882.

42587.55.5 Rivière, Henri. La jeunesse d'un désespére. Paris, 1882.

X Cg 38525.50 Rotrou, Jean de. Théâtre choisi. Paris, 1882. 2v.

37547.6.3 Rousse, J. Poésies bretonnes: au pays de Retz, poèmes italiens et bretons. Paris, 1882.

FL 6047.11 Rousseau, J.J. Jean-Jacques Rousseau. 2. Aufl. v.1-2. Langensalza, 1882-83.

42535.20 Saint-Victor, Paul de. Hommes et dieux. Paris, 1882.

37574.42.5 Saintsbury, George. French lyrics. London, 1882.

37574.42A Saintsbury, George. French lyrics. London, 1882.

37542.15 Saintsbury, George. Short history of French literature. Oxford, 1882.

37542.15.2 Saintsbury, George. Short history of French literature. Oxford, 1882.

FL 398.79 Samson, J.I. Mémoires. Paris, 1882.

42578.35 Sarcey, Francisque. Misères d'un fonctionnaire chinois. Paris, 1882.

42546.28 Sardou, Victorien. L'oncle Sam. Paris, 1882.

42546.29.8 Sardou, Victorien. La perle noire. Paris, 1882.

38528.13.5A Satyre Ménippée de la vertu du catholicon. Paris, 1882.

Htn 42556.29.35* Saulière, Auguste. Les leçons conjugales, contes lestes. 4. éd. Paris, 1882.

X Cg 39534.32 Scarron, Paul. Le roman comique. Paris, 1882.

42548.26.7 Scribe, E. La bataille de dames. Paris, 1882.

42587.58.9 Ségur, Sophie. Le Général Dourakine. Paris, 1882.

42587.58.8.5 Ségur, Sophie. Les malheurs de Sophie. 14. éd. Paris, 1882.

37547.90 Semmig, Herman. Kultur- und Litteraturgeschichte der Französischen Schweiz und Savoyens. Zürich, 1882.

42546.33.5 Silvestre, Armand. Le pays des roses. Paris, 1882.

41586.30.12.4 Soumet, A. The gladiator...performed by Salvini. N.Y., 1882.

38526.27.9 Stecher, J. Oeuvres de Jean Lemaire de Belges. Louvain, 1882. 4v.

1882 - cont.

37596.26.5 Stengel, E. La cancun de Saint Alexis. Marburg, 1882.

42556.19.5 Sully-Prudhomme, R.F.A. Poésies. Paris, 1882.

38588.19 Théâtre de Dufresny. Paris, 1882.

42583.21 Theuriet, André. Madame Heurteloup. (La bête noire). Paris, 1882.

42583.25.3 Theuriet, André. Les mauvais ménages. Paris, 1882.

42583.28 Theuriet, André. Sauvageonne. Paris, 1882.

41563.27.2 Toepffer, Rodolphe. Nouvelles genevoises. Paris, 1882.

39568.16 Torneaux, M. Grimm; la bibliothèque et les papiers. Paris, 1882.

FL 399.71.9 Touché, Raoul. Les premières illustrées. v.1-6. Paris, 1882-87. 3v.

42546.31.12 Uchard, Mario. Un Jossier. La fiammina contre Odette. Paris, 1882.

42584.47 Ulbach, Louis. La confession d'un abbé. Paris, 1882.

42587.65.12 Vachette, Eugène. Les petites comédies du vice. Paris, 1882.

40526.69.5 Vadé, Jean Joseph. La pipe casée. Paris, 1882.

42548.52 Verconsin, Eugène. Saynètes et comédies. Paris, 1882.

42582.18 Verne, Jules. The giant raft. N.Y., 1882. 2v.

42583.50.30 Véron, Pierre. La mascarade de l'histoire. Paris, 1882.

41564.3.75 Vigny, Alfred de. Cinq-Mars. Paris, 1882. 2v.

41564.19 Vigny, Alfred de. Théâtre complet. Paris, 1882.

37536.10 Villemain, A.F. Cours de littérature française. Paris, 1882. 2v.

Mol 623.1 Wasserzieher, E. Die tragischen Zuge bei Molière. Neustadt, 1882.

Mon 133.1 Wendell, H. Etude sur la langue des essais. Stockholm, 1882.

42587.72 Witt, Henriette Guizot de. Par monts et par vaux. Paris, 1882.

42584.9.15 Zola, Emile. Albine, or The abbe's temptation. Philadelphia, 1882.

42584.3.7 Zola, Emile. L'assommoir. Photoreproduction. Philadelphia, 1882.

42584.22 Zola, Emile. Documents littéraires. Paris, 1882.

42584.23.70 Zola, Emile. The mysteries of the court of Louis Napoléon. Philadelphia, 1882.

42584.20 Zola, Emile. Pot-Bouille. Philadelphia, 1882.

1883

X Cg 39544.9 Adolph, Carl. Voltaire et le théâtre de Shakespeare. Sorau, 1883.

37565.15.3 Albert, Paul. Littérature française au XVIII siècle. Paris, 1883.

37561.18 Aubertin, Charles. Histoire de la littérature françaises au moyen âge. Paris, 1883. 2v.

42542.5.15 Augier, Emile. Les effrontés. Paris, 1883.

42542.3.5 Augier, Emile. Théâtre complet. v.3. lost 1947. Paris, 1883-86. 6v.

38526.48.45 Aulard, F.A. Les théories dramatiques de Jean de Schelandre. Poitiers, 1883.

42586.14.9.5 Badin, Adolphe. Un parisien chez les russes. Paris, 1883.

40594.3 Balzac, Honoré de. Vie privée. Le contract de mariage. Paris, 1883.

42554.9 Banville, Théodore de. Mes souvenirs. Paris, 1883.

42554.2 Banville, Théodore de. Odes funambulesques. Paris, 1883.

42554.10 Banville, Théodore de. Paris vécu. Paris, 1883.

41522.2.35 Barbey d'Aurevilly, Jules. Memoranda. Paris, 1883.

41522.2.25 Barbey d'Aurevilly, Jules. Les ridicules du temps. 5. éd. Paris, 1883.

42554.12 Barbier, Auguste. Ïambes et poèmes. 33e éd. Paris, 1883.

42554.12.40 Barbier, Auguste. Souvenirs personnels et silhouettes contemporaines. Paris, 1883.

42554.14 Barracand, L. Lamartine et la muse. Paris, 1883.

42563.22.14.24 Belot, Adolphe. Le testament de César Girodot. 12. éd. Paris, 1883.

42512.6 Bernard-Derosne, Léon. Types et travers. Paris, 1883.

37572.28 Bernardin, N.M. Morceaux choisis des classiques français. Paris, 1883.

38536.25A Besant, Walter. Readings in Rabelais. London, 1883.

42563.28.15 Biart, Lucien. Entre deux océans. Paris, 1883.

42563.28.37 Biart, Lucien. Le secret de José. Paris, 1883.

X Cg 41574.21 Biré, Edmond. Victor Hugo avant 1830. Paris, 1883.

FL 6138.83 Borgeaud, C. Jean-Jacques Rousseau's Religionsphilosophie. Genève, 1883.

42542.29.137 Bornier, Henri de. La lizardière. Paris, 1883.

38557.32.9 Bossuet, J.B. Choix de sermons. Paris, 1883.

38557.27A Bossuet, J.B. Oraisons funèbres. Paris, 1883.

FL 6128.83.2 Bougeault, A. Étude sur l'état mental de Jean-Jacques Rousseau. Paris, 1883.

43544.2.30 Bouret, G. Les Broussailles. Paris, 1883.

Htn 37567.15* Bourget, Paul. Essais de psychologie contemporaine. Paris, 1883.

37567.15 Bourget, Paul. Essais de psychologie contemporaine. Paris, 1883.

38527.13 Bourgoin, Auguste. Valentin Conrart. Paris, 1883.

38576.6.2 Boursault, Edme. Théâtre choisi. Paris, 1883.

42563.38 Bouvier, Alexis. Etienne Marcel. Paris, 1883.

38528.14.9 Brantôme, P. de B. de. Vie des dames galantes. Paris, 1883.

FL 390.5.10 Brazier, Nicolas. Chroniques des petits théâtres de Paris. Paris, 1883. 2v.

42524.17 Brunetière, F. Le roman naturaliste. Paris, 1883.

42524.17.2 Brunetière, F. Le roman naturaliste. Paris, 1883.

39586.18.10 Chamfort, S.R.N. Oeuvres choisies. Paris, 1883-85. 3v.

Htn 38511.22* Chandos, the herald. Le prince noir. London, 1883.

38511.22.2 Chandos, the herald. Le prince noir. London, 1883.

40586.11.27 Chateaubriand, F.A.R. Atala, René, Le dernier Abencérage. Paris, 1883.

42565.4.7 Cherbuliez, Victor. L'aventure de Ladislas Bolski. 7. éd. Paris, 1883.

42565.9.4 Cherbuliez, Victor. Le comte Kostia. 10. éd. Paris, 1883.

42565.13.2 Cherbuliez, Victor. La ferme du choquard. Paris, 1883.

42565.13 Cherbuliez, Victor. La ferme du Choquard. Paris, 1883.

42565.18 Cherbuliez, Victor. Hommes et choses du temps présent. Paris, 1883.

42565.55.125 Cladel, Léon. Le deuxième mystère de l'incarnation. 4. éd. Paris, 1883.

42565.55.70 Cladel, Léon. Pierre patient. Paris, 1883.

42586.31.30 Claretié, J. Monsieur le ministre. 3. éd. Paris, 1883.

41596.2.10 Clouard, Maurice. Bibliographie des oeuvres d'Alfred de Musset. Paris, 1883.

Chronological Listing

1883 - cont.

Htn	FL 398.7.30*	Colombier, Marie. The life...of Sarah Barnum. London, 1883? 2 pam.
	FL 398.7.29	Colombier, Marie. Les mémoires de Sarah Barnum. Paris, 1883.
	42554.21	Coppée, François. Vingt contes nouveaux. Paris, 1883.
	40532.1	Cordier, Henri. Bibliographie des oeuvres de Beaumarchais. Paris, 1883.
	38575.34	Corneille, Pierre. Le menteur et Rodogune. Paris, 1883.
	39533.18	Cotin, Charles. La satyre des satyres. Paris, 1883.
	Mol 853.5	Cotin. La satyre des satyres. Paris, 1883.
	FL 398.48	Criticisms of Eugénie Legrand in America. N.Y., 1883?
	43554.26.100	Cros, Charles. L'homme propre. Paris, 1883.
	42554.26.95	Cros, Charles. L'homme propre. Paris, 1883.
	37561.31	Darmesteter, Arsène. Cours de littérature française du moyen âge. Paris, 1883.
	42566.22	Daudet, Alphonse. L'évangéliste; roman parisien. Paris, 1883.
	42566.22.5	Daudet, Alphonse. L'évangéliste; roman parisien. 38. éd. Paris, 1883.
	FL 382.90	Delvau, A. Le théâtre érotique français sous le bas-empire. Paris, 1883.
	37543.28	Deschanel, Émile. Le romantisme des classiques. Paris, 1883.
	FL 398.17.11	D'Heylli, Georges. Delaunay. Paris, 1883.
	40536.7.30	Doberenz, Heinrich. La Marteliere und seine Bearbeitung Schillerscher Dramen auf den Theater der französischen Revolution. Löbau, 1883.
	Mol 880.1	Dryden, J. Plays from Molière. London, 1883.
	38526.7	Du Bellay, Joachim. Lettres de Joachim Du Bellay. Paris, 1883.
	42568.19.3	Du Boisgobey, Fortuné. Le collier d'acier. 2. éd. Paris, 1883.
	42568.19.4	Du Boisgobey, Fortuné. Le collier d'acier. 3. éd. Paris, 1883.
	42586.38.15	DuCamp, M. Souvenirs littéraires. Paris, 1883. 2v.
	42515.43	Dufour, Théophile. Lettres à Quinet sous l'empire. 1849-1866. Paris, 1883.
	42542.69.5	Dumanoir, M. Le gentilhomme pauvre. N.Y., 1883.
	42543.16.11	Dumas, Alexandre. Camille. Indianapolis, 1883.
	42543.16	Dumas, Alexandre. La dame aux camélias. Paris, 1883.
	42543.14.9	Dumas, Alexandre. Demi-monde; comedia. Madrid, 1883.
	41538.51	Dumas, Alexandre. Théâtre complet. v.3-25. Paris, 1883. 11v.
	41538.51.3	Dumas, Alexandre. Théâtre complet. v.8. Paris, 1883.
	41538.55.17	Dumas, Alexandre. Le vicomte de Bragelonne. v.1-6. Paris, 1883. 3v.
	Mol 604.5	Dumoustier, L. Molière, auteur et comédien. Paris, 1883.
	42563.45.4	Durand, Alice M.C.F. Dosia. 42. éd. Paris, 1883.
	42563.45.2.5	Durand, Alice M.C.F. Dosia. 44. éd. Paris, 1883.
	42563.49.5	Durand, Alice M.C.F. Louis Breuil. Histoire d'un pautouflard. Paris, 1883.
	42563.64	Durand, Alice M.C.F. Le voeu de Nadia. Paris, 1883.
	40516.20.2	Eaux fortes pour illustrer les contes. Paris, 1883.
	42568.23.100	Eekhoud, Georges. Kees doorik. Bruxelles, 1883.
	42568.30.810	Enault, Louis. Christine. N.Y., 1883.
	42572.10.15	Erckmann, Emile. La guerre. Cambridge, 1883.
	38528.8	Estienne, Henri. Deux dialogues du nouveau langage françois, italianizé. Paris, 1883. 2v.
	37596.16	Étienne, E. La vie Saint Thomas le martir. Paris, 1883.
	Mol 250.9.2	Fage, R. Molière et les limousins. Limoges, 1883.
	Mol 250.9	Fage, R. Molière et les limousins. Limoges, 1883.
NEDL	FL 375.35	Faguet, Émile. La tragédie française au XVI siècle. Paris, 1883.
	38524.20	Faifeu, Pierre. La legende joyeuse. Paris, 1883.
	37596.13A	Fath, Fritz. Die Lieder des Castellans von Coucy. Heidelberg, 1883.
	37596.68	Feilitzen, Hugo. Liver del juise. Photoreproduction. Upsala, 1883.
	42575.28	Feuillet, Octave. La fée. N.Y., 1883.
	42575.39.40	Feuillet, Octave. Un roman parisien. 3. éd. Paris, 1883.
	37555.100	Fobler, A. Vom Französischen Versbau alter und neuer Zeit. Leipzig, 1883.
	38526.46.305	Gasté, A. Noels et vaudevires de manuscrit de Jehan Porée. Caen, 1883.
	41542.16	Gautier, Théophile. Souvenirs de théâtre. Paris, 1883.
	41542.18.7	Gautier, Théophile. Voyage en Espagne. Paris, 1883.
	42566.16	Gerstmann, A. Alphonse Daudet. Berlin, 1883.
	41541.8.13	Girardin, Delphine Gay. La joie fait peur. Paris, 1883.
	40516.20	Godard d'Aucour, Claude. Contes de Godard d'Aucour. Paris, 1883.
	37574.27	Godefroy, Frédéric. Morceaux choisis des poètes et prosateurs français du IXe au XVIe siècle. Paris, 1883.
Htn	40516.25.20*	Gourdan, Alexandrine E. Correspondance de Madame Gourdan. Bruxelles, 1883.
	40535.18	Graffigny, Françoise d'Issembourg d'Happoncourt de. Lettres. Paris, 1883.
	38543.14	Granges de Surgères, Anatole. Traductions en langues étrangères des réfléxions ou sentences et maximes morales de La Rochefoucauld. Paris, 1883.
	37596.81	Grebel, Max. Le tornoiment antéchrist par Huon de Mery. Inaug. Diss. Leipzig, 1883.
	40528.9	Gresset, Jean B. Poésies choisies. Paris, 1883.
	Mon 117.1	Grimm, F.M. de. Voyages et essais de Montaigne. Cahors, 1883.
	39544.45	Hagmann, J.G. Ueber Voltaires "Essai sur les moeurs". Leipzig, 1883.
	42576.40.302	Halévy, Ludovic. L'abbé Constantin. 54. éd. Paris, 1883.
NEDL	42576.40.400A	Halévy, Ludovic. Criquette. 23. éd. Paris, 1883.
	42576.40.355	Halévy, Ludovic. Deux mariages. Paris, 1883.
	42576.40.368	Halévy, Ludovic. La famille Cardinal. Paris, 1883.
	39532.5.7	Hamilton, Anthony. Mémoires du chevalier de Grammont. Paris, 1883.
	38587.23	Hardy, Alexandre. Théâtre. v.1-5. Marburg, 1883. 4v.
	40515.5.86	Herpin, C.A.L. Une femme du monde au XVIIIe siècle; dernières années de Madame d'Epinay. Paris, 1883.
	40515.5.86.2	Herpin, C.A.L. Une femme du monde au XVIIIe siècle; dernières années de Madame d'Epinay. 2e éd. Paris, 1883.
	40515.5.86.3	Herpin, C.A.L. Une femme du monde au XVIIIe siècle; dernières années de Madame d'Epinay. 3e éd. Paris, 1883.
	40515.5.85.4	Herpin, C.A.L. Une femme du monde au XVIIIe siècle. La jeunesse de Madame d'Epinay. 4e éd. Paris, 1883.
	42543.69.15	Hervilly, Ernest. Vent d'ouest, comédie, et La soupière. N.Y., 1883.
Htn	42576.65.11*	Heusy, Paul. Un coin de la vie de misère. Paris, 1883.
	39545.6	Hugo, Victor. Oration on Voltaire. N.Y., 1883.

1883 - cont.

	42554.65.7	Hugues, Clovis. Les jours de combat; poésies. Paris, 1883.
	Mol 608.8.2	Humbert, C. Deutschlands Urteil über Molière. Oppeln, 1883.
	Mol 608.8	Humbert, C. Deutschlands Urteil über Molière. Oppeln, 1883.
	41593.92	Jouin, Henri A. L'Ardoisé, poésie. Paris, 1883.
	38524.18	Julyot, Ferry. Les élégies de la belle fille. Paris, 1883.
NEDL	37596.63	Koschwitz, E. Karls des grossen Reise nach Jerusalem und Constantin. Heilbronn, 1883.
	Mol 611.4	Krause, H. Wycherley und seine französischen Quellen. Halle, 1883.
	38551.74	Krause, K.E. Beitrage zur Würdigung Fénelons als praktischer Theologe. Freiburg, 1883.
	42544.28.2	Labiche, Eugène. La grammaire. N.Y., 1883.
	42544.28	Labiche, Eugène. La grammaire. N.Y., 1883.
	42544.26.2	Labiche, Eugène. Le voyage de Monsieur Perrichon. N.Y., 1883.
	38564.31	La Bruyère, J. de. Les caractères. Paris, 1883. 2v.
	FL 391.100	Lacour, Leopold. Gaulois et parisiens. Paris, 1883.
	39526.33.10	La Fontaine, Jean de. Fables. Paris, 1883.
	39524.7.15F	La Fontaine, Jean de. Fables. Paris, 1883. 2v.
	39525.14	La Fontaine, Jean de. Oeuvres. v.1-11 and album. Paris, 1883. 12v.
	42544.31	Lapointe, A. Le cousin César. Paris, 1883.
	38543.10.30	La Rochefoucauld, François. Maximes. Paris, 1883.
	38543.5	La Rochefoucauld, François. Oeuvres complètes. Paris, 1883. 2v.
	FL 365.25	Lelion-Damièms, L. Le bréviare des comédiens. Paris, 1883.
	40517.31.7	Le Prince de Beaumont, M. Magasin des enfans. Paris, 1883. 2v.
	39586.26	Lescure, M. de. Rivarol et la société française. Paris, 1883.
	41586.17.9	Leuven, Adolphe de. La poupee de Nuremberg. Paris, 1883.
	Mol 612.9	Leveaux, A. L'enseignement moral dans les comédies de Molière. Compiègne, 1883.
	Mol 855.12.5	Le livre abominable de 1665. Ménard. Paris, 1883. 2v.
	40516.28.6.2	Louvet de Couvral, J.B. Les aventures du chevalier de Faublas. v.1-4. Bruxelles, 1883. 2v.
	Mol 612.14	Luder, H.A. Carlo Goldini in seinem Verhältnis zu Molière. Oppeln, 1883.
	Mol 713.1	Mahrenholtz, R. Molière: Einführung in Leben und Werke. Heilbronn, 1883.
	39545.21	Mahrenholtz, R. Voltaire im Urteile der Zeitgenossen. Oppeln, 1883.
	42577.11.6	Malot, Hector. Sans famille. v.2. 40. éd. Paris, 1883.
	42555.48	Manuel, Eugène. Pages intimes, poésies. Washington, 1883.
	39594.3.32	Marat, J.P. Eloge de Montesquieu. Libourne, 1883.
	40535.27	Marivaux, Pierre Carlet de Chamblain de. Théâtre choisi. Paris, 1883.
	42577.12	Marsonnière, J.L. de la. Un drama au Logis de la Lycorne. London, 1883.
	38524.19	Martin, Nicolas. Les Noelz et Chansons. Paris, 1883.
	42577.2.25	Maupassant, Guy de. Mlle Fifi. Paris, 1883.
	42577.4.29.7	Maupassant, Guy de. Une vie. (L'humble vérite). 19. éd. Paris, 1883.
	42545.10.11.7	Meilhac, Henri. Froufrou. Indianapolis, 1883.
	42587.22.10	Ménard, Louis. Histoire des Israélites d'après l'exégèse biblique. Paris, 1883.
	41555.20.3	Mérimée, Prosper. Carmen. 13. éd. Paris, 1883. 7 pam.
	37542.21	Merlet, Gustave. Études littéraires sur Racine, Corneille, Molière, Chanson de Roland. Paris, 1883. 2v.
	42533.11A	Mézières, A. En France XVIIIe et XIXe siècles. Paris, 1883.
	42533.12	Mézières, A. Hors de France; Italie, Espagne. Paris, 1883.
	42587.27.10	Michel, Adolphe. Le roman d'un vieux garçon. 3. éd. Paris, 1883.
	38511.8	Milet, Jacques. L'istoire de la destruction de Troye la grant. Marburg, 1883.
	42545.27.9	Millanvoye, B. Le diner de Pierrot. 2e éd. Paris, 1883.
	FL 382.32.4	Mirbeau, Octave. Le comédien. 4e ed. Paris, 1883.
	FL 382.32.7	Mirbeau, Octave. Le comédien. 7e ed. Paris, 1883.
	Mol 62.30	Molière, Jean Baptiste Poquelin. Ausgewählte Lustspiele...Bierling. Stuttgart, 1883. 3v.
	Mol 171.30	Molière, Jean Baptiste Poquelin. Le bourgeois gentilhomme...Figuière. Paris, 1883.
	Mol 171.31	Molière, Jean Baptiste Poquelin. Le bourgeois gentilhomme...Pellisson. Paris, 1883.
	Mol 211.38	Molière, Jean Baptiste Poquelin. Les femmes savantes...Vapereau. Paris, 1883.
	Mol 235.24	Molière, Jean Baptiste Poquelin. Le médecin malgré lui...Fasnacht. London, 1883.
	Mol 235.23	Molière, Jean Baptiste Poquelin. Le médecin malgré lui...Gasc. London, 1883.
	Mol 245.56	Molière, Jean Baptiste Poquelin. Le misanthrope. Livet. Paris, 1883.
	Mol 18.83	Molière, Jean Baptiste Poquelin. Werke...Laun. 2e Aufl. v.1-5. Leipzig, 1883-87.
	42545.29	Monnier, Henry. Un détraqué. Paris, 1883.
	Mon 28.15.5	Montaigne, Michel de. Extraits. Paris, 1883.
	42533.15A	Montégut, Émile. Nos morts contemporains. 1. sér. Paris, 1883.
	37575.420	Les muses du foyer de l'opéra. Bruxelles, 1883.
X Cg	41596.19.5	Musset, Alfred de. Nouvelles et contes. Paris, 1883.
	41596.18.9F	Musset, Alfred de. Oeuvres. Paris, 1883.
	42587.37.08	Musset, Paul de. Lui et elle. Paris, 1883.
	42587.37.1	Mystere, J.E.B. Histoire scandaleuse de la famille d'Orléans. Paris, 1883?
	38513.55	Mystère de Saint Eustache joué en 1504. Gap, 1883.
	42578.29.13	Ohnet, Georges. La comtesse Sarah. 21. éd. Paris, 1883.
	42578.29.15	Ohnet, Georges. La comtesse Sarah. 45. éd. Paris, 1883.
	40542.33	O'Meara, Kathleen. Frederic Ozanam, his life and works. 3. American ed. N.Y., 1883.
	37571.29	Pagès, Alphonse. Les grands poètes français. Paris, 1883.
	42541.24	Pailleron, Édouard. Le monde où l'on s'ennuie. Paris, 1883.
	Mol 855.15	Panégyrique de l'école des femmes. Paris, 1883.
	Mol 855.15.2	Panégyrique de l'école des femmes. Paris, 1883.
	37543.32	Parnajon, Félix de. Histoire de la littérature française. Paris, 1883.

Chronological Listing

1883 - cont.

	38521.18	Pellisier, Georges. La vie et les oeuvres de Du Bartas. Paris, 1883.
	Mol 735.6	Perrin, E. Deux portraits de Molière. Paris, 1883.
	FL 365.105	Perrin, Émile. Étude sur la mise en scène. Paris, 1883.
	37596.18	Petit, Louis. Les satires. Paris, 1883.
Htn	42515.15*	Poulet-Malassis, A. Bibliographie descriptive et anecdotique des ouvrages. Paris, 1883.
	38585.28.5	Racine, Jean. Esther. N.Y., 1883.
	40556.21A	Raynal, Paul de. Les correspondents de J. Joubert, 1785-1822. Paris, 1883.
	38527.29	Réaume, Eugene. Étude sur Agrippa d'Aubigné. Paris, 1883.
	42556.17.7	Rebière, Gratien. Conference sur Sully-Prudhomme. Bergerac, 1883.
	37585.5	Regnier, A. Théâtre classique. Paris, 1883.
	42515.27.6A	Renan, Ernest. Histoire des origines du christianisme. Index général. Paris, 1883.
	42515.30.452	Renan, Ernest. L'islamisme et la science. 2. éd. Paris, 1883.
	42515.30.495	Renan, Ernest. Le judaisme comme race et comme religion. Paris, 1883. 3 pam.
	42515.30.490	Renan, Ernest. Le judaisme et le christianisme. Paris, 1883. 2 pam.
	42515.30.732	Renan, Ernest. Recollections of my youth. London, 1883.
	42515.30.731	Renan, Ernest. Recollections of my youth. N.Y., 1883.
	42515.30.710	Renan, Ernest. Souvenirs d'enfance et de jeunesse. Paris, 1883.
	39544.25.3	Renard, Georges. Vie de Voltaire. Paris, 1883.
Htn	40524.28.20*	Restif de la Bretonne, Nicolas E. Monsieur Nicolas. Paris, 1883. 14v.
	42556.22.5	Richepin, Jean. Le pavé. Paris, 1883.
	FL 6128.83	Ritter, E. Conseil de Genève jugeant les oeuvres de Rousseau. Genève, 1883.
Htn	42581.40*	Robida, A. Le voyage de M. Dumollet. Paris, 1883.
	42556.32.65	Rollinat, Maurice. Dans les brandes. Paris, 1883.
	42558.40	Ronchaud, Louis de. Poèmes dramatiques. Paris, 1883.
	38525.51	Rotrou, Jean de. Théâtre choisi. Paris, 1883.
	42578.66.30	Rouslane, V. (pseud.). Le juif de Sofievka. Paris, 1883.
	FL 6046.12.10	Rousseau, J.J. Émile ou De l'éducation. Boston, 1883.
	FL 6001.883	Rousseau, J.J. Oeuvres complètes. v.1- Paris, 1883-95.
	39594.30.6	St. Pierre, J.H.B. de. Paul and Virginia. Boston, 1883.
	37574.42.2A	Saintsbury, George. French lyrics. N.Y., 1883.
	37586.3	Sammlung Französisches Neudrucke. v.3-6. Heilbronn, 1883.
	41557.9.42.25	Sand, George. Correspondance, 1812-1876. 4. ed. Paris, 1883-92. 6v.
	41557.8.97	Sand, George. Les maîtres mosaistes. Paris, 1883.
	41557.9.31.4	Sand, George. La petite Fadette. Paris, 1883.
	41557.23.6	Sandeau, Jules. Marianna. 14e éd. Paris, 1883.
	42546.24.2	Sardou, Victorien. Divorçons. Paris, 1883.
	39534.30	Scarron, Paul. Virgile travesti. Oppeln, 1883.
	42548.26.9	Scribe, E. The ladies battle. N.Y., 1883.
	42546.34.14	Silvestre, Armand. Madame Dandin et Mademoiselle Phryné. Paris, 1883.
	42546.34.15	Silvestre, Armand. Les mélancolies d'un joyeux. Paris, 1883.
	42546.34.8	Silvestre, Armand. Pour faire rire; gauloiseries contemporaines. Paris, 1883.
	42546.34.13	Silvestre, Armand. Les tocasson. Paris, 1883.
	42516.16	Sorel, Albert. Essais d'histoire et de critique. Paris, 1883.
	41558.62.5	Souvestre, Émile. Le mémorial de famille. Paris, 1883.
	42548.76	St. Louis in chains; drama. Baltimore, 1883.
	42583.17.9	Theuriet, André. Le journal de Tristan. Paris, 1883.
	42583.33	Theuriet, André. Michel Verneuil. Paris, 1883.
	42583.29.3	Theuriet, André. Sous-bois. Paris, 1883.
	41557.10.5	Thomas, Bertha. George Sand. Boston, 1883.
	37562.16	Tolle, Konrad. Das Betheuern und Beschwöven in Altromanischen Poesie. Erlangen, 1883.
	37556.22	Toudouze, G. Albert Wolff. Paris, 1883.
	42536.49	Troubat, Jules. Le blason de la révolution. Paris, 1883.
	Mol 745.6	Ubalde. Le secret du masque de fer. Bordeaux, 1883. 3 pam.
	Mol 870.34	Valade, Léon. Les papillotes. Paris, 1883.
	37542.11.90	Van Laun, Henri. History of French literature. London, 1883.
	37543.29	Vapereau, L.G. Éléments d'histoire de la littérature française. Paris, 1883. 2v.
	42576.57.1A	Viaud, Julien. Mon frère Yves. Paris, 1883.
	41564.3.77	Vigny, Alfred de. Cinq-Mars. N.Y., 1883.
	Mol 805.2	Vitu, Auguste. Le jeu de paume des Mestayers. Paris, 1883.
	Mol 623.2	Waschow, J. Molière et ses prédécesseurs. Oppeln, 1883.
	42587.84.31	Zaccone, Pierre. Un duel à mort. Paris, 1883.
	42584.4	Zola, Emile. Au bonheur des dames. Paris, 1883.

1884

	42562.14	About, Edmond. De Pontoise à Stamboul. Paris, 1884.
	42562.6.20	About, Edmond. Germaine. 3e séries. Paris, 1884.
	42562.35	About, Edmond. Selections. London, 1884.
	42586.6.5	Achard, Amédée. Brunes de blondes. Paris, 1884.
	Mol 601.1F	Achkinasi, M. Molière, ses traducteurs en Russie. Paris, 1884.
	37576.20	Alamanach des petits jeux floraux de Marseille, pour 1884-1885. Marseille, 1884-85.
	37563.17	Alaux, J.E. La langue et la littérature franc du XVe au XVIIe siècle. Paris, 1884.
	42566.16.10	Albalat, A. L'amour chez Alphonse Daudet. 3. éd. Paris, 1884.
	37566.27	Albert, Paul. La littérature française au 19th siècle. Paris, 1884. 2v.
	41578.36	Alexandre, Charles. Souvenirs sur Lamartine. Paris, 1884.
	42553.32	Amiel, Henri F. Fragments d'un journal intime. Genève, 1884. 2v.
	42586.8	Arène, Paul. Oeuvres. Paris, 1884.
	37593.64.10	Bahlsin, L. Adam de la Halle. Marburg, 1884.
	40594.16	Balzac, Honoré de. Études philosophiques. La peau de chagrin. Paris, 1884.
	40594.18	Balzac, Honoré de. Études philosophiques. Sur Catherine de Médici. Louis Lambert. Paris, 1884.
	40594.21	Balzac, Honoré de. Oeuvres de jeunesse. Argon le pirate. Jame la pale. Paris, 1884.
	40594.24	Balzac, Honoré de. Oeuvres de jeunesse. L'héritière de birague. Paris, 1884.
	40597.32.4	Balzac, Honoré de. La peau de chagrin. Paris, 1884.
	40594.15	Balzac, Honoré de. Vie de campagne. Le médecin de campagne. Paris, 1884.

1884 - cont.

	40594.8	Balzac, Honoré de. Vie de province. Illusions perdues. v.1-2. Paris, 1884.
	40594.6	Balzac, Honoré de. Vie de province. Les célibataires. v.12.- Paris, 1884.
	40594.11	Balzac, Honoré de. Vie parisienne. César Berotteau. La maison Nuchingen. Paris, 1884.
	40594.4	Balzac, Honoré de. Vie privée. Beatrix. Honorine. Paris, 1884.
	40594.1	Balzac, Honoré de. Vie privée. La maison du Chat-qui-Pelote. Paris, 1884.
	42554.8	Banville, Théodore de. Contes héroiques. Paris, 1884.
	42554.3	Banville, Théodore de. Nous tous. Paris, 1884.
	42586.19	Baudoux, F. Bigarrures par F. Baudoux. Bruxelles, 1884.
	37596.3A	Beaumanoir, P. de. Oeuvres poétique. Paris, 1884-85. 2v.
	40532.4.20	Beaumarchais, Pierre A.C. de. Le barbier de Séville. Paris, 1884.
	42513.16	Beausacq, Marie Josephine. Maximes de la vie. Paris, 1884.
	42542.28.7	Becque, Henri. Le frisson; fantasie rimée. Paris, 1884.
	42563.22.14.25	Belot, Adolphe. Le testament de César Girodot. N.Y., 1884.
	38526.4	Béreau, Jacques. Oeuvres poétiques de Jacques Béreau. Paris, 1884.
	40528.10	Bernard, Pierre Joseph. Poésies choisies. Paris, 1884.
	FL 6128.84.2	Berthoud, F. Jean-Jacques Rousseau et le pasteur de Montmollin. Fleurier, 1884.
	Mol 870.35	Bertol-Graivil. Maître et valets. Paris, 1884.
	40582.24.6	Beyle, Henri. Le rouge et le noir. Paris, 1884. 3v.
	42563.28.13	Biart, Lucien. Le pensativo. Paris, 1884.
	42563.28.41	Biart, Lucien. Le roi des prairies. Paris, 1884.
	38512.100	Bible. O.T. Psalms. French (Old French). Le Psautier de Metz. Paris, 1884.
	42563.23.21.10	Bloy, Léon. Propos d'un entrepreneur de démolitions. Paris, 1884.
Htn	FL 384.61*	Borbey d'Aurevilly, Jules. Les vielles actrices. Paris, 1884.
	41522.65.5	Borel, d'Hauterive, Petrus. Rapsodies. Avec une eau-forte d'Adrien Aubry. Bruxelles, 1884.
	38557.39	Bossuet, J.B. Fac-simile du sermon sur le jugement dernier. Paris, 1884.
	42542.42.5	Bouché, Jacques. Gallet et le Caveau, 1698-1757. v.1-2. Paris, 1884.
	42542.30.11	Bouchor, Maurice. L'Aurore. Paris, 1884.
	Mol 855.6	Boursault, E. Le medecin volant. Paris, 1884.
	38576.5	Boursault, Edme. Le medicine volant. Paris, 1884.
	37596.27.2	Braunis, Julius. Über...der altfranzösischen Cancun de St. Alexis. Kiel, 1884.
	38551.21	Broglie, Emmanuel de. Fénelon a Cambrai 1699-1715. Paris, 1884.
	37558.29	Brunel, Lucien. Les philosophes et l'Académie française. Paris, 1884.
	42524.14	Brunetière, F. Histoire et littérature. Paris, 1884. 3v.
	42586.29.3	Caraguel, J. Le Boul' Mich'. 2. éd. Paris, 1884.
	42521.19.24	Casoli, Pier. Di Luigi Veuillot. Modena, 1884.
	39586.18	Chamfort, S.R.N. Oeuvres. Paris, 1884.
	38521.50	Chardon, Henri. La vie de Rotrou mieux connue. Paris, 1884.
	40586.11.30F	Chateaubriand, F.A.R. Atala. N.Y., 1884.
	40527.16.5	Chenier, André. Poésies. Paris, 1884.
	38525.27	Cherrier, Henri. Bibliographie de Mathurin Régnier. Paris, 1884.
	42554.26.33	Circello, marquis de. Entretiens poétiques. Firenze, 1884.
	42565.55.20	Cladel, Léon. Kerkader garde-barrière. Paris, 1884.
	37567.31	Claretie, J. Célébrités contemporaines. A. Dumas. Paris, 1884.
	37567.30	Claretie, J. Célébrités contemporaines. Victor Hugo. Paris, 1884.
	42586.30.52	Claudin, G. Mes souvenirs, les boulevards de 1840-1870. 2. éd. Paris, 1884.
	37596.56	Cloetta, Wilhelm. Alfassungszeit und Überlieferung das Poème moral. Erlangen, 1884.
	FL 398.7.27	Colombier, Marie. Les mémoires de Sarah Barnum. Paris, 1884.
	FL 398.7.28	Colombier, Marie. The memoirs of Sarah Barnum. N.Y., 1884.
	42554.23.5	Coppée, François. La maison de Molière; poésie. Paris, 1884.
	Mol 270.19A	Coquelin, C. Tartuffe. Paris, 1884.
	42561.13.25	Craven, Pauline. Le travail d'une ame. 4e éd. Paris, 1884.
	37558.39	D., Y. "The forty immortals". N.Y., 1884.
	42566.20	Daudet, Alphonse. Contes choisis. Paris, 1884.
	42566.21.7	Daudet, Alphonse. Contes du lundi. Paris, 1884.
	42566.24.8	Daudet, Alphonse. Fromont jeune et Risler ainé. Paris, 1884.
	42566.52.27	Daudet, Alphonse. The immortal or One of the forty. Chicago, 1884.
	42566.30.8	Daudet, Alphonse. Numa Roumestan. Paris, 1884.
	42566.34	Daudet, Alphonse. Sapho. Paris, 1884.
	40528.12	De Bonnard, C. Poésies diverses. Paris, 1884.
	42548.8	Delair, Paul. Les contes d'à présent. Paris, 1884.
	42542.63.2	Dellard, P. Un amour de Wateau. Valenciennes, 1884.
	38585.8	Deschanel, Émile. Racine. Paris, 1884. 2v.
	Mol 604.3	Despine, P. La science du coeur humain. Paris, 1884.
	37567.27	Desprez, Louis. L'évolution naturaliste. Paris, 1884.
	40535.5.21	Destouches, Philippe Néricault. Théâtre choisi. Paris, 1884.
	39564.13	Diderot, Denis. Le nevue de Rameau. Paris, 1884.
	39564.8	Diderot, Denis. Oeuvres choisies. Paris, 1884.
	FL 360.60.20	Dreyfus, Abraham. Mellan kulisserna. Visby, 1884.
	42568.9.5	Droz, Gustave. Une femme gênante. 26. éd. Paris, 1884.
	42568.11.2	Droz, Gustave. Monsieur, madame et bébé. 126. éd. Paris, 1884.
	42568.13A	Droz, Gustave. Tristesses et sourires. Paris, 1884.
	42568.18.9	Du Boisgobey, Fortuné. Le secret de Berthe. v.1-2. Paris, 1884.
	42541.8.15	Dumanior, P.F.P. Les invalides du mariage. Paris, 1884.
	41539.10	Dumas, Alexandre. Le monument de Alexandre Dumas, oeuvre de Gustave Doré. Paris, 1884.
	41538.53.75	Dumas, Alexandre. De tre musketerer. Kjøbenhavn, 1884.
	41538.64	Dumas, Alexandre. Oi treis somatophylakes. En Athènais, 1884. 2v.
	42554.29.200.5	Dupuy, E. Les parques. Paris, 1884.

1884 - cont.

42563.44.3 Durand, Alice M.C.F. Un crime. Paris, 1884.
42563.55.10 Durand, Alice M.C.F. L'ingénue. 6. éd. Paris, 1884.
42568.22 Durny, Georges. Andrée. Paris, 1884.
37596.73 Eberhardt, Paul. Der Lucidaire Gilleberts. Halle, 1884.
37541.30 Engel, Eduard. Psychologie der französischen Literatur. Wien, 1884.
Mon 116.1 Feis, Jacob. Shakespeare and Montaigne. London, 1884.
42575.51.2 Feuillet, Octave. La veuve. Le voyageur. 16. éd. Paris, 1884.
42575.51.4 Feuillet, Octave. La veuve. Le voyageur. 24. éd. Paris, 1884.
42575.51.3 Feuillet, Octave. La veuve. Le voyageur. 30. éd. Paris, 1884.
42575.51 Feuillet, Octave. La veuve. Le voyageur. 30. éd. Paris, 1884.
FL 397.82 Fischbach, Gustave. Le théâtre de Strasbourg et la dotation apffel. Strasbourg, 1884.
Htn 42576.36* Flaubert, Gustave. Lettres à George Sand. Paris, 1884.
42576.35.8A Flaubert, Gustave. Lettres à George Sand précédées d'une étude par Guy de Maupassant. Paris, 1884.
37596.10A Foerster, Wendelin. Christian von Troyes sämtliche Werke. Halle, 1884-1932. 5v.
42575.53.48 Fould, W. de (Mme.). Le sphinx aux perles. Paris, 1884.
38588.22 Fournel, Victor. Petites comédies, rare et curieuses de 17e siècle. Paris, 1884. 2v.
42586.52.5A Fouvielle, Wilfred de. L'espion aérien. Paris, 1884.
39566.125 François, L. Lettres à M. Bizot de Fonteny. Langres, 1884.
42576.61.55 Frémine, Charles. Vieux airs et jeunes chansons. Paris, 1884.
42571.24 Gaboriau, Emile. L'argent des autres. Paris, 1884. 2v.
42571.25 Gaboriau, Emile. La corde au cou. Paris, 1884.
FL 398.14 Gaillet, Eugène. La vie de Marie Pigeonnier (Marie Colombier). Paris, 1884.
37562.26 Garreaud, L. Causeries...sur le moyen âge littéraires de la France. Paris, 1884. 2v.
41542.26 Gautier, Théophile. Caprices et zigzags. Paris, 1884.
41542.25 Gautier, Théophile. L'Orient. Paris, 1884. 2v.
41542.30.90 Gautier, Théophile. Poésies complètes. Paris, 1884-85. 2v.
37565.96 Géruzez, Eugéne. Histoire de la littérature française, 1789-1800. 8e éd. Paris, 1884.
41539.5 Glinel, Charles. Alexandre Dumas et son oeuvre. Reims, 1884. 2v.
37555.310 Gosset, A. Manual of French prosody...use of Engish students. London, 1884.
42576.40.305 Halévy, Ludovic. L'abbé Constantin. 62. éd. Paris, 1884.
37547.5 Halgan, Stéphane. Anthologie des poètes breton du XVIIe siècle. Nantes, 1884.
41574.23 Hartmann, K.A.M. Victor Hugo. Leipzig, 1884.
FL 358.84A Hawkins, F. Annals of the French stage. London, 1884. 2v.
Htn 42543.62.85* Hennique, Léon. L'accident de Monsieur Hébert. Paris, 1884.
42543.65.10 Hermant, Abel. M. Rabosson. Paris, 1884.
40515.5.86.5 Herpin, C.A.L. Une femme du monde au XVIIIe siècle; dernières années de Madame d'Epinay. 5e éd. Paris, 1884.
38525.8.5 Herting, A. Der Versbau Etienne Jodelle's. Kiel, 1884.
42576.67.2 Hervieu, Paul. La bêtise parisienne. Paris, 1884.
FL 398.56.20 Heulhard, A. Jean Monnet. Paris, 1884.
FL 398.74.78 Houssaye, A. La comédienne. 8e ed. Paris, 1884.
37558.36 Houssaye, Arsène. Histoire de 41me fauteuil. Paris, 1884.
41572.40 Hugo, Victor. Les chansons des rues et des lois. Paris, 1884.
NEDL 41573.18.12 Hugo, Victor. La légende des siecles. 1e série. Paris, 1884.
41572.28.15 Hugo, Victor. Les orientales. Les feuilles d'automne. Les chants du crépuscule. Paris, 1884.
41572.33.5 Hugo, Victor. Théâtre. Paris, 1884. 3v.
41572.30.12 Hugo, Victor. Les voix intérieures. Les rayons et les ombres. Paris, 1884.
Mol 608.9 Humbert, C. Englands Urteil über Molière. Leipzig, 1884.
42588.10 Isidore Baurel. Paris, 1884.
FL 6128.84 Jansen, A. Jean-Jacques Rousseau als Musiker. Berlin, 1884.
37565.25 Joret, Charles. Des rapports intellectuels et littéraires. Paris, 1884.
37558.33.5 Kerviler, René. Bibliographie chronologique. Saint-Nazaire, 1884.
42544.26.3 Labiche, Eugène. Le voyage de Monsieur Perrichon. 3e éd. N.Y., 1884.
42514.18.7A Laboulaye, Edouard. Derniers contes bleus. Paris, 1884.
Htn 39526.31* La Fontaine, Jean de. Fables of La Fontaine. Boston, 1884.
41522.17.8 Laporte, A. Baudelaire et Roger de Beauvoir; bibliographie. Paris, 1884.
42554.11.2 Laporte, A. Théodore de Banville. Paris, 1884.
37530.66 Laporte, Antoine. Bibliographie contemporaine. Paris, 1884-90. 7v.
Htn 40597.7* Laporte, Antoine. Honoré de Balzac. Étude bibliographique. Paris, 1884.
41522.3 La Porte, Antonio. Barbey d'Aurevilly et ses oeuvres. Paris, 1884.
FL 361.29 La Rounat, C. Études dramatiques. Le théâtre français. Paris, 1884.
42555.33.50 Leconte, Léon. La sorciere de Baincthum. St. Omer, 1884.
37567.26 Lermina, J. Le mouvement littéraire en France en 1882-1883. Paris, 1884.
42513.74 Leroy-Beaulieu, A. Un homme d'etat Russe. Paris, 1884.
37574.14.5 Louandre, Charles. Chefs-d'oeuvres des conteurs français. Paris, 1884.
38575.105 Maillet du Boullay, Charles. La maison de pierre Corneille au petit Couronne. Rouen, 1884.
40556.27.5 Maistre, Joseph de. Oeuvres complètes. Lyon, 1884. 14v.
40528.11 Malfilâtre, J.C.L. de C. de. Poésies. Paris, 1884.
40526.22 Malfilâtre, J.C.L. de C. de. Poésies. Paris, 1884.
37596.69.2 Mann, M.F. Der Physiologus des Philipp von Thaün und seine Quellen. Halle, 1884.
38526.32.4 Marguerite d'Angoulême. L'Heptaméron des nouvelles. Paris, 1884.
42557.4.50 Mariéton, Paul. Joséphin Soulary et la pléiade lyonnaise: Victor de Laprade. Paris, 1884.
42545.9.14 Martel de Janville, S.G. Autour du mariage. 47e éd. Paris, 1884.

1884 - cont.

42555.49.150 Marth, Frédéric. Poésies de F. Marth. Paris, 1884.
Htn 42577.3.10* Maupassant, Guy de. Au soleil. Paris, 1884.
42577.2.3 Maupassant, Guy de. Miss Harriet. Paris, 1884.
42577.4.1 Maupassant, Guy de. Les soeurs Rondoli. Paris, 1884.
42577.4 Maupassant, Guy de. Une vie. Paris, 1884.
Mol 171.32 Molière, Jean Baptiste Poquelin. Le bourgeois gentilhomme...Clapin. Cambridge, 1884.
Mol 171.33 Molière, Jean Baptiste Poquelin. Le bourgeois gentilhomme...Moriarty. London, 1884.
Mol 211.40 Molière, Jean Baptiste Poquelin. Les femmes savantes...Livet. Paris, 1884.
Mol 211.40.2 Molière, Jean Baptiste Poquelin. Les femmes savantes...Livet. Paris, 1884.
Mol 251.36 Molière, Jean Baptiste Poquelin. Les précieuses ridicules. Lang. Oxford, 1884.
Mol 251.37 Molière, Jean Baptiste Poquelin. Les précieuses ridicules. Larroumet. Paris, 1884.
Mol 251.35 Molière, Jean Baptiste Poquelin. Les précieuses ridicules. Livet. Paris, 1884.
Mol 251.35.2 Molière, Jean Baptiste Poquelin. Les précieuses ridicules. Livet. Paris, 1884.
Mol 130.3 Molière, Jean Baptiste Poquelin. Sobranie sochinenii. Sankt Peterburg, 1884.
FL 398.56.15 Monnet, Jean. Mémoires de Jean Monnet. Paris, 1884.
42555.52 Monnier, Marc. Novelle napoletane. 2. ed. Milano, 1884.
42555.52.10 Monnier, Marc. La renaissance, de Dante à Luther. Paris, 1884.
42533.16A Montégut, Émile. Nos morts contemporains. 2. sér. Paris, 1884.
38513.19.7 Moreau, Georges. Grande pastorale de Noël. Drame-mystère. Tours, 1884.
41596.22.5 Musset, Alfred de. La confession d'un enfant du siècle. Paris, 1884.
41596.12.5A Musset, Alfred de. Premières poésies. 1829-1835. Paris, 1884.
42578.17.200 Niboyet, Paulin. La vierge de Belem. Paris, 1884.
37536.15 Nisard, Désiré. Histoire de la littérature française. v.2-4. 12. éd. Paris, 1884. 3v.
42578.27 Noriac, Jules. Paris tel qu'il est. Paris, 1884.
37576.547 Le nouveau décaméron. 2e, 5e, 9e journée. Paris, 1884-87.
42578.30.20 Ohnet, Georges. Der Hüttenbesitzer. v.1-2. Stuttgart, 1884.
42578.29.5 Ohnet, Georges. Lise Fleuron. Paris, 1884.
42578.30 Ohnet, Georges. Le maître de forges. Paris, 1884.
42578.30.10 Ohnet, Georges. Serge Panine. Paris, 1884.
37562.12.26 Otten, G. Ueber die Caesur im altfranzösischen. Greifswald, 1884.
37596.66 Paris, Gaston. Le lai de l'oiselet. Poème français du XIIIe siècle. Paris, 1884.
38511.29 Parmentier, J. Le henno de Reuchlin et la farce de Maistre Pathelin. Paris, 1884.
39544.33.2 Parton, James. Life of Voltaire. 4th ed. Boston, 1884. 2v.
40573.3.50 Peignot, Gabriel. Lettres inédites. Dijon, 1884.
42578.30.47 Peladan, J. Etudes passionnelles de décadence. 2. éd. Paris, 1884.
37543.25 Petit de Julleville, L. Leçons de littérature française. Paris, 1884.
42587.46.2 Peyrebrune, G. de. Une séparation. Paris, 1884.
41587.18.5 Picard, Louis Benoît. Les deux ménages. Paris, 1884.
40567.2 Piedagnel, A. Jules Janin. Paris, 1884.
40567.40.3 Piedagnel, Alexander. Jules Janin. 3. éd. Paris, 1884.
40536.20.25 Piron, Alexis. Voyage à Beaune. Paris, 1884.
Mol 616.3 Pohlisch, B. Patoisformen in Molières Lustspielen. Halle, 1884.
42556.12 Pontgibaud. Normandies, ou Le décaméron Normand. Caen, 1884.
38585.19.1.5 Racine, Jean. Andromaque; tragédie. Paris, 1884.
37595.33 Raynaud, Gaston. Bibliographie des chansonniers français des XIIIe et XIXe siècles. Paris, 1884.
38587.8.7 Regnard, Jean François. Le joueur, comédie en cinq actes. London, 1884.
42515.30.410 Renan, Ernest. Nouvelles études d'histoire religieuse. Paris, 1884.
40524.31 Restif de la Bretonne, Nicolas E. La vie de mon père. Paris, 1884.
42578.31.120 Revillon, T. La bourgeoise pervertie. Paris, 1884.
42556.22.10F Richepin, Jean. Les blasphèmes. Paris, 1884.
42556.22.8 Richepin, Jean. Nana-Sahib. Paris, 1884.
42578.19.14 Rod, Edouard. La femme d'Henri Vauneau. Paris, 1884.
FL 6041.84 Rousseau, J.J. Émile ou De l'éducation. Paris, 1884.
FL 6002.884 Rousseau, J.J. Morceaux choisis. Paris, 1884.
41557.8.102.3 Sand, George. La mare au diable. Paris, 1884.
FL 384.60 Sarcey, F. Comédiens et comédiennes. Théâtres divers. Paris, 1884.
42546.29.3 Sardou, Victorien. La perle noire. N.Y., 1884.
42546.29 Sardou, Victorien. La perle noire. N.Y., 1884.
42546.16.5 Sardou, Victorien. Théâtre. Paris, 1884-98. 2v.
37596.73.5 Schladebach, H. Das Elucidarium des Honorius Augustodunensis. Leipzig, 1884.
42546.40.110 Scholl, Aurélien. Denise. Paris, 1884.
42546.47.30 Sonal, Marc. Le sonnet d'Arvers. Paris, 1884.
41558.26 Soulié, Frédéric. Aventures d'un jeune cadet de famille. Paris, 1884.
42583.31 Theuriet, André. Tante Aurélie. Paris, 1884.
37543.31 Tivier, H. Histoire de la littérature française. Paris, 1884.
42547.7.15 Uchard, Mario. Mademoiselle Blaisot. 10e ed. Paris, 1884.
Htn 42581.33* Vallès, Jules. Jacques Vingtras. L'enfant. Paris, 1884.
42547.10.21 Vallette, Marguerjte. Monieur Vénus. Bruxelles, 1884.
37543.30 Vapereau, L.G. Esquise d'histoire de la littérature française. Paris, 1884.
42521.3 Veuillot, Louis. Correspondance. Paris, 1884. 9v.
42576.57.2 Viaud, Julien. Mon frère Yves. Paris, 1884.
42584.25.75 Vibe, J. Nogle bemaerkninger i anledning af naturalismen. Kristiania, 1884.
37576.330 Villeneuve-Guibert, Gaston. Le portefeuille de Madame Dupin. Paris, 1884.
38514.18.9 Villon, François. Le Jargon du XV siècle. Onze ballades. Paris, 1884.
37562.57.5 Vising, J. Sur la versification Anglo-Normande. Upsala, 1884.
FL 383.57 Vitu, Auguste. Le mille et une nuits du théâtre. Paris, 1884-94. 9v.
Mol 723.1 Warburg, K. Molière; en Lefnadsteckning. Stockholm, 1884.

1884 - cont.

	37564.35	Weinberg, Gustav. Das französische Schäferspiel in der 17th Jahrhundert. Frankfurt, 1884.
	42584.3.8	Zola, Emile. L'assommoir. Paris, 1884.
	42584.23.6.5	Zola, Emile. La joie de vivre. Paris, 1884.
	42584.23.6	Zola, Emile. La joie de vivre. Paris, 1884.
	42584.12.17	Zola, Emile. Nais Micoulin. Paris, 1884.
	37555.210	Zschalig, H. Die Verslehren von Fabri, du Pont...Alteren Geschichte der franz Poetik. Leipzig, 1884.

1885

	37595.5	Abailard, Pierre. Lettres complètes d'Abélard et d'Héloise. Paris, 1885?
	42562.9.5	About, Edmond. Lettres d'un bon jeune homme à sa cousine Madeleine. Paris, 1885.
	42562.13.3	About, Edmond. La mère de la marquise. N.Y., 1885.
	42562.31	About, Edmond. Le nez d'un notaire. 13. éd. Boston, 1885.
	42562.31.1	About, Edmond. Le nez d'un notaire. 14. éd. Boston, 1885.
	42562.38.14.60	Adam, Paul. Chair molle; roman naturaliste. Bruxelles, 1885.
	42542.1.11.25	Alexandre, André. Le sonneur de Biniou. Paris, 1885.
	37596.26.10	Aléxius, Saint. Légend. La vie de Saint Aléxis. Paris, 1885.
X Cg	37596.26.10.5	Aléxius, Saint. Légend. La vie de Saint Aléxis. Paris, 1885.
	42553.32.75	Amiel, Henri F. Amiel's journal. London, 1885.
	42553.32.2	Amiel, Henri F. Fragments d'un journal intime. Genève, 1885. 2v.
	FL 361.32	Audebrand, P. Petits mémoirs d'une stalle d'orchestre. Paris, 1885.
	37594.20	Augustin, Friedrich. Sprachliche Untersuchung über die Werke Henri d'Andelis. Inaug. Diss. Marburg, 1885.
	37591.15	Aumeric. La passion Sainte Catherine. Paris, 1885.
	42553.68	Baillet, Eugène. Chansons et petits poèmes. Paris, 1885.
	40594.20	Balzac, Honoré de. Les contes drolatiques. v. 1-3. Paris, 1885.
	40597.15.6	Balzac, Honoré de. Le cousin Pons. Paris, 1885.
	40596.13.26	Balzac, Honoré de. The Duchess de Langeais. Boston, 1885.
	40597.36.9	Balzac, Honoré de. Les Parisiens en Province. Paris, 1885.
	40597.29.4.75	Balzac, Honoré de. Père Goriot. Boston, 1885.
	40597.29.4.4	Balzac, Honoré de. Le père Goriot. Paris, 1885.
	40597.29.4.3	Balzac, Honoré de. Père Goriot. Paris, 1885.
	40594.7	Balzac, Honoré de. Vie de province. Les parisiens en province. Paris, 1885.
	42554.5.2	Banville, Théodore de. Contes bourgeois. Paris, 1885.
	42554.8.2	Banville, Théodore de. Lettres chimeriques. Paris, 1885.
	41522.42	Bernard, Charles de. Le noeud gordien. Paris, 1885.
	42542.29.90	Beudin, J.F. Pedro el negro. Madrid, 1885.
	40582.8.7	Beyle, Henri. La chartreuse de Parme. Paris, 1885.
	42563.28.9	Biart, Lucien. Le fleuve d'or. Paris, 1885.
	37596.127A	Bible. N.T. Gospels Nicodemus. Trois versions rimées de l'evangile Nicodime. Paris, 1885.
	Mol 860.51	Billard, E. La vocation de Molière. Paris, 1885.
	41539.4A	Blaze Bury, H. Alexandre Dumas, sa vie, son temps, son oeuvre. Paris, 1885.
	FL 397.115.82	Body, Albin. Le théâtre et la musique à Spa au temps passé et au temps présent. 2. éd. Bruxelles, 1885.
	40587.5	Bona, Félix de. Chateaubriand, sa vie et ses écrits. Lille, 1885.
	38557.33	Bossuet, J.B. Choix de sermons. Paris, 1885.
	38557.27.10	Bossuet, J.B. Oraisons funèbres. Paris, 1885.
	38557.27.15	Bossuet, J.B. Oraisons funèbres. Paris, 1885?
	42563.37.5A	Bourget, Paul. Cruelle énigme. Paris, 1885.
	42563.37.40	Bourget, Paul. L'irréparable. 3. éd. Paris, 1885.
	42587.73.5	Bouton, Victor. Lettre à Madame de Witt. Paris, 1885.
	42587.39.5	Cantacuzène-Altieri, Olga. Fleur de Neige. Paris, 1885.
	FL 6128.85	Ceresole, V. Jean-Jacques Rousseau à Venise, 1743-1744. Genève, 1885.
	42563.71	Challamel, August. Souvenirs d'un hugolâtre; la génération de 1830. Paris, 1885.
	42564.56	Chapuis, Ernest. Récits et légendes de Franche-Comté. Paris, 1885.
	40527.16.8	Chenier, André. Oeuvres poétiques. Paris, 1885.
	42565.55.75	Cladel, Léon. Léon Cladel et sa kyrielle de chiens. Paris, 1885.
	42565.55.120	Cladel, Léon. Petits cahiers. Paris, 1885.
	37543.27	Collas, Louis. Histoire de la littérature française. Paris, 1885.
	38526.17.19	Collischonn, G.A.O. Jacques Grévin's Tragödie "Caesar". Inaug. Diss. Marburg, 1885.
Htn	37556.21.11*	Contades, G. L'homme au camélia Lautour-Megeray. Argentan, 1885.
	37572.48A	Contes de Figaro. Paris, 1885.
	38575.33.4	Corneille, Pierre. Horace; a tragedy. N.Y., 1885.
	40534.29	Crébillon, Prosper Jolyot de. Théâtre complet. Paris, 1885.
	FL 383.34	Crémieux, A. Autographes. Paris, 1885.
Htn	42561.15*	Daudet, Alphonse. Fromont jeune et Risler ainé. Paris, 1885. 2v.
	42566.20.13	Daudet, Alphonse. Le siège de Berlin. N.Y., 1885.
	42567.30.5	Daudet, Ernest. Le roman de Delphine. Paris, 1885.
	37596.45.3	Davids, Fritz. Über Form und Sprache der Gedichte Thibaults IV. Braunschweig, 1885.
	38585.8.2	Deschanel, Émile. Racine. Paris, 1885. 2v.
	37565.29	Desnoiresterres, Gustave. La comédie satirique au XVIIIe siècle. Paris, 1885.
	42542.66.5	Dreyfus, A. On his devoted head. N.Y., 1885.
	37543.12	Droz, T. L'ésprit Gaulois dans la littérature française. Zürich, 1885.
	42543.16.10.5	Dumas, Alexandre. La dame aux camélias. N.Y., 1885.
	42543.16.30	Dumas, Alexandre. Denise; pièce en quatre actes. 3e éd. Paris, 1885.
	40597.2.300	Du Pontavice de Heussey, Robert. Balzac en Bretagne. Rennes, 1885.
	42563.44.4	Durand, Alice M.C.F. Un crime. 12. éd. Paris, 1885.
	42563.45.5	Durand, Alice M.C.F. Dosia. 4. éd. N.Y., 1885.
	42563.48.15	Durand, Alice M.C.F. Idylles. N.Y., 1885.
	42563.48.10	Durand, Alice M.C.F. Idylles. Paris, 1885.
	42524.50	Duret, T. Critique d'avant-garde. Paris, 1885.
	42568.23.14.42	Duval, Paul. Modernités. Paris, 1885.
	38528.8.2	Estienne, Henri. Deux dialogues du nouveau langage françois, italianizé. Paris, 1885. 2v.
	42574.15.3	Fabre, Ferdinand. Barnabé. Paris, 1885.
	42574.19	Fabre, Ferdinand. Lucifer. Paris, 1885.
	42554.32.10	Fabre Des Essarts, L.E.J. Humanité. Paris, 1885.

1885 - cont.

	37564.32.50	Faguet, Émile. Les grands maitres du dix-septième siècle. Paris, 1885.
	38527.63	Favre, Jules. Olivier de Magny. Paris, 1885.
	38554.322.65	Fénelon, F. de S. de la Mothe. De l'existence de Dieu. Paris, 1885.
	42576.28.39	Flaubert, Gustave. Madame Bovary. Paris, 1885.
	42576.28.38	Flaubert, Gustave. Madame Bovary. Paris, 1885.
	42576.16	Flaubert, Gustave. Oeuvres complètes. Paris, 1885. 8v.
	42576.33.2	Flaubert, Gustave. Trois contes. 7. éd. Paris, 1885.
	37591.25	Foerster, Wendelin. Li sermon Saint Bernart. Erlangen, 1885.
	Mol 213.5	Follioley, L. Les femmes savantes. Tours, 1885.
	37564.20	Follioley, Léopold. Histoire de la littérature française. 5e éd. Tours, 1885. 3v.
	42586.54.4	Fouquier, Henry. La sagesse parisienne. Paris, 1885.
	37564.38	Fournel, Victor. De Malherbe a Bossuet. Paris, 1885.
	Mol 606.5	Fournier, E. Étude sur la vie et les oeuvres de Molière. Paris, 1885.
	Mol 606.5.2	Fournier, E. Études sur la vie et les oeuvres de Molière. Paris, 1885.
	42571.28	Gaboriau, Emile. Le crime d'Orcival. Paris, 1885.
	42571.31	Gaboriau, Emile. Les esclaves de Paris. Paris, 1885. 2v.
	43616.2.36F	Gautier, Judith. Poèmes de la libellule. Paris, 1885.
	41542.11.3	Gautier, Théophile. Mademoiselle de Maupin. Paris, 1885.
	42554.45	Ghil, René. Légende d'âmes et de sangs. Paris, 1885.
	42575.57	Goncourt, Edmond de. En 18... Paris, 1885.
	42575.67	Goncourt, Jules de. Lettres. Paris, 1885.
	42543.60.15	Grandmougin, Charles. Yvonne. Paris, 1885.
	40517.37.10	Gueulette, T.S. Parades inédites. Paris, 1885.
	FL 395.215	Gueullette, C. Répetoire de la comédie-française, 1883-1891. Paris, 1885-92. 8v.
	42543.62.24	Guiard, Emile. Feu de paille. Paris, 1885.
	FL 394.85PF	Guillaumot, Auguste E. Costumes de la comédie française. Paris, 1885.
	37596.24A	Hamel, A.G. van. Romans de charité et misère. Paris, 1885. 2v.
	Mol 608.16	Hartmann, C. Einfluss Molière auf Dryden's...Dichtungen. Leipzig, 1885.
	41555.39.5	Haussonville, Gabriel Paul. Prosper Mérimée. Paris, 1885.
	42541.17	Hennequin, Alfred. La femme à papa. N.Y., 1885.
	42576.14.55	Houssaye, Arsène. Les confessions. 1830-1880. Paris, 1885-1891. 6v.
	42576.14.10	Houssaye, Arsène. Contes pour les femmes. v.1-2,5. Paris, 1885-1886.
Htn	37596.108*	Hue Archevesque. Les dits de Hue Archevesque. Paris, 1885.
	37596.108.2	Hue Archevesque. Les dits de Hue Archevesque. Rouen, 1885.
	40526.8.20	Hülsen, R. André Chénier. Berlin, 1885.
	41573.40.10	Hugo, Victor. L'oeuvre complète de Victor Hugo; extraits. Paris, 1885.
	41571.2	Hugo, Victor. Oeuvres de Victor Hugo. Paris, 1885-91. 29v.
	41574.48	Hugo, Victor. Propos de table recueillis par R. Lesclide. 3e éd. Paris, 1885.
	41573.37	Hugo, Victor. Translations from the poems of Victor Hugo. London, 1885.
	Mol 608.14	Humbert, C. Molière, Vater der deutschen Schauspielkunst. Berlin, 1885.
	FL 6128.85.2	Jansen, A. Documents sur Jean-Jacques Rousseau, 1762-1765. Genève, 1885.
	FL 6128.85.3	Jansen, A. Jean-Jacques Rousseau als Botaniker. Berlin, 1885.
	38527.45	Jensen, A. Syntactische Studien zu Robert Garnier. Kiel, 1885.
	40556.20.18	Joubert, Joseph. Pensées of Joubert. Paris, 1885. 2v.
	Mol 611.1	Kayser, H. Zur Syntax Molières. Kiel, 1885.
	FL 398.74.56	Kennard, Nina H. Rachel. London, 1885.
	38514.58.2	Koch, F. Leben und Werke der Christine de Pisan. Goslar, 1885.
	37564.16	Koerting, H. Geschichte des französischen Romans im XVII Jahrhunderts. Leipzig, 1885. 2v.
	38587.29	Kownatzki, F.A. Essai sur Hardy. Tilsit, 1885.
	37595.14	Krensnir, Adolf. Rustebrief's Gedichte. Wolfenbüttel, 1885.
	42544.26.4	Labiche, Eugène. Le voyage de Monsieur Perrichon. London, 1885.
	38564.35	La Bruyère, J. de. The characters. London, 1885.
	38564.35.3	La Bruyère, J. de. The "characters". N.Y., 1885.
	41578.30.4	Lamartine, Alphonse. Raphael. Paris, 1885.
	42514.26	Lanfrey, P. Correspondance. Paris, 1885. 2v.
	Mol 803.1	Larroumet, G. Une famille des comédiens au XVIIe siècle, les Béjart. Paris, 1885.
	Mol 870.36	Legendre, L. Célimène. Paris, 1885.
	42513.80	Leroy-Beaulieu, A. Les catholiques liberaux. Paris, 1885.
	41574.48.2	Lesclide, Richard. Propos de table de Victor Hugo. 4e éd. Paris, 1885.
	37597.11.6	Lorenz, F.W. Der Stil in Maistre Wace's Roman de Rou. Leipzig, 1885.
	42555.42.25	Lys, Georges de. Les tubereuses. Paris, 1885.
	39544.34	Mahrenholtz, R. Voltaires Leben und Werke. Oppeln, 1885.
	40588.41	Maistre, Xavier. La jeune sibérienne. Cambridge, 1885.
	40588.41.2	Maistre, Xavier. La jeune sibérienne. London, 1885.
	40588.47.1	Maistre, Xavier. Journey round my room. Edinburgh, 1885.
	40588.47	Maistre, Xavier. Journey round my room. Edinburgh, 1885.
	41595.70.100	Manso, C. Sonnets d'automne. Paris, 1885.
	37572.32	Marcou, F.L. Morceaux choisis des classiques français poètes. 27. éd. Paris, 1885.
	37572.31	Marcou, F.L. Morceaux choisis des classiques français prosateurs. Paris, 1885.
	42576.76.14	Margueritte, Paul. Tous quatre. Paris, 1885.
	Mon 175.2	Marionneau, C. Visite aux ruines du Chateau de Montaigne. Bordeaux, 1885.
	42545.6.350	Marot, Gaston. Les Francais au Tonkin. Paris, 1885.
	39544.25	Maugras, Gaston. La vie de Voltaire. Paris, 1885.
	42577.4.2	Maupassant, Guy de. Bel-ami. Paris, 1885.
	42577.4.5.2	Maupassant, Guy de. Contes du jour et de la nuit. Paris, 1885.
	42577.4.3	Maupassant, Guy de. Monsieur Parent. Paris, 1885.
	38526.37	Maynard, F. de. Oeuvres poétiques. Paris, 1885. 3v.
	38527.24	Mazon, A. Notice sur la vie et les oeuvres d'Achille Gamon. Lyon, 1885.

Chronological Listing

1885 - cont.

	Mol 613.3	Meier, D. Vergleich und Metapher in den Lustspielen Molières. Marburg, 1885.
	42545.11	Meilhac, Henri. La duchesse Martin. Boston, 1885.
	42555.58.2	Mendès, Catulle. Les contes du rouet. 6e éd. Paris, 1885.
	42555.58.34	Mendès, Catulle. Les poésies. v.1-7. Paris, 1885.
	38525.92	Merlet, L.V.C. Notice biographique sur Jean Rotrou. Chartres, 1885.
	37596.30.2A	Meyer, Paul. Fragments d'une vie de Saint Thomas de Canterbury. Paris, 1885.
	Mol 165.42	Molière, Jean Baptiste Poquelin. L'avare...Marcou. Paris, 1885.
	Mol 215.31	Molière, Jean Baptiste Poquelin. Les Fourberies de Scapin...Scheffler. Bielefeld, 1885.
	Mol 246.30.5	Molière, Jean Baptiste Poquelin. De menschenhater. Thijm. Amsterdam, 1885.
	Mol 60.23	Molière, Jean Baptiste Poquelin. Molière in outline...F.C. Brewster. Philadelphia, 1885.
	Mol 230.9	Molière, Jean Baptiste Poquelin. Receptio publicus unius juvenis medici...Hillemacher. 5e éd. Paris, 1885.
	Mol 268.67	Molière, Jean Baptiste Poquelin. Le Tartuffe. Boully. Paris, 1885.
	42555.53.10	Monnier, Marc. La réforme, de Luther à Shakespeare. Paris, 1885.
	37565.47	Monselet, Charles. Oubliés et dédaignés. Paris, 1885.
	42577.13.22	Montépin, X. de. Deux amours; Hermine. Paris, 1885.
	Mol 745.5A	Monval, G. Recueil sur la mort de Molière. Paris, 1885.
	42577.38.100	Morin, Louis. Histories d'autrefois. v.2,3. Paris, 1885- 2v.
	42577.40.100	Muller, Eugène. La m:ionette. Paris, 1885.
	41596.12.8A	Musset, Alfred de. Poésies nouvelles. 1836-1852. Paris, 1885.
	39527.4.25	Nicolardot, Louis. La Fontaine et la comédie humaine suivi du langage des animaux. 2e éd. Paris, 1885.
	37572.37	O'connor, B.F. Choix de contes contemporains. N.Y., 1885.
	42578.29.12	Ohnet, Georges. La grande marnière. 38. éd. Paris, 1885.
	41557.10.27	Owen, E.T. Notes on the Petite Fadette of George Sand. Madison, 1885.
	37562.11.3	Paris, Gaston. La poésie du moyen âge. Paris, 1885.
	37562.11	Paris, Gaston. La poésie du moyen âge. Paris, 1885-1895. 2v.
	FL 397.75	Paris, Louis. Le théâtre à Reims. Reims, 1885.
	FL 358.85	Parodi, D.A. Le théâtre en France. Paris, 1885.
	40573.3.55	Peignot, Gabriel. Lettres inédites au Docteur Bourée. Dijon, 1885.
	FL 6049.3	Peltzer, P. Jean-Jacques Rousseau's Glaubensbekenntniss des Vikars aus Savoyen. Köln, 1885.
	FL 370.55	Petit de Julleville, L. Les comédiens en France au Moyen Age. Paris, 1885.
	41522.56.5	Piépape, Léonce de. Charles de Bernard sa vie, ses oeuvres. Paris, 1885.
	42534.31.10	Pontmartin, A.F. de. Mes mémoires. Paris, 1885-86. 2v.
	41574.73	Prensa associada de Santo Domingo. Victor Hugo. Santo Domingo, 1885.
Htn	40521.9F*	Prévost, Antoine F. Histoire de Manon Lescaut et du chevalier des Grieux. Paris, 1885.
	40522.9.10	Prévost, Antoine F. Histoire du chevalier des Grieux et de Manon Lescaut. Paris, 1885.
	40535.31.9	Printzen, W. Marivaux. Sein Leben, sein Werke. Münster, 1885.
	38527.45.5	Procop, W. Syntactische Studien zu Robert Garnier. Eichstätt, 1885.
	42578.31.90	Puaux, N.A.E. L'abbaye de la vallée d'Arc. 2. éd. Paris, 1885.
	38536.19A	Rabelais, F. Les cinq livres de F. Rabelais. Paris, 1885. 4v.
	38585.19.60	Racine, Jean. Athalie; tragédie. 10th éd. London, 1885.
	38583.3.15	Racine, Jean. Oeuvres. Paris, 1885. 8v.
	38585.43.50	Racine, Jean. Les plaideurs. N.Y., 1885.
	42587.53	Regnier, Marie S. Une aventure d'hier. Paris, 1885.
	42515.29.707	Renan, Ernest. Marc-Aurèle et la fin du monde antique. 5. éd. n.p., 1885.
	42556.27.35	Renaud, A. Drames du peuple. Paris, 1885.
	42556.22.12	Richepin, Jean. Les blasphèmes. 28e éd. Paris, 1885.
NEDL	FL 6046.13.30	Rousseau, J.J. Emile; or Concerning education. Boston, 1885.
	38512.48	Rühlemann, Otto. Altfranzösischen Lebens Gregor des Grossen. Halle, 1885.
	38527.22.30	Salis, Arnold von. Agrippa d'Aubigné. 2e Aufl. Heidelberg, 1885.
	41557.8.61.10	Sand, George. Le compagnon du tour de France. Paris, 1885. 2v.
	41557.9.46.3	Sand, George. La mare au diable. London, 1885.
	41557.9.46.2	Sand, George. La mare au diable. N.Y., 1885.
	42578.34	Sarcey, Francisque. Souvenirs de jeunesse. Paris, 1885.
	42541.35	Sardou, Victorien. Divorçons. N.Y., 1885.
	42546.25	Sardou, Victorien. L'ecureuil. Paris, 1885.
	42535.5	Savine, Albert. Les étapes d'un naturaliste. Paris, 1885.
	42535.22.60	Scherer, Edmond. Études sur la littérature contemporaine. Paris, 1885-95. 10v.
	Mol 619.11	Schmidt, H. Das Pronomen bei Molière. Kiel, 1885.
	38537.13	Schwarz, Gottlieb. Rabelais und Fischart. Winterthur, 1885.
	41586.30.12.5	Soumet, A. The gladiator...performed by Salvini. N.Y., 1885.
	FL 362.20	Souriau, Maurice. De la convention dans la tragedie classique. Paris, 1885.
	42587.61	Summer, Mary. La jeunesse de 1830. Paris, 1885.
Htn	40524.2*	Tencin, Claudine A.G. de. Mémoires du Comte de Comminges. Paris, 1885.
	42583.26.15	Theuriet, André. Péché mortel. Paris, 1885.
	37596.5	Tjaden, H.P. Untersuchungen über die Poetik Rutebeufs. Marburg, 1885.
	37555.301.11	Tobler, A. Le vers français ancien et moderne. Paris, 1885.
	42581.33.5	Vallès, Jules. L'enfant. Paris, 1885.
	37542.12	Van Laun, Henri. History of French literature. v.1-3. N.Y., 1885.
	42547.11.17	Vaucaire, Maurice. Arc-en-ciel. Paris, 1885.
	38527.9	Vauquelin de la Fresnaye, Jean. L'art poétique. Paris, 1885.
Htn	42581.11.2*	Verne, Jules. Mathias Sandorf. Paris, 1885.
	42582.24.9	Verne, Jules. The tour of the world in eighty days. Chicago, 1885.
	42582.44	Verne, Jules. The vanished diamond. London, 1885.

1885 - cont.

	42558.15	Villemer-Delormel. Les chansons d'Alsace-Lorraine. Paris, 1885.
	Mol 740.2	Vitu, Auguste. La maison des Poquelins et la maison de Regnard aux piliers des Halles. Paris, 1885.
	42522.10	Vogüé, E.M. de. Histoires d'hiver. Paris, 1885.
	40524.35	Voisenon, Claude Henri. Contes légers. Paris, 1885.
	Mon 132.4.5	Voizard, E. Étude sur la langue de Montaigne. Photoreproduction. Paris, 1885.
	Mon 132.4	Voizard, E. Étude sur la langue de Montaigne. Thèse. Paris, 1885.
	39545.64	Voltaire, François Marie Arouet de. Zadig. Paris, 1885.
	42547.23	Weill, Alexandre. Mon théâtre. Paris, 1885.
	42587.84.36	Zaccone, Pierre. L'inconnu de Belleville. Paris, 1885.
	42584.4.9	Zola, Emile. Le capitaine Burle. Paris, 1885.
	42584.23.9.2	Zola, Emile. Germinal. Paris, 1885.
X Cg	42584.12.13	Zola, Emile. Mystères de Marseille. Paris, 1885.
	42584.12.22.8	Zola, Emile. Nana. 129. éd. Paris, 1885.

1886

	42562.5	About, Edmond. Le buste. N.Y., 1886.
	42562.16.13	About, Edmond. Le roi des Montagnes. Paris, 1886.
	42562.16.14	About, Edmond. Le roi des Montagnes. 2e éd. N.Y., 1886.
	42586.4.5	Achard, Amédée. Les campagnes d'un roué. Paris, 1886.
	37597.28	Amiens, Gerard von. Der Roman von Escanor. Tübingen, 1886.
	42542.23	Augier, Émile. Le post-scriptum. Paris, 1886.
	Mol 702.2	Baluffe, A. Molière inconnu; sa vie. Paris, 1886.
	40596.14.5	Balzac, Honoré de. After-dinner stories. N.Y., 1886.
	40596.13.14	Balzac, Honoré de. César Birotteau. Boston, 1886.
	40594.19	Balzac, Honoré de. Études analytiques. Physiologie du mariage. Paris, 1886.
	40594.17	Balzac, Honoré de. Études philosophiques. L'enfant maudit. Les Marana. Paris, 1886.
	40596.13.34	Balzac, Honoré de. Eugénie Grandet. Boston, 1886.
	40596.13.74	Balzac, Honoré de. Pére Goriot. Boston, 1886.
	40597.29.4.45	Balzac, Honoré de. Père Goriot. N.Y., 1886.
	40594.5	Balzac, Honoré de. Vie de province. Ursule Mirouët. Eugène Grandet. Paris, 1886.
	42554.6.5.3	Banville, Théodore de. Socrate et sa femme. 3d ed. Paris, 1886.
	41522.1.4.2	Barbey d'Aurevilly, Jules. Le chevalier des Touches. Paris, 1886.
	FL 362.2	Barthélemy, C. Histoire de la comédie en France. Paris, 1886.
	38514.69.4	Becker, Karl. Die Mysterien le Siège d'Orléans. Marburg, 1886.
	Mol 602.5	Berg, Peter. Die Syntax des Verbums bei Molière. Kiel, 1886.
	42542.29.13	Bergerat, Émile. Ours et fours; théâtre en chambre. Paris, 1886. 2v.
	41522.38.10	Bernard, Charles de. Gerfaut. Paris, 1886.
	37548.140	Bibliographie nationale. Bruxelles, 1886-1910. 4v.
	41561.27	Blondel, A. Rodolphe Toepffer, l'écrivain, l'artiste et l'homme. Paris, 1886.
	37595.3.10	Bonghi, Ruggero. Eloisa: studio. Città di Castello, 1886.
	37541.32	Bornhak, G. Geschichte der Französischen Literatur. Berlin, 1886.
	42541.7.5	Bornier, Henri de. La fille de Roland. N.Y., 1886.
Htn	38557.28*	Bossuet, J.B. Oraisons funèbres. Paris, 1886.
	37574.25A	Both-Hendriksen, Louis. La triade française, A. de Musset, Lamartine, et Victor Hugo. Boston, 1886.
	40528.13	Boufflers, S. de. Poésies diverses. Paris, 1886.
	42563.37.7	Bourget, Paul. Un crime d'amour. Paris, 1886.
	37567.15.2	Bourget, Paul. Nouveaux essais de psychologie contemporaine. Paris, 1886.
	38576.7.5	Boursault, Edme. Lettres à Babet. Paris, 1886.
	Mol 803.3	Chardon, H. Nouveau documents. v.1. Paris, 1886.
	38528.33	Chenevière, A. Bonaventure des Periers. Sa vie, ses poésies. Paris, 1886.
	40532.25	Chévrier, Maurice. Discours sur Beaumarchais. Paris, 1886.
	42565.55.84	Cladel, Léon. Mi-diable. Paris, 1886.
	42565.55.30	Cladel, Léon. Titi Föyssac IV dit la république et la chrétienté. Paris, 1886.
	42586.31.20	Claretié, J. La canne de M. Michelet. Paris, 1886.
Htn	40545.30.81*	Contades, Gerard de. Armand Malitourne. Argentan, 1886.
	Mol 800.7	Copin, A. Histoire des comédiens de la troupe de Molière. Paris, 1886.
	Mol 800.6	Copin, A. Histoire des comédiens de la troupe de Molière. Paris, 1886.
	Mol 870.39	Copin, A. Molière chez Conti. Paris, 1886.
	42554.26.2	Coppée, François. Théâtre 1881-85. Paris, 1886.
	38575.34.2	Corneille, Pierre. Nicomède. Paris, 1886.
	38575.31.4	Corneille, Pierre. Polyeucte. London, 1886.
	42565.100	Courtois, Edgar. Cancans de plage. Paris, 1886.
	42566.19.5	Daudet, Alphonse. Aventures prodigieuses de Tartarin. Paris, 1886.
	42566.20.1	Daudet, Alphonse. Contes choisis. La fantaisie et l'histoire. Paris, 1886.
Htn	42566.35.3*	Daudet, Alphonse. Tartarin sur les Alpes. Paris, 1886.
	42566.35.3.5	Daudet, Alphonse. Tartarin sur les Alpes. Paris, 1886.
	42566.35.4A	Daud-t, Alphonse. Tartarin sur les Alpes. Paris, 1886.
	FL 377.27	Degenhardt, E. Die Metaphor bei den Vorläufern Molière's, 1612-1654. Marburg, 1886.
	FL 6113.12	Delestre, M. Catalogue d'une précieuse collection de lettres autographes comprenant une correspondance de Jean-Jacques Rousseau. Paris, 1886.
	42535.22.9	Delzant, A. Paul de Saint-Victor. Paris, 1886.
	37538.27	Demogeot, Jacques Claude. Histoire de la littérature française. Paris, 1886.
	42545.69.14	Dennery, Adolphe Philippe. Le Cid. Paris, 1886.
	37567.121	Derôme, L. Causeries d'un amie des livres. Paris, 1886-1887.
	42542.64.9	Déroulède, Paul. Marches et sonneries. Paris, 1886.
	41593.29.3.8	Desbordes-Valmore, Marceline. Oeuvres poétiques. Paris, 1886?-1922. 4v.
	Mol 870.37	d'Hervilly, E. Molière en prison. Paris, 1886.
	38562.27	Doncieux, G. Le père Bouhours. Paris, 1886.
	42568.19.17	Du Boisgobey, Fortuné. Porte close. Paris, 1886.
	42568.18	Du Boisgobey, Fortuné. Rubis sur l'ongle. Paris, 1886.
	42568.19.15.3	Du Boisgobey, Fortuné. La voilette bleue. 3. éd. Paris, 1886.
	Mon 68.8	Du Boys, E. Une nouvelle lettre de Montaigne. Paris, 1886.
	42556.21.100	Duchesne, J. Un heritier de Brizeux. Rennes, 1886.

1886 - cont.

	41538.20	Dumas, Alexandre. La dame de volupté. v.1-2. Paris, 1886.
	41538.20.2	Dumas, Alexandre. Les demoiselles de St. Cyr. London, 1886.
	42563.44.5	Durand, Alice M.C.F. Clairefontaine. 2. éd. Paris, 1886.
	42563.62	Durand, Alice M.C.F. Cleopatra. Boston, 1886.
	42563.63	Durand, Alice M.C.F. Dosia's daughter. Boston, 1886.
	41593.32.10.50	Durand, Claude. La chanson des Vignerons. Niort, 1886.
	42568.23.14.30	Duval, Paul. Très russe. Paris, 1886.
	FL 360.23	Edwards, H.S. Famous first representations. London, 1886.
	42554.31.20	Eggis, Étienne. Poésies. Neuchâtel, 1886.
	42568.25.5	Enault, Louis. Carine. N.Y., 1886.
	Mol 870.38	Ephraim, A. La première du "Misanthrope". Paris, 1886.
	42543.29.5	Erckmann, Émile. L'ami Fritz. N.Y., 1886.
	42572.3.7	Erckmann, Emile. Le blocus. N.Y., 1886.
	42572.24	Erckmann, Emile. Madame Thérèse. N.Y., 1886.
	42554.32	Fabie, François. La poésie des bêtes. Paris, 1886.
	42574.14.3	Fabre, Ferdinand. L'abbé Tigrane. Paris, 1886.
	37596.67	Faut, Carl. L'image du monde; poème du XIIIe siècle. Upsala, 1886.
	42575.38.10	Feuillet, Octave. Aliette. (La morte). N.Y., 1886.
	42575.38.8	Feuillet, Octave. La morte. 13. éd. Paris, 1886.
	42575.38.9	Feuillet, Octave. La morte. 98. éd. Paris, 1886.
	37578.48.5	Finod, J. de. A thousand flashes of French wit, wisdom. N.Y., 1886.
	42576.33.75	Flaubert, Gustave. Par les champs et par les grèves. Paris, 1886.
	37565.53	Fournel, Victor. De Jean-Baptiste Rousseau à André Chénier. Études litteraires et morales sur le XVIIIe siècle. Paris, 1886.
	42524.61	Frary, Raoul. Mes tiroirs. Paris, 1886.
	42571.26	Gaboriau, Emile. La clique dorée. Paris, 1886.
	42576.63.50	Gagneur, L. (Mme.). Pour être aimée. Paris, 1886.
	Mol 607.1	Gallert, G. Über den Gebrauch des Infinitions bei Molière. Halle, 1886.
	42554.40.50	Gauthiez, Pierre. Les voix errantes. Paris, 1886.
	41542.14.2	Gautier, Théophile. Portraits contemporains. Paris, 1886.
	42554.39	Gérard, Albert. Poésies, rêves, regrets, hommages, foyers et récits. Paris, 1886.
	42554.47	Gnafron fils (pseud.). Théâtre. Lyon, 1886.
	42575.64	Goncourt, Edmond de. Pages retrouvées. Paris, 1886.
	42543.54.16	Gondinet, Edmond. Un parisien. Paris, 1886.
Htn	43625.3.39*	Gourmont, Rémy de. Merlette. Paris, 1886.
	40597.2.450	Gozlan, Léon. Balzac intime. Paris, 1886.
	42554.48	Grandmougin, C. Rimes de combat. Paris, 1886.
	38514.67	Gröhler, H. Über Richard Ros' mittenglische Übersetzung des Gedichtes von Alain Chartier, La belle dame sans mercy. Breslau, 1886.
	42576.64.5	Grousset, P. Le capitaine Trafalgar. Paris, 1886.
	42525.7.19A	Grousset, R. Oeuvres posthumes. Paris, 1886.
	42576.40.306	Halévy, Ludovic. L'abbé Constantin. N.Y., 1886.
	42554.51	Harel, Paul. Aux champs. Paris, 1886.
	41574.29	Hartmann, K.A.M. Zeittafel zu Victor Hugos Leben und Werken. Oppeln, 1886.
	42541.17.5	Hennequin, Alfred. Lili. Paris, 1886.
	37565.33	Hennet, Léon. Le régiment de la Calotte. Paris, 1886.
	37542.27	Henry, A. Les auteurs français. Paris, 1886.
	42576.67.8	Hervieu, Paul. Les yeux verts. Paris, 1886.
	42584.31	Hetzel, P.J. Maroussia. 11. éd. Paris, 1886.
	37562.12.8	Heune, W. Die Casus im Mittelfranzösischen. Greifswald, 1886.
	42576.14.75	Houssaye, Arsène. Philosophers and actresses. N.Y., 1886. 2v.
	37567.42A	Houssaye, Henry. Les hommes et les idées. Paris, 1886.
	41571.32.3.3	Hugo, Victor. Ninety-three. London, 1886.
	41574.7	Hugo, Victor. Oeuvres complètes. La fin de Satan. 2d ed. Paris, 1886.
	41574.8	Hugo, Victor. Oeuvres complètes. Théâtre en liberté. Paris, 1886.
	41573.8	Hugo, Victor. Rasgos de Victor Hugo por Manuel Delofen y Leonard. Habana, 1886.
	41573.26.9	Hugo, Victor. Ruy Blas. N.Y., 1886.
	FL 396.68.3	Hugot, Eugène. Histoire...du théâtre du Palais-Royal, 1784-1884. Paris, 1886.
	FL 396.68	Hugot, Eugène. Histoire littéraire, critique et anecdotique du théâtre du Palais-Royal, 1784-1884. Paris, 1886.
	37564.40	Jacquet, A. La vie littéraire dans un ville de Province sous Louis XIV. Paris, 1886.
	FL 398.74.57	Kennard, Nina H. Rachel. Boston, 1886.
	41557.10.200	Kirpichnikov, A.I. Dve biografii: Zhorzh Zand i Genrikh Geine. Moskva, 1886.
	42543.16.27.25	Korvin-Krukovskii, P. Die Danischeffs. Leipzig, 1886.
	38514.27.5	Kuhl, F. Die Allegorie bei Charles d'Orleans. Marburg, 1886.
	38564.32	La Bruyère, J. de. Les caractères. Paris, 1886.
Htn	39524.5*	La Fontaine, Jean de. Fables. Paris, 1886-87. 4v.
	41578.5.5	Lamartine, Alphonse de. Harmonies poétiques et religieuses. Paris, 1886.
	41578.9	Lamartine, Alphonse de. Nouvelles méditations poétiques. Paris, 1886.
	41578.7A	Lamartine, Alphonse de. Premières méditations poétiques. Paris, 1886.
	42587.12.25	Lapauze, Jeanne. Le mariage de Gabrielle. N.Y., 1886.
	Mol 730.9	Larroumet, G. Molière, l'homme et le comédien. Paris, 1886.
	42544.24.16	Lavedan, Henri. Reine janvier. Paris, 1886.
	42555.36.5A	Leconte de Lisle, C.M.R. Oeuvres. Paris, 1886.
	37562.25.3	Lecoy de la Marche, A. La chaire française au moyen âge. 2. éd. Paris, 1886.
	42541.20.9	Legouvé, Ernest. Soixante ans de souvenirs. Paris, 1886. 2v.
	42544.33.20	Lemaître, Jules. Sérénus. Paris, 1886.
	37563.35	Lenient, Charles. La satire en France au XVIe siècle. v.2. Paris, 1886.
	40512.12.4A	LeSage, Alain René. Adventures of Gil Blas of Santillane. Edinburgh, 1886. 3v.
	40512.34.4	LeSage, Alain René. Historia de Gil Blas de Santillana. N.Y., 1886.
	Mol 712.4	Loiseleur, J. Molière, nouvelles controverses. Orleans, 1886.
	42587.15.10	Lubomirski, Jozef. Tzar, archiduchesse et Burgraves. Paris, 1886.
	42555.42.1100	Mac-Nab, Maurice. Poèmes mobiles, monlogues. Paris, 1886.
	40588.49.1	Maistre, Xavier. A noctural expedition round my room. Edinburgh, 1886.
	40588.49	Maistre, Xavier. A nocturnal expedition round my room. Edinburgh, 1886.
	37543.8.5	Marcillac, F. Manuel d'histoire de la littérature française. Genève, 1886.
	42576.76.12	Margueritte, Paul. La confession posthume. Paris, 1886.
	42555.49.12	Mariéton, Paul. La viole d'amour. Paris, 1886.
	Mol 765.4	Marmottan, P. Molière rue Richelieu. Paris, 1886.
X Cg	39544.24	Maugras, Gaston. Voltaire et J.J. Rousseau. Paris, 1886.
	42577.4.28	Maupassant, Guy de. La petite roque. Paris, 1886.
	41574.24	A memento of Victor Hugo. n.p., 1886.
	42555.58.4	Mendès, Catulle. Contes choisis. Paris, 1886.
	41555.22.15	Mérimée, Prosper. Colomba. Paris, 1886.
	42587.27.79	Michel, Louise. Mémoires, écrits par elle-même. Paris, 1886.
	42587.27.15	Michel, Louise. Les microbes humains. Paris, 1886.
	Mol 165.54	Molière, Jean Baptiste Poquelin. L'avare...Pellisson. 3e éd. Paris, 1886.
	Mol 171.35	Molière, Jean Baptiste Poquelin. Le bourgeois gentilhomme...Livet. Paris, 1886.
	Mol 171.35.2	Molière, Jean Baptiste Poquelin. Le bourgeois gentilhomme...Livet. Paris, 1886.
	Mol 171.34	Molière, Jean Baptiste Poquelin. Le bourgeois gentilhomme...Tarver. London, 1886?
	Mol 195.30	Molière, Jean Baptiste Poquelin. L'école des femmes...Scheffler. Bielefeld, 1886.
	Mol 211.42	Molière, Jean Baptiste Poquelin. Les femmes savantes...Masson. Oxford, 1886.
	Mol 215.32	Molière, Jean Baptiste Poquelin. Les Fourberies de Scapin...Gasc. London, 1886.
	Mol 245.57	Molière, Jean Baptiste Poquelin. Le misanthrope. Cambridge, 1886.
	Mol 245.58	Molière, Jean Baptiste Poquelin. Le misanthrope. Boully. Paris, 1886.
	Mol 18.86	Molière, Jean Baptiste Poquelin. Oeuvres complètes...Louandre. Paris, 1886-87. 8v.
	Mon 18.86.2	Montaigne, Michel de. Essais. Motheau et Jouaust. Paris, 1886-89. 7v.
	Mon 18.86.3A	Montaigne, Michel de. Essais. Motheau et Jouaust. Paris, 1886-89. 7v.
	Mon 30.5	Montaigne, Michel de. Essayes. Florio (Morley). London, 1886.
Htn	Mon 30.5.2*	Montaigne, Michel de. Essays. Florio (Morley). London, 1886.
	42555.61	Moréas, Jean. Les cantilènes. Paris, 1886.
	42545.44.10	Moreau, Émile. Matapan; comédie en trois actes. Paris, 1886.
	Mol 713.8	Morf, H. Zeittafel zu Vorlesungen über Molière. Bern, 1886.
	39566.12.3	Morley, John. Diderot and the encyclopaedists. London, 1886. 2v.
	FL 6118.73.5A	Morley, John Morley. Rousseau. London, 1886. 2v.
	FL 6118.73.3	Morley, John Morley. Rousseau. 3. ed. Boston, 1886. 2v.
	42577.13.45F	Mouton, Eugène. Histoire de l'invalide à la tête de bois. Paris, 1886.
	38514.58.5	Müller, Ernst. Zur Syntax der Christine de Pisan. Greifswald, 1886.
X Cg	41596.12.9	Musset, Alfred de. Poésies nouvelles. 1836-1852. Paris, 1886.
	42555.63.3	Nadaud, G. Contes, scènes et récits. Paris, 1886.
	39526.41	Netter, Abraham. La Fontaine et Descartes, ou Les deux rats. Paris, 1886.
	42578.29.6	Ohnet, Georges. Les dames de croix-mort. Paris, 1886.
	37551.61	Paris, G. La poésie française au 15 siècle. Paris, 1886.
	42578.30.45	Peladan, J. La décadence latine. v. 2-4, 6-10, 12-19. Paris, 1886-1926. 16v.
	FL 371.15.3	Petit de Julleville, L. La comédie et les moeurs en France. Paris, 1886.
	FL 370.57	Petit de Julleville, L. Répertoire du théâtre comique en France au Moyen Age. Paris, 1886.
	FL 376.11	Picot, Émile. Le monologue dramatique dans l'ancien théâtre français. Paris, 1886-88.
	37567.246	Pipitone-Federico, G. Il naturalismo contemporaneo in letteratura. Palermo, 1886.
	38514.57A	Pisan, Christine de. Oeuvres poétiques. Paris, 1886- 3v.
	37594.14	Poème moral. Photoreproduction. Erlangen, 1886.
	42541.31	Ponsard, François. Le lion amoureux. London, 1886.
	38526.46.350	Poupo, Pierre. Poésies diverses tirées de la muse chrestienne. Paris, 1886.
	42556.14	Pradels, O. Chansons. Paris, 1886.
	40522.9.52	Prévost, Antoine F. The history of Manon Lescaut. v.1-3. Edinburgh, 1886.
	40522.9.7	Prévost, Antoine F. Manon Lescaut. London, 1886.
	40522.9.6	Prévost, Antoine F. The story of Manon Lescaut. N.Y., 1886.
	42587.50.10.5	Quellien, N. Loin de Bretagne. Paris, 1886.
NEDL	38585.19	Racine, Jean. Andromaque. Paris, 1886.
	38582.22	Racine, Jean. Ausgewählte Tragödien. Leipzig, 1886.
	38585.27	Racine, Jean. Britannicus. London, 1886.
	38585.34	Racine, Jean. Iphigénie. London, 1886.
	38527.47	Raeder, Hans. Die Tropen und Figuren bei Robert Garnier. Wandsbeck, 1886.
	38564.45	Rahstede, H.G. Ueber La Bruyère und seine Charaktere. Oppeln, 1886.
Htn	37596.74*	Raynaud, Gaston. Un nouveau dit des femmes. Paris, 1886.
	Mon 28.16	Réaume, E. Rabelais et Montaigne pédagogues. Paris, 1886.
	38537.10	Réaume, Eugène. Rabelais et Montaine pédagogues. Paris, 1886.
	42587.50.65	Rebell, Hugues. Les Méprisants. Paris, 1886.
	38587.8.14	Regnard, Jean François. Le légataire universel, le bal. Paris, 1886.
	41563.33.10	Relove, P.M. La vie et les oeuvres de Toepffer. Paris, 1886.
	42515.30.5	Renan, Ernest. L'abbesse de Jouarre. 21. éd. Paris, 1886.
	42515.30.193	Renan, Ernest. Dialogues et fragments philosophiques. Paris, 1886.
	42515.30.615.2	Renan, Ernest. Le prètre de Nemi. 3. éd. Paris, 1886.
	42515.30.615	Renan, Ernest. Le prètre de Nemi. 6. éd. Paris, 1886.
Htn	42515.30.570*	Renan, Ernest. 1802; dialogue des morts. Paris, 1886.
	Mol 880.28	Richepin, J. Monsieur Scapin. Paris, 1886.
	42556.22.15	Richepin, Jean. La mer. Paris, 1886.
	42556.32.45	Rollinat, Maurice. L'abime; poésies. Paris, 1886.
	FL 6021.86	Rousseau, J.J. Les confessions. Paris, 1886.
	39594.30.7	St. Pierre, J.H.B. de. Paul et Virginie. Paris, 1886.
	42535.22	Saint-Victor, Paul de. Anciens et modernes. Paris, 1886.

1886 - cont.

40575.37.10 Sainte-Beuve, Charles A. Premiers lundis. Paris, 1886-94. 3v.
41557.9.46 Sand, George. La mare au diable. N.Y., 1886.
42546.23.5 Sardou, Victorien. Andrea; comedia. Madrid, 1886.
42546.30.33 Sardou, Victorien. Patrie. Paris, 1886.
Mon 28.17 Saucerotte, C. L'esprit de Montaigne. Paris, 1886.
42514.4.10 Sbarbaro, Pietro. Laboulaye, un fonditore di caratteri. Rome, 1886.
40535.7.3 Schoepke, P.T. Philippe Nericault Destouches et son théâtre. Leipzig, 1886.
42581.33.83 Séché, Léon. Portraits à l'encre:Jules Vallès. Paris, 1886.
38546.36.8 Sévigné, Marie de R.C. Lettres choisies de Madame de Sévigné. Lille, 1886.
41558.44.9 Souvestre, Émile. Au coin du feu. London, 1886.
40597.5 Spoelberch de Lovenjoul, Charles. Histoire des oeuvres de Honoré de Balzac. Paris, 1886.
42587.60 Sternon, P. Les moines et les sorcières d'Ancy. Nancy, 1886.
37562.12.23 Stramwitz, E. Ueber Strophen- und Versenjambement im altfranzösischen. Greifswald, 1886.
37544.10 Süpfle, Theodor. Geschichte des deutschen Kultureinflusses auf Frankreich. v.1-2. Gotha, 1886-90. 3v.
41574.26 Swinburne, A.C. A study of Victor Hugo. London, 1886.
FL 364.55 Taphanel, A. Le théâtre de Saint-Cyril. Versailles, 1886.
39527.29 Tarver, Francis. Fables de La Fontaine. London, 1886.
FL 396.56.9 Thelmier. Histoire du théâtre Montparnasse. Paris, 1886.
42583.20 Theuriet, André. Bigarreau. Paris, 1886.
42557.5.250 Thiebault, Henry. Chants d'un français; patrie. Alger, 1886.
37551.10 Tougard, A. L'Hellénisme dans les écrivains du Moyen-Age. Paris, 1886.
37562.17 Trebe, J. H.H. Les trouvères et leurs exhortations aux croisades. Leipzig, 1886.
41574.147 Ulbach, Louis. La vie de Victor Hugo. Paris, 1886.
42553.34 Vadier, Berthe. Henri Frédéric Amiel. Paris, 1886.
42557.10.9 Vard, A. Heures noires et nuits blanches. Paris, 1886.
41586.15.85 Vauthier, Gabriel. Essai sur la vie et les oeuvres de Népomucène Lemercier. Thèse. Photoreproduction. Toulouse, 1886.
42581.34 Vaux, Ludovic de. Légende de Montford-la-Cane. Paris, 1886.
42581.2.2 Verne, Jules. Un billet de loterie. Paris, 1886.
Htn 42581.2* Verne, Jules. Un billet de loterie. Paris, 1886.
Htn 42581.22* Verne, Jules. Robur le conquérant. Paris, 1886.
42521.18.4 Veuillot, Louis. Les libres penseurs. 7. éd. Paris, 1886.
42576.49 Viaud, Julien. Fleurs d'ennui. Paris, 1886.
42576.50 Viaud, Julien. Le mariage de Loti. Paris, 1886.
42576.52.2 Viaud, Julien. Pêcheur d'Islande. 6. éd. Paris, 1886.
42576.53 Viaud, Julien. Le roman d'un Spahi. Paris, 1886.
42557.22.20 Vielé-Griffin, F. Les cygnes. Alean-Levy, 1886.
Htn 42547.18.6* Villiers de l'Isle Adam, Auguste. L'amour suprême. Paris, 1886.
42547.25 Weill, Alexandre. Mes romans. Paris, 1886. 2v.
38513.66 Wimmer, Georg. Prolegomena zu einer kritischen Bearbeitung. Marburg, 1886.
42584.3.9 Zola, Emile. L'assommoir. Paris, 1886.
42584.12.7 Zola, Emile. Madeleine Férat. Paris, 1886.
42584.23.7.2 Zola, Emile. L'oeuvre. Paris, 1886.
42584.23.7 Zola, Emile. L'oeuvre. Paris, 1886.
X Cg 42584.4.5 Zola, Emile. Soirées de Medan. Paris, 1886.

1887

42562.17.6 About, Edmond. Le roi des Montagnes. Paris, 1887.
42562.37.210 Achkinasi, M. La chasse aux juifs, histoire d'hier et d'aujourd'hui. 2e éd. Paris, 1887.
FL 6118.87 Aleksyeef, A.S. Etiudy o J.J. Rousseau, 1741-1762. Moskva, 1887.
41578.61 Alexandre, Charles. Madame de Lamartine. Paris, 1887.
42553.32.5A Amiel, Henri F. Fragments d'un journal intime. Genève, 1887. 2v.
38526.50 Andrieu, Jules. Théophile de Viau. Paris, 1887.
Mol 755.7 Angot, A. Les Pocquelin ecclésiastiques. Mamers, 1887.
38576.21 Arnaud, C. Étude sur la vie et les oeuvres de l'abbé d'Aubignac (Hédelin François). Paris, 1887.
42561.9 Arréat, Lucien. Journal d'un philosophe. Paris, 1887.
39527.28 Aubertin, Charles. Fables de La Fontaine. Paris, 1887.
42558.11 Bader, Clarisse. La comtesse Jeanne. Paris, 1887.
Mol 755.6.5 Baluffe, A. Le père de Molière. n.p., 1887.
40596.13.4 Balzac, Honoré de. The alkahest. Boston, 1887.
40596.13.18 Balzac, Honoré de. The country doctor. Boston, 1887.
40597.29.4.50 Balzac, Honoré de. Père Goriot. N.Y., 1887.
40596.13.62 Balzac, Honoré de. The two brothers. Boston, 1887.
40594.9 Balzac, Honoré de. Vie parisienne. Les courtisanes. Vautrin. Paris, 1887.
40594.12 Balzac, Honoré de. Vie parisienne. Les parents pauvres. Paris, 1887.
40594.14 Balzac, Honoré de. Vie politique. Le député d'Arcis. Paris, 1887.
40594.2 Balzac, Honoré de. Vie privée. Mémoires de deux jeunes mariées. Paris, 1887.
42554.1.2 Banville, Théodore de. Le forgeron. Paris, 1887.
42554.9.2 Banville, Théodore de. Madame Robert. Paris, 1887.
40513.16 Barberet, V. LeSage et le théâtre de la foire. Nancy, 1887.
37566.12.15 Barbey d'Aurevilly, J.A. Les philosophes et les écrivains religieux. Paris, 1887.
41522.4.9 Baudelaire, Charles. Oeuvres posthumes et correspondances inédites. Paris, 1887.
42542.29.14.15 Bergerat, Émile. Le livre de Caliban. Paris, 1887.
37572.28.2 Bernardin, N.M. Morceaux choisis des classiques français. Paris, 1887.
42542.29.98 Bisson, Alexandre. Ma gouvernante; comédie. Paris, 1887.
38546.52 Boissier, G. Mme. de Sévigné. London, 1887.
38546.51.3 Boissier, G. Mme. de Sévigné. 2. éd. Paris, 1887.
42563.24 Boisson, Firmin. Jean de la lune. Paris, 1887.
42524.12 Bonneau, A. Curiosa. Essais critiques de littérature. Paris, 1887.
42563.37.41 Bourget, Paul. André Cornélis. Paris, 1887.
42563.37.3 Bourget, Paul. Mensonges. Paris, 1887.
Mol 728.15 Bricauld de Verneuil, E. Molière à Poiteurs en 1648. Paris, 1887.
42586.29.4 Caraguel, J. Les Barthozouls. Paris, 1887.
41557.10.6A Caro, Elme. George Sand. Paris, 1887.
FL 6135.10 Castellant, A. Jean-Jacques Rousseau. Paris, 1887.

1887 - cont.

40517.1.9 Caylus, Anne C.P. Correspondance inédite. Paris, 1887. 2v.
42562.50 Celières, Paul. The startling exploits of Dr. J.B. Luiès. N.Y., 1887.
40597.8A Cerfberr, Anatole. Répertoire de la comédie humaine de H. de Balzac. Paris, 1887.
40542.25 Chauveau, Pierre. Frédéric Ozanam. Montréal, 1887.
37542.26 Chauvin, A. La littérature française par les critiques contemporaines. Paris, 1887-1888. 2v.
42565.55.90 Cladel, Léon. Gueux de marque. 2. éd. Paris, 1887.
42565.55.35 Cladel, Léon. N'a-qu'un-oeil. Paris, 1887.
42586.31 Claretié, J. Candidat. Paris, 1887.
42524.34 Contades, G. de. Portraits et fantaisies. Paris, 1887.
FL 398.84.9 Copin, Alfred. Études dramatiques; Talma et la révolution. Paris, 1887.
FL 398.84.8 Copin, Alfred. Talma et l'empire. Paris, 1887.
42554.23.6 Coppée, François. Arrière Saison. Paris, 1887.
42586.32.5.2 Coquelin, Ernest. Le rire. Paris, 1887.
42586.32.5 Coquelin, Ernest. Le rire. 5. éd. Paris, 1887.
42586.32.5.3 Coquelin, Ernest. Le rire. 6. éd. Paris, 1887.
38575.34.6.5 Corneille, Pierre. Polyeucte. London, 1887.
38575.34.6 Corneille, Pierre. Polyeucte par Felix Hermon. Paris, 1887.
Mol 853.5.2 Cotin. La satyre des satyres. Paris, 1887.
37563.17.9 Darmesteter, Arsène. Le seizième siècle en France. v.1-2. 3e éd. Paris, 1887.
42566.64.5 Daudet, Alphonse. Les amoureuses. Paris, 1887.
42566.51.2A Daudet, Alphonse. La Belle-Nivernaise; story of an old boat. London, 1887.
42566.51.5 Daudet, Alphonse. La Belle-Nivernaise; story of an old boat. N.Y., 1887
42566.34.2.5 Daudet, Alphonse. Sapho. Paris, 1887.
42566.34.2.10 Daudet, Alphonse. Sappho. Paris, 1887.
42566.20.13.5 Daudet, Alphonse. Le siège de Berlin. N.Y., 1887.
42566.19.7.50 Daudet, Alphonse. Tartarin de Tarascon. n.p., 1887.
42566.19.7 Daudet, Alphonse. Tartarin de Tarascon. Paris, 1887.
42566.19.7.10 Daudet, Alphonse. Tartarin de Tarascon. Paris, 1887.
42566.19.8A Daudet, Alphonse. Tartarin of Tarascon. London, 1887.
42566.35.23A Daudet, Alphonse. Tartarin on the Alps. London, 1887.
42566.35.22 Daudet, Alphonse. Tartarin on the Alps. London, 1887.
37591.31.9 Davids, S. Strophen- und Versbau der Lieder des Kastellans von Coucy. Hamburg, 1887.
41593.29.2 Désaugiers, M.A. Théâtre. Paris, 1887.
40526.34 Desnoiresterres, G. Le chevalier Dorat. Paris, 1887.
Mol 870.22 d'Hervilly, E. Cinq anniversaires de Molière. Paris, 1887.
37597.6.3 Doinel, Jules. Guy Fabi et Guillaume Rebrachien. Orléans, 1887.
42542.66 Dreyfus, A. Jouons la comédie. Paris, 1887.
42568.11 Droz, Gustave. Monsieur, madame et bébé. Paris, 1887.
38537.25.11 Dubouchet, A. François Rabelais à Montpellier 1530-1538. Montpellier, 1887.
42542.66.70 Dugué, Ferdinand. Théroigne; drame en 5 actes, en vers. Paris, 1887.
41524.3 Dumas, Alexandre. Comte de Monte Cristo. v.1-6. Paris, 1887. 3v.
41538.68.30 Dumas, Alexandre. La comtesse de Charny. v.1-6. Paris, 1887. 3v.
42543.19.30 Dumas, Alexandre. Francillon. 28e éd. Paris, 1887.
42543.16.5F Dumas, Alexandre. The lady with the camellias. London, 1887.
41538.52 Dumas, Alexandre. Théâtre complet. v.8. Paris, 1887.
42563.44.6 Durand, Alice M.C.F. Count Xavier. Boston, 1887.
42563.63.5 Durand, Alice M.C.F. La fille de Dosia. 27. éd. Paris, 1887.
42568.21 Durandal, Pierre. Le vengeur de Montcalm. Paris, 1887.
42568.23.14.52 Duval, Paul. Les griseries. Paris, 1887.
Mol 193.14 Engel, Karl. Die Don Juan - Sage auf der Bühne. Oldenburg, 1887.
42572.24.2 Erckmann, Emile. Madame Thérèse. N.Y., 1887.
42574.31 Fabre, Ferdinand. Madame Fuster. Paris, 1887.
37566.30.9 Faguet, Émile. Dix-neuvième siècle; études littéraires. Paris, 1887.
37566.30.20 Faguet, Émile. Dix-neuvième siècle; études littéraires. Paris, 1887.
Mon 116.2 Favre, J. (Mrs.). Montaigne, moraliste et pedagogue. Paris, 1887.
Htn 42575.49.15* Feuillet, Octave. Le roman d'un jeune homme pauvre. Paris, 1887.
42576.35 Flaubert, Gustave. Correspondance. Paris, 1887-1892. 4v.
42571.14 France, Anatole. Nos enfants; scènes de la ville et des champs. Paris, 1887.
37542.30A Frankfurter neuphilologische Beitrage. Frankfurt, 1887.
37551.11 Fremy, E. L'Académie des Derniers Valois. Paris, 1887.
Mol 570.4 Fritsche, H. Molière Studien. 2. Aufl. Berlin, 1887.
42571.23 Gaboriau, Emile. L'affaire Lerouge. Paris, 1887.
42571.30 Gaboriau, Emile. Le dossier numéro 113. Paris, 1887.
38514.40 Gasté, Armand. Olivier Basselin et le Vau de vire. Paris, 1887.
41542.11.50 Gautier, Théophile. Mademoiselle de Maupin. London, 1887.
42554.44.20 Ghil, René. Legendes de rêve et de sang. Paris, 1887.
42575.63 Goncourt, Edmond de. Idées et sensations. Paris, 1887.
38576.7.32 Grawe, Ludwig. Edme Boursault Leben und Werke. Inaug. Diss. Lingen, 1887.
42576.39 Guiches, Gustave. Céleste Prudhomat. Paris, 1887.
42576.40 Guiches, Gustave. L'ennemi. Paris, 1887.
40566.13 Guizot, François Pierre Guillaume. Le temps passé. Paris, 1887. 2v.
42576.40.308F Halévy, Ludovic. L'abbé Constantin. Paris, 1887.
42576.40.415 Halévy, Ludovic. Princesse. Paris, 1887.
42543.62.38 Haraucourt, Edmond. Amis. Paris, 1887.
42576.65.4 Hardÿ de Périni, Edouard. Contes de garnison. Paris, 1887.
42543.62.91 Hennique, Léon. Esther Brandès. Paris, 1887.
42543.62.90 Hennique, Léon. Jacques Damour. Paris, 1887.
42543.62.94 Hennique, Léon. Poeuf. Paris, 1887.
42587.1.15 Hermant, A. Le cavalier Miserey. Paris, 1887.
42576.67.6 Hervieu, Paul. L'inconnu. Paris, 1887.
38537.11 Heulhard, Arthur. Rabelais légiste. Paris, 1887.
41574.77 Hugo, Adele. Victor Hugo. N.Y., 1887.
41573.30.10 Hugo, Victor. Dramatic works. London, 1887.
41573.32.9 Hugo, Victor. Hernani. N.Y., 1887.
41571.16.6 Hugo, Victor. Les misérables. Boston, 1887. 5v.
41571.16.1 Hugo, Victor. Les misérables. N.Y., 1887.

1887 - cont.

41571.32.2 Hugo, Victor. Les misérables. v.1-4. v.5 lost 1921. Boston, 1887. 5v.

41571.41 Hugo, Victor. Les misérables. v.2-5. v.1 lost 1929. London, 1887. 5v.

41574.9 Hugo, Victor. Oeuvres inédites. Choses vues, 1815-35. Paris, 1887.

41573.37.3 Hugo, Victor. Translations from the poems of Victor Hugo. N.Y., 1887?

41573.37.2 Hugo, Victor. Translations from the poems of Victor Hugo. 2d ed. London, 1887.

42576.65.80.25 Huysmans, Joris Karl. Un dilemme. Paris, 1887.

38575.20 Jacobi, Philipp. Syntactische Studien über Pierre Corneille. Giessen, 1887.

37565.18 Jeanroy-Felix, Victor. Nouvelle histoire de la littérature française pendant la revolution. Paris, 1887.

Mol 860.52.2 Jouin, Henry. Corneille et Lulli. Paris, 1887.

Mol 711.1A Kreiten, W. Molière's Leben und Werke. Freiburg, 1887.

38526.27 Labé, Louise Charly. Oeuvres. Paris, 1887. 2v.

38564.35.11 La Bruyère, J. de. Des ouvrages de l'Ésprit. Paris, 1887.

FL 358.87 Lacroix, Paul. Le théâtre. Mystères. Paris, 1887.

Mol 860.52 La Motte, M. de. Molière au berceau. Paris, 1887.

38521.14 Lange, Paul. Über Ronsards Franciade. Wurzen, 1887.

40535.19.200 Lanson, Gustave. Nivelle de La Chaussée et la comédie larmoyante. Paris, 1887.

42544.3.9 Lapommeraye, H. de. La critique de Francillon. Paris, 1887.

Mol 612.5 Larroumet, G. La comédie de Molière. Paris, 1887.

Mol 612.4 Larroumet, G. La comédie de Molière. Paris, 1887.

37562.18 Lecoy de la Marche, A. Le treizième siècle littéraire et scientifique. Lille, 1887.

42541.21 Legouvé, Ernest. Soixante ans de souvenirs. Paris, 1887. 2v.

37567.32A Lemaître, Jules. Les contemporains. 9. éd. Paris, 1887-1899. 8v.

38527.5 Lemercier, Aimé Prosper. Étude sur Jean Vauquelin. Nancy, 1887.

41593.12.15 Le Mouel, Eugène. Bonnes gens de Bretagne. Paris, 1887.

42587.14.20 Lepic, Adèle. L'ombra. N.Y., 1887.

40515.9 Lespinasse, J.J.E. de. Lettres. Paris, 1887.

39566.22 Leyds, J.J.C. Principaux écrits religieuse à la personne...de Diderot. Paris, 1887.

FL 382.37 L'Homme, François. Études sur le théâtre contemporain. Paris, 1887.

37578.49 Lutaud, Auguste. Le Parnasse hippocratique. Paris, 1887.

42576.76.18 Margueritte, Paul. Maison ouverte. Paris, 1887.

42576.76.13 Margueritte, Paul. Pascal Géfosse. Paris, 1887.

FL 397.115.50 Martiny, Jules. Histoire du théâtre de Liège depuis son origine jusqu'à nos jours. Liège, 1887.

37574.26.10A Masson, Gustave. La lyre française. London, 1887.

FL 365.17 Maugras, Gaston. Les comédiens hors la loi. Paris, 1887.

42577.4.26A Maupassant, Guy de. Contes et nouvelles. Paris, 1887.

Mol 713.4 Mazzoni, G. La vita de Molière. n.p., 1887.

42555.58.12 Mendès, Catulle. L'homme tout nu. Paris, 1887.

42555.58.23 Mendès, Catulle. La première maîtresse; roman contemporain. Paris, 1887.

42548.73 Les mendiantes. Cambridge, 1887.

FL 377.28 Mennechet, E. Théâtre français classique. N.Y., 1887.

42555.49.27 Merrill, S Les gammes. Paris, 1887.

Htn Mol 698.2* Moland, Louis. Molière, sa vie et ses oeuvres. Paris, 1887.

Mol 698.2.3 Moland, Louis. Molière sa vie et ses oeuvres. Paris, 1887.

Mol 165.46 Molière, Jean Baptiste Poquelin. L'avare...Boully. Paris, 1887.

Mol 165.43 Molière, Jean Baptiste Poquelin. L'avare...Cotte. N.Y., 1887.

Mol 165.44 Molière, Jean Baptiste Poquelin. L'avare...Livet. Paris, 1887.

Mol 165.45 Molière, Jean Baptiste Poquelin. L'avare...Pontsevrez. Paris, 1887.

Mol 171.36 Molière, Jean Baptiste Poquelin. Le bourgeois gentilhomme...Cotte. N.Y., 1887.

Mol 171.37 Molière, Jean Baptiste Poquelin. Le bourgeois gentilhomme...Gasté. Paris, 1887.

Mol 201.30 Molière, Jean Baptiste Poquelin. L'escole des maris...Schefflr. Bielefeld, 1887.

Mol 211.43 Molière, Jean Baptiste Poquelin. Les femmes savantes...Henry. Paris, 1887.

Mol 235.27 Molière, Jean Baptiste Poquelin. Le médecin malgré lui; Mariage forcé; Le sicilien. Paris, 1887.

Mol 246.5.6 Molière, Jean Baptiste Poquelin. Der Misanthrop. Werther. Essen, 1887.

Mol 245.59 Molière, Jean Baptiste Poquelin. Le misanthrope. Livet. Paris, 1887.

Mol 245.60 Molière, Jean Baptiste Poquelin. Le misanthrope. Pélissier. Paris, 1887.

Mol 251.40 Molière, Jean Baptiste Poquelin. Les précieuses ridicules. Larroumet. Paris, 1887.

Mol 251.42 Molière, Jean Baptiste Poquelin. Les précieuses ridicules. Reynier. Paris, 1887.

Mol 251.43 Molière, Jean Baptiste Poquelin. Les précieuses ridicules. Scheffler. Bielefeld, 1887.

Mol 268.69 Molière, Jean Baptiste Poquelin. Le Tartuffe. Livet. n.p., 1887.

Mon 31.37.9 Montaigne, Michel de. Works. Wight. Boston, 1887. 4v.

37543.90A Montégut, E. Mélanges critiques. Paris, 1887.

42577.36 Monteil, E. La grande Babylone. Paris, 1887.

Mol 820.4 Monval, G. Le laquais de Molière. Paris, 1887.

Mol 713.7.2 Monval, G. Lettres au Mercure sur Molière. Paris, 1887.

Mol 713.7 Monval, G. Lettres au Mercure sur Molière. Paris, 1887.

Mol 870.40 Moreau, E. Protestation. Paris, 1887.

42543.1 Moreau, F. Le code civil et le théâtre contemporain. Paris, 1887.

42543.44.50 Morens, Antonio de. Refutacion al drama de Alfredo Gassier "Juárez ó la guerra de Mexico". Mexico, 1887.

FL 397.79.15 Mugrier, F. Le théâtre en Savoie. Chamberg, 1887.

41596.14.5 Musset, Alfred de. Oeuvres posthumes. Paris, 1887.

41596.12.12 Musset, Alfred de. Premières poésies, 1829-1835. Paris, 1887.

41596.12.10 Musset, Alfred de. Premières poésies. 1829-1835. Paris, 1887.

39544.270 Nicolardot, L. Ménage et finances de Voltaire. Paris, 1887. 2v.

42578.29.7 Ohnet, Georges. Noir et rose. Paris, 1887.

1887 - cont.

42541.24.10 Pailleron, Édouard. Le monde où l'on s'ennuie. Thèse. N.Y., 1887.

37562.11.2 Paris, Gaston. La poésie du moyen âge. Paris, 1887.

42534.12.23 Pavie, V. Oeuvres choisies précédées d'une notice biographique par René Bazin. Paris, 1887. 2v.

42587.43 Pène, Henry de. Trop belle. Paris, 1887.

37555.27.5 Pfuhl, H. Untersuchungen ueber die Roudeaux und Virelais des XIV und XV Jahrhunderts. Regimonti, 1887.

39594.3.35 Pietsch, Theodor. Über das Verhältnis der politischen Theorie, Locke's zu Montesquieu. Breslau, 1887.

38511.25A Pra, Siboud. Le mystère des trois doms joué à Romans en MDIX. Lyon, 1887.

42545.100 Prével, Jules. L'amour mouillé. Paris, 1887.

42515.40 Quinet, E. (Mme.). Edgar Quinet avant l'exil. Paris, 1887.

38537.32.5A Rabelais, F. The life of Gargantua and the heroic deeds of Pantagruel. 4. éd. London, 1887.

38585.19.1.3 Racine, Jean. Andromaque. Les plaideurs. Paris, 1887.

38585.20 Racine, Jean. Athalie. Paris, 1887.

38585.44 Racine, Jean. Les plaideurs. Paris, 1887.

42578.18.4 Racot, A. Le capitaine Muet. Paris, 1887.

Mol 193.13 Récy, René de. Don Juan, le antenaire et la légende. Paris, 1887. 5 pam.

38587.8.9 Regnard, Jean François. Les joueur. Les folies amoureuses. Paris, 1887.

FL 361.35.2 Regnier, P. Souvenirs et études de théâtre. 2e ed. Paris, 1887.

FL 361.35.3 Regnier, P. Souvenirs et études de théâtre. 3e ed. Paris, 1887.

42515.30.220 Renan, Ernest. Discours et conférences. Paris, 1887.

42515.30.222 Renan, Ernest. Discours et conférences. 2. éd. Paris, 1887.

42578.31.86 Richet, C. Possessions. Paris, 1887.

37572.33 Roche, Antoine. Les prosateurs français. Paris, 1887.

41569.16 Le roman de mes fredaines. Bruxelles, 1887.

38524.36 Ronsard, P. de. Oeuvres. Paris, 1887. 6v.

42578.22 Rosny, J.H. Le bilatéral. Paris, 1887.

42514.37 Roziere, E. de. Bibliographie des oeuvres de M. François Mignet. Paris, 1887.

37556.21.14 Runge, H. Courtilz de Sandras und die Anfänge des Mercure historique et politique. Inaug. Diss. Halle, 1887.

42546.15.21 St. Geniès, Richard. Le club des Braconniers. Paris, 1887.

42587.59 Sainte-Croix, C. de. Contempler. Paris, 1887.

41557.19.21 Sandeau, Jules. Mademoiselle de la Seiglière. 5. ed. London, 1887.

37542.25 Sandras, Étienne G. Leçons sur l'histoire de la littérature française. Paris, 1887.

42546.23.35 Sardou, Victorien. Daniel Rochat. 11e ed. Paris, 1887.

42546.30.30 Sardou, Victorien. Patrie. Paris, 1887.

39568.20 Scherer, E. Melchior Grimm. Paris, 1887.

FL 6138.87 Schmidt, Otto. Rousseau und Byron. Greifswald, 1887.

41588.3.4 Scribe, Eugène. Adrienne Lecouvreur. Bielefeld, 1887.

42546.34.25 Silvestre, Armand. Au pays des souvenirs. 3. éd. Paris, 1887.

42546.34 Silvestre, Armand. Contes incongrus et fantaisies galantes. Paris, 1887.

40554.17 Simon, Jules. Victor Cousin. Paris, 1887.

39594.17 Sorel, Albert. Montesquieu. London, 1887.

41541.2 Spoelberch de Lovenjoul, Charles. Histoire des oeuvres de Théophile Gautier. Paris, 1887. 2v.

Mol 619.7 Stapfer, P. Molière et Shakespeare. Paris, 1887.

37555.532 Stengel, E. Verwendung, Bau und Auwendung der romanischen Zehn-Silbners. Frankfurt, 1887.

Mol 619.9 Stichling, O.W. Molière und kein Ende. Berlin, 1887.

41569.18 T....., baroness de. Mystère. Bruxelles, 1887.

42583.35.10 Tardieu, J.R. Pour une épingle. London, 1887.

42584.25 Ten Brink, Jan. Emile Zola und seine Werke. Braunschweig, 1887.

37585.3 Théâtre classique. Paris, 1887.

FL 395.263 Thierry, E. La comédie-française pendant les deux sièges, 1870-1871. Paris, 1887.

42547.4.15 Thurwanger, Joseph. Quatre comédies. Paris, 1887.

42557.6 Tiercelin, Louis. Les anniversaires. Poèmes. Paris, 1887.

38537.19.9 Töpel, Carl. Syntaktische Untersuchungen zu Rabelais. Oppeln, 1887.

40597.2.155 Tours, France. Statue de Honoré de Balzac à Tours. Paris, 1887.

41565.37 Vacquerie, Auguste. Souvent homme varie. Paris, 1887.

42582.30 Verne, Jules. Underground city. Philadelphia, 1887.

41564.23 Vigny, Alfred de. La canne de jonc. Cambridge, 1887.

41564.3.80 Vigny, Alfred de. Cinq-Mars. v.1-2. London, 1887.

42587.70.21 Weill, Alexandre. Paris mensonge. Paris, 1887-1888.

37594.10 Wendahl, C.A. Si vers de la mort (Poème artésien anonyme du milieu du XIIIe siècle). Lund, 1887.

42587.84.41 Zaccone, Pierre. La dame d'Auteuil. Paris, 1887.

37597.16.10 Zetsche, A.W. Über den I. Teil der Bearbeitung des "Roman de Brut" des Wace durch Robert Mannyng of Brunne. Inaug. Diss. Reudnitz, 1887.

Htn 42584.23.50* Zola, Emile. Renée, pièce en cinq actes. Paris, 1887.

42584.19.5.2 Zola, Emile. La terre. Paris, 1887.

1888

37595.8.5 Abailard, Pierre. Lettres amoureuses d'Héloise. Paris, 1888.

42562.5.1 About, Edmond. Le buste. N.Y., 1888.

42562.12.2A About, Edmond. Les mariages de Paris. Paris, 1888.

42562.13.4 About, Edmond. La mère de la marquise. N.Y., 1888.

42562.37.5 Achard, Amédée E. Mademoiselle d'Esparo. Paris, 1888.

42542.1.11.19 Alexandre, André. Le sac. Paris, 1888.

42542.1.12 Alexis, Paul. La fin de Lucie Pellegrin. Paris, 1888.

42542.1.20 Ancey, Georges. Monsieur Lamblin. Paris, 1888.

42562.38.54.5 Arnould, Arthur. La revancha de Clodión. Madrid, 1888.

41593.12.30 Augier, E. Brizeux et Mistral. Brest, 1888.

42542.4.5 Augier, Émile. The adventuress. N.Y., 1888.

42542.10.2 Augier, Émile. Le gendre de M. Poirier. Paris, 1888.

40596.14A Balzac, Honoré de. After-dinner stories. N.Y., 1888.

40597.14.7.1 Balzac, Honoré de. César Birotteau. Boston, 1888.

40596.13.20 Balzac, Honoré de. Cousin Bette. Boston, 1888.

40597.35.100 Balzac, Honoré de. La femme et l'amour. 2. éd. Paris, 1888.

40596.13.52 Balzac, Honoré de. Modeste Mignon. Boston, 1888.

42554.4.2 Banville, Théodore de. Les belles poupées. Paris, 1888.

42554.8.8 Banville, Théodore de. Gringoire; comédie en un acte en prose. London, 1888.

Chronological Listing

1888 - cont.

41522.2.23 Barbey d'Aurevilly, Jules. Ce qui ne meurt pas. Paris, 1888. 2v.
42554.12.4 Barbier, Auguste. Iambes et poèmes. 35e éd. Paris, 1888.
42563.15.7A Barrès, Maurice. Le Quartier Latin, ces messieurs, ces dames. Paris, 1888.
41522.13.9.6 Baudelaire, Charles. Les fleurs du mal. Paris, 1888.
40532.7.30 Beaumarchais, Pierre A.C. de. El casamiento de Figaro. N.Y., 1888.
37555.520 Becker, A. Zur Geschichte der Vers Libres. Halle, 1888.
42563.22.14.30 Belot, Adolphe. Le testament de César Girodot. N.Y., 1888.
42542.29.29.3 Bernhardt, S. (Mme.). L'aveu. Paris, 1888. 2v.
41592.31.5A Betts, Craven L. Songs from Béranger. N.Y., 1888.
42514.3 Bigelow, John. Edward Laboulaye. N.Y., 1888.
38546.51.10 Boissier, G. Mme. de Sévigné. Chicago, 1888.
38546.51.5A Boissier, G. Mme. de Sévigné. 3. éd. Paris, 1888.
42542.29.121 Bonnetain, P. En mer. Paris, 1888.
FL 395.245 Boucheron, M. La divine comédie française. Paris, 1888.
42542.30.25 Bouchor, Maurice. Dieu le Vent. Paris, 1888.
41574.149 Boulanger, Louis. Costumes dessinés par Louis Boulanger pour La Esmeralda. Paris, 1888.
38575.12.5 Bouquet, F. Points obscurs..de la vie de Pierre Corneille. Paris, 1888.
FL 6059.2 Brunel, L. La nouvelle Héloise et Mme. d'Houdetot. Paris, 1888.
37557.19 Caro, E. Poètes et romanciers. Paris, 1888.
41557.10.6.5 Caro, Elme. George Sand. Chicago, 1888.
41557.10.14 Caro, Elme. George Sand. London, 1888.
42563.80.120 Champsaur, Félicien. Les éreintés de la vie. Paris, 1888.
40587.955 Chateaubriand, Celeste Buisson (de Lavigne) (Mme.). Lettres inédites à M. Clausel de Coussergues. Bordeaux, 1888.
42565.9.20 Cherbuliez, Victor. La vocation du comte Ghislain. Paris, 1888.
37562.31 Child, T. Christmas mystery in the fifteenth century. n.p., 1888.
37595.36A Chrestien de Troyes. Cliges. v.1-2. Halle, 1888.
37597.12 Christine de Pizan. Les epistres sur le roman de la rose. Neuburg, 1888.
42565.55.94 Cladel, Léon. Effigies d'inconnus. Paris, 1888.
42565.55.100 Cladel, Léon. Raca. Paris, 1888.
40515.51 Claretie, Léo. Florian. Paris, 1888.
40534.22.3 Collin d'Harleville, J.F. Le vieux célibataire. Paris, 1888.
37596.34 Colvin, Mary N. Lautliche Untersuchung der Werke Roberts von Blois. Zürich, 1888.
40553.9 Constant de Rebecque, Benjamin. Lettres. Paris, 1888.
42586.32.5.15 Coquelin, Ernest. Pirouettes. Paris, 1888.
42542.53.75 Corneau, André. Belle-petite; comédie. Paris, 1888.
38575.34.3 Corneille, Pierre. Nicomède. Paris, 1888.
39544.10.6 Cunisset-Carnot, Paul. La querelle du président de Brosses, avec Voltaire. Dijon, 1888.
38576.32.5 Dannheiser, E. Studien zu Jean de Mairet's Leben und Werken. Sudwigshafen, 1888.
42566.15.5 Darzens, Rodolphe. L'amante du Christ. Paris, 1888.
42566.39 Daudet, Alphonse. Choix de contes. Boston, 1888.
42566.19.15 Daudet, Alphonse. Difesa di Tarascona. 2. ed. Napoli, 1888.
42566.52 Daudet, Alphonse. L'immortel; moeurs parisiennes. Paris, 1888.
42566.52.20 Daudet, Alphonse. One of the "forty". N.Y., 1888.
42566.32.10 Daudet, Alphonse. Robert Helmont, journal d'un solitaire. Paris, 1888.
42566.34.3A Daudet, Alphonse. Sapho. Paris, 1888.
Htn 42566.54*A Daudet, Alphonse. Souvenirs d'un homme de lettres. Paris, 1888.
42566.35.4.5 Daudet, Alphonse. Tartarin sur les Alpes. Paris, 1888.
42566.62.2 Daudet, Alphonse. Thirty years of Paris and my literary life. London, 1888.
42566.40.5A Daudet, Alphonse. Trente ans de Paris à travers ma vie et mes livres. Paris, 1888.
Mol 604.2 Degenhardt, E. Die Metapher bei den Vorlaufern Molière's. Marburg, 1888.
38567.21 Delaporte, P.V. L'art poétique. Lille, 1888. 3v.
Mon 114.5 Dembski, M. Montaigne und Voiture. Greifswald, 1888.
X Cg 38567.10 Deschanel, Émile. Boileau, Charles Perrault. Paris, 1888.
40526.34.50 Dorat, C.J. The kisses. London, 1888.
43576.4.32 Du Bois-Melly, Charles. The history of Nicolas Muss. N.Y., 1888.
FL 6118.88.2 Ducros, L. Jean-Jacques Rousseau. Paris, 1888.
42541.8 Dumanior, P.F.P. Don Caesar de Bazan. N.Y., 1888.
42543.16.30.15 Dumas, Alexandre. Denise. 31. éd. Paris, 1888.
41538.56.20 Dumas, Alexandre. Louis XV et sa cour. Paris, 1888. 2v.
41538.61.5A Dumas, Alexandre. Mèmoires d'un médecin, Joseph Balsamo. Paris, 1888-89. 5v.
41538.53.95 Dumas, Alexandre. Twenty years after. Boston, 1888. 2v.
NEDL 41528.17 Dumas, Alexandre. Vingt ans après. Paris, 1888. 3v.
42563.55.4 Durand, Alice M.C.F. Perdue. N.Y., 1888.
Mol 605.1 Ehrhard, A. Les comédies de Molière en Allemagne. Paris, 1888.
37541.28 Engel, Eduard. Geschichte der Französischen Literatur. 2. Aufl. Leipzig, 1888.
42573.13 Erckmann, Emile. L'ami Fritz. N.Y., 1888.
42572.10.17 Erckmann, Emile. La guerre. Cambridge, 1888.
42572.21 Erckmann, Emile. Le juif polonais. N.Y., 1888.
37596.41 Evers, Robert W. Dan Michel's Ayenbite of Inwyt. Erlangen, 1888.
39531.17 Fabre, A. Les ennemis de Chapelain. Paris, 1888.
38575.14 Faguet, Émile. Corneille. Paris, 1888.
38554.518.40 Fénelon, F. de S. de la Mothe. Lettre sur les occupations de l'Académie Française. Paris, 1888.
38553.15.4.38 Fénelon, F. de S. de la Mothe. Selections. Boston, 1888.
42576.31 Flaubert, Gustave. Salammbô. Paris, 1888.
42576.36.12 Fleuriot, Zenaide Marie A. Armelle Traher. 6. éd. Paris, 1888.
42576.3.30F Flore, Jeanne. Histoire de la belle Rosemonde et du preux chevalier Andro. Paris, 1888.
38562.20.15 Fontenelle, B. Le B. de. Choix d'éloges. Paris, 1888.
38528.25.20 Frank, Félix. Léxique de la langue de Bonaventure des Periers. Paris, 1888.
X Cg 38528.25.20 Frank, Félix. Léxique de la lanque de Bonaventure des Periers. Paris, 1888.
42576.61.100 Frescaly, Marcel. Nouvelles algériennes. Paris, 1888.
38526.14.150 Garaby, Antoine. Satires inédites. Rouen, 1888.

1888 - cont.

42513.39.15 Gasparin, V.B.C. de. Under French skies. N.Y., 1888.
43616.2.33 Gautier, Judith. La marchande de sourires. Paris, 1888.
41542.28 Gautier, Théophile. Les vacances du Lundi. Paris, 1888.
FL 395.247 Giffard, P. La vie au théâtre. Paris, 1888.
42576.6.6 Ginisty, Paul. Crime et châtiment. Paris, 1888. 4 pam.
Mol 870.43 Godin, Eugène. La lyre de Cahors. Paris, 1888.
Htn 42575.72.3* Goncourt, Edmond de. Germinie Lacerteux. Paris, 1888.
42575.68.1 Goncourt, Edmond de. Journal des Goncourt. Paris, 1888-1917. 9v.
42575.65 Goncourt, Edmond de. Préfaces et manifestes. Paris, 1888.
42575.64.50 Goncourt, Edmond de. Préfaces et manifestes littéraires. Paris, 1888.
43625.89.3100 Goudeau, Émile. Dix ans de Bonème. Paris, 1888.
Mol 853.3 Gueret, G. La promenade de Saint-Cloud. Paris, 1888.
42576.40.330F Halévy, Ludovic. The abbé Constantin. London, 1888.
42576.40.328 Halévy, Ludovic. L'abbé Constantin. Paris, 1888.
43631.75.111 Harel, Paul. Sous les pommiers. 2. éd. Paris, 1888.
X Cg FL 379.31 Hawkins, F. The French stage in the 18th century. Photoreproduction. London, 1888. 2v.
42576.67.3 Hervieu, Paul. Deux plaisanteries. Paris, 1888.
Htn Mol 698.1* Houssaye, A. Molière, sa femme et sa fille. Paris, 1888.
41572.8.70 Hugo, Victor. History of a crime. N.Y., 1888.
41573.13 Hugo, Victor. Hoi Athlioi.' v.1-2,3-5. en Athenais, 1888. 2v.
41571.12.2 Hugo, Victor. Les misérables. N.Y., 1888.
41571.31.5A Hugo, Victor. The man who laughs. Boston, 1888. 2v.
41571.32.3.2 Hugo, Victor. Ninety-three. Boston, 1888.
41571.32.3 Hugo, Victor. Ninety-three. Boston, 1888.
41573.23.10A Hugo, Victor. Notre Dame. Boston, 1888.
41571.32.4 Hugo, Victor. Notre-Dame de Paris. Boston, 1888. 2v.
41573.23.1 Hugo, Victor. Notre Dame de Paris. v.1-2. Boston, 1888.
41572.20.5 Hugo, Victor. Quatre-vingt-treize. N.Y., 1888.
41571.32.5 Hugo, Victor. The toilers of the sea. Boston, 1888. 2v.
41573.17.4 Hugo, Victor. The toilers of the sea. Boston, 1888. 2v.
41573.17.3 Hugo, Victor. The toilers of the sea. Boston, 1888. 2v.
41571.43A Hugo, Victor. The toilers of the sea. London, 1888. 2v.
37564.37 Janet, Paul. Les passions et les caractères dans la littérature du XVIIe siècle. Paris, 1888.
37556.22.3 Joze, V. Les marechieux de la chronique: H. Rochefort, A. Scholl, A. Wolff. Paris, 1888.
41544.6.10 Karr, Alphonse. Encore les femmes. 2. éd. Paris, 1888.
FL 398.74.60 Kennard, Nina H. Rachel. Boston, 1888.
40527.19.100 Kerviler, R. Olivier Morvan, 1754-1794. St. Brieuc, 1888.
42544.28.10 Labiche, Eugène. Un chapeau de paille d'Italie. Paris, 1888.
42544.27.25 Labiche, Eugène. La grammaire, comédie-vaudeville. 5. éd. London, 1888.
39526.31.5 La Fontaine, Jean de. Fables, précédées d'une notice biographique. Paris, 1888.
41578.32 Lamartine, Alphonse. Graziella. Paris, 1888.
Mol 870.41 Lambert, A. Une collaboration. Paris, 1888.
Mol 612.3 Larocque, J. La plume et le pouvoir au XVIIe siècle. Paris, 1888.
NEDL 38557.16 Lebarq, J. Histoire critique de la prédication de Bossuet. Lille, 1888.
38575.13 Lemaitre, Jules. Corneille et la poetique d'Aristote. Paris, 1888.
FL 360.28.2 Lemaitre, Jules. Impressions de théâtre. Sér. 1,5. Paris, 1888- 2v.
FL 360.28 Lemaitre, Jules. Impressions de théâtre. Sér. 1-11. Paris, 1888-1920. 11v.
42576.43.30 Lemonnier, Camille. La comédie des jouets. Paris, 1888.
41593.12.7 Le Mouel, Eugène. Stances à Brizeux. Paris, 1888.
FL 379.30 Lenient, C. La comédie en France au XVIIIe siècle. Paris, 1888. 2v.
Htn 37530.10.25* Le Petit, Jules. Bibliographie des principales éditions originales d'ecrivains français. Paris, 1888.
42566.16.25 Le Roux, H. Notre patron, Alphonse Daudet. Paris, 1888.
42513.75 Leroy-Beaulieu, A. La France, La Russie et l'Europe. Paris, 1888.
FL 377.6 Levertin, Oscar. Studier ofver fars och farsörer i frankrike. Upsala, 1888.
37555.32 Loise, Ferdinand. Histoire de la poésie...en France. Paris, 1888.
42576.72.3 Lombard, Jean. L'agonie. Paris, 1888.
42577.6 Malot, Hector. Folie d'amour. Paris, 1888.
42545.6.151 Maques, Melville G. Gustave the professor. Boston, 1888.
39534.36.30 Marillot, Paul. Scarron. Thèse. Paris, 1888.
42545.6.250 Martin, Alexis. Les débuts de Corneille. Paris, 1888.
42555.49.21 Martin, Gabriel. Les cantiques impies. Paris, 1888.
41574.25.2A Marzials, Frank T. Life of Victor Hugo. London, 1888.
37562.2 Masson, Gustave. French literature. London, 1888.
42577.4.15 Maupassant, Guy de. Clair de lune. Paris, 1888.
42577.4.17.5 Maupassant, Guy de. Pierre et Jean. Paris, 1888.
Htn 42571.47F* Maupassant, Guy de. Pierre et Jean. Paris, 1888. 2v.
42577.4.17.6 Maupassant, Guy de. Pierre et Jean. 7. éd. Paris, 1888.
NEDL 42577.4.24 Maupassant, Guy de. Le rosier de Madame Husson. Paris, 1888.
42577.4.24.5 Maupassant, Guy de. Le rosier de Madame Husson. Paris, 1888.
42577.4.29.5 Maupassant, Guy de. Sur l'eau. Paris, 1888.
42545.10.5 Meilhac, Henri. Barbe-bleue. Paris, 1888.
42555.58.45 Mendès, Catulle. L'en vers des feuilles. 6. éd. Paris, 1888.
42555.58.15 Mendès, Catulle. Grande Maguet. Paris, 1888.
FL 6133.2 Metzger, A. La conversion de Mme. de Warens. Paris, 1888.
FL 6132.3 Metzger, A. Les pensées de Mme. de Warens. Lyon, 1888.
42545.27.5 Mikhaël, Ephraim. Le cor fleuri. Paris, 1888.
Mol 165.46.5 Molière, Jean Baptiste Poquelin. L'avare...de Vere. N.Y., 1888.
Mol 181.20A Molière, Jean Baptiste Poquelin. Dépit amoureux...Vitu. Paris, 1888.
Mol 195.32 Molière, Jean Baptiste Poquelin. L'école des femmes...Saintsbury. Cambridge, 1888.
Mol 205.20 Molière, Jean Baptiste Poquelin. L'étourdi...Vitu. Paris, 1888.
Mol 228.30 Molière, Jean Baptiste Poquelin. Le malade imaginaire...Gasc. London, 1888.
Mol 245.61 Molière, Jean Baptiste Poquelin. Le misanthrope. Aulard. Paris, 1888.

1888 - cont.

Htn Mol 8.88* Molière, Jean Baptiste Poquelin. Oeuvres. Paris, 1888-96. 31v.
Mol 252.2 Molière, Jean Baptiste Poquelin. The precious ridiculous. N.Y., 1888.
Mol 252.2.1 Molière, Jean Baptiste Poquelin. The precious ridiculous. N.Y., 1888.
Mol 8.88.2 Molière, Jean Baptiste Poquelin. Six plays, with introduction. Paris, 1888.
Mol 268.128 Molière, Jean Baptiste Poquelin. Tartuffe, or The imposter. N.Y., 1888.
Mol 268.70 Molière, Jean Baptiste Poquelin. Le Tartuffe. Gasc et Holmes. London, 1888.
Mol 268.71 Molière, Jean Baptiste Poquelin. Le Tartuffe. Mayer. Paris, 1888.
42543.1.17 Moniquet, P. Les idées de Alexandre Dumas fils. Paris, 1888. 2 pam.
Mon 28.18 Montaigne, Michel de. Extraits. Réaume. Paris, 1888.
42533.14.5 Montégut, Émile. Libres opinions morales et historiques. Paris, 1888.
Mol 880.36 Mouton, E. L'affaire Scapin. Paris, 1888.
37596.27.4 Müller, Paul. Studien über drei dramatisch Bearbeitungen der Alexinslegende. Berlin, 1888.
42577.32.28 Murger, Henry. Scenes from the life of Bohemia. Indianapolis, 1888?
41596.18.13 Musset, Alfred de. Three novelettes and Valentine's wager, a comedy. Photoreproduction. N.Y., 1888.
42578.5.30 Noir, Louis Salmon. La banque juive. Paris, 1888.
42578.30.35 Ohnet, Georges. Volonté. Paris, 1888.
42541.25 Pailleron, Édouard. La souris. Paris, 1888.
38557.24.110 Panov, Ioann I. Bossiuet i ego propovedi. Sankt Peterburg, 1888.
37562.22A Paris, Gaston. La littérature française au moyen âge. Paris, 1888.
42578.30.46 Peladan, J. Istar. v.1-2. Paris, 1888.
42587.46 Peyrebrune, G. de. Les frères Colombe. N.Y., 1888.
37593.61A Philippe de Navarre. Les quatres âges de l'homme. Paris, 1888.
38514.46 Piaget, Arthur. Martin Le Franc. Lausanne, 1888.
41587.13.25 Picard, Louis Benoît. Mediocre et rampant. Halle, 1888.
37567.347 Plomert, J. Petit glossaire pour servir à l'intelligence des auteurs décadents et symbolistes. Paris, 1888.
42555.73.100F Popelin, Claudius. Un livre de sonnets. Paris, 1888.
41593.12.5 Quellien, Narcisse. Bardit lu sur la tombe de Brizeux au cimetière du Barnel. Paris, 1888.
42515.40.2 Quinet, E. (Mme.). Edgar Quinet avant l'exil. Paris, 1888.
38537.33A Rabelais, F. The sequel to Pantagruel. London, 1888.
38537.31 Rabelais, F. Three good giants. Boston, 1888.
38585.33 Racine, Jean. Iphigénie. Paris, 1888.
42578.31.110 Radet, L. Le siège de Montargis, 1427. Montargis, 1888.
42515.30.250A Renan, Ernest. Drames philosophiques. Paris, 1888.
42515.29.369 Renan, Ernest. Saint Paul. Paris, 1888.
42515.29.30A Renan, Ernest. Vie de Jésus. 19. éd. Paris, 1888.
37596.46A Renaut, Le Trouvère. Le roman de galerent. Montpellier, 1888.
Mol 755.8 Révérend du Mesnil, E. François de Molière, Anne Picardet. Charolles, 1888.
40562.16 Ricard, Antoine l'abbé. Lacordaire. Paris, 1888.
Mol 880.29 Richepin, J. Monsieur Scapin. Paris, 1888.
Htn 42556.22.20* Richepin, Jean. Miarka, la fille à l'ourse. Paris, 1888.
37574.44 Robertet, G. Poètes lyriques du XIXe siècle. Paris, 1888. 2v.
42578.19.8.1 Rod, Edouard. Giacome Leopardi. Études sur le 19. siècle. Lausanne, 1888.
42578.19.8 Rod, Edouard. Giacome Leopardi. Études sur le 19. siècle. Paris, 1888.
42578.20.5 Rosny, J.H. Les corneilles. Paris, 1888.
42578.22.2 Rosny, J.H. Marc Fane. Paris, 1888.
FL 6046.12.13 Rousseau, J.J. Emile, or Concerning education. Boston, 1888.
38537.19.10 Saenger, S. Syntaktische Untersuchungen zu Rabelais. Halle, 1888.
38514.49A St. Bernard de Menthon. Le mystère de Saint Bernard de Menthon. Paris, 1888.
FL 391.90 Saint-Mor, Guy de. Paris sur scène. Saison, 1886-87. 2e ed. Paris, 1888.
Htn 38512.8F* Saint-Pierre. Novella e poesie francesi inedite o rarissime del secolo XIV. Firenze, 1888.
X Cg 42546.15.25 Salandri, Gaston. La prose. Paris, 1888.
42546.15.26 Salandri, Gaston. La prose. Paris, 1888.
40597.1 Saltres, Edgar E. Balzac. Boston, 1888.
37586.4 Sammlung Französisches Neudrucke. v.7-8. Heilbronn, 1888. 2v.
37586.5 Sammlung Französisches Neudrucke. v.9. Heilbronn, 1888.
41557.9.74 Sand, George. Indiana. Philadelphia, 1888.
41557.8.103 Sand, George. La mare au diable. Paris, 1888.
41557.19.3 Sandeau, Jules. Helena de la Seiglière. N.Y., 1888.
41557.19.5 Sandeau, Jules. Helena de la Seiglière. N.Y., 1888.
42546.26.6.2 Sardou, Victorien. Les pattes de mouche. N.Y., 1888.
38527.49 Schmidt-Wartenberg, H.M. Seneca's influence on Robert Garnier. Darmstadt, 1888.
42578.36.4 Schultz, Jeanne. La neuvaine de Colette. Paris, 1888.
42578.36.30 Schultz, Jeanne. Was der heilige Joseph vermag. Stuttgart, 1888.
37597.31 Seeger, Hermann. Über die Sprache des Guillaume le Clerc de Normandie. Halle, 1888.
42587.58.12 Ségur, Sophie. Un bon petit diable. Paris, 1888.
38513.19.5 Serrigny, Ernest. La representation d'un mystère de Saint Martin à Seurre en 1496. Dijon, 1888.
42546.34.5 Silvestre, Armand. Fabliaux gaillards. Paris, 1888.
42546.34.7 Silvestre, Armand. Gauloiseries nouvelles. Paris, 1888.
Htn 42546.34.10* Silvestre, Armand. Le nu au salon de 1888-1890. v.1,2,4,5,10. Paris, 1888-92. 5v.
40554.19 Simon, Jules. Victor Cousin. Chicago, 1888.
37596.49A Söderhjelm, Werner. De Saint Laurent. Paris, 1888.
39594.17.3 Sorel, Albert. Montesquieu. Chicago, 1888.
FL 360.25 Soubies, Albert. Une première par jour. Paris, 1888.
Mol 619.6 Souriau, M. La versification de Molière. Paris, 1888.
41558.67.8 Souvestre, Émile. An attic philosopher in Paris. N.Y., 1888.
40596.4.11 Spoelberch de Lovenjoul, Charles. Histoire des oeuvres de H. de Balzac. 3. éd. Paris, 1888.
41561.11 Sue, Eugène. Le Juif errant. Paris, 1888.
39527.5.2A Taine, Hippolyte. La Fontaine et ses fables. 11e éd. Paris, 1888.

1888 - cont.

FL 355.700 Théâtre d'application, Paris. Cultures et acteurs; catalogue de l'exposition. Paris, 1888. 2 pam.
FL 391.95 Théâtre fin de siècle 1881-1888. Paris, 1888?
42583.33.22 Theuriet, André. Contes de la forêt. Paris, 1888.
37548.28 Thibaut, F. Marguerite d'Autriche et Jehan Lemaire de Belges. Paris, 1888.
Mol 870.42 Tiercelin, L. Le rire de Molière. Paris, 1888.
42578.52.23 Tinseau, Léon de. Ma cousine Pot-au-feu et, Le mariage au gant. 6. éd. Paris, 1888.
42578.56.5 Toutain, Paul. Chez nos ancêtres. Paris, 1888.
42578.58.5 Uchard, Mario. My uncle Barbassou. London, 1888.
42584.47.25 Ulbach, Louis. La csardas. 2. éd. Paris, 1888.
42587.65.9 Vachette, Eugène. Lilie, Tutue, Bebeth. Paris, 1888.
38546.54 Vallery-Radot. Mme. de Sévigné. Paris, 1888.
38526.9.25 Venema, Johannes. Über die "Soltane". Inaug. Diss. Marburg, 1888.
42582.23 Verne, Jules. North against South. London, 1888.
39544.37 Vernier, Léon. Étude sur Voltaire Grammairien. Thèse. Paris, 1888.
42576.56.15 Viaud, Julien. From lands of exile. N.Y., 1888.
42576.55.4 Viaud, Julien. Madame Chrysanthème. London, 1888.
Htn 42576.55.5* Viaud, Julien. Madame Chrysanthème. Paris, 1888.
42576.55.6 Viaud, Julien. Madame Chrysanthème. Paris, 1888.
42557.28 Vicaire, Gabriel. Le miracle de St. Nicolas. Paris, 1888.
42584.52 Vincent, Jacques. Ce que femme veut. Paris, 1888.
Htn 42584.24.6.10* Vizetelly, E.A. Extracts principally from English classics. London, 1888.
39545.37.6 Voltaire, François Marie Arouet de. Candide, or The optimist. London, 1888.
39544.27.3.7 Voltaire, François Marie Arouet de. Lettres d'amour...Louis Malard. Paris, 1888. 2v.
FL 365.60.5 Wattendorff, L. Essai sur l'influence que Shakespeare a exercée sur la tragédie. Coblenz, 1888.
42587.70.4 Weill, Alexandre. Épitres cinglantes à M. Drumont. Paris, 1888.
42587.70.5 Weill, Alexandre. L'esprit de l'esprit. Paris, 1888.
37596.93 Werth, Hermann. Über die ältesten französischen Übersetzungen mittelalterlicher Jagd- (Beiz-) Lehrbücher. Inaug. Diss. Göttingen, 1888.
40525.9 Wespy, Paul. Der graf Tressan. Leipzig, 1888.
41573.26.15F Wogel, J. Grandes scèces de Ruy Blas. Paris, 1888.
39594.18 Zévort, Edgar. Montesquieu. London, 1888.
42584.13 Zola, Emile. Une campagne. 1880-81. Paris, 1888.
42584.23.9 Zola, Emile. Germinal. Paris, 1888.
42584.10.20 Zola, Emile. The girl in scarlet. London, 1888.
42584.11.9 Zola, Emile. Jacques Damour. Paris, 1888.
42584.19.7 Zola, Emile. La terre. Chicago, 1888.
42584.19.4.50 Zola, Emile. Le rêve. Philadelphia, 1888.

1889

42553.60 Amanieux, M. La révolution. Paris, 1889.
42553.33 Amiel, Henri F. Amiel's journal. London, 1889.
42542.1.21 Ancey, Georges. L'ecole des veufs. Paris, 1889.
42542.1.18 Ancey, Georges. Les inséparables. Paris, 1889.
42542.10.4 Augier, Émile. Le gendre de M. Poirier. 2. ed. London, 1889.
42542.8.2A Augier, Émile. Maître Guérin. Paris, 1889.
42515.35.18 Auzies, Célestin. Les origines de la Bible et M. Ernest Renan. Paris, 1889.
Mol 702.1 Baluffe, A. Autour de Molière. Paris, 1889.
40596.13.10 Balzac, Honoré de. Bureaucracy. Boston, 1889.
40597.14.7.2 Balzac, Honoré de. César Birotteau. Boston, 1889.
Htn 40591.20* Balzac, Honoré de. Les chouans. Paris, 1889.
40597.35.166 Balzac, Honoré de. Cousin Bette. Boston, 1889.
40597.20.3 Balzac, Honoré de. Eugénie Grandet. Boston, 1889.
40597.26A Balzac, Honoré de. Louis Lambert. Boston, 1889.
40596.13.56 Balzac, Honoré de. Seraphita. Boston, 1889.
42554.1.07 Banville, Théodore de. Les cariatides. Paris, 1889.
42554.1.25 Banville, Théodore de. Oeuvres. Paris, 1889.
42554.6.5.5 Banville, Théodore de. Socrates and his wife. 1st ed. N.Y, 1889.
41522.1.2 Barbey d'Aurevilly, Jules. Une histoire sans nom. Paris, 1889.
41522.2.5 Barbey d'Aurevilly, Jules. Pensées détachées. Paris, 1889.
41522.2.9 Barbey d'Aurevilly, Jules. Polemiques d'hier. 2. éd. Paris, 1889.
42524.10 Bardoux, A. Études d'un autre temps. Paris, 1889.
42554.14.100 Barrucand, V. Une partie d'échecs. Paris, 1889.
Htn 42563.26.10* Bauer, Henry. Une comédienne; scènes de la vie de théâtre. Paris, 1889.
42563.26.10.5 Bauer, Henry. Une comédienne. Paris, 1889.
37578.85 Beausacq, M.J. Le livre d'or de la comtesse Diane. Paris, 1889.
Mol 602.3 Bennewitz, A. Molière's Einfluss auf Congreve. Leipzig, 1889.
41592.31.4 Béranger, P.J. de. Béranger's poems. Philadelphia, 1889.
Htn 42542.29.12* Bergerat, Émile. L'amour en république. Paris, 1889.
42542.29.81 Berton, Pierre. Les jurons de Cadillac. Paris, 1889.
NEDL 39574.29 Bertrand, Joseph. D'Alembert. Paris, 1889.
40582.13 Beyle, Henri. Lamiel. Paris, 1889.
37543.60 Birch-Hirschfeld, A. Geschichte der französischen Literatur. Stuttgart, 1889.
42563.23.35 Bloy, Léon. Un brelan d'excommuniés. Paris, 1889.
38512.17.9 Blume, F. Metrik Froissarts. Greifswald, 1889.
38566.22 Boileau Despréaux, Nicolas. Oeuvres de Boileau. Paris, 1889.
38566.17.15 Boileau Despréaux, Nicolas. Oeuvres poétiques. Paris, 1889.
42512.7.3 Bois, Georges. Au temps de la ballade. Paris, 1889.
42563.26.15 Boissie, A. Dragona y escarcela; novela francesa. Habana, 1889.
42542.29.120 Bonnetain, P. La pelote. Paris, 1889.
42542.29.145 Borrelli, V. Alain Chartier. Paris, 1889.
38557.34 Bossuet, J.B. Sermons. Paris, 1889.
42563.37.15 Bourget, Paul. Etudes et portraits. Paris, 1889. 3v.
37564.30 Bourgoin, Auguste. Les maitres de la critique au XVIIeme siècle. Paris, 1889.
38512.41A Bozon, Nicole. Les contes moralisés. Paris, 1889.
42512.14 Broglie, Albert de. Histoire et diplomatie. Paris, 1889.
37557.13A Brunetière, F. Études critiques sur l'histoire de la littérature française. Série 1-9. Paris, 1889-1932. 9v.
42524.15 Brunetière, F. Questions de critique. Paris, 1889.
42561.13 Cahun, Léon. Adventures of Captain Mago. N.Y., 1889.

1889 - cont.

39544.305 Carel, George. Voltaire und Goethe als Dramatiker. v.1-2. Berlin, 1889-98.
42542.49 Céard, Henry. Les résignés. Paris, 1889.
40586.13 Chateaubriand, F.A.R. Atala. Paris, 1889.
40526.7.6 Chenier, André. Poésies choisies. 2e éd. Paris, 1889.
42565.55.5 Cladel, Léon. L'ancien. Paris, 1889.
42565.55.109 Cladel, Léon. Seize morceaux de litterature. Paris, 1889.
38527.9.30 Contades, Gérard de. Le cabaliste. Argentan, 1889.
42554.22.40 Coppée, François. Henriette. Paris, 1889.
42554.19.3 Coppée, François. Le pater. Paris, 1889?
38575.29.2.7 Corneille, Pierre. Le Cid. N.Y., 1889.
38574.12.5 Corneille, Pierre. Oeuvres des deux Corneille. Paris, 1889. 2v.
38575.34.7 Corneille, Pierre. Polyeucte. London, 1889.
42566.23.3 Daudet, Alphonse. Les femmes d'artistes. Paris, 1889.
42566.52.25 Daudet, Alphonse. The immortal. N.Y., 1889.
42566.26.2.10 Daudet, Alphonse. Jack. Paris, 1889.
42566.63.2 Daudet, Alphonse. Recollections of a literary man. London, 1889.
42566.27.15F Daudet, Alphonse. The struggle for life. n.p., 1889.
42566.40 Daudet, Alphonse. Trente ans de Paris. Paris, 1889.
42566.40.2 Daudet, Alphonse. Trente ans de Paris à travers ma vie et mes livres. Paris, 1889.
42567.39 Daudet, Ernest. Apostate. N.Y., 1889.
FL 360.5 De Lapommeraye, H. Conférences...du théâtre Nationale de l'Odéon. Paris, 1889. 14v.
42575.89 Delzant, A. Les Goncourt. Paris, 1889.
42542.63.3 Demesse, H. Les mères rivales. Paris, 1889.
42554.29.4.5 Déroulède, Paul. Refrains militaires. Paris, 1889.
42524.38 Desjardins, Paul. Esquisses et impressions. Paris, 1889.
42568.19.19 Du Boisgobey, Fortuné. Doctor Villagos. N.Y., 1889.
41538.69.15 Dumas, Alexandre. Le Chevalier de Maison Rouge. Paris, 1889. 2v.
41538.16.4.2 Dumas, Alexandre. The count of Monte Cristo. Boston, 1889. 4v.
41538.22 Dumas, Alexandre. Episodes from Pepin et Charlemagne. London, 1889.
41538.20.8.3 Dumas, Alexandre. The forty five. Boston, 1889. 2v.
41538.20.28 Dumas, Alexandre. The forty-five. Boston, 1889. 2v.
41538.21 Dumas, Alexandre. La bouillie de la comtesse Berthe. London, 1889.
41538.29.2.3 Dumas, Alexandre. Marguerite de Valois. Boston, 1889. 2v.
41538.53.24.3 Dumas, Alexandre. The three musketeers. Boston, 1889. 2v.
41538.53.1 Dumas, Alexandre. Les trois mousquetaires. Boston, 1889.
41538.55.19 Dumas, Alexandre. The vicomte de Bragelonne. Boston, 1889. 6v.
Mol 704.1A Durand, H. Molière. Paris, 1889.
FL 361.39 Edwards, Henry S. Idols of the French stage. London, 1889. 2v.
FL 361.40 Edwards, Henry S. Idols of the French stage. 2d ed. London, 1889. 2v.
42543.29 Erckmann, Émile. L'ami Fritz. N.Y., 1889.
38537.15 Eriches, Ludwig. Les grandes et inestimables chroniques de Gargantua und Rabelais. Strassburg, 1889.
39533.8.30 Fabre, Antonin. Lexique de la langue de Chapelain. Paris, 1889.
42575.3 Fage, Émile. Causeries limousines. Paris, 1889.
39526.28 Faguet, Émile. La Fontaine. Paris, 1889.
FL 383.55 Faguet, Émile. Notes sur le théâtre contemporain. ser. 1-3. Paris, 1889-1891. 3v.
42575.27.5 Feuillet, Octave. Le divorce de Juliette. Paris, 1889.
42543.41 Figuies, L. La science au théâtre, comédies. Paris, 1889. 2v.
42543.41.2 Figuies, L. La science au théâtre, drames. Paris, 1889.
42575.53.28.10 Flammarion, Camille. Uraine. Paris, 1889.
42576.63.7.1 France, Anatole. Le crime de Sylvestre Bonnard. Paris, 1889.
37557.20A France, Anatole. La vie littéraire. v.1,3-4. Paris, 1889. 3v.
37555.560 Fuster, Charles. Les poètes du clocher. Paris, 1889.
41542.30 Gautier, Théophile. Partie carrée. Paris, 1889.
41542.31A Gautier, Théophile. Poésies complètes. Paris, 1889-90. 2v.
Mon 117.2 Georgov, Ivan. Montaigne als vertreter des Relativismus. Leipzig, 1889.
37567.194 Gille, Philippe. La bataille littéraire, 1875-1894. Paris, 1889-94. 7v.
42576.65 Glouvet, Jules de. Histoires du vieux temps. Paris, 1889.
NEDL 42575.59 Goncourt, Edmond de. Madame Gervaisais. Paris, 1889.
40535.7 Graziano, Joseph. Essai sur la vie et les oeuvres de Destouches. Frauenfeld, 1889.
37541.11 Grignard, Jean. Nos gloires littéraires. Bruxelles, 1889.
42576.37.50 Grosclaude, E. Les joies du plein air. Paris, 1889.
37562.57 Guerlich, Robert. Bemerkungen über den Versbau der Anglonormannen. Breslau, 1889.
42543.62.23.5 Guiard, Emile. Poésies. Paris, 1889.
42576.11.20 Guillemot, Maurice. Lettres d'un amant. Paris, 1889.
42576.40.312 Halévy, Ludovic. L'abbé Constantin. N.Y., 1889.
39532.13.8 Hamilton, Anthony. Memoires of the Count de Grammont. London, 1889. 2v.
37543.35 Hémon, Félix. Cours de littérature. v.1-25. Paris, 1889-93. 8v.
FL 398.39.2 Houssaye, Arsène. Behind the scenes of comédie française. London, 1889.
FL 398.39 Houssaye, Arsène. Behind the scenes of comédie française. Philadelphia, 1889.
41571.40A Hugo, Victor. The man who laughs. London, 1889. 2v.
41571.42A Hugo, Victor. Ninety-three. London, 1889. 2v.
41573.23.4 Hugo, Victor. Notre Dame de Paris. Boston, 1889. 2v.
41573.55 Hugo, Victor. Victor Hugo de la jeunesse. Paris, 1889.
42576.66.4 Huysmans, Joris Karl. Certains. Photoreproduction. Paris, 1889.
37558.12 Jacquinet, P. Les femmes de France. Paris, 1889.
37562.12 Jeanroy, Alfred. De nostratibus medii aevi poetis. Paris, 1889.
37561.27.1 Jeanroy, Alfred. Les origines de la poésie lyrique en France au moyen âge. Paris, 1889.
37561.27 Jeanroy, Alfred. Les origines de la poésie lyrique en France au moyen âge. 1. éd. Paris, 1889.
42587.10.5 Julliot, François de. Mademoiselle Solange. N.Y., 1889.
37543.39.9 Junker, Heinrich P. Grundriss des Geschichte der französischen Litteratur. Münster, 1889.

1889 - cont.

37551.36.2 Kerviler, René. Bretagne à l'Academie Française. Paris, 1889.
37562.33 Kuttner, Max. Das Naturgefühl der Altfranzösen und sein Einfluss auf ihre Dichtung. Berlin, 1889.
40562.27 Lacordaire, Jean Baptiste Henri. Le Père Lacordaire. Paris, 1889.
38544.27.35 La Fayette, Marie M. La Princesse de Clèves. Paris, 1889.
FL 383.25 Laforet, L.P. Le carillon théâtral. Paris, 1889.
FL 379.30.3 Lanson, G. La comédie au XVIIIe siècle. Paris, 1889.
FL 6128.89.2 Lebasteur, H. Essai sur le caractère de Jean-Jacques Rousseau. Chambéry, 1889.
43688.8.60 Le Goffic, Charles. Amour breton. Paris, 1889.
37567.32.5 Lemaître, Jules. Les contemporains. 4e serie. 8e éd. Paris, 1889.
42587.14.22 Lepic, Adèle. Marchand d'allumettes. Paris, 1889?
40512.33.5 LeSage, Alain René. Historia de Gil Blas de Santillana. N.Y., 1889.
41522.3.12 Maffre de Baugé, Achille. J. Barbey d'Aurevilly. Toulouse, 1889.
FL 6118.89 Mahrenholtz, R. Jean-Jacques Rousseau. Leben, Geistesentwickelung und Hauptwerke. Leipzig, 1889.
42577.11.2 Malot, Hector. Episodes from Sans famille. London, 1889.
Mon 175.3 Malvezin, T. Notes sur la maison d'habitation de Montaigne. Bordeaux, 1889.
Mol 270.19.5 Mantegazza, P. Il secolo Tartufo. Milano, 1889.
42576.76.16 Margueritte, Paul. Jours d'épreuve. Paris, 1889.
42555.49.19 Mariéton, Paul. Hellas. Paris, 1889.
42577.4.29.5.3 Maupassant, Guy de. Afloat. London, 1889.
42577.4.10A Maupassant, Guy de. Fort comme la mort. Paris, 1889.
42577.4.25 Maupassant, Guy de. Histoire d'une fille de ferme. Paris, 1889.
42577.4.21 Maupassant, Guy de. La main gauche. Paris, 1889.
42577.2.2 Maupassant, Guy de. La maison Tellier. Paris, 1889.
42577.2.3.5 Maupassant, Guy de. Miss Harriet. Paris, 1889.
42577.4.19.5 Maupassant, Guy de. The odd number. N.Y., 1889.
42577.4.19.2A Maupassant, Guy de. The odd number. N.Y., 1889.
42577.4.27 Maupassant, Guy de. Yvette. Paris, 1889.
42545.10.9 Meilhac, Henri. La vie Parisienne. Paris, 1889.
42555.58.28 Mendès, Catulle. Le cruel berceau. Paris, 1889.
FL 6128.89.3 Mentha, F.H. Discours sur le système politique de Rousseau. Neuchâtel, 1889.
41555.22.1.3 Mérimée, Prosper. Chronique du règne de Charles IX. Paris, 1889.
41555.7.10 Mérimée, Prosper. Letters to an incognita. N.Y., 1889.
42545.21.10 Méténier, Oscar. La casserole. Paris, 1889.
FL 383.85F Mobisson. Costumes of the modern stage. pt.1-5. London, 1889-91.
FL 6128.89 Mörbius, P.J. Jean-Jacques Rousseau's Krankheitsgeschichte. Leipzig, 1889.
Mol 165.47 Molière, Jean Baptiste Poquelin. L'avare...Gasc. London, 1889.
Mol 165.48 Molière, Jean Baptiste Poquelin. L'avare...Humbert. Leipzig, 1889.
Mol 165.48.2 Molière, Jean Baptiste Poquelin. L'avare...Humbert: Anmerkungen. Leipzig, 1889.
Mol 165.49 Molière, Jean Baptiste Poquelin. L'avare...Lavigne. Paris, 1889.
Mol 165.50 Molière, Jean Baptiste Poquelin. L'avare...Masson. 12th ed. London, 1889.
Mol 171.39 Molière, Jean Baptiste Poquelin. Le bourgeois gentilhomme...Schele de Vere. N.Y., 1889.
Mol 185.10 Molière, Jean Baptiste Poquelin. Dom Garcie de Navarre...Vitu. Paris, 1889.
Mol 201.32A Molière, Jean Baptiste Poquelin. L'escole des maris...Vitu. Paris, 1889.
Mol 245.62 Molière, Jean Baptiste Poquelin. Le misanthrope. Brette. London, 1889.
Mol 18.89 Molière, Jean Baptiste Poquelin. Oeuvres complètes...Louandre. Paris, 1889. 3v.
Mol 880.1.3 Molière, Jean Baptiste Poquelin. Plays froms Molière, by English dramatists. London, 1889.
Mol 251.45 Molière, Jean Baptiste Poquelin. Les précieuses ridicules. Vitu. Paris, 1889.
Mol 261.25 Molière, Jean Baptiste Poquelin. Sganarelle. Vitu. Paris, 1889.
Mol 268.74 Molière, Jean Baptiste Poquelin. Le Tartuffe. Lavigne. Paris, 1889.
Mon 28.19 Montaigne, Michel de. De l'institution des enfants. Paris, 1889.
Htn Mon 30.6* Montaigne, Michel de. Essayes. McCarthy. London, 1889. 2v.
Mon 45.5A Montaigne, Michel de. Journal du voyage. Ancona. Castello, 1889.
37567.58 Morice, C. La littérature de tout à l'heure. Paris, 1889.
41596.18.40 Musset, Alfred de. Théâtre. Paris, 1889-1891. 4v.
42545.45.6 Najac, Émile de. Babie; a comedy in three acts. Boston, 1889.
41596.3 Nienkirchen, Friedrich. Alfred de Mussets Gedicht::Sur la Paresse. Inaug. Diss. Berlin, 1889.
40572.31 Nisard, Désiré. Oegrè somnia. Paris, 1889.
42578.29.50 Ohnet, Georges. Dernier amour. 68. éd. Paris, 1889.
42578.29.3 Ohnet, Georges. Dr. Rameau. N.Y., 1889.
42578.29.2 Ohnet, Georges. Dr. Rameau. Philadelphia, 1889.
42545.62 Pailleron, Edouard. Amours et haines. Paris, 1889.
42545.63.5 Pailleron, Edouard. Le monde ou l'on s'ennuie. 38. éd. Paris, 1889.
39544.33.3 Parton, James. Life of Voltaire. 6. ed. Boston, 1889. 2v.
37562.20 Pilz, Oskar. Beiträge zur Kenntnis der altfranzösischen Fableaux. Stettin, 1889.
FL 378.15 Poctevin, A. Le théâtre de la foire. Paris, 1889.
42534.35 Pontmartin, A.F de. Péchés de vieillesse. Paris, 1889.
40539.15.47 Potocki, Jan. Voyage en Turquia et en Egypte. 2. éd. Varsovie, 1889.
37567.110.9 Les premières armes du symbolisme. Paris, 1889.
42578.31.65 Prévost, Marcel. Mademoiselle Jaufre. Paris, 1889.
42576.65.2.80 Quesnay de Beaurepaire, Jules. Marie Fougère. 18. éd. Paris, 1889.
42515.41 Quinet, E. (Mme.). Edgar Quinet avant l'exil. Paris, 1889.
38585.19.2 Racine, Jean. Andromaque. London, 1889.
38585.26 Racine, Jean. Britannicus. Paris, 1889.
38585.29 Racine, Jean. Esther. Paris, 1889.
38583.6.12 Racine, Jean. Théâtre complet. Paris, 1889.
37548.15 Rambert, Eugène. Écrivains de la Suisse romande. Lausanne, 1889.

1889 - cont.

	42535.11	Rambert, Eugène. Études de littérature alpestre. Lausanne, 1889.
	38514.51A	Raynaud, G. Rondeaux et autres poésies du XVe siècle. Paris, 1889.
NEDL	42515.23	Reinach, Joseph. Études de littérature et d'histoire. Paris, 1889.
	42515.29.270	Renan, Ernest. Les apotres. Paris, 1889.
	40524.28.100	Restif de la Bretonne, Nicolas E. Mes inscripions journal intime de Restif de la Bretonne, (1780-1787). Paris, 1889.
	38587.28	Rigal, Eugène. Alexandre Hardy. Paris, 1889.
	Mol 875.9	Roger-Milés, L. L'Agnès moderne. Paris, 1889.
	FL 6031.89	Rousseau, J.J. Du contrat social. Paris, 1889.
	FL 6048.35.5	Rousseau, J.J. Profession of faith of a Savoyard vicar. N.Y., 1889.
	42578.31.1100	Ruyters, André. La correspondance du Mauvais-Riche. Bruxelles, 1889.
	42542.2.7	Saint-Victor, P. Le théâtre contemporaine, Émile Augier. Paris, 1889.
	40587.19	Sainte-Beuve, Charles. Chateaubriand. Paris, 1889. 2v.
	37574.42.10	Saintsbury, George. French lyrics. N.Y., 1889.
	37542.16A	Saintsbury, George. Short history of French literature. Oxford, 1889.
	41557.8.50.5	Sand, George. Les amours de l'Age d'or. Paris, 1889.
	38546.107	Saporta, Gaston. La famille de Madame de Sévigné. Paris, 1889.
	Mol 880.17	Scènes du Tartuffe di Gigli. Paris, 1889.
	38513.23	Schaumburg, K. La farce de Pathelin. Paris, 1889.
	FL 6138.89	Schneider, Karl. Rousseau und Pestalozzi. 4. Aufl. Berlin, 1889.
Htn	42546.34.9*	Silvestre, Armand. Le nu au champ de mars. Paris, 1889.
	39594.17.4	Sorel, Albert. Montesquieu. 2. éd. Paris, 1889.
	41586.30.12.6	Soumet, A. The gladiator...performed by Salvini. N.Y., 1889.
	37567.113	Sprouck, M. Les articles litteraires. Paris, 1889.
	38537.12	Stapfer, Paul. Rabelais. Paris, 1889.
	41561.15.22	Sue, Eugène. Wandering Jew. London, 1889. 3v.
	37567.33	Tellier, Jules. Nos poètes. Paris, 1889.
NEDL	37573.22	Tiercelin, Louis. Le Parnasse Breton contemporain. Paris, 1889-
	42578.52.78	Tinseau, Léon de. Alain de Kerisel. 4. éd. Paris, 1889.
	42578.52.5	Tinseau, Léon de. L'attelage de la marquise. N.Y., 1889.
	42578.56.10	Toutain, Paul. Testament d'un moderne. Paris, 1889.
	37555.531	Trüger, E. Geschichte der Alexandriners. Leipzig, 1889.
	38585.44.20	Tüchert, Aloys. Racine und Heliodor. Zweibrücken, 1889.
	38546.53	Vallery-Radot. Mme. de Sévigné. Paris, 1889.
Htn	42557.19.90*	Verlaine, Paul. Parallèlement. Paris, 1889.
	42582.13.8	Verne, Jules. From the earth to the moon. N.Y., 1889.
	42581.16.10	Verne, Jules. Le tour du monde en quatre-vingt jours. N.Y., 1889.
	41564.3.85	Vigny, Alfred de. Cinq-Mars. Boston, 1889.
	38514.21.4	Villon, François. Le Jargon et Jobelin, avec un dictionnaire analytique. Paris, 1889.
Htn	42581.35*	Vogué, E.M. Le portrait du Louvre. Paris, 1889.
	39545.67.5	Voltaire, François Marie Arouet de. Zaire; tragédie. London, 1889.
	39545.67	Voltaire, François Marie Arouet de. Zaire. Paris, 1889.
	FL 6138.78.5	Vuy, J. Origine des idées politiques de Rousseau. Genève, 1889.
	42587.70.16	Weill, Alexandre. Mes poésies d'amour de jeunesse. Paris, 1889.
	42587.70.19	Weill, Alexandre. La nouvelle Phèdre. Paris, 1889.
	FL 382.45	Weiss, Jean Jacques. Le théâtre et les moeurs. 3. ed. Paris, 1889.
	37596.93.5	Werth, Hermann. Altfranzösische Jagdlehrbücher. Halle, 1889.
	Mol 870.44	Zidler, G. Le baiser à Molière. Paris, 1889.
	42584.7.2	Zola, Emile. Nouveaux contes à Ninon. Paris, 1889.

189-

	40596.21	Balzac, Honoré de. Les chouans. Paris, 189-?
	40532.4.25	Beaumarchais, Pierre A.C. de. Le barbier de Séville. Paris, 189-.
	38566.17.20	Boileau Despréaux, Nicolas. Oeuvres poétiques. Paris, 189-?
	42559.12	Champsaur, F. La chanson du Moulin à Vent. Paris, 189-.
	42554.23.15	Coppée, François. Severo Torelli. N.Y., 189-?
	38575.34.11	Corneille, Pierre. Pompée. 5e éd. Paris, 189-.
	42566.18.5	Daudet, Alphonse. Les amoureuses. Paris, 189-?
	42566.24.15	Daudet, Alphonse. Fromont, Jr., and Risler, Sr. Chicago, 189-?
	42566.27.4	Daudet, Alphonse. Lettres de mon moulin. Paris, 189-?
	42566.32.15	Daudet, Alphonse. Robert Helmont, journal d'un solitaire. Paris, 189-?
	42566.33.5	Daudet, Alphonse. Les rois en exil. Paris, 189-?
	42566.35.27	Daudet, Alphonse. Tartarin on the Alps. Philadelphia, 189-?
	42543.15.8.5	Dumas, Alexandre. Camille. N.Y., 189-.
	42543.15.8.10	Dumas, Alexandre. Camille. Philadelphia, 189-.
	41538.61.15	Dumas, Alexandre. Memoirs of a physician. Chicago, 189-.
	41538.53.123	Dumas, Alexandre. Ten years later. N.Y., 189-?
	41538.53.24.5	Dumas, Alexandre. The three musketeers. N.Y., 189-?
Htn	42563.44.5.10*	Durand, Alice M.C.F. Clairefontaine. 12. éd. Paris, 189-.
	41542.21.10	Gautier, Théophile. Stronger than death, or Spirite. Chicago, 189-.
	42576.40.333	Halévy, Ludovic. The abbé Constantin. Chicago, 189-.
	42576.40.334	Halévy, Ludovic. The abbé Constantin. N.Y., 189-.
	42554.55.5	Heredia, J.M. de. Les trophées. Paris, 189-.
	38537.46F	Heulhard, Arthur. Rabelais. 2. éd. Paris, 189-?
	41572.7.17	Hugo, Victor. Hans of Iceland. Boston, 189-?
	41571.16.7	Hugo, Victor. Les misérables. Boston, 189-? 5v.
	41571.31	Hugo, Victor. The man who laughs. Boston, 189-? 2v.
	41573.18.4	Hugo, Victor. Ninety-three. Boston, 189-? 2v.
	41573.23.3	Hugo, Victor. Notre Dame de Paris. Boston, 189-?
	41573.17.6	Hugo, Victor. The toilers of the sea. Boston, 189-?
	41573.51	Hugo, Victor. The works. Boston, 189-.
	42576.70.300	Lepsinasse, L. de. Toute à l'amour. Paris, 189-?
	38526.32.13	Marguerite d'Angoulême. The Heptaméron. N.Y., 189-?
	38526.32.14	Marguerite d'Angoulême. The Heptaméron. Philadelphia, 189-?
	38526.32.21	Marguerite d'Angoulême. The Heptaméron. Philadelphia, 189-. 2v.
	42576.76.16.2	Margueritte, Paul. Jours d'épreuve. 7. éd. Paris, 189-?
	42545.9.26	Martel de Janville, S.G. Autour du divorce. Paris, 189-.
	42545.9.30	Martel de Janville, S.G. Petit Bob. Paris, 189-.

189- - cont.

NEDL	42577.4.24.7	Maupassant, Guy de. Le rosier de Madame Husson. Paris, 189-?
	42577.4.4.2	Maupassant, Guy de. Sur l'eau. Paris, 189-?
	41555.20.70	Mérimée, Prosper. Carmen. Philadelphia, 189-?
	41555.29.25	Mérimée, Prosper. The house of a traitor. London, 189-.
	38567.14	Morillot, Paul. Boileau. Paris, 189-.
	37556.24A	Morillot, Paul. Le roman en France depuis 1610 jusqu'à nos jours. Paris, 189-?
	41596.13.1A	Musset, Alfred de. Poésies. Paris, 189-?
	42578.31.27.5	Prévost, Marcel. L'automne d'une femme. 53. éd. Paris, 189-.
	38536.20.3	Rabelais, F. Five books of the lives...of Gargantua. Philadelphia, 189-.
	38536.18.55	Rabelais, F. Works. London, 189-?
	42556.22.162	Richepin, Jean. Les caresses. Paris, 189-?
	42578.22.8.7	Rosny, J.H. Hellhorn de l'armée du salut. Paris, 189-?
	FL 6026.8.5	Rousseau, J.J. The confessions. Philadelphia, 189-. 2v.
	41588.14.10	Scribe, Eugène. Das Glas Wasser, oder Ursachen und Wirkungen. Leipzig, 189-.
	42556.19.9A	Sully-Prudhomme, R.F.A. Poésies 1865-1866. Paris, 189-?
	37576.537	Terrible tales. Paris, 189-?
	42559.97	Xanrof, Léon. Chansons d'étudiants. Paris, 189-.
	42584.23.9.30	Zola, Emile. Germinal. Philadelphia, 189-? 2v.
	42584.23.6.25	Zola, Emile. How jolly life is! Paris, 189-?
	42584.3.12	Zola, Emile. L'assommoir. v.2. Philadelphia, 189-?
	42584.12.25	Zola, Emile. Nana. Philadelphia, 189-? 2v.
	42584.20.5	Zola, Emile. Pot-Bouille. Philadelphia, 189-? 2v.
	42584.23.4.25	Zola, Emile. The rush for the spoil. Paris, 189-?

1890

	42562.7.5	About, Edmond. La Grèce contemporaine. Paris, 1890.
	42562.38.3	Adam, Paul. L'essence de soleil. Paris, 1890.
	42542.1.13.10	Alexis, Paul. Monsieur Betey. Paris, 1890.
	42542.1.17	Ancey, Georges. Grand'mère. Paris, 1890.
	42542.18.5	Augier, Émile. Les Fourchambault. 23. éd. Paris, 1890.
	40596.13.28	Balzac, Honoré de. Fame and sorrow. Boston, 1890.
	40596.13.58	Balzac, Honoré de. Sons of the soil. Boston, 1890.
	42554.6.2	Banville, Théodore de. L'âme de Paris. Paris, 1890.
	42554.8.8.5	Banville, Théodore de. Gringoire; comédie en un acte en prose. Paris, 1890.
	42554.8.15	Banville, Théodore de. Le sang de la coupe. Paris, 1890.
	42554.3.2	Banville, Théodore de. Sonnailles et clochettes. Photoreproduction. Paris, 1890.
Htn	41522.2.27*	Barbey d'Aurevilly, Jules. Amaidée: poeme en prose. Paris, 1890.
	42515.35.26.2	Barrès, Maurice. Huit jours chez M. Renan. 2. éd. Paris, 1890.
	40597.5.2	Barriere, Marcel. L'oeuvre de Honoré de Balzac. Paris, 1890.
	38563.10	Bayle, Pierre. Choix de la correspondance. Copenhague, 1890.
	42563.5.100	Beaubourg, Maurice. Contes pour les assassins. Paris, 1890.
	Mol 602.2	Becker, Joseph. Die Entwickelung der Dienerrolle bei Molière. Strassburg, 1890.
	42542.28	Becque, Henri. Théatre complet. Paris, 1890.
	37591.37	Bédier, J. Le lai de l'ombre. Freiburg, 1890.
	42563.22.11	Belot, Adolphe. Folies de jeunesse. Paris, 1890.
	Mol 602.4	Bennewitz, A. Congreve und Molière. Leipzig, 1890.
NEDL	38587.30	Beraneck, Jules. Senèque et Hardy. Leipzig, 1890.
	40582.40	Beyle, Henri. Vie de Henri Brulard, autobiographie. Paris, 1890.
	38557.25.75	Bossuet, J.B. Oeuvres oratoires. Lille, 1890. 6v.
	Mol 870.45	Bouchinet, A. Le docteur Mascarille. Paris, 1890.
	42542.30.9	Bouchor, Maurice. Noël ou Le mystère de la nativité. Paris, 1890.
	42563.37.2.5	Bourget, Paul. Mensonges. Paris, 1890.
	38576.4.7	Boursault, Edme. Les Bavardes. Paris, 1890.
	42524.16	Brunetière, F. Nouvelles questions de critique. Paris, 1890.
	37544.8	Brunetière, Ferdinand. L'évolution des genres dans l'histoire de la littérature. Paris, 1890.
	37596.88.3	Burckhardt, A. Über den Lothringer Reimpsalter. Inaug. Diss. Halle, 1890.
	42542.49.5	Céard, Henry. Tout pour l'honneur. Paris, 1890.
	42586.29.110	Chabrier, Jean. La gamelle. Paris, 1890.
NEDL	FL 6128.90	Chatelain, D. La folie de Jean-Jacques Rousseau. Neuchâtel, 1890.
	42565.27	Cherbuliez, Victor. Une gageure. Paris, 1890.
	42565.27.5	Cherbuliez, Victor. Une gageure. 6. éd. Paris, 1890.
	42565.17.3	Cherbuliez, Victor. L'idée de Jean Têterol. 7. éd. Paris, 1890.
	42565.55.40	Cladel, Léon. Urbains et ruraux. Paris, 1890.
	40513.27	Claretie, Leo. LeSage. Paris, 1890.
	42554.23.7	Coppée, François. Disillusion. N.Y., 1890.
	42554.20.7	Coppée, François. Ten tales. N.Y., 1890.
	42554.20.5	Coppée, François. Ten tales. N.Y., 1890.
	42554.23.26	Coppée, François. Toute une jeunesse. 12e éd. Paris, 1890.
	42554.23.29	Coppée, François. The wanderer. N.Y., 1890.
	40583.6	Cordier, H. Stendhal et ses amis. Evreux, 1890.
	38575.33.2	Corneille, Pierre. Horace. N.Y., 1890.
	38575.34.4	Corneille, Pierre. Nicomède. Paris, 1890.
	Mol 253.7	Dalimier, H. A propos des Précieuses ridicules. Saint-Lo, 1890.
	42542.64.27.80	Darien, Georges. Les vrais sous-offs; réponse à M. Descaves. Paris, 1890.
	42542.60.5	Darmont, A. Argument of the play of Pauline Blanchard. N.Y., 1890.
	42566.23.4A	Daudet, Alphonse. Artists'.wives. London, 1890.
	42566.52.5	Daudet, Alphonse. L'immortel; moeurs parisiennes. Paris, 1890.
	42566.26.2.5	Daudet, Alphonse. Jack. London, 1890.
	42566.24.26	Daudet, Alphonse. Kings in exile. London, 1890.
NEDL	42566.48	Daudet, Alphonse. La lutte pour la vie. Paris, 1890.
NEDL	42566.48.2	Daudet, Alphonse. La lutte pour la vie. Paris, 1890.
	42566.28.1A	Daudet, Alphonse. Port-Tarascon. Paris, 1890.
	42566.33.6A	Daudet, Alphonse. Les rois en exil. Paris, 1890.
	42566.20.14	Daudet, Alphonse. Le siège de Berlin. N.Y., 1890.
	42542.62.25	Delacour, A. Le retour du Japon. N.Y., 1890.
	42586.35.5	Delpit, Albert. Toutes les deux. Paris, 1890.
	42542.64.5	Déroulède, Paul. Histoire d'amour. Paris, 1890.
	42542.64.27	Descaves, Lucien. Les chapons. Paris, 1890.
Htn	38526.71*	De Vaynes, J.H.L. A Huguenot garland. Hertford, 1890.

Chronological Listing

1890 - cont.

37543.33 Doumic, René. Éléments d'histoire littéraire. Paris, 1890.
42542.66.7 Dreyfus, A. La gifle. N.Y., 1890.
42568.11.5 Droz, Gustave. Monsieur, madame et bébé. 149. éd. Paris, 1890.
37565.14 Du Bled, Victor. Le prince de ligne et ses contemporains. Paris, 1890.
42586.38.5 DuCamp, M. Mémoires d'un suicidé. Paris, 1890.
41542.4 Du Camp, Maxime. Théophile Gautier. Paris, 1890.
FL 6128.90.3 Dufour, L. Les ascendants de Jean-Jacques Rousseau. Genève, 1890.
41538.2.6 Dumas, Alexandre. Ange Pitou. v.1-2. Boston, 1890.
41538.69.20 Dumas, Alexandre. The Chevalier de Maison-Rouge. Boston, 1890.
42543.13.50 Dumas, Alexandre. The Clemenceau case. N.Y., 1890.
41538.16.7 Dumas, Alexandre. Count of Monte Cristo. Boston, 1890. 4v.
41538.23 Dumas, Alexandre. Episodes from Aventures de Lyderic. London, 1890.
41538.4 Dumas, Alexandre. Iza's love letters. N.Y., 1890.
41538.16.8.43 Dumas, Alexandre. La comtesse de Charny. Boston, 1890. 4v.
42543.12.15 Dumas, Alexandre. Nouveaux entr'actes. 5. éd. Paris, 1890.
41538.63.32 Dumas, Alexandre. The queen's necklace. Boston, 1890. 2v.
41538.53.24 Dumas, Alexandre. The three musketeers. Boston, 1890. 2v.
41538.53A Dumas, Alexandre. Les trois mousquetaires. Boston, 1890.
41538.53.100 Dumas, Alexandre. Twenty years after. Boston, 1890.
41538.55.20 Dumas, Alexandre. Vicomte de Bragelonne; or Ten years later. Boston, 1890.
41538.55.22 Dumas, Alexandre. Le vicomte de Bragelonne. v.1-6. Paris, 1890. 3v.
41574.33 Dupuy, Ernest. Victor Hugo. Paris, 1890.
41574.32 Dupuy, Ernest. Victor Hugo. Paris, 1890.
42563.45.3A Durand, Alice M.C.F. Dosia. N.Y., 1890.
42563.55.5 Durand, Alice M.C.F. Le passé. Paris, 1890.
42568.22.5 Durny, Georges. Fin de rêve. Paris, 1890.
42568.26 Enault, Louis. Le chien du capitaine. N.Y., 1890.
38537.17 Ernst, Karl. Syntaktische Studien zu Rabelais. Greifswald, 1890.
42574.14.2 Fabre, Ferdinand. L'abbé Tigrane. Paris, 1890.
42574.17 Fabre, Ferdinand. Un illuminé. Paris, 1890.
42543.38.32 Fabre, Joseph. Jeanne d'Arc. Paris, 1890.
37565.36.20 Faguet, Émile. Dix-huitième siècle. Paris, 1890.
37565.36.9 Faguet, Émile. Dix-huitième siècle. 4e éd. Paris, 1890.
38553.27.15 Fénelon, F. de S. de la Mothe. Aventures de Télémaque. Paris, 1890.
FL 6138.90 Fester, R. Rousseau und der deutsche Geschichtsphilosophie. Stuttgart, 1890.
42575.30.10 Feuillet, Octave. An artist's honor. Chicago, 1890.
42575.30.5 Feuillet, Octave. Honneur d'artiste. Paris, 1890.
42575.51.25 Feuillet, Octave. Vie de Polichinelle et ses nombreuses aventures. Paris, 1890.
43607.2.30 Fèvre, Henry. En detresse. Paris, 1890.
42575.53.28 Flammarion, Camille. Urania. Boston, 1890.
42575.53.28.5 Flammarion, Camille. Uranie. N.Y., 1890.
37543.22.3 Fleury, Jean. Histoire élémentaire de la littérature française. 8. éd. Paris, 1890.
42586.54.3 Fouquier, Henry. Le roman d'une conspiration. Paris, 1890.
42576.63.7.35 France, Anatole. The crime of Sylvestre Bonnard. N.Y., 1890.
42576.62.28.10 France, Anatole. Tales from a mother of pearl casket. N.Y., 1890.
42571.34 Gaboriau, Emile. La vie infernale. 9. éd. Paris, 1890. 2v.
41542.5.2 Gautier, Théophile. Oeuvres. Paris, 1890. 3v.
37596.38A Gautier d'Arras. Oeuvres. Paris, 1890. 2v.
43617.7.30 Génin, Auguste. Poèmes aztèques...1884-1889. Paris, 1890.
42576.6.7 Ginisty, Paul. Deux tourtereaux. Paris, 1890.
NEDL 37548.9 Godet, Philippe. Histoire littéraire de la Suisse Française. Paris, 1890.
NEDL FL 398.13.10 Goncourt, E. de. Mademoiselle Clairon. Paris, 1890.
42575.62.12 Goncourt, Edmond de. Soeur Philomène. Paris, 1890.
FL 6118.90 Grand-Carteret, J. Jean-Jacques Rousseau jugé par les Français d'aujourd'hui. Paris, 1890.
42535.22.95 Gréard, Octave. Edmond Scherer. Paris, 1890.
42543.56.30 Grenet-Dancourt, Ernest. La scène à faire. Paris, 1890.
37596.44 Guillaume le Clerc. Le bestiaire. Leipzig, 1890.
37567.41 Hennequin, E. Quelques ecrivains français. Photoreproduction. Paris, 1890.
42543.62.92 Hennique, Léon. Amour. Paris, 1890.
42576.67.5.12 Hervieu, Paul. Flirt. N.Y., 1890.
42576.67.5.10 Hervieu, Paul. Flirt. Paris, 1890.
41572.45 Hugo, Victor. Les contemplations. Paris, 1890? 2v.
Htn 41574.11* Hugo, Victor. Oeuvres inédites. En voyage. Alps et Pyrénées. Paris, 1890.
41573.34 Hugo, Victor. Oeuvres poétiques. Odes. Paris, 1890.
41573.22.4 Hugo, Victor. Quatre-vingt-treize. N.Y., 1890.
41572.21 Hugo, Victor. Quatre-vingt-treize. Paris, 1890? 4v.
41573.16.5 Hugo, Victor. Les travailleurs de la mer. N.Y., 1890.
37596.91 Irmer, Eugen. Die altfranzösische Bearbeitung der Formula honestae vitae des Martin von Braga. Halle, 1890.
FL 397.114.100 Isnardon, Jacques. Le théâtre de la monnaie depuis sa fondation jusqu'à nos jours. Bruxelles, 1890.
37572.25 Jacquinet, P. Lettres choisies du dix-septième siècle. Paris, 1890.
37595.36.2 Jesus Christ Altprovenzalische Marienklage. v.3-4. Halle, 1890.
41541.21 Kerardven, L. Guionrac'h. Chronique bretonne. Nantes, 1890.
38537.16 Klett, Adolf. Lexikographische Beiträge zur Rabelais Gargantua. Bühl, 1890.
37596.27.3 Kötting, Georg. Studien über altfranzösische Bearbeitungen der Alexinslegende. Trier, 1890.
37597.33.9 Krause, A. Bemerkungen zu den Gedichten des Bendouin und des Jean de Condé. Berlin, 1890.
38526.13.2 Kreutzberg, P. Die Grammatik Malherbe's nach dem "Commentaire sur Desportes". Neisse, 1890.
37572.26 Labbé, M.J. Choix de lettres du XVIIIe siècle. Paris, 1890.
42544.27.12 Labiche, Eugène. La grammaire: comédie. N.Y., 1890.
42514.16.7A Laboulaye, Édouard. Abdallah. Chicago, 1890.

1890 - cont.

38543.32 Lacroix, L. Quid de instituendo principe senserit Vayerius. Paris, 1890.
38544.27.450 La Fayette, Marie M. Mémoire de Mme. de La Fayette. Paris, 1890.
39527.29.2 La Fontaine, Jean de. Fables. London, 1890.
37562.12.28 Langlois, Ernest. De artibus rhetoricae rhythmicae. Parisiis, 1890.
FL 6039.6 Larmartine, A. de. Jean-Jacques Rousseau, son faux. Paris, 1890.
38514.53.5 La Sale, Antoine de. L'hystoyre...du Petit Jehan de Saintré. Paris, 1890.
37556.25 Le Breton, André. Le roman au dix septième siècle. Photoreproduction. Paris, 1890.
42576.68.150 Lecomte du Nouÿ, H.O. (Mme.). Amitié amoureuse. Paris, 1890.
37566.44.15 Le Goffic, Charles. Les romanciers d'aujourd'hui. Paris, 1890.
37555.318 Le Goffie, C. Nouveau traité de versification française. Paris, 1890.
Mol 880.37 Le Mercier de Neuville. Le sac de Scapin. 3. éd. Paris, 1890.
Mol 825.11 Léon-Petit. Les médecins de Molière. Paris, 1890.
42576.45.12 Le Roux, H. Les fleurs à Paris. Paris, 1890.
42513.79 Leroy-Beaulieu, A. La revolution et le liberalisme. Paris, 1890.
40512.34 LeSage, Alain René. Historia de Gil Blas de Santillana. N.Y., 1890.
37544.7 Lintilhac, Eugène. Précis historique et critique de la littérature française. Paris, 1890. 2v.
37562.18.5 Loubier, Jean. Das Ideal der männlichen Schönheit bei den altfranzösischen XIII Jahrhunderts. Halle, 1890.
42526.7.25 Lucas, Hippolyte. Portraits et souvenirs littéraires. Paris, 1890.
42545.3.4.2 Maeterlinck, Maurice. Serres chaudes. Bruxelles, 1890.
38576.28.2 Mairet, Jean de. Silva. Bamberg, 1890.
42576.76.11 Margueritte, Paul. Amants. Paris, 1890.
40535.25.30 Marivaux, Pierre Carlet de Chamblain de. Oeuvres choisies. Paris, 1890.
42577.4.2.15 Maupassant, Guy de. Bel-ami. N.Y., 1890.
42577.4.20 Maupassant, Guy de. L'inutile beauté. Paris, 1890.
42577.4.11 Maupassant, Guy de. Notre coeur. Paris, 1890.
42577.33 Maurel, André. Candeur. Paris, 1890.
42555.58.25 Mendès, Catulle. La vie et la mort d'un clown. L'argent de Papiol. Paris, 1890.
41555.22.2 Mérimée, Prosper. A chronicle of the reign of Charles IX. London, 1890.
41555.23.2 Mérimée, Prosper. Colomba. London, 1890.
41555.29 Mérimée, Prosper. Episodes from Mateo Falcone. London, 1890.
37572.36.2 Merrill, S. Pastels in prose. N.Y., 1890.
37572.36.3 Merrill, S. Pastels in prose. N.Y., 1890.
37572.36.4 Merrill, S. Pastels in prose. N.Y., 1890.
37572.36A Merrill, S. Pastels in prose. N.Y., 1890.
Mol 165.53 Molière, Jean Baptiste Poquelin. L'avare...Gosset. London, 1890.
Mol 171.40 Molière, Jean Baptiste Poquelin. Le bourgeois gentilhomme...Humbert. Leipzig, 1890.
Mol 171.40.2 Molière, Jean Baptiste Poquelin. Le bourgeois gentilhomme...Humbert. Anmerkungen. Leipzig, 1890.
Mol 178.15 Molière, Jean Baptiste Poquelin. La critique de l'École des femmes...Vitu. Paris, 1890.
Mol 195.34 Molière, Jean Baptiste Poquelin. L'école des femmes...Vitu. Paris, 1890.
Mol 208.25 Molière, Jean Baptiste Poquelin. Les facheux...Vitu. Paris, 1890.
Mol 221.12 Molière, Jean Baptiste Poquelin. L'impromptu de Versailles...Vitu. Paris, 1890.
37557.17 Monselet, Charles. Curiosités littéraires. Paris, 1890.
FL 383.77 Montégat, Émile. Dramaturges et romansiers. Paris, 1890.
Mol 800.8 Monval, G. Premier registre de La Thorillière. Paris, 1890.
FL 395.20 Monval, Georges. Premier registre de La Thorillière (1663-1664). Paris, 1890.
41595.33 Moreau, Hégésippe. Oeuvres complètes. Paris, 1890. 2v.
FL 6133.6 Mugnier, F. Mme. de Warens et Jean-Jacques Rousseau. Paris, 1890.
42545.44.30 Mullem, Louis. Une nouvelle école. Paris, 1890.
NEDL 41596.18.3A Musset, Alfred de. Comedies. London, 1890.
41596.13 Musset, Alfred de. Premières poésies. 1829-1835. Paris, 1890.
42578.30.13 Ohnet, Georges. Serge Panine. Paris, 1890.
41596.4.3 Oliphant, Cyril F. Alfred de Musset. Edinburgh, 1890.
42545.63.6 Pailleron, Edouard. Le monde ou l'on s'ennuie. 46. éd. Paris, 1890.
39578.8 Paléologue, Maurice. Vauvenargues. Paris, 1890.
42542.2 Parigot, H. Émile Augier. Paris, 1890.
37562.22.2 Paris, Gaston. La littérature française au moyen âge. 2. éd. Paris, 1890.
38537.19.5 Platen, Eugen. Syntaktische Untersuchungen zu Rabelais. Leipzig, 1890.
42541.30 Ponsard, François. L'honneur et l'argent. N.Y., 1890.
42534.35.5 Pontmartin, A.F. de. Episodes littéraires. Paris, 1890.
42545.88.55 Porto-Riche, G. L'infidèle. Paris, 1890.
FL 366.77 Pougin, Arthur. Le théâtre à l'exposition universelle de 1889. Paris, 1890.
Mol 616.4 Prevost, G. Le peuple dans Molière. n.p., 1890.
42556.4 Quillard, Pierre. La gloire du verbe 1885-90. Paris, 1890.
38585.34.15 Racine, Jean. Iphigénie. Paris, 1890.
42535.11.2 Rambert, Eugène. Études littéraires. Lausanne, 1890. 2v.
42535.11.4 Rambert, Eugène. Mélanges. Lausanne, 1890.
42556.21 Raynaud, Ernest. Les cornes du Faune. Paris, 1890.
42515.30.35 Renan, Ernest. L'avenir de la science. Pensées de 1848. 4. éd. Paris, 1890.
42515.30.313 Renan, Ernest. L'ecclésiaste. 3. éd. Paris, 1890.
42515.30.550 Renan, Ernest. Melanges d'hisoire et de voyages. Paris, 1890.
42515.25.10 Renan, Ernest. Pages choisies. Paris, 1890.
42556.22.25 Richepin, Jean. Le cadet. Paris, 1890.
Htn 42556.22.150* Richepin, Jean. Les débuts de César Borgia. Paris, 1890.
42556.22.17 Richepin, Jean. La mer. Paris, 1890.
42556.22.30 Richepin, Jean. Les morts bizarres. Paris, 1890.
38585.11 Robert, Pierre. La poètique de France. Paris, 1890.

1890 - cont.

37565.31.2 Rocafort, J. Les doctrines littéraires de l'encyclopedie. Paris, 1890.
42578.19.5 Rod, Edouard. Scènes de la vie cosmopolite. Paris, 1890.
42578.19.5.3 Rod, Edouard. Scènes de la vie cosmopolite. 2. éd. Paris, 1890.
42578.19.6 Rod, Edouard. Trois coeurs. Paris, 1890.
42578.19.6.3 Rod, Edouard. Les trois coeurs. 3. éd. Paris, 1890.
NEDL 38525.19 Ronsard, Pierre de. Oeuvres choisies. Paris, 1890.
42578.21 Rosny, J.H. Le termite. Paris, 1890.
43758.27.100 Ruffin, Alfred. Poésies variees et nouvaux chats. Paris, 1890.
41568.11.18 Saintine, Joseph Xavier Boniface. Picciola. Chicago, 1890.
41557.9.69 Sand, George. The bagpipers. Boston, 1890.
41557.9.48.4 Sand, George. The haunted pool. N.Y., 1890.
41557.9.46.10 Sand, George. La mare au diable. N.Y., 1890.
41557.8.105 Sand, George. Le marquis de Villemer. Paris, 1890.
42546.30 Sardou, Victorien. Argument of the play of La Tosca. Paris, 1890.
37596.90 Schauer, Karl. Textkritische Beiträge zu den coutumes du Beauvaisis des Philippe de Beaumanoir. Halle, 1890.
41588.15.8.10 Scribe, Eugène. Bataille de dames, ou Un duel en amour. 2. éd. London, 1890.
Mol 840.1 Sebillot, P. Molière et les traditions populaires. Yannes, 1890.
42546.32.9 Serment, Julien. Ki-Ki-ri-ki; japone-asmeria en un acto. Madrid, 1890.
42546.34.6 Silvestre, Armand. Les faceties de Cadet-Bitard. Paris, 1890.
Mol 875.10 Souza, R. de. Toinette à Molière. Paris, 1890.
42578.52.10 Tinseau, Léon de. L'attelage de la marquise, le secret de l'abbé Césaire. Paris, 1890.
42578.52.79.8 Tinseau, Léon de. Strass et diamants. 8. éd. Paris, 1890.
37567.39 Tissot, Ernest. Les evolutions de la critique française. Paris, 1890.
42557.10 Valabrèque, Antony. La chanson de l'hiver. Paris, 1890.
Htn 42576.50.5* Viaud, Julien. Barahu or The marriage of Loti. N.Y. 1890.
42576.54 Viaud, Julien. Le roman d'un enfant. 33. éd. Paris, 1890.
42557.29 Vicaire, Gabriel. L'heure enchantée. Paris, 1890.
Mol 870.46 Villetard, A. Monsieur Dorine. Paris, 1890.
42547.16 Villiers de l'Isle Adam, Auguste. Axel. Paris, 1890.
Htn 42547.20.5* Villiers de l'Isle Adam, Auguste. Chez les passants. Paris, 1890.
39545.69 Voltaire, François Marie Arouet de. Zaïre-Mérope. Chefs-d'oeuvre dramatiques. Paris, 1890.
40597.9.1 Wedmore, F. Life of H. de Balzac. London, 1890.
40597.9A Wedmore, F. Life of H. de Balzac. London, 1890.
42587.70.14 Weill, Alexandre. Introduction à mes mémoires. Paris, 1890.
42587.70.9 Weill, Alexandre. Julie Verrier, une arrière-petite soeur de Jeanne d'Arc. Paris, 1890.
42587.70.12 Weill, Alexandre. Mes contemporains. Paris, 1890.
42587.73 Witt, Henriette Guizot de. Les bourgeois de Calais. Paris, 1890.
42547.37 Wolff, Pierre. Jacques Bouchard. Paris, 1890.
42559.97.5 Xanrof, Léon. Chansons sans-gène. Paris, 1890.
42584.23.3 Zola, Emile. La bête humaine. Paris, 1890.
NEDL 42584.23.3.2 Zola, Emile. La bête humaine. Paris, 1890.
42584.9.5 Zola, Emile. La faute de l'abbé Mouret. Paris, 1890.
42584.19 Zola, Emile. Le rêve. Paris, 1890.
X Cg 42584.19.15 Zola, Emile. Le voeu d'une morte. Paris, 1890.

1891

42562.5.2 About, Edmond. Le buste. N.Y., 1891.
42562.38.2 Adam, Paul. En décor. Paris, 1891.
37565.36 Albert, Maurice. La littérature française sous la révolution. Paris, 1891.
38526.25.150 Allais, Gustave. De Franciades epica fabula in posteriore XVImi saeculi parte. Paris, 1891.
42553.33.1 Amiel, Henri F. Gems from Amiel's journal. N.Y., 1891.
40596.21.8 Balzac, Honoré de. The chouans. Chicago, 1891.
40597.19.3 Balzac, Honoré de. Eugénie Grandet. Paris, 1891.
40596.13.38 Balzac, Honoré de. An historical mystery. Boston, 1891.
40597.24.50A Balzac, Honoré de. The lily of the valley. Boston, 1891.
40597.28.4 Balzac, Honoré de. Le lys dans la vallée. Paris, 1891.
40597.28.5 Balzac, Honoré de. Le lys dans la vallée. Paris, 1891.
40597.32.4.5 Balzac, Honoré de. La peau de chagrin. Paris, 1891.
40596.13.66A Balzac, Honoré de. Ursula. Boston, 1891.
40597.34.5.20 Balzac, Honoré de. Ursule Mirouet. Paris, 1891.
42554.6.3 Banville, Théodore de. Marcelle Rabe. Paris, 1891.
37566.12 Barbey d'Aurevilly, J.A. Les oeuvres et les hommes. Paris, 1891-1898. 6v.
41522.2.12 Barbey d'Aurevilly, Jules. Dernières polémiques. 2. éd. Paris, 1891.
42548.3 Barbier, J.P. Jeanne d'Arc. Paris, 1891.
39596.21 Barine, Arvède. Bernardin de St. Pierre. Paris, 1891.
42563.20 Barrès, Maurice. Le jardin de Bérénice. Paris, 1891.
FL 6118.91 Beaudouin, H. Jean-Jacques Rousseau, la vie et les oeuvres. Paris, 1891. 2v.
37572.28.3 Bernardin, N.M. Morceaux choisis des classiques français. Paris, 1891.
Mol 860.53 Bernede, A. La vocation de Poquelin. Paris, 1891.
38526.9 Bertaut, Jean. Les oeuvres poétiques. Paris, 1891.
FL 6039.4 Bertrand, A. Le texte primitif du Contrat social. Paris, 1891.
37562.12.11 Binet, H. Le style de la lyrique courtoise en France. Paris, 1891.
41574.21.2 Biré, Edmond. Victor Hugo après 1830. Paris, 1891. 2v.
42542.29.102 Bisson, Alexandre. Le député de Bombignac. 2. éd. Paris, 1891.
38525.21 Bizos, G. Ronsard. Paris, 1891.
38557.48.70 Bossuet, J.B. De la connaissance de Dieu et de soi-même. Paris, 1891.
FL 6113.4 Boston. Public Library. Titles of books added 1891. (Rousseau). Boston, 1891.
42542.31.5 Bouilhet, Louis. Oeuvres. Paris, 1891.
42563.37.10 Bourget, Paul. Nouveaux pastels. Paris, 1891.
42563.37.9.5 Bourget, Paul. Pastels of men. Boston, 1891.
42563.37.11 Bourget, Paul. Physiologie de l'amour moderne. Paris, 1891.
38576.7 Boursault, Edme. Lettres par E. Colombey. Paris, 1891.
37574.25.4 Bowen, Benjamin Lester. Introduction to modern French lyrics. Boston, 1891.
Mol 270.21 Brunetière, F. Tartuffe. Paris, 1891. 4 pam.

1891 - cont.

38528.28.9 Brunot, F. De Philiberti Bugnonii vita et eroticis versibus. Lugduni, 1891.
38523.15A Brunot, Ferdinand. Doctrine de Malherbe. Paris, 1891.
FL 6138.91 Buffenoir, H. Jean-Jacques Rousseau et les femmes. Paris, 1891.
38514.23.155 Byvanck, W.G.C. Un poéte inconnu de la Société de François Villon. Paris, 1891.
42554.17.40 Carrère, Jean. Ce qui renait toujours. Vanves, 1891.
41578.55 Chamborant de Périssat, Albert. Lamartine inconnu. Paris, 1891.
40586.20 Chateaubriand, F.A.R. Les martyrs. Paris, 1891.
42554.18.32 Chatillon, Auguste de. La grand' pinte. Paris, 1891.
37595.36.3.5 Chrestien de Troyes. Yvain. Halle, 1891.
37595.36.3 Chrestien de Troyes. Yvain. v.5-6. Halle, 1891.
42565.55.45 Cladel, Léon. Ompdrailles le tombeau-des-lutteurs. Paris, 1891.
37596.7 Clédat, Léon. Rutebeuf. Paris, 1891.
37596.124 Conon de Béthune. Chansons. Helsingfors, 1891.
42554.22.30 Coppée, François. Poésies, 1886-1890. Paris, 1891.
42554.20 Coppée, François. Ten tales. N.Y., 1891.
42554.26.1 Coppée, François. Théâtre 1879-81. Paris, 1891?
38575.29.3 Corneille, Pierre. Le Cid. London, 1891.
38575.33.12 Corneille, Pierre. Le menteur. London, 1891.
38575.34.7.5 Corneille, Pierre. Polyeucte. Boston, 1891.
37555.314 Crouslé, L. Éléments de versification française. Paris, 1891.
Htn 42566.38* Daudet, Alphonse. L'Obstacle. Paris, 1891.
42566.28.2 Daudet, Alphonse. Port-Tarascon. London, 1891.
42566.28.4 Daudet, Alphonse. Port-Tarascon. N.Y., 1891.
42566.19.8.78 Daudet, Alphonse. Tartarin de Tarascon. Paris, 1891.
NEDL 37564.41 Delaporte, P.V. Du merveilleux dans la littérature française sous le règne de Louis XIV. Paris, 1891.
39527.6 Delboulle, A. Les fables de La Fontaine. Paris, 1891.
38581.22 Delfour, S.C. La Bible dans Racine. Paris, 1891.
FL 398.37 D'Héricault, C. Une reine de théâtre souvenirs de jeunesse. Paris, 1891.
X Cg 39564.14 Diderot, Denis. Rameau's nephew, and d'Alembert's dream. Paris, 1891.
42542.65.42 Donnay, Maurice. Eux. Paris, 1891.
37543.33.2 Doumic, René. Histoire de la littérature française. Paris, 1891.
Mol 880.1.5 Dryden, J. Plays from Molière. London, 1891.
42568.19.8 Du Boisgobey, Fortuné. The high roller. N.Y., 1891.
42542.66.55 Dugué, Ferdinand. Théâtre complet. Paris, 1891-94. 10v.
41530.333 Dumas, Alexandre. The black tulip. Boston, 1891.
41530.332 Dumas, Alexandre. Le chevalier d'Harmental. Boston, 1891.
42543.16.7.05 Dumas, Alexandre. La dame aux camélias. N.Y., 1891.
41538.37 Dumas, Alexandre. Gabrielle de belle-isle. N.Y., 1891.
41538.8A Dumas, Alexandre. The memoirs. London, 1891. 2v.
41530.334 Dumas, Alexandre. The page of the duke of Savoy. Boston, 1891. 2v.
41530.331 Dumas, Alexandre. The regent's daughter. Boston, 1891.
41530.335 Dumas, Alexandre. The two Dianas. Boston, 1891. 3v.
42563.55.4.5 Durand, Alice M.C.F. Perdue. N.Y., 1891.
42568.23 Duval, Paul. Sonyeuse. Paris, 1891.
39533.8.2 Émile de Molènes. La Pucelle ou La France delivrée. Paris, 1891. 2v.
42568.30.800 Enault, Louis. Carine. Boston, 1891.
42568.30 Enault, Louis. Tragiques amours. Paris, 1891.
42572.24.3 Erckmann, Emile. Madame Thérèse. Boston, 1891.
37561.28 Études romanes dédiées a G. Paris. Paris, 1891.
37566.28 Faguet, Émile. Politiques et moralistes du dix-neuvième siècle. v.3. Paris, 1891.
FL 1018.97.21 Ferrand, David. La musse normande de David Ferrand. Rouen, 1891-94. 5v.
37556.28 Flinckslieck, F. Zur Entwicklungsgeschichte der Realismus im französischen Roman des 19 Jahrhunderts. Marburg, 1891.
42554.33.19 Fontainas, A. Crépuscules. Paris, 1891.
43611.1.30 Fort, Paul. La petite Bête; comédie en une route. Paris, 1891.
42576.63.7.65 France, Anatole. Sylvestre Bonnard's forbrydelse. Kristiana, 1891.
37567.34 Frommel, Gaston. Esquisses contemporaines. Lausanne, 1891.
37562.12.13 Galino, T. Musique et versification française. Leipzig, 1891.
42543.44.20 Gassier, Alfred. Alceste. Paris, 1891.
41542.32 Gautier, Théophile. La nature chez elle et ménagerie intime. Photoreproduction. Paris, 1891.
37595.36.4 Gautier D'Arras. Ille und Galeron. v.7-8. Halle, 1891.
37543.34 Gazier, A. Petite histoire de la littérature française. Paris, 1891.
42575.55 Goncourt, Edmond de. Charles Demailly. Paris, 1891.
NEDL 42575.68 Goncourt, Edmond de. Journal des Goncourt. v.2-9. Paris, 1891. 8v.
42575.61 Goncourt, Edmond de. Renée Mauperin. Paris, 1891.
42575.62 Goncourt, Edmond de. Soeur Philomène. Paris, 1891.
42543.60.25 Grandmougin, Charles. Aryénis. Paris, 1891.
42576.11 Guillemot, Jules. Florimond. Paris, 1891.
37593.64 Guy, Henry. Essai sur la vie...du trouvère Adam de la Halle. Paris, 1891.
38544.27.510 Haussonville, Gabriel. Mme. de La Fayette. Paris, 1891.
37555.57 Hecq, Gaëtan. La ballade et ses dérivés. Bruxelles, 1891.
42576.67.4 Hervieu, Paul. L'exorcisée. Paris, 1891.
42576.14.58 Houssaye, Arsène. Les confessions. 1830-1880. Paris, 1891. 6v.
42576.14.105 Houssaye, Arsène. Histoires romanesques. Paris, 1891.
41572.7.19 Hugo, Victor. Hans of Iceland. Boston, 1891.
41573.32.11 Hugo, Victor. Hernani. Boston, 1891.
41574.10 Hugo, Victor. Oeuvres inédites. Dieu. Paris, 1891.
41573.28.5 Hugo, Victor. Torquemada drama. México, 1891.
37566.30 Huret, Jules. Enquète sur l'évolution littéraire. Paris, 1891.
39566.26 Ipsen, Knud. Diderot, hans liv og hans gerning. København, 1891.
41596.4 Janzé, Alix C.C. Étude et récits sur Alfred de Musset. Paris, 1891.
FL 377.31 Kenne, C.H. Formulas in the language of the French poet-dramatists of the 17th century. Boston, 1891.
37564.17A Koerting, H. Geschichte des französischen Romans im XVII Jahrhunderts. Leipzig, 1891.
FL 6067.76 Krueger, G. Fremde Gedanken in J.J. Rousseaus ersten Discours. Braunschweig, 1891.
42514.20 Laboulaye, Edouard. Contes choisis. Paris, 1891.
38557.22.10 La Broise, R. de. Bossuet et la Bible. Paris, 1891.

Chronological Listing

1891 - cont.

38544.27.55 La Fayette, Marie M. The Princess of Cleves. Boston, 1891. 2v.
37555.650 La Grasserie, Raoul de. De la césure. Vannes, 1891.
37597.12.20 Langlois, Ernest. Origines et sources du roman de la rose. Photoreproduction. Paris, 1891.
38557.17 Lanson, G. Bossuet. Paris, 1891.
42584.25.10 Laporte, A. Naturalisme ou l'immortalité littéraire. Paris, 1891.
43687.84.120 La Tailhède, Raymond de. Ode à Jean Moréas. Moissac, 1891.
42544.22 Lavedan, Henri. Une famille. Paris, 1891.
42544.31.26 Lecomte, Georges. La meule. Paris, 1891.
42576.68.40 Le Corbeiller, Maurice. Les fourches caudines. Paris, 1891.
42544.33 Lemaître, Jules. Le députe Leveau. Paris, 1891.
42544.33.30 Lemaître, Jules. Mariage blanc. Paris, 1891.
38575.17 Lodge, Lee Davis. A study in Corneille. Baltimore, 1891.
39532.18.5 Loret, Jean. La muse historique. Index. Paris, 1891.
42555.42 Lutel, Paul. La légende de Campagne. Paris, 1891.
42545.3.43 Maeterlinck, Maurice. Blind. The Intruder. Washington, 1891.
42545.1.9 Maeterlinck, Maurice. Blind. The intruders. Washington, 1891.
42545.3A Maeterlinck, Maurice. La princesse Maleine. 5e éd. Bruxelles, 1891.
42545.3.1 Maeterlinck, Maurice. La princesse Maleine. 9e éd. Bruxelles, 1891.
42545.2A Maeterlinck, Maurice. Les sept princesses. Bruxelles, 1891.
42555.43.80 Mallarmé, Stéphane. Pages. Bruxelles, 1891.
42576.76.15 Margueritte, Paul. La force des choses. Paris, 1891.
Mol 247.18 Markheim, H.W.G. Molière and the misanthrope. Oxford, 1891.
39598.8 Marmontel, J.F. Memoirs. Paris, 1891. 3v.
39598.8.5 Marmontel, J.F. Memoirs. Paris, 1891.
42545.9.40 Martel de Janville, S.G. Un raté. 12. éd. Paris, 1891.
37558.17 Mason, Amelia Gere. The woman of the French salons. N.Y., 1891.
FL 382.24.15 Matthews, J.B. French dramatists of the 19th century. N.Y., 1891.
42577.4.30 Maupassant, Guy de. La maison Tellier. Paris, 1891.
42577.4.9 Maupassant, Guy de. Musotte. Paris, 1891.
FL 376.9 Meier, Konrad. Über die Didotragödien des Jodelle. Zwickau, 1891.
42559.54.10 Mensy, Victor. Chansons modernes. Paris, 1891.
Htn 43698.76.120* Merrill, Stuart. Les fastes. Paris, 1891.
38514.37 Meschinot, Jean. Les lunettes des princes. Nantes, 1891.
42545.21.12 Méténier, Oscar. Les voyous au théâtre. Bruxelles, 1891.
42577.42 Meunier, Levallois (Mme.). Le roman du Mont Saint Michel, 1364. Paris, 1891.
42559.54.5 Meusy, Victor. Chansons d'hier et d'aujourd'hui. Paris, 1891.
Mol 165.56 Molière, Jean Baptiste Poquelin. L'avare...Marandet. Paris, 1891.
Mol 165.55 Molière, Jean Baptiste Poquelin. L'avare...Pellisson. 5e éd. Paris, 1891.
Mol 171.33.2 Molière, Jean Baptiste Poquelin. Le bourgeois gentilhomme; comedie. Boston, 1891.
Mol 171.41 Molière, Jean Baptiste Poquelin. Le bourgeois gentilhomme...Gasté. Paris, 1891.
Mol 191.10 Molière, Jean Baptiste Poquelin. Dom Juan...Monval. Paris, 1891.
Mol 229.20 Molière, Jean Baptiste Poquelin. Dos cartas autógrafas é inéditas de Blanco White y El enfermo de aprehension. Sevilla, 1891.
Mol 228.34 Molière, Jean Baptiste Poquelin. Le malade imaginaire...Friese. Bielefeld, 1891.
Mol 231.25 Molière, Jean Baptiste Poquelin. Le mariage forcé...Vitu. Paris, 1891.
Mol 235.29 Molière, Jean Baptiste Poquelin. Le médecin malgré lui...Gasc. Boston, 1891.
Mol 245.63 Molière, Jean Baptiste Poquelin. Le misanthrope. Boston, 1891.
Mol 245.64 Molière, Jean Baptiste Poquelin. Le misanthrope. Boully. Paris, 1891.
Mol 245.65 Molière, Jean Baptiste Poquelin. Le misanthrope. Markheim. Oxford, 1891.
NEDL Mol 8.91 Molière, Jean Baptiste Poquelin. Oeuvres choisies. Paris, 1891.
Mol 251.49 Molière, Jean Baptiste Poquelin. Les précieuses ridicules. Braunholtz. Cambridge, 1891.
Mol 251.51 Molière, Jean Baptiste Poquelin. Les précieuses ridicules. Dupuis. London, 1891.
Mol 251.48 Molière, Jean Baptiste Poquelin. Les précieuses ridicules. Fasnacht. London, 1891.
Mol 251.50 Molière, Jean Baptiste Poquelin. Les précieuses ridicules. Gasc. London, 1891.
Mol 255.15 Molière, Jean Baptiste Poquelin. La princesse d'Élide. Vitu. Paris, 1891.
Mol 18.91 Molière, Jean Baptiste Poquelin. Théâtre. v.1-11. Paris, 1891-95. 4v.
Mon 30.7 Montaigne, Michel de. The essayes of Michael Lord of Montaigne. Florio. London, 1891.
42577.13.15 Montal, Marie. L'idéal de Germaine. Paris, 1891.
38527.31.3A Montchrétien, Antoine de. Les tragédies. Paris, 1891.
39594.3.15 Montesquieu, C.L. de S. Der Geist der Gesetze von Montesquieu. Leipzig, 1891.
FL 6133.3 Montet, A. de. Madame de Warens et le pays de Vaud. Lausanne, 1891.
42555.62 Moréas, Jean. Le pélerin passionné. Paris, 1891.
39566.12.4 Morley, John. Diderot and the encyclopaedists. London, 1891. 2v.
FL 6118.73.6 Morley, John Morley. Rousseau. v.2. N.Y., 1891.
41596.13.2 Musset, Alfred de. Poésies nouvelles. 1836-1852. Paris, 1891.
X Cg 38527.47.5 Mysing, O. Robert Garnier und die antike Tragödie. Leipzig, 1891.
37562.12.18 Naetebus, G. Die nicht-lyrischen Strophenformen des altfranzösischen. Leipzig, 1891.
37567.7.2 Nisard, Desiré. Essais sur l'ecole romantique. Paris, 1891.
42578.29.120 Ohnet, Georges. Dette de haine. Paris, 1891.
41564.33 Paléologue, Maurice. Alfred de Vigny. Paris, 1891.
41574.145 Pelletan, Camille. Victor Hugo, homme politique. Paris, 1891.

1891 - cont.

41547.11.5 Pigault-Lebrun, C.A.G.R. de. La folie espagnole. Paris, 1891.
FL 372.13.5 Piolin, D. Paul. Le thèatre Chrétien dans le Maine. Mamers, 1891.
38514.57.3A Pisan, Christine de. Le dit de la rose. Halle, 1891.
42534.32 Pontmartin, A.F. de. Derniers Samedis. Paris, 1891-92. 3v.
42578.31.15 Pradels, O. Les desserts gaulois. Paris, 1891.
42578.31.63 Prévost, Marcel. La confession d'un amant. Paris, 1891.
42578.18.3.10 Rabusson, Henry. Hallali! 5. éd. Paris, 1891.
37544.12 Rahstede, Georg. Wanderungen durch und französischen Litteratur. Oppeln, 1891.
38557.19.10 Rébelliau, A. Bossuet historien du protestantisme. Thèse. Paris, 1891.
42556.24 Régnier, Henri de. Episodes. Paris, 1891.
38514.21.7 Reichel, H. Syntaktische Studien zu Villon. Leipzig, 1891.
42515.30.96 Renan, Ernest. Le cantique des cantiques. 6. éd. Paris, 1891.
42515.30.51 Renan, Ernest. The future of science. Boston, 1891.
42515.30.54 Renan, Ernest. The future of science. London, 1891.
42515.29.710 Renan, Ernest. Marc-Aurèle et la fin du monde antique. 6. éd. Paris, 1891.
42556.27.90 Retté, Adolphe. Thulé des brumes. Paris, 1891.
42556.22.35 Richepin, Jean. Le mage; opera en cinq actes. Paris, 1891.
42556.22.40 Richepin, Jean. Truandailles. Paris, 1891.
FL 6128.91 Ritter, E. Isaac Rousseau. Paris, 1891.
37596.33.8 Robert de Blois. Floris et Liriope. Leipzig, 1891.
42578.19.2 Rod, Edouard. La course à la mort. 4. éd. Paris, 1891.
42578.19.2.4 Rod, Edouard. La course à la mort. 5. éd. Paris, 1891.
42578.19.3 Rod, Edouard. Nouvelles romandes. Paris, 1891.
42578.19 Rod, Edouard. Le sens de la vie. Paris, 1891.
Mol 870.47 Roger-Milés, L. Alceste converti. Paris, 1891.
42578.20 Rosny, J.H. Daniel Valgraive. Paris, 1891.
37548.13 Rossel, Virgile. Histoire littéraire de la Suisse romande. Geneva, 1891. 2v.
FL 6026.8.10 Rousseau, J.J. The confessions of Jean-Jacques Rousseau. London, 1891. 2v.
FL 6002.891 Rousseau, J.J. Lectures choisies. Paris, 1891.
FL 397.34.15 Rousset, Henry. Le théâtre à Grenoble, 1500-1890. Grenoble, 1891.
39534.36.2 Roy, Emile. La vie et les oeuvres de Charles Soral. Paris, 1891.
40575.21 Sainte-Beuve, Charles A. Portraits of men. London, 1891.
40575.20.7 Sainte-Beuve, Charles A. Portraits of women. London, 1891.
37567.43 Sainte-Croix, C. de. Moeurs littéraires. Paris, 1891.
37556.27 Saintsbury, George. Essays on French novelists. London, 1891.
41557.8.112.10 Sand, George. Nanon. Paris, 1891.
41557.19.23 Sandeau, Jules. Mademoiselle de la Seiglière. Boston, 1891.
42546.25.35 Sardou, Victorien. Les ganaches. Paris, 1891.
42546.26.6.5 Sardou, Victorien. Les pattes de mouche. Paris, 1891.
Mol 193.16 Schädel, O. Ein Beitrag zur Don Juan-Litteratur. Bensheim? 1891?
37565.35.2 Scherer, Edmond. Etudes sur la littérature au XVIIIe siècle. Paris, 1891.
39586.32 Scherer, Edmond H.A. Études sur la littérature au XVIIIe siècle. Paris, 1891.
42546.34.19 Silvestre, Armand. Les ailes d'or. Paris, 1891.
42546.33 Silvestre, Armand. Grisélidis. Paris, 1891.
Htn 42546.33.2* Silvestre, Armand. Grisélidis. Paris, 1891.
42584.37.30 Simon, Jules. Nouveaux mémoires des autres. Paris, 1891.
38514.60 Le songe veritable. Paris, 1891.
38526.28.3 Stecher, J. Notice Jean Lemaire de Belges. Bruxelles, 1891.
38525.95 Steffens, Georg. Rotrou-Studien. Oppeln, 1891.
Mol 619.10 Sundermann, A. Aus Molières Dichtung. Berlin, 1891.
42583.33.30 Theuriet, André. Charme dangereux. Paris, 1891.
42578.56.15 Toutain, Paul. La fin d'une âme. Paris, 1891.
42557.19.110 Verlaine, Paul. La bonne chanson. Paris, 1891.
42557.19.40 Verlaine, Paul. Mes hopitaux. Paris, 1891.
42557.19.55 Verlaine, Paul. Les uns et les autres. Paris, 1891.
42582.21 Verne, Jules. Mistress Branican. N.Y., 1891.
42521.15 Veuillot, Louis. Ca et la. Paris, 1891. 2v.
38525.96 Vianey, Joseph. Deux sources inconnues de Rotrou. Dole, 1891.
42576.52.5 Viaud, Julien. Islandski Ribari. Zagreb, 1891.
42576.55 Viaud, Julien. Le livre de la pitié. Paris, 1891.
42522.6 Vogüé, E.M. de. Spectacles contemporains. Paris, 1891.
39544.27.3 Voltaire, François Marie Arouet de. Lettres choisies. 6th ed. Paris, 1891.
39545.32.25 Voltaire, François Marie Arouet de. Zadig and other tales. London, 1891.
42547.34 Wolff, Pierre. Leurs filles. Paris, 1891.
37557.26 Wuscher, Gottlieb. Der Einfluss der englischen Ballad- en Poesie. Trogen, 1891.
42559.97.10 Xanrof, Léon. Chansons à rire. Paris, 1891.
38526.42.15 Zilch, Georg. Der Gebrauch des französischen Pronomens in der 2. Hälfte des XVI. Jahrhunderts. Heppenheim, 1891.
42584.12 Zola, Emile. L'argent. Paris, 1891.
42584.4.3 Zola, Emile. Au bonheur des dames. Paris, 1891.
42584.12.5 Zola, Emile. Das Geld. v.1-2. 2. Aufl. Stuttgart, 1891.

1892

42562.24 About, Edmond. Le dix-neuvième sièle. Paris, 1892.
42562.13.5 About, Edmond. La mère de la marquise. N.Y., 1892.
42562.17.2 About, Edmond. Le roi des Montagnes. N.Y., 1892.
37562.284 Ahlström, Axel. Studier i den fornfranska lais-litteraturen. Upsala, 1892.
38523.16 Allais, Gustave. Malherbe et la poésie française. Paris, 1892.
42553.62.30 Amoric, Amédée. Les vibrations. Paris, 1892.
42558.100 Les amours des anges. Paris, 1892.
42542.1.16.5 Ancey, Georges. La dupe. Paris, 1892.
37567.40 Audebrand, P. Petits mémoires du XIXe siècle. Paris, 1892.
42561.8 Augustin, Marie. Le macandal. Nouvelle Orleans, 1892.
40596.13.2 Balzac, Honoré de. Albert Savarus. Boston, 1892.
40597.11.10 Balzac, Honoré de. Beatrix. Paris, 1892.
40596.24 Balzac, Honoré de. The country doctor. N.Y., 1892.
40597.24.5 Balzac, Honoré de. Histoire des Treize. Paris, 1892.
40597.34.2 Balzac, Honoré de. Une ténébreuse affaire. Paris, 1892.

1892 - cont.

42554.6.6 Banville, Théodore de. Dans la fournaise. Paris, 1892.
42554.2.2 Banville, Théodore de. Odes funambulesques. Paris, 1892.
FL 371.27 Bapst, G. Etudes sur les mystères au Moyen Age. Paris, 1892.
42563.18.10 Barrès, Maurice. Le culte du moi. Examen de trois idéologies. Paris, 1892.
42563.16.12 Barrès, Maurice. Toute licence saufe, contre l'amour. Paris, 1892.
42563.21.52 Bazin, René. A blot of ink. London, 1892.
Mol 875.11 Bertal, G. Molière. Paris, 1892.
38514.140 Bertrand de Broussillon, A. René d'Orange, poète du Bas-Maine. Laval, 1892.
40582.11.5 Beyle, Henri. Lettres intimes. 2. éd. Paris, 1892.
40582.38 Beyle, Henri. Souvenirs d'égotisme. Paris, 1892.
38542.30 Blessebois, P.C. Pastorale tirée des oeuvres satyriques (1676). Alençon, 1892.
38527.59 Bonnefon, Paul. Oeuvres complètes d'Estienne de La Boëtie. Paris, 1892.
42542.29.122 Bonnetain, P. Passagère. 7. éd. Paris, 1892.
FL 383.133 Borbey d'Aurevilly, Jules. Théâtre contemporain, 1870-1883. Paris, 1892.
Htn 38557.70* Bossuet, J.B. Témoignage sur la vie et les vertus éminentes de Monsieur Vincent de Paul. Paris, 1892.
37530.11.8 Boston Public Library. Works of fiction in the French language. Boston, 1892.
42542.30 Bouchor, Maurice. La dévotion à St. André. Paris, 1892.
40526.30 Boufflers, Stanislas de. Oeuvres choisies. Paris, 1892.
42563.37.16.2 Bourget, Paul. Cosmopolis. Paris, 1892.
37567.15.4 Bourget, Paul. Nouveaux essais de psychologie contemporaine. Paris, 1892.
42563.37.9.10 Bourget, Paul. Pastels of men. Boston, 1892.
42563.37.12 Bourget, Paul. La terre promise. Paris, 1892.
37573.36.20 Bournand, F. L'eloquence et la littérature chrétiennes. Lyon, 1892?
38576.11.2 Brueys, D.A. de. L'avocat Pathelin. London, 1892.
FL 358.92 Brunetière, F. Conférences de l'Odéon. Les époque du théâtre français (1636-1850). Paris, 1892.
FL 360.91 Brunetiére, F. Les epoques du théâtre français, 1636-1850. Paris, 1892.
42524.18 Brunetière, F. Le roman naturaliste. Paris, 1892.
37566.32 Byvanck, W.G.C. Un hollandais à Paris en 1891. Sensations de literature. Paris, 1892.
42563.68 Cabot, Adrien. Le marquis de Saint-Etienne. Paris, 1892.
42586.28 Caro, E. Amour de jeune fille. Paris, 1892.
42563.39.600 Carol, Jean. Honneur est sauf. Paris, 1892.
42546.31.16 Chadourne, A. La collaboration au théâtre. Paris, 1892.
38526.10.8.15 Chassignet, Jean Baptiste. Sonnets franc-comtois, inédits. Paris, 1892.
40586.13.5 Chateaubriand, F.A.R. Atala. Paris, 1892.
FL 366.9 Chatillon, Louis. Anastasie et sa besace. Paris, 1892.
42576.12.20 Cherbonnel, Alice. My uncle and my curé. N.Y., 1892.
FL 397.115.32 Claeys, Prosper. Histoire du théâtre à Gand. Gand, 1892. 3v.
42586.31.5 Claretié, J. L'Américaine. Paris, 1892.
37558.16 Colombey, Emile. Ruelles, salons, et cabarets. Paris, 1892. 2v.
37547.30 Contades, Gérard de. Bagnoles. (Souvenirs littéraires). Alençon, 1892.
42554.21.17 Coppée, François. Les vrais riches. Paris, 1892.
38575.34.7.7 Corneille, Pierre. Polyeucte. Cambridge, 1892.
38575.31.4.2 Corneille, Pierre. Polyeucte. London, 1892.
42566.15 Danville, Gaston. Les infinis de la chair. Paris, 1892.
42542.60.10 Darmont, A. Argument of the play of Leah. N.Y., 1892.
42566.23.5 Daudet, Alphonse. Artists' wives. London, 1892.
42566.20.2 Daudet, Alphonse. Contes choisis. La fantaisie et l'histoire. Paris, 1892.
42566.22.7 Daudet, Alphonse. L'évangéliste; roman parisien. Paris, 1892.
42566.63 Daudet, Alphonse. Recollections from a literary man. London, 1892.
42566.32.26 Daudet, Alphonse. Robert Helmont, diary of a recluse. London, 1892.
42566.32.25 Daudet, Alphonse. Robert Helmont, diary of a recluse. London, 1892.
42566.46.2A Daudet, Alphonse. Rose et Ninette. Paris, 1892.
42566.20.15 Daudet, Alphonse. Le siège de Berlin. N.Y., 1892.
42566.41 Daudet, Alphonse. Trois contes choisis. Boston, 1892.
FL 397.56 Declève, Jules. Le théâtre à Mons. Mons, 1892.
42586.35.7.3 Delpit, Albert. Belle-Madame. 5. éd. Paris, 1892.
42561.18 Descaves, Lucien. Sous-offs. Paris, 1892.
37584.19 Desmahis, J.F.E. de C. Chefs-d'oeuvre des auteurs comiques. Paris, 1892.
FL 397.3.9 Despierres, G. (Mme.). Le théâtre et les comédiens à Alençon 16 et 17 siècle. Paris, 1892.
39564.6 Diderot, Denis. Lectures choisies par H. Parigot. Paris, 1892.
39527.6.5 Disprés, Armand. Les éditions illustrées des fables de La Fontaine. Paris, 1892.
37567.35 Doumic, René. Portraits d'écrivains. Paris, 1892.
41538.69.25 Dumas, Alexandre. Le Chevalier de Maison-Rouge. Paris, 1892. 2v.
41538.16.4.3 Dumas, Alexandre. Le comte de Monte Cristo. Paris, 1892.
41530.315 Dumas, Alexandre. The romances of Alexandre Dumas. Boston, 1892-97. 45v.
41538.66.10 Dumas, Alexandre. The son of Porthos or The death of Aramis. N.Y., 1892.
41538.66 Dumas, Alexandre. The son of Porthos or The death of Aramis. N.Y., 1892.
NEDL 42543.9 Dumas, Alexandre. Théâtre complet. 7. série. Paris, 1892.
41538.53.26 Dumas, Alexandre. The three musketeers. N.Y., 1892.
41538.48.20 Dumas, Alexandre. The two Dianas. Boston, 1892. 2v.
37564.36 Dupuy, Adrien. Histoire de la littérature française (au XVIIe siècle). Paris, 1892.
39594.3.50 Durkheim, E. Quid secundatus politicae scientiae. Burdigalae, 1892.
Mol 260.10 Erdmann, H. Molière's Psyché. Insterburg, 1892.
42515.35.299F Ernest Renan, 1823-1892. Paris, 1892.
39545.7 Espinasse, F. Life of Voltaire. London, 1892.
42543.29.55 Eude, Emile. Poëmes johanniques. Paris, 1892.
42574.25 Fabre, Ferdinand. Sylviane. Paris, 1892.
37565.37 Faguet, Emile. XVIII siècle. Etudes littéraires. Paris, 1892.
40583.26 Farges, Louis. Stendhal diplomate. Paris, 1892.
38553.15.4.45 Fénelon, F. de S. de la Mothe. Selections from Fénelon. Boston, 1892.
Htn 42576.22.2* Flaubert, Gustave. Hérodias. Paris, 1892.

1892 - cont.

Htn 42576.22* Flaubert, Gustave. Hérodias. Paris, 1892.
39574.30 Förster, Max. Beiträge zur Kenntnis des Characters und der Philosophie d'Alemberts. Hamburg, 1892.
FL 377.33 Fournel, Victor. Le théâtre au XVIIe siècle. Paris, 1892.
42576.62.27.5 France, Anatole. L'étui de nacre. 2. éd. Paris, 1892.
42576.62.5 France, Anatole. Le livre de mon ami. Paris, 1892.
42576.62.5.10 France, Anatole. Le livre de mon ami. 16. éd. Paris, 1892.
38537.13.9 Frantzen, J.J.A.A. Kritische Bemerkungen zu Fischarts Übersetzung von Rabelais' Gargantua. Inaug. Diss. Strassbourg, 1892.
38525.22.5 Froger, L. Les premières poésies de Ronsard. Mamers, 1892.
42586.62 Gauthier-Villars, Henry. L'année fantaisiste. Paris, 1892.
41542.11.5 Gautier, Théophile. Mademoiselle de Maupin. Paris, 1892.
41542.34 Gautier, Théophile. Voyage en Italie. Paris, 1892.
42576.4 Gevin-Cassal. Souvenirs du Sundgau. Paris, 1892.
FL 360.75 Ginisty, P. Choses et gens de théâtre. Paris, 1892.
42576.64.10 Gramont, Louis de. Simone. Paris, 1892.
42543.60 Grandmougin, Charles. Le Christ. Paris, 1892.
42543.60.3F Grandmougin, Charles. L'enfant Jésus. Paris, 1892.
42543.60.20 Grandmougin, Charles. Le réveillon. Paris, 1892.
37556.26.5 Griswold, W.M. A descriptive list of novels...relating to life in France. Cambridge, 1892.
42543.61.5 Guinon, Albert. Deux pièces. Seul et À qui la faute? Paris, 1892.
42576.40.375 Halévy, Ludovic. Karikari. 11. éd. Paris, 1892.
40527.18 Harassti, Jules. La poésie d'André Chenier. Paris, 1892.
37551.31 Hecq, Gaëtan. Le lai, le virelai, le rondeau. Bruxelles, 1892.
42576.67.5 Hervieu, Paul. Flirt. Paris, 1892.
41571.16.2 Hugo, Victor. Les misérables. v.1 lost 1931. N.Y., 1892. 2v.
41574.12 Hugo, Victor. Oeuvres inédites. En voyage. France et Belgique. Paris, 1892.
41573.22.2 Hugo, Victor. Quatre-vingt-treize. Boston, 1892.
41572.22 Hugo, Victor. Quatre-vingt-treize. N.Y., 1892.
39544.189 Ingersoll, R.G. Oration on Voltaire. London, 1892.
38551.72A Janet, Paul. Fénelon. Paris, 1892.
42554.66 Jouy, Jules. La muse à bébé. Paris, 1892.
42543.71 Jullien, Jean. Le théâtre vivant. Paris, 1892. 2v.
37578.53.16A Kalendrier des Bergers. Le compost et kalendrier des bergiers. The kalender of shepherdes. v.1-3. London, 1892.
37544.15 Keene, H.G. The literature of France. London, 1892.
37544.15.5 Keene, H.G. The literature of France. N.Y., 1892.
39527.36 La Fontaine, Jean de. L'amour et psyché. Paris, 1892.
39527.29.7 La Fontaine, Jean de. Fables. London, 1892.
41578.32.12 Lamartine, Alphonse. Graziella. Chicago, 1892.
41578.28 Lamartine, Alphonse. Jocelyn. Paris, 1892.
41578.9.5 Lamartine, Alphonse de. Nouvelles méditations poétiques. Paris, 1892.
38567.12A Lanson, Gustave. Boileau. Paris, 1892.
FL 360.30 Larroumet, G. Etudes d'histoire et de critique dramatique. Paris, 1892.
42544.24.7.5 Lavedan, Henri. La critique du prince d'Aurec. 2e éd. Paris, 1892.
42554.16 Le Braz, A. La chanson de la Bretagne. Rennes, 1892.
42544.5.5 Legouvé, Ernest. La cigale chez les fourmis. Boston, 1892.
40597.2.2 Lemer, Julien. Balzac. Paris, 1892.
42587.14.21 Lepic, Adèle. Pour l'honneur! Paris, 1892.
42576.45.5 Le Roux, H. Marins et soldats. Paris, 1892.
39596.22 Lescure, M. de. Bernardin de St. Pierre. Paris, 1892.
40556.33 Lescure, M. de. Le Comte Joseph de Maistre et sa famille. Paris, 1892.
40587.7 Lescure, M.F.A. de. Chateaubriand. Paris, 1892.
X Cg 38575.15 Liéby, A. Corneille. Etudes sur le théâtre classique. Paris, 1892.
37542.23A Lintilhac, Gustave. Supplément aux études littéraires de G. Merlet. Paris, 1892.
42546.31.7 Macchetta, B.R. (Mrs.). Victorien Sardou, poet, author, and member of the Academy of France. London, 1892.
42545.1.2 Maeterlinck, Maurice. Les aveugles. 3. éd. Bruxelles, 1892.
42545.3.3.1 Maeterlinck, Maurice. Pélléas et Mélisande. 2e éd. Bruxelles, 1892.
42533.1 Marchand, Alfred. Poetes et penseurs. Paris, 1892.
37543.8.9 Marcillac, F. Manuel d'histoire de la littérature française. 11. éd. Genève, 1892.
42577.12.5 Marenches, E. Hermine. 2. éd. Paris, 1892.
42576.76.10 Margueritte, Paul. Le cuirassier blanc. Paris, 1892.
42576.76.17 Margueritte, Paul. Ma grande. Paris, 1892.
42576.76.19 Margueritte, Paul. Sur le retour. Paris, 1892.
37574.26.12 Masson, Gustave. La lyre française. London, 1892.
42577.34 Masson-Forestier, A. Pour une signature. Paris, 1892.
38512.91 Matheolus. Les lamentations. Paris, 1892. 2v.
42577.4.10.5 Maupassant, Guy de. Fort comme la mort. Paris, 1892.
39596.23 Maury, Fernand. Etude sur la vie et les oeuvres de Bernardin de St. Pierre. Paris, 1892.
42545.6 Mazel, Henri. La fin des dieux. Paris, 1892.
X Cg 42555.58.26 Mendès, Catulle. Le joyeuses commères de Paris. Paris, 1892.
NEDL 42555.58 Mendès, Catulle. Poésies. Photoreproduction. Paris, 1892. 3v.
37596.25.2 Merguet, V. Anglo-Normannischen religiösen Dramas Adam. Konigsberg, 1892.
42545.24 Meurice, Paul. Fanfan la Tulipe. Paris, 1892.
37596.126A Meyer, Paul. Le chansonnier français de Saint Germain-des-Près. Tom.1. Paris, 1892.
38537.14A Millet, René. Les grands écrivains français. Rabelais. Paris, 1892.
Mol 713.5 Moland, L. Vie de Jean Baptiste Poquelin Molière. Paris, 1892.
Mol 155.30 Molière, Jean Baptiste Poquelin. L'amour médecin...Monval. Paris, 1892.
Mol 171.43 Molière, Jean Baptiste Poquelin. Le bourgeois gentilhomme...Gasc. London, 1892.
Mol 171.33.3 Molière, Jean Baptiste Poquelin. Le bourgeois gentilhomme...Moriarty. London, 1892.
Mol 211.46 Molière, Jean Baptiste Poquelin. Les femmes savantes...Gasc. London, 1892.
Mol 211.48 Molière, Jean Baptiste Poquelin. Les femmes savantes...Marandet. Paris, 1892?

1892 - cont.

Mol 211.47 Molière, Jean Baptiste Poquelin. Les femmes savantes...Roche. London, 1892.
Mol 236.70 Molière, Jean Baptiste Poquelin. Lou medecin maugratéu. Avignon, 1892.
Mol 228.35 Molière, Jean Baptiste Poquelin. Le malade imaginaire...Humbert. 3e éd. Paris, 1892?
Mol 235.28 Molière, Jean Baptiste Poquelin. Le médecin malgré lui...Monval. Paris, 1892.
Mol 62.33 Molière, Jean Baptiste Poquelin. Meisterwerke...Fulda. Stuttgart, 1892.
Mol 241.5 Molière, Jean Baptiste Poquelin. Mélicerte...Monval. Paris, 1892.
Mol 245.66 Molière, Jean Baptiste Poquelin. Le misanthrope. Lavigne. Paris, 1892.
Mol 245.67 Molière, Jean Baptiste Poquelin. Le misanthrope. Monval. Paris, 1892.
Mol 245.68 Molière, Jean Baptiste Poquelin. Le misanthrope. Pellisson. 4. éd. Paris, 1892.
Mol 245.69 Molière, Jean Baptiste Poquelin. Le misanthrope. Scheffler. Bielefeld, 1892.
Mol 251.52 Molière, Jean Baptiste Poquelin. Les précieuses ridicules. Figuière. Paris, 1892.
Mol 265.20 Molière, Jean Baptiste Poquelin. Le sicilien. Monval. Paris, 1892.
Mol 268.78 Molière, Jean Baptiste Poquelin. Le Tartuffe. Friese. Bielefeld, 1892.
Mol 18.92 Molière, Jean Baptiste Poquelin. Théâtre complet. Paris, 1892. 8v.
38585.13 Monceaux, Paul. Racine. Paris, 1892.
37567.155 Monselet, Charles. Petits memoires littéraires. Paris, 1892.
Mon 30.8A Montaigne, Michel. Essays. Florio (Saintsbury). London, 1892-93. 3v.
39594.9 Montesquieu, C.L. de S. Mélanges inédits de Montesquieu. Bordeaux, 1892.
Htn 39594.14.3* Montesquieu, C.L. de S. The Persian letters. London, 1892. 2v.
39594.14.4A Montesquieu, C.L. de S. The Persian letters. London, 1892. 2v.
39531.18 Mühlan, Alois. Jean Chapelain als litterarischer Kritiker. Strassburg, 1892.
38513.16 Mystères du Moyen-Age. Mystères liturgiques. Paris, 1892.
42578.16 Narrey, Charles. Voyage autour du dictionnaire. Paris, 1892.
37548.33.10 Nautet, Francis. Histoire des lettres Belges d'éxpression française. v.1-2. Bruxelles, 1892?
37596.20.2 Orpen, Goddard H. Song of Dermont and the Earl. Oxford, 1892.
37561.26 Paris, Gaston. Les origines de la poésie lyrique en France au moyen âge. Paris, 1892.
39544.33.4 Parton, James. Life of Voltaire. 7. ed. Boston, 1892. 2v.
42578.30.50 Peladan, J. La queste du Graal. Paris, 1892?
37556.26 Perret, Émile. Le roman. Étude morale. Lausanne, 1892.
40522.9.8 Prévost, Antoine F. Manon Lescaut. Paris, 1892.
42578.31.25 Prévost, Marcel. Lettres de femmes. 20. éd. Paris, 1892.
42578.31.25.2 Prévost, Marcel. Lettres de femmes. 21. éd. Paris, 1892.
42578.18 Quillot, Maurice. L'entrainé. Paris, 1892.
38531.11 Rabelais, F. Works. London, 1892. 2v.
38585.43 Racine, Jean. Phèdre. London, 1892.
38585.49 Racine, Jean. Théâtre complet. Paris, 1892.
37562.42 Rauschmaier, A. Über den figürlichen Gebrauch der Zahlen in altfranzösischen Litteratur. Erlangen, 1892.
42587.50.60 Rebell, Hugues. Baisers d'ennemis. Paris, 1892.
42515.30.435 Renan, Ernest. Feuilles détachées. 8. éd. Paris, 1892.
42515.30.438 Renan, Ernest. Feuilles détachées. 13. éd. Paris, 1892.
42515.34.75 Renan, Ernest. Recollections and lettres of Ernest Renan. N.Y., 1892.
42587.52.2 Renard, Jules. Sourires pincés. Paris, 1892.
38576.12.42.80 Reynier, Gustave. Thomas Corneille, sa vie et son théâtre. Paris, 1892.
41578.44 Reyssié, Félix. La jeunesse de Lamartine. Paris, 1892.
42556.22.45 Richepin, Jean. Par la glaive; drame. Paris, 1892.
42578.31.85 Richet, C. A la recherche de la gloire. Paris, 1892.
FL 370.62 Rigal, E. De l'établissement de la tragédie en France. Paris, 1892.
37573.21 Rion, Aldine. Les femmes poètes bretonnes. Nantes, 1892.
42578.19.4 Rod, Edouard. La sacrifiée. Paris, 1892.
40583.7 Rod, Edouard. Stendhal. Photoreproduction. Paris, 1892.
42556.32.35 Rollinat, Maurice. La nature; poésies. Paris, 1892.
FL 6015.10 Rothschild, H. de. Lettres inédites de Jean-Jacques Rousseau. Paris, 1892.
FL 6002.892 Rousseau, J.J. Extraits en prose. Paris, 1892.
FL 6002.892.2 Rousseau, J.J. Morceaux choisis. Paris, 1892.
42587.56.100 Saint-Aulaire, Auguste. Gilda. Paris, 1892.
39595.20.50 St. Pierre, J.H.B. de. Paul and Virginia. N.Y., 1892.
41574.70 Saint-Victor, P. de. Victor Hugo. Paris, 1892.
40575.38 Sainte-Beuve, Charles A. Essays. London, 1892.
37542.16.5 Saintsbury, George. A short history of French literature. 4. ed. Oxford, 1892.
37572.30.2 Saintsbury, George. Specimens of French literature. Oxford, 1892.
42546.15.27 Salandri, Gaston. La ronçon. Paris, 1892.
FL 6138.92.2 Salomon, Otto. Förelasningar öfver Jean-Jacques Rousseau. Göteborg, 1892.
41557.8.135 Sand, George. Germain's marriage. N.Y., 1892.
41557.9.47 Sand, George. La mare au diable. Boston, 1892.
41557.9.48 Sand, George. La mare au diable. Boston, 1892.
41557.19.12 Sandeau, Jules. Mademoiselle de la Seiglière. 7. ed. London, 1892.
42578.34.2 Sarcey, Francisque. Souvenirs d'age mûr. Paris, 1892.
42546.30.7.3 Sardou, Victorien. Fédora. Milano, 1892.
Htn 39534.32.6* Scarron, Paul. The comical romance and other tales. London, 1892. 2v.
39534.32.5A Scarron, Paul. The comical romance and other tales. London, 1892. 2v.
42578.36.2 Schultz, Jeanne. Jean de Kerdren. N.Y., 1892.
42587.58.7 Ségur, Sophie. Pauvre blaise. Paris, 1892.
NEDL 41568.17.1 Sénancour, Étienne Pivert de. Obermann. Par s, 1892.
NEDL 41568.17.1A Sénancour, Étienne Pivert de. Obermann. Paris, 1892.
Htn 38537.25.26* Silvestre, Armand. Le nu de Rabelais. Paris, 1892.
42546.34.16 Silvestre, Armand. Pour les amants. Paris, 1892?
41558.67.10 Souvestre, Émile. An attic philosopher in Paris. N.Y., 1892.
37555.306 Souza, R. de. Le rythme poétique. Paris, 1892.

1892 - cont.

41571.16.5 Sozialistische Einheitsparti. Die Bedeutung der Arbeiten des Genossen Stalin. v.3-5. v.1-2 lost 1931. Boston, 1892. 5v.
FL 6138.92 Spitzer, A. Natur und Naturgemässheit bei Jean-Jacques Rousseau. Leipzig, 1892.
38521.39 Sporleder, Carl. Über Montchrestiens "Escossoise." Marburg, 1892.
37555.312 Sully, R.F.A. Réfléxions sur l'art des vers. Paris, 1892.
Mol 719.4 Süss, O. Questionnaire sur vie et oeuvres de Molière. Strehlen, 1892.
41561.21 Tchernychev, A. Oeuvres choisies. Paris, 1892.
42578.52.15 Tinseau, Léon de. Faut-il aimer? 11. éd. Paris, 1892.
42578.52.20 Tinseau, Léon de. Mon oncle Alcide. 6. éd. Paris, 1892.
42578.52.75 Tinseau, Léon de. Thérèse de Guilliane. N.Y., 1892.
42578.56.20 Toutain, Paul. Dialogues des vivants. Paris, 1892.
42584.11.8 Urien, Carlos M. La débâcle. Buenos Aires, 1892.
42547.11.14 Vaucaire, Maurice. Un beau soir. Paris, 1892.
42582.25 Verne, Jules. The tour of the world in eighty days. Chicago, 1892.
42582.25.4 Verne, Jules. The tour of the world in eighty days. N.Y., 1892.
42582.25.3 Verne, Jules. The tour of the world in eighty days. N.Y., 1892.
42576.57.18 Viaud, Julien. The book of pity and of death. N.Y., 1892.
42576.51 Viaud, Julien. Fantôme d'Orient. Paris, 1892.
42576.54.4 Viaud, Julien. Pêcheur d'Islande. 107. éd. Paris, 1892.
41564.3.70 Vigny, Alfred de. Cinq-Mars. Boston, 1892. 3v.
41564.4.9A Vigny, Alfred de. Cinq-Mars. London, 1892.
38514.21.3 Villon, François. Le jargon Jobelin de Maistre François Villon. Paris, 1892.
38514.20.2A Villon, François. Oeuvres complètes. Paris, 1892.
38514.20.27 Villon, François. Poems. London, 1892.
43824.84.120 Vitta, Émile. Vere l'étoile. Paris, 1892.
42522.5 Vogüé, E.M. de. Regards historiques et littéraires. Paris, 1892.
37562.13 Weidinger, Anton. Die Schäferlyrik der französischen Vorrenaissance. München, 1892-1893.
37557.24 Weigand, Wilhelm. Essays (Voltaire, Rousseau, etc.). München, 1892.
42587.70.17 Weill, Alexandre. Dix fables oubliées de La Fontaine. Paris, 1892.'
42587.70.18 Weill, Alexandre. Le nouvel Isaïe. Paris, 1892.
42587.70.23 Weill, Alexandre. Le parole nouvelle. 5. éd. Paris, 1892.
FL 390.60 Weiss, Jean Jacques. Trois années de théâtre, 1883-1885. Paris, 1892-96. 4v.
42547.38 Wolff, Pierre. Les maris de leurs filles. Paris, 1892.
40597.2.30 Wormeley, K.P. A memoir of Honoré de Balzac. Boston, 1892.
42584.11 Zola, Emile. La débâcle. Paris, 1892.

1893

42562.38.14.50 Adam, Paul. L'automne. Paris, 1893.
37596.3.2 Albert, A.C. Die Sprache Philippes de Beaumanoir in seinen poetischen Werken. Erlangen, 1893.
39574.27.2 Alembert, J. Le Rond d'. Discours préliminaire de l'encyclopédie. Paris, 1893.
42542.1.13 Alexis, Paul. Charles Demailly. Paris, 1893.
37558.13 Alq, Louise. Anthologie féminine. Paris, 1893.
42553.33.2 Amiel, Henri F. Amiel's journal. N.Y., 1893. 2v.
42562.38.15 Ardel, H. Coeur de sceptique. Paris, 1893.
42562.38.17 Ardel, H. Près du bonheur. N.Y., 1893.
42586.9 Arène, Paul. La chèvre d'or. Paris, 1893.
42586.11.15 Assollant, A. Récits de la vieille France. Boston, 1893.
38527.21 Audiat, L. Prosper mérimée et son édition de Foeneste. La Rochelle, 1893.
Mol 870.48 Augé de Lassus, L. La Saint Jean. Paris, 1893.
42562.55 Auriol, G. Histoire de rire. Paris, 1893?
42586.14.9 Badin, Adolphe. Minine et Pojarski. Paris, 1893.
42536.34.10 Bailleu, Paul. Hippolyte Taine. n.p., 1893?
40596.13.8 Balzac, Honoré de. The brotherhood of consolation. Boston, 1893.
40596.13.36 Balzac, Honoré de. A great man of the provinces in Paris. Boston, 1893.
40596.13.135 Balzac, Honoré de. The human comedy. N.Y., 1893. 3v.
40596.13.44 Balzac, Honoré de. Lost illusions. Boston, 1893.
40596.13.78 Balzac, Honoré de. Ursula. Boston, 1893.
40596.13.68 Balzac, Honoré de. The village rector. Boston, 1893.
42554.3.5 Banville, Théodore de. Esope; comédie en trois actes. Paris, 1893.
FL 358.93FA Bapst, Germain. Essai sur l'histoire du théâtre. Paris, 1893.
41522.1.4 Barbey d'Aurevilly, Jules. Le chevalier des Touches. Paris, 1893.
40587.8 Bardoux, A. Chateaubriand. Paris, 1893.
41596.1.2 Barine, Arvède. Alfred de Musset. Paris, 1893.
42563.16.10 Barrès, Maurice. L'ennemi des lois. Paris, 1893.
42542.27.26.10 Barrière, Théodore. Zerstreut (Tête de linotte). Leipzig, 1893.
40532.7.15 Beaumarchais, Pierre A.C. de. Le mariage de Figaro. Paris, 1893?
38526.28 Becker, P.A. Jean Lemaire. Der erste humanistische Dichter Frankreichs. Strassburg, 1893.
37562.21 Bédier, Joseph. Les fabliaux. Paris, 1893.
42542.29.77 Berr de Turique, J. Madame Agnès. Paris, 1893.
42563.23.76 Bloy, Léon. Sueur de sang, 1870-1871. Paris, 1893.
40526.51.50 Boccage, Marie Anne F. du. La Colombiade. Lisboa, 1893.
38566.32 Boileau Despréaux, Nicolas. Le Lutrin. Poetry. Paris, 1893.
Mol 860.54 Bois, George. Racine à Chevreuse. Paris, 1893.
37555.317 Boissière, G. Notions de versification française. Paris, 1893.
Mon 142.1 Bonnefon, P. Montaigne; l'homme et l'oeuvre. Bordeaux, 1893.
42563.37.6 Bourget, Paul. Un coeur de femme. Paris, 1893.
42563.37.16.4 Bourget, Paul. Cosmopolis. N.Y., 1893.
37567.15.3 Bourget, Paul. Essais de psychologie contemporaine. 9e éd. Paris, 1893.
42563.37.14A Bourget, Paul. Un scrupule. Paris, 1893.
42563.39.310 Brown, Alphonse. La station aérienne. Paris, 1893.
NEDL 39533.20.15 Brun, P.A. Savinien de Cyrano de Bergerac, sa vie et ses oeuvres. Paris, 1893.
38511.23 Bullrich, G. Über Charles d'Orléans. Berlin, 1893.
37595.36.5 Caravajal, B. de. La bandolera de Flandes. v.9-10. Halle, 1893.

1893 - cont.

42554.18 Cazalis, Henry. L'illusion par Jean Lahor. Paris, 1893. 2v.
40596.4.12 Cerfberr, Anatole. Répertoirs de la Comédie humaine de H. de Balzac. Paris, 1893.
42586.29.100 Chabrier, Jean. Aller et retour. Paris, 1893.
42554.18.9 Chambrun, Marie Jean de. La comtesse de Chambrun, ses poésies. Paris, 1893.
39544.35 Champion, E. Voltaire. Études critiques. Paris, 1893.
42565.32 Cherbuliez, Victor. Le secret du précepteur. Paris, 1893.
FL 6118.93A Chuquet, A. Jean-Jacques Rousseau. Paris, 1893.
41584.41.3 Cim, A. En pleine gloire; histoire d'une mystification. Paris, 1893.
Mol 603.5 Comte, Charles. Les stances libres dans Molière. Versailles, 1893.
42542.53.25 Coolus, R. Le menage Brésile. Paris, 1893.
42586.32.20 Coster, Charles de. La legende d'Ulenspiegel. Bruxelles, 1893.
42542.58.9 Curel, François de. L'amour brode. Paris, 1893.
37563.18 Darmesteter, Arsène. Le seizième siècle. 5e éd. Paris, 1893.
42566.20.5A Daudet, Alphonse. Contes de Daudet including "La Belle-Nivernaise".2. éd. N.Y., 1893.
42566.24.27 Daudet, Alphonse. Kings in exile. London, 1893.
42566.27.13 Daudet, Alphonse. Letters from my mill. N.Y., 1893.
42566.34.5 Daudet, Alphonse. Sapho. Paris, 1893.
42566.62 Daudet, Alphonse. Thirty years of Paris and my literary life. London, 1893.
42515.35.71 Delaporte, V. L'"Apothéose" de Renan. Paris, 1893.
37567.44 Delille, Edward. Some French writers. London, 1893.
40556.31 Descostes, François. Joseph de Maistre. Paris, 1893. 2v.
Mol 560.15 Despois, P. Oeuvres de Molière. Paris, 1893.
42515.35.72 Desportes, Henri. Ernest Renan, sa vie et son oeuvre. Paris, 1893.
FL 382.57 Doumic, René. De scribe à Ibsen. Paris, 1893.
42586.38 DuCamp, M. Le crépuscule. Paris, 1893.
42586.38.20 DuCamp, M. Literary recollections. London, 1893. 2v.
43576.14.2100 Ducros, Emmanuel. Paris. Paris, 1893.
41538.10.6 Dumas, Alexandre. The chevalier d'Harmental. Boston, 1893.
41538.10.5 Dumas, Alexandre. The chevalier d'Harmental. Boston, 1893.
41538.20.6 Dumas, Alexandre. Les deux Diane. Paris, 1893. 3v.
41538.20.8.7 Dumas, Alexandre. The forty five. Boston, 1893.
41538.20.8.5 Dumas, Alexandre. The forty five. Boston, 1893.
41538.20.30A Dumas, Alexandre. The forty-five. v.1-2. Boston, 1893.
41538.29.2.5A Dumas, Alexandre. Marguerite de Valois. Boston, 1893.
41538.29.3 Dumas, Alexandre. Marguerite de Valois. Boston, 1893.
41538.61.18 Dumas, Alexandre. Memoirs of a physician. Boston, 1893. 3v.
41538.115 Dumas, Alexandre. Olympe de Cleves. Boston, 1893. 2v.
41530.339 Dumas, Alexandre. Olympe de Clèves. Boston, 1893. 2v.
41538.110 Dumas, Alexandre. The page of the duke of Savoy. Boston, 1893. 2v.
41538.63.31 Dumas, Alexandre. The queen's necklace. Boston, 1893. 2v.
41538.24.26 Dumas, Alexandre. The regent's daughter. Boston, 1893.
41529.50 Dumas, Alexandre. Romances. Boston, 1893-95. 54v.
NEDL 42543.11.7 Dumas, Alexandre. Théâtre complet. Paris, 1893-96. 7v.
41538.53.25 Dumas, Alexandre. The three musketeers. Boston, 1893. 2v.
41538.53.103 Dumas, Alexandre. Twenty years after. Boston, 1893. 2v.
Mol 605.2.2 Eloesser, A. Die älteste deutsche Übersetzung Molièrescher Lustspiele. Berlin, 1893.
Mol 605.2 Eloesser, A. Die älteste deutsche Übersetzung Molièrescher Lustspiele. Berlin, 1893.
Htn 42554.30* Elskamp, Max. Salutations. Bruxelles, 1893.
42575.39.50 Feuillet, Octave. A Parisian romance. N.Y., 1893.
40597.9.2 Flat, Paul. Essais sur Balzac. Paris, 1893.
42561.23 Fleury, Jules. The faience violin. N.Y., 1893.
40516.63A Ford, Clarence. The life and letters of Madame de Kruedener. London, 1893.
37543.53 Fortier, Alcée. Histoire de la littérature française. N.Y., 1893.
42586.53.25 Fouillée, A. (Mme.). Les enfants patriots. Boston, 1893.
42576.61 Franay, Gabriel. Mon chevalier. Paris, 1893.
41578.45 France, A. L'Elvire de Lamartine. Paris, 1893.
42576.62.7.3 France, Anatole. Les opinions de M. Jérôme Coignard. Paris, 1893.
42576.62.5.90 France, Anatole. La rôtisserie de la reine Pédauque. Paris, 1893.
42576.61.50 Frémine, Charles. La chanson du pays; récits normands. Paris, 1893.
38557.20 Freppel, Charles Émile. Bossuet et l'éloquence sacrée au XVIIe siècle. Paris, 1893. 2v.
38557.24.115 Gasté, Armand. Bossuet en Normandie. Caen, 1893.
NEDL FL 372.18.9 Gasté, Armand. Les drames liturgiques de la Cathédrale de Rouen. Evreux, 1893.
43616.89.3100 Gaud, Auguste. Au pays natal. Niort, 1893.
Mon 117.4 Gauthiez, P. Etudes sur le XVIe siècle. Paris, 1893.
43616.2.37 Gautier, Judith. Fleurs d'Orient. Paris, 1893.
43616.2.34 Gautier, Judith. Le vieux de la montagne. Paris, 1893.
Htn 41541.4.6* Gautier, Théophile. Le roi Candaule. Paris, 1893.
FL 398.35.12 Goncourt, Edmond de. La Guimard. Paris, 1893.
43625.3.71 Gourmont, Rémy de. Le fantome. Paris, 1893.
43625.3.67 Gourmont, Rémy de. Théodat. Paris, 1893.
42543.60.16 Grandmougin, Charles. L'empereur 1807-1821. Paris, 1893.
42515.35.122A Grant Duff, M.E. Ernest Renan. London, 1893.
40517.38.8 Gueulette, T.S. Thousand and one quarters of an hour. London, 1893.
42576.40.371 Halévy, Ludovic. La famille Cardinal. Paris, 1893.
42576.40.410 Halévy, Ludovic. Mariette. Paris, 1893.
42576.40.382 Halévy, Ludovic. A marriage for love. N.Y., 1893.
39527.6.10 Hédé-Haüy, A. Les illustrations des contes de La Fontaine. Paris, 1893.
NEDL 42554.55 Heredia, J.M. de. Les trophées. Paris, 1893.
42576.67.9 Hervieu, Paul. Les paroles restent. Paris, 1893.
42576.67.7 Hervieu, Paul. Peints par eux-mêmes. Paris, 1893.
37567.9.3 James, Henry. French poets and novelists. 2nd ed. London, 1893.
37567.38.2 Klein, Félix. Nouvelles tendances en religion et en littérature. Paris, 1893.

1893 - cont.

42543.16.27.5 Korvin-Krukovskii, P. Les Danicheff. Paris, 1893.
41584.29.40 La Borderie, Arthur de. Une illustration rennaise. Rennes, 1893.
41578.5.10 Lamartine, Alphonse de. Harmonies poétiques et religieuses. Paris, 1893.
37557.28 Larroumet, G. Études de littérature et d'art. Paris, 1893. 3v.
NEDL 37557.28 Larroumet, G. Études de littérature et d'art. v.4. Paris, 1893.
42544.31.25 Lecomte, Georges. Mirages. Paris, 1893.
37596.24.3 Leendertz, P. Het middelnederlandsche leerdicht rinclus. Amsterdam, 1893.
42544.31.35 Lefebure, H. Conte bleu. Paris, 1893.
42513.77 Leroy-Beaulieu, A. La papauté. Paris, 1893.
40513.28A Lintilhac, E. LeSage. Paris, 1893.
38575.31.10 Lippold, F. Bemerkungen zu Corneilles Cinna. Zwickan, 1893.
37571.31 Le livre d'or des annales politiques et littéraires. Paris, 1893.
42544.34.25.30 Lorde, André de. Monsieur, Madame et les autres. Paris, 1893.
Htn 42544.34.39* Louys, Pierre. Lêda. Paris, 1893.
42526.7 Lucas, Hippolyte. Chants de divers pays. Nantes, 1893.
41574.30 Mailleau, L. Victor Hugo. Paris, 1893.
42555.43 Mallarmé, Stéphane. Vers et prose. Paris, 1893.
Mol 613.2 Mangold, W. Archivalische Notizen zur franzosischen Literatur des 17. Jahrhunderts. Berlin, 1893.
42555.49.9 Marés, Roland de. Ariettes douloureuses. Paris, 1893.
42576.76.25 Margueritte, Paul. La mouche. Paris, 1893.
42576.76.21 Margueritte, Paul. Le tourmenté. Paris, 1893.
42577.4.26.2 Maupassant, Guy de. Contes et nouvelles. Paris, 1893.
42577.2.5 Maupassant, Guy de. La maison Tellier. Paris, 1893.
42577.4.29 Maupassant, Guy de. La paix du ménage. Paris, 1893.
42577.4.27.5 Maupassant, Guy de. Yvette. 18. éd. Paris, 1893.
37593.63 Meienriers, Richard. Adam de la Halle's Spiel, "Robin und Marion". München, 1893.
40539.20 Mercier, Barthelemy. Merceriana. Paris, 1893.
Mol 161.35 Molière, Jean Baptiste Poquelin. Amphitryon...Monval. Paris, 1893.
Mol 165.58 Molière, Jean Baptiste Poquelin. L'avare...Friese. Bielefeld, 1893.
Mol 165.59 Molière, Jean Baptiste Poquelin. L'avare...Monval. Paris, 1893.
Mol 218.20 Molière, Jean Baptiste Poquelin. George Dandin...Monval. Paris, 1893.
Mol 228.36 Molière, Jean Baptiste Poquelin. Le malade imaginaire...Pellisson. Paris, 1893.
Mol 245.54.3 Molière, Jean Baptiste Poquelin. Le misanthrope. Fasnacht. 2. éd. London, 1893.
Mol 18.93A Molière, Jean Baptiste Poquelin. Oeuvres complètes...Fournier. Paris, 1893. 12v.
Mol 251.54 Molière, Jean Baptiste Poquelin. Les précieuses ridicules. Jacquinet et Boully. Paris, 1893.
Mol 251.55 Molière, Jean Baptiste Poquelin. Les précieuses ridicules. Vapereau. 4. éd. Paris, 1893.
Mol 268.79 Molière, Jean Baptiste Poquelin. Le Tartuffe. Boully. Paris, 1893.
Mol 38.93 Molière, Jean Baptiste Poquelin. Théâtre choisi...Albert. 5e éd. Paris, 1893.
37596.77.5 Mondeville, H. de. Chirurgie de maitre H. de Mondeville. Paris, 1893.
Mon 18.93 Montaigne, Michel de. Essais, lettres, journal de voyage. 5e éd. Paris, 1893.
Mon 28.21 Montaigne, Michel de. Les essais. Paris, 1893.
Mon 28.20 Montaigne, Michel de. Essais. Paris, 1893.
Mon 30.9 Montaigne, Michel de. Essays. Florio (Chubb). London, 1893.
42533.14.10 Montégut, Émile. Esquisses littéraires. Paris, 1893.
Mol 803.4 Monval, G. Un comédien amateur d'art. Michel Baron. Paris, 1893.
42555.61.15 Moréas, Jean. Autant en emporte le vent. Paris, 1893.
41596.25 Musset, Alfred de. Frédéric et Bernerette. Paris, 1893.
42555.63.130 Nibor, Yann. Chansons et récits de mer. Paris, 1893?
39526.37 Noelle, A. Beiträge zum Studium der Fabel. Cuxhaven, 1893.
Mon 125.1 Owen, John. Skeptics of the French Renaissance. London, 1893.
FL 382.92 Parigot, Hippolyte. Le théâtre d'hier. Paris, 1893.
42545.69.5 Parodi, A. Théâtre. Paris, 1893. 2v.
40556.32A Paulhan, F. Joseph de Maistre. Paris, 1893.
37566.29.5 Pellissier, G. Essais de littérature contemporaine. Paris, 1893.
42515.35.223 Perraud, A. À propos de la mort et des funérailles de M. Ernest Renan. 2. éd. Paris, 1893.
37543.25.5 Petit de Julleville, L. Leçons de littérature française. 9. éd. Paris, 1893.
42587.49 Poictevin, Francis. Tout bas. Paris, 1893.
40522.9.9 Prévost, Antoine F. Manon Lescaut. Boston, 1893. 2v.
42578.31.27 Prévost, Marcel. L'automne d'une femme. Paris, 1893?
40573.22 Pyat, Félix. The rag-picker of Paris. 4. ed. N.Y., 1893.
42585.70 Quesada, G. de. Patriotismo; cuentos de guerra. N.Y., 1893.
38536.18.5 Rabelais, F. Oeuvres. 3. éd., v.1; 2. éd., v.2. Paris, 1893. 2v.
NEDL 38531.12 Rabelais, F. Works. London, 1893. 2v.
42578.18.3 Rabusson, Henry. Sans entraves. Paris, 1893.
38585.19.4 Racine, Jean. Andromaque, tragédie. London, 1893.
38585.20.2 Racine, Jean. Athalie. London, 1893.
42515.29.410A Renan, Ernest. L'antéchrist. 5. éd. Paris, 1893.
42515.29.370 Renan, Ernest. Saint Paul. 13. éd. Paris, 1893.
42515.30.718 Renan, Ernest. Souvenirs d'enfance et de jeunesse. Paris, 1893.
42515.30.720 Renan, Ernest. Souvenirs d'enfance et de jeunesse. 26. éd. Paris, 1893.
42515.30.404 Renan, Ernest. Studies in religious history. 2. ser. London, 1893?
42515.30.405 Renan, Ernest. Studies of religious history. London, 1893.
42515.29.35 Renan, Ernest. Vie de Jésus. 23. éd. Paris, 1893.
42587.50.1203 Renard, Georges. Un exilé. 3. éd. Paris, 1893.
NEDL 41574.28 Renouvier, Charles. Victor Hugo. Paris, 1893.
42556.27.150 Riffard, Léon. Pièces et morceaux. Paris, 1893.
41578.38 Rod, Edouard. Lamartine. Paris, 1893.
42578.19.7 Rod, Edouard. La vie privée de Michel Teissier. Paris, 1893.

Chronological Listing

1893 - cont.

FL 6031.93 Rousseau, J.J. Contrat social. Paris, 1893.
FL 6047.4 Rousseau, J.J. Emil oder über Erziehung. Langensalza, 1893. 2v.
FL 6036.10 Rousseau, J.J. The social contract. N.Y., 1893.
43757.94.1120 Roux, Paul. L'âme noire du prieur blanc. Paris, 1893.
42548.71 Le Rubicon. Paris, 1893.
41568.11.20 Saintine, Joseph Xavier Boniface. Picciola. N.Y., 1893.
41557.9.36 Sand, George. Convent life of George Sand. Boston, 1893.
41557.9.46.5 Sand, George. La mare au diable. London, 1893.
41557.9.81A Sand, George. Marianne. N.Y., 1893.
41557.9.48.7 Sand, Goerge. The haunted pool. N.Y., 1893.
FL 390.65 Sarcey, Francisque. Paris vivant; le théâtre. Paris, 1893.
42578.35.5 Sarcey, Francisque. Recollections of middle life. London, 1893.
42578.35.6 Sarcey, Francisque. Recollections of middle life. N.Y., 1893.
42546.30.7.9 Sardou, Victorien. Fédora. N.Y., 1893.
39534.33 Scarron, Paul. Jodelet Duelliste und seine spanischen Quellen. Erlangen, 1893.
42578.36.17 Schultz, Jeanne. The story of Colette. N.Y., 1893.
FL 398.80 Séchan, C. Souvenirs d'un homme de théâtre. Paris, 1893.
37565.41 Séché, L. Éducateurs et moralistes. Paris, 1893.
41558.68A Souvestre, Émile. An attic philosopher in Paris. N.Y., 1893.
37555.23 Sudre, Léopold. Publii Ovidii Nasonis Metamorphoseon Libros. Paris, 1893.
42578.52.25 Tinseau, Léon de. Ma cousine Pot-au-feu et, Le mariage au gant. 16. éd. Paris, 1893.
42578.52.30 Tinseau, Léon de. Maître Gratien. 4. éd. Paris, 1893.
37555.313 Tisseur, C. Modestes observations sur l'art de versifier. Lyon, 1893.
39534.36 Toldo, Pierre. Ce que Scarron doit aux auteurs burlesques d'Italie. Paris, 1893.
39564.18 Tolemache, B.L. Diderot's thoughts on art and style. London, 1893.
42578.56.25 Toutain, Paul. Ascension. Paris, 1893.
38541.16 Urbain, Charles. Nicolas Coeffeteau Dominican. Paris, 1893.
42547.11.15 Vaucaire, Maurice. Le poète et le financier. Paris, 1893.
42547.11.13 Vaucaire, Maurice. Valet de coeur. Paris, 1893.
Htn 42557.19.70* Verlaine, Paul. Élégies. Paris, 1893.
Htn 42557.19.45* Verlaine, Paul. Mes prisons. Paris, 1893.
Htn 42557.19.30* Verlaine, Paul. Odes en son honneur. Paris, 1893.
42582.32 Verne, Jules. Die Familie ohne Namen. v.1-2. Wien, 1893.
42576.47.30 Viaud, Julien. Aziyadé. 22. éd. Paris, 1893.
42576.57 Viaud, Julien. L'exilée. Paris, 1893.
42576.56 Viaud, Julien. Madame Chrysanthème. 15. éd. Paris, 1893.
42576.57.4.2 Viaud, Julien. Matelot. Paris, 1893.
42557.22 Vielé-Griffin, F. La chevauchée d'Yeldis et autres poèmes (1892). Paris, 1893.
42587.66.19 Vigné d'Octon, P. Les angoisses du Docteur Combalas. Paris, 1893.
41564.5 Vigny, Alfred de. Cinq-Mars. London, 1893.
42547.18 Villiers de l'Isle Adam, Auguste. Premières poésies 1856-1858. Bruxelles, 1893.
42522.10.2 Vogüé, E.M. de. Coeurs Russes. Paris, 1893.
39544.28.5 Voltaire, François Marie Arouet de. Lettres choisies. Paris, 1893. 2v.
41583.32.20 Vuacheux, Ferdinand. Casimir Delavigne. Havre, 1893.
42584.11.5 Zola, Emile. La débâcle. Paris, 1893.
42584.13.2 Zola, Emile. Le docteur Pascal. Paris, 1893.
42584.13.5 Zola, Emile. Le docteur Pascal. Paris, 1893.
42584.1.25 Zola, Emile. The experimental novel. N.Y., 1893.
X Cg 42584.17.3 Zola, Emile. Le roman expérimental. Paris, 1893.
42584.11.25 Zola, Emile. Slom. [La débâcle]. Beograd, 1893.

1894

FL 391.102 Aderer, A. Le théâtre à Côté. Paris, 1894.
37543.10.2 Albert, Paul. La littérature française des origines au XVIe siècle. 8. éd. Paris, 1894.
39574.27.3 Alembert, J. Le Rond d'. Discours préliminaire de l'encyclopédie. Paris, 1894.
FL 395.155 Alencon, Edouard d'. Masque i besace. Roma, 1894.
41564.35 Alfred de Vigny et la poésie politique. Paris, 1894.
Mol 870.48.2 Augé de Lassus, L. Les grands maîtres mis en petites comédies. 2. éd. Paris, 1894.
42562.38.100.5 Auschitsky, Daniel. L'épiscopat sous le joug. Paris, 1894.
40596.13.12 Balzac, Honoré de. Cathérine de Médici. Boston, 1894.
40596.13.72 Balzac, Honoré de. César Birotteau. Boston, 1894.
40596.13.42 Balzac, Honoré de. The lily of the valley. Boston, 1894.
40596.13.64 Balzac, Honoré de. Memoirs of two young married women. Boston, 1894.
42561.9.10 Barrès, M. Une journée parlementaire. Paris, 1894.
41522.13.9.8 Baudelaire, Charles. Les fleurs du mal. Paris, 1894.
42563.22.75 Beer, Guillaume (Mme.). La voie douloureuse. Paris, 1894.
41574.21.3 Biré, Edmond. Victor Hugo après 1852. Paris, 1894.
42542.30.8 Bouchor, Maurice. Les mystères d'Elensis. Paris, 1894.
42542.30.20 Bouchor, Maurice. Les mystères d'Éleusis, en quatre tableaux, en vers. Paris, 1894.
42563.37.16A Bourget, Paul. Cosmopolis. Paris, 1894.
42563.37.15.5 Bourget, Paul. Extraits choisis des oeuvres. Boston, 1894.
Htn 42563.37.17* Bourget, Paul. Un saint. Paris, 1894.
Htn 42563.37.18* Bourget, Paul. Steeple-chase. Paris, 1894.
NEDL 38525.5.3 Brachet, Auguste. Morceaux choisis...du XVIe siècle. 7e éd. Paris, 1894.
37543.109 Brisson, A. Portraits intimes. Paris, 1894. 5v.
37544.67 Brun, Felix. L'alouette; histoire littéraire d'un petit oiseau. Meulan, 1894.
37567.45 Brunetière, Ferdinand. L'evolution de la poésie lyrique en France au dix-neuvième siècle. Paris, 1894. 2v.
Mol 165.63 Bué, H. The new conversational French reader. London, 1894.
FL 6128.94 Buffenois, H. Une journée à Ermenonville. n.p., 1894.
42542.47.65 Busnach, W. L'assommoir. Paris, 1894.
42557.5.85 Cazals, F.A. Laurent Tailhade. Paris, 1894.
42554.18.12 Champon, C. Chansons nouvelles. Paris, 1894.
NEDL 40586.18.13 Chateaubriand, F.A.R. Génie du Christianisme. v.1-2. Paris, 1894.
42586.31.14 Claretié, J. La frontière. Paris, 1894.
X Cg 40513.26 Claretie, Leo. LeSage. Paris, 1894.
41596.4.2 Claveau, A. Alfred de Musset. Paris, 1894.
40556.34 Cogordan, G. Joseph de Maistre. Paris, 1894.

1894 - cont.

X Cg 38575.26.10 Corneille, Pierre. Le Cid. N.Y., 1894.
37567.391.4 Crane, T.F. Le romantisme français, 1824-1848. 4. éd. N.Y., 1894.
38512.13A Darmesteter, Mary. Froissart. Paris, 1894.
42566.55 Daudet, Alphonse. Entre les frises et la rampe. Paris, 1894.
42566.24.17 Daudet, Alphonse. Fromont jeune et Risler ainé. Paris, 1894.
42566.17.100A Daudet, Alphonse. Morceaux choisis d'Alphonse Daudet. Boston, 1894.
42566.31.10 Daudet, Alphonse. Le petit chose. N.Y., 1894.
42566.35.25 Daudet, Alphonse. Tartarin on the Alps. N.Y., 1894.
41583.28.9 Delavigne, Casimir. Louis XI. London, 1894.
42554.29.4.10 Déroulède, Paul. Chants du paysan. Paris, 1894.
42542.64.15 Descamps, E. Afrika; preisgekröntes Drama in fünf Aufzügen. Münster, 1894.
37557.35A Deschamps, G. La vie et les livres. Série 1-5. Paris, 1894. 5v.
37567.52 Deschamps, Gaston. La vie et les livres. Paris, 1894. 6v.
42554.29.6 Destrée, O.G. Poèmes sans rimes. London, 1894.
43568.85 Dieulefit, J. Contes celtiques. Paris, 1894.
42588.4 Dilettantes. Paris, 1894.
42542.65.11 Donnay, Maurice. Phryné. Paris, 1894.
42576.15.60 Doublet, G. La composition de Salambô. Toulouse, 1894.
37567.35.2 Doumic, René. Écrivains d'aujourd'hui. Paris, 1894.
38521.11 Du Bellay, Joachim. Oeuvres choisies. Paris, 1894.
39566.7A Ducros, Louis. Diderot - l'homme et l'écrivain. Paris, 1894.
41538.2.7 Dumas, Alexandre. Ange Pitou. Boston, 1894. 2v.
41538.70 Dumas, Alexandre. The Chevalier de Maison-Rouge. Paris, 1894. 2v.
41538.125 Dumas, Alexandre. The companions of Jehu. Boston, 1894. 2v.
41530.336 Dumas, Alexandre. The companions of Jehu. Boston, 1894. 2v.
41530.321 Dumas, Alexandre. The company of Jehu. Boston, 1894.
41538.150 Dumas, Alexandre. The company of Jehu. Boston, 1894.
41529.100.3 Dumas, Alexandre. The company of Jehu. Boston, 1894. 2v.
41538.16.8.48 Dumas, Alexandre. Comtesse de Charny. Boston, 1894. 3v.
41538.16.6 Dumas, Alexandre. Count of Monte Cristo. Boston, 1894. 3v.
41538.16.5A Dumas, Alexandre. Count of Monte Cristo. Boston, 1894. 3v.
41538.16.6.5 Dumas, Alexandre. Count of Monte Cristo. N.Y., 1894. 2v.
41538.20.8.10 Dumas, Alexandre. La dame de Monsoreau. v.1-2. Boston, 1894?
41529.76 Dumas, Alexandre. The duke's page. Boston, 1894. 2v.
41529.101.10 Dumas, Alexandre. The first republic. Boston, 1894. 2v.
41530.320 Dumas, Alexandre. The first republic. Boston, 1894.
41538.140 Dumas, Alexandre. The first republic. v.1-2. Boston, 1894.
41538.20.32 Dumas, Alexandre. The forty-five. v.1-2. Boston, 1894?
41525.20 Dumas, Alexandre. Impressions de voyage. Excursions sur les bords du Rhin. Paris, 1894.
41538.61.20 Dumas, Alexandre. Joseph Balsamo. Chicago, 1894.
41538.28.50 Dumas, Alexandre. The last Vendée. Boston, 1894.
41538.28.52 Dumas, Alexandre. The last Vendée. Boston, 1894.
41538.28.54 Dumas, Alexandre. The last Vendée. v.1-2. Boston, 1894.
41538.18.10 Dumas, Alexandre. Le chevalier de Maison-Rouge. Boston, 1894.
41529.77 Dumas, Alexandre. Olympe de Clèves. Boston, 1894. 2v.
41530.338 Dumas, Alexandre. The she-wolves of Machecoul. Boston, 1894. 2v.
41538.120 Dumas, Alexandre. The she-wolves of Machecoul and The Corsican brothers. Boston, 1894. 2v.
41538.10.8 Dumas, Alexandre. The chevalier d'Harmental. Boston, 1894?
42543.2 Dumas, Alexandre. Théâtre complet. 3. éd. Paris, 1894. 2v.
41538.53.27F Dumas, Alexandre. The three musketeers. N.Y., 1894. 2v.
41538.53.5F Dumas, Alexandre. Les trois mousquetaires. Paris, 1894. 2v.
41529.78 Dumas, Alexandre. The two Dianas. Boston, 1894. 3v.
41530.337 Dumas, Alexandre. The Whites and the Blues. Boston, 1894. 2v.
41538.83 Dumas, Alexandre. The whites and the blues. Boston, 1894. 2v.
42547.15.5 Du Pontairce de Heussey, R. Villiers de l'Isle Adam. London, 1894.
42568.23.14.35 Duval, Paul. Yanthis. Paris, 1894.
42554.31.100 Eichthal, Eugène d'. A la musique; sonnets. Chartres, 1894.
39577.80 Ellis, Henry. The centenary of Condorcet. London, 1894?
42573.20.5 Erckmann, Emile. Invasion of France in 1814. N.Y., 1894.
42573.25.4 Erckmann, Emile. The plebiscite or A miller's story of the war. N.Y., 1894.
42543.29.50 Eude, Émile. Le nouveau mystère du siège d'Orléans. Orléans, 1894.
42543.38.16 Fabre, Émile. Comme ils sont tous. Paris, 1894.
37563.20 Faguet, Emile. Seizième siècle; études littéraires. Paris, 1894.
FL 397.66.14 Fernand-Michel, P. Le théâtre antique d'Orange. Paris, 1894.
FL 397.66.15 Fernand-Michel, P. Le théâtre antique d'Orange. 2nd ed. Paris, 1894.
42571.18 Feuillet, Octave. Quelques années de ma vie. Paris, 1894.
42575.52.2 Feuillet, Octave. Quelques années de ma vie. Paris, 1894.
42575.52 Feuillet, Octave. Quelques années de ma vie. 4. éd. Paris, 1894.
42586.48.5 Feval, Paul H. Contes de Bretagne. Limoges, 1894.
41555.37 Filon, A. Mérimée et ses amis. Paris, 1894.
42576.19 Flaubert, Gustave. Un coeur simple. Paris, 1894.
NEDL 42576.35.2 Flaubert, Gustave. Correspondance. Paris, 1894-1905.
37543.22.4 Fleury, Jean. Histoire élémentaire de la littérature française. 9. éd. Paris, 1894.
40535.15.2 Font, Auguste. Favart l'opéra comique. Paris, 1894.
40537.54 Fouéré-Macé, M.E. Époque révolutionnaire; curiosités historiques. Rennes, 1894.
42576.62.10.2 France, Anatole. Le lys rouge. 2. éd. Paris, 1894.

Chronological Listing

1894 - cont.

42576.62.10.2.5 France, Anatole. Le lys rouge. 24. éd. Paris, 1894.
38527.43 Garnier, Robert. Cornelia von Thomas Kyd. München, 1894.
42554.40.55 Gauthiez, Pierre. Deux poèmes. Paris, 1894.
43616.2.42 Gautier, Judith. Iskender, histoire persane. Paris, 1894.
X Cg 41542.8.7 Gautier, Théophile. Émaux et camées. Paris, 1894.
Htn 41541.4* Gautier, Théophile. Une nuit de Cléopatre. Paris, 1894.
42543.45.60 Gavault, Paul. Le passant. Paris, 1894.
42576.5 Gebhart, Emile. Autour d'une tiare, 1075-1085. Paris, 1894.
43617.77.100 Germain, André. Famille! Paris, 1894.
42543.57 Goury, G. Vercingetorix. Paris, 1894.
37541.10 Goutier, Léon. La littérature catholique et nationale. Bruges, 1894.
40517.38 Gueulette, T.S. Transmigrations of the Mandarin Fum-Hoam. London, 1894.
40517.38.2 Gueulette, T.S. Transmigrations of the Mandarin Fum-Hoam. London, 1894.
42576.40.428A Halévy, Ludovic. Parisian point of view. N.Y., 1894.
42576.40.426 Halévy, Ludovic. Parisian point of view. N.Y., 1894.
42576.40.429 Halévy, Ludovic. Parisian point of view. N.Y., 1894.
42576.40.425 Halévy, Ludovic. Parisian point of view. N.Y., 1894.
42576.40.385 Halévy, Ludovic. Les petites Cardinal. 49. éd. Paris, 1894.
Htn 42543.62.47* Haraucourt, Edmond. L'effort. Paris, 1894.
38576.19.3.2 Hauteroche, N. le B. de. Crispin médecin. Paris, 1894.
42543.64.5 Hermant, Abel. La carrière. Paris, 1894.
38585.16.100 Houben, H. Der Chor in den Tragödien des Racine. Düsseldorf, 1894.
41572.7.18 Hugo, Victor. Hans of Iceland. Boston, 1894.
NEDL 41573.32.10 Hugo, Victor. Hernani. N.Y., 1894-
41573.26.17 Hugo, Victor. Ruy Blas. Boston, 1894.
41573.48 Hugo, Victor. Works. Boston, 1894.
38537.19 Huguet, Edmond. Étude sur la syntax de Rabelais. Paris, 1894.
FL 6138.94 Izoulet, Jean. De Jean-Jacques Rousseau (Jean-Jacques Rousseau) utrum misopolis fuerit an philopolis. Paris, 1894.
39527.4.13 Jahnow, Alfred. Beobachtungen über La Fontaine's Fabeln. Strehlen, 1894. 2v.
37594.13 Jarry, L. Deux chansons normandes. Orléans, 1894.
37543.40 Junker, Heinrich P. Grundriss des Geschichte der französischen Litteratur. Münster, 1894.
FL 398.74.66 Kennard, Nina H. Rachel. London, 1894.
39545.18.5 Klemperer, W. Voltaire und die Judin. Berlin, 1894.
38527.46 Körner, Paul. Der Versbau Robert Garniers. Berlin, 1894.
Mon 28.22 La Brière, L. de. Montaigne chrétien. Paris, 1894.
41564.36.5 Lafond, Paul. Alfred de Vigny en Béarn. Pau, 1894.
39525.5 La Fontaine, Jean de. Oeuvres diverses. Paris, 1894.
41578.34.5 Lamartine, Alphonse. Philosophie et littérature. Paris, 1894.
NEDL 38557.18 Lanson, G. Bossuet. Paris, 1894.
X Cg 40535.31.10 Larroumet, Gustave. Marivaux. Paris, 1894.
42513.60.2 Laveleye, Emile de. Essais et études. 1st serie, 1861-75, 2d serie, 1875-82, 3d serie 1883-1892. Paris, 1894. 3v.
41586.8.5 Laya, Léon. Le duc job; comédie en quatre actes et en prose. Paris, 1894.
42576.42.9 Le Barillier, Berthe. Le mime Barthylle. Paris, 1894.
41593.12.9 Le Mouel, Eugène. Kèmenes. Paris, 1894.
37555.31 Lenient, Charles. La poésie patriotique en France dans les temps modernes. Paris, 1894. 2v.
37573.594.5 Leune, Albert. Difficult modern French. Boston, 1894.
37542.24 Lintilhac, Gustave. Études littéraires sur les classiques français de G. Merlet. Paris, 1894. 2v.
38527.31.9 Lücken, E. Zur Syntax Montchrétiens. Darmstadt, 1894.
Htn FL 380.12* Lumiere, Henry. Le théâtre français pendant la révolution. Paris, 1894.
42545.3.2 Maeterlinck, Maurice. Alladine et Palomides. 2e éd. Bruxelles, 1894.
42545.3.2.5 Maeterlinck, Maurice. Alladine et Palomides. 4e éd. Bruxelles, 1894.
42545.3.3.5 Maeterlinck, Maurice. Pélléas et Mélisande. N.Y., 1894.
42545.3.7.6 Maeterlinck, Maurice. Plays. Ser. 1. Chicago, 1894.
38526.32.20 Marguerite d'Angoulême. The Heptaméron. London, 1894. 5v.
42576.76.22 Margueritte, Paul. Ame d'enfant. Paris, 1894.
42576.76.27 Margueritte, Paul. L'avril. Paris, 1894.
42555.49.22 Martin, Gabriel. Les poésies fantaisistes. Paris, 1894.
37555.18.9 Martonne, Alfred de. Le sonnet dans midi de la France. Aix, 1894.
42577.34.6 Masson-Forestier, A. La jambe coupée. Paris, 1894.
42577.1.05 Maupassant, Guy de. Contes de la bécasse. 6. éd. Paris, 1894.
42577.4.20.10 Maupassant, Guy de. L'inutile beauté. 26. éd. Paris, 1894.
42577.4.11.5 Maupassant, Guy de. Notre coeur. 69. éd. Paris, 1894.
37543.73 Mazzoni, Guido. Il teatro della rivoluzione. Bologna, 1894.
42545.10.26 Meilhac, Henri. Gotte. Paris, 1894.
42545.10.20 Meilhac, Henri. Ma camarade. Paris, 1894.
42545.10.33 Meilhac, Henri. Pepa. Paris, 1894.
41555.23.2.5 Mérimée, Prosper. Colomba. London, 1894.
41555.23.3 Mérimée, Prosper. Colomba. N.Y., 1894.
42545.21.11 Méténier, Oscar. Demi-castors. Paris, 1894.
Mol 151.15 Molière, Jean Baptiste Poquelin. Les amants magnifiques...Monval. Paris, 1894.
Mol 165.60 Molière, Jean Baptiste Poquelin. L'avare...Boully. Paris, 1894.
Mol 165.62 Molière, Jean Baptiste Poquelin. L'avare...Henckels. Boston, 1894.
Mol 165.61 Molière, Jean Baptiste Poquelin. L'avare. Boston, 1894.
Mol 171.46 Molière, Jean Baptiste Poquelin. Le bourgeois gentilhomme...Monval. Paris, 1894.
NEDL Mol 60.25 Molière, Jean Baptiste Poquelin. Comedies...Mathew. 3rd ed. London, 1894.
Mol 211.50 Molière, Jean Baptiste Poquelin. Les femmes savantes...Figuière. 2e éd. Paris, 1894.
Mol 211.51 Molière, Jean Baptiste Poquelin. Les femmes savantes...Henry. Paris, 1894.
Mol 211.52 Molière, Jean Baptiste Poquelin. Les femmes savantes...Pellisson. 6e éd. Paris, 1894.
Mol 211.53 Molière, Jean Baptiste Poquelin. Les femmes savantes...Scheffler. Bielefeld, 1894.
Mol 215.36 Molière, Jean Baptiste Poquelin. Les Fourberies...de Scapin...Gasc. London, 1894.
Mol 248.35 Molière, Jean Baptiste Poquelin. M. de Pourceaugnac. Monval. Paris, 1894.

1894 - cont.

Mol 245.73 Molière, Jean Baptiste Poquelin. Le misanthrope. Braunholtz. Cambridge, 1894.
Mol 60.26A Molière, Jean Baptiste Poquelin. Molière...K.P. Wormeley. Boston, 1894-97. 6v.
Mol 18.94 Molière, Jean Baptiste Poquelin. Oeuvres complètes. v.1-3,4-6,7-9,10-12,15-16. Paris, 1894. 5v.
Mol 251.56 Molière, Jean Baptiste Poquelin. Les précieuses ridicules. A. Dupuis. London, 1894.
Mol 268.81 Molière, Jean Baptiste Poquelin. Le Tartuffe. Monval. Paris, 1894.
Mol 268.82 Molière, Jean Baptiste Poquelin. Le Tartuffe. Pellisson. 4. éd. Paris, 1894.
42584.25.5.5 Moncoq. Réponse complète au Lourdes de Emile Zola. Caen, 1894.
37567.46 Monod, Gabriel. Renan, Taine, Michelet. Paris, 1894.
Mon 31.42 Montaigne, Michel de. Essays. Hazlitt. v.1-2. N.Y., 1894?
Mon 28.18.3 Montaigne, Michel de. Extraits. Réaume. Paris, 1894.
40526.8 Morillot, Paul. André Chénier. Paris, 1894.
38513.7 Mostert, Wilhelm. Das Mystère de Saint Genis. Marburg, 1894.
41596.16.10 Musset, Alfred de. Mélanges de littérature. Paris, 1894.
41556.30 Nodier, Charles. Inès de las Sierras. Paris, 1894.
42555.66.55 Nolhac, Pierre de. Paysage de France et d'Italie. Paris, 1894.
42545.46 Normand, J. La muse qui trotte. Paris, 1894.
42555.68.130 Olivaint, Maurice. Fleurs du Mé-kong; poésies. Paris, 1894.
42556.37.30 Pagnerre, Edmond. Poésies. Fécamp, 1894?
FL 360.45 Parigot, H. Génie et Métier. Paris, 1894.
42578.30.52 Peladan, J. Comment on devient artiste; ésthétique. Paris, 1894.
37576.539 Pène Du Bois, H. French folly in maxims of philosophy. N.Y., 1894.
42578.31.28.2 Prévost, Marcel. Les demi-vièrges. 45. éd. Paris, 1894.
42578.31.28 Prévost, Marcel. Les demi-vièrges. 60. éd. Paris, 1894.
42578.31.26 Prévost, Marcel. Nouvelles lettres de femmes. 11. éd. Paris, 1894.
42578.31.26.5 Prévost, Marcel. Nouvelles lettres de femmes. 22. éd. Paris, 1894.
37567.151 Pujo, Maurice. Le règne de la grâce. Paris, 1894.
42578.18.12 Rameau, Jean. Mademoiselle Azur. Paris, 1894.
42578.18.5 Rameau, Jean. La rose de Grenade. Paris, 1894.
42587.50.85 Rebell, Hugues. Union des trois aristocraties. Paris, 1894.
42556.24.5 Régnier, Henri de. Contes à soi-même. Paris, 1894.
39566.8A Reinach, Joseph. Diderot. Paris, 1894.
42515.27.8 Renan, Ernest. Histoire des origines du christianisme. v.2. Paris, 1894.
42515.25.14 Renan, Ernest. Pages choisies. 9. éd. Paris, 1894.
Mol 870.49 Rengade, J. Novus doctor. Paris, 1894.
42556.22.50 Richepin, Jean. Vers la joie; conte bleu. Paris, 1894.
43756.66.100 Riotor, Léon. Le parabolain. Paris, 1894.
42578.19.8.10A Rod, Edouard. Études sur le 19. siècle. 2. éd. Paris, 1894.
42578.19.33A Rod, Edouard. Michel Teissier. Paris, 1894.
42578.19.10.5A Rod, Edouard. La seconde vie de Michel Teissier. Paris, 1894.
42578.19.10 Rod, Edouard. La seconde vie de Michel Teissier. Paris, 1894.
42578.19.9 Rod, Edouard. Le silence. Paris, 1894.
42578.19.9.5 Rod, Edouard. Le silence. 12. éd. Paris, 1894.
42578.22.170 Rosny, J.H. L'impérieuse bonté. Paris, 1894.
42578.22.8.16 Rosny, J.H. Renouveau. Paris, 1894.
42546.15.22 St. Geniès, Richard. Place au théâtre! 3e éd. Paris, 1894.
40576.3.5 Sainte-Beuve, Charles A. Causeries du lundi. 3. éd. Paris, 1894.
37543.21.15 Saintsbury, George. Primer of French literature. 3. ed. Oxford, 1894.
41557.9.26 Sand, George. The countess of Rudolstadt. N.Y., 1894.
41557.9.64 Sand, George. François the waif. N.Y., 1894.
41557.9.66 Sand, George. François the waif. N.Y., 1894.
41557.9.5 Sand, George. Pages choisies des Grands Écrivains. Paris, 1894.
41557.19.15 Sandeau, Jules. Mademoiselle de la Seiglière. London, 1894.
42546.24.6 Sardou, Victorien. Divorçons! 22e éd. Paris, 1894.
38527.31.10 Scholl, Sigmund. Die Vergleiche in Montchrétiens Tragödien. Nördlingen, 1894.
37591.24.5 Schulze, A. Predigten des St. Bernhard. Tübingen, 1894.
42587.57.34 Schwob, Marcel. Le livre de Monelle. Paris, 1894.
37596.4.5 Sepet, M. Un drame religieux du Moyen Âge. Paris, 1894.
42566.16.4 Sherard, R.H. Alphonse Daudet. London, 1894.
37567.51 Spoelberch de Lovenjoul, Charles. Les lundis d'un chercheur. Paris, 1894.
40592.32 Staël Holstein, Anne Louise. Corinne, or Italy. Philadelphia, 1894. 2v.
43779.24.3110 Stéphane, Marc. Savants devis et joyeux rythmes d'un buveur de soleil. Paris, 1894.
42536.11 Taine, Hippolyte. Derniers essais de critique et d'histoire. Paris, 1894.
Htn 42547.1* Thalasso, Adolphe. L'art. Paris, 1894.
42583.33.21 Theuriet, André. Paternité. Paris, 1894.
42557.6.5 Tiercelin, Louis. Trois drames en vers. Paris, 1894.
42578.52.35 Tinseau, Léon de. Le chemin de Damas. Paris, 1894.
42557.7 Tisseur, Clair. Pauca Paucis. Lyon, 1894.
37555.301.2 Tobler, A. Vom Französischen Versbau alter und neuer Zeit. 3. Aufl. Leipzig, 1894.
42578.56.30 Toutain, Paul. Multiple vie. Paris, 1894.
37573.594 Van Daell, Alphonse Naus. An introduction to French authors. Boston, 1894.
Htn 42557.19.20* Verlaine, Paul. Dans les limbes. Paris, 1894.
Htn 42557.19.25* Verlaine, Paul. Dédicaces. Paris, 1894.
42557.20 Verlaine, Paul. Epigrammes. Paris, 1894.
42581.10.5 Verne, Jules. L'île mystèrieuse. Paris, 1894.
Mol 622.2 Veselovskii, A. Etiudy i Kharateristiki. Moskva, 1894.
X Cg 42576.52.9 Viaud, Julien. An Iceland fisherman. N.Y., 1894.
39545.66.80 Voltaire, François Marie Arouet de. Zadig et micromégas. London, 1894.
38537.25.18 Walter, Dott. Rabelais e la circulazione del sangue. Genova, 1894.
39544.167 Wheeler, J.M. Voltaire; a sketch of his life and work with selections from his writings. London, 1894.
40596.13 Wormeley, K.P. A memoir of Honoré de Balzac. Boston, 1894.
42559.97.15 Xanrof, Léon. L'amour et la vie. Paris, 1894.

Chronological Listing

1894 - cont.

42584.8.9 Zola, Emile. La conquête de Plassans. Paris, 1894.

42584.13.105 Zola, Emile. Lourdes. Paris, 1894.

42584.13.100 Zola, Emile. Lourdes. Paris, 1894.

37574.57 Zuccaro, L. L'Italie dans la poèsie française contemporaine. Milano, 1894.

1895

42578.30.80 Aeschylus. Sâr Peladan. Paris, 1895.

37565.15.6 Albert, Paul. Littérature française au XVIIIe siècle. Paris, 1895.

42515.35.8 Allier, Raoul. La philosophie d'Ernest Renan. Paris, 1895.

42562.65.5 Aubanel, Henry. Historiettes. Paris, 1895.

38527.20 Aubigné, Théodore Agrippa d'. Avantures du Baron de Foeneste. v.1-2. Paris, 1895.

Mon 112.6 Bailey, W.H. Shakespeare and Montaigne. Manchester, 1895.

43537.50.130 Baldensperger, F. Mezza voie. Paris, 1895.

40596.12.2 Balzac, Honoré de. At the sign of the cat and racket. London, 1895.

40597.37 Balzac, Honoré de. At the sign of the cat and racket. London, 1895.

40596.13.6 Balzac, Honoré de. Béatrix. Boston, 1895.

40596.12.7 Balzac, Honoré de. The Chouans. London, 1895.

40597.38 Balzac, Honoré de. The chouans. London, 1895.

40596.13.110 Balzac, Honoré de. Comédie humaine. London, 1895-98. 40v.

40597.40 Balzac, Honoré de. The country doctor. London, 1895.

40596.13.22 Balzac, Honoré de. A daughter of Eve. Boston, 1895.

40596.12.14A Balzac, Honoré de. Eugénie Grandet. London, 1895.

40597.19.15 Balzac, Honoré de. Eugénie Grandet. N.Y., 1895.

40597.77A Balzac, Honoré de. Ferragus, chief of the Devorants. Boston, 1895.

40596.12.31A Balzac, Honoré de. The guest of the absolute. London, 1895.

40596.13.100 Balzac, Honoré de. Honoré de Balzac. v.1-49,51-53. Philadelphia, 1895-1900. 52v.

40596.13.76 Balzac, Honoré de. The lily of the valley. Boston, 1895.

40596.13.46 Balzac, Honoré de. Lucien de Rubempré. Boston, 1895.

40596.13.50 Balzac, Honoré de. The marriage contract. Boston, 1895.

40596.13.114 Balzac, Honoré de. Novels. Philadelphia, 1895-1900. 50v.

40596.16 Balzac, Honoré de. Pages choisies. Paris, 1895.

40597.42 Balzac, Honoré de. The quest of the absolute. London, 1895.

40596.13.70 Balzac, Honoré de. Sons of the soil. Boston, 1895.

40596.13.60 Balzac, Honoré de. A start in life. Boston, 1895.

40596.12.37 Balzac, Honoré de. Ursule Mirouet. London, 1895.

40597.43 Balzac, Honoré de. Ursule Mirouet. London, 1895.

40597.39 Balzac, Honoré de. The wild ass's skin. London, 1895.

40596.12.38 Balzac, Honoré de. The wild ass's skin. London, 1895.

38547.9 Banti, Charlotte. L'Amyntas du Tasse et l'Astrée d'Honoré d'Urfé. Milan, 1895.

43537.6.33 Barbusse, Henri. Pleureuses. Paris, 1895.

40554.21 Barthélemy-Saint Hilaire, J. Victor Cousin, sa vie, sa correspondance. Paris, 1895. 3v.

42563.26.11 Bauer, Henry. Mémoires d'un jeune homme. Paris, 1895.

FL 398.7.7 Becque, Henry. Souvenirs d'un auteur dramatique. Paris, 1895.

41592.27 Béranger, P.J. de. Songs of France. Philadelphia, 1895.

37567.50 Bérenger, H. L'aristocratie intellectuelle. Paris, 1895.

40582.8.8.2 Beyle, Henri. Chartreuse de Parme. N.Y., 1895. 3v.

Htn 40582.8.8* Beyle, Henri. Chartreuse de Parme. N.Y., 1895. 3v.

40582.24.2 Beyle, Henri. Le rouge et le noir. Paris, 1895. 2v.

37567.55 Biré, Edmond. Histoire et littérature. Lyon, 1895.

42584.25.12 Boissarie, P.G. Zola. Paris, 1895.

42542.29.115 Boniface, Maurice. La tante Léontine. 2. éd. Paris, 1895.

37567.47 Bordeaux, H. La vie et l'art. Ames modernes. Paris, 1895.

42542.29.136 Bornier, Henri de. La fille de Roland. N.Y., 1895.

42554.15.9 Bouchaud, P. de. Rythmes et nombres. Paris, 1895.

42542.30.13 Bouchor, Maurice. Les symboles. Paris, 1895.

42586.23 Bounières, R. de. Lord Hyland. Histoire véritable. Paris, 1895.

38543.3A Bourdeaux, J. La Rochefoucauld. 1930. Paris, 1895.

X Cg 37567.15.10 Bourget, Paul. Essais de psychologie contemporaine. 9e éd. Paris, 1895.

42563.37.12.25 Bourget, Paul. The land of promise. N.Y., 1895.

42563.37.17.5 Bourget, Paul. A saint. Boston, 1895.

38523.17 Bourrienne, Gustave. Malherbe, Points obscurs de sa vie Normande. Paris, 1895.

42542.47.16 Brieux, Eugène. La rose bleue. Paris, 1895.

37543.102 Brisson, A. La comédie littéraire. Paris, 1895.

42566.17 Brivois, Jules. Essai de bibliographie des oeuvres de Daudet. Paris, 1895.

37567.45.4 Brunetière, Ferdinand. L'evolution de la poésie lyrique en France au dix-neuvième siècle. 2. éd. Paris, 1895.

37567.36.2 Brunetière, Ferdinand. Nouveaux essais sur la littérature contemporaine. Paris, 1895.

FL 6128.95.2 Buffenois, H. Jean-Jacques Rousseau et ses visiteurs. Paris, 1895.

42586.52.12 Caillot-Duval (pseud.). Correspondance philosophique de Caillot-Duval. Nancy, 1895.

Mol 870.51 Caristie-Martel. Célimène aux enfers. Paris, 1895.

41592.10 Causeret, Charles. Béranger. Paris, 1895.

FL 6049.4 Censori, V. Dei criteri educativi di J.J. Rousseau. Tivoli, 1895.

40585.420 Chateaubriand, F.A.R. Lectures choisies de Chateaubriand. Paris, 1895.

42554.18.15 Chavanne, A. Murmures. Paris, 1895.

42554.18.90 Clarens, J.P. L'éternelle douleur. Paris, 1895.

39566.6.2 Collignon, Albert. Diderot, sa vie et ses oeuvres, sa correspondance. Paris, 1895.

37543.42.5 Collignon, Albert. La vie littéraire. Paris, 1895.

42576.15.9 Commauville, Carol. Souvenirs sur Gustave Flaubert. Paris, 1895.

39545.2.5 Condorcet, Marie Jean A.N.C. Vie de Voltaire. Paris, 1895.

40553.9.45 Constant de Rebecque, Benjamin. Journal intime et lettres à sa famille et à ses amis. Paris, 1895.

42524.34.10 Contades, G. de. Flers (souvenirs litteraires). Discours. Alençon, 1895.

42554.19 Coppée, François. Pour la Couronne. Drame en cinq actes, en vers. Paris, 1895.

42559.13.5 Couyba, Charles Maurice. Nouvelles chansons, rêves, joies, regrets. Paris, 1895.

42513.3 Darmesteter, James. Selected essays. Boston, 1895.

1895 - cont.

38512.13.2 Darmesteter, Mary. Froissart. N.Y., 1895.

42566.53A Daudet, Alphonse. La petite paroisse. Moeurs conjugales. Paris, 1895.

42566.34.6 Daudet, Alphonse. Sapho. N.Y., 1895.

42566.19.8.79 Daudet, Alphonse. Tartarin de Tarascon. N.Y., 1895.

41583.27.15 Delavigne, Casimir. Les enfans d'Edouard. Cambridge, 1895.

37567.74 Delfour, L.C. La religion des contemporains. Paris, 1895. 4v.

FL 398.17.15 Desclée, Aimée. Lettres. 3e éd. Paris, 1895.

FL 398.17.16 Desclée, Aimée. Lettres de Aimée Desclée à Fanfan. Paris, 1895.

40556.31.2 Descostes, François. Joseph de Maistre pendant la révolution. Tours, 1895.

41557.10.15 Devaux, A. George Sand; étude à laquelle l'académie française a décerneé le prix d'éloquence en 1894. Paris, 1895.

38527.72 Le dict des jardiniers. Paris? 1895?

38528.8.8 Dieterle, Hans. Henri Estienne. Strassburg, 1895.

43573.14.55 Docquois, G. Bêtes et gens de lettres. Paris, 1895.

42524.42 Doumic, René. La vie et les moeurs au jour le jour. Paris, 1895.

41529.90 Dumas, Alexandre. Ange Pitou. Boston, 1895. 2v.

41529.85 Dumas, Alexandre. Ascanio. Boston, 1895. 2v.

41538.5.15 Dumas, Alexandre. Ascanio. Boston, 1895.

41538.5.16 Dumas, Alexandre. Ascanio. Boston, 1895.

41538.5.50 Dumas, Alexandre. The ball of snow, to which is added Sultanetta. Boston, 1895.

41529.85.20A Dumas, Alexandre. Black. The story of a dog. Boston, 1895.

41538.70.85 Dumas, Alexandre. The black tulip. Boston, 1895.

41538.42 Dumas, Alexandre. Celebrated crimes. Philadelphia, 1895. 8v.

41529.55 Dumas, Alexandre. The celebrated crimes of history. N.Y., 1895. 8v.

41529.100 Dumas, Alexandre. The companions of Jehu. Boston, 1895. 2v.

41538.96 Dumas, Alexandre. La guerre des femmes. Paris, 1895. 2v.

41529.91 Dumas, Alexandre. Memoirs of a physician. v.2-3. v.1 lost 1931. Boston, 1895. 2v.

41538.100 Dumas, Alexandre. Tales of the Caucasus. Boston, 1895.

41538.95 Dumas, Alexandre. The war of women. Boston, 1895.

41529.101 Dumas, Alexandre. The whites and the blues. Boston, 1895. 2v.

40531.16 Dutrait, Maurice. Étude sur la vie de Crébillon (1674-1762). Bordeaux, 1895.

38537.13.5 Ellmer, W. Rabelais' Gargantua und Fischarts Geschichtklitterung. Weimar, 1895.

42515.35.89A Espinasse, Francis. Life of Ernest Renan. London, 1895.

42543.38.9 Fabre, Emile. L'argent, comédie en quatre actes. Paris, 1895.

39544.31 Faguet, Emile. Voltaire. Paris, 1895.

42576.17.5 Flaubert, Gustave. Pages choisies. Paris, 1895.

FL 6138.95.5 Fleuriaux, J. Jean-Jacques Rousseau; sa vie, ses oeuvres. Bruxelles, 1895.

Mol 825.12 Folet, H. Molière et la médecine de son temps. Lille, 1895.

42576.60.510 Fonsegrive, G.L. Lettres d'un curé de canton. Paris, 1895.

42586.54.2 Foulon de Vaulx, A. Les floraisons fanées. Paris, 1895.

42576.62.13.2 France, Anatole. Le jardin d'Epicure. Paris, 1895.

42576.62.7 France, Anatole. Les opinions de M. Jérôme Coignard. Paris, 1895.

42576.62.12 France, Anatole. Le puits de Sainte Claire. Paris, 1895.

37551.50 Franqueville, Charles. Le premier siècle de l'Institut de France 1795-1895. Paris, 1895. 2v.

38512.11A Froissart, Jean. Méliador. Paris, 1895. 3v.

37597.22 Fuhrken, G.E. De David li prophecie. Halle, 1895.

42576.38.2100 Galland, C. De Mazas à Jérusalem. Paris, 1895.

41542.8.10 Gautier, Théophile. Emaux et camées. Paris, 1895.

41542.5.5 Gautier, Théophile. Lectures littéraires. Pages choisies des grands écrivains. Paris, 1895.

42576.79.30 Geruzez, Paul. A pied, à cheval, en voiture. Paris, 1895.

42576.6.5 Ginisty, Paul. Louis XVII. Paris, 1895.

37548.10 Godet, Philippe. Histoire littéraire de la Suisse Française. 2. éd. Paris, 1895.

Htn 43625.3.46* Gourmont, Rémy de. Phocas; (collection de l'Ymagier). Paris, 1895.

42571.41.10 Grousset, P. Schoolboy days in Japan. Boston, 1895.

42576.40.340 Halévy, Ludovic. The abbé Constantin. N.Y., 1895.

42576.40.341 Halévy, Ludovic. The abbé Constantin. N.Y., 1895.

42576.40.342 Halévy, Ludovic. The abbé Constantin. N.Y., 1895.

37557.25 Hallard, J.H. Gallica and other essays. London, 1895.

Mol 608.3 Hamel, F.A. Molière-Syntax. Halle, 1895.

40562.17 Haussonville, Gabriel Paul Othenin de Cléron. Lacordaire. Paris, 1895.

42543.62.55 Heller, Louie R. André Chénier. N.Y., 1895.

38512.50 Henry VII. Les voeux de l'Epervier. Metz, 1895.

Htn 42554.55.2* Heredia, J.M. de. Les trophées. Paris, 1895.

42576.67.12.15 Hervieu, Paul. L'armature. Paris, 1895.

41574.16 Hugo, Victor. Victor Hugo's letters to his wife. Boston, 1895.

42554.65.5 Hugues, Clovis. Le mauvais larron. Paris, 1895.

FL 379.75 Ivanov, I.I. Politicheskaia rol' frantsuzskago teatra. Moskva, 1895.

38546.27 Janet, Paul. Les lettres de Mme. de Grignan. Paris, 1895.

42576.67.46 Jicé, Michel. Fleurs d'Israël. Photoreproduction. Paris, 1895.

37567.700 Jourdain, Frantz. Les décorés, ceux qui ne le sont pas. Paris, 1895.

37597.37 Keidel, George C. Romance and other studies. No.1: Evangile aux femmes; an old French satire on women. Diss. Baltimore, 1895.

37597.38 Keidel, George C. Romance and other studies. No.1: Evangile aux femmes; an old French satire on women. Diss. Baltimore, 1895.

FL 398.74.62 Kennard, Nina H. Rachel. Boston, 1895.

40587.53 Kervile, René. Essai d'une bio-bibliographie de Chateaubriand. Vannes, 1895.

Mol 611.3 Köhler, I. Molières und Fenelons Stellung. Plauen, 1895.

42514.22.2 Laboulaye, Edouard. The spaniel-prince. Liverpool, 1895.

39527.2.2 Lafenestre, Georges. La Fontaine. Paris, 1895.

39526.31.10 La Fontaine, Jean de. Fables. London, 1895.

Mol 870.50 Lambert, A. Vieux camerades. Paris, 1895.

Chronological Listing

1895 - cont.

37572.25.13 Lanson, G. Choix de lettres du XVIIIe siècle. 4. éd. Paris, 1895.
37543.38 Lanson, Gustave. Histoire de la littérature française. Paris, 1895.
37543.37 Lanson, Gustave. Hommes et livres. Études morales et littéraires. Paris, 1895.
Mon 152.1 Lanusse, M. Montaigne. Paris, 1895.
41574.175 Larroumet, Gustave. La maison de Victor Hugo. Paris, 1895.
42544.24.20 Lavedan, Henri. Une cour. Paris, 1895.
42544.24.50 Lavedan, Henri. Leur coeur. 18e éd. Paris, 1895.
37567.49 Lazare, B. Figures contemporains. Paris, 1895.
39586.27 Le Breton, André. Rivarol; sa vie, ses idées, son talent. Paris, 1895.
42555.36 Leconte de Lisle, C.M.R. Derniers poèmes. Paris, 1895.
42544.33.19 Lemaître, Jules. L'âge difficile. N.Y., 1895.
39545.22.5 Leon, Henri. Les tragédies de Voltaire. Paris, 1895.
42544.34.6 Lepelletier, E. Madame Sans-Gêne. Boston, 1895.
42544.34.5 Lepelletier, E. Madame Sans-Gêne. N.Y., 1895.
42576.45 Le Roux, H. Le festéjadon. Récits du sud. Paris, 1895.
42555.38.110 Letalle, Abel. La poésie de l'enfance. Paris, 1895.
42555.38.100 Letalle, Abel. La revanche des fleurs. Paris, 1895.
42576.46.30 Létang, Louis. Le lieutenant Philippe. Les deux frères. Paris, 1895.
42576.46.31 Létang, Louis. Le supplice d'un père. Les deux frères. Paris, 1895.
Mol 612.12 Linder, F. Henry Fieldings dramatische Werke. Leipzig, 1895.
37564.28.2 Livet, C.L. Précieux et précieuses. Paris, 1895.
Mol 570.10 Livet, Charles L. Lexique de la langue de Molière. Paris, 1895-97. 3v.
Mol 570.10.2 Livet, Charles L. Lexique de la langue de Molière. Paris, 1895-97. 3v.
41555.54 Loennbohm, K. Prosper Mérimée. Helsingissä, 1895.
37564.39 Longhaye, R.P.G. Histoire de la littérature française aux dix-septième siècle. Paris, 1895- 4v.
37562.20.5 Loth, Johannes. Die Sprichwörter und Sentenzen der altfranzösischen Fabliaux. Greifenberg, 1895-1896.
42575.80A Lowndes, Marie A. (Belloc). Edmond and Jules de Goncourt. London, 1895.
42575.81 Lowndes, Marie A. (Belloc). Edmond and Jules de Goncourt. N.Y., 1895. 2v.
41586.17.50 Lucas, Hyppolite. Rachel; drama em 4 actos, em verso. Lisboa, 1895.
FL 6128.95 MacDonald, F. Studies in the France of Voltaire and Rousseau. London, 1895.
42545.3.7.7 Maeterlinck, Maurice. Plays. 2d ed. Chicago, 1895.
42545.3.4 Maeterlinck, Maurice. Serres chaudes. Bruxelles, 1895.
40588.55 Maistre, Xavier. Chapitre inédit d'histoire littéraire et bibliographique. Genève, 1895.
42555.43.5 Mallarmé, Stéphane. Oxford, Cambridge. La musique et les lettres. Paris, 1895.
42555.49.3 Manuel, Eugène. Poésies du foyer et de l'école. Paris, 1895.
42576.76.24 Margueritte, Paul. Fors l'honneur. Paris, 1895.
42576.76.27.5A Margueritte, Paul. L'avril. N.Y., 1895.
42576.76.26 Margueritte, Paul. Simple histoire. Paris, 1895.
39598.9A Marmontel, J.F. Memoirs. London, 1895. 2v.
39598.11A Marmontel, J.F. Moral tales. London, 1895.
42545.9.2 Martel de Janville, S.G. Ces bons Normands. Paris, 1895.
42545.9.2.5 Martel de Janville, S.G. Ces bons Normands. 17e éd. Paris, 1895.
42545.9.19 Martel de Janville, S.G. Chiffon's marriage. N.Y., 1895.
42545.9.20 Martel de Janville, S.G. Chiffon's marriage. 2d ed. N.Y., 1895.
42545.9.24 Martel de Janville, S.G. A Gallic girl. N.Y., 1895.
42545.9.23 Martel de Janville, S.G. Le mariage de Chiffon. 36e éd. Paris, 1895.
37558.46 Martin, Jules. Nos Académiciens. Académie Française. Portraits et Biographies. Paris, 1895.
FL 384.80 Martin, Jules. Nos artistes. Paris, 1895.
39544.24.15 Maugras, Gaston. Voltaire et J.J. Rousseau. Wien, 1895.
42545.10.29 Meilhac, Henri. Ma cousine. N.Y., 1895.
38525.21.3A Mellerio, Louis. Lexique de Ronsard. Paris, 1895.
42587.22.8 Ménard, Louis. Poèmes et rêveries d'un paien mystique. Paris, 1895.
41555.21 Mérimée, Prosper. Crónica del reinado de Carlos IX. Valparaíso, 1895.
41555.29.30 Mérimée, Prosper. Helmiä. Helsingissä, 1895.
43698.76.110 Merrill, Stuart. Petits poèmes d'automne. Paris, 1895.
37596.174 Meyer, Paul. Notice sur le manuscrit de la bibliothèque nationale. Paris, 1895.
42514.35 Mignet, F.A.M. Lectures littéraires. Pages choisies des grands écrivains. Mignet. Paris, 1895.
42557.12 Mockel, Albert. Émile Verhaeren avec une note biographique. Paris, 1895.
Mol 165.65 Molière, Jean Baptiste Poquelin. L'avare...Boully. Paris, 1895.
Mol 171.47 Molière, Jean Baptiste Poquelin. Le bourgeois gentilhomme...Fischer. Bielefeld, 1895.
Mol 175.5 Molière, Jean Baptiste Poquelin. La comtesse d'Escarbagnas...Monval. Paris, 1895.
Mol 211.55 Molière, Jean Baptiste Poquelin. Les femmes savantes...Monval. Paris, 1895.
Mol 211.36.5 Molière, Jean Baptiste Poquelin. Les femmes savantes. London, 1895.
Mol 215.37 Molière, Jean Baptiste Poquelin. Les Fourberies de Scapin...Monval. Paris, 1895.
Mol 228.39 Molière, Jean Baptiste Poquelin. Le malade imaginaire...Fasnacht. London, 1895.
Mol 228.40 Molière, Jean Baptiste Poquelin. Le malade imaginaire...Friese. Bielefeld, 1895.
Mol 245.74 Molière, Jean Baptiste Poquelin. Le misanthrope. Boully. Paris, 1895.
Mol 251.58A Molière, Jean Baptiste Poquelin. Les précieuses ridicules. Davis. Boston, 1895.
Mol 48.95 Molière, Jean Baptiste Poquelin. Principales scènes. Paris, 1895?
Mol 258.20 Molière, Jean Baptiste Poquelin. Psyché. Monval. Paris, 1895.
Mol 268.84 Molière, Jean Baptiste Poquelin. Le Tartuffe. Figuière. 2. éd. Paris, 1895.
Mon 28.23 Montaigne, Michel de. Extraits. Klein. Paris, 1895.
Mon 45.10 Montaigne, Michel de. L'Italia alla fine del secolo XVI. Lapi, 1895.

1895 - cont.

42555.60 Montesquiou-Fezensac, Robert de. Le parcours du rêve au souvenir. Paris, 1895.
38526.13 Mucha, Oscar. Über Stil und Sprache von Philippe Desportes. Hamburg, 1895.
41596.18.6.5 Musset, Alfred de. Comédies et proverbes. Paris, 1895. 3v.
41596.18.6A Musset, Alfred de. Selection from poetry and comedies. Boston, 1895.
41596.18.5.15A Musset, Alfred de. A selection from the poetry and comedies of Alfred de Musset. Boston, 1895.
Htn Mol 614.1* Nash, F.H. The commedia dell'arte. n.p., 1895.
FL 383.18.5 Nebout, Pierre. Le drame romantique. Thèse. Photoreproduction. Paris, 1895.
41556.22 Nodier, Charles. Trilby, the fairy of Argyle. 1st ed. Boston, 1895.
42545.46.10 Normand, J. L'amiral. Paris, 1895.
37541.21 Odin, A. Genèse des grands hommes. Gens des lettres françaises modernes. Paris, 1895. 2v.
42578.29.110 Ohnet, Georges. La dame en gris. 67. éd. Paris, 1895.
40556.35 Paillette, C. La politique de Joseph de Maistre. Paris, 1895.
Mol 210.10 Pech, R. Les fâcheux de Molière comparés à son Misanthrope. Königshütte, 1895.
42578.30.58 Peladan, J. Les fils des étoiles. Beauvais, 1895.
42578.30.70 Peladan, J. Le livre spectre politique. Paris, 1895.
X Cg 37567.48 Pellissier, G.J.M. Nouveaux essais de littérature contemporaine. Paris, 1895.
39586.19.9 Pellisson, M. Chamfort. Paris, 1895.
42556.36.30 Potez, Henri. Jours d'autre fois. Paris, 1895.
42541.31.9 Pottecher, Maurice. Le diable marchand de Goutte. Nancy, 1895.
40522.9.13 Prévost, Antoine F. Histoire de Manon Lescaut et du chevalier des Grieux. Paris, 1895.
42578.31.25.5 Prévost, Marcel. Lettres de femmes. Paris, 1895?
42578.31.30 Prévost, Marcel. Notre compagne. Paris, 1895.
42578.31.30.2 Prévost, Marcel. Notre compagne. Paris, 1895.
38513.18 Quedenfeldt, Gustav. Die Mysterien des heilige Sebastian. Berlin, 1895.
38585.44.5 Racine, Jean. Les plaideurs. London, 1895.
42578.18.6 Rameau, Jean. La chevelure de Madeleine. Paris, 1895.
40556.21.5 Raynal, Paul de. Correspondance de J. Joubert. 9. éd. Paris, 1895.
42556.23 Read, Henri Charles. Poésies. Paris, 1895.
41522.18.120 Rechert, E. Charles Baudelaire und die Modernen. Wien, 1895.
42556.27.13 Régnier, Henri de. Aréthuse. Paris, 1895.
NEDL 42556.26 Régnier, Henri de. Poèmes (1887-1892). Paris, 1895.
42556.27.12 Regnier, Henri de. Le trèfle noir. Paris, 1895.
42515.30.535 Renan, Ernest. Ma soeur Henriette. Paris, 1895.
42515.30.545 Renan, Ernest. My sister Henrietta. Boston, 1895.
42515.29.45 Renan, Ernest. Vie de Jésus. 58. éd. Paris, 1895.
42556.27.70 Retté, Adolphe. L'archipel en fleurs. Paris, 1895.
42556.27.67 Retté, Adolphe. Similitudes. Paris, 1895.
42556.27.75 Retté, Adolphe. Trois dialogues nocturnes. Paris, 1895.
37572.45A Rinder, Edith N. The massacre of the innocents and other tales. Chicago, 1895.
37543.39 Robert, P. Études sur l'histoire de la littérature française. Paris, 1895.
42578.19.11 Rod, Edouard. Les roches blanches. Paris, 1895.
42578.19.11.3A Rod, Edouard. Les roches blanches. 21. éd. Paris, 1895.
42546.8.15 Rodenbach, G. La vocation. Paris, 1895.
38546.33.2 Roger, Jules. Madame de Sévigné malade. Paris, 1895.
38525.21.2 Rosenbauer, A. Die poetischen Theorien der Plejadi nach Ronsard und Dubellay. Erlangen, 1895.
42578.31.3100 Roujon, Henry. Miremonde. Paris, 1895.
37547.6 Rousse, J. La poésie bretonne au XIXe siècle. Paris, 1895.
41557.9.48.8 Sand, George. The haunted pool. N.Y., 1895.
41557.9.32.8 Sand, George. La petite Fadette. Boston, 1895.
42546.30.20.2 Sardou, Victorien. Arguments of the play of Mme. Sans-Gêne. N.Y., 1895.
42546.30.19.10 Sardou, Victorien. Madame Sans-Gêne. N.Y., 1895.
42546.30.19.9 Sardou, Victorien. Madame Sans-Gêne. N.Y., 1895.
42546.20.5 Sardou, Victorien. Rabagas; comedia en cinco actos. Valparaiso, 1895.
37555.38.5 Schlaeger, G. Studien über das Tagelied. Jena, 1895.
41588.3.12 Scribe, Eugène. Une chaîne. London, 1895.
42515.35.237 Séailles, G. Ernest Renan. Paris, 1895.
42546.33.9 Silvestre, Armand. Argument of "Izeyl". N.Y., 1895. 2v.
37596.52.2 Simon, Philipp. Jacques d'Amiens. Berlin, 1895.
FL 394.97 Soubies, A. La comédie française, 1825-1894. Paris, 1895.
FL 395.150 Soubies, A. La comédie-française depuis l'époque romantique, 1825-1894. Paris, 1895.
41558.66.10 Souvestre, Émile. Un philosophe sous les toits. London, 1895.
41558.73 Souvestre, Émile. Le serf. Cambridge, 1895.
Mol 619.7.3 Stapfer, P. Molière et Shakespeare. 3. éd. Paris, 1895.
Mon 129.1.2 Stapfer, P. Montaigne. Paris, 1895.
Mon 129.1 Stapfer, P. Montaigne. Paris, 1895.
39527.5.10 Taine, Hippolyte. La Fontaine et ses fables. 13e éd. Paris, 1895.
42576.15.10 Tarver, J.C. Gustave Flaubert as seen in his works and correspondence. N.Y., 1895.
FL 6138.95A Texte, J. Jean-Jacques Rousseau et...cosmopolitisme littéraire. Paris, 1895.
37556.24.7 Toldo, Piètro. Contributo allo studio della novella francese del XVe XVI secolo. Roma, 1895.
40536.34 Tronchin, François. Le Conseiller François Tronchin et ses amis. (1704-1798). Paris, 1895.
37597.35 L'urban cortese. Pisa, 1895.
42547.11.20 Vaucaire, Maurice. Le panier d'argenterie. Paris, 1895.
Htn 42557.20.9*A Verlaine, Paul. Confessions, notes autobiographiques. Paris, 1895.
42557.21 Vielé-Griffin, F. Poèmes et poésies. Paris, 1895.
38514.21.5 Villon, François. Le Jargon de François Villon. Paris, 1895.
42522.16 Vogüé, E.M. de. Russian portraits. N.Y., 1895.
42587.70.7 Weill, Alexandre. Epapée alsacienne. Paris, 1895.
42587.70.26 Weill, Alexandre. Robbin et Nonne. Paris, 1895.
40597.9.12 Wormeley, K.P. A memoir of Honoré de Balzac. Boston, 1895.
42584.11.13 Zola, Emile. Jacques Damour. Boston, 1895.

Chronological Listing

1896

42562.38.14.39 Adam, Paul. Le cuivre. Paris, 1896.
42562.38.14.14 Adam, Paul. La force du mal. Paris, 1896.
37593.62 Adam de la Halle. Le jeu de Robin et Marion. n.p., 1896.
37593.64.11 Adam de la Halle. La revue Dunord. n.p., 1896.
42586.7.25 Aicard, Jean. Notre-dame-d'amour. Paris, 1896.
37556.29.15 Albalat, A. Ouvriers et procédés. Paris, 1896.
38526.47.14 Arnould, Louis. Racan. Paris, 1896.
38527.28.3 Aubigné, Théodore Agrippa d'. Les tragiques. Paris, 1896.
40597.45 Balzac, Honoré de. The Atheist's mass. London, 1896.
40596.12.3A Balzac, Honoré de. The atheist's mass. London, 1896.
40596.12.4A Balzac, Honoré de. A bachelor's establishment. London, 1896.
40597.47 Balzac, Honoré de. A bachelor's establishment. London, 1896.
40596.12.5 Balzac, Honoré de. Beatrix. London, 1896.
40596.12.9 Balzac, Honoré de. The country parson. London, 1896.
40596.13.24 Balzac, Honoré de. The deputy of Arcis. Boston, 1896.
40596.13.32 Balzac, Honoré de. Gabseck. Boston, 1896.
40596.13.30 Balzac, Honoré de. The gallery of antiquities. Boston, 1896.
40597.46 Balzac, Honoré de. La grande Bretêche. London, 1896.
40597.55 Balzac, Honoré de. A Harlot's progress. London, 1896. 2v.
40596.12.18 Balzac, Honoré de. A harlot's progress. London, 1896. 2v.
40596.13.40 Balzac, Honoré de. Juana. Boston, 1896.
40596.13.112 Balzac, Honoré de. La comédie humaine. Philadelphia, 1896-1900. 45v.
40596.12.17 Balzac, Honoré de. La grande Bretêche and other stories. London, 1896.
40596.12.25A Balzac, Honoré de. Modeste Mignon. London, 1896.
40596.12.26 Balzac, Honoré de. Old Goriot. Photoreproduction. London, 1896.
40596.12.28A Balzac, Honoré de. The peasantry. London, 1896.
40597.54 Balzac, Honoré de. The peasantry. London, 1896.
40597.53 Balzac, Honore de. Pierrette and The Abbé Birotteau. London, 1896.
40596.12.29A Balzac, Honoré de. Pierrette and the Abbé Birotteau. London, 1896.
40596.12.6 Balzac, Honoré de. The rise and fall of César Biroteau. London, 1896.
40597.52 Balzac, Honoré de. The unknown masterpiece. London, 1896.
40596.12.36 Balzac, Honoré de. The unknown masterpiece and other stories. London, 1896.
40597.34.6 Balzac, Honoré de. Ursula. Paris, 1896.
42563.5.120 Beaubourg, Maurice. La saison au Bois de Boulogne. Paris, 1896.
42542.29.9 Bergerat, Émile. Le capitaine fracassé. Paris, 1896.
38528.16.8.25 Béroalde de Verville. L'histoire véritable, ou Le voyage des princes fortunez. Paris, 1896.
42554.13.250 Berrichon, Paterne. Le vin maudit; petits poèmes. Paris, 1896.
38563.13 Betz, Louis P. Pierre Bayle. Zürich, 1896.
37555.325.3 Bibesco, Alex. La question du vers français. Paris, 1896.
42586.21.29 Bigot, Charles (Mme.). La tâche du petit Pierre. N.Y., 1896.
42571.10 Blaze de Bury, Y. Anatole France. n.p., 1896.
37548.39.10 Bloch, Maurice. Femmes d'Alsace; souvenirs littéraires. Paris, 1896.
38546.51.20 Boissier, G. Mme. de Sévigné. 4. éd. Paris, 1896.
38514.38 Borderie, A. de. Jean Meschinot. Sa vie et ses oeuvres. Paris, 1896.
38557.31.5 Bossuet, J.B. Oraison funèbre de Henriette d'Angleterre. Paris, 1896.
FL 355.710 Bouchot, Henri. Catalogue des dessins relatifs à l'histoire du théâtre. Paris, 1896.
42563.37.19 Bourget, Paul. Une idylle tragique. Paris, 1896.
42563.37.31 Bourget, Paul. A tragic idyl. N.Y., 1896.
39527.2.5 Broc, V. de. La Fontaine moraliste. Paris, 1896.
NEDL 42559.9 Bruant, A. Chansons et monologues. Paris, 1896-97.
42524.13.5 Brunetière, F. La renaissance de l'idéalisme. Paris, 1896.
42524.18.2 Brunetière, F. Le roman naturaliste. 7. éd. Paris, 1896.
42554.18.2 Cazalies, Henry. Les quatrains d'Al Ghazali. Paris, 1896.
42557.14.8 Cazals, F.A. Paul Verlaine. v.1-2. Paris, 1896.
42563.80.110 Champsaur, Félicien. Pierrot et sa conscience. Paris, 1896.
38514.26 Charles d'Orleans. Poésies complètes. Paris, 1896. 2v.
40585.410 Chateaubriand, F.A.R. Pages choisies. Paris, 1896.
42565.6 Cherbuliez, Victor. Après fortune faite. Paris, 1896.
37595.36.7A Chrestien de Troyes. Erec und Enide. v.13. Halle, 1896.
42586.31.13 Claretié, J. La divette. Paris, 1896.
FL 6128.96.2 Claretie, L. Jean-Jacques Rousseau et ses amies. Paris, 1896.
Mol 870.53 Claretie, L. Le prêcheur converti. Paris, 1896.
FL 370.65 Clédat, Léon. Le théâtre en France au Moyen Age. Paris, 1896.
37543.42 Collignon, Albert. La religion des lettres. Paris, 1896.
42542.53.10 Coolus, R. Raphael. Paris, 1896.
42554.23.33 Coppée, François. Le coupable. Paris, 1896.
42554.23.14A Coppée, François. On rend l'argent. N.Y., 1896.
42554.19.2 Coppée, François. Le pater. Boston, 1896.
38575.27.3 Corneille, Pierre. Le Cid. 8. éd. Paris, 1896.
38575.26.8 Corneille, Pierre. Corneille's the Cid. Harrisburg, 1896.
38575.31.25 Corneille, Pierre. Don Sanche d'Arragon. Comédie hèroique. Paris, 1896.
42559.13 Couyba, Charles Maurice. Chansons rouges. Paris, 1896.
42542.58.40 Curel, François de. La figurante. Paris, 1896.
42566.43 Daudet, Alphonse. L'enterrement d'une étoile. Paris, 1896.
42566.58A Daudet, Alphonse. In the midst of Paris. N.Y., 1896.
42566.51.6 Daudet, Alphonse. La Belle-Nivernaise; story of an old boat. Boston, 1896.
42566.63.5 Daudet, Alphonse. Recollections of a literary man. London, 1896.
42566.35.28 Daudet, Alphonse. Tartarin on the Alps. London, 1896.
42566.62.5 Daudet, Alphonse. Thirty years of Paris and my literary life. London, 1896.
42567.38 Daudet, Ernest. Poussière du passé. Paris, 1896.
NEDL 43565.5.65 Daudet, Léon A. Les idées en marche. Paris, 1896.
43565.5.60 Daudet, Léon A. Vingt-neuf mois d'exil. Paris, 1896.
43565.5.90 Daudet, Léon A. Le voyage de Shakespeare. Paris, 1896.
39527.2.6 Delaporte, Louis. La philosophie de La Fontaine. Paris, 1896.

1896 - cont.

38514.58.8 Delisle, Léopold. Notice sur les sept psaumes allegorises de Christine de Pisan. Paris, 1896.
38551.23 Delmont, T. Fénelon et Bossuet. Paris, 1896.
42542.64.10 Déroulède, Paul. Messire du gueselin. 4. éd. Paris, 1896.
Htn 41593.29.3.10* Desbordes-Valmore, Marceline. Correspondance intime de Marceline Desbordes-Valmore. Paris, 1896. 2v.
42586.40.7 Deschamps, G. Chemin fleuri. Paris, 1896.
42586.40.5 Deschamps, G. Chemin fleuri. 3. éd. Paris, 1896.
Mol 870.52 d'Hervilly, E. L'hommage de Flipote. Paris, 1896.
42542.65.9 Donnay, Maurice. Lysistrata. Paris, 1896.
42542.65.90 Dorian, Tola. Mineur et soldat. Paris, 1896.
37558.41 Doucet, Camille. A l'institut rapports annuels (1886-1894). Paris, 1896.
37543.41 Doumic, René. Études sur la littérature française. Paris, 1896. 6v.
37567.53 Doumic, René. Les jeunes. Etudes et portraits. Paris, 1896.
43576.14.2110 Ducros, Emmanuel. Poèmes du midi. Paris, 1896.
41538.5.20 Dumas, Alexandre. Ascanio. v.1-2. Boston, 1896.
41538.14.10 Dumas, Alexandre. Le collier de la reine. Paris, 1896. 3v.
42543.15.15 Dumas, Alexandre. La dame aux camélias. Paris, 1896.
Htn 42543.20* Dumas, Alexandre. Ilka. Paris, 1896.
42543.16.8A Dumas, Alexandre. La signora dalle camelie. N.Y., 1896.
41538.63.60 Dumas, Alexandre. Six years later, or Taking the Bastile. N.Y., 1896.
41529.107.4.2 Dumas, Alexandre. Taking the Bastile (Ange Pitou]. v.1-2. N.Y., 1896?
41538.53.32 Dumas, Alexandre. The three musketeers. v.1-2. N.Y., 1896.
43576.1.42 Dumas, André. La galante surprise. Paris, 1896.
43576.57.120 Dumur, Louis. Pauline. Paris, 1896.
42568.23.8 Duval, Paul. Une femme par jour. Paris, 1896.
42568.23.7 Duval, Paul. M. de Bougrelon. Paris, 1896.
42568.23.120 Eekhoud, Georges. Burch mitsu. Bruxelles, 1896.
37596.75 Ehrismann, Henri. Le sermon des plaies. Strasbourg, 1896.
38513.9 Erler, Otto. Das Mystère de Saint Denis...und seine Quelle. Marburg, 1896.
37567.61 Felgeres, Charles. Essais d'histoire et de littérature. Paris, 1896.
Htn 37573.596* Feminies; huit chapitres inédits dévoués à la femme. Paris, 1896.
42575.52.10 Feuillet, Octave. Souvenirs et correspondances. 3. éd. Paris, 1896.
42576.33.9.5 Flaubert, Gustave. Bouvard and Pécuchet. London, 1896.
X Cg 42576.20.5 Flaubert, Gustave. L'education sentimentale. Paris, 1896.
42576.28.6 Flaubert, Gustave. Madame Bovary. Philadelphia, 1896. 2v.
42576.23.9 Flaubert, Gustave. De serzoeking san den H. Antonius. Amsterdam, 1896.
37567.56 Fonsegrive, G.L. Les livres et les idées, 1894-1895. Paris, 1896.
42586.54.2.5 Foulon de Vaulx, A. Les vaines romances. Paris, 1896.
37543.43 Fouquet, Férnand. A travers la vie. Paris, 1896.
42576.62.10.2.8 France, Anatole. Le lys rouge. 36. éd. Paris, 1896.
42576.63.15 France, Anatole. Poésies. Paris, 1896.
42543.45.75 Gavault, Paul. Plutus. Paris, 1896.
41567.19.5 Geoffroy, J. Louis. Napoléon apocryphe, 1812-1852. Paris, 1896?
42575.54 Goncourt, Edmond de. Pages choisies des auteurs contemporains. Paris, 1896.
42575.76 Goncourt, Edmond de. Première amoureuse. Paris, 1896.
Htn 37567.60.2* Gourmont, Rémy de. Le livre des masques. 1e éd. Paris, 1896.
42571.41.12 Grousset, P. Schoolboy days in France. Boston, 1896.
40513.10 Haack, Gustav. Untersuchungen zur Quellenkunde von LeSage's "Gil Blas." Kiel, 1896.
40522.12 Harrisse, Henry. L'Abbé Prévost. Histoire de sa vie et ses oeuvres. Paris, 1896.
42587.1 Heard, John. Esquisses mexicaines. Paris, 1896.
37562.12.5 Hecq, G. La poétique française. Paris, 1896.
42525.8 Hello, Ernest. Le siècle, les hommes et les idées. Paris, 1896.
37543.36 Hémon, Félix. Études littéraires et morales. Paris, 1896.
38543.3.5 Hémon, Félix. La Rochefoucauld. Paris, 1896.
42543.68.20 Hennequin, Alfred. A woman of sense and a hair powder plot. N.Y., 1896.
42554.55.30 Heredia, J.M. de. Salut à l'empereur. Paris, 1896.
42543.65.7 Hermant, Abel. La meute. Paris, 1896.
42576.14.65 Houssaye, Arsène. Souvenirs de jeunesse. Paris, 1896. 2v.
41573.32.18 Hugo, Victor. Herani, ó el pundonor castellano. Habana, 1896.
41574.16.5 Hugo, Victor. Letters of Victor Hugo to his family. Boston, 1896. 2v.
41573.17.2 Hugo, Victor. The toilers of the sea. London, 1896.
37555.616 Johannesson, Fritz. Zur Lehre vom französischen Reim. Berlin, 1896. 2v.
42543.73 Josz, Virgile. Rembrandt. Paris, 1896.
38527.25 Kaiser, Hermann. Über die Schöpfungsgedichte des Chr. de Gamon und Agrippa d'Aubigné. Bremen, 1896.
37596.27.6 Keidel, George C. An old French prose version of La vie de St. Aléxis. Baltimore, 1896.
42554.71 Kerhalvé, Sylvane de. Branches d'épines. Nantes, 1896.
41593.27 Kremer, A.R. Sprachliche Untersuchungen über J.M. Delille. Bonn, 1896.
42544.30 Labiche, Eugène. Moi. Comédie en trois actes. Boston, 1896.
38544.27.42 La Fayette, Marie M. La Princesse de Clèves. Boston, 1896.
38544.27.40 La Fayette, Marie M. La Princesse de Clèves. Boston, 1896.
42555.3 La Grasserie, R. de. La nature. Poésies. Paris, 1896.
37569.434 La Jeunesse, Ernst. Les nuits. Paris, 1896.
37574.55.5 Lamartine, Alfred. Love songs of France, from original of De Musset. N.Y., 1896.
37575.635 Lang, Andrew. Ballads and lyrics of old France. Portland, 1896.
42576.41.10 Lantoine, Albert. Elisçuah. Paris, 1896.
42544.24.21 Lavedan, Henri. Leur beau physique. Paris, 1896.
42544.24.52 Lavedan, Henri. Leurs soeurs. Paris, 1896.
42544.24.22 Lavedan, Henri. Petites fêtes. 9e éd. Paris, 1896.
42544.24.26 Lavedan, Henri. Les petites visites. 4e éd. Paris, 1896.
43688.7.945 Lebey, André. Chansons grises. Paris, 1896.
37567.622 Le Blond, Maurice. Essai sur le naturisme. Paris, 1896.

1896 - cont.

37542.29 Le Fèvre-Deumier, J. Critique littéraire (1825-1845). Paris, 1896.
38526.33.2 Lefranc, Abel. Les dernières poésies de Marguerite de Navarre. Paris, 1896.
42554.38 Le Guyader, Frédéric. L'ére bretonne. Paris, 1896.
42544.33.29 Lemaître, Jules. La bonne Hélène. Paris, 1896.
42544.32.5A Lemaître, Jules. Moreaux choisis. Boston, 1896.
38525.6 Lemercier, A.P. Chefs-d'oeuvre des poètes du XVIe siècle. Paris, 1896.
FL 382.42 Lencon, Hippolyte. Le théâtre nouveau. Paris, 1896.
42576.44 Le Roux, H. Ô mon passé. Mémoires d'un enfant. Paris, 1896.
40511.9 LeSage, Alain René. Pages choisies. Paris, 1896.
37561.36 Lyons. Les trois génies de la chaire Bossuet, Bourdaloue. Nice, 1896.
FL 377.37 Maatz, Anton. Der Einfluss des heroisch-galanten Romans. Rostock, 1896.
NEDL 42545.3.6 Maeterlinck, Maurice. Aglavaine et Selysette. Paris, 1896.
42545.3.7.8 Maeterlinck, Maurice. Plays. Ser. 2. Chicago, 1896.
42545.3.5 Maeterlinck, Maurice. Le trésor des humbles. 3e éd. Bruxelles, 1896.
43697.34.270 Magre, Maurice. Le retour. Toulouse, 1896.
42576.76.23 Margueritte, Paul. L'eau qui dort. Paris, 1896.
42576.76.28 Margueritte, Paul. L'essor. Paris, 1896?
42576.76.20 Margueritte, Paul. Le jardin du passé. Paris, 1896.
42576.76.29 Margueritte, Paul. La pariétaire. Paris, 1896.
42555.49.13 Mariéton, Paul. Le livre de mélancolie. Paris, 1896.
42545.9.6 Martel de Janville, S.G. A professional lover. N.Y., 1896.
42545.9.7 Martel de Janville, S.G. Those good Normans. Chicago, 1896.
38524.36.2 Marty-Laveaux, C. La Pléiade françoise. Appendice. Paris, 1896. 2v.
42577.34.5 Masson-Forestier, A. Remords d'Avocat. Paris, 1896.
42555.2 Mauclair, C. Jules Laforgue. Paris, 1896.
41555.20.4 Mérimée, Prosper. Carmen. Boston, 1896.
42514.36 Mignet, F.A.M. Pages choisies de Mignet. Paris, 1896.
37555.615 Möllman, J. Der Homonyme Reim im Französischen. Münster, 1896.
42545.28.9.20 Moinaux, Georges. La vie de Caserne. Paris, 1896?
Mol 211.57 Molière, Jean Baptiste Poquelin. Les femmes savantes...Fortier. Boston, 1896.
Mol 228.41.2 Molière, Jean Baptiste Poquelin. Le malade imagimaire...Monval. Paris, 1896.
Mol 228.41 Molière, Jean Baptiste Poquelin. Le malade imaginaire...Monval. Paris, 1896.
Mol 62.35 Molière, Jean Baptiste Poquelin. Meisterwerke...Fulda. 2e Aufl. Stuttgart, 1896.
Mol 48.96 Molière, Jean Baptiste Poquelin. Le misanthrope...fragments...Boitel. Paris, 1896.
NEDL Mol 245.75 Molière, Jean Baptiste Poquelin. Le misanthrope. Figuière. 4. éd. Paris, 1896.
Mol 18.96 Molière, Jean Baptiste Poquelin. Oeuvres...Bon marché. Paris, 1896. 2v.
Mol 251.32.5 Molière, Jean Baptiste Poquelin. Les précieuses ridicules. London, 1896.
Mol 48.96.2 Molière, Jean Baptiste Poquelin. Scènes choisies...Thirion. Paris, 1896.
Mol 268.89 Molière, Jean Baptiste Poquelin. Le Tartuffe des comédiens. Régnier. Paris, 1896.
Mol 268.89.2 Molière, Jean Baptiste Poquelin. Le Tartuffe des comédiens. Régnier. 2. éd. Paris, 1896.
42584.25.5 Moncoq. Tribunal du bon sens public. Réponse à Rome de Zola. Caen, 1896.
Mon 35.5 Montaigne, Michel de. Essays. Breslau, 1896.
Mon 28.24 Montaigne, Michel de. Pages choisies. Thiery. Paris, 1896.
39594.2.5 Montesquieu, C.L. de S. Extraits de l'esprit des lois. Paris, 1896.
43701.62.150 Montfort, Eugène. Sylvie, ou Les émois passiones. Paris, 1896.
42555.60.130 Montgomery, Lucy Ditte de. Rondels-sonnets; poésies philosophiques. 3e éd. Paris, 1896.
FL 393.52 Montorgueil, G. Les déshabilles au théâtre. Paris, 1896.
42555.60.330 Montoya, Gabriel. Chansons naïves et pérverses. 2. éd. Paris, 1896.
FL 6118.73.7 Morley, John Morley. Rousseau. London, 1896. 2v.
41596.19.10 Musset, Alfred de. Nouvelles. Paris, 1896.
41596.13.4 Musset, Alfred de. Premières poésies. Paris, 1896.
42578.17.25 Naurouze, Jacques. A travers la tourmente. Paris, 1896.
Htn 41543.11* Nerval, Gerard de. Sylvie: Souvenirs du Valois. Portland, 1896.
42555.63.135 Nibor, Yann. La chanson des cols bleus; chants populaires de la flotte française. Paris, 1896.
41556.31 Nodier, Charles. La neuvaine de la Chandeleur. Paris, 1896.
39544.36A Nourrisson, Jean Félix. Voltaire et le Voltairianisme. Paris, 1896.
40587.8.5 Pailhès, G. Chateaubriand: sa femme et ses amis. Bordeaux, 1896.
37556.31 Pajot, Henri. Le paysan dans la littérature française. Paris, 1896.
37567.57 Paris, Gaston. Penseurs et poètes. Paris, 1896.
37595.42 Paris, Gaston. Récits extraits des poètes et prosateurs du Moyen Âge. Paris, 1896.
37597.29.2 Péan Gatineau. Leben und Wunderthaten des Heiligen Martin. Tübingen, 1896.
42578.30.55 Peladan, J. Le prince de Byzance. Paris, 1896.
37534.7 Petit de Julleville, L. Histoire de la langue et de la littérature française. v.1-3,5-8. Paris, 1896. 7v.
38514.72A Piaget, A. Oeuvres poétiques de Guillaume Alexis. Paris, 1896. 3v.
37563.21 Piéri, Marius. Le pétrarquisme au XVIe siècle. Marseille, 1896.
42578.31.95 Pierret, Emile. Les crimes passionnels. Paris, 1896.
FL 390.70.2 Pougin, A. Acteurs et actrices d'autrefois. Paris, 1896.
42578.31.7 Pouvillon, E. Mademoiselle Clémence. Paris, 1896.
42578.31.69 Prévost, Marcel. Le mariage de Julienne. Paris, 1896.
38585.19.5 Racine, Jean. Andromaque. Paris, 1896.
38585.20.4 Racine, Jean. Athalie. London, 1896.
38585.20.5A Racine, Jean. Athalie. Paris, 1896.
NEDL 38585.43.7 Racine, Jean. Phaedra. N.Y., 1896?
FL 391.110 Raphanel, Jean. Histoire anecdotique des théâtres de Paris. Paris, 1896.
42515.34.20A Renan, Ernest. Brother and sister. N.Y., 1896.

1896 - cont.

42515.30.80 Renan, Ernest. Caliban. N.Y., 1896.
42515.34.10 Renan, Ernest. Lettres intimes, 1842-1845. 3. éd. Paris, 1896.
42515.30.733 Renan, Ernest. The poetry of the Celtic races. London, 1896.
42587.52.32 Renard, Jules. La demande. Paris, 1896.
42587.51.55 Renard, Jules. La maîtresse. Paris, 1896.
42578.31.2100 Rennes, Gaston. La roulotte. Paris, 1896.
42556.27.76 Retté, Adolphe. La forêt bruissante. Paris, 1896.
42556.27.82 Retté, Adolphe. Promenades subversives. Paris, 1896.
41557.10.7 Revon, Michel. George Sand. Paris, 1896.
Htn 42556.22.55* Richepin, Jean. Les étapes d'un réfractaire. Paris, 1896.
FL 6128.96 Ritter, E. Famille et jeunesse de Jean-Jacques Rousseau. Paris, 1896.
42578.19.13 Rod, Edouard. Dernier refuge. Paris, 1896.
42578.19.13.3 Rod, Edouard. Dernier refuge. 6. éd. Paris, 1896.
42578.19.13.6 Rod, Edouard. Dernier refuge. 12. éd. Paris, 1896.
42578.19.7.3A Rod, Edouard. La vie privée de Michel Teissier. 10. éd. Paris, 1896.
37555.42 Rosières, Raoul. Recherches sur la poésie contemporaine. Paris, 1896.
42578.22.8.14 Rosny, J.H. Elem d'Asie. Paris, 1896.
Htn FL 6026.8.15* Rousseau, J.J. The confessions. n.p., 1896. 2v.
FL 6026.8.16 Rousseau, J.J. The confessions of Jean-Jacques Rousseau. n.p., 1896. 2v.
FL 6031.96 Rousseau, J.J. Contrat social. Paris, 1896.
FL 6002.896 Rousseau, J.J. Extraits de J.J. Rousseau publiés avec une introduction et des notes par L. Brunel. 3. éd. Paris, 1896.
FL 6077.5 Rousseau, J.J. Lettre à Mr. d'Alembert sur les spectacles. Paris, 1896.
41557.8.15.5 Roy, Just J.E. The recluse of Rambouillet. N.Y., 1896.
42587.56.602 Saillens, R. Récits et allégories. 2. éd. Neuchatel, 1896.
42535.20.10 Saint-Victor, Paul de. Hommes et dieux. 9. éd. Paris, 1896.
40575.39A Sainte-Beuve, Charles A. Selected essays. Boston, 1896.
41557.9.48.14 Sand, George. The devil's pool. Boston, 1896.
NEDL 41557.9.30.4 Sand, George. Fadette. N.Y., 1896.
41557.8.117.10 Sand, George. Le peche de monsieur Antoine. Paris, 1896. 2v.
42546.29.25 Sardou, Victorien. Argument of Gesmonda. N.Y., 1896.
42546.30.26 Sardou, Victorien. Les femmes fortes, comédie. Paris, 1896.
42587.57.7 Schwob, Marcel. Spicilège. Paris, 1896.
42587.57.6 Schwob, Marcel. Spicilège. 2. éd. Paris, 1896.
42516.9 Secrétan, Charles. Essais de philosophie et de littérature. Lausanne, 1896.
42546.34.12 Silvestre, Armand. Les aurores lointaines; poésies nouvelles. Paris, 1896.
42546.34.28 Silvestre, Armand. Trente sonnets pour mademoiselle Bartet. Paris, 1896.
42535.25.31 Simon, P.M. Temps passé. 2e éd. Paris, 1896.
37595.36.6 Sordello de Goito. Vita e poesie. v.11-12. Halle, 1896.
39594.17.5 Sorel, Albert. Montesquieu. Deutsch von Adolf Kressner. Berlin, 1896.
40597.2.7 Spoelberch de Lovenjoul, Charles. Un roman d'amour. Paris, 1896.
Mon 178.2A Stapfer, P. La famille et les amis de Montaigne. Paris, 1896.
42556.20 Sully-Prudhomme, R.F.A. La nymphie des bois de Versailles. Paris, 1896.
42536.12 Taine, Hippolyte. Essais de critique et d'histoire. Paris, 1896.
43787.2.100 Téramond, Edmond Gautier. Les joies de la possession. Paris, 1896.
37575.116 Terrebasse, Humbert de. Poésies dauphinoises du XVIIe siècle. Lyon, 1896.
42583.33.10 Theuriet, André. Fleur de Nice. Paris, 1896.
42583.33.25 Theuriet, André. Josette. Paris, 1896.
37567.59A Tolstoi, Léon. Zola-Dumas. Guy de Maupassant. Paris, 1896.
42584.25.100 Toulouse, E. Enquête médico-psychologique, Emile Zola. Paris, 1896.
42587.64.3100 Uzanne, Octave. Contes de la vingtième année. Paris, 1896.
42557.11.1 Verhaeren, Émile. Poèmes. v.1-3. Paris, 1896-1904.
Htn 42557.19.35* Verlaine, Paul. Invectives. Paris, 1896.
38525.27.5 Vianey, Joseph. Mathurin Régnier. Paris, 1896.
42576.56.30 Viaud, Julien. Le désert. 45. éd. Paris, 1896.
42576.52.11 Viaud, Julien. An Iceland fisherman. N.Y., 1896.
42576.52.10 Viaud, Julien. An Iceland fisherman. 159. ed. N.Y., 1896.
42576.47 Viaud, Julien. Pages choisies. Paris, 1896.
37555.43 Vigié-Lecocq, E. La poésie contemporaine, 1884-1896. Paris, 1896.
42547.17 Villiers de l'Isle Adam, Auguste. Elën. Paris, 1896.
42547.22 Villiers de l'Isle Adam, Auguste. Tribulst Bonhornet. Photoreproduction. Paris, 1896.
42522.8 Vogüé, E.M. de. Devant le siècle. Paris, 1896.
42548.67 Voisine, A. Le moblot du 33e épisode de la guerre de 1870. Le Mans, 1896.
37596.79 Wagner, Philipp. Gillon le Muisi. Brünn, 1896.
39544.27.4 Wege, Bernhard. Der Prozess Calas im Briefwechsel Voltaires. Berlin, 1896.
37543.100 Wells, B.W. Modern French literature. Boston, 1896.
41596.3.2 Werner, Moritz. Kleine Beiträge zur Würdigung Alfred de Mussets. Berlin, 1896.
40597.2.9 Wright, T.F. Balzac and Swedenborg. Boston, 1896.
42584.3.10 Zola, Emile. L'assommoir. Paris, 1896.
42584.14.3A Zola, Emile. Rome. N.Y., 1896. 2v.
42584.14.2 Zola, Emile. Rome. Paris, 1896.

1897

42562.38.14.8 Adam, Paul. Le vice filial. Paris, 1897.
37596.23.7A Adam. Reimpredigt. Halle, 1897.
41592.2 Aigoin, L. Notice sur Félix Arvers. Paris, 1897.
37567.148 Allais, Gustave. Quelques vues générales sur le romantisme français. Paris, 1897.
42542.19.5 Augier, Émile. Le jouer de flute. Paris, 1897.
42542.25 Augier, Émile. La pierre de touche. London, 1897.
42542.3.7 Augier, Émile. Théâtre complet. Boston, 1897. 7v.
42562.38.100 Auschitsky, Daniel. Dans les couloirs du Vatican. Paris, 1897.

Chronological Listing

1897 - cont.

37596.88 Baker, Alfred T. Die versifizierte Übersetzung der Französischen Bibel. Cambridge, 1897.
40597.57 Balzac, Honoré de. About Catherine de Medici. London, 1897.
40596.12 Balzac, Honoré de. About Catherine de Medici. London, 1897.
40596.12.10 Balzac, Honoré de. Cousin Betty. London, 1897.
40597.64 Balzac, Honoré de. Cousin Pons. London, 1897.
40596.12.11 Balzac, Honoré de. Cousin Pons. London, 1897.
40596.12.12 Balzac, Honoré de. A daughter of Eve. London, 1897.
40596.15.3 Balzac, Honoré de. A daughter of Eve and Letters of two brides. London, 1897.
40597.56 Balzac, Honoré de. A distinguished provincial at Paris. London, 1897.
40596.12.13 Balzac, Honoré de. A distinguished provinicial at Paris. London, 1897.
40597.19.7 Balzac, Honoré de. Eugénie Grandet. Philadelphia, 1897.
40597.58 Balzac, Honoré de. The lily of the valley. London, 1897.
40596.12.20 Balzac, Honoré de. The lily of the valley. London, 1897.
40596.12.21 Balzac, Honoré de. Lost illusions. London, 1897.
40597.59 Balzac, Honoré de. Lost illusions. London, 1897.
40597.68 Balzac, Honoré de. A marriage settlement. London, 1897.
40596.12.22 Balzac, Honoré de. A marriage settlement. London, 1897.
40596.12.32 Balzac, Honoré de. The seamy side of history. London, 1897.
40597.61 Balzac, Honoré de. The seamy side of history. London, 1897.
40597.62 Balzac, Honoré de. Seraphita. London, 1897.
40596.12.33 Balzac, Honoré de. Seraphita and other stories. London, 1897.
40596.12.35 Balzac, Honoré de. The unconscious mummers. London, 1897.
40597.66 Balzac, Honoré de. The unconscious mummers. London, 1897.
40597.63 Balzac, Honoré de. A woman of thirty. London, 1897.
40596.12.39 Balzac, Honoré de. A woman of thirty. London, 1897.
42554.6.5 Banville, Théodore de. Socrate et sa femme. Paris, 1897.
41522.2.63 Barbey d'Aurevilly, Jules. Rhythmes oubliés. Paris, 1897.
Mol 820.2 Bernardin, N.M. Un mari d'actrice au XVIIe siècle. Paris, 1897.
42542.29.75 Berr de Turique, J. Comme ils sont tous. Paris, 1897.
42556.28.100 Berrichon, P. La vie de Jean Arthur Rimbaud. Photoreproduction. Paris, 1897.
Mol 870.56 Bertheroy, J. Aristophane et Molière. Paris, 1897.
37565.39 Bertrand, L. La-fin du classicisme. Paris, 1897.
40597.2.5 Bire, Edmond. Honoré de Balzac. Paris, 1897.
42566.14.5 Bishop, Maria Catherine. Madame Craven née La Ferronays. Paris, 1897.
Mol 860.55 Blémont, E. Molière en bonne fortune. Paris, 1897.
Mol 875.12 Blémont, E. La soubrette de Molière. Paris, 1897.
38512.52 Bohnstedt, K.R. Vie Saint Nicholas altfranzösisches Gedicht. Erlangen, 1897.
FL 398.6.50F Bonnefont, G. Mademoiselle Bartet. Paris, 1897.
37567.47.2 Bordeaux, H. La vie et l'art. Sentiments et idées de ce temps. Paris, 1897.
42541.7.7 Bornier, Henri de. La fille de Roland. Paris, 1897.
42563.27 Bosc, Jean. Le vice marin. Paris, 1897.
38557.34.9 Bossuet, J.B. Instruction sur les états d'oraison. Paris, 1897.
38557.30 Bossuet, J.B. Oraisons funèbres. Paris, 1897.
37574.25.3 Both-Hendriksen, Louis. La triade française, A. de Musset, Lamartine et Victor Hugo. Boston, 1897.
42586.24 Boubée, Simon. La jeunesse de Tartufé. Paris, 1897. 2v.
42542.30.35 Bouchor, Maurice. Le mariage de Papillonne. Paris, 1897.
38551.24 Boulve, L. Der l'Hellénisme chez Fénelon. Paris, 1897.
39526.44 Boulvé, Leon. De Fontanio Platonis studioso. Thesim. Paris, 1897.
42563.37.33 Bourget, Paul. Recommencements. Paris, 1897.
42563.37.20 Bourget, Paul. Voyageuses. Paris, 1897.
38557.23 Bourseaud, H.M. Histoire et description des MS. set des éditions originales des ouvrages de Bossuet. Paris, 1897.
42563.38.503 Bovet, M.A. Partie du pied gauche. 5. éd. Paris, 1897.
37574.25.5 Bowen, Benjamin Lester. Introduction to modern French lyrics. Boston, 1897.
38526.10.5 Boysson, Richard de. Un humaniste toulousain Jéhan de Boysson, 1505-1559. Paris, 1897.
37567.20.5 Brandes, Georg. Die Reaktion in Frankreich. 5e Aufl. Leipzig, 1897.
38523.18A Broglie, Albert. Malherbe. Paris, 1897.
42512.16 Broglie, Albert de. Histoire et politique. Paris, 1897.
NEDL Mol 825.13 Brown, A.M. Molière and his medical associations. London, 1897.
42524.22 Capperon, J. Notes d'art et de littérature. Paris, 1897.
37567.62 Carez, F. Auteurs contemporains. Liége, 1897.
Mon 143.2 Carlyle, T. Montaigne, and other essays. London, 1897.
42563.66 Catacuzène-Altiéri, Olga. Croquis russes. Paris, 1897.
37567.515 Charbonnel, Victor. Les mystiques dans la littérature présente. 1. série. Paris, 1897.
Mol 820.3 Cherot, R.P.H. Le Béarnais professeur de seconde de Molière. Auch, 1897.
43553.53.100 Cim, Albert. Cesarin. Paris, 1897.
42565.55.105 Cladel, Léon. Juive-errante. Paris, 1897.
42586.31.9 Claretié, J. Brichanteau. Boston, 1897.
38526.9.20 Contades, G. de. Les prédécesseurs de Bertaut. Alençon, 1897.
42542.53.5 Coolus, R. L'enfant malade. Paris, 1897.
42554.23.35 Coppée, François. Le coupable. Paris, 1897.
42554.23.8 Coppée, François. La grève des forgerons; poème. 25e éd. N.Y., 1897.
42554.19.4 Coppée, François. Le pater. Boston, 1897.
37576.535 Cupid's capers, by the chief French artists. Boston, 1897.
42566.31.4 Daudet, Alphonse. Le petit chose. Paris, 1897.
42566.45 Daudet, Alphonse. Le trésor d'Arlatan. Paris, 1897.
42568.56.110 Demolder, Eugène. Quatuor. Paris, 1897.
42554.29.3 Depont, L. Sérénites. Paris, 1897.
42542.64.6 Déroulède, Paul. Le mort de Hoche. Paris, 1897.
40535.32.5A Deschampe, Gaston. Marivaux. Paris, 1897.
FL 362.25 Des Granges, C.M. De scenico soliloquio. Thèse. Paris, 1897.
42586.41 Desjardin, P.A. Les mystères de Constantinople. Paris, 1897.
42586.41.5 Desjardin, P.A. Les secrets d'Yildiz. Paris, 1897.
39564.6.5 Diderot, Denis. Extraits. Paris, 1897.
FL 397.66.16 Digonnet, F. Le théâtre antique d'Orange. Avignon, 1897.
42568.50.100 Dollivet, Louis. Sale juif. Paris, 1897.
FL 382.57.10 Doumic, René. Essais sur le théâtre contemporain. Paris, 1897.

1897 - cont.

Htn 37543.45.5* Dowden, Edward. A history of French literature. N.Y., 1897.
42554.29.8.10 Druilhet, Georges. Au temps des lilas. Paris, 1897.
FL 6128.97 Dubois, A. Jean-Jacques Rousseau au champ du moulin. Neuchâtel, 1897.
42515.35.77 Duclaux, A.M.F.R. The life of Ernest Renan. Boston, 1897.
41538.90 Dumas, Alexandre. Agénor de Mauléon. Boston, 1897. 2v.
41538.75A Dumas, Alexandre. The brigand. Boston, 1897.
41538.17.3 Dumas, Alexandre. Chauvelin's will; The woman with the velvet necklace, Blanche de Beaulieu. Boston, 1897.
41538.6 Dumas, Alexandre. Cherubino y Celestini. Madrid, 1897.
41529.4 Dumas, Alexandre. The count of Monte Cristo. v.3-4. v.1-2 lost 1931. Boston, 1897. 2v.
41538.20.8.15 Dumas, Alexandre. The forty five. Boston, 1897. 2v.
41538.29.3.8 Dumas, Alexandre. Marguerite de Valois. Boston, 1897. 2v.
41538.17 Dumas, Alexandre. Monsieur de Chauvelin's will; The woman with the velvet necklace. Boston, 1897.
41538.17.2 Dumas, Alexandre. Monsieur de Chauvelin's will; The woman with the velvet necklace. Boston, 1897.
41538.12 Dumas, Alexandre. Pages choisies des grands écrivains. Paris, 1897.
41529.86 Dumas, Alexandre. Sylvandire. Boston, 1897.
41538.105 Dumas, Alexandre. Sylvandire. Boston, 1897.
41529.1A Dumas, Alexandre. The three musketeers. Boston, 1897. 2v.
41529.2A Dumas, Alexandre. Twenty years after. Boston, 1897.
41529.3 Dumas, Alexandre. Vicomte de Bragelonne; or, Ten years later. v.3-6. v.1 lost 1931. Boston, 1897.
42568.23.14.47 Duval, Paul. Loreley. Paris, 1897.
42568.23.9 Duval, Paul. L'ombre ardente; poésies. Paris, 1897.
42572.8.10 Erckmann, Emile. The count of Nideck. Boston, 1897.
42572.24.5 Erckmann, Emile. Madame Thérèse. Boston, 1897.
37596.78 Everlien, Hermann. Über Judas Machabee von Gautier de Belle Perche. Halle, 1897.
39531.17.2 Fabre, A. Les ennemis de Chapelain. Paris, 1897.
42565.72.4 Favre de Coulevain, Hélène. American nobility. N.Y., 1897.
40562.32 Fesch, P. Lacordaire journaliste, 1830-1848. Paris, 1897.
Mol 606.2 Fest, O. Der Miles Gloriosus in der französischen Komödie. Erlangen, 1897.
FL 363.15 Fest, Otto. Der miles gloriosus in der französischen Komödie. Erlangen, 1897.
FL 394.99PF Figaro Illustré. La comédie française. Paris, 1897.
37567.209 Fisher, M. A group of French critics. Chicago, 1897.
42576.60.500 Fonsegrive, G.L. Le journal d'un évêque. Paris, 1897. 2v.
40597.2.740 Ford, Mary Hanford Finney. Balzac's Seraphita; the mystery of sex. Chicago, 1897.
42586.54.1 Foulon de Vaulx, A. La vie eteinte. Paris, 1897.
42576.62.160 France, Anatole. Discours de réception. Paris, 1897.
42576.62.13 France, Anatole. Le jardin d'Epicure. Paris, 1897.
42576.62.10 France, Anatole. Le lys rouge. Paris, 1897.
NEDL 42576.62.11 France, Anatole. Le mannequin d'osier. Paris, 1897.
42576.62.8.1 France, Anatole. L'orme du mail. 57. éd. Paris, 1897.
42554.37.50 Fret, L.J. Le pape de Mortagne. 2e éd. La Chapelle-Montligeon, 1897.
38527.44 Garnier, Robert. Countess of Pembroke's Antoine. Photoreproduction. Weimar, 1897.
X Cg 41542.9.5 Gautier, Théophile. Fortunio. Paris, 1897.
41542.11.8 Gautier, Théophile. Mademoiselle de Maupin. Philadelphia, 1897. 2v.
42543.45.50 Gavault, Paul. Le petit Guignol. Paris, 1897.
42576.36.15 Gay, Ernest. Fille de comtesses. Paris, 1897?
43619.24.170 Ghéon, Henri. Les campagnes simples la solitude de l'été. Paris, 1897.
42554.46.3 Gielkens, Émile. Au roi. Bruxelles, 1897.
42575.95 Goncourt, Edmond de. Bibliothèque des Goncourt. 18ème siècle. Paris, 1897.
42575.93 Goncourt, Edmond de. Livres modernes, ouvrages. Paris, 1897.
42543.53A Gondinet, Edmond. Théâtre complet. Paris, 1897. 6v.
NEDL 43625.3.31 Gourmont, Rémy de. Les chevaux de Diomède. 3e éd. Paris, 1897.
43625.3.31 Gourmont, Rémy de. Les chevaux de Diomède. 5e éd. Paris, 1897.
Htn 43625.3.59* Gourmont, Rémy de. Le vieux roi. Paris, 1897.
FL 383.12 Granges, C.M. de. Geoffroy et la critique dramatique 1800-1814. Paris, 1897.
Mol 860.55.5 Griselin, J. Alliance. Paris, 1897.
40517.38.12 Gueulette, T.S. The thousand and one quarters of an hour. N.Y., 1897.
42576.40.5 Guiches, Gustave. Snob. Paris, 1897.
39534.40 Harmaud, R. Essai sur la vie et les oeuvres de Georges de Brébeuf, 1617?-1661. Paris, 1897.
FL 6138.97 Haymann, F. Begriff der volonté générale. Leipzig, 1897.
37543.46 Henry, A. Histoire de la littérature française. Paris, 1897.
37558.21 Henry, Stuart. Hours with famous Parisians. Chicago, 1897.
42554.64.31 Herold, A.F. Images tendres et merveilleuses. Paris, 1897.
40526.8.10 Hildebrandt, P. Bemerkungen zu André Chénier. Berlin, 1897.
NEDL 41572.60.5 Hugo, Victor. La fin de Satan. Paris, 1897.
41572.60.10 Hugo, Victor. The last days of a condemned. London, 1897.
41573.5 Hugo, Victor. Morceaux choisis. Paris, 1897.
NEDL 41573.25.3 Hugo, Victor. La préface de Cromwell. Paris, 1897?
37572.39 Huguet, E. Portraits et récits extraits des prosateurs du XVIe siècle. Paris, 1897.
38557.22.17 Ingold, A.M.P. Bossuet et le Jansénisme. Paris, 1897.
42587.8 Jeannin, J. Contes des champs et des rues. Paris, 1897.
37593.63.5 Jiersot, Julien. Sur le jeu de Robin et Marion d'Adam de la Halle (XIIIe siècle). Paris, 1897.
38514.68 Joret-Desclosières, G. Un écrivain national au XVe siècle Alain Chartier. Paris, 1897.
37567.146 Jullien, Adolphe. Le romantisme et l'éditeur Rendual. Paris, 1897.
NEDL 42554.68 Kahn, Gustave. Le livre d'images. Paris, 1897.
42554.68.22 Kahn, Gustave. Premiers poèmes. 2e éd. Paris, 1897.
FL 375.50 Klein, Friedrich. Das Chor in den wichtigsten Tragödien der Französischen Renaissance. Leipzig, 1897.
Mol 237.10 Kugel, A. Untersuchungen zu Molière's Médecin malgré lui. Berlin, 1897.

1897 - cont.

42576.41.5 La Bédollièrre, E.G. de. Storia di un Gatto. Firenze, 1897.
42544.27 Labiche, Eugène. Un jeune homme pressé. Paris, 1897.
38564.32.5 La Bruyère, J. de. Les caractères. Paris, 1897.
40562.28 Lacordaire, Jean Baptiste Henri. Mgr. d'Hulst et le P. Lacordaire. Paris, 1897.
43687.3.30 Lafagette, R. d'E. Symphonies pyrénéennes. Paris, 1897.
41564.36 Lafond, Paul. Alfred de Vigny en Béarn. Photoreproduction. Paris, 1897.
39526.31.12F La Fontaine, Jean de. Fables. Tours, 1897.
41578.28.5 Lamartine, Alphonse. Jocelyn. Paris, 1897.
41578.5.13 Lamartine, Alphonse de. Harmonies poétiques et religieuses. Paris, 1897.
41578.7.3 Lamartine, Alphonse de. Premières méditations poétiques. Paris, 1897.
42526.4 Larroumet, G. Petits portraits et notes d'art. Paris, 1897.
42544.24.3 Lavedan, Henri. Les deux noblesses. (Drama). Paris, 1897.
42544.24.15 Lavedan, Henri. Les jeunes. Paris, 1897.
42554.16.4 Le Braz, A. Pâques d'Islande. Paris, 1897.
38521.36 Lefranc, Abel. Marguerite de Navarre et le platonisme de la renaissance. Paris, 1897.
42576.14.800 Lemaitre, Ernest. Arsène Houssaye. Reims, 1897.
37567.32.10 Lemaître, Jules. Les contemporains. Paris, 1897-1903. 7v.
42557.14.6 Lepelletier, E. Paul Verlaine et ses contemporains. Paris, 1897.
42576.45.4 Le Roux, H. Le maître de l'heure. Paris, 1897.
42513.82 Leroy-Beaulieu, A. L'antisémitisme. Paris, 1897.
42513.76 Leroy-Beaulieu, A. Études Russes et européennes. Paris, 1897.
41568.15 Levallois, Jules. Un précurseur: Sénancour. Paris, 1897.
42555.33.100 Levey, Henry J.M. Le pavillon. Paris, 1897.
Mol 728.20F L'Hérault. L'Hérault-Artiste à Molière. Paris, 1897.
FL 6138.97.2 Lincoln, C.H. Rousseau and the French revolution. Philadelphia, 1897.
42545.3.6.4 Maeterlinck, Maurice. Aglavaine and Selysette. London, 1897.
42545.3.5.5 Maeterlinck, Maurice. The treasure of the humble. N.Y., 1897.
Mol 613.1 Maffre de Bauge, A. Molière et le régionalisme. Paris, 1897.
42577.11.1 Malot, Hector. Capi et sa troupe. London, 1897.
Htn 38526.28.100* Marbeuf, P. de. Recueil des vers de Pierre de Marbeuf. Rouen, 1897.
38526.33.3A Marguerite d'Angoulême. The mirror of the sinful soul. London, 1897.
42576.76.30 Margueritte, Paul. Le carnaval de Nice. Paris, 1897.
42576.76.31 Margueritte, Paul. Poum; aventures d'un petit garçon. Paris, 1897.
42545.9.45 Martel de Janville, S.G. Bijou. Paris, 1897.
FL 384.90 Martin, Jules. Nos auteurs et compositeurs dramatiques. Paris, 1897.
42545.6.35 Mazel, Henri. Le Khalife de Carthage. Paris, 1897.
42545.10.7 Meilhac, Henri. Les brigands. Paris, 1897.
Htn FL 385.54* Mendes, C. L'art au théâtre. Paris, 1897-1900. 3v.
X Cg 42555.58.4.5 Mendès, Catulle. Contes choisis. Paris, 1897.
41555.23.70 Mérimée, Prosper. Colomba. N.Y., 1897.
43698.76.140 Merrill, Stuart. Poèmes, 1887-1897. Paris, 1897.
42533.13 Mézières, A. Morts et vivants. Paris, 1897.
FL 397.8.5 Minier, H. Le théâtre à Bordeaux, étude historique. Bordeaux, 1897.
Mol 165.66 Molière, Jean Baptiste Poquelin. L'avare...Braunholtz. Cambridge, 1897.
Mol 251.60 Molière, Jean Baptiste Poquelin. Les précieuses ridicules. Pellisson. 2. éd. Paris, 1897.
Mol 48.97 Molière, Jean Baptiste Poquelin. Scènes choisies...Cahen. Paris, 1897.
37596.77 Mondeville, H. de. La chirurgie. Paris, 1897. 2v.
Mon 30.10A Montaigne, Michel de. Essays. Florio. London, 1897. 5v.
Mol 713.6.2 Monval, G. Chronologie Moliéresque. Paris, 1897.
Mol 713.6 Monval, G. Chronologie Moliéresque. Paris, 1897.
42555.61.5 Moréas, Jean. Les cantilènes. Paris, 1897.
38526.10 Mugnier, F. La vie et les poésies de Jean de Boyssomé. Paris, 1897.
37566.148 Muhlfeld, Lucien. Le monde oú L'on imprime. Paris, 1897.
41596.17.15 Musset, Alfred de. Comédies et proverbes. Paris, 1897-1899. 3v.
41596.19.15 Musset, Alfred de. Contes. Paris, 1897.
41596.14.10 Musset, Alfred de. Oeuvres posthumes. Paris, 1897.
37555.308 Nebout, P. Gallici Versus metrica ratio facultati. Paris, 1897.
Htn 42558.50* Noël, fait en manière de dialogue. Orléans, 1897.
FL 397.9 Notice illustré sur le théâtre du peuple de Bussang. Paris, 1897.
41574.232 Nuse, P. Victor Hugo als Dramatiker. Berlin, 1897.
42578.29.100 Ohnet, Georges. Le curé de Favières. 3. éd. Paris, 1897.
37555.18.5 Olmsted, E.W. The sonnet in French literature. Ithaca, 1897.
38511.33 Ovidius. Phaetonfabel im Ovide moralise. Bern, 1897.
42545.68.15 Pailleron, Edouard. Pièces et morceaux. Paris, 1897.
Htn 38524.28* Palinodz. Chantz royaulx. Facsimile. Paris, 1897.
37572.38.5 Paris, Gaston. Chrestomathie du moyen âge. Paris, 1897.
37566.29.4 Pellissier, G. Literary movement in France during 19th century. N.Y., 1897.
FL 396.30 Péricaud, L. Le théâtre des funambules. Paris, 1897.
43740.1.60 Philippe, Charles Louis. Quatre histoires de pauvre amour. Paris, 1897.
41557.10.9 Plauchut, Edmond. Autour de Nohant. Lettres de Barbes à George Sand. Paris, 1897.
41557.10.19 Pompery, A. de. Un ami de George Sand. Paris, 1897.
37555.38 Potez, H. L'élégie en France avant le romantisme. Paris, 1897.
FL 390.70 Pougin, A. Acteurs et actrices d'autrefois. Paris, 1897?
42578.31.26.10 Prévost, Marcel. Dernières lettres de femmes. Paris, 1897.
42578.31.32 Prévost, Marcel. Le jardin secret. 32. éd. Paris, 1897.
42578.31.32.5 Prévost, Marcel. Le jardin secret. 53. éd. Paris, 1897.
42578.31.25.20 Prévost, Marcel. Letters of women. N.Y., 1897.
42556.4.15 Quillard, Pierre. La lyre. 29. éd. Paris, 1897.
38585.20.16A Racine, Jean. Athalie. Cambridge, 1897.
38585.43.3 Racine, Jean. Phèdre, tragédie en cinq actes. London, 1897.
43752.59.120 Randon, G. Les soliloques du pauvre. 6. éd. Paris, 1897.

1897 - cont.

37596.16.5 Raoul de Houdenc. Sämtliche Werke. Halle, 1897-1909. 2v.
42556.23.2 Read, Henri Charles. Poésies. 4. éd. Paris, 1897.
42587.50.70 Rebell, Hugues. La Nichina. Paris, 1897.
42556.21.5 Reboux, P. Les matinales. Paris, 1897.
43753.9.150 Reboux, Paul. Les Matinoles. Paris, 1897.
42556.27.5 Régnier, Henri de. La canne de Jaspe. Paris, 1897.
42556.26.3 Régnier, Henri de. Poèmes (1887-1892). Paris, 1897.
42515.29.475 Renan, Ernest. Antichrist. Boston, 1897.
42556.27.50 Replat, J. Feuilles d'album. Annecy, 1897.
42556.27.74 Rette, Adolphe. Campagne première. Paris, 1897.
38526.14.75 Reure, Odon Claude. Le bibliographie Antoine Du Verdier. Paris, 1897.
FL 398.35.5 Robert, Louis de. The eternal enigma. Romance in the life of Yvette Guilbert. N.Y., 1897.
42578.19.29 Rod, Edouard. Les idées morales du temps présent. Paris, 1897.
42578.19.15 Rod, Edouard. L'innocente. Paris, 1897.
42578.19.12 Rod, Edouard. Là-haut. Paris, 1897.
42578.19.12.3 Rod, Edouard. Là-haut. 14. éd. Paris, 1897.
42578.19.1.5A Rod, Edouard. Le sens de la vie. 13. éd. Paris, 1897.
42578.19.7.5 Rod, Edouard. La vie privée de Michel Teissier. Paris, 1897.
42546.8 Rodenbach, G. Le voile. Paris, 1897.
42556.29.5 Romberg, E. Au Louvre. Paris, 1897.
42578.22.10.45 Rosny, J.H. La flûte de Pan. Paris, 1897.
42578.22.8.10 Rosny, J.H. Nornai. Paris, 1897.
42578.22.8.12 Rosny, J.H. Nouvel amour. Paris, 1897.
42578.22.8.13 Rosny, J.H. La tentatrice. Paris, 1897.
37543.105 Rossel, V. Histoire de la littérature française hors de France. Paris, 1897.
37543.106 Rossel, V. Histoire des relations littéraires entre France et l'Allemagne. Paris, 1897.
42546.15.11 Rostand, Edmond. Pour la Grèce. Paris, 1897.
FL 6096.2 Rousseau, J.J. Un testament littéraire. Paris, 1897.
43757.92.175 Roussel, Raymond. La doublure. 2. éd. Paris, 1897.
40576.4.5 Sainte-Beuve, Charles A. Seven of the Causeries du lundi. N.Y., 1897.
37542.17.5 Saintsbury, George. A short history of French literature. 5th ed. Oxford, 1897.
41557.9.24.20 Sand, George. Consuelo. Boston, 1897. 2v.
41557.9.42 Sand, George. Lettres à Alfred de Musset et à St. Beuve. Paris, 1897.
41557.8.113.10 Sand, George. Narcisse. Paris, 1897.
38526.51 Schirmacher, K. Théophile de Viau. Sein Leben und seine Werke (1591-1626). Leipzig, 1897.
41588.15.2.2 Scribe, Eugène. Contes de la Reine de Navarre. Bielefeld, 1897.
Mol 270.24.2 Socin, A. Zur Metrik emiger ins Arabische übersetzter Dramen Molière's. Leipzig, 1897?
Mol 270.24 Socin, A. Zur Metrik emiger ins Arabische übersetzter Dramen Molière's. Lipsiae, 1897?
43775.91.100 Souza, R. de. Sources vers la fleure. Paris, 1897.
Mon 108.3 Spalikowski, E. Dictionnaire medical de Montaigne. Paris, 1897.
40597.2.6 Spoelberch de Lovenjoul, Charles. Autour de Honoré de Balzac. Paris, 1897.
41557.10.10 Spoelberch de Lovenjoul, Charles. La veritable histoire de "Elle et lui". Paris, 1897.
38585.16.310 Stapfer, Paul. Racine et Victor Hugo. 6. éd. Paris, 1897.
37566.7.5A Thieme, Hugo P. La littérature française du dix neuvième siècle. Paris, 1897.
42557.6.10 Tiercelin, Louis. Sur la harpe, poésies, 1886-1896. Paris, 1897.
42587.63.50 Torquet, A. Au seuil de l'espoir. Paris, 1897.
40525.6 Tressan, L.E. Souvenirs de comte de Tressan. Versailles, 1897.
42547.10.630 Valabrèque, D. Le quatorzième convive. 3. éd. Paris, 1897?
Htn 42557.20.15* Verlaine, Paul. Paul Verlaine; correspondance et documents inédits relatifs à son livre "Quinze jours en Hollande". La Haye, 1897.
42587.66.50 Verly, Hippolyte. Les socialistes au pouvoir. Paris, 1897.
42576.56.3 Viaud, Julien. Madame Chrysanthème. London, 1897.
42576.57.3.2 Viaud, Julien. Ramuntcho. N.Y., 1897.
42576.57.3 Viaud, Julien. Ramuntcho. Paris, 1897.
42576.47.5 Viaud, Julien. Selections from Pierre Loti. N.Y., 1897.
42576.54.20 Viaud, Julien. Les trois dames de la Kasbah. Paris, 1897.
42557.24 Vielé-Griffin, F. La clarté de vie. Paris, 1897.
42547.18.9 Villiers de l'Isle Adam, Auguste. La révolte. Photoreproduction. Paris, 1897.
37595.36.8 Vincenz, Beauvais. La estoria. v.14. Halle, 1897.
42522.13 Vogüé, E.M. de. Jean d'Agrève. Paris, 1897.
37563.31 Voigt, J. Das Naturgefühl in der Literatur der französischen Renaissance. Berlin, 1897.
39545.33.4 Voltaire, François Marie Arouet de. Voltaire's prose. Boston, 1897.
39543.50 Voltaire, François Marie Arouet de. The whole prose romances. Philadelphia, 1897-98. 3v.
42584.10.3 Zola, Emile. His Excellency. N.Y., 1897.
42584.13.115 Zola, Emile. Lourdes. v. 1-2. N.Y., 1897.
42584.23.75 Zola, Emile. A page of love. Philadelphia, 1897. 2v.
42584.1.8 Zola, Emile. Pages choisies des auteurs contemporains. Paris, 1897.
40526.8.9 Zyromski, E. De A. Chenerio poeta. Paris, 1897.
41578.46 Zyromski, E. Lamartine, poète lyrique. Paris, 1897.

1898

40575.3.5 Académie Française, Paris. Inauguration du monument élève à la memoire de Sainte-Beuve. Paris, 1898. 2 pam.
43513.1.37 Acker, Paul. Dispensé de l'article 23. Paris, 1898.
42562.38.14.22 Adam, Paul. Lettres de Malaisie; roman. Paris, 1898.
42562.38.14.35 Adam, Paul. Les tentatives passionnées. 5e éd. Paris, 1898.
42562.38.14.36 Adam, Paul. Le triomphe des médiocres. 4e éd. Paris, 1898?
37565.36.4 Albert, Maurice. La littérature française sous la révolution. Paris, 1898.
FL 398.75.10 Alexandre, Arsène. Suzanne Reichenberg. Paris, 1898.
42542.1.13.5 Alexis, Paul. Celle qu'on n'épouse pas. Paris, 1898.
39544.24.5 Allier, Raoul. Voltaire et Calas. Paris, 1898.
42542.1.15 Ancey, Georges. L'avenir. Paris, 1898.
42553.52 Anglés, Augustin. Les écloses. Paris, 1898.

Chronological Listing

1898 - cont.

NEDL	37573.25	Anthologie des poètes français du XIXe siècle. Paris, 1898. 4v.
	38571.21	Ayer, Charles C. Tragic heroines of Pierre Corneille. Strassburg, 1898.
	40597.14.7.5	Balzac, Honoré de. César Birotteau. Boston, 1898.
	40597.13	Balzac, Honoré de. Les chouans. Paris, 1898.
	40596.13.73	Balzac, Honoré de. Cousin Pons. Boston, 1898.
	40596.12.15	Balzac, Honoré de. A father's curse. London, 1898.
	40597.71	Balzac, Honoré de. A father's curse and other stories. London, 1898.
	40597.73	Balzac, Honoré de. A gondreville mystery. London, 1898.
	40596.12.16	Balzac, Honoré de. A Gondreville mystery. London, 1898.
	40596.12.19	Balzac, Honoré de. The jealousies of a country town. London, 1898.
	40597.69	Balzac, Honoré de. The jealousies of a country town. London, 1898.
	40597.28.7	Balzac, Honoré de. La maison du chat-qui-pelote. Paris, 1898.
	40597.72A	Balzac, Honoré de. The member for Arcis. London, 1898.
	40596.12.23	Balzac, Honoré de. The member for Arcis. London, 1898.
	40596.12.24	Balzac, Honoré de. The middle classes. London, 1898.
	40597.75	Balzac, Honoré de. The middle classes. London, 1898.
	40597.67	Balzac, Honoré de. Parisians in the country. London, 1898.
	40596.12.27	Balzac, Honoré de. Parisians in the country. London, 1898.
	40596.12.30	Balzac, Honoré de. A princess's secrets. London, 1898.
	40597.74	Balzac, Honoré de. A princess's secrets. London, 1898.
	40597.84.1	Balzac, Honoré de. Seraphita. Boston, 1898.
	40597.70	Balzac, Honoré de. The thirteen. London, 1898.
	40596.12.34	Balzac, Honoré de. The thirteen. London, 1898.
	41567.12	Bardoux, Agénor. Étude sociales et politiques, La duchesse de Duras. Paris, 1898.
	37555.316	Barneville, P. de. Le rythme dans la poésie française. Paris, 1898.
	43537.4.30	Bataille, Henry. Ion Sang précédé de La Lépreuse. 2. éd. Paris, 1898.
	41522.6.30	Baudelaire, Charles. Výbor z malých básní v prose. Praha, 1898.
	40532.5	Beaumarchais, Pierre A.C. de. Le barbier de Séville. Boston, 1898.
	37556.12.15	Belfort, Roland. Johnny Crapand and his journals. London, 1898.
	FL 382.55	Benoist, Antoine. Essais de critique dramatique. Paris, 1898.
	42542.29.28.35	Bernard, Tristan. Sous toutes reserves. Paris, 1898.
	43538.9.50	Berthaut, Léon. Rose-Blanche. Havre, 1898.
	37566.7A	Blaze de Bury, Yetta. French literature of to-day. Boston, 1898.
	Mol 860.57	Blémont, E. Théâtre Molièresque et Cornélien. Paris, 1898.
	42563.23.15	Blondel, Auguste. The revenge of Lucas Helm. Philadelphia, 1898.
	42563.23.19	Bloy, Léon. Le mendiant ingrat. Bruxelles, 1898.
	42512.7	Bois, Georges. Souvenirs et fantaisies. Causeries du Dimanches. 2. ser. Paris, 1898.
	Mon 142.1.5A	Bonnefon, P. Montaigne et ses amis. Paris, 1898. 2v.
	38557.31.9	Bossuet, J.B. Oraison funèbre de Henriette-Marie de France. Paris, 1898.
	42563.37.21	Bourget, Paul. Complications sentimentales. Paris, 1898.
	42563.37.22	Bourget, Paul. Sa duchesse bleue. Paris, 1898.
	42563.38.508	Bovet, M.A. Petites rosseries. 5. éd. Paris, 1898.
	42542.47.10	Brieux, Eugène. Resultat des courses. Paris, 1898.
	37564.42	Broc, Hervé de. Propos littéraires. Paris, 1898.
	42524.13	Brunetière, F. L'art et la morale. Paris, 1898.
	37557.16	Brunetière, F. Essays in French literature. London, 1898.
	37543.47.10	Brunetière, Ferdinand. Manual of the history of French literature. N.Y., 1898.
	Mon 112.5	Bruns, Ivo. Montaigne und die Alten. Kiel, 1898.
	37595.36.9	Charlemagne. Romance. Latin. Gesta Karoli Magni. v.15. Halle, 1898.
	42565.17.5	Cherbuliez, Victor. Jacquine Vanesse. Paris, 1898.
	43554.7.40	Clemenceau, Georges. Au pied du Sinaï. Paris, 1898.
	42554.18.50	Clément, Jean B. Cent chansons nouvelles. Paris, 1898?
	42555.40.52	Contades, G. Gustave Le Vavasseur, bibliographie de ses oeuvres (1840-1896). Alençon, 1898.
	42555.40.53	Contades, G. Gustave Le Vavasseur; débuts litteraires. Alençon, 1898.
	42554.23.16	Coppée, François. La bonne souffrance. N.Y., 1898.
	42554.26.3A	Coppée, François. Théâtre 1885-95. Paris, 1898.
	Mol 603.6	Cordier, H. Molière jugé par Stendhal. Paris, 1898.
	37530.11	Cornu, Sophie. List of French fiction. Boston, 1898.
	42554.14	Cousin, Victor. Pages choisies. Paris, 1898.
	Mol 870.57	Croze, J.L. Les bergers de Molière. Paris, 1898.
	42566.15.9	Darzens, Rodolphe. Le roman d'un clown. Paris, 1898.
	42566.24.18	Daudet, Alphonse. Fromont and Risler. N.Y., 1898.
	42566.49.4	Daudet, Alphonse. The head of the family. N.Y., 1898.
	42566.29.7	Daudet, Alphonse. The Nabob. N.Y., 1898. 2v.
	42566.17.40A	Daudet, Alphonse. The works of Alphonse Daudet. Boston, 1898-1900. 24v.
	42566.16.100	Daudet, Léon. Alphonse Daudet. To which is added the Daudet family. Boston, 1898.
	FL 6138.98A	Davidson, T. Rousseau and education according to nature. N.Y., 1898.
	37566.146.10	Delaporte, Louis. Pastels et figurines. 2. éd. Paris, 1898.
	42542.64.18	Descaves, Lucien. La cage. Paris, 1898.
	42542.65.5	Donnay, Maurice. La douloureuse. Paris, 1898.
	FL 398.4.12	Douglas, R.B. Sophie Arnould. Paris, 1898.
	37555.45	Doumic, R. La poésie lyrique en France au dix-neuvième siècle. Montréal, 1898.
	42515.35.78	Duclaux, A.M.F.R. The life of Ernest Renan. 2. ed. London, 1898.
	42515.35.76	Duclaux, A.M.F.R. La vie de Ernest Renan. Paris, 1898.
	FL 6128.98	Dufour, E. Jacob Vernes, 1728-1791. Genève, 1898.
	42543.15.18	Dumas, Alexandre. La dame aux camélias. Paris, 1898.
	41538.61.16	Dumas, Alexandre. Memoirs of a physician. N.Y., 1898.
	42543.22.5	Dumas, Alexandre. La question d'argent. Boston, 1898.
NEDL	42543.10	Dumas, Alexandre. Théâtre complet. 8. série. Paris, 1898.
NEDL	40535.35	Dupont, Paul. Houdar de La Motte. Paris, 1898.
	38521.6A	Durand-Lapie, P. Saint-Amant, son temps...1594-1661. Paris, 1898.
	42568.23.14.45	Duval, Paul. Princesse d'Italie. Paris, 1898.
Htn	42554.30.1*	Elskamp, M. Enluminures; paysages, heures, vies, chansons, grotesques. Bruxelles, 1898.
	42554.30.3	Elskamp, M. Le louange de la vie. 2e éd. Paris, 1898.
	42573.27.50	Erckmann, Emile. The blockade of Phalsburg. N.Y., 1898.
	42572.11.22	Erckmann, Emile. The conscript; a story of the French war of 1813. N.Y., 1898.
	42573.20.7	Erckmann, Emile. Invasion of France in 1814. N.Y., 1898.
	42572.24.7	Erckmann, Emile. Madame Thérèse. N.Y., 1898.
	42573.25.4.5	Erckmann, Emile. The plebiscite. N.Y., 1898.
	42572.32.8	Erckmann, Emile. Waterloo. N.Y., 1898.
	42543.28.1100	Eudel, Paul. Le mort récalcitrant. Paris, 1898.
	42543.38.11	Fabre, Émile. Le bien d'Autrue. Paris, 1898.
	FL 360.55	Faguet, Émile. Drame ancien, drame modern. Paris, 1898.
	43606.89.55	Faure, Gabriel. Berthe de Provence. Paris, 1898.
	41555.38	Filon, A. Mérimée et ses amis. Paris, 1898.
	FL 382.65A	Filon, Augustin. De Dumas à Rostand. Paris, 1898.
	42586.49	Filon, Augustin. Garrick's pupil. Chicago, 1898.
	FL 382.65.3	Filon, Augustin. The modern French drama. London, 1898.
	43611.1.25.2	Fort, Paul. Montagne, forêt. 2. éd. II. Paris, 1898.
	43611.1.25.3	Fort, Paul. Roman de Louis XI. 2. éd. III. Paris, 1898.
Htn	42576.62.65*	France, Anatole. La leçon bien apprise. Paris, 1898.
	42576.62.11.2	France, Anatole. Le mannequin d'osier. 44. éd. Paris, 1898.
	42576.62.8	France, Anatole. L'orme du mail. Paris, 1898.
	42576.62.9	France, Anatole. Pages choisies. Paris, 1898.
	42576.63.650	France, H. Sous le bournous. Paris, 1898.
	39594.19.3	Gäbler, H. Studien zu Montesquieus Persischen Briefen. Chemnitz, 1898.
	42576.64.105	Gallet, Louis. The adventures of Cyrano de Bergerac. N.Y., 1898.
	41555.56.81	Galley, Jean B. Un romantique oublié, Antonin Moine, 1796-1849. Saint-Etienne, 1898.
	38575.28.5	Gasté, Armand. La querelle du Cid, pièces et pamphlets. Paris, 1898.
	43616.2.38	Gautier, Judith. Khou-n-Atonou; fragments d'un papyrus. Paris, 1898.
Htn	41542.37.18*	Gautier, Théophile. La mille et deuxième nuit. Paris, 1898.
	42576.5.11	Gebhart, Emile. Au son des cloches, contes et légendes. 2. éd. Paris, 1898.
	43622.24.30	Glesener, Edmond. Histoire de M. Aristide Truffaut. Paris, 1898.
	42575.54.5	Goncourt, Edmond de. Selections from Edmond and Jules de Goncourt. N.Y., 1898.
	43625.3.42	Gourmont, Rémy de. D'un pays Lointain. 2e ed. Paris, 1898.
	41593.34.22	Guérin, Maurice de. Journal, lettres et poèmes avec l'assentiment. 22. éd. Paris, 1898.
	37555.322	Guillaume, Juleo. Le vers français et les prosodies modernes. Bruxelles, 1898.
	42576.38.1100	Guillemain, E. Autour de la trahison. Paris, 1898.
	42543.62	Guinon, Albert. Les jobards. Paris, 1898.
	42576.40.344	Halévy, Ludovic. The abbé Constantin. N.Y., 1898.
	38512.115.50	Hanf, G. Über Guillaume de Machauts Voir-dit. Halle, 1898.
	42543.62.32	Haraucourt, Edmond. Don Juan de Mañara. Paris, 1898.
	FL 6138.98.3	Haymann, F. Jean-Jacques Rousseau Sozialphilosophie. Leipzig, 1898.
Htn	Mol 608.5*	Henning, G.N. Molières doctrine. n.p., 1898.
	42554.56	Heredia, J.M. de. Sonnets. San Francisco, 1898.
	42543.67	Hermant, Abel. Les transatlantiques. Paris, 1898.
	40515.5.85.7	Herpin, C.A.L. Une femme du monde au XVIIIe siècle. La jeunesse de Madame d'Épinay. 7e éd. Paris, 1898.
	41573.32.14	Hugo, Victor. Hernani; a drama. London, 1898.
	41574.8.5	Hugo, Victor. Oeuvres posthumes. Correspondance, 1815-1882. Paris, 1898. 2v.
	42576.65.27	Huysmans, Joris Karl. La Bièvre et Saint-Séverin. Paris, 1898.
	37595.34	Jeanroy, Alfred. Chansons et dits artésiens du XIIIe siècle. Bordeaux, 1898.
	42576.67.100	Karélis, André. Mémoires d'un fou. Paris, 1898.
	39527.25.10	La Fontaine, Jean de. Fables choisies. N.Y., 1898?
	42555.9	Lalot, Émile. Poésies. Paris, 1898.
	38514.60.75	La Marche, Olivier de. Le chevalier délibéré. London, 1898.
	41578.32.4	Lamartine, Alphonse. Graziella. Chicago, 1898.
	41578.9.6	Lamartine, Alphonse de. Nouvelles méditations poétiques. Paris, 1898.
	38575.19	Lanson, G. Corneille. Paris, 1898?
	42576.46.17	Lapauze, Jeanne L. Comédienne. Paris, 1898.
	42576.15.330	Lapierre, Charles. Esquisse sur Flaubert intime. Evreux, 1898.
	38585.14	Larroumet, Gustave. Racine. Paris, 1898.
	43687.89.9110	Lautrec, Gabriel de. Poèmes en prose. Paris, 1898.
	42554.16.5	Le Braz, A. Pâques d'Islande. Paris, 1898.
	37556.34A	Le Breton, A. Le roman au dix-huitième siècle. Paris, 1898.
	41593.12	Lecigne, C. Brizeux. Sa vie et ses oeuvres. Paris, 1898.
	38521.37A	Lefranc, Abel. Les idées réligieuses de Marguerite de Navarre. Paris, 1898.
	37543.55	Legouvé, E. Dernier travail derniers souvenirs. Paris, 1898.
	42544.8.2	Legouvé, Ernest. Il migliore amico della donna. Roma, 1898.
	FL 6138.98.4	Leipmann, M. Die Rechtsphilosophie des Jean-Jacques Rousseau. Berlin, 1898.
	42559.49	Lemercier, Eugène. Autor du Moulin chansons de la batte. Paris, 1898.
	FL 382.35	Lenient, C. La comédie en France au XIX siècle. Paris, 1898. 2v.
	40511.29	LeSage, Alain René. The history of Gil Blas of Santillana. Philadelphia, 1898. 3v.
	42526.5.5	Lhomme, F. La comédie d'aujourd'hui. Paris, 1898.
	43690.1.50	Lichtenberger, A. Mon petit Trott. Paris, 1898.
	FL 360.80	Lintilhac, E. Conférences dramatiques. Paris, 1898.
	Mol 728.18A	Loquin, A. Molière à Bordeaux vers 1647 et en 1656. Paris, 1898. 2v.
	42544.34.25.10	Lorde, André de. Dans la nuit. Paris, 1898.
	42544.34.25.15	Lorde, André de. Madame Blanchard. Paris, 1898.
	42544.34.28.2	Louys, Pierre. Les chansons de Bilitis. 14. éd. Paris, 1898.
	42544.34.28	Louys, Pierre. Les chansons de Bilitis. 15. éd. Paris, 1898.
	42544.34.29.5	Louys, Pierre. La femme et le pantin. 20e éd. Paris, 1898.
	Mon 152.2A	Lowndes, M.E. Michel de Montaigne. Cambridge, 1898.
	42545.3.42.5A	Maeterlinck, Maurice. Les aveugles. 8e éd. Bruxelles, 1898.

1898 - cont.

42545.3.3.2 Maeterlinck, Maurice. Pélléas et Mélisande. 7e éd. Bruxelles, 1898.
42545.3.5.3 Maeterlinck, Maurice. Le trésor des humbles. 14e éd. Paris, 1898.
42545.3.8.1 Maeterlinck, Maurice. Wisdom and destiny. N.Y., 1898.
42546.12 Magne, Émile. Les erreurs de documentation de Cyrano de Bergerac. Paris, 1898.
X Cg 37556.32 Maigron, Louis. Le roman historique à l'époque romantique. Paris, 1898.
42577.11.2.5 Malot, Hector. Episodes from Sans famille. London, 1898.
42577.11.25 Malot, Hector. Pages choisies. Paris, 1898.
38512.17 Mann, G. Die Sprache Froissarts auf Grund seiner Gedichte. Halle, 1898.
37596.82 Mann, W. Die Lieder des Dichters Robert de Raius gewannt la Chivre. Halle, 1898.
39527.37 Marchain, R. Les distractions de La Fontaine. Paris, 1898.
42576.76.32 Margueritte, Paul. Le désastre. Paris, 1898.
Mol 860.56 Marsolleau, L. Le dernier madrigal. Paris, 1898.
42545.9 Martel de Janville, S.G. Israel. Paris, 1898.
42545.9.8 Martel de Janville, S.G. Journal d'un grinchu. Paris, 1898.
42545.9.3 Martel de Janville, S.G. Miquette. Paris, 1898.
42557.14 Martrin-Donos, Charles. Verlaine intime. Paris, 1898.
42577.34.7 Masson-Forestier, A. Angoisses de Juge. Paris, 1898.
40587.17 Maurel, Andre. Essai sur Chateaubriand. Paris, 1898.
42555.58.5 Mendès, Catulle. Médée; tragédie. Paris, 1898.
NEDL 37566.37 Meunier, G. Le Bilan littéraire du XIXe siècle. Paris, 1898.
37558.34 Michel, H. Le quarantième fauteuil. Paris, 1898.
42545.28 Mirbeau, Octave. Les mauvais bergers. Paris, 1898.
Mol 212.15.5 Molière, Jean Baptiste Poquelin. Femmes savantes. Leipzig, 1898. 2 pam.
Mol 211.59 Molière, Jean Baptiste Poquelin. Les femmes savantes. 8e éd. Paris, 1898.
Mol 232.9 Molière, Jean Baptiste Poquelin. De gedwongen Knecht...J.J.G. Wahlen. Nijmegen, 1898.
X Cg Mol 246.3.5 Molière, Jean-Baptiste Poquelin. The great French triumvirate. Constable. London, 1898.
Mol 38.98 Molière, Jean Baptiste Poquelin. Théâtre choisi...Léna. Paris, 1898.
Mol 166.25 Molière, Jean Baptiste Poquelin. De vrek...T.H. de Beer. 's Gravenhage, 1898.
Mon 35.5.2 Montaigne, Michel de. Essays. Breslau, 1898.
Mon 30.10.3A Montaigne, Michel de. Essays. Florio. v.2-6. London, 1898. 5v.
40575.4 Morel, L. Études littéraires Sainte-Beuve...Pascal. Zurich, 1898.
Htn 42577.13.40* Morvan, L. The secret of Fougereuse. Boston, 1898.
NEDL 41596.26 Musset, Alfred de. Lorenzaccio, drame. Paris, 1898.
42578.30.15 Ohnet, Georges. La fille du député. N.Y., 1898.
43737.94.110 Pawlowski, Gaston William Adam de. On se moque de nous. Paris, 1898.
37567.48.5 Pellissier, G.J.M. Etudes de littérature contemporaine. 1e et 2e série. Paris, 1898. 2v.
42578.30.75 Petitcolin, André. Arvor. Paris, 1898.
37567.72 Pica, V. Letteratura d'eccezione. Milan, 1898.
38521.34 Pinvert, L. Jacques Grévin. Paris, 1898.
42545.80 Ply, H. Les chevaliers d'Eppes. Chauny, 1898.
41593.29.3.50 Pougin, Arthur. La jeunesse de Mme. Desbordes-Valmore. Paris, 1898.
42578.31.34 Prévost, Marcel. Trois nouvelles. 23. éd. Paris, 1898.
42578.31.34.5 Prévost, Marcel. Trois nouvelles. 36. éd. Paris, 1898.
41564.44 Prudhomme, S. À Alfred de Vigny sonnet. Paris, 1898.
37567.150 Pujo, Maurice. Essais de critique générale. Paris, 1898.
42587.50.10 Quellien, N. Contes et nouvelles du Pays-de-Tréguier. Paris, 1898.
38585.20.6 Racine, Jean. Athalie. Boston, 1898.
38585.23 Racine, Jean. Bajazet. Paris, 1898.
42587.50.75 Rebell, Hugues. La femme qui a connu l'Empereur. Paris, 1898.
42556.21.6 Reboux, P. Les iris noirs. Paris, 1898.
43753.9.130 Reboux, Paul. Les iris noirs. Paris, 1898.
37567.63 Recolin, Charles. L'anarchie littéraire. Paris, 1898.
42515.29.280A Renan, Ernest. The apostles. Boston, 1898.
42515.34.25 Renan, Ernest. E. Renan et M. Berthelot. Paris, 1898.
42515.30.151 Renan, Ernest. Lectures on the influence of the institution...of Rome. 4. ed. London, 1898.
42587.52.23 Renard, Jules. Le plaisir de rompre. Paris, 1898.
42556.27.66 Retté, Adolphe. Oeuvres complètes. Paris, 1898.
42556.27.86 Retté, Adolphe. XIII idylles diaboliques. Paris, 1898.
42556.21.2100 Reynold, Berthe. Jardins suspendus. Paris, 1898.
42556.22.60 Richepin, Jean. La martyre. Paris, 1898.
43757.5.110 Robert, Louis de. La première femme. Paris, 1898.
42578.19.16.3 Rod, Edouard. Le ménage du pasteur Naudié. Paris, 1898.
42578.19.16 Rod, Edouard. Le ménage du pasteur Naudié. Paris, 1898.
42578.22.10.40 Rosny, J.H. Amour étrusque. Paris, 1898.
42578.22.8.11 Rosny, J.H. La silencieuse. Paris, 1898.
Mol 618.2 Rossmann, G. Der Aberglaube bei Molière. Burg, 1898.
42546.14.3A Rostand, Edmond. Cyrano de Bergerac. Boston, 1898.
42546.14A Rostand, Edmond. Cyrano de Bergerac. N.Y., 1898.
42546.13.3 Rostand, Edmond. Cyrano de Bergerac. N.Y., 1898.
42546.13.2.3 Rostand, Edmond. Cyrano de Bergerac. N.Y., 1898.
42546.14.1.5A Rostand, Edmond. Cyrano de Bergerac. N.Y., 1898.
42546.13.1.6 Rostand, Edmond. Cyrano de Bergerac. N.Y., 1898.
42546.13.1.4 Rostand, Edmond. Cyrano de Bergerac. Paris, 1898.
42546.13.1.2 Rostand, Edmond. Cyrano de Bergerac. Paris, 1898.
42546.13.1.7 Rostand, Edmond. Cyrano de Bergerac. Paris, 1898.
42546.13 Rostand, Edmond. Cyrano de Bergerac. Paris, 1898.
42546.13.6.5 Rostand, Edmond. Cyrano de Bergerac. Paris, 1898.
42546.13.6 Rostand, Edmond. Cyrano de Bergerac. Paris, 1898.
42546.13.5 Rostand, Edmond. Cyrano de Bergerac. Paris, 1898.
42546.14.7 Rostand, Edmond. The story of Cyrano de Bergerac. N.Y., 1898.
42546.14.8.75 Rostand, Edmond. Syrano de Mperzerak. en Peiraiei, 1898.
43757.98.100 Royère, Jean. Exil daré; poésies. Paris, 1898.
FL 398.74.70 Samson, J.I. (Mme.). Rachel et Samson. 3e ed. Paris, 1898.
41557.9.62 Sand, George. François le Champi. Paris, 1898.
41557.8.105.5 Sand, George. Le marquis de Villemer. Paris, 1898.
38544.27.520 Scheuer, Ernst. Frau von La Fayette. Bonn, 1898.
40522.14 Schroeder, V. L'Abbé Prévost. Sa vie - ses romans. Paris, 1898.
42578.36.16 Schultz, Jeanne. Colette. N.Y., 1898.
42587.57.5 Schwob, Marcel. The children's crusade. Boston, 1898.
38512.67 Sieper, Ernst. Les échecs amoureux. Weimar, 1898.

1898 - cont.

42546.34.23 Silvestre, Armand. Belles histoires d'amour. Paris, 1898.
42546.34.11 Silvestre, Armand. Les tendresses; poésies nouvelles. Paris, 1898.
42543.1.25 Soreau, Georges. La vie de la dame aux camélias. Paris, 1898.
42516.16.2 Sorel, Albert. Nouveaux essais d'histoire et de critique. Paris, 1898.
42566.49 Soutien de la famille, moeurs contemporaines. Paris, 1898.
41558.68.5 Souvestre, Émile. An attic philosopher in Paris. N.Y., 1898.
38557.24 Stapfer, Paul. La grande prédication chrétienne en France. Paris, 1898.
37543.49 Tenarg, Paul. Nos bons auteurs. Paris, 1898.
Mol 213.13 Tendering, T. Molière's Femmes savantes. Hamburg, 1898.
43788.5.240 Tharaud, Jérôme. Le coltineur débile. Paris, 1898.
42583.17.7 Theuriet, André. Pages choisies. Paris, 1898.
42583.33.28 Theuriet, André. Le refuge. Paris, 1898.
37555.530 Thieme, H.P. The technique of the French Alexandrine. n.p., 1898.
42578.50.5 Töpffer, Rodolphe. La bibliothèque de mon oncle. N.Y., 1898.
42578.56.35 Toutain, Paul. Rustres. Paris, 1898.
38525.36.9 Tristan L'Hermite, F. Le page disgracié. Paris, 1898.
38575.18.3 Trollope, H.M. Corneille and Racine. Edinburgh, 1898.
42547.10.25 Vallette, Marguerite. L'heure sexuelle. Paris, 1898?
42547.13 Verhaeren, Émile. The dawn. London, 1898.
FL 1029.87 Verkvitz, Wilhelm. Tractate zur Unterweisung in der Anglo-Normannischen Briefschreibkunst. Greifswald, 1898.
42576.57.5 Viaud, Julien. Figures et choses qui passaient. Paris, 1898.
42576.57.4 Viaud, Julien. Matelot. Paris, 1898.
42557.25.100 Vielé-Griffin, F. Phocas le jardinier. Paris, 1898.
41564.15.5 Vigny, Alfred de. Poésies complètes. Paris, 1898.
42587.66.25 Villecrose, Julien. Les lamentations du peuple. Paris, 1898.
42522.14 Vogüé, E.M. de. Histoire et poésie. Paris, 1898.
37563.30 Voigt, J. Das Naturgefühl in der Literatur der französischen Renaissance. Berlin, 1898.
42584.23.2 Zola, Emile. Une page d'amour. Paris, 1898.
42584.23.10.7 Zola, Emile. Paris. N.Y., 1898. 2v.
42584.23.10.2 Zola, Emile. Paris. Paris, 1898.
42584.23.10.4 Zola, Emile. Paris. Paris, 1898.
42584.23.10 Zola, Emile. Paris. Paris, 1898.
42584.19.2 Zola, Emile. Le rêve. Paris, 1898.
42584.14.5 Zola, Emile. Rome. N.Y., 1898. 2v.

1899

42562.38.4 Adam, Paul. La force. Paris, 1899.
FL 384.95PF Appiello, Leonetto. Nos actrices. 4. ed. Paris, 1899.
42553.53.100 Arnaud, Robert. Les dires de celui qui passe. Alger, 1899.
40596.13.80.27 Balzac, Honoré de. Catherine de Medici. Boston, 1899.
40597.90 Balzac, Honoré de. The celibates. Philadelphia, 1899.
40597.91 Balzac, Honoré de. César Birotteau. Philadelphia, 1899.
40597.92 Balzac, Honoré de. The country doctor. Philadelphia, 1899.
40597.93 Balzac, Honoré de. Cousin Betty. Philadelphia, 1899.
40596.13.80.19 Balzac, Honoré de. Cousin Pons. Boston, 1899.
40596.17.5 Balzac, Honoré de. Le curé de Tours. Boston, 1899.
40597.94A Balzac, Honoré de. The deputy for Arcis. Philadelphia, 1899.
40597.95 Balzac, Honoré de. A distinguished provincial at Paris. Philadelphia 1899.
40597.96 Balzac, Honoré de. Eugénie Grandet. Philadelphia, 1899.
40597.99 Balzac, Honoré de. The jealousies of a country town. Philadelphia, 1899.
40596.13.80.31 Balzac, Honoré de. Juana, and other stories. Boston, 1899.
40597.100 Balzac, Honoré de. Modeste Mignon. Philadelphia, 1899.
40597.101A Balzac, Honoré de. Muse of the department. Philadelphia, 1899.
40596.9 Balzac, Honoré de. Oeuvres posthumes. Lettres à l'étrangère (1833-1842). Paris, 1899. 2v.
40597.102A Balzac, Honoré de. The peasantry. Philadelphia, 1899.
40597.103 Balzac, Honoré de. Seraphita. Philadelphia, 1899.
40596.13.80.5 Balzac, Honoré de. A start in life. Boston, 1899.
40597.98 Balzac, Honoré de. The harlot's progress. Philadelphia, 1899.
40597.104 Balzac, Honoré de. The wild ass's skin. Philadelphia, 1899.
40597.105 Balzac, Honoré de. A woman of thirty. Philadelphia, 1899.
37566.13 Barbey d'Aurevilly, J.A. Les oeuvres et les hommes. 3rd series. Paris, 1899.
42563.16.9 Barrès, Maurice. Un amateur d'âmes. Paris, 1899.
37596.2.6 Bauer, Fritz. Das personal Pronomen in le Pelerinage de vie humaine de Guileville. Würzburg, 1899.
42563.5.110 Beaubourg, Maurice. Les joueurs de boules de Saint-Mandé. Paris, 1899.
42554.13.1100 Bengy-Puyvallée, A. de. Emaux sur or. Paris, 1899.
37567.64 Bérenger, H. La France intellectuelle. Paris, 1899.
37593.63.9 Berger, R. Canchoirs und Partures des...Adam de la Halle. Halle, 1899.
42542.29.14.9 Bergerat, Émile. Plus que reine. 3. éd. Paris, 1899.
42542.29.28.190 Bernard, Tristan. Franches lippées. Paris, 1899.
38566.24 Boileau Despréaux, Nicolas. Oeuvres poétiques. 19. éd. Paris, 1899.
42542.29.124 Bordise, S. Bureau de renseignements, ouvert à une heure. Paris, 1899.
Htn 38557.31* Bossuet, J.B. Oraisons funèbres du Prince de Condé. Paris, 1899.
42542.30.6 Bouchor, Maurice. Poèmes et récits. Paris, 1899.
42542.30.10 Bouchor, Maurice. Tobie. Paris, 1899.
42563.39.5 Boylesve, René. Mlle Cloque. Paris, 1899.
43545.89.100 Braunt, A. Dans la rue. Paris, 1899?
37543.47.5 Brunetière, Ferdinand. Manuel de l'histoire de la littérature française. Paris, 1899.
42584.25.170 Burrows, H. Zola. London, 1899.
37574.115 Canfield, Arthur G. French lyrics. N.Y., 1899.
37574.115.3 Canfield, Arthur G. French lyrics. N.Y., 1899.
38514.64.6 Chartier, Alain. Le curial. Halle, 1899.
40586.28 Chateaubriand, F.A.R. Memoires d'outre-tombe. v.1-4,6. Paris, 1899. 5v.
40526.7A Chénier, André. Oeuvres poétiques. Paris, 1899. 2v.
42586.27.30 Cherot, Henri. Bourdaloue. Paris, 1899.

Chronological Listing

1899 - cont.

38527.35.5 Christie, R.C. Etienne Dolet. London, 1899.
38528.8.9 Clément, S. Henri Estienne et son oeuvre française. Paris, 1899.
37596.80 Colonna, Egidio. Li livres du gouvernement des rois. N.Y., 1899. 2v.
42542.53.13 Coolus, R. Coeurblette. Paris, 1899.
38575.29.4 Corneille, Pierre. Le Cid. Tournai, 1899.
38575.25 Corneille, Pierre. Le Cid. Horace. Polyeucte. Scènes choisies...par M. Bouchor. Paris, 1899.
38537.26 Coutaud, Albert. La pedagogie de Rabelais. Paris, 1899.
39544.40 Crouslé, L. La vie et les oeuvres de Voltaire. Paris, 1899. 2v.
42542.58.10 Curel, François de. L'invitée. Paris, 1899.
42542.58.35 Curel, François de. La nouvelle idole. Photoreproduction. Paris, 1899.
39533.20.9A Cyrano de Bergerac. Le pedant joué. Boston, 1899.
39533.20.5 Cyrano de Bergerac. Voyage to the moon. N.Y., 1899.
42566.24.28 Daudet, Alphonse. Kings in exile. N.Y., 1899.
42566.51.10 Daudet, Alphonse. La Belle-Nivernaise; story of an old boat. Philadelphia, 1899.
42566.53.5 Daudet, Alphonse. The little parish church. N.Y., 1899.
42566.56 Daudet, Alphonse. Notes sur la vie. Paris, 1899.
38513.19.9 David, Carl. Die drei Mysterien des heiligen Martin von Tours. Frankfurt am Main, 1899.
FL 379.41 Dejob, C. Les femmes dans la comédie française et italienne au XVIIIe siècle. Paris, 1899.
42567.100 Delattre, Louis. Marionnettes rustiques montrant les bonnes petites gens à leurs métiers. Liège, 1899.
42548.71.20 La demoiselle de compagnie. N.Y., 1899.
NEDL Mol 704.2 Des Granges, René. La querelle de Molière et de Boursault. Paris, 1899.
42542.65.13.2 Donnay, Maurice. Le torrent, in four acts. N.Y., 1899.
42542.65.13 Donnay, Maurice. Le torrent. Paris, 1899.
37567.35.5 Doumic, René. Contemporary French novelists. N.Y., 1899.
42515.35.80 Duclaux, A.M.F.R. The life of Ernest Renan. Boston, 1899.
41538.16.8.3 Dumas, Alexandre. The count of Monte Cristo. Boston, 1899. 2v.
41538.52.9 Dumas, Alexandre. Don Juan de Marana; Kean; Riquillo. Paris, 1899.
41538.29.9 Dumas, Alexandre. A marriage of convenience. London, 1899.
41538.29.11 Dumas, Alexandre. A marriage of convenience. N.Y., 1899.
41538.24.28 Dumas, Alexandre. The regent's daughter. Boston, 1899.
41529.105.4.5 Dumas, Alexandre. Ten years later. N.Y., 1899.
41538.53.32.10 Dumas, Alexandre. The three musketeers. N.Y., 1899.
38526.37.11 Durand-Lapie, Paul. François Maynerd et François Menard. Paris, 1899.
42572.11.23 Erckmann, Emile. The conscript; a story of the French war of 1813. N.Y., 1899.
43598.84.140 Estaunié, Édouard. Le ferment. Paris, 1899.
42554.32.5 Fabie, François. Vers la maison. Paris, 1899.
42574.5.31 Fabre, Aristide. La pipe de Philibert. Paris, 1899.
FL 6138.99 Fährmann, E. Jean-Jacques Rousseau's Naturanschauung. Plauen, 1899.
X Cg 42576.15.11 Faguet, Emile. Flaubert. Paris, 1899.
43606.89.67 Faure, Gabriel. Fleurs rouges. Paris, 1899.
42576.33.6 Flaubert, Gustave. Trois contes. Paris, 1899.
42576.36.11 Fleuriot, Zenaide Marie A. Z.M.A. Fleuriot. Paris, 1899.
42576.62.14A France, Anatole. L'anneau d'améthyste. Paris, 1899.
42576.62.11.5 France, Anatole. Le mannequin d'osier. 46. éd. Paris, 1899.
42576.62.15 France, Anatole. Pierre Nozière. Paris, 1899.
42576.62.15.5 France, Anatole. Pierre Nozière. 29. éd. Paris, 1899.
42576.62.15.2 France, Anatole. Pierre Nozière. 36. éd. Paris, 1899.
38521.31 Garrisson, C. Théophile et Paul de Viau. Paris, 1899.
Mol 878.1 Geffroy, G. Salut à Molière. Paris, 1899.
42554.46.5 Gielkens, Émile. Camille. Bruxelles, 1899.
41574.36 Glachant, P. Papiers d'autrefois. Paris, 1899.
Htn 43625.3.76* Gourmont, Rémy de. Ici commence le poème des St. du Paradis. Paris, 1899.
42543.60.5 Grandmougin, Charles. Visions chrétiennes. Paris, 1899.
Htn 42576.40.79* Guillemot, Maurice. Entr'actes de pierres. Paris, 1899.
Mon 117.3 Guizot, G. Montaigne, etudes et fragments. Paris, 1899.
42576.40.338 Halévy, Ludovic. L'abbé Constantin. Boston, 1899.
39532.7.10 Hamilton, Anthony. Four Facardins. London, 1899.
41596.4.25 Hendreich, Otto. Alfred de Musset, ein Vertreter des "esprit gaulois". Berlin, 1899.
42543.62.96 Hennique, Léon. Minnie Brandon. Paris, 1899.
42543.64.10 Hermant, Abel. Théâtre des deux mondes. Paris, 1899.
42554.64.50 Herold, A.F. Savitri. Paris, 1899.
41573.32.15 Hugo, Victor. Hernani. 12. ed. London, 1899.
41573.23.11 Hugo, Victor. The hunchback of Notre Dame. Boston, 1899.
41574.13.6 Hugo, Victor. Memoirs. N.Y., 1899.
41574.13.5 Hugo, Victor. Memoirs. N.Y., 1899.
39545.6.3 Hugo, Victor. Oration on Voltaire. Portland, Me., 1899.
Mol 608.15 Humbert, C. Zu Molière's Leben und Werken. Bielefeld, 1899.
FL 398.7.17.5 Huret, Jules. Sarah Bernhardt. London, 1899.
42576.65.24 Huysmans, Joris Karl. Pages catholiques. Paris, 1899.
42554.65.130 Ibels, André. Talentiers; ballades libres. Paris, 1899.
43667.51.90 Jaloux, Edmond. L'agonie de l'amour. Paris, 1899.
42554.66.100 John, Pantaléon. Les secrets du coeur, poésies diverses. Toulouse, 1899.
38514.68.2 Joret-Desclosières, G. Un écrivain national au XVe siècle Alain Chartier. Paris, 1899.
38557.2.5 Jovy, Ernest. Bossuet...et Pierre du Laurens. n.p., 1899.
Mol 870.58 Jubin, G. Molière et Cyrano. Paris, 1899.
41583.32.25 Klinger, Ludwig. Über die Tragödien Casimir Delavignes. pt.1-3. Waldenburg, 1899-1907.
41557.10.16A Komarova, V.D. George Sand, sa vie et ses oeuvres 1804-1876. Paris, 1899-1926. 4v.
42576.42 Labusquière, John. L'autrefois; récits de Gascogne et d'ailleurs. Paris, 1899.
38523.21.25 Lair, J. Recherches sur une maison de Paris ou demeura Malherbe. Caen, 1899.
FL 360.30.2 Larroumet, G. Nouvelle études d'histoire et de critique dramatique. Paris, 1899.
40536.23 Laservière, Joseph de. Un professeour d'ancien régime le Père Charles Porée (1676-1741). Paris, 1899.
42544.24.30 Lavedan, Henri. Nocturnes. 12e éd. Paris, 1899.
38537.25.6 Le Double, A. Rabelais anatomiste et physiologiste. Paris, 1899.
42548.48 Legouvé, Ernest. Théâtre de campagne. ser. 9. Paris, 1899.
42576.45.3 Le Roux, H. Gens de poudre. Paris, 1899.

1899 - cont.

42555.40.55 Le Vavasseur, G. Inauguration du buste de Gustave Le Vavasseur. Alençon, 1899.
Mol 612.10 Levinstein, K. Christian Weise und Molière. Berlin, 1899.
Htn 42544.34.29* Louys, Pierre. La femme et le pantin. Paris, 1899.
42544.34.42 Louys, Pierre. Mimes des courtisanes de Lucien. 6e éd. Paris, 1899.
42584.24.5 Macdonald, A. Emile Zola. Study of his personality. Washington, 1899.
42545.3.6.3 Maeterlinck, Maurice. Aglavaine et Selysette. 7e éd. Paris, 1899.
42545.3.7.2 Maeterlinck, Maurice. Alladine and Palomides. Chicago, 1899.
42545.3.7 Maeterlinck, Maurice. Alladine and Palomides. Interior. The death of Tintagiles. London, 1899.
42545.3.5.6 Maeterlinck, Maurice. The treasure of the humble. N.Y., 1899.
42577.11.2.10 Malot, Hector. Episodes from Sans famille. Boston, 1899.
42576.76.34 Margueritte, Paul. Femmes nouvelles. Paris, 1899.
42576.76.33 Margueritte, Paul. La poste des neiges. Barcelone, 1899.
41596.4.13 Martellet, Adèle C. Dix ans chez Alfred de Musset. Paris, 1899.
42545.20.15 Massonneau, F. Étude sentimentale; coeurs blessés. N.Y., 1899.
42577.4.12 Maupassant, Guy de. Le père Milon, contes inédits. Paris, 1899.
42545.10.21 Meilhac, Henri. Décoré. Paris, 1899.
42545.10.8 Meilhac, Henri. La grande-duchesse de Gérolstein. Paris, 1899.
37573.599 Méras, Baptiste. Cinq histoires. N.Y., 1899.
41555.22.1.5 Mérimée, Prosper. Chronique du règne de Charles IX. Boston, 1899.
41555.23.5 Mérimée, Prosper. Colomba. Boston, 1899.
41555.6.15 Mérimée, Prosper. Lettres à une inconnue. Paris, 1899. 2v.
Mol 171.50 Molière, Jean Baptiste Poquelin. Le bourgeois gentilhomme...Jacquinet. Paris, 1899.
Mol 171.50.2 Molière, Jean Baptiste Poquelin. Le bourgeois gentilhomme...Jacquinet. Paris, 1899.
Mol 211.60 Molière, Jean Baptiste Poquelin. Les femmes savantes...Pille. Paris, 1899.
Mol 239.1.5 Molière, Jean Baptiste Poquelin. Le médecin volant...colvé des jardins. Paris, 1899.
Mol 245.81 Molière, Jean Baptiste Poquelin. Le misanthrope. Eggert. Boston, 1899.
Mol 245.80 Molière, Jean Baptiste Poquelin. Le misanthrope. Eggert. Boston, 1899.
Mol 251.63 Molière, Jean Baptiste Poquelin. Les précieuses ridicules. Toy. Boston, 1899.
Mol 251.63.2 Molière, Jean Baptiste Poquelin. Les précieuses ridicules. Toy. Boston, 1899.
Mol 48.99.2 Molière, Jean Baptiste Poquelin. Scènes choisies...Bouchor. Paris, 1899-1900. 2v.
Mol 48.99 Molière, Jean Baptiste Poquelin. Scènes choisies...Bouchor. Paris, 1899-1900. 2v.
37573.599.10 Mont, Paul de. Modernités. Almelo, 1899.
Mon 32.6 Montaigne, Michel de. Education of children. N.Y., 1899.
39593.30 Montesquieu, C.L. de S. Pensées et fragments inédits de Montesquieu. Bordeaux, 1899.
39594.3.7 Montesquieu, C.L. de S. The spirit of laws. N.Y., 1899. 2v.
FL 370.67.10 Mortensen, Johan. Medeltidsdramit i Frankrike. Göteborg, 1899.
41596.22.10 Musset, Alfred de. La confession d'un enfant du siècle. Paris, 1899.
41596.13.7 Musset, Alfred de. Poésies nouvelles, 1836-1852. Paris, 1899.
41596.13.5 Musset, Alfred de. Premières poésies, 1829-1835. Paris, 1899.
40587.20 Nantes, France. Société des Bibliophiles Bretons. Le cinquantenaire des funérailles de Chateaubriand. Nantes, 1899.
38514.69 Oliver, T.E. Jacques Milet's Drama "La destruction de Troye la Grant". Heidelberg, 1899.
42555.68.330 Paban, Adolphe. Les roses de Kerné. Paris, 1899.
41539.6 Parigot, Hippolyte. Le drame d'Alexandre Dumas. Paris, 1899.
37547.22 Paris, Gaston. La littérature Normande avant annexion. (912-1204). Paris, 1899.
37597.29.5 Péan Gatineau. Das altfranzösische Martinsleben. Helsingfors, 1899.
42545.75.30 Picard, André. Franchise. Paris, 1899.
FL 360.88 Pottecher, Maurice. Le théâtre du peuple. Paris, 1899.
42515.44 Quinet, E. (Mme.). Cinquante ans d'amitié. Paris, 1899.
37547.58 Quirielle, Roger de. Bio-bibliographie des écrivains anciens du Bourbonnais. Moulins, 1899.
42587.50.68 Rebell, Hugues. L'espionne impériale. Paris, 1899.
42556.25 Régnier, Henri de. Premiers poèmes. Paris, 1899.
42556.25.5 Régnier, Henri de. Premiers poèmes. 10e éd. Paris, 1899?
42556.27.8 Régnier, Henri de. Le tréfle blanc. Paris, 1899.
42515.30.630 Renan, Ernest. Prière sur l'acropole. Paris, 1899.
42556.27.89 Retté, Adolphe. La seule nuit. Paris, 1899.
42556.22.65 Richepin, Jean. Les truands. Paris, 1899.
42587.55.9 Rivoire, André. Berthe aux grands pieds. Paris, 1899.
NEDL 37555.50 Robert, Pierre. Les poètes du XIXe siècle. Période romantique. Paris, 1899.
42578.19.2.5 Rod, Edouard. La course à la mort. 6. éd. Paris, 1899.
42578.19.8.2 Rod, Edouard. Nouvelles études sur le 19. siècle. Paris, 1899.
42578.19.16.10 Rod, Edouard. Pastor Naudie's young wife. Boston, 1899.
43757.50.343 Rolland, Romain. Le triomphe de la raison; drame. Paris, 1899.
42556.32.50 Rollinat, Maurice. Paysages et paysans. Paris, 1899.
42578.22.160 Rosny, J.H. L'aiguille d'or. 2. éd. Paris, 1899.
42546.14.2A Rostand, Edmond. Cyrano de Bergerac. N.Y., 1899.
42546.15.6.11 Rostand, Edmond. La princesse Lointaine. Paris, 1899.
42546.15 Rostand, Edmond. The romancers. N.Y., 1899.
42546.15.5 Rostand, Edmond. Les romanesques. Paris, 1899.
FL 6002.899 Rousseau, J.J. Petits chefs-d'oeuvres. Paris, 1899.
42578.31.130 Saint-Pol Roux. La dame à la faulx. 2. éd. Paris, 1899.
41557.9.95.2 Sand, George. Mauprat. Boston, 1899.
41557.9.31.5 Sand, George. La petite Fadette. N.Y., 1899.
41557.30.10 Sandeau, Jules. Madeleine: a story of French love. Chicago, 1899.
38514.28 Sauerstein, Paul. Charles d'Orleans und die englische Übersetzung seiner Dichtungen. Halle, 1899.

1899 - cont.

38557.45.10 Scheiding, O. Bossuets Stellung zur Reformatiobewegung. Hamburg, 1899.
Mol 619.3 Schneegans, H. Groteske Satire bei Molière? Halle, 1899.
Mol 598.20F Schneegans, H. Molière als Satiriker. München, 1899.
42578.36.10A Schultz, Jeanne. La neuvaine de Colette. N.Y., 1899.
Mon 129.2 Schwabe, P. Michel de Montaigne als philosophischer Charakter. Hamburg, 1899.
38585.5 Séché, Léon. Port-Royal des Champs, petit manuel...suivi de Racine à Port-Royal. Paris, 1899.
43765.21.35 Sée, Edmond. Les miettes. Paris, 1899.
37567.626 Segard, Achille. Itineraire fantaisiste. Paris, 1899.
42587.58.8.10 Ségur, Sophie. Les malheurs de Sophie. Paris, 1899.
38546.43 Sévigné, Marie de R.C. Letters. Boston, 1899.
FL 396.52 Soubies, Albert. Histoire du théâtre-lyrique, 1851-70. Paris, 1899.
42563.18.276 Suarès, André. Barrès. Paris, 1899.
41563.20 Suberwick, de (Mme.). Geheimnisse der Inquisition. Budapest, 1899.
37596.155 Suchier, W. Über das altfranzösische Gedicht von der Zerstörung Jerusalems. Inaug. Diss. Halle, 1899.
FL 6138.95.2A Texte, J. Jean-Jacques Rousseau and the cosmopolitan spirit in literature. London, 1899.
37555.60 Théret, Auguste. Littérature du Berry; Poésie XVIe, XVIIe et XVIIIe siècles. Paris, 1899.
42557.5.255 Thiebault, Henry. Nouveaux chants d'un français. Alger, 1899.
38524.50 Thresor du sonet. XVIe-XVIIe siècles. Macon, 1899-
37564.58 Toinet, R. Notes pour servir à l'histoire littérature du XVIIe siècle. v.3-4. Tulle, 1899- 2v.
42587.63.100 Toudouze, Gustave. Madame Lambelle. N.Y., 1899.
39564.24 Tourneux, M. Diderot et Catherine II. Paris, 1899.
40555.31.5 Ulrich, O. Charles de Villers. Leipzig, 1899.
38557.2 Urbain, Charles. Bossuet. Paris, 1899.
37551.70 Vaganay, H. Bibliographie des sonnets françaises du XIXe siècle. Louvain, 1899.
38537.23 Vallat, Gustave. Rabelais sa vie, son génie et son oeuvre. Paris, 1899.
42547.11.5 Vaucaire, Maurice. Les girouettes. Paris, 1899.
42547.11.12 Vaucaire, Maurice. Petit chagrin. Paris, 1899.
37595.36.10 Vega Carpio, Lape Felix de. Los Guzmanes. v.16. Halle, 1899.
42557.11.2 Verhaeren, Émile. Poems. Photoreproduction. London, 1899.
42557.11.23 Verhaeren, Émile. Les visages de la vie. Bruxelles, 1899.
X Cg 42557.18.4 Verlaine, Paul. Oeuvres complètes. Paris, 1899- 2v.
42576.57.6 Viaud, Julien. Reflets sur la sombre route. 10. éd. Paris, 1899.
41564.5.7 Vigny, Alfred de. Cinq-mars. London, 1899.
41564.5.5 Vigny, Alfred de. Cinq-Mars. Paris, 1899.
41564.28 Vigny, Alfred de. Imperial grandeur or the family. n.p., 1899.
Htn 42584.24.6* Vizetelly, E.A. With Zola in England. London, 1899.
39545.26.50 Voltaire, François Marie Arouet de. Essays and criticisms. N.Y., 1899.
39545.54A Voltaire, François Marie Arouet de. La pucelle, the maid of Orleans. London, 1899. 2v.
37597.39 Wachter, Hermann. Der Springer unserer lieben Frau. Erlangen, 1899.
42522.32 Warney, H. Le chemin d'espérance. Paris, 1899.
FL 6138.99.2 Windenberger, J.L. Système politique étrangère de Jean-Jacques Rousseau. Paris, 1899.
37555.39 Zimmermann, O. Die Totenklage in den altfranzösischen Chansons de Geste. Berlin, 1899.
42584.11.7 Zola, Emile. La débâcle. Boston, 1899.
42584.12.34 Zola, Emile. Les quatre évangiles, fécondité. Paris, 1899.
42584.14.6 Zola, Emile. Rome. London, 1899.
40516.59.10 Zollinger, Oskar. Louis Sébastien Mercier als Dramatiker und Dramaturg. Strassburg, 1899.

19-

42562.35.10 About, Edmond. The twins. London, 19- .
43531.7.33.10 Aubert, Octave Louis. Le baléer-brô. St. Brieuc, 19- .
42554.50.16A Baldersperger, F. Charles Guérin et son oeuvre lyrique. n.p., 19- .
40597.35.70 Balzac, Honoré de. Catherine de Medici. N.Y., 19- .
40597.14.6.10 Balzac, Honoré de. César Birotteau. London, 19- .
40597.14.4 Balzac, Honoré de. César Birotteau. N.Y., 19- .
40596.21.10 Balzac, Honoré de. The chouans. Chicago, 19- ?
40597.20.4 Balzac, Honoré de. Eugénie Grandet. London, 19- .
40597.32.55 Balzac, Honoré de. A harlot's progress. N.Y., 19- .
40597.29.4.60 Balzac, Honoré de. Old Goriot. N.Y., 19- .
40597.33.5 Balzac, Honoré de. La recherche de l'absolu. Paris, 19- .
40596.15.14 Balzac, Honoré de. Short stories. N.Y., 19- .
40596.15.12 Balzac, Honoré de. Short stories. N.Y., 19- .
40597.31.5 Balzac, Honoré de. The two young brides. London, 19- .
40597.32.6.5 Balzac, Honoré de. The wild ass's skin. N.Y., 19- .
40596.13.122 Balzac, Honoré de. Works. N.Y., 19- . 6v.
41522.2.70 Barbey d'Aurevilly, Jules. Du dandysme et de G. Brummell. Memoranda. Paris, 19- ?
42563.21.47 Bazin, René. Madame Corentine. Paris, 19- .
40532.7.40 Beaumarchais, Pierre A.C. de. Essai sur le genre dramatique. Paris, 19- ?
40532.14.15 Beaumarchais, Pierre A.C. de. Théâtre choisi. Paris, 19- ?
42542.29.15.5 Bernard, Tristan. L'anglais tel qu'on le parle. Paris, 19- .
41573.15 Berret, Paul. Le moyen age dans la légende des siècles et les sources de Victor Hugo. Paris, 19- .
41522.58.15 Bertrand, Louis Le keepsake fantastique. Paris, 19- .
38566.36.2A Boileau Despréaux, Nicolas. Les héros de Roman. Dialogue. Boston, 19- .
38557.31.30 Bossuet, J.B. Oraisons funèbres. Paris, 19- ?
43545.3.1100 Brame, Hector. Illusion et vérité. Poissy, 19- .
FL 398.7.41 Brisson, Adolphe. Phèdre et Mme. Sarah Bernhardt. Paris, 19- ?
40597.2.13.5 Brunetière, F. Honoré de Balzac. N.Y., 19- .
37567.45.10 Brunetière, Ferdinand. L'evolution de la poésie lyrique en France au dix-neuvième siècle. 10. éd. Paris, 19- . 2v.
43547.77.100 Burnat-Provins, Marguerite. Le livre pour toi. 7. éd. Paris, 19- ?
40597.2.21 Calippe, Charles. Balzac, ses idées sociales. Reims, 19- ?
42554.17.50 Cantacuzène, C.A. Considerations lyriques. Paris, 19- .
43550.77.3100 Carrot, Antoine. Premiers matins; poèmes. Lyon, 19- .

19- - cont.

40516.6.7 Cazotte, Jacques. Amores do diabo; romance. 2. ed. Porto, 19- .
37563.55 Chamard, Henri. La doctrine et l'oeuvre de la Pléiade. Paris, 19- . 2v.
40586.28.5 Chateaubriand, F.A.R. Mémoires d'outre-tombe. Paris, 19- . 6v.
42576.12.12 Cherbonnel, Alice. Mon oncle et mon curé. Paris, 19- ?
42576.12.10 Cherbonnel, Alice. Mon oncle et mon curé. 140. éd. Paris, 19- .
41553.110 Clement, J. Charles Paul de Kock and the Bourgeoisie of Paris,. n.p., 19- ?
43556.49.110 Colette, Sidonie Gabrielle. L'entrave. Paris, 19- .
43556.49.120 Colette, Sidonie Gabrielle. L'éther consolateur. Paris, 19- .
43556.49.130 Colette, Sidonie Gabrielle. Ledos, tapissier. Paris, 19- .
43556.49.140 Collette, Sidonie Gabrielle. Les vrilles de la vigne. 19e éd. Paris, 19- .
FL 398.7.85 Colombier, Marie. Voyages de Sarah Bernhardt en Amerique. Paris, 19- ?
42554.23.19 Coppée, François. Contes rapides. Henriette. Paris, 19- ?
42554.23.21 Coppée, François. Une idylle pendant le siège. Paris, 19- ?
42554.23.23 Coppée, François. Longues et prèves. Paris, 19- ?
42554.23.25 Coppée, François. Toute une jeunesse. Paris, 19- ?
NEDL 38575.33.7 Corneille, Pierre. Horace. London, 19- .
42559.14 Couyba, Charles Maurice. Stances à Manon. Paris, 19- .
42566.27.10 Daudet, Alphonse. Lettres de mon moulin. Paris, 19- ?
42566.29.25 Daudet, Alphonse. The Nabob. London, 19- .
42566.30.10 Daudet, Alphonse. Numa Roumestan. 1. éd. Paris, 19- .
42566.34.11 Daudet, Alphonse. Sapho. Paris, 19- .
42566.34.12 Daudet, Alphonse. Sapho. Paris, 19- . 3v.
42566.34.10 Daudet, Alphonse. Sapho. Paris, 19- .
42566.35.8 Daudet, Alphonse. Tartarin sur les Alpes. Paris, 19- .
42566.65 Daudet, Julia R.C. Fragments d'un livre inèdit. Paris, 19- ?
37574.75 Dorchain, Auguste. Les cent meilleurs poèmes, lyriques, de la langue française. Philadelphia, 19- .
43574.1.40 Drouot, Paul. L'oeillet rouge. Alençon, 19- .
38526.6.15 Du Bellay, Joachim. Les regrets. Paris, 19- .
42568.19.16 Du Boisgobey, Fortuné. El caballero rompe y rasga. v.1-2. N.Y., 19- ?
41529.111.9 Dumas, Alexander. The regent's duaghter. N.Y., 19- .
41529.111.2A Dumas, Alexander. The black tulip. N.Y., 19- .
41529.107.6 Dumas, Alexandre. The chevalier de Maison Rouge. N.Y., 19- .
41529.112 Dumas, Alexandre. The Chevalier d'Harmental. Boston, 19- .
41538.10.10 Dumas, Alexandre. The chevalier d'Harmental. Boston, 19- ?
41529.109.2 Dumas, Alexandre. Chicot, the jester (La dame Monsoreau). N.Y., 19- .
Htn 41538.3.5* Dumas, Alexandre. The comtesse de Saint-Géran. N.Y., 19- ?
Htn 41538.3* Dumas, Alexandre. The comtesse de Saint-Géran. N.Y., 19- .
41529.111.8 Dumas, Alexandre. The conspirators or The chevalier d'Harmental. N.Y., 19- .
41530.324 Dumas, Alexandre. The count of Monte Christo or, the adventures of Edmond Dantes. v.1-4. Boston, 19- ? 2v.
41529.112.2 Dumas, Alexandre. The count of Monte Cristo. v.1-4. Boston, 19- . 2v.
41529.107.5 Dumas, Alexandre. The countess de Charny. N.Y., 19- .
41529.112.4 Dumas, Alexandre. La dame de Monsoreau. v.1-2. Boston, 19- .
41538.20.8.25 Dumas, Alexandre. La dame de Monsoreau. v.1-2. Boston, 19- ?
41538.16.12 Dumas, Alexandre. Edmond Dantès. Chicago, 19- .
41538.20.50 Dumas, Alexandre. The forty-five. v.1-2. Boston, 19- ?
41529.112.6 Dumas, Alexandre. The forty-five. v.1-2. Boston, 19- .
41529.109.3 Dumas, Alexandre. The forty-five guardsmen. N.Y., 19- .
41538.61.25 Dumas, Alexandre. Joseph Balsamo. Chicago, 19- ?
41529.107.1 Dumas, Alexandre. Joseph Balsamo. N.Y., 19- .
41538.54.20 Dumas, Alexandre. The man in the iron mask. London, 19- ?
41529.105.6A Dumas, Alexandre. The man in the iron mask. N.Y., 19- .
41529.112.8 Dumas, Alexandre. Marguerite de Valois. Boston, 19- .
41538.29.3.20 Dumas, Alexandre. Marguerite de Valois. Boston, 19- ?
41529.109.1 Dumas, Alexandre. Marguerite de Valois. N.Y., 19- .
41529.107.2A Dumas, Alexandre. The memoirs of a physician. N.Y., 19- .
41529.111.5 Dumas, Alexandre. The page of the duke of Savoy. N.Y., 19- .
41529.111.4 Dumas, Alexandre. The page of the Duke of Savoy. N.Y., 19- .
41529.107.3 Dumas, Alexandre. The queen's necklace. N.Y., 19- .
41530.322 Dumas, Alexandre. The regent's daughter. Boston, 19- ?
41538.24.30 Dumas, Alexandre. The regent's daughter. N.Y., 19- ?
41529.112.10 Dumas, Alexandre. The regent's daughter. The black tulip. Boston, 19- .
41529.107.4 Dumas, Alexandre. Taking the Bastile (Ange Pitou). N.Y., 19- .
41538.53.125 Dumas, Alexandre. Ten years later. N.Y., 19- .
41529.105.1A Dumas, Alexandre. The three guardsmen. N.Y., 19- .
41538.53.33 Dumas, Alexandre. The three guardsmen. N.Y., 19- ?
41538.53.33.5 Dumas, Alexandre. The three guardsmen. N.Y., 19- .
41530.323 Dumas, Alexandre. The three musketeers. Boston, 19- ?
41538.53.35 Dumas, Alexandre. The three musketeers. London, 19- .
41538.53.34 Dumas, Alexandre. The three musketeers. N.Y., 19- . 2v.
41538.53.8 Dumas, Alexandre. Les trois mousquetaires. Paris, 19- .
41538.70.90 Dumas, Alexandre. La tulipe noire. Paris, 19- ?
41529.112.12 Dumas, Alexandre. Twenty years after. Boston, 19- .
41529.105.2 Dumas, Alexandre. Twenty years after. N.Y., 19- .
41538.53.114 Dumas, Alexandre. Twenty years after. v.1-2. Boston, 19- ?
41529.111.6 Dumas, Alexandre. The two Dianas. N.Y., 19- .
41529.111.7 Dumas, Alexandre. The two Dianas. N.Y., 19- .
41538.55.25 Dumas, Alexandre. The vicomte de Bragelonne. N.Y., 19- ?
41538.55.35 Dumas, Alexandre. The vicomte de Bragelonne. v.1,2-3,4-5. Boston, 19- . 3v.
41529.112.14 Dumas, Alexandre. The vicomte de Bragelonne. v.1,2-5. Boston, 19- . 3v.
41538.85 Dumas, Alexandre. The whites and the blues. N.Y., 19- ?
37572.26.3 Les epistoliers du XVIIIe siècle. Paris, 19- ?
37544.25.8 Faguet, Émile. Les dix commandements de l'amitié. 8. éd. Paris, 19- .
37566.31.10 Faguet, Émile. Dix-neuvième siècle. Paris, 19- .

19- - cont.

37564.32.20 Faguet, Émile. Dix-septième siècle. Paris, 19- .
37564.32.22 Faguet, Émile. Dix-septième siècle. Paris, 19- .
37564.32.8 Faguet, Émile. Dix-septième siècle. Paris, 19- .
37563.20.7 Faguet, Émile. Seizième siècle; études littéraires. Paris, 19- .
FL 398.7.31 Farewell American tour...Sarah Bernhardt...1905-06. N.Y., 19- ?
40535.15.3.5 Favart, Charles S. Polichinelle, comte de Paonfier. N.Y., 19- .
42565.70.5 Favre de Coulevain, Hélène. Eve victorieuse. Paris, 19- ?
42575.35.5 Feuillet, Octave. Un mariage dans le monde. Paris, 19- ?
42586.48.15 Feval, Paul H. O corcunda ou Um drama da regencia. Rio de Janeiro, 19- . 2v.
43607.2.31 Fèvre, Henry. L'honneur; roman. Paris, 19- .
42576.33.5A Flaubert, Gustave. Trois contes. Paris, 19- ?
42576.63.7.38A France, Anatole. The crime of Sylvestre Bonnard. N.Y., 19- ?
42586.56.25 Fromentin, Eugène. Dominique. Montréal? 19- .
42571.23.2 Gaboriau, Emile. The Lerouge case. N.Y., 19- ?
41542.11.6 Gautier, Théophile. Mademoiselle de Maupin. Paris, 19- ?
40588.18.10 Genlis, S.F.D. de St. Le siège de la Rochelle. N.Y., 19- .
43625.6.33 Gosselin, L.L.T. Légendes de Noël. Paris, 19- ?
42576.40.347 Halévy, Ludovic. L'abbé Constantin. Philadelphia, 19- ?
37572.9 Half-hours with the best French authors. N.Y. 19- ?
39544.155.2 Hall, Evelyn B. The life of Voltaire. 3d ed. N.Y., 19- . 2v.
42554.55.10 Heredia, J.M. de. Les trophées. Paris, 19- .
42587.1.17 Hermant, A. Le cavalier Miserey. Paris, 19- .
43632.77.100 Hervieu, Louise. Sangs; roman. Paris, 19- .
42576.67.18.5 Hervieu, Paul. Théâtre complet. Paris, 19- . 4v.
41572.2.10 Hugo, Victor. L'année terrible. Paris, 19- .
41572.24.10 Hugo, Victor. Les contemplations. Paris, 19- .
41571.30.2 Hugo, Victor. Les feuilles d'automne. Paris, 19- .
41572.8.76 Hugo, Victor. History of a crime. Boston, 19- ?
41572.8.75 Hugo, Victor. History of a crime. N.Y., 19- ? 2v.
41572.8.77 Hugo, Victor. History of a crime. N.Y., 19- .
41573.23.12 Hugo, Victor. The hunchback of Notre Dame. Chicago, 19- .
41571.40.15 Hugo, Victor. The laughing man. N.Y., 19- .
41572.17 Hugo, Victor. Le Rhin. Boston, 19- . 2v.
41571.16.8 Hugo, Victor. Les misérables. N.Y., 19- . 2v.
41571.17.1 Hugo, Victor. Les misérables. Oeuvres complètes. Paris, 19- . 4v.
41573.17.7 Hugo, Victor. Things seen. N.Y., 19- .
41571.32.6 Hugo, Victor. The toilers of the sea. Chicago, 19- ?
43668.3.100 Jeanne, Paul. Brume de soleil, poésies. Paris, 19- .
37575.440 Junges Frankreich. München, 19- .
41578.160 Jussieu de Senevier, Charles B. En marge de la vie de Lamartine. Paris, 19- .
38544.26.20 La Fare, C.A. The unpublished poems of the...1644-1712. N.Y., 19- .
38544.27.45 La Fayette, Marie M. La Princesse de Clèves. London, 19- .
Htn 39527.10.60* La Fontaine, Jean de. Tales and novels. London, 19- .
41578.34.2 Lamartine, Alphonse. Raphael. Paris, 19- .
41577.11.35 Lamartine, Alphonse de. Chefs-d'oeuvre poétiques. Paris, 19- .
41577.12.5 Lamartine, Alphonse de. Recueillements poétiques. Boston, 19- ?
38543.19.40 La Rochefoucauld, François. Reflections, or sentences and moral maxims. N.Y., 19- .
42544.24.18 Lavedan, Henri. Le lit. Paris, 19- .
42576.41.20.10 Le Blanc, Maurice. The frontier. London, 19- .
42554.16.14 Le Braz, A. La terre du passé. 5e éd. Paris, 19- ?
37556.36.2 Le Breton, A. Le roman français au XIXe siècle avant Balzac. Paris, 19- ?
42555.34.4 Leconte de Lisle, C.M.R. Poèmes antiques. Paris, 19- .
42544.33.22 Lemaître, Jules. Myrrha, vierge et martyre. Paris, 19- .
42544.33.12.5 Lemaître, Jules. Révoltée. Paris, 19- ?
43688.61.702 Lenormand, Henri René. Three plays. N.Y., 19- ?
42545.010 Maeterlinck, Maurice. Morceaux choisis. Paris, 19- .
43697.79.5100 Marty, Jean. La chanson des vingt ans; poèmes. Paris, 19- .
43697.81.1100 Masset, G. Le jardin du Scarabée. Paris, 19- .
42577.1.1.5 Maupassant, Guy de. Contes de la bécasse. Paris, 19- .
42577.4.26.5 Maupassant, Guy de. Contes et nouvelles. N.Y., 19- ?
42577.4.29.35 Maupassant, Guy de. Mademoiselle Perle, and other stories. London, 19- ?
42577.4.7 Maupassant, Guy de. Mouche. Paris, 19- ?
41555.29.5 Mérimée, Prosper. Mateo Falcone. Strasbourg, 19- ?
42545.26.52 Michaud, H. Une héroïne. N.Y., 19- ?
42545.26.50 Michaud, H. Ma bonne. N.Y., 19- ?
42545.28.16 Moinaux, Georges. Un client sérieux. Paris, 19- ?
42545.28.26 Moinaux, Georges. Les gaîtés de l'escadron. Paris, 19- .
Mol 171.55 Molière, Jean Baptiste Poquelin. Le bourgeois gentilhomme; comédie-ballet. Strasbourg, 19- .
43701.61.1100 Montier, Edward. Les mois. n.p., 19- ?
41596.18.6.10 Musset, Alfred de. Comédies et proverbes. Paris, 19- ? 2v.
41596.22.7 Musset, Alfred de. La confession d'un enfant du siècle. Paris, 19- ?
41596.20.5 Musset, Alfred de. Contes. Paris, 19- ?
41596.16.15 Musset, Alfred de. Mélanges de littérature et de critique. Paris, 19- ?
41596.19.7 Musset, Alfred de. Nouvelles. Paris, 19- ?
41596.14.15 Musset, Alfred de. Oeuvres posthumes. Paris, 19- ?
41596.13.10 Musset, Alfred de. Poésies nouvelles. Paris, 19- ?
41596.13.8 Musset, Alfred de. Premières poésies. Paris, 19- ?
41596.18.14 Musset, Alfred de. Three plays. Fantasio. On ne badine pas avec l'amour. Carmosine. London, 19- ?
Htn 43709.3.23* Noailles, Anna, E. Poésies. Paris, 19- .
42578.30.30 Ohnet, Georges. Felipe Derblay. Buenos Aires, 19- .
40522.9.14 Prévost, Antoine F. Histoire de Manon Lescaut et du chevalier des Grieux. Vienne, 19- ?
38536.18.57 Rabelais, F. Works. London, 19- .
38537.29.5A Rabelais, F. The works of Rabelais faithfully translated from the French. n.p., 19- .
38585.29.5 Racine, Jean. Esther; tragédie, 1689. Heitz, 19- .
FL 6026.8.25 Rousseau, J.J. The confessions of Jean-Jacques Rousseau. N.Y., 19- ?
37557.75 Roustan, M. La lettre; évolution du genre. Paris, 19- ?
39595.22.5 St. Pierre, J.H.B. de. Paul and Virginia. Boston, 19- .
39595.22.13 St. Pierre, J.H.B. de. Paul et Virginie. Paris, 19- .
41557.9.24.25 Sand, George. Consuelo. N.Y., 19- .

19- - cont.

42546.30.22.5 Sardou, Victorien. Argument of the play Thermidor. N.Y., 19- ?
41522.3.10.5 Seillière, E. Barbey d'Aurevilly. Halle, 19- .
43775.2.30 Souvestre, Pierre. La fiacre de nuit. Paris, 19- .
41561.2.5 Sue, Eugène. Arthur. Paris, 19- . 2v.
41561.2.10 Sue, Eugène. The knight of Malta. Paris, 19- .
41563.16.20 Sue, Eugène. The mysteries of Paris. Boston, 19- . 3v.
41561.2.15 Sue, Eugène. The mysteries of Paris. Paris, 19- .
41561.2.20 Sue, Eugène. The seven cardinal sins, avarice and anger. Paris, 19- .
41561.2.25 Sue, Eugène. The seven cardinal sins, envy. Paris, 19- .
41561.2.30 Sue, Eugène. The seven cardinal sins, luxury and gluttony. Paris, 19- .
41561.2.35 Sue, Eugène. The seven cardinal sins, pride. Paris, 19- . 2v.
41561.2.40 Sue, Eugène. The wandering Jew. Paris, 19- . 3v.
42583.23.2 Theuriet, André. La chanoinesse. Paris, 19- ?
37596.71.2 Thibaud de Montmorency, seigneur de Marly. Vers sur la mort. Paris, 19- .
40516.63.10 Turquan, Joseph. La baronne de Kruedener (1766-1824) d'après des documents inédits. Paris, 19- .
42547.10.32 Vandérem, F. Les deux rives; roman. 18e éd. Paris, 19- .
V43500.317 Vérane, Léon. Bars; poèmes. Toulon, 19- ?
V43500.319 Vérane, Léon. Les étoiles noires; poèmes. Toulon, 19- ?
42557.11.27 Verhaeren, Émile. Hymnen an das Leben. Leipzig, 19- .
42582.22.4 Verne, Jules. Michael Strogoff. N.Y., 19- ?
42582.25.12 Verne, Jules. The tour of the world in eighty days. N.Y., 19- ?
42576.57.3.1 Viaud, Julien. Ramuntcho. Paris, 19- .
42576.53.10 Viaud, Julien. The romance of a Spahi. N.Y., 19- .
39545.37.10 Voltaire, François Marie Arouet de. Voltaire, Candide. N.Y., 19- ?
39545.32.20 Voltaire, François Marie Arouet de. Zadig and other romances. London, 19- .
42557.20.145 Zweig, Stefan. Verlaine. Berlin, 19- .

190-

42553.27 Amiel, Henri F. Amiel's journal. N.Y., 190-?
40597.15.110 Balzac, Honoré de. Le cousin Pons. N.Y., 190- .
40596.13.121 Balzac, Honoré de. The works of Honoré de Balzac. N.Y., 190-. 16v.
43537.11.30 Barraute du Plessio. Les 13 cauchemars. n.p., 190-?
42563.36.279 Bordeaux, Henry. Le pays natal. 9. éd. Paris, 190-?
40597.2.14 Canabès, Augustin. Balzac ignoré. 2. éd. Paris, 190-?
37563.18.5 Darmesteter, Arsène. Le seizième siècle. 8e éd. Paris, 190-?
41529.51 Dumas, Alexandre. Works. N.Y., 190-? 18v.
42573.25.10 Erckmann, Emile. The plebiscite or A miller's story of the war. N.Y., 190-?
42576.62.27.8 France, Anatole. L'étui de nacre. Paris, 190-?
41542.35.5 Gautier, Théophile. Le roman de la momie. Paris, 190-.
41573.37.10 Hugo, Victor. Poems. Boston, 190-?
43667.51.280 Jaloux, Edmond. Le boudoir de Proserpine. Paris, 190-?
42576.76.32.4 Margueritte, Paul. Les braves gens. Paris, 190-?
43697.83.110 Masson, Emile. Lettre d'un répétiteur en congé. Paris, 190-.
42577.1.20 Maupassant, Guy de. Contes choisis. Paris, 190-?
Mol 925.2 Molière en images. n.p., 190-?
Mon 30.10.15 Montaigne, Michel de. Essays of Montaigne. London, 190-?
40542.33.5 O'Meara, Kathleen. Frederic Ozanam. N.Y., 190-?
43743.3.30 Porré, Emmanuel. Fantaisus. Paris, 190-?
43752.3.30 Rabier, Benjamin A. La tranquillité des parents. Paris, 190-?
FL 6026.10.15A Rousseau, J.J. The confessions of Jean-Jacques Rousseau. N.Y., 190-?
40592.33 Staël Holstein, Anne Louise. Corinne, or Italy. N.Y., 190-.
42556.19.13 Sully-Prudhomme, R.F.A. Poésies. Paris, 190-?
42556.19.11 Sully-Prudhomme, R.F.A. Poésies. Épaves. Paris, 190-?
42582.25.10 Verne, Jules. Around the world in eighty days. N.Y., 190-?

1900

42562.38.8 Adam, Paul. Basile et Sophia. Paris, 1900.
37595.36.11 Adam de la Halle. Canchons. v.17. Halle, 1900.
FL 393.12A Albert, Maurice. Les théâtres de la foire. Paris, 1900.
38514.21.14 Alheim, Pierre d'. La passion de Maître François Villon. Paris, 1900.
41592.2.5 Arvers, Félix. Poésies. Paris, 1900.
37567.93 Asse, Eugène. Les petits romantiques. Paris, 1900.
37556.12.5 Avenel, Henri. Histoire de la presse française depuis 1789 jusqu'à nos jours. Paris, 1900.
43537.9.30 Ballieu, A.J. Jean Linquiet. Paris, 1900.
40596.13.80.32 Balzac, Honoré de. Balzac, a memoir. Boston, 1900.
40597.14.6 Balzac, Honoré de. César Birotteau. N.Y., 1900.
40596.13.80.20 Balzac, Honoré de. The chouans. Boston, 1900.
40596.13.80.24 Balzac, Honoré de. The country doctor. Boston, 1900.
40596.13.80.18 Balzac, Honoré de. Cousin Bette. Boston, 1900.
40596.10.7A Balzac, Honoré de. Honoré de Balzac. Boston, 1900.
40596.13.125 Balzac, Honoré de. Honoré de Balzac. N.Y., 1900. 22v.
40596.13.80.34 Balzac, Honoré de. Letters to Madame Hanska. Boston, 1900.
40596.10.5 Balzac, Honoré de. Letters to Mme. Hanska. Boston, 1900.
40596.13.80.9 Balzac, Honoré de. The lily of the valley. Boston, 1900.
40595.7 Balzac, Honoré de. Oeuvres complètes. Paris, 1900-02. 49v.
40597.32.4.10 Balzac, Honoré de. La peau de chagrin. Paris, 1900.
40596.13.80.26 Balzac, Honoré de. Sons of the soil. Boston, 1900.
40597.35.140 Balzac, Honoré de. Splendeurs et misères des courtisanes. Paris, 1900. 2v.
40597.13.2 Balzac, Honoré de. The Chouans. N.Y., 1900.
41522.2.34 Barbey d'Aurevilly, Jules. Premier memorandum, 1836-1838. 3. éd. Paris, 1900.
42563.16.15 Barrès, Maurice. L'appel au soldat. Paris, 1900.
NEDL 42563.16.14 Barrès, Maurice. L'appel au soldat. Paris, 1900.
43537.5.31 Barrière, M. Le nouveau Don Juan. Paris, 1900. 3v.
42563.21.30 Bazin, René. La terre qui meurt. Paris, 1900.
37551.65 Beaujon, Georges. Contribution à l'histoire de la poésie lyrique française contemporaine. Bâle, 1900.
40556.23 Beaunier, André. La jeunesse de Joseph Joubert. Paris, 1900.

1900 - cont.

	42542.29.8	Bergerat, Émile. Théâtre. 2. éd. Paris, 1900.
	37596.34.5	Berlit, O. Die Sprache des altfranzösischen Dichters Robert von Blois. Halle, 1900.
	42542.29.34	Bernstein, H. Le marché. Paris, 1900.
	42563.23.7.60	Berthet, E.B. The catacombs of Paris. Westminster, 1900.
	40587.22	Bertrin, G. La sincérité religieuse de Chateaubriand. Paris, 1900.
	38531.17	Birch Hirschfeld, A. Das Fümfte Buch das Pantagruel. Lipsiae, 1900-01.
	42563.23.9	Blanc, Thérèse. Tchelovek. Paris, 1900.
	Mol 728.11	Bleton, Auguste. Molière à Lyon. Lyon, 1900?
	42563.32.700	Blouët, Paul. Woman and artist. N.Y., 1900.
Htn	42563.23.30*	Bloy, Léon. Le fils de Louis XVII. 3. éd. Paris, 1900.
	37567.70	Bordeaux, H. Les ecrivains et les moeurs (1897-1900). 2e éd. Paris, 1900.
	41557.10.12	Born, Max. George Sand's Sprache in dem Romane Les maîtres sonneurs. Teil 1. Berlin, 1900.
	42542.29.138	Bornier, Henri de. France...d'abord! Paris, 1900.
	43544.4.45	Botrel, Théodore. Contes du Lit-Clos. Paris, 1900.
	42542.30.12	Bouchor, Maurice. La première vision de Jeanne d'Arc. Paris, 1900.
	42563.37.23	Bourget, Paul. Domestic dramas. N.Y., 1900.
	43544.7.30	Bout de Charlemont, H. Cigale. Monographie. 2. éd. Avignon, 1900.
	37595.45	Brandin, L. Inedita der altfranzösischen Liederhandschrift Pb5 bibliothèque nationale 846. Berlin, 1900.
	40583.10	Brun, Pierre. Henry Beyle-Stendhal. Grenoble, 1900.
	42554.17.60	Cantacuzène, C.A. Cinglons les souvenirs et cinglons vers les rêves. Paris, 1900.
	42564.1.9	Capus, Alfred. Qui perd gagne. Paris, 1900.
	40597.8.4	Cerfberr, Anatole. Compendium. Honoré de Balzac's Comédie humaine. Philadelphia, 1900.
	40597.8.3	Cerfberr, Anatole. Repertory of la comédie humaine de H. de Balzac. N.Y., 1900.
	39586.19	Chamfort, S.R.N. Pensées - maximes - anecdotes - dialogues. Paris, 1900.
	Mon 113.2	Champion, E. Introduction aux essais de Montaigne. Paris, 1900.
	Mol 603.8	Claretie, Jules. Shakspere and Molière. N.Y., 1900.
	43554.7.32	Clemenceau, Georges. Au fil des jours. Paris, 1900.
	42554.18.55	Clément, Jean B. La chanson populaire. Paris, 1900.
	41596.2.15	Clouard, Maurice. Documents inedits sur Alfred de Musset. Paris, 1900.
	40583.11	Comment a vécu Stendhal. Paris, 1900.
	42542.53.14	Coolus, R. Le marquis de Carabas. Paris, 1900.
	42554.21.12	Coppée, François. Tales for Christmas. Boston, 1900.
	38575.34.4.15	Corneille, Pierre. Nicomède. London, 1900.
	38575.33.35	Corneille, Pierre. Rodogune. Paris, 1900.
	42542.54.75	Crisafulli, H. Le bonnet de coton. Paris, 1900.
	42542.58.30	Curel, François de. Les fossiles. Paris, 1900.
	42566.26.2.15	Daudet, Alphonse. Jack. Boston, 1900. 2v.
	42566.26.2.17	Daudet, Alphonse. Jack. Boston, 1900. 2v.
	42566.26.2.18	Daudet, Alphonse. Jack. N.Y., 1900. 2v.
	42566.27.14	Daudet, Alphonse. Letters from my mill. Boston, 1900.
	42566.31.25	Daudet, Alphonse. Little what's his name. Boston, 1900.
	42566.31.27	Daudet, Alphonse. Little what's his name. N.Y., 1900.
	42566.17.250	Daudet, Alphonse. Memories of a man of letters. Boston, 1900.
	42566.17.255	Daudet, Alphonse. Memories of a man of letters. N.Y., 1900.
	42566.30.15	Daudet, Alphonse. Numa Roumestan. Boston, 1900.
	42566.30.12	Daudet, Alphonse. Numa Roumestan. N.Y., 1900.
	42566.28.6	Daudet, Alphonse. Port-Tarascon. N.Y., 1900.
	42566.49.10	Daudet, Alphonse. The support of the family. Boston, 1900.
	42566.49.12	Daudet, Alphonse. The support of the family. N.Y., 1900.
	42566.19.8.95	Daudet, Alphonse. Tartarin of Tarascon. Boston, 1900.
	42566.19.8.97	Daudet, Alphonse. Tartarin of Tarascon. N.Y., 1900.
	37555.56	Davidson, F.J.A. Ueber den Ursprung und die Geschichte der Französischen Ballade. Halle, 1900.
	FL 6138.98.1	Davidson, T. Rousseau and education according to nature. N.Y., 1900.
	Mol 230.12	Debove, G.M. Le malade imaginaire. Paris, 1900.
	FL 397.53.5	Deschamps, Robert. Le théâtre au Mans. Maniers, 1900.
	Mol 870.59	Des Essarts, E. L'illustre théâtre. Moulins, 1900.
	39564.17	Diderot, Denis. Rameau's Neffe...Studien in Goethes Übersetzung. Berlin, 1900.
	42568.2.38	Didier, Charles. The romance of l'Aiglon. N.Y., 1900.
	42568.2.36	Didier, Charles. The romance of l'Aiglon. N.Y., 1900.
	37585.25	Dieulafoy, J. Le théâtre dans l'intimité. Paris, 1900.
	42542.65.100	Doucet, J. Notre ami Pierrot. Paris, 1900.
	43576.4.30	Du Bois-Melly, Charles. "Ceux de Genève." 2. éd. Genève, 1900.
	37565.31.5	Ducros, L. Les encyclopédistes. Paris, 1900.
	42543.16.30.20	Dumas, Alexandre. Denise. Paris, 1900.
	41538.20.45	Dumas, Alexandre. The forty-five guardsmen. N.Y., 1900.
	41538.20.8.23	Dumas, Alexandre. La dame de Monsoreau. Boston, 1900.
	41538.20.8.20A	Dumas, Alexandre. La dame de Monsoreau. N.Y., 1900.
	41538.29.3.18	Dumas, Alexandre. Marguerite de Valois. N.Y., 1900.
	41538.29.3.15	Dumas, Alexandre. Marguerite de Valois. N.Y., 1900.
	41538.170	Dumas, Alexandre. Marie Stuart à Lochleven. N.Y., 1900.
	41538.53.37	Dumas, Alexandre. The three musketeers. N.Y., 1900.
	42573.20.15	Erckmann, Emile. Invasion of France in 1814. N.Y., 1900.
	42573.20.10	Erckmann, Emile. Invasion of France in 1814. N.Y., 1900.
	42573.25.5	Erckmann, Emile. The plebiscite or A miller's story of the war. N.Y., 1900.
	42543.36	Fabius de Champville, G. Cyrano Farceur. Paris, 1900.
	42565.70.3	Favre de Coulevain, Hélène. Eve victorieuse. Paris, 1900.
	38554.350.275	Fénelon, F. de S. de la Mothe. Concerning education. N.Y., 1900.
	42575.23	Feuillet, Octave. Théâtre complet. Paris, 1900. 5v.
	43611.1.25.5	Fort, Paul. L'amour marin. V. Paris, 1900.
	43611.1.25.4	Fort, Paul. Les idylles antiques et les hymnes. 2. éd. IV. Paris, 1900.
	42586.54	Foulon de Vaulx, A. Madame de Lauraguais. Paris, 1900.
Htn	42576.62.16*	France, Anatole. Clio. Paris, 1900.
	42576.62.26	France, Anatole. Filles et garçons. Paris, 1900?
Htn	42576.62.75*	France, Anatole. Jean Gutenberg. Paris, 1900.
	42571.15F	France, Anatole. Nos enfants; scènes de la ville et des champs. Paris, 1900.
	37567.68	Frédérix, G. Trente ans de critique. Paris, 1900. 2v.
	42571.30.7	Gaboriau, Emile. File no. 113. N.Y., 1900.
	42571.28.3	Gaboriau, Emile. The mystery of Orcival. N.Y., 1900.
	42571.24.6	Gaboriau, Emile. Other people's money. N.Y., 1900.

1900 - cont.

	41574.230	Ganser, F. Beiträge zur Beurteilung des Verhältnisses. Inaug. Diss. Heidelberg, 1900.
	41574.38	Garson, J. L'évolution Napoléonienne de Victor Hugo sous la restauration. Paris, 1900.
	43616.2.35	Gautier, Judith. Les princesses d'amour. Paris, 1900.
	41542.5	Gautier, Théophile. Works of Théophile Gautier. N.Y., 1900-03. 24v.
	FL 6119.00	Gehrig, H. Jean-Jacques Rousseau. Leben und Schriften. Leipzig, 1900. 3v.
	42554.46.6	Gielkens, Émile. Camille. Bruxelles, 1900.
	37547.3	Gourcuff, O. de. Gens de Bretagne, histoire et littérature, prose et poésie. Paris, 1900.
	37556.21.15	Gourmont, P. Les petites revues. Paris, 1900.
	42554.49	Gregh, F. La beauté de vivre. Paris, 1900.
	40515.57	Günther, E. Die Quellen der Fabeln Florians. Plauen, 1900.
	FL 383.20	Guex, Jules. Le théâtre et la société française. Vevey, 1900.
	37593.64.9	Guy, Henry. Bibliographie critique du trouvère Adam de la Halle. Toulouse, 1900.
	37593.64.5	Guy, Henry. Le trouvère Adam de la Halle. Paris, 1900.
	Mol 870.60	Henriquet, S. La voix du rêve. Paris, 1900.
	42554.55.9	Heredia, J.M. de. The trophies, sonnets. Boston, 1900.
	42543.65	Hermant, Abel. L'empreinte. Paris, 1900.
	42543.65.6	Hermant, Abel. Le Fanbourg. Paris, 1900.
	42554.64.45	Herold, A.F. Au hasard des chemins, poèmes. Paris, 1900.
	37572.25.5	Herriot, Édouard. Lettres choisies du XVII siècle. Paris, 1900.
	37562.20.7	Herrmann, F. Schilderung...der gesellschaftliche Verhältnisse Frankreichs in der Fabliauxdichtung des XII und XIII Jahrhunderts. Coburg, 1900.
	42576.67.18	Hervieu, Paul. Oeuvres::théâtre. v.1,3-4. Paris, 1900?-09. 3v.
	39594.19.21	Holmes, Oliver W. Montesquieu. N.Y., 1900.
	41573.25.4	Hugo, Victor. La préface de Cromwell and Hernani. Chicago, 1900.
	41573.25.4.2	Hugo, Victor. La préface de Cromwell and Hernani. Chicago, 1900.
	41571.32.1	Hugo, Victor. The man who laughs. Boston, 1900. 2v.
	41573.6	Hugo, Victor. Morceaux choisis. Paris, 1900.
	43638.34.100	Hugues, Clovis. La chanson de Jehanne Darc. Paris, 1900.
	42563.18.85	Jacquet, René. Notre maître Maurice Barrès. Paris, 1900.
	42584.23.12	Johannis, A.J. de. A proposito del libro di Emile Zola "Fecondita". Firenze, 1900.
	42554.65.231	Joncières, L. de. Tanagra. Paris, 1900.
	37543.63.27	Kastner, Leon Emile. Short history of French literature. London, 1900.
	37543.63.25	Kastner, Leon Emile. Short history of French literature. N.Y., 1900.
	42547.15.7	Kraemer, Alexio von. Villiers de l'Isle Adam. Thèse. Helsingfors, 1900.
	37555.304	La Grasserie, R. de la. Des principes scientifiques de la versification française. Paris, 1900.
	41578.32.5	Lamartine, Alphonse. Graziella. Boston, 1900.
	41578.9.7	Lamartine, Alphonse de. Nouvelles méditations poétiques. Paris, 1900.
	41578.7.2A	Lamartine, Alphonse de. Premières méditations poétiques. Paris, 1900.
	37543.48	Lanson, Gustav. Dějiny novodobé literatury francouzské. pt. 1-2. Praha, 1900.
	38543.19.43	La Rochefoucauld, François. Maxims. N.Y., 1900.
	38543.19.42	La Rochefoucauld, François. Reflections, or sentences and moral maxims. N.Y., 1900.
	38557.14.5	Le Bidois, G. De comoedia...quid judicaverit Bossuetius. Paris, 1900.
	42554.16.6.5	Le Braz, A. Au pays des pardons. Paris, 1900?
	42554.16.12	Le Braz, A. Le gardien du feu. Paris, 1900.
	FL 396.69	Lecomte, L.H. Histoire des théâtres. Le panorama dramatique, 1821-23. Paris, 1900.
	FL 398.19	Lecomte, L.H. Marie Dorval. Paris, 1900.
	FL 398.63.30	Lecomte, L.H. Odry et ses oeuvres.Paris, 1900.
	FL 398.84.11	Lecomte, L.H. Talma en paradis. Paris, 1900.
	FL 382.40	Lecomte, Louis H. Napoléon et l'empire racontés par le théâtre. Paris, 1900.
	43688.35.130	Le Grand, Maurice. La nouvelle cuisinière bourgeoise. Paris, 1900.
	42555.39.35	Lemoyne, André. La mare aut chevreuils. Paris, 1900.
	42576.45.6	Le Roux, H. Ménélik et nous. Paris, 1900.
	42576.46	Le Roy, Eugène. Jacquou le croquant. Paris, 1900.
	37555.55	Levrault, L. L'épopée (Évolution du genre). Paris, 1900.
	43690.24.100	Lienard, Albert. A l'ombre du portique. Paris, 1900.
	38513.14.4.5	Loewinski, Henri. Die Lyrik in den Miracles de Notre Dame. Berlin, 1900.
	38513.40	Lohmann, N. Untersuchungen über J. Louvets 12 Mysterien. Greifswald, 1900.
	37597.9.7A	Lorris, Guillaume de. The romance of the rose. London, 1900. 3v.
	42544.36.15	Loyson, Paul H. L'Évangile du Sang. 2e éd. Genève, 1900.
	37555.28	Madeleine, J. Quelques poètes Français des XVIe et XVIIe siècles à Fontainebleau. Fontainebleau, 1900.
	42545.3.5.7	Maeterlinck, Maurice. The treasure of the humble. N.Y., 1900.
	42545.3.8.7	Maeterlinck, Maurice. Wisdom and destiny. N.Y., 1900.
	38537.24	Mättig, J. Über den Einfluss der heimischen volkstümlichen literatur auf Rabelais. Leipzig, 1900.
	42576.76.32.2	Marguerite, Paul. Les tronçons du glaive. Paris, 1900.
	42545.9.16	Martel de Janville, S.G. Trop de chic. Paris, 1900.
	FL 377.41A	Martinenche, E. La comédie espagnole en France de Hardy à Racine. Paris, 1900.
	42577.1.10	Maupassant, Guy de. Huit contes choisis. Boston, 1900.
	42577.1.12	Maupassant, Guy de. Huit contes choisis. Boston, 1900.
	42545.11.10A	Meilhac, Henri. Théâtre de Meilhac et Halévy. Paris, 1900. 8v.
X Cg	42555.58.24	Mendès, Catulle. Les braises du cendrier. Paris, 1900.
	42555.58.1130	Mérat, Albert. Triolets des parisiennes de Paris. Paris, 1900.
	42555.58.1120	Mérat, Albert. Vers le soir. Paris, 1900.
	42555.49.25	Merrill, S. Les quatre saisons. 2. éd. Paris, 1900.
	Mol 165.69	Molière, Jean Baptiste Poquelin. L'avare...M. Levi. Boston, 1900.
	Mol 166.2.76	Molière, Jean Baptiste Poquelin. L'avare...M.Levi. Boston, 1900.
	Mol 211.61	Molière, Jean Baptiste Poquelin. Les femmes savantes...Lanson. Paris, 1900.
	Mol 211.61.2	Molière, Jean Baptiste Poquelin. Les femmes savantes...Lanson. Paris, 1900.

Chronological Listing

1900 - cont.

Mol 19.00 Molière, Jean Baptiste Poquelin. Oeuvres complètes. Oxford, 1900.
Htn Mol 19.00.2* Molière, Jean Baptiste Poquelin. Oeuvres complètes. Oxford, 1900. 4v.
Mol 251.64 Molière, Jean Baptiste Poquelin. Les précieuses ridicules. Lanson. Paris, 1900.
Mol 268.99 Molière, Jean Baptiste Poquelin. Le Tartuffe. Gasc. Boston, 1900.
FL 394.105 Monval, Georges. Liste alphabétique des societaires (de la comédie-française). Paris, 1900.
FL 6132.5 Mugnier, F. Nouvelles lettres de Mme. Warens. Paris, 1900.
38575.17.5 Mulert, A. Pierre Corneille auf der englischen Bühne. Erlangen, 1900.
37555.29 Neff, T.L. La satire des femmes dans la poésie lyrique française du Moyen Âge. Paris, 1900.
42587.37.9 Nion, François de. Les derniers Trianons. Paris, 1900.
42578.29.80 Ohnet, Georges. Gens de la noce. Paris, 1900.
39545.22.6 Olivier, J.J. Voltaire et les comédiens. Paris, 1900.
42548.71.10 Olympe Dunoyer ou La jeunesse de Voltaire. Paris, 1900.
40556.23.35 Pailhès, Gabriel. Du nouveau sur J. Joubert. Paris, 1900.
42587.40.10 Paul, Viteau. Notre premiere école. Paris, 1900.
43792.90.140 Perdicras (pseud.). Le metier d'Amant, roman. Paris, 1900.
42515.35.213 Platzhoff, L.E. Ernest Renan. Dresden, 1900.
37573.26 Potter, Henry Austin. Dix contes modernes des meilleurs auteurs du jour. Boston, 1900.
42578.31.36 Prévost, Marcel. Frédérique. Paris, 1900.
42578.31.38 Prévost, Marcel. Léa. Paris, 1900.
FL 361.42 Prost, J.C.A. Famille d'artistes: les Thénards. Paris, 1900.
FL 360.60 Quet, Édouard. La puissance du théâtre en France. Paris, 1900.
42515.69 Quinet, Edgar. Lettera alla marchesa Arconati Visconti. Città di Castello, 1900.
38536.20.5 Rabelais, F. Gargantua and Pantagruel. v.2. London, 1900.
38585.19.9 Racine, Jean. Andromaque. Iphigénie. Athalie. Paris, 1900. 2v.
42578.18.10 Rameau, Jean. Le dernier bateau. Paris, 1900.
42587.50.80 Rebell, Hugues. La camorra. Paris, 1900.
38557.19 Rébelliau, A. Bossuet. Paris, 1900.
42556.26.29.15 Régnier, Henri de. La double maîtresse; roman. 13. éd. Paris, 1900.
42556.27.100 Renimal, Paul. Chansons. Paris, 1900.
41574.35 Renouvier, Charles. Victor Hugo le philosophe. Paris, 1900.
43756.3.30 Richepin, Jacques. La reine de Tyr. Paris, 1900.
41574.37 Rigal, Eugène. Victor Hugo poète epique. Paris, 1900.
42587.55.45 Rivoire, André. La peur de souffrir. Paris, 1900.
FL 397.7.25 Robert, Ulysse. Les origines du théâtre à Besançon. n.p., 1900.
37567.156 Roberto, Diego de. Poeti francesi contemporanei. Milano, 1900.
37597.26.85 Rohnström, Johan Otto. Étude sur Jehan Bodel. Thèse. Uppsala, 1900.
43757.48.100 Roland, Claude. L'aiguilleur. Paris, 1900.
42546.10.4 Rostand, Edmond. L'aiglon. Paris, 1900.
42546.10.4.5 Rostand, Edmond. L'aiglon. Paris, 1900.
42546.14.9 Rostand, Edmond. The fantasticks. London, 1900.
42546.14.10 Rostand, Edmond. The fantasticks. N.Y., 1900.
42546.10.5A Rostand, Edmond. L'aiglon. N.Y., 1900.
42546.11.5 Rostand, Edmond. L'aiglon. N.Y., 1900.
42546.10.6 Rostand, Edmond. L'aiglon. N.Y., 1900.
42546.11A Rostand, Edmond. L'aiglon. N.Y., 1900.
42546.15.6.12 Rostand, Edmond. La princesse Lointaine. Paris, 1900.
FL 6022.00 Rousseau, J.J. Les confessions. Paris, 1900.
FL 6042.00 Rousseau, J.J. Émile ou De l'éducation. Paris, 1900.
FL 6042.05 Rousseau, J.J. Émile ou De l'éducation. Paris, 1900.
FL 6052.00 Rousseau, J.J. La nouvelle Héloise. Paris, 1900.
43757.92.160 Roussel, Raymond. Chiquenaude. Paris, 1900.
43892.7 Saint Mary Magdalen; a drama. Philadelphia, 1900.
40576.3.9 Sainte-Beuve, Charles A. Causeries du lundi. Paris, 1900.
41557.9.31.7 Sand, George. La petite Fadette. N.Y., 1900.
FL 382.77 Sarcey, Francisque. Quarante ans de théâtre. Paris, 1900-1902. 8v.
42546.12.9 Schenk, A. Études sur la Rime dans Cyrano de Bergerac. Kiel, 1900.
42556.30.40 Schuré, Edouard. Le théâtre de l'ame. Paris, 1900.
37567.69 Segard, A. Les voluptueux et les hommes d'action. Paris, 1900.
FL 6133.4 Serand, J. L'habitation de Mme. de Warens à Annecy. Annecy, 1900.
FL 6133.5 Serand, J. Nouveaux documents sur Mme. de Warens. n.p., 1900.
38546.37 Sévigné, Marie de R.C. Lettres. Paris, 1900.
37556.21.5 Söderhjehn, A. Le régime de la presse pendant la révolution française. Helsingforo, 1900-01. 2v.
41558.56 Souvestre, Émile. Le mari de Madame de Solange. Boston, 1900.
43780.5.320 Suarès, André. Airs; 5 livres de poèmes. Paris, 1900.
37541.33 Suchier, H. Geschicihte der Französischen Literatur. Leipzig, 1900.
41561.18 Sue, Eugène. The knight of Malta. N.Y., 1900.
43787.77.100 Terre, J. Echos de Chine. Shanghai, 1900.
43788.5.117 Tharaud, Jérôme. La lumière. Paris, 1900.
37567.67 Thompson, Vance. French portraits. Boston, 1900.
39527.4.12 Uhlemayr, B. Der Einfluss La Fontaine's auf die Englische Fabeldichtung der 18. Jahrhundert. Nürnberg, 1900.
42547.10.22 Vallette, Marguerite. La jongleuse. 4e éd. Paris, 1900.
42557.11.7 Verhaeren, Émile. Le cloitre. 2. éd. Bruxelles, 1900.
42557.25.150 Vielé-Griffin, F. La légende ailée de Wieland le forgeron. Paris, 1900.
41596.1.5 Vincens, Cécile. Alfred de Musset. 3. éd. Paris, 1900.
37564.28.7 Vincent, Leon. Hôtel de Rambouillet and The précieuses. Boston, 1900.
42522.7 Vogüé, E.M. de. Le rappel des ombres. Paris, 1900.
Mol 207.5 Weidler, W. Das Verhältnis von Mrs. Antlivrés. Halle, 1900.
Mol 623.5.2 Weiss, J.J. Molière. Paris, 1900.
Mol 623.5 Weiss, J.J. Molière. Paris, 1900.
41583.32.15 Wetzig, Reinold. Studie über die Tragödien Casimir Delavignes. Leipzig, 1900.
37591.25.5 Wiese, Leo. Die Sprache der Dialoge des Papetes Gregor. Halle, 1900.
42584.23.11A Zola, Emile. Fruitfullness. N.Y., 1900.

1900 - cont.

42584.12.50 Zola, Emile. Les quatre évangiles, fécondité. Paris, 1900.

1901

NEDL 37595.9.5 Abailard, Pierre. Love letters. London, 1901.
42586.6.12 Achard, Amédée. The golden fleece. Boston, 1901.
42586.6.10 Achard, Amédée. The golden fleece. Boston, 1901.
42562.38.14.29 Adam, Paul. Robes rouges. Paris, 1901.
42586.7.21 Aicard, Jean. King of Carveargue. Philadelphia, 1901.
42542.1.11.5 Ajalbert, Jean. A fleur de peau. Paris, 1901.
42546.15.9 Arnold, N. Edmond Rostands "Princesse Lointaine" und "Samaritaine". Arnstadt, 1901.
38526.47.9 Arnould, S. Un gentil homme de lettres au XVIIe siècle. Racan. Paris, 1901.
42553.72 Baldenne, F. En marge de la vie. Paris, 1901.
40596.114 Balzac, Honoré de. About Catherine de Medici. Boston, 1901.
40596.50 Balzac, Honoré de. About Catherine de Médici. N.Y., 1901.
40597.35.72 Balzac, Honoré de. About Catherine de Medici and Gambara. Boston, 1901.
40596.102 Balzac, Honoré de. At the sign of the cat and racket. Boston, 1901.
40596.115 Balzac, Honoré de. Béatrix. Boston, 1901.
40596.116 Balzac, Honoré de. The Chouans. Boston, 1901.
40596.51 Balzac, Honoré de. The Chouans. N.Y., 1901.
40596.8.74A Balzac, Honoré de. Cinq scènes de la comédie humaine. Boston, 1901.
40596.117 Balzac, Honoré de. The country parson. Boston, 1901.
40596.111 Balzac, Honoré de. Cousin Betty. Boston, 1901.
40596.107 Balzac, Honoré de. A daughter of Eve. Boston, 1901.
40596.15.5 Balzac, Honoré de. A daughter of Eve and other stories. N.Y., 1901.
40596.53 Balzac, Honoré de. A distinguished provincial at Paris. N.Y., 1901.
40596.113 Balzac, Honoré de. The dramas. Boston, 1901.
40596.19 Balzac, Honoré de. The dramatic works. Chicago, 1901. 2v.
40596.105 Balzac, Honoré de. Eugénie Grandet. Boston, 1901.
40596.54 Balzac, Honoré de. Eugénie Grandet. N.Y., 1901.
40597.19.18 Balzac, Honoré de. Eugénie Grandet. Paris, 1901?
40596.106 Balzac, Honoré de. The lily of the valley. Boston, 1901.
40596.55 Balzac, Honoré de. The lily of the valley. N.Y., 1901.
40596.112 Balzac, Honoré de. Lost illusions. Boston, 1901.
40596.57 Balzac, Honoré de. Lost illusions. N.Y., 1901.
40597.35.85.1 Balzac, Honoré de. Lost illusions. A distinguished provincial at Paris. Boston, 1901.
40596.11 Balzac, Honoré de. Love letters. London, 1901. 2v.
40596.104 Balzac, Honoré de. The magic skin. Boston, 1901.
40597.29.1.3 Balzac, Honoré de. La maison du chat-qui-pelote. Paris, 1901.
40596.110 Balzac, Honoré de. A marriage settlement. Boston, 1901.
40596.109 Balzac, Honoré de. The member for Arcis. Boston, 1901.
40597.75.10 Balzac, Honoré de. The middle classes. Boston, 1901.
40596.56 Balzac, Honoré de. Old Goriot. N.Y., 1901.
40596.30 Balzac, Honoré de. Parisian life. N.Y., 1901. 9v.
40597.29.3.80 Balzac, Honoré de. Père Goriot. The marriage contract. Boston, 1901.
40597.32.13.9 Balzac, Honoré de. The physiology of marriage. Boston, 1901.
40596.58 Balzac, Honoré de. A princess's secrets. N.Y., 1901.
40596.101 Balzac, Honoré de. The rise and fall of César Birotteau. Boston, 1901.
40596.103 Balzac, Honoré de. Scenes from a courtesans's life. Boston, 1901.
40596.108 Balzac, Honoré de. The thirteen. Boston, 1901.
40596.59 Balzac, Honoré de. Ursule Mirouëtt. N.Y., 1901.
40595.10 Balzac, Honoré de. Works. v.11 lost 1966. Boston, 1901. 34v.
42563.21.74.5 Bazin, René. Les oberlé. Paris, 1901.
FL 398.6.15 Bellanger, J. Les matinées Ballande. Paris, 1901.
42542.29.14 Bergerat, Émile. La Pompadour. Paris, 1901.
37557.50 Bernard, A. Le sermon au XVIII siècle. Paris, 1901.
FL 360.65 Bernardin, N.M. Devant le Rideau. Paris, 1901.
40526.8.5 Bertheroy, J. Eloge de André Chénier. Paris, 1901.
42563.23.8.5 Bertrand, Louis. La cina. 3. éd. Paris, 1901.
40582.9.17 Beyle, Henri. The chartreuse of Parma. N.Y., 1901.
40582.9.16 Beyle, Henri. The chartreuse of Parma. N.Y., 1901.
37596.84A Bible. French. (Old). N.T. Revelation. L'apocalypse en français au XIIIe siècle. Paris, 1901. 2v.
38585.16 Bidois, Georges le. La vie la tragédie de Racine. Paris, 1901.
43540.1.30 Billaud, V. Jeune amour. Paris, 1901.
37556.20 Biré, E. La presse royale de 1830 à 1852, Alfred Nettement sa vie et ses oeuvres. Paris, 1901.
37555.324 Bock, Moriz. Über Vergleiche...bei einigen altfranzösischen Dichtern. Linz, 1901.
38575.16.5 Böhm, J. Die dramatischen Theorien Pierre Corneilles. Berlin, 1901.
38566.26.7 Boileau Despréaux, Nicolas. Art poétique...Bibliothèque nationale. Paris, 1901. 2v.
41583.15.6 Bonjour, Casimir. Oeuvres. Paris, 1901.
41583.15 Bonjour, Casimir. Théâtre. Paris, 1901. 3v.
41557.10.11 Born, Max. George Sand's Sprache in dem Romane Les maîtres sonneurs. Berlin, 1901.
42563.37.8.20 Bourget, Paul. The disciple. N.Y., 1901.
42563.37.8.5 Bourget, Paul. Le disciple. Paris, 1901.
42563.37.21.25 Bourget, Paul. The screen. N.Y., 1901.
42536.27 Boutmy, E. Taine, Scherer, Laboulaye. Paris, 1901.
42563.39.10 Boylesve, René. La becquée. Paris, 1901.
X Cg 37564.44 Brun, P. Autour du dix-septième siècle. Grenoble, 1901.
42524.16.6 Brunetière, F. Discours académiques. Paris, 1901.
38525.90 Buchetmann, F.E. Jean de Rotrou's Antigone und ihre Quellen. Erlangen, 1901.
38551.24.4 Cagnac, Moïse. Fénelon directeur de conscience. Paris, 1901.
42586.52.9 Caillot-Duval (pseud.). Les mystifications de Caillot-Duval. Paris, 1901.
FL 6139.01 Campayré, G. Jean-Jacques Rousseau et l'éducation de la nature. Paris, 1901.
Mol 603.2 Canora, Jean. Molière moraliste. Paris, 1901.
42542.48 Capus, Alfred. La bourse ou la vie. Paris, 1901.
42542.48.11 Capus, Alfred. Rosine. 2. éd. Paris, 1901.
38526.45.15 Catalogue des ouvrages...de Guy du Faur Signeur de Pibrac. Orléans, 1901.

1901 - cont.

38514.64.9 Chartier, Alain. Dialogus familiaris amici et sodalis. Halle, 1901.
37547.6.5 Chateau-Verdun, Marie de. Legendes bretonnes et autres récits. 2. éd. Lille, 1901.
40586.13.10 Chateaubriand, F.A.R. Atala and René. Chicago, 1901.
40556.37 Chavanne, Paul. Les idées de Joseph de Maistre. Angers, 1901.
40526.7.8 Chénier, André. Poésies. Paris, 1901.
43552.25.1100 Chevalier, Toussaint. Parisiens aux États-Unis. Cincinnati? 1901.
43552.26.105 Chevrillon, André. Études anglaises. 2e éd. Paris, 1901.
FL 397.71 Clouzot, Henri. L'ancien théâtre en Poitou. Niort, 1901.
42542.53.12 Coolus, R. Les amants de Sazy. Paris, 1901.
42542.54 Corneille, P. Richelieu. Paris, 1901.
37565.46 Coulanges, A. de. La chaire française au dix-huitième siècle. Paris, 1901.
38514.58.20 Coville, Alfred. Sur une ballade de Christine de Pisan. n.p., 1901.
42542.58.6 Curel, François de. L'envers d'une sainte. Paris, 1901.
Mol 604.1 Danschacher, H. Molière's Monomanen. Fürth, 1901.
42566.27.12 Daudet, Alphonse. Letters from my mill. Boston, 1901.
42566.21.25 Daudet, Alphonse. Monday tales. Boston, 1901.
42566.31.12 Daudet, Alphonse. Le petit chose. N.Y., 1901.
42576.63.745 Delaporte, Louis. Anatole France. Tours, 1901.
37566.146 Delaporte, Louis. Quelques-uns. 1. série. 5. éd. Paris, 1901.
FL 398.17.12 Delaunay, Louis A. Souvenirs. Paris, 1901.
38557.22 Delmont, T. Autour de Bossuet. Paris, 1901. 2v.
42575.53 Deries, Léon. Octave Feuillet. Saint-Lô, 1901.
42542.64.27.5 Descaves, Lucien. La colonne. 4. éd. Paris, 1901.
Mol 853.2A Déscente de l'ame de Molière dans les Champs-Élysées. Paris, 1901.
42568.2.37 Didier, Charles. The romance of l'Aiglon. N.Y., 1901.
42568.2.35A Didier, Charles. The romance of l'Aiglon. N.Y., 1901.
38567.17 Dreyfus-Brisac, E. Un faux classique. Nicolas Boileau. Paris, 1901.
42568.14 Droz, Gustave. The registered letter. Boston, 1901.
37551.66 Dubedout, E. Le sentiment chrétien dans la poésie romantique. Paris, 1901.
37558.117 Duboul, Axel. Les deux siècles de l'académie des jeux floraux. Toulouse, 1901. 2v.
41538.24.2 Dumas, Alexandre. Episodes from Monte-Cristo. London, 1901. 2v.
41538.53.36A Dumas, Alexandre. The three guardsmen. N.Y., 1901.
41538.53.105 Dumas, Alexandre. Twenty years after. N.Y., 1901.
41538.53.104 Dumas, Alexandre. Twenty years after. N.Y., 1901.
43576.1.35 Dumas, André. Paysages. Paris, 1901.
43576.5.30F Dupond, J. Légendes et histoires Trivoltiennes. Trevoux, 1901.
37562.12.16 Enneccerus, M. Versbau und gesanglicher Vortrag des ältesten Französischen Liedes. Frankfurt, 1901.
42573.28 Erckmann, Emile. The blockade of Phalsburg. N.Y., 1901.
NEDL 37565.37.6 Faguet, Émile. XVIII siècle. Études littéraires. Paris, 1901.
38554.737.40 Fénelon, F. de S. de la Mothe. Réponse inédite à Bossuet. Paris, 1901.
37595.36.50 Foerster, Wendelin. Romanische Bibliothek. 2. Aufl. v.1,5,6,8,13. Halle, 1901-03. 5v.
42554.37 Fontenelle, F. La chanson du cidre. Rennes, 1901.
37562.14.6 Forkert, F.M. Beiträge zu den Bildern...auf Grund der Miracles de Nostre Dame. Bonn, 1901.
43611.2.30 Fouquier, Henry. Philosophie parisienne. Paris, 1901.
42576.62.17A France, Anatole. Monsieur Bergeret à Paris. Paris, 1901.
37576.16.1 French belles-lettres from 1640 to 1870. N.Y., 1901.
37576.16 French belles lettres from 1640 to 1870. Washington, 1901.
42571.30.9 Gaboriau, Emile. File no. 113. N.Y., 1901.
42571.32.10 Gaboriau, Emile. The honor of the name. N.Y., 1901.
42571.32.2 Gaboriau, Emile. Monsieur Lecoq. N.Y., 1901.
42571.28.4 Gaboriau, Emile. The mystery of Orcival. N.Y., 1901.
42571.24.7 Gaboriau, Emile. Other people's money. N.Y., 1901.
42571.23.3 Gaboriau, Emile. The widow Lerouge. N.Y., 1901.
FL 398.7.18 Gallus, A. Sarah Bernhardt: her artistic life. N.Y., 1901.
43620.2.33 Gide, André. Le roi Candaule. Paris, 1901.
42536.28 Giraud, V. Essai sur Taine; son oeuvre et son influence. Fribourg, 1901.
42543.48 Giron, A. Un soir des saturnales. Paris, 1901.
37566.80 Gregh, Fernand. La fenêtre ouverte. Paris, 1901.
FL 1028.116.100 Gregorius I, the Great, Saint, Pope. Dialogues, translated into Angle-Norman French by Angier. Strassburg, 1901.
37548.17 Gribble, Francis. Lake Geneva and its literary landmarks. Westminster, 1901.
37548.18 Gribble, Francis. Lake Geneva and its literary landmarks. Westminster, 1901.
42576.64.4 Grin, Henri L. Incroyables aventures de L. de Rougemont. Paris, 1901.
43671.59.100 Gung, E. La vie européenne au Tonkin. Paris, 1901.
38526.3.5.200 Hamon, Auguste. Un grand rhétoriqueur poitevin. Thèse. Paris, 1901.
37557.23A Harper, G.M. Masters of French literature. N.Y., 1901.
38514.56.5 Henckenkamp, F. Les quinze joyes de mariage. Halle, 1901.
37594.19 Henri d'Andeli. Le Lai d'Aristote. Rouen, 1901.
42554.57.5 Heredia, J.M. de. Les trophées. Paris, 1901?
42571.37.90 Hervieu, Paul. La course du flambeau. 9. éd. Paris, 1901.
41574.15 Hugo, Victor. Lettres à la fiancée. 1820-1822. Paris, 1901.
41574.15.30 Hugo, Victor. The love letters of Victor Hugo. N.Y., 1901.
41574.14 Hugo, Victor. Post-scriptum de ma vie. Paris, 1901.
41573.22.3 Hugo, Victor. Quatre-vingt-treize. Boston, 1901.
39545.6.5 Hugo, Victor. Voltaire oration. Chicago, 1901.
FL 382.47 Huret, Jules. Loges et coulisses. Paris, 1901.
FL 6091.76.10 Istel, Edgar. Jean-Jacques Rousseau als Komponist seiner lyrischen scene Pygmalion. Leipzig, 1901.
40516.60.90 Jacobus X (pseud.). Le Marquis de Sade et son oeuvre devant la science. Paris, 1901.
37591.41 Jeanroy, Alfred. Lais et descorts français du XIIIe siècle. Texte et musique. Paris, 1901.
FL 395.220 Joannidès, A. La comédie française. Paris, 1901-1925. 18v.
FL 394.107 Joannidès, A. La comédie-française de 1680-1900. Paris, 1901.
37564.71 Johnson, A. Étude sur...littérature...du XVIIe siècle. Thèse. Paris, 1901.
37564.70A Johnson, A. Lafosse Otway, Saint-Real. Paris, 1901.
40526.27 Josz, V. Clavel d'Haurimonts. Paris, 1901.

1901 - cont.

37543.63.29 Kastner, Leon Emile. Short history of French literature. N.Y., 1901.
38525.22.7 Köhler, F. Die Allitteration bei Ronsard. Erlangen, 1901.
42514.18.5 Laboulaye, Edouard. Contes bleus. Boston, 1901.
37530.18 La Chèvre, F. Bibliographie des recueils collectifs de poésies publiés de 1597 à 1700. Paris, 1901-05. 4v.
42544.32 Lamaître, Jules. Opinions à répandre. Paris, 1901.
38514.62 La Marche, Olivier de. Le triumphe des dames. Rostock, 1901.
42576.46.24 Lapauze, Jeanne L. Fiancée d'outre-mer. Péril d'amour. Justice mondaine. Une mère. 7. éd. Paris, 1901.
37556.22.50 Lavalley, G. Études sur la presse en Normandie. Paris, 1901-10. 2v.
42563.23.4 Le Berre, Léon. Fleurs de Basse-Bretagne. Rennes, 1901.
42554.16.10.5 Le Braz, A. Le sang de la Sirène. Paris, 1901.
42554.16.13 Le Braz, A. La terre du passé. 2e éd. Paris, 1901?
37556.36 Le Breton, A. Le roman français au dix-neuvième siècle. pt. 1. Paris, 1901.
42576.68.160 Lecomte du Nouÿ, H.O. (Mme.). L'amour est mon péché. Paris, 1901?
38514.42.10 Le Houx, Jean. Le livre des chants nouveaux de Vau de vire. Rouen, 1901.
40512.36 LeSage, Alain René. The bachelor of Salamanca. Boston, 1901.
42544.34.60.5A Louys, Pierre. Les aventures de Roi Pausole. Paris, 1901.
42544.34.28.3 Louys, Pierre. Les chansons de Bilitis. Paris, 1901.
Htn 42544.34.33* Louys, Pierre. L'homme de pourpre. Paris, 1901.
42545.3.13.3 Maeterlinck, Maurice. The life of the bee. 4. ed. London, 1901.
42545.3.8.2 Maeterlinck, Maurice. Wisdom and destiny. N.Y., 1901.
43697.34.160 Magre, Maurice. Le poème de la jeunesse. Paris, 1901.
37543.92 Maillard, F. Le requiem des gens de lettres. Paris, 1901.
42587.16.13 Maindron, M. Blancador l'avantageux. Paris, 1901.
40556.28.6 Maistre, Joseph de. Pages choisies. Paris, 1901.
40588.43.15A Maistre, Xavier. Voyage autour de ma chambre. Cambridge, 1901.
42563.23.117 Martineau, René. Un vivant et deux morts. Villiers de l'isle-Adam, 1901.
Mol 270.28 Matić, Tomo. Molière's Tartuffe. Berlin, 1901. 11 pam.
42526.14 Mauclair, C. L'art en silence. Photoreproduction. Paris, 1901.
42577.4.14 Maupassant, Guy de. Les dimanches d'un bourgeois de Paris. Paris, 1901.
42577.4.29.8A Maupassant, Guy de. Une vie. Paris, 1901.
42545.10.22 Meilhac, Henri. Rip. Paris, 1901.
41555.23.73A Mérimée, Prosper. Colomba and Carmen. The French classical romances. N.Y., 1901.
42545.21.14 Méténier, Oscar. Son poteau. Paris, 1901.
FL 6139.01.5 Mettrier, Henri. L'impot et la milice dans Jean-Jacques Rousseau et Mably. Thèse. Paris, 1901.
43699.2.30 Mitchell, Georges. La maison: pièce en trois actes. Paris, 1901.
42555.59.110 Mithouard,A. Le tourment de l'unité. Paris, 1901.
41574.60 Moell, O. Beiträge zur Geschichte...der "Orientales" von Victor Hugo. Mannhein, 1901.
Mol 165.70 Molière, Jean Baptiste Poquelin. L'avare...Lanson. Paris, 1901.
Mol 165.71 Molière, Jean Baptiste Poquelin. L'avare. London, 1901.
Mol 215.45 Molière, Jean Baptiste Poquelin. Les Fourberies...de Scapin. London, 1901.
Mol 62.37 Molière, Jean Baptiste Poquelin. Meisterwerke...Fulda. 3e Aufl. Stuttgart, 1901.
Mol 251.65 Molière, Jean Baptiste Poquelin. Les précieuses ridicules. (The temple Molière). London, 1901.
42587.36 Moreau, H.C. L'un ou l'autre. Paris, 1901
42587.36.5 Morgan, Jean. Thérèse Heurtot. Paris, 1901.
42542.2.5 Morillot, Paul. Émile Augier, 1820-1889. Grenoble, 1901.
37555.575 Müller, Oskar. Die Technik des romantischen Verses. Berlin, 1901.
41596.18.15A Musset, Alfred de. Trois comédies: Fantasio, On ne badine pas avec l'amour, Il faut qu'une porte soit ouverte ou fermée. Boston, 1901.
41596.18.16 Musset, Alfred de. Trois comédies: Fantasio, On ne badine pas avec l'amour, Il faut qu'une porte soit ouverte ou fermée. Boston, 1901.
43709.3.100 Noailles, Anna E. La coeur innombrable. Paris, 1901?
Mol 615.2 Oettinger, W. Das Komische bei Molière. Strassburg, 1901.
42578.29.60 Ohnet, Georges. Le brasseur d'affaires. Paris, 1901.
42578.30.25 Ohnet, Georges. La ténébreuse. Paris, 1901.
38514.21.6A Paris, Gaston. François Villon. Paris, 1901.
39533.32.5 Patin, Guy. Correspondance. Paris, 1901.
37567.48.10 Pellissier, G.J.M. Le mouvement littéraire contemporain. 2e éd. Paris, 1901.
Htn 41578.35.135* Per le nozze Grancini Lamarre. Firenze, 1901.
FL 360.65.5 Pergameni, H. Le théâtre politique en France depuis 1789. Bruxelles, 1901.
39594.13.3 Persian and Chinese letters; being the lettres persanes. Washington, 1901.
38537.16.5 Pfeffer, G. Beiträge zum Wortschatz des 3. Buches Rabelais. Marburg, 1901.
37562.20.9 Pillet, A. Das Fableau von den trois bossus Ménestrels. Halle, 1901.
43743.37.100 Polhes, Alban de. Le parfum de l'Amphore. Paris, 1901.
FL 6129.01 Pougin, A. Jean-Jacques Rousseau. Paris, 1901.
42578.31.61 Prévost, Marcel. Chonchette. Paris, 1901.
42578.31.28.6 Prévost, Marcel. Les demi-vièrges. Paris, 1901.
42578.31.57A Prévost, Marcel. Le domino jaune. Paris, 1901.
42578.31.40 Prévost, Marcel. L'heureux ménage. 55. éd. Paris, 1901.
X Cg 42584.10.6 Ramond, F.C. Les personnages des Rougon-Macquart. Paris, 1901.
42556.26.21 Régnier, Henri de. Figures et caractères. 3. éd. Paris, 1901.
42556.27.88 Retté, Adolphe. Lumières tranquilles. Paris, 1901.
42554.41 Risson, Paul. La vie et l'oeuvre de Gelu. Avignon, 1901.
43756.2.30 Rivollet, G. Alkestis. Paris, 1901.
37594.16 Robert de Ho. Les enseignements. Paris, 1901.
42578.19.17 Rod, Edouard. Mademoiselle Annette. Paris, 1901.
42546.8.5 Rodenbach, G. Le mirage. Paris, 1901.
42546.11.6 Rostand, Edmond. L'aiglon. N.Y., 1901.
42546.11.2 Rostand, Edmond. L'aiglon. N.Y., 1901.
FL 6026.18 Rousseau, J.J. Confessions. n.p., 1901. 2v.
FL 6026.8.20 Rousseau, J.J. The confessions. v.1,3-4. n.p., 1901. 3v.
Mon 128.2 Ruel, E. Du sentiment artistique dans la morale de Montaigne. Paris, 1901.

Chronological Listing

1901 - cont.

FL 382.75 Saint-Auban, Émile de. L'idée sociale au théâtre. Paris, 1901.

38551.116 St. Cyres, S.H.N. François de Fénelon. London, 1901.

37542.17 Saintsbury, George. A short history of French literature. 6th ed. Oxford, 1901.

42556.29.11 Samain, Albert. Le chariot d'or. Paris, 1901.

38551.120 Sanders, E.K. Fénelon. London, 1901.

42546.30.20 Sardou, Victorien. Madame Sans-Gêne. London, 1901.

42546.30.19.12 Sardou, Victorien. Madame Sans-Gêne. N.Y., 1901.

42546.30.20.1 Sardou, Victorien. Madame Sans-Gêne. N.Y., 1901.

FL 366.32 Sauton, Maurice. L'engagement théâtre. Thèse. Paris, 1901.

39591.21 Schwarcz, J. Montesquieu und die Verantwortlichkeit der Räthe des Monarchen. Leipzig, 1901.

41568.17.2 Sénancour, Étienne Pivert de. Obermann. Cambridge, 1901. 2v.

FL 370.75 Sepet, Marius. Origines catholiques de théâtre moderne. Paris, 1901.

40537.13 Sieby, A. Etude sur le théâtre de Marie Joseph Chénier. Paris, 1901.

37567.329.25 Skerlitch, Jean. L'opinion publique en France d'après la poésie politique et sociale de 1830 à 1848. Diss. Lausanne, 1901.

41574.39 Sleumer, A. Die Dramen Victor Hugos. Berlin, 1901.

40597.2.8 Spoelberch de Lovenjoul, Charles. La genése d'un roman de Balzac: Les paysans. Paris, 1901.

40575.5.5 Spoelberch de Lovenjoul, V. de. Sainte-Beuve inconnu. Paris, 1901.

42535.34 Stapfer, Paul. Des réputations littéraires. Paris, 1901. 2v.

41574.45.10 Stapfer, Paul. Victor Hugo et la grande poésie satirique en France. Paris, 1901.

38537.35 Stein, H. Un Rabelais apocryphe de 1549. Paris, 1901.

FL 6129.01.5 Stoppoloni, A. Le donne nella vita di G.G. Rousseau. Roma, 1901.

42547.2 Thénard, J. (Mme.). Marie Antoinette et son cercle. Paris, 1901.

FL 6129.01.2 Thomas, L. Grange-canal et Jean-Jacques Rousseau. Genève, 1901.

37555.41 Thurau, G. Der Refrain in der französischen Chanson. Berlin, 1901.

42578.56.40 Toutain, Paul. Contes normands. Paris, 1901.

42547.5.40 Trarieux, Gabriel. Sur la foi des étoiles. Paris, 1901.

42547.18.10 Van der Meulen, C.J.C. The revolt and The escape. London, 1901.

42547.11 Vaucaire, Maurice. Amoureuse Anitié. Paris, 1901.

42557.11.10 Verhaeren, Émile. Philippe II; drame. Paris, 1901.

42576.52.15.1 Viaud, Julien. An Iceland fisherman. N.Y., 1901.

42576.52.15 Viaud, Julien. An Iceland fisherman. N.Y., 1901.

42576.52.4.20 Viaud, Julien. Pêcheur d'Islande. Bielefeld, 1901.

42576.54.5A Viaud, Julien. The story of a child. Boston, 1901.

43824.25.1100 Vieu, R. La petite énigme. Paris, 1901.

38575.20.5A Vincent, Leon H. Corneille. Boston, 1901.

38575.20.7 Vincent, Leon H. Corneille. Boston, 1901.

37558.42A Vincent, Leon H. The French Academy. Cambridge, 1901.

39543.16 Voltaire, François Marie Arouet de. The works of Voltaire. Paris, 1901. 42v.

39545.32.30 Voltaire, François Marie Arouet de. Zadig and other tales. London, 1901.

FL 6059.3 Vreeland, W.V.D. Rapport litteraire entre Genève et l'Angleterre. Genève, 1901.

Mol 270.29 Waechter, A. Les sources du Tartuffe de Molière. Erfurt, 1901.

37563.4 Wahlund, Karl. Kronologiskt ordnade geografiska schemata. Uppsala, 1901.

42584.13.25 Zola, Emile. Doctor Pascal. N.Y., 1901.

42584.23.13 Zola, Emile. Labor. N.Y., 1901.

42584.23.19.5 Zola, Emile. Madame Neigeon. Paris, 1901.

42584.23.37 Zola, Emile. Rome. v.1-2. N.Y., 1901.

1902

42562.33.2 About, Edmond. The king of the mountains. N.Y., 1902.

42513.48.9 Adam, Juliette. The romance of my childhood and youth. N.Y., 1902.

42562.38.14.9 Adam, Paul. L'année de Clarisse. Paris, 1902.

42562.38.14.13 Adam, Paul. L'infant d'Austerlitz. Paris, 1902.

FL 393.13 Albert, Maurice. Les théâtres des boulevards. Paris, 1902.

37566.27.5 Albert, Paul. La littérature française au 19th siècle. Paris, 1902. 2v.

37567.76 Alméras, H. de. Avant la gloire. Leurs débuts. Paris, 1902.

42553.32.50 Amiel, Henri F. Daily maxims from Amiel's journal. N.Y., 1902.

40596.26 Balzac, Honoré de. The best of Balzac. N.Y., 1902.

40597.35.106 Balzac, Honoré de. Le colonel Chabert. Paris, 1902.

40597.15.105 Balzac, Honoré de. Le cousin Pons. Boston, 1902.

40597.32.6.50 Balzac, Honoré de. The magic skin. The hidden masterpiece. Boston, 1902.

40597.31.6 Balzac, Honoré de. Memoires of two young brides. N.Y., 1902. 2v.

41522.2.20 Barbey d'Aurevilly, Jules. Lettres à Léon Bloy. Paris, 1902.

38546.23 Batereau, A. Georges de Scudéry als Dramatiker. Leipzig, 1902.

41522.12.17 Baudelaire, Charles. Gedichte in Vers und Prosa. Leipzig, 1902.

37596.87 Baudler, A. Guiot von Provins, seine Gönner. Halle, 1902.

37555.62 Beaunier, A. La poésie nouvelle. Paris, 1902.

37555.61 Bercy, L. de. Montmartre et ses chansons. Paris, 1902.

FL 393.15 Bernardin, N.M. La comédie italienne en France et les théâtres de la foire et du boulevard. Paris, 1902.

42587.22.13 Berthelot, Philippe. Louis Ménard et son oeuvre. Paris, 1902.

41522.58.5 Bertrand, Louis. Gaspard de la nuit. Paris, 1902.

38521.7 Bible. O.T. Psalms. French. Paraphrases. Le pseautier Huguenot du XVIe siècle. Paris, 1902.

42563.23.36 Bloy, Léon. Exégèse des lieux commus. v.1-2. Paris, 1902..

FL 375.55 Böhm, Karl. Beiträge zur Kenntnis des Einflusses Seneca's...Französischen Tragödien. Erlangen, 1902.

38566.36A Boileau Despréaux, Nicolas. Les héros de Roman. Dialogue. Boston, 1902.

43544.5.31 Boulenger, Marcel. Opinions choisies. Paris, 1902.

1902 - cont.

42563.37.57 Bourget, Paul. L'eau profonde. Les pas dans les pas. Paris, 1902.

37566.33 Brandes, G. L'Ecole romantique en France. Paris, 1902.

42542.47 Brieux, Eugène. Les avaries. Paris, 1902.

42542.47.5 Brieux, Eugène. Le Berceau. 2. éd. Paris, 1902.

42542.47.18 Brieux, Eugène. Les bienfaiteurs. Paris, 1902.

42542.47.14 Brieux, Eugène. L'ecole des belles-mères. Paris, 1902.

42542.47.15 Brieux, Eugène. L'engrenage. Paris, 1902.

42542.47.6.25 Brieux, Eugène. Les remplacantes. Paris, 1902.

41574.41A Brunetière, F. Victor Hugo. Paris, 1902. 2v.

FL 6015.11 Buffenoir, H. Jean-Jacques Rousseau et Henriette. Paris, 1902.

FL 6129.02.4 Buffenois, H. Les charmettes et Jean-Jacques Rousseau. Paris, 1902.

FL 366.12 Cahuet, Albéric. La liberté en France et a l'etranger. Paris, 1902.

42555.37.4 Calmettes, F. Un demi siècle littéraire. Leconte de Lisle et ses amis. Paris, 1902.

42542.48.10 Capus, Alfred. La veine. Paris, 1902.

42586.28.5 Casale, F. Chanteclair. Paris, 1902.

41555.39 Chambon, F. Notes sur Prosper Mérimée. Paris, 1902.

42587.22.12 Champion, E. Le tombeau de Louis Ménard. Paris, 1902.

42563.80 Champsaur, Félicien. Le semeur d'amour, roman hindou. Paris, 1902.

39533.9.5 Chapelle, C.E.L. Voyage d'Encausse. Caen, 1902.

NEDL 40586.29 Chateaubriand, F.A.R. Memoirs of...Chateaubriand. London, 1902. 6v.

42565.31.7 Cherbuliez, Victor. Samuel Brohl and company. N.Y., 1902. 2v.

42576.15.235 Christensen, Hjalmar. Gustave Flaubert. Kjøbenhavn, 1902.

40583.12 Chuquet, A. Stendhal-Beyle. Paris, 1902.

FL 384.97 Claretie, Jules. Profils de théâtre. Paris, 1902.

41574.40 Claretie, Jules. Victor Hugo. Paris, 1902.

41574.30.10 Comitato italiano per celebrazioni il centenario di Victor Hugo. Il centenario di Victor Hugo a Roma. Roma, 1902.

42542.58.7 Curel, François de. La fille sauvage. Paris, 1902.

FL 6139.02.2 Dalleggio, A. Beiträge zur Psychologie Jean-Jacques Rousseau's. Jena, 1902.

42566.26.3 Daudet, Alphonse. Jack. Boston, 1902.

42566.29.23A Daudet, Alphonse. The Nabob. N.Y., 1902.

42566.35.24 Daudet, Alphonse. Tartarin on the Alps. London, 1902.

41539.20 Davidson, A.F. Alexandre Dumas (père) his life and works. Westminster, 1902.

41539.1A Davidson, Arthur F. Alexandre Dumas, (père) his life and works. Philadelphia, 1902.

37546.10 Deberre, E. La vie littéraire à Dijon au XVIIIe siècle. Paris, 1902.

43566.48.150 Delarue-Mardrus, Lucie. Ferveur. Paris, 1902.

FL 397.58 Destranges, E. Le théâtre à Nantes, 1430-1901. Paris, 1902.

42586.36.9 Divat, Joseph. Les dieux d'or. Paris, 1902.

42542.65.12 Donnay, Maurice. La Vrille. Paris, 1902.

42542.65.110 Doucet, J. Tales of the spinner. N.Y., 1902.

37567.35.1 Doumic, René. Portraits d'écrivains. Paris, 1902.

38585.43.9 Dreyfus-Brisac, E. Phèdre et Hippolyte ou Racine moraliste. Paris, 1902.

38563.15 Dubois, L. Bayle et la tolérance. Photoreproduction. Paris, 1902.

38563.15.2 Dubois, L. Bayle et la tolérance. Thèse. Paris, 1902.

41538.71.5 Dumas, Alexandre. The black tulip. N.Y., 1902.

41538.28.15 Dumas, Alexandre. Journeys with Dumas. Boston, 1902.

41538.47.10 Dumas, Alexandre. The king's gallant. N.Y., 1902.

42543.15.8.12 Dumas, Alexandre. The lady of the camellias. London, 1902.

42543.15.8.13A Dumas, Alexandre. The lady of the camellias. N.Y., 1902.

42568.23.6 Duval, Paul. Coins de Bysance. Le vice errant. 13. éd. Paris, 1902.

42586.42.9 Epry, C. L'ecume. Paris, 1902.

42572.11.30 Erckmann, Emile. The conscript; a story of the French war of 1813. N.Y., 1902.

42572.32.10 Erckmann, Emile. Waterloo. N.Y., 1902.

37567.71 Ernest-Charles, J. La littérature française d'aujourd'hui. Paris, 1902.

43598.84.230 Estaunié, Édouard. L'épave. Paris, 1902.

40527.19.5 Faguet, E. André Chenier. Paris, 1902.

42565.70.6 Favre de Coulevain, Hélène. Eve triumphant. N.Y., 1902.

42575.50.4A Feuillet, Octave. The romance of a poor young man. N.Y., 1902.

42576.28.12 Flaubert, Gustave. Madame Bovary. N.Y., 1902.

43611.1.25.6 Fort, Paul. Paris sentimental. 2. éd. VI. Paris, 1902.

41596.34 Foss, Ernst. Die "Nuits" von Alfred de Musset. Berlin, 1902.

Htn 42576.62.70* France, Anatole. Histoire de Dona Maria d'Avalos. Paris, 1902.

42576.63.23 France, Anatole. La liberté par l'étude. Paris, 1902.

42576.62.50 France, Anatole. Madame de Luzy. Paris, 1902.

Htn 42576.62.50* France, Anatole. Madame de Luzy. Paris, 1902.

Htn 42576.63.11* France, Anatole. Mémoires d'un volontaire. Paris, 1902.

37556.40 Franche, Paul. Le prêtre dans le roman français. Paris, 1902.

38551.22.5 Funk-Brentano, F. Fénelon. Paris, 1902.

42554.75.80 Fuster, Charles. Par les chemins de Bretagne et les routes de France. St. Etienne, 1902.

42571.28.6 Gaboriau, Emile. The mystery of Orcival. N.Y., 1902.

37596.85A Gace Brulé. Chansons. Paris, 1902.

38546.6 Gasté, A. Madeleine de Scudéry et le dialogue des héros de roman. Rouen, 1902.

40587.9.5 Gautier, P. Qua familiaritate Chateaubriand. Andigavis, 1902.

41542.7.5 Gautier, Théophile. Captain Fracasse. N.Y., 1902.

40588.21.75 Genlis, S.F.D. de St. Lettres inédites de Mme. de Genlis à son fils. Paris, 1902.

42554.45.10 Ghil, René. Le pantoun des pantoun; poème javanais. Paris, 1902.

42576.6.17 Ginisty, Paul. Lendemains d'amour. Paris, 1902.

42536.29 Giraud, V. Taine. Paris, 1902.

40527.19 Glachant, Paul. André Chenier Critique et critiqué. Paris, 1902.

41574.46 Glanchant, P. Essai critique sur le théâtre de Victor Hugo. Les drames en vers. Paris, 1902.

42586.68.2.5 Gobineau, Arthur de. Nachgelassene Schriften. Alexandre le Macédonien. 2. Aufl. Strassburg, 1902.

38526.10.17 Gohin, F. De Lud. Charondae, vita et versibus. Lutetiae Parisiorum, 1902.

42575.61.15 Goncourt, Edmond de. Renée Mauperin. N.Y., 1902.

37576.602 Gossez, Alphonse Marius. Poètes du Nord. Paris, 1902.

1902 - cont.

37596.21.5 Gross, Max. Geffrei Gaimar. Die Komposition seiner Reimchroniek. Erlangen, 1902.
42576.40.9 Guiches, Gustave. Le nuage. Paris, 1902.
42576.40.346 Halévy, Ludovic. L'abbé Constantin. 219. éd. Paris, 1902.
42576.40.343 Halévy, Ludovic. Abbé Constantin and Le marriage for love. N.Y., 1902.
42543.62.29 Haraucourt, Edmond. Héro et Léandre. Paris, 1902.
42543.62.37 Haraucourt, Edmond. Les naufragés. Paris, 1902.
NEDL 42554.57 Heredia, J.M. de. The trophies. London, 1902.
42576.67.11 Hervieu, Paul. Théroigne de Méricourt. Paris, 1902.
38531.14 Heulhard, Arthur. Une lettre fameuse. Paris, 1902.
FL 6139.02 Höffding, H. Rousseau und seine Philosophie. Stuttgart, 1902.
38576.7.30 Hoffmann, A. Edme Boursault nach seinem Leben und in seinen Werken. Metz, 1902.
41574.13.40 Hugo, Goerges Victor. Mon Grand-Père. Paris, 1902.
41573.31 Hugo, Victor. Dernière gerbe. Paris, 1902.
41573.23.13A Hugo, Victor. Notre Dame de Paris. N.Y., 1902.
41573.23.5.5A Hugo, Victor. Notre Dame de Paris. N.Y., 1902. 2v.
37596.2.10 Hultman, J.E.E. Guillaume de Deguileville. Upsala, 1902.
42576.65.31 Huysmans, Joris Karl. Esquisse biographique sur Don Bosco. n.p., 1902.
Mon 105.7F Ives, G.B. Bibliography of the essays. Boston, 1902-04.
37555.44 Jouffret, M. De Hugo à Mistral. Leipzig, 1902.
37567.73 Kahn, Gustave. Symbolistes et décadents. Paris, 1902.
42544.1.75 Kerambars, Charles de. Velléda la druidesse de l'Ile de Sein. Vannes, 1902.
FL 377.43 Kingler, O. Die Comédie-Italienne in Paris nach der Sammlung von Gherardi. Strassburg, 1902.
41553.33.7 Kock, Charles Paul de. Sister Anne. Boston, 1902.
41553.33.8 Kock, Charles Paul de. Sister Anne. Boston, 1902. 2v.
42586.63 Kretzer, E. Joseph Arthur, Graf von Gobineau. Leipzig, 1902.
37562.70 Kühn, Oscar. Ueber Erwähnung und Schilderung von Körperlichen Krankheiten und Körpergebrechen in altfranzösischen Dichtungen. Breslau, 1902.
40535.19.100 La Chaussée, Pierre Claude Nivelle de. Freundeschule. Naumburg, 1902.
43687.16.100 Lacuzon, A. Eternité. Paris, 1902. 2v.
38512.32.10 La Tour-Landry, Geoffrey de. The book of thenseygnementes and techynge. London, 1902.
42584.24.7 L'Aurore. 6 Oct. 1902. Funeral of Emile Zola. Paris, 1902.
42544.24.6.5F Lavedan, Henri. Le marquis de Priola. (Drama). Paris, 1902.
42576.42.10 Le Barillier, Berthe. Les vièrges de Syracuse. Paris, 1902.
43688.14.3140 Leclèrc, Tristan. Le livre d'esquisses. Paris, 1902.
42576.68.155 Lecomte du Nouÿ, H.O. (Mme.). Incertidumbre por H.L.N. Buenos Aires, 1902.
42555.35.15 Leconte de Lisle, C.M.R. Premières poésies et lettres intimes. Paris, 1902.
Mol 875.13 Lefebvre, Henri. La revanche de Thomas Diafoirus. Paris, 1902.
41574.42 Legay, T. Victor Hugo jugé par son siècle. Paris, 1902.
42544.5.8 Legouvé, Ernest. La cigale chez les fourmis. Boston, 1902.
43688.35.180 Le Grand, Maurice. L'honorable Conque. Paris, 1902?
42544.33.26 Lemaître, Jules. Quatre discours. Paris, 1902.
FL 398.49.35 Lemounier, A. Les mille et un souvenirs d'un Homme de théâtre. Paris, 1902.
39598.40 Lenel, S. Un homme de lettres au XVIIIe siècle. Marmontel. Paris, 1902.
42544.34.6.20 Lepelletier, E. Il giuramento d'Orsini. Milano, 1902.
FL 398.84.12 Leport, Charles. Étude critique sur l'opération de Talma comme traitement de l'ascite. Thèse. Paris, 1902.
42566.16.155 Lestienne, Pierre. Un regard sur Alphonse Daudet. Roubaix, 1902.
43693.1.30 Loison, F. Les reflets. Paris, 1902.
42576.72 Lombard, Jean. Byzance. Paris, 1902.
37558.18 Longuemare, P. de. Une famille d'auteurs aux 16e, 17e et 18e siècles. Les Sainte-Marthe. Paris, 1902.
41574.30.5 Mabilleau, L. Victor Hugo. Paris, 1902.
42545.3.10A Maeterlinck, Maurice. The Buried temple. N.Y., 1902.
42545.3.13.5 Maeterlinck, Maurice. The life of the bee. N.Y., 1902.
42545.3.11 Maeterlinck, Maurice. Monna Vanna. Paris, 1902.
42545.3.3.8 Maeterlinck, Maurice. Pélléas et Mélisande. Leipzig, 1902.
42545.3.7.20 Maeterlinck, Maurice. The plays. Chicago, 1902. 2v.
42545.3.9A Maeterlinck, Maurice. Sister Beatrice and Ardiane and Barbe Bleue. N.Y., 1902.
42545.3.9.25 Maeterlinck, Maurice. Le Temple Enseveli. Paris, 1902.
42545.3.5.11 Maeterlinck, Maurice. Le trésor des humbles. 31. éd. Paris, 1902.
42545.3.8.3A Maeterlinck, Maurice. Wisdom and destiny. N.Y., 1902.
39594.19 Marcus, W. Die Darstellung der französische Zustände in Montesquieus Lettres persanes...der Wirklichkeit. Breslau, 1902.
42576.76.44.5 Margueritte, Paul. Le jardin du roi. 9. éd. Paris, 1902?
42555.49.14 Mariéton, Paul. Hippolyta. Paris, 1902.
43697.75.7510 Marnière, Jeanne. L'aile. Paris, 1902.
37548.32 Masoin, F. Histoire de la littérature française en Belgique de 1815 à 1830. Bruxelles, 1902.
41571.5 Méaulle, L.F. (Mme.). Victor Hugo 1802-1902. Paris, 1902.
41578.48 Mehnert, K. Ueber Lamartines politische Gedichte. Erlangen, 1902.
42545.18.20 Meilhac, Henri. Ma cousine. Paris, 1902. 3 pam.
37551.67 Mendès, Catulle. Rapport...sur le mouvement poétique français de 1867 à 1900. Paris, 1902.
38526.48.2.75 Mennung, A.G.H.A. J.F. Sarasin's Leben und Werke. v.1-2. Halle, 1902-04.
42555.58.1210 Mérat, Albert. Chansons et madrigaux. Paris, 1902.
42555.58.1140 Mérat, Albert. Les joies de l'heure. Paris, 1902.
42555.58.1110 Mérat, Albert. Vers oubliés. Paris, 1902.
Mol 245.94 Molière, Jean Baptiste Poquelin. Le misanthrope. F. Spencer. London, 1902.
Mol 60.30 Molière, Jean Baptiste Poquelin. Plays in French...A.R. Waller. v.2-4. London, 1902-03. 3v.
37596.145 Monaci, E. Francese antico. Roma, 1902.
Mon 31.43A Montaigne, Michel de. Essays. Cotton (Hazlitt). London, 1902. 4v.
Mon 30.11F Montaigne, Michel de. Essays. Florio. Boston, 1902-04. 3v.
Htn 39594.14.5* Montesquieu, C.L. de S. Histoire veritable publiée d'après un nouveau manuscrit. Bordeaux, 1902.

1902 - cont.

42555.61.20 Moréas, Jean. Feuillets. Paris, 1902.
42555.61.35 Moréas, Jean. Le voyage de Grèce. Paris, 1902.
41596.20.10 Musset, Alfred de. Contes et nouvelles. Paris, 1902.
43707.2.30 Nils, A. La terre de la beauté. Paris, 1902.
39544.119 Obser, Karl. Voltaires Beziehungen zu der Markgräfen Karoline Luise von Baden-Durlach und dem Karlsruber Hofe. Heidelberg, 1902.
42578.29.70 Ohnet, Georges. Le crépuscule. 17. éd. Paris, 1902.
41574.17.10 Ouayle, W.A. A hero. Jean Valjean. Cincinnati, 1902.
41539.7 Parigot, Hippolyte. Alexandre Dumas père. Paris, 1902.
38525.21.5 Perdrizet, Pierre. Ronsard et la réforme. Paris, 1902.
38563.32 Perrault, C. Histoire de Peau d'Âne; conte de ma mère Layç. Londres, 1902.
38513.32A Picot, Émile. Recueil général des soties. Paris, 1902. 3v.
42546.12.10 Platow, Hans. Die Personen von Rostands Cyrano de Bergerac. Erlangen, 1902.
Mol 870.9.5 Ponsard, F. Le mariage d'Angélique. Paris, 1902.
38513.3 Pottier, L. La vie et histoire de madame Saint Barbe. Laval, 1902.
FL 395.102 Pougin, Arthur. La comédie française et la révolution. Paris, 1902.
42578.31.43 Prévost, Marcel. Lettres à Françoise. 39. éd. Paris, 1902?
42541.3 Rambeau, A. Augier's L'aventurière of 1848 and 1860. Boston, 1902.
42578.18.11 Rameau, Jean. Ame fleurie. Paris, 1902.
37563.78 Rebell, H. Les inspiratrices de Balzac, Stendhal, Mérimée. Paris, 1902.
42563.37.80 Reggio, A. L'oeuvre de M. Paul Bourget. Paris, 1902.
42556.26.18 Régnier, Henri de. Le bon plaisir. 2e éd. Paris, 1902.
42515.34.5 Renan, Ernest. Lettres du séminaire, 1838-1846. 3. éd. Paris, 1902.
42515.30.728A Renan, Ernest. Souvenirs d'enfance et de jeunesse. Boston, 1902.
38514.21.12 Reure. Simple conjecture sur les origines paternelles de François Villon. Paris, 1902.
41574.57 Reuve, Paul. Victor Hugo. Paris, 1902.
42556.22.47 Richepin, Jean. Par la glaive. Paris, 1902.
FL 6129.02.3 Ritter, E. La parenté de Jean-Jacques Rousseau, 1614. Genève, 1902.
41574.44 Roedel, P. Victor Hugo und der conservateur littéraire. Heidelberg, 1902.
43757.50.359 Rolland, Romain. Le 14 juillet. Paris, 1902.
X Cg 42578.22.7.12 Rosny, J.H. Les deux femmes. 5. éd. Paris, 1902.
42546.15.10 Rostand, Edmond. Un soir à Hernani. Paris, 1902.
43757.89.3100 Rouart, Eugène. La victime. Paris, 1902.
NEDL FL 6036.11.7 Rousseau, J.J. The social contract. 3. ed. London, 1902.
NEDL FL 370.77 Roy, Emile. Études sur le théâtre français du XIV et du XV siècle. Paris, 1902.
38513.2.9 Roy, Emile. Le jour du jugement. Mystère français sur le grande schisme. Paris, 1902.
38551.110 Sackebant, X. Fénelon et le Seminaire de Cambrai d'après des documents la plupart inédits. Cambrai, 1902.
43761.41.140 St. Georges de Bouhelier. Les chants de la vie ardente. Paris, 1902.
NEDL 39532.30 Samfiresco, Elvire. Ménage. Paris, 1902.
41557.9.90.5 Sand, George. Antonia. Boston, 1902.
41557.9.96A Sand, George. Mauprat. N.Y., 1902.
Mol 719.2 Schneegans, H. Molière. Berlin, 1902.
42556.30.42 Schuré, Edouard. Le théâtre de l'ame. 2. série. Paris, 1902.
41564.37 Séché, Léon. Alfred de Vigny et son temps. Paris, 1902.
38575.13.5A Segall, J.B. Corneille and the Spanish drama. N.Y., 1902.
41539.1.5 Spurr, H.A. The life and writings of Alexandre Dumas, 1802-70. London, 1902.
41539.1.6 Spurr, H.A. The life and writings of Alexandre Dumas, 1802-70. N.Y., 1902.
37596.92 Steuer, Wilhelm. Die altfranzösische Histoire de Joseph; kritischerText. Erlangen, 1902.
42557.5.35 Tailhade, Laurent. Discours civiques. Paris, 1902.
42536.32 Taine, Hippolyte. Hippolyte Taine, sa vie et sa correspondance. Paris, 1902. 4v.
42536.32.50 Taine, Hippolyte. Life and letters of Hippolyte Taine 1828-1852. Westminster, 1902. 3v.
38537.25.17 Talant, L. Rabelais et la réforme. Cahors, 1902.
42583.33.5 Theuriet, André. Contes de la Marjolaine. Paris, 1902.
FL 6061.76 Thomas, L. Allégorie: la dernière phase de la pensée religieuse. Lausanne, 1902.
FL 6129.02.2 Thomas, L. Genève, Rousseau et Voltaire, 1775-1778. Genève, 1902.
42536.45 Troubat, Jules. Essais critiques. Paris, 1902.
42537.16 Vayssière, Georges André. Les prairies d'argent et le bosquet de la rime. Paris, 1902.
42557.18.25 Verlaine, Paul. Gedichte. Berlin, 1902.
42557.18 Verlaine, Paul. Oeuvres complètes. Paris, 1902. 5v.
42576.52.20 Viaud, Julien. An Iceland fisherman. N.Y., 1902.
42576.57.50 Viaud, Julien. Lives of two cats. Boston, 1902.
42547.18.5 Villiers de l'Isle Adam, Auguste. L'Eve future. Paris, 1902.
Mol 722.3A Vincent, L.H. Molière. Boston, 1902.
Mol 722.3.5 Vincent, L.H. Molière. Boston, 1902.
37574.37 Vingtrinier, J. Chants et chansons des soldats de France. Paris, 1902.
43824.2.38 Vivien, Renée. Brumes de Fjords. Paris, 1902.
42537.20 Weiss, J.J. Notes et impressions. Paris, 1902.
38521.19.9 Weller, P. Joshuah Sylvesters englische Übersetzungen der religiösen Epen des Du Bartas. Tübingen, 1902.

1903

42553.3 Ackermann, L. Pensées d'une solitaire. Paris, 1903.
42562.38.13 Adam, Paul. Au soleil de juillet, 1829-30. 13e éd. Paris, 1903.
42562.38.14.10 Adam, Paul. La bataille d'Uhde. 6e éd. Paris, 1903.
42562.38.14.30 Adam, Paul. La ruse, 1827-1828. Paris, 1903.
42542.1.9 Adenis, E. Le chevalier qui donna sa femme au diable. Paris, 1903.
41571.5.9 Alexandre, A. La maison de Victor Hugo. Paris, 1903.
41574.49 Allais, G. Les debuts dramatiques de Victor Hugo. Paris, 1903.
37567.76.2 Alméras, H. de. Avant la gloire. Leurs débuts. Paris, 1903.
42562.62 Almeras, Henri d'. Le citoyen Machavoine. Paris, 1903.
37576.530 Alvarado, H.A. Piedras preciosas. San José, 1903.
42553.43 Angellier, A. À l'amie perdue. Paris, 1903.

Chronological Listing

1903 - cont.

42553.44 Angellier, A. Le chemin des saisons. Paris, 1903.
37567.40.7 Audebrand, P. Lauriers et cyprès. Paris, 1903.
37571.41 Aux pecheurs Bretons. Paris, 1903.
40596.13.126.5 Balzac, Honoré de. Honoré de Balzac. N.Y., 1903.
40596.13.126 Balzac, Honoré de. Honoré de Balzac. N.Y., 1903.
40597.31.3 Balzac, Honoré de. Memoires de deux jeunes mariées. Paris, 1903?
40597.36 Balzac, Honoré de. Une page perdue. Paris, 1903.
42554.8.5 Banville, Théodore de. Gringoire. 5th ed. London, 1903.
43537.6.32 Barbusse, Henri. Les suppliants. Paris, 1903.
42586.14.40.10 Bascle de Lagrèze, Gaston. La lune rousse. Tours, 1903.
38551.36.40 Bastier, Paul. Fénelon. Paris, 1903.
42562.38 Batilliat, Marcel. Paul Adam. Paris, 1903.
42563.21.33 Bazin, René. Contes de bonne Perrette. Paris, 1903.
42563.21.61 Bazin, René. Le guide de l'empereur. Paris, 1903.
42563.21.39 Bazin, René. Les Noellet. 9. éd. Paris, 1903?
42563.21.50 Bazin, René. Une tache d'encre. Paris, 1903.
40516.58 Béclard, S. Sébastien Mercier, sa vie, son oeuvre, son temps. Paris, 1903.
37557.12 Bédier, Joseph. Études critiques. Paris, 1903.
FL 385.7.15 Bernheim, Adrien. Trente ans de théâtre. Paris, 1903. 5v.
42542.29.33 Bernstein, H. Joujou. Paris, 1903.
42563.23.8.15 Bertrand, Louis. Le rival de Don Juan. 6. éd. Paris, 1903.
38528.2 Bever, A. van. Les poètes satyriques des XVIe et XVIIe siècles. Paris, 1903.
40587.44 Blennerhassett, C. Chateaubriand. Mainz, 1903.
42563.23.45 Bloy, Léon. Les dernières colonnes de l'église. 3. éd. Paris, 1903.
42563.37.41.5 Bourget, Paul. André Cornélis. Paris, 1903.
42563.38.525 Bovet, M.A. Ballons rouges. Paris, 1903.
42515.35.40 Brauer, H.G.A. The philosophy of Ernest Renan. Madison, 1903.
42542.47.6 Brieux, Eugène. Blanchette. Paris, 1903.
42542.47.7 Brieux, Eugène. Les remplacantes. Paris, 1903.
42524.16.8 Brunetière, F. Discours de combat. Paris, 1903.
38551.24.5 Cagnac, Moïse. Fénelon directeur de conscience. 2. éd. Paris, 1903.
42542.48.3 Capus, Alfred. Les deux ecoles. Paris, 1903.
41578.68.15 Cenzatti, G. Alfonso de Lamartine et l'Italie. Livorno, 1903.
37557.48 Charbonnel, J. Roger. Essai sur l'apologetique littéraire du XVII siècle a nos jours. Paris, 1903.
39531.14 Chardon, H. Scarron inconnu. Paris, 1903. 2v.
40586.34 Chateaubriand, F.A.R. Un dernier amour de René; correspondance. Paris, 1903.
43552.24.200 Chérau, Gaston. Monseigneur voyage. 5e éd. Paris, 1903.
38513.23.5 Chevaldin, E.E. Les jargons de la farce de Pathelin. Paris, 1903.
37566.145 Chevalier, Adrian. Humbles essais. Paris, 1903.
42578.26 Chevalier, Adrian. Paul Ravenel. Paris, 1903?
37567.84 Cim, Albert. Le dîner des gens de lettres. Paris, 1903.
43556.49.187 Colette, Sidonie Gabrielle. Claudine à Paris. 92e éd. Paris, 1903.
43556.49.186 Colette, Sidonie Gabrielle. Claudine en ménage. 112e éd. Paris, 1903.
43556.49.185 Colette, Sidonie Gabrielle. Claudine s'en va. 20e éd. Paris, 1903.
43556.50.2100 Collin, Isi. La valée heureuse. Paris, 1903.
42542.53.6 Coolus, R. Lucette. Paris, 1903.
43556.89.110 Coullet-Tessier, Antonine. Poésies d'une enfant. Paris, 1903.
42542.58.8 Curel, François de. Le repas du Lion. Paris, 1903.
42546.31.10 Dante. London, 1903.
42566.17.50A Daudet, Alphonse. Alphonse Daudet. N.Y., 1903.
42566.17.48A Daudet, Alphonse. Alphonse Daudet. N.Y., 1903.
Mon 30.80 Dieckow, F. John Florio's Englische Übersetzung Montaignes. Strasburg, 1903.
37567.35.4 Doumic, René. Écrivains d'aujourd'hui. Paris, 1903.
37567.82 Doumic, René. Hommes et idées du XIXe siècle. Paris, 1903.
38514.56.7 Dressler, A. Die Chantilly Handschrift der "Quinze joyes de mariage". Greifswald, 1903.
38521.10 Du Bellay, Joachim. Oeuvres complètes. Paris, 1903. 4v.
41538.16.8.50 Dumas, Alexandre. The countess de Charny. N.Y., 1903.
41524.11.8 Dumas, Alexandre. Dame de Monsoreau. Paris, 1903.
41538.61.30 Dumas, Alexandre. Joseph Balsamo. N.Y., 1903.
41538.18.5 Dumas, Alexandre. Le chevalier de Maison-Rouge. N.Y., 1903.
41538.63.33 Dumas, Alexandre. The queen's necklace. N.Y., 1903.
41538.71 Dumas, Alexandre. La tulipe noire. N.Y., 1903?
43576.95.100 Dumas, Charles. L'Eau souterraine. Paris, 1903.
37543.66 Dumesnil, G. L'âme et l'évolution de la littérature. Paris, 1903. 2v.
38514.56.10 Une énigme d'histoire littéraire. Paris, 1903.
42573.25.15 Erckmann, Emile. The plebiscite. N.Y., 1903.
43597.59.105 Ernest-Charles, J. Les samedis litteraires. Paris, 1903-05. 5v.
42574.36 Fabre, Ferdinand. Ma jeunesse. Paris, 1903.
FL 360.55.5 Faguet, Émile. Drame ancien, drame modern. Paris, 1903.
43606.41.110 Faillet, Georges. Ixion; poème. Paris, 1903.
42543.40.11 Fauchois, R. Louis XVII, drame en 5 actes. Paris, 1903.
42565.72.33 Favre de Coulevain, Hélène. Sur la branche. 126. éd. Paris, 1903.
42565.72.35 Favre de Coulevain, Hélène. Sur la branche. 145. éd. Paris, 1903.
42576.16.50 Flaubert, Gustave. Gustave Flaubert. N.Y., 1903.
38514.56.8 Fleig, Arthur. Der Treperel-Druck der Quinze joyes de mariage. Greifswald, 1903.
37543.22.5 Fleury, Jean. Histoire élémentaire de la littérature française. Paris, 1903.
FL 398.29 Flore, C. (Mlle.). Mémoirs de Mlle. Flore. Paris, 1903.
42586.52 Foley, Charles. La soif rouge Madame de Lamballe. Paris, 1903.
43611.1.25.7 Fort, Paul. Les hymnes de feu. VII. Paris, 1903.
42576.62.2.3 France, Anatole. Balthasar. Paris, 1903.
42515.35.105 France, Anatole. Discours prononcé à l'inauguration de la statue d'Ernest Renan. Paris, 1903.
42576.62.20 France, Anatole. Sur la pierre blanche. 41. éd. Paris, 1903. 2v.
42571.34.5 Gaboriau, Emile. File no. 113. N.Y., 1903.
41542.5.25 Gautier, Théophile. Théophile Gautier. N.Y., 1903.
41542.5.27 Gautier, Théophile. Théophile Gautier. N.Y., 1903.
42543.45.56 Gavault, Paul. Les Dupont. Paris, 1903.

1903 - cont.

42543.45.90 Gavault, Paul. L'enfant du miracle. Paris, 1903.
42543.45.80 Gavault, Paul. L'inconnue. Paris, 1903.
42554.46.9 Gielkens, Émile. Le progrès; poèmes. Bruxelles, 1903.
41574.46.2 Glachant, P. Essai critique sur le théâtre de Victor Hugo. Les drames en prose. Paris, 1903.
42586.68.10 Gobineau, Arthur de. Alexander in Weimar. Bayreuth, 1903.
42586.65.3 Gobineau, Arthur de. La renaissance. Paris, 1903.
42576.64.3 Goron, Marie F. El ahorcado de Passy. Madrid, 1903.
43626.5.4100 Grave, J. Malfaiteurs. Paris, 1903.
42554.11.5 Grein, Heinrich. Studien über den Reim bei Théodore de Banville. Kiel, 1903.
38521.33 Grente, Georges. Jean Bertant. 1552-1611. Paris, 1903.
37597.10.2 Guillon, Félix. Jean Clopinel dit de meung. Le roman de la rose. Photoreproduction. Paris, 1903.
42543.62.9 Guinon, Albert. Le jong. Paris, 1903.
39544.155.20 Hall, Evelyn B. The life of Voltaire. 3d ed. N.Y., 1903.
39532.13.9A Hamilton, Anthony. Memoires of Count Grammont. London, 1903.
40597.2.10 Hanotaux, Gabriel. La jeunesse de Balzac. Paris, 1903.
38576.12.21 Hausding, Curt. Jean Galhert de Campistron. Leipzig, 1903.
42543.62.75 Hennequin, Maurice. Heureuse. Paris, 1903.
FL 366.33 Hesse, André. Code pratique du théâtre. Paris, 1903.
38514.44.10 Hoepffer, Ernst. Eustache Deschamps. Strassburg, 1903.
FL 375.57 Holl, Fritz. Das politische Tendenzdrama des 16 Jahrhunderts in Frankreich. Erlangen, 1903.
FL 6119.03A Hudson, H.W. Rousseau and naturalism in life and thought. N.Y., 1903.
38575.19.5 Huszár, Guil. Pierre Corneille et le théâtre Espagnol. Photoreproduction. Paris, 1903.
FL 370.79 Jacobsen, J.P. Det komiske dramas. København, 1903.
43667.51.380 Jaloux, Edmond. Le triomphe de la frivolité. Paris, 1903.
43667.1.32 Jammes, Francis. Le deuil des primevères 1898-1900. 5. éd. Paris, 1903.
37555.18 Jasinski, Max. Histoire du sonnet en France. Douai, 1903.
38557.24.10 Jovy, Ernest. Études et recherches sur Jacques Benigne Bossuet. Vitry-le-François, 1903.
37555.208 Kastner, L.E. History of French versification. Oxford, 1903.
41553.38.5 Kock, Charles Paul de. The barber of Paris. v.1-2. Boston, 1903.
41553.65 Kock, Charles Paul de. The child of my wife. Boston, 1903.
42514.18.6 Laboulaye, Edouard. Contes bleus. Boston, 1903.
43687.26.110 Lafargue, Marc. L'age d'or. 2e éd. Paris, 1903.
39527.29.23 La Fontaine, Jean de. Fables. London, 1903.
39527.29.25 La Fontaine, Jean de. Fifty fables. N.Y., 1903.
41578.6.20 Lamartine, Alphonse de. Premières méditations poétiques. Paris, 1903.
38576.14.83 Langheim, O. De Visé. Inaug. Diss. Wolfenbüttel, 1903.
FL 398.47 Lassouche, J.P. Mémoires anecdotiques. Paris, 1903.
Htn 42576.42.12* Le Barillier, Berthe. La danseuse de Pompei. Paris, 1903.
42542.65.50 Le Brun, R. Maurice Donnay. Paris, 1903.
41539.2 Lecomte, L. Henry. Alexandre Dumas, 1802-70, sa vie intime, ses oeuvres. Paris, 1903.
43688.15.120 Leconte, S.C. Le tentation de l'homme. Paris, 1903.
42544.33.28 Lemaître, Jules. Nouvel état d'esprit. Paris, 1903.
42576.45.7 Le Roux, H. Business and love. N.Y., 1903.
41557.10.13 Le Roy, Albert. George Sand et ses amis. 2e éd. Paris, 1903.
40515.8.15 Lespinasse, J.J.E. de. Lettres. Paris, 1903.
40515.11A Lespinasse, J.J.E. de. Lettres. Paris, 1903.
38526.22.2 Leykauff, A. François Habert's Leben und Weltanschauung. Naumberg, 1903.
37567.80 Lionnet, J. L'evolution des idées chez quelques-uns de nos contemporains. Paris, 1903.
42515.35.158 Le livre d'or de Renan. Paris, 1903.
42544.34.53.5A Louys, Pierre. Sanguines. Paris, 1903.
41557.10.17 Lumbroso, A. Gli amanti di Venezia, Georgio Sand e Alfredo de Musset. Roma, 1903.
42586.29.9 Maël, Pierre (pseud.). Mademoiselle Pompon. Tours, 1903.
42545.3.15.8 Maeterlinck, Maurice. Joyzelle. Leipzig, 1903.
X Cg 42545.3.15 Maeterlinck, Maurice. Joyzelle. Paris, 1903.
X Cg 42545.3.15.6 Maeterlinck, Maurice. Joyzelle. Paris, 1903.
X Cg 42545.3.15.4 Maeterlinck, Maurice. Joyzelle. Paris, 1903.
42545.3.11.20 Maeterlinck, Maurice. Monna Vanna. Leipzig, 1903.
42545.3.11.4 Maeterlinck, Maurice. Monna Vanna. N.Y., 1903.
42545.3.11.3 Maeterlinck, Maurice. Monna Vanna. N.Y., 1903.
42545.3.8.5 Maeterlinck, Maurice. Wisdom and destiny. N.Y., 1903.
41542.4.65 Marcel, H. Essai sur Théophile Gautier. Paris, 1903.
38526.32.22 Marguerite d'Angoulême. The Heptaméron. London, 1903. 2v.
42576.76.35 Margueritte, Paul. L'eau souterraine. Paris, 1903.
41557.10.160 Mariéton, Paul. Une histoire d'amour. 38. éd. Paris, 1903.
39598.9.5 Marmontel, J.F. Memoirs of Marmontel. Paris, 1903.
43697.79.120 Mary, André. Symphonies pastorales. Pithiviers, 1903.
37574.26.14 Masson, Gustave. La lyre française. London, 1903.
42577.3.25 Maupassant, Guy de. Au soleil or African wanderings. N.Y., 1903.
42577.1.24 Maupassant, Guy de. The complete short stories. n.p., 1903.
42577.4.10.12 Maupassant, Guy de. Fort comme la mort and other tales. N.Y., 1903.
42577.1.60 Maupassant, Guy de. Guy de Maupassant, an introduction by Arthur Symone. N.Y., 1903.
42577.4.29.50 Maupassant, Guy de. The life of Maupassant. London, 1903. 17v.
Htn 42577.4.30.1* Maupassant, Guy de. The life work of Maupassant. London, 1903. 17v.
42577.4.11.25 Maupassant, Guy de. Notre coeur, Yvette, a selection from the writings of G. de Maupassant. N.Y., 1903.
42577.4.19.8 Maupassant, Guy de. The odd number, thirteen tales. N.Y., 1903.
42577.4.17.10 Maupassant, Guy de. Pierre et Jean and other tales. N.Y., 1903.
42577.1.30 Maupassant, Guy de. Short stories of the tragedy and comedy of life. N.Y., 1903.
42577.4.4.15 Maupassant, Guy de. Sur l'eau and other tales. N.Y., 1903.
42555.58.31 Mendès, Catulle. Méphistophéla. Paris, 1903.
37567.152 Mendes, Catulle. Le mouvement poétique française de 1867-1900. Paris, 1903.
42555.58.1180 Mérat, Albert. La rance et la mer. Paris, 1903.
42555.58.1160 Mérat, Albert. Les trente-six dédicaces pour Les trente-six quatrains à madame. Paris, 1903.

1903 - cont.

42555.58.1100 Mérat, Albert. Les trente-six quatrains à madame. Paris, 1903.
41555.20.8 Mérimée, Prosper. Carmen. N.Y., 1903.
41555.18.2 Mérimée, Prosper. Prosper Mérimée. N.Y., 1903.
41555.18 Mérimée, Prosper. Prosper Mérimée. N.Y., 1903.
42555.65 Michard, d'Humias L. Le roi Grallon. Paris, 1903.
37563.23.9 Michaut, G. Quibus rationibus Sainte-Beuve opus suum de 16th seculo. Lutetia Parisiorum, 1903.
40575.5.9.2 Michaut, G. Sainte-Beuve avant Les "Lundis". Fribourg, 1903.
40575.5.9 Michaut, G. Sainte-Beuve avant Les "Lundis". Paris, 1903.
38537.14.2 Millet, René. Les grands écrivains français. Rabelais. Paris, 1903.
Mon 50.1 Montaigne, Michel de. Journal. Waters. London, 1903. 3v.
Mon 31.44 Montaigne, Michel de. Selected essays. Cotton. N.Y., 1903.
39544.32.7 Morley, John. Voltaire. London, 1903.
FL 370.80 Mortensen, Johan. Le théâtre français au Moyen Age. Paris, 1903.
42546.12.43 Mügge, O. Edmond Rostand als Dramatiker. Friedeberg, 1903.
41596.18.7 Musset, Alfred de. A selection from the poetry and comedies. Boston, 1903.
38514.56.15 Nève, Joseph. Antoine de la Sale, sa vie et ses ouvrages. Paris, 1903.
42587.37.10 Nion, François de. Bellefleur. Paris, 1903.
37567.79 Nordan, Max. Vus du Dehors. Paris, 1903.
FL 6119.03.2 Nourrisson, J.F. Jean-Jacques Rousseau et le Rousseauisme. Paris, 1903.
FL 366.60 Oeuvre française de trente ans de théâtre, 1902-1912. Paris, 1903- 2v.
42578.29.90 Ohnet, Georges. Marchand de poison. Paris, 1903.
43748.19.100 Ordonneau, Maurice. Le jockey malgré lui. Paris, 1903.
41564.33.5 Paléologue, Maurice. Alfred de Vigny. 2. ed. Paris, 1903.
37562.22.9A Paris, Gaston. Mediaeval French literature. London, 1903.
37596.54.5 Paris, Gaston. La vie de Saint Aléxis. Paris, 1903.
41522.16 Patterson, Arthur S. L'influence d'Edgar Poe sur Charles Baudelaire. Thèse. Grenoble, 1903.
38513.15 Pein, E. Untersuchungen über die Verfasser der Passion und der Vengence. Greifswald, 1903.
42578.30.53 Peladan, J. Oedipe et le sphinx. 4. éd. Paris, 1903.
42545.28.8 Pilon, E. Octave Mirbeau. Paris, 1903.
37591.25.4 Pope, Mildred K. Étude sur la langue de Frère Angier. Paris, 1903.
42545.88.60 Porto-Riche, G. Bonheur manqué. Paris, 1903.
42578.31.46 Prévost, Marcel. Cousine Laura. Paris, 1903.
41578.47 Quentin-Bauchart, P. Lamartine homme politique. Paris, 1903.
43625.3.80 Querlon, Pierre de. Rémy de Gourmont. Paris, 1903.
38536.24.15 Rabelais, F. Pantagruel. Paris, 1903.
43752.59.100 Randon, G. Les soliloques du pauvre. 5. éd. Paris, 1903.
42546.31 Rebell, Hugues. Victorien Sardou. Paris, 1903.
42556.26.28 Régnier, Henri de. Les vacances d'un jeune homme sage. 9. éd. Paris, 1903.
42515.29.715 Renan, Ernest. Marcus Aurelius. London, 1903.
37567.66.5 Retté, A. Le symbolisme. Anecdotes et souvenirs. Paris, 1903.
42556.27.78 Retté, Adolphe. Mémoires de Diogène. Paris, 1903.
37563.29 Revue de la renaissance, organ international des amis du XVIe siècle et de la Pléiade. Paris, 1903.
38537.1 Revue des études Rabelaisiennes. Paris, 1903. 10v.
43756.3.65 Richepin, Jacques. Cadet Roussel comédie en trois actés en vers. Paris, 1903.
42578.19.18 Rod, Edouard. L'inutile effort. Paris, 1903.
FL 375.56 Roemer, Matthaus. Der Aberglaube bei den Dramatikern des 16. Jahrhunderts. München, 1903.
37597.28.6 Römermann, A. Über das Verhältnis der Handschrift D von Girard d'Amiens'Cheval de fust. Greifswald, 1903.
43757.50.570 Rolland, Romain. Le temps viendra. Paris, 1903?
42556.32.55 Rollinat, Maurice. En errant. Paris, 1903.
38525.18.3A Ronsard, Pierre de. Songs and sonnets of Pierre de Ronsard. Boston, 1903.
42546.12.20 Rostand, Edmond. Discours de réception à l'Académie Française. Paris, 1903.
42546.15.6 Rostand, Edmond. Les romanesques. Boston, 1903.
42546.15.8.5 Rostand, Edmond. La Samaritaine. Paris, 1903.
FL 6026.19 Rousseau, J.J. Confessions. London, 1903.
FL 6032.03 Rousseau, J.J. Du contrat social. Paris, 1903.
42584.25.140 Runge, E. Emile Zola. Schlawe, 1903.
40575.7.5 Sainte-Beuve, Charles A. Lettres inédites. Paris, 1903.
41564.38 Sakellarides, Emma. Alfred de Vigny. Paris, 1903.
NEDL 42556.29.17 Samain, Albert. Au jardin de l'infante. 7. éd. Paris, 1903.
42544.33.80 Sansot-Orland, E. Jules Lemaître. Paris, 1903.
42578.34.5 Sarcey, Francisque. Journal de jeunesse. Paris, 1903.
42546.32 Sartène, Jean. Le hotteu. Paris, 1903.
37556.36.3 Schmidt, Bertha. Esquisses littéraires. Karlsruhe, 1903.
37596.146 Schmidt, R. Die Lieder des Andrieu contredit d'Arras. Inaug. Diss. Halle, 1903.
37596.79.7 Schmidt, W. Untersuchung der Reime in den Dichtungen dess Abte Gilles Li Muisis. Inaug. Diss. Leipzig, 1903.
FL 397.3.12 Schoen, Henri. Le théâtre Alsacien. Strasbourg, 1903.
FL 397.3.12.5 Schoen, Henri. Le théâtre populaire en Alsace. Paris, 1903.
38514.17 Scholl, Sigmund. Guillaume Tardif und seine französische Übersetzung. Kempten, 1903.
37596.10.95 Schulz, Otto. Die Darstellung psychologischer Vorgange in den Romanen des Kristian von Troyes. Inaug. Diss. Breslau, 1903.
Mol 820.5 Schwartz, F. Somaize und seine Précieuses ridicules. Königsberg, 1903.
FL 383.125 Sebille, Henri. Toute la troupe. Paris, 1903.
41568.17.5A Sénancour, Étienne Pivert de. Obermann. London, 1903.
41538.18 Senotre, G. Le vrai chevalier de Maison-Rouge. Paris, 1903.
43892.9 Sijenna. Humble Moisson; poésies. Paris, 1903.
42586.62.15 Solenière, Eugène de. Willy. 2. éd. Paris, 1903.
42587.59.9 Soyez-Le Roy, Lettice. Infelice. Paris, 1903.
43776.41.190 Spire, André. Lacité présente, poèmes 1892-1902. Paris, 1903.
37567.83 Spoelberch de Lovenjoul, Charles. Bibliographie et littérature. Paris, 1903.
41574.63 Stange, Paul. Le Cid dans la poèsie lyrique de Victor Hugo. Erfurt, 1903.

1903 - cont.

37596.92.2 Steuer, Wilhelm. Die altfranzösische Histoire de Joseph; kritischer Text. Erlangen, 1903.
40583.21 Stryienski, C. Histoire des oeuvres de Stendhal. Paris, 1903.
41563.16.15 Sue, Eugène. The mysteries of Paris. v.1-6. N.Y., 1903. 3v.
37543.65 Suran, T. Les ésprits directeurs de la pensée française. Paris, 1903.
39594.19.5 Tchernoff, J. Montesquieu et J.J. Rousseau. Paris, 1903.
41596.4.9 Teissier, O. Alfred de Musset. Documents généalogiques. Draguignan, 1903.
FL 6135.4 Thomas, L. La réhabilitation publique de Jean-Jacques Rousseau. Genève, 1903.
FL 6129.03 Thorolfsson, S. Jean-Jacques Rousseau. Reykjavik, 1903.
38525.22.4 Tiersot, J. Ronsard et la musiques de son temps. Paris, 1903.
42578.51.21 Tinayre, Marcelle. La maison du péché. Paris, 1903.
42578.51.30 Tinayre, Marcelle. La rançon. Paris, 1903.
43789.98.100 Tizé, Bertrand de. Sansonnets. Photoreproduction. Rennes, 1903.
37555.301.3 Tobler, A. Vom Französischen Versbau alter und neuer Zeit. 4. Aufl. Leipzig, 1903.
42547.5.30 Trarieux, Gabriel. La guerre au village. Paris, 1903.
FL 395.250 Truffier, Jules C. La comédie-française, 1902. Paris, 1903.
37573.718 Vallée, Léon. La sarabande. Paris, 1903. 2v.
43822.3.30 Vandelbourg, R.H. de. La châine des heures. Paris, 1903.
42557.19.10 Verlaine, Paul. Jadis et naguère. Paris, 1903.
42557.19 Verlaine, Paul. Oeuvres posthumes. Paris, 1903.
42521.19.10 Veuillot, E. Louis Veuillot. Paris, 1903. 3v.
43824.2.43 Vivien, Renée. Du vert au violet. Paris, 1903.
43824.2.30 Vivien, Renée. Études et préludes. 2e éd. Paris, 1903.
43824.2.46 Vivien, Renée. Évocations. Paris, 1903.
39545.32 Voltaire, François Marie Arouet de. Pages choisies. Paris, 1903.
Htn 42584.25.23* Vouvier, Bernard. L'oeuvre de Zola. Genève, 1903.
42547.32 Wolff, Pierre. Celles qu'on respecte. Paris, 1903.
42584.23.16 Zola, Emile. Truth. N.Y., 1903.
42584.23.45A Zola, Emile. Truth. 2d ed. N.Y., 1903.

1904

42513.47 Adam, Juliette. Mes premières armes littéraires et politiques. Paris, 1904.
42513.47.15 Adam, Juliette. My literary life. London, 1904.
42513.47.10 Adam, Juliette. My literary life. N.Y., 1904.
42562.38.14.37 Adam, Paul. Le tropeau de Clarisse. 12e éd. Paris, 1904.
43514.25.210 Aderer, A. l'inévitable amour. Paris, 1904.
42542.1.11 Ajalbert, Jean. La fille Elisa. Paris, 1904.
42542.1.11.35 Ajalbert, Jean. Maître Lacombasse. Paris, 1904.
42586.62.9 Albert, Henri. Willy. Paris, 1904.
FL 396.56 Artus, M. Le théâtre Montmarte. Paris, 1904.
42545.90 Aubrun, R.G. Péladan. Paris, 1904.
42578.30.90.2 Aubrun, René Georges. Peladan. 2. éd. Paris, 1904.
42556.35.50 Aubry, Georges Jean. Essai sur Jules Tellier. Paris, 1904.
40596.13.130.1 Balzac, Honoré de. The comédie humaine. N.Y., 1904. 5v.
40597.31.8 Balzac, Honoré de. The comédie humaine: Memoirs of two young married women and Albert Savarus. Boston, 1904.
40597.23.101 Balzac, Honoré de. An historical mystery. Boston, 1904.
Htn 40597.32.13.7* Balzac, Honoré de. The physiology of marriage. London, 1904.
40597.32.13.5 Balzac, Honoré de. The physiology of marriage. London, 1904.
37555.52 Barat, E. Le style poétique et la révolution romantique. Paris, 1904.
41522.2.65 Barbey d'Aurevilly, Jules. Romanciers d'hier et d'avant hier. Paris, 1904.
39594.3.31 Barckhausen, Henri. Montesquieu, l'esprit des loix et les archives. Bordeaux, 1904.
39596.21.2 Barine, Arvède. Bernardin de St. Pierre. Paris, 1904.
42563.16.32 Barrès, Maurice. Quelques cadences. 2. éd. Paris, 1904.
42563.16 Barrès, Maurice. La Vierge assassinée. Paris, 1904.
43537.5.30 Barrière, M. L'art des passions. Paris, 1904.
43537.4.55 Bataille, Henry. L'enchantement. Paris, 1904.
41522.4.8 Baudelaire, Charles. Novellen und kleine Dichtungen in Prosa. Minden in Westfalen, 1904.
41522.5.10 Baudelaire, Charles. Werke. Minden in Westfalen, 1904-10. 5v.
42576.43.65 Bazalgette, Léon. Camille Lemonnier. Paris, 1904.
42544.19.15 Bazin, René. Dicours de reception sur Ernest Legouvé. Paris, 1904.
42563.21.42 Bazin, René. Donatienne. 31. éd. Paris, 1904.
42563.21.45 Bazin, René. Pages choisies. Paris, 1904.
42563.21.48 Bazin, René. Récits de la plaine et de la montagne. 14. éd. Paris, 1904.
42563.21.51 Bazin, René. Une tache d'encre. 34. éd. Paris, 1904?
42534.3.2 Bédier, J. Bibliographie des travaux de Gaston Paris. Paris, 1904.
42534.3 Bédier, J. Bibliographie des travaux de Gaston Paris. Paris, 1904.
42534.4 Bédier, J. Hommage à Gaston Paris. Paris, 1904.
37555.40 Belloc, Hilaire. Avril: being essays on the poetry of the French renaissance. London, 1904.
FL 6139.04 Benrubi, J. Jean-Jacques Rousseaus ethisches Ideal. Langensalza, 1904.
Mol 197.9 Bernardin, N.M. L'école des femmes. Paris, 1904.
42542.29.76 Berr de Turique, J. Lettres posthumes. Paris, 1904.
42542.29.78 Berr de Turique, J. Le Maroquin. Paris, 1904.
42545.3.400 Bever, A. v. Maurice Maeterlinck. Paris, 1904.
37574.880 Bever, Adolphe van. Les conteurs libertins du XVIIIe siècle. Paris, 1904.
42534.36 Biré, E. A. de Pontmartin, sa vie et ses oeuvres. 1811-1890. Paris, 1904.
42542.29.103 Bisson, Alexandre. Le député de Bombignac; comédie. Paris, 1904.
41574.50 Blanchard, Alexandre. Le théâtre de Victor Hugo et la parodie. Amiens, 1904.
42554.14.50 Blanchon, Pierre. Solitude; poésies. Paris, 1904.
38566.56 Boileau Despréaux, Nicolas. The satires. Glasgow, 1904.
42542.37.10 Bois, Jules. Hippolyte couronné. Paris, 1904.
42563.37.28.5 Bourget, Paul. Un divorce. Paris, 1904.
42563.38.510 Bovet, M.A. A l'assault de la vie. Paris, 1904.
42563.38.520 Bovet, M.A. Autour de l'étendard. Paris, 1904.
42542.47.23 Brieux, Eugène. Argument of La robe rouge. N.Y., 1904.

Chronological Listing

1904 - cont.

42542.47.13 Brieux, Eugène. La couvée. Paris, 1904.
42542.47.17 Brieux, Eugène. La déserteuse. Paris, 1904.
42542.47.20 Brieux, Eugène. Maternité. Paris, 1904.
42542.47.20.5 Brieux, Eugène. Maternité. 6. éd. Paris, 1904.
37562.40 Brix, Clemens. Richard I., Herzog von der Normandie der französischen Litteratur. Münster, 1904.
37543.61 Broc, V. de. Paysages poétiques et littéraires. Paris, 1904.
42524.16.18 Brunetière, F. Variétés liettéraires. 2. éd. Paris, 1904.
FL 6135.5 Buffenoir, H. Les tombeaux de Rousseau et de Voltaire. Paris, 1904.
FL 6129.04 Buffenois, H. Jean-Jacques Rousseau à Montmorency. Paris, 1904.
42542.47.75 Caillavet, G.A. La Montansier. Paris, 1904.
37567.7.5 Canat, R. Du sentiment de la solitude morale chez les romantiques. Paris, 1904.
40593.28 Canat, René. Quae de Graecis Mme. de Staël scripserit. Andegavis, 1904.
37565.45 Candel, Jules. Les prédicateurs français dans la première moitié du XVIIIe siècle. Paris, 1904.
38575.17.6A Canfield, Dorothea F. Corneille and Racine in England. N.Y., 1904.
42542.48.15 Capus, Alfred. L'adversaire. Paris, 1904.
42542.48.2 Capus, Alfred. La chatelaine. Paris, 1904.
X Cg 41541.36 Cartier, J. Un intermediaire entre la France et l'Allemagne, G. de Nerval. Genève, 1904.
37564.43.5 Chamaillard, E. La poésie et les poètes devant Pascal. Paris, 1904.
Mol 247.15 Chantavoino, S. Le misanthrope. n.p., 1904.
43556.49.235 Colette, Sidonie Gabrielle. Dialogues de bêtes. Paris, 1904.
43556.50.1100 Collin, Sullian. La mort des fleurs. Paris, 1904.
38523.19 Counson, A. Malherbe et ses sources. Liège, 1904.
42542.54.4 Courson de la Villeneuve, R. de. Théâtre. Paris, 1904.
43565.5.175 Daudet, Léon A. La France en Darme. Paris, 1904.
43565.89.5100 Dauguet, Marie. Par l'amour. Paris, 1904.
37573.654 David-Sauvageat, A. Morceaux choisis des classiques français. Paris, 1904.
Mol 604.6 Davignon, St. Molière et la vie. Photoreproduction. Paris, 1904.
42542.61.15 Decourcelle, Adrien. I dine with my mother. N.Y., 1904.
42568.56.100 Demolder, Eugène. L'arche de Monsieur Cheunus. Paris, 1904.
37564.50 Desjardins, Paul. La méthode des classiques française Corneille-Poussin-Pascal. Paris, 1904.
42513.22 Didon, Henri. Lettres du R.P. Didon de l'Ordre prêcheurs à Mlle. Thérèse Vianzane. Paris, 1904.
42542.65.3 Donnay, Maurice. L'autre danger. Paris, 1904.
42542.65.21 Donnay, Maurice. L'escalade. Paris, 1904.
42542.65.10 Donnay, Maurice. Oiseaux de passage. Paris, 1904.
42554.29.100 Ducoté, E. La prairie en fleurs, 1895-1902. Paris, 1904.
42554.29.150 Dujardin, E. Le délassement du guerrier. Paris, 1904.
41538.11.5 Dumas, Alexandre. Chicot the jester. N.Y., 1904.
41538.54.25 Dumas, Alexandre. The man in the iron mask. N.Y., 1904.
41538.63.34 Dumas, Alexandre. The queen's necklace. N.Y., 1904.
41538.85.10 Dumas, Alexandre. The whites and the blues. N.Y., 1904.
FL 397.8 Durieu, Jules. Les samedis littéraires du théâtre discours d'ouverture. Bordeaux, 1904.
42568.23.14.49 Duval, Paul. Deux heures du matin. Paris, 1904.
37567.367 Eloesser, A. Literarische Porträts aus dem modernen Frankreich. Berlin, 1904.
38567.27 Englander, D. La Xe satire de Boileau comparée à la VIe de Juvénal. Berlin, 1904.
FL 367.15 Eyriès, Eugène. Les idées médicales dans le théâtre contemporain. Montpellier, 1904.
37544.22.2 Faguet, Emile. Propos littéraires. 2. séries. Paris, 1904.
42565.70 Favre de Coulevain, Hélène. Eve victorieuse. Paris, 1904.
42555.59.25 Féret, C.T. Les cendres d'Ernest Millet. Alençon, 1904. 2 pam.
42554.32.15 Ferrières, G. La belle matinée. Paris, 1904.
Mol 730.2 Fischmann, P. Molière als Schauspieldirektor. Halle, 1904.
42576.16.27 Flaubert, Gustave. Best known works. N.Y., 1904.
42576.24.5 Flaubert, Gustave. The candidate. v. 8. Chicago, 1904.
42576.16.26 Flaubert, Gustave. Complete works. N.Y., 1904.
42576.16.52 Flaubert, Gustave. Works. N.Y., 1904.
42568.23.23 Fleischmann, Hector. Le massacre d'une amazone. Paris, 1904.
42575.53.29 Formont, M. La grande amoureuse. 5. éd. Paris, 1904.
42576.62.18 France, Anatole. Crainquebille. Putois. Riquet. Paris, 1904.
42576.63.7.3 France, Anatole. Le crime de Sylvestre Bonnard. N.Y., 1904.
42576.63.5 France, Anatole. Le crime de Sylvestre Bonnard. N.Y., 1904.
42576.62.135A France, Anatole. La vie littéraire. Paris, 1904. 4v.
42576.62.135.3 France, Anatole. La vie littéraire. v. 3. Paris, 1904?
42586.55.5 Frapié, L. La maternelle. Paris, 1904.
39598.42 Freund, Max. Die moralischen Erzählungen Marmontels. Halle, 1904.
FL 398.30.15 Fusil, Louise. Souvenirs d'une actrice. Paris, 1904.
42554.70.65 Fuster, Charles. La prose et les vers de Jean Plémeur. Paris, 1904.
42571.32.14 Gaboriau, Emile. The honor of the name. N.Y., 1904.
42571.32.3 Gaboriau, Emile. Monsieur Lecoq. N.Y., 1904.
42571.28.5 Gaboriau, Emile. The mystery of Orcival. N.Y., 1904.
41574.605 Garson, Jules. L'évolution démocratique de Victor Hugo. Bruxelles, 1904.
42544.34.80 Gaubert, E. Pierre Louys. 2e éd. Paris, 1904.
42543.45.35 Gavault, Paul. Les femmes de Paille. Paris, 1904.
42543.45.25 Gavault, Paul. Fin de rêve. Paris, 1904.
42525.7 Gazier, A. Mélanges de littérature et d'histoire. Paris, 1904.
39568.19 Georges, Karl A. Friedrich Melchior Grimm als Kritiker. Leipzig, 1904.
NEDL 38547.10 Germa, B. L'Astrée d'Honoré d'Urfé. Sa composition. Son influence. Paris, 1904.
37555.89.10 Ghil, René. Oeuvre. En méthode à l'oeuvre. Thèse. Paris, 1904.
40597.2.151 Gilbert, E. Balzac à vingt ans. Bruxelles, 1904.
40587.11 Giraud, Victor. Chateaubriand. Paris, 1904.
42586.65.5.2 Gobineau, Arthur de. Die Rénaissance. Leipzig, 1904.
40535.32.9 Golubev, Viktor. Marivaux' Lustspiele in deutschen Übersetzungen des 18. Jahrhunderts. Heidelberg, 1904.

1904 - cont.

43616.2.80A Gourmont, R. de. Judith Gautier. Paris, 1904.
37555.305.6 Grammont, M. Le vers français ses moyen d'éxpression son harmonie. Paris, 1904.
FL 382.50 Granges, C.M. La comédie et les moeurs, 1815-1848. Paris, 1904.
42563.37.83 Grappe, G. Paul Bourget. Paris, 1904.
42554.49.3 Gregh, F. Les clartés humaines. Paris, 1904.
41522.3.9 Grele, Eugene. Jules Barbey d'Aurevilly, sa vie et son oeuvre. Caen, 1904. 2v.
42586.76 Guillaumin, Emile. La vie d'un simple. Paris, 1904.
42543.61 Guinon, Albert. Décadence. Paris, 1904.
40536.20.80 Hagen, Diedrich. Alexis Pirons Dramen. Inaug. Diss. Leipzig, 1904.
42543.62.30 Haraucourt, Edmond. La passion. Paris, 1904.
FL 6139.04.8 Hartmann, E. Jean-Jacques Rousseaus Einfluss auf J.H. Campe. Inaug.-Diss. Nevenburg, 1904.
40535.23.13 Henriet, Maurice. Letellier, auteur dramatique forain. Château-Thierry, 1904.
42543.63.5 Hermant, Abel. Confession d'un homme d'aujourd'hui. Paris, 1904.
Mon 118.2 Herzberg, Curt. Die skeptischen, naturalischen und rigoristischen Elemente in Montaignes ethischen Anschauugen. Inaug. Diss. Leipzig, 1904.
38514.44.11 Hoepffer, Ernst. Eustache Deschamps. Strassburg, 1904.
41574.87 Hofmannsthal, Hugo. Victor Hugo. Berlin, 1904.
37548.35 Horrent, D. Écrivains belges d'aujourd'hui. 1. série. Bruxelles, 1904.
41572.4.5 Hugo, Victor. Jargal. Oxford, 1904.
41571.1 Hugo, Victor. Roman. Paris, 1904-24. 9v.
41574.51 Huguet, E. Le sens de la forme dans les métaphores de Victor Hugo. Paris, 1904.
40535.2.25 Humbert, H. Delisle de la Drévetière. Berlin, 1904.
43667.51.220 Jaloux, Edmond. Les sangsues. 2. éd. Paris, 1904.
37567.9.5 James, Henry. French poets and novelists. London, 1904.
37561.27.2 Jeanroy, Alfred. Les origines de la poésie lyrique en France au moyen âge. 2. éd. Paris, 1904.
37574.745 Jenkins, T.A. Longer French poems. N.Y., 1904.
40586.18.9 Julien, servant of Chateaubriand. Itinéraire de Paris à Jérusalem. Paris, 1904.
40586.18.6 Julien, servant of Chateaubriand. Itinéraire de Paris à Jérusalem. 3. éd. Paris, 1904.
41553.34.5 Kock, Charles Paul de. André the Savoyard. N.Y., 1904.
41553.30.25 Kock, Charles Paul de. Gustave. Boston, 1904.
Mon 121.1 Kühn, Emil. Die Bedeutung Montaignes für unsere Zeit. Strassburg, 1904.
43687.59.1100 Langlade, Emile. A travers la Haine, poèmes dramatiques. Paris, 1904.
37562.36 Laur, Franz. Ueber Krankenbehandlung und Heilkunde in der Litteratur des alten Frankreichs. Arnstadt, 1904.
42544.25 Lavedan, Henri. Verennes. Paris, 1904.
37596.95 Lavesne, Douin de. Trubert, altfranzösischer Schelmenroman. Dresden, 1904.
42556.27.33.800 Leautaud, P. Henri de Régnier. Paris, 1904.
42563.22.9 Le Beaumont, Maurice. Gringalette. Paris, 1904.
42571.11.3 Le Brun, R. Anatole France. Paris, 1904.
42571.11 Le Brun, R. Anatole France. Paris, 1904.
FL 398.56.9 Lecomte, L.H. La Montansier. Ses aventures, 1730-1820. Paris, 1904.
42536.34 Lefèvre, E. Hippolyte Taine de l'Académie Française. Paris, 1904.
37564.59 Legouvé, Ernest. Dernières pages recueillies, 1898-1903. Evreux, 1904.
X Cg FL 383.21 Le Roy, Albert. L'aube du théâtre romantique. 3. ed. Paris, 1904.
40512.12.7 LeSage, Alain René. The adventures of Gil Blas. London, 1904. 4v.
43688.83.1100 Lésu, B.J. Amoureuses confidences. Paris, 1904.
38526.22 Leykauff, A. François Habert. Leipzig, 1904.
40597.8.5 Lhomer, J. Balzac dans l'intimité et les types de la comédie humaine. Paris, 1904.
42526.5 Lhomme, F. La comédie d'aujourd'hui. Paris, 1904.
38588.17 Lindemann, F. Die Operntexte Philippe Quinaults. Leipzig, 1904.
FL 359.04 Lintilhac, E. Histoire générale du théâtre en France. Paris, 1904. 5v.
42545.3.6.5 Maeterlinck, Maurice. Aglavaine and Selysette. London, 1904.
42545.3.12.3A Maeterlinck, Maurice. The double garden. N.Y., 1904.
42545.3.200 Maeterlinck, Maurice. Le double jardin. Paris, 1904.
42545.3.7.11 Maeterlinck, Maurice. Drei mystische Spiele. 2. Aufl. Leipzig, 1904.
42545.3.5.4 Maeterlinck, Maurice. Le trésor des humbles. 33e éd. Paris, 1904.
42545.3.37.10 Maeterlinck, Maurice. Das Wunder des heiligen Antonius. Jena, 1904.
42587.16.10 Maindron, M. Monsieur de Clérambon. Paris, 1904.
42587.27.85 Malato, Charles. Luisa Michel; la vita, le oper e l'azione rivoluzionaria. Roma, 1904.
43697.59.120 Mandin, L. Les sommeils. Paris, 1904.
38513.6.5 Manz, G. Li jus de Saint Nicholas des A. Jean Bodel. Erlangen, 1904.
42576.76.32.6 Margueritte, Paul. La commune. Paris, 1904.
43697.75.7500 Marnière, Jeanne. Le livre d'une amoureuse. Paris, 1904.
Htn 42555.49.23* Martin, Gabriel. Les poésies fantaisistes. Paris, 1904.
42555.58.7 Mendès, Catulle. Le carnaval fleuri. Paris, 1904.
42555.58.1190 Mérat, Albert. Quelques pages avant le livre. Paris, 1904.
41555.23.9 Mérimée, Prosper. Colomba. Gotha, 1904.
43698.78.2100 Merys, J.A. Solitude. Paris, 1904.
42545.28.7.21 Mirbeau, Octave. Le jardin des supplices. Paris, 1904.
Mol 165.75 Molière, Jean Baptiste Poquelin. L'avare...M. Levi. Boston, 1904.
Mol 19.04 Molière, Jean Baptiste Poquelin. Oeuvres complètes. Paris, 1904? 3v.
Mol 60.31.5 Molière, Jean Baptiste Poquelin. Plays. N.Y., 1904.
FL 6129.04.2 Montaigu, A. Démêlés du comte de Montaigu. Paris, 1904.
39594.13.5 Montesquieu, C.L. de S. Lettres persanes. Paris, 1904.
38564.40 Morillot, P. La Bruyère. Paris, 1904.
Mon 154.1 Neyrac, J. Montaigne. Bergerac, 1904.
42545.45.15 Nigond, Gabriel. L'Ombre des pins. Paris, 1904.
Mon 124.1A Norton, Grace. Early writings of Montaigne. N.Y., 1904.
Mon 124.1.5A Norton, Grace. Studies in Montaigne. N.Y., 1904.
38557.1.5 Paris. Bibliothèque Nationale. Département des imprimés. Catalogue des ouvrages de Bossuet. Paris, 1904.
42555.68 Paté, Lucien. Les souffles libres. Paris, 1904.
38513.25 Pathelin. Maistre Pierre Pathelin Hystorié. Paris, 1904.

Chronological Listing

1904 - cont.

38526.43 Peletier, Jacques. Oeuvres poétiques. Paris, 1904.
41574.34 Pellier, H. La philosophie de Victor Hugo. Paris, 1904.
42545.95.15 Pottecher, M. La passion de Jeanne d'Arc. Paris, 1904.
42578.31.5 Pouvillon, E. Jep. Paris, 1904.
42578.31.48 Prévost, Marcel. La plus faible. 5. éd. Paris, 1904.
42542.48.25 Quet, E. Alfred Capus. Paris, 1904.
38536.20.10 Rabelais, F. Five books of the lives...of Gargantua and his son Pantagruel. London, 1904. 3v.
38536.1 Rabelais, F. Pantagruel. Paris, 1904.
38536.24.9A Rabelais, F. Selections from Gargantua. N.Y., 1904.
42534.4.10 Rajna, Pio. Gaston Paris; discorso letto alla R. Accademia della Crusca. Firenze, 1904.
42578.18.7 Rameau, Jean. La jungle de Paris. Paris, 1904.
42578.18.9 Rameau, Jean. Zarette. Paris, 1904.
FL 398.84.13 Regnault-Warin, J.J. Mémoires sur Talma. Paris, 1904.
42556.26.25 Régnier, Henri de. Les rencontres de M. de Bréot. Paris, 1904.
42587.52.5 Renard, Jules. Carrots. London, 1904.
42587.52.6 Renard, Jules. Carrots. London, 1904.
42587.52.19 Renard, Jules. Comédies. Paris, 1904.
42587.52.15 Renard, Jules. L'écornifleur. Paris, 1904.
37596.97 Restori, A. La gaite de la Tor. Messina, 1904.
FL 376.18 Reuter, Otto. Der Chor in den Französischen Tragödie. Berlin, 1904.
43756.3.55 Richepin, Jacques. Falstaff. Paris, 1904.
37596.151 Richter, Max. Die Lieder des altfranzösischen Lyrikers Jehan de Nurvile. Halle, 1904.
39527.4.18 Richter, R. La Fontaine et Lamolle. Elbogen, 1904.
42587.55.10 Rivoire, André. Le chemin de l'oubli. Paris, 1904.
42578.19.19 Rod, Edouard. Un vainqueur. Paris, 1904.
FL 398.77 Roll, Maximin. Souvenirs d'un Claqueur et d'un Figurant. Paris, 1904.
43757.50.490 Rolland, Romain. La montespan. Paris, 1904.
42556.32.40 Rollinat, Maurice. Ruminations; proses d'un solitaire. Paris, 1904.
FL 6026.10A Rousseau, J.J. The confessions. Edinburgh, 1904. 2v.
43757.92.150 Roussel, Raymond. La vue. Paris, 1904.
38511.10.9 Roy, Emile. Le mystère de la passion en France du XIVe au XVIe siècle. Paris, 1904.
43757.98.110 Royère, Jean. Eurythmies. Paris, 1904.
42546.15.22.10 St. Geniès, Richard. L'amour sans phrases. Paris, 1904.
40575.7.7 Sainte-Beuve, Charles A. Correspondance inédite de Sainte-Beuve avec M. et Mme. Juste Olivier. 3. éd. Paris, 1904.
40575.15 Sainte-Beuve, Charles A. Le livre d'or de Sainte-Beuve. Paris, 1904.
40575.18.8 Sainte-Beuve, Charles A. Portraits of the seventeenth century. N.Y., 1904.
40575.18A Sainte-Beuve, Charles A. Portraits of the seventeenth century. N.Y., 1904. 2v.
41557.9.42.5A Sand, George. Correspondance; publiée intégralement. Bruxelles, 1904.
41557.10.18 Sand, George. Correspondance...Gustave Flaubert. 5e éd. Paris, 1904.
41557.9.42.7 Sand, George. Correspondance de George Sand et d'Alfred de Musset. Bruxelles, 1904.
41557.10.18.5 Sand, George. Correspondance entre George Sand et Gustave Flaubert. Paris, 1904.
41557.10.18.3 Sand, George. Correspondance entre George Sand et Gustave Flaubert. Paris, 1904.
41557.9.94.2 Sand, George. Mauprat. Paris, 1904.
41557.9.53 Sand, George. Souvenirs et idées. Paris, 1904.
37555.303 Saran, F. Der Rhythmus der Französischen Verses. Halle, 1904.
42546.27.6 Sardou, Victorien. La sorcière. Paris, 1904.
42546.27.5 Sardou, Victorien. La sorcière. Paris, 1904.
40553.10 Sauris, Georges de. Benjamin Constant et les idées libérales. Paris, 1904.
42556.30.45 Schuré, Edouard. Précurseurs et révoltés. Paris, 1904.
40575.5.13 Séché, Leon. Sainte-Beuve. Paris, 1904. 2v.
40525.1 Sénac de Meilhan, G. L'émigré. Paris, 1904.
42525.8.81 Serre, J. Ernest Hello, l'homme, le penseur, l'écrivain. Paris, 1904?
41574.43.5 Simon, G. L'enfance de Victor Hugo. Paris, 1904.
41574.122.10 Simon, Gustave. Visite à la maison de Victor Hugo. 4e éd. Paris, 1904.
43775.89.110 Souchon, Paul. La beauté de Paris, poèmes. Paris, 1904.
43779.24.3100 Stéphane, Marc. Aphorismes, boutades et cris de révolte. Paris, 1904.
41563.13 Sue, Eugène. The pilgrim's shell. N.Y., 1904.
42556.18 Sully-Prudhomme, R.F.A. Oeuvres. Paris, 1904.
42536.32.52 Taine, Hippolyte. Life and letters of Hippolyte Taine 1828-52. Westminster, 1904-08. 2v.
42559.84.5 Taravel, Antoine. L'amour chante. Paris, 1904.
42583.33.15 Theuriet, André. Souvenirs des vertes saisons. Paris, 1904.
38537.25 Thuasne, L. Étude sur Rabelais. Paris, 1904.
37563.24A Tilley, Arthur A. Literature of the French renaissance. Cambridge, 1904. 2v.
42578.52.50 Tinseau, Léon de. La princesse errante. Montréal, 1904.
42578.52.45A Tinseau, Léon de. Le secrétaire de Madame la duchesse. Paris, 1904.
42578.52.40 Tinseau, Léon de. La valise diplomatique. Paris, 1904.
42587.63.55 Torquet, A. Force ennemie. 7. éd. Paris, 1904.
42587.63.60 Torquet, A. Hiers bleus. Paris, 1904.
42578.56.45 Toutain, Paul. Les hôtes de l'estuaire. Paris, 1904.
38527.29.9 Trenel, J. L'element biilique dans l'oeuvre poétique d'Aubigné. Paris, 1904.
42587.66.9 Vedel, Emile. L'Ile d'Epouvante. Paris, 1904.
X Cg 42557.15.5 Verlaine, P. Choix de poésies. Paris, 1904.
Htn 42557.19.80* Verlaine, Paul. Hombres (hommes). Paris, 1904.
42557.16 Verlaine, Paul. Poems. London, 1904.
42557.18.15 Verlaine, Paul. Poésies religieuses. Paris, 1904.
FL 360.72 Veuillot, François. Les prédicateurs de la scène. Paris, 1904.
43823.98.100 Veyrin, Emile. L'embarquement pour Cythère. Paris, 1904.
42557.29.5 Vicaire, Gabriel. Livingstone. Paris, 1904.
43824.2.41 Vivien, Renée. La dame à la louve. Paris, 1904.
42584.24.6.5 Vizetelly, E.A. Emile Zola. London, 1904.
42522.18 Vogüé, E.M. de. Sous l'horizon. Paris, 1904.
37596.94 Wiese, Leo. Die Lieder des Blondel de Nesle. Dresden, 1904.
41551.25 Wiese, Oskar. Kritische Beiträge zur Geschichte der Jugend und Jugendwerke. Olenburg, 1904.
Mol 560.18 Wohlfeil, P. Die deutschen Molière Übersetzungen. Frankfurt, 1904.

1904 - cont.

FL 398.6.25 Young, B. Michel Baron. Paris, 1904.
42515.35.293 Ys, René d'. Ernest Renan en Bretagne d'après des documents nouveaux. 3. éd. Paris, 1904.
43858.1.62 Zamacois, Miguel. Bohémos. Paris, 1904.
37596.50.9 Zarifopol, Paul. Kritischer Text der Lieder Richards de Fournival. Halle, 1904.

1905

42562.38.5 Adam, Paul. Combats. Paris, 1905.
42562.38.14.31 Adam, Paul. Le serpent noir. 17e éd. Paris, 1905.
FL 382.97 Aderer, Adolph. Hommes et chosis de théâtre. Paris, 1905.
43522.48.110 Allard, Roger. La divine aventure. Lille, 1905.
FL 379.52 Alméras, Henri d'. Les théâtres libertins au XVIIIe siècle. Paris, 1905.
42542.1.19 Ancey, Georges. Ces Messieurs. Paris, 1905.
42553.40 Angellier, A. Les dialogues d'amour. Paris, 1905. 2v.
37567.192 Annuaire des gens de lettres et des dessinateurs 1905. Paris, 1905.
37574.697 Anthologie des poètes français XIXe siècle. Paris, 1905.
37555.120 Anzalone, Ernesto. Su la poesia satirica in Francia e in Italia nel secolo XVI. Catania, 1905.
43528.2.30F Arquillière. La grand famille. Paris, 1905.
38527.17 Aubigné, Théodore Agrippa d'. Oeuvres poétiques choisies. Paris, 1905.
42526.18 Aubry, G.J. Camille Mauclair. Paris, 1905.
37567.40.5 Audebrand, P. Derniers jours de La Bohème. Paris, 1905.
40596.21.12 Balzac, Honoré de. The chouans. Boston, 1905.
40596.15.25 Balzac, Honoré de. Contes choisis. London, 1905.
NEDL 37557.11 Balzo, C. L'Italia nella letterature francese. Roma, 1905.
42515.35.27 Barry, William. Ernest Renan. London, 1905.
42515.35.27.2A Barry, William. Ernest Renan. N.Y., 1905.
43537.4.70 Bataille, Henry. La marche nuptiale. Paris, 1905.
37576.560.5 Bazin, R. The ink-stain (Tache d'encre). Paris, 1905.
42563.21.54 Bazin, René. L'isolée. 29. éd. Paris, 1905.
FL 393.20 Beaulieu, H. Les théâtres du boulevard du crime. Paris, 1905.
40532.5.7A Beaumarchais, Pierre A.C. de. The barber of Seville. London, 1905.
43538.14.48 Beckett, Samuel. Le Roi Tobol. Paris, 1905.
41584.29.80 Bellier-Dumaine, C. Alexandre Duval et son oeuvre dramatique. Paris, 1905.
37576.560.10A Bernard, Charles de. Gefaut. Paris, 1905.
42542.29.31 Bernstein, H. Le Bercail. Paris, 1905.
42542.29.31.3 Bernstein, H. Le Bercail. Paris, 1905.
42542.29.42 Bernstein, H. La rafale. Paris, 1905.
38537.25.180 Besant, W. Rabelais. Edinburgh, 1905.
40582.17 Beyle, Henri. Mémoires d'un touriste. Oxford, 1905.
42542.29.94 Bilhaud, P. Le gaut. Paris, 1905.
38525.22.6.5 Binet, Claude. Critical edition of the Discours de la vie de Pierre de Ronsard. Philadelphia, 1905.
38525.22.6 Binet, Claude. Critical edition of the Discours de la vie de Pierre de Ronsard. Philadelphia, 1905.
37576.560.15A Blanc, T. de S. (Mme.). Jacqueline. Paris, 1905.
42563.23.18 Bloy, Léon. Belluaires et Porchers. Paris, 1905.
42556.29.30 Bocquet, Léon. Albert Samain; sa vie, son oeuvre. Paris, 1905.
38563.18 Bolin, W. Pierre Bayle, sein Leben und seine Schriften. Stuttgart, 1905.
42563.36.30 Bordeaux, Henry. La petite mademoiselle. Paris, 1905.
43544.4.32.2 Botrel, Théodore. Chansons de chez nous. Paris, 1905.
42563.37.16.8 Bourget, Paul. Cosmopolis. Paris, 1905.
42554.16.20 Boutelleau, Georges. Le banc de Pierre. Paris, 1905.
FL 396.90 Boutet, R. Les variétés, 1850-1870. Paris, 1905.
42563.39.15 Boylesve, René. Le bel avenir. 3. éd. Paris, 1905.
42542.47.12 Brieux, Eugène. L'armature. Paris, 1905.
42542.47.28 Brieux, Eugène. L'armature. Paris, 1905.
42542.47.19 Brieux, Eugène. L'evasion. Paris, 1905.
42546.27.8 Byrne, C.A. La sorcière. N.Y., 1905.
X Cg FL 379.51 Capon, Gaston. Les théâtres clandestins. Paris, 1905.
42542.48.5 Capus, Alfred. Monsieur Piégois. Paris, 1905.
42542.48.23 Capus, Alfred. Monsieur Piegois. Paris, 1905.
42542.48.7 Capus, Alfred. Notre Jeunesse. Paris, 1905.
42542.48.4 Capus, Alfred. Théâtre: Brignol et sa fille, et petites folles. Paris, 1905.
FL 371.40A Carnahan, D.H. The prologue in the old French and Provencal mystery. New Haven, 1905.
38563.14A Cazes, A. Pierre Bayle. Paris, 1905.
42563.80.100 Champsaur, Félicien. Dinah Samuel. Paris, 1905.
Mol 803.3.2 Chardon, H. Nouveau documents. v.2. Paris, 1905.
38527.48.5 Chardon, Henri. Robert Garnier; sa vie, ses poésies inédites. Paris, 1905.
40586.13.12 Chateaubriand, F.A.R. Atala. Boston, 1905.
43552.25.4120 Chevalier, Adrien. Sur le seuil. Paris, 1905.
41578.152 Citoleux, Marc. La poésie philosophique au XIXe siècle; Lamartine. Thèse. Paris, 1905.
42565.54.265 Cladel, Judith. La vie de Léon Cladel. Paris, 1905.
37576.560.20 Claretie, J. Prince Zilah (Le prince Zilah). Paris, 1905.
FL 364.26 Claretie, L. Histoire des théâtres de société. Paris, 1905.
37543.63 Claretie, Léo. Histoire de la littérature française. Paris, 1905. 5v.
42554.18.65 Cohendy, Claude. Visions d'Hellas. Paris, 1905.
37576.560.25A Coppée, F. A romance of youth. Paris, 1905.
38526.10.13 Corrozet, Gilles. Hecatomgraphie. Paris, 1905.
40534.34 Crébillon, Claude Prosper Jolyot de. Das Spiel des Zufalls am Kaminfeuer. Leipzig, 1905.
42542.55 Croisset, Francis de. Théâtre. Paris, 1905. 2v.
39533.20.12 Cyrano de Bergerac. Lettres d'amour. Paris, 1905.
37576.560.30A Daudet, A. Fromont and Risler. Paris, 1905.
42567.23.5 Daudet, Ernest. L'espionne. Paris, 1905.
42554.29.5 Despax, E. La maison des Glycines. Paris, 1905.
40587.32 Dick, Ernst. Plagiats de Chateaubriand. Bern, 1905.
42542.65.7 Donnay, Maurice. L'affranchie. Paris, 1905.
42542.65.9.1 Donnay, Maurice. Lysistrata. Paris, 1905.
41577.14 Doumic, R. Lettres d'Elvire à Lamartine. Paris, 1905.
Mon 144.1 Dowden, E. Michel de Montaigne. London, 1905.
Mon 144.1.1 Dowden, E. Michel de Montaigne. Philadelphia, 1905.
37596.104 Drivernoy, E. Le tournoi de Chauvenoy en 1285. Paris, 1905.
37576.560.31 Droz, Gustave A.G. Monsieur. Paris, 1905.
42554.29.8 Druilhet, Georges. Les haltes sereines. Paris, 1905.
FL 6076.77 Dufour, T. Les institutions chimiques de Jean-Jacques Rousseau. Genève, 1905.
42543.16.7.08 Dumas, Alexandre. La dame aux camélias. N.Y., 1905.

Chronological Listing

1905 - cont.

42543.19.12 Dumas, Alexandre. La femme de Claude. N.Y., 1905.
42576.15.12 Dumesnil, René. Flaubert. Paris, 1905.
41574.42.5 Dupuy, E. La jeunesse des romantiques. Paris, 1905.
42543.38 Fabre, Emile. Les ventres dorés. Paris, 1905.
42543.38.13 Fabre, Emile. Les ventres dorés. Paris, 1905.
37544.22.3 Faguet, Emile. Propos littéraires. 3. séries. Paris, 1905.
38514.59.5A The farce of Master Pierre Patelin. Boston, 1905.
38514.44.12 Fehse, Erich. Sprichwort und Sentenz bei Eustache Deschamps. n.p., 1905.
FL 6119.05 Feller, L. Jean-Jacques Rousseau de sa vie et de ses oeuvres. Paris, 1905.
43607.76.2100 Fernand. Saint-Pierre. Fort-de-France, 1905.
42576.28.14 Flaubert, Gustave. Madame Bovary. Paris, 1905.
42576.61.5 Franay, Gabriel. Comme dans un conte. Paris, 1905.
37576.560.35 France, A. The red lily (le lis rouge). Paris, 1905.
42576.63.13 France, Anatole. A la lumière. Paris, 1905.
Htn 42576.62.23* France, Anatole. Crainquebille. Paris, 1905.
42576.62.27.10 France, Anatole. L'étui de nacre. Paris, 1905.
42576.62.20.5 France, Anatole. Sur la pierre blanche. 43. éd. Paris, 1905. 2v.
37557.6 Franz, Arthur. Das literarische Portrat in Frankreich. Leipzig, 1905.
FL 398.56.10 Fromagot, P. Le théâtre de Versailles et la Montansier. Versailles, 1905.
37556.10A Funck-Brentano, F. Les nouvellistes. 2. éd. Paris, 1905.
37565.66 Funck-Brentano, T. Les sophistes français. Paris, 1905.
39534.22.9 Furetière, Antoine. Unsere biederen stadtleut...Deutsch von E. Meyer. Leipzig, 1905.
37556.22.5 Gärtner, J. Das Journal etranger und seine Bedeutung...in Frankreich. Mainz, 1905.
FL 6129.05 Gaidau, E. Le lieu de naissance de Jean-Jacques Rousseau. Genève, 1905.
37562.6 Galpin, S.L. Cortois and Vilain. New Haven, 1905.
42543.44.2 Gandillot, Leon. Vers l'amour. Paris, 1905.
42543.44 Gandillot, Leon. Vers l'amour. Paris, 1905.
43616.74.100 Gardilanne, Paule de. Le dernier rêve du duc d'Enghien. Paris, 1905.
43616.83.110 Gasquet, Joachim. Dionysos. Paris, 1905.
42568.23.15 Gaubert, E. Jean Lorrain. (Paul Duval). Paris, 1905.
41542.11.17 Gautier, Théophile. Mademoiselle de Maupin. Paris, 1905.
42543.45.70 Gavault, Paul. Une affaire scandaleuse. Paris, 1905.
37564.46 Gelin, H. Une famille poitevine d'Ecrivains illustres. Niort, 1905.
42586.68.5 Gobineau, Arthur de. Pages choisies, précédées d'une étude. 2. éd. Paris, 1905.
37557.21A Gosse, E. French profiles. N.Y., 1905.
42555.62.25 Gourmont, J. de. Jean Moréas. Paris, 1905.
42543.60.12 Grandmougin, Charles. Le sang du Calvaire. Paris, 1905.
FL 383.100 Gratacap, M. Le théâtre français comtemporain. Vienne, 1905.
42554.49.7 Gregh, F. L'or des minutes. Paris, 1905.
41571.5.17 Gregh, Fernand. Étude sur Victor Hugo. Paris, 1905.
40575.5.4 Grojean, Oscar. Sainte-Beuve a Liege. Lettres et documents inédits. Bruxelles, 1905.
37572.53 Guerlac, Othon. Selections from standard French authors. Boston, 1905.
39544.155.5 Hall, Evelyn B. The life of Voltaire. 3d ed. N.Y., 1905?
39544.155 Hall, Evelyn B. The life of Voltaire. 3d ed. N.Y., 1905.
42543.62.39 Haraucourt, Edmond. Les Oberlé. Paris, 1905.
42543.62.31 Haraucourt, Edmond. Les Oberlé. Paris, 1905.
42543.62.40 Haraucourt, Edmond. Les Oberlé. Paris, 1905.
42545.3.460 Heine, Selma. Maeterlinck. Berlin, 1905.
FL 371.41 Heinze, Paul. Die Engel auf der mittelalterlichen Mysterienbühne Frankreichs. Inaug. Diss. Griefswald, 1905.
37594.11 Hélinandus. Les vers de la mort. Paris, 1905.
40597.2.250 Helm, W. Aspects of Balzac. N.Y., 1905.
42543.63 Hermant, Abel. La belle Madame Héber. Paris, 1905.
42541.18.5 Hermant, Abel. Les transatlantiques. Paris, 1905.
42541.18.5.2 Hermant, Abel. Les transatlantiques. Paris, 1905.
38512.68 Höfler, Hans. Les échecs amoureux. Neustadt, 1905.
37562.12.30 Holborn, G. Wortaccent und Rhythmus. Greifswald, 1905.
41571.1.7 Hugo, Victor. En voyage. Paris, 1905-10.
41571.1.3 Hugo, Victor. Poésie. Paris, 1905-35. 12v.
41571.1.5 Hugo, Victor. Théâtre. Paris, 1905-34. 6v.
41574.51.2 Huguet, E. La couleur...et l'ombre dans les métaphores de Hugo. Paris, 1905.
43638.99.100 Huzard, A. de B. (Mme.). Comment s'en vont les reines. Paris, 1905.
38526.8.10A Ingraham, E.S. The sources of Les amours de Jean Antoine de Baif. Columbus, 1905.
43667.51.80 Jaloux, Edmond. Le jeune homme au masque. Paris, 1905.
Htn 40597.8.6* James, Henry. The question of our speech. Boston, 1905.
42543.70 Janvier, A. Théâtre. Paris, 1905. 4v.
38512.26A Jean le Seneschal. Les cent ballades. Poème du XIVe siècle. Paris, 1905.
Mol 610.4 John, A. Les traits conventionnels de domestiques de Molière. Meiningen, 1905-06.
38512.69 Jordan, Otto. Jehan du Vingnai und sein Kirchenspiegel. Halle, 1905.
39545.56 Die Jungfrau von Orleans. Boston, 1905.
38512.31 Kehrmann, Alexander. Die deutsche Übersetzung der Novellen des Ritters vom Turn. Inaug. Diss. Marburg, 1905.
42544.2.7 Kistemaekers, Henry. Théâtre de rire et de larmes. Paris, 1905.
42544.26.5 Labiche, Eugène. Le voyage de Monsieur Perrichon. Boston, 1905.
38562.22A Laborde-Milaa, A. Fontenelle. Paris, 1905.
Mol 860.59 Lafenestre, Pierre. La farce du medecin; comédie. Paris, 1905.
40526.62 Laignel, Jean B.J. La fête de Louisee. Rouen, 1905.
41578.32.15 Lamartine, Alphonse. Graziella. Chicago, 1905.
42576.46.15 Lapauze, Jeanne L. La force du passé. Paris, 1905.
Htn 42576.46.21* Lapauze, Jeanne L. La masque d'amour. Paris, 1905.
37567.92 Lardanchet, H. Les enfants perches du romantisme. Paris, 1905.
40587.12 Latreille, C. Chateaubriand. Paris, 1905.
42544.24.2 Lavedan, Henri. Le duel. Paris, 1905.
42544.24.2.2 Lavedan, Henri. Le duel. 30. éd. Paris, 1905.
40597.2.12 Le Breton, A. Balzac; l'homme et l'oeuvre. Paris, 1905.
FL 390.90 Lecomte, L.H. Histoire des théâtres de Paris, 1402-1904. v.1. Paris, 1905.
FL 390.91 Lecomte, L.H. Histoire des théâtres de Paris, 1838-1904. v.2. Paris, 1905.
38531.16 Lefranc, A. Les navigations de Pantagruel. Paris, 1905.

1905 - cont.

37562.35 Leibecke, O. Der verabredete Zweikampf in der altfranzösischen Litteratur. Göttingen, 1905.
42544.33.14F Lemaître, Jules. Bertrade. Paris, 1905.
42544.33.13.5 Lemaître, Jules. Bertrade. Paris, 1905.
42544.33.6 Lemaître, Jules. En marge des vieux livres. Paris, 1905-08. 2v.
42544.33.15F Lemaître, Jules. La massière. Paris, 1905.
42576.46.7 Le Roy, Eugène. Le moulin du Frau. Paris, 1905.
43690.24.110 Lienard, Albert. Les voiles blanches. Paris, 1905.
42577.4.32 Lumbroso, A. Souvenirs sur Maupassant. Rome, 1905.
37596.41.5 Lusner, L. La somme des vices et des vertus. Wien, 1905.
40525.45 Mackrodt, J. Die Romanze vom sire de Criqui. Halle, 1905.
42545.3.11.4.5 Maeterlinck, Maurice. Monna Vanna. N.Y., 1905.
42545.01 Maeterlinck, Maurice. Théâtre. Bruxelles, 1905-1908. 3v.
42545.3.13 Maeterlinck, Maurice. La vie des abeilles. Paris, 1905.
39534.36.5 Magne, Emile. Scarron et son milieu. Paris, 1905.
38576.29.6 Mairet, Jean de. La Sylvie. Paris, 1905.
38576.29.5 Mairet, Jean de. La Sylvie. Paris, 1905.
37576.560.40 Malot, H. Conscience (Conscience). Paris, 1905.
39544.47 Mangold, Wilhelm. Voltaires Rechtsstreit mit dem Könglichen Schutzjuden Hirschel 1751. Berlin, 1905.
41539.8.2 Mansfield, M.F. Dumas' Paris. Boston, 1905.
42576.76.36 Margueritte, Paul. Le prisme. Paris, 1905.
42576.76.41 Margueritte, Paul. Quelques idées. Paris, 1905.
FL 376.19 Marsan, Jules. La pastorale dramatique en France. Paris, 1905.
37576.560.45A Massa, Philippe de. Zibeline. Paris, 1905.
42559.53 Masson, A. Pour les quais. Paris, 1905.
43697.89.9100 Maurey, Max. Asile de nuit. Paris, 1905.
42555.58.9 Mendès, Catulle. Scarron; comédie tragique. Paris, 1905.
42555.58.21 Mendès, Catulle. Scarron. Paris, 1905.
FL 382.52 Méré, Charles. La tragédie contemporaine. Paris, 1905.
41555.23.10 Mérimée, Prosper. Colomba. London, 1905.
X Cg 37556.45 Merlant, J. Le roman personnel. Paris, 1905.
40575.5.10 Michaut, G. Études sur Sainte-Beuve. Paris, 1905.
40575.5.27 Michaut, G. Le livre d'amour de Sainte-Beuve. Paris, 1905.
FL 394.112 Moeller van den Bruck, A. Das Théâtre français. Berlin, 1905.
42544.2.8.5 Moinaux, G. La conversion d'Alceste; et L'instinct par Henry Kistemaeckers. Paris, 1905.
Mol 870.62 Moinaux, G. La conversion d'Alceste. Paris, 1905.
Mol 228.51 Molière, Jean Baptiste Poquelin. Le malade imaginaire...E.W. Olmsted. Boston, 1905.
Mol 251.70 Molière, Jean Baptiste Poquelin. Les précieuses ridicules. Truffier. Paris, 1905.
NEDL Mol 268.116 Molière, Jean Baptiste Poquelin. Le Tartuffe. Paris, 1905.
Mol 268.117A Molière, Jean Baptiste Poquelin. Le Tartuffe. Dreyfus. Brisac. Paris, 1905.
Mol 268.120.2A Molière, Jean Baptiste Poquelin. Le Tartuffe. Wright. Boston, 1905.
Mol 39.05 Molière, Jean Baptiste Poquelin. Théâtre classique populaire. Paris, 1905.
43701.5.30 Monnerot Dumaine, M. Le baronne d'Armilly. Paris, 1905.
Mon 31.46 Montaigne, Michel de. Essays. Cotton. London, 1905. 3v.
X Cg 38527.31.5 Montchrétien, Antoine de. La reine d'Escosse. Paris, 1905.
42555.61.30 Moréas, Jean. Les stances. Paris, 1905.
37576.560.50 Musset, A. de. Confession of a child of the century. Paris, 1905.
43709.3.120 Noailles, Anna E. La domination. 14e éd. Paris, 1905?
42578.29.11 Ohnet, Georges. La conquérante. Paris, 1905.
42578.29.11.5 Ohnet, Georges. La conquérante. 3. éd. Paris, 1905.
38527.29.10 Palmgren, V. Observations sur l'infinitif dans Agrippa d'Aubigné. Stockholm, 1905.
Mol 716.3 Peisert, P. Molière's Leben in Bühnenarbeitungen. Halle, 1905.
42578.30.63 Peladan, J. Sémiramis. Paris, 1905.
37568.43 Pellissier, G. Études de littérature et de morale contemporaines. Paris, 1905.
37595.36.12 Perrin d'Angicourt. Lieder. v.18. Halle, 1905.
38526.14.40 Philipp, K. Pierre Du Ryers Leben und dramatische Werke. Zwickau, 1905.
42576.76.80 Pilon, Edmond. Paul et Victor Margueritte. Paris, 1905.
43743.37.110 Polhes, Alban de. Le petit. Paris, 1905.
41578.49 Poplawsky, T.A. von. L'influence d'Ossian sur l'oeuvre de Lamartine. Heidelberg, 1905.
39544.39 Popper, Josef. Voltaire. Dresden, 1905.
42578.31.50 Prévost, Marcel. L'accordeur aveugle. Paris, 1905.
38536.26A Rabelais, F. Five books of Gargantua and his son Pantagruel. N.Y., 1905.
38536.18.85 Rabelais, F. Hours with Rabelais. London, 1905.
38536.1.2 Rabelais, F. L'isle sonante. Paris, 1905.
38585.20.9 Racine, Jean. Athalie. Paris, 1905.
38585.43.6 Racine, Jean. Phaedra. N.Y., 1905?
42578.18.13 Rameau, Jean. Brimborion. Paris, 1905.
42556.21.2 Raynaud, Ernest. La couronne des jours. Paris, 1905.
42587.50.90 Rebell, Hugues. Gringalette. Paris, 1905.
42556.27.7 Régnier, Henri de. Le passé vivant. Paris, 1905.
43753.2.32 Régnier, M.L.A. de. Esclave. Paris, 1905.
42587.52.35 Renard, Jules. Bucoliques. Paris, 1905.
42524.19.9 Richard, L.R. Ferdinand Brunetière. Paris, 1905.
42556.22.70 Richepin, Jean. Don Quichotte. Paris, 1905.
42556.22.71 Richepin, Jean. Don Quichotte. Paris, 1905.
42587.55.42 Rivoire, André. Il était une bergère. Paris, 1905.
41557.10.8 Rocheblave, S. George Sand et sa fille, d'après leur correspondance inédite. Paris, 1905.
41557.10.8.5 Rocheblave, S. George Sand et sa fille. Paris, 1905.
42578.19.20 Rod, Edouard. L'indocile. Paris, 1905.
42546.15.7 Rostand, Edmond. La princesse Lointaine. Paris, 1905.
42546.15.7.2 Rostand, Edmond. La princesse Lointaine. Paris, 1905.
42546.15.8.2 Rostand, Edmond. La Samaritaine. Paris, 1905.
42546.15.8 Rostand, Edmond. La Samaritaine. Paris, 1905.
FL 6047.3 Rousseau, J.J. Emil oder über die Erziehung. Wien, 1905.
FL 6081.70 Rousseau, J.J. Lettere dalla montagna. Milan, 1905.
NEDL FL 6001.885 Rousseau, J.J. Oeuvres complètes. v.1-8,11-13. Paris, 1905. 6v.
FL 6002.905 Rousseau, J.J. Pages choisies des grands écrivains. 7. ed. Paris, 1905.
39595.22.7 St. Pierre, J.H.B. de. Paul et Virginie. London, 1905.
40575.18.15 Sainte-Beuve, Charles A. Portraits of the 18th century, historic and literary. N.Y., 1905. 2v.

1905 - cont.

40575.18.10 Sainte-Beuve, Charles A. Portraits of the 18th century, historic and literary. v.1-2. N.Y., 1905.
40575.18.20 Sainte-Beuve, Charles A. Portraits of the 18th century. N.Y., 1905.
40575.16.5 Sainte-Beuve, Charles A. Profils anglais. London, 1905.
43761.49.160 Salmon, André. Poèmes. Paris, 1905.
42556.29.18 Samain, Albert. Au jardin de l'infante. Paris, 1905.
42556.29.15 Samain, Albert. Aux flancs du vase. Paris, 1905.
42556.29.12 Samain, Albert. Le chariot d'or. Paris, 1905.
40597.2.11 Sandars, Mary F. Honoré de Balzac. His life and writings. N.Y., 1905.
42546.27.10 Sardou, Victorien. La sorcière. N.Y., 1905.
42578.35.100 Sarton, Georges. Une vie de poète. Gand, 1905.
42557.12.30 Schlaf, J. Emile Verhaeren. Berlin, 1905.
37596.99 Schmidt, A. La vie saint Franchois. Diss. Leipzig, 1905.
37596.98 Schmidt, A. La vie saint Franchois. Diss. Viersen, 1905.
42578.36.15 Schultz, Jeanne. La neuvaine de Colette. N.Y., 1905.
42556.30.43 Schuré, Edouard. Le théâtre de l'ame. 3. série. Paris, 1905.
38516.26 Schwob, Marcel. Le parnasse satyrique du XVe siècle. Paris, 1905.
40515.14 Ségur, Pierre. Julie de Lespinasse. Paris, 1905.
37587.30 Société des textes français modernes. Sketch of the purpose of the society. Mâcon, 1905.
37576.560.55 Souvestre, É. An "attic" philosopher. Paris, 1905.
41574.45.5 Stapfer, Paul. Victor Hugo à Guernesey. Paris, 1905.
40583.39 Stryienski, Casimir. Soirées du Stendhal club. Paris, 1905.
40583.40 Stryienski, Casimir. Soirées du Stendhal Club. 2. éd. Paris, 1905-08. 2v.
37576.560.60 Theuriet, A. A woodland queen (Reine des bois). Paris, 1905.
37567.107 Tiercelin, Louis. Bretons de lettres. Paris, 1905.
Mol 720.6 Trollope, H.M. The life of Molière. London, 1905.
38525.14.2 Vaganay, H. Pierre de Ronsard. Oeuvres poétiques. Lyon, 1905.
42582.13.10 Verne, Jules. From the earth to the moon. N.Y., 1905.
42582.9.4 Verne, Jules. A journey to the center of the earth. N.Y., 1905.
42582.22.7 Verne, Jules. Michael Strogoff. N.Y., 1905.
37576.560.65A Viaud, J. Madame Chrysanthème. Paris, 1905.
37576.560.70A Vigny, A. Cinq-mars. Paris, 1905. 2v.
Htn 38514.18.5* Villon, François. Le Petit et le Grant Testament. Paris, 1905.
38514.20.28.5 Villon, François. Poems. Portland, 1905.
39545.75 Voltaire, François Marie Arouet de. Un accte inédit d'un opéra de Voltaire. Upsala, 1905.
39545.67.8A Voltaire, François Marie Arouet de. Zadig and other stories. Boston, 1905.
39545.32.35 Voltaire, François Marie Arouet de. Zadig and other stories. Boston, 1905.
37562.45A Voretzsch, Carl. Einführung in das Studium der altfranzösischen Literatur. Halle, 1905.
41574.16.10A Wack, Henry W. The romance of Victor Hugo and Juliette Drouet. N.Y., 1905.
42584.25.425 Wiegler, Hans. Geschichte und Kritik der Theorie des Milieus bei Emile Zola. Inaug. Diss. Rostock, 1905.
40535.23.9 Wienhold, Hans. Lemierre's Tragödien. Leipzig, 1905.
FL 361.45 Williams, H. Noel. Queens of the French stage. London, 1905.
FL 361.45.5 Williams, H. Noel. Queens of the French stage. N.Y., 1905.
FL 374.5 Witkowski, Gustave Joseph. Les médecins au théâtre. Paris, 1905.
37585.33 Wogue, Jules. La comédie aux XVIIe et XVIIIe siècle. Paris, 1905.
42547.29 Wolff, Pierre. L'age d'aimer. Paris, 1905.
42547.29.5 Wolff, Pierre. L'age d'aimer. Paris, 1905.
42584.23.77 Zola, Emile. A love episode. Paris, 1905?
42584.23.10.5 Zola, Emile. Paris. London, 1905.
42584.1.15 Zola, Emile. Selections from Emile Zola. N.Y., 1905.

1906

42562.38.6 Adam, Paul. Les lions. Paris, 1906.
42562.38.9 Adam, Paul. Les mouettes. Paris, 1906.
42562.38.14.27 Adam, Paul. La parade amoureuse. 4e éd. Paris, 1906.
42562.38.14.32 Adam, Paul. Soir. 3e éd. Paris, 1906.
42542.1.100 Albin de Cigala, Celestin. Le Christ-Roi. Paris, 1906.
42553.33.2.2 Amiel, Henri F. Amiel's journal. N.Y., 1906. 2v.
43528.61.220 Arnoux, Alexandre. L'allée des mortes; poèmes. Paris, 1906.
43528.1.30F Arnyvèlde, G. La courtisane. Paris, 1906.
40596.13.131 Balzac, Honoré de. La comédie humaine. N.Y., 1906. 7v.
40597.34.7 Balzac, Honoré de. Ursula. The vicar of Tours. Boston, 1906.
40597.32.6 Balzac, Honoré de. The wild ass's skin. London, 1906.
42554.6.4 Banville, Théodore de. Le baiser. Paris, 1906.
41522.2.45 Barbey, d'Aurevilly, Jules. Poésie et poètes. 3. éd. Paris, 1906.
41522.2.38 Barbey d'Aurevilly, Jules. Deuxième memorandum (1838) et quelques pages de 1864. Paris, 1906.
42542.27.21.15 Barrière, Théodore. Les faux bonshommes. Paris, 1906.
41522.13.4 Baudelaire, Charles. Les fleurs du mal. Paris, 1906.
41522.15 Baudelaire, Charles. Lettres 1841-1866. Paris, 1906.
41522.13A Baudelaire, Charles. Poems. London, 1906?
38526.48.29 Baur, Albert. M. Scève et la renaissance lyonnaise. Paris, 1906.
38539.2.50 Bayer, Albert. Jean Pierre Camus; sein Leben und seine Romae. Inaug. Diss. Leipzig, 1906.
42563.22.3 Beaume, G. La bourrasque. Paris, 1906.
43538.11.40 Beaunier, André. Les souvenirs d'un peintre. Paris, 1906.
FL 6119.06 Belcourt, V. Petite vie du grand Jean-Jacques Rousseau. Paris, 1906.
42542.29.28.50 Bernard, Tristan. Triple patte. Paris, 1906.
43538.3.30 Bernède, A. Sous l'Epaulette. Paris, 1906.
42542.29.32 Bernstein, H. Le détour. Paris, 1906.
42542.29.41 Bernstein, H. La griffe. Paris, 1906.
42542.29.30 Bernstein, H. La Rafael. Paris, 1906.
40517.18.9 Besenval, Pierre V. de. Erzählungen. Leipzig, 1906.
37575.779 Bever, Adolphe van. Contes et conteurs gaillards au XVIIIe siècle. Paris, 1906.
40582.20.25 Beyle, Henri. Roma. 1. ed. Roma, 1906.
42542.29.104 Bisson, Alexandre. Le député de Bombignac; comédie. Paris, 1906.

1906 - cont.

42547.15.9 Bloy, Leon. La resurrection de Villiers de l'Isle Adam. Paris, 1906.
NEDL FL 385.8.100 Blum, Leon. Au théâtre réflexions critiques. Paris, 1906-1911. 4v.
43543.88.100 Blum, Léon. En listant. Paris, 1906.
42554.14.200 Bocquet, Léon. Les cygnes noirs; poèmes 1899-1903. Paris, 1906.
38561.61 Boileau-Despréaux, Nicolas. Satires, commentées par lui-même. Paris, 1906.
42563.34.100 Boissière, A. Clara Bill, danseuse. Paris, 1906.
Mon 112.8 Bond, R.W. Montaigne. London, 1906.
42554.15 Bonnard, Abel. Les familiers. Paris, 1906.
42563.36.40 Bordeaux, Henry. Paysages romanesques. 5. éd. Paris, 1906.
42563.36.35 Bordeaux, Henry. Les Roquevillard. Paris, 1906.
37597.10.7 Bourdillon, F.W. The early editions of the roman de la rose. London, 1906.
43544.10.30 Bourgeois, E. Mariage d'argent. 2. ed. Paris, 1906.
FL 6139.06.10A Brédif, L. Du caractère intellectuel et moral de Jean-Jacques Rousseau. Paris, 1906.
38513.53 Briand, François. Quatre histoires...sur quatre évangiles. Paris, 1906.
42542.47.11 Brieux, Eugène. Les Hannetons. Paris, 1906.
43545.41.200 Brillaud de Laujardière, C. Péril jaune. Paris, 1906.
42563.36.550 Britsch, Amédée. Henry Bordeaux. Paris, 1906.
40597.2.13A Brunetière, F. Honoré de Balzac. 1799-1850. Paris, 1906.
40597.2.13.2 Brunetière, F. Honoré de Balzac. 1799-1850. Philadelphia, 1906.
40597.2.13 Bruntière, F. Honoré de Balzac. 1799-1850. Paris, 1906.
FL 6139.06.2 Buffenoir, H. Jean-Jacques Rousseau, jugé par Chateaubriand. Genève, 1906.
FL 393.25A Cain, G. Anciens théâtres de Paris (Boulevard). Paris, 1906.
42542.48.20 Capus, Alfred. L'attentat. Paris, 1906.
42542.48.16 Capus, Alfred. L'attentat. Paris, 1906.
Htn FL 385.11.5* Capus, Alfred. Notre époque et le théâtre. Paris, 1906.
42542.48.22 Capus, Alfred. Ses passagères. Paris, 1906.
37567.86 Casella, G. La nouvelle littérature, 1895-1905. Paris, 1906.
X Cg 37567.90 Cassagne, Albert. La théorie de l'art pour l'art en France chez les derniers romantiques. Paris, 1906.
42584.25.145 Castaneda, P. Emilio Zola. Guatemala, 1906.
42542.49.9 Céard, Henry. Terrains à vendre au bord de la mer. Paris, 1906.
NEDL 40586.14 Chateaubriand, F.A.R. Atala. Paris, 1906.
40586.28.7 Chateaubriand, F.A.R. Mémoires d'outre-tombe, 1814-1815. Oxford, 1906.
Mol 703.6A Chatfield-Taylor, Herbert C. Molière; a biography. N.Y., 1906.
Mol 703.6.5A Chatfield-Taylor, Herbert C. Molière, a biography. N.Y., 1906.
42565.10 Cherbuliez, Victor. La vocation du comte Ghislain. 8. éd. Paris, 1906.
43552.25.4140 Chevalier, Adrien. La mésaventure de M. de Chanqueyras. Paris, 1906.
37596.10.35 Chrestien de Troyes. Yvain. Der Löwenritter. 3. Aufl. Halle, 1906.
FL 6118.93.3 Chuquet, A. Jean-Jacques Rousseau. 3. ed. Paris, 1906.
42551.7 Citoleux, Marc. Mme Ackermann. Paris, 1906.
FL 373.6 Cohen, Gustave. Histoire de la mise en scène dans le théâtre religieux français du Moyen Age. Paris, 1906.
42565.59 Commings, Marie Aimery. Le voluptueux voyage. Paris, 1906.
42542.53 Coolus, R. Antoinette Sabrier. Paris, 1906.
42542.53.16 Coolus, R. L'enfant chérie. Paris, 1906.
38575.31.8 Corneille, Pierre. Cinna; tragédie. Nouvelle éd. Paris, 1906.
38575.34.8.9 Corneille, Pierre. Polyeucte. Boston, 1906.
42542.55.10 Croisset, Francis de. La bonne intention. Paris, 1906.
42542.55.2 Croisset, Francis de. Le tour de main. Paris, 1906.
42542.58.5 Curel, François de. Le coup d'Aile. Paris, 1906.
Mol 560.16 Currier, T.F. Catalogue of the Molière collection. Cambridge, 1906.
Mol 513.1.1 Currier, T.F. Index to Le Molieriste. Cambridge, 1906.
Mol 513.1.3 Currier, T.F. Index to Le Molieriste. Cambridge, 1906.
43565.1.30 Daireaux, M. Ses pénitents noirs. Paris, 1906.
42566.22.10 Daudet, Alphonse. L'évangéliste; roman parisien. Paris, 1906?
42566.19.8.65 Daudet, Alphonse. Tartarin de Tarascon. London, 1906.
43565.5.35 Daudet, Léon A. Les primaires. Paris, 1906.
37567.85A Davies, Thomas R. French romanticism and the press: the Globe. Cambridge, 1906.
42586.36.3 Demond, G. Jean de Précour. Une page d'histoire. Paris, 1906.
37596.102.3 Denis Piramus. La vie seint Edmund le Rei. Philadelphia, 1906.
42542.64.25 Descaves, Lucien. La préférée. Paris, 1906.
43566.82.100 Des Rieux, L. Héculie. Paris, 1906.
38563.17A Dévolve, J. Religion, critique et philosophie positive chez Pierre Bayle. Paris, 1906.
42542.65.14.2 Donnay, Maurice. Education de prince. Paris, 1906.
42542.65.6 Donnay, Maurice. Paraitre. Paris, 1906.
37574.75.3 Dorchain, Auguste. Les cent meilleurs poèmes. 4. éd. Paris, 1906.
37543.118 Doumic, René. Histoire de la littérature française. 23. éd. Paris, 1906.
Mon 144.1.3 Dowden, E. Michel de Montaigne. Philadelphia, 1906.
39533.20.16 Dübi, H. Cyrano de Bergerac (1619-1655) sein Leben. Bern, 1906.
40524.32 Dühren, E. Rétif de la Bretonne. Berlin, 1906.
41538.91 Dumas, Alexandre. Agénor de Mauléon. London, 1906. 2v.
41538.53.40 Dumas, Alexandre. The three musketeers. London, 1906.
43576.95.120 Dumas, Charles. L'ombre et les proies. Paris, 1906.
43576.56.100 Dumont-Wilden, L. Les soucis des derniers soirs. Bruxelles, 1906.
38526.13.500 Durand, Estienne. Méditations. Paris, 1906.
43554.5.80 Durel, P. Leo Claretie. Paris, 1906.
38575.23.110 Écorcheville, J. Corneille et la musique. Paris, 1906.
42586.63.7 Eulenburg-Hertefeld, P. Graf Arthur Gobineau. Strassburg, 1906.
37596.10.90 Euler, H. Recht und Staat in den Romanen des Cretien von Troyes. Inaug. Diss. Marburg, 1906.
42543.38.5 Fabre, Émile. La vie publique. Paris, 1906.
FL 385.26.5 Faguet, Emile. Propos de théâtre. Series 1-5. Paris, 1906. 5v.

Chronological Listing

1906 - cont.

43606.78.120 Farrère, Claude. Les civilisés. 25. éd. Paris, 1906.
42565.71 Favre de Coulevain, Hélène. L'île inconnue. Paris, 1906.
42565.72 Favre de Coulevain, Hélène. Noblesse américaine. Paris, 1906.
41543.21 Ferrières, G. Gerard de Nerval, la vie et l'oeuvre, 1808-1855. Paris, 1906.
42586.48.25 Feval, Paul H. La fée des gréves. Boston, 1906.
FL 6139.06.3 Findeisen, Hermann. Die philosophischen Grundgedanken der Pädagogiks Jean-Jacques Rousseaus. Borna, 1906.
42576.35.48 Flaubert, Gustave. Lettres à sa nièce Caroline. Paris, 1906.
37595.36.51 Foerster, Wendelin. Romanische Bibliothek. 3. Aufl. Halle, 1906-28. 3v.
43611.1.25.8 Fort, Paul. Coxcomb, ou l'Homme tout nu tombé. VIII. Paris, 1906.
42576.61.6 Franay, Gabriel. Comme dans un conte. Paris, 1906.
Htn 42576.62.24* France, Anatole. Au petit bonheur. Paris, 1906. 2 pam.
Htn 42576.63.12* France, Anatole. Le jonglevr de Notre-Dame. Paris, 1906.
Htn 42576.62.60* France, Anatole. Sainte Euphrosine. Paris, 1906.
42576.62.3.5 France, Anatole. Thaïs. Paris, 1906.
42576.63.20 France, Anatole. Vers les temps meilleurs. v.1-3. Paris, 1906.
41574.52 Fréminet, E. Les sources grecques des trois cents. Paris, 1906.
37558.53 Gassier, Émile. Les cinq cents immortels. Paris, 1906.
37596.106 Gastoué, A. Le drame liturgique les vierges sages et folles. Paris, 1906.
42554.26.25 Gaubert, E. François Coppée. Paris, 1906.
41542.37.8.5 Gautier, Théophile. One of Cleopatra's nights. N.Y., 1906.
37556.37 Gerhardt, Max. Der Aberglaube in der Französischen Novelle des 16. Jahrhunderts. Schöneberg, 1906.
42554.44.9 Ghil, René. Oeuvre. Paris, 1906. 4v.
41541.6.15 Girardin, Delphine Gay. Choix de lettres parisiennes. Oxford, 1906.
37555.323 Gladow, J. Vom französischen Versbau neuerer Zeit. Berlin, 1906.
37597.29.9 Göderhjehn, T. Die Sprache in dem altfranzösischen Martinsleben des Péan Gatineau aus Tours. Helsingfors, 1906.
FL 6049.6 Görland, A. Rousseau als Klassiker des Sozialpädagogik. Gotha, 1906.
37555.53 Gonon, Jean F. Histoire de chanson Stephanoise et Forézienne. St. Étienne, 1906.
42576.15.13 Gould, G.M. A biographic clinic on Gustave Flaubert. Philadelphia, 1906.
43625.3.37 Gourmont, Rémy de. Lilith, suivi de Théodat. 2. éd. Paris, 1906.
37543.95.2 Gourmont, Rémy de. Promenades littéraires. Série 2. Paris, 1906.
Htn FL 395.255* Grandval, C. De la comédie-française aux boulevards. Paris, 1906.
42586.31.25 Grappe, G. Jules Claretié. Paris, 1906
42586.78 Guillaumin, Emile. Albert Manceau Adjudant. Paris, 1906.
42543.61.9 Guinon, Albert. Le partage. Paris, 1906.
FL 6002.906.2 Guy, J. Jean Jacques Rousseau. Paris, 1906.
38526.25.5 Haacke, M. Un précurseur de Molière [Pierre de Larivey]. Halle, 1906.
37596.109 Hard af Segerstad, Kerstin. Quelques commentaires sur la plus ancienne chanson d'états française, Le livre des Manièrs. Uppsala, 1906.
42543.64 Hermant, Abel. Les grands bourgeois. Paris, 1906.
42571.37.2 Hervieu, Paul. Le réveil, L'énigme. 6. éd. Paris, 1906.
42571.37 Hervieu, Paul. Le réveil. 13. éd. Paris, 1906.
42587.4.105 Hudry-Menos, J. (Mme.). Ames cévenoles. Paris, 1906.
41573.5.10 Hugo, Victor. Morceaux choisis. Paris, 1906?
41573.23.5.10 Hugo, Victor. Notre Dame de Paris. Oxford, 1906.
41573.53 Hugo, Victor. Works. N.Y., 1906. 7v.
43667.51.170 Jaloux, Edmond. L'école des mariages. Paris, 1906.
43667.78.110 Jarry, Alfred. Ubu sur la butte. Paris, 1906.
37562.37 Junge, A. Ueber Gerichtsbeamte...in der Litteratur des alten Frankreich. Göttingen, 1906.
38576.11.19 Koch, J. Brueys und Palaprat und ihre dramatischen Werke. Dresden, 1906.
38564.32.9 La Bruyère, J. de. Les caractères. Paris, 1906.
38567.12.10 Lanson, Gustave. Boileau. 3. éd. Paris, 1906.
FL 360.30.3 Larroumet, G. Études de critique dramatique. Paris, 1906. 2v.
FL 6139.06 Lassudrie-Duchêne, G. Jean-Jacques Rousseau et le droit des gens. Paris, 1906.
42544.23.5 Lavedan, Henri. Le bon temps. (Roman). Paris, 1906.
42544.24.2.3 Lavedan, Henri. Le duel. 2. éd. Paris, 1906.
42544.24.13 Lavedan, Henri. Le nouveau jeu. Paris, 1906.
37576.505 Lazare, Jules. Contes et nouvelles des meilleurs auteurs contemporains. Boston, 1906.
42576.42.15 Le Barillier, Berthe. Les délices de Mantoue. Paris, 1906.
42555.37 Lebloud, M.A. Leconte de Lisle. Paris, 1906.
38575.15.5 LeBrun, Roger. Corneille devant trois siècles. Paris, 1906.
42545.28.802 Le Brun, Roger. Georges Courteline. Paris, 1906.
37596.130 LeCompte, I.C. The sources of the Anglo-French comentary on the proverbs of Solomon. Collegeville, Pa., 1906.
FL 390.92 Lecomte, L.H. Histoire des théâtres de Paris. Le théâtre histoire. v.3. Paris, 1906.
42544.33.7 Lemaître, Jules. En marge des vieux livres. Paris, 1906.
42544.33.12.3 Lemaître, Jules. Révoltée, Le député, Le veau, Mariage blanc, Flipote. Paris, 1906.
FL 6129.06.3 Lenz, K.G. Über Rousseaus Verbindung mit Weibern. Berlin, 1906.
NEDL 42576.46.5 Le Roy, Eugène. Au pays des pierres. Paris, 1906.
40515.9.15 Lespinasse, J.J.E. de. Coresspondance entre Mlle. de Lespinasse et le comte de Guibert. Paris, 1906.
40515.9.9.5 Lespinasse, J.J.E. de. Lettres. Paris, 1906.
40515.9.9 Lespinasse, J.J.E. de. Lettres. Paris, 1906.
43688.4.30 Levaillant, M. Le miroir d'Étain. Paris, 1906.
43693.2.30 Lorquise, C. Les invectives. Paris, 1906.
42544.34.32.5 Louys, Pierre. Aphrodite. Paris, 1906.
FL 6119.06.5 MacDonald, F. Jean-Jacques Rousseau, a new criticism. London, 1906. 2v.
42545.3.5.20 Maeterlinck, Maurice. Der Schotz der Armen. 3. Aufl. Jena, 1906.
42545.3.9.3 Maeterlinck, Maurice. Sister Beatrice and Ardiane and Barbe Bleue. N.Y., 1906.
42545.3.13.9A Maeterlinck, Maurice. The swarm. N.Y., 1906.

1906 - cont.

43697.34.180 Magre, Maurice. Les livres et le secret. Paris, 1906.
38562.23 Maigron, L. Fontenelle. Paris, 1906.
42576.76.37 Margueritte, Paul. Sur le vif. Paris, 1906.
37583.600 Marnière, Jeanne. Théâtre de madame. Paris, 1906.
42577.12.9 Martin, Victor. Sous la terreur. Paris, 1906.
Mol 613.7 Martinenche, E. Molière et le théâtre espagnol. Paris, 1906.
37564.52 Martino, Pierre. L'Orient dans la littérature française au XVIIe et au XVIIIe siècle. Paris, 1906.
43697.79.130 Mary, André. Les sentiers du paradis. Paris, 1906.
Mol 713.13A Marzials, F.J. Molière. London, 1906.
42577.1.1A Maupassant, Guy de. Contes de la bécasse. Paris, 1906.
42577.4.10.7 Maupassant, Guy de. Fort comme la mort. Paris, 1906.
42555.58.22 Mendès, Catulle. Glatigny. Paris, 1906.
42555.58.22.5 Mendès, Catulle. Glatigny. Paris, 1906.
42555.58.27 Mendès, Catulle. St. Thérése. Paris, 1906.
42555.58.20 Mendès, Catulle. La vierge d'Avila. Paris, 1906.
38523.3.9 Mensch, J. Das Tier in der Dichtung Marots. Leipzig, 1906.
38523.3.10 Mensch, J. Das Tier in der Dichtung Marots. Naumburg, 1906.
41555.2 Mérimée, Prosper. Ausgewählte Novellen. Leipzig, 1906.
37596.103 Metcke, Albert. Die Lieder des altfranzösischen Lyrikers Gille le Vinier. Halle, 1906.
38514.69.6 Meyer, A. Das Kulturhistorische in Le mystère du Siège d'Orléans. Leipzig, 1906.
40547.14.17 Michelet, Jules. Pages choisies des grands écrivains. 9. éd. Paris, 1906.
42545.28.7.45 Mirbeau, Octave. Le journal d'une femme de chambre. Paris, 1906.
Mol 171.59 Molière, Jean Baptiste Poquelin. Le bourgeois gentilhomme. London, 1906.
Mol 211.72 Molière, Jean Baptiste Poquelin. Les femmes savantes. Strasbourg, 1906.
Mol 245.90 Molière, Jean Baptiste Poquelin. Le misanthrope. Strasbourg, 1906.
Mol 216.30.5 Molière, Jean Baptiste Poquelin. De schelmenstreken van Scapin. Amsterdam, 1906.
Mol 268.121 Molière, Jean Baptiste Poquelin. Le Tartuffe. Matzke. N.Y., 1906.
Mol 268.120A Molière, Jean Baptiste Poquelin. Le Tartuffe. Wright. Boston, 1906.
Mon 19.06F Montaigne, Michel de. Les essais. Bordeaux, 1906-33. 5v.
Mon 19.06.3F Montaigne, Michel de. Essais. Paris, 1906-31. 3v.
Mon 45.9 Montaigne, Michel de. Journal du voyage. Laritrey. Paris, 1906.
42555.61.42 Moréas, Jean. Paysages et sentiments. Paris, 1906.
42555.61.39 Moréas, Jean. Trois nouveaux contes de la vielle France. Paris, 1906.
43701.2.30 Mounet-Sully, J. La vieillesse de Don Juan. Paris, 1906.
41596.35.2 Musset, Alfred de. Il faut qu'une porte soit ouverte ou fermée. Paris, 1906.
41596.13.13 Musset, Alfred de. Poésies choisies. Oxford, 1906.
41596.13.11A Musset, Alfred de. Poésies nouvelles. Paris, 1906.
Mon 124.1.6A Norton, Grace. Le plutarque de Montaigne. Boston, 1906.
43731.1.30 Oudinot, C. Chaîne anglaise. Paris, 1906.
37574.67 Payne, John. Flowers of France. The romantic period. 19th century. London, 1906. 2v.
Htn 37574.67* Payne, John. Flowers of France. The romantic period. 19th century. London, 1906. 2v.
FL 6129.06.2 Perrin, L. Rousseau à Motiers-Travers et sa lapidation. Fleurier, 1906.
38567.23 Petersen, Karl. Die Urteile Boileaus über die Dichter seiner Zeit. Kiel, 1906.
43740.1.34 Philippe, Charles Louis. Croquignole. Paris, 1906.
42545.77 Picard, André. Jeunesse. Paris, 1906.
37563.26 Picot, Émile. Les français italianisants au XVIe siècle. Paris, 1906. 2v.
43743.2.55 Poizat, A. Le cyclope. Paris, 1906.
38537.25.7 Precicou, A. Rabelais et les Limosins. Limoges, 1906.
40522.4.5 Prévost, Antoine F. Geschichte einer Neugriechin. Leipzig, 1906.
42578.31.52.5A Prévost, Marcel. Monsieur et Madame Moloch. Paris, 1906.
42578.31.52 Prévost, Marcel. Monsieur et Madame Moloch. 58. éd. Paris, 1906.
42566.16.145 Die Pseudogenres bei Alphonse Daudet. Inaug. Diss. Borna, 1906.
38585.34.25 Racine, Jean. Iphigénie. 8. éd. Paris, 1906.
38585.44.9 Racine, Jean. Les plaideurs. Boston, 1906.
37567.138 Rageot, Gaston. Le succès, auteurs et public. Paris, 1906.
42578.18.8 Rameau, Jean. La bonne étoile. Paris, 1906.
37596.102 Ravenel, Florence L. La vie seint Edmund le Rei. Philadelphia, 1906.
42556.27.9 Régnier, Henri de. La sandale ailée 1903-1905. Paris, 1906.
42556.26.27 Régnier, Henri de. Sujets et paysages. 4. éd. Paris, 1906.
40516.41 Reinhäckel, R.P. Madame de Charriere. Weida, 1906.
42515.25.60 Renan, Ernest. Cahiers de jeunesse. 2. éd. Paris, 1906. 2v.
42515.29.75 Renan, Ernest. Vie de Jésus. 101. éd. Paris, 1906?
42587.52.9 Renard, Jules. La lanterne sourde. Paris, 1906.
42578.31.4100 Renkin, Jean-François. Ecrits wallons. Liège, 1906?
42556.27.80 Retté, Adolphe. Poésies, 1892-1906. Paris, 1906.
40536.33 Rey, A. La vieillesse de Sedaine. Paris, 1906.
43756.1.30 Riche, D. Le Prétexte. Paris, 1906.
42556.22.75 Richepin, Jean. L'aimé. Paris, 1906.
42556.22.80 Richepin, Jean. La chanson des gueux. Paris, 1906.
42587.55.20 Rivoire, André. Le songe de l'amour. Paris, 1906.
FL 6129.06.4 Rod, É. L'affaire Jean-Jacques Rousseau. Paris, 1906.
42578.19.23 Rod, Edouard. Le réformateur. Paris, 1906.
43757.50.131 Rolland, Romain. Jean Christophe. Photoreproduction. Paris, 1906-07. 4v.
43757.90.1100 Rouger, Henri. La retraite fleuril. Paris, 1906.
FL 6042.06 Rousseau, J.J. Émile ou De l'éducation. Paris, 1906.
41578.91 Roustan, Marius. Lamartine et les Calhaliques Lyonnais. Paris, 1906.
FL 395.260 Rouveyre, A.L.M. La comédie-française. Paris, 1906.
NEDL 40597.2.20 Roux, Fernand. Balzac, jurisconsulte et criminaliste. Paris, 1906.
42578.19.45 Roz, F. Edouard Rod. Paris, 1906.
37567.87 Sageret, J. Les grands convertis. Paris, 1906.
43761.41.180 St. Georges de Bouhelier. Le roi sans couronne. Paris, 1906.

1906 - cont.

39595.22.8 St. Pierre, J.H.B. de. Paul et Virginie. Boston, 1906.
40576.12 Sainte-Beuve, Charles A. Livre d'amour. Paris, 1906.
40575.18.22 Sainte-Beuve, Charles A. Portraits of the 18th century. N.Y., 1906. 2v.
42546.30.21 Sardou, Victorien. La piste. Paris, 1906.
42546.30.22 Sardou, Victorien. Thermidor. Paris, 1906.
37565.30.6 Sargent, George H. The French revolution and Napoleon in literature and caricature. n.p., 1906.
37596.92.7 Sass, Ernst. L'estoire Joseph. Dresden, 1906.
37596.92.6 Sass, Ernst. L'estoire Joseph. Halle, 1906.
43761.4.30 Saulnay, S. de. Ombres colorées. Paris, 1906.
FL 6002.906 Schroeder, V. Jean Jacques Rousseau morceaux choisis. Paris, 1906.
41578.50 Séché, Léon. Lamartine de 1816 à 1830. Paris, 1906.
FL 6029.4 Sehinz, A. Confessions de Jean-Jacques Rousseau. Paris, 1906.
FL 6119.06.7 Sommerfelt, V. Jean-Jacques Rousseau. Kristiania, 1906.
42515.35.244 Sorel, Georges. Le système historique de Renan. Paris, 1906.
43775.89.100 Souchon, Paul. Le Dieu nouveau. Paris, 1906.
42587.59.8 Soyez-Le Roy, Lettice. Coeur fier. Lille, 1906.
37595.16.5 Stimming, Albert. Die altfranzösische Motette der Bamberger Handschrift. Dresden, 1906.
38537.25.9 Stoppoloni, A. Francesco Rabelais. Roma, 1906.
FL 6119.06.8 Stoppoloni, A. Gian Giacomo Rousseau. Roma, 1906.
Mon 129.3 Strowski, F. Montaigne. Paris, 1906.
40553.10.70 Tambour, Ernest. Benjamin Constant à Luzarches. Versailles, 1906.
42559.84 Taravel, Antoine. La chanson sentimentale. Paris, 1906.
43788.5.100 Tharaud, Jérôme. Dingley, l'illustre écrivain. Paris, 1906.
38514.21.20 Thomas, Louis. Les dernières leçons de Marcel Schwob sur François Villon. Paris, 1906.
42578.51.20A Tinayre, Marcelle. La maison du péché. 40. éd. Paris, 1906.
42578.52.55 Tinseau, Léon de. Les étourderies de la chanoinesse. Paris, 1906.
42578.56.50 Toutain, Paul. Terriens. Paris, 1906.
38525.5.9 Ulrich, J. Proben der französischen Novellistik des 16. Jahrhunderts. Leipzig, 1906.
43822.51.100 Valmy-Baysse, Jean. La vie enchantée; poèmes, 1902-05. Paris, 1906.
FL 6039.14 Vecchio, G. Su la teoria del Contratto sociale. Bologna, 1906.
42557.11 Verhaeren, Emile. Poèmes. Paris, 1906. 3v.
42557.18.30 Verlaine, Paul. Ausgewählte Gedichte. Leipzig, 1906.
37564.118 Vial, Francisque. Idées et doctrines littéraires du XVIIe siècle. Paris, 1906.
42576.57.7.2A Viaud, Julien. Les désenchantées. Paris, 1906.
42576.57.7.5A Viaud, Julien. Les désenchantées. 67. éd. Paris, 1906.
42576.57.7.15 Viaud, Julien. Disenchanted. N.Y., 1906.
42576.56.4 Viaud, Julien. Madame Chrysanthème. 82. éd. Paris, 1906?
42557.23 Vielé-Griffin, F. Plus loin. Paris, 1906.
43824.49.210 Vildrac, Charles. Poèmes, 1905. Lille, 1906.
38527.67 Vion d'Alibray, Charles. Oeuvres poétiques. Paris, 1906.
38542.12 Vogler, H. Die literargeschichtlichen Kenntnisse und Urteile des J.L.G. de Balzac. Altona, 1906.
39543.68 Voltaire, François Marie Arouet de. Voltaire: seine Persönlichkeit in seinen Werken. Stuttgart, 1906.
37574.625 Walch, G. Anthologie des poètes français contemporains. Paris, 1906. 2v.
37573.30 Walch, Gerard. Anthologie des poètes français contemporains, 1866-1907. Paris, 1906-32. 4v.
37556.46 Waldberg, M. Der empfindsame Roman in Frankreich. Strassburg, 1906.
42515.41.5 Wenderoth, O. Der junge Quinet und seine Übersetzungen und...Ideen. Erlangen, 1906.
FL 361.45.2 Williams, H. Noel. Later queens of the French stage. London, 1906.
38525.9 Wyndham, George. Ronsard and la Pléiade with selections from poetry. London, 1906.
Mon 136.1 Zangroniz, J. de. Montaigne, Amyot et Saliat. Paris, 1906.
42584.23.4.2 Zola, Emile. La curée. Paris, 1906.
42584.21.25 Zola, Emile. Théâtre. Paris, 1906.

1907

42562.38.11 Adam, Paul. Les coeur untiles. Paris, 1907.
42562.38.14.11 Adam, Paul. Les coeurs nouveaux. 5e éd. Paris, 1907.
42562.38.14.19 Adam, Paul. Les images sentimentales. 4e éd. Paris, 1907.
42562.38.14.20 Adam, Paul. Irène et les eunugues. 16e éd. Paris, 1907.
42562.38.7 Adam, Paul. Les monettes. Paris, 1907.
42562.38.12 Adam, Paul. Le mystère des foules. 4e éd. Paris, 1907. 2v.
38546.66.10A Aldis, Janet. The queen of letter writers, Marquise de Sévigné. N.Y., 1907.
43522.41.200 Alibert, François Paul. L'arbue qui saigne. Carcassonne, 1907.
42586.9.5 Arène, Paul. La gueuse parfumée. Paris, 1907.
X Cg 37555.65 Bailey, John C. The claims of French poetry. London, 1907.
42524.9 Baldensperger, F. Études d'histoire littéraire. 1. série. Paris, 1907.
40596.22 Balzac, Honoré de. Père Goriot. Boston, 1907.
40597.34.8 Balzac, Honoré de. Ursula. The vicar of Tours. Boston, 1907.
37544.30.2 Balzo, Carlo del. L'Italia nella letteratura francese. Torino, 1907.
41522.2.15 Barbey d'Aurevilly, Jules. Letteres à une amie, 1880-1887. Paris, 1907.
42554.12.20 Barbier, Auguste. Iambes et poèmes. Oxford, 1907.
42541.6.9 Bataille, Henry. Poliche. Paris, 1907.
41522.13.9.30 Baudelaire, Charles. Blumen des Bösen. Leipzig, 1907.
42586.14.55 Baudry, J. (Mme.). Devant l'obstacle. Paris, 1907.
42557.12.5 Bazalgette, S. Emile Verhaeren. Paris, 1907.
42563.21.42.5 Bazin, René. Donatienne. Paris, 1907.
37562.47 Becker, P.A. Grundriss der altfranzösischen Literatur. Heidelberg, 1907.
42563.22.14.19 Belot, Adolphe. El secreto terrible. Madrid, 1907.
42542.29.21.5 Bernard, Tristan. Sa soeur; pièce en trois actes. Paris, 1907.
42542.29.29 Bernhardt, S. (Mme.). Adrienne. Paris, 1907.
FL 398.7.19A Bernhardt, Sarah. Ma double vie. Mémoires de Sarah Bernhardt. Paris, 1907.
FL 398.7.15 Bernhardt, Sarah. Memories of my life. N.Y., 1907.

1907 - cont.

FL 398.7.15.8 Bernhardt, Sarah. My double life. London, 1907.
42542.29.40 Bernstein, H. Le voleur. Paris, 1907.
42542.29.40.5 Bernstein, H. Le voleur. Paris, 1907.
42563.23.8.20 Bertrand, Louis. L'invasion. Paris, 1907.
40582.21.5A Beyle, Henri. Racine et Shakespeare. Oxford, 1907.
42542.29.99 Bisson, Alexandre. Les plumes du Paon. Paris, 1907.
38566.32.2 Boileau Despréaux, Nicolas. Le Lutrin. Paris, 1907.
FL 397.66.17 Boissy, G. La dramaturgie d'Orange. Paris, 1907.
FL 6139.07.5 Bonnard, R. Prétendu individualisme de Jean-Jacques Rousseau. Paris, 1907.
42577.4.33 Bosson, O. Guy de Maupassant. London, 1907.
42563.37.35A Bourget, Paul. L'émigré. Paris, 1907.
41568.15.25 Bouyer, Raymond. Obermann, précurseur et musicien. Paris, 1907.
38513.3.6 Brandenburg, Max. Die festen Strophengebilde...des Mystère de Saint Barbe. Griefswald, 1907.
42541.7.12 Brieux, Eugène. La Française, comédie en trois actes. Paris, 1907.
42541.7.11 Brieux, Eugène. La Française. Paris, 1907.
42542.47.7.2 Brieux, Eugène. Les remplacantes. 8. éd. Paris, 1907.
37547.37 Brun, Charles. Littératures provinciales. Paris, 1907.
42524.16.9 Brunetière, F. Discours de combat. Paris, 1907.
42524.16.9.2 Brunetière, F. Discours de combat. Paris, 1907.
42524.16.9.3 Brunetière, F. Discours de combat. Paris, 1907.
37572.54 Buffum, D.L. French short stories. N.Y., 1907.
37572.54.5 Buffum, D.L. French short stories. 2. ed. N.Y., 1907.
FL 6139.01.3 Campayré, G. Jean-Jacques Rousseau and education from nature. N.Y., 1907.
42542.48.8 Capus, Alfred. Les passagères. Paris, 1907.
42578.22.800 Casella, Georges. J.H. Rosny. Paris, 1907.
38512.37 Casola, Nicola da. Attila, poema franco-italiano per G. Bertoni. Friburgo, 1907.
X Cg 38514.29 Champion, Pierre. Le manuscrit autographe de Charles d'Orleans. Paris, 1907.
NEDL 40586.14.3 Chateaubriand, F.A.R. Atala, René, Le dernier Abencérage. Paris, 1907?
40586.66 Chateaubriand, F.A.R. La jeunesse de Chateaubriand. Oxford, 1907.
38511.26 Chatelain, H. Le mistere de Saint Quentin. St. Quentin, 1907.
43552.23.100 Chemin, Emile. Jean des Brebis. Paris, 1907.
40526.7.7 Chénier, André. Poésies choisies. Oxford, 1907.
42565.8 Cherbuliez, Victor. La bête. Paris, 1907.
42565.31.8 Cherbuliez, Victor. Samuel Brohl et Cie. 9. éd. Paris, 1907.
FL 373.6.10 Cohen, Gustave. Geschichte der Inszenierung im geistlichen Schauspiele des Mittelalters in Frankreich. Leipzig, 1907.
42542.53.9 Coolus, R. Coeur à coeur. Paris, 1907.
42554.23.17 Coppée, François. La bonne souffrance. N.Y., 1907.
42554.22.4A Coppée, François. Poésies. Paris, 1907. 6v.
42554.22.35 Coppée, François. Poésies choisies de François Coppée. Oxford, 1907.
38575.33.8 Corneille, Pierre. Horace. 7 éd. Paris, 1907.
42541.7.15 Croisset, F. de. Paris - New York. Paris, 1907.
FL 6139.07.9 Culcasi, C. Gli Influssi Italiani nell' Opera di G.G. Rousseau. Roma, 1907.
43565.2.30 Dampierre, J. de. La couronne de Sierre. Paris, 1907.
38542.16 Daniel, W.M. Saint-Evremond en Angleterre. Versailles, 1907.
39594.18.5A Dargan, E.P. The aesthetic doctrine of Montesquieu. Baltimore, 1907.
38542.12.6 Declareuil, J. Idées politiques de Guez de Balzac. Paris, 1907.
42542.61 Decourcelle, P. Après le pardon. Paris, 1907.
43566.45.100 Delacour, André. Les oasis. Paris, 1907.
Mon 190.2 Delacroix, Raymond. Montaigne, malade et médecin. Lyon, 1907.
38551.20 Delphanque, A. Fénelon et la doctrine de l'amour. Lille, 1907.
38551.47.15 Delplanque, A. Fénelon et la doctrine de l'amour pur d'après sa correspondance avec ses principaux amis. Lille, 1907.
40527.27 Demachy, Jacques François. Histoires et contes. Paris, 1907.
42554.29.2 Deniker, N. Poèmes. Paris, 1907.
42545.69.15 Dennery, Adolphe Philippe. Les deux orphelines. Paris, 1907.
42545.69.20 Dennery, Adolphe Philippe. Martyre. Paris, 1907.
38526.11.15 Des Masures, Louis. Tragédies saintes. Paris, 1907.
42542.64.40 Devore, G. La sacrifiée. Paris, 1907.
38527.50.12 Dezeimeris, R. Sur l'objectif réel du discours d'Estienne de La Boétie de la servitude volontaire. Bordeaux, 1907.
42542.65.8 Donnay, Maurice. Amants. 13. éd. Paris, 1907.
42542.65.14 Donnay, Maurice. Education de prince. Paris, 1907.
37574.75.4 Dorchain, Auguste. Les cent meilleurs poèmes. Paris, 1907.
37576.500A Dow, Louis Henry. Quelques contes des romanciers naturalistes. Boston, 1907.
37576.500.3 Dow, Louis Henry. Quelques contes des romanciers naturalistes. Boston, 1907.
37547.45 Droux, Georges. La chanson lyonnaise. Lyon, 1907.
38525.22.8 Dufay, Pierre. Le portrait, le buste et l'épitaphe de Ronsard au musée de Plois. Paris, 1907.
FL 6096.3 Dufour, T. Le testament de Jean-Jacques Rousseau. Genève, 1907.
41539.12 Dumas, Alexandre. My memoirs. N.Y., 1907-09. 6v.
37544.34 Edwards, Matilda Betham. Literary rambles in France. London, 1907.
42572.22.10 Erckmann, Emile. Le juif polonais. Paris, 1907.
42541.13.12 Fabre, Emile. La maison d'argile. Paris, 1907.
42541.13.15 Fabre, Emile. Timon d'Athenes. Paris, 1907.
FL 397.88 Fage, René. Un demi-siècle de théâtre à Tulle, 1800-1850. Brive, 1907.
37543.127 Faguet, E. Amours d'hommes de lettres. Paris, 1907.
37543.129 Faguet, E. A literary history of France. London, 1907.
37544.22.4 Faguet, Emile. Propos littéraires. 4. séries. Paris, 1907.
41583.32 Fauchier Delavigne, M. Casimir Delavigne intime. Paris, 1907.
38554.524A Fénelon, F. de S. de la Mothe. Fénelon et Mme. Guyon. Paris, 1907.
Mol 247.17 Ferchlandt, H. Molière's Misanthrop und seine englischen Nachahmungen. Inaug. Diss. Halle, 1907.
42556.17 Fons, Pierre. Sully-Prudhomme. Paris, 1907.
Mon 170.3 Fränkel, R. Montaignes Stellung zum Staat und zur Kirche. Leipzig, 1907.

Chronological Listing

1907 - cont.

42576.62.9.10 France, Anatole. Chez Anatole France. Paris, 1907.
42576.63.7.7 France, Anatole. Le crime de Sylvestre Bonnard. Paris, 1907.
42576.62.30.5 France, Anatole. Les désirs de Jean Servien. Paris, 1907.
43612.58.100 Franche, Paul. Le legende dovée des Bêtes. Paris, 1907.
42586.57 Fromentin, Eugène. Dominik. Leipzig, 1907.
42576.15.27 Fusco, Antonio. La filosofia dell'arte in Gustavo Flaubert. Messina, 1907.
42547.10.15 Gaubert, Ernest. Rachilde. Paris, 1907.
X Cg 41542.11.7 Gautier, Théophile. Mademoiselle de Maupin. Paris, 1907.
42543.45.8 Gavault, Paul. Mlle Josette, ma femme. Paris, 1907.
42543.45.8.2 Gavault, Paul. Mlle Josette, ma femme. Paris, 1907.
43616.98.3100 Gazel, Louis. Pro patria. Hanoi, 1907.
Mol 194.2 Gendarme de Bévotte, Georges. Le Festin de Pierre avant Molière. Paris, 1907.
Mol 194.2.2 Gendarme de Bévotte, Georges. Le Festin de Pierre avant Molière. Thèse. Paris, 1907.
43617.7.31 Génin, Auguste. Poèmes aztèques. 2. éd. México, 1907.
42563.18.80 Gillouin, René. Maurice Barrès. Paris, 1907.
37543.79 Giraud, Victor. Livres et questions d'aujourd'hui. Paris, 1907.
42576.64.2 Goron, Marie F. The truth about the case. Philadelphia, 1907.
43625.3.35 Gourmont, Rémy de. Epilogues; reflect sur la vie, 1895-1912. 3e éd. Paris, 1907-16. 6v.
37556.21.9 Grages, C.M. des. La presse littéraire sur la restauration, 1815-1830. Paris, 1907.
42571.41.5 Grousset, P. Mémoires d'un collégien. N.Y., 1907.
37596.27.8 Guéry, Charles. Guillaume Aléxis dit le bon moine. Eveux, 1907.
42576.40.16 Guiches, Gustave. Chacun sa vie. Paris, 1907.
42576.40.15 Guiches, Gustave. Chacun sa vie. Paris, 1907.
42576.40.13 Guiches, Gustave. Chacun sa vie. Paris, 1907.
42543.61.19 Guinon, Albert. Son père. Paris, 1907.
42541.13.35 Guirand, Edmond. Anna Karénine. Paris, 1907.
39544.155.10 Hall, Evelyn B. The life of Voltaire. 3d ed. N.Y., 1907.
42543.62.50 Haraucourt, Edmond. Circé. Paris, 1907.
42543.62.33 Haraucourt, Edmond. Le peur. Paris, 1907.
38526.1.9 Hartmann, Hans. Guillaume des Autels (1529-1581?). Zürich, 1907.
37557.22.5 Heiss, Hanns. Studien und einige Beziehungen zur der deutschen und der französischen Literatur. Erlangen, 1907.
42543.63.9 Hermant, Abel. La discorde. Paris, 1907.
42541.18.6 Hermant, Abel. Les Jacobines. Paris, 1907.
42543.65.9 Hermant, Abel. Monsieur de Courpière. Paris, 1907.
38513.50 Hinriche, B. Le mystère de Saint Remi. Greifswald, 1907.
41571.1.9 Hugo, Victor. Histoire. Paris, 1907. 2v.
41574.14.25A Hugo, Victor. Victor Hugo's intellectual autobiography. N.Y., 1907.
Mol 608.17 Huszár, G. Molière et l'Espagne. Paris, 1907.
42576.65.29 Huysmans, Joris Karl. Les soeurs Vatard. Paris, 1907.
38513.14.5 Intemann, F. Das Verhältnis des "Nouveau Testament" von Geffroi de Paris zu der "Conception Notre-Dame von Wace". Greifswald, 1907.
39534.36.9 Janicki, J. Les comedies de Paul Scarron. Posen, 1907.
NEDL 38525.7.9 Jodelle, d'Estienne. Les amours and autres poésies. Paris, 1907.
38526.43.9 Jugé, C. Jacques Peletier du Mans. Paris, 1907.
38526.10.19 Juge, Clement. Nicolas Denisot du mans. Paris, 1907.
38587.15.10 Juyot, Joseph. Le poete Jean François Regnard en son chateau de Quelon. Paris, 1907.
FL 382.53 Kahn, Armand. Le théâtre social en France de 1870 à nos jours. Paris, 1907.
37543.64 Kastner, Leon Emile. Short history of French literature. N.Y., 1907.
39532.15.5 Kissenberth, Wilhelm. Antoine d'Hamilton; sein Leben und seine Werke. Berlin, 1907.
42544.2.5 Kistemaekers, Henry. La rivale. Paris, 1907.
42544.2.8 Kistemaekers, Henry. La rivale. Paris, 1907.
38576.21.30 Kretschmar, Amo. Madame de Villedieu. Weida, 1907.
38513.45 Kruse, Kurt. J. Michel: Das Mystère de la passion Jesu Crist. Greifswald, 1907.
37596.107 Langfors, Artur. Li regres nostre dame. Paris, 1907.
42576.41.4 La Bédollièrre, E.G. de. Histoire de la mère Michel et de son chat. Boston, 1907.
42514.18.9 Laboulaye, Edouard. Contes bleus. Boston, 1907.
41578.23 Lamartine, Alphonse de. Le manuscrit de ma mère. Paris, 1907.
41578.7.4 Lamartine, Alphonse de. Premières mèditations poétiques. Strasbourg, 1907?
41577.12 Lamartine, Alphonse de. Recueillements poétiques. Paris, 1907.
FL 376.21 Lancaster, H.C. The French tragi-comedy. Baltimore, 1907.
42576.46.22 Lapauze, Jeanne L. Madame l'ambassadrice. 10. éd. Paris, 1907.
37567.88A Lasserre, Pierre. Le romantisme français. Paris, 1907.
Htn 42576.68.25* La Vaudère, Jane de. Les prêtresses de Mylitta. Paris, 1907.
43687.90.3100 Lavclanet, François. Corinne, moeurs haïtiennes. Port-au-Prince, 1907.
42544.24.2.4 Lavedan, Henri. Le duel. Paris, 1907.
38526.10.18 Lechèvre, Frédéric. Le prince des libertins du XVIIe siècle: Jacques Vallée Des Barreaux, sa vie et ses poésies, 1599-1673. Paris, 1907.
FL 390.93 Lecomte, L.H. Histoire des théâtres de Paris. Le théâtre national, 1793-4. v.4. Paris, 1907.
FL 390.94 Lecomte, L.H. Histoire des théâtres de Paris. Les Nouveautés. v.5. Paris, 1907.
FL 6119.07.3 Lemaitre, J. Jean-Jacques Rousseau. N.Y., 1907.
42557.14.5.1 Lepelletier, E. Paul Verlaine; sa vie, son oeuvre. 2. éd. Paris, 1907.
42557.14.5 Lepelletier, E. Paul Verlaine. Paris, 1907.
42541.21.12 Leroux, G. La maison des juges. Paris, 1907.
42555.40.9 Le Roy, G. La chanson du pauvre. Paris, 1907.
40512.12.5A LeSage, Alain René. Adventures of Gil Blas of Santillane. v.2. London, 1907.
42576.46.35 Le Tersec, M.J.E.M. Âmes de soldats. Paris, 1907.
42544.34.19 Lorde, André de. Terre d'Epouvante. Paris, 1907.
38537.25.13 Loviot, L. Au pays de Rabelais. Paris, 1907.
37596.105 McKibben, G.F. The eructavit; an old French poem. Baltimore, 1907.
42545.3.50A Maeterlinck, Maurice. Chrysanthemums and other essays. N.Y., 1907.
42545.3.16.5 Maeterlinck, Maurice. Die Intelligenz der Blumen. Jena, 1907.

1907 - cont.

42545.3.14.5A Maeterlinck, Maurice. The measure of the hours. N.Y., 1907.
42545.3.3.7 Maeterlinck, Maurice. Pélléas et Mélisande. N.Y., 1907.
38576.21.29 Magne, Émile. Madame de Villedieu. Paris, 1907.
37567.89 Maillard, F. La cité des intellectuels. Paris, 1907.
43697.3.30 Mandelstamm, V. L'amoral. Paris, 1907.
43697.59.130 Mandin, L. Ombres voluptueuses. Paris, 1907.
42577.37 Marmier, Xavier. Les fiancés du Spitzberg. Oxford, 1907.
39531.28 Martin de Pinchesne, E. La chronique des Chapons et des Gélinottes du Mans. Paris, 1907.
42584.25.6 Martineau, H. Le roman scientifique d'Emile Zola. Paris, 1907.
43697.79.150 Mary, André. Les profondeurs de la forêt. Paris, 1907.
42577.2.30 Maupassant, Guy de. Mlle Fifi. Paris, 1907.
42577.4.29.5.5 Maupassant, Guy de. Sur l'eau. Paris, 1907.
42577.4.30.3 Maynial, É. Maupassant. Berlin, 1907.
42577.4.31.40 Maynial, Édouard. Maupassant. Berlin, 1907.
42577.4.31.35 Maynial, Édouard. La vie et l'oeuvre de Guy de Maupassant. 4. éd. Paris, 1907.
FL 6139.07.7 Mensch, E. Jean-Jacques Rousseau der Philosoph das Naturrechts. Berlin, 1907.
Mon 153.2 Merezhkovskiĭ, Dimitriĭ S. The life-work of Montaigne. London, 1907.
41555.20.7A Mérimée, Prosper. Carmen. Boston, 1907.
41555.2.10 Mérimée, Prosper. Contes et nouvelles. Oxford, 1907.
41568.15.6 Merlant, G. Sénancour. Paris, 1907.
38512.65 Mettlich, Josef. Die Schachpartie in der Prosabearbeitung der allegorisch-didaktischen Dichtung "Les eschez amoureux." Münster, 1907.
38585.5.9 Michaut, G. La Bérénice de Racine. Paris, 1907.
38528.17.9 Mojsisovics, E. von. Jean Passerat. Halle, 1907.
Mol 165.80 Molière, Jean Baptiste Poquelin. L'avare. Ann Arbor, 1907.
Mol 205.40 Molière, Jean Baptiste Poquelin. L'étourdi. London, 1907.
Mol 211.73 Molière, Jean Baptiste Poquelin. Les femmes savantes. London, 1907.
Mol 225.89 Molière, Jean Baptiste Poquelin. La jalousie du Barbouille. London, 1907.
Mol 60.31A Molière, Jean Baptiste Poquelin. Plays in French...A.R. Waller. Edinburgh, 1907. 3v.
Mon 19.07 Montaigne, Michel de. Essais de Montaigne. Paris, 1907-09. 4v.
Mon 30.13 Montaigne, Michel de. Essays. Florio. N.Y., 1907.
42555.61.9 Moréas, Jean. Poèmes et sylves 1886-96. N.Y., 1907.
42555.61.8 Moréas, Jean. Premières poésies 1883-86. 3e éd. N.Y., 1907.
37543.68 Mornet, D. Le sentiment de la nature en France. Paris, 1907.
37555.501 Mornet, Daniel. L'alexandrin français...XVIIIe siècle. Toulouse, 1907.
43702.89.2100 Mouézy-Eon, A. Les nuits du Hampton-Club. Paris, 1907.
37562.71 Müller, Martin. Minne und Dienst. Inaug. Diss. Marburg, 1907.
37588.8 La muse française...Jules Marsan, 1823-24. Paris, 1907-09. 2v.
41596.18.10 Musset, Alfred de. Les chefs-d'oeuvre lyriques. Paris, 1907.
41596.18.7.5 Musset, Alfred de. Comédies et proverbes. Paris, 1907.
41596.9 Musset, Alfred de. Correspondance. 1827-1857. Paris, 1907.
41596.9.2 Musset, Alfred de. Correspondance. 1827-1857. Paris, 1907. 2v.
41596.19.12.5 Musset, Alfred de. Novelleja. Helsinki, 1907.
41596.2.5 Le Mussetiste. Ann. 1-12. v.1-2. Paris, 1907-1918.
42545.45.50 Nigond, Gabriel. Nouveaux contes de la Limousine. Paris, 1907.
43709.3.130 Noailles, Anna E. Les éblouissements. Paris, 1907.
40592.60 Nolde, Elizabeth. Madame de Staël and Benjamin Constant. N.Y., 1907.
43709.77.1100 Normand, Gilles. Les barbacoles; moeurs scolaires et provinciales. Paris, 1907?
42568.23.16 Normandy, G. Jean Lorrain. (Paul Duval). Paris, 1907.
42578.29.8 Ohnet, Georges. La dixième muse. Paris, 1907.
42578.30.2 Ohnet, Georges. Le maître de forges. Paris, 1907?
38513.15.2 Oldörp, Bernhard. Untersuchungen über das Mystère "La vengeance nostre seigneur". Greifswald, 1907.
FL 398.49.5 Olivier, J.J. Henri-Louis Lekain. Paris, 1907.
37573.682 The Oxford book of French verse. Oxford, 1907.
37562.22.5 Paris, Gaston. Esquisse historique de la littérature française au moyen âge. Paris, 1907.
37595.42.6 Paris, Gaston. Récits extraits des poètes et prosateurs du Moyen Âge. 6. éd. Paris, 1907.
38513.24.5 Pathelin. Maistre Pierre Pathelin. Paris, 1907.
Htn 42587.40.9* Paul, Viteau. Sornettes. Paris, 1907.
Htn 37574.65* Payar, John. Flowers of France. The renaissance period. 16th century. London, 1907.
37574.65 Payne, John. Flowers of France. 16th century. London, 1907.
FL 363.12 Peirce, W.T. The bourgeois from Moliére to Beaumarchais. Columbus, Ohio, 1907.
42545.69.12 Petit-Favre. Le drapeau. Épernay, 1907.
43743.37.120 Polhes, Alban de. L'enfant du Temple. Paris, 1907.
43743.1.30 Porché, François. A chaque jour. Paris, 1907.
37578.94 Porchère, Samuel. Musée-dictionnaire d'originalités. 2. éd. Saint-Etienne, 1907.
42545.85 Porto-Riche, G. Théâtre d'amour. Paris, 1907.
40522.9.14.5 Prévost, Antoine F. Manon Lescaut. Strasbourg, 1907.
42556.26.6 Régnier, Henri de. Poèmes, 1887-1892. 6. éd. Paris, 1907-1925.
41574.28.5 Renouvier, Charles. Victor Hugo. 5. ed. Paris, 1907.
42556.27.65 Retté, Adolphe. Du diable à dieu. Paris, 1907.
42541.31.15 Richepin, J. La marjolaine. pt. 1-2. Paris, 1907.
42556.22.90 Richepin, Jean. Le chemineau. Paris, 1907.
42578.19.21 Rod, Edouard. L'incendie. Paris, 1907.
42578.19.7.9 Rod, Edouard. La vie privée de Michel Teissier. Paris, 1907.
38525.22.10 Ronsard, Pierre de. Amours de Cassandre. Paris, 1907.
38525.20.29A Ronsard, Pierre de. Les chefs d'oeuvres lyriques. Paris, 1907.
38525.20.9 Ronsard, Pierre de. Livret de folastries. Paris, 1907.
38525.88A Rotrou, Jean de. Saint Genest and Venceslas. Boston, 1907.
FL 6027.4 Rousseau, J.J. Bekenntnisse. Berlin, 1907.
FL 6017.3 Rousseau, J.J. Briefe in Answahl. Genf, 1907.
FL 6047.75 Rousseau, J.J. Emil. Přerově, 1907.
43757.98.140 Royère, Jean. Soeur de narcisse nue. Paris, 1907.

1907 - cont.

38526.47.30 Saint-Amant, Marc Antoine Gérard. Oeuvres. Paris, 1907.
FL 6119.07.5 Saint-Pierre, B. de. Jean-Jacques Rousseau, vie et ouvrages. Paris, 1907.
40575.16.10 Sainte-Beuve, Charles A. Profils anglais. 2. ed. London, 1907.
43761.49.150 Salmon, André. Les féeries. Paris, 1907.
42546.30.19 Sardou, Victorien. Madame Sans-Gêne. Paris, 1907.
42546.30.5 Sardou, Victorien. Théodora. Paris, 1907.
42586.63.3 Schemann, Ludwig. Die Gobineau-Sammlung zu Strassburg. Strassburg, 1907.
42586.63.6 Schemann, Ludwig. Graf Arthur Gobineau. Stuttgart, 1907.
37555.36 Scudéry, M. de. De la poésie française jusqu'à Henry Quatrième. Paris, 1907.
41596.4.12 Séché, L. Alfred de Musset. Paris, 1907. 2v.
40515.14.3 Ségur, Pierre. Julie de Lespinasse. Paris, 1907?
38546.36.12 Sévigné, Marie de R.C. Lettres choisies. Paris, 1907.
42577.4.6 Shippee, L.B. Stories from French realists. N.Y., 1907.
Mol 193.25 Siccardi, V. Les Don Juan célèbres. Asti, 1907.
37556.22.6 Sichel, J. Die Englische Literatur im Journal Etranger. Darmstadt, 1907.
37543.110 Sourian, Maurice. Moralistes et poètes. Paris, 1907.
37596.150 Spanke, J. Zwei altfranzösische Minnesinger. Inaug. Diss. Leipzig, 1907.
43780.5.280 Suarès, André. Bouclier du Zodiaque. Paris, 1907.
42557.5.10 Tailhade, Laurent. Poèmes élégiaques. Paris, 1907.
39545.21.3A Tallentyre, S.G. The friends of Voltaire. N.Y., 1907.
38526.2.30 Tenner, Fritz. François le Metel de Boisrobert als Dramatiker und Nachahmer des spanischen Dramas. Leipzig, 1907.
43788.5.140 Tharaud, Jérôme. La ville et les champs, 1870-71. 8e éd. Paris, 1907.
43788.22.100 Thémer. Coccinelle. Paris, 1907.
X Cg 38526.49.3 Théophile de Viau. Oeuvres. Paris, 1907.
37566.7.9 Thieme, Hugo P. Guide bibliographique de la littérature française de 1800 à 1906. Paris, 1907.
37530.65A Thième, Hugo Paul. Guide bibliographique de la littérature française de 1800 à 1906. Paris, 1907.
38537.25.8 Thuasne, L. Rabelais et Villon. Paris, 1907.
38537.25.5A Tilley, Arthur. François Rabelais. Philadelphia, 1907.
37543.72 Traccanaglia, G. Contributo allo studio dell'Italianismo in Francia. Lodi, 1907.
39532.33 Triaire, P. Lettres de Gui Patin, 1630-1672. Paris, 1907.
43816.1.30 Urville, G. d'. Spectacles et rêves. Paris, 1907.
43822.2.30 Vallery-Radot, Robert. Les grains de myrrhe, 1904-06. Paris, 1907.
43822.9.40 Vandervelden, Joseph. La rançon de l'âme. Gand, 1907.
42547.12.10 Veber, Pierre. Une passade. Paris, 1907.
43823.1.30 Vérola, P. Les nuages de pourpre. Paris, 1907.
42555.37.5.5 Vianey, Joseph. Les sources de Leconte de Lisle. Montpellier, 1907.
42557.21.4 Vielé-Griffin, F. Poèmes et poésies. 4. éd. Paris, 1907.
41564.22 Vigny, Alfred de. Héléna. Paris, 1907.
43824.2.58 Vivien, Renée. Chansons pour mon ombre. Paris, 1907.
43824.2.56 Vivien, Renée. Le Christ, Aphrodite et M. Pépin. Paris, 1907.
38542.2.15 Voiture, Vincent. Stances, sonnets, rondeaux et chansons. Paris, 1907.
39545.90 Voltaire, François Marie Arouet de. Contes choisis. London, 1907.
42576.15.100 Wassermann, J.S. Flaubert; ein Selbstporträt nach seinen Briefen. Berlin, 1907.
37555.617 Wentzel, Julius. Uber den Reim in der neueren französischen Dichtung. Borsdorf, 1907.
42541.56 Wolff, Pierre. Le ruisseau. Paris, 1907.
43858.1.31 Zamacois, Miguel. Les bouffons. Paris, 1907.
43858.1.30 Zamacois, Miguel. Redites-nous quelque chose! 4e éd. Paris, 1907.
42584.2.10 Zola, Emile. Correspondance. Paris, 1907. 2v.
42584.2 Zola, Emile. Correspondance. Lettres de jeunesse. Paris, 1907.
42584.1.9 Zola, Emile. Pages choisies des auteurs contemporains. Paris, 1907.
42584.23.39 Zola, Emile. Rome. N.Y., 1907.
42584.9.10 Zola, Emile. The sin of the abbé Mouret. London, 1907.
42556.17.9 Zyromski, Ernest. Sully-Prudhomme. Paris, 1907.

1908

42566.16.35 A. Daudet, 1840-1897. Paris, 1908?
37567.131.5 Amicis, Edmondo de. Ritratti letterari. Milano, 1908.
42512.4.9 Amis, Henri. Jours passés. Paris, 1908.
42553.42 Angellier, A. Les episodes. Paris, 1908-09. 2v.
42553.47.5 Angellier, A. Pages choisies de Auguste Angellier. Oxford, 1908.
42562.38.16 Ardel, H. L'été de Guillemette. 6e éd. Paris, 1908.
38526.48.20 Ashton, H. Du Bartas en Angleterre. Paris, 1908.
43529.3 Aulnoye, P. de. Le Lieutenant de Trémazan. Paris, 1908.
38557.21.5 Autour d'une brochure. Sept lettres...Bossuet. Paris, 1908.
43532.2.30 Avèze, André. Immoralité du Christianisme. Paris, 1908.
40596.23 Balzac, Honoré de. Balzac; sein Weltbild aus den Werken. Stuttgart, 1908.
40597.15.5 Balzac, Honoré de. Le cousin Pons. Paris, 1908.
40596.45 Balzac, Honoré de. Le député d'Arcis. Paris, 1908.
40596.13.132 Balzac, Honoré de. La comédie humaine. v.7A lost 1947. N.Y., 1908. 13v.
40597.32.6.10 Balzac, Honoré de. The wild ass's skin. London, 1908.
Htn 41522.2.68* Barbey d'Aurevilly, Jules. Les dédicaces a la main de J. Barbey d'Aurevilly. Paris, 1908.
Htn 41522.2* Barbey d'Aurevilly, Jules. Lettres à Trebutien. Paris, 1908. 2v.
41522.2.40 Barbey d'Aurevilly, Jules. Voyageurs et romanciers. Paris, 1908.
38527.54 Barrère, J. Estienne de La Boëtie contre Nicolas Machiavel. Bordeaux, 1908.
42563.18.75 Barrés, Maurice. Vingt-cinq années de vie littéraire. Paris, 1908.
43537.4.31 Bataille, Henry. Théâtre - Le Masque - La Marche nuptiale. Paris, 1908.
41522.4.9.2 Baudelaire, Charles. Oeuvres posthumes et correspondances inédites. Paris, 1908.
FL 383.130 Bayet, Jean. La société des auteurs et compositeurs dramatiques. Paris, 1908.
42563.21.60 Bazin, René. Le mariage de Mademoiselle Gimel. Paris, 1908.

1908 - cont.

42563.21.63 Bazin, René. Mémoires d'une veille fille. 18. éd. Paris, 1908.
42563.21.55 Bazin, René. The nun. N.Y., 1908.
42563.21.35 Bazin, René. Redemption. N.Y., 1908.
38513.65 Becker, Rudolf. Das "La Genesi de Nostre Dame Sainte Marie". Griefswald, 1908.
42542.29.16 Bernard, Tristan. Les jumeaux de Brighton. Paris, 1908.
42542.29.28 Bernard, Tristan. Théâtre. Paris, 1908-39. 7v.
42542.29.49 Bernstein, H. Bakkarat; ein Stück in drei Aufzügen. Leipzig, 1908.
42542.29.36 Bernstein, H. Israël. Paris, 1908.
42542.29.35 Bernstein, H. Samson. Paris, 1908.
40597.2.620 Bertaut, Jules. Balzac anecdotique. Paris, 1908.
42555.58.75 Bertrand, A. Catulle Mendès. Paris, 1908.
37556.52 Bethleem, L. Romans à lire et romans à proscrire. Cambrai, 1908.
40582.33 Beyle, Henri. Correspondance of Stendhal (1800-1842). Paris, 1908. 3v.
40582.31 Beyle, Henri. Journal de Stendhal. Paris, 1908.
40582.7.5 Beyle, Henri. Stendhal (Henri Beyle). 4. éd. Paris, 1908.
43540.2.30 Biollay, Maurice. L'affranchie. Paris, 1908.
37556.36.9 Biré, Edmond. Romans et romanciers contemporains. Paris, 1908.
42542.29.105 Bisson, Alexandre. Mariage d'etoile. Paris, 1908.
42563.23.24 Bloy, Léon. Celle qui pleure. Paris, 1908.
43544.1.30 Bonchamps, G. de. Vieux miroirs. Paris, 1908.
42554.15.2 Bonnard, Abel. Les histoires: La sous préfête; Le prince persan. Paris, 1908.
42554.15.3 Bonnard, Abel. Les royautés; poèmes. Paris, 1908.
42563.18.290 Bonnefon, Jean de. M. Auguste Maurice Barrès. Paris, 1908.
FL 383.132 Borbey d'Aurevilly, Jules. Le théâtre contemporain, 1866-1869. Paris, 1908-1909. 3v.
42542.30.17 Bouchor, Maurice. Cinq pièces, en un acte. Paris, 1908.
42542.30.29 Bouchor, Maurice. Il faut mourir. Paris, 1908.
43544.5.32 Boulenger, Marcel. Nos élégances. Paris, 1908.
42542.46 Bourget, Paul. Un divorce; pièce en trois actes. Paris, 1908.
42542.46.2 Bourget, Paul. Un divorce; pièce en trois actes. Paris, 1908.
42563.37.29A Bourget, Paul. L'émigré. Paris, 1908.
42563.37.46 Bourget, Paul. The weight of the name. Boston, 1908.
42563.39.20 Boylesve, René. Mon amour. 8. éd. Paris, 1908.
42563.39.25 Boylesve, René. Le parfum des îles Borromées. Paris, 1908.
42576.63.25.10A Brandes, G. Anatole France. N.Y., 1908.
42542.47.5.2 Brieux, Eugène. Le Berceau. Paris, 1908.
42542.47.21 Brieux, Eugène. Simone. Paris, 1908.
FL 6129.08 Buffenois, H. Causeries familial sur Jean-Jacques Rousseau. Paris, 1908.
42542.47.76.2 Caillavet, G.A. L'amour veille. Paris, 1908.
42542.47.77 Caillavet, G.A. Le roi. Paris, 1908.
42542.47.77.5 Caillavet, G.A. Le roi. 22. éd. Paris, 1908.
FL 398.11 Capon, G. Les Vestries Vestris family. Paris, 1908.
42542.48.9 Capus, Alfred. Les deux hommes. Paris, 1908.
42542.48.45 Carré, Michel. La courtisane de Corinthe. Paris, 1908.
38511.23.5 Champion, Pierre. Charles d'Orléans joueur d'echecs. Paris, 1908.
42547.15 Chapoutot, H. Villiers de l'Isle Adam. Paris, 1908.
40586.14.3.5 Chateaubriand, F.A.R. Atala, René, Le dernier Abencérage. 3. ed. London, 1908.
40586.20.40.3 Chateaubriand, F.A.R. Os martyres. 3. ed. Lisboa, 1908. 2v.
37555.550 Chatelain, Henri. Recherches sur le vers français au XVe siècle. Paris, 1908.
40526.4.25 Chénier, André. Les chefs d'oeuvre lyriques. 2e éd. N.Y., 1908.
40526.4.5 Chénier, André. Oeuvres complètes. Paris, 1908-20. 3v.
42587.36.15 Chenin, Emile. Le rouet d'ivoire; enfances lorrains. Paris, 1908?
43552.25.4130 Chevalier, Adrien. Au gré de l'heure. Paris, 1908.
40517.44 Choderlos de Laclos, Pierre A.F. Poesies. Paris, 1908.
37576.560.22 Claretie, J. Prince Zilah. N.Y., 1908.
39544.50A Collins, J.C. Voltaire, Montesquieu and Rousseau in England. London, 1908.
Mon 113.3 Compayré, G. Montaigne and education of the judgement. N.Y., 1908.
42542.53.15 Coolus, R. Les rendez-vous strasbourgeois, et autres. Paris, 1908.
42565.62 Corday, Michel. Mariage de demain. Paris, 1908.
38575.27.4 Corneille, Pierre. Le Cid. 13. éd. Paris, 1908.
40586.35 La correspondance de Chateaubriand avec sa femme. Paris, 1908.
42554.18.5 Crouzet-Benaben, J. Jean Lahor. Paris, 1908.
37565.42 Cushing, Mary G. Pierre le tourneur. [Translator]. N.Y., 1908.
39533.20.10 Cyrano de Bergerac. Le pedant joué. Paris, 1908.
42542.60.9 Dartigues, L. Répudiée. Paris, 1908.
42566.21.20 Daudet, Alphonse. Monday tales. N.Y., 1908.
39535.33.5 Dauxménil. Mémoires pour servir à l'histoire. Paris, 1908.
38511.30 Débat de l'ame et du corps. Basel, 1908.
42542.61.9 Decourcelle, P. Service secret. Paris, 1908.
40516.25.30 Defrance, Eugène. La maison de Madame Gourdan. Paris, 1908.
43566.48.160 Delarue-Mardrus, Lucie. La figure de proue. Paris, 1908.
37556.21.30 Delfour, L.C. La presse contre l'église. 2. éd. Paris, 1908.
39564.8.2 Diderot, Denis. Oeuvres choisies. Paris, 1908. 2v.
42542.65.19 Donnay, Maurice. Ailleurs. Paris, 1908.
42542.65.18 Donnay, Maurice. Chères madames. Paris, 1908.
42542.65.16A Donnay, Maurice. La patronne. Paris, 1908.
FL 382.57.15 Doumic, René. Le théâtre nouveau. Paris, 1908.
42587.70.50 Dreyfus, Robert. Alexandre Weill. Paris, 1908.
37576.560.32 Droz, Gustave A.G. Monsieur, madame et bébé. N.Y., 1908.
X Cg 38526.48.24 Du Bartas, Guillaume de Salluste. The divine weeks of Josuah Sylvester. Waukesha, 1908.
38526.6.5 Du Bellay, Joachim. Oeuvres poétiques. Paris, 1908-1931. 7v.
42576.65.13.145 Du Bourg, Antoine. Huysmans intime. Paris, 1908.
41530.300 Dumas, Alexandre. Works. v.1, 3-7. N.Y., 1908.
43576.53.100 Dumas, Roger. Hélène. Paris, 1908.
42554.29.200 Dupuy, E. Poèmes. Paris, 1908.

Chronological Listing

1908 - cont.

Mol 605.6 Enderlein, Erich. Zur Bedeutungsentwicklung des bestimmten Artikels im Französischen mit besonderer Molières. Marburg, 1908.
42554.30.9 Errera, Léo. Recueil d'oeuvres. v.3. Bruxelles, 1908.
42565.74A Favre de Coulevain, Hélène. Au coeur de la vie. 69. éd. Paris, 1908.
37562.90 Fellinger, F. Das Kind in der altfranzösischen Literatur. Göttingen, 1908.
42576.15.14 Fischer, E.W. Etudes sur Flaubert inédit. Leipzig, 1908.
42576.23.4 Flaubert, Gustave. La première tentation de Saint-Antoine. Paris, 1908.
42543.42 Flers, Robert de. L'eventail. Paris, 1908.
42576.36.11.15 Fleuriot, Zenaide Marie A. Loyauté. 5. éd. Paris, 1908.
42564.55.9 Fleury, Jules. Un coin de littérature sous le second empire, Sainte-Beuve et Champfleury. Paris, 1908.
43611.62.100 Fons, Pierre. La divinité quotidienne; poèmes. Paris, 1908.
38562.18.9A Fontenelle, B. Le B. de. Histoire des Oracles. Paris, 1908.
43611.1.25.9 Fort, Paul. Ballades françaises. Ile-de-France. IX. Paris, 1908.
42576.62.21.5A France, Anatole. L'île des pingouins. Paris, 1908.
42576.62.21.8 France, Anatole. L'île des pingouins. Paris, 1908.
42576.62.13.5 France, Anatole. Le jardin d'Épicure. 41. éd. Paris, 1908?
FL 376.22 Friedrich, Ernst. Die Magie im Französischen Theater 16. und 17. Jahrhunderts. Leipzig, 1908.
39531.17.9 Furetière, A. The poésies diverses. Baltimore, 1908.
42571.34.7 Gaboriau, Emile. File no. 113. N.Y., 1908.
42571.32.5 Gaboriau, Emile. Monsieur Lecoq. N.Y., 1908.
43616.41.100 Gaillard de Champris, Henry. Sur quelques idéalistes. Paris, 1908.
41584.50.15 Gaillardet, Frédéric. La tour de Nesle. Paris, 1908.
38527.37.50 Galtier, Octave. Etienne Dolet. Paris, 1908.
41542.5.7 Gautier, Théophile. Stories. N.Y., 1908.
42543.45 Gavault, Paul. Le bonheur de Jacqueline. Paris, 1908.
42543.45.65 Gavault, Paul. Napoléon malgré lui. Paris, 1908.
42543.45.40 Gavault, Paul. La petite Madame Dubois. Paris, 1908.
42543.46 Geffroy, Gustave. L'apprentie. Paris, 1908.
FL 398.32 George, Marguerite Joséphine Weimer. Mémoires inédits. Paris, 1908.
43617.4.62 Géraldy, Paul. La comédie des familles. Paris, 1908.
43617.4.48 Géraldy, Paul. La fantaisie. Paris, 1908.
43617.4.30 Géraldy, Paul. Les petites ames. Paris, 1908.
Htn 43709.3.800* Gillouin, René. La Comtesse Mathieu de Noailles. Paris, 1908.
FL 6113.5 Girardin, Fernand. Iconographie de Jean-Jacques Rousseau. Paris, 1908.
42586.65.5 Gobineau, Arthur de. Die Rénaissance. Strassburg, 1908.
43625.3.63 Gourmont, Rémy de. Couleurs. Paris, 1908.
FL 6119.08.5 Graham, H. Grey. J.J. Rousseau; ego zhin' i...sreda. Moskva, 1908.
42576.37.40 Grave, Jean. Terre libre. Paris, 1908.
X Cg FL 6129.08.3 Gribblo, F. Rousseau and the women he loved. N.Y., 1908.
40536.32 Günther, L. L'oeuvre dramatique de Sedaine. Thèse. Paris, 1908.
38512.115A Guillaume de Machaut. Oeuvres. Paris, 1908-11. 3v.
43628.1.34F Guitry, Sacha. Le scandale de Monte-Carlo. Paris, 1908.
37596.128 Gutbier, J. Bruchstack einer lateinischen mit französischen Sätzen. Halle, 1908.
42557.20.230 Haessler, E. Paul Verlaine. Finsterwalde, 1908.
43631.1.30 Halary, P. Du vallon au sommet. Paris, 1908.
39532.13.12 Hamilton, Anthony. Memoires of Count Grammont. Edinburgh, 1908. 2v.
42543.62.35 Haraucourt, Edmond. L'ame nue. Paris, 1908.
42543.62.36 Haraucourt, Edmond. Seul. Paris, 1908.
42576.65.9.5 Harry, Myriam (pseud.). L'île de volupté. Paris, 1908?
V42576.65.5.5 Harry, Myriam (pseud.). Jeruzsálem meghóditasa. Budapest, 1908. 2v.
Mol 608.18 Heller, Kurt. Michel de Montaigne's Einfluss auf die Aerztestücke Molière's. Diss. Jena, 1908.
38525.34.17 Henke, Karl. Syntaktische Untersuchungen zu Guillaume Bouchets "Serées". Marburg, 1908.
37555.29.12 Hensel W. Die Vögel in der provenzalischen und nordfranzösischen Lyrik des Mittelalters. Erlangen, 1908.
42554.55.25 Heredia, J.M. de. Los trofeos. Madrid, 1908.
37562.2.9 Hertel, Adolf. Verzauberte Örtlichkeiten und Gegenstände in der altfranzösischen erzählenden Dachtung. Hannover, 1908.
41564.40 Hoegen, W. Die Menschheitsdichtungen der französichen Romantiker Vigny-Lamartine-Hugo. Darmstadt, 1908.
41573.16 Hugo, Victor. The laughing man. London, 1908.
41573.23.6 Hugo, Victor. Notre Dame de Paris. London, 1908.
41573.23.7 Hugo, Victor. Notre Dame de Paris. London, 1908?
41573.26.10 Hugo, Victor. Ruy Blas. Paris, 1908?
41573.17 Hugo, Victor. The toilers of the sea. London, 1908.
41573.54A Hugo, Victor. Works. N.Y., 1908. 7v.
42576.65.19 Huysmans, Joris Karl. Croquis parisiens. Paris, 1908.
42576.65.22 Huysmans, Joris Karl. De tout. Paris, 1908.
42576.65.26 Huysmans, Joris Karl. En ménage. Paris, 1908.
42576.65.28.2 Huysmans, Joris Karl. Là-bas. Paris, 1908.
42576.65.23 Huysmans, Joris Karl. Trois eglises et trois primitifs. Paris, 1908.
43638.99.105 Huzard, A. de B. (Mme.). Princesses de science. 26. éd. Paris, 1908.
37567.9.7 James, Henry. French poets and novelists. London, 1908.
40515.15 Jebb, Camilla. A star of the salons. London, 1908.
40515.15.4 Jebb, Camilla. A star of the salons. N.Y., 1908.
42576.65.13.7 Jørgensen, Johannes. J.K. Huysmans. Mainz, 1908.
40532.34 Jones, Florence N. Beaumarchais and Plautus the sources of the Barbier de Séville. Chicago, 1908.
40556.36 Joseph de Maistre et Blacas. Paris, 1908.
39566.28 Kassner, R. Denis Diderot. Berlin, 1908.
42544.2.8.9 Kistemaekers, Henry. Monsieur Dupont Chauffeur. Paris, 1908.
Mol 611.5 Klatt, W. Molières Bezichungen zum Stirtendrama. Berlin, 1908.
Mol 611.5.5 Klatt, W. Molières Bezichungen zum Stirtendrama. Diss. Göttingen, 1908.
FL 6139.08.5 Krausbauer, Theodor. Rousseaus Pädogogik und ihre nach, bis auf die Neuzeit. 3. ed. Minden, 1908.
37567.114 Küchler, W. Französische Romantik. Heidelberg, 1908.
37596.52.5 Kühlhorn, G. Das Verhältnis der Art d'amors les Jacques d'Amiens zu Ovido Ars amatoria. Inaug. Diss. Weida, 1908.
42544.26.5.8 Labiche, Eugène. Le voyage de Monsieur Perrichon. Boston, 1908.

1908 - cont.

39544.52 Lachèore, F. Voltaire mourant. Paris, 1908.
43687.2.35 Lafon, André. Poèmes provinciaux. Roubaix, 1908.
Mol 612.17 Langer, Carl. Molières Ideen über die Frauenerzichung. Inaug. Diss. Berlin, 1908.
37556.24.5 Langlois, E. Nouvelles françaises inédites du 15e siècle. Paris, 1908.
37543.38.2 Lanson, Gustave. Histoire de la littérature française. 10. éd. Paris, 1908.
38543.10.18 La Rochefoucauld, François. Les maximes. 2. éd. Londres, 1908.
38526.27.5.55 La Taille, Jean de. Jean de La Taille und sein Saül le furieux. Leipzig, 1908.
FL 397.11 Lavalley, G. La censure théâtrale à Caen en l'an VII. Caen, 1908.
42544.23.6 Lavedan, Henri. Bon an, Malan. Paris, 1908. 7v.
42576.42.11 Le Barillier, Berthe. Le journal de Marguerite Plantin. Paris, 1908.
43688.14.3130 Leclèrc, Tristan. Le valet de coeur. Paris, 1908.
FL 390.95 Lecomte, L.H. Histoire des théâtres de Paris. Les jeux gymniques. v.6. Paris, 1908.
FL 390.96 Lecomte, L.H. Histoire des théâtres de Paris. Les variétés Amus. v.7. Paris, 1908.
41555.43 Lefebvre, Alphonse. La célèbre inconnue de Prosper Mérimée. Paris, 1908.
NEDL 38585.14.5 Lemaitre, J. Jean Racine. 15e éd. Paris, 1908.
38585.14.7 Lemaitre, Jules. Jean Racine. 21e éd. Paris, 1908.
X Cg 38585.14.7 Lemaitre, Jules. Jean Racine. 21e éd. Paris, 1908.
43688.61.140 Lenormand, Henri René. Le réveil de l'instinct. Paris, 1908.
42584.25.9 Lepelletier, E. Emile Zola. Paris, 1908.
43688.1.30.5 Leroux, Gaston. The mystery of the yellow room. N.Y., 1908.
43688.1.30.6 Leroux, Gaston. The mystery of the yellow room. N.Y., 1908.
40512.58.15 LeSage, Alain René. The bachelor of Salamanca. N.Y., 1908.
40587.25 Lescure, M.F.A. de. Chateaubriand. Paris, 1908.
40515.12 Lespinasse, J.J.E. de. Die Liebesbriefe der Julie, 1773-1776. München, 1908.
FL 394.115 Lollée, F. La maison de Molière. Paris, 1908.
42544.34.25.20 Lorde, André de. Une leçon à la salpétrière. Tableau dramatique. Paris, 1908.
37573.11.5A Lucas, St. John. The Oxford book of French verse, XIII-XIX centuries. Oxford, 1908.
42545.3.47 Maeterlinck, Maurice. Interior. London, 1908.
42545.3.3.6A Maeterlinck, Maurice. Pélléas et Mélisande. N.Y., 1908.
42545.5 Manquat, Maurice. Tout se pays. Paris, 1908.
41539.8 Mansfield, M.F. Dumas' Paris,. Boston, 1908.
Mol 713.11.5 Mantzius, K. Molière. Paris, 1908.
41578.51A Marechal, Christian. Le véritable "Voyage en Orient" de Lamartine d'après manuscrits. Paris, 1908.
42576.76.38 Margueritte, Paul. L'autre. Paris, 1908.
42576.76.4 Margueritte, Paul. Souvenirs de jeunesse. Paris, 1908.
42545.9.22 Martel de Janville, S.G. Le mariage de Chiffon. Paris, 1908.
42587.19.75 Médins, F. L'arnice qui souffre. Paris, 1908.
38576.12.39 Meinel, Friedrich. Samuel Chappuzeau. Inaug. Diss. Borna, 1908.
38587.15 Menasci, G. Nuovi saggi di letterature francese. Regnard. Livorno, 1908.
NEDL 42555.58.10 Mendès, Catulle. Théâtre en prose. Paris, 1908.
42576.15.85 Merezhkovskii, D.S. The life-work of Flaubert. London, 1908.
41555.29.10 Mérimée, Prosper. Mateo Falcone and other stories. London, 1908.
42545.21.5 Méry, J. La bête féroce. Paris, 1908.
43699.3.30 Mille, Pierre. Barnavaux et quelques femmes. 8. éd. Paris, 1908.
42545.28.7A Mirbeau, Octave. Le foyer. Paris, 1908.
Mol 165.82 Molière, Jean Baptiste Poquelin. L'avare. Ann Arbor, 1908.
Mol 165.83 Molière, Jean Baptiste Poquelin. L'avare. Strasbourg, 1908?
Mol 181.30 Molière, Jean Baptiste Poquelin. Dépit amoureux. London, 1908.
Mol 212.3 Molière, Jean Baptiste Poquelin. Les femmes savantes. N.Y., 1908.
Mol 245.96 Molière, Jean Baptiste Poquelin. Le misanthrope. London, 1908.
NEDL Mol 60.32 Molière, Jean Baptiste Poquelin. Molière. N.Y., 1908. 2v.
Mol 261.40 Molière, Jean Baptiste Poquelin. Sganarelle. London, 1908.
Mol 269.70.5 Molière, Jean Baptiste Poquelin. Tartuf. A. Mascras. Barcelona, 1908.
Mol 39.08 Molière, Jean Baptiste Poquelin. Théâtre choisi. 6e éd. Paris, 1908.
Mon 30.14 Montaigne, Michel de. Essays. Florio. London, 1908. 3v.
Mon 35.10 Montaigne, Michel de. Gesammelte Schriften. München, 1908. 8v.
Mon 35.9 Montaigne, Michel de. Versuche. Berlin, 1908.
42555.60.9 Montesquiou-Fezensac, Robert de. Assemblée de notables. Paris, 1908.
42555.60.12 Montesquiou-Fezensac, Robert de. Les paons. Paris, 1908.
37567.105 Moréas, J. Esquisses et souvenirs. Paris, 1908.
42577.14.40 Murger, Henry. Le bonhomme jadis. Paris, 1908.
41596.22.75 Musset, Alfred de. The confession of a child of the century. N.Y., 1908.
41596.18.45 Musset, Alfred de. Le théâtre d'Alfred de Musset. Strasbourg, 1908.
42545.45.10 Népoty, L. L'Oreille. Fendue. Paris, 1908.
40526.21.80 Nietzelt, Otto. La Grange-Chancel als Tragiken. Inaug. Diss. Leipzig, 1908.
Mon 124.1.7A Norton, Grace. Montaigne (influence of). Boston, 1908.
Mon 124.1.8A Norton, Grace. The spirit of Montaigne. Boston, 1908.
41578.57 Olliver, M.T.E. Valentine de Lamartine. Paris, 1908.
43723.51.110 Ollone, Charles. Heures chantantes. Paris, 1908. 2v.
37595.36.13 Pavla, Saint. La vie Sainte Paule. v.19. Halle, 1908.
39544.48A Pellissier, G. Voltaire, philosophe. Paris, 1908.
X Cg 38546.24 Perrier, E. Scudéry et sa soeur à Marseille. Valence, 1908.
42545.69.9 Petitdidier, L.E. Théâtre légendaire. Paris, 1908.
43667.1.835 Pilon, Edmond. Francis Jammes et le sentiment de la nature. Paris, 1908.
41555.40 Pinvert, L. Sur Mérimée. Paris, 1908.

1908 - cont.

	38514.57.4	Pisan, Christine de. The book of the duke of true lovers. London, 1908.
	38514.57.4.5	Pisan, Christine de. The book of the duke of true lovers. N.Y., 1908.
	37574.525A	La poésie symboliste. Paris, 1908.
Htn	FL 398.70PF*	Porel, Paul. Souvenirs d'un vieil homme de théâtre. Paris, 1908.
	42545.86	Porto-Riche, G. Amoureuse. Paris, 1908.
	42545.95	Pottecher, M. Le château de Hans. Paris, 1908.
	42578.31.59	Prévost, Marcel. La fausse bourgeoise. Paris, 1908.
	42578.31.54	Prévost, Marcel. Histoire de la dame potelée. Paris, 1908.
	42578.31.44	Prévost, Marcel. Lettres à Françoise mariée. 44. éd. Paris, 1908.
	38514.75	Le prisonnier desconforté. Paris, 1908.
	FL 6139.08.10	Puibaraud, L. Le gouvernement direct chez J.J. Rousseau. Poitiers, 1908.
	42515.74	Quinet, Edgar. France et Allemagne. Oxford, 1908.
	38585.20.9.5	Racine, Jean. Athalie. London, 1908.
	38521.25.5	Radouant, R. Guillaume du Vair. Paris, 1908.
	37596.17.3	Raoul de Houdenc. Songs d'enfer...La voie de paradis. Photoreproduction. Paris, 1908.
	38544.27.530A	Rea, Lilian. The life and times of Marie Madeleine countess of La Fayette. London, 1908.
	42556.26.24	Régnier, Henri de. La peur de l'amour. 6. éd. Paris, 1908.
	42556.26.26	Régnier, Henri de. Les scrupules de Sganarelle. 5. éd. Paris, 1908.
	42556.27.84	Retté, Adolphe. Le régne de la bête. Paris, 1908.
	37556.50A	Reynier, G. Le roman sentimental avant l'Astrée. Paris, 1908.
	42556.22.82	Richepin, Jean. La belle au bois dormant. Paris, 1908.
	Mol 618.4	Rigal, E. Molière. Paris, 1908. 2v.
	42587.55.11	Rivoire, André. Le bon roi Dagobert. Paris, 1908.
	42578.19.24	Rod, Edouard. Aloÿse Valérien. Paris, 1908.
	40588.7.20	Rösler, G. Beiträge zur Kenntnis von Mme. Cottin. Inaug. Diss. Leipzig, 1908.
	43757.50.193	Rolland, Romain. Jean-Christophe à Paris; La foire sur la place. 4e éd. Paris, 1908.
	43757.50.203	Rolland, Romain. Jean-Christophe à Paris: Antoinette. 3. éd. Paris, 1908.
	42556.30.85	Romeuf, L. de. Edouard Schuré. Paris, 1908.
	38525.20.5	Ronsard, Pierre de. Selected poems. Oxford, 1908.
	FL 363.10	Rottenbacher, L. Die französischen Virginia. Dramen. Dessau, 1908.
	FL 6007.5	Rousseau, J.J. Jean-Jacques Rousseau: in seinen Werken. Stuttgart, 1908.
	42587.56.105	Saint-Aulaire, Auguste. Un prosélyte de l'amour. Paris, 1908.
	41556.35	Salomon, Michel. Charles Nodier et le groupe romantique. Paris, 1908.
	39534.43	Sansrefus, G. Gaultier Garguille. Caen, 1908.
	42546.30.6	Sardou, Victorien. L'affaire des poisons. Paris, 1908.
	42546.30.7	Sardou, Victorien. Fédora. Paris, 1908.
	37543.253	Sauvebois, Gaston. Après le naturalisme. Paris, 1908.
	39534.34	Scarron, Paul. Poésies diverses. Paris, 1908.
	38526.48.39	Schelandre, J. de. Tyr et Sidon ou Les funestes amours de Belcar. Paris, 1908.
	42545.3.410	Schlaf, J. Maurice Maeterlinck. Berlin, 1908.
	37597.19.9	Schneider, Oskar. Die Verbalformen bei Wace. Halle, 1908.
	38513.14.9	Schroeder, R. Handschriftenverhältnis und Text der altfranzösischen Achtsilbnerredaktionen der "Heirat Mariae". Greifswald, 1908.
	42556.30.3	Schuré, Edouard. Femmes inspiratrices et poètes annonciateurs. Paris, 1908.
	37555.29.9	Schwarzkopf, F. Coulanges, Chanlien und La Fare. Leipzig, 1908.
	40515.50	Schwenke, Walter. Florians Beziehungen zur deutschen Literatur. Weida, 1908.
	FL 385.80	Séché, Alphonse. L'evolution du théâtre comtemporain. Paris, 1908.
	41555.47	Séché, L. Hortense Allart de Méritens. Paris, 1908.
	38513.3.5	Seefeldt, P. Studien über die...Fassungen...des ältesten Mystère français de Saint Barbe en deux journées. Griefswald, 1908.
NEDL	37567.91	Seillière, E. Le mal romantique. Paris, 1908.
	38521.71	Sesportes, Philippe. Le mariage. Texte de 1573, 1583, 1585, 1586. Macon, 1908.
	42556.33	Severin, F. Poèmes. Paris, 1908.
	FL 6002.908	Simond, C. Jean-Jacques Rousseau. Paris, 1908.
	38512.70	Snavely, G.E. Aesopic fables in the Mireoir historial of Jehan de Vignay. Baltimore, 1908.
	38514.56.4	Soderhjelm, W. Les inspirateurs des Quinze joyes de mariage. n.p., 1908-09.
	42546.46	Sorbets, G. La Rencontre. Paris, 1908.
	42554.28.15	Sorel, A.E. Auguste Dorchain. Paris, 1908.
	42516.17	Sorel, Albert. Pages normandes. Paris, 1908.
	43776.41.160	Spire, André. Versets et vous riez. Poèmes juifs. 2. éd. Paris, 1908.
	37556.36.5	Stephens, Winifred. French novelists of today. London, 1908.
	37563.6	Sturel, R. Jacques Amyot. Paris, 1908.
	37567.66.2	Symons, Arthur. The symbolist movement in literature. N.Y., 1908.
	42557.5.45	Tailhade, Laurent. La corne et l'épée. Paris, 1908.
	42583.33.16	Theuriet, André. Colette. 12. éd. Paris, 1908.
	42547.4.9	Thurner, Georges. Le passe partour. Paris, 1908.
	37564.55	Tilley, Arthur Augustus. From Montaigne to Molière. London, 1908.
	42578.51.10.2	Tinayre, Marcelle. Avant l'amour. Paris, 1908.
	42578.51.15	Tinayre, Marcelle. Hellé. 9. éd. Paris, 1908?
	42578.51.25	Tinayre, Marcelle. L'oiseau d'orage. 3. éd. Paris, 1908?
	42578.51.5	Tinayre, Marcelle. La vie amoureuse de François Barbazauges. 15. éd. Paris, 1908?
	42578.52.60	Tinseau, Léon de. Le port d'attache. 6. éd. Paris, 1908.
	42547.5	Trarieux, Gabriel. L'alibi. Paris, 1908.
	37597.15.6	Ulrich, Alfred. Über das Verhältnis von Wace's Roman. Erlangen, 1908.
	42547.12	Veber, Pierre. Qui perd gagne, d'après le roman d'A. Capus. Paris, 1908.
Htn	38575.22.5*	Verdier, P. Additions à la bibliographie Cornelienne. Rouen, 1908.
	42557.11.5	Verhaeren, Emile. Les forces tumultueuses. Paris, 1908.
	42557.11.6	Verhaeren, Emile. Les villes tentaculaires. Paris, 1908.
	42557.15.8	Verlaine, Paul. Choix de poésies. Paris, 1908.

1908 - cont.

	38557.1	Verlaque, V. Bibliographie raisonnée des oeuvres de Bossuet. Paris, 1908.
	42584.50	Vernet, Nancy. Dix ans de coulisses. Paris, 1908.
	Mol 825.14	Vialard, M.J. Essai médical sur Molière. Bordeaux, 1908.
	42576.57.8	Viaud, Julien. Ramuntcho. Paris, 1908.
	41564.24.8	Vigny, Alfred de. Chatterton. Oxford, 1908.
	43824.1.30	Vilade, J. de. Sur un thème éternel. Paris, 1908.
	43824.49.160	Vildrac, Charles. Images et mirages. Paris, 1908.
	Mon 132.5.2	Villey, P. Les livres d'histoire moderne utilisés par Montaigne. Paris, 1908.
	Mon 132.5	Villey, P. Les livres d'histoire moderne utilisés par Montaigne. Thèse. Paris, 1908.
NEDL	Mon 132.5.6	Villey, P. Les sources et l'évolution des essais de Montaigne. Paris, 1908.
	Mon 132.5.5	Villey, P. Les sources et l'évolution des essais de Montaigne. v.1-2. Thèse. Paris, 1908.
	38526.27.5.55.1	Werner, Andreas. Jean de La Taille und sein Saül le furieux. Naumburg, 1908.
	40555.31	Wittmer, L. Charles de Villers, 1765-1815. Genève, 1908.
	FL 372.18.5	Young, Carl. Contributions to the history of liturgical drama at Rouen. Chicago, 1908.
	FL 6139.08	Zabel, E. Die soziale Bedeutung von J.J. Rousseaus Erziehungstheorie. Quedlinburg, 1908.
	43858.1.33	Zamacois, Miguel. The jesters. N.Y., 1908.

1909

	43519.11.100	Aicard, Jean. La poesie. Paris, 1909.
	43537.4.85	Amiel, Denys. Henry Bataille. Paris, 1909.
	38568.903	L'amour de Madeleine. Paris, 1909?
	41578.68.25	Artensi, M. Lamartine, le poète et l'Italie. Città de Castello, 1909.
NEDL	38526.8.12	Auge-Chiquet, Mathieu. La vie, les idées et l'oeuvres de Baif. Paris, 1909.
	38526.8.5	Baif, Jean Antoine de. Les amours. Paris, 1909.
	40596.13.130	Balzac, Honoré de. La comédie humaine. N.Y., 1909. 7v.
	40597.14.70	Balzac, Honoré de. Short stories. Little French masterpieces. N.Y., 1909.
	37566.13.20	Barbey d'Aurevilly, J.A. Philosophes et écrivains. Paris, 1909.
	41522.2.55	Barbey d'Aurevilly, Jules. Critiques diverses. 3. éd. Paris, 1909.
	41522.1.3.10	Barbey d'Aurevilly, Jules. Poussieres. Paris, 1909.
	43537.4.75	Bataille, Henry. Le scandale. Paris, 1909.
	42513.25.80	Baudry, Joséphine. Une Bretonne de lettres; la comtesse Jégou Du Laz. Heunebont, 1909.
	42563.21.71.5A	Bazin, René. La barrière. Paris, 1909.
	42563.21.40	Bazin, René. This, my son. N.Y., 1909.
	42524.41	Beaufils, Edouard. René Doumic. Paris, 1909.
	40532.5.3	Beaumarchais, Pierre A.C. de. Le barbier de Séville. Ann Arbor, 1909.
	37595.18.5	Bedier, J. Les chansons de croisade. Paris, 1909.
	42542.29	Beniére, L. Papillon, dit Lyonnais le Juste. Paris, 1909.
	41592.34	Béranger, P.J. de. Oeuvres inédites. Paris, 1909.
	42542.29.28.160	Bernard, Tristan. Contes de Caliban. Paris, 1909.
	42557.20.290	Bersancourt, Albert de. Paul Verlaine. Paris, 1909.
	42542.29.80	Berton, Pierre. La rencontre. Paris, 1909.
	43543.88.110	Blum, Léon. Nouvelles conversations de Goethe avec Eckermann, 1887-1900. Paris, 1909.
	42542.37	Bois, Jules. La furie. Paris, 1909.
	37558.26	Boissier, G. L'académie française. Paris, 1909.
	38576.11.35	Boissière, G. Urbain Chevreau, 1613-1701 Moit, 1909.
	42563.36.55	Bordeaux, Henry. La croisée des chemins. 49. éd. Paris, 1909.
	42563.36.50	Bordeaux, Henry. Portraits de femmes et d'enfants. Paris, 1909.
	38557.37	Bossuet, J.B. Correspondance. v.1-9,11-14. Paris, 1909-23. 12v.
	FL 390.82	Bossuet, Pierre. Histoire des théâtres nationaux. Paris, 1909.
	41593.29.3.56	Boulenger, Jacques. Marceline Desbordes-Valmore d'après ses papiers inédits. Paris, 1909?
	43544.6.30	Boulenger, Jacques. Ondine Valmore. Paris, 1909.
	42563.39.30	Boylesve, René. Le meilleur ami. Paris, 1909.
	39544.65	Brandes, Georg. Voltaire in seinem Verhältnis zu Friedrich dem Grossen. Berlin, 1909.
	42557.20.310	Braun, Thomas. Paul Verlaine en Ardennes. Paris, 1909.
	42542.47.22	Brieux, Eugène. Suzette. Paris, 1909.
	38576.11.3	Brueys, D.A. de. L'avocat Pathelin. N.Y., 1909.
	38514.4	Bruyant, Jean. Le livre du Chastel de labour. n.p., 1909.
	FL 6119.09	Buffenoir, H. Le prestige de Jean-Jacques Rousseau. Paris, 1909.
	42542.48.12A	Capus, Alfred. L'oiseau blessé. Paris, 1909.
	40588.7.10	Cardaillac, Ferdnand de. Madame Cottin à Bigoire. Paris, 1909.
	43550.3.30	Castanier, Prosper. El loto del Ganges. Paris, 1909.
	43550.83.100	Castiaux, P. Joie vagabonde. Paris, 1909.
	42554.18.3	Cazalis, Henry. Oeuvres choisies, précédées d'une biographie. Paris, 1909.
	FL 6139.09.5A	Champion, E. Jean-Jacques Rousseau et la révolution Française. Paris, 1909.
	37574.13	La chanson française du XVe au XXe siècle. Paris, 1909.
	37591.42F	Le chansonnier de l'Arsenal (trouvères du XIIe et XIIIe siècle). Paris, 1909.
	38514.26.10	Charles d'Orleans. Poème, ballades, caroles, chansons, complaintes, rondeaux. Paris, 1909.
	40587.952	Chateaubriand, Celeste Buisson (de Lavigne) (Mme.). Cahiers. Paris, 1909.
	38511.26.5	Chatelain, H. Le mistere de Saint Quentin. St. Quentin, 1909.
	38523.21	Chevreau, Urbain. Remarque sur les poésies de Malherbe. Niort, 1909.
	37596.10.13	Chrestien de Troyes. Eric und Emile. Halle, 1909.
	37596.10.4A	Chrestien de Troyes. Philomena. Paris, 1909.
	43554.5.30	Claretie, L. Sourires litteraires. Paris, 1909.
	37596.7.2	Clédat, Léon. Rutebeuf. 2. éd. Paris, 1909.
Htn	43556.1.120*	Cocteau, Jean. La lampe d'Aladin. Paris, 1909.
	37576.23	Comfort, W.W. Les maîtres de la critique littéraire au XIVe siècle. Boston, 1909.
	38575.27.5	Corneille, Pierre. Le Cid. London, 1909.
	38575.34.8.14	Corneille, Pierre. Polyeucte. Boston, 1909.
NEDL	38574.19	Corneille, Pierre. Théâtre choisi illustré. Paris, 1909.
	38576.12.42.95	Coutil, Léon. IIe Centenaire de Thomas Corneille né à Rouen, le 20 août, 1625. Les Andelys, 1909.
	42542.55.5	Croisset, Francis de. Arsène Lupin. Paris, 1909.

Chronological Listing

1909 - cont.

42542.58.6.5 Curel, François de. L'envers d'une sainte. 4. éd. Paris, 1909.
42566.31.15 Daudet, Alphonse. Le petit chose. Paris, 1909?
42566.39.25 Daudet, Alphonse. Short stories. N.Y., 1909.
42542.61.12 Decourcelle, P. Le roy sans royaume. Paris, 1909.
39594.19.11 Dedieu, J. Montesquieu et la tradition politique. Paris, 1909.
41583.28.12 Delavigne, Casimir. Louis XI. London, 1909.
42576.15.30 Descharmes, René. Flaubert. Paris, 1909.
39564.6.9 Diderot, Denis. Extraits. Paris, 1909.
42542.65.17 Donnay, Maurice. La clairière. Paris, 1909.
42542.65.9.2 Donnay, Maurice. Lysistrata. Paris, 1909.
37574.75.15 Dorchain, Auguste. Chefs-d'oeuvre lyriques de F. de Malherbe et de l'école classique. v.2. Paris, 1909.
42555.37.6 Dornis, J. Essai sur Leconte de Lisle. 2e éd. Paris, 1909.
40535.35.5 Dost, G. Houdar de La Motte...Theoretiker. Weida, 1909.
41557.10.23 Doumic, René. George Sand. Paris, 1909.
37562.50 Doutrepont, G. La littérature française à la cour des ducs de Burgoyne. Paris, 1909.
FL 391.130 Dreyfus, R. Petite histoire de la revue de fin d'année. Paris, 1909.
38526.37.10 Drouhet, Charles. Le poète François Mainard (1583-1646). Paris, 1909.
38526.37.9 Drouhet, Charles. Tableau des lettres du poète François Mainard. Paris, 1909.
43576.4.31 Du Bois-Meilly, Charles. Eve de la Pasle; épisode de la guerre. 2. éd. Genève, 1909.
38528.21.9 Du Fail, Noël. Das Leben und die Werke. Borna, 1909.
41574.65 Dufay, P. Victor Hugo à vingt ans. Paris, 1909.
41538.53.10 Dumas, Alexandre. Les trois mousquetaires. Paris, 1909.
43576.57.140 Dumur, Louis. Les trois demoiselles du père Marie. Paris, 1909.
37576.560.28 Ernst, Paul. Altfranzösische Novellen. Leipzig, 1909. 2v.
43598.84.150 Estaunié, Édouard. L'empreinte. Paris, 1909.
43598.84.160 Estaunié, Édouard. La vie secrète. Paris, 1909.
42543.37 Fabre, Émile. Les vainqueurs. Paris, 1909.
43606.78.100 Farrère, Claude. La bataille. Paris, 1909.
42543.40.9 Fauchois, R. Beethoven et la fille de Pilate. Paris, 1909.
43606.89.50 Faure, Gabriel. Paysages passionnés. Paris, 1909.
38571.16 Les fêtes du IIIe centenaire de Pierre Corneille. Rouen, 1909.
42576.33.9.3 Flaubert, Gustave. Bouvard und Pécuchet. Minden, 1909.
42576.19.5 Flaubert, Gustave. Un coeur simple. Paris, 1909.
FL 378.5 Fleischhammer, Alfred. Der Provinziale in der FranzösischenKomödie von 1650 bis 1750. Halle, 1909.
42543.42.20 Flers, Robert de. L'ane de Buridan; comédie en trois actes. Paris, 1909?
42543.42.5 Flers, Robert de. L'ane de Buridan. Paris, 1909.
42542.64.12 Florent-Matter, Eugène. Paul Déroulède. Paris, 1909.
38562.17 Fontenelle, B. Le B. de. Pages choisies des grands écrivains. Paris, 1909.
43611.1.25.10 Fort, Paul. Mort cerf. X. Paris, 1909.
42576.63.7.45 France, Anatole. The crime of Sylvestre Bonnard. London, 1909.
42576.63.18 France, Anatole. Les sept femmes de la Barbe-Bleue. Paris, 1909.
43612.60.100 Francisci, Carlo. Fantasies littéraires. Perugia, 1909.
38513.62 Franke, Ernst. Untersuchung über Le mistere. Griefswald, 1909.
37596.111A Freine, Simund de. Les oeuvres. Paris, 1909.
37556.11 Funck-Brentano, F. Figaro et ses devanciers. Paris, 1909.
42571.28.10 Gaboriau, Emile. The mystery of Orcival. N.Y., 1909.
40545.20 Galley, J.B. Claude Fauriel. Saint-Etienne, 1909.
43616.83.120 Gasquet, Joachim. Les printemps; poèmes. Paris, 1909.
37596.143 Gast, Erich. Die beidenRedaktionen des "Évangile de l'enfence". Greifswald, 1909.
43616.2.30 Gautier, Judith. Le collier des jours: le second rang du collier. Paris, 1909.
43616.2.30.5 Gautier, Judith. Le collier des jours: le troisième rang du collier. 5. éd. Paris, 1909.
42543.45.5 Gavault, Paul. La petite chocolatière. Paris, 1909.
38567.15 Geissler, A. Die Theorien Boileaus. Leipzig, 1909.
43617.5.32 Géniaux, Charles. Le voueur. Paris, 1909.
39534.5.9 Gérard-Gailly, E. Bussy-Rabutin; sa vie, ses oeuvres. Paris, 1909.
42576.37 Gheusi, P.B. L'opéra romanesque. Paris, 1909.
42554.46.7 Gielkens, Émile. David. Bruxelles, 1909.
37556.30.5 Gilbert, Eugène. Le roman en France pendant le XIXe siècle. Paris, 1909.
40597.2.595 Gillette, Fredericka B. Title index to the works of Honoré de Balzac. Boston, 1909.
42543.47 Giocosa, J. Comme les feuilles. Paris, 1909.
43620.74.145 Giraudoux, Jean. Provinciales. Paris, 1909.
42586.65.6 Gobineau, Arthur de. Michelangelo. Strassburg, 1909.
37543.95.3 Gourmont, Rémy de. Promenades littéraires. Série 3. Paris, 1909.
40587.34.2 Gribble, Francis. Chateaubriand and his court of women. N.Y., 1909.
Htn 40587.34* Gribble, Francis. Chateaubriand and his court of women. N.Y., 1909.
42554.50.9.40 Guérin, C. L'homme intérieur. 3e ed. Paris, 1909.
41593.36 Guérin, Maurice de. Le centaure, la bacchante, glaucus. Paris, 1909.
37596.118 Guesnon, A. La bataille d'enfer et de paradise. Paris, 1909.
38512.115.14 Guillaume de Machaut. Poésies lyriques. Paris, 1909. 2v.
40583.18 Gunnel, D. Stendhal et l'Angleterre. Paris, 1909.
42543.62.34 Haraucourt, Edmond. Trumaille et Pélisson. Paris, 1909.
40575.5.14A Harper, George M. Charles Augustin Sainte-Beuve. Philadelphia, 1909.
42543.63.3 Hermant, Abel. Chronique du cadet de Coutras. Paris, 1909.
42543.65.19 Hermant, Abel. Trains de luxe. Paris, 1909.
38526.21.19 Héroet, A. Oeuvres poétiques. Paris, 1909.
42543.69.5 Hervieu, Paul. Connais-toi. Paris, 1909.
42543.69 Hervieu, Paul. La course du flambeau. Paris, 1909.
42543.69.13 Hervieu, Paul. Enchained, a play in 3 acts. n.p., 1909.
41571.3.90 Hugo, Victor. Poèmes choisis 1822-1865. London, 1909.
41573.26.11 Hugo, Victor. Ruy Blas. Boston, 1909.
41573.26.1 Hugo, Victor. Ruy Blas. N.Y., 1909.
41573.26 Hugo, Victor. Ruy Blas. N.Y., 1909.

1909 - cont.

37572.39.5 Huguet, E. Portraits et récits extraits des prosateurs du XVIe siècle. Paris, 1909.
37591.46 Huon le Roi de Cambrai. La vie de Saint Quentin. Helsingfors, 1909.
42576.65.21 Huysmans, Joris Karl. Sainte Lydwine de Schiedam. Paris, 1909.
43638.99.110 Huzard, A. de B. (Mme.). Les dames du palais. Paris, 1909.
43667.50.100 Jallade, E.J. A vol d'oiseau. N.Y., 1909.
43667.51.120 Jaloux, Edmond. Le reste est silence. Paris, 1909.
37596.112 Jenkins, T.A. Eructairt. Dresden, 1909.
40556.20.9 Joubert, Joseph. Pensées. Paris, 1909.
37543.40.5 Junker, Heinrich P. Grundriss der Geschichte der französischen Literatur. 6. Aufl. Münster, 1909.
41553.70 Kock, Charles Paul de. La demoiselle du cinquième. Paris, 1909.
42514.21 Laboulaye, Edouard. Fairy tales. London, 1909.
42514.22.10 Laboulaye, Edouard. Prince charming. Polo, Ill., 1909.
38521.30 Lachèvre, Frédéric. Le procès du poète Thèophile de Viau. v.2. Paris, 1909.
Mol 712.7 Lafenestre, G. Molière. Paris, 1909.
42555.1 Laforgue, Jules. Oeuvres complètes. 4. éd. v.1 lost 1947. Paris, 1909. 5v.
41578.29 Lamartine, Alphonse. Josselin inédit. Paris, 1909.
38557.2.40 Lambin, G. Les rapports de Bossuet avec l'Angleterre. Paris, 1909.
42514.25 Lamy, E. Au service des idées et des lettres. Paris, 1909.
38564.43 Lange, Maurice. La Bruyère. Paris, 1909.
37597.26.80 Langlade, Emile. Jehan Bodel. Paris, 1909.
38575.19.3 Lanson, G. Corneille. 3. éd. Paris, 1909.
37530.116 Lanson, Gustave. Manuel bibliographique. Paris, 1909-14. 5v.
37530.115 Lanson, Gustave. Manuel bibliographique. v.2-3. Paris, 1909-14. 2v.
38526.25.100 Laudun d'Aigaliers, P. de. L'art poétique français. Toulouse, 1909.
41564.39A Lauvrière, E. Alfred de Vigny, sa vie et son oeuvre. Paris, 1909.
42544.24.35 Lavedan, Henri. La haute. 20e éd. n.p., 1909.
42544.24.10 Lavedan, Henri. Sire. Paris, 1909.
42546.15.24 Le Blond, M. St. Georges de Bouhélier. Paris, 1909.
40587.14 Le Braz, A. Au pays d'exil de Chateaubriand. Paris, 1909.
40587.14.2 Le Braz, A. Au pays d'exil de Chateaubriand. 2. éd. Paris, 1909.
FL 390.97 Lecomte, L.H. Histoire des théâtres de Paris. Les folies-nouvelles. v.8. Paris, 1909.
37567.95 Ledigne, C. Le Fléan romantique. Photoreproduction. Paris, 1909.
37596.166 Le Duc de Danmartin, Herbert. Folque de Candie. Dresden, 1909-36. 3v.
42544.31.40 Legendre, Louis. Pylade. Paris, 1909.
FL 6119.09.5 Lemaitre, J. Jean-Jacques Rousseau. Paris, 1909.
43688.54.100 LeMercier d'Erm, C. Les exiles; poèmes. Paris, 1909.
42557.20.255 Lepelletier, Edmond. Paul Verlaine. London, 1909?
41595.5 Le Poittevin, Alfred. Oeuvres inédites. Paris, 1909.
43688.1.39 Leroux, Gaston. The double life. N.Y., 1909.
43688.1.32.5 Leroux, Gaston. The perfume of the lady in black. N.Y., 1909.
43688.77.100 Leroy-Allais, J. Marie-Rose au couvent. Paris, 1909.
42544.34.20 Lorde, André de. Théâtre d'Epouvante. Paris, 1909.
FL 380.15 Lunel, E. Le théâtre et la révolution. Paris, 1909.
42557.11.170 Mabille de Poncheville, André. Gedichte. Stuttgart, 1909.
42586.29.10 Maël, Pierre (pseud.). César Borgia. Paris, 1909.
42545.3.18.1 Maeterlinck, Maurice. The blue bird. London, 1909.
42545.3.18A Maeterlinck, Maurice. The blue bird. N.Y., 1909.
42545.3.12.4 Maeterlinck, Maurice. The double garden. London, 1909.
42545.3.19.15A Maeterlinck, Maurice. Macbeth. Paris, 1909.
38526.2.31 Magne, E. Le plaisant Abbé de Boisrobert. Paris, 1909.
40588.39.15 Maistre, Xavier. Oeuvres complètes. Paris, 1909.
43792.1.30 Marchandeau, Marcel. La pâque des roses, 1900-1908. Paris, 1909.
42576.76.43F Margueritte, Paul. La flamme. Paris, 1909.
42576.46.50 Mariel, Jean. Pierre Loti. Paris, 1909.
41566.2 Marquiset, A. Le vicomte d'Arlincourt. Paris, 1909.
42563.37.84 Marsan, Eugène. Les cannes de Paul Bourget. Niort, 1909.
37567.595 Marten, Miloš (pseud.). Kniha silných. Praha, 1909.
42578.51.250 Martin-Mamy, Eugène. Marcelle Tinayre. Paris, 1909.
43788.65.2805 Martineau, Henri. Louis Thomas. Niort, 1909.
42563.18.285 Massis, Henri. La pensée de Maurice Barrès. Paris, 1909.
43697.83.120 Masson, Emile. Les rebelles. Paris, 1909.
42577.1.3 Maupassant, Guy de. Works. N.Y., 1909. 10v.
42577.4.30.4 Maupassant, Guy de. The works of Guy de Maupassant. v.1,3-10. N.Y., 1909. 9v.
Htn 42577.4.30.2* Maupassant, Guy de. The works of Maupassant. v.2-4,6,7,9,10. N.Y., 1909. 7v.
37562.12.20 Melchior, G. Der Achtsilbler in der altfranzösischen Dichtung mit Ausschluss der Lyrik. Leipzig, 1909.
40583.15A Mélia, Jean. La vie amoureuse de Stendhal. Paris, 1909.
42555.58.19A Mendès, Catulle. L'Impératrice. Paris, 1909.
43698.76.130 Merrill, Stuart. Une voix dans la foule. Paris, 1909.
41568.15.5 Michaut, G. Sénancour, ses amis et ses ennemis. Paris, 1909.
Mol 185.15 Molière, Jean Baptiste Poquelin. Dom Garcie de Navarre...Vitu. London, 1909.
Mol 262.2.5 Molière, Jean Baptiste Poquelin. Esgauarel l'amour Melge. Barcelona, 1909.
Mol 211.74 Molière, Jean Baptiste Poquelin. Les femmes savantes. 2e éd. Paris, 1909.
Mol 268.126 Molière, Jean Baptiste Poquelin. Le Tartuffe. J. Arnavon. Paris, 1909.
42545.44 Moreau, Émile. Le procès de Jeanne d'Arc. Paris, 1909.
39545.15 Morize, A. L'apologie du Luxe au XVIIIe siècle. "Le mondain et ses sources". Paris, 1909.
43701.77.2110 Mortier, Alfred. Le temple sans idoles. Paris, 1909.
42577.23.10 Murger, Henry. Le pays latin. Paris, 1909.
41596.8.16.2 Musset, Alfred de. Poésies. Strasbourg, 1909.
42545.45.35 Nigond, Gabriel. Kéroubinos. Paris, 1909.
37567.101 Nonnenberg-Chun, M. Der französischen Philhell...Jahrhundert. Berlin, 1909.
43723.51.130 Ollone, Charles. Soeur Marie-Odile. 2nd éd. Paris, 1909.
38513.57 Ostrowski, Otto. Le mystère de Saint Crespin et Crispinien. Greifswald, 1909.
42541.25.5A Pailleron, Édouard. La souris, comédie. 29e éd. Paris, 1909?
42515.35.204 Parigot, Hippolyte. Renan. Paris, 1909.

Chronological Listing

1909 - cont.

37562.22.3 Paris, Gaston. La littérature française au moyen âge. 4. éd. Paris, 1909.
42563.18.280 Pastourel, Léonce. Egotisme et acceptation. Paris, 1909.
38513.22.9 Pathelin. La farce de maître Pathelin. Paris, 1909?
37567.94 Pavie, A. Médaillons romantiques. Paris, 1909.
38563.29 Perrault, C. Mémoires de ma vie. Paris, 1909.
39545.13 Petkovic, J. Voltaire's Tragödie, "La morte de César verglichen mit Shakespere" Julius Cäsar. Wien, 1909.
38537.25.14A Plattard, G. L'invention...dans l'oeuvre de Rabelais. Paris, 1909.
FL 6139.09 Pons, A.A. Jean-Jacques Rousseau et le théâtre. Genève, 1909.
37562.32 Pons, S. Les poèmes vaudois et les mystères provençaux du XVe siècle. Pinerolo, 1909.
43743.1.32 Porché, François. Au loin, peut-être. Poèmes. Paris, 1909.
42578.31.48.90 Prévost, Marcel. Pierre et Thérèse. 23. éd. Paris, 1909.
42576.63.26 Raphaël, Cor. M. Anatole France et la pensée contemporaine. Paris, 1909.
38557.19.13 Rébelliau, A. Bossuet historien du protestantisme. 3. éd. Paris, 1909.
42556.26.29 Régnier, Henri de. Les amants singuliers. 7. éd. Paris, 1909.
42556.27.10 Régnier, Henri de. Couleur du temps. Paris, 1909.
42556.27.11 Régnier, Henri de. La flambée. Paris, 1909.
37596.107.3 Reiche, Paul. Beiträge zu Artur Långfors Ausgabe des Regret Notre Dame. Inaug. Diss. Berlin, 1909.
42515.30.729A Renan, Ernest. Souvenirs d'enfance et de jeunesse. Boston, 1909.
37567.103 Retinger, J.H. Le conte fantastique dans le romantisme français. Paris, 1909.
FL 398.74.305 Reuilly, Jean de. Le Raucourt et ses amies. Paris, 1909.
FL 6129.09 Rey, A. Jean-Jacques Rousseau dans la Vallée de Montmorency. Paris, 1909.
42556.22.95 Richepin, Jean. Braves gens. Paris, 1909.
42556.22.85A Richepin, Jean. La route d'émerande. Paris, 1909.
42578.19.25A Rod, Edouard. Les unis. Paris, 1909.
FL 6039.5 Rodet, St. Le contrat social...de Jean-Jacques Rousseau. Paris, 1909.
43757.50.213 Rolland, Romain. Jean-Christophe à Paris: Dans la maison. 10e éd. Paris, 1909.
43757.50.360 Rolland, Romain. Le 14 juillet. Paris, 1909.
43757.55.110 Romilly, Edouard. Vers l'effort. Paris, 1909.
42578.22.10.55 Rosny, J.H. Marthe Baraquin. 8. éd. Paris, 1909.
42546.15.20 Rothschild, Henri de. La rampe et les deux visages. Paris, 1909.
40597.1.8 Ruxton, G. La dilecta de Balzac. Paris, 1909.
42546.15.23 St. Georges de Bouhélier. La tragédie royale. Paris, 1909.
40576.4.15 Sainte-Beuve, Charles A. Causeries du lundi. London, 1909-11. 8v.
41557.9.28.10 Sand, George. Elle et lui. 6e éd. Paris, 1909.
42546.24.7 Sardou, Victorien. Divorçons. Chicago, 1909.
42546.30.8 Sardou, Victorien. La Tosca. Paris, 1909.
42578.35.105 Sarton, Georges. La chaîne d'or. Mons, 1909.
FL 6139.09.3 Schinz, A. Jean-Jacques Rousseau a forerunner of pragmatism. Chicago, 1909.
38527.29.11 Schwerd, Karl. Vergleich, Metapher...in den "Tragiques" des Agrippa d'Aubigné. Leipzig, 1909.
39566.96 Séché, A. Diderot. Paris, 1909?
37567.98 Séché, Alphonse. Au temps du romantisme. Paris, 1909.
37588.9 Séché, L. Le cénacle de la muse française, 1823-1827. Paris, 1909.
40575.5.15 Séché, Leon. Madame d'Arbouville...1846-1850. Paris, 1909.
40587.23 Souriau, Maurice. Les idées morales de Chateaubriand. 2. éd. Paris, 1909.
43780.5.190 Suarès, André. Lais et cônes. Paris, 1909.
FL 6138.95.4 Texte, J. Jean-Jacques Rousseau et les origines de cosmopolitisme littéraire. 2. éd. Paris, 1909.
FL 396.50.2 Thalasso, A. Le théâtre libre. Paris, 1909.
42583.33.17.5 Theuriet, André. Jean-Marie. Antwerpen, 1909.
37567.135 Thorold, Algar L. Six masters in disillusion. London, 1909.
42578.51.10 Tinayre, Marcelle. Avant l'amour. 13. éd. Paris, 1909?
42578.51.35 Tinayre, Marcelle. La rebelle. 39. éd. Paris, 1909?
38513.61 Tinius, Fritz. Studium über das Mystère de Saint Clement. Griefswald, 1909.
42578.52.77 Tinseau, Léon de. Sur les deux rives. 13. éd. Paris, 1909?
40546.21 Tocqueville, Alexis de. Correspondance...et A. de Gobinean, 1843-1859. Paris, 1909.
42547.5.5 Trarieux, Gabriel. La dette, trois actes. Paris, 1909.
38525.36.7 Tristan L'Hermite, F. Oeuvres.. Paris, 1909.
38525.36.8 Tristan L'Hermite, F. Les plaintes d'Acante et autres oeuvres. Paris, 1909.
38525.35.23 Tristan L'Hermite, F. Tristan L'Hermite; les amours, la lyre. 3e éd. Paris, 1909.
38547.3 Urfé, Honoré d'. Oeuvres poétiques choisies. Paris, 1909.
40534.16.25 Urschlecter, Hans. Die vornehme französische Frau des XVIII Jahrhunderts...Proverbes dramatiques. n.p., 1909.
43822.11.30 Văcărescu, Elena. Amor vincit. Paris, 1909.
42547.12.3 Veber, Pierre. Les grands. Paris, 1909.
42557.11.9 Verhaeren, Emile. Deux drames: Le cloitre, Philippe II. Paris, 1909.
42557.11.8 Verhaeren, Emile. Deux drames: Le cloitre, Philippe II. 3. éd. Paris, 1909.
37565.43 Vial, F. Idées et doctrines littéraires du XVIII siècle. Paris, 1909.
37563.21.5 Vianey, J. Le pétrarquisme en France au XVIe siècle. Montpellier, 1909.
X Cg 42576.56.5 Viaud, Julien. Madame Chrysanthème. 97. éd. Paris, 1909?
Mon 132.5.10 Villey, P. Montaigne a-t-il lu le traité de l'education de J. Sadolet? Paris, 1909.
38514.21.5.2A Villon, François. Le Jargon de François Villon. Paris, 1909.
Htn 41581.17* Virely, A. René-Charles Guilbert de Pixerécourt, 1773-1844. Paris, 1909.
43824.2.51 Vivien, Renée. Poèmes en prose. Paris, 1909.
39545.65.5 Voltaire, François Marie Arouet de. Zadig. Strasbourg, 1909.
39566.31 Voss, K.J. von. Diderots Moralphilosophie. Halle, 1909.
37543.85 Wilmotte, M. Études des critiques sur la tradition littéraire en France. Paris, 1909.
42547.35 Wolff, Pierre. Le lys. Paris, 1909.
42547.35.10 Wolff, Pierre. Le lys. Paris, 1909.

1909 - cont.

Mol 860.60 Yvan, A. Jardin de Molière. Paris, 1909.

191-

43537.6.58 Barbusse, Henri. L'enfer. Paris, 191-?
Htn 42563.17.15* Barrès, Maurice. Comprendre des américains, c'est les aimer et les honorer. n.p., 191-?
Htn 42563.17.16* Barrès, Maurice. Le secteur américain de la bataille. n.p., 191-.
42542.29.46 Bernstein, H. Le detour. Israel. Paris, 191-.
38523.13.5 Bible. O.T. Psalms. French. Psaumes, avec les mélodies. Strasbourg, 191-?
42542.47.80.2 Caillavet, G.A. La belle aventure. Paris, 191-.
43552.25.4110 Chevalier, Adrien. Paroles pendant l'orage. Paris, 191-?
40553.5.25 Constant de Rebecque, Benjamin. Adolphe. Paris, 191-?
41538.53.110 Dumas, Alexandre. Twenty years after. N.Y., 191-?
41538.55.30 Dumas, Alexandre. Le vicomte de Bragelonne, ou Dix ans plus tard. Paris, 191-? 5v.
37544.23.2 Faguet, Emile. Les dix commandements de la vieillesse. 2. éd. Paris, 191- .
37564.32.15 Faguet, Emile. Dix-septième siècle. Paris, 191-?
37567.279.5 Faguet, Emile. Politiques et moralistes du dix-neuvieme siècle. Paris, 191-?
43606.78.160 Farrère, Claude. Fumée d'opium. 16. éd. Paris, 191-?
43606.78.170 Farrère, Claude. L'homme qui assassina. 71. éd. Paris, 191-?
43606.78.180 Farrère, Claude. Mademoiselle Dax jeune fille. 34. éd. Paris, 191-?
43606.78.200 Farrère, Claude. Les petites alliées. 42. éd. Paris, 191-?
42576.62.18.10 France, Anatole. Crainquebille. Putois. Riquet. 64. éd. Paris, 191-?
42576.62.4.2 France, Anatole. Jocaste et Le chat maigre. Paris, 191-?
42576.62.4.6 France, Anatole. Jocaste et Le chat maigre. Paris, 191-?
42576.62.10.2.10 France, Anatole. Le lys rouge. 156. éd. Paris, 191-?
42571.23.5 Gaboriau, Emile. El proceso Lerouge. 2a ed. Madrid, 191-.
42543.45.85 Gavault, Paul. Madame Flirt. Paris, 191-.
42576.67.10.5 Hervieu, Paul. Les tenailles. Paris, 191-.
41573.32.16 Hugo, Victor. Hernani. Paris, 191-.
41573.36.3 Hugo, Victor. Odes et ballades. Paris, 191-.
43638.99.107 Huzard, A. de B. (Mme.). Princesses de science. 47. éd. Paris, 191- ?
40597.6.15 Keim, A. Balzac. (Los grandes hombres). Paris, 191-?
38526.26.70 Labé, Louise Charly. Die vierundzwanzig Sonette der Louïze Labé, Lyoneserin, 1555. Leipzig, 191-.
37572.32.10 Marcou, F.L. Morceaux choisis des classiques français poètes. Paris, 191-?
37572.31.10 Marcou, F.L. Morceaux choisis des classiques français prosateurs. Paris, 191-?
40535.27.6 Marivaux, Pierre Carlet de Chamblain de. Théâtre. Paris, 191-? 2v.
42577.4.29.6 Maupassant, Guy de. Mont Oriol. Paris, 191-.
43698.1.30 Mendès, Jane C. La ville Merveilleuse, Rio de Janeiro, poèmes. Paris, 191-.
Mol 155.40 Molière, Jean Baptiste Poquelin. L'amour médecin. Strasbourg, 191-?
Mol 248.45 Molière, Jean-Baptiste Poquelin. M. de Pourceaugnac. Strasbourg, 191-?
Mol 251.90 Molière, Jean Baptiste Poquelin. Les précieuses ridicules. C.H. Page. Paris, 191-?
42545.44.4 Moreau, Emile. Argument of the play Le procès de Jeanne d'Arc. N.Y., 191-?
41556.11.5 Nodier, Charles. Contes fantastiques. Paris, 191-?
37562.22.4.5 Paris, Gaston. La littérature française au moyen âge. 6e éd. Paris, 191-?
43745.1.30 Psichari, Ernest. L'Appel des Armes. 18. éd. Paris, 191-.
42556.26.24.5 Régnier, Henri de. La peur de l'amour. 18. éd. Paris, 191-.
38575.33.9 Roosbroeck, Gustave L. van. The genesis of Corneille's Mélite. Vinton, 191-.
40597.2.19 Royaumont, Louis de. Balzac et la société des gens de lettres 1833-1913. Paris, 191-?
41558.66.16 Souvestre, Emile. Un philosophe sous les toits. Paris, 191-?
41558.66.15 Souvestre, Emile. Un philosophe sous les toits. Paris, 191-?
43822.11.50 Văcărescu, Elena. Le sortilège. 3e éd. Paris, 191-.
42557.11.39 Verhaeren, Emile. Helenas Heimkehr; Drama in vier Akten. Leipzig, 191-.

1910

42513.47.5 Adam, Juliette. Après l'abandon de la revanche. Paris, 1910.
43514.25.110 Aderer, A. Comme ils sont tous. Paris, 1910.
42562.38.48 Aimard, Gustave. The Indian scout. London, 1910.
43522.4.110 Alanic, Mathilde. Bal blanc. Paris, 1910.
Mon 111.1 Armaingand, A. Montaigne Pamphlétaire. Paris, 1910.
42566.16.50 Ashlemann, L.A. La société française d'après l'oeuvre d'Alphonse Daudet. Thèse. Paris, 1910.
42586.14.6.15 Audoux, M. Le chaland de la reine. Nevers, 1910.
42586.14 Audoux, M. Marie-Claire. Paris, 1910.
42542.10.5.9 Augier, Emile. Le gendre de M. Poirier. Boston, 1910.
42524.9.2A Baldensperger, F. Etudes d'histoire littéraire. 2d ser. Paris, 1910.
40597.19.30 Balzac, Honoré de. Eugénie Grandet. London, 1910.
40597.20.6 Balzac, Honoré de. Eugénie Grandet. Strassbourg, 1910.
40596.16.10 Balzac, Honoré de. Pages sociales et politiques. Paris, 1910.
42555.62.9 Barrès, M. Adieu à Moréas. Paris, 1910.
42563.16.8 Barrès, Maurice. Du sang, de la volupté et de la mort. Paris, 1910.
42563.16.11 Barrès, Maurice. L'ennemi des lois. Paris, 1910.
37562.20.10 Barth, Bruno. Liebe und Ehe im altfranzösischen Fabel. Berlin, 1910.
42586.14.40.5 Bascle de Lagrèze, Gaston. Zurückgekehrt. Einsiedeln, 1910.
43537.4.33F Bataille, Henry. Le Songe d'un Soir d'Amour. Paris, 1910.
43537.4.65 Bataille, Henry. La vierge folle. Paris, 1910.
42563.21.71 Bazin, René. The barrier. N.Y., 1910.
43538.1.30 Beauduin, Nicolas. La divine folie. Paris, 1910.
40587.36 Beaunier, André. Trois amies de Chateaubriand. Paris, 1910.
42542.28.6 Becque, Henri. Les polichinelles. Paris, 1910.
42542.28.5 Becque, Henri. Les polichinelles. Paris, 1910.

Chronological Listing

1910 - cont.

42575.8 Bellemare, Louis de. Le coureur des bois. 16. éd. Paris, 1910. 2v.
42556.22.120 Benelli, Sem. La beffa. Paris, 1910.
42554.13.150 Bengoechea, Alfred de. L'orgueilleuse. Paris, 1910.
37576.560.12 Bernard, Charles de. Gerfaut. N.Y., 1910.
38575.28.7 Bernard, G. Le Cid espagne et le Cid français. Lille, 1910.
42542.29.18 Bernard, Tristan. Le costand des Epinettes. Paris, 1910.
42542.29.17 Bernard, Tristan. Le danseur inconnu. Paris, 1910.
38588.33 Bernhard, A. Die Parodie..."Chapelain decoiffée". Leipzig, 1910.
38588.34 Bernhard, A. Die Parodie..."Chapelain decoiffée". Inaug. Diss. Naumberg, 1910.
41574.125.6 Berret, Paul. La philosophie de Victor Hugo (1854-1859). Paris, 1910.
42563.21.80 Bersaucourt, A. de. René Bazin. Paris, 1910.
42542.47.40 Bertrand, A. Eugène Brieux. Paris, 1910.
42563.23.8.25 Bertrand, Louis. Les bains de Phalère. Paris, 1910.
FL 355.65.2 Bethleem, Louis. Les pièces de théâtre. Paris, 1910.
40534.13 Bièvre, G. Mareschal de. Le marquis de Bièvre. Paris, 1910.
43540.60.120 Binet-Valmer, Gustave. Lucien. Paris, 1910.
37542.28.9 Biré, E. Dernières causeries historiques et littéraires. 3. éd. Lyon, 1910.
42542.29.101 Bisson, Alexandre. Nick Carter. Paris, 1910.
38565.21.6 Boileau Despréaux, Nicolas. Oeuvres. Paris, 1910?
FL 386.504 Bordeau, Henry. La vie au théâtre, 1907-1921. Paris, 1910-1921. 5v.
42563.36.65.10 Bordeaux, Henry. La robe de laine. Paris, 1910.
42563.36.65A Bordeaux, Henry. La robe de laine. 59. éd. Paris, 1910.
42542.44 Bourdet, Édouard. Le Rubicon. Paris, 1910. 2 pam.
37576.560.17 Bourgée, Paul. Cosmopolis. N.Y., 1910.
42542.46.5 Bourget, Paul. La barricade. Paris, 1910.
42563.37.42 Bourget, Paul. La barricade chronique de 1910. Paris, 1910.
42542.46.7 Bourget, Paul. Un cas de conscience. Paris, 1910.
42563.37.45 Bourget, Paul. La dame qui a perdu son peintre. Paris, 1910.
42524.12.9 Brédif, L. Mélanges. Paris, 1910.
38551.39 Bremond, Henri. Apologie pour Fénelon. Paris, 1910.
42542.47.18.5 Brieux, Eugène. Les bienfaiteurs. 4. éd. Paris, 1910.
42542.47.6.5 Brieux, Eugène. Blanchette. 14. éd. Paris, 1910.
42542.47.32.5 Brieux, Eugène. Discours de réception à l'Académie Française. Paris, 1910.
42542.47.15.2 Brieux, Eugène. L'engrenage. Paris, 1910.
42542.47.9.2 Brieux, Eugène. Les trois filles de M. Dupont. 3. éd. Paris, 1910.
37556.56 Brun, Charles. Le roman social en France au XIXe siècle. Paris, 1910.
42515.35.42 Brunetière, Ferdinand. Cinq lettres sur Ernest Renan. Paris, 1910.
37595.114 Butler, Isabel. Tales from the old French. Boston, 1910.
38553.10 Cagnac, M. Lettres inédites de Fénelon. Paris, 1910.
38551.24.15 Cagnac, Moïse. Fénelon. Études critiques. Paris, 1910.
42542.47.78 Caillavet, G.A. Le bois sacré. Paris, 1910.
42542.48.13 Capus, Alfred. Un auge. Paris, 1910.
42542.48.17 Capus, Alfred. L'aventurier. Paris, 1910.
42542.48.14 Capus, Alfred. Les deux écoles. Paris, 1910.
38511.22.5 Chandos, the herald. Life of the black prince. Oxford, 1910.
40536.20.85 Chaponnière, Paul. Piron; sa vie et son oeuvre. Genève, 1910.
41522.69.600 Charlieu, H. de. La marseillaise. Paris, 1910.
40586.18.14 Chateaubriand, F.A.R. O genio do Christianismo. 6a ed. Porto, 1910. 2v.
42565.9.5A Cherbuliez, Victor. Le comte Kostia. Paris, 1910.
42565.22.5 Cherbuliez, Victor. Oliver Maugant. 9. éd. Paris, 1910.
38539.2.500 Cholières, Nicolas de. Oeuvre. Paris, 1910.
42586.31.15 Claretié, J. Preuse Zilah. N.Y., 1910.
42563.18.305 Clouard, Henri. La cocarde de Barrès. Paris, 1910.
43556.1.30 Cocteau, Jean. Le Prince Frivole. Paris, 1910.
FL 373.10 Cohen, Gustave. L'évolution de la mise en scène dans le théâtre français. Lille, 1910.
43556.49.150 Colette, Sidonie Gabrielle. La vagabonde. 5e éd. Paris, 1910.
43556.2.31 Colomb, F. L'Écrin. Paris, 1910.
42542.53.11 Coolus, R. Une femme passa. Paris, 1910.
40513.1 Cordier, Henri. Essai bibliographique sur les oeuvres d'Alain René LeSage. Paris, 1910.
38575.34.1.5 Corneille, Pierre. Le menteur. Paris, 1910.
42586.32.210 Coster, Charles de. Tyll Ulenspiegel und Lamm Goedzak. 2. Aufl. Jena, 1910.
42542.55.7 Croisset, Francis de. Le feu du voisin. Paris, 1910.
39533.20.4.5 Cyrano de Bergerac. L'autre monde ou Les états et empires de la lune. Dresden, 1910.
37567.102 Daudet, A. (Mme.). Souvenirs autour d'un groupe littéraire. Paris, 1910.
42566.21.9 Daudet, Alphonse. Contes du lundi. Paris, 1910.
42566.35.10 Daudet, Alphonse. Tartarin sur les Alpes. London, 1910.
43566.45.110 Delacour, André. Le rayonnement. Paris, 1910.
43566.5.35 Détanger, Émile. La barque annamite. Paris, 1910.
43566.91.100 Devoncaux, Marie. Le jardin symbolique. Macon, 1910.
FL 6119.10 Dide, A. Jean-Jacques Rousseau. Le protestantisme et la Révolution française. Paris, 1910.
37574.75.6 Dorchain, Auguste. Les cent meilleurs poèmes. Paris, 1910.
43574.1.30 Drouot, Paul. Sous le vocable du chien. (Poèmes). Paris, 1910.
43576.6.250 Duhamel, Georges. Selon ma loi. Paris, 1910.
41529.57 Dumas, Alexandre. Celebrated crimes. N.Y., 1910. 8v.
41564.45 Dupuy, Ernest. Alfred de Vigny. Paris, 1910-12. 2v.
43576.3.31 Duquesnel, F. A la flamme de Paris. Paris, 1910.
43576.82.105 Dussap, J.V. (Mme). Ma conscience en robe rose. 16. éd. Paris, 1910.
43598.68.90 Espardés, Georges. Les demi solde. Paris, 1910.
38512.90 L'estoire de Griseldis. (1395). Paris, 1910.
42586.63.8 Eulenburg-Hertefeld, P. Gobineau und die deutsche Kultur. Leipzig, 1910.
42543.38.10 Fabre, Émile. César Birotteau. Paris, 1910.
FL 6129.10 Faguet, E. Les amies de Rousseau. Paris, 1910.
FL 6139.10 Faguet, E. Rousseau artiste. Paris, 1910.
FL 6139.10.5 Faguet, E. Rousseau penseur. Paris, 1910.
40525.22 Les faits et gestes du vicomte de Nantel: ma vie de garçon. Paris, 1910.
37596.113 Faral, E. Mimes français du XIIIe siècle. Paris, 1910.
FL 398.74.82 Faucignyy-Lucinge, A. Rachel et son temps. Paris, 1910.

1910 - cont.

42565.73.5A Favre de Coulevain, Hélène. On the branch. N.Y., 1910.
38554.522.5 Fénelon, F. de S. de la Mothe. Spiritual counsels from the letters of Fénelon. 1st-2nd series. London, 1910.
37573.37.5 Ferrières, Gauthier. Anthologie des écrivains français du XVIIIe siècle; prose. Paris, 1910.
42543.41.9 Feydeau, Georges. On purge Bébé! Paris, 1910.
42576.34.12 Flaubert, Gustave. Der Büchernarr. Hannover, 1910.
42576.17 Flaubert, Gustave. Notes de voyages. Paris, 1910. 2v.
42576.16.15 Flaubert, Gustave. Oeuvres de jeunesse inédites. Paris, 1910. 3v.
42576.23.8 Flaubert, Gustave. The temptation of St. Anthony. N.Y., 1910.
FL 398.74.83 Fleischmann, H. Rachel intime. Paris, 1910.
42543.43 Fonson, F. Le mariage de Mlle Beulemans. Paris, 1910.
43611.1.25.11 Fort, Paul. Tristesse de l'homme. XI. Paris, 1910.
42576.63.7.100 France, Anatole. Aux étudiants. Paris, 1910.
42576.63.7.103 France, Anatole. Aux étudiants. 3. éd. Paris, 1910.
42576.62.107 France, Anatole. On life and letters. 1st series. London, 1910.
42586.55.9 Frapié, L. La maternelle. Paris, 1910.
43612.2.32 Fraudet, René. Montmartre. Paris, 1910.
42571.32.7 Gaboriau, Emile. Monsieur Lecoq. N.Y., 1910.
42571.24.12 Gaboriau, Emile. Other people's money. N.Y., 1910.
42571.23.4 Gaboriau, Emile. The widow Lerouge. N.Y., 1910.
FL 379.57 Gaiffe, F. Étude sur le drame en France au XVIIIe siècle. Paris, 1910.
42542.2.10 Gaillard de Champris, Henry. Émile Augier et la comédie sociale. Paris, 1910.
42543.44.9 Ganem, C. Antar. Paris, 1910.
41542.8.3 Gautier, Théophile. Émaux et camées. Paris, 1910.
41542.37.9 Gautier, Théophile. One of Cleopatra's nights. N.Y., 1910.
FL 6113.5.2 Girardin, Fernand. Iconographie des oeuvres de Jean-Jacques Rousseau. Paris, 1910.
FL 398.34 Got, M. Journal de Edmond Got. 2e ed. Paris, 1910. 2v.
37558.14.30 Gourmont, Jean de. Muses d'aujourd'hui. Paris, 1910.
37567.104 Gribble, Francis. The passions of the French romantics. London, 1910.
41574.158 Grillet, Claudius. Le Bible dans Victor Hugo d'après de nombreux tableaux de concordance. Lyon, 1910.
41574.55 Guiard, A. Virgile et Victor Hugo. Paris, 1910.
41574.107 Guiard, Amédée. La fonction du poète; étude sur Victor Hugo. Thèse. Paris, 1910.
FL 398.35 Guilbert, Yvette. Yvette Guilbert. Struggles and victories. London, 1910.
FL 359.10 Guillemot, J. L'évolution de l'idée dramatique. Paris, 1910.
37555.21 Guy, H. Histoire de la poésie française au XVIe siècle. Paris, 1910. 2v.
42576.40.345 Halévy, Ludovic. The abbé Constantin. N.Y., 1910.
39544.155.15 Hall, Evelyn B. The life of Voltaire. 3d ed. N.Y., 1910.
39578.3 Hamel, Frank. An eighteenth century marquise. London, 1910.
39532.13.13 Hamilton, Anthony. Memoires of the court of Charles II, by Count de Grammont. Memoires of the courts of Europe. v.4. N.Y., 1910.
42545.3.420 Harry, Gérard. Maurice Maeterlinck. London, 1910.
Mol 608.16.10 Hartmann, H. Die literarische Satire bei Molière. Diss. Tübingen, 1910.
40517.31.50 Hazard, Paul. Journal de Ginguené, 1807-1808. Paris, 1910.
42543.65.75 Hermant, Abel. Le fremier pas. Paris, 1910.
42543.69.12 Hervieu, Paul. Enchained, a play in 3 acts. n.p., 1910.
38512.75 Hoepffner, E. La prise amoureuse. Dresden, 1910.
42557.14.7 Hommage à Verlaine. Paris, 1910.
38514.59.3 Hoochstraten, M.H. van. Die Evangelien van den Spinrocke. 's Gravenhage, 1910.
41573.30.7 Hugo, Victor. Dramas. v.1-4. Boston, 1910. 2v.
41571.15.3 Hugo, Victor. Les misérables. London, 1910.
41571.16.10 Hugo, Victor. Les misérables. v.1-5. Boston, 1910? 3v.
41571.31.10 Hugo, Victor. The man who laughs. v.1-2. Boston, 1910?
41571.32.3.5 Hugo, Victor. Ninety-three. v.1-2. Boston, 1910?
41573.23.6.3 Hugo, Victor. Notre Dame de Paris. v.1-2. Boston, 1910?
42576.65.14 Huysmans, Joris Karl. En route. Paris, 1910.
Htn 42576.65.30* Huysmans, Joris Karl. Prières et pensées chrétiennes. Lyon, 1910.
43638.99.112 Huzard, A. de B. (Mme.). Les dames du palais. 20. éd. Paris, 1910.
43667.1.35 Jammes, Francis. Clairières dans le ciel 1902-1906. 3. éd. Paris, 1910.
38511.41A Le jardin de plaisance. Paris, 1910-25. 2v.
FL 370.79.5 Jocobsen, J.P. Essai sur les origines de la comédie en France au Moyen-Age. Paris, 1910.
43670.94.170 Jouve, Pierre Jean. Les muses romaines et florentines. Paris, 1910.
42544.2.6 Kistemaekers, Henry. Le marchand de bonheur. Paris, 1910.
37543.122 Kouta, A.K. The history of French literature. N.Y., 1910.
FL 383.180 Labarthe, Gustave. Le théâtre pendant les jours au siège et de la commune. Paris, 1910.
41596.51.50 Lafond, Paul. L'aube romantique. 2. éd. Paris, 1910.
42555.8.33 Laforest, Edmond. Sonnets. Paris, 1910.
41578.1 Lamartine, Alphonse de. La chute d'un ange. Paris, 1910.
37597.11.8 Langlois, E. Les manuscrits du roman de la rose. Lille, 1910.
39544.46.10 Lanson, Gustave. Voltaire. 2. éd. Paris, 1910.
42576.46.23 Lapauze, Jeanne L. Du sang dans les ténèbres. Paris, 1910.
FL 6129.25 Larsson, Hans. Rousseau och Pestalozzi. Lund, 1910.
38514.53.9 La Sale, Antoine de. Histoire...du Petit Jehan de Saintré. Paris, 1910.
38525.21.8 Laumonier, P. La vie de Pierre de Ronsard. Paris, 1910.
43687.89.3110 Lavaud, Guy. Des fleurs, pourquoi. Paris, 1910.
40597.2.15 Lawton, Fred. Balzac. London, 1910.
42576.42.20 Le Barillier, Berthe. La passion d'Héloïse et d'Abélard. Paris, 1910.
42576.41.21.4 Le Blanc, Maurice. The blonde lady. N.Y., 1910.
42576.41.23.5A Le Blanc, Maurice. 813. Paris, 1910.
FL 390.98 Lecomte, L.H. Histoire des théâtres de Paris. Théâtre de la cité, 1792-1807. Paris, 1910.
43688.15.100 Leconte, S.C. L'esprit qui passe. 3e éd. Paris, 1910.
41593.41 Lefranc, A. Maurice de Guérin d'après des documents inedits. Paris, 1910.
38551.79 Lemaître, Jules. Fénelon. Pairs, 1910.
42544.33.35 Lemaître, Jules. Lettres à mon ami, 1909. Paris, 1910.

1910 - cont.

	42544.33.18F	Lemaître, Jules. Le mariage de Telemaque. Paris, 1910.
	38514.21.9	Le Pileur, L. Les maladies de Vénus dans l'oeuvre de François Villon. Paris, 1910.
	43688.1.37	Leroux, Gaston. Le fantôme de l'opéra. Paris, 1910.
X Cg	43688.1.30.3	Leroux, Gaston. Le mystère de la chambre jaune. Paris, 1910.
	43688.4.40	Levaillant, M. Le temple interieur. Paris, 1910.
	38557.22.6	Longuemare, E. Bossuet et la société française. Paris, 1910.
	42544.34.25	Lorde, André de. Bagnes d'enfants. Paris, 1910.
	42544.34.45.10	Louys, Pierre. Woman and puppet. N.Y., 1910.
	42545.3.18.40	Maeterlinck, Maurice. Der blaue Vogel. 6. Aufl. Berlin, 1910.
	42545.3.18.2	Maeterlinck, Maurice. The blue bird. London, 1910.
	42545.3.18.3	Maeterlinck, Maurice. The blue bird. N.Y., 1910.
	42545.3.128	Maeterlinck, Maurice. The inner beauty. London, 1910.
	42545.3.22	Maeterlinck, Maurice. Mary Magdalene. London, 1910.
	42545.3.22.5A	Maeterlinck, Maurice. Mary Magdalene. N.Y., 1910.
X Cg	42545.3.20.5	Maeterlinck, Maurice. L'oiseau bleu. Paris, 1910.
	42545.3.20.3	Maeterlinck, Maurice. L'oiseau bleu. Paris, 1910.
	42545.3.9.5	Maeterlinck, Maurice. Sister Beatrice and Ardiane and Barbe Bleue. N.Y., 1910.
X Cg	37567.96	Maigron, L. Le romantisme et les moeurs. Paris, 1910.
	42587.16.11	Maindron, M. La gardienne de l'idole noire. Paris, 1910.
	42555.43.2	Mallarmé, Stéphane. Vers et prose. Paris, 1910.
	42576.76.39	Margueritte, Paul. Nos tréteaux. Paris, 1910.
	43697.75.1100	Margyl, George. Dessus-Dessous. Paris, 1910.
	43697.77.190	Martin du Gard, Roger. L'une de nous. Paris, 1910.
	42514.39.2	Masson, Frédéric. Au jour le jour. 2. éd. Paris, 1910.
	38585.17	Masson-Forestier, Alfred. Autour d'un Racine ignoré. Paris, 1910.
	Mol 713.14A	Matthews, B. Molière his life and his works. N.Y., 1910.
	38551.19	Maugain, G. Documenti bibliografici e critici...del Fénelon in Italia. Paris, 1910.
	42577.4.29.10A	Maupassant, Guy de. Francesca and Carlotta Rondoli. N.Y., 1910.
	42577.2.5.10	Maupassant, Guy de. Madame Tellier's establishment, and stories. N.Y., 1910.
	42577.4.3.6	Maupassant, Guy de. Monsieur Parent and short stories. N.Y., 1910.
	42577.2.4	Maupassant, Guy de. The window, and short stories. N.Y., 1910.
	40583.24	Mélia, Jean. Les idées de Stendhal. Paris, 1910.
	42555.58.29	Mendès, Catulle. Zo'har; roman contemporain. Paris, 1910.
	Mol 613.8A	Miles, D.H. The influence of Molière on restoration comedy. N.Y., 1910.
	37576.610.5F	La misère sociale de la femme d'après les écrivains. Paris, 1910.
	42545.28.110	Moinaux, Georges. Les balances. Paris, 1910?
	Mol 171.62	Molière, Jean Baptiste Poquelin. Le bourgeois gentilhomme. N.Y., 1910.
	Mol 211.75	Molière, Jean Baptiste Poquelin. Les femmes savantes. Paris, 1910.
	Mol 228.60	Molière, Jean Baptiste Poquelin. Le malade imaginaire. Ann Arbor, 1910.
	Mol 245.98	Molière, Jean Baptiste Poquelin. Le misanthrope. Lausm. 2. éd. Paris, 1910.
	Mol 251.80	Molière, Jean Baptiste Poquelin. Les précieuses ridicules. Paris, 1910.
	38514.6	Molinier, H.J. Essai biographique et littéraire sur Octovien de Saint-Gelays. Rodez, 1910.
	38526.47.45	Molinier, H.J. Mellin de Saint-Gelays (1490-1558). Rodez, 1910.
	Mon 30.16A	Montaigne, Michel de. Essays. London, 1910. 3v.
	42576.15.42	Moore, Thomas S. Art and life. (Flaubert and Blake). London, 1910.
	42555.61.31	Moréas, Jean. Les stances. 6e éd. Paris, 1910.
	42555.61.45	Moréas, Jean. Variations sur la vie et les livres. Paris, 1910.
	42545.44.9	Moreau, Émile. Madame Margot. Paris, 1910.
	42545.44.2	Moreau, Émile. Le procès de Jeanne d'Arc. Paris, 1910.
	38526.17.9	Morel, L. Jean Ogier de Gombauld: sa vie, son oeuvre. Neuchâtel, 1910.
	42577.32.10	Murger, Henry. Scènes de la vie de Bohème. Paris, 1910.
	41596.35.5	Musset, Alfred de. Il faut qu'une porte soit ouverte ou fermée. London, 1910.
	41596.35.6	Musset, Alfred de. Il faut qu'une porte soit ouverte ou fermée. London, 1910.
	41596.9.4A	Musset, Alfred de. Lettres d'amour à Aimée d'Alton. Paris, 1910.
	42545.45.7	Najac, Raoul de. Maman; drame zoologique en deux actes et un prologue. n.p., 1910.
	42545.45.16	Nigond, Gabriel. 1812. v.1-2. Paris, 1910.
NEDL	40562.20	Noble, P.H.D. Le P. Lacordaire. Paris, 1910.
	37595.18.6	Oeding, F. Das altfranzösische Kreuzlied. Braunschweig, 1910.
	43723.51.100	Ollone, Charles. Théâtre en prose. Paris, 1910.
	37562.22.4	Paris, Gaston. Mélanges de littérature française du moyen âge. Paris, 1910. 2v.
	37562.22.4.1A	Paris, Gaston. Mélanges de littérature française du moyen âge. v.1-2. Paris, 1910-1912.
	42545.75	Picard, André. L'ange gardien. Paris, 1910.
	42545.76	Picard, André. La fugitive. Paris, 1910.
	43741.59.4120	Pinguet, Auguste. Nouveaux poèmes de l'Anjou. Angers, 1910.
Htn	38536.24.20*	Plan, Pierre Paul. Une réimpression ignorée du Pantagruel de Dresde. Paris, 1910.
	38537.25.16	Plattard, Jean. L'oeuvre de Rabelais. Paris, 1910.
	43743.2.45	Poizat, A. Saül; Antigone. Paris, 1910.
	42545.95.25	Pottecher, M. La clairière aux abeilles. Paris, 1910.
	42545.105	Prévost, M. Pierre et Thérèse. Paris, 1910.
	42578.31.37	Prévost, Marcel. Féminités. Paris, 1910.
	38575.17.9	Raab, Rudolf. Pierre Corneille in deutschen Ubersetzungen. Heidelberg, 1910.
	38536.1.4	Rabelais, F. Lettres écrites. Paris, 1910.
	38536.1.3	Rabelais, F. Le quatre livres de Pantagruel. Paris, 1910.
	38585.19.6	Racine, Jean. Andromaque. Boston, 1910.
	38585.35	Racine, Jean. Iphigénie. Paris, 1910.
	38585.43.4.12	Racine, Jean. Phaedre. Boston, 1910.
	FL 398.74.115	Racovita, Elena von Donniges. Princesse et comédienne; souvenirs de ma vie. Paris, 1910.
	38537.25.15	Ravà, B. L'art de Rabelais. Rome, 1910.
	40536.24.15	Reboul, Jacques. Un grand précurseur des romantiques, Ramond, 1755-1827. Nice, 1910.
	43753.9.123	Reboux, Paul. A la manière de Octave Mirbeau. Paris, 1910.

1910 - cont.

	37562.21.10	Recueil de fabliaux. Paris, 1910.
	42556.26.22	Régnier, Henri de. Le mariage de minuit. Paris, 1910.
	38526.11.9	Reibetanz, A. Jean Desmarets de Saint Sorlin, sein Leben. Leipzig, 1910.
	42587.52.40	Renard, Jules. La Bigote. Paris, 1910.
	42578.31.105	Reschal, A. Les derniers exploits de Maud. Paris, 1910.
	38547.1	Reure, O.C. Le vie et les oeuvres de Honoré d'Urfé. Paris, 1910.
	42556.22.100	Richepin, Jean. La glu. Paris, 1910.
	42556.22.22	Richepin, Jean. Miarka, la fille à l'ourse. Paris, 1910.
	38588.17.5	Richter, Erich. Philippe Quinault sein Leben. Leipzig, 1910.
	42546.6.9	Rivoire, A. Mon ami Teddy. Paris, 1910.
	42546.6.10	Rivoire, A. Mon ami Teddy. Paris, 1910.
	37558.44	Robertson, D.M. The French Academy. N.Y., 1910.
	38527.30.5	Rocheblave, S. Agrippa d'Aubigné. Paris, 1910.
	42578.19.26	Rod, Edouard. Le glaive et le bandeau. Paris, 1910.
	43757.50.710.2	Rolland, Romain. Jean-Christophe: Dawn, morning, youth, revolt. N.Y., 1910.
	43757.50.710	Rolland, Romain. Jean-Christophe: Dawn, morning, youth, revolt. N.Y., 1910.
	43757.50.233	Rolland, Romain. Jean-Christophe - la fin du voyage. Les amies. 7e éd. Paris, 1910.
	43757.3.30	Romains, Jules. Un être en marche. Paris, 1910.
	43757.3.100	Romains, Jules. Manuel de déification. Paris, 1910.
	38525.22.11	Ronsard, Pierre de. Amours de Pierre de Ronsard Vandomois. Paris, 1910.
	42578.20.2	Rosny, J.H. Les audacieux. Paris, 1910.
	42578.22.10.100	Rosny, J.H. La vague rouge. Paris, 1910.
	42578.22.140	Rosny, J.H. Les xipéhuz. Paris, 1910.
	42546.15.13.7	Rostand, Edmond. Chantecler; pièce en quatre actes, en vers. Paris, 1910.
	42546.15.13.3A	Rostand, Edmond. Chantecler. N.Y., 1910.
	42546.15.13.5	Rostand, Edmond. Chantecler. Paris, 1910.
	42546.15.13	Rostand, Edmond. Chantecler. Paris, 1910.
	42546.15.13.4	Rostand, Edmond. Chantecler. Paris, 1910.
	42546.15.13.2	Rostand, Edmond. Chantecler. Paris, 1910.
	42546.15.13.1	Rostand, Edmond. Chantecler. Paris, 1910.
	42546.15.13.6A	Rostand, Edmond. Chantecler. Paris, 1910.
	42546.15.12	Rostand, Edmond. Chantecler. pts.1-4. Paris, 1910.
	43757.83.70	Rostand, Maurice. Conversation avec la gloire. Paris, 1910.
	42547.22.80	Rougemont, E. de. Villiers de l'Isle Adam, biographie et bibliographie. Paris, 1910.
	43757.9.30	Roüpnel, Gaston. Nono. Paris, 1910.
	39532.4.15	Rousseau, J.B. Correspondance de J.B. Rousseau et de Brossette. Paris, 1910. 2v.
	FL 6022.10	Rousseau, J.J. Confessions. Paris, 1910.
	FL 6015.13	Rousseau, J.J. Correspondance avec L. Usteri. Zurich, 1910.
	FL 6085.5	Rousseau, J.J. Le nouveau Dédale, 1742. Genève, 1910.
	42576.63.795	Rumeau, Jacques. Anatole France et Sully-Prudhomme. Bordeaux, 1910.
	38526.47.35	Ruutz-Rees, Caroline. Charles de Sainte-Marthe. N.Y., 1910.
	40575.10.5	Sainte-Beuve, Charles A. Poésies complètes. Paris, 1910.
	43761.49.170	Salmon, André. Le calumet; poèmes. Paris, 1910.
	41557.9.67	Sand, George. François the Champi. Oxford, 1910.
	41557.9.44.20	Sand, George. Les maîtres sonneurs. Oxford, 1910.
NEDL	41557.29.10	Sandeau, Jules. Madeleine. Paris, 1910.
	Mon 178.12	Schiff, M. La fille d'alliance de Montaigne et Mario de Gournay. Paris, 1910.
	43763.1	Schwob, M. Bagatelle. Paris, 1910.
	37555.315	Sebillet, T. Art poétique françoys. Paris, 1910.
	37555.315.2	Sebillet, T. Art poétique françoys. Paris, 1910.
	41541.19	Séché, L. Delphine Gay, Mme. de Girardin. Paris, 1910.
	37567.115	Séché, L. La jeunesse dorée sous Louis-Philippe. Paris, 1910.
	40535.22.5	Segitz, Conrad. Marc Antoine Le Grand. Erlangen, 1910.
	41522.3.10	Seillière, E. Barbey d'Aurevilly. Paris, 1910.
	37556.24.6	Söderhjelm, W. La nouvelle française au XVe siècle. Paris, 1910.
	41558.68.20	Souvestre, Émile. An attic philosopher in Paris. N.Y., 1910.
	43776.41.170	Spire, André. J'ai trois robes distinguées. Paris, 1910.
	37596.38.9	Stevenson, W.M. Der Einfluss des Gautier d'Arras auf die altfranzösische Kunstepils. Göttingen, 1910.
	FL 373.9	Stuart, D.C. Stage decoration in France in the Middle Ages. N.Y., 1910.
	41578.54	Sugier, S. Lamartine - étude morale. Paris, 1910.
	42557.5.57	Tailhade, Laurent. La forêt. Paris, 1910.
	42557.5.9	Tailhade, Laurent. Poèmes aristophanesques. 3. éd. Paris, 1910.
	42547.4.10	Thurner, Georges. Gaby. Paris, 1910.
	42545.3.555	Tille, Vaclav. Maurice Maeterlinck; analyticna studie. V Praze, 1910.
	37555.301.5	Tobler, A. Vom Französischen Versbau alter und neuer Zeit. 5. Aufl. Leipzig, 1910.
	Mol 620.2	Toldo, P. L'oeuvre de Molière. Turin, 1910.
	40575.5.29	Troubat, Jules. La salle à manger de Sainte-Beuve. Paris, 1910.
	42557.11.3.5	Verhaeren, Émile. Ausgewählte Gedichte. Leipzig, 1910.
	42582.42	Verne, Jules. Hier et demain. Paris, 1910?
	42576.57.10.9	Viaud, Julien. Le chateau de la Belle-au-Bois-Dormant. Paris, 1910.
	42576.57.7.20	Viaud, Julien. Disenchanted. N.Y., 1910.
	42576.57.9.5	Viaud, Julien. Egypt. N.Y., 1910.
	42576.56.5.5	Viaud, Julien. Madame Chrysanthème. N.Y., 1910.
	42576.52.4.2	Viaud, Julien. Pêcheur d'Islande. Paris, 1910? 2v.
	42557.30	Vibert, Théodore. Les Girondins. Paris, 1910.
	43824.4.30	Villetard, P. Les amoureuses. Paris, 1910.
	42547.18.7	Villiers de l'Isle Adam, Auguste. L'évasion; drame. 2e éd. Paris, 1910.
	38514.18.7	Villon, François. Oeuvres le Petit et le Grant Testament, poésies diverses. Paris, 1910.
	43824.2.48	Vivien, Renée. Le vent des vaisseaux. Paris, 1910.
	37574.72	Watrin, Eugène. Echos poétiques de Lorraine. 2. éd. Guénange, 1910.
	Mol 698.11	Wechssler, E. Molière als Philosoph. Marburg, 1910.
	37597.27	Weydig, Otto. Beiträge zur Geschichte des Mirakelspiels. Inaug. Diss. Erfurt, 1910.
	43833.1.33	Weyl, Fernand. Au temps d'Adrien. Paris, 1910.
	43833.1.31	Weyl, Fernand. L'illustration théatrale. Paris, 1910.
	43833.1.32	Weyl, Fernand. Joconde; fantaisie en deux actes. Paris, 1910.

Chronological Listing

1910 - cont.

	Mol 723.3	Wolff, Max I. Molière der Dichter und sein Werk. München, 1910.
	42547.33	Wolff, Pierre. Les marionnettes. Paris, 1910.
	43858.1.32.5	Zamacois, Miguel. La fleur merveilleuse. Paris, 1910.
	43858.1.32	Zamacois, Miguel. La fleur merveilleuse. Paris, 1910.
	42584.19.3	Zola, Emile. Le rêve. Paris, 1910.

1911

	42562.29.2	About, Edmond. Les mariages de Paris. Paris, 1911.
	42562.38.14.5	Adam, Paul. La ville inconnue. 3. éd. Paris, 1911.
	43517.1.30	Aguétant, P. La vieille terre. Belley, 1911.
	42542.1.11.30	Ajalbert, Jean. Raffin Su-Su. Paris, 1911.
	37596.114	Aldebrandin de Sienne. Le régime du corps. Paris, 1911.
	42553.39	Angellier, A. Dans la lumière antique. Les scènes. Paris, 1911.
	42586.14.6	Audoux, M. Marie-Claire. N.Y., 1911.
	42586.14.5	Audoux, M. Marie-Claire. N.Y., 1911.
	42586.14.3	Audoux, M. Marie-Claire. Paris, 1911.
	40596.13.130.2	Balzac, Honoré de. The comédie humaine. N.Y., 1911. 4v.
	40597.19.22	Balzac, Honoré de. Eugénie Grandet. Paris, 1911.
	37562.65	Bardenwerper, K. Die Anwendung fremder Sprachen und Mundarten in den französischen Farcen. Halle, 1911.
	37567.111.2	Barre, A. Bibliographique poésie symboliste. Paris, 1911.
	37567.111	Barre, A. Le symbolisme. Paris, 1911.
	42541.6.10	Bataille, Henry. L'enfant de l'amour. Paris, 1911.
	38563.6A	Bayle, Pierre. Pensées diverses sur la Cornète. Paris, 1911. 2v.
	42563.21.58	Bazin, René. Le blé qui lève. Paris, 1911?
	43538.1.33	Beauduin, Nicolas. Les deux regnes. Paris, 1911.
	40532.14.10	Beaumarchais, Pierre A.C. de. Théâtre illustré. Bibliothèque Larousse. Paris, 1911?
	37562.21.6	Bédier, Joseph. Les fabliaux. 3. éd. Paris, 1911.
	42578.35.20	Behrens, H. Francisque Sarceys Theaterkritik. Greifswald, 1911.
	FL 385.7	Benoist, A. Le théâtre d'aujourd'hui. Paris, 1911. 2v.
	43538.2.30	Benoit, F. Foire aux paysages. Paris, 1911.
	41592.19	Béranger, P.J. de. Les chansons de Béranger, morceaux choisis. London, 1911.
	42542.29.10	Bergerat, Émile. Souvenirs d'un enfant de Paris. Paris, 1911. 2v.
	43538.76.2100	Bernard, O. Quand l'amour voyage. Paris, 1911.
	42542.29.28.150	Bernard, Tristan. L'intrús (Le danseur inconnu). Barcelona, 1911.
	43538.4.30	Bernardin, N.M. L'Abbé Frifillis. Paris, 1911.
	42542.29.29.7	Bernhardt, S. (Mme.). Un coeur d'homme. Paris, 1911. 2 pam.
	42542.29.45	Bernstein, H. Après moi. Paris, 1911.
	40582.32	Beyle, Henri. Journal d'Italie. Paris, 1911.
	37596.115	Bible. Anglo-Norman. O.T. Samuel. Li quatre livre des Reis. Dresden, 1911.
	42556.16.3	Billigheimer, S. Das religiöse Leben Sully-Prudhommes. Freiburg, 1911.
X Cg	42542.29.106	Bisson, Alexandre. Les surprises du divorce. Paris, 1911.
	38566.26.9	Boileau Despréaux, Nicolas. L'art poétique. 7. éd. Paris, 1911.
	42542.37.15	Bois, Jules. Les deux Hélène. Paris, 1911.
	42563.36.32	Bordeaux, Henry. Die kleine Mamsell. N.Y., 1911.
	40516.6.10	Bourgeois, Armand. Pages inédites ou ignorées sur Cazotte. Paris, 1911.
	42563.37.8.7A	Bourget, Paul. Le disciple. Paris, 1911.
	42563.37.32	Bourget, Paul. L'envers du décor. Paris, 1911.
	42563.37.30	Bourget, Paul. Le tribun. Paris, 1911.
Htn	FL 6139.11*	Boyd, William. The educational theory of Jean-Jacques Rousseau. London, 1911.
	42556.16	Brangsch, W. Philosophie und Dichtung bei Sully-Prudhomme. Berlin, 1911.
	42542.47.25A	Brieux, Eugène. Three plays. London, 1911.
	42542.47.39.15A	Brieux, Eugène. Three plays. N.Y., 1911.
	40539.15.20	Brückner, Alexander. Jana hr. Potockiego i zasługi naukowe. Warszawa, 1911.
	FL 6129.02.5	Buffenois, H. Les charmettes et Jean-Jacques Rousseau. Paris, 1911.
	42542.47.79.3	Caillavet, G.A. Primerose. Paris, 1911.
	37567.109	Canat, René. La renaissance de la Grèce antique (1820-1850). Paris, 1911.
	Mon 113.4	Cancalon. L'esprit positif et scientifique dans Montaigne. Paris, 1911.
	37567.65.10	Cario, Louis. L'exotisme. 2e éd. Paris, 1911.
	38514.23.165	Catani, Nazzareno. La misère et la sensualité de Villon. Crema, 1911.
	42557.14.9	Cazals, F.A. Les derniers jours de Paul Verlaine. Paris, 1911.
	40586.28.12	Chateaubriand, F.A.R. Mémoires d'outre-tombe. Paris, 1911.
	40585.412	Chateaubriand, F.A.R. Pages choisies: La correspondance. Paris, 1911.
	38576.21.31	Chatenet, H.E. Le roman...Mme. de Villedieu (1632-1683). Paris, 1911.
	38567.18	Chiarini, M. Nicolas Boileau Despréaux. Imola, 1911.
	37563.28	Chinard, G. L'exotisme américain dans la littérature française au XVIe siècle. Paris, 1911.
X Cg	37563.28	Chinard, G. L'exotisme américain dans la littérature française au XVIe siècle. Paris, 1911.
	37595.36.14A	Chrestien de Troyes. Wilhelm von England. v.20. Halle, 1911.
	38514.30A	Cigada, Sergio. Vie de Charles d'Orleans (1394-1465). Milano, 1911.
NEDL	43554.2	Claudel, Paul. Théâtre. Serie 1. Paris, 1911. 4v.
	37548.232	Congrès national des oeuvres intellectuelles de langue française, 1st,Brussels, 1910. Premier congrès national des oeuvres intellectuelles de langue française. Huy, 1911.
	42542.53.50	Copeau, Jacques. Les frères Karamazov. Paris, 1911.
	37571.50	Côte, Léon. La flore littéraire du Dauphiné. Grenoble, 1911. 3v.
	37596.116	Courtois d'Arras jeu du XIIIe siècle. Paris, 1911.
	42566.20.10	Daudet, Alphonse. Neuf contes choisis. N.Y., 1911.
	42566.19.8.25	Daudet, Alphonse. Tartarin de Tarascon. Boston, 1911.
	42566.66.19.8.25	Daudet, Alphonse. Tartarin de Tarascon. Boston, 1911.
	42566.36.15	Daudet, Alphonse. Théâtre. 3e série. Paris, 1911.
	40545.21	De Mohl, O. Correspondance de Fauriel et Mary Clarke. Paris, 1911.

1911 - cont.

	39527.4.14	De Rochambeau, Achille Lacroix. Bibliographie des oeuvres de La Fontaine. Paris, 1911.
	41593.29.3.5	Desbordes-Valmore, Marceline. Lettres inedites. 1812-1857. Paris, 1911?
	42514.28.105	Descogs, Pedro. A travers l'oeuvre de M. Maurras. Paris, 1911.
	42542.64.60	Dieudonne, R. Messieurs les ronds-de-cuir. Paris, 1911.
	42543.16.7.1	Dumas, Alexandre. La dame aux camélias. N.Y., 1911.
	41538.16.15	Dumas, Alexandre. Edmond Dantès. N.Y., 1911.
	41596.4.15	Dumoulin, M. Les ancêtres d'Alfred de Musset. Paris, 1911.
	37565.31.6	Dupont-Chatelain, M. Les encyclopédistes et les femmes. Paris, 1911.
	43576.3.30F	Duquesnel, F. La fille. Paris, 1911.
	42563.60	Durand, Alice M.C.F. Mon chien Bop et ses amis. Paris, 1911.
	38539.6	Du Vair, Guillaume. Actions et traictez oratoires. Paris, 1911.
	42524.55	Duval, Maurice. Émile Faguet. Le critique, le moraliste. Paris, 1911.
	37567.139	Edwards, Matilda. French men, women and books. Chicago, 1911.
	42572.11.25	Erckmann, Emile. The history of a conscript of 1813 and Waterloo. London, 1911.
	42543.38.12	Fabre, Émile. Les sauterelles. Paris, 1911.
	37543.124	Faguet, E. En lisant les beaux vieux livres. Paris, 1911.
	37543.124.2	Faguet, E. En lisant les beaux vieux livres. 2. éd. Paris, 1911.
	FL 6119.10.3A	Faguet, E. Vie de Rousseau. Paris, 1911.
	43606.1.30	Falk, H. Poèmes brefs, idylles et comédies. Paris, 1911.
	43606.78.100.5	Farrère, Claude. La bataille. 8. éd. Paris, 1911.
	43606.78.190	Farrère, Claude. La maison des hommes vivants. 27. éd. Paris, 1911.
	42543.40.10	Fauchois, R. Rivoli. Paris, 1911.
	42565.72.2	Favre de Coulevain, Hélène. Noblesse américaine. 61. éd. Paris, 1911?
	42565.71.50	Favre de Coulevain, Hélène. The unknown isle. London, 1911.
	37573.37.4	Ferrières, Gauthier. Anthologie des écrivains français du XVIIe siècle; poésie. Paris, 1911.
	37573.37.3	Ferrières, Gauthier. Anthologie des écrivains français du XVIIe siècle; prose. Paris, 1911.
	37573.37.6	Ferrières, Gauthier. Anthologie des écrivains français du XVIIIe siècle; poésie. Paris, 1911.
	42543.41.10	Feydeau, Georges. Occupe-toi d'Amélie! Paris, 1911.
	43609.1.30	Fiel, Marthe. Sur le sol d'Alsace. Paris, 1911.
	42576.23.7	Flaubert, Gustave. The temptation of St. Anthony. N.Y., 1911.
	42543.42.11	Flers, Robert de. Miquette et sa mère. Paris, 1911.
	42543.42.6	Flers, Robert de. Papa. Comédie en trois actes. Paris, 1911.
	42555.12.25	Fleury, E. Hippolyte de La Morvonnais. Paris, 1911.
	42554.35	Floupette, A. Les déliquescences. Paris, 1911.
	40562.45.15	Folghera, J.D. L'apologétique de Lacordaire. Paris, 1911.
	43611.1.25.12	Fort, Paul. L'aventure éternelle. Livre I. XII. Paris, 1911.
	38513.60	Fourmann, J. Über die Uberlieferung und den Versbau des Mystère. Erlangen, 1911.
	42576.62.105	France, Anatole. Honey-bee. London, 1911.
	42576.62.21.7	France, Anatole. L'île des pingouins. 107. éd. Paris, 1911.
	42576.62.13.7	France, Anatole. Le jardin d'Epicure. 54. éd. Paris, 1911?
	43616.1.30	Ganay, E. de. Le fleures du silence. Paris, 1911.
	43616.83.130	Gasquet, Joachim. Le paradis retrauvé. Paris, 1911.
	43616.2.45	Gautier, Judith. La fille du ciel. 10. éd. Paris, 1911.
	42543.45.30	Gavault, Paul. Family-hotel. Paris, 1911.
	43617.3.30	Genty, R. Les âmes légères. Paris, 1911.
	37567.140	Ghéon, Henri. Nos directions. Paris, 1911.
X Cg	43620.2.32	Gide, André. L'immoraliste. 4. éd. Paris, 1911.
	37543.80.2	Giraud, Victor. Les maîtres de l'heure. Paris, 1911-
	43620.74.165	Giraudoux, Jean. L'école des indifférents. Paris, 1911.
	42586.68.9	Gobineau, Arthur de. Alexander. 3. Aufl. Strassburg, 1911.
	42586.68.2	Gobineau, Arthur de. Nachgelassene Schriften. Briefe. 2. Aufl. Strassburg, 1911.
	42576.37.35	Gorsse, H. de. Cinq semaines en aéroplane. Paris, 1911.
	43625.3.30	Gourmont, Rémy de. Le chemin de velours. 5e ed. Paris, 1911.
	43625.3.30.5	Gourmont, Rémy de. Le chemin de velours. 60e éd. Paris, 1911.
	43625.3.43	Gourmont, Rémy de. Pèlerin du silence. 5e ed. Paris, 1911.
	37574.775	Grautoff, Otto. Die lyriche Bewegung im gegenwärtigen Frankreich. Jena, 1911.
	FL 398.74.85	Gribble, F. Rachel, her stage life and real life. London, 1911.
NEDL	FL 398.74.85	Gribble, F. Rachel, her stage life and real life. London, 1911.
	FL 398.74.86	Gribble, F. Rachel, her stage life and real life. N.Y., 1911.
	38551.65.20	Griselle, Eugène. Fénelon; études historiques. Paris, 1911.
	42554.50.11	Guérin, C. La semeur de cendres 1898-1900. 6e éd. Paris, 1911.
	41593.34.25	Guérin, Maurice de. Journal, lettres et poèmes. 25. éd. Paris, 1911.
	42543.61.10	Guinon, Albert. Le bonheur. Paris, 1911.
	42543.62.25	Guiraud, E. Marie-Victoire. Paris, 1911.
	42543.62.20	Guitry, Sacha. Le veilleur de nuit. Paris, 1911.
	Mol 270.34	Hähnel, Oskar. Die Tendenz von Molières Tartuffe in der fronziösischen Kritik. Inaug. Diss. Mannheim, 1911.
	39532.5.8	Hamilton, Anthony. Der Chevalier von Grammont. München, 1911. 2v.
	39545.18.2	Hamley, E.B. Voltaire. Edinburgh, 1911.
	42543.63.10	Hermant, Abel. La biche relancée. Paris, 1911.
	42554.64.40	Herold, A.F. La route fleurie. Paris, 1911.
	37543.74	Hervier, M. Les écrivains français jugés par leurs contemporains. Paris, 1911- 4v.
	38544.1	Hill, H.W. La Calprenède's romances and restoration drama. Chicago, 1911.
	41573.5.15	Hugo, Victor. Morceaux choisis. Paris, 1911.
	41571.3.95	Hugo, Victor. The poetry of Victor Hugo. Boston, 1911.
	43638.99.115	Huzard, A. de B. (Mme.). Le métier de roi. Paris, 1911.
	39532.4.45	Hyrvoix de Landosle, A. Jean-Baptiste Rousseau. Paris, 1911.

Chronological Listing

1911 - cont.

37556.58 Jakob, M. Gustave. L'illusion et le désillusion dans le roman réaliste français. Paris, 1911.
43667.1.34 Jammes, Francis. De l'angelus de l'aube à l'angelus du soir 1888-1897. 5. éd. Paris, 1911.
43667.1.31 Jammes, Francis. Les géorgiques chrétiennes. Paris, 1911.
43667.1.33 Jammes, Francis. Le triomphe de la vie 1900-1901. 3. éd. Paris, 1911.
43667.53.100 Janot, Paul. Le théâtre chrétien. Paris, 1911.
43667.78.170 Jarry, Alfred. Gestes et opinions du docteur Faustroll. Paris, 1911.
43670.94.230 Jouve, Pierre Jean. Les aéroplanes. Paris, 1911.
43670.94.160 Jouve, Pierre Jean. Les ordres qui changent. Paris, 1911.
FL 398.42.5 Judith, Julie B. La vie d'une grande comédienne. Paris, 1911.
40536.18.15 Junge, Ernest. Charles François Panard. Leipzig, 1911.
38514.80 Klein, A. Die altfranzösischen Minnefragen. Marburg, 1911.
FL 375.65 Kohler, E. Entwicklung des Biblischen Dramas des XVI Jahrhunderts. Leipzig, 1911.
FL 6139.11.5 Krstitsch, M. Rousseaus pädagogische Ansichten im lichte der Gegenwartigen Erziehungswissenschaft. Zürich, 1911.
FL 6129.11 Künzler, Fritz. Die Ermitage-Zeit als ein Markstein in Rousseaus Leben. Solothurn, 1911.
42544.30.15 Labiche, Eugène. Monsieur Pickwick. Paris, 1911.
42544.26.6 Labiche, Eugène. Le voyage de Monsieur Perrichon. Boston, 1911.
38521.30.2 Lachèvre, Frédéric. Disciplines et successeurs de Théophile de Viau. Paris, 1911.
38521.30.3 Lachèvre, Frédéric. Une seconde revision des oeuvres du poète Théophile de Viau. Paris, 1911.
41578.63 Lacretelle, Pierre de. Les origines et la jeunesse de Lamartine. 1790-1812. Paris, 1911.
38544.27.46 La Fayette, Marie M. La Princesse de Clèves. Paris, 1911.
41578.5.12 Lamartine, Alphonse de. Harmonies poétiques et religieuses. Paris, 1911.
37555.311 Landry, E. La théorie du rythme et le rythme du français déclamé. Paris, 1911.
42544.3.25 Laroze, L. Le respect de l'amour. Paris, 1911.
38525.20.260 Laumonier, P. Tableau chronologique des oeuvres de Ronsard. 2e éd. Paris, 1911.
42544.24.11 Lavedan, Henri. Le gout du vice. Paris, 1911.
42576.41.20 Le Blanc, Maurice. La frontière. Paris, 1911.
42576.41.23 Le Blanc, Maurice. 813. Garden City, 1911.
37593.64.12A Le Bossi, A. Le jeu de la feuille. Paris, 1911.
43688.15.110 Leconte, S.C. Le masque de fer. Paris, 1911.
42576.15.15 Lehmann, R. Die Formelemente des Stils von Flaubert. Marburg, 1911.
43688.49.100 Le Leu, Louis. Récits d'un siècle. Paris, 1911.
37556.80 Lemonnier, L. Populisme. Paris, 1911.
42544.20 Lengyel, M. Le typhon. Paris, 1911.
43688.1.33.10 Leroux, Gaston. The phantom of the opera. N.Y., 1911.
43688.1.33.11 Leroux, Gaston. The phantom of the opera. N.Y., 1911.
43688.3.30 Lestrange, R. Le miroir enchanté. Paris, 1911.
43688.91.110 Level, Maurice. The grip of fear. N.Y., 1911.
37556.35.13 Levrault, Léon. La satire. Paris, 1911?
37574.54 Lewis, Charles B. La lyre d'amour. Anthology of French love poems. London, 1911.
43690.24.130 Lienard, Albert. Les esclaves. Paris, 1911.
37558.55 Loliée, Frédéric. L'Académie française devant l'opinion. Paris, 1911.
FL 398.7.22 London Coleseum. Mme. S. Bernhardt season. Prospectus. London, 1911.
37597.9.17 Lorris, Guillaume de. The romaunt of the rose. London, 1911.
Htn 42544.34.28.5* Louys, Pierre. Les chansons de Bilitis. Paris, 1911.
42544.36 Loyson, Paul H. L'apôtre. Paris, 1911.
42545.3.6.20 Maeterlinck, Maurice. Aglavaine and Selysette. Jena, 1911.
42545.3.6.2 Maeterlinck, Maurice. Aglavaine et Selysette. N.Y., 1911.
42545.3.18.30 Maeterlinck, Maurice. The blue bird. London, 1911.
42545.3.18.5A Maeterlinck, Maurice. The blue bird. N.Y., 1911.
42545.3.32 Maeterlinck, Maurice. Death. 3d ed. London, 1911.
42545.3.127A Maeterlinck, Maurice. The inner beauty. Chicago, 1911.
42545.3.125 Maeterlinck, Maurice. The inner beauty. N.Y., 1911.
42545.3.15.25 Maeterlinck, Maurice. Joyzelle. N.Y., 1911.
42545.3.21 Maeterlinck, Maurice. L'oiseau bleu. Paris, 1911.
42545.3.3.9 Maeterlinck, Maurice. Pélléas and Mélisande, Alladine and Palomides, Home. N.Y., 1911.
42545.3.1.3 Maeterlinck, Maurice. Princess Maleine. N.Y., 1911.
42545.3.9.6 Maeterlinck, Maurice. Sister Beatrice and Ardiane and Barbe Bleue. N.Y., 1911.
42545.01.5 Maeterlinck, Maurice. Théâtre. Bruxellles, 1911-12. 3v.
42545.3.7.15 Maeterlinck, Maurice. Three plays. London, 1911.
42545.3.5.9 Maeterlinck, Maurice. The treasure of the humble. London, 1911.
38542.3.5 Magne, Emile. Voiture et les origines de l'hotel de Rambouillet. 1597-1635. Paris, 1911.
X Cg 37567.96.5 Maigron, L. Le romantisme et la mode. Paris, 1911.
42587.16.14.5 Maindron, M. Ce bon M. de Véragues. Paris, 1911.
42576.76.13.10 Margueritte, Paul. Pascal Géfosse. Paris, 1911.
38575.23.35 Mariolle-Pilté, R. La descendance des Corneille. Paris, 1911.
38523.10.25 Marot, Clément. Oeuvres. Paris, 1911.
38523.8 Marot, Clément. Oeuvres. v.1,4,5. Paris, 1911-31. 3v.
37555.500 Martinon, Philippe. Les Strophes, étude historique et critique. Paris, 1911.
43697.79.140 Mary, André. Le cantique de la Seine. Paris, 1911.
41578.77 Masson, Pierre M. Lamartine. Paris, 1911.
42577.4.8.15 Maupassant, Guy de. The Horla, Miss Harriet, Little Louise Roque and other stories. London, 1911.
42577.4.3.5 Maupassant, Guy de. Monsieur Parent. London, 1911.
42577.4.17.15 Maupassant, Guy de. Pierre and Jean, Father and son, Boitelle and other stories. London, 1911.
42577.4.10.8 Maupassant, Guy de. Strong as death and other stories. London, 1911.
43697.88.600 Mauriac, François. L'adieu à l'adolescence. Paris, 1911.
40583.23 Mélia, Jean. Stendhal et ses commentateurs. Paris, 1911.
42533.10 Mézières, A. Pages d'automne. Paris, 1911.
40587.26 Michel, E. Chateaubriand. Paris, 1911. 2v.
40583.28 Mino, F. Saggio di uno studio su lo Stendhal. Napoli, 1911.
37555.67 Miomandre, F. Figures d'hier et d'aujourd'hui. Paris, 1911.

1911 - cont.

42545.28.6 Mirbeau, Octave. Les affaires sont les affaires. Paris, 1911.
42545.28.9.40 Moinaux, Georges. La cruche. Paris, 1911.
Mol 165.88 Molière, Jean Baptiste Poquelin. L'avare. N.Y., 1911.
Mol 60.22.5 Molière, Jean Baptiste Poquelin. Dramatic works. v.2. London, 1911.
Mol 211.77 Molière, Jean Baptiste Poquelin. Les femmes savantes...M.P. Brush. N.Y., 1911.
Mol 62.54 Molière, Jean Baptiste Poquelin. In Deutscher Sprache...O. Hauser. Berlin, 1911-12. 2v.
Mol 60.34 Molière, Jean Baptiste Poquelin. The Kiltartan Molière by Lady Gregory. Dublin, 1911.
Mol 235.49A Molière, Jean Baptiste Poquelin. Le médecin malgré lui...R.L. Hawkins. Boston, 1911.
Mol 62.39 Molière, Jean Baptiste Poquelin. Meisterwerke...Fulda. 5e Aufl. Stuttgart, 1911.
Mon 31.50 Montaigne, Michel de. Essays. Cotton (Hazlitt). 2. ed. London, 1911. 3v.
42545.44.3 Moreau, Émile. Argument of the play Le procès de Jeanne d'Arc. N.Y., 1911.
43701.4.30 Morice, Charles. Il est ressuscité! 3e éd. Paris, 1911.
43701.4.37 Morice, Charles. The re-appearing. N.Y., 1911.
40526.70 Müller, Max. Jean Joseph Vadé (1719-1757) und das Vaudeville. Griefswald, 1911.
41543.16 Nerval, Gerard de. Correspondance (1830-1855). Paris, 1911.
42545.45.40 Nigond, Gabriel. Perlot; pièce en un acte. Paris, 1911.
43723.51.140 Ollone, Charles. La victoire aileé. Paris, 1911.
37562.60 Oulmont, Charles. Les débats du Clerc et du chevalier. Paris, 1911.
38526.18.10 Oulmont, Charles. Étude sur la langue de Pierre Gringore. Paris, 1911.
38526.18.9 Oulmont, Charles. Pierre Gringore. Paris, 1911.
42545.63.7 Pailleron, Edouard. Le monde ou l'on s'ennuie. Boston, 1911.
X Cg 37596.54.9 Paris, Gaston. La vie de Saint Aléxis. Paris, 1911.
42578.30.72 Peladan, J. Das allmächtige Gold. München, 1911.
37565.48 Pellisson, M. Les hommes de lettres au XVIIIe siècle. Paris, 1911.
43738.3.30 Pelsener, A. Dans le vent des hélices. Grand, 1911.
43738.76.160 Pergaud, Louis. La revanche du corbeau. Paris, 1911.
40537.14 Peters, Ernst. Marie Joseph Chénier als Kritiker. Leipzig, 1911.
42586.9.15 Petry, L. Paul Arène, ein Dichter der Provence. Halle, 1911.
43740.1.38 Philippe, Charles Louis. Faits divers. Nevers, 1911.
43740.1.32 Philippe, Charles Louis. Lettres de jeunesse à Henri Vandeputte. Paris, 1911.
39533.34 Pic, P. Guy Patin. Paris, 1911.
43743.2.31 Poizat, A. Classicisme et Catholicisme. Paris, 1911.
43743.2.50 Poizat, A. Méléagre et Atalante. Paris, 1911.
43743.1.31 Porché, François. Humus et Poussière. Poèmes. Paris, 1911.
42545.87 Porto-Riche, G. Le vieil homme. Paris, 1911.
42545.95.40 Pottecher, M. Le mystère de Judas Iscariote. Paris, 1911.
39544.102 Price, W.R. Symbolism of Voltaire's novels. N.Y., 1911.
38536.24.25 Rabelais, F. Rabelais médecin: notes et commentaires. Paris, 1911.
38583.12.10 Racine, Jean. Dramatic works. v.2. London, 1911.
38583.14 Racine, Jean. Oeuvres inconnues. n.p., 1911.
38587.10.20 Regnard, Jean François. Les folies amoureuses. Paris, 1911.
Htn 42522.3* Régnier, H. de. Discours de réception à l'academie française. Paris, 1911.
42556.26.20 Régnier, Henri de. La cité des eaux. Paris, 1911.
42556.27.1 Régnier, Henri de. Les jeux rustiques et divins. 8. éd. Paris, 1911.
42556.27.6.8 Régnier, Henri de. Les médailles d'Argile. 8e éd. Paris, 1911.
42556.26.22.89 Régnier, Henri de. Le miroir des heures. 7e éd. Paris, 1911.
42556.26.23 Régnier, Henri de. Le miroir des heures. 8. éd. Paris, 1911.
42556.27.7.2 Régnier, Henri de. Le passé vivant. Paris, 1911.
42556.27.9.7 Régnier, Henri de. La sandale ailée 1903-1905. 7e éd. Paris, 1911.
40524.27.55 Restif de la Bretonne, Nicolas E. Oeuvre. Paris, 1911-22. 2v.
37567.106 Retinger, J.H. Histoire de la littérature française du romantisme à nos jours. Paris, 1911.
38546.23.5 Reumann, R. Georges de Scudéry als Epiker. Coburg, 1911.
40536.21.30 Richard, Achille. Les suppliants. Paris, 1911.
FL 376.25 Rigal, E. De Jodelle à Molière. Tragédie. Paris, 1911.
43757.5.30 Robert, Louis de. Le roman du malade. Paris, 1911.
42515.35.226 Roberto, Diego de. Renan. Torino, 1911.
41574.53 Rochette, A. L'alexandrin chez Victor Hugo. Paris, 1911.
38527.47.9 Rolland, J. La tragédie française au XVIe siècle. "Les juifves". Photoreproduction. Paris, 1911.
43757.50.711A Rolland, Romain. Jean-Christophe: Dawn, morning, youth, revolt. N.Y., 1911.
43757.50.243 Rolland, Romain. Jean-Christophe - la fin du voyage. Le buisson ardent. 4e éd. Paris, 1911?
43757.50.245 Rolland, Romain. Jean-Christophe - la fin du voyage. Le buisson ardent. 11e éd. Paris, 1911?
43757.50.720 Rolland, Romain. Jean-Christophe in Paris. The market place, Antoinette,The house. N.Y., 1911.
43757.50.721A Rolland, Romain. Jean-Christophe in Paris. The market place, Antoinette,The house. N.Y., 1911.
42556.32.60 Rollinat, Maurice. Les bêtes. Paris, 1911.
43757.3.285 Romains, Jules. L'armée dans la ville. Paris, 1911.
43757.3.32 Romains, Jules. Mort de quelqu'un; roman. Paris, 1911.
37596.117 Roques, M. Le garçon et l'aveugle. Paris, 1911.
42545.3.450 Rose, Henry. On Maeterlinck. London, 1911.
42546.15.14 Rostand, Edmond. Les musardises. Paris, 1911.
42546.15.7.5 Rostand, Edmond. La princesse Lointaine. Paris, 1911.
42546.15.7.6 Rostand, Edmond. La princesse Lointaine. Paris, 1911.
43757.83.73 Rostand, Maurice. Poèmes. Paris, 1911.
FL 6002.911 Rousseau, J.J. Extraits. Paris, 1911.
FL 6015.14 Rousseau, J.J. Lettres inédites à Mmes. Boy de La Tour. Paris, 1911.
FL 6005.20 Rousseau, J.J. Minor educational writings of Jean-Jacques Rousseau. London, 1911.
43761.41.120 St. Georges de Bouhelier. Carnaval des enfants. Paris, 1911.
39595.23 St. Pierre, J.H.B. de. Paul et Virginie suivi de La chaumière indienne. Paris, 1911?

1911 - cont.

40575.7.35 Sainte-Beuve, Charles A. Lettres inédites de Sainte-Beuve à Charles Labitte, 1834-45. Paris, 1911.
41557.8.134 Sand, George. Thoughts and aphorisms from her work. London, 1911.
40546.11 Schemann, L. Alexis de Tocqueville. Stuttgart, 1911.
37556.72 Schomaum, E. Französische Utopisten und ehr Frauenideal. Berlin, 1911.
Mol 193.30 Schröder, Theodor. Die Quellen des "Don Juan" von Molière. Inaug. Diss. Halle, 1911.
FL 391.155 Schuermann, Joseph L. Secret de coulisses. Paris, 1911.
38513.23.10 Schumacher, Joseph. Studien zur Farce Pathelin. Rostock, 1911.
41578.62 Séché, Léon. Les amitiés de Lamartine. 1e série. Paris, 1911.
42587.58.8.15 Ségur, Sophie. Les malheurs de Sophie. Paris, 1911.
41569.20 Les sérails de Londres. Paris, 1911.
37562.34 Shishmarev, V. Lirika i liriki...istorii frantsii. Paris, 1911.
Mon 159.2A Sichel, E. Michel de Montaigne. London, 1911.
Mon 129.4A Sichel, E. Michel de Montaigne. N.Y., 1911.
37574.71 Société havraise d'etudes diverses. L'abeille havraise. Havre, 1911.
FL 385.82 Sorel, A.E. Essais de psychologie dramatique. Paris, 1911.
43775.1.30 Sorel, Albert E. L'écueil. 4. éd. Paris, 1911.
43776.41.180 Spire, André. Vers les routes absurdes. Paris, 1911.
41574.67 Stölten, O. Die Entwicklung des bildlichen Ausdrucks in der Sprache Victor Hugos. Jena, 1911.
42536.33 Taine, Hippolyte. Sein Leben in Briefen. v.1-2. Berlin, 1911.
FL 398.83 Talma, F.J. Lettres d'amour inédits de Talma à la princesse Pauline Bonaparte. Paris, 1911.
42577.4.42 Tassart, François. Souvenir sur Guy de Maupassant. Paris, 1911.
43788.55.100 Tharaud, Jérôme. La maîtresse servante. Paris, 1911.
42545.3.440.2 Thomas, Edward. Maurice Maeterlinck. N.Y., 1911.
38514.21.8 Thuasne, L. Villon et Rabelais. Paris, 1911.
42578.51.37 Tinayre, Marcelle. Douceur de vivre. Paris, 1911.
42578.51.40 Tinayre, Marcelle. La douceur de vivre. 27. éd. Paris, 1911.
42578.52.65 Tinseau, Léon de. Le finale de la symphonie. Paris, 1911.
37567.270 Tissot, Ernest. Nouvelles princesses de lettres. Paris, 1911.
37530.27 Toinet, R. Essai d'une liste alphabètique des auteurs. Tulle, 1911.
43792.89.2100 Toucas-Massillon, Edmond. Saturnin. Paris, 1911.
42587.16.16 Toussaint, R.J. Mademoiselle. 4. éd. Paris, 1911.
42547.5.9 Trarieux, Gabriel. La brebis perdue. Paris, 1911.
42547.5.10 Trarieux, Gabriel. Un soir. Paris, 1911.
43822.1.30 Valentin, A. Je dirae sur la route. Paris, 1911.
FL 6119.11 Vallette, G. J.J. Rousseau Génevois. Paris, 1911.
42547.10.29 Vandérem, F. Cher maître. Paris, 1911.
42547.12.4 Veber, Pierre. La gamine. Paris, 1911.
42557.11.2.17 Verhaeren, Émile. Poèmes. 7. éd. Paris, 1911.
42582.4 Verne, Jules. Works. N.Y., 1911. 15v.
42576.51.3 Viaud, Julien. Fantôme d'Orient. Paris, 1911?
42576.57.4.3 Viaud, Julien. Matelot. Paris, 1911?
41564.1.5 Vigny, Alfred de. Journal d'un poete. Paris, 1911.
Mon 132.5.9A Villey, P. L'influence de Montaigne...de Locke. Paris, 1911.
Mon 132.5.7 Villey, P. Montaigne a-t-il en quelque influence sur François Bacon? Paris, 1911-12.
38514.20.11A Villon, François. Oeuvres. Paris, 1911.
37555.47 Visau, T. de. L'attitude du lyrisme contemporain. Paris, 1911.
42522.20 Vogüé, E.M. de. Trois drames de l'histoire de Russie. Paris, 1911.
40575.2.5 Voizard, F. Sainte-Beuve l'homme et l'oeuvre. Paris, 1911.
37596.144 Wallheinke, Arndt. Die "Vers de le mort" von Robert le Clerc. Inaug. Diss. Weida, 1911.
38567.8 Walter, Ulrich. Boileaus Wirkung auf seine englischen Zeitgenossen. Inaug. Diss. Strassburg, 1911.
37597.12.5 Ward, C.F. Epistles on romance of the rose. Chicago, 1911.
Mol 723.4 Wechssler, E. Über die Bezichungen von Weltanschauung...Molière und V. Hugo. Marburg, 1911.
40597.2.390 Weigand, W. Stendhal und Balzac; essays. Leipzig, 1911.
42547.36 Wolff, Pierre. L'amour défendu. Paris, 1911.
43858.1.65 Zamacois, Miguel. L'arche de Noé. Paris, 1911.
40534.11 Zimmermann, Erich. Pierre-Laurent Buirette de Belloy, sein Leben und seine Tragödien. Leipzig, 1911.
42584.23.57 Zola, Emile. For a night. The maid of the dawber. Philadelphia, 1911.
42584.23.79 Zola, Emile. Love's chase. N.Y., 1911.

1912

37543.114 Abry, E. Histoire illustrée de la littérature française. Paris, 1912.
42562.38.14.46 Adam, Paul. Le trust. 6e éd. Paris, 1912.
NEDL 42586.7.20 Aicard, Jean. L'âme d'un enfant. Paris, 1912?
39574.27.20 Alembert, J. Le Rond d'. Einleitung in die französische Enzyklopädie von 1751. Leipzig, 1912.
43522.41.220 Alibert, François Paul. Le buisson ardent. Paris, 1912.
42553.47 Angellier, A. Oeuvres posthumes. Paris, 1912.
38513.58 Ante, Elizabeth. Sprachliche Untersuchung der Mysterien La passion d'Arnoul Gréban. Inaug. Diss. Darmstadt, 1912.
43524.1 Anthelme, P. L'honneur japonais. Paris, 1912.
43528.3.30 Arnaud, Simone. Myrdhin; opéra-légende. Paris, 1912.
Mol 213.16 Arnavon, Jacques. La mise en scène des femmes savantes. Paris, 1912.
38526.21.29 Arnoux, J. Un précurseur de Ronsard, Antoine Héroët. Digne, 1912.
42586.14.8 Audoux, M. Valserine. N.Y., 1912.
43532.1.30 Avril, R. d'. L'Arbu des Fées. Paris, 1912.
43536.1.30 Azaïs, Marcel. La Chevauchée Nocturne. 2e éd. Paris, 1912.
37566.41A Babbitt, Irving. Masters of modern French criticism. Boston, 1912.
37566.41.5 Babbitt, Irving. Masters of modern French criticism. Boston, 1912.
43537.1.30 Bailly, F. Rimes galantes. Paris, 1912.
41564.46A Baldensperger, F. Alfred de Vigny. Parjs, 1912.
40596.8 Balzac, Honoré de. Comédie humaine. Études de moeurs. Scènes de la vie privée. Paris, 1912-13. 7v.

1912 - cont.

40597.35.101 Balzac, Honoré de. La femme et l'amour. Paris, 1912.
40596.15.20 Balzac, Honoré de. Morceaux choisis. Paris, 1912.
41522.2.30 Barbey d'Aurevilly, Jules. Fragment à mettre en tête du Joseph Delorme que je dois donner. Paris, 1912.
FL 6135.8.5A Barrés, Maurice. Le bi-centenaire de Jean-Jacques Rousseau. Paris, 1912.
42563.20.18 Barrès, Maurice. Pour nos églises. Paris, 1912.
43537.78.103 Barry, Léon. Au delà du Bonheur. 3e éd. Paris, 1912?
40542.28 Baudrillart, Alfred. Frédéric Ozanam. Paris, 1912.
43537.3.30 Baye, B. de. Le Temple du Rêve. Paris, 1912.
42563.21.42.7 Bazin, René. Donatienne. Paris, 1912.
43538.11.50 Beaunier, André. Discours adressé aux élèves du collège Stanislas le 24 décembre 1911. Bruges, 1912.
38521.19.5 Beekman, A. Influence de Du Bartas. Poitiers, 1912.
37555.146 Beer, Guillaume (Mme.). La sensibilité dans la poésie française contemporaine, 1885-1912. Paris, 1912.
37574.920 Bernard, Jean Marc. Pages politiques des poètes français. Paris, 1912.
42542.29.20 Bernard, Tristan. L'accord parfait. Paris, 1912.
42542.29.22 Bernard, Tristan. On nait esclave. Paris, 1912.
42542.29.23 Bernard, Tristan. Le petit café. Paris, 1912.
Mol 602.9 Berneburg, E. Charakterkomik bei Molière. Marburg, 1912.
Mol 602.9.5 Berneburg, E. Charakterkomik bei Molière. Diss. Marburg, 1912.
37594.12.15 Bernhardt, A. Die altfranzosische Helinandstrophe. Münster, 1912.
42542.29.37 Bernstein, H. L'assaut. Paris, 1912.
42542.29.38 Bernstein, H. Le détour. Paris, 1912.
42554.50 Bersancourt, A. de. Charles Guérin. Paris, 1912.
41574.82 Bersaucourt, Albert. Les pamphlets contre Victor Hugo. Paris, 1912.
NEDL 37556.68 Bertaut, Jules. Les romanciers du nouveau siècle. Paris, 1912.
42576.15.16 Bertrand, L. Gustave Flaubert. 3. éd. Paris, 1912.
NEDL 40582.29 Beyle, Henri. L'abbesse de Castro. Paris, 1912.
40582.12 Beyle, Henri. La chasse au bonheur. Paris, 1912.
42576.65.13.2 Blandin, H. J.K. Huysmans. Paris, 1912.
37562.5.10 Boer, C. de. La Normandie et la renaissance. Groningue, 1912.
42542.37.5 Bois, Jules. Nail. Paris, 1912.
38557.5.6 Bonet, Pierre. Bossuet moraliste. Paris, 1912.
42524.12.5 Bonnefou, Jean de. Dans les débris et sur les ruines. Paris, 1912.
42566.16.12 Bonnet, B. Le "baile" Alphonse Daudet. Paris, 1912.
42563.36.70A Bordeaux, Henry. La neige sur les pas. Paris, 1912.
42563.36.70.2 Bordeaux, Henry. Nieve sobre las huellas. Paris, 1912.
38557.36 Bossuet, J.B. Six lettres originales. Paris, 1912.
43544.4.33 Botrel, Théodore. Les alouettes. Paris, 1912.
43544.4.39 Botrel, Théodore. Chansons de clochers-à-jour. Paris, 1912.
41542.4.70 Boucher, Henri. Iconographie générale de Théophile Gautier. Paris, 1912.
43544.5.33 Boulenger, Marcel. Le marché aux fleurs. Paris, 1912.
43544.87.2100 Boulestin, X.M. Le frequentations de Maurice. Paris, 1912.
42563.37.76 Bourget, Paul. La crise. Paris, 1912.
37567.136 Bourget, Paul. Pages de critique et de doctrine. Paris, 1912. 2v.
FL 6119.12.7 Bouvier, B. Jean-Jacques Rousseau. Genève, 1912.
42563.39.35 Boylesve, René. Madeleine, jeune femme. 26. éd. Paris, 1912.
39534.38 Brébeuf, Georges de. Entretiens solitaires. Paris, 1912.
42542.47.3 Brieux, Eugène. Damaged goods. N.Y., 1912.
42542.47.26 Brieux, Eugène. La foi. Paris, 1912.
42542.47.39.20 Brieux, Eugène. Three plays. 4. ed. N.Y., 1912.
42524.16.10 Brunetière, F. Lettres de combat. Paris, 1912.
38512.63 Brush, H.R. La bataille de Trente. Chicago, 1912.
42542.47.79 Caillavet, G.A. Primerose. Paris, 1912.
39545.11 Canssy, F. Voltaire Seigneur de village. Paris, 1912.
42542.48.18 Capus, Alfred. En garde. Paris, 1912.
42542.48.19 Capus, Alfred. Les favorites. Paris, 1912.
42542.48.24 Capus, Alfred. Les moeurs du temps. Paris, 1912. 2v.
Htn 43550.1.30* Carco, Francis. La Bohème et mon coeur. n.p., 1912.
40587.902 Caud, Lucile (de Chateaubriand) de (Mme.). Oeuvres de Lucile de Chateaubriand. Paris, 1912.
37567.120 Charlier, G. Le sentiment de la nature chez les romantiques français. Paris, 1912.
38514.64.10 Chartier, Alain. Die französische Version von Alain Chartiers Dialogus familiaris. Rossleben, 1912.
40586.32 Chateaubriand, F.A.R. Correspondance générale. Paris, 1912-1924. 5v.
43552.6.100 Chateaubriant, Alphonse de. Monsieur des Lourdinés. Paris, 1912.
43552.9.100 Chatelain, U.V. Le double destin. Paris, 1912.
42576.12.30 Cherbonnel, Alice. Un obstacle. 5. éd. Paris, 1912.
43600.25.100 Chevalier, Adrien. Sous le ciel changeant. Paris, 1912.
38512.10.50 Les chroniqueurs français: Villehardouin, Froissart, Joinville, Commines. Paris, 1912.
42553.49.5 Clement, Louis. Auguste Angellier, son oeuvre poétique. Lille, 1912.
43554.3.30 Clerc, C. Les oasis. London, 1912.
41578.65 Cochin, Henry. Lamartine et la Flandre. Paris, 1912.
43556.1.31 Cocteau, Jean. La Dance de Sophocles. Paris, 1912.
38526.10.15 Collas, Georges. Jean Chapelain, 1595-1674. Paris, 1912.
38575.28.9 Collas, Georges. Les sentiments de l'Académie français sur la tragi-comédie du Cid. Paris, 1912.
43556.2.30 Colomb, F. L'Ame éparse. Paris, 1912.
43556.53.1100 Combette, Bernard. Des hommes. Paris, 1912.
42576.65.13.40 Coquiot, G. La vrai J.K. Huysmans. Paris, 1912.
42542.55.8 Croisset, Francis de. Le coeur dispose. Paris, 1912.
42542.58.37 Curel, François de. La nouvelle idole. 7. éd. Paris, 1912.
37596.148 Danne, F. Das altfranzösische Ebrulfsleben. Inaug. Diss. Erlangen, 1912.
43565.3.30 Darmet, L. Prés du Piano Fermé, 1909-11. Paris, 1912.
41574.54 Davidson, Arthur F. Victor Hugo; his life and work. Philadelphia, 1912.
40536.13 Delfarge, D. La vie et l'oeuvre de Palissot. Paris, 1912.
42568.2.5 Deschard, Marie. La prima lucia. Madrid, 1912.
42576.15.34 Descharmes, René. Autour de Flaubert. Photoreproduction. Paris, 1912. 2v.
40535.2.16 Desforges, Pierre Jean Baptiste. Mémoires du poète libertin (1798). Paris, 1912.
43612.61.800 Discours prononcé sur la tombe de Henri Franck. n.p., 1912?
43568.91.130 Divoire, F. L'amoureux. Paris, 1912.

1912 - cont.

Mol 860.61F	Donnay, M. Le ménage de Molière. Paris, 1912. 2v.
42542.65.1	Donnay, Maurice. Théâtre. Paris, 1912. 6v.
41578.64	Doumic, R. Les grands écrivains français, Lamartine. Paris, 1912.
43573.98.1100	Doysié, Abel. Heures de France et d'exil. Paris, 1912.
43574.1.31	Droüet, Marcel. L'ombre qui tourne; poèmes. Paris, 1912.
FL 6113.6	Du Bus, Charles. L'exposition Jean-Jacques Rousseau à la bibliothèque nationale. Paris, 1912.
41538.11.10	Dumas, Alexandre. Chicot the jester. London, 1912.
41538.61.10	Dumas, Alexandre. Memoirs of a physician. N.Y., 1912.
42543.25.18	Dumas, Alexandre. Une visite de noces. Paris, 1912.
43576.1	Dumas, André. Esther, Princesse d'Israël. Paris, 1912.
40515.14.15	Élica, G. Un après-midi chez Julie de Lespinasse. 2e éd. Paris, 1912.
37541.29	Engel, Eduard. Geschichte der Französischen Literatur. 8. Aufl. Leipzig, 1912.
37574.660	Engwer, T. Choix de poésies françaises. Bielefeld, 1912.
42545.3.880	Esch, Maximilian. L'oeuvre de Maurice Maeterlinck. Paris, 1912.
41556.37	Fach, Theodor. Naturschilderung bei Charles Nodier. Halle, 1912.
37543.125	Faguet, E. En lisant les beaux vieux livres. Paris, 1912.
42565.70.8	Favre de Coulevain, Hélène. Eve triumphant. N.Y., 1912.
42565.74.5	Favre de Coulevain, Hélène. The heart of life. N.Y., 1912.
42565.72.3	Favre de Coulevain, Hélène. Noblesse américaine. 66. éd. Paris, 1912.
FL 377.53	Feichtinger, W.M. Die Rolle des Vertrauten in der klassischen Tragödie der Franzözen. Wien, 1912.
37556.38	Flake, O. Der französische Roman und die Novelle. Leipzig, 1912.
FL 385.28.9	Flat, P. Figures du théâtre contemporain. Paris, 1912. 2v.
42543.42.9	Flers, Robert de. Le roi. L'ange du foyer. Paris, 1912.
38528.21.10	Förster, Richard. Die sogenannten facetiösen Werke Noëls du Faill. Halle, 1912.
37595.36.52A	Foerster, Wendelin. Romanische Bibliothek. 4. Aufl. v.1,5. Halle, 1912. 2v.
39527.43	La Fontaine. Paris, 1912.
43611.1.25.13	Fort, Paul. Montlhéry-la-bataille. 3. éd. Livre II. XIII. Paris, 1912.
43611.1.25.14	Fort, Paul. Vivre en Dieu. 2. éd. Livre III. XIV. Paris, 1912.
42576.62.22A	France, Anatole. Les dieux ont soif. Paris, 1912.
42576.62.22.5	France, Anatole. Les dieux ont soif. Paris, 1912. 3v.
42576.62.105.2	France, Anatole. Honey-bee. 2. ed. London, 1912.
42576.62.5.30	France, Anatole. Le livre de mon ami. 116. éd. Paris, 1912?
42576.62.8.5	France, Anatole. L'orme du mail. Paris, 1912?
42576.62.6.2	France, Anatole. La rôtisserie de la reine Pédauque. Paris, 1912.
42576.62.3.7	France, Anatole. Thaïs. 109. éd. Paris, 1912?
42543.44.15	Gassier, Alfred. Théâtre romantique. Paris, 1912.
42586.62.30	Gauthier-Villars, Henry. L'implaquable Siska. Paris, 1912?
37596.122	Gautier de Dargies. Chansons et descorts. Paris, 1912.
42543.45.6	Gavault, Paul. Le bonheur sous la main. Paris, 1912.
42543.45.7	Gavault, Paul. L'idée de Françoise. Paris, 1912.
38526.11.11	Gebhardt, Rudolf. Jean Desmarets de Saint Sorlin als dramatischer Dichter. Leipzig, 1912.
42576.5.5	Gebhart, Emile. Petits mémoires. Paris, 1912.
37558.115	Gélis, F. de. Histoire critique des jeux floraux. Toulouse, 1912.
42554.40	Gendry, Eugène. Fleurs d'arvor. St. Servan, 1912.
43617.1.30	Gérard, Rosemonde. Un bon petit diable. Paris, 1912.
43617.2	Gerbidon, M.M. Une affaire d'or. Paris, 1912.
37567.128	Giraud, V. Maîtres d'autrefois et d'aujourd'hui. Paris, 1912.
37543.80	Giraud, Victor. Les maîtres de l'heure. 3. éd. Paris, 1912.
40587.15	Giraud, Victor. Nouvelles études sur Chateaubriand. Paris, 1912.
42586.65.5.1	Gobineau, Arthur de. Die Rénaissance. Leipzig, 1912.
43625.3.41.15	Gourmont, Rémy de. A night in the Luxembourg. Boston, 1912.
43625.3.41	Gourmont, Rémy de. Nuit au Luxembourg. 4e ed. Paris, 1912.
37543.95.4	Gourmont, Rémy de. Promenades littéraires. Série 4. Paris, 1912.
40593.27	Grahl-Schulze, Elisabeth. Die Anschauungen der Frau von Staël über das Wesen und die Aufgaben der Dichtung. Inaug. Diss. Neuminster, 1912.
FL 6119.12	Gran, G. Jean-Jacques Rousseau. Edinburgh, 1912.
FL 361.50	Gribble, F. Romances of the French theatre. London, 1912.
39545.12.5	Gröschl, K. Die Deutschen Übersetzungen Voltaire'schen Tragöden. Prag, 1912.
42554.50.9	Guérin, C. Le coeur solitaire. 5e éd. Paris, 1912.
42554.50.10	Guérin, C. L'homme intérieur 1901-05. 4e éd. Paris, 1912.
43628.1.30	Guitry, Sacha. Un beau mariage. Paris, 1912.
43628.1.35F	Guitry, Sacha. Jean III. Paris, 1912.
42513.42	Guyau, J.M. Pages choisies. Paris, 1912.
40597.2.17	Haas, J. H. Balzacs Scènes de la vie privée von 1830. Halle, 1912.
37567.272	Halflants, Paul. Religion et littérature. 2e éd. Bruxelles, 1912.
39527.4.90	Hamel, Frank. Jean de La Fontaine. N.Y., 1912.
41586.28.9	Hartog, W.G. Guilbert de Pixerécourt, sa vie, son mélodrame. Thèse. Paris, 1912.
41586.28.12	Heel, Franz. Guilbert de Pixerécourt. Erlangen, 1912.
43632.59.100	Hennebois, C. La loi de vivre. Clérmont-Ferrand, 1912.
42543.63.7	Hermant, Abel. Coutras voyage. Paris, 1912.
42543.66	Hermant, Abel. Essais de critique. Paris, 1912.
42543.65.37	Hermant, Abel. Les renards. Paris, 1912.
FL 385.37	Héros, Eugène. Le théâtre anecdotique. Paris, 1912.
42543.69.14.5	Hervilly, Ernest. Sayonava, or The testing of the poet. Brooklyn, 1912.
FL 6139.12.5	Höffding, H. Jean-Jacques Rousseau et sa philosophie. Paris, 1912.
FL 6139.12.4	Höffding, H. Jean-Jacques Rousseau og hans filosofi. København, 1912.
41572.4.8	Hugo, Victor. Bug-Jargal. Paris, 1912.
41571.17.5	Hugo, Victor. Les misérables. pt. 1, 2-3,4,5. Paris, 1912. 4v.
41573.21.30	Hugo, Victor. Notre Dame de Paris, 1482. Paris, 1912? 2v.

1912 - cont.

41572.29.7	Hugo, Victor. Le roi s'amuse. Paris, 1912.
FL 381.10	Huszar, G. L'influence de l'Espagne sur le théâtre. Photoreproduction. Paris, 1912.
42576.65.29.5	Huysmans, Joris Karl. Les soeurs Vatard. Paris, 1912?
37556.58.2	Jakob, M. Gustave. L'illusion et la désillusion dans le roman réaliste français. (1851-1890). Paris, 1912.
43667.1.30	Jammes, Francis. Les géorgiques chrétiennes. 4. éd. Paris, 1912.
42563.18.105	Jary, Jacques. Essai sur l'art et la psychologie de Maurice Barrès. 2. éd. Paris, 1912.
FL 6139.12.8	Jean-Jacques Rousseau. Paris, 1912.
43670.1.30	Jouglet, René. Les roses sur la vie. Paris, 1912.
FL 377.54A	Jourdain, E.F. An introduction to the French classical drama. Oxford, 1912.
43670.94.220	Jouve, Pierre Jean. Présences. Paris, 1912.
37555.515	Kahn, Gustave. Le vers libre. 3. éd. Paris, 1912.
38512.88	Karl, Louis. Un moraliste...Jean Dupin. Paris, 1912.
42544.2.4	Kistemaekers, Henry. Le flambée. Paris, 1912.
37576.412	Klincksieck, Friedrich. Der Brief in der französischen Literatur des 19. Jahrhunderts; eine Auswahl. Halle, 1912.
42575.82	Koehler, Erich. Edmond und Jules de Goncourt. Leipzig, 1912.
37596.120	Långfors, Artur. Huon le Roi, Le vair palefroi. Paris, 1912.
43687.7.100	Labeur, F. Jean Klein, légionnaire. Paris, 1912.
42544.26.7	Labiche, Eugène. Le voyage de Monsieur Perrichon. Paris, 1912.
41595.30.2	Ladoué, Pierre. Millevoye. La vie et l'oeuvre. Paris, 1912.
41595.30	Ladoué, Pierre. Millevoye. 1782-1816. Paris, 1912.
43687.2.32A	Lafon, André. L'élève Gilles. Récit. 17e éd. Paris, 1912.
43687.2.30	Lafon, André. L'elève Gilles. Récit. 26e éd. Paris, 1912.
43687.27.100	La Forest-Divonne, P. de. La cité des lampes. Paris, 1912.
38514.57.5A	Laigle, Mathilde. Le livre des trois vertues de Christine de Pisan. Paris, 1912.
42555.33	Langel, A. Flammes et cendres. Paris, 1912.
37543.38.3	Lanson, Gustave. Histoire de la littérature française. Paris, 1912.
42576.46.20	Lapauze, Jeanne L. Au tournant des jours. Paris, 1912.
42563.37.98	Lardeur, F.J. La vérité psychologique et morale dans les romans de M. Paul Bourget. Paris, 1912.
38543.10.19	La Rochefoucauld, François. Maximes. London, 1912.
41522.3.11	Laurentie, F. Sur Barbey d'Aurevilly. 2. éd. Paris, 1912.
42576.41.21	Le Blanc, Maurice. Le bouchon de cristal. Paris, 1912.
42576.41.20.5	Le Blanc, Maurice. The frontier. N.Y., 1912.
43688.2.30	Le Cardonnel, Louis. Poèmes. 4e éd. Paris, 1912.
FL 390.99	Lecomte, L.H. Histoire des théâtres de Paris. Les fantaisies-parisiennes. v.9. Paris, 1912.
37555.48A	Légouis, Émile. Défense de la poésie française a l'usage des lectures anglaises. Londres, 1912.
39594.19.15	Leir-Malvano, E. Montesquieu et Machiavelli. Paris, 1912.
43688.5.30	Lemaitre, C. Eiou qu'y va le trachi. Caen, 1912.
42544.33.21	Lemaître, Jules. Les rois. Paris, 1912.
43688.1.30F	Leroux, Gaston. Le mystère de la chambre jaune. Paris, 1912.
37596.84.5	Loh, Hugo. Histoires tirées de l'ancien testament. Münster, 1912.
38525.11	Longnon, Henri. Pierre de Ronsard. Paris, 1912.
42544.34.25.5	Lorde, André de. Cauchemars. Paris, 1912.
42544.36.9	Loyson, Paul H. L'apostolo; tragedia moderna. Milano, 1912.
43697.6.61	Machard, Alfred. Les cent gosses. Paris, 1912.
NEDL 42545.3.31	Maeterlinck, Maurice. Death. N.Y., 1912.
42545.3.13.12	Maeterlinck, Maurice. The life of the bee. N.Y., 1912.
42545.3.150A	Maeterlinck, Maurice. On Emerson. N.Y., 1912.
43697.34.100	Magre, Maurice. Comediante. Paris, 1912.
37556.32.5	Maigron, Louis. Le roman historique à l'époque romantique. Paris, 1912.
42587.16.14	Maindron, M. Dariolette. Paris, 1912.
NEDL 42587.16.11	Maindron, M. Saint-Cendre. Paris, 1912.
40588.41.10	Maistre, Xavier. La jeune sibérienne. Boston, 1912.
42576.67.25	Malherbe, H. Paul Hervieu. Paris, 1912.
43697.2.30	Mallarmé, C. Le Ressac. Paris, 1912.
43697.59.100	Mandin, L. Ariel esclave. Paris, 1912.
37563.32	Mansuy, A. Le monde slave et les classiques français. Paris, 1912.
42563.23.143	Marches de Provence. Fascicule spécial consacré à Léon Bloy. Marseille, 1912.
NEDL 40563.26	Marquiset, Alfred. Ballanche et Mme. d'Hautefeuille. Lettres inédites. Paris, 1912.
37567.119	Marsau, J. La bataille romantique. Paris, 1912.
FL 6129.12.5	Martin-Decaen, A. Le Marquis René de Girardin, 1735-1808. Paris, 1912.
40583.37	Martineau, Henri. Litinéaire de Stendhal. Paris, 1912.
37555.500.2	Martinon, Philippe. Les strophes. Paris, 1912.
42554.18.7	Masbrenier, J.L. L'oeuvre de Jean Lahor. n.p., 1912.
37558.59A	Masson, Frédéric. L'Académie française, 1629-1793. Paris, 1912.
38567.22	Maugain, Gabriel. Boileaux et l'Italie. Paris, 1912.
40587.24	Maurras, Charles. Chateaubriand, Michelet, Saint-Beuve. Paris, 1912.
37543.81	Maury, L. Classiques et romantiques. Paris, 1912.
37543.77	Mercereau, Alex. La littérature et les idées nouvelles. Paris, 1912.
FL 6139.12.9	Mertaut, J. Un entretien inconnu de George Sand et de Flaubert sur Jean-Jacques Rousseau. Montpellier, 1912.
FL 6129.12	Meynier, A. Jean-Jacques Rousseau révolutionnaire. Paris, 1912.
41568.17.3	Michaut, G. De Sénancour. Obermann. Paris, 1912. 2v.
43699.3.29	Mille, Pierre. Louise et Barnavaux. Paris, 1912.
43699.3.34	Mille, Pierre. Sur la vaste terre. 6. éd. Paris, 1912.
Mol 182.9.5	Molière, Jean Baptiste Poquelin. Ta erotika poiemata. Athenai, 1912.
Mol 219.6	Molière, Jean Baptiste Poquelin. George Dandin...Karl Vollmöller. Leipzig, 1912.
Mol 172.5	Molière, Jean Baptiste Poquelin. Le bourgeois gentilhomme. N.Y., 1912.
Mol 60.27	Molière, Jean Baptiste Poquelin. Molière. Boston, 1912-1919. 6v.
Mol 252.3	Molière, Jean Baptiste Poquelin. The precious ridiculous. N.Y., 1912.
Mol 62.60	Molière, Jean Baptiste Poquelin. Sämtliche Werke...P.A. Becker. v.1-3,4-6. Leipzig, 1912. 2v.

Chronological Listing

1912 - cont.

Mol 269.3.25 Molière, Jean Baptiste Poquelin. Tartuffe. C.H. Page. N.Y., 1912.
Mol 269.4A Molière, Jean Baptiste Poquelin. Tartuffe. C.H. Page. N.Y., 1912.
Mon 28.27A Montaigne, Michel de. Textes choisis. Paris, 1912.
42555.61.7 Moréas, Jean. Iphigénie. 5e éd. N.Y., 1912.
37555.68 Moréas, Jean. Réflexions sur quelques poètes. Paris, 1912.
37596.147 Müller, Herbert. Sprachliche Untersuchung der Apokalypse der Kerr-Handschrift. Inaug. Diss. Münster, 1912.
43703.73.100 Murat, A. Le livre de poésie. Paris, 1912.
37597.32.5 Muset, Colin. Les chansons. Paris, 1912.
41596.8.9 Musset, Alfred de. Les chefs-d'oeuvre lyriques. Paris, 1912.
42545.45.11 Népoty, L. Les petits. Paris, 1912.
42545.45.13 Nigond, Gabriel. Théâtre. 2e éd. Paris, 1912.
42543.1.10 Noel, C.M. Les idées sociales dans le théâtre de Alexandre Dumas fils. Paris, 1912.
Htn Mon 108.8F* Norton, Grace. Index of the names in Montaigne's essays. Cambridge, 1912.
Htn Mon 108.7F* Norton, Grace. Lexique de la langue de Montaigne. Cambridge, 1912. 3v.
Htn Mon 108.5F* Norton, Grace. Lexique de la langue de Montaigne. Cambridge, 1912. 5v.
43715.39.100 Ochse, J. D'île en île. Paris, 1912.
43718.27.100 Offel, H. Le retour aux lumières. Paris, 1912.
42578.29.9 Ohnet, Georges. La serre de l'aigle. Paris, 1912.
37562.22.4.10 Paris, Gaston. Mélanges de littérature française du moyen âge. v. 1-2. Paris, 1912.
42584.25.15A Patterson, J.G. A Zola dictionary, the characters of the Rougon-Macquart novels of Emile Zola. N.Y., 1912.
40522.18 Pauli, F. Die philosophischen Grundanschauungen in den Romanen des Abbé Prévost. Marburg, 1912.
37566.29.3 Pellissier, G. Le mouvement littéraire au XIXe siècle. 9e éd. Paris, 1912.
37567.118 Pellissier, G. Le réalisme du romantisme. Paris, 1912.
43740.1.43 Philippe, Charles Louis. Mutter und Kind. Berlin, 1912.
43741.51.100 Pilon, Edmond. Sites et personnages. Paris, 1912.
FL 6119.12.5 Plan, P.P. Jean-Jacques Rousseau. 3. éd. Paris, 1912.
37571.70 Poëtes français, première anthologie. Paris, 1912.
42545.88 Porto-Riche, G. Un drame sous Philippe II. Paris, 1912.
42545.88.43 Porto-Riche, G. Zubiri. Paris, 1912.
40587.27 Potiquet, François Albert. Chateaubriand; l'anatomie de ses formes et ses amies. Paris, 1912.
43743.92.110 Pouvourville, Albert de. L'Annam sanglant. Paris, 1912.
40522.9.17 Prévost, Antoine F. Manon Lescaut. Paris, 1912?
40522.9.15 Prévost, Antoine F. Manon Lescaut. Paris, 1912.
42578.31.49 Prévost, Marcel. Pierre et Thérèse. Paris, 1912.
37571.71 Prosateurs français, deuxième anthologie. Paris, 1912.
38536.17 Rabelais, F. Oeuvres. Paris, 1912-31. 5v.
42578.18.14 Rameau, Jean. La route bleue. Paris, 1912.
43752.2.30 Rateau, Jules. Noël Breton. Paris, 1912.
37556.39 Rauchfuss, Arthur. Der französische Hirtenroman am Ende des 18. Jahrhunderts. Leipzig, 1912.
42557.20.280 Raynaud, Ernest. L'assomption de Paul Verlaine. Paris, 1912.
43753.9.125 Reboux, Paul. A la manière de Octave Mirbeau. 2. serie et 1. serie. Paris, 1912.
37543.83 Reckzch, E. Beitrage zur Entwicklungsgeschichte des Frauenideals in der französischenLiteratur am Ausgang der Mittelalter. Greifswald, 1912.
43753.33.1100 Regismanset, Charles. La vaine chanson. Paris, 1912.
38587.8.15 Regnard, Jean François. Le légataire universel. Austin, 1912.
42556.26.31 Régnier, Henri de. L'Amphisbène. 2e éd. Paris, 1912.
42556.26.30 Régnier, Henri de. La double maîtresse. Paris, 1912.
42556.26.33 Régnier, Henri de. Pour les mois d'hiver. Paris, 1912.
38525.22.62 Régnier, Mathurin. Oeuvres complètes. Paris, 1912?
Mon 128.3 Rey-Pailhade, E. de. Montaigne philosophie-moraliste, étude. Toulouse, 1912.
37556.66 Reynier, G. Origines du roman réaliste. Photoreproduction. Paris, 1912.
37596.119A Richier. La vie de S. Remi, poème. London, 1912.
43756.69.100 Ripert, Émile. La terre des lauriers. Paris, 1912.
42546.6.12 Rivoire, A. Pour vivre heureux. Paris, 1912.
38527.27 Rocheblave, S. La vie d'un hiros Agrippa d'Aubigné. Paris, 1912.
42545.88.135 Roger-Marx, Claude. G. de Porto-Riche. Paris, 1912.
41588.15.10 Rolland, J. Les comédies politiques d'Eugène Scribe. Paris, 1912.
43757.50.450 Rolland, Romain. L'humble vie héroique. Paris, 1912.
43757.50.251 Rolland, Romain. Jean-Christophe - la fin du voyage. La nouvelle journée. 2e éd. Paris, 1912?
43757.50.253 Rolland, Romain. Jean-Christophe - la fin du voyage. La nouvelle journée. 5e éd. Paris, 1912.
43757.50.254 Rolland, Romain. Jean-Christophe - la fin du voyage. La nouvelle journée. 6. éd. Paris, 1912.
43757.50.722 Rolland, Romain. Jean-Christophe in Paris. The market-place, Antoinette, The house. N.Y., 1912.
42578.22.120 Rosny, J.H. La mort de la terre. Paris, 1912.
FL 6024.5 Rousseau, J.J. N'a jamais eu d'enfants. Nice, 1912.
43757.2 Roux, M.X. L'enjôleuse. Paris, 1912.
41557.10.60 Ruggeberg, J. Die Persönlichkeit George Sands in ihren Werken. Inaug. Diss. Bonn, 1912.
FL 6119.12.15 Sahlin, Enar. Jean-Jacques Rousseau; en levnadsteckning. Uppsala, 1912.
37557.38.10 Saillard, G. Essai sur la fable en France au dix-huitième siècle. Toulouse, 1912.
40515.52 Saillard, G. Florian, sa vie - son oeuvre. Toulouse, 1912.
38542.26 Saint-Evremond, C. de M. de S.D. Schriften und Briefe. München, 1912. 2v.
43761.41.130 St. Georges de Bouhelier. La romance de l'homme. Paris, 1912.
38526.47.40 Saint-Pavin, Denis Sanguin de. Poésies choisies. Paris, 1912.
37543.21.30 Saintsbury, George. Primer of French literature. 5. ed. Oxford, 1912.
37572.55 Salon bleu d'Arthénice par son ombre. 2. éd. Paris, 1912.
FL 360.12 Samson, J.I. L'art théâtral. Paris, 1912.
40597.1.9 Sattler, Hermann. H. de Balzacs Roman La peau de chagrin. Halle, 1912.
43761.3.30 Savignon, André. Filles de la pluie. Paris, 1912.
42586.63.3.5 Schemann, Ludwig. Neues aus der Welt Gobineaus. Hildburghausen, 1912.

1912 - cont.

39533.6.9 Searles, C. Catalogue de tous les livres de feu M. Chapelain. Stanford, 1912.
41574.68 Séché, L. Victor Hugo et les poètes. Paris, 1912. 2v.
43765.21.40 Sée, Edmond. La Brebis. Paris, 1912.
42535.23 Segur, M. de. Parmi les Cyprès et les Lauriers. Paris, 1912.
38563.22.25 Serrurier, C. Pierre Bayle en Hollande. Apeldoorn, 1912.
41586.21.80 Sessler, Georg. Die Komödien Mazères'. Diss. Heidelberg, 1912.
38563.19 Smith, H.E. The literary criticism of Pierre Bayle. Albany, 1912.
37543.255 Smith, Mabell S.C. The spirit of French letters. N.Y., 1912.
43775.89.4110 Soulages, Gabriel. Ce bougre d'original. n.p., 1912?
37555.216 Souza, Robert de. Du rythme en français. Paris, 1912.
42587.59.10 Soyez-Le Roy, Lettice. Amour et vaillance. Lille, 1912.
37543.172 Strachey, Giles Lytton. Landmarks in French literature. London, 1912?
37543.170A Strachey, Giles Lytton. Landmarks in French literature. N.Y., 1912.
43779.1.30 Stradiot, J. À la Venvole. Paris, 1912.
37566.40 Strowski, F. Tableau de la littérature française au XIXe siècle. Paris, 1912.
43780.5.260 Suarès, André. Sur la vie. v.3. Paris, 1912.
42577.4.43 Tassart, François. Recollections of Guy de Maupassant. London, 1912.
FL 6135.9 Tauro, Giacomo. À l'occasion du second centenaire de la naissance de Rousseau. Rome, 1912.
43788.5.108 Tharaud, Jérôme. La fête arabe. Paris, 1912.
43788.5.110 Tharaud, Jérôme. La fête arabe. 4e éd. Paris, 1912.
Mol 39.12 Thirion, E. Théâtre choisi de Molière. Paris, 1912.
42545.3.440 Thomas, Edward. Maurice Maeterlinck. 2d ed. N.Y., 1912.
41522.18.485 Thomas, Louis. Curiosités sur Baudelaire. Paris, 1912.
FL 6139.12 Tiersot, J. Jean-Jacques Rousseau. Paris, 1912.
42557.14.10 Tournoux, G.A. Bibliographie verlainienne. Leipzig, 1912.
39594.19.12 Tournyol du Clos, Jean. Les idées financières de Montesquieu. Paris, 1912.
42547.5.11A Trarieux, Gabriel. L'escapade. Paris, 1912.
43795.77.1100 Turpin, René. Willy Jones apprenti. Paris, 1912.
43811.1.30 Ulmes, T. de. Pension de famille. Paris, 1912.
43822.9.30 Vandervelden, Joseph. Les nocturnes. Bruxelles, 1912.
42557.15.10 Verlaine, Paul. Choix de poésies. Paris, 1912.
37555.514 Verrier, Paul. L'isochronisme dans le vers français. Paris, 1912.
42576.57.12 Viaud, Julien. Carmen Sylva. N.Y., 1912.
42576.56.9 Viaud, Julien. The daughter of heaven. N.Y., 1912..
42557.25 Vielé-Griffin, F. La lumière de grèce. Paris, 1912.
Mon 132.5.11 Villey, P. Encore un livre italien de la bibliothèque de Montaigne. Florence, 1912.
38524.56 Villey, P. Les sources d'idées. Textes choisis et commentées. Paris, 1912.
37567.112 Vincent, Francis. Ames d'aujourd'hui. Paris, 1912.
42522.19 Vogüé, E.M. de. Pages choisies. Paris, 1912.
38526.3.7 Vulliod, A. La femme docteur (Bougeant). Lyon, 1912.
FL 6139.12.7 Wasmuth, E. Jean-Jacques Rousseau. Leipzig, 1912.
37556.33.5 Wells, B.W. A century of French fiction. N.Y., 1912.
37548.36 Wilmotte, M. La culture française en Belgique. Paris, 1912.
41595.30.5 Wirthwein, Theodora. Die Elegie bei Millevoye. Diss. Darmstadt, 1912.
37543.57A Wright, C.H. Conrad. A history of French literature. N.Y., 1912.
37556.63 Wurzbach, W. von. Geschichte des französischen Romans. Heidelberg, 1912.
37596.121 Zipperling, C. Das altfranzösische Fablel du Vilain Mire. Halle, 1912.

1913

42562.31.50 About, Edmond. Le nez d'un notaire. Paris, 1913.
37543.114.2 Abry, E. Histoire illustrée de la littérature française. 2. éd. Paris, 1913.
43513.1.30F Acker, Paul. La victoire. pt.1-3. Paris, 1913. 3 pam.
42562.38.14.21 Adam, Paul. Jeunesse et amours de M. Henricourt. Paris, 1913.
42562.38.10 Adam, Paul. Stéphanie. Paris, 1913.
37596.27.9 Aléxius, Saint. Légend. Die altfranzösische Prosareision des Aléxiuslégende. Berlin, 1913.
42576.36.25 Allmendinger, J.F. Die Romanschriftstellerin Sophie Gay. Rottenburg, 1913.
43526.65.280 Apollinaire, Guillaume. La Roma des Borgia. Paris, 1913.
41583.7.100 Artois, Armand d'. Papa flirt. Paris, 1913.
40542.18 Auer, Heinrich. Friedrich Ozanam, der Gründer des Vinzenz-Vereins. Freiburg, 1913.
43537.50.100 Baldensperger, F. Contes et récits vosgiens. Paris, 1913.
40596.8.2 Balzac, Honoré de. Comédie humaine. Études de moeurs. Scènes de la vie de province. Paris, 1913. 5v.
40596.8.3 Balzac, Honoré de. Comédie humaine. Études de moeurs. Scènes de la vie parisienne. Paris, 1913-14. 8v.
40596.25 Balzac, Honoré de. Contes philosophiques. London, 1913?
40597.29.5.3A Balzac, Honoré de. Father Goriot. London, 1913.
40597.81 Balzac, Honoré de. Gobseck et Jésus Christ en Flandre. N.Y., 1913.
40596.8.50 Balzac, Honoré de. Napoléon par Balzac; récits et épisodes du Premier Empire tirés de la "Comédie Humaine". Paris, 1913.
40597.29.4.20 Balzac, Honoré de. Père Goriot. Paris, 1913.
39594.12.9 Barckhausen, Henri. Montesquieu; Lettres persanes. Paris, 1913. 2v.
42563.17.2 Barrès, Maurice. Colette Baudoche. Paris, 1913.
42563.16.13 Barrès, Maurice. La colline inspirée. Paris, 1913.
42515.35.26.5A Barrès, Maurice. Huit jours chez M. Renan. Paris, 1913.
43537.4.35F Bataille, Henry. Les flambeaux. Paris, 1913.
43537.4.32F Bataille, Henry. Le Phalène. Paris, 1913.
43537.89.2160 Baumann, Émile. Le baptême de Pauline Ardel. Paris, 1913.
39545.21.5 Baumgärtner, G. Voltaire auf der englischen Bühne des 18 Jahrhunderts. Strassburg, 1913.
39566.190 Beaurepaire, Edmond. Les logis de Diderot. Photostat of an article in Revue de français. v.17. n.p., 1913.
37530.11.10 Beaurepaire-Froment, Paul de. Pour le régionalisme. Paris, 1913.
42542.28.3 Becque, Henri. The vultures, The woman of Paris. N.Y., 1913.
38526.47.23 Begemann, H. M. Christian Roses geistliche Schauspiele S. Theophania und Holofern, 1647/8. Berlin, 1913.

Chronological Listing

1913 - cont.

41595.10.15 Beranger, Alphonse. Lettres inédites à Pierre Lebrun et à Mme. Lebrun. Paris, 1913.
43538.75.2100 Bernard, Jean-Marc. Subtegmine fagi; amours, bergeries et jeux. Paris, 1913.
42542.29.25 Bernard, Tristan. Les phares soubigou. Paris, 1913.
42542.29.43 Bernstein, H. Le secret. Paris, 1913.
37567.125 Bersaucourt, A. de. Études et recherches. 2e éd. Paris, 1913.
Mol 602.12 Besing, Max. Molières Einfluss auf das englische Lustspiel bis 1700. Diss. Borna, 1913.
FL 366.57 Bex, Maurice. Contribution à l'histoire du salaire au théâtre en France de 1658. Paris, 1913.
40582.2.10 Beyle, Henry. Vie de H. Brulard. Paris, 1913. 2v.
42542.29.110 Bisson, Alexandre. Chateau historique! 6. éd. Paris, 1913.
42563.36.94 Bordeaux, Henry. La maison morte. Paris, 1913.
42563.36.75 Bordeaux, Henry. La nouvelle croisade des enfants. Paris, 1913.
42563.36.60.2 Bordeaux, Henry. La peur de vivre. 100. éd. Paris, 1913.
42542.29.135.25 Bornier, Henri de. Oeuvres choisies. Paris, 1913.
37597.10.8 Bourdillon, F.W. A Vérard fragment of the roman de la rose. London, 1913.
42563.39.40 Boylesve, René. La marchande de petits pains. 10. éd. Paris, 1913.
38512.42 Bozon, Nicole. Metaphoro of Brother Bozon. London, 1913.
38557.25.60 Bremond, H. Bossuet. Paris, 1913. 3v.
42576.65.13 Bricaud, Joanny. Huysmans occultiste et magicien. Paris, 1913.
42542.47.31 Brieux, Eugène. Les avaries. 33. éd. Paris, 1913.
42542.47.33A Brieux, Eugène. Blanchette and the escape. Boston, 1913.
42542.47.27 Brieux, Eugène. La femme seule. Paris, 1913.
42542.47.8.2 Brieux, Eugène. La robe rouge. Paris, 1913.
42542.47.39A Brieux, Eugène. Three plays; Maternity, Three daughters, Damaged goods. 7. ed. N.Y., 1913.
42542.47.39.3A Brieux, Eugène. Three plays. 6. ed. N.Y., 1913.
42542.47.9.3 Brieux, Eugène. Les trois filles de M. Dupont. 4. éd. Paris, 1913.
43545.41.500 Brival-Gaillard, C. Les sept aventures de Madame Lafarge. Brive, 1913.
38543.22 Brix, Ernst. Die Entwicklungsphasen der Maximen La Rochefoucaulds. Inaug. Diss. Erlangen, 1913.
38557.22.9 Brunetière, F. Bossuet. Paris, 1913.
42524.16.12 Brunetière, F. Science et la religion. Paris, 1913.
37567.36.5 Brunetière, Ferdinand. Essais sur la littérature contemporaine. Paris, 1913.
FL 6129.13 Buffenois, H. Les portraits de Jean-Jacques Rousseau. Paris, 1913.
38526.47.33 Buls, Johannes. Das Naturgefühl bei Saint-Amant. Rostock, 1913.
40583.53 Burger, Jakob. Stendhal-Beyle und die franzözische Romantik. Marburg, 1913.
42542.48.21 Capus, Alfred. Hélène Ardouin. Paris, 1913.
FL 385.11 Capus, Alfred. Le théâtre. Paris, 1913.
43550.83.110 Castiaux, P. Lumières du monde. Paris, 1913.
43551.48.100 Celarié, H. Petite "novia" une Française en Espagne. Paris, 1913.
38514.23.5A Champion, P. François Villon, sa vie et son temps. Paris, 1913. 2v.
38514.26.40 Charles d'Orleans. Rondeaux choisis. Paris, 1913.
39544.27.11 Charrot, C. Quelques notes sur la "Correspondance" de Voltaire. Paris, 1913.
37564.63 Chinard, G. L'Amérique et le rève exotique. Paris, 1913.
X Cg 37564.63 Chinard, G. L'Amérique et le rève exotique. Paris, 1913.
43552.63.100 Chobanian, Arshag. La vie et la rève. Paris, 1913.
37596.10.2.5 Chrestien de Troyes. Arthurian romances. London, 1913.
42586.31.9.5 Claretié, J. Brichanteau. Paris, 1913.
43554.2.37.15 Claudel, Paul. Arte poetica. Milano, 1913.
X Cg 43554.2.32 Claudel, Paul. Cinq grandes odes. Paris, 1913.
43554.2.31 Claudel, Paul. Connaissance de l'est. 4e éd. Paris, 1913.
38526.16.25 Claus, F. Jean Godard, Leben und Werke (1564-1630). Greifswald, 1913.
43554.4.31 Clermont, Emile. Laure. Paris, 1913.
37567.123 Clouard, H. Les disciplines. Paris, 1913.
41578.66 Cognets, Jean des. La vie intérieure de Lamartine. Paris, 1913.
40553.9.64.3 Constant de Rebecque, Benjamin. Adolphe. Paris, 1913.
39566.35A Cru, Robert L. Diderot as a disciple of English thought. N.Y., 1913.
FL 6139.13 Cuendet, W. La philosophie religieuse de Jean-Jacques Rousseau et ses sources. Genève, 1913.
43565.4.30 Dargel, Henri. Trois farces antiques d'après Plaute. Paris, 1913.
42566.17.9 Daudet, Alphonse. Pages choisies des grands écrivains. 6. éd. Paris, 1913.
42542.61.10 Decourcelle, P. La rue du Sentier. Paris, 1913.
39591.22 Dedieu, J. Montesquieu. Paris, 1913.
38512.64 De Laigue, R. Le combat des trente et les champions. n.p., 1913.
43566.3.30 Delaquys, Georges. Le beau couchant. Paris, 1913.
43566.53.2100 Demange, Charles. Lettres d'italie. Paris, 1913.
43566.75.140 Derème, Tristan. La flûte fleurie. Paris, 1913.
42542.64.27.20 Descaves, Lucien. Philémon, vieux de la vieille. 19. éd. Paris, 1913.
42542.64.26 Descaves, Lucien. La saignée. Paris, 1913.
43566.89.110 Deubel, Léon. Régner. Paris, 1913.
39564.11.10 Diderot, Denis. La religieuse. Paris, 1913.
V37574.500 Diez Canedo, Enrique. La poesía francesa moderna. Madrid, 1913.
42563.37.120A Dimnet, E. Paul Bourget. London, 1913.
43780.5.815 Dommartin, Henry. Suarès. Paris, 1913.
42542.65.20 Donnay, Maurice. Les eclaireuses. Paris, 1913.
FL 382.57.3 Doumic, René. De scribe à Ibsen. Paris, 1913.
43576.7.60 Du Bois, Albert. La conquête d'Athènes (l'apôtre Paul). Paris, 1913.
43576.7.80 Du Bois, Albert. La dernière dulcinée (Cervantès). Paris, 1913.
43576.7.40 Du Bois, Albert. Hélène et Penelope (Homère). Paris, 1913.
43576.7.95 Du Bois, Albert. Lord Byron (l'aristocrate). Paris, 1913.
43576.7.75 Du Bois, Albert. Rabelais; poème comique en trois actes. Paris, 1913.
41571.5.10 Dubois, P. Bio-bibliographie de Victor Hugo de 1802-25. Paris, 1913. 10v.
41574.72 Dubois, P. Victor Hugo, ses idées religieuses, 1802-25. Paris, 1913.

1913 - cont.

40535.21.25 Duffo, F.A. J.J. Lefranc, poète et magistrat. Thèse. Paris, 1913.
37567.133 Du Fresnois, André. Une année de critique. Paris, 1913.
43554.2.830 Duhamel, Georges. Paul Claudel, le philosophe, le poête. Paris, 1913.
42554.29.160 Dujardin, É. Poésies. Paris, 1913.
37544.10.5 Dupouy, Auguste. France et Allemagne: littératures comparées. Paris, 1913.
41564.45.5 Dupuy, Ernest. Alfred de Vigny, la vie et l'oeuvre. Paris, 1913.
37568.30 Dupuy, Ernest. Poètes et critiques. Paris, 1913.
43576.2.30F Dusserre, A. Jean et Louise. pt. 1-3. Paris, 1913.
X Cg 37575.18 Les elegantes. Paris, 1913.
37574.660.5 Engwer, T. Choix de poésies françaises. Ergänzungsband. 8. Aufl. Leipzig, 1913.
40597.2.16 Fagnet, E. Balzac. Paris, 1913.
39527.4.17A Faguet, E. La Fontaine. Paris, 1913.
37543.128 Faguet, E. Petite histoire de la littérature française. Paris, 1913.
38575.14.5 Faguet, Émile. En lisant Corneille. Paris, 1913.
43606.78.220 Farrère, Claude. Thomas l'Agnelet. 2. éd. Paris, 1913.
43606.78.222 Farrère, Claude. Thomas l'Agnelet. 19. éd. Paris, 1913.
43606.2.30 Faure, A. Justin Pinard. 2. éd. Paris, 1913.
42565.72.5A Favre de Coulevain, Hélène. American nobility. N.Y., 1913.
42576.15.35 Ferrère, E.L. L'esthétique de Gustave Flaubert. Thèse. Paris, 1913.
42543.40.7 Ferrier, Paul. Yvonic. Paris, 1913.
37573.37.2.5 Ferrières, Gauthier. Anthologie des écrivains français des XVe et XVIe siècles; poésie. Paris, 1913.
37573.37.1 Ferrières, Gauthier. Anthologie des écrivains français des XVe et XVIe siècles. Prose. Paris, 1913.
39526.40 Fischer, W.P. The literary relations between La Fontaine and the "Astrée" of Honoré d'Urfé. Philadelphia, 1913.
42576.21 Flaubert, Gustave. Dictionnaire des idées reçues. Parjs, 1913.
43610.1.30F Fleg, Edmond. Le trouble-fête. Paris, 1913.
42543.42.7.5 Flers, Robert de. L'habit vert; comédie. 4e éd. Paris, 1913. 2 pam.
42543.42.7 Flers, Robert de. L'habit vert. Paris, 1913.
37595.36.53A Foerster, Wendelin. Romanische Bibliothek. Halle, 1913.
43611.1.25.15 Fort, Paul. Chansons. 2. éd. XV. Paris, 1913.
43611.1.21 Fort, Paul. Choix de ballades françaises. Paris, 1913.
37543.53.5 Fortier, Alcée. Histoire de la littérature française. N.Y., 1913.
39544.27.9 Foulet, L. Correspondance de Voltaire. Paris, 1913.
42576.63.15.90 France, Anatole. La comédie de celui qui épousa une femme muette. Paris, 1913.
42576.63.16 France, Anatole. La comédie de celui qui épousa une femme muette. 18. éd. Paris, 1913.
42576.63.7.10 France, Anatole. Le crime de Sylvestre Bonnard. Paris, 1913?
42576.62.7.7 France, Anatole. Les opinions de M. Jérôme Coignard. 56. éd. Paris, 1913.
FL 6113.17F François, A. L'exposition iconographique. Genève, 1913.
40596.28 Frary, Léon. Selon Balzac; le coeur humain. Paris, 1913.
43612.2.34 Fraudet, René. Blanche Câline. Paris, 1913.
43612.2.33 Fraudet, René. L'homme qui assassina. Paris, 1913.
43612.2.45 Fraudet, René. L'homme qui assassina. 4. éd. Paris, 1913.
42554.62 Fromm, Heinrich. Les Trophées von José Maria de Heredia. Inaug. Diss. Greifswald, 1913.
42571.34.16 Gaboriau, Emile. Baron Trigault's vengeance, sequel to The count's millions. N.Y., 1913.
42571.34.22 Gaboriau, Emile. Caught in the net. N.Y., 1913.
42571.34.24 Gaboriau, Emile. The clique of gold. N.Y., 1913.
42571.34.12 Gaboriau, Emile. The count's millions. N.Y., 1913.
42571.34.18 Gaboriau, Emile. Within an inch of his life. N.Y., 1913.
40546.9 Gaschet, R. Paul Louis Courier et la restauration. Paris, 1913.
43616.3.30 Gaubert, E. L'amour Marié. Paris, 1913.
42576.5.7 Gebhart, Emile. D'Ulysse à Panurge. 4. éd. Paris, 1913.
Mol 607.8 Gillet, J.E. Molière en Angleterre 1660-1670. Paris, 1913.
43620.51.50 Gillouin, René. Essais de critique litteraire et philosophique. Paris, 1913.
FL 398.7 Ginisty, P. Mlle. Gogo, Mlle. Beaumenard, 1730-1799. Paris, 1913.
41564.2 Giraud, J. Alfred de Vigny oeuvres choisies. Paris, 1913.
42586.65.5.4 Gobineau, Arthur de. Die Rénaissance. Berlin, 1913.
42586.65.5.6A Gobineau, Arthur de. The renaissance. N.Y., 1913.
42586.65.5.3 Gobineau, Arthur de. Die Rénaissance. Strassburg, 1913.
NEDL 42575.71.25 Goncourt, Edmond de. Germinie Lacerteux. Paris, 1913.
43625.3.73 Gourmont, Rémy de. La petite ville; paysages. Paris, 1913.
37543.95.5 Gourmont, Rémy de. Promenades littéraires. Série 5. Paris, 1913.
37555.305.7 Grammont, M. Le vers français ses moyen d'expression son harmonie. Paris, 1913.
43626.3.2100 Gramont, Sanche de. Antérôs. Paris, 1913.
42576.40.17 Guiches, Gustave. Vouloir. Paris, 1913.
43628.1.31 Guitry, Sacha. La prise de Berg-op-Zoom. Paris, 1913.
42546.12.21A Haraszti, J. Edmond Rostand. Paris, 1913.
38557.24.23 Hardy, Georges. Le "De civitate Dei" source principale du "Discours sur l'histoire universelle". Paris, 1913.
42546.31.5 Hart, J.A. Sardou and the Sardou plays. Philadelphia, 1913.
41586.28.10 Hartog, W.G. Guilbert de Pixerécourt, sa vie, son mélodrame. Paris, 1913.
40593.48 Haussonville, Gabriel Paul Othenin de Cléron. Le Prince Auguste de Prusse, Madame de Staël, et Madame Récamier. Paris, 1913.
37574.46 Henning, G.N. Representative French lyrics of the 19th century. Boston, 1913.
37567.126 Henriot, Emile. A quoi rêvent les jeunes gens. Paris, 1913.
42554.58 Heredia, J.M. de. Les trophées. 5. éd. Paris, 1913.
42543.65.50 Hermant, Abel. La fameuse comédienne. 7e éd. Paris, 1913?
Htn 42576.67.13* Hervieu, Paul. Bagatelle. Paris, 1913.
42543.69.7.15 Hervieu, Paul. The labyrinth. N.Y., 1913.
37548.38.15 Heumann, A. Le mouvement littéraire belge d'expression française. Paris, 1913.
41564.53 Huber, Richard. Alfred de Vigny als Philosoph. Marburg, 1913.
41573.32.17 Hugo, Victor. Hernani, Marion de Lorme. Paris, 1913-15.
41571.15.5 Hugo, Victor. Les misérables; a novel. London, 1913.

1913 - cont.

41573.26.30 Hugo, Victor. Ruy Blas, Les Burgraves, Marion de Lorme. Paris, 1913.
41571.1.11 Hugo, Victor. Souvenirs. Paris, 1913. 2v.
41573.17.5 Hugo, Victor. The toilers of the sea. London, 1913.
37596.107.5 Huon le Roi de Cambrai. Huon le Roi de Cambrai. Paris, 1913.
43638.99.125 Huzard, A. de B. (Mme.). Les sables mouvants. Paris, 1913.
43667.1.36 Jammes, Francis. Feuilles dans le vent. Paris, 1913.
37596.135A Jean Renart. Lai de l'ombre. Paris, 1913.
43670.94.190 Jouve, Pierre Jean. Parler. 2. série. Paris, 1913.
43670.99.110 Jozercan, K. Le champ de bataille. Poitier, 1913.
38525.21.10 Jusserand, J.J. Ronsard. Paris, 1913.
42544.2.8.7 Kistemaekers, Henry. L'embuscade. Paris, 1913.
42544.2.8.6 Kistemaekers, Henry. L'exilée. Paris, 1913.
42544.2.8.8 Kistemaekers, Henry. L'occident. Paris, 1913.
40587.28 Körding, Hermann. Chateaubriand als Versdichter. Berlin, 1913.
42514.17 Laboulaye, Edouard. Abdallah. N.Y., 1913.
38564.32.15 La Bruyère, J. de. Les caractères. Paris, 1913.
39527.29.26 La Fontaine, Jean de. Fables. Paris, 1913.
39527.35 La Fontaine, Jean de. Psyché. Paris, 1913.
43687.4.30F Lagros de Langeron, G. Un roman de théâtre. pts.1-4. Paris, 1913.
FL 366.35 Lailler, Jean. Le contrat de représentation théatrale. Paris, 1913.
38526.14.45 Lancaster, H.C. Pierre Du Ryer, dramatist. Washington, 1913.
37573.33 Lanson, Gustave. Anthologie des poètes nouveaux. 3. éd. Paris, 1913.
38543.10.20A La Rochefoucauld, François. Maximes. Paris, 1913.
42544.24.12 Lavedan, Henri. Servir. Paris, 1913.
43688.7.100 Lebesgue, P. Les servitudes. Paris, 1913.
43688.7.930 Lebey, André. Sur la route sociale. Paris, 1913. 2v.
42576.41.62 Le Blanc, Maurice. Confessions of Arsène Lupin. Garden City, 1913.
42576.41.60 Le Blanc, Maurice. Confessions of Arsène Lupin. N.Y., 1913.
42576.41.21.8A Le Blanc, Maurice. The crystal stopper. Garden City, 1913.
43688.8.15 Le Goffic, Charles. Poésies complètes. Paris, 1913.
FL 6119.07.3.5 Lemaitre, J. Jean-Jacques Rousseau. 32. éd. Paris, 1913?
42544.33.16F Lemaître, Jules. Kismet. Paris, 1913.
40575.5.40 Lemaitre, Jules. Les péchér de Sainte-Beuve. Paris, 1913.
37575.787 Lemercier d'Erm, Camille. Les ballades d'amour du XIIe siècle à nos jours choix. Paris, 1913.
42584.25.7 Lemm, S. Zur Entstehungsgeschichte von Emile Zolas Rougon-Macquart. Halle, 1913.
43688.1.31F Leroux, Gaston. Alsace. Paris, 1913.
40512.48 LeSage, Alain René. The adventures of Gil Blas of Santillane. N.Y., 1913.
41584.35 Le Senne, C. Charles Guillaume Étienne. Paris, 1913.
43688.4.31 Levaillant, M. Pierres saintes::Versailles. Paris, 1913.
43688.28.100 Lévrier, Léonce. À bâtons, rompus. Paris, 1913.
40527.18.5 Lewy, Fritz. Zur Verbalmmetapher bie André Chenier. Inaug. Diss. Strassburg, 1913.
43690.24.120 Lienard, Albert. Le collier des heures. Paris, 1913.
37555.533 Lote, George. L'Alexandrin Français d'après la phonetique expérimental. Paris, 1913.
37555.502.2F Lote, Georges. L'alexandrin d'après la phonétique expérimentale. 2. éd. Paris, 1913. 3v.
42544.34.45 Louys, Pierre. Woman and puppet. N.Y., 1913.
41542.4.6 Luitz, Friedrich. Die Ästhetik von Théophile Gautier. Inaug. Diss. Freiburg, 1913.
37555.315.5 Lukin, Erich. Du Bellay's Deffence...in ihrem Verhältnis zu Sebillet's Art poetique. Inaug. Diss. Oldenburg, 1913.
43697.6.55 Machard, Alfred. Titine. Paris, 1913.
42545.3.23 Maeterlinck, Maurice. Marie-Magdeleine. Paris, 1913.
42545.3.23.5 Maeterlinck, Maurice. Marie-Magdeleine. Paris, 1913.
42545.3.11.22 Maeterlinck, Maurice. Monna Vanna. Jena, 1913.
42545.3.11.5A Maeterlinck, Maurice. Monna Vanna. N.Y., 1913.
42545.3.30 Maeterlinck, Maurice. Le mort. Paris, 1913.
42545.3.60 Maeterlinck, Maurice. Our friend the dog. N.Y., 1913.
42545.3.5.10 Maeterlinck, Maurice. The treasure of the humble. N.Y., 1913.
43697.34.170 Magre, Maurice. Les belles de nuit. Paris, 1913.
42577.11.7 Malot, Hector. Sans famille. 2. ed. N.Y., 1913.
42563.16.13.5 Mangenot, Eugène. La colline inspirée. Paris, 1913.
37556.70 Martino, P. Le roman réaliste. Paris, 1913.
42514.28.210 Maurras, Charles. Charles Maurras et la critique des lettres. Paris, 1913.
42576.15.48 Maynial, E. La jeunesse de Flaubert. Paris, 1913.
42545.10.24 Meilhac, Henri. L'autographe. Paris, 1913.
42515.35.172 Michaelis, Paul. Philosophie und Dichtung bei Ernest Renan. Berlin, 1913.
39527.4.16 Michant, G. La Fontaine. Paris, 1913. 2v.
43699.3.735 Mille, Pierre. Two little Parisians. London, 1913.
43699.1.30 Millet, P. Jenny s'en va-t-en-querre. Paris, 1913.
Mol 613.6 Molière, commenté d'après les observations de nos meilleurs critiques. Paris, 1913. 2v.
Mol 166.3 Molière, Jean Baptiste Poquelin. L'avare...C.H. Page. Photoreproduction. N.Y., 1913.
Mol 246.4 Molière, Jean Baptiste Poquelin. Le misanthrope. C.H. Page. N.Y., 1913.
Mol 19.13 Molière, Jean Baptiste Poquelin. Oeuvres complètes. v.1,3-6. Paris, 1913? 5v.
39544.32.8 Morley, John. Voltaire. London, 1913.
40536.27.9 Mühle, M. B.J. Saurin. Sein Leben und seine Werke. Inaug. Diss. Dresden, 1913.
37567.124 Muller, J. Les tendances présentes de la littérature française. Paris, 1913.
41596.32.10F Musset, Alfred de. La nuit venitienne. Paris, 1913.
41596.13.9 Musset, Alfred de. Poésies nouvelles. Londres, 1913.
43709.3.140 Noailles, Anna E. De la rive d'Europe à la rive d'Asie. Paris, 1913.
43709.3.170 Noailles, Anna E. Les vivants et les morts. Paris, 1913.
40535.19.17 Noël, Georges. Madame de Grafigny, 1695-1758. Paris, 1913.
42578.29.10 Ohnet, Georges. The eagle's talon. N.Y., 1913.
Mol 173.4 Oliver, Thomas E. Notes on the Bourgeois gentilhomme. n.p., 1913.
43723.51.120 Ollone, Charles. Nouvelles heures chantantes. Paris, 1913.
37595.72 Oulmont, Charles. La poésie française du Moyen Âge, XIe-XVe siècles. Paris, 1913.

1913 - cont.

40542.14 Ozanam, Antoine F. Deux oeuvres de jeunesse de F. Ozanam. Lyon, 1913.
37562.22.5.2 Paris, Gaston. Esquisse historique de la littérature française au moyen âge. 2. éd. Paris, 1913.
FL 372.19 Pas, Justine de. Mystères et jeux scéniques à St. Omer. Lille, 1913.
Htn 37574.68* Payne, John. Flowers of France. 19th and 20th centuries. London, 1913. 2v.
37574.68 Payne, John. Flowers of France. 19th and 20th centuries. London, 1913. 2v.
42578.30.74 Peladan, J. St. Francis of Assisi. London, 1913.
FL 6135.8.3 Per il IIe centenario di G.G. Rousseau. Genova, 1913.
37565.50 Petermann, B. Streit um Vers und Prosa in der französischen Literatur des XVIII Jahrhundert. Halle, 1913.
43740.1.36 Philippe, Charles Louis. Bübü, roman. Berlin, 1913.
43740.1.31 Philippe, Charles Louis. Charles Blanchard. Paris, 1913.
43740.1.33 Philippe, Charles Louis. Croquignole. Leipzig, 1913?
38524.87 Picot, E. Recueil de pièces historiques imprimées dans les provinces françaises au XVIe siècle. Paris, 1913.
42578.30.150 Pilon, E. Portraits de sentiments. Paris, 1913.
43743.2.30F Poizat, A. Sophonisbe. Paris, 1913.
42555.72.130 Pomairols, Charles de. Poèmes choisis. Paris, 1913.
42578.31.56 Prévost, Marcel. Les anges gardiens. Paris, 1913.
42578.31.56.5 Prévost, Marcel. Les anges gardiens. Paris, 1913.
43747.50.110 Puliga, H.C.S. Retour du flat. Paris, 1913.
FL 380.40 Quentin, Henri. Le théâtre sous la terreur (théâtre de la peur), 1793-1794. Paris, 1913.
41578.47.10 Quentin-Bauchart, P. Lamartine et la politique étrangère de la révolution de février. Paris, 1913.
43757.13.100 Rachebrune, A. Le calvaire de Islam. Paris, 1913.
38583.8.15 Racine, Jean. Théâtre choisi. 8. éd. Paris, 1913.
43752.1.30F Rageot, G. La voix qui q'est tué. pt.1-4. Paris, 1913.
43752.59.122 Randon, G. Les soliloques du pauvre. Paris, 1913.
43753.9.127 Reboux, Paul. A la manière de Racine. 3. serie. Paris, 1913.
42556.26.43 Régnier, Henri de. Le plateau de laque. Paris, 1913.
40583.45 La revue critique des idées et des livres. v.20. Paris, 1913.
41591.24.40 Rimpler, Karl. Jacques Delille als beschreibend-didaktischer Dichter. Inaug. Diss. Weida, 1913.
43756.2.31 Rivollet, G. Bénédicte. Paris, 1913.
43756.2.32 Rivollet, G. Jerusalem! Paris, 1913.
39527.4.15 Roche, Louis. La vie de Jean de La Fontaine. 2. éd. Paris, 1913.
42546.8.35 Rodenbach, G. Die dramatischen Werke. München, 1913.
41578.68 Rolla, C. Lamartine et l'Italie. Novare, 1913.
43757.50.713 Rolland, Romain. Jean-Christophe: Dawn, morning, youth, revolt. N.Y., 1913.
43757.50.731 Rolland, Romain. Jean Christophe: Journey's end, Love and friendship, The burning bush, The new dawn. N.Y., 1913.
43757.50.730A Rolland, Romain. Jean-Christophe - Journey's end: Love and friendship, The burning bush, The new dawn. N.Y., 1913.
FL 360.90 Rolland, Romain. Le théâtre du peuple. Paris, 1913.
43757.3.31 Romains, Jules. Odes et prières. Paris, 1913.
43757.3.46 Romains, Jules. La vie unanime. Paris, 1913.
42546.11.15 Rostand, Edmond. L'aiglon, drame en six actes. N.Y., 1913.
42546.15.13.25 Rostand, Edmond. The story of Chanticleer. N.Y., 1913.
43757.83.80 Rostand, Maurice. Page de la vie. Paris, 1913.
43757.4.30 Rougé, P. de. Épaves. Paris, 1913.
FL 6021.13.2 Rousseau, J.J. Les confessions. v.1-2,4. Paris, 1913. 3v.
FL 6042.13 Rousseau, J.J. Émile. Paris, 1913.
38542.12.5 Sabrié, J.B. Les idées religieuse de J.L. Guez de Balzac. Paris, 1913.
FL 6139.13.3 Sakmann, P. Jean-Jacques Rousseau. Berlin, 1913.
41557.9.94.5 Sand, George. Mauprat. Paris, 1913.
Mol 619.12 Sanlaville, F. Molière et le Droit. Paris, 1913.
42586.63.6.5 Schemann, Ludwig. Gobineau. Strassburg, 1913. 2v.
FL 6039.9 Schinz, Albert. La question du "Contrat social". Paris, 1913.
37596.152 Schmidt, J. Le jugement d'amours. Inaug. Diss. Borna, 1913.
42545.84 Schrenker, H. Ponsard als Dramatiker und Lyriker. Inaug. Diss. Borna, 1913.
38526.27.35 Schroeder, F. Claude Le Petit; sein Leben. Wismar, 1913.
43763.40.100 Schwaeblé, René. Chez Satan pages à l'index possession. Paris, 1913.
37555.72 Séché, A. Les caractères de la poésie contemporaine. Paris, 1913.
43757.50.850 Seippel, Paul. Romain Rolland, l'homme et l'oeuvre. Paris, 1913.
43775.90.100 Souday, Paul. Les livres du temps. 2. éd. Paris, 1913.
43775.89.4100 Soulages, Gabriel. L'idylle vénitienne. Paris, 1913.
37596.153 Steppuhn, A. Das Fabel vom Prestre comporte und seine Versionen. Inaug. Diss. Königsburg, 1913.
37567.134 Stewart, H.F. The romantic movement in French literature. Cambridge, 1913.
43780.5.330 Suarès, André. Cressida. Paris, 1913.
43780.5.240 Suarès, André. Essais. Paris, 1913.
43780.5.270 Suarès, André. Idées et visions. Paris, 1913.
43780.5.350 Suarès, André. Portraits. Paris, 1913.
43780.7.100 Suberville, Jean. Deux pièces jouées au front. 2. éd. Paris, 1913.
37541.33.2 Suchier, H. Geschichte der Französischen Literatur. Leipzig, 1913. 2v.
40597.2.335 Taine, H.A. Balzac. Leipzig, 1913.
43785.2.20 Taravel, Antoine. La douce chanson. Paris, 1913.
42578.52.72 Tinseau, Léon de. Le duc Rollon. London, 1913.
42578.52.70 Tinseau, Léon de. Le duc Rollon. Paris, 1913.
41522.18 Turquet-Milnes, G. The influence of Baudelaire in France and England. London, 1913.
43822.2.31 Vallery-Radot, Robert. Homme de désir. Paris, 1913.
43827.89.110 Vaudoyer, J.L. Poésies. Paris, 1913.
40584.13 Vauthier, G. Villemain. 1790-1870. Paris, 1913.
42557.11.4.20 Verhaeren, Émile. Les blés mouvants; poèmes. Paris, 1913.
Htn 42557.19.100* Verlaine, Paul. Romances sans paroles. Harlaam, 1913.
42581.20.15 Verne, Jules. Voyage au centre de la terre. London, 1913.
43823.78.100 Verrier, A. Le croisie train de plaisir. Angers, 1913.
42576.47.40 Viaud, Julien. Aziyadé. Paris, 1913?
42576.57.7.10 Viaud, Julien. Disenchanted. N.Y., 1913.
42557.30.80 Vibert, Paul Théodore. Le cinquantenaire des Girondins, 1860-1910. Paris, 1913.
NEDL 41564.1.7 Vigny, Alfred. Stello. Paris, 1913.

1913 - cont.

41564.5.15 Vigny, Alfred de. Cinq-Mars. Paris, 1913.
41564.1.4 Vigny, Alfred de. Daphné. Paris, 1913.
41564.31.40 Vigny, Alfred de. Lettres inédites d'Alfred de Vigny. Bordeaux, 1913.
41564.1.30 Vigny, Alfred de. Oeuvres complètes. Paris, 1913-14. 13v.
41564.15.10 Vigny, Alfred de. Poésies complètes. Paris, 1913.
42547.17.35A Villiers de l'Isle Adam, Auguste. Le nouveau monde. Paris, 1913.
38514.20.19A Villon, François. The poems of François Villon. London, 1913.
39545.35.15 Voltaire, François Marie Arouet de. Candide, ou L'optimisme. Paris, 1913.
39545.48 Voltaire, François Marie Arouet de. Voltaires orphelin de la Chine. Dresden, 1913.
37562.45.2 Voretzsch, Carl. Einführung in das Studium der altfranzösischen Literatur. Halle, 1913.
FL 363.20 Warland, H. Die literargeschichtliche Entwickelung des französischen Harleken. Inaug. Diss. Köln, 1913.
43833.77.100 Werth, Léon. La maison blanche. Paris, 1913.
FL 370.90 Wiedenhofen, A. Beiträge zur Entwicklungsgeschichte der Französischen Farce. Münster, 1913.
FL 398.97 X. Ce que mes jolis yeux ont vu. Paris, 1913.
42557.12.8 Zweig, Stefan. Emile Verhaeren. 2. Aufl. Leipzig, 1913.
42557.20.150 Zweig, Stefan. Paul Verlaine. Boston, 1913.

1914

43513.1.31 Acker, Paul. Les Demoiselles Bertram. Paris, 1914.
40556.39 Albalat, A. Joseph de Maistre. Lyon, 1914.
38525.5.30 Allem, Maurice (pseud.). Anthologie poétique française XVIe siècle. Paris, 1914?
43526.65.290 Apollinaire, Guillaume. Les trois Don Juan. Paris, 1914.
40583.34 Arbelet, Paul. La jeunesse de Stendhal. Paris, 1914.
FL 385.4.25 Ascoli, Alfredo. Il diritto privato nel teatro contemporaneo francese ed italiano. Milano, 1914.
40597.29.1.10A Balzac, Honoré de. At the sign of the cat and racket. N.Y., 1914.
40596.8.4 Balzac, Honoré de. Comédie humaine. Études de moeurs. Scénes de la vie politique. Paris, 1914.
40597.20.5 Balzac, Honoré de. Eugénie Grandet. Boston, 1914.
40597.20.7 Balzac, Honoré de. Eugénie Grandet. N.Y., 1914.
40597.20.19 Balzac, Honoré de. Eugénie Grandet. N.Y., 1914.
40597.29.4.12 Balzac, Honoré de. Father Goriot. N.Y., 1914.
40597.32.8 Balzac, Honoré de. The magic skin. N.Y., 1914.
41578.67 Barrès, Maurice. L'abdication du poète. Paris, 1914.
42563.15 Barrès, Maurice. Maurice Barrès, recueil de morceaux chosis. Paris, 1914?
FL 6139.14 Bartissol, Carlos. Sources des idées médicales de Rousseau. Paris, 1914.
Mol 270.31 Baumal, Francis. La genèse du Tartufe. Paris, 1914.
42563.21.66 Bazin, René. Gingolphe l'abandonné. 11. éd. Paris, 1914.
43538.11.60 Beaunier, André. La revolté. Paris, 1914.
37555.73 Bellessort, André. Sur les grands chemins de la poésie classique. Paris, 1914.
FL 6133.7 Benedetto, L.F. Madame de Warens, d'après de nouveaux documents. Paris, 1914.
42542.29.27 Bernard, Tristan. Les deux Canards. Paris, 1914.
42542.29.26 Bernard, Tristan. Jeanne Doré. Paris, 1914. 2 pam.
FL 377.56 Bernardin, N.M. Les chefs du choeur: Corneille, Molière, Racine, Boileau. Paris, 1914.
40597.2.18 Bernheim, P. Balzac und Swedenborg. Berlin, 1914.
41593.27.5 Berthaoldt, Ludwig. Jacques Delille. Inaug. Diss. Nürnberg, 1914.
FL 384.100 Berton, Pierre. Souvenirs de la vie de théâtre. Paris, 1914.
42563.23.8.35 Bertrand, Louis. Le sang des races. 8. éd. Paris, 1914.
40582.2.25 Beyle, Henri. Vies de Haydn de Mozart et de Métastase. Paris, 1914.
37567.127 Bisi, A. L'Italie et le romantisme français. Milan, 1914.
FL 6059.5 Blatz, Heinrich. Die Aufnahme der nouvelle Héloise. Heidelberg, 1914.
40583.33 Blum, Léon. Stendhal et le beylisme. Paris, 1914.
42563.36.49 Bordeaux, Henry. The awakening. N.Y., 1914.
39526.55 Borri, Vittorio Ferruccio. Le novelle del Decameron, imitate da La Fontaine. Trieste, 1914.
43544.4.35 Botrel, Théodore. Le fils de la veuve. 5. éd. Paris, 1914?
43544.3.30 Bouillon, V. Autour d'une vieille église. Paris, 1914.
41543.22.10 Boulenger, Jacques. Au pays de Gerard de Nerval. Paris, 1914.
42563.37.34.2F Bourget, Paul. Le démon de midi. pts. 1-6. Paris, 1914. 6v.
42563.37.34 Bourget, Paul. Le démon du midi. Paris, 1914. 2v.
42563.37.4 Bourget, Paul. Mensonges. Paris, 1914.
FL 398.28.12 Bourgogne, Jean de. Un comédien d'autrefois. Paris, 1914.
42542.47.32 Brieux, Eugène. Bourgeois aux champs. Paris, 1914.
42542.47.39.5A Brieux, Eugène. Three plays. London, 1914.
Htn FL 355.55* Brunet, Charles. Tables des pièces de théâtre. Paris, 1914.
42542.47.80 Caillavet, G.A. La belle aventure. Paris, 1914.
41564.50 Calvet, J. Alfred de Vigny. Paris, 1914.
43550.55.110 Cami, Henri. L'home à la tête d'epingle. Paris, 1914.
42542.48.24.5 Capus, Alfred. L'institut de beauté. Paris, 1914.
37596.169 Carlé, Theodor. Der altfranzösische Dichter Garnier von Pont-Sainte-Maxence und seine Zeit. Münster, 1914.
40586.8 Chateaubriand, F.A.R. Pensées. Paris, 1914.
40527.17 Chenier, André. Oeuvres inédites. Paris, 1914.
42587.36.23 Chenin, Emile. Les etudiants. 2. éd. Paris, 1914.
43600.25.110 Chevalier, Adrien. Mémoires d'outre-tombe d'Hannibal Châtaignier. Paris, 1914.
39585.1.10A Chevrier, F.A. Un roman satyrique du XVIIIe siècle: Le Colporteur. Paris, 1914.
38524.64 Choix de poésies politiques et satiriques du temps de la Fronde. Strasbourg, 1914.
43554.2.30 Claudel, Paul. L'annonce faite à Marie. 9e éd. Paris, 1914.
Htn 43554.2.69* Claudel, Paul. Le chemin de la croix. Anvers, 1914.
43554.2.34 Claudel, Paul. Deux poèmes d'été. 3e éd. Paris, 1914.
43554.2.31.5 Claudel, Paul. The East I know. New Haven, 1914.
43554.2.370.10 Claudel, Paul. Théâtre. 3e éd. Paris, 1914.
43554.6.30 Clément-Janin, Noël. Judith vaincue. Paris, 1914.
42554.26.24 Coppée, François. Lettres à sa mère et sa soeur 1862-1908. 6e éd. Paris, 1914.
42565.63 Corday, Michel. Un remous, nouvelle. Paris, 1914.
40582.2.5 Cordier, Henri. Bibliographie Stendhalienne. Paris, 1914.

1914 - cont.

42586.32.200 Coster, Charles de. De legende en de heldhaftige, vroolijke en roemrijke daden van Uilenspiegel. Amsterdam, 1914.
42542.55.9F Croisset, Francis de. L'épervier. Paris, 1914.
42542.58.12F Curel, François de. Le danse devant le miroir. Paris, 1914.
42524.19.15 Curtus, Ernst Robert. Ferdinand Brunetière. Strassburg, 1914.
38511.11.5 Dannenberger, Otto. Bilder des bürgerlich hauslichen Lebens in Frankreich. Mannheim, 1914.
42566.19.8.70 Daudet, Alphonse. Tartarin de Tarascon. Paris, 1914.
42566.19.8.80 Daudet, Alphonse. Tartarin de Tarascon. 1st ed. N.Y., 1914.
42567.37 Daudet, Ernest. De la terreur au consulat. Paris, 1914.
37543.144.4 Des Granges, C.M. Histoire illustrée de la littérature française. 2. éd. Paris, 1914.
39564.8.12 Diderot, Denis. Diderot. Notice de Jacques Marlord. Paris, 1914.
39564.8.9A Diderot, Denis. Diderot pensées philosophiques le nevue de Rameau. Paris, 1914.
FL 378.10 Dollfus, Paul. Reines de théâtre. Paris, 1914.
41596.4.17 Donnay, Maurice. Alfred de Musset. Paris, 1914.
42557.12.60 Doutrepont, G. Les débuts littéraires d'Emile Verhaeren à Louvain. Bruxelles, 1914.
Htn 43574.65.120* Droin, Alfred. Du sang sur la masquée, poésies. Paris, 1914.
43576.7.50 Du Bois, Albert. L'Aphrodite et le Khéroub (Ézékiel). Paris, 1914.
43576.7.85 Du Bois, Albert. Betty Hatton; pièce. Paphnuce Smith; comédie (Shakespeare). Paris, 1914.
43576.7.45 Du Bois, Albert. Gazelle de l'Aurore! (David). Paris, 1914.
42542.64.13 Ducray, C. Paul Déroulède, 1846-1914. Paris, 1914.
43576.91.84 Duvernois, Henri. La maison des confidences. Paris, 1914.
42576.15.17 Elliott monographs. v.1-4. Flaubert. Baltimore, 1914.
FL 6139.14.5 Eppensteiner, Friedrick. Rousseaus Einfluss. Inaug. Diss. Tübingen, 1914.
37567.71.5 Ernest-Charles, J. Essais critiques. Paris, 1914.
43598.84.170 Estaunié, Édouard. Les choses voient; roman. Paris, 1914.
37566.48 Estève, Louis. L'hérédité romantique dans la littérature contemporaine. 2e éd. Paris, 1914.
42543.38.14 Fabre, Émile. Un grand bourgeois. Paris, 1914.
Mol 606.7.5A Faguet, E. En lisant Molière. 5. éd. Paris, 1914.
40575.5.3 Faguet, E. La jeunesse de Sainte-Beuve. Paris, 1914.
42576.15.11.5 Faguet, Emile. Flaubert. Boston, 1914.
43606.87.170 Fauchois, René. Le miracle. Paris, 1914.
43606.87.180 Fauchois, René. Nocturne. Paris, 1914.
42565.75.10 Favre de Coulevain, Hélène. The wonderful romance. N.Y., 1914.
38554.518.46 Fénelon, F. de S. de la Mothe. Lettre à l'Académie. 6. éd. Paris, 1914.
38554.526.10 Fénelon, F. de S. de la Mothe. Spiritual letters: letters to men. N.Y., 1914.
42543.41.11 Feydeau, Georges. La dame de chez Maxim. v.1-2. Paris, 1914-19.
37564.65 Fidao-Justiniani, J.E. L'Esprit classique et le preciosité au XVIIe siècle. Paris, 1914.
38546.62 Fitzgerald, C. Dictionary of Madame de Sévigné. London, 1914. 2v.
37566.46 Florian-Parmentier, Ernest. La littérature et l'epoque, histoire de la littérature française. Paris, 1914.
43610.66.100 Floris, A.C. Le mystère. N.Y., 1914.
37595.36.21A Foerster, Wendelin. Kristian von Troyes. Halle, 1914.
43611.1.25 Fort, Paul. Ballades françaises. 1. série. I. Paris, 1914.
43611.1.25.16 Fort, Paul. Les nocturnes. XVI. Paris, 1914.
42576.62.20.10 France, Anatole. Allocution prononcée. London, 1914?
42576.62.110 France, Anatole. On life and letters. 2d series. London, 1914.
42576.62.25.5A France, Anatole. La révolte des anges. Paris, 1914.
42576.62.25.3 France, Anatole. La révolte des anges. 15. éd. Paris, 1914.
42576.62.25.7 France, Anatole. La révolte des anges. 72. éd. Paris, 1914.
42584.25.8.2 Franke, Carl. Emile Zola als romantischer Dichter. Marburg, 1914.
42584.25.8 Franke, Carl. Emile Zola als romantischer Dichter. Marburg, 1914.
43612.5.110 Fraudet, René. Aphrodite. Paris, 1914.
40534.16.22 Friedrich, Kurt. Carmontelle und seine Proverbes dramatiques. Inaug. Diss. Halle, 1914.
42543.45.10F Gavault, Paul. Ma tante d'Honfleur: comédie-bouffe. Paris, 1914.
42543.45.9 Gavault, Paul. Le mannequin. Paris, 1914.
43616.4.30 Gayet, A. Le Roman de Claude D'Antioche. Paris, 1914.
38529.12 La gazette de 1609. Paris, 1914.
38557.12 Gazier, Augustin. Bossuet et Lois XIV (1662-1704). Paris, 1914.
43617.1.31 Gérard, Rosemonde. La marchande d'allumettes. Paris, 1914.
43620.2.64 Gide, André. Die Rückkehr des verlorenen Sohnes. Leipzig, 1914.
37543.130 Gillot, Hubert. La querelle des anciens et des modernes. Thèse. Nancy, 1914.
FL 379.45 Ginisty, Paul. Mémoires et souvenirs de comédiennes, XVIIIe siècle. Paris, 1914.
43622.1.30 Gleize, Lucien. Le veau d'or, comédie satirique. Paris, 1914.
37595.46 Glixelli, Stefan. Les cinq poèmes des trois morts et des trois vifs. Paris, 1914.
43625.2.30 Gorsse, Henry. Le procureur Hallers: quatre actes. Paris, 1914.
37557.21.10 Gosse, E. French profiles. N.Y., 1914.
43625.3.32 Gourmont, Rémy de. Un coeur virginal. 5e ed. Paris, 1914.
43625.3.34 Gourmont, Rémy de. Divertissement. 2e ed. Paris, 1914.
NEDL 38543.3.9 Graudsaignes D'Hauterise, R. Le pessimisme de La Rochefoucauld. Paris, 1914.
43757.50.920 Grautoff, Otto. Romain Rolland. Frankfurt, 1914.
43626.1.30F Grillet, G. Rachel. Paris, 1914.
41574.56 Guimbaud, Louis. Victor Hugo et Juliette Drouet. Paris, 1914.
43628.41.1100 Guinle, A. Un prête rendu. N.Y., 1914.
43628.2.30 Gurval, A. Evit ar vreiziz! Pour les bretons! Dinard? 1914.
42576.40.290 Halévy, Ludovic. Morceaux choisis de Ludovic Halévy. N.Y., 1914.

Chronological Listing

1914 - cont.

43631.2.30 Hamp, Pierre. La peine des hommes; le rail. 4. éd. Paris, 1914.
43687.6.80 Harlor. Leopold Lacour, biographie critique. Paris, 1914?
42576.65.8F Harry, Myriam (pseud.). La petite fille de Jérusalem. v. 1-4. Paris, 1914.
40513.12 Heinz, Hans. Gil Blas und das zeitgenossische Leben in Frankreich. Inaug. Diss. Erlangen, 1914.
43632.2.30.5 Hellem, Charles. Sabotage; a play. Easton, 1914.
43632.1.30 Hennequin, M. Mon bébé! Paris, 1914.
37563.39 Henningsen, W. Das Verhältnis der französischen Plejadendichtung zur älteren französischen Literatur. Kiel, 1914.
37594.18.50 Henri d'Andeli. The battle of the seven arts. Berkeley, 1914.
43632.6.140 Henriot, Emile. La flamme et les cendres. Paris, 1914.
42543.65.11 Hermant, Abel. Le joyeux garçon. Paris, 1914.
42543.65.7.10 Hermant, Abel. La meute, Sylvie. Paris, 1914.
37594.23 Hilka, Alfons. Ein bisher unbekanntes Narcissusspiel. Breslau, 1914.
43757.50.980 Hochstaelter, M. Essai sur l'oeuvre de Romain Rolland. Paris, 1914.
37563.103 Homén, Olaf. Studier i fransk klassicism. v. 1-2. Helsingfors, 1914-1916.
42576.65.80.21 Huysmans, Joris Karl. Marthe; histoire d'une fille. Paris, 1914.
37596.142 Ilvonen, Eero. Parodies de thèmes pieux dans la poésie française du moyen âge. Thèse. Helsingfors, 1914.
37546.14 Jeanroy, Alfred. La poésie académique à Toulouse au XIVe et au XVe siècles. Toulouse, 1914.
43738.1.83 Johannet, René. Les Lettres. Péguy et ses Cahiers. Paris, 1914.
40556.18.25 Joubert, Joseph. Joubert; textes choisis. Paris, 1914.
43673.77.1100 Kermen, de (Mme.). Clairvoyante. N.Y., 1914.
39594.19.14 Klemperer, Victor. Montesquieu. Heidelberg, 1914-15. 2v.
38526.10.16.5 Kunckel, C. Leben und Werke Charles Cotin's. Strassburg, 1914.
38521.30.4 Lachèvre, Frédéric. Les recueils collectifs de poésies. Paris, 1914.
40562.9 Lacordaire, Jean Baptiste Henri. Correspondence inédite de R.P. Lacordaire. Paris, 1914.
Mol 730.10 Lacour, L. Les maitresses et la femme de Molière. Paris, 1914.
X Cg 41578.9.10 Lamartine, Alphonse de. Nouvelles méditations poétiques. Paris, 1914.
37572.25.14 Lanson, G. Choix de lettres du XVIIIe siècle. 9. éd. Paris, 1914.
43687.75.190 Larguier, Léo. Orchestres. Paris, 1914.
43687.5.30 Laudet, F. La vie qui passe. Paris, 1914.
42544.24.7.3A Lavedan, Henri. Three modern plays from the French: The prince d'Aurec. N.Y., 1914.
43687.91.110 La Ville de Mirmont, Jean de. Les dimanches de Jean Dézert. Paris, 1914.
42576.42.14 Le Barillier, Berthe. La couronne d'épines. Paris, 1914.
42576.41.70 Le Blanc, Maurice. The teeth of the tiger. N.Y., 1914.
42576.41.23.10 Le Blanc, Maurice. 813. 4. éd. Paris, 1914.
37563.40 Lefranc, A. Grands ecrivains français. Paris, 1914.
43688.1.35.10 Leroux, Gaston. The secret of the night. N.Y., 1914.
42513.95 Leroy-Beaulieu, A. Discours prononcés à l'inauguration du monument. n.p., 1914.
NEDL 37555.54 Levrault, L. Le genre pastoral. Paris, 1914.
43690.24.140 Lienard, Albert. Cléopâtre. Paris, 1914.
37597.9.9A Lorris, Guillaume de. Le roman de la rose. Paris, 1914-24. 5v.
43693.89.3021 Louis, Fernand. Oeuvres poetiques. Vierzon, 1914.
43694.1.30 Lugné-Poe, A. Les cinq messieurs de Francfort. Paris, 1914.
42545.3.29 Maeterlinck, Maurice. The intruder and other plays. N.Y., 1914.
42545.3.28 Maeterlinck, Maurice. The intruder and other plays. N.Y., 1914.
42545.3.41 Maeterlinck, Maurice. The massacre of the innocents. London, 1914.
42545.3.26.5 Maeterlinck, Maurice. Our eternity. N.Y., 1914.
42545.3.170 Maeterlinck, Maurice. The unknown guest. N.Y., 1914.
43697.2.31 Mallarmé, C. Eome fa l'onda. Milano, 1914.
43697.59.110 Mandin, L. Les saisons ferventes. Paris, 1914.
42578.31.74 Mannes, Elisabeth. Marcel Prévosts Ansicht über die Frauen. Inaug. Diss. Bonn, 1914.
41543.22 Marie, Aristide. Gerard de Nerval, le poète, l'homme. Paris, 1914.
42586.57.79 Martino, P. Fromentin. Alger, 1914.
37564.66A Merlant, J. De Montaigne a Vauvenargues. Paris, 1914.
42587.26.603 Meyer, A. Ce qu'il faut taire. 3. éd. Paris, 1914.
Mol 613.9 Meyier, F. de. Molière en zijn vijanden. n.p., 1914.
38576.12.42.85 Michaelis, Georg. Die Sogenannten "comédies espagnoles" des Thomas Corneille. Berlin, 1914.
43699.3.31 Mille, Pierre. Caillon et Tili. 9. éd. Paris, 1914.
43699.3.32 Mille, Pierre. Le monarque. 8. éd. Paris, 1914.
Mol 171.69 Molière, Jean Baptiste Poquelin. Le bourgeois gentilhomme. Boston, 1914.
Mol 195.45 Molière, Jean Baptiste Poquelin. L'école des femmes. Strasbourg, 1914.
Mol 228.64 Molière, Jean Baptiste Poquelin. Le malade imaginaire...Heitz et Mündel. Strasbourg, 1914.
Mol 245.103 Molière, Jean Baptiste Poquelin. Le misanthrope. G. Arnavon. Paris, 1914.
38542.16.6 Mollenhauer, Ernst. Saint-Evremond als Kritiker. Greifswald, 1914.
38542.16.5 Mollenhauer, Ernst. Saint-Evremond als Kritiker. Greifswald, 1914.
Mon 28.26 Montaigne, Michel de. Oeuvres choisis. Radouant. Paris, 1914.
Mon 28.25A Montaigne, Michel de. Selections from Montaigne. Wright. Boston, 1914.
39591.18A Montesquieu, C.L. de S. Correspondance. Paris, 1914. 2v.
43701.74.4110 Morax, R. Tell. Lausanne, 1914.
37563.42A Morf, H. Geschichte der französischen Literatur im Zeitalter der Renaissance. 2. Aufl. Strassburg, 1914.
42577.15.2 Murger, Henry. Le bonhomme jadis. Paris, 1914?
43703.80.140 Muselli, Vincent. Les travaux et les jeux. Paris, 1914.
38551.88.30 Navatel, Ludovic. Fénelon; la confrérie secrète du pur amour. Paris, 1914.
38525.22.16 Nolhac, Pierre de. La dernière amour de Ronsard. Paris, 1914.

1914 - cont.

37562.22.4.2 Paris, Gaston. La littérature française au moyen âge. 5e éd. Paris, 1914.
38514.59.6.5 Pathelin. Master Pierre Patelin. Boston, 1914.
38514.59.6A Pathelin. Master Pierre Patelin. Boston, 1914.
42555.69.15 Paul, Jules. Les sept errants de Lan-Illtud. Paris, 1914.
40582.2.110 Paupe, Adolphe. La vie littéraire de Stendhal. Paris, 1914.
37574.66.5 Payne, John. Flowers of France. The classical period. 17th and 18th century. London, 1914.
43738.1.30 Péguy, Charles. Ève. Paris, 1914.
42578.30.73 Peladan, J. Das unbekannte Schicksal. München, 1914.
Mol 616.5 Pellisson, M. Les comédies-ballets de Molière. Paris, 1914.
37556.31.5 Peters, Rudolf. Der Bauer im Französischen Roman. Inaug. Diss. Strassburg, 1914.
38528.21.11 Philipot, E. Essai sur le style et la langue de Noël du Fail. Paris, 1914.
38528.21.12 Philipot, E. La vie et l'oeuvre litteraire de Noël du Fail. Paris, 1914.
43741.1.30 Pierrelle, C. Les Pierres qui vivent. Paris, 1914.
41556.38 Pinquad, Léonce. La jeunesse de Charles Nodier. Besançon, 1914.
43743.1.45 Porché, François. Le dessous du masque. Paris, 1914.
42568.23.800 Puymbrouck, H. von. Georges Eekhoud en zijn werk. Antwerpen, 1914.
42578.18.3.5 Rabusson, Henry. Gogo et cie, une famille de la bourgeoisie. Paris, 1914.
37596.168 Raoul de Soissons. Lieder. Herausgegeben von Emil Winkler. Halle, 1914.
42556.21.4 Raynaud, Ernest. Les deux Allemagne. Paris, 1914.
42556.26.30.2 Régnier, Henri de. La double maîtresse. 26e éd. Paris, 1914.
42556.26.32 Régnier, Henri de. Romaine Mirmault. Paris, 1914.
43753.2.31 Régnier, M.L.A. de. Le séducteur. 13. éd. Paris, 1914.
42515.25.30 Renan, Ernest. Fragments intimes et romanesques. Paris, 1914.
42556.27.68 Retté, Adolphe. Quand l'ésprit souffle. 3e éd. Paris, 1914.
37564.150 Reynier, Gustave. Le roman réaliste au XVIIe siècle. Paris, 1914.
40536.21.27 Richard, Achille. Judas. Paris, 1914.
43756.3.75 Richepin, Jacques. Le minaret. Paris, 1914.
37555.12 Ritter, Otto. Die Geschichte des französischen Balladenformen. Halle, 1914.
42563.37.96 Rivasso, R. de. L'unité d'une pensée. Paris, 1914.
42546.6.14 Rivoire, A. Le plaisir des jours. Paris, 1914.
43757.50.762 Rolland, Romain. Above the battlefield. Cambridge, 1914.
43757.3.190 Romains, Jules. The death of a nobody. N.Y., 1914.
38525.14.9 Ronsard, Pierre de. Oeuvres complètes. Paris, 1914-19. 8v.
38525.12.20 Ronsard, Pierre de. Oeuvres complètes. Paris, 1914-48. 18v.
38525.21.20 Ronsard, Pierre de. Pierre de Ronsard. Paris, 1914.
37543.132 Roques, Mario. Précis d'histoire de la littérature française des origines à nos jours. Citta di Castelle, 1914.
42578.22.25 Rosny, J.H. La force mystérieuse. Paris, 1914.
FL 6048.49.17 Rousseau, J.J. La "Profession de foi du Vicaire Savoyard". Paris, 1914.
FL 6048.49.14 Rousseau, J.J. La "Profession de foi du Vicaire Savoyard". Thèse. Fribourg, 1914.
FL 6002.914A Rousseau, J.J. Selections from the work of J.J. Rousseau. C. Gauss. Princeton, 1914.
38526.47.35.3 Ruutz-Rees, Caroline. Charles de Sainte-Marthe. Paris, 1914.
38545.20.5 Saint Réal, César V. de. Histoire de Dom Carlos. Halle, 1914.
41557.9.60 Sand, George. François le Champi. N.Y., 1914.
37574.108A Sarolea, C. Anthologie des poètes lyriques français. Paris, 1914.
40597.2.23 Schätzle, Anselm. Balzac als Naturalist. Inaug. Diss. Heidelberg, 1914.
42586.63.6.6 Schemann, Ludwig. Quellen und Untersuchungen zum Leben Gobineaus. Strassburg, 1914-1919. 2v.
41574.75 Schenck, E.M. La part de Charles Nodier de la formation des idées de Victor Hugo. Paris, 1914.
41593.42 Schneegans, F. Maurice de Guérin. Strassburg, 1914.
40536.31.7 Sedaine, Michel Jean. Le philosophe sans le scavoir. N.Y., 1914.
42576.15.25 Seillière, Ernest. Le romantisme des réalistes. Paris, 1914.
41574.122 Simon, Gustave. La vie d'une femme. 2e éd. Paris, 1914.
42515.35.243 Soman, Mariette. La formation philosophique d'Ernest Renan. Thèse. Paris, 1914.
43775.90.105 Souday, Paul. Les livres du temps. 2. série. Paris, 1914.
39544.180 Steiner, Rudolf. Voltaire vom Gesichtspunkte der Geisteswissenschaft. Berlin, 1914.
37573.669 Stewart, Hugh F. The French romanticists. Cambridge, Eng., 1914.
Htn 41574.85* Swinburne, Algernon C. A study of Victor Hugo's "Les Misérables". London, 1914.
42557.5.50 Tailhade, Laurent. Les commerages de Tybalt. Paris, 1914.
FL 398.84.16 Talma. Paris, 1914.
43787.1.45 Tendron, Marcel. Deux essais. Paris, 1914.
43787.1.30 Tendron, Marcel. Le peuple de la mer. Paris, 1914.
42542.64.13.5 Tharaud, J. La morte de Paul Déroulède. Paris, 1914.
42542.64.13.10 Tharaud, J. Paul Déroulède. Paris, 1914.
43822.11.40 Văcărescu, Elena. La dormeuse éveillée. Paris, 1914.
43822.4.30 Variot, Jean. Les hasards de la guerre. 5e éd. Paris, 1914.
42547.12.5 Veber, Pierre. Un fils d'Amérique; comédie. Paris, 1914.
42557.11.38 Verhaeren, Émile. Drei Dramen. 2. Aufl. Leipzig, 1914.
42582.25.75 Verne, Jules. Il giro del mondo in ottanta giorni. Milano, 1914.
42576.57.4.5 Viaud, Julien. Matelot. Paris, 1914.
42557.25.120 Vielé-Griffin, F. Voix d'Ionie. 2. éd. Paris, 1914.
41564.1.6 Vigny, Alfred de. Servitude et grandeur militaire. Paris, 1914.
41564.5.20 Vigny, Alfred de. Cinq-Mars. Paris, 1914-22.
41564.1.3 Vigny, Alfred de. Cinq Mars ou conjuration sous Louis XIII. Paris, 1914. 2v.
41564.30 Vigny, Alfred de. Lettres inédites de Alfred Vigny au marquis. Paris, 1914.
41564.2.5 Vigny, Alfred de. Morceaux choisis. Paris, 1914.
41564.15.20 Vigny, Alfred de. Poèmes: Livre mystique. Livre antique. Livre moderne. Poèmes philosophiques. Paris, 1914.

1914 - cont.

X Cg	41564.16.10	Vigny, Alfred de. Poèmes antiques et modernes. Paris, 1914.
	41564.7.5	Vigny, Alfred de. Servitude et grandeur militaires. Paris, 1914.
	38514.20.3	Villon, François. Oeuvres. 2e éd. Paris, 1914.
	37566.166	Voloshin, M.A. Liki tvorchestve. Sankt Peterburg, 1914.
	39545.26.5	Voltaire, François Marie Arouet de. Oeuvres inédites. Paris, 1914.
	42557.12.90A	Zweig, Stefan. Émile Verhaeren. Boston, 1914.
	42557.12.9	Zweig, Stefan. Émile Verhaeren. London, 1914.

1915

	43524.85.103	Anouilh, Jean. Colombe. 2. ed. Paris, 1915.
	43524.85.100	Antelme, J. Soldats de France, simples esquisses. 3. ed. Paris, 1915.
	42542.12	Augier, Émile. Four plays. N.Y., 1915.
	40597.29.4.65	Balzac, Honoré de. Father Goriot. N.Y., 1915.
	40597.32.7	Balzac, Honoré de. The magic skin. N.Y., 1915.
	42554.5.10	Banville, Théodore de. Charming Léandre; a comedy in one act. N.Y., 1915.
	42563.20.40	Barrès, Maurice. Pages choisies. Paris, 1915.
	42563.21.69A	Bazin, René. Récits du temps de la guerre. 19. éd. Paris, 1915.
	43538.1.31	Beauduin, Nicolas. L'offrande héroïque; poèmes. Neuilly, 1915?
	43538.7.33	Benjamin, René. Les soldats de la guerre. Paris, 1915.
	42542.29.40.15	Bernstein, H. The thief. Garden City, 1915.
	37574.647	Bever, Adolphe van. Poètes d'aujourd'hui. Paris, 1915-17. 2v.
	37548.38	Bithell, Jethro. Contemporary Belgian literature. London, 1915.
	43543.5.110	Blanche, Jacques Émile. Cahiers d'un artiste. v.1,3,5-6. Paris, 1915. 4v.
	42563.36.61	Bordeaux, Henry. The fear of living. N.Y., 1915.
	42563.36.37	Bordeaux, Henry. The will to live. N.Y., 1915.
	43544.4.31	Botrel, Théodore. Chansons de route. Paris, 1915.
	43544.4.30	Botrel, Théodore. Les chants du bivouac. Paris, 1915.
	42554.15.35	Botrel, Théodore. Songs of Brittany. Boston, 1915.
	42542.30.9.15	Bouchor, Maurice. A Christmas tale, in one act. N.Y., 1915.
	42563.37.36A	Bourget, Paul. Le sens de la mort. Paris, 1915.
	42542.47.34	Brieux, Eugène. The plays of Eugène Brieux. Boston, 1915.
	37572.54.10	Buffum, D.L. Contes français. N.Y., 1915.
	43550.55.115	Cami, Henri. Le poilu aux mille trucs. Paris, 1915.
	43550.56.110	Cammaerts, E. Belgian poèms, chants patriotiques et autres poèmes. London, 1915.
	43550.56.112A	Cammaerts, E. Belgian poèms, chants patriotiques et autres poèmes. London, 1915.
	42542.64.13.15	Chevé. Au chevet d'un héros. Paris, 1915.
	FL 383.115	Clark, B.H. Contemporary French dramatists. Cincinnati, 1915.
	37583.615	Clark, Barrett Harper. Four plays of the free theater: the fossils. Cincinnati, 1915.
	43554.2.37	Claudel, Paul. Art poetique. 3e éd. Paris, 1915.
	43554.2.33	Claudel, Paul. Corona benignitatis anni Dei. 4e éd. Paris, 1915.
	43554.2.36A	Claudel, Paul. La nuit de Noël 1914. Paris, 1915.
	43554.2.38	Claudel, Paul. Trois poemes de guerre. 7e éd. Paris, 1915.
	37575.525	Contes véridiques de tranchées, 1914-1915. Paris, 1915.
	FL 6129.15	Cordier, Leopold. Jean-Jacques Rousseau und der Calvinismus. Inaug. Diss. Heidelberg, 1915.
	38526.25.15	Cox, E.M. Notes, critical and bibliographical. London, 1915.
	37596.29.5	Cristal und Clarie. Dresden, 1915.
	43566.5.31	Détanger, Émile. Hiên le maboul. 4e éd. Paris, 1915.
	42542.65.23	Donnay, Maurice. Lovers; The free woman; They. N.Y., 1915.
	37576.555	Dorchain, A. The twelve best short stories in the French language. London, 1915.
	42554.28.10	Dorchain, Auguste. Hymne aux cloches de pâques 1915. Paris, 1915.
	41574.16.8.10	Drouet, Juliette. Juliette Drouet's love-letters to Victor Hugo. 2d ed. London, 1915.
	42557.20.320	Dugas, Marcel. Feux de Bengale à Verlaine glorieux. Montreal, 1915.
	41538.16.8.5	Dumas, Alexandre. Count of Monte Cristo. N.Y., 1915. 2v.
	41538.63.35	Dumas, Alexandre. The queen's necklace. London, 1915.
	41538.53.45	Dumas, Alexandre. The three musketeers. N.Y., 1915.
	43584.92.100	Edwards, Émile. Journal d'un habitant de Constantinople (1914-1915). Paris, 1915.
	41555.42	Falke, E. Die romantischen Elemente in Prosper Mérimées Roman und Novellen. Halle, 1915.
	38554.9	Fénelon, F. de S. de la Mothe. Explication des articles d'Issy. Paris, 1915.
	43611.4.30	Foley, Charles. La guerre vécue. Paris, 1915.
	37530.7	Foulet, Lucien. A bibliography of medieval French literature for college libraries. New Haven, 1915.
	42576.63.17A	France, Anatole. The man who married a dumb wife. N.Y., 1915.
	42576.62.140	France, Anatole. Sur la voie glorieuse. 15. éd. Paris, 1915.
	41522.17.7	Gautier, T. Charles Baudelaire. N.Y., 1915.
	42576.63.28	George, W.L. Anatole France. London, 1915.
	42576.63.120A	George, W.L. Anatole France. N.Y., 1915.
	43617.4.47	Géraldy, Paul. Le grand-père. Paris, 1915.
	38576.7.95	Goehlert, Ernst. Abbé Claude Boyer. Leipzig, 1915.
	37574.69	González Martínez, Enrique. Jardines de Francia. México, 1915.
	37548.37	Gourmont, Remy de. La Belgique littéraire. 4. éd. Paris, 1915.
	43625.3.49.3	Gourmont, Rémy de. Pendant l'orage. Paris, 1915.
	43625.3.44	Gourmont, Rémy de. Sixtine. 4e ed. Paris, 1915.
	43757.50.1230	Guilbeaux, Henri. Pour Romain Rolland. Genève, 1915.
	37596.2.3	Guillaume de Deguilleville. Die pilger Fahrt des traumenden Mönchs. Berlin, 1915.
	FL 386.501	Guillot de Saix, Léon. Le théâtre de demain. Paris, 1915.
	37596.123	Guiot de Provins. Les oeuvres de Guiot de Provins. Manchester, 1915.
	38526.22.5.80	Hammerschmidt, Wilhelm. Amadis Jamyn; sein Leben und seine Werke. Weimar, 1915.
	43631.2.79.5	Hamp, Pierre. La victoire de la France sur les Français. 6. éd. Paris, 1915.

1915 - cont.

	37596.102.5	Haxo, Henry E. Denis Piramus; La vie seint Edmunt. Chicago, 1915.
	37556.16.25	Hemfrich, Paul. Le journal littéraire de La Haye, 1713-1737. Berlin, 1915.
	43632.6.300	Henriot, Émile. Bellica. Paris, 1915.
	42543.65.15	Hermant, Abel. Heures de guerre de la famille Valadier. 15e éd. Paris, 1915.
	42543.65.14	Hermant, Abel. Heures de guerre de la famille Valadier. 18e éd. Paris, 1915.
	42543.69.8	Hervieu, Paul. The trail of the torch; play in 4 acts. N.Y., 1915. 2v.
	41574.16.8	Hugo, Victor. Juliette Drouet's love letters to V. Hugo. London, 1915.
	39544.55	Hurn, A.S. Voltaire et Balingbroke. Thèse. Paris, 1915.
	40593.39	Jaeck, Emma Gertrude. Madame de Staël. N.Y., 1915.
	37567.145	Jäger, Karl. Der Empirestil in der schöngeistigen Literatur Frankreichs. Griefswald, 1915.
	37596.170	Jodoc, Saint. La vie Saint Joce; eine altfranzösische Heiligenlegende. Greifswald, 1915.
	41574.93	Joussain, André. Le pittoresque dans le lyrisme et et dans l'épopée. Thèse. Paris, 1915.
	43670.94.210	Jouve, Pierre Jean. Vous êtes des hommes, 1915. Paris, 1915.
	37556.73	Killen, Alice M. Roman "terrifiant" de Walpole à Anne Radcliffe et son influence sur la littérature française jusqu'en 1840. Paris, 1915.
	37556.73.2	Killen, Alice M. Le roman "terrifiant" ou roman "noir". Thèse. Paris, 1915.
	41578.7.9	Lamartine, Alphonse de. Méditations poétiques. Paris, 1915. 2v.
	43687.7.30	Lambert, M. de. Debout les morts! n.p., 1915.
	42544.24.21.5	Lavedan, Henri. Leur beau physique. Paris, 1915.
	43688.1.34	Leroux, Gaston. Bride of the sun. N.Y., 1915.
	40512.80	LeSage, Alain René. Crispin, rival of his master. N.Y., 1915.
	39534.22.50	Leuschner, Kurt. Antoine Furetière. Inaug. Diss. Erlangen, 1915.
	37596.138	Li romans dou lis. N.Y., 1915.
	37555.75	Lowell, Amy. Six French poets, studies in contemporary literature. N.Y., 1915.
	42545.3.3.14	Maeterlinck, Maurice. Pélléas and Mélisande. N.Y., 1915.
	37555.329	Martinon, P. Dictionnaire méthodique...des rimes françaises. 6. éd. Paris, 1915.
	37567.132	Matthey, Hubert. Essai sur le merveilleux dans la littérature française depuis 1800. Paris, 1915.
	42545.10.42	Meilhac, Henri. Panurge's sheep. N.Y., 1915.
	39544.70	Meinhardt, G. Voltaire und seine Sekretäre. Inaug. Diss. Berlin, 1915.
	41555.20.75	Mérimée, Prosper. Carmen based on Prosper Mérimée's story. N.Y., 1915.
	39594.19.17	Michel, Ernst Friedrich. Die anthropogeographischen Anschauung Montesquieus. Inaug. Diss. Heidelberg, 1915.
	43699.3.705	Mille, Pierre. Barnavaux. London, 1915.
	43699.3.745	Mille, Pierre. Joffre chaps and some others. London, 1915.
	43699.3.725	Mille, Pierre. Under the tricolour. London, 1915.
	Mol 252.3.15	Molière, Jean Baptiste Poquelin. The affected young ladies. N.Y., 1915.
	Mol 172.5.40	Molière, Jean Baptiste Poquelin. The merchant gentleman (le bourgeois gentilhomme). N.Y., 1915.
	Mon 30.15	Montaigne, Michel de. Essays. London, 1915.
	Mon 32.7	Montaigne, Michel de. Montaigne's essay on friendship. Boston, 1915.
	43701.62.100	Montfort, Eugène. La belle-enfant. Paris, 1915?
	40551.25.5	Moulinié, Henri. De Bonald. Thèse. Paris, 1915.
	40551.20	Moulinié, Henri. Lettres inédites du Vicomte de Bonald...à Madame Victor de Sèze. Thèse. Paris, 1915.
	41574.39.5	Mrodzinsky, Rektor Carl. Die deutschen Übersetzungen der dramatischen Hauptwerke Victor Hugos. Inaug. Diss. Halle, 1915.
	42545.3.360	Pastore, A. Filosofia e poesia nell'opere di Maurizio Maeterlinck. Genova, 1915.
Htn	37574.66*	Payne, John. Flowers of France. The classical period. 17th and 18th century. London, 1915.
	42515.44.22F	Pellegrini, Carlo. Edgar Quinet e la litteratura italiana. Pisa, 1915.
	42515.44.20	Pellegrini, Carlo. Edgar Quinet e l'Italia. Roma, 1915.
X Cg	42556.26.25.2	Régnier, Henri de. Les rencontres de M. de Bréot. Paris, 1915.
	43753.1.30	Reinach, J. Récits et portraits contemporains. Paris, 1915.
	42556.22.105	Richepin, Jean. Proses de guerre. Paris, 1915.
	43757.50.712	Rolland, Romain. Jean-Christophe: Dawn, morning, youth, revolt. N.Y., 1915.
	43757.50.732A	Rolland, Romain. Jean-Christophe: Journey's end, Love and friendship, The burning bush, The new dawn. N.Y., 1915.
	43757.50.723A	Rolland, Romain. Jean-Christophe in Paris: The market-place, Antoinette, The house. N.Y., 1915.
NEDL	FL 6002.915	Rousseau, J.J. Political writings, edited from the original manuscripts...text in French. v.1-2. Cambridge, Eng., 1915. 2v.
	39576.30	Ruplingen, André. Un representant provincial de l'esprit philosophique au XIIIe siècle...C. Bordes. Lyon, 1915.
	41578.72	Sachs, Eva. Les idées sociales de Lamartine jusqu'a 1848. Thèse. Paris, 1915.
	42546.30.31A	Sardou, Victorien. Patrie! Historical drama in five acts. Garden City, 1915.
	43738.1.910	Seippel, Paul. Un poète français tombé au champ d'honneur: Charles Péguy. Paris, 1915.
	38587.31	Sirich, Edward Hinman. Study in syntax of Alexandre Hardy. Baltimore, 1915.
	43780.5.290	Suarès, André. Italie, Italie. Paris, 1915.
	43738.1.915	Suarès, André. Péguy. Paris, 1915.
	42545.3.430	Taylor, U. Maurice Maeterlinck; a critical study. N.Y., 1915.
	43787.2.30	Teramond, Guy de. Mystery of Lucien Delorme. N.Y., 1915.
	42578.51.45	Tinayre, Marcelle. La veillée des armes. Le départ:août 1914. Paris, 1915.
	40553.10.5	Ullmann, Helene. Benjamin Constant und seine Beziehungen zum deutschen Geistesleben. Marburg, 1915.
	40553.10.4	Ullmann, Helene. Benjamin Constant und seine Beziehungen zum deutschen Geistesleben. Inaug. Diss. Marburg, 1915.
	40535.14.28	Ulrich, Erich. Charles B. Fagan's Lustspiele. Inaug. Diss. Dresden, 1915.
	43822.4.40	Variot, Jean. Petits écrits de 1915. Paris, 1915.
	42557.11.13	Verhaeren, Émile. Cloister. Boston, 1915.

Chronological Listing

1915 - cont.

42557.11.13.2 Verhaeren, Émile. The cloister. London, 1915.
42547.13.2 Verhaeren, Émile. The dawn. Boston, 1915.
42557.11.15 Verhaeren, Émile. Deux drames: Le cloitre, Philippe II. 7. éd. Paris, 1915.
42557.11.2.15 Verhaeren, Émile. Poems. London, 1915.
42576.54.3A Viaud, Julien. Le roman d'un enfant. Paris, 1915.
43824.3.30 Villeroy, A. La vierge de Lutée (St. Geneviève). Paris, 1915?
39544.28.30 Voltaire, François Marie Arouet de. Lettres philosophiques. v.1-2. éd. Paris, 1915-
Mol 730.11 Wechssler, E. Molière als Philosoph. 2e. Aufl. Marburg, 1915.
43833.1.30 Weyl, Fernand. Prière dans la nuit; drame en un acte. Paris, 1915.
38541.25 Woelffel, Paul. Die Reisebilder in den Romanen la Calprenèdes. Greifswald, 1915.
42557.12.10 Zweig, Stefan. Émile Verhaeren. London, 1915.

1916

37543.114.3 Abry, E. Histoire illustrée de la littérature française. 3. éd. Paris, 1916.
38575.28.9.5 Académie française, Paris. Les sentiments de l'Académie française sur le Cid. Minneapolis, 1916.
42562.38.14.38 Adam, Paul. Dans l'air qui tremble. Paris, 1916.
37569.3 Adam, Paul. La littérature et la guerre. Paris, 1916.
43874.5 Au bruit du canon; contes véridiques, 1916. Paris, 1916.
42582.2 Bachmann, Hans. Das englishe Sprachgut in den Romanen Jules Vernes. Greifswald, 1916. 2v.
41522.2.60 Barbey d'Aurevilly, Jules. L'ensorcelée. Paris, 1916.
43537.6.29 Barbusse, Henri. Le feu (journal d'une escouade). Paris, 1916.
41578.75 Barthow, Louis. Lamartine, orateur. Paris, 1916.
43537.4.37 Bataille, Henry. Beau voyage, poésies. Paris, 1916.
43537.4.36 Bataille, Henry. La divine tragédie. Paris, 1916.
42563.21.72 Bazin, René. Aujourd'hui et demain. Paris, 1916.
43538.7.32 Benjamin, René. La guerre sous le ciel de France. Paris, 1916.
43538.76.9100 Bérénice (pseud.). Le jardin de Marrès. Paris, 1916.
37543.306 Bernardin, N.M. Du XVe au XXe siècle. Paris, 1916.
43538.8.30 Bertrand, Adrien. L'appel du sol. Paris, 1916.
40582.8.9 Beyle, Henri. Chartreuse de Parme. Paris, 1916.
40582.25.45 Beyle, Henri. The red and the black. London, 1916.
43543.1.31 Blois, Louis A. La vocation. Roman. 7. éd. Paris, 1916.
39545.19.5 Boissier, R. La mort de Voltaire. Thèse. Paris, 1916.
43544.5.40 Boulenger, Marcel. Sur un tambour. Paris, 1916.
42563.37.37.5 Bourget, Paul. The night cometh. N.Y., 1916.
42563.37.37 Bourget, Paul. Le sens de la mort. Paris, 1916.
43544.89.1100 Boutet, Frédéric. Victor et ses amis. Paris, 1916.
37530.28 Bowerman, S.G. Recent French literature; an annotated list of books recommended for libraries. Chicago, 1916.
42563.39.130 Boylesve, René. A gentlewoman of France. N.Y., 1916.
39544.65.10 Brandes, Georg. François de Voltaire. Kjøbenhavn, 1916-17. 2v.
42542.47.27.5 Brieux, Eugène. Woman on her own, False gods and The red robe. London, 1916.
43547.1.30 Buisson, Benjamin. Les Helléniques de Landor et autre poèmes. Paris, 1916.
42566.16.9 Burns, Mary. La langue d'Alphonse Daudet. Thèse. Paris, 1916.
Mol 213.14 Campbell, R.W. Studies in modern languages. Oxford, 1916.
37555.716 Chalons, Vincent. Règles de la poésie française. Paris, 1916.
43554.2.39 Claudel, Paul. Autres poëmes. 2e éd. Paris, 1916.
43554.2.705 Claudel, Paul. The tidings brought to Mary. New Haven, 1916.
43556.49.565 Colette, Sidonie Gabrielle. La paix chez les bêtes. Paris, 1916.
38574.16 Corneille, Pierre. Théâtre. Paris, 1916. 2v.
42542.58.11 Curel, François de. A false saint. Garden City, 1916.
43565.5.32 Daudet, Léon A. La vermine du monde de l'éspionnage allemand. Paris, 1916.
43565.5.30 Daudet, Léon A. La vermine du monde de l'éspionnage allemand. Paris, 1916.
39564.11.15 Diderot, Denis. La religieuse. Paris, 1916.
39564.12 Diderot, Denis. La religiosa. Paris, 1916.
FL 376.30 Dietschy, Charlotte. Die "dame d'intrigue". Inaug. Diss. Basel, 1916.
38557.5.9 Dimier, Louis. Bossuet. Paris, 1916.
42542.65.22 Donnay, Maurice. L'impromptu du paquetage, pièce en un acte. Paris, 1916.
42542.65.24 Donnay, Maurice. Le théatre aux armées. Paris, 1916.
38546.59 Dorbec, Prosper. L'hotel carnavale et marquis de Sévigné. Paris, 1916.
43576.95.110 Dumas, Charles. Stellus. Paris, 1916.
43606.78.210 Farrère, Claude. Quatorze histoires de soldats. Paris, 1916.
43606.87.160 Fauchois, René. L'Augusta. Paris, 1916.
43611.1.25.18 Fort, Paul. Deux chaumières au pays de l'Yveline. XVIII. Paris, 1916.
43611.1.25.19 Fort, Paul. Poèmes de France. 1. série. XIX. Lausanne, 1916.
42576.62.47 France, Anatole. Amycus et Célestin. N.Y., 1916.
42576.62.31 France, Anatole. Opinion sociales. Paris, 1916. 2 pam.
38576.39.80 Franz, Henry. Palaprat; son temps, ses oeuvres. Paris, 1916.
43612.2.65 Fraudet, René. Prelude aux poèmes du coq. Paris, 1916.
Htn Mol 925.7F* French and Co., N.Y. The comedies of Molière; tapestries. N.Y., 1916?
42586.56.20 Fromentin, Eugène. Dominique. Paris, 1916.
43616.51.102 Galopin, Arnould. Les poilus de la 9e. Paris, 1916?
41542.7.8 Gautier, Théophile. Captain Fracasse. Boston, 1916.
41542.29.5 Gautier, Théophile. Un trio de romans. Paris, 1916.
FL 360.9 Gavault, Paul. Conférence de l'Odéon (1915-1916). Paris, 1916.
43625.3.33 Gourmont, Rémy de. La culture des idées. 7e ed. Paris, 1916.
43625.3.50 Gourmont, Rémy de. Dans la tourmente. Paris, 1916.
43625.3.36 Gourmont, Rémy de. Histoires magiques. 4. éd. Paris, 1916.
43625.3.49 Gourmont, Rémy de. Pendant l'orage. Paris, 1916.
37543.95 Gourmont, Rémy de. Promenades littéraires. 6. éd. Paris, 1916.
43625.3.45 Gourmont, Rémy de. Songe d'une femme. 5e ed. Paris, 1916.
42545.3.815 Griggs, E.H. Maeterlinck. N.Y., 1916.

1916 - cont.

37556.36.10 Guérard, Albert L. Five masters of French romance. N.Y., 1916?
42576.40.348A Halévy, Ludovic. L'abbé Constantin. Boston, 1916.
43631.76.1100F Harispe, Pierre. La divine tragédie. Paris, 1916.
37591.30.25 Hasselmann, Fritz. Über die quellen de Chronique rimée von Philippe Mousket. Göttingen, 1916.
38526.14.130A Hawkins, R.L. Maistre Charles Fontaine, parisien. Cambridge, 1916.
37562.79 Heldt, Elisabeth. Französische Virelais aus dem 15. Jahrhundert. Halle, 1916.
Htn 43632.3.30* Hémon, Louis. Maria Chapdelaine. Montréal, 1916.
43625.4.80 Henzey, Juliette. Lucie Felix-Faure Goyan. Paris, 1916.
42543.65.12 Hermant, Abel. L'autre aventure du joyeux garçon. Paris, 1916.
FL 6139.16.5 Hofer, Cuno. L'influence de Jean-Jacques Rousseau sur le droit de la guerre. Genève, 1916.
42576.65.80.10 Huysmans, Joris Karl. Le drageoir aux épices. Paris, 1916.
43667.14.150 Jacob, Max. Le cornet à Dés. Paris, 1916.
43667.14.150.2 Jacob, Max. Le cornet à Dés. 2. éd. Paris, 1916.
43667.1.39 Jammes, Francis. Cinq prières pour le temps de la guerre. Paris, 1916.
43667.1.38 Jammes, Francis. Le rosaire au soleil. 9. éd. Paris, 1916.
38514.38.5 Kerdaniel, Edouard L. Un soldat-poète du XVe siècle Jehan Meschinot. Paris, 1916.
43757.50.860 Key, Ellen. Själarnas neutralitet. Stockholm, 1916.
42513.42.9 Kiesow, Julius. Die philosophische Lyrik von Guyau und Lahor. Greifswald, 1916.
FL 379.65A Kurz, Harry. European characters in French drama. N.Y., 1916.
37543.38.6 Lanson, Gustave. Histoire de la littérature française. 13. éd. Paris, 1916.
42576.41.26 Le Blanc, Maurice. L'éclat d'obus. Paris, 1916.
43688.14.115 Leclerc, Marc. La passion de notre frère le poilu. Paris, 1916.
43688.1.35 Leroux, Gaston. Les étranges noces de Rouletabille. Paris, 1916.
42576.44.3 Le Roux, H. Au champ d'honneur. Paris, 1916.
40512.43 LeSage, Alain René. Histoire de Gil Blas de Santillane. Chicago, 1916.
38526.28.9 Lingendes, J. de. Oeuvres poétiques. Manchester, 1916.
38526.28.10 Lingendes, J. de. Oeuvres poétiques. Paris, 1916.
42544.36.5 Loyson, Paul H. The apostle; modern tragedy in 3 acts. Garden City, 1916.
43697.6.40 Machard, Alfred. La guerre des mômes. Paris, 1916.
42545.3.34 Maeterlinck, Maurice. Les débris de la guerre. Paris, 1916.
42545.3.35 Maeterlinck, Maurice. Les débris de la guerre. Paris, 1916.
42545.3.33 Maeterlinck, Maurice. Les débris de la guerre. Paris, 1916.
42545.3.9.10 Maeterlinck, Maurice. Sister Beatrice and Ardiane and Barbe Bleue. N.Y., 1916.
42545.3.8.4 Maeterlinck, Maurice. Wisdom and destiny. N.Y., 1916.
42576.74.100 Mahon, Patrice. Monsieur Pierre. Paris, 1916-17.
42576.76.40 Margueritte, Paul. L'embusqué. Paris, 1916.
40535.27.7 Marivaux, Pierre Carlet de Chamblain de. Théâtre. Paris, 1916-17. 2v.
41568.26.50 Marx, Ludwig. Claude Tillier als Romanschriftsteller. Inaug. Diss. Heidelberg, 1916.
43697.82.160 Massis, Henri. Impressions de guerre. Paris, 1916.
43745.1.125 Massis, Henri. La vie d'Ernest Psichari. Paris, 1916.
FL 6139.16.2 Masson, Pierre M. La religion de Jean-Jacques Rousseau. Paris, 1916. 3v.
FL 6139.16 Masson, Pierre M. La religion de Jean-Jacques Rousseau. Thèse. Paris, 1916.
Mol 713.14.5 Matthews, B. Molière his life and his works. N.Y., 1916.
42577.12.78 Maygrier, Raymond. Le dernier Faust. Paris, 1916.
41555.23.12 Mérimée, Prosper. Colomba. Boston, 1916.
43699.3.45 Mille, Pierre. En croupe de Bellone. Paris, 1916.
43699.3.715 Mille, Pierre. Louise and Barnavaux. London, 1916.
43699.3.33 Mille, Pierre. Sous leur dictée. 5. éd. Paris, 1916.
Mol 269.70.10 Molière, Jean Baptiste Poquelin. Tartufo: comedia refundida. Barcelona, 1916.
42566.16.15 Mülbrecht, K. Die Dramatisierungen der daudetschen Romane. Inaug. Diss. Königsburg, 1916.
37575.526 Nouveaux contes veridiques des tranchées, 1914-1916. Paris, 1916.
37596.171 Paris. Bibliothèque nationale. Eine altfranzösische Bearbeitung biblischer Stoffe. Halle, 1916.
43738.1.5 Péguy, Charles. Oeuvres complètes. v.1-16. Paris, 1916-52. 15v.
43738.2.30 Perrier, Martial. Aux jardins d'Aspasie. Paris, 1916.
43740.1.65 Philippe, Charles Louis. Contes du matin. Paris, 1916.
43743.1.33 Porché, François. L'arrêt sur la marne. Paris, 1916.
43743.1.47 Porché, François. Nous poèmes choisis. Paris, 1916.
43743.75.100 Porché, François. Le poème de la tranchée. Paris, 1916.
42545.95.55 Pottecher, M. Les chants de la tourmente. Paris, 1916.
43743.91.130 Pourtalès, Guy de. A mes amis suisses. Paris, 1916.
42578.31.58A Prévost, Marcel. L'adjudant Benoît. Paris, 1916.
43745.1.31 Psichari, Ernest. Le voyage du centurion. Paris, 1916.
37544.32 Ravà, Béatrix. Venise dans la littérature française. Paris, 1916.
43753.2.30 Régnier, M.L.A. de. Jeune fille. Paris, 1916.
42577.4.35 Reuel, Fritz. Maupassant als Physiognomiker. Inaug. Diss. Marburg, 1916.
42587.55.30 Rivoire, André. L'humble offrande. Paris, 1916.
43738.1.905 Roberty, Jules Émile. Charles Péguy. Paris, 1916.
42578.19.22.10 Rod, Edouard. L'ombre s'étend sur la montagne. 1. éd. Paris, 1916.
42578.22.15 Rosny, J.H. Perdus? Paris, 1916.
43779.52.100 St. Lys, Odette. L'auberge. Londres, 1916.
43761.7.30 Samain, Alfred. Contes. 22e éd. Paris, 1916.
41557.10.21 Sand, George. La langue et le style rustique de George Sand dans les champêtres. Paris, 1916.
41557.9.48.9 Sand, George. La mare au diable. N.Y., 1916.
38526.48.31 Scève, Maurice. Délie, object de plus haulte vertu. Paris, 1916.
43763.37.1100 Schewaebel, Joseph. La pentecôte à Arras, 1915. Paris, 1916.
FL 6129.16 Schinz, Albert. Jean-Jacques Rousseau et le libraire. Genève, 1916.
43765.31.150 Ségalen, Victor. Peintures. Paris, 1916.
43765.77.1110 Sertillanges, Antonin Gilbert. Aux morts de la guerre. Paris, 1916.

1916 - cont.

43765.77.1100 Sertillanges, Antonin Gilbert. Prière de la femme française pendant la guerre. Paris, 1916.
37530.193 Société Littéraire de France. Catalogue de la Société Littéraire de France. Paris, 1916.
43892.5A Sous les obus; contes véridiques, 1914-1916. Paris, 1916.
38514.21.16 Stacpoole, H. De Vere. François Villon, his life and times. N.Y., 1916.
43780.5.300 Suarès, André. Angleterre. Paris, 1916.
43780.5.310 Suarès, André. Ceux de Verdun. Paris, 1916.
37555.211 Thieme, Hugo P. Essai sur l'histoire du vers français. Paris, 1916.
Htn 42547.10.20* Vallette, Marguerite. Théâtre. Paris, 1916.
42547.10.18 Vallette, Marguerite. La tour d'amour. Paris, 1916.
42557.11.4.50 Verhaeren, Émile. The plays of Émile Verhaeren. Boston, 1916.
42557.11.14 Verhaeren, Émile. Poèmes legendaires de Flandre. Paris, 1916.
42582.28.10 Verne, Jules. Twenty thousand leagues under the sea. N.Y., 1916.
42576.57.10.20 Viaud, Julien. La hyéne enragée. Paris, 1916.
41564.1.2A Vigny, Alfred de. Poésies. Paris, 1916.
41564.1 Vigny, Alfred de. Thèâtre. Paris, 1916.
43757.50.900 Vogt, W. A propos du moins Romain der Rollands furieux. Paris, 1916.
42587.69.50 Wagner, Charles. Trois contes et deux histoires pour amuser les petits et faire penser les grands. Paris, 1916.
38526.37.100 Werth, Werner. François de Molière. Inaug. Diss. Berlin, 1916.
38516.8 Wright, Charles H.C. French verse of the XVI century. Boston, 1916.
43858.1.59 Zamacois, Miguel. L'ineffacable, La grande guerre. Paris, 1916.
42584.19.4 Zola, Emile. Le rêve. Paris, 1916.

1917

43513.1.32 Acker, Paul. L'oislau vainquer; roman. Paris, 1917.
42562.38.14 Adam, Paul. La terre qui tonne; France, Italie. 5e éd. Paris, 1917.
37593.63.10 Adam de la Halle. Les partures Adam; les jeux partis. Paris, 1917.
42586.7.16.5 Aicard, Jean. Maurin des Maures. Paris, 1917?
43520.54.1100 Aimé, Henri. Le bandeau sur le front. Paris, 1917.
41522.17.9A Aubry, G. Jean. Baudelaire et Honfleur. Paris, 1917.
43529.4.30 Audigier, Camille. La terre qui renaît. Paris, 1917.
37556.148 Bacourt, P. de. French of today. N.Y., 1917.
42515.42.11 Bär, Georg. Edgar Quinets Ahasvérus und seine Beziehungen zu Quinets Geschichtsphilosophie. Inaug. Diss. Rostock, 1917.
40596.13.80.10 Balzac, Honoré de. Ursula. Boston, 1917.
43537.6.30.2 Barbusse, Henri. Under fire. N.Y., 1917.
43537.8.30 Barranx, Serge. Notre France! Paris, 1917.
42563.15.5 Barrès, Maurice. En regardant au fond descrevasses. Paris, 1917.
42563.16.7 Barrès, Maurice. Leurs figures. Paris, 1917.
41522.17.13 Barthou, Louis. Autour de Baudelaire. Paris, 1917.
43537.4.38 Bataille, Henry. L'Amazone: Les flambeaux. Paris, 1917.
43537.4.80A Bataille, Henry. Ecrits sur le théâtre. 2e éd. Paris, 1917.
41522.13.32 Baudelaire, Charles. Douze poèmes. Paris, 1917.
41522.13.5 Baudelaire, Charles. Les fleurs du mal. Paris, 1917.
42563.21.73 Bazin, René. La closerie de champdolent. 9. éd. Paris, 1917.
43538.11.35 Beaunier, André. Figures d'autrefois. Paris, 1917.
Htn 43538.7.33.5* Benjamin, René. Les soldats de la guerre. Paris, 1917.
43538.6.32 Berger, Marcel. Jean Darboise auxiliaire. Paris, 1917.
43538.6.30 Berger, Marcel. Le miracle du feu; roman. Paris, 1917.
43538.6.700 Berger, Marcel. The ordeal by fire. N.Y., 1917.
42542.29.44 Bernstein, H. Élévation; piece en trois actes. Paris, 1917.
43538.8.35 Bertrand, Adrien. L'orage sur le jardin de candide. Paris, 1917.
43538.8.37 Bertrand, Adrien. Le verger de Cypris. Paris, 1917.
42563.23.8.30 Bertrand, Louis. Mademoiselle de Jessincourt. Paris, 1917.
42576.65.13.4 Besse, Jean M. Joris Karl Huysmans. Paris, 1917.
43543.2.30 Blancard, Jules César. La carmagnole. St. Paul, 1917.
43543.1.30 Blois, Louis A. Contes pour lire au crepuscule. Paris, 1917.
37574.645 Bodkin, Thomas. May it please your lordship. Dublin, 1917.
42563.37.38 Bourget, Paul. Lazarine. Paris, 1917.
42563.39.50 Boylesve, René. Le bonheur à cinq sous. Paris, 1917.
42563.39.50.6 Boylesve, René. Le bonheur à cinq sous. 6. éd. Paris, 1917.
42563.39.45 Boylesve, René. Tu n'es plus rien. Paris, 1917.
38512.94 Brasdefer, Jean. Pamphile et Galatie. Thèse. Paris, 1917.
38526.17.100 Brenier de Montmorand, Antoine F.J.H.L. Anne de Graville. Paris, 1917.
38525.21.25 Buhler, Karl. Ronsard und seine Stellung zur mittelalterlichen französischen Litteratur. Inaug. Diss. Frankfurt, 1917.
43547.1.31 Buisson, Benjamin. Teutoniana. Paris, 1917.
43547.77.110 Burnat-Provins, Marguerite. Poèmes de la Boule de Verre. Paris, 1917.
42546.27.9 Byrne, C.A. The sorceress. Boston, 1917.
42586.63.2 Cartellieri, A. Gobineau. Strassburg, 1917.
40586.36 Chateaubriand, F.A.R. A propos de la naissance du duc de Chateaubriand (Bordeaux). Paris, 1917.
38551.43.6 Chérel, Albert. Fénelon au XVIIIe siècle en France. Supplément. Fribourg, 1917.
X Cg 38551.43.5 Chérel, Albert. Fénelon au XVIIIe siècle en France (1715-1820). Paris, 1917.
41522.17.12 Le cinquantenaire de Charles Baudelaire. Paris, 1917.
43554.2.790 Claudel, Paul. Die Musen. Leipzig, 1917.
43554.4.35 Clermont, Emile. Histoire d'Isabelle. Paris, 1917.
43556.49.420 Colette, Sidonie Gabrielle. Les heures lonques, 1914-1917. Paris, 1917.
40546.8.61 Courier de Méré, Paul Louis. Lettres et pamphlets. Paris, 1917?
38514.21.17 Cox, Edwin Marion. The ballads of François Villon. London, 1917.
43565.6.30 Dautrin, E. L'envolée (roman). 11. éd. Paris, 1917.
43566.54.107 Demians d'Archimbaud, M. A travers la tourmente. Une vie intime. Paris, 1917.
41522.18.405A Dérieux, H. Baudelaire; trois essais. Bale, 1917.

1917 - cont.

42542.65.36 Donnay, Maurice. Lettres à une dame blanche. Paris, 1917.
43574.41.110A Drieu La Rochelle, Pierre. Interrogation. Poèmes. Paris, 1917.
FL 6129.08.6 Dueros, L. Jean-Jacques Rousseau de Genève à l'Hermitage, 1757-1765. Paris, 1917.
37575.205 Dumont-Wilden, Louis. Anthologie des écrivains belges. Paris, 1917.
43576.69.100 Dupin, Jules. Journal, 1905-1915. Montbrison, 1917.
38526.1.35 Eckhardt, Alex. Reandremy Belleau. Budapest, 1917.
42568.23.115 Eekhoud, Georges. The new Carthage. N.Y., 1917.
43598.84.180 Estaunié, Édouard. Solitudes; roman. Paris, 1917.
42576.67.30 Estéve, Edmond. Paul Hervieu; conteur, moraliste. Paris, 1917.
43606.78.240 Farrère, Claude. La veille d'armes. Paris, 1917.
43606.89.35 Faure, Gabriel. Paysages littéraires. Série 1-2. Paris, 1917-1918. 2v.
38553.15.5 Fénelon, F. de S. de la Mothe. Fénelon inédit. Vitry-le-France, 1917.
42576.28.1.3 Flaubert, Gustave. Madame Bovary. Paris, 1917.
43611.4.50 Foley, Charles. Sylvette et son blessé. Paris, 1917.
43611.3.31 Fonson, Jean F. La demoiselle de magasin. Paris, 1917.
43611.3.30 Fonson, Jean J. La kommandantur. Paris, 1917.
43611.1.25.21 Fort, Paul. L'alouette. 3. éd. XXI. Paris, 1917.
43611.1.25.40 Fort, Paul. Que j'ai de plaisir d'être français. Paris, 1917.
43611.1.32.2 Fort, Paul. Si peau d'âne m'était. 4. éd. Paris, 1917.
43611.1.25.17 Fort, Paul. Si peau d'âne m'était conté. 3. éd. XVII. Paris, 1917.
42576.62.150 France, Anatole. The human tragedy. London, 1917.
42576.62.10.15 France, Anatole. The red lily. N.Y., 1917.
42576.62.10.16A France, Anatole. The red lily. N.Y., 1917.
43612.61.100 Franck, Henri. La danse devant l'Arche. 4. éd. Paris, 1917.
43613.45.100 Frison-Roche, Roger. Retour à la montagne. Paris, 1917.
42576.63.29 Garrison, F.W. The democracy of Anatole France. N.Y., 1917.
41542.20.10 Gautier, Théophile. Nouvelles. Paris, 1917.
37562.77 Gelzer, H. Nature zum Einfluss der Scholastik auf den altfranzösischen Roman. Halle, 1917.
43617.4.32.5 Géraldy, Paul. La guerre, Madame. 34. éd. Paris, 1917.
43617.4.32 Géraldy, Paul. La guerre, Madame. 47. éd. Paris, 1917.
43617.4.33 Géraldy, Paul. Les noces d'argent. Paris, 1917.
43617.4.31 Géraldy, Paul. Toi et moi. 30. éd. Paris, 1917.
43617.4.32.10 Géraldy, Paul. The war Madame. N.Y., 1917.
43617.6.30 Germain, André. Renée Vivien. Paris, 1917.
37576.35 Ginisty, Paul. Anthologie du journalisme du XVIIe siècle à nos jours. Paris, 1917.
37567.60.3 Gourmont, Rémy de. Le livre des masques. v.1: 10. éd.; v.2: 6. éd. Paris, 1917. 2v.
43625.3.47 Gourmont, Rémy de. Physique de l'amour. Paris, 1917.
43628.39.100 Guilbeaux, H. Du champs des horreurs. Genève, 1917.
42513.42.5 Guyau, M. Vers d'un philosophe. 9. éd. Paris, 1917.
43631.2.62 Hamp, Pierre. Gens. 5. éd. Paris, 1917.
42543.65.8 Hermant, Abel. Histoire amoureuse de Fanfan. Paris, 1917.
42543.65.39 Hermant, Abel. Histoires héroïques de mon ami Jean. Paris, 1917.
42543.69.9 Hervieu, Paul. The trail of the torch; play in 4 acts. Garden City, 1917.
Mol 730.13 Heussler, Otto. Molières religiöse Ueberzeugung. Greifswald, 1917.
39564.29.7 Hirn, Yrjö. Diderot. Stockholm, 1917.
38513.23.7 Holbrook, Richard T. Étude sur Pathelin. Baltimore, 1917.
43638.99.120 Huzard, A. de B. (Mme.). Mirabelle de pampelune. Paris, 1917.
43667.1.37 Jammes, Francis. Le roman de lièvre. 11. éd. Paris, 1917.
37562.73 Jessel, Marie. Strophenbau und Liedbildung in der altfranzösischen Kunstlyrik des 12. und 13. Jahrhunderts. Greifswald, 1917.
38529.8 Jones, Léonard Chester. Simon Goulart. Genève, 1917.
38585.14.9 Jovy, Ernest. De Royer-Collard à Racine. Saint-Dizier, 1917.
42555.37.3 Keiser, Gustav A. Stilstudien zu Leconte de Lisle. Halle, 1917.
37555.20.9 Langfors, Arthur. Les incipit des poèmes français. Paris, 1917.
43687.84.110 La Tailhède, Raymond de. Hymne pour la France. Paris, 1917.
42576.65.13.5 Lavalée, G. Essai sur la pyschologie morbide de Huysmans. Thèse. Paris, 1917.
42576.41.75A Le Blanc, Maurice. The golden triangle. N.Y., 1917.
43688.14.120 Leclerc, Marc. Les souvenirs de tranchées d'un poilu. Paris, 1917.
42544.31.20 Lecomte, Georges. Les lettres au service de la patrie. Paris, 1917.
43688.8.30 Le Goffic, Charles. Le crucifié de Keraliès. Paris, 1917.
43688.8.65 Le Goffic, Charles. Sans nouvelles. Paris, 1917.
38526.8.7 Lehmann, Johanna. Baifs dichterische Vorstellung von Meer und Wasser. Greifswald, 1917.
37563.41 Loviot, Louis. Auteurs et livres anciens, XVIe et XVIIe siècles. Paris, 1917.
43697.6.52 Machard, Alfred. Bout-de-bibi. Paris, 1917.
42545.3.10.5 Maeterlinck, Maurice. The Buried temple. N.Y., 1917.
42545.3.15.32 Maeterlinck, Maurice. Joyzelle. N.Y., 1917.
42555.43.9 Mallarmé, Stéphane. Divagations. Paris, 1917.
42545.9.5 Martel de Janville, S.G. Les flanchards. 14. éd. Paris, 1917.
41522.17.14 Mauclair, Camille. Charles Baudelaire, sa vie. Paris, 1917.
42577.2.4.5 Maupassant, Guy de. Mad, and other stories. N.Y., 1917.
42577.2.5.15 Maupassant, Guy de. Madame Tellier's establishment and family, and other stories. N.Y., 1917.
42577.2.35 Maupassant, Guy de. Mllé Fifi, and other stories. N.Y., 1917.
42577.4.19.25 Maupassant, Guy de. The second odd number. N.Y., 1917.
42555.37.5 Maurer, Chlothilde. Das persönliche Element in den Werken Leconte de Lisles. Inaug. Diss. Heidelberg, 1917.
41557.10.17.5 Maurras, C. Les amants de Venise, George Sand et Musset. Paris, 1917.
43699.65.105 Miomandre, Francis de. La saison des dupes. Paris, 1917.
43699.74.100 Mirat, Paul. Le chanson des épées. Paris, 1917.
42557.12.40 Mockel, Albert. Un poète de l'énergie. Paris, 1917.
Mol 171.57 Molière, Jean Baptiste Poquelin. Le bourgeois gentilhomme; comédie-ballet. Paris, 1917?
Mon 39.5 Montaigne, Michel de. Páginas escogidas. Madrid, 1917.
39594.6.45 Montesquieu, C.L. de S. Considérations sur les causes...décadence. 4e éd. Paris, 1917.

Chronological Listing

1917 - cont.

42555.60.4 Montesquiou-Fezensac, Robert de. Majeurs et mineurs. Paris, 1917.
FL 360.92 Mortier, Alfred. Dramaturgie de Paris. Paris, 1917.
43701.2.80 Mounet-Sully, J. Souvenirs d'un tragédien. Paris, 1917.
41596.18.5.10 Musset, Alfred de. Barberine. Paris, 1917.
NEDL 41596.18.8.25 Musset, Alfred de. Comédies et proverbes. v.2. Paris, 1917?
41596.18.8 Musset, Alfred de. Morceaux choisis. Paris, 1917.
43705.1.30 Nadaud, Marcel. Les derniers mousquetaires. Paris, 1917.
43705.1.32 Nadaud, Marcel. La guerre aérienne; chignole. Paris, 1917.
43705.1.31 Nadaud, Marcel. Ma p'tite femme. Paris, 1917.
FL 398.20.7 Olivier, Jean J. (pseud.). Madame Dugazon de la comédie-italienne, 1755-1821. Paris, 1917.
37567.160 Osmont, Anne. Le mouvement symboliste. Paris, 1917.
37574.362 Petits poèmes érotiques du XVIIIe siècle. Paris, 1917.
41578.93 Pirazzini, Agide. The influence of Italy on the literary career of Alphonse de Lamartine. N.Y., 1917.
37573.619.25A Poèmes des poilus. Boston, 1917.
42578.22.50 Rosny, J.H. L'énigme de Givreuse. Paris, 1917.
FL 6090.50 Rousseau, J.J. A lasting peace through the federation of Europe. London, 1917.
39567.9 Rubensohn, Georg. Die "Coresspondance littéraire". Inaug. Diss. Berlin, 1917.
37555.76 Rudmose-Brown, T. French literary studies. Dublin, 1917.
43892.13 Sainte Seductre; an inner view of the Boche at Bay. N.Y., 1917.
37556.27.5A Saintsbury, George. A history of the French novel. London, 1917-19. 2v.
37542.17.7 Saintsbury, George. A short history of French literature. 7th ed. Oxford, 1917.
43780.5.230 Saurès, André. Remarques. v.1-12. Paris, 1917-18. 2v.
FL 372.16 Schäfer, Johannes. Das Pariser Reformationsspiel...1524. Inaug. Diss. Halle, 1917.
42542.47.41 Scheifley, W.H. Brieux and contemporary French history. N.Y., 1917.
37530.194 Société Littéraire de France. Catalogue de la Société Littéraire de France. Paris, 1917.
38514.21.16.5 Stacpoole, H. De Vere. François Villon. N.Y., 1917.
42513.48.10 Stephens, Winifred. Madame Adam. N.Y., 1917.
43780.5.170 Suarès, André. Sur la mort de mon frère. Paris, 1917.
X Cg 38525.36.2.5 Tristan L'Hermite, F. La Mariane, tragédie. Paris, 1917.
37573.617 Turpin, Georges. Les poètes de la guerre. v.1-2. Paris, 1917.
37548.37.5 Turquet-Milnes, G. Some modern Belgian writers. N.Y., 1917.
43822.2.32 Vallery-Radot, Robert. Le réveil de l'esprit. Paris, 1917.
41522.17.10 Vandérem, Fernand. Baudelaire et Sainte-Beuve. Paris, 1917.
37565.51 Van Tieghem, P. L'année littéraire, 1754-1790. Thèse. Paris, 1917.
43822.5.30 Vanzype, Gustave. Mother nature. Progress. 2 Belgian plays. Boston, 1917.
42557.11.60 Verhaeren, Émile. Afternoon. N.Y., 1917.
42557.11.4.5 Verhaeren, Émile. Choix de poèmes. 6. éd. Paris, 1917.
42557.11.4.10 Verhaeren, Émile. Choix de poèmes. 13. éd. Paris, 1917.
42557.11.20 Verhaeren, Émile. Les flammes hautes. 9. éd. Paris, 1917.
42557.11.19 Verhaeren, Émile. Quinze poèmes. Paris, 1917.
42557.11.55 Verhaeren, Émile. The sunlit hours. N.Y., 1917.
42576.51.5 Viaud, Julien. Quelques aspects du vertige mondial. Paris, 1917.
41557.10.20 Vincent, L. George Sand et l'amour. Paris, 1917.
37575.325 Weber-Silvain, L. Anthologie de prosateurs romands de J.J. Rousseau à nos jours. Lucerne, 1917.
43833.87.50 Wetterlé, Émile. Au service de l'ennemi. Paris, 1917.
37562.75 Wood, Mary M. The spirit of protest in Old French literature. N.Y., 1917.

1918

37543.114.4A Abry, E. Histoire illustrée de la littérature française. Paris, 1918.
37596.23.9 Adam (Mystery). Le mystère d'Adam. Manchester, 1918.
42524.19.12 Allard, Louis. Ferdinand Brunetière. n.p., 1918?
X Cg 38524.70 Allem, Maurice (pseud.). Anthologie poétique française XVIe siècle. Paris, 1918. 2v.
37596.64.15 Allen, H.E. Mystical lyrics of Mannuel des Pechiez. N.Y., 1918.
43528.61.120 Arnoux, Alexandre. Abisag. Paris, 1918.
43528.88.110 Artus, Louis. La maison ou Fou. Paris, 1918.
43531.7.33 Aubert, Octave Louis. Contes d'un Breton adoptif. St. Brieuc, 1918?
43537.13.30 Bachelin, H. Le serviteur. Paris, 1918.
40597.29.4.25 Balzac, Honoré de. Old Goriot. London, 1918.
41522.1.10.15 Barbey d'Aurevilly, Jules. Poussières. Paris, 1918.
43537.6.29.10 Barbusse, Henri. Le feu. Paris, 1918.
43537.6.56 Barbusse, Henri. The inferno. N.Y., 1918.
43537.6.31A Barbusse, Henri. Nous autres. v.1-3. Paris, 1918.
43537.6.30.5A Barbusse, Henri. Under fire. N.Y., 1918.
43537.6.50 Barbusse, Henri. We others. N.Y., 1918.
FL 383.60 Baret, Charles. Le théâtre en province. Paris, 1918.
42563.18.23 Barrès, Maurice. The faith of France. Boston, 1918.
43537.12.30 Basly, Émile. Le martyre de Lens. Paris, 1918.
FL 386.502 Bataille, Henry. Le théâtre après la guerre. Paris, 1918.
43537.84.100 Bataille, Michel. Le chapeau de velours. 2e éd. Paris, 1918.
41522.4.5 Baudelaire, Charles. Baudelaire choisie, poésie. Lyon, 1918.
41522.13.6 Baudelaire, Charles. Les fleurs du mal. Paris, 1918.
41522.4.6 Baudelaire, Charles. J. Barbey d'Aurevilly prose. Paris, 1918.
41522.4.10 Baudelaire, Charles. Lettres inédites a sa mère. Paris, 1918.
40556.23.5 Beaunier, André. Joseph Joubert et la révolution. Paris, 1918.
43538.59.110 Benda, Julien. Le bouquet de Glycère. Paris, 1918.
43538.7.30 Benjamin, René. Le Major Pipe et son père. 8. éd. Paris, 1918.
43538.6.710 Berger, Marcel. The secret of the Maine, how Sergeant Aritsch saved France. N.Y., 1918.
38514.23.10 Bernard, Jean Marc. François Villon, 1431-1463. Paris, 1918.
43538.76.2110 Bernard, O. A la visite. Paris, 1918.
43538.76.2120 Bernard, O. Le petit Don Juan. Paris, 1918.

1918 - cont.

40588.70.2 Berthier, Alfred. Xavier de Maistre. Lyon, 1918.
40588.70 Berthier, Alfred. Xavier Maistre. Thèse. Lyon, 1918?
37574.28.12 Bever, A. van. Les poètes du terroir du XVe siècle au XXe siècle. v.1,3-4. Paris, 1918. 3v.
43540.3.30 Billy, André. Scènes de la vie littéraire à Paris. Paris, 1918.
43543.13.145 Bloch, J.R. Et cie. 4. éd. Paris, 1918.
42563.23.32 Bloy, Léon. Dans les ténèbres. 2. éd. Paris, 1918.
37543.11.5 Bordeaux, Henry. Les pierres du foyer. Paris, 1918.
43544.75.705 Borel, Marguerite Appeli. The man who survived. N.Y., 1918.
43544.4.32 Botrel, Théodore. Chansons de chez nous. Paris, 1918.
42554.15.35.5 Botrel, Théodore. Folk songs of Brittany. New Haven, 1918.
42563.37.39 Bourget, Paul. Némésis. Paris, 1918.
FL 374.6 Boutarel, M. La médecine dans notre théâtre comique. Caen, 1918.
FL 370.16 Boutarel, Maurice. "Mires, fisisciens, navrés" dans notre théâtre...XVIe siècle. Thèse. Caen, 1918.
42574.37 Bowen, Ray Preston. The novels of Ferdinand Fabre. Thesis. Boston, 1918.
43544.98.101 Boyer, Lucien. La chanson des poilus. Paris, 1918.
42563.39.46 Boylesve, René. You no longer count. N.Y., 1918.
42542.47.36 Brieux, Eugène. Artists' families. N.Y., 1918.
39544.44 Bruce, H.L. Voltaire on the English stage. Berkeley, 1918.
43547.77.120 Burnat-Provins, Marguerite. Nouveaux poèmes de la Boule de Verre. Paris, 1918.
42522.25.80 Cagnat, René. Notice sur la vie et les travaux de Charles Jean Melchior le marquis de Vogüé. Paris, 1918.
43550.56.105 Cammaerts, E. A ma patrie enchainée; poèmes. Bruxelles, 1918.
43550.56.100 Cammaerts, E. Messines and other poems. N.Y., 1918.
43552.26.115 Chevrillon, André. Nouvelles études anglaises. 2e éd. Paris, 1918.
40587.40 Chinard, Gilbert. L'exotisme américain dans l'oeuvre de Chateaubriand. Photoreproduction. Paris, 1918.
43554.2.43 Claudel, Paul. Le pain dur. 6e éd. Paris, 1918.
Htn 43554.2.71* Claudel, Paul. Sainte Cecile. Paris, 1918.
43554.7.33 Clemenceau, Georges. Le voile du bonheur. Paris, 1918.
43556.1.280 Cocteau, Jean. Le coq et l'arlequin. Paris, 1918.
42563.39.840 Codet, Louis. César Capéran ou La tradition. Paris, 1918.
42554.23.6.5 Coppée, François. Avant la grande guerre. Paris, 1918.
38575.37 Corneille, Pierre. L'illusion comique. Strasbourg, 1918?
43557.2.100 Crabos, Pierre G. La forêt des Cippes. Paris, 1918. 2v.
41574.88 Cüppers, Franz Maria. Der Gottesgedanke bei Victor Hugo. Inaug. Diss. Marburg, 1918.
37567.143 Curtius, Ernst Robert. Die literarischen Wegbereiter des neuen Frankreich. Potsdam, 1918.
42566.19.8.85 Daudet, Alphonse. Tartarin de Tarascon. Boston, 1918.
43877.5 De la somme à Verdun et sur le front d'Orient. Paris, 1918.
42575.114 Deffoux, Léon. L'immortalité littéraire selon M. de Goncourt. Paris, 1918.
42577.4.34 Defoux, Léon. Guy de Maupassant. Paris, 1918.
43566.43.100 Dekobra, Maurice. Sammy, volontaire américain. Paris, 1918.
40583.36 Delacroix, Henri. La psychologie de Stendhal. Paris, 1918.
43566.50.5100 Dellac, Louis. La princesse qui ne sourit plus. Paris, 1918.
43566.6.30 Delly, M. (pseud.). Le mystère de Ker-Even. Paris, 1918.
43566.4.30 Delvert, Charles Laurent. Quelques héros. Paris, 1918.
43566.81.100 Desjardins, J. Iokonoshi, conte japonais. Paris, 1918.
43568.91.110 Divoire, F. Marathon. Paris, 1918.
38526.6.9 Du Bellay, Joachim. Poésies françaises et latines. Paris, 1918. 2v.
42555.37.7 Ducros, Jean. Le retour de la poésie française. Paris, 1918.
FL 6129.08.7 Dueros, L. Jean-Jacques Rousseau de Genève à l'Hermitage, 1765-1778. Paris, 1918.
43576.6.32 Duhamel, Georges. Compagnons. 4. éd. Paris, 1918.
43593.91.100 Envin, Guy. Du fond de l'ombre. Paris? 1918.
43606.89.3100 Faure-Favier, Louise. Six contes et deux rêves. Paris, 1918.
37573.37.2 Ferrières, Gauthier. Anthologie des écrivains français des XVe et XVIe siècles; poésie. Paris, 1918.
37573.37 Ferrières, Gauthier. Anthologie des écrivains français des XVe et XVIe siècles; prose. Paris, 1918.
38537.25.21 Fiume, Cordelia del. De l'influence de quelques auteurs italiens sur...Rabelais. Firenze, 1918.
43611.1.25.22 Fort, Paul. La lanterne de priollet. XXII. Paris, 1918.
42576.62.10.3 France, Anatole. Le lys rouge. 209. éd. Paris, 1918.
42576.63.22.4 France, Anatole. Le petit Pierre. 102. éd. Paris, 1918.
42576.62.21.40 France, Anatole. The six greatest novels of Anatole France. 1. ed. Garden City, N.Y., 1918.
FL 396.90.50 Frank, Waldo. The art of the Vieux Colonibier. Paris, 1918.
43612.2.30 Fraudet, René. Le crime de Sylvestre Bonnard. Paris, 1918.
37594.33 Friedivagner, M. Die Vengeance Raguidel. Halle, 1918.
37555.77 Fusil, C.A. La poésie scientifique. Thèse. Paris, 1918.
43616.75.100 Garenne, A. La forêt tra. Paris, 1918.
41542.11.12 Gautier, Théophile. Mademoiselle de Maupin. N.Y., 1918.
41542.11.13 Gautier, Théophile. Mademoiselle de Maupin. N.Y., 1918.
FL 360.9.2 Gavault, Paul. Conférence de l'Odéon. 2. sér (1916-17). Paris, 1918.
43617.5.31 Géniaux, Charles. Le cyprès; a novel. Paris, 1918.
43617.5.30 Géniaux, Charles. La passion d'Armelle Louanais. Paris, 1918.
43617.7.35 Génin, Auguste. Vers pour la France. México, 1918.
43620.2.34.5 Gide, André. Nouveaux prétextes. 4. éd. Paris, 1918.
43620.1.30 Gilbert, Oscar P. Lumière entrevue. Paris, 1918.
42576.6.9 Ginisty, Paul. La chartreuse de Parme. Paris, 1918.
42586.68.3 Gobineau, Arthur de. Kleinere anthropologisch-historische und politische Schriften. Strassburg, 1918.
43625.3.69 Gourmont, Rémy de. M. Croquant. Paris, 1918.
43628.1.32 Guitry, Sacha. Deburau; comédie. Paris, 1918.
37530.20 Hague. Bibliotheek. Catalogus der Fransche taal-en-letterkunde. v.1-5. Den Haag, 1918-19. 4v.
43738.1.80 Halévy, D. Charles Péguy et les Cahiers de la Quinzaine. Paris, 1918.
42576.15.19 Hamilton, Arthur. Sources of the religious element in Flaubert's Salambô. Diss. Baltimore, 1918.

Chronological Listing

1918 - cont.

43631.2.32 Hamp, Pierre. La peine des hommes; marée fraiche vin de champagne. 3. éd. Paris, 1918.
43631.2.36A Hamp, Pierre. La peine des hommes; travail invincible. 10. éd. Paris, 1918.
42543.62.45 Haraucourt, Edmond. Shylock. Paris, 1918.
38526.1.25 Harvitt, Hélène. Eustorg de Beaulieu, a disciple of Marot. Lancaster, 1918.
37556.27.25 Hawkins, R.L. Review of Saintsbury's History of the French novel. N.Y., 1918.
43632.6.100 Henriot, Émile. Valenti. Paris, 1918.
42543.65.13 Hermant, Abel. Le rival inconnu. Paris, 1918.
41573.36.9 Hudson, William H. Victor Hugo and his poetry. London, 1918.
41573.5.20 Hugo, Victor. Morceaux choisis. Paris, 1918.
43667.14.110 Jacob, Max. Le phanerogame. Paris, 1918.
43667.51.40 Jaloux, Edmond. Fumées dans la campagne. Paris, 1918.
43667.51.50 Jaloux, Edmond. L'incertaine. Paris, 1918.
43667.1.40 Jammes, Francis. Monsieur le curé d'Ozeron. 11. éd. Paris, 1918.
43667.1.50 Jammes, Francis. Rayons de miel. Paris, 1918.
37595.33.2A Jeanroy, Alfred. Bibliographie sommaire des chansonniers français du Moyen Âge. Paris, 1918.
43670.94.205 Jouve, Pierre Jean. Danse des morts. 2. éd. La Chaux de Fonds, 1918.
41596.4.125 Koskenniemi, V.A. Alfred de Musset. Porvoo, 1918.
39527.32 La Fontaine, Jean de. La Fountaines Fabler. København, 1918.
41578.33 Lamartine, Alphonse. Saül, tragédie. Paris, 1918.
43752.59.130 Landre, Jeanne. Loin des balles. Paris, 1918.
43687.74.100 Larbaud, Valéry. Enfantines. 9e éd. Paris, 1918.
43687.75.200 Larguier, Léo. Les heures déchirées; notes du front. Paris, 1918.
43687.88.3100 Lavaud, Guy. Sur un vieux livre de marine. Paris, 1918.
42544.24.8 Lavedan, Henri. Les sacrifices. Paris, 1918.
NEDL 42576.41.24 Le Blanc, Maurice. Le triangle d'or. Paris, 1918.
43688.14.100 Leclerc, Marc. The passion of our brother, the poilu. Berkeley, Calif.? 1918?
37555.24 Lefèvre, Frédéric. La jeune poésie française. Paris, 1918.
43753.58.1800 Le Mercier d'Erm, Camille. Jean-Michel Renaitour. Paris, 1918.
39564.25 Leo, Werner. Diderot als Kunstphilosophie. Inaug. Diss. Erlangen, 1918.
38521.30.5 Le Petit, Claude. Oeuvres libertines. Paris, 1918.
42576.44.4 Le Roux, H. On the field of honor. Boston, 1918.
37573.618 Les Humbles. Anthologie des Humbles. Paris, 1918.
37543.133 Levi, Angelo Raffaello. Histoire de la littérature française depuis les origines jusqu'à nos jours. Venise, 1918.
37574.43 Lewisohn, Ludwig. The poets of modern France. N.Y., 1918.
37596.160 L'ordene de chevalerie; an old French poem. Thesis. Chicago, 1918.
43738.1.920 Mabille de Poncheville, André. Charles Péguy et sa mère. Paris, 1918.
43697.6.65 Machard, Alfred. Bout-de-bibi. Paris, 1918.
43697.6.30 Machard, Alfred. Le massacre des innocents. Paris, 1918.
43697.6.58 Machard, Alfred. Popaul et Virginie. Paris, 1918.
43697.74.9110 Madrus, Joseph Charles. La reine de Saba. Paris, 1918.
42545.3.18.22A Maeterlinck, Maurice. The betrothal. N.Y., 1918.
42545.3.40 Maeterlinck, Maurice. Deux contes: Le massacre des innocents. Onirologie. Paris, 1918.
42545.3.46 Maeterlinck, Maurice. Intérieur; pièce. Paris, 1918.
42545.3.37 Maeterlinck, Maurice. The miracle of St. Anthony. N.Y., 1918.
42545.3.8.6 Maeterlinck, Maurice. Wisdom and destiny. N.Y., 1918.
43697.34.190 Magre, Maurice. La montée aux enfers. Paris, 1918.
42545.9.10 Martel de Janville, S.G. Ceux qui s'en f.... Paris, 1918.
42577.1.32 Maupassant, Guy de. Selected short stories. N.Y., 1918.
43697.89.100 Maurois, André. Les silences du Colonel Bramble. Paris, 1918.
43699.65.110 Miomandre, Francis de. Voyages d'un sedentaire. Paris, 1918.
42545.28.7.40 Mirbeau, Octave. La pipe de cidre. Paris, 1918.
42545.28.7.12 Mirbeau, Octave. La vache tachetée. Paris, 1918.
NEDL 42545.28.9.9 Moinaux, Georges. Théâtre. v.2. Paris, 1918.
Mol 165.95A Molière, Jean Baptiste Poquelin. L'avare. Manchester, 1918.
Mol 268.130 Molière, Jean Baptiste Poquelin. Le Tartuffe. N.Y., 1918.
43701.76.2100 Morand, Pierre. Patria vietrix. Paris, 1918.
43705.1.30.5 Nadaud, Marcel. The flying poilu. London, 1918.
43737.94.100 Pawlowski, Gaston William Adam de. Signaux à l'ennemi. Paris, 1918.
37572.65 Petite anthologie des auteurs gais contemporains. Paris, 1918.
37574.515 Pound, Ezra. A study in French poets. N.Y., 1918.
41522.17.20 Raynaud, Ernest. Baudelaire et la religion du Dandysme. Paris, 1918.
37567.66.7 Raynaud, Ernest. La mêlée symboliste, 1870-1910. pts. 1-3. Paris, 1918-22. 3v.
42556.27.2 Régnier, Henri de. 1914-1916. Poésies. 2. éd. Paris, 1918.
43753.90.110 Reverdy, P. La balle au bond. Marseille, 1918.
43753.90.100 Reverdy, P. Les jockeys camoufle's; trois poèmes. Paris, 1918.
43756.3.31 Richepin, Jacques. La guerre et l'amour. Paris, 1918.
43757.50.760 Rolland, Romain. The people's theater. N.Y., 1918.
FL 360.90.3 Rolland, Romain. The people's theater. N.Y., 1918.
38525.22.12 Ronsard, Pierre de. Amours de Pierre de Ronsard. Paris, 1918. 2v.
FL 6032.18 Rousseau, J.J. Du contrat social. Manchester, 1918.
37567.485 Roy, C. La critique littéraire. Québec, 1918.
38526.48.30 Scève, Maurice. La saulsaye; eglogue de la vie solitaire. Paris, 1918.
38546.41 Sévigné, Marie de R.C. Selected letters. Manchester, 1918.
37543.134 Simek, Otokar. Dějiny literatury francouzské v obrysech. Praha, 1918. 4v.
43792.90.130 Toulet, Paul Jean. Comme une fantaisie. Coutonges-sur-l'Autize, 1918.
43792.91.110 Toussaint, Franz. Le tapis de Jasmins. Paris, 1918.
X Cg 42514.28.115 Truc, Gonzague. Charles Maurras et son temps. Paris, 1918.
43822.6.30 Vallotton, Benjamin. The heart of Alsace. N.Y., 1918.
43827.89.105 Vaudoyer, J.L. Les permissions de Clément Bellin. Paris, 1918.

1918 - cont.

42557.11.4.15 Verhaeren, Émile. Les blés mouvants; poèmes. 11. éd. Paris, 1918.
FL 397.52.25 Vermorel, Jean. Quelques petits théâtres Lyonnais des XVIIIe et XIXe siècles. Lyon, 1918.
37567.142 Vial, Francisque. Idées et doctrines littéraires du XIXe siècle. Paris, 1918.
41564.16.12 Vigny, Alfred de. Poèmes choisis. Manchester, 1918.
43824.52.105 Villèle, A. de. Allemand d'Amérique. 3e éd. Paris, 1918.
43824.3.35 Villeroy, A. Le lion devenu vieux; comédie. Paris, 1918.
38514.18.10A Villon, François. Jargon. Boston, 1918.
39545.92 Voltaire, François Marie Arouet de. Contes choisis. Paris, 1918.
Mol 723.5 Weddigen, Eduard. Volkstümliche Rede und Lebensweisheit bei Molière. Inaug. Diss. Marburg, 1918.
41578.76A Whitehouse, Henry R. The life of Lamartine. Boston, 1918.
37562.85 Winkler, E. Französische Dichter des Mittelalters. Wien, 1918.
43858.1.55 Zamacois, Miguel. L'avant-scène D. Paris, 1918.
42584.9.8 Zola, Emile. La faute de l'abbé Mouret. Paris, 1918.

1919

43514.24.1100 Adès, Albert. Le livre de Goha le simple. Paris, 1919.
FL 6139.19.7 Alessiani, Paolina. Rousseau et il metodo Montessori. Fermo, 1919.
37574.380 Allem, M. Anthologie poétique française. Paris, 1919.
43524.34.100 Angot, E. Dames du grand siècle. Paris, 1919.
42578.35.17 Anna, Luigi de. Francisque Sarcey. Florence, 1919.
43526.65.794 Apollinaire, Guillaume. Pasmo. Praha, 1919.
40582.2.115 Arbelet, P. La jeunesse de Stendhal. Paris, 1919. 2v.
FL 6139.19A Babbitt, Irving. Rousseau and romanticism. Boston, 1919.
37568.14 Baldensperger, F. L'avant-guerre dans la littérature française. Paris, 1919.
39544.104A Ballantyne, A. Voltaire's visit to England, 1726-1729. London, 1919.
41522.2.21 Barbey d'Aurevilly, Jules. Le cachet d'onyx. Lea, 1831-1832. Paris, 1919.
43537.6.39A Barbusse, Henri. Light. N.Y., 1919.
41574.59 Barthou, Louis. Les amours d'un poète. Paris, 1919.
43537.4.40 Bataille, Henry. Les soeurs d'amour. Paris, 1919.
41522.13.7 Baudelaire, Charles. Les fleurs du mal. Paris, 1919.
42563.21.75 Bazin, René. Les nouveaux oberlé. 15. éd. Paris, 1919.
42563.21.75.5 Bazin, René. Les nouveaux oberlé. 104. éd. Paris, 1919.
43538.60.100 Benjamin, René. L'hôtel des ventes. Paris, 1919.
NEDL 43538.61.30 Benoît, Pierre. L'Atlantide. Paris, 1919.
42542.29.28.20 Bernard, Tristan. Le taxe fantôme. Paris, 1919.
43538.9.30 Berthaut, Léon. Soldats de Jeanne d'Arc. Paris, 1919.
40582.12.45 Beyle, Henri. Armance. Paris, 1919.
40582.2.30 Beyle, Henri. Rome, Naples. Paris, 1919. 2v.
38521.30.6 Blot-l'Église, Claude de Chouvigny. Chansons libertines. Paris, 1919.
42563.23.20.5 Bloy, Léon. L'invendable. 4. éd. Paris, 1919.
42563.23.20.7 Bloy, Léon. L'invendable. 5. éd. Paris, 1919.
42563.23.21.5 Bloy, Léon. Le pélerin de l'absolu. 4. éd. Paris, 1919.
42563.23.21 Bloy, Léon. Le vieux de la montagne. 4. éd. Paris, 1919.
42563.23.21.2 Bloy, Léon. Le vieux de la montagne. 5. éd. Paris, 1919.
38566.26.14 Boileau Despréaux, Nicolas. L'art poétique. Cambridge, 1919.
42521.24 Bontoux, G. Louis Veuillot et les mauvais maîtres des XVIe, XVIIe et XVIIIe siècles. Paris, 1919.
V43500.33 Bouchaud, Pierre de. Les fêtes de la victoire; 14 juillet 1919. Nior, 1919.
42542.35.25 Bouilhet, Louis. Sous peine de mort. Thèse. Rouen, 1919.
43544.5.43 Boulenger, Marcel. Les trois graces. Paris, 1919.
42563.37.44 Bourget, Paul. Le justicier. Paris, 1919.
42563.37.48 Bourget, Paul. Laurence Albani. Paris, 1919.
43544.9.30 Boussus, M. L'armoire de citronnier; almanach 1919. Paris, 1919.
41593.13.230 Boyer d'Agen, J.A.B. Les sept paraliponienes à la Divine Comédie. Paris, 1919.
Htn 42563.39.4* Boylesve, René. Discours prononcés. Paris, 1919.
42563.39.55 Boylesve, René. Le médecin des dames de Néans. Paris, 1919.
42563.39.60 Boylesve, René. Sainte Marie des fleurs. 14. éd. Paris, 1919.
37573.219 Bremond, Henri. Anthologie des écrivains catholiques. Paris, 1919.
43787.78.1100 Brienne, Maxine. Gustave Téry et son oeuvre. Paris, 1919.
37555.149 Carco, Francis. La poésie. Paris, 1919.
43554.2.810 Casnati, F. Paul Claudel e i suoi drammi. Como, 1919.
42542.49.15 Céard, Henry. Sonnets de guerre, 1914-1918. Paris, 1919.
43551.59.110 Cendrars, Blaise. Dix-neuf poèmes élastiques. Paris, 1919.
43551.59.100 Cendrars, Blaise. Du monde entier. Paris, 1919.
43552.3.140 Chaine, Pierre. Les commentaires de Ferdinand. Paris, 1919.
37555.78 Chaix, Marie-Antoinette. La correspondance des arts dans la poésie contemporaine. Paris, 1919.
43552.4.4110 Charasson, H. Attente, 1914-1917. Paris, 1919.
37555.83 Charbonnier, F. La poésie française et les guerres de religion (1560-1574). Paris, 1919.
42514.28.130 Charles Maurras; poems, portraits. Aix-en-Provence, 1919.
43552.5.1210 Chartier, Émile. Les marchands de sommeil. Paris, 1919.
40526.7.10 Chénier, André. Poésies. Lyon, 1919.
43552.25.4100 Chevalier, Adrien. Avant et après l'orage. Paris, 1919.
40517.44.5 Choderlos de Laclos, Pierre A.F. Les liaisons dangereuses. 17. éd. Paris, 1919.
43554.2.41 Claudel, Paul. La messe la-bas. 7e éd. Paris, 1919.
43554.2.49 Claudel, Paul. L'otage; drama. 8e éd. Paris, 1919.
43554.2.55 Claudel, Paul. L'ours et la lune. 4e éd. Paris, 1919.
43554.2.66 Claudel, Paul. Three poems of the war. New Haven, 1919.
43554.7.31 Clemenceau, Georges. Aux embuscades de la vie. Paris, 1919.
43554.7.30 Clemenceau, Georges. Les plus forts, roman contemporain. Paris, 1919.
43554.7.30.2 Clemenceau, Georges. The strongest. N.Y., 1919.
42586.32.7 Coster, Charles de. Briefe an Elisa. Leipzig, 1919.
42542.58 Curel, François de. Théâtre complet. Paris, 1919-1922. 6v.
42566.34.15A Daudet, Alphonse. Sappho and Manon Lescaut. N.Y., 1919.
43565.5.40 Daudet, Léon A. Dans la lumière. Paris, 1919.
43566.42.100 Dejean, Georges. La confession d'un légionnaire. Paris, 1919.
42557.14.12 Delahaye, Ernest. Documents relatifs à Paul Verlaine. Paris, 1919.

Chronological Listing

1919 - cont.

	43566.6.35	Delly, M. (pseud.). La petite chanoinesse. Paris, 1919.
	42542.64.19	Descaves, Lucien. L'imagier d'Epinal. 3. éd. Paris, 1919.
	42542.64.60.8	Dieudonne, R. La bonne aventure. Paris, 1919.
	42542.65.9.5	Donnay, Maurice. Lysistrata. Paris, 1919.
	37555.335	Dorchain, Auguste. L'art des vers. Paris, 1919.
	43573.76.50	Dorgelès, Roland. Le cabaret de la Belle Femme. Paris, 1919.
	43573.76.35	Dorgelès, Roland. Les croix de bois. Paris, 1919.
	43576.7.70	Du Bois, Albert. Bérénice l'hérodienne (Juvenal). Paris, 1919.
	43576.7.55	Du Bois, Albert. Le casque de la déesse (Démosthènes). Paris, 1919.
	43576.7.30	Du Bois, Albert. L'herodienne. Paris, 1919.
	43576.7.90	Du Bois, Albert. Si Dieu n'éxistait pas...! (Voltaire). Paris, 1919.
	43576.7.100	Du Bois, Albert. Victor Hugo; poème scénique en trois actes. Paris, 1919.
	37568.10	Duclaux, Agnes Mary Frances. Twentieth century French writers. London, 1919.
	43576.6.31	Duhamel, Georges. Civilisation, 1914-1917. 28. éd. Paris, 1919.
	43576.6.200	Duhamel, Georges. Élévation et mort d'Armand Branche. Paris, 1919.
	43576.6.30	Duhamel, Georges. Lapointe et Ropiteau. Genève, 1919.
	43576.6.105	Duhamel, Georges. La lumière: pièce en quatre actes. 2. éd. Paris, 1919.
	42554.29.165	Dujardin, E. De Stephane Mallarmé au prophete Ezéchiel. Paris, 1919.
	37567.144	Eccles, Francis Yvon. La liquidation du romantisme. Oxford, 1919.
Htn	43878.5*	Eridan. Paris, 1919.
	43598.13.102	Escholier, R. Dansons la trompeuse. 4. éd. Paris, 1919.
	37597.10.9	Ettmayer, Karl R. Der Rosenroman. Heidelberg, 1919.
	43606.76.120	Fargue, Léon P. Poèmes suivis de Pour la musique. 4. éd. Paris, 1919.
	43607.76.110	Féret, Charles Théophile. L'arc d'Ulysse. Paris, 1919.
	37573.37.12	Ferrières, Gauthier. Anthologie des écrivains français contemporaines. v.1-2. Paris, 1919.
	37573.37.7	Ferrières, Gauthier. Anthologie des écrivains français du XIXe siècle; prose. v.1-2. Paris, 1919-20.
	42576.32.5	Flaubert, Gustave. Die Sage von Sankt Julian dem Gastfreien. Potsdam, 1919.
	42576.31.7	Flaubert, Gustave. Salammbô. N.Y., 1919.
	43610.22.110	Fleg, Edmond. Le mur des pleurs; poème. Paris, 1919.
	43610.22.120	Fleg, Edmond. Le Psaume de la terre promise. Genève, 1919.
	43611.1.25.43	Fort, Paul. Barbe-Bleue, Jeanne d'Arc et mes amours. Paris, 1919.
	43611.1.25.25	Fort, Paul. Chansons à la Gauloise sur la vie, le rêve, et l'amour. XXV. Paris, 1919.
	43611.1.25.23	Fort, Paul. Les enchanteurs. XXIII. Paris, 1919.
	42576.62.11.10	France, Anatole. Le mannequin d'osier. Paris, 1919?
	42576.63.22A	France, Anatole. Le petit Pierre. Paris, 1919.
	42576.63.9	France, Anatole. Le petit soldat de plomb. Paris, 1919.
	42576.62.6.5	France, Anatole. La rôtisserie de la reine Pédauque. 118. éd. Paris, 1919.
	42576.62.135.5	France, Anatole. La vie littéraire. 2. série. Paris, 1919?
	43612.3.30	Frappa, Jean José. L'idée; roman. Paris, 1919.
	43612.5.170	Fraudet, René. La nuit sur le Rhin. Paris, 1919.
	FL 360.9.3	Gavault, Paul. Conférence de l'Odéon. 3. sér (1917-18). Paris, 1919.
	43619.24.120	Ghéon, Henri. L'homme né de la guerre. 3. éd. Paris, 1919.
	43620.2.41	Gide, André. Prétextes. 18. éd. Paris, 1919.
	43620.1.35	Gilbert, Oscar P. L'humble bonheur. Paris, 1919.
	43620.51.40	Gillouin, René. Idées et figures d'aujourd'hui. Paris, 1919.
Htn	43620.74.155*	Giraudoux, Jean. Adieu à la guerre. Paris, 1919.
	42556.29.27	Gobin, Ferdinand. L'oeuvre poétique de Albert Samain. Paris, 1919.
	39527.4.20	Godchot, Simon. La Fontaine et St. Augustin. Paris, 1919.
	39566.140	Goll, Iwan. Die drei guten Geister Frankreichs. 2. Aufl. Berlin, 1919.
	42575.59.10	Goncourt, Edmond de. Madame Gervaisais. Paris, 1919.
	42575.61.25	Goncourt, Edmond de. Renée Mauperin. N.Y., 1919?
	43625.3.52	Gourmont, Rémy de. Lettres d'un satyre. 7e éd. Paris, 1919.
	43625.3.51	Gourmont, Rémy de. Les pas sur le sable. Paris, 1919.
	43626.4.100	Granvilliers, J. de. Le prix de l'homme. Paris, 1919-1920.
	43626.2.30	Grivet, A. Néron. Paris, 1919.
	43627.23.100	Gsell, P. Les gosses dans les ruines. Paris, 1919.
	41593.36.2	Guérin, Maurice de. Der Kentauer. Leipzig, 1919.
	42586.76.9	Guillaumin, Emile. The life of a simple man. N.Y., 1919.
	43628.1.38	Guitry, Sacha. Pasteur. Paris, 1919.
	43738.1.82	Halévy, D. Charles Péguy et les Cahiers de la Quinzaine. Paris, 1919.
	43631.2.38	Hamp, Pierre. La peine des hommes; les métiers blessés. 2. éd. Paris, 1919.
	43632.6.270	Henriot, Émile. Le diable à l'hôtel. Paris, 1919.
	42543.65.35	Hermant, Abel. L'aube ardente. 9e éd. Paris, 1919.
	42554.64.35	Herold, A.F. Guillaume le petit. Paris, 1919.
	43537.6.80	Hertz, Henri. Henri Barbusse. Paris, 1919.
	42576.67.15	Hervieu, Paul. Le destin est maître. Paris, 1919.
	37543.135	Hudson, W.H. Short history of French literature. London, 1919.
	41573.36.7	Hugo, Victor. Chefs-d'oeuvre lyriques. London, 1919.
	38543.27.50	Igel, Johann. René Le Pays, sein Leben und seine Werke. Inaug. Diss. Nürmberg, 1919.
	43667.14.100	Jacob, Max. La défense de Tartufe. Paris, 1919.
	43667.51.100	Jaloux, Edmond. Les amours perdues. Paris, 1919.
	37567.9.10	James, Henry. French poets and novelists. London, 1919
	43667.1.44	Jammes, Francis. La noël de mes enfants. Paris, 1919.
	43667.1.43	Jammes, Francis. La rose. Paris, 1919.
	43667.1.42	Jammes, Francis. Une vierge. Paris, 1919.
	43667.1.41	Jammes, Francis. La vierge. Paris, 1919.
	37544.45	Jensen, Emeline Maria. The influence of French literature on Europe. Boston, 1919.
	37543.136	Joliet, L. Précis illustré de la littérature française. Paris, 1919.
	38514.85	Kerdaniel, Edouard L. de. Un rhetorique, André de la Vigne. Paris, 1919.
	42548.28.20	Labiche, Eugène. La poudre aux yeux. N.Y., 1919.
	42544.26.20	Labiche, Eugène. Le voyage de Monsieur Perrichon. Boston, 1919.

1919 - cont.

	42555.1.3	Laforgue, Jules. Poésies complètes. v.3. 6. éd. Paris, 1919.
	43752.59.140	Landre, Jeanne. Bob et Bobette. Paris, 1919.
	FL 398.52.45	Lassalle, E. Comédiens et amateurs. Montréal, 1919.
	43687.83.125	Lasserre, Pierre. Le romantisme français. Paris, 1919.
	43687.88.3110	Lavaud, Guy. Imageries des mers. Paris, 1919.
	37548.38.6	Lazzeri, Gerolamo. Interpreti dell'anima Belga. Belogna, 1919.
	42554.16.8	Le Braz, A. Du soleil et de la brume. 5e éd. Paris, 1919.
	37566.44.5	Le Goffic, Charles. La littérature française aux XIX et XX siècle. Paris, 1919. 2v.
	43688.8.31	Le Goffic, Charles. Passions celtes. Paris, 1919?
	43688.54.130	LeMercier d'Erm, C. La guerre? Paris, 1919.
	43688.54.120	LeMercier d'Erm, C. Le poème de Paris nocturne. Paris, 1919.
	42576.46.2	Le Roy, Eugène. Jacquou the rebel. N.Y., 1919.
	42542.36.100	Letellier, L. Louis Bouilhet, 1821-1869. Thèse. Rouen, 1919.
	37557.38	Levrault, Léon. La fable. Paris, 1919.
	43690.1.85	Lichtenberger, A. Le coeur est le même. Paris, 1919.
	42575.91	Loesch, Georg. Die impressionistische Syntax der Goncourt. Inaug. Diss. Nürnberg, 1919.
	42544.34.23	Lorde, André de. Théâtre de la peur. Paris, 1919.
	42544.34.32.10	Louys, Pierre. Aphrodite. n.p., 1919.
	43697.14.350	MacOrlan, Pierre. Bob, bataillonnaire. Paris, 1919.
	42545.3.18.25	Maeterlinck, Maurice. The betrothal. London, 1919.
	42545.3.38	Maeterlinck, Maurice. Le bourgmestre de Stilmonde. Paris, 1919.
	42545.3.39A	Maeterlinck, Maurice. The burgomaster of Stilemonde. N.Y., 1919.
	42545.3.13.8	Maeterlinck, Maurice. The children's life of the bee. N.Y., 1919.
	42545.3.13.7	Maeterlinck, Maurice. The life of the bee. N.Y., 1919.
	42545.3.36	Maeterlinck, Maurice. Le miracle de Saint Antoine. Paris, 1919.
	42545.3.45	Maeterlinck, Maurice. Mountain paths. N.Y., 1919.
	42545.3.44	Maeterlinck, Maurice. Les sentiers dans la montagne. Paris, 1919.
	43697.1.30	Margrot, Jean H. Paris en l'an 3000. Paris, 1919?
Htn	40535.29.7*	Marivaux, Pierre Carlet de Chamblain de. Le jeu de l'amour. Paris, 1919?
	43697.78.110	Martinet, Marcel. Les temps Maudits. 3d ed. Paris, 1919.
	43697.83.100	Masson, Émile. Le livre des hommes et leurs paroles inouies. 2e éd. Paris, 1919?
	FL 382.24.20	Matthews, J.B. French dramatists of the 19th century. 5. ed. N.Y., 1919.
	42577.2.6	Maupassant, Guy de. Love, and other stories. N.Y., 1919.
	42577.2.40	Maupassant, Guy de. Mlle Fifi. Boston, 1919.
	43697.88.320	Mauriac, François. La robe prétexte. Paris, 1919?
	43697.98.35	Mayran, Camille (pseud.). Histoire de Gotton Connixloo. 10. éd. Paris, 1919.
	43699.51.24	Milosz, Oscar Vladislas. Wybór poezji. Poznań, 1919.
	43699.65.210	Miomandre, Francis de. La cabane d'amour. Paris, 1919.
	42545.28.7.13	Mirbeau, Octave. Chez l'illustre écrivain. Paris, 1919.
	42545.28.7.11	Mirbeau, Octave. La pipe et cidre. Paris, 1919.
	Mol 60.22	Molière, Jean Baptiste Poquelin. Dramatic works...C.H. Wall. London, 1919. 3v.
	42555.60.7	Montesquiou-Fezensac, Robert de. Un moment du pleur éternel. Paris, 1919.
	43703.80.100	Muselli, Vincent. Les masques; sonnets heroi-comiques. Paris, 1919.
	43705.1.55	Nadaud, Marcel. Birds of a feather. Garden City, 1919.
	43705.1.34	Nadaud, Marcel. Frangipane. Paris, 1919.
	43709.41.100	Noir, Jacques. Les maledictions. Paris, 1919.
	42545.46.5	Normand, J. Les drapeaux déployés. Paris, 1919.
	43723.51.125	Ollone, Charles. Dernières heures chantantes. Paris, 1919.
	37596.160.2	Ordene de chevalerie. L'ordene de chevalerie; an old French poem. Norman, 1919.
	42545.63.9	Pailleron, Edouard. Le monde ou l'on s'ennuie. 130e éd. Paris, 1919?
	37566.43	Pailleron, M.L. (Mme.). François Buloz. Paris, 1919.
	40536.18.50	Patrat, Joseph. L'anglais. Paris, 1919.
	43737.98.100	Paz, M.L. (Mme.). Femme. Paris, 1919.
	37572.43.3	Pellissier, G. Le XVIIe siècle par les textes. 2. éd. Paris, 1919.
	43738.74.105	Perdriel-Vaissière, Jeanne. La complainte des jeunes filles qui ne seront pas épousées. 5e éd. Paris, 1919.
	V43500.245	Picabia, Francis. Pensées sans langage; poème. 4. ed. Paris, 1919.
NEDL	42547.15.15	Pierredon, Georges. Notes sur Villiers de l'Isle Adam. Paris, 1919.
	42576.65.13.15	Poinsot, Maffei C. Les logis de Huysmans. Paris, 1919.
	41574.89	Poinsot, Maffeo C. Auprès de Victor Hugo. Paris, 1919.
X Cg	37567.66.9	Poizat, Alfred. Le symbolisme de Baudelaire à Claudel. Paris, 1919.
	FL 6139.19.5	Pons, Jacques. L'éducation en Angleterre entre 1750 et 1800. Paris, 1919.
	43743.1.34	Porché, François. La jeune fille. Paris, 1919.
	43743.1.35	Porché, François. La jeune fille. Paris, 1919.
	43743.1.55	Porché, François. Le poème de la delivrance. Paris, 1919.
	43744.64.120	Prody, Alfred. Les reflets; poèmes. Brive, 1919.
	43744.67.45	Proust, Marcel. Pastiches et mélanges. 28. éd. Paris, 1919.
	42578.18.15	Rameau, Jean. Les mains blanches. 4. éd. Paris, 1919.
	42556.26.35A	Régnier, Henri de. Histoires incertaines. 9e éd. Paris, 1919.
	43756.3.35	Richepin, Jacques. La grève des femmes. Paris, 1919.
	42556.22.110A	Richepin, Jean. Poèmes durant la guerre, 1914-18. Paris, 1919.
	42556.22.3	Richepin, Jean. Théâtre en vers. Paris, 1919-21. 3v.
Htn	42556.28.15F*	Rimbaud, Jean Arthur. Poésies. Paris, 1919.
	43757.50.1090	Rolland, Romain. Colas Breugnon. N.Y., 1919.
	43757.50.392	Rolland, Romain. Colas Breugnon. 39e éd. Paris, 1919.
	FL 360.90.4	Rolland, Romain. The people's theatre. London, 1919.
	43757.50.558	Rolland, Romain. Les precurseurs. Paris, 1919.
	43757.50.533	Rolland, Romain. Voyage musical aux pays du passé. Paris, 1919.
	42556.32.70	Rollinat, Maurice. Fin d'oeuvre. Paris, 1919.
	43757.3.33	Romains, Jules. Europe. 2e éd. Paris, 1919.
	Mol 718.1	Rondel, Auguste. Commémoration de Molière, Racine, Corneille, Shakespeare et Cervantes à la comédie française. Paris, 1919.
	42578.22.40	Rosny, J.H. L'appel du bonheur. Paris, 1919.
	42578.22.45	Rosny, J.H. Et l'amour ensuite. Paris, 1919.

1919 - cont.

42546.14.5.10 Rostand, Edmond. Cyrano de Bergerac. N.Y., 1919.
FL 6047.7 Rousseau, J.J. Emil oder über die Erziehung. Potsdam, 1919.
43757.98.120 Royère, Jean. Par la lumière peints. Paris, 1919.
V43500.275 Royère, Jean. La poésie de Mallarmé. Paris, 1919?
43761.41.100 St. Georges de Bouhelier. O Edipe, roi de Thébes. Paris, 1919.
43761.41.110 St. Georges de Bouhelier. La vie d'une femme. Paris, 1919.
42556.29.16 Samain, Albert. Aux flancs du vase. Paris, 1919.
42556.29.25 Samain, Albert. Polypheme; deux actes en vers. 11. éd. Paris, 1919.
41557.10.22 Sand, George. George Sand et le Berry. Paris, 1919. 2v.
42586.63.4.5 Schemann, Ludwig. Fünfundzwanzig Jahre Gobineau. Strassburg, 1919.
42514.28.150 Ségard, Achille. Les hommes d'action. Paris, 1919.
37567.91.5 Seillière, E. Les étapes du mysticisme passionel. Paris, 1919.
42515.42.9 Seillière, Ernest. Edgar Quinet et le mysticisme démocratique. Paris, 1919.
42576.63.45 Shanks, Lewis Piaget. Anatole France. Chicago, 1919.
41539.9 Simon, Gustave. Histoire d'une collaboration. Paris, 1919.
42555.44.11 Soula, Camille. La poésie et la pensée de Stéphane Mallarmé, essai sur l'hermétisme Mallarmé. Paris, 1919.
Mol 619.13 Sous le masque de Molière. Louis XIV et Molière. Paris, 1919.
43776.41.120 Spire, André. Poèmes juifs. Genève, 1919.
43776.41.100 Spire, André. Le secret. Paris, 1919.
42546.12.23 Suberville, J. Le théâtre d'Edmond Rostand. Paris, 1919.
37567.66.3 Symons, Arthur. The symbolist movement in literature. N.Y., 1919.
43788.5.120 Tharaud, Jérôme. Une relève. Paris, 1919.
42583.33.18 Theuriet, André. L'abbé Daniel. N.Y., 1919.
43789.3.100 Tian, André. Nouveaux poèmes. Lyon, 1919.
38525.36.5 Tristan L'Hermite, F. La mort de Sénèque. Paris, 1919.
42587.65.12.5 Vachette, Eugène. Les petites comédies du vice. Paris, 1919?
42587.65.13 Vachette, Eugène. Les petits drames de la vertu. Paris, 1919.
Htn 43822.49.390* Valéry, Paul. La soirée avec M. Teste. Paris, 1919.
42547.10.39 Vandérem, F. Le miroir de lettres. Paris, 1919-29. 8v.
43827.89.140 Vaudoyer, J.L. Les papiers de Cléonthe. Paris, 1919.
43822.89.110 Vautel, Clément. La réouverture. Paris, 1919.
42557.11.16 Verhaeren, Émile. Les ailes rouges de la guerre. Poèmes. 19. éd. Paris, 1919.
42557.11.13.10 Verhaeren, Émile. Cloister. Boston, 1919.
42557.20.75 Verlaine, Paul. Frauen. Hannover, 1919.
42576.56.8 Viaud, Julien. Madame Prune. N.Y., 1919.
42576.52.4.3 Viaud, Julien. Pêcheur d'Islande. Paris, 1919?
42576.57.13 Viaud, Julien. Prime jeunesse. Paris, 1919.
41564.8.5 Vigny, Alfred de. Military servitude and grandeur. N.Y., 1919.
38514.20.5 Villon, François. Les oeuvres de François Villon. Paris, 1919.
43823.82.100 Virt, Marie Louise. Le rayon dans l'ombre; poèmes. Calais, 1919?
43824.2.54 Vivien, Renée. Vagabondages. Paris, 1919?
39544.27.10A Voltaire, François Marie Arouet de. Voltaire in his letters. N.Y., 1919.
39527.7.5 Vossler, Karl. La Fontaine und sein Fabelwirk. Heidelberg, 1919.
38551.124.5 Wieser, Max. Deutsche und romanische Religiösitat. Berlin, 1919.
42547.40 Wolff, Pierre. Le voile déchiré. Paris, 1919.
43858.1.35 Zamacois, Miguel. Monsieur Césarin. Paris, 1919.
43858.1.34 Zamacois, Miguel. Monsieur Césarin. Paris, 1919.

192-

43513.1.35 Acker, Paul. Les exilés. Paris, 192-.
42586.14.6.10 Audoux, M. Marie-Claire. Paris, 192-.
40597.14.61 Balzac, Honoré de. Droll stories. N.Y., 192-.
42542.29.28.10 Bernard, Tristan. Too much of a good thing. Bangkok, 192-?
43538.76.7110 Bernouard, F. La berlue rayonnante. Paris, 192-.
42563.37.11.4 Bourget, Paul. Physiologie de l'amour moderne. Paris, 192-?
42563.39.100 Boylesve, René. L'enfant à la balustrade. Paris, 192-.
42563.39.115 Boylesve, René. Je vous ai désirée un soir. Paris, 192-.
43566.75.130 Derème, Tristan. Le quatorze juillet, ou Petit art de rimer. Paris, 192-.
41538.53.51 Dumas, Alexandre. The three musketeers. N.Y., 192-?
42568.23.10 Duval, Paul. La maison Philibert. Paris, 192-.
37555.355 Fabre d'Olivet, A. Un manuscrit inédit de Fabre d'Olivet. Paris, 192-?
X Cg 37566.28.5 Faguet, Émile. Politiques et moralistes du dix-neuvième siècle. Paris, 192-.
42576.33.11 Flaubert, Gustave. The legend of Saint Julian. London, 192-?
40515.30.75 Florian, Jean P.C. de. Les arlequinades. Strasbourg, 192-.
37555.519 Florian Parmentier, Ernest. Essai de codification du vers libre. Paris, 192-?
43620.35.110 Gilbert de Voisins, Auguste. L'enfant qui prit peur. Paris, 192-.
39527.29.15 La Fontaine, Jean de. Fables choisies. Paris, 192-?
42555.35.50 Leconte de Lisle, C.M.R. Poèmes antiques. Paris, 192-.
42555.35.75 Leconte de Lisle, C.M.R. Poèmes tragiques. Paris, 192-.
43688.35.110 Le Grand, Maurice. Fables nouvelles. Paris, 192-.
43688.54.110 LeMercier d'Erm, C. Léda. 3e éd. Dinard, 192-.
40535.29.2 Marivaux, Pierre Carlet de Chamblain de. Les fausses confidences; comédie. London, 192-?
Mol 235.50 Molière, Jean Baptiste Poquelin. Le médecin malgré lui. Paris, 192-.
Mon 32.20 Montaigne, Michel de. Love and marriage, being Montaigne's essay "Sur des vers de Virgil". Florence, 192-?
43701.74.100 Morand, Paul. Lewis et Irène. Paris, 192-.
42577.32.25 Murger, Henry. The Latin quarter. N.Y., 192-.
43709.3.180 Noailles, Anna E. L'ombre des jours. Paris, 192-.
42545.85.2 Porto-Riche, G. Théâtre d'amour. 19e éd. Paris, 192-?
43528.53.140 Rapa-nui; novela. Madrid, 192-?
42587.55.34 Rivoire, André. Oeuvres. Poèmes d'amour. Paris, 192-.
43757.50.105 Rolland, Romain. Jean-Christophe. Paris, 192-? 4v.

192- - cont.

43757.50.412 Rolland, Romain. Liluli. 2e éd. Paris, 192-.
43757.50.402.5A Rolland, Romain. Pierre et Luce. Paris, 192-.
42578.22.190 Rosny, J.H. Vamireh. Paris, 192-?
43763.2.38 Schopfer, Jean. Ariane. London, 192-.
Htn 43799.5.110* Tzara, Tristan. Sept manifestes Dada. Paris, 192-.
38514.20.28A Villon, François. Poems. N.Y., 192-.

1920

Htn 37596.39.5* Abbott, C.C. Nine songs from the 12th century French. Chelsea, 1920.
42562.38.14.55 Adam, Paul. Le temps et la vie: Le lion d'Arras. Paris, 1920.
37574.302 Adam, Pierre. Étude sur le vocabulaire du chansonnier historique. Thèse. Nancy, 1920.
38526.7.10 Addamiano, Natale. Delle opere poetiche francesi di Joachim Du Bellay. Cagliari, 1920.
42586.7.17.5 Aicard, Jean. L'illustre maurin. Paris, 1920.
37543.390.4 Albalat, Antoine. Comment il faut lire les auteurs classiques français de Villon à Victor Hugo. 4. éd. Paris, 1920.
37566.50 Albalat, Antoine. Souvenirs de la vie littéraire. Paris, 1920.
37558.130 Anglade, J. Les origines du Gai Savoir. Paris, 1920.
37573.36 Anthologie des indépendants. Paris, 1920.
43527.3.120 Aragon, Louis. Feu de foie. Paris, 1920.
43528.14.100 Arcos, René. Das Gemeinsame. Leipzig, 1920.
37555.79 Arreat, Lucien. Nos poètes et la pensée de leur temps. Paris, 1920.
37564.102.10 Atkinson, Geoffroy. The extraordinary voyage in French literature before 1700. N.Y., 1920.
42586.14.6.20 Audoux, M. Marie Claire's workshop. N.Y., 1920.
43529.5.30 Audoux, Marguerite. L'atelier de Marie-Claire. Paris, 1920.
43529.5.30.5 Audoux, Marguerite. L'atelier de Marie-Claire. Paris, 1920.
42542.6.3 Augier, Émile. Le fils de Giboyer. Paris, 1920?
40596.8.5 Balzac, Honoré de. Comédie humaine. Études de moeurs. Scènes de la vie militaire. Paris, 1920.
40596.15.10 Balzac, Honoré de. Short stories. N.Y., 1920.
40597.14.75 Balzac, Honoré de. Short stories. N.Y., 1920?
Htn 41522.2.58* Barbey d'Aurevilly, Jules. Disjecta membra. Paris, 1920.
43537.6.34 Barbusse, Henri. Clarté; roman. Paris, 1920.
43745.1.120 Barres, Maurice. Le tombeau d'Ernest Psichari au seuil de la forêt des Ardennes. Paris, 1920.
FL 385.6 Basch, Victor. Études d'esthétique dramatique. Ser. I. Paris, 1920.
43537.4.39 Bataille, Henry. L'animateur. Paris, 1920.
43537.4.43 Bataille, Henry. La quadrature de l'amour. Paris, 1920.
41522.13.12 Baudelaire, Charles. Journaux intimes. Paris, 1920.
42563.21.46.5 Bazin, René. Pierre and Joseph. N.Y., 1920.
43538.11.33 Beaunier, André. L'amour et les secret. Paris, 1920.
38528.37 Beauxoncles, Charles T. de. Oeuvres satyriques. 1. éd. Paris, 1920.
42576.15.20 Benedetto, Luigi F. Le origini di Salammbô. Firenze, 1920.
43538.7.37 Benjamin, René. Amadou, bolcheviste. Paris, 1920.
43538.61.33 Benoît, Pierre. L'Atlantide; roman. Paris, 1920.
43538.61.59 Benoît, Pierre. Koenigsmark. 55. éd. Paris, 1920.
43538.61.39A Benoît, Pierre. L'Atlantida. (L'Atlantide). N.Y., 1920.
43538.61.50 Benoît, Pierre. Pour Don Carlos. Paris, 1920.
42542.29.24 Bernard, Tristan. Les petites curieuses. Paris, 1920.
42542.29.29.10 Bernhardt, S. (Mme.). Petit idole. Paris, 1920.
42542.29.60 Berr, Georges. Monsieur Beverley. Paris, 1920.
37556.36.13 Bertaut, Jules. Le roman nouveau. Paris, 1920.
41596.66.2 Berthier, Alfred. Le poète savoyard Jean-Pierre Veyrat, 1810-1844. Paris, 1920.
Htn 41596.66.3* Berthier, Alfred. Le poète savoyard Jean-Pierre Veyrat. Paris, 1920.
41522.58.10 Bertrand, Louis. Gaspard de la nuit. 8. éd. Monte-Carlo, 1920.
42563.23.8.40 Bertrand, Louis. Pépète et Balthasar. 4. éd. Paris, 1920.
42563.23.8.45 Bertrand, Louis. Pépète et Balthasar. 7. éd. Paris, 1920.
37556.52.7 Bethleem, L. Romans à lire et romans à proscrire. 7. éd. Paris, 1920.
37548.39.5 Bever, A. van. Anthologie littéraire de l'Alsace et de la Lorraine. Paris, 1920.
43540.99.100 Bizet, René. L'aventure aux quitares. Paris, 1920.
43761.41.800 Blanchart, Paul. St. Georges de Bouhelier, son oeuvre. Paris, 1920.
43543.13.200 Bloch, J.R. Carnaval est mort. Paris, 1920.
42563.23.23 Bloy, Léon. La porte des humbles. 4. éd. Paris, 1920.
38566.17.12 Boileau Despréaux, Nicolas. Oeuvres poétiques. 12. éd. Paris, 1920.
37573.643A Boni, Albert. The modern book of French verse in English translations. N.Y., 1920.
42544.33.50 Bordeaux, H. Jules Lemaître, avec huit gravures. Paris, 1920.
42563.36.20 Bordeaux, Henry. Une doctrine de vie; extraits de l'oeuvre de Henry Bordeaux. Paris, 1920.
42563.36.80.3 Bordeaux, Henry. La vie recommence, la résurrection de la chair. Paris, 1920.
42563.36.80 Bordeaux, Henry. La vie recommence, la résurrection de la chair. Paris, 1920.
42563.36.80.5 Bordeaux, Henry. La vie recommence, la résurrection de la chair. Paris, 1920.
38557.50 Bossuet, J.B. Lettres sur l'éducation du Dauphin. Paris, 1920.
38562.31A Bouhours, D. Entretiens d'Ariste et d'Eugène. Paris, 1920.
42563.37.43 Bourget, Paul. Anomalies. Paris, 1920.
37567.15.5 Bourget, Paul. Essais de psychologie contemporaine. Paris, 1920. 2v.
40583.50 Bourget, Paul. Stendhal. Paris, 1920.
42563.39.75 Boylesve, René. Alcindor, ou suite à la leçon d'amour. Paris, 1920.
42563.39.70 Boylesve, René. La leçon d'amour dans un parc. 8. éd. Paris, 1920.
42563.39.65 Boylesve, René. Nyphes dansant avec des satyres. 9. éd. Paris, 1920.
42563.39.67 Boylesve, René. Nyphes dansant avec des satyres. 13. éd. Paris, 1920.
42542.47.35F Brieux, Eugène. Les américains chez nous. Paris, 1920.
43547.77.140 Burnat-Provins, Marguerite. Heures d'hiver. Paris, 1920.
42542.47.90 Caillavet, G.A. La belle aventure. Paris, 1920?
FL 390.80 Cain, Georges. Anciens théâtres de Paris. Paris, 1920.

Chronological Listing

1920 - cont.

42542.48.24.10 Capus, Alfred. La traversée. Paris, 1920.
43550.1.50 Carco, Francis. Petits airs. Paris, 1920.
43550.84.100 Castier, Jules. Rother like...some endeavours to assume the mantles of the great. London, 1920.
40517.1.17 Caylus, Anne C.P. Oeuvres badines et galantes du Conte de Caylus. Paris, 1920.
43552.2.110 Chadourne, Louis. L'inquiète adolescence. Paris, 1920.
43552.3.100 Chaine, Pierre. L'étrange aventure de M. Martin-Péquet. Paris, 1920.
37555.80 Chamard, H. Les origines de la poésie française de la renaissançe. Photoreproduction. Paris, 1920.
40583.55 Champion, Edouard. Hommage à Stendhal. Abbeville, 1920.
FL 385.12.50 Chandler, Frank W. The contemporary drama of France. Boston, 1920.
37555.82 Charbonnier, F. La poésie française et les guerres de religion. Thèse. Paris, 1920.
38525.22.13 Charlier, Gustave. Un amour de Ronsard: "Austrée". Paris, 1920.
43552.3.4120 Charpentier, Henry. Le poème d'Armageddon. Paris, 1920.
43552.25.5100 Charpentier, Leon. Les transmigrations de Yo-Tcheon. Paris, 1920.
43552.3.3100 Charpentier, O. Les vierges de Mai. Paris, 1920.
40586.50 Chateaubriand, F.A.R. Voyage au Mont-Blanc. Grenoble, 1920.
43552.24.110 Chérau, Gaston. Valentine Pacquault. Paris, 1920.
42576.12.35 Cherbonnel, Alice. Les deux sommets. Paris, 1920.
43600.25.120 Chevalier, Adrien. La retraite de M. de Pluviane. Paris, 1920.
43552.26.110 Chevrillon, André. Études anglaises. 4e éd. Paris, 1920.
43554.2.40 Claudel, Paul. The city. New Haven, 1920.
43554.2.63 Claudel, Paul. Le père humiliè. 5e éd. Paris, 1920.
43554.2.60 Claudel, Paul. Protée. Paris, 1920.
43554.7.42 Clemenceau, Georges. Au pied du Sinaï. Paris, 1920.
43554.7.55 Clemenceau, Georges. The surprises of life. Garden City, 1920.
43556.1.330 Cocteau, Jean. Carte blanche. Paris, 1920.
37548.55.2 Cohen, Gustave. Ecrivains français en Hollande. Paris, 1920.
37548.55 Cohen, Gustave. Écrivains français en Hollande. Thèse. Paris, 1920.
38513.70 Cohen, Gustave. Mystères et moralités du manuscrit 617 de Chantilly. Paris, 1920.
38513.70.5 Cohen, Gustave. Mystères et moralités du manuscrit 617 de Chantilly. Thèse. Paris, 1920.
43556.49.160 Colette, Sidonie Gabrielle. Chéri, roman. 85e éd. Paris, 1920.
38575.31.35 Corneille, Pierre. La galerie du Palais. London, 1920.
42586.32.11 Coster, Charles de. Flemish legends. London, 1920.
42586.32.8 Coster, Charles de. Die Hochzeitsreise, Zoulets Heirat. Berlin, 1920.
42586.32.65 Coster, Charles de. Tyll Ulenspiegel. München, 1920.
40546.8.9 Courier de Méré, Paul Louis. Paul Louis Courier; a selection from the works. Manchester, 1920.
42542.58.13F Curel, François de. L'ame en folie. Paris, 1920.
37567.143.2 Curtius, Ernst Robert. Die literarischen Wegbereiter des neuen Frankreich. 2. Aufl. Potsdam, 1920.
38576.12.44.10 Dancourt, Florent C. Le chevalier à la mode. Strassbourg, 1920.
43565.5.155 Daudet, Léon A. Souvenirs de milleux littéraires. Paris, 1920.
43566.9.100 Debout, J. Les voix de Jeanne d'Arc. Paris, 1920.
43566.27.100 Deffes, Louis. Epevas poétiques et dramatiques. 1. ser. 1. éd. Tarbes, 1920.
37567.180 Deffoux, Léon. Le group de Médan. Paris, 1920.
43566.7.30 Deval, Jacques. Une faible femme. Paris, 1920.
43573.14.50 Docquois, G. La rôtisserie de la reine Pédauque. Paris, 1920.
42542.65.25 Donnay, Maurice. La chasse à l'homme. Paris, 1920.
42542.65.26 Donnay, Maurice. Dialogues d'hier. Paris, 1920.
42542.65.28 Donnay, Maurice. Le roi Candaule. Paris, 1920.
43574.41.130 Drieu La Rochelle, Pierre. Fond de cantine. 4. éd. Paris, 1920.
43574.1.45 Drouot, Paul. Les derniers vers de Paul Drouot. Paris, 1920.
43576.5.110 Dubech, Lucien. Poèmes pour Aricil. Paris, 1920.
41555.39.10 Du Bos, Charles. Notes sur Mérimée. Paris, 1920.
37568.10.2 Duclaux, Agnes Mary Frances. Twentieth century French writers. N.Y., 1920.
43576.6.120 Duhamel, Georges. Dans l'ombre des statues. 4. éd. Paris, 1920.
43576.6.78 Duhamel, Georges. Élégies. 5. éd. Paris, 1920.
43576.6.35 Duhamel, Georges. L'oeuvres des athlètes. 5. éd. Paris, 1920.
37569.3.10 Duliamel, Georges. Guerre et littérature. Paris, 1920.
43576.1.31 Dumas, André. Le premier couple. Paris, 1920.
43576.57.100 Dumur, Louis. Nach Paris! Paris, 1920.
42568.21.5 Duranty, Louis E.E. La cause de beau Guillaume. Paris, 1920.
43576.6.800 Durtain, Luc. Georges Duhamel. Paris, 1920.
43576.77.165 Durtain, Luc. Le retour des hommes. 2. éd. Paris, 1920.
43593.30.100 Enfrey, L.M. Le livre des harems. Paris, 1920.
43598.54.115 Esménard, Jean d'. Thi-Bâ, fille d'Annam. Paris, 1920.
43598.84.116 Estaunié, Édouard. L'ascension de M. Baslévre. Paris, 1920.
37567.202 Évrard, E. Nos mandarins. Tourcoing, 1920.
42541.13.16 Fabre, Émile. La maison sous l'orage. Paris, 1920.
42543.37.5 Fabre, Émile. Théâtre. v.1-2,4-5. Paris, 1920-21. 4v.
43606.41.100 Faillet, Georges. La prière des quarante heures ou les XIV stations sous l'horloge du destin. Paris, 1920.
38526.47.37 Farmer, A.J. Les oeuvres françaises de Scevole de Sainte Marthe, 1536-1623. Toulouse, 1920.
38526.47.37.2 Farmer, A.J. Les oeuvres françaises de Scevole de Sainte Marthe, 1536-1623. Thèse. Toulouse, 1920.
43606.78.110.5 Farrère, Claude. Bêtes et gens qui s'aimèrent. Paris, 1920.
43606.78.110 Farrère, Claude. Bêtes et gens qui s'aimèrent. Paris, 1920.
43606.78.130 Farrère, Claude. Les condamnés à mort. Paris, 1920.
43606.78.150 Farrère, Claude. La dernière déesse. Paris, 1920.
43606.78.280 Farrère, Claude. Roxelane. Paris, 1920.
43606.78.250 Farrère, Claude. La vieille histoire. Paris, 1920.
43606.89.40 Faure, Gabriel. Les amants enchainées. Paris, 1920.
40583.60 Faure, Gabriel. Au pays de Stendhal. Grenoble, 1920.
40587.128 Fauré, Gabriel. Chateaubriand et l'Occitanienne. Paris, 1920.

1920 - cont.

42565.71.10 Favre de Coulevain, Hélène. L'île inconnue. 174. éd. Paris, 1920.
42565.72.6 Favre de Coulevain, Hélène. Nobleza americana. Paris, 1920.
37596.7.5 Feger, G. Rutebeufs Kritik an den Zuständen seiner Zeit. Inaug. Diss. Freiburg, 1920.
38553.27.21 Fénelon, F. de S. de la Mothe. Aventures de Télémaque. Paris, 1920?
38553.27.20 Fénelon, F. de S. de la Mothe. Aventures de Télémaque. Paris, 1920. 2v.
37575.161 Féret, Charles Théophile. Anthologie critique des poètes normands de 1900 à 1920. Paris, 1920.
37573.37.8 Ferrières, Gauthier. Anthologie des écrivains du XIXe siècle; poésie. v.1-2. Paris, 1920.
NEDL 37573.37.10 Ferrières, Gauthier. Anthologie des écrivains français contemporaines; poésie. Paris, 1920.
NEDL 37573.37.9 Ferrières, Gauthier. Anthologie des écrivains français contemporaines; prose. Paris, 1920.
37567.99 Finch, M.B. The origins of French romanticism. London, 1920.
43609.79.100 Fischer, Max. Dans l'ascenseur. Paris, 1920.
43610.1.35F Fleg, Edmond. La maison du bon Dieu. Paris, 1920.
40515.30.35 Florian, Jean P.C. de. Fables, précédées d'un étude sur la fable suivies de Tuth et de Tobie. Paris, 1920.
43611.4.40 Foley, Charles. Pernette en escapade. Paris, 1920.
43611.1.25.73 Fort, Paul. Ballades françaises. 1. série. 8. éd. Paris, 1920.
43611.5.30 Fournier, Alain. Le grand meaulnes. Londres, 1920.
42576.63.7.20 France, Anatole. Le crime de Sylvestre Bonnard. 141. éd. Boston, 1920.
42576.62.21.15 France, Anatole. L'île des pingouins. 175. éd. Paris, 1920.
42576.62.13.10 France, Anatole. Le jardin d'Epicure. 93. éd. Paris, 1920.
42576.62.29 France, Anatole. Les opinions de M. Jérôme Coignard. 114e éd. Paris, 1920.
42576.62.29.5 France, Anatole. Les opinions de M. Jérôme Coignard. 129. éd. Paris, 1920.
42576.62.29.10 France, Anatole. Les opinions de M. Jérôme Coignard recueillies. Paris, 1920.
42576.63.18.5 France, Anatole. The seven wives of Bluebeard. London, 1920.
42576.62.115 France, Anatole. Under the rose. London, 1920.
FL 6059.4 François, Alexis. Le premier baiser de l'amour. Genève, 1920.
43612.2.43 Fraudet, René. L'appassionate. Paris, 1920.
43612.2.35 Fraudet, René. Colette Baudoche. Paris, 1920.
43612.2.31 Fraudet, René. La maison cernée. Paris, 1920.
43616.9.21 Gabory, Georges. Coeurs à prendre. Poèmes. Paris, 1920.
38512.141 Gaston III Phoebus, Count of Foix. Le livre des oraisons de Gaston Phébus. Paris, 1920.
FL 360.9.4 Gavault, Paul. Conférence de l'Odéon. 4. sér. (1918-19). Paris, 1920.
43617.5.33 Géniaux, Charles. La victoire du bled; nouvelles. n.p., 1920.
43619.24.100 Ghéon, Henri. La farce du pendu dépendu. Paris, 1920.
43619.24.130 Ghéon, Henri. Le miroir de Jésus. Paris, 1920.
37555.89 Ghil, René. La tradition de poésie scientifique. Paris, 1920.
40597.2.615 Gigli, Guiseppe. Balzac in Italia. Milano, 1920.
43620.1.40 Gilbert, Oscar P. Le triomphe de la haine. Florence, 1920.
42576.6.11 Ginisty, Paul. L'histoire singulière de Mlle Leblanc. Paris, 1920.
43620.74.135 Giraudoux, Jean. Adorable Clio. Paris, 1920.
38523.19.2 Gosse, Edmund W. Malherbe and the classical reaction in the 17th century. Oxford, 1920.
42542.28.50 Got, Ambroise. Henry Becque, sa vie et son oeuvre. Paris, 1920.
Htn 43625.3.77* Gourmont, Rémy de. La patience de Griseledis. Paris, 1920.
37543.137.5 Grenier, Abel. Histoire de la littérature française. 5. éd. Paris, 1920.
42515.35.124 Guilloux, Pierre. L'esprit de Renan. Paris, 1920.
43628.1.37 Guitry, Sacha. Béranger. Paris, 1920.
43628.1.36 Guitry, Sacha. Béranger. Paris, 1920.
43628.1.33F Guitry, Sacha. Mon père avait raison. Paris, 1920.
43631.2.40 Hamp, Pierre. La peine des hommes; la victoire mécanniciene. 6. éd. Paris, 1920.
43631.2.34 Hamp, Pierre. La peine des hommes; l'enquête. 6. éd. Paris, 1920.
43631.2.42 Hamp, Pierre. La peine des hommes; les chercheurs d'or. 8. éd. Paris, 1920.
40597.8.10 Hastings, Walter Scott. The drama of Honoré de Balzac. Menasha, Wis., 1920.
43632.6.280 Henriot, Émile. Omphale. n.p., 1920.
42543.65.25 Hermant, Abel. La journée brève. Paris, 1920.
41573.18.15 Hugo, Victor. Legende des siècles. Paris, 1920-27. 6v.
41573.25.5 Hugo, Victor. La préface de Cromwell. Berlin, 1920.
42576.65.16 Huysmans, Joris Karl. En route. N.Y., 1920.
43667.51.110 Jaloux, Edmond. Au-dessus de la ville. Paris, 1920.
43667.51.250 Jaloux, Edmond. L'éventail de crêpe. Paris, 1920.
43667.1.55 Jammes, Francis. Le bon Dieu chez les enfants. Paris, 1920.
43667.1.45 Jammes, Francis. Le poète rustique. 5. éd. Paris, 1920.
39568.23 Jones, A.C. Friederich Melchior Grimm. Wiesbaden, 1920.
43670.80.100 Joseph-Renaud, J. Le clavecin hanté. Paris, 1920.
41574.93.2 Joussain, André. Le pittoresque dans l'esthétique de Victor Hugo. Paris, 1920.
43757.50.810A Jouve, Pierre J. Romain Rolland vivant, 1914-1919. Paris, 1920.
43670.94.100 Jouve, Pierre Jean. Heures livre de la grâce. Genève, 1920.
37556.16 King, Helen Maxwell. Les doctrines littéraires de la quotidienne, 1814-30. Durham, N.C., 1920.
37556.16.2 King, Helen Maxwell. Les doctrines littéraires de la quotidienne, 1814-30. Northampton, Mass., 1920.
41578.71 Kool, Jacob Heye. Les premières meditations en Hollande. Paris, 1920.
43757.50.840 Küchler, W. Romain Rolland. 2. Aufl. Würzburg, 1920.
38564.25.50 La Bruyère, J. de. La Bruyère avec introduction, bibliographique, notes. Paris, 1920.
38521.30.7 Lachèvre, Frédéric. Mélanges. Paris, 1920.
43687.15.200 Lacretelle, Jacques de. La vie inquiète de Jean Hermelin. 15e éd. Paris, 1920.

1920 - cont.

39527.42.10 La Fontaine, Jean de. Lettres de Jean de La Fontaine à sa femme sur un voyage des Paris en limosin. Paris, 1920.
42555.1.20 Laforgue, Jules. Chroniques parisiennes. Paris, 1920.
43687.53.130 Lamandé, André. Sous le clair regard d'Athéné. Paris, 1920.
38544.1.5 Lancaster, Henry Carrington. La Calprenède, dramatist. Chicago, 1920?
FL 362.12A Lanson, Gustav. Esquisse d'une histoire de la tragédie française. N.Y., 1920.
43687.83.100 Lasserre, Pierre. Les chapelles litteraires. Paris, 1920.
43687.83.130 Lasserre, Pierre. Henri de Sauvelade, roman. Paris, 1920?
42544.24.45 Lavedan, Henri. La belle histoire de Geneviève. Paris, 1920.
42544.24.40 Lavedan, Henri. Le chemin du salut. I, Inène Olette. Paris, 1920.
39582.30 La Villeherve, Bertran de. Francois-Thomas de Baculard d'Arnaud. Paris, 1920.
42555.36.13 Leconte de Lisle, C.M.R. Les erinnyes. Paris, 1920.
43688.35.100 Le Grand, Maurice. Les avis de l'oncle Bertrand. Paris, 1920.
40515.5.90 Legros, A. Madame d'Épinay, valenciennoise. Valenciennes, 1920.
38575.23.5 Le Guiner, Jeanne. Les femmes dans les tragédies de Corneille. Paris, 1920.
42544.33.20.5A Lemaître, Jules. Serenus and other stories. London, 1920.
38523.3.5 Lerber, Walther de. L'influence de Clement Marot aut XVIIme et XVIIIme siècles. Lausanne, 1920.
43688.1.38 Leroux, Gaston. Le capitaine Hyx. Paris, 1920.
38557.22.12 Letellier, Albert. Bossuet. Paris, 1920.
43688.89.105 Leuba, J. L'aile de feu, roman. Paris, 1920.
43688.91.100 Level, Maurice. Tales of mystery and horror. N.Y., 1920.
43689.4.100 Lhande, Pierre. Les mouettes. 9e éd. Paris, 1920.
43690.1.63 Lichtenberger, A. Le petit roi. Paris, 1920.
43690.1.70 Lichtenberger, A. La petite soeur de Trott. Paris, 1920.
43693.3.30 Loumaye, Marcel. L'ombre de la guerre; poème. Bruxelles, 1920.
42544.34.50 Louys, Pierre. Byblis, Leda, A new pleasure. N.Y., 1920.
Htn 42544.34.28.20* Louys, Pierre. The songs of Bilitis. n.p., 1920.
42584.25.240 Lugones, Leopoldo. Emilio Zola. Buenos-Aires, 1920.
40575.5.18 MacClintock, Lauder. Sainte-Beuve's critical theory and practice after 1849. Chicago, 1920.
40575.5.17 MacClintock, Lauder. Sainte-Beuve's critical theory and practice after 1849. Chicago, 1920.
43697.14.150 MacOrlan, Pierre. Le nègre Léonard et maître Jean Mullin. 4. ed. Paris, 1920.
43697.14.340 MacOrlan, Pierre. Petit manuel du parfait aventurier. Paris, 1920.
42545.3.13.10 Maeterlinck, Maurice. The life of the bee. N.Y., 1920.
39533.23 Magne, Émile. Un ami de Cyrano de Bergerac, le chavalier de Lignières. Paris, 1920.
43697.34.110 Magre, Maurice. La mort enchaînée. Paris, 1920.
FL 397.8.25 Mahelot, L. Le mémoire de Mahelot...de l'hôtel de Bourgogne. Paris, 1920.
42555.43.6 Mallarmé, Stéphane. Vers de circonstance. 6. éd. Paris, 1920.
43547.77.800 Malo, Henri. Marguerite Burnat-Provins. Paris, 1920.
37576.550 Manley, Edward. Eight French stories. Boston, 1920.
41578.79 Marie, Margueritte. Le roman d'une grande âme. Paris, 1920.
42555.49.11 Mariéton, Paul. Paul Mariéton d'après sa correspondance. Paris, 1920. 3v.
42545.9.12 Martel de Janville, S.G. Les amoureux. Paris, 1920.
42545.9.11 Martel de Janville, S.G. Le monde à côté. Paris, 1920.
43697.77.180 Martin du Gard, Roger. Le testament du Père Leleu. Paris, 1920.
37567.175 Martineau, René. Promenades biographiques, Flaubert, Barbey. Paris, 1920.
42577.3.50 Maupassant, Guy de. Contes normands. Paris, 1920.
42577.4.23.10 Maupassant, Guy de. The inheritance. N.Y., 1920.
42577.2.4.3 Maupassant, Guy de. Mad, and short stories. N.Y., 1920.
42577.4.29.9A Maupassant, Guy de. Une vie. N.Y., 1920?
37566.147 Maurevert, Georges. Quelques gentilshommes de lettres. Lyon, 1920.
43697.88.840 Mauriac, François. De quelques coeurs inquiets. Paris, 1920.
43697.89.560 Maurois, André. Les bourgeois de Witzheim. Paris, 1920.
43697.89.103 Maurois, André. Le Général Bramble. Paris, 1920.
43697.89.102 Maurois, André. Les silences du Colonel Bramble. Paris, 1920.
43697.98.40 Mayran, Camille (pseud.). L'épreuve du fils. Paris, 1920.
43697.98.702 Mayran, Camille (pseud.). The story of Gotton Connixloo. N.Y., 1920.
43697.99.2100 Mazaud, Émile. La folle journée; comédie en un acte. Paris, 1920.
43698.41.100 Meiss, H. Choses d'Alsace. Nice, 1920.
37543.149 Mélanges d'histoire littéraire et de philologie offerts à M. Bernard Bouvier. Genève, 1920.
43698.75.120 Méré, Charles. Les conquérants. Paris, 1920.
41555.23.78 Mérimée, Prosper. Colomba. N.Y., 1920.
40583.187 Mérimée, Prosper. H.B. par un des quarante. Paris, 1920.
43699.73.100 Miguel, P. Le philatéliste. Toulouse, 1920.
43699.3.35 Mille, Pierre. Histoires exotiques et merveilleuses. Paris, 1920.
43699.3.48 Mille, Pierre. Trois femmes. Paris, 1920.
42545.28.7.14 Mirbeau, Octave. Un gentilhomme. Paris, 1920.
Mol 211.80A Molière, Jean Baptiste Poquelin. Les femmes savantes...C.H.C. Wright. N.Y., 1920.
Mol 247.23 Molière, Jean Baptiste Poquelin. Le misanthrope. 6. éd. Paris, 1920.
Mol 39.20 Molière, Jean Baptiste Poquelin. Théâtre choisi. 5e éd. Paris, 1920.
Htn Mon 19.06.5F* Montaigne, Michel de. Essais. v.4. mss. notes. Paris, 1920.
42555.60.2 Montesquiou-Fezensac, Robert de. Les pas effacés. Mémoires. v.1-3. Paris, 1920.
43701.62.120 Montfort, Eugène. Un coeur vierge, roman. Paris, 1920.
38546.57 Montigny, Maurice. En voyageant avec Mme. de Sévigné. Paris, 1920.
42555.61.37 Moréas, Jean. Le septième livre des stances. Paris, 1920.
42556.17.5 Morice, Henri. L'esthétique de Sully-Prudhomme. Thèse. Vannes, 1920.
42556.17.3 Morice, Henri. La poésie de Sully-Prudhomme. Paris, 1920.
42556.17.3.2 Morice, Henri. La poésie de Sully-Prudhomme. Thèse. Paris, 1920.
39544.53 Muller, D. Les rentes viagères. Paris, 1920.
42576.15.145 Muoni, Guido. Gustavo Flaubert. Roma, 1920.

1920 - cont.

41543.10 Nerval, Gerard de. De Paris à Cythère. Paris, 1920.
43709.3.150 Noailles, Anna E. Les forces éternelles. Paris, 1920.
42584.24.8 Oehlert, Richard. E. Zola als Theatherdichter. Berlin, 1920.
40592.88 Onerva, L. (pseud.). Madame de Staël. Porvoossa, 1920.
37562.12.14F Ovidio, F. d'. Studii sulla più antica versificazione francese; memoria. Roma, 1920.
37562.12.15 Ovidio, F. d'. Studii sulla più antica versificazione francese. Milan? 1920.
43737.41.100 Paillot, F. Les trois maitresses de M. de Frivolac. Paris, 1920.
43737.98.110 Paz, M.L. (Mme.). Woman. N.Y., 1920.
42578.30.65 Peladan, J. Le livre secret. Paris, 1920.
38526.32.55 Pellegrini, C. La prima opera di Margherita di Navarra. Catania, 1920.
38526.32.50 Pellegrini, C. La prima opera di Margherita di Navarra. Catania, 1920.
43738.77.104 Pérochon, Ernest. Nêne. Paris, 1920.
43738.77.90 Pérochon, Ernest. Nêne. Paris, 1920.
37573.620 Pévost, Ernest. Le livre épique. Paris, 1920.
43611.5.150 Pilon, Edmond. Alain-Fournier. Abbeville, 1920.
43741.59.4140 Pinguet, Auguste. Le poème, 1918. Angers, 1920.
42545.88.40 Porto-Riche, G. Anatomie sentimentale. Paris, 1920?
42578.31.60 Prévost, Marcel. Mon cher Tommy. Paris, 1920.
42578.31.62 Prévost, Marcel. La nuit finira. 30. éd. Paris, 1920. 2v.
43744.64.100 Prody, Alfred. La légende du Bois de la Fage. Aurillac, 1920.
43889.77 Les propos d'Alain. 3e éd. Paris, 1920. 2v.
38536.18.15A Rabelais, F. Oeuvres de Rabelais. Paris, 1920. 2v.
38536.25.5 Rabelais, F. Readings selected by W.F. Smith. Cambridge, Eng., 1920.
38585.20.12 Racine, Jean. Athalie. Paris, 1920.
43752.51.110 Ramel-Cals, Jeanne. La grande aventure. Paris, 1920.
43752.51.100 Ramel-Cals, Jeanne. La ronde. Paris, 1920.
43752.98.120 Raynal, Paul. Le maître de son coeur. Paris, 1920.
43753.9.140 Reboux, Paul. Chonchon. Paris, 1920.
38587.10.10 Regnard, Jean François. La provençale. Paris, 1920.
42556.26.39 Régnier, Henri de. La pécheresse. 7e éd. Paris, 1920.
42556.26.40 Régnier, Henri de. La pécheresse. 15e éd. Paris, 1920.
37596.136.20 Renauld de Beaujeu. Les amours de Frêne et Galeran. Paris, 1920.
43755.3.100 Rhaïs, Elissa. Le Café-Chontant, Kerkeb, Noblesse arabe. 2. éd. Paris, 1920.
42576.15.22 Riddell, Agnes R. Flaubert and Maupassant. Chicago, 1920.
42576.15.21 Riddell, Agnes R. Flaubert and Maupassant. Thesis. Chicago, 1920.
42587.55.14 Rivoire, André. Juliette et Roméo. Paris, 1920.
42587.55.12 Rivoire, André. Roger Bontemps. Paris, 1920.
43757.13.3100F Roche, Juliette. Demi cercle. Paris, 1920.
43752.38.100 Rohblenbeck, G. L'année glorieuse, 1914; roman. Bruxelles, 1920.
43757.50.425 Rolland, Romain. Aux peuples assasinés. Paris, 1920?
43757.50.422A Rolland, Romain. Clerambault, histoire d'une conscience libre pendant la guerre. 18e éd. Paris, 1920.
43757.50.560 Rolland, Romain. Les precurseurs. Paris, 1920.
43757.50.532 Rolland, Romain. Voyage musical au pays du passé. Paris, 1920.
43757.3.35 Romains, Jules. Cromedeyre-le-Vieil. 3e éd. Paris, 1920.
43757.3.282 Romains, Jules. Le voyage des amants. 3. éd. Paris, 1920.
38525.20.9.2 Ronsard, Pierre de. Livret de folastries à janot parisien. Paris, 1920.
42578.22.95 Rosny, J.H. L'amoureuse aventure. Paris, 1920.
42578.22.10 Rosny, J.H. Le félin géant. 5. éd. Paris, 1920.
FL 6090.25A Rousseau, J.J. L'état de guerre et projet de paix perpetuelle. N.Y., 1920.
NEDL FL 6002.920.4 Rousseau, J.J. Morceaux choisis. 4. ed. Paris, 1920.
Mol 860.62 Rovetta, G. Molière e sua moglie. Milano, 1920.
40583.65 Sabatier, Pierre. Equisse de la morale de Stendhal. Paris, 1920.
42575.83A Sabatier, Pierre. L'esthétique des Goncourt. Paris, 1920.
42575.87 Sabatier, Pierre. L'esthétique des Goncourt. Thèse. Paris, 1920.
40575.22.20 Sainte-Beuve, Charles A. Madame de Pontivy. Paris, 1920.
43761.51.100 Salomon, Michel. Portraits et paysages. Paris, 1920.
42546.30.19.5 Sardou, Victorien. Madame Sans-Gêne. Milano, 1920.
37568.15A Schinz, Albert. French literature of the great war. N.Y., 1920.
43763.2.35 Schopfer, Jean. Ariane. Paris, 1920[1921]
42578.36.5 Schultz, Jeanne. La neuvaine de Colette. 143. éd. Paris, 1920.
41588.12.5 Scribe, Eugène. Mon étoile. Bielefeld, 1920.
38546.9.9 Scudéry, Madeleine de. La promenade de Versailles. Paris, 1920.
41557.10.24 Seillière, Ernest. George Sand. Paris, 1920.
37567.170 Smith, Maxwell A. L'influence des Lakistes sur les romantiques français. Paris, 1920.
37567.170.2 Smith, Maxwell A. L'influence des Lakistes sur les romantiques français. Thèse. Paris, 1920.
Htn 43775.90.7100* Soupault, Philippe. Rose des vents. Paris, 1920.
43776.41.110 Spire, André. Tentations. Paris, 1920.
39585.18.10 Suard, Amelie. Essais de mémoires sur M. Suard. Paris, 1920.
41522.18.10 Symons, Arthur. Charles Baudelaire; a study.. N.Y., 1920.
43788.5.150 Tharaud, Jérôme. L'ombre de la croix. Paris, 1920.
43788.5.130 Tharaud, Jérôme. Un royaume de Dieu. 24e éd. Paris, 1920.
43788.41.100 Thibaudet, Albert. Trente ans de vie française. Paris, 1920-23. 4v.
Mon 194.5 Thiele, Ernst A. Montaigne und Locke. Leipzig, 1920.
37574.40 Thorley, Wilfrid Charles. Fleurs-de-lys...French poetry. Boston, 1920.
42578.51.54 Tinayre, Marcelle. Perséphone. Paris, 1920.
42578.51.55 Tinayre, Marcelle. Perséphone. 13. éd. Paris, 1920.
39544.77 Tochander, R. Fremdes Sprachgut im Wortschatze Voltaires. Paris, 1920.
43792.90.150 Toulet, Paul Jean. Les contes de Béhanzigue. Paris, 1920.
38547.7 Urfé, Honoré d'. L'Astrée de Honoré d'Urfé. pt. 1, book 1-8,9-12. Strassbourg, 1920?
38547.11 Urfé, Honoré d'. Un épisode de l'Astrée. Les amours d'Alcedon. Paris, 1920.
43822.10.30 Vaillat, Léandre. Le peintre et l'amant. Paris? 1920.
43822.49.115 Valéry, Paul. Charmes. Paris, 1920.
43822.6.15 Vallotton, Benjamin. Ceux de Barivier. Lausanne, 1920.
43822.8.30 Vaudoyer, Jean L. Le dernier rendez-vous. Paris, 1920.
42557.11.18 Verhaeren, Émile. Hélène de Sparte. 4. éd. Paris, 1920.

Chronological Listing

1920 - cont.

42557.11.17 Verhaeren, Émile. Toute la Flandre. Paris, 1920. 3v.

37567.396 Verlaine, P. Les poètes maudits. Paris, 1920.

42557.20.5 Verlaine, Paul. Fêtes galantes. Paris, 1920.

FL 6049.12 Vial, Francisque. La doctrine l'éducation de Jean-Jacques Rousseau. Paris, 1920.

42576.56.6.5 Viaud, Julien. Japan (Madame Chrysanthème). N.Y., 1920.

42576.56.6 Viaud, Julien. Madame Chrysanthème. 187. éd. Paris, 1920.

42576.52.4.5 Viaud, Julien. Pêcheur d'Islande. N.Y., 1920.

42576.52.4.15 Viaud, Julien. Pêcheur d'Islande. N.Y., 1920.

43824.16.100 Vidal, B. Fleurs de montagne. n.p., 1920?

41564.24.10 Vigny, Alfred de. Chatterton. Strasbourg, 1920.

43824.49.130 Vildrac, Charles. Chants du désespéré, 1914-1920. Paris, 1920.

43824.49.100 Vildrac, Charles. Le paquebot Tenacity. 2e éd. Paris, 1920.

38514.18.11 Villon, François. Les ballads en jargon du manuscrit de Stockholm. Groningen, 1920.

43824.5.30 Vindry, F. Dahut. Lyon, 1920.

43824.67.150 Vioux, Marcelle. Une enlisée. Paris, 1920.

Mon 132.5.15 Vivier, P. Montaigne, auteur scientifique. Paris, 1920?

41574.91 Vodoz, J. "Roland". Paris, 1920.

38547.14 Werner, Ernst. Die Dastellung des Empfindungslebens in der "Astrée" des Honoré d'Urfé. Inaug. Diss. Nürmberg, 1920.

37564.60A Wright, Charles H.C. French classicism. Cambridge, 1920.

1921

43512.2 Abadie, C.A. La nouveaux riches. Paris, 1921.

37558.65 Académie française, Paris. Anthologie de l'Académie française. Paris, 1921. 2v.

42562.38.4.7 Adam, Paul. La force. Paris, 1921. 2v.

37543.143 Adami, J. Précis de littérature avec de nombreuses citations. Paris, 1921.

37596.54.10 Aléxius, Saint. Légend. La vie de Saint Aléxis. 3. éd. Paris, 1921.

43522.41.110 Alibert, François Paul. Le devil des muses. Carcassonne, 1921.

43757.50.950 Altamira, D.R. La nueva literatura pacifista el "Clerambault" de Romain Rolland. Madrid, 1921.

43523.41.100 Amiel, Denys. La souriante Madame Beudet. Paris, 1921.

FL 396.50.5 Antoine, André. "Mes souvenirs" sur le théâtre-libre. Paris, 1921.

43526.65.145 Apollinaire, Guillaume. L'enchanteur pourrissant. Paris, 1921.

43528.61.210 Arnoux, Alexandre. La nuit de Saint Barnabé. Paris, 1921.

43531.7.4100 Aubert, Denise. Les année heureuses. 2. éd. Paris, 1921.

37564.62 Bailly, A. L'école classique française. Paris, 1921.

40597.200 Balzac, Honoré de. Jesus Christus in Flandern. Potsdam, 1921.

42554.8.9 Banville, Théodore de. Gringoire. N.Y., 1921.

43537.6.60 Barbusse, Henri. Le couteau entre les clents. Paris, 1921.

43537.6.35 Barbusse, Henri. Quelques coins du coeur. Genève, 1921.

42563.16.6.2 Barrès, Maurice. Amori et dolori sacrum. Paris, 1921.

43537.4.41 Bataille, Henry. L'homme à la rose. Paris, 1921.

43537.4.42 Bataille, Henry. La tendresse; pièce. Paris, 1921.

X Cg 41522.13.8.3 Baudelaire, Charles. Les fleurs du mal. Paris, 1921.

41522.13.8 Baudelaire, Charles. Les fleurs du mal. Paris, 1921.

40556.39.10 Baussan, Charles. Joseph de Maistre et l'idée de l'orde. Paris, 1921.

42563.21.74 Bazin, René. Les oberlé. 289. éd. Paris, 1921.

38544.27.540 Beaunier, André. La jeunesse de Mme. de La Fayette. Paris, 1921.

42546.12.30 Bédier, Joseph. Discours de réception à l'Académie Française. Paris, 1921.

FL 6133.8 Benedetto, L.F. Madame de Warens. Firenze, 1921.

43538.61.40 Benoît, Pierre. Le lac salé. Paris, 1921.

43538.74.110.2 Béraud, Henri. Le vitriol de lune; roman. Paris, 1921.

43538.74.110 Béraud, Henri. Le vitriol de lune; roman. Paris, 1921.

43538.10.30 Bernard, Jean J. Le feu qui reprend mal; pièce. Paris, 1921.

43538.76.1140 Bernard, Jean-Marc. Haut-Vivarais d'hiver. Saint-Félicen-en-Vivarais, 1921.

37567.196 Bersaucourt, A. de. Au temps des parnassiens. Paris, 1921?

43538.77.1100 Berton, Henry. Le coeur effeuillé. Paris, 1921.

41596.4.19 Betheder-Matibet, M. L'influence de Shakespeare sur Musset. Paris, 1921.

Htn 40582.8.10* Beyle, Henri. La chartreuse de Parme. Paris, 1921. 3v.

40582.34 Beyle, Henri. Stendhal, lettres à Pauline. Paris, 1921.

38542.29.5 Blessebois, P.C. Oeuvre. Paris, 1921.

42563.23.22 Bloy, Léon. Au seuil de l'apocalypse. 5. éd. Paris, 1921.

42563.23.20 Bloy, Léon. Quatre ans de captivité à Cochons-sur-Marne. 4. éd. Paris, 1921. 2v.

42556.29.36 Bocquet, Léon. Albert Samain. 6. éd. Paris, 1921.

38526.2.15 Boisrobert, F. le M. de. Epistre en vers. Paris, 1921. 2v.

43544.57.100 Bompard, J. L'étrangère. Paris, 1921.

43757.50.820 Bonnerot, Jean. Romain Rolland; sa vie, son oeuvre. Paris, 1921.

X Cg 42543.1.11 Bonney, M.T. Les idées morales dans le théâtre d'Alexandre Dumas fils. Thèse. Quimper, 1921.

42563.36.90 Bordeaux, Henry. Ménages d'après guerre. Paris, 1921.

42563.36.85 Bordeaux, Henry. La vie recommence. La chair et l'esprit. Paris, 1921.

42563.36.85.5 Bordeaux, Henry. La vie recommence. La chair et l'esprit. Paris, 1921.

38557.59.155 Bossuet, J.B. Sermon sur la mort. Paris, 1921.

Mon 112.9 Bouillier, Victor. La renommée de Montaigne en Allemagne. Paris, 1921.

43544.6.35 Boulenger, Jacques. Mais l'art est difficite! v.1-2. Paris, 1921.

43544.5.35 Boulenger, Marcel. Marguerite. Paris, 1921.

42563.37.6.10 Bourget, Paul. Un coeur de femme. Paris, 1921.

42563.37.47 Bourget, Paul. Un drame dans le monde. Paris, 1921.

42563.37.50 Bourget, Paul. L'écuyère. Paris, 1921.

42563.39.85 Boylesve, René. Le carrosse aux deux lézards verts. Paris, 1921.

42563.39.80 Boylesve, René. Le dangereux jeune homme. 5. éd. Paris, 1921.

42563.39.90 Boylesve, René. Elise. 12. éd. Paris, 1921.

42563.39.95 Boylesve, René. La jeune fille bien élevée. 11. éd. Paris, 1921.

43545.3.110 Brandenburg, A.J. Niobé. Paris, 1921.

1921 - cont.

42542.47.1 Brieux, Eugène. Théâtre complet. Paris, 1921-29. 9v.

41583.17.50 Brifaut, Charles. Souvenirs d'un académicien. Paris, 1921. 2v.

40597.2.25 Burton, John M. Honoré de Balzac and his figures of speech. Baltimore, 1921.

40597.2.26 Burton, John M. Honoré de Balzac and his figures of speech. Princeton, N.J., 1921.

37567.109.5 Canat, René. La littérature française au XIXe siècle. Paris, 1921. 2v.

37576.621.15 Cario, L. La pensée française. Paris, 1921.

40516.6.8 Cazotte, Jacques. Le diable amoureux. Paris, 1921.

FL 385.12.51A Chandler, Frank W. The contemporary drama of France. Boston, 1921.

43552.7.6100 Chapuis, Lucien. La gerbe enrubannée. Paris, 1921.

43667.78.900 Chassé, C. Sous le masque d'Alfred Jarry. Paris, 1921.

43552.16.100 Chavannes, Eduard. Fables chinoises du IIIe au VIIIe siècle. Paris, 1921.

40575.5.25 Choisy, Louis F. Sainte-Beuve, l'homme et la poète. 4. éd. Paris, 1921.

39532.15 Clark, Ruth. Anthony Hamilton. London, 1921.

43554.2.93 Claudel, Paul. Ode jubilaire pour le six-centième anniversaire de la mort de Dante. Paris, 1921.

43556.1.785 Cocteau, Jean. Cock and harlequin. London, 1921.

42563.39.805 Codet, Louis. La fortune de Bécot. Paris, 1921.

37596.124.5A Conon de Béthune. Chansons. Paris, 1921.

42542.53.51 Copeau, Jacques. Les frères Karamazov. Paris, 1921.

42565.64 Corday, Michel. En libre grâce; nouvelle. Paris, 1921.

40534.31 Crébillon, Claude Prosper Jolyot de. L'oeuvre de Crébillon le fils: Tableau des moeurs du temps dans les différents ages de la vie. Paris, 1921.

42542.55.1 Croisset, Francis de. Théâtre. v.3. Paris, 1921?

43557.66.120 Crommelynck, Fernand. Les amants puerits. 2e éd. Paris, 1921.

43557.66.100 Crommelynck, Fernand. Le cocu magnifique. Paris, 1921.

42542.58.14 Curel, François de. La comédie du génie. Paris, 1921.

42563.18.150 Curtius, F.R. Maurice Barrès und die geistigen Grundlagen des französischen Nationalismus. Bonn, 1921.

42567.28.5 Daudet, Ernest. Souvenirs de mon temps. Paris, 1921.

37558.119 Dawson, John C. Toulouse in the renaissance. pt. 1. N.Y., 1921.

41566.36.5 Delécluze, E.J. Mademoiselle Justine de Liron. Paris, 1921.

43566.54.110 Demians d'Archimbaud, M. La vie continue. Paris, 1921.

41593.29.3.16 Desbordes-Valmore, Marceline. Albums à Pauline. Oeuvres manuscrites. Paris, 1921.

37543.144 Des Granges, C.M. Illustrated history of French literature. Paris, 1921.

39564.22 Diderot, Denis. Diderot et l'abbé Barthélemy. Paris, 1921.

39564.17.5 Diderot, Denis. Entretien entre d'Alembert et Diderot. Paris, 1921.

42542.65.8.5F Donnay, Maurice. Amants. Paris, 1921.

43573.75.100 Doreau, François-Marie. Une de mes vies. Paris, 1921.

43573.76.55 Dorgelès, Roland. Wooden crosses. N.Y., 1921.

43574.41.190 Drieu La Rochelle, Pierre. État civil. Paris, 1921.

41574.71 Duclaux, A.M.F. (Mrs.). Victor Hugo. London, 1921.

38528.20.10 Du Fail, Noël. Propos rustiques. Paris, 1921.

38588.20.15 Dufresny, Charles Rivière. Amusements sérieux et comiques. Paris, 1921.

43606.89.81 Dujet, A. Gabriel Faure. Paris, 1921.

38545.22A Dulong, Gustave. L'abbé de Saint Réal; étude sur les rapports. Paris, 1921. 2v.

43576.77.200 Durtain, Luc. Face à face. Paris, 1921.

FL 394.120 Dussane, B. (Mme.). La comédie-française. Paris, 1921.

43576.91.150 Duvernois, Henri. The holidays; a book of gay stories. London, 1921.

43576.91.35F Duvernois, Henri. Morte la bête. Paris, 1921.

43598.13.100 Escholier, R. Cantegril. Paris, 1921.

42554.32.7 Fabie, François. Oeuvres. Poésies, 1905-18. Paris, 1921.

43606.9.100 Fabrici, Delphi. Das Gespenst. Berlin, 1921.

37543.520 Faguet, Émile. Histoire de la littérature française. Paris, 1921. 2v.

41538.53.57 Fairbanks, Douglas. The three musketeers. N.Y., 1921.

40587.126 Fauré, Gabriel. Les amours de Chateaubriand et de Madame de Vichet. Saint-Félicien-en-Vivarais, 1921.

43606.89.70 Faure, Gabriel. Mon lycée. Saint-Félicien-en-Vivarais, 1921.

38554.523 Fénelon, F. de S. de la Mothe. Spiritual letters, letters to women. London, 1921.

42576.28.5 Flaubert, Gustave. Madame Bovary. Paris, 1921.

42576.17.27 Flaubert, Gustave. Madame Bovary. Paris, 1921.

42576.31.9 Flaubert, Gustave. Salammbô. Paris, 1921.

42576.33.7 Flaubert, Gustave. Trois contes. Paris, 1921.

V43500.95 Flers, Robert de. Discours de reception à l'Academie française le 16 juin 1921. Paris, 1921.

42543.42.8F Flers, Robert de. Le retour; comédie. Paris, 1921.

40597.1.12 Floyd, J.H. Women in the life of Balzac. N.Y., 1921.

43611.4.35 Foley, Charles. Fleur d'ombre. Paris, 1921.

43611.1.25.48 Fort, Paul. Aux pays des Moulins. Paris, 1921.

43611.1.25.26 Fort, Paul. Hélène en fleur. 4. éd. XXVI. Paris, 1921.

43611.1.25.76 Fort, Paul. Selected poems and ballads. N.Y., 1921.

FL 6129.21 Foster, E.A. Le dernière séjour de Rousseau à Paris, 1770-1778. Northampton, 1921.

FL 6129.21.5 Foster, E.A. Le dernière séjour de Rousseau à Paris, 1770-1778. Northampton, 1921.

42576.62.2.5 France, Anatole. Balthasar. 61. éd. Paris, 1921.

42576.62.180A France, Anatole. Les contes de Jacques Tournebroche. Paris, 1921.

42576.62.30 France, Anatole. Les désirs de Jean Servien. 60. éd. Paris, 1921.

42576.62.28 France, Anatole. L'étui de nacre. 107. éd. Paris, 1921.

42576.63.10 France, Anatole. Le miracle de la pie. Paris, 1921.

42576.62.17.10A France, Anatole. Monsieur Bergeret in Paris. London, 1921.

42576.62.15.10 France, Anatole. Pierre Nozière. 87. éd. Paris, 1921.

42576.62.6.3 France, Anatole. La rôtisserie de la reine Pédauque. 381. éd. Paris, 1921.

43612.2.36 Fraudet, René. La bataille. Paris, 1921.

43741.51.800 Gahisto, Manoel. Edmond Pilon. Paris, 1921.

43616.41.110 Gaillard de Champris, Henry. Anniversaires et pèlerinages. Québec, 1921.

43616.51.1110 Galtier-Boissière, Jean. Loin de la rifflette. Paris, 1921.

43616.83.100 Gasquet, Joachim. Il y a une volupté dans la douleur. Paris, 1921.

1921 - cont.

37568.25 Gaultier, Paul. Les maîtres de la pensée française. Paris, 1921.
37595.47 Gennrich, Friedrich. Rondeaux, Virelais und Ballanden. Dresden, 1921. 2v.
43617.4.35F Géraldy, Paul. Aimer. Paris, 1921.
43620.2.21 Gide, André. Morceaux choisis. 27. éd. Paris, 1921.
43620.2.46 Gide, André. Les nourritures terrestres. 32. éd. Paris, 1921.
43620.3.30 Gilbert, M. Celle qui s'en va. v.1-4. Paris, 1921.
41593.29.9.50 Girard, Henri. Bourgeois dilettante...E. Deschamps. Paris, 1921.
41593.29.9.51 Girard, Henri. Un bourgeois dillettante...Émile Deschamps. Thèse. Paris, 1921. 2 pam.
37543.80.5 Giraud, Victor. Les ecrivains et soldats. Paris, 1921.
43745.1.80 Goichon, A.M. (Mlle.). Ernest Psichari d'après des documents inédits. 9. éd. Paris, 1921.
38511.22.9 Gollancz, Israel. Some observations on a manuscript of the life and feats of arms of Edward, prince of Wales. London, 1921.
42575.56.5 Goncourt, Edmond de. Chérie. Paris, 1921.
43625.6.30 Gosselin, L.L.T. Les grognards; comédie. Paris, 1921.
37566.140 Gourmont, Rémy de. The book of masks. Boston, 1921.
43625.3.79.15A Gourmont, Rémy de. Decadence and other essays on the culture of ideas. N.Y., 1921.
NEDL 43625.3.55 Gourmont, Rémy de. Lettres à l'Amazone. 11e éd. Paris, 1921.
43625.3.57 Gourmont, Rémy de. Lettres à Sixtine. 4e éd. Paris, 1921.
43625.3.58 Gourmont, Rémy de. Petits crayons. Paris, 1921.
40556.26.5 Goyau, Georges. La pensée religieuse de Joseph de Maistre. Paris, 1921.
41593.34.40 Guérin, Maurice de. Le cahier vert. Paris, 1921.
43628.1.85 Guitry, Sacha. Le comédien. Paris, 1921.
43628.1.49 Guitry, Sacha. Deburau. N.Y., 1921.
43628.1.44 Guitry, Sacha. Je t'aime. Paris, 1921.
43628.99.100.5F Guyot, C. La toison d'or. Paris, 1921.
38546.60 Hallays, André. Madame de Sévigné. Paris, 1921.
37548.38.10 Hamelius, P. Introduction à la littérature française et flamande de Belgique. Bruxelles, 1921.
43631.2.63.25 Hamp, Pierre. People. N.Y., 1921.
43631.2.51 Hamp, Pierre. Vieille histoire. 4. éd. Paris, 1921.
40597.2.10.5 Hanotaux, Gabriel. La jeunesse de Balzac. Paris, 1921.
40522.20 Havens, G.R. The Abbé Prévost and English literature. Baltimore, 1921.
40522.20.5 Havens, G.R. The Abbé Prévost and English literature. Princeton, 1921.
43632.3.32A Hémon, Louis. Maria Chapdelaine. N.Y., 1921.
43632.3.35 Hémon, Louis. Maria Chapdelaine. N.Y., 1921.
43632.3.33 Hémon, Louis. Maria Chapdelaine. N.Y., 1921.
43632.3.31 Hémon, Louis. Maria Chapdelaine. N.Y., 1921.
43632.3.31.5A Hémon, Louis. Maria Chapdelaine. N.Y., 1921.
43632.3.40A Hémon, Louis. Maria Chapdelaine. N.Y., 1921.
43632.3.30.5 Hémon, Louis. Maria Chapdelaine. Paris, 1921.
43632.3.30.8 Hémon, Louis. Maria Chapdelaine. Paris, 1921.
43632.3.31.6 Hémon, Louis. Maria Chapdelaine. Toronto, 1921.
43632.3.30.15 Hémon, Louis. Maria Chapdelaine. 297. éd. Paris, 1921.
43632.3.30.20 Hémon, Louis. Maria Chapdelaine. 509. éd. Paris, 1921.
43632.3.30.25 Hémon, Louis. Maria Chapdelaine. 688. éd. Paris, 1921.
43632.6.230 Henriot, Émile. Les temps innocents. Paris, 1921.
42543.65.30 Hermant, Abel. Le crépuscule tragique. Paris, 1921.
37597.10.11 Högberg, Paul. Une édition rarissime du Roman de la rose. n.p., 1921.
41573.23.6.5 Hugo, Victor. Notre Dame de Paris. London, 1921.
37596.120.5 Huon le Roi de Cambrai, 13th cent. Huon le Roi, Le vair palefroi. 2. éd. Paris, 1921.
43667.14.140 Jacob, Max. Le laboratoire central; poésies. Paris, 1921.
43667.14.180 Jacob, Max. Le roi de Béotie. 4. éd. Paris, 1921.
43667.51.130 Jaloux, Edmond. L'ennemi des femmes. Paris, 1921.
43667.51.60 Jaloux, Edmond. La fin d'un beau jour. Paris, 1921.
43667.1.46 Jammes, Francis. Le livre de Saint Joseph. Paris, 1921.
43667.1.25 Jammes, Francis. Mémoires. Paris, 1921-23. 3v.
43667.1.105 Jammes, Francis. Le tombeau de Jean de la Fontaine suivi de poèmes mésurés. 3. éd. Paris, 1921.
43667.78.100 Jarry, Alfred. Ubu roi. Paris, 1921.
37598.5A Jeanroy, Alfred. Chansons satiriques et bachiques du XIIIe siècle. Paris, 1921.
43738.1.85 Johannet, René. Itinéraires d'intellectuels. Paris, 1921.
40556.20.7 Joubert, Joseph. Lettres à Madame de Vintimille. Paris, 1921.
43670.89.100 Jouhandeau, M. La jeunesse de Théophile. 4. éd. Paris, 1921.
43670.94.200 Jouve, Pierre Jean. Toscanes. Genève, 1921.
43670.99.100 Jozercan, K. Le voeu. Poitier, 1921.
42544.2.8.10 Kistemaeckers, Henry. La passante. Paris, 1921.
38564.36.5 La Bruyère, J. de. Extraits des caractères de La Bruyère. Paris, 1921.
38521.30.8 Lachèvre, Frédéric. Les oeuvres libertines de Cyrano de Bergerac. Paris, 1921. 2v.
FL 361.60 Lacour, Léo. Les premières actrices françaises. Paris, 1921.
42555.1.9A Laforgue, Jules. Dragées, Charles Beaudelaire, Tristan Corbiere. Paris, 1921.
42555.1.10 Laforgue, Jules. Exil, poésie, spleen. Paris, 1921.
42555.1.35 Laforgue, Jules. Moralités légendaires. Paris, 1921.
41578.14 Lamartine, Alphonse de. Poèmes choisies. Manchester, 1921.
43687.59.100 Landry, Eugène. Oeuvres choisies. Macon, 1921.
41522.18.480 Lang, Georges E. Charles Baudelaire jugé par Ernest Feydeay. Paris, 1921.
37530.40 Lanson, Gustave. Manuel bibliographique de la littérature française moderne. v.1-2. Paris, 1921.
43687.77.1120 Larrouy, Maurice. Rafaël Gatouna, Français d'occasion; roman. Paris, 1921.
43687.83.120 Lasserre, Pierre. Portraits et discussions. Paris, 1921?
42544.24.40.2 Lavedan, Henri. Le chemin du salut. II, Gaudias. v.1-2. Paris, 1921.
37543.249 Le Bidois, Georges. L'honneur au miroir de nos lettres. Paris, 1921.
42576.41.30 Le Blanc, Maurice. The three eyes. N.Y., 1921.
43688.2.57 Le Cardonnel, Louis. A Sainte Térèse de Jésus. Saint-Félicien-en-Vivarais, 1921.
43688.14.3120 Leclèrc, Tristan. L'éscarbille d'or. Paris, 1921.
43688.14.3110 Leclèrc, Tristan. Humoresques. Amiens, 1921.
43688.27.100 Lefebvre, L. La prière d'un homme. Paris, 1921.
37596.117.5 Le Garçon et L'Aveugle. Le garcon et l'aveugle, jeu du XIIIe siècle. 2. éd. Paris, 1921.
43688.8.32 Le Goffic, Charles. L'abbesse du Guérande. Paris, 1921.

1921 - cont.

43688.8.18 Le Goffic, Charles. Poésies complètes. Paris, 1921.
40526.65 Le Laé, Claude Marie. La vie les oeuvres comiques. Paris, 1921.
37574.300 Lély, Gilbert. Chefs-d'oeuvre des poètes galants du XVIIIe siècle. Paris, 1921.
FL 6119.07.4 Lemaitre, J. Jean-Jacques Rousseau. Paris, 1921.
43688.61.100 Lenormand, Henri René. Le simoun. Paris, 1921.
43688.61.110 Lenormand, Henri René. Théâtre complet. Paris, 1921-1938. 9v.
43688.4.45 Levaillant, M. Des vers d'amour. Paris, 1921.
43688.4.33 Levaillant, M. La porte secrète. Paris, 1921.
43688.91.104 Level, Maurice. Crises; tales of mystery and horror. 3rd ed. London, 1921.
37569.54 Lievre, Pierre. Esquisses critiques. 1e Série. Paris, 1921.
42542.64.13.35 Ligue des patriotes. La glorification de Déroulède à Metz. Paris, 1921.
42544.34.21F Lorde, André de. Napoléonette. Paris, 1921.
37597.9.15F Lorris, Guillaume de. Der Roman von der Rose. Wien, 1921.
Mol 612.16 Lyonnet, H. Les "premières" de Molière. Paris, 1921.
37576.621 Macklin, A.E. Twenty nine short stories. London, 1921.
42545.3.48 Maeterlinck, Maurice. L'hôte inconnu. Paris, 1921.
42545.3.21.6 Maeterlinck, Maurice. Sininen lintu. Porvoossa, 1921.
V43500.187 Magallon, Xavier de. L'ombre. Paris, 1921.
43697.34.130 Magre, Maurice. Sin, féerie chinoise. Paris, 1921.
43697.74.101.5 Maran, René. Batouala. Paris, 1921.
43697.74.102 Maran, René. Batouala. Paris, 1921.
43697.74.100 Maran, René. Batouala. Paris, 1921.
43697.74.101 Maran, René. Batouala. Paris, 1921.
43697.74.103 Maran, René. Batouala. Paris, 1921.
43697.75.100 Marcel, Gabriel. Le coeur des autres. Paris, 1921.
42576.77.10 Marguerite, Victor. Leilah. Paris, 1921.
40535.29.15 Marivaux, Pierre Carlet de Chamblain de. Le spectateur français. Paris, 1921.
43697.78.3130 Marsan, Eugène. Amazones. Abbeville, 1921.
43697.78.120 Martinet, Marcel. La nuit. Paris, 1921.
42562.38.1 Mauclair, C. Paul Adam, 1862-1920. Paris, 1921.
43697.89.104 Maurois, André. Les silences du Colonel Bramble. Paris, 1921.
42514.28.32 Maurras, Charles. Inscriptions. Paris, 1921.
43697.99.110 Mazade, Fernand. De sable et d'or; poèmes. Paris, 1921.
40575.5.11 Michaut, G. Sainte-Beuve. Paris, 1921.
43699.3.40 Mille, Pierre. Memoires d'un dada besogneux. 7. éd. Paris, 1921.
42545.28.3 Mirbeau, Octave. Théâtre. Paris, 1921. 2v.
Mol 228.70 Molière, Jean Baptiste Poquelin. Le malade imaginaire. Paris, 1921?
Mol 62.53 Molière, Jean Baptiste Poquelin. Sämtliche Werke. München, 1921. 6v.
38527.9.25 Mongreclien, Georges. Étude sur la vie et l'oeuvre de Nicolas Vauquelin. Paris, 1921. 2 pam.
42555.60.3 Montesquiou-Fezensac, Robert de. Les délices de capharnaüm. Paris, 1921.
Htn 42555.60.8* Montesquiou-Fezensac, Robert de. Diptyque de Flandre. Triptyque de France. Paris, 1921.
42555.60.10 Montesquiou-Fezensac, Robert de. Élus et appelés. Paris, 1921.
43701.62.170 Montfort, Eugène. La soirée perdue. Abbeville, 1921.
37556.23.50 Morillot, Paul. Le roman français durant l'époque classique (1610-1800). London, 1921.
41596.4.21 Moroncine, E. Alfred de Musset e l'Italia. Milano, 1921.
42515.35.177 Mott, Lewis F. Ernest Renan. N.Y., 1921.
42545.45.11.3F Népoty, L. La cigale ayant aimé. Paris, 1921.
41543.8.10 Nerval, Gerard de. La bohème galante. Paris, 1921.
42576.35.10 Nesselstrauss, B. Flauberts Briefe, 1871-1880. Halle, 1921.
42545.45.17F Nigond, Gabriel. Sophie Arnould. v.1-2. Paris, 1921.
43709.3.134 Noailles, Anna E. Les éblouissements. 34e éd. Paris, 1921.
41556.18.5 Nodier, Charles. The luck of the bean-rows. London, 1921.
41556.28 Nodier, Charles. Moi-même. Paris, 1921.
38525.22.15 Nolhac, Pierre de. Ronsard et l'humanisme. Paris, 1921.
42587.37.8 Noussanne, H. de. Un foyer, un pays, un ciel. Paris, 1921.
43709.89.30 Nouveau, Germain. Valentines et autres vers. Paris, 1921.
38539.85 L'oeuvres des conteurs français. Paris, 1921.
38512.145.2 Orsier, Joseph. Un ambassadeur de Savoie en Angleterre. 2e éd. Paris, 1921.
43730.85.100 Otte, Guy. Fleurs d'oubli, fleurs des champs, fleurs d'amour, fleurs fanées. Louhans, 1921.
38526.42.10 Palissy, B. Recepte veritable. Strasbourg, 1921.
37572.38.10 Paris, Gaston. Chrestomathie du moyen âge. 13. éd. Paris, 1921?
38514.21.6.5 Paris, Gaston. François Villon. 3e éd. Paris, 1921.
43737.89.1130 Paulhan, Jean. Le pont traversé. Paris, 1921.
43738.49.110 Pellerin, Jean. La romance du retour. Paris, 1921.
43738.60.100 Pemjian, L. Cyrano de Bergerac. Paris, 1921.
43738.76.170 Pergaud, Louis. Les rustiques. Paris, 1921.
43738.77.100 Pérochon, Ernest. Nêne. Paris, 1921?
43740.1.47 Philippe, Charles Louis. Le Père Perdrix. Paris, 1921.
37543.187 Pilon, Edmond. Figures françaises et littéraires. Paris, 1921.
43743.59.100 Ponchon, Raoul. La muse au carbaret. Paris, 1921.
43743.75.110 Porché, François. Les commandiments du destin. Paris, 1921.
43743.1.39 Porché, François. La Dauphine; comédie. Paris, 1921.
38537.25.40 Porto, Filippo. Studi Rabelesiani. Catania, 1921.
42545.88.5 Porto-Riche, G. Le passé; comédie. Paris, 1921.
38585.40A Racine, Jean. Mithridate. Chicago, 1921.
43752.57.780 Ramuz, Charles Ferdinand. Es geschehen Zeichen; roman. Basel, 1921.
43752.57.100 Ramuz, Charles Ferdinand. Salutation paysanne et autres morceaux. Genève, 1921.
43752.57.775 Ramuz, Charles Ferdinand. Die Sühne in feuer Gedichte und Novellen. Basel, 1921.
38587.9.10 Regnard, Jean François. Chefs d'oeuvres dramatiques. Paris, 1921?
42556.27.20 Régnier, Henri de. Portraits et souvenirs. 5e éd. Paris, 1921.
42556.27.30 Régnier, Henri de. Vestigia flammae. Paris, 1921.
42515.30.330 Renan, Ernest. Essai psychologique sur Jésus-Christ. Paris, 1921.
42515.25.40 Renan, Ernest. Pages françaises. Paris, 1921.
42515.25.24 Renan, Ernest. Páginas escogidas. 2a. ser. San José, 1921.
42587.51.27 Renard, Jules. Nos frères farouches. 2. éd. Paris, 1921.

Chronological Listing

1921 - cont.

42587.51.25	Renard, Jules. L'oeil Clair suivi de chroniques théâtrales et divers inédits. Paris, 1921.
42563.39.05	Revon, M. René Boylesve. Paris, 1921.
43753.99.2110	Reynaud, J. Polymnie. St. Félicien, 1921.
43755.3.110	Rhaïs, Elissa. Les juifs. Paris, 1921.
42556.22.115	Richepin, Jean. Le coin des fous. Paris, 1921.
42556.28.125	Rimbaud, Isabelle. Reliques. 3e éd. Paris, 1921.
42556.28.75	Rimbaud, Jean Arthur. Leben und Dichtung. 2. Aufl. Leipzig, 1921.
42587.55.27	Rivoire, André. Fleurs de cendre. Paris, 1921.
FL 6119.21	Roland-Holst, Henriette. Jean-Jacques Rousseau. München, 1921.
43757.50.767	Rolland, Romain. Clerambault; the story of an independent spirit during the war. N.Y., 1921.
43757.50.21	Rolland, Romain. Pages choisis. v. 2, 2. éd. Paris, 1921. 2v.
43757.50.402	Rolland, Romain. Pierre et Luce. 11e éd. Paris, 1921.
38525.20.65	Ronsard, Pierre de. La bouquinade et autres gaillardises. Paris, 1921.
38525.18.5	Ronsard, Pierre de. Sonnets pour Hélène. Paris, 1921.
42578.22.10.65	Rosny, J.H. Les pures et les impures. v.1-2. Paris, 1921.
42578.22.35	Rosny, J.H. Torches et lumignons. Paris, 1921.
42546.14.5.60	Rostand, Edmond. Cyrano de Bergerac. N.Y., 1921.
42546.15.15A	Rostand, Edmond. La dernière nuit de Don Juan. Paris, 1921.
42541.31.25F	Rostand, Edmond. La dernière nuit de Don Juan. Paris, 1921.
38547.2A	Rostand, Edmond. Deux romanciers de Provence. Paris, 1921.
42546.10.2	Rostand, Edmond. Plays of Edmond Rostand. N.Y., 1921. 2v.
43757.83.33	Rostand, Maurice. La gloire. Paris, 1921.
43757.83.30	Rostand, Maurice. La messe de cinq heures. Paris, 1921.
42546.15.20.3F	Rothschild, Henri de. Le caducée; pièce. Paris, 1921.
43757.33.100	Rougier, Paul. La victoire. Paris, 1921.
FL 6002.921A	Rousseau, J.J. Vie et oeuvres de Jean-Jacques Rousseau. Boston, 1921.
41587.20.160	Rousseau, Pierre Joseph. Die Portierfrau. Berlin, 1921.
38537.25.25	Sainéau, Lazar. L'histoire naturelle et les branches connexes dans l'oeuvre de Rabelais. Paris, 1921.
38542.26.5	Saint Evremond, C. de M. de S.D. Critique littéraire. Paris, 1921.
43761.49.240	Salmon, André. L'amant des Amazones. Paris, 1921.
43761.49.110	Salmon, André. Peindre. Paris, 1921.
43761.49.180	Salmon, André. Ventes d'amour. Paris, 1921.
42556.29.19	Samain, Albert. Oeuvres. Paris, 1921- 3v.
40516.59	San-Giorgiu, J. Sébastien Merciers dramaturgische Ideen im "Sturm und Drang." Inaug. Diss. Basel, 1921.
38557.22.15	Sanders, E.K. Jacques Benigne Bossuet. London, 1921.
43761.6.30	Sarment, Jean. Le pêcheur d'hombres; comédie. Paris, 1921.
43761.5.30	Savoir, Alfred. La huitième femme de Barbe-bleue. Paris, 1921.
43763.3.30	Schneider, Édouard. Le dieu d'Argile. Paris, 1921.
43763.2.45	Schopfer, Jean. Petite ville. Paris, 1921.
43763.2.30	Schopfer, Jean. Quand la terre trembla; roman. v.1-4. Paris, 1921.
42556.30.5	Schuré, Edouard. Le double. 4. éd. Paris, 1921.
42587.57.4	Schwob, Marcel. Oeuvres. Paris, 1921. 2v.
43765.21.30	Sée, Edmond. Un ami de jeunesse. Paris, 1921. 2 pam.
43765.31.120	Ségalen, Victor. Les immemoriaux. Paris, 1921.
42543.1.12	Seillière, E. L'évolution passionnelle dans le théâtre contemporain. Paris, 1921.
FL 6139.21	Seillière, Ernest. Jean-Jacques Rousseau. Paris, 1921.
38544.1.10	Seillière, Ernest. Le romancier du Grand Condé. Paris, 1921.
40575.5.70	Seilliere, Ernest. Saint-Beuve agent, juge et complice de l'evolution romantique. Paris, 1921.
43765.77.2100	Serstevens, Albert t'. Petites trilogies. Paris, 1921.
43780.7.110	Suberville, Jean. Le Dieu inconnu. 2. éd. Paris, 1921?
42557.5.40	Tailhade, Laurent. Les reflets de Paris, 1918-19. Paris, 1921.
42556.35.30	Tellier, Jules. Les deux paradis d'Abd-er-Rhaman. Paris, 1921.
Mol 620.4	Tiersot, Julien. La musique dans la comédie de Molière. Paris, 1921?
Mol 620.3A	Tilley, Arthur. Molière. Cambridge, 1921.
42578.51.60	Tinayre, Marcelle. Les lampes voilées, Laurence-Valentine. 19. éd. Paris, 1921.
42578.51.35.10	Tinayre, Marcelle. La rebelle. Paris, 1921.
43792.90.105	Toulet, Paul Jean. Les contrerimes. Paris, 1921.
38585.16.10	Truc, Gonzague. Le cas Racine. Paris, 1921.
FL 395.270	Truffier, Jules C. Comédie-française, 1914-1918. Paris, 1921.
37568.20	Turquet-Milnes, G. Some modern French writers. N.Y., 1921.
42547.10.23	Vallette, Marguerite. Les Rageac. Paris, 1921.
43822.89.120	Vautel, Clément. Les folies bourgeoises. Paris, 1921.
42557.11.25	Verhaeren, Émile. Les heures du soir. 7. éd. Paris, 1921.
42557.18.20	Verlaine, Paul. Poèmes saturniens. Paris, 1921.
40556.39.15	Vermale, François. Notes sur Joseph de Maistre inconnu. Chambéry, 1921.
43824.4.36F	Villetard, P. Le château sous les roses; roman. v. 1-4. Paris, 1921.
43824.4.43	Villetard, P. M. et Mme. Bille. Paris, 1921?
43824.4.40	Villetard, P. Monsieur Bille dans la tourmente. Paris, 1921.
38523.3.12	Villey, Pierre. Tableau chronologique des publications de Marot. Paris, 1921.
42556.32.90	Vinchon, Émile. Maurice Rollinat. Paris, 1921.
39545.105	Voltaire, François Marie Arouet de. Das lächeln Voltaires, ein Buch in dise Zeit. Leipzig, 1921.
37562.46	Voretzsch, Carl. Altfranzösisches Lesebuch zur Erlänterung der altfranzösischen Literaturgeschichte. Halle, 1921.
37574.605	Walch, G. Poètes d'hier et d'aujourd'hui. Paris, 1921.
37562.35.10	Witthoff, Johannes. Motiv des Zweikampfes zwischen Vater und Sohn. Nürnberg, 1921.
42547.44	Wolff, Pierre. Les ailes brisées. Paris, 1921.
42547.42	Wolff, Pierre. Le chemin de Damas. Paris, 1921.
42547.28	Wolff, Pierre. Théâtre. Paris, 1921.
42584.23.35	Zola, Emile. Poèmes lyriques. Paris, 1921.
43757.50.800	Zweig, Stefan. Romain Rolland. Frankfurt, 1921.
41593.36.10	Zyromski, Ernest. Maurice de Guérin. Paris, 1921.

1922

37543.114.10	Abry, E. Histoire illustrée de la littérature française. 7. éd. Paris, 1922.
Mol 878.3	Academie Française, Paris. Fêtes du tricentenaire de la naissance de Molière. Paris, 1922
37596.175	Aitken, Marion Y.H. Étude sur le Miroir...de Robert de Gretham. Thèse. Paris, 1922.
43522.41.120	Alibert, François Paul. Odes. Paris, 1922.
37543.146	Allain, Maurice. Histoire générale de littérature française. Paris, 1922.
43523.41.775	Amiel, Denys. La sorridente signora Beudet. Milano, 1922.
43523.41.103	Amiel, Denys. La souriante Madame Beudet. Paris, 1922.
42553.32.25	Amiel, Henri F. Fragments d'un journal intime. Genève, 1922. 3v.
FL 6139.22	Amiel, Henri F. Jean-Jacques Rousseau. N.Y., 1922.
NEDL Mol 601.3	Angot, E. Roles et caractères dans les comédies de Molière. Paris, 1922.
37569.165	Annuaire international des lettres et des arts. Carcassonne, 1922.
43526.65.135	Apollinaire, Guillaume. La fin de Babylone. Paris, 1922.
42562.38.15.25	Ardel, H. Un conte bleu. 29e éd. Paris, 1922.
43528.88.120	Artus, Louis. Le vin de ta vigne. Paris, 1922.
38544.27.550	Ashton, Harry. Mme. de La Fayette, sa vie et ses oeuvres. Cambridge, Eng., 1922.
37564.102.15A	Atkinson, Geoffroy. The extraordinary voyage in French literature from 1700 to 1720. Paris, 1922.
40587.35	Audwin, M. Supernaturalism and satanism in Chateaubriand. Chicago, 1922.
FL 6077.80	Ayres, E.H. Histoire de l'impression et de la publication de la lettre à d'Alembert de Jean-Jacques Rousseau. Menasha, 1922.
42563.8	Bac, Ferdinand. La volupté romaine. Paris, 1922.
40596.8.6	Balzac, Honoré de. Comédie humaine. Études de moeurs. Scènes de la vie de campagne. Paris, 1922-23. 4v.
40597.36.5	Balzac, Honoré de. Traité de la vie elegante suivi de la théorie de la démarche. Paris, 1922.
43537.72.100	Baranger, Léon. A la terrasse. Paris, 1922.
41574.607	Barbey d'Aurevilly, Jules. Victor Hugo. Paris, 1922.
42563.16.13.20	Barrès, Maurice. La colline inspirée. Paris, 1922.
42563.16.13.25	Barrès, Maurice. La colline inspirée. Paris, 1922.
42563.19.5	Barrès, Maurice. Un homme libre. Paris, 1922.
42563.20.15	Barrès, Maurice. Un jardin sur l'Oronte. 28. éd. Paris, 1922.
43537.80.100	Baschet, Jacques. Le refuge. pt. 1. Paris, 1922.
43537.4.45	Bataille, Henry. La chair humaine. Paris, 1922.
43537.4.47	Bataille, Henry. Notre image. Paris, 1922.
43537.4.44	Bataille, Henry. La possession. Paris, 1922.
43537.4.42.5	Bataille, Henry. La tendresse. L'homme à la rose. Paris, 1922.
43537.4.6	Bataille, Henry. Théâtre complet. Paris, 1922-30. 12v.
41522.13.8.4	Baudelaire, Charles. Les fleurs du mal. Münich, 1922.
41522.6	Baudelaire, Charles. Les fleurs du mal. Paris, 1922.
43537.89.2100	Baumann, Émile. Job le prédestiné. Paris, 1922.
37567.204	Beaume, G. Au pays des lettres. Parmi les vivants et les morts. Paris, 1922.
42542.28.2.10	Becque, Henri. Théâtre complet. Paris, 1922-24. 2v.
42542.28.2.12	Becque, Henri Théâtre complet. Paris, 1922. 2v.
Mol 602.11	Beekom, W.L. van. De la formation intellectuelle et morale de la femme, d'après Molière. Thèse. Paris, 1922.
43538.7.34	Benjamin, René. Les plaisirs du hasard. Paris, 1922.
43538.7.35	Benjamin, René. Les plaisirs du hasard. Paris, 1922.
43538.74.100A	Béraud, Henri. Martyre de l'obèse. Paris, 1922.
43538.10.31	Bernard, Jean J. Le feu qui reprend mal; pièce en trois actes. Paris, 1922.
43538.10.35	Bernard, Jean J. Martine; pièce. Paris, 1922.
42542.29.28.15	Bernard, Tristan. My love, Mon amour. Paris, 1922.
42542.29.48	Bernstein, H. Judith. Paris, 1922.
41557.10.26	Bertaut, Jules. Une amitie romantique. Paris, 1922?
41596.66.10	Berthier, Alfred. Le désaccord Veyrat-Raymond, 1841-1843. Paris, 1922.
43538.81.120	Beslou, Jaime de. Les cloches de Saint-Amarain. Paris, 1922.
40582.7.25	Beyle, Henri. Stendhal (Henri Beyle). 2. éd. Paris, 1922.
40582.2.40	Beyle, Henri. Vie du Rossini. Paris, 1922. 2v.
37569.2	Billy, André. La muse aux besicles. Photoreproduction. Paris, 1922.
42563.23.25	Bloy, Léon. Lettres à sa fiancée. Paris, 1922.
38546.52.10	Boissier, G. Mme. de Sévigné. 10. éd. Paris, 1922.
42575.53.7	Bordeaux, A. La jeunesse d'Octave Feuillet, 1821-1890. 9. éd. Paris, 1922.
42563.36.100	Bordeaux, Henry. Le fantôme de la rue Michel-Ange. Paris, 1922.
42563.36.96	Bordeaux, Henry. The house that died. N.Y., 1922.
42563.36.105	Bordeaux, Henry. Le lac noir, ou Le sorcier de Myans. Paris, 1922.
42563.36.95	Bordeaux, Henry. La maison morte. Paris, 1922.
41522.64.40	Borel d'Hauterive, Petrus. Champavert. Paris, 1922.
41522.67.30	Borel d'Hauterive, Petrus. Rhapsodies. Paris, 1922.
43544.109.100	Bouchardon, Pierre. Le mystère du chateau de Chamblas. Paris, 1922.
Mon 112.9.5	Bouillier, Victor. La fortune de Montaigne en Italie et en Espagne. Paris, 1922.
42542.44.7	Bourdet, Édouard. L'heure du berger. Paris, 1922.
42542.44.5	Bourdet, Édouard. L'heure du berger. Paris, 1922.
Htn 42576.15.37*	Bourget, Paul. Gustave Flaubert. Discours. Paris, 1922.
42563.37.53	Bourget, Paul. Nouvelles pages de critique et de doctrine. Paris, 1922. 2v.
43544.89.100	Bousquet, Joë. Comédienne. Paris, 1922.
43544.88.100	Boussac de Saint-Marc, A. Le loup de Gubbio. Paris, 1922.
43544.88.101	Boussac de Saint-Marc, A. Le loup de Gubbio. Paris, 1922.
43544.90.100	Bouvelet, Jehan. Barbe-blonde. Paris, 1922.
43620.2.80	Braak, Sybrandi. André Gide et l'âme moderne. Amsterdam, 1922?
43545.3.120	Brandenburg, A.J. Le poème royal. Paris, 1922.
42542.47.37	Brieux, Eugène. L'avocat. Paris, 1922.
38514.52.10	Bronarski, Alphonse. Le petit Jehan de Saintré, une énigme littéraire. Florence, 1922.
43537.34.100	Bugnet, Charles. Le collier de pierres de lune. Paris, 1922.
43547.77.130	Burnat-Provins, Marguerite. Contes en vingt lignes. Saint-Raphaël, 1922.
38576.48.50	Bussom, Thomas W. The life and dramatic works of Pradon. Paris, 1922.
38576.48.52	Bussom, Thomas W. A rival of Racine. Paris, 1922.

1922 - cont.

38527.41.2 Busson, Henri. Dans l'orbe de la pléiade. Charles d'Espinay évêque de Dol. Thèse. Paris, 1922.
42563.23.8.80 Cabeen, David C. The African novels of Louis Bertrand. Thesis. Philadelphia, 1922.
38526.45.30.2 Cabos, Alban. Guy du Faur de Pibrac. Paris, 1922.
38526.45.30 Cabos, Alban. Guy du Faur de Pibrac. Thèse. Paris, 1922.
39527.4.45 Cacudi, N. La Fontaine, imitateur de Boccace. Bari, 1922.
43550.1.32 Carco, Francis. L'homme traqué. Paris, 1922.
37566.60 Carrere, Jean. Les mauvais maîtres. Paris, 1922.
41522.17.40 Cerini, Matteo. La poesia di Carlo Baudelaire. Catania, 1922.
43552.1.115 Chabaneix, Philippe. Les tendres amies. Paris, 1922.
43552.2.100 Chadourne, Louis. Accords, suivi d'autres poèmes. 4e éd. Paris, 1922.
39586.19.1 Chamfort, S.R.N. Maximes et pensées de Chamfort. Paris, 1922.
43554.4.3100 Charasson, Henriette. Jules Tellier. Paris, 1922.
43552.5.100 Chardonne, Jacques. L'épithalame. Paris, 1922. 2v.
43552.5.103 Chardonne, Jacques. L'épithalame. Paris, 1922. 2v.
43552.5.105 Chardonne, Jacques. L'épithalame. v. 1-2. Paris, 1922.
43552.5.2110 Charles-Étienne. Léon dit Léonie. Paris, 1922.
43552.3.6100 Charpentier, Léon. L'épopée de la vieille Ecosse. Paris, 1922.
40586.55 Chateaubriand, F.A.R. Amour et vieillesse. Paris, 1922.
43606.89.88 Chevalier, Adrien. L'Italie de Gabriel Faure. Saint-Félicien-en-Vivarais, 1922.
37555.385A Clarke, Charles C. Concerning French verse. New Haven, 1922.
43554.2.65 Claudel, Paul. Poëmes de guerre, 1914-1916. Paris, 1922.
43554.8.100 Clauzel, R. La maison au soleil. pts. 1-2. Paris, 1922.
43554.7.45 Clemenceau, Georges. At the foot of Sinai. N.Y., 1922.
41574.95 Clement-Janin, Noël. Victor Hugo en exil. 5e éd. Paris, 1922.
43701.77.3100 Clouard, Henri. Aurel. Paris, 1922.
43556.1.46 Cocteau, Jean. Vocabulaire, poèmes. Paris, 1922.
43556.49.161 Colette, Sidonie Gabrielle. Chéri. Paris, 1922.
43556.49.180 Colette, Sidonie Gabrielle. La maison de Claudine. Paris, 1922.
42557.27 Corbel, H. Un poéte, Gabriel Vicaire (1848-1900). Paris, 1922.
38574.23 Corneille, Pierre. Théâtre choisi. Paris, 1922.
39586.21.6 Cornou, François. Elie Fréron, 1718-1776. Paris, 1922.
42586.32.100 Coster, Charles de. The legend of Ulenspiegel and Lamme Gaedzak. Garden City, N.Y., 1922. 2v.
37596.243 Courtois d'Arras. Courtois d'Arras, jeu du XIIIe siècle. Paris, 1922.
42554.26.100 Cros, Charles. Le coffret de santal. 4e éd. Paris, 1922.
42542.58.16 Curel, François de. Le coup d'aile. Paris, 1922.
42542.58.18 Curel, François de. L'ivresse du sage. Paris, 1922.
43565.5.160 Daudet, Léon A. Les dicts et pronostiquations d'Alcofribas deuxième. Paris, 1922.
43565.5.80 Daudet, Léon A. Les oeuvres dans les hommes. Paris, 1922.
42542.61.17 Decourcelle, P. L'autre fils. Paris, 1922.
42566.16.160 Degoumois, Léon. L'Algérie d'Alphonse Daudet. Genève, 1922.
38521.30.9 Dehénault, Jean. Les oeuvres de Jean Dehénault. Paris, 1922.
43566.48.210 Delarue-Mardrus, Lucie. L'ex-voto. Paris, 1922.
FL 384.115 Delini, J. Nos vedettes. Paris, 1922.
40575.5.60 Deschamps, Jules. Sainte-Beuve et les sillage de Napoleon. Liège, 1922.
37543.144.30.5 Des Granges, C.M. Précis de littérature française. 17. éd. Paris, 1922.
39564.23 Diderot, Denis. Ist er gut? Ist er böse? Dresden, 1922.
43568.91.140 Divoire, F. Orphée. Paris, 1922.
37555.521 Dondo, M.M. Vers libre, a logical development of France verse. Thesis. Paris, 1922.
42542.65.27 Donnay, Maurice. La belle angevine. Paris, 1922.
41557.10.23.2 Doumic, René. George Sand. Paris, 1922.
FL 6139.19.2F Draper, John N. The summa of romanticism. N.Y.? 1922?
43574.65.100 Droin, Alfred. A l'ombre de Saint-Odile. Paris, 1922.
37567.17 Dugas, L. Les grands timides; J.J. Rousseau, Constant, Chateaubriand. Paris, 1922.
37555.109 Duhamel, G. Les poètes et la poésie 1912-1914. Paris, 1922.
43576.6.190 Duhamel, Georges. Carré et Lerondeau. Paris, 1922.
43576.6.180 Duhamel, Georges. Le combat. 4. éd. Paris, 1922.
43576.6.130 Duhamel, Georges. Lettres d'Auspasie. Paris, 1922.
37555.554 Dujardin, Édouard. Les premiers poètes du vers libre. Paris, 1922.
41574.234 Dullaert, M. Victor Hugo à Bruxelles. Bruxelles, 1922.
43576.1.45 Dumas, André. Ma petite Yvette. Paris, 1922.
37566.65 Duquesnel, Félix. Souvenirs littéraires. Paris, 1922.
43576.77.175 Durtain, Luc. Douze cent mille. 5. éd. Paris, 1922.
43576.91.40 Duvernois, Henri. La dame de bronze et le monsieur de cristal. Paris, 1922.
43576.91.35.2F Duvernois, Henri. Morte la bête. Paris, 1922. 2 pam.
42513.48.25 Eliott, A. Madame Adam (Juliette Lamber)...1870-71. Paris, 1922.
41593.17.3.55 Enfield, D.E. A lady of the salons. The story of Louise Colet. London, 1922.
43598.84.108 Estaunié, Édouard. L'appel de la route. Paris, 1922.
43598.84.130 Estaunié, Édouard. "Bonne dame". Paris, 1922.
38526.14.100 Esternod, C. d'. L'espadon satyrique. 1e éd. Paris, 1922.
37557.51 Étienne, S. Le genre romanesque en France. Paris, 1922.
Mol 825.15 Farez, Paul. Les médecins de Molière. Paris, 1922.
43606.78.230 Farrère, Claude. Trois promenades. Paris, 1922.
43606.89.65 Faure, Gabriel. Printemps. Paris, 1922.
43606.89.100 Fauré-Fremiet, P. Le souffle du désordre. Paris, 1922.
43607.76.120 Féret, Charles Théophile. Les couronnes. Paris, 1922.
42521.19.3 Fernessole, Pierre. Les origines littéraires de Louis Veuillot (1813-1843). Paris, 1922.
41564.55 Fierini, Mario. Alfred de Vigny; saggio critico. Bari, 1922.
42576.35.3 Flaubert, Gustave. Correspondance. Paris, 1922-1925. 4v.
42576.17.31 Flaubert, Gustave. L'éducation sentimentale. Paris, 1922.
42576.17.28 Flaubert, Gustave. Salammbô. Paris, 1922.
42576.17.29 Flaubert, Gustave. La tentation de Saint-Antoine. Paris, 1922.
37578.44 Fleuret, Fernand. Les satires françaises du XVIe siècle. Paris, 1922. 2v.
41522.17.35A Flottes, Pierre. Baudelaire. Paris, 1922.
38562.18.15 Fontenelle, B. Le B. de. L'ésprit de Fontenelle. Paris, 1922.

1922 - cont.

43611.1.25.29 Fort, Paul. L'arbre à poèmes. XXIX. Paris, 1922.
43611.1.47 Fort, Paul. Ballades françaises. v.1-5, 7-15. Paris, 1922-53. 14v.
43611.1.50 Fort, Paul. Florilège des Ballades françaises. Paris, 1922.
43611.1.25.53 Fort, Paul. Louis XI, curieux homme. Paris, 1922.
42576.62.6.30 France, Anatole. At the sign of the reine Pédauque. London, 1922.
42576.63.17.3 France, Anatole. The man who married a dumb wife. N.Y., 1922.
42576.63.19 France, Anatole. Les matinées de la villa Saïd. 91. éd. Paris, 1922.
42576.62.88 France, Anatole. Les noces corinthiènnes. Paris, 1922.
42576.62.112 France, Anatole. On life and letters. 3d series. London, 1922.
42576.62.100 France, Anatole. The opinions of Anatole France. N.Y., 1922.
42576.63.21 France, Anatole. La vie en fleur. Paris, 1922.
42576.63.21.6 France, Anatole. La vie en fleur. 53. éd. Paris, 1922.
38525.9.5 Franchet, Henri. Le poète et son oeuvre d'après Ronsard. Thèse. Paris, 1922.
38513.47 Frank, Grace. La passion du Palatinus - Mystère du XIVe siècle. Paris, 1922.
43612.3.35 Frappa, Jean José. Molière. Paris, 1922.
Mol 870.63 Frappa, Jean José. Molière: pièce. Paris, 1922.
43612.2.39 Fraudet, René. L'insoumise. Paris, 1922.
43612.2.37 Fraudet, René. Le reflet. Paris, 1922.
43616.59.100 Gandéra, Felix. Atout...coeur. Paris, 1922.
FL 363.28 Garçon, Émile. Du crime...avec l'art dramatique. Paris, 1922.
NEDL 37596.30.1 Garnier de Pont Sainte Maxence. La vie de Saint Thomas le martyr. Lund, 1922.
42543.45.46 Gavault, Paul. Monsieur l'Adjoint. Paris, 1922.
FL 394.115.10 Genest, E. La maison de Molière. Paris, 1922.
43617.59.220 Genevoix, Maurice. Rémi des rauches. Paris, 1922.
43617.4.36 Géraldy, Paul. Aimer. Paris, 1922.
43617.4.38 Géraldy, Paul. Carnet d'un auteur dramatique. Paris, 1922.
43619.24.110 Ghéon, Henri. Le débat de Nicolazia entre Sainte Anne et le recteur. Paris, 1922.
43620.2.60 Gide, André. Saül. Paris, 1922.
37548.38.20 Gilles, M. Histoire des lettres françaises de Belgique des origines à nos jours. Bruxelles, 1922.
Htn FL 382.80* Ginisty, Paul. France d'antan: le théâtre romantique. Paris, 1922.
41541.8.15 Girardin, Delphine Gay. La joie fait peur. Bielefeld, 1922.
42563.18.90 Giraud, Victor. Les maîtres de l'heure: Maurice Barrès. Paris, 1922.
43620.74.145.8 Giraudoux, Jean. Provinciales. 8. éd. Paris, 1922.
43620.74.106 Giraudoux, Jean. Siegfried et le limousin. 17. éd. Paris, 1922.
42543.49.6 Glatigny, Albert. Poésies complètes. Paris, 1922?
Htn 43625.3.250* Gourmont, Jean de. Bibliographie des oeuvres de Rémy de Gourmont. Paris, 1922.
43625.3.48 Gourmont, Rémy de. Le puits de la vérité. Paris, 1922.
43625.3.79.25 Gourmont, Rémy de. Very woman. N.Y., 1922.
38526.17.12 Grévin, Jacques. Théâtre complet et poésies choises. Paris, 1922.
43628.1.42 Guitry, Sacha. L'amour masqué. Paris, 1922.
38526.22.01 Habert, François. Le philosophe parfaict, et Le temple de vertu. Thèse. Paris, 1922.
39527.7.10 Hallays, André. Jean de La Fontaine. Paris, 1922.
43631.2.44 Hamp, Pierre. La peine des hommes; le cantique des cantiques. 3. éd. Paris, 1922. 2v.
43631.2.46 Hamp, Pierre. La peine des hommes; un nouvel honneur. 4. éd. Paris, 1922.
NEDL 37565.60 Hatzfeld, H. Geschichte der französischen Aufklärung. München, 1922.
43632.6.240 Henriot, Émile. Aquarelles. Paris, 1922.
FL 380.30 Hérissay, Jacques. Le monde des théâtres pendant la révolution, 1789-1800. Paris, 1922.
42571.38 Hervieu, Paul. La course du flambeau. Boston, 1922.
41574.34.5 Heugel, Jacques. Essai sur la philosophie de Victor Hugo. Paris, 1922.
42572.85 Hinzelin, E. Erckmann-Chatrian. Paris, 1922.
43633.1.35 Hirsch, Charles H. La danseuse rouge. 6. éd. Paris, 1922.
41573.2 Hugo, Victor. Le conservateur littéraire 1819-1821. pt. 1,2. Paris, 1922-38. 4v.
41572.24.9A Hugo, Victor. Les contemplations. Paris, 1922. 3v.
43644.4.100 Icard, Renaud. Le livre d'amour. Lyon, 1922.
43667.14.130 Jacob, Max. Art poétique. Paris, 1922.
43667.51.140 Jaloux, Edmond. L'éscalier d'or. Paris, 1922.
43667.51.230 Jaloux, Edmond. Les profondeurs de la mer. 24. éd. Paris, 1922.
43667.1.48 Jammes, Francis. Le poète et l'inspiration. Neines, 1922.
FL 6139.22.5 Johnson, Mary L. Contemporary opinion of Rousseau in English periodicals. Thesis. Raleigh, N.C., 1922.
37596.64.10 Kjellman, Hilding. La deuxième collection anglo-normande des miracles de la Saint Vierge. Paris, 1922.
42557.5.80 Kolney, Fernand. Laurent Tailhade. Paris, 1922.
42544.26.1 Labiche, Eugène. Théâtre complet. Paris, 1922-23. 10v.
38527.60.5 La Boétie, Estienne de. Discours de la servitude volontaire. Paris, 1922.
42533.17.25 Laborde-Milau, A. Un essayiste, Emile Montégut, 1825-1895. Paris, 1922.
37555.20.15 Lachèvre, F. Bibliographie des recueils collectifs de poésies du XVI siècle. Paris, 1922.
38521.30.10 Lachèvre, Frédéric. Les successeurs de Cyrano de Bergerac. n.p., 1922.
38521.30.4.2 Lachèvre, Frédéric. Supplément. Additions et corrections. Les recueils collectifs de poésies. Supplément. Paris, 1922.
41574.160 Lacretelle, Pierre de. La véritable édition originale des Châtiments. Paris, 1922.
38513.26.10 Lacroix, Paul. Recueil de farces. Paris, 1922?
39527.2.3 Lafenestre, Georges. La Fontaine. 5e éd. Paris, 1922.
38543.30.5 La Mothe le Vayer, F. de. Deux dialogues faits à l'imitation des anciens. Paris, 1922.
37569.1 Lang, André. Voyage en zigzags dans la république des lettres. Paris, 1922.
38567.12.15 Lanson, Gustave. Boileau. 6. éd. Paris, 1922.
43687.75.100 Larguier, Léo. L'après-midi chez l'antiquaire. Paris, 1922.

Chronological Listing

1922 - cont.

37567.185	Lasserre, Pierre. Cinquante ans de pensée français. 7e éd. Paris, 1922.
43687.83.110	Lasserre, Pierre. La promenade insolite. 11e éd. Paris, 1922.
43537.76.100	Le Bargy, C.G.A. Une danseuse est morte. Paris, 1922. 2 pam.
42578.49.80	Lebey, André. Jean de Tinan, souvenirs et correspondance. Paris, 1922.
42576.41.25	Le Blanc, Maurice. The eight strokes of the clock. N.Y., 1922.
42576.41.35	Le Blanc, Maurice. The tremendous event. N.Y., 1922.
37547.2	Leclerc, Marc. Poètes angevins d'aujourd'hui. Paris, 1922.
42555.36.790	Leconte de Lisle, C.M.R. Erinii. St. Petersburg, 1922.
43688.49.110	Le Leu, Louis. La semence sanglante. Paris, 1922.
38585.14.7.5	Lemaitre, Jules. Jean Racine. Paris, 1922.
43688.59.50	Lenéru, Marie. Journal. 9e éd. v.1-2. Paris, 1922.
43688.59.45	Lenéru, Marie. Journal of Marie Lenéru. Paris, 1922. 2v.
43688.59.100	Lenéru, Marie. La paix. Paris, 1922.
40587.42	Levaillant, Maurice. Splendeurs et misères de Chateaubriand. 3. éd. Paris, 1922.
Mol 712.8	Levi, Cesare. Molière. Roma, 1922.
43690.1.80	Lichtenberger, A. Notre Minnie. 30e éd. Paris, 1922.
37596.17.5	Livingston, C.H. Li dis Raoul Hosdaing. n.p., 1922.
42544.34.24	Lorde, André de. Théâtre rouge. 3e éd. Paris, 1922.
42557.11.175	Mabille de Poncheville, André. Deux maisons du poète. Gand, 1922?
42557.11.171	Mabille de Poncheville, André. Fünf Erzählungen. Leipzig, 1922.
43697.6.50	Machard, Alfred. Titine, histoire d'un viol. Paris, 1922.
37576.621.3	Macklin, A.E. Twenty nine tales from the French. N.Y., 1922.
42545.3.135	Maeterlinck, Maurice. The great secret. N.Y., 1922.
42545.3.22.10	Maeterlinck, Maurice. Mary Magdalene. Paris, 1922.
Mol 713.16	Magne, Emile. Une amie inconnue de Molière. 3. éd. Paris, 1922.
43697.34.800	Magre, Maurice. L'oeuvre amoureuse et sentimentale de Maurice Magre. Paris, 1922.
43697.3.35	Mandelstamm, V. New York. pt.1-4. Paris, 1922.
43697.74.104	Maran, René. Batouala. N.Y., 1922.
43697.75.4130	Marchon, Albert. Sous le signe de la vierge. Paris, 1922.
43697.74.2100	Margueritte, Lucie Paul. A jolie fille, joli garçon. Paris, 1922.
42576.77.11	Margueritte, Victor. La garconne. Paris, 1922.
41522.67.80	Marie, Aristide. Petrus Borel, le lycanthrope. Paris, 1922.
40535.29.17	Marivaux, Pierre Carlet de Chamblain de. La provinciale. Genève, 1922.
43697.77.3100	Marmouset. Au lion tranquille. Paris, 1922.
42545.9.50	Martel de Janville, S.G. Souricette. Paris, 1922.
37567.190	Martinenche, E. Histoire de l'influence espagnole sur la littérature française. Paris, 1922.
43697.79.190	Mary, André. Le livre des idylles et passe-temps. Paris, 1922.
43709.3.815	Masson, G.A. La Comtesse de Noailles, son oeuvre. Paris, 1922.
43611.1.100	Masson, Georges A. Paul Fort. Paris, 1922.
43697.82.2100	Massot, Pierre de. De Mallarmé à 391. Saint-Raphaël, 1922.
38529.60	Mathorez, J. Mathurine et les libelles publiés sous son nom. Paris, 1922.
37567.66.11	Mauclair, Camille. Servitude et grandeur litteraires. Paris, 1922.
42577.1.4	Maupassant, Guy de. Oeuvres complètes. Paris, 1922-1932. 29v.
43697.89.410	Maurois, André. Les discours du Docteur O'Grady. Paris, 1922.
43697.89.710	Maurois, André. General Bramble. N.Y., 1922.
37567.198A	Maurras, C. Romantisme et révolution. Paris, 1922.
42514.28.50	Maurras, Charles. Pages littéraires choisies. 5. éd. Paris, 1922.
43757.50.830	Maxe, Jean. Le bolchevisme littéraire. Paris, 1922.
37573.622	Mélanges. Paris, 1922.
43698.75.100F	Méré, Charles. La flamme. Paris, 1922.
41586.23.20	Méry, Joseph. Quatre nouvelles humoristiques. Paris, 1922.
Mol 713.15A	Michaut, G. La jeunesse de Molière. Paris, 1922.
43698.203.100	Michelet, M. Marraine de guerre. N.Y., 1922.
43699.3.42	Mille, Pierre. Myrrhine, courtisane et martyre. Paris, 1922.
43699.65.130	Miomandre, Francis de. Ces petits messieurs. 7. éd. Paris, 1922.
43699.65.220	Miomandre, Francis de. Les taupes. Paris, 1922.
Mol 878.5	Modern Languages. Molière tercentenary, special no. v.3. no. 6. London, 1922.
42545.28.19.5	Moinaux, Jules. Les deux sourds; comédie en un acte. Paris, 1922.
Mol 191.30	Molière, Jean Baptiste Poquelin. Dom Juan. Strasbourg, 1922.
38557.49.40	Monod, A. La controverse de Bossuet et de R. Simon au sujet de la "Version de Trévoux". Strasbourg, 1922.
43886.10	Monsier Jalabert. Paris, 1922.
Mon 19.22	Montaigne, Michel de. Les essais de Michel de Montaigne. Paris, 1922-23. 3v.
Mon 28.30	Montaigne, Michel de. Montaigne. Preface de Anatole France. Paris, 1922.
42555.60.6	Montesquiou-Fezensac, Robert de. Le mort remontant. Paris, 1922.
42555.60.13	Montesquiou-Fezensac, Robert de. La trépidation. Paris, 1922.
37568.40A	Montfort, Eugène. Vingt-cinq ans de littérature française. Paris, 1922-1926. 2v.
37543.145A	Morize, André. Problems and methods of literary history. N.Y., 1922.
37530.177	Morize, André. Survey of French periodicals. n.p., 1922.
FL 6118.73.9	Morley, John Morley. Rousseau. London, 1922. 2v.
41596.8.16	Musset, Alfred de. Premières poésies, 1828-1833. Paris, 1922.
43705.83.120	Natanson, J. L'enfant truque. Paris, 1922.
43705.2.35	Naudeau, Ludovic. Plaisir du Japon. pts. 1-2. Paris, 1922.
41543.17.25	Nerval, Gerard de. Daughters of fire. N.Y., 1922.
42545.45.18	Nigond, Gabriel. Sophie Arnould. Paris, 1922.
37543.178	Nitze, W. Albert. A list of French literature from the earliest times to the great war. N.Y., 1922.

1922 - cont.

Location	Call number	Entry
	42555.67	Nolhac, Pierre de. Ausonia Victrix. Abbeville, 1922.
	42545.62.9	Pailleron, Edouard. L'autre motif. Paris, 1922.
	37555.87	Pardo Bazan, E. El lirismo en la poesia francesca. Madrid, 1922?
	41542.4.10	Patch, Helen E. The dramatic criticism of Théophile Gautier. Diss. Bryn Mawr, 1922.
	43738.50.100	Pellerin, J.V. 32 décembre suivi de quelques mirlitons antérieurs. Paris, 1922.
	FL 361.65	Péricaud, L. Le panthéon des comédiens. Paris, 1922.
	43738.77.700	Pérochon, Ernest. Nêne. N.Y., 1922.
	43738.83.100	Pesquidoux, J.D. Sur la glèbe. Paris, 1922.
	43741.21.100	Piéchaud, M. Mademoiselle Pascal. Paris, 1922.
	43741.50.1100	Pillet, Roger. Les oraisons amoureuses de Jeanne Aurélie Grivolin. Paris, 1922.
	43741.88.102	Pittard, Hélène (Mme.). Le nouveau déluge. Paris, 1922.
	43741.88.100	Pittard, Hélène (Mme.). Le nouveau déluge. pts.1-5. Paris, 1922.
	43743.2.35	Poizat, A. Circé. Paris, 1922.
	43743.1.41	Porché, François. Le chevalier de Colomb. Paris, 1922.
	43743.90.110	Pourrat, Henri. Gaspard des Montagnes. Paris, 1922.
	42578.31.64	Prévost, Marcel. Les Don Juanes. 53. éd. Paris, 1922.
	38583.11	Racine, Jean. Lettres à son fils. Paris, 1922.
	38585.40.15	Racine, Jean. Mithridate; tragédie. Chicago, 1922.
	41522.18.12	Raynaud, Ernest. Charles Baudelaire. Paris, 1922.
	43753.90.150	Reverdy, P. Cravates de Chanvre Illustré d'eauxfortes. Paris, 1922.
	42556.22.130	Richepin, Jean. Les glas. Paris, 1922.
	42556.28.10	Rimbaud, Jean Arthur. Oeuvres complètes. Paris, 1922. 3v.
	37574.77A	Ritchie, R.L.G. French verse from Villon to Verlaine. London, 1922.
	43756.90.120	Rivière, Jacques. Aimée. 15. éd. Paris, 1922.
	43756.2.40	Rivollet, G. Les Phéniciennes. Paris, 1922.
	43757.50.431A	Rolland, Romain. L'âme enchantée. v. 1-2; v. 3, pt. 1-2; v. 4, pt. 1-3. Paris, 1922-33. 7v.
	43757.50.702A	Rolland, Romain. Pierre and Luce. N.Y., 1922.
	43757.50.300	Rolland, Romain. Les vaincus; drame. Anvers, 1922.
	43757.3.37	Romains, Jules. Lucienne. 14e éd. Paris, 1922.
	43757.3.79	Romains, Jules. Quand le navire. 47e éd. Paris, 1922.
	37597.42	Roman des romans. Deux poèmes moraux anglo-français. Le roman des romans et le sermon de vers. Paris, 1922.
	38525.20.25A	Ronsard, Pierre de. Ronsard lyrique et amoureux. Paris, 1922.
	42578.22.10.50	Rosny, J.H. Dans la nuit des coeurs. Paris, 1922.
	42546.15.16	Rostand, Edmond. Le cantique de l'aile. Paris, 1922.
	42546.14.5.62	Rostand, Edmond. Cyrano de Bergerac. Garden City, 1922.
	42546.14.8.15	Rostand, Edmond. Cyrano von Bergerac. Stuttgart, 1922.
	43757.83.34A	Rostand, Maurice. La gloire. Paris, 1922.
	43757.83.35	Rostand, Maurice. La mort de Molière. Paris, 1922. 3 pam.
	41522.17.25	Rougemout, Edouard de. Commentaires graphologiques sur Charles Boudelaire. Paris, 1922.
X Cg	FL 6002.922	Rousseau, J.J. Extraits publiés avec une introduction. L. Brunel. 13. éd. Paris, 1922.
	FL 6024.10	Rousseau, J.J. Jean-Jacques Rousseau en Savoie; Annecy, chambéry, les charmettes. Chambéry, 1922.
	38557.24.15	Rouvier, Frédèric. Le coeur du Maitre d'après Bossuet. Lille, 1922.
X Cg	38537.18.5	Sainéau, L. La langue de Rabelais. Paris, 1922-23. 2v.
	43761.41.5100	St. Sorny. Bicchii. Paris, 1922.
	Mol 719.10	Salza, Livia. Molière nel III centenario della sua nascita. Novara, 1922.
	41593.16.10	Samie, Lucy. À l'aube du romanticisme, Chênedollé and Extraits du journal de Chênedollé. Thèse. v.1-2. Caen, 1922.
	43761.6.32	Sarment, Jean. Le mariage d'Hamlet. Paris, 1922.
	37574.355	Sauvage, R.N. Poesies latines et française sur la convalescence de Louis XV (1744). Rouen, 1922.
	43761.5.32	Savoir, Alfred. Bauco! Paris, 1922.
	43763.38.216	Schlumberger, Jean. Le camarade infidèle. 21. éd. Paris, 1922.
	43763.40.3120	Schwab, Raymond. La conquête de la joie. Paris, 1922.
	40597.8.15	Seillière, Ernest. Balzac et la morale romantique. Paris, 1922.
	37555.13.5	Sévrette, Gaston. Les vieilles chansons des pays de France. Paris, 1922.
	39533.22.5	Sorel, Charles. La jeunesse de Francion, texte de 1626. Paris, 1922.
	FL 6119.22	Stark, Georg. Rousseau und das Gefühl. Schwabach, 1922.
	37568.35	Strowski, F. La rénaissance littéraire. 4e éd. Paris, 1922.
	42557.5.55	Tailhade, Laurent. Petits memoires de la vie. Paris, 1922.
	Mon 170.2.5	Taylor, J.S. Montaigne and médicine. N.Y., 1922.
	43788.5.190	Tharaud, Jérôme. La randonnée de Samba Diouf. Paris, 1922.
	43788.5.170A	Tharaud, Jérôme. Tragédie de Ravaillac. Paris, 1922.
NEDL	42576.15.40	Thibaudet, A. Gustave Flaubert. Paris, 1922.
	37563.24.10	Tilley, Arthur A. Studies in the French renaissance. Cambridge, 1922.
	42578.51.50	Tinayre, Marcelle. Le bouclier d'Alexandre. Paris, 1922. 2 pam.
	42578.51.67	Tinayre, Marcelle. Priscille Séverac. 8. éd. Paris, 1922.
	42578.51.70	Tinayre, Marcelle. Priscille Séverac. 11. éd. Paris, 1922.
	43822.49.170	Valéry, Paul. Le serpent. Paris, 1922.
	39544.68	Valles, Charles de. La propriété du coeur de Voltaire. Paris, 1922.
	37566.55	Valois, Georges. D'un siècle à l'autre. 3e éd. Paris, 1922.
	43822.4.35	Variot, Jean. La belle de Haguenau; comédie. Paris, 1922.
	43822.89.130	Vautel, Clément. Mademoiselle Sans-Gêne. Paris, 1922.
	42557.11.50	Verhaeren, Emile. La multiple splendeur; poèmes. 21. éd. Paris, 1922.
	42557.20.7	Verlaine, Paul. Correspondance. Paris, 1922-29. 3v.
	42557.18.10	Verlaine, Paul. Gesammelte Werke in zwei Bänden. Leipzig, 1922. 2v.
	37567.147	Viatte, Auguste. Le catholicisme chez les romantiques. Paris, 1922.
	42576.52.4.25	Viaud, Julien. Pêcheur d'Islande. Boston, 1922.
	42557.25.110	Vielé-Griffin, F. Couronne offerte a la muse romaine. Paris, 1922.
	42557.25.130	Vielé-Griffin, F. La rose au flot, légende du Paitou. Paris, 1922.

1922 - cont.

38543.34 Viguié, Pierre. L'honnête homme au XVIIe siècle le Chevalier de Méré. Paris, 1922.
38514.20.14.25 Villon, François. Les lais. Paris, 1922.
37573.28.5 Walch, Gerard. Antologie des poètes français contemporains, 1866-1914. Paris, 1922-24. 3v.
42584.23.300 Zola, Emile. Das Glück der Familie Rougon. München, 1922.
42584.23.340 Zola, Emile. Nana. München, 1922.
42584.23.320 Zola, Emile. Die Sünde des Abbé Mouret. München, 1922.

1923

43514.5.100 Adam, Juliette. La chanson des nouveaux époux. Paris, 1923.
37593.62.23A Adam de la Halle. Adam le Bossu. Paris, 1923.
37593.62.24A Adam de la Halle. Adam le Bossu. 2. éd. Paris, 1923.
37543.143.5 Adami, J. Précis de littérature avec de nombreuses citations. 2. éd. Paris, 1923.
43522.41.130 Alibert, François Paul. Eglogues. Paris, 1923.
43522.41.210 Alibert, François Paul. Elégies romaines. Paris, 1923.
FL 382.84A Allard, Louis. La comédie de moeurs en France au XIXe siècle. Cambridge, Mass., 1923.
43523.41.110 Amiel, Denys. Le voyageur. Paris, 1923.
42557.14.11 Aressy, Lucien. La dernière bohème, Verlaine et son milieu. Paris, 1923.
43528.56.100 Armont, Paul. L'école des cocottes. Paris, 1923.
Mol 601.5 Arnavon, J. La représentation de la comédie classique. Paris, 1923.
FL 398.7.33 Arthur, George. Sarah Bernhardt. London, 1923.
FL 371.60 Axelson, Angelica. Supernatural beings in the French medieval dramas...miracles of the Virgin. Copenhagen, 1923.
37566.67A Bacourt, Pierre de. French literature during the last half century. N.Y., 1923.
43537.50.110 Baldensperger, F. La croisée des routes; poesies, 1901-1914. Paris, 1923.
Htn 40597.33.9* Balzac, Honoré de. Les cahiers balzaciens. v.1-4, 5-8. Paris, 1923-28. 2v.
40597.32.75 Balzac, Honoré de. La Rabouilleuse. Paris, 1923.
38526.22.12 Banachévitch, N. Jean Bastier de La Péruse, 1529-1554. Paris, 1923.
40597.2.38 Barnes, Helen E. A study of the variations between the original and the standard editions of Balzac's Les Chouans. Chicago, 1923.
38527.60.7 Barrère, Joseph. L'humanisme et la politique. Paris, 1923.
42563.16.20 Barrès, Maurice. Dante, Pascal et Renan. Paris, 1923.
42515.35.26 Barrès, Maurice. Ernest Renan. Abbeville, 1923.
43537.4.60 Bataille, Henry. Vers préférés. Paris, 1923.
41522.6.2 Baudelaire, Charles. Quelques-uns de mes contemporains. Paris, 1923.
Mol 730.15 Baumal, F. Molière, auteur précieux. Paris, 1923.
42563.21.76A Bazin, René. Il était quatre petits enfants. 14. éd. Paris, 1923.
42563.21.76.5 Bazin, René. Il était quatre petits enfants. 54. éd. Paris, 1923.
42563.21.70 Bazin, René. Stéphanette. 21. éd. Paris, 1923.
37543.152F Bedier, Joseph. Histoire de la littérature française illustrée. Paris, 1923. 2v.
42556.30.81 Beer, G. (Mme.). Un celte d'Alsace; la vie...d'Edouard Schuré. Paris, 1923.
43538.61.62 Benoît, Pierre. Koenigsmark. 221. éd. Paris, 1923.
FL 398.7.19.9 Bernhardt, Sarah. Ma double vie; mémoires. Paris, 1923. 2v.
FL 398.7.15.5 Bernhardt, Sarah. Memories of my life. N.Y., 1923.
43538.9.40 Berthaut, Léon. Les amants de Tereul. Paris, 1923.
FL 398.7.35.5 Berton, Thérèse M. The real Sarah Berndardt, as I knew her. London, 1923.
41522.58.12 Bertrand, Louis. Le keepsake fantastique. Paris, 1923.
43538.81.110 Beslière, Jean. Le page mutilé. Paris, 1923.
43538.81.100 Beslou, Jaime de. Idéologues. Paris, 1923.
37576.623.10 The best French short stories of 1923, 1924, 1926, 1927 and the yearbook of the French short stories. Boston, 1923-28. 4v.
40582.9.20A Beyle, Henri. Chartreuse of Parma. London, 1923.
40582.2.15 Beyle, Henri. Journal. Paris, 1923.
40582.2.16 Beyle, Henri. Journal. Paris, 1923.
40582.2.35 Beyle, Henri. Le rouge et le noir. Paris, 1923. 2v.
43540.7.100 Bibescu, M.L. Isvor, le pays des saules. 5. éd. v.1-2. Paris, 1923.
43526.65.915 Billy, André. Apollinaire vivauf. Paris, 1923.
43540.74.100 Birabeau, André. Un jour de folie. Paris, 1923.
38547.13 Bochet, Henri. L'Astrée...formation de la littérature. Genève, 1923.
37569.50 Bocquet, Léon. Les destinées mauvaises. Amiens, 1923.
43544.51.100 Bollaert, A.A.J. Le porlu de l'etoile (meditations). N.Y., 1923.
42563.36.110 Bordeaux, Henry. Yamilé sous les cèdres. Paris, 1923.
43544.74.100 Bordeaux, P.H. Sur la route de Pabmyre. Paris, 1923.
43544.4.37 Botrel, Théodore. Chansons de chez nous. Paris, 1923.
43544.4.41 Botrel, Théodore. Chansons en sabots. Paris, 1923.
42542.44.10 Bourdet, Edouard. L'homme enchaîné. Paris, 1923.
42563.37.55 Bourget, Paul. La geôle. Paris, 1923.
42563.37.79 Bourget, Paul. Le roman des quatres. Paris, 1923.
38526.10.7 Boysson, Jéhan de. Les trois centuries. Toulouse, 1923.
38526.10.7.2 Boysson, Jéhan de. Les trois centuries. Thèse. Toulouse, 1923.
43545.3.130 Brandenburg, A.J. L'immortelle bien-aimée. Paris, 1923.
43545.3.100 Brandenburg, A.J. Un jeune légionnaire. N.Y., 1923.
43545.4.100 Branson, K.A. La petite illustration. Paris, 1923.
42542.47.38 Brieux, Eugène. L'enfant; comédie. Paris, 1923.
43547.76.100 Burnet, Etienne. Soin de icônes. Paris, 1923.
38527.41 Busson, Henri. Charles d'Espinay évêque de Dol, et son oeuvre poétique (1531?-1591). Paris, 1923.
37543.148A Butler, Kathleen J. A history of French literature. London, 1923. 2v.
43550.40.100 Cahuet, Albéric. Le missel d'amour. pt.1-3. Paris, 1923.
FL 385.14.5 Capeau, Jacques. Etudes d'art dramatique; critiques d'une autre temps. Paris, 1923.
FL 385.14 Capeau, Jacques. Etudes d'art dramatique; critiques d'une autre temps. 2e ed. Paris, 1923.
FL 385.14.8 Capeau, Jacques. Etudes d'art dramatique; critiques d'une autre temps. 7e ed. Paris, 1923.
43550.1.210 Carco, Francis. Rieu qu'une femme. Paris, 1923.
42576.57.115 Cario, Louis. Pierre Loti aux armées. Paris, 1923.
39545.21.4 Chabrillan, A. Une amie de Voltaire; madame de Saint-Julien. Paris? 1923.

1923 - cont.

39586.19.2 Chamfort, S.R.N. Chamfort; produits de la civilization perfectionnes. 10e éd. Paris, 1923?
37562.32.10 Champion, P. Histoire poétique du XVe siècle. Paris, 1923. 2v.
38525.21.15 Charbonnier, F. Pamphlets: Protestants contre Ronsard, 1560-1577. Paris, 1923.
38514.26.25A Charles d'Orleans. Poésies. Paris, 1923-24. 2v.
Mol 270.32 Charlier, Gustave. Le premier "Tartuffe". Paris, 1923.
38514.64.8 Chartier, Alain. Le quadriloque invectif. Paris, 1923.
43552.6.110 Chateaubriant, Alphonse de. La brière; roman. 309e éd. Paris, 1923.
43552.6.108 Chateaubriant, Alphonse de. La brière. 277e éd. Paris, 1923.
43554.2.50 Claudel, Paul. L'otage. Paris, 1923.
43556.1.795 Cocteau, Jean. A call to order. N.Y., 1923.
43556.1.33A Cocteau, Jean. Le grand écart. 7e éd. Paris, 1923.
43556.49.200 Colette, Sidonie Gabrielle. Le blé en herbe. Paris, 1923.
43556.49.182 Colette, Sidonie Gabrielle. La maison de Claudine. Paris, 1923.
43556.49.154 Colette, Sidonie Gabrielle. La vagabonde. Paris, 1923.
43556.49.145 Colette, Sidonie Gabrielle. Les vrilles de la vigne. Paris, 1923.
42542.53.17 Coolus, R. L'autruche; comédie en 3 actes. Paris, 1923.
42542.53.60 Copeau, Jacques. La maison natale. Paris, 1923.
38575.34.9.20 Corneille, Pierre. Polyeucte. N.Y., 1923.
42556.28.115 Coulon, Marcel. Le problème de Rimbaud, poéte maudit. Nîmes, 1923.
42542.58.20 Curel, François de. Terre inhumaine. Paris, 1923.
43565.88.100 Datz, Philippe P. Jours fériés. Paris, 1923.
43565.92.100 David, A. Le roman du plaisir. Paris, 1923.
42542.28.53 Dawson, E.A. Henry Becque, sa vie et son théâtre. Paris, 1923.
37558.120 Dawson, John C. Toulouse in the renaissance. N.Y., 1923.
42556.28.120 Delahaye, Ernest. Rimbaud, l'artiste et l'être moral. Paris, 1923.
43566.48.220 Delarue-Mardrus, Lucie. Marie, fille-mère; roman. Paris, 1923.
43566.87.100 Delbrel, Jean-Emile. Gine. Paris, 1923.
43566.51.300 Delteil, Joseph. Choléra par Joseph Delteil. Paris, 1923.
43566.76.130 Derennes, Charles. La fontaine jouvence. Paris, 1923.
40556.26.50 Dermenghem, E. Joseph de Maistre, mystique. Paris, 1923.
41593.29.3.15 Desbordes-Valmore, Marceline. Marceline Desbordes-Valmore et ses amis lyonnais. Paris, 1923.
41593.29.10 Deschamps, E. Un manifeste du romantisme. Paris, 1923.
37543.144.5 Des Granges, C.M. Histoire illustrée de la littérature française. 8. éd. Paris, 1923.
43566.83.120 Des Vallières, Jean. Essais sur le théâtre. v. 1-2. Paris, 1923-25.
38526.18.12 Dittmann, W. Pierre Gringore als Dramatiker. Berlin, 1923.
37566.71 Dix causeries françaises. Paris, 1923.
37556.31.9 Dordan, E. Le paysan français d'après les romans du XIXe siècle. Thèse. Toulouse, 1923.
43620.2.2 Doré, R. Les livres d'André Gide. Abbeville, 1923.
42584.25.21 Doucet, Fernand. L'esthétique d'Emile Zola et son application à la critique. Den Haag, 1923.
FL 382.82 Draper, F.W.M. Rise and fall of the French romantic drama. London, 1923.
43822.49.965 Droin, Alfred. M. Paul Valéry et la tradition poétique française. Paris, 1923.
38526.6.19 Du Bellay, Joachim. Les amours de Faustine. Amiens, 1923.
43576.12.100 Duc, R. Eux et nous. Paris, 1923.
37574.95 Duhamel, Georges. Anthologie de la poésie lyrique...XVe-XIXe. Leipzig, 1923.
39585.5.10 Dulaurens, H.J. L'Arretin. v.1-2. Rouen, 1923.
43576.57.110 Dumur, Louis. Les défaitistes, roman. Paris, 1923.
43576.70.110 Du Plessys, M. Odes olympiques. Paris, 1923.
43576.91.42 Duvernois, Henri. Seule. Paris, 1923. 2 pam.
43598.13.120 Escholier, R. La nuit; roman. Paris, 1923.
43598.84.700 Estaunié, Edouard. Call of the road. N.Y., 1923.
43598.84.100 Estaunié, Edouard. L'infirme aux mains de lumière. Paris, 1923.
37565.55 Estève, E. Etudes de littérature préromantique. Paris, 1923.
FL 383.16 Evans, D.O. Les problèmes d'actualité au théâtre, 1827-1850. Thèse. Paris, 1923.
FL 382.88 Evans, David O. Le drame moderne à l'époque romantique. Paris, 1923.
43606.8.100 Fabre, Lucien. Rabevel, ou le mal des ardents. Paris, 1923. 3v.
37555.31.50 Faguet, Emile. Histoire de la poésie française de la renaissance au romantisme. Paris, 1923-26. 11v.
42555.37.6.10 Falshaw, Gladys. Leconte de Lisle et l'Inde. Thèse. Paris, 1923.
43606.78.705 Farrère, Claude. The house of the secret. N.Y., 1923.
42543.40.15 Fauchois, R. Comédies. Paris, 1923. 2v.
FL 6129.23.5 Faure, Gabriel. Jean-Jacques Rousseau en Dauphine, 1768-1770. Grenoble, 1923.
43606.89.102 Fauré-Fremiet, P. Le souffle du désordre. Paris, 1923.
42521.19.2 Fernessole, Pierre. Bio-biliographie de la jeunesse de Louis Veuillot, 1813-1843. Thèse. Tarbes, 1923.
42521.19 Fernessole, Pierre. Les origines littéraires de Louis Veuillot, 1813-1843. Thèse. Paris, 1923.
37563.56 Festugière, Jean. La philosophie de l'amour de Marsile Fecin. Coimbra, 1923.
43609.79.110 Fischer, Max. Estelle. London, 1923.
42576.17.26 Flaubert, Gustave. Bouvard et Pécuchet. Paris, 1923.
42576.20.19 Flaubert, Gustave. L'éducation sentimentale. Paris, 1923.
42543.42.10 Flers, Robert de. Monsieur Brotonneau. Paris, 1923.
42543.42.12 Flers, Robert de. Les vignes du Seigneur; comédie. Paris, 1923.
37578.45 Fleuret, Fernand. Les satires françaises du XVIIe siècle. Paris, 1923. 2v.
40515.47A Florian, Jean P.C. de. Mémoires d'un jeune Espagnol...lettres à Mme. de La Briche. Paris, 1923.
43611.1.25.58 Fort, Paul. Les compères du Roi Louis. Paris, 1923.
41564.55.100 France, Anatole. Alfred de Vigny. Paris, 1923.
42576.62.28.7 France, Anatole. L'étui de nacre. Paris, 1923.
42576.62.28.5 France, Anatole. L'étui de nacre. Paris, 1923.
42576.62.13.15 France, Anatole. The garden of Epicurus. N.Y., 1923.
42576.62.15.75 France, Anatole. Pierre Nozière. London, 1923.
42576.62.6.8 France, Anatole. The queen Pédauque. N.Y., 1923.
42576.62.3.20 France, Anatole. Thaïs. Paris, 1923.
43612.2.41 Fraudet, René. La gardienne; pièce en 4 actes. Paris, 1923.
FL 6119.23 Fusil, C.A. Rousseau juge de Jean-Jacques. Paris, 1923.

Chronological Listing

1923 - cont.

42576.63.32 Gaffiot, M. Les théories sociales d'Anatole France. Alger, 1923.
42576.63.32.2 Gaffiot, M. Les théories sociales d'Anatole France. Thèse. Alger, 1923.
43616.52.100.5 Galzy, Jeanne. Les allonges. 35. éd. Paris, 1923.
43616.52.100 Galzy, Jeanne. Les allonges. 56. éd. Paris, 1923.
43616.62.100 Gantillon, Simon. Cyclone, pièce en deux actes. Paris, 1923.
38527.42.5 Garnier, Robert. Oeuvres complètes. Paris, 1923. 2v.
38527.42.10 Garnier, Robert. Oeuvres complètes. Paris, 1923. 2v.
43616.2.39 Gautier, Judith. Mémoires d'un éléphant blanc. 7. éd. Paris, 1923.
41542.33.10 Gautier, Théophile. Romans et contes. Paris, 1923.
42543.45.15 Gavault, Paul. Manu militari! Paris, 1923.
42576.36.50 Geffroy, G. Cécile Pommier. pt. 1-2. Paris, 1923. 2v.
37575.450 Genest, Emile. Les belles citations de la littérature française. le série. Paris, 1923.
43617.5.34 Géniaux, Charles. La résurrection d'Aphrodite; roman. Paris, 1923.
43617.7.40 Génin, Auguste. Legendes et recits du Mexique ancien. Paris, 1923?
43617.4.57 Géraldy, Paul. Le prélude. Paris, 1923.
43617.4.31.10 Géraldy, Paul. Toi et moi. Paris, 1923.
43617.74.100 Gérard, Rosemonde. Les pipeaux. Paris, 1923.
37567.165 Ghil, René. Les dates et les oeuvres; symbolisme et poésie scientifique (1883-1922). Paris, 1923.
42515.32.5 Girard, Henri. Bibliographie des oeuvres de Ernest Renan. Paris, 1923.
37543.150 Giraud, Victor. Moralistes français. Paris, 1923.
43620.74.720 Giraudoux, Jean. My friend from Limousin. N.Y., 1923.
43620.74.290 Giraudoux, Jean. La prière sur la tour Eiffel. Paris, 1923.
43620.74.730 Giraudoux, Jean. Suzanne and the Pacific. N.Y., 1923.
42543.49.7 Glatigny, Albert. Lettres d'Albert Glatigny à Théodore de Bainville. Paris, 1923.
42575.59.15 Goncourt, Edmond de. Madame Gervaisais. Paris, 1923?
37576.21 Gorceix, Septime. Le miroir de la France. Paris, 1923.
43625.3.65 Gourmont, Rémy de. L'ombre d'une femme; pièce. Paris, 1923.
43625.3.75 Gourmont, Rémy de. 1874-1880. Journal intime et inédit. Paris, 1923.
42554.49.10 Gregh, F. Couleur de la vie. Paris, 1923.
42543.1.20 Gros, Johannes. Une page du romantisme galant; A. Dumas et Marie Duplessis. Paris, 1923.
40597.2.37 Guérard, A.L. Honoré de Balzac et la Comédie Humaine. Houston, 1923?
42554.50.12 Guérin, C. Premiers et derniers vers. Paris, 1923.
41593.33.85 Guérin, Maurice de. Le centaure. 7. éd. Paris, 1923.
42586.76.15 Guillaumin, Emile. Ispoved'. Moskva, 1923.
42543.62.26 Guiraud, E. Vautrin. Paris, 1923.
43628.1.40 Guitry, Sacha. Un sujet de roman. Paris, 1923.
41574.56.3 Haggard, A.C.P. Victor Hugo; his work and his love. N.Y., 1923.
43631.2.60 Hamp, Pierre. L'art et le travail. Paris, 1923.
43631.2.63 Hamp, Pierre. Gens. Paris, 1923.
43631.2.64 Hamp, Pierre. La maison avant tout pièce. Paris, 1923.
42576.65.9 Harry, Myriam (pseud.). Les amants de Sion. 12. éd. Paris, 1923.
38537.25.30 Hatzfield, H. François Rabelais. München, 1923.
43631.89.100 Haurigot, Paul. Alphonsine. Paris, 1923.
43632.51.100 Heller, Maximilienne. La mer rouge; roman. Paris, 1923.
43632.3.65 Hémon, Louis. La belle que voilà. Paris, 1923.
43632.3.50 Hémon, Louis. My fair lady. N.Y., 1923.
43632.1.32 Hennequin, M. La sonnette d'alarme. Paris, 1923.
43632.6.160 Henriot, Emile. Livres et portraits. Paris, 1923.
FL 397.72.5 Herelle, Georges. Etudes sur le théâtre basque. La répresentation des pastorales. Paris, 1923.
39564.29 Hermand, Pierre. Les idées morales de Diderot. Paris, 1923.
43632.77.2100 Hermant, A. La vie littéraire. Paris, 1923-28. 2v.
42543.64.15A Hermant, Abel. Dernier et premier amour. Paris, 1923.
42543.65.6.25 Hermant, Abel. Le loyal serviteur. 17e éd. Paris, 1923.
42543.65.10.15 Hermant, Abel. Le proces du très honorable lord. 2e éd. Paris, 1923.
42543.65.17 Hermant, Abel. Le suborneur. 18e éd. Paris, 1923.
43632.82.100 Hesse, Raymond. Riquet à la houppe et ses compagnons. Paris, 1923.
42556.27.33.805 Hounert, Robert. Henri de Régnier. Paris, 1923.
43638.31.100 Hugard, Jane. Ces demoiselles de l'opéra. Paris, 1923.
41573.23.14 Hugo, Victor. The hunchback of Notre Dame. N.Y., 1923.
42543.69.75 Humières, Robert. Théâtre. Paris, 1923.
37555.93 Hytier, Jean. Le plaisir poétique: étude de psychologie. Thèse. Paris, 1923.
37555.91 Hytier, Jean. Les téchniques modernes du vers français. Paris, 1923.
42554.63 Ibrovac, Miodrag. José Maria de Heredia, sa vie, son oeuvre. Paris, 1923.
42554.63.2 Ibrovac, Miodrag. José Maria de Heredia, sa vie, son oeuvre. Thèse. Paris, 1923.
42554.63.6 Ibrovac, Miodrag. Les sources des "Trophées". Thèse. Paris, 1923.
43667.14.200 Jacob, Max. Filibuth; ou La montre en or. Paris, 1923.
40525.11.2 Jacoubet, Henri. Le comte de Tressan et les origines du genre troubadour. Thèse. Paris, 1923.
40525.11 Jacoubet, Henri. Le comte de Tressan et les origines du genre troubadour. Thèse. Paris, 1923.
43667.51.340 Jaloux, Edmond. L'amour de Cécile Fougères. Paris, 1923.
43667.51.105 Jaloux, Edmond. Les amours perdues. 20. éd. Paris, 1923.
43667.51.70 Jaloux, Edmond. L'ésprit des livres. 1. série. Paris, 1923.
43667.1.49A Jammes, Francis. Cloches pour deux mariages, le mariage basque, le mariage de raison. 12. éd. Paris, 1923.
43667.1.85 Jammes, Francis. Le deuxième livre des quatrains. Paris, 1923.
43667.1.80 Jammes, Francis. Le premier livre des quatrains. Paris, 1923.
43765.13.800 Jean-Desthieux, F. Alphonse Séché. Paris, 1923.
42536.40 Jean-Desthieux, F. Taine, son oeuvre. Paris, 1923.
37596.38.30 Jehan le teinturier d'Arras. Le mariage des sept arts. Paris, 1923.
43672.39.100 Kahn, G. La pépinière du Luxembourg. Paris, 1923.
43672.40.100 Karagueuz, Effendi. Le chah du Mahboulistan. Paris, 1923.
43674.23.100 Khaïry, M. Les batailles intérieures. Paris, 1923.

1923 - cont.

37556.73.3 Killen, Alice M. Le roman "terrifiant" ou roman "noir". 2. éd. Paris, 1923.
42544.2.8.18 Kistemaekers, Henry. En bombe. Paris, 1923.
42544.2.8.14 Kistemaekers, Henry. L'esclave errante; pièce en 3 actes. Paris, 1923.
42544.2.8.12 Kistemaekers, Henry. Le roi des palaces; comédie en 4 actes. Paris, 1923.
43687.15.712 Lacretelle, Jacques de. Silbermann. N.Y., 1923.
43687.15.120 Lacretelle, Jacques de. Silbermann. 79e éd. Photoreproduction. Paris, 1923.
42555.1.6 Laforgue, Jules. Oeuvres complètes, mélanges posthumes. 8. éd. Paris, 1923.
43687.51.1110 Lalou, René. Le chef. Paris, 1923.
37566.69 Lalou, René. Histoire de la littérature française contemporaine (1870 à nos jours). Paris, 1923.
37543.38.10F Lanson, Gustave. Histoire illustrée de la littérature française. Paris, 1923. 2v.
43687.68.100 Lapaire, Hugues. La treille en fleur. 2e éd. Paris, 1923.
41556.34.4 Larat, Jean. Bibliographie critique des oeuvres de Charles Nodier. Paris, 1923.
41556.34.2 Larat, Jean. Biblioographie critique des oeuvres de Charles Nodier. Thèse. Paris, 1923.
41556.34 Larat, Jean. La tradition et l'exotisme dans l'oeuvre de Charles Nodier, 1780-1844. Thèse. Paris, 1923.
NEDL 41556.34.3 Larat, Jean. La tradition et l'exotisme dans l'oeuvre de Charles Nodier. Paris, 1923.
43687.74.145 Larbaud, Valéry. Les poésies de A.O. Barnabooth. 18e éd. Paris, 1923.
42515.35.155.5 Lasserre, Pierre. Renan et nous. Paris, 1923.
37567.210 Latzarus, M.T. La littérature enfantine en France dans la seconde moitié du XIXe siècle. Thèse. Paris, 1923.
38525.21.9.5 Laumonier, P. Ronsard poète lyrique. 2. ed. Paris, 1923.
37574.602 La Vaissière, Robert de. Anthologie poétique du XXe siècle. v.1-2. Paris, 1923.
42544.24.40.3 Lavedan, Henri. Le chemin du salut. III, Panteau. v.1-2. Paris, 1923.
43885.10 La Vrille. Le journal d'une masseuse. Paris, 1923.
40583.107 Lebègue, Raymond. Étude bibliographique sur armance. Paris, 1923.
FL 383.17 Le Breton, André. Le théâtre romantique (1829-1843). Paris, 1923?
41564.54.5 Lednicki, W. Alfred de Vigny. Warszawa, 1923.
43688.35.140 Le Grand, Maurice. Le jardin des bêtes et des plantes. Paris, 1923.
38512.102 Le laie Bible. Le laie Bible, a poem of the fourteenth century. N.Y., 1923.
43688.53.100 Le Marchand, A. Raoul de Fougères. Rennes, 1923.
43688.61.710 Lenormand, Henri René. Failures. N.Y., 1923.
43688.61.125 Lenormand, Henri René. Failures. N.Y., 1923.
42557.14.5.5 Lepelletier, E. Paul Verlaine. 7. éd. Paris, 1923.
42555.39.1120 Lerberghe, C. van. Entrevisions suivi des poèmes posthumes. Paris, 1923.
43688.1.42 Leroux, Gaston. Chéri-Bibi and Cecily. London, 1923.
43688.1.44 Leroux, Gaston. Missing men. N.Y., 1923.
40512.38 LeSage, Alain René. LeSage: Historia de Gil Blas de Santillana. Boston, 1923.
FL 397.114 Liebrecht, Henri. Histoire du théâtre français à Bruxelles au XVIIe et au XVIIIe siècle. Paris, 1923.
37555.340 Limbosch, R. Le principe et l'évolution du vers français. Bruxelles, 1923-24. 3 pam.
38516.22A Löpelmann, M. Die Liederhandschrift des Cardinals de Rohan. Göttingen, 1923.
43693.59.100 Londres, A. Au bagne. Paris, 1923.
38575.23.9 Lyonnet, Henry. Les "premières" de Pierre Corneille. Paris, 1923.
37576.623.5 Macklin, A.E. Five striking stories. London, 1923.
43697.14.131 MacOrlan, Pierre. La Vénus internationale. 6e ed. Paris, 1923.
43697.14.130 MacOrlan, Pierre. La Vénus internationale. 13e ed. Paris, 1923.
42545.3.49 Maeterlinck, Maurice. The cloud that lifted and the power of the dead. N.Y., 1923.
X Cg 38543.24.5 Magne, Emile. Le vrai visage de La Rochefoucauld. 3. éd. Paris, 1923.
40556.28.5 Maistre, Joseph de. Les carnets. Lyon, 1923.
42576.57.105 Mallet, Frédéric. Pierre Loti; son oeuvre. Paris, 1923.
X Cg 43697.75.120 Marcel, Gabriel. L'iconoclaste. Paris, 1923.
38526.34.25 Marguerite d'Angoulême. Comédies. Strasbourg, 1923.
42576.77.31 Marguerite, Victor. Le compagnon. Paris, 1923.
43697.76.100 Marquet, Jean. Nestor, patron pêcheur. Paris, 1923.
43697.78.3120 Marsan, Eugène. Passantes. Paris, 1923.
43697.77.100 Martin du Gard, Roger. Les Thibault. v.1-8. Paris, 1923-40. 10v.
37567.214 Martino, Pierre. Le naturalisme français (1870-1895). Paris, 1923.
42515.36.169A Massis, Henri. Jugements. Paris, 1923.
42515.35.169 Massis, Henri. Jugements. 1. ser. Paris, 1923.
42576.63.33 Masson, G.A. Anatole France, son oeuvre. Paris, 1923.
42577.1.2 Maupassant, Guy de. Works. N.Y., 1923. 10v.
43697.88.530 Mauriac, François. Le fleuve de feu. Paris, 1923[1939]
43697.88.520 Mauriac, François. Genitrix. Paris, 1923.
43697.88.210 Mauriac, François. Les péloueyne: le baiser au lépreux. Paris, 1923.
43698.60.100 Ménez, F. L'envoûté. Paris, 1923.
43698.75.102 Méré, Charles. Le vertige. Paris, 1923.
37576.623 Michaud, R. Conteurs français d'aujourd'hui. Boston, 1923.
Mol 800.15 Michaut, G. Les débuts de Molière à Paris. Paris, 1923.
39544.220 Michelmore, G. and Co. Voltaire. London, 1923.
37567.211 Mignon, Maurice. Les affinites intellectuelles de l'Italie et de la France. Paris, 1923.
FL 370.82 Mignon, N. Études sur le théâtre français et italien de la renaissance. Paris, 1923.
43699.65.140 Miomandre, Francis de. Écrit sur l'eau. Paris, 1923.
42545.28.7.30A Mirbeau, Octave. Contes de la chaumiere. Paris, 1923.
Mol 245.103.3 Molière, Jean Baptiste Poquelin. Le misanthrope. Paris, 1923.
Mon 30.16.3 Montaigne, Michel de. Essays. London, 1923. 3v.
39594.14.2 Montesquieu, C.L. de S. Persian letters. London, 1923.
43701.62.115 Montfort, Eugène. L'oubli des morts, roman. 9. éd. Paris, 1923.
43701.74.715 Morand, Paul. Open all night. N.Y., 1923.
42555.61.10 Moréas, Jean. Oeuvres. Paris, 1923-26. 2v.
37530.177.2 Morize, André. Survey of French periodicals of literary interest. Supplement. n.p., 1923.
39544.32.10A Morley, John. Voltaire. London, 1923.

Chronological Listing

1923 - cont.

37530.35 Moura, Édouard. Catalogue de beaux livres. Paris, 1923.
43703.74.100 Muraz, Gaston. Sous le grand soleil, chez les primitifs. Coulommiers, 1923.
41596.8.17 Musset, Alfred de. Poésies nouvelles, 1833-1852. Paris, 1923.
Htn 43753.58.702* New bodies for old. N.Y., 1923.
43709.3.220 Noailles, Anna E. Les innocentes. Paris, 1923.
43709.75.100 Nogelet, Francis. Fresques du souvenir. Paris, 1923.
37566.43.2 Pailleron, M.L. (Mme.). François Buloz et ses amis: les derniers romantiques. Paris, 1923.
43737.60.110 Pange, P.L.M. Le beau jardin. Paris, 1923.
43738.49.100 Pellerin, Jean. Le bouquet inutile. 8e éd. Paris, 1923.
43738.49.120 Pellerin, Jean. Cécile et ses amours; roman. Paris, 1923?
37583.623 Pellissier, Georges. Anthologie du théâtre français contemporain. 3. éd. Paris, 1923.
43740.1.45 Philippe, Charles Louis. Der alte Perdrix. München, 1923.
43740.1.40 Philippe, Charles Louis. Die gute Madeleine und die arme Marie. München, 1923.
43740.1.30.5 Philippe, Charles Louis. La mère et l'enfant. 14e éd. Paris, 1923.
43741.21.110 Piéchaud, M. Le sommeil des amants. Paris, 1923.
43741.59.4130 Pinguet, Auguste. La chanson de l'Anjou. Paris, 1923.
38537.25.16.3 Plattard, Jean. L'adolescence de Rabelais en Poitow. Paris, 1923.
42515.35.214.5 Poincaré, R. Ernest Renan. Abbeville, 1923.
42515.35.214 Poincaré, Raymond. Ernest Renan. Paris, 1923.
43743.2.40 Poizat, A. Électre. Paris, 1923.
42515.35.215 Pommier, Jean. Renan d'après des documents inédits. Paris, 1923.
42545.85.5 Porto-Riche, G. Théâtre complet. Paris, 1923. 2v.
43743.83.100 Postel-Vinay, G. Refrains d'Espagne traduits. Paris, 1923.
37558.125 Praviel, Armand. Histoire anecdotique des jeux floraux. Toulouse, 1923.
43744.41.775 Privat, Maurice. L'avuenturiera dagli occhi verdi. Firenze, 1923.
FL 6129.23 Proal, Louis. La psychologie de Jean-Jacques Rousseau. Paris, 1923.
42578.31.78 Psichari, Jean. Typesses. Paris, 1923.
37573.724 Quatre poèmes de Francis Carco, Philippe Chabaneix, Tristan Dereme et Vincent Muselli. Paris, 1923.
43752.18.110 Radiguet, Raymond. Le diable au corps, roman. 122. éd. Paris, 1923.
43752.57.170 Ramuz, Charles Ferdinand. La séparation des races. Paris, 1923.
43528.53.132 Rapa-nui. 8e éd. Paris, 1923.
42556.21.3 Raynaud, Ernest. Souvenirs de police. Paris, 1923. 3v.
43753.30.102 Regis, L. Bastos le hardi. Paris, 1923.
Htn 38514.15.10* Regnier, Jehan. Les fortunes et adversitez. Paris, 1923.
38514.15.10.2A Regnier, Jehan. Les fortunes et adversitez. Paris, 1923.
43753.2.31.10 Régnier, M.L.A. de. Le séducteur. Paris, 1923.
43574.1.81 Regnier, Paul. Paul Drouot. Paris, 1923.
43753.58.1100 Renaitour, Jean Michel. L'enfant chaste. Paris, 1923.
42515.34.15 Renan, Ernest. Nouvelles lettres intimes, 1846-1850. Paris, 1923.
42515.36.10 Renan, Ernest. Valentine de Milan; Christene de Suède. Abbeville, 1923.
42556.22.140 Richepin, Jean. Interludes. Paris, 1923.
37548.38.9 Ridder, André de. La littérature flamande contemporaine. 1890-1923. Anvers, 1923.
41522.3.110 Risolo, Michel. Barbey d'Aurevilly. Napoli, 1923.
42578.31.122 Robida, A. Le trésor de Carcassonne. Paris, 1923?
42546.8.41 Rodenbach, G. Oeuvres. Paris, 1923-25. 2v.
42536.30 Roe, F.C. Taine et l'Angleterre. Paris, 1923.
42536.31 Roe, F.C. Taine et l'Angleterre. Thèse. Paris, 1923.
43757.50.763 Rolland, Romain. The montespan. N.Y., 1923.
43757.50.778 Rolland, Romain. Peter und Lutz. München, 1923.
43757.50.352 Rolland, Romain. Théâtre de la révolution: 14 juillet - Danton - Les loups. 5e éd. Paris, 1923?
43757.50.785 Rolland, Romain. Vidas ejemplares: Beethoven - Miguel Angel - Tolstoi. México, 1923.
37597.42.5 Roman des romans. Le roman des romans. Princeton, 1923.
38525.14.25 Ronsard, Pierre de. La fleur des musiciens. Paris, 1923.
38525.14.15 Ronsard, Pierre de. La fleur des poésies. v.1-2,3-4. Paris, 1923. 2v.
38525.14.5 Ronsard, Pierre de. Oeuvres complètes. Paris, 1923-25. 7v.
42546.14.5.63 Rostand, Edmond. Cyrano de Bergerac. N.Y., 1923.
43757.83.63 Rostand, Maurice. Les insomnies. Paris, 1923.
43757.83.40 Rostand, Maurice. Le masque de fer; pièce...en vers. Paris, 1923.
43757.83.37 Rostand, Maurice. Le phénix. Paris, 1923.
FL 6015.16 Rousseau, J.J. Matériaux pour la correspondance. Paris, 1923.
43757.98.130 Royère, Jean. Quiétude. Paris, 1923.
37543.167 Rudler, Gustave. Les techniques de la critique et de l'histoire littéraires en littérature française moderne. Oxford, 1923.
V43500.283 Ruet, Noël. L'ombre et le soleil. Bruxelles, 1923.
43761.41.190 St. Georges de Bouhelier. La tragédie de Tristan et Iseult. Paris, 1923.
40575.23 Sainte-Beuve, Charles A. Literarische Portraits aus dem Frankreich. Frankfurt, 1923. 2v.
FL 6139.13.3.2 Sakmann, P. Jean-Jacques Rousseau. 2. Aufl. Leipzig, 1923.
43761.59.103 Sandy, Isabelle. Andorra, ou Les hommes d'Airain. Paris, 1923.
43761.59.100 Sandy, Isabelle. Andorra, ou Les hommes d'Airain. v.1-4. Paris, 1923.
43761.6.15 Sarment, Jean. Le mariage d'Hamlet. 4e éd. Paris, 1923.
43761.6.38 Sarment, Jean. Les six grimaces de Don Juan. Paris, 1923.
43761.3.35 Savignon, André. Le secret des laux. v.1-3. Paris, 1923.
43761.5.34 Savoir, Alfred. La couturière de Lunéville; comédie. Paris, 1923.
43761.5.36 Savoir, Alfred. La nouvelle Héloise; comédie. Paris, 1923.
43763.3.32 Schneider, Édouard. Le dieu d'Argile. Paris, 1923.
43763.2.40 Schopfer, Jean. Mademoiselle Bourrat. Paris, 1923.
43763.41.107 Schultz, Yvonne. Les nuits de fer. Roman. Paris, 1923.
42587.57.35 Schwob, Marcel. Le livre de Monelle. Paris, 1923.
43744.67.80.5 Scott-Moncrieff, Charles Kenneth. Marcel Proust; an English tribute. Photoreproduction. N.Y., 1923.
38546.21.14 Scudéry, Madeleine de. Isabelle, Grimaldi, princesse de Monaco; roman. 4. éd. Paris, 1923.

1923 - cont.

43765.21.51 Sée, Édmond. L'indiscret; comédie en trois actes. Paris, 1923.
42584.25.20 Seillière, Ernest. Emile Zola. Paris, 1923.
38546.36.16 Sévigné, Marie de R.C. Lettres choisies, suivis d'un choix de lettres. Paris, 1923.
38546.36.15A Sévigné, Marie de R.C. Lettres choisies, suivis d'un choix de lettres. v.1-2. Paris, 1923?
37572.57 Sirich, E.H. Harper's French anthology, XVII-XVIII-XIX centuries. N.Y., 1923.
Htn Mol 878.7.3* Société des Auteurs Dramatiques. Tricentenaire de Molière: recueil des discours. Paris, 1923.
Mol 878.7 Société des Auteurs Dramatiques. Tricentenaire de Molière: recueil des discours. Paris, 1923.
43775.74.100 Sorbets, G. L'embrassement. Paris, 1923.
43776.41.140 Spire, André. Fourisseur. Paris, 1923.
37564.61A Stewart, H.F. The classical movement in French literature. Cambridge, Eng., 1923.
38525.11.5 Storer, Walter Henry. Virgil and Ronsard. Thesis. Paris, 1923.
37543.98.2A Strachey, Giles Lytton. Landmarks in French literature. N.Y., 1923.
41596.4.170 Suarès, André. Alfred de Musset au théâtre. Abbeville, 1923.
Htn 40583.75* Suarès, André. Stendhal, Verlaine, Baudelaire, Gérard de Nerval et autres gueux. Paris, 1923.
42556.21.280 Tacconi, Ilde Brando. Un poeta dei paria. Zara, 1923.
42556.35 Tellier, Jules. Ses oeuvres publiées par Raymond de la Tailhède. Paris, 1923. 2v.
43788.5.103 Tharaud, Jérôme. Un drame de l'automne. Paris, 1923.
43788.5.250 Tharaud, Jérôme. La maison des Mirabeau. Félicien-en-Vivarais, 1923.
43788.23.100 Thénon, Georges. La revue du vaudeville. Paris, 1923.
43822.49.930 Thibaudet, Albert. Paul Valéry. Paris, 1923.
37564.55.2 Tilley, Arthur Augustus. From Montaigne to Molière. 2nd ed. Cambridge, 1923.
42578.51.65 Tinayre, Marcelle. La légende de Duccio et d'Orsette. Paris, 1923.
43792.90.180 Toulet, Paul Jean. Les demoiselles la mortagne. Paris, 1923.
43792.90.160 Toulet, Paul Jean. Les tendres ménages, roman. Paris, 1923.
FL 382.70.5 Trotain, M. Les scènes historiques; étude du théâtre livresque à la veille du drame romantique. Thèse. Paris, 1923.
FL 382.70 Trotain, M. Les scènes historiques; étude du théâtre livresque à la veille du drame romantique. Thèse. Paris, 1923.
37569.4 Varillou, Pierre. Enquête sur les maîtres de la jeune littérature. Paris, 1923.
43827.89.100 Vaudoyer, J.L. La reine évanouie. Paris, 1923.
43822.89.142 Vaulet, Clément. Mon curé chez les riches. Paris, 1923.
43822.89.140 Vautel, Clément. Mon curé chez les riches. Paris, 1923.
42557.19.15 Verlaine, Paul. Bonheur. Paris, 1923.
42557.18.5 Verlaine, Paul. Poésies complètes. Paris, 1923-26. 7v.
42557.18.52 Verlaine, Paul. Vers. 3. éd. Munich, 1923.
42576.57.17 Viaud, Julien. Un jeune officier pauvre. Paris, 1923.
42576.57.15 Viaud, Julien. Un jeune officier pauvre. pt. 1-4. Paris, 1923.
42557.21.14 Vielé-Griffin, F. Choix de poèmes. Paris, 1923.
42557.22.10 Vielé-Griffin, F. Le domaine royal; discours lyriques. Paris, 1923.
41564.5.65 Vigny, Alfred de. Cinq-Mars. N.Y., 1923.
43824.49.700 Vildrac, Charles. A book of love. N.Y., 1923.
43566.48.800 Villers, Emilie de. Lucie Delarue-Mardrus. Paris, 1923.
38523.3.15A Villey, Pierre. Marot et Rabelais, avec une table chronologique des oeuvres de Marots. Paris, 1923.
38514.20.15A Villon, François. Oeuvres. Paris, 1923. 3v.
38514.20.17 Villon, François. Oeuvres. 3. éd. Paris, 1923.
38514.20.25 Villon, François. Le poésie. Torino, 1923.
43824.2.35 Vivien, Renée. Poèmes. Paris, 1923.
40526.31.10 Webster, Nestor H. (Mrs.). The chevalier de Boufflers. N.Y., 1923.
37556.23.40 Wilmotte, Maurice. De l'origine du roman en France. Paris, 1923.
37564.109 Wollstein, Rose H. English opinions of French poetry, 1660-1750. N.Y., 1923.
42584.23.345 Zola, Emile. Am häuslichen Herd. München, 1923.
42584.23.310 Zola, Emile. Der Bauch von Paris. München, 1923.
42584.23.335 Zola, Emile. Ein Blatt der Liebe. München, 1923.
42584.23.315 Zola, Emile. Die Froberung von Plassans. München, 1923.
42584.23.11.25 Zola, Emile. Fruitfullness. Garden City, 1923.
42584.23.360 Zola, Emile. Germinal. München, 1923.
42584.23.305 Zola, Emile. Die Jagdbeute. München, 1923.
42584.23.355 Zola, Emile. Die Lebensfreude. München, 1923.
42584.23.370 Zola, Emile. Mutter Erde. München, 1923.
42584.23.350 Zola, Emile. Das Paradies der Damen. München, 1923.
42584.23.325 Zola, Emile. Seine Excellenz Eugen Rougon. München, 1923.
42584.21.20 Zola, Emile. Théâtre. Paris, 1923.
42584.23.330 Zola, Emile. Der Totschläger. München, 1923.
42584.23.390 Zola, Emile. Der Zusammenbruch. München, 1923.
40575.5.140 Zweig, Stefan. Sainte-Beuve. Frankfurt, 1923.

1924

43512.75.100 Achard, Marcel. Voulez-vous jouer avec moâ? Trois actes. 4. ed. Paris, 1924.
43513.75.100 Acremant, Germaine (Paulain). La hutte d'acajou. Paris, 1924.
43520.54.695 Aimery de Pierrebourg, M.J.G. Cleopatra. Garden City, 1924.
43520.54.704 Aimery de Pierrebourg, M.J.G. The life and death of Cleopatra. 1st ed. Garden City, 1924.
43522.41.140 Alibert, François Paul. Le cantique sur la calline. Paris, 1924.
43524.15.100 Andard, Louis. En roulotte a travers l'inde catholique. Paris, 1924.
38528.29 Angot, Robert. Les éxercices de ce temps. Paris, 1924.
38537.25.45 Anna, Luigi de. Rabelais e la sua epopea burlesca. Firenze, 1924.
FL 398.84.27 Antoine, André. La vie amoureuse de François Joseph Talma. Paris, 1924.
43527.3.280 Aragon, Louis. Le libertinage. 7. éd. Paris, 1924.
40583.382 Arbelet, Paul. Les amours romantiques de Stendhal et de Victorine. Paris, 1924.
43528.48.100 Arland, Marcel. Étienne. Paris, 1924.

Chronological Listing

1924 - cont.

43528.58.2120 Arnac, Marcel. Le brelan de joie. 205e éd. Paris, 1924.
39526.47 Arnould, Louis. La terre de France chez La Fontaine, bêtes et gens. Tours, 1924.
40597.2.34 Arrigon, L.J. Les débuts littéraires d'Honoré de Balzac. 2. éd. Paris, 1924.
40597.2.310 Arüss, A. Le joli page de Balzac. Paris, 1924.
41588.15.15 Arvin, Neil Cole. Eugène Scribe and the French theatre, 1815-1860. Cambridge, 1924.
37573.619 Association des écrivains combattants. Anthologie des écrivains morts à la guerre, 1914-1918. Amiens, 1924-26. 5v.
37564.102 Atkinson, Geoffroy. Les relations de voyages du XVIIIe siècle et l'évolution des idees. Paris, 1924.
42576.65.13.70 Aubault de la Haulte Chambre, G. J.K. Huysmans. 2. éd. Paris, 1924.
42562.38.80 Aubier, F. C'est Venus tout entière. Paris, 1924.
43531.10.110 Aubry, Octave. Le roi perdu (Louis XVIII retrouvé). Paris, 1924.
42542.8.25 Augier, Émile. Maître Guérin. N.Y., 1924.
38525.4 Aynard, J. Les poëtes lyonnais. Paris, 1924.
FL 6139.19.4 Babbitt, Irving. Rousseau and romanticism. Boston, 1924.
42584.25.85 Baillot, Alex. Emile Zola. Paris, 1924.
40597.29.4 Balzac, Honoré de. Le père Goriot. Paris, 1924.
42554.8.10 Banville, Théodore de. Gringoire. Paris, 1924?
43538.74.6100 Barbey, Bernard. Lt coeur gros. Paris, 1924.
43537.74.100 Barde, André. Pépé: comédie. Paris, 1924.
42563.20.30 Barrès, Maurice. Une enquête aux pays du levant. Paris, 1924. 2v.
42563.20.25 Barrès, Maurice. Quelques lettres politiques inédites. Paris, 1924.
43537.5.35 Barrière, M. Le sang d'Asmodée. Paris, 1924.
42557.12.15 Baudouin, C. Psychoanalysis and aesthetics. (A study of symbolism in works of Verhaeren). N.Y., 1924.
43537.2.1030 Bauer, G. Il faut parler le premier. Ahbenitle, 1924.
40556.23.9 Beaunier, André. Le roman d'une amitié. 3. éd. Paris, 1924.
NEDL 42542.28.05 Becque, Henri. Oeuvres complètes. Paris, 1924. 7v.
40597.2.32 Bellessort, A. Balzac et son oeuvres. 6. éd. Paris, 1924.
43538.7.40 Benjamin, René. Le soliloque de Maurice Barrès. Paris, 1924.
41522.18.565 Bennett, Joseph D. Baudelaire, a criticism. Princeton, 1924.
43538.61.63 Benoît, Pierre. Koenigsmark. 268. éd. Paris, 1924.
43538.74.220 Béraud, Henri. La croisade des langues figures. Paris, 1924.
43538.74.180 Béraud, Henri. Lazare; roman. Paris, 1924.
43538.10.45 Bernard, Jean J. Le printemps des autres. Paris, 1924.
42542.29.27.5 Bernard, Tristan. Féerie bougeoise; roman. Paris, 1924.
42557.12.20 Bersaucourt, A. de. Émile Verhaeren, son oeuvre. Paris, 1924.
41578.40.49 Bert, Paul. Lamartine, homme sociale. Paris, 1924.
FL 398.7.35 Berton, Thérèse M. The real Sarah Bernhardt. N.Y., 1924.
FL 398.7.34 Berton, Thérèse M. The real Sarah Bernhardt. N.Y., 1924.
43538.81.1100 Beslière, Jean. Marguerite Fauquenoy. Paris, 1924.
43538.82.110 Besnard, Lucien. L'homme qui n'est pas plus de ce monde. Paris, 1924.
43538.82.100 Besnard, Lucien. Je veux revoir ma Normandie; pièce. Paris, 1924.
FL 355.65 Bethleem, Louis. Les pièces de théâtre. Paris, 1924.
40582.8.4 Beyle, Henri. De l'amour. Paris, 1924.
40582.2.43 Beyle, Henri. Histoire de la peinture en Italie. Paris, 1924. 2v.
43540.7.700 Bibescu, M.L. Isvor. N.Y., 1924.
37556.21.20 Billy, A. Le monde des journaux, tableau de la presse française contemporaine. Paris, 1924.
43540.74.110 Birabeau, André. La fleur d'oranger; comédie. Paris, 1924.
42563.23.40 Bloy, Léon. Mon journal. Paris, 1924. 2v.
43544.60.5110 Bonjean, François Joseph. Mansour. 13. éd. Paris, 1924.
43544.71.100 Bopp, Leon. Jean Darien. Paris, 1924.
42563.36.125 Bordeaux, Henry. La chartreuse du reposoir. Paris, 1924.
42563.36.125.5 Bordeaux, Henry. La chartreuse du reposoir. Paris, 1924.
42563.36.150 Bordeaux, Henry. The gardens of Omar. N.Y., 1924.
42563.36.107 Bordeaux, Henry. Le lac noir, ou Le sorcier de Myans. Paris, 1924.
42563.18.125A Bordeaux, Henry. Le retour de Barrès à sa terre. Paris, 1924.
38557.54.25 Bossuet, J.B. Panegyrics of the Saints, from French of Bossuet and Bourdaloue. London, 1924.
43544.83.100 Bost, Pierre. Hercule et mademoiselle. 4. éd. Paris, 1924.
42563.37.78 Bourget, Paul. Coeur pensif ne sait où il va. Paris, 1924.
42563.37.60 Bourget, Paul. The goal. N.Y., 1924.
42563.37.39.5 Bourget, Paul. Némésis. Paris, 1924.
37543.140.5 Braunschvig, Marcel. Notre littérature étudiée dans les textes. v.2. 2. éd. Paris, 1924.
42563.18.130 Bremond, H. Maurice Barrès. Paris, 1924.
37569.40.8 Breton, André. Manifeste du surréalisme. Paris, 1924.
Htn 37569.40.8* Breton, André. Manifeste du surréalisme. Paris, 1924.
43545.41.6100 Brillant, Maurice. L'amour sur les treteaux. Paris, 1924. 2v.
42576.63.41.5A Brousson, Jean J. Anatole France en pantoufles. 15. éd. Paris, 1924.
42576.63.41 Brousson, Jean J. Anatole France en pantoufles. 89. éd. Paris, 1924.
39535.62A Le cabinet satyrique. Paris, 1924. 2v.
38514.57.50 Campbell, P.G.C. L'épêtre d'Othea; étude sur les sources de Christine de Pisan. Thèse. Paris, 1924.
37564.73 Cauchie, Maurice. Documents pour server à l'histoire littéraire du XVIIe siècle. Paris, 1924.
43551.59.320 Cendrars, Blaise. Kodak. 5e éd. Paris, 1924.
39586.19.7 Chamfort, S.R.N. Caractères et anecdotes. Paris, 1924.
43552.3.7100 Champion, Pierre. Françoise au Calvaire. 18e éd. Paris, 1924.
38525.22.45.15A Champion, Pierre. Pierre de Ronsard et Amadis Jamyn; leur autographs. Paris, 1924.
38537.25.35 Chappell, A.F. The enigma of Rabelais, an essay in interpretation. Cambridge, 1924.
43552.5.2150 Charles-Étienne. Notre-Dame de Lesbos. Paris, 1924.
40586.45.25 Chateaubriand, F.A.R. Les aventures du dernier Abencérage. Strasbourg, 1924?
43552.6.103 Chateaubriant, Alphonse de. Monsieur des Lourdinés. Paris, 1924.
40526.7.2 Chénier, André. Oeuvres poétiques. Paris, 1924. 2v.

1924 - cont.

43552.24.100 Chérau, Gaston. La maison de Patrice Perrier; roman. v. 1-4. Paris, 1924.
43552.25.4150 Chevalier, Adrien. Sur l'autre versant. Paris, 1924.
43552.41.110 Chivas-Baron, C. Folie exotique (en brousse sedang), roman. Paris, 1924.
40517.44.8 Choderlos de Laclos, Pierre A.F. Dangerous acquaintances. London, 1924.
41564.54A Citoleux, Marc. Alfred de Vigny. Paris, 1924.
42586.31.72 Claretié, J. Souvenirs du diner Bixio. Paris, 1924.
43554.24.100 Clerc, Henri. L'epreuve du bonheur; pièce. Paris, 1924.
37555.52.5 Clouard, H. La poésie française moderne des romantiques à nos jours. Paris, 1924.
43556.1.360 Cocteau, Jean. Les mariés de la Tour Eiffel. Paris, 1924.
38525.22.20 Cohen, Gustave. Ronsard; sa vie et son oeuvre. Photoreproduction. Paris, 1924.
43556.49.510 Colette, Sidonie Gabrielle. Aventures quotidiennes. Paris, 1924.
43556.49.210 Colette, Sidonie Gabrielle. La femme cachée. Paris, 1924.
43556.74.100 Cordés, C. Les feux sur le Léban. Paris, 1924.
38526.10.12 Corrozet, Gilles. Le compte du rossignol. Paris, 1924.
38526.10.2 Corrozet, Gilles. Le compte du rossignol. Paris, 1924.
43557.24.100 Cremieux, Benjamin. XXe siècle. Paris, 1924.
43557.66.102 Crommelynck, Fernand. Le cocu magnifique. Milano, 1924.
40524.23.27 Crosby, Emily A. Une romancière oubliée, Mme. Riccoboni...ses oeuvres. Paris, 1924.
40524.23.25 Crosby, Emily A. Une romancière oubliée, Mme. Riccoboni. Thèse. Paris, 1924.
42542.58.38 Curel, François de. La nouvelle idole, pièce en trois actes. N.Y., 1924.
43565.5.100 Daudet, Léon A. Le drame des Jardies, 1877-1882. 13. éd. Paris, 1924.
41557.10.18.15 David, Henri C.E. Flaubert and George Sand in their correspondance. Chicago, 1924.
37566.86 Deffoux, Léon. Le groupe de Medau; Émile Zola. Paris, 1924.
42576.15.150 Degoumois, L. Flaubert à l'école de Goethe. Genève, 1924.
43566.43.150 Dekobra, Maurice. Mon coeur au ralenti. Paris, 1924.
43566.48.230 Delarue-Mardrus, Lucie. La mère et le fils. Paris, 1924.
43566.51.302 Delteil, Joseph. Les cinq sens, roman. Paris, 1924.
43566.53.100 Demasy, Paul. Jésus de Nazareth. Paris, 1924.
41593.29.3.12 Desbordes-Valmore, Marceline. Lettres de Marceline. Paris, 1924. 2v.
43566.7.35 Deval, Jacques. Le bien-aimé; pièce. Paris, 1924.
43568.91.100 Divoire, F. Marathon. Paris, 1924.
43568.91.156 Divoire, F. Stratégie littéraire. Paris, 1924.
42542.65.29 Donnay, Maurice. Le geste. Paris, 1924.
40566.5 Doudan, Ximénès. Des révolutions du gout. Paris, 1924.
43574.41.100 Drieu La Rochelle, Pierre. Plainte contre inconnu. Paris, 1924.
41593.70.80 Dufay, Pierre. Celui dout ou ne parle pas, Eugène Hugo, sa vie, sa folie, ses oeuvres. Paris, 1924.
43576.6.95 Duhamel, Georges. La journée des aveux. Paris, 1924.
43576.6.60 Duhamel, Georges. Le Prince Jaffar. 20. éd. Paris, 1924.
42554.29.155 Dujardin, É. Les lauriers sont coupés. Paris, 1924.
38545.21 Dulong, Gustave. L'abbé de Saint Réal. Paris, 1924. 2 pam.
42543.16.7.25A Dumas, Alexandre. La dame aux camélias. N.Y., 1924.
43576.70.100 Du Plessys, M. Le feu sacré. Paris, 1924.
43576.77.210 Durtain, Luc. Perspectives. Paris, 1924.
43576.77.183 Durtain, Luc. La source rouge. 3. éd. Paris, 1924.
38523.3.27 Duvergie, J. L'hérésie de Clément Marot, 1524-1527. Chartres, 1924.
43576.91.44 Duvernois, Henri. Le club des canards mandarins; comédie. Paris, 1924.
43576.91.46 Duvernois, Henri. La guitare et le jazz-band. Paris, 1924.
39544.53.15 Ellissen, O.A. Voltaire als Denker. v.3. Leipzig, 1924.
43598.54.700 Esménard, Jean d'. The red gods. N.Y., 1924.
43598.84.192 Estaunié, Édouard. Le labyrinthe. Paris, 1924.
43598.84.200 Estaunié, Édouard. Un simple. Paris, 1924.
43606.8.120 Fabre, Lucien. Bassesse de Venise. Paris, 1924.
37596.10.85 Fabriek, P. La construction relative dans Chréstien de Troyes. Amsterdam, 1924.
38524.826 Farce nouvelle. Strassbourg, 1924.
43606.78.210.5 Farrère, Claude. Quatorze histoires de soldats. Paris, 1924.
43606.78.720 Farrère, Claude. Thomas the Lambkin. N.Y., 1924.
42543.40.12 Fauchois, R. Mozart; comédie. Paris, 1924.
42563.18.115 Faure-Biguet, Jacques N. Maurice Barrès, son oeuvre, portrait et autographe. Paris, 1924.
40535.15.3A Favart, Charles S. Polichinelle, comte de Paonfier. Paris, 1924.
40597.2.28 Fees, Gilbert M. The correspondence of physical and material factors with character in Balzac. Thesis. Philadelphia, 1924.
43607.76.130 Féret, Charles Théophile. Le verger des muses et des satyres bouquins. Paris, 1924.
42576.23.5 Flaubert, Gustave. La tentation de Saint-Antoine. Paris, 1924.
V43500.97 Flers, Robert de. Le roi. L'ange du foyer. Paris, 1924?
38512.109 Fletcher, Frank. Études sur la langue des voeux du Paon. Thèse. Paris, 1924.
43610.25.100 Fleuret, Fernand. Les derniers plaisirs, histoire espagnole. Paris, 1924.
43610.25.102 Fleuret, Fernand. Les derniers plaisirs. Paris, 1924.
V43500.103 Forges, Lucien. Limbes; poesies; suivies de poèmes en prose. Paris, 1924.
43611.1.35 Fort, Paul. Ysabeau. Paris, 1924.
43611.5.50 Fournier, Alain. Miracles. Paris, 1924.
42576.62.120 France, Anatole. Anatole France à la béchellerie. Paris, 1924.
42576.62.2.6 France, Anatole. Balthasar. N.Y., 1924.
42576.63.8.20 France, Anatole. The Latin genius. London, 1924.
42576.62.10.4 France, Anatole. Le lys rouge. 426. éd. Paris, 1924.
42576.63.17.5 France, Anatole. The man who married a dumb wife. N.Y., 1924.
42576.63.24.35 France, Anatole. The merrie tales of Jacques Tournebroche. N.Y., 1924.
42576.62.38.5 France, Anatole. My friend's book. London, 1924.
42576.62.38 France, Anatole. My friend's book. N.Y., 1924.
42576.62.113 France, Anatole. On life and letters. 4th series. London, 1924.
42576.63.22.5 France, Anatole. Le petit Pierre. 197. éd. Paris, 1924.
42576.62.40A France, Anatole. Representative stories. Boston, 1924.
42576.62.25.10 France, Anatole. The revolt of the angels. London, 1924.

Chronological Listing

1924 - cont.

42576.62.6.6 France, Anatole. La rôtisserie de la reine Pédauque. 296. éd. Paris, 1924.
42576.62.3.15 France, Anatole. Thaïs. 314. éd. Paris, 1924.
43620.2.430 Gabory, G. André Gide, son oeuvre. Paris, 1924.
43616.41.120 Gaillard de Champris, Henry. Les heroiques et les tristes. Québec, 1924.
43616.62.110 Gantillon, Simon. Maya. Paris, 1924.
43616.83.2150 Gastine, Louis. Le roi - soleil s'amus. Paris, 1924.
43617.4.40 Géraldy, Paul. Si je voulais. Paris, 1924.
FL 6049.10 Gerdil, G.S. L'anti-Emilio. Firenze, 1924.
37569.68A Germain, A. De Proust à dada. Paris, 1924.
43617.77.120 Germain, André. Pèlerinages européens. 6. éd. Paris, 1924.
43620.2.38.13 Gide, André. Corydon. Paris, 1924.
43620.2.48 Gide, André. Incidences. 11. éd. Paris, 1924.
43620.2.65 Gide, André. Le retour de l'enfant prodigue. 6. éd. Paris, 1924.
43620.2.36.5 Gide, André. Strait is the gate (la porte étroite). N.Y., 1924.
43620.73.100 Girard, Georges. Les vainqueurs. 3. éd. Paris, 1924.
43620.74.420 Giraudoux, Jean. Juliette au pays des hommes. Paris, 1924.
43620.74.270 Giraudoux, Jean. Visite chez le prince. Paris, 1924.
41572.24.15 Glotz, R. Les variantes des contemplations. Thèse. Paris, 1924.
42587.58.90 Gobillot, René. La comtesse de Ségur. Allençon, 1924.
42586.67.20 Gobineau, Arthur de. Le prisonnier chanceux. Paris, 1924.
43625.3.79 Gourmont, Rémy de. Dernières pensées inédites. Paris, 1924.
43625.3.78 Gourmont, Rémy de. Pensées inédites. Paris, 1924.
37556.34.5 Green, F.C. La peinture des moeurs de la bonne société dans le roman français de 1715-1761. Paris, 1924.
37556.34.7 Green, F.C. La peinture des moeurs de la bonne société dans le roman français de 1715-1761. Thèse. Paris, 1924.
37568.265.2 Greshoff, Jan. Latijnsche lente. 2. Druk. Leiden, 1924.
37568.128 Greshoff, Jean. Mengelstoffen op het gebied der fransche letterkunde. Maastricht, 1924.
37566.55.2 Gressent, A.G. D'un siècle à l'autre. Paris, 1924.
43628.41.6110 Guinle, Alexandre. La lyre couronnée. Paris, 1924.
37543.157 Haas, Joseph. Kurzgefasste französische Literaturgeschichte von 1549-1900. Halle, 1924-27. 4v.
43631.2.55 Hamp, Pierre. La peine des hommes. Paris, 1924.
V42576.65.8.5 Harry, Myriam (pseud.). Den lille pige fra Jerusalem. Kjobenhavn, 1924.
37555.529 Hatzfeld, H. Die französische Renaissance-Lyrik. München, 1924.
FL 6139.24 Haymann, Franz. Weltbürgertum und Vaterlandsliebe in der Staatslehre Rousseau und Fichtes. Berlin, 1924.
43632.3.43 Hémon, Louis. Colin-Maillard. 17. éd. Paris, 1924.
43632.3.45 Hémon, Louis. Colin-Maillard. 64. éd. Paris, 1924.
43632.3.70 Hémon, Louis. The journal of Louis Hémon. N.Y., 1924.
43632.3.42.2 Hémon, Louis. Maria Chapdelaine. N.Y., 1924.
43632.6.122 Henriot, Émile. Aricie Brun, ou Les vertus bourgeoises. Paris, 1924.
43632.6.120 Henriot, Émile. Aricie Brun, ou Les vertus bourgeoises. Paris, 1924.
43632.6.290 Henriot, Émile. L'instant et le souvenir. Paris, 1924.
40583.77 Henriot, Émile. Stendhaliana. Paris, 1924.
42545.88.130 Henry-Marx. Georges de Porto-Riche. Paris, 1924.
42554.54.10 Heredia, J.M. de. Poésies complètes. Paris, 1924.
FL 398.35.20 Houville, Gerard d' (pseud.). Lucien Guitry. Paris, 1924.
41572.24.20 Hugo, Victor. Essai sur la psychologie des variantes des "Contemplations". Thèse. Paris, 1924.
42576.65.28.5 Huysmans, Joris Karl. Down there. N.Y., 1924.
42576.65.20.5 Huysmans, Joris Karl. The oblate. London, 1924.
43659.88.100 Istrati, Panait. Oncle Anghel. 24. éd. Paris, 1924.
43667.14.160 Jacob, Max. L'homme de chair et l'homme reflet. 2. éd. Paris, 1924.
43667.51.260 Jaloux, Edmond. Le rayon dans le brouillard. Paris, 1924.
43667.1.90 Jammes, Francis. Le troisième livre des quatrains. Paris, 1924.
40597.2.255 Jarry, P. Le dernier logis de Balzac. Paris, 1924.
FL 371.70 Jeanroy, A. Le théâtre religieux en France du XIe au XIIe siècles. Paris, 1924.
40597.2.40 Joseph, S.D.L. Les souvenirs et l'esprit napoléoniens chez Balzac. Thèse. Paris, 1924.
43670.89.110 Jouhandeau, M. Les Pincengrain. Paris, 1924.
43670.94.110 Jouve, Pierre Jean. Prière. Paris, 1924.
42576.43.50 Kiepert, Alexander. Camille Lemonnier und seine Romane. Inaug. Diss. Greifswald, 1924.
42544.2.8.16 Kistemaekers, Henry. L'amour. Paris, 1924.
38526.26.75 Labé, Louise Charly. De sonnetten van Lovize Labé. Maastricht, 1924.
42548.29.9 Labiche, Eugène. Les petis oiseaux. N.Y., 1924.
38527.58.10 La Boétie, Estienne de. Über freiwillige Knechtschaft. Berlin, 1924.
38521.30.11 Lachèvre, Frédéric. Les derniers libertines. Paris, 1924.
38544.26 La Fare, C.A. Poésies inédites du marquis de la Fare. Paris, 1924.
43687.26.120 Lafargue, Marc. Ode aux jeunes filles de Vendôme pour qu'elles aillent récitant Ronsard aux Bords du Loir. Paris, 1924.
38544.27.453 La Fayette, Marie M. Lettres de M.M. Pioche de la Vergne. London, 1924.
39527.29.63 La Fontaine, Jean de. Le songe de vaux. Paris, 1924.
42576.63.165 Lahy-Hollebecque, M. Anatole France et la femme. Paris, 1924.
37566.70.5 Lalou, René. Contemporary French literature. N.Y., 1924.
37566.69.5A Lalou, René. Histoire de la littérature française contemporaine (1870 à nos jours). Paris, 1924.
42586.63.70A Lange, Maurice. Le comte Arthur de Gobineau. London, 1924.
43687.74.113 Larbaud, Valéry. Amants, heureux amants. 12e éd. Paris, 1924.
43687.74.115 Larbaud, Valéry. Amants, heureux amants. 17e éd. Paris, 1924.
43687.77.1110 Larrouy, Maurice. Le révolté. Paris, 1924.
41578.40.10 Latreille, Camile. Lamartine, poète politique. Lyon, 1924.
37567.210.5 Latzarus, M.T. La littérature enfantine en France dans la seconde moitié du XIXe siècle. Thèse. Paris, 1924.
38525.21.7 Laumonier, P. Ronsard et sa province; anthologie régionale. Paris, 1924.
42546.12.25 Lautier, André. Edmond Rostand, son oeuvre, portrait et autographe. Paris, 1924.

1924 - cont.

42576.41.40 Le Blanc, Maurice. La comtesse de Cagliostro. Paris, 1924.
V43500.167 Lebrau, Jean. Le ciel sur la garrigue. Paris, 1924.
43688.2.55 Le Cardonnel, Louis. De l'une à l'autre aurore, poèmes. Paris, 1924.
37568.58 Lefèvre, Frédéric. Une heure avec... Série 1. Paris, 1924.
37568.58.3 Lefèvre, Frédéric. Une heure avec... Série 1. 13e éd. Paris, 1924.
37568.58.7 Lefèvre, Frédéric. Une heure avec... Série 2. 16e éd. Paris, 1924.
41595.15 Le Fevre-Deumier, J. Les vespres de l'abbaye du val. Paris, 1924.
38526.27.17 Lemaire de Belges, Jean. Jean Lemaire de Belges (um 1473 - um 1515). Berlin, 1924.
FL 360.28.10 Lemaitre, Jules. Theatrical impressions. London, 1924.
43688.61.150 Lenormand, Henri René. A l'ombre du mal. Paris, 1924.
41595.5.10 Le Poittevin, Alfred. Une promenade de Belial et oeuvres inédites. Paris, 1924.
40512.3.50 LeSage, Alain René. Diavolul schiop. Bucuresti, 1924.
40587.25.7 Lescure, M.F.A. de. Chateaubriand. 7. éd. Paris, 1924?
37569.54.2 Lievre, Pierre. Esquisses critiques. 2e Série. Paris, 1924.
43690.88.100 Litschfousse, V. Alain, ou Les vertus guerrières. Paris, 1924.
38526.70.100 Livingston, C.H. Les cent nouvelles nouvelles de Philippe de Vigneulles. Paris, 1924.
43788.65.2800 Llona, Victor. Notes sur Louis Thomas. Paris, 1924.
42544.34.25.25 Lorde, André de. Les drames célèbres du Grand-guignol. Paris, 1924.
43694.11.120 Lucchini, Pierre. Notre-Dame de la sagesse. 24. éd. Paris, 1924.
38585.16.60 Lyonnet, Henry. Les "premières" de Jean Racine. Paris, 1924.
42545.3.11.2 Maeterlinck, Maurice. Monna Vanna. Paris, 1924.
39534.36.05 Magne, Émile. Bibliographie générale des oeuvres de Scarron. Paris, 1924.
39534.36.7 Magne, Émile. Scarron et son milieu. Paris, 1924.
43697.34.200 Magre, Maurice. La porte du mystère. Paris, 1924.
43697.48.2100 Malaurie, Albert. La femme de Judas. Paris, 1924.
42555.44.7 Mallarmé, Stéphane. Lettres de Mallarmé à Aubanel et Mistral. Saint-Felicien-en-Vivarais, 1924.
42555.43.3.3 Mallarmé, Stéphane. Poésies. Paris, 1924?
41541.20.15 Malo, Henri. Une muse et sa mère, Delphine Gay de Girardin. Paris, 1924.
42576.77.15 Margueritte, Victor. The bachelor girl. N.Y., 1924.
42576.77.35 Margueritte, Victor. Le couple. Paris, 1924.
38525.22.25 Martellière, Jean. Pierre de Ronsard gentilhomme vandomois. Paris, 1924.
37555.504 Martin, Eugène-Louis. Les symétries du français littéraire. Thèse. Paris, 1924.
37555.504.2 Martin, Eugène-Louis. Les symétries du français littéraire. Thèse. Paris, 1924.
43697.76.9140 Martin du Gard, Maurice. Impertinences; portraits contemporains. Paris, 1924.
42563.23.135 Martineau, René. Léon Bloy. Paris, 1924.
38585.14.11 Martinez Ruiz, José. Racine y Molière. Madrid, 1924.
43697.79.180 Mary, André. Les rondeaux. Mesnil, 1924.
42515.35.169.5A Massis, Henri. Jugements. 2. sér. Paris, 1924.
43697.85.100 Masson, G.A. Ou le parfait plagiaire. Paris, 1924.
42577.4.28.25 Maupassant, Guy de. Little roque and other stories. N.Y., 1924.
42577.1.50 Maupassant, Guy de. Saint Anthony, and other stories. N.Y., 1924.
43697.89.8100 Maurel, Gérard. La route ardente. Paris, 1924.
42576.63.145A Maurras, Charles. Anatole France, politique et poète. Paris, 1924.
37567.344A Maurras, Charles M.P. Poètes. Paris, 1924.
42576.63.790 May, James Lewis. Anatole France, the man and his work. London, 1924.
43698.74.110 Mercier, Louis. Les cinq mystères joyeux. Saint-Félicien, 1924.
43698.74.100 Mercier, Louis. Lazare le ressucité suivi de Ponce Pilate. Paris, 1924.
43698.75.130 Méré, Charles. La danse de minuit. Paris, 1924.
43698.75.110 Méré, Charles. Le prince Jean; pièce en 4 actes. Paris, 1924.
42556.30.35 Merlin. (Romance). French. 1924. Schuré. Merlin l'énchanteur, légende dramatique, trilogie. Paris, 1924.
39583.2.5 Micard, Étienne. Écrivain académique au XVIIIe siècle, Antoine L. Thomas. Thèse. Paris, 1924.
39583.2 Micard, Étienne. Un écrivain académique au XVIIIe siècle. Paris, 1924.
43699.3.58 Mille, Pierre. L'illustre partonneau. Paris, 1924.
43699.50.21 Millien, Achille. Anthologie du poète nivernais. Fortin, 1924.
43699.51.100 Milosz, Oscar Vladislas. Ars magna. Paris, 1924.
43699.65.100 Miomandre, Francis de. La jeune fille au jardin. Paris, 1924.
Mol 219.25 Molière, Jean Baptiste Poquelin. George Dandin. Paris, 1924.
Mol 252.3.25 Molière, Jean Baptiste Poquelin. Les précieuses ridicules. Toronto, 1924.
Mon 28.35 Montaigne, Michel de. De l'institution des enfants. Paris, 1924.
Mon 19.24 Montaigne, Michel de. Essais. Paris, 1924-29. 6v.
Htn 42557.14.3* Montel, François. Bibliographie de Paul Verlaine. Paris, 1924.
43701.63.130.5 Montherlant, Henry de. Les onze devant la porte dorée. Paris, 1924.
43701.63.130 Montherlant, Henry de. Les onze devant le porte darée. 24e éd. Paris, 1924.
43701.63.340 Montherlant, Henry de. Le paradis à l'ombre des épées. Paris, 1924.
43701.74.370 Morand, Paul. Les amis nouveaux. Paris, 1924.
43701.74.390 Morand, Paul. La fleur double. Paris, 1924.
43701.74.735 Morand, Paul. Green shoots. N.Y., 1924.
43701.74.110A Morand, Paul. Poèmes, 1914-1924. 3e éd. Paris, 1924.
37542.32 Mornet, Daniel. Histoire de la littérature et de la pensée française. Paris, 1924.
37566.98 Mornet, Daniel. Histoire de la littérature et de la pensée françaises. Paris, 1924.
43701.82.110 Mossé, Armand. Les reliefs. Paris, 1924.
43709.3.190 Noailles, Anna E. Poème de l'amour. Paris, 1924.
37555.85 Noblet, Albert. La poésie lyrique en France des origines à 1914. Londres, 1924.

Chronological Listing

1924 - cont.

37555.350 Olovsson, Halvar. Étude sur les rimes de trois poétes romantiques. Thèse. Lund, 1924.

37566.43.5 Pailleron, M.L. (Mme.). François Buloz et ses amis de 1885 a nos jours. Paris, 1924.

37567.212 Partridge, E. The French romantics' knowledge of English literature (1820-1848). Paris, 1924.

43738.77.140 Pérochon, Ernest. Les gardiennes. Paris, 1924.

43738.2.35 Perrier, Martial. Ma version de la maison cernée. Paris, 1924.

43738.85.100 Peter, René. Pouche, comedie en trois actes. Paris, 1924.

43741.24.1100 Pierre-Quint, Léon. Décheances aimables. Paris, 1924.

43741.88.105 Pittard, Hélène (Mme.). Le nouvel Adam. pts.1-5. Paris, 1924.

38526.48.29.5 Plattard, Jean. La vie et l'oeuvre de Scévole de Sainte-Marthe. Paris, 1924.

37596.64.5 Poem on the assumption. Cambridge, 1924.

FL 361.70 Poizat, Alfred. Les maitres du théâtre, d'Eschyle à Curel. Paris, 1924. 2v.

37567.66.9.2 Poizat, Alfred. Le symbolisme. Paris, 1924.

43743.89.100 Pouget, P. L'autre bataille. Paris, 1924.

43744.25.6100 Praviel, Armand. The murder of Monsieur Fualdes. N.Y., 1924.

V43500.247 Prévost, Ernest. Le livre de l'immortelle amie. Paris, 1924.

42578.31.64.5 Prévost, Marcel. The Don Juanes. N.Y., 1924.

43744.67.41 Proust, Marcel. Within a budding grove. N.Y., 1924.

41568.1.25 Rabbé, Alphonse. Album d'un pessimiste. Le centaure. Le naufrage. L'adolescence. Paris, 1924.

43752.57.130 Ramuz, Charles Ferdinand. La guérison des maladies. 13. éd. Paris, 1924.

40536.22.29 Randon de Malboissière, G.F. Lettres de Geneviève de Malboissière à Adélaïde Méliand, 1761-1766. Thèse. Paris, 1924.

43752.11.100 Raucat, Thomas. L'honorable partie de campagne. Paris, 1924.

43752.11.102 Raucat, Thomas. L'honorable partie de campagne. 2. éd. Paris, 1924.

43752.11.110 Raucat, Thomas. L'honorable partie de campagne. 8. éd. Paris, 1924.

43752.98.100 Raynal, Paul. Le tombeau sous l'Arc de Triomphe; tragédie. Paris, 1924.

42556.26.34 Régnier, Henri de. Scènes mythologiques. Paris, 1924.

43753.2.55 Régnier, M.L.A. de. Le chou. Paris, 1924.

42557.12.70 Regoyos, Dario de. La espaṇa negra de Verhaeren. Madrid, 1924.

Htn 40524.28.30* Restif de la Bretonne, Nicolas E. Monsieur Nicolas. Paris, 1924-25. 4v.

40524.31.25 Restif de la Bretonne, Nicolas E. La vie de mon père. Paris, 1924.

37596.32.75 La résurrection du Sauveur. Strasbourg, 1924.

42556.27.92 Retté, Adolphe. La basse-cour d'Apollon. Paris, 1924.

43753.90.2100 Réval, Gabrielle. La chaîne des dames. Paris, 1924.

Htn 43753.90.130* Reverdy, P. Les épaves du ciel. Paris, 1924.

42545.28.7.80 Revon, M. Octave Mirbeau, son oeuvre. Paris, 1924.

43606.78.810 Revon, Maxime. Claude Farrère, son oeuvre. Paris, 1924.

43753.98.100 Rey, Ę. Ce que femme veut. Paris, 1924.

42545.88.120 Rey, Étienne. Georges de Porto-Riche. Abbeville, 1924.

FL 370.100 Reyval, Albert. L'église et le théâtre. Paris, 1924.

43756.3.45 Richepin, Jacques. Mon coeur. Paris, 1924.

42556.28.208 Rickword, Edgell. Rimbaud; the boy and the poet. N.Y., 1924.

42556.28.207 Rickword, Edgell. Rimbaud. London, 1924.

42587.55.39 Rivoire, André. La cousine Émile. Abbeville, 1924.

38525.22.45.25 Rocher, E. Pierre de Ronsard, prince des poètes, 1524-1585. Paris, 1924.

42577.4.37 Rolland, J. Guy de Maupassant. Paris, 1924.

43757.50.413.5 Rolland, Romain. Liluli. Frankfurt, 1924.

43757.50.768 Rolland, Romain. Mahatma Gandhi. N.Y., 1924.

Htn 43757.50.510* Rolland, Romain. Mahatma Gandhi. Paris, 1924.

43757.50.530 Rolland, Romain. Musiciens d'autrefois. 9e éd. Paris, 1924.

43757.3.38 Romains, Jules. Knock, ou Le triomphe de la médicine. Paris, 1924.

43757.3.40 Romains, Jules. Knock, ou Le triomphe de la médicine. 2e éd. Paris, 1924.

43757.3.40.2 Romains, Jules. Knock, ou Le triomphe de la médicine. 24e éd. Paris, 1924.

43757.3.41 Romains, Jules. Monsieur le Trouhadec saisi, par la débauche. Paris, 1924.

37555.370 Romains, Jules. Petit traité de versification. 9. éd. Paris, 1924.

38525.20.23 Ronsard, Pierre de. Discours des misères de ce temps à la Royne mere du Roy. Paris, 1924.

38525.20.21 Ronsard, Pierre de. Poésies. Paris, 1924.

38525.20.26 Ronsard, Pierre de. Poésies choisies. Paris, 1924.

38525.18.3.20 Ronsard, Pierre de. Songs and sonnets of Pierre de Ronsard. Boston, 1924.

42578.22.10.70 Rosny, J.H. L'amour d'abord. Paris, 1924.

42578.22.30 Rosny, J.H. L'assassin surnaturel. Paris, 1924.

42578.22.200 Rosny, J.H. Les autres vies et les autres mondes. Paris, 1924.

42546.14.5.50A Rostand, Edmond. Cyrano de Bergerac. N.Y., 1924.

43757.83.45 Rostand, Maurice. Le secret du sphinx; pièce en vers. Paris, 1924.

FL 6015.17A Rousseau, J.J. Correspondance général de Jean-Jacques Rousseau. Paris, 1924-34. 20v.

FL 6046.14.5 Rousseau, J.J. Rousseau's estimate of the manual arts. Paris, 1924.

FL 6036.11.5 Rousseau, J.J. The social contract. London, 1924.

43757.98.150 Royère, Jean. Poésies. Amiens, 1924.

42555.2.10 Ruchon, François. Jules Laforgue, 1860-1887. Genève, 1924.

43761.42.3100 St. Prix, J. de. Lettres. Paris, 1924.

43761.58.100 Sandre, Thierry. Le chèvre feuille. Paris, 1924.

43761.58.105 Sandre, Thierry. Le chèvre feuille. 26e éd. Paris, 1924.

42546.29.10 Sardou, Victorien. La perle noire. N.Y., 1924.

43761.6.35 Sarment, Jean. Je suis trop grand pour moi; pièce. Paris, 1924.

43761.6.16 Sarment, Jean. Je suis trop grand pour moi. Paris, 1924.

37594.8 Sarrasin, Jean. Lettre à Nicolas Arrode (1249). Paris, 1924.

38528.13.7 Satyre Ménippée; ou La vertu du catholicon. Paris, 1924.

43761.89.100 Saunier, R. Deux hommes, une femme. Paris, 1924.

43761.5.38 Savoir, Alfred. La grande-duchesse et le garçon d'étage. Paris, 1924.

1924 - cont.

43763.38.110 Schlumberger, Jean. Un homme heureux. 11. éd. Paris, 1924.

43763.2.21 Schopfer, Jean. Théâtre: Mademoiselle Bourrat. Paris, 1924.

37543.245 Schwarz, H.S. An outline history of French literature. N.Y., 1924.

42587.57.75 Schwob, Marcel. Imaginary lives. N.Y., 1924.

43765.21.43 Sée, Edmond. La dépositaire. Paris, 1924.

42576.46.60 Serban, Nicolas. Pierre Loti. Paris, 1924.

40597.2.77 Serval, M. Autor d'Eugénie Grandet d'après des documents inédits. Paris, 1924.

42576.63.710 Sherman, Stuart Puth. Anatole France. N.Y., 1924?

37543.165A Smith, M. Short history of French literature. N.Y., 1924.

39533.22.15 Sorel, Charles. Histoire comique de Francion. Photoreproduction. Paris, 1924-31. 4v.

39533.22.20 Sorel, Charles. Oeuvres galante. Paris, 1924.

43775.90.7165 Soupault, Philippe. Les frères Durandeau, roman. 10. éd. Paris, 1924.

40586.24.100 Spring, H.P. Chateaubriand at the crossways. N.Y., 1924.

37567.226 Strowski, F. Tableau de la littérature française au XIXe siècle et au XXe siècle. Paris, 1924.

37567.226.3 Strowski, F. Tableau de la littérature française au XIXe siècle et au XXe siècle. Paris, 1924.

42557.5.15 Tailhade, Laurent. Laurent Tailhade intime. 2. éd. Paris, 1924.

42557.5.30 Tailhade, Laurent. La médaille qui s'efface. Paris, 1924.

38571.22 Tastevin, Maria. Les héroines de Corneille. Paris, 1924.

43788.5.195 Tharaud, Jérôme. The long walk of Samba Diouf. N.Y., 1924.

43788.5.122 Tharaud, Jérôme. Une relève. 30e éd. Paris, 1924.

43788.5.700 Tharaud, Jérôme. The shadow of the cross. N.Y., 1924.

42576.65.13.65 Thérive, André. J.K. Huysmans, son oeuvre. Paris, 1924.

42563.18.160 Thibaudet, A. Les princes lorrains. 12. éd. Paris, 1924.

41522.18.96 Thibaudet, Albert. Intérieurs. 6. éd. Photoreproduction. Paris, 1924.

Mol 560.20 Thuasne, L. Les privilèges des éditions originales de Molière. Paris, 1924.

42545.3.470 Timmerman, B. Le Spinozisme de Maeterlinck. Proefschrift. Zalt-Bommel, 1924.

43893.2 Le tombeau de Michel Abadie. Nevers, 1924.

37573.625 Tondo, M.M. Pathelin, et autres pièces. N.Y., 1924.

42587.63.65 Torquet, A. Poèmes triviaux et mystiques. Paris, 1924.

43792.90.61 Toulet, Paul Jean. Lettres à Madame Bulteau. Paris, 1924.

41555.43.25 Trahard, Pierre. La jeunesse de Prosper Mérimée. Thèse. Paris, 1924.

37556.15.100 Trahard, Pierre. Une revue oubliée, La revue poétique du XIXe siècle, 1835. Thèse. Paris, 1924.

40583.72 Trompeo, Pietro Paolo. Nell'Italia romantica sulle orme di Stendhal. Roma, 1924.

42576.63.150 Truc, G. Anatole France, l'artiste et le penseur. Paris, 1924.

43822.49.125 Valéry, Paul. Eupalinos, ou L'architecte, précédé de L'ame et la danse. 29e éd. Paris, 1924.

43822.49.128 Valéry, Paul. Eupalinos, ou L'architecte, précédé de L'ame et la danse. 45e éd. Paris, 1924.

43822.49.100 Valéry, Paul. Variété. Paris, 1924.

43822.49.102 Valéry, Paul. Variété. 29e éd. Paris, 1924.

39533.8.35 Van Roosbroeck, G.L. Chapelain décoiffe. Baltimore, 1924.

43827.89.135 Vaudoyer, J.L. La maitresse et l'amie. Paris, 1924.

43827.89.120 Vaudoyer, J.L. Peau d'ange. Paris, 1924.

43822.89.170 Vaulet, Clément. Madame ne vent pas d'enfant. Paris, 1924.

43822.89.100 Vautel, Clément. Candide; pièce...(d'après le roman de Voltaire). Paris, 1924.

43823.50.100 Velleroy, Guy. Le feu grégois. Paris, 1924.

41542.4.20 Velthius, H.E.A. Théophile Gautier; l'homme - l'artiste. Middelburg, 1924.

42557.11.35 Verhaeren, Émile. A la vie qui s'éloigne. 9. éd. Paris, 1924.

42557.11.45 Verhaeren, Émile. Five tales. N.Y., 1924.

42557.19.50 Verlaine, Paul. Sagesse. Paris, 1924.

43824.3.100 Vialar, Paul. L'âge de caison. Paris, 1924.

Htn 42576.57.35* Viaud, Julien. Journal intime. Paris, 1924.

42576.57.20 Viaud, Julien. Lettres de Pierre Loti. Paris, 1924.

42576.57.22 Viaud, Julien. Lettres de Pierre Loti à madame Juliette Adam 1880-1922. Paris, 1924.

42576.57.45 Viaud, Julien. Pierre Loti; notes of my youth. Garden City, N.Y., 1924.

42576.54.3.5 Viaud, Julien. Le roman d'un enfant. Paris, 1924.

42576.3.5 Viaud, Julien. Le roman d'un enfant. Paris, 1924.

42576.57.2.9 Viaud, Julien. A tale of Brittany. N.Y., 1924.

42557.21.20 Vielé-Griffin, F. Oeuvres. Paris, 1924-30. 4v.

41564.26 Vigny, Alfred de. Les destinées. Paris, 1924.

38514.20.32 Villon, François. The retrospect of François Villon. London, 1924.

39545.55.5 Voltaire, François Marie Arouet de. Orleanskais devstvennitsa. Moskva, 1924. 2v.

43833.1.45 Weyl, Fernand. La pure courtisane. Paris, 1924.

43833.1.35 Weyl, Fernand. La sonate à Kreutzer. Paris, 1924.

37567.208A Whitridge, A. Critical ventures in modern French literature. N.Y., 1924.

42547.46 Wolff, Pierre. Après l'amour. Paris, 1924.

43858.1.45 Zamacois, Miguel. Suzanne et les deux vieillards. Paris, 1924.

Htn 38514.18.25* Ziwes, Armand. Le Grant Testament et le Petit. Paris, 1924.

42584.23.380 Zola, Emile. Die Bestie im Menschen. München, 1924.

42584.23.395 Zola, Emile. Doktor Pascal. München, 1924.

42584.23.385 Zola, Emile. Das Geld. München, 1924.

42584.23.375 Zola, Emile. Der Traum. München, 1924.

42584.23.365 Zola, Emile. Das Werk. München, 1924.

1925

37595.9.25 Abailard, Pierre. Letters of Abélard and Héloise. London, 1925.

37595.9.24 Abailard, Pierre. Love letters of Abélard and Héloise. London, 1925.

37543.114.14 Abry, E. Histoire illustrée de la littérature française. 7. éd. Paris, 1925.

37596.23.11 Adam (Mystery). Das altfranzösische Adamsspiel. Photoreproduction. Paris, 1925.

38525.22.45.20 Addamiano, Natale. Il rinascimento in Francia. Palermo, 1925.

43874.99.30 Les âges de la vie. v. 1-3. Paris, 1925-

Chronological Listing

1925 - cont.

	39544.82	Aldington, Richard. Voltaire; the republic of letters. London, 1925.
	43522.41.150	Alibert, François Paul. La guirlande lyrique. Paris, 1925.
	43523.41.181	Amiel, Denys. Théâtre: Le voyageur. v.1. Paris, 1925.
	42553.33.5	Amiel, Henri F. En drömmares dagbok. Stockholm, 1925.
	43524.19.100	André, Louis. La mysterieuse Baronne de Feuchères. Paris, 1925.
	37574.80	Anthologie de la nouvelle poésie française. Paris, 1925.
	41578.103	Antoir, J. Les manuscrits d'Antoir, l'ami Lamartine. Paris, 1925.
	43526.65.100A	Apollinaire, Guillaume. Calligrammes. Paris, 1925.
	43526.65.120	Apollinaire, Guillaume. Il y a. Paris, 1925.
	43528.58.2100	Arnac, Marcel. 83 centiméntres d'ovenhure. Paris, 1925.
	43528.86.70	Artaud, Antonin. L'ombilic des limbes. Paris, 1925.
	41543.20	Audiat, Pierre. L'Aurélia de Gerard de Nerval. Thèse. Paris, 1925.
	43576.6.805	Aveline, Claude. Les ouvrages de Georges Duhamel. Paris, 1925.
	43537.13.35	Bachelin, H. La cornemuse de Saulieu. Paris, 1925.
	43537.42.140	Bainville, Jacques. Tyrrhenus. Saint-Pélicien-en-Vivarais, 1925.
	37567.216	Baldensperger, F. Sensibilité musicale et romantisme. Paris, 1925.
	40596.8.7	Balzac, Honoré de. Comédie humaine. Études philosophiques. Paris, 1925-27. 5v.
	40597.14.54	Balzac, Honoré de. Les contes drolatiques. Paris, 1925. 2v.
	40597.79	Balzac, Honoré de. Cromwell. v.1-2. Paris, 1925.
	40597.32.13.6	Balzac, Honoré de. The physiology of marriage. London, 1925.
	41522.1.7	Barbey d'Aurevilly, Jules. The diaboliques. N.Y., 1925.
	41522.2.42	Barbey d'Aurevilly, Jules. Disjesta membra. Paris, 1925.
X Cg	43537.6.37	Barbusse, Henri. Les enchainements. v.1. Paris, 1925.
	43537.6.37	Barbusse, Henri. Les enchainements. v.2. Paris, 1925.
	42563.18.7	Barrès, Maurice. Sous l'oeil des barbares. Paris, 1925.
	41578.87	Barthou, Louis. Autour de Lamartine. Paris, 1925.
	41578.126	Barthou, Louis. Victor Hugo. Abbeville, 1925.
	41522.6.4A	Baudelaire, Charles. L'art romantique. Paris, 1925.
	43537.89.100A	Baudouin, C. Contemporary studies. N.Y., 1925.
	Mol 270.33	Baumal, Francis. Tartuffe et ses avatars. Paris, 1925.
	43537.89.2130	Baumann, Émile. L'immolé. Paris, 1925.
	40515.15.7	Beaunier, André. La vie amoureuse de Julie de Lespinasse. Paris, 1925.
	42576.63.75	Bédé, Albert. Anatole France vu par la critique d'aujourd'hui. Paris, 1925.
	37562.21.8	Bédier, Joseph. Les fabliaux. 4. éd. Paris, 1925.
Htn	38514.23.15*	Beebe, Lucius M. François Villon, certain aspects. Cambridge, Mass., 1925.
	39544.106A	Bellessort, A. Essai sur Voltaire; cours professé à la Société des conférences. Paris, 1925.
	V43500.18	Bénal, Henri. Le chemin du mirage; poèmes. Bordeaux, 1925.
	43538.59.100	Benda, Julien. Billets de Sirius. Paris, 1925.
	40597.2.42.2	Benjamin, René. La prodigieuse vie d'Honoré de Balzac. Paris, 1925.
	40597.2.42A	Benjamin, René. La prodigieuse vie d'Honoré de Balzac. Paris, 1925.
	43538.61.65	Benoît, Pierre. Le puits de Jacob. Paris, 1925.
	43538.61.66	Benoît, Pierre. Le puits de Jacob. Paris, 1925.
	43538.3.35	Benoit, Pierre André. Les guerres d'enfer et l'avenir de l'intelligence. Félicien-en-Vivarais, 1925.
	37543.558	Bérard, Léon. Au service de la pensée française. Paris, 1925.
	43538.74.150	Béraud, Henri. Au Capucin Gourmand. Paris, 1925.
	37548.38.7	Berger, Lya. Les femmes poètes de la Belgique. Paris, 1925.
	43538.76.6100	Berl, Emmanuel. Meditation sur un amour défunt. Paris, 1925.
	43538.10.50	Bernard, Jean J. Théâtre. Paris, 1925.
	42542.29.28.25	Bernard, Tristan. Autour du ring (tableau de la boxe). Paris, 1925.
	42542.29.28.60	Bernard, Tristan. L'ecole des quinquagénaires. Paris, 1925. 3 pam.
	42542.29.50	Bernstein, H. La galerie des glaces, pièce en trois actes. Paris, 1925.
	42556.29.32	Bersaucourt, A. de. Albert Samain; son oeuvre. Paris, 1925.
	43538.78.100	Berton, René. Le precurseur. Paris, 1925.
	42563.23.8.50	Bertrand, Louis. Jean Perbal, roman. 20. éd. Paris, 1925.
	43538.88.100	Betz, Maurice. L'incertain; roman. Paris, 1925.
	40582.2.45	Beyle, Henri. Armance, ou Quelques scènes d'un salon de Paris en 1827. Paris, 1925.
	40582.9.26	Beyle, Henri. The charterhouse of Parma. N.Y., 1925. 2v.
	40582.9.25	Beyle, Henri. The charterhouse of Parma. N.Y., 1925.
	40582.2.47	Beyle, Henri. Racine et Shakspeare. Paris, 1925. 2v.
	43540.60.110	Binet-Valmer, Gustave. Quand ils furent nus. Paris, 1925.
	43540.74.120	Birabeau, André. Chiffarton; comédie. Paris, 1925.
	42563.18.140	Blanc-Péridier, A. La route ascendante de Maurice Barrès. Paris, 1925.
	43543.13.130	Bloch, J.R. Levy. 5. éd. Paris, 1925.
	42563.23.37	Bloy, Léon. Le pal. Paris, 1925.
	42563.23.34	Bloy, Léon. Le symbolisme de l'apparition, 1879-1880. Paris, 1925.
	37569.50.10	Bocquet, Léon. La commemoration des morts. Amiens, 1925.
	37597.26.60	Bodel, Jehan. Jean Bodel, trouvère artésien du XIIIe siècle. Paris, 1925.
	42556.29.28	Bonneau, G. Albert Samain, poète symboliste. Thèse. Paris, 1925. 2 pam.
	42553.34.5	Bopp, Leon. Henri Frédéric Amiel. Thèse. Paris, 1925.
	42563.36.220	Bordeaux, Henry. L'amour et le bonheur. Paris, 1925.
	42563.18.126	Bordeaux, Henry. L'appel du divin ou Maurice Barrès en Orient. Paris, 1925.
	42563.36.115	Bordeaux, Henry. Les jeux dangereux. Paris, 1925-26.
	41522.3.15	Bordeaux, Henry. Le Walter Scott Normand. Paris, 1925.
	38537.1.15	Boulenger, Jacques. Rabelais. Paris, 1925.
	42563.37.63	Bourget, Paul. Conflits intimes. Paris, 1925.
	40534.19.50	Bouvier, Armand. Le poete Colardeau, 1732-1776. Orléans, 1925.
	42553.34.10	Bouvier, B. Henri Frédéric Amiel. Stockholm, 1925.
	42563.37.87	Bowman, E.M. The early novels of Paul Bourget. N.Y., 1925.
	42563.39.12	Boylesve, René. La becquée. N.Y., 1925.
	37543.140.7	Braunschvig, Marcel. Notre littérature étudiée dans les textes. 3. éd., v.1.; 2. éd., v.2. Paris, 1925. 2v.

1925 - cont.

	41593.49.25	Bremond, Henri. Le roman et l'histoire d'une conversion. Paris, 1925.
	FL 398.7.36	Bron, Ludovic. Sarah Bernhardt. Paris, 1925.
	42576.63.40A	Brousson, Jean J. Anatole France himself. Philadelphia, 1925.
	38514.44.15	Bruins, Jan Gerard. Observation sur la langue d'Eustache Deschamps. Amsterdam, 1925.
	42556.11.7	Brujère, M. Jean Reboul de Nimes 1796-1864; sa vie et ses oeuvres. Thèse. Paris, 1925.
	39564.28	Busnelli, Manlio D. Diderot et l'Italie. Paris, 1925.
	39564.27	Busnelli, Manlio D. Diderot et l'Italie. Thèse. Paris, 1925.
	43550.40.110	Cahuet, Albéric. Régime Romani. Paris, 1925.
	43550.55.100	Cami, Henri. Les exploits galants du baron de Crac. Paris, 1925.
	43550.65.102	Capy, M. L'amour roi. Paris, 1925.
	43550.1.40	Carco, Francis. Perversite; roman. Paris, 1925.
	43550.74.100	Carco, Francis. Visite à Saint-Lazare. Paris, 1925.
	37595.52	Cary, Henry F. The early French poets. N.Y., 1925.
	43550.82.260	Cassou, Jean. Eloge de la folie. Paris, 1925.
	43537.4.90	Catalogne, Gerard de. Henry Bataille. Paris, 1925.
	V43500.55	Cazin, Paul. L'hôtellerie du Bacchus sans tête. Paris, 1925.
	41578.165	Cerf, Léon. Le reliquaire de Lamartine. Paris, 1925.
	38525.22.45.10F	Champion, Pierre. Contribution à l'histoire de la société polie, Ronsard et Villeroy. Paris, 1925.
Htn	38536.22.11*	Champion, Pierre. Deux publications lyonnais de 1532 (Les grandes et inestimables croniques). Paris, 1925.
	38525.22.30	Champion, Pierre. Ronsard et son temps. Paris, 1925.
	43552.3.9135	Chamson, André. Roux le bandit. Paris, 1925.
	37595.49	Le chansonnier d'Arras. Paris, 1925.
	43552.3.4130F	Charpentier, Henry. Océan pacifique; poème. Paris, 1925.
	42554.11.15	Charpentier, John. Théodore de Banville. Paris, 1925.
	40515.2.25	Charrière, Isabella A. Four tales by Zélide. London, 1925.
	40515.2.26	Charrière, Isabella A. Four tales by Zélide. N.Y., 1925.
	43552.24.1100	Chérade, R. Possebleu. 4e éd. Paris, 1925.
	43552.41.100	Chivas-Baron, C. Three women of Annam. N.Y., 1925.
	38546.61	Clarie, Henriette. Madame de Sévigné. Paris, 1925.
	38567.25	Clark, A.F. Bruce. Boileau and the French classical critics in England. (1660-1830). Paris, 1925.
	43554.2.83	Claudel, Paul. Morceaux choisis. Paris, 1925.
	43744.67.950	Clermont-Tonnerre, E. de G. Robert de Montesquiou et Marcel Proust. Paris, 1925.
	43625.3.100	Coalon, Marcel. L'enseignement de Rémy de Gourmont. Paris, 1925.
	43556.1.50A	Cocteau, Jean. Poésie, 1916-1923. Paris, 1925.
	42563.39.820	Codet, Louis. Louis l'Indulgent. Paris, 1925.
	42563.39.830	Codet, Louis. La petite chiquette. 3. éd. Paris, 1925.
	FL 371.75.2	Cohen, Gustave. Le livre de conduite du régisseur. Paris, 1925.
	FL 371.75	Cohen, Gustave. Le livre de conduite du régisseur. Strasbourg, 1925.
	43556.49.188	Colette, Sidonie Gabrielle. Claudine à Paris. Paris, 1925.
	43556.49.188.1	Colette, Sidonie Gabrielle. Claudine à Paris. Paris, 1925.
	43556.49.240	Colette, Sidonie Gabrielle. Dialogues de bêtes. Paris, 1925.
	Mon 113.5	Coppin, Joseph. Étude sur la grammaire et le vocabulaire de Montaigne. Thèse. Lille, 1925.
	Mon 113.5.3	Coppin, Joseph. Étude sur le grammaire et le vocabulaire de Montaigne. Lille, 1925.
	Mon 82.2.1	Coppin, Joseph Leon. Montaigne. Lille, 1925.
	Mon 82.2	Coppin, Joseph Leon. Montaigne. Thèse. Lille, 1925.
	42565.64.15	Corday, Michel. Des histoires. Paris, 1925.
	42557.20.220	Coulon, Marcel. Au coeur de Verlaine et de Rimbaud. Paris, 1925.
	42555.1.90	Cuisinier, Jeanne. Jules Laforgue. Paris, 1925.
	37568.48.2	Curtius, Ernst R. Französischer Geist im neuen Europa. Stuttgart, 1925.
	37568.48	Curtius, Ernst R. Französischer Geist im neuen Europa. Stuttgart, 1925.
	40545.7	Custine, A. Lettres inédites au Marquis de la Grange. Paris, 1925.
	43560.82.700	Custot, Pierre. Sturly. Boston, 1925.
	37569.270F	Czerefkow, S. Les ecrivains chez eux. Paris, 1925.
	43565.5.27	Daudet, Léon A. Memoirs. N.Y., 1925.
	43565.5.255	Daudet, Léon A. Oeuvre philosophique: l'hérédo. Paris, 1925.
	43565.5.145	Daudet, Léon A. Le róman et les nouveaux écrivains. Paris, 1925.
	43566.2.30	Deberly, Henri. L'ennemi des siens. Paris, 1925.
	37596.19.25	Dedecek, U.L. Étude littéraire de Li hystore de Julius Cesar. Philadelphia, 1925.
	43566.43.715	Dekobra, Maurice. Wings of desire. N.Y., 1925.
	43566.48.100	Delarue-Mardrus, Lucie. Graine au vent. Paris, 1925.
	42567.110	Delattre, Louis. Du côté de l'ombre. Bruxelles, 1925.
	43566.53.110	Demasy, Paul. La cavalière Elsa. Paris, 1925.
	43566.71.110	Deprat, Jacques. Le conquérant, roman, présenté par Claude Farrère. Paris, 1925.
	43566.75.200	Derème, Tristan. La bride et le cheval. Tarbes, 1925.
	43566.75.120	Derème, Tristan. La verdure dorée. 11. éd. Paris, 1925.
	43566.76.125	Derennes, Charles. Premières poésies. Paris, 1925. 2v.
	38525.20.250	DeRicci, S. Catalogue d'une collection unique des editions orginales de Ronsard. Paris, 1925.
	41593.29.3.25	Desbordes-Valmore, Marceline. Poésies. Paris, 1925.
	41593.29.3.59	Descaves, Lucien. La vie amoureuse de Marceline Desbordes-Valmore. Paris, 1925.
	37555.6	Desfeuilles, Paul. Dictionnaire de rimes. Paris, 1925.
	43566.79.100	Des Gachons, J. "Huit heures" de M. Colbert. Paris, 1925.
	43566.79.110	Des Gachons, J. Nicolas Poussin: Triptyque. Paris, 1925.
	42576.63.60	Des Hons, Gabriel. Anatole France et Racine. Paris, 1925.
	38526.12.35	Desportes, Philippe. Oeuvres. pts.1-2. Strasbourg, 1925.
	41593.31.10	Dierx, Léon. Oeuvres complètes. Paris, 1925. 2v.
	41574.97.5	Ditchy, Jay Karl. La mer dans l'oeuvre littéraire de Victor Hugo. Paris, 1925.
	41574.97	Ditchy, Jay Karl. La mer dans l'oeuvre littéraire de Victor Hugo. Inaug. Diss. Paris, 1925.
	42542.65.30	Donnay, Maurice. Un homme léger. Paris, 1925.
	43573.76.36	Dorgelès, Roland. Les croix de bois. Paris, 1925.
	43573.76.45	Dorgelès, Roland. Montmartre. Paris, 1925.
	37569.5	Dubech, L. Les chefs de file de la jeune génération. Paris, 1925.

1925 - cont.

43576.5.120 Dubech, Lucien. La douceur de vivre. Saint-Félicien, 1925.
FL 386.609A Dubech, Lucien. Le théâtre, 1918-1923. Paris, 1925.
38526.6.17 Du Bellay, Joachim. Les regrets. Paris, 1925.
43576.7.35 Du Bois, Albert. Le secret de la ville des 3 Cypres. pt. 1-2. Paris, 1925.
38585.16.25 Duclaux, A. (Mme.). The life of Racine. London, 1925.
38585.16.24A Duclaux, A. (Mme.). The life of Racine. N.Y., 1925?
Htn FL 6113.10* Du Four, Théophile. Recherches bibliographique sur les oeuvres imprimées de Jean-Jacques Rousseau. Paris, 1925. 2v.
43576.6.70 Duhamel, Georges. La Belle-Étoile. Paris, 1925.
43576.6.315 Duhamel, Georges. Delibérations. Paris, 1925.
43576.6.115 Duhamel, Georges. Le dernier. Paris, 1925.
37556.78 Duhamel, Georges. Essai sur le roman. Paris, 1925.
Htn 43576.6.140* Duhamel, Georges. Suite Hollandaise. Paris, 1925.
42543.16.14 Dumas, Alexandre. Camille. N.Y., 1925.
41538.145 Dumas, Alexandre. A life's ambition. Philaldelphia, 1925?
42568.23.12 Duval, Paul. Prométhée. Paris, 1925.
43576.91.50 Duvernois, Henri. Edgar. Paris, 1925.
43576.91.48 Duvernois, Henri. L'élève Chocotte. Paris, 1925.
38527.29.15 Ellerbroek, G.G. Observations sur la langue de l'histoire universelle de Théodore Agrippa d'Aubigné. Enschede, 1925.
42563.18.135 Empaytaz, F. Reconnaissance à Barrès. Paris, 1925.
42572.24.15 Erckmann, Emile. Madame Thérèse. Paris, 1925.
43598.13.135 Escholier, R. Quand on conspire; roman. 39. éd. Paris, 1925.
43598.84.183 Estaunié, Édouard. Solitudes; roman. Paris, 1925.
42556.17.11 Estéve, Edmund. Sully-Prudhomme. Paris, 1925.
43697.78.3100 Eugène Marsan par Charles Maurras. Lyon, 1925.
38513.92 La farce d'Esopet et du couturier. Paris, 1925.
38539.18.10 Faret, Nicolas. L'honeste homme, ou L'art de plaire à la cour. Thèse. Photoreproduction. Paris, 1925.
43606.89.63 Faure, Gabriel. Pages lyriques. Saint-Félicien-en-Vivarais, 1925.
37566.72A Fäy, Bernard. Panorama de la littérature contemporaine. Paris, 1925.
NEDL 37566.72.2 Fäy, Bernard. Panorama de la littérature contemporaine. 11. éd. Paris, 1925.
FL 355.73 Ferrari, Luigi. Traduzioni italiane del teatro. Paris, 1925.
FL 355.73.5 Ferrari, Luigi. Traduzioni italiane del teatro tragico françese nei secoli XVII e XVIII. Paris, 1925.
43609.58.1100 Firaud, Georges. Herma. Paris, 1925.
38524.63 Fleuret, F. Les amoureux passe-temps. Paris, 1925.
37563.12.5 Fleury, Claude. Dialogues...sur l'éloquence judiciare (1664). Thèse. Paris, 1925.
Mol 706.5 Flutre, F. Molière. Paris, 1925.
40566.10 Fontaney, Antoine. Journal intime. Paris, 1925.
37566.74 Forst-Battaglia, O. Die französische Literatur der Gegenwart, 1870-1924. Wiesbaden, 1925.
43611.1.45 Fort, Paul. Anthologie des ballades françaises, 1897-1920. Paris, 1925.
43611.1.25.63A Fort, Paul. Fantômes de chaque jour. Paris, 1925.
43565.5.820 Fournier, Paul. L'entrevue de Léon Daudet. Paris, 1925.
42576.62.95 France, Anatole. Anatole France himself. London, 1925.
42576.62.96 France, Anatole. Anatole France himself. N.Y., 1925.
42576.62.32.5A France, Anatole. Dernières pages inédites. 12. éd. Paris, 1925.
42576.62.97 France, Anatole. Franciana. Bruxelles, 1925.
42576.62.35 France, Anatole. Le livre de mom ami. 309. éd. Paris, 1925.
42576.62.5.40 France, Anatole. Le livre de mon ami. N.Y., 1925.
42576.62.10.7 France, Anatole. Le lys rouge. Paris, 1925.
42576.62.145 France, Anatole. Mother of pearl. N.Y., 1925.
42576.62A France, Anatole. Oeuvres complètes. Paris, 1925-1935. 25v.
42576.62.21.20 France, Anatole. Penguin island. London, 1925.
42576.62.100.5 France, Anatole. Pensées d'Anatole France. Paris, 1925.
42576.62.3.25 France, Anatole. Thaïs. N.Y., 1925?
43612.59.705 Francis, Robert (pseud.). The wolf at the door. Boston, 1925.
FL 397.161 Fransen, Jan. Les comédiens français en Hollande au XVIIe et au XVIIIe siècles. Paris, 1925.
42586.55.15 Frapié, L. Gamins de Paris. Paris, 1925.
43612.2.47 Fraudet, René. L'homme a l'hispano. Roman 1-5. Paris, 1925.
43612.5.100 Fraudet, René. La menace; pièce en quatre actes. Paris, 1925.
38585.8.12 Fubini, Mario. Jean Racine é la critica delle sue tragédie. Torino, 1925.
40516.11.35 Galli de Bibiena, J. The fairy doll. London, 1925.
42586.62.20 Gauthier-Villars, Henry. Souvenirs littéraires et autres. Paris, 1925.
43617.59.100 Genevoix, Maurice. Raboliot. 89. éd. Paris, 1925.
43617.4.43 Géraldy, Paul. Robert et Marianne. 17. éd. Paris, 1925.
43617.1.35 Gérard, Rosemonde. La robe d'un soir. Paris, 1925.
43619.24.160 Ghéon, Henri. Le comédien et la grâce. Paris, 1925.
43620.2.79.160 Gide, André. Caractères. Paris, 1925.
43620.2.53 Gide, André. Les faux-monnayeurs. Paris, 1925.
NEDL 43620.2.70 Gide, André. Le prométhée mal enchainé. Paris, 1925.
43620.2.37.5 Gide, André. The Vatican swindle. N.Y., 1925.
40583.79 Giglio, A. Stendhal e la letteratura italiana. Milano, 1925.
43620.3.55 Gilbert, M. Le joug, roman. Paris, 1925.
FL 364.125 Ginisty, Paul. Le théâtre de la rue. Paris, 1925.
42576.63.88 Girard, Georges. La jeunesse d'Anatole France, 1844-1876. Paris, 1925.
43620.73.1100 Girard, Pierre. Lord Algernon. Paris, 1925.
40587.57 Giraud, Victor. Le christianisme de Chateaubriand. Paris, 1925. 2v.
40587.37 Giraud, Victor. Passions et romans d'autrefois. Paris, 1925.
42586.67.5 Gobineau, Arthur de. Five oriental tales. N.Y., 1925.
43745.1.82 Goichon, A.M. (Mlle.). Ernest Psichari d'après des documents inédits. Paris, 1925.
43625.3.62 Gourmont, Rémy de. La fin de l'art. Paris, 1925.
43625.3.64 Gourmont, Rémy de. Fin de promenade et trois autres contes. Paris, 1925.
43625.3.37.2 Gourmont, Rémy de. Lilith. Paris, 1925.
43625.3.72 Gourmont, Rémy de. Les nouvelles dissociations. Paris, 1925.
43625.3.79.20 Gourmont, Rémy de. A virgin heart. N.Y., 1925.
40542.30 Goyau, Georges. Frédéric Ozanam. Paris, 1925.
43626.3.100 Grangié, E. Gracieuse au béret bleu. Paris, 1925.

1925 - cont.

FL 366.38 Grante, Marcel. Protection legale des oeuvre dramatique. Paris, 1925.
37597.42.9 Gros, Gaston. L'amour dans le roman de la rose. Paris, 1925.
37596.2.3.15 Guillaume de Deguilleville. Die pilger Fahrt des traumenden Mönchs. Bonn, 1925.
42543.62.27 Guiraud, E. Une femme. Paris, 1925.
43628.1.46 Guitry, Sacha. Une étoile nouvelle. Paris, 1925.
43628.5.100 Gustalla, P. Gérar. Paris, 1925.
41593.48.10 Guttinguer, Ulric. Arthur. Paris, 1925.
43630.6.100 Gybal, André. Luxure. Paris, 1925.
41578.40.20 Hazard, Paul. Lamartine. Paris, 1925.
43632.3.47 Hémon, Louis. Blind man's buff. N.Y., 1925.
43632.6.210 Henriot, Émile. Histoires morales. Paris, 1925.
43632.6.165 Henriot, Émile. Livres et portraits. 2. éd. Paris, 1925.
43632.6.250 Henriot, Émile. Vignettes et allégories. Paris, 1925.
39544.72 Herman, G. Voltaires dramatische Arbeitsweise. Inaug. Diss. Erfurt, 1925.
37556.19.10 Hinter den Kulissen des französischen Journalismus. Berlin, 1925.
43633.1.50 Hirsch, Charles H. La marieuse. Paris, 1925.
Htn 41574.109* Hofmannsthal, H. Versuch über Victor Hugo. München, 1925.
43756.90.803 Hommage à Jacques Rivière, 1886-1925. Paris, 1925.
39585.18 Hunter, Alfred C. J.B.A. Suard; un introducteur de la littérature anglaise en France. Paris, 1925.
39585.17.50 Hunter, Alfred C. J.B.A. Suard; un introducteur de la littérature anglaise en France. Thèse. Paris, 1925.
37596.107.7 Huon le Roi de Cambrai. Oeuvres. Paris, 1925.
42576.65.80.3 Huysmans, Joris Karl. The cathedral. London, 1925.
39582.31 Inklaar, Derk. François-Thomas de Baculard d'Arnaud. 's-Gravenhage, 1925.
37567.358 Iorga, N. Quatre figures françaises en lumière roumaine discours commémoratifs. Bucarest, 1925.
43667.51.180 Jaloux, Edmond. L'alcyone. 24. éd. Paris, 1925.
43667.51.210 Jaloux, Edmond. Le coin des cyprès. Paris, 1925.
43667.1.95 Jammes, Francis. Le quatrième livre des quatrains. Paris, 1925.
43667.1.247 Jammes, Francis. Les Robinsons basques. 11. éd. Paris, 1925.
43667.75.100 Jardin, Renée. Nostalgie. St. Raphael, 1925.
40566.10.10 Jasinski, René. Une amitié amoureuse; Marie Nodier et Fontaney. Paris, 1925.
37596.135.10A Jean Renart. Galeran de Bretagne. Paris, 1925.
37561.27.4 Jeanroy, Alfred. Les origines de la poésie lyrique en France au moyen âge. 3e éd. Paris, 1925.
38525.7.15A Jodelle, d'Estienne. Cleopâtre captive; tragédie. Paris, 1925.
42576.63.155 Johannet, René. Anatole France, est-il grand écrivain? Paris, 1925.
43670.94.140 Jouve, Pierre Jean. Les mystérieuses noces. Paris, 1925.
43670.94.249 Jouve, Pierre Jean. Paulina, 1880. 9. éd. Paris, 1925.
42513.45.50A Jusserand, J.J. The school for ambassadors. N.Y., 1925.
37567.343 Kahn, Gustave. Silhouettes littéraires. Paris, 1925.
42576.63.410 Kahn, Maurice. Le père d'Anatole France. Paris, 1925.
Mol 611.8 Kapp, Max. Die Frauengestalten in Molières Werken. Halle, 1925.
40526.63 Kerby, W.M. The life, diplomatic career and literary activities of Nicolas Germain Léonard. Paris, 1925.
42544.2.8.20 Kistemaekers, Henry. La nuit est à nous. Paris, 1925.
38526.27.05 Koczorowski, S.P. Louise Labé; étude littéraire. Paris, 1925.
Mol 810.5 Kohler, Pierre. Autour de Molière. L'ésprit classique. Paris, 1925.
40526.8.12 Kramer, C. André Chénier et la poésie parnassiene - Leconte de Lisle. Paris, 1925.
40527.19.10 Kramer, Cornelie. André Chenier et la poésie parnassienne. Reims, 1925.
38526.26.30 Labé, Louise Charly. The debate between Folly and Cupid. London, 1925.
43687.15.240 Lacretelle, Jacques de. La belle journée. Paris, 1925.
43687.15.110 Lacretelle, Jacques de. La Bonifas. 29e éd. Paris, 1925.
38544.27.10 La Fayette, Marie M. Oeuvres de Madame de la Fayette. Paris, 1925-30. 3v.
39527.29.20 La Fontaine, Jean de. Choix de fables. Paris, 1925.
39527.29.89 La Fontaine, Jean de. Fables de La Fontaine; cent fables choisies. Paris, 1925.
43744.67.1062 Laget, Auguste. Le roman d'une vocation; Marcel Proust. Marseille, 1925.
37566.70A Lalou, René. Histoire de la littérature française contemporaine (1870 à nos jours). Paris, 1925.
41578.28.10 Lamartine, Alphonse. Jocelyn. Paris, 1925.
41578.34.3 Lamartine, Alphonse. Raphäel; notices et annotations par Georges Roth. Paris, 1925.
41578.5.14 Lamartine, Alphonse de. Harmonies poétiques et religieuses. Paris, 1925.
41578.7.15 Lamartine, Alphonse de. Méditations poétiques. Paris, 1925.
41577.12.10 Lamartine, Alphonse de. Recueillements poétiques. Paris, 1925.
41557.10.45 Langlade, J. La dernière manière de George Sand. Paris, 1925.
37543.38.11F Lanson, Gustave. Histoire illustrée de la littérature française. 2. éd. Paris, 1925-1926. 2v.
38543.10.15A La Rochefoucauld, François. Mémoires. Paris, 1925.
42515.35.155 Lasserre, Pierre. La jeunesse d'Ernest Renan. Paris, 1925-32. 3v.
43687.89.8100 Lauzanne, Stéphane. La table qui parle. Paris, 1925.
42576.41.55 Le Blanc, Maurice. La vie extravagante de Balthazar. Paris, 1925.
43688.10.100 Lebrau, Jean. Témoignage. St. Félicien-en-Vivarais, 1925.
43688.11.1100 Lecache, B. Jacob. Paris, 1925.
43688.2.45 Le Cardonnel, Louis. Carmina sacra. 11e éd. Paris, 1925.
42544.31.15 Lecomte, Jules. Un scandale littéraire. Paris, 1925.
42555.36.15 Leconte de Lisle, C.M.R. Contes en prose. Paris, 1925.
37568.58.10 Lefèvre, Frédéric. Une heure avec... Série 3. Paris, 1925.
37568.58.12 Lefèvre, Frédéric. Une heure avec... Série 3. 4e éd. Paris, 1925.
43625.3.85 Legrand, André. Rémy de Gourmont son oeuvre. Paris, 1925.
40546.9.20 Lelarge, André. Paul Louis Courier. Paris, 1925.
43688.57.55 Lemonnier, L. L'amour intredit. Paris, 1925.
43688.59.130 Lenéru, Marie. Le bonheur des autres. Paris, 1925.
43688.61.170 Lenormand, Henri René. L'armée secrète suivi de fidélité et du juge intérieur. 6e éd. Paris, 1925.
43688.61.787 Lenormand, Henri René. Stimmen aus dem Dunkel. Berlin, 1925.

Chronological Listing

1925 - cont.

	38543.27.15	Le Pays, René. Nouvelles oeuvres suivies du dialogue de l'amour et de la raison. Paris, 1925.
	38543.27.17	Le Pays, René. Un précieux pient par lui-mème. Portrait de M. Le Pays. Thèse. Paris, 1925.
	42563.18.120	Lesourd, Paul. La terre et les morts de Maurice Barrès. Paris, 1925.
	43688.83.100	Le Stanc, Yves. Chansons de mon village. Paris, 1925.
	43688.91.1100	Levy, Jacob. Juifs d'aujourd'hui, les Pollaks. Paris, 1925.
	42514.28.180	Liévre, Pierre. Maurras. Paris, 1925.
	40597.2.119	Louis, Paul. Les types sociaux chez Balzac et Zola. Paris, 1925.
	42544.34.31	Louys, Pierre. La femme et le pantin. Paris, 1925.
	Mol 750.25	Lyonnet, Henry. Mademoiselle Molière. Paris, 1925.
	43697.6.33	Machard, Alfred. Wolf man. N.Y., 1925.
	38547.12	McMahon, Mary C. (Sister). Aesthetics and art in the Astrée of Honoré d'Urfé. Washington, D.C., 1925.
	43697.14.179	MacOrlan, Pierre. Les pirates de l'avenue du Rhum. 9e ed. Paris, 1925.
	40532.2	Macpherson, Harriet D. Editions of Beaumarchais in New York City. N.Y., 1925.
	43697.34.240	Magre, Maurice. Priscilla d'Alexandrie; roman. Paris, 1925.
	43697.34.230	Magre, Maurice. La tendre camarade. Roman. Paris, 1925?
	43697.34.120A	Magre, Maurice. La vie amoreuse de Messaline. Paris, 1925.
	42555.43.45	Mallarmé, Stéphane. Igitur, ou La folie d'Elbehnon. Paris, 1925.
	41541.20.5	Malo, Henri. La gloire de Vicomte de Launay. Paris, 1925.
	43697.52.3100	Malteste, Louis. Lucile et Ginette ou Les vierges folles. Paris, 1925?
	43697.75.110	Marcel, Gabriel. La chapelle ardente. Paris, 1925.
	43697.75.140	Marcel, Gabriel. La quatuor en fa dièse. Paris, 1925.
	39566.130	Marcel, Louis. La mort de Diderot. Paris, 1925.
	FL 394.127	Marcerou, Louis. La comédie française, l'association des comédiens français. Thèse. Paris, 1925.
	43697.75.4000	Marchon, Albert. Le bachelier sans vergogne. 13e ed. Paris, 1925.
	38526.32.25	Marguerite d'Angoulême. The Heptaméron. N.Y., 1925.
Htn	38512.110*	Marguerite de Beaujeu. Les heures de Marguerite de Beaujeu. Paris, 1925.
	43697.76.1108	Mars, Antony. Les deux pigeons. 8. éd. Paris, 1925.
	43697.78.3110	Marsan, Eugène. Le nouvel amour. Paris, 1925.
	41574.105	Martin, Eugène-Louis. Les symétries de la prose dans les principaux romans de Victor Hugo. Thèse. Paris, 1925.
	43697.76.9120	Martin du Gard, Maurice. Feux tournants; nouveaux portraits contemporains. Paris, 1925.
	42554.26.810	Martineau, René. Tristan Corbière. Paris, 1925.
	42577.4.29.6.5	Maupassant, Guy de. Mont Oriol. Paris, 1925?
	43697.88.100	Mauriac, François. Le désert de l'amour. Paris, 1925.
	43697.89.550	Maurois, André. Arabesques. Paris, 1925.
	43697.89.450	Maurois, André. Captains and kings. N.Y., 1925.
	43697.89.110	Maurois, André. Dialogues sur le commandement. Paris, 1925.
	42514.28.59.50	Maurras, Charles. La musique intérieure. 50. éd. Paris, 1925.
	41578.68.35	Mengin, U. Lamartine à Florence, 1825-1828. Grenoble, 1925.
	43698.75.180	Méré, Charles. Par la farce. Paris, 1925.
	43698.75.140	Méré, Charles. La tentation. Paris, 1925.
	38526.7.15	Merrill, R.V. Platonism of Joachim Du Bellay. Chicago, 1925.
	43698.76.100A	Merrill, Stuart. Prose et vers; oeuvres posthumes. Paris, 1925.
	FL 377.70	Mersmann, A. Das "Schauspiel im Schauspiel" im französischen Drama des XVII Jahrhunderts. Münster, 1925.
	42533.17.28	Meunier, Pierre-Alexis. Émile Montégut. Paris, 1925.
	42533.17.27	Meunier, Pierre-Alexis. Émile Montégut. Thèse. Paris, 1925. 2 pam.
NEDL	Mol 713.15.5A	Michaut, G. Les luttes de Molière. Paris, 1925.
	40587.47	Miller, Meta Helena. Chateaubriand and English literature. Baltimore, 1925.
	43699.65.200	Miomandre, Francis de. Contes des cloches de cristal. Paris, 1925.
	Mol 19.25	Molière, Jean Baptiste Poquelin. Oeuvres de Molière illustrées des gravoures anciennes. Paris, 1925-29. 7v.
	Mol 216.64.5	Molière, Jean Baptiste Poquelin. Le trappolerie de Scapino. Palermo, 1925.
	FL 6119.25	Monglond, A. Vies préromantiques. Paris, 1925.
Htn	Mon 32.25.2*	Montaigne, Michel de. Essays. Cambridge, 1925. 4v.
	Mon 32.25A	Montaigne, Michel de. Essays. Cambridge, 1925. 4v.
	43701.62.140	Montfort, Eugène. La maîtresse américaine. Paris, 1925.
	43701.63.360	Montherlant, Henry de. Chant funèbre pour les morts de verdun. 11. éd. Paris, 1925.
	43701.74.705	Morand, Paul. Closed all night. 2nd ed. London, 1925.
	43701.74.170	Morand, Paul. L'Europe gallante. 82e éd. Paris, 1925.
	43701.76.100	Morienval, H. Sorciere de Montepilloy. Paris, 1925.
Htn	41596.23.25*	Morley, Christopher. Two fables. Garden City, N.Y., 1925.
	37543.68.15	Mornet, D. Histoire des grandes oeuvres de la littérature française. Paris, 1925.
	40575.5.85A	Mott, L.F. Saint-Beuve. N.Y., 1925.
	40515.57.5	Mueller, H.W. Der Fabeldichter Florian. Wesel, 1925.
	37555.148	Nanteuil, Jacques. L'inquiétude religieuse et les poètes d'aujourd'hui. Paris, 1925.
	43705.83.130	Natanson, J. L'âge heureux. Paris, 1925.
	41543.13	Nerval, Gerard de. Jemmy. London, 1925.
	41543.4.30	Nerval, Gerard de. La Pandora. Paris, 1925.
	38514.115	Nesson, Pierre de. Pierre de Nesson et ses oeuvres. Paris, 1925.
	42578.17.400	Neveux, P. Louis. Golo. 10. éd. Paris, 1925.
	42555.66.5	Nolhac, Pierre de. Poèmes de France et d'Italie. Paris, 1925.
	40583.81	Novati, Francesco. Stendhal e l'anima italiana. Milano, 1925.
	42547.22.85	Palgen, R. Villiers de l'Isle Adam, auteur dramatique. Paris, 1925.
	43737.56.100	Pampelonne, Roger de. Carnet lyrique. Saint-Félicien-en-Vivarais, 1925.
	37567.153A	Parker, Clifford S. The defense of the child by French novelists. Menasha, 1925.
	43737.83.140	Passeur, Steve. La maison ouverte. Paris, 1925.
	38514.59.15	Pathelin. The farce of the worthy Master Pierre Patelin. N.Y., 1925.
	43738.77.120	Pérochon, Ernest. Huit gouttes d'opium. Paris, 1925.
	43738.83.112	Pesquidoux, J.D. Le livre de raison. 18e éd. Paris, 1925.
	37597.26.50	Philpot, J.H. Maistre Wace. London, 1925.

1925 - cont.

38525.22.42	Photiades, C. Ronsard et son luth. 4e éd. Paris, 1925.
37576.625	Picard, Gaston. Nos ecrivains definis par eux-mêmes. Paris, 1925.
41587.17.20	Picard, Louis Benoit. Les marionnettes. London, 1925.
43744.67.82A	Pierre-Quint, Léon. Marcel Proust, sa vie, son oeuvre. 7. éd. Paris, 1925.
43744.67.81	Pierre-Quint, Léon. Marcel Proust. Paris, 1925.
43741.98.110	Pize, Louis. Les muses champètres. Paris, 1925.
43743.59.1100	Ponet, Marthe Bordeaux. Un drame d'enfant. Paris, 1925.
43743.75.120	Porché, François. Les butors et la finette. 8. éd. Paris, 1925.
43743.1.43	Porché, François. La vierge au grand coeur. Paris, 1925.
43743.89.2100	Poulaille, H. Ames neuves. Paris, 1925.
43743.90.210	Pourrat, Henri. A la belle Bergère. Paris, 1925.
43743.90.2120	Pourrat, Henri. La combe délaissée. Saint-Félicien-en-Vivarais, 1925.
42578.31.66	Prévost, Marcel. Sa maitresse et moi. Paris, 1925.
43744.41.2100	Prin, Armand de. La vierge au sourire. Paris, 1925.
43744.64.110	Prody, Alfred. Par les sentes; poèmes. Brive, 1925.
43744.67.79	Proust, Marcel. Comment débuta Marcel Proust; lettres inédites. Paris, 1925.
43744.67.41.20	Proust, Marcel. The Guermantes way. N.Y., 1925.
43744.69.100	Proust, Pierre Henry. La maison aux mille fenêtres; poems. Paris, 1925.
42515.35.216	Psichari, Jean. Ernest Renan. Paris, 1925.
42578.31.80	Psichari, Jean. Fioretti per Francesca. Paris, 1925.
38585.27.9	Racine, Jean. Britannicus. N.Y., 1925.
43752.57.110	Ramuz, Charles Ferdinand. L'amour du monde. Paris, 1925.
43752.57.143	Ramuz, Charles Ferdinand. Joie dans le ciel. Paris, 1925.
43752.57.785	Ramuz, Charles Ferdinand. Das Regiment des Bösen; roman. Zürich, 1925.
40536.22.30	Randon de Malboissière, G.F. Une jeune fille au XVIIIe siècle. Lettres...à Adélaïde Méliand, 1761-1766. Paris, 1925.
38525.22.45.30	Rayon, E. Ronsard en France et dans la région de Brie-Gatinais. Melun, 1925.
43556.49.860	Reboux, Paul. Colette, ou Le génie du style. Paris, 1925.
42556.27.30.45	Régnier, Henri de. Proses datées. 8e éd. Paris, 1925.
43753.2.60	Régnier, M.L.A. de. Paris et les voyages. Paris, 1925.
38543.27.55	Rémy, Gabriel. Un précieux de Province au XVIIe siècle, René Le Pays. Thèse. Paris, 1925.
42515.34.50	Renan, Ernest. Lettres à son frère Alain. Paris, 1925.
42515.25.25	Renan, Ernest. Páginas escogidas. 3a. ser. San José, 1925.
42587.51.7	Renard, Jules. Debuts littéraires, 1883-1890. Paris, 1925.
42587.51.5	Renard, Jules. Journal inédit, 1887-1910. Paris, 1925-1927. 5v.
37596.135.15	Renart, Jean. Le roman de l'écoufle. Paris, 1925.
FL 6139.25	Rice, R.A. Rousseau and the poetry of nature in eighteenth century France. Northampton, 1925.
37569.20	Riviere, Jacques. Études: Baudelaire, Paul Claudel, André Gide. 10e éd. Paris, 1925.
43756.2.35	Rivollet, G. Les trois grâces. n.p., 1925.
FL 398.47.60	Rivollet, Georges. Adrienne Lecouvreur. Paris, 1925.
43757.32.100	Roger-Marx, Claude. Simili. Paris, 1925.
43757.50.750A	Rolland, Romain. Annette and Sylvie. v.1. N.Y., 1925.
43757.50.110	Rolland, Romain. Jean-Christophe. Paris, 1925-1927. 10v.
43757.50.440	Rolland, Romain. Le jeu de l'amour et de la mort. Paris, 1925.
43757.50.444	Rolland, Romain. Le jeu de l'amour et de la mort. Paris, 1925.
43757.50.442	Rolland, Romain. Le jeu de l'amour et de la mort. Paris, 1925.
43757.50.766.2	Rolland, Romain. Les loups. Paris, 1925.
43757.50.776	Rolland, Romain. Ein Spiel von Tod und Liebe. Erlenbach, 1925.
43757.50.752A	Rolland, Romain. Summer. v.2. N.Y., 1925.
43757.50.310	Rolland, Romain. Les tragédies de la foi. 9e éd. Paris, 1925.
43757.3.37.5	Romains, Jules. Lucienne. N.Y., 1925.
43757.3.44	Romains, Jules. Le mariage de le Trouhadec. Paris, 1925.
43757.3.90	Romains, Jules. Ode génoise. Paris, 1925.
38525.22.40.5	Ronsard et son temps. Paris, 1925.
38525.22.40	Ronsard et son temps. Paris, 1925.
42578.22.10.30	Rosny, J.H. La courtisane triomphante. Paris, 1925.
42578.22.8.18	Rosny, J.H. La fille d'affaires. Paris, 1925.
42546.15.7.42	Rostand, Edmond. The far princess. N.Y., 1925.
43757.83.47	Rostand, Maurice. L'archange. Paris, 1925.
43757.83.60	Rostand, Maurice. L'homme que j'ai tué. Paris, 1925.
43757.83.100	Rostand, Maurice. La nuit des amants. Paris, 1925.
43757.89.4120	Rouff, Marcel. L'homme et la montagne. Paris, 1925.
42576.63.160	Roujon, Jacques. La vie et les opinions d'Anatole France. Paris, 1925.
FL 6046.10.15	Rousseau, J.J. Émile or Education. London, 1925.
FL 6052.25	Rousseau, J.J. La nouvelle Héloise. Paris, 1925- 4v.
43757.92.113	Roussel, Raymond. L'étoile au front. 3. éd. Paris, 1925.
43757.98.160	Royère, Jean. Clartes sur la poésie. Paris, 1925.
37576.557	Rudmose-Brown, T.B. French short stories. Oxford, 1925.
43566.75.800	Ruet, Noël. Derèmiana, ou Jeux, impromptus et divertissements de Tristan Derème. Seraing, 1925.
V43500.279	Ruet, Noël. L'Escarpolette fleurie; poèmes. Bruxelles, 1925.
37596.4.10	Rutebeuf. Le miracle de Théophile. Paris, 1925.
43761.41.5110	St. Sorny. Palaces. Paris, 1925.
43761.49.190A	Salmon, André. Une orgil à Saint-Petersbourg. Paris, 1925.
43761.6.40	Sarment, Jean. Madelon. Paris, 1925.
43763.2.54	Schopfer, Jean. La fin d'un monde. Paris, 1925.
37595.91	Schwartzkopff, W. Sagen und Geschichten aus dem Alten Frankreich und England. München, 1925.
38525.22.35	Schweinitz, M. de. Les épitaphes de Ronsard. Paris, 1925.
38525.22.34	Schweinitz, M. de. Les épitaphes de Ronsard. Thèse. Paris, 1925.
42587.57.38	Schwob, Marcel. Coeur double. Paris, 1925.
42587.57.30	Schwob, Marcel. La lampe de Psyché. 9. éd. Paris, 1925.
41522.18.435	Séché, A. Charles Baudelaire. Paris, 1925.
43765.21.32	Sée, Edmond. Le bel amour. Paris, 1925.
42576.63.170	Ségur, N. Conversations avec Anatole France ou Les mélancolies de l'intelligence. Paris, 1925.
41574.83	Seilliere, Ernest. Du quiétisme au socialisme romantique. Paris, 1925.
41568.17.25	Sénancour, Étienne Pivert de. Aldomen. Paris, 1925.
40597.2.78	Serval, M. Une amie de Balzac. Paris, 1925.

Chronological Listing

1925 - cont.

37583.625.5 Setchanove, L.J. Five French comedies. Boston, 1925.
37583.625 Setchanove, L.J. Four French comedies. Boston, 1925.
FL 382.86 Smith, Hugh Allison. Main currents of modern French drama. N.Y., 1925.
FL 398.47.65 Sorel, Cécile. La vie amoureuse d'Adrienne Lecouvreur. Paris, 1925.
38525.22.45 Sorg, Roger. Cassandre ou Le secret de Ronsard. Paris, 1925.
43775.90.7170 Soupault, Philippe. En joue, roman. Paris, 1925.
37595.36.22 Spanke, Hans. Eine altfranzösische Liedersammlung. Halle, 1925.
37564.85 Strowski, F.J. La sagesse française: Montaigne, Saint François de Sales, Descartes. Paris, 1925.
43780.5.200 Suarès, André. Polyxène. Paris, 1925.
43780.5.250 Suarès, André. Sur la vie. Paris, 1925. 2v.
43780.69.100 Supervielle, Jules. Gravitations. 3. éd. Paris, 1925.
42557.5.22 Tailhade, Laurent. Poésies posthumes. Paris, 1925.
43788.5.175 Tharaud, Jérôme. La vie et la mort de Déroudèda. 34e éd. Paris, 1925.
42583.33.32 Theuriet, André. L'oncle Scipion. Paris, 1925. 3 pam.
43788.25.100 Thévenin, Léon. La robe sans couture. Paris, 1925.
37596.42.5A Thibaut I, King of Navarre. Les chansons de Thibaut de champagne roi de Navarre. Paris, 1925.
41568.25.70 Tillier, Claude. De l'Espagne. Paris, 1925.
40583.158 Tiltoni, T. Arrigo Beyle (Stendhal). Torino, 1925.
43792.90.170 Toulet, Paul Jean. Quatre contes. Paris, 1925.
37567.218 Trabard, P. Le romantisme; défini par "Le globe". Paris, 1925.
37556.15.105 Trahard, Pierre. Une revue oubliée. Paris, 1925.
38525.36.12 Tristan L'Hermite, F. Les amours et autres poesies. Paris, 1925.
43880.87.100 Les trois. L'initiation de reine Dermine. Paris, 1925.
43554.2.825 Truc, Gonzague. Paul Claudel, portrait et autographe. Paris, 1925.
FL 398.54 Truffier, J. Mélinque; le comédien, l'Homme. Paris, 1925.
38547.7.5A Urfé, Honoré d'. L'Astrée. Lyon, 1925-28. 5v.
Mon 161.10 Valeri, Diego. Montaigne. Roma, 1925.
43822.49.745 Valéry, Paul. An evening with Mr. Teste. Paris, 1925.
42547.15.12 Van der Meulen, C.J.C. L'idéalisme de Villiers de l'Isle Adam. Amsterdam, 1925.
43827.89.130 Vaudoyer, J.L. Raymonde Mangematin. Paris, 1925.
43822.89.150 Vaulet, Clément. Mon curé chez les pauvres. Paris, 1925.
FL 398.79.5 Veber, Pierre. Samson. Paris, 1925.
39545.29.15 Vezinet, F. Autour de Voltaire. Paris, 1925.
42576.57.30 Viaud, Julien. Journal intime par Pierre Loti. v.2. Paris, 1925-29.
42576.57.19 Viaud, Julien. Le livre de la pitié et de la mort. Paris, 1925.
42576.56.7 Viaud, Julien. Madame Chrysanthème. Paris, 1925.
42576.57.2.3 Viaud, Julien. Mon frère Yves. Paris, 1925.
42557.27.5 Vicaire, Jean. Bibliographie de Gabriel Vicaire d'après les notes recueilles par G. Vicaire. Paris, 1925.
42557.25.140 Vielé-Griffin, F. La sagesse d'Ulysse, orné d'une composition de K.-X. Roussel. Paris, 1925.
41564.1.2.5 Vigny, Alfred de. Poésies complètes. Paris, 1925.
43824.49.110 Vildrac, Charles. Madame Béliard. Paris, 1925.
43824.49.140 Vildrac, Charles. Poèmes de l'abbaye suivis de esquisse d'un pégase. Paris, 1925.
42547.16.3 Villiers de l'Isle Adam, Auguste. Axel. London, 1925.
41556.41 Vodoz, Jules. "Les fes aux miettes." Paris, 1925.
39545.32.15 Voltaire, François Marie Arouet de. Selections from Voltaire with explanatory comment. N.Y., 1925.
39545.32.27 Voltaire, François Marie Arouet de. Zadig, an Oriental history. Photoreproduction. Cincinnati, 1925.
37562.45.10 Voretzsch, Carl. Einführung in das Studium der altfranzösischen Literatur. Halle, 1925.
40526.31 Webster, Nestor H. (Mrs.). Chevalier de Boufflers. London, 1925.
40526.31.5A Webster, Nestor H. (Mrs.). The chevalier de Boufflers. N.Y., 1925.
37543.57.5 Wright, C.H. Conrad. A history of French literature. N.Y., 1925.
37574.760 Young, C.E. Anthology of French lyric poetry. Chicago, 1925.
41574.99 Yperloon, J.C. Les traductions hollandaises des poésies lyriques de Victor Hugo jusqu'en 1885. Bussum, 1925.
38514.21.25 Yve-Plessis, R. La psychose de François Villon. Paris, 1925.
43858.1.37 Zamacois, Miguel. Seigneur Pohchinelle. Paris, 1925.
42584.11.8.50 Zola, Emile. The downfall. N.Y., 1925.

1926

37543.114.15 Abry, E. Histoire illustrée de la littérature française. 7. éd. Paris, 1926.
43512.75.110 Achard, Marcel. Je ne vous aime pas. 4. ed. Paris, 1926.
37596.25.10A Adam (Mystery). Adam...play of 12th century. Seattle, 1926.
FL 391.15 Aghion, Max. Le théâtre à Paris au XVIIIe siècle. Paris, 1926.
43822.49.185 Aguettant, Louis. Les dialogues de Paul Valéry. Saint-Félicien-en-Vivarais, 1926.
43520.54.700 Aimery de Pierrebourg, M.J.G. Cleopatra. Garden City, 1926.
43522.4.100 Alanic, Mathilde. En treinte du passe. Paris, 1926.
43522.41.170 Alibert, François Paul. Le chemin sur la mer. Paris, 1926.
43522.49.110 Alleman, Jeanne. Le goéland. 14. ed. Paris, 1926.
Mol 601.13 American Academy of Arts and Letters. Proceedings at the commemoration of the 300th anniversary of the birth of Molière. N.Y., 1926.
43523.41.180 Amiel, Denys. La carcasse. Paris, 1926.
37574.100 Anderson, Frederick. Illustrations of early French literature, 1100-1600. Boston, 1926.
37576.626A Anthologie de la nouvelle prise française. Paris, 1926.
43526.65.793 Apollinaire, Guillaume. Kacir e spoie. Praha, 1926.
43526.65.792 Apollinaire, Guillaume. Prsytireswvy. Praha, 1926.
43527.3.390 Aragon, Louis. Le mouvement perpétuel. Paris, 1926.
40583.85 Arbelet, Paul. Stendhal épicier. Paris, 1926.
43528.48.175 Arland, Marcel. Nonique. Paris, 1926.
43528.53.1100 Armagnac, M.M. d'. La carrière Bolcheviste d'Alexis Jourouskine. Paris, 1926.
43528.58.2110 Arnac, Marcel. Saint-Lettres. Paris, 1926.
43531.10.100 Aubry, Octave. Le lit du roi. Paris, 1926.
43531.14.100 Auclair, Marcelle. Changer d'etoile. Paris, 1926.

1926 - cont.

41543.5.1 Audiat, Pierre. L'Aurelia de Gerard de Nerval. Paris, 1926.
42542.10.5.13 Augier, Émile. Le gendre de M. Poirier. Boston, 1926.
43606.89.82 Aurenche, Louis. L'oeuvre de Gabriel Faure. Paris, 1926.
43536.5.100 Azaïs, Marcel. Le chemin des gardies. Paris, 1926.
42576.65.13.19 Bachelin, H. J.K. Huysmans du naturalisme littéraire. Paris, 1926.
37543.154 Badaire, J. Précis de littérature française. Boston, 1926.
43537.42.130 Bainville, Jacques. Nouveau dialogue dans le salon d'Alienor. Paris, 1926.
43537.42.150 Bainville, Jacques. Polioute. Liège, 1926.
40563.22.10 Ballanche, Pierre Simon. La vielle des expiations (livres IV à VII). Paris, 1926.
40596.27A Balzac, Honoré de. Complete novelettes. N.Y., 1926.
40597.14.16 Balzac, Honoré de. Les contes drolatiques. Paris, 1926.
40597.29.3 Balzac, Honoré de. Un ménage de garçon. Paris, 1926.
40597.29.5.6 Balzac, Honoré de. Old Goriot. London, 1926.
41522.1.1.5 Barbey d'Aurevilly, Jules. Un prêtre marié. Paris, 1926. 2v.
41522.2.54 Barbey d'Aurevilly, Jules. Une vieille maîtresse. Paris, 1926. 2v.
41522.17.42 Barrès, Maurice. La folie de Charles Baudelaire. Paris, 1926.
42563.19.15 Barrès, Maurice. Le mystère en pleine lumière. Paris, 1926.
41522.12.15 Baudelaire, Charles. Baudelaire, prose and poetry. N.Y., 1926.
41522.18.15 Baudelaire, Charles. Dernières lettres inédites à sa mère. Paris, 1926.
41522.13.8.70 Baudelaire, Charles. Les fleurs du mal. N.Y., 1926.
41522.6.6 Baudelaire, Charles. Petits poèmes en prose. Oeuvres complètes. Paris, 1926.
43537.89.2140 Baumann, Émile. Le signe sur les mains. 7. éd. Paris, 1926.
42563.21.79 Bazin, René. Baltus le lorrain. Paris, 1926.
38523.3.30 Becker, P.A. Clément Marot sein Leben und seine Dichtung. München, 1926.
37567.223 Belis, A. La critique française a la fin du XIXe siècle. Paris, 1926.
43744.67.1068 Benoist-Mechin, J.G.P.M. La musique et l'immortalite dans l'oeuvre de Marcel Proust. Paris, 1926.
43538.61.70A Benoît, Pierre. Alberte. Paris, 1926.
40575.5.35 Benoit-Levy, Edmond. Sainte-Beuve et Mme. Victor Hugo. Paris, 1926.
43538.74.115 Béraud, Henri. Le bois du templier pendu. Paris, 1926.
43538.76.102 Bernanos, Georges. Sous le soleil de Satan. Paris, 1926.
43538.76.100A Bernanos, Georges. Sous le soleil de Satan. Paris, 1926.
42542.29.28.180 Bernard, Tristan. Mémoires. Paris, 1926.
42542.29.28.30 Bernard, Tristan. Un perdreau de l'année; comédie en trois actes. Paris, 1926.
42542.29.65 Berr, Georges. Azais, comédie en trois actes. Paris, 1926.
FL 398.74.92 Berthon, Louis. Rachel. Paris, 1926.
41522.58.20 Bertrand, Louis. Oeuvres poétiques. Paris, 1926.
41522.58.22 Bertrand, Louis. Oeuvres poétiques. Thèse. Paris, 1926.
40597.2.149 Bettelheim, A. Balzac, eine Biografie. München, 1926.
43538.88.130 Betz, Maurice. Le démon impur; roman. Paris, 1926.
Htn 42557.14.4* Bever, A. van. Bibliographie et iconographie de Paul Verlaine. Paris, 1926.
40582.2.50 Beyle, Henri. De l'amour. Paris, 1926. 2v.
40582.2.55 Beyle, Henri. Lucien Leuwen. Paris, 1926-27. 4v.
37577.40 Bienstock, J.W. Le bonheur du jour. Paris, 1926.
43540.83.100 Bisson, André. Le rosaire; piece en trois actes et quatre tableaux. Paris, 1926.
43543.13.102 Bloch, J.R. Dernier empereur. 3. éd. Paris, 1926.
43543.1.35 Blois, Louis A. Au soleil d'or. Paris, 1926.
38543.23.35 Bochénski, Aleksander. Nienawiść i miłość La Rochefoucauld. Warszawa, 1926.
39526.50 Boillot, Félix. Les impressions sensorielles chez La Fontaine. Paris, 1926.
FL 396.54 Boissard, M. Le théâtre de Maurice Boissard, 1907-1923. v.1, 4. ed; v.2, 8. ed. Paris, 1926-45. 2v.
42576.63.86 Bölöni, I.M.J. (Mme.). Rambles with Anatole France. Philadelphia, 1926.
38512.57 Bonet, Honoré. L'apparicion maistre Jehan de Meun. Paris, 1926.
38512.57.5 Bonet, Honoré. L'apparicion maistre Jehan de Meun. Thèse. Strasbourg, 1926.
42563.36.120 Bordeaux, Henry. Les jeux dangereux. Paris, 1926.
42563.36.60.3 Bordeaux, Henry. La peur de vivre. N.Y., 1926.
FL 6139.26 Boschann, Johannes. Die Spontaneitätsidee bei Jean-Jacques Rousseau. Inaug. Diss. Berlin, 1926?
37595.58 Bossuat, Robert. Drouart la Vache, traducteur d'André le chapelain (1290). Thèse. Paris, 1926.
38557.25.80 Bossuet, J.B. Oeuvres oratoires. Paris, 1926-27. 7v.
43544.83.140 Bost, Pierre. Voyage de l'esclave. Paris, 1926.
43544.89.9100 Boudry, Robert. Le valet de coeur. Paris, 1926.
40526.30.35 Boufflers, Stanislas de. The queen of Golconda. London, 1926.
41593.29.3.55 Boulenger, Jacques. Marceline Desbordes-Valmore. Paris, 1926.
42542.44.25A Bourdet, Édouard. Captive. N.Y., 1926.
42542.44.29 Bourdet, Édouard. La prisonnière. Paris, 1926.
42542.44.31 Bourdet, Édouard. La prisonnière. Paris, 1926.
42542.44.30 Bourdet, Édouard. La prisonnière. 6. éd. Paris, 1926.
42563.37.65 Bourget, Paul. Le danseur mondain. Paris, 1926.
42563.37.59 Bourget, Paul. Nos actes nous suivent. pt.1-6. Paris, 1926-27.
37567.237 Bouteron, Maral. Muses romantiques. Paris, 1926.
42563.39.105 Boylesve, René. Les deux romanciers. Paris, 1926.
42563.39.72 Boylesve, René. Les nouvelles leçons d'amour dans un parc. Paris, 1926.
37566.77A Braunschvig, M. La littérature française contemporaine. Paris, 1926.
37564.93A Bray, René. La formation de la doctrine classique en France. Thèse. Dijon, 1926.
43545.23.3100 Bremond, Charles. Le train de plaisir. Paris, 1926.
42542.47.39.10 Brieux, Eugène. Famille Lavolette. Paris, 1926.
42576.63.42 Brousson, Jean J. Anatole France en pantoufles. Paris, 1926.
X Cg 43546.82.100 Bustros, Éveline. La main d'Allah. 11. éd. Paris, 1926.
FL 363.38 Calvet, Jean. Les types universéls dans la littérature française. Paris, 1926.
43550.1.35A Carco, Francis. Le roman de François Villon. Paris, 1926.
FL 6049.13 Carrara, Vincenza. Jean-Jacques Rousseau. Firenze, 1926.

Chronological Listing

1926 - cont.

42556.28.110 Carré, Jean Marie. La vie aventureuse de Jean Arthur Rimbaud. Paris, 1926.
37530.195F Carteret, Léopold. Manuscrits de Pierre Louys et de divers auteurs contemporains. Paris, 1926.
43551.59.135 Cendrars, Blaise. L'ABC du cinéma. Paris, 1926.
43551.59.290 Cendrars, Blaise. Eloge de la vie dangereuse. Paris, 1926.
43551.59.280 Cendrars, Blaise. L'eubage aux antipodes de l'unite. Paris, 1926.
43551.59.260 Cendrars, Blaise. Profond aujourd'hui. Paris, 1926.
42576.63.65A Cerf, Barry. Anatole France, the degeneration of a great artist. N.Y., 1926.
43552.1.120 Chabaneix, Philippe. Recuerdos. La Rochelle, 1926.
38526.27.18 Champion, P. Le canonicat pour Jean Lemaire de Belges à Lyon. Lyon, 1926.
38514.53.12 Champion, Pierre. Le manuscrit d'auteur du Petit Jehan de Saintré. Paris, 1926.
42587.57.82 Champion, Pierre. Marcel Schwob. Paris, 1926.
43552.4.100 Chantel, L. Le silence. Paris, 1926.
43552.5.2100 Charles-Etienne. Les épices libertines. Paris, 1926.
39544.84A Chase, C.B. Young Voltaire. N.Y., 1926.
40586.45.28 Chateaubriand, F.A.R. Les aventures du dernier Abencérage. Paris, 1926. 2v.
43552.6.140 Chateaubriant, Alphonse de. Le baron du Puydreau. Paris, 1926.
43552.24.190 Chérau, Gaston. Le vent du destin. Paris, 1926.
42563.18.145 Cheydleur, F.D. Maurice Barrès. v.1-2. n.p., 1926.
43554.2.785 Claudel, Paul. Der Bürge. Hellerau, 1926.
43554.2.78 Claudel, Paul. La jeune fille Violaine. Paris, 1926.
38537.25.62 Clement, N.H. The influence of the Arthurian romances on the five books of Rabelais. Berkeley, 1926.
37567.255 Clerc, Charly. Le génie du paganisme. Paris, 1926.
43556.13.100 Cochet, Marie A. Le sommeil du solipsiste. Bruxelles, 1926.
43556.1.37A Cocteau, Jean. Lettre à Jacques Maritain. Paris, 1926.
42563.39.800 Codet, Louis. Poèmes et chansons. 2. éd. Paris, 1926.
NEDL FL 373.6.5 Cohen, Gustave. Histoire de la mise en scène dans le théâtre religieux français du Moyen Age. Paris, 1926.
37544.9 Cohnen, Theodor. Der Rhein in der französischen Literatur. Inaug.-Diss. Bonn, 1926.
43556.49.170 Colette, Sidonie Gabrielle. La fin de Chéri. Paris, 1926.
43556.49.229 Colette, Sidonie Gabrielle. La retraite sentimentale. Paris, 1926.
43556.50.110 Colling, Alfred. L'iroguois; roman. Paris, 1926.
38513.25.10 Cons, Louis. L'auteur de la farce de Pathelin. Princeton, N.J., 1926.
42586.32.50 Coster, Charles de. Die Geschichte von Ulenspiegel und Lamme Goedzak und ihren heldenmässigen, fröhlichen und glorreichen Abenteuern. München, 1926. 2v.
FL 397.8.15 Courteault, P. La révolution et les théâtres à Bordeaux d'après des documents inédits. Paris, 1926.
43557.25.105 Crevel, René. La mort difficile. 2e éd. Paris, 1926.
42542.58.25 Curel, François de. La viveuse et le moribund; trois actes. Paris, 1926.
42566.29.21 Daudet, Alphonse. Le Nabab. Paris, 1926.
42566.33.9 Daudet, Alphonse. Les rois en exil. Paris, 1926.
43565.5.250 Daudet, Léon A. Léon Daudet. Paris, 1926.
43565.5.25 Daudet, Léon A. Memoirs. London, 1926.
43822.49.3 Davis, Ronald. Bibliographie des oeuvres de Paul Valéry (1895-1925). Paris, 1926.
43822.49.900A De l'art pour tous à l'art pour l'art. Valéry ou Boileau? Paris, 1926.
43566.2.35 Deberly, Henri. Supplice de Phédre. Paris, 1926.
43566.2.36 Deberly, Henri. Le supplice de Phédre. 13e éd. Paris, 1926.
43566.2.37 Deberly, Henri. Le supplice de Phédre. 60. éd. Paris, 1926.
43566.2.38 Deberly, Henri. Le supplice de Phédre. 90. éd. Paris, 1926.
FL 6129.26 De Crue de Stoutz, Francis. L'ami de Rousseau et des Necker. Paul Moultou à Paris en 1778. Paris, 1926.
43566.53.120 Demasy, Paul. Dalilah. Paris, 1926.
37555.365 Derème, Tristan. Guirlande pour deux vers de Gérard de Neroal. Saint-Félicien-en-Vivarais, 1926.
43566.76.110 Derennes, Charles. La matinée du faune, 1906-1926. Paris, 1926.
42542.64.27.10 Descaves, Lucien. Le coeur ébloui. Paris, 1926.
37572.56 Des Granges, C. Pages de littérature française (1800-1920). Paris, 1926.
43566.7.40 Deval, Jacques. La rose de septembre. Paris, 1926.
37567.141.10 Dondey, Théophile. Feu et flamme. Paris, 1926.
42542.65.35 Donnay, Maurice. Autour du Chat Noir. Paris, 1926.
41596.4.7 Donnay, Maurice C. La vie amoureuse d'Alfred de Musset. Paris, 1926.
43573.76.39 Dorgelès, Roland. Partir. Paris, 1926.
37543.200 Doutrepont, Georges. Les types populaires de la littérature française. pt. 1. Bruxelles, 1926-27. 2v.
43744.67.818A Dreyfus, R. Marcel Proust a dix-sept ans. Paris, 1926.
43744.67.815 Dreyfus, R. Souvenirs sur Marcel Proust. Paris, 1926.
37595.57 Dronart la Vache. Le livres d'amour de Dronart la Vache. Thèse. Paris, 1926.
FL 394.129 Dubech, Lucien. La comédie-française d'aujourd'hui. Paris, 1926.
38585.8.7 Dubech, Lucien. Jean Racine politique. Paris, 1926.
43576.13.100 Duchêne, Ferdinand. Kamir; roman d'une femme Arabe. Paris, 1926.
FL 360.97 Duhamel, G. Essai sur une renaissance dramtique. Paris, 1926.
43576.6.125 Duhamel, Georges. Ballades. Paris, 1926.
43576.6.88 Duhamel, Georges. Lettres au Patagon. 11. éd. Paris, 1926.
43576.6.50 Duhamel, Georges. La Pierre d'Horeb. 5. éd. Paris, 1926.
43576.6.135 Duhamel, Georges. Les plaisirs et les jeux. v.1-2. Paris, 1926. 3v.
42543.16.35 Dumas, Alexandre. Le démi-monde. Paris, 1926.
41538.53.14A Dumas, Alexandre. Les trois mousquetaires. N.Y., 1926.
42568.23.13 Duval, Paul. Portraits littéraires et mondains. Paris, 1926.
43576.90.100 Duverne, René. Victime expiatoire. Paris, 1926.
42574.38 Duviard, Ferdinand. Ferdinand Fabre, 1827-1898. Thèse. Cahors, 1926.
40597.2.60 Duviard, Ferdinand. Un prédécesseur de Ferdinand Fabre. Cahors, 1926.
42568.23.105 Eekhoud, Georges. La faneuse d'amour. Paris, 1926.
43591.89.110A Eluard, Paul. Capitale de la douleur. Paris, 1926.
43598.13.102.5 Escholier, R. Dansons la trompeuse. Paris, 1926.

1926 - cont.

41574.115A Escholier, Raymond. Victor Hugo, artiste. Paris, 1926.
43598.84.190 Estaunié, Édouard. Le labyrinthe. Paris, 1926.
43598.84.220 Estaunié, Édouard. Le silence dans la campagne. 20. éd. Paris, 1926.
43606.78.140 Farrère, Claude. Le dernier dieu. Paris, 1926.
43606.87.190 Fauchois, René. La paix des familles. Paris, 1926.
Mon 116.35 Faure, Élie. Montaigne et ses trois premiers-nés. Paris, 1926.
42576.35.50A Flaubert, Gustave. Correspondance. Paris, 1926-1935. 9v.
43610.24.100 Flers, Robert de. Les nouveaux messieurs. Paris, 1926.
42543.42.15 Flers, Robert de. Romance. Paris, 1926.
43610.25.140 Fleuret, Fernand. Soeur Félicité. Paris, 1926.
42555.37.6.15 Flottes, Pierre. L'influence d'Alfred de Vigny sur Leconte de Lisle. Thèse. Paris, 1926.
41564.35.9 Flottes, Pierre. La pensée politique et sociale d'Alfred de Vigny. Thèse. Strasbourg, 1926.
37567.315 Flutre, Fernand. Le romantisme. Paris, 1926.
43611.4.45 Foley, Charles. Femmes aimantes, femmes aimées. Paris, 1926.
43611.59.100 Fondmarin, H. Nos précieuses ridicules. Paris, 1926.
43611.1.25.34 Fort, Paul. Le camp du drap d'or. XXXIV. Paris, 1926.
37555.102 Fort, Paul. Histoire de la poésie française depuis 1850. Paris, 1926.
43611.5.32 Fournier, Alain. Le grand meaulnes. Paris, 1926.
42576.62.130 France, Anatole. Anatole France at home. N.Y., 1926.
42576.63.7.25 France, Anatole. Le crime de Sylvestre Bonnard. 314. éd. Paris, 1926.
42576.63.7.26 France, Anatole. Le crime de Sylvestre Bonnard. 317. éd. Paris, 1926.
42576.63.7.55 France, Anatole. The crime of Sylvestre Bonnard. N.Y., 1926.
42576.62.45A France, Anatole. Golden tales of Anatole France. N.Y., 1926.
42576.63.17.10 France, Anatole. The man who married a dumb wife. N.Y., 1926.
42576.62.3.26 France, Anatole. Thaïs. N.Y., 1926.
43612.61.110 Franck, Henri. Lettres à quelques amis. Paris, 1926.
43612.2.50 Fraudet, René. L'eau du Nil; roman. Paris, 1926.
43614.1.100 Fua, Albert. Le triomphe de satan. Paris, 1926.
41522.17.33 Fumet, Stanislas. Notre Baudelaire. Paris, 1926.
43744.67.810A Gabory, Georges. Essai sur Marcel Proust. Paris, 1926.
43615.1.330 Gadala, Marie-Therese. Tels que je les vois. Paris, 1926.
FL 395.222 Gaulot, Paul. Le foyer de la comédie française, 1870-1900. Paris, 1926.
42577.4.40 Gelzer, Heinrich. Guy de Maupassant. Heidelberg, 1926.
43617.5.39 Géniaux, Charles. Les feux s'eteigneut. Paris, 1926.
43617.4.45 Géraldy, Paul. Robert et Marianne. Paris, 1926.
FL 397.114.105 Gersdorff, Arthur. Théâtre royal de la monnaie 1856-1926. Bruxelles, 1926.
43619.24.140 Ghéon, Henri. Les propos interrompus. Paris, 1926.
43620.2.49 Gide, André. Numquid et tu? Paris, 1926.
41574.102 Giese, W.F. Victor Hugo, the man and the poet. N.Y., 1926.
43620.35.120 Gilbert de Voisins, Auguste. Les miens. Paris, 1926.
37568.86 Gillouin, René. Esquisses litteraires et morales. 5e éd. Paris, 1926.
FL 398.8 Ginisty, Paul. Bocage. Paris, 1926.
37567.340 Girard, Henri. Le centenaire du premier cénacle romantique de la "Muse française". Paris, 1926.
43620.74.100 Giraudoux, Jean. Bella. Paris, 1926.
43620.74.125 Giraudoux, Jean. Elpénor. 34. éd. Paris, 1926.
43620.74.230 Giraudoux, Jean. Simon le pathétique. 30. éd. Paris, 1926.
42586.66.25 Gobineau, Arthur de. The dancing girl of Shamokha. N.Y., 1926.
43625.19.340 Godoy, Armand. Stéle pour Charles Baudelaire. Paris, 1926.
42543.51.25 Gohier, Urbain. Spartacus. Paris, 1926.
43625.49.160 Goll, Claire. Der Neger Jupider raubt Europa. Basel, 1926.
43625.3.41.20 Gourmont, Rémy de. A night in the Luxembourg. N.Y., 1926.
Htn 37543.96* Gourmont, Rémy de. Promenades littéraires. 6. série. Paris, 1926.
38546.49.10 Grignan, Françoise M. Lettres choisies. Paris, 1926.
43626.41.21 Grimard, Luc. Sur ma flûte de bambou; poèmes. Paris, 1926.
FL 379.82 Grohmann, W. Die pronominalen Anredeformen in Drama des 18. Jahrhunderts. Inaug. Diss. Leipzig, 1926.
38588.17.10 Gros, Etienne. Philippe Quinault; sa vie et son oeuvre. Thèse. Paris, 1926.
38588.17.8 Gros, Etienne. Philippe Quinault; sa vie et son oeuvre. Thèse. Paris, 1926.
42554.50.4 Guérin, C. Oeuvres. Paris, 1926-30. 3v.
43628.1.50 Guitry, Sacha. Deburau. Paris, 1926.
43628.1.48 Guitry, Sacha. Mozart; comédie en trois actes. Paris, 1926.
37596.109.5 Hård af Segerstad, Kerstin. Sur les dieux des Sarrasins dans les chansons de geste du XIIe siècle. Uppsala, 1926.
37567.273 Halflants, Paul. Religion et littérature. 3e éd. Louvain, 1926.
38563.33 Hallays, André. Les Perrault. 2. éd. Paris, 1926.
38563.33.2 Hallays, André. Les Perrault. 3. éd. Paris, 1926.
43632.6.167 Henriot, Émile. L'enfant perdu. Paris, 1926.
42554.59 Heredia, J.M. de. Les trophées. Paris, 1926.
FL 397.72.7 Herelle, Georges. Études sur le théâtre basque. Les pastorales à sujets tragediques considérées littérairement. Paris, 1926.
43632.98.100 Heyrand, Charles. Le coeur gagne. Paris, 1926.
42576.63.55 Huard, George. Anatole France et le quai Malaquais. Paris, 1926.
42576.66.3.10 Huysmans, Joris Karl. Against the grain. Paris, 1926.
43638.99.130 Huzard, A. de B. (Mme.). Aujourd'hui. Paris, 1926.
43643.23.103 Ibals, A. La maison de l'enfer. Paris, 1926.
43659.88.710 Istrati, Panait. Kyra kyralina. N.Y., 1926.
43667.14.330 Jacob, Max. Le nom. Paris, 1926.
39583.30 Jacquart, Jean. L'abbé Trublet, critique et moraliste, 1697-1770. Paris, 1926.
39583.18 Jacquart, Jean. L'abbé Trublet, critique et moraliste, 1697-1770. Thèse. Paris, 1926.
39583.23 Jacquart, Jean. La correspondance de l'abbé Trublet. Thèse. Paris, 1926.
39583.20.5 Jacquart, Jean. La correspondance de l'abbé Trublet. Thèse. Paris, 1926.
41578.74 Jacquemin, Juliette. Lamartine, ses origins Franc-comtoises. Lyon, 1926.

Chronological Listing

1926 - cont.

43667.51.200 Jaloux, Édmond. L'âge d'or. Paris, 1926.

43667.51.190 Jaloux, Édmond. L'ami des jeunes filles. Paris, 1926.

43667.51.240 Jaloux, Édmond. O toi que j'eusse aimée. 23. éd. Paris, 1926.

43667.1.115 Jammes, Francis. Ma france poétique. 4. éd. Paris, 1926.

43667.1.65 Jammes, Francis. Oeuvres. v.5. Paris, 1926.

43667.1.60 Jammes, Francis. Trente-six femmes. 6. éd. Paris, 1926.

41555.46 Johnstone, G.H. Prosper Mérimée, a mask and a face. London, 1926.

43670.40.100 Joignet, M. La rivière d'argent. Blois, 1926.

43670.94.410 Jouve, Pierre Jean. Nouvelles noces. Paris, 1926.

42554.68.10 Kahn, Gustave. Contes juifs. Paris, 1926.

43673.82.100 Kessel, Jacques. Le triplace. Paris, 1926.

42544.33.52 Knopf, A. Jules Lemaître als Dramatiker. Inaug. Diss. Leipzig, 1926.

FL 6139.26.5 Kühl, Erich. Die Natur des Menschen und die Struktur der Erzishung bei Rousseau und Pestalozzi. Inaug. Diss. n.p., 1926.

39544.49 Labriola, A. Voltaire e la filosofia della liberazione. Napoli, 1926.

38564.32.25 La Bruyère, J. de. Les caractères. Paris, 1926.

42577.4.32.5 Lacaze-Duthiers, Gerard de. Guy de Maupassant, son oeuvre. Paris, 1926.

40562.10 Lacordaire, Jean Baptiste Henri. Pages choisies. 7. éd. Paris, 1926?

37564.68 Lacour, L. Richelieu dramaturge et ses collaborateurs. Paris, 1926.

43687.15.285 Lacretelle, Jacques de. Trebuchet. Liège, 1926.

38544.27.295 La Fayette, Marie M. Histoire de la Princesse de Monpensier. Paris, 1926.

39527.33.26 La Fontaine, Jean de. Les amours de psyché, opuscules et lettres. Paris, 1926.

39526.29.15 La Fontaine, Jean de. Fables. Paris, 1926.

41578.81 Lamartine, Alphonse. Lettere inedite di Alphonse de Lamartine alla marchesa di Barolo. Torino, 1926.

40517.50.10 Lamorlière, J.R. de. Angola: an Eastern tale. London, 1926.

38512.97A Langfors, Arthur. Recueil général des jeux-partis français. v.1-2. Paris, 1926.

37543.38.13 Lanson, Gustave. Histoire de la littérature française. 19. éd. Paris, 1926?

43687.74.125 Larbaud, Valéry. Fermina Márquez. 8e éd. Paris, 1926.

43822.49.924 Larbaud, Valery. Paul Valéry et la Méditerranée. 1. éd. Maestricht, 1926.

43687.75.110 Larguier, Léo. Sabine. pt.1-2. Paris, 1926.

43687.77.3100 La Rochefoucauld, Edmée (de Fels). Nombres. Paris, 1926.

FL 398.20.8 La Roux, Hugues. La Dugazon. Paris, 1926.

42514.28.155 Larpent, G. Pour connaître Charles Maurras. Paris, 1926.

41595.31.50 Larrebat, J. Poesies Gasconnes. Paris, 1926.

38514.55.13 La Sale, Antoine de. The fifteen joys of marriage. London, 1926.

38514.53.15 La Sale, Antoine de. Le Petit Jehan de Saintré. Paris, 1926.

43687.83.115 Lasserre, Pierre. Le secret d'Abélard. Paris, 1926.

39586.27.5 Latzarus, L. La vie paresseuse de Rivarol. Paris, 1926.

43688.9.100 Lebrau, Jean. La rumeur des pins. Paris, 1926.

43688.14.3100 Leclèrc, Tristan. Schéhérazade. Amiens, 1926.

43822.49.995 Lefévre, Fréderic. Entretiens avec Paul Valéry. Paris, 1926.

40597.2.295 Léger, C. Eve de Balzac d'après des documents. Paris, 1926.

38546.64 Lemoine, Jean. Madame de Sévigné. Paris, 1926.

42576.43.35 Lemonnier, Camille. Un mâle. Paris, 1926.

43688.59.110A Lenéru, Marie. Les affranchis. Paris, 1926.

43688.61.160 Lenormand, Henri René. Le lâche. Paris, 1926.

40512.65 LeSage, Alain René. Les aventures du flibustier Beauchêne. N.Y., 1926.

43688.83.110 Le Stanc, Yves. Chansons du flot le long des grèves. Paris, 1926.

43757.50.1000A Liber amicorum Romain Rolland. Zürich, 1926.

43885.15 Luc-Cyl (pseud.). Le beau chanteur du Boris's bar. Paris, 1926.

43694.59.101 Lunel, Armand. Nicolo-Peccair. Paris, 1926.

37564.80 Luschka, W.H. Die Rolle des Fortschrittsgedankens in der Poetik und Literarischen Kritik der Franzosen. Inaug. Diss. München, 1926.

38544.27.565 Magne, Émile. Madame de La Fayette en ménage. Paris, 1926.

43697.34.250 Magre, Maurice. La luxure de Grenade; roman. Paris, 1926.

38523.30.10 Malherbe, François de. Les poésies de Malherbe. Paris, 1926.

41584.55.150 Maloigne, M. Jacques Grévin, sa vie, son oeuvre. Laval, 1926.

43697.52.160 Malraux, André. La tentation de l'Occident. 12 éd. Paris, 1926.

43744.67.800A Marcel Proust. Paris, 1926.

43697.75.3010 Marchand, L. Mon gosse de père. Paris, 1926.

41543.4.25 Marie, Aristide. Bibliographie des oeuvres de Gerard de Nerval. Paris, 1926.

42514.28.165 Maritain, Jacques. Une opinion sur Charles Maurras. Paris, 1926.

43556.1.41A Maritain, Jacques. Réponse à Jean Cocteau. Paris, 1926.

43697.78.3140 Marsan, Eugène. Notre costume. Liège, 1926.

FL 385.53 Marsan, Jules. Théâtre d'hier et d'aujourd'hui. Paris, 1926.

43697.76.2700 Martel, D. de. Silhouettes of Peking. Peking, 1926.

43697.77.705 Martin du Gard, Roger. The Thibaults. N.Y., 1926- 2v.

42563.23.116 Martineau, René. Autour de Léon Bloy. Paris, 1926.

38525.22.45.43 Maugain, Gabriel. Ronsard en Italie. Paris, 1926.

43744.67.993 Mauriac, F. Proust. Paris, 1926.

43697.88.610 Mauriac, François. Fabien. Paris, 1926.

43697.4.40 Mauriac, François. La province. Paris? 1926.

43756.90.855 Mauriac, François. Le tourment de Jacques Rivière. Strasbourg, 1926.

43697.89.105 Maurois, André. Bernard Quesnay. Paris, 1926.

43697.89.160 Maurois, André. Bernard Quesnay. 31. éd. Paris, 1926.

43697.89.705A Maurois, André. Mape; the world of illusion. N.Y., 1926.

43697.89.115 Maurois, André. Meïpe; ou La délivrance. Paris, 1926.

43697.89.115.10 Maurois, André. Meïpe; ou La délivrance. 9. éd. Paris, 1926.

43697.89.117 Maurois, André. Meïpe; ou La délivrance. 44. éd. Paris, 1926.

43697.89.104.9 Maurois, André. Les silences du Colonel Bramble. Paris, 1926.

1926 - cont.

43697.89.104.10 Maurois, André. Les silences du Colonel Bramble. Paris, 1926.

42563.37.130 Maurras, Charles. Un jubilé. Liège, 1926.

37558.19 Maurras, Çharles. Le romantisme féminin. Paris, 1926.

37543.415 Maynial, Édouard. Précis de littérature française. Paris, 1926.

43697.98.55 Mayran, Camille (pseud.). Hiver. Paris, 1926.

43697.99.100 Mazade, Fernand. Les poèmes de Sainte-Marthe. Paris, 1926.

43698.75.150 Méré, Charles. Le lit nuptial. Paris, 1926.

41555.12.10 Mérimée, Prosper. La guzla, ou choix de poésies illyriques. Strasbourg, 1926?

41555.34 Mérimée, Prosper. Pages choisies. Paris, 1926.

NEDL 42545.28.11 Moinaux, Georges. Théâtre. v.1. Paris, 1926.

Mol 220.5 Molière, Jean Baptiste Poquelin. Un ancêtre italien de George Dandin. n.p., 1926?

Mol 166.6 Molière, Jean Baptiste Poquelin. L'avaro...N. Cacudi. Firenze, 1926.

Mol 19.26 Molière, Jean Baptiste Poquelin. Oeuvres de Molière. Paris, 1926-29. 10v.

Mol 60.31.12 Molière, Jean Baptiste Poquelin. Plays...A.R. Waller. Edinburgh, 1926. 8v.

Mol 212.15.75 Molière, Jean Baptiste Poquelin. Le saccenti...Alceste Bisi. Firenze, 1926.

43701.75.100 Moreno, M. La statue de sel et le bonhomme de neige. Paris, 1926.

43701.76.110 Morienval, H. Dans la lande de Kermar. Paris, 1926.

37564.87.5 Morley, Grace Louise (McCann). Le sentiment de la nature en France dans la première moitié du dix-septième siècle. Nemours, 1926.

37564.87 Morley, Grace Louise (McCann). Le sentiment de la nature en France dans la 1e moitié de 17me siècle. Thèse. Nemours, 1926.

42557.20.315 Moroy, Elie. La guirlande de Verlaine. Genève, 1926.

43701.82.100 Mossé, Armand. L'hôtesse du Panthéon. Paris, 1926.

39574.33 Muller, Maurice. Essai sur la philosophie de Jean d'Alembert. Paris, 1926.

39574.32 Muller, Maurice. Essai sur la philosophie de Jean d'Alembert. Thèse. Paris, 1926.

41596.8.15 Musset, Alfred de. Oeuvres complètes. Paris, 1926-1935. 4v.

43705.84.100 Natanson, L.A. Vieille renommée. Paris, 1926.

41543.4.27 Nerval, Gerard de. Petits chateaux de bohême. Paris, 1926.

38537.25.50 Nicati, William. Rabelais notre maitre, son oeuvre, sa doctrine, le pantagruelisme. Marseille, 1926.

38525.22.45.35A Nolhac, Pierre de. La vie amoureuse de Pierre de Ronsard. Paris, 1926.

42577.4.31.5 Normandy, G. Guy de Maupassant. Paris, 1926.

38526.27.07 O'Connor, D. Louise Labé, sa vie et son oeuvre. Paris, 1926.

38526.27.09 O'Connor, D. Louise Labé. Thèse. Abbeville, 1926.

43728.56.100 Ormoy, Marcel. Le coeur lourd suivi de sept élégies. Paris, 1926.

43731.18.100 Oudiane, S. Chants de la Caravane. Paris, 1926.

37574.90 The Oxford book of French verse, 13th - 20th centuries. Oxford, 1926.

43737.34.100 Pagnol, Marcel. Les marchands de gloire. Paris, 1926.

X Cg 37556.36.15 Palache, J.G. Four novelists of the old regime. N.Y., 1926.

37596.3.10 Paris, Gaston. Le soir de Beaumanoir. Paris, 1926.

43737.83.1100 Pastre, J.L.G. La neuvième croisade. 8e éd. Paris, 1926.

43822.49.915 Paul Valéry. Paris, 1926.

42578.30.67 Peladan, J. Modestie et vanité. Paris, 1926.

37543.120.5 Pellissier, Georges. Précis de l'histoire de la littérature française. Paris, 1926.

43738.76.3100 Pericard, Jacques. J'ai huit enfants. Paris, 1926.

43741.24.100 Pierron, S. Le bateau Dématé suivi de l'auberge Délaissée. Bruxelles, 1926.

42563.18.320 Pilon, Edmond. Maurice barrès, souvenirs, notes et fragments de lettres inédites. Saint-Félicion, 1926.

43741.88.110 Pittard, Hélène (Mme.). Celui qui voit; roman. pts.1-4. Paris, 1926.

37567.213 Porcelli, Giacomo. Letterature italiano...nella critica francese (1830-1848). Firenze, 1926.

43822.49.940 Porché, F. Paul Valéry et la poésie pure. Paris, 1926.

41522.17.23 Porché, François. La vie douloureuse de Charles Baudelaire. Paris, 1926.

42545.95.50 Pottecher, M. Un d'eux, nommé Jean. Paris, 1926.

42576.63.70 Pouquet, J.M. (Mme.). Le salon de madame Arman de Caillavet. Couloummiers, 1926.

42576.63.71 Pouquet, J.M. (Mme.). Le salon de madame Arman de Caillavet. Paris, 1926.

43743.90.150 Pourrat, Henri. Le mauvais garçon. 10. éd. Paris, 1926.

43743.92.100 Pouvourville, Albert de. Le mal d'argent, les livres de la brousse. Paris, 1926.

38546.33.5 Pradel, Genès. Madame de Sévigné en Bourbonnais. Montluçon, 1926.

Mon 159.5 Prévost, Jean. La vie de Montaigne. 8. éd. Paris, 1926.

42578.31.83 Psichari, Jean. Le crime de Lazarina. Paris, 1926.

38588.16.2 Quinault, Philippe. La mère coquette. Paris, 1926.

38588.16.1 Quinault, Philippe. La mère coquette ou Les amants brouillés. Thèse. Paris, 1926.

38585.40.50A Racine, Jean. Mithridate. Medford, 1926.

43752.1.47 Rageot, G. Sens unique. Paris, 1926.

43752.57.160 Ramuz, Charles Ferdinand. La grande peur dans la montagne. Paris, 1926.

43752.57.120 Ramuz, Charles Ferdinand. Pour ou contre. Paris, 1926.

39533.15.40 Raynal, Marie-Aline. La nouvelle française de Segrais à Mme. de la Fayette. Thèse. Paris, 1926.

38544.27.570 Raynal, Marie-Aline. Le talent de Mme. de La Fayette. Thèse. Paris, 1926.

37563.24.15 Redenbacher, F. Die Novellistik der französischen Hoch-Renaissance. Inaug. Diss. München, 1926.

42556.27.18 Régnier, Henri de. Contes pour chacun de nous. Paris, 1926.

42556.27.15 Régnier, Henri de. L'escapade; roman. 10e éd. Paris, 1926.

43753.2.40 Régnier, M.L.A. de. Le temps d'aimer. 29. éd. Paris, 1926.

42515.34.35 Renan, Ernest. Correspondence, 1846-1871. Paris, 1926. 2v.

42515.30.730 Renan, Ernest. Sur Corneille, Racine et Bossuet. Paris, 1926.

42587.51.11 Renard, Jules. Les Clopartes. II. Chroniques, 1885-1893. Paris, 1926.

Chronological Listing

1926 - cont.

42587.51.13 Renard, Jules. Coquecigrues suivies de buceliques. Paris, 1926.
42587.51.9 Renard, Jules. L'écornifleur suivi de la lanterne sourde. Paris, 1926.
42587.51.15 Renard, Jules. Poil de Carotte, le roman et la pièce suivi des histoires naturelles. Paris, 1926.
42587.51.17 Renard, Jules. Ragotte, suivi de La maîtresse. Paris, 1926.
40556.26.55 Rheinlaender, Eduard. Die Geschichtsphilosophie des Grafen Joseph de Maistre. Inaug. Diss. Elberfeld, 1926.
37575.207 Ridder, André de. Anthologie des écrivains flamands contemporains. Anvers, 1926.
43756.69.120 Ripert, Émile. Le poème d'Assise. 2. éd. Paris, 1926.
43756.69.130A Ripert, Émile. Poèmes d'Amerique. Abbeville, 1926.
43756.90.110 Rivière, Jacques. Correspondance, 1907-1914. Paris, 1926.
43756.90.100 Rivière, Jacques. Jacques Rivière et Alain Fournier: correspondance, 1905-1914. 5. éd. Paris, 1926- 2v.
41574.130 Robertson, Mysie E.I. L'epithète dans les oeuvres lyriques de Victor Hugo. Paris, 1926.
FL 355.75 Rolland, Joachim. Le théâtre comique en France avant le XVe siècle. Paris, 1926.
43757.50.333 Rolland, Romain. Aërt, drame. Paris, 1926?
43757.50.394A Rolland, Romain. Colas Breugnon. 78e éd. Paris, 1926.
43757.50.769 Rolland, Romain. The game of love and death. N.Y., 1926.
43757.50.725 Rolland, Romain. Jean-Christophe in Paris. N.Y., 1926.
43757.50.414 Rolland, Romain. Liluli. 39e éd. Paris, 1926.
43757.50.512A Rolland, Romain. Mahatma Gandhi. 53e éd. Paris, 1926.
Htn 43757.50.470* Rolland, Romain. Pâques fleuries. Paris, 1926.
43757.50.472 Rolland, Romain. Pâques fleuries. Paris, 1926.
43757.50.354A Rolland, Romain. Théâtre de la révolution. 9e éd. Paris, 1926.
43757.50.580 Rolland, Romain. Le théâtre du peuple. Paris, 1926.
43757.50.312 Rolland, Romain. Les tragédies de la foi. 12e éd. Paris, 1926.
43757.50.990 Der Romain Rolland Almanach. Frankfurt, 1926.
43757.3.48 Romains, Jules. Dictateur. Paris, 1926.
43757.3.48.2 Romains, Jules. Le dictateur. Demetrios. 2. éd. Paris, 1926.
43891.5 Le roman des quatre par Paul Bourget. v.2. Paris, 1926.
43757.55.100 Romilly, Édouard. Théâtre. 3e éd. Paris, 1926.
38525.20.27 Ronsard, Pierre de. Les amours. Paris, 1926. 3v.
43688.61.800 Rops, Daniel. Sur le théâtre de Henri René Lenormand. Paris, 1926.
42578.22.150 Rosny, J.H. Les beaux yeux de Paris. Paris, 1926.
42578.22.10.35 Rosny, J.H. Une jeune fille à la page. Paris, 1926.
43757.83.49 Rostand, Maurice. Deserteuse. Paris, 1926.
43757.89.4110 Rouff, Marcel. Sur le quai Wilson. Paris, 1926.
FL 6002.926 Rousseau, J.J. Pages choisies. 15. éd. Paris, 1926.
43757.92.130 Roussel, Raymond. La poussière de soleils. Paris, 1926.
41571.5.12 Rudwin, M.J. Bibliographie de Victor Hugo. Paris, 1926.
41574.128.5 Rudwin, Maximilien. Satan et le satanisme dans l'oeuvre de Victor Hugo. Paris, 1926.
41574.128 Rudwin, Maximilien. Satan et le satanisme dans l'oeuvre de Victor Hugo. Thèse. Paris, 1926.
43744.67.1070 Ruskin, John. La Bible d'Amiens. 9e éd. Paris, 1926.
43628.1.500 Sacha Guitry. Paris, 1926.
40576.7 Sainte-Beuve, Charles A. Les grands écrivains français. (XVIe siècle). Paris, 1926. 2v.
40575.12 Sainte-Beuve, Charles A. Mes poisons, cahiers intunes inédits. Paris, 1926.
43761.49.133 Salmon, André. Créances, 1905-1910: Les clés ardentes - Féeries - Le calumet. 3e éd. Paris, 1926.
43761.49.120 Salmon, André. Venus dans la balance. Paris, 1926.
41557.10.35 Sand, George. Journal intime. Paris, 1926.
43761.58.110 Sandre, Thierry. Mousseline. Paris, 1926.
38526.48.2.25 Sarasin, Jean F. Oeuvres rassemblées. Paris, 1926. 2v.
43761.6.50 Sarment, Jean. As tu du coeur. Paris, 1926.
43761.6.20 Sarment, Jean. La couronne de carton. Paris, 1926.
43761.6.17 Sarment, Jean. Madelon. Paris, 1926.
43761.6.19 Sarment, Jean. Le pêcheur d'ombres. Paris, 1926.
43761.6.18 Sarment, Jean. Les plus beaux yeux du monde. Paris, 1926.
43761.6.45 Sarment, Jean. Les plus beaux yeux du monde. Paris, 1926.
37555.710 Sauvage, Marcel. Poésie du temps. Marseille, 1926.
FL 6059.10 Schinz, Albert. Date d'achèvement de La nouvelle Héloise. Baltimore, 1926.
38537.25.90 Schmidt, Konrad. Rabelais, als Artz in seinen Roman "Gargantua und Pantagruel". Greifswald, 1926.
43763.41.100 Schultz, Yvonne. La flamme sur le rampart. v.1-4. Paris, 1926.
40515.2.36.6 Scott, Geoffrey. The portrait of Zélide. N.Y., 1926.
42542.28.55 Sée, Edmond. Henry Becque, ou Servitude et grandeur dramatiques. 4. éd. Paris, 1926.
37574.658 Shipley, J.T. Modern French poetry. N.Y., 1926.
37596.181A Le siège de Barbastre. Paris, 1926.
FL 398.49.33 Silvain, Eugene. Frédérick Lemaitre. Paris, 1926.
43769.59.100 Sindral, J. Mars cover. 5. éd. Paris, 1926.
37587.34 Société des anciens textes français. Compte rendu de la séance tenue à Paris. Paris, 1926.
39544.59 Sonet, E. Voltaire et l'influence anglaise. Thèse. Rennes, 1926.
38546.66 Sonnié-Moret, P. La marquise de Sévigné. Paris, 1926.
42555.44.13A Soula, Camille. La poésie et la pensée de Stéphane Mallarmé. Paris, 1926.
43775.90.7210 Soupault, Philippe. Carte postale. Paris, 1926.
38526.27.40 Spaak, Paul. Jean Lemaire de Belges. Paris, 1926.
43776.41.150 Spire, André. Refuges. Paris, 1926.
41522.59 Sprietsma, Cargill. Louis Bertrand dit Aloysius Bertrand, 1807-1841. Paris, 1926.
41522.59.2 Sprietsma, Cargill. Louis Bertrand dit Aloysius Bertrand, 1807-1841. Thèse. Paris, 1926.
43554.2.815 Ste. Marie Perrin, E. Introduction à l'oeuvre de Paul Claudel. Paris, 1926.
43780.5.220 Suarès, André. Haï Kaï d'Occident. Paris, 1926.
43780.5.340 Suarès, André. Saint Juin de la Primevère. Nimes, 1926.
43780.69.130 Supervielle, Jules. Le voleur d'enfants. 5. éd. Paris, 1926.
42557.5.12A Tailhade, Laurent. Lettres à sa mère, 1874-1891. Paris, 1926.
FL 6119.14.2 Tarozzi, Guiseppi. Gian Giacomo Rousseau. 2. ed. Roma, 1926.
42556.29.33 Temborius, H. Albert Samains Leben, Persönlichkeit und Stil. Inaug. Diss. Oberlahnstein, 1926.
43738.1.860 Tharaud, J. Notre cher Péguy. Paris, 1926. 2v.
38526.49.4A Théophile de Viau. Oeuvres poétiques. Paris, 1926.

1926 - cont.

43788.24.170 Thérive, André. Le retour d'Amazan ou Une histoire de la littérature française. 3e éd. Paris, 1926.
FL 363.35 Thiel, M.A. Figure de Saül. Amsterdam, 1926.
42578.51.75 Tinayre, Marcelle. Figures dans la nuit. Paris, 1926.
42578.51.72 Tinayre, Marcelle. Saint Jean, libérateur. Paris, 1926.
43792.89.100 Toudouze, G.G. Parmi les loups. Paris, 1926.
43792.90.190 Toulet, Paul Jean. Notes de littérature. Paris, 1926.
42542.48.27 Treich, Léon. L'esprit d'Alfred Capus. 3. éd. Paris, 1926.
42542.65.62 Treich, Léon. L'esprit de Maurice Donnay. Paris, 1926.
39586.27.10 Treich, Léon. L'esprit de Rivarol. Paris, 1926.
37578.70 Treich, Léon. Histoires littéraires. 8. éd. Paris, 1926.
38585.8.5 Truc, Gonzague. Jean Racine, l'oeuvre, l'artiste, l'homme et le temps. Paris, 1926.
42557.8 Truffier, J.C. L'échéance. Paris, 1926.
37563.48 Turner, Robert. Didon dans la tragédie de la renaissance italienne et française. Thèse. Paris, 1926.
43795.78.100 Turquet-Milnes, G. From Pascal to Proust. N.Y., 1926.
42577.4.31.20 Urtel, H. Guy de Maupassant. München, 1926.
43822.49.460 Valéry, Paul. Propos sur l'intelligence. Paris, 1926.
43822.49.340 Valéry, Paul. Rhumbs. Paris, 1926.
43822.49.100.5 Valéry, Paul. Variété. 27e éd. Paris, 1926.
43822.89.160 Vaulet, Clément. Je suis un affreux bourgeois. Paris, 1926.
42547.12.30 Veber, Pierre. L'aventure. Paris, 1926.
42557.11.40 Verhaeren, Émile. Impressions. Paris, 1926. 3v.
42576.57.9.15 Viaud, Julien. La mort de Philae. 55. éd. Paris, 1926.
41564.21 Vigny, Alfred de. Théâtre. Paris, 1926. 2v.
43824.49.120 Vildrac, Charles. Le pèlerin; pièce en un acte. Paris, 1926.
43824.49.240 Vildrac, Charles. Recits. Paris, 1926.
43824.84.100 Vitta, Émile. Le lac des pleurs et quelques autres poésies nouvelles. Paris, 1926.
41522.18.45A Vivier, Robert. L'originalité de Baudelaire. Bruxelles, 1926.
38526.70.145 Vivonne, H. de. Les chansons de Callianthe. Paris, 1926.
39545.65.8 Voltaire, François Marie Arouet de. Zadig ou la destinée. Oxford, 1926.
38585.16.105 Vossler, Karl. Jean Racine. München, 1926
40556.35.10A Vulliaud, Paul. Joseph de Maistre, franc-maçon. Paris, 1926.
FL 363.30.5 Wade, Ira O. "Philosophe" in French drama of 18th century. Princeton, N.J., 1926.
FL 363.30 Wade, Ira O. "Philosophe" in French drama of 18th century. Princeton, 1926.
FL 6128.15.5 Wagner, Sigmund von. L'ile de Saint-Pierre, ou l'ile de Rousseau...Pierre Kohler. Lausanne, 1926.
FL 396.50.10A Waxman, S.M. Antoine and the théâtre-libre. Cambridge, 1926.
41574.135 Weil, Felix. Victor Hugo et Richard Wagner. Thèse. Zofingue, 1926.
38512.76 Weingärtner, Paul. Quellenverhältnis und Allegorie in der Prise amoureuse des Jehan Acart de Headin. Inaug. Diss. Würzburg, 1926.
FL 398.19.5 Weyl, Fernand. Madame Dorval. Paris, 1926.
37543.160A Wright, C.H.C. Background of modern French literature. Boston, 1926.
42584.19.75 Zola, Emile. Pot-Bouille. Paris, 1926-28. 2v.
42584.23.60 Zola, Emile. Two novelettes: Shell-fish and For a night of love. N.Y., 1926.

1927

43514.4.110 Adam, Juliette. Les olivieres triampheront; roman. Paris, 1927.
42576.15.95A Albalat, A. Gustave Flaubert et ses amis. Paris, 1927.
43522.41.160 Alibert, François Paul. La prairie aux narcisses. Marseille, 1927.
42553.32.7 Amiel, Henri F. Fragments d'un journal intime. Paris, 1927. 2v.
42553.33.9 Amiel, Henri F. Philine, fragments inédits du journal intime. Paris, 1927.
41568.1.75 Andrieux, Louis. Alphonse Rabbé. Thèse. Paris, 1927.
43528.48.153 Arland, Marcel. Les âmes en peine. Paris, 1927.
Mon 105.10 Armaingand, A. Bibliothèque du Dr. A. Armaingand. Paris, 1927.
42542.28.58 Arnaoutovich, A. Henry Becque; sa biographie, son observation, sa philosophie. Paris, 1927. 3v.
42542.28.60 Arnaoutovitch, A. Henry Becque. Thèse. Paris, 1927. 2v.
42542.28.61 Arnaoutovitch, A. Henry Becque devant ses contemporains et devant la postérite. Thèse. Paris, 1927.
40597.9.5 Arrigon, L.J. Les années romantiques de Balzac. Paris, 1927.
43528.86.67 Artaud, Antonin. Correspondance avec Jacques Riviere. Paris, 1927.
Mol 701.4 Ashton, Harry. A preface to Molière. N.Y., 1927.
38526.45.35 Auacker, Robert d'. Les traductions d'Antoine Stettler. Berne, 1927.
43531.10.120 Aubry, Octave. Le roman de Napoléon. Paris, 1927.
38547.18.3 Badolle, Maurice. Anne d'Urfé, l'homme, le poète. Thèse. Paris, 1927.
40597.2.48 Baldensperger, F. Orientations étrangères chez Honoré de Balzac. Paris, 1927.
40596.11.25 Balzac, Honoré de. Balzac and Souverain. An unpublished correspondence. Garden City, 1927.
40596.8.8 Balzac, Honoré de. Comédie humaine. Études analytiques. Paris, 1927. 2v.
40597.29.4.80 Balzac, Honoré de. Père Goriot. Boston, 1927.
42563.20.5 Barrès, Maurice. Le jardin de Bérénice. Paris, 1927.
41522.14.10 Baudelaire, Charles. Poèmes d'amour de Baudelaire. Paris, 1927.
38544.27.620 Beaunier, André. L'amie de La Rochefoucauld. Paris, 1927.
37563.59 Becker, A. Aus Frankreichs Frührenaissance. München, 1927.
37563.58 Becker, A. Aus Frankreichs Frührenaissance. München, 1927.
43538.17.100A Bedel, Maurice. Jerome, 60 latitude nord. 26. éd. Paris, 1927.
40575.5.37 Bellessort, A. Sainte-Beuve et le 19te siècle. Paris, 1927.
43538.7.60 Benjamin, René. La force de la Sorbonne. Paris, 1927.
43538.61.108 Benoît, Pierre. Le Roi lepreux. Paris, 1927.
43538.74.210 Béraud, Henri. La flaneur salarié. Paris, 1927.
42542.29.28.45 Bernard, Tristan. Les moyens du bord. Paris, 1927.
42542.29.70 Berr, Georges. Maître Bolbec et son mari. Paris, 1927.

Chronological Listing

1927 - cont.

41574.125	Berret, Paul. Victor Hugo. Paris, 1927.
38557.24.28	Bertault, Philippe. Bossuet intime. Paris, 1927.
43538.9.35	Berthaut, Léon. Lueurs dans l'infini. St. Brienc, 1927.
38551.37	Bertolino, A. La politica economica di Fénelon e il pensiero politico el economico del suo tiempo. Siena, 1927.
43538.82.120	Besnard, Lucien. Le coeur portage. Paris, 1927.
43538.82.130	Besnard, Lucien. Dans l'ombre du harem. Paris, 1927.
43538.88.160	Betz, Maurice. La fille qui chante. Paris, 1927.
40582.3.3	Beyle, Henri. La chartreuse de Parme. Paris, 1927. 2v.
40582.8.4.15	Beyle, Henri. On love. N.Y., 1927.
40582.36	Beyle, Henri. Une position sociale. Paris, 1927.
40582.23.30	Beyle, Henri. Rome. Paris, 1927.
40582.3.27	Beyle, Henri. Le rouge et le noir. Paris, 1927. 2v.
40582.3.30A	Beyle, Henri. Vie de Henri Bruland. Paris, 1927. 2v.
37568.55	Billy, André. La littérature française contemporaine. Paris, 1927.
43540.74.125	Birabeau, André. Le chemin des écoliers. Paris, 1927.
43540.83.110	Bisson, André. Le chatelaine de Shenstone. Paris, 1927.
FL 393.3	Bizet, René. L'époque du music-hall. Paris, 1927.
43543.13.190	Bloch, J.R. Les chasses de Renaut. 9. éd. Paris, 1927.
43543.13.100	Bloch, J.R. Dernier empereur. Paris, 1927.
43543.13.220	Bloch, J.R. Forces monde. Paris, 1927.
42576.63.87	Bölöni, I.M.J. (Mme.). Promenades d'Anatole France. Paris, 1927.
43544.60.5100	Bonjean, François Joseph. El Azhar. 6. éd. Paris, 1927.
42563.36.202	Bordeaux, Henry. La fée de Port-Cross ou La voie sans retour. Paris, 1927.
42563.36.73	Bordeaux, Henry. La neige sur les pas. Paris, 1927.
42577.4.35.3	Borel, Pierre. Le destin tragique de Guy de Maupassant d'après des documents originaux. Paris, 1927.
38557.36.27	Bossuet, J.B. Lettres. Paris, 1927.
42563.37.59.4	Bourget, Paul. Nos actes nous suivent. v.2. Paris, 1927.
FL 398.26.7	Bouvet, Charles. Cornélie Falcon. Paris, 1927.
43544.94.170	Bove, Emmanuel. Armand. Paris, 1927.
42563.39.110	Boylesve, René. Feuilles tombées. Paris, 1927.
41564.55.5	Brach, Paul. La destinée du comte Alfred de Vigny. Paris, 1927.
38528.14.10	Brantôme, P. de B. de. Recueil d'aulcunes rymes de mes jeunes amours. Paris, 1927.
37564.65.15	Bray, René. La formation de la doctrine classique en France. Paris, 1927.
38575.23.26	Bray, René. La tragédie cornélienne devant al critique classique. Thèse. Dÿon, 1927.
38575.23.25	Bray, René. La tragédie cornélienne devant la critique classique. Paris, 1927.
42541.7.12.5	Brieux, Eugène. La Française. N.Y., 1927.
43545.41.7110	Brimont, Renée. L'arche. Paris, 1927.
37572.54.7	Buffum, D.L. French short stories. 2. ed. N.Y., 1927.
37572.59	Bush, Stephen H. Sixteenth century French anthology. Boston, 1927.
43550.40.120	Cahuet, Albéric. Les amants du lac; roman. v.1-4. Paris, 1927.
37569.10	Calvet, J. Le renouveau catholique dans la littérature contemporaine. Paris, 1927.
37555.106	Cameron, Margaret M. L'influence des saisons de Thomson sur la poésie déscriptive en France (1759-1810). Thèse. Paris, 1927.
37555.106.5	Cameron, Margaret M. L'influence des saisons de Thomson sur la poésie déscriptive en France (1759-1810). Paris, 1927.
43550.1.188	Carco, Francis. De Montmartre au Quartier Latin. Paris, 1927.
43550.1.20	Carco, Francis. Poèmes retrouvés, 1904-1923. Paris, 1927.
38537.25.60	Causeret, Charles. Ce qu'il faut connaître de Rabelais. Paris, 1927.
V43500.57	Cazin, Paul. Lubies. Paris, 1927.
43551.59.160	Cendrars, Blaise. Le plan de l'Aiguille. 49e éd. Paris, 1927.
43552.2.1110	Chadourne, Marc. Vasco. Paris, 1927.
37574.105	Chamberlain, B.H. Huit siècles de poésie française. Paris, 1927.
FL 395.220.5	Champion, E. La comédie française. Paris, 1927-1937. 5v.
43552.3.9100	Chamson, André. Les hommes de la route. 27e éd. Paris, 1927.
43552.5.115	Chardonne, Jacques. Le chant du bienheureux. Paris, 1927.
37567.395	Charpentier, John. Le symbolisme. Paris, 1927.
43552.5.1110A	Chartier, Emile. Les idées et les âges. Paris, 1927. 2v.
42576.77.85	Charton, Jean C. Victor Margueritte. Paris, 1927.
43552.6.705	Chateaubriant, Alphonse de. The peat-cutters. N.Y., 1927.
43552.66.100	Chollet, Louis. La flamme errante. Paris, 1927.
43822.49.1430	Clauzel, Raymond. Trois introductions à Paul Valéry. La Rochelle, 1927.
43554.7.50	Clemenceau, Georges. Au soir de la pensée. Paris, 1927.
43556.1.89	Cocteau, Jean. Les enfants terribles. 65e éd. Paris, 1927.
43556.1.60	Cocteau, Jean. Opéra, oeuvres poétiques, 1925-1927. Paris, 1927.
43556.1.70	Cocteau, Jean. Orphée. Paris, 1927.
43556.49.775	Colette, Sidonie Gabrielle. Cats, dogs and I. N.Y., 1927.
FL 397.53.50	Combarnous, V. L'histoire du Grand-théâtre de Marseille, 31 Octobre 1778 - 13 Novembre 1919. Marseille, 1927.
40556.12	Combes de Patris, B. Une muse romantique, Pauline de Flaugergues et son oeuvre. Paris, 1927.
40553.8.25	Constant de Rebecque, Benjamin. Les chevaliers. Paris, 1927.
43557.61.110	Constantin-Weyer, Maurice. Cavelier de La Salle. 5e éd. Paris, 1927.
42542.53.54A	Copeau, Jacques. The brothers Karamazov. Garden City, N.Y., 1927.
42576.63.83	Corday, Michel. Anatole France après ses confidences. Paris, 1927.
43743.59.800	Coulon, Marcel. Raoul Ponchon. Paris, 1927.
38557.24.25	Courten, C. de. Bossuet e il suo "Discours sur l'histoire universelle" 1627-1704. Milano, 1927.
40534.34.13	Crébillon, Claude Prosper Jolyot de. The sofa; a moral tale. London, 1927.
38575.23.30	Cretin, Roger. Les images dans l'oeuvre de Corneille. Thèse. Caen, 1927.
38571.22.5	Cretin, Roger. Les imagines dans l'oeuvre de Corneille. Paris, 1927.
38575.23.32	Cretin, Roger. Lexique comparé des metaphores dans le théâtre de Corneille et de Racine. Thèse. Caen, 1927.
43557.25.120	Crevel, René. Babylone. Paris, 1927.
43557.25.115	Crevel, René. L'esprit contre la raison. Marseille, 1927.
42542.55.15	Croisset, Francis de. Le docteur miracle. Paris, 1927.
42542.55.25	Croisset, Francis de. Les nouveaux messieurs. Paris, 1927.
42542.58.45	Curel, François de. Orage mystique. Paris, 1927.
39533.20.7	Cyrano de Bergerac. Voyages to the moon and the sun. London, 1927.
42542.28.70	Damianov, H. L'oeuvre de Becque au théatre. Thèse. Grenoble, 1927.
43565.60.100	Daniel-Rops, Henry. Notre inquietude, essais. 3. ed. Paris, 1927.
42566.19.8.76	Daudet, Alphonse. Tartarin de Tarascon. London, 1927.
42566.35.6	Daudet, Alphonse. Tartarin sur les Alpes. Paris, 1927.
43565.98.100	Day, G. Rapsodies en mauve. Paris, 1927.
43566.8.100	Debille, Léon. La légende du roi d'un jour. Paris, 1927.
43877.25	Decalandrier ou, De l'autobus Passy-Bourse à la poesie pure. Paris, 1927.
42576.65.13.21	Deffoux, Léon. J.K. Huysmans sous divers aspects. Paris, 1927.
43566.3.40	Delaquys, Georges. Le marchand de lunettes. Paris, 1927.
43566.51.320	Delteil, Joseph. The Poilus. N.Y., 1927.
43566.52.140	Demaison, André. Le pacha de Tombouctou. Paris, 1927.
43566.75.240	Derème, Tristan. Le livre de Clymène; élégies. Paris, 1927.
43566.75.260	Derème, Tristan. Toulouse. Paris, 1927.
43566.75.110	Derème, Tristan. Le zodiaque ou Les étoiles sur Paris. Paris, 1927.
Htn 38525.20.253*	DeRicci, S. Catalogue of a unique collection of early editions of Ronsard. London, 1927.
42545.42.50	Desfeuilles, P. Charles Monselet et la critique anecdotique. Thèse. Paris, 1927.
43566.79.115	Des Gachons, J. M. de Buffon sur les terrasses. Paris, 1927.
42576.63.61	Des Hons, Gabriel. Anatole France et Racine. Paris, 1927.
41542.4.3	Dillingham, L.B. The creative imagination of Théophile Gautier. Diss. Bryn Mawr, 1927?
37567.196.5	Ditchy, Jay K. Le thème de la mer chez les parnassiens. Paris, 1927.
37574.75.8	Dorchain, Auguste. Les cent meilleurs poèmes. Paris, 1927.
37574.75.9	Dorchain, Auguste. Les cent meilleurs poèmes. Philadelphia, 1927.
43576.9.96	Du Bos, Charles. Approximations. 2. série. Paris, 1927.
42568.19.21	Ducasse, I.L. Oeuvres complètes du Comte de Lautréamont. Paris, 1927.
43576.6.65	Duhamel, Georges. Confession de minuit. 35. éd. Paris, 1927.
43576.6.260	Duhamel, Georges. Mémorial de Cauchois. Paris, 1927.
43576.1.38	Dumas, André. A propos. Paris, 1927.
43576.6.802	Durtain, Luc. Georges Duhamel. Paris, 1927.
43576.77.100A	Durtain, Luc. Quarantième étage. 8. éd. Paris, 1927.
43576.91.65	Duvernois, Henri. Comédies en un acte. Paris, 1927.
43576.91.74	Duvernois, Henri. Maxime. Paris, 1927.
37573.706	Écrits. Paris, 1927.
39578.11	Eggli, Edmond. L'érotique comparée de C. de Villers, 1806. Thèse. Paris, 1927.
39578.12	Eggli, Edmond. L'érotiques comparée de C. de Villers, 1806. Paris, 1927.
42572.2.15	Erckmann, Emile. L'ami Fritz. Paris, 1927.
43598.84.208	Estaunié, Édouard. Tels qu'ils furent; roman. Paris, 1927.
43598.84.210	Estaunié, Édouard. Tels qu'ils furent; roman. 40. éd. Paris, 1927.
43554.4.85	Études et souvenirs sur Émile Clermont. Paris, 1927.
42543.40.20	Fauchois, R. La leçon de Talma. Paris, 1927.
43606.89.60	Faure, Gabriel. Amours romantiques. Paris, 1927.
43606.97.102	Fay, Bernard. Faites vos jeux. Paris, 1927.
43606.97.100	Fay, Bernard. Faites vos jeux. 7. éd. Paris, 1927.
37566.72.10	Fäy, Bernard. Since Victor Hugo. Boston, 1927.
43822.49.905	Fernandat, René. Paul Valéry. Paris, 1927.
43822.49.920A	Fisher, H.A.L. Paul Valéry. Oxford, 1927.
42576.34	Flaubert, Gustave. Par les champs et par les grèves. Paris, 1927.
42576.30.6	Flaubert, Gustave. Salambô. N.Y., 1927.
42576.31.30	Flaubert, Gustave. Salammbô. Paris, 1927.
42576.34.5	Flaubert, Gustave. Théâtre. Paris, 1927.
42543.41.150	Flers, P.L. Le bon Désaugiers. Paris, 1927.
43610.25.110	Fleuret, Fernand. Falourdin. Paris, 1927.
41564.35.5	Flottes, Pierre. La pensée politique et sociale d'Alfred de Vigny. Paris, 1927.
41574.164	Flutre, Fernand. Victor Hugo. Paris, 1927.
43611.1.25.68	Fort, Paul. L'or. Paris, 1927.
42576.62.5.42	France, Anatole. Le livre de mon ami. N.Y., 1927.
37583.400	Francheville, Robert. Mirliton du romantisme. Paris, 1927.
43612.3.40	Frappa, Jean José. À Paris. Paris, 1927.
41522.18.25	Freund, Cayetan. Der Vers Baudelaires. Inaug. Diss. München, 1927.
43616.41.1100	Gaillard, André. Le fond du coeur. Marseille, 1927.
38526.14.142	Gamon, Christophe de. Excerpte, prélection de Juliette Roche. Paris, 1927.
41542.8.5	Gautier, Théophile. Émaux et camées. Paris, 1927.
41542.37.12	Gautier, Théophile. One of Cleopatra's nights. N.Y., 1927.
41542.35.10	Gautier, Théophile. Le roman de la momie. Paris, 1927.
42543.45.20	Gavault, Paul. La dette. Paris, 1927.
37556.9	Gehring, Christian. Die Entwicklung des politischen Urtzblatts in Deutschland. Inaug. Diss. Leipzig, 1927.
43617.4.90	Géraldy, Paul. Ihr Mann (Son Mari). Berlin, 1927.
43617.4.50	Géraldy, Paul. Son mari. Paris, 1927.
43620.2.79.190	Gide, André. Voyage au Congo. 23. éd. Paris, 1927.
43620.3.34	Gilbert, M. Le silence de Cambridge. v.1-2. Paris, 1927.
40526.51.105	Gill-Mark, Grace. Une femme de lettres au XVIIIe siècle, Anne Marie du Boccage. Paris, 1927.
40526.51.100	Gill-Mark, Grace. Une femme de lettres au XVIIIe siècle, Anne-Marie du Boccage. Thèse. Paris, 1927.
43822.49.945	Gillet, Martin Stanislas. Paul Valéry et la métaphysique. Paris, 1927.
37567.276	Giraud, Jean. L'école romantique française. Paris, 1927.
37569.36	Giraud, V. Les maîtres de l'heure. 4e éd. Paris, 1927?
43620.74.101	Giraudoux, Jean. Bella. N.Y., 1927.
43620.74.310	Giraudoux, Jean. Eglantine. 43. éd. Paris, 1927.

Chronological Listing

1927 - cont.

42586.68.15 Gobineau, Arthur de. Études critiques, 1844-1848. Paris, 1927.
40515.2.35 Godet, Philippe. Madame de Charrière et ses amis (1740-1805). Lausanne, 1927.
43625.19.101 Godoy, Armand. Le carnaval de Schumann. Paris, 1927.
43625.19.105 Godoy, Armand. Triste et tendre. Paris, 1927.
37568.74 Gómez Carrillo, E. La nueva literatura francesa. Madrid, 1927.
37543.96.5 Gourmont, Rémy de. Promenades littéraires. 7. série. Paris, 1927.
37567.234 Grant, Elliott M. French poetry and modern industry, 1830-1870. Cambridge, 1927.
40524.32.45 Grasilier, Leonce. Restif de la Bretonne. Paris, 1927.
43626.22.123 Green, Julien. Adrienne Mesurat. Paris, 1927.
43626.22.110 Green, Julien. Adrienne Mesurat. Paris, 1927.
43626.22.120 Green, Julien. Adrienne Mesurat. Paris, 1927.
43626.22.705 Green, Julien. Avarice house. n.p., 1927.
43626.41.100 Grimard, Luc. Ritournelles; poèmes. Paris, 1927.
42544.33.55 Grimm, L. Lemaître als Kritiker des französischen Theaters. Inaug. Diss. Nürnberg, 1927.
FL 398.35.10 Guilbert, Yvette. La chanson de ma vie. Paris, 1927.
FL 398.35.9 Guilbert, Yvette. La chanson de ma vie. Paris, 1927.
38542.12.9 Guillaumie, Gaston. J.L. Guez de Balzac et la prose française. Paris, 1927.
38542.12.11A Guillaumie, Gaston. J.L. Guez de Balzac et la prose française. Thèse. Paris, 1927.
43628.41.100 Guillet, L. Films narquois. 50 fables. Paris, 1927.
41574.120 Guimbaud, Louis. Victor Hugo et Madame Biard. Paris, 1927.
42543.62.28 Guiraud, E. Le bonheur de jour. Paris, 1927.
43631.2.68 Hamp, Pierre. La maison. 3. éd. Paris, 1927.
43822.49.908 Hanotaux, Gabriel. Réponse au discours de M. Paul Valéry. Paris, 1927.
40583.95.3 Hazard, Paul. La vie de Stendhal. 25. éd. Paris, 1927.
43632.3.42 Hémon, Louis. Maria Chapdelaine. N.Y., 1927.
39544.98 Henriot, E. Voltaire et Frederic II. Paris, 1927.
43632.6.110 Henriot, Émile. Éloge de la curiosité. Paris, 1927.
43632.6.170 Henriot, Émile. Livres et portraits. 4. éd. Paris, 1927.
43698.78.805 Henry, M.L. La contribution d'un Américain au symbolisme français. Paris, 1927.
42555.49.50 Henry, M.L. Stuart Merrill. Thèse. Paris, 1927.
42554.60 Heredia, J.M. de. Translations from José Maria de Heredia. N.Y., 1927.
42584.25.345 Herriot, Edouard. Emile Zola et son oeuvre. Paris, 1927.
43697.74.9120 Histoire charmante de l'adolescent sucre d'amour. Paris, 1927.
43606.76.835 Hommage à Léon-Paul Fargue. Paris, 1927.
41557.10.125A Howe, M.J. George Sand. N.Y., 1927.
37555.510 Hudson, Margaret E. The juxtaposition of accents at the rime in French versification. Thesis. Philadelphia, 1927.
41571.32.15 Hugo, Victor. Havets arbetare. Stockholm, 1927. 2v.
41571.16.9 Hugo, Victor. Les misères. Paris, 1927. 2v.
43638.35.100 Huguet, Auguste. La caresse des soirs. Paris, 1927.
43659.88.110 Istrati, Panait. Famille Perlmutter. Paris, 1927.
38543.26.80 Ivanoff, N. La marquise de Sablé et son salon. Thèse. Paris, 1927.
37567.392 Jaloux, Edmond. De Pascal à Barrès. 3. éd. Paris, 1927.
42578.31.70 Jansen, Gretl. Frauenpsychologie und Frauenpädagogik bei Marcel Proust. Würzburg, 1927.
43667.79.100 Jarry, P. Étudiants et grisettes romantiques. Paris, 1927.
37595.34.5 Jeanroy, Alfred. Anthologie des troubadours, XIIe-XIIIe siècles. Paris, 1927.
39566.38 Johansson, J.V. Études sur Denis Diderot. Göteborg, 1927.
43670.89.330 Jouhandeau, M. Prudence Hautechaumee. 3. éd. Paris, 1927.
43670.94.120 Jouve, Pierre Jean. Le monde désert. 3. éd. Paris, 1927.
42576.63.415 Kahn, Maurice. Anatole France et Emile Zola. Paris, 1927.
43673.83.100 Kessel, Joseph. Les coeurs purs. 6. éd. Paris, 1927.
38513.96 Kleine, Félix. Sept comédies du Moyen-Âge. Paris, 1927.
38567.41 Kopal, Josef. Literarni teorie Boileau na. Praha, 1927.
38542.30.25 Lachèvre, Frédéric. La Casanova du XVIIIe siècle: Pierre Corneille Blessebois, normand (1646?-1700?). Paris, 1927.
43687.15.190 Lacretelle, Jacques de. Aparté: Colère - Jour de colère - Dix jours à Ermenonville. 14e éd. Paris, 1927.
43687.15.280 Lacretelle, Jacques de. Le cachemire écarlate. Paris, 1927.
43687.15.61 Lacretelle, Jacques de. Letters espagnoles. Paris, 1927.
39524.7.5 La Fontaine, Jean de. Fables. Paris, 1927. 2v.
Mon 152.4 Lamandé, André. La vie gaillarde et sage de Montaigne. Paris, 1927.
37567.240 Lamartine, A. de. Portraits et salons romantiques. Paris, 1927.
41578.32.7 Lamartine, Alphonse. Graziella. Paris, 1927.
37543.38.30 Lanson, Gustave. L'idéal française dans la littérature. Paris, 1927.
43687.65.110 Lanza del Vasto, Joseph Jean. Conquiste di vento. Firenze, 1927.
43687.71.130 Laporte, René. Le dîner chez Olga. Paris, 1927.
38526.21.31 Larbaud, V. Notes sur Antoine Héroët et Jean de Lingendes. Paris, 1927.
43687.74.170 Larbaud, Valéry. Caderno. Paris, 1927.
43687.74.155 Larbaud, Valéry. Crayons de couleurs. Liège, 1927.
43687.74.135 Larbaud, Valéry. Jaune, bleu, blanc. Paris, 1927.
43556.49.880 Larnac, Jean. Colette. Paris, 1927.
38543.10.12 La Rochefoucauld, François. La première rédaction des maximes. Paris, 1927.
43687.77.1130 Larrouy, Maurice. Sirènes et Tritons, le roman du sous-marin. Paris, 1927.
37567.88.10 Lasserre, Pierre. Des romantiques à nous. 6e éd. Paris, 1927.
43687.89.100 Launay, Louis de. La voie sacrée. Paris, 1927.
43687.89.3120 Lavaud, Guy. Sous le signe de l'eau. Paris, 1927.
42584.25.350 Le Blond, Maurice. Les projets littéraires d'Emile Zola au moment de sa mort. Paris, 1927.
41578.124 Lecomte, G. Lamartine. Abbeville, 1927.
37568.58.14 Lefèvre, Frédéric. Une heure avec... Série 4. 6e éd. Paris, 1927.
43554.2.820 Lefévre, Frédéric. Les sources de Paul Claudel. Paris, 1927.
38521.30.15 Lefèvre, Louis R. La vie de Cyrano de Bergerac. Paris, 1927.
40597.9.10 Léger, Charles. À la recherche de Balzac. Paris, 1927.
43688.35.150 Le Grand, Maurice. Le kiosque à musique. Paris, 1927.
43688.60.130 Leiris, Michel. Le point cardinal. Paris, 1927.
43688.59.112 Lenéru, Marie. Les affranchis. Paris, 1927.
43688.59.120 Lenéru, Marie. La maison sur le roc. Paris, 1927.

1927 - cont.

38526.27.30 Le Petit, Claude. La chronique scandaleuse, ou Paris ridicule. Paris, 1927.
43688.1.25 Leroux, Gaston. Mister Flou. Paris, 1927.
42576.46.3 Le Roy, Eugène. Jacquou le croquant. 37. éd. Paris, 1927.
43688.76.100 Le Roy, Florian. Bonne soeur des chemins. Paris, 1927.
37563.52 Levengood, S.L. The use of color in the verse of the Pléiade. Diss. Paris, 1927.
43690.1.34 Lichtenberger, A. Des enfants dans un jardin; nouvelle. Paris, 1927.
42586.32.505 Liebrecht, Henri. La vie et le rêve de Charles de Coster. Bruxelles, 1927.
37555.95 Liefde, C.L. de. Le Saint-Simonisme dans la poésie française entre 1825 et 1865. Haarlem, 1927.
41578.40.30 Lima-Barbosa, Mario de. Lamartine et le Brésil. Paris, 1927.
43693.48.100 L'Olagne, Jean. La collina ronde. Paris, 1927.
42544.34.65 Louys, Pierre. Psyché. Paris, 1927.
Htn 42544.34.55* Louys, Pierre. The twilight of the nymphs. Philadelphia, 1927.
42544.34.28.15 Louys, Pierre. A vida amorosa de Bilitis. Lisboa, 1927.
41596.4.29 Lyonnet, Henry. Les "premières" de Alfred de Musset. Paris, 1927.
39591.23 Lypschutz, Michael. Montesquieu als Geschichtsphilosophie. Inaug. Diss. Strasbourg, 1927.
43697.14.370 MacOrlan, Pierre. Chronique des jours désespérés. Paris, 1927.
43697.14.390 MacOrlan, Pierre. La danse macabre. Paris, 1927.
43697.14.290 MacOrlan, Pierre. Les jeux du demi-jour. 4e ed. Paris, 1927.
43697.14.120 MacOrlan, Pierre. Le quai des brumes. 2e ed. Paris, 1927.
42545.3.15.30 Maeterlinck, Maurice. Joyzelle. Paris, 1927.
38547.15 Magendie, Maurice. Du nouveau sur l'Astrée. Paris, 1927.
43697.34.140 Magre, Maurice. Arlequin. Paris, 1927.
43697.34.260 Magre, Maurice. Le mystére du tigre. Paris, 1927.
43697.34.280 Magre, Maurice. Le roman de Confucius. Paris, 1927.
43697.48.100 Malan, Jean. Vingt poèmes de la nuit. Marseille, 1927.
38527.90 Marcel, P. Jean Martin. Paris, 1927.
43697.75.3000 Marchand, L. Nous ne sommes plus des enfants. Paris, 1927.
42576.77.43 Margueritte, Victor. Ton corps est à toi. Paris, 1927.
37556.75.5 Massis, Henri. En marge de "Jugements". Paris, 1927.
43752.18.805 Massis, Henri. Raymond Radiguet. Paris, 1927.
41522.18.20 Mauclair, Camille. La vie amoureuse de Charles Baudelaire. Paris, 1927.
42577.4.1.3 Maupassant, Guy de. Les soeurs Rondoli. Paris, 1927?
43697.88.500 Mauriac, François. Le désert de l'amour; roman. Paris, 1927.
43697.4.35.5 Mauriac, François. Thérèse Desqueyroux. Photoreproduction. Paris, 1927.
43697.89.390 Maurois, André. Les anglais. Paris, 1927.
43697.89.742 Maurois, André. Bernard Quesnay. N.Y., 1927.
43697.89.380 Maurois, André. La conversation. Paris, 1927.
43697.89.195A Maurois, André. Petite histoire de l'espèce humaine. Paris, 1927.
41574.555 Maurras, Charles. Lorsque Hugo eut les cent ans. Paris, 1927.
38526.37.6 Maynard, F. de. Poésies de François Maynard. Paris, 1927.
42576.15.45 Maynial, E. Flaubert et son milieu. Paris, 1927.
37574.106 Mazade, F. Anthologie des poètes français des origines à nos jours. Paris, 1927-28. 4v.
43698.75.160 Méré, Charles. Berlioz. Paris, 1927.
41555.1.3 Mérimée, Prosper. Carmen, Arsène Guillot, L'abbé Aubain. Paris, 1927.
41555.20.20 Mérimée, Prosper. Carmen. Arsène Guillot. Paris, 1927.
41555.1.12 Mérimée, Prosper. Lettres a Viollet-le-duc (documents inédits), 1839-1870. Paris, 1927.
41555.23.15 Mérimée, Prosper. Mateo Falcone. Colomba. Paris, 1927.
41555.1.25 Mérimée, Prosper. Oeuvres en trois volumes. Paris, 1927. 3v.
41555.1 Mérimée, Prosper. Premiers essais (1823-1824) théâtre de Clara Gazul (1825-1830). Paris, 1927.
41578.114 Michaud-Lapeyre, M.R. Lamartine à Tresserve. Chambéry, 1927.
39544.64A Minderhoud, H.J. La Henriade. Proefschrift. Paris, 1927.
42545.28.7.50 Mirbeau, Octave. Les grimaces et quelques autres chroniques. Paris, 1927.
37584.24 Mistral, Frédéric. Un poète bilingué, Adolph Dumas, 1806-1861. Paris, 1927.
42545.28.9.10 Moinaux, Georges. Théâtre. Paris, 1927. 2v.
Htn 37567.283* Monda, Maurice. Bibliographie des poètes maudits. Paris, 1927. 2v.
FL 361.72 Mongrédien, Georges. Les grands comédiens du XVIIe siècle. Paris, 1927.
42545.42.10 Monselet, Charles. Lettres de Monselet à Lesclide, juin-octobre, 1846. Thèse. Paris, 1927.
Mon 19.28 Montaigne, Michel de. Essais de Messire Michel de Montaigne. Paris, 1927-30. 7v.
43701.62.130 Montfort, Eugène. Ceasar Casteldor. Paris, 1927.
43701.63.740A Montherlant, Henry de. The bullfighters. N.Y., 1927.
43701.63.550 Montherlant, Henry de. Lettre sur le serviteur châtié. Paris, 1927.
43701.74.725 Morand, Paul. Europe at love. N.Y., 1927.
43701.74.120 Morand, Paul. Lampes à arc. Paris, 1927.
43701.74.155 Morand, Paul. Le voyage. Paris, 1927.
42555.61.25 Moréas, Jean. Oeuvres en prose. Paris, 1927.
40587.66.5 Moreau, Pierre. Chateaubriand, l'homme et la vie. Paris, 1927.
43701.74.290 Morland, Paul. Bouddha vivant. Paris, 1927.
37566.99.2 Mornet, Daniel. Histoire de la littérature et de la pensée françaises contemporaines, 1870-1927. Paris, 1927.
42576.65.13.140 Mugnier, Arthur. J.K. Huysmans à la trappe. Paris, 1927.
Mol 613.11 Mullins, Marjorie. La famille au XVIIe siècle, d'après le théâtre de Molière. Thèse. Toulouse, 1927.
40524.17.300 Nerciat, A.R. Oeuvre. Paris, 1927. 2v.
41543.12.10 Nerval, Gerard de. Aurélia. Paris, 1927.
41543.10.20 Nerval, Gerard de. Le cabaret de la mère Saguet. Paris, 1927.
41543.10.10 Nerval, Gerard de. La sonate du diable. Paris, 1927.
41543.12.3 Nerval, Gerard de. Voyage en Orient. Paris, 1927-30. 3v.
43707.91.100 Nivoix, Paul. Eve toute nue. Paris, 1927.
43709.3.260 Noailles, Anna E. L'honneur de souffrir. 23e éd. Paris, 1927.
43709.3.113 Noailles, Anna E. Le visage émerveillé. 31e éd. Paris, 1927.

Chronological Listing

1927 - cont.

37555.315.8 Noo, Hendrik de. Thomas Sebillet. Proefschrift. Utrecht, 1927.
43709.77.103 Normand, S. Cinq femmes sur un gatere. 6e éd. Paris, 1927.
42568.23.18 Normandy, G. Jean Lorrain. (Paul Duval). Paris, 1927.
43822.49.1380 Noulet, Emilie. Paul Valéry. Bruxelles, 1927.
41574.615 Nusinov, Isaak M. Problema istoricheskoqo romana; V. Giugo i A. Frans. Moskva, 1927.
V43500.221 Ormoy, Marcel. Carrefours. Paris, 1927.
V43500.229 Ormoy, Marcel. Le visage retrouvé. Paris, 1927.
43737.34.110 Pagnol, Marcel. Jazz. Paris, 1927.
40575.5.20 Pailleron, M.L. (Mme.). Sainte-Beuve à seize ans. Paris, 1927.
41542.4.30 Palache, John. Gautier and the romantics. London, 1927.
37568.52 Palmarocchi, R. Letteratura francese contemporanea. Rome, 1927.
V43500.231 Parrot, Louis. Cornemuse de l'orage; poèmes. Tours, 1927.
38526.42.11 Parthenay, C. Ballets allégoriques en vers 1592-1593. Paris, 1927.
43737.83.120 Passeur, Steve. Pas encore; la traversée de Paris à la Nage. 4e éd. Paris, 1927.
37556.18.12 Petric, D.S. Le groupe littéraire de la Minerve française. 1818-1820. Paris, 1927.
43740.1.35 Philippe, Charles Louis. Bubu de Montparnasse. Paris, 1927.
38514.58.9 Pinet, Marie-Josèphe. Christine de Pisan, 1364-1430. Paris, 1927.
38514.58.10 Pinet, Marie-Josèphe. Christine de Pisan, 1364-1430. Thèse. Paris, 1927.
37572.58 Plattard, Jean. Anthologie du XVIl siècle français. London, 1927.
43743.90.2110 Pourrat, Henri. Dans l'herbe des trois vallees. Paris, 1927.
43743.90.4120 Pourtal de Ladevèze, Jean. Fragments. Paris, 1927.
43744.2.100 Prado, Jacques. Balises. Paris, 1927.
40597.2.50 Preston, E. Recherches sur la technique de Balzac. Paris, 1927.
40522.6.15 Prévost, Antoine F. L'abbé Prévost, mémoires et avantures d'un homme de qualité qui s'est retiré du monde. Paris, 1927.
40522.6.16 Prévost, Antoine F. Mémoires et avantures d'un homme de qualité qui s'est retiré de monde. Paris, 1927.
42578.31.66.5 Prévost, Marcel. His mistress and I. N.Y., 1927.
43744.67.50 Proust, Marcel. Chroniques. 12. éd. Paris, 1927.
43744.67.39 Proust, Marcel. Cities of the plain. N.Y., 1927. 2v.
37596.10.100 Putz, Rudolf. Chrestiens "Yvain" und Hartmanns "Iwein". Neustrelitz, 1927.
42576.77.80 Quesada, Ernesto. Victor Margueritte. Paris, 1927.
38536.18.23 Rabelais, F. Oeuvres. Paris, 1927-1928. 4v.
43752.57.295 Ramuz, Charles Ferdinand. La faneuse dans son pre. Paris, 1927.
43752.57.795 Ramuz, Charles Ferdinand. Das grosse Grauen in den Bergen. Stuttgart, 1927.
43752.11.120 Raucat, Thomas. The honorable picnic. N.Y., 1927.
38525.20.255 Raymond, M. Bibliographie critique de Ronsard en France, 1550-1585. Paris, 1927.
38525.14.4 Raymond, Marcel. Bibliographie critique de Ronsard. Paris, 1927.
38525.22.45.41 Raymond, Marcel. L'influence de Ronsard sur la poésie française (1550-1585). Paris, 1927. 2v.
38525.22.45.40 Raymond, Marcel. L'influence de Ronsard sur la poésie française (1550-1585). Thèse. Paris, 1927.
38587.8.20 Regnard, Jean François. Le légataire universel. Manchester, 1927.
42556.27.3 Régnier, Henri de. Le pavillon fermé. Paris, 1927.
43753.2.50 Régnier, M.L.A. de. L'inconatante. Paris, 1927.
42515.30.40 Renan, Ernest. Voyages; Italie, 1849. Paris, 1927.
42587.51.19 Renard, Jules. Comédies. Paris, 1927. 2v.
42587.51.23 Renard, Jules. Correspondance inédite. Paris, 1927. 2v.
42587.52.25 Renard, Jules. Journal. Paris, 1927. 4v.
42587.51.21 Renard, Jules. Le Vigneron dans sa vigne suivi de propos littéraires et mots d'écrit. Paris, 1927.
43753.58.100 Renard, M. Celui qui n'a pas tue. Paris, 1927.
43753.90.120 Reverdy, P. Le gaut de crin. Paris, 1927.
43755.3.120 Rhaïs, Elissa. Par la voix de la musique. 16. éd. Paris, 1927.
43756.7.100 Ribemont-Dessaignes, Georges. Le bar du lendemain. Paris, 1927.
42556.28.30 Rimbaud, Jean Arthur. À Douai et à Charleville. Paris, 1927.
42556.28.74 Rimbaud, Jean Arthur. Gesammelte Werk. Leipzig, 1927.
43756.91.100 Rivière, P.L. La route. Paris, 1927.
43757.8.4100 Robin, Gilbert. La prison de soie. Paris, 1927.
43757.50.753 Rolland, Romain. Mother and son. v.3. N.Y., 1927.
43757.50.534 Rolland, Romain. Musiciens d'aujourd'hui. 12e éd. Paris, 1927.
43757.50.590 Rolland, Romain. Vie de Michel-Ange. 11e éd. Paris, 1927.
43757.3.50 Romains, Jules. Jean le Maufranc. Paris, 1927.
43757.3.40.5A Romains, Jules. Knock, ou Le triomphe de la médicine. N.Y., 1927.
37573.637 Roosbroeck, Gustave L. van. An anthology of modern French poetry. N.Y., 1927.
37567.260 Rosny, J.H. Mémoires de la vie littéraire. Paris, 1927.
42546.10.8 Rostand, Edmond. L'aiglon. New Haven, 1927.
41578.40.15 Roth, Georges. Lamartine et la Savoie, extraits situés et commentés. Chambéry, 1927.
43757.89.4100 Rouff, Marcel. Les étranglés. Paris, 1927.
43757.91.100 Rouquette, Louis-Frédéric. La chanson du pays. Paris, 1927.
FL 6094.8 Rousseau, J.J. Les rêveries d'un promeneur solitaire. Paris, 1927.
FL 6094.15 Rousseau, J.J. The reveries of a solitary. London, 1927.
43625.3.96 Rouveyre, A.L.M. Le reclus et le retors; Gourmont et Gide. Paris, 1927.
42555.44.15A Royère, Jean. Mallarmé. Paris, 1927.
37567.96.8 Rudwin, Max. Romantisme et satanisme. Paris, 1927.
37543.175 Sáenz Hayes, Ricardo. Perfiles y caracteres. Buenos Aires, 1927.
37563.43 Saineanu, L. Problèmes littéraires du seizième siècle. Paris, 1927.
38542.24.5 Saint Evremond, C. de M. de S.D. Oeuvres. Paris, 1927. 3v.
40597.2.115 Saint-Germès, M. Balzac considéré comme historien du droit. Besançon, 1927.
43761.41.6100 St. René, Martin. La carnyx d'Airain. Paris, 1927.

1927 - cont.

38585.8.17 Saint-René Taillandier, Madeleine M.L. (Mme.). Racine. Paris, 1927.
40576.8 Sainte-Beuve, Charles A. Les grands écrivains français (XVIIe siècle). Paris, 1927-30. 5v.
40575.26.15 Sainte-Beuve, Charles A. Volupté. Paris, 1927. 2v.
43667.14.800F Salmon, André. Max Jacob, poète, peintre, mystique et homme de qualité. Paris, 1927.
43761.59.105 Sandy, Isabelle. Les soutanes vertes. Paris, 1927.
43761.6.65 Sarment, Jean. Leopold le bien-aimé. Paris, 1927.
38526.48.34 Scève, Maurice. Oeuvres poétiques complètes. Paris, 1927.
41557.10.110 Schermerhorn, E.W. The seven strings of the lyre...George Sand. Boston, 1927.
FL 6139.27.5 Schinz, A. La pensée religieuse de Rousseau et ses récents interprètes. Paris, 1927.
43763.38.160 Schlumberger, Jean. Césaire ou La puissance de l'ésprit. Paris, 1927.
43763.38.230 Schlumberger, Jean. Dialogues avec le corps endormi. Paris, 1927.
43763.38.150 Schlumberger, Jean. L'enfant qui s'accuse. Paris, 1927.
43763.2.37 Schopfer, Jean. Ariane. N.Y., 1927.
43757.50.870 Schüler, G. Studien zur Romain Rollands "Colas Breugnon". Inaug. Diss. Erlangen, 1927.
41557.10.31 Schutz, A.H. Peasant vocabulary in works of George Sand. Columbia, 1927.
37569.15 Schwartz, W.L. The imaginative interpretation of the Far East in modern French literature, 1800-1925. Paris, 1927.
42543.1.28A Schwarz, H.S. Alexandre Dumas fils dramatist. N.Y., 1927.
40515.2.36.4A Scott, Geoffrey. The portrait of Zélide. N.Y., 1927.
40515.14.8 Ségur, Pierre. Julie de Lespinasse. N.Y., 1927.
42575.98 Seillière, E. Les Goncourt moralistes. 2. éd. Paris, 1927.
38546.36.4 Sévigné, Marie de R.C. Lettres choisies. 3e éd. Paris, 1927.
42576.15.50 Shanks, Lewis P. Flaubert's youth, 1821-1845. Baltimore, 1927.
42554.11.9 Siciliano, Italo. Dal romanticismo al simbolismo. Torino, 1927.
42576.63.80 Smith, Helen B. The skepticism of Anatole France. Paris, 1927.
39594.19.48 Smoleński, W. Monteskjusz w polsce w XVIII. Warszawa, 1927.
43620.2.83A Sonday, Paul. André Gide. 2. éd. Paris, 1927.
43744.67.85 Sonday, Paul. Marcel Proust. Paris, 1927.
43822.49.912 Sonday, Paul. Paul Valéry. Paris, 1927.
43526.65.815 Soupault, P. Guillaume Apollinaire. Marseille, 1927.
43775.90.7152 Soupault, Philippe. Le coeur d'or. 12. éd. Paris, 1927.
43775.90.7240 Soupault, Philippe. Histoire d'un blanc. Paris, 1927.
37567.249 Souriau, Maurice. Histoire du romantisme en France. Paris, 1927. 2v.
42557.12.25 Starkie, Enid. Les sources du lyrisme dans la poésie d'Émile Verhaeren. Thèse. Paris, 1927.
42576.63.48A Stewart, H.L. Anatole France, the Parisian. N.Y., 1927.
43788.5.198 Tharaud, Jérôme. En Bretagne; essais ornés de compositions originales. Paris, 1927.
42563.18.275 Tharaud, Jérôme. Un grand maître n'est plus. Liège, 1927.
43788.5.160F Tharaud, Jérôme. La Rose de Sâron. Paris, 1927.
43788.5.162 Tharaud, Jérôme. La Rose de Sâron. Paris, 1927.
37567.233 Thérive, André. Du siècle romantique. Paris, 1927.
43788.24.158 Thérive, André. Les souffrances perdues. 12e éd. Paris, 1927.
42576.63.35 Thomas, André. Les conceptions sociales d'Anatole France. Thèse. Paris, 1927.
42543.41.80 Treich, Léon. L'esprit de Georges Feydeau. Paris, 1927.
39545.22.10 Treich, Léon. L'esprit de Voltaire. Paris, 1927.
Htn 43822.49.110* Valéry, Paul. Album de vers anciens. Paris, 1927.
43822.49.120 Valéry, Paul. Discours de réception à l'Académie française. Paris, 1927.
42576.65.13.180 Valéry, Paul. Huysmans, eau-forte de C. Jovas. Paris, 1927.
43822.49.105A Valéry, Paul. Variety. N.Y., 1927.
37567.305 Van Roosbroeck, G.L. The legend of the decadents. N.Y., 1927.
43822.8.40 Vaudoyer, Jean L. La bien-aimée. Paris, 1927.
38571.26 Vedel, Valdemar. Fransk Klassik. København, 1927.
42582.22.14.25 Verne, Jules. The mysterious island. N.Y., 1927.
42521.2 Veuillot, Louis. Louis Veuillot; pages choisies. Paris, 1927.
42576.56.7.5 Viaud, Julien. Madame Chrysanthème. Paris, 1927?
38514.20.14 Villon, François. Oeuvres complètes de Villon. Paris, 1927.
43824.84.110 Vitta, Émile. La promenade franciscaine. Paris, 1927.
43826.3.100 Vlaminck, Maurice de. Histoires et poèmes de mon époque. Paris, 1927.
43827.50.100 Vollard, Ambroise. Sainte Monique. Paris, 1927.
39543.51 Voltaire, François Marie Arouet de. The complete romances of Voltaire. N.Y., 1927.
39545.46.3.8 Voltaire, François Marie Arouet de. L'ingénu. Paris, 1927.
39544.27.30A Voltaire, François Marie Arouet de. A letter to James Boswell...Feb. 11, 1765. N.Y., 1927.
39544.27.21 Voltaire, François Marie Arouet de. Lettres. N.Y., 1927.
39545.115 Voltaire, François Marie Arouet de. La princesse de Babylone. Paris, 1927.
39542.32.15 Voltaire, François Marie Arouet de. Théâtre de Voltaire. Paris, 1927. 2v.
41539.15 Wilke, Heinz. Alexandre Dumas, père, als Dramatiker. Inaug. Diss. München, 1927.
Mon 162.15 Willis, Irene C. Montaigne. N.Y., 1927.
37564.112 Wilson, N.S. The French classic age. London, 1927.
43858.90.120 Zavie, Émile. La course aux rebelles. 5e éd. Paris, 1927.
42584.1.5 Zola, Emile. Les oeuvres completes. Paris, 1927-1929. 49v.
42557.12.11 Zweig, Stefan. Erinnerungen an Émile Verhaeren. Leipzig, 1927.
41593.29.3.63 Zweig, Stefan. Marceline Desbordes-Valmore. Leipzig, 1927.

1928

FL 398.74.76 Agate, James E. Rachel. London, 1928.
42576.63.95 Ajzensztejn, Max. La femme et l'amour dans l'oeuvre d'Anatole France. Thèse. Toulouse, 1928.
39574.28 Alembert, J. Le Rond d'. Discours sur la philosophie prononcé par d'Alembert le 3 decembre 1768. N.Y., 1928.

1928 - cont.

42582.2.5 Allotte de la Fuÿe, Marguerite. Jules Verne, sa vie, son oeuvre. 4. éd. Paris, 1928.

42582.2.8 Allotte de la Fuÿe, Marguerite. Jules Verne. 6. éd. Paris, 1928.

Mol 268.141 Alméras, Henri d'. Le Tartuffe de Molière. Amiens, 1928.

40597.2.57 Altszyler, Hélène. La genèse et le plan des caractères dans l'oeuvre de Balzac. Paris, 1928.

40597.2.55 Altszyler, Hélène. La genèse et le plan des caractères dans l'oeuvre de Balzac. Paris, 1928.

43523.41.182 Amiel, Denys. Théâtre: L'engrenage. v. 2. Paris, 1928.

43524.19.110 André, Paul. Aurore et crepuscule. Paris, 1928.

43620.2.165 André Gide. Paris, 1928.

FL 396.64.5 Antoine, André. Mes souvenirs sur le théâtre Antoine. 1e ed. Paris, 1928.

FL 396.64.8 Antoine, André. Mes souvenirs sur le théâtre Antoine. 12e ed. Paris, 1928.

43526.65.110 Apollinaire, Guillaume. La flaneur des deux rives. 5. ed. Paris, 1928.

40583.322 Arbelet, Paul. Premier voyage de Stendhal au pays des comediennes. Paris, 1928.

43528.58.100 Arnal, Emilie. L'Hôte Divin. Paris, 1928.

38527.19.10 Aubigné, Théodore Agrippa d'. Sa vie à ses enfants. 4e éd. Photoreproduction. Paris, 1928.

43531.10.700 Aubry, Octave. The emperor falls in love. N.Y., 1928.

43532.41.100 Avilla, Francis d'. Chansons tristes. Paris, 1928.

42555.45.100 Aymonier, Camille. Xavier marmier, sa vie. Besançon, 1928.

37567.281 Baale-Uittenbosch, A.E.M. Les poétesses dolentes du romantisme. Haarlem, 1928.

43537.12.100 Bach-Sesley, J. L'humble et merveilleux évangile de la pucelle. Brignais, 1928.

43537.18.100 Badin, Charles. Tetus Pallade, le muletier; roman. v. 1-2. Paris, 1928.

40596.22.5A Balzac, Honoré de. Le père Goriot. N.Y., 1928.

40597.36.12A Balzac, Honoré de. Théâtre II. La maratre. Le faiseur. Paris, 1928.

40597.2.65 Balzac mis à nu. Paris, 1928.

41522.2.52 Barbey d'Aurevilly, Jules. Une vieille maîtresse. Paris, 1928. 2v.

41522.2.61 Barbey d'Aurveilly, Jules. L'ensorcelée. Paris, 1928.

40597.5.5 Barriere, P. Honoré de Balzac. Thèse. Paris, 1928. 2 pam.

41522.6.8 Baudelaire, Charles. Les paradis artificiels. Paris, 1928.

40552.4 Beaulieu, Camille. Vie et travaux de Burgaud des Marets, philologue, bibliophile et poète saintongeais. La Rochelle, 1928.

40532.17 Beaumarchais, Pierre A.C. de. Lettres à Madame de Godeville, 1777-79. Paris, 1928.

FL 366.40 Béchet, H. Les impots sur les spectacles. Thèse. Paris, 1928.

43538.17.710 Bedel, Maurice. Jerome; or, The latitude of Cove. N.Y., 1928.

43538.17.110 Bedel, Maurice. Molinoff, Indre-et-Loire. Paris, 1928.

43538.36.105 Béhaine, René. Histoire d'une société. Paris, 1928. 16v.

43625.3.88.5 Bencze, Eugène. La doctrine esthétique de Rémy de Gourmont. Toulouse, 1928.

43625.3.88 Bencze, Eugène. La doctrine esthétique de Rémy de Gourmont. Thèse. Toulouse, 1928.

43538.5.35 Benda, Julien. La fin de l'éternel. 4. éd. Paris, 1928.

43538.5.50 Benda, Julien. Prosperee, au Les amants. Paris, 1928.

37576.50 Benjamin, L.S. Great French short stories. N.Y., 1928.

43538.7.65 Benjamin, René. Antoine enchâiné. Paris, 1928.

43709.3.805 Benjamin, René. Au soleil de la poésie. Paris, 1928.

43538.61.35 Benoît, Pierre. L'Atlantide. Paris, 1928.

41574.183 Benoît-Lévy, E. La jeunesse de Victor Hugo. Paris, 1928.

43538.74.190 Béraud, Henri. La gerbe d'or. Paris, 1928.

39527.4.30 Berèrne, Tristan. Sous les troènes du Beárn. St. Felicien, 1928.

43538.76.230 Bernanos, Georges. Madame Dargent. Paris, 1928.

43538.76.235 Bernanos, Georges. Une nuit. Paris, 1928.

42542.29.175 Bernard, Tristan. Decadence et grandeur. Paris, 1928.

42542.29.28.145 Bernard, Tristan, Le voyage imprevu. Paris, 1928.

37565.78 Bertaut, Jules. Égéries du XVIIIe siècle. Paris, 1928.

42563.23.8.55 Bertrand, Louis. La nouvelle éducation sentimentale. 13. éd. Paris, 1928.

43537.4.875 Besançon, Jacques B. Essai sur le théâtre d'Henry Bataille. Groninque, 1928.

40517.18.9.5 Besenval, Pierre V. de. Spleen. London, 1928.

41553.115 Beyer, Friedrich. Der Romanschriftsteller Charles Paul de Kock und seine Welt. Inaug. Diss. Barmen, 1928.

Htn FL 379.34* Beyier, Agne. Recueil de plusieurs fragments des premières comédies italiennes. Paris, 1928.

40582.12.50 Beyle, Henri. Armance. N.Y., 1928.

40582.3.24 Beyle, Henri. Racine et Shakespeare. Paris, 1928.

40582.3.25 Beyle, Henri. Romans et nouvelles. Paris, 1928. 2v.

40582.3.32 Beyle, Henri. Vies de Haydn, de Mozart. Paris, 1928.

43540.7.110A Bibescu, M.L. Catherine-Parish. N.Y., 1928.

37568.55.2 Billy, André. La littérature française contemporaine. 2e éd. Paris, 1928.

43540.3.50 Billy, André. Route cavalière de la solitude. Paris, 1928.

43540.74.220 Birabeau, André. Le jardin aux vingt-cinq allées. Paris, 1928.

FL 6139.28 Bitsilli, P.M. Jean-Jacque Rousseau et la démocratie. Sofia, 1928.

41543.22.5 Bizet, René. La double vie de Gerard de Nerval. Paris, 1928.

37569.25.5 Blanche, J.E. Mes modéles. Paris, 1928.

37569.25 Blanche, J.E. Mes modéles. 2. éd. Paris, 1928.

38565.21.5 Boileau Despréaux, Nicolas. Oeuvres de Boileau. Paris, 1928.

38565.21.10 Boileau Despréaux, Nicolas. Oeuvres de Boileau. Paris, 1928-29. 5v.

41541.20.21 Bondy, François de. Une femme d'esprit en 1830, madame de Girardin. Paris, 1928.

41522.18.35 Bonfantini, Mario. Vita, opere e pensieri di Charles Baudelaire. 2. ed. Novara, 1928.

43744.67.90A Bonnet, Henri. Deux etudes sur Marcel Proust. Arras, 1928.

42563.36.160 Bordeaux, Henry. Andromède et le monstre. Paris, 1928.

42563.36.170 Bordeaux, Henry. Le calvaire de Cimiez. Paris, 1928.

42563.18.127 Bordeaux, Henry. Maurice Barrès à Pau, 11 décembre 1926. Pau, 1928.

V43500.35 Bouchor, Maurice. Confession de foi; poème. Paris, 1928.

1928 - cont.

42556.28.355 Bouet, Paul. Fantaisies sur deux ardennais: Arthur Rimbaud, Hippolyte Taine. Paris, 1928.

37543.191 Boulenger, J. Le touriste littéraire. 5. éd. Paris, 1928.

42542.44.32 Bourdet, Édouard. Vient de paraître. Paris, 1928.

X Cg 43620.74.800 Bourdet, M. Jean Giraudoux, son oeuvre. Paris, 1928.

43544.89.1110 Boutet, Frédéric. Je jeune homme du rez-de-chaussée. Paris, 1928.

43544.94.150 Bove, Emmanuel. La coalition. Paris, 1928.

43544.94.160 Bove, Emmanuel. Coeurs et visages. Paris, 1928.

43544.94.180 Bove, Emmanuel. Henri Duchemin et ses ombres. Paris, 1928.

37543.140.15 Braunschvig, Marcel. La littérature française contemporaine. 2. éd. Paris, 1928.

37543.140.8 Braunschvig, Marcel. Notre littérature étudiée dans les textes. 5. éd. Paris, 1928-29. 2v.

40563.24A Bredin, Claude Julien. Un ami de Ballanche. Correspondence...avec Ballanche. Thèse. Paris, 1928.

43545.22.2100 Brégé, Louis. Sonnets marins. Paris, 1928?

40587.70 Briod, Blaisé. L'homérisme de Chateaubriand. Paris, 1928.

42584.25.30 Brown, Sidney B. La peinture des métiers et des moeurs professionnelles dans les romans de Zola. Thèse. Montpellier, 1928.

38588.17.15 Buijtendorp, Johannes B.A. Philippe Quinault; sa vie, ses tragédies et ses tragi-comédies. Amsterdam, 1928.

43550.40.105 Cahuet, Albéric. Mademoiselle de Milly; roman. v.1-2. Paris, 1928.

FL 6029.7 Calemard, J. L'édition originale des Confessions de Jean-Jacques Rousseau. Paris, 1928.

FL 363.39 Calvet, Jean. Les types universéls dans la littérature française. series 1-2. Paris, 1928. 2v.

42554.17.55 Cantacuzène, C.A. Les automnes complémentaires; anamorphoses. Paris, 1928.

43550.1.44 Carco, Francis. Images cachées. Paris, 1928.

V43500.53 Carco, Francis. La légende et la vie d'Utrillo. Paris, 1928.

43550.1.700 Carco, Francis. Perversity. Chicago, 1928.

43550.1.127 Carco, Francis. Rue Pigalle. Paris, 1928.

43550.1.75 Carco, Francis. Les vrais de vrai. Paris, 1928.

42556.28.111 Carré, Jean Marie. Les deux Rimbaud. Paris, 1928.

40526.84 Cassier, François. Un poète nivernais de XVIII siècle: l'Abbé François Cassier, 1721-1772. Nevers, 1928.

43550.82.270 Cassou, Jean. Le pays qui n'est à personne. Paris, 1928.

39544.96 Celarié, H. Monsieur de Voltaire. Paris, 1928.

43551.59.39 Cendrars, Blaise. Petits contes nègres. Paris, 1928.

V43500.61 Chabaneix, Philippe. Comme des songes. Paris, 1928.

43552.2.1102 Chadourne, Marc. Vasco. N.Y., 1928.

43552.2.1100 Chadourne, Marc. Vasco. N.Y., 1928.

37556.73.10 Chaplyn, Marjorie. Le roman mauresque en France de Zayde au Dernier Abencérape. Thèse. Nemours, 1928.

37576.220 Chapman, P.A. An anthology of seventeenth century French literature. Princeton, 1928.

43552.5.2120 Charles-Étienne. Les désexués. Paris, 1928?

43552.5.2130 Charles-Étienne. La nuit perverse. Paris, 1928.

43552.3.4100 Charpentier, Henry. Signes. Saint-Felicien-en-Vivarais, 1928.

37544.38 Chassée, Charles. Styles et physiologie. Paris, 1928.

42565.26.8 Cherbuliez, Victor. La revanche de Joseph Noirel. Paris, 1928.

37596.10.2.15 Chrestien de Troyes. Arthurian romances. London, 1928.

43554.2.89A Claudel, Paul. Positions et propositions. 4e éd. Paris, 1928-1934. 2v.

FL 382.100 Clement-Janin, N. Drames et comédies romantiques. Paris, 1928.

40517.54.25 Cobb, Lillian. Pierre-Antoine de la Place, sa vie, et son oeuvre, 1707-1793. Paris, 1928.

40516.15.15 Cobb, Lillian. Pierre-Antoine de La Place, sa vie et son oeuvre (1707-1793). Thèse. Paris, 1928.

43556.1.100 Cocteau, Jean. Oedipe-roi. Paris, 1928.

43537.4.87 Cogo, Guido. L'amore nei drammi di Henry Bataille. Palermo, 1928.

FL 370.84A Cohen, Gustave. Le théâtre en France au Moyen Age. Paris, 1928-31. 2v.

43556.49.460 Colette, Sidonie Gabrielle. Le voyage égoïste. Paris, 1928.

37576.415 Comfort, W.W. French romantic prose. N.Y., 1928.

40553.9.50 Constant de Rebecque, Benjamin. Journal intime, 1804-1816. Paris, 1928.

43557.61.106.2 Constantin-Weyer, Maurice. Un homme se penche sur son passé. 211e éd. Paris, 1928.

43557.61.106 Constantin-Weyer, Maurice. Un homme se penche sur son passé. 214e éd. Paris, 1928.

42542.53.22 Coolus, R. Les vacances de Paques Coeurblette. Paris, 1928.

39564.29.5 Corday, Michel. La vie amoureuse de Diderot. Paris, 1928.

42586.32.110 Coster, Charles de. The legend of Ulenspiegel in the land of Flanders and elsewhere. London, 1928.

42586.32.30 Coster, Charles de. La legende et les aventures héroiques. Bruxelles, 1928.

42542.55.20 Croisset, Francis de. La livrée de M. le Comte. Paris, 1928.

37564.106 Crump, Phyllis Eirene. Nature in the age of Louis XIV. London, 1928.

43744.67.965 Curtius, E.R. Marcel Proust. Paris, 1928.

43565.41.2100 Dainville, Blanche. Au fil des jours. Paris, 1928?

40532.25.6 Dalséme, René. La vie de Beaumarchais. 6. éd. Paris, 1928.

42566.19.8.74A Daudet, Alphonse. Tartarin de Tarascon. Boston, 1928.

42514.28.145 Daudet, Léon. Charles Maurras et son temps. Paris, 1928.

43565.5.140 Daudet, Léon A. Mélancholie. Paris, 1928.

43566.43.160 Dekobra, Maurice. Sérénade au bourreau. Paris, 1928.

43566.45.120 Delacour, André. Le voyage à l'étoile. Paris, 1928.

43566.47.100 Delaporte, M. Sonnets. Paris, 1928.

42556.28.130 Delattre, Jean Luc. Le déséquilibre mental d'Arthur Rimbaud, 1854-1891. Paris, 1928.

43566.51.390 Delteil, Joseph. De J.J. Rousseau à Mistral. Paris, 1928.

42576.8.50 Demarquette, J. J.A. Gleizes et son influence sur le mouvement naturaliste. Thèse. Paris, 1928.

40587.75 Dempsey, Madeleine. A contribution to the study of the sources of the "Génie du christianisme". Thèse. Paris, 1928.

43566.75.100 Derème, Tristan. Le ballet des muses. Paris, 1928.

43566.75.220 Derème, Tristan. L'enfant perdu, poème. Paris, 1928.

43566.76.100 Derennes, Charles. Le noces sur la banquise. Paris, 1928.

41593.29.3.20 Desbordes-Valmore, Marceline. Poèmes et proses. Paris, 1928.

42542.64.27.15 Descaves, Lucien. Les fruits de l'amour. Paris, 1928.

Chronological Listing

1928 - cont.

37567.196.10 Desonay, Fernand. La rêve Hellénique chez les poètes parnassiens. Louvain, 1928.

37567.196.12 Desonay, Fernand. Le rêve Hellénique chez les poètes parnassiens. Paris, 1928.

43566.7.45 Deval, Jacques. Ventöse. Paris, 1928.

43568.65.100 Dion-Lévesques, Rosaire. En égrenant le chapelet des jours. Montréal, 1928.

43568.91.120 Divoire, F. Itinéraire. Paris, 1928.

43568.91.158 Divoire, F. Stratégie littéraire. Evreux, 1928.

42542.65.18.5 Donnay, Maurice. Chères madames. 9. éd. Paris, 1928.

40516.63.15 Drygalski, Irma von. Juliane von Krüdener; der Roman eines Lebens. Jena, 1928.

43576.7.1100 Dubé, Théodore. Pétales effeuillés de ma pensée. Étampes, 1928.

43576.5.100 Dubech, Lucien. Poèmes. Paris, 1928.

43576.7.105 Du Bois, Albert. Le dernier vol de l'alouette. Paris, 1928. 2 pam.

43576.9.43 Du Bos, Charles. Extraits d'un journal, 1908-1928. Paris, 1928.

42557.14.42 Dugas, Marcel. Verlaine; essai. Paris, 1928.

43576.6.145 Duhamel, Georges. Entretien sur l'esprit européen. Paris, 1928.

43576.6.150 Duhamel, Georges. Les sept dernières plaies. Paris, 1928.

41538.47.8A Dumas, Alexandre. Henri III et sa cour. Paris, 1928.

42576.15.57 Dumesnil, René. En marge de Flaubert. Paris, 1928.

42576.15.54 Dumesnil, René. La publication de "Madame Bovary". Amiens, 1928.

42576.15.55 Dumesnil, René. La publication de "Madame Bovary". 3. éd. Amiens, 1928.

43877.20 Dunois, D. (pseud.). Georgette Garou. Paris, 1928.

43576.91.52 Duvernois, Henri. L'invité. Paris, 1928.

42542.65.64 Duvernois, Henri. Maurice Donnay. Paris, 1928.

43576.91.58 Duvernois, Henri. Le professor. Paris, 1928.

43792.90.805 Dyssord, J. L'aventure de Paul Jean Toulet. 4e éd. Paris, 1928.

43579.82.100 Dyssord, Jacques. On frappe à la porte. Paris, 1928.

43701.63.840 Empaytaz, F. Essai sur Montherlant. n.p., 1928.

41574.143A Escholier, Raymond. La vie glorieuse de Victor Hugo. Paris, 1928.

43598.84.120 Estaunié, Édouard. L'ascension de M. Baslèvre. Paris, 1928.

42557.12.75 Estève, Edmond. Un grand poète de la vie moderne, Émile Verhaeren. Paris, 1928.

37567.279A Faguet, Émile. Politicians and moralists of the nineteenth century. Boston, 1928.

43688.5.5805 Faillet, G. Lettres à Paul Léautaud. Paris, 1928.

43606.76.200 Fargue, Léon P. Banalité. Paris, 1928.

43606.76.102 Fargue, Léon P. Épaisseurs. Paris, 1928.

43606.89.45 Faure, Gabriel. Heures romanesques. Paris, 1928.

42546.12.40 Faure, Paul. Vingt ans d'intimite avec Edmond Rostand. Paris, 1928.

43606.98.130 Fayard, Jean. Oxford et Margaret. Paris, 1928.

43607.75.100 Ferdinand, Roger. Chatard et Cie. Paris, 1928.

43607.76.100 Féret, Charles Théophile. La Normandie exaltée. 2. éd. Paris, 1928.

38537.25.55 Fetzer, Herman. The book of Rabelais. Garden City, 1928.

43607.27.705 Feval, P. Martyr to the queen. N.Y., 1928.

43607.27.700 Feval, P. The mysterious cavalier. N.Y., 1928.

42586.48.7 Feval, Paul H. Contes de Bretagne. Paris, 1928.

42545.3.480 Fidler, F. The bird that is blue. London, 1928.

42576.17.25 Flaubert, Gustave. Correspondance. Paris, 1928. 3v.

42555.44.190 Fontainas, André. De Stéphane Mallarmé à Paul Valery. Paris, 1928.

37567.287 Fontainas, André. Mes souvenirs du symbolisme. 3e éd. Paris, 1928.

43611.75.2100 Forge, Henry de. Le fils de joie. Paris, 1928.

41578.40.25 Fournet, Charles. Lamartine et ses amis suisses. Paris, 1928.

43611.5.40 Fournier, Alain. The wanderer. N.Y., 1928.

43611.5.44 Fournier, Alain. The wanderer (Le grand meaulnes). N.Y., 1928.

FL 6139.28.5 Frässdorf, W. Die psychologischen Anschauungen Jean-Jacques Rousseau. Inaug. Diss. Langensalza, 1928.

42576.62.22.29 France, Anatole. The gods are athirst. N.Y., 1928.

42576.62.10.8 France, Anatole. Le lys rouge. Paris, 1928?

43612.63.100 Franzoni, F. Le printemps tragique; poems. Paris, 1928.

43612.2.55 Fraudet, René. Les amants de Paris. Paris, 1928.

43612.2.60 Fraudet, René. Deux fois vingt ans, roman. 102. éd. Paris, 1928.

40524.32.5A Funck-Bretano, F. Restif de la Bretonne. Paris, 1928.

39586.19.15 Gabor, Georg. Die Misanthropie Chamforts. Inaug. Diss. Berlin, 1928.

43616.51.100 Galopin, Arnould. Le bacille. Paris, 1928.

43616.62.705 Gantillon, Simon. Maya; a play. N.Y., 1928.

43616.62.706 Gantillon, Simon. Maya. N.Y., 1928.

40546.9.10 Gaschet, R. Les aventures d'un écrivain, Paul Louis Courier. Paris, 1928.

43616.83.115 Gasquet, Joachim. Des chants de l'amour et des hymnes. Paris, 1928.

42586.62.25 Gauthier-Villars, Henry. Contes sans feuilles de vigne. Paris, 1928.

43617.4.34 Géraldy, Paul. Les noces d'argent. Paris, 1928.

43617.4.55 Géraldy, Paul. Theater. v.2. Berlin, 1928.

43617.78.2100 Gervais, Albert. Une fille de H'an. Paris, 1928.

42554.44.15 Ghil, René. Choix de poèmes. Paris, 1928.

43620.2.79.72 Gide, André. Le retour du Tchad. 29. éd. Paris, 1928.

FL 382.110 Giesse, Hermann. Die Engländer in der französischen Komödie des 19. Jahrhunderts. Diss. n.p., 1928.

43620.49.1100 Gillet, Louis. Amitiés littéraires. Paris, 1928.

42536.34.6 Giraud, V. Hippolyte Taine; études et documents. Paris, 1928.

43554.4.83 Giraudoux, J. Marche vers Clermont avec un portrait de l'auteur par Alereuff. Paris, 1928.

43620.74.108 Giraudoux, Jean. Siegfried. Paris, 1928.

43620.74.107 Giraudoux, Jean. Siegfried. 16. éd. Paris, 1928.

43620.74.390 Giraudoux, Jean. Le sport. Paris, 1928.

43622.66.100 Glotz, René. À mon gré. Paris, 1928.

43625.19.100 Godoy, Armand. Le carnaval de Schumann. Paris, 1928.

43625.19.110 Godoy, Armand. Hosanna sur le sistre. Paris, 1928.

43625.19.120 Godoy, Armand. Monologue de la tristesse et colloque de la joie. 5e éd. Paris, 1928.

37543.192 Gottschalk, Walter. Die humoristische Gestalt in der französischen Literatur. Heidelburg, 1928.

42563.18.260 Gouhier, H. Notre ami Maurice Barrès. Paris, 1928.

43626.4.1100 Grasset, P. L'échauffourée du métro. Paris, 1928.

1928 - cont.

43626.22.740 Green, Julien. Christine, suivi de Léviathan. Paris, 1928.

43626.22.722A Green, Julien. The closed garden. N.Y., 1928.

43626.22.102 Green, Julien. Mont-Cinère. Paris, 1928.

37595.11.10 Grimes, Evie M. The lays of Desiré, Graclant, and Mehon. N.Y., 1928.

42576.65.13.23 Grolleau, C. Un logis de J.K. Huysmans. Paris, 1928.

42514.28.65 Groos, René. Esquisses: Charles Maurras, M. Proust, G.B. Shaw. Paris, 1928.

43822.49.918 Gueguen, P. Paul Valéry. Paris, 1928.

43628.23.110 Guéhenno, Jean. Caliban parle. 10e éd. Paris, 1928.

42576.63.105 Guillaume, Louis. Le cerveau d'Anatole France. Tours, 1928.

41574.56.2 Guimbaud, Louis. Les orientales de Victor Hugo. Amiens, 1928.

37596.203 Guiot de Dijon. Les chansons attribuées à Guiot de Dijon et Jocelin. Paris, 1928.

37596.203.5 Guiot de Dijon. Critical edition of poems attributed to Guiot de Dijon and Jocelin de Dijon. Paris, 1928.

43628.44.100 Guislain, J.M. Pan et syrinx. Toulouse, 1928.

43628.1.60 Guitry, Sacha. Jean de la Fontaine. Paris, 1928.

43628.1.53 Guitry, Sacha. Un miracle. Paris, 1928.

Mol 607.12 Gulkind, K.S. Molière und das komische Drama. Halle, 1928.

43631.41.100 Hain, Georges. Le cyprès sur l'Azur. Paris, 1928.

39532.13.15 Hamilton, Anthony. Memoires of Count Grammont. London, 1928.

43631.2.63.10 Hamp, Pierre. Gens. Paris, 1928.

43631.2.70 Hamp, Pierre. Monsieur l'administrateur. 3. éd. Paris, 1928.

42586.32.500 Hanse, Joseph. Charles de Coster. Louvain, 1928.

43631.75.100 Harel, Paul. Poèmes à la gloire du Christ. Paris, 1928.

43631.77.100 Harlaire, André. En croix. Paris, 1928.

42576.65.10 Harry, Myriam (pseud.). Le petit prince de Syrie. Paris, 1928.

42576.65.7.5 Harry, Myriam (pseud.). Siona à Berlin. Paris, 1928.

40587.65 Hart, Charles R. Chateaubriand and Homer. Baltimore, 1928.

37597.22.5 Hawkins, R.L. The manuscripts of the roman de la rose in the libraries of Harvard and Yale Universities. n.p., 1928.

NEDL 41596.4.35 Henriot, Émile. Alfred de Musset. Paris, 1928.

43632.6.260 Henriot, Émile. Esquisses d'X. Paris, 1928.

43632.6.130 Henriot, Émile. Poésies. Paris, 1928.

FL 397.72 Herelle, Georges. Études sur le théâtre basque. Le répertoire du théâtre tragique. Paris, 1928.

42563.39.09 Hermant, Abel. Discours de la réception à l'académie française. Paris, 1928.

37573.223 Hilka, Alfons. Drei Erzählungen aus dem didaktischen Epos. Halle, 1928.

Mol 250.5.5 Hodges, J.C. Authorship of Squire Trelooby. London, 1928.

37543.475 Hofmiller, Josef. Franzosen. München, 1928.

38514.72.15 Holbrook, Richard T. Guillaume Alexis et Pathelin. Berkeley, Calif., 1928.

41555.43.30 Hovenkamp, Jan W. Mérimée et la couleur locale. Nijmegen, 1928.

FL 6139.27A Hubert, René. Rousseau et l'encyclopédie. Paris, 1928.

41573.23.17 Hugo, Victor. Notre Dame de Paris, 1492. London, 1928.

41573.17.8A Hugo, Victor. Tristesse d'Olympio. Paris, 1928.

42576.65.17 Huysmans, Joris Karl. En route. Paris, 1928.

42576.65.18 Huysmans, Joris Karl. Oeuvres complètes de J.K. Huysmans. v.1-18. Paris, 1928-34. 23v.

43628.99.105 Huzard, A. de B. (Mme.). Rose, madame, roman inédit. Paris, 1928.

37556.74 Hytièr, Jean. Les romans de l'individu constant. Paris, 1928.

43659.88.170 Istrati, Panait. Les chardons du Baragan. Paris, 1928.

43667.14.170 Jacob, Max. Le cabinet noir. 4. éd. Paris, 1928.

43667.1.70 Jammes, Francis. Diane. Paris, 1928.

43667.1.226 Jammes, Francis. Janot-poète. 8. éd. Paris, 1928.

FL 398.17.5 Janin, Jules. Deburau. N.Y., 1928.

43667.75.110 Jardin, Renée. Appareillage. Paris, 1928.

43667.98.100 Jay, Marcel. Sur les voies romaines; poésies. Reims, 1928.

39576.2 Johnston, Elsie. Le marquis d'Argens, sa vie et ses oeuvres. Paris, 1928.

42584.25.81A Josephson, M. Zola and his time. Garden City, 1928.

42584.25.80A Josephson, M. Zola and his time. N.Y., 1928.

43670.1.35 Jouglet, René. Colombe. Paris, 1928.

43670.89.180 Jouhandeau, M. Opales. 5. éd. Paris, 1928.

43670.94.130 Jouve, Pierre Jean. Noces. Paris, 1928.

Htn 38585.14.8* Jovy, Ernest. Une contribution indirecte à l'histoire de Racine. Paris, 1928.

37543.193 Kayer, Hermann. Das Problem der gesellschaftlichen Entwurzelung in der FranzösischenLiteratur. Inaug. Diss. Stuttgart, 1928.

38526.2.4.25 Keegstra, Pieter. Abraham sacrifiant de Théodore de Bèze. Proefschrift. Den Haag, 1928.

43673.76.100 Kerdyk, René. Sentiments. Paris, 1928.

43673.77.100 Kerpenhir, Jean de. Anna Calvé. Paris, 1928.

43673.83.240 Kessel, Joseph. La femme de maison. Paris, 1928.

43673.83.180 Kessel, Joseph. Nouveaux contes. Paris, 1928.

42555.62.30 Kroll, Heinrich. Studien über den Versaufbau in "Les stances" von Jean Moréas. Inaug. Diss. Swinemünde, 1928.

42556.28.135 Krollman, Clara. Arthur Rimbaud; ein Deutungsversuch. Inaug. Diss. Bonn, 1928.

38526.26.50 Labé, Louise Charly. Oeuvres complètes. Maestricht, 1928.

38564.32.28 La Bruyère, J. de. Les caractères. Paris, 1928. 3v.

41586.28.11 Lacey, Alexander. Pixerécourt and the French romantic drama. Toronto, 1928.

37530.68 Lachèvre, Frédéric. Bibliographie sommaire de l'Almanach des Muses (1765-1833). Paris, 1928.

Mol 730.19 Lacour, L. Molière acteur. Paris, 1928.

43687.15.270 Lacretelle, Jacques de. Études. Paris, 1928.

41574.152 Lacretelle, Pierre de. Vie politique de Victor Hugo. Paris, 1928.

43687.26.100 Lafargue, Marc. Les plaisirs et les regrets. Paris, 1928.

40532.25.15 Lafon, Roger. Beaumarchais, le brillant armateur. Paris, 1928.

42555.1.55 Laforgue, Jules. Six moral tales. Photoreproduction. N.Y., 1928.

43620.2.88 Laloro, René. André Gide. Strassbourg, 1928.

42543.1.35 Lamy, Pierre. Le théâtre de Alexandre Dumas fils. Thèse. Paris, 1928.

43687.69.100 Lapaquellerie, Yvon. La princesse Tarakanov. Paris, 1928.

1928 - cont.

43687.74.105 Larbaud, Valéry. A.O. Barnabooth. 22e éd. Paris, 1928.
38526.47.11 Larbaud, Valery. Notes sur Racan. Maestricht, 1928.
43687.75.125 Larguier, Léo. Avant le déluge, souvenirs. 10e éd. Paris, 1928.
43687.75.120 Larguier, Léo. Les Bonaparte. n.p., 1928.
43687.75.115 Larguier, Léo. Les gardiens; nouvelle. Paris, 1928.
43687.77.3110 La Rochefoucauld, Edmée (de Fels). La vie humaine par Gilbert Mauge (pseud.). Paris, 1928.
41586.3.5 Latouche, Henri de. La reine d'Espagne. Paris, 1928.
41574.17.5 Laube, Herbert David. The story of Jean Valjean. Geneva, N.Y., 1928.
42544.24.2.5 Lavedan, Henri. Le duel. N.Y., 1928.
37548.215 Lebel, Roland. Études de littérature coloniale. Paris, 1928.
43688.6.100 Lebert, E.M. Le masque de la vie. N.Y., 1928.
41574.140 Le Breton, André Victor. La jeunesse de Victor Hugo. Paris, 1928.
43688.2.35 Le Cardonnel, Louis. Oeuvres. Paris, 1928-1929. 2v.
38557.24.105 Le Dieu, François. Les dernières années de Bossuet. v.1-2. Paris, 1928-29.
43688.27.110 Lefebvre, L. Prières. Paris, 1928.
43688.30.110 Le Franc, Marie. The whisper of a name. Indianapolis, 1928.
Htn 38514.46.5* Le Franc, Martin. L'estrif de fortune et de vertu. Bruxelles, 1928.
37574.632 Le Goffic, Charles. Les poètes de la mer de moyen âge à nos jours. Paris, 1928.
37574.102 Le Goffir, Charles. Les poètes de la mer du moyen age à nos jours. Paris, 1928.
43688.33.100 Legrand, Ignace. La patrie interieure. Paris, 1928.
39566.22.5 Le Gras, Joseph. Diderot er l'encyclopédie. Amiens, 1928.
38512.89.5 Le ménagier de Paris. The goodman of Paris. London, 1928.
38512.89.10 Le ménagier de Paris. The goodman of Paris. N.Y., 1928.
39535.37 L'enclos, Anne. Lettres de Ninon de L'enclos. Paris, 1928.
43688.61.700 Lenormand, Henri René. Three plays: The dream doctor, Man and his phantoms, The coward. London, 1928.
43688.65.100 Léon-Martin, L. L'ascension d'Élise amour. Paris, 1928.
42557.18.800A Le Rouge, Gustave. Verlainiens et décadents. Paris, 1928.
38551.76.10A Leroy, Maxime. Fénelon. Paris, 1928.
40512.3.12 LeSage, Alain René. Le diable boiteux. Paris, 1928.
42555.67.80 Levaillant, M. Pierre de Nolhac. Paris, 1928.
37574.642 Lévy, Jules. Les hydropathes. Paris, 1928.
38514.20.50 Lewis, D.B. Wyndham. François Villon; a documented survey. London, 1928.
38514.20.52 Lewis, D.B. Wyndham. François Villon; a documented survey. N.Y., 1928.
38514.20.54A Lewis, D.B. Wyndham. François Villon. Garden City, 1928.
38514.20.53A Lewis, D.B. Wyndham. François Villon. N.Y., 1928.
43690.1.45 Lichtenberger, A. Léïla si blanche. Paris, 1928.
43566.78.100 Lind, M. Un parnassien universitaire...Emmanuel Des Essarts. Thèse. Paris, 1928.
42544.34.26 Lorde, André de. Mon curé chez les riches. Paris, 1928.
37597.5.10 Lorris, Guillaume de. Le roman de la rose. Paris, 1928.
37597.9.12 Lorris, Guillaume de. Le roman de la rose. Paris, 1928.
41539.13.12 Lucas-Dubreton, Jean. The fourth musketeer. N.Y., 1928.
41539.13.10 Lucas-Dubreton, Jean. The fourth musketeer. N.Y., 1928.
41539.13 Lucas-Dubreton, Jean. La vie d'Alexandre Dumas. 15. éd. Paris, 1928.
43694.11.110 Lucchini, Pierre. Weltuntergang. München, 1928.
43694.88.100 Lutz, Émile. Poèmes errants. Paris, 1928.
43697.14.360 MacOrlan, Pierre. Rue Saint-Vincent. Paris, 1928.
42545.3.52 Maeterlinck, Maurice. The life of space. London, 1928.
42545.3.140 Maeterlinck, Maurice. La vida del espacio. Montevideo, 1928.
42577.11.75 Malot, Hector. The little sister. N.Y., 1928.
43697.75.3020 Marchand, L. J'ai tué. Paris, 1928.
43697.75.4120 Marchon, Albert. L'impasse. Paris, 1928.
42576.76.45 Margueritte, Paul. La cité des fauves. Paris, 1928.
42576.77.39 Margueritte, Victor. Le bétail humain. Paris, 1928.
37574.607 Martin, Dorothy. Sextette. London, 1928.
38551.83.16 Martin, Henri G. Fénelon en Hollande. Amsterdam, 1928.
38551.83.15 Martin, Henri G. Fénelon en Hollande. Amsterdam, 1928.
43697.76.9150 Martin du Gard, Maurice. Vérités du moment. Paris, 1928.
43697.77.130 Martin du Gard, Roger. La gonfle. Paris, 1928.
43697.77.240 Martin du Gard, Roger. Noizemont-les-Vierges. Liège, 1928.
43697.79.100 Mary, André. Poèmes (1903-1928). Paris, 1928.
37547.9 Matern, Erich. Die Bourgogne in den liedern ihrer Dichter. Saalfeld, 1928.
40563.27 Mauduit, Roger. Ballanche le vieillard et le jeune homme. Thèse. Paris, 1928.
43697.88.150 Mauriac, François. La chair et le sang; roman. Paris, 1928.
43697.88.380 Mauriac, François. Préséances. Paris, 1928.
37556.79 Mauriac, François. Le roman. Paris, 1928.
NEDL 43697.88.722 Mauriac, François. Thérèse. N.Y., 1928.
38585.16.30A Mauriac, François. La vie de Jean Racine. Paris, 1928.
43697.89.743 Maurois, André. Bernard Quesnay. Paris, 1928.
43697.89.133 Maurois, André. Climats. Paris, 1928.
43697.89.130 Maurois, André. Climats. 229. éd. Paris, 1928.
43697.89.120 Maurois, André. Contact. Maestricht, 1928.
43697.89.790 Maurois, André. The next chapter. 1. éd. N.Y., 1928.
43697.89.400 Maurois, André. Le pays des trente-six mille volontés. Paris, 1928.
37567.198.10 Maurras, C. Un débat sur le romantisme. Paris, 1928.
FL 381.15 Melcher, Edith. Stage realism in France between Diderot and Antoine. Diss. Bryn Mawr, 1928.
43698.74.3100 Mercier, André Charles. Le coeur et les sens. Paris, 1928.
43698.74.112 Mercier, Louis. Verginis corona. 2. éd. Paris, 1928.
43698.75.170 Méré, Charles. Le carnaval de l'amour. Paris, 1928.
41555.1.7 Mérimée, Prosper. Portraits historiques et littéraires. Paris, 1928.
43698.78.100 Mery, Andrée. Weekend. Adaptée de l'anglais. Paris, 1928.
38513.14.3.10 Mielot, Jean. Miracles de Nostre Dame. Strasbourg, 1928.
43699.65.170 Miomandre, Francis de. La naufragée; roman. Paris, 1928.
Mol 246.3.9 Molière, Jean-Baptiste Poquelin. The misanthrope of Molière. Boston, 1928.
Mon 153.20 Montagnon, F. Trois portraits de Montaigne. Paris, 1928.
Mon 19.28.5 Montaigne, Michel de. Les essais. Paris, 1928? 6v.
Mon 30.28 Montaigne, Michel de. Essays. v.1,3. London, 1928. 2v.
Mon 30.16.7 Montaigne, Michel de. Essays of Michael lord of Montaigne. London, 1928. 3v.

1928 - cont.

Mon 45.20 Montaigne, Michel de. Journal de voyage en Italie. Paris, 1928-29. 2v.
43701.63.310 Montherlant, Henry de. Pages de tendresse. Paris, 1928.
40556.37.5 Montmasson, J. L'idée de Providence d'après Joseph de Maistre. Thèse. Lyon, 1928.
43701.74.360 Morand, Paul. Excelsior, U.S.A. Liège, 1928.
43701.74.400 Morand, Paul. Syracusse, U.S.A. Paris, 1928.
40575.5.50 Morin, Georges. Sainte-Beuve, etudiant en medecine. Thèse. Lyon, 1928.
37566.99 Mornet, Daniel. Histoire de la littérature et de la pensée françaises contemporaines (1870-1925). 2e éd. Paris, 1928.
FL 6059.15 Mornet, Daniel. La nouvelle Héloise; étude et analyse. Paris, 1928.
41596.24.5 Musset, Alfred de. On ne badine pas avec l'amour. Evanston, 1928.
40587.82 Napione, T. Studi sulla fortuna di Chateaubriand nella letteratura e nell'arte italiana. Torino, 1928.
41543.17.4 Nerval, Gerard de. Les filles du feu. Paris, 1928.
41543.12.15 Nerval, Gerard de. Nouvelles et fantaisies. Paris, 1928.
41543.6 Nerval, Gerard de. Poésie et théâtre. Paris, 1928.
43705.95.100 Newsom, J.D. Garde à vous! A novel. Garden City, N.Y., 1928.
37543.179.5 Nitze, W. Albert. A history of French literature from earliest times to the present. N.Y., 1928.
43709.3.250 Noailles, Anna E. La nouvelle espérance. Paris, 1928.
43709.3.240 Noailles, Anna E. Poèmes d'enfance. Paris, 1928.
43709.23.100 Noël, Marie. Les chansons et les heures. Paris, 1928.
39526.58 Nohain, Franc. La vie amoureuse de Jean de La Fontaine. Paris, 1928.
37567.193 Noli, Mlle. Les romantiques français et l'Italie. Thèse. Dijon, 1928.
FL 363.42 Norman, H.L. Swindlers and rouges in French drama. Chicago, 1928.
40535.45.1 Oláh, Liliane. Une grande dame, auteur dramatique et poète au XVIIIe siècle, Madame de Montesson. Thèse. Paris, 1928.
40535.45 Oláh, Liliane. Une grande dame, auteur dramatique et poète au XVIIIe siècle, Madame de Montesson. Paris, 1928.
V43500.227 Ormoy, Marcel. Poèmes pour des fantômes. Saint-Félicien-en-Vivarais, 1928.
42546.12.35 Page, Dorothy. Edmond Rostand et la légende napoléonienne dans L'aiglon. Thèse. Paris, 1928.
43738.76.100 Pergaud, Louis. Poèmes. Paris, 1928.
43738.83.115 Pesquidoux, J.D. Le livre de raison. 16e éd. Paris, 1928.
37596.190 Pettersen, Holger. La vie de saint Eustàche. Paris, 1928.
43740.1.62 Philippe, Charles Louis. Lettres à sa mère. Paris, 1928.
43744.67.824 Pierre-Quint, Léon. Le comique et le mystère chez Proust. Paris, 1928.
43744.67.820A Pierre-Quint, Léon. Comment travaillait Proust. Paris, 1928.
43741.50.100A Pillionnel, J.H. Poèmes d'Amérique. Paris, 1928.
43741.59.4100 Pinguet, Auguste. Le cantique de la mer. Angers, 1928.
43741.98.100 Pize, Louis. Chansons du pigeonnier. Paris, 1928.
38537.25.65 Plattard, Jean. Vie de François Rabelais. Paris, 1928.
37573.632 La poésie d'aujourd'hui; anthologie nouvelle. Paris, 1928.
43743.48.1100 Poldès, Leo. L'éternel ghetto. Paris, 1928.
42545.28.810 Portail, Jean. Georges Courteline, l'humoriste Français. Paris, 1928.
43743.90.4110 Pourtal de Ladevèze, Jean. Desseins. Paris, 1928.
38527.19.20 Prévost, Jean. Agrippa d'Aubigné: sa vie à ses enfants. 2e éd. Paris, 1928.
Htn 43744.67.850* Proust, Marcel. Lettres à Madame Scheikévitch. Paris, 1928.
43744.67.65 Proust, Marcel. Quelques lettres de Marcel Proust. Paris, 1928.
43744.67.62.5 Proust, Marcel. Quelques lettres de Marcel Proust à Jeanne. Paris, 1928.
38526.47.5 Racan, Honorat de Bueil. Poésies lyriques profanes. Maestricht, 1928.
38585.44.15 Racine, Jean. The litigants. London, 1928.
43752.1.46 Rageot, G. Prise de vues. 3. éd. Paris, 1928.
41557.10.40 Raya, Maurace. George Sand. Paris, 1928.
43752.98.700 Raynal, Paul. The unknown warrior. N.Y., 1928.
42556.26.19.5 Régnier, Henri de. Le bon plaisir. Les vacances d'un jeune homme sage. v.1-2. Paris, 1928.
42556.27.30.5 Régnier, Henri de. Flamma tenax, 1922-1928. 3e éd. Paris, 1928.
42556.27.25 Régnier, Henri de. Sept médailles amoureuses. Paris, 1928.
43753.2.36 Régnier, M.L.A. de. La vie amoureuse de la belle Hélène. Paris, 1928.
42515.35.224 Renard, Edmond. Renan; les étapes de sa pensée. Paris, 1928.
42521.23 Renault, Jules. Louis Veuillot. Paris, 1928.
FL 397.114.5 Renieu, Lionel. Histoire des théâtres de Bruxelles. Paris, 1928. 2v.
43755.3.130 Rhaïs, Elissa. Le sein blanc. Paris, 1928.
43756.24.100 Rienzi, Raymond. Le gamin passionné. Paris, 1928.
43757.5.100 Robert, Louis de. De Loti à Proust. Paris, 1928.
37596.27.12 Rösler, Margarete. Sankt Alexius Altfranzösische Legendendichtung des 11 Jahrhunderts. Halle, 1928.
43757.50.537 Rolland, Romain. Goethe und Beethoven. Zürich, 1928.
43757.50.482 Rolland, Romain. Les léonides. Paris, 1928.
43757.50.480 Rolland, Romain. Les léonides. Paris, 1928.
43757.50.403 Rolland, Romain. Pierre et Luce. 40e éd. Paris, 1928.
43757.50.538 Rolland, Romain. Vie de Beethoven. 15e éd. Paris, 1928.
43757.50.555 Rolland, Romain. La vie de Tolstoi. Paris, 1928.
43757.3.60 Romains, Jules. Chants des dix années (1914-1924). 3e éd. Paris, 1928.
43757.3.53 Romains, Jules. Europe. Paris, 1928.
43757.3.40.8 Romains, Jules. Knock, ou Le triomphe de la médicine. 33e éd. Paris, 1928.
42536.35.2 Rosca, Dumitru D. L'influence de Hegel sur Taine. Paris, 1928.
42536.35 Rosca, Dumitru D. L'influence de Hegel sur Taine théoricien de la connaissance et de l'art. Thèse. Paris, 1928.
42578.22.180 Rosny, J.H. La fille des rocs. Paris, 1928.
42578.22.60 Rosny, J.H. La guerre du feu. Paris, 1928.
43757.83.90 Rostand, Maurice. Morbidezza. Paris, 1928.
43757.83.55 Rostand, Maurice. Napoléon IV. Paris, 1928.
43757.83.53 Rostand, Maurice. Napoléon IV. Paris, 1928.
43757.83.56 Rostand, Maurice. Napoléon IV. Paris, 1928.
43757.89.4130 Rouff, Marcel. Jubabau. Paris, 1928.
43757.91.110 Rouquette, Louis-Frédéric. La bête bleue. Paris, 1928.
FL 6037.28 Rousseau, J.J. Il contratto sociale. Messina, 1928.

Chronological Listing

1928 - cont.

	FL 6080.7	Rousseau, J.J. Lettres à Mr. de Malesherbes. London, 1928.
	42514.28.160	Roux, Marie. Charles Maurras et le nationalisme de l'action française. Paris, 1928.
	43757.97.102	Royer, L.C. La maitresse noire. Paris, 1928.
	Mol 618.5	Rudolph, M. Der Aufbau der Komödien bei Molière. Inaug. Diss. Leipzig, 1928.
	40515.56	Rühfel, Fritz. Florians Bearbeitung der Galatea des Cervantes. Inaug. Diss. München, 1928.
	43758.24.140	Ruet, Noël. Le musicien du coeur. Liège, 1928.
	Mol 618.6	Rummel, W. Die Berücksichtigung der Schauspieler bei Molières Schaffen. Inaug. Diss. Leipzig, 1928.
	43761.49.144	Salmon, André. Carreaux, 1918-1921. 4e éd. Paris, 1928.
	42556.29.21	Samain, Albert. Oeuvres choisies. Paris, 1928.
	41557.9.30.10	Sand, George. Little Fadette. A domestic story. N.Y., 1928.
	43761.89.5100	Saurat, Denis. Tendances. Paris, 1928.
	FL 6139.28.10	Schaad, Herbert. Der Ausbruch der Geisteskrankeit Jean-Jacques Rousseau's und ihre Anzeichen in seinen letzten Werken und Briefen. Inaug. Diss. Erlangen, 1928.
	43763.38.120	Schlumberger, Jean. Les yeux de dix-huit ans. 3. éd. Paris, 1928.
	38513.73	Schneegans, F.E. Le théâtre édifiant en France aux XIVe et XVe siècles. Paris, 1928.
	43763.3.38	Schneider, Edouard. L'exaltation. Paris, 1928.
	37567.356	Schneider, H. Deutsche Art und Sitte im Spiegel französischer...Jahren 1830-1870. Inaug. Diss. Köln, 1928.
	43763.41.105	Schultz, Yvonne. L'idylle passionnée. v.1-2. Paris, 1928.
	42587.57.4.5	Schwob, Marcel. Oeuvres completes de Marcel Schwob. Paris, 1928.
	43765.6.100	Sébastien, R. La chapelle des Saints-Anges, roman. Paris, 1928.
	41522.18.360	Séché, Alphonse. La vie des Fleurs du mal. Amiens, 1928.
	43765.21.47	Sée, Edmond. Le métier d'amant. Paris, 1928. 2 pam.
	FL 385.80.15	Sée, Edmond. Le théâtre français contemporain. Paris, 1928.
	40597.2.69	Segar, Friéderic. Un maitre de Balzac. Paris, 1928.
	43765.34.100	Segonzac, R. La légende de Flarinda. 4. éd. Paris, 1928.
	41586.3.11	Ségu, Fréderic. Un maitre de Balzac méconnu, H. de Latouche. Paris, 1928.
	43765.35.100	Seguin, Hélène. Le miroir de Clélie. Paris, 1928.
	FL 6049.14	Sertz, Edwin. Werte, Wertarten und ihre Rangordung in Jean-Jacques. Diss. Giessen, 1928.
Htn	38546.41.15*	Sévigné, Marie de R.C. Memoranda of memorabilia. Oxford, 1928.
	43769.50.100	Silvester, Charles. Le vent du Gauffre. Paris, 1928.
	43769.52.100	Silvy, René. Le chemin de nuage. Toulouse, 1928.
	37555.115	Smith, Nina. L'accord de la science et de la poésie dans la seconde moitié du XIXe siècle. Thèse. Ligugé, 1928.
	42556.29	Soto, Rafael Arcangel. Un olvidado precursor del modernismo francés. N.Y., 1928.
	37567.393	Souday, Paul. Les romantiques à l'Académie. Paris, 1928.
	43775.90.7134	Soupault, Philippe. Les dernières nuits de Paris. 4. éd. Paris, 1928.
	43775.90.7230	Soupault, Philippe. Terpsichore. Paris, 1928.
	40592.50A	Staël Holstein, Anne Louise. Lettres à B. Constant. Paris, 1928.
	37596.25.13	Stone, N. A translation of Chapter XI-XVI of the pseudo-Augustinian sermon against Jews, pagans. Seattle, 1928.
	37564.98	Storer, Mary E. Un épisode littéraire de la fin du XVIIe siècle. Paris, 1928.
	37564.98.5	Storer, Mary E. Un épisode littéraire de la fin du XVIIIe siècle. Thèse. Paris, 1928.
	43780.69.120	Supervielle, Jules. Saisir. Paris, 1928.
	41595.11	Szwarc, Herc. Un précurseur du romantisme. Thèse. Dijon, 1928.
	FL 398.84.30	Talma, F.J. Correspondance avec Mme. de Staäl. Paris, 1928.
	Mon 130.3	Tauro, Giacomo. Montaigne. Milano, 1928.
	39544.56A	Thaddeus, V. Voltaire, genius of mockery. N.Y., 1928.
	43788.3.100	Thaly, Daniel. Chants de l'Atlantique. Paris, 1928.
	42563.18.170	Tharaud, Jérôme. Mes années chez Barrès. Paris, 1928.
	37567.103.25	Tharp, J.B. The fantastic short story in France, 1850-1900. n.p., 1928.
	43788.24.140	Thérive, André. Sans âme. Paris, 1928.
	41568.26.3	Tillier, Claude. Mon oncle Benjamin. N.Y., 1928.
	FL 398.42.2	Tisseau, P. Une comédienne, Marie-Elisabeth Joly. Paris, 1928.
	41574.176	Tomov, T.S. Eziku i stilu vu "Legendata na věkovetě". Sofiia, 1928.
	41555.43.26	Trahard, Pierre. Prosper Mérimée de 1834 à 1853. Paris, 1928.
	43793.5.100	Traz, R. de. La puritaine et l'amour. Paris, 1928.
	41564.55.16	Traz, Robert de. Alfred de Vigny. Paris, 1928.
	42515.35.259	Tronchon, Henri. Ernest Renan et l'étranger. Paris, 1928.
	43795.82.100	Tustes, Albert. Les sirènéennes. Paris, 1928.
	38547.7.20A	Urfé, Honoré d'. Le premier des grands romans français l'Astrée. Paris, 1928.
Htn	43822.49.135*	Valéry, Paul. Réponses. Saint-Félicien-en-Vivarais, 1928.
	43667.78.810	Vallette, M.E. Alfred Jarry. Paris, 1928.
	42547.10.24	Vallette, Marguerite. Le prisonnier. Paris, 1928.
	43827.89.125	Vaudoyer, J.L. Premières amours. Paris, 1928.
	43827.89.115	Vaudoyer, J.L. Rayons croisés, Léonardesques, Héliade, A. Thamar Karsavina. Paris, 1928.
	43827.89.117	Vaudoyer, J.L. Rayons croisés, Léonardesques, Héliade. Paris, 1928.
	37567.147.10	Viatte, Auguste. Les sources occultes du romantisme, illuminisme, théosophie, 1770-1820. Paris, 1928. 2v.
	37567.147.5	Viatte, Auguste. Les sources occultes du romantisme, illuminisme, théosophie, 1770-1820. Thèse. Paris, 1928. 2v.
	42576.48.25	Viaud, Julien. Constantinople. N.Y., 1928?
	42576.57.36	Viaud, Julien. Journal intime. v. 1-3. Paris, 1928.
	43824.49.150	Vildrac, Charles. Livre d'amour. 12e éd. Paris, 1928.
	43824.49.113	Vildrac, Charles. Madame Béliard. Paris, 1928.
	38557.24.32	Villemot, Henri. Bossuet et notre temps. Dijon, 1928.
	38514.21.2.5	Villon, François. The complete works of François Villon. N.Y., 1928. 2v.
	39545.95	Voltaire, François Marie Arouet de. An essay upon the civil wars of France. Westport, 1928.
	39578.8.5A	Wallas, May. Luc de Clapiers, marquis de Vauvenargues. Cambridge, 1928.
	43832.77.100	Warnod, A. Lina de Montparnasse. Paris, 1928.
	Mol 623.6	Warsitz, Franz V. Erweiterte Barbeitung...nomenatque omen. Inaug. Diss. Breslau, 1928.
	42566.16.17	Wenzel, D. Der literarische Impressionismus dargestellt an der Prosa Alphonse Daudets. Inaug. Diss. München, 1928.
	43833.1.40	Weyl, Fernand. La vie amoureuse de Ninon de Lanclos. Paris, 1928.
	40526.60.5	Wilson, Aileen. Fontanes, 1757-1821. Paris, 1928.
	40526.60	Wilson, Aileen. Fontanes, 1757-1821. Thèse. Paris, 1928.
	39584.39	Wright, Katheryn Thorne. Germain François Poullain de Saint Foix. Cleveland, 1928.
	43576.6.810	Zehrer, Hanns. George Duhamel. Inaug. Diss. Oettingen, 1928.
	41593.29.3.65	Zweig, Stefan. Marceline Desbordes-Valmore, son oeuvre. Paris, 1928.

1929

40597.2.167	Abraham, Pierre. Balzac. Paris, 1929.
43512.75.120	Achard, Marcel. Jean de la hune. Paris, 1929.
43514.32.100	Aegerter, E. Poèmes d'Europe. Paris, 1929.
38567.48	Albalat, Antoine. L'art poétique de Boileau. Paris, 1929.
39574.27.5	Alembert, J. Le Rond d'. Discours préliminaire de l'encyclopédie. 5e éd. Paris, 1929.
FL 385.3	Alibert, F.P. La renaissance de la tragedie. Carcassonne, 1929?
43522.41.100	Alibert, François Paul. Les plus beaux poèmes. Carcassonne, 1929.
43522.48.100	Allard, Roger. Poésies légéres, 1911-1927. 2. ed. Paris, 1929.
43522.49.100	Alleman, Jeanne. L'áréne brûlante. Paris, 1929.
38528.29.10	Angot, Robert. Oeuvres satyriques. Paris, 1929.
37576.615	Anthologie des essayistes français contemporains. Paris, 1929.
43524.87.100	Antoine, André. L'ennemie. Paris, 1929.
42576.63.115	Antoniu, A. Anatole France, critique littéraire. Thèse. Nancy, 1929.
43527.3.310	Aragon, Louis. La grande gaîté. Paris, 1929.
43528.48.110	Arland, Marcel. L'ordre. 28e éd. Paris, 1929. 3v.
43518.56.100	Armont, Paul. L'amoureuse aventure. Paris, 1929.
Mol 601.5.10	Arnavon, J. Molière, notre contemporain. Paris, 1929.
41563.18.5	Atkinson, Nora. Eugène Sue et le roman. Feuilleton. Nemours, 1929.
41563.18	Atkinson, Nora. Eugène Sue et le roman. Feuilleton. Thèse. Nemours, 1929.
43531.9.100	Aubrun, Jacques. Le lys brisé et poèmes divers. 2e éd. Paris, 1929.
43740.1.87	Bachelin, Henri. Charles Louis Philippe, 1874-1909. Paris, 1929.
43537.42.100	Bainville, Jacques. Jaco et Tori; roman. Paris, 1929.
43537.42.120	Bainville, Jacques. Le jardin des lettres. Paris, 1929. 2v.
43537.49.100	Baldassera, P. Recois mon coeur. Paris, 1929.
41564.46.5	Baldensperger, F. Alfred de Vigny. 7e éd. Paris, 1929.
40597.19.25	Balzac, Honoré de. Eugénie Grandet. Paris, 1929.
40596.8.10	Balzac, Honoré de. Théâtre. Paris, 1929. 2v.
43537.6.45A	Barbusse, Henri. I saw it myself. N.Y., 1929.
43537.6.46	Barbusse, Henri. Tatsachen. Berlin, 1929.
39543.802	Barr, Mary M.H. A century of Voltaire study...1825-1925. N.Y., 1929.
42563.18.70	Barrès, Maurice. Mes cahiers. Paris, 1929-57. 14v.
42563.18.25	Barrès, Maurice. The sacred hill. N.Y., 1929.
42575.53.10	Barresen, A. Le théâtre d'Octave Feuillet, 1821-1890. Thèse. Paris, 1929.
FL 385.6.2	Basch, Victor. Études d'esthétique dramatique. Ser. I. 2e ed. Paris, 1929.
37595.60	Bastin, Julia. Recueil général des Isopets. Paris, 1929-30. 2v.
41522.14.40	Baudelaire, Charles. Conseils aux jeunes litterateurs. Paris, 1929.
41522.13.8.10	Baudelaire, Charles. Les fleurs du mal. Paris, 1929.
41522.4.5.8	Baudelaire, Charles. Morceaux choisis; poëmes et proses. 8. éd. Paris, 1929.
38557.24.36	Baumann, E. Bossuet. Paris, 1929.
38557.24.37	Baumann, E. Bossuet. 19. éd. Paris, 1929.
43537.90.100	Bausil, Albert. Poèmes d'amour et d'autonne. Paris, 1929.
42563.21.49	Bazin, René. Davidée Birot. Paris, 1929.
42563.21.77	Bazin, René. Le roi des archers. Paris, 1929.
40532.16A	Beaumarchais, Pierre A.C. de. Lettres inédites de Beaumarchais. Paris, 1929.
42566.16.130	Beaume, Georges, Les lettres de mon moulin d'Alphonse Daudet. Paris, 1929.
43538.17.700	Bedel, Maurice. Molinoff; or, The count in the kitchen. N.Y., 1929.
37596.135.30	Bédier, Joseph. La tradition manuscrite du Lai de l'ombre. Paris, 1929.
43538.18.100	Bédier, Joseph. Tristan et Iseut. Paris, 1929.
43744.67.930A	Bell, Clive. Proust. N.Y., 1929.
43538.61.140	Benoît, Pierre. Erromango. Paris, 1929.
37568.54.3	Berl, Emmanuel. Mort de la morale bourgeoise. 9e éd. Paris, 1929.
37568.54	Berl, Emmanuel. Mort de la pensée bourgeoise. Paris, 1929.
43538.76.200	Bernanos, Georges. Le joie. Paris, 1929.
42542.29.28.70	Bernard, Tristan. Jules, Juliette et Julien. Paris, 1929.
37596.198	Bernart Marti, Robert. Les poésies de Bernart Marti. Paris, 1929.
42542.29.55	Bernstein, H. Félix. Paris, 1929.
40597.2.191	Bertault, Philippe. Balzac et la musique religieuse. Paris, 1929.
43538.78.110	Berton, René. La lumière dans le tombeau (Gott mit uns!). Paris, 1929.
43538.78.120	Berton, René. Le roi du cuir. Paris, 1929.
37574.648	Bever, Adolphe van. Poètes d'aujourd'hui. Paris, 1929. 3v.
40582.3.9	Beyle, Henri. Histoire de la peinture en Italie. Paris, 1929. 2v.
40582.13.50A	Beyle, Henri. Lamiel. N.Y., 1929.
40582.3.13	Beyle, Henri. Lucien Leuwen. Paris, 1929. 3v.
40582.2.60	Beyle, Henri. Napoléon. Paris, 1929. 2v.
40582.25.8	Beyle, Henri. Le rouge et le noir. Paris, 1929. 2v.
40582.3.31	Beyle, Henri. Vie de Rossini. Paris, 1929. 2v.
37568.56	Billy, André. La littérature française contemporaine. 3e éd. Paris, 1929.
FL 398.4.25	Billy, André. La vie amoureuse de Sophie Arnould. Paris, 1929.

1929 - cont.

43540.74.130 Birabeau, André. Dejeuner d'amoureux. Paris, 1929. 3 pam.
42563.18.225 Blanc-Péridier, A. Maurice Barrès. Paris, 1929.
43543.4.100 Blanchet, Alfred. L'homme de la jungle; roman colonial. Paris, 1929.
43543.13.715 Bloch, J.R. "- + Co.". N.Y., 1929.
43544.14.110 Bocquet, L. Les branches Lourdes, poèmes, 1903-1910. 3. éd. Paris, 1929.
43544.87.100 Bodet, Lucien. Fantasques. Paris, 1929.
V43500.29 Bollery, Joseph. Un grand ecrivain français méconnu: Leon Bloy. La Rochelle, 1929.
42563.36.260 Bordeaux, Henry. Sous les pins aroles. Paris, 1929.
37547.9.10 Bouchard, Marcel. De l'humanisme à l'encyclopédie. Thèse. Paris, 1929.
43544.89.9110 Boudry, Robert. Toussaint Vezzani. Paris, 1929.
43544.14.100 Bouquet, L. Crucifixiones. Paris, 1929.
42563.89.40 Bourges, Elémir. Sous la hache. Paris, 1929.
42563.37.51 Bourget, Paul. Au service de l'ordre. Paris, 1929.
42563.37.34.8 Bourget, Paul. Le démon de midi. Paris, 1929.
42563.37.34.7 Bourget, Paul. Le démon de midi. tom.2. Paris, 1929.
42563.37.73 Bourget, Paul. On ne voit pas les coeurs. Le soupçon. La vérité délivre. Paris, 1929.
42563.37.11.5 Bourget, Paul. Physiologie de l'amour moderne. Paris, 1929.
40597.2.240 Bouteron, M. La véritable image de Madame Hanska. Paris, 1929.
43544.90.110 Bouvelet, Jehan. Au clair de la lune. Paris, 1929.
43544.94.140 Bove, Emmanuel. L'amour de Pierre Neuhart. Paris, 1929.
40583.134 Boylesve, René. Réflexions sur Stendhal. Paris, 1929.
43545.4.2100 Bramson, Fru Karen A. Nous, les barbares. Paris, 1929.
37543.140.20 Braunschvig, Marcel. La littérature française contemporaine étudiée dans les textes. 3. éd. Paris, 1929.
39527.26.10 Brays, René. Les fables de La fontaine aves un index de tous les noms cités. Paris, 1929.
FL 379.86 Brenner, Clarence D. L'histoire nationale dans la tragédie française du XVIIIe siècle. Berkeley, Calif., 1929.
41593.36.15 Brodnitz, Lili-Charlotte. Maurice de Guérin. Inaug. Diss. Jena, 1929.
42555.37.6.20 Brown, Irwing. Leconte de Lisle. N.Y., 1929.
43547.76.110 Burnet, Etienne. Essences: Paul Valéry et l'unité de l'esprit. Paris, 1929.
43550.50.100 Callias, S. de. Jeanne d'Arc répond. Paris, 1929.
42576.63.230 Calmettes, Pierre. La grande passion d'Anatole France. Paris, 1929.
43550.57.100 Camp, Jean. Vin nouveau. 7. éd. Paris, 1929.
43550.1.31 Carco, Francis. La Bohème et mon coeur. 5. éd. Paris, 1929.
43550.1.220 Carco, Francis. Huit jours à Seville. Paris, 1929.
43550.1.45 Carco, Francis. Images cachées. Paris, 1929.
37556.76 Carkes, I. Le roman familial a la fin du XIXe siècle. Thèse. Montpellier, 1929.
FL 6129.29 Casotti, Mario. Il moralismo di G.G. Rousseau. Milano, 1929?
43551.59.140 Cendrars, Blaise. Les confessions de Dan Yack. Paris, 1929.
43552.1.100 Chabaneix, Philippe. Le bouquet d'Ophélie. Paris, 1929.
Htn FL 375.70* Chamard, H. La tragédie de la renaissance. Paris, 1929-30.
43552.3.9190 Chamson, André. The road. N.Y., 1929.
43552.3.9130 Chamson, André. Roux the bandit. N.Y., 1929.
43552.5.107 Chardonne, Jacques. Les Varais, roman. Paris, 1929.
43552.5.2140 Charles-Etienne. Manon l'ortie; roman. Paris, 1929.
40586.21.15 Chateaubriand, F.A.R. Renato. Bruxelles, 1929.
43756.90.850 Chauvet, Alice. Essai sur Jacques Rivière et Alain-Fournier. Mont-de-Marsan, 1929.
42565.8.15 Cherbuliez, Victor. La bête. Paris, 1929.
42565.28.15 Cherbuliez, Victor. Le roman d'une honnête femme. Paris, 1929.
41574.170 Chesnier du Chessne, A. Le "Ronsard" de Victor Hugo. Paris, 1929.
43552.25.3100 Chevrier, M. Les trois premiers livres des chants. Paris, 1929.
43554.2.98 Claudel, Paul. L'oiseau noir dans la soleil levant. 4e éd. Paris, 1929.
43554.2.165 Claudel, Paul. Le soulier de satin. 21e éd. Paris, 1929. 2v.
38546.23.15 Clerc, Charles. Un matamore des lettres. Paris, 1929.
41543.22.15 Clouard, Henri. La destinée tragique de Gerard de Nerval. Paris, 1929.
42563.18.190 Cohen, G. Le dernier projet littéraire de Maurice Barrès. Abbéville, 1929.
Htn 43556.49.163* Colette, Sidonie Gabrielle. Chéri. Paris, 1929.
43556.49.189 Colette, Sidonie Gabrielle. Claudine a l'école. Paris, 1929.
43556.49.260 Colette, Sidonie Gabrielle. La seconde; roman. Paris, 1929.
38551.45 Compigny des Bordes, A. de. Fénelon et le chevalier de Ramsay. Paris, 1929.
40553.7.15 Constant de Rebecque, Benjamin. Adolphe; suivi de lettres choisies de Benjamin Constant. Paris, 1929.
38575.23.123PF Corneille, Pierre. Les autographies de Pierre Corneille. Paris, 1929.
38575.26.15 Corneille, Pierre. Corneille's Le Cid. N.Y., 1929.
43556.89.100 Coullet-Tessier, Antonine. Marthe. Paris, 1929.
42557.20.225 Coulon, Marcel. Verlaine, poète saturnien. Paris, 1929.
42556.28.118 Coulon, Marcel. La vie de Rimbaud et de son oeuvre. Paris, 1929.
43744.67.970A Crémieux, Benjamin. Du côte de Marcel Proust. Paris, 1929.
43557.25.110 Crevel, René. Êtes-vous fous? Paris, 1929.
40532.25.7 Dalséme, René. Beaumarchais. 1. American ed. N.Y., 1929.
42566.64 Daudet, Alphonse. Oeuvres complètes illustrées. Paris, 1929-1931. 20v.
42566.17.45A Daudet, Alphonse. Works. N.Y., 1929.
43565.5.56 Daudet, Léon A. Paris vécu. Paris, 1929-30. 2v.
43565.5.45 Daudet, Léon A. Le voyage de Shakespeare. 5e éd. Paris, 1929.
37567.215 Deffaux, L.L. Le naturalisme. Paris, 1929.
37558.70 Deffoux, L. Chronique de l'académie Goncourt. Paris, 1929.
43566.48.110 Delarue-Mardrus, Lucie. Amaint; roman. pt.1-3. Paris, 1929.
43566.48.130 Delarue-Mardrus, Lucie. Hortensia dégénéré, roman. Paris, 1929.
43566.50.100 Delétang, Marie. Nocturnales. Paris, 1929.
43566.49.100 Delétang-Tardif, Y. Eclats; poèmes. Paris, 1929.

1929 - cont.

43566.6.40 Delly, M. (pseud.). Une misére dorée, roman. Paris, 1929.
43566.52.100 Demaison, André. Le livre des bêtes qu'on appelle sauvages. Paris, 1929.
40515.5.10 D'Épinay, Louise F. Lettere inedite, 1769-1772. Bari, 1929.
43566.75.210 Derème, Tristan. L'étoile de poche. Maestricht, 1929.
43566.75.150 Derème, Tristan. Patachou, petit garçon. 28. ed. Paris, 1929.
43566.75.250 Derème, Tristan. Poèmes des Colombes. Paris, 1929.
43566.80.2100 Deslandes, Pierre. Harmonies. Lausanne, 1929.
40535.5.25 Destouches, Philippe Néricault. Deux comédies de Destouches. Cambridge, Eng., 1929.
43566.89.100A Deubel, Léon. Oeuvres. Paris, 1929.
43566.7.50 Deval, Jacques. Une tant belle fille. Paris, 1929.
42542.65.37 Donnay, Maurice. L'ascension de Virginie. Paris, 1929.
42542.65.2.5 Donnay, Maurice. Le retour de Jérusalem. Paris, 1929.
39594.19.23.5 Doods, Muriel. Les récits de voyages. Thèse. Paris, 1929.
39594.19.23 Doods, Muriel. Les récits de voyages. Thèse. Paris, 1929.
37544.36 Dorbee, Prosper. Les lettres française dans leurs contacts avec l'atelier de l'artiste. Paris, 1929.
43573.76.72 Dorgelès, Roland. Souvenir sur les croix de bois. Paris, 1929.
43574.41.120A Drieu La Rochelle, Pierre. Une femme a sa fenêtre. 14. éd. Paris, 1929.
43574.65.110 Droin, Alfred. La triple symphonie. Paris, 1929.
FL 384.110 Dubeux, Albert. Acteurs: Julia Bartet, Mounet-Sully. Paris, 1929.
43576.9.97 Du Bos, Charles. Approximations. 3. série. Paris? 1929.
X Cg 43576.6.160 Duhamel, Georges. Le club des Lyonnais; roman. 34. éd. Paris, 1929.
42563.18.95 Duhourcau, F. La voix interieure de Maurice Barrès d'après ses cahiers. Paris, 1929.
41530.310 Dumas, Alexandre. On board the Emma. London, 1929.
43576.58.120 Dunan, Renée. Les amantes du diable. Paris, 1929.
42526.9 Dupire, Noël. Bibliographie des travaux de Ernest Langlois. Paris, 1929.
FL 398.14.62 Dussane, (Mme.). La célimène de thermidor, Louis Cordat, 1760-1813. Paris, 1929.
43576.91.68 Duvernois, Henri. La fugue. Paris, 1929.
43591.89.100 Éluard, Paul. L'amour, la poesie. 5. éd. Paris, 1929.
42563.18.100 Engeraud, R. Aux fontaines de Barrès. Paris, 1929.
43598.54.100 Esménard, Jean d'. Le soleil d'Ethiopie. Paris, 1929.
41564.55.15 Estève, E. Alfred de Vigny. Paris, 1929.
43606.76.100A Fargue, Léon P. Espaces. 5. éd. Paris, 1929.
43606.76.110A Fargue, Léon P. Sous la lamp. 4. éd. Paris, 1929.
40535.15.9 Favart, Charles S. L'empirique. N.Y., 1929.
37566.72.5 Fäy, Bernard. Panorama de la littérature contemporaine. Paris, 1929.
Mol 706.8 Fernandez, Ramon. La vie de Molière. 2. éd. Paris, 1929.
43607.77.100 Ferret, Gilles. La sarabande ensorcelée; poèmes. Paris, 1929.
37564.65.5 Fidao-Justiniani, J.E. Qu'est-ce qu'un classique? Paris, 1929.
43824.84.800 Fillon, Amélie. L'oeuvre imprimée et inédite d'Émile Vitta. Paris, 1929?
42576.34.10 Flaubert, Gustave. Bibliomania. Evanston, 1929.
42576.31.15 Flaubert, Gustave. Salammbô. N.Y., 1929.
42576.17.30 Flaubert, Gustave. Trois contes. Paris, 1929.
43610.22.100 Fleg, Edmond. Le marchand de Paris. Paris, 1929.
Htn 43610.22.700* Fleg, Edmond. The wall of weeping. London, 1929.
41574.162 Flemming, Hans. Mit Victor Hugo im alten Paris. Inaug. Diss. Berlin, 1929.
43610.25.1100 Fleury, René-Albert. Quelques musiques encore. Limoges, 1929.
42555.37.6.12 Flottes, Pierre. Le poète Leconte de Lisle. Paris, 1929.
42557.12.45 Fontaine, André. Verhaeren et son oeuvre. Paris, 1929.
38562.17.5 Fontenelle, B. Le B. de. Fontenelle. Paris, 1929?
V43500.119 Fourcade, Claude. Les fugitives. Paris, 1929.
42576.62.21.22 France, Anatole. Penguin island. 11. éd. N.Y., 1929.
38537.25.86A France, Anatole. Rabelais. London, 1929.
38537.25.85 France, Anatole. Rabelais. Paris, 1929.
42576.62.3.30 France, Anatole. Thaïs. N.Y., 1929.
37565.76 Francois, A. Les origines lyriques de la phrase moderne. Paris, 1929.
43612.5.120 Fraudet, René. Auprès de ma blonde. 167. éd. Paris, 1929.
43612.5.140 Fraudet, René. La côte des dieux. Paris, 1929.
40522.19 Friedrich, Hugo. Abbé Prévost in Deutschland. Heidelburg, 1929.
FL 398.52 Galipaux, Félix. Les Luguet, une dynastie des comédiens. Paris, 1929.
43616.52.110 Galzy, Jeanne. Le retour dans la vie. Paris, 1929.
41542.9.4 Gautier, Théophile. Émaux et camées. Paris, 1929.
NEDL 41542.18.15 Gautier, Théophile. L'España de T. Gautier. Thèse. Paris, 1929.
41542.14.25 Gautier, Théophile. Souvenirs romantiques. Paris, 1929.
43617.66.100 George, Nancy. La chalegane. Paris, 1929.
43617.67.115 Georges-Michel, Michel. Les Montparnos. Paris, 1929.
43617.72.100 Géraldy, Paul. L'homme de jolie. Paris, 1929.
43617.90.100 Gével, Claude. Cher les hommes. Paris, 1929.
43619.24.150 Ghéon, Henri. Le jeux de l'enfer et du ciel, roman. Paris, 1929. 3v.
43619.24.205 Ghéon, Henri. The secret of the curé d'Ars. N.Y., 1929.
43620.2.75 Gide, André. L'école des femmes. 44. éd. Paris, 1929.
43620.2.79.85 Gide, André. Un esprit non prévenu. Paris, 1929.
43620.2.73 Gide, André. Paludes. 16. éd. Paris, 1929.
43620.2.78 Gide, André. Robert. Supplement à L'école des femmes. Paris, 1929.
43620.2.43 Gide, André. Si le grain ne meurt. 48. éd. Paris, 1929.
43620.2.44 Gide, André. Le voyage d'Urien suivi de Paludes. Paris, 1929.
43620.33.100 Gignoux, Régis. La castiglione. Paris, 1929.
43620.35.100 Gilbert de Voisins, Auguste. L'absence et le retour. Paris, 1929.
43620.66.120 Giono, Jean. Colline. 29 éd. Paris, 1929.
43620.66.100A Giono, Jean. Un de Baumugnes. Paris, 1929.
43620.66.705 Giono, Jean. Hill of destiny. N.Y., 1929.
43620.74.4100 Giraud, V. Portraits d'ames. Paris, 1929.
43620.74.115 Giraudoux, Jean. Amphitryon 38. Photoreproduction. Paris, 1929.
43625.19.130 Godoy, Armand. Le drame de la passion. 2e éd. Paris, 1929.
43625.19.140 Godoy, Armand. Foch. Paris, 1929.
43625.19.170 Godoy, Armand. Quatre nocturnes. Paris, 1929.
39527.4.35 Gohin, Ferdinand. L'art de La Fontaine dans ses fables. St. Vivarais, 1929.
43625.49.130 Goll, Claire. Une perle, roman. 21e éd. Paris, 1929.

Chronological Listing

1929 - cont.

42575.78 Goncourt, Edmond de. Manette Salomon. Paris, 1929?

41539.22 Gorman, H.S. The incredible marquis, Alexandre Dumas. N.Y., 1929.

37574.637 Gossez, Alphonse Marius. Les poètes du XXe siècle. Paris, 1929-36. 2v.

43757.50.880 Gotzfried, J.L. Der heroische Idealismus bei Romain Rolland. Inaug. Diss. Freudenstadt, 1929.

43625.3.38 Gourmont, Rémy de. Rémy de Gourmont; selections. N.Y., 1929.

40597.3.15 Gozlan, Léon. Balzac in slippers. N.Y., 1929.

43626.5.100 Grasset, B. La chose littéraire. 13. éd. Paris, 1929.

38526.22.5.86 Graur, Theodosia. Un disciple de Ronsard, Amadis Jamyn. Paris, 1929.

38526.22.5.85 Graur, Theodosia. Un disciple de Ronsard, Amadis Jamyn. Thèse. Paris, 1929.

43626.22.155 Green, Julien. The dark journey. N.Y., 1929.

43626.22.130 Green, Julien. Léviathan, roman. Paris, 1929.

41574.157 Grillet, Claudius. Victor Hugo spirite. Lyon, 1929.

X Cg 38543.23.15 Grubbs, Henry A. The originality of La Rochefoucauld's Maxims. Diss. Paris, 1929.

41593.36.7 Guérin, Maurice de. From centaur to cross. N.Y., 1929.

FL 398.35.7 Guilbert, Yvette. La passante émerveillée. Paris, 1929.

37596.45.25 Guillaume d'Oye. La vie de Saint Thibaut. N.Y., 1929.

42576.46.10 Guillaumie, G. Eugène Le Roy, 1836-1907. Bordeaux, 1929.

43628.1.70 Guitry, Sacha. Histoires de France. Paris, 1929.

43628.1.65 Guitry, Sacha. Mariette ou Comment on écrit l'histoire. Paris, 1929.

43631.2.48 Hamp, Pierre. La peine des hommes; mes métiers. 8. éd. Paris, 1929.

43744.67.1375 Hansen, H.P.E. Syntesen af Marcel Prousts vaerk. København, 1929.

43576.77.810 Harpe, J. L'influence des inventions scientifiques modernes sur le renouvellement des images dans les romans de Luc Durtain. San Francisco, 1929.

39596.26 Hawkins, Richmond L. Bernardin de St. Pierre and Peale's Philadelphia Museum. n.p., 1929.

40522.17A Hazard, Paul. Études critiques sur Manon Lescaut. Chicago, 1929.

40583.102 Hazard, Paul. Stendhal (Henri Beyle). N.Y., 1929.

Mol 708.2 Heiss, Hanns. Molière. Leipzig, 1929.

43632.50.100 Hellens, Franz. La femme partages. Paris, 1929.

43632.7.100 Herbert, Huberte. Elle en est, ma chère. Paris, 1929.

42554.55.12 Heredia, J.M. de. The trophies. N.Y., 1929.

42587.1.20 Hermant, A. Amour de tête. Paris, 1929.

43738.1.95 Hommage à Charles Péguy. 2nd éd. Paris, 1929.

43576.6.815 Humbourg, P. Georges Duhamel. Paris, 1929.

42576.65.40 Huysmans, Joris Karl. Croquis parisiens à Vau-l'Eau. Paris, 1929.

43744.67.1066A Jacob, Jean. Marcel Proust, son oeuvre. Paris, 1929.

43667.14.120 Jacob, Max. Cinématoma. 2. éd. Paris, 1929.

37567.310 Jacoubet, Henri. Le genre troubadour et les origines françaises du romantisme. Paris, 1929.

43667.1.125 Jammes, Francis. La divine douleur. Paris, 1929.

43667.1.290 Jammes, Francis. Les nuits qui me chantent. Paris, 1929.

41542.4.25 Jasinski, René. Les années romantiques de Théophile Gautier. Paris, 1929.

41542.4.26 Jasinski, René. Les années romantiques de Théophile Gautier. Thèse. Paris, 1929.

37596.136.25 Jean Renart. Les amours de Frêne et Galeran. Paris, 1929.

43668.4.100 Jeanson, Henri. Toi que j'ai tant aimée. Paris, 1929.

43668.36.100 Jehan, Auguste. Nouvelles méditation versaillaises. Paris, 1929.

39534.36.15 Jéramec, Jacques. La vie de Scarron. 4th éd. Paris, 1929.

43670.91.100 Joubert, Marcel P. Mazarinades. Paris, 1929.

43670.89.250 Jouhandeau, M. Astaroth. 4. éd. Paris, 1929.

43670.94.150 Jouve, Pierre Jean. Le paradis perdu. Paris, 1929.

42554.68.15 Kahn, Gustave. Images bibliques; poèmes. Paris, 1929.

42586.63.12 Kaufmann, Josef. Gobineau und die Kultur des Abendlandes. Inaug. Diss. Duisburg, 1929.

FL 6129.29.10 Kehrwald, Max. Jean-Jacques Rousseau's Religionsphilosophie und moralischreligiöse Erziehungsmaxime. Inaug. Diss. München, 1929.

43673.83.165 Kessel, Joseph. Dames de Californie. Paris, 1929.

43673.83.130 Kessel, Joseph. L'équipage. 159. éd. Paris, 1929.

43673.83.250 Kessel, Joseph. Vent de sable. Paris, 1929.

37543.190 King, Donald L. L'influence des sciences physiologiques. Thèse. Paris, 1929.

43752.57.910 Kohler, Pierre. L'art de Ramuz. Genève, 1929.

39544.92 Kozminski, L. Voltaire, financier. Thèse. Paris, 1929.

Mol 611.9 Küchler, Walther. Molière. Leipzig, 1929.

37530.67 Lachèvre, Frédéric. Bibliographie sommaire des keepsakes. v.1-2. Paris, 1929.

37530.69 Lachèvre, Frédéric. Glanes bibliographiques et littéraires. Paris, 1929. 2v.

43687.15.100 Lacretelle, Jacques de. Amour nuptial. 25e éd. Paris, 1929.

43687.15.220 Lacretelle, Jacques de. Histoire de Paolo Ferrani. Paris, 1929.

43687.15.703 Lacretelle, Jacques de. Marie Bonifas. N.Y., 1929.

43687.15.125 Lacretelle, Jacques de. Silbermann. 105e éd. Paris, 1929.

39527.10.65 La Fontaine, Jean de. Tales and novels. N.Y., 1929.

43687.29.100 Lafourcode, Georges. Édéa et autres poèmes. La Cailor, 1929.

FL 377.75A Lancaster, H.C. History of French dramatic literature in 17th century. v.1-5. Baltimore, 1929-32. 9v.

43687.60.100 Lang, André. Fragile. Paris, 1929.

37543.37.10 Lanson, Gustave. Études d'histoire littéraire. Paris, 1929.

43687.74.150 Larbaud, Valéry. Allen. Paris, 1929.

43687.74.220 Larbaud, Valéry. Deux artistes lyriques. Paris, 1929.

43687.74.1100 Lardanchet, Armand. Le mauvais ange. Paris, 1929.

41578.88 Larguier, Leo. Alphonse de Lamartine. Paris, 1929.

37558.14.20 Larnac, Jean. Histoire de la littérature féminine en France. 4. éd. Paris, 1929.

43687.77.1100 Larrouy, Maurice. Les nostalgiques. Paris, 1929.

41578.90.5 Lasbordes, Henriette. La poèsie des souvenirs d'enfance chez Lamartine. Thèse. Paris, 1929.

41578.90 Lasbordes, Henriette. La poèsie des souvenirs d'enfance chez Lamartine. Thèse. Paris, 1929.

43687.83.145 Lasserre, Pierre. Faust en France. Paris, 1929.

43687.83.135 Lasserre, Pierre. Trente années de vie littéraire. Paris, 1929.

43687.91.100 La Ville de Mirmont, Jean de. L'horizon chimérique. Paris, 1929.

43688.5.5130 Léautaud, Paul. Passe-temps. 8e éd. Paris, 1929.

1929 - cont.

38513.19.4.10 Lebegue, Raymond. Le mystère des actes des apôtres. Thèse. Paris, 1929.

FL 371.77 Lebègue, Raymond. La tragédie religieuse en France; les debuts, 1514-1573. Paris, 1929.

FL 371.77.5 Lebègue, Raymond. La tragédie religieuse en France; les debuts, 1514-1573. Thèse. Paris, 1929.

43688.7.935 Lebey, André. Disques et pellicules. Paris, 1929.

41578.138 Lebey, André. Lamartine dans ses horizons. Paris, 1929.

43688.9.110 Lebrau, Jean. Couleur de Vigne et d'Olivier. Paris, 1929.

43688.15.2120 Leconte, Henri. Dieux et Dieu, poèmes. Paris, 1929.

42555.34.15 Leconte de Lisle, C.M.R. Poèmes barbares. Paris, 1929?

41574.172 Le Dû, M.A. Le groupement ternaire dans la prose de Victor Hugo. Thèse. Paris, 1929.

41574.172.5 Le Dû, M.A. La répétition symétrique dans l'Alexandrin de Victor Hugo. Thèse. Paris, 1929.

37568.58.15 Lefèvre, Frédéric. Une heure avec... Série 5. 7e éd. Paris, 1929.

38563.58 Legauz, Pierre. Caractères véritables ou Recherche de la vérité dans les moeurs des hommes. Paris, 1929.

42544.33.8 Lemaître, Jules. On the margins of old books. N.Y., 1929.

42546.12.38 Lemke, Ottilie. Der historische Hintergrund. Inaug. Diss. Leipzig, 1929.

41522.18.410 Lemonnier, Léon. Enquêtes sur Baudelaire. Paris, 1929.

43688.1.30.15 Leroux, Gaston. The mystery of the yellow room. N.Y., 1929.

40583.110 Leroy, Maxime. Stendhal politique. Paris, 1929.

40512.27.10 LeSage, Alain René. Histoire de Gil Blas. Boston, 1929.

42545.3.820 Le Sidaner, Louis. Maurice Maeterlinck. Paris, 1929.

37556.77 Levaux, Léopold. Romanciers. Paris, 1929.

39544.235 Lewis, J. Voltaire. N.Y., 1929.

37569.54.3 Lievre, Pierre. Esquisses critiques. Paris, 1929.

43690.25.120 Lièvre, Pierre. Ouvrages galants et moraux. Paris, 1929.

43744.67.1060 Lima, Jorge de. Dois en saios. Maceio, 1929.

43693.13.100 Lochac, Emmanuel. Le promenoir des élégies. Paris, 1929.

43693.89.100 Louwyck, J.H. Retour de flamme. Paris, 1929.

38575.23.40 Lyonnet, Henry. Le Cid de Corneille. Paris, 1929.

43697.6.45 Machard, Alfred. Kunder unter sich. Rudolstadt, 1929.

43697.13.100 Mackay, Helen E. Patte-Blanche. Paris, 1929.

43697.14.160 MacOrlan, Pierre. Le chant de l'equipage. 2e ed. Paris, 1929.

43697.14.420 MacOrlan, Pierre. Nuits aux bouges. Paris, 1929.

43697.14.11 MacOrlan, Pierre. Oeuvres poétiques complètes. Paris, 1929.

43697.14.280 MacOrlan, Pierre. Selections sur ondes courtes. Paris, 1929.

42545.3.190 Maeterlinck, Maurice. Berniquel. Paris, 1929.

42545.3.210 Maeterlinck, Maurice. La grande féerie. Paris, 1929.

38567.1 Magne, Émile. Bibliographie générale des oeuvres de Nicolas Boileau Despréaux. Paris, 1929. 2v.

43697.34.710A Magre, Maurice. The kingdom of Lu. N.Y., 1929.

Htn 43697.34.700* Magre, Maurice. Messalina. N.Y., 1929.

Htn 42584.25.35* Mallarmé, Stéphane. Dix-neuf lettres de Stéphane Mallarmé à Emile Zola. Paris, 1929.

43697.52.100 Malraux, André. Les conquérants. Paris, 1929.

43697.52.740 Malraux, André. The conquerors. N.Y., 1929.

42576.77.21 Margueritte, Victor. Au fil de l'heure, poésies. Paris, 1929.

43697.4.30 Mariotti, Jean. Au fil des jours. Paris, 1929.

43697.77.1100 Mariotti, Jean. Au fil des jours. Paris, 1929.

37567.480 Marsan, Jules. Bohême romantique. Paris, 1929.

43697.78.4100 Marsaux, Lucien. Le carnaval des Vendanges. Paris, 1929.

43697.76.3110 Martet, Jean. Dolorès, roman. Paris, 1929. 3 pam.

43697.88.732 Mauriac, François. Destinies. N.Y., 1929.

43697.88.160 Mauriac, François. Dieu et Mammon. Paris, 1929.

43697.88.580 Mauriac, François. L'enfant chargé de chaînes. Paris, 1929.

43697.88.370 Mauriac, François. Mes plus lointains souvenirs. Paris, 1929.

43697.88.410 Mauriac, François. La nuit du bourreau de soi-même. Paris, 1929.

43697.88.110 Mauriac, François. Trois récits. 33. éd. Paris, 1929.

43697.89.762A Maurois, André. Atmosphere of love. N.Y., 1929.

43697.89.520 Maurois, André. Fragments d'un journal de vacances. Paris, 1929.

43697.89.320 Maurois, André. Les mondes imaginaires. Paris, 1929.

43697.89.780 Maurois, André. A voyage to the island of the Articoles. N.Y., 1929.

43698.51.100 Melon, Joseph. L'archange remember. Paris, 1929.

38543.33.15 Méré, Antoine G. Les conversations du Chevalier de Méré avec le maréchal de Clerambault. Paris, 1929.

41555.1.5 Mérimée, Prosper. Dernières nouvelles. Paris, 1929.

41555.27.20 Mérimée, Prosper. Théâtre de Clara Gazul. Paris, 1929.

37562.98 Merlino, Camillo P. The French studies of Mario Equicola (1470-1525). Berkeley, Calif., 1929.

40535.32.12 Meyer, E. Marivaux. Paris, 1929.

43699.12.100 Michel, André. Le clavecin mal tempéré suivi de la jungle du livre. Montpellier, 1929.

43699.49.100 Millet, Marcel. Cote coeur; prix des poètes, 1929. Paris, 1929.

43699.65.230 Miomandre, Francis de. Le jeune homme des palaces. Paris, 1929.

43699.65.180A Miomandre, Francis de. Oriental l'aventure de Therese Beauchamps. N.Y., 1929.

43699.65.120 Miomandre, Francis de. La vie amoureuse de Vénus, déesse de l'amour. Paris, 1929.

42545.28.7.20 Mirbeau, Octave. Le jardin des supplices. Paris, 1929.

43701.73.100 Mois, André. Neptune - Paris. Paris, 1929.

Mol 60.38 Molière, Jean Baptiste Poquelin. Comedies. London, 1929. 2v.

Mol 181.40 Molière, Jean Baptiste Poquelin. Dépit amoureux. Cambridge, 1929.

Mol 211.80.9 Molière, Jean Baptiste Poquelin. Les femmes savantes...C.H.C. Wright. N.Y., 1929.

Mol 229.10 Molière, Jean Baptiste Poquelin. Il malato immaginario. Torino, 1929.

Mol 19.29 Molière, Jean Baptiste Poquelin. Oeuvres complètes. Paris, 1929-30. 6v.

Mol 252.3.35 Molière, Jean Baptiste Poquelin. Les précieuses ridicules, Le Tartuffe - Le misanthrope. N.Y., 1929.

Mol 172.5.25 Molière, Jean Baptiste Poquelin. The would-be nobleman (Le bourgeois gentilhomme). London, 1929.

37565.72 Monglond, André. Histoire intérieure du préromantisme français de l'abbé Prevosta Jouvert. Thèse. Grenoble, 1929. 2v.

37565.74 Monglond, André. Projets d'une bibliographie methodique. Grenoble, 1929.

1929 - cont.

38585.16.275 Mongredien, Georges. Athalée. Paris, 1929.
Mon 50.29 Montaigne, Michel de. The diary of Montaigne's journey to Italy in 1580 and 1581. London, 1929.
Mon 50.30A Montaigne, Michel de. The diary of Montaigne's journey to Italy in 1580 and 1581. N.Y., 1929.
Mon 28.40 Montaigne, Michel de. Les essais de Michel de Montaigne. Paris, 1929.
39594.14.20 Montesquieu, C.L. de S. Considérations sur les richesses de l'Espagne. Paris, 1929.
39594.13.7 Montesquieu, C.L. de S. Lettres persanes. Paris, 1929. 2v.
39593.10 Montesquieu, C.L. de S. Montesquieu. Paris, 1929.
43701.63.100 Montherlant, Henry de. Les bestiaires. Paris, 1929.
43701.63.320 Montherlant, Henry de. Hispano-moresque. Paris, 1929.
43701.63.370 Montherlant, Henry de. Les îles de la felicité. Paris, 1929.
43701.63.110 Montherlant, Henry de. Le songe. Paris, 1929.
42577.32.50 Montorgueil, George. Henry Murger, romancier de la Bohème. Paris, 1929.
43701.74.125 Morand, Paul. Le Rhône en hydroglisseur. Paris, 1929.
FL 6139.29.5 Moreau-Rendu, S. L'idée de Bonté naturelle chez Jean-Jacques Rousseau. Paris, 1929.
37556.16.50 Morgan, B. Histoire du journal des Scavane depuis 1665 jusqu'en 1701. Paris, 1929.
37543.196 Morienval, Jean. De Pathelin à Ubu. Paris, 1929.
37565.86 Mornet, Daniel. French thought in the eighteenth century. N.Y., 1929.
43701.77.2100 Mortier, Alfred. Le souffleur de bulles. Paris, 1929.
43705.83.100 Natanson, J. Je t'attendais. Paris, 1929.
40524.32.10 Naughton, A. Le tableau des moeurs dans les romans de Restif de la Bretonne. Thèse. Paris, 1929.
37574.110 Néel, Henri Charles. French anthology. N.Y., 1929.
37558.4 Neré, F. Il maggio delle fate a altri scritti di letteratura francesse. Novara, 1929.
41543.15 Nerval, Gerard de. Les illuminés. Paris, 1929.
41543.15.5 Nerval, Gerard de. Les illuminés. Paris, 1929.
41543.10.30 Nerval, Gerard de. Lorely. Paris, 1929.
43707.91.110 Nivoix, Paul. Amours. Paris, 1929.
38537.25.70A Nock, Albert J. Francis Rabelais, the man et his work. N.Y., 1929.
42555.66.25 Nolhac, Pierre de. Le testament d'un Latin. Paris, 1929.
39578.8.15 Norman, S.M. Vauvenargues d'après sa corrrespondance. Toulouse, 1929.
42514.28.220 Oberson, Gabriel. La politique de Charles Maurras. Olten, 1929.
43723.88.100 Oltramare, G. L'escalier de service. Paris, 1929.
V43500.219 Ormoy, Marcel. Le bonheur est dans une île. Lille? 1929.
V43500.223 Ormoy, Marcel. Elegies secrètes et marines. Sainte Marguerite de la Mer, 1929.
38514.155.5 Ovide moralisé. Le commentaire de Copenhague. Amsterdam, 1929.
40517.60 Panard, C.F. Alzirette; an unpublished parody of Voltaire's Alzire. N.Y., 1929.
43737.74.100 Paraf, P. Quand Israël aima. 8e éd. Paris, 1929.
37576.629 Pargment, M.S. Trente trois contes et nouvelles. N.Y., 1929.
43737.83.100 Passeur, Steve. Suzanne. Paris, 1929.
43738.41.120 Peisson, Edouard. Le courrier de la mer blanche. Paris, 1929.
43738.41.100 Peisson, Edouard. Hans le marin. Paris, 1929.
43738.76.110 Pergaud, Louis. De Goupil à Margot. 42e éd. Paris, 1929.
43738.77.110 Pérochon, Ernest. Le crime étrange de Lise Balzan. Paris, 1929.
43741.4.100 Piat, P. Inquiétudes. Paris, 1929.
42568.19.23 Pierre, Q.L. Le comte de Lautréamont. Marseille, 1929.
43741.64.100 Pioch, Georges. La paix inconnue et dolente. Paris, 1929.
43741.75.100 Pirey Saint-Alby. A première vue. 9e éd. Paris, 1929.
FL 1109.71.10 Poème moral. Le poème moral, traité de vie chretienne ecrit dans la région wallonne vers l'an 1250. Liège, 1929.
40587.88 Poirier, Alice. Les notes critiques d'Avramiotti sur le voyage en Grèce de Chateaubriand. Thèse. Paris, 1929.
37569.46 Porché, F. Poètes français depuis Uerlaine. Paris, 1929.
43620.2.90 Poucel, Victor. L'esprit d'André Gide. Paris, 1929.
43743.90.100 Pourrat, Henri. La ligne vente. 4. éd. Paris, 1929.
43744.25.110 Prévost, Jean. Dix-huitième année. 4. éd. Paris, 1929.
43744.25.140 Prévost, Jean. Polymnie. Paris, 1929.
42578.31.67 Prévost, Marcel. L'homme vierge. Paris, 1929.
39544.100 Prod'homme, J.G. Voltaire raconté par ceux qui l'ont vu. Paris, 1929.
43744.67.42 Proust, Marcel. The captive. 2. ed. N.Y., 1929.
43744.67.38.5 Proust, Marcel. Du coté de chez Swann. Paris, 1929. 2v.
43744.67.62 Proust, Marcel. Quelques lettres de M. Proust à Jeanne. Paris, 1929.
38537.25.80 Putnam, Samuel. François Rabelais, man of the Renaissance. N.Y., 1929.
37567.322 Quennell, Peter. Baudelaire and the symbolists. London, 1929.
38514.55.15 Les quinze joyes de mariage. Paris, 1929.
43738.1.105 Quoniam, Théodore. De la sainteté de Péguy. Paris, 1929.
38537.34 Rabelais, F. The heroic deeds of Gargantua and Pantagruel. London, 1929. 2v.
38536.18.17 Rabelais, F. Oeuvres complètes de Rabelais. Paris, 1929. 5v.
38526.47.6 Racan, Honorat de Bueil. Les bergeries et autres poésies lyriques. Paris, 1929.
38585.47.15 Racine, Jean. Bérénice. Manchester, 1929.
38583.11.10 Racine, Jean. Lettres d'Uzès. Uzès, 1929.
38583.8.25 Racine, Jean. Théâtre de 1664 à 1667. Paris, 1929.
41578.89 Raronneaux, Alfred. Lamartine, romancier populaire et social. Thèse. Lyon, 1929.
43752.85.100 Ratel, Simonne. Trois parmi les autres. Paris, 1929.
37567.625 Rebell, Hugues (pseud.). Le culte des idoles. Paris, 1929.
43753.9.170 Reboux, Paul. Bamboulina. Paris, 1929.
43753.33.100 Régnier, Pierre. Colombine ou La grande semaine. Paris, 1929.
40571.4.50 Remise d'une epée d'academicien à M.A. Lefranc. Nogent-le-Rotrou, 1929.
43753.90.140 Reverdy, P. Flaques de verre. 4. éd. Paris, 1929.
37566.76A Revue des deux mondes. Le livre du centenaire. Paris, 1929.
38575.28.10 Reynier, Gustave. Le Cid de Corneille. Paris, 1929.
43756.12.4100 Richard, Gaston Charles. La maison des trois marches noires. Paris, 1929.

1929 - cont.

37558.14.10 Richardson, Lula. The forerunners of feminism in French literature. Diss. Baltimore, 1929.
43756.69.110 Ripert, Émile. Le train bleu, poèmes. Paris, 1929.
37574.77.10A Ritchie, R.L.G. French verse from Villon to Verlaine. London, 1929.
42587.55.24 Rivoire, André. Le désir et l'amour. Paris, 1929.
43757.7.100 Robert, V.A. Mes dieux sont morts. Paris, 1929.
43757.8.3100 Robin, E. Accuse, live-for. Paris, 1929.
38526.10.8.28 Roche, Louis P. Claude Chappuys (?-1575). Paris, 1929.
38526.10.8.28.5 Roche, Louis P. Claude Chappuys (?-1575). Thèse. Poitiers, 1929.
43757.50.520A Rolland, Romain. Essai sur la mystique et l'action de l'Inde viviante. v. 1-2. pt. 1-2. Paris, 1929-30. 2v.
43757.50.777 Rolland, Romain. Die Leoniden. Frankfurt, 1929.
43757.50.765 Rolland, Romain. Les leonides. N.Y., 1929.
43757.50.413.10 Rolland, Romain. Palmsonntag. Frankfurt, 1929.
43757.50.550 Rolland, Romain. Vie de Tolstoi. Paris, 1929.
42556.28.310 Rolland de Reneville, A. Rimbaud le voyant. Paris, 1929.
43757.3.82 Romains, Jules. Boën, ou La possession des biens. Paris, 1929.
43757.3.77 Romains, Jules. Le dieu des corps. 81e éd. Paris, 1929.
43757.3.75 Romains, Jules. Lucienne. 68e éd. Paris, 1929.
43757.3.70 Romains, Jules. Volpone, en collaboration avec Stefan Zweig d'après Ben Jonson. 2e éd. Paris, 1929.
37567.324 Le romantisme et les lettres par Ferdinand Brunot, Daniel Mornet, Paul Hazard. Paris, 1929.
42578.22.210 Rosny, J.H. Les plaisirs passionnés. Paris, 1929.
42546.15.7.10 Rostan,d Edmond. La princesse Lointaine. Paris, 1929.
42546.14.5.70A Rostand, Edmond. Cyrano de Bergerac. N.Y., 1929.
42546.13.1.3 Rostand, Edmond. Cyrano de Bergerac. Paris, 1929.
42546.15.15.25 Rostand, Edmond. The last night of Don Juan. Yellow Springs, Ohio, 1929.
43757.83.105 Rostand, Maurice. Le dernier tzar...en vers. Paris, 1929.
40587.80 Rouff, Marcel. La vie de Chateaubriand. 3. éd. Paris, 1929.
43757.89.100 Roukhomousky, Suzanne. Le temple d'argile. Paris, 1929.
42586.63.60 Rowbothan, Arnold H. The literary works of Count de Gobineau. Paris, 1929.
40597.05 Royce, W.H. A Balzac bibliography. Chicago, 1929.
37555.375 Royère, Jean. Le musicisme; Boileau, La Fontaine, Baudelaire. Paris, 1929.
42556.28.105 Ruchon, François. Jean Arthur Rimbaud; sa vie, son oeuvre, son influence. Paris, 1929.
42556.29.29 Russell, F. L'art d'Albert Samain. Thèse. Toulouse, 1929.
40516.60.78 Sade, D.A.F. de. Corespondance inédite du Marquis de Sade. Paris, 1929.
39595.22.10A St. Pierre, J.H.B. de. Paul and Virginia. N.Y., 1929.
40575.7.15 Sainte-Beuve, Charles A. Correspondance littéraire. Paris, 1929.
40575.7.25 Sainte-Beuve, Charles A. Sainte Beuve et Alfred de Vigny; lettres. Paris, 1929.
38526.47.200 Salel, H. Hugues Salel de Cazals-en-Quercy, 1504-1553. Paris, 1929.
41557.9.48.10A Sand, George. The devil's pool. London, 1929.
41557.9.31.10 Sand, George. La petite Fadette. N.Y., 1929.
43761.59.110 Sandy, Isabelle. Le dieu noir, roman. pt.1-3. Paris, 1929.
42546.30.40 Sardou, Victorien. Nos intimes! Paris, 1929.
43761.6.70 Sarment, Jean. Sur mon beau navire. Paris, 1929.
41574.137 Saurat, Denis. La religion de Victor Hugo. Paris, 1929.
37567.196.20 Saurian, M. Histoire du parnasse. Paris, 1929.
43761.90.25 Sauvage, C. Oeuvres. Paris, 1929.
39534.35.20 Scarron, Paul. Scarron et sa Gazette Burlesque. Paris, 1929.
37555.49 Schaffer, A. Parnassus in France; currents and cross-currents in nineteenth-century French lyric poetry. Austin, 1929.
41574.185 Schenk, Rudolf. Die sprachmechanischen Grundlagen der Bildersprache in der Lyrik Victor Hugos. Würzburg, 1929.
43667.1.805 Schilla, Alfred. Francis Jammes. Inaug. Diss. Saalfeld, 1929.
FL 6139.29.10 Schinz, A. La pensée de Jean-Jacques Rousseau. Paris, 1929.
37556.16.40 Schmitt, Jakob. Die Literaturpolitik der "Revue des deux mondes" von 1850 bis 1870. Inaug. Diss. Marburg, 1929.
43620.2.81 Schulz, Wilhelm. Der Stil André Gides (Teildruck). Inaug. Diss. Marburg, 1929.
38546.22.45 Scudéry, Georges de. Le prince déguise. N.Y., 1929.
43765.31.110 Ségalen, Victor. Équipée, de Pékin aux marches Thibétaines. Paris, 1929.
43765.31.100 Ségalen, Victor. Équipée, voyage au pays du réel. Paris, 1929.
FL 6119.29 Sells, Arthur L. The early life and adventures of Jean-Jacques Rousseau, 1712-1740. Cambridge, 1929.
37530.45 Société des Libraires et Éditeurs de la Suisse Romande, Geneva. Catalogue des ouvrages de langue française publiée en Suisse, 1910-1927. n.p., 1929.
43775.1.35 Sorel, Albert. E. Regine et nous, roman. pt.1-3. Paris, 1929.
38557.24.40 Souday, Paul. Bossuet. Liège, 1929.
43775.90.120 Souday, Paul. Les livres du temps. Paris, 1929.
43775.90.7120 Soupault, Philippe. Le grand homme. 2. éd. Paris, 1929.
43775.90.7702 Soupault, Philippe. Last nights of Paris. N.Y., 1929.
43776.41.130 Spire, André. Poèmes de Laire. Paris, 1929.
37555.338 Spoerri, Theophil. Französische Metrik. München, 1929.
41556.42 Stadelmann, J. Charles Nodier im Urteil seiner Zeitgenossen. Inaug. Diss. n.p., 1929.
38567.30 Stein, Henricus J.A. Boileau en Hollande. Nijmegon, 1929.
43780.5.210 Suarès, André. Variables. Paris, 1929.
43785.9.705 Taboureau, Jean. Bourru, soldier of France. N.Y., 1929.
37530.55 Taupin, René. L'interprétation américaine de la poésie française contemporaine. Paris, 1929.
43788.5.105 Tharaud, Jérôme. La chronique des frères ennemis. Paris, 1929.
37567.196.15 Therive, A. Le parnasse. Paris, 1929.
43788.24.100 Thérive, André. La charbon ardent. 9e éd. Paris, 1929.
42553.34.20 Thibaudet, A. Henri Frédéric Amiel; ou, La part du rêve. Paris, 1929.
37597.11.10 Thuasne, Louis. Le roman de la rose. Paris, 1929.
43789.48.100 Tillac, Charles. Essai de joie. Paris, 1929.
37565.70A Tilley, Arthur. Decline of the age of Louis XIV. Cambridge, 1929.
41555.36.5 Trahard, Pierre. Bibliographie des oeuvres de Prosper Mérimée. Paris, 1929.
FL 383.17.15 Treille, Marguerite. Le conflit dramatique en France de 1823 a 1830. Paris, 1929.

Chronological Listing

1929 - cont.

43793.24.100 Trezel, Germain. Les feux du prisme. Paris, 1929.
43799.5.100 Tzara, Tristan. De nos oiseaux. Paris, 1929?
43822.49.359 Valéry, Paul. Littérature. Paris, 1929.
43822.49.400 Valéry, Paul. Remarques extérieures. Paris, 1929.
43822.49.104 Valéry, Paul. Variété II. Paris, 1929.
43822.6 Vallotton, Benjamin. Nous sommes fort. Quel est ton pays. v.1. Paris, 1929.
43822.51.3100 Valschaerts, Jean. Points de vue. Louvain, 1929.
43822.87.100 Vaucher, N.Z. (Mme.). L'oasis sentimentale; poèmes. Paris, 1929.
43822.89.180 Vaulet, Clément. La grande rafle. Paris, 1929.
Mol 622.5 Vedel, Valdemar. Molière. København, 1929.
43709.89.805 Verane, Léon. Humilis. Paris, 1929.
42557.19.5 Verlaine, Paul. Oeuvres posthumes. Paris, 1929. 3v.
42557.26 Vermersch, Eugene. Florilège. Paris, 1929.
42576.57.25 Viaud, Julien. Correspondance inédite, 1865-1904. Paris, 1929.
42576.57.3.20 Viaud, Julien. A tale of the Pyrenees (Ramuntcho). N.Y., 1929?
38513.14.7 Vingt miracles de Notre Dame. Paris, 1929.
43824.67.100 Vioux, Marcelle. Les amours d'Héloïse et d'Abélard. Paris, 1929.
37555.125 Vittoz, René. Essai sur les conditions de la poésie pure. Paris, 1929.
43826.3.110 Vlaminck, Maurice de. Tournant dangereux. Paris, 1929.
42577.4.44 Voivenel, Paul. Sous le signe de la P.G. Paris, 1929.
39545.35.20 Voltaire, François Marie Arouet de. Candide. N.Y., 1929.
39545.80 Voltaire, François Marie Arouet de. The white bull. London, 1929.
39545.32.37 Voltaire, François Marie Arouet de. Zadig. N.Y., 1929.
39545.65.10 Voltaire, François Marie Arouet de. Zadig. Thèse. v.1-2. Paris, 1929.
38516.28 Wallis, N.H. Anonymous French verse. London, 1929.
43833.1.75 Weyl, Fernand. Three gallant plays: A Byzantine afternoon, Beauty and the beast, The slippers of Aphrodite. N.Y., 1929.
38526.22.4 Wichert, Hans. François Habert und der christliche Humanismus. Inaug. Diss. Elberfeld, 1929.
FL 382.115 Wiener, Francis. La vie parisienne au théâtre. 14e éd. Paris, 1929.
FL 6139.29A Wright, Ernest Hunter. The meaning of Rousseau. London, 1929.
41522.18.40 Wright, Malcolm. The role of the auditive sense in Baudelaire's works. Thesis. Philadelphia, 1929.
43858.90.100 Zavie, Emile. Les beaux soirs de l'Iran. 4e éd. Paris, 1929.
43858.90.110 Zavie, Emile. Les dieux de la tribu. 4e éd. Paris, 1929.
43757.50.802 Zweig, Stefan. Romain Rolland. Frankfurt, 1929.
43757.50.804 Zweig, Stefan. Romain Rolland. Paris, 1929.

193-

43531.9.110 Aubrun, Jacques. La guerre; poème. Paris, 193-?
43697.89.820 Bakeless, John. André Maurois. N.Y., 193-.
42576.65.13.55 Belleville, F. La conversion de M. Huysmans. Bourges, 193-?
38514.26.50 Charles d'Orleans. Chansons. Blaricum, 193-.
43607.30.105 Fels, Andrée. Mademoiselle Colifichet, modes. 4. éd. Paris, 193-.
42576.28.35 Flaubert, Gustave. Madame Bovary. N.Y., 193-.
42576.23.7.5 Flaubert, Gustave. The temptation of St. Anthony. N.Y., 193-?
40516.60.84.5 Gorer, G. The devil's disciple. Paris, 193-?
43631.49.100 Halla, Bernard. Maximes. Paris, 193-.
42544.33.7.10 Lamaître, Jules. En marge des vieux livres. v.1-2. Paris, 193-?
43687.59.1110 Langlade, Emile. Le livre des tristesses et des drames. Paris, 193-?
37555.55.10 Levrault, L. La poésie lyrique des origines. Paris, 193-.
38514.23.31 Marthold, E. de. François Villon. Roma, 193-.
40597.2.97 Meissner, Emmy. Die soziologische Fragestellung bei Balzac. Inaug. Diss. Darmstadt, 193-.
43687.62.800 Morize, André. Reconnaissance à Gustave Lanson. Cambridge, Mass.? 193-?
43738.50.120 Pellerin, J.V. Têtes de rechange. Intimité. Paris, 193-?
42545.95.20 Pottecher, M. La passion de Jeanne d'Arc. Paris, 193-?
42526.10.80 Renaud, Jacques. Maurice le blond. Paris, 193-?
38525.20.49 Ronsard, Pierre de. Hymne des daimons. Thèse. Paris, 193-?
37543.212 Roustan, M. La littérature française par la dissertation. Paris, 193-. 4v.
43761.1.701 Sandoz, Maurice Yves. Fantastic memories. London, 193-.
43763.2.50.5 Schopfer, Jean. Mayerling, the love and tragedy of a crown prince. London, 193-.
43757.50.806 Zweig, Stefan. Romain Rolland élete. Budapest, 193-?

1930

43744.67.835 Abraham, P. Proust; recherches sur la création intellectuelle. Paris, 1930.
37567.675 Ábrangi, Tibor. A francia szinbolizmes lirái formaé. Budapest, 1930.
43512.75.130 Achard, Marcel. La belle marineere. Paris, 1930.
42576.63.100 Ahlstrom, A. Le Moyen Age dans l'oeuvre d'Anatole France. Paris, 1930.
42576.63.98 Ahlstrom, A. Le Moyen Age dans l'oeuvre d'Anatole France. Thèse. Paris, 1930
37562.95 Ahsmann, H.P.J.M. Le culte de la sainte Vierge et la littérature française profane du moyen âge. Utrecht, 1930.
38526.7.35 Ambrière, F. Joachim Du Bellay. Paris, 1930.
43523.41.183 Amiel, Denys. Théâtre: L'image. v. 3. Paris, 1930.
42553.33.11 Amiel, Henri F. Philine, from the unpublished journals. Boston, 1930.
FL 386.402 Antonini, Giacomo. Il teatro contemporaneo in Francia. Milano, 1930.
43744.67.837 Aressy, Lucien. A la recherche de Marcel Proust. Paris, 1930.
43528.48.183 Arland, Marcel. Ou le coeur se partage. Paris, 1930.
43528.48.142 Arland, Marcel. La route obscure. 4. éd. Paris, 1930.
42542.1.35 Arnault, L. Attilio Regolo e Fiesco. Ferrara, 1930.
Mol 701.4.10 Ashton, Harry. Molière. Photoreproduction. London, 1930.
V43500.17 Audiberti, Jacques. L'empire et la trappe; poems. Paris, 1930.
43531.33.100 Augiu, Gladys. Son juif; roman. Paris, 1930.
42563.37.86 Autin, Albert. Le disciple de Paul Bourget. Paris, 1930.

1930 - cont.

43532.23.190 Aveline, Claude. La vie de Philippe Denis. v. 1-2. Paris, 1930.
43535.53.100 Aymard, C.E. Les précurseurs. Paris, 1930.
43535.54.149 Aymé, Marcel. La rue sans nom. 19e éd. Paris, 1930.
43535.54.100 Aymé, Marcel. Le Table-aux-Crevés. 39e éd. Paris, 1930.
43537.41.100 Bailly, A. Néron. Paris, 1930.
43537.50.5 Baldensperger, F. Publications. Paris, 1930.
40596.8.12 Balzac, Honoré de. Contes drolatiques. Paris, 1930. 2v.
40597.20.29 Balzac, Honoré de. Eugénie Grandet. Boston, 1930.
40597.14.6.20 Balzac, Honoré de. Histoire de la grandeur et la décadence de César Birotteau. Paris, 1930.
40596.9.10 Balzac, Honoré de. Lettres à l'étrangère. Paris, 1930. 4v.
40597.29.4.10 Balzac, Honoré de. Le père Goriot. Paris, 1930.
40596.18.12 Balzac, Honoré de. Le théâtre inédit de Honoré de Balzac. Paris, 1930.
40596.18.10 Balzac, Honoré de. Le théâtre inédit de Honoré de Balzac. Thèse. Paris, 1930.
X Cg 43744.67.830 Bandieu, Arnaud. Marcel Proust. Paris, 1930.
42576.46.53 Bargone, C. Pierre Loti. Paris, 1930.
43537.89.2120 Baumann, Emile. Abel et Cain. Paris, 1930.
37562.100 Beardwood, Jane. Rhymes of Latin and French words in Old French. Thesis. Philadelphia, 1930.
39586.22.5 Béarn, P. Grimod de la Reynière. 4. éd. Paris, 1930.
43538.17.120 Bedel, Maurice. Philippine. 23. éd. Paris, 1930.
37530.60 Belgium. Ministère des Sciences et des Arts. Les lettres belges d'expression française 1830-1930. Bruxelles, 1930.
41574.139 Bellesart, André. Victor Hugo. Paris, 1930.
42557.20.160 Benéteau, André. Étude sur l'inspiration et l'influence de P. Verlaine. Diss. Washington, 1930.
43538.61.75 Benoît, Pierre. Le soleil de minuit; roman. pt.1-4. Paris, 1930.
43538.61.75.2 Benoît, Pierre. Le soleil de minuit. Paris, 1930.
38585.16.35 Bentmann, F. Die Geschichte der Racine-Kritik in der französischen Romantik. Wertheim, 1930.
43538.74.116 Béraud, Henri. The wood of the hanging templar. N.Y., 1930.
42582.2.70 Berenguer, Carisomo Arturo. Julio Verne. Buenos-Aires, 1930.
37555.81.10 Berger, Bruno. Vers rapportés. Karlsruhe, 1930.
42542.29.28.40 Bernard, Tristan. L'école des charlatans. Paris, 1930.
42542.29.28.90 Bernard, Tristan. Langrevin père et fils. Paris, 1930.
42542.29.28.80 Bernard, Tristan. Sketches radiophoniques. Paris, 1930.
42542.29.28.110 Bernard, Tristan. Théâtre sans directeur. Paris, 1930.
42542.29.62 Berr, Georges. Miss France; comédie en quatre actes. Paris, 1930.
43538.77.6102 Berry, André. Chante fable de Murielle et d'Alain. Paris, 1930.
43538.78.3100 Berton, Henry. Horizons proches. Paris, 1930.
43538.78.3110 Berton, Henry. Sur l'autre rive. Paris, 1930.
37556.21.17 Beuchat, C. La revue contemporaine, 1885-1886. Thèse. Paris, 1930.
42578.19.50 Beuchat, Charles. Edouard Rod et le cosmopolitisme. Paris, 1930.
42578.19.48 Beuchat, Charles. Edouard Rod et le cosmopolitisme. Thèse. Paris, 1930.
40582.8.15 Beyle, Henri. La chartreuse de Parme. Paris, 1930.
40582.25.9A Beyle, Henri. Le rouge et le noir. N.Y., 1930.
40582.3.19 Beyle, Henri. Molière. Paris, 1930.
40582.3.20 Beyle, Henri. Napoléon. Paris, 1930. 2v.
40582.3.33 Beyle, Henri. Voyage dans le midi de la France. Paris, 1930.
FL 386.500 Bidou, Henry. L'année dramatique. Paris, 1930. 2v.
43744.67.980A Billy, Robert de. Marcel Proust; lettres et conversations. Paris, 1930.
43540.74.140 Birabeau, André. Promesse des fleurs; histoires d'enfants. Paris, 1930.
43540.74.805A Birabeau, André. Revelation. N.Y., 1930.
FL 383.123.3 Bissell, Clifford H. Les conventions du théâtre Bourgeois contemporain en France, 1887-1914. Paris, 1930.
FL 383.123 Bissell, Clifford H. Les conventions du théâtre Bourgeois contemporain en France, 1887-1914. Paris, 1930.
42542.28.65 Blanchart, Paul. Henry Becque, son oeuvre. Paris, 1930.
43543.5.100 Blanche, Jacques Emile. Aymeris. Paris, 1930.
FL 385.8.50 Bloch, J.R. Destin du théâtre. 6e éd. Paris, 1930.
43543.13.110 Bloch, J.R. Offrande à la musique. Paris, 1930.
41574.179 Bohland, Werner. "Les rayons et les ombres" von Victor Hugo. Inaug. Diss. Berlin, 1930.
39586.8.60 Bondeli, Julie von. Die Briefe von Julie Bondeli an J.G. Zimmermann. Leipzig, 1930.
42524.19.17 Bondy, Louis Joseph. Le classicisme de Ferdinand Brunetière. Diss. Baltimore, 1930.
37569.27 Bonneau, Georges. Le symbolisme dans la poésie française contemporaine. Paris, 1930.
42563.36.180 Bordeaux, Henry. Tuilette. Paris, 1930.
42563.36.190 Bordeaux, Henry. Visages français. Paris, 1930.
43544.74.112 Bordeaux, P.H. Antaram de Trébizonde. Paris, 1930.
38557.53.200.60 Bossuet, J.B. L'église et le théâtre. Paris, 1930.
38557.60.110 Bossuet, J.B. Traité de la concupiscence. Paris, 1930.
37547.9.11 Bouchard, Marcel. De l'humanisme à l'encyclopédie. Paris, 1930.
43544.89.6100 Bouju, Paul M. Vers anciens et nouveaux. Paris, 1930.
42563.37.75 Bourget, Paul. La vengeance de la vie. Paris, 1930.
37548.19 Bouvier, J.B. Essai sur l'histoire intellectuelle. (Du romantisme à Genève). Paris, 1930.
40597.2.80 Bouvier, René. Balzac, homme d'affaires. Paris, 1930.
39544.94.5A Brandes, Georg. Voltaire. N.Y., 1930. 2v.
43545.5.100 Brauquier, L. Eau douce pour naveres. Paris, 1930.
43545.23.3110 Bremond, Charles. Le compartiment des chasseurs. Paris, 1930.
38585.16.40 Brémond, Henri. Racine et Valéry. Paris, 1930.
43545.24.230 Breton, André. L'immaculée conception. Paris, 1930.
Htn 37569.40.10* Breton, André. Second manifeste du surréalisme. Paris, 1930.
43545.91.110 Brunet, G. Evocation littéraires. Paris, 1930.
39534.1.30 Bussy-Rabutin. Histoire amoureuse des Gaules. Paris, 1930. 2v.
43550.40.130 Cahuet, Albéric. Irène, femme inconnue; roman. v.1-3. Paris, 1930.
37573.648 Cairo. Egyptian University. Anthologie de prose française. La Caire, 1930.
42563.23.80 Calleye, Hubert. L'âme de Léon Bloy. Paris, 1930.
37544.68 Calvet, Jean. L'enfant dans la littérature française. Paris, 1930.

Chronological Listing

1930 - cont.

	38526.7.30	Cameron, Alice. The influence of Ariosto's epic and lyric poetry on Ronsard and his group. A portion of a diss. Baltimore, 1930.
	43550.1.240	Carco, Francis. Au coin des rues. Dessins en couleurs d'Henri Mirande. Paris, 1930.
	41574.181	Carli, Antoino de. L'Italia nell'opera di Victor Hugo. Torino, 1930.
	41596.12.80	Cassou, Jean. Les nuits de Musset. Paris, 1930.
	43551.59.120	Cendrars, Blaise. Rhum. 24e éd. Paris, 1930.
	43552.2.1120	Chadourne, Marc. Cécile de La Folie. Paris, 1930.
	41563.33	Champonniere, Paul. Notre Toepffer. Lausanne, 1930.
	43552.3.9140	Chamson, André. The crime of the just. N.Y., 1930.
	37573.310	Chapman, Percy A. An anthology of eighteenth century French literature. Princeton, 1930.
	43552.5.109	Chardonne, Jacques. Eva, ou Le journal interrompu. 10e éd. Paris, 1930.
	37555.150	Charpentier, J. L'évolution de la poésie lyrique. Paris, 1930.
	38527.38.5	Chassaigne, Marc. Etienne Dolet. Paris, 1930.
	40586.14.5	Chateaubriand, F.A.R. Atala, or The love and constancy of two savages in the desert. Stanford, 1930.
	40586.14.10	Chateaubriand, F.A.R. Atala, René. Paris, 1930.
	42556.28.215	Chisholm, A.R. The art of Arthur Rimbaud. Melbourne, 1930.
	43566.51.380	Choisy, Maryse. Delteil tout nu. Paris, 1930.
	43554.2.145	Claudel, Paul. Feuilles de saints. 13e éd. Paris, 1930.
	43554.7.38	Clemenceau, Georges. Figures de Vendée. Paris, 1930.
	43554.24.110	Clerc, Henri. Le beau metier. Paris, 1930.
	43556.1.141	Cocteau, Jean. Opium. Paris, 1930.
	43556.1.250	Cocteau, Jean. La voix humaine, piece en un acte. 7e éd. Paris, 1930.
	43556.37.110	Cohen, Albert. Solal. Paris, 1930.
	43556.49.725	Colette, Sidonie Gabrielle. Chéri. N.Y., 1930.
	43556.49.173	Colette, Sidonie Gabrielle. La fin de Chéri. Paris, 1930.
	43556.49.705A	Colette, Sidonie Gabrielle. Mitsou, or How girls grow wise. N.Y., 1930.
	40553.7.20	Constant de Rebecque, Benjamin. Adolfo. Bruxelles, 1930.
	42542.53.19	Coolus, R. Pardon, madame, comédie en trois actes. Paris, 1930.
	42586.32.40	Coster, Charles de. Légendes flamandes. Bruxelles, 1930?
	38512.17.15	Coulton, G.G. The chronicler of European chivalry. (Froissart). London, 1930.
	42557.25.180	Cours, Jean de. Francis Vielé-Griffin. Paris, 1930.
	40534.34.20A	Crébillon, Claude Prosper Jolyot de. Lettres de la Marquise de M*** au comte de R***. Paris, 1930.
	42554.29.4.110	Da Guerrois, C. Dans le monde des fantomes. Paris, 1930.
	42554.29.4.120	Da Guerrois, C. Fleur d'abime. Paris, 1930.
	42566.27.8A	Daudet, Alphonse. Lettres de mon moulin. Paris, 1930.
Htn	42566.59*	Daudet, Alphonse. Pages inconnues. Paris, 1930.
	43565.5.50	Daudet, Léon A. Flammes. Paris, 1930.
	43565.91.100	Davet, Michel. Le prince qui m'aimait. Paris, 1930.
	43566.43.120	Dekobra, Maurice. Le geste de Phryné; amours exotiques. 43. éd. Paris, 1930.
	43566.43.720	Dekobra, Maurice. The sphinx has spoken. N.Y., 1930.
	43566.43.110	Dekobra, Maurice. Venus on wheels. N.Y., 1930.
	43687.28.705	De La Fouchardière, Georges de. Poor sap. N.Y., 1930.
	42557.14.14	Delahaye, Ernest. Verlaine. Paris, 1930.
	43566.48.180	Delarue-Mardrus, Lucie. Les sept douleurs d'octobre. Paris, 1930.
	43566.50.3100	Delly, M. (pseud.). Entre deux âmes. Paris, 1930.
	43566.6.50	Delly, M. (pseud.). Le maître de silence. Paris, 1930-32. 2v.
	43566.51.100	Delorme, Hugues. Zoo (vers). Paris, 1930.
	43566.51.310	Delteil, Joseph. Don Juan. Paris, 1930.
	43566.52.120	Demaison, André. La comédie animale. 16e éd. Paris, 1930.
	43566.77.100	Desaulnier, G. Les lois qui chantent. Montreal, 1930.
	37573.40	Des Granges, Charles M. Morceaux choisis des auteurs français du moyen âge à nos jours. 23. éd. Paris, 1930.
	43566.81.4140	Desnos, Robert. Corps et biens. Paris, 1930.
	43566.89.61	Deubel, Léon. Lettres de Léon Deubel (1897-1912). Paris, 1930.
	43566.7.55	Deval, Jacques. Etienne; pièce en trois actes. Paris, 1930.
	39564.9.5	Diderot, Denis. Lettres à Sophie Volland. Paris, 1930. 3v.
	37567.325	Dijon. Université. Faculté des Lettres. En l'honneur du romantisme. Dijon, 1930.
	Mol 247.21	Doumic, René. Le misanthrope de Molière; étude et analyse. Paris, 1930.
	43574.1.35	Drouot, Paul. Eurydice, deux fois perdue. Paris, 1930.
	43573.76.800	Dubeux, Albert. Roland Dorgelès. Paris, 1930.
	37556.16.45	DuBled, V. Le salon de la "Revue des deux mondes". Paris, 1930.
	43576.15.1100	Ducrocq, Georges. La belle Libanaise. Le journal de Soleiman. Paris, 1930.
	43576.6.210	Duhamel, Georges. Scènes de la vie future. 45. éd. Paris, 1930.
	41538.73	Dumas, Alexandre. Antony; drame en cinq actes. Paris, 1930.
	41538.53.112	Dumas, Alexandre. Twenty years after. London, 1930.
	40553.10.8	Dumont-Wilden, L. La vie de Benjamin Constant. 11. éd. Paris, 1930.
	43576.58.115	Dunan, Renée. Pope Joan. London, 1930.
	41555.45	Dupouy, Auguste. Carmen de Mérimée. Paris, 1930.
	43576.77.130	Durtain, Luc. Dieux blancs, hommes jaunes. Paris, 1930.
	43576.91.90	Duvernois, Henri. Apprentissages. Paris, 1930.
	42543.1.23	Dyssord, J. La vie amoureuse de la dame aux camelias. Paris, 1930.
	42577.34.18	Ehmke, W. Masson-Forestier, sein Leben und sein Werk. Inaug. Diss. Altdöbern, 1930.
	39544.108	Emmrich, Hanna. Zur Behandlung des Judentums bei Voltaire. Inaug. Diss. Breslau, 1930.
	37544.40	Engel, Claire Eliane. La littérature alpestre en France et en Angleterre. Chambéry, 1930.
	43606.78.173	Farrère, Claude. L'homme qui assassina. N.Y., 1930.
	41592.10.15	Faur, Léon. La vie en chansons de Béranger. Paris, 1930.
	42586.63.14	Faure-Biguet, J.N. Gobineau. Paris, 1930.
	41557.10.175	Ferra, Bartomen. Chopin i George Sand a la Cartoixa de Valldemossa. Ciutat de Mallorca, 1930.
	43607.80.100	Fessy, A. L'ange de la patrie. Paris, 1930.
	37596.65.5	Fitz Warine, Fulk. Fouke Fitz Warin. Paris, 1930.
	43610.28.100	Flad, Albert. Le feu dérobé. Paris, 1930.
	42576.28.30	Flaubert, Gustave. Madame Bovary. N.Y., 1930.
	42576.28.98	Flaubert, Gustave. Madame Bovary. Paris, 1930.
	42576.33.8.7	Flaubert, Gustave. Trois contes. Paris, 1930.

1930 - cont.

	43610.25.120	Fleuret, Fernand. Jim Click où La merveilleuse invention. 4. éd. Paris, 1930.
	43611.5.80	Fombeure, Maurice. Homage à Alain-Fournier. Paris, 1930.
	37569.56	Fontainas, André. Dans la lignée de Baudelaire. Paris, 1930.
	42576.60.1100	Forbin, Victor. Mes aventures sous les tropiques. Paris, 1930?
	43611.5.70	Fournier, Alain. Lettres au petit B. Paris, 1930.
	42576.63.7.30	France, Anatole. Le crime de Sylvestre Bonnard. N.Y., 1930.
	38512.104	Frank, Grace. Le livre de la passion. Paris, 1930.
	42586.56.15	Fromentin, Eugène. Dominique. N.Y., 1930.
	37569.52	Gandon, Yves. Mascardes litteraires. Paris, 1930.
	FL 398.10	Gaulot, Paul. Les trois Brohan. Paris, 1930.
	41542.7.15	Gautier, Théophile. Le capitaine Fracasse. N.Y., 1930.
	41542.7.10	Gautier, Théophile. Le capitaine Fracasse. Paris, 1930. 2v.
	41542.9.8	Gautier, Théophile. Fortunio et autres nouvelles...1833-1849. Paris, 1930.
	41542.11.15	Gautier, Théophile. Mademoiselle de Maupin. Paris, 1930.
	37575.455	Genest, Emile. Les belles citations de la littérature française suggérées par les mots et les idées. Paris, 1930.
	43617.4.75	Géraldy, Paul. L'amour; or, The art of love. N.Y., 1930.
	42576.15.70	Gérard-Gailly, Emile. Flaubert et "Les fantômes de Trouville". Paris, 1930.
	43620.2.79.40	Gide, André. L'affaire Redureau. Paris, 1930.
	43620.2.67	Gide, André. André Walter. Paris, 1930.
	43620.2.47	Gide, André. Les nourritures terrestres. 49. éd. Paris, 1930.
	43620.2.33.10	Gide, André. Le roi Candaule. 13. éd. Paris, 1930.
	43620.33.110	Gignoux, Régis. Le prof' d'anglais. Paris, 1930.
	42576.6.15	Ginisty, Paul. Souvenirs de journalisme et de théâtre. Paris, 1930.
	43620.66.330	Giono, Jean. Manosque-des-Plateaux. Paris, 1930.
	43620.66.350	Giono, Jean. Présentation de pan. Paris, 1930.
	40542.20	Girard, H. Un catholique romantique: F. Ozanam. Paris, 1930.
	43620.74.710A	Giraudoux, Jean. Siegfried; a play in four acts. N.Y., 1930.
	39527.4.22	Godchot, Simon. La Fontaine et Sénèque. Saint-Cloud, 1930.
	43625.19.160	Godoy, Armand. Le brasier mystique. Paris, 1930.
	43625.19.150	Godoy, Armand. Les litanies de la vierge. Paris, 1930.
	37596.204	Göring, Werner. Untersuchung der Sprache des Roman de silence von Heldris de Cornualle. Inaug. Diss. Halle, 1930.
	42575.71.35	Goncourt, Edmond de. Germinie Lacerteux. Paris, 1930.
	43625.90.100	Gourbeyre, L. Contes et légendes d'Uzège. Uzès, 1930.
	37565.68.2	Green, Frederick C. French novelists. N.Y., 1930.
	43626.22.140	Green, Julien. Le voyageur sur la terre. Paris, 1930.
	40597.2.230	Gribble, F. Balzac, the man and the lover. London, 1930.
	41539.17	Gribble, F.H. Dumas, father and son. London, 1930.
	40597.2.95	Griffith, B. Balzac aux Etats-Unis. Thèse. Paris, 1930?
	41593.33.50	Guérin, Maurice de. Oeuvres. Paris, 1930. 2v.
	43628.42.160	Guilloux, Louis. Dossier confidentiel. Paris, 1930.
	41574.120.10	Guimbaud, Louis. La mère de Victor Hugo, 1772-1821. Paris, 1930.
	FL 398.7.37	Hahn, Reynaldo. La grande Sarah. Paris, 1930.
	37543.505	Haškovec, P.M. Francouzské kapitaly. Praha, 1930.
	43631.98.705	Hazard, Paul. A souvenir of Chicago. Paris, 1930?
	37567.126.10	Henriot, Emile. Romanesques et romantiques. Paris, 1930.
	42543.64.20	Hermant, Abel. Last and first love. N.Y., 1930.
	41574.34.10	Heugel, J. Essai sur la philosophie de Victor Hugo. Paris, 1930.
	41578.99	Hinrichs, M.S. Ètude sur le cours familier de littérature de Lamartine. Thèse. Strasbourg, 1930.
	38514.68.10	Hirschel, Grete. Le livre des quatre dames von Alain Chartier. Inaug. Diss. Wertheim, 1930.
	42576.57.95	Hirschmann-Guenzel, Gustav. Der Todesgedanke bei Pierre Loti. Hamburg, 1930.
	FL 6139.12.6A	Höffding, H. Jean-Jacques Rousseau and his philosophy. New Haven, 1930.
	42557.12.50	Hoersch, Anton. Der Stil Émile Verhaerens. Inaug. Diss. Dillingen, 1930.
	43636.61.100	Honnert, Robert. Les désirs. 6. éd. Paris, 1930.
	41572.7.20	Hugo, Victor. Han de Islandia. Barcelona, 1930.
	37578.75	L'humour est enfant de Paris. Paris, 1930.
X Cg	42576.66.3	Huysmans, Joris Karl. Against the grain. N.Y., 1930.
	40535.14.505	Iacuzzi, Alfred. The European vogue of Favart. N.Y., 1930.
	42575.100	Immergluck, M. La question sociale dans l'oeuvre des Goncourt. Paris, 1930.
	42575.99	Immergluck, M. La question sociale dans l'oeuvre des Goncourt. Thèse. Strasbourg, 1930.
	43659.88.140	Istrati, Panait. Le pêcheur d'éponges. Paris, 1930.
	43667.48.100	Jalabert, Pierre. La coupe d'Ambroisie, poèmes. Paris, 1930.
	43667.1.135	Jammes, Francis. Champêteries et méditations. Paris, 1930.
	43667.1.165	Jammes, Francis. Leçons poétiques. 3. éd. Paris, 1930.
	40597.2.93	Jarblum, Irène. Balzac et la femme étrangère. Thèse. Paris, 1930.
	40597.2.83	Jarblum, J. Balzac et la femme étrangère. Paris, 1930.
	Mon 170.5	Jaunssen, H.J.J. Montaigne fideiste. Nijmegen, 1930.
	38514.20.18	Jeanroy, A. Deux manuscrits de François Villon. Paris, 1930.
	37543.136.5	Joliet, L. Précis illustré de la littérature française. 3. éd. Paris, 1930.
	38526.34.100	Jourda, Pierre. Marguerite d'Angoulême...1492-1549. Paris, 1930. 2v.
	38526.34.98	Jourda, Pierre. Marguerite d'Angoulême...1492-1549. Thèse. Paris, 1930. 2v.
	38526.34.101	Jourda, Pierre. Répertoire analytique et chronologique de la correspondance de Marguerite d'Angoulême. Paris, 1930.
	38526.34.102	Jourda, Pierre. Répertoire analytique et chronologique de la correspondance de Marguerite d'Angoulême. Paris, 1930.
	43671.50.100	Jullien, J. Casanova a Nîmes. Uzés, 1930.
	37578.53.20	Kalendrier des Bergers. The calendar and compost of shepherds from the original. London, 1930.
	38526.42.10.35	Keeler, M.J. Étude sur la poésie et sur le vocabulaire de Loys Papon. Washington, D.C., 1930.
	43673.83.110	Kessel, Joseph. La rage au ventre. Paris, 1930.
	43556.49.800	Koberle, M. Moderne Tendenzen in Colette's Sprache. Inaug. Diss. München, 1930.

Chronological Listing

1930 - cont.

42544.26.35 Labiche, Eugène. Le voyage de Monsieur Perrichon. Paris, 1930.
42576.63.730 Lacretelle, Jacques de. A la rencontre de France. Paris, 1930.
43687.15.170 Lacretelle, Jacques de. Le retour de Silbermann. 10e éd. Paris, 1930.
43687.15.172 Lacretelle, Jacques de. Le retour de Silbermann. 24e éd. Paris, 1930.
39527.29.27 La Fontaine, Jean de. Fables. N.Y., 1930.
39527.29.3 La Fontaine, Jean de. Fables de La Fontaine. v.1-2. Paris, 1930.
Htn 43687.50.110* Lallier, Roger. Tante Elastine. Paris, 1930.
43687.53.100 Lamandé, André. Les leviers de commande. 9e éd. Paris, 1930.
43752.59.800 Landre, Jeanne. Les soliloques du pauvre de Jehran-Rictus. Paris, 1930.
43687.60.110 Lang, André. Les trois Henry. Paris, 1930.
37543.38.15 Lanson, Gustave. Manuel illustrée d'histoire de la littérature française. 2. éd. Paris, 1930.
42556.32.81 Lapaire, Hugues. Rollinat, poète et musicien. Paris, 1930.
43693.76.100 Lariot de la Salle, C. Coeur transparent. Paris, 1930.
38514.54.50 La Sale, Antoine de. Le paradis de la reine Sibylle. Paris, 1930.
38512.32.20 La Tour-Landry, Geoffrey de. The book of the knight of La Tour-Landry. London, 1930?
40532.25.10 Latzarus, Louis. Beaumarchais. Paris, 1930.
43687.88.100 Laubiès, Charles. Musique de danse; poèmes. Grenoble, 1930.
43687.89.3100 Lavaud, Guy. Poétique du ciel. Paris, 1930.
43688.15.2100 Leconte, Henri. Le Musulman blanc. Paris, 1930.
43688.15.2110 Leconte, Henri. La vie des spectres. Paris, 1930.
43688.2.231 Le Franc, M. Le poste sur la dune. Paris, 1930.
43688.8.40 Le Goffic, Charles. La double confession. 18e éd. Paris, 1930.
43688.8.50 Le Goffic, Charles. La payse, roman. Paris, 1930.
43688.35.120 Le Grand, Maurice. Le chapeau chinois. Paris, 1930.
43688.35.160 Le Grand, Maurice. Dites-nous quelque chose de Franc-Nohain (pseud.). Paris, 1930.
38546.33.10 Lemoine, J. Madame de Sévigné aux Rochers;...1669-1676. Rennes, 1930.
43688.57.50 Lemonnier, L. Le baiser de Satan. Paris, 1930.
40553.10.35 Léon, Paul L. Benjamin Constant. Paris, 1930.
38526.22.14.10 Livingston, C.H. Un disciple de Clément Marot. Paris, 1930.
42544.34.27 Lorde, André de. Mon curé chez les pauvres. Paris, 1930.
41574.177 Lote, Georges. En préface à "Hernani" cent ans d'après. Paris, 1930.
42544.34.32.8 Louys, Pierre. Aphrodite. Paris, 1930.
42544.34.28.10 Louys, Pierre. Les chansons de Bilitis. Paris, 1930.
42544.34.31.5 Louys, Pierre. La femme et le pantin. Paris, 1930.
37556.22.10 Lovering, S. L'activité intellectuelle de l'Angleterre d'après l'ancien "Marcure de France", 1672-1778. Thèse. Paris, 1930.
41595.2.82 Lucas-Dubreton, Jean. Lacenaire, ou Le romantisme de l'assassinat. Paris, 1930.
FL 398.52.35 Lugné, P.A. Le sot du tremplin. 3e éd. Paris, 1930.
41574.197 Lyonnet, Henry. Les premières de Victor Hugo. Paris, 1930.
43697.14.410 MacOrlan, Pierre. Contes de la pipe en terre. Paris, 1930?
42545.3.8.15 Maeterlinck, Maurice. La sagesse et la destinée. Paris, 1930.
38542.3.7 Magne, Émile. Voiture et l'hotel de Rambouillet. Paris, 1930.
43697.34.150A Magre, Maurice. Confessions sur les femmes, l'amour. Paris, 1930.
41574.225 Maison de Victor Hugo, Paris. Victor Hugo raconte par l'image. Paris, 1930?
43697.52.140 Malraux, André. La voie royale. 50e ed. Paris, 1930.
42563.37.90 Mannoni, Paul. Les idées sociales dans l'oeuvre de Paul Bourget. Thèse. Oran, 1930.
43697.74.106 Maran, René. Batouala. Bonibooks. N.Y., 1930.
43697.75.3030 Marchand, L. Durand, bijoutier. Paris, 1930.
FL 1106.5 Maréchal, Lucien. Anthologie des poètes wallons namurois. Namur, 1930.
42576.77.45 Margueritte, Victor. Le chant du berger. Paris, 1930.
42545.9.13 Martel de Janville, S.G. Ces bons docteurs. Paris, 1930.
43697.76.3140 Martet, Jean. La mort du tigre. Paris, 1930.
FL 386.602 Martin du Gard, Maurice. Carte rouge. Paris, 1930.
43697.77.140 Martin du Gard, Roger. Devenir! 3e éd. Paris, 1930.
42557.14.16 Martino, P. Verlaine. Paris, 1930.
FL 6139.30 Marzano, L. L'unità di pensiero nell'opera di Gian-Giacomo Rousseau. Palermo, 1930.
42577.2.8 Maupassant, Guy de. Boule de suif. Paris, 1930.
39578.3.25 Maurel, André. La marquise de Châtelet, amie de Voltaire. Paris, 1930.
43697.88.120 Mauriac, François. Ce qui était perdu, roman. Paris, 1930.
43697.88.323 Mauriac, François. La robe prétexte. Paris, 1930.
43697.89.772 Maurois, André. Conversation. N.Y., 1930.
43697.89.370 Maurois, André. Relativisme. Paris, 1930.
42514.28.52 Maurras, Charles. De Demas à César. v.1-2. Paris, 1930.
42556.28.102 Méléra, M. (Mme.). Rimbaud. 6e éd. Paris, 1930.
38543.33.5 Méré, Antoine G. Oeuvres complètes. Paris, 1930. 3v.
41555.20.21 Mérimée, Prosper. Carmen. Arsène Guillot. Paris, 1930.
41555.20.25 Mérimée, Prosper. Carmen et autres nouvelles. Boston, 1930.
41555.1.14 Mérimée, Prosper. Études anglo-américaines. Paris, 1930.
41555.1.10 Mérimée, Prosper. Lettres à Francisque Michel (1848-1870). Journal de Prosper Mérimée (1860-1868). Paris, 1930.
41555.7.50 Mérimée, Prosper. Lettres de Prosper Mérimée à la comtesse de Montijó. Paris, 1930. 2v.
43698.83.100 Mestrallet, Jean Marie. Rythmes épars. Paris, 1930.
41571.5.15 Michaux, F. Essais bibliographiques concernant les oeuvres de V. Hugo...pendant l'exil. Paris, 1930.
40597.2.73 Milatchitch, Douchan Z. Le théatre de Honoré de Balzac d'après des documents nouveaux et inédits. Thèse. Paris, 1930.
40597.2.74 Milatchitch, Douchan Z. Le théâtre de Honoré de Balzac d'après des documents nouveaux et inédits. Paris, 1930.
37556.84.5 Mille, Pierre. The French novel. 1. ed. Philadelphia, 1930.
37556.84 Mille, Pierre. Le roman français. 4. éd. Paris, 1930.
42555.58.280 Minassian, Jean. Un poète. Paris, 1930.

1930 - cont.

FL 6077.82 Moffat, M.M. La controverse sur la moralité du théatre après la lettre à d'Alembert de Jean-Jacques Rousseau. Thèse. Paris, 1930.
FL 6129.30 Moffat, M.M. Rousseau et la querelle du théatre au XVIIIe siècle. Paris, 1930.
Mol 64.15 Molière, Jean Baptiste Poquelin. Commedie scelte. Milano, 1930.
Mol 229.8 Molière, Jean Baptiste Poquelin. De ingeheelde zieke. Kortrijk, 1930.
Mol 245.103.5 Molière, Jean Baptiste Poquelin. Le misanthrope de Molière. Paris, 1930.
Mol 19.30 Molière, Jean Baptiste Poquelin. Molière; sa vie, son oeuvres. Paris, 1930. 6v.
Mol 252.3.30 Molière, Jean Baptiste Poquelin. Molière's masterpieces, Les précieuses ridicules and Le médecin malgré lui. N.Y., 1930.
Mol 269.4.10F Molière, Jean Baptiste Poquelin. Tartuffe. C.H. Page. Leipzig, 1930.
37565.72.5 Monglond, André. Le préromantisme français. Grenoble, 1930. 2v.
Mon 19.30.5 Montaigne, Michel de. Essais. Paris, 1930-31. 6v.
Mon 19.30 Montaigne, Michel de. Les essais de Michel de Montaigne. Paris, 1930. 3v.
38563.22.10 Montgomery, F.K. La vie et l'oeuvre du père Buffier. Paris, 1930.
43701.63.590 Montherlant, Henry de. Au petit mutilé. Paris, 1930.
37563.27.50 Moore, W.G. La réforme allemande et la littérature française. Strasbourg, 1930.
37563.27.48 Moore, W.G. La réforme allemande et la littérature française. Thèse. Strasbourg, 1930.
43701.74.430 Morand, Paul. A la fregate. Paris, 1930.
43701.74.105 Morand, Paul. Champions du monde. Paris, 1930.
43701.74.140 Morand, Paul. Fermé la nuit. 140e éd. Paris, 1930.
43701.74.718 Morand, Paul. Open all nignt. N.Y., 1930.
37542.32.10 Mornet, Daniel. Déjiny, sou debého pisemn a mýsleni francouzckébo 1870-1927. Praha, 1930.
43701.90.100 Morucci, P.F. Charts tithonievs. Paris, 1930.
43703.80.110 Muselli, Vincent. Les sonnets à Philis. Paris, 1930.
37543.204 Navarre, Charles. Les grands écrivains étrangers. Paris, 1930.
Htn 43620.2.160* Naville, Arnold. Notes bibliographiques sur l'oeuvre de André Gide. Paris, 1930.
43706.55.105 Némirovsky, Irène. Le bal. 22e éd. Paris, 1930.
43706.55.700 Némirovsky, Irène. David Golden. N.Y., 1930.
38525.97 Neri, F. La sorte del Rotrou. Torino, 1930.
41543.12.12 Nerval, Gerard de. Aurélia, ou Le rêve et la vie. Paris, 1930.
41543.10.40 Nerval, Gerard de. Le marquis de Fayolle. Paris, 1930.
43709.3.200 Noailles, Anna E. Choix de poésies. Paris, 1930.
43709.3.210 Noailles, Anna E. Exactitudes. Paris, 1930.
V43500.225 Ormoy, Marcel. Mon plus tendre climat. Lourmarin de Provence, 1930.
43737.34.120 Pagnol, Marcel. Topaze; pièce en quatre actes. Paris, 1930.
37566.43.15 Pailleron, M.L. (Mme.). François Buloz et ses amis;...la revue des deux mondes et la comédie française. Paris, 1930.
37566.43.10 Pailleron, M.L. (Mme.). François Buloz et ses amis;...la vie littéraire sous L. Phillippe. Paris, 1930.
40536.22.180A Palinger, E.H. Pierre Charles Roy, playwriter. N.Y., 1930.
Mol 716.5A Palmer, John. Molière. N.Y., 1930.
37567.320 Paris. Bibliothèque Nationale. Le romantisme. Paris, 1930.
38526.28.5.55 Parker, R.A. Claude de l'Estoille, poet and dramatist, 1597-1652. Part of a Diss. Baltimore, 1930.
43737.83.110 Passeur, Steve. L'acheteuse. Paris, 1930.
43737.83.112 Passeur, Steve. L'acheteuse. 3e éd. Paris, 1930.
43737.89.1140 Paulhan, Jean. Le guerrier appliqué. Lausanne, 1930.
43737.89.2110 Pauphilet, Albert. Suite romanesque. Paris, 1930.
38526.15.81 Pellet, E.J. Gabriel Gilbert, 1620?-1680? Baltimore, 1930.
37530.125 Perceau, L. Bibliographie du roman érotique au XIXe siècle. v.1-2. Paris, 1930.
38524.78 Perceau, Louis. Mathurin Regnier et les satyriques. Paris, 1930.
43738.78.100 Perse, Saint-John. Anabasis; a poem. London, 1930.
Mol 716.4 Picco, Francesco. Molière. Firenze, 1930.
40513.29 Pierson, O.P. The dramatic works of Alain-René LeSage and analytical and comparative study. Urbana, 1930.
43741.88.115 Pinget, Robert. Les amours de Corinne. Paris, 1930.
43741.59.4150 Pinguet, Auguste. Oeuvres; poèmes 1910-1930. Angers, 1930.
40587.86 Poirier, Alice. Les idées artistiques de Chateaubriand. Thèse. Paris, 1930.
43743.62.110 Pons, Justin. Jours et nuits de Paris. Paris, 1930.
41522.18.110 Porché, F. Der Leidensweg des Dichters Baudelaire. Berlin, 1930.
43892.11 Porche, Simone Benda. Le désordre. Paris, 1930.
42545.88.35 Porto-Riche, G. Le marchand d'estampes. Paris, 1930.
42545.88.25 Porto-Riche, G. Les vrais dieux. Paris, 1930. 2 pam.
42545.95.60 Pottecher, M. L'appel des sirènes. Paris, 1930.
43743.90.115 Pourrat, Henri. Les vaillances. Paris, 1930.
40522.9.20 Prévost, Antoine F. Histoire du chevalier des Grieux et de Manon Lescaut. N.Y., 1930.
43744.25.102 Prévost, Jean. Les frères Bouquinquant. Paris, 1930.
43744.25.100 Prévost, Jean. Les frères Bouquinquant. 16. éd. Paris, 1930.
42578.31.55 Prévost, Marcel. Voici ton maître. Paris, 1930.
37576.22 Prior, O.H. Morceaux choisis des penseurs français du XVIe au XIXe siècle. Paris, 1930.
43744.67.61 Proust, Marcel. Comment parut "Du Côte de chez Swann". Paris, 1930.
43744.67.63 Proust, Marcel. Lettres à Robert de Montesquiou, 1893-1921. Paris, 1930.
43744.67.41.5 Proust, Marcel. Within a budding grove. N.Y., 1930.
Htn 43744.67.77* Proust, Marcel. 47 lettres inédites...à Walter Berry. Paris, 1930.
43747.50.100 Puliga, H.C.S. La maison de la peur. Paris, 1930.
37574.510 Quelques chefs-d'oeuvres de la poésie française. Paris, 1930?
43750.41.1100 Quinton, René. Maximes sur la guerre. Paris, 1930.
38526.47.7 Racan, Honorat de Bueil. Poésies. Paris, 1930-37. 2v.
43752.85.712 Ratel, Simonne. Love's not enough. N.Y., 1930.

Chronological Listing

1930 - cont.

43822.49.955 Rauhut, Franz. Paul Valéry, Geist und Mythos. München, 1930.
42556.27.30.85 Régnier, Henri de. Le voyage d'amour ou L'initiation venitienne. 2e éd. Paris, 1930.
38525.26.20A Régnier, Mathurin. Oeuvres complètes. Paris, 1930.
43753.58.110 Renard, M. La jeune fille du yacht. pt.1-3. Paris, 1930.
43528.53.150 Les réprouvés. Paris, 1930.
40524.28.75 Restif de la Bretonne, Nicolas E. Monsieur Nicolas. London, 1930-31. 6v.
Htn 40524.27.50* Restif de la Bretonne, Nicolas E. L'oeuvre. Paris, 1930-32. 9v.
40524.27.51 Restif de la Bretonne, Nicolas E. L'oeuvre de Restif de la Bretonne. Paris, 1930-32. 9v.
43756.7.110 Ribemont-Dessaignes, Georges. Adolescence. Paris, 1930.
39578.8.13 Richard, Pierre. La vie de Vauvenargues. 5th ed. Paris, 1930.
39534.36.20 Richardson, L.T. Lexique de la langue des oeuvres burlesques de Scarron. Thèse. Aix-en-Provence, 1930.
42556.28.87 Rimbaud, Jean Arthur. Dílo. Praha, 1930.
42556.28.77 Rimbaud, Jean Arthur. Leben, Werk, Briefe. Berlin, 1930.
42556.28.385 Rivière, Jacques. Rimbaud. Paris, 1930.
43757.7.3100 Robert, Louis de. De l'amour a la sagesse, suivi de réflexions sur M. Proust. Paris, 1930.
Htn 43757.50.595* Rolland, Romain. Paroles de Renan à un adolescent. n.p., 1930.
43757.50.539 Rolland, Romain. Zivot Beethovenuv. Praha, 1930.
43757.3.55 Romains, Jules. Donogoo; un prologue. Paris, 1930.
43757.3.65 Romains, Jules. Pièces en un acte. 3. éd. Paris, 1930.
42578.22.155 Rosny, J.H. Les amours tragiques de la première princesse de Lamballe. Paris, 1930.
40597.2.220 Rosny, J.H. La vie amoureuse de Balzac. Paris, 1930.
42546.13.1.5 Rostand, Edmond. Cyrano de Bergerac. Paris, 1930.
43757.83.61 Rostand, Maurice. L'homme que j'ai tué. Paris, 1930.
FL 6032.30 Rousseau, J.J. Du contrat social. 5. ed. Paris, 1930.
40597.05.2 Royce, W.H. A Balzac bibliography. Indexes. Chicago, 1930.
V43500.281 Ruet, Noël. Musique de chambre. Sainte Marguerite de la Mer, 1930.
38537.18.10 Sainéau, Lazar. L'influence et la réputation de Rabelais. Paris, 1930.
38526.47.32 Saint-Amant, Marc Antoine Gérard. Oeuvres poétiques. Photoreproduction. Paris, 1930.
39595.22.15 St. Pierre, J.H.B. de. Paul et Virginie. Paris, 1930.
39594.30.10 St. Pierre, J.H.B. de. Paul et Virginie. Paris, 1930.
40576.9.5 Sainte-Beuve, Charles A. Auteurs dramatiques et poètes. Paris, 1930.
40576.10 Sainte-Beuve, Charles A. Philosophes et essayistes. Paris, 1930. 3v.
40576.9 Sainte-Beuve, Charles A. Romanciers et moralistes. Paris, 1930.
41557.9.65 Sand, George. The country waif. London, 1930.
41557.9.48.12 Sand, George. The devil's pool. London, 1930.
41557.9.48.15 Sand, George. La mare au diable. Paris, 1930.
43761.6.75 Sarment, Jean. Bobard. Paris, 1930.
43761.5.40 Savoir, Alfred. La fuite en avant. 3. éd. Paris, 1930.
FL 376.20 Schaberth, F.W. Das komische Element in der französischen Tragikomödies. Inaug. Diss. Nürnberg, 1930.
43763.2.50 Schopfer, Jean. L'amour en Russie. Paris, 1930.
43763.2.39 Schopfer, Jean. Ariane, jeune fille russe. Paris, 1930.
43763.41.110 Schultz, Yvonne. Le sampanier de la Baie d'Along. Paris, 1930.
41578.97 Schulz, J. Lamartines Jugend und Bildungsgang. Inaug. Diss. München, 1930.
38546.22.26 Scudéry, Georges de. La mort de Caesar. N.Y., 1930.
38512.17.20A Sears, F.S. Froissart, chronicler and poet. London, 1930.
43765.21.37 Sée, Edmond. Les miettes. Paris, 1930.
FL 385.80.10 Sée, Edmond. Le mouvement dramatique. 1. ser. Paris, 1930.
42535.22.90 Seilliere, Ernest. Romantisme et démocratie romantique. Paris, 1930.
37569.29 Sénéchal, Christian. L'Abbaye de Créteil. Paris, 1930.
40587.91 Servien, Pius. Lyrisme et structures sonores. Thèse. Paris, 1930.
40587.90 Servien, Pius. Lyrisme et structures sonores. Thèse. Paris, 1930.
37548.145 Seyn, Eugene. Dictionnaire des écrivains belges. Bruges, 1930-31. 2v.
41522.18.130 Shanko, L.P. Baudelaire flesh and spirit. Boston, 1930.
43769.48.100 Silva, Édouard. La vie et la mort. Paris, 1930.
37556.12.10 Sirel, Louis. Journalisme et droit. Thèse. Toulouse, 1930.
43775.90.110 Souday, Paul. Les livres du temps. 3. série. Paris, 1930.
37595.62 Streng Renbonen, W.O. Les estampies françaises. Paris, 1930.
37530.50 Strong, Lois. Bibliography of Franco-Spanish literary relations until the XIXth century. N.Y., 1930.
42556.28.335 Štyrský, J. Život J.A. Rimbauda. Praha, 1930.
41564.55.25 Summers, V.A. L'orientalisme d'Alfred de Vigny. Paris, 1930.
41564.55.23 Summers, V.A. L'orientalisme d'Alfred de Vigny. Thèse. Paris, 1930.
42563.23.82 Termier, Pierre. Introduction á Léon Bloy. Paris, 1930.
FL 391.17 Le théâtre à Paris au XVIIIe siècle. Paris, 1930.
43788.24.165 Thérive, André. La revanche; roman. Paris, 1930.
39544.90 Torrey, N.L. Voltaire and the English deists. New Haven, 1930.
41555.43.27 Trahard, Pierre. La vieillesse de Prosper Mérimée, 1854-1870. Paris, 1930.
37567.326 Tronchon, Henri. Romantisme et préromantisme. Paris, 1930.
42556.28.300 Vaillant, J. Rimbaud. Paris, 1930.
43822.49.228 Valéry, Paul. El cementerio marino. Paris, 1930.
43822.49.360 Valéry, Paul. Littérature. Paris, 1930.
43822.49.23 Valéry, Paul. Morceaux choisis; prose et poésie. Paris, 1930.
43822.49.172 Valéry, Paul. Poésies. Paris, 1930.
43822.49.103 Valéry, Paul. Variété II. Paris, 1930.
42581.33.25 Vallès, Jules. Souvenirs d'un étudiant pauvre. 6. éd. Paris, 1930.
43611.5.60 Valloton, Henri. Lettres d'Alain-Fournier à sa famille. Paris, 1930.
43822.6.5 Vallotton, Benjamin. Suspects. Quel est ton pays. v.2. Paris, 1930.
FL 398.67 Vaudoyer, J.L. Alice Ozy, ou L'asposie moderne. Paris, 1930.
43823.74.100 Vérane, Léon. Le livre des passe-temps. Paris, 1930.
42557.18.3 Verlaine, Paul. Oeuvres complètes. Paris, 1930. 5v.
43823.76.3100 Verne, Maurice. Musées de voluptés. 78e éd. Paris, 1930.
38526.7.25 Vianey, Joseph. Les regrets de Joachim Du Bellay. Paris, 1930.
43824.25.702 Vignaud, J. Venus. N.Y., 1930.
43824.49.170 Vildrac, Charles. La brouille. Paris, 1930.
43824.49.260 Vildrac, Charles. Vitrines. Paris, 1930.
40592.90 Villa-Urrutia, W.R. Mujeres de antaño. Madame de Staël. Madrid, 1930.
43824.3.40 Villeroy, A. La double passion. Paris, 1930.
38514.20.35A Villon, François. Works. London, 1930.
43824.67.120 Vioux, Marcelle. Le désert victorieux. Paris, 1930.
39542.35 Voltaire, François Marie Arouet de. Contes et romans. Paris, 1930. 4v.
39545.37.30 Voltaire, François Marie Arouet de. Extraits. Paris, 1930.
39545.32.17 Voltaire, François Marie Arouet de. Selections from Voltaire. N.Y., 1930.
43744.67.1064 Wegener, Alfons. Impressionismus und Klassizismus im Werke Marcel Prousts. Frankfurt, 1930.
FL 398.19.7 Weyl, Fernand. Madame Dorval par Nozière (pseud.). Paris, 1930.
38547.15.10 Winkler, Egon. Komposition und Liebestheorieen der "Astrée" des Honoré d'Urfé. Diss. Oblau, 1930.
42545.38.75 Wolerum, H. Das literarische Werk Henri Monnier's. Inaug. Diss. Lauf, 1930.
37548.38.25 Woodbridge, B.M. Le roman belge contemporain. Bruxelles, 1930.
43620.2.95 Yang, T.L. L'attitude d'André Gide. Thèse. Lyon, 1930.
37556.16.47 Zdraveva, B.V. Les origines de la revue des deux mondes et les littératures européennes, 1831-1842. Thèse. Sophia, 1930.
37565.31.15 Zeller, Hugo. Die Grammatik in der grossen französischen Enzyklopädie. Inaug. Diss. Weisswasser, 1930.
42584.14.12 Zola, Émile. Rome. v.1-2. Paris, 1930.

1931

37566.84 Abraham, P. Avec in texte inédit de Balzac. 4e éd. Paris, 1931.
37566.84.5 Abraham, P. Creatures chez Balzac. Paris, 1931.
43514.41.100 Adine, France. La cité sur l'Arno. Bruxelles, 1931.
37596.26.18 Aléxius, Saint. Légend. The life of Saint Aléxis. N.Y., 1931.
43522.41.180 Alibert, François Paul. Le plainte de Calypas. Paris, 1931.
43523.41.120 Amiel, Denys. Décalage. Paris, 1931.
42553.32.10 Amiel, Henri F. Fragments d'un journal intime. Paris, 1931.
37568.76.5A Arland, Marcel. Essais critiques. 6e éd. Paris, 1931.
43528.56.110 Armant, Paul. Ces messieurs de la Santé. Paris, 1931.
43528.59.100 Arnaud, René. Trois pages d'histoire. Paris, 1931.
43528.61.127 Arnoux, Alexandre. Carnet de route du Juif errant. 11. éd. Paris, 1931.
V43500.15 Arrou, Pierre. Les logis de Leon Bloy. Paris, 1931.
42563.23.160 Arrou, Pierre. Les logis de Léon Bloy. Paris, 1931.
39594.19.42 Assollant, G. Montesquieu; les lettres persanes. Paris, 1931.
41578.107 Assollant, Georges. Lamartine, premières meditations poetiques. Paris, 1931.
43532.23.200 Aveline, Claude. Trois histoires de la nuit. Paris, 1931.
FL 6129.31.5 Baillods, Jules. L'ile de Saint-Pierre. Neuchâtel, 1931.
42545.3.490 Bailly, A. Maeterlinck. Paris, 1931.
37567.187 Bain, M.I. Les voyageurs français en Écosse, 1770-1830. Paris, 1931.
37567.186 Bain, M.I. Les voyageurs français en Écosse, 1770-1830. Thèse. Paris, 1931.
40597.35.80 Balzac, Honoré de. Le médecin de campagne. Paris, 1931.
40597.29.5.8 Balzac, Honoré de. Old Goriot. London, 1931.
40597.29.4.15 Balzac, Honoré de. Père Goriot. N.Y., 1931.
41522.60 Banner, F. Aloysius Bertrand's Gaspard de la nuit als Wortkunstwerk. Inaug. Diss. Augsburg, 1931.
38526.9.50 Bassecourt, Claude de. Trage-comédie pastoralle. Bruxelles, 1931.
42542.29.56 Bathille, Pierre. Henry Bernstein, son oeuvre. Paris, 1931.
42584.25.50 Batilliat, M. Emile Zola. Paris, 1931.
41522.13.8.72A Baudelaire, Charles. Flowers of evil. N.Y., 1931.
42563.21.53 Bazin, René. Magnificat. Paris, 1931.
43744.67.910 Beckett, Samuel. Proust. London, 1931.
43538.18.110 Bédier, Joseph. Cheyalerie. Tours, 1931.
38512.17.25 Bekkers, F.H.H.A. Étude sur l'emploi que Froissart fait de la préposition. Amsterdam, 1931.
43540.60.100 Benet-Valmer, Gustave. Le desir, roman. Paris, 1931.
43554.2.800 Benoist-Méchin, Jacques. Bibliographie des oeuvres de Paul Claudel. Paris, 1931.
42563.36.555 Benoit, Pierre. Henry Bordeaux. Paris, 1931.
38585.16.35.5 Bentmann, F. Die Geschichte der Racine-Kritik in der französischen Romantik. Wertheim, 1931.
40587.105 Bérenger, Henry. Chateaubriand; héros de l'aventure romantique. Paris, 1931.
41593.12.20 Bernard, D. Autour de Brizeux. Quimper, 1931.
42542.29.28.100 Bernard, Tristan. Un ami d'Argentine. Paris, 1931.
37556.96 Bertuccioli, A. Les origines du roman maritime français. Livorno, 1931.
43538.88.140 Betz, Maurice. Rossignol du Japon. Paris, 1931.
40582.25.10 Beyle, Henri. Le rouge et le noir. N.Y., 1931.
40582.3.22 Beyle, Henri. Pensées. Paris, 1931. 2v.
40582.3.29 Beyle, Henri. Théâtre. Paris, 1931. 3v.
FL 394.131 Bib (pseud.). La comédie française vue par Bib. Paris, 1931.
38539.3.275 Bichemaier, Karl. Die Preziositöt das senimentalen Romane des Sieur des Escuteaux. Wertheim, 1931.
38526.2.4.100 Billard, C. Gaston de Foix. N.Y., 1931.
43540.74.150 Birabeau, André. Côte d'Azur. Paris, 1931.
42568.23.150 Black, G.W. Bibliographie de Georges Eekhoud. Boston, 1931.
40597.2.89 Blanchard, Marc. La champagne et ses habitants dans l'oeuvre de Honoré de Balzac. Thèse. Paris, 1931.
40597.2.91 Blanchard, Marc. Témoignages et jugements sur Balzac. Thèse. Paris, 1931.
43543.13.156 Bloch, J.R. Destin du siècle. 6. éd. Paris, 1931.
43543.13.705 Bloch, J.R. A night in Kurdistan. N.Y., 1931.
X Cg 42563.36.60.5 Bordeaux, Henry. La peur de vivre. Paris, 1931.
42563.36.48 Bordeaux, Henry. Les yeux qui s'ouvrent. Paris, 1931.

Chronological Listing

1931 - cont.

37583.405 Borgerhoff, J.L. Nineteenth century French plays. N.Y., 1931.
37562.250 Bossuat, R. Le moyen âge. Paris, 1931.
43544.88.3100 Bourcier, E. La guerre du Tonkin. Paris, 1931.
42542.44.40 Bourdet, Édouard. Le sexe faible; pièce en trois actes. Paris, 1931.
42542.44.42 Bourdet, Édouard. Le sexe faible. 10. éd. v.1-9. Paris, 1931.
43544.90.7100 Bouvier, André. Le collier. Lausanne, 1931.
43544.94.130 Bove, Emmanuel. Journal écrit en hiver. Paris, 1931.
43744.67.1120 Boylesve, René. Quelques échanges et témoignages. Paris, 1931.
41578.95 Brimont, R. de B. Autour de "Graziella". Paris, 1931.
40597.2.87 Buttke, Erika. Balzac als Dichter des modernen Kapitalismus. Inaug. Diss. Berlin, 1931.
43550.55.120 Cami, Henri. Christophe Colomb. Paris, 1931.
43550.57.110 Camp, Jean. Le cid est revenu. Paris, 1931.
42576.63.110A Carias, Léon. Anatole France. Paris, 1931.
FL 6139.31 Carton, Paul. Le faux naturisme de Jean-Jacques Rousseau. Paris, 1931.
43550.82.250 Cassou, Jean. Comme une grande image. Paris, 1931.
37564.114 Caudwell, H. Introduction to French classicism. London, 1931.
43551.59.705 Cendrars, Blaise. Panama, or The adventure of my seven uncles. N.Y, 1931.
43552.3.2700 Chambe, René. Still a woman. N.Y., 1931.
43552.5.130 Chardonne, Jacques. Claire; roman. Paris, 1931.
43552.6.5100 Charlier, Gustave. De Ronsard à Victor Hugo. Bruxelles, 1931.
40583.114 Charlier, Gustave. Stendhal et ses amis belges. Paris, 1931.
FL 6119.31.3 Charpentier, John. Jean-Jacques Rousseau ou Le démocrate par dépit. Paris, 1931.
FL 6119.31 Charpentier, John. Rousseau, the child of nature. N.Y., 1931.
43552.5.8100 Chaumeix, André. Le fauteuil de Clemenceau. Paris, 1931.
43556.49.805A Chauvière, Claude. Colette. Paris, 1931.
43552.24.170 Chérau, Gaston. Toi. Paris, 1931.
43554.2.105 Claudel, Paul. La cantate à trois voix. Paris, 1931.
43554.2.305 Claudel, Paul. The satin slipper. New Haven, 1931.
42556.28.340 Clauzel, Raymond. Une saison en enfer et Arthur Rimbaud. Paris, 1931.
43556.1.92 Cocteau, Jean. Les enfants terribles. Paris, 1931.
Htn 43556.1.140* Cocteau, Jean. Opium, journal d'une desintoxication. Paris, 1931.
37596.10.110 Cohen, Gustav. Un grand romancier d'amour et d'aventure au XII siècle. Paris, 1931.
43556.49.165 Colette, Sidonie Gabrielle. Chéri. Paris, 1931.
43556.49.185.5A Colette, Sidonie Gabrielle. Claudine s'en va. Paris, 1931.
43556.185.5A Colette, Sidonie Gabrielle. Claudine s'en va. Paris, 1931.
43556.49.710 Colette, Sidonie Gabrielle. The gentle libertine. N.Y., 1931.
43556.49.290 Colette, Sidonie Gabrielle. La naissance du jour. Paris, 1931.
43556.49.730 Colette, Sidonie Gabrielle. Renée la vagabonde. 1st ed. Garden City, N.Y., 1931.
43556.49.715 Colette, Sidonie Gabrielle. Young lady of Paris. N.Y., 1931.
42576.15.295 Commanville, C. Succession de Mme Franklin Grout-Flaubert. Paris, 1931.
42557.12.55 Commémoration d'Émile Verhaeren à Saint Cloud 4 juillet 1931. Paris, 1931.
38524.72A Cons, Louis. Anthologie littéraire de la renaissance française. N.Y., 1931.
41574.123 Constans, Charles. Leopoldine Hugo. Beziers, 1931.
41574.124 Constans, Charles. Leopoldine Hugo. Beziers, 1931.
40553.7.10 Constant de Rebecque, Benjamin. Adolphe. Le cahier rouge. Paris, 1931.
40553.9.7 Constant de Rebecque, Benjamin. Lettres de Benjamin Constant à sa famille. Paris, 1931[1932]
40582.3.45 Constantin, Abraham. Idées italiennes sur quelques tableaux célèbres. 2. éd. Paris, 1931.
FL 396.90.52 Copeau, J. Souvenirs du Vieux-Colonibier. Paris, 1931.
FL 6129.31 Cornelissen, A.J.M. Calvijn en Rousseau. Nijmengen, 1931.
37569.62 Crémieux, B. Inventaires. Paris, 1931.
38526.2.4.125 Dabney, L.E. Claude Billard. Baltimore, 1931.
42554.29.4.130 Da Guerrois, C. Musique de rêve. Paris, 1931.
43565.50.100 Dalize, René (pseud.). Au Zanzi des coeurs. Paris, 1931.
43598.84.800 Daniel Rops, Henry. Édouard Estaunié. Paris, 1931.
42566.60 Daudet, Alphonse. La doulou; la vie; extraits des carnets inédits. Paris, 1931.
42566.27.9 Daudet, Alphonse. Lettres de mon moulin. Paris, 1931.
40583.118 David, Maurice. Stendhal; sa vie, son oeuvre. Paris, 1931.
37562.25.15 Davy, M.M. Les sermons universitaires parisiens de 1250-1251. Paris, 1931.
42584.25.255 Deffoux, Léon. La publication de L'assommoir. Paris, 1931.
43566.48.120 Delarue-Mardrus, Lucie. Le batard; vie de Guillaume le conquerant. Paris, 1931.
43566.53.130 Demasy, Paul. La tragédie d'Alexandre. Paris, 1931.
43528.53.160 Le demon bleu. Paris, 1931. 2v.
42576.15.66 Demorest, D.L. A travers les plans, manuscrits et dossiers de Bouvard et Pécuchet. Thèse. Paris, 1931.
42576.15.64 Demorest, D.L. L'expression figurée et symbolique dans l'oeuvre de Gustave Flaubert. Thèse. v.1. Paris, 1931. 2v.
43566.75.230 Derème, Tristan. Les compliments en vers de Patachou. Paris, 1931.
41593.29.3.7 Desbordes-Valmore, Marceline. Les greniers et la guitare de Marceline. Paris, 1931.
41593.29.3.1 Desbordes-Valmore, Marceline. Poésies complètes. Paris, 1931-1932. 2v.
38514.56.25 Desonay, F. Nouvelles notes autographes d'Antoine de la Sale. Paris, 1931.
43566.90.100 Deval, Jacques. Marie galante, roman. Paris, 1931.
39564.61 Diderot, Denis. Correspondance inédite. Paris, 1931. 2v.
43554.2.935 Dieckmann, H. Die Kunstanschauung Paul Claudel's. München, 1931.
39566.36 Dieckmann, H. Stand und Probleme der Diderot-Forschung. Bonn, 1931.
40587.93 Döhner, Kurt. Zeit und Ewigkeit bei Chateaubriand. Inaug. Diss. Marburg, 1931.

1931 - cont.

41539.19 Döling, Erich. Alexandre Dumas pères Subjektivismus in seinen Dramen aus der Zeit der Romantik. Inaug. Diss. Halle, 1931.
41522.18.60 Dufay, Pierre. Autour de Baudelaire. Paris, 1931.
43576.6.430 Duhamel, Georges. L'Alsace entrevue. Strasbourg, 1931.
43576.6.345 Duhamel, Georges. Geographie cordiale de l'Europe. 82. éd. Paris, 1931.
43576.6.170 Duhamel, Georges. Pages de mon carnet. Paris, 1931.
38526.13.270 Du Hamel, J. d. The earliest French play about America. N.Y., 1931.
43877.10 Dunois, D. (pseud.). A lover returns. N.Y., 1931.
37562.120 Dupin, Henri. La courtoisie au moyen âge. Paris, 1931.
43576.71.100 Dupony, A. L'homme de la palud. Paris, 1931.
37556.82 Dupuy, Aimé. Un personnage nouveau du roman français, l'enfant. Thèse. Paris, 1931.
43576.77.110 Durtain, Luc. Captain O.K.; roman. Paris, 1931.
43576.91.54 Duvernois, Henri. Beauté. Paris, 1931.
43576.91.86 Duvernois, Henri. Les soeurs Hortensias; roman. Paris, 1931.
43576.93.110 Duwez, Maurice. Arsène et Chrysostome. Bruxelles, 1931.
43586.86.100 Eftimiu, Victor. Le nain du théâtre français. Paris, 1931.
42572.11.15 Erckmann, Emile. Histoire d'un conscrit de 1813. Paris, 1931.
43598.13.110 Escholier, R. L'herbe d'amour; roman. Paris, 1931.
41574.143.15 Escholier, Raymond. Victor Hugo raconté par ceux qui l'ont vu. Paris, 1931.
38513.22.11 La farce du pâté et de la tarte, tres bonne effort joyeuse à quatre personnages. 10. éd. Paris, 1931.
43606.78.710 Farrère, Claude. Black opium. N.Y., 1931.
43606.88.100A Fauconnier, H. Malaisie. N.Y., 1931.
40583.112 Faure, Gabriel. Stendhal, compagnon d'Italie. Paris, 1931.
43606.98.108 Fayard, Jean. Mal d'amour; roman. 15. éd. Paris, 1931.
43606.98.120 Fayard, Jean. Mes maîtresses. Paris, 1931.
FL 396.66 Fischer, Carlos. Les costumes de l'opéra. Paris, 1931.
42581.33.81 Flink, G. Jules Vallès. Inaug. Diss. Berlin, 1931.
37555.131 Fontains, A. Tableau de la poésie française d'aujourd'hui. Paris, 1931.
42557.14.25 Fontains, André. Verlaine-Rimbaud. Paris, 1931.
42524.58.05 Foulché-Delbosc, Isabel. Bibliografia de Raymond Foulché-Delbosc (1864-1929). Madrid, 1931.
43611.89.100 Foulon, Pierre. Angkor dans la forêt. Hanoi, 1931.
FL 386.603 Fox, Mary Constantia. The miracle and the mystère in France in the last decade, 1920-30. Urbana, Ill., 1931.
42576.62.6.10 France, Anatole. At the sign of the reine Pédauque. N.Y., 1931.
42576.62.6.25 France, Anatole. The romance of the queen Pédauque. N.Y., 1931.
43612.5.130 Fraudet, René. Le voleur de femmes. Paris, 1931.
41578.145 Fréjaville, Gustave. Les méditations de Lamartine. Paris, 1931.
42542.2.15 Friedrich, W. Die Entwicklung Émile Augiers bis zu seinen Sittendramen. Inaug. Diss. Zwickau, 1931.
FL 362.6 Gaiffe, Felix A. Le rire et la scène française. Paris, 1931.
43757.50.500 Gandhi, M.K. Vie de M.-K. Gandhi écrite par lui-même. 7e éd. Paris, 1931.
V43500.129 Garnier, Georges Louis. Le songe dépouillé. Paris, 1931.
43687.83.805 Gasgtowtt, A.M. Pierre Lasserre, 1867-1930. Paris, 1931.
FL 398.7.39.6 Geller, G.G. Sarah Bernhardt. 6e éd. Paris, 1931.
43617.59.110 Genevoix, Maurice. Rroû, roman. Paris, 1931.
43617.66.110 George, Nancy. Jeux d'été; nouvelle. Paris, 1931.
43617.66.1100 Georges-Michel, Michel. Left bank. N.Y., 1931.
43617.1.40 Gérard, Rosemonde. Les papillotes. Paris, 1931.
42555.59.100 Gerding, A. Adrien Mithouard. Inaug. Diss. n.p., 1931.
43618.90.100 Gevers, Marie. La comtesse des Dignes; roman. pt.1-3. Paris, 1931.
42543.1.40 Gheorghin, O. Le théâtre de Dumas fils et la société contemporaine. Thèse. Nancy, 1931.
43620.2.56A Gide, André. Divers. Paris, 1931.
43620.2.79.2 Gide, André. Si le grain ne meurt. Paris, 1931.
40575.5.80 Giese, William F. Sainte-Beuve, a literary portrait. Madison, 1931.
43620.3.36 Gilbert, M. Camille eu Le reflet de Rome; roman. pt.1-3. Paris, 1931.
42542.59.82 Gilbert de Voisins, Auguste. François de Curel. Paris, 1931.
42576.6.20 Ginisty, Paul. Lettres galantes du chevalier de Faques. Paris, 1931.
43620.66.170 Giono, Jean. Le grand troupeau. 24. éd. Paris, 1931.
43620.74.430 Giraudoux, Jean. Mirage de Bessines. Paris, 1931.
38526.16.265 Godefroy, J.E. La vie de Dom Simplicien Gody. Vienne, 1931.
43625.19.180 Godoy, Armand. Le poème de l'Atlantique. Paris, 1931.
FL 379.88 Grannis, V.B. Dramatic parody in eighteenth century France. N.Y., 1931.
37565.68.5 Green, Frederick C. Eighteenth-century France. N.Y., 1931.
43626.22.150 Green, Julien. L'autre sommeil. Paris, 1931.
42546.12.45 Grieve, J.W. L'oeuvre dramatique d'Edmond Rostand. Paris, 1931.
42546.12.44 Grieve, J.W. L'oeuvre dramatique d'Edmond Rostand. Thèse. Paris, 1931.
43628.23.100 Guéhenno, Jean. Conversion à l'humain. Paris, 1931.
43667.1.810 Guidetti, A. Francis Jammes. Torino, 1931.
43628.1.75 Guitry, Sacha. Frans Hals ou "L'Admiration". Paris, 1931.
42514.28.200 Gurian, Waldemar. Der integrale Nationalismus. Frankfurt, 1931.
43628.98.100 Guyon-Cesbron, J. Désaxés; roman. Paris, 1931.
42576.15.75 Haas, Eugen. Flaubert und die Politik. Inaug. Diss. Biella, 1931.
41574.187 Heimbecher, H.J. Victor Hugo und die Ideen der grossen französischen Revolution. (Teildruck). Inaug. Diss. Berlin, 1931.
41574.191 Hennig, E. Die ethische Wertung des Kindes hei Victor Hugo. Inaug. Diss. Charlottenburg, 1931.
41556.43 Henry-Rosier, M. La vie de Charles Nodier. 2e éd. Paris, 1931.
43632.76.145 Hériat, Philippe. L'innocent. 31. éd. Paris, 1931.
42543.65.55 Hermant, Abel. Eddy et Paddy. Paris, 1931.
42543.65.66 Hermant, Abel. Les épaves; roman. Paris, 1931.
37530.74 Hilka, Alfons. Französische Philologie. Göttingen, 1931.
37578.80 Histoires parisiennes. Paris, 1931.
43638.7.705 Hubermont, P. Thirteen men in the mine. N.Y., 1931.
41573.23.20 Hugo, Victor. Notre Dame de Paris. v.1-2. N.Y., 1931.

Chronological Listing

1931 - cont.

41571.3.25 Hugo, Victor. L'oeuvre de Victor Hugo; poesie, prose, théâtre. Paris, 1931.
42576.66.3.5 Huysmans, Joris Karl. Against the grain. N.Y., 1931.
42565.54.225 Ingersoll, J.D. Les romans régionalistes de Léon Cladel. Thèse. Toulouse, 1931.
43757.3.180 Israël, M. Jules Romains. 3e éd. Paris, 1931.
43659.88.700 Istrati, Panait. The bitter orange tree. N.Y., 1931.
43625.3.90 Jacob, P.E. Rémy de Gourmont. Thesis. Urbana, 1931.
43667.1.145 Jammes, Francis. L'arc en ciel des amours. Paris, 1931.
43667.1.196 Jammes, Francis. L'école buissonnière. 2. éd. Paris, 1931.
42566.16.120 Jolly, Maria. Die Stilmittel Alphonse Daudets in der Schilderung der Provence. Wertheim am Main, 1931.
37562.13.9A Jones, W.P. The pastourelle. Cambridge, 1931.
FL 6119.31.10A Josephson, M. Jean-Jacques Rousseau. N.Y., 1931.
43670.89.300 Jouhandeau, M. Le journal du coiffeur. 2. éd. Paris, 1931.
40583.116 Jourda, Pierre. Stendhal raconté par ceux qui l'ont vu. Paris, 1931.
42584.25.115 Jouvenel, B. de. Vie de Zola. Paris, 1931.
43757.50.890 Kaempffer, A. Romain Rolland's Frauengestalten. Inaug. Diss. Charlottenburg, 1931.
43740.1.85 Kellermann, W. Studien zu Charles Louis Philippe. Wertheim am Main, 1931.
43740.1.81 Kerber, Karl. Charles Louis Philippe. Inaug. Diss. Leipzig, 1931.
43673.83.190 Kessel, Joseph. Le coup de grâce. Paris, 1931.
41522.18.115 Klassen, P. Baudelaire; weet und gegenwelt. Weimar, 1931.
38525.11.10 Klengel, Alice. Pierre de Ronsards Hymnendichtung. Inaug. Diss. Leipzig, 1931.
43757.50.910 Krakowski, B. La psychologie des peuples allemand et juif dans les romans de Romain Rolland. Thèse. Toulouse, 1931.
FL 381.17 Kromsigt, A.L.C. Le théâtre biblique à la veille du romantisme (1789-1830). Zutphen, 1931.
38557.24.80 La Batut, G. de. Oraison funèbre d'Henriette d'Angleterre par Bossuet. Paris, 1931.
41522.18.53 Laforque, R. L'échec de Baudelaire. Paris, 1931.
43687.38.1100 La Hire, Jean de. La prisonnière du Dragon Rouge. Paris, 1931?
Htn 43687.50.120* Lallier, Roger. L'ami Géo. Niort, 1931.
43687.53.110 Lamandé, André. L'affaire Soulacroux. Paris, 1931.
43822.49.925A Larbaud, Valery. Paul Valéry. Paris, 1931.
37596.32.80 La Résurrection du Sauveur. La résurrection du Sauveur. Paris, 1931.
43697.89.805 Larg, David G. André Maurois. London, 1931.
43687.75.180 Larguier, Léo. Le père Corot. 4e éd. Paris, 1931.
43709.3.820 Larnac, Jean. Comtesse de Noailles. Paris, 1931.
38543.6.5 La Rochefoucauld, François. Maximes et réfléxions morales. Paris, 1931.
38514.54.15 La Sale, Antoine de. Little John of Saintré. London, 1931.
43687.83.140 Lasserre, Pierre. Mise au point. 2e éd. Paris, 1931.
43687.88.110 Laubiès, Charles. Symphonie pastorale; poèmes. Grenoble, 1931.
43687.88.2705 Laubreaux, Alin. Mulatto Johnny. N.Y., 1931.
42544.24.55 Lavedan, Henri. Bonne-étoile; roman. Pt.1-4. Paris, 1931.
40597.2.85 Leathers, V.L. L'Espagne et les Espagnols dans l'oeuvre d'Honoré de Balzac. Paris, 1931.
40597.2.84 Leathers, V.L. L'Espagne et les Espagnols dans l'oeuvre d'Honoré de Balzac. Thèse. Paris, 1931.
37548.65 Lebel, Roland. Histoire de la littérature coloniale en France. Paris, 1931.
42545.3.536 Leblanc, Georgette. Souvenirs. Paris, 1931.
42576.41.45 Le Blanc, Maurice. Man of miracles. N.Y., 1931.
42584.25.135 Le Blond-Zola, Denise. Emile Zola raconté. Paris, 1931.
43688.17.100 Lécuyer, A.H. (Mme.). Soledad; roman. pt.1-3. Paris, 1931.
42576.65.13.27A Lefèvre, F. Entretiens sur J.K. Huysmans. Paris, 1931.
43688.8.35 Le Goffic, Charles. Les pierres-vertes. Paris, 1931.
43688.8.21 Le Goffic, Charles. Poésies complètes. Paris, 1931-32. 2v.
43688.33.120 Legrand, Ignace. Renaissance. Paris, 1931.
43688.35.105 Le Grand, Maurice. Fables. Paris, 1931.
42522.23 Le Meur, Léon. L'adolescence et la jeunesse d'Eugéne Melchior de Vogüé. Thèse. Paris, 1931.
37556.22.25 Levron, J. La presse Creusoise au XIXe siècle. Limoges, 1931.
40534.19.150 Levy, Bernard. The unpublished plays of Carolet. N.Y., 1931.
43688.92.100 Lévy, Sarah. Henri und Sarah; Roman. Berlin, 1931.
37548.33 Liebrecht, Henri. Histoire illustrée de la littérature belge de langue française. 2. éd. Bruxelles, 1931.
38511.10.5 Le livre des Mestiers. pt.1-6. Brugea, 1931.
42544.34.60 Louys, Pierre. Les aventures du Roi Pausole. Paris, 1931.
42544.34.70 Louys, Pierre. Contes choisis. Paris, 1931.
41522.18.50 Loving, Pierre. Gardener of evil. N.Y., 1931?
43694.14.100 Luciète, C. La guerre des cerveaux. Paris, 1931.
FL 398.52.37 Lugné, P.A. Acrobaties; tremplin. 3e éd. Paris, 1931.
43697.14.100 MacOrlan, Pierre. La bandera. 4e ed. Paris, 1931.
43697.14.110 MacOrlan, Pierre. La cavalière Elsa. 29. ed. Paris, 1931.
43697.34.220 Magre, Maurice. Le sang de Toulouse. Paris, 1931.
38512.112 Maillart, Jean. Le roman du comte d'Anjou. Paris, 1931.
42555.43.90 Mallarmé, Stéphane. Posie. Praha, 1931.
37567.390 Mann, Heinrich. Geist und Tat. Berlin, 1931.
41558.30A March, Harold. Frédéric Soulié, novelist and dramatist. New Haven, 1931.
42545.9.35 Martel de Janville, S.G. Le coup du lapin. Paris, 1931.
42545.9.25 Martel de Janville, S.G. Le joyeuse enfance de la IIIe République. Paris, 1931.
43697.77.150 Martin du Gard, Roger. Confidence africaine. Paris, 1931.
43697.82.100 Massis, Henri. Evocations; souvenirs, 1905-1911. Paris, 1931.
43697.82.102 Massis, Henri. Evocations; souvenirs. Paris, 1931-
42563.21.82 Mauriac, F. René Bazin. Paris, 1931.
43697.88.4110 Maurice, Martin. Heureux ceux qui ont faim. Paris, 1931.
43697.89.500 Maurois, André. L'Amérique inattendue. Paris, 1931.
43697.89.140A Maurois, André. Fragment d'un journal (aout-septembre 1930) relativisme suite par André Maurois. Paris, 1931.
43697.89.180 Maurois, André. Le peseur d'âmes. 75. éd. Paris, 1931.
43697.89.712 Maurois, André. The weigher of souls. N.Y., 1931.
42514.28.53 Maurras, Charles. Au signe de flore. Paris, 1931.
42514.28.45 Maurras, Charles. Les plus belles pages de Maurras. Paris, 1931.
42514.28.49 Maurras, Charles. Principes. Paris, 1931.
42563.37.88 Maurray, C. Triptyque de Paul Bourget, 1895-1900-1923. Paris, 1931.

1931 - cont.

43697.99.120 Mazade, Fernand. Féerie. Uzès, 1931.
43698.52.100 Mélot du Dy, Robert. A l'amie dormante. Paris, 1931.
43698.61.100 Ménot, Alfred. Charmes du souvenir. Paris, 1931.
41555.20.85 Mérimée, Prosper. Carmen based on Prosper Mérimée's story. N.Y., 1931.
41555.23.25 Mérimée, Prosper. Çolomba. N.Y., 1931.
41555.1.16 Mérimée, Prosper. Études de littérature russe. Paris, 1931-32. 2v.
41555.1.18 Mérimée, Prosper. La Jaquerie suivie de La famille de Carvajal. Paris, 1931.
41555.7.60 Mérimée, Prosper. Lettres de Mérimée à la famille Delessert publiées. Paris, 1931.
38516.20.5 Michault, Pierre. Le doctrinal du temps présent de Pierre Michault (1466). Thèse. Paris, 1931.
37569.17 Mieille, Paul. Pages de bibliographie pyrénéenne. Paris, 1931.
41556.44 Mönch, Walter. Charles Nodier, Zusammenhang von Erlebnis - Übertragung. Inaug. Diss. Berlin, 1931.
41556.45 Mönch, Walter. Charles Nodier und die deutsche und englische Literatur. Berlin, 1931.
Mol 162.50 Molière, Jean Baptiste Poquelin. Amfitrione; commedia. Lauciano, 1931.
Mol 165.96 Molière, Jean Baptiste Poquelin. L'avare. Paris, 1931.
Mol 60.42 Molière, Jean Baptiste Poquelin. Four Molière comedies. London, 1931.
Mon 19.31.5 Montaigne, Michel de. Essais. Paris, 1931. 6v.
Mon 19.31 Montaigne, Michel de. Essais. Livre. Paris, 1931-32. 6v.
Mon 30.31 Montaigne, Michel de. Essays. Florio. London, 1931. 2v.
Mon 45.25 Montaigne, Michel de. Journal de voyage de Michel Seigneur de Montaigne. Paris, 1931.
Mon 37.50 Montaigne, Michel de. Saggi scetti. Torino, 1931.
43701.76.1100 Morand, Germaine. La douloureuse enfance. Paris, 1931.
43701.74.200 Morand, Paul. Papiers d'identité. Paris, 1931.
43701.74.1100 Morane, P. Sybie. Paris, 1931.
42577.39.100 Mossé, Armand. Un dieu sur la terre? Paris, 1931.
43701.82.120 Mossé, Armand. Monsieur Homais. Paris, 1931.
42546.31.30 Mouly, Georges. Vie prodigieuse de Victorien Sardou. Paris, 1931.
43738.1.100 Mounier, E. La pensée de Charles Péguy. pts.1-2. Paris, 1931.
Htn 43703.80.130* Muselli, Vincent. L'étrange interview. Argenteuil, 1931.
V43500.209 Muselli, Vincent. Léon Bloy, ou Celui qui exagère. La Rochelle, 1931.
43703.80.150 Muselli, Vincent. Les strophes de contre-fortune. Paris, 1931.
41596.18.25 Musset, Alfred de. Comédies et proverbes. Paris, 1931. 2v.
41596.13.15 Musset, Alfred de. Poèmes choisies. Manchester, 1931.
41543.8.12 Nerval, Gerard de. La bohème galante. Paris, 1931.
41543.17 Nerval, Gerard de. Les filles du feu. Paris, 1931. 2v.
41543.17.2 Nerval, Gerard de. Les filles du feu. Le rêve et la vie. Paris, 1931.
41543.7.5 Nerval, Gerard de. Gerard de Nerval. 10e éd. Paris, 1931.
37557.7 Nitsche, Karl. Die Bedeutung derBiographie für die Kulturproblematik des Gegenwärtigen Frankreichs. Berlin, 1931.
39533.20.18 Normano, J.F. A neglected Utopian::Cyrano de Bergerac, 1619-1655. n.p., 1931.
FL 6139.31.5 Nourrisson, Paul. Jean-Jacques Rousseau et Robinson Crusot. Paris, 1931.
37574.90.5A The Oxford book of French verse, 13th - 20th centuries chosen by St. John Lucas. 2. ed. Oxford, 1931.
43737.34.130 Pagnol, Marcel. Marius; pièce en quatre actes. Paris, 1931.
42545.68.75 Paternostro, A.L. Edouard Pailleron, 1834-1899. Paris, 1931.
38513.24.10 Pathelin. Maître Pierre Pathelin. Paris, 1931.
37597.16.25 Pelan, Margaret. L'influence du Brut de Wace. Paris, 1931.
43687.29.800 Pesquidoux, J.D. Le duc de La Force. Paris, 1931.
39594.19.27 Petersen, Karl. Die Satzverbindung bei Montesquieu. Inaug. Diss. n.p., 1931.
43741.88.120 Pinget, Robert. Le chercheur d'ondes; roman. pts.1-2. Paris, 1931.
43741.59.4110 Pinguet, Auguste. Le jardin des quatrains. Angers, 1931.
43741.98.120 Pize, Louis. Les feux de septembre. Paris, 1931.
38527.30.8 Plattard, Jean. Une figure de premier plan dans nos lettres de la renaissance. Photoreproduction. Paris, 1931.
38537.25.16.11 Plattard, Jean. Guide illustré au pays de Rabelais. Paris, 1931.
38537.25.16.7 Plattard, Jean. Life of François Rabelais. N.Y., 1931.
42545.95.10 Pottecher, M. Le secret de la montagne. Paris, 1931?
42545.95.45 Pottecher, M. T'es pris, Grillot! Paris, 1931?
40515.52.5 Pourrat, Henri. Le bosquet pastoral. Florian. 6. éd. Paris, 1931.
37543.198 Preissig, E. Der Völkergedanke. Brunn, 1931.
40522.9.53 Prévost, Antoine F. The history of Manon Lescaut. N.Y., 1931.
40522.9.77 Prévost, Antoine F. The history of the chevalier des Grieux and of Manon Lescaut. London, 1931.
43744.25.120 Prévost, Jean. Nous marchons sur la mer. 5. éd. Paris, 1931.
37567.328 Prévost, Jean L. Les épicuriens français. 2e éd. Paris, 1931.
42578.31.68 Prévost, Marcel. Her master. N.Y., 1931.
43744.67.66 Proust, Marcel. Lettres à la comtesse de Noailles, 1901-1919. Paris, 1931.
43744.67.43 Proust, Marcel. Time regained. London, 1931.
37567.193.55 Pujarniscle, E. Philoxène. Paris, 1931.
39578.8.11 Rabow, Hans. Die zehn Schaffensjahre des Vauvenargues. Inaug. Diss. Berlin, 1931.
43752.11.124 Raucat, Thomas. The honorable picnic. London, 1931.
43753.9.180 Reboux, Paul. Colin, ou Les voluptés tropicales. Paris, 1931.
Mon 128.4 Rech, Bruno. Grundbegriffe und Wertbegriffe bei Michel de Montaigne. Inaug. Diss. Berlin, 1931.
37567.327 Régnier, Henri de. Faces et profils. Souvenirs sur Villiers de l'Isle-Adam. Paris, 1931.
42556.27.30.65 Régnier, Henri de. Nos rencontres. 3. éd. Paris, 1931.
43753.2.45 Régnier, M.L.A. de. Les poésies de Gérard d'Hauville [pseud.]. Paris, 1931.
42515.25.50 Renan, Ernest. Travaux de jeunesse, 1843-1844. Paris, 1931.

Chronological Listing

1931 - cont.

43756.3.85F Richepin, Jacques. L'affaire Dreyfus. Paris, 1931.
43756.3.87 Richepin, Jacques. L'affaire Dreyfus. Paris, 1931.
43757.8.100 Robinet, Auguste. Cagayous, ses meilleures histoires. Paris, 1931.
38563.20 Robinson, Howard. Bayle the sceptic. N.Y., 1931.
43757.50.115A Rolland, Romain. Jean Christophe. Paris, 1931-32. 4v.
43757.50.775 Rolland, Romain. Menschen auf der Strasse. Stuttgart, 1931.
43757.50.536 Rolland, Romain. Les origines du théâtre lyrique moderne. Paris, 1931.
43757.3.95 Romains, Jules. Morceaux choisis. 2e éd. Paris, 1931.
43757.3.275 Romains, Jules. Musse. 8. éd. Paris, 1931.
43757.3.205A Romains, Jules. Problèmes d'aujourd'hui. Paris, 1931.
43756.90.805 Roos, E.G. de. Het essayistisch werk van Jacques Rivière. Amsterdam, 1931.
42584.25.45 Rost, W.H. German criticism of Zola, 1875-1893. N.Y., 1931.
42546.14.5.75 Rostand, Edmond. Cyrano de Bergerac. N.Y., 1931.
43757.83.110 Rostand, Maurice. Le général Boulanger. Paris, 1931.
42546.15.20.5 Rothschild, Henri de. Le grand patron. Paris, 1931.
43757.88.100 Rouff, Marcel. La vie de fête sans le second empire. Paris, 1931.
41557.10.50 Rouget, M.T. George Sand "socialiste." Lyon, 1931.
41557.10.49 Rouget, M.T. George Sand "socialiste." Thèse. Lyon, 1931.
FL 6026.11 Rousseau, J.J. Confessions of Jean-Jacques Rousseau. London, 1931. 2v.
42556.30.90 Roux, A. In memoriam Edouard Schuré. Paris, 1931.
40515.15.10 Royde-Smith, N. The double heart. N.Y., 1931?
43758.24.120 Ruet, Noël. Cercle magique. Paris, 1931.
37568.140 Rumilly, Robert. Littérature française moderne. Montréal, 1931.
38542.25.15 Saint Evremond, C. de M. de S.D. La comédie des académistes. N.Y., 1931.
43761.41.150 St. Georges de Bouhelier. Le sang de Danton. Paris, 1931.
39578.8.25 Saintville, G. Quelques notes sur Vauvenargues. Paris, 1931.
37573.240 Schinz, Albert. Seventeenth century French readings. N.Y., 1931.
37567.323 Schinzel, E. Natur und Natursymbolik bei Poe. Inaug. Diss. Düren, 1931.
43763.38.100 Schlumberger, Jean. Saint-Saturnin. Paris, 1931.
FL 6139.31.10 Schreiben, P. Gedanken- und Satzverbindung bei Jean-Jacques Rousseau. Inaug. Diss. Regenslenrg, 1931.
38512.17.30 Schreijir, Willem. Étude sur la négation dans les chroniques de Froissart. Amsterdam, 1931.
43765.17.100 Sedeyn, Émile. Nihilia; nouvelle. Paris, 1931.
41596.4.40 Sedgwick, H.D. Alfred de Musset, 1810-1857. Indianapolis, 1931.
41586.3.9 Ségu, Fréderic. H. de Latouche, 1785-1851. Paris, 1931.
41586.3.10A Ségu, Fréderic. H. de Latouche et son intervention dans les arts. Paris, 1931.
38526.35.150 Seider, M.H. Anne de Marquets poétesse religieuse du XVIe siècle. Thèse. Washington, 1931.
41522.18.65 Seillière, E. Baudelaire. Paris, 1931.
43744.67.860 Seillière, E. Marcel Proust. Paris, 1931.
42576.65.13.31A Seillière, Ernest. J.K. Huysmans. Paris, 1931.
43769.54.110A Simenon, Georges. Un crime en Hollande. Paris, 1931.
43769.54.100 Simenon, Georges. Un crime en Hollande. Paris, 1931.
43769.54.120A Simenon, Georges. La tête d'un homme. Paris, 1931.
42555.44.12 Soula, Camille. La poésie et la pensée de Stéphane Mallarmé. Paris, 1931.
39544.175 Spitzer, Leo. Einige Voltaire-Interpretationen. Marburg, 1931.
43779.3.100 Stalla-Bourdillon, Jules. Au foyer de la comédie-française. Marseille, 1931.
37555.127 Stewart, Jean. Poetry in France and England. London, 1931.
38539.3.310 Sullivan, Sister M. St. F. Étienne du Trouchet. Washington, 1931.
43787.1.35 Tendron, Marcel. La belle Eugénie, roman. Paris, 1931.
43788.5.180 Tharaud, Jérôme. L'oiseau d'or. Paris, 1931.
37569.97.5 Therive, A. Galerie de ce temps. Paris, 1931.
43788.24.110 Thérive, André. Noir et or. Paris, 1931.
37555.81 Thibaut de Maisières, Maury. Les poèmes inspirés du début de la genèse a l'époque de la renaissance. Louvain, 1931.
40583.130 Thihaudet, Albert. Stendhal. Paris, 1931.
FL 6049.16 Tieng-yd'n, Liang. L'éducation masculine et l'éducation féminine selon Jean-Jacques Rousseau. Thèse. Dijon, 1931.
42578.51.85 Tinayre, Marcelle. L'ennemie intime. Paris, 1931.
37564.116 Trahard, P. Les maîtres de la sensibilité français au XVIIe siècle (1715-1789). Paris, 1931-1933. 4v.
38524.827 Trois farces du recueil de Londres. Rennes, 1931.
43822.41.100A Vaillant-Couturier, Paul. The French boy. Philadelphia, 1931.
43822.49.10A Valéry, Paul. L'ame et la danse, Eupalinos ou l'architecte. Paris, 1931.
43822.49.11A Valéry, Paul. Monsieur Teste. Paris, 1931.
Htn 43822.49.165* Valéry, Paul. Moralités. Paris, 1931.
43822.49.16 Valéry, Paul. Pièces sur l'art. Paris, 1931.
NEDL 43822.49.173 Valéry, Paul. Poésies. 10e éd. Paris, 1931.
43822.49.155A Valéry, Paul. Regards sur le monde actuel. Paris, 1931.
43822.6.10 Vallotton, Benjamin. Et voici la France. Quel est ton pays. v.3. Paris, 1931.
42547.10.35 Vandérem, F. La bibliophile nouvelle. Paris, 1931-33. 2v.
43822.76.100 Varney, Charles. Igor Youriewitch. Paris, 1931.
37555.228 Verrier, Paul. Le vers français. Paris, 1931-32. 3v.
42576.52.4.10 Viaud, Julien. Pêcheur d'Islande. N.Y. 1931.
43824.49.200 Vildrac, Charles. Découvertes. 13e éd. Paris, 1931.
Htn 43895.5* Villiot, Jean de (pseud.). Black lust. N.Y., 1931.
38514.20.40A Villon, François. Book of François Villon. Boston, 1931.
38514.20.45 Villon, François. Oeuvres de François Villon. Paris, 1931.
39542.35.15 Voltaire, François Marie Arouet de. Voltaire and the enlightenment. N.Y., 1931.
39545.33.25 Voltaire, François Marie Arouet de. Voltaire and the enlightenment selections. N.Y., 1931.
37562.102 Voretzsch, Carl. Introduction to the study of Old French literature. Halle, 1931.
37562.102.5 Voretzsch, Carl. Introduction to the study of Old French literature. N.Y., 1931.
FL 6119.31.5 Vulliamy, Colwyn E. Rousseau. London, 1931.
37555.129 Wann, Harry Vincent. Tradition of the homeric simile in 18th century French poetry. Diss. Terre Haute, Ind., 1931.

1931 - cont.

42553.34.30 Weck, René de. Amiel ou La noix creuse. Lausanne, 1931.
40597.2.410 Weith, Otto. Romantisches im Theater Honoré de Balzac's. Wertheim, 1931.
Mol 623.7.10 Wheatley, K.E. Molière and Terence. Austin, 1931.
Mol 623.7 Wheatley, K.E. Molière and Terence. Austin, 1931.
37530.70A Williams, Ralph C. Bibliography of the seventeenth-century novel in France. N.Y., 1931.
37573.631 Wolfenstein, Alfred. Hier Schreit Paris. Berlin, 1931.
37567.66.10 Woolley, G. Richard Wagner et le symbolisme français. Paris, 1931.
42548.57 Xanrof, Léon. La mécanique de l'esprit. Paris, 1931.
43852.89.125 Yourcenar, Marguerite. La nouvelle Eurydice. Paris, 1931.

1932

37595.64 Abbott, C.C. Early mediaeval French lyrics. London, 1932.
43512.75.140 Achard, Marcel. Domino; comedie en trois actes. Paris, 1932.
43611.5.83 Ahting, Georg. Henri Alain-Fournier, 1886-1914. Inaug. Diss. Barssel, 1932.
37596.215 Aimon de Varennes. Florimont. Göttingen, 1932.
43522.41.190 Alibert, François Paul. Epigrammes. Paris, 1932.
V43500.11 Allem, Maurice (pseud.). La poésie de l'amour; anthologie poetique du moyen âge à nos jours. Paris, 1932.
43523.41.130 Amiel, Denys. L'âge du fer. Paris, 1932.
42553.33.15 Amiel, Henri F. Essais critiques. Paris, 1932.
43554.2.835 Angenendt, Paul. Eine syntaktisch-stilistiche Untersuchung der Werke P. Claudels. Inaug. Diss. Bonn, 1932.
FL 391.120 Antoine, André. Le Théâtre. Paris, 1932-1933. 2v.
40597.9.8 Arrigon, L.J. Balzac et la "contessa". Paris, 1932.
38564.51 Assollant, Georges. La Bruyère, les caractères. Paris, 1932.
38527.28.6A Aubigné, Théodore Agrippa d'. Les tragiques. Paris, 1932-33. 4v.
37556.19.50 Awtrey, H. La presse Anglo-Americaine de Paris. Thèse. Paris, 1932.
40597.35.105 Balzac, Honoré de. Le colonel Chabert. Paris, 1932.
40597.14.67 Balzac, Honoré de. Droll stories; thirty tales. N.Y., 1932. 3v.
40597.20.25A Balzac, Honoré de. Eugénie Grandet. N.Y., 1932.
40597.29.4.55 Balzac, Honoré de. Père Goriot. Washington, 1932.
40597.32.80 Balzac, Honoré de. La Rabouilleuse. Paris, 1932.
42584.25.55 Barbusse, H. Zola. 9. éd. Paris, 1932.
42542.65.70 Bathilles, P. Maurice Donnay. Paris, 1932.
41522.4.15 Baudelaire, Charles. Lettres à sa mère. Paris, 1932.
41522.12.10 Baudelaire, Charles. Oeuvres en collaboration. Paris, 1932.
FL 363.46 Baudin, Maurice. Les bâtards au théâtre en France de la renaissance à la fin du XVIIIe siècle. Baltimore, 1932.
42563.21.36.25 Bazin, René. De toute son âme. Paris, 1932.
39566.40 Beck, Fritz. Die dramatischen Entwürfe Denis Diderots. Inaug. Diss. Kallmünz, 1932.
43538.17.125A Bedel, Maurice. Zulfu. 58. éd. Paris, 1932.
42514.28.70.2 Benjamin, René. Charles Maurras, ce fils de la mer. Paris, 1932.
42514.28.70 Benjamin, René. Charles Maurras, ce fils de la mer. Paris, 1932.
43538.74.160 Béraud, Henri. Les Lurons de Sabolas. Paris, 1932.
43538.10.38 Bernard, Jean J. Martine; play. London, 1932.
42542.29.28.120 Bernard, Tristan. Le sauvage. Paris, 1932.
42542.29.28.130 Bernard, Tristan. Le sexe fort. Paris, 1932.
43538.77.1110 Berton, Henry. L'humaine rumeur. Paris, 1932.
38512.2 Bertoni, G. Liriche di Oton de Grandson. Genève, 1932.
42563.23.8.60 Bertrand, Louis. Hippolyte porte-couronnes. 2. éd. Paris, 1932.
37556.52.10 Bethleem, L. Romans à lire et romans à proscrire. 11. éd. Paris, 1932.
43538.88.150 Betz, Maurice. Le ressac. Paris, 1932.
40582.3.8 Beyle, Henri. Écoles italiennes de peinture. Paris, 1932. 3v.
40582.3.14 Beyle, Henri. Mélanges d'art. Paris, 1932.
40582.2.65 Beyle, Henri. Mémoires d'un touriste. Paris, 1932-33. 3v.
40582.25.12 Beyle, Henri. Le rouge et le noir. Paris, 1932.
39566.37 Billy, André. Diderot. Paris, 1932.
43540.74.160 Birabeau, André. Baisers perdus. Paris, 1932.
43543.13.170 Bloch, J.R. Sybilla. 8. éd. Paris, 1932.
43543.13.785 Bloch, J.R. Vom Sinn unseres Jahrhunderts. Berlin, 1932.
43744.67.870A Blondel, Charles. La psychographie de Marcel Proust. Paris, 1932.
43543.89.100 Blum, René. Les amours du poête. Paris, 1932.
42563.37.92 Börner, M. Die "Conversion" Bourgets. Inaug. Diss. Stettin, 1932.
38566.54.10A Boileau Despréaux, Nicolas. Satires. Paris, 1932.
37567.300.5 Bouvier, Émile. Initiation a la littérature d'aujourd'hui. Paris, 1932.
43544.94.100 Bove, Emmanuel. Mes amis; roman. Paris, 1932.
42542.49.81 Brand, R.F. Henry Céard. Ithaca, 1932.
42577.32.60 Brauns, Walter. Die Lyrik Henry Murgers. Inaug. Diss. Coburg, 1932.
37567.331 Bray, René. Chronologie du romantisme (1804-1830). Paris, 1932.
43527.3.800 Breton, André. Misère de la poésie. Paris, 1932.
43545.24.110 Breton, André. Le revolver à cheveux blancs. Paris, 1932.
43545.39.100 Briand, C. Aliaga; roman. Paris, 1932.
42576.63.43 Brousson, Jean J. Les vêpres de l'avenue Hoche. Paris, 1932.
42584.25.60 Bruneau, Alfred. A l'ombre d'un grand coeur. Paris, 1932.
41596.4.65 Brunet, V. Le lyrisme d'Alfred de Musset. Thèse. Toulouse, 1932.
42576.65.13.175 Brunner, Henriette. En marge d'Arebours de J.K. Huysmans. Paris, 1932.
42554.30.7 Brussels. Bibliothèque Royale. Exposition Max Elskamp 1862-1931. Bruxelles, 1932.
37543.201 Bruyère, Jean. Histoire littéraire des gens de métier en France. Paris, 1932.
40597.2.88 Buttke, Erika. Balzac als Dichter des modernen Kapitalismus. Berlin, 1932.
43550.40.140 Cahuet, Albéric. Saint Hélène petite ile. v.1-4. Paris, 1932.
37556.90 Cailliet, Émile. The themes of magic in nineteenth century French fiction. Paris, 1932.
38571.22.10 Calvet, J. Polyenete de Corneille. Paris, 1932.
43550.55.130 Cami, Henri. Pssitt et Pchutt. Paris, 1932.

1932 - cont.

42563.37.94 Carco, F. Paul Bourget, suivi de pages inédites et de l'histoire du XXXIII fauteuil. Paris, 1932.
43550.1.135 Carco, Francis. Jésus-la-Caille. Paris, 1932.
37567.329 Carr, P. Days with the French romantics in the Paris of 1830. London, 1932.
38562.23.10 Carré, J.R. La philosophie de Fontenelle. Paris, 1932.
38562.23.8 Carré, J.R. La philosophie de Fontenelle ou Le sourire de la raison. Thèse. Paris, 1932.
38537.25.130 Carvalho, R. de. Rabelais et le rire de la renaissance. Paris, 1932.
43550.82.2100 Castro, Germaine. Passage. Paris, 1932.
43552.3.9164 Chamson, André. Héritages; roman. 10e éd. Paris, 1932.
43552.5.110 Chardonne, Jacques. L'amour du prochain. Paris, 1932.
37569.265 Charensol, G. Comment ils ecrivent. Paris, 1932.
43552.3.4110 Charpentier, Henry. Odes et poèmes. Paris, 1932.
40586.21.50 Chateaubriand, F.A.R. Les Natchez. Baltimore, 1932.
43667.78.815 Chauveau, Paul. Alfred Jarry. Paris, 1932.
43552.7.100 Chauviré, R. Mademoiselle de Boisdauphin. pt. 1-3. Paris, 1932.
43552.24.120 Chérau, Gaston. L'enfant du pays; roman. pt. 1-4. Paris, 1932.
43552.24.180 Chérau, Gaston. Le monstre. Paris, 1932.
43552.24.2100 Chessin, S. de. La valse aux enfers. pt. 1-2. Paris, 1932.
42576.63.125A Chevalier, H.M. The ironic temper; Anatole France. N.Y., 1932.
40517.44.7 Choderlos de Laclos, Pierre A.F. Les liaisons dangereuses. Paris, 1932.
43822.49.1375 Choux, Jean. Michel-Ange et Paul Valéry. Paris, 1932.
41564.55.30 Clarke, S.H. The works of Vigny judged by his contemporaries. Toulouse, 1932.
43556.1.150 Cocteau, Jean. Essai de critique indirecte. Paris, 1932.
43556.1.110 Cocteau, Jean. Morceaux choisis, poèmes. Paris, 1932.
43556.15.100 Coculesco, Pius S. Introduction à une manière d'être. Paris, 1932.
38525.22.23 Cohen, Gustave. Ronsard; sa vie et son oeuvre. Paris, 1932.
43556.49.190 Colette, Sidonie Gabrielle. Ces plaisirs. Paris, 1932.
38574.23.5 Corneille, Pierre. Théâtre choisi. Paris, 1932. 2v.
38514.56.18A Coville, Alfred. Jean Petit. Paris, 1932.
38526.10.17.75 Cretin, Guillaume D. Oeuvres poétiques. Paris, 1932.
42542.55.35 Croisset, Francis de. Il était une fais. Paris, 1932.
42542.55.30 Croisset, Francis de. Pierre ou Jack. Paris, 1932.
43566.28.100 Daffoux, L. Pipe-en-Boise, témoin de la commune. Paris, 1932.
37564.120.5 Dallas, D.F. Le roman français de 1660 a 1680. Paris, 1932.
37564.120 Dallas, D.F. Le roman français de 1660 a 1680. Thèse. Paris, 1932.
40597.2.136A Dargan, Edwin P. Honoré de Balzac. Chicago, 1932.
40597.2.135A Dargan, Edwin P. Studies in Balzac's realism. Chicago, 1932.
42566.34.30 Daudet, Alphonse. Sappho. N.Y., 1932.
43565.91.110 Davet, Michel. Une lampe sur la marche. Paris, 1932.
41593.36.32 Decahors, E. Maurice de Guérin, essai de biographie psychologique. Thèse. Paris, 1932.
41593.36.30 Decahors, E. Maurice de Guérin. Paris, 1932.
FL 6139.32 Dedeck-Héry, E. Jean-Jacques Rousseau et le projet de constitution pour la corse. Thèse. Philadelphia, 1932.
43566.43.140 Dekobra, Maurice. La volupté éclairant le monde, roman. Paris, 1932.
43566.46.100 Delance, Georges. Bluff; comédie en trois actes. Paris, 1932.
37556.21.25 Demaison, A. Les voix de la France. Paris, 1932.
42542.64.19.10F Descaves, Lucien. L'humble Georgin. Paris, 1932.
37556.255 Desnitskii, Vasilii A. Frantsuzskii realisticheskii roman XIX veka. Leningrad, 1932.
42576.63.24.100 Desvanges, A. Livres, manuscrits dessins...manuscrits d'Anatole France. Paris, 1932.
43566.90.110 Deval, Jacques. Mademoiselle. Paris, 1932.
43566.7.60 Deval, Jacques. Signor Bracoli. Paris, 1932.
43688.59.810 Dissen, Maria. Marie Lenéru. Inaug. Diss. Gelsenkirchen, 1932.
X Cg 40587.92 Dollinger, Albert. Les études historiques de Chateaubriand. Paris, 1932.
40587.92.5 Dollinger, Albert. Les études historiques de Chateaubriand. Thèse. Strasbourg, 1932.
43573.76.43 Dorgelès, Roland. Le château des brouillards, roman. Paris, 1932.
40597.2.99 Drucker, P. The critical doctrine of Honoré de Balzac. Colorado Springs, 1932.
39544.170 Dubas, V. Voltaire. Kaunas, 1932.
43576.7.115 Du Bois, Albert. Corsica. Paris, 1932.
43576.9.100 Du Bos, Charles. Approximations. 5. série. Paris, 1932.
43576.6.31.10 Duhamel, Georges. Civilisation, 1914-1917. 79. éd. Paris, 1932.
43576.6.255 Duhamel, Georges. Querelles de famille. 13. éd. Paris, 1932.
NEDL 43576.6.215 Duhamel, Georges. Tel qu'en lui-même...roman. Paris, 1932.
42576.15.59 Dumesnil, René. Gustave Flaubert, l'homme et l'oeuvre. Paris, 1932.
40583.136 Dumolard, Henry. Autour de Stendhal. Grenoble, 1932.
43576.57.130 Dumur, Louis. Les loups rouges. Paris, 1932.
38514.71.88 Dupire, Noël. Etude critique des manuscrits et éditions des poésies de Jean Molinet. Thèse. Paris, 1932.
38514.71.90 Dupire, Noël. Étude critique des manuscrits et éditions des poésies de Jean Molinet. Paris, 1932.
38514.71.85 Dupire, Noël. Jean Molinet: la vie. Paris, 1932.
38514.71.83 Dupire, Noël. Jean Molinet: la vie - les oeuvres. Thèse. Paris, 1932.
38526.28.280 Durel, L.C. L'oeuvre d'Andre Mareschal. Baltimore, 1932.
41563.18.25 Edler, Erich. Eugène Sue und die deutsche Mysterienliteratur. Berlin, 1932.
39544.110 Engemann, W. Voltaire und China. Inaug. Diss. Leipzig, 1932.
42573.35 Erckmann, Emile. Erckmann et Chatrian par Erckmann seul. Thèse. Metz, 1932.
42572.20.15 Erckmann, Emile. L'invasion ou Le fou Yégoff. Paris, 1932.
43598.84.240 Estaunié, Édouard. Madame Clapain. Paris, 1932.
42576.63.37 Evelpidi, C. Anatole France, critique social. Paris, 1932.
43526.65.805 Fabureau, H. Guillaume Apollinaire, sa oeuvre. Paris, 1932.

1932 - cont.

40597.2.142 Faillettaz, E. Balzac et le monde des affaires. Diss. Lausanne, 1932.
43606.87.110 Fauchois, René. Prenez garde à la peinture. Paris, 1932.
43606.98.105 Fayard, Jean. Mal d'amour; roman. 7. éd. Paris, 1932.
43607.76.4100 Fernandez, Ramon. Le pari. Paris, 1932.
40583.120 Fineshriber, William H. Stendhal, the romantic rationalist. Princeton, 1932.
37596.236.10 Flutre, Fernand. Li fait des Romains dans les litteratures française et italienne du XIIIe au XVIe siècle. Thèse. Paris, 1932.
37596.236.15 Flutre, Fernand. Les manuscrits des faits des Romains. Thèse. Paris, 1932.
38514.23.18 Foschini, Antonio. L'avventura di Villon. Milano, 1932.
43611.94.100 Fowlie, W.A. Mausolée de choses mortes. Paris, 1932.
42576.63.24.30 France, Anatole. Anatole France, très rare collection des oeuvres. Paris, 1932.
42576.62.3.35 France, Anatole. Thaïs. N.Y., 1932?
43612.5.160 Fraudet, René. Zigoël. Paris, 1932.
43612.41.120 Frick, Louis de Gonzague. Vibones. Paris, 1932.
FL 6119.32 Fusil, C.A. La contagion sacrée ou Jean-Jacques Rousseau de 1778 à 1820. Paris, 1932.
41542.31.5 Gautier, Théophile. Poésies complètes de T. Gautier. v.1-3. Paris, 1932.
43617.4.60 Géraldy, Paul. Christine; pièce en quatre actes. Paris, 1932.
42576.15.72 Gérard-Gailly, Émile. L'unique passion de Flaubert:"Madame Arnoux". Paris, 1932.
43620.2.5 Gide, André. Oeuvres complètes. Paris, 1932-39. 15v.
43620.2.65.2 Gide, André. Le retour de l'enfant prodigue. 25. éd. Paris, 1932.
43620.66.130 Giono, Jean. Solitude de la pitié. 20. éd. Paris, 1932.
42536.28.5 Giraud, V. Essai sur Taine; son oeuvre et son influence. 7e éd. Paris, 1932.
42524.19.20 Giraud, Victor. Brunetière. Paris, 1932.
40587.11.10 Giraud, Victor. Chateaubriand. Paris, 1932.
38529.35A Girault, F. The tale of Gargantua and King Arthur. Cambridge, 1932.
42543.49.15 Glatigny, Albert. Lettres inédites. Rouen, 1932.
43625.19.190 Godoy, Armand. Marcel; poème dramatique. Paris, 1932.
41543.4.29 Goethe, J.W. von. Les deux Faust de Goethe. Paris, 1932.
42544.30.80 Gordon, Zina. Labiche et son oeuvre. Thèse. Toulouse, 1932.
43626.22.200 Green, Julien. Épaves. Paris, 1932.
43626.22.105 Green, Julien. The strange river. N.Y., 1932.
42554.49.8 Gregh, F. La gloire du coeur, poèmes. Paris, 1932.
43693.88.805 Grosse, Karl B. Emile Joseph Lotte. Inaug. Diss. Jena, 1932.
38539.28.50 Grubbs, H.A. Damien Mitton, 1618-1690. Princeton, 1932.
41593.36.3 Guérin, Maurice de. Le centaure et la bacchante. Thèse. Paris, 1932.
43628.41.6120 Guinle, Alexandre. Atalante. Orphée. Paris, 1932.
43667.1.815 Gutheil, Werner. Francis Jammes als Symbolist und Katholik. Inaug. Diss. Marburg, 1932.
37543.318 Guyer, Foster E. The main stream of French literature. Boston, 1932.
FL 398.7.38 Hahn, Reynoldo. Sarah Bernhardt. London, 1932.
41593.36.25 Harcourt, B. Maurice de Guérin et le poème en prose. Paris, 1932.
41578.101 Harris, Ethel. Lamartine et le peuple. Thèse. Paris, 1932.
42545.3.419 Harry, Gérard. La vie et l'oeuvre de Maurice Maeterlinck. Paris, 1932.
42576.65.10.15 Harry, Myriam (pseud.). La divine chanson. Paris, 1932.
43631.90.110 Hautier, Raoul. L'oiseau phénix. La Louvière, 1932.
41574.187.5 Heimbecher, H.J. Victor Hugo und die Ideen der grossen französischen Revolution. Berlin, 1932.
42562.38.1.10 Heinen, F.H. Das Frankreichbild im Werke Paul Adams, 1862-1920. Inaug. Diss. Bochum-Langendreer, 1932.
FL 363.44 Hill, L.A. The Tudors in French drama. Baltimore, 1932.
38525.8.10 Horváth, K.A. Étienne Jodelle. Budapest, 1932.
38575.23.45 Hoyer, Luise. Die Anrede in Corneille Dramen. Inaug. Diss. Berlin, 1932.
42544.33.60 Hucke, S. Jules Lemâitre als Erzähler. Inaug. Diss. Schwelm, 1932.
41572.23.10 Hugo, Victor. Les châtiments. Paris, 1932.
41571.3.100 Hugo, Victor. Poèmes choisis. Manchester, 1932.
43638.99.150 Huzard, A. de B. (Mme.). Cher coeur humain! Paris, 1932.
Mol 609.1 Ilutowicz, S. Le peuple dans le théâtre de Molière. Thèse. Toulouse, 1932.
43667.51.320 Jaloux, Édmond. La balance faussée. Paris, 1932.
43667.1.206 Jammes, Francis. L'antigyde, ou Élie de Nacre. 5. éd. Paris, 1932.
37596.205 Jean de la Chapele de Bois. Le conte Dou Barril. New Haven, 1932.
43670.89.120 Jouhandeau, M. L'amateur d'imprudence. Paris, 1932.
43670.89.310 Jouhandeau, M. Tite-le-Long. 6. éd. Paris, 1932.
43673.83.220 Kessel, Joseph. Bas-fonds. Paris, 1932.
43673.83.175 Kessel, Joseph. Fortune carrée. Paris, 1932.
43673.83.210 Kessel, Joseph. Nuits de Montmartre. Paris, 1932.
43673.83.200 Kessel, Joseph. Wagon-lit. 7. éd. Paris, 1932.
40554.22 Knoop, B. Victor Cousin, Hegel und die französische Romantik. Inaug. Diss. Oberviechtach, 1932.
43687.15.140 Lacretelle, Jacques de. Sabine. 6e éd. Paris, 1932.
39525.15.25 La Fontaine, Jean de. Fables, contes et nouvelles. Paris, 1932.
41522.18.55 Laforgue, R. The defeat of Baudelaire. London, 1932.
43687.50.130 Lallier, Roger. Promenons-nous par les airs. Paris, 1932.
43687.58.4100 Landais, Puisné. Durandeau de Shanghai et quelques autres, roman. Paris, 1932.
37543.38.18 Lanson, Gustave. Manuel d'histoire de la littérature française. 4. éd. Paris, 1932.
43687.69.110 Lapaquellerie, Yvon. Été indieu; roman. pt.1-2. Paris, 1932.
38543.6.7 La Rochefoucauld, François. Réflexions ou Sentences et maximes morales. Paris, 1932.
43688.59.805 Lavaud, S. Marie Lenéru. Thèse. Paris, 1932.
42545.3.535A Leblanc, Georgette. Souvenirs; my life with Maeterlinck. N.Y., 1932.
37573.686 Lecompte, I. Anthology of modern French literature. N.Y., 1932.
43688.27.120 Lefebvre, L. Rectificatione. Paris, 1932.
43688.33.121 Legrand, Ignace. Renaissance. Paris, 1932.
37567.338 Lehrmann, Kuno. Das Humanitätsideal der sozialistischromantischen Epoche Frankreichs. Inaug. Diss. Würzburg, 1932.

Chronological Listing

1932 - cont.

38526.27.14 Lemaire de Belges, Jean. La plainte du désiré. Paris, 1932.
42554.26.27 Le Meur, Léon. La vie et l'oeuvre de François Coppée. Thèse. Paris, 1932.
40512.44.2 LeSage, Alain René. Gil Blas. Paris, 1932.
43885.20 Lettres à Lucilia. Paris, 1932.
37556.35.2 Levrault, Léon. Le roman des origines à nos jours. Paris, 1932?
FL 359.32 Levrault, Léon. Le théâtre des origines à nos jours. Paris, 1932.
42544.34.32.12 Louys, Pierre. Aphrodite; Ancient manners. N.Y., 1932.
42544.34.28.30 Louys, Pierre. Collected works. N.Y., 1932.
43697.14.400 MacOrlan, Pierre. Quartier réservé. 13. ed. Paris, 1932.
42545.3.160 Maeterlinck, Maurice. L'araignée de verre. Paris, 1932.
43886.5 Magd-Abril (pseud.). Nos voisins de campagne; nouvelle. Paris, 1932.
37556.120 Magendie, M. Le roman français au XVIIe siècle. Paris, 1932.
43697.53.705 Malvil, A. The seven stars. N.Y., 1932.
40535.29.4 Marivaux, Pierre Carlet de Chamblain de. Les fausses confidences; comédie. L'épreuve; comédie. Paris, 1932?
37596.71.10 Marly, T. de M. Les vers de Thibaud de Marly. Thèse. Paris, 1932.
40583.122 Marsan, Jules. Stendhal. Paris, 1932.
43697.76.3120 Martet, Jean. Les portes du desert. v.1-3. Paris, 1932.
43697.77.160 Martin du Gard, Roger. Un taciturne. 6e ed. Paris, 1932.
42553.34.15 Matthews, John. Amiel et la solitude. Thèse. Annemasse, 1932.
43566.89.805 Maunty, G. Léon Deubel (1879-1913) sein Leben und sein Dichten. Inaug. Diss. Velbert, 1932.
43697.88.180 Mauriac, François. Commencements d'une vie. Paris, 1932.
43697.88.140A Mauriac, François. Le noeud de vipères; roman. Paris, 1932.
43697.88.130 Mauriac, François. Pèlerins. Paris, 1932.
43697.88.4100 Maurice, Martin. Die Revolution der Reichen. Berlin, 1932.
43697.89.360 Maurois, André. L'Anglaise et d'autres femmes. Paris, 1932.
43697.89.148 Maurois, André. Le cercle de famille; roman. 174. éd. Paris, 1932.
43697.89.150 Maurois, André. Le cercle de famille; roman. 193. éd. Paris, 1932.
43697.89.152 Maurois, André. Le cercle de famille. Paris, 1932.
43697.89.145A Maurois, André. Le côté de Chelsea. 14. éd. Paris, 1932.
43697.89.750 Maurois, André. The family circle. London, 1932.
43697.89.156 Maurois, André. The family circle. N.Y., 1932.
43697.89.200 Maurois, André. Mes songes que voici. 46. éd. Paris, 1932.
43697.89.440 Maurois, André. A private universe. N.Y., 1932.
39544.123.5 Maurois, André. Voltaire. London, 1932.
42514.28.38 Maurras, Charles. Ironie et poésie. St. Félicien-en-Vivarais, 1932.
42514.28.54 Maurras, Charles. Prologue d'un essai sur la critique. Paris, 1932.
43697.98.3100 May, Janine. La jeune fille au masque; roman. Paris, 1932.
43697.100.120 Mazeline, Guy. Les coups. Paris, 1932.
43698.25.150 Meersch, M. van der. La maison dans la dune. Paris, 1932.
40542.31.10 Mejecaze, F. Essai de synthèse des idées. Lyon, 1932.
40542.31 Mejecaze, F. Frédéric Ozanam et l'eglise catholique. Lyon, 1932.
42587.22.5 Ménard, Louis. Lettres inédites. Paris, 1932.
41555.20.95 Mérimée, Prosper. Carmen. Gand, 1932.
43699.82.100 Mistler, Jean. La maison du Docteur Clifton. Paris, 1932.
42545.28.27 Moinaux, Georges. Les plus belles pages de Courteline. Paris, 1932.
Mol 19.32 Molière, Jean Baptiste Poquelin. Théâtre complet. Paris, 1932. 10v.
Mon 45.15 Montaigne, Michel de. Journal de voyage en Italie par la Suisse et l'Allemagne. Paris, 1932.
39594.2.15 Montesquieu, C.L. de S. Montesquieu. Paris, 1932.
43701.62.160 Montfort, Eugène. Choix de proses. Paris, 1932.
43701.74.145 Morand, Paul. L'art de mourer. Paris, 1932.
43701.74.162 Morand, Paul. Flèche d'Orient. 5e éd. Paris, 1932.
43701.74.160 Morand, Paul. Flèche d'Orient. 35e éd. Paris, 1932.
43701.74.150 Morand, Paul. Le voyageur et l'amour. Paris, 1932.
37567.330 Moreau, P. Le classicisme des romantiques. Paris, 1932.
37567.330.5 Moreau, P. Le classicisme des romantiques. Thèse. Paris, 1932.
37565.49.3 Mornet, Daniel. Le romantisme en France au XVIII siècle. 3e éd. Paris, 1932.
43702.89.100 Mourguet, M. Amitié; pièce en trois actes et quatre tableaux. Paris, 1932.
41596.16.50 Musset, Alfred de. Comédies et nuits. N.Y., 1932.
43704.8.35 Nabert, Jeanne. Le cavalier de le mer. Paris, 1932.
43697.89.210A Ni ange, ni bête. N.Y., 1932.
43709.3.42 Noailles, Anna E. Le livre de ma vie. Paris, 1932.
40597.2.270 Noiset, L. Balzac et les femmes. Paris, 1932.
42555.66.50 Nolhac, Pierre de. Contes philosophiques. Paris, 1932.
42555.66.30 Nolhac, Pierre de. Laus Florentiae. Fano, 1932.
38567.31 Noss, Mary T. La sensibilité de Boileau. Thèse. Paris, 1932.
40556.39.20 Ostrogorsky, C. Joseph de Maistre and seine Lehre von der Höchseten Macht und ihren Trägern. Helsingfors, 1932.
43737.75.100 Paret, T. Dans la mêlée. Paris, 1932.
FL 377.82 Pascoe, M.E. Les drames religieux du milieu du XVIIe siècle 1636-1650. Paris, 1932.
FL 377.78 Pascol, M.E. Les drames religieux du milieu du XVIIe siècle. No. 36-1650. Paris, 1932.
37595.78 Pauphilet, A. Contes du jongleur. Paris, 1932.
41542.4.35 Payr, B. Théophile Gautier und E.T.A. Hoffmann. Berlin, 1932.
43738.41.140 Peisson, Edouard. Parti de Liverpool. 37e éd. Paris, 1932.
43738.83.120 Pesquidoux, J.D. Le livre de raison. 12e éd. Paris, 1932.
37530.72 Peyre, Henri. Bibliographie critique de l'Hellénisme en France de 1843 à 1870. New Haven, 1932.
37530.71 Peyre, Henri. Bibliographie critique de l'Hellénisme en France de 1843 à 1870. Thèse. New Haven, 1932.
42587.22.15 Peyre, Henri. Louis Ménard, 1822-1901. New Haven, 1932.
42587.22.17 Peyre, Henri. Louis Ménard (1822-1901). Thèse. New Haven, 1932.
38575.24 Pierre Corneille. Münster, 1932.
43741.50.110 Pillionnel, J.H. Les graminées; poèmes. Paris, 1932.
37564.53 Pinot, V. La Chine et la formation de l'esprit philosophique en France 1640-1740. Thèse. Paris, 1932.

1932 - cont.

38514.57.10 Pisan, Christine de. The book of fayttes of armes and of chyvalrye. London, 1932.
38537.25.16.20 Plattard, Jean. François Rabelais. Paris, 1932.
41522.6.20 Poe, Edgar Allan. Histoires extraordinaires. Oeuvres complètes de Charles Baudelaire. Paris, 1932.
41522.18.70 Pommier, J. La mystique de Baudelaire. Paris, 1932.
43743.1.49 Porché, François. La race errante. Paris, 1932.
38557.1.15F Porcher, Jean. Catalogue des manuscrits de Bossuet de la collection Henri de Rothschild. Paris, 1932.
43743.92.120 Pouvourville, Albert de. A vingt-neuf agent secret. Paris, 1932.
38546.33.8 Pradel, Genès. Madame de Sévigné en Provence. Montluçon, 1932.
43744.67.69A Proust, Marcel. Lettres à Monsieur et Madame Sydney Schiff. Paris, 1932.
43747.32.100 Puget, C.A. La ligne de coeur. Paris, 1932.
39578.8.20 Rabow, Hans. Die zehn Schaffensjahre des Vauvenargues. Berlin, 1932.
42578.18.16 Rameau, Jean. Flore. Paris, 1932.
43752.57.251 Ramuz, Charles Ferdinand. Farinet. Paris, 1932.
43752.98.130 Raynal, Paul. Au soleil de l'instinct. Paris, 1932.
43753.9.100 Reboux, Paul. Madame se meurt! Madame est morte! Paris, 1932.
37556.86 Refort, Lucien. La caricature littéraire. Paris, 1932.
42556.27.30.75 Régnier, Henri de. Choix de poèmes. Paris, 1932.
37596.10.120 Reinhard, J.R. Chréstien de Troyes. Ann Arbor, 1932.
43753.58.120 Renard, M. Le professeur Krantz. Paris, 1932.
41596.4.50 Rickey, H. Wynn. Musset Shakespearien. Thèse. Bordeaux, 1932.
42556.28.70A Rimbaud, Jean Arthur. Prose poems from Les illuminations. London, 1932.
Mon 190.1 Rodríguez Portillo, M. La medicina y los médicos vistos por Montaigne. Barcelona, 1932.
43757.50.740A Rolland, Romain. The revolt of the machines: or, Invention run wild; a motion picture fantasy. Ithaca, 1932.
43757.50.665 Rolland, Romain. Romain Rolland Malwida von Meyseukug. Stuttgart, 1932.
43757.3.85A Romains, Jules. Les hommes de bonne volonté. Paris, 1932-44. 27v.
43757.3.110 Romains, Jules. Puissances de Paris. 7. éd. Paris, 1932.
43757.3.260 Romains, Jules. La vision extra-rétinienne et le sens paroptique. 3. éd. Paris, 1932.
42578.22.10.90 Rosny, J.H. Les destins contraires. Paris, 1932.
42578.22.20 Rosny, J.H. Les femmes des autres. Paris, 1932.
42578.22.90 Rosny, J.H. Passion et bonheur. Paris, 1932.
42578.22.10.25 Rosny, J.H. Sabine et son père. Paris, 1932.
42578.22.55 Rosny, J.H. Un voleur. pt. 1-2. Paris, 1932.
41574.182 Rosso, A.T. L'ispirazione Hughiana nel Carducci. Torino, 1932.
43757.83.120 Rostand, Maurice. Une jeune fille espagnole. Paris, 1932.
43757.92.190 Roussel, Raymond. Impressions d'Afrique. Paris, 1932.
43757.92.143 Roussel, Raymond. Nouvelles impressions d'Afrique suivies de l'ame de Victon Hugo. 3. éd. Paris, 1932.
43757.98.170 Royère, Jean. Frantans. 1e série. Paris, 1932.
43761.39.705A St. Exupéry, A. de. Night flight. N.Y., 1932.
42546.30.45 Sardou, Victorien. Carlin; roman. Paris, 1932.
43761.6.80 Sarment, Jean. Le plancher der vaches. Paris, 1932.
39566.42 Scheyer, Alice. Diderot als universaler Denker. Inaug. Diss. Berlin, 1932.
43763.38.700 Schlumberger, Jean. Saint Saturnin. N.Y., 1932.
38542.16.10 Schmidt, A.M. Saint-Evremond ou L'humaniste impur. Paris, 1932.
40597.2.103.2 Schöll, Erwin. César Birotteau. Wertheim, 1932.
40597.2.103 Schöll, Erwin. César Birotteau. Inaug. Diss. Wertheim, 1932.
38585.16.140 Schröder, R.A. Racine und die deutsche Humanität. München, 1932.
37574.415 Schwartz, W.L. French romantic poetry. 1. ed. N.Y., 1932.
42576.46.70 Schweickert, E. Pierre Loti und André Gide, zwei Arten von Exotisten. Inaug. Diss. München, 1932.
43620.2.465 Schwob, René. Le vrai drame d'André Gide. Paris, 1932.
42576.46.75 Scribner, H.M. Pierre Loti. Thèse. Poitiers, 1932.
42545.88.115 Sée, Edmond. Porto-Riche. Paris, 1932.
42568.2.44 Sellards, John. Dans le sillage du romantisme: Charles Didier. 1805-1864. Thèse. Paris, 1932.
V43500.299 Sentenac, Paul. Gaspard Maillol. Paris, 1932?
43769.54.705 Simenon, Georges. The death of Monsieur Gallet. N.Y., 1932.
43769.54.350 Simenon, Georges. La nuit du carrefour. Paris, 1932.
43769.54.280 Simenon, Georges. Le passager du Palarlys. Paris, 1932.
43769.54.260 Simenon, Georges. Les 13 énigmes. Paris, 1932.
43775.74.110 Sorbets, G. La colombe poignardie. Paris, 1932.
43775.74.120 Sorbets, G. La maison verte. Paris, 1932.
43744.67.895 Souza, S. de. L'influence de Ruskin sur Proust. Thèse. Montpellier, 1932.
43554.4.81.2 Spiegel, E. Emile Clermont, 1880-1916. Wertheim, 1932.
43554.4.81 Spiegel, E. Emile Clermont (1880-1916). Inaug. Diss. Würzburg, 1932.
42586.63.16 Spring, G.M. The vitalism of Count de Gobineau. N.Y., 1932.
37555.135 Strauss, L. Uebersetzungen italienischer Dichtwerke in Frankreich zwischen 1789 und 1820. Inaug. Diss. Stuttgart, 1932.
39585.18.20 Suard, Jean. Lettres inédites de Suard à Wilkes. Berkeley, 1932.
43780.69.152 Supervielle, Jules. La belle au bois. 2. éd. Paris, 1932.
40597.1.6 Surville, L. A une amie de province, lettres. Paris, 1932.
43785.89.100 Taupin, René. Quatre essais indifferents pour une esthétique de l'inspiration. Paris, 1932.
Mon 130.4 Tavera, François. L'idée d'humanité dans Montaigne. Paris, 1932.
43788.5.115 Tharaud, Jérôme. Les bien aimées. Paris, 1932.
43788.24.120 Thérive, André. Anna. Paris, 1932.
Mol 720.7A Thuillier, R. La vie maladive de Molière. Paris, 1932.
43792.75.110 Torres, Henry. Édition speciale. Paris, 1932.
42535.22.85 Tremblay, Napoléon. La critique littéaire d'Edmond Scherer. Tuscon, 1932?
42535.22.85.5 Tremblay, Napoléon. La critique littéraire d'Edmond Scherer. Menasha, Wis., 1932.
43793.41.110 Trintziers, René. Fin et commencement. Paris, 1932.
37596.210 Trois aveugles de compiègne. Cortrebarbe. Paris, 1932.
41596.4.55 Tuong, N.M. Essai sur la valeur dramatique du théâtre d'Alfred de Musset. Thèse. Montpellier, 1932.
42554.14.325 Tuong Nguyen Manh. Jules Boissière 1863-1897. Thèse. Montpellier, 1932.

Chronological Listing

1932 - cont.

43799.5.190 Tzara, Tristan. Où boivent les loups. Paris, 1932.
43822.49.229 Valéry, Paul. El cementerio marino. Montevideo, 1932.
43822.49.425 Valéry, Paul. Choses tues. Paris, 1932.
43822.49.725 Valéry, Paul. Eupalinos; or The architect. London, 1932.
43822.49.705 Valéry, Paul. The graveyard by the sea. Philadelphia, 1932.
43822.49.166 Valéry, Paul. Moralités. Paris, 1932.
43822.50.1100 Vallerey, G. Les chansons de l'esclave. Bordeaux, 1932.
42581.33.10 Vallès, Jules. Jacques Vingtras, le bachelier. Paris, 1932.
43822.51.110 Valmy-Baysse, Jean. Le coeur et les yeux; poèmes. Paris, 1932.
39533.8.37 Van Roosbroeck, G.L. Chapelain décoiffe. N.Y., 1932.
43812.89.100 Vaunois, L. Le roman de Louis XIII. Paris, 1932.
43823.77.100 Verneuil, Louis. La banque Nemo. Paris, 1932.
43823.77.110 Verneuil, Louis. Une femme ravie; pièce en quatre actes. Paris, 1932.
38525.22.45.84 Vianey, Joseph. Les odes de Ronsard. Paris, 1932.
NEDL Mon 132.5.25 Villey, P. Les essais de Michel de Montaigne. Paris, 1932.
38526.70.150 Vivonne, H. de. Poésies de Heliette de Vivonne. Paris, 1932.
37562.46.2 Voretzsch, Carl. Altfranzösisches Lesebuch. 2. Aufl. Halle, 1932.
Mol 622.4 Vree, T.J. van. Les pamphlets et libelles litteraires contre Molière. Thèse. Paris, 1932?
37597.17.20 Wace, Maistre. La vie de Sainte Marguerite. Paris, 1932.
43611.5.125 Wall, Eva von der. Alain-Fournier. Hamburg, 1932.
38526.20.50 Whittem, Arthur F. Two fable collections. [Les fables morales de Philibert Guide]. Cambridge, 1932.
38527.31.12 Willner, Kurt. Montchrétiens Tragödien und die stoische Lebensweisheit. Berlin, 1932.
38527.31.11 Willner, Kurt. Montchrétiens Tragödien und die stoische Lebensweisheit. Inaug. Diss. Berlin, 1932.
37573.667 Wilson, C.I. Modern French prose, 1918-1928. London, 1932.
43744.67.890 Wolters, Klaus. Marcel Proust im literarischen Urteil seiner Zeit. Inaug. Diss. München, 1932.
41593.36.35 Wouden-Veldkamrp, J.M. von. Maurice de Guérin. Proefschrift. Amsterdam, 1932.
40587.156 Zdziechowski, M. Chateaubriand i Napoleon. Wilno, 1932.
40562.45.10 Zeller, Renée C.T. Lacordaire. Paris, 1932.
42581.33.85 Zévaès, A.B. Jules Vallès, son oeuvre. Paris, 1932.

1933

43512.75.150 Achard, Marcel. La femme en blanc. Paris, 1933.
37596.27.15 Aléxius, Saint. Légend. La vie de Saint Aléxis. Paris, 1933.
FL 382.84.5 Allard, Louis. La comédie de moeurs en France au XiXe siècle. v.2. Paris, 1933.
43523.41.184 Amiel, Denys. Théâtre: L'age du fer. v. 4. Paris, 1933.
43523.41.140 Amiel, Denys. Trois et une. Paris, 1933.
43527.3.100 Aragon, Louis. The red front. Chapel Hill, 1933.
42513.48.15 Arndt, Dora. Juliette Adam. Inaug. Diss. Würzburg, 1933.
FL 377.85 Auerbach, E. Das französische Publikum des 17. Jahrhunderts. München, 1933.
42545.95.30 Auvray, R. Le sotré de Noël. Remiremont, 1933?
43535.54.105 Aymé, Marcel. La jument verte. 80e éd. Paris, 1933.
42584.25.65 Baer, Elisabeth. Das Weltbild Zolas in den Quatre Evangiles. Inaug. Diss. München, 1933.
40597.35.145 Balzac, Honoré de. Un inédit de Balzac. Paris, 1933.
38542.4.20 Balzac, J.L.G. de. Les premières lettres de Guez de Balzac, 1618-1627. Paris, 1933-34. 2v.
41522.18.75 Bandy, W.T. Baudelaire judged by his contemporaries, 1845-1867. N.Y., 1933.
42584.25.53 Barbusse, H. Zola. 1. ed. N.Y., 1933.
Htn FL 398.7.42* Baring, Maurice. Sarah Bernhardt. London, 1933.
43776.41.810 Barnshaw, Stanley. André Spire and his poetry. Philadelphia, 1933.
37597.43.5 La bataille de Caresme et de Charnage. Paris, 1933.
43537.88.100 Baty, Gaston. Crime et chatiment. Paris, 1933.
41522.13.9.29 Baudelaire, Charles. Flowers of evil. N.Y., 1933.
41522.14.25 Baudelaire, Charles. Le salon de 1845 de Charles Baudelaire. Thèse. Toulouse, 1933.
43537.89.2150 Baumann, Émile. La symphonie du désir. Paris, 1933.
43745.1.85 Becherer, Walter. Ernest Psichari in seiner psychologischen Entwicklung. Inaug. Diss. Leipzig, 1933.
37555.140 Bejot, Amédée. L'évolution poétique en France. Paris, 1933.
Mon 112.10 Belleli, M.L. Modernita di Montaigne. Roma, 1933.
43628.1.510 Benjamin, R. Sacha Guitry, roi du théâtre. Paris, 1933.
43538.61.85 Benoît, Pierre. Fort-de-France. Paris, 1933.
43538.74.200 Béraud, Henri. Ciel du serie. Paris, 1933.
43538.74.102 Béraud, Henri. Le martyre de l'obèse; roman. Paris, 1933.
42563.23.6 Bernard, T. Paris secret. Paris, 1933.
42542.29.28.140 Bernard, Tristan. Le prince charmant. v.1-2. Paris, 1933.
42542.29.52 Bernstein, H. Mélo. Paris, 1933.
43538.77.6103 Berry, André. La corheille de Ghislaine. Paris, 1933.
43538.77.6100 Berry, André. Lais de Gascogne. Paris, 1933.
40582.8.17 Beyle, Henri. La chartreuse de Parme. v.1-2. Paris, 1933.
40582.3.5 Beyle, Henri. Correspondance. Paris, 1933-34. 10v.
40582.3.15 Beyle, Henri. Mélanges de littérature. Paris, 1933. 3v.
40582.3.16 Beyle, Henri. Mélanges de politique et d'histoire. Paris, 1933. 2v.
43540.74.170 Birabeau, André. Ma soeur de luxe. Paris, 1933.
43543.13.120 Bloch, J.R. La nuit kurde. Paris, 1933.
43543.13.210 Bloch, J.R. Offrande à la politique. 9. éd. Paris, 1933.
42563.23.29 Bloy, Léon. Lettres à René Martineau. Paris, 1933.
42563.23.26 Bloy, Léon. Lettres à Véronique. Paris, 1933.
42556.29.34 Bocquet, Léon. Autour d'Albert Samain. Paris, 1933.
41574.215 Boer, J.P.C. Victor Hugo et l'enfant. Wassenaar, 1933.
42576.63.130 Boillot, Félix. L'humour d'Anatole France. Paris, 1933.
42563.36.290 Bordeaux, Henry. Amitiées étrangères. Paris, 1933.
42563.36.210 Bordeaux, Henry. Ginette. Paris, 1933.
43544.75.100 Borel, Marguerite Appeli. Ruth. pt.1-2. Paris, 1933.
43822.49.960 Bosanquet, Theodora. Paul Valéry. London, 1933.
41542.4.50 Boschot, Adolphe. Théophile Gautier. Paris, 1933.
43544.82.100 Bosschère, Jean de. Satan l'obscur, roman. Paris, 1933.
43544.4.71 Botrel, Théodore. Les mémoires d'un barde Breton. Paris, 1933.
42563.37.51.2 Bourget, Paul. Au service de l'ordre. ser. 2. Paris, 1933.
42563.37.68 Bourget, Paul. L'honneur du nom. Paris, 1933.

1933 - cont.

42524.58.81 Bourlaud, B.P. Raymond Foulché-Delbosc, 1864-1929. N.Y., 1933.
43544.94.110 Bove, Emmanuel. Le meurtre de Suzy Pommier; roman. 21. éd. Paris, 1933.
38575.23.50 Braun, Ernst. Die Stellung des Dichters Pierre Corneille zu den "Remarques" des Grammatikers Vaugelas. Inaug. Diss. Kaiserslautern, 1933.
42576.65.13.50 Brennan, Donal. La conversion de J.K. Huysmans et son oeuvre religieuse. Thèse. Montpellier, 1933.
43545.24.130 Breton, André. Le pas perdus. 6. ed. Paris, 1933.
39544.62.10 Breuer, J. Claude François Nonnott S.J. Inaug. Diss. Werl, 1933.
40583.124 Brussaly, Manuel. The political ideas of Stendhal. N.Y., 1933.
38526.22.5.90 Cameron, Alice. The influence of Ariosto's epic and lyric poetry on the work of Amadis Jamyn. Baltimore, 1933.
43550.1.55 Carco, Francis. L'ombre, roman. Paris, 1933.
43550.1.110 Carco, Francis. Palace Égypte; roman. Paris, 1933.
43550.1.31.10 Carco, Francis. Pour faire suite a la Bohème et mon coeur. Paris, 1933.
43744.67.1052 Casnati, Francesco. Proust. Brescia, 1933.
39568.23.10 Cazes, André. Grimm et les encyclopédistes. Paris, 1933.
39568.23.8 Cazes, André. Grimm et les encyclopédistes. Thèse. Paris, 1933.
37569.42 Chaigne, L. Vies et oeuvres d'écrivains. Paris, 1933-38. 4v.
43552.3.9175 Chamson, André. L'auberge de l'abîme; roman. 18e éd. Paris, 1933.
43552.3.9178 Chamson, André. The Mountain Tavern. N.Y., 1933.
43552.4.4100 Charasson, H. En chemin de fer; piece en un acte. Paris, 1933.
43552.6.4100 Charles, Jacques. Le journal d'une figurante, roman de moeurs du music hall. Paris, 1933.
38514.23.35 Charpentier, L. François Villon, le personnage. Paris, 1933.
37595.4.10 Charrier, Charlotte. Héloise dans l'histoire et dans la légende. Paris, 1933.
37595.4.8 Charrier, Charlotte. Héloise dans l'histoire et dans la légende. Thèse. Paris, 1933.
40586.28.55 Chateaubriand, F.A.R. En marge des mémoires d'outre-tombe. Paris, 1933.
40586.28.50 Chateaubriand, F.A.R. En marge des mémoires d'outre-tombe. Thèse. Paris, 1933.
43552.6.120A Chateaubriant, Alphonse de. La réponse du Seigneur. 58e éd. Paris, 1933.
37568.234 Chauveau, Paul. Caractéres. Paris, 1933.
43554.2.140 Claudel, Paul. Ways and crossways. N.Y., 1933.
43556.1.71 Cocteau, Jean. Orphée. London, 1933.
43822.49.950 Cohen, G. Essai d'explication du cimetière marin. Paris, 1933.
37597.12.25 Cohen, G. Le roman de la rose. Paris, 1933.
43556.49.112 Colette, Sidonie Gabrielle. L'entrave. Paris, 1933.
37583.410 Comfort, William W. French romantic plays. N.Y., 1933.
43606.89.86 Conrazier, Joseph. Gabriel Faure. Paris, 1933.
40553.9.12 Constant de Rebecque, Benjamin. Correspondance de Benjamin Constant et d'Anna Lindsay. Paris, 1933.
42555.44.20 Cooperman, H. The aesthetics of Stéphane Mallarmé. Photoreproduction. N.Y., 1933.
38574.23.10 Corneille, Pierre. Corneille inconnu. München, 1933.
42542.55.40 Croisset, Francis de. Le vol nuptial. Paris, 1933.
40597.2.106 Curtius, E.R. Balzac. Paris, 1933.
39533.20.2 Cyrano de Bergerac. Oeuvres diverses. Paris, 1933.
43566.13.100 Declercq, A. L'envers vaut l'endroit. Paris, 1933.
FL 377.80 Deierkauf-Holsboer, Sophie Wilma. L'histoire de la mise en scène dans le théâtre français de 1600 à 1657. Thèse. Paris, 1933.
FL 377.80.5 Deierkauf-Holsboer, Sophie Wilma. L'histoire de la mise en scène dans le théâtre français de 1600 à 1657. Thèse. Paris, 1933.
37575.105 Delzangles, Fernand. Biographies et morceaux choisies d'écrivains d'Auvergne. Aurillac, 1933.
43566.52.110 Demaison, André. Les hommes sur le wharf. Paris, 1933.
40515.5.32 D'Epinay, Louise F. Gli ultimi anni della signora d'Épinay. Bari, 1933.
41593.29.3.4 Desbordes-Valmore, Marceline. Choix de poésies. Paris, 1933.
37543.144.10 Des Granges, C.M. Histoire illustrée de la littérature française. 3. éd. Paris, 1933.
38514.23.25 Desonay, F. Villon. Paris, 1933.
43566.82.7730 Destouches, Louis Ferdinand. L'église. Paris, 1933.
43566.83.100 Des Vallières, Jean. Les hommes sans nom, roman. Paris, 1933.
43566.90.120 Deval, Jacques. Lundi huit heures. Paris, 1933.
43625.19.810 Devaux, André. Armand Godoy. Paris, 1933.
37567.332 Doolittle, Dorothy. The relations between literature and mediaeval studies in France, 1826-1860. Diss. Bryn Mawr, 1933.
43697.88.810 DuBas, C. François Mauriac et la problème du romancier catholique. Paris, 1933.
43576.6.67 Duhamel, Georges. Confession de minuit. N.Y., 1933.
43576.6.295 Duhamel, Georges. L'humaniste et l'automate. Paris, 1933.
43576.6.220A Duhamel, Georges. Le notaire du Havre. 51. éd. Paris, 1933.
Mol 704.4 Duhamel, R. Le rire et les larmes de Molière. Paris, 1933.
43576.39.100 Duhourcau, F. L'enfant de la victoire. N.Y., 1933.
42577.4.46 Dumesnil, René. Guy de Maupassant. Paris, 1933.
X Cg 43877.15 Dunois, D. (pseud.). Suspicion. N.Y., 1933.
40587.94.5 Durry, M.J. La vieillesse de Chateaubriand, 1830-1848. Paris, 1933. 2v.
40587.94 Durry, M.J. La vieillesse de Chateaubriand, 1830-1848. Thèse. Paris, 1933. 2v.
FL 363.48 Dussane, B. (Mme.). Le comédien sans parodoxe. Paris, 1933.
42568.23.14 Duval, Paul. Un second oratoire. Dijon, 1933.
43576.91.82 Duvernois, Henri. A l'ombre d'une femme. Paris, 1933.
43576.91.72 Duvernois, Henri. Jeanne. Paris, 1933.
43757.50.930 Dvorak, Robert. Das ethische und das asthetische bei Romain Rolland. Inaug. Diss. Boltrop, 1933.
37567.334 Eggli, Edmond. Le débat romantique en France, 1813-1830. Paris, 1933.
37569.30 Ehrhard, J.E. Le roman français depuis Marcel Proust. Paris, 1933?
43591.89.130 Éluard, Paul. Comme deux gouttes d'eau. Paris, 1933.
39566.41 Engelmayer, Otto. Romantische Lendenzen im Künstlerischen. Inaug. Diss. München, 1933.

Chronological Listing

1933 - cont.

V43500.85 Éon, Francis. Suite à Perséphone. Paris, 1933.
42572.14.4 Erckmann, Emile. Histoire d'un paysan. Paris, 1933. 3v.
43606.87.531 Fauconnier, G.A.M. Claude, roman. 99. éd. Paris, 1933.
43606.88.103 Fauconnier, H. Malaisie. Paris, 1933.
43607.75.110 Ferdinand, Roger. Trois pour cent. Paris, 1933.
40597.2.110 Ferguson, M.B. La volonté dans la "Comedie humaine" de Balzac. Paris, 1933.
43822.49.907 Fernandat, René. Autour de Paul Valéry. Grenoble, 1933.
41522.18.80 Ferran, André. L'esthetique de Baudelaire. Paris, 1933.
41522.18.79 Ferran, André. L'esthetique de Baudelaire. Thèse. Paris, 1933.
43556.49.870 Fillon, Amélie. Colette. Paris, 1933.
43744.67.960A Fiser, Emeric. L'esthétique de Marcel Proust. Paris, 1933.
43611.1.25.36 Fort, Paul. La conquête de l'Angleterre. Paris, 1933.
42576.62.22.35 France, Anatole. The gods are athirst. London, 1933.
42576.62.21.25 France, Anatole. Penguin island. N.Y., 1933.
43612.59.103 Francis, Robert (pseud.). La grange aux trois belles. 14. éd. Paris, 1933.
42576.15.80 Frejlich, Hélène. Flaubert d'après sa correspondance. Thèse. Paris, 1933.
38525.98 Fries, Wilhelm. Der Stil der Theaterstücke Rotrous. Inaug. Diss. Würzburg, 1933.
FL 379.92.15 Fuchs, Max. La vie théâtrale en province au XVIIIe siècle. Paris, 1933-
40542.23 Galopin, Eugène. Essai de bibliographie chronologique sur Antoine-Frédéric Ozanam. Paris, 1933.
37569.53 Gandon, Yves. Imageries critiques. Paris, 1933.
41596.4.47 Gastinel, Pierre. Le romantisme d'Alfred de Musset. Paris, 1933.
38546.33.15 Gazier, Cécile. Madame de Sévigné. Paris, 1933.
42557.14.35 Gedeon, Jolán. La fortune intellectuelle de Verlaine. Szeged, 1933.
FL 398.7.40 Geller, G.G. Sarah Bernhardt. London, 1933.
43618.90.110 Gevers, Marie. Madame Orpha, ou La sérénade de mai. pt. 1-2. Paris, 1933.
43620.74.195 Giraudoux, Jean. Intermezzo; comédie en trois actes. Paris, 1933.
37573.662 Glanes d'Esculape. Nice, 1933.
37556.88 Glaser, Hellmuth. Studien zur Entwicklungsgeschichte des französischen Bauernromans von Rétif de la Bretonne zum Naturalismus. Inaug. Diss. Neirode, 1933.
42586.68.63 Gobineau, Arthur de. Correspondance entre Gobineau et le comte de Prakesch-Osten (1854-1876). 4. éd. Paris, 1933.
43625.19.200 Godoy, Armand. Ite, missa est. 5e éd. Paris, 1933.
43625.19.202 Godoy, Armand. Ite, missa est. 9e éd. Paris, 1933.
43625.3.94 Goedecke, Renate. Der philosophische Gehalt in Rémy de Gourmonts Gesamtwerk. Inaug. Diss. Dresden, 1933.
38547.1.10 Goudard, M.L. Étude sur les épistres morales d'Honoré d'Urfé. Washington, 1933.
41574.205 Graef, Karl. Die wirkungsvollen Abschlüsse in der Lyrik Victor Hugos. Eine psychologische-genetische Stiluntersuchung. Gekrönte Preis. Wertheim, 1933.
37576.633 Green, F.C. French stories of the 19th and 20th centuries. London, 1933.
41574.285 Gregh, Fernand. L'oeuvre de Victor Hugo. Paris, 1933.
41574.189 Gregoire, E. L'astronomie dans l'oeuvre de Victor Hugo. Liège, 1933.
43626.23.1120 Grenier, Jean. Les îles. Paris, 1933.
37547.45.10 Grosclaude, P. La vie intellectuelle a Lyon dans la deuxième moitié du XVIIIe siècle. Thèse. Paris, 1933.
FL 6129.33 Grosclaude, Pierre. Jean-Jacques Rousseau à Lyon. Lyon, 1933.
FL 6129.33.5 Grosclaude, Pierre. Jean-Jacques Rousseau à Lyon. Thèse. Lyon, 1933.
FL 362.22 Hainleén, G. Die vorromantischen Angriffe in Frankreich auf die klassische Tragödie. Inaug. Diss. Jena, 1933.
37548.16 Hasler, A. Les vaudois et le sentiment de la nature à l'époque préromantique et romantique. Thèse. Dijon, 1933.
43631.90.100 Hautier, Raoul. Réconciliation. La Louvière, 1933.
39544.352 Havens, George R. Voltaire's marginalia on the pages of Rousseau. Columbus, 1933.
37572.25.10A Hawkins, Richmond L. Newly discovered French letters of the 17th, 18th, and 19th centuries. Cambridge, 1933.
43780.5.805 Helmke, Bruno. André Suarès als Denker und Künster. inaug. -Diss. Coburg, 1933.
43632.6.220 Henriot, Émile. Le pénitent de Psalmodi. Paris, 1933.
43632.76.135 Hériat, Philippe. L'araignée du matin. Paris, 1933.
43632.76.110 Hériat, Philippe. La main tendue. Paris, 1933.
43744.67.880A Hier, Florence. La musique dans l'oeuvre de Marcel Proust. N.Y., 1933.
43554.2.840 Hirschberger, T. Der drei Fassungen von Claudels "Annonce faite à Marie". Diss. Breslau, 1933.
Mon 210.15A IVe centenaire de la naissance de Montaigne, 1533-1933. Conferences. Bordeaux, 1933.
43667.51.330 Jaloux, Edmond. Le demon de la vie. Paris, 1933.
43667.51.87 Jaloux, Edmond. La grenade mordue. Paris, 1933.
43667.1.216 Jammes, Francis. Pipe, chien. 5. éd. Paris, 1933.
FL 362.23 Jördens, W. Die französischen Odipusdramen. Inaug. Diss. Bochum, 1933.
37562.104 Jones, P.J. Prologue and epilogue in Old French lives of saints before 1400. Thesis. Philadelphia, 1933.
43670.1.40 Jouglet, René. Tulipe. Paris, 1933.
43670.89.260 Jouhandeau, M. Binche-ana. 6. éd. Paris, 1933.
43670.89.220 Jouhandeau, M. Élise. Paris, 1933.
43670.89.210 Jouhandeau, M. Monsieur Godeau marié. 2. éd. Paris, 1933.
43670.89.140 Jouhandeau, M. Véronicana. Paris, 1933.
38585.14.10 Jovy, Ernest. La bibliothèque des Racines; Jean, Jean-Baptiste et L. Racine. Paris, 1933.
43674.24.110 Kher, Amy. Salma et son village. Paris, 1933.
43744.67.1054 Kinds, Edmond. Etude sur Marcel Proust. Paris, 1933.
42563.18.109 King, S.M. Maurice Barrès; la pensée allemande et le problème du Rhin. Thèse. Paris, 1933.
42563.18.110 King, S.M. Maurice Barrès; la pensée allemande et le problème du Rhin. Thèse. Paris, 1933.
37544.73 Knauer, K. Studien zur Geschichte der Farbenbestimmung van den Anfangen vis gegenEnde des 18. Jahrhundert. Genève, 1933.
40597.06 Korwin-Piotrowska, S. Balzac en Pologne. Paris, 1933.
40597.06.5 Korwin-Piotrowska, S. Balzac en Pologne. Thèse. Paris, 1933.
40597.2.101 Korwin-Piotrowska, S. Balzac et le monde slave. Paris, 1933.
40597.2.100 Korwin-Piotrowska, S. Balzac et le monde slave. Thèse. Paris, 1933.

1933 - cont.

38587.32 Kranzfelder, H.R. Die Hirtendichtung und die dramiatischen Pastoralen Alexandre Hardy's. Inaug. Diss. Würzburg, 1933.
38526.26.80 Labé, Louise Charly. Sechs Sonnette. Hamburg, 1933.
37530.69.10 Lachèvre, Frédéric. Nouvelles glanes bibliographiques et littéraires. Paris, 1933.
43687.15.146 Lacretelle, Jacques de. Les fiançailles. 11e éd. Paris, 1933.
43687.15.145 Lacretelle, Jacques de. Les fiançailles. 24e éd. Paris, 1933.
43687.51.1100 Lalou, René. Le clavecin non tempéré. Paris, 1933.
43687.53.120 Lamandé, André. Les jeux du mensonge. Paris, 1933.
43687.56.2100 Lamoureux, Tristan. L'enfant livré aux hommes. Paris, 1933.
43687.71.120 Laporte, René. Le somnambule. Paris, 1933.
43687.74.130 Larbaud, Valéry. Le gouverneur de Kerguelen. Abbeville, 1933.
42544.25.81 Lavedan, Henri. Avant l'oubli; un enfant rêveur. Pt.1-3. Paris, 1933.
42544.25.90 Lavedan, Henri. Avant l'oubli. Paris, 1933-37. 3v.
FL 398.91 Lavedan, Henri. Volange, comédien de la Foire, 1756-1808. Paris, 1933.
40583.132 Le Breton, André V. Le rouge et le noir de Stendhal. Paris, 1933?
43688.1.3700 Leclerc, Marc. "Honorably discharged". Boston, 1933.
42555.54.80 Lloyd, W. Xavier Marmier. Diss. Washington, 1933.
42555.45.105 Lloyd, Wildon. Xavier Marmier: poet and traveler. Washington, 1933.
39533.22.81 Loch, Philipp. Charles Sorel als literarischer Kritiker. Inaug. Diss. Würzburg, 1933.
37597.5.15 Lorris, Guillaume de. Le roman de la rose. Paris, 1933.
FL 362.18 Loukoutch, K. La tragédie religieuse classique en France. Thèse. Paris, 1933.
FL 376.26 Loukovitch, Kosta. L'évolution de la tragédie religieuse classique en France. Paris, 1933.
FL 398.52.39 Lugné, P.A. Sous les étoiles. 6e éd. Paris, 1933.
39544.112A McGhee, D.M. Voltairian narrative devices as considered in author's Contes philosophiques. Menasha, 1933.
43554.2.816A Madaule, Jacques. Le génie de Paul Claudel. 2e éd. Paris, 1933.
40583.152 Madini, P. Stendhal a Milano e il Casino degli Andeghee. Milano, 1933.
43697.74.9100 Madrus, Joseph Charles. L'oiseau des hauteurs. Paris, 1933.
42555.43.10A Mallarmé, Stéphane. La dernière mode. N.Y., 1933.
43697.52.110 Malraux, André. La condition humaine. Paris, 1933.
42555.47 Manuel, Eugène. Pendant la gueurre poésies. Washington, 1933.
43744.67.1058 Maranini, Lorenzo. Proust, arte e conoscenza. Firenze, 1933.
37575.605 Maritain, J. "Les iles". Paris, 1933.
43697.77.708 Martin du Gard, Roger. The Thibaults. London, 1933-34. 2v.
43697.77.120 Martin du Gard, Roger. Vieille France. 15e éd. Paris, 1933.
43697.88.160.1 Mauriac, François. Dieu et Mammon. Paris, 1933.
43697.88.240 Mauriac, François. Le mystère frontenac. 88. ed. Paris, 1933.
43697.88.300 Mauriac, François. Petits essais de psychologie religieuse. 6. ed. Paris, 1933.
43697.88.162 Mauriac, François. Le romancier et ses personnages. Paris, 1933.
43697.88.710 Mauriac, François. Vipers' tangle. London, 1933.
43822.49.935 Maurois, A. Introduction à la méthode de Paul Valéry. Paris, 1933.
43697.89.151 Maurois, André. Le cercle de famille; roman. Paris, 1933.
43698.25.110 Meersch, M. van der. Quand les sirènes se Tausint. Paris, 1933.
42576.15.90 Melang, Walter. Flaubert als Begründer des literarischen Impressionismus in Frankreich. Inaug. Diss. Emsdetten, 1933.
43698.75.190 Méré, Charles. Un homme du nord. Paris, 1933.
41555.22.1.15 Mérimée, Prosper. Chronique du règne de Charles IX. Paris, 1933.
41555.7.120 Mérimée, Prosper. Lettres de Prosper Mérimée à la comtesse de Boigne. Paris, 1933.
41555.24.15 Mérimée, Prosper. Mosaique. Paris, 1933.
43698.78.110 Mery, Andrée. Cinq à sept. Paris, 1933.
37573.633A Michaud, Régis. Vingtième siècle. N.Y., 1933.
42557.12.35 Mockel, Albert. Émile Verhaeren. Paris, 1933.
37555.133 Mönch, Walter. Frankreichs Dichtung von der Renaissance zur Gegenwart im Spiegel geistesgeschichtlicher Probleme. Berlin, 1933.
Mol 202.20 Molière, Jean Baptiste Poquelin. Molière i "L'escola des maritas. Barcelona, 1933.
Mol 60.46 Molière, Jean Baptiste Poquelin. Three Molière plays; Tartufe, Scapin the Trickster, The School for wives. London, 1933.
Mon 19.33 Montaigne, Michel de. Essais. Texte. Argenteuil, 1933.
Mon 30.33A Montaigne, Michel de. Essayes. N.Y., 1933.
38544.28.31 Montauban, Jacques P. de. Les aventures et le mariage de Panurge (1674). Baltimore, 1933.
43701.63.170 Montherlant, Henry de. Les morts perdues. Abbeville, 1933.
43701.63.140 Montherlant, Henry de. La relève du matin. Paris, 1933.
43701.74.380 Morand, Paul. Mes débuts. Paris, 1933.
43701.74.240 Morand, Paul. Rococo. 5e éd. Paris, 1933.
37567.336.5 Moraud, Marcel. Le romantisme français en Angleterre de 1814 a 1848. Paris, 1933.
37567.336 Moraud, Marcel. Le romantisme français en Angleterre de 1814 a 1848. Thèse. Paris, 1933.
40587.97 Moreau, Pierre. La conversion de Chateaubriand. Paris, 1933.
37567.66.15 Morrissette, B.A. Les aspects fondamentaux de l'esthétique symboliste. Thèse. Clermont-Ferrand, 1933.
FL 386.604 Mortier, Alfred. Quinze ans de théâtre, 1917-1932. Paris, 1933.
41596.32 Musset, Alfred de. Les deux "André del Sarto". Thèse. Rouen, 1933.
42524.19.25 Nanteuil, Jacques. Ferdinand Brunetière. Paris, 1933.
38562.23.15 Neumüller, Josef. Fontenelles Stil im Lichte des Satzverknüpfung. Inaug. Diss. Murnan, 1933.
43706.98.100 Neyrac, Pierre. L'indifférence perdue. Paris, 1933.
43709.21.100 Noé, Yvan. Teddy and partner, pièce en trois actes. Paris, 1933.
42555.66.40 Nolhac, Pierre de. Le rameau d'or. Paris, 1933.
43714.8.700 Obey, André. Lucrece. N.Y., 1933.

Chronological Listing

1933 - cont.

37568.231 Ocvirk, Anton. Razgovori. V Ljubljana, 1933.

37567.341 Orliac, Antoine. La cathédrale symboliste. Paris, 1933-48. 2v.

43731.16.100 Oudard, G. Prosze Pana. Paris, 1933.

Mol 560.22 Paris. Bibliothèque Nationale. Catalogue des ouvrages de Molière. Paris, 1933.

38537.20.50 Paris. Bibliothèque Nationale. Rabelais; exposition organisée à l'occasion du quatrième centenaire de la publication de Pantagruel. Paris, 1933.

37530.185 Paris. Bibliothèque Sainte-Geneviève. Collection Doucet. Première exposition du 21 Juin du 15 Juillet. Paris, 1933.

43625.19.820 Pasquali, P.S. Armand Godoy. Paris, 1933.

43738.1.152.10 Péguy, M. La decheance de l'or. Paris, 1933?

38513.14.4.15 Penn, Dorothy. The staging of the "Miracles de Nostre Dame par personnages" of M. Cangé. N.Y., 1933.

37575.725 Pia, Pascal. Bouquet poétique des medecins. Paris, 1933.

43741.21.120 Piéchaud, M. Le favori. Paris, 1933.

43620.2.105 Pierre-Quint, L. André Gide: sa vie. Paris, 1933.

43741.88.130 Pittard, Hélène (Mme.). Jean-Jacques ou Le promeneur solitaire. Paris, 1933.

Mon 156.2A Plattard, J. Montaigne et son temps. Paris, 1933.

41522.6.12 Poe, Edgar Allan. Nouvelles historiques extraordinaires. Paris, 1933.

42515.35.215.7 Pommier, Jean. La jeunesse cléricale d'Ernest Renan. Paris, 1933.

42515.35.215.5 Pommier, Jean. La jeunesse cléricale d'Ernest Renan. Thèse. Strasbourg, 1933.

42576.43.55A Pope, F.R. Nature in the work of Camille Lemonnier. N.Y., 1933.

42557.20.180 Porché, F. Verlaine. Paris, 1933.

42545.95.35 Pottecher, M. Jean de Calais. Paris, 1933.

42546.12.50 Premsela, M.J. Edmond Rostand. Amsterdam, 1933.

43744.67.38.20 Proust, Marcel. A la recherche du temps perdu. v.3-5, pt.1-3. Paris, 1933-35. 3v.

43744.67.41.15 Proust, Marcel. The Guermantes way. N.Y., 1933.

43744.67.72A Proust, Marcel. Lettres à P. Lanallée. Paris, 1933.

43744.67.44.5 Proust, Marcel. Remembrance of things past. v.3. N.Y., 1933.

43744.67.52 Proust, Marcel. Sus mejores páginas. Santiago, 1933.

43745.1.90 Psichari, H. Ernest Psichari, mon frere. Paris, 1933.

38583.6.20A Racine, Jean. Théâtre. Paris, 1933. 2v.

43752.1.36 Rageot, G. Tels que nous sommes. Paris, 1933.

43620.2.110 Rauch, Erich. Zur Freundschaftsproblem im Leben und Werk André Gides. Inaug. Diss. Jena, 1933.

42584.25.70 Rauch, Franz. Das Verhältnis der Evangelien E. Zolas zu dessen früheren Werken. Inaug. Diss. Nürnberg, 1933.

37555.52.12 Raymond, Marcel. De Baudelaire au surréalisme. Paris, 1933.

41539.05 Reed, Frank W. A bibliography of Alexandre Dumas père. London, 1933.

42556.27.30.25 Régnier, Henri de. De mon temps. 3e éd. Paris, 1933.

42556.27.32 Régnier, Henri de. Poems from The winged sandal. Boston, 1933.

42587.51.35 Renard, Jules. Monsieur Vernet; comédie en deux actes. Paris, 1933.

43757.32.110 Roger-Marx, Claude. Dimanche; comédie en un acte. Paris, 1933.

37565.80 Rohrer, B. Das Erdbeben von Lissabon in der französischen Literatur des achtzehnten Jahrhunderts. Inaug. Diss. Heidelberg, 1933.

43757.50.754 Rolland, Romain. The death of a world. v.4. N.Y., 1933.

43757.3.130A Romains, Jules. Men of good will. N.Y., 1933-46. 14v.

43757.3.210 Romains, Jules. Problèmes européens. Paris, 1933.

40553.10.12 Romieu, André. Benjamin Constant et l'esprit européen. Thèse. Paris, 1933.

42578.22.155.5 Rosny, J.H. La cité infernale. Paris, 1933.

42546.14.5.73 Rostand, Edmond. Cyrano de Bergerac. Washington, 1933.

FL 6022.33 Rousseau, J.J. Les confessions. Argenteuil, 1933.

FL 6094.8.5 Rousseau, J.J. Les rêveries du promeneur solitaire. Paris, 1933.

39566.150 Saenger, H. Juden und Altes Testament bei Diderot. Wertheim, 1933.

43761.41.160 St. Georges de Bouhelier. Napoléon. Paris, 1933.

43761.6.90 Sarment, Jean. Peau d'Espagne. Paris, 1933.

42554.16.18 Schienemann, W. Anatole Le Braz und die Bretonen. Inaug. Diss. Königsberg, 1933.

37562.106 Schilperoort, G. Le commerçant dans la litérature française du moyen âge (Caractère, Vie, position sociale). Proefschrift. Groningen, 1933.

43763.38.201 Schlumberger, Jean. L'inquiète paternité. Paris, 1933.

42582.2.15 Schmökel, Gerda. Die Belebheit des Stils in der Darstellung des Jules Verne. Breslau, 1933.

42572.86.5 Schoumacker, L. Erckmann-Chatrian. Thèse. Strasbourg, 1933.

43763.39.5100 Schreiber, Isabelle G. Nouvelles petites fables. Villefranche-de-Rouergue, 1933.

43620.2.100 Schreiber, Lotte. Leben und Denken im Werk von André Gide. Berlin, 1933.

43620.2.98 Schreiber, Lotte. Leben und Denken im Werk von André Gide. Inaug. Diss. Berlin, 1933.

FL 377.44 Schwartz, I.A. The commedia dell'arte and its influence on French comedy in the seventeenth century. Paris, 1933.

38526.48.75 Sconin, Adrin. L'oeuvre poétique d'Adrien Sconin. Paris, 1933.

43544.14.800 Secret, M.N. Léon Bocquet. Paris, 1933.

37567.91.15 Seillière, E. Sur la psychologie du romantisme-français. Paris, 1933.

42568.2.46 Sellards, John. Dans le sillage du romantisme: Charles Didier. 1805-1864. Thèse. Paris, 1933.

42563.37.100 Selring, Anna L. La pensée de M. Paul Bourget. L'exotisme, 1852-1902. Grenoble, 1933.

37569.32 Semiontek, H. D'enfant et la littérature enfantine contemporaine en France. Thèse. Toulouse, 1933.

37568.62A Sénéchal, C. Les grands courants de la littérature française contemporaine. Paris, 1933.

42572.86 Shoumacker, L. Erckmann-Chatrian. Paris, 1933.

43769.54.160 Simenon, Georges. Le coup de lune. Paris, 1933.

43769.54.130 Simenon, Georges. L'écluse. Paris, 1933.

43769.54.380 Simenon, Georges. Les fiancailles de Mr. Hire. Paris, 1933.

43769.54.140 Simenon, Georges. Les gens d'en face. Paris, 1933.

43769.54.240 Simenon, Georges. M. Gallet décédé. Paris, 1933.

40534.23.81 Skinner, L.H. Collin d'Harleville, 1755-1806. N.Y., 1933.

41564.31.10 Sorrento, Luigi. Correspondance. Paris, 1933.

41522.18.90 Starkie, Enid. Baudelaire. N.Y., 1933.

41596.4.60 Steis, Alois. Das Motiv des Ennui bei Alfred de Musset. Inaug. Diss. Würzburg, 1933.

42543.55.81 Stolle, Hermann. Das Komische bei Gondinet. Inaug. Diss. Rostock, 1933.

42586.63.65 Strasbourg. Bibliotheque national et universaire. Exposition à l'occasion du cinquantième anniversaire de la mort d'Arthur de Gobineau (10-30 nov. 1932.). Paris, 1933.

37563.54 Strowski, Fortunat. La Pléiade; la doctrine et l'oeuvre poétique. v.1-2. Paris, 1933.

39594.19.33 Struck, Walter. Montesquieu als Politiker. Berlin, 1933.

43780.69.193 Supervielle, Jules. L'enfant de la haute mer. 8. éd. Paris, 1933.

40553.10.20 Talma, Julie C. (Mme.). Lettres de Julie Talma à Benjamin Constant. Paris, 1933.

43787.1.40 Tendron, Marcel. La maison du pas périlleux, roman. Paris, 1933.

38526.49.15 Théophile de Viau. Pyrame et Thisbe. Strasbourg, 1933.

37530.145 Thieme, H.P. Bibliographie de la littérature française de 1800 à 1930. Paris, 1933. 3v.

41574.200 Thomas, John H. L'Angleterre dans l'oeuvre de Victor Hugo. Thèse. Paris, 1933.

39533.15.55 Tipping, W.M. Jean Regnaud de Segrais, l'homme et son oeuvres. Paris, 1933.

39533.15.50 Tipping, W.M. Jean Regnaud de Segrais. Thèse. Paris, 1933.

41557.10.70 Toesca, Maurice. Le plus grand amour de George Sand. Thèse. Paris, 1933.

41542.4.45 Tuin, H. van der. L'évolution psychologique, esthétique et littéraire de T. Gautier. Amsterdam, 1933.

41542.4.44 Tuin, H. van der. L'évolution psychologique, esthétique et littéraire de T. Gautier. Thèse. Amsterdam, 1933.

39586.27.15 Vadasz, E.B. Studien zu Rivarol. Inaug. Diss. Berlin, 1933.

43822.49.12A Valéry, Paul. Album de vers anciens. Paris, 1933.

43822.49.330 Valéry, Paul. De la diction des vers. Paris, 1933.

43822.49.440 Valéry, Paul. L'idée fixe. Paris, 1933.

37574.360 Van Roosbroeck, G.L. Unpublished poems by Voltaire. N.Y., 1933.

39578.8.30 Vauvenagues, L. de C. Lettres inédites de Vauvenargues et de son frère Cadet. Paris, 1933.

41557.10.245 Venskstern, Nataliia. Zhorzh Sand. Moskva, 1933.

42582.28.25 Verne, Jules. Twenty thousand leagues under the sea. N.Y., 1933.

Mon 161.5 Villey, P.J. Montaigne. Paris, 1933.

Htn 38514.20.21* Villon, François. Two ballades transcribed from the French of Master François Villon. Rugby, 1933.

43824.67.110 Vioux, Marcelle. La nuit en flammes. pt. 1-2. Paris, 1933.

37597.24.10 Wace, Maistre. The conception Nostre Dame of Wace. Menasha, 1933.

40583.126 Wagner, Wolfgang. Stendhals Beziehung zum 18. Jahrhundert und sein Werk. Inaug. Diss. Dresden, 1933.

38537.25.110 Watson, Francis. Laughter for Pluto. London, 1933.

42583.33.81 Weiss, Karl. Die Landschaftschilderung bei André Theuriet. Inaug. Diss. Rostock, 1933.

43576.77.812 Wessely, Trude. Ein Europäer, Luc Durtain. Brünn, 1933.

41564.55.33 Whitridge, A. Alfred de Vigny. London, 1933.

37569.197 Wilhelm, J. Das Fortleben des Gallikanismus in der französischen Literatur der Gegenwart. München, 1933.

FL 391.135 Winkler, E.G. Moderne Französische Klassikeraufführungen auf Pariser Bühnen. Inaug. Diss. Stuttgart, 1933.

43598.84.810 Zapf, Hasso. Syntaktische Eigentümlichkeiten in den Werken Edouard Estaunié's. Inaug. Diss. Borna, 1933.

42556.32.85 Zevaès, A.B. Maurice Rollinat, son oeuvre. Paris, 1933.

1934

37595.9.75 Abailard, Pierre. Epistolario completo. Palermo, 1934.

37595.7.20 Abailard, Pierre. Traduction de la première épitre de Pierre Abélard (l'histoire calamitatum). Thèse. Paris, 1934.

43512.75.160 Achard, Marcel. Petrus. Paris, 1934.

FL 6129.34 Aimery de Pierrebough, M.T.G. Jean-Jacques Rousseau et les femmes. 9. éd. Paris, 1934.

37596.26.23 Aléxius, Saint. Légend. Saint Alexis; étude. Paris, 1934.

FL 383.87 Allevy, M.A. La mise en scène en France dans la première moitié du dix-neuvième siècle. Paris, 1934.

43527.3.140 Aragon, Louis. Les cloches de Bâle. Paris, 1934.

43527.3.110 Aragon, Louis. Hourra l'Oural. Paris, 1934.

38546.6.15 Aragonnès, Claude. Madeleine de Scudéry, reine du Tendre. Paris, 1934.

40583.86 Arbelet, Paul. Stendhal du pays des comédiennes. Grenoble, 1934.

43528.48.130 Arland, Marcel. Les vivants. 7e éd. Paris, 1934.

40536.32.5 Arnoldson, Louise Parkinson. Sedaine et les musiciens de son temps. Thèse. Paris, 1934.

43528.61.110 Arnoux, Alexandre. Poésie du hasard. Paris, 1934.

43535.54.115 Aymé, Marcel. Le nain. 28e éd. Paris, 1934.

40597.19.55 Balzac, Honoré de. Eugénie Grandet. Paris, 1934. 2v.

40596.11.35 Balzac, Honoré de. Letters to his family, 1809-1850. Princeton, 1934.

41522.1.6 Barbey d'Aurevilly, Jules. Les diaboliques. Paris, 1934.

41574.199 Batault, G. Le pontéfe de la démagogie, Victor Hugo. Paris, 1934.

41522.13.35 Baudelaire, Charles. Petits poèmes en prose (Le spleen de Paris). Paris, 1934.

40532.14.25 Beaumarchais, Pierre A.C. de. Théâtre. Paris, 1934.

37565.79 Beck, T.J. Northern antiquities in French learning and literature, 1755-1855. N.Y., 1934-35. 2v.

43538.14.740 Beckett, Samuel. More pricks than kicks. London, 1934.

38585.16.120 Becthum le Ducq, M. Défense de Racine. Paris, 1934.

43538.51.100 Belloni, Georges. La porte d'ivoire. Paris, 1934.

43538.74.240 Béraud, Henri. Pavés rouges. Paris, 1934.

37568.114 Berger, Marcel. Le style au microscope. Série 1. Paris, 1934.

40517.7.35 Bergmann, H. Madame d'Aulnoy und Spanien. Inaug. Diss. Würzburg, 1934.

43757.9.805 Bernhardt, M. Gaston Roüpnel und Burg. Inaug. Diss. Würzburg, 1934.

42542.29.72 Berr, Georges. Mon crime! Comédie en deux actes. Paris, 1934.

37595.34.25F Bibliothèque Nationale, Paris. Mss. (Fr. 19152). Le manuscrit 19152 du Fonds français de la bibliothèque nationale. Paris, 1934.

1934 - cont.

43554.2.845 Bindel, Victor. Claudel. Paris, 1934.
41574.195 Blanchard, M. Marie-Tudor; essais sur les sources...avec notes...de Victor Hugo. Paris, 1934.
41578.113 Boeniger, Y. Lamartine et le sentiment de la nature. Paris, 1934.
38566.54.15 Boileau Despréaux, Nicolas. Satires. Paris, 1934.
V43500.27 Bollery, Joseph. Un grand ecrivain français mal connu: Léon Bloy. La Rochelle, 1934.
42563.36.245 Bordeaux, Henry. Le chêne et les roseaux. Paris, 1934.
42563.36.230 Bordeaux, Henry. Episodes de la vie littéraire. Paris, 1934.
42542.44.35 Bourdet, Édourd. Les temps difficiles. Paris, 1934.
43545.24.140 Breton, André. Point der jour. 3. éd. Paris, 1934.
37564.124 Brown, H. Scientific organizations in seventeenth century French (1620-1680). Baltimore, 1934.
37562.108 Bruel, Andrée. Romans français du moyen âge; essais. Paris, 1934.
41557.10.65 Brugger, Irene. Frauentypen bei George Sand. Inaug. Diss. Ochsenfurt, 1934.
42545.88.102 Brugmans, H. Georges de Porto-Riche. Paris, 1934.
42545.88.100 Brugmans, H. Georges de Porto-Riche. Proefschrift. Paris, 1934.
40597.2.109 Büchsenschütz, Heinz. Balzac im Spiegel seines Briefwechsels. Inaug. Diss. Marburg, 1934.
43547.34.120 Bugnet, Georges. Siraj, étranges relations. Montréal, 1934.
43550.40.150 Cahuet, Albéric. La nuit espagnole. v.1-3. Paris, 1934.
37547.18 Calmon, Jean. Essai de bibliographie du département de lot. pt. 1-4. Cahors, 1934-47. 2v.
40583.142 Caraccio, Armand. Stendhal et les promenades dans Rome. Thèse. Paris, 1934.
43550.1.230 Carco, Francis. Amitie avec Joulet. Paris, 1934.
43550.1.100 Carco, Francis. La lumière noire; roman. Paris, 1934.
43550.1.60 Carco, Francis. Mémoires d'une autre vie. Paris, 1934.
43550.1.800A Champion, E. La poésie de Carco. Paris, 1934.
43701.63.895 Champion, Édouard. Montherlant vivant. Paris, 1934.
43552.3.9153 Chamson, André. L'année des vaincus. 9. éd. Paris, 1934.
43552.5.145 Chardonne, Jacques. Les destinées sentimentales, roman. Paris, 1934.
43552.5.150 Chardonne, Jacques. La femme de Jean Barnery. Paris, 1934.
43552.5.152 Chardonne, Jacques. Pauline, roman. Paris, 1934.
43552.5.9100 Charles, Gilbert. Les signes de la nuit, 1920-1932. Paris, 1934.
43552.5.1100 Chartier, Émile. Propos de littérature. Paris, 1934.
40586.13.15 Chateaubriand, F.A.R. Atala. Paris, 1934.
43552.24.130 Chérau, Gaston. Sa destinée. v. 1-2. Paris, 1934.
38551.43.10 Chérel, Albert. Fénelon. Paris, 1934.
37564.63.2A Chinard, G. L'Amérique et le rève exotique. Paris, 1934.
37555.180 Chisholm, A.R. Towards Hérodiade. Melbourne, 1934.
37596.10.25 Chrestien de Troyes. Cliges. Halle, 1934.
37595.36.7.5 Chrestien de Troyes. Erec und Enide. 3. Aufl. Halle, 1934.
37596.10.30 Chrestien de Troyes. Le manuscrit d'Annonay. Paris, 1934.
43620.66.840 Ciossek, Heinz Hermann. Jean Giono. Bottrop, 1934.
43554.2.115 Claudel, Paul. Écoute, ma fille. 29e éd. Paris, 1934.
43554.2.400 Claudel, Paul. La legende de Prakriti. Paris, 1934.
FL 6139.34 Cobban, Alfred. Rousseau and the modern state. London, 1934.
43556.1.190 Cocteau, Jean. La machine infernale. 7e éd. Paris, 1934.
40517.39.5 Coderre, A.D. L'oeuvre romanesque de Thomas Simon Gueullette (1683-1766. Thèse. Montpellier, 1934.
43556.49.278 Colette, Sidonie Gabrielle. Duo. Paris, 1934.
Htn 43556.49.305* Colette, Sidonie Gabrielle. La jumelle noire. Paris, 1934.
43557.61.150 Constantin-Weyer, Maurice. Un sourir dans la tempête. Paris, 1934.
42513.48.20 Cormier, Manon. Madame Juliette Adam. Bordeaux, 1934.
38574.8.15 Corneille, Pierre. Théâtre. Paris, 1934. 2v.
38525.22.45.50 Cornelia, W.B. The classical sources of the nature references in Ronsard's poetry. N.Y., 1934.
37542.34.5 Cournot, A.A. Considérations sur la marche des idées. Paris, 1934. 2v.
39544.114 Crist, C.M. The dictionnaire philosophique portatif and the early French deists. Brooklyn, 1934.
43557.66.130 Crommelynck, Fernand. Une femme qu'a le coeur trop petit. Paris, 1934.
38528.14.81 Crucy, François. Brantôme. Paris, 1934.
37556.92 Cumings, E.K. The literary development of the romantic fairy tale in France. Diss. Bryn Mawr, 1934.
38526.27.5.101 Daley, Tatham A. Jean de la Taille, 1533-1608. Paris, 1934.
38526.27.5.100 Daley, Tatham A. Jean de la Taille, 1533-1608. Thèse. Paris, 1934.
43565.60.120 Daniel-Rops, Henry. Mort, où est ta victoire? Roman. Paris, 1934.
37563.17.7 Darmesteter, Arsène. Morceaux choisis des...écrivains du XVIe siècle. 21e éd. Paris, 1934.
43565.5.170 Daudet, Léon A. La police politique. Paris, 1934.
42563.23.175 Debran, Isabelle. A mon oncle Léon Bloy. La Rochelle, 1934. 2v.
43566.48.170 Delarue-Mardrus, Lucie. L'enfant au coq. Paris, 1934.
43566.75.190 Derème, Tristan. Le paisson rouge. 4. ed. Paris, 1934.
40587.96 Deschamps, Jules. Chateaubriand en Angleterre. Paris, 1934.
43566.82.7714A Destouches, Louis Ferdinand. Journey to the end of the night. Boston, 1934.
X Cg 43566.82.7110 Destouches, Louis Ferdinand. Voyage au tout de la nuit; roman. Paris, 1934.
43566.82.7110 Destouches, Louis Ferdinand. Voyage au tout de la nuit; roman. Paris, 1934.
43566.7.65 Deval, Jacques. Prière pour les vivants. Paris, 1934.
43566.90.130 Deval, Jacques. Tovaritch. Paris, 1934.
43573.76.60 Dorgelès, Roland. Si c'était vrai. Paris, 1934.
37543.118.5 Doumic, René. Histoire de la littérature française. Paris, 1934.
41522.3.19 Doyon, R.L. Barbey d'Aurevilly, amoureux et dupe. Paris, 1934.
43574.41.160 Drieu La Rochelle, Pierre. La comédie de Charleroi. 7. éd. Paris, 1934.
43576.6.340 Duhamel, Georges. Discours aux nuages. 19. éd. Paris, 1934.
43576.6.222A Duhamel, Georges. Le jardin des bêtes sauvages 11. éd. Paris, 1934.
43576.6.310 Duhamel, Georges. Remarques sur les mémoires imaginaires. 5. éd. Paris, 1934.

1934 - cont.

43576.6.224 Duhamel, Georges. Vue de la Terre Promise. 4. éd. Paris, 1934.
43576.6.224.3 Duhamel, Georges. Vue de la Terre Promise. 11. éd. Paris, 1934.
37574.365 Dumas, André. Anthologie des poètes français du XVIIIe siècle. Paris, 1934.
43576.68.100 Dupays, Paul. Au-dessus de la vie. Paris, 1934.
43576.68.110 Dupays, Paul. L'hiver. 3. éd. Paris, 1934.
43576.68.120 Dupays, Paul. Qualités et tendances. Paris, 1934.
43576.74.100 Duran, Michel. Liberté provisoire. Paris, 1934.
42544.33.65 Durrière, G. Jules Lemaître et le théâtre. Paris, 1934.
42544.33.31 Durrière, G. Productions et variantes dramatiques inédites de Jules Lemaître. Thèse. Paris, 1934.
43591.89.120 Éluard, Paul. La rose publique. Paris, 1934.
43592.69.110 Empeirikos, Alexandros. Physionomies. Paris, 1934.
40583.140 Enste, Egon. Stendhal als Schilderer der Sitten seiner Zeit. Inaug. Diss. Bochum-Langendrer, 1934.
43593.88.100 Entrevaux, V. d'. La vie secrète de Geraldine Deguith. pt. 1-3. Paris, 1934.
42572.22.50 Erckmann, Emile. Loïs, histoire d'une petite bohémienne. Paris, 1934.
37568.72 Eremburg, I.G. Duhamel, Gide, Malraux, Moraud, Romains, Unamuno. 2e éd. Paris, 1934.
Htn 37530.64.5* Escoffier, M. Le mouvement romantique, 1788-1850. Paris, 1934.
37530.64 Escoffier, M. Le mouvement romantique, 1788-1850. Paris, 1934.
43598.68.100 Espardés, Georges. Rocroy, Victoire du Cid. Paris, 1934.
37567.333 Evans, R.L. Les romantiques français et la musique. Paris, 1934.
37567.333.5 Evans, R.L. Les romantiques français et la musique. Thèse. Paris, 1934.
41596.45.81 Fahmy, Dorrya. Charles Poncy: poète-macon, 1821-1891. Thèse. Paris, 1934.
41557.10.75 Fahmy, Dorrya. George Sand, auteur dramatique. Thèse. Paris, 1934.
43606.87.120 Fauchois, René. La dame aux gants verts. Paris, 1934.
43606.89.75 Faure, Gabriel. Pages choisies de Gabriel Faure. Paris, 1934.
43526.65.810 Fettweks, C. Apollinaire en Ardenne. Bruxelles, 1934.
43744.67.885 Feuillerat, A. Comment Marcel Proust a composé son roman. New Haven, 1934.
39544.116 Fischer, E. Voltaire als Paedagoge. Inaug. Diss. Leipzig, 1934.
42556.28.295 Fontaine, A. Génie de Rimbaud. Paris, 1934.
V43500.105 Forot, Charles. Charmes des jours; poèmes. Saint-Félicien-en-Vivarais, 1934.
43611.89.1110 Fourest, G. La nègresse blonde. 7. éd. Paris, 1934.
43612.59.110 Francis, Robert (pseud.). Le bateau-refuge. 41. éd. Paris, 1934.
43612.59.120 Francis, Robert (pseud.). La maison de vivre. 21. éd. Paris, 1934.
37556.94 Fraser E.M. Le renouveau religieux d'après le roman français de 1886 à 1914. Thèse. Paris, 1934.
FL 379.90 Fredrick, E.C. The plot and its construction in 18th century criticism of French comedy. Diss. Bryn Mawr, 1934.
42576.46.80 Friderich, Emmy. Baskenland und Basken bei Pierre Loti. Inaug. Diss. Würzburg, 1934.
38514.44.20 Frise, F. Allegorische und mythologische Gestalten in den Dichtungen Eustache Deschamps'. Inaug. Diss. Bottrop, 1934.
41542.35.15 Gautier, Théophile. Le roman de la momie. Paris, 1934.
43617.5.45 Géniaux, Charles. Le choc des races. Paris, 1934.
41593.17.3.60 Gérard-Gailly, E. Autour de Gustave Flaubert, les véhémences de Louise Colet. Paris, 1934.
42545.3.530 Gerardino, A. La théâtre de Maeterlinck. Thèse. Paris, 1934.
43617.85.100 Getten, Gilbert. La lyre ardente. Paris, 1934.
40593.29 Gibelin, Jean. L'esthétique de Schelling et l'Allemagne de Madame de Staël. Paris, 1934.
40593.29.5 Gibelin, Jean. L'esthétique de Schelling et l'Allemagne de Madame de Staël. Thèse. Clermont-Ferrand, 1934.
43620.2.68 Gide, André. Pages de journal (1929-1932). Paris, 1934.
43620.2.68.2 Gide, André. Pages de journal (1929-1932). 12. éd. Paris, 1934.
43620.2.79.70 Gide, André. Perséphone. Paris, 1934.
43620.2.31.5 Gide, André. La porte étroite. Paris, 1934.
40587.95 Gillot, Hubert. Chateaubriand; ses idées, son action, son oeuvre. Paris, 1934.
43620.66.390 Giono, Jean. Le chant du mode. Paris, 1934.
43620.74.240 Giraudoux, Jean. Combat avec l'ange. 13. éd. Paris, 1934.
43620.74.167 Giraudoux, Jean. L'école des indifférents. Paris, 1934.
43620.74.110 Giraudoux, Jean. Fin de Siegfried. Paris, 1934.
42586.65.4A Gobineau, Arthur de. La renaissance. Paris, 1934. 2v.
43625.19.210 Godoy, Armand. Du cantique des cantiques au chemin de la Croix. Paris, 1934.
43625.19.153A Godoy, Armand. Les litanies de la vierge. Avec une lithographie de M. Lydis. Paris, 1934.
37596.2.4 Goetze, F. Untersuchungen über die Pilgerfahrt des träumenden Mönchs. Marburg, 1934.
43620.2.268A Gouiran, É. André Gide. Paris, 1934.
40597.2.107 Grafe, Hans. Die Frauengestalten im Werke Honoré de Balzac's. Inaug. Diss. Zeulenroda, 1934.
37573.50 Les grands écrivains de France illustrés. v.1-2. pts.1-6. Paris, 1934-38. 5v.
37583.634 Grant, E.M. Chief French plays of the nineteenth century. 1. ed. N.Y., 1934.
43626.22.710 Green, Julien. Dreamer. N.Y., 1934.
43626.22.170 Green, Julien. Le visionnaire. Paris, 1934.
39568.6.2 Grimm, F.M. von. Correspondance inédite, 1794-1800 du Baron Grimm au comte de Findlater. Thèse. Paris, 1934.
39568.6 Grimm, F.M. von. Correspondance inédite, 1794-1801...au comte de Findlater. Paris, 1934.
43626.67.100 Groslier, G. Monsieur de la garde, roi. pt.1-2. Paris, 1934.
37568.67 Gross, René. Les lettres. Paris, 1934.
43628.1.80 Guitry, Sacha. Faisons un rêve. Paris, 1934.
43628.1.90 Guitry, Sacha. La jalousie. Paris, 1934.
43628.1.105 Guitry, Sacha. Souvenirs. Paris, 1934.
43628.1.23 Guitry, Sacha. Théâtre. Paris, 1934-35. 2v.
37596.26.30 Hahnel, Kurt. Sprachliche Untersuchung zur Alexius-Handschrift "V". Inaug. Diss. Coburg, 1934.
39544.160 Harper, H.H. Voltaire. Boston, 1934?
FL 6139.34.5A Hendel, C.W. Jean-Jacques Rousseau, moralist. London, 1934. 2v.

Chronological Listing

1934 - cont.

43632.76.105	Hériat, Philippe. La foire aux garçons. 3. éd. Paris, 1934.
40516.63.20	Hermant, A. Madame de Kruedener. Paris, 1934.
43620.2.115	Hofmann, M. Der Moralist André Gide. Inaug. Diss. Würzburg, 1934.
FL 383.95	Hsi-Wen, Tsao. La question d'argent dans le théâtre français sous le second empire. Thèse. Paris, 1934.
41571.1.13	Hugo, Victor. Philosophie. Paris, 1934-37. 2v.
37567.193.15	Hung Cheng Fu. Un siècle d'influence chinoise sur la littérature française (1815-1930). Thèse. Paris, 1934.
41586.26.281	Hupperts, F.D. Edouard Ourliac, 1813-1848. Groningen, 1934.
43659.88.120	Istrati, Panait. Méditerranée lever du soleil. 12. éd. Paris, 1934.
43659.88.130	Istrati, Panait. Présentation des Haïdouce. Paris, 1934.
43667.51.290	Jaloux, Edmond. Déssins aux trois crayons. Paris, 1934.
43667.1.335	Jammes, Francis. Le crucifix du poète. Paris, 1934.
42515.35.145	Jaspar, M.H. Ernest Renan et sa republique. Paris, 1934.
38524.871.10	John, Hans. Pompee. Inaug. Diss. Nürnberg, 1934.
43670.89.320	Jouhandeau, M. Chamin adour. Paris, 1934-41. 3v.
43670.89.270	Jouhandeau, M. Images de Paris. 6. éd. Paris, 1934.
37564.122	Karpa, Louise. Themen der franzözischen Lyrik im 17. Jahrhundert. Inaug. Diss. Homburg-Saar, 1934.
42546.12.55	Katz, Elly. L'esprit français dans le théâtre d'Edmond Rostand. Thèse. Paris, 1934.
42584.25.365	Kleman, Mikhail K. Emil' Zola. Leningrad, 1934.
42584.25.91	Kneer, G. Das Familienproblem in Emile Zola's Rougon-Macquart. Bechstein, 1934.
42584.25.90	Kneer, G. Das Familienproblem in Emile Zola's Rougon-Macquart. Inaug. Diss. Wertheim, 1934.
FL 386.403	Knowles, Dorothy. La réaction idéaliste au théâtre depuis 1890. Paris, 1934.
43683.62.100	Kunstler, Charles. Les amours de François Villon. Paris, 1934.
38564.32.35	La Bruyère, J. de. Oeuvres complètes. Paris, 1934.
43687.15.153	Lacretelle, Jacques de. Les aveux étudiés. Paris, 1934.
38544.27.47	La Fayette, Marie M. La Princesse de Clèves. Paris, 1934.
39525.15	La Fontaine, Jean de. Contes et nouvelles en vers. Paris, 1934. 2v.
39525.15.2A	La Fontaine, Jean de. Fables choisies, mises en vers. Paris, 1934. 2v.
41595.2.80	Lapaquellerie, Yvon. Lacenaire. Paris, 1934.
42555.32.5	Laprade, Victor de. Lettres inédites de Victor de Laprade à Charles Alexandre, 1852-1871. Thèse. Lyon, 1934.
43687.75.170	Larguier, Léo. Roses de papier. Paris, 1934.
38526.27.03	Larnac, Jean. Louise Labé, la belle cordière de Lyon (1522?-1566). Paris, 1934.
42544.25.83	Lavedan, Henri. Avant l'oubli écrire. Paris, 1934.
43688.17.110	Lécuyer, A.H. (Mme.). Le printemps sous l'orage; roman. pts.1-3. Paris, 1934.
43688.33.110	Legrand, Ignace. A sa lumière. Paris, 1934.
42544.33.64	Lemaître, Jules. Jules Lemaître et le théâtre. Thèse. Paris, 1934.
37567.193.30	Lichtenberger, M. Ecrivains français en Égypte contemporaine 1870 à nos jours. Thèse. Paris, 1934.
38585.16.50	Lichtenstein, J. Racine, poète biblique. Paris, 1934.
43576.6.820	Linsenmaier, W. Die Darstellung des Menschen in Georges Duhamels Roman "Deux Hommes". Inaug. Diss. Würzburg, 19
42576.15.115	Lombard, A. Flaubert et Saint-Antoine. Paris, 1934.
40587.98	Longi, Olga. La terre et les morts dans l'oeuvre de Chateaubriand. Thèse. Baltimore, 1934.
41592.10.20	Lucas-Dubreton, J. Béranger. Paris, 1934.
43697.14.140	MacOrlan, Pierre. A bord de l'Étoile-Matutine. 3e ed. Paris, 1934.
37567.193.50	Malleret, L. L'exotisme indochinois dans la littérature française depuis 1860. Paris, 1934.
43697.52.705	Malraux, André. Man's fate. N.Y., 1934.
37569.40.60	Mangeat, Guy. Histoire du surréalisme. Bruxelles, 1934.
38526.34.530A	Margarete of Austria. Albums poétiques. Cambridge, 1934.
43697.77.8100	Martin, Maurice. Le Triptyque. Bordeaux, 1934.
42513.23.79	Martin, René. Bibliographie de Charles Dollfus (Mulhouse, 1827. Paris, 1913.) Thèse. Gap, 1934.
42513.23.81	Martin, René. La vie et l'oeuvre de Charles Dollfus. Mulhouse, 1827. Paris, 1913. Thèse. Gap, 1934.
43697.78.130	Martinet, Marcel. Chants du passages. Paris, 1934.
40583.144	Martino, Pierre. Stendhal. Paris, 1934.
41574.211	Matt, Hildegard. Das visuelle Element in der Kunst Victor Hugos betrachtet an seinen Bildern. Inaug. Diss. Freiburg, 1934.
43697.88.310	Mauriac, François. Discours de réception à l'Académie française et Réponse de M. André Chaumeix. Paris, 1934.
43697.88.190A	Mauriac, François. Journal. Paris, 1934-1953. 5v.
43697.89.340	Maurois, André. L'instinct du bonheur. 18. éd. Paris, 1934.
43697.100.700	Mazeline, Guy. The wolves. N.Y., 1934.
43698.25.705	Meersch, M. van der. When the looms are silent. N.Y., 1934.
37573.650	Mélanges de litterature, philosophie et histoire offerts à M. Louis Arnould. Poitiers, 1934.
37543.220	Mélanges de philologie d'histoire et de littérature offerts a Joseph Vianey. Paris, 1934.
FL 391.7.8	Mélèse, Pierre, Répertoire analytique des documents contemporains d'information...théâtre à Paris sous Louis XIV. Thèse. Paris, 1934.
FL 391.7.10	Mélèse, Pierre. Répertoire analytique des documents contemporains d'information...théâtre à Paris sous Louis XIV. Paris, 1934.
FL 391.7.2	Mélèse, Pierre. Le théâtre et le public à Paris sous Louis XIV, 1659-1715. Thèse. Paris, 1934.
FL 391.7	Mélèse, Pierre. Le théâtre et le public à Paris sous Louis XIV. Paris, 1934.
41555.7.110	Mérimée, Prosper. Lettres de Mérimée à Ludovic Vitet. Paris, 1934.
41555.9.20	Mérimée, Prosper. Romans et nouvelles. Paris, 1934.
41555.31	Mérimée, Prosper. The slave ship. Evanston, 1934.
43698.78.120	Mery, Andrée. Les jeux sont faits. Paris, 1934.
FL 6139.34.15	Meyer, Hans. Rousseau und Shelley; ein typologischer Vergleich. Inaug. Diss. Würzburg, 1934.
37568.60A	Michaud, Régis. Modern thought and literature in France. N.Y., 1934.
42576.35.4	Miller, L.G. Index de la correspondance de G. Flaubert. Strasbourg, 1934.
Mol 191.35	Molière, Jean Baptiste Poquelin. Dom Juan. Cambridge, Eng., 1934.
Mon 32.34.5	Montaigne, Michel de. Essays. N.Y., 1934-36. 3v.
Mon 32.34	Montaigne, Michel de. Selected essays. Manchester, 1934.

1934 - cont.

Location	Call number	Entry
	43701.63.160	Montherlant, Henry de. Les célibataires; roman. 63e éd. Paris, 1934.
	43701.63.163	Montherlant, Henry de. Les celibataires. 90e éd. Paris, 1934.
	43701.63.732	Montherlant, Henry de. Les lepreuses, roman. Paris, 1934.
	38526.42.20	Moore, M.J. Estienne Pasquier. Thèse. Poitiers, 1934.
	43701.74.270	Morand, Paul. France la doulce. Paris, 1934.
	42563.21.97	Moreau, Abel. René Bazin et son oeuvre romanesque. Auxerre, 1934.
	42563.21.95	Moreau, Abel. René Bazin et son oeuvre romanesque. Thèse. Auxerre, 1934.
	37556.20.70	Morienval, J. Les créateurs de la grande presse en France. Paris, 1934.
	42545.88.109	Müller, W. Georges de Porto-Riche, 1849-1930; l'homme, le poète, le dramaturge. Thèse. La Flèche, 1934.
	42545.88.110	Müller, W. Georges de Porto-Riche, 1849-1930. Paris, 1934.
Htn	43703.80.120*	Muselli, Vincent. Les sonnets moraux. Autun, 1934.
	41596.18.29	Musset, Alfred de. Comédies et proverbes. Paris, 1934. 2v.
	41596.18.28	Musset, Alfred de. Comédies et proverbes. Paris, 1934.
	41596.22.15	Musset, Alfred de. La confession d'un enfant du siècle. Paris, 1934.
	41596.18.35	Musset, Alfred de. Théâtre complete; comédies et proverbes. Paris, 1934.
	43709.3.230	Noailles, Anna E. Derniers vers et poèmes d'enfance. 9e éd. Paris, 1934.
	38537.25.74	Nock, Albert J. A journey into Rabelais's France. N.Y., 1934.
	38537.25.73	Nock, Albert J. A journey into Rabelais's France. N.Y., 1934.
	FL 383.89	Nostrand, H.L. Le théâtre antique et à l'antique en France de 1840 à 1900. Thèse. Paris, 1934.
	FL 383.90A	Nostrand, H.L. Le théâtre antique et à l'antique en France de 1840 à 1900. Thèse. Paris, 1934.
	43728.50.100	Orliac, J. Le deuxième mari de Lady Chatterly. Paris, 1934.
	43737.34.140	Pagnol, Marcel. Fanny. Paris, 1934.
	37595.34.15	Palfrey, T.R. Medieval French literature. N.Y., 1934.
	43737.52.100	Paluel-Marmont, A.P.H.J. Sud. Paris, 1934.
	37555.12.10	Papin, M.D. La ballade. Grenoble, 1934.
	V43500.233	Parrot, Louis. Misery farm, poèmes. n.p., 1934.
	41557.9.75	Parturier, Maurice. Une expérience of Lélia. Paris, 1934.
	38513.48	La passion d'Autun. Paris, 1934.
	41539.21	Pearce, G.R. Dumas Père. London, 1934.
	43738.1.70.5	Péguy, Charles. Prières. 2nd éd. Paris, 1934.
	43738.41.160	Peisson, Edouard. Une femme. Paris, 1934.
	43738.76.5100	Périn, Cécile. Dicté par une ombre. Paris, 1934.
	43738.77.130	Pérochon, Ernest. Les endiablés. Paris, 1934.
	37547.28	Pérouse, Gabriel. Causeries sur l'histoire littéraire de la Savoie. Chambery, 1934. 2v.
	37558.66	Peter, René. Vie secrète de l'académie française. Paris, 1934-38. 4v.
	43738.81.2100	Petibon, Andrée. Sur le chemin du rêve. Paris, 1934.
	37574.650	Petite anthologie poétique du surréalisme. Paris, 1934.
	43741.2.100	Piachaird, R.L. La tragédie de Coriolan. Paris, 1934.
	43741.51.110	Pilon, Edmond. Dans le buisson des lettres. Paris, 1934.
	41522.6.14	Poe, Edgar Allan. Aventures d'Arthur Gordon Pym. Paris, 1934.
	43743.1.60	Porché, François. Vers, 1928-1933. Paris, 1934.
	42545.95.5	Pottecher, M. Le bourdon de Herlisheim. Paris, 1934.
	42545.95.2	Pottecher, M. Le château de Hans. Paris, 1934?
X Cg	43744.67.38.15	Proust, Marcel. A la recherche du temps perdu. v.1-8. Paris, 1934-39. 16v.
	43744.67.44	Proust, Marcel. Remembrance of things past. v.2-4. N.Y., 1934. 3v.
	43750.24.160	Queneau, Raymond. Gueule de Pierre. 3. éd. Paris, 1934.
	38536.25.15	Rabelais, F. L'Abbage de Thélème. Paris, 1934.
	38536.18.60	Rabelais, F. Rabelais; the fine books and minor writings. v.1. 2. ed. Cambridge, Eng., 1934.
	43752.85.702	Ratel, Simonne. The house in the hills. N.Y., 1934.
	Mon 128.4.5	Rech, Bruno. Grundbegriffe und Wertbegriffe bei Michel de Montaigne. Inaug. Diss. Berlin, 1934.
	43753.3.32	Régnier, P. L'abbaye d'Evolayne. Paris, 1934.
	42515.30.634	Renan, Ernest. Prière sur l'acropole. Manchester, 1934.
	41574.207	Reymann, E. Victor Hugos Stellung zur Frau. Inaug. Diss. Coburg, 1934.
	42542.59.84	Richter, Kurt. François de Curel, ein Beitrag zur französischen dramatischen Literatur um die Jahrhundertwende. Inaug. Diss. Grimma, 1934.
	43757.4.1100	Robert, Louis de. La servante sans gages. Paris, 1934.
	43757.7.5100	Robert-Dumas, Charles. Ceux du S.R. Deuxieme bureau. Paris, 1934.
	43757.50.755	Rolland, Romain. A world in birth. v.5. N.Y., 1934.
	38525.20.40	Ronsard, Pierre de. Sonnets pour Hélène. London, 1934.
	42578.22.165	Rosny, J.H. Les arrivistes. Paris, 1934.
	42578.22.130	Rosny, J.H. Les compagnons de l'univers. 9. éd. Paris, 1934.
	42578.22.8.25	Rosny, J.H. Eyrimah. Paris, 1934.
	42578.22.70	Rosny, J.H. L'initiation de Diane. Paris, 1934.
	43757.83.130	Rostand, Maurice. L'homme que j'ai fait naitre; roman. Paris, 1934.
	43697.89.810	Roya, Maurice. André Maurois. Paris, 1934.
	V43500.277	Ruet, Noël. L'anneau de feu. Mézières, 1934.
	37596.4.15	Rutebeuf. Le miracle de Théophile. Paris, 1934.
	43761.41.170	St. Georges de Bouhelier. Jeanne d'Arc. Paris, 1934.
	43761.42.100	St. Helièr, Monique. Bois-mort. 13e éd. Paris, 1934.
	39595.22.20	St. Pierre, J.H.B. de. Paul et Virginie suivi de La chaumière indienne. Paris, 1934.
	41522.18.335	Samuel, Paul de. Baudelaire. Brussel, 1934.
	42546.16.10	Sardou, Victorien. Théâtre complet. Paris, 1934. 15v.
	43761.6.100	Sarment, Jean. La couronne de carton. Paris, 1934.
	43761.6.110	Sarment, Jean. Le discours des prix; pièce en 3 actes. Paris, 1934.
	42542.28.75	Schilling, Ida. Frauentypen in den Dramen von Henry Becque. Inaug. Diss. Würzburg, 1934.
	43763.38.130	Schlumberger, Jean. Sur les frontiers religieuses. Paris, 1934.
	38527.50.10	Schmidt, Hans. Estienne de La Boétie's "Discours de la servitude volontaire". Inaug. Diss. Marburg, 1934.
	42576.15.130	Schollmeyer, V. Gustave Flaubert in seinem Verhältnis zu Michel de Montaigne. Griefswald, 1934.
	41542.4.40	Schulz, Agnes. Die Sprachkunst Théophile Gautiers. Inaug. Diss. Bochum-Langendreer, 1934.

Chronological Listing

1934 - cont.

41578.40.39 Schwabbauer, W. Lamartines "Graziella". Inaug Diss. Bielefeld, 1934.
42555.13.10 Séchaud, Pierre. Victor de Laprade: l'homme, son oeuvre poétique. Thèse. Paris, 1934.
42576.63.140 Seillière, Ernest. Anatole France, critique de son temps. Paris, 1934.
42576.63.135 Seillière, Ernest. La jeunesse d'Anatole France. Paris, 1934.
38526.70.20 Shaw, Helen A. Conrad Badius and the Comedie du Pape Malade. Diss. Philadelphia, 1934.
37556.18.25 Shumway, A.E. A study of the Minerva française. (Feb. 1818-Mar. 1920). Diss. Philadelphia, 1934.
38514.23.20 Siciliano, Italo. François Villon et les thèmes poétiques de Moyen-Âge. Paris, 1934.
FL 398.82 Silvain, Jean. Tel etait Silvain. Paris, 1934.
43769.54.170 Simenon, Georges. L'homme de Londres. Paris, 1934.
43769.54.185 Simenon, Georges. Les suicidés. 72. éd. Paris, 1934.
43775.90.7180 Soupault, Philippe. Les moribonds. 7. éd. Paris, 1934.
38542.26.12 Spalatin, Krsto. Saint Evremond. Thèse. Zagreb, 1934.
FL 6139.34.10 Spink, J.S. Jean-Jacques Rousseau et Genève. Paris, 1934.
FL 6139.34.8 Spink, J.S. Jean-Jacques Rousseau et Genève. Thèse. Paris, 1934.
37569.135 Stolpe, Sven. Den kristna talangen; transka essayer. Stockholm, 1934.
37576.210 Storer, M.E. Contes de fées du grand siècle. N.Y., 1934.
43780.69.110 Supervielle, Jules. Les amis inconnus. 3. éd. Paris, 1934.
42563.18.180 Thieville, H.L. La pensée de Maurice Barrès. Paris, 1934.
41574.201 Thomas, J.H. L'Angleterre dans l'oeuvre de Victor Hugo. Paris, 1934.
42522.23.5 Tillmann, Erich. Eugène Melchior de Vogüé. Inaug. Diss. Bochum-Langendreer, 1934.
42578.51.90 Tinayre, Marcelle. Chateau en limousin. v.1-3. Paris, 1934.
V43500.309 Tortel, Jean. Jalons; esthétique. Paris, 1934.
38525.35.30A Tristan L'Hermite, F. Le parasite. Paris, 1934.
38557.24.45 Truc, Gonzague. Bossuet et le classicisme religieux. Paris, 1934.
42576.65.13.47 Trudgian, Helen. L'esthétique de J.K. Huysmans. Paris, 1934.
42576.65.13.45 Trudgian, Helen. L'évolution des idées esthétiques de J.K. Huysmans. Thèse. Paris, 1934.
41574.193 Turner, R.E. The sixteenth century in Victor Hugo's inspiration. N.Y., 1934.
FL 363.50 Tzoneff, Stoyan. L'homme d'argent au théâtre français jusqu'à la révolution. Thèse. Gap, 1934.
43822.49.179 Valéry, Paul. Pièces sur l'art. Paris, 1934.
43822.49.370F Valéry, Paul. Sémiramis. Paris, 1934.
43822.49.13 Valéry, Paul. Variété. Paris, 1934-37. 2v.
40587.100 Vallese, R.E. (Mme.). Le thème de la mer dans l'oeuvre de Chateaubriand. Thèse. Milano, 1934.
37575.161.5 Vaneille, Jean Louis. Les poètes bas-normands. Saint-Lo, 1934.
39578.8.38 Vauvenargues, L. de C. Réflexions et maximes. Paris, 1934.
43823.75.105 Vercel, Roger. Capitaine Conan. Paris, 1934.
43823.75.730 Vercel, Roger. In sight of Eden. 1st ed. N.Y., 1934.
42556.28.123 Verlaine, Paul. Rimbaud. 4e éd. Paris, 1934.
43823.77.120 Verneuil, Louis. L'école des contribuables. Paris, 1934.
43823.77.130 Verneuil, Louis. Pile ou face. Paris, 1934.
43823.77.1100 Vert, Marie Louise. Refoulement. Paris, 1934.
38514.20.20 Villon, François. Oeuvres. Paris, 1934.
38514.20.15.10 Villon, François. Oeuvres. Paris, 1934.
43824.2.21 Vivien, Renée. Poésies complètes. Paris, 1934. 2v.
39544.27.3.3 Voltaire, François Marie Arouet de. Lettres choisies. 18e éd. Paris, 1934.
37565.98 Wais, Kurt K.T. Das antiphilosophische Weltbild des französischen Sturm und Drang, 1760-1789. Berlin, 1934.
42555.62.35 Weber, Julia. Jean Moréas und die französische Tradition. Inaug. Diss. Nürnberg, 1934.
42576.65.13.35 Weise, C. J.K. Huysmans Beziehungen zur Malerei. Inaug. Diss. Bochum-Langendreer, 1934.
38543.31.10 Wickelgren, F.L. La Mothe le Vayer. Paris, 1934.
38543.31.8 Wickelgren, F.L. La Mothe le Vayer. Thèse. Paris, 1934.
40566.6.100 Witmeur, Claire. Ximénès Doudan, sa vie et son oeuvre. Liège, 1934.
42563.21.87 Wood, John S. Un aspect du mouvement traditionaliste et social dans la littérature française contemporaine. Thése. Paris, 1934.
42563.21.88 Wood, John S. Un aspect du mouvement traditionaliste et social dans la littérature française contemporaine. Paris, 1934.
37556.15.120 Wood, K.L. Criticism of French romantic literature in the Gazette de France 1830-1848. Philadelphia, 1934.
41593.27.10 Zatuska, A. Poezja opisowa Delille a w Polsce. Kraków, 1934.
40587.157 Zdziechowski, M. Chateaubriahd i Bourbonowie. Wilno, 1934.
38551.128 Zermati, D.J. La place de Fénelon dans l'histoire des doctrines économiques. Thèse. Alger, 1934.

1935

38526.51.10 Adam, Antoine. Théophile de Viau et la libre pensée française en 1620. Paris, 1935.
38526.51.9 Adam, Antoine. Théophile de Viau et la libre pensée française en 1620. Thèse. Paris, 1935.
37593.62.40 Adam de la Halle. Le jeu de Robin et Marion. Paris, 1935.
40575.5.147 Allem, Maurice. Sainte-Beuve et "Volupte". Paris, 1935.
43523.41.185 Amiel, Denys. Théâtre: Trois et une. v. 5. Paris, 1935.
42553.33.65 Amiel, Henri F. La jeunesse d'Henri Frédéric Amiel. Paris, 1935.
42553.33.3 Amiel, Henri F. The private journal of Henri F. Amiel. N.Y., 1935.
43620.2.79.194 André Gide et notre temps. Paris, 1935.
37574.656 Année poétique. Album de l'Année poétique. Paris, 1935.
43524.67.100 Anouilh, Jean. Y'avait un prisonnier. Paris, 1935.
42576.15.105 Anweiler, J. Die stilistische Funktion der medi:inischen und naturwissenschaftlichen Fachausdrücke in Flauberts "Madame Bovary". Inaug. Diss. Heidelberg, 1935?
43526.65.795 Apollinaire, Guillaume. Básně. Praha, 1935.
43527.3.300 Aragon, Louis. Pour un réalisme socialiste. Paris, 1935.
43528.35.100 Argyll, Claude. Escale aux Mascareignes. Paris, 1935.
43528.48.195 Arland, Marcel. La vigie. Paris, 1935.
43528.80.100 Arschat, P. La nuit sur Mytilene. Paris, 1935.

1935 - cont.

41574.203 Ascoli, G. Reponse à quelques détracteurs de Victor Hugo. Paris, 1935.
37563.62A Atkinson, G. Les nouveaux horizons de la renaissance française. Paris, 1935.
38526.47.33.5 Aubin, R.A. Saint-Amant as "preromantic". n.p., 1935.
FL 386.605 Aykroyd, Phyllis. The dramatic art of La compagnie des quinze. London, 1935.
43535.54.160 Aymé, Marcel. Maison basse. 2e éd. Paris, 1935.
FL 6139.35 Baldanzi, E.R. Il pensiero religioso di Gian Giacomo Rousseau. Firenze, 1935.
40596.8.25 Balzac, Honoré de. La comédie humaine. Paris, 1935-37. 10v.
40596.11.45 Balzac, Honoré de. Correspondance inédite avec Madame Zulma Carraud (1829-1850). Paris, 1935.
40597.19.45 Balzac, Honoré de. Evgeniia Grande. Moskva, 1935.
40596.8.14 Balzac, Honoré de. Oeuvres diverses. Paris, 1935-38. 3v.
41574.560 Barbier, Henry. L'ame et dieu. Paris, 1935.
43537.77.100 Barle, F. Le coeur passionne. Paris, 1935.
41574.212 Bauer, H.F. Les "Ballades" de Victor Hugo. Thèse. Paris, 1935.
37576.305 Bayet, Albert. Les écrivains politiques du XVIIIe siècle. 5. éd. Paris, 1935.
43538.17.140 Bedel, Maurice. L'alouette aux nuages. Paris, 1935.
42542.28.80 Behrens, A. Henry Becque als Kritiker. Inaug. Diss. Würzburg, 1935.
43538.5.40 Benda, Julien. Délice d'éleuthère. 4. éd. Paris, 1935.
38526.13.273 Bergounioux, L.A. Un poète quercynois du XVIe siècle; Guillaume Du Buys, 1520?-1594. Thèse. Paris, 1935.
37569.48A Bermardini, Ada. Simbolisti e decadenti. Roma, 1935.
43538.10.55 Bernard, Jean J. Nationale 6. Paris, 1935.
43538.76.2130 Bernard, O. Les comédiens ambulants. Paris, 1935.
43538.76.2140 Bernard, O. La petite pharmacienne. Paris, 1935.
40582.3.6 Beyle, Henri. Courrier anglais. Paris, 1935-36. 5v.
43540.7.120 Bibescu, M.L. Egalité. pt.1-3. Paris, 1935.
38523.13.10 Bible. O.T. Psalms. French. Les pseaumes mis en rime françoise. Kassel, 1935.
Mon 112.11 Billeskov Jansen, F.J. Sources vives de la pensée de Montaigne. Copenhague, 1935.
43540.84.100 Bitard-Viaud, M. De mon coeur à ton coeur. Paris, 1935.
43744.67.1170 Blackert, H. Der Aufbau der Kunstwirklichkeit. Berlin, 1935.
42563.23.20.2 Bloy, Léon. Quatre ans de captivité à Cochons-sur-Marne. 7. éd. v. 1-2. Paris, 1935.
Mon 112.12 Boase, Alan Martin. The fortunes of Montaigne. London, 1935.
42563.36.257 Bordeaux, Henry. Le pays sans ombre. Paris, 1935.
37562.253 Bossuat, R. La littérature morale au moyen âge. Paris, 1935.
42563.37.7.8 Bourget, Paul. A love crime. Paris, 1935.
42576.63.175 Braidant, Charles. Du Boulangisme au Panama. Paris, 1935.
37568.68.2 Brasillach, R. Portraits. Paris, 1935.
37568.68 Brasillach, R. Portraits. 4e éd. Paris, 1935.
43545.5.110 Breitman, M. Le pilote, avec deux dessins d'Etienne Bouchaud. Tunis, 1935.
43699.3.805 Brendel, Hans. Pierre Mille und die koloniale Frage in Frankreich. Inaug. Diss. Jena, 1935.
41574.565 Brunet, Georges. Victor Hugo. Paris, 1935.
43548.75.100 Byrch, Rita. Amor, in memoriam. Paris, 1935.
40587.930 Cahuet, Albéric. Lucile de Chateaubriand. Paris, 1935.
43744.67.875A Capasso, Aldo. Marcel Proust. Milano, 1935.
X Cg 39544.130 Carré, J.R. Réflexions sur l'Anti-Pascal de Voltaire. Paris, 1935.
42545.3.500 Cartwright, F. (Mrs.). Amerikanische Gedanken in den literarischen Werken Maeterlincks. Inaug. Diss. n.p., 1935.
FL 382.160 Cecchi, A. Il teatro francese. Milano, 1935.
43552.3.9110 Chamson, André. Barren harvest. London, 1935.
43552.3.9184 Chamson, André. Les quatre éléments. 10e éd. Paris, 1935.
43552.3.5100 Charpent, John. Les grands Templiers. Paris, 1935.
40583.146 Chartier, E. Stendhal. Paris, 1935.
40597.2.210 Chartier, Émile. En lisant Balzac. Paris, 1935.
40586.21.10 Chateaubriand, F.A.R. René. Paris, 1935.
43552.24.150 Chérau, Gaston. Le mulet de Phidias. Paris, 1935.
38526.58.10 Choptrayanovitch, G. Étienne Tabourot des accords, 1549-1590. Thèse. Dijon, 1935.
43552.67.100 Chottès, Lucien. Premières étreintes. Paris, 1935.
37596.10.2.20 Chrestien de Troyes. Arthurian romances. N.Y., 1935.
37542.37 Cinq cents ans de littérature française. Paris, 1935.
37555.153 Citoleux, M. La voie royale de la poésie française. Paris, 1935.
43554.2.320 Claudel, Paul. Conversations dans le Loir et Cher. Paris, 1935.
43554.2.125 Claudel, Paul. Le livre de Christophe Colomb. 16e éd. Paris, 1935.
43556.1.180 Cocteau, Jean. Portraits - souvenir, 1900-1914. 6e éd. Paris, 1935.
43556.1.88 Cocteau, Jean. Soixante dessins pour les enfants terribles. 6e éd. Paris, 1935.
43556.49.440 Colette, Sidonie Gabrielle. Prisons et paradis. Paris, 1935.
43556.49.580 Colette, Sidonie Gabrielle. Sido. Paris, 1935.
42563.39.07 Corporon-Bédard, Y. La vie provinciale dans l'oeuvre de René Boylesve. Thèse. Toulouse, 1935.
43757.3.325 Cuisenier, André. Jules Romains et l'unanimisme. Paris, 1935-48. 2v.
37555.257 Danilin, Iu. Iv. Poety Iul'skoi revoliutsii. Moskva, 1935.
41557.10.220 Davray, Jean. George Sand et les amants. Paris, 1935.
43625.19.825 Deambrosis Martins, Carlos. Armando Godoy, poeta Francés. Santiago, 1935.
37596.5.10 Dehm, C. Studien zu Rutebeuf. Inaug. Diss. Würzburg, 1935.
X Cg 43566.43.705 Dekobra, Maurice. Bedroom eyes. N.Y., 1935.
43566.48.5100 Delcassan, R. Fables pour illustrer les temps actuels. Paris, 1935.
41596.42.5 Delhorbe, C. Juste et Caroline Olivier. Neuchâtel, 1935.
43566.56.100 Demonts, L. Superbea vitae. Paris, 1935.
43566.71.100 Deprat, Jacques. Le capitaine du Fai-Tsi-Long. Paris, 1935.
43566.75.161 Derème, Tristan. Le violon des muses. Paris, 1935.
43566.75.160 Derème, Tristan. Le violon des muses. 5e ed. Paris, 1935.
37569.44 Derieux, Henry. La poesie française contemporaine, 1885-1935. 2. éd. Paris, 1935.
43566.90.140 Deval, Jacques. L'âge de Juliette. Paris, 1935.

Chronological Listing

1935 - cont.

38514.44.25 Dickmann, A. Eustache Deschamps als Schilderer der Sitten seiner Zeit. Inaug. Diss. Bochum, 1935.
39564.10.75A Diderot, Denis. Supplément au voyage de Bougainville. Paris, 1935.
40587.99 Diem, Heidi. Das Bild Deutschlands in Chateaubriands Werk. Bern, 1935.
37544.65 Dimier, L. Le nationalisme littéraire et ses mefaits chez les français. Paris, 1935.
43573.77.100 Dorly, P.A. Amis; pièce en un acte. pt.1-2. Paris, 1935.
38513.72 Droz, Eugenie. Le recueil Trepperel. Paris, 1935. 2v.
38526.48.15.10 Du Bartas, Guillaume de Salluste. Works. Chapel Hill, 1935-38. 3v.
43576.7.125 Du Bois, Albert. Le sourire du roi des juifs. Paris, 1935.
39596.30 Duchêne, Albert. Les rêveries de Bernardin de St. Pierre. Paris, 1935.
40516.4.15 Ducray-Duminil, F.G. Las tardes de la Granja. Madrid, 1935.
42557.14.40 Dugas, Marcel. Verlaine; ensayo. La Habana, 1935.
43576.6.226.10 Duhamel, Georges. La nuit de la Saint-Jean. Paris, 1935.
43576.6.226 Duhamel, Georges. La nuit de la Saint-Jean. 37. éd. Paris, 1935.
43576.68.130 Dupays, Paul. Heureuses dispositions et déviations de principes. Londres, 1935.
43576.68.140 Dupays, Paul. La paix mondiale. Londres, 1935.
43576.68.150 Dupays, Paul. Vers la paix par le travail. Londres, 1935.
43576.86.100 Dutheil, Marcel. Gretel Wiesbach; roman. v.1-3. Paris, 1935.
43576.91.76 Duvernois, Henri. Rouge! Paris, 1935.
37567.346 Eckardt, Hans. Die Musikausschauung der französischen Romantik. Kassel, 1935.
38526.27.08 Elfert, Anna. Die Dichtung der Louise Labé. Inaug. Diss. Ahlen, 1935.
Htn 37543.206* Ellis, Havelock. From Rousseau to Proust. Boston, 1935.
42572.3.8 Erckmann, Emile. Le blocus. Paris, 1935.
FL 6139.35.5 Erdmann, Karl D. Das Verhältnis von Staat und Religion nach der Sozialphilosophie Rousseaus. Berlin, 1935.
37596.235 Faits Des Romains. Li fet des Romains compilé ensemble de Saluste et de Suetoine et de Lucan. Paris, 1935-38. 2v.
FL 398.74.90 Falk, Bernard. Rachel. London, 1935.
43606.87.1110 Fauconnier, G.A.M. Les étangs de la double. Paris, 1935.
40597.2.111 Ferguson, M.B. La volonté dans la "Comedie humaine" de Balzac. Thèse. Paris, 1935.
41557.10.100 Ferra, Bartomeu. Chopin and George Sand in Majorca. Palma de Mallorca, 1935.
43757.50.940 Fest, Otto. Stilistische Untersuchungen zu Romain Rolland's "Pierre et Luce". Inaug. Diss. Borna, 1935.
39544.122 Fitch, R.E. Voltaire's philosophic procedure. Thesis. Forest Grove, 1935.
43610.25.130 Fleuret, Fernand. De Ronsard à Baudelaire. Paris, 1935.
43611.89.1100 Fourest, G. Le géranium ovipare. Paris, 1935.
37555.142 Fraenkel, C. Studien zur sozialen Arbeiterlyrik in Frankreich von Beginn des 19. Jahrhundert bis zum Ausbruch des Weltkrieges. Inaug. Diss. Breslau, 1935.
43612.59.112 Francis, Robert (pseud.). Les mariés de Paris. 11. éd. Paris, 1935.
FL 370.86 Frappier, Jean. Le théâtre comique au Moyen Âge. Paris, 1935.
42557.12.65 Frets, Huberta. L'élément germanique dans l'oeuvre d'Émile Verhaeren. Paris, 1935.
42557.12.64 Frets, Huberta. L'élément germanique dans l'oeuvre d'Émile Verhaeren. Thèse. Paris, 1935.
37568.64 Friedrich, Hugo. Das antiromantische Denken im modernen Frankreich. München, 1935.
40532.25.20 Frischauser, Paul. Beaumarchais. N.Y., 1935.
42563.23.165 Fumet, Stanislas. Mission de Léon Bloy. Paris, 1935.
37576.635 Gallaud, J.S. Ten favorite French stories. N.Y., 1935.
43616.83.2140 Gastine, Louis. Les nuits galantes du Régent. Paris, 1935.
43616.83.2120 Gastine, Louis. Orgies gauloises. Paris, 1935?
43616.83.2100 Gastine, Louis. Plaisirs féodaux. Paris, 1935.
43616.83.2110 Gastine, Louis. Souveraines et princesses d'amour. Paris, 1935.
43616.83.2130 Gastine, Louis. Voluptés Gallo-Romaines. Paris, 1935.
43667.1.820 Gauss, H. Francis Jammes in sienem Verhältnis zur Antike. Inaug. Diss. Quakenbrück, 1935.
FL 377.83 Geisler, K. Das Nachwirken des Mimus in der satirischen und burlesken Literatur Frankreichs in 17. Jahrhunderts. Inaug. Diss. Würzburg, 1935.
43617.66.120 George, Nancy. Une aventure de Don Juan. Paris, 1935.
43617.4.65 Géraldy, Paul. Do, mi, sol, do! Paris, 1935.
42546.12.56 Gérard, R. Edmond Rostand. Paris, 1935.
43618.90.120 Gevers, Marie. Le voyage de frère Jean. Paris, 1935.
43620.7.100 Gibert, Charles. Poèmes vagabonds. Paris, 1935. 2v.
43620.2.79.10 Gide, André. If it die. N.Y., 1935.
43620.2.58 Gide, André. Les nouvelles nourritures. 15. éd. Paris, 1935.
43620.2.79A Gide, André. Si le grain ne meurt. 68. éd. Paris, 1935.
43620.3.40 Gilbert, M. Trois jours et trois nuits. v.1-3. Paris, 1935.
43822.49.946 Gillet, Martin Stanislas. Paul Valéry et la métaphysique. Paris, 1935.
43620.66.172 Giono, Jean. Le grand troupeau. 25. éd. Paris, 1935.
43620.66.160 Giono, Jean. Jean Le Bleu. 27. éd. Paris, 1935.
42576.63.190A Giraud, V. Anatole France. Paris, 1935.
40575.5.90 Giraud, V. La vie secrète de Sainte-Beuve. Paris, 1935.
43620.74.202 Giraudoux, Jean. La guerre de Troie n'aura pas lieu. Paris, 1935.
43620.74.200 Giraudoux, Jean. La guerre de Troie n'aura pas lieu. Paris, 1935.
43625.19.220 Godoy, Armand. Le chemin de la Croix. Paris, 1935.
43625.19.222 Godoy, Armand. Le chemin de la Croix. 3. éd. Paris, 1935.
43625.19.705 Godoy, Armand. Dal contico dei cantici alla via della croce. Milano, 1935.
43625.19.710A Godoy, Armand. The drama of the passion. London, 1935.
43625.19.133 Godoy, Armand. Le drame de la passion. Paris, 1935.
43625.19.107 Godoy, Armand. Triste et tendre. 2e éd. Paris, 1935.
39527.4.50 Gohin, Ferdinand. Les comédies attribuées à La Fontaine. Paris, 1935.
Mon 117.6 Gracey, P. Montaigne et la poésie. Thèse. Paris, 1935.
37574.405 Grant, E.M. French poetry of the nineteenth century. N.Y., 1935.
41574.209 Grant, E.M. Victor Hugo during the second republic. Northampton, 1935.

1935 - cont.

37567.345 Grillet, Claudius. Le diable dans la littérature au XIXe siècle. Paris, 1935.
43565.5.825 Groh, Hans. Der publizistische Stil des Léon Daudet. Inaug. Diss. Bottrop, 1935.
42587.52.80 Guichard, Léon. L'oeuvre et l'ame de Jules Renard. Paris, 1935.
42587.52.79 Guichard, Léon. L'ouevre et l'ame de Jules Renard. Thèse. Paris, 1935.
43628.1.405A Guitry, Sacha. If memory serves. Garden City, 1935.
43628.1.95 Guitry, Sacha. Un tour au paradis (le renard et la grenouille). Paris, 1935.
42564.55.15 Händel, H. Champfleury, sein Leben und Werk. Inaug. Diss. Borna, 1935
42563.21.84 Hafner, H.K. René Bazin peintre de la vie rurale. Thèse. Paris, 1935.
39544.62.5 Hajdu, Pál. Egy fejezet a Jézus Tarsaság Voltaire elleni Küzdelméböl. Budapest, 1935.
42576.40.271 Halévy, Ludovic. Carnets. Paris, 1935- 2v.
42554.50.15 Hanson, J.B. Le poète Charles Guérin. Thèse. Paris, 1935.
37555.137 Harrison, Ruth. An approach to French poetry. London, 1935.
40563.15 Haufe, Heinz. Jean-Jacques Ampère, 1800-1864. Inaug. Diss. Dresden, 1935.
43631.51.100 Haunaert, Louis. Journal d'une femme. Bruxelles, 1935.
37574.46.5 Henning, G.N. Representative French lyrics of the 19th century. Boston, 1935.
42524.9.81 Hergěsić, I. Zapadmjački pogledi na književnost. Zagreb, 1935.
42543.65.70 Hermant, Abel. Souvenirs de la vie mondaine. Paris, 1935.
43632.78.100 Hervilliez, G. d'. A louer meublé. Paris, 1935.
37594.48.5 Hoepffner, E. Les Lais de Marie de France. Paris, 1935.
40556.39.25 Holdsworth, F. Joseph de Maistre et l'Angleterre. Paris, 1935.
40556.39.24 Holdsworth, F. Joseph de Maistre et l'Angleterre. Thèse. Paris, 1935.
43537.89.2805 Holthoff, R. Émile Baumann und seine Bedeutung für die heuitige Zeit. Diss. Jena, 1935.
37556.15.10A Hunt, Herbert J. Le socialisme et le romantisme, étude de la presse 1830-1848. Oxford, 1935.
43667.1.825 Irsch, Anni. Die Themen der Lyrik von Francis Jammes. Inaug. Diss. Bochum, 1935.
43659.88.160 Istrati, Panait. La maison Thüringer. Paris, 1935.
37556.137 Jacoubet, Henri. Varietés de histoire littéraire de methodologie. Paris, 1935.
43667.15.100 Jacquemaine, M. Monime reine de pont, roman 1870-1885. Paris, 1935.
43667.1.155 Jammes, Francis. De tout temps à jamais. 3. éd. Paris, 1935.
37543.67 Jan, E.F. von. Die Landschaft des französischen Menschen. Weimar, 1935.
43670.1.50 Jouglet, René. Soleil-levant. v.1-3. Paris, 1935.
43670.89.240 Jouhandeau, M. Algèbre des valeurs morales. Paris, 1935.
43670.94.180 Jouve, Pierre Jean. Sueur de sang. Paris, 1935.
43670.94.400 Jouve, Pierre Jean. Ténèbre. Paris, 1935.
37556.16.75 Kanonenberg, H. Die Zeitung "L'avenir" (Paris 1830-1831). Inaug. Diss. Marburg, 1935.
43673.83.120 Kessel, Joseph. Une balle perdue. 33. éd. Paris, 1935.
43673.83.140 Kessel, Joseph. Le repos de l'équipage. 5. éd. Paris, 1935.
38564.49 Klaus, Hermann. Jean de la Bruyère. Inaug. Diss. Berlin, 1935.
43620.2.120 Klippstein, P. Die Begriffswelt von André Gide. Inaug. Diss. Berlin, 1935.
40539.15.25 Kotwicz, Władysław. Jan hr. Potocki i jego podróz do Chin. Wilno, 1935.
37567.193.45 Krieg, Wera. Griechenland und der Orient. Inaug. Diss. Würzburg, 1935.
43687.15.150 Lacretelle, Jacques de. Années d'espérance. 14e éd. Paris, 1935.
43687.15.155 Lacretelle, Jacques de. La monnaie de plomb. 2e éd. Paris, 1935.
39527.10.20 La Fontaine, Jean de. Nouvelles en vers, tirée de Bocace et de l'Ariosle. Paris? 1935.
43687.27.110A La Forest-Divonne, P. de. Bénediction. 53e éd. Paris, 1935.
41578.32.10 Lamartine, Alphonse. Graziella. Campobasso, 1935.
42566.16.30 Lancier, E. Kind und junger Mensch in den Werken Alphonse Daudets. Inaug. Diss. Bochum, 1935.
43687.58.2100 Landry, Charles François. La légende de St. Nitouche. Uzès, 1935.
37569.1.5 Lang, André. Tiers de siecle. Paris, 1935.
42536.36 Langwieler, W. Hippolyte Taine. Inaug. Diss. Heidelberg, 1935.
37543.38.21A Lanson, Gustave. Manuel d'histoire de la littérature française. 4. éd. Paris, 1935.
43687.70.100 Laparcerie-Richepin, Cora. La vraie Carmen. Paris, 1935.
42563.23.128 Laquerrière, A. Biblio-iconographie de Léon Bloy. Paris, 1935.
41522.100.85 Larbaud, Valery. Théophile Dondey de Santeny. Tunis, 1935.
38543.10.40 La Rochefoucauld, François. Les maximes suivies des réfléxions diverses. Paris, 1935.
38514.51.50 La Sale, Antoine de. Oeuvres complètes. Liège, 1935- 2v.
43687.79.100 La Salle, B. de. La pierre philosophale. Paris, 1935.
43822.49.975 Latour, Jane de. Examen de Valéry. Paris, 1935.
V43500.155 La Tour du Pin, Patrice de. L'enfer; poème avec la fac-similé d'un feuillet manuscrit. Tunis, 1935.
42576.41.65 Le Blanc, Maurice. Wanton Venus. N.Y., 1935.
43688.2.240 Le Franc, M. Hélier, fèls des bois; roman. Paris, 1935.
37574.120 Legge, J.G. Chanticleer; a study of the French Muse. London, 1935.
42554.38.10 Le Guyader, Frédéric. L'ére bretonne. 3. éd. Quimper, 1935.
37596.135.40 Lejeune-Dehousse, R. L'oeuvre de Jean Renart. Liége, 1935.
43688.61.130 Lenormand, Henri René. Crépuscule du théâtre. Paris, 1935.
42568.23.20 Léon-Gauthier, P. Jean Lorrain. (Paul Duval). Thèse. Paris, 1935.
40512.44.3 LeSage, Alain René. Histoire de Gil Blas de Santillane. Paris, 1935. 2v.
43688.88.100 Létraz, Jean de. Bichon. Paris, 1935.
Mol 612.18 Leupold, W. Die aristotelische Lehre in Molières Werken. Berlin, 1935.

Chronological Listing

1935 - cont.

39544.118	Libby, M.S. The attitude of Voltaire to magic and the sciences. N.Y., 1935.
37562.110	Lifschitz-Golden, M. Les juifs dans la littérature française du moyen âge. N.Y., 1935.
42543.1.45	Linge, Tore. La conception de l'amour dans le drame de Dumas fils et d'Ibsen. Paris, 1935.
42543.1.43	Linge, Tore. La conception de l'amour dans le drame de Dumas fils et d'Ibsen. Thèse. Paris, 1935.
39544.126	Lowenstein, R. Voltaire. Diss. Baltimore, 1935.
43694.11.2100	Lucas, Wilfrid Louis Eugène. Les cavaliers de Dieu. Paris, 1935.
41557.10.80	Lüdicke, Heinz. George Sand als Heimatdichterin. Inaug. Diss. Leipzig, 1935.
Mon 152.3	Lugli, Vittorio. Montaigne. Milano, 1935.
38527.14.10	Mabille de Poncheville, A. Valentin Conrart, le père de l'Académie française. Paris, 1935.
43697.14.190	MacOrlan, Pierre. Marquerite de la nuit. Paris, 1935.
42545.3.93	Maeterlinck, Maurice. Vor dem grossen Schweigen. Berlin, 1935.
43697.33.100	Magne, Émile. Naissance de l'Academie Française. Paris, 1935.
43697.49.100	Malèque, J. Augustin, où Le maître est lá. v.1-2. Paris, 1935.
43697.52.710A	Malraux, André. The royal way. N.Y., 1935.
43697.52.130	Malraux, André. Le temps du mépris. 5e ed. Paris, 1935.
V43500.191	Marca, René. Capitales. Paris, 1935.
43697.75.4110	Marchon, Albert. Trésor en Espagne. 6. éd. Paris, 1935.
43697.75.6100	Mardelle, M. Pierruche au soleil. Paris, 1935.
40535.27.10	Marivaux, Pierre Carlet de Chamblain de. Théâtre. Paris, 1935. 2v.
43697.76.3130	Martet, Jean. La partie de boules. v.1-4. Paris, 1935.
43697.79.160	Mary, André. Le livre nocturne. Paris, 1935.
38585.16.45	Maulnier, Thierry. Racine. Paris, 1935.
43697.88.470	Mauriac, François. La fin de la nuit. Paris, 1935.
43697.88.420A	Mauriac, François. Le mal. Paris, 1935.
43697.89.765	Maurois, André. Ricochets. N.Y., 1935.
39544.124A	Maurois, André. Voltaire. 60e éd. Paris, 1935.
43698.25.135	Meersch, M. van der. Invasion 14; roman. Paris, 1935.
37544.53	Mélanges de littérature d'histoire et de philologie offerts a Paul Laumonier. Paris, 1935.
43698.62.100	Menuau, Georges. Choc en retour. Paris, 1935.
43698.74.2100	Mercier, Max. Conscience. Paris, 1935.
41522.3.25	Merz, F. Das psychologisch-problematische bei Barbey d'Aurevilly und seine Wurzeln. Inaug. Diss. Bielefeld, 1935.
V43500.205	Messiaen, Alain. Les rues s'allongent comme des plaintes. Paris, 1935.
43698.200.105	Michaux, Henri. La nuit remue. 2. éd. Paris, 1935.
37566.75	Millequant, P. Tableau de la littérature française du romantisme à nos jours. Berlin, 1935.
Mol 195.50	Molière, Jean Baptiste Poquelin. L'école des femmes; comédie. Paris, 1935.
Mol 39.35A	Molière, Jean Baptiste Poquelin. The principal comedies of Molière. N.Y., 1935.
Mol 19.35	Molière, Jean Baptiste Poquelin. Théâtre de 1655 à 1660. Paris, 1935.
42545.38.21	Monnier, Henry. Morceaux choisis. Paris, 1935.
Mon 32.35A	Montaigne, Michel de. The autobiography...selected...by M. Lowenthal. Boston, 1935.
43701.63.150	Montherlant, Henry de. Service inutile. 9e éd. Paris, 1935.
FL 379.94	Moore, A.P. The Genre Paissard and the French stage of the eighteenth century. N.Y., 1935.
43701.74.255	Morand, Paul. Rond-point des Champs-Elysées. 10e éd. Paris, 1935.
37543.207	Mornet, D. A short history of French literature. N.Y., 1935.
43705.83.110	Natanson, J. L'été; comédie en 3 actes. Paris, 1935.
43706.55.124	Némirovsky, Irène. Le vin de solitude; roman. Paris, 1935.
37564.128	Ninow, Otto. Die Komposition des französischen idealistischen Romans im 17. Jahrhundert nach seinen Hauptvertretern. Inaug. Diss. Halle, 1935.
43688.61.810	Oria, José A. El teatro de Lenormand. Buenos Aires, 1935.
43737.34.150	Pagnol, Marcel. Merlusse. Paris, 1935.
38514.50.5	Paris, Gaston. Chansons du XVe siècle. Paris, 1935.
37555.139	Patterson, W.F. Three centuries of French poetic theory 1328-1630. pt.1-4. Ann Arbor, 1935. 2v.
43554.2.850	Paul Claudel; l'homme, le chrétien, l'oeuvre. Juvisy, 1935.
43738.41.130	Peisson, Edouard. Le chalutier 304. Paris, 1935.
43620.2.130	Pell, E.E. André Gide; l'evolution de sa pensée religieuse. Thèse. Grenoble, 1935.
43738.97.140	Peyre, Joseph. Coups durs. 11e éd. Paris, 1935.
43738.97.110	Peyre, Joseph. Sang et lumières. Paris, 1935.
43741.11.100	Pic, M. La Féerie interieure; poèmes. Paris, 1935.
43744.67.826	Pierre-Quint, Léon. Marcel Proust. Paris, 1935.
43741.50.2100	Piller, Pedro R. El prófugo. Valencia, 1935. 2 pam.
43741.50.120	Pillionnel, J.H. Les tragiques de l'après-guerre (1918-21). Paris, 1935.
43741.88.140	Pittard, Hélène (Mme.). Le nouveau Lazare. pts.1-3. Paris, 1935.
38557.24.50	Polenghi, M. Benigno Bossuet. Torino, 1935.
43743.75.130	Porché, François. Un roi, deux dames et un valet. Paris, 1935.
Mon 194.10	Porteau, Paul. Montaigne et la vie pédagogique de son temps. Thèse. Paris, 1935.
Mon 194.11	Porteau, Paul. Montaique et la vie pédagogique de son temps. Paris, 1935.
43743.98.1100	Pozzi, C. Peau d'âme. Paris, 1935.
40522.9.55	Prévost, Antoine F. Manon Lescaut. N.Y., 1935.
42542.59.88	Pronier, Ernest. La vie et l'oeuvre de François de Curel. Paris, 1935.
43744.67.75A	Proust, Marcel. Lettres à Walter Berry. Paris, 1935.
43752.57.140	Ramuz, Charles Ferdinand. Joie dans le ciel. 23. éd. Paris, 1935.
43752.85.110	Ratel, Simonne. Le raison vert. Paris, 1935.
37558.67.10	Le rayon annuaire du cercle français de l'université Fordham à New York, 1935. N.Y., 1935?
41558.30.5	Reinholdt, H. Die moralischen, religiösen und sozialen Ideen in den Romanen Frédéric Souliés. Inaug. Diss. Münster, 1935.
43753.99.2100	Reynaud, J. Delpheca. St. Félicien, 1935.
38575.42	Rivaille, L. Pierre Corneille, correcteur de ses premières. Thèse. Paris, 1935.

1935 - cont.

43756.87.100	Rivière, Isabelle. Le bouquet de roses rouges. 8. éd. Paris, 1935.
42514.28.120	Roche, A.V. Les idées traditionalistes en France et le traditionisme de Charles Maurras. Urbana, 1935.
43757.50.670	Rolland, Romain. Par la révolution. Paris, 1935.
42584.25.105	Romains, J. Zola et son exemple. Paris, 1935.
43757.3.140	Romains, Jules. Le vin blanc de la villette. 13e éd. Paris, 1935.
FL 398.17.50	Ronzis, R. de. Aimée Desclée. Roma, 1935.
42557.12.80	Rosenbaum, Ruth. Die Natur in der Lyrik Verhaerens. Inaug. Diss. Borna, 1935.
42578.22.110	Rosny, J.H. La sauvage aventure. Paris, 1935.
42578.22.10.60	Rosny, J.H. Le vampire de Bethnal Green. Paris, 1935.
42578.22.105	Rosny, J.H. La vengeance. Paris, 1935.
42546.15.7.40	Rostand, Edmond. The far princess. Boston, 1935.
42581.33.90	Rouchon, Ulysse. La vie bruyante de Jules Vallès. St. Etienne, 1935-37. 2v.
43757.92.120	Roussel, Raymond. Comment j'ai écrit certains de mes livres. Paris, 1935.
43761.44.110	St. Soline, Claire. D'une haleine. Paris, 1935.
40575.7.20	Sainte-Beuve, Charles A. Correspondance générale recueillie classée. Paris, 1935-58. 16v.
V43500.289	Salonne, Marie Paule. L'ossuaire charnel. Saint-Brieuc, 1935.
40535.14.510	Salvatore, P.J. Favart's unpublished plays. N.Y., 1935.
43761.6.130	Sarment, Jean. L'impromptu de Paris. Paris, 1935.
43761.6.120	Sarment, Jean. Madame Quinze. Paris, 1935.
37568.66A	Saurat, Denis. Modernes. Paris, 1935.
43763.38.140	Schlumberger, Jean. Histoire de quatre potiers. Paris, 1935.
41522.18.85	Schröer, C. Les petits poèmes en prose von Baudelaire. Inaug. Diss. Leipzig, 1935.
37567.339	Schwarz, Adam. Studien zum Fortschritts- und Humanitätsgedanken in der französischen Romantik. Inaug. Diss. Würzburg, 1935.
37567.215.10	Schwesinger, M. Die Literarischen und Buchhändlerischen Erfalge des naturalistischen Romans des 19. Jahrhundert im französischen Publikum. Inaug. Diss. Miltenberg, 1935.
37558.127	Ségu, F. L'académie des jeux floraux. Paris, 1935-36. 2v.
42586.14.6.50	Seybold, Betty. Leben und Werke von Marguerite Audoux. Inaug. Diss. Würzburg, 1935.
FL 394.134	Siaud, Simon. La comédie française, son statut juridique. Thèse. Lyon, 1935.
43769.54.220	Simenon, Georges. Les Pitard. 38. éd. Paris, 1935.
43769.54.365	Simenon, Georges. Quartier nègre. 39 éd. Paris, 1935.
37530.90	Société des lettres et des arts. Association des amis de Sequana. Lectures françaises; catalogue. Paris, 1935.
43775.75.100	Sorel, G. Propos de Georges Sorel. Paris, 1935.
37569.38	Stansbury, M.H. French novelist of today. Philadelphia, 1935.
42542.29.125	Stewart, Nancy. La vie et l'oeuvre d'Henri de Bornier. Paris, 1935.
42541.6.55	Stewart, Nancy. La vie et l'oeuvre d'Henri de Bornier. Thèse. Paris, 1935.
43779.41.1100	Stiénon du Pré, Jean André. Alterable délice. Saint-Félicien-en-Vivarais, 1935.
37566.88	Stock, P.V. Mémorandum d'un éditeur. Paris, 1935.
42586.63.20	Streidl, R. Gobineau in der französischen Kritik. Inaug. Diss. Würzburg, 1935.
43688.7.805	Striegler, H. Philéas Lebesgue, ein Dichter der Pikardie. Inaug. Diss. Engelsdorf, 1935.
43780.5.110	Suarès, André. Trois hommes. Paris, 1935.
42576.15.41A	Thibaudet, A. Gustave Flaubert. 6. éd. Paris, 1935.
37569.40.40	Topass, J. La pensée en révolte, essai sur le surrealisme. Photoreproduction. Bruxelles, 1935.
V43500.311	Trente poèmes de Philippe Chabaneix. Paris, 1935.
43793.67.150	Troyat, Henri. Le vivier. Paris, 1935.
43822.49.14A	Valéry, Paul. Discours. Paris, 1935.
43822.49.415	Valéry, Paul. État de la vertu. Paris, 1935.
43822.49.175	Valéry, Paul. Poésies. 34e éd. Paris, 1935.
42581.33.15	Vallès, Jules. Jacques Vingtras, l'insurgé, 1871. Paris, 1935.
42581.33.30	Vallès, Jules. Les réfractaires. Paris, 1935.
37530.80	Varillon, F. Bibliographie élémentaire de littérature française. Paris, 1935.
38571.26.10	Vedel, Valdemar. Deux classiques Français. Paris, 1935.
43823.75.200	Vercel, Roger. Remorques; roman. Paris, 1935.
42557.11.4	Verhaeren, Émile. Choix de poèmes. 39. éd. Paris, 1935.
42583.11.7	Verne, Jules. Hector Servadac. N.Y., 1935.
43823.77.140	Verneuil, Louis. L'amant de Madame Vidal. Paris, 1935.
43823.77.150	Verneuil, Louis. Dora Nelson, un film de Louis Verneuil. pt.2. Paris, 1935.
41564.14.10	Vigny, Alfred de. Le journal d'un poète. Paris, 1935.
Mon 132.5.20	Villey, P. Montaigne devant la postérité. Paris, 1935.
38514.20.15.13	Villon, François. Oeuvres. Paris, 1935.
43824.59.120	Vilmorin, L. de. Histoire d'aimer. 11e éd. Paris, 1935.
43556.49.810	Voigt, W. Colette, Leben und Werk. Inaug. Diss. Jena, 1935.
37565.82	Werner, Erich. Das Literarische Porträt in Frankreich im 18. Jahrhundert. Inaug. Diss. Leipzig, 1935.
41522.3.22	Werner, J. Die aristokratische Lebensanschauung von Jules Barbey d'Aurevilly. Inaug. Diss. Berlin, 1935.
42555.44.25	Winkel, Joseph. Mallarmé-Wagner-Wagnerismus. Inaug. Diss. Bückeburg, 1935.
Mon 133.2	Wittkomer, E. Die Form der Essais von Montaigne. Diss. Berlin, 1935.
38525.22.45.55A	Wolfe, Humbert. Ronsard and French romantic poetry. Oxford, 1935.
FL 371.79A	Wright, J.G. A study of the themes of the resurrection in the mediaeval French drama. Bryn Mawr, 1935.
41555.48	Yu, Hous Jali. Prosper Mérimée, romancier et nouvelliste. Thèse. Lyon, 1935.
42584.19.4.10	Zola, Emile. Le rêve. Paris, 1935.
37558.67	1635-1935. Trois siècles de l'académie française. Paris, 1935.

1936

43512.75.170	Achard, Marcel. Noix de coco. Paris, 1936.
42557.20.170	Adam, Antoine. Le vrai Verlaine; essai psychanalytique. Paris, 1936.
42557.20.172	Adam, Antoine. Le vrai Verlaine; essai psychanalytique. Thèse. Paris, 1936.
37596.23.20A	Adam (Mystery). Le jeu d'Adam et Ève. Paris, 1936.

1936 - cont.

37596.26.25 Aléxius, Saint. Légend. La vita di S. Alessio. Firenze, 1936.
37574.167 Almeida, G. de. Poetas de França. São Paulo, 1936.
43523.41.150 Amiel, Denys. La femme en fleur. Paris, 1936.
40587.101 André-Vincent, P. Les idées politiques de Chateaubriand. Montpellier, 1936.
40587.102 André-Vincent, P. Les idées politiques de Chateaubriand. Montpellier, 1936.
37574.654 Anthologie des poètes de la N.R.F. 8. éd. Paris, 1936.
43527.3.250 Aragon, Louis. Anciet, ou Le panorama. 8. éd. Paris, 1936.
43527.3.130 Aragon, Louis. Les beaux quartiers. 9th ed. Paris, 1936.
43527.3.705 Aragon, Louis. The bells of Basel. N.Y., 1936.
43528.53.100 Armandy, A. L'arc-en-ciel de lume. Paris, 1936.
43528.60.100 Arnauld, C. Anthologie Celine Arnauld. Bruxelles, 1936.
43528.60.110 Arnauld, C. Heures intactes. Bruxelles, 1936.
43528.88.100 Artus, Louis. Mon mal et moi; roman. Paris, 1936.
37567.352 Asztrik, G. Index romain et littérature française à l'époque romantique. Budapest, 1936.
38527.28.15 Aubigné, Théodore Agrippa d'. Les tragiques. Paris, 1936.
42542.10.5.17 Augier, Émile. Le gendre de M. Poirier. Boston, 1936.
42542.10.5.15 Augier, Émile. Le gendre de M. Poirier. N.Y., 1936.
43532.23.100 Aveline, Claude. Le prisonnier. Paris, 1936.
43535.54.110 Aymé, Marcel. Le moulin de la sourdine. 35e éd. Paris, 1936.
40553.10.25 Bach, W. Benjamin Constant und die Politik, 1767-1802. Inaug. Diss. Engelsdorf, 1936.
40596.16.50 Balzac, Honoré de. Sténie ou les erreurs philosophiques. Paris, 1936.
40597.83 Balzac, Honoré de. Sténie ou Les erreurs philosophiques. Paris, 1936.
38542.9 Balzac, J.L.G. de. Oeuvres choisies. Paris, 1936.
43537.73.102 Barbarin, George. Jesusa de Guipuzcoa. Paris, 1936.
43537.73.100 Barbarin, George. Jesusa de Guipuzcoa. pt. 1-2. Paris, 1936.
37547.70 Barrière, P. La vie intellectuelle en Périgord, 1550-1800. Bordeaux, 1936.
43537.88.110 Baty, Gaston. Madame Bovary; vingt tableaux adaptés. Paris, 1936.
41522.13.8.78 Baudelaire, Charles. Flowers of evil. 3. ed. N.Y., 1936.
41574.213 Bauer, H.F. Les "Ballades" de Victor Hugo. Paris, 1936.
42563.21.27 Bazin, René. Etapes de ma vie. Paris, 1936.
42563.21.70.5 Bazin, René. Stéphanette. N.Y., 1936.
43538.13.100 Beaumont, G. La longue nuit. Paris, 1936.
41543.22.20 Beguin, Albert. Gerard de Nerval. Paris, 1936.
43822.49.980A Bendz, E. Paul Valéry et l'art de la prose. Göteborg, 1936.
37556.116 Benedek, A. A francia szellemesség a XVIII században. Budapest, 1936.
Mol 702.8 Benjamin, R. Molière. 21e éd. Paris, 1936.
43538.61.80 Benoît, Pierre. Saint Jean d'Arce. Paris, 1936.
43538.74.250 Béraud, Henri. Trois ans de colère. Paris, 1936.
38526.13.275 Bergounioux, L.A. Guillaume Du Buys, 1520?-1594. Paris, 1936.
43538.76.105A Bernanos, Georges. Journal d'un curé de campagne. Paris, 1936.
43538.76.110 Bernanos, Georges. Journal d'un curé de campagne. Paris, 1936.
42563.37.81 Bernonille, G. Paul Bourget. Paris, 1936.
43538.76.7100 Bernouard, F. Franchise militaire. 2. éd. Paris, 1936.
42542.29.54 Bernstein, H. Espoir; pièce en cinq actes. Paris, 1936.
42542.29.68 Berr, Georges. Les fontaines lumineuses. Paris, 1936.
43538.77.3100 Berthault, François. Vaisseaux solaires. Paris, 1936.
42563.23.8.77 Bertrand, Louis. The art of suffering. N.Y., 1936.
42563.23.8.65 Bertrand, Louis. Sur la route du sud. 8. éd. Paris, 1936.
40582.8.20 Beyle, Henri. La charteuse de Parme. Paris, 1936.
40582.3.17 Beyle, Henri. Mélanges intimes et Marginalia. Paris, 1936. 2v.
FL 398.7.44 Binet-Valmer, G. Sarah Bernhardt. Paris, 1936.
43540.74.180 Birabeau, André. Fiston; comédie en quatre actes. Paris, 1936.
43543.13.230 Bloch, J.R. Naissance d'une culture. 7. éd. Paris, 1936.
41596.4.70 Bock, M. Symbolistisches in den Dramen von Alfred de Musset. Inaug. Diss. Berlin, 1936.
42554.14.210 Bocquet, Léon. La lumière d'Hellas. Paris, 1936.
38565.21.15 Boileau Despréaux, Nicolas. Boileau. Paris, 1936.
43544.55.100 Bommart, Jean. Blanc et rouge. Paris, 1936.
FL 378.22 Borgerhoff, E.B.O. The evolution of liberal theory and practice in the French theater, 1680-1757. Diss. Princeton, 1936.
37595.68 Bossaut, R. La poésie lyrique au Moyen Âge. Paris, 1936.
38557.30.36 Bossuet, J.B. Oraisons funèbres. Argenteuil, 1936.
43544.87.5100 Bourdet, E. Margot. Paris, 1936.
43544.89.110 Bousquet, Joë. La tisane de Sarments. Paris, 1936.
42563.38.517 Bovet, M.A. Noces blanches. 3. éd. Paris, 1936.
42563.39.028 Boylesve, René. Varia. Paris, 1936.
FL 391.144A Brasillach, Robert. Animateurs de théâtre. Paris, 1936.
43545.4.4230 Brasillach, Robert. Le marchand d'oiseaux. Paris, 1936.
37569.40.20 Breton, André. What is surrealism? London, 1936.
42584.25.300 Brulat, P. Histoire populaire de Emile Zola. Paris, 1936.
FL 6139.36.5 Brunello, Bruno. Gian Giacomo Rousseau. Modena, 1936.
43545.91.100 Brunet, G. Ombres vivantes. Paris, 1936.
42563.18.245 Busse, Curt-Ulrich. Das regionalistische Programm bei Maurice Barrès dargestellt nach den Werken seiner Période de l'énergie nacionale. Inaug. Diss. Bochum, 1936.
37576.637 Calvert, C.V. The French newspaper. London, 1936.
42563.23.85 Carton, Paul. Un héro de Dieu, Léon Bloy. Paris, 1936.
43550.82.105 Cassou, Jean. Les massacres de Paris. 12. éd. Paris, 1936.
42563.21.100 Catta, Tony. Un romancier de vraie France, René Bazin. Paris, 1936.
37569.58 Cavallucci, G. Quelques maîtres d'aujourd'hui. Naples, 1936.
42565.48.12 Celières, A. Victor Cherbuliez::romancier, publiciste, philosophe. Thèse. Paris, 1936.
V43500.65 Chabaneix, Philippe. D'un coeur sombre et secret; poèmes. Saint-Félicien-en-Vivarais, 1936.
37569.42.5 Chaigne, L. Vie et oeuvres d'écrivains. Paris, 1936.
43552.3.110 Chaine, Pierre. L'heure H...; comédie en trois actes. Paris, 1936.
39533.8.15 Chapelain, Jean. Opuscules critiques publiés. Paris, 1936.
43552.5.180 Chardonne, Jacques. Porcelaine de Limoges. Paris, 1936.
41557.10.120 Charpentier, J. George Sand. 11. ed. Paris, 1936.
43552.5.1120.5 Chartier, Émile. Histoire de mes pensées. 3e éd. Paris, 1936.

1936 - cont.

43552.5.1120 Chartier, Émile. Histoire de mes pensées. 7e éd. Paris, 1936.
40586.28.65 Chateaubriand, F.A.R. Deux livres des mémoires d'outre-tombe. Paris, 1936. 2v.
40586.20.10 Chateaubriand, F.A.R. Les martyrs. Paris, 1936.
43552.24.162 Chérau, Gaston. Le petit Dagrello. Paris, 1936.
43552.25.2100 Chevallier, Gabriel. Clochemerle. 280e éd. Paris, 1936.
37596.9.75 Chrestien de Troyes. Oeuvres choises. Paris, 1936.
38526.12.85 Cioranescu, A. Les imitations de l'Arioste de Philippe Desportes. Paris, 1936.
38539.2.5100 Ciorxenescu, A. Les Romans de la princesse de Conti. Paris, 1936.
43554.2.155 Claudel, Paul. Figures et paraboles. 8e éd. Paris, 1936.
43554.2.231 Claudel, Paul. Toi, qui es-tu? Paris, 1936.
37565.88 Clayton, Vista. The prose poem in French literature of the eighteenth century. N.Y., 1936.
43556.1.710 Cocteau, Jean. The infernal machine. London, 1936.
38537.25.230 Cohen, Gustave. Rabelais. Paris, 1936?
43556.49.450 Colette, Sidonie Gabrielle. Morceaux choisis. Paris, 1936.
43556.49.21 Colette, Sidonie Gabrielle. Textes choisis de Colette. Paris, 1936.
43556.49.155 Colette, Sidonie Gabrielle. La vagabonde. Paris, 1936.
43556.54.100 Comert, Marguerit. Poèmes de retour eternal. Paris, 1936.
38514.23.50 Cons, Louis. Etat présent des études sur Villon. Paris, 1936.
43556.77.41 Corpechot, Lucien. Souvenirs d'un journaliste. Paris, 1936-1937. 3v.
42547.15.20 Daireaux, Max. Villiers de l'Isle Adam, l'homme et l'oeuvre. Paris, 1936.
42556.28.210 Daniel-Rops, Henry. Rimbaud. Paris, 1936.
FL 383.215 Danilin, Iurii Iv. Teatral'naia zhizn' v epokhu parizhskoi kommuny. Moskva, 1936.
43565.5.165 Daudet, Léon A. Bréviaire de journalisme. Paris, 1936.
43565.92.7140 Davray, Jean. Fraicheur; roman. Paris, 1936.
43565.89.6100 Davzat, Albert. Poèmes de la douleur et du souvenir. Paris, 1936.
37565.92 Dedieu, J. Les philosophes du XVIIIe siècle. Paris, 1936.
43566.3.50 Delaquys, Georges. Saint Barbe-Bleue. pt. 1-2. Paris, 1936.
43566.48.140 Delarue-Mardrus, Lucie. L'amour attend. v. 1-3. Paris, 1936.
37569.80 Delourme, P. Trente-cinq années de politique religieuse. Paris, 1936.
37573.679 Demeur, L. Pages choisies des écrivains français de Belgique. Bruxelles, 1936.
43566.82.7840 Denoël, Robert. Apologie de mort à crédit. Paris, 1936.
43566.75.170 Derème, Tristan. L'escargot bleu. Paris, 1936.
43566.79.130 Des Gachons, J. La grande fable de J. de la Fontaine. Paris, 1936.
38526.12.50 Desportes, Philippe. Les imitations de l'Arioste. Paris, 1936.
38526.12.49 Desportes, Philippe. Les imitations de l'Arioste. Thèse. Paris, 1936.
43566.82.7100 Destouches, Louis Ferdinand. Mort à crédit. Paris, 1936.
43625.19.813 Devaux, André. Armand Godoy. Paris, 1936.
43566.94.100 Devaux, P. La lanque verte, suivie des propos de l'affranchi. Paris, 1936.
39564.8.15 Diderot, Denis. Diderot's writings on the theatre. Cambridge, Eng., 1936.
38526.13.215A Diller, Georges E. Les dames des Roches. Diss. Paris, 1936.
40526.8.60 Dimoff, Paul. La vie et l'oeuvre d'André Chénier jusqu'à la révolution française, 1762-1790. Thèse. Paris, 1936. 2v.
40526.8.61 Dimoff, Paul. La vie et l'oeuvre d'André Chénier jusqu'à la révolution française, 1762-1790. Paris, 1936. 2v.
37562.140 Don, Blanche H. The varying attitude toward women in French literature of the fifteenth century. N.Y., 1936.
Mon 170.4 Dréano, M. La pensée religieuse de Montaigne. Thèse. Paris, 1936.
43574.41.140 Drieu La Rochelle, Pierre. Beloukia, roman. Paris, 1936.
38526.6.13 Du Bellay, Joachim. La defense et illustration de la langue française. Paris, 1936.
43576.7.130 Du Bois, Albert. Notre déesse. Paris, 1936.
38514.58.15 Du Castel, F.P.D. Ma grand-mère, Christine de Pisan. Paris, 1936.
37574.301 Dufay, Pierre. L'enfer des classiques. Paris, 1936.
43576.6.420 Duhamel, Georges. Discours de réception de M. Georges Duhamel. Paris, 1936.
43576.6.243 Duhamel, Georges. Le notaire du Havre. Paris, 1936.
43576.6.380 Duhamel, Georges. Tables de mon jardin. Paris, 1936.
42555.44.30 Dujardin, E. Mallarmé par un des siens. Paris, 1936.
37556.16.60 Dumas, G. Histoire du journal de Thévaux depuis 1701 jusqu'en 1762. Thèse. Paris, 1936.
42576.15.53 Dumesnil, René. "L'éducation sentimentale" de Gustave Flaubert. Paris, 1936.
43576.68.160 Dupays, Paul. Efforts. Londres, 1936.
43576.68.190 Dupays, Paul. L'été. Paris, 1936.
43576.68.170 Dupays, Paul. La femme. n.p., 1936.
43576.68.180 Dupays, Paul. Le printemps. Paris, 1936.
43576.74.110 Duran, Michel. Trois...six...neuf...; comédie en trois actes. Paris, 1936.
43576.77.155 Durtain, Luc. Suite brasileira. São Paulo, 1936.
Mol 704.5 Dussame, Béatrix. Un comédien nommé Molière. Paris, 1936.
42568.23.14.10 Duval, Paul. La ville empoisonnée. Paris, 1936.
37556.16.43 DuVal, T.E. The subject of realism in the Revue des deux mondes (1831-1863). Philadelphia, 1936.
43576.89.100 Duvant, Albert. Nida et chansons. Paris, 1936.
43576.91.70 Duvernois, Henri. Crapotte. Paris, 1936.
37543.500A Ellis, Havelock. From Rousseau to Proust. London, 1936.
43591.89.705 Éluard, Paul. Thorns of thunder. London, 1936.
43593.88.110 Entrevaux, V. d'. Compagnons de chaine. pt. 1-3. Paris, 1936.
42572.27.10 Erckmann, Emile. Maître Gaspard Fix. Paris, 1936.
42556.28.145 Étiemble, René. Rimbaud. Paris, 1936.
37567.619 Evans, David Owen. Le roman social sous la monarchie de juillet. Paris, 1936.
42543.38.18 Fabre, Émile. La rabouilleuse. Paris, 1936.
37576.636.10 Fage, André. Anthologie des conteurs d'aujourd'hui. Paris, 1936.
42586.63.40 Falk, Reinhold. Die weltanschauliche Problematik bei Gobineau. Inaug. Diss. Rostock, 1936.
43607.76.4110 Fernandez, Ramon. L'homme est-il humain? Paris, 1936.
43697.88.805 Fillon, Amédie. François Mauriac. Paris, 1936.

1936 - cont.

39586.21.300 Finke, Hans. Les fréres parfaict. Inaug. Diss. Dresden, 1936.
42576.28.50 Flaubert, Gustave. Madame Bovary. Paris, 1936. 2v.
42576.33.8 Flaubert, Gustave. Trois contes. Paris, 1936.
42576.33.8.3 Flaubert, Gustave. Trois contes. Paris, 1936.
42554.33.41 Fontainas, A. Confession d'un poète. Paris, 1936.
43611.1.39A Fort, Paul. L'arlequin de plomb. Paris, 1936.
V43500.115 Fourcade, Claude. De flamme et d'ombre. Paris, 1936.
43611.5.28 Fournier, Alain. Le grand meaulnes. Paris, 1936.
43611.94.110 Fowlie, W.A. Matines et vers, 1933-1935. Paris, 1936.
43612.4.1100 Francillon, Clarisse. Béatrice et les insectes. Paris, 1936.
43612.58.6100 Francis, Louis. La neige de Galatie. 7. éd. Paris, 1936.
37544.43 Fransen, J. Iets over vergelijkende literatuurstudie, Perioden en Invaloeden. Groningen, 1936.
43612.5.150 Fraudet, René. Le lieutenant de Gibraltar. Paris, 1936.
42576.15.83 Frejlich, Hélène. Les amants de Mantes, Flaubert et Louise Calet. Paris, 1936.
40529.31.85 Fusil, Casimir Alexandre. Sylvain Maréchal. Paris, 1936.
37562.170 Gambier, H. Les trois grands siècles du moyen âge (XIe-XIIe-XIIIe). Treviso, 1936.
37563.66 Gambier, Henri. Italie et renaissance poétique en France. Padova, 1936.
37596.30.10 Garnier de Pont Sainte Maxence. La vie de Saint Thomas Becket. Paris, 1936.
37597.12.15 Garvey, C. The syntax of the declinable words in the roman de la rose. Washington, 1936.
38585.16.65 Geleerd, Sara. Les traductions hollandaises de Racine au XVIIe et au XIIIe siècles. Zutphen, 1936.
43619.24.200 Ghéon, Henri. Chants de la vie et la foi, 1897-1934. Paris, 1936.
43619.24.180 Ghéon, Henri. Le pauvre sous l'escalier. 25. éd. Paris, 1936.
43619.24.210 Ghéon, Henri. The secret of the curé d'Ars. London, 1936.
43620.2.72 Gide, André. Genevieve. 31. éd. Paris, 1936.
43620.2.69 Gide, André. Nouvelles pages de journal, 1932-35. Paris, 1936.
43620.1.58 Gilbert, Oscar P. Mollenard. 8. éd. Paris, 1936.
38539.13.81 Ginzl, W. Puget de La Serre. Inaug. Diss. Rostock, 1936.
43620.66.140 Giono, Jean. Le chant du monde. 39. éd. Paris, 1936.
43620.66.150 Giono, Jean. Que ma joie demeure; roman. Paris, 1936.
43620.66.190 Giono, Jean. Les vraies richesses. Paris, 1936.
37543.326 Glasser, R. Studien zur Geschichte des französischen Zeitbegriffs. München, 1936.
42586.68.66 Gobineau, Arthur de. Lettres à deux athéniennes, 1868-1881. Athènes, 1936.
42556.28.150 Godchot, S. Arthur Rimbaud, ne varietur. Nice, 1936-37. 2v.
43625.19.230 Godoy, Armand. Rome. Paris, 1936.
43626.5.140 Grasset, B. Commentaires. Paris, 1936.
43626.22.160 Green, Julien. Miniat. Paris, 1936.
37555.144 Gregh, F. Portrait de la poésie française au XXe siècle. Paris, 1936.
42587.52.73 Guichard, Léon. L'interprétation graphique. Thèse. Paris, 1936.
42587.52.75 Guichard, Léon. L'interpretation graphique cinématographique et musicale des oeuvres de Jules Renard. Paris, 1936.
41542.4.55 Guillaumie-Reicher, G. Théophile Gautier et l'Espagne. Thèse. Ligugé, 1936.
41574.636 Guillaumie-Reicher, Gilberte. Le voyage de Victor Hugo en 1843: France, Espagne, Pays basque. Paris, 1936.
41578.111 Guillemin, H. Le Jocelyn de Lamartine. Thèse. Paris, 1936.
43628.42.112 Guillevic, Eugène. Le sang noir. 31e éd. Paris, 1936.
43628.42.100 Guilloux, Louis. Histoires de brigands. Paris, 1936.
43628.41.6100 Guinle, Alexandre. Visage de la France. Paris, 1936.
43628.1.406 Guitry, Sacha. If memory serves. Garden City, 1936.
43628.1.100 Guitry, Sacha. Quand jouons-nous la comédie! Paris, 1936.
43628.99.100 Guyot, C. La légende de la ville d'Ys, d'après les anciens textes. Paris, 1936.
FL 6119.36 Guyot, Charly. De Rousseau à Mirabeau. Neuchâtel, 1936.
37563.64 Haag, H. Der Gestaltwandel der Kupplerin in der französischen Literatur des 16. und 17. Jahrhunderts. Marburg, 1936.
42524.19.30 Hacking, Elton. Ferdinand Brunetière. Madison, 1936.
43631.2.50 Hamp, Pierre. Marée fraiche. 5. éd. Paris, 1936.
37565.90 Hastings, H. Man and beast in French thought of the eighteenth century. Baltimore, 1936.
40517.23.50 Heilmann, E. Charles Pinot Duclos, ein Literat des 18. Jahrhunderts und seine Beziehungen zu Rousseau. Inaug. Diss. Würzburg, 1936.
FL 6139.36 Hellweg, Martin. Der Begriff des Gewissens bei J.J. Rousseau. Marburg, 1936.
43632.6.180A Henriot, Émile. Tout va finir. Paris, 1936.
42555.58.80 Herlihy, J.F. Catulle Mendès: critique dramatique et musical. Thèse. Paris, 1936.
42543.65.60 Hermant, Abel. Chroniques de Lancelot du temps. (1933-1936). Paris, 1936-38. 2v.
38567.35 Hervier, M. L'art poétique de Boileau. Paris, 1936.
43633.1.40 Hirsch, Charles H. L'homme aux sangliers. Paris, 1936.
37562.190 Hoffmann, K. Themen der französischen Lyrik im 12. und 13. Jahrhundert. Inaug. Diss. Freiburg, 1936.
40535.32.15 Holzbecher, Karl. Denkart und Denkform von Pierre de Marivaux. Inaug. Diss. Berlin, 1936.
41571.17.10 Hugo, Victor. Les chandeliers de l'évêque; episodes des misérables de Victor Hugo. Boston, 1936.
42576.65.80.15 Huysmans, Joris Karl. La cathédrale, chartres. London, 1936.
43659.88.150 Istrati, Panait. Le bureau de placement. Paris, 1936.
43667.14.21 Jacob, Max. Morceaux choisis. Paris, 1936.
43667.14.220 Jacob, Max. Saint Matorel. 3. éd. Paris, 1936.
43667.51.300 Jaloux, Edmond. La chute d'Icare. Paris, 1936.
43667.1.175 Jammes, Francis. Dieu, l'âme et le sentiment. 13. éd. Paris, 1936.
43667.1.170 Jammes, Francis. Le pélerin de Lourdes. 9. éd. Paris, 1936.
43667.1.185 Jammes, Francis. Sources. Paris, 1936.
43670.83.104 Josset, André. Élizabeth, la femme sans homme. Paris, 1936.
43670.83.100 Josset, André. Élizabeth, la femme sans homme. Paris, 1936.
43670.89.190 Jouhandeau, M. Le saladier. 2. éd. Paris, 1936.
V37573.730 Journées du livre. Dans le jardin des lettres: parni nos auteurs contemporains. Paris, 1936.
43743.2.81 Just, Otto. Alfred Poizat. Inaug. Diss. Borna, 1936.

1936 - cont.

37567.343.10 Kahn, Gustave. Les origines du symbolisme. Paris, 1936.
41578.109 Kaiser, P. Lamartine und die Musik. Inaug. Diss. München, 1936.
37574.145 Kastner, L.E. A book of French verse from Marot to Mallarme. Cambridge, Eng., 1936.
43673.83.230 Kessel, Joseph. La passante du sans-souci. Paris, 1936.
37596.10.130 Königer, H. Die Darstellung der Personen bei Chrétien de Troyes. Inaug. Diss. München, 1936.
38575.23.65 Krauss, Werner. Corneille als politischer Dichter. Marburg, 1936.
42566.16.40 Kroff, Alexander. Alphonse Daudet et la Provence. Thèse. Paris, 1936.
37543.228 Krüger, P. Fransk litteraer kritik indtil 1830. København, 1936.
43687.15.210 Lacretelle, Jacques de. Le demie-dieu on le voyage de Grèce. Paris, 1936.
43687.15.130 Lacretelle, Jacques de. L'écrivain public. 14e éd. Paris, 1936.
41554.15.10 Lacroix, Paul. My republic. Chicago, 1936.
37566.95 Lafargue, P. Critiques littéraires. Paris, 1936.
43687.27.705 La Forest-Divonne, P. de. Benediction. N.Y., 1936.
41578.29.50 Lamartine, Alphonse. Les visions. Paris, 1936.
41578.29.48 Lamartine, Alphonse. Les visions. Thèse. Paris, 1936.
43687.89.2100 La Varende, Jean de. Pays d'Ouche, 1740-1933. Paris, 1936.
38526.12.81 Lavaud, J. Un poète de cour. Paris, 1936.
38526.12.80 Lavaud, J. Un poète de cour au temps des derniers valois. Philippe Desportes, 1546-1606. Thèse. Paris, 1936.
42544.25.85 Lavedan, Henri. Avant l'oubli. Paris, 1936.
41564.55.40 Lebbin, E. Alfred de Vignys Beziehungen zu England und zur englischen Literatur. Inaug. Diss. Halle, 1936.
43688.15.5705 Le Corbeau, A. The forest giant. Garden City, 1936.
38575.23.55 Le Corbeiller, A. Pierre Corneille intime. Paris, 1936.
37544.49 Leib, H. Les cas de mésalliances dans le roman et le théâtre. Thèse. Berlin, 1936.
38575.23.42 Lemoine, Jean. La première du Cid, le théâtre, les interprètes d'après des documents inédits. Paris, 1936.
43688.61.240 Lenormand, Henri René. Les ratés. Paris, 1936?
43688.79.110 Lescure, Pierre de. Tendresse inhumaine. Paris, 1936.
39533.22.85 Letsch, Karl. La vraie histoire comique de Francion von Charles Sorel. Inaug. Diss. Bielefeld, 1936.
40586.28.63 Levaillant, M. Deux livres des mémoires d'outre-tombe. Paris, 1936. 2v.
40587.42.8 Levaillant, Maurice. Chateaubriand, Madame Récamier et les mémoires d'outre-tombe, 1830-1850. Thèse. Paris, 1936.
40587.42.10 Levaillant, Maurice. Chateaubriand, Madame Récamier et les mémoires d'outre-tombe. Paris, 1936.
39594.3.40 Levi, L.M. The political doctrine of Montesquieu's Esprit des lois. N.Y., 1936.
37569.40.30 Levy, Julien. Surrealism. N.Y., 1936.
41574.217 Ley-Deutsch, M. Le gueux chez Victor Hugo. Thèse. Paris, 1936.
39566.43 Luppol, I.K. Diderot. Paris, 1936.
43632.3.85 McAndrew, A. Louis Hémon: sa vie et son oeuvre. Thèse. Paris, 1936.
43554.2.813 Madaule, Jacques. Le drame de Paul Claudel. 2e éd. Paris, 1936.
42545.3.90 Maeterlinck, Maurice. Before the great silence. N.Y., 1936.
42545.3.100 Maeterlinck, Maurice. The hour-glass. N.Y., 1936.
42545.3.110 Maeterlinck, Maurice. L'ombre des ailes. Paris, 1936.
42545.3.70 Maeterlinck, Maurice. Pigeons and spiders (the water spider). N.Y., 1936.
42545.3.80 Maeterlinck, Maurice. Le sablier. Paris, 1936.
43697.33.110F Magne, Emile. La princesse Adélaïde ou L'amoureuse contrariée. Paris, 1936.
38576.27.31 Magnon, J. de. Tite: a tragi-comedy. Diss. Baltimore, 1936.
38523.30.15A Malherbe, François de. Poésies. Paris, 1936-37. 2v.
43697.52.715 Malraux, André. Days of wrath. N.Y., 1936.
43697.52.708 Malraux, André. Man's fate. N.Y., 1936.
43697.75.3040 Marchand, L. La vie est si courte. Paris, 1936.
38526.34.30 Marguerite d'Angoulême. La coche. Strasbourg, 1936.
37567.342 Marie, Aristide. La forêt symboliste; esprits et visages. Paris, 1936.
37564.126A Marni, A. Allegory in the French heroic poem of the seventeenth century. Princeton, 1936.
43697.76.9110 Martin du Gard, Maurice. Caractères et confidences. Paris, 1936.
43697.76.9100 Martin du Gard, Maurice. Harmonies critiques. Paris, 1936.
43697.80.1100 Maschino, Blanche. La chaine des temps. Paris, 1936.
43697.80.1110 Maschino, Blanche. Eros: la science et le rêve. Paris, 1936.
43697.80.1120 Maschino, Blanche. Le fléau divin: Némésis, poèmes. Paris, 1936.
43745.1.100 Massis, Henri. Notre ami Psichari. Paris, 1936.
43697.88.350 Mauriac, François. L'education des filles. Paris, 1936.
43697.4.45 Mauriac, François. Genitrix. 66e éd. Paris, 1936.
43697.89.176 Maurois, André. Le livre moderne illustré. Paris, 1936.
43697.89.25 Maurois, André. Textes choisis. Paris, 1936.
43697.100.150 Mazeline, Guy. Les îles du matin. Paris, 1936.
43698.25.130 Meersch, M. van der. L'empreinte du Dieu. Paris, 1936.
37576.636 Mélanges offerts à M. Abel Lefranc par ses élèves et ses amis. Paris, 1936.
38576.14.81 Mélèse, P. Donneau de Visé, fondateur du Mercure Galant. Paris, 1936.
41555.7.130 Mérimée, Prosper. Lettres de Prosper Mérimée à madame de Beaulaincourt, 1866-1870. Paris, 1936.
V43500.199 Messiaen, Alain. C'était toi, le démon! Paris, 1936.
38564.53 Michaut, G. La Bruyère. Paris, 1936.
43698.200.140 Michaux, Henri. Voyage en Grande Garabagne. Paris, 1936.
40547.14.10 Michelet, Jules. Pages littéraires. Paris, 1936.
37563.68 Mönch, Walter. Die italienische Platonrenaissance und ihre Bedeutung für Frankreichs Literatur. Berlin, 1936.
37565.84 Mohrenschildt, D.S. Russia in the intellectual life of eighteenth-century France. N.Y., 1936.
Mol 19.36 Molière, Jean Baptiste Poquelin. Théâtre. Paris, 1936?
38514.71.25 Molinet, J. Les faictz et dictz de Jean Molinet. Paris, 1936-39. 3v.
38526.34.110 Molnar, R. A Francia élet a Heptaméronban. Pécs, 1936.
43744.67.940 Monkhouse, E. La révélation de Marcel Proust. Thèse. Paris, 1936.
Mon 28.58 Montaigne, Michel de. Des livres. Paris, 1936.
Mon 28.56 Montaigne, Michel de. Du pedantisme. Paris, 1936.

Chronological Listing

1936 - cont.

43701.63.120 Montherlant, Henry de. Les jeunes filles, roman. Paris, 1936.
43701.63.120.5 Montherlant, Henry de. Les jeunes filles, roman. 3e éd. Paris, 1936.
43701.63.120.10 Montherlant, Henry de. Les jeunes filles, roman. 39e éd. Paris, 1936.
43701.63.720 Montherlant, Henry de. Perish in their pride. N.Y., 1936.
43701.63.121 Montherlant, Henry de. Pitié pour les femmes. Paris, 1936.
43701.74.135 Morand, Paul. Bug O'Shea. Dessins de Louis Icart. Paris, 1936.
43701.74.180A Morand, Paul. Les extravagants. 13e éd. Paris, 1936.
41564.55.35 Moreau, P. Les "destinées" d'Alfred de Vigny. Paris, 1936.
39544.132 Morehouse, A.R. Voltaire and Jean Meslier. New Haven, 1936.
41557.10.85 Moret, M.M. Le sentiment religieux chez George Sand. Thèse. Paris, 1936.
37543.68.25 Mornet, D. La littérature française enseignée par la dissertation. Paris, 1936.
37543.207.2 Mornet, D. A short history of French literature. N.Y., 1936.
FL 6139.36.10 Mühlenkamp, I. Der Begriff der Revolution bei Jean-Jacques Rousseau im Rahmen der Grundbegriffe seines Systems. Inaug. Diss. Leipzig, 1936.
40536.4.50 Mühlhofer, L. Abbé Jean Bernard Le Blanc, seine Leben und Werke. Inaug. Diss. Würzburg, 1936.
38585.16.55 Müller, Curt. Die "Phlldra" Racines. Inaug. Diss. Leipzig, 1936.
38526.27.45 Munn, K.M. A contribution to the study of Jean Lemaire de Belges. Diss. N.Y., 1936.
41596.26.10 Musset, Alfred de. La genèse de Lorenzaccio. Paris, 1936.
41596.26.9 Musset, Alfred de. La genèse de Lorenzaccio. Thèse. Paris, 1936.
42555.44.35 Naumann, W. Der Sprachgebrauch Mallarmé's. Inaug. Diss. Marburg, 1936.
39544.128A Naves, Alfred. Voltaire. N.Y., 1936.
43706.55.116 Némirovsky, Irène. Jézabel, roman. Paris, 1936.
42555.62.40 Niklaus, R. Jean Moréas, poète lyrique. Paris, 1936.
39566.51 Oestreicher, Jean. La pensée politique. Vincennes, 1936.
43688.61.812 Oria, José A. El teatro de Lenormand. Buenos Aires, 1936.
37562.180A Pagès, A. La poésie française en Catalogne du XIIIe siècle a la fin du XVe. Toulouse, 1936.
42576.15.110 Pantke, A. Gustave Flauberts Tentation de Saint-Antoine. Inaug. Diss. Engelsdorf, 1936.
37567.319 Paris. Bibliothèque Nationale. Cinquantenaire du symbolisme. Paris, 1936.
37544.56 Paul Emile, Sister. Le renouveau Marial dans la littérature française. Ottawa, 1936.
38523.3.32 Pauphilet, A. Clément Marot. Paris, 1936.
43737.89.2100 Pauphilet, Albert. Arc-en-ciel. Paris, 1936.
43738.41.150 Peisson, Edouard. Gens de mer. Paris, 1936.
43738.41.171 Peisson, Edouard. Mer baltique, roman. Paris, 1936.
43738.41.200 Peisson, Edouard. Mer baltique. Paris, 1936.
37555.226 Pellissier, Georges. Traité théorique et historique de versification française. 2. éd. Paris, 1936?
43738.77.150 Pérochon, Ernest. Milon. Paris, 1936.
43738.77.2100 Perrier, A. Gravitation. Paris, 1936.
43738.83.43 Pesquidoux, J.D. La harde. Paris, 1936.
Mon 126.2 Peyre, Albert. Du prestige de la pensée. Paris, 1936.
43738.97.120 Peyre, Joseph. L'homme de choc. 19e éd. Paris, 1936.
43738.97.153 Peyre, Joseph. Tema. Paris, 1936.
43740.66.100 Photiades, Vassily. Marylène. Paris, 1936.
43742.41.110 Plisnier, Charles. Mariages. Paris, 1936.
41522.6.16 Poe, Edgar Allan. Eureka, La Genèse d'un poème. Paris, 1936.
37597.52 Poème du XIIIme siècle en l'honneur de la vierge. Mons, 1936.
43743.77.1100 Portal, Georges. Un protestant. Paris, 1936.
43743.90.140 Pourrat, Henri. Toucher terre. Uzès, 1936.
38546.33.9 Pradel, Genès. Madame de Sévigné en Provence. Paris, 1936.
40597.2.113 Priault, A. Balzac avant la Comédie humaine, 1818-1829. Paris, 1936.
40597.2.112 Priault, A. Balzac avant la Comédie humaine, 1818-1829. Thèse. Paris, 1936.
43744.67.39.5 Proust, Marcel. Cities of the plain. London, 1936. 2v.
43744.67.38.10 Proust, Marcel. Du coté de chez Swann. 156. éd. Paris, 1936. 2v.
43744.67.76 Proust, Marcel. Lettres à Madame et Monsieur Émile Straus. Paris, 1936.
38514.55.20 Quinze joyes de mariage. Les quinze joyes de mariage. Paris, 1936.
38583.12.25A Racine, Jean. The best plays of Racine. Princeton, 1936.
38583.11.50 Racine, Jean. Poesies. Paris, 1936.
43752.1.40 Rageot, G. Pleine eau. v.1-2. Paris, 1936.
43752.57.797 Ramuz, Charles Ferdinand. Der bergsturz. München, 1936.
43752.57.300 Ramuz, Charles Ferdinand. Le cirque. Lausanne, 1936.
43752.57.150 Ramuz, Charles Ferdinand. Derborence. 18. éd. Paris, 1936.
42576.46.12 Rau, Erich. Das Périgord und seine Bewohner in den Romanen Eugène Le Roys. Inaug. Diss. Emsdetten, 1936.
37567.66.8A Raynaud, Ernest. En marge de la mêtée symboliste. 2e éd. Paris, 1936.
37569.40.50 Read, Herbert. Surrealism. London, 1936.
42543.49.20 Reymond, Jean. Albert Glatigny; la vie, l'homme, le poète. Paris, 1936.
42543.49.18 Reymond, Jean. Albert Glatigny: la vie, l'homme, le poète. Thèse. Paris, 1936.
43753.99.100 Reymond, M.L. Le miracle. Neuchâtel, 1936.
43743.90.130 Ringelmann, A. Henri Pourrat, geb. 1887. Inaug. Diss. Würzburg, 1936.
38575.23.67 Rivaille, Louis. Les débuts de Pierre Corneille. Paris, 1936.
38575.23.66 Rivaille, Louis. Les débuts de Pierre Corneille. Thèse. Paris, 1936.
37562.160 Röhl, G. Die idyllisch-ländlichen Motive in der altfranzösischen Literatur. Inaug. Diss. Rostock, 1936.
43757.50.460 Rolland, Romain. Compagnons de route. Paris, 1936.
42578.22.100 Rosny, J.H. Dans le calme et dans la tempête. Paris, 1936.
42578.22.10.20 Rosny, J.H. Les plus belles pages de J.H. Rosny. Paris, 1936.
FL 6002.936 Rousseau, J.J. Extraits, publiés avec une introduction. Paris, 1936.

1936 - cont.

FL 6002.936.5 Rousseau, J.J. Extraits des oeuvres autobiographiques. Paris, 1936.
37569.87 Rousseaux, A. Ames et visages du XXe siècle. 6e éd. 2. Série. Paris, 1936.
37555.512 Rudrauf, L. Rime et sex. Tartu, 1936.
42563.21.93 Ruppe, Fritz. Das Problem der Landflucht im heutigen Frankreich und seine Aktualität im Werke René Bazins. Inaug. Diss. Jena, 1936.
42546.12.57 Ryland, H. The sources of the play Cyrano de Bergerac. N.Y., 1936.
43620.2.125 Sachs, Maurice. André Gide. Paris, 1936.
FL 382.83 Sächer, H. Die Melodramatik und das romantische Drama in Frankreich. Inaug. Diss. Borna, 1936.
40597.2.114 Saint-Germès, M. Balzac considéré comme historien du droit. Thèse. Besançon, 1936.
43761.48.140 Salacrou, Armand. L'inconnue d'Arras. Paris, 1936.
37544.47 Samsami, N.D. L'Iran dans la littérature française. Paris, 1936.
37544.46 Samsami, N.D. L'Iran dans la littérature française. Thèse. Paris, 1936.
43761.59.120F Sandy, Isabelle. Quand les loups ont faim. Paris, 1936.
43761.6.140F Sarment, Jean. Le voyage a Biarritz. Paris, 1936.
43761.3.40 Savignon, André. Une femme dans chaque port. Paris, 1936.
37565.120 Schalk, Fritz. Einleitung in die Encyclopädie der französischen Aufklärung. München, 1936.
38575.23.69A Schlumberger, J. Plaisir à Corneille. 5th éd. Paris, 1936.
FL 6039.12 Schwarz, Erich. Freiheit und Staatsomnipotenz in Rousseaus "Contrat social". Inaug. Diss. Schramberg, 1936.
42563.23.87 Seillière, Ernest, Léon Bloy. Paris, 1936.
42576.15.125 Servais, T.H. Gustave Flauberts Urteile über die französische Literatur in seiner "Correspondance". Inaug. Diss. Münster, 1936.
FL 394.135 Siaud, Simon. La comédie française, son histoire, son statut. Paris, 1936.
41557.33.10 Silver, Mabel. Jules Sandeau; l'homme et la vie. Thèse. Paris, 1936. 10v.
43769.54.315 Simenon, Georges. Le charretier de la providence. Paris, 1936.
43769.54.210 Simenon, Georges. Pietr-le-Letton. Paris, 1936.
43744.67.900 Spagnoli, J.J. The social attitude of Marcel Proust. N.Y., 1936.
43776.42.705 Spitz, J. Sever the earth. London, 1936.
37566.88.10 Stock, P.V. Mémorandum d'un éditeur. 2e serie. Paris, 1936.
43780.5.150 Suarès, André. Valeurs. 9. éd. Paris, 1936.
43780.69.140 Supervielle, Jules. Bolivar. 5. éd. Paris, 1936.
40524.32.20 Tabarant, A. Le vrai visage de Restif de la Bretonne. Paris, 1936.
43788.24.130 Thérive, André. Fils du jour, roman. Paris, 1936.
37543.208 Thibaudet, A. Histoire de la littérature française de 1789 à nos jours. Paris, 1936.
42562.36.5 Thiebaut, Marcel. Edmond About. 9e éd. Paris, 1936.
40575.5.100 Thomas, Jean. Sainte-Beuve et l'école normale, 1834-1867. Paris, 1936.
38546.33.25 Tilley, A. Madame de Sévigné. Cambridge, Eng., 1936.
42578.51.100 Tinayre, Marcelle. Sainte Marie du feu. Paris, 1936.
43792.90.110 Toulet, Paul Jean. Vers inedits. Paris, 1936.
40556.45 Treves, P. Joseph de Maistre. Milano, 1936.
38525.36.25 Tristan L'Hermite, F. La folie du sage. Paris, 1936.
43793.67.140 Troyat, Henri. Grandeur nature. Paris, 1936.
43795.51.100 Tuloup, A. Aphrodite moderne; roman. Rennes, 1936.
FL 385.88 Turcotte, S.J. Les gens d'affaires sur la scène française de 1870 à 1914. Paris, 1936.
FL 363.52 Turcotte, S.J. Les gens d'affaires sur la scène française de 1870 à 1914. Thèse. Paris, 1936.
37562.130 Tuschen, A. Die Taufe in der altfranzösischen Literatur. Inaug. Diss. Wanne-Eickel, 1936.
37596.45.30 Two old French poems on St. Thibaut. New Haven, 1936.
43816.53.110 Urmatt, F. La damnation de Georges Bruckner. Paris, 1936.
43822.49.15A Valéry, Paul. L'idée fixe. Paris, 1936.
43822.49.190A Valéry, Paul. La jeune parque. Paris, 1936.
43822.49.177 Valéry, Paul. Poésies. 40e éd. Paris, 1936.
43822.49.106 Valéry, Paul. Variété III. Paris, 1936.
43757.3.300 Vasse, P. Jules Romains et les médicins. Paris, 1936.
39578.8.40 Vauvenargues, L. de C. Réflexions et maximes. Cambridge, Eng., 1936.
37567.348 Venzac, G. De Chateaubriand à Barrès aux pays de leur enfance. Paris, 1936.
43823.75.110 Vercel, Roger. Léna, roman. Paris, 1936.
43823.77.160 Verneuil, Louis. Vive le roi! pts.1-2. Paris, 1936.
37543.210 Verriest, Léon. L'évolution de la littérature française. N.Y., 1936.
43824.49.180 Vildrac, Charles. Michel Auclair. 18e éd. Paris, 1936.
38514.20.15.20 Villon, François. Les deux testaments et les ballades de François Villon. Paris, 1936.
39545.46.3.10 Voltaire, François Marie Arouet de. L'ingénu. Paris, 1936.
37574.135 Wais, Kurt. Doppelfassungen Französischer Lyrik von Marot bis Valéry. Halle, 1936.
FL 1022.5 Walberg, Emanuel. Quelques aspects de la littérature anglo-normande. Paris, 1936.
38543.34.5 Wilhelm, Kurt. Chevalier de Méré und sein Verhaltnis zu Blaise Pascal. Berlin, 1936.
43620.2.150 Wittrock, W. Der Gottesbegriff im Werk André Gides. Inaug. Diss. Marburg, 1936.
FL 371.73 Wright, E.A. The dissemination of the liturgical drama in France. Bryn Mawr, Pa., 1936.
43848.76.705 Yergath, A. The weaver by the Nile. Portland, 1936.
41596.51.35 Zévaès, A.B. Eugène Pottier et "L'International". Paris, 1936.

1937

43744.67.1020 Abatangel, L. Marcel Proust et la musique. Paris, 1937.
43523.5.100 Amat, J.C. Malespine. pt. 1-2. Paris, 1937.
39544.150 Amato, J. La grammaire et le lexique de Voltaire. Palermo, 1937?
43744.67.1040 Ames, Van Meter. Proust and Santayana; the aesthetic way of life. Chicago, 1937.
43523.41.160 Amiel, Denys. Ma liberte! Paris, 1937.
41522.18.395 Anhegger, G. Der Spleen bei Charles Baudelaire. Zürich, 1937.
43524.67.110 Anouilh, Jean. Le voyageur sans bagage. Paris, 1937.
42514.28.135 Arbellot, Simon. Maurras, homme d'action. Paris, 1937.

Chronological Listing

1937 - cont.

43528.48.120 Arland, Marcel. Les plus beaux de nos jours. 2e éd. Paris, 1937.
43528.53.110 Armandy, A. Le padrão; roman. Paris, 1937.
43528.74.100 Arrault, Albert. Eugénie Grandet. Paris, 1937.
43528.86.65A Artaud, Antonin. Les nouvelles revelations de l'être. Paris, 1937.
43531.18.1200 Audiberti, Jacques. Race des hommes. Paris, 1937.
42586.14.7 Audoux, M. Marie-Claire. Paris, 1937.
40546.9.15 Axthelm, M.S. Paul Louis Courier. Inaug. Diss. Jena, 1937.
43535.54.130 Aymé, Marcel. Gustalin; roman. 14e éd. Paris, 1937.
39527.4.55 Bailly, A. La Fontaine. Paris, 1937.
37543.218 Bainville, J. Lectures; préface de Charles Maurras. Paris, 1937.
40596.36 Balzac, Honoré de. The student's Balzac. N.Y., 1937.
43688.2.90 Barrelle, Georges. Le pelerin lyrique, Entretiens avec Louis Le Cardonnel au Palias du Roure. Paris, 1937.
42563.17.12 Barrès, Maurice. Les deracinés. Paris, 1937. 2v.
38575.23.75 Al Bassir, Mahdi. Le lyrisme de Corneille. Thèse. Montpellier, 1937.
42563.18.255 Bauer, Bernhard. Versuch über Inhalt. Stassburg, 1937.
43537.89.1200 Bauër, Gérard. Les billets de guermantes. Paris, 1937. 2v.
39598.42.5 Bauer, H. Jean-François Marmontel als Literarkritiker. Inaug. Diss. Dresden, 1937.
43537.98.3100 Bayvet, Henri. Dimanche matin. Paris, 1937.
37576.502A Bédé, J.A. Quelques textes naturalistes. N.Y., 1937.
38525.5.25 Bégne, C. Les humanistes français. Paris, 1937.
43538.5.70 Benda, Julien. La jeunesse d'un clerc. 8. éd. Paris, 1937.
43538.5.45A Benda, Julien. Précision. (1930-1937). 4. éd. Paris, 1937.
43538.5.75 Benda, Julien. Un régulier dans le siècle. Paris, 1937.
40597.2.43 Benjamin, René. La prodigieuse vie d'Honoré de Balzac. Paris, 1937.
43538.62.100 Benoit-Guyod, Georges. Histoires de gendarmes. 6. éd. Paris, 1937.
43538.76.712 Bernanos, Georges. The diary of a country priest. N.Y., 1937.
42542.29.28.170 Bernard, Tristan. La partie de bridge. Paris, 1937.
42542.29.53 Bernstein, H. Le coeur. Paris, 1937.
42535.22.12 Beuchat, Charles. Paul de Saint-Victor, sa vie, son oeuvre. Paris, 1937.
40582.9.28 Beyle, Henri. The charterhouse of Parma. N.Y., 1937.
40582.3.10 Beyle, Henri. Journal. Paris, 1937. 5v.
40582.9.15 Beyle, Henri. La chartreuse de Parme. N.Y., 1937.
40582.25.15 Beyle, Henri. Le rouge et le noir. v.1-2. Paris, 1937.
38527.29.18 Bietenbeck, K. Der Dichter Agrippa d'Aubigné als Kritiker seiner Zeit. Inaug. Diss. Borken, 1937.
43540.50.100 Billot, F. Mensonges. Paris, 1937.
43540.74.190 Birabeau, André. Pamplemousse. Paris, 1937.
43540.83.120 Bisson, André. Le pur de gloire. Paris, 1937.
Mon 112.13 Blasberg, H. Die Wortstellung bei Montaigne. Inaug. Diss. Bochum-Langendreer, 1937.
43543.13.140 Bloch, J.R. Et compagnie. 6. éd. Paris, 1937.
43543.88.116 Blum, Léon. Nouvelles conversations de Goethe avec Eckermann. 6. éd. Paris, 1937.
38566.63 Boileau Despréaux, Nicolas. Épitres. Paris, 1937.
42554.15.4 Bonnard, Abel. Savoir aimer. Paris, 1937.
40575.1.10 Bonnerot, Jean. Bibliographie de l'oeuvre de Sainte-Beuve. Paris, 1937- 3v.
42563.36.240 Bordeaux, Henry. Le maître de l'amour. Paris, 1937.
42563.36.340 Bordeaux, Henry. Le parrain. Paris, 1937.
37572.38.35 Bossuat, A. Les chroniqueurs français du moyen âge. Paris, 1937-
38557.53.260 Bossuet, J.B. Méditations sur l'évangile. Paris, 1937. 2v.
43544.87.5110 Bourdet, E. Fric-frac; pièce en cinq actes. Paris, 1937.
FL 398.12.30 Boyer, William. The romantic life of Maurice Chevalier. London, 1937.
43545.4.4100 Brasillach, Robert. Comme le temps passe. Paris, 1937.
43545.4.7100 Braunschwig, M. Regards interieurs. Paris, 1937.
40575.5.95 Bray, René. Sainte-Beuve à l'Académie de Lausanne. Paris, 1937.
38562.23.20 Breinbauer, S.A. Bedingungssätze bei Fontenelle. Inaug. Diss. Würzburg, 1937.
43545.41.7100 Brimont, Renée. Les fileuses. Paris, 1937.
43545.42.100A Brisson, P. Du meilleur av pire. Paris, 1937.
42576.65.13.60 Bron, L. Huysmans d'après des documents inédits. Paris, 1937.
42587.50.125 Brückmann, J. Hugues Rebell, ein Vorkämpfer des französischen Nationalismus. Inaug. Diss. Bonn, 1937.
39566.44 Brugmans, H. Diderot, 1710-1784. Amsterdam, 1937.
43545.89.6100 Brunet, Romain. Violet, indigo, bleu. Paris, 1937.
FL 6139.37 Buckner, M.L. A contribution to the study of the descriptive technique of Jean-Jacques Rousseau. Baltimore, 1937.
43667.1.830 Burckhardt, H. Natur und Heimat bei Francis Jammes. Inaug Diss. Würtzburg, 1937.
43550.40.160 Cahuet, Albéric. La femme aux images. pt.1-3. Paris, 1937.
43550.40.170 Cahuet, Albéric. Pontcarral. Paris, 1937.
38523.21.30 Celles, J. de. Malherbe; sa vie. Paris, 1937.
V43500.63 Chabaneix, Philippe. Le désir et les ombres. Paris, 1937.
43552.2.1130 Chadourne, Marc. Dieu créa d'abord Lilith. Paris, 1937.
43552.5.120 Chardonne, Jacques. Romanesques; roman. Paris, 1937.
43552.5.122 Chardonne, Jacques. Romanesques. Paris, 1937.
41578.40.43 Charlier, G. Aspects de Lamartine. Paris, 1937.
41522.18.100 Charpentier, John. Baudelaire. Paris, 1937.
40597.2.144A Chartier, Émile. Avec Balzac. 7. éd. Paris, 1937.
43552.5.1045 Chartier, Émile. Les saisons de l'esprit. Paris, 1937.
43552.5.1170 Chartier, Émile. Souvenirs de guerre. Paris, 1937.
43552.24.140 Chérau, Gaston. Séverin Dunastier. pt. 1-3. Paris, 1937.
43552.24.113 Chérau, Gaston. Valentine Pacquault. Paris, 1937. 2v.
43745.1.110 Chevalier, I. La vocation de Psichari. Le Sarte, 1937.
43552.25.2102 Chevallier, Gabriel. Clochemerle. 305e éd. Paris, 1937.
43552.25.2103 Chevallier, Gabriel. The scandals of Clochemerle. N.Y., 1937.
Mon 113.15A Citoleux, Marc. Le vrai Montaigne, théologien et soldat. Paris, 1937.
43554.2.310 Claudel, Paul. Les aventures de Sophie. Paris, 1937.
43554.23.100 Clément, Colette Grunbaum. Éblouissement; pièce en trois actes et quatre tableaux. Paris, 1937.
43554.63.100 Clo, Jean. Les frères perdus. Nancy, 1937.

1937 - cont.

43556.1.170 Cocteau, Jean. Les chevaliers de la table ronde. 13e éd. Paris, 1937.
43556.1.160 Cocteau, Jean. Mon premier voyage. 18e éd. Paris, 1937.
43556.49.220A Colette, Sidonie Gabrielle. Bella-vista. Paris, 1937.
40575.5.110 Combe, T.G.S. Sainte-Beuve poète et les poètes anglais. Thèse. Bordeaux, 1937.
42586.63.25 Combris, A. La philosophie des races du comte de Gobineau. Paris, 1937.
42586.63.24 Combris, A. La philosophie des races du comte de Gobineau. Thèse. Paris, 1937.
FL 398.56.50 Cottier, E. Le comédien Auvergant, Montdory. Clermont-Ferrand, 1937.
43688.2.81 Coulon, Marcel. Louis Le Cardonnel, poète et prêtre. Uzès, 1937.
38514.56.20 Coville, Alfred. Le petit Jehan de Saintré. Paris, 1937.
39544.136 Crouvezier, G. La vie de Voltaire. Paris, 1937.
37569.64 Dagher, J.A. L'Orient dans la littérature française d'après guerre 1919-1933. Beyrouth, 1937.
42576.63.185 Dargan, E.P. Anatole France, 1844-1896. N.Y., 1937.
42566.61.25 Daudet, Alphonse. Father Gaucher's elixir. Ormond Beach, Fla., 1937.
41574.27.10 Daudet, Léon. La tragique existence de Victor Hugo. Paris, 1937.
43566.47.5100 Delaquys, Georges. La naissance de Tristan. Paris, 1937.
37596.220 Des Grantz geanz; an Anglo-Norman poem. Oxford, 1937.
43566.82.7720 Destouches, Louis Ferdinand. Mea culpa and the life works of Semmelweis. Boston, 1937.
39564.6.15 Diderot, Denis. Diderot. London, 1937.
39564.9.15 Diderot, Denis. Lettre adressée à un magistrat sur le commerce de la librairie. Paris, 1937.
42563.23.90 Dillinger, W. Das Frankreichbild im Werke Léon Bloys, 1846-1917. Inaug. Diss. Düsseldorf, 1937.
V43538.76.1145 Dobraczynski, Jan. Bernanos pouriciopisatz. Lublin, 1937.
42542.65.40 Donnay, Maurice. Mes débuts à Paris. 2. éd. Paris, 1937.
43620.50.805 Dopagne, G. Maurice Gauchez. Bruxelles, 1937.
43574.41.150 Drieu La Rochelle, Pierre. Rêveuse bourgeoisie. 13. éd. Paris, 1937.
43576.9.102 Du Bos, Charles. Approximations. 7. série. Paris, 1937.
43576.6.128 Duhamel, Georges. Défense des lettres. 22. éd. Paris, 1937.
43576.6.228.5 Duhamel, Georges. Le désert de Bièvres. 13. éd. Paris, 1937.
43576.6.228 Duhamel, Georges. Le désert de Bièvres. 26. éd. Paris, 1937.
43576.6.270 Duhamel, Georges. Deux patrons, suivi de vie et mort d'un héros de roman. Paris, 1937.
43576.6.230 Duhamel, Georges. Les maîtres. 26. éd. Paris, 1937.
43576.6.21 Duhamel, Georges. Textes choisis de Georges Duhamel. Paris, 1937.
43576.6.225 Duhamel, Georges. Vue de la Terre Promise. Paris, 1937.
43576.6.830 Duhamel et nous. Paris, 1937.
42576.15.8 Dumesnil, René. Bibliographie de Gustave Flaubert. Paris, 1937.
43576.68.200 Dupays, Paul. L'automne. Paris, 1937.
43576.77.120 Durtain, Luc. Le mari singulier. Paris, 1937.
Mol 865.5 Dussane, B. (Mrs.). An actor named Molière. N.Y., 1937.
43576.86.110 Dutheil, Marcel. La passion de Puisjoli. v.1-2. Paris, 1937.
43576.91.80 Duvernois, Henri. La maison Camille. Paris, 1937.
43537.98.805 Eicke, W.A. Léon Bazalgette, 1873-1929. Inaug. Diss. Bonn, 1937.
43537.98.809 Eicke, W.A. Léon Bazalgette, 1873-1929 und seine Anschaunungen über Latinität udn Germanentum. Bonn, 1937.
43591.89.251 Éluard, Paul. Les animaux et leurs hommes, les hommes et leurs animaux. Paris, 1937.
43591.59.251 Éluard, Paul. Les animaux et leurs hommes, les hommes et leurs animaux. Paris, 1937.
43591.89.210 Éluard, Paul. Quelques-uns des mots qui jusqu'ici m'étaient mysterieusement interdits. Paris, 1937.
43606.87.113 Fauchois, René. Prenez garde à la peinture. N.Y., 1937.
43606.89.4 Faure, Gabriel. Oeuvres. Saint-Félicien-en-Vivarais, 1937. 8v.
Mol 606.9 Fellows, O.E. French opinion of Molière 1800-1850. Diss. Providence, 1937.
42563.37.102 Feuillerat, A. Paul Bourget. Paris, 1937.
43697.89.815 Fillon, A.F. André Maurois. Paris, 1937.
39531.18.10 Fischer, H. Antoine Funetière, 1619-1688. Berlin, 1937.
43610.4.100 Flament, A. L'enchanteresse errante, la Malibran. Paris, 1937.
42576.46.85 Flottes, P. Le drame intérieur de Pierre Loti. Paris, 1937.
42557.20.190 Fontaine, A. Verlaine, homme de lettres. Paris, 1937.
37555.230 Formont, M. Le vers français. Paris, 1937.
V43500.109 Forot, Charles. Epigrammes; quatrains, 1920-1930. Valence-sur-Rhône, 1937.
43611.1.27 Fort, Paul. Joies désolées et tristesses consolées. Paris, 1937.
43611.4.91 Fouchet, Max Pol. Simples sans vertu. Alger, 1937.
42544.34.85 Franke, Karl. Pierre Louys. Inaug. Diss. Bonn, 1937.
43613.25.100 Fresnay, Pierre. L'écurie Watson. Paris, 1937.
42566.16.45 Fricker, E. Alphonse Daudet et la société au second empire. Paris, 1937.
43687.83.810 Frohock, W.M. Pierre Lasserre. Thesis. Ann Arbor, 1937.
42586.56.10 Fromentin, Eugène. Dominique. Paris, 1937.
39527.4.65 Garnier, L. La vie de notre Bon Jehan de La Fontaine contée par l'image. Château-Thierry, 1937.
42521.19.20 Gauthier, E. Le vrai Louis Veuillot. Paris, 1937.
43617.40.100 Gehri, Alfred. Sixième etage. Paris, 1937.
43617.66.130 George, Nancy. Cinq a sept. Paris, 1937.
42563.39.025 Gérard-Gailly, Emile. Notes sur René Boylesve. Paris, 1937.
40556.26.60 Gianturco, Elio. Joseph de Maistre and Giambattista Vico (Italian roots of De Maistre's political culture). Washington, 1937.
43620.2.79.15 Gide, André. Amyntas. Paris, 1937.
43620.1.60 Gilbert, Oscar P. Courrier d'Asie. 5. éd. Paris, 1937.
39566.46 Gillot, H. Denis Diderot. Paris, 1937.
43620.66.302 Giono, Jean. Batailles dans la montagne. Paris, 1937.
43620.66.110 Giono, Jean. Refus d'obeissances. 30. éd. Paris, 1937.
43620.66.180 Giono, Jean. Regain. 37. éd. Paris, 1937.
43620.66.710 Giono, Jean. The song of the world. N.Y., 1937.
37544.58 Giraud, V. Le problème religieux et l'histoire de la littérature française. Paris, 1937.
43620.74.210 Giraudoux, Jean. Electre; pièce en deux actes. Paris, 1937.
43620.74.212 Giraudoux, Jean. Electre. Paris, 1937.

1937 - cont.

43620.74.220 Giraudoux, Jean. L'impromptu de Paris. 4. éd. Paris, 1937.
43620.74.460 Giraudoux, Jean. Supplément au voyage de Cook. Paris, 1937.
43625.19.163 Godoy, Armand. Le brasier mystique. 3e éd. Paris, 1937.
43625.19.240 Godoy, Armand. Trois poèmes de Saint Jean de la Croix. Paris, 1937.
42543.51.72 Gohier, Urbain. Mon jubilé, après cinquante années de journalisme, 1884-1934. 3e éd. Paris, 1937.
39527.4.37 Gohin, Ferdinand. La Fontaine. Paris, 1937.
42575.69.25 Goncourt, Edmond de. The Goncourt journals, 1851-1870. Garden City, 1937.
37555.305.12 Grammont, M. Le vers français; ses moyens d'éxpression son harmonie. 4. éd. Paris, 1937.
Htn 38511.11.1.5* Greban, Arnoul. Le mystère de la nativité de Nostre Saulveur Jhesu Christ. Paris, 1937.
43626.22.103 Green, Julien. Mont-Cinère. N.Y., 1937.
43626.25.100 Grente, Georges. Ecrits et paroles. Paris, 1937.
40597.2.117A Grib, V. Balzac. N.Y., 1937.
37562.200 Gröber, G. Geschichte der mittelfranzösischen Literatur. 2e Aufl. Berlin, 1937. 2v.
43628.23.125 Guéhenno, Jean. Journal d'un homme de 40 ans. Paris, 1937.
43631.49.110 Halla, Bernard. L'inconnue du lac. v.1-2. Paris, 1937.
43631.2.52 Hamp, Pierre. La peine des hommes. 10. éd. Paris, 1937.
43631.78.705 Hart, R.E. The poet of the Indian Ocean. Portland, 1937.
43752.57.805 Hartmann, A. C.F. Ramuz, Mensch, Werk und Landschaft. Inaug. Diss. Dresden, 1937.
38539.2.57 Hartmann, B. Jean Pierre Camus, Erziehung und Erbauung in seinen Unterhaltungsschriften. Inaug. Diss. München, 1937.
38516.10.25 Heilemann, K. Der Wortschatz von Georges Chastellain. Inaug. Diss. Grimma, 1937.
38516.10.30 Hemmer, K. Georges Chastellain (1405-75). Inaug. Diss. Lengerich, 1937.
40587.103 Hey, Paula. Chateaubriand und Pascal. Inaug. Diss. Würzburg, 1937.
37562.210 Holmes, U.T. A history of Old French literature from the origins to 1300. N.Y., 1937.
V43500.137 Houdelot, Robert. Le temps perdu. Paris, 1937.
37596.38.12 Hüppe, W. Der Sprachstil Gautiers von Arras. Inaug. Diss. Bochum, 1937.
41571.1.15 Hugo, Victor. Actes et paroles. Paris, 1937-40. 3v.
40588.30.125 Hundrup, M.A. Die Romane der Mme de Souza in problemgeschichtlicher Schau. Inaug. Diss. Emsdetten, 1937.
37564.131 Irmen, F. Liebe und Freudschaft in der französischen Literatur der 17. Jahrhunderts. Inaug. Diss. Speyer, 1937.
43620.2.140 Iseler, P. Les débuts d'André Gide. Paris, 1937.
42565.48.11 Istrati, Marie Anne. Victor Cherbuliez et le cosmopolitisme. Paris, 1937.
41593.17.3.50 Jackson, J.F. Louise Colet et ses amis littéraires. New Haven, 1937.
37544.51 Jones, P.M. French introspectives from Montaigne to André Gide. Cambridge, Eng., 1937.
38585.16.70 Karl, Ludwig. Jean Racine. Wien, 1937.
43673.83.155 Kessel, Joseph. La rose de Java. 28. éd. Paris, 1937.
38546.74 Kögel, T. Bilder bei Mme. de Sévigné. Inaug. Diss. Würzburg, 1937.
40575.5.105 Kötz, Kurt. Das Frankreichbild im Werke Sainte-Beuve's. Inaug. Diss. Bochum-Langendreer, 1937.
43738.1.120 Krakowski, E. Deux poètes de l'heroïsme: Charles Péguy et Stanislaw Wyspiański. Paris, 1937.
38537.25.140 Kummer, G. Das Nachwirken der antiken komischen Dichtung in denWerken von Rabelais. Berlin, 1937.
38537.25.138 Kummer, G. Das Nachwirken der antiken komischen Dichtung in den Werken von Rabelais. Inaug. Diss. Berlin, 1937.
43687.50.100 Lallier, Roger. Pages d'amitiés. Paris, 1937.
43697.77.815 Lalon, René. Roger Martin du Gard. 5e éd. Paris, 1937.
43687.59.2100 Langhade, Jane. Reflets. Beyrouth, 1937.
43687.79.110 La Salle, B. de. Les forces cachées. Paris, 1937.
43687.89.2110 La Varende, Jean de. Nez-de-Auir, gentilhomme d'amour. Paris, 1937.
42584.25.110 Le Blond, Maurice. La publication de La Terre. Paris, 1937.
42545.3.510 Lecat, Maurice. Le Maeterlinckianisme. Bruxelles, 1937-
42545.3.515 Lecat, Maurice. L'ombre des Ailes de Maeterlinck. Bruxelles, 1937.
41564.55.50 Le Clercq, J.G.C. L'inspiration biblique dans l'oeuvre poétique d'Alfred de Vigny. Thèse. Annemasse, 1937.
V43500.185 Le Sidaner, Louis. La condition de l'écrivain; essai. Paris, 1937.
37575.28 Lestrange, R. Les animaux dans la littérature. Gap, 1937.
43697.52.805 Levin, Harry. Tragedy and revolution. n.p., 1937.
37562.220 Lewels, M. Theologische Streifzüge durch die altfranzösische Literatur. Vechte, 1937.
37595.34.60 Linskill, Joseph. Saint Léger. Paris, 1937.
37595.34.59 Linskill, Joseph. Saint Léger. Thèse. Paris, 1937.
42576.63.24.110 Lion, J. Anatole France à l'exposition internationale de 1937. Paris, 1937.
40571.25 Lobinger, M. Un précurseur de la littérature comparée; Nicolas Martin. Szeged, 1937.
43694.13.100 Luchaire, J. Altitude 3,200. Paris, 1937.
43694.59.110 Lunel, Armand. Jérusalem a Carpentras. 5e éd. Paris, 1937.
40553.10.30 Luz León, José de la. Benjamin Constant o El donjuanismo intelectual. Habana, 1937.
41522.17.8.15 Maggs Bros., London. Éditions originales et autographes de Charles Baudelaire, Paul Verlaine. Paris, 1937.
43697.74.110 Maran, René. Le livre de la brousse. Paris, 1937.
Mol 193.35 Maranini, L. Morte e commedia di Don Juan. Bologna, 1937.
43697.75.3050 Marchand, L. Trois valses. Paris, 1937.
43738.1.115 Margenburg, E. Charles Péguy; ein Beitrag zur Geschichts-Philosophie. Berlin, 1937.
37567.119.10A Marsau, J. Autour du romantisme. Toulouse, 1937.
42563.23.180 Mas, Edouard. Léon Bloy, son oeuvre, portrait et autographe. Paris, 1937.
43697.80.1130 Maschino, Blanche. Ephémère; poèmes. Paris, 1937.
43697.80.1140 Maschino, Blanche. Rhéa. Paris, 1937.
43744.67.920 Massis, H. Le drame de Marcel Proust. Paris, 1937.
43697.82.110 Massis, Henri. L'honneur de servir. Paris, 1937.
43697.89.3100 Maulvault, Lucien. El requête. Paris, 1937.
43697.4.50 Mauriac, François. Le baiser au lépreux. Paris, 1937.
43697.89.220 Maurois, André. La machine à lire les pensées. 46. éd. Paris, 1937.
43697.89.190 Maurois, André. Victoria Regina. Paris, 1937.

1937 - cont.

42514.28.58 Maurras, Charles. La deutelle du rempart, 1886-1936. Paris, 1937.
42545.6.50 Mazel, Henri. Le serment, 1848-1852. Paris, 1937.
43697.100.135 Mazeline, Guy. Bêtafeu, roman. 13. éd. Paris, 1937.
43698.25.100 Meersch, M. van der. L'élu, roman. Paris, 1937.
43698.25.712 Meersch, M. van der. Invasion. N.Y., 1937.
43698.35.100 Mégret, C. Les anthropophages. 7. ed. Paris, 1937.
37544.60 Mello Franco, A.A. de. O indio brasileiro e a revolução francesa. Rio de Janeiro, 1937.
41555.7.140 Mérimée, Prosper. Lettres aux antiquaires de l'Ouest, 1836-1869. Poitiers, 1937.
41555.7.150 Mérimée, Prosper. Merime v pis'makh k Dubenskoi. Moskva, 1937.
V43500.201 Messiaen, Alain. Le miroir vivant; proses. Paris, 1937.
V43500.203 Messiaen, Alian. Orages; poèmes romantiques. Paris, 1937.
41578.115 Michaud-Lapeyre, M.R. Itinéraire des sites Lamartiniens de Savoie. Chambéry, 1937.
43699.3.70 Mille, Pierre. Les aventuriers. 9. éd. Paris, 1937.
38575.28.15 Milon, F.J. Le troisième centenaire du "Cid". Paris, 1937.
43699.51.110 Milosz, Oscar Vladislas. Dix-sept poèmes de Milosz. Tunis, 1937.
43699.65.145 Miomandre, Francis de. Écrit sur de l'eau. Paris, 1937.
43699.65.160 Miomandre, Francis de. Olympe et ses amis; roman. Paris, 1937.
42542.28.85 Möller, G. Henry Becque und Eugène Brieux. Inaug. Diss. Breslau, 1937.
42545.28.25 Moinaux, Georges. Les gaîtés de l'escadron. Paris, 1937.
42545.28.9.32 Moinaux, Georges. Messieurs les ronds-de-cuir. Paris, 1937.
Mol 171.69.25 Molière, Jean Baptiste Poquelin. Le bourgeois gentilhomme. Paris, 1937.
43576.6.825 Mondor, H. Lettre et images pour Georges Duhamel. Paris, 1937.
43701.59.150 Monfreid, Henri de. Abdi. Paris, 1937.
43701.59.100 Monfreid, Henri de. Le roi des abeilles. 23. éd. Paris, 1937.
Mon 28.42 Montaigne, Michel de. L'apologie de Raymond Sebond. Paris, 1937.
Mon 28.41 Montaigne, Michel de. L'apologie de Raymond Sebond. Thèse. Paris, 1937.
43701.63.122 Montherlant, Henry de. Le démon du vien. Paris, 1937.
43701.63.540 Montherlant, Henry de. Fléche du sud. Paris, 1937.
43701.63.121.5 Montherlant, Henry de. Pitié pour les femmes. 96e éd. Paris, 1937.
43632.3.87 Montigny, L.T. de. La revanche de Maria Chapdelaine. Montréal, 1937.
43701.74.228 Morand, Paul. Le réveille matin. 8e éd. Paris, 1937.
43701.74.1110 Morane, P. Poèmes imparfaits. Paris, 1937.
38514.130 Le mors de la pomme. N.Y., 1937.
43703.73.110 Murat, A. Vivre encore. Uzès, 1937.
43703.77.100 Muro, A.L.B. de Baumarchais de. Legends of France and Spain. Stanford, 1937.
41596.8.18 Musset, Alfred de. La confession d'un enfant du siècle. Paris, 1937.
43707.98.705 Nizan, Paul. Trojan horse. London, 1937.
43709.21.110 Noé, Yvan. "Christian"; pièce en trois actes. Paris, 1937.
37556.98A O'Brien, J. The novel of adolescence in France. N.Y., 1937.
V43500.215 Olivier, Pascale. Le chant perdu dans le silence. Abbeville, 1937.
43728.56.110 Ormoy, Marcel. La terrasse sur la mer; poèmes. Paris, 1937.
37555.152 Orth, Hildegard. Der Todesgedanke in der französischen Lyrik des 19. Jahrhunderts. Inaug. Diss. Ochsenfurt, 1937.
38513.24.15 Pathelin. La farce de Maître Pathelin. Paris, 1937.
38514.59.12 Pathelin. Maistre Pierre Pathelin, farce du XV siècle. 2e éd. Paris, 1937.
37543.216 Pauphilet, Albert. Le moyen âge. Paris, 1937.
43738.1.57 Péguy, Charles. De Jean Coste. Paris, 1937.
43738.1.25 Péguy, Charles. Morceaux choisies. 30e éd. Paris, 1937.
43738.41.110 Peisson, Edouard. Le pilate, roman. Paris, 1937.
43738.76.112 Pergaud, Louis. De Goupil à Margot. 60e éd. Paris, 1937.
43738.76.130 Pergaud, Louis. La guerre des boutons. 41e éd. Paris, 1937.
43738.83.110 Pesquidoux, J.D. Le livre de raison. 27e éd. Paris, 1937.
FL 371.58 Petzold, H. Das französische Jesus Christus-Drama nach dem Verfall der mittelalterlichen Misterienspile, 1539-1936. Inaug. Diss. Dresden, 1937.
37573.250 Peyre, Henri. Seventeenth century French prose and poetry. Boston, 1937.
43738.97.130 Peyre, Joseph. Roc-Gibraltar. 10e éd. Paris, 1937.
43740.41.100 Philippe, A. L'acier; roman. Paris, 1937.
38526.46.100 Pierre de Laval. Les rimes de Pierre de Laval. Bordeaux, 1937.
41522.3.28 Pinthus, H. Die Normandie in Barbey d'Aurevillys Romanen. Jena, 1937.
43742.5.100 Plateau, J. Poésie. Hasselt, Belgique, 1937.
43742.41.100 Plisnier, Charles. Faux passeports. Paris, 1937.
43742.41.103 Plisnier, Charles. Faux passeports. 133e éd. Paris, 1937.
41522.6.18 Poe, Edgar Allan. Histoires grotesques et sérieuses. Paris, 1937.
37530.97 Popa, N.I. Memoriu de titluri şi lucrari. Iaşi, 1937.
41564.55.45 Popova, I.M. L'orignilité de l'oeuvre d'Alfred de Vigny. Thèse. Toulouse, 1937.
38526.42.10.75 Posadowsky-Wehner, K. Jean Parmentier, 1494-1529. München, 1937.
41596.51.25 Pottier, Eugène. Chants révolutionnaires. Paris, 1937.
43743.90.120 Pourrat, Henri. La veillée de novembre. Uzès, 1937.
43743.90.4100 Pourtal de Ladevèze, Jean. D'un mirage secret. Paris, 1937.
43743.91.108 Pourtalès, Guy de. La pêche miraculeuse; roman. 58. éd. Paris, 1937.
43743.91.100 Pourtalès, Guy de. La pêche miraculeuse. 47. éd. Paris, 1937.
43744.1.1100 Pradelle, François. Le dit du grant pin. Paris, 1937.
43744.25.130 Prévost, Jean. La chasse du matin. 6. éd. Paris, 1937.
42515.35.217A Psichari, H. Renan d'après lui-même. Paris, 1937.
43750.24.180 Queneau, Raymond. Chêne et chien. Paris, 1937.
43750.24.140 Queneau, Raymond. Odile. Paris, 1937.
Htn 38536.19.25* Rabelais, F. Gargantua. Dijon, 1937.
38526.47.8.10 Racan, Honorat de Bueil. Poésies. v.2. Paris, 1937.
43752.98.140 Raynal, Paul. Napoléan unique. Paris, 1937.
38526.24.20 Reese, H.R. La Mesnadière's poétique (1639). Diss. Baltimore, 1937.

Chronological Listing

1937 - cont.

38525.27.15 Reger, K.F. Mathurin Régniers literargeschichtliche Bedeutung. Inaug. Diss. München, 1937.
42556.28.165 Reitz, H. Impressionistische und expressionistische Stilmittel bei A. Rimbaud. Inaug. Diss. München, 1937.
43753.57.100 Remy, J. La grande lutte. Paris, 1937.
42556.28.35 Rimbaud, Jean Arthur. Ébauches. 2e éd Paris, 1937.
42556.28.14 Rimbaud, Jean Arthur. Oeuvres. Paris, 1937.
43756.90.130 Rivière, Jacques. A la trace de Dieu. 28. éd. Paris, 1937.
43756.90.103 Rivière, Jacques. Jacques Rivière et Alain Fournier: correspondance, 1905-1914. Paris, 1937. 4v.
37567.580 Roche, A.V. Les idées traditionalistes en France de Rivard à Charles Maurras. Urbana, 1937.
39544.142 Rochwood, R.O. The cult of Voltaire to 1791; a revolutionary deity, 1789 - May 30, 1791. Chicago, 1937.
43757.11.100 Rogissart, Jean. Mervale; roman. Paris, 1937.
43757.50.542 Rolland, Romain. Gefährten meines Weges. Zürich, 1937.
43757.50.766 Rolland, Romain. The wolves. N.Y., 1937.
43757.3.225 Romains, Jules. The body's rapture. N.Y., 1937.
43757.3.200 Romains, Jules. The boys in the back room. N.Y., 1937.
43757.3.150 Romains, Jules. Les copains. 71e éd. Paris, 1937.
43757.3.270A Romains, Jules. L'homme blanc. Paris, 1937.
43757.3.105 Romains, Jules. Pour l'esprit et la liberté. 11e éd. Paris, 1937.
37556.108 Rosier, R. Le couple moderne à travers le roman contemporain. Thèse. Bordeaux, 1937.
42578.22.10.80 Rosny, J.H. Un banquier. Paris, 1937.
43757.88.3100 Rougemont, Denis de. Journal d'un intellectuel. Paris, 1937.
FL 6016.5 Rousseau, J.J. Citizens of Geneva. N.Y., 1937.
FL 6024.15 Rousseau, J.J. Selections from the confession and rêveries d'un promeneur solitaire. N.Y., 1937.
43757.89.8100 Roussel, Romain. La vallée sans printemps. Paris, 1937.
43757.89.8101 Roussel, Romain. Le vallée sans printemps. Paris, 1937.
37544.70 Rudwin, M.J. Les écrivains diaboliques de France. Paris, 1937.
43761.9.100 Sabouraud, R. Sur les pas de Montaigne. Paris, 1937.
39594.30.12 St. Pierre, J.H.B. de. Paul et Virginie. N.Y., 1937.
38514.23.40 Saisset, L. Le Grand Testament de François Villon. Paris, 1937.
43761.48.100 Salacrou, Armand. "Atlas-hotel" (version défintive). Pièce en trois actes. Paris, 1937.
37543.214 Sammartino, P. Survey of French literature. N.Y., 1937.
42584.25.120 Schildbach, W. Die Dramatisierung des naturalistischen Romans bei Emile Zola. Inaug. Diss. Halle, 1937.
37569.70 Schildener, E.H. Jüdische Bestrebungen im Spiegel französischer Literatur der Gegenwart. Inaug. Diss. Borna, 1937.
43763.38.223 Schlumberger, Jean. Essais et dialogues. 6. éd. Paris, 1937.
41557.7.81 Schüler, Helene. Louis Reybauds Roman: "Jérôme Paturot à la recherche d'une position sociale" im Spiegel seiner Zeit. Inaug. Diss. Würzhurg, 1937.
43763.41.120 Schultz, Yvonne. Au fond d'un temple Hindou. v.1-2. Paris, 1937.
41564.55.54 Schweitzer, A. Die Darstellungskunst in A. de Vignys historischem Roman Cinq-Mars. Inaug. Diss. Emsdetten, 1937.
40597.2.121 Scott, Mary W. Art and artists in Balzac's Comédie humaine. Chicago, 1937.
37565.94 Seeber, E.D. Anti-slavery opinion in France during the second half of the eighteenth century. Baltimore, 1937.
37565.94.5 Seeber, E.D. Anti-slavery opinion in France during the second half of the eighteenth century. Baltimore, 1937.
37567.442 Senechal, Christian. La Pologne de 1830 à 1846. Paris, 1937.
38525.22.45.60A Silver, Isidore. The Pindaric odes of Ronsard. Paris, 1937.
43769.54.205 Simenon, Georges. L'assassin. 22. éd. Paris, 1937.
43769.54.275 Simenon, Georges. Le blanc à lunettes. 24. éd. Paris, 1937.
43769.54.325 Simenon, Georges. Le testament Donadien. 18. éd. Paris, 1937.
38557.24.55 Simpson, W.J.S. A study of Bossuet. London, 1937.
37543.238 Smith, H.E. Masters of French literature. N.Y., 1937.
43731.16.110 Sokol Slobodskoë (pseud.). La conquête du pôle nord. Paris, 1937.
43775.49.100 Soleillant, M. À la claire fontaine. Uzès, 1937.
43775.90.7110 Soupault, Philippe. Poésies complètes 1917-1937. Paris, 1937.
41574.219 Spiegelberg, W.E. Einheit und Vielheit bei Victor Hugo. Inaug. Diss. Lengerich, 1937.
40592.52 Staël Holstein, Anne Louise. Lettres inédites à Juste Constant de Rebecque. Paris, 1937.
43779.68.100 Stor, K. Les nouvelles histoires Marseillaises de Marius. Paris, 1937?
37596.10.140 Strassberg, S. Die Entführung und Befreiung der Konigin Ginevra. Inaug. Diss. Berlin, 1937.
43780.69.795 Supervielle, Jules. Bosque sin horas. Montévideo, 1937.
43780.69.183 Supervielle, Jules. Le forçat innocent. 4. éd. Paris, 1937.
Htn 37530.105* Talvart, Hector. Bibliographie des auteurs modernes de langue française, 1801-1936. v.2-3,6-10. Paris, 1937. 7v.
42543.1.50A Taylor, F.A. The theatre of Alexandre Dumas fils. Oxford, 1937.
38526.34.105A Telle, E.V. L'oeuvre de Marguerite d'Angoulême. Toulouse, 1937.
38526.34.104 Telle, E.V. L'oeuvre de Marguerite d'Angoulême. Thèse. Toulouse, 1937.
42515.44.30 Tronchon, Henri. Le jeune Edgar Quinet. Paris, 1937.
43793.67.110 Troyat, Henri. La clef de voûte. Paris, 1937.
38516.10.15 Urwin, K. Georges Chastellain. Paris, 1937.
38516.10.14 Urwin, K. Georges Chastellain. Thèse. Paris, 1937.
40562.30 Vaast, E. Lacordaire et ses conférences de Notre Dame. Paris, 1937.
38514.23.45 Valéry, Paul. Villon et Verlaine. Maestricht, 1937.
42581.33.7 Vallès, Jules. Jacques Vingtras. L'enfant. Paris, 1937.
43823.75.100 Vercel, Roger. Sous le pied de l'archange. Paris, 1937.
42557.11.160 Verhaeren, Emile. A Marthe Verhaeren; 219 lettres. 2. éd. Paris, 1937.
37565.43.5 Vial, F. Idées et doctrines littéraires du XVIII siècle. 10e éd. Paris, 1937.
43824.3.2100 Vialatte, A. Badonce et les créatures. Uzès, 1937.
43824.59.100 Vincent, R. Campagne. Paris, 1937.
43824.67.130 Vioux, Marcelle. Anne de Boleyn, la favorite-vierge d'Henri VIII. Paris, 1937.
43824.90.100 Vivan, M. Village noir. Paris, 1937.
43826.11.100 Vocance, J. Le livre des Haï-Kaï. Paris, 1937.
39543.40 Voltaire, François Marie Arouet de. Fragments on India. Lahore, 1937.
41593.36.40 Wauner, M. Versuch über den Stil Maurice de Guérins. Wädenswil, 1937.
37567.350.2 Weinberg, Bernard. French realism; the critical reaction, 1830-1870. N.Y., 1937.
37567.350 Weinberg, Bernard. French realism; the critical reaction, 1830-1870. Diss. Chicago, 1937.
41542.4.60 Weiss, Edith. Natur und Landschaft bei Théophile Gautier. Inaug. Diss. Würzburg, 1937.
40597.2.123 Wenger, Jared. The Province and the provinces in the work of Honoré de Balzac. Diss. Princeton, 1937.
43526.65.820 Wolf, E. Guillaume Apollinaire und das Rhineland. Inaug. Diss. Bonn, 1937.
43744.67.1010A Zaeske, Käthe. Der Stil Marcel Prousts. Emsdetten, 1937.
42584.23.9.25 Zola, Emile. Germinal. N.Y., 1937.

1938

43511.76.100 Abril, M. L'homme abandonné. v. 1-2. Paris, 1938.
43512.75.180 Achard, Marcel. "Le corsaire". Paris, 1938.
41557.10.17.10 Adam, A. Le secret de l'aventure vénitienne. Paris, 1938.
37595.34.40 Agnes, Saint, Legend. The Old French lives of St. Agnes. Cambridge, 1938.
42555.44.43A Aish, D.A.K. La métaphore dans l'oeuvre de S. Mallarmé. Paris, 1938.
42555.44.42 Aish, D.A.K. La métaphore dans l'oeuvre de S. Mallarmé. Thèse. Paris, 1938.
37567.354 Ajalhert, J. Mémoires en Vrac, 1880-1890. Paris, 1938.
41538.47.25 Albertin. Edition critique d'une mise en scène romantique. Paris, 1938.
41538.47.24 Albertin. Edition critique d'une mise en scène romantique. Paris, 1938.
43522.31.100 Algan, Lauzence. Rue de la Roquette. Paris, 1938.
FL 383.86 Allevy, M.A. La mise en scène en France. Thèse. Paris, 1938.
43523.41.200 Amiel, Denys. Famille. Paris, 1938.
42553.48.10 Angellier, A. Auguste Angellier. Paris, 1938.
43527.3.710 Aragon, Louis. Residential quartier. N.Y., 1938.
43528.56.120 Armont, Paul. Le valet-maitre. Paris, 1938.
43528.57.100 Arnaud, Michel. Manière de Blanc. Paris, 1938.
Mol 230.14 Arnavon, Jacques. Le malade imaginaire de Molière. Paris, 1938.
43531.8.6100 Aubret, M. Les jeux de minuit. Paris, 1938.
43535.54.720 Aymé, Marcel. The green mare. London, 1938.
43535.54.120 Aymé, Marcel. Silhouette du scandale. Paris, 1938.
43537.42.110 Bainville, Jacques. Chroniques. Paris, 1938.
40597.1.2 Barbery, B. Henry de Balzac, ou une double famille. Paris, 1938.
42563.16.13.35 Barrès, Maurice. La colline inspirée. Paris, 1938.
42563.20.7 Barrès, Maurice. Le jardin de Bérénice. Paris, 1938.
42544.19.50 Barts, E. Gabriel-Jean-Baptiste Legouvé. Inaug. Diss. Berlin, 1938.
43537.82.100 Bassan, Jean. Juliette. Paris, 1938.
Htn 43538.14.720* Beckett, Samuel. Murphy. London, 1938.
43538.36.705 Béhaine, René. The survivors. N.Y., 1938.
43538.7.39 Benjamin, René. Chronique d'un temps troublé. Paris, 1938.
43538.76.120A Bernanos, Georges. Les grands cimetieres sous la lune. Paris, 1938.
42542.29.55.15 Bernstein, H. Le cap des tempêtes. Paris, 1938.
42542.29.55.10 Bernstein, H. Le voyage. Paris, 1938.
42542.29.73 Berr, Georges. Le train pour Venise. Paris, 1938.
38536.27 Bertoni, G. Rabelais; espisodi scelti. Modena, 1938-
42563.23.8.70 Bertrand, Louis. Mes années d'apprentissage. 5. éd. Paris, 1938.
40582.19.15 Beyle, Henri. Promenades dans Rome. Paris, 1938-40. 3v.
40582.25.35 Beyle, Henri. Scarlet and black. London, 1938. 2v.
40582.7.30 Beyle, Henri. Stendhal. 4. éd. Paris, 1938.
37569.29.5 Bidal, M.L. Les écrivains de l'abbaye. Paris, 1938.
43540.74.200 Birabeau, André. Chaleur du sein. Paris, 1938.
42563.18.215 Bley, Liselotte. Auffassung und Gestaltung des Problems der Entwurzlung in Maurice Barrès. Heidelberg, 1938.
40575.5.165 Bo, Carlo. Delle imagini giovanili di Sainte-Beuve. Firenze, 1938.
42557.20.340 Bollery, Joseph. Un séjour ignoré de Verlaine en Belgique. La Rochelle, 1938.
43544.71.110 Bopp, Leon. Liassons du monde. Paris, 1938.
40583.148.5 Bosselaers, R. Le cas Stendhal, une mise au point. Paris, 1938.
40583.148 Bosselaers, R. Le cas Stendhal, une mise au point. Paris, 1938.
43544.88.7100A Bourgeois, A. Ballades louisianaises. Houston, 1938.
40597.2.128 Bouvier, R. Les comptes dramatiques de Balzac. Paris, 1938.
V43500.49 Boyé, Maurice Pierre. Nuées; poèmes. Paris, 1938.
42514.28.100 Boyer, Noël. Charles Maurras en prison. Paris, 1938?
43752.57.810 Brandner, G. C.F. Ramuz, der Dichter des Waadtlandes. Inaug. Diss. Würzberg, 1938.
38575.23.72 Brasillach, Robert. Pierre Corneille. Paris, 1938.
V43500.51 Briant, Theophile. Sabatrion. Paramé, 1938.
38546.78A Brodin, P. Madame de Sévigné. N.Y., 1938.
43576.6.855 Broe, Axel. Georges Duhamel. København, 1938.
43547.34.110 Bugnet, Georges. Voix de la solitude. Montréal, 1938.
40535.22.8 Burnet, M.S. Marc Antoine Legrand...1673-1728. Paris, 1938.
40535.22.6 Burnet, M.S. Marc Antoine Legrand...1673-1728. Thèse. Paris, 1938.
40535.22.9 Burnet, M.S. Marc Antoine Legrand. Paris, 1938.
42542.27.26.100A Byam, E.C. Théodore Barrière. Baltimore, 1938.
42542.27.26.105 Byam, E.C. Théodore Barrière. Thesis. Baltimore, 1938.
37544.55 Cabanes, A. Autour de la vie de Bohème. Paris, 1938.
43744.67.805 Cabeen, D.C. A selected bibliography of works on Proust for a small library. N.Y., 1938?
39534.32.4 Cadorel, Raymond. Le roman comique. Paris, 1938.
37567.360 Cain, J. Ehanche et premiers éléments d'un musée de la littérature. Paris, 1938.
43550.1.65 Carco, Francis. A voix basse. Paris, 1938.
43550.1.130 Carco, Francis. L'homme de minuit. Paris, 1938.
43550.1.120 Carco, Francis. Les innocents. Paris, 1938.
43550.1.70 Carco, Francis. Montmartre à vingt-ans. Paris, 1938.

1938 - cont.

39544.130.10 Carré, J.R. Consistance de Voltaire. Paris, 1938.
37555.155 Cazamian, L. Retour d'un Anglicisant à la poésie française. Oxford, 1938.
43551.59.130 Cendrars, Blaise. Histoires vraies. Paris, 1938.
43551.59.156 Cendrars, Blaise. La vie dangereuse. 6e éd. Paris, 1938.
40597.2.133 Césari, P. Étude critique des passions dans l'oeuvre de Balzac. Paris, 1938.
40597.2.132 Césari, P. Étude critique des passions dans l'oeuvre de Balzac. Thèse. Paris, 1938.
FL 398.42.9 Cézan, Claude. Louis Jouvet et le théâtre d'aujourd'hui. Paris, 1938.
43552.2.120 Chadourne, Louis. Terre de chanaan. Paris, 1938.
37573.638 Chaigne, L. Anthologie de la renaissance catholique. Paris, 1938-39. 2v.
43552.3.120 Chaine, Pierre. Ray Blas 38. Paris, 1938.
43552.5.140 Chardonne, Jacques. Le bonheur de Barbezieux. Paris, 1938.
37548.26 Charlier, Gustave. Les lettres françaises de Belgique. Bruxelles, 1938.
41596.4.75 Charpentier, J. Alfred de Musset. Paris, 1938.
39544.144 Charpentier, J. Voltaire. Paris, 1938.
43552.5.1135 Chartier, Émile. Esquisses de l'homme. 8e éd. Paris, 1938.
43552.6.715 Chateaubriant, Alphonse de. Gehalte Kraft. Karlsruhe, 1938.
43552.6.125 Chateaubriant, Alphonse de. Les pas ont chanté. 4e éd. Paris, 1938.
43822.49.990 Chisholm, A.R. An approach to M. Valéry's Jeune parque. Melbourne, 1938.
43688.2.85 Christofour, R. Louis Le Cardonnel. Paris, 1938.
43528.53.120 La cité profonde. Paris, 1938.
43620.66.820 Clarke, Katherine A. Le lyrisme dans l'oeuvre de Jean Giono. Thèse. Grenoble, 1938.
43554.2.170 Claudel, Paul. Un poète regarde la croix. 18e éd. Paris, 1938.
43554.24.120 Clerc, Henri. La femme de César. Paris, 1938.
43556.37.104 Cohen, Albert. Mangeclous. 7e éd. Paris, 1938.
43556.37.105 Cohen, Albert. Mangeclous. 8e éd. Paris, 1938.
43556.49.280 Colette, Sidonie Gabrielle. Duo. Paris, 1938.
43556.49.400 Colette, Sidonie Gabrielle. L'envers du music-hall. Rio de Janeiro, Brasil, 1938.
38563.22.30 Courtines, L.P. Bayle's relations with England and the English. N.Y., 1938.
41522.3.32 Creed, Elizabeth. Le dandysme de Jules Barbey d'Aurevilly. Paris, 1938.
41522.3.31 Creed, Elizabeth. Le dandysme de Jules Barbey d'Aurevilly. Thèse. Paris, 1938.
43744.67.1056 Cremonte, Lelio. Proust. Firenze, 1938.
42576.65.13.75 Cressot, M. La phrase et le vocabulaire de J.K. Huysmans. Paris, 1938.
42576.65.13.74 Cressot, M. La phrase et le vocabulaire de J.K. Huysmans. Thèse. Paris, 1938.
37556.100 Dangelzer, Joan Yvonne. La description du milieu dans le roman français de Balzac à Zola. Thèse. Paris, 1938.
43565.60.130 Daniel-Rops, Henry. L'ame obscure. Paris, 1938.
43565.60.110 Daniel-Rops, Henry. La maladie des sentiments. Paris, 1938. 2v.
43565.5.120 Daudet, Léon A. Les Lys sanglants. Paris, 1938.
43565.5.70 Daudet, Léon A. Tièvres de Camargue. 17e éd. Paris, 1938.
43566.48.190 Delarue-Mardrus, Lucie. Fleurette. pt. 1-3. Paris, 1938.
43566.48.400 Delarue-Mardrus, Lucie. Mes mémoires. Paris, 1938.
37576.655 Demeur, L. Pages choisies des ecrivains français de Belgique. 2. éd. Bruxelles, 1938.
43566.75.180 Derème, Tristan. Le poème des griffons. 7. éd. Paris, 1938.
41578.117A Dérieux, H. Lamartine, raconté par ceux qui l'ont vu. Paris, 1938.
37556.118 Deschamp, J.G. The history of French children's books. Paris, 1938.
43566.82.7705 Destouches, Louis Ferdinand. Death on the installment plan. Paris, 1938.
Htn 43566.82.7130* Destouches, Louis Ferdinand. L'école des cadavres. 48e éd. Paris, 1938.
42568.19.21.10 Ducasse, I.L. Oeuvres complètes; les chants de Maldoror. Paris, 1938.
42568.19.21.5 Ducasse, I.L. Oeuvres complètes. Paris, 1938.
40587.108 Duchemin, Marcel. Chateaubriand; essais de critique et d'histoire littéraire. Paris, 1938.
43576.6.238.6 Duhamel, Georges. Cécile parmi nous. 15. éd. Paris, 1938.
43576.6.238 Duhamel, Georges. Cécile parmi nous. 21. éd. Paris, 1938.
43576.6.290 Duhamel, Georges. Le dernier voyage de Candide suivi d'un choix de nouvelles. Paris, 1938.
43576.6.710 Duhamel, Georges. The Pasquier chronicles. N.Y., 1938.
42554.29.170A Dujardin, É. We'll to the woods no more. Norfolk, 1938.
FL 398.6.55 Duleux, Albert. Julia Bartet. Paris, 1938.
43576.74.120 Duran, Michel. Barbara. Paris, 1938.
43576.77.140 Durtain, Luc. L'étape nécessaire. Paris, 1938.
43756.69.805 Elliott, B. Émile Ripert, poète et humaniste de Provence. Avignon, 1938.
43591.89.140 Éluard, Paul. Cours naturel. Paris, 1938.
43620.74.810 Escande de Messières, R. Le role de l'ironie dans l'oeuvre de Giraudoux. N.Y.? 1938.
37555.5.6 Espèner-Scott, J.G. (Mrs.). Claude Fauchet; sa vie, son oeuvre. Thèse. Paris, 1938.
V43500.87 Estang, Luc. Au delà de moi-même. Paris, 1938.
38546.22.15.37 Farinholt, V.C. A critical edition of Georges de Scudéry's L'amour tyrannique. Chicago, 1938.
37555.5.5 Fauchet, C. Recueil de l'origine de la langue et poésie française. Paris, 1938.
37555.5.4 Fauchet, C. Recueil de l'origine de la langue et poésie française. Thèse. Paris, 1938.
43606.87.130 Fauchois, René. Le chirurgien de Jauvence. Paris, 1938.
43606.88.110 Fauconnier, H. Visions. Paris, 1938.
43606.89.72 Faure, Gabriel. Pages choisies. Vienne, 1938.
43607.75.120 Ferdinand, Roger. Le Président Haudecoeur. Paris, 1938.
37564.133A Feugère, A. Le mouvement religieux dans la littérature du XVIIe siècle. Paris, 1938.
42576.25 Flaubert, Gustave. Two tales of Flaubert. N.Y., 1938.
43611.1.58 Fort, Paul. Expo 37, suivi de Raymonde aux yeux verts. Paris, 1938.
38516.4.25A Francon, M. Poèmes de transition, XVe et XVIe siècles. Cambridge, 1938.
43613.65.100 Fromentin, A. Paroles volées à l'écoute. Paris, 1938.
41593.3.80 Gallagher, M. Baour-Lormian. Diss. Philadelphia, 1938.
37569.53.10 Gandon, Yves. Le démon du style. Paris, 1938.
42554.44.12 Ghil, René. Oeuvres complètes. Paris, 1938. 3v.

1938 - cont.

40597.2.130 Gillot, H. Balzac, le médecin de campagne. Paris, 1938.
43620.66.122 Giono, Jean. Colline. 32. éd. Paris, 1938.
43620.66.200 Giono, Jean. Naissance de l'Odyssée. Paris, 1938.
43620.66.210 Giono, Jean. Le poids du ciel. Paris, 1938.
37567.375A Giraud, V. De Chateaubriand à Brunetière. Paris, 1938.
38585.16.86 Giraudoux, J. Racine. Cambridge, 1938.
43620.74.705 Giraudoux, Jean. Amphitryon 38. N.Y., 1938.
43620.74.250 Giraudoux, Jean. Cantique des cantiques. Paris, 1938.
39527.4.60A Giraudoux, Jean. Les cinq tentations de La Fontaine. Paris, 1938.
39527.4.62 Giraudoux, Jean. Les cinq tentations de La Fontaine. 20e éd. Paris, 1938.
43620.74.440A Giraudoux, Jean. Pour ce onze novembre. Paris, 1938.
43757.3.310 Glässer, E. Denkform und Gemeinschaft bei Jules Romains. Berlin, 1938.
43625.19.182 Godoy, Armand. Le poème de l'Atlantique. Paris, 1938.
42576.65.13.112 Grassl, M. Die Musik in den Werken des J.K. Huysmans. München, 1938.
43626.22.43A Green, Julien. Journal. v.7. Paris, 1938.
43626.23.100 Grellet-Dumazeau, Albert. Vieux bourbonnais. Moulins, 1938.
41578.118 Grillet, C. La Bible dans Lamartine. Lyon, 1938.
40517.39.15 Gueulette, J.E. Un magistrat du XVIIIe siècle. Paris, 1938.
40517.39.14 Gueulette, J.E. Un magistrat du XVIIIe siècle. Thèse. Paris, 1938.
FL 396.41.7 Gueullette, T.S. Notes et souvenirs sur le théâtre-italien au XVIIIe siècle. Paris, 1938.
FL 396.41.6 Gueullette, T.S. Notes et souvenirs sur le théâtre-italien au XVIIIe siècle. Thèse. Paris, 1938.
37543.225 Guillaume, M.M. Histoire de la littérature française. Lyon, 1938.
41543.32 Guiraud, Alexandre. Pélage. Paris, 1938.
42556.28.169 Hackett, Cecil A. Le lyrisme de Rimbaud. Thèse. Paris, 1938.
38585.16.75 Haley, Marie P. Racine and the Art poètique of Boileau. Baltimore, 1938.
43631.2.77 Hamp, Pierre. Enquêtes Guevles noires. Paris, 1938.
37562.96 Hanm, Gertrud. Das altfranzösische Gedicht zu Mariae Hemmelfahrt...Beziehungen. Inaug. Diss. Würzburg, 1938.
Mon 170.20 Hay, C.H. Montaigne. Poitiers, 1938.
Mon 170.19 Hay, C.H. Montaigne. Thèse. Poitiers, 1938.
43632.78.110 Hervilliez, G. d'. Mouvement judiciaire. Pt. 1-3. Paris, 1938.
41574.223A Hooker, K.W. The fortunes of Victor Hugo in England. N.Y., 1938.
37596.240 Hugues de Berzy. La "Bible" au seigneur de Berzé. Paris, 1938.
37596.240.5 Hugues de Berzy. La "Bible" au seigneur de Berzé. Thèse. Paris, 1938.
37563.72 Hulubei, A. L'églogue en France au XVIe siècle. Paris, 1938.
37563.72.2 Hulubei, A. L'eglogue en France au XVIe siècle. Thèse. Paris, 1938.
43620.2.155 Hytier, Jean. André Gide. 3. éd. Alger, 1938.
43659.1.100 Isaac, J. Les joyeuses histoires juives. Paris, 1938.
42577.4.48 Jackson, Samuel. Guy de Maupassant. London, 1938.
43667.51.356 Jaloux, Edmond. L'oiseau-lyre; roman. 6. éd. Paris, 1938.
43667.1.230 Jammes, Francis. La légende de l'aile, ou Marie-Élisabeth. Uzes, 1938.
43756.90.815 Jans, A. La pensée de Jacques Rivière. Bruxelles, 1938.
38551.73.2 Joppin, G. Fénelon et la mystique de pur amour. Thèse. Paris, 1938.
38551.73 Joppin, G. Fénelon et la mystique du pur amour. Paris, 1938.
38539.2.60 Joppin, G. Une querelle autour de l'amour pur, Jean Pierre Camus. Paris, 1938.
38539.2.59 Joppin, G. Une querelle autour de l'amour pur, Jean Pierre Camus. Thèse. Paris, 1938.
40556.21.15 Joubert, Joseph. Les carnets de Joseph Joubert. Paris, 1938.
43670.89.290 Jouhandeau, M. Le jardin de Cordoue. 3. éd. Paris, 1938.
37544.48 Jourda, P. L'éxotisme dans la littérature française depuis Chateaubriand. Paris, 1938. 2v.
43670.94.2100 Jouvenel, Renard de. Commune mésure; chroniques. Paris, 1938.
43670.95.100 Jouvet, Louis. Réflexions du comédien. Paris, 1938.
43566.82.7820 Keminski, H.E. Céline en chemise brune. Paris, 1938.
40515.2.36 Kimstedt, C. Frau von Charrière, 1740-1805; ihre Gedankenwelt und ihre Beziehungen zur französischen und deutschen Literatur. Berlin, 1938.
40515.2.36.2 Kimstedt, C. Frau von Charrière, 1740-1805. Inaug. Diss. Berlin, 1938.
40597.2.102 Korwin-Piotrowska, S. L'etrangère, Eveline Hanska de Balzac. Paris, 1938.
38512.42.25 Küter, Egon. Die Predigtmarlein (contes moralisés) des Fr. Nicole Bozon. Werl in Westfalen, 1938.
42556.27.33.810 Lacretelle, Jacques de. Discours de réception de M. Jacques de Lacretelle à l'Academie Francaise. Paris, 1938.
43687.15.25 Lacretelle, Jacques de. Morceaux choisis. 5e éd. Paris, 1938.
39527.42 La Fontaine, Jean de. Discours à Madame de la Sablière. Paris, 1938.
39527.29.10 La Fontaine, Jean de. La Fontaine: récits et dialogues. Paris, 1938. 2v.
43687.75.135 Larguier, Léo. Les trésors de Palmyre. Paris, 1938.
43687.84.100 La Tailhède, Raymond de. Poésies. Paris, 1938.
40575.5.160 Lausanne. Université. Hommage à Sainte-Beuve. Lausanne, 1938.
43687.89.9100 Lautrec, Gabriel de. Souvenirs des jours sans souci. Paris, 1938.
43687.89.2140 La Varende, Jean de. Le centaure de Dieu. Paris, 1938.
43687.89.2130 La Varende, Jean de. Les manants du roi. Paris, 1938.
42544.25.88 Lavedan, Henri. Avant l'oubli; les beaux soirs. Pt.1-3. Paris, 1938.
42576.41.85 Le Blanc, Maurice. Arsène Lupin, gentleman-cambrioleur. Boston, 1938.
43688.30.100 Le Franc, Marie. Pecheurs de Gaspésie. Paris, 1938.
42515.35.159 Lefrance, A. Ernest Renan en Italie. Paris, 1938.
37569.60 Lemaitre, G. Four French novelists. London, 1938.
37547.103 Lissorgues, Marcellin. Les grands écrivains, écrivains d'Auvergne et du Velay. Aurillac, 1938.
37548.20 Littératures de la Suisse. Paris, 1938.
38537.25.145 Lote, Georges. La vie et l'oeuvre de François Rabelais. Aix-en-Provence, 1938.

Chronological Listing

1938 - cont.

39566.45 Luc, Jean. Diderot, l'artiste et le philosophe. Paris, 1938.
37596.7.15 Lucas, H. Les poésies personnelles de Rutebeuf. Thèse. Strasbourg, 1938.
43694.11.100 Lucchini, Pierre. Colère sur Paris. Paris, 1938.
43697.34.210 Magre, Maurice. Le trésor des Albigeois. Paris, 1938.
43697.41.100 Maindron, M. Monsieur de Puymonteil. Paris, 1938.
43697.52.730 Malraux, André. Days of hope. London, 1938.
43697.52.785 Malraux, André. La esperanza. Santiago de Chile, 1938.
43697.52.725 Malraux, André. Man's hope. N.Y., 1938.
43697.75.150 Marcel, Gabriel. Le dard; pièce en trois actes. Paris, 1938.
Htn 38526.35.6.5* Maréchal, Antoine. Le railleur. N.Y., 1938.
38514.68.200 Margny, J. de. L'aventurier. Paris, 1938.
43697.75.7100 Marguerette, L.P. (Mme.). Nous attendons l'imperatrice. Paris, 1938.
37595.70 Marichal, R. Le théâtre en France au Moyen Âge, 12ème et 13ème siècles. Paris, 1938.
43697.75.8100 Marois, P. Rowena. Paris, 1938.
38523.6.50 Marot, Clément. L'edition originale de la deploration sur le trespas de feu messire Florimond Robertet. Paris, 1938.
41574.221 Marsan, Jules. Le centenaire de Tristesse d'Olympio. Toulouse, 1938.
41522.3.34 Martineau, R. Aspects méconnus de Barbey d'Aurevilly. Paris, 1938.
42577.1.70 Maupassant, Guy de. Chroniques, études. Paris, 1938.
43697.87.100 Maurette, Marcelle. Madame Capet. Paris, 1938.
43697.88.331 Mauriac, François. Asmodée. Paris, 1938.
43697.88.172A Mauriac, François. Plongées. Paris, 1938.
40587.110.5A Maurois, André. Chateaubriand, poet, statesman, lover. N.Y., 1938.
40587.110.6A Maurois, André. Chateaubriand. Paris, 1938.
39544.124.10 Maurois, André. Voltaire. N.Y., 1938.
43697.89.1000 Mauron, Marie. Le quartier Mortisson. 1. éd. Paris, 1938.
38551.83.50 May, James L. Fénelon; a study. London, 1938.
43697.100 Mazeline, Guy. Le panier flottant; roman. 10. éd. Paris, 1938.
41555.7.160 Mérimée, Prosper. Lettres à Fanny Lagden. Paris, 1938.
41555.7.180 Mérimée, Prosper. Lettres à la duchesse de Castiglione-Colonna. Paris, 1938.
Mon 123.5 Michaut, G. Montaigne: De la vanité. Paris, 1938.
43620.66.805 Michelfelder, C. Jean Giono et les religions de la terre. 5. éd. Photoreproduction. Paris, 1938.
43744.67.1000 Milon, F.J. Proust, Valéry et le plaisir de la lecture. Paris, 1938.
43699.51.120 Milosz, Oscar Vladislas. La clef de l'apocalypse. Paris, 1938.
37563.68.5 Mönch, Walter. Frankreichs Literatur im XVI Jahrhundert. Berlin, 1938.
43701.61.100 Monnier, Thyde. Le pain des pauvres; roman. Paris, 1938.
43701.63.180A Montherlant, Henry de. L'équinoxe de septembre. 21e éd. Photoreproduction. Paris, 1938.
43701.63.126 Montherlant, Henry de. Les Olympiques. 65e éd. Paris, 1938.
43701.63.250 Montherlant, Henry de. Pasiphaé. Paris, 1938.
43701.63.710 Montherlant, Henry de. Pity for women. N.Y., 1938.
41563.18.30 Moosy, John. Les idées sociales d'Eugène Sue. Thèse. Paris, 1938.
43701.74.204A Morand, Paul. L'heure qu'il est. 4e éd. Paris, 1938.
43701.74.210 Morand, Paul. Isabeau de Bavière, femme de Charles VI. Paris, 1938.
42557.20.210 Morotini, C. Das Lebensgefühl Paul Verlaines in Sagesse. Lengerich, 1938.
43702.88.100 Mounet, L.R. L'ombre sur l'avenir. Paris, 1938.
FL 6119.38 Mowot, R.B. Jean-Jacques Rousseau. Bristol, 1938.
39534.12.25 Mühll, E. von der. Denis Veiras et son histoire des Sévarambes, 1677-1679. Diss. Paris, 1938.
40522.20.12 Müller, W. Die Grundbegriffe der gesellschaftlichen Welt in den Werken des Abbé Prévost. Marburg, 1938.
37597.32.10 Muset, Colin. Les chansons de Colin Muset. 2. éd. Paris, 1938.
41596.16.25 Musset, Alfred de. Oeuvres complètes en prose. Paris, 1938.
39544.145 Naves, Raymond. Le goût de Voltaire. Thèse. Paris, 1938?
39544.147 Naves, Raymond. Voltaire et l'encyclopédie. Paris, 1938.
43706.55.138 Némirovsky, Irène. La proie, roman. Paris, 1938.
37543.179.7A Nitze, W. Albert. A history of French literature. 3. ed. N.Y., 1938.
43707.98.100 Nizan, Paul. La conspiration. Paris, 1938.
43822.49.985A Noulet, Emilie. Paul Valéry; études suivi de Fragments des mémoirs d'un poème par P. Valéry. Paris, 1938.
41557.10.90A Pailleron, M.L. George Sand; histoire de sa vie. Paris, 1938. 3v.
42545.3.541 Palleske, S.O. Maurice Maeterlinck en Allemagne. Paris, 1938?
42545.3.540 Palleske, S.O. Maurice Maeterlinck en Allemagne. Thèse. Strasbourg, 1938.
38526.34.115 Pauphilet, A. Marguerite de Navarre. Paris, 1938.
43738.1.46 Péguy, Charles. Souvenirs. 12e éd. Paris, 1938.
40593.32 Pellegrini, C. Madame de Staël. Firenze, 1938.
FL 379.97 Petersen, C.E. The doctor in French drama, 1700-1775. N.Y., 1938.
37568.70 Peyre, H. Hommes et oeuvres du XXe siècle. Paris, 1938.
43738.98.100 Peyret-Chappuis, Charles de. "Frenesie"; pièce en trois actes. Paris, 1938.
37556.103 Phythian, M.T. La géographie des Alpes françaises dans les romanciers contemporains. Thèse. Grenoble, 1938.
37567.189 Pichon, Jules E. Promenades littéraires en Tchécoslovaquie. Grenoble, 1938.
43741.23.100 Pierhal, A. Jeunes morts chéris des dieux. Paris, 1938.
37569.85 Pierrefeu, Jean de. Les beaux livres de notre temps. Paris, 1938.
39544.138 Pignet, G. La vérité sur la vie amoureuse de M. de Voltaire. Paris, 1938.
38544.1.15 Pitou, Spire. La Calprenède's Faramond. Baltimore, 1938.
38523.3.35 Plattard, J. Clément Marot, 1518. Paris, 1938.
38523.3.36A Plattard, J. Marot, sa carrière poétique, son oeuvre. Paris, 1938.
37563.15.55 Plattard, Jean. La renaissance des lettres en France de Louis XII à Henri IV. 3e éd. Paris, 1938.
43742.41.130 Plisnier, Charles. Sacre. Paris, 1938.
37573.645A Poètes contemporains. Paris, 1938.
43743.98.100 Poydenot, H. Impasse de l'avenir. Paris, 1938.
43744.67.39.10A Proust, Marcel. Cities of the plain. 1. ed. N.Y., 1938.
38544.46.35A Pure, Michel. La prétieuse, ou Le mystère des ruelles. Paris, 1938. 2v.

1938 - cont.

43750.24.230 Queneau, Raymond. Les enfants du Limon. 7. éd. Paris, 1938.
42563.37.105 Raffetto, R. L'évolution du roman de Paul Bourget. Thèse. Toulouse, 1938.
42576.46.90 Rafter, B.B. La femme dans l'oeuvre de Pierre Loti. Thèse. Paris, 1938.
43752.1.45 Rageot, G. Anne-Jeanne; roman. v.1-3. Paris, 1938.
43744.67.59 Raphael, N.P. Introduction à la correspondance de M. Proust. Leiden, 1938.
43744.67.60A Raphael, N.P. Introduction à la correspondance de Marcel Proust. Paris, 1938.
42515.29.720 Renan, Ernest. Vie de Jésus. Paris, 1938.
37596.136.15 Renauld de Beaujeu. Le lai d'Ignaurès ou lai du prisonnier. Bruxelles, 1938.
37569.47 Richli-Bidal, L. Après le symbolisme. Thèse. Paris, 1938.
43611.5.87 Rivière, I.F. (Mme.). Images d'Alain-Fournier par sa soeur Isabelle. Paris, 1938.
43757.50.732.10A Rolland, Romain. Jean-Christophe. N.Y., 1938.
38525.14.11 Ronsard, Pierre de. Oeuvres complètes. Paris, 1938. 2v.
37566.93 Ross, W. Das Bild der römischen Kaiserzeit in der französischen Literatur des 19. Jahrhunderts. Inaug-diss. Bochum, 1938.
42546.13.1.10 Rostand, Edmond. Cyrano de Bergerac. Paris, 1938.
43757.91.4100 Rousseau, B. Quatre contes. Bruxelles, 1938.
FL 6015.6 Rousseau, J.J. Les plus belles lettres de Jean-Jacques Rousseau et de ses correspondants choisies par Jules Baillods. Neuchâtel, 1938.
43757.94.105 Roux, F. de. Brune; roman. 23e éd. Paris, 1938.
37567.66.20 Rudler, M.G. Parnassiens symbolistes et décadents. Paris, 1938.
43761.5.3100 Sabatier, P. "Tu crois avoir airué". Paris, 1938.
43761.41.200 St. Georges de Bouhelier. Le roi soleil. Paris, 1938.
38546.33.30 Saint-René Taillandier, M.M.L.C. (Mme.). Madame de Sévigné et sa fille. Paris, 1938.
43761.59.125 Sandy, Isabelle. Nuits Andorranes. Paris, 1938.
43761.6.150 Sarment, Jean. Othello. Paris, 1938.
37594.9 Sarrasin, Jean. Le roman du Hem. Paris, 1938.
43761.78.103A Sartre, Jean Paul. La nausée. 13e éd. Paris, 1938.
37566.90 Saurat, D. Perspectives. Paris, 1938.
43761.89.5700 Saurat, Denis. The end of fear. London, 1938.
42536.37.5 Schaepdryner, C.J.R.B. de. Hippolyte Taine. Proefschrift. Paris, 1938.
42536.37 Schaepdryner, K. de. Hippolyte Taine. Paris, 1938.
40592.1.5A Schazmann, Paul E. Bibliographie des oeuvres de Mme. de Staël. Paris, 1938.
37563.74 Schmidt, Albert Marie. La poésie scientifique en France au seizième siècle. Thèse. Paris, 1938?
37563.75 Schmidt, Albert Marie. La poésie scientifique en France au 16e siècle. Paris, 1938.
38546.33.20 Schmidt, M. Madame de Sévigné. Inaug. Diss. München, 1938.
FL 6139.38 Sciaky, G. Il problema dello stato nel pensiero del Rousseau. Firenze, 1938.
41522.18.125 Seguin, M. Génie des fleurs du mal. Paris, 1938.
43769.50.110 Silvester, Charles. Mère et fils. Paris, 1938.
43769.54.290 Simenon, Georges. Au rendez-vous des terre-neuves. Paris, 1938.
43769.54.345 Simenon, Georges. La danseuse du Gai-Moulin. Paris, 1938.
43769.54.430 Simenon, Georges. L'homme qui regardait passer les trains. Paris, 1938.
43769.54.335 Simenon, Georges. Le Marie du port. 22. éd. Paris, 1938.
43769.54.196 Simenon, Georges. Les rescapés du Télémaque. 16. éd. Paris, 1938.
43769.54.155A Simenon, Georges. Les soeurs Lacroix. 22. éd. Paris, 1938.
43769.54.305 Simenon, Georges. Le suspect. 19. éd. Paris, 1938.
43769.54.235 Simenon, Georges. Touriste de bananes, ou Les dimanches de Tahiti. 18. éd. Paris, 1938.
43769.54.250 Simenon, Georges. Les trois crimes de mes amis. Paris, 1938.
41522.18.105 Soupault, P. Baudelaire. Paris, 1938.
FL 6139.38.5 Spell, J.R. Rousseau in the Spanish world before 1833. Austin, 1938.
37567.370 Stahl, A. Die Schilderung des Sterbens im französischen Roman des 19. Jahrhunderts. Inaug. Diss. Württemberg, 1938.
42556.28.160 Starkie, Enid. Rimbaud en Abyssinie. Paris, 1938.
42576.15.260 Stein, H.A. Die Legenstandswelt im Werke Flauberts. Bleicherode am Harz, 1938.
39544.140 Stern, Jean. Belle et Bonne, une fervente amie de Voltaire, 1757-1822. Paris, 1938.
40597.2.125 Stevenson, N.W. Paris dans la Comédie humaine de Balzac. Paris, 1938.
40597.2.124 Stevenson, N.W. Paris dans la Comédie humaine de Balzac. Thèse. Paris, 1938.
37565.31.25 Stofflet, D.E. Les "Encyclopédistes" et la Franco-Maçonnerie. Paris, 1938?
42555.13.15 Strasser, R. Victor de Laprade, ein Dichter des Lyonnais. Inaug. Diss. Würzburg, 1938.
Mon 159.25 Strowski, F. Montaigne. Paris, 1938.
43780.5.63 Suarès, André. Cette âme ardente. Paris, 1938.
43780.5.100 Suarès, André. Trois grands vivants. Paris, 1938.
43780.69.203 Supervielle, Jules. L'arche de Noé. 6. éd. Paris, 1938.
43780.69.162 Supervielle, Jules. La fable du monde. 3. éd. Paris, 1938.
43780.69.173 Supervielle, Jules. L'homme de la pampa. 8. éd. Paris, 1938.
43780.69.213 Supervielle, Jules. Le survivant. 5. éd. Paris, 1938.
42557.12.85 Sussex, R.T. L'idée d'humanité chez Émile Verhaeren. Paris, 1938.
42557.12.84 Sussex, R.T. L'idée d'humanité chez Émile Verhaeren. Thèse. Paris, 1938.
37543.232 Thibaudet, A. Réflexions sur la littérature. 5. éd. Paris, 1938.
43788.41.110A Thibaudet, Albert. Réflexions sur le roman. 6e éd. Paris, 1938.
39566.48 Thomas, Jean. L'humanisme de Diderot. 2e éd. Paris, 1938.
38526.66.75 Thomas, Jean. Isabelle; tragédie imitée de l'Arioste. Thèse. Paris, 1938.
41539.23 Thompson, J.A. Alexandre Dumas père and Spanish romantic drama. University, La., 1938.
39544.90.5 Torrey, N.L. The spirit of Voltaire. N.Y., 1938.
37566.97 Tran Van Tung. L'école de France. Hanoi, 1938.
FL 6119.38.5 Trintzius, R. La vie privée de Jean-Jacques Rousseau. Paris, 1938.

1938 - cont.

43793.67.100 Troyat, Henri. L'araigne. Paris, 1938.
43793.67.130 Troyat, Henri. Faux jour. 41 bois originaux d'Irène Kolsky. Paris, 1938.
43793.89.100 Truck, Robert Paul. Heures folles. Lille, 1938.
43816.53.100 Urmatt, F. Les possédés du Saint-Esprit. Paris, 1938.
43822.41.110 Vaillant-Couturier, Paul. Poésie; oeuvres choisies. Paris, 1938.
Htn 43822.49.380* Valéry, Paul. Discours aux chirurgiens. Paris, 1938.
43822.49.17A Valéry, Paul. Les divers essais sur Leonard de Vinci. Paris, 1938.
43822.49.210A Valéry, Paul. Introduction à la poétique. 11e éd. Paris, 1938.
43822.49.156A Valéry, Paul. Regards sur le monde actuel. Paris, 1938.
43822.49.715 Valéry, Paul. Variety. 2nd series. N.Y., 1938.
42547.10.38 Vandérem, F. Gens de qualité. Paris, 1938.
43823.75.705A Vercel, Roger. Tides of Mont St. Michel. N.Y., 1938.
43823.78.1100 Véry, Pierre. Série de sept. 7e éd. Paris, 1938.
39578.8.27 Vial, F. Une philosophie et une morale du sentiment, Luc de Clapiers, marquis de Vauvenargues. Paris, 1938.
37574.150 Vianey, J. Chefs d'oeuvre poétiques du XVIe siècle. 5. éd. Paris, 1938.
37569.66 Vignaud, J. L'esprit contemporain. Paris, 1938.
43824.49.190 Vildrac, Charles. L'air du temps. Paris, 1938.
43824.50.100 Villars, M. Les deux Madame Carroll. Paris, 1938.
43824.59.105 Vincent, R. Campagne. 119e éd. Paris, 1938.
40583.299 Vinogradov, Anatolii K. Stendal' i ego vremia. Moskva, 1938.
38557.24.60 Virely, A. Bossuet. Macon, 1938.
39544.27.13 Voltaire, François Marie Arouet de. Lettres d'Alsace à sa nièce Madame Denis. Paris, 1938.
39545.61.33 Voltaire, François Marie Arouet de. Le temple du goût. Paris, 1938.
42555.44.40A Wais, K.K.T. Mallarmé. München, 1938.
37544.75 Wandruszka von Wanstetten, M.W. Nord und Süd in französischen Geistesleben. Diss. Jena, 1938.
37567.380 Weis, E. Der Elsässer im Französischen Roman des 19. und 20. Jahrhunderts. Inaug. Diss. Tübingen, 1938.
FL 1022.15 West, C.B. Courtisie in Anglo-Norman literature. Oxford, 1938.
Mol 623.8 Wilcox, John. The relation of Molière to restoration comedy. N.Y., 1938.
40583.150 Wurm, J. Die Kunstanschauung von Henri Beyle-Stendhal. Inaug. Diss. Battrop, 1938.
43852.89.180 Yourcenar, Marguerite. Les songes et les sorts. Paris, 1938.

1939

43513.75.114 Acremant, Germaine (Paulain). Ces dames aux chapeaux verts. Paris, 1939.
43513.75.120 Acremant, Germaine (Paulain). La route mouvante. Paris, 1939.
41522.18.140 Adriani, B. Baudelaire und Georges. Berlin, 1939.
42515.36.8 Alfaric, Prosper. Les manuscrits de la Vie de Jésus. Paris, 1939.
Mol 268.150 Alméras, Henri d'. Le Tartuffe, ou L'imposteur. Paris, 1939.
43523.41.210 Amiel, Denys. La maison monestier. Paris, 1939.
37543.279 André, Paul. Survivants. Neuchâtel, 1939?
43738.1.130 Archambault, P. Charles Péguy; images d'une vie héroïque. St. Amand, 1939.
43528.53.113 Armandy, A. Le padrão. Paris, 1939.
40597.2.139 Aubrée, E. Balzac à fougères. Paris, 1939.
43531.42.100 Aujard, Dominique. Le chant interrompu. Paris, 1939.
43535.54.125 Aymé, Marcel. Le boeuf clandestin; roman. 24e éd. Paris, 1939.
41555.49 Bac, F. Mérimée inconnu. Paris, 1939.
42568.19.22 Bachelard, G. Lautréamont. Paris, 1939.
42524.9.3 Baldensperger, F. Études d'histoire littéraire. 3. série. Paris, 1939.
42524.9.4 Baldensperger, F. Études d'histoire littéraire. 4. série. Paris, 1939.
38585.16.84.10 Baldensperger, F. Racine et la tradition romanesque. Paris, 1939.
38585.16.84 Baldensperger, F. La souplesse du monosyllable dans diction de Racine. n.p., 1939.
41522.6.25 Bandy, William T. A word index to Baudelaire's poems. Madison, 1939.
40536.10.290 Barts, E. Gabriel Jean-Baptiste Legouvé, ein vergessener Dichter der Revolutionszeit. Berlin, 1939.
43537.88.120 Baty, Gaston. Dulcinée; tragi-comédie en deux parties et huit tableaux. Paris, 1939.
41522.5.30 Baudelaire, Charles. Juvenilia; oeuvres posthumes. Paris, 1939-52. 3v.
43537.89.2110 Baumann, Émile. L'excommunié. Paris, 1939.
43538.36.715 Béhaine, René. The conquest of life. London, 1939.
43538.61.110 Benoît, Pierre. Notre-Dame de Tortose, roman. Paris, 1939.
43538.76.140 Bernanos, Georges. Scandale de la vérité. 4. éd. Paris, 1939.
43538.77.8100 Berthet, Jean. Les vacances d'Apollon. Paris, 1939.
42563.23.8.75 Bertrand, Louis. Jérusalem. 4. éd. Paris, 1939.
37567.378 Beuchat, Charles. De Restif à Flaubert, ou Le naturalisme en Marche. Paris, 1939.
43538.89.100 Beucler, André. La fleur qui chante; roman. Paris, 1939.
40582.9.18 Beyle, Henri. La chartreuse de Parme. Paris, 1939.
43540.7.140 Bibescu, M.L. Feuilles de calendrier. Paris, 1939.
43540.7.712 Bibescu, M.L. Katia. N.Y., 1939.
43540.24.100 Biette, E. Aux mille mers, j'ai navigué. Paris, 1939.
43540.74.815 Birabeau, Andre. Dame nature. N.Y., 1939.
43540.74.210 Birabeau, André. Le nid. Paris, 1939.
42563.23.50 Bloy, Léon. La femme pauvre. 31. éd. Paris, 1939.
38565.21.25 Boileau Despréaux, Nicolas. Épitres, Art poétique, Lutrin. Paris, 1939.
V43500.25 Bollery, Joseph. Biblio-iconographie de Villiers de l'Isle-Adam. Paris, 1939.
42563.36.250 Bordeaux, Henry. La cendre chaude. v.1-3. Paris, 1939.
39594.19.49 Bordeaux. Bibliothèque Municipale. Exposition des manuscrits de Montesquieu acguis à la vente du 23 février 1939 accompagnés d'un choix de livres. Bordeaux, 1939.
43544.80.785 Borrély, Maria. Das Letze feuer. Zürich, 1939.
43544.80.787 Borrély, Maria. Mistral. Zürich, 1939.
V43500.47 Boyé, Maurice Pierre. Chevreuse et ses environs. Paris, 1939.
43545.4.4110 Brasillach, Robert. Les sept couleurs. Paris, 1939.

1939 - cont.

41542.7.65 Bruneau, Charles. Explication de Théophile Gautier: Emaux et camées. Paris, 1939.
41574.227 Buchanan, D.W. Les sentiments religieux de Victor Hugo de 1825 à 1848. Thèse. Besançon, 1939.
42514.28.140 Buthman, W.C. The rise of integral nationalism in France. N.Y., 1939.
43616.2.85 Camacho, M. Judith Gautier, sa vie et son oeuvres. Thèse. Paris, 1939.
43550.58.110 Camus, Albert. Noces. Paris, 1939.
43550.1.31.2 Carco, Francis. La Bohème et mon coeur. Paris, 1939.
42557.20.240 Carco, François. Verlaine. Paris, 1939.
38524.90 Cart, A. La poésie française au XVII siècle, 1594-1630. Paris, 1939.
43550.78.100 Cartonde Wiart, H. Souvenirs littéraires. Paris, 1939.
43550.82.112 Cassou, Jean. Légion; roman. 9. éd. Paris, 1939.
43552.3.9200 Chamson, André. La galève. Paris, 1939.
37574.668.5 Charpentier, John. Fleurs du jardin lyrique. 3. éd. Paris, 1939.
43552.5.1102 Chartier, Émile. Propos de littérature. 7e éd. Paris, 1939.
43552.6.8100 Chaude, Antonin. La bouquetière de Saint-Jean. Toulon, 1939.
Mol 603.9 Chaumartin, H. Gens de Molière. Vienne, 1939.
43552.23.5100 Chenal, A. La cité des ombres. Paris, 1939.
40536.24.75 Chevalier, A. Rulhière, Jean-Jacques Rousseau et la comédie de caractere de 1770 à 1778. Thèse. Paris, 1939.
43552.25.2110 Chevallier, Gabriel. Sainte-Colline. 192e éd. Paris, 1939.
38585.16.80 Clark, Alexander Frederick Bruce. Jean Racine. Cambridge, 1939.
43554.2.350 Claudel, Paul. L'épée et le miroir. 15e éd. Paris, 1939.
43554.2.190 Claudel, Paul. Jeanne d'Arc au bûcher. Paris, 1939.
43554.2.280F Claudel, Paul. La mystique des pierres precieuses. Paris, 1939.
42514.28.75 Clavière, M. Charles Maurras, ou la restauration des valeurs humaines. Paris, 1939.
37567.382 Clement, N.H. Romanticism in France. N.Y., 1939.
43556.1.97 Cocteau, Jean. Les enfants terribles. 18e éd. Paris, 1939.
43556.50.100 Colling, Alfred. Demain, relâche. Paris, 1939.
37573.652 Cooper, N. A first anthology of French poetry. Oxford, Eng., 1939.
38563.22.60A Cowdrick, Ruth Elizabeth. The early reading of Pierre Bayle. Scottdale, Pa., 1939.
38514.56.9 Cressot, M. Vocabulaire des Quinze joyes de mariage. Thèse. Paris, 1939.
43565.8.102 Dabit, E. Journal intime, 1928-1936. 2. ed. Paris, 1939.
43565.5.130A Daudet, Léon A. Mes idées esthétiques. 6. éd. Paris, 1939.
37548.32.5 Dautrepont, G. Histoire illustrée de la littérature française en Belgique. Bruxelles, 1939.
43565.92.7000 Davray, Jean. L'eau trouble. Paris, 1939.
42547.22.95 Deenen, M. Le merveilleux dans l'oeuvre de Villiers de l'Isle Adam. Paris, 1939.
43566.32.700 Degée, Olivier. Jean Clarambaux; a novel by Jean Tousseul (pseud.). Philadelphia, 1939.
43566.3.60 Delaquys, Georges. La grande mademoiselle. Paris, 1939.
42553.49 Delattre, Floris. La personnalité d'Auguste Angellier. Paris, 1939-44. 2v.
42578.19.55 Delhorbe, C. Edouard Rod d'après des documents inédits. Neuchatel, 1939.
43568.4.100 Diamant-Berger, M. Baignoire "B"; pièce en deux actes. Paris, 1939.
43574.41.173 Drieu La Rochelle, Pierre. Gilles; roman. 10. éd. Paris, 1939.
41574.16.15 Drouet, Juliette. Autour de "Ruy Blas"; lettres inédites de Juliette Drouet à Victor Hugo. Paris, 1939.
43576.6.300A Duhamel, Georges. Le combat contre les ombres. 30. éd. Paris, 1939.
43576.6.229 Duhamel, Georges. Le désert de Bièvres. Paris, 1939.
43576.6.720A Duhamel, Georges. In defence of letters. N.Y., 1939.
43576.77.190 Durtain, Luc. La guerre n'éxiste pas...roman de 1914-1916. Paris, 1939.
43576.91.53 Duvernois, Henri. L'invité. Paris, 1939.
43591.89.24 Éluard, Paul. Chanson complète. Paris, 1939.
40522.21 Engel, Claire E. Figures et aventures du XVIIIe siècle. Paris, 1939.
40587.115 Evans, J. Chateaubriand; a biography. London, 1939.
40553.10.40 Fabre-Luce, A. Benjamin Constant. Paris, 1939.
V43500.91 Fargue, Leon Paul. Le piéton de Paris. Paris, 1939.
37543.236 Fay, E.G. A new outline of French literature with reading references. Ithaca, 1939.
41574.245 Fecarotta, F. L'elemento storico del "Cromwell" di Victor Hugo. Palermo, 1939.
43744.67.1110 Ferré, André. Geographie de Marcel Proust. Paris, 1939.
43744.67.1115 Ferré, André. Géographie de Marcel Proust avec index des noms de lieux et des termes géographiques. Thèse. Paris, 1939.
42576.28.55A Flaubert, Gustave. Madame Bovary. London, 1939.
39594.3.45 Fletcher, F.T.H. Montesquieu and English politics, 1750-1800. London, 1939.
42562.38.1.20 Fogelberg, T. La langue et le style de Paul Adam. Thèse. Paris, 1939.
43611.94.120 Fowlie, W.A. Intervalles. Paris, 1939.
43745.1.105A Fowlie, Wallace. Ernest Psichari. N.Y., 1939.
37563.70 Françon, Marcel. Notes sur l'esthétique de la femme au 16e siècle. Cambridge, Mass., 1939.
42576.15.140 Freienmuth von Helms, E.E. German criticism of Gustave Flaubert,1857-1930. N.Y., 1939.
43612.63.6130 Freminville, René Marie de la Poix de. Abandons de postes. Paris, 1939.
38525.22.45.70 Frey, Dora E. Le genre elegiaque dans l'oeuvre de Ronsard. Inaug. Diss. Liège, 1939.
37556.110 Friedrich, Hugo. Die Klassiker des französischen Romans. Leipzig, 1939.
37564.135 Ganter, P. Das literarische Porträt in Frankreich im 17. Jahrhundert. Berlin, 1939.
43617.4.85 Géraldy, Paul. Duo; pièce en trois actes d'après le roman de Colette. Paris, 1939.
43620.2.79.25 Gide, André. L'evolution du théâtre. Manchester, 1939.
43620.2.69.5 Gide, André. Journal, 1889-1939. Paris, 1939.
37573.55 Gifford, G.H. La France à travers les siècles. N.Y., 1939.
43620.66.775 Giono, Jean. Bergschlacht. Stockholm, 1939.
43620.66.720 Giono, Jean. Harvest. N.Y., 1939.
43620.66.220 Giono, Jean. Precisions. 18. éd. Paris, 1939.

Chronological Listing

1939 - cont.

37530.160 Giraud, Jeanne. Manuel de bibliographie littéraire pour les 16, 17 et 18 siècle français. Paris, 1939-

43620.74.250.7 Giraudoux, Jean. Cantique des cantiques. 7. éd. Paris, 1939.

43620.74.280 Giraudoux, Jean. Choix des éleves. Paris, 1939.

43620.74.540 Giraudoux, Jean. Choix des études. Paris, 1939.

43620.74.260 Giraudoux, Jean. Ondine; pièce en trois actes. Paris, 1939.

43620.74.260.2 Giraudoux, Jean. Ondine. Paris, 1939.

43625.19.250 Godoy, Armand. À Milosz. Lausanne, 1939.

37595.75 Gossart, A.M. Contes et récits; extraits des prosateurs et poètes du Moyen Âge mis en français moderne. Paris, 1939.

43626.22.50 Green, Julien. Personal record, 1928-1939. N.Y., 1939.

37555.700 Gregh, Fernand. Portrait de la poésie moderne de Rimbaud et Valéry. Paris, 1939.

FL 6139.39.10 Grusemann, Hans. Die Natur-Kulturantithese bei Delisle de la Drévetière und J.J. Rousseau. Lengerich, 1939.

42586.76.20 Guillaumin, Emile. La vie d'un simple. Moulins, 1939.

42576.15.155 Guillemin, Henri. Flaubert devant la vie et devant Dieu. Paris, 1939.

41543.22.25 Haedens, Kleber. Gerard de Nerval; ou La sagesse romantique. Paris, 1939.

42543.62.52 Haraucourt, Edmond. Le livre de mon chien. Paris, 1939.

37569.170 Haseganu, I. La France dans l'oeuvre poétique des écrivains roumains contemporains de langue français. Thèse. Cluj, 1939.

43632.6.150 Henriot, Émile. Le livre de mon père. Paris, 1939.

43632.76.125 Hériat, Philippe. Les enfants gâtés. 148. éd. Paris, 1939.

43632.78.120 Hervilliez, G. d'. La donation. Paris, 1939.

43776.41.820 Hommage à André Spire. Paris, 1939.

41573.23.25 Hugo, Victor. The hunchback of Notre Dame. N.Y., 1939.

41573.26.31 Hugo, Victor. Ruy Blas. Paris, 1939.

37563.72.6 Hulubei, A. Repertoire des églogues en France au XVIe siècle, époque des valois, 1515-1589. Thèse. Paris, 1939.

37563.72.5 Hulubei, A. Repertoire des églogues en France au XVIe siècle, Paris, 1939.

43667.51.360 Jaloux, Edmond. La capricieuse. Le pèlerin, La surprise. 6. éd. Paris, 1939.

42575.105 Jarman, L.M. The Goncourt brothers::modernists in abnormal psychology. Albuquerque, 1939.

37556.22.43 Jones, K. La revue Britannique, son histoire et son action littéraire, 1825-1840. Paris, 1939.

37556.22.40 Jones, K. La revue Britannique, son histoire et son action littéraire, 1825-1840. Thèse. Paris, 1939.

37530.11.20 Jones, S.P. A list of French prose fiction from 1700 to 1750. N.Y., 1939.

FL 375.75 Jonker, G.D. Le protestantisme et le théâtre de langue française au XVIe siècle. Groningen, 1939.

43620.66.810 Josiponici, J. Lettre à Jean Giono. Paris, 1939.

43670.1.60 Jouglet, René. La nuit magique; nouvelle. Paris, 1939.

43709.3.825 Kirseck, Ilse. Anna Elisabeth, comtesse de Noailles. Inaug. Diss. Jena, 1939.

39567.15 Krakeur, L.G. La correspondance de Diderot. N.Y., 1939.

40593.35 Lacretelle, P. Madame de Staël et les hommes. Paris, 1939.

43687.25.100 Lafforest, Roger de. Les figurants de la mort, roman. Paris, 1939.

37569.90 Lafourcade, G. Notes sur le roman français contemporain. Buffalo? 1939.

43667.1.850 La Phalange. Francis Jammes. Paris, 1939.

38543.19.50 La Rochefoucauld, François. Maxims. London, 1939.

41564.55.63 LaSalle, Bertrand de. Alfred de Vigny. Paris, 1939.

38526.27.5.60 La Taille, Jean de. De l'art de la tragédie. Manchester, 1939.

43687.87.102A La Tour du Pin, Patrice de. La quête de joie. Paris, 1939.

41522.3.37 LaVarende, J. de. Grands normands. Rouen, 1939.

42545.3.375 Lecat, Maurice. Bibliographie de Maurice Maeterlinck. Bruxelles, 1939.

42545.3.376 Lecat, Maurice. Maurice Maeterlinck en Pantoufles. Bruxelles, 1939.

41522.3.40 Le Corbeille, A. Les diaboliques de Barbey d'Aurevilly. Paris, 1939.

43688.17.120 Lécuyer, A.H. (Mme.). Cris dans le ciel. Paris, 1939.

42576.46.99 Lefèvre, R. Les désenchantées de Pierre Loti. Paris, 1939.

43697.89.830 Lemâitre, George Édouard. André Maurois. Stanford, 1939.

37543.263 Le Maître, Henry. Essai sur le mythe de psyche dans la littérature française. Thèse. Persan, 1939.

43688.59.55 Lenéru, Marie. Journal de Marie Lenéru. Paris, 1939.

40587.42.12 Levaillant, Maurice. Chateaubriand. 2. éd. Paris, 1939.

43689.25.100 Lhermier, Pierre. Le couvent dans la montagne, roman. Paris, 1939.

43690.25.110 Lièvre, Pierre. La vie et le roman. Paris, 1939.

43538.18.805 Lot, F. Joseph Bédier, 1864-1938. Paris, 1939.

43693.89.110 Louwyck, J.H. Danse pour ton ombre! Paris, 1939. 3 pam.

42563.23.205 Loveilhe, Jacques. Léon Bloy, son oeuvre, sa mission. La Rochelle, 1939.

39527.65 Lugli, Vittorio. Il prodigio di La Fontaine. Messina, 1939.

37556.112 Lukács, Zsuzsanna. A féltékenység elemzése az ujabb francia regényben. Budapest, 1939.

41522.18.162 Macchia, Giovanni. Baudelaire critico. Firenze, 1939.

FL 391.140 McKee, K.N. The rôle of the priest on the Parisian stage during the French revolution. Thesis. Baltimore, 1939.

42545.3.115 Maeterlinck, Maurice. La grande porte. Paris, 1939.

43697.48.3110 Malaquais, Jean. Les javanais. Paris, 1939.

43697.59.1100 Maneil, Adrian van. Essais sur notre monde. Paris, 1939.

37569.105 Manuel de la littérature catholique en France de 1870 à nos jours. Paris, 1939.

38526.34.35A Marguerite d'Angoulême. Comédie de la nativité de Jesus Christ. Paris, 1939.

38526.32.40 Marguerite d'Angoulême. Das Heptaméron. Lübeck, 1939.

43697.77.710 Martin du Gard, Roger. The Thibaults. N.Y., 1939.

43697.88.340 Mauriac, François. Les maisons fugitives. Paris, 1939.

43697.89.153 Maurois, André. Le cercle de famille. Le livre moderne illustré. Paris, 1939.

40587.110.7 Maurois, André. Chateaubriand. Paris, 1939.

43697.89.230 Maurois, André. Discours de réception à l'Académie française. Paris, 1939.

43697.100.110 Mazeline, Guy. L'amour soi-même; roman. 40. éd. Paris, 1939.

43698.35.110 Mégret, C. Les fausses compagnies. Paris, 1939.

1939 - cont.

43698.58.3120 Menanteau, Pierre. L'arbre et la maison. Preuilly-sur-Claise, 1939.

43688.58.100 Menanteau, Pierre. L'arbre et la maison. Preuilly-sur-Claise, 1939.

38585.16.115 Mersch, Ernest. Racine et nous, 1639-1939. Liége, 1939.

37596.10.150 Micha, Alexandre. La tradition manuscrite des romans de Chréstien de Troyes. Paris, 1939.

37596.10.149 Micha, Alexandre. La tradition manuscrite des romans de Chréstien de Troyes. Thèse. Paris, 1939.

40535.32.20 Michaut, G. Marivaux; Jeu de l'amour et du hasard. Paris, 1939.

Mol 19.35.3 Molière, Jean Baptiste Poquelin. Théâtre de 1661 à 1663. Paris, 1939.

37564.28.10 Mongrédien, Georges. Les précieux et les précieuses. Paris, 1939.

Mon 28.45 Montaigne, Michel de. Discours de la servitude volontaire, lettres, éphémérides, notes marginales. Paris, 1939.

Mon 32.39 Montaigne, Michel de. The living thoughts of Montaigne. 1. ed. N.Y., 1939.

Mon 28.48A Montaigne, Michel de. Les pages immortelles de Montaigne. Paris, 1939.

38527.31.8.2 Montchrétien, Antoine de. Aman; a critical edition. Thesis. Philadelphia, 1939.

39594.15.25 Montesquieu, C.L. de S. Manuscrits de Montesquieu. Paris, 1939.

43701.74.193 Morand, Paul. Réflexes et réflexions. 6. éd. Paris, 1939.

Mon 123.6 Moreau, P. Montaigne; l'homme et l'oeuvre. Paris, 1939.

Mol 167.15 Morin, L. Les ancêtres de "L'avare" de Molière. Troyes, 1939.

37556.22.30.5 Morino, L. La nouvelle revue française dans l'histoire des lettres. Paris, 1939.

37556.22.30 Morino, L. La nouvelle revue française dans l'histoire des lettres. 6. éd. Paris, 1939.

37569.93 Mornet, D. Introduction à l'étude des écrivains français d'aujourd'hui. Paris, 1939.

41596.64.800 Müller, P.O. Jules Tellier. Appenzell, 1939.

38546.27.5 Murbach, Janet M. La vrai visage de la comtesse de Grignan. Toulouse, 1939.

43706.55.140 Némirovsky, Irène. Deux, roman. Paris, 1939.

FL 363.58 Newton, W. Le thème de phèdre et d'Hippolyte dans la littérature française. Thèse. Paris, 1939.

V43500.211 Nollet, Genevieve. Discontinu. Dinard, 1939.

41568.26.60 O'Hara, F.P. Claude Tillier, sa vie et ses oeuvres. Thèse. Paris, 1939.

40556.39.27 Omodeo, A. Un reazionario, il conte J. de Maistre. Bari, 1939.

43728.3.100 Orain, André. Les égarés, roman. Paris, 1939.

FL 6139.39 Pahlmann, Franz. Mensch und Staat bei Rousseau. Berlin, 1939.

42544.33.66 Parsell, J.R. L'esthetique de Jules Lemaître. Minneapolis, 1939.

37567.387 Pauly, M.H. Les voyageurs-français en Irlande au temps du romantisme. Thèse. Paris, 1939.

37595.34.20 Pauphilet, A. Poètes et romanciers du Moyen Âge. Paris, 1939.

43738.1.27 Péguy, Charles. La France. Paris, 1939.

43738.41.175 Peisson, Edouard. La carte marine. 4e éd. Paris, 1939.

43738.77.160 Pérochon, Ernest. Babette et ses frères. Paris, 1939.

43757.50.540 Peshkov, A.M. Eux et nous. Paris, 1939.

37596.67.25 Petite philosophie. A critical edition of la Petite Philosophie. Diss. Chicago, 1939.

43738.97.103 Peyre, Joseph. Matterhorn. Paris, 1939.

43738.98.110 Peyret-Chappuis, Charles de. Feu Monsieur Pic. Paris, 1939.

43741.88.150 Pittard, Hélène (Mme.). La vallée perdue; roman. pts.1-3. Paris, 1939.

37563.45 Plattard, Jean. La renaissance des lettres pour françois. Paris, 1939.

38537.25.16.15A Plattard, Jean. La vie et l'oeuvre de Rabelais. Paris, 1939.

43742.41.120 Plisnier, Charles. Meurtres. v.1,2,4,5. Paris, 1939. 4v.

43744.67.1050 Pommier, J.J.M. La mystique de Marcel Proust. Paris, 1939.

39566.192 Pommier, Jean. Diderot avant Vincennes. Paris, 1939.

41596.51.37 Pottier, Eugène. Internatsional. Moskva, 1939.

37558.22 Proszwimmer, K. A Francia if júsági irodalom a XVIII szazadban és a XIX század elején. Budapest, 1939.

40516.59.25 Pusey, W.W. Louis-Sébastien Mercier in Germany. N.Y., 1939.

43750.24.104 Queneau, Raymond. Un rude hiver. 4. éd. Paris, 1939.

38536.24.6 Rabelais, F. Gargantua. Paris, 1939.

38583.20 Racine, Jean. Fedra, Andromaca, Britanico, Ester. Buenos Aires, 1939. 2v.

37573.445 Rat, Maurice. Contes et récits du XIXe siècle. Paris, 1939.

40597.2.820 Reizov, Boris G. Tvorchestvo Bal'zaka. Leningrad, 1939.

43753.88.100 Retté, M. Les fils de Mammon. N.Y.? 1939.

42556.28.17 Rimbaud, Jean Arthur. Poésies. 4e éd. Paris, 1939.

42556.28.43 Rimbaud, Jean Arthur. A season in hell; une saison en enfer. Norfolk, Conn., 1939.

42556.28.80 Rimbaud, Jean Arthur. Some poems of Rimbaud. N.Y., 1939.

43687.70.110 Riollet, M. La bête; pièce en un acte. Paris, 1939. 3 pam.

Mon 170.24 Riveline, Maurice. Montaigne et l'amitié. Paris, 1939.

Mon 170.23 Riveline, Maurice. Montaigne et l'amitié. Thèse. Paris, 1939.

FL 6139.39.5 Robert, Ella. Rousseau és a zene. Budapest, 1939.

43757.10.100 Robida, Michael. Les trenandour; roman. Paris, 1939.

43757.53.100 Román, José. Mes souvenirs de Chasseur de chez Maxim's. Paris, 1939.

38525.20.50A Ronsard, Pierre de. Hymne des daimons. Paris, 1939?

37567.196.25 Rosenberg, Z. La persistance du subjectivisme chez les poètes parnassiens. Thèse. Paris, 1939.

42578.22.115 Rosny, J.H. Les instincts. Paris, 1939.

41557.10.57 Rouget, M.T. Essai sur l'évolution psychologique et littéraire de George Sand. Thèse. Lyon, 1939.

41557.10.55 Rouget, M.T. George Sand et l'Italie. Thèse. Lyon, 1939.

43757.9.110 Roüpnel, Gaston. Le vieux garain. Paris, 1939.

FL 6005.30A Rousseau, J.J. The living thoughts of Rousseau. N.Y., 1939.

Mon 159.30 Sáenz Hayes, R. Miguel de Montaigne, 1533-1592. Buenos Aires, 1939.

43761.39.117 St. Exupéry, A. de. Vol de nuit. N.Y., 1939.

X Cg 43761.39.115 St. Exupéry, A. de. Vol de nuit. Paris, 1939.

43761.39.721 St. Exupéry, A. de. The wild garden. 1st ed. N.Y., 1939.

1939 - cont.

43761.39.715A St. Exupéry, A. de. Wind, sand and stars. N.Y., 1939.
V43500.293 Sandelion, Jeanne. D'un amour tué. Paramé, 1939.
V43500.295 Sandelion, Jeanne. D'un amour vivant. Paramé, 1939.
40526.32.10 Schäfer, K. François Joachim de Pierre. Inaug. Diss. Dresden, 1939.
37572.70 Schinz, A. Nineteenth century French readings. N.Y., 1939. 2v.
43763.41.130 Schultz, Yvonne. La divine inconnue. pts.1-2. Paris, 1939.
38575.23.80 Schwartz, W.L. The sentential in the dramas of Corneille. Stanford, 1939.
38546.23.20 Schweitzer, J.W. Georges de Scudéry's Almahide. Baltimore, 1939.
41568.19.10 Sénancour, Étienne Pivert de. Rêveries sur la nature primitive de l'homme. Paris, 1939-40.
37556.16.48 Server, A.W. L'Espagne dans la revue des deux mondes (1829-1848). Thèse. Paris, 1939.
43765.89.100 Seuphor, Michel. Les évasions d'Olivier Trickmanshoh. Paris, 1939.
40583.1.25 Silomon, Karl H. Stendhal in Deutschland; ein bibliographischer Versuch. Murnau, 1939.
43769.54.375 Simenon, Georges. Le bourgemestre. 5. éd. Paris, 1939.
38543.24.10 Sivasriyananda, W. L'éspecurisme de La Rochefoucauld. Thèse. Paris, 1939.
43775.14.100 Socorri, C. (Mme.). Fabienne; pièce en trois actes. Paris, 1939.
42584.25.130 Sondel, B.S. Zola's naturalistic theory with particular reference to the drama. Chicago, 1939.
43744.67.1030 Souza, S. La philosophie de Marcel Proust. Paris, 1939.
40597.2.860 Spitzer, Márta. Balzac zsidó alakjai. Budapest, 1939.
40597.2.315 Spitzer, Márta. Les juifs de Balzac. Budapest, 1939.
39584.20.25 Sproull, G.M. The critical doctrine of Jean-François de La Harpe. Chicago, 1939.
42556.28.173 Starkie, Enid. Arthur Rimbaud. N.Y., 1939.
42576.15.135A Steegmüller, F. Flaubert and Madame Bovary. N.Y., 1939.
43779.15.100 Steiman, S.A. L'assassin habite au 21. Paris, 1939.
38528.14.83 Stevens, L.C. La langue de Brantôme. Paris, 1939.
37562.230A Studies in French language and mediaeval literature. Manchester, 1939.
37564.210 Tableau de la littérature française. Paris, 1939.
37574.155 Talagrand, Jacques. Introduction à la poésie française. Paris, 1939.
37569.97F Therive, A. Lettre de Paris. n.p., 1939.
37543.232.5 Thibaudet, A. Réflexions sur la critique. 5. éd. Paris, 1939.
38526.66.77 Thomas, Jean. Isabelle; tragédie imitée de l'Arioste. Paris, 1939.
V43500.303 Thomé, Jules René. Images. Paramé, 1939.
37556.105 Toursch, V. L'enfant français à la fin du XIXe siècle d'après ses principaux romanciers. Thèse. Paris, 1939.
43793.67.145 Troyat, Henri. La fosse commune. Paris, 1939.
42587.64.75 Uzès, A. de R. Souvenirs. Paris, 1939.
43822.49.25 Valéry, Paul. Conférences. Paris, 1939.
43822.49.200 Valéry, Paul. Poésie et pensée abstraite. Oxford, 1939.
39566.50 Venturi, F. Jeunesse de Diderot, 1713-1753. Paris, 1939.
43823.75.125 Vercel, Roger. Jean Villemeur. Paris, 1939.
42557.20.5.2 Verlaine, Paul. Fêtes galantes. Paris, 1939.
42557.18.40 Verlaine, Paul. Parallèlement. Paris, 1939.
42557.18.21 Verlaine, Paul. Poèmes saturniens. Paris, 1939.
42557.19.51 Verlaine, Paul. Sagesse. Paris, 1939.
43823.77.170 Verneuil, Louis. La femme de ma vie. Paris, 1939.
37564.118.5 Vial, Francisque. Idées et doctrines littéraires du XVIIe siècle. Paris, 1939.
37563.21.10 Vianey, J. Les prostateure du XVIe siècle. Paris, 1939.
39527.4.75 Vianey, Joseph. La psychologie de La Fontaine. Paris, 1939.
42576.57.3.10 Viaud, Julien. Ramuntcho. Boston, 1939.
43824.24.30 Viel, R. Notre-Dame de la paix; roman. Paris, 1939.
41596.4.80 Villiers, André. La vie privée d'Alfred de Musset. Paris, 1939.
43824.59.110 Vincent, R. Blanche. 2e éd. Paris, 1939.
39545.34.3 Voltaire, François Marie Arouet de. Contes. I. Paris, 1939.
39544.28.50 Voltaire, François Marie Arouet de. Lettres philosophiques. Paris, 1939.
38528.8.12 Weber, E. Die Bedeutung der Analogie für die Beschäftigung Henri Estiennes. Marburg, 1939.
43833.13.42 Weck, René de. Souvenirs littéraires. 2e éd. Paris, 1939.
37595.95 Wickelgren, F.L. Some gems of early lyrical poetry. Gloucester, 1939.
37562.195 Wilmotte, M. L'epopée française, origine et élaboration. Paris, 1939.
43757.50.960A Wilson, R.A. The pre-war biographies of Romain Rolland and their place in his work and the period. London, 1939.
43852.89.110 Yourcenar, Marguerite. Le coup de grâce. 8e éd. Paris, 1939.
43861.77.113 Zermatten, Maurice. Unnützes Herz; Roman. Einsiedeln, 1939.

194-

43537.88.3100 Baudry, Édouard. Rue principale. Montréal, 194-?
43554.67.1100 Cloup, François. Sur le chemin de Crête. Paris, 194-.
43556.49.727 Colette, Sidonie Gabrielle. The twilight of the gods. Hanley, 194-.
43611.95.100 Fowlie, W.A. La pureté dans l'art. Montréal, 194-.
43620.66.250 Giono, Jean. Pondeur des jous. Alger, 194-.
43620.74.295 Giraudoux, Jean. Sodome et Gomorrhe; pièce en deux actes. Paris? 194-.
43626.66.100 Groodt-Adant, J. de. Les fruits du combat. Anvers, 194-?
37543.263.1 Lemaître, Henri. Essai sur le mythe de Psyché dans la littérature française des origines à 1890. Paris, 194-.
43744.67.46 Proust, Marcel. Retratos de pintores y de músicos. Madrid, 194-.
43753.58.1130 Renaitour, Jean Michel. Poésie de l'histoire. Paris, 194-.
43780.69.21 Supervielle, Jules. A poesia de Jules Supervielle; estudo. Lisboa, 194-.
37575.161.10 Vaneille, Jean Louis. Les vieux maitres de la littérature bas-normands. Saint-Lo, 194-?
43823.77.11 Verneuil, Louis. Théâtre complet. N.Y., 194-. 4v.
39545.35.25 Voltaire, François Marie Arouet de. Candide. N.Y., 194-?

1940

37558.75 Adler, Wolfgang. Hassdichtung in Frankreich. Berlin, 1940.
43757.50.970 Aguirre, M. Palabras en Juan Cristobal. La Habana, 1940.
43744.67.1051A Alden, D.W. Marcel Proust and his French critics. Los Angeles, 1940.
42582.2.10 Allott, Kenneth. Jules Verne. London, 1940?
43738.1.132 Archambault, P. Péguy: la patrie charnelle et la cité du Dieu. Paris, 1940.
42563.37.115 Austin, L.J. Paul Bourget, sa vie et son oeuvre jusqu'en 1889. Paris, 1940.
42563.37.114 Austin, L.J. Paul Bourget, sa vie et son oeuvre jusqu'en 1889. Thèse. Paris, 1940.
38585.16.315 Bady, René. Portrait de Jean Racine. Fribourg, 1940.
43537.50.120 Baldensperger, F. Cassandre. Los Angeles, 1940.
43537.50.41 Baldensperger, F. Une vie parmi d'autres. Paris, 1940.
40596.38 Balzac, Honoré de. Balzac's Le message. Cambridge, Mass., 1940.
40596.35 Balzac, Honoré de. Ferragus. Boston, 1940.
40597.29.5.10A Balzac, Honoré de. Old Goriot. London, 1940.
40597.32.13.15 Balzac, Honoré de. Physiologie du mariage. Paris, 1940.
43538.61.115 Benoît, Pierre. Les environs d'Aden. Paris, 1940.
FL 6139.40.10 Benrubi, Isaak. L'idéal moral chez Rousseau, Mme. de Staël et Amiel. pt.1. Benrubi. Paris, 1940.
FL 6139.40.5 Bernadiner, B.M. Sotsial' no-politicheskaia Filosofiia Zh.Zh. Russo. Voronezh, 1940.
43538.76.715 Bernanos, Georges. Star of Satan. London, 1940.
41578.122 Bertrand, L. Lamartine. Paris, 1940.
43538.88.120 Betz, Maurice. Dialogues des prisonniers, 1940. Paris, 1940.
38525.22.45.65 Bishop, M. Ronsard, prince and poet. London, 1940.
43544.18.110A Bodin, Jean. Théâtre. Paris, 1940- 2v.
41564.55.75 Bonnefoy, Georges. La pensée religieuse et moral. Paris, 1940.
42563.36.74 Bordeaux, Henry. La neige sur les pas. Paris, 1940.
43544.80.786 Borrély, Maria. Das Dorf ohne Sonne. Zürich, 1940.
41578.73 Bouchard, Marcel. Lamartine; ou, Le sens de l'amour. Paris, 1940.
42563.89.33 Bourges, Elémir. La nef. Paris, 1940.
40597.2.137 Bowen, R.P. The dramatic construction of Balzac's novels. Eugene, 1940.
37573.671 Braibant, Marcel. Les paysans d'aujourd'hui. Anthologie d'auteurs contemporaine. 10. éd. Paris, 1940.
43550.1.31.20 Carco, Francis. Bohème d'artiste. Paris, 1940.
43550.1.76 Carco, Francis. Heures d'Égypte. 6. éd. Avignon, 1940.
43544.59.100 La cavalcade héroique. Paris, 1940.
43551.59.165 Cendrars, Blaise. D'oultremer à l'indigo. Paris, 1940.
Mol 735.8 Chapman, P.A. The spirit of Molière; an interpretation. Princeton, 1940.
43552.5.160 Chardonne, Jacques. Chronique privée. Paris, 1940.
40526.4.20 Chénier, André. Oeuvres complètes. Paris, 1940.
37557.60 Cherel, Albert. La prose poétique française. 3. éd. Paris, 1940.
43556.1.195 Cocteau, Jean. Les monstres sacrés. Paris, 1940.
43556.49.250 Colette, Sidonie Gabrielle. Chambre d'hôtel. Paris, 1940.
43556.49.167 Colette, Sidonie Gabrielle. Chéri; roman. 2e éd. Rio de Janeiro, 1940.
FL 6119.40A Cresson, André. Jean-Jacques Rousseau; sa vie, son oeuvre, avec un exposé de sa philosophie. Paris, 1940.
38585.16.130 Crouzet, Paul. Tout Racine ici, à Port-Royal. Paris, 1940.
43565.60.145 Daniel-Rops, Henry. L'épee de feu; roman. Paris, 1940.
42566.16.75A Daudet, Léon. Quand vivait mon père; souvenirs inédits sur Alphonse Daudet. 11. éd. Paris, 1940.
38514.51.80 Desonay, F. Antoine de la Sale. Liège, 1940.
38523.3.40 Dettmer, Gustav. Die Geisteshaltung Clément Marots. Inaug. Diss. Bottrop, 1940.
43567.89.100 Dhumez, H. Ma cigalière. Cannes, 1940.
38576.13.30 Donneau de Vizé, Jean. Trois comédies. Paris, 1940.
Mon 114.9 Dow, N. The concept and term "nature" in Montaigne's essays. Philadelphia, 1940.
38585.16.26 Duclaux, A. (Mme.). Racine. Paris, 1940.
43576.6.730 Duhamel, Georges. Cécile Pasquier. N.Y., 1940.
43576.6.350A Duhamel, Georges. Les jumeaux de Vallangoujard. Boston, 1940.
43576.6.330 Duhamel, Georges. Suzanne et les jeunes hommes. Paris, 1940.
41530.345 Dumas, Alexandre. The alchemist. San Francisco, 1940.
43757.3.330 Ehrenfels, Walter. Das unanimistische Bewusstsein im Werke Jules Romains'. Berlin, 1940.
42584.25.340 Eikhengol'ts, M. Tvorcheskaia laboratoriia Zolia. Moskva, 1940.
43592.53.190 Emmanuel, Pierre. Élégies. Paris, 1940.
43606.78.195 Farrère, Claude. La onzième heure; roman. Paris, 1940.
42576.23.6.5 Flaubert, Gustave. La tentation de Saint-Antoine. Paris, 1940.
43610.24.5100 Fleurange, Claude. Mon frère Jack, R.A.F.; roman. Paris, 1940.
37567.197 Fourcassié, Jean. Le romantisme et les Pyrénées. Thèse. Paris, 1940.
Mon 116.40 Frame, Donald Murdoch. Montaigne in France, 1812-1852. N.Y., 1940.
41593.14.30 Frey, Hugo. Max Buchon et son oeuvre. Thèse. Besancon, 1940.
43617.2.3100 Genet, Louis. Les signets du missel. Paris, 1940.
41578.40.45 George, A.J. Lamartine and romantic unanimism. N.Y., 1940.
43620.66.700 Giono, Jean. Joy or man's desiring. N.Y., 1940.
43626.5.110 Grasset, B. Une rencontre. Paris, 1940.
41593.36.8 Guérin, Maurice de. Der Kentauer. Leipzig, 1940.
41578.120A Guillemin, H. Lamartine, l'homme et l'oeuvre. Paris, 1940.
38526.48.28.30 Guore, A.E. The language of Du Bartas. Seattle, 1940.
37567.389 Guyette, M.A. The moniteur universel and romanticism, 1813-1830. Thesis. Urbana, Ill., 1940.
43631.03.100 Haedens, Kléber. Une jeune serpente; roman. 4. éd. Paris, 1940.
39586.27.25 Harris, G.W. Antoine Rivarol, journalist of the French revolution. Oxford, 1940.
37583.640A Harvitt, H.J. Representative plays from the French theatre of today. Boston, 1940.
37567.385 Hazard, P. Quatre études; Baudelaire, romantiques, sur un cycle poétique. N.Y., 1940.
41573.23.8 Hugo, Victor. Notre Dame de Paris. N.Y., 1940.
41541.5.80 Iraizoz y de Villar, Antonio. Emilio de Girardin y el periodismo moderno. Habana, 1940.

1940 - cont.

42555.67.90 Karraker, I.O. Pierre de Nolhac: poet, historian and scholar. Urbana, 1940.

38523.3.50 Kinch, Charles E. La poésie satirique de Clément Marot. Paris, 1940.

38523.3.45 Kinch, Charles E. La poésie satirique de Clément Marot. Thèse. Paris, 1940.

37562.240 Koch, Marie Pierre. An analysis of the long prayers in Old French literature with special reference to the "Biblical-creed-narrative" prayers. Diss. Washington, 1940.

37556.246 Lacher, W. Le réalisme dans le roman contemporain. 2. éd. Genève, 1940.

39527.29.50 La Fontaine, Jean de. Fables, contes et nouvelles. Paris, 1940.

42547.22.90 Lanfredini, Dina. Villiers de l'Isle Adam (1838-1889) studio critico. Firenze, 1940.

43687.62.2100 Lanteuil, H. de. Trois poèmes. Rio de Janeiro, 1940.

42555.26.5 Laprade, Victor de. Psyché. Thèse. Paris, 1940.

38544.26.100 La Rüe, C. Oraisons funèbres. Paris, 1940.

43687.89.2120 La Varende, Jean de. Man d'Arc. Paris, 1940.

43697.82.800 Leitolf, Otto. Die Gedankenwelt von Henri Massis. Berlin, 1940.

38512.120 LeMote, J. de. La voie d'enfer et de paradis. Diss. Washington, 1940.

43744.67.1080 Leon, D. Introduction to Proust. London, 1940.

40575.5.120 Leroy, Maxime. La pensée de Sainte-Beuve. Paris, 1940.

40556.27.115 Maistre, Joseph de. Une politique expérimentale. Paris, 1940.

42555.43.30 Mallarmé, Stéphane. Herodias. Prairie City, Ill., 1940.

43697.76.5100 Mari, Jeanne. Le sens de la terre. Gap, 1940.

42566.16.55 Martinet, Y. Alphonse Daudet (1840-1897). Gap, 1940.

42577.4.28.51 Maupassant, Guy de. Lettres de Guy de Maupassant à G. Flaubert par Pierre Borel. Avignon, 1940.

40562.40 Mauriac, François. Lacordaire et nous. 24e éd. Paris, 1940.

37593.62.80 Mayer, Gilbert. Léxique des oeuvres d'Adam de la Halle. Paris, 1940.

40597.2.180 Mayer, Gilbert. La qualification affective dans les romans d'Honoré de Balzac. Thèse. Paris, 1940.

39533.20.22 Meder, Maria. Das Weltbild in Cyrano de Bergeracs Roman L'autremonde. Mannheim, 1940.

43698.25.120 Meersch, M. van der. Pêcheurs d'hommes. Paris, 1940.

37543.87 Mélanges de philologie et d'histoire littéraire. Paris, 1940.

42563.18.205 Mercanton, Jacques. Poésie et religion dans l'oeuvre de Maurice Barrès Lausanne, 1940.

Mol 68.5 Molière, Jean Baptiste Poquelin. Tartufo, o El impostor; La escuela de los maridos; El burgues gentilhombre. Buenos Aires, 1940.

42557.20.250 Mondor, Henri. L'amitié de Verlaine et Mallarmé. 8. éd. Paris, 1940.

43701.63.735 Montherlant, Henry de. Costals and the Hippogniff. N.Y., 1940.

43701.63.200 Montherlant, Henry de. Paysage des olympiques. Paris, 1940.

37530.95 Morize, A. General view of French literature. Ann Arbor, 1940.

37564.175 Mornet, Daniel. Histoire de la littérature française classique. Paris, 1940.

37562.265 Nyström, Urban. Poèmes français sur les biens d'un ménage depuis l'Oustillement au villain du XIIIe siècle jusqu'aux Controverses de Gratien du Pont. Thèse. Helsinki, 1940.

FL 6139.40 Osborn, A.M. Rousseau and Burke. London, 1940.

43738.1.160 Péguy, Pierre. Pour connaître la pensée de Péguy. Paris? 1940.

43738.41.170 Peisson, Edouard. Mer baltique, roman. Paris, 1940.

42563.37.110 Pelletier, Séverin. La nature et la grâce chez Paul Bourget. Montréal, 1940.

40597.04 Perre, P. Les préfacons belges. Bruxelles, 1940.

38575.23.105 Pietsch, Franz. Der Einfluss der Ethik Corneilles auf seine Zeitgenassen. Inaug. Diss. n.p., 1940.

40587.120 Pigasse, J. L'Occitanienne et sa soeur. Albi, 1940.

43747.60.100 Punj, Alain. Lettres d'un Samoyède. Thonon-Les-Bains, 1940?

37597.34.15 Ralph, D.M. Jean de Meun, the Voltaire of the middle ages. Urbana, 1940.

43752.57.11 Ramuz, Charles Ferdinand. Oeuvres complètes. Lausanne, 1940-41. 23v.

43752.57.180 Ramuz, Charles Ferdinand. Si le soleil ne revenait pas; roman. Lausanne, 1940.

42576.46.11 Ratoret, P. Le paysan et le paysage dans l'oeuvre de Eugène Le Roy. Thèse. Sadiac, 1940.

43753.9.110 Reboux, Paul. Liszt, ou Les amours romantiques. Paris, 1940.

43625.92.800 Rees, G. Rémy de Gourmont. Thèse. Paris, 1940.

43753.90.160 Reverdy, P. Antologia poética. Tokio, 1940.

42576.63.195 Roberts, E.C. The educational ideals of Anatole France. Urbana, 1940.

43757.11.110 Rogissart, Jean. Le fer et la forêt. Paris, 1940.

43757.3.135 Romains, Jules. The aftermath. London, 1940.

43761.39.717 St. Exupéry, A. de. Wind, sand and stars. N.Y., 1940.

38585.8.19 Saint-René Taillandier, Madeleine M.L. (Mme.). Racine. 4e éd. Paris, 1940.

38585.16.90 Savory, D.L. Jean Racine. London, 1940.

42566.16.14 Saylor, G.R. Alphonse Daudet as a dramatist. Diss. Philadelphia, 1940.

37569.95 Schinz, A. L'année littéraire mil neuf cent trente-neuf. n.p., 1940.

37583.640.5 Schwarz, Henry S. Lever de Rideau. N.Y., 1940. 6 pam.

38585.16.110 Segond, Joseph. Psychologie de Jean Racine. Paris, 1940.

41557.10.95 Seyd, Felizia. Romantic rebel. N.Y., 1940.

42576.15.120 Seznec, Jean. Les sources de l'épisode des dieux dans "La tentation de Saint-Antoine". Paris, 1940.

39534.7.10A Silin, Charles I. Benserade and his Ballets de cour. Baltimore, 1940.

39534.7.9 Silin, Charles I. Benserade and his Ballets de cour. Diss. Baltimore, 1940.

43769.54.710 Simenon, Georges. Maigret to the rescue. London, 1940.

43769.54.752 Simenon, Georges. The patience of Maigret. N.Y., 1940.

43775.89.3100 Sounac, Denis. L'Hagion-Oros. Marseille, 1940.

39594.19.45 Spurlin, P.M. Montesquieu in America, 1760-1801. University, La., 1940.

Htn 38526.26.88* Steeg, Gertrud von. Louise Labé. Baruth, 1940.

38539.2.70 Sufuma, Louis. Les histoires dévotes de Jean Pierre Camus. Paris, 1940.

43788.5.200 Tharaud, Jérôme. Discours de réception de Jérôme Tharaud à l'Académie française. Paris, 1940.

37543.208.5 Thibaudet, A. Histoire de la littérature française de 1789 à nos jours. Rio de Janeiro, 1940- 2v.

37543.232.7 Thibaudet, A. Réflexions sur la littérature. 8. éd. Paris, 1940.

41539.25 Todd, R. The laughing mulatto. London, 1940?

43793.67.160 Troyat, Henri. Judith Madrier. Paris, 1940.

43822.49.230 Valéry, Paul. Cementerio marino. Caracas, 1940.

43822.49.232 Valéry, Paul. El cementerio marino. Santiago, 1940.

39578.8.42 Vauvenargues, L. de C. The reflections and maxims. London, 1940.

43823.75.715 Vercel, Roger. Troubled waters, a novel. N.Y., 1940.

42557.19.113 Verlaine, Paul. La bonne chanson. Paris, 1940.

42557.19.117 Verlaine, Paul. Romances sans paroles. Paris, 1940.

43824.3.135 Vialar, Paul. La rose de la mer. Paris, 1940.

43824.3.130 Vialar, Paul. Rose of the sea. N.Y., 1940.

38514.20.30 Villon, François. Poems. Oxford, 1940.

41522.56 Wal, Jan S. van der. Charles de Bernard, 1804-1850. Purmerend, 1940.

41584.35.10 Wicks, C.B. Charles-Guillaume Étienne. Baltimore, 1940.

38585.16.95 William, E.E. Racine depuis 1885. Baltimore, 1940.

43861.77.102 Zermatten, Maurice. Erzählungen aus dem Walliser Hochland. Einsiedeln, 1940.

1941

40583.160 Alciatore, J. Stendhal et Helvetius. Thesis. Chicago, 1941.

37596.27.10 Aléxius, Saint. Légend. Sankt Alexius. 2. Aufl. Halle, 1941.

39566.52 Allison, J.M.S. Concerning the education of a prince. New Haven, 1941.

43526.65.125 Apollinaire, Guillaume. Il y a. n.p., 1941.

43527.3.715 Aragon, Louis. The century was young. N.Y., 1941.

37573.671.5 Arland, Marcel. Le paysan français à travers la littérature. 2. éd. Paris, 1941.

42577.4.49.115 Artinian, Artine. Maupassant criticism in France, 1880-1940. N.Y., 1941.

43697.89.840 Auriant (pseud.). Un écrivain original. Paris, 1941.

37574.212 Aury, Dominique. Poètes précieux et baroques du XVIIe siècle. Angers, 1941.

37568.78 Baldensperger, F. La littérature française entre les deux guerres, 1919-1939. Los Angeles, 1941.

39566.22.10 Barker, J.E. Diderot's treatment of the Christian religion in the encyclopédia. N.Y., 1941.

43537.77.2106A Baroncelli, J. de. Vingt-six hommes, récit. 6e éd. Paris, 1941.

41522.13.8.25 Baudelaire, Charles. Les fleurs du mal. Paris, 1941.

43538.1.220 Béalu, Marcel. Coeur vivant. Paris, 1941.

43538.1.335 Béarn, Pierre. Mains sur la mère. Paris, 1941.

37565.110 Bellessort, A. Dix-huitième siècle et romantisme. Paris, 1941.

43538.7.49 Benjamin, René. Le printemps tragique. Paris, 1941.

43538.61.90 Benoît, Pierre. Le désert de Gobi, roman. Paris, 1941.

40588.22 Bertaut, Jules. Madame de Genlis. Paris, 1941.

40534.15.25 Billardon, Louis E. Vashington, ou La liberté du Nouveau Monde. Princeton, N.J., 1941.

43540.3.40 Billy, André. Le double assassinat de la maison du Boeuf. Genève, 1941.

41564.55.60 Bird, Charles W. Alfred de Vigny's Chatterton. Los Angeles, 1941.

43543.3.100 Blanchi, J.P. Naissance et mort de la comédie. Paris, 1941.

43543.41.100 Blin, Louis. Le père Simard. Avignon, 1941.

38566.57 Boileau Despréaux, Nicolas. Les premières satires, I-IX. Lille, 1941.

43544.60.100 Bonnamy, George. L'état-major s'en va-t-en guerre. 2. éd. Paris, 1941.

42563.36.286 Bordeaux, Henry. La sonate au clair de lune. Paris, 1941.

43544.82.110 Bosschère, Jean de. Peacocks and other mysteries. N.Y., 1941.

37573.664 Bovée, A.G. Promenades littéraires et historiques. N.Y., 1941.

43545.4.4195 Brasillach, Robert. Notre avant-guerre. Paris, 1941.

43545.4.4180 Brasillach, Robert. Le procès de Jeanne d'Arc. 5. éd. Paris, 1941.

43545.41.5100 Brion, Marcel. Le théâtre des esprits. Fribourg, 1941.

38557.24.85 Calvet, Jean. Bossuet. Paris, 1941.

37574.115.10 Canfield, Arthur G. French poems. N.Y., 1941.

43550.1.80 Carco, Francis. Nostalgie de Paris. Genève, 1941.

38512.37.5 Casola, Nicola da. La guerra d'Attila. Modena, 1941. 2v.

41574.500 Castelnau, Jacques. Adèle Hugo. Paris, 1941.

V43500.59 Chabaneix, Philippe. Au souvenir de Federico Garcia Lorca. n.p., 1941.

43552.4.5100 Charbonneau, Robert. Ils possideront la terre. Montreal, 1941.

43552.5.165 Chardonne, Jacques. Voir la figure. Paris, 1941.

43738.1.52 Charles Péguy. Angouleme, 1941.

40586.40 Chateaubriand, F.A.R. Chateaubriand. Grenoble, 1941.

43552.25.100 Chevalier, Claude R. Destin, roman. Saint-Etienne, 1941.

43552.25.2120 Chevallier, Gabriel. Ma petite amie Pomme. 170e éd. Paris, 1941.

43552.25.2115 Chevallier, Gabriel. Sainte-Colline. 262e éd. Paris, 1941.

41574.530 Ciana, Albert. Victor Hugo. Genève, 1941.

43554.2.226 Claudel, Paul. Toi, qui es-tu? 55e éd. Paris, 1941.

43554.67.100 Clos-Jouve, H. Le prétoire dans la boutique. Lyon, 1941.

43556.1.260A Cocteau, Jean. Allégories. Paris, 1941.

43556.1.175 Cocteau, Jean. Dessins en marge du texte des Chevaliers de la table ronde. Paris, 1941.

43556.49.350 Colette, Sidonie Gabrielle. Journal à rebours. Paris, 1941.

43556.49.270 Colette, Sidonie Gabrielle. Julie de Carneilhan. 24e éd. Paris, 1941.

43556.49.41 Colette, Sidonie Gabrielle. Mes cahiers. Paris, 1941.

43556.49.480 Colette, Sidonie Gabrielle. Le pur et l'impur. Paris, 1941.

40553.7.6 Constant de Rebecque, Benjamin. Adolphe. Manchester, 1941.

42542.55.45 Croisset, Francis de. La côte de Jade. Paris, 1941.

43565.53.1100 Damase, Jean. La comédie héroique. Paris, 1941.

43566.43.178 Dekobra, Maurice. Emigrés de luxe, roman. 8e éd. N.Y., 1941.

43566.50.6100 Delmelle, Joseph. Vingt ans. Bruxelles, 1941.

1941 - cont.

43566.52.130 Demaison, André. Trois histoires de Bêtes. Avignon, 1941.
43566.80.100 Des Cars, Guy. L'officier sans nom. Cannes, 1941.
42576.65.13.89 Descaves, Lucien. Les dernières années. 4. éd. Paris, 1941.
43566.82.7150 Destouches, Louis Pierre. Les beaux draps. Paris, 1941.
38585.16.135 Dimier, Louis. Racine perdu et retrouvé. Paris, 1941.
43822.49.1015A Dresden, Samuel. L'artiste et l'absolu, Paul Valéry et Marcel Proust. Assen, 1941.
42576.46.97 Du Coglay, M. Le vrai Loti. 2. éd. Tunis, 1941.
43576.6.320 Duhamel, Georges. Les confessions sans pénitence. Paris, 1941.
43576.75.100 Duret, Roger-Léon. Demain. Ambilly-Annemane, 1941.
42555.37.10 Empeirikos, A. Leconte de Lisle. Thonon-les-Bains, 1941.
43595.89.100 Epuy, M. Initiation méridionale. La Chaux-de-Fonds, 1941.
43606.76.180 Fargue, Léon P. Haute solitude. Paris, 1941.
42555.44.55 Faure, Gabriel. Mallarmé à Tournon. Grenoble, 1941.
37543.247 Fess, Gilbert Malcolm. The American revolution in creative French literature (1775-1937). Columbia, 1941.
41522.18.135 Feuillerat, A. Baudelaire et la belle aux cheveux d'or. New Haven, 1941.
37543.240 Feuillerat, A. Studies by members of the French department of Yale University. New Haven, 1941.
37567.66.25 Fiser, Emeric. Le symbole littéraire. Paris, 1941.
43744.67.962 Fiser, Emeric. La théorie du symbole littéraire et Marcel Proust. Paris, 1941.
43610.68.700 Florez, C. de. Put a log on the fire. N.Y., 1941.
42582.2.30 Frank, Bernard. Jules Verne et ses voyages, d'après l'ouvrage biographique Marguerite Allotte de la Fuÿe. Paris, 1941.
43612.63.6120 Freminville, René Marie de la Poix de. Marines, nouvelles. N.Y., 1941.
38585.16.155 Freudeman, Erika R. Das Adjektiv und seine Ausdruckswerte im Stils Racine. Berlin, 1941.
43616.41.1110 Gaillard, André. Oeuvres complètes. Marseille, 1941.
42576.65.13.80 Garcon, Maurice. Huysmans inconnu. Paris, 1941.
40597.2.145 Garrett, H.T. Clothes and character. Philadelphia, 1941.
43616.87.100 Gattefossé, René M. Paradis; société anonyme. Lyon, 1941.
43616.98.100 Gazave, Jean. Romain Apuech; roman. Lyon, 1941.
43617.67.100 Georges-Michel, Michel. Nulle part dans le monde. N.Y., 1941- 2v.
43617.67.110 Georges-Michel, Michel. Star...roman d'une demoiselle de cinéma. N.Y., 1941.
43617.76.100 Germain, Philippe. Trois époques, roman (novembre 1940). Lyon, 1941.
43619.24.220 Ghéon, Henri. La jambe noire, roman. Paris, 1941.
43698.200.800 Gide, Andre P.G. Decouvrons Henri Michaux. Gallimard, 1941.
42581.33.87 Gilles, Gaston. Jules Vallès, 1832-1885. Paris, 1941.
42581.33.95 Gilles, Gaston. Jules Vallès. v.1-2. Paris, 1941.
43625.27.145 Goffin, Robert. Les cavaliers de la deroute, roman. 9. éd. N.Y., 1941.
43625.27.110 Goffin, Robert. Le chat sans tête, roman. N.Y., 1941.
43625.27.100 Goffin, Robert. Le fusillé de Dunkerque. N.Y., 1941.
43625.27.120 Goffin, Robert. Le nouveau sphinx, roman. N.Y., 1941.
43625.45.100 Goldorp V. Un prince franc-maçon, le duc d'Orleans; roman historique. Paris, 1941.
43625.49.110 Goll, Claire. Éducation barbare. N.Y., 1941.
43625.49.100 Goll, Claire. Le tombeau des amants inconnus. N.Y., 1941.
42576.37.37 Gorsse, H. de. La jeunesse de Cyrano de Bergerac. N.Y., 1941.
40597.3.12 Gozlan, Léon. Balzac en pantoufles. Paris, 1941?
43626.22.180 Green, Julien. Varouma. N.Y., 1941.
39532.4.50 Grubbs, H.A. Jean-Baptiste Rousseau. Paris, 1941.
37556.127 Haedens, Kléber. Paradoxe sur le roman. Marseille, 1941.
FL 374.10 Harvey, H.G. The theatre of the Basoche. Cambridge, 1941.
FL 374.15 Hermann, Tage. Den latinske tradition i det førklassiske franske drama. København, 1941.
41573.36.40 Hugo, Victor. Les années funestes, 1852-1870, Dernière Gerbe. Paris, 1941.
37555.156 Hunt, Herbert J. The epic in 19th century France. Oxford, 1941.
42556.27.33.815 Jaloux, Edmond. Souvenirs sur Henri de Régnier. Lausanne, 1941.
43667.51.310 Jaloux, Edmond. Le vent souffle sur la flamme. Fribourg, 1941.
40535.32.25 Jamieson, Ruth K. Marivaux. Morningside Hts., N.Y., 1941.
43667.52.105 Janon, René. Les salopards, roman. 5. éd. Alger, 1941.
43668.4.1100 Jean, Yves. Tourmentes. Avignon, 1941.
43671.61.100 Juniac, L. de. Impressions. Paris, 1941.
40553.10.45 Kerchove, Arnold de. Benjamin Constant. Bruxelles, 1941.
FL 383.170 Kovatchévitch, M. Le sort artistes français et russes en 1812 et le décret de Moscou. Clemont-Ferrand, 1941.
43687.15.180 Lacretelle, Jacques de. L'heure qui change. Genève, 1941.
37569.115 Lalou, René. Le roman français depuis 1900. Paris, 1941.
38527.56 Lambin, Denys. Lettres galantes de Denys Lambin, 1552-1554. Paris, 1941.
FL 395.30 Lancaster, H.C. The comédie française, 1680-1701. Baltimore, Md., 1941.
43687.62.2780 Lanteuil, H. de. Logaritmos IX poemas. Rio de Janeiro, 1941.
43687.73.100 Laquiere, Maurice. Fortunée, la juive, roman. Paris, 1941.
40536.4.40 Le Blanc, J.B. Un voyageur-philosophe au XVIIIe siècle; l'abbé Jean-Bernard Le Blanc. Cambridge, 1941.
V43500.163 Lebrau, Jean. Alphabet du bestiaire. Preuilly-sur-Claise, 1941.
43688.29.100 Lefèvre, Fréderic. Monsieur Maubenoît. Avignon, 1941.
43688.31.100 Le Gac, Pierre-Marie. La victoire sans ailes. Paris, 1941.
37544.82 Lehrmann, C. L'élément juif dans la littérature française. 2. éd. Zürich, 1941.
38526.27.7.5 Le Loyer, Pierre. Pierre Le Loyer's version of the Ars amatoria. Chapel Hill, 1941.
37569.110A Lemaitre, G. From cubism to surrealism in French literature. Cambridge, 1941.
43688.68.100 LeNormand, Michelle. La maison aux phlox. N.Y., 1941.
40575.5.123 Leroy, Maxime. La politique de Sainte-Beuve. Paris, 1941.
43690.1.50.20 Lichtenberger, A. Trott. N.Y., 1941.
38568.855 McKee, David Rice. Simon Tyssot de Patot and the 17th century background of critical deism. Thesis. Baltimore, 1941.
42513.7.5 McNeil, P.A. Notes on the works of F. Denis, 1798-1890. Washington, 1941.
43697.32.100 Magermans, Rémy. La maladie dans la tour. Bruxelles, 1941.
37576.631 March, H. Types of the French short story. N.Y., 1941.

1941 - cont.

43697.76.6100 Maritain, Raïssa. Les grandes amitiés. N.Y., 1941-1944. 2v.
38523.3.80 Marot, Clément. Marot et sons temps. Angers, 1941.
43697.76.110 Marquet, Jean. Master Lou Po To. Avignon, 1941.
43697.77.730 Martin du Gard, Roger. Summer 1914. N.Y., 1941.
43697.82.127 Massis, Henri. Les idées restent. Lyon, 1941.
42577.1.25 Maupassant, Guy de. The complete short stories. N.Y., 1941.
42577.1.36 Maupassant, Guy de. Short stories. N.Y., 1941.
43697.88.200 Mauriac, François. La pharisienne. Paris, 1941.
37569.26A Maurois, A. Études littéraires. N.Y., 1941-44.
43697.89.715 Maurois, André. The silence of Colonel Bramble. N.Y., 1941.
42555.44.164 Mauron, Charles. Mallarmé l'obscur. Paris, 1941.
41555.7.40 Mérimée, Prosper. Correspondance générale. Paris, 1941. 17v.
43699.65.150 Miomandre, Francis de. Le fil d'Ariane. Avignon, 1941.
42555.44.63 Mondor, Henri. Vie de Mallarmé. 3e éd. Paris, 1941.
37573.60 Montagne. Grenoble, 1941.
Mon 28.54 Montaigne, Michel de. Annotations sur les annales de Nicole Gills. Paris, 1941.
Mon 39.10 Montaigne, Michel de. Ensayos. Buenos Aires, 1941. 4v.
39594.14.25 Montesquieu, C.L. de S. Cahiers (1716-1755). 22. ed. Paris, 1941.
43701.63.280 Montherlant, Henry de. Le solstice de juin. 36. éd. Paris, 1941.
43701.74.265 Morand, Paul. Chroniques de l'homme maigre, suivies de propos d'hier. 15. éd. Paris, 1941.
39566.58 Mornet, Daniel. Diderot; l'homme et l'oeuvre. Paris, 1941.
37569.182 Morrow, Christine. Le roman irréaliste dans les littératures contemporaines de langues française et anglaise. Toulouse, 1941.
41596.26.5 Musset, Alfred de. Lorenzaccio. Manchester, 1941.
37564.165 Neubert, Fritz. Die französische Klassik und Europa. Stuttgart, 1941.
38575.94 Neukomm, Gerda. Formwerdung und Formzerfall bei Pierre Corneille. Zürich, 1941.
Mon 154.2 Nicolai, A. Montaigne intimé. Paris, 1941.
V43500.213 Norge, Géo. Joie aux âmes. Bruxelles, 1941.
37597.46 Paré, G.M. Le roman de la rose et la scolastique courtoise. Paris, 1941.
37595.34.23 Pauphilet, A. Jeux et sapience du Moyen Âge. Paris, 1941.
43738.1.66.15 Péguy, Charles. Notre Dame. 17e éd. Paris, 1941.
43738.1.68.20 Péguy, Charles. Saints de France. 40e éd. Paris, 1941.
43738.1.152 Péguy, M. Le destin de Charles Péguy. 2e éd. Paris, 1941.
43738.41.210 Peisson, Edouard. L'aigle de mer. Paris, 1941.
38528.95 Le petit oeuvre d'amour et gaige d'amytié. François Roussin. Paris, 1941.
37543.242 Peyre, Henri. L'influence des littératures antiques. New Haven, 1941.
43744.67.1130 Polanšcak, Antun. La peinture du décor et de la nature chez Marcel Proust. Thèse. Paris, 1941.
41522.17.23.10 Porché, François. Baudalaire et la présidente. Genève, 1941.
43743.90.2100 Pourrat, Henri. Georges. Paris? 1941.
43743.91.120 Pourtalès, Guy de. Les contes du milieu du monde. Fribourg, 1941.
43743.91.110 Pourtalès, Guy de. Saints de Pierre. Fribourg, 1941.
FL 396.50.15 Prince, Felix. André Antoine et la renouveau du théâtre, 1880-1900. Amsterdam, 1941.
43750.24.170 Queneau, Raymond. Les temps mêles. 10. éd. Paris, 1941.
37556.114 Randall, E.S. The Jewish character in the French novel, 1870-1914. Menasha, 1941.
40583.162 Ravel, Louis. Stendhal, curieux homme. Avignon, 1941.
43753.12.100 Recamier, E. L'enfant blond. Avignon, 1941.
43753.18.100 Redier, A. Le capitaine. Lyon, 1941.
43697.77.825 Rice, H.C. Roger Martin du Gard and the world of the Thibaults. N.Y., 1941. 2v.
38514.20.70 Rice, W.H. The European ancestry of Villon's Satirical testaments. N.Y., 1941.
43756.13.100 Richer, C. Le dernier voyage du "Pembroke". Paris, 1941.
43757.3.160A Romains, Jules. Grace encore pour la terre! N.Y., 1941.
43757.3.25 Romains, Jules. Morceaux choisis. N.Y., 1941.
43757.3.115 Romains, Jules. Une vue des choses. N.Y., 1941.
42546.13.15 Rostand, Edmond. Cyrano de Bergerac. Mount Vernon, 1941.
37563.84A Rouillard, Clarence D. The Turk in French history, thought, and literature (1520-1660). Paris, 1941.
40597.2.146 Saba, Jean. Balzac as a social historian. Urbana, 1941.
43620.2.175 Schäppi, Max. Wesen und Formen der Selbstdarstellung im Jugendwerk André Gides. Luzern, 1941.
FL 6113.16 Schinz, Albert. État présent des travaux sur Jean-Jacques Rousseau. N.Y., 1941.
43763.38.240 Schlumberger, Jean. Talons. Montréal, 1941.
43763.40.3100 Schwob, René. Cinq mystères en forme de rétable. Montréal, 1941.
43738.1.140 Secrétain, R. Péguy. N.Y., 1941.
FL 362.35 Sharon d'Obremer, M.A. Les rôles des femmes dans la comédie française de Moliére à Marivoux. Paris, 1941.
43769.54.748 Simenon, Georges. Maigret keeps a rendez-vous. N.Y., 1941.
43769.54.710.5 Simenon, Georges. Maigret to the rescue. N.Y., 1941.
FL 6129.41 Speerli, Leonore. Rousseau and Zürich. Brugg, 1941.
39566.54 Steel, Eric M. Diderot's imagery. Thesis. N.Y., 1941.
43779.41.104 Stiebel, G. Décadence et grandeur. Alger, 1941.
43780.69.785 Supervielle, Jules. La desconocida del Sena. Buenos Aires, 1941.
38525.22.45.83 Thibault, G. Bibliographie des poésies de Pierre de Ronsard. Paris, 1941.
42586.63.28 Thomas, Louis. Arthur de Gobineau, inventeur du racisme, 1816-1882. Paris, 1941.
42555.62.45 Thomas, Louis. Souvenirs sur Moréas. Paris, 1941.
43556.49.815 Trahard, P. L'art de Colette. Paris, 1941.
FL 355.90A Travers, S. Catalogue of nineteenth century French theatrical parodies. N.Y., 1941.
42575.90 Traz, Georges de. Edmond et Jules de Goncourt. Paris, 1941.
43793.67.128 Troyat, Henri. Le jugement de Dieu. 14e éd. Paris, 1941.
43556.49.875 Truc, Gonzague. Madame Colette. Paris, 1941.
43822.49.290 Valéry, Paul. Mauvaises pensées et autres. Marseille, 1941.
43822.49.256A Valéry, Paul. Mélange. n.p., 1941.
43822.49.255 Valéry, Paul. Mélange. 11e éd. Montrouge, 1941.
43822.49.220 Valéry, Paul. La politique de l'esprit. Manchester, 1941.
43822.49.267 Valéry, Paul. Tel quel. Paris, 1941-43.

Chronological Listing

1941 - cont.

43822.89.190 Vautel, Clément. "Mon film". Souvenirs d'un journaliste. Paris, 1941.
43822.49.1000 Venettis, Jean. Exégèse poétique de l'Ebauche d'un serpent de Paul Valéry. Paris, 1941.
43823.75.120 Vercel, Roger. La clandestine. Paris, 1941.
38514.20.33 Villon, François. The free meals of François Villon and his companions and The monologue of the free archer of Baignollet. Paris, 1941.
38514.20.31 Villon, François. Poésies. Paris, 1941.
39545.4.10 Wade, Ira Owen. Voltaire and Madame du Chatelet. Princeton, 1941.
FL 355.90.5 Weingarten, J.A. Modern French dramatists. N.Y., 1941.
42584.3.20 Zola, Emile. The best known works of Emile Zola. N.Y., 1941.

1942

37593.62.42 Adam de la Halle. Rondeaux à trois voix égales. Paris, 1942.
43527.3.180 Aragon, Louis. Brocéliande; poème. Neuchâtel, 1942.
43527.3.320 Aragon, Louis. Cantique a Elsa. Alger, 1942.
43527.3.150 Aragon, Louis. Le crève-coeur. London, 1942.
43527.3.152 Aragon, Louis. Le crève-coeur. N.Y., 1942?
43527.3.210.5 Aragon, Louis. Les yeux d'Elsa. Paris, 1942.
43528.48.200 Arland, Marcel. Heimaterde. Dessau, 1942.
42547.22.135 Aubry, Georges Jean. Une amitie exemplaire. Paris, 1942.
43531.18.1240 Audiberti, Jacques. La nouvelle origine. 4. éd. Paris, 1942.
42584.25.155 Auriant (pseud.). La véritable histoire de "Nana". Paris, 1942.
43531.76.23 Aurient (pseud.). Fragments. Bruxelles, 1942.
42584.24.9 Baeza, R. Centenario de Emile Zola, 1840-1902. Buenos-Aires, 1942.
40597.36.7 Balzac, Honoré de. Traité de la prière. Thèse. Paris, 1942.
42554.10.5 Banville, Théodore de. Les stalactites de Théodore de Banville. Thèse. Paris, 1942.
41566.36.15 Baschet, Robert. E.J. Delécluze, témoin de son temps, 1781-1863. Paris, 1942.
41566.36.20 Baschet, Robert. E.J. Delécluze. Thèse. Paris, 1942.
37583.642.5 Baty, Gaston. Trois p'tits tours et puis s'en vont. Paris, 1942.
41522.13.9.15 Baudelaire, Charles. Les fleurs du mal. Oxford, 1942.
41522.13.9.17A Baudelaire, Charles. Les fleurs du mal. 2. éd. Paris, 1942.
41522.14.30 Baudelaire, Charles. The mirror of Baudelaire. Norfolk, Conn., 1942.
40583.4 Benedetto, L.F. Arrigo Beyle milanese. Firenze, 1942.
43538.74.170 Béraud, Henri. Sans hoine et sans crainte. Paris, 1942.
V43500.19 Bérimont, Luc. Malisette; roman. Paris, 1942.
40597.2.171 Bertault, Philippe. Balzac et la religion. Thèse. Paris, 1942.
38526.2.2 Beys, Charles. Les illustres fous of Charles Beys. Baltimore, 1942.
42515.13 Bisson, L.A. Amedée Pichot, a romantic Prometheus. Oxford, 1942.
43544.21.100 Boecop-Malye, M. Jardin 26. Montréal, 1942.
38566.5 Boileau Despréaux, Nicolas. Dialogues. Paris, 1942.
38566.40 Boileau Despréaux, Nicolas. Dissertation sur la Joconde. Paris, 1942.
38566.66 Boileau Despréaux, Nicolas. Lettres à Brossette. Paris, 1942.
37555.525 Bougier, Marie. Essai sur la renaissance de la poésie catholique. Thèse. Sète, 1942.
V43500.41 Bouhier, Jean. Dompter le fleuve. Niort, 1942.
38537.1.20 Boulenger, Jacques. Rabelais. Paris, 1942.
38567.37 Bray, René. Boileau; l'homme et l'oeuvre. Paris, 1942.
43752.57.815 Bringolf, I. Bibliographie de l'oeuvre de C.F. Ramuz. Lausanne, 1942.
Mol 702.9.5 Brisson, P. Molière. Paris, 1942.
37568.82 Brodin, Pierre. Les écrivains français de l'entre-deux-guerres. Montreal, 1942.
37573.34 Brøndal, Viggo. Franske digte fra Renaissancen til vore dage. København, 1942.
43545.90.105 Brunet, Berthelot. Chacun sa vie. Montréal, 1942.
37569.40.70 Calas, Nicolas. Confound the wise. N.Y., 1942.
43550.58.173 Camus, Albert. Le mythe de Sisyphe. Paris, 1942.
41593.31.81 Camus-Clavier, M.L. Le poète Léon Dierx, 1838-1912. Thèse. Moret-sur-Loing, 1942.
43550.74.2100 Caraco, Albert. Le mystère d'Eusèbe. Buenos Aires, 1942.
42544.34.87 Cardinne-Petit, R. Pierre Louys intime. Paris, 1942.
38514.23.55 Castelnau, J. François Villon. Paris, 1942.
39566.56 Charles, M.L. The growth of Diderot's fame in France from 1784 to 1875. Thesis. Bryn Mawr, 1942.
43552.25.2105 Chevallier, Gabriel. Clochemerle. 452e éd. Paris, 1942.
43554.2.240 Claudel, Paul. Cent phrases pour éventails. Paris, 1942.
43554.2.23 Claudel, Paul. Gedichte. Basel, 1942.
43554.2.360 Claudel, Paul. L'histoire de Tobie et de Sara. Paris, 1942.
43554.2.180 Claudel, Paul. Presence et prophetie. Fribourg, 1942.
37563.55.15 Clements, R.J. Critical theory and practice of the Pléiade. Cambridge, 1942.
43556.15.110 Coculesco, Pius S. Orient, suivi de Leeds Servien. Montreal, 1942.
FL 386.503 Coindreau, Maurice Edgar. La farce est jouée. N.Y., 1942.
43556.49.470 Colette, Sidonie Gabrielle. De ma fenêtre. Paris, 1942.
38526.10.9.15 Collerye, Roger de. Roger de Collerye et ses poésies dolentes. Paris, 1942.
43556.61.1100 Conrad, Florence. Camarades de Combat. N.Y., 1942.
FL 360.95 Copeau, Jacques. Le théâtre populaire. 2. éd. Paris, 1942.
42556.27.92.800 Cornell, W.K. Adolphe Retté, 1863-1930. New Haven, 1942.
43690.54.800 Coster, Sylvain de. De l'existentialisme...poète R. Limbosch. Bruxelles, 1942.
40545.28 Côte, Léon. Achille, allier, historien, conteur, imagier bourbonnais, 1807-1836. Thèse. Moulins, 1942.
40597.2.147 Crain, William L. An introduction to a critical edition of Le secret des Ruggieri. Chicago, 1942.
40597.2.134 Dargan, Edwin P. The evolution of Balzac's Comédie humaine. Chicago, 1942.
43566.43.180 Dekobra, Maurice. Le roman d'un lâche; roman. N.Y., 1942.
41566.36.10 Delécluze, E.J. Imperessions romaines. Paris, 1942.
41564.55.70 Dorval, Marie. Lettres à Alfred de Vigny. Paris, 1942.
37567.417 Dumont, Francis. Naissance du romantisme contemporain. Paris, 1942.

1942 - cont.

37544.77 Dupouy, Auguste. Géographie des lettres françaises. Paris, 1942.
43592.53.210 Emmanuel, Pierre. Orphiques. Paris, 1942.
37556.13.30 Ester, Carl d'. Die Presse Frankreichs im eigenen Urteil, 1540-1940. Stuttgart, 1942.
42576.67.35 Fahmy, Sabri. Paul Hervieu, sa vie et son oeuvre. Thèse. Marseille, 1942.
43606.76.170 Fargue, Léon P. Refuges. Paris, 1942.
43606.76.140 Fargue, Léon P. Trois poèmes. Paris, 1942.
38528.25.10A Febvre, Lucien. Origène et des Periers ou l'énigme du Cymbalum mundi. Paris, 1942.
37574.367.2 Fellows, Otis E. The age of enlightenment. N.Y., 1942.
42586.48.75 Feval, Paul H. Ar pesk aour. Roazhon, 1942.
41522.18.150 Fleury, René Albert. Huit ans de lutte pour le buste de Baudelaire. Paris, 1942.
V43500.99 Fombeure, Maurice. Chansons de la grande hune. Paris, 1942.
V43500.101 Fombeure, Maurice. D'amour et d'aventure. Paris, 1942.
41578.40.27 Fournet, Charles. Lamartine-Roi. Neuchatel, 1942.
43616.63.21 Ganzo, Robert. Poèmes. Paris, 1942.
43616.77.104 Garr, Max. Le chant de Weyla; la voix. N.Y., 1942.
43616.87.110 Gattefossé, René M. Le roman de Marthe, la salyenne. Lyon, 1942.
42563.21.103 Gelson, Mary Aline. An analysis of the realistic elements in the novels of René Bazin. Thesis. Washington, 1942.
37562.286 Gennrich, Fredrich. Zwei altfranzösische Lais. Torino, 1942.
43554.2.855 Gillet, Louis. Claudel présent. Fribourg, 1942.
43620.66.310 Giono, Jean. Triomphe de la vie. 28. éd. Paris, 1942.
43625.27.135 Goffin, Robert. Sabotages dans le ciel, roman. N.Y., 1942.
43625.49.700 Goll, Claire. My sentimental zoo. Mt. Vernon, 1942.
40553.10.10 Gougelot, Henri. L'idée de liberté. Thèse. Melun, 1942.
43626.22.715 Green, Julien. Memories of happy days. N.Y., 1942.
37595.80 Groult, Pierre. Anthologie de la littérature française du Moyen Âge. Gembloux, 1942-43. 2v.
41578.119 Guillemin, H. Connaissance de Lamartine. Fribourg, 1942.
FL 6119.42.5 Guillemin, Henri. Les philosophes contre Jean-Jacques. 5. éd. Paris, 1942.
43628.42.170 Guilloux, Louis. Le pain des rèves; roman. 28. éd. Paris, 1942.
37566.101 Guthrie, R. French literature and thought since the revolution. N.Y., 1942.
37576.623.15 Guyer, F.E. Vingt contes favoris. N.Y., 1942.
37562.260 Heft, D. Proverbs and sentences in fifteenth-century French poetry. N.Y., 1942.
42554.55.8 Heredia, J.M. de. Les trophées. Cambridge, Eng., 1942.
43620.74.935 Hoest, Gunvar. L'oeuvre de Jean Giraudoux. Oslo, 1942.
38514.68.15 Hoffman, E.J. Alain Chartier. N.Y., 1942.
41571.1.17 Hugo, Victor. Ocean and Tas de Pierres. Paris, 1942.
43667.51.21 Jaloux, Edmond. Les saisons littéraires. Fribourg, 1942. 2v.
42515.35.147 Jaspar, M.H. Le genie liberal de la France. N.Y., 1942.
41574.237 Josephson, Matthew. Victor Hugo. Garden City, 1942.
43620.2.184 Kaas-Albarda, Maria. André Gide et son journal. Arnhem, 1942.
43620.2.185 Kaas-Albarda, Maria. André Gide et son journal. Arnhem, 1942.
43674.24.100 Kher, Amy. Mes soeurs. Le Caire, 1942.
37555.160 Krieser, Jules. Les ascendances romantiques du surnaturalisme contemporain. Thèse. Paris, 1942.
38527.60.6A La Boétie, Estienne de. Anti-dictator. N.Y., 1942.
39525.5.10 La Fontaine, Jean de. Oeuvres diverses. v.2. Paris, 1942.
41577.14.10 Lamartine, Alphonse de. Lettres des années sombres, 1853-1867. Fribourg, 1942.
43687.20.100 Lannes, Roger. La peine capitale. Paris, 1942.
37548.30 Lejeune-Dehousse, Rita. Histoire sommaire de la littérature Wallone. 2. éd. Bruxelles, 1942.
FL 1102.5.2 Lejeune-Dehousse, Rita. Histoire sommaire de la littérature wallonne. 2. ed. Bruxelles, 1942.
40512.44 LeSage, Alain René. Histoire de Gil Blas de Santillane. v.1-2. Paris, 1942.
37574.662 López-Narváez, C. La voz en el eco. Bogota, 1942.
38526.28.60 Lorgnier, Louis. Un homme à la mode. Amiens, 1942.
43744.67.1090 Luidner, D. Marcel Proust. Stanford, 1942.
39544.88 Maestro, Marcello T. Voltaire and Beccaria as reformers of criminal law. Thesis. N.Y., 1942.
42545.3.205 Maeterlinck, Maurice. L'autre monde. N.Y., 1942.
43697.45.700 Makhali-Phal. The young concubine. N.Y., 1942.
42555.43.15 Mallarmé, Stéphane. L'art pour tous. Aurora, N.Y., 1942.
42587.52.85 Mardin, Pierre. La langue et le style de Jules Renard. Thèse. Paris, 1942.
43697.76.6110 Maritain, Raïssa. We have been friends together. N.Y., 1942-45. 2v.
38524.19.5 Martin, Nichlas. Noelz et Chansons. Annecy, 1942.
43697.79.170 Mary, André. Rimes et bacchanales. Paris, 1942.
43697.89.240 Maurois, André. Cinq visages de l'amour. N.Y., 1942.
43697.89.722 Maurois, André. I remember, I remember. N.Y., 1942.
43697.89.41A Maurois, André. Memoires. N.Y., 1942. 2v.
43697.89.720 Maurois, André. A time for silence. N.Y., 1942.
38567.26 Miller, J.R. Boileau en France au dix-huitième siècle. Baltimore, 1942.
43701.60.100 Monnier, Mathilde. Dispersion, poèmes. N.Y., 1942.
Mon 45.22 Montaigne, Michel de. Journal de voyage en Italie. Paris, 1942.
43701.63.270 Montherlant, Henry de. La vie en forme de proue. 24. éd. Paris, 1942.
43701.74.300 Morand, Paul. Feu m. le duc. Genève, 1942.
43701.74.280 Morand, Paul. Petit théâtre. Paris, 1942.
42577.4.31.30 Morand, Paul. Vie de Guy de Maupassant. Paris, 1942.
37564.175.5 Mornet, Daniel. Histoire de la littérature française classique, 1660-1700. 2. éd. Paris, 1942.
37596.245 Nardin, Pierre. Lexique compare des fabliaux Jean Bedel. Paris, 1942.
39544.147.7 Naves, Raymond. Voltaire, l'homme et l'oeuvre. Paris, 1942.
41574.241 O'Connor, M.I. A study of the sources of Han d'Islande and their significance in the literary development of Victor Hugo. Thesis. Washington, 1942.
43738.1.64 Péguy, Charles. Pensées. 100. éd. Paris, 1942.
43738.1.47 Péguy, Charles. Souvenirs. Paris, 1942.
43738.80.100 Perron-Louis, G. Lettres du prisonnier. Paris, 1942.
43738.78.200 Perse, Saint-John. Poème à l'étrangère. n.p., 1942?
38514.57.15 Pisan, Christine de. The epistle of Othea to Hector. Philadelphia, 1942.
43743.60.110 Ponge, Francis. Le parti pris des choses. Paris, 1942.

1942 - cont.

43743.98.530A Pozner, Vladimir. The edge of the sword. N.Y., 1942.
40582.13.60 Prevost, Jean. Essai sur les sources de Lamiel. Lyon, 1942.
40583.175 Prévost, Juan. La création chez Stendhal. Sagittaire, 1942.
FL 398.7.70 Pronier, Ernest. Sarah Bernhardt. Genève, 1942.
43744.67.64 Proust, Marcel. Lettres à une amie. Manchester, 1942.
43750.25.1100 Quey, Georges. Bar-Tabac. Villencuve-les-Avignon, 1942.
37543.281 Raymond, Marcel. Génies de France. Neuchâtel, 1942.
37583.642 Rhodes, Solomon A. The contemporary French theater. N.Y., 1942.
42556.28.82 Rimbaud, Jean Arthur. Selected verse poems. London, 1942.
43757.3.236 Romains, Jules. Salsette decouvre l'Amerique. N.Y., 1942.
43757.3.235 Romains, Jules. Salsette discovers America. N.Y., 1942.
38525.18.30 Ronsard, Pierre de. Amours de Marie. Paris, 1942.
FL 6094.8.10 Rousseau, J.J. Les rêveries d'un promeneur solitaire. Manchester, 1942.
FL 6139.44.2 Sacheli, Calogero. Rousseau. 2. ed. Messina, 1942.
43761.39.710A St. Exupéry, A. de. Flight to Arras. N.Y., 1942.
39595.22.30 St. Pierre, J.H.B. de. Paul et Virginie suivi de La chaumière indienne. Manchester, 1942.
Mol 560.25A Saintonge, Paul F. Fifty years of Molière studies. Baltimore, 1942.
37567.400 Schmidt, Albert M. La littérature symboliste (1870-1900). 1. éd. Paris, 1942.
40516.6.80A Shaw, E.P. Jacques Cazotte, 1719-1792. Cambridge, 1942.
43780.69.220 Supervielle, Jules. Le petit bois. México, 1942.
43780.69.350 Supervielle, Jules. Poèmes de la France malheureuse. Neuchâtel, 1942.
Mon 105.3 Tannenbaum, Samuel A. Michel Eyquem de Montaigne. N.Y., 1942.
41563.28.1.20 Toepffer, Rodolphe. Nouvelles. v.1,2-3. Genève, 1942. 2v.
Mon 130.5.4 Toffanir, Giuseppe. Montaigne e l'idea classica. 2. ed. Bologna, 1942.
39578.8.44.5 Vauvenargues, L. de C. Oeuvres choisies de Vauvenargues. Paris, 1942.
42557.20.5.3 Verlaine, Paul. Fêtes galantes; La bonne chanson. Manchester, 1942.
42557.19.32 Verlaine, Paul. Odes en son honneur. Paris, 1942.
43823.76.2100 Vermorel, Claude. Jeanne avec nous; pièce en quatre actes. Paris, 1942.
FL 398.7.46 Verneuil, Louis. La vie merveilleuse de Sarah Bernhardt. N.Y., 1942.
41574.239A Viatte, Auguste. Victor Hugo et les illuminés de son temps. Montreal, 1942.
42576.57.3.5 Viaud, Julien. Pincelados vascas. Buenos Aires, 1942.
43538.18.810 Vinaver, E. Hommage a Bédier. Manchester, 1942.
43824.67.140 Vioux, Marcelle. Jeanne d'arc. Paris, 1942.
38539.8.25 Wadsworth, P.A. The novels of Gomberville; critical study of Palexandre and Cythérée. New Haven, 1942.
39544.187 Waterman, Mina. Voltaire, Pascal and human destiny. Thesis. N.Y., 1942.
37556.23.45 Wilmotte, Maurice. Origines du roman en France. Photoreproduction. Paris, 1942.
40597.2.148 Wilson, Rachel. Variations in Le cure de Tours. Chicago, 1942.
42555.44.75A Woolley, Grange. Stéphane Mallarmé, 1842-1898. Madison, 1942.
43863.55.100 Zimmermann, J.P. Cantique de notre terre. Neuchatel, 1942.

1943

43526.65.830 Aegerter, E. Guillaume Apollinaire. Paris, 1943.
43527.3.261 Aragon, Louis. Le musée Grévin. Paris, 1943.
42556.28.220 Arnoult, Pierre. Rimbaud. Paris, 1943.
38527.17.20 Aubigné, Théodore Agrippa d'. Prose. Neuchâtel, 1943. 2v.
43531.8.4110 Aubray, T. Ouvrir des yeux. 3. éd. Paris, 1943.
42576.15.165 Auriant (pseud.). Koutchauk-hauem, l'almée de Flaubert. 4. éd. Paris, 1943.
37574.643 Aury, D. Anthologie de la poésie religieuse française. 8. éd. Paris, 1943.
43535.54.220 Aymé, Marcel. Le passe-muraille. 190e éd. Paris, 1943.
43620.66.815 Bady, René. Le problème de la jaie. Fribourg, 1943.
40597.35.210 Balzac, Honoré de. Monographie de la presse parisienne. Paris, 1943.
41522.13.8.30 Baudelaire, Charles. Les fleurs du mal. Buenos Aires, 1943.
41574.243 Baudouin, Charles. Psychoanalyse de Victor Hugo. Genève, 1943.
43538.1.445 Beauvoir, Simone de. L'invitée. 29. éd. Paris, 1943.
43538.61.120 Benoît, Pierre. Seigneur, j'ai tout prevu...roman. Paris, 1943.
43538.74.120 Béraud, Henri. Qu'as-tu fait de ta jeunesse? Paris, 1943.
43538.76.152 Bernanos, Georges. Le chemin de la Croix-des-Ames. "Les cahiers de la victoire II". Rio de Janeiro, 1943.
43538.76.150 Bernanos, Georges. Monsieur Ouine. Rio de Janeiro, 1943.
43538.76.740 Bernanos, Georges. Reflexions sur le cas de conscience français. Alger, 1943?
41522.58.17 Bertrand, Louis. Gaspard de la nuit. Paris, 1943.
40582.3.40 Beyle, Henri. Lettres à Stendhal. Paris, 1943. 2v.
39566.37.5 Billy, André. Vie de Diderot. Paris, 1943.
43543.8.110 Blanchot, Maurice. Faux pas. Paris, 1943.
43544.18.100 Bodin, Jean. L'immortelle. 1. éd. Paris, 1943.
38566.65 Boileau Despréaux, Nicolas. Lettres à Racine et à divers. Paris, 1943.
42576.65.13.170 Bossier, Herman. Un personage de roman. Bruxelles, 1943.
43545.30.100 Breugnot, A.L. La faire d'embrouille. Alger, 1943.
FL 386.607 Brisson, Pierre Anatole François. Le théâtre des années folles. Genève, 1943.
37569.125 Brodin, Pierre. Maîtres et temoins de l'entre-deux-guerres. N.Y., 1943.
43823.75.2110A Bruller, Jean. La marche à l'étoile. Paris, 1943[1945]
43823.75.2202 Bruller, Jean. Le silence de la mer. N.Y., 1943.
43545.90.100 Brunet, Berthelot. Le mariage blanc d'Armandine. Montréal, 1943.
37567.680 Cailliet, Émile. La tradition littéraire des idéologues. Philadelphia, 1943. 2v.
43550.52.100 Calvet, Jean. Témoins de la conscience française. Paris, 1943.
43550.56.700 Cammaerts, E. Upon this rock. N.Y., 1943.
40542.35 Cassidy, J.F. Frederic Ozanam; a study in sanctity and scholarship. Dublin, 1943.

1943 - cont.

43552.5.135 Chardonne, Jacques. Attachements (chronique privée). 19e éd. Paris, 1943.
40517.44.2 Choderlos de Laclos, Pierre A.F. Oeuvres complètes. 2. éd. Paris, 1943.
37576.643A Chroniques interdites. v.1-2. Paris, 1943-44[1945]
43565.5.800 Clavière, M. Léon Daudet, ou Le contre-courant d'une décadence. Paris, 1943.
43556.1.310 Cocteau, Jean. Renaud et Armide. 9e éd. Paris, 1943.
43556.49.295 Colette, Sidonie Gabrielle. Le képi. Paris, 1943.
43556.49.245 Colette, Sidonie Gabrielle. Sept dialogues de bêtes. 71e éd. Paris, 1943.
37558.135A Cook, Mercer. Five French Negro authors. Washington, 1943.
37569.120 Cooper, C.B. Women poets of the twentieth century in France. N.Y., 1943.
39545.4.15 Coptrajanov, Djordje. Essai sur Candide. Skopie, 1943.
42586.32.45 Coster, Charles de. The glorious adventures of Tyl Ulenspiegel. N.Y., 1943.
Mon 114.10.2 Dédéyan, C. Montaigne dans le romantisme Anglo-Saxon. Thèse. v.1-2. Paris, 1943.
39594.19.11.5 Dedieu, J. Montesquieu; l'homme et l'oeuvre. Paris, 1943.
40597.2.157 Dedinsky, B.H. Development of the scheme of the Comédie humaine. Chicago, 1943.
43566.43.200 Dekobra, Maurice. Lune de miel à Shanghaï. N.Y., 1943.
43566.43.190 Dekobra, Maurice. La madone à Hollywood. N.Y., 1943.
V43500.83 Delétang-Tardif, Yanette. Edellina, ou Les pouvoirs de la musique. Niort, 1943.
43566.6.45 Delly, M. (pseud.). Esclave...ou reine? Paris, 1943.
37547.101 Desayniard, J. L'Auvergne dans les lettres contemporaines. Saint-Félicien, 1943.
39564.17.10 Diderot, Denis. Selected writings. N.Y., 1943.
37567.409 Dinar, André. La croisade symboliste. Paris, 1943.
43752.59.810 Doyon, René Louis. Jehan Rictus devant lui-même. Paris, 1943.
43574.41.235 Drieu La Rochelle, Pierre. L'homme à cheval, roman. 26. éd. Paris, 1943.
38526.6.18 Du Bellay, Joachim. Les regrets. Genève, 1943.
42568.19.21.15 Ducasse, I.L. Maldoror. (Les chants de Maldoror). n.p., 1943?
42554.29.175 Dujardin, É. De l'ancêtre mythique au chef moderne. London, 1943.
38567.39 Dumesnil, René. Boileau. Paris, 1943.
37555.390 Eigeldinger, Marc. Le dynamisme de l'image dans la poésie française. Neuchâtel, 1943.
40597.2.245 Emery, Leon. Balzac. Paris, 1943.
43592.53.125 Emmanuel, Pierre. La colombe. Fribourg, 1943.
43592.53.250 Emmanuel, Pierre. Prière d'Abraham. Neuchâtel, 1943.
43598.82.100 Estang, Luc. Invitation a la poésie. Marseille, 1943.
43598.82.130 Estang, Luc. Le mystère apprivoisé. Marseille, 1943.
43607.74.1110 Feraudy, Jacqueline de Gourcy. Chrysanthèmes. Paris, 1943.
40597.2.280 Fernandez, R. Balzac. Paris, 1943.
37543.257 Fernandez, R. Itinéraire française. Paris, 1943.
43611.53.170 Fombeure, Maurice. Manille coinchée. Issy-les-Moulineaux, 1943.
40526.59.10 Fontanes, Louis. Correspondance de Louis de Fontanes et de Joseph Joubert. Paris, 1943.
43740.1.83 Fourchambault, Jacques de. Charles Louis Philippe. Paris, 1943.
37568.84 Fowlie, Wallace. Clowns and angels. N.Y., 1943.
V43500.123 Frenaud, André. Les rois-mages; poèmes. Villeneuve-les-Avignon, 1943.
43616.77.110 Garr, Max. Histoire d'un chien d'émigrées et autres histoires. N.Y., 1943.
42577.4.49.110 Gaudefroy-Demomlynes, L. La femme dans l'oeuvre de Maupassant. Thèse. Paris, 1943.
43617.67.120 Georges-Michel, Michel. Autres personnalités que j'ai connues. N.Y., 1943.
43620.2.79.30 Gide, André. Attendu que. Alger, 1943.
43620.2.45.5A Gide, André. Interviews imaginaires. N.Y., 1943.
43620.2.37.3 Gide, André. Lafcadio's adventures. (Les caves du Vatican . N.Y., 1943.
37548.137 Gille, Valère. La jeune Belgique au hasard des souvenirs. Bruxelles, 1943.
42576.43.57 Gilles, Maurice. Camille Lemonnier. Bruxelles, 1943.
41522.18.145 Gilman, M. Baudelaire, the critic. N.Y., 1943.
43620.66.280 Giono, Jean. L'eau vine, contes. 23. éd. Paris, 1943.
43620.66.230 Giono, Jean. Théâtre de Jean Giono. Paris, 1943.
37556.12.34 Goedorp, Victor. Figures du temps: Eugène Lautier, G. Lenotri. Paris, 1943.
43625.27.130 Goffin, Robert. La colombe de la Gestapo. N.Y., 1943.
39572.25 Grases, Pedro. Notas sobre filologia. Caracas, 1943.
43628.25.100 Guerdan, L. Des minarets aux gratte-ciel. N.Y., 1943.
FL 6119.43 Guillemin, Henri. Un homme. Genève, 1943.
43631.89.110 Haurigot, Paul. Théâtre. v.2. Paris, 1943-
37575.685 L'Honneur des poètes. v.1-2. Paris, 1943-44.
41573.32.19 Hugo, Victor. Hernani. Paris, 1943.
41571.16.15 Hugo, Victor. Les misérables. N.Y., 1943.
40583.167 Jacoubet, Henri. Stendhal. Paris, 1943.
43667.1.45.5 Jammes, Francis. Le poète rustique. Paris, 1943.
FL 398.7.48 Jochamowitz, A. Sarah Bernhardt en Lima. Lima, 1943?
43670.89.200 Jouhandeau, M. Monsieur Godeau intime. Paris, 1943.
43670.89.160 Jouhandeau, M. Nouvelles chroniques maritales. Paris, 1943.
43670.89.170 Jouhandeau, M. L'oncle Henri. Paris, 1943.
43670.94.260 Jouve, Pierre Jean. Vers majeurs. Fribourg, 1943.
43673.83.162 Kessel, Joseph. L'armée des ombres. Alger, 1943.
41542.80 Lader, M.K. The life and novels of Léon Gozlan. Philadelphia, 1943.
39527.29.35 La Fontaine, Jean de. Fables à calorier. pt. 1-3,4-6. Montréal, 1943. 2v.
37555.158 Lalou, René. Les étapes de la poésie française. 1. éd. Paris, 1943.
43687.51.100 Laloy, Louis. Trois drames de l'Asie. Neuchâtel, 1943.
41577.13.5 Lamartine, Alphonse de. Correspondance générale de 1830 à 1848. Paris, 1943- 2v.
43687.20.104 Lannes, Roger. Argelés. Paris, 1943.
V43500.159 Lebesgue, Philéas. Florilège de poésie rustique. Blainville-sur-Mer, 1943?
43688.2.50 Le Cardonnel, Louis. Louis Le Cardonnel à San Remo. Grenoble, 1943.
42555.36.14 Leconte de Lisle, C.M.R. Poèmes choisis. Manchester, 1943.
43688.35.170 Le Grand, Maurice. L'art de vivre. Paris, 1943.
43688.60.100 Leiris, Michel. Haut mal. Paris, 1943.
43688.61.230 Lenormand, Henri René. Les Pitoëff. Paris, 1943.

Chronological Listing

1943 - cont.

43689.89.100 L'Huillier, Georges. Mars! Drame lyrique en vers. N.Y., 1943.
40535.32.55 Luethi, K. Les femmes dans l'oeuvre de Marivaux. Bienne, 1943.
42584.25.152 Luquet, A. Vida e obras de Zola. Porto, 1943.
43697.48.3700 Malaquais, Jean. Men from nowhere. N.Y., 1943.
42555.43.75A Mallarmé, Stéphane. Élucidation du poème Un coup de dés jamais. Neuchâtel, 1943.
42555.43.3.5 Mallarmé, Stéphane. Stéphane Mallarmé: poésies choisies. Londres, 1943.
43620.2.170A Mann, Klaus. André Gide and the crisis of modern thought. N.Y., 1943.
38526.32.45 Marguerite d'Angoulême. L'Heptaméron. Paris, 1943.
40556.39.33 Mary Alphonsus, mother. The influence of Joseph de Maistre on Baudelaire. Thesis. Bryn Mawr, 1943.
43697.87.2100 Matthey, P.L. Poésies, 1910-1942. Lausanne, 1943.
43697.88.215A Mauriac, François. Le cahier noir. Paris, 1943.
43697.88.216 Mauriac, François. Le cahier noir. Paris, 1943[1944]
43697.89.723 Maurois, André. Call no man happy. London, 1943.
43697.89.250 Maurois, André. Espoirs et souvenirs. N.Y., 1943.
43697.89.730A Maurois, André. Toujours l'inattendu arrive. N.Y., 1943.
42576.15.49 Maynial, E. Flaubert. Paris, 1943.
43698.75.3105 Merglen, Albert. Groupe franc. 5. éd. Paris, 1943.
42557.20.275 Micha, Alexandre. Verlaine et les poètes symbolistes. Paris, 1943.
37556.12.20 Mitton, F. La presse française. Paris, 1943-45. 2v.
39545.22.15 Moench, W. Voltaire und Freidrich der Grosse. Stuttgart, 1943.
43701.63.905 Mohrt, Michel. Montherlant, homme libre. 16. éd. Paris, 1943.
Mol 19.35.5 Molière, Jean Baptiste Poquelin. Théâtre 1664-1665. Paris, 1943.
42555.44.70 Mondor, Henri. Vie de Mallarmé. 10. éd. Paris? 1943.
Mon 32.43 Montaigne, Michel de. Selected essays. N.Y., 1943.
38527.31.8.5 Montchrétien, Antoine de. Les lacenes; a critical edition. Philadelphia, 1943.
43701.74.320 Morand, Paul. Propos des 52 semaines. Genève, 1943.
38585.16.125 Moreau, Pierre. Racine, l'homme et l'oeuvre. Paris, 1943.
41522.13.8.85 Morgan, Edwin. Flower of evil. N.Y., 1943.
37555.517 Morier, Henri. Le rythme du vers libre symboliste. Genève, 1943-44. 3v.
Mol 713.17 Mornet, Daniel. Molière. Paris, 1943.
41543.22.30 Nerval, Gerard de. Lettres d'amour à Jenny Colon. Bruxelles, 1943.
43706.97.100 Neveux, Georges. Théâtre. Paris, 1943-
42557.12.100 Olivero, F. Il contrasto nella lirica di Émile Verhaeren. Torino, 1943.
43738.1.50A Péguy, Charles. Basic verities. N.Y., 1943.
43738.1.62 Péguy, Charles. Notre seigneur. Paris, 1943.
37543.241 Peyre, Henri. Essays in honor of Albert Feuillerat. New Haven, 1943.
43741.25.230 Pieyre de Mandiargues, André. Dans les années sordides. Monaco, 1943.
38557.24.65 Pissère, Robert. Les idées politiques de Bossuet. Thèse. Montpellier, 1943.
43742.41.150 Plisnier, Charles. Ave genitrix. Fribourg, 1943.
43742.41.155 Plisnier, Charles. Ave genitrix. Paris, 1943.
43742.41.170 Plisnier, Charles. Hospitalité. Fribourg, 1943.
43743.57.700A Poncins, G. de M. Home is the hunter. N.Y., 1943.
37555.159 Poulaille, Henry. La fleur des chansons d'amour. Paris, 1943.
43743.90.160 Pourrat, Henri. Vent du Mars. Paris, 1943.
43743.98.531A Pozner, Vladimir. First harvest. N.Y., 1943.
43743.98.430 Pozner, Vladimir. Les gens du pays. N.Y., 1943.
40522.9.60 Prévost, Antoine F. Manon Lescaut. Oxford, 1943. 2v.
37556.125 Prévost, Jean. Problèmes du roman. Lyon, 1943.
43747.32.130 Puget, C.A. Théâtre. Paris, 1943-46. 3v.
43747.53.100 Pulsifer, S.F.N. Fighting French ballads. N.Y., 1943.
43750.24.130 Queneau, Raymond. Pierrot mon ami. 24. éd. Paris, 1943.
38585.43.8 Racine, Jean. Phèdre. Manchester, 1943.
37574.720 Ramuz, C. Anthologie de la poésie française. Paris, 1943. 2v.
40583.164 Raya, Gino. Stendhal. Modena, 1943.
42556.28.45A Rimbaud, Jean Arthur. Oeuvres complètes. Buenos Aires, 1943.
43757.7.3061 Robert, Louis de. Lettres à Paul Faure (1898-1937). Paris, 1943.
FL 398.3.50 Rochefort, C. Le film de mes souvenirs. Paris, 1943.
42546.13.1.15 Rostand, Edmond. Cyrano de Bergerac. Oxford, 1943.
FL 6032.43 Rousseau, J.J. Du contrat social. Paris, 1943.
37543.243 Rousseaux, André. Le monde classique. Paris, 1943.
V43500.273 Rousselot, Jean. Refaire la nuit; poèmes. Niort, 1943.
43761.39.713.2 St. Exupéry, A. de. The little prince. N.Y., 1943.
43761.39.713A St. Exupéry, A. de. The little prince. N.Y., 1943.
43761.39.130 St. Exupéry, A. de. Le petit prince. N.Y., 1943.
43761.48.110 Salacrou, Armand. Théâtre. v.1-7. Paris, 1943-47. 5v.
42584.25.150 Salvan, A.J. Zola aux Etats-Unis. Providence, 1943.
V43500.291 Samain, Albert. Poèmes pour la grande amie. 10. ed. Paris, 1943.
43763.38.170 Schlumberger, Jean. Nouveaux jalons. Marseille, 1943.
43763.38.185 Schlumberger, Jean. Théâtre. 3. éd. Paris, 1943.
43765.32.110 Seghers, Pierre. Le chien de pique. Neuchâtel, 1943.
42576.23.15 Seznec, Jean. Saint-Antoine et les monstres. N.Y., 1943.
37576.639.5 Speare, M.E. Great French short stories. Cleveland, 1943.
43779.77.105 Strouski, Fortunat. Les libérateurs. Rio de Janeiro, 1943.
43788.65.120 Thomas, E. Contes d'Auxois. Paris, 1943.
37547.75 Trigon, Jean de. Portraits et médaillons morlaisiens Morlaix, France. Brest, 1943.
43793.42.135 Triolet, Elsa. Les amants d'Avignon. Paris, 1943[1945]
43793.42.180 Triolet, Elsa. Le cheval blanc; roman. Paris, 1943.
43793.42.200 Triolet, Elsa. Mille regrets. Paris, 1943.
43822.49.350 Valéry, Paul. Poesía de Paul Valéry. Mexico, 1943.
37573.72 Varney, J.M.V. Ecrivains français; extraits. N.Y., 1943.
39544.28.60 Voltaire, François Marie Arouet de. Lettres philosophiques. Oxford, 1943.
42582.2.35A Waltz, G.H. Jules Verne. N.Y., 1943.
43775.75.800 Wanner, J. Georges Sorel et la décadence. Lausanne, 1943.
37543.445 Yetkin, S.K. Edebî meslekler. Istanbul, 1943.

1944

37574.167.2 Almeida, G. de. Poetas de França. 2. ed. São Paulo, 1944.
43524.36.100 Angreville, M. d'. Les lilas refleuriront. N.Y., 1944.
43527.3.220 Aragon, Louis. Aurelien, roman. 31. ed. Paris, 1944.
43527.3.155 Aragon, Louis. Le crève-coeur. Paris, 1944.
43527.3.270 Aragon, Louis. Le crime contre l'esprit. Paris, 1944.
37543.259 Arland, Marcel. Le promeneur. Paris, 1944.
43528.61.140 Arnoux, Alexandre. Rhône, mon fleuve. Paris, 1944.
43532.23.121 Aveline, Claude. Le temps mort. Paris, 1944.
42576.63.200A Axelrad, J. Anatole France. N.Y., 1944.
43535.54.170 Aymé, Marcel. Vogue la galère. Paris, 1944.
40597.34.5.5 Balzac, Honoré de. Ursule Mirouet. Paris, 1944.
40597.2.159.2 Bardèche, Maurice. Balzac, romancier. Bruxelles, 1944.
37574.670 Barker, Arthur. Twelve more echoes. Wellington, 1944.
41522.13.9.20 Baudelaire, Charles. Flores das "Flores do mal". Rio de Janeiro, 1944.
41522.13.9.25 Baudelaire, Charles. Las flores del mal. México, 1944.
43538.1.465 Beauvoir, Simone de. Pyrrhus et Cinéas. Paris, 1944.
43738.1.175 Béguin, A. La prière de Péguy. Neuchatel, 1944.
42563.23.92A Béguin, Albert. Léon Bloy l'impatient. Fribourg, 1944.
43538.74.230 Béraud, Henri. Les raisons d'un silence. Paris, 1944.
43538.76.154 Bernanos, Georges. Le chemin de la Croix-des-Ames (1941-1942). "Les cahiers de la victoire IV". Rio de Janeiro, 1944.
43538.76.720 Bernanos, Georges. Plea for liberty. N.Y., 1944.
41578.123 Bertrand, L. Lamartine. Paris, 1944.
40597.2.153 Billy, André. Vie de Balzac. Paris, 1944. 2v.
38525.22.6.10 Binet, Claude. Discours de la vie de Pierre de Ronsard. Paris, 1944.
43543.13.160 Bloch, J.R. Toulon. Moscou, 1944.
37574.540 Bo, Carlo. Anthologia del surrealism. Milano, 1944.
37569.40.215 Bo, Carlo. Bilancio del surrealismo. Padova, 1944.
43822.49.957 Bolle, Louis. Paul Valéry. Fribourg en Swisse, 1944.
43556.1.803A Boni, Gianni. Cocteau e la poetica del film. Roma, 1944.
40597.2.275 Bonnet-Roy, F. Balzac, les médecins. Paris, 1944.
43698.25.820 Bordes, Elis. Le drame spirituel dans l'oeuvre de Maxence van der Meersch. 3. éd. Tourcoing, 1944.
42577.4.35.5 Borel, Pierre. Maupassant et l'androgyne. Paris, 1944.
V43500.37 Bouhier, Jean. Calcaire, 1942-1944. n.p., 1944?
43823.75.2710 Bruller, Jean. Put out the light. London, 1944.
43823.75.2203 Bruller, Jean. Le silence de la mer. Paris, 1944.
43823.75.2700A Bruller, Jean. The silence of the sea. N.Y., 1944.
Mon 112.14 Brunschvicq, L. Descartes et Pascal; lectures de Montaigne. N.Y., 1944.
43550.56.705 Cammaerts, E. The flower of grass. London, 1944.
43550.1.140 Carco, Francis. L'ami des peintres, souvenirs. Genève, 1944.
42557.20.241 Carco, François. Verlaine. Paris, 1944.
43550.82.140 Cassou, Jean. Trente-trois sonnets composés au secret. Paris, 1944.
42556.28.185 Castelnau, Jacques. Rimbaud. Paris, 1944.
43551.80.190 Cesbron, Gilbert. Les innocents de Paris. Paris, 1944.
43552.4.30 Chantal, S. Dieu ne dort pas; roman. N.Y., 1944.
43552.5.125 Chardonne, Jacques. L'amour c'est beaucoup plus que l'amour. Paris, 1944.
37548.26.2 Charlier, Gustave. Les lettres françaises de Belgique. Bruxelles, 1944.
38514.64.8.5 Chartier, Alain. Le quadriloque invectif. Paris, 1944.
43552.5.3100 Chassé, Charles. Les contes de la Lande. Paris, 1944.
37595.36.3.10 Chrestien de Troyes. La chevalier au lion. 4. éd. Paris, 1944.
43554.2.25 Claudel, Paul. Pages de prose. 23e éd. Paris, 1944.
37573.677 Clot, René Jean. L'exil français. Alger, 1944.
43744.67.1072 Coelho, Ruy. Proust e introducão ao método crítico. São Paulo, 1944.
43556.49.430 Colette, Sidonie Gabrielle. La chatte; roman. 123e éd. Paris, 1944.
43556.49.310 Colette, Sidonie Gabrielle. Gigi. Lausanne, 1944.
43556.49.330 Colette, Sidonie Gabrielle. Paris de ma fenêtre. Genève, 1944.
41539.27 Constantin-Weyer, Maurice. L'aventure vécue de Dumas père. Genève, 1944.
38575.37.10 Corneille, Pierre. L'illusion comique. Manchester, 1944.
42563.37.112 Correa Pastene, M. Los caminos de Roma. Santiago, 1944.
37547.14.5 Cuzacq, René. Autour de l'école Gaston-Phébus (1897-1919). Bayonne, 1944.
42566.16.85 Daudet, Lucien. Vie d'Alphonse Daudet. 17. éd. Gallinard, 1944.
43565.92.105 David, A. Amour charnel de la patrie. N.Y., 1944.
Mon 114.10 Dédéyan, C. Montaigne chez ses amis Anglo-Saxons. Paris, 1944? 2v.
Mon 59.7 Dedeyan, Charles. Essai sur le Journal de voyage de Montaigne. Paris, 1944.
43566.43.210 Dekobra, Maurice. Les lèvres que mentent. Montréal, 1944.
43566.77.2100 Des Baux, C. Les bacchantes; tragédie. Alexandrie, 1944.
43566.82.7140 Destouches, Louis Ferdinand. Guignol's band; roman. Paris? 1944.
43566.82.7145 Destouches, Louis Pierre. Guignol's band; roman. Paris, 1944- 2v.
37556.133 Dinar, André. A la recherche de romans d'amour. 4. éd. Paris, 1944.
43573.76.70 Dorgelès, Roland. Route des tropiques. Paris, 1944.
43576.6.354 Duhamel, Georges. Biographie de mes fantômes. Paris, 1944.
43576.6.217A Duhamel, Georges. Chronique des saisons amères, 1940-1943. 13. éd. Paris, 1944.
43576.6.31.5 Duhamel, Georges. Civilisation française. Paris, 1944.
43576.6.46 Duhamel, Georges. Deux hommes. Paris, 1944.
43576.6.112 Duhamel, Georges. Journal de Salavin; roman. Paris, 1944.
37578.90 Duliani, Mario. Deux heures de fou rire. Montréal, 1944.
41538.80 Dumas, Alexandre. The journal of Madame Giovanni. N.Y., 1944.
41578.40.51 Dupouy, Auguste. Elvire. Paris, 1944.
37596.255 Ellebaut. Anticlaudien. Washington, 1944.
43592.53.150 Emmanuel, Pierre. Cantos. Neuchâtel, 1944.
43592.53.220F Emmanuel, Pierre. Le poète fou. Monaco, 1944.
43592.53.100 Emmanuel, Pierre. Sodome. Fribourg, 1944.
43592.53.155 Emmanuel, Pierre. Tombeau d'Orphée. Fribourg, 1944.
Mol 728.11.5 Farnoux-Reynaud, Lucien. L'aventure comique. Lyon, 1944.
43606.87.140 Fauchois, René. Vitrail, un acte. Paris, 1944.
38526.32.60 Febvre, Lucien. Autour de l'Heptaméron. 2e éd. Paris, 1944.
43822.49.907.5 Fernandat, René. Autour de Paul Valéry. Grenoble, 1944.
41522.18.137 Feuillerat, A. Baudelaire et sa mère. Montréal, 1944.
42576.31.20 Flaubert, Gustave. Salammbô. London, 1944.
42576.31.25 Flaubert, Gustave. Salammbô. Paris, 1944. 2v.
42576.33.8.5 Flaubert, Gustave. Trois contes. Montréal, 1944.

Chronological Listing

1944 - cont.

43611.1.80 Fort, Paul. Mes mémoires. Paris, 1944.
43611.5.34 Fournier, Alain. Le grand meaulnes. Londres, 1944.
37568.88 Fowlie, Wallace. The spirit of France. London, 1944.
42576.63.18.7F France, Anatole. Il miracolo del grande S. Nicola. Torino, 1944.
43612.58.1100 France, Naira. Exil. London, 1944.
43612.64.100 Frémont, Jean. L'ascension et d'autres poèmes. Oxford, 1944.
FL 379.92.20 Fuchs, Max. Lexique des troupes de comédiens au XVIIIe siècle. Paris, 1944.
43616.7.30 Gaberel, Henri. Tombeau pour un amour médiéval. Porrentruy, 1944.
43616.78.740 Gary, Romain. Forest of anger. London, 1944.
43617.67.130 Georges-Michel, Michel. Bohème a New York. N.Y., 1944.
43617.67.135 Georges-Michel, Michel. Dames éstranges. Montréal, 1944.
FL 360.93 Gheon, Henri. L'art du théâtre. Montréal, 1944.
43620.2.45.20 Gide, André. Entrevistas imaginarias. Bogotá, 1944.
43620.2.45.15 Gide, André. Imaginary interviews. 1. American ed. N.Y., 1944.
43620.2.68.10 Gide, André. Pages de journal. Alger, 1944.
43620.74.360 Giraudoux, Jean. Le film de Béthanie. Paris, 1944.
43620.74.325 Giraudoux, Jean. Littérature. Paris, 1944.
43625.19.260 Godoy, Armand. De vêpres à matines. Fribourg, 1944.
43699.51.800 Godoy, Armand. Milosz. Fribourg, 1944.
43625.27.140 Goffin, Robert. Passeports pour l'au-delá. N.Y., 1944.
43626.22.717 Green, Julien. Memories of happy days. London, 1944.
37566.105 Grosse, Pierre de. Villegiatures romantiques. Paris, 1944.
43626.68.100 Grout, Marius. Passage de l'homme; roman. Paris, 1944.
43628.23.135 Guéhenno, Jean. Dans la prison. Paris, 1944.
37555.235 Henriot, Émile. De Turold à André Chenier. Lyon, 1944.
37543.310A Hoog, A. Littérature en Silesie. Paris, 1944.
43667.14.25 Jacob, Max. Max Jacob, mystique et martyr. Paris, 1944.
43670.89.510 Jouhandeau, M. Chroniques maritales. Paris, 1944.
43670.94.280 Jouve, Pierre Jean. Gloire, 1940. Fribourg, 1944.
43670.94.270 Jouve, Pierre Jean. La vierge de Paris. Fribourg, 1944.
42576.63.220 Jusselin, M. Aïeux et parents beaucerons d'Anatole France. Chartres, 1944.
43673.83.160 Kessel, Joseph. L'armée des ombres. N.Y., 1944.
43673.83.158A Kessel, Joseph. Army of shadows. N.Y., 1944.
41577.14.15 Lamartine, Alphonse de. Lettres inédites, 1821-1851. 7. éd. Porrentruy, Switzerland, 1944.
43687.75.145 Larguier, Léo. Mes vingt ans et moi. Paris, 1944.
43687.75.160 Larguier, Léo. Petites histories pour bibliophiles. Paris, 1944.
41564.55.65 LaSalle, Bertrand de. Alfred de Vigny. Paris, 1944.
40587.145 Lathion, Lucien. Chateaubriand et Goethe en Valais. Sierre, 1944.
FL 375.83 Lebègue, Raymond. La tragédie française de la renaissance. Bruxelles, 1944.
43688.33.50 Legrand, Ignace. Deux nouvelles du passé. London, 1944.
42563.23.100 Léon Bloy, études. Toulouse, 1944.
42563.23.95 Léon Bloy. Neuchâtel, 1944.
38525.22.45.80 Lewis, D.B.W. Ronsard. London, 1944.
42563.23.114.5 Lory, M.J. Léon Bloy et son époque. Paris, 1944.
43738.1.190 Mabille de Poncheville, A. Jeunesse de Péguy. Paris, 1944.
39527.70 Macé, Alcide. La Fontaine et Horace. Rennes, 1944.
43697.48.3120 Malaquais, Jean. Coups de barre. N.Y., 1944.
43697.77.111 Martin du Gard, Roger. Les Thibault. v.1-8. Montréal, 1944. 9v.
43697.78.5100 Martin Saint-René (pseud.). Les années maudites. Paris, 1944.
41522.18.157 Massin, Jean. Baudelaire devant la donleur. Paris, 1944.
43745.1.101 Massis, Henri. Notre ami Psichari. Paris, 1944.
43697.88.230 Mauriac, François. Les anges noirs. Paris, 1944.
43697.88.390 Mauriac, François. Ne pas se renier. Alger, 1944.
43697.89.221 Maurois, André. La machine à lire les pensées. N.Y., 1944.
43697.89.718 Maurois, André. Seven faces of Love. N.Y., 1944.
42514.28.11 Maurras, Charles. Poesie et verite. Lyon, 1944.
43698.200.130 Michaux, Henri. L'espace du dedans. Paris, 1944.
43698.205.100 Michelin, M. Les riches heures. N.Y., 1944.
43699.51.13 Milosz, Oscar Vladislas. Oeuvres complètes. v.1-5, 8. Fribourg, 1944-1946. 5v.
39594.2.30 Montesquieu, C.L. de S. De l'esprit des lois. Paris, 1944-45.
39594.2.25 Montesquieu, C.L. de S. Extraits sur la loi, la liberté et le gouvernment anglais. Princeton, 1944.
39594.14.30 Montesquieu, C.L. de S. Le spicilège, un carnet inédit. Paris, 1944.
43701.63.190 Montherlant, Henry de. Fils de personne, fils des autres, un incompris. Bruxelles, 1944.
43701.63.195 Montherlant, Henry de. Fils de personne. 33. éd. Paris, 1944.
43701.63.350 Montherlant, Henry de. Un incompris. Paris, 1944.
43620.74.845 Morand, Paul. Adieu à Giraudoux. Porrentruy, 1944.
43701.75.6102 Morgan, C. La marque de l'homme. Paris, 1944.
41522.13.8.86 Morgan, Edwin. Flower of evil, a life of Charles Baudelairę. London, 1944.
37555.157A Noulet, E. Études littéraires. Mexique, 1944.
43731.50.100 Oulmont, Charles. Message personnel. Lisboa, 1944.
40593.45 Pange, P.L.M. de B. Le dernier amour de Madame de Staël d'après des documents inédites. Genève, 1944.
43738.1.60 Péguy, Charles. Deux voix françaises. Paris, 1944.
43738.1.60.2 Péguy, Charles. Deux voix françaises. Paris, 1944.
43738.1.56 Péguy, Charles. Men and saints. N.Y., 1944.
43738.79.100 Perrier, F. La garde montante. N.Y., 1944.
37567.394 Picard, Roger. Le romantisme social. N.Y., 1944.
FL 1102.6.2 Piron, Maurice. Les lettres wallonnes contemporaines. 2. ed. Tournai, 1944.
43742.41.140 Plisnier, Charles. Une voix d'or. Freibourg en Swisse, 1944.
41596.4.90 Pommier, Jean. Variétés sur Alfred de Musset et son théâtre. Paris, 1944?
43743.57.100 Poncins, G. de M. Jean Menadieu. N.Y.? 1944.
40583.170 Poppe, Roger. Stendhal à Rome. Paris, 1944.
43744.1.100 Praag, Siegfried Emanuel van. Fille de France. Londres, 1944.
43744.5.110 Prassinos, Gisèle. Le feu maniaque. Paris, 1944.
39598.44A Price, Lawrence M. The vogue of Marmontel on the German stage. Berkeley, 1944.
43747.53.102 Pulsifer, S.F.N. L'esprit de la France. N.Y., 1944.
43750.24.150 Queneau, Raymond. Loin de Rueil. Paris, 1944.
38536.26.4 Rabelais, F. Five books of Gargantua and Pantagruel. N.Y., 1944.

1944 - cont.

38585.48 Racine, Jean. Principes de la tragédie en marge de la poétique d'Aristote. Manchester, 1944.
FL 386.608 Radine, Serge. Essais sur le théâtre, 1919-1939. Genève-Annemasse, 1944.
43752.21.100 Raeders, Georges. La découverte du nouveau monde. Rio de Janeiro, 1944.
43752.57.710 Ramuz, Charles Ferdinand. The end of all men. N.Y., 1944.
43752.57.280 Ramuz, Charles Ferdinand. La guerre dans le Haut-Pays. Lausanne, 1944.
43752.57.275 Ramuz, Charles Ferdinand. Histoire du soldat. Lausanne, 1944.
43752.57.190 Ramuz, Charles Ferdinand. Vie de Samuel Belet. Paris, 1944.
42576.63.205 Reissig, L. Anatole France. Buenos Aires, 1944.
42515.30.695 Renan, Ernest. Les sciences de la nature et les sciences historiques. Princeton, 1944.
37564.160 Reynold, Gonzague. Le XVIIe siècle. Montréal, 1944.
43756.12.100 Richard, Marius. La Rapee. Paris, 1944.
37564.145 Riva Agüero, José de la. Estudios sobre literatura francesca. Lima, 1944.
43757.12.100 Roblès, Emmanuel. Travail d'homme. Alger, 1944.
37566.111 Rolland de Renéville, A. Univers de la parole. 5. éd. Paris, 1944.
43757.3.86 Romains, Jules. Bertrand de ganges. N.Y., 1944.
43757.3.240 Romains, Jules. Retrouver la foi. N.Y., 1944.
42546.15.20.6 Rothschild, Henri de. Un côeur sur le gril; pièce en quatre actes. Pôrto, 1944.
43738.1.165 Rousseaux, A. Le prophete Péguy. pts.2,4-5. Neuchatel, 1944-1945. 2v.
43757.96.100 Roy, Claude. La mer à boire. Paris, 1944.
FL 6139.44 Sacheli, Calogero. Rousseau. 2. ed. Messina, 1944.
43761.39.140.5 St. Exupéry, A. de. Lettre à un otage. 26. éd. Paris, 1944.
43761.44.100 St. Soline, Claire. Et l'enfant que je fus. Paris, 1944.
43761.1.700 Sandoz, Maurice Yves. Fantastic memories. Garden City, N.Y., 1944.
43761.92.100 Savarion, A. Visages et paysages du Marias Poitevin. Paris, 1944.
37555.49.10 Schaffer, A. The genres of Parnassian poetry. Baltimore, Md., 1944.
38514.23.75 Schneider, Pierre B. Étude sur la criminalité de François Villon. Lausanne, 1944.
43763.2.52 Schopfer, Jean. Mayerling. Paris, 1944.
39566.60 Seillière, Ernest. Diderot. Paris, 1944.
43769.54.715 Simenon, Georges. Escape in vain. N.Y., 1944.
43822.49.1010 Sørensen, Hans. La poésie de Paul Valéry. Thesis. Aarhus, 1944.
43775.90.7710 Soupault, Philippe. Ode to bombed London. Algiers, 1944.
43775.90.7175 Soupault, Philippe. Tous ensemble au bout du monde. Algers, 1944.
43776.41.200 Spire, André. Poèmes d'ici et de là-bas. N.Y., 1944.
38544.27.585 Styger, Flora. Essai sur l'oeuvre de Mme. de La Fayette. Affoltems, 1944.
43780.69.230 Supervielle, Jules. Choix de poèmes. Buenos Aires, 1944.
43620.74.820 Tavernier, René. Hommage à Giraudoux. Paris? 1944?
40556.23.15 Tessoneau, Rémy. Joseph Joubert. Thèse. Paris, 1944.
43788.5.230 Tharaud, Jérôme. Les contes de la Vierge. Paris, 1944.
FL 370.104.5 Thiry, Paul. Le théâtre français au Moyen Age. 2. ed. Bruxelles, 1944.
42547.22.87 Thomas, Louis. Le vrai Villiers de l'Isle Adam. Paris, 1944.
37574.170 Thorley, W.C. The French muse. London, 1944.
41563.29.10 Toepffer, Rodolphe. Le Presbytère. Genève, 1944. 2v.
41563.32.10 Toepffer, Rodolphe. Rosa et Gertrude. Genève, 1944.
40516.6.82 Trintzius, R. Jacques Cazotte. 2. éd. Paris, 1944.
43822.49.790 Valéry, Paul. Cuatra maestros franceses: Stendhal - Baudelaire - Verlaine - Mallarmé. Bogotá, 1944.
41596.4.85 Van Tieghem, Philippe. Musset, l'homme et l'oeuvre. Paris, 1944.
42557.18.35 Verlaine, Paul. Paralelamente a Paul Verlaine. São Paulo, 1944.
42557.20.8 Verlaine, Paul. Verlaine. Basel, 1944.
42582.40 Verne, Jules. Julio Verne y America. Buenos-Aires, 1944.
FL 398.8.5 Verneuil, Louis. Rideau à neuf heures. N.Y., 1944-
41557.10.105 Viens, Claude P. George Sand and Gustave Planche: unpublished correspondence. Providence, 1944.
38514.23.85 Villon, François. Villon. Fribourg, 1944.
39544.28.100 Voltaire, François Marie Arouet de. Voltaires Briefwechsel mit Friedrich dem Grossen. Berlin, 1944.
38513.19.15 Whittredge, R. La nativité et le geu des trois roys. Bryn Mawr, Pa., 1944.
37548.22 Ziégler, Henri de. La Suisse littéraire d'aujourd'hui. Lisboa, 1944.

1945

43514.3.100 Adam, George. A l'appel de la liberté. Paris, 1945.
37568.92 Aegerter, E. Au temps de Guillaume Appollinaire. Paris, 1945.
43515.79.100 Aeschimann, Paul. La terre et l'ange; poèmes. Paris, 1945.
FL 398.7.55 Agate, May. Madame Sarah. London, 1945.
43523.5.105 Amat, J.C. Malespine; roman. Montréal, 1945.
43524.22.100 André-May, Pierre. Le matin. Paris, 1945.
43524.67.140 Anouilh, Jean. Le bal des voleurs. Grenoble, 1945.
43524.67.130A Anouilh, Jean. Pièces noires. 36. éd. Paris, 1945.
43524.67.120 Anouilh, Jean. Pièces roses. 29. éd. Paris, 1945.
43527.3.720 Aragon, Louis. Aragon, poet of the French resistance. N.Y., 1945.
43527.3.21 Aragon, Louis. Aragon, une étude par Claude Roy. Paris, 1945.
43527.3.242 Aragon, Louis. En étrange pays dans mon pays lui-même. Monaco, 1945.
43527.3.170 Aragon, Louis. Le paysan de Paris. 11. éd. Paris, 1945.
43757.94.1800 Aragon, Louis. Saint Paul Roux, ou L'espoir. Paris, 1945.
43527.3.160A Aragon, Louis. Servitude et grandeur des Français scénes des années terribles. Paris, 1945.
43527.3.190 Aragon, Louis. Les yeux d'Elsa. Neuchâtel, 1945.
43527.3.210 Aragon, Louis. Les yeux d'Elsa. Paris, 1945.
Mol 601.5.15 Arnavon, J. Morale de Molière. Paris, 1945.
43528.68.150 Arp, Hans. Le blanc aux pieds de nègre. Paris, 1945.
40597.2.162 Arrault, Albert. Madame de Berny; éducatrice de Balzac. Tours, 1945.
43620.2.225 Aubry, G.J. André Gide et la musique. Paris, 1945.
43532.23.130 Aveline, Claude. Dans Paris retrouvé. Paris, 1945.

Chronological Listing

1945 - cont.

43532.23.110 Aveline, Claude. Les devoirs de l'esprit. 3e éd. Paris, 1945.
43532.23.120 Aveline, Claude. Le temps mort. Paris, 1945.
37573.675 Bady, René. L'âme française à travers la littérature. Lausanne, 1945.
40532.25.30 Bailly, Auguste. Beaumarchais. 12. éd. Paris, 1945.
37556.21.50 Balch, M. A survey of the Paris daily press. Paris, 1945.
37567.398 Baldensperger, F. La critique et l'histoire en France. N.Y., 1945.
40597.14.6.15 Balzac, Honoré de. César Birotteau. Montréal, 1945.
40596.47 Balzac, Honoré de. Le chef-d'oeuvre inconnu. Genève, 1945.
43537.70.100 Barbier, René. Marie Pietrot. Paris, 1945.
37574.535 Bastos, V. Anthologie de la poésie française moderne. Buenos Aires, 1945.
37563.77 Bates, B.W. Literary portraiture in the historical narrative of the French renaissance. N.Y., 1945.
41522.13.9.27 Baudelaire, Charles. Les fleurs du mal. Paris, 1945.
41522.13.40 Baudelaire, Charles. Mon coeur mis à nu. Mexico, 1945.
40556.39.40 Bayle, Francis. Les idées politiques de Joseph de Maistre. Paris, 1945.
40532.3.40 Beaumarchais, Pierre A.C. de. Beaumarchais. Montréal, 1945.
43538.1.435 Beauvoir, Simone de. Les bouches inutiles; pièce en deux actes et huit tableaux. 5. éd. Paris, 1945.
37576.645A Becker, Belle. Bedside book of famous French stories. N.Y., 1945.
41543.22.23A Beguin, Albert. Gerard de Nerval. Paris, 1945.
37555.40.10 Belloc, Hilaire. Avril, being essays on the poetry of the French renaissance. London, 1945.
43538.5.85 Benda, Julien. Exercise d'un enterré vif (juin 1940 - août 1944). 4. éd. Genève, 1945.
37568.94.10 Benda, Julien. La France byzantine,...essai d'une psychologie originelle du littérature. 12e éd. Paris, 1945.
43538.61.130 Benoît, Pierre. Martine Juillet. Montréal, 1945.
43538.61.160 Benoît, Pierre. Le sentier couvert. Montréal, 1945.
FL 398.7.50 Berendt, Rachel. Sarah Bernhardt en mi recuerdo. Buenos Aires, 1945.
43538.76.730 Bernanos, Georges. The open mind. London, 1945.
FL 363.60 Bernard, Rene. Le bègue sur la scène française. Paris, 1945.
43822.49.1005 Berne-Joffroy, A. Présence de Valéry. Paris, 1945.
FL 398.7.60 Bernhardt, L.S. Sarah Bernhardt. Paris, 1945.
40582.14.12 Beyle, Henri. Lucien Leuwen. Monaco, 1945. 2v.
43540.7.130 Bibescu, M.L. Images d'Epinal. Paris, 1945.
43540.3.67 Billy, André. La terrasse du Luxembourg. Paris, 1945.
43543.6.100 Blanchard, André. Capitale. Paris, 1945.
42563.23.55 Bloy, Léon. Inédits de Léon Bloy. Montréal, 1945.
42555.44.100 Bo, Carlo. Mallarmé. Milano, 1945.
43556.49.895 Boncompain, Claude. Colette. Lyon, 1945?
43544.60.110 Bonnamy, George. Souvenirs d'un pseudo vaincu. Paris, 1945.
43544.81.100 Bory, Jean Louis. Mon village à l'heure allemandi; roman. N.Y., 1945.
43544.83.130A Bost, Pierre. La haute fourche. Paris, 1945.
43544.83.120 Bost, Pierre. Monsieur L'admiral va bientôt mourir. 9. éd. Paris, 1945.
43544.99.100 Bourgeois, André. René Boylesve. Paris, 1945.
43526.65.840 Bourgois, A. Rene Borflesve. 4th ed. Paris, 1945.
43544.94.120 Bove, Emmanuel. Le piège. Paris, 1945.
42563.23.110 Brady, M.R. Thought and style in the works of Léon Bloy. Thesis. Washington, 1945.
43545.24.160 Breton, André. L'amour Lou. Paris, 1945.
43545.24.100 Breton, André. Arcane 17. N.Y., 1945.
43545.24.150A Breton, André. Nadja. 10. éd. Paris, 1945.
42576.57.80 Broden, Pierre. Loti. Montréal, 1945.
43823.75.2100 Bruller, Jean. Le songe. Paris, 1945.
43744.67.1140 Buchet, E.E. Ecrivains intelligents du XXe siècle. Paris, 1945.
43526.65.850 Cadou, René G. Testament d'Apollinaire temoignage. Paris, 1945.
40526.74.2 Campion, Charles Michel. Oeuvres de Charles Michel Campion. Bloomington, 1945.
43550.58.63 Camus, Albert. Lettres à un ami allemand. Paris, 1945.
43550.58.112 Camus, Albert. Noces. 11. éd. Paris, 1945.
41522.3.26 Canu, Jean. Barbey d'Aurevilly. 7. éd. Paris, 1945.
40556.47 Caponigri, A.R. Some aspects of the philosophy of Joseph de Maistre. Chicago, 1945.
43550.1.150 Carco, Francis. Jésus-la-Caille, roman. Paris, 1945.
43550.82.120 Cassou, Jean. Le centre du monde. Paris, 1945.
37568.90 Catalogne, G. de. Les compagnons du spirituel: Mauriac - Massis - Ducattillon. Montréal, 1945.
39586.19.6 Chamfort, S.R.N. La jeune Indienne. Princeton, 1945.
43552.3.9120 Chamson, André. Le puits des miracles, roman. 50e éd. Paris, 1945.
42514.28.73 Chandet, Henriette. Le procés Maurras. Lyon, 1945.
43552.4.1010 Chaponnière, P. Pensées et arrière-pensées. Boudry, 1945.
43552.4.7100 Chapron, Marcel. Un chouan fulgurant. Paris, 1945.
43552.4.2140 Char, René. Le marteau sans maitre. Paris, 1945.
43552.4.2110 Char, René. Seuls demeurent. Paris, 1945.
43552.4.5110 Charbonneau, Robert. Fontile; roman. Montreal, 1945.
43552.5.1150 Chartier, Emile. Les aventures du coeur. Paris, 1945.
40586.28.75 Chateaubriand, F.A.R. Mémoires d'outre-tombe. Paris, 1945.
43744.67.1100 Chernowitz, M.E. Proust and painting. N.Y., 1945.
43554.2.380 Claudel, Paul. Deux farces lyriques. 10e éd. Paris, 1945.
43554.2.63.5 Claudel, Paul. Le père humiliè. 10e éd. Paris, 1945.
43554.2.64 Claudel, Paul. Poèmes et paroles durant la guerre de trente ans. Paris, 1945.
43554.2.710 Claudel, Paul. Three plays; The hostage, Trusts, The humiliation of father. Boston, 1945.
42576.64.4.5 Clune, Frank. The greatest liar on earth. Melbourne, 1945.
43556.1.205 Cocteau, Jean. Leone. Paris, 1945.
43556.1.65 Cocteau, Jean. Poèmes. Lausanne, 1945.
43556.1.200 Cocteau, Jean. Poésie critique. Paris, 1945.
43701.2.82 Cocteau, Jean. Portrait de Mounet-Sully. Paris, 1945.
43556.49.61 Colette, Sidonie Gabrielle. Une amitié inattendue. Paris, 1945.
43556.49.186.10 Colette, Sidonie Gabrielle. Claudine en ménage. Paris, 1945.
43556.49.315 Colette, Sidonie Gabrielle. Gigi. Paris, 1945.
40553.9.55 Constant de Rebecque, Benjamin. Journal intime. 2. éd. Monaco, 1945.
X Cg 38575.27.20 Corneille, Pierre. Le Cid. Lyon, 1945.

1945 - cont.

38575.33.25A Corneille, Pierre. Rodogune. Paris, 1945.
38574.23.7 Corneille, Pierre. Théâtre choisi. Montreal, 1945. 2v.
38524.100 Dans les jardins de la poésie française. Seizième siècle. Paris, 1945.
43565.5.150 Daudet, Léon A. L'heure qui tourne. Paris, 1945.
43738.1.180 David, M. Initiation à Charles Péguy. Paris, 1945.
43565.92.7100 Davray, Jean. Les complaintes. Paris, 1945.
43566.14.100 Decour, Jacques. Comme je vous en donne l'exemple. Paris, 1945.
43566.36.110 Deharme, Lise. Cette année-la. 3e éd. Paris, 1945.
43566.43.115 Dekobra, Maurice. A Paris, tous les deux. Journal d'un Yankee entre deux guerres. N.Y., 1945.
43566.43.42 Dekobra, Maurice. La perruche bleue; journal d'une courtisane sous la terreur nazie. N.Y., 1945.
38526.1.35.20 Delacourcelle, D. Le sentiment de l'art dans la Bergerie de Remy Belleau. Oxford, 1945.
43566.48.200 Delarue-Mardrus, Lucie. Le roi des reflets. Paris, 1945.
43763.38.805 Delcourt, Marie. Jean Schlumberger. 2. éd. Paris, 1945.
43566.51.2100 Delvaille, A. Charlas intimas de "Trebla". San José, 1945.
43566.53.6100 Demêtre, Marie E. Histoire simples de gens simples pour gens simples. Paris, 1945.
43566.59.100 Deneveure, J. The last supper of nations. N.Y., 1945.
43566.32.800 Denuit, Désiré. Jean Tousseul. Bruxelles, 1945.
37575.650 Díez-Canedo, E. La poesía francesa del romanticismo al superrealismo. Buenos Aires, 1945.
43757.50.1025 Doisy, Marcel. Romain Rolland, 1866-1944. Bruxelles, 1945.
37575.160 Drouillet, Jean. Anthologie des poètes nivernais. Moulins, 1945.
38526.6.45 Du Bellay, Joachim. Les antiquitez de Rome et les regrets. Paris, 1945.
43620.74.830 Du Genêt, Gabriel. Jean Giraudoux. Paris, 1945.
43576.6.355 Duhamel, Georges. Biographie de mes fantômes, 1901-1906. Paris, 1945.
43576.6.375 Duhamel, Georges. Georges Duhamel dans ses plus beaux textes. Montréal, 1945.
43576.6.360 Duhamel, Georges. Inventaire de l'abîme, 1884-1901. Paris, 1945.
43576.6.370 Duhamel, Georges. Lieu d'asile. Paris, 1945.
43576.6.365 Duhamel, Georges. Lieu d'asile. 32. éd. Paris, 1945.
43576.54.120 Dumaine, Philippe. Cortèges. Paris, 1945.
42576.15.12.5 Dumesnil, René. Le grand amour de Flaubert. Genève, 1945.
43576.68.3100 Dupé, Gilbert. Le bateau à soupe. 29. éd. Paris, 1945.
FL 361.75 Dussane, B. Reines de théâtre, 1633-1941. Montréal, 1945.
38539.6.5 Du Vair, Guillaume. De la sainte philosophie. Paris, 1945.
43822.49.1025 Eigeldinger, Marc. Paul Valéry. Neuchâtel, 1945.
43591.89.200 Eluard, Paul. Doubles d'ombre. Paris, 1945.
43591.89.330 Eluard, Paul. Une longue réflexion amoureuse. Neuchâtel, 1945.
43591.89.150 Eluard, Paul. Les malheurs des immortels. Paris, 1945.
43591.89.180 Eluard, Paul. Poésie et vérité. Bruxelles, 1945.
43591.89.170F Eluard, Paul. Souvenirs de la maison des fous. Paris, 1945.
43592.53.200 Emmanuel, Pierre. Combats avec tes défenseurs. Paris, 1945.
43592.53.110 Emmanuel, Pierre. Jour de colère. Alger, 1945.
38511.34 Engels, Joseph. Etudes sur l'Ovide moralisé. Groningen, 1945.
43598.82.160 Estang, Luc. Les béatitudes. Paris, 1945.
43604.73.100 Eyquem, Marie T. Jeunes filles au soleil. Paris, 1945.
43606.78.260 Farrère, Claude. La seconde porte. Paris, 1945.
43526.65.835 Faure-Favier, Louise. Souvenirs sur Guillaume Apollinaire. Paris, 1945. 2v.
38554.526.20 Fénelon, F. de S. de la Mothe. Spiritual letters. Cornwall-on-Hudson, 1945.
43607.74.1100 Feraudy, Jacqueline de Gourcy. Marguerites, herbes fleuries; poèmes. Paris, 1945.
43609.24.100 Fieschi, P. Fête foraine. Paris, 1945.
42576.28.60 Flaubert, Gustave. Madame Bovary. Paris, 1945. 2v.
V43500.107 Forot, Charles. Dix sonnets. Paris, 1945.
43611.88.100 Fougère, Jean. Un don comme l'amour. Paris, 1945.
37574.725 La France nouvelle. Paris, 1945.
43612.22.110 Frédérique, André. Histoires blanches. 2. éd. Paris? 1945.
FL 370.102 Fuchs, Max. France des origines à la periode classique. Paris, 1945.
42525.8.82 Fumet, Stanislas. Ernest Hello. Paris, 1945.
43591.89.800 Gaffé, René. Paul Eluard. Paris, 1945.
38527.42.3.30 Garnier, Robert. Les Juifves, tragédie. Paris, 1945.
43616.76.100 Garo, Joseph. Pages d'évadé. Paris, 1945.
42563.18.210 Garreau, Albert. Barrès, défenseur de la civilization. Paris, 1945.
43616.78.110 Gary, Romain. Education européenne. Paris, 1945.
43616.1.8100 Gautier, Jean Jacques. L'oreille. Paris, 1945.
FL 396.64.1 Genty, Raymond. Les souterrains de l'Odéon. Paris, 1945.
40563.28 George, Albert J. Pierre-Simon Ballanche. Syracuse, 1945.
38514.68.18 Gerig, John L. On a review. N.Y., 1945.
43620.2.79.80 Gide, André. Jeunesse. Neuchâtel, 1945.
43526.65.825 Giedion-Welcher, C. Die neue Realität bei Guillaume Apollinaire. Bern, 1945.
43620.40.100 Gilliard, Edmond. Journal, 1930-1945. Lausanne, 1945. 2v.
43620.74.350 Giraudoux, Jean. Armistice à Bordeaux. Monaco, 1945.
43620.74.510 Giraudoux, Jean. D'exil. Paris, 1945.
43620.74.410 Giraudoux, Jean. La France sentimentale. 18. éd. Paris, 1945.
43620.74.30 Giraudoux, Jean. Théâtre complet. Neuchâtel, 1945-53. 16v.
43625.27.150 Goffin, Robert. Patrie de la poèsie. Montréal, 1945.
41557.10.130 Grebanier, F.V. The life of the heart. N.Y., 1945.
41557.10.132A Grebanier, F.V. The life of the heart. 4. ed. N.Y., 1945.
42554.49.20 Gregh, F. La couronne perdue et retrouvée. Paris, 1945.
43628.41.5100 Guillot, René. Contes de la Brousse fauve. Grenoble, 1945.
38524.98 Hasselmann, Jules. Les conteurs français du XVIe siécle. Paris, 1945.
37565.105 Henriot, Emile. Courrier littéraire, XVIIIe siècle. Paris, 1945. 2v.
43757.3.335 Hommage à Jules Romains pour son soixantième anniversaire. Paris, 1945.
43757.50.1006A Hommage à Romain Rolland. Genève, 1945.
43620.74.840 Honlet, Jacques. Le théâtre de Jean Giraudoux. Paris, 1945.

1945 - cont.

V43500.135 Houdelot, Robert. Sept poèmes de guerre. Paris, 1945.

43697.88.825 Hourdin, Georges. Mauriac, romancier chrétien. 2. éd. Photoreproduction. Paris, 1945.

42576.57.83 Hublard, M.J.C. L'attitude religieuse de Pierre Loti. Thèse. Fribourg, 1945.

41573.39.25 Hugo, Victor. La Belgique vue par Victor Hugo. Bruxelles, 1945.

41571.19.10 Hugo, Victor. Cosette et Marius. Boston, 1945.

42576.65.25.7 Huysmans, Joris Karl. La cathédrale. Paris, 1945.

43638.99.140 Huzard, A. de B. (Mme.). Grand mère. Paris, 1945.

43659.65.100 Isolle, Jacques. Chronique de Saint-Macé. Angers, 1945.

43667.14.190 Jacob, Max. Conseils à un jeune poète. 2. éd. Paris, 1945.

43667.14.210 Jacob, Max. Derniers poèmes en vers et en prose. Paris, 1945.

43611.5.81 Jöhr, Walter. Alain-Fournier, le paysage d'une âme. Thèse. Neuchâtel, 1945.

37567.405 Johandsen, Svend. Le symbolisme; étude sur le style des symbolistes français. Copenhague, 1945.

43670.95.110A Jouvet, Louis. Préstiges et perspectives du théâtre, français, quatre ans de tournée en Amérique latine, 1941-1945. 5. éd. Paris, 1945.

42557.12.140 Kunel, Maurice. Verlaine et Rimbaud en Belgique. Liège, 1945.

FL 6129.45 Labrousse, Roger. Rousseau y su tiempo. La Plata, 1945.

43687.26.2100 Laffont, G. De Dunkerque à Hambourg. Marseille, 1945.

FL 377.75.10 Lancaster, H.C. Sunset, a history of Parisian drama in the last years of Louis XIV, 1701-1715. Baltimore, 1945.

41597.58.3 Lanusse, A. Creole voices; poems in French by free men of color. Washington, 1945.

43687.65.100 Lanza del Vasto, Joseph Jean. Principes et préceptes du retour à l'évidence. Paris, 1945.

43744.67.1125 Larcher, P.L. Le parfum de Combray. Paris, 1945.

38543.10.45 La Rochefoucauld, François. Les maximes. Paris, 1945.

43687.78.6021 Lassaigne, Assia. L'Idiote du village. Paris, 1945.

41564.39.5 Lauvrière, E. Alfred de Vigny, sa vie et son oeuvre. Paris, 1945. 2v.

V43500.157 Lavaud, Guy. Marseillaise reviens! 25 juin 1940 - 25 août 1944. Paris, 1945.

43688.5.5110 Léautaud, Paul. Marly-le-Roy et environs. Paris, 1945.

V43500.161 Lebois, André. Partage des eaux. Fougères, 1945.

37576.641 Le Figaro, Paris. Suites françaises. N.Y., 1945. 2v.

43688.33.700 Legrand, Ignace. The embassy train. London, 1945.

38575.22.10 Lemonnier, Leon. Corneille. Paris, 1945.

43688.59.58 Lenéru, Marie. Journal. 7e éd. Paris, 1945.

43688.61.795 Lenormand, Henri René. El hombre y sus fantasmas. 2e éd. Buenos Aires, 1945.

42576.65.13.95 Letters, Francis J.H. Joris Karl Huysmans, a study. Westmead, 1945?

37576.325 Lettres choisies du XVIIIe siècle. Le Cavie, 1945.

37576.215 Lettres du XVIIe siècle. Paris, 1945.

43688.90.100 Levaux, Léopold. Quand Dieu parle. Bruxelles, 1945.

40583.178 Litto, Victor del. Bibliographie stendhalienne, 1938-1943. Grenoble, 1945. 6v.

42544.34.28.25 Louys, Pierre. Les poëmes de Pierre Louys. Paris, 1945. 2v.

41555.43.40 Luppé, A.M.P. Mérimée. Paris, 1945.

X Cg 38513.75 Magariños, S. Farsas francesas de la edad media. Madrid, 1945.

40575.5.125 Mahieu, Robert G. Sainte-Beuve aux Etats-Unis. Princeton, 1945.

42555.43.1 Mallarmé, Stéphane. Oeuvres complètes. Paris, 1945.

42555.43.3.1 Mallarmé, Stéphane. Poésies. 126. éd. Paris, 1945.

43697.52.745 Malraux, André. La lutte avec l'ange. Genève, 1945.

43697.52.2140 Malraux, Clara. Portrait de Grisélidis. Paris, 1945.

37556.21.45 Manevy, Raymond. Histoire de la presse, 1914 à 1939. Paris, 1945.

43697.61.100 Manoir, Georges. Monsier de Falindor. Paris, 1945.

37569.118 Manoll, Michel. Introduction à la poésie d'aujourd'hui. n.p., 1945.

43697.75.165 Marcel, Gabriel. L'horizon. Paris, 1945.

43697.75.2100 Marcenac, Jean. A merveille. Paris, 1945.

X Cg 43697.75.2000 Marcenac, Jean. Le cavalier de Coupe. Paris, 1945.

38526.32.6 Marguerite d'Angoulême. L'Heptaméron des nouvelles de la reine de Navarre. Paris, 1945-46. 4v.

40535.27.15 Marivaux, Pierre Carlet de Chamblain de. Les chefs-d'oeuvre de Marivaux. Rio de Janeiro, 1945.

38523.12.10 Marot, Clément. Dialogue de deux amoureux. Paris, 1945.

43697.77.9105 Martin, François. L'ange de la mort. 5. éd. Paris, 1945.

40583.37.5 Martineau, Henri. L'oeuvre de Stendhal. Paris, 1945.

37567.411 Martinet, E. Princes de lettres. Genève, 1945.

37566.103 Martino, Pierre. L'époque romantique en France, 1815-1830. Paris, 1945.

41522.18.155 Massin, Jean. Baudelaire "Entre Dieu et Satan". Paris, 1945.

43697.86.120 Masson, Loÿs. La lumière nait le mercredi. Paris, 1945?

43697.86.110 Masson, Loÿs. Le requis civil, roman. 8. éd. Paris, 1945.

43697.89.3110 Maulvault, Lucien. Les saintes colères. Paris, 1945.

42577.4.25.5 Maupassant, Guy de. Maalaispiika ja perhetyttö. Helsinki, 1945.

42577.4.29.9.5 Maupassant, Guy de. Naiskohtalo. Helsinki, 1945.

43697.87.110 Mauretti, Marcelle. Le roi Christine. Paris, 1945.

43556.1.800 Mauriac, C. Jean Cocteau. Paris, 1945.

40597.2.174 Mauriac, Claude. Aimer Balzac. Liege, 1945.

40597.2.173 Mauriac, Claude. Aimer Balzac. Paris, 1945.

37568.94.15 Mauriac, Claude. La trahison d'un clerc. Paris, 1945.

43697.88.330 Mauriac, François. Asmodée. Paris, 1945.

43697.4.55 Mauriac, François. Les mal aimes. Paris, 1945.

43697.88.42 Mauriac, François. Pages de journal. Monaco, 1945.

43697.88.250 Mauriac, François. La rencontre avec Barrès. Vanves, 1945.

43697.88.325 Mauriac, François. La robe prétexte. Paris, 1945.

43697.89.300 Maurois, André. Eisenhower. Paris, 1945.

43697.89.270 Maurois, André. Etudes américaines. N.Y., 1945.

43697.89.310 Maurois, André. Franklin. Paris, 1945.

43697.89.260 Maurois, André. Terre promise, roman. N.Y., 1945.

43697.89.775 Maurois, André. Woman without love. 1. éd. N.Y., 1945.

42514.28.125 Maurras, Charles. Le procès de Charles Maurras. Lyon, 1945.

43697.99.130 Mazade, Fernand. La rose. Paris, 1945.

43698.53.100 Membré, Henri. Petit-Bourgeois. Monaco, 1945.

43698.75.2105 Merglen, Albert. Mission spéciale en France. 3. éd. Grenoble, 1945.

41555.20.105 Mérimée, Prosper. Carmen. Monaco, 1945.

37575.9 Mesnard, Pierre. De Villon à Rimbaud. Alger, 1945.

1945 - cont.

41543.22.165 Messiaen, Pierre. Gerard de Nerval. Paris? 1945.

43698.83.2100 Mestre, Jean B. Jehanne chez ses bons amis de Compiègne. Compiègne, 1945.

39544.186 Meyer, A.E. Voltaire: man of justice. N.Y., 1945.

43698.200.135 Michaux, Henri. Un barbare en Asie. 9. éd. Paris, 1945.

43698.200.115 Michaux, Henri. Épreuves. Paris, 1945.

Mol 165.109 Molière, Jean Baptiste Poquelin. L'avare...R.A. Wilson. London, 1945.

Mol 245.104 Molière, Jean Baptiste Poquelin. Le misanthrope. R.A. Wilson. London, 1945.

Mol 268.155 Molière, Jean Baptiste Poquelin. Tartuffe (1669) avec une notre biographique. Paris, 1945.

43554.2.875 Molitor, André. Aspects de Paul Claudel. Paris, 1945.

43701.6.35 Monnerot, Jules. On meurt les yeux ouverts. 8. éd. Paris, 1945.

43701.61.120 Monnier, Thyde. Les Desmichels. Paris, 1945-57. 7v.

39594.13.35 Montesquieu, C.L. de S. Lettres persanes. Paris, 1945.

37556.122 Moore, Margaret. Les doctrines littéraires du constitutionnel (1815-1830) leurs rapports avec la politique. Chicago, Ill., 1945.

37569.155 Morel, Robert. La littérature clandestine 1940-1944. Périgueux, 1945.

43701.2.32PF Mounet-Sully, J. The modern cupid. Boston, 1945.

43757.50.1004 Mühlestein, H. Geist und Politik, Romain Rolland's politische Sendung. Zürich, 1945.

43703.75.105 Murciaux, Christian. La fontaine de vie. 2. éd. Paris, 1945.

41596.8.20 Musset, Alfred de. La confession d'un enfant du siècle. Lille, 1945.

39544.190 O'Flaherty, K. Voltaire. Cork, 1945.

FL 398.66 Oswald, Marianne. One small voice. N.Y., 1945.

43737.74.3100 Parain, Brice. La mort de Jean Modec. Paris, 1945.

38575.23 Paris. Bibliothèque Nationale. Objets exposés à le second centenaire à Pierre Corneille. Paris, 1945.

43737.80.110 Parrot, Louis. Paille noire des étables. Paris, 1945.

43822.49.1090 Paul Valéry. Ciudad Trujillo, 1945.

43738.1.50.5 Péguy, Charles. Basic verities. 4th ed. N.Y., 1945.

43554.2.865 Perche, Louis. Claudel et les cinq grandes odes. Périgueux, 1945.

43738.78.130 Perse, Saint-John. Exil. Paris, 1945.

FL 385.69 Peter, René. Le théâtre et la vie sous la troisième République. Paris, 1945-1947. 2v.

37578.92 Picard, André L. Quelques mots de France. N.Y., 1945.

37544.85 Picard, Roger. Artifices et mystifications littéraires. Montréal, 1945.

43741.12.100 Picasso, Pablo. Le désir attrapé par la queue. Paris, 1945.

37583.645A Pillement, Georges. Anthologie du théâtre français contemporain. Paris, 1945-48. 3v.

37585.40 Pillemont, Georges. Anthologie du théâtre français contemporain. Paris, 1945.

43742.41.160 Plisnier, Charles. Héloise. Paris, 1945.

41522.18.72 Pommier, J. Dans les chemins de Boudelaire. Paris, 1945.

43744.67.78 Proust, Marcel. Quatre lettres de Marcel Proust à ses concierges. Genève, 1945.

43750.26.105 Quesnel, Joseph. Tirelire. Paris, 1945.

37556.13.25 Quéval, Jean. Première page, cinquième collone. 19. éd. Paris, 1945.

42554.50.17 Quinche, Philippe. Les thèmes principaux de l'oeuvre poétique de C. Guérin. Thèse. Zofingue, 1945.

38585.19.9.5 Racine, Jean. Andromaque. Paris, 1945.

43752.57.41 Ramuz, Charles Ferdinand. Journal, 1896-1942. Paris, 1945.

43752.57.245 Ramuz, Charles Ferdinand. Taille de l'homme. 13. éd. Paris, 1945.

43752.57.265 Ramuz, Charles Ferdinand. Vers. Lausanne, 1945.

43752.98.110 Raynal, Paul. Le tombeau sous l'Arc de Triomphe. Paris, 1945.

37568.98 Regards sur l'art contemporain. Bruxelles, 1945.

42515.25.70 Renan, Ernest. Ernest Renan et l'Allemagne. N.Y., 1945.

V43500.251 Renard, Jean Claude. Juan. Toulouse, 1945.

43753.90.190 Reverdy, P. Plupart du temps. 5. éd. Paris, 1945.

43753.99.4100 Reynaud, J.C. Une etoile qui nait; roman. Paris, 1945.

42556.28.48 Rimbaud, Jean Arthur. Oeuvres. Paris, 1945.

42556.28.47 Rimbaud, Jean Arthur. Oeuvres complètes. Paris, 1945.

42556.28.43.10 Rimbaud, Jean Arthur. A season in hell. Norfolk, Conn., 1945.

42556.28.43.25 Rimbaud, Jean Arthur. A season in hell and The drunken boat. Norfolk, Conn., 1945.

43744.67.1135 Rivane, Georges. Influence de l'asthme sur l'oeuvre de Marcel Proust. Paris, 1945.

43757.10.10 Robida, Michael. Botemry. Paris, 1945.

41555.44.5 Roger, G. Prosper Mérimée et la Corse. Alger, 1945.

43757.32.1100 Roger, René. Le diapason de l'orage. Paris, 1945.

43738.1.170 Rolland, R. Péguy. Paris, 1945. 2v.

43757.50.770 Rolland, Romain. Roland and Tagore. Calcutta, 1945.

43757.50.597 Rolland, Romain. Le seuil. Genève, 1945.

43757.3.245 Romains, Jules. Retrouver la foi. Paris, 1945.

42578.22.75 Rosny, J.H. Le destin de Marin Lafaille. Paris, 1945.

38575.23.85 Rostand, François. L'imitation de soi chez Corneille. Paris, 1945.

42546.15.19.5 Rostand, Maurice. Charlotte et Macimilien. Paris, 1945.

43757.3.5100 Roud, Gustave. Air de la solitude. Lausanne, 1945.

FL 6067.8 Rousseau, J.J. Discours sur les sciences et les arts. Paris, 1945.

43758.17.100 Rudel, Yves M. Johnny de Roscoff. Paris, 1945.

41557.9.35.10 Sand, George. Histoire de ma vie. Paris, 1945.

43761.1.710 Sandoz, Maurice Yves. The maze. 1st ed. Garden City, 1945.

43761.78.210A Sartre, Jean Paul. L'âge de raison, roman. Paris, 1945.

43761.78.180A Sartre, Jean Paul. Le sursis, roman. v.2. Paris, 1945.

43763.38.123 Schlumberger, Jean. Les yeux de dix-huit ans. 8. éd. Paris, 1945.

43763.41.6110 Scipion, Robert. Prête-moi ta plume. 7. éd. Paris, 1945.

43763.42.100 Scize, Pierre. Vingt dieux de république. Lyon, 1945.

43765.32.120 Seghers, Pierre. Le domaine public. Paris, 1945.

40525.2.25 Sénac de Meilhan, G. Portraits et caractères. Paris, 1945.

42556.28.189 Silvain, R. Rimbaud, le précurseur. Paris, 1945.

43769.54.385 Simenon, Georges. La fuite de M. Monde, roman. Paris, 1945.

43769.54.720 Simenon, Georges. The shadow falls. London, 1945.

43769.64.100 Sjöberg, Henri. Hors paison à Vichy. Paris, 1945.

43775.52.100 Soleymieu, Jacques (pseud.). Dimanche. N.Y., 1945.

41564.48 Sorrento, Luigi. Lettura e illustrazione critica della poesia di Alfred de Vigny. Milano, 1945.

Chronological Listing

1945 - cont.

42555.44.14 Soula, Camille. Gloses sur Mallarmé. Paris, 1945.
42544.30.85 Soupault, Philippe. Eugène Labiche, sa vie, son oeuvre. Paris, 1945.
38526.48.155 Sponde, Jean de. Oeuvre poétique pour le premier fois réunie en un volume. Paris, 1945.
43787.78.200 Téry, Simone. Où l'aube se lève. N.Y., 1945.
43788.65.110 Thomas, E. Le champ libre; roman. Paris, 1945.
41563.32.25 Toepffer, Rodolphe. Voyages en zigzag. Genève, 1945-52. 7v.
41557.10.73 Toesca, Maurice. Une autre George Sand. Paris, 1945.
43792.91.105 Toussaint, Franz. Sentiments distingués. 16e éd. Paris, 1945.
FL 362.5 Une tradition théâtrale. Paris, 1945.
43793.42.140 Triolet, Elsa. Les amants d'Avignon. Paris, 1945.
43793.42.170 Triolet, Elsa. Le mythe de la baronne Mélanie. Neuchâtel, 1945.
43793.42.100 Triolet, Elsa. Le premier accroc coûte deux francs. Paris, 1945.
43793.42.120 Triolet, Elsa. Six entre autres. Lausanne, 1945.
Mon 160.1 Truc, Gonzague. Montaigne. Paris, 1945.
39544.195 Trudel, Marcel. L'influence de Voltaire au Canada. Montreal, 1945. 2v.
37567.415 Tuzet, Hélène. Voyageurs français en Sicile. Thèse. Paris, 1945.
37567.413 Tuzet, Hélène. Voyageurs français en Sicile au temps du romantisme. Paris, 1945.
43822.49.410F Valéry, Paul. Le physique du livre. Paris, 1945.
FL 394.137 Valmy-Baysse, J. Naissance et vie de la comédie-française...1402-1945. Paris, 1945.
43822.8.60 Vaudoyer, Jean L. Italiennes. Paris, 1945.
37574.693 Vaunois, Louis. Les poètes de la vie. Paris, 1945.
V43500.321 Vérane, Léon. La fête s'loigne. Paris, 1945.
43823.80.100 Verdet, André. Souvenirs du présent. Paris, 1945.
42557.11.26 Verhaeren, Émile. Les heures claires. Paris, 1945.
43823.76.110 Verne, Marc. Marie Villarceaux; un roman d'amour. Haiti, 1945.
FL 398.8.10 Verneuil, Louis. Rideau à neuf heures. Paris, 1945.
38514.20.15.28 Villon, François. Oeuvres complètes. Grenoble, 1945.
38514.20.31.3 Villon, François. Poésies. Paris, 1945.
43824.59.130 Vincent, R. Seigneur. Paris, 1945.
43827.91.100 Voisin, Joseph. Fontaine revient. Moulins, 1945.
39545.35.40 Voltaire, François Marie Arouet de. Candide. Oxford, 1945.
39544.25.10 Voltaire, François Marie Arouet de. Mémoires pour servir à la vie. Paris, 1945.
43830.39.100 Wahl, J.A. Poèmes. Montréal, 1945.
42515.35.285 Weiler, Maurice. La pensée de Renan. Grenoble, 1945.
43833.41.1100 Weiss, Louise. La Marseillaise. Paris, 1945-1947. 2v.

1946

V43500.7 Aeschimann, Paul. Feux d'automne. Dizains précédés d'un Choix de poèmes, 1918-1944. Paris, 1946.
43517.2.100 Agadjanian, G. La vallee des ombres. N.Y., 1946.
43738.1.205 Ageorges, Joseph. La sublime folie de Charles Péguy. Paris, 1946.
NEDL 37543.267 Akademiia nauk SSSR. Institut literatury. Istoriia frantsuzskoi literatury. Moskva, 1946.
37576.646 Aldington, Richard. Great French romances. London, 1946.
43522.25.100 Alexandre, Maxime. Echoes intimes; poèmes. Paris, 1946.
37596.27.14 Aléxius, Saint. Légend. La vie de Saint Aléxis. Oxford, 1946.
Mol 268.145 Alméras, Henri d'. Le Tartuffe de Molière. Paris, 1946.
43822.49.1075 Andouard, Y. Recherche de Paul Valéry. Albi, 1946.
43761.39.805 Anet, Daniel. Antoine de St. Exupéry. Paris, 1946.
43524.67.700 Anouilh, Jean. Antigone. N.Y., 1946.
43524.67.22 Anouilh, Jean. Nouvelles pièces noires. Paris, 1946.
43526.65.160 Apollinaire, Guillaume. Estudio preliminar y paginas. Buenos Aires, 1946.
Htn 43526.65.150* Apollinaire, Guillaume. Les mamelles des Tirésias. 1st ed. Paris, 1946.
43527.3.722 Aragon, Louis. Aragon, poet of resurgent France. London, 1946.
43527.3.200 Aragon, Louis. La diare française. Paris, 1946.
43527.3.260 Aragon, Louis. Le musée Grévin. Paris, 1946.
43527.3.780 Aragon, Louis. Vstrechi; rasskazy. Moskva, 1946.
43620.2.200 Archambault, Paul. Humanité d'André Gide. Paris, 1946.
43528.86.61 Artaud, Antonin. Lettres de Rodez. Paris, 1946.
43531.19.110 Audry, Colette. On jour perdant. 3. éd. Paris, 1946.
43537.48.100 Balain, Blanche. Temps loinlain. Paris, 1946.
42576.46.14 Ballot, Marc. Eugène Le Roy. Bordeaux, 1946.
40597.35.110 Balzac, Honoré de. Albert Savarus. Oran, 1946.
40596.17.10 Balzac, Honoré de. Le curé de Tours. Tours, 1946.
40596.31 Balzac, Honoré de. Le curé de ville. Montréal, 1946.
40597.35.85 Balzac, Honoré de. Les illusions perdues. Paris, 1946.
40597.29.1.4 Balzac, Honoré de. La maison du chat-qui-pelote. Montréal, 1946?
40597.29.4.57 Balzac, Honoré de. Père Goriot and Eugénie Grandet. 1. ed. N.Y., 1946.
40597.35.125 Balzac, Honoré de. Le rendez-vous. Tours, 1946.
41522.13.45 Bandelaire, Charles. Ecrits intimes. Paris, 1946.
43537.77.1100 Baron, Jacques. Le noir de l'azur. Paris, 1946.
41522.13.12.10 Baudelaire, Charles. Ecrits intimes. Paris, 1946.
41522.13.8.90 Baudelaire, Charles. Flowers of evil. Norfolk, 1946.
41522.6.10 Baudelaire, Charles. Les paradis artificiels suivis des journeaux intimes. Lausanne, 1946.
41522.13.3 Baudelaire, Charles. Poèmes. Paris, 1946.
41522.12.20 Baudelaire, Charles. Selected poems. London, 1946.
43537.88.2100 Baudy, Nicolas. Le piano d'Arlequin. Paris, 1946.
43538.1.460 Beauvoir, Simone de. Le sang des autres; roman. Paris, 1946.
43538.1.440 Beauvoir, Simone de. Tous les hommes sont mortels, roman. Paris, 1946.
43611.5.89 Becker, Aimé. Itinèraire spirituel d'Alain-Fournier. Paris, 1946.
43538.25.100 Beer, Jean de. Tombeau de Jean Giraudoux. Paris, 1946.
40597.2.175 Béguin, Albert. Balzac visionnaire, Propositions. Genève, 1946.
43667.14.805 Belaval, Yvon. La rencontre avec Max Jacob. Paris, 1946.
43538.76.755 Bernanos, Georges. The crime. London, 1946.
43538.76.735 Bernanos, Georges. Joy. N.Y., 1946.
43538.76.151 Bernanos, Georges. Monsieur Ouine. Paris, 1946.
43538.10.53 Bernard, Jean J. Théâtre. Paris, 1946.
43538.76.4100 Bernardine, T. Le chef-d'oeuvre de Claude Harmel. Paris, 1946.

1946 - cont.

40597.2.190A Bertault, Philippe. Balzac, l'homme et l'oeuvre. Paris, 1946.
40582.12.53 Beyle, Henri. Armance. Paris, 1946.
40582.5 Beyle, Henri. Cent y soixante petits faits vrais. Paris, 1946.
40582.9.40 Beyle, Henri. La chartreuse de Parme. Paris, 1946.
40582.10.5 Beyle, Henri. Chroniques italiennes. Paris, 1946.
43540.3.80 Billy, André. Mort prochaine. Paris, 1946.
43543.1.4105 Blanc, Julien. Seule, la vie. v.1-2. Paris, 1946-47.
42563.23.43 Bloy, Léon. Le désespéré. Paris, 1946.
42563.23.44 Bloy, Léon. Léon Bloy. Paris, 1946.
37575.327 Boccard, Eugène de. Anthologie des poètes de la Suisse romande. Paris, 1946.
43544.12.100 Bochot, Pierre. Chez eux. Paris, 1946.
43544.18.120 Bodin, Jean. Armel. Paris, 1946.
43544.60.2120 Bonnefoy, Yves. Traité du pianiste. Paris, 1946.
43744.67.1150 Bonnet, Henri. Le progrès spirituel dans l'oeuvre de Marcel Proust. v.1-2. Paris, 1946-
42563.36.300 Bordeaux, Henry. Appolline. Paris, 1946.
42563.36.310 Bordeaux, Henry. Cas de conscience. Paris, 1946.
43544.73.100 Bordeaux, Henry. Un crime sous le directoire. Paris, 1946.
43544.101.110 Borne, Alain. Poèmes à Lislei. Paris, 1946.
43544.81.2105 Bosco, Henri. L'âne Culotte; roman. 21. éd. Paris, 1946.
43544.81.2700 Bosco, Henri. The farm theotime. London, 1946.
43544.4.47 Botrel, Théodore. Souvenirs d'un barde errant. Paris, 1946.
42557.20.155 Bouhier, Jean. Verlaine et l'amour. Bruxelles, 1946.
42563.37.34.15 Bourget, Paul. Le démon de midi. Paris, 1946.
42563.37.77.15 Bourget, Paul. L'étape. Paris, 1946.
43544.90.5100 Bourhis, Andrée. La fleur enchantée. Paris, 1946.
43544.8.30 Bousquet, Joe. Le meneur de lune. 4. éd. Paris, 1946.
43545.2.100 Braibant, Charles. Irène Soubeyran. Paris, 1946.
43545.4.4120 Brasillach, Robert. Poèmes de Fresnes. Louvain, 1946.
37543.140.12 Braunschvig, Marcel. Notre littérature étudiée dans les textes. Paris, 1946. 2v.
37574.687 Bray, René. Anthologie de la poésie precieuse de Thibaut de Champagne à Giraudoux. Paris, 1946.
43744.67.87 Bret, Jacques. Marcel Proust. Genève, 1946.
43619.24.810 Brochet, Henri. Henri Ghéon. Paris, 1946.
43823.75.2720 Bruller, Jean. Guiding star. London, 1946.
43823.75.2120 Bruller, Jean. Les ormes de la nuit. Paris, 1946.
43823.75.2130 Bruller, Jean. Portrait d'une amitié. Paris, 1946.
Mol 602.13 Bruyelle, Roland. Les personnages de la comédie de Molière. Paris, 1946.
43547.13.100 Bucline, Jean. Lili bat. Paris, 1946.
Mon 59.10 Buffum, Imbrie. L'influence du voyage de Montaigne sur les essais. Diss. Princeton, 1946.
43547.50.100 Bulliard, Paul. La chanson simple; poèmes. Paris, 1946.
43550.48.1100 Caland, Laurence. Si peu d'amour. Paris, 1946.
43550.58.100A Camus, Albert. L'étranger. N.Y., 1946.
43550.58.705 Camus, Albert. The outsider. London, 1946.
43550.58.700 Camus, Albert. The stranger. 1. American ed. N.Y., 1946.
42576.15.175 Canu, Jean. Flaubert, auteur dramatique. Paris, 1946.
38551.41A Carcassone, E. Fénelon, l'homme et l'oeuvre. Paris, 1946.
42576.63.112 Carias, Léon. Les carnets intimes d'Anatole France. Paris, 1946.
37555.200 Carter, M.E. The role of the symbol in French romantic poetry. Washington, 1946.
43550.82.130 Cassou, Jean. Les enfants sans âge. Paris, 1946.
42584.25.147 Castelnau, Jacques. Zola. Paris, 1946.
37543.275 Castex, Pierre. Manuel des études littéraires françaises. v.1-6. Paris, 1946-50.
43550.98.100 Cayrol, Jean. Poèmes de la nuit et du brouillard. Paris, 1946.
43551.50.100 Celly, R. Un ami pour rien. Paris, 1946.
43551.59.170 Cendrars, Blaise. Dan-Yacks: le plan de l'Aiguille. Paris, 1946.
43551.59.310 Cendrars, Blaise. La main coupée. Paris, 1946.
43551.79.105 Césaire, Aimé. Les armes miraculeuses. 2e éd. Paris, 1946.
38514.23.65A Chaney, Edward F. François Villon in his environment. Oxford, 1946.
43552.4.30.5 Chantal, S. Dieu ne dort pas. Paris, 1946.
37576.646.5 Chapelan, Maurice. Anthologie du poème en prose. Paris, 1946.
43552.4.2105 Char, René. Feuillets d'Hypnos. 3e éd. Paris, 1946.
43576.9.810 Charles Du Bos. Toulouse, 1946?
38537.25.165 Charpentier, John. Rabelais. Paris, 1946.
43552.4.8120 Charpier, Jacques. Paysage du salut. Paris, 1946.
40586.17.15 Chateaubriand, F.A.R. Itinéraire de Paris à Jérusalem. Baltimore, 1946. 2v.
FL 398.12 Chevalier, Maurice. Ma route et mes chansons. Paris, 1946.
43554.2.340 Claudel, Paul. Le chemin de la croix. Paris, 1946.
43554.2.119 Claudel, Paul. Écoute, ma fille. Fribourg, 1946.
43554.2.210 Claudel, Paul. Le livre de Job. Paris, 1946.
43554.2.245 Claudel, Paul. L'oeil éconte. Paris, 1946.
43554.2.200 Claudel, Paul. Partage de midi. Lausanne, 1946.
43554.2.89.5 Claudel, Paul. Positions et propositions. Paris, 1946-1948. 2v.
41522.3.45 Clermont-Tonnerre, Élisabeth de. Barbey d'Aurevilly. Paris, 1946.
42566.16.90 Clogenson, Y.E. Alphonse Daudet. Paris, 1946.
37548.3 Closset, François. Dictionnaire des littérateurs. Bruxelles, 1946.
43556.1.217 Cocteau, Jean. La belle et la bête. 37e éd. Paris, 1946.
43556.1.230 Cocteau, Jean. La crucifixion, poème. Paris, 1946.
43556.1.12 Cocteau, Jean. Oeuvres complètes. Lausanne, 1946-1957. 11v.
37595.81A Cohen, Gustave. Anthologie de la littérature française du Moyen Âge. Paris, 1946.
37569.130 Cohen, Gustave. Ceux que j'ai connus. Montréal, 1946.
43556.49.2100 Coléno, Alica. Le quai des Indes; roman. Paris, 1946.
43556.49.360 Colette, Sidonie Gabrielle. Chambre d'hôtel. Paris, 1946.
43556.49.370 Colette, Sidonie Gabrielle. L'étoile vesper. Genève, 1946.
43556.49.410 Colette, Sidonie Gabrielle. Le tendron; nouvelle. Paris, 1946.
43556.49.380 Colette, Sidonie Gabrielle. Trois...six...neuf. Paris, 1946.
43556.49.156 Colette, Sidonie Gabrielle. La vagabonde. Paris, 1946.
40553.7.25 Constant de Rebecque, Benjamin. Adolphe. Paris, 1946.
43557.61.130 Constantin-Weyer, Maurice. Le bar de San Miguel. Paris, 1946.

1946 - cont.

43557.61.120	Constantin-Weyer, Maurice. Les compagnons de la boule. Paris, 1946.
42542.53.65	Copeau, Jacques. Le petit pauvre. 3. éd. Paris, 1946.
38575.33.40	Corneille, Pierre. Rodogune; tragédie. Paris, 1946.
43556.82.700	Cossery, Albert. Men God forgot - a circle edition. Berkeley, 1946.
43557.66.1100	Cros, Guy-Charles. Mon soleil nouveau, serivi de Soleils anciens. Paris, 1946.
43560.78.100	Curtis, Jean Louis. Les jeunes hommes. Paris, 1946.
43560.78.150	Curtis, Jean Louis. Siegfried. Paris, 1946.
38526.39.45	Daele, Rose M. Nicolas de Montreux (Ollenix du Mont-Sacre . N.Y., 1946.
43565.60.700	Daniel-Rops, Henry. Death, where is the victory? London, 1946.
43565.60.170	Daniel-Rops, Henry. Quêtes de Dieu. Paris, 1946.
43565.2.3110	Darbon, Jean F. Les suspects. 3e éd. Paris, 1946.
43565.92.7130	Davray, Jean. La fin du premier acte. Paris, 1946.
40524.32.30	Dawes, C.R. Restif de la Bretonne, 1734-1806. London, 1946.
37543.510	Debidour, V.H. Saveurs des lettres. Paris, 1946.
43566.43.730	Dekobra, Maurice. Paradise in Montparnasse. N.Y., 1946.
43566.48.1100	Delafosse, B. Le songe du poète. Paris, 1946.
40556.26.52	Dermenghem, E. Joseph de Maistre, mystique. Paris, 1946.
43566.81.4100	Desnos, Robert. Choix de poèmes. Paris, 1946.
43566.82.4110	Desternes, J. Clarière de la vie. 3. éd. Paris, 1946.
43566.93.700	Devaulx, N. The tailor's cake. London, 1946.
43568.17.100	Didelot, R.F. Au soleil de la Brousse. Paris, 1946.
43524.67.803	Didier, J. A la rencontier de Jean Anouilh. Liege, 1946.
43568.23.100	Diego, C. Un homme sans l'occident. Paris, 1946.
42576.15.170	Digeon, Claude. Le dernier visage de Flaubert. Paris, 1946.
37576.647	Dix nouvelles par Edmond Teissor. Paris, 1946.
43573.78.100	Dorsinville, Roger. Barrières; pièce en trois actes. Haïti, 1946.
43573.89.100	Doucet, Jacques. Lustrales. Porrentruy, 1946.
38524.105	Driano, Maturin. La Pléiade. Angers, 1946.
43574.68.100	Drouin, Henri. Les plus belles années. 22. éd. Paris, 1946.
38526.6.7	Du Bellay, Joachim. Oeuvres choisies. Paris, 1946.
43738.1.185	Dubois-Dumée, J.P. Solitude de Péguy. Paris, 1946.
43576.9.42	Du Bos, Charles. Journal. Paris, 1946-59. 9v.
42515.38.30	Dubreuil, Léon. Rosmapamon. [Renan, E.]. Paris, 1946.
41574.287	Dubuc, A. Villeguier dans la vie et l'oeuvre de Victor Hugo. Rouen, 1946.
42568.19.21.12	Ducasse, I.L. Oeuvres complètes. Paris, 1946.
43822.49.1095	Duchesne-Guillemin, J. Essai sur La jeune parque de Paul Valéry. Bruxelles, 1946.
43537.6.85	Duclos, Jacques. Henri Barbusse. Paris, 1946.
41543.22.43A	Ducray, C. Gerard de Nerval. Paris, 1946.
43576.15.100	Ducreux, Louis. Les clefs du ciel. Paris, 1946.
37565.100	Dufrenoy, Marie L. L'Orient romanesque en France, 1704-1789. Montréal, 1946-1947. 2v.
37574.95.5	Duhamel, Georges. Anthologie de la poésie lyrique en France. Paris, 1946.
43576.6.305	Duhamel, Georges. Le combat contre les ombres. Paris, 1946.
43576.6.390	Duhamel, Georges. Souvenirs de la vie du paradis. Lausanne, 1946.
43576.6.395	Duhamel, Georges. Souvenirs de la vie du paradis. Paris, 1946.
43576.6.740	Duhamel, Georges. Suzanne and Joseph Pasquier. London, 1946.
FL 398.20.15	Dullin, Charles. Souvenirs et notes de travail d'un acteur. Paris, 1946.
41538.130	Dumas, Alexandre. Ma revolution de 1830. Paris, 1946.
42576.15.56	Dumesnil, René. Madame Bovary de Gustave Flaubert. Paris, 1946.
43576.91.67	Duvernois, Henri. Comédies en un acte. 3. éd. Paris, 1946.
37569.177	Écrivains dans le siècle; étude sur Georges Bernanos, Paul Claudel, Georges Duhamel and others. Toulouse, 1946?
37564.155	Edelman, Nathan. Attitudes of 17th century France toward the Middle Ages. N.Y., 1946.
38525.7.80	Ellis, Lowell Bryce. Estienne Jodelle; Cleopâtre captive, a critical edition. Philadelphia, 1946.
43591.89.195	Éluard, Paul. Choix de poèmes. Paris, 1946.
43591.89.220	Éluard, Paul. Liberté. Paris, 1946.
43591.89.160	Éluard, Paul. Le lit, la table. Genève, 1946.
43591.89.290	Éluard, Paul. Les nécessités de la vie. Paris, 1946.
43591.89.270	Éluard, Paul. Paul Éluard. 2. éd. Clichy, 1946.
43591.89.165	Éluard, Paul. Poésie ininterrompue. Paris, 1946. 2v.
43592.53.130	Emmanuel, Pierre. La poète et son Christ 1938. Neuchâtel, 1946.
43592.53.155.5	Emmanuel, Pierre. Tombeau d'Orphée. Paris, 1946.
43592.53.135	Emmanuel, Pierre. Tristesse o ma patrie. Paris, 1946.
43598.82.118	Estang, Luc. Le passage du seigneur. 12. éd. Paris, 1946.
37562.270	Études romanes dédiées à Mario Roques, pas ses amis, collegues et élèves de France. Paris, 1946.
42586.57.90	Evans, Arthur R. The literary art of Eugène Fromentin. Baltimore, 1946.
43604.19.100	Eydoux, Emmanuel. Abraham l'hébreu et Samuel le voyant. Neuchâtel, 1946.
43606.8.110	Fabre, Lucien. Dieu est innocent. Paris, 1946.
43606.10.100	Fabre-Luce, Alfred. Hors d'atteinte. Paris, 1946.
V43500.89	Faillet, Georges. Vers et prose. Blainville-sur-Mer, 1946.
37569.160	Farges, Marcel. Poètes des temps présents. Paris, 1946.
43822.49.1070	Fargue, L. Rue de Villejust. Paris, 1946.
43606.76.130	Fargue, Léon P. Meandres. Genève, 1946.
40587.125	Fauré, Gabriel. Essais sur Chateaubriand. Grenoble, 1946.
42555.44.56	Faure, Gabriel. Mallarmé à Tournon. Paris, 1946.
43620.2.180	Fayer, M. Harry. Gide, freedom and Dostoevsky. Burlington, 1946.
43607.75.130	Ferdinand, Roger. Les derniers seigneurs. Paris, 1946.
43607.75.150	Ferdinand, Roger. Théâtre. Paris, 1946. 2v.
43610.4.110	Flament, A. Le bal Pré-Catelan. 5. éd. Paris, 1946.
42576.19.15	Flaubert, Gustave. Un coeur simple. Monaco, 1946.
42576.35.15	Flaubert, Gustave. Lettres inédites à Tourgueneff. Monaco, 1946.
42576.28.65	Flaubert, Gustave. Madame Bovary. Monaco, 1946.
42576.28.70	Flaubert, Gustave. Madame Bovary. Paris, 1946.
43611.75.110	Forestier (pseud.). Les langes. 8. éd. Paris, 1946.
43611.1.45.2	Fort, Paul. Anthologie des ballades françaises. Paris, 1946.

1946 - cont.

V43500.111	Fort, Paul. Ballades françaises. v. 9-13. Paris, 1946-1949. 5v.
43611.88.110	Fougère, Jean. Flo. Paris, 1946.
42556.28.182	Fowlie, Wallace. Rimbaud. London, 1946.
42556.28.180	Fowlie, Wallace. Rimbaud. N.Y., 1946.
38526.7.40	François, A. Les sonnets suisses de Joachim Du Bellay. Lausanne, 1946.
42586.55.12	Frapié, L. La vedette à l'école. Paris, 1946.
43612.63.4100	Fréminville, Claude de. Des vies exemplaires; roman. Paris, 1946.
43612.63.6100	Freminville, René Marie de la Poix de. Rien que la mer. Paris, 1946.
37574.666	Gaese, William F. French lyrics, in English verse. Madison, 1946.
43616.78.130	Gary, Romain. Tulipe. 2. éd. Paris, 1946.
43616.89.100	Gaubert, Léo. Amnésie. Paris, 1946.
43616.90.100	Gaucheron, Jacques H. La grande épitaphe - misère. Paris, 1946.
41542.11.75	Gautier, Théophile. La préface de Mademoiselle de Maupin. Paris, 1946.
43620.2.45.30	Gide, André. Deux interviews imaginaires. Paris, 1946.
43620.2.52	Gide, André. Journal. Paris, 1946.
43620.2.66	Gide, André. Le retour. Paris, 1946.
43620.2.79.60	Gide, André. Souvenirs littéraires et problèmes actuels. Beyrouth, 1946.
43620.2.50.5	Gide, André. Thésée. Paris, 1946.
43620.2.50	Gide, André. Thésée. 1. ed. N.Y., 1946.
43620.2.79.55	Gide, André. Le traité du Narcisse. Lausanne, 1946.
37574.685	Giedion-Welcker, C. Poètes à l'Ecart. Bern, 1946.
43524.67.800	Gignoux, H. Jean Anouilh. Paris, 1946.
43554.2.870	Gillet, Louis. Claudel, Peguy. Paris, 1946.
43620.66.730	Giono, Jean. Blue boy. N.Y., 1946.
37556.129	Giraud, V. La critique littéraire. Paris, 1946.
43620.74.400	Giraudoux, Jean. Aventures de Jérôme Bardim, roman. Paris, 1946.
43620.74.340	Giraudoux, Jean. La film de la duchesse de Langlois. Montreal, 1946.
43620.74.330	Giraudoux, Jean. La folle de Chaillot. Paris, 1946.
43620.74.195.2	Giraudoux, Jean. Intermezzo. Neuchâtel, 1946.
43620.74.187	Giraudoux, Jean. Judith, tragédie en trois actes. Paris, 1946.
43620.74.420.25	Giraudoux, Jean. Juliette au pays des hommes. Paris, 1946.
43620.74.380	Giraudoux, Jean. Portrait de la Renaissance. Paris, 1946.
37573.315	Gnostiques de la révolution. Paris, 1946. 2v.
42586.64.5	Gobineau, Arthur de. Les Pléiades. Monaco, 1946.
43625.19.270	Godoy, Armand. Mon fils! Mon fils! Fribourg, 1946.
43625.49.710F	Goll, Claire. Diary of a horse. Brooklyn, 1946.
42575.107	Goncourt, Edmond de. Hommage à Edmond et Jules de Goncourt à l'occasion du 50ème anniversaire de la mort de Edmond de Goncourt. Paris, 1946.
37595.83	Grands poètes français: le Moyen Âge. Lausanne, 1946.
38546.49.15	Grignan, Françoise M. Madame de Sévigné, her letters and her world. London, 1946.
38585.16.150	Grimmer, G. Andromaque de Racine. Paris, 1946.
43626.66.1120	Grosjean, Jean. Terre du temps. Paris, 1946.
40597.2.205	Grossman, L.P. Balzac en Russie. Paris, 1946.
38585.16.145A	Guéguen, Pierre. Poésie de Racine. Paris, 1946.
FL 398.35.11	Guilbert, Yvette. Autres temps, autres chants. 12. éd. Paris, 1946.
41578.121	Guillemin, H. Lamartine et la question sociale (documents inédits). Genève, 1946.
43628.41.3100	Guillevic, Eugène. Fractures. Paris, 1946.
37555.395	Gutmann, René A. Introduction à la lecture des poètes français. Paris, 1946.
43752.57.825	Guyot, Charly. Comment lire C.F. Ramuz. Paris, 1946.
43738.1.82.10	Halévy, D. Péguy and les Cahiers de la Quinzaine. London, 1946.
43631.2.75	Hamp, Pierre. Et avec ça, Madame? Paris, 1946.
37548.135A	Hanlet, C. Les écrivains belges contemporains de langue française. Liège, 1946- 2v.
42543.62.52.5	Haraucourt, Edmond. Mémoires des jours et des gens. Paris, 1946.
43631.76.2100	Harley, Jean. La paix des collines. Bordeaux, 1946.
42544.33.68	Harry, Myriam. La vie Jules Lemaître. Paris, 1946.
43631.89.120	Haurigot, Paul. Napoléon noir. Paris, 1946.
41555.52	Healy, Dennis M. Mérimée et les Anglais. Thèse. Paris, 1946?
43744.25.2800	Henriot, Émila. Le fautenial de Marcel Prévost. Paris, 1946.
37555.240	Henriot, Émile. De Lamartine à Valéry. Lyon, 1946.
40597.2.195	Hirschfell, G.J. Balzac und Delacroix. Inaug. Diss. Saint-Louis, 1946.
37575.755	Un hommage à la poésie. Nantes, 1946.
43545.4.4800	Isorni, J. Le procès Robert Brasillach. Paris, 1946.
42556.28.197	Izambard, Georges. Rimbaud tel que je l'ai connu. Paris, 1946.
43667.14.230	Jacob, Max. Max Jacob. Lyon, 1946.
37543.285	Jaloux, Edmond. Introduction à l'histoire de la littérature française. v.1-2. Genève, 1946-47.
43667.1.78	Jammes, Francis. Choix de poésies chrétiennes. Paris, 1946.
43667.1.260	Jammes, Francis. Élegies et autres vers. Lausanne, 1946.
43667.1.270	Jammes, Francis. Poèmes choisis. Paris, 1946.
43667.1.300.25	Jammes, Francis. Le roman du lièvre. 54. éd. Paris, 1946.
43698.25.800	Jans, Adrien. A la rencontre de Maxence van der Meersch. n.p., 1946.
43667.76.100	Jarlot, Gérard. Les armes blanches. 8. éd. Paris, 1946.
43668.4.110	Jeanson, Henri. Entrée des artistes. Paris, 1946.
37555.705	Jelínek, H. Podobizny básníků sladké Francie. Praha, 1946.
38525.7.20	Jodelle, d'Estienne. Cleopâtre captive. Philadelphia, 1946.
40583.172	Josephson, Matthew. Stendhal. Garden City, 1946.
43670.94.290	Jouve, Pierre Jean. Défense et illustration. Paris, 1946.
43554.2.860	Jouve, Raymond. Comment lire Paul Claudel. Paris, 1946.
41563.33.20	Kossmann, Friedrich K.H. Rodolphe Toepffer. Rotterdam, 1946.
43687.8.100	Labbe, Jean. Croisières. Paris, 1946.
43687.15.230	Lacretelle, Jacques de. Ideés dans un chapeau. Monaco, 1946.
43687.15.250	Lacretelle, Jacques de. Le pour et le contre, roman. Genève, 1946. 2v.
38544.27.60	La Fayette, Marie M. La Princesse de Clèves. Paris, 1946.
39526.33.27F	La Fontaine, Jean de. Douze fables. Agen, 1946.
39527.29.55	La Fontaine, Jean de. Fables. Londres, 1946.

Chronological Listing

1946 - cont.

39525.15.5 La Fontaine, Jean de. Fables choisies, mises en vers. Paris, 1946.
42555.1.30 Laforgue, Jules. Stéphane Vassiliew. Vésenaz près Genève, 1946.
37568.80.5 Lalou, René. Histoire de la littérature française contemporaine. v.2. 3e éd. Paris, 1946.
38514.60.85A La Marche, Olivier de. Le chevalier délibéré. Washington, 1946.
43687.58.2120 Landry, Charles François. La merle de novembre. 7e éd. Paris, 1946.
43687.75.155 Larguier, Léo. La curiosité. Paris, 1946.
43687.77.100 Larronde, Olivier. Les barricades mystérieuses. Paris? 1946.
43687.92.100 Lautère, Adrienne. Madame d'Aulnoy et sa mère; roman. Paris, 1946.
43688.5.5100 Léautaud, Paul. Choix de pages de Paul Léautaud. Paris, 1946.
43688.8.1100 Lebel, Roland. La porte d'or. Paris, 1946.
38527.49.5 Lebèque, R. Robert Garnier, Les juives. v.1-2. Paris, 1946.
43688.17.139 Lécuyer, A.H. (Mme.). Lettres anonymes. 19e éd. Paris, 1946.
37543.273 Ledésert, R.P.L. Histoire de la littérature française des origines à l'époque contemporaine. London, 1946-47. 2v.
42563.23.102 Lefèbvre, Louis. Léon Bloy. Paris, 1946.
43688.29.110 Lefèvre, Fréderic. Ce vagabond. Paris, 1946.
43688.34.110 Legrand, Jean. Journal de Jacques. 5e éd. Paris, 1946.
43688.60.120 Leiris, Michel. L'âge d'homme. 7e éd. Paris, 1946.
43688.60.110 Leiris, Michel. Aurora, roman. Paris, 1946.
43620.2.190 Lepoutre, Raymond. André Gide. Paris, 1946.
43688.88.110 Létraz, Jean de. Descendez! On vous demande. Paris, 1946.
43757.50.1010 Levy, Arthur R. L'idéalisme de Romain Rolland. Thèse. Paris, 1946.
41557.10.135 L'Hopital, Madeleine. La notion d'artiste chez George Sand. Paris, 1946.
43690.1.800 Lichtenberger, M. Le message de André Lichtenberger. 2. éd. Paris, 1946.
FL 394.52 Lindsay, Frank W. Dramatic parody by marionettes in 18th century Paris. Thesis. N.Y., 1946.
43565.60.810 Lobet, Marcel. À la rencontre de Daniel-Rops. n.p., 1946.
43693.75.100 Lorenz, Paul. Notre-Dame de thermidor. Paris, 1946.
43693.75.110 Lorenz, Paul. Le tombeau de Paul Valéry. Paris, 1946.
38514.23.60 Maas, P.M. François Villon. Utrecht, 1946.
41522.18.165 Macchia, Giovanni. Baudelaire e la poetica della Malinconia. Napoli, 1946.
37543.269 Madaule, Jacques. Reconnaissances. v.3. Paris, 1946.
43697.31.100 Magali (pseud.). L'enveloppe aux cachets bleus. Montréal, 1946.
43697.88.821 Majault, J. Mauriac et l'art du roman. Paris, 1946.
42555.43.35 Mallarmé, Stéphane. Propos sur la poésie. Monaco, 1946.
43697.52.120 Malraux, André. Scènes choisies. Paris, 1946.
Mol 613.12A Mandach, André. Molière et la comédie de moeurs en Angleterre. Neuchâtel, 1946.
37567.390.10 Mann, Heinrich. Geist und Tat. Weimar, 1946.
43697.61.1100 Manot, Léon. Ce verbe et ce silence. Paris, 1946.
43822.49.1085 Marcailhou d'Aymeric, A.L.A.C. Paul Valéry. Thèse. Toulouse, 1946.
38526.34.40 Marguerite d'Angoulême. Théâtre profane. Paris, 1946.
FL 362.23.10 Marignac, A. de. Les imitations françaises de l'Oedipé Roi de Saphocle. Le Caire, 1946?
43761.39.800 Marill, René. St. Exupéry. Paris, 1946.
40535.27.20 Marivaux, Pierre Carlet de Chamblain de. Théâtre complet. v.1-2. Paris, 1946.
38523.12.15 Marot, Clément. Choix de poèmes. Lyon, 1946.
43697.76.4100 Mars, Claire. Dans l'ombre fraîche. Paris, 1946.
42576.65.13.100 Martineau, René. Autour de J.K. Huysmans. Bruges, 1946.
V43500.193 Martinet, Marcel. Florilège poétique. Blainville-sur-Mer, 1946.
43822.49.1035A Mascagni, P. Initation à Paul Valéry. Paris, 1946.
42577.2.10 Maupassant, Guy de. Boule de suif, and other stories. Harmondsworth, 1946.
42577.4.7.15 Maupassant, Guy de. Caresses. London, 1946.
42577.1.22 Maupassant, Guy de. Contes choisis. Angers, 1946.
42577.4.5.10 Maupassant, Guy de. Contes des beaux jours. Rouen, 1946.
43697.52.807 Mauriac, Claude. Malraux. Paris, 1946.
43697.88.260 Mauriac, François. Les chemins de la mer. Paris, 1946.
43697.88.725 Mauriac, François. God and Mammon. London, 1946.
43697.88.726 Mauriac, François. A woman of the Pharisies. London, 1946.
43697.89.42 Maurois, André. Journal. (États-Unis, 1946). Paris, 1946.
43697.89.290 Maurois, André. Toujours l'inattendu arrive. Paris, 1946.
42514.28.77A Maurras, Charles. Le procès de Charles Maurras. Paris, 1946.
43697.98.4100 Mazéas, Gaulven. Kosmanomothéos. Paris, 1946.
43697.100.148 Mazeline, Guy. Le souffle de l'été. Paris, 1946.
43698.35.120 Mégret, C. L'absent. Paris, 1946.
42556.28.104 Méléra, M. (Mme.). Resonances autour de Rimbaud. Paris, 1946.
37562.272 Merk, J. Die literarische Gestaltung der altfranzösischen Heiligerleben. Affaltern, 1946.
43698.200.120 Michaux, Henri. Au pays de la magie. London, 1946.
43698.200.19 Michaux, Henri. Henri Michaux, un étude. Paris, 1946.
40547.14.15 Michelet, Jules. Michelet. Genève, 1946.
43699.3.710 Mille, Pierre. Barnavaux et quelques femmes. Paris, 1946.
43699.51.17 Milosz, Oscar Vladislas. Oeuvres complètes. v.3-5. Paris, 1946- 3v.
42545.28.7.70 Mirbeau, Octave. Diary of a chambermaid. N.Y., 1946.
Mol 161.36 Molière, Jean Baptiste Poquelin. Amphitryon; comédie. Paris, 1946.
Mol 165.110 Molière, Jean Baptiste Poquelin. L'avare. Paris, 1946.
Mol 228.85 Molière, Jean Baptiste Poquelin. Le malade imaginaire. London, 1946.
Mol 166.4 Molière, Jean Baptiste Poquelin. The miser. Iowa City, Iowa, 1946.
Mol 268.160 Molière, Jean Baptiste Poquelin. Le Tartuffe. H. Ashton. Oxford, 1946.
Mol 19.35.7 Molière, Jean Baptiste Poquelin. Théâtre 1666 à 1668. Paris, 1946.
Mol 172.5.35 Molière, Jean Baptiste Poquelin. The would-be gentleman. Chicago, 1946.
42555.44.73 Mondor, Henri. Vie de Mallarmé. 19. éd. Paris, 1946.
38546.3 Mongrédien, Georges. Madeleine de Scudéry et son salon. Paris, 1946.
Mon 32.46 Montaigne, Michel de. The essays of Montaigne. N.Y., 1946.

1946 - cont.

Mon 45.24 Montaigne, Michel de. Journal de voyage en Italie. Paris, 1946.
41574.255 Monteamor, H.H. Victor Hugo. Rosario, 1946.
39594.13.40 Montesquieu, C.L. de S. Lettres persanes. Paris, 1946.
43701.63.135 Montherlant, Henry de. Aux fontaines du désir. Paris, 1946.
43701.63.290 Montherlant, Henry de. Encore un instant de bonheur. Paris, 1946.
43701.63.210 Montherlant, Henry de. L'exil, pièces en trois actes. Paris, 1946.
43701.63.120.15 Montherlant, Henry de. Les jeunes filles, roman. Paris, 1946.
43701.63.185 Montherlant, Henry de. Malatesta. Lausanne, 1946.
43701.63.145 Montherlant, Henry de. Le petite infante de Castille. Paris, 1946.
43701.63.430 Montherlant, Henry de. Sur les femmes. Sceaux, 1946.
42563.18.220 Moreau, Pierre. Maurice Barrès. Paris, 1946.
42557.14.95 Morice, L. Verlaine. Paris, 1946.
43701.76.6100 Morisseau-Leroy, F. Récolte. Port-au-Prince, 1946.
42577.32.30 Moss, Arthur. The legend of the Latin quarter. N.Y., 1946.
43552.4.2800 Mounin, G. Avez-vous lu Char? 2e éd. Paris, 1946.
41522.18.160 Mouquet, Jules. Baudelaire en 1848. Paris, 1946.
43703.73.3110 Muray, Jean. La déesse. Paris, 1946.
42577.32.20 Murger, Henry. Scènes de la vie de Bohème. Paris, 1946.
41596.17.25 Musset, Alfred de. Alfred de Musset. v.1-2. Lyon, 1946.
41596.37 Musset, Alfred de. Le chandelier. Paris, 1946.
41596.19.12 Musset, Alfred de. Nouvelles. Lille, 1946.
43705.9.100 Nabonne, Bernard. La meunière de Javel. Paris, 1946.
43705.83.140 Natanson, J. Manigances. Paris, 1946.
43706.52.100 Nelly, Luce. Chansons de douceur et d'automne. Paris, 1946.
41543.11.7 Nerval, Gerard de. Sylvie, souvenirs du Valois. Paris, 1946.
41543.11.12 Nerval, Gerard de. Sylvie. Monaco, 1946.
41543.11.9 Nerval, Gerard de. Sylvie. Montréal, 1946.
42515.32.10 Novak, O. Renanova theorie slohu. Praha, 1946.
V43500.217 Olivier, Pascale. Proses. Frontispice et bandeau de Charles Bernard. Albi, 1946.
37558.74 Osborne, Nancy F. The doctor in the French literature of the sixteenth century. N.Y., 1946.
41557.10.140 Paillou, Paul H. La vie émouvante de George Sand. Paris, 1946.
43697.88.817 Palonte, Alain. Mauriac, le roman et la vie. Paris, 1946.
43737.65.100 Panet, Edmond. Le poète Edmond Panet. Pierrefitte, 1946.
43737.59.100 Panneel, Henry. Contes et légendes du pays de Flandre. Paris, 1946.
37556.131 Paraf, Pierre. L'information. Paris, 1946.
43822.49.1120 Paris. Bibliothèque Sainte-Geneviève. Collection Doucet. Catalogue de l'exposition Paul Valéry. Paris, 1946?
42557.20.295 Paris. Bibliothèque Ste. Geneviève. Collection Doncet. Catalogue de l'exposition Paul Verlaine. Paris, 1946.
37574.664 Parisot, Henri. Les poètes voyagent. Paris, 1946.
43822.49.1105 Parize, J.H. Essai sur la pensée et l'art de Paul Valéry. Paris, 1946.
43822.49.916A Paul Valéry, vivant. Marseille, 1946.
43737.89.1120 Paulhan, Jean. La métromanie. Paris, 1946.
43738.1.59 Péguy, Charles. Clio. Paris, 1946.
43738.1.30.10 Péguy, Charles. Les tapisseries Ève. Paris, 1946.
43738.1.152.5 Péguy, M. Le destin de Charles Péguy. 12e éd. Paris, 1946.
43738.78.140 Perse, Saint-John. Exil. Paris, 1946.
43738.78.190F Perse, Saint-John. Vents. Paris, 1946.
FL 6139.46 Petruzzellis, N. Il pensiero politico e pedagogico. Milano, 1946.
37569.150 Peyrade, Jean. Recherche de la joie. Paris, 1946.
V43500.241 Peyre, Sully-André. Le grand-père que j'ai en songe. Genève, 1946.
43738.99.100 Pezet, Jacques. Symphonie héroïque; roman. Paris, 1946.
43739.23.100 Pfeiffer, Jean. Traité de l'aventure. Paris, 1946.
43740.1.35.5 Philippe, Charles Louis. Bubu de Montparnasse. Monte Carlo, 1946.
43697.52.865A Picon, Gaëlan. André Malraux. 13. éd. Paris, 1946.
43744.67.83 Pierre-Quint, Léon. Marcel Proust. Paris, 1946.
42576.65.13.98 Pirard, Pierre. Huysmans. Paris, 1946.
37573.673 Les plëiades. Paris, 1946.
43742.41.115 Plisnier, Charles. Mariages, roman. Paris, 1946-48. 2v.
43742.41.220 Plisnier, Charles. Mes bien-aimés. Paris, 1946.
43822.49.1045 Pommier, Jean. Paul Valéry et la création littéraire. Paris, 1946.
NEDL 41522.17.23.15 Porché, François. Baudelaire. Paris, 1946.
43743.77.3100 Porquet, André. Le ciel dans les poches. Paris, 1946.
39527.4.80 Pradier, M. La vie de Jean de La Fontaine. Paris, 1946.
43744.24.21 Prévert, Jacques. Histoires. Paris, 1946.
40522.9.30 Prévost, Antoine F. Histoire du chevalier des Grieux et de Manon Lescaut. Paris, 1946.
43744.67.74 Proust, Marcel. Lettres à Madame C. Paris, 1946.
41522.3.42 Quéru, Hermann Albert. Le dernier grand seigneur. Paris, 1946.
38536.1.1 Rabelais, F. Pantagruel. Paris, 1946.
38537.30.15 Rabelais, F. The portable Rabelais. N.Y., 1946.
43752.57.260 Ramuz, Charles Ferdinand. Le régne de l'esprit malin. Lausanne, 1946.
43752.57.210 Ramuz, Charles Ferdinand. Les servants et autres nouvelles. Lausanne, 1946.
43752.57.700 Ramuz, Charles Ferdinand. The triumph of death. Paris, 1946.
37558.70.5 Ravon, Georges. L'académie Goncourt en dix couverts. Avignon, 1946.
43822.49.1020 Raymond, Marcel. Paul Valéry et la tentation de l'esprit. Neuchâtel, 1946.
43752.98.150 Raynal, Paul. A souffert sous Ponce Pilate. 7. éd. Paris, 1946.
42587.52.8 Renard, Jules. Carrots. London, 1946.
43688.2.83 Richard, Noël. Louis Le Cardonnel et les revues symbolistes. Paris, 1946.
38564.55 Richard, Pierre. La Bruyère et ses "Caractères". Amiens, 1946.
43756.3.60 Richepin, Jacques. L'image obstinée. Paris, 1946.
42556.28.50 Rimbaud, Jean Arthur. Oeuvres complètes. Paris, 1946.
42556.28.72 Rimbaud, Jean Arthur. Prose poems from the Illuminations. N.Y., 1946.
42556.28.53 Rimbaud, Jean Arthur. Sämtliche Gedichte. Heidelberg, 1946.

1946 - cont.

42556.28.40 Rimbaud, Jean Arthur. Une saison en enfer. Montréal, 1946.

43526.65.855 Rimes et Raisons. Guilleaume Apollinaire. Abbi, 1946.

43756.55.1100 Rimière, Edmond. Conte crépusculaire. Paris, 1946.

43757.10.120 Robida, Michael. Le temps de la longue patiense. Paris, 1946.

43757.12.1100 Roché, Louis. Si proche et lointaine. Paris, 1946.

43757.50.1020 Rolano-Holst, Henriëtte. Romain Rolland. Amsterdam, 1946.

43757.50.733 Rolland, Romain. De Jean Christophe à Colas Breugnon; pages de journale de Romain Rolland. Paris, 1946.

43757.50.605 Rolland, Romain. Le périple. Paris, 1946.

43757.50.1008 Rolland, Romain. Das Romain Rolland Buch. Zürich, 1946.

V43500.257 Rolland de Renéville, André. La nuit, l'esprit. Paris, 1946.

43757.3.250 Romains, Jules. Le colloque de novembre. Paris, 1946.

43757.3.80 Romains, Jules. Quand le navire. 81e éd. Paris, 1946.

43757.3.298 Romains, Jules. Réception de M. Jules Romains. Paris, 1946.

38525.20.10A Ronsard, Pierre de. Lyrics. London? 1946.

38525.20.15 Ronsard, Pierre de. Poèmes choisis et commentes par André Barlier. Oxford, 1946.

43757.73.100 Roques, Jeanne. La vie sentimentale de George Sand. Paris, 1946.

42546.15.3.30 Rostand, Edmond. Chantecler. Paris, 1946.

FL 6067.10A Rousseau, J.J. Jean-Jacques Rousseau; discours sur les sciences et les arts. N.Y., 1946.

37543.243.10 Rousseaux, André. Le monde classique. Paris, 1946.

43738.1.87 Roussel, J. Mesure de Péguy. Paris, 1946.

V43500.265 Rousselot, Jean. La mansarde; poèmes en prose. Millau? 1946.

43667.14.807 Rousselot, Jean. Max Jacob. 6. éd. Paris, 1946.

43757.94.1110 Roux, Paul. L'ancienne à la coiffe innombrable. Nantes, 1946.

43757.94.1100 Roux, Paul. Anciennetés...réposoirs de procession. n.p., 1946.

40597.2.169 Royce, William H. Balzac as he should be read. N.Y., 1946.

42556.28.187 Ruchon, F. Rimbaud. Vésenaz-Genève, 1946.

42584.25.160 Rufener, Helen L. Biography of a war novel: Zola's "La débacle". Morningside Heights, 1946.

39544.200 Russell, Trusten Wheeler. Voltaire, Dryden and heroic tragedy. N.Y., 1946.

37595.85 Rutebeuf. Onze poèmes concernant la croisade. Paris, 1946.

37543.251 Saintsbury, George. French literature and its masters. 1. ed. N.Y., 1946.

43761.47.100 Sales, Henri. Almanach. Paris, 1946.

42556.29.6 Samain, Albert. Albert Samain et Francis James. Paris, 1946.

43550.58.805 Sartre, J.P. Explication de L'étranger. n.p., 1946.

43761.78.705 Sartre, Jean Paul. The flies (Les mouches) and In camera (Huis clos). London, 1946.

43761.78.120 Sartre, Jean Paul. Morts sans sepulture. Lausanne, 1946.

43761.78.710A Sartre, Jean Paul. Portrait of the anti-semite. N.Y., 1946.

43761.78.110 Sartre, Jean Paul. La putain respectueuse. 12. éd. Paris, 1946.

43761.89.5710 Saurat, Denis. Death and the dreamer. London, 1946.

37568.66.5A Saurat, Denis. Modern French literature. London, 1946.

43761.89.5105 Saurat, Denis. Tendances ideas françaises. Paris, 1946.

43697.52.2100 Savane, Marcel. André Malraux. Paris, 1946.

43763.36.100 Scheler, Lucien. La lampe tempête. Paris, 1946.

43620.2.260 Schildt, G. Gide och människan, en studie. Stockholm, 1946.

40542.34 Schimberg, Albert P. The great friend: Frederick Ozanam. Milwaukee, 1946.

42576.15.185 Schöne, Maurice. La langue de Flaubert. Paris, 1946?

43763.40.3110 Schwob, René. Mistère de Jeanne d'Arc. Paris, 1946.

43769.54.725 Semenon, Georges. Lost moorings. London, 1946.

43765.80.100 Serge, Victor (pseud.). Les derniers temps. Montréal, 1946. 2v.

42576.46.13 Shaw, Marjorie. L'histoire du Périgord dans l'oeuvre d'Eugène Le Roy. Thèse. Dijon, 1946.

FL 398.81 Sorel, Cécile. Les belles heurs de ma vie. Monaco, 1946.

37555.212 Suberville, Jean. Histoire et théorie de la versification française. 2. éd. Paris, 1946.

42571.11.7 Suffel, Jacques. Anatole France. Paris, 1946.

42586.57.81 Suire, Louis. Le paysage charentais. La Rochelle, 1946.

42563.18.175 Tharaud, Jérôme. Le roman d'Aïssé. Paris, 1946.

43788.5.205 Tharaud, Jérôme. Vers d'almanach. Paris, 1946.

38526.49.20 Théophile de Viau. La maison de Sylvia. n.p., 1946.

43789.49.100 Tillard, Paul. On se bat dans la ville. Paris, 1946.

43792.40.150 Toesca, Maurice. L'esprit du coeur. Paris, 1946.

43792.70.100 Topliceano, Roxane. Bagatelles et autres. Paris, 1946.

Mol 720.8 Toudouze, Georges G. Molière. Paris, 1946.

43793.41.105 Trintziers, René. La grande peur. Grenoble, 1946.

43793.42.110 Triolet, Elsa. Personne ne m'aime. Paris, 1946.

42576.65.13.106 Tupigny, J.P. Le sentiment heraldique dans l'oeuvre de J.K. Huysmans. Paris, 1946.

37564.180 Turnell, Martin. The classical moment. Norfolk, 1946.

43799.5.120A Tzara, Tristan. Terre sur terre. Genève, 1946.

43799.5.140 Tzara, Tristan. Vingt-cinq-et-un poèmes. Paris, 1946.

43822.11.60 Văcărescu, Elena. Memorial sur le mode mineur. Paris, 1946.

43822.50.100 Vailland, Roger. Drôle de jeu. Paris; 1946.

43822.49.275F Valéry, Paul. L'ange. Paris, 1946.

43822.49.280 Valéry, Paul. Mon Faust. Paris, 1946.

43822.49.150 Valéry, Paul. Monsieur Teste. Paris, 1946.

43822.49.171 Valéry, Paul. Poésies. Paris, 1946.

38525.100 Valle Abad, F. del. Influencia española sobre la literatura francesa. Avila, 1946.

43598.84.815 Vallery-Radot, Pasteur. Discours de réception de M. Pasteur Vallery-Radot à l'Académie Française. Paris, 1946.

37543.261 Van Tieghem, Philippe. Petite histoire des grandes doctrines littéraire sen France. Paris, 1946.

43823.74.110 Vérane, Léon. La calanque au soleil. Paris, 1946.

42557.19.115 Verlaine, Paul. La bonne chanson. Paris, 1946.

42557.20.10 Verlaine, Paul. Confessions. Paris, 1946.

42557.20.5.7 Verlaine, Paul. Fêtes galantes. Paris, 1946.

42557.19.12 Verlaine, Paul. Jadis et naguère. Paris, 1946.

42557.19.95 Verlaine, Paul. Parallèlement. Paris, 1946.

42557.19.21 Verlaine, Paul. Poèmes choisis. Paris, 1946.

42557.18.23 Verlaine, Paul. Poèmes saturniens. London, 1946.

42557.18.22 Verlaine, Paul. Poèmes saturniens. Paris, 1946.

42557.19.120 Verlaine, Paul. Romances sans paroles. Paris, 1946.

42557.19.52 Verlaine, Paul. Sagesse. Paris, 1946.

1946 - cont.

37568.102 Vettard, Camille. Du côté de chez. Albi, 1946.

43824.3.140 Vialar, Paul. La mort est un commencement. Paris, 1946. 8v.

43824.3.150 Vialar, Paul. Une ombre. Paris, 1946.

38525.22.45.85 Vianey, Joseph. Les odes de Ronsard. Paris, 1946.

43824.49.230 Vildrac, Charles. Lazare. Paris, 1946.

43824.49.220 Vildrac, Charles. Théâtre. 8e éd. Paris, 1946. 2v.

38514.20.22 Villon, François. Ballades. London, 1946.

38514.20.15.30A Villon, François. Oeuvres. Paris, 1946.

39544.28.15 Voltaire, François Marie Arouet de. Lettres choisies. v.1-2. Paris, 1946.

39544.28.65 Voltaire, François Marie Arouet de. Lettres philosophiques. Oxford, 1946.

39545.37.18.30 Voltaire, François Marie Arouet de. Satirical dictionary of Voltaire. Mt. Vernon, N.Y., 1946.

39545.110 Voltaire, François Marie Arouet de. Sémiramis; tragédie. Paris, 1946.

39545.32.40 Voltaire, François Marie Arouet de. Zadig; ou La destinée. Paris, 1946.

40587.152 Walker, Thomas Capell. Chateaubriand's natural scenery. Baltimore, 1946.

43837.77.100 Wurmser, André. L'enfant enchainé. Paris, 1946.

42584.25.165 Zévaès, A.B. Zola. Paris, 1946.

43863.50.100 Zilkha, Berthie. La voie et les detours; roman. N.Y., 1946.

42584.23.9.27 Zola, Emile. Germinal. v.1-2. Paris, 1946.

42584.23.83 Zola, Emile. The masterpiece. N.Y., 1946.

41574.275 Zumthor, Paul. Victor Hugo. 7. éd. Paris, 1946.

40597.2.165A Zweig, Stefan. Balzac. N.Y., 1946.

40597.2.164 Zweig, Stefan. Balzac. Stockholm, 1946.

1947

43511.67.100 About, Pierre Edmond. L'ombre verte. N.Y., 1947.

40526.80 Affolter, Hans. Un jurisconsulte bernois, poète français, Sigismond Louis de Lerber. Bienne, 1947.

43620.2.195 Ames, Van Meter. André Gide. Norfolk, 1947.

42525.8.84 Angwerd, P.M. L'oeuvre d'Ernest Hello. Thèse. Sarnen, 1947.

43738.1.225 Anice, Robert. Péguy. Bruges, 1947?

43526.65.170 Apollinaire, Guillaume. Le poète assassine. Paris, 1947.

Mol 601.18 Apollonio, Mario. Molière. 2. ed. Brescia, 1947.

43527.3.41 Aragon, Louis. Chroniques du belcants. Genève, 1947.

43527.3.727 Aragon, Louis. Deux poètes d'aujourd'hui. Paris, 1947.

43527.3.240 Aragon, Louis. En étrange pays dans mon pays lui-même. Paris, 1947.

43527.3.725 Aragon, Louis. Passengers of destiny. London, 1947.

43527.3.230 Aragon, Louis. Les voyageurs de l'impériale. Paris, 1947.

41522.18.180A Aressy, Lucien. Les dernières années de Baudelaire. Paris, 1947.

42557.14.11.9 Aressy, Lucien. Verlaine et la dernière bohème. 9. éd. Paris, 1947.

37574.112 Arland, M. Anthologie de la poésie française. Paris, 1947.

Mol 193.40 Arnavon, Jacques. Le Don Juan de Molière. Copenhague, 1947.

Mol 193.40.2 Arnavon, Jacques. Le Don Juan de Molière. Thèse. Copenhague, 1947.

41522.18.170 Arnold, Paul. Le Dieu de Baudelaire. Paris, 1947.

43528.61.180 Arnoux, Alexandre. L'amour des trois oranges. Paris, 1947.

40597.2.163 Arrault, Albert. La Touraine de Baleac. Tours, 1947.

41574.270 Audiat, Pierre. Ainsi vécut Victor Hugo. Paris, 1947.

37574.643.25 Aury, D. Poètes d'aujourd'hui. Paris, 1947.

43535.54.190 Aymé, Marcel. Lucienne et le boucher. 5e éd. Paris, 1947.

43535.54.135.15 Aymé, Marcel. Le vin de Paris. 29e éd. Paris, 1947.

37569.40.75 Balakian, Anna E. Literary origins of surrealism. N.Y., 1947.

40596.8.30 Balzac, Honoré de. La comédie humaine. v.4-6,8,10-15,20. Paris, 1947. 11v.

40597.35.130 Balzac, Honoré de. L'eglise. Paris, 1947.

NEDL 40597.35.131 Balzac, Honoré de. L'eglise. Paris, 1947.

40597.19.35 Balzac, Honoré de. Eugénie Grandet. Tours, 1947.

40597.35.120 Balzac, Honoré de. L'illustre Gaudissart. Tours, 1947.

40597.28.20 Balzac, Honoré de. Le lys dans la vallée. Tours, 1947.

40597.35.95 Balzac, Honoré de. Maître Cornélius. Tours, 1947.

40597.21.10 Balzac, Honoré de. Les parisiens comme ils sont, 1830-1846. Genève, 1947.

40597.85 Balzac, Honoré de. Vautrin. Paris, 1947.

41522.2.39 Barbey d'Aurevilly, Jules. Journal (memoranda). Paris, 1947.

40583.176A Bardèche, M. Stendhal Romancier. Paris, 1947.

38562.18.25 Bauchard, Marcel. L'histoire des Oracles de Fontenelle. Paris, 1947.

41522.4.20 Baudelaire, Charles. Correspondance générale. Paris, 1947-53. 6v.

41522.13.12.5 Baudelaire, Charles. Intimate journals. Hollywood, 1947.

41522.13.8.95 Baudelaire, Charles. Paris spleen, 1869. N.Y., 1947.

41522.13.50 Baudelaire, Charles. Le spleen de Paris. Paris, 1947.

43538.13.2100 Becker, Yves. Puisque voici la joie. Paris, 1947.

42563.23.93 Béguin, Albert. Léon Bloy; a study in impatience. N.Y., 1947.

37543.330 Bénac, Henri. Études sur les chefs-d'oeuvre de la littérature française. Paris, 1947-48. 2v.

42566.16.95 Benoit-Guyod, G. Alphonse Daudet. Paris, 1947.

41592.29.25 Béranger, P.J. de. One hundred songs of Pierre-Jean de Béranger. London, 1947.

43538.75.110 Bergmans, Simone. Le patrémoine secret. Bruxelles, 1947.

V43500.21 Bérimont, Luc. Sur la terre, qui est au ciel. Preuilly-sur-Claise, 1947.

43538.76.11 Bernanos, Georges. Oeuvres. Paris, 1947. 6v.

43538.10.65 Bernard, Jean J. Le pain rouge. Paris, 1947.

41578.40.48 Bert, Paul. Lamartine "homme social", son action dans la région natale. Paris, 1947.

37567.428 Bertaut, Jules. L'époque romantique. Paris, 1947.

42576.15.190 Bertrand, G.E. Les jours de Flaubert. Paris, 1947.

43606.76.800 Beucler, André. Dimanche avec Léon-Paul Fargue. Paris, 1947.

40582.12.55 Beyle, Henri. Armance. Paris, 1947.

40582.3.42 Beyle, Henri. Cent soixante-quatorze lettres à Stendhal. Paris, 1947. 2v.

40582.10.10 Beyle, Henri. Chroniques italiennes. Paris, 1947.

40582.13.65 Beyle, Henri. Lamiel. Paris, 1947.

40582.8.4.20 Beyle, Henri. On love. N.Y., 1947.

1947 - cont.

37596.10.160 Bezzola, Rito R. Le sens de l'aventure et de l'amour. Chréstien de Troyes. Paris, 1947.
43744.67.70 Bibescu, M.L.L. Le voyageur voilé: Marcel Proust. Lettres au duc de Guiche. Genève, 1947.
43540.3.55 Billy, André. Les beaux jours de Barbezon. Paris, 1947.
43554.2.847 Bindel, Victor. Claudel et nous. Tournai, 1947.
43688.61.820 Blanchart, Paul. Le théâtre de Henri René Lenormand. Paris, 1947.
43543.8.1100 Blancpain, Marc. Le solitaire. Paris, 1947.
42563.23.27 Bloy, Léon. Correspondance. Paris, 1947.
42563.23.33 Bloy, Léon. Histoires désobligeantes. Monaco, 1947.
42563.23.16.3 Bloy, Léon. Histoires désobligeantes. Paris, 1947.
42563.23.16.1 Bloy, Léon. Je m'accuse. Paris, 1947.
42563.23.16.4 Bloy, Léon. Lettres aux Montchal inédites. v. 1-3. Paris, 1947-48.
42563.23.70A Bloy, Léon. Pilgrim of the absolute. N.Y., 1947.
42563.23.16.2 Bloy, Léon. Le salut par les Juifs. Paris, 1947.
42563.23.75 Bloy, Léon. The woman who was poor. N.Y., 1947.
40583.33.3 Blum, Léon. Stendhal et le beylisme. 3. éd. Paris, 1947.
42563.23.104 Bollery, Joseph. Léon Bloy. Paris, 1947-53. 3v.
41522.3.55 Bonnes, J.P. Le bonheur du masque. Tournai, 1947.
42563.36.320 Bordeaux, Henry. Le jeu de massacre. Paris, 1947.
42563.36.65.20 Bordeaux, Henry. La robe de laine. Paris, 1947.
43544.101.100 Borne, Alain. L'eau fine. Paris, 1947.
43544.81.2130 Bosco, Henri. La fattoria. Milano, 1947.
43544.81.2120 Bosco, Henri. Le mas théotime. Paris, 1947.
37574.705 Bournet, S. Anthologie des poètes français du Sud-Est de 1900 à nos jours. Lyon, 1947.
38512.42.5 Bozon, Nicole. Three saints' lives. N.Y., 1947.
38512.2.5 Braddy, Haldeen. Chaucer and the French poet Graunson. Baton Rouge, La., 1947.
38526.48.16.9 Braspart, Michel. Du Bartas, Poète chrétien. Neuchâtel, 1947.
FL 383.165 Braun, Sidney D. The courtisane in the French theatre from Hugo to Becque. Baltimore, Md., 1947.
37543.140.17 Braunschvig, Marcel. La littérature française contemporaine. 11. éd. Paris, 1947.
Htn FL 355.7* Brenner, C.D. A bibliographical list of plays in the French language, 1700-1789. Berkeley, Calif., 1947.
43545.23.100 Brenner, J. La minute heureuse. Paris, 1947.
43545.24.100.5 Breton, André. Arcane 17 entré d'ajours. Paris, 1947.
37569.40.15 Breton, André. Les manifestes du surréalisme. Paris, 1947.
43688.14.800 Bruel, André. Marc Leclerc, 1874-1946. Angers, 1947.
37569.145 Brugmans, H. Zoekend frankrijk. Amsterdam, 1947.
43823.75.2715 Bruller, Jean. Three short novels. 1st ed. Boston, 1947.
43547.12.700 Buchet, E.E. Children of wrath. London, 1947.
37530.100 Cabeen, David C. A critical bibliography of French literature. Syracuse, 1947-56. 5v.
39594.15.5 Cabeen, David Clark. Montesquieu: a bibliography. N.Y., 1947.
43550.48.100 Calet, Henri. Trente à quarante. Paris, 1947.
43550.58.770 Camus, Albert Sivulliner. Helsingissa, 1947.
43550.58.715A Camus, Albert. Caligula. London, 1947.
43550.58.115 Camus, Albert. Noces. Photoreproduction. Paris, 1947.
43550.58.120 Camus, Albert. La peste. 81. éd. Paris, 1947.
40583.142.10 Caraccio, Armand. Variétés Stendhaliennes. Grenoble, 1947.
37567.419 Carré, Jean Marie. Les écrivains français et le mirage allemand. Paris, 1947.
37576.647.10 Castex, Pierre. Anthologie du conte fantastique français. Paris, 1947.
43550.98.120 Cayrol, Jean. Je vivrai l'amour des autres. v.1-2,3. Neuchâtel, 1947. 2v.
43550.98.110 Cayrol, Jean. Passe temps de l'homme et des oiseaux. Neuchâtel, 1947.
43551.59.800 Cendrars, Blaise. Blaise Cendrars. Paris, 1947.
43551.59.190 Cendrars, Blaise. Moravagine; roman. Paris, 1947.
43551.59.105 Cendrars, Blaise. Poésies complètes. Paris, 1947.
43551.79.140 Césaire, Aimé. Cahier d'un retour au pays natal. N.Y., 1947.
43551.80.21 Cesbron, Gilbert. Oeuvres romanesques. Lausanne, 1947. 12v.
43552.1.21 Chabaneix, Philippe. Poèmes choisis. Paris, 1947.
43738.1.200 Chabanon, A. La poétique de Charles Péguy. Paris, 1947.
40593.37 Chanson, P. Le mariage d'amour selon Madame de Staël. Paris, 1947.
43552.5.1140 Chartier, Émile. Humanites. Paris, 1947.
43667.78.910 Chassé, C. Dans les coulisses de la gloire. Paris, 1947.
42555.44.82 Chassé, Charles. Lueurs sur Mallarmé. Paris, 1947.
40586.28.85 Chateaubriand, F.A.R. Incidences, digression philosophique. Paris, 1947.
40586.21.12 Chateaubriand, F.A.R. René. Lille, 1947.
43554.2.880 Chonez, Claudine. Introduction à Paul Claudel. Paris, 1947.
39527.4.85A Clarac, Pierre. La Fontaine. Paris, 1947.
43752.57.835A Claudel, P. Du côté de chez Ramuz. Neuchâtel, 1947.
43554.2.300 Claudel, Paul. Contacts et circonstances. 17e éd. Paris, 1947.
43554.2.330 Claudel, Paul. Discours et remerciements. 2e éd. Paris, 1947.
43554.2.260 Claudel, Paul. L'endormie. Neuchâtel, 1947.
43554.2.714 Claudel, Paul. Lord, teach us to pray. London, 1947.
43554.2.250 Claudel, Paul. La perle noire. Paris, 1947.
43554.2.223 Claudel, Paul. La rose et le rosaire. Paris, 1947.
43554.2.220 Claudel, Paul. La rose et le rosaire. Paris, 1947.
43554.2.370 Claudel, Paul. Théâtre. Paris, 1947-1948. 2v.
43554.2.230 Claudel, Paul. Toi, qui es-tu? Paris, 1947.
43554.2.270 Claudel, Paul. Visages radieux. 7e éd. Paris, 1947.
37568.99 Clouard, Henri. Histoire de la littérature française. Paris, 1947. 2v.
43556.1.300 Cocteau, Jean. L'aigle à deux têtes, trois actes. Paris, 1947.
43556.1.290 Cocteau, Jean. La difficulté d'être. Paris, 1947.
43556.1.245 Cocteau, Jean. Le foyer des artistes. Paris, 1947.
43556.1.703 Cocteau, Jean. The typewriter. London, 1947.
43556.15.120 Coculesco, Pius S. Sagesse et poésie. Paris, 1947.
43556.49.168 Colette, Sidonie Gabrielle. Chéri. Genève, 1947.
43556.49.340 Colette, Sidonie Gabrielle. L'ingénue libertine. Lausanne, 1947.
43556.49.298 Colette, Sidonie Gabrielle. Le képi. Paris, 1947.
43556.49.390 Colette, Sidonie Gabrielle. Le toutounier. 100e éd. Paris, 1947.
42576.15.305 Colling, Alfred. Gustave Flaubert. Paris, 1947.
42554.26.130 Corbière, Tristan. Les amours jaunes. Paris, 1947.
42554.26.120 Corbière, Tristan. Poems. N.Y., 1947.

1947 - cont.

43556.74.1100 Cordonnié, Paul. Heurtoirs; poèmes. Paris, 1947.
43556.82.705 Cossery, Albert. The house of certain death. London, 1947.
Mon 113.10A Cresson, Andre. Montaigne. Paris, 1947.
42566.31.22 Daudet, Alphonse. Le petit chose. Paris, 1947.
41574.277 Delande, Jean. Victor Hugo à Hauteville House. Paris, 1947.
43619.24.800 Deléglise, M. Le théâtre d'Henri Ghéon. Sion, 1947.
37574.691 Denux, Roger. Ces roses-ci; sonnets. Isey-les-Monlineaux, 1947.
42576.65.13.91 Descaves, Lucien. Deux amis, J.K. Huysmans et l'abbé Mugnier. Paris, 1947.
43566.82.7707A Destouches, Louis Ferdinand. Death on the installment plan. N.Y.? 1947.
39564.20.105 Diderot, Denis. Jacques, le fataliste, et son maîte. Paris, 1947.
39564.15 Diderot, Denis. Le nevue de Rameau. Paris, 1947.
39564.11.20 Diderot, Denis. La religieuse. Paris, 1947.
FL 386.405 Doisy, Marcel. Le théâtre français contemporain. Bruxelles, 1947.
43620.74.835 Domec, Pierre. En pensée avec Giraudoux...les cahiers de Claudies. Genève, 1947.
43565.5.805 Dresse, Paul. Léon Daudet. Paris, 1947.
38526.6.61 Du Bellay, Joachim. Divers jeux rustiques. Genève, 1947.
38526.6.60 Du Bellay, Joachim. Divers jeux rustiques. Lille, 1947.
38526.6.63 Du Bellay, Joachim. Divers jeux rustiques. Paris, 1947.
43620.2.415 Du Bos, Charles. Le dialogue avec André Gide. Paris, 1947.
43822.49.1095.10 Duchesne-Guillemin, J. Étude de Charmes de Paul Valéry. Bruxelles, 1947.
43576.6.400 Duhamel, Georges. Consultation aux pays d'Islam. Paris, 1947.
43576.6.413 Duhamel, Georges. La musique consolatrice. Monaco, 1947.
43576.6.275 Duhamel, Georges. La nuit d'orage. Paris, 1947.
43576.6.55 Duhamel, Georges. La Pierre d'Horeb. 31. éd. Paris, 1947.
43576.6.138 Duhamel, Georges. Les plaisirs et les jeux. Paris, 1947.
43576.6.285 Duhamel, Georges. Semailles au vent. Monaco, 1947.
43576.6.287 Duhamel, Georges. Semailles au vent. Montréal, 1947.
43576.6.405 Duhamel, Georges. Le temps de la recherche. Paris, 1947.
43576.6.219 Duhamel, Georges. Tribulations de l'éspérance. Paris, 1947.
41538.135 Dumas, Alexandre. Une nuit a Florence. Paris, 1947.
41538.30.10 Dumas, Alexandre. Pauline. Paris, 1947.
37555.527 Dupouy, A. La poésie de la mer. Paris, 1947.
41539.30 Duriline, S. Alexander Dumas Perè en Russie. Paris, 1947.
38516.4.35 Duviard, Ferdinaud. Antologie des poètes français. Paris, 1947.
43620.2.370 Eckhoff, Lorentz. André Gide. Oslo, 1947.
43626.22.800 Eigeldinger, Marc. Julien Green et la lentation de l'irréel. Paris, 1947.
43591.89.240 Éluard, Paul. Le livre ouvert (1938-1944). Paris, 1947.
37574.545 Eluard, Paul. Le Meilleur choix de poèmes. Paris, 1947.
43592.53.160 Emmanuel, Pierre. Chansons du dé à coude. Paris, 1947.
43592.53.140 Emmanuel, Pierre. La liberté guide nos pas. Paris, 1947.
43592.53.180 Emmanuel, Pierre. Qui est cet homme. 3. éd. Paris, 1947.
43538.76.800 Estang, Luc. Présence de Bernanos. Paris, 1947.
43599.41.147 Étiemble, René. L'enfant de choeur. 7. éd. Paris, 1947.
43599.41.100 Etiemble, René. Six essais sur trois tyrannies. Paris, 1947.
40556.23.20 Evans, Joan. The unselfish egoist; a life of Joseph Joubert. London, 1947.
FL 398.7.8 Fabre, E. De Tholie à Melpoméne. Paris, 1947.
42555.37.20 Fairlie, Alison. Leconte de Lisle's poems on the Barbarian races. Cambridge, Eng., 1947.
43606.76.120.10 Fargue, Léon P. Poèmes. 11. éd. Paris, 1947.
43606.76.150 Fargue, Léon P. Portrait de famille. Paris, 1947.
38553.15.4.50 Fénelon, F. de S. de la Mothe. Christian perfection. N.Y., 1947.
V43500.93 Féret, Charles Theophile. Poèmes normands. Saint-Vaast-la-Houge, 1947.
43620.74.850 Fink, Werner M. Jean Giraudoux; Glück und Tragik. Inaug. Diss. Basel, 1947.
40583.185 Flake, Otto. Versuch über Stendhal. München, 1947.
42576.20.20 Flaubert, Gustave. L'éducation sentimentale. v. 1-2. Paris, 1947.
42576.35.20 Flaubert, Gustave. Lettres choisies. Paris, 1947.
42576.33.105A Flaubert, Gustave. Three tales. Norfolk, 1947.
37596.247 Floriant et Florete. Florian et Florete. Ann Arbor, 1947.
42577.4.31.10 Fodéré, René. Maupassant, est-il mort fau? Paris, 1947.
43611.53.130 Fombeure, Maurice. J'apprivoise par jeu. Paris, 1947.
43611.53.180 Fombeure, Maurice. Sortilèges vus de près. Paris, 1947.
41522.18.190 Fondane, B. Baudelaire et l'experience du Gouffre. Paris, 1947.
43611.63.100 Fontaine, Anne. Prismes. Fribourg, 1947.
FL 367.10 Forkey, Leo O. The role of money in French comedy during the reign of Louis XIV. Baltimore, 1947.
43738.1.2 Fossier, Andrée. Tables analytiques des oeuvres de Péguy. Paris, 1947.
37569.123A Fowlie, W. Jacob's night. N.Y., 1947.
42576.62.125 France, Anatole. Anatole France à la béchellerie. Paris, 1947.
42576.62.21.31 France, Anatole. L'île des pingouins. Paris, 1947.
43554.2.885 Francia, Ennio. Paul Claudel. Brescia, 1947.
42557.14.45 Furtado, Diogo. Verlaine. Lisboa, 1947.
43616.17.110 Gadenne, Paul. Le vent noir. Paris, 1947.
41563.33.25 Gagnebin, Marianne. Rodolphe Toepffer. Neuchâtel, 1947.
40526.8.35 Galzy, Jeanne. Vie intime d'André Chénier. Paris, 1947.
43616.62.700 Gantillon, Simon. Vessel of wrath. N.Y., 1947.
37575.670 Ganzo, R. Cinq poètes assassinés. Paris, 1947.
43616.63.100 Ganzo, Robert. Langage, poèmes. Paris, 1947.
42576.65.13.104 Garreau, Albert. J.K. Huysmans. Tournai, 1947.
43761.39.815 Gascht, André. L'humanisme cosmique d'Antoine de St. Exupéry. Bruges, 1947.
41542.8.25 Gautier, Théophile. Émaux et camées. Lille, 1947.
42556.28.192 Gengoux, Jacques. La symbolique de Rimbaud. Paris, 1947.
40592.80.5 Gennari, G. Le premier voyage de Madame de Staël en Italie. Paris, 1947.
40592.80 Gennari, G. Le premier voyage de Madame de Staël en Italie et la genèse de Corinne. Thèse. Paris, 1947.
43620.2.38.12 Gide, André. Corydon. 88. éd. Paris, 1947.
43620.2.30.4 Gide, André. Isabelle. N.Y., 1947.
43620.2.30.3 Gide, André. Isabelle. N.Y., 1947.
43620.2.69.21 Gide, André. Journals. London, 1947. 4v.
43620.2.69.20A Gide, André. Journals. N.Y., 1947-48. 4v.
43822.49.1030 Gide, André. Paul Valéry. Paris, 1947.
43620.2.39A Gide, André. Prétextes. Paris, 1947.

Chronological Listing

1947 - cont.

43620.2.59.5	Gide, André. Le procès, pièce tirée du roman de Kafka. 17. éd. Paris, 1947.
43620.2.79.65	Gide, André. Théâtre complete. v.1-8. Neuchâtel, 1947-49. 4v.
43620.66.102	Giono, Jean. Un de Baumugnes. Paris, 1947.
43620.66.260	Giono, Jean. Noe; chroniques. Paris, 1947.
43620.66.240	Giono, Jean. Un roi sans divertissement. Paris, 1947.
43620.66.270	Giono, Jean. Le voyage en calèche. Monaco, 1947.
43620.74.370	Giraudoux, Jean. L'Apollon de Bellac. Paris, 1947.
43620.74.450	Giraudoux, Jean. Pour une politique urbaine. Paris, 1947.
43620.74.740	Giraudoux, Jean. The madwoman of Chaillot. N.Y., 1947.
38524.115	Grands poètes français. Lausanne, 1947. 2v.
43626.22.210	Green, Julien. Si j'étais vous. Paris, 1947.
42554.49.15	Gregh, F. L'âge d'or. Paris, 1947.
37574.695	Gregh, Fernand. Sonnets du temps jadis. Paris, 1947.
38562.23.25	Gregoire, Franz. Fontenelle. Thèse. Nancy, 1947.
43757.50.1120	Greshoff, Jan. Sans famille. 1. druk. Amsterdam, 1947.
43626.66.5120	Grosclaude, Pierre. L'éternelle escorte; poèmes. Paris, 1947.
41593.36.6	Guérin, Maurice de. La centaure, la bacchante. Lausanne, 1947.
41593.33.55	Guérin, Maurice de. Oeuvres complètes. v.1-2. Paris, 1947.
41574.120.15	Guimbaud, Louis. En cabriolet vers l'Académie. Paris, 1947.
43628.1.78	Guitry, Sacha. Quatre ans d'occupations. Paris, 1947.
43628.1.110	Guitry, Sacha. Toutes reflexions faites. Paris, 1947.
43628.85.140	Guth, Paul. Quarante contre un. Paris, 1947.
40597.2.200A	Guyon, Bernard. La pensée politique et sociale de Balzac. Paris, 1947.
43738.1.82.12	Halévy, D. Péguy and les Cahiers de la Quinzaine. 1st ed. N.Y., 1947.
43757.50.1060	Hellwig, Hans. Romain Rolland. Lübeck, 1947.
43632.61.1100	Henry, Jean Marcel. Girondenes, poésies. Bordeaux, 1947.
37569.140	Heppenstall, R. The double image. London, 1947.
41593.36.45	Heuschele, Otto. Maurice de Guérin, Leben und Werk, eines Dichter. Bühl, 1947.
43631.98.800	Hommage à Paul Hazard. Paris, 1947?
41571.1.19	Hugo, Victor. Correspondance. Paris, 1947-52. 4v.
41571.16.20	Hugo, Victor. Les misérables. Garden City, 1947.
41574.15.20	Hugo, Victor. Victor Hugo et ses correspondants. Paris, 1947.
37548.23	Humbert, Jean. La poésie au pays de Gruyère. Bienne, 1947.
43638.53.100	Humbourg, Pierre. Le miroir sans tain. Paris, 1947.
42576.66.2.5	Huysmans, Joris Karl. A rebours. Paris, 1947.
42576.66.4.30	Huysmans, Joris Karl. Les foules de Lourdes. Paris, 1947.
37555.523	Isou, Isidore. Introduction à une nouvelle poésie. Paris, 1947.
43667.14.290	Jacob, Max. Méditations religieuses. Paris, 1947.
43667.1.250	Jammes, Francis. Clara d'Ellebeuse. Lausanne, 1947.
43667.1.280	Jammes, Francis. Heures chrétiennes. Paris, 1947.
43667.1.310	Jammes, Francis. Lettres inédites. Paris, 1947.
37543.265A	Jasinski, René. Histoire de la littérature française. Paris, 1947. 2v.
43670.89.130	Jouhandeau, M. Essai sur moi-même. Paris, 1947.
37555.540	Jouve, P.J. Apologie du poète. Paris, 1947.
43670.94.300	Jouve, Pierre Jean. Aventure de Catherine Crachat. Paris, 1947.
43744.67.1160	Kinds, Edmond. Marcel Proust. Paris, 1947.
42577.4.49.140	Kirkbride, R. de Levington. The private life of Guy de Maupassant. N.Y., 1947.
40516.60.95	Klossowski, P. Sade mon prochain. Paris, 1947.
38526.26.77	Labé, Louise Charly. Love sonnets. N.Y., 1947.
43620.2.230	Lafille, Pierre. Rencontre avec André Gide. Gap, 1947.
39526.33.30	La Fontaine, Jean de. Fables vom Jean de la Fontaine. Friburg, 1947.
42555.1.8	Laforgue, Jules. Oeuvres complètes. Paris, 1947. 2v.
43687.30.100	Lafue, P. Fumées sur la ville. Paris, 1947.
FL 395.15.5	La Grange, C.V. Le registre de La Grange. Paris, 1947. 2v.
37568.80.10	Lalou, René. Histoire de la littérature française contemporaine. v.1-2. Paris, 1947.
37574.715	Lalow, René. Les plus beaux poémes français. 2. éd. Paris, 1947.
41522.18.205	Landa, M.T. de. Charles Baudelaire. México, 1947.
42576.65.13.102	Langé, Gabriel U. En la fête de J.K. Huysmans. Fécamp, 1947.
43822.49.1065	Lannes, Roger. Appel à Paul Valéry. Paris, 1947.
38543.11.10	La Rochefoucauld, François. Réfléxions. Porrentruy, 1947.
43687.87.120	La Tour du Pin, Patrice de. Une somme de poésie. Paris, 1947. 3v.
43688.5.5120	Léautaud, Paul. Propos d'un jour. Paris, 1947.
37563.81	Lebègue, Raymond. La poésie française de 1560 à 1630. v.1-2. Paris, 1947.
42554.16.12.5	Le Braz, A. Le gardien du feu. Paris, 1947.
41596.57.10	Lebreton, Dagmar R. Chahta-Ima. Baton Rouge, 1947.
37576.8	LeClerc de la Herverie, B. Les plus belles lettres d'amour française. Paris, 1947.
38526.27.13A	Lemaire de Belges, Jean. La concorde des deux langages. Paris, 1947.
43688.52.705	Lemarchand, Jacques. Genevieve. London, 1947?
43688.52.700	Lemarchand, Jacques. Parenthesis. 1st American ed. N.Y., 1947.
37556.80.10	Lemonnier, L. Edgar Poe et les conteurs français. Paris, 1947.
43744.25.3800	Lenglin, Jeanne. Le poète de la tendresse, Ernest Prévost, sa vie, son oeuvre. Paris, 1947.
39544.310	Leningrad. Universitet. Vol'ter. Leningrad, 1947.
43688.61.190	Lenormand, Henri René. Les coeurs anxieux. Paris, 1947.
43688.68.110	LeNormand, Michelle. Enthousiasme. Montréal, 1947.
40575.5.124	Leroy, Maxime. Vie de Sainte-Beuve. Paris, 1947.
40597.2.185A	Levin, Harry. Toward Balzac. Norfolk, 1947.
42568.19.24	Linder, Hans R. Lautréamont, sein Werk und sein Weltbild. Affaltern am Albis, 1947.
38514.23.77	Lôo, Pierre. Villon; étude psychologique et médico-legale. Paris, 1947.
42544.34.60.10	Louys, Pierre. Les aventures du Roi Pausole. Lausanne, 1947.
38514.23.70	Macworth, Cecily. François Villon. London, 1947.
43554.2.814	Madaule, Jacques. Le drame de Paul Claudel. 3e éd. Paris, 1947.
42545.3.155	Maeterlinck, Maurice. The great beyond. N.Y., 1947.
43697.33.1100	Magnusson, André. Chansons d'écorces. Bruxelles, 1947.

1947 - cont.

42555.43.70	Mallarmé, Stéphane. Gedichte. Zweisprachige Ausg. Freiburg, 1947.
43697.52.170	Malraux, André. Romans. Paris, 1947.
43697.52.735	Malraux, André. A second Griselda. London, 1947.
43697.52.2700	Malraux, Clara. A second Griselda. London, 1947.
43697.75.115A	Marcel, Gabriel. Théâtre comique. Paris, 1947.
42521.26	Marconcini, Federico. Luigi Veuillot, atleta della penna, 1813-1883. Alba, 1947.
37555.161	Maria Consolato, mother. Christ in the poetry of Lamartine, Vigny, Hugo and Musset. Bryn Maur, 1947.
40535.30.35	Marivaux, Pierre Carlet de Chamblain de. La vie de Marianne. Paris, 1947.
43697.77.4110	Martin, Marietta. Adieu temps. Neuchâtel, 1947.
43744.67.1155	Martin-Deslias, N. Idealisme de Marcel Proust. Montpellier, 1947.
37548.132	Matthews, A.J. La Wallonie, 1886-1892. N.Y., 1947.
43697.86.2100	Maulnier, Thierry. La course des rois. Paris, 1947.
42577.4.2.30	Maupassant, Guy de. Bel-ami. Cleveland, 1947.
43554.2.890	Maurer, Lily Elsa. Gestalt und Bedeutung der Frau im Werke Paul Claudel's "Abhandlung". Zürich, 1947.
43744.67.992	Mauriac, F. Du coté de chez Proust. Paris, 1947.
43697.88.218	Mauriac, François. Le cahier noir. Paris, 1947.
43697.88.165	Mauriac, François. Le jeune homme. Paris, 1947.
43697.88.41A	Mauriac, François. Journal. Paris, 1947.
43697.88.280	Mauriac, François. Réponse à Paul Claudel. Vanves, 1947.
43697.88.270	Mauriac, François. Trois grands hommes devant Dieu. Paris, 1947.
43697.88.715	Mauriac, François. Vipers' tangle. N.Y., 1947.
37569.26.3	Maurois, A. Études littéraires. v.1-2. Paris, 1947.
43697.89.330A	Maurois, André. Les mondes impossibles. Paris, 1947.
43697.89.350	Maurois, André. Premiers contes. Rouen, 1947.
43697.89.280	Maurois, André. Retour en France. N.Y., 1947.
43697.89.325	Maurois, André. Sept visages de l'amour. 2. éd. Paris, 1947.
41555.20.110	Mérimée, Prosper. Carmen. Paris, 1947.
41555.23.35	Mérimée, Prosper. Colomba. Paris, 1947.
41522.18.200	Messiaen, Pierre. Sentiment chrétien et poésie française. Baudelaire, Verlaine, Rimbaud. Paris, 1947.
37567.111.15	Michaud, Guy. La doctrine symboliste. Paris, 1947.
37567.420.2	Michaud, Guy. Message poétique du symbolisme. Paris, 1947. 3v.
37567.420	Michaud, Guy. Message poétique du symbolisme. v.1-2,3. Paris, 1947. 2v.
40547.14.20	Michelet, Jules. Pages choisies. v.1-2. Paris, 1947.
42545.28.40	Moinaux, Georges. Boubouroche. n.p., 1947.
42545.28.60	Moinaux, Georges. Les femmes d'amis. n.p., 1947.
Mol 171.70	Molière, Jean Baptiste Poquelin. Le bourgeois gentilhomme. Boston, 1947.
Mol 245.105	Molière, Jean Baptiste Poquelin. Le misanthrope. Boston, 1947.
Mol 245.106	Molière, Jean Baptiste Poquelin. Le misanthrope. Oxford, 1947.
Mol 19.35.9	Molière, Jean Baptiste Poquelin. Théâtre, 1668-1669. Paris, 1947.
43620.2.250	Mondor, H. Les premiers temps d'une amitié; Andre Gide et Paul Valéry. Monaco, 1947.
42555.44.66	Mondor, Henri. Mallarmé, documents iconographiques. Genève, 1947.
37564.170A	Mongrédien, G. La vie littéraire au XVII siècle. Paris, 1947.
Mon 28.52	Montaigne, Michel de. De la vanité; essai. Paris, 1947.
Mon 32.47	Montaigne, Michel de. The essays of Michel de Montaigne. N.Y., 1947. 3v.
Mon 28.50	Montaigne, Michel de. Trois essais. Paris, 1947.
39593.15	Montesquieu, C.L. de S. Montesquieu, 1689-1755. Genève, 1947.
37555.301.12	Monteverdi, Angelo. L'epopea francese. Roma, 1947.
43701.63.390	Montherlant, Henry de. L'art et la vie. Paris, 1947.
43701.63.103	Montherlant, Henry de. Les bestiaires. Monaco, 1947.
43701.63.230	Montherlant, Henry de. Carnets XXIX à XXXV. Paris, 1947.
43701.63.122.10	Montherlant, Henry de. Le démon du vien. Paris, 1947.
43701.63.330	Montherlant, Henry de. Il y a encore des paradis. Sceaux, 1947.
43701.63.123.7	Montherlant, Henry de. Les lepreuses. Paris, 1947.
43701.63.260	Montherlant, Henry de. Le maître de Santiago. 53e éd. Paris, 1947.
43701.63.243	Montherlant, Henry de. Pages catholiques. Paris, 1947.
43701.63.121.10	Montherlant, Henry de. Pitié pour les femmes. Paris, 1947.
43701.63.220	Montherlant, Henry de. La reine morte. Paris, 1947.
43701.74.30	Morand, Paul. Montociel. Genève, 1947.
37564.175.10	Mornet, Daniel. Histoire de la littérature française classique. 3. éd. Paris, 1947.
FL 398.74.94	Morrison, P. Rachel. London, 1947.
37597.12.35	Müller, Franz Walter. Der Rosenroman und der lateinische Averroismus des 13. Jahrhunderts. Frankfurt, 1947.
43703.80.160	Muselli, Vincent. Les convives. Paris, 1947.
41596.27	Musset, Alfred de. Il ne faut jurer de rien. Paris, 1947.
41543.6.5	Nerval, Gerard de. Poésies. Paris, 1947.
41543.6.10	Nerval, Gerard de. Poésies. 2. éd. Mermod, 1947.
41543.11.15	Nerval, Gerard de. Sylvie. Paris, 1947.
37576.648	New writing. French stories from New writing. London, 1947.
37543.277	Noblot, Jean. Les époques des lettres françaises. Paris, 1947- 2v.
43709.23.25	Noël, Marie. Chants et psaumes d'automne. Paris, 1947.
43737.34.170	Pagnol, Marcel. Discours de récéption à l'Académie française le 27 mars 1947. Paris, 1947.
43737.34.210	Pagnol, Marcel. La fille du puisatier. Lyon, 1947.
43737.34.160	Pagnol, Marcel. Notes sur le rire. Paris, 1947.
42556.28.195	Paillou, Paul. Arthur Rimbaud. Paris, 1947.
37574.420	Palfrey, F.R. Petite anthologie. N.Y., 1947.
37577.6	Pange, Pauline L.M. de B. Lettres de femmes du XIXe siècle. Monaco, 1947.
37597.12.30	Paré, Gérard. Les idées et les lettres au XIIIe siècle. Montréal, 1947.
37575.655	Paulhan, Jean. La patrie se fait tous les jours. Paris, 1947.
43737.89.3100	Pauline, Julia. Poèmes pour vous. Paris, 1947.
41557.10.145	Paz, Magdeleine L. La vie d'un grand homme George Sand. Paris, 1947.
43738.1.81	Péguy, Charles. Péguy et les Cahiers. Paris, 1947.
43697.88.819	Pell, Elsie. François Mauriac in search of the infinite. N.Y., 1947.
41574.250.5	Pendell, William D. Victor Hugo's acted dramas. Thesis. Baltimore, 1947.

Chronological Listing

1947 - cont.

41574.250 Pendell, William D. Victor Hugo's acted dramas and the contemporary press. Baltimore, 1947.
37595.82 Pernond, Régine. La poésie médiévale française. Paris, 1947.
43738.78.3100 Perruchot, Henri. Patrice. Paris? 1947.
43738.78.160 Perse, Saint-John. Anabase. Paris, 1947.
43738.97.1240 Peyrefitte, Roger. Mademoiselle de Murville. Paris, 1947.
43741.11.3100 Picabia, Francis. Choix de poèmes. Paris, 1947.
43741.10.100 Picard, G. Pour lire entre les lignes. Paris, 1947.
43741.13.100 Pichette, Henri. Apoèmes. Paris, 1947.
43741.49.100 Pillement, Georges. Les femmes ont le coeur sur la main. Paris, 1947.
42563.23.97 Polimeni, E. Léon Bloy, the pauper prophet. London, 1947.
43743.60.100 Ponge, Francis. Le carnet du bois de pins. Lausanne, 1947.
41522.18.342 Porché, François. Baudelaire. Paris, 1947.
43744.5.100 Prassinos, Gisèle. Le rêve. Paris, 1947.
42576.63.24.115 Premsela, Martin Jacob. Anatole France en Hollande. La Haye, 1947.
43744.24.23 Prévert, Jacques. Paroles. Paris, 1947.
43745.1.28 Psichari, Ernest. Lettres du Centurion. Paris, 1947.
43745.1.33 Psichari, Ernest. Le voyage du centurion. Paris, 1947.
42515.35.217.5 Psichari, H. Renan et la guerre de 70. Paris, 1947.
43750.24.110 Queneau, Raymond. Exercices de style. 3. éd. Paris, 1947.
38536.29 Rabelais, F. La grande et vraye pronostication nouvelle. Paris, 1947.
38536.18.25 Rabelais, F. Oeuvres complètes. Bruxelles, 1947. 3v.
38536.28.5 Rabelais, F. Pantagruel's prognostication. Oxford, 1947.
38536.24.40 Rabelais, F. Le quart livre...Pantagruel. Genève, 1947.
38536.38 Rabelais, F. Sunren Gargantuan hirmuinen elämä. Jyväshylä, 1947.
38585.23.40 Racine, Jean. Bajazet. Paris, 1947.
38583.11.60 Racine, Jean. Intimité de Racine. Le Raincy, 1947.
43752.57.220 Ramuz, Charles Ferdinand. Adieu à beaucoup de personnages et autres nouveaux. Lausanne, 1947.
43752.57.200 Ramuz, Charles Ferdinand. Nouvelles. Paris, 1947.
43752.57.230 Ramuz, Charles Ferdinand. Passage du poète. Lausanne, 1947.
43752.57.255 Ramuz, Charles Ferdinand. Présence de la mort. Lausanne, 1947.
43752.57.705 Ramuz, Charles Ferdinand. When the mountain fell. N.Y., 1947.
37555.52.15 Raymond, Marcel. De Baudelaire au surréalisme. Paris, 1947.
42515.34.40 Renan, Ernest. Lettres familières, 1851-1871. Paris, 1947.
42515.25.5 Renan, Ernest. Oeuvres complètes. Paris, 1947-49. 10v.
43756.12.3110 Richard, Lucien. Fables humoristiques. Avignon, 1947.
43756.12.3100 Richard, Lucien. Sketches et monologues fantaisistes. Avignon, 1947.
FL 364.75.5 Richard, P.J. Montaigne comédien et le théâtre des Jésuites. Valence-sur-Rhone, 1947.
41543.22.35 Richer, Jean. Gerard de Nerval et les doctrines ésotériques. Paris, 1947.
43697.88.815 Rideau, Emile. Comment lire François Mauriac. Paris, 1947.
42556.28.83 Rimbaud, Jean Arthur. Four poems. Denver, 1947.
42556.28.19 Rimbaud, Jean Arthur. Poésies. Paris, 1947.
43756.90.148 Rivière, Jacques. Nouvelles études. 9. éd. Paris, 1947.
37575.660 Roger, G. L'ame de la corse à travers la littérature française. Alger, 1947.
43757.50.732.5 Rolland, Romain. Journey within. N.Y., 1947.
43757.50.61 Rolland, Romain. Lettres à un combattant de la resistance. Paris, 1947.
43757.50.602 Rolland, Romain. La révolte des machines. Paris, 1947.
43757.50.599 Rolland, Romain. Souvenirs de jeunesse (1866-1900). Lausanne, 1947.
43757.3.78 Romains, Jules. Le dieu de corps. 125e éd. Paris, 1947.
43757.3.165 Romains, Jules. Grace encore pour la terre. Paris, 1947.
43757.3.185 Romains, Jules. Le problème numéro un. Paris, 1947.
38525.20.28 Ronsard, Pierre de. Les amours. 1. ed. Milano, 1947.
38525.18.7 Ronsard, Pierre de. Sonnets pour Hélène. Paris, 1947.
43757.88.3110 Rougemont, Denis de. Les personnes du drame. Paris, 1947.
FL 6022.47 Rousseau, J.J. Les confessions. Paris, 1947.
FL 6032.47 Rousseau, J.J. Du contrat social. Genève, 1947.
FL 6036.13.15 Rousseau, J.J. The social contract. N.Y., 1947.
37568.96 Rousseaux, André. Portraits littéraires choisis. Genève, 1947.
40535.32.30 Roy, Claude. Lire Marivaux. Neuchâtel, 1947.
42557.20.215 Ruchon, Francois. Verlaine; documents iconographiques. Vésenaz, 1947.
40516.60.5 Sade, D.A.F. de. Idée sur les romans. 4. ed. Paris, 1947.
43761.43.105 St. René Taillandier, M.M.L. Ce monde disparu. Paris, 1947-
38546.82 Saint René Taillandier, M.M.L.C. (Mme.). Adieu! Paris, 1947.
43761.7.40 Samain, Albert. Le chariot d'or. Paris, 1947.
42556.29.20 Samain, Albert. La petite princesse Gélide. Paris, 1947.
43554.2.895 Samson, J. Paul Claudel. Genève, 1947.
43576.6.845 Santelli, C. Georges Duhamel. Paris, 1947.
41522.18.175 Sarte, Jean Paul. Baudelaire. 17. éd. Paris, 1947.
43743.60.815 Sartre, Jean-Paul. L'homme et les choses. Paris, 1947.
43761.78.715A Sartre, Jean Paul. The reprieve. 1st American ed. N.Y., 1947.
43761.78.130A Sartre, Jean Paul. Théâtre. 35. éd. Paris, 1947-
37564.187 Saulnier, Verdun L. La littérature française du siècle classique, 1610-1715. 2. éd. Paris, 1947.
37576.647.5 Saurat, Denis. Angels and beasts. London, 1947.
39534.34.10 Scarron, Paul. Poésies diverses. Paris, 1947- 2v.
38526.48.35 Scève, Maurice. Maurice Scève. Paris, 1947.
42555.44.78A Scherer, Jacques. L'expression littéraire dans l'oeuvre de Mallarmé. Paris, 1947.
43765.32.100 Seghers, Pierre. Le futur anterieur. Paris, 1947.
37574.689 Seghers, Pierre. Poésie, 39-45. London, 1947.
41568.17.10 Sénancour, Étienne Pivert de. Obermann; texte original de 1804. Grenoble, 1947. 3v.
43769.54.713 Simenon, Georges. Affairs of destiny. London, 1947.
43769.54.390 Simenon, Georges. Au bout du rouleau. Paris, 1947.
43769.54.733 Simenon, Georges. Black rain. N.Y., 1947.
43769.54.740 Simenon, Georges. The first-born. N.Y., 1947.
43576.6.835 Simon, Pierre-Henri. Georges Duhamel. Paris, 1947.
37574.700 Société des poètes français. Anthologie de la Société des poètes français. Paris, 1947.
43775.90.7125 Soupault, Philippe. Le grand homme, roman. Paris, 1947.
38526.48.150 Sponde, Jean de. Stances et sonnets de la mort. Paris, 1947.
42556.28.178.3 Starkie, Enid. Arthur Rimbaud. N.Y., 1947.
43780.69.250 Supervielle, Jules. A la nuit. Neuchâtel, 1947.
43780.69.240 Supervielle, Jules. Choix de poèmes. Paris, 1947.
37543.283 Talagrand, J. Languages. Lausanne, 1947.
38585.16.48 Talagrand, J. Racine. 32e éd. Paris, 1947.
FL 386.406 Talmon-Gros, Walter. Das moderne französische Theater. München, 1947.
43554.2.910 Thomas, J. Paul Claudel der Mensch und Dichter. Trier, 1947.
37574.175 Thorley, W.C. The French muse. 3. ed. London, 1947.
41557.10.72 Toesca, Maurice. The other George Sand. London, 1947.
43793.42.130 Triolet, Elsa. Les amants d'Avignon. Paris, 1947.
43793.42.190 Triolet, Elsa. Dessins animés. Paris, 1947.
43793.42.150 Triolet, Elsa. Les fantômes armés; roman. Paris, 1947.
43793.42.700 Triolet, Elsa. A fine of 200 francs. N.Y., 1947.
43793.64.100 Trofimoff, André. Au jardin des muses françaises. Paris, 1947.
43793.67.180 Troyat, Henri. Les vivants, pièce en trois actes. Paris, 1947.
FL 377.84 Turnell, Martin. The classical moment. London, 1947.
43799.5.130 Tzara, Tristan. Morceaux choisis. Paris, 1947.
43799.5.150 Tzara, Tristan. Le surréalisme et l'après-guerre. 3e éd. Paris, 1947.
43822.49.795 Valéry, Paul. Anfion. Buenos Aires, 1947.
43822.49.300 Valéry, Paul. Mauvaises pensées et autres. 30e éd. Paris, 1947.
43822.49.710 Valéry, Paul. Monsieur Teste. 1st American ed. N.Y., 1947.
43822.49.310 Valéry, Paul. Souvenirs poétiques. 2e éd. Paris, 1947.
43822.49.106.10 Valéry, Paul. Variété IV. Paris, 1947.
43823.75.210 Vercel, Roger. Au large de l'Eden. Paris, 1947.
43823.75.710 Vercel, Roger. Madman's memory. N.Y., 1947.
42557.19.122 Verlaine, Paul. Romances sans paroles. Paris, 1947.
42545.45.80 Vesvre, Hilaire de. Gabriel Nigond. Verneuil-sur-Igneraie, 1947.
42576.57.40 Viaud, Julien. Pierre Loti; quelques fragments du journal intime. Paris, 1947.
41564.27 Vigny, Alfred de. Les destinées. Paris, 1947.
38514.18.30 Villon, François. The testaments of François Villon. London, 1947.
39545.35.47A Voltaire, François Marie Arouet de. Candide, ou L'optimisme. N.Y., 1947.
39545.4.12 Wade, Ira Owen. Studies on Voltaire. Princeton, 1947.
37543.271 Waite, Vincent. An approach to French literature. London, 1947.
40526.8.30 Walter, Gérard. André Chénier. 10. éd. Paris, 1947.
37558.77 Yates, F.A. The French academies of the sixteenth century. London, 1947.
42556.28.290 Zech, Paul. Jean Arthur Rimbaud. Berlin, 1947.

1948

37564.195 Adam, Antoine. Histoire de la littérature française au XVIII siècle. Paris, 1948-1951. 5v.
37576.648.5 Alden, Douglas W. Introduction to French masterpieces. N.Y., 1948.
41596.4.95 Allem, M. Alfred de Musset. Grenoble, 1948.
42553.32.90 Amiel, Henri F. Journal intime, années 1839 à 1848. Genève, 1948. 2v.
43757.3.255 L'amitié, par Charles Vildrac, André Cuisenier, Pierre Labracherie. Paris, 1948.
43526.65.200 Apollinaire, Guillaume. Ombre de mon amour. 3. ed. Genève, 1948.
43526.65.108 Apollinaire, Guillaume. Les onze mille verges. En Hallander, 1948.
43526.65.190 Apollinaire, Guillaume. Poésies libres. Amsterdam, 1948.
43554.7.85 Applebaum, Samuel. Clemenceau. N.Y., 1948.
43527.3.157 Aragon, Louis. Le nouveau crève-coeur, poèmes. 13. éd. Paris, 1948.
43528.48.240 Arland, Marcel. Faire le point. Paris, 1948.
43528.60.120 Arnauld, C. Rien qu'une étoile. Paris, 1948.
38512.140 Arnould, Emile Jules F. Étude sur Le livre des saintes medecines du duc Henri de Lancastre. Paris, 1948.
40597.2.163.5 Arrault, Albert. Madame de Berny; le premier amour de Balzac. Tours, 1948.
43528.86.110A Artaud, Antonin. Pour en finir avec le jugement de dieu. Paris, 1948.
38527.22 Aubigné, Théodore Agrippa d'. Le printemps. Lille, 1948.
43531.18.100 Audiat, Pierre. Les ravages; roman. Paris, 1948.
43531.18.1140 Audiberti, Jacques. Théâtre. v.3, 3. éd. Paris, 1948. 5v.
42566.16.105 Auriant (pseud.). Quatre héros d'Alphonse Daudet. Paris, 1948.
43532.23.140 Aveline, Claude. Pegomancie. Paris, 1948.
43535.54.700 Aymé, Marcel. The transient hour. London, 1948.
43535.54.230 Aymé, Marcel. Travelingue. 90e éd. Paris, 1948.
43535.54.180 Aymé, Marcel. Uranus, roman. Paris, 1948.
43535.54.181 Aymé, Marcel. Uranus. Paris, 1948.
43535.54.270 Aymé, Marcel. Le vaurien. 20e éd. Paris, 1948.
43537.42.41 Bainville, Jacques. Journal. Paris, 1948-49. 3v.
40597.31.2 Balzac, Honoré de. La femme de trente ans. Paris, 1948.
37563.79 Baridon, S.F. La Pléiade française. Milano, 1948.
42563.16.25 Barrès, Maurice. Du sang, de la volupté et de la mort. Paris, 1948.
41522.5.15 Baudelaire, Charles. Oeuvres. Paris, 1948.
38563.21 Bayle, Pierre. Pierre Bayle. Paris, 1948.
43537.99.100 Bazin, Hervé. Vipère au poing, roman. Paris, 1948.
43538.1.450 Beauvoir, Simone de. L'Amérique au jour le jour. Paris, 1948.
43538.14.2100 Beck, Béatrix. Barmy. Paris, 1948.
40524.32.40 Bégue, A. État présent des études sur Restif de la Bretonne. Paris, 1948.
42563.23.94 Béguin, Albert. Léon Bloy, mystique de la douleur. Paris, 1948.
41564.55.80 Bélanger, D. Les séjours d'Alfred de Vigny en Charante. Angoulême, 1948.
37569.180 Bendz, E.P. Visages d'écrivains. Paris, 1948.
43538.50.21 Bengoechea, Hernando de. Hernando de Bengoechea, ou L'âme d'un poète. Paris, 1948.
37565.118A Bénichou, P. Morales du grand siècle. 3. éd. Paris, 1948.
37558.70.10 Benjamin, René. La galère des Goncourt. Paris, 1948.
43538.7.52 Benjamin, René. Le vin, lumière du coeur. Paris, 1948.
43538.75.100 Bergmans, Simone. Le collier d'épines. Gand, 1948.

Chronological Listing

1948 - cont.

43538.10.705 Bernard, Jean J. The sulky five, five plays. London, 1948.
43620.74.860 Beucler, A. Les instants de Giraudoux. Genève, 1948.
40582.8.4.10 Beyle, Henri. De l'amour. Paris, 1948.
40582.13.70 Beyle, Henri. Lamiel. Paris, 1948.
40582.38.5 Beyle, Henri. Souvenirs d'égotisme. Paris, 1948.
43687.87.800 Biéville-Nayant. Patrice de La Tour du Pin. Paris, 1948.
43543.8.100 Blanchot, Maurice. L'arrêt de mort. 6. éd. Paris, 1948.
43543.8.140 Blanchot, Maurice. Le Très-Haut. 5. éd. Paris, 1948.
41522.18.195 Blin, Georges. Le sadisme de Baudelaire. Paris, 1948.
43543.13.180 Bloch, J.R. Toulon et autres pièces. Paris, 1948.
42563.23.16.6 Bloy, Léon. La chevalière de la mort. Paris, 1948.
42563.23.16.5 Bloy, Léon. Le désespéré. v. 1-2. Paris, 1948.
42563.23.16.7 Bloy, Léon. Le mendiant ingrat. v.1-12. Paris, 1948-49. 6v.
38514.58.25 Boldingh-Goemans, W.L. Christine de Pisan. Rotterdam, 1948.
43544.60.1100 Bonmariage, Sylvein. L'amour songé. Paris, 1948.
43544.60.120 Bonnamy, George. Resistantialisme. Paris, 1948.
42563.36.330 Bordeaux, Henry. La lumière au bout du chemin. Paris, 1948.
42563.36.46 Bordeaux, Henry. Les yeux qui s'ouvrent. Paris, 1948?
39594.19.50 Bordeaux. Bibliothèque Municipale. Montesquieu et l'esprit des lois. Bordeaux, 1948.
43544.81.2110 Bosco, Henri. Malicroix; roman. 25. éd. Paris, 1948.
43544.81.2250 Bosco, Henri. Sylvius. Paris, 1948.
37562.257 Bossuat, R. La poésie lyrique en France au XVe siècle. v.1-3. Paris, 1948.
38557.60.10 Bossuet, J.B. Traité du libre-arbitre. Tucumán, 1948.
43544.87.2700 Boulestin, X.M. Ease and endurance. London, 1948.
37564.28.15A Bray, René. La préciosité et les précieux. Paris, 1948.
43545.24.220 Breton, André. La lampe dans l'horloge. Paris, 1948.
43545.24.120 Breton, André. Martinique, charmeuse de serpents. Paris, 1948.
43545.24.170 Breton, André. Poèmes. 8. éd. Paris, 1948.
37564.190 Busson, H. La religion des classiques. 1. éd. Paris, 1948.
38526.42.30 Butler, R. Nationales und universales Denken in Werke Estienne Pasquiers. Basel, 1948.
43526.65.845 Cadeau, R.G. Guillaume Apollinaire. Nantes, 1948.
37555.170 Camagna, E.M. Le epopee francesi. Messina, 1948.
43550.58.200 Camus, Albert. L'état de siege. 23. éd. Paris, 1948.
43550.58.130A Camus, Albert. Le malentendu. 32. éd. Paris, 1948.
43550.58.724 Camus, Albert. The plague. N.Y., 1948.
43550.58.720 Camus, Albert. The plague. N.Y., 1948.
42557.20.245 Carco, François. Verlaine, poète maudit. Paris, 1948.
37567.426 Cassou, Jean. Le quarante-huitard. Paris, 1948.
43551.59.180 Cendrars, Blaise. Bourlinguer. Paris, 1948.
43551.80.700 Cesbron, Gilbert. No plaster saint. London, 1948.
43552.3.9220 Chamson, André. Histoires de Tabusse. Paris, 1948.
43552.3.9105 Chamson, André. L'homme qui marchait devant moi, roman. Paris, 1948.
43552.3.9210 Chamson, André. Si la parole a quelque pouvoir. Genève, 1948.
43552.4.2130 Char, René. Fete des arbres et du Chasseur. Paris, 1948.
43552.4.2240 Char, René. Fureur et mystère. 3. éd. Paris, 1948.
43552.4.5120 Charbonneau, Robert. Les désirs et les jours. Montreal, 1948.
43552.5.170 Chardonne, Jacques. Chimériques. Monaco, 1948.
43552.5.170.5 Chardonne, Jacques. Chimériques. Monaco, 1948.
37567.424 Charlier, Gustave. Le mouvement romantique en Belgique, 1815-1850. Bruxelles, 1948- 2v.
40583.200 Chartier, E. Stendhal. Paris, 1948.
40585.415 Chateaubriand, F.A.R. François René de Chateaubriand: Choix de textes. Monaco, 1948.
40586.28.10 Chateaubriand, F.A.R. Mémoires de ma vie. Paris, 1948.
40586.28.82 Chateaubriand, F.A.R. Mémoires d'outre-tombe. Paris, 1948.
41563.18.35 Chaunu, P. Eugène Sue et la seconde République. 1. ed. Paris, 1948.
43552.12.100 Chavance, L. Le corbeau. Paris, 1948.
43552.7.2112 Chazal, Malcolm de. Sens-plastique. 2e éd. Paris, 1948.
37543.287 Chazel, Pierre. Figures de proue; de Corneille à Valéry. Neuchâtel, 1948.
43697.75.810 Chenn, Joseph. Le théâtre de Gabriel Marcel. Paris, 1948.
43552.25.2700 Chevallier, Gabriel. The Euffe inheritance. London, 1948.
43554.2.32.10 Claudel, Paul. Cinq grandes odes. 43e éd. Paris, 1948.
43554.2.130 Claudel, Paul. Paul Claudel interroge le Cantique des Cantiques. Paris, 1948.
43554.2.720 Claudel, Paul. Poetic art. N.Y., 1948.
43554.2.290 Claudel, Paul. Sous le signe du dragon. Paris, 1948.
43744.67.955 Clermont-Tonnerre, E. de G. Marcel Proust. Paris, 1948.
43556.1.80 Cocteau, Jean. Antigone. Les mariés de la Tour Eiffel. Paris, 1948.
43556.1.715 Cocteau, Jean. The eagle has two heads. London, 1948.
43556.1.65.5 Cocteau, Jean. Poèmes. Paris, 1948.
43556.1.340 Cocteau, Jean. Le rappel à l'ordre. Paris, 1948.
43556.1.370 Cocteau, Jean. Le sang d'un poète. Paris, 1948.
43556.1.270 Cocteau, Jean. Théâtre. Paris, 1948- 2v.
FL 370.84.5 Cohen, Gustave. Le théâtre en France au Moyen-Age. Paris, 1948.
43556.49.490 Colette, Sidonie Gabrielle. Mitsou, ou Comment l'esprit vient aux filles. Paris, 1948.
43556.49.11 Colette, Sidonie Gabrielle. Oeuvres complètes. Paris, 1948-1950. 15v.
43757.50.1045 Connes, G. The tragedy of Romain Rolland. Buffalo, 1948.
43557.61.140 Constantin-Weyer, Maurice. Pronunciamiento. Paris, 1948.
38575.31.9.35 Corneille, Pierre. Cinna. Paris, 1948.
38575.31.9.30 Corneille, Pierre. Cinna. Paris, 1948.
39544.215 Crésson, André. Voltaire. Paris, 1948.
43761.39.810 Crisnoy, Maria de. Antoine de St. Exupéry. Paris, 1948.
43620.2.258 Davet, Yvonne. Autour des Nourritures terrestres. Paris, 1948.
FL 397.82.6 Deck, Panteléon. Histoire du théâtre français à Strasbourg. Strasbourg, 1948.
FL 397.82.5 Deck, Panteléon. Histoire du théâtre français à Strasbourg. Thèse. Strasbourg, 1948.
43611.5.92 Dedeyan, Christian. Alain-Fournier et la réalité secrète. Paris, 1948.
41566.36.3 Delécluze, E.J. Journal de Delécluze. 2. ed. Paris, 1948.
FL 6139.48.2 Derathé, Robert. Le rationalisme de Jean-Jacques Rousseau. Thèse. Paris, 1948.
FL 6139.48 Derathé, Robert. Le rationalisme de Jean-Jacques Rousseau. 1. éd. Paris, 1948.
43757.50.1035 Descotes, M. Romain Rolland. Paris, 1948.

1948 - cont.

37543.144.25 Des Granges, C.M. Histoire de la littérature française des origines à nos jours. 43. éd. Paris, 1948.
43566.93.100 Devaulx, N. Le pressoir mystique. Neuchâtel, 1948.
43752.57.830 Dichamp, Marius. Ramuz. Paris, 1948.
37543.296 Dieckmann, Heinz. Von Villon bis Eluard. Saarbrücken, 1948.
40583.190 Dollot, René. Stendhal, journaliste. Paris, 1948.
37569.366 Dreher, S. Bibliographie de la littérature française, 1930-39. Lille, 1948-49.
43576.6.750 Duhamel, Georges. Light on my days; an autobiography. London, 1948.
37542.38 Duhamel, Roger. Littérature. Montréal, 1948-
41525.29 Dumas, Alexandre. Impressions de voyage en Suisse. N.Y., 1948.
42576.15.315 Dumesnil, René. Flaubert. Vésenaz, 1948.
37596.249 Edward, the Confessor, King of England, Saint. Legend. La vie d'Edouard le confesseur. Uppsala, 1948.
43591.89.280 Éluard, Paul. Corps mémorable. Paris, 1948.
43591.89.235 Éluard, Paul. Poèmes politiques. 15. éd. Paris, 1948.
43591.89.21 Éluard, Paul. Premiers poèmes. Lausanne, 1948.
43591.89.810 Emmanuel, P. Le Je universel chez Paul Éluard. Paris, 1948.
43592.53.170 Emmanuel, Pierre. Poésie raison ardente. 3. éd. Paris, 1948.
43592.53.240 Emmanuel, Pierre. Le poète fou suivi de élégies. Boudry, 1948.
42555.62.50 Empeirikos, A. Les étapes de Jean Moréas. Lausanne, 1948.
43822.49.1100 Eschmann, E.W. Paul Valéry. Herrliberg, 1948.
43697.75.800A Existentialisme chrétien: Gabriel Marcel. Paris, 1948.
43576.6.840 Falls, W.F. Le message humain de Georges Duhamel. Paris? 1948.
43606.15.100 Fardoulis-Lagrange, Michel. Le texte inconnu. Paris, 1948.
43744.67.1137 Fardwell, F.V. Landscape in the works of Marcel Proust. Washington, 1948.
43606.74.100 Farge, Yves. L'escalier. Paris, 1948.
FL 6119.48 Faure, Gabriel. Essais sur Jean-Jacques Rousseau. Grenoble, 1948.
42575.21.2 Feydeau, Ernest. Fanny. 2. éd. Paris, 1948.
42543.41.20 Feydeau, Georges. Théâtre complet. v.1,2-3,4-5,6-7,8,9. Paris, 1948. 6v.
43609.88.100 Fitz-George, France. Chansons pour rien. Lausanne, 1948.
42576.35.30 Flaubert, Gustave. Lettres de Grèce. Paris, 1948.
42576.35.25 Flaubert, Gustave. Lettres inédites à Maxime du Camp. Sceaux, 1948.
42576.34.15 Flaubert, Gustave. Voyages. Paris, 1948. 2v.
43611.53.150 Fombeure, Maurice. Les godillots sont lourds. 17. éd. Paris, 1948.
43611.63.110 Fontaine, Anne. Nausicaa, avec une rose de Henri Mondor. Fribourg, 1948.
37586.34 Fox, J.H. Robert de Blois. Paris? 1948?
37596.34.10 Fox, John Howard. Robert de Blois, et narrative;...Son oeuvre didactique. Paris? 1948?
39544.210 Francis, L. La vie privée de Voltaire. Paris, 1948.
41574.260 Froment-Guieysse, G. Victor Hugo. v.1-2. Paris, 1948.
37569.175A Garaudy, Roger. Literature of the graveyard. N.Y., 1948.
43617.78.140 Genêt, Jean. Poèmes. Lyon, 1948.
43738.83.800 Genevoix, Maurice. Discours de réception de Maurice Genevoix à l'Académie française. Paris, 1948.
43620.2.32.15 Gide, André. The immoralist. N.Y., 1948.
43620.2.69.15 Gide, André. Journal. Paris, 1948.
43620.2.51.5 Gide, André. Journal des faux-monnayeurs. 44. éd. Paris, 1948.
43620.2.79.45 Gide, André. Récits, roman, soties. Paris, 1948. 2v.
43620.2.79.75 Gide, André. Rencontres. Neuchâtel, 1948.
43620.2.79.35 Gide, André. Théâtre. Paris, 1948.
43620.2.50.10 Gide, André. Theseus. London, 1948.
39544.345 Gielly, L.J. Voltaire. Genève, 1948.
43611.5.95 Gillet, Henri. Alain-Fournier. Paris, 1948.
43620.66.300 Giono, Jean. Batailles dans la montagne; roman. 73. éd. Paris, 1948.
Mol 157.5 Girard, Joseph. A propos de "L'amour médecin". Paris, 1948.
43620.74.1130 Giraudoux, Jean Pierre. Pas assez de silence. Paris, 1948.
43756.90.820 Gisi, Martha. Die Entwicklung des Moralbegriffs bei Jacques Rivière. Freiburg, 1948.
42556.28.265 Goffin, Robert. Rimbaud et Verlaine vivants. Paris, 1948?
42556.28.209 Graaf, Daniel. Arthur Rimbaud. Assen, 1948.
43545.24.820 Gracq, J. André Breton. Paris, 1948.
43626.70.110 Gracq, Julien. Le roi pêcheur. Paris, 1948.
40575.5.130 Grosclaude, P. Sainte-Beuve et Marceline Desbordes-Valmore. Paris, 1948.
FL 6029.8 Guéhenno, Jean. Jean-Jacques. Paris, 1948-52. 3v.
43752.57.865 Guenther, W. C.F. Ramuz. Bern, 1948.
37575.208 Guiette, Robert. Poètes français de Belgique de Verhaeren au surréalisme. Manteau, 1948.
41578.121.10 Guillemin, H. Lamartine en 1848. 1. éd. Paris, 1948.
39527.4.100 Guillet, L. Divers visages de La Fontaine. Paris, 1948.
42556.28.171 Hackett, Cecil A. Rimbaud l'enfant. Paris, 1948.
41578.128 Harcourt, B. Lamartine, Barbey d'Aurevilly et Paul de Saint Victor en 1848. Paris, 1948.
37566.107 Henriot, Émile. Courrier littéraire, XIXe siècle. v.1-2. Paris, 1948.
37558.150 Henriot, Émile. Les livres du second rayon. Paris, 1948.
37597.44 Henry, Albert. L'oeuvre lyrique d'Henri III, duc de Brabant. Brugge, 1948.
43632.75.700 Herbart, Pierre. Halcyon. London, 1948.
43636.64.110 Hoog, Armand. L'accident. Paris, 1948.
43556.1.860 Hugo, V.M. Ruy Blas. Paris, 1948.
42515.37.20 Inauguration du Musée Renan. Paris, 1948.
43565.90.800 Inial, M.F. Henri Davignon. Washington, 1948.
43545.24.850 Isou, Isidore. Réflexiions sur André Breton. Paris, 1948.
37568.104 Jamet, Claude. Images mêlées de la littérature et du théâtre. Paris, 1948.
43667.1.320 Jammes, Francis. Correspondance, 1893-1938 de Francis Jammes et André Gide. 8. éd. Paris, 1948.
37574.835 Janet, Gaston. Poètes de Paris et de l'Ile de France. Paris, 1948.
43667.78.13 Jarry, Alfred. Oeuvres complètes. Monte-Carlo, 1948. 8v.
40532.7.20 Jasinski, René. Le mariage de Figaro. v.1-3. Paris, 1948.
37591.37.10A Jean, Renast. Le lai de l'ombre. Edinburgh, 1948.
43670.89.400 Jouhandeau, M. Don Juan. Paris, 1948.

Chronological Listing

1948 - cont.

43670.89.340 Jouhandeau, M. La faute plutôt que le scandale. Paris, 1948.
43670.89.230 Jouhandeau, M. Mémorial. Paris, 1948. 6v.
43670.89.150 Jouhandeau, M. Ménagerie domestique. 6. éd. Paris, 1948.
38537.25.170 Jourda, P. La Gargantua de Rabelais. Paris, 1948.
43670.94.125 Jouve, Pierre Jean. Génie. Paris, 1948.
43670.94.310 Jouve, Pierre Jean. Histoires sanglantes. Paris, 1948.
37573.704 Klemperer, V. Die moderne französische Prosa. 3. Aufl. Leipzig, 1948.
42556.28.201 Küchler, Walter. Arthur Rimbaud. Heidelberg, 1948.
42556.28.201.5 Küchler, Walter. Trunkene und gläubige Dichtung. Iserlohn, 1948.
V43500.149 La Croix, Robert de. Migrations; poèmes. Nantes, 1948.
39527.29.60 La Fontaine, Jean de. Fables. Paris, 1948.
38514.60.90 La Marche, Olivier de. Den camp vander doot. Antwerpen, 1948.
42563.23.106 Langlois, G. Un mendiant de la souffrance, Léon Bloy. Ottawa, 1948.
43687.74.180 Larbaud, Valéry. Ce vice impuni. 9e éd. Paris, 1948.
43687.74.190 Larbaud, Valéry. Enfantines. 27e éd. Paris, 1948.
41542.4.90 Larguier, Léo. Théophile Gautier. Paris, 1948.
41557.10.155 Larnac, Jean. George Sand révolutionnaire. Paris, 1948.
37568.106 Larnac, Jean. La littérature française d'aujourd'hui. Paris, 1948.
43687.87.110 La Tour du Pin, Patrice de. La contemplation errante. Paris, 1948.
43687.87.700 La Tour du Pin, Patrice de. The dedicated life in poetry. London, 1948.
43687.90.100 Laude, Jean. Entre deux morts. Paris, 1948.
V43500.173 Le Cunff, Louis. La ville exsangue. Paramé, 1948.
37574.550 LeDantec, Y. La guirlande des muses françaises. Paris, 1948.
43688.60.160 Leiris, Michel. La règle du jeu. Paris, 1948- 3v.
38526.27.15 Lemaire de Belges, Jean. Les épîtres de l'amant vert. Lille, 1948.
V43500.183 Le Rossignol, Edouard. Contes normandes et gaulois. Saint-Vaast-la-Hougue, 1948.
43688.88.120 Létraz, Jean de. La fessei. Paris, 1948.
42513.26.80 Linden, Jacobus Petrus van der. Alphonse Esquiros. Heerlem, 1948.
38537.78 Lindfors-Nordin, Elsa G. Berne, berner, expressions rabelaisiennes. Stockholm, 1948.
38585.16.163 Lion, Fernand. Les rêves de Racine. 6. éd. Paris, 1948.
37543.300F Littérature française. Paris, 1948-49. 2v.
37567.434 Lugli, V. Jules Renard ed altri amici. Messina, 1948.
41578.150 Luppe Albert, M.P. Les travaux et les jours d'Alphonse de Lamartine. Paris, 1948.
41555.42.5 Lyon, Sylvia. The life and times of Prosper Mérimée. N.Y., 1948.
43697.11.100 MacDann, Pierre. Fragments. Auxerre, 1948.
43697.14.200 MacOrlan, Pierre. Dinah Miami. Paris, 1948.
42545.3.215 Maeterlinck, Maurice. Bulles bleues, souvenirs heureux. Monaco, 1948.
42555.43.28 Mallarmé, Stéphane. Dix poèmes. Lille, 1948.
42555.44.8 Mallarmé, Stéphane. Les lettres; poésie, philosophie. Paris, 1948.
43697.52.180 Malraux, André. Les noyers de l'Altenburg. Paris, 1948.
43620.2.172 Mann, Klaus. André Gide. Zürich, 1948.
43620.2.171 Mann, Klaus. André Gide and the crisis of modern thought. London, 1948.
43744.67.1145A March, Harold. The two worlds of Marcel Proust. Philadelphia, 1948.
38543.21.5 Marchand, J. Bibliographie générale raisonée de La Rochefoucauld. Paris, 1948.
42587.37.4.10 Martin, René. La vie d'un grand journaliste Auguste Nefftzer. Besançon, 1948-1953. 2v.
40583.180 Martineau, H. Petit dictionnaire stendhalien. Paris, 1948.
43620.2.245 Massis, Henri. D'André Gide à Marcel Proust. 8. éd. Lyon, 1948.
43697.86.2120 Maulnier, Thierry. Esquisses littéraires. Paris? 1948.
43697.88.292 Mauriac, François. Passage du Malin. Paris, 1948.
43697.88.735 Mauriac, François. The unknown sea. N.Y., 1948.
43697.89.727A Maurois, André. From my journal. 1st ed. N.Y., 1948.
43697.89.45 Maurois, André. Journal d'un tour en Amerique latine. Paris, 1948.
43697.89.47 Maurois, André. Memoires. Paris, 1948-
43697.89.510 Maurois, André. Patapoufs and Filifers. Boston, 1948.
42514.28.60 Maurras, Charles. Réponse à André Gide. Paris, 1948.
38575.23.90 May, G.C. Tragédie cornélienne, tragédie racionienne. Urbana, 1948.
43698.25.140 Meersch, M. van der. Le coeur pur. Paris, 1948.
43698.25.715 Meersch. M. van der. Bodies and souls. N.Y., 1948.
37567.422.7 Meeüs, Adrien des. Les romantisme. 7e éd. Paris, 1948.
40583.195 Mérimée, Prosper. H.B. Texte de l'édition originale de 1850. Paris, 1948.
42576.15.195 Merker, Emil. Flaubert. Urack, 1948.
V43500.197 Messiaen, Alain. Bestiaire mystique. Preuilly-sur-Claise, 1948.
43698.200.125 Michaux, Henri. Ailleurs. Paris, 1948.
43698.200.21 Michaux, Henri. Henri Michaux. Paris, 1948.
43698.200.110 Michaux, Henri. Nous deux encore, 1948. Paris, 1948.
42555.44.84 Miomandre, F. de. Mallarmé. Mulhouse, 1948.
42545.28.7.73 Mirbeau, Octave. Torture garden. N.Y., 1948.
42545.28.90 Moinaux, Georges. Ah! Jeunesse et autres contes. Paris, 1948.
42545.28.50 Moinaux, Georges. Un client sérieux. n.p., 1948.
42545.28.25.10 Moinaux, Georges. Les gaîtés de l'escadron. Paris, 1948.
42545.28.80 Moinaux, Georges. Les linottes. n.p., 1948.
42545.28.9.35 Moinaux, Georges. Messieurs les ronds-de-cuir. n.p., 1948.
42545.28.70 Moinaux, Georges. Le train de 8h. 47. n.p., 1948.
Mol 196.5A Molière, Jean Baptiste Poquelin. The school for wives. Dublin, 1948.
43822.49.1265 Mondor, Henri. L'heureuse rencontre de Valéry et Mallarmé. Paris, 1948.
42555.44.68 Mondor, Henri. Histoire d'un faune. 9. éd. Paris, 1948.
43822.49.1050A Mondor, Henri. Trois discours pour Paul Valéry. 7e éd. Paris, 1948.
43822.49.1055 Monod, Jules P. Regard sur Paul Valéry. Lausanne, 1948.
Mon 35.6 Montaigne, Michel de. Die Essais und das Raisetagebuch. Stuttgart, 1948.
Mon 32.48 Montaigne, Michel de. Essays. Hillesborough, Calif., 1948.
Mon 45.26 Montaigne, Michel de. Journal de voyage en Italie par la Suisse et l'Allemagne. Paris, 1948.

1948 - cont.

Mon 178.3A Montaigne, Michel de. Le livre de raison de Montaigne. Paris, 1948.
Mon 32.34.3 Montaigne, Michel de. Selected essays. 2. ed. Manchester, 1948.
Htn 39594.14.10* Montesquieu, C.L. de S. Histoire veritable. Lille, 1948.
43526.65.900 Montfort, Eugene. Apollinaire travesti. Paris, 1948.
43701.63.502 Montherlant, Henry de. Carnets, XLII et XLIII. Paris, 1948.
43620.74.855 Morand, Paul. Giraudoux. Genève, 1948.
43701.75.105 Moreno, M. Souvenirs de ma vie. Paris, 1948.
39594.3.55 Morgan, Charles. The liberty of thought and the separation of powers. Oxford, 1948.
43744.67.95 Mouton, Jean. Le style de Marcel Proust. Paris, 1948.
38575.23.95 Nadel, O. Le sentiment de l'amour dans l'oeuvre de Corneille. Thèse. Paris, 1948.
37530.165 National Book League. A thousand years of French books. London, 1948.
37576.650 New writing. Modern French stories. N.Y., 1948?
43714.8.100 Obey, André. Théâtre. v.1- 2e éd. Paris, 1948-
43723.18.703A Oldenbourg, Zoé. The world is not enough. N.Y., 1948.
38585.7.10 Orgel, Vera. A new view of the plays of Racine. London, 1948.
43745.1.112 Pacheco, M.J. Ernest Psichari, um neto de Renan. Lisboa, 1948.
43737.83.130 Passeur, Steve. 107'. Paris, 1948.
43737.89.700 Pauwels, Louis. Not into clean hands. London, 1948.
43738.1.3 Péguy, Charles. Lettre à Franklin Bouillon. Paris, 1948.
43738.1.63 Péguy, Charles. Oeuvres poétiques complétes. Paris, 1948.
43738.1.61 Péguy, Charles. Situations. Paris, 1948.
37562.274 Pei, Mario A. French precursors of the Chauson de Roland. N.Y., 1948.
43738.78.150 Perse, Saint-John. Éloges. Paris, 1948.
43745.1.87 Peyrade, J. Psichari. Paris, 1948.
43738.97.1100 Peyrefitte, Roger. L'oracle. Paris, 1948.
43741.12.700 Picasso, Pablo. Desire. N.Y., 1948.
43741.13.150 Pichette, Henri. Les Epiphanies. Paris, 1948.
43538.76.820 Picon, G. Georges Bernanos. Paris, 1948.
43742.41.180 Plisnier, Charles. Nicole Arnaud. Paris, 1948.
37567.438 Pommier, J. Les écrivains devant la revolution de 1848. 1. éd. Paris, 1948.
43743.60.120 Ponge, Francis. Poèmes. Paris, 1948.
37543.290 Pons, Roger. L'Yseult a violaine. Paris, 1948.
38524.122A Porteau, Paul. Contes. Paris, 1948.
43743.90.180 Pourrat, Henri. Le trésor des contes. v.1-13. Paris, 1948-53. 11v.
38537.25.155 Powys, John C. Rabelais. London, 1948.
43744.67.80.2 Proust, Marcel. A un ami. Paris, 1948.
43744.67.20 Proust, Marcel. Marcel Proust; a selection. London, 1948.
43744.67.57 Proust, Marcel. Maxims. N.Y., 1948.
43744.67.56 Proust, Marcel. Pleasures and regrets. N.Y., 1948.
43750.24.700 Queneau, Raymond. A hard winter. London, 1948.
43750.24.240 Queneau, Raymond. L'instant fatal. 4. éd. Paris, 1948.
43750.24.120 Queneau, Raymond. Saint Glinglin. 10. éd. Paris, 1948.
43750.24.720 Queneau, Raymond. The skin of dreams. N.Y., 1948.
43750.24.190 Queneau, Raymond. Les ziaux. Paris, 1948.
43752.57.250 Ramuz, Charles Ferdinand. Farinet, ou La fausse monnaie. Paris, 1948.
43752.57.708 Ramuz, Charles Ferdinand. What is man. N.Y., 1948.
42587.52.70 Renard, Jules. Hunting with the Fox. Oxford, 1948.
43753.90.170 Reverdy, P. Le livre de mon bord. Paris, 1948.
Mol 213.20 Reynier, G. Les femmes savantes de Molière. Paris, 1948.
42556.28.25 Rimbaud, Jean Arthur. Oeuvres complètes. Lausanne, 1948. 2v.
43756.90.104 Rivière, Jacques. Correspondance, 1905-1914. Paris, 1948. 2v.
43757.50.65A Rolland, Romain. Choix de lettres. Paris, 1948.
43757.50.525 Rolland, Romain. La vie de Vivekananda et l'évangile universel. v. 1-2. Paris, 1948.
43757.3.72 Romains, Jules. Choix de poèmes. 7. éd. Paris, 1948.
38525.20.45 Ronsard, Pierre de. Sonnets d'amour. Mainz, 1948.
43757.83.140 Rostand, Maurice. Confession d'un demi-siècle. Paris, 1948.
FL 6077.8 Rousseau, J.J. Lettre à Mr. d'Alembert sur les spectacles. Lille, 1948.
FL 6094.8.25 Rousseau, J.J. Les rêveries du promeneur solitaire. Genève, 1948.
FL 6094.8.15 Rousseau, J.J. Les rêveries du promeneur solitaire. Lille, 1948.
FL 6094.10 Rousseau, J.J. Les rêveries du promeneur solitaire. Paris, 1948.
37543.243.5 Rousseaux, André. Le monde classique. Paris, 1948.
V43500.269 Rousselot, Jean. Odes à quelques-uns: Supervielle, Van Gogh, Eluard, Max Jacob, Modigliani, Apollinaire, Holderlin, Voronca, Lorca. Paris, 1948.
43554.2.900 Rywalski, P. La Bible, dans l'oeuvre littéraire de Paul Claudel. Thèse. Porrentruy, 1948.
43554.2.903 Rywalski, P. Claudel et la Bible. Porrentruy, 1948.
40516.60.30 Sade, D.A.F. de. Morceaux choisis. Paris, 1948.
43761.39.152A St. Exupéry, A. de. Citadelle. 71. éd. Paris, 1948.
40587.19.10 Sainte-Beuve, Charles. Chateaubriand et son groupe littéraire. Paris, 1948.
40575.7.40 Sainte-Beuve, Charles A. Lettres à deux amies. Paris, 1948.
41557.9.73.2 Sand, George. Indiana. Paris, 1948.
41557.9.49.10 Sand, George. Le marquis de Villemer. Paris, 1948.
43761.78.712A Sartre, Jean Paul. Anti-semite and Jew. N.Y., 1948.
43761.78.720 Sartre, Jean Paul. The chips are down. N.Y., 1948.
43761.78.170 Sartre, Jean Paul. L'engrenage. 2. éd. Paris, 1948.
43761.78.745.2 Sartre, Jean Paul. Intimacy, and other stories. N.Y., 1948.
43761.78.160 Sartre, Jean Paul. Les mains sales. 50e éd. Paris, 1948.
43761.78.230 Sartre, Jean Paul. Visages. Paris, 1948.
43761.78.770 Sartre, Jean Paul. The wall. N.Y., 1948.
38526.48.29.10 Saulnier, Verdum L. Maurice Scève. Paris, 1948-49. 2v.
38526.48.29.11 Saulnier, Verdum L. Maurice Scève. v.1-2. Paris, 1948-49.
37595.89 Sbordone, F. Festi ed appunti per lo studio del medioevo francese. Napoli, 1948-
43763.38.190 Schlumberger, Jean. Stéphane le Glorieux. 14. éd. Paris, 1948.
38575.23.102 Schneider, R. Corneilles Ethos in der Ära Ludwigs XIV, 1-10 Tourend. Baden-Baden, 1948.
42563.89.85 Schwab, Raymond. La vie d'Elémir Bourges. Paris, 1948.
41543.22.40 Sebillotte, L. Le secret de Gerard de Nerval. Paris, 1948.

Chronological Listing

1948 - cont.

40587.130 Séchelles, R. Chateaubriand et l'âme celte. St. Brieuc, 1948.
42563.37.122 Secor, Walter. Paul Bourget and the nouvelle. N.Y., 1948.
41522.3.50 Seguin, J.P. Barbey d'Aurevilly. Avranches, 1948.
37567.432 Siciliano, Italo. Lirici francesi dell'ottocento. Venezia, 1948.
43769.54.730 Simenon, Georges. Magnet of doom. London, 1948.
41574.280 Souchon, Paul. Les deux femmes de Victor Hugo. Paris, 1948.
42556.28.179 Starkie, Enid. Das trunkene Schiff. Hamburg, 1948.
43780.5.120 Suarès, André. Voici l'homme. Paris, 1948.
43780.69.280 Supervielle, Jules. Robinson. Paris, 1948.
43785.75.100 Tardieu, Jean. Jours pétrifés, 1942-1944. Paris, 1948.
38557.24.95 Terstegge, G. Providence as Idée-Maîtresse in the works of Bossuet. Washington, 1948.
37569.97.10 Therive, A. Moralistes de ce temps. Paris, 1948.
43788.67.100 Thouy, Louis. Au diapason de la raison pure. Aurillac, 1948?
42515.35.252 Tielrooy, J.B. Ernest Renan. Amsterdam, 1948.
43752.57.820 Tissot, André. C.F. Ramuz. Neuchâtel, 1948.
40546.24 Tocqueville, Alexis de. Recollections. London, 1948.
43737.36.810 Toesca, M. Jean Paulhan. Paris, 1948.
43792.24.100 Toetenel, Albert. Florilège. Paris, 1948.
42576.46.105 Traz, Robert de. Pierre Loti. Paris, 1948.
43793.42.160 Triolet, Elsa. L'inspecteur de ruines; roman. Paris, 1948.
43793.67.170 Troyat, Henri. La case de l'Oncle Sam. Paris, 1948.
43793.67.190 Troyat, Henri. Le sac et la cendre; roman. Paris, 1948.
43793.89.1100 Truchot, Robert. Ephemeres et noctuelles. Rouen, 1948?
43620.2.264 Uhlig, Helmut. André Gide. Berlin, 1948.
43822.50.700 Vailland, Roger. Playing for keeps. Boston, 1948.
43822.50.710 Vailland, Roger. Playing with fire. London, 1948.
43822.49.720 Valéry, Paul. Reflections on the world today. N.Y., 1948.
43822.49.107 Valéry, Paul. Variété V. Paris, 1948.
43822.49.320 Valéry, Paul. Vues. Paris, 1948.
42547.10.27 Vallette, Marguerite. Quand j'etais jeune. Paris, 1948.
38537.25.175 Valot, S. Regardons vivre François Rabelais. Paris, 1948.
42515.35.275 Van Jieghem, Philippe. Renan. Paris, 1948.
43761.78.800 Varet, Gilbert. L'ontologie de Sartre. 1. éd. Paris, 1948.
43823.75.132 Vercel, Roger. La caravane de Paques. Paris, 1948.
43823.75.720 Vercel, Roger. Northern lights. N.Y., 1948.
43823.75.5100 Verfrey, Maurice Michel. La chanson des rivages; poèmes. Paris, 1948.
42557.19.130 Verlaine, Paul. Louise Leclercq. Söcking, 1948.
42557.18.45 Verlaine, Paul. Oeuvres complètes. Paris, 1948-53. 5v.
42557.19.54 Verlaine, Paul. Sagesse. Paris, 1948.
42557.17 Verlaine, Paul. Selected poems. Berkeley, 1948.
42557.12.95 Vermeulen, G. Les débuts d'Émile Verhaeren. Bruxelles, 1948.
41564.1.25A Vigny, Alfred de. Oeuvres complètes. Paris, 1948. 2v.
42586.32.510 Voorde, Urbain van de. Charles de Coster's Ulenspiegel. Nijmegen, 1948.
43752.57.840 Voyenne, B. C.F. Ramuz et la sainteté de la terre. Paris, 1948.
43830.39.110 Wahl, J.A. Poésie, pensée, perception. Paris, 1948.
Mon 133.3 Weiler, M. La pensée de Montaigne. Paris, 1948.
37569.193 Weinert, H. Dichtung aus dem Glauben. Hamburg, 1948.
43757.50.1040 Weiss, H. Romain Rolland. Berlin, 1948.
38512.17.40 Wilmatte, M. Froissart. Bruxelles, 1948.
38575.23.125 Zanghi, Rosario. Introduzione a Cinna di Corneille. Torino, 1948.
43761.39.820 Zeller, Renée C.T. La vie secrète d'Antoine. Paris, 1948.
43752.57.875 Zermatten, Maurice. C.F. Ramuz. Neuchâtel, 1948.

1949

43512.75.195 Achard, Marcel. Histoires d'amour. 2. ed. Paris, 1949.
FL 386.802 Ambrière, Francis. La galerie dramatique, 1945-1948. Paris, 1949.
43524.67.105 Anouilh, Jean. Ardèle. Paris, 1949.
43526.65.180 Apollinaire, Guillaume. Couleur du temps. Paris, 1949.
43526.65.210 Apollinaire, Guillaume. La femme assise. 11. ed. Paris, 1949.
43527.3.290 Aragon, Louis. Les communistes. Paris, 1949-1951. 5v.
43528.86.63 Artaud, Antonin. Supplement aux Lettres de Rodez. Paris, 1949.
43687.74.800 Aubry, G.J. Valéry Larbaud. Monaco, 1949.
43531.29.100 Aufrère, Gaston Henry. Fleurs de guerre et d'exil; poèmes. Paris, 1949.
43535.54.210 Aymé, Marcel. La belle image. 58e éd. Paris, 1949.
43535.54.260 Aymé, Marcel. Le confort intellectual. Paris, 1949.
43535.54.705 Aymé, Marcel. The fable and the flesh. London, 1949.
43535.54.710 Aymé, Marcel. The miraculous barber. London, 1949.
38585.16.175 Bailly, A. Racine. Paris, 1949.
40597.15.125 Balzac, Honoré de. Le cousin Pons. Paris, 1949.
40597.35.163 Balzac, Honoré de. La cousine Bette. Paris, 1949.
40597.35.91 Balzac, Honoré de. La duchesse de Langeais. Paris, 1949.
40597.35.90 Balzac, Honoré de. La duchesse de Langeais. Paris, 1949.
40597.32.10 Balzac, Honoré de. The fatal skin. London, 1949.
40596.43 Balzac, Honoré de. Les idées de Balzac. Genève, 1949-50. 2v.
40596.6 Balzac, Honoré de. L'oeuvre de Balzac. Paris, 1949-53. 16v.
FL 398.6.20 Barrault, J.L. Réflexions sur le théâtre. Paris, 1949.
41574.283 Barrère, Jean Bertrand. La fantaisie de Victor Hugo. Paris, 1949. 3v.
Mon 142.2 Barrière, P. Montaigne, gentilhomme français. 2. éd. Bordeaux, 1949.
41522.13.12.15 Baudelaire, Charles. Journaux intimes. Paris, 1949.
41522.4.7 Baudelaire, Charles. Selected critical studies. Cambridge, Eng., 1949.
43537.99.110 Bazin, Hervé. La tête contre les murs. 51e éd. Paris, 1949.
42555.44.200 Beausire, Pierre. Mallarmé. Lausanne, 1949.
43538.1.470 Beauvoir, Simone de. She came to stay. London, 1949.
43538.13.3100 Beckers, Alain. Sonnets. Bruxelles, 1949.
43538.76.810 Béguin, Albert. Georges Bernanos. Neuchâtel, 1949.
43538.36.710 Béhaine, René. Day of glory. London, 1949.
43822.49.1150 Bémol, Maurice. Paul Valéry. Thèse. Clermont-Ferrand, 1949.
43538.61.190 Benoît, Pierre. Le casino de Barbazon. Montréal, 1949.
37568.112 Berger, Marcel. Le style au microscope. Série 2. v.1-2,3,4. Paris, 1949-1952. 3v.

1949 - cont.

43538.76.160 Bernanos, Georges. Dialogues des carmélites. Neuchâtel, 1949.
43538.76.170 Bernanos, Georges. Les enfants humiliés. 16. éd. Paris, 1949.
40597.2.215 Bernes, Pierre. Exposition commemorative du cent cinquantieme anniversaire de Balzac. Paris, 1949.
FL 398.7.65 Bernhardt, L.S. Sarah Bernhardt. London, 1949.
43576.9.800 Bertocci, A.P. Charles Du Bos and English literature. N.Y., 1949.
37566.109A Beuchat, C. Histoire du naturalisme français. Paris, 1949. 2v.
40582.38.70 Beyle, Henri. Memoirs of an egotist. London, 1949.
40582.38.25 Beyle, Henri. Memoirs of egotism. N.Y., 1949.
40582.25.40 Beyle, Henri. Stendhal's The red and the black. Philadelphia, 1949.
40582.40.2 Beyle, Henri. Vie de Henry Brulard. Paris, 1949. 2v.
43540.7.150 Bibescu, M.L. Prince Imperial. London, 1949.
43744.67.71 Bibescu, M.L.L. The veiled wanderer, Marcel Proust. London, 1949.
37547.80 Billy, A. Fontainebleau. Paris, 1949.
43540.3.69 Billy, André. Le balcon au bord de l'eau. Paris, 1949.
43540.3.85 Billy, André. Malvina. Paris, 1949.
43543.8.120 Blanchot, Maurice. La part du feu. 6. éd. Paris, 1949.
43543.14.700 Bloch-Michel, J. The witness. N.Y., 1949.
42563.23.16.8 Bloy, Léon. La femme pauvre. v. 1-2. Paris, 1949.
43544.103.100 Bolle, Louis. La faucille et la Carandie. Paris, 1949.
38512.57.10 Bonet, Honoré. The tree of battles. Cambridge, Mass., 1949.
43544.81.2115 Bosco, Henri. Le roseau et la source. Paris, 1949.
42556.28.204 Bouillane de Lacoste, Henry de. Rimbaud et le problème des illuminations. Paris, 1949.
42556.28.203 Bouillane de Lacoste, Henry de. Rimbaud et le problème des illuminations. Paris, 1949.
42556.28.211 Breton, André. Flagrant délit. Paris, 1949.
43545.42.110 Brisson, P. Autre temps. Paris, 1949.
43823.75.2140A Bruller, Jean. Le songe. Paris, 1949.
37575.695 Bryen, C. Anthologie de la poésie naturelle. Paris, 1949.
38585.60 Cambier, Maurice. Racine et Madame de Maintenon. Bruxelles, 1949.
43550.56.710 Cammaerts, E. The devil takes the chair. London, 1949.
43550.1.190 Carco, Francis. De Montmartre au Quartier Latin. Paris, 1949.
43550.1.170 Carco, Francis. Morsure; roman. 11. éd. Paris, 1949.
43550.1.180 Carco, Francis. Morsure. 12. éd. Paris, 1949.
43550.1.160 Carco, Francis. Mortefontaine. Paris, 1949.
43550.1.125 Carco, Francis. Rue Pigalle. Paris, 1949.
43550.76.1100 Carion, Daniel. L'homme cassé. Paris, 1949.
43698.200.810 Caulon, P. de. Henri Michaux. Neuchâtel, 1949.
43551.59.200 Cendrars, Blaise. La fin du monde. Paris, 1949.
43551.59.210 Cendrars, Blaise. L'homme foudroyé. Paris, 1949.
41564.55.95 Cesare, Raffaele de. Intorno a servitude et grandeur militaires di A. de Vigny. Arona, 1949.
43552.3.9147 Chamson, André. Le crime des justes. 32. éd. Paris, 1949.
43552.4.2115 Char, René. Claire, théâtre de verdure. Paris, 1949.
43552.4.2120 Char, René. Dehors la nuit est gouvernée. Paris, 1949.
38514.64.33 Chartier, Alain. La belle dame sans mercy et les poésies lyriques. 2e éd. Lille, 1949.
43552.5.1165 Chartier, Émile. Entretiens au bord de la mar. 5. éd. Paris, 1949.
40586.28.84 Chateaubriand, F.A.R. Mémoires d'outre-tombe. 2. éd. Paris, 1949-50. 2v.
40585.1.5 Chateaubriand en Amérique; essai de bibliographie. n.p., 1949?
43552.7.2126 Chazal, Malcolm de. La vie filtrée. 6e éd. Paris, 1949.
41522.18.215 Chérix, Robert B. Commentaire des Fleurs du mal. Genève, 1949.
FL 398.12.5 Chevalier, Maurice. The man in the straw hat. N.Y., 1949.
43761.39.825 Chevrier, Pierre A. Antoine de St. Exupéry. 13. éd. Paris, 1949.
40524.32.35 Childs, J. Restif de la Bretonne. Paris, 1949.
43554.2.390 Claudel, Paul. Accompagnements. 3e éd. Paris, 1949.
43554.2.375 Claudel, Paul. Le bestiaire spirituel. Lausanne, 1949.
43554.2.37.25A Claudel, Paul. Commentaire à l'Art poétique. Paris, 1949.
43554.2.410 Claudel, Paul. Correspondance, 1899-1926. Paris, 1949.
43554.2.200.5 Claudel, Paul. Partage de midi. 12e éd. Paris, 1949.
43554.2.168 Claudel, Paul. Le soulier de satin. Paris, 1949.
43556.1.320 Cocteau, Jean. Lettre aux Américains. Paris, 1949.
43556.1.350 Cocteau, Jean. Maalesh. 16e éd. Paris, 1949.
43556.1.275 Cocteau, Jean. Théâtre de poche. Paris, 1949.
38513.80 Cohen, Gustave. Recueil de farces françaises inédites du XVe siècle. Cambridge, Mass., 1949.
37562.276 Cohen, Gustave. La vie littéraire en France au moyen âge. Paris, 1949.
42555.44.86 Cohn, Robert G. Mallarmé's un coup de dés. New Haven, 1949.
43556.49.500 Colette, Sidonie Gabrielle. Le fanal bleu. Paris, 1949.
43556.49.530 Colette, Sidonie Gabrielle. Journal intermittent. Paris, 1949.
40553.9.10 Constant de Rebecque, Benjamin. Lettres à un ami; Benjamin Constant et Madame de Staël. Neuchâtel, 1949.
42554.26.140 Corbière, Tristan. Litanie du sommeil et autres poèmes. Paris, 1949.
42554.26.110 Corbière, Tristan. Poèmes, choisis et présentés. Paris, 1949.
38575.80 Corneille, Pierre. Clitandre. Lille, 1949.
38575.34.60 Corneille, Pierre. La mort de solon. Paris, 1949.
43556.82.705.5A Cossery, Albert. The house of certain death. N.Y., 1949.
38575.23.100.5 Couton, Georges. La vieillesse de Corneille. Paris, 1949.
38575.23.100 Couton, Georges. La vieillesse de Corneille. Thèse. Paris, 1949.
39566.65 Cresson, A. Diderot. Paris, 1949.
42515.37.25 Cresson, A. Ernest Renan. Paris, 1949.
40583.329 Davray, J. Notre Stendhal. Paris, 1949.
42556.28.199 Debray, Pierre. Rimbaud, le magicien désabusé. Paris, 1949.
X Cg 37542.46 Decahors, E. Histoire de la littérature française. Paris, 1949. 2v.
40575.5.127 Decreus-Van Liefland, Juliette. Sainte-Beuve et la critique des auteurs féminins. Paris, 1949.
43566.49.2100 Del Dongo, Fabrice. Amitiés, mes belles etoiles! Monte-Carlo, 1949.
43566.82.7160 Destouches, Louis Ferdinand. Casse-pipe. Paris, 1949.
43566.82.7712 Destouches, Louis Ferdinand. Journey to the end of the night. N.Y., 1949?

1949 - cont.

37596.253 Dialogue de Saint Julien et son disciple. Dialogue de saint Julien et son disciple. Oxford, 1949.
39564.10.90 Diderot, Denis. Les pages immortelles de Diderot. Paris, 1949.
39566.75 Diderot studies. Syracuse, N.Y., 1949-52. 13v.
42566.16.110 Dobie, G. Alphonse Daudet. London, 1949.
39544.230 Donvez, J. De quoi vivait Voltaire. Paris, 1949.
43565.60.800 Dournes, P. Daniel-Rops. Paris, 1949.
43573.98.100 Doyon, René L. Éloge du maquereau. Paris, 1949.
43574.75.100 Druon, Maurice. Mégarée. Paris, 1949.
38526.6.18.5 Du Bellay, Joachim. Les regrets. Paris, 1949.
42545.28.800 Dubeux, Albert. La curieuse vie de Georges Courteline. Paris, 1949.
43709.3.830 Du Bos, C. La comtesse de Noailles et le climat du génie. Paris, 1949.
37596.135.12 Dubs, Ingeborg. Galeran de Bretagne. Bern, 1949.
42586.9.20 Duche, Rene. La carque et le style de Paul Arène. Paris, 1949.
43576.14.100 Ducros, C. Inès de Castro. Paris, 1949.
43576.6.100 Duhamel, Georges. La passion de Joseph Pasquier. Paris, 1949.
43576.6.325 Duhamel, Georges. La pesée des âmes. Paris, 1949.
43576.6.745 Duhamel, Georges. Suzanne; Joseph. N.Y., 1949.
41538.185 Dumas, Alexandre. Captain Marion. Christchurch, N.Z., 1949.
37567.418 Dumont, Francis. Les petits romantiques français. Ligugé? 1949.
43576.76.100 Durry, Marie-Jeanne. La cloison courbe. Paris, 1949.
FL 6059.20 Ellis, M.B. Julie, ou la nouvelle Héloise. Toronto, 1949.
43591.89.260 Éluard, Paul. Une leçon de morale, poèmes. 4. éd. Paris, 1949.
43606.76.160 Fargue, Léon P. Etc. Genève, 1949.
43606.78.270 Farrère, Claude. Jab, siècle XX; roman. Paris, 1949.
38554.518.55 Fénelon, F. de S. de la Mothe. Letters from Cambrai written to the Contess de Montberon. Cornwall-on-Hudson, 1949.
39544.44.20 Fenger, H. Voltaire et le théâtre anglais. Copenhague, 1949.
41557.10.102 Ferra, Bartomeu. Chopin y George Sand en Mallorca. Palma de Mallorca, 1949.
38514.150 Ferrier, J. L'histoire de Messire Guido. Manchester, Eng., 1949.
42576.28.80 Flaubert, Gustave. Madame Bovary. Paris, 1949.
42576.28.75 Flaubert, Gustave. Madame Bovary. 1. ed. Philadelphia, 1949.
43625.19.817 Fontaine, Anne. L'Herbier d'Armand Godoy. Fribourg, 1949.
42555.44.96.5 Fowlie, Wallace. Mallarmé as Hamlet. Yonkers, N.Y., 1949.
42576.63.20.8 France, Anatole. Vers les temps meilleurs. Paris, 1949-3v.
42576.62.135.10 France, Anatole. La vie littéraire. 3. éd. 5. série. Paris, 1949.
43612.35.100 Frédérix, P. On ne vit qu'une fois; roman. Paris, 1949.
43612.23.110 Frénaud, André. Poemas de dessaus le plancher. Paris, 1949.
Mon 116.45 Friedrich, Hugo. Montaigne. Bern, 1949.
43613.45.700 Frison-Roche, Roger. First on the rope. London, 1949.
43616.41.2100 Gaillard, Robert. Louisiane; roman. Paris, 1949.
43616.62.112 Gantillon, Simon. Maya. Paris, 1949.
38527.43.10 Garnier, Robert. Bradamante. Paris, 1949.
38527.42.3.32 Garnier, Robert. Les Juifves. Paris, 1949.
43616.78.170 Gary, Romain. Le grand vestiaire. Paris, 1949.
43617.78.190 Genêt, Jean. L'enfant criminel et Adame Miroir. Paris, 1949.
43617.78.100 Genêt, Jean. Haute surveillance. 6. éd. Paris, 1949.
43617.78.110 Genêt, Jean. Journal au voleur. 12. éd. Paris, 1949.
43617.59.120 Genevoix, Maurice. Cyrille. Paris, 1949.
43617.80.100 Gengenbach, E. Judas. Paris, 1949.
43620.2.79.50 Gide, André. Feuillets d'automne. Paris, 1949.
43620.2.47.5 Gide, André. Fruits of the earth. London, 1949.
43620.2.69.23 Gide, André. Journals. N.Y., 1949. 4v.
43620.2.31 Gide, André. La porte étroite. 7. éd. Paris, 1949.
43620.2.35.50 Gide, André. Two symphonies. N.Y., 1949.
37574.710 Gide, André Paul Guillaume. Anthologie de la poésie française. Paris, 1949.
37574.710.5 Gide, André Paul Guillaume. Anthologie de la poésie française. Paris, 1949.
43757.50.60 Gillet, Louis. Correspondance entre Louis Gillet et Romain Rolland. Paris, 1949. 2v.
43620.66.340 Giono, Jean. Les âmes fortes. Paris, 1949.
43620.66.320 Giono, Jean. Mort d'un personnage. Paris, 1949.
43620.66.155 Giono, Jean. Que ma joie demeure; roman. Paris, 1949.
43620.66.290 Giono, Jean. Le serpent d'étoiles. 30. éd. Paris, 1949.
37568.122 Girard, M. Guide illustré de la littérature française moderne. Paris, 1949.
43625.19.280 Godoy, Armand. Rossignol. Paris, 1949.
43625.19.290 Godoy, Armand. Sonnets pour l'aube. Paris, 1949.
43625.46.100 Gos, C. Song of the high hills. London, 1949.
43626.72.100 Greeff, E. La nuit est ma lumière. Paris, 1949.
43744.67.995 Green, Frederick C. The mind of Proust. Cambridge, Eng., 1949.
43626.22.725 Green, Julien. If I were you. 1st ed. N.Y., 1949.
37574.555 Gregh, F. Sonnets d'hier et d'aujourd'hui. Paris, 1949.
43738.1.201 Gremminger, E. Charles Péguy. Olten, 1949.
FL 6139.49 Groethuysen, B. Jean-Jacques Rousseau. 4. éd. Paris, 1949.
40597.2.290 Guignard, R. Balzac et Issoudun. Issoudun, 1949
43628.41.3110 Guillevic, Eugène. Les chansons d'Antonin Blond. Paris, 1949.
43628.42.120 Guilloux, Louis. Le jeu de patience. Paris, 1949.
37543.302 Haedens, K. Une histoire de la littérature française. Paris, 1949.
37543.292 Hartoy, M. d'. De l'inouisme et de quelques autres complexes en littérature. Avignon, 1949.
41556.46 Held, Mariette. Charles Nodier. Bienne, 1949.
37594.35 Henri d'Arci. Vitas patrum. Washington, 1949[1950]
43598.84.805 Hok, Ruth E. Édouard Estaunié. Thesis. N.Y., 1949.
41572.52 Hugo, Victor. Pages d'amour de Victor Hugo. Paris, 1949.
43667.14.61A Jacob, Max. Choix de lettres de Max Jacob à Jean Cocteau. Paris, 1949.
43667.78.120 Jarry, Alfred. La revanche de la nuit. Paris, 1949.
43670.59.110 Jones, Philippe. Grand largue. Bruxelles, 1949.
43670.94.115 Jouve, Pierre Jean. Diadème. Paris, 1949.
43757.50.845 Küchler, W. Romain Rolland. 3. Aufl. Frankfurt, 1949.
38585.16.170 Lacretelle, Pierre de. La vie privée de Racine. Paris, 1949.

1949 - cont.

43620.2.262 Lang, Renée. André Gide et la pensée allemande. Paris, 1949.
43687.60.4100 Laniez, Gabriel. Désert, suivi de cinq élégies. Paris, 1949.
43822.49.1080 La Rochefoucauld, Edmée de Fels. Images de Paul Valéry. Strasbourg, 1949.
43687.89.2150 La Varende, Jean de. Le miracle de Janvier. Paris, 1949.
FL 375.80 Lawton, H. Handbook of French Renaissance dramatic theory. Manchester, Eng., 1949.
39564.35 Lefebure, H. Diderot. Paris, 1949.
43737.36.800 Lefebve, M.J. Jean Paulhan. Paris, 1949.
43688.53.3100 Lemaitre, Gaston. Des vers. Postface d'André Gressier. Paris, 1949.
43688.61.180 Lenormand, Henri René. Les confessions d'un auteur dramatique. Paris, 1949-1953. 2v.
43688.61.200 Lenormand, Henri René. L'enfant des sables. Paris, 1949.
43688.87.100 Leopold, E. Poèmes. Paris, 1949.
42557.14.60 Linhardt, A. Dichter und Vagabund. Wien, 1949.
40583.206 Liprandi, Claude. Stendhal. Avignon, 1949.
37574.895 Le livre des sonnets. Paris, 1949.
Htn 40593.43* Lonchamp, F.C. L'oeuvre imprimé de Madame Germaine de Staël. Genève, 1949.
37596.10.155A Loomis, R.S. Arthurian tradition and Chréstien de Troyes. N.Y., 1949.
43693.75.120 Lorenz, Paul. Les monstres innocents. Paris, 1949.
37597.9.20 Lorris, Guillaume de. Le roman de la rose. 8. éd. Paris, 1949.
37555.165A Lote, Georges. Histoire du vers français. Paris, 1949-51. 2v.
39566.70 Lücke, T. Denis Diderot. Berlin, 1949.
37574.730 Lugli, V. Da Villon a Valéry. Messina, 1949.
37574.122 Lugli, Vittorio. Da Villon a Valéry; il libro della poesia francese. Messina, 1949.
43694.59.120 Lunel, Armand. Les amandes d'Aix. Paris, 1949.
43697.48.3730 Malaquais, Jean. World without visa. London, 1949.
42555.44.2 Mallarmé, Stéphane. Correspondance inédite de Stéphane Mallarmé et Henry Roujon. Genève, 1949.
X Cg 42555.43.3.2 Mallarmé, Stéphane. Poésies. 108. éd. Paris, 1949.
43697.62.700 Marchal, L. The Mesh. N.Y., 1949.
37568.108 Marill, René. La révolte des écrivains d'aujourd'hui. Paris, 1949.
40535.30.55 Marivaux, Pierre Carlet de Chamblain de. Romans. Paris, 1949.
40535.27.25 Marivaux, Pierre Carlet de Chamblain de. Théâtre complet. Paris, 1949.
43697.76.7100 Marker, C. Le coeur net. Paris, 1949.
38516.45 Martin, C.B.W. A few early French verses done into English. Albany, 1949.
43697.77.720 Martin du Gard, Roger. Jean Barois. N.Y., 1949.
42515.38.10 Massis, Henri. Portrait de Monsieur Renan. Paris, 1949.
43697.85.110 Masson, G.A. A la façon de Jean Anouilh. Paris, 1949.
43545.24.800 Maureac, P. André Breton. Paris, 1949.
37543.294 Mauriac, F. Mes grands hommes. Monaco, 1949.
43697.88.740 Mauriac, François. The desert of love. London, 1949.
43697.88.360 Mauriac, François. Orages. Paris, 1949.
43744.67.105 Maurois, André. A la recherche de Marcel Proust. 60. éd. Paris, 1949.
42514.28.79 Maurras, Charles. Inscriptions sur nos ruines. Paris, 1949.
43697.97.700 Maximoff, Mateo. The Ursitory. London, 1949.
38585.16.165 May, Georges C. D'Ovide à Racine. Paris, 1949.
43698.25.775 Meersch, M. van der. Drama um Direktor Bramburger. Luzern, 1949.
43698.25.720 Meersch, M. van der. The poor girl. London, 1949.
43698.58.4110 Ménard, René. L'arbre et l'horizon. Paris, 1949.
37543.304 Merquiol, A. La côte d'Azur dans la littérature française. Nice? 1949.
43698.200.700 Michaux, Henri. A barbarian in Asia. N.Y., 1949.
43698.200.160 Michaux, Henri. La vie dans les plis. 4. ed. Paris, 1949.
43699.76.100 Mitaud, J. Hate de vivre. Paris, 1949.
43701.39.110 Mohrt, Michel. Mon royaume pour un cheval. Paris, 1949.
42545.28.100 Moinaux, Georges. La vie de ménage. Paris, 1949.
Mol 19.49 Molière, Jean Baptiste Poquelin. Oeuvres complètes. Paris, 1949. 11v.
Mol 19.35.11 Molière, Jean Baptiste Poquelin. Théâtre, 1669-1670. Paris, 1949.
37569.377 Monnerot, Jules. La poésie moderne et le sacré. Paris, 1949.
Mon 31.50.1 Montaigne, Michel de. Essays. Cotton (Hazlitt). N.Y., 1949.
39592.21 Montesquieu, C.L. de S. Oeuvres complètes. Paris, 1949-51. 2v.
39594.3.8 Montesquieu, C.L. de S. The spirit of the laws. v.1-2. N.Y., 1949.
43701.63.300 Montherlant, Henry de. Demain il fera jour. Pasiphaé. 3. éd. Paris, 1949.
43701.63.145.10 Montherlant, Henry de. Le petite infante de Castille, historiette. 40e éd. Paris, 1949.
37558.13.12 Mooij, A.L.A. Caractères principaux. Groningen, 1949.
Mol 613.10 Moore, W.G. Molière. Oxford, 1949.
37556.21.65 Mottin, Jean. Histoire politique de la presse, 1944-1949. Paris, 1949.
43705.91.700 Navel, Georges. Man at work. London, 1949.
43620.2.163 Naville, Arnold. Bibliographie des écrits de André Gide, jusqu'en 1952. Paris, 1949.
43620.2.162 Naville, Arnold. Bibliographie des écrits de André Gide. Paris, 1949.
37543.308 Neubert, Fritz. Geschichte der französischen Literatur. Tübingen, 1949.
40553.10.49 Nicolson, H.G. Benjamin Constant. Garden City, 1949.
40553.10.50 Nicolson, H.G. Benjamin Constant. London, 1949.
43709.89.32 Nouveau, Germain. Le calepin du mendiant. Précédé d'autres poèmes, vers inédits. Paris, 1949.
43714.8.710 Obey, André. Noah. London, 1949.
43554.2.905 O'Flaherty, K.M.J. Paul Claudel and "The tidings". Cork, 1949.
43728.25.710 Orieux, J. Fontagre. London, 1949.
43737.34.180 Pagnol, Marcel. Critique des critiques. Paris, 1949.
43737.89.100 Pauwels, Louis. Les voies de petite communication. Paris, 1949.
43822.49.1060A Pelmont, Raoul. Paul Valéry et les beaux-arts. Cambridge, Mass., 1949.
43738.81.180 Perret, Jacques. Ernest le rebelle; roman. Paris, 1949.
43738.81.100 Perret, Jacques. Objets perdus. 10e éd. Paris, 1949.
37558.67.20 Peter, René. L'académie française et le XX siècle. Paris, 1949.

Chronological Listing

1949 - cont.

42556.28.205 Petitfills, P. L'oeuvre et visage d'Arthur Rimbaud. Paris, 1949.
40597.2.225 Pfeiffer, C.L. Taste and smell in Balzac's novels. Tucson, 1949.
43740.1.50 Philippe, Charles Louis. Marie Donadieu. London, 1949.
37573.684 Picon, Gaëtan. Panorama de la nouvelle littérature française. Paris, 1949.
FL 398.70.20 Pitoëff, Georges. Notre théâtre. Paris, 1949.
43742.41.190 Plisnier, Charles. Vertu du désordre. Paris, 1949.
37565.125 Poulet, Georges. Études sur le temps humain. Edinburgh, 1949.
43743.90.170 Pourrat, Henri. L'école buissonnière. Paris, 1949.
43744.67.67 Proust, Marcel. Letters. N.Y., 1949.
43744.67.80 Proust, Marcel. Letters to a friend. London, 1949.
43744.67.73 Proust, Marcel. Lettres à André Gide. Neuchâtel, 1949.
43744.67.68 Proust, Marcel. Lettres de Marcel Proust à Bibesco. Lausanne, 1949.
43750.20.100 Queffélec, Henri. Le bout du monde. Paris, 1949.
38536.25.16 Rabelais, F. L'Abbaye de Thélème. Genève, 1949.
38536.33 Rabelais, F. Gargantua. Paris, 1949.
38536.23.10 Rabelais, F. Le vroy Gargantua. Paris, 1949.
43752.18.700 Radiguet, Raymond. The devil in the flesh. London, 1949.
37557.42 Rambaud, L. L'éloquence française. Lyon, 1949? 2v.
43752.59.110 Randon, G. Le coeur populaire. Paris, 1949.
41522.18.220 Ratermanis, J.B. Étude sur le style de Baudelaire. Bade, 1949.
43753.90.180 Reverdy, P. Main d'oeuvre. Paris, 1949.
42556.28.55 Rimbaud, Jean Arthur. Lettre du baron de Petdechevré à son secretaire au château de Saint-Magloire. Genève, 1949.
42546.8.40 Rodenback, G. Choix de poésies. Paris, 1949.
43757.3.57 Romains, Jules. Le moulin et l'hospice. Paris, 1949.
43757.3.58 Romains, Jules. Le moulin et l'hospice. Paris, 1949.
43757.3.265 Romains, Jules. Paris des Hommes de bonne volonté. Paris, 1949.
38525.20.24 Ronsard, Pierre de. Discours des misères de ce temps. Paris, 1949.
38525.20.22 Ronsard, Pierre de. Poésies. Lausanne, 1949.
37543.132.5A Roques, Mario. Études de littérature française. Lille, 1949.
FL 6022.49 Rousseau, J.J. Les confessions. Paris, 1949. 2v.
V43500.263 Rousselot, Jean. L'homme en proie. Paris, 1949.
37568.110 Roy, C. Descriptions critiques. Paris, 1949- 5v.
43757.96.116 Roy, Claude. Clefs pour l'Amerique. 6. éd. Paris, 1949.
38526.48.140 Ruchon, J. La vie et l'oeuvre de Jean de Sponde. Genève, 1949.
37596.4.2 Rutebeuf. Le miracle de Théophile. 2. éd. Paris, 1949.
43701.63.800 Saint-Pierre, M. Montherlant. Paris, 1949.
40575.41 Sainte-Beuve, Charles A. Oeuvres. Paris, 1949. 2v.
FL 6139.49.10 Saloni, Alfredo. Rousseau. Milano, 1949.
41522.18.210A Sartre, J.P. Baudelaire. London, 1949.
43761.78.730 Sartre, Jean Paul. The diary of Antoine Roquentin. London, 1949.
43761.78.240 Sartre, Jean Paul. La mort dans l'âme, roman. Paris, 1949.
43761.78.735A Sartre, Jean Paul. Nausea. Norfolk, 1949.
43761.78.190A Sartre, Jean Paul. Situations. Paris, 1949- 7v.
43761.78.740 Sartre, Jean Paul. Three plays. London, 1949.
43761.78.624 Sartre, Jean Paul. Three plays. 1st American ed. N.Y., 1949.
43761.78.725 Sartre, Jean Paul. What is literature? N.Y., 1949.
37543.370 Sauro, Antoine. Études françaises d'esthétique. Napoli, 1949.
38526.48.32 Scève, Maurice. Sixty poems. N.Y., 1949.
43620.2.261 Schildt, G. Gide et l'homme. Paris, 1949.
43765.80.110 Serge, Victor (pseud.). L'affaire Toulaév. Paris, 1949.
42576.15.181 Seznec, Jean. Nouvelles études sur "La tentation de Saint-Antoine". London, 1949.
43769.27.100 Signoret, E. Chants vers la berge. Paris, 1949.
43769.54.735 Simenon, Georges. Black rain. London, 1949.
43769.54.707 Simenon, Georges. A wife of sea. London, 1949.
38514.23.80 Sommer, Ernst. Villon. Berlin, 1949.
43775.89.2100 Soubiran, André. Les hommes en blanc. Paris, 1949-51. 3v.
41574.280.5 Souchon, Paul. Victor Hugo. Paris, 1949.
43775.90.7190 Soupault, Philippe. Chansons. Rolle, 1949.
38526.48.150.5 Sponde, Jean de. Les amours et la mort. Paris, 1949.
38526.48.157 Sponde, Jean de. Poésies. Genève, 1949.
42577.4.38 Steegmüller, F. Maupassant, a lion in the path. N.Y., 1949.
37543.289 Studies in French language, literature and history presented to R.L. Graime Ritchie. Cambridge, Eng., 1949.
43780.5.130 Suarès, André. Hélène chez Archimèdes. Paris, 1949.
37596.23.6 Suchier, Hermann. Zwei altfranzösische Reimpredigten. Halle, 1949.
43780.69.109 Supervielle, Jules. Gravitations, poèmes. 13. éd. Paris, 1949.
43780.69.270 Supervielle, Jules. Oublieuse mémoire. Paris, 1949.
43780.69.300 Supervielle, Jules. Shéhérazade. 3. éd. Paris, 1949.
43780.69.130.10 Supervielle, Jules. Le voleur d'enfants. 8. éd. Paris, 1949.
37547.85 Susini, Jean. Histoire littéraire des Cévennes. Thèse. Alès, 1949.
40588.7.30 Sykes, L.C. Madame Cottin. Oxford, 1949.
43783.85.100 Syte, Raymond. Mots a personne; litanies parisiennes. Paris, 1949.
38557.24.70 Tans, J.A.G. Bossuet en Hollande. Thèse. Maastricht, 1949.
38557.24.71 Tans, J.A.G. Bossuet en Hollande. Thèse. Paris, 1949?
43744.67.1165 Tauman, L. Marcel Proust. Paris, 1949.
43744.67.1166 Tauman, L. Marcel Proust. Thèse. Paris, 1949.
43620.2.395 Teppe, Julien. Sur le purisme d'André Gide. Paris, 1949?
40597.2.265 Tersteeg, J. Honoré de Balzac en drie vrouwen. 's Gravenhage, 1949.
43738.1.91 Tharaud, J. Pour les fidèles de Péguy. Paris, 1949.
37585.45 Le théâtre picard. Abbeville, 1949.
38526.62.10 Théophile de Viau. Oeuvres choisies. Paris, 1949.
V43500.305 Thomé, Jules René. Le poème de la Meuse. Charleville, 1949.
43792.40.100 Toesca, Maurice. Deux contes. Paris? 1949.
V43500.315 Trolliet, Gilbert. L'inespéré. Genève, 1949.
40583.202 Tusero, Clemente. Stendhal. 1. ed. Verona, 1949.
43799.5.160 Tzara, Tristan. Phases. Paris, 1949.
37575.675 Valette, R. Hippocrate et la muse. Paris, 1949.
37543.298A Van Tieghem, Philippe. Histoire de la littérature française. Paris, 1949.

1949 - cont.

42557.19.18 Verlaine, Paul. Bonheur. Paris, 1949.
42557.19.19 Verlaine, Paul. Bonheur. Thèse. Paris, 1949.
43823.78.1700 Véry, Pierre. In what strange land? London, 1949.
43824.3.160 Vialar, Paul. Le bouc étourdi. Paris, 1949.
42515.37.30 Vié, L. Renan, la guerre de 70. Paris, 1949.
41564.14.15 Vigny, Alfred de. Journal d'un poète. Paris, 1949.
43824.49.250 Vildrac, Charles. D'après l'écko. Paris, 1949.
37569.188 Villard, E. La poésie patriotique de l'arrière en France et la guerre de 1914-1918. La Chaux-de-Fonds, 1949.
38514.20.8 Villon, François. Oeuvres complètes. Mulhouse, 1949.
39543.60 Voltaire, François Marie Arouet de. The portable Voltaire. N.Y., 1949.
43792.90.810 Waezer, P.A. Paul Jean Toulet. Paris, 1949.
37595.87 Wagner, R.L. Textes d'étude. Lille, 1949.
43833.20.100 Weil, Simone. Le pesânteur et la grâce. Paris, 1949.

195-

FL 398.43 Brisebarre, Jean Bernard. L'acteur Joanny et son journal inédit. Paris, 195-.
43591.89.621 Éluard, Paul. Selected writings. Norfolk, Conn., 195-.
43606.75.1100 Farell, Dominique. Ellipse. Paris, 195-?
43688.27.4100 Lefeuvre, Jean. Une petite espérance. Paris, 195-.
43822.49.1250 Michel, Pierre. Valéry. pts.1-2. Paris, 195-.
FL 355.705 Paris. Bibliotheque de l'Arsenal. Art and action. Paris, 195-.
42514.28.175 Santos, Arlindo Veiga dos. Maurras. Sao Paulo, 195-?

1950

43512.12.100 Abellio, R. Les yeux d'Ezéchiel sont ouverts. 12. ed. Paris, 1950.
43514.6.100 Adamov, Arthur. La parodie. Paris, 1950.
43744.67.1195 Adér-Winkler, E. Marcel Proust: Op zaek naar het volmaakte. 's-Graveland, 1950.
43524.67.160 Anouilh, Jean. La répétition; ou, L'amour puni. Genève, 1950.
43524.67.710 Anouilh, Jean. Ring-round the moon. London, 1950.
38524.125 Antoine, G. Le XVIe siècle. Paris, 1950.
43526.65.115 Apollinaire, Guillaume. Alcools. Paris, 1950.
43526.65.260 Apollinaire, Guillaume. Que faire? Paris, 1950.
43526.65.105 Apollinaire, Guillaume. Selected writings. N.Y., 1950.
43757.50.1055 Arcos, René. Romain Rolland. Paris, 1950.
40535.32.32 Arland, M. Marivaux. 4. éd. Paris, 1950.
42576.57.110 Atabinen, Resit Saffet. Pierre Loti. Istanbul, 1950.
FL 365.50 Attinger, Gustave. L'esprit de la commedia dell'arte dans le théâtre français. Paris, 1950.
43531.18.1150 Audiberti, Jacques. La pluie sur les boulevards. Angers, 1950.
43532.23.700 Aveline, Claude. Prisoner barn. London, 1950.
43535.54.715 Aymé, Marcel. The barkeep of Blemont. 1st ed. N.Y., 1950.
43535.54.240 Aymé, Marcel. Clérambard. Paris, 1950.
43537.50.115 Baldensperger, F. Rimes d'exil et d'espoir. Paris, 1950.
40597.35.200A Balzac, Honoré de. Un début dans la vie. Genève, 1950.
40597.35.155 Balzac, Honoré de. Falthurne. Paris, 1950.
40596.11.40 Balzac, Honoré de. Lettres à sa famille, 1809-1850. Paris, 1950.
40597.35.115 Balzac, Honoré de. Mademoiselle du Vissard. Paris, 1950.
40596.17.30 Balzac, Honoré de. The vicar of Tours. London, 1950.
FL 398.6.20.5 Barrault, J.L. Une troupe et ses auteurs. Paris, 1950.
41522.13.8.92 Baudelaire, Charles. The flowers of evil. N.Y., 1950.
41522.14.35 Baudelaire, Charles. My heart laid bare. London, 1950.
43537.89.110 Baudouin, C. The myth of modernity. London, 1950.
39566.85 Belavel, Y. L'esthétique sans paradox de Diderot. Paris, 1950.
41539.33 Bell, A. Alexandre Dumas. London, 1950.
43538.5.90 Benda, Julien. Les cahiers d'un clerc. 3. éd. Paris, 1950.
40583.4.10 Benedetto, L.F. La Parma di Stendhal. Firenze, 1950.
43538.75.120 Bergmans, Simone. Faligan. Bruxelles, 1950.
43538.76.750 Bernanos, Georges. Tradition of freedom. London, 1950.
43538.76.751 Bernanos, Georges. Tradition of freedom. N.Y., 1950.
43538.76.1100 Bernard, Marc. Une journée tout simple. 5. éd. Paris, 1950.
40597.2.235 Bertaut, Jules. La vie privée de Balzac. Paris, 1950.
40582.12.57 Beyle, Henri. Armance, ou Quelques scènes d'un salon de Paris en 1827. Paris, 1950.
40582.14.15 Beyle, Henri. Lucien Leuwen. Paris, 1950.
40582.38.75 Beyle, Henri. Souvenirs d'égotisme. Paris, 1950.
43540.8.100 Bibes, Jacques. Crier le jour. Paris, 1950.
43540.3.45 Billy, André. Le narthex. Paris, 1950.
43543.8.130 Blanchot, Maurice. Thomas l'obscur. 5. éd. Paris, 1950.
42563.23.16.9 Bloy, Léon. Celle qui pleure. Paris, 1950.
42563.23.16.10 Bloy, Léon. Le pal. part 1. Paris, 1950.
42576.15.205A Bonwit, M. Gustave Flaubert et le principe d'impossibilité. Berkeley, 1950.
41543.22.50 Borgal, C. De quoi vivait Gerard de Nerval. Paris, 1950.
37564.200A Borgerhoff, E. The freedom of French classicism. Princeton, 1950.
43544.81.2260 Bosco, Henri. Irénée; roman. Paris, 1950.
43544.81.2190 Bosco, Henri. Un rameau de la nuit. Paris, 1950.
43544.82.120 Bosschère, Jean de. Heritiers de l'abêne. Paris, 1950.
V43500.43 Bouhier, Jean. Pour l'amour de Colette. Nantes, 1950.
37574.765 Bouquet, G. Trésor de la poésie française. Paris, 1950-52. 2v.
42563.39.040 Bourgeois, André. René Boylesve et le problème de l'amour. Lille, 1950.
42563.89.30 Bourges, Elémir. Le crépuscule des dieux. Paris, 1950.
43544.106.100 Boutelleau, G. Ventriloques, roman. Paris, 1950.
43544.105.100 Boyer, François. The secret game. London, 1950.
43545.41.3100 Brencoutt, A. Le vert paradis. Paris, 1950.
43744.67.1180 Briand, C. Le secret de Marcel Proust. Paris, 1950.
37556.147 Bridenne, J.J. La littérature française d'imagination scientifique. Paris, 1950.
43823.75.2170 Bruller, Jean. Plus ou moins homme. Paris, 1950.
43823.75.2150 Bruller, Jean. Les yeux et la lumière. Paris, 1950.
43550.48.710 Calet, Henri. Young man of Paris. 1. ed. N.Y., 1950.
43550.58.160A Camus, Albert. Actuelles. Paris, 1950-58. 2v.
43550.58.140 Camus, Albert. Les justes. Paris, 1950.
43550.58.150 Camus, Albert. Le minotaure. Paris, 1950.
43550.58.721 Camus, Albert. The plague. N.Y., 1950.
43545.24.810 Carrouges, M. André Breton. 5. éd. Paris, 1950.
37574.425 Cassell's anthology of French poetry. London, 1950.
40597.2.305 Cazenove, M. Le drame de Balzac. Paris, 1950.
V43500.67 Chabaneix, Philippe. Les nocturnes. Lyon, 1950.
43552.4.2125 Char, René. Les matinaux. Paris, 1950.

Chronological Listing

1950 - cont.

40586.13.20 Chateaubriand, F.A.R. Atala. Paris, 1950.
40586.17.20 Chateaubriand, F.A.R. Journal de Jérusalem. Paris, 1950.
43552.6.130 Chateaubriant, Alphonse de. Écrits de l'autre rive. Paris, 1950.
43552.13.100 Chaulot, Paul. Comme un vivant. Paris, 1950.
40526.4.23 Chénier, André. Oeuvres complètes. Paris, 1950.
38524.120 Chesney, K. Fleurs de rhétorique. Oxford, 1950.
FL 398.12.2 Chevalier, Maurice. Ma route et mes chansons. Paris, 1950-57. 9v.
43552.25.2710 Chevallier, Gabriel. Mascarade. London, 1950.
43552.40.100 Chiha, Michel. Essais. v. 1-2. Beyrouth, 1950-
38514.60.180 Claneria, C. Le chevalier délibéré. Zaragoza, 1950.
37567.465 Clark, Mary Ursula. The cult of enthusiasm in French romanticism. Washington, 1950.
43554.2.725 Claudel, Paul. The eye listens. N.Y., 1950.
43554.2.430 Claudel, Paul. Une voix sur Israel. Paris, 1950.
40583.204 Clewes, Howard. Stendhal. London, 1950.
43556.1.720 Cocteau, Jean. Diary of a film. N.Y., 1950.
43556.1.806 Cocteau, Jean. Jean Cocteau. Bruxelles, 1950.
37562.276.10 Cohen, Gustave. Tableau de la littérature française médiévale. Paris, 1950.
43556.49.520 Colette, Sidonie Gabrielle. Chats [de Colette]. Paris, 1950.
43556.50.6100 Colin, Paul. Les jeux sauvages, roman. Paris, 1950.
42554.26.132 Corbière, Tristan. Les amours jaunes. Paris, 1950.
38575.75 Corneille, Pierre. Mélite. Lille, 1950.
38516.50 Currey, R.N. Formal spring. London, 1950.
43560.78.110 Curtis, Jean Louis. Haute ecole. Paris, 1950.
37548.210 Cuzacq, René. L'époque contemporaine. Mont-de-Marsan, 1950.
43565.60.150 Daniel-Rops, Henry. Where angels pass. London, 1950.
42576.65.13.108 Daoust, J. Les débuts bénédictins. Paris, 1950.
42555.44.91A Davies, Gardner. Les poèmes commémoratifs de Mallarmé. Thèse. Paris, 1950.
42555.44.90 Davies, Gardner. Les "Tombeaux" de Mallarmé. Paris, 1950.
43565.90.110 Davignon, Henri. Un penitent de Furnes. Paris, 1950.
40583.208 Debraye, H. Stendhal. Genève, 1950.
FL 6139.50 Derathé, Robert. Jean-Jacques Rousseau et la science politique de son temps. Thèse. Paris, 1950.
FL 6139.50.2 Derathé, Robert. Jean-Jacques Rousseau et la science politique de son temps. 1. éd. Paris, 1950.
41593.29.3.6 Desbordes-Valmore, Marceline. Poèmes choises. Paris, 1950.
40597.2.260 Descaves, Pierre. Les centjours de M. de Balzac. Paris, 1950.
42586.42.4 Desprez, Louis. Lettres inédites de Louis Desprez à Emile Zola. Thèse. Paris, 1950?
43566.82.7125 Destouches, Louis Ferdinand. Scandale aux Abysses. Paris, 1950.
39564.15.10 Diderot, Denis. Le nevue de Rameau. Genève, 1950.
39564.15.11 Diderot, Denis. Le nevue de Rameau. Thèse. Genève, 1950.
39564.8.7 Diderot, Denis. Pensées philosophiques. Genève, 1950.
40529.31.90 Dommanget, M. Sylvain Maréchal. Paris, 1950.
43573.89.110 Doucet, Jacques. La vue seconde. Paris, 1950.
42563.23.108 Dubois, E.T. Portrait of Léon Bloy. London, 1950.
43576.9.61 Du Bos, Charles. Lettres de Charles Du Bos et réponses de André Gide. Paris, 1950.
42568.19.21.14 Ducasse, I.L. Oeuvres complètes. Paris, 1950.
41538.160 Dumas, Alexandre. The wolf leader. Philadelphia, 1950.
37569.195 Dumay, R. Mort de la littérature. Paris, 1950.
43576.69.1100 Dupin, Jacques. Cendrier du voyage. Paris, 1950.
42576.15.200 Durry, M. Flaubert et ses projets inédits. Paris, 1950.
43576.87.100 Dutourd, Jean. Une tête de chien. Paris, 1950.
43545.24.830 Eigeldinger, Marc. André Breton. Neuchâtel, 1950.
43591.89.302 Eluard, Paul. Le dur désir de durer. Paris, 1950.
43591.89.301 Eluard, Paul. Le dur désir de durer. Philadelphia, 1950.
43591.89.310 Eluard, Paul. Tout dire. Paris, 1950.
43592.53.230 Emmanuel, Pierre. Car enfin je vous aime. Neuchâtel, 1950.
43592.53.705 Emmanuel, Pierre. The universal singular. London, 1950.
42556.28.145.5 Etiemble, René. Rimbaud. Paris, 1950.
V37575.791 Fischer, Jan O. Manifesty francouzských realisti XIX. a XX. století. Praha, 1950.
42576.35.35 Flaubert, Gustave. Letters. London, 1950.
42576.35.40 Flaubert, Gustave. Lettres inédites à Raoul Duval. Paris, 1950.
42576.28.85 Flaubert, Gustave. Madame Bovary. Harmondsworth, 1950.
43611.53.140 Fombeure, Maurice. Les étoiles brûlées. 4. éd. Paris, 1950.
43611.63.120 Fontaine, Anne. Le premier jour. Paris, 1950.
40597.2.285 Forest, H. L'esthétique du roman balzacien. Paris, 1950.
37596.9.80 Fotich, T. The narrative tenses in Chrestien de Troyes. Washington, 1950.
37569.184 Fowlie, W. Age of surrealism. N.Y., 1950.
43613.45.701 Frison-Roche, Roger. First on the rope. 1. American ed. N.Y., 1950.
37530.110 Fromm, H. Bibliographie deutscher Ubersetzungen. Baden-Baden, 1950-53. 6v.
41557.10.150 Galzy, J. George Sand. Paris, 1950.
43616.89.2100 Gautier-Vignal, Louis. Lyncée. Paris, 1950.
42555.44.92.5 Gengoux, J. Le symbolisme de Mallarmé. Paris, 1950.
42555.44.92 Gengoux, J. Le symbolisme de Mallarmé. Thèse. Paris, 1950.
42556.28.213 Gengoux, Jacques. La pensée poétique de Rimbaud. Paris, 1950.
42556.28.213.5 Gengoux, Jacques. La pensée poétique de Rimbaud. Thèse. Paris, 1950.
38512.125 Geoffroi de Paris. Six historical poems, written in 1314-1318. Chapel Hill, 1950.
43619.23.21 Ghelderode, Michel de. Théâtre. 5. éd. Paris, 1950. 5v.
43619.24.700 Ghéon, Henri. St. Anne and the gouty rector. 1. ed. N.Y., 1950.
43620.2.37.7 Gide, André. Les caves de Vatican. Paris, 1950.
43620.2.38.20 Gide, André. Corydon. 1. English ed. N.Y., 1950.
43620.2.79.95 Gide, André. If it die. London, 1950.
43620.2.52.10 Gide, André. Journal, 1942-1949. 57. éd. Paris, 1950.
43620.2.79.110 Gide, André. Littérature engagée. Paris, 1950.
43620.2.77A Gide, André. The school for wives. 1. ed. N.Y., 1950.
43620.2.79.125 Gide, André. Souvenirs de la cour d'assises. 14. éd. Paris, 1950.
43620.2.79.90 Gide, André. Two legends: Oedipus and Theseus. N.Y., 1950.
FL 6129.50.5 Gilliard, E. De Rousseau à Jean-Jacques. Lausanne, 1950.
43620.55.100 Gilson, Paul. Ballades pour fantômés. Paris, 1950.
43620.74.196 Giraudoux, Jean. The enchanted. N.Y., 1950.

1950 - cont.

37569.186 Gmelin, H. Der französische Zyklenroman der Gegenwart. Heidelberg, 1950.
37576.650.5 Goodyear, R.G. Two centuries of French short stories. London, 1950.
43626.70.100 Gracq, Julien. A dark stranger. N.Y., 1950?
43626.22.220 Green, Julien. Moïra. Paris, 1950.
43626.66.1132 Grosjean, Jean. Hypostases. 2e éd. Paris, 1950.
43626.74.100 Groussard, Serge. La femme sans passé. 83e éd. Paris, 1950.
41593.36.9 Guérin, Maurice de. Der Kentauer. Wiesbaden, 1950.
42555.2.20A Guichard, L. Jules Laforgue et ses poésies. Paris, 1950.
43550.58.810 Guido, B. Los dos Albertos en la novela contempóranea. Rosario, 1950.
42587.6 Guille, F.V. François-Victor Hugo et son oeuvre. Paris, 1950.
40516.60.80 Heine, Maurice. Le Marquis de Sade. Paris, 1950.
43632.50.130 Hellens, Franz. Testament. Paris, 1950.
37567.430 Hemmings, F.W.J. The Russian novel in France. London, 1950.
43632.61.2100 Henry, Fernand. Passages des oiseaux. Paris, 1950.
43566.82.7800 Hindus, M. Crippled giant. N.Y., 1950.
43545.22.800 Hogarth, H. Henri Bremond. London, 1950.
42578.31.88 Hommage à Jean Psichari. Paris, 1950.
38557.24.75 Hüppi, Beda. Versuch über den Stil Bossuets. Freiburg, 1950.
41573.18.20 Hugo, Victor. La légende des siècles. Paris, 1950.
41571.3.88 Hugo, Victor. Oeuvres choisies. Paris, 1950. 2v.
FL 383.150 Ihrig, G.P. Heroines in French drama of the romantic period. N.Y., 1950.
43652.46.150 Ikor, Roger. A travers nos déserts. Paris, 1950.
43757.50.1050 Ilbert, Werner. Traum und Tat. Halle, 1950.
43659.67.110 Isou, Isidore (pseud.). Les journeaux des dieux. Paris, 1950.
43659.67.100 Isou, Isidore (pseud.). Précisions sur ma poésie et moi. Paris, 1950.
43667.51.370 Jaloux, Edmond. La constellation. Genève, 1950.
43667.1.330 Jammes, Francis. Le poème d'ivonie et d'amour. Paris, 1950.
37567.436 Jean, Marcel. Genèse de la pensée moderne dans la littérature française. Paris, 1950.
43670.89.370 Jouhandeau, M. La ferme en folie. Paris, 1950.
43670.89.350 Jouhandeau, M. L'imposteur. Paris, 1950.
43670.89.360 Jouhandeau, M. Un monde. 4. éd. Paris, 1950.
38523.3.55 Jourda, Pierre. Marot, l'homme et l'oeuvre. Paris, 1950.
43670.94.135 Jouve, Pierre Jean. Ode. Paris, 1950.
40553.10.46 Kerchove, Arnold de. Benjamin Constant. Paris, 1950.
43673.83.280 Kessel, Joseph. Le tour du malheur. Paris, 1950. 4v.
37562.278 Ketcham, H. Nature in Old and Middle French poetry. Williamsport, Pa., 1950.
43677.66.120 Klossowski, Pierre. La vocation suspendue; roman. Paris, 1950.
38585.16.195.2 Knight, Roy Clement. Racine et la Grèce. Thèse. Paris, 1950.
FL 396.90.52.5 Kurtz, Maurice. Jacques Copeau. Paris, 1950.
38526.26.82 Labé, Louise Charly. Sonnets. Toronto, 1950.
38526.26.84 Labé, Louise Charly. The twenty-four love sonnets. London, 1950.
38526.26.78 Labé, Louise Charly. Die vierundzwanzig Sonette der Louïze Labé. Wiesbaden, 1950.
43687.14.115 Lacour, José André. Notre peau, mélodrame en 3 actes. Paris, 1950.
38544.27.63 La Fayette, Marie M. La Princesse de Clèves. Genève, 1950.
38544.27.65 La Fayette, Marie M. The Princesse de Cleves. London, 1950.
39527.42.5 La Fontaine, Jean de. Discours à Madame de la Sablière sur l'âme des animaux. Genève, 1950.
42563.18.230 Lalou, René. Maurice Barrès. Paris, 1950.
43687.56.100A La Mure, P. Moulin Rouge. N.Y., 1950.
FL 379.250 Lancaster, H.C. French tragedy in the time of Louis XV and Voltaire. Baltimore, 1950.
37575.690 La Nef. Almanach surréaliste du demi-siècle. Paris, 1950.
43687.61.100 L'Anselme, Jean. Cahier d'histoires naturelles. Paris, 1950.
43701.63.875 Laprade, Jacques de. Le théâtre de Montherlant. Paris, 1950.
43744.24.85 Lapsley, Mary. Jacques Prévert. N.Y., 1950.
43687.74.11 Larbaud, Valéry. Oeuvres complètes. Paris, 1950- 9v.
43687.80.700 Larthomas, P.H. Meeting. London, 1950.
38525.21.30A Lebègue, Raymond. Ronsard. Paris, 1950.
43688.7.11 Lebesque, Philéas. Oeuvres poetiques. Méru, 1950-52. 3v.
43667.78.800 Lebois, André. Alfred Jarry l'irremplaçable. Paris, 1950.
40583.132.5 Le Breton, André. Le rouge et le noir de Stendhal. Paris, 1950.
V43500.171 Le Cunff, Louis. Aux cent routes du Ponant. Paris, 1950.
V43500.175 Le Dantec, Yves Gérard. L'Éden futur. Paris, 1950.
FL 1022.10 Legge, Mary Dominica. Anglo-Norman in the cloisters. Edinburgh, 1950.
37567.111.20A Lehmann, Andrew G. The symbolist aesthetic in France. Oxford, 1950.
43688.82.100 Lesort, Paul André. The searcher of hearts. London, 1950.
39594.19.70 Loehring, Martin. Montesquieu. Wiesbaden, 1950.
Mol 612.19 Loiselot, J.L. De quoi vivait Molière. Paris, 1950.
39566.80 Loy, J.R. Diderot's determined fatalist. N.Y., 1950.
43697.14.145 MacOrlan, Pierre. Le bal du pont du Nord. 9. ed. Paris, 1950.
43697.14.220 MacOrlan, Pierre. Chanson de charme pour Faux-Nez. Paris, 1950.
37556.141 Magny, C.E. Histoire du roman français depuis 1918. Paris, 1950-
43697.37.1110 Mahélin, Yves. Six voyages sur une corde tendue. Paris, 1950.
42553.34.25 Maranón, Gregorio. Amiel. 7. ed. Madrid, 1950.
43554.9.30 Marcenac, J. La beauté du Diable racontée. Paris, 1950.
43752.57.845 Marclay, R. C.F. Ramuz et le Valais. Lausanne, 1950.
43780.5.820 Marseilles. Exposition. André Suarès. Catalogue de l'exposition André Suarès. Saint-Maur, 1950.
40583.37.10 Martineau, Henri. Le calendrier de Stendhal. Paris, 1950.
40583.37.15 Martineau, Henri. Nouvelles soirées du Stendhal-club. Paris, 1950.
43697.79.110 Mary, André. Forêteries. Paris, 1950.
43697.86.130 Masson, Loÿs. Icare; ou, Le voyage. Paris, 1950.
43697.88.2100 Maurel, Christian. Pont de l'étoile. Paris, 1950.
43744.67.994 Mauriac, F. Proust's way. N.Y., 1950.

1950 - cont.

43697.88.745 Mauriac, François. A kiss for the leper. London, 1950.

43744.67.107A Maurois, André. Proust. 1. ed. N.Y., 1950.

43744.67.106 Maurois, André. The quest for Proust. London, 1950.

42555.44.105 Mauron, Charles. Introduction à la psychanalyse de Mallarmé. Neuchâtel, 1950.

42514.28.78 Maurras, Charles. Le mont de saturne. n.p., 1950.

43697.100.20 Mazeline, Guy. Le roman des Jobourg. Paris, 1950- 5v.

42545.38.80A Melcher, Edith. The life and times of Henry Monnier. Cambridge, 1950.

43698.58.4100 Ménard, René. Hymnes à la présence solitaire. Paris, 1950.

43698.75.7100 Merle, Robert. Flamines. 2. éd. Paris, 1950.

43752.57.850 Mermod, H.L. Album C.F. Ramuz. Lausanne, 1950.

43698.200.150 Michaux, Henri. Passages, 1937-1950. Paris, 1950.

43698.200.710A Michaux, Henri. Selected writings. N.Y., 1950.

43699.12.2100 Michel, Simonne. Poèmes. Paris, 1950.

43701.1.30 Molaine, Pierre. Les orgues de l'enfer. Paris, 1950.

Mol 161.37 Molière, Jean Baptiste Poquelin. Amphitryon; comédie. Genève, 1950.

Mol 19.35.13 Molière, Jean Baptiste Poquelin. Théâtre de l'annee 1671. Paris, 1950.

Mol 713.20 Mongrédien, George. La vie privée de Molière. Paris, 1950.

39594.2.32 Montesquieu, C.L. de S. De l'esprit des lois. Paris, 1950- 2v.

39592.20 Montesquieu, C.L. de S. Oeuvres complètes. Paris, 1950. 3v.

43701.63.400 Montherlant, Henry de. Celles qu'on prend dans ses bras. 28e éd. Paris, 1950.

43701.63.380 Montherlant, Henry de. Notes sur mon théâtre. Paris, 1950.

43701.63.10 Montherlant, Henry de. Le théâtre complet. v.1-6. Neuchâtel, 1950-51. 3v.

FL 6139.49.5A Mornet, Daniel. Rousseau. Paris, 1950.

37555.123.2 Muller, A. La poésie religieuse catholique de Marot à Malherbe. Paris, 1950.

37555.123 Muller, A. La poésie religieuse catholique de Marot à Malherbe. Thèse. Paris, 1950.

43706.74.100 Ner, Henri. Jeanne d'Arc et sa mère. Paris, 1950.

41543.12.5 Nerval, Gerard de. Voyage en Orient. v.1-4. Paris, 1950. 2v.

Mon 170.28 Nicolai, Alexandre. Les belles amies de Montaigne. Paris, 1950.

43707.3.120 Nimier, Roger. Le hussard bleu. 30e éd. Paris, 1950.

43697.88.827 North, R.L. Le catholicisme dans l'oeuvre de François Mauriac. Paris, 1950.

42555.44.88A Noulet, E. L'oeuvre poétique de Stéphane Mallarmé. Paris, 1950.

43822.49.986 Noulet, Emilie. Paul Valéry. Bruxelles, 1950.

43738.1.240 Onimus, Jean. L'image dans Éve. Thèse. Paris, 1950.

38585.16.190 Orcibal, Jean. La genèse d'Esther et d'Athalie...Racine. Paris, 1950.

40542.13 Ozanam, Antoine F. Una peregrinación al país del Cid. Buenos Aires, 1950.

37556.21.6 Palfrey, T. Le Panorama littéraire de l'Europe. Evanston, 1950.

43737.74.3110 Parain, Brice. La mort de Socrate. Paris, 1950.

42576.57.85 Paris, Bibliothèque nationale. Pierre Loti. Paris, 1950.

40597.2.325 Paris. Bibliotheque nationale. Honoré de Balzac. Paris, 1950.

42545.3.545 Pasquier, Alexandre. Maurice Maeterlinck. Bruxelles, 1950.

37543.320 Paulhan, J. Les fleurs de tarbes, ou La terreur dans les lettres. 12. éd. Paris, 1950.

43738.1.75 Péguy, Charles. The mystery of the charity of Joan of Arc. N.Y., 1950.

43738.1.215 Péguy, M. Pourquoi Péguy fonda les "Cahiers". Paris, 1950.

43738.81.150 Perret, Jacques. Un homme perdu. Paris, 1950.

43738.97.1725 Peyrefitte, Roger. Special friendships. N.Y., 1950.

40597.2.340 Peytel, A. Balzac. Paris, 1950.

43741.13.110 Pichette, Henri. Lettres arc-en-ciel. Paris, 1950.

43741.13.130 Pichette, Henri. Le point vélique. Paris, 1950.

43741.13.120 Pichette, Henri. Rond-point. Paris, 1950.

41568.15.7 Pizzorusso, A. Sénancour. Messina, 1950.

40597.2.320 Ponceau, A. Paysages et destins balzaciens. Paris, 1950.

40539.15.13 Potocki, Jan. Rękopis znaleziony w Saragossie. Warszawa, 1950. 3v.

43632.3.89 Potuin, Damase. Le roman d'un roman. Québec, 1950.

43743.90.190 Pourrat, Henri. L'homme à la peau de loup. Neuchâtel, 1950.

43744.24.23.7 Prévert, Jacques. Paroles. Paris, 1950.

43744.41.4100 Priou, J.N. Jeux de massacre. Paris, 1950.

Htn 43744.67.54* Proust, Marcel. Le Balzac de Monsieur de Guermantes. Neuchâtel, 1950.

43744.67.58 Proust, Marcel. Letters. London, 1950.

43750.24.200 Queneau, Raymond. Batons. Paris, 1950.

43750.24.710 Queneau, Raymond. Pierrot. London, 1950.

37555.52.20 Raymond, Marcel. From Baudelaire to surrealism. N.Y., 1950.

42515.30.685 Renan, Ernest. La réforme intellectuelle et morale. Cambridge, 1950.

43753.58.2100 Renard, J.C. Haute-mer. Paris, 1950.

37571.75 Revel, Bruno. Introduzione alla letteratura francese. Milano, 1950- 3v.

Mon 128.6 Revel, Bruno. Verso un saggio di Montaigne. Varese, 1950.

42545.28.805 Richards, M.L. Le comique de Courteline. Montreal, 1950.

42545.28.805.2 Richards, M.L. Le comique de Courteline. Montreal, 1950.

42556.28.65 Rimbaud, Jean Arthur. Lettre du voyant. Paris, 1950.

FL 380.50 Rivoire, J.A. Le patriotisme dans le théâtre serieux de la révolution (1789-1799). Thèse. Paris, 1950.

43670.89.800 Rocle, Henri. Marcel Jouhandeau et ses personnages. Paris, 1950.

FL 6129.50 Roddier, Henri. Jean-Jacques Rousseau en Angleterre au XVIIIe siècle. Paris, 1950.

FL 6129.50.10 Roddier, Henri. Jean-Jacques Rousseau en Angleterre au XVIIIe siècle. Thèse principale. Paris, 1950.

43757.50.675 Rolland, Romain. Romain Rolland et la Belgique. Bruxelles, 1950.

Mol 618.7A Romano, D. Essai sur le comique de Molière. Berne, 1950.

43757.58.21 Rondeau-Luzeau, Lucie. Le livre du souvenir: Témoignage, 1914-1918. Paris, 1950?

43757.73.2100 Roques, René. Ici on est heureux. Paris, 1950.

38525.65.10 Rotrou, Jean de. Cosroès. Paris, 1950.

42555.44.94 Roulet, Claude. Nouveaux éléments de poétique mallarméenne. Neuchâtel, 1950.

39544.240 Roulet, L.E. Voltaire et les Bernois. Neuchâtel, 1950.

FL 6085.10 Rousseau, J.J. Le nouveau Dédale. 1. ed. Pasadena, Calif., 1950.

43757.92.2110 Rousselot, Jean. Le coeur bronzé. Paris, 1950.

V43500.259 Rousselot, Jean. Deux poèmes. Bruxelles, 1950.

V43500.267 Rousselot, Jean. Les moyens d'existence; poèmes. Limoges, 1950.

43761.39.725 St. Exupéry, A. de. The wisdom of the sands. N.Y., 1950.

43761.48.120 Salacrou, Armand. Poof. Paris, 1950.

43701.63.810 Sandelion, J. Montherlant et les femmes. Paris, 1950.

43761.56.110 Sandoz, Maurice Yves. The house without windows. London, 1950.

43761.56.100 Sandoz, Maurice Yves. On the verge. 1st ed. Garden City, 1950.

41522.18.355 Sartre, J.P. Baudelaire. Norfolk, 1950.

43761.78.750 Sartre, Jean Paul. Iron in the soul. London, 1950.

FL 377.86.5 Schérer, Jacques. La dramaturgie classique en France. Paris, 1950?

FL 377.86 Schérer, Jacques. La dramaturgie classique en France. Paris, 1950.

39544.225 Schilling, B.N. Conservative England and the case against Voltaire. N.Y., 1950.

43763.38.250 Schlumberger, Jean. Éveils. Paris, 1950.

43765.31.130 Ségalen, Victor. René Leys. Paris, 1950.

FL 6113.18 Sénelier, J. Bibliographie générale des oeuvres. Paris, 1950.

43765.80.700 Serge, Victor (pseud.). The case of Comrade Tulayer. 1. éd. Garden City, 1950.

38585.16.185 Siciliano, Italo. Racine. Padova, 1950.

39527.4.95 Siegfried, André. La Fontaine, machiavel français. Paris, 1950.

43769.54.750 Simenon, Georges. Maigret on holiday. London, 1950.

43769.54.717 Simenon, Georges. Poisoned relation. London, 1950.

43769.54.723 Simenon, Georges. The snow was black. 1. ed. N.Y., 1950.

43769.54.708 Simenon, Georges. Strange inheritance. London, 1950.

43701.63.870 Simon, P.H. Procés du héros. Paris, 1950.

43769.55.100 Simoncelly, Hermine. Le grand collège. Paris, 1950.

40525.36.5 Une soeur aînée d'Atala: Odérahi, histoire américaine. Paris, 1950.

37573.688 Southwell, K. Signposts in French literature. London, 1950.

43757.50.5 Starr, W.T. A critical bibliography of published writings of Romain Rolland. Evanston, Ill., 1950.

43779.24.100 Stéphane, R. Portrait de l'aventurier. Paris, 1950.

FL 6129.55 Stutzer, H. Jean-Jacques Rousseau und die Schweiz. Basel, 1950.

43780.5.140 Suarès, André. Minos et Pasiphoé. Paris, 1950.

43780.69.135 Supervielle, Jules. The colonel's children. London, 1950.

43780.69.260 Supervielle, Jules. Contes et poèmes. Edinburgh, 1950.

43780.69.290 Supervielle, Jules. Premiers pas de l'univers. Paris, 1950.

37574.573 Taylor, A.C. A book of French verse. 5. ed. Carlton 1950.

39586.19.10 Teppe, Julien. Chamfort; sa vie, son oeuvre, sa pensée. Paris, 1950.

43620.2.266A Thomas, L. André Gide. London, 1950.

42577.4.31.15 Thoraval, J. L'art de Maupassant. Paris, 1950.

42577.4.31.16 Thoraval, J. L'art de Maupassant. Thèse. Paris, 1950.

43792.93.100 Toursky, Alexandre. Christine. Paris, 1950.

37544.88 Trigon, Jean de. Histoire de la littérature enfantine. Paris, 1950.

42554.26.800 Trigon, Jean de. Tristan Corbière. Paris, 1950.

37562.11.10 Trofimoff, A. Poètes français avant Ronsard. Paris, 1950.

43793.67.200 Troyat, Henri. Étrangers sur la terre. Paris, 1950.

37556.143A Turnell, Martin. The novel in France. London, 1950.

38526.52.5 Tyard, Pontus. Le solitaire premier. Lille, 1950.

40597.2.330 U.N.E.S.C.O. Hommage à Balzac. Paris, 1950.

42555.44.98 Valéry, P. Écrits divers sur Stéphane Mallarmé. Paris, 1950.

43822.49.405 Valéry, Paul. Histoires brisées. Paris, 1950.

43822.8.50 Vaudoyer, Jean L. Italie retrouvée. Paris, 1950.

43667.51.805 Vaudoyer, Jean Louis. Discours de réception à l'Académie Française. Paris, 1950.

43537.6.95 Verbyts'kyi, P.P. Polum"ianyi propahandyst velykoho zhovtnia. Kharkiv, 1950.

43823.75.740 Vercel, Roger. The Easter fleet. N.Y., 1950.

43823.75.140 Vercel, Roger. La fosse aux vents. v.2. Paris, 1950.

43823.75.150 Vercel, Roger. Les 4 temps vus par les écrivains du demi-siècle. n.p., 1950.

42557.20.20A Verlaine, Paul. Confessions of a poet. London, 1950.

43824.6.150 Vigée, Claude. La lutte avec l'ange. Paris, 1950.

38514.20.29 Villon, François. Poems. London, 1950.

39544.27.28 Voltaire, François Marie Arouet de. Correspondance avec les Tondrin. Paris, 1950.

39544.27.3.9 Voltaire, François Marie Arouet de. Lettres inédites aux Tranchin. v.1,2-3. Genève, 1950. 2v.

39543.19 Voltaire, François Marie Arouet de. Romans et contes. Paris, 1950.

39544.27.25 Voltaire, François Marie Arouet de. Voltaire's England. London, 1950.

39545.27.10 Voltaire, François Marie Arouet de. Voltaire's micromégas. Princeton, 1950.

42576.63.158 Walton, L. Anatole France. Durham, 1950.

38524.110A Weinberg, B. Critical prefaces of the French renaissance. Evanston, Ill., 1950.

43833.41.110 Weingarten, Romain. Le théâtre de la chrysalide. Paris, 1950.

38537.25.185 Willcocks, M.P. The laughing philosopher. London, 1950.

43837.77.25 Wurmser, André. Un homme vient au monde. Paris, 1950. 8v.

1951

38514.175 Alisandre l'Orfelin. Alixandre l'Orphelin. Manchester, Eng., 1951.

37572.26.20 Angel, P. Lettres inédites sur l'inquiétude moderne. Paris, 1951.

43524.67.730 Anouilh, Jean. Antigone and Eurydice. London, 1951.

43524.67.720 Anouilh, Jean. Ardèle. London, 1951.

43524.67.280 Anouilh, Jean. L'invitation au château. Paris, 1951.

43526.65.103 Apollinaire, Guillaume. Lettres à sa marraine, 1915-1918. Paris, 1951.

37576.651 Arland, M. La prose française. Paris, 1951-

43528.48.260 Arland, Marcel. Lettres de France. Paris, 1951.

43530.5 Attal, J.P. Il y avait trois clowns. Paris, 1951.

Chronological Listing

1951 - cont.

43531.8.4120	Aubray, T. Un seul chemin. Paris, 1951.
43535.54.725	Aymé, Marcel. The second face. London, 1951.
43535.54.320	Aymé, Marcel. La Youirve. Paris, 1951.
43537.1.1030	Bailby, Léon. Souvenirs. Paris, 1951-
40597.47.5	Balzac, Honoré de. A bachelor's establishment. London, 1951.
40596.11.30	Balzac, Honoré de. Correspondance avec Zulma Carraud. 5. éd. Paris, 1951.
40597.35.81	Balzac, Honoré de. Le médecin de campagne. Paris, 1951.
FL 398.6.20.2	Barrault, J.L. Reflections on the theatre. London, 1951.
41522.12.13	Baudelaire, Charles. Pensées de Baudelaire. Paris, 1951.
42563.21.34	Bazin, René. Contes de bonne Perrette. Tours, 1951.
42545.3.525	Beachboard, R. Le théâtre de Maeterlinck aux États-Unis. 2. éd. Thèse. Paris, 1951.
43538.1.210	Béalu, Marcel. La pérégrination fantasque. Paris, 1951.
43538.14.140	Beckett, Samuel. Melone meurt. Paris, 1951.
43538.17.130	Bedel, Maurice. Le mariage des couleurs. 4. éd. Paris, 1951.
43538.74.140	Béraud, Henri. Quinze jours avec la mort. Paris, 1951.
FL 393.50	Bercy, Anne de. A Montmartre, le soir; cabarets et chansonniers d'Hier. Paris, 1951.
37569.40.80	Berger, P.C. Bilanz des Surrealismus. Caburg, 1951.
43538.91.100	Bérimont, Luc. Les mots germent la nuit. Paris, 1951.
43538.76.180	Bernanos, Georges. Un mauvais rêne. Paris, 1951.
42525.8.86	Bertin, G.M. L'essere e il nulla in Ernest Hello. 1. ed. Milano, 1951.
40582.13.55	Beyle, Henri. Lamiel. London, 1951.
40582.4.130	Beyle, Henri. Oeuvres complètes. Paris, 1951-56. 25v.
40582.7.40	Beyle, Henri. Stendhal par lui même. Paris, 1951.
43540.7.720	Bibescu, M.L. The sphinx of Bagatelle. London, 1951.
37567.450	Billy, André. L'époque 1900. Paris, 1951.
43540.3.35	Billy, André. Pudeur. Paris, 1951.
38543.22.20A	Bishop, Morris. The life and adventures of La Rochefoucauld. Ithaca, 1951.
43543.6.110	Blanchard, André. Petit bestiaire moral et fabuleux. Paris, 1951.
43543.8.150	Blanchot, Maurice. Au moment voulu. Paris, 1951.
43543.59.700	Blond, Georges. The plunderers. N.Y., 1951.
42563.23.17	Bloy, Léon. Pages. Paris, 1951.
37568.116	Boisdeffre, P. de. Métamorphose de la littérature. Paris, 1951. 2v.
42576.15.220	Bopp, Léon. Commentaire sur Madame Bovary. Neuchâtel, 1951.
42563.36.350	Bordeaux, Henry. Histoire d'une vie. Paris, 1951. 12v.
42577.4.35.4	Borel, Pierre. Le vrai Maupassant. Genève, 1951.
42566.16.115A	Bornecque, J.H. Les années d'apprentissage d'Alphonse Daudet. Paris, 1951.
43544.81.110	Bory, Jean Louis. Fragile. London, 1951.
43544.81.2135	Bosco, Henri. Hyacinthe. 19. éd. Paris, 1951.
43554.89.100	Bosquet, A. Syncopes. Paris, 1951.
43544.89.2100	Bosquet, Alain. Langue morte. Paris, 1951.
43544.89.2230	Bosquet, Alain. Syncopes. Paris, 1951.
38512.42.10	Bozon, Nicole. Seven more poems. N.Y., 1951.
37573.700	Bradley, R.F. Eight centuries of French literature. N.Y., 1951.
43545.4.4130	Brasillach, Robert. Les quatre jeudis. Paris, 1951.
38585.16.180	Brereton, G. Jean Racine. London, 1951.
37569.190	Breton, V.M.F. Claudel, Mauriac et Cie. Paris, 1951.
43545.89.3100	Bruckberger, R.M. The stork and the jewels. N.Y., 1951.
43823.75.2121	Bruller, Jean. Les ormes de la nuit et La puissance du jour. Paris, 1951.
43823.75.2205A	Bruller, Jean. Le silence de la mer. N.Y., 1951.
38527.29.20	Buffum, Imbrie. Agrippa d'Aubigné's Les tragiques. New Haven, 1951.
37574.740	Burt, P. Paris et ses poètes. Paris, 1951.
43550.19.110	Cadou, René Guy. Les biens de ce monde. Paris, 1951.
43550.58.700.5	Camus, Albert. The stranger. N.Y., 1951.
38539.2.30	Camus, Jean P. Agathonphile, récit de philargayrippe. Genève, 1951.
37567.196.14	Canat, René. L'Hellénisme des romantiques. v.1-2. Paris, 1951-53.
40583.142.5	Caraccio, Armand. Stendhal, l'homme et l'oeuvre. Paris, 1951.
38539.96	Cartigny, J. de. The wandering knight. Seattle, 1951.
43550.82.160	Cassou, Jean. Suite. Paris, 1951.
37556.145	Castex, Pierre. Le conte fantastique en Frnce de Nodier à Maupassant. Paris, 1951.
43552.1.130	Chabaneix, Philippe. Pour une morte. Gap, 1951.
43552.4.2160	Char, René. A une serenité crispée. Paris, 1951.
43552.4.2150	Char, René. Le soleil des eaux. Paris, 1951.
43552.5.106	Chardonne, Jacques. Oeuvres complètes. Paris, 1951- 6v.
43552.68.100	Charpentier, Gabriel. Les amitiés errantes. Paris, 1951.
40586.35.10	Chateaubriand, F.A.R. Lettre à M. de Fontanes sur la campagne romaine. Genève, 1951.
40586.20.20A	Chateaubriand, F.A.R. Les martyres de Dioclétien. Paris, 1951.
43552.6.115	Chateaubriant, Alphonse de. Lettres à la chrétienté mourante. Paris, 1951.
41522.18.230	Cladel, Judith. Maître et disciple. Paris, 1951.
43556.1.725	Cocteau, Jean. The human voice. London, 1951.
43556.1.72	Cocteau, Jean. Orphée. Paris, 1951.
FL 373.6.6	Cohen, Gustave. Histoire de la mise en scène dans le théâtre religieux français du Moyen Age. Paris, 1951.
37562.276.15	Cohen, Gustave. Littérature française du moyen âge. Bruxelles, 1951.
42555.44.86.2	Cohn, Robert G. L'oeuvre de Mallarmé. Paris, 1951.
43556.49.725.5	Colette, Sidonie Gabrielle. Cheri, and The last of Chéri. London, 1951.
43556.49.740	Colette, Sidonie Gabrielle. Creatures great and small. London, 1951.
43556.49.735	Colette, Sidonie Gabrielle. Short novels. N.Y., 1951.
43620.2.282	Combelle, L. Je dois à André Gide. Paris, 1951.
37574.426	Conder, Alan. A treasury of French poetry. N.Y., 1951.
40553.7.30	Constant de Rebecque, Benjamin. Cecile. Paris, 1951.
FL 1101.5	Coppe, Paul. Dictionnaire bio-bibliographique des littérateurs d'expression wallone, 1622 à 1950. Gembloux, 1951.
37543.460	Cordie, Carlo. Saggi e studi di letteratura francese. Padova, 1951.
43697.88.830	Cormeau, Nelly. L'art de François Mauriac. Paris, 1951.
37567.440	Cornell, William Kenneth. The symbolist movement. New Haven, 1951.
38575.23.100.10	Couton, Georges. Corneille et la Fronde. Clermont, 1951.

1951 - cont.

42536.26	Cresson, André. Hippolyte Taine. 1. éd. Paris, 1951.
37562.280	Crosland, J.R. The Old French epic. Oxford, 1951.
43560.78.710	Curtis, Jean Louis. The forests of the night. N.Y., 1951.
43560.78.130	Curtis, Jean Louis. Les forêts de la nuit. Paris, 1951.
40597.2.106.5	Curtius, E.R. Balzac. 2. Aufl. Bern, 1951.
37556.21.2	Dahl, F. Les débuts de la presse française. Göteborg, 1951.
43833.20.800	Davy, M.M. The mysticism of Simone Weil. London, 1951.
43566.10.100	Debû-Bredel, Jacques. Sous la cendre. Paris, 1951.
43566.49.110	Delétang-Tardif, Y. La nuit des temps. Paris, 1951.
V43500.81	Delétang-Tardif, Yanette. L'éclair et le temps. Limoges, 1951?
42555.44.92.10	Delfel, Guy. L'esthétique de Stéphane Mallarmé. Paris, 1951.
40515.5.35	D'Épinay, Louise F. Histoire de Madame de Montbrillant. 1. éd. Paris, 1951. 3v.
43620.2.274	Derais, F. L'envers du journal de Gide. Paris, 1951.
40597.2.610	Descaves, Pierre. Le president Balzac. Paris, 1951.
43554.2.920	Dessaintes, M. Paul Claudel et L'annonce faite à Marie. Bruxelles, 1951.
43568.4.110	Diamant-Berger, M. Poèmes d'Everlor. Paris, 1951.
39564.9.10	Diderot, Denis. Lettre sur les avengles. Genève, 1951.
39563.6	Diderot, Denis. Oeuvres. Paris, 1951.
39564.7.4	Diderot, Denis. Oeuvres romanesques. Paris, 1951.
39564.10.20	Diderot, Denis. Le rêve le d'Alembert. Paris, 1951.
39564.10.18	Diderot, Denis. Le rêve le d'Alembert. Thèse. Paris, 1951.
39566.95	Dieckmann, H. Inventaire du fonds vandeul et inédits de Diderot, Genève, 1951.
41557.10.170	Dolléans, E. George Sand. Paris, 1951.
43574.41.180	Drieu La Rochelle, Pierre. Récit secrèt. n.p., 1951.
41574.300	Drouet, J. Mille et une lettres d'amour à Victor Hugo. 4. éd. Paris, 1951.
43576.9.2100	Du Bouchet, André. Air. Paris, 1951.
43576.6.335	Duhamel, Georges. Cri des profondeurs. Paris, 1951.
43576.54.100	Dumaine, Philippe. Ame. Paris, 1951.
43576.54.110	Dumaine, Philippe. Arpents secrets. Villeneuve, 1951.
FL 386.805	Dussane, Beatrix. Notes de théâtre, 1940-1950. Lyon, 1951.
42515.35.82	Dussaud, R. L'oeuvre scientifique d'Ernest Renan. Paris, 1951.
43576.87.700	Dutourd, Jean. A dog's head. London, 1951.
38539.6.10	Du Vair, Guillaume. The moral philosophie of the Stoicks. New Brunswick, N.J., 1951.
43591.89.196	Éluard, Paul. Choix de poèmes. Paris, 1951.
43591.89.320	Eluard, Paul. La jarre peut-elle être plus belle que l'eau? Paris, 1951.
37574.545.5	Eluard, Paul. Première anthologie vivante de la poésie du passé. v..1-2. Paris, 1951.
43592.41.100	Émié, Louis. Romancero du profil perdu. Paris, 1951.
43592.53.260	Emmanuel, Pierre. Babel. Paris, 1951.
43592.69.100	Empeirikos, Alexandros. Poèmes inutiles. Genève, 1951.
42582.2.40	Escarch, R. Voyage à travers le monde vernien. Bruxelles, 1951.
43598.82.140	Estang, Luc. Cherchant qui devores. Paris, 1951.
42536.34.20	Eustis, A.A. Hippolyte Taine and the classical genius. Berkeley, 1951.
40597.2.375	Evans, Henri. Louis Lambert et la philosophie de Balzac. Paris, 1951.
37569.189	Evnina, E.M. Literatura frantsuzskogo soprotivleniia. Moskva, 1951.
Mol 606.10	Fabre, Émile. Notre Molière. Paris, 1951.
38554.326.110	Fénelon, F. de S. de la Mothe. Dialogues on eloquence. Princeton, 1951.
42575.21.15	Feydeau, Ernest. Mémoires d'une jeune fille de bonne famille. Paris, 1951.
40583.339	Fischer, Jan O. Stendhal, první soudce kapitalismu. Praha, 1951.
FL 6049.18	Flores d'Arcais, G. Il problema pedagogico nell'Emilio di G.G. Rousseau. Padova, 1951.
39544.255	Flowers, Ruth C. Voltaire's stylistic transformation of Rabelaisian satirical devices. Washington, 1951.
V43500.121	Fourcade, Claude. Magie de septembre. Paris, 1951.
42576.62.22.40	France, Anatole. The gods are athirst. London, 1951. 2v.
40583.214	François-Poncet, Andre. Stendhal in Braunschweig. Mainz, 1951.
43613.45.710	Frison-Roche, Roger. The grand crevasse. 1. American ed. N.Y., 1951.
42556.28.217	Fusero, C. Vita e poesia di Rimbaud, Milano, 1951.
37567.452	Gandon, Y. Cent ans de jargon. Paris, 1951.
43616.79.110	Gascar, Pierre. Le visage clos. Paris, 1951.
40586.28.64	Gautier, Jean Maurice. L'exotisme américain dans l'oeuvre de Chateaubriand. Manchester, 1951.
43709.89.800	Genevieve. Collection Doucet. Catalogue de l'exposition Germain, nouveau, 1851-1951. Paris, 1951.
43617.77.110	Germain, Andre. La bourgeosée qui brûle. Paris, 1951.
43619.25.100	Gheorghiu, Georges. Livre du nouveau Job. Paris, 1951.
43620.2.79.105	Gide, André. The counterfeiters. 1. ed. N.Y., 1951.
43620.2.79.77	Gide, André. Et nunc manet in te. Neuchâtel, 1951.
43620.2.79.115	Gide, André. The immoralist. N.Y., 1951.
43620.2.37.4	Gide, André. Lafcadio's adventures. N.Y., 1951.
43620.2.47.10	Gide, André. Les nourritures terrestres et les nouvelles nourritures. Paris, 1951.
43620.2.79.130	Gide, André. The secret drama of my life. Paris, 1951.
43620.55.110	Gilson, Paul. Poèmes. Paris, 1951.
43620.66.370	Giono, Jean. Accompagnés de la flute. Perigneux, 1951.
43620.66.360.5	Giono, Jean. Les grands chemins. 23. éd. Paris, 1951.
43620.66.355	Giono, Jean. Le hussard sur le toit. 32. éd. Paris, 1951.
43620.74.470	Giraudoux, Jean. La française et la France. Paris, 1951.
40516.20.10	Godard d'Aucour, Claude. Themidor. Heidenheim, 1951.
43625.19.275	Godoy, Armand. Colloque de la joie. 3e éd. Paris, 1951.
43625.19.300	Godoy, Armand. Les sept jours de la rose. Paris, 1951.
43738.1.800	Goldie, R. Vers un héroïsme intégral dans la lignée de Péguy. Paris, 1951.
43625.49.140	Goll, Claire. Les larmes pétrifiées. Paris, 1951.
FL 371.80	Goodman, H.P. Original elements in the French and German Passion plays. Thesis. Bryn Mawr, Pa., 1951.
43576.9.815	Gouhier, Marie Anne. Charles Du Bos. Paris, 1951.
38527.100	Graces de la Bugne. Le roman des deduis. Karlshamn, 1951.
43626.70.130	Gracq, Julien. La littérature à l'estomac. Paris, 1951.
43626.70.120	Gracq, Julien. Le rivage des syrtes. Paris, 1951.
43626.22.730	Green, Julien. Moïra. London, 1951.
42554.49.17	Gregh, F. L'age d'Airain; souvenirs 1905-25. Paris, 1951.
43626.74.110	Groussard, Serge. Talya. 4e éd. Paris, 1951.
43628.2.5	Guastalla, P.R. Journal, 1940-44. Paris, 1951.

1951 - cont.

43620.2.272	Guerard, Albert Joseph. André Gide. Cambridge, 1951.
41574.290	Guillemin, H. L'humour de Victor Hugo. Neuchâtel, 1951.
43697.89.845	Guiry, S. La pensée d'André Maurois. Paris, 1951.
40597.2.202	Guyon, Bernard. La création littéraite chez Balzac. Paris, 1951.
37594.19.15	Henri d'Andeli. Le lai d'Aristote. Paris, 1951.
37558.150.5	Henriot, Émile. Portraits de femmes d'Héloise à Katherine Mansfield. Paris, 1951.
43576.6.850	Héron de Villefosse, A. Chronique de Paris. Paris, 1951.
42576.15.58	Herval, René. Les véritables origine de "Madame Bovary". Paris, 1951.
43744.67.1175	Holdane, C.F. Marcel Proust. London, 1951.
V43500.133	Hommage à Max Jacob, avec des inedits de Max Jacob, et la collaboration de Jean Cassou. Bordeaux, 1951.
37556.149	Hubert, R.R. The Dreyfus affair and the French novel. Thesis. Cambridge, Mass., 1951.
41571.16.25	Hugo, Victor. Les misérables. Paris, 1951.
41572.24.40	Hugo, Victor. Pierres. Genève, 1951.
41574.14.20	Hugo, Victor. Victor Hugo par lui-même. Paris, 1951.
43638.55.100	Humeau, E. L'épreuve au soleil. Paris, 1951.
43643.23.2100	Ibels, J.C. Le péril de vivre. Paris, 1951.
43667.14.65	Jacob, Max. Les cahiers Max Jacob. v.1-5. Paris? 1951-
43667.14.64	Jacob, Max. Lettres à un ami; correspondance 1922-1937. Paris, 1951.
37530.120A	Jaffe, A.H. Bibliography of French literature in American magazines in the 18th century. East Lansing, 1951.
37573.255	Jan, E. von. Classicisme français. Leipzig, 1951.
43667.78.700	Jarry, Alfred. Ubu roi. London, 1951.
Mol 247.19	Jasinski, René. Molière et le misanthrope. Paris, 1951.
37555.175	Jones, Percy Mansel. The background of modern French poetry. Cambridge, Eng., 1951.
43670.1.70	Jouglet, René. Les paysans. Paris, 1951.
43670.89.460	Jouhandeau, M. De l'abjection. Paris, 1951.
43670.89.390	Jouhandeau, M. Éloge de la volupté. Paris, 1951.
43670.89.590	Jouhandeau, M. Léonora; ou Dangers de la vertu. Paris, 1951.
43670.89.430	Jouhandeau, M. Portraits de famille. Paris, 1951.
43670.93.100	Jourdan. Midi à mes portes. Paris, 1951.
43673.78.100	Kerchove, Arnold de. N. poèmes. Paris, 1951.
38585.16.195	Knight, Roy Clement. Racine et la Grèce. Paris, 1951.
42587.52.90	Knodel, A.J. Jules Renard as critic. Berkeley, 1951.
42577.4.32.20	Lacassagne, J. Guy de Maupassant et son Mal. Lyon, 1951.
38544.27.66	La Fayette, Marie M. The Princess of Cleves. N.Y., 1951.
FL 386.177	Lalou, René. Le théâtre en France depuis 1900. Paris, 1951.
43544.81.2800	Lambert, Jean. Un voyageur des deux mondes. Paris, 1951.
V43500.153	Lamireau, Gilbert. Traduit du sang. Limoges, 1951?
43687.63.100	Langevin, André. Crade de la nuit. Montreal, 1951.
43687.71.110	Laporte, René. Le gant de fer et le gant de velours. Paris, 1951.
43687.80.710	Larthomas, P.H. Solitaire. Boston, 1951.
42576.15.225	Laumet, Lucien. La sensibilité de Flaubert. Alençon, 1951.
43687.89.1700	Laurent, Jacques. Goribon's folly. London, 1951.
40556.35.20	Laurent, Jules. Joseph de Maistre. Monte-Carlo, 1951.
43688.5.5140	Léautaud, Paul. Entretiens avec Robert Mallet. 18e éd. Paris, 1951.
37563.78.5	Lebègue, Raymond. La poésie française de 1560 à 1630. v.1-2. Paris, 1951.
43688.61.210	Lenormand, Henri René. Renée. N.Y., 1951.
43688.61.220	Lenormand, Henri René. Troubles. Paris, 1951.
39566.97	Les Cahiers Haut-Marnais. Cahier Diderot. Chaumont, 1951.
43690.90.2100	Lévis Mano, Guy. Il n'y a pas plus solitaire que la nuit. Paris, 1951.
38551.137	Little, Katherine D. François de Fénelon. N.Y., 1951.
37598.10	Livingstone, C.H. Le jongleur Gautier le leu. Cambridge, 1951.
FL 6039.15	Lo Gatto Napolitano, M. Il contratto sociale di Gian Giacomo Rousseau. Napoli, 1951.
42563.23.114	Lory, M.J. La pensée religieuse de Léon Bloy. Thèse. Bruges, 1951.
43694.8.100	Lubin, Armen. Sainte patience. 4. éd. Paris, 1951.
41578.155	Lucas-Dubreton, Jean. Lamartine. Paris, 1951.
42555.43.27	Mallarmé, Stéphane. Poems. N.Y., 1951.
42545.38.90	Marash, J.G. Henry Monnier. London, 1951.
43697.74.3100	Marceau, Félicien. Capri. 9. ed. Paris, 1951.
43697.74.3162	Marceau, Félicien. Chair et cuir. 2. ed. Paris, 1951.
43697.75.125	Marcel, Gabriel. Rome n'est plus dans Rome. Paris, 1951.
43620.2.288	Marill, R. L'odyssée d'André Gide. Paris, 1951.
43697.76.7110	Marker, C. The forthright spirit. London, 1951.
38523.11	Marot, Clément. Les chansons de Clément Marot. Paris, 1951.
38523.12.3	Marot, Clément. Oeuvres complètes. Paris, 1951?
38514.70.5	Martial de Paris. Les arrêts d'amour. Paris, 1951.
43620.2.286	Martin du Gard, Roger. Notes sur André Gide. Paris, 1951.
37595.93	Mary, André. La fleur de la poésie française depuis les origines jusqu'à la fin du XV siècle. Paris, 1951.
42514.28.80	Massis, H. Maurras et notre temps. v.1-2. Paris, 1951.
43697.84.100	Masson, R. Oranges vertes. Paris, 1951.
41542.4.80.10	Matoré, G. Le vocabulaire de la prose littéraire de 1833 à 1845. Thèse. Genève, 1951.
41542.4.80A	Matoré, G. Le vocabulaire et la société sous Louis-Philippe. Genève, 1951.
42577.4.28.55	Maupassant, Guy de. Correspondance inédite. Paris, 1951.
43620.2.278	Mauriac, Claude. Conversations avec André Gide. Paris, 1951.
37543.294.5	Mauriac, F. Men I hold great. N.Y., 1951.
43697.88.440	Mauriac, François. Le feu sur la terre. Paris, 1951.
43697.88.12	Mauriac, François. Oeuvres complètes. Paris, 1951- 12v.
43697.88.400	Mauriac, François. Le sagouin. Paris, 1951.
43697.88.750	Mauriac, François. That which was lost. London, 1951.
43697.89.430	Maurois, André. Ce que je crois. Paris, 1951.
43697.89.11	Maurois, André. Oeuvres complètes. Paris, 1951. 16v.
43697.89.735	Maurois, André. The return of doctor O'Grady. London, 1951.
42514.28.30	Maurras, Charles. Tragi-comédie de ma surdité. Aix-en-Provence, 1951.
39566.90	May, Georges C. Quatre visages de Denis Diderot. Paris, 1951.
43698.25.725	Meersch, M. van der. The bellringer's wife. London, 1951.
43698.25.160	Meersch, M. van der. Corps et ames. Paris, 1951.
43620.74.865	Meister, G. Gesalt und Bedeutung. Diss. Rorschoch, 1951.
37563.83	Mélanges d'histoire littéraire de la renaissance offerts à Henri Chamard. Paris, 1951.

1951 - cont.

39544.186.3	Meyer, A.E. Voltaire. London, 1951.
43698.200.200F	Michaux, Henri. Mouvements. Paris, 1951.
43699.75.100	Miracle, Anne. Poèmes et leurs dessina. Paris, 1951.
Mol 205.25	Molière, Jean Baptiste Poquelin. L'estourdi, ou Les contretemps. Lille, 1951.
42514.27.10	Mondor, Henri. Eugène Lefébure. 8. éd. Paris, 1951.
43744.67.1190	Monnin-Hornung, J. Proust et la peinture. Genève, 1951.
Mon 28.60	Montaigne, Michel de. Montaigne par lui-même. Paris, 1951.
Mon 28.50.5	Montaigne, Michel de. Trois essais. Paris, 1951.
39594.2.34	Montesquieu, C.L. de S. Vom Geist der Gesetze. n.p., 1951. 2v.
43701.63.745	Montherlant, Henry de. The master of Santiago. 1st American ed. N.Y., 1951.
43701.63.410	Montherlant, Henry de. La ville dont le prince est un enfant. 37. éd. Paris, 1951.
38526.10.8.17	Müller, A. Un poète religieux du XVIe siècle. Paris, 1951.
38526.10.8.17.2	Müller, A. Un poète religieux du XVIe siècle. Thèse. Paris, 1951.
40553.7.27	Murry, J.M. The conquest of death. London, 1951.
43707.3.100	Nimier, Roger. Amour et néant. 2e éd. Paris, 1951.
43538.76.830	Nostitz, I. von. Georges Bernanos. Speyer, 1951.
43620.2.284	Nouvelle Revue Française. Hommage à André Gide. Paris, 1951.
42584.25.180	Nowakowski, Jan. Spór o Zolę zu Polsce. Wrocław, 1951.
43620.2.270	Painter, G.D. André Gide. London, 1951.
39566.12.5A	Paris. Bibliothèque nationale. Diderot et l'encyclopédie. Paris, 1951.
43737.89.1100	Paulhan, Jean. Les causes célèbres. Paris, 1951.
37557.76.10	Paulhan, Jean. Petite préface à toute critique. Paris, 1951.
V43500.237	Pédoja, Marcel. Flamme rouge. Blainville-sur-Mer, 1951.
43761.39.830	Pellissier, G. Les cinq visages de St. Exupéry. Paris, 1951.
43738.81.110	Perret, Jacques. Bande à part. Paris, 1951.
41522.18.270	Peyre, Henri. Connaissance de Baudelaire. Paris, 1951.
43738.97.1110	Peyrefitte, Roger. Les ambassades. Paris, 1951.
43738.97.1700	Peyrefitte, Roger. Diplomatic conclusions. Paris, 1951.
39534.36.25	Phelps, N.F. The queen's invalid. Baltimore, 1951.
43740.1.55	Philippe, Charles Louis. Bubu of Montparnasse. N.Y., 1951.
37574.560	Les poètes de la Commune. Paris, 1951.
43743.90.200	Pourrat, Henri. Le chasseur de la nuit. Paris, 1951.
42515.44.35A	Powers, Richard H. Edward Quinet. Dallas, 1951.
43752.57.855	Présence de Ramuz. Haute-Savoie, 1951.
43744.24.50	Prévert, Jacques. Grand bal du printemps. Lausanne, 1951.
43744.24.65	Prévert, Jacques. Spectacle. 46. éd. Paris, 1951.
40522.9.65	Prévost, Antoine F. Manon Lescaut. Harmondsworth, 1951.
39533.20.25	Pujos, Charles. Le double visage de Cyrano de Bergerac. Agen, 1951.
43750.27.100	Queneau, J. Adieu chansons. Paris, 1951.
43750.24.210	Queneau, Raymond. Le dimanche de la vie. 13. éd. Paris, 1951.
38536.31	Rabelais, F. Gargantua. Paris, 1951.
38583.3.20	Racine, Jean. Oeuvres complètes. Paris, 1951.
38583.6.30	Racine, Jean. Théâtre. Paris, 1951-52. 5v.
43524.67.805	Radine, S. Anouilh, Lenormand, Salacrou. Genève, 1951.
43752.57.285	Ramuz, Charles Ferdinand. Besoin de grandeur. Lausanne, 1951.
43752.57.270	Ramuz, Charles Ferdinand. Chant de notre Rhône. Lausanne, 1951.
43752.57.787	Ramuz, Charles Ferdinand. Die Geschichte vom Soldaten. Zürich, 1951.
43752.57.132	Ramuz, Charles Ferdinand. La guérison des maladies. Lausanne, 1951.
43761.39.840	Rauch, Karl. Antoine de St. Exupéry. 2. Aufl. Esslinger, 1951.
43753.99.1100	Rebatet, L. Les deux étendards. 18. éd. Paris, 1951. 2v.
43738.1.220	Reclus, M. Le Péguy que j'ai connu. Paris, 1951.
38523.3.60	Regius, Karl. Untersuchungen zum Übersetzerstil Clément Marots. Diss. Scwarzenbach, 1951.
43757.50.1167	Relgis, Eugen. Romain Rolland. Montevideo, 1951.
Mon 128.5	Renart, F. Zigzags dans les parterres de Montaigne. Paris, 1951.
43753.59.100	Rendinger, C.M. Eutretiens de Chevremont. Paris, 1951.
41543.22.45	Rhodes, Solomon. Gerard de Nerval. N.Y., 1951.
43756.13.110	Richer, C. Ti-Coyo and his shark. London, 1951.
37556.195	Roger, Georges. Situation du roman régionaliste français. Paris, 1951.
43757.49.100	Rolin, Dominique. Les enfants pérdus. Paris, 1951.
43757.50.43	Rolland, Romain. Inde. Paris, 1951.
43757.50.30	Rolland, Romain. Richard Strauss et Romain Rolland. Paris, 1951.
43822.49.1160	Romain, W.P. Paul Valéry. Paris, 1951.
43757.3.215	Romains, Jules. La douceur de la vie lithographie originale de Heuze. Paris, 1951.
38525.20.60	Ronsard, Pierre de. Le second livre des amours. Genève, 1951.
43757.82.700	Rossi, J.B. The false start. London, 1951.
FL 6042.51	Rousseau, J.J. Émile. 16. éd. Paris, 1951.
37543.243.15	Rousseaux, André. Le monde classique. 3. série. Paris, 1951.
43757.92.2140	Rousselot, Jean. Les papiers. Paris, 1951.
43757.93.700	Roussin, André. The little hut. London, 1951.
43761.39.835	Roy, Jules. Passion de St. Exupéry. Paris, 1951.
43554.2.915	Ryan, Mary. Introduction to Paul Claudel. Dublin, 1951.
37543.312	Sage, Pierre. Le bon prêtre dans la littérature française d'Amadis de Gaule au Génie du christianisme. Genève, 1951.
43761.78.755	Sartre, Jean Paul. Troubled sleep. 1st American ed. N.Y., 1951.
38526.7.45	Saulnier, V.L. Du Bellay. Paris, 1951.
41539.36	Saunders, E. The prodigal father. London, 1951.
39534.32.4.5	Scarron, Paul. Le roman comique. v.1-2. Paris, 1951.
43763.36.2100	Schehadé, Georges. Monsieur Bob'le. 4. éd. Paris, 1951.
Mon 129.5	Sclafert, C. L'ame religieuse de Montaigne. Paris, 1951.
43765.80.120	Serge, Victor (pseud.). Mémoires d'un révolutionnaire, 1901-1941. Paris, 1951.
42556.33.10	Severin, F. Poèmes. Paris, 1951.
42576.15.215	Seznec, Jean. Flaubert à l'exposition de 1851. Oxford, 1951.
43769.54.745	Simenon, Georges. The heart of a man. 1. American ed. N.Y., 1951. 2v.
43769.54.415	Simenon, Georges. Quarante-cinq degrés à l'ombre. Paris, 1951.

Chronological Listing

1951 - cont.

43769.54.775 Simenon, Georges. The strangers in the house. London, 1951.
37569.40.200 Simon, P.H. L'homme en procès. 3. ed. Neuchâtel, 1951.
38551.112 Société historique et archéologique du Périgord, Périgueux. III centenaire de la naissance de Fénelon. Périgueux, 1951.
37543.324 Sofer, Johann. Die Antike in der französischen Geistesgeschichte. Wien, 1951.
37596.106.5 Sponsus. Le Sponsus. 1. éd. Paris, 1951.
43780.5.61 Suarès, André. Correspondance. 2. éd. Paris, 1951.
43780.69.320 Supervielle, Jules. Boire à la source. Paris, 1951.
43780.69.310 Supervielle, Jules. Naissances. Paris, 1951.
43780.69.710 Supervielle, Jules. The survivor. London, 1951.
43576.91.800 Taffel, Abram. The prose fiction and dramatic works of Henri Duvernois. N.Y., 1951.
43785.75.110 Tardieu, Jean. Monsieur. Paris, 1951.
43788.5.125 Tharaud, Jérôme. La double confidence. Paris, 1951.
38526.49.2 Théophile de Viau. Oeuvres poétiques. Genève, 1951. 2v.
38585.16.200 Tielrooy, J.B. Jean Racine. Amsterdam, 1951.
40546.20.10 Tocqueville, Alexis de. Oeuvres. Paris, 1951-53. 15v.
43793.42.715 Triolet, Elsa. The white horse. London, 1951.
43793.67.700A Troyat, Henri. My father's house. N.Y., 1951.
43793.67.210 Troyat, Henri. La tête sur les épaules. Paris, 1951.
37556.143.5 Turnell, Martin. The novel in France. N.Y., 1951.
43822.50.110 Vailland, Roger. Un jeune homme seul. Paris, 1951.
43822.49.735 Valéry, Paul. Dance and the soul. London, 1951.
43822.49.710.3 Valéry, Paul. Monsieur Teste. London, 1951.
43822.49.722 Valéry, Paul. Reflections on the world today. London, 1951.
42581.33.35 Vallès, Jules. La rue à Londres. Paris, 1951.
43822.74.100 Varasteh, Khosro. Rapsodie persane, roman. Paris, 1951.
42557.19.150F Verwey, Albert. Twee portretten van Paul Verlaine. Amsterdam, 1951.
43824.3.170 Vialar, Paul. L'éperon d'Argent. Paris, 1951.
43824.7.100 Victor, P.E. Poèmes esquimaux. Paris, 1951.
43824.6.100 Vigée, Claude. Avent. Paris, 1951.
38585.16.205 Vinaver, E. Racine et la poésie tragique. Paris, 1951.
39543.18 Voltaire, François Marie Arouet de. Choix de contes. Cambridge, Eng., 1951.
37548.155 Weber-Perret, M. Écrivains romands 1900-1950. Lausanne, 1951.
43833.20.20 Weil, Simone. Cahiers. Paris, 1951- 3v.
43833.98.100 Weygand, J. Légionnaire. Paris, 1951.
Htn 43852.89.120* Yourcenar, Marguerite. Mémoires d'Hadrien. Paris, 1951.
42563.18.300 Zarach, Alphonse, Bibliographie barrésienne, 1881-1948. Paris, 1951.
43699.51.805 Zidonis, G.I. Oscar Vladislas de L. Milosz. Paris, 1951.
42584.23.85 Zola, Emile. Piping hot. N.Y., 1951.

1952

40588.72 Académie...Chambery. Xavier de Maistre. Chambéry, 1952.
43512.75.200 Achard, Marcel. Le moulin de la galette. Paris, 1952.
43526.65.860 Adéma, Marcel. Guilleaume Apollinaire le mal-aime. Paris, 1952.
40583.160.5 Alciatore, J. Stendhal et Helvetius. Genève, 1952.
42562.60 Allais, Alphonse. Littéralement. Paris, 1952.
38551.130 Amis des lettres, Paris. Fénelon et son temps. Paris, 1952.
40586.20.55 Andlau, Beatrix. Chateaubriand et Les martyrs. Thèse. Paris, 1952.
38539.2.65 Angers, J.E. Du stoicisme chrétien à l'humanisme chrétien. Meaux? 1952.
43524.67.750 Anouilh, Jean. Colombe. London, 1952.
43524.67.740 Anouilh, Jean. Legend of lovers. N.Y., 1952.
43524.67.760 Anouilh, Jean. Thieves carnival. London, 1952.
43524.67.115 Anouilh, Jean. La valse des toréadors. Paris, 1952.
37573.702 Anthologie de la poésie française depuis le surréalisme. Paris, 1952.
37574.755 Anthologie 52. Paris, 1952.
43526.65.220 Apollinaire, Guillaume. Casanova. Paris, 1952.
43526.65.155 Apollinaire, Guillaume. Le guetteur melancolique. Paris, 1952.
43526.65.250 Apollinaire, Guillaume. Tendre comme le souvenir. Paris, 1952.
43526.65.230 Apollinaire, Guillaume. Textes inédits. Genève, 1952.
41574.294 Aragon, L. Hugo. Paris, 1952.
43528.48.125 Arland, Marcel. La consolation du voyageur. Paris, 1952.
43528.48.205 Arland, Marcel. Essais et nouveaux essais critique. Paris, 1952.
43528.61.150 Arnoux, Alexandre. Les crimes innocents. Paris, 1952.
43528.86.69 Artaud, Antonin. Lettres d'Antonin Artaud à Jean-Louis. Paris, 1952.
38527.22.3 Aubigné, Théodore Agrippa d'. Le printemps. Genève, 1952.
43531.18.1110 Audiberti, Jacques. Marie Dubois. 2. éd. Paris, 1952.
43535.54.735 Aymé, Marcel. Clérambard. London, 1952.
43535.54.730 Aymé, Marcel. The house of men. London, 1952.
43535.54.250 Aymé, Marcel. La tête des autres. Paris, 1952.
43535.54.740 Aymé, Marcel. The wonderful farm. London, 1952.
37563.85 Bailly, A. La vie littéraire sous la renaissance. Paris, 1952.
43544.41.100 Baisdeffre, Pierre de. Les fins dernieres. Paris, 1952.
40597.2.360 Balzac, le livre du centenaire. Paris, 1952.
42557.20.260A Barnecque, J.H. Études verlainiennes. Paris, 1952. 2v.
43537.77.5110 Baroche, Jacques. Chants d'amour. Paris, 1952.
42555.6.80 Barquissau, R. Le poète Lacaussade et l'exotisme tropical. Paris, 1952.
41522.13.14 Baudelaire, Charles. Baudelaire par lui-même. Paris, 1952.
41522.13.8.40 Baudelaire, Charles. Les fleurs du mal. London, 1952.
41522.13.8.96 Baudelaire, Charles. Poems. London, 1952.
43537.99.120 Bazin, Hervé. Lève-toi et marche. Paris, 1952.
43538.1.225 Béalu, Marcel. Ocarina. Paris, 1952.
43538.1.480 Beauvoir, Simone de. America day by day. London, 1952.
43538.14.120 Beckett, Samuel. En attendant Godot. Paris, 1952.
43822.49.1152 Bémol, Maurice. Variations sur Valéry. Sarrebruck, 1952. 2v.
43538.5.100 Benda, Julien. Mémoires d'infra-tombe. Paris, 1952.
43538.61.81 Benoît, Pierre. Le prêtre Jean. Paris, 1952.
43538.90.100 Berl, Emmanuel. Sylvia. 13. éd. Paris, 1952.
43538.76.760 Bernanos, Georges. The fearless heart. London, 1952.
43538.77.7100 Berson, Simone. Les rencontres imaginaires. Paris, 1952.
42578.30.85 Bertholet, E. La pensée et les secrets du Sâr Joséphin Peladan. Neuchatel, 1952. 4v.

1952 - cont.

40582.13.57 Beyle, Henri. Lamiel. Norfolk, 1952.
40582.3.25.2 Beyle, Henri. Romans et nouvelles. Bottin, 1952. 2v.
40582.6.5 Beyle, Henri. To the happy few; selected letters. London, 1952.
43540.7.112 Bibescu, M.L. Catherine-Paris. Genève, 1952.
43540.7.105 Bibescu, M.L. La vie d'une amitié. Paris, 1952. 3v.
42584.25.225 Bibliothèque Nationale, Paris. Emile Zola. Paris, 1952.
41571.5.19 Bibliothèque nationale, Paris. Victor Hugo. Paris, 1952.
40575.5.132A Billy, A. Sainte-Beuve. Paris, 1952- 2v.
43543.14.100 Bloch-Michel, J. La fuite en Egypte. 7. éd. Paris, 1952.
43543.59.710 Blond, Georges. Goddess Island. London, 1952.
42563.23.28 Bloy, Léon. Lettres intimes. Paris, 1952.
37574.735 Boase, A.M. The poetry of France from André Chénier to Pierre Emmanuel. London, 1952.
43544.19.100 Boden, Paul. Les amants du Theil. Paris, 1952.
43697.52.815A Boisdeffre, O. de. André Malraux. Paris, 1952.
43544.58.100 Bonaparte, Marie. A la memoire des disparus. London, 1952.
43544.81.120 Bory, Jean Louis. Un Noël à la Tyrolienne. Paris, 1952.
43544.81.2125 Bosco, Henri. Antonin. 31. éd. Paris, 1952.
43544.89.2112 Bosquet, Alain. La grande éclipse. 7. éd. Paris, 1952.
V43500.39 Bouhier, Jean. De mille endroits. Paris, 1952.
43544.108.100 Boulle, Pierre. Le pont de la rivière Kwai. Paris, 1952.
41557.10.180 Boury, F. De quoi vivait George Sand. Paris, 1952.
41574.292A Boussel, P. De quoi vivait Victor Hugo. Paris, 1952.
43544.107.100 Boutron, Michel. Hans. London, 1952.
43545.4.4150 Brasillach, Robert. Lettres écrites en prison. Paris, 1952.
43545.24.210 Breton, André. Entretiens 1913-1952. 7. éd. Paris, 1952.
42584.25.250 Brown, Calvin S. Repetition in Zola's novels. Athens, Georgia, 1952.
43545.89.3130 Bruckberger, R.M. Golden goat. N.Y., 1952.
43545.89.3110 Bruckberger, R.M. One sky to share. N.Y., 1952.
43823.75.2160 Bruller, Jean. Les animaux dénaturés. Paris, 1952.
42557.14.65 Bruneau, C. Verlaine. Paris, 1952.
FL 6129.52 Burgelin, Pierre. La philosophie de l'existence de Jean-Jacques Rousseau. Paris, 1952.
FL 6129.52.2 Burgelin, Pierre. La philosophie de l'existence de Jean-Jacques Rousseau. Thèse. Paris, 1952.
43550.19.100 Cadou, René Guy. Hélène, ou Le règne végétal. Paris, 1952-53. 2v.
43550.1.33 Carco, Francis. L'homme traqué. Saverne, 1952.
43550.82.170 Cassou, Jean. La rose et la vin. Paris, 1952.
43701.63.820 Castay, Marcel. Les heritiers de la couronne. Paris, 1952.
41564.55.85 Castex, Pierre. Vigny. Paris, 1952.
43744.67.1200 Castro, C. Marcel Proust. Madrid, 1952.
43744.67.1205 Cattaui, Georges. Marcel Proust. Paris, 1952.
43550.98.210 Cayrol, Jean. Les mots sont aussi des demeures. Neuchâtel, 1952.
43550.98.160 Cayrol, Jean. Le vent de la memoire, roman. Neuchâtel, 1952.
41574.308 Celarie, H. Victor Hugo amoureux. Paris, 1952.
43551.59.220 Cendrars, Blaise. Blaise Cendrars vous parle. Paris, 1952.
43551.80.100 Cesbron, Gilbert. Les saints vont en enfer. Paris, 1952.
FL 397.87 Cézan, Claude. Le Grenier de Toulouse tel que je l'ai on. Toulouse, 1952.
42515.17 Champagne, Paul. Nouvel essai sur Octane Pirmez. Gembloux, 1952.
43552.3.8100 Champigny, Robert. Dépôt. Paris, 1952.
43552.3.9230 Chamson, André. On ne voit pas les coeurs. 6e éd. Paris, 1952.
43552.4.2200 Char, René. La paroi et la prairie. Paris, 1952.
43552.4.2700 Char, René. Poems. Roma, 1952.
43552.5.1175 Chartier, Emile. Propos d'un Normand. Paris, 1952. 5v.
43545.24.840 Chastre, V. André Breton. n.p., 1952.
43552.18.100 Chédid, Andrée. Le sommeil délivré. 8e éd. Paris, 1952.
37569.40.197 Chiare, Joseph. Contemporary French poetry. Manchester, 1952.
40517.44.10A Choderlos de Laclos, Pierre A.F. Dangerous acquaintances. Norfolk, Conn., 1952.
37596.10.2.25 Chrestien de Troyes. Romans. Paris, 1952. 4v.
43822.49.1290 Christensen, Alfred. Paul Valéry. Oslo, 1952.
43554.4.2100 Clappier, L. Festung Königsberg. Köln, 1952.
43554.2.412 Claudel, Paul. The correspondence, 1899-1926 between Paul Claudel and André Gide. N.Y., 1952.
43554.2.11 Claudel, Paul. Oeuvres complètes. Paris, 1952-53. 26v.
43554.2.435 Claudel, Paul. La ravissement de Scapin. n.p., 1952.
43556.1.380.5 Cocteau, Jean. Bacchus; pièce en trois actes. 14e éd. Paris, 1952.
43556.1.390 Cocteau, Jean. Le chiffre sept. Paris, 1952.
43556.1.62 Cocteau, Jean. Opéra. Paris, 1952.
43556.49.320 Colette, Sidonie Gabrielle. Gigi. N.Y., 1952.
43556.49.745 Colette, Sidonie Gabrielle. Julie de Carneilhan. London, 1952.
38562.23.35 Consentini, John W. Fontenelle's art of dialogue. N.Y., 1952.
40553.7.30.2 Constant de Rebecque, Benjamin. Cecile. London, 1952.
40553.9.60 Constant de Rebecque, Benjamin. Journaux intimes. Paris, 1952.
40553.9.5 Constant de Rebecque, Benjamin. Lettres à Bernadotte. Genève, 1952.
38575.85 Corneille, Pierre. The chief plays of Corneille. Princeton, 1952.
43556.82.712 Cossery, Albert. The lazy one. London, 1952.
43556.82.710 Cossery, Albert. The lazy ones. N.Y., 1952.
39566.100 Crocker, L.G. Two Diderot studies. Baltimore, 1952.
43556.49.750 Crottet, R. Stranded in heaven. London, 1952.
43560.78.700 Curtis, Jean Louis. Lucifer's dream. London, 1952.
43744.67.966 Curtius, E.R. Marcel Proust. Berlin, 1952.
37568.118 Curtius, Ernst R. Französischen Geist im zwanzigsten Jahrhundert. Bern, 1952.
43560.90.110 Cuvelier, F. Psycalè. Bruxelles, 1952.
FL 375.84 Dabney, Lancaster Eugene. French dramatic literature in the reign of Henri IV. Austin, Texas, 1952.
43565.89.100 Daumal, René. Le mont analogue. 2. éd. Paris? 1952.
42555.39.1195 Davignon, Henri. Charles van Lerberghe et ses amis. Bruxelles, 1952.
39544.28.3 Delattre, A. Répertoire chronologique des lettres de Voltaire. Chapel Hill, 1952.
FL 397.34.25 Delucinge, Edmond. Grenoble et son théâtre, de Molière à nos jours. Grenoble, 1952.

Chronological Listing

1952 - cont.

38525.22.45.90	Desonay, F. Ronsard. Bruxelles, 1952. 3v.
37548.180	Desonay, Fernand. Cinquante ans de littérature Belge. Bruxelles, 1952.
43566.82.7112	Destouches, Louis Ferdinand. Voyage au tout de la nuit. 3. éd. Paris, 1952.
43566.93.705	Devaulx, N. Sainte Barbegrise. 5. éd. Paris, 1952.
42556.28.225	Dhôtel, A. Rimbaud. 5. éd. Paris, 1952.
42556.28.225.2	Dhôtel, A. Rimbaud et la révolte moderne. 2. éd. Paris, 1952.
43567.79.100	Dhôtel, André. Bernard le paresseux. 5. ed. Paris, 1952.
39564.7.20A	Diderot, Denis. Textes choisis. v.1-3, 6. Paris, 1952- 4v.
43822.49.1170	Doisy, M. Paul Valéry. Paris, 1952.
43573.76.40	Dorgelès, Roland. Portraits sans retouche. Paris, 1952.
43573.98.41	Doyon, René L. Mémoire d'homme. Paris, 1952.
Mon 114.7.5	Dréano, M. La renommée de Montaigne en France au XVIII siècle. Angers, 1952.
Mon 114.12	Dresden, Samuel. Montaigne, de spelende wijsgeer. Leiden, 1952.
43574.75.710	Druon, Maurice. The rise of Simon Lachaume. 1. ed. N.Y., 1952.
43576.6.725	Duhamel, Georges. Patrice Periot. London, 1952.
41538.53.60	Dumas, Alexandre. The three musketeers. Harmondsworth, 1952.
41578.130	Dumont, F. De guoi vivait Lamartine. Paris, 1952.
37577.35	Dupee, F.W. Great French short novels. N.Y., 1952.
43576.74.2140	Duras, Marguerite. Le marin de Gibraltar. Paris, 1952.
43576.74.2100	Duras, Marguerite. The seawall. N.Y., 1952.
43576.87.110	Dutourd, Jean. Au bon beurre. Paris, 1952.
41522.18.240	Eigeldinger, Marc. Le platonisme de Baudelaire. Neuchâtel, 1952.
43591.89.315	Éluard, Paul. Le phénix. Paris, 1952.
43591.89.198	Éluard, Paul. Poèmes pour tous. Paris, 1952.
43591.89.22	Éluard, Paul. Selected writings. London, 1952.
40597.2.246	Emery, Leon. Balzac en sa création. Lyon, 1952?
41574.505	Escande de Messières, R. Le journal de l'exil d'Adèle Hugo. N.Y., 1952.
43599.41.110	Étiemble, René. Hygiène des lettres. Paris, 1952-55. 4v.
42556.28.145.8	Étiemble, René. Le mythe de Rimbaud. v.1,2,5. 2e éd. Paris, 1952. 3v.
43606.10.41	Fabre-Luce, Alfred. Journal 1951. Paris, 1952.
40532.38	Filippini, F. Figaro. n.p., 1952.
43609.83.700	Fisson, Pierre. No memorial. London, 1952.
42576.16.60	Flaubert, Gustave. L'oeuvre de Flaubert. Paris, 1952.
42576.16.62	Flaubert, Gustave. Oeuvres. Paris, 1952. 2v.
43611.53.110	Fombeure, Maurice. Les patron-minet. Paris, 1952.
43611.63.130	Fontaine, Anne. Par-dessus la haie. Paris, 1952.
43552.5.1810	Foulquie, P. Alain. Paris, 1952.
V43500.117	Fourcade, Claude. Du côté de l'aurore. Paris, 1952.
42563.18.235	Frandon, I.M. L'orient de Maurice Barrès. Genève, 1952.
42563.18.236	Frandon, I.M. L'orient de Maurice Barrès. Paris, 1952.
37543.314	The French mind. Studies in honour of Gustave Rudler. Oxford, 1952.
42584.25.185	Freville, J. Zola, semeur d'orages. Paris, 1952.
43613.45.720	Frison-Roche, Roger. The lost crevasse. London, 1952.
43613.45.740	Frison-Roche, Roger. The lost trail of the Sahara. 1. American ed. N.Y., 1952.
43697.52.810A	Frohock, W.M. André Malraux and the tragic imagination. Stanford, 1952.
37575.700F	Galtier-Bossière, Jean. Anthologie de la poésie argotique. Paris, 1952.
43616.60.120	Ganne, Gilbert. Interviews impubliables. Paris, 1952.
43616.64.100	Garnier, Christine. White people smile at me. London, 1952.
38527.42.20	Garnier, Robert. La troade antigone. Paris, 1952.
43616.78.140	Gary, Romain. Les couleurs du jours. 7. éd. Paris, 1952.
43617.78.12A	Genêt, Jean. Oeuvres complètes. Paris, 1952. 4v.
43617.59.130	Genevoix, Maurice. L'aventure est en nous. Paris, 1952.
FL 362.40	Germain, F. Une tragédie. v.1-2. Paris, 1952?
43619.24.710	Ghéon, Henri. The comedian. London, 1952.
43619.24.730	Ghéon, Henri. The marriage of St. Francis. London, 1952.
43619.24.720	Ghéon, Henri. The marvellous history of St. Bernard. London, 1952.
43619.24.230	Ghéon, Henri. Oedipe. Paris, 1952.
43620.2.79.135.5	Gide, André. Ainsi soit-il, ou Les jeux sont faits. 31. éd. Paris, 1952.
43620.2.38.25	Gide, André. Corydon. London, 1952.
43620.2.79.150	Gide, André. Et nunc manet in te and Intimate journal. London, 1952.
43620.2.71	Gide, André. Lettres à un sculpteur. Paris, 1952.
43620.2.79.155	Gide, André. Logbook of the coiners. London, 1952.
43620.2.79.140	Gide, André. Madeleine. N.Y., 1952.
43620.2.79.120A	Gide, André. My theater. 1. American ed. N.Y., 1952.
43620.2.37.6	Gide, André. The Vatican cellars. London, 1952.
43620.66.380	Giono, Jean. Le Moulin de Pologne. Paris, 1952.
43620.74.480.5	Giraudoux, Jean. Les contes d'un matin. 4. éd. Paris, 1952.
43620.74.490	Giraudoux, Jean. Visitations. Paris, 1952.
43788.41.800	Glauser, A. Albert Thibaudet et la critique créatrice. Paris, 1952.
43757.50.1070A	Grappin, P. Le bund neues Naterland. Lyon, 1952.
43626.66.1150	Grosjean, Jean. Le livre du juste. Paris, 1952.
38526.19.5	Groulot, Arsène. Arsène Groulot. Torino, 1952. 2v.
42554.49.55	Guaita, Stanislas de. Lettres inédites de Stanislas de Guaita. Neuchâtel, 1952.
43628.23.145	Guéhenno, Jean. Voyages. Paris, 1952.
43628.41.3140	Guillevic, Eugène. Terre à bonheur. Paris, 1952.
43628.42.130	Guilloux, Louis. Absent de Paris. 7. éd. Paris, 1952.
37597.42.20A	Gunn, A.M.F. The mirror of love. Lubbock, Texas, 1952.
37574.565	Hackett, C.A. Anthology of modern French poetry. Oxford, 1952.
41522.18.245	Hamelin, Jacques. La réhabilitation judiciaire de Baudelaire. Paris, 1952.
40553.10.55	Hasselrot, Bengt. Nouveaux documents sur Benjamin Constant et Mme de Staël. Copenhague, 1952.
37542.42	Hatzfeld, H. Literature through art. N.Y., 1952.
41574.306	Hawana. Oficina del Histanador de la Cuidad. Homenaje a Victor Hugo. La Habana, 1952.
43632.50.110	Hellens, Franz. Mélusine. Paris, 1952.
43632.50.120	Hellens, Franz. Una. Paris, 1952.
43822.49.1140	Henry, Albert. Language et poésie chez Paul Valéry. Paris, 1952.
43620.2.280	Herbart, P. A la recherche d'André Gide. 13. éd. Paris, 1952.

1952 - cont.

38575.23.108	Herland, Louis. Horace. Paris, 1952.
43703.80.800	Hommage à Vincent Muselli. Hommage à Vincent Muselli. Paris, 1952.
43524.67.809	Hoogland, C. Den briljante Anouilh. Stockholm, 1952.
41573.7	Hugo, Victor. Avez-vous lu Victor Hugo? Paris, 1952.
41573.33.5	Hugo, Victor. Les orientales. Paris, 1952. 2v.
41574.13.20	Hugo, Victor. Souvenirs personnels. Paris, 1952.
42576.65.13.116	Huysmans et l'abbé Mugnier à Saint-Thomas d'Aquin. Coulommiers? 1952.
43667.1.842	Inda, J.P. Francis Jammes. Lyon, 1952.
43667.1.843	Inda, J.P. Francis Jammes. Thèse. Lyon, 1952.
43667.1.840A	Inda, J.P. Francis Jammes du faune au patriache. Thèse. Lyon, 1952.
43667.51.245	Jaloux, Edmond. Essences. Paris, 1952.
43667.78.140	Jarry, Alfred. L'amour absolu. Paris, 1952.
43544.82.800	Jean de Boschère. Paris, 1952.
41522.18.235	Jones, Percy Mancell. Baudelaire. Cambridge, 1952.
41522.18.250	Jouanne, R. Baudelaire et Poulet-Malassis. Alençon, 1952.
43670.89.380	Jouhandeau, M. Nouveau bestiaire. 2. éd. Paris, 1952.
43670.95.120	Jouvet, Louis. Témoignages sur le théâtre. Paris, 1952. 2v.
37568.120	Kanters, R. Des écrivains et des hommes. Paris, 1952.
38585.16.250	Knight, Roy Clement. Racine, convention and classicism. Swansea, 1952.
43617.78.800	Konkel, M.H. Sister René Fernantat. Washington, 1952.
37557.46	Krafft, J.G. Essai sur l'ésthétique de la prose. Paris, 1952.
38564.32.33	La Bruyère, J. de. Les caractères. v.1-2. Paris, 1952.
41595.2.10	Lacenaire, Pierre François. Memoirs. London, 1952.
42586.57.85	Lagrange, André. L'art de Fromentin. Paris, 1952.
FL 6139.52	Lama, E. Rousseau. Milano, 1952.
V43500.151	Lamireau, Gilbert. La clef de voûte. Paris, 1952.
43687.74.200	Larbaud, Valéry. Gaston d'Ercoule. Paris, 1952.
43687.87.140	La Tour du Pin, Patrice de. La vie recluse en poésie. Paris, 1952.
43687.89.1100	Laurent, Jacques. Neuf perles de culture. 19e éd. Paris, 1952.
42547.22.100	Lebais, A. Villiers de l'Isle Adam. Neuchâtel, 1952.
38537.25.215	Lebègue, R. Rabelais. Tübingen, 1952.
43744.67.996	Le Bidois, Robert. L'inversion du sujet dans la prose contemporaine. Paris, 1952.
43744.67.996.2	Le Bidois, Robert. L'inversion du sujet dans la prose contemporaine. Thèse. Paris, 1952.
42563.89.80	Lebois, André. Les tendences du symbolisme à travers l'oeuvre d'Elémir Bourges. Thèse. Paris, 1952.
43744.67.1210	Le Disque Vert. Hommage à Marcel Proust. Bruxelles, 1952.
40516.60.86	Lély, Gilbert. Vie du Marquis de Sade. 2. éd. Paris, 1952.
43688.61.720	Lenormand, Henri René. The rising. London, 1952.
42555.39.1100	Lerberghe, C. van. La chanson d'Eve. Paris, 1952.
37543.345	Leroy, Jules. Saint-Germain-des Prés. Paris, 1952.
FL 397.111.10	Lilar, Suzanne. Soixante ans de théâtre belge. Bruxelles, 1952.
43620.2.294	Lime, M. Gide. Paris, 1952.
37567.448	Lion, F. Der französische Roman in neunzehnten Jahrhundert. Stendhal, 1952.
FL 398.42.15	Lipnitzky, Haim E.B. Images de Louis Jouvet. Paris, 1952.
43556.49.820A	Loos, Anita. Gigi. N.Y., 1952.
40597.9.15	Lotte, F. Dictionnaire biographique des personnages fictifs de La Comédie humaine. Paris, 1952.
43738.76.800	Louis Pergaud. Besançon, 1952?
42544.36.20	Loyson, Paul H. Mystique du liberalisme. Paris, 1952.
40597.2.355	Lukács, G. Balzac und der Französische Realismus. Berlin, 1952.
43550.58.815	Luppé, Robert de. Albert Camus. Paris, 1952.
43697.14.310	MacOrlan, Pierre. Picardie; roman. Paris, 1952.
42546.8.80	Maes, Pierre. Georges Rodenbach. Gembloux, 1952.
42555.43.40	Mallarmé, Stéphane. Igitur ou La folie d'Elbehnon. 7. éd. Paris, 1952.
43697.2.2100	Mallet, Robert. Amour mot de passe. Paris, 1952.
43697.2.1700	Mallet-Joris, Françoise (pseud.). The illusionists. N.Y., 1952.
43697.52.145	Malraux, André. La voie royale. Paris, 1952.
43697.52.720	Malraux, André. The walnut trees of Altenburg. London, 1952.
40597.2.565	Mancisidor, José. Balzac. México, 1952.
43709.23.820	Manoll, Michael. Marie Noël. Paris, 1952.
V43500.189	Manoll, Michel. Louisfert-en-poesie. Vitry-sur-Seine, 1952.
43697.74.3110	Marceau, Félicien. L'homme du roi. 4. ed. Paris, 1952.
43697.75.160	Marcel, Gabriel. Les coeurs avides. Paris, 1952.
43697.75.700	Marcel, Gabriel. A man of God. London, 1952.
43620.2.276A	March, H. Gide and the Hound of Heaven. Philadelphia, 1952.
40583.212	Martineau, Henri. Le coeur de Stendhal. Paris, 1952. 2v.
37543.294.10	Mauriac, F. Great men. London, 1952.
43697.88.430	Mauriac, François. Galigaï. Paris, 1952.
43697.88.765	Mauriac, François. The knot of vipers. London, 1952.
43697.88.60	Mauriac, François. Lettres ouvertes. Monaco, 1952.
43697.88.760	Mauriac, François. The little misery. London, 1952.
43697.88.770A	Mauriac, François. The loved and the unloved. N.Y., 1952.
43697.88.755	Mauriac, François. The weakling and the enemy. N.Y., 1952.
43697.89.432	Maurois, André. Ce que je crois. Paris, 1952.
41557.10.165	Maurois, André. Lélia. 80. éd. Paris, 1952.
39544.124.20	Maurois, André. Voltaire. London, 1952.
42514.28.35	Maurras, Charles. La balance interieure. 3. éd. Lyon, 1952.
42514.28.40	Maurras, Charles. Le guignon français. Roanne, 1952.
43697.98.50	Mayran, Camille (pseud.). Larmes et lumière à Oradour. Paris, 1952.
V43500.195	Menanteau, Pierre. Le cheval de l'aube. Paris, 1952.
43698.58.4120	Ménard, René. La terre tourne. Paris, 1952.
41555.7.190	Mérimée, Prosper. Une amitié littéraire. Paris, 1952.
39566.105	Mesnard, P. Le cas Diderot. Paris, 1952.
37567.715	Michaud, Guy. Le romantisme. Paris, 1952.
43698.200.170	Michaux, Henri. Nouvelles de l'étranger. Paris, 1952.
43556.1.810	Millecam, J.P. L'étaile de Jean Cocteau. Monaco, 1952.
42556.28.251	Miller, Henry. Rimbaud. Lausanne, 1952.
43699.61.100	Minne, Jules. Séve bantoue. Bruxelles, 1952.
Mol 172.9	Molière, Jean Baptiste Poquelin. The burgher in purple. St. Albans, 1952.
Mol 115.1	Molière, Jean Baptiste Poquelin. Dzieła. Warszawa, 1952. 6v.
43701.63.440	Montherlant, Henry de. Le fichier parisien. Paris, 1952.

Chronological Listing

1952 - cont.

43703.80.190 Muselli, Vincent. Les douze pas des muses. Paris, 1952.
37568.126 Nadeau, M. Littérature présente. Paris, 1952.
43769.54.800 Narcejac, T. The art of Simenon. London, 1952.
37543.322 Nathan, J. La littérature et les écrivains. Paris, 1952?
41543.4.5 Nerval, Gerard de. Oeuvres. Paris, 1952. 2v.
37543.308.10 Neubert, Fritz. Studien zur vergleichenden Literaturgeschichte. Berlin, 1952.
43707.3.700 Nimier, Roger. The blue Hussar. London, 1952.
43709.80.170 Nourissier, François. La vie parfaite. Paris, 1952.
43552.5.1800A Nouvelle Revue Française. Hommage a Alain. Paris, 1952.
43688.7.11.1 Oeuvres poétiques. Méru, 1952?
43737.36.100 Paulhan, Jean. L'aveuglette. Paris, 1952.
43738.1.68.25 Péguy, Charles. Jeanne d'Arc. Paris, 1952.
43738.1.19 Péguy, Charles. Pages choisies. Paris, 1952.
43738.1.54 Péguy, Charles. Par ce demi-clair matin. Paris, 1952.
43738.76.2024 Périer, Odilon Jean. Poèmes. 4e éd. Paris, 1952.
43833.20.810 Perrin, J.M. Simone Weil. Paris, 1952.
37569.185 Pesis, B.A. Frantsuzskaia progressivnaia literatura v bor'be za mir i demokratiiu. Moskva, 1952.
43738.97.160 Peyre, Joseph. Guadalquivir. Paris, 1952.
43741.13.140 Pichette, Henri. Nucléa. Paris, 1952.
43741.24.3100 Pierre, Henri. Les carnets blancs. Poèmes. Genéve, 1952-67. 3v.
43620.2.105.5 Pierre-Quint, L. André Gide. 15. éd. Paris, 1952.
43741.59.3180 Pinget, Robert. Mahu. Paris, 1952.
43620.2.292 Planche, H. Le problème de Gide. Paris, 1952.
43743.60.130 Ponge, Francis. L'Araignée. Paris, 1952.
43743.60.140 Ponge, Francis. La rage de l'expression. Lausanne, 1952.
43743.61.100 Potier, André. Un français à l'école americaine. Paris, 1952.
37565.124 Poulet, Georges. Études sur le temps humain. Paris, 1952- 4v.
43743.98.440 Pozner, Vladimir. Qui a tuè H.O. Burrell? Paris, 1952.
43620.2.300 Prétexte. Cahier André Gide. Bruxelles, 1952.
43744.24.40 Prévert, Jacques. Guignal. Lausanne, 1952.
43744.24.55 Prévert, Jacques. Lettre des Iles Baladar. Paris, 1952.
40522.9.35 Prévost, Antoine F. Histoire du chevalier des Grieux et de Manon Lescaut. Paris, 1952.
37569.205 Prévost, J.L. Le prêtre. 3. éd. Paris, 1952.
37567.446 Priddin, Deirdre. The art of the dance in French literature. London, 1952.
43744.67.48 Proust, Marcel. Jean Santeuil. 19. éd. Paris, 1952. 3v.
43750.20.700 Queffélec, Henri. Island priest. 1. ed. N.Y., 1952.
43750.24.220 Queneau, Raymond. Si tu t'imagines. 13. éd. Paris, 1952.
38536.32 Rabelais, F. Pantagruel. Paris, 1952.
38585.20.13 Racine, Jean. Athalie. Paris, 1952.
43752.18.12A Radiguet, Raymond. Oeuvres complètes. Paris, 1952.
37555.52.17 Raymond, Marcel. De Baudelaire au surréalisme. Paris, 1952.
Htn 43753.58.1110* Renaitour, Jean Michel. Robert Le Pieux. Paris, 1952.
43698.25.810 Reus, Robert. Portrait morpho-psychologique de Maxence van der Meersch. Aurillac, 1952.
43753.99.5700 Reynolds, P. When and if. N.Y., 1952.
41543.22.47 Rhodes, Solomon. Gerard de Nerval, 1808-1855. London, 1952.
43756.14.100 Ricquebourg, F. Hai-Kaï d'Indochine. Paris, 1952.
42556.28.84 Rimbaud, Jean Arthur. The drunken boat. London, 1952.
42556.28.19.10 Rimbaud, Jean Arthur. Poésies. Paris, 1952.
37596.10.170 Ritchie, R.L.G. Chrétien de Troyes and Scotland. Oxford, 1952.
42584.25.420 Robert, Guy. Emile Zola. Paris, 1952.
42584.25.415 Robert, Guy. La terre d'Emile Zola. Paris, 1952.
42584.25.416 Robert, Guy. La terre d'Emile Zola. Thèse. Paris, 1952.
43757.12.150 Roblès, Emmanuel. La vérité est morte. Paris, 1952.
43757.50.41A Rolland, Romain. Le cloître de la rue d'Ulm. Paris, 1952.
43757.50.680 Rolland, Romain. Journal des années de guerre. Paris, 1952.
43757.3.299 Romains, Jules. Jules Romains. Paris, 1952.
37543.316 Romains, Jules. Saints de notre calendrier. Paris, 1952.
43757.3.280 Romains, Jules. Tussles with time. London, 1952.
38525.16.10 Ronsard, Pierre de. Les odes. Paris, 1952.
42546.13.20 Rostand, Edmond. Cyrano de Bergerac. Milano, 1952.
43757.83.2100 Rostand, Jean. Page d'un moraliste. Paris, 1952.
43757.83.65 Rostand, Maurice. La lettre à Dieu. Paris, 1952.
Htn FL 6094.20* Rousseau, J.J. Les rêveries du promeneur solitaire. Paris, 1952.
43757.96.140 Roy, Claude. Le parfait amour. Paris, 1952.
43757.96.4110 Roy, Jules. Beau sang. Paris, 1952.
43758.70.100 Rupied, J. Élysée, 1928-34. Paris, 1952.
37596.8.10 Rutebeuf. Poèmes concernant l'Université de Paris. Paris, 1952.
43761.13.100 Sachs, Maurice. Abracadalera. 7. éd. Paris, 1952.
43761.13.110 Sachs, Maurice. Derriere cinq barreaux. 6. éd. Paris, 1952.
43738.78.815 Saillet, Maurice. Saint-John Perse. Paris, 1952.
43761.49.200 Salmon, André. Les étoiles dans l'encrier. Paris, 1952.
43761.78.260 Sartre, Jean Paul. Le diable et le bon dieu. Paris, 1952.
43761.78.760 Sartre, Jean Paul. Lucifer and the Lord. London, 1952.
43761.78.622.5 Sartre, Jean Paul. No exit (Huis clos). N.Y., 1952.
38523.3.65 Saulnier, V.L. Les élégies de Clément Marot. Paris, 1952.
43763.36.2106 Schehadé, Georges. Les poésies. 6. éd. Paris, 1952.
43765.32.21 Seghers, Pierre. Poèmes choisis, 1939-52. Paris, 1952.
43765.80.130 Serge, Victor (pseud.). Carnets. Paris, 1952.
43822.49.1130 Sewell, E. Paul Valéry. Cambridge, Eng., 1952.
43769.54.738 Simenon, Georges. The Burgomaster of Furnes. London, 1952.
43769.54.780 Simenon, Georges. The girl in the past. 1. American ed. N.Y., 1952.
43769.54.395 Simenon, Georges. Tante Jeanne. Paris, 1952.
43769.56.2130 Simon, Claude. Gulliver, roman. Paris, 1952.
43775.76.100 Soriana, M. L'enclume ou Le marteau. Paris, 1952.
43822.49.1190 Soulairol, Jean. Paul Valéry. Paris, 1952.
41571.16.3 Sozialistische Einheitsparti. Die Bedeutung der Arbeiten des Genossen Stalin. Berlin, 1952.
43744.67.1185A Spalding, P.A. A reader's handbook. London, 1952.
42576.15.210 Spencer, P. Flaubert. London, 1952.
40592.54 Staël Holstein, Anne Louise. Lettres de Madame de Staël à Madame Récamier. Paris, 1952.
37555.332 Suchier, W. Französische Verslehre auf historischer Grundlage. Tübingen, 1952.
43611.5.104 Suire, Pierre. Les raisons du Grand Meaulnes. Riort, 1952.
43785.75.140 Tardieu, Jean. La première personne du singulier. Paris, 1952.
FL 386.278 Le théâtre contemporain. Paris, 1952.

1952 - cont.

37564.215 Tortel, Jean. Le préclassicisme français. Paris, 1952.
43792.91.120 Toussaint, Franz. Lénine inconnu. Paris, 1952.
43793.42.710 Triolet, Elsa. The inspector of ruins. London, 1952.
43793.67.700.2 Troyat, Henri. My father's house. London, 1952.
43793.67.220 Troyat, Henri. La neige en deuil. Paris, 1952.
40515.5.95 Valentino, Henri. Madame d'Epinay, 1726-1783. Paris, 1952.
43822.49.118 Valéry, Paul. Charmes. 4e éd. Paris, 1952.
43822.49.420 Valéry, Paul. Lettres à quelques-uns. 5e éd. Paris, 1952.
43822.82.100 Vasseur, Pierre. Tunique; poèmes. Paris, 1952.
43823.75.760 Vercel, Roger. La Hourie. Paris, 1952.
43823.77.700 Verneuil, Louis. Affairs of state. N.Y., 1952.
43824.3.180 Vialar, Paul. La chasse aux hommes! Paris, 1952-1953. 10v.
43824.6.110A Vigée, Claude. Aurore souterraine. Paris, 1952.
41564.31.20 Vigny, Alfred de. Lettres d'un dernier amour. Genève, 1952.
43620.2.290 Vila Selma, José. André Gide y Paul Claudel. Madrid, 1952.
38514.20.29.5 Villon, François. Poems. London, 1952.
43824.54.100 Vilmorin, Louise de. Juilletta. London, 1952.
41522.18.48 Vivier, Robert. L'originalité de Baudelaire. Bruxelles, 1952.
39545.120 Voltaire, François Marie Arouet de. Notebooks. Genève, 1952. 2v.
39544.28.80 Voltaire, François Marie Arouet de. Voltaire. Genève, 1952.
39527.4.105A Wadsworth, P.A. Young La Fontaine. Evanston, 1952.
42555.44.92.15 Wais, K.K.T. Mallarmé. 2. Aufl. München, 1952.
43833.20.700 Weil, Simone. Gravity and grace. N.Y., 1952.
43833.20.715 Weil, Simone. Notebooks. London, 1952-55. 2v.
43550.1.810 Weiner, S.S. Francis Carco. N.Y., 1952.
43835.23.100 Wiehn, P. Vade-mecum du petit homme d'état. Paris, 1952.
42584.25.175 Wilson, Angus. Emile Zola. London, 1952.
43852.89.130 Yourcenar, Marguerite. Alexis. Paris, 1952.
43861.2.700 Zeraffa, Michel. The living and the lost. London, 1952.
FL 6119.52 Ziegenfuss, U. Jean-Jacques Rousseau. Erlangen, 1952.
FL 6139.52.5 Ziegenfuss, W. Jean-Jacques Rousseau. Erlanzen, 1952.
42584.25.195A Zola, Emile. Zola par lui-même. Paris, 1952.

1953

42557.20.265 Adam, Antoine. Verlaine. Paris, 1953.
38525.6.10 Allem, Maurice (pseud.). Sonnets du XVIe siècle. Grenoble, 1953.
42582.2.9 Allotte de la Fuÿe, Marguerite. Jules Verne, sa vie, son oeuvre. Paris, 1953.
42582.2.9.2 Allotte de la Fuÿe, Marguerite. Jules Verne, sa vie, son oeuvre. Paris, 1953.
38563.22.35 André, P. La jeunesse de Bayle. Genève, 1953.
43524.67.118A Anouilh, Jean. L'alouette. Paris, 1953.
43524.67.170 Anouilh, Jean. Medée. Paris, 1953.
43524.67.780 Anouilh, Jean. Pièces brillantes. Paris, 1953.
43526.65.116 Apollinaire, Guillaume. Alcools. Paris, 1953.
43527.3.330 Aragon, Louis. Le neveu de M. Duval. Paris, 1953.
43528.58.1100 Arnaud, G. Le salaire de la peur. Paris, 1953.
43528.67.100 Arout, Gabriel. La dame de Tréfle. Paris, 1953.
43528.86.100 Artaud, Antonin. Vie et mort de satan le feu. Paris, 1953.
FL 1026.2 Aspin, Isabel Stewart Tod. Anglo-Norman political songs. Oxford, 1953.
41522.18.275 Asselineau, Charles. Baudelaire et Asselineau. Paris, 1953.
38537.25.205 Association des amis de Rabelais et de La Devinière. Quatrième centenaire de la mort de Rabelais. Tours, 1953.
38537.25.190 Association d'humanisme et Renaissance. François Rabelais. Genève, 1953.
43529.7.30 Astorg, Bertrand d'. D'amour et d'amitié. Paris, 1953.
43531.7.3110 Aubert, Claude. Persiennes. [Poèmes]. Boudry, 1953.
43531.18.2100 Audisio, Gabriel. Danger de vie. Limoges, 1953.
43535.54.21 Aymé, Marcel. Contes et novelles. Paris, 1953.
43535.54.745 Aymé, Marcel. The secret stream. London, 1953.
43537.42.42 Bainville, Jacques. Journal inédit (1914). Paris, 1953.
38526.52.80 Baridon, S.F. Pontus de Tyard. Milano, 1953.
43554.2.925A Barjon, Louis. Paul Claudel. Paris, 1953.
43537.84.3100 Bataille, Roger. Les mains de l'éte. Alger, 1953.
43537.99.130 Bazin, Hervé. Humeurs. Paris, 1953.
37574.870 Bealu, Marcel. Anthologie de la poésie feminine. Paris, 1953.
42514.28.110 Beau de Loménie, Emanuel. Maurras et son système. Bourg, 1953.
40532.7.35 Beaumarchais, Pierre A.C. de. Le mariage de Figaro. Paris, 1953.
40516.60.82 Beauvoir, S. de. Must we burn De Sade? London, 1953.
43538.14.2710 Beck, Béatrix. The passionate heart. N.Y., 1953.
43538.14.2700 Beck, Béatrix. The priest. London, 1953.
43538.14.100 Beckett, Samuel. L'innommable. Paris, 1953.
43538.14.110 Beckett, Samuel. Molloy. Paris, 1953.
43538.14.730A Beckett, Samuel. Watt. 1. ed. Paris? 1953.
43538.74.130 Béraud, Henri. Les derniers beau jours. Paris, 1953.
43538.76.765 Bernanos, Georges. Night is darkest. London, 1953.
43538.76.1110 Bernard, Marc. Vacanes. Paris, 1953.
43757.3.340 Berry, Madeleine. Jules Romains. Paris, 1953.
43538.78.2100 Bertin, Célia. La dernière innocence. Paris, 1953.
40582.16.5 Beyle, Henri. Mémoires d'un touriste. Paris, 1953. 2v.
40582.25.29 Beyle, Henri. The red and the black. N.Y., 1953.
40582.25.31 Beyle, Henri. The red and the black. N.Y., 1953.
40582.40.5 Beyle, Henri. Vie de Henry Brulard. Paris, 1953.
43709.3.845 Bibliothèque Nationale, Paris. Anna de Noailles; exposition de manuscripts, livres et documents. Paris, 1953.
41555.36 Bibliothéque nationale, Paris. Prosper Mérimée; exposition. Paris, 1953.
43543.8.170 Blanchot, Maurice. Celui qui ne m'accompagnait pas. Paris, 1953.
43742.41.800 Bodart, R. Charles Plisnier. Paris, 1953.
43620.2.304 Bongs, Rolf. Das Antlitz André Gides. Düsseldorf, 1953.
37543.385 Bornecque, P.H. La France et sa littérature. Lyon, 1953-57. 2v.
43544.81.2210 Bosco, Henri. L'enfant et la rivière. Paris, 1953.
43544.89.2120 Bosquet, Alain. Ni singe. Paris, 1953.
43544.109.41 Bouchardon, Pierre. Souvenirs. Paris, 1953.
38526.48.29.20 Boutang, Pierre. Commentaire sur quarante-neuf dizains de la Délie. Paris, 1953.
43545.1.1100 Bradley, J. Frenchie. Paris, 1953.

1953 - cont.

43545.4.4140	Brasillach, Robert. Six heures à perdre. Paris, 1953.
43545.24.190	Breton, André. La clé des champs. Paris, 1953.
43545.24.180	Breton, André. Ode à Charles Fourier. Paris, 1953.
38526.10.8.4	Bruès, Guy de. Dialogues. Baltimore, 1953.
43823.75.2725	Bruller, Jean. You shall know them. 1st ed. Boston, 1953.
FL 6139.53	Bruno, A. Illuminismo e romanticismo in Rousseau e in Hegel. Bari, 1953.
43547.34.100	Bugnet, Georges. La forêt. Montréal, 1953.
43546.37.30	Buhet, Gil. The bouey siege. London, 1953.
43550.6.140	Cabanis, José. L'auberge fameuse, roman. Paris, 1953.
43550.48.700	Calet, Henri. Monsieur Paul. 1. ed. N.Y., 1953.
43550.58.725	Camus, Albert. The rebel. London, 1953.
40542.36	Camus, L.Y. Frédéric Ozanam. Paris, 1953.
FL 6129.53.5	Carlsen, Olaf. Rousseau og Dannmark. Aarhus, 1953.
43550.82.150	Cassou, Jean. Recueil. Rodg, 1953.
40539.10	Cellier, Léon. Fabre d'Olivet. Thèse. Paris, 1953.
43551.59.265	Cendrars, Blaise. Noel aux quatre coins du monde. Paris, 1953.
43551.80.710	Cesbron, Gilbert. Saints in hell. London, 1953.
39586.19.3.5	Chamfort, S.R.N. Maximes et pensées caractères, ancedotes. Paris, 1953. 2v.
43552.3.8110	Champigny, Robert. L'intermonde. Paris, 1953.
43552.4.2061	Char, René. Lettera amorosa. Paris, 1953.
42514.28.86	Charles Maurras. Paris, 1953.
38526.10.8.16	Chassignet, Jean Baptiste. Le mespris de la vie et consolation contre la mort. Genève, 1953.
37598.15	Chastie-musart. Il poemetto Chastie-musart della Vaticana. Messina, 1953.
43552.6.45	Chateaubriant, Alphonse de. Fragments d'une confession. Paris, 1953.
43552.18.150	Chédid, Andrée. Textes pour le vivant. Paris, 1953.
40517.44.25	Choderlos de Laclos, Pierre A.F. Laclos, par lui-même. Paris, 1953.
43554.3.100	Clairal, V. Zone dangereuses. Paris, 1953.
37574.770	Clancier, G.E. De Rimbaud au surréalisme. Paris, 1953.
43554.2.445	Claudel, Paul. Trois figures saintes pour le temps actuel. Paris, 1953.
37530.135	Clouzat, M. Guide du bibliophile français. Biographie pratique des oeuvres littéraires français. Paris, 1953.
37530.135.5	Clouzat, M. Guide du bibliophile français. Notions générales des bibliophiles pratique. Paris, 1953.
43556.1.32	Cocteau, Jean. Le bel indifférent. Paris, 1953.
43556.1.815	Cocteau, Jean. Démarche d'un poète. München, 1953.
43556.1.395	Cocteau, Jean. Journal d'un inconnu. Paris, 1953.
42576.65.13.118	Cogny, Pierre. J.K. Huysmans à la recherche de l'unité. Thèse. Paris, 1953.
FL 397.110.25	Cohen, G. Le théâtre français en Belgique au Moyen Age. Bruxelles, 1953.
43556.49.755	Colette, Sidonie Gabrielle. My mother's house and Sido. London, 1953.
43556.58.100	Conchon, Georges. Les grandes lessives. Paris, 1953.
39571.30	Condillac, E.B. de. Lettres inédites à Gabriel Cramer. 1. éd. Paris, 1953.
40553.8.50	Constant de Rebecque, Benjamin. Cecile. Norfolk, 1953.
42554.26.133	Corbière, Tristan. Les amours jaunes. Paris, 1953.
39594.19.55	Cotta, S. Montesquieu e la scienza della società. Tornio, 1953.
38575.23.115	Couton, Georges. Réalisme de Corneille. Paris, 1953.
42514.28.87	Cromier, Aristide. Mes entretiens de prêtre avec Charles Maurras. Paris, 1953.
43556.49.825	Crosland, M. Madame Colette. London, 1953.
43560.90.100	Cuvelier, F. Dieu n'habite pas au 74. Malines, 1953.
FL 385.16	Daniels, May. The French drama of the unspoken. Edinburgh, 1953.
42576.65.13.109	Daoust, J. J.K. Huysmans, directeur de conscience. Fécamp, 1953.
43565.89.105	Daumal, René. Essais et notes. v.1- Paris, 1953-
42555.44.89	Davies, Gardner. Vers une explication rationnelle du coup de dés. Paris, 1953.
43697.88.836	De Bordeaux à Stockholm. Bordeaux, 1953.
43566.48.2100	Delarge, Léon. Reflets d'une âme. Liège, 1953.
43566.81.4120	Desnos, Robert. De l'érotisme. Paris, 1953?
43566.81.4110	Desnos, Robert. Domaine public. Paris, 1953.
39564.8.20	Diderot, Denis. Diderot par lui-même. Paris, 1953.
39564.20.110	Diderot, Denis. Jacques, le fataliste, et son maîte. Paris, 1953.
FL 6139.53.5	Di Napoli, G. Il pensiero di Gian Giacomo Rousseau. Dreocae, 1953.
43697.89.850	Droit, Michel. André Maurois. Paris, 1953.
FL 365.110	Drugis, N. Le decor de théâtre en France du Moyen Age, à 1925. Paris, 1953.
38526.6.8	Du Bellay, Joachim. Oeuvres choisies. Paris, 1953.
43576.9.2110	Du Bouchet, André. Sans couvercle. Paris, 1953.
43620.2.306	Dubourg, M. Eugène Dabit et André Gide. Paris, 1953.
42568.19.21.16	Ducasse, I.L. Oeuvres complètes. Paris, 1953.
43576.6.755	Duhamel, Georges. Cry out of the depths. London, 1953.
43576.6.425	Duhamel, Georges. Les espoirs et les épreuves. Paris, 1953.
43576.71.2100	Dupré, Guy. Les fiancées sont froides. Paris, 1953.
43576.74.1700	Durafour, Michel. Bettina. London, 1953.
43576.74.2130	Duras, Marguerite. Les petits chevaux de Trequinia. Paris, 1953.
39594.3.50.5A	Durkheim, E. Montesquieu et Rousseau. Paris, 1953.
40597.2.380	Durry, M.J. Balzac, un début dans la vie. Paris, 1953.
42576.57.120	Ekstroem, Per G. Evasions et désespérances de Pierre Loti. Thèse. Göteborg, 1953.
43591.66.100	Elot, Maryse. Symphonie des Antilles. Malines, 1953.
37574.545.10	Eluard, Paul. La poésie du passé. Paris, 1953-54. 3v.
43592.53.185	Emmanuel, Pierre. L'ouvrier de la onzième heure. Paris, 1953.
43593.33.700	Englebert, O. The wisdom of Father Pecquet. London, 1953.
43597.79.100	Ersam, Roger. L'éspoir et les ombres. Paris, 1953.
41574.298	Escholier, R. Un amant de génie. Paris, 1953.
42556.28.145.10	Etiemble, René. Le mythe de Rimbaud. Paris, 1953. 2v.
42544.34.90	Farrere, C. Mon ami Pierre Louys. Paris, 1953.
43606.87.150	Fauchois, René. Délices des mourants. Paris, 1953.
43822.49.1110	Felici, Noël. Regards sur Valéry. Paris, 1953.
43757.92.800	Ferry, Jean. Une étude sur Raymond Roussel. Paris, 1953.
43609.50.110	Filiatrault, Jean. Terres stériles; roman. Québec, 1953.
42576.35.45	Flaubert, Gustave. Selected letters. N.Y., 1953.
43611.53.100	Fombeure, Maurice. Pendant que vous dormez. Paris, 1953.
43611.63.140	Fontaine, Anne. Le cerf-volant. Paris, 1953.
43611.88.120	Fougère, Jean. Un cadeau utile. Paris, 1953.
42555.44.96	Fowlie, Wallace. Mallarmé. Chicago, 1953.

1953 - cont.

42556.28.183	Fowlie, Wallace. Rimbaud's Illuminations. London, 1953.
42576.62.34	France, Anatole. Paita. Hämeenlinna, 1953.
37565.135	French thought in the eighteenth century. London, 1953.
42571.34.8	Gaboriau, Emile. File no. 113. London, 1953.
41539.38	Gaillard, Robert. Alexandre Dumas. Paris, 1953.
43616.58.150	Gandon, Yves. La ville invisible. Paris, 1953.
Mol 707.30	Garcon, Maurice. Sous le masque de Molière. 2. éd. Paris, 1953.
43616.79.100	Gascar, Pierre. Les bêtes. Paris, 1953.
42521.19.22	Gauthier, E. Le génie satirique de Louis Veuillot. Lyon, 1953.
43616.1.8700	Gautier, Jean Jacques. The bridge of asses. London, 1953.
43616.98.1100	Gay-Lussac, Bruno. La mort d'un prêtre. Paris, 1953.
43744.67.1325	Germain, André. Les clés de Proust. Paris, 1953.
43619.23.35	Ghelderode, Michel de. La flandre est un songe. Bruxelles, 1953.
43611.5.100	Gibson, Robert. The quest of Alain-Fournier. London, 1953.
43620.2.79.145A	Gide, André. Marshlands and Prometheus Misbound. London, 1953.
43620.2.79.146	Gide, André. Marshlands and Prometheus Misbound. N.Y., 1953.
43620.2.79.165	Gide, André. The return of the prodigal. London, 1953.
43620.40.110	Gilliard, Edmond. Outre journal. Lausanne, 1953.
37548.160	Gilsone, Robert. Les influences Anglo-Saxonnes sur les lettres françaises de Belgique de 1850 à 1880. Bruxelles, 1953.
43620.74.3100	Girard, H. Le salaire de la peur. Paris, 1953.
43620.74.500	Giraudoux, Jean. Pour Lucrèce. Paris, 1953.
43622.41.110	Glissant, Edouard. Un champ d'iles. Paris, 1953.
37530.130	Golden, H.H. Modern French literature and language. Cambridge, Mass., 1953.
40516.60.84	Gorer, G. The life and ideas of the Marquis de Sade. London, 1953.
37557.55	Gotaas, Mary C. Bossuet and Vieira. Washington, 1953.
43625.89.110	Gourfinkel, N. L'autre patrie. Paris, 1953.
43625.89.100	Gourfinkel, N. Naissance d'un monde. Paris, 1953.
43626.5.120	Grasset, B. Textes choisis. Paris, 1953.
43626.22.230	Green, Julien. Sud, pièce en trois actes. Paris, 1953.
43626.66.1100	Grosjean, Jean. Fils de l'homme. 2e éd. Paris, 1953.
43628.24.100	Guérin, R. Les poupées. 2. éd. Paris, 1953.
43628.25.2100	Guersant, M. Jean-Paul. Paris, 1953.
38526.26.86	Guidici, Enzo. Influssi italiani nel Débat di Louise Labé. Roma, 1953.
43628.43.100	Guigues, Louis Paul. Lisbeth. Paris, 1953.
43628.42.180	Guilloux, Louis. La maison du peuple, suivi de Compagnons. Paris, 1953.
43822.49.1260	Guiraud, P. Langage et versification d'après l'oeuvre de Paul Valéry. Paris, 1953.
43822.49.1260.2	Guiraud, P. Langage et versification d'après l'oeuvre de Paul Valéry. Thèse. Paris, 1953.
37569.220F	Guiraud, Pierre. Index du vocabulaire du symbolisme. v.1-3, 5, 7. v.4 lost 1969. Paris, 1953- 5v.
43552.5.805	Guitard-Auviste, G. La vie de J. Chardonne. Paris, 1953.
43631.21.100	Haedrich, Marcel. Les évangiles de la vie. Paris, 1953.
42587.58.80	Hedouville, M. de. La comtesse de Ségur et les siens. Paris, 1953.
42584.25.190	Hemmings, F.W.J. Emile Zola. Oxford, 1953.
43632.3.75	Hémon, Louis. Monsieur Repois et la Némésis. Paris, 1953.
37566.108	Henriot, Emile. Courrier littéraire, XIX siècle. Paris, 1953.
41596.4.38	Henriot, Emile. L'enfant du siècle, Alfred de Musset. Paris, 1953.
42563.23.112	Heppenstall, Rayner. Léon Bloy. Cambridge, 1953.
FL 385.38	Hobson, H. The French theatre of to-day. London, 1953.
43636.89.110	Hougron, Jean. Mort en fraude. 100. éd. Paris, 1953.
43636.89.100	Hougron, Jean. Reap the whirlwind. N.Y., 1953.
43636.94.100	Howlett, J. Un temps pour rien. Paris, 1953.
41522.18.255A	Hubert, Judd David. L'ésthétique des Fleurs du mal. Genève, 1953.
43638.7.810	Hubert, R.R. La cité borgne. Paris, 1953.
41573.32.70	Hugo, Victor. Carnets intimés, 1870-1871. 7. ed. Paris, 1953.
42576.65.80.50A	Huysmans, Joris Karl. Lettres inédites à Emile Zola. Genève, 1953.
43822.49.1180	Hytier, Jean. La poétique de Valéry. Paris, 1953.
43761.39.845	Ibert, J.C. Antoine de St. Exupéry. Paris, 1953.
43656.59.100	Ionesco, Eugène. Théâtre. Paris, 1953.
43667.11.100	Jaccottet, Philippe. L'effrail et autres poésies. Paris, 1953.
43667.14.63	Jacob, Max. Correspondance. Paris, 1953. 2v.
43667.14.260	Jacob, Max. Lettres à Bernard Esdras. Gosse. Paris, 1953.
43667.14.240	Jacob, Max. Poèmes de morven le Gaëlique. Paris, 1953.
43744.24.25	Jacques Prévert parmi nous. Labastide-Rouairoux, 1953?
43744.67.997	Jaloux, Edmond. Avec Marcel Proust, suivi de dix-sept lettres inedites de Proust. Paris, 1953.
43667.78.130	Jarry, Alfred. L'objet aimé. Paris, 1953.
43667.78.160	Jarry, Alfred. Le surmale. Paris, 1953.
38514.160	Jean de Garencières. Le chevalier poète Jehan de Garencières, 1372-1415. pts.1-2. Paris, 1953.
43670.89.410	Jouhandeau, M. Carnet du professeur. Paris, 1953.
43670.89.440	Jouhandeau, M. Dernières années et mort de Véronique. Paris, 1953.
43670.89.420	Jouhandeau, M. Galande. Paris, 1953.
43670.89.700	Jouhandeau, M. Marcel and Elise. N.Y., 1953.
43670.89.560	Jouhandeau, M. Notes sur la magie et le vol. Paris, 1953.
43670.98.100	Joyau-Dormoy, Alice. Chart des isles. Paris, 1953.
42536.34.30	Kahn, S.J. Science and aesthetic judgment. London, 1953.
42536.34.30.2	Kahn, S.J. Science and aesthetic judgment. N.Y., 1953.
37597.24.15	Keller, H.E. Etude descriptive sur le vocabulaire de Wace. Diss. Berlin, 1953.
43677.66.100	Klossowski, Pierre. Roberte ce coir. Paris, 1953.
38551.74.20	Kraus, J. Fénelon. Baden Baden, 1953.
Mol 611.10	Krauss, W. Molière und das Problem des Verstehens. Düsseldorf, 1953.
38526.27.8.5	La Ceppède, Jean de. Essai sur la vie et l'oeuvre de Jean de La Ceppède. Genève, 1953.
43687.15.260	Lacretelle, Jacques de. Deux coeurs simples. Paris, 1953.
42515.38.25	La Ferla, Guiseppe. Renan, politico. Torino, 1953.
43611.5.110	Lampo, Hubert. De roman van een roman. Antwerpen, 1953.
FL 379.253	Lancaster, H.C. French tragedy in the reign of Louis XVI and the early years of the French revolution. Baltimore, 1953.
43697.88.842	Landry, Anne G. Represented discourse in the novels of F. Mauriac. Washington, 1953.
43687.63.110	Langevin, André. Poussière sur la ville. Montreal, 1953.

Chronological Listing

1953 - cont.

43740.1.89 Lanoizelée, L. Charles Louis Philippe, l'homme, l'écrivain. Paris, 1953.

37543.38.40 Lanson, Gustave. Histoire de la littérature française. Paris, 1953.

37543.38.25 Lanson, Gustave. Manuel illustré d'histoire de la littérature française. Paris, 1953.

38526.27.4.9 Larivey, P. de. Les esprits. Paris, 1953.

FL 6129.53 Lathion, Lucien. Jean-Jacques Rousseau et le Valais. Lausanne, 1953.

43687.89.1110 Laurent, Jacques. Lucrezia Borgia. 2d ed. Milano, 1953.

43688.9.120 Lebrau, Jean. Impasse du romarin. Paris, 1953.

V43500.179 Lefèvre, Raymonde. Poèmes pour une ombre. Paris? 1953.

40575.5.135 LeHir, Yves. L'originalité littéraire de Sainte-Beuve dans Volupte. Paris, 1953.

42563.21.105 Leighton, J.H. René Bazin et l'Alsace. Strasbourg, 1953.

42563.21.105.2 Leighton, J.H. René Bazin et l'Alsace. Thèse. Strasbourg, 1953.

43688.77.2100 Leroux, S. Le roi bafoué. Paris, 1953.

43690.54.100 Limbosch, R. Sisyphe. v.1-3. Bruxelles, 1953.

43693.7.100 Lobet, M. Les croisés belges à Constantinople. Bruxelles, 1953?

40536.24.25 Lourdes. Musée Pyrénéen. Exposition L.F.E. Ramond, 1755-1827, Lourdes, 1953. Pau, 1953.

43693.98.100 Lozère, T. Nous n'irons plus au bois. Paris, 1953.

43620.2.296 McLaren, J.C. The theatre of André Gide. Baltimore, 1953.

43697.14.210 MacOrlan, Pierre. Chansons pour accordéon. Paris, 1953.

43697.14.260 MacOrlan, Pierre. La lanterne sourde. 6e ed. Paris, 1953.

42545.3.21.5 Maeterlinck, Maurice. L'oiseau bleu. Paris, 1953.

43697.48.3720 Malaquais, Jean. Le gaffeur. Buchet, 1953.

42555.43.37 Mallarmé, Stéphane. Propos sur la poésie. Monacoville, 1953.

43697.2.1710 Mallet-Joris, Françoise (pseud.). Into the labyrinth. Paris, 1953.

43697.52.42 Malraux, André. Malraux par lui-même. Paris, 1953.

43697.52.2110 Malraux, Clara. Par de plus longs chemins. Paris, 1953.

43697.61.6100 Manoll, Michel. Thérèse; ou La solitude dans la ville. Paris, 1953.

43697.74.3130 Marceau, Félicien. Bergère légère, roman. 8. ed. Paris, 1953.

42576.57.90 Marchand, Henri. En relisant Loti. Alger, 1953.

43697.76.2100 Marill, René. Les hommes traqués. Paris, 1953.

43761.78.820A Marill, René. Jean-Paul Sartre. Paris, 1953.

43524.67.807 Marsh, E.J. Jean Anouilh. London, 1953.

38557.24.78 Martimort, A.G. Le gallicanisme de Bossuet. Paris, 1953.

38557.24.78.2 Martimort, A.G. Le gallicanisme de Bossuet. Thèse. Paris, 1953.

43620.2.286.2 Martin du Gard, Roger. Notes on André Gide. London, 1953.

43620.2.286.20 Martin du Gard, Roger. Recollections of André Gide. N.Y., 1953.

43697.78.5160 Martin Saint-René (pseud.). Précis de poésie, pour servir à la composition rationnelle. Paris, 1953. 2 pam.

43697.78.5120 Martin Saint-René (pseud.). La veillée aux étoiles. Paris, 1953.

43697.84.700 Masson, R. Green oranges. 1st American ed. N.Y., 1953.

37568.94.15.5 Mauriac, Claude. Hommes et idées d'aujourd'hui. Paris, 1953.

43697.88.450 Mauriac, François. Écrits intimes. Genève, 1953.

43697.88.780 Mauriac, François. Letters on art and literature. N.Y., 1953.

43697.88.775 Mauriac, François. The mask of innocence. N.Y., 1953.

43697.88.45 Mauriac, François. Mauriac par lui-même. Paris, 1953.

41557.10.168 Maurois, André. Lélia. N.Y., 1953.

43697.89.61 Maurois, André. Lettres à l'inconnue. Paris, 1953.

43697.89.785 Maurois, André. My Latin-American diary. London, 1953.

42514.28.46 Maurras, Charles. Pascal puni. Paris, 1953.

42514.28.48 Maurras, Charles. Votre bel aujourd'hui. Paris, 1953.

43698.25.730 Meersch, M. van der. The dynamite factory. London, 1953.

43698.75.7110 Merle, Robert. La mort est mon métier. Paris, 1953.

42555.44.110A Michaud, Guy. Mallarmé. Paris, 1953.

43699.12.110 Michel, André. Amants bissextils, suivi de soupir au demeurant des pauses. Montpellier, 1953.

43701.39.100 Mohrt, Michel. Le serviteur fidèle. Paris, 1953.

43701.41.1100 Moirant, René. Parure de pauvre homme. n.p., 1953.

43701.1.30.5 Molaine, Pierre. Strange laughter. N.Y., 1953.

Mol 166.4.5 Molière, Jean Baptiste Poquelin. The miser, and Coxcombs in petticoats. St. Albans, 1953.

43701.59.110 Monfreid, Henri de. Le serpent rouge. Paris, 1953.

43701.60.2100 Monnier, Adrienne. Les gazettes d'Adrienne Monnier. Paris, 1953.

Mon 19.53 Montaigne, Michel de. Essais. Brie-Comte-Robert, 1953- 3v.

Mon 28.62 Montaigne, Michel de. Selected works. N.Y., 1953.

39593.20A Montesquieu, C.L. de S. Montesquieu par lui-même. Paris, 1953.

43701.63.41A Montherlant, Henry de. Montherlant par lui-même. Paris, 1953.

38537.54 Montpellier, France. Musée Fabre. Expositon commémorative du 400me anniversaire de la mort de François Rabelais. Montpellier, 1953.

43701.74.740 Morand, Paul. The flagellant of Seville. London, 1953.

41574.520 Moscow. Vsesoiuznaia gosudarstvennaia biblioteka inostrannoi literatury. Bibliografiia russkikh perevodov proizvedenii Viktora Giugo. Moskva, 1953.

43697.52.820 Mounier, E. L'espoir des desespérés. Paris, 1953.

37564.220 Mourgues, O. de. Metaphysical. Oxford, 1953.

42514.28.82 Mourre, M. Charles Maurras. Paris, 1953.

43761.78.812 Murdoch, Iris. Sartre. Cambridge, Eng., 1953.

43761.78.810 Murdoch, Iris. Sartre. New Haven, 1953.

41596.18.17 Musset, Alfred de. Textes dramatiques inedits. Paris, 1953.

43744.67.1505 Nathan, Jacques. La morale de Proust. Paris, 1953.

39564.30 Nedergaard, Leif. Diderot, filosoffens liv og virke. København, 1953.

43744.67.1215 Newman, Pauline. Marcel Proust et l'existentialisme. Thèse. Paris, 1953.

43706.105.100 Nguyen-Tien-Lang. Les chemins de la révolte. Paris, 1953.

43537.6.87 Nikolaev, V.N. Anri Barbius. Moskva, 1953.

43707.3.702 Nimier, Roger. The blue Hussar. N.Y., 1953.

43707.3.110 Nimier, Roger. Histoire d'un amour. 13e éd. Paris, 1953.

42556.28.230 Noulet, E. Le premier visage de Rimbaud. Bruxelles, 1953.

43709.89.25 Nouveau, Germain. Oeuvres poétiques. 5e éd. Paris, 1953. 2v.

43620.2.298 O'Brien, J. Portrait of André Gide. 1. ed. N.Y., 1953.

43737.34.190 Pagnol, Marcel. Angèle. Paris, 1953.

43737.74.3120 Parain, Brice. Sur la dialectique. Paris, 1953.

43737.80.100 Parrot, Louis. Oeil de fumée. Niort, 1953.

1953 - cont.

38514.59.7 Pathelin. Maistre Pierre Pathelin. Genève, 1953.

38514.59.20 Pathelin. Mistrz Piotr Pathelin. Warszawa, 1953.

38523.3.90 Patocchi, Pericle. Quando Marot traduceva Petrarca. Lugano, 1953.

43738.1.77 Péguy, Charles. L'esprit de système. Paris, 1953.

43738.1.58 Péguy, Charles. Un poète l'a dit. 10e éd. Paris, 1953.

43738.41.220 Peisson, Edouard. Capitaines de la route de New York. Paris, 1953.

43833.20.870 Perrin, Joseph Marie. Simone Weil as we knew her. London, 1953.

43738.78.21A Perse, Saint-John. Oeuvre poétique. Paris, 1953. 2v.

43738.78.740F Perse, Saint-John. Winds. N.Y, 1953.

39527.4.115 Petit, Léon. La Fontaine et Saint-Evremond. Toulouse, 1953.

43738.97.1120 Peyrefitte, Roger. La fin des ambassades. Paris, 1953.

43738.99.2100 Pezeril, D. Rue Notre Dame. N.Y., 1953.

37573.684.5 Picon, Gaëtan. Panorama de la nouvelle littérature française. Paris, 1953.

43741.25.130 Pieyre de Mandiargues, André. Marbre. Paris, 1953.

FL 6015.18 Plan, P.P. Table de la correspondance général de Jean-Jacques Rousseau. Genève, 1953.

43742.41.210 Plisnier, Charles. L'homme et les hommes. Paris, 1953.

42514.28.170 Points et contrepoints. Hommage à Charles Maurras. Paris, 1953.

42584.25.230 Présence de Zola. Paris, 1953.

43744.24.45 Prévert, Jacques. L'opera de la lune. Lausanne, 1953.

40522.9.36 Prévost, Antoine F. Histoire du chevalier des Grieux et de Manon Lescaut. Genève, 1953.

41522.18.260 Prévost, Jean. Baudelaire. Paris, 1953.

37567.328.5 Prévost, Jean L. Le prêtre ce héros de roman. 2. éd. Paris, 1953.

43697.75.820 Prini, Pietro. Gabriel Marcel et la méthodologie de l'invérifiable. Paris, 1953.

43744.67.79.20 Proust, Marcel. Correspondance avec sa mère. Paris, 1953.

43744.67.68.2 Proust, Marcel. Letters to Antoine Bibesco. London, 1953.

43744.67.999 Proust, Marcel. Marcel Proust par lui-même. Paris, 1953.

43752.18.710 Radiguet, Raymond. Count d'Orgel. N.Y., 1953.

43752.34.100 Ragon, Michel. Drôles de métiers. Paris, 1953.

37544.141 Ragon, Michel. Histoire de la littérature ouvrière du Moyen Âge à nos jours. Paris, 1953.

42555.1.80A Ramsey, Warren. Jules Laforgue and the ironic inheritage. N.Y., 1953.

43753.58.1120 Renaitour, Jean Michel. Le tombeau de Tibulle. Paris, 1953.

42587.51.30 Renard, Jules. Correspondance. Paris, 1953.

42575.109A Ricatte, Robert. La création romanesque chez les Goncourt. Paris, 1953.

V43500.253 Rieder, Violette. Ex-voto. Rodez? 1953.

38526.32.65 Ritter, R. Les solitudes de Marguerite de Navarre. Paris, 1953.

43757.6.100 Robbe-Grillet, Alain. Les gommes. Paris, 1953.

43697.88.832 Robichon, J. François Mauriac. Paris, 1953.

43757.8.2100 Robin, Armand. Poésie non traduite. 3. éd. Paris, 1953. 20v.

43757.12.2100 Roché, Henri Pierre. Jules et Jim. Paris, 1953.

40597.2.365 Rogers, S. Balzac and the novel. Madison, 1953.

43757.3.295 Romains, Jules. Maisons. Paris, 1953.

38525.20.62 Ronsard, Pierre de. Les bacchanales. Genève, 1953.

43757.83.2110 Rostand, Jean. La vie. Paris, 1953.

FL 6005.40 Rousseau, J.J. Political writings containing The social contract. Edinburgh, 1953.

43738.1.87.5 Roussel, J. Charles Péguy. Paris, 1953.

V43500.261 Rousselot, Jean. Homme, c'est ta grandeur. n.p., 1953.

43757.92.2100 Rousselot, Jean. Poèmes choises. Paris, 1953.

37564.225 Rousset, Jean. La littérature de l'âge baroque en France. Paris, 1953.

FL 398.77.100 Roussin, A. Patience et impatience. Genève, 1953.

41557.10.280 Ryelandt, Christophe. Malgrétout. George Sand et les Ardennes. Mézières, 1953.

43761.5.4110 Sabatier, Robert. Alain et le nègre. Paris, 1953.

43761.13.641 Sachs, Maurice. Day of wrath. London, 1953.

40516.60.50 Sade, D.A.F. de. Cahiers personnels, 1803-1804. Paris, 1953.

40516.60.65 Sade, D.A.F. de. Le carillon de Vincennes. Paris, 1953.

40516.60.55 Sade, D.A.F. de. Histoire secrète d'Isabelle de Bavière. Paris, 1953.

43761.39.150 St. Exupéry, A. de. Carnets. 18. éd. Paris, 1953.

43761.39.140 St. Exupéry, A. de. Lettre à un otage. Paris, 1953.

43761.39.142 St. Exupéry, A. de. Lettres à l'âmie inventée. Paris, 1953.

43761.39.141 St. Exupéry A. de. Lettres de jeunesse. 55. éd. Paris, 1953.

43761.48.130 Salacrou, Armand. Les invités du Bon Dieu. Paris, 1953.

41557.10.185 Salomon, P. George Sand. Paris, 1953.

41557.10.18.10 Sand, George. Correspondance inédite. 8. éd. Paris, 1953.

43761.77.113 Sarraute, Nathalie. Martereau. 3. éd. Paris, 1953.

38527.29.25 Sauerwein, H.A. Agrippa d'Aubigné's Les tragiques. Baltimore, 1953.

37563.87 Saulnier, Verdun L. La littérature française de la renaissance. 3. éd. Paris, 1953.

37566.113 Sauro, A. Il mito del romanticismo francese. Bari, 1953.

43763.37.2100 Schehadé, Laurice. La fille royale et blanche. Paris, 1953.

38524.135 Schmidt, A.M. Poètes du XVI siècle. Paris, 1953.

37543.328 Schneider, Pierre. La voix vive. Paris, 1953.

43738.1.230 Servais, Y. Charles Péguy. Cork, 1953.

38546.36.25 Sévigné, Marie de R.C. Lettres. Paris, 1953- 3v.

43769.54.773 Simenon, Georges. No vacation for Maigret. Roslyn, 1953.

43769.54.755 Simenon, Georges. The stain on the snow. London, 1953.

40597.2.520 Smith, Stephen R.B. Balzac et l'Angleterre. Londres, 1953.

FL 398.81.20 Sorel, Cécile. Cécile Sorel. London, 1953.

43775.89.2700 Soubiran, André. The doctors. N.Y., 1953.

43775.90.7200 Soupault, Philippe. Sans phrases. Paris, 1953.

43776.41.210 Spire, André. Poèmes d'hier et d'aujourd'hui. Paris, 1953.

43620.2.302A Starkie, Enid. André Gide. Cambridge, Eng., 1953.

39527.4.110 Sutherland, M. La Fontaine. London, 1953.

43785.77.100 Tarpiniau, Armen. Le chant et l'ombre. Paris, 1953.

41563.25.10 Toepffer, Rodolphe. Mélanges sur les beaux-arts. Genève, 1953. 2v.

43792.40.130 Toesca, Maurice. Le fantassin à cheval. Paris, 1953.

43620.74.870 Tonssaint, F. Jean Giraudoux. Paris, 1953.

Chronological Listing

1953 - cont.

FL 395.280	Touchard, P.A. Six années de comédie française. Paris, 1953.
43792.89.1700	Tourville, A. de. Wedding dance. N.Y., 1953.
43744.67.1290	Trahard, P. L'art de Marcel Proust. Paris, 1953.
37543.332	Trnka, J. A propos d'une traduction. Paris, 1953.
43793.67.710	Troyat, Henri. The mountain. London, 1953.
41522.18.225	Turnell, M. Baudelaire. London, 1953.
41522.18.226	Turnell, M. Baudelaire. Norfolk, Conn., 1953.
43756.90.825	Turnell, M. Jacques Rivière. Cambridge, Eng., 1953.
43799.5.180	Tzara, Tristan. La face intérieure. Paris, 1953.
39543.65	Vail, F. Voltaire, sa vie et son oeuvre, avec textes complèts annotés. Paris, 1953.
43822.50.715	Vailland, Roger. Expérience du drame. Paris, 1953.
43822.49.106.2	Valéry, Paul. Variété III. 50e éd. Paris, 1953.
42514.28.84	Vallat, X.J. Charles Maurras. Paris, 1953.
43697.49.800	Varin, G. Foi perdue et retrouvée. Fribourg, 1953.
43823.2.35	Védrès, Nicole. Les cordes rouges, roman. Paris, 1953.
43823.75.750	Vercel, Roger. Ride out the storm. N.Y., 1953.
43823.75.160	Vercel, Roger. Visage perdu. Paris, 1953.
43537.6.90	Vidal, A. Henri Barbusse. Paris, 1953.
41564.7.10	Vigny, Alfred de. The military necessity. N.Y., 1953.
38514.20.29.10	Villon, François. Seven poems. n.p., 1953.
39544.28.75A	Voltaire, François Marie Arouet de. Correspondance. Genève, 1953-64. 107v.
39545.61.33.2	Voltaire, François Marie Arouet de. Le temple du goût. 2. éd. Genève, 1953.
43822.49.1220	Walzer, P.O. La poésie de Valéry. Genève, 1953.
42584.20.10	Zola, Emile. Restless house. N.Y., 1953.

1954

37595.9.101	Abailard, Pierre. Die Leidensgeschichte, und der Briefwechsel mit Heloisa. 2. Aufl. Heidelberg, 1954.
37595.7.25	Abailard, Pierre. The story of Abélard's adversities. Toronto, 1954.
43512.74.100	Abrassart, Lucy. La quête de lumière. Malines en Belgique, 1954.
43693.41.1100	Academie...Bordeaux. Academie nationale des sciences, belles-lettres, et arts de Bordeaux. Réception de M. Jean Loiseau a l'Academie. Bordeaux, 1954.
43757.7.6100	Academie...Bordeaux. Academie nationale des sciences, belles-lettres et arts de Bordeaux. Réception de M. Paul de Robert à l'academie. Bordeaux, 1954.
43697.89.860	Académie Bordeaux. Réception de M. André Maurois de l'Académie française à l'Académie nationale des sciences, belles lettres et arts de Bordeaux, 18 mai 1953. Bordeaux, 1954.
43526.65.860.5	Adéma, Marcel. Apollinaire. London, 1954.
V43500.9	Albert-Birot, P. Poèmes à l'autre moi. Paris, 1954.
43522.48.1100	Allain-Cornic, Pierre. Fugues. Paris, 1954.
42562.60.7	Allais, Alphonse. Cinquante cinq contes d'Alphonse Allais. Paris, 1954.
42562.60.5	Allais, Alphonse. Les zèbres. n.p., 1954.
40575.5.145	Allem, Maurice. Portrait de Sainte-Beuve. Paris, 1954.
43522.51.100	Alloo, Gustave. A poignardé ma vie. Malines, 1954.
43524.20.100	André, Alix. Ordre du prince. Paris, 1954.
43524.67.152	Anouilh, Jean. Antigone. Paris, 1954.
43524.67.142	Anouilh, Jean. Le bal des voleurs. Paris, 1954.
43524.67.180	Anouilh, Jean. Cécile, ou L'école des pères. Paris, 1954.
43524.67.770A	Anouilh, Jean. Mademoiselle Colombe. N.Y., 1954.
43524.79.100	Ans, Geneviève d'. Lui. Paris, 1954?
43526.65.800	Apollinaire, Guillaume. Apollinaire par lui-même. Paris, 1954.
37574.795	Aragon, L. Journal d'une poésie nationale. Lyon, 1954.
40583.220	Aragon, L. La lumière de Stendhal. Paris, 1954.
43527.3.340	Aragon, Louis. Les yeux et la mémoire. 7. éd. Paris, 1954.
43528.7.100	Arbellot, Simon. Journaliste! Paris, 1954.
43528.48.210	Arland, Marcel. Nouvelles lettres de France. Paris, 1954.
V43500.13	Arnold, Jacques. Sonate de la Marne. Paris, 1954.
43528.61.160	Arnoux, Alexandre. Royaume des ombres. Paris, 1954.
43529.8.30	Aspel, Pauline. Goût d'une autre terre. Paris, 1954.
43529.6.30	Astier de la Vigerie, E. L'été n'en finit pas. Paris, 1954.
FL 6119.54.5	Atene, Paolo. Gian Giacomo Rousseau. Genova, 1954.
43531.7.2100	Aubier, D. La nourriture du feu. Paris, 1954.
Mol 601.20	Audiberti, J. Molière. Paris, 1954.
43531.18.1100	Audiberti, Jacques. Les jardins et les fleures. 7. éd. Paris, 1954.
43535.54.360	Aymé, Marcel. Autres contes de chat perché. Paris, 1954.
43535.54.280	Aymé, Marcel. Les quatre vérités. Paris, 1954.
37573.708	Bagaert, Jean. Les lettres françaises. Paris, 1954-58. 3v.
43544.41.110	Baisdeffre, Pierre de. Des vivants et des morts. Paris, 1954.
43537.51.100	Ballot-Léna, Bernard. Saisons; poèmes. Paris, 1954.
43538.76.850	Balthasar, H.U. von. Bernanos. Köln, 1954.
40597.35.10	Balzac, Honoré de. Louis Lambert. Paris, 1954.
43537.74.1100	Barbier, Jean Joël. Irradiante. Paris, 1954.
38526.22.6	Baridon, Silvio F. Claude de Kerquefinen. Genève, 1954.
42563.14.5	Barrès, Maurice. Barrès. Paris, 1954.
41522.13.14.5	Baudelaire, Charles. Baudelaire. Paris, 1954.
43537.99.140	Bazin, Hervé. L'huile sur le feu. Paris, 1954.
43752.57.860	Beaujon, E. La vision du peintre chez Ramuz. Bondy, 1954.
43554.2.940	Beaumont, Ernest. The theme of Beatrice in the plays of Claudel. London, 1954.
43538.1.452	Beauvoir, Simone de. L'Amérique au jour le jour. Paris, 1954.
43538.1.455	Beauvoir, Simone de. Le Mandarins. 248. éd. Paris, 1954.
43538.14.2720	Beck, Béatrix. Des accommodements avec le ciel. Paris, 1954-55.
43620.2.325	Beigbeder, M. André Gide. Paris, 1954.
38526.1.35.18	Belleau, R. La bergerie. Genève, 1954.
43538.51.120	Belloni, Georges. Sous le signe du Bélier. Paris, 1954.
43538.76.41A	Bernanos, Georges. Bernanos par lui-même. Paris, 1954.
43538.76.712.5	Bernanos, Georges. The diary of a country priest. N.Y., 1954.
37565.78.5	Bertaut, Jules. La vie littéraire en France au XVIIIe siècle. Paris, 1954.
43538.78.2110	Bertin, Célia. Contre-champ. Paris, 1954.
42563.23.8.72	Bertrand, Louis. Mes ambassades. Paris, 1954.
43538.83.100	Bésus, Roger. Cet homme qui vous aimait, roman. Paris, 1954.
43538.89.110	Beucler, André. Le carnet de vengeance. Paris, 1954.
43606.76.810	Beucler, André. The last of the Bohemians. N.Y., 1954.

1954 - cont.

40582.34.5	Beyle, Henri. The private diaries of Stendhal. Garden City, 1954.
40582.11.20	Beyle, Henri. The private journals of Stendhal. Kentfield, Calif., 1954.
41557.9.70	Biblioteque nationale, Paris. George Sand. Paris, 1954.
40556.22	Bibliothèque National. Paris. Joseph Joubert. Paris, 1954.
42575.112	Billy, André. Les frères Goncourt. Paris, 1954.
43543.3.1100	Blanc, Louis. Feuillets épars, poèmes. Paris, 1954.
40583.260	Blin, Georges. Stendhal et les problémes du roman. Paris, 1954.
43543.66.100	Blondel. La peau l'aurochs. Paris, 1954.
41596.4.100	Blum, Arlette. L'expression poetique des souvenirs chez Alfred de Musset. Paris, 1954.
V43500.23	Bluteau, Jeanne. Chansons de la Baie d'Audierne. Paris, 1954.
43556.49.835	Bonmariage, Sylvain. Willy, Colette et moi. n.p., 1954.
43544.60.2100	Bonnefoy, Yves. Du mouvement et de l'immobilité de Douve. Paris, 1954.
43544.60.3100	Bonnet, M.R. Enfance, limousine. Paris, 1954.
43701.63.850	Bordonove, G. Henry de Montherlant. Paris, 1954.
43544.81.130	Bory, Jean Louis. Une vie de château. Paris, 1954.
43544.81.2140	Bosco, Henri. L'antiquaire. 21. éd. Paris, 1954.
43544.82.130	Bosschère, Jean de. Contes de la neige et de la nuit. Blainville-sur-Mer, 1954.
43544.108.700	Boulle, Pierre. The bridge over the River Kwai. N.Y., 1954.
FL 398.9.10A	Bourgeois, J. Toute ma vie. v.1-2. Paris, 1954.
43544.90.2100	Bourricaud, Jean. Coordonnées 44-54. Paris, 1954.
40597.2.405	Bouteron, M. Études balzaciennes. Paris, 1954.
43544.105.110	Boyer, François. La gare du ciel. Paris, 1954.
FL 391.145	Brasillach, Robert. Animateurs de théâtre. Paris, 1954.
43545.4.4170	Brasillach, Robert. Berenice. Paris, 1954.
43545.5.1100	Brassens, Georges. La Mauvaise reputation. Paris, 1954.
Mol 602.14	Bray, René. Molière. Paris, 1954.
43545.42.3100	Brisville, Jean Claude. La présence réelle. Paris, 1954.
37568.82.10	Brodin, Pierre. Présences contemporaines. Paris, 1954-57. 3v.
40583.13	Brombert, V.H. Stendhal et la voie oblique. New Haven, 1954.
43823.75.2730A	Bruller, Jean. Borderline. London, 1954.
43823.75.2180	Bruller, Jean. Les pas dans la sable. Paris, 1954.
43546.87.30	Butor, Michel. Passage de Mitar. Paris, 1954.
43550.6.130	Cabanis, José. Juliette Bonviolle. Paris, 1954.
43550.42.100	Cailloux, René. L'eternelle Phèdre. Cavaillon, 1954.
43550.41.1100	Caizergues, Jacques. Ritournelles pour traversée. Paris, 1954.
43550.48.110	Calet, Henri. Les deux bouts. 2. éd. Paris, 1954.
37543.203.10	Calvet, Jean. Le bestiaire de la littérature française. Paris, 1954.
43550.58.180	Camus, Albert. L'été. Paris, 1954.
43550.58.190	Camus, Albert. Le malentendu. 59. éd. Paris, 1954.
43545.89.800	Carco, F. La belle epoque au temps de Braunt. Paris, 1954.
38537.25.200	Carpenter, N.C. Rabelais and music. Chapel Hill, 1954.
37569.40.210	Carrouges, M. Les machines celibataires. Paris, 1954.
43550.77.100	Carrouges, M. Les portes Dauphines. Paris, 1954.
FL 6139.54	Cassirer, E. The question of Jean-Jacques Rousseau. N.Y., 1954.
42563.23.120A	Cattaui, G. Léon Bloy. Paris, 1954.
43550.98.130	Cayrol, Jean. L'espace d'une nuit. Neuchâtel, 1954.
37555.655	Cellier, Léon. L'épopée romantique. Paris, 1954.
43551.80.110	Cesbron, Gilbert. Chiens perdus sans callier. Paris, 1954.
43538.76.840	Chaigne, L. Georges Bernanos. Paris, 1954.
43738.1.235	Challaye, F. Péguy socialiste. Paris, 1954.
43552.3.9240	Chamson, André. Le chiffre de nos jours. 24e éd. Paris, 1954.
43552.4.2170	Char, René. A la santé du serpent. Paris, 1954.
43552.4.2661	Char, René. Leaves of Hypnos (extracts) and Lettera amorosa. Roma, 1954.
43552.4.6100	Chardonnal, U.B. Au village. Le Puy-en-Velaz, 1954.
43552.5.190	Chardonne, Jacques. Lettres à Roger Niumier. 6e éd. Paris, 1954.
43552.5.1125	Chartier, Émile. Definitions. 6e éd. Paris, 1954?
43552.5.1025	Chartier, Émile. Philosophie. Paris, 1954. 2v.
42555.44.82.5	Chassé, Charles. Les clés de Mallarmé. Paris, 1954.
43552.5.4021	Chauffin, Yvonne. Les Ramboult. v. 1-4. Paris, 1954-1956. 2v.
43554.2.930	Chiari, J. The poetic drama of Paul Claudel. London, 1954.
43552.69.100	Chraibi, Driss. Le passé simple: roman. Paris, 1954.
37595.36.7.10	Chrestien de Troyes. Erec et Enide. Paris, 1954.
43554.2.450	Claudel, Paul. L'échange. Paris, 1954.
43554.2.440	Claudel, Paul. Mémoires improvisés. 6e éd. Paris, 1954.
42524.19.35	Clerk, J.G. La pensée de Ferdinand Brunètiere. Paris, 1954.
43556.1.105	Cocteau, Jean. Clair-obscur. Monaco, 1954.
42563.39.810	Codet, Louis. The fortunes of Bécot. London, 1954.
43556.49.25	Colette, Sidonie Gabrielle. Colette. Paris, 1954.
37556.14.20	Colletet, F. Les journaux pour enfants. Paris, 1954.
43556.61.2100	Conte, Arthur. Les oiseaux n'y savent pas chanter. Paris, 1954.
42554.26.135	Corbière, Tristan. Selections from Les amours jaunes. Berkeley, 1954.
38574.25	Corneille, Pierre. Corneille par lui-même. Paris, 1954.
38575.33.10	Corneille, Pierre. La veuve. Genève, 1954.
43556.76.100	Cornélus, Henri. Bakonji, les chefs. Aalter, 1954.
39566.110	Crocker, L.G. The embattled philosopher. East Lansing, 1954.
42554.26.80	Cros, Charles. Oeuvres complètes. Paris, 1954.
43556.49.826	Crosland, M. Colette. 1st American ed. N.Y., 1954.
Htn 42557.12.2*	Culot, Jean-Marie. Bibliographie de Émile Verhaeren. Bruxelles, 1954.
43560.78.120	Curtis, Jean Louis. Les justes causes. Paris, 1954.
40597.2.400	Dagneud, R. Les éléments populaires dans le lexique de la comédie humaine d'Honoré de Balzac. Paris, 1954.
43565.41.110	Daix, Pierre. La dernière forteresse. Paris, 1954.
43565.41.100	Daix, Pierre. Un tueur roman. Paris, 1954.
37567.454	Dale, E.H. La poésie française en Angleterre. Paris, 1954.
43565.60.1100	Daninos, Pierre. Les carnets du Major W. Marmaduke Thompson. Paris, 1954.
43701.63.860	Datain, Jean. Montherlant et le mystère malalesta. Alencon, 1954.
43565.89.120	Daumal, René. La grande beuverie. Paris, 1954.

Chronological Listing

1954 - cont.

43565.89.110 Daumal, René. Poésie noire, poésie blanche; poèmes. Paris, 1954.
43565.89.7100 Dauphin, Marcel. Boisrond Tonnerre. Port-au-Prince, 1954.
43620.2.385 Dauvigny, Alain. André Gide au l'impossible morale. Bordeaux, 1954.
43565.90.120 Davignon, Henri. Souvenirs d'un écrivain belge, 1879-1945. Paris, 1954.
43833.20.830 Davy, M.M. Introduction au message de Simone Weil. Paris, 1954.
42556.28.245 Decaunes, Luc. Arthur Rimbaud. Paris, 1954.
FL 396.53 Deierkauf-Holsboer, Sophie Wilma. Le théâtre du Marais. Paris, 1954. 2v.
43611.5.115 Delettrez, J.M. Alain-Fournier et le grand meaulnes. Paris, 1954.
43620.2.330 Delmas-Marsalet, M. Jean Yves. La culpabilité morbile d'André Gide. Bordeaux, 1954.
Mol 604.8 Descaves, Pierre. Molière en U.R.S.S. Paris, 1954.
43566.82.7740 Destouches, Louis Ferdinand. Guignol's band. Hartford, Conn., 1954.
43566.90.1100 Devaré, U. Zariné. N.Y., 1954.
43567.79.110 Dhôtel, André. Le maître de pension. Paris, 1954.
43568.6.120 Dib, Mohammed. Algérie. Paris, 1954-61. 3v.
39564.8.25 Diderot, Denis. Mystification. Paris, 1954.
FL 398.15 Doisy, Marcel. Jacques Copeau. Paris, 1954.
43573.77.1700 Dorp, J. van. The sable lion. N.Y., 1954.
43573.89.5100 Douce, Paul. Nous serons un seul corps. Paris, 1954.
40583.356 Drevet, Camille. Le dauphiné de Stendhal. Gap, 1954.
37530.150 Drevet, M.L. Bibliographie de la littérature française. Genève, 1954-55.
43556.1.820 Dubourg, P. Dramaturgie de Jean Cocteau. Paris, 1954.
43833.20.840 Dugnion-Secretan, Perle. Simone Weil. Neuchâtel, 1954.
43576.6.756 Duhamel, Georges. Cry out of the depths. Boston, 1954.
43576.6.760 Duhamel, Georges. Refuges de la lecture. Paris, 1954.
43761.78.840 Dumas, Alexandre. Kean. London, 1954.
43576.53.2100 Dumay, Raymond. Fannie en Orient. Paris, 1954.
43576.57.1100 Dumur, Guy. Le matin de leurs jours. Paris, 1954.
43576.72.100 Dupuy, Michel. La source et le feu. Montréal, 1954.
43576.74.2120 Duras, Marguerite. Des journées entières. Paris, 1954.
43576.90.1100 Duvignaud, Jean. Le piège. 2. éd. Paris, 1954.
43667.1.845 Dyson, Rose M. Les sensations et la sensibilité chez Francis Jammes. Genève, 1954.
43591.89.185 Éluard, Paul. Les sentiers et les routes de la poésie. 5. éd. Paris, 1954.
43667.14.810 Emié, Louis. Dialogues avec Max Jacob. Paris, 1954.
39564.17.20 Encyclopédie of Diderot. The encyclopédie of Diderot. Cambridge, Eng., 1954.
40593.40 Escarpit, R. L'Angleterre dans l'oeuvre de Madame de Staël. Paris, 1954.
43598.82.150 Estang, Luc. Les fontaines du grand abime. Paris, 1954.
43598.82.170 Estang, Luc. Les stigmates. Paris, 1954.
42556.28.145.12 Étiemble, René. Le mythe de Rimbaud. v.2. 4e éd. Paris, 1954.
43626.22.825 Fangara, A. L'existence dans les romans de Julien Green. Roma, 1954.
37576.654 Farouche à quatre feuilles. Paris, 1954.
43822.49.1240 Faure, G. Paul Valéry, méditerranéen. Paris, 1954.
38552.12.10 Fénelon, F. de S. de la Mothe. Oeuvres spirituelles. Paris, 1954.
37556.13.40 Feron, B. Feu la presse libre? Paris, 1954.
37556.155 Ferrier, J.M. Forerunners of the French novel. Manchester, 1954.
43609.83.710 Fisson, Pierre. Fever in Mexico. London, 1954.
42576.35.50.1A Flaubert, Gustave. Correspondance. Supplément. Paris, 1954. 4v.
42576.21.5 Flaubert, Gustave. Dictionary of accepted ideas. Norfolk, 1954.
42576.21.10 Flaubert, Gustave. A dictionary of platitudes. London, 1954.
43610.66.2100 Florenne, Yves. Antigone. Paris, 1954.
42576.63.715 Florian, L. Anatole France. Budapest, 1954.
42555.37.6.25 Flottes, Pierre. Leconte de Lisle. Paris, 1954.
42576.62.90 France, Anatole. Anatole France par lui-même. Paris, 1954.
40583.215 François-Poncet, Andre. Stendhal a Genève. Neuchâtel, 1954.
42563.18.238 Frandon, I.M. Assassins et danseurs mystiques. Genève, 1954.
42563.18.239 Frandon, I.M. Assassins et danseurs mystiques. Thèse. Abbéville, 1954.
FL 370.106 Frank, Grace. The medieval French drama. Oxford, 1954.
37562.297 Frappier, Jean. La poésie lyrique en France au XII et XIII siècle. Paris, 1954.
38523.33.5 Fromilhague, R. Malherbe. Paris, 1954.
38523.33.6 Fromilhague, R. Malherbe. Thèse. Paris, 1954.
38523.33 Fromilhague, R. La vie de Malherbe. Paris, 1954.
38523.33.2 Fromilhague, R. La vie de Malherbe. Thèse. Paris, 1954.
43616.74.1100 Garçon, Maurice. Plaidoyers chimériques. Paris, 1954.
43616.89.6100 Gaultier, Yvette. Mes vérités. Paris, 1954.
43617.78.150 Genêt, Jean. Les bonnes. Sceaux, 1954.
43617.78.700 Genêt, Jean. The maids. N.Y., 1954.
43617.59.140 Genevoix, Maurice. Fatou cissé, roman. Paris, 1954.
40588.21.50 Genlis, S.F.D. de St. Dernières lettres d'amour. Paris, 1954.
43617.78.1011 Gervais, Maurice. Oeuvres complètes. Paris, 1954-
43611.5.102 Gibson, Robert. The quest of Alain-Fournier. New Haven, 1954.
43620.66.740 Giono, Jean. The horseman on the roof. 1. American ed. N.Y., 1954.
43620.66.400 Giono, Jean. Voyage en Italie. 38. éd. Paris, 1954.
43620.74.103 Giraudoux, Jean. Bella. Paris, 1954.
43620.74.750 Giraudoux, Jean. Ondine. N.Y., 1954.
43620.74.21 Giraudoux, Jean. Théâtre. Paris, 1954. 2v.
43620.74.1100 Giraudoux, Jean Pierre. Débuts au théâtre. Paris, 1954.
43625.17.1100 Godeau, Georges L. Rictus. Paris, 1954.
43625.19.115 Godoy, Armand. Bréviaire. Paris, 1954.
43626.5.6100 Graveraux, Hubert. Devenir; ou, La destinée de l'homme. Paris, 1954?
43626.22.190 Green, Julien. L'ennem. Paris, 1954.
43626.22.11A Green, Julien. Oeuvres complètes. Paris, 1954. 10v.
41574.304 Gregh, F. Victor Hugo: sa vie, son oeuvre. Paris, 1954.
43626.66.5100 Grosclaude, Pierre. Vers quel rendez-vous? Paris, 1954.
43628.23.140 Guéhenno, Jean. Aventures de l'esprit. 19. éd. Paris, 1954.
43628.24.3100 Guéridon, Roland. Rien que la vie. Paris, 1954.
37597.45 Guger, F.E. Romance in the making. N.Y., 1954.
43628.41.3120 Guillevic, Eugène. Trente et un sonnets. Paris, 1954.

1954 - cont.

43628.42.140 Guilloux, Louis. Parpagnacco. 7. éd. Paris, 1954.
43628.1.120 Guitry, Sacha. Et Versailles vous est conté. Paris, 1954.
43628.1.125 Guitry, Sacha. Si Versailles m'était conté. Paris, 1954.
43628.85.100 Guth, Paul. Le naïf sous les drapeaux. Paris, 1954.
37569.215.5 Guyard, M.F. La Grande-Bretagne dans le roman français, 1914-1940. Paris, 1954.
37569.215 Guyard, M.F. L'image de la Grande-Bretagne dans le roman français. Paris, 1954.
40556.23.25 Halda, Bernard. Joseph Joubert, ou De la perfection. Paris, 1954.
43788.5.800 Halevy, D. Eloge de Jérôme Tharaud. Paris, 1954.
38525.22.45.95 Hallowell, R.E. Ronsard and the conventional Roman elegy. Urbana, 1954.
43631.76.700 Hardy, René. The sword by God. London, 1954.
43632.50.180 Hellens, Franz. Comme le raisin promis pour la vendange. Lyon, 1954.
43632.50.140 Hellens, Franz. Mémoires d'Elseneur. Paris, 1954.
37566.106 Henriot, Émile. Courrier littéraire, XIX siècle. Paris, 1954.
43701.63.830 Henry de Montherlant et son oeuvre. Paris, 1954?
Mol 496.1 Henusse, Theodor. Une pièce de Molière inconnue. Bruxelles, 1954.
42563.23.112.2 Heppenstall, Rayner. Léon Bloy. Cambridge, 1954.
43744.67.1220 Hindus, M. The Proustian vision. N.Y., 1954.
43709.23.800 Hommage à Marie Noël. Paris, 1954.
43636.89.130 Hougron, Jean. Blaze of the sun. London, 1954.
43636.89.120 Hougron, Jean. Les portes de l'aventure. Paris, 1954.
43638.7.800 Hubert, R.R. Asymptotes. Paris, 1954.
41574.14.30 Hugo, Victor. Journal. Paris, 1954.
43638.92.100 Huwart, Louis. L'odeur de notre amour. Malines, 1954.
43648.32.100 Igé, Jean. Jour le jour; poèmes. Paris, 1954.
43656.59.105 Ionesco, Eugène. Théâtre. 2. éd. Paris, 1954- 4v.
43667.14.250 Jacob, Max. Ballades. Paris, 1954.
41578.132 Jallaguier, B. Les idées politiques et sociales d'Alphonse de Lamartine. Montpellier, 1954.
43667.51.375 Jaloux, Edmond. Visage français. Paris, 1954.
43697.88.834 Jarrett-Kerr, M. François Mauriac. Cambridge, England, 1954.
43697.88.834.2 Jarrett-Kerr, M. François Mauriac. New Haven, 1954.
37574.790 Jones, P.M. Modern French verse. Manchester, Eng., 1954.
V43500.139 Joseph, Roger. Chants alternés pour deux déesses; poèmes. Orléans, 1954.
43670.89.450 Jouhandeau, M. Ana de Madame Apremont. 6. éd. Paris, 1954.
43670.89.610 Jouhandeau, M. Confidences. Paris, 1954.
43670.94.330 Jouve, Pierre Jean. En miroir. Paris, 1954.
43670.94.320 Jouve, Pierre Jean. Langue. Paris, 1954.
43670.95.130 Jouvet, Louis. Le comédien désincarné. Paris, 1954.
V43500.141 Julien. De la même forme que l'eau. Paris, 1954.
38546.90 Kauffmann, Lida. Die Briefe der Madame de Sévigné. Köln, 1954.
43761.39.855 Kessel, Patrick. La vie de St. Exupéry. Paris, 1954.
37565.140 Klemperer, V. Geschichte der französischen Literatur im 18. Jahrhundert. Berlin, 1954.
42587.28.80 Knowles, R.E. Victor-Emile Michelet. Thèse. Paris, 1954.
43681.3.100 Krakowsky, Georges. Le passenger, roman. Malines, 1954.
43683.5.30 Kues, Maurice. Le dire et le penser. Genève, 1954.
43620.2.310 Lafille, P. André Gide, romancier. Paris, 1954.
39527.29.30 La Fontaine, Jean de. Fables. N.Y., 1954.
41578.1.5 Lamartine, Alphonse de. La chute d'un ange. Genève, 1954.
41578.1.6 Lamartine, Alphonse de. La chute d'un ange. Thèse. Genève, 1954.
40535.19.800 Landois, Paul. The first French tragédie bourgeoise Silvie. Baltimore, 1954.
42576.65.13.114 Laner, James. The first decadent. London, 1954.
42586.14.6.55 Lanoizelée, Louis. Marguerite Audoux. Paris, 1954.
42584.25.200 Lanoux, A. Bonjour, Monsieur Zola. Paris, 1954.
43687.61.1125 Lanoux, Armand. La licorne. Paris, 1954.
43687.71.100 Laporte, René. La tête haute. Paris, 1954.
43822.49.1082 La Rochefoucauld, Edmée de Fels. Paul Valéry. Paris, 1954.
43687.89.1120 Laurent, Jacques. Le petit canard. Paris, 1954.
43688.5.5150 Léautaud, Paul. Journal littéraire. Paris, 1954-1956. 19v.
FL 375.83.2 Lebègue, Raymond. La tragédie française de la renaissance. 2. éd. Bruxelles, 1954.
V43500.169 Lebrau, Jean. Couleur de cèpe et de colchique. Bruxelles, 1954.
43688.13.5100 Leclère, Paul. Ecce vita. Paris, 1954?
43761.39.860 Le Hir, Y. Fantasie et mystique dans Le petit prince de St. Exupéry. Paris, 1954.
43688.49.1100 Lely, Gilbert. Ma civilisation. Paris, 1954.
43659.67.800 Lemaître, M. Isidore Isou. Paris, 1954.
43688.53.1110 Lemaitre, Maurice. Qu'est-ce que le lettrisme? Paris, 1954.
43688.52.100F Lemarchand, Jacques. L'odyssée d'Ulysse. Paris, 1954.
38537.36 Lenoir, P. Quelques aspects de la pensée de Rabelais. Paris, 1954.
42555.39.1110 Lerberghe, C. van. Lettres à une jeune fille. Bruxelles, 1954.
38575.90 Leroy, L. Polyeucte et la critique. Abbaye de Pontigny, 1954.
41574.310 Levaillant, M. La crise mystique de Victor Hugo (1843-1856) d'après des documents inédits. Paris, 1954.
43636.55.1100 L'homme du fonds des camps. Le raisin de Tokay. Malines, 1954.
43690.54.110 Limbosch, R. Il disait. Bruxelles, 1954.
38551.140 Lombard, Alfred. Fénelon et le retour a l'antique au XVIIIe siècle. Neuchâtel, 1954.
37597.9.23 Lorris, Guillaume de. Le roman de la rose. Milano, 1954-57. 2v.
43693.89.7100 Loudet, Louis. Soleils broyés. Paris, 1954.
40542.40 Louvain. Université catholique. Foundation Jules Besucci. Frédéric Ozanam. Louvain, 1954.
43526.65.865 Luca, A.T. Guillaume Apollinaire. Monaco, 1954.
43694.82.100 Lusreyran, Jacques. Et la lumière fût. Paris, 1954.
43697.8.1100 Mabit, Jacqueline. Couleur banlieue. Malines, 1954.
37565.145 McGhee, D.M. Fortunes of a tale. Menasha, Wisconsin, 1954.
43697.14.230 MacOrlan, Pierre. Poésies documentaires complètes. Paris, 1954.
40583.358 Maione, Italo. Due profili: Stendhal, G. de Nerval. Napoli, 1954.
43697.48.3112 Malaquais, Jean. Les javanais. Paris, 1954.
43697.48.3710 Malaquais, Jean. The joker. Garden City, 1954.

Chronological Listing

1954 - cont.

43697.61.4100 Manoury, Paul. Feuilles au vent et branches mortes. Evreux? 1954-
43697.61.2100 Mansour, Joyce. Cris. Paris, 1954.
43697.74.3700 Marceau, Félicien. The King's man. London, 1954.
43697.75.5700 Marchal, L. The sage of Canudos. London, 1954.
43620.2.320 Marchand, Max. Le complexe pedagogique et didactique d'André Gide. Oran, 1954.
38526.34.45 Margarete of Austria. Gedichte Margarethe's von Osterreich. Wien, 1954.
43697.76.6120 Maritain, Raïssa. Au creux du rocher. Paris, 1954.
40535.27.55 Marivaux, Pierre Carlet de Chamblain de. Marivaux, par lui-même. Paris, 1954.
43697.77.740 Martin du Gard, Roger. The postman. London, 1954.
41595.22.26 Martin-Maillefer, P.D. Los novios de Caracas, poema eclectico en dos cantos. Caracas, 1954.
43697.78.5130 Martin Saint-René (pseud.). Le sang des dieux. Paris, 1954.
37548.165 Martinet, E. Portraits d'écrivains romands contemporains. 2. série. Neuchâtel, 1954.
43697.78.140 Martinet, Marcel. Eux et moi. Monte-Carlo, 1954.
37567.220.13 Martino, Pierre. Parnasse et symbolisme. 9e éd. Paris, 1954.
43556.49.830 Maulnier, Thierry. Introduction à Colette. Paris, 1954.
43697.86.2110 Maulnier, Thierry. La maison de la nuit. Paris, 1954.
43822.49.1230 Maurer, K. Interpretation zur späteren Lyrik Paul Valérys. München, 1954.
43697.88.460 Mauriac, François. L'agneau. Paris, 1954.
43697.88.795 Mauriac, François. Paroles catholiques. Paris, 1954.
43697.88.785 Mauriac, François. The river of fire. London, 1954.
41574.302A Maurois, André. Olympio. Paris, 1954.
37568.132 Maurras, C. Maîtres et témoins de ma vie d'esprit. Paris, 1954.
42514.28.47 Maurras, Charles. Oeuvres capitales. Paris, 1954. 4v.
39566.92 May, Georges C. Diderot et la religieuse. 11. éd. New Haven, 1954.
38523.3.70 Mayer, C.A. Bibliographie des oeuvres de Clément Marot. v.1-2. Genève, 1954.
43620.74.875 Mercier-Campiche, M. Le théâtre de Giraudoux. Paris, 1954.
43698.75.7700 Merle, Robert. Death is my trade. London, 1954.
43698.200.180 Michaux, Henri. Face aux verrous. Paris, 1954.
43699.65.190 Miomandre, Francis de. Rencontres dans la nuit. Bienne, 1954.
43701.33.100 Mogin, Georges. La langue verte. Paris, 1954.
Mol 192.2 Molière, Jean Baptiste Poquelin. Don Juan. St. Albans, 1954.
Mol 19.54 Molière, Jean Baptiste Poquelin. Oeuvres complètes. Paris, 1954-56. 3v.
FL 6119.54 Mondolfo, R. Rousseau e la conscienza moderna. 1. ed. Firenze, 1954.
42555.44.115 Mondor, Henri. Mallarmé lycéen. Paris, 1954.
V43500.207 Monod, François. Exercices preliminaires. Lyon, 1954.
39594.08 Montesquieu, C.L. de S. Catalogue de la bibliothèque de Montesquieu. Genève, 1954.
39594.13.45 Montesquieu, C.L. de S. Lettres persanes. Genève, 1954.
43701.63.420 Montherlant, Henry de. L'histoire d'amour de la Rose de Sable. Paris, 1954.
43701.63.450 Montherlant, Henry de. Port-Royal. 73. éd. Paris, 1954.
43701.74.429 Morand, Paul. L'eau sous les ponts. 9. éd. Paris, 1954.
43606.75.800 Morgan, Claude. Yves Farge. Paris, 1954.
39566.72 Mortier, Roland. Diderot en Allemagne, 1750-1850. 1. éd. Paris, 1954.
43576.9.805 Mouton, J. Charles Du Bos. Paris, 1954.
43703.80.180 Muselli, Vincent. La barque allait. Paris, 1954.
37568.124 Nathan, J. Histoire de la littérature comtemporaine. Paris, 1954.
38537.25.220 Naudon, Paul. Rabelais. Paris, 1954.
41543.8.15 Nerval, Gerard de. La bohème galante. Paris, 1954.
43707.3.710 Nimier, Roger. Children of circumstance. London, 1954.
43709.23.120 Noël, Marie. L'âme en peine. Paris, 1954.
43714.8.110 Obey, André. Le joueur de triangle. Paris, 1954.
43620.2.6 O'Brien, J. Index détaillé des quinze volumes. Asnières, 1954.
43723.18.710 Oldenbourg, Zoé. The corner stone. London, 1954.
43723.18.100 Oldenbourg, Zoé. La pierre angulaire. 188. éd. Paris, 1954.
43731.85.120 Out-el-Kouloub. La nuit de la destinée. Paris, 1954.
38514.155 Ovide moralisé. Ovide moralisé en prose. Amsterdam, 1954.
37568.130 Paribatra, M. Le romantisme contemporain. Thèse. Paris, 1954.
42556.28.235 Paris. Bibliothèque nationale. Arthur Rimbaud. Paris, 1954.
43737.82.100 Passeur, Delia. Aux jeunes et aux vieux. Limoges, 1954.
43738.1.45 Péguy, Charles. Lettres et entretiens. Paris, 1954.
43738.49.102 Pellerin, Jean. Le bouquet inutile. Paris, 1954.
43738.76.140 Pergaud, Louis. Oeuvres. Paris, 1954.
43738.81.700 Perret, Jacques. The wind in the sails. London, 1954.
Mon 156.10 Peursen, C.A. van. Michel de Montaigne. Paris, 1954.
43738.97.1710 Peyrefitte, Roger. Diplomatic diversions. 2nd ed. London, 1954.
43738.97.1720 Peyrefitte, Roger. South from Naples. London, 1954.
FL 398.74.96 Piechaud, M. La vie privée de Rachel. Paris, 1954.
43744.67.1230 Pierre-Quint, Léon. Proust et la stratégie littéraire. Paris, 1954.
38585.16.210 Pommier, Jean. Aspects de Racine. Paris, 1954.
40522.9.40 Prévost, Antoine F. Histoire du chevalier des Grieux et de Manon Lescaut. Bordeaux, 1954.
43744.67.38.16 Proust, Marcel. A la recherche du temps perdu. Paris, 1954- 3v.
43744.67.51 Proust, Marcel. Contre Sainte-Beuve. 15. éd. Paris, 1954.
43744.67.21 Proust, Marcel. Marcel Proust. Paris, 1954.
43744.67.44.10 Proust, Marcel. Pages choisies. Paris, 1954.
37583.654A Puccioni, O.F. The French theater since 1930. Boston, 1954.
43750.20.110 Queffélec, Henri. Un homme d'Ouessant. Paris, 1954.
38583.18 Racine, Jean. Poésies religieuses inconnues. Landerman, 1954.
43761.39.865 Racky, E.A. Die Auffassung vom Menschen. Weisbaden, 1954.
43752.54.100 Rameau-Renevey, Camille. Juvéniles et magistrale présences. Chagny-en-Bourgogue, 1954.
43752.70.130 Rapin, Simone. La trêve de Dieu. Genève, 1954?
43757.50.1125 Relgis, Eugen. El hombre libre frente a la barbarie totalitaria. Montevideo, 1954.
43744.67.1225 Remacle, M. L'élément poétique dans A la Recherche du temps perdu de Marcel Proust. Bruxelles, 1954.
37567.475 Richard, J.P. Littérature et sensation. Paris, 1954.

1954 - cont.

43756.13.115 Richer, C. Son of Ti-Coyo. 1. American ed. N.Y., 1954.
V43500.255 Rieder, Violette. Limonaire; douze airs pour orgue de barbarie. Saint-Félicien, 1954.
42556.28.52 Rimbaud, Jean Arthur. Oeuvres complètes. Paris, 1954.
43757.12.110 Roblès, Emmanuel. Frederica. Paris, 1954.
43757.12.160 Roblès, Emmanuel. Montserrat. Paris, 1954.
41557.10.190 Roger, G. Les maîtres sonneurs de George Sand. Paris, 1954.
43757.50.62 Rolland, Romain. Printemps romain. Paris, 1954.
43757.3.290 Romains, Jules. Examen de conscience des Français. Paris, 1954.
43757.57.100 Romus, André. Voix dans le labyrinthe. Paris, 1954.
38525.20.28.3 Ronsard, Pierre de. Les amours. v.1-2. Paris, 1954.
43757.92.2120 Rousselot, Jean. Une fleur de sang. Paris, 1954.
43757.92.2130 Rousselot, Jean. Il n'y a pas d'exil. Paris, 1954.
V43500.271 Rousselot, Jean. Le pain se fait la nuit. Oran, 1954.
43757.96.210 Roy, Claude. Un seul poème. 6. éd. Paris, 1954.
37574.825 Roy, Claude. Trésor de la poésie populaire française. Paris, 1954.
43757.96.4103 Roy, Jules. Le navigateur. 47. éd. Paris, 1954.
43757.96.4707 Roy, Jules. Return from hell. 2d ed. London, 1954.
37557.41 Rutten, A. Les grands orateurs belges depuis 1830. Bruxelles, 1954.
43758.87.100 Ruttgers, Paul. Silences en moi. Paris, 1954.
43761.5.4100 Sabatier, Robert. Le marchand de sable. Paris, 1954.
40516.60.45 Sade, D.A.F. de. Adelaide of Brunswick. Washington, 1954.
40516.60.60 Sade, D.A.F. de. Monsieur le 6. Paris, 1954.
43761.31.100 Sagan, Françoise. Boujour tristesse. Paris, 1954.
43761.78.765 Sartre, Jean Paul. In the mesh. London, 1954.
43761.78.280 Sartre, Jean Paul. Le mur. Paris, 1954.
43761.78.622.10 Sartre, Jean Paul. No exit (Huis clos) a play in one act. N.Y., 1954.
40536.27.35 Saurin, Bernard J. Mirza and Fatima. London, 1954.
37567.456 Sauro, A. La lingua poetica in Francia. Bari, 1954.
43822.49.1200A Scarfe, F. The art of Paul Valéry. London, 1954.
43763.36.2110 Schehadé, Georges. La soirée des proverbes. Paris, 1954.
40532.36 Scherer, J. La dramaturgie de Beaumarchais. Paris, 1954.
38557.24.90 Schmittlein, R. L'aspect politique du différend Bossuet-Fénelon. Bade, 1954.
Mon 129.6 Schon, Peter M. Vorformen des Essays in Antike und Humanismus. Wiesbaden, 1954.
37562.290 Scivoletto, Nino. Spiritualitá medioevale e tradizione scolastica nel secolo XII en Francia. Napoli, 1954.
43765.90.100 Sénac, Jean. Poèmes. 3. éd. Paris, 1954.
43765.76.100 Sernin, André. L'apprenti philosophe. Paris, 1954.
43769.54.765 Simenon, Georges. Across the street. London, 1954.
43769.54.770 Simenon, Georges. Inspector Maigret and the strangled stripper. 1. ed. Garden City, 1954.
43769.54.722 Simenon, Georges. Tidal wave. Garden City, 1954.
43769.56.2110 Simon, Claude. Le sacré du printemps, roman. Paris, 1954.
43775.89.2710A Soubiran, André. The healing oath. N.Y., 1954.
38526.48.160 Sponde, Jean de. Meditation, avec un Essai de poèmes chretiens. Paris, 1954.
41522.67.82 Starkie, E. Petrus Borel. London, 1954.
41522.67.83 Starkie, E. Petrus Borel. Norfolk, 1954.
43620.2.303 Starkie, Enid. André Gide. New Haven, 1954.
42556.28.157A Starkie, Enid. Athur Rimbaud. Oxford, 1954.
43779.23.1100 Sten, Oliven. Le passant démesuré. Paris, 1954.
43822.49.1210 Suckling, N. Paul Valéry. London, 1954.
41522.18.265 Sugar, L. de. Baudelaire et R.M. Rilke. Paris, 1954.
42577.4.33.10 Sullivan, E.D. Maupassant the novelist. Princeton, 1954.
43687.54.800 Synthèses; revue mensuelle internationale, Bruxelles. Maurice Lambilliotte. Bruxelles, 1954?
43785.75.130 Tardieu, Jean. Une voix sans personne. Paris, 1954.
43785.76.100 Taricat, Jacques. Médailles; poèmes. Paris, 1954.
FL 6139.54.10 Testa, Aldo. Sulle orme di Rousseau. Mazara, 1954.
43620.2.315 Theis, Raimund. Untersuchungen über "Poesie" und "Kunst" bei André Gide. Köln, 1954.
37543.335 Tielrooy, J.B. Verkenningen in het land der literatuur. Groningen, 1954.
43792.40.120 Toesca, Maurice. Le dernier cri d'un homme, roman. Paris, 1954.
43792.40.110 Toesca, Maurice. L'expérience amoureuse. Paris, 1954.
42577.4.49.125 Togeby, K. L'oeuvre de Maupassant. Copenhague, 1954.
43833.20.820 Tomin, E.W.F. Simone Weil. Cambridge, Eng., 1954.
43793.67.230 Troyat, Henri. Les semailles et les moissons. Paris, 1954.
37567.460 Valeri, D. Il simbolismo francese da Nerval a de Régnier. Padova, 1954.
43822.49.152 Valéry, Paul. Monsieur Teste. Paris, 1954.
43822.58.1100 Vandamme, Robert. Briser te convient. Malines, 1954.
42576.63.210 Vandegans, A. Anatole France. Paris, 1954.
43822.90 Vauthier, Jean. Théâtre. Paris, 1954-
43823.25.100 Veraldi, Gabriele. La machine humaine. 80. éd. Paris, 1954.
43823.75.180 Vercel, Roger. L'île des revenants, roman. Paris, 1954.
42577.4.49.130 Vial, André. La genése d'"Une vie". Paris, 1954.
42577.4.49.131 Vial, André. La genése d'"Une vie". Thèse. Paris, 1954.
42577.4.49.135 Vial, André. Guy de Maupassant et l'art du roman. Thèse. Paris, 1954.
43824.3.175 Vialar, Paul. The silver spur. London, 1954.
43824.3.2110 Vialatte, A. Fruit of the Congo. London, 1954.
43824.6.120 Vigée, Claude. La corne du grand pardon, poème. Paris, 1954.
41564.31.30 Vigny, Alfred de. Lettres à Brizeux. Paris, 1954.
42547.21.5 Villiers de l'Isle Adam, Auguste. Contes cruels. Paris, 1954-
42547.17.25 Villiers de l'Isle Adam, Auguste. Réliqués. Paris, 1954.
43824.54.110 Vilmorin, Louise de. L'alphabet des aveux. Paris, 1954.
43824.54.115 Vilmorin, Louise de. Les belles amours, roman. Paris, 1954.
43824.54.105 Vilmorin, Louise de. Madame de. Paris, 1954.
43824.58.1100 Vinçotte, J.H. Le bouguet dans l'incendie. Paris, 1954.
37555.190A Vivier, Robert. Et la poésie fut langage. Bruxelles, 1954.
V43500.323 Voisard, Alexandre. Écrit sur un mur. Porrentruy, 1954.
38524.110.5 Weinberg, B. French poetry of the renaissance. N.Y., 1954.
43833.98.110 Weygand, J. Goumier de l'Atlas. Paris, 1954.
FL 6129.54 Wille, Hans J. Die Gefährtin. 2. Aufl. Berlin, 1954.
37555.15 Winegarten, R. French lyric poetry. Manchester, 1954.
37530.140 Woledge, Brian. Bibliographie des romans et nouvelles en prose française antérieurs. Genève, 1954.
43848.76.100 Yerlès, Pierre. Peintures de craie. Malines, 1954.
43852.89.140 Yourcenar, Marguerite. Électre, ou La chute des masques. Paris, 1954.

Chronological Listing

1954 - cont.

43852.89.700A Yourcenar, Marguerite. Memoirs of Hadrian. N.Y., 1954.
38543.22.30 Zeller, Mary F. New aspects of style in the Maxims of La Rochefoucauld. Washington, 1954.
38514.18.12 Ziwes, Armand. Le jargon de François Villon. Paris, 1954. 2v.
42584.23.90 Zola, Emile. The kill. N.Y., 1954.
37562.288 Zumthor, Paul. Histoire littéraire de la France médiévale. 1. éd. Paris, 1954.

1955

42557.20.268 Adam, Antoine. Verlaine. Paris, 1955.
43697.77.4800 Adam-Rosé, L. La vie de Marietta Martin. Paris, 1955.
43514.6.110 Adamov, Arthur. Théâtre. v.1, 4. éd.; v.2, 3. éd. Paris, 1955. 4v.
43744.67.1280 Adan, Antoine. Marcel Proust. Paris, 1955.
43514.24.2100 Aderca Bouton, Juliette. Ce rire a traversé le bois. Malines, 1955.
39574.27.25 Alembert, J. Le Rond d'. Einleitung zur Enzyklopädie von 1751. Hamburg, 1955.
43522.98.1100 Alzin, Josse. Ce rein miraculeux. Malines, 1955.
43554.2.950 Andrieu, J. La foi dans l'oeuvre de Paul Claudel. Paris, 1955.
38525.5.15 Anthologie des poètes du seizième siècle. Paris, 1955.
43526.65.240 Apollinaire, Guillaume. Anecdotiques. 5. ed. Paris, 1955.
43526.65.101 Apollinaire, Guillaume. Calligrammes. Paris, 1955.
43528.32.100 Arger, Hubert. De cinabre et d'ombre. Paris, 1955.
37543.350 Arland, Marcel. La grâce d'écrire. 2. éd. Paris, 1955.
42556.28.222 Arnoult, Pierre. Rimbaud. Paris, 1955.
43528.61.170 Arnoux, Alexandre. Le seigneur de l'heure, recit. Paris, 1955.
42577.4.49.116 Artinian, Artine. Pour et contre Maupassant. Paris, 1955.
43531.18.1120 Audiberti, Jacques. L'Abhumanisme. 2. éd. Paris, 1955.
43531.18.1130 Audiberti, Jacques. La beauté de l'amour. Paris, 1955.
43531.18.1184 Audiberti, Jacques. Le cavalier seul. Paris, 1955.
43744.67.109 Autret, Jean. L'influence de Ruskin sur la vie. Genève, 1955.
43532.41.1100 Avicenne, Paul. Feuilles des hommes. Maliness, 1955.
42555.44.130 Ayda, Adile. Le drame interieur de Mallarmé. Istanbul, 1955.
43536.74.1100 Azra, Georges. L'ame sous le sexe. Malines, 1955.
38546.85 Bailly, A. Madame de Sévigné. Paris, 1955.
43537.41.1100 Baiocchi, A. Acquetinte. Sarzana, 1955.
42576.65.13.120 Baldick, Robert. The life of J.K. Huysmans. Oxford, 1955.
40597.14.6.18 Balzac, Honoré de. César Birotteau. N.Y., 1955.
40596.7.2 Balzac, Honoré de. Oeuvres. n.p., 1955-63. 28v.
43537.77.5100 Baroche, Jacques. Au bois cruel. Paris, 1955.
43537.82.2100 Basson, Pierre. Chemin d'homme. Paris, 1955.
41522.13.9.28 Baudelaire, Charles. The flowers of evil. Norfolk, 1955.
41522.13.8.50 Baudelaire, Charles. Les fleurs du mal; 14 poems. Baltimore, 1955.
41522.6.7 Baudelaire, Charles. The mirror of art. London, 1955.
41522.5.20 Baudelaire, Charles. Oeuvres complètes. Paris, 1955. 2v.
43538.1.215 Béalu, Marcel. La rivièra. Aulnay-sous-Bois, 1955?
43538.1.442 Beauvoir, Simone de. All men are mortal. 1. ed. Cleveland, 1955.
43538.1.500 Beauvoir, Simone de. Privilèges. 9. éd. Paris, 1955.
43538.14.750 Beckett, Samuel. Molloy. Paris, 1955.
43538.14.130 Beckett, Samuel. Nouvelles et textes pour rien. Paris, 1955.
38512.130 Bell, Dora M. Étude sur le songe du vieil pèlerin de Philippe de Mézières. Genève, 1955.
43822.49.1154 Bémol, Maurice. La parque et le serpent. Paris, 1955.
43833.20.850 Berger, Herman. De gedachtenwereld van Simone Weil. Antwerpen, 1955.
39594.19.65 Berlin, Isaiah. Montesquieu. London, 1955?
43538.76.190 Bernanos, Georges. Dialogue d'ombres. Paris, 1955.
43538.76.220 Bernanos, Georges. La France contre los robots. Paris, 1955.
43538.76.151.3 Bernanos, Georges. Monsieur Ouine. 1. éd. Paris? 1955.
42542.29.28.800 Bernard, J.J. Mon père Tristan Bernard. Paris, 1955.
43538.76.1120 Bernard, Marc. Salut. 8. éd. Paris, 1955.
39544.250 Besterman, Theodore. Travaux sur Voltaire. Genève, 1955- 88v.
43606.76.820 Beucler, André. Poet of Paris. London, 1955.
40582.4.155A Beyle, Henri. Oeuvres intimes de Stendhal. Paris, 1955.
40582.34.6 Beyle, Henri. The private diaries of Stendhal. London, 1955.
43626.66.1140 Bible. O.T. Prophets. Les prophètes. Paris, 1955.
FL 398.13.50 Bibliographie des oeuvres de Gustave Cohen. Paris, 1955.
38523.36 Bibliotèque Nationale, Paris. Malherbe et les poétes de son temps. Paris, 1955.
43552.5.1855 Bibliothèque Nationale, Paris. Alain. Exposition de manuscrits, de livres et de divers souvenirs. Paris, 1955.
42557.11.165 Bibliothèque nationale, Paris. Emile Verhaeren. Paris, 1955.
41543.21.80 Bibliothèque nationale, Paris. Gerard de Nerval. Paris, 1955.
40575.5.180 Bibliothèque nationale, Paris. Sainte-Beuve. Paris, 1955.
43543.4.3100 Blanchard, Maurice. Le pain, la lumière. Paris, 1955.
43543.14.710 Bloch-Michel, J. The flight into Egypt. N.Y., 1955.
43543.14.113 Bloch-Michel, J. Journal du Désordre. 4. éd. Paris, 1955.
43543.67.100 Blondin, Antoine. L'humeur vagabonde. Paris, 1955.
43544.18.130 Bodin, Jean. Reconstitution de la Mêlée. Chambéry, 1955.
40583.394 Boncompain, Claude. Stendhal; ou, La double vie de Henri Beyle. Paris, 1955.
37564.235 Bonfantini, Mario. La letteratura francese del XVII secolo. Napoli, 1955.
39594.19.53 Bordeaux. Bibliothèque Municipale. Montesquieu. Bordeaux, 1955.
43611.5.105 Borgal, Clément. Alain-Fournier. Paris, 1955.
43544.81.140 Bory, Jean Louis. Clio dans les blés. Paris, 1955.
43544.81.2150 Bosco, Henri. Les Balesta. 5. éd. Paris, 1955.
43544.81.2710 Bosco, Henri. The dark bough. London, 1955.
43544.89.2130 Bosquet, Alain. Quel royaume oublié? Paris, 1955.
43544.108.710 Boulle, Pierre. Not the glory. N.Y., 1955.
43544.89.3100 Bourniquel, Camille. Le blé sauvage. Paris, 1955.
43544.106.110 Boutelleau, G. Les fétiches. Paris, 1955.
43545.4.4160 Brasillach, Robert. Journal d'un homme occupé. Paris, 1955.
43744.67.1235A Brée, Germaine. Marcel Proust and deliverance from time. New Brunswick, N.J., 1955.
43545.24.200 Breton, André. Les vases communicants. Paris, 1955.
43537.6.105 Brett, Vladimir. Henri Barbusse a oblas jeho díla a činnosti u nás. Praha, 1955.

1955 - cont.

42566.66 Bruyère, Marcel. La jeunesse d'Alphonse Daudet. Paris, 1955.
43546.37.35 Buhet, Gil. The story-teller. London, 1955.
37576.655.5 Burger, H.C. La France d'hier et d'aujourd'hui. Melbourne, 1955.
43546.76.100 Burniaux, Constant. L'autocar. Bruxelles, 1955?
37543.203 Calvet, Jean. Histoire de la littérature française. Paris, 1955- 10v.
43550.58.735.5 Camus, Albert. The myth of Sisyphus, and other essays. N.Y., 1955.
43550.58.735 Camus, Albert. The myth of Sisyphus. 1. American ed. N.Y., 1955. 2v.
43550.70.2100 Caplandres, Pierre Arnaud. Ici repose...(un cemetière imaginaire). 1. éd. Paris, 1955.
43550.1.22 Carco, Francis. Poésies complètes. Paris, 1955.
43550.77.2110 Caroutch, Yvonne. Les veilleurs endormis. Paris, 1955.
43550.75.3100 Carrez, Michel. Arsenal du jour, poèmes. Paris, 1955.
38525.38 Carriat, A. Bibliographie des oeuvres de Tristan L'Hermite. Limoges, 1955.
38525.38.10 Carriat, A. Tristan. Limoges, 1955.
43550.79.1100 Casazza, Jean. Virginité. Paris, 1955.
43550.82.180 Cassou, Jean. Le livre de Lazare. Paris, 1955.
43550.90.100 Cavens, A. Perspectives. Malines, 1955.
43550.98.140 Cayrol, Jean. Pour tous les temps. Paris, 1955.
43550.98.2100 Cazalis, Marc. La marche au cercueil. Paris, 1955.
37543.340 Cazamian, Louis. A history of French literature. Oxford, 1955.
42557.12.120 Černý, V. Emile Verhaeren a jeho místo v dějinách volného verse. Praha, 1955.
43552.2.1140 Chadourne, Marc. Le mal de Colleen. Paris, 1955.
43552.3.130 Chaine, Pierre. Le Duc Assassin. Paris, 1955.
43552.3.8120 Champigny, Robert. Brûler. Paris, 1955.
43552.4.2190 Char, René. Poèmes des deux années, 1953-1954. Paris, 1955.
43552.4.2180 Char, René. Recherche de la base et du sommet. Paris, 1955.
43552.4.8100 Charpier, Jacques. Mythologie du vent. Paris, 1955.
43552.5.1020 Chartier, Emile. Vingt et une scenes de comedie. Paris, 1955.
43552.7.4100 Chastel, Lou. Lumières. Paris, 1955.
43552.6.135 Chateaubriant, Alphonse de. Cahiers, 1906-1951. 2e éd. Paris, 1955.
43552.18.140 Chédid, Andrée. Jonathan, roman. Paris, 1955.
43552.18.130 Chédid, Andrée. Textes pour la terre aimée. Paris, 1955.
43552.24.3100 Cherry, Dominique. Sixieme sens. Paris, 1955.
43552.25.2104 Chevallier, Gabriel. Clochemerle-Babylon. London, 1955.
42557.12.105 Christophe, L. Émile Verhaeren. Paris, 1955.
43553.3 Cingria, Charles Albert. Charles Albert Cingria. Genève, 1955.
43553.3.100 Cingria, Charles Albert. Xénia et le diamant. Lyon, 1955.
41539.42 Clanard, Henri. Alexandre Dumas. Paris, 1955.
43554.2.465 Claudel, Paul. L'aime la Bible. Paris, 1955.
43554.2.455 Claudel, Paul. Lettres sur la Bible au R.P.R. Paroissin. Paris, 1955.
43554.7.38.5 Clemenceau, Georges. Figures de Vendée. Halle, 1955.
43556.49.840 Cocteau, Jean. Colette. Paris, 1955.
43556.1.35A Cocteau, Jean. Discours de réception. 8e éd. Paris, 1955.
43556.1.410 Cocteau, Jean. Jean Cocteau. Paris, 1955.
38513.70.10 Cohen, Gustave. Anthologie du drame liturgique en France au Moyen-Âge. Paris, 1955.
43556.49.540 Colette, Sidonie Gabrielle. Belles saisons. Paris, 1955.
43556.49.732 Colette, Sidonie Gabrielle. The vagabond. N.Y., 1955.
38523.37 Comité aixois du 4e centenaire de la naissance de Malherbe. Malherbe et la Provence. Aix-en-Provence, 1955.
42545.3.550 Compere, Gaston. Le théâtre de Maurice Maeterlinck. Bruxelles, 1955.
40553.9.65 Constant de Rebecque, Benjamin. Adolphe. Paris, 1955.
40553.9.70 Constant de Rebecque, Benjamin. Benjamin et Rosalie de Constant. Paris, 1955.
37530.155 Cordie, Carlo. Avviamento allo studio della lingua e della letteratura francese. Milano, 1955.
43556.82.715 Cossery, Albert. Mendiants et orgueilleux. Paris, 1955.
43556.89.6100 Courtir, Charles. Sonnets pour Orphée. Paris, 1955.
43556.1.830 Crosland, M. Jean Cocteau. London, 1955.
43560.78.1100 Cury, Maurice. Vert-quatre. Paris, 1955.
37566.178 D'Aló, Oresto A. Algunos hombres, algunas ideas: Amiel, Renán, Becher, Ingenieros. Santa Fe, 1955.
38551.152 Danielou, Madeleine C. Fénelon et le duc de Bourgogne. Paris, 1955.
43565.60.1110A Daninos, Pierre. The notebooks of Major Thompson. 1st American ed. N.Y., 1955.
43565.61.1100 Dansart, Olivier. Mouvements, poèmes. Paris, 1955.
43565.76.100 Dariel, Jean-Loup. Les cahiers d'Olivier. Paris, 1955.
42586.33.100 Darien, Georges. Le voleur. Sceaux, 1955.
43565.90.5100 Daveau, René Raoul. Le mendiant d'eau pure. Paris, 1955.
43788.41.810 Davies, J.C. L'oeuvre critique d'Albert Thibaudet. Genève, 1955.
43565.97.100 Dax, Claire. Au long du jour. Paris, 1955.
43620.74.880 Debidour, V.H. Jean Giraudoux. Paris, 1955.
38544.27.575A Dédéyan, Charles. Madame de La Fayette. Paris, 1955.
43566.29.100 Defosse, Marcel. Les masques du destin. Paris, 1955.
43566.36.120 Deharme, Lise. Le poids d'un oiseau. Paris, 1955.
43697.52.825 Delhomme, Jeanne. Temps et destin. 2. éd. Paris, 1955.
43620.2.340 Delmas-Marsalet, M. Jean Yves. André Gide l'enchainé. Bordeaux, 1955.
40535.32.36 Deloffre, Frédéric. Une préciosité nouvelle, Marivaux et le Marivaudage. Thèse. Paris, 1955.
40535.32.35 Deloffre, Frédéric. Une préciosité nouvelle. Paris, 1955.
43566.62.105 Déon, Michel. Tout l'amour du monde. Paris, 1955-
43566.76.3100 Dermèze, Yves. Le mess ager du roi Henri. Paris, 1955.
FL 396.80 Derval, Paul. The Folies Bergère. London, 1955.
FL 383.160 Descotes, M. Le drame romantique et ses grands createurs, 1827-1839. Paris, 1955.
43566.81.7100 Desmeuzes, Jean. Les marches de la brume. Paris, 1955.
43566.81.4130 Desnos, Robert. Chantefables et Chantefleurs. Paris, 1955.
43566.82.7170 Destouches, Louis Ferdinand. Entretiens avec le professeur Y. Paris, 1955.
43567.79.140 Dhôtel, André. La chronique fabuleuse. Paris, 1955.
43567.79.120 Dhôtel, André. Mémoires de Sebastien. Paris, 1955.
43567.79.130 Dhôtel, André. Le pays, ou L'on n'arrive jamais. Paris, 1955.
39564.61.5 Diderot, Denis. Correspondance. Paris, 1955. 16v.
39564.10.76 Diderot, Denis. Supplément au voyage de Bougainville. Genève, 1955.

Chronological Listing

1955 - cont.

43744.67.1270 Donze, Roland. Le comique dans l'oeuvre de Marcel Proust. Neuchâtel, 1955.
38526.6.18.10 Du Bellay, Joachim. Les regrets. Paris, 1955.
43576.9.5100 Dubois, Frédèric. La part du feu. Paris, 1955.
43544.71.120 Duckworth, C. A study of Leon Bopp. Genève, 1955.
43576.6.765 Duhamel, Georges. L'archange de l'aventure. Paris, 1955.
43576.6.460 Duhamel, Georges. Vie et aventures de Salavin. Paris, 1955. 5v.
43576.53.1100 Dumas, Hubert. Passeport pour l'unique frontière. Paris, 1955.
40583.225 DuParc, Yves. Dans le sillage de Stendhal. Lyon, 1955.
43576.87.705 Dutourd, Jean. The best butter. N.Y., 1955.
43576.87.130 Dutourd, Jean. Doucin. 18. éd. Paris, 1955.
43576.87.140 Dutourd, Jean. Le petit Don Juan. Paris, 1955.
43576.88.100 Dutreil, Nicole. Le miel acide. 5. éd. Paris, 1955.
42554.30.4 Elskamp, M. L'amitié de Max Elskamp et d'Albert Mockel. Bruxelles, 1955.
43592.53.270 Emmanuel, Pierre. Visage nuage. Paris, 1955.
43757.50.1080 Europe. Revue Mensuelle. Romain Rolland. Paris, 1955.
40526.8.55 Fabre, Jean. André Chénier, l'homme et l'oeuvre. Paris, 1955.
43606.76.190 Fargue, Léon P. Pour la peinture. Paris, 1955.
43606.91.100 Favre, André. L'acier victorieux. Avignon, 1955.
40583.295 Feuillade, J.H. Notes sur Stendhal. Paris, 1955.
43609.50.100 Filiatrault, Jean. Chaînes. Montréal, 1955.
42576.16.30 Flaubert, Gustave. Flaubert. Paris, 1955.
43610.22.140 Fleg, Edmond. Ecoute, Israël. Paris, 1955.
43611.53.120 Fombeure, Maurice. Une forêt de charme. Paris, 1955.
38562.20.20 Fontenelle, B. Le B. de. Entretiens sur la pluralité des mondes. Oxford, 1955.
43611.76.1100 Forneret, Xavier. Le diamant de l'herbe. Paris, 1955.
41584.43.5 Forneret, Xavier. Le diamant de l'herbe. Paris, 1955.
37574.780 Fowlie, W. Mid-century French poets. N.Y., 1955.
Mon 116.42 Frame, Donald Murdoch. Montaigne's discovery of man. N.Y., 1955.
43744.67.1240 France. Direction genérale des relations culturelles. Marcel Proust and his time. London, 1955.
FL 394.140 France in the United States Monthly. A special issue in honor of the first appearance in the United States of the Comédie française. N.Y., 1955.
42584.25.215 Frandon, Ida Marie. Autour de Germinal. Genève, 1955.
43612.65.100 Frank, Bernard. L'illusion comique. Paris, 1955.
39566.115 Fredman, A.G. Diderot and Sterne. N.Y., 1955.
43612.41.110 Frick, Louis de Gonzague. Abrupta nubes. Paris, 1955.
43612.41.100 Frick, Louis de Gonzague. Statures lyriques. Paris, 1955.
39534.20.10 Furetière, Antoine. Le Roman bourgeois. Paris, 1955?
43616.17.100 Gadenne, Paul. L'invitation chez les Stirl. 6. éd. Paris, 1955.
43616.41.2110 Gaillard, Robert. Images du neilleur des mondes. Givors, 1955.
V43500.127 Gali, Christian. Hectares de Paris. Paris, 1955.
37575.705 Gallotti, Jean. Le Paris des poètes et des romanciers. Paris, 1955.
37568.138 Garnier, C. L'homme et son personnage. Paris, 1955.
43822.49.1275 Garrigue, F. Goeth et Valéry. Paris, 1955.
43616.79.220 Gascar, Pierre. Les femmes. Paris, 1955.
43616.79.120 Gascar, Pierre. La graine. 17. éd. Paris, 1955.
43538.76.870 Gaucher, Guy. Le thème de la mort dans les romans de Georges Bernanos. Paris, 1955.
41574.510 Gaudon, J. Victor Hugo. Paris, 1955.
37566.115 George, A.J. The development of French romanticism. Syracuse, N.Y., 1955.
43620.2.10 Gide, André. André Gide - Paul Valéry. 14. éd. Paris, 1955.
43620.48.100 Gilbert-Lecomte, Roger. Testament. Paris, 1955.
43620.66.750 Giono, Jean. The malediction. N.Y., 1955.
43620.66.410 Giono, Jean. Notes sur l'affaire Dominici. 3. éd. Paris, 1955.
43620.74.1110 Giraudoux, Jean Pierre. Ce n'est pas Angeline. Paris, 1955.
43622.23.100 Glejser, Herbert. La rencontre à l'aube. Malines, 1955.
43622.41.120 Glissant, Edouard. La terre inquiète. Paris, 1955.
43625.19.310 Godoy, Armand. Monologue de la Tristesse. Paris, 1955.
43752.18.800 Goesch, Keith. Raymond Radiguet. Paris, 1955.
37558.155 Goldmann, L. Le dieu caché. Paris, 1955.
42575.71.30 Goncourt, Edmond de. Germinie Lacerteux. N.Y., 1955.
43625.91.100 Govy, G. Le moissonneur d'Epines. Paris, 1955.
38585.16.215 Grasclaude, P. Le renoncement de Jean Racine. Paris, 1955.
43626.5.130 Grasset, B. Evangile de l'édition selon Péguy. Paris, 1955.
43626.23.1130 Grenier, Jean. Lexique. Paris, 1955.
FL 6119.55 Grien, J. Charles. Jean-Jacques Rousseau. Cambridge, 1955.
Mol 707.5 Grimarest, J.L. La vie de Monsieur de Molière. Paris, 1955.
37565.150 Grundpositionen der franzözischen Aufklärung. 1. Aufl. Berlin, 1955.
FL 6049.20 Guarnieri, Primo. L'educazione femmile nel pensiero di G.G. Rousseau. Adria, 1955.
41522.18.280 Guex, André. Art baudelairien. Lausanne, 1955.
43757.50.1100 Gugenheim, S. Romain Rolland e l'Italia. Milano, 1955.
43554.2.945 Guillemin, H. Claudel et son art d'ecrire. 2e éd. Paris, 1955.
41564.55.90 Guillemin, Henri. M. de Vigny. 7. ed. Paris, 1955.
FL 355.40 Guiraud, P. Index du vocabulaire du théâtre classique. v.1-4. Paris, 1955- 19v.
FL 355.40F Guiraud, P. Index du vocabulaire du théâtre classique. v.5-6. Paris, 1955. 2v.
43628.1.115 Guitry, Sacha. Napoléon. Paris, 1955.
43628.85.110 Guth, Paul. Le naïf aux quarante enfants. Paris, 1955.
41574.320 Guyer, F.E. The Titan. N.Y., 1955.
43631.03.110 Haedens, Kléber. Adieu â la rose. 5. éd. Paris, 1955.
43631.45.100 Halsdorf, Denyse. Poèmes d'adolescence. Paris, 1955.
39586.11.4 Hampton, John. Nicolas Antoine Boulanger et la science de son temps. Genève, 1955.
43632.50.162 Hellens, Franz. Fantômes vivants. 2. éd. Paris, 1955.
37566.108.5 Henriot, Émile. Courrier littéraire, XIX-XX siècles. Paris, 1955.
43632.79.100 Hertz, Henri. Tragédie des temps volages. Paris, 1955.
37556.12.40 Hisard, Claude. Histoire de la spoliation de la presse française. Paris, 1955.
37569.210 Hubbard, L.J. The individual and the group in French literature since 1914. Washington, 1955.
38557.24.100 Hubert, Jean. Manuscrits de J.B. Bossuet. Melun, 1955.
41573.49 Hugo, Victor. Victor Hugo s'amuse. Paris, 1955.

1955 - cont.

43638.83.110 Huszar, Étienne. J'ai éteint le soleil. Malines, 1955.
43638.83.100 Huszar, Étienne. La raison d'être. Malines, 1955.
42576.65.80.22 Huysmans, Joris Karl. Marthe; histoire d'une fille. Paris, 1955.
43652.46.100 Ikor, Roger. Les fils d'Avrom. Paris, 1955.
43757.50.1048 Ilberg, Werner. Der schwere Weg. Schwerin, 1955.
42584.25.220 Jagmetti, Antoinette. La bête humaine d'Emile Zola. Genève, 1955.
42562.60.80 Jakovsky, Anatole. Alphonse Allais, le tueur à gags. Paris, 1955.
43744.67.1250 Jauss, Hans R. Zeit und Erinnerung in Marcel Prousts A la recherche du temps perdu. Heidelberg, 1955.
38525.7.25 Jodelle, d'Estienne. L'Eugene. Milano, 1955.
43670.79.100 Josa, Solange Claude. Soleil de cendres. Paris, 1955.
43670.89.470 Jouhandeau, M. Contes d'enfer. 4. éd. Paris, 1955.
43671.51.2100 Julian, E. Poèmes et chansons. Avignon, 1955.
37543.360 Kemp, Robert. La vie des livres. Paris, 1955. 2v.
V43500.143 Klingsor, Tristan (pseud.). Florilège poétique. Blainville-sur-Mer, 1955.
37542.52 Kohler, Pierre. Histoire de la littérature française. Lausanne, 1955. 3v.
38526.26.85 Labé, Louise Charly. Il canzoniere. Parma, 1955.
43687.14.100 Lacour, José André. Confession interdite. Paris, 1955.
43687.26.5100 Lafond, Madeleine. Au tonkin. Lezay, 1955.
42584.25.210 Lanoux, A. Zola. London, 1955.
38585.16.220 Lapp, John C. Aspects of Racinian tragedy. Toronto, 1955.
43687.74.210 Larbaud, Valéry. Journal, 1912-1935. 2e éd. Paris, 1955.
43687.74.700 Larbaud, Valéry. Poems of a multimillionaire. N.Y.? 1955.
43687.77.3120 La Rochefoucauld, Edmée (de Fels). Choix de poèmes. Paris, 1955.
43538.1.457 Lå Vouldie. Mme. Simone de Beauvoir et ses "Mandarins". Paris, 1955.
38523.3.75 Leblanc, Paulette. La poésie religieuse de Clément Marot. Thèse. Paris, 1955.
41596.4.105 Lefebvre, Henri. Alfred de Musset. Paris, 1955.
38537.37 Lefebvre, Henri. Rabelais. Paris, 1955.
38525.99 Leiner, W. Etude stylistique et litteraire de Venceslas. Saarbrücken, 1955.
43688.89.1100 Leuck, René Georges. La nuit en cause. Paris, 1955.
43688.93.100 Levy, Jacques. Journal et correspondance. Grenoble, 1955.
42533.19.25 L'Hopital, Suzanne Aline. Joseph Milsand. Dijon, 1955.
43554.2.955 Lindemann, R. Kreuz und Eros. Paul Claudels. Frankfurt, 1955.
40583.178.5 Litto, Victor del. En marge des manuscrits de Stendhal. Paris, 1955.
43693.89.6100 Louve, Annie. Route barrée, poèmes. Paris, 1955.
43694.8.120 Lubin, Armen. Transfert nocturne. 4. éd. Paris, 1955.
43697.14.240 MacOrlan, Pierre. La trádition de minuit. 2e ed. Paris, 1955.
41578.134 Magnien, Emil. Dans l'intimité de Lamartine. Macon, 1955.
43620.2.335 Mahias, C.J. La vie d'André Gide. Paris, 1955.
43697.2.2110 Mallet, Robert. Une mort ambiguë. 7. éd. Paris, 1955.
43697.52.112 Malraux, André. La condition humaine. Paris, 1955.
37556.21.46 Manevy, Raymond. La presse da la III république. Paris, 1955.
43697.61.2110 Mansour, Joyce. Déchirures. Paris, 1955.
40597.2.385 Marceau, F. Balzac et son monde. 6. ed. Paris, 1955.
43697.74.3120 Marceau, Félicien. Les élans du coeur. 94. ed. Paris, 1955.
43697.75.145 Marcel, Gabriel. Croissez et multipliez. Paris, 1955.
43697.75.155 Marcel, Gabriel. L'homme problematique. Paris, 1955.
43697.75.135A Marcel, Gabriel. Mon temps n'est pas le vôtre. Paris, 1955.
43697.79.3100 Mariabère, Jean. Sténogrammes, le troisième livre des poèmes. Casablanca, 1955.
43738.1.245 Marie-Louis, Mère. Culte marial de Charles Péguy. Nicolet, Quebec, 1955.
43697.76.5 Mariel, Anne. Lola Montés. Paris, 1955.
41543.22.80 Marill, René. Gerard de Nerval. Paris, 1955.
40535.28.3 Marivaux, Pierre Carlet de Chamblain de. Le petit-maître corrigé. Genève, 1955.
43697.78.1100 Martin-Chauffier, Simone. La première personne. Paris, 1955.
43697.77.220 Martin du Gard, Roger. Oeuvres complétes. Paris, 1955. 2v.
43697.78.5150 Martin Saint-René (pseud.). Bleu, blanc, rouge. Paris, 1955.
43697.78.2100 Martine, Claude. La vie de palace. 4. ed. Paris, 1955.
42577.4.2.16 Maupassant, Guy de. Bel-ami. London, 1955.
42577.1.26 Maupassant, Guy de. The complete short stories. 1. ed. Garden City, 1955.
42577.1.14 Maupassant, Guy de. Huit contes choisis. Halle, 1955.
43697.88.790 Mauriac, François. Flesh and blood. N.Y., 1955.
43697.88.700 Mauriac, François. The lamb. N.Y., 1955.
43697.88.50 Mauriac, François. Le pain vivant. Paris, 1955.
43554.2.960 Maurocordato, A. L'ode de Paul Claudel. Genève, 1955?
41539.40 Maurois, André. Alexandre Dumas. 1. ed. N.Y., 1955.
43697.89.707 Maurois, André. Robert et Elizabeth Browning. Paris, 1955.
40535.31.30 Meister, Anna. Zur Entwicklung Marivaux. Diss. Bern, 1955.
43698.55.110 Memmi, Albert. Agar. Paris, 1955.
43698.55.100 Memmi, Albert. The pillar of salt. N.Y., 1955.
41596.4.115 Merlant, J.C. Le moment de Lorenzaccio dans le destin de Musset. Athènes, 1955.
38516.20.10 Michault, Pierre. Van den drie boinde danssen. Amsterdam, 1955.
42576.57.88 Millvard, K.G. L'oeuvre de Pierre Loti et l'esprit "Fin de siécle". Paris, 1955.
43701.41.700 Moinot, Pierre. The royal hunt. N.Y., 1955.
43701.1.35 Molaine, Pierre. Satan. Paris, 1955.
Mol 246.42.5 Molière, Jean Baptiste Poquelin. The misanthrope. 1. ed. N.Y., 1955.
42556.28.240 Mondor, Henri. Rimbaud. 2. éd. Paris, 1955.
43701.59.130 Monfreid, Henri de. Pilleurs d'épaves. Paris, 1955.
43701.59.120 Monfreid, Henri de. Wahauga. Paris, 1955.
43701.62.2041 Montguerre, Jean-Marc. Journées, 1954-1955. Paris, 1955.
43701.63.230.5 Montherlant, Henry de. Carnets XXII à XXVIII. Paris, 1955.
43701.63.22 Montherlant, Henry de. Théâtre. Paris? 1955.
43701.63.460 Montherlant, Henry de. Un voyageur solitaire est un diable. Monaco, 1955.
43822.49.1295 Morawska, L. Studium o jezyku poezji Pawła Valéry. Lublin, 1955.
40584.5.80 Mortier, Roland. Un précurseur de Madame de Staël: Charles Vanderbourg, 1765-1827. Paris, 1955.

Chronological Listing

1955 - cont.

42582.2.3 Moscow. Vsesoiuznaia gosudarstvennaia biblioteka. Inostrannoi literatury. Zhiul' Vern. Moskva, 1955.
43701.79.100 Moussy, Marcel. Les mauvais sentiments. Paris, 1955.
37568.135 Nanteuil, Jacques. Le fanal exhaussé. Niort, 1955.
41574.535 Nikolaev, V.N. V. Giugo. Moskva, 1955.
43709.23.125 Noël, Marie. Le judgement de Don Juan. Paris, 1955.
42556.27.92.810 Nuyens, A.J. De heilige van het symbolisme. Antwerpen, 1955.
43714.5.100 Obaldia, René de. Tamerlan des coeurs. Paris, 1955.
43714.8.120A Obey, André. Noe. Boston, 1955.
43729.85.100 Oster, Pierre. Le champ de mai. Paris, 1955.
43731.85.110 Out-el-Kouloub. Harem. Paris, 1955.
43738.1.79A Péguy, Charles. Une amitié française. Paris, 1955.
43738.1.73 Péguy, Charles. Deuxième élégie XXX. 4e éd. Paris, 1955.
43738.41.180 Peisson, Edouard. Dieu te juge! Paris, 1955.
43738.51.100 Pelliot, Marianne. La chevelur de Bérénice. Paris, 1955.
43738.76.150 Pergaud, Louis. Correspondance. Paris, 1955.
43738.79.2100 Perrin, André. Mario. Paris, 1955.
37568.145 Perroud, R. De Mauriac a gli esistenzialisti. Milano, 1955.
37569.225 Perruchot, H. La haine des masques. Paris, 1955.
37555.205 Perticucci Bernardini, Ada. Dal simbolismo all'esistenzialismo. Roma, 1955.
37556.150A Peyre, Henri. The contemporary French novel. N.Y., 1955.
43738.97.1130 Peyrefitte, Roger. Les clés de Saint-Pierre. Paris, 1955.
43744.67.828 Pierre-Quint, Léon. Le combat de Marcel Proust. Paris, 1955.
43744.67.1245 Piroué, Georges. Par les chemins de Marcel Proust. Neuchâtel, 1955.
FL 398.50 Pitoeff, A. Ludmilla. Paris, 1955.
43743.50.2100 Poliza, Elena. Croisée. Buenos Aires, 1955.
43743.50.100 Pomier, Jean. Creations en litterature. Paris, 1955.
43743.62.2100 Pons, Maurice. Virginales nouvelles. Paris, 1955.
38585.16.225 Port Royal, France. Musée national des Granges de Port Royal. Racine et Port-Royal. Paris, 1955.
43822.49.1280 Poulain, Gaston. Paul Valéry. Montpellier, 1955.
40597.2.395 Pradalié, G. Balzac historien. 1. éd. Paris, 1955.
43744.24.30 Prévert, Jacques. Lumières d'homme. Paris, 1955.
43744.24.35 Prévert, Jacques. La pluie et le beau temps. 42. éd. Paris, 1955.
43744.67.53 Proust, Marcel. Marcel Proust et Jacques Rivière. Paris, 1955.
43620.66.825 Pugnet, Jacques. Jean Giono. Paris, 1955.
43747.90.100 Puvis de Chavannes, Henri. Le ciel dans mon coeur. Paris, 1955.
37576.655.10 Queneau, R. Anthologie des jeunes auteurs. Paris, 1955.
43744.24.80 Quéval, Jean. Jacques Prévert. Paris, 1955.
38537.33.25 Rabelais, F. The history of Gargantua and Pantagruel. Harmondsworth, Middlesex, 1955.
38536.18.30.2 Rabelais, F. Oeuvres complètes. Paris, 1955.
43752.70.110 Rapin, Simone. Une jeune fille juive. Monte-Carlo, 1955.
37564.230 Raymond, Marcel. Baroque et renaissance poétique. Paris, 1955.
37595.36.24 Raynaud, Gaston. Bibliographie des altfranzösischen Liedes. Leiden, 1955.
43753.61.1100 Renoux, Isaïe. Feuilles de flammes, poèmes. Paris, 1955.
41574.325 Revel, Bruno. Victor Hugo. Milano, 1955.
37567.470 Revue des Sciences Humaines. Autour du symbolisme. Lille, 1955.
42555.44.155 Reyes, Alfonso. Mallarmé entre nosotros. México, 1955.
41543.6.80A Richard, J.P. Poésie et profondeur. Paris, 1955.
40562.45 Ridel, Jean. Lacordaire. Rennes, 1955.
42556.28.86 Rimbaud, Jean Arthur. Pages choisies. Paris, 1955.
43757.6.110 Robbe-Grillet, Alain. Le voyeur. Paris, 1955.
40522.22 Roddier, Henri. L'Abbé Prévost. Paris, 1955.
43757.50.270 Rolland, Romain. Jean-Christophe et Armel. Lyon, 1955.
43757.50.685 Rolland, Romain. Romain Rolland. Paris, 1955.
43757.3.296 Romains, Jules. A Frenchman examines his conscience. London, 1955.
43757.3.286 Romains, Jules. Passagers de cette planète. Paris, 1955.
38525.20.283 Ronsard, Pierre de. Amori. Firenze, 1955.
38525.17.10 Ronsard, Pierre de. Pierre de Ronsard et ses musiciens. Paris, 1955.
43526.65.890 Rouseyne, A.L.M. Amour et poesie d'Apollinaire. Paris, 1955.
FL 6026.20 Rousseau, J.J. The confessions. N.Y., 1955.
FL 6003.5 Rousseau, J.J. Ecrits autobiographiques. Paris, 1955.
FL 6094.8.20 Rousseau, J.J. Rêveries du promeneur solitaire. Paris, 1955.
FL 6067.15A Rousseau, J.J. Über Kunst und Wissenschaft. Hamburg, 1955.
43551.59.810 Rousselot, J. Blaise Cendrars. Paris, 1955.
43757.93.710 Roussin, André. Le mari. Monaco, 1955.
39544.260 Rowe, Constance. Voltaire and the state. N.Y., 1955.
43757.96.120 Roy, Claude. A toit ou à raison. 7. éd. Paris, 1955.
43757.96.4170 Roy, Jules. La femme infidèle. Paris, 1955.
43757.96.4700 Roy, Jules. The navigator. 1st American ed. N.Y., 1955.
41522.18.285 Ruff, Marcel A. Baudelaire. Paris, 1955.
41522.18.290 Ruff, Marcel A. L'esprit du mal et l'esthétique baudelairienne. Paris, 1955.
41522.18.291 Ruff, Marcel A. L'esprit du mal et l'esthétique baudelairienne. Paris, 1955.
39566.22.8 Rzadkowska, E. Encyklopedia i Diderot w polskiem oświeceniu. Wrocław, 1955.
43761.5.4130 Sabatier, Robert. Les fêtes solaires. Paris, 1955.
43761.5.4140 Sabatier, Robert. Le grût de la cendre. Paris, 1955.
43761.5.4700 Sabatier, Robert. The little barrier. London, 1955.
43761.13.120 Sachs, Maurice. Histoire de John Cooper d'Albany. 6. éd. Paris, 1955.
43761.31.700A Sagan, Françoise. Bonjour tristesse. N.Y., 1955.
43761.39.145 St. Exupéry, A. de. Lettres à sa mère. 2. éd. Paris, 1955.
40575.11.5 Sainte-Beuve, Charles A. Cahier de notes grecques. Chapel Hill, 1955.
43761.56.120 Sandoz, Maurice Yves. Imitation des Sonnets from the Portuguese. Genève, 1955.
43550.58.806 Sartre, J.P. Literary and philosophical essays. London, 1955.
43761.78.203 Sartre, Jean Paul. Les jeux sont faits. Paris, 1955.
43761.78.630 Sartre, Jean Paul. Literary and philosophical essays. London, 1955.
43761.78.41A Sartre, Jean Paul. Sartre. Paris, 1955.
43761.89.5110 Saurat, Denis. Encaminament catar. Tolosa, 1955.
42555.44.120 Sauriau, M. Le mystère de Mallarmé. Lille, 1955.
37555.195 Sayce, R.A. The French biblical epic in the seventeenth century. Oxford, 1955.

1955 - cont.

43763.39.110 Schneider, Pierre. Les cinq saisons. Paris, 1955.
43763.41.3100 Scialom, Marc. Journal d'été. Paris, 1955.
43765.31.140 Ségalen, Victor. Stèles. Paris, 1955.
37567.505 Siciliano, Italo. Romanticismo francese. Venezia, 1955.
39527.4.120 Siegfried, André. La Fontaine. Paris, 1955.
43769.54.785 Simenon, Georges. Maigret and the burglar's wife. London, 1955.
37596.260 Smeets, Jean Robert. La chevalerie de Judas Macabé. Assen, 1955.
37569.200A Smith, T.M. Transatlantic migration. Durham, 1955.
41557.10.275 Spire, Thérèse M. Les romantiques et la musique: le cas George Sand. Paris, 1955.
43626.22.810 Stokes, S.E. Julien Green and the thorn of Puritanism. N.Y., 1955.
43780.5.160 Suarès, André. Ignorées du destinataire. Paris, 1955.
43780.69.340 Supervielle, Jules. Bolivar. 2. éd. Paris, 1955.
43780.69.330 Supervielle, Jules. Le jeune homme du dimanche et des autres jours. 3. éd. Paris, 1955.
43822.49.1270 Sutcliffe, J.E. La pensée de Paul Valéry. Paris, 1955[1954]
43785.75.120 Tardieu, Jean. Théâtre de chambre. Paris, 1955.
43792.40.140 Toesca, Maurice. A la grâce de Dieu. Paris, 1955.
43792.40.410 Toesca, Maurice. A la grace de Dieu. Paris, 1955.
37569.40.65 Torre, G. de. Qué es el superrealismo. Buenos Aires, 1955.
43792.90.115 Toulet, Paul Jean. Journal et voyages. Paris, 1955.
37567.525 Trautner, Erich. Das Bild des Priesters in der französischen Literatur des 19. und 20. Jahrhunderts. München, 1955.
V43500.313 Trolliet, Gilbert. La colline. Paris, 1955.
37583.655 Turgeon, F. Quatre pièces moderne en un acte. N.Y., 1955.
43799.5.170 Tzara, Tristan. Parler seul. Paris, 1955.
43822.49.192 Valéry, Paul. La jeune parque. 2e éd. Paris, 1955.
42581.33.31 Vallès, Jules. Les réfractaires. Paris, 1955.
43822.90.100 Vauthier, Jean. Le personage combattent; ou, Fortissimo. Paris, 1955.
FL 377.150 Vedier, Georges. Origine et évolution de la dramaturgie néo-classique. 1. ed. Paris, 1955.
FL 391.150 Veinstein, André. Du théâtre libre au théâtre Louis Jounct;...1887-1934. Paris, 1955.
41574.312 Venzac, Geraud. Les origines religieuses de Victor Hugo. Paris, 1955.
41574.315 Venzac, Geraud. Les premiers maîtres de Victor Hugo. Paris, 1955.
42555.37.5.6 Vianey, Joseph. Les poèmes barbares de Leconte de Lisle. Paris, 1955.
41596.67.10 Viennet, J.P.G. Journal. Paris, 1955.
FL 385.90.5A Vilar, Jean. De la tradition théâtrale. Paris, 1955.
43620.66.830 Villeneuve, R. de. Jean Giono. Avignon, 1955.
43824.54.120 Vilmorin, Louise de. Histoire d'aimer. 11e éd. Paris, 1955.
38585.16.206 Vinaver, E. Racine and poetic tragedy. Manchester, 1955.
43827.92.100 Voëlin, Henri. Les saints innocents. Porrentruy, 1955.
43827.41.100 Voidies, Jean Pierre. Irène, poèmes. Paris, 1955.
39545.35.42 Voltaire, François Marie Arouet de. Candido. Trodotto, 1955.
39545.46.3.15 Voltaire, François Marie Arouet de. L'ingénu. Paris, 1955.
39544.27.3.10 Voltaire, François Marie Arouet de. Voltaire. Paris, 1955.
43833.20.120 Weil, Simone. Venise sauvée. Paris, 1955.
42584.23.415 Zola, Emile. La fortune des Rougon. Paris, 1955.
42584.12.36 Zola, Emile. Nana. Paris, 1955.
42584.12.33 Zola, Emile. Nana. Paris, 1955.
42584.10.25 Zola, Emile. Savage Paris. London, 1955.

1956

42557.12.115 Académie...Brussels. Académie royale de langue et de littérature françaises, Brussels. Le centenaire d'Émile Verhaeren, 1855-1955. Bruxelles, 1956.
42562.37.9 Achard, Amédée E. Les chevauchées de M. de la Guerche. Paris, 1956.
43512.75.210 Achard, Marcel. Le mal d'amour. Paris, 1956.
37575.710 Actualité de la poésie. Paris, 1956.
39544.285 Addamiano, Natale. Voltaire. Roma, 1956.
43514.23.100 Adenis, Henri. Les viviers du cri. Paris, 1956.
43517.3.35 Aguilar, Paul Jean. Poèmes simples. Paris, 1956.
42576.65.13.124 Aimery, Christiane. Joris-Karl Huysmans. Paris, 1956.
42562.60.6 Allais, Alphonse. A dire et à lire. Paris, 1956.
43522.47.100 Allard L'Olivier, Audal. Les luminaires. Monte Carlo, 1956.
42582.2.9.5 Allotte de la Fuÿe, Marguerite. Jules Verne. 1st American ed. N.Y., 1956.
37569.40.205 Alquie, F. Philosophie du surrealisme. Paris, 1956.
43523.41.2100 Amila, John. Le 9 de pique. Paris, 1956.
43524.67.690 Anouilh, Jean. The lark. N.Y., 1956.
43524.67.790 Anouilh, Jean. The lark. N.Y., 1956.
43524.67.190 Anouilh, Jean. Ornifle. Paris, 1956.
43524.67.210 Anouilh, Jean. Pièces brillantes. Paris, 1956.
43526.65.270 Apollinaire, Guillaume. Oeuvres poetiques. Paris, 1956.
43527.3.350 Aragon, Louis. Le roman inachevé. Paris, 1956.
42586.9.10 Arène, Paul. Poémes provenceaux. London, 1956.
42586.9.12 Arène, Paul. Provenzalische Novellen. Halle, 1956.
43528.61.175 Arnoux, Alexandre. Le rossignol napolitain. Paris, 1956.
43528.86.13 Artaud, Antonin. Oeuvres complètes. Paris, 1956- 8v.
43531.18.1160 Audiberti, Jacques. La pouplé. Paris, 1956.
43531.19.120 Audry, Colette. Soledad. Paris, 1956.
41543.22.65 Aunos y Pérez, Eduardo. Gerard de Nerval et ses énigmes. Paris, 1956.
41522.18.295 Austin, L.J. L'univers poétique de Baudelaire. Paris, 1956.
Mol 173.5 Ayda, Adile. Un diplomate turc auprès du Roi Soleil. Istanbul, 1956.
43537.14.100 Backer, A.M. de. Les étoiles de novembre. Paris, 1956.
43537.1.2030 Baissette, Gaston. Ces grappes de ma vigne. Paris, 1956.
40597.47.10 Balzac, Honoré de. The bachelor's house. N.Y., 1956.
40596.7.5A Balzac, Honoré de. Balzac par lui-même. Paris, 1956.
40597.51 Balzac, Honoré de. Béatrix. N.Y., 1956.
40597.50 Balzac, Honoré de. The country parson. N.Y., 1956.
40597.49 Balzac, Honoré de. Modeste Mignon. N.Y., 1956.
43554.2.1100 Barrault, Jean Z. Adieu à Claudel. Viernheim, 1956.
41522.13.30 Baudelaire, Charles. Baudelaire critique d'art. Paris, 1956.

Chronological Listing

1956 - cont.

41522.13.25	Baudelaire, Charles. Curiosités esthétiques. Lausanne, 1956.
41522.13.8.38	Baudelaire, Charles. The essence of laughter. N.Y., 1956.
43537.98.5100	Bayo, Gérard. Nostalgies pour paradis; poèmes. Paris, 1956.
43537.99.150	Bazin, Hervé. Qui j'ose aimer. Paris, 1956.
43537.98.4100	Bazin, Jean. Tristie, poèmes. Paris, 1956.
43538.1.200.5	Béalu, Marcel. Marcel Béalu. Rodez, 1956.
43538.1.205	Béalu, Marcel. Les messagers clandestins. Paris, 1956.
43538.1.340	Béarn, Pierre. Dialogues de mon amour. v.1-4. Paris, 1956.
43756.90.830	Beaulieu, Paul. Jacques Rivière. Paris, 1956.
43538.1.490A	Beauvoir, Simone de. The Mandarins. Cleveland, 1956.
43538.14.760	Beckett, Samuel. Malone dies. N.Y., 1956.
38551.135	Bédoyere, M. de la. The archbishop and the lady. London, 1956.
38539.80	Belliévre, C. Souvenirs de voyages en Italie et en Orient. Genève, 1956.
37569.203	Benac, Henri. Écrivains français vivants. Alegre, 1956.
43538.61.3100	Benoit-Guyod, Jeanne. Le chant des pierres. Paris, 1956.
43538.90.110	Berl, Emmanuel. Présence des morts. Paris, 1956.
43538.76.257	Bernanos, Georges. Le crépuscule des vieux. 7. éd. Paris, 1956.
43538.76.8100	Bernard-Luc, Jean. Les amants novices. Paris, 1956.
43538.93.100	Berrin, Lucien. Taille-douce. Paris, 1956.
43538.84.100	Bessy, Maurice. Voici le temps des assassins. Paris, 1956.
40582.23.25	Beyle, Henri. Rome. Paris, 1956.
43822.49.1285	Bibliothèque nationale, Paris. Paul Valéry. Paris, 1956.
43620.74.885	Bidal, M.L. Giraudoux tel qu'en lui-même. Paris, 1956.
37568.57	Billy, André. L'epoque contemporaine. Paris, 1956.
42575.112.5	Billy, André. Vie des frères Goncourt. Monaco, 1956. 3v.
43543.4.2100	Blanchet, Louis. Le feu est dans la ville. Magné, 1956.
43543.4.2110	Blanchet, Louis. Le revé des bagnards. Magné, 1956.
42563.23.60	Bloy, Léon. Journal. Paris, 1956. 4v.
37543.615	Bonneau, Georges. Mélanges critiques. Ankara, 1956.
43544.81.2160	Bosco, Henri. L'Âne Culotte. Tours, 1956.
43544.81.2200	Bosco, Henri. Le renard dans l'île. Paris, 1956.
43544.89.2021	Bosquet, Alain. Trois poètes. Paris, 1956.
43632.50.810	Bosschère, J. de. Franz Hellens. Lyon, 1956.
38557.47.265	Bossuet, J.B. L'établissement du texte de la defensio declarationis de Bossuet. Paris, 1956.
43544.89.4100	Boucharlat, René. De dessous les eaux. Paris, 1956.
43544.111.100	Boucher, Maurice. Quand l'âme est absente. Paris, 1956.
43544.89.7100	Bouchet, Paul. Hu Gadam. Paris, 1956.
43544.108.705	Boulle, Pierre. Face of a hero. N.Y., 1956.
V43500.45	Bourquin, Francis. Paysages du coeur. Bienne, 1956.
37555.74	Brereton, G. An introduction to the French poets. London, 1956.
42556.28.270	Briet, Suzanne. Rimbaud, notre prochain. Paris, 1956.
41598.14	Brochon, Pierre. Béranger et son temps. Paris, 1956. 2v.
43545.89.3120	Bruckberger, R.M. Madeleine et Judas. Chambéry, 1956.
43823.75.2206	Bruller, Jean. Colères, roman par Vercors (pseud.). Paris, 1956.
43823.75.2190	Bruller, Jean. Les divagations d'un français en Chine. Paris, 1956.
43823.75.2735A	Bruller, Jean. The insurgents. 1st ed. N.Y., 1956.
43566.81.4800	Buchole, Rosa. L'évolution poétique de Robert T. Desnos. Bruxelles, 1956.
43550.6.160	Cabanis, José. Le fils; roman. Paris, 1956.
43550.12.1100	Cachera, André. Le porcelet de Delphes. Poems. Paris, 1956?
43550.20.100	Cadou, Hélène. Le bonheur du jour. Paris, 1956.
38523.38	Caen, France. Malherbe et son temps. Caen, 1956.
Mol 703.7	Cairncross, John. New light on Molière. Genève, 1956.
43550.58.210	Camus, Albert. La chute, récit. 64. éd. Paris, 1956.
43556.51.1800	Caradec, François. Christophe Colomb. Paris, 1956.
FL 368.15	Carré, Ambrosius M. L'église s'est-elle réconciliée avec le théâtre? Paris, 1956.
42547.22.105	Castex, Pierre. Contes cruels. Paris, 1956.
43744.67.1350	Cattaui, Georges. Marcel Proust. Genève, 1956-
43550.98.150	Cayrol, Jean. Le deménagement. Paris, 1956.
39544.368	Ceitac, Jane. L'affaire des natifs et Voltaire. Genève, 1956.
39544.280	Ceitac, Jane. Voltaire et l'affaire des natifs. Genève, 1956.
40542.37	Celier, Léonce. Frédéric Ozanam. Paris, 1956.
41543.22.51	Cellier, Léon. Gerard de Nerval. Paris, 1956.
43551.52.100	Celly, Jean Jacques. Fanfare. Paris, 1956.
43551.59.240	Cendrars, Blaise. Emmène-moi au bout du monde; roman. Paris, 1956.
43551.59.230	Cendrars, Blaise. La fin du monde. Paris, 1956.
43551.79.120	Césaire, Aimé. Cahier d'un retour au pays natal. Paris, 1956.
43551.79.110	Césaire, Aimé. Et les chiens se taisaient. Paris, 1956.
43551.80.120	Cesbron, Gilbert. Vous verrez le ciel ouvert. Paris, 1956.
42515.38	Chaix-Ruy, J. Ernest Renan. Paris, 1956.
43552.3.9250	Chamson, André. Adeline Venician. Paris, 1956.
FL 6139.56	Chapman, J.W. Rousseau, totalitarian or liberal? N.Y., 1956.
43552.4.2210	Char, René. En trente-trois morceaux. Paris, 1956.
43552.4.2710	Char, René. Hypnos waking. N.Y., 1956.
43552.5.200	Chardonne, Jacques. Matinales. Paris, 1956.
37543.365	Charlier, Gustave. De Montaigne à Verlaine. Bruxelles, 1956.
43552.4.8110	Charpier, Jacques. Le fer et le Laurier. Paris, 1956.
43552.5.1177	Chartier, Emile. Propos. Paris, 1956. 2v.
43552.13.110	Chaulot, Paul. L'herbe de chaque escale. Paris, 1956.
43552.18.110	Chédid, Andrée. Terre et poésie. Paris, 1956.
43552.23.1100	Chenorg, Léon. Sable et cendres, poèmes. Paris, 1956.
42555.44.135	Chiari, Joseph. Symbolisme from Poe to Mallarmé. London, 1956.
43752.57.870	Cingria, Hélène. Ramuz. Bienne, 1956.
38585.16.235	Claudel, Paul. Conversation sur Jean Racine. Paris, 1956.
43554.2.370.5	Claudel, Paul. Théâtre. Paris, 1956.
43554.2.460	Claudel, Paul. La ville. Paris, 1956.
43744.67.1260A	Cocking, J.M. Proust. London, 1956.
FL 398.9.11	Cocteau, Jean. Adieu à Mistinguett. Liège, 1956.
43556.1.415	Cocteau, Jean. Le discours de Strasbourg. Metz, 1956.
43556.1.405	Cocteau, Jean. Le discours d'Oxford. Paris, 1956.
43556.1.745	Cocteau, Jean. The hand of a stranger. London, 1956.
43556.1.740	Cocteau, Jean. Journals. 1st ed. N.Y., 1956.
43556.1.400	Cocteau, Jean. Maalesh. London, 1956.

1956 - cont.

43556.1.750	Cocteau, Jean. La machine à écrire. Paris, 1956.
43556.1.755	Cocteau, Jean. Paris album, 1900-1914. London, 1956.
43556.1.65.10	Cocteau, Jean. Poèmes. 5e éd. Paris, 1956.
FL 370.84.10	Cohen, Gustave. Études d'histoire du théâtre en France au Moyen Âge et à la renaissance. Paris, 1956.
38525.22.24	Cohen, Gustave. Ronsard; sa vie et son oeuvre. Paris, 1956.
43556.49.760	Colette, Sidonie Gabrielle. Claudine at school. London, 1956.
43556.49.722	Colette, Sidonie Gabrielle. The ripening seed. N.Y., 1956.
43556.49.550	Colette, Sidonie Gabrielle. La treille muscate. Lausanne, 1956.
39594.19.75	Congrès Montesquieu, Bordeaux. Actes du congrès. Bordeaux, 1956.
37574.885	Cordone, Jacques. Les muses chez Thémis. Paris, 1956.
42514.28.88	Cormier, Aristide. La vie interieure de Charles Maurras. Paris, 1956.
43557.66.110	Crommelynck, Fernand. Théâtre complet. Paris, 1956-
37562.280.5	Crosland, J.R. Medieval French literature. Oxford, 1956.
43560.78.140	Curtis, Jean Louis. L'échelle de soie. Paris, 1956.
43560.78.160	Curtis, Jean Louis. Un saint au néon. Paris, 1956.
43560.78.715	Curtis, Jean Louis. The side of the angels. N.Y., 1956.
43560.78.1110	Cury, Maurice. Mine d'or, suivi de Petits poèmes pour un enfant triste. Paris, 1956.
43560.81.100	Cusin, Pierre. Remords. Paris, 1956.
43565.41.120	Daix, Pierre. Les embarras de Paris. Paris, 1956.
43565.60.160	Daniel-Rops, Henry. Nocturnes. Paris, 1956.
43565.60.1200	Daninos, Pierre. Passeport pour la nuit; ou, Le roi-sommeil. Paris, 1956.
43565.60.1190	Daninos, Pierre. Le secret du Major Thompson. Paris, 1956.
43565.76.700	Dariel, Jean Loup. Oliver kept a diary. London, 1956.
43565.93.100	Darnal, J.C. Ce soir on joue guignol. Paris, 1956.
43701.63.865	Datain, Jean. Montherlant et l'héritage. Paris, 1956.
43565.89.1100	Dauberoille, H. L'eternel paradoxe. Paris, 1956.
43556.1.840	Dauven, Jean. Jean Cocteau chez les sirenes. Monaco, 1956.
43565.90.1100	Davallon, A. Le train par la tête. Paris, 1956.
43833.20.835	Davy, M.M. Simone Weil. Paris, 1956.
40513.38	Dédéyan, Charles. A.R. LeSage. v.1-2. Paris, 1956.
38585.16.245	Dédéyan, Charles. La Phèdre de Racine. Paris, 1956.
39544.315	Dédéyan, Charles. Voltaire et la pensée anglaise. Paris, 1956.
40583.255	De'de'yuan, Charles. Stendhal et les chroniques italiennes. Paris, 1956.
43566.48.8100	Delamare, G. Vingt années sans guerre, 1919-1939. Paris, 1956.
43757.83.2800	Delaunay, Albert. Jean Rostand. Paris, 1956.
43620.2.350	Delay, J.P.L. La jeunesse d'André Gide. Paris, 1956. 2v.
41596.53.30	Delfolie, Valéry. La Marseillaise. Montmorillon, 1956.
43566.50.1100	Dell'Aid. Présence. Paris, 1956.
43566.52.160	Demaison, André. Les lions du Kalahari. Paris, 1956.
43566.57.100	Demorest, J.J. Les passionnés ont vécu. Paris, 1956.
43566.62.100	Déon, Michel. Les trompeuses espérances. Paris, 1956.
43566.81.7110	Desmeuzes, Jean. Les roses vertes. Paris, 1956.
43566.83.110	Des Vallières, Jean. Le chevalier de la Camargue. Paris, 1956.
43567.79.150	Dhôtel, André. L'île aux oiseaux de fer. Paris, 1956.
43568.66.100	Diop, D. Coups de pilons. Paris, 1956.
43573.16.100	Dodat, François. Etrusques. Paris, 1956.
43573.76.38	Dorgelès, Roland. Tout est à vendre, roman. Paris, 1956.
43574.70.100	Drouet, Minou. First poems. London, 1956.
43738.1.250	Dru, Alexander. Péguy. London, 1956.
43574.75.720	Druon, Maurice. The iron king. London, 1956.
43574.75.750	Druon, Maurice. Les rois maudits. Paris, 1956. 6v.
43574.75.730	Druon, Maurice. The strangled queen. London, 1956.
43576.9.2120	Du Bouchet, André. Le moteur lbanc. Paris, 1956.
42568.19.21.6	Ducasse, I.L. Oeuvres complètes; les chants de Maldoror. Paris, 1956.
43576.6.770	Duhamel, Georges. Les compagnons de l'Apocalypse. Paris, 1956.
41538.9A	Dumas, Alexandre. The road to Monte Cristo. N.Y., 1956.
38527.40	Dupérier, Scipion. Harangue pour le prince de Joinville. Paris, 1956.
37544.105	Dupuy, Aimé. L'Algérie dans les lettres d'éxpression française. Paris, 1956.
37544.100	Dupuy, Aimé. La Tunisie dans les lettres d'éxpression française. Paris, 1956.
43576.74.2112	Duras, Marguerite. Le square. Paris, 1956.
41543.22.60	Durry, M.J. Gerard de Nerval et le mythe. Paris, 1956.
43526.65.910A	Durry, M.J. Guillaume Apollinaire. Paris, 1956.
43576.87.710A	Dutourd, Jean. Five a.m. N.Y., 1956.
43576.87.150	Dutourd, Jean. Les taxis de la Marne. 6. éd. Paris, 1956.
42556.28.260	Eaubonne, F. d'. La vie passionnee d'Arthur Rimbaud. Paris, 1956.
43591.89.325	Éluard, Paul. Léda. 2. éd. Lausanne, 1956.
Mol 705.1	Emery, Léon. Molière. Lyon, 1956.
43592.53.710	Emmanuel, Pierre. The mad poet. Baltimore, 1956.
43597.55.100	Ermin, France. Les beaux départs. Paris, 1956.
38537.25.210	Études rabelaisiennes. Genève, 1956. 9v.
39594.19.60	Eyland, J.M. Montesquieu chez ses notaires de la Brede. Bordeaux, 1956.
38526.26.90	Fargue, Léon Paul. Louise Labé. Liège, 1956.
43607.78.100	Ferré, Léo. Poète. Paris, 1956.
43609.79.1100	Fischer, Pierre. Paroles simples. Paris, 1956.
42576.31.35	Flaubert, Gustave. Salammbô. London, 1956.
43612.4.102	France, Claire. Les enfants qui s'aiment; roman. Montréal, 1956.
43744.67.1255	François, S. Le dandysme et Marcel Proust. Bruxelles, 1956.
37568.175	Frank, Bernard. Le dernier des mohicans. Paris, 1956.
43612.23.100	Frenaud, André. Passage de la visitation. Paris, 1956.
43612.23.1100	Frénouville, Anne. Thalassa; poèmes. Paris, 1956.
43617.6.1100	Gabalda, Jean. Mortes avant l'été, poèmes. Paris, 1956.
43616.59.2775	Gangateau, Alfredo. Poesía. Quito, 1956.
43616.63.23	Ganzo, Robert. L'oeuvre poétique. Paris, 1956.
43616.78.150	Gary, Romain. Les racines du ciel, roman. 271. éd. Paris, 1956.
43616.79.700	Gascar, Pierre. Beasts and men. 1. ed. Boston, 1956.
41543.22.70	Gaulmier, Jean. Gerard de Nerval et Les filles du feu. Paris, 1956.
37596.38.2	Gautier d'Arras. Ille et Galeron. Paris, 1956.
43617.78.120	Genêt, Jean. Le balcon. Décines, 1956.
43617.78.130	Genêt, Jean. Miracle de la rose. 2. éd. Décines, 1956.

Chronological Listing

1956 - cont.

37573.690 Genève, par Lydia Kerr. Hors-texte de Fanny Gianini. Genève, 1956.
38512.126 Geoffroi de Paris. La chronique métrique attribuée à Geoffroy de Paris. Paris, 1956.
38512.126.2 Geoffroy de Paris. La chronique métrique attribuée à Geoffroy de Paris. Thèse. Strasbourg, 1956.
43617.74.2100 Gérard, Jean. Poèmes déchirés. Paris, 1956.
43620.7.1100 Gibelin, Colette. Appel. Paris, 1956.
43620.2.69.22 Gide, André. The journals of André Gide. 1. ed. N.Y., 1956. 2v.
43620.55.120 Gilson, Paul. Ce qui me chante. Paris, 1956.
43620.66.760A Giono, Jean. The Dominici affair. London, 1956.
43620.66.420 Giono, Jean. Giono par lui-même. Paris, 1956.
43620.66.165 Giono, Jean. Jean Le Bleu. Paris, 1956.
43620.66.185 Giono, Jean. Regain. Paris, 1956.
43620.74.765 Giraudoux, Jean. Tiger at the gates. N.Y., 1956.
43620.75.100 Girou, Jean. Trencavel et la louve de cennantier. Paris, 1956.
43622.41.130 Glissant, Edouard. Les Indes. Paris, 1956.
43622.41.100 Glissant, Edouard. Soleil de la conscience. Paris, 1956.
FL 6139.56.20 Glum, Friedrich. Jean-Jacques Rousseau. Stuttgart, 1956.
42586.66.20 Gobineau, Arthur de. Nouvelles. Paris, 1956. 2v.
43625.19.320 Godoy, Armand. Sonnets pour Don Juan. Paris, 1956.
42555.44.125 Goffin, Robert. Mallarmé vivant. Paris, 1956.
38585.16.240 Goldmann, Lucien. Jean Racine. Paris, 1956.
43625.49.720 Goll, Claire. Diary of a horse. N.Y., 1956.
42575.75.2 Goncourt, Edmond de. La fille Elisa. Paris, 1956.
42575.69.30 Goncourt, Edmond de. Journal. Monaco, 1956. 22v.
38551.145.10 Goré, Jeanne-Lydie. La notion d'indifférence chez Fénelon et ses sources. Paris, 1956.
38551.145 Goré, Jeanne-Lydie. La notion d'indifférence chez Fénelon et ses sources. 1. éd. Grenoble, 1956.
43626.22.240 Gorkine, M. Julien Green. Paris, 1956.
43744.67.1340 Goron, Lucien. Le Combray de Marcel Proust et son horizon. Toulouse, 1956?
43556.49.851 Goudeket, Maurice. Près de Colette. Paris, 1956.
37573.455 Govaert, Marcel. Les lettres françaises. Anvers, 1956.
41522.18.300 Grava, Arnolds. L'aspect metaphysique du mal dans l'oeuvre littéraire de Charles Baudelaire et d'Edgar Alleunde. Lincoln, 1956.
38513.19.20 Gréban, Arnoul. The true mistery of the nativity. London, 1956.
43626.22.250 Green, Julien. Le malfaiteur. Paris, 1956.
42554.49.25 Gregh, F. L'age de fer; souvenirs 1925-1955. Paris, 1956.
43626.66.1110 Grosjean, Jean. Majestés et passants. Paris, 1956.
43744.67.1305 Guichard, Léon. Introduction à la lecture de Proust. Paris, 1956.
42555.39.1180 Guillaume, Jean. Essai sur la valeur exégétique du substantif dans les Entrevisions. Bruxelles, 1956.
37543.535 Guillemin, Henri. A vrai dire. Paris, 1956.
43628.41.6130 Guinle, Alexandre. Pour Béatrice. Paris, 1956.
43628.41.2100 Guiraud, G. Henri de. Aux frontières de l'enfer. Paris, 1956.
41578.136 Guyard, M.F. Alphonse de Lamartine. Paris, 1956.
43631.22.100 Haeffely, Claude. Le sommeil et la neige. Montréal, 1956.
43556.1.850 Hagen, Friedrich. Zwischen Stern und Spiegel. München, 1956.
37567.490 Hamelin, J. Hommes de lettres inculpés. Paris, 1956.
43631.50.100 Hàn, Françoise. Cité des hommes (1951-1955). Paris, 1956.
43631.76.705 Hardy, René. Bitter victory. London, 1956.
43632.14.100 Hecquet, Stephen. Anne. Paris, 1956.
43632.50.21 Hellens, Franz. Choix de poèmes. v.1-2. Paris, 1956.
43632.50.150 Hellens, Franz. Style et caractère. Bruxelles, 1956.
43632.59.1100 Henein, Georges. Le seuil interdit. Paris, 1956.
43632.76.700 Hériat, Philippe. The spoiled children. N.Y., 1956.
41522.18.305 Horner, Lucie. Baudelaire. Genève, 1956.
38585.16.265 Hubert, J.D. Essai d'exégèse racinienne. Paris, 1956.
41574.225.5 Hugo, Paris Maison de Victor. Victor Hugo. Paris, 1956.
41573.32.76 Hugo, Victor. Claude Gueux. Thèse. Paris, 1956.
41573.32.75 Hugo, Victor. Claude Gueux. 1. ed. Paris, 1956.
43761.39.880 Huguet, Jean. St. Exupéry; ou, L'enseignement du désert. Paris, 1956.
37563.60.1 Humanisme et renaissance, table 1934-1940. Genève, 1956.
43638.53.110 Humbourg, Pierre. Mort de vieillesse. Paris, 1956.
42514.28.95 Hupin, Gérard. Charles Maurras. Paris, 1956.
42576.65.80.55 Huysmans, Joris Karl. Lettres inédites à Edmond de Toncourt. Paris, 1956.
43667.14.270 Jacob, Max. Esthétique de Max Jacob. Paris, 1956.
43670.59.100 Jones, Philippe. Amour et autres visages. Paris, 1956.
43670.89.480 Jouhandeau, M. Jaunisse. Paris, 1956.
43670.89.600 Jouhandeau, M. Nouvelles images de Paris, suivies de remarques sur les visages. 3. éd. Paris, 1956.
40583.240 Journées Stendhaliennes internationales. Journées Stendhaliennes internationales de Grenoble. Paris, 1956.
43670.94.340 Jouve, Pierre Jean. Lyrique. Paris, 1956.
43670.94.800 Jouve, Pierre Jean. Pierre Jean Jouve. Paris, 1956.
43670.94.2110 Jouvenel, Renard de. Il n'y a pas d'oubli. Paris, 1956.
39586.27.30 Juenger, Ernst. Rivarol. Frankfurt, 1956.
43551.79.800 Juin, Hubert. Aimé Cesairé. Paris, 1956.
37569.290 Kamras, Hugo. Om Proust och vägra till. Stockholm, 1956.
FL 360.98 Kemp, Robert. La vie du théâtre. Paris, 1956.
43673.83.167 Kessel, Joseph. Le temps de l'espérance. 100. éd. Paris, 1956. 6v.
43675.24.100 Kihm, Jean Jacques. Eloge de l'ombre. Paris, 1956.
37566.125 Klemperer, Victor. Geschichte der französischen Literatur im 19. und 20. Jahrhunderts. Berlin, 1956- 2v.
38526.26.83 Labé, Louise Charly. Die Liebesgedichte einer schönen Lyoneser Seilerin namens Louize Labé. Rudolstadt, 1956.
43687.14.110 Lacour, José André. La mort en ce jardin. Paris, 1956.
42555.1.60 Laforgue, Jules. Selected writings. N.Y. 1956.
43687.53.1110 Lambert, Jean. Tobiolo. Paris, 1956.
43687.63.122 Langevin, André. Le temps des hommes; roman. 2. éd. Montreal, 1956.
43687.61.1110 Lanoux, Armand. Le Commandant Watrin. Paris, 1956.
43687.61.1120 Lanoux, Armand. Le photographe délirant. Paris, 1956.
43687.65.101 Lanza del Vasto, Joseph Jean. Principes et préceptes du retour à l'évidence. Paris, 1956.
43687.71.2100 Laporte, Geneviève. Sous le manteau de feu. Paris, 1956.
43709.3.835 La Rochefoucauld, E. Anna de Noailles. Paris, 1956.
43687.89.4100 Laugier, Jean. L'espace muet. Paris, 1956.
43687.89.5100 Laurencin, Marie. Le carnet des nuits. Genève, 1956.
43688.5.5170 Léautaud, Paul. Lettres à ma mère. Paris, 1956.
43688.5.5160 Léautaud, Paul. Le petit am:. Paris, 1956.
37543.395 Lebel, Roland. Le Maroc dans les lettres d'éxpression française. Paris, 1956.
43688.11.100 Le Breton, Alain. Car pour Rome. Paris, 1956.

1956 - cont.

43688.16.100 Lecoeur, Yves. L'escalier de J.P. Sartre. 3e éd. Paris, 1956.
40597.2.420 Lecuyer, Maurice A.F. Balzac et Rabelais. Paris, 1956.
43688.27.3100 Lefévre, Raymonde. Le plus secret tombeau. Paris, 1956.
43556.49.845 LeHardouin, M. Colette. Paris, 1956.
37555.245 Le Hir, Yves. Esthétique et structure du vers français. Paris, 1956.
43688.60.140 Leiris, Michel. Bagatelles végétales. Paris, 1956.
43688.94.100 Lequenne, F. Les pères naturel. Paris, 1956.
43554.2.965 Lerch, Emil. Versuchung und Gnade. Wien, 1956.
40592.82 Levaillant, M. Une amitié amoureuse. Paris, 1956.
43688.96.100 Lévy, Edmond. La fin du premier jour. 5e éd. Paris, 1956.
43688.95.100 Levy, Paul. Ici tombe la nuit. Paris, 1956.
38525.6.5 Lockert, Lacy. The chief rivals of Corneille and Racine. Nashville, 1956.
43693.53.100 Lombard-Maurog, G. Le temps revient. Paris, 1956.
37597.9.16 Lorris, Guillaume de. Der Rosenroman. Berlin, 1956.
43693.89.1110 Louwe, Pierre. Les instants d'une vie. Paris, 1956.
43694.11.4110 Lucasserie, Louis de. Broutilles; poèmes. Paris, 1956.
37543.375 Luzi, Mario. Aspetti della generazione napoleonica. Parma, 1956.
43697.14.250 MacOrlan, Pierre. Malice. 5. ed. Paris, 1956.
43554.2.814.5 Madaule, Jacques. Paul Claudel. Paris, 1956.
42555.43.20 Mallarmé, Stéphane. Selected prose, poems, essays, and letters. Baltimore, 1956.
43697.2.1140 Mallet-Joris, Françoise (pseud.). Cordélia. Paris, 1956.
43697.2.1120 Mallet-Joris, Françoise (pseud.). Les mensonges. Paris, 1956.
43697.2.1720 Mallet-Joris, Françoise (pseud.). The red room. N.Y., 1956.
43697.52.741 Malraux, André. The conquerors. Boston, 1956.
43697.52.210 Malraux, André. Les voix du silence. Paris, 1956.
43697.54.100 Mammeri, M. The sleep of the just. London, 1956.
37556.21.45.5 Manevy, Raymond. L'évolution des formules de présentation de la presse quotidienne. Paris, 1956.
37556.21.45.6 Manevy, Raymond. L'évolution des formules de présentation de la presse quotidienne. Paris, 1956.
43697.61.2120 Mansour, Joyce. Jules César. Paris, 1956.
43550.58.825 Maquet, Albert. Albert Camus. Paris, 1956.
43620.2.321 Marchand, Max. Du Marquis de Sade à André Gide. Oran, 1956.
42582.2.95 Marcucci, Edmondo. Les illustrations des voyages extraordinaires de Jules Verne. Paris, 1956.
Htn 38526.33.2.5* Marguerite d'Angoulême. La navire. Paris, 1956.
40583.230 Marill, Francine. Le naturel chez Stendhal. Paris, 1956.
40583.231 Marill, Francine. Le naturel chez Stendhal. Thèse. Paris, 1956.
40583.236 Marill, Francine. Stendhal et le sentiment. Thèse. Paris, 1956.
40583.235 Marill, Francine. Stendhal et le sentiment religieux. Paris, 1956.
37568.108.5 Marill, René. Bilan littéraire du XXe siècle. Paris, 1956.
43757.92.2800 Marissel, André. Jean Rousselot. Rodez, 1956.
40535.29.40 Marivaux, Pierre Carlet de Chamblain de. Le Télémaque travesti. Genève, 1956.
43697.77.4100 Martin, Marietta. Cahiers. v.1-2. Paris, 1956.
43697.78.5110 Martin Saint-René (pseud.). Une lyre tendue à tous les vents du ciel! Paris, 1956.
43697.78.8100 Martinon, R. Messages secrets de la nature. Chauny, 1956.
43697.86.140 Masson, Loÿs. Les tortues. Paris, 1956.
43697.18.100 Maud'huit, R. Les poèmes d'Orlando de la Folie. Paris, 1956-
42577.2.5.20 Maupassant, Guy de. La maison Tellier. Urbiro?, 1956.
42577.4.29.60A Maupassant, Guy de. Maupassant, journaliste et chroniqueur. Paris, 1956.
43697.88.55 Mauriac, François. The stumbling block. London, 1956.
40587.110.9 Maurois, André. René. Paris, 1956.
43697.89.460 Maurois, André. Les roses de septembre. Paris, 1956.
41574.303 Maurois, André. Victor Hugo. London, 1956.
40517.23.80 Meister, Paul. Charles Duclos. Genève, 1956.
40517.23.82 Meister, Paul. Charles Duclos. Genève, 1956.
42563.39.030 Ménard, Jean. L'oeuvre de Boylesve avec des documents inédits. Paris, 1956.
37574.858 Ménard, René. Le livre des arbres. Paris, 1956.
37575.720 Mermod, Françaişe. La Provence. Lausanne, 1956.
38528.38.35 Meylan, Henri. Epitres du coq à l'âne. Genève, 1956.
43698.200.190 Michaux, Henri. Misérable miracle. Monaco, 1956.
42556.28.250 Miller, Henry. The time of the assassins. Norfolk, 1956.
43744.67.1275A Miller, M.L. Nostalgia. Boston, 1956.
43699.51.25 Milosz, Oscar Vladislas. Poèmes. Paris, 1956.
43701.80.100 Mogin, Jean. Pâtures du silence. Paris, 1956.
Mol 60.44 Molière, Jean Baptiste Poquelin. Six prose comedies. London, 1956.
42563.18.315 Mondor, Henri. Maurice Barrès avant le Quartier Latin. Paris, 1956.
43701.63.490 Montherlant, Henry de. Les auligny. Paris, 1956.
43701.63.470 Montherlant, Henry de. Brocéliande. 10. éd. Paris, 1956.
43701.63.480 Montherlant, Henry de. Carnets XIX à XXI. Paris, 1956.
43701.74.2100 Mordreuc, Jean. An distro. Paris, 1956.
43701.75.3100 Moreau, Martial. Arc en ciel. Paris, 1956.
40587.66 Moreau, Pierre. Chateaubriand, l'homme et l'oeuvre. Paris, 1956.
42556.28.255A Morrissette, Bruce A. The great Rimbaud forgery. St. Louis, 1956.
43527.3.805 Moscow. Vsesoiuznaia gosudarstvennaia biblioteka inostrannykh literatur. Lui Aragon; bio-bibliograficheskii ukazatel'. Moskva, 1956.
43701.87.1100 Mottier, Christian. Ville pour guitare. Paris, 1956.
43701.89.100 Mourgue, Gerard. Chateau-fer. Paris, 1956.
37543.355 Natoli, Glauco. Figure e problemi della cultura francese. Messina, 1956.
43706.74.105 Ner, Henri. J'ai nom Eliacin. Paris, 1956.
43707.14.100 Nicolas, André. Je ne suis pas si vilaine. Fontenay-le-Comte, 1956.
43538.5.800 Niess, R.J. Julien Benda. Ann Arbor, 1956.
43707.58.100 Ninck, Roger. Les couteaux du destin. Paris, 1956.
43709.23.21 Noël, Marie. L'oeuvre poétique. Paris, 1956.
37569.260 Nourissier, François. Les chiens à fouetter. Paris, 1956.
43709.80.100 Nourissier, François. Les orphelins d'Auteuil. Paris, 1956.
43728.54.110 Ormesson, Jean d'. L'amour est un plaisir, roman. Paris, 1956.
43737.34.200 Pagnol, Marcel. Judas. Paris, 1956.
43574.70.800 Parinaud, A. L'affaire Minou Drouet. Paris, 1956.

Chronological Listing

1956 - cont.

37574.815	Paris, Jean. Anthologie de la poésie nouvelle. Monaco, 1956.
38526.42.13.10	Pasquier, Étienne. Choix de lettres sur la littérature, la langue et la traduction. Genève, 1956.
V43500.235	Paysan, Catherine. Écrit pour l'âme des cavaliers. Paris, 1956.
43738.1.76	Péguy, Charles. The mystery of the holy innocents. N.Y., 1956.
43738.78.155	Perse, Saint-John. Éloges. N.Y., 1956.
43738.97.1140	Peyrefitte, Roger. Les amitiés particulières. Paris, 1956.
43738.97.1150	Peyrefitte, Roger. Jeunes proies. Paris, 1956.
38585.18.60	Picard, Raymond. La carrière de Jean Racine. 3. éd. Paris, 1956.
38585.18.60.5	Picard, Raymond. La carrière de Jean Racine d'après les documents contemporains. Thèse. Paris, 1956.
38585.18.65	Picard, Raymond. Corpus Racinianum. Paris, 1956.
38585.18.70	Picard, Raymond. Corpus Racinianum. Thèse. Paris, 1956.
43741.25.100	Pieyre de Mandiargues, André. Le lis de mer. Paris, 1956.
43741.59.3150	Pinget, Robert. Graal flibuste. Paris, 1956.
43741.89.100	Piroué, Georges. Chansons à dire. Paris, 1956.
37565.155	Pizzorusso, Arnaldo. Studi sulla letteratura dell'età preromantica in Francia. Pisa, 1956.
42587.52.95	Pollitzer, Marcel. Jules Renard. Paris, 1956.
39594.19.100	Polska Akademii Nauk. Komitet Nauk Prawnych. Monteskiusz i jegodzieło. Wrocław, 1956.
40532.40	Pomeau, R. Beaumarchais. Paris, 1956.
39544.275	Pomeau, René. La religion de Voltaire. Paris, 1956.
39544.275.2	Pomeau, René. La religion de Voltaire. Thèse. Paris, 1956.
40532.42	Pooschwitz, G. von. Introduction à l'étude du vocabulaire de Beaumarchais. Stockholm, 1956.
43743.77.100	Portejoie, Pierre. J'appelle les hommes. Paris, 1956.
40539.15.14	Potocki, Jan. Rękopis znaleziony w Saragossie. Warszawa, 1956.
37565.126	Poulet, Georges. Studies in human time. Baltimore, 1956.
43743.89.1100	Poulet, Robert. La lanterne magique. Paris, 1956.
43743.98.450	Pozner, Vladimir. Deuil en 24 heures. Paris, 1956.
43526.65.870	Precchioni, P. Le thème du Rhin dans l'inspiration de Guillaume Apollinaire. Paris, 1956.
43744.67.68.5	Proust, Marcel. Letters to his mother. London, 1956.
43744.67.74.5	Proust, Marcel. Lettres à Reynaldo, Halm. 5. éd. Paris, 1956.
43744.67.40.15A	Proust, Marcel. Swann's way. N.Y., 1956.
42515.36.217	Psichari, Henriette. La prière sur l'Acropole et ses mystères. Paris, 1956.
43745.1.34	Psichari, Lucien. Le chien et la pierre. Paris, 1956.
41578.140	Puls, Hans. Die Musikauffassung der französischen Romantiker. Saarbrücken? 1956?
43750.20.120	Queffélec, Henri. Un feu s'allume sur la mer. Paris, 1956.
43550.58.820	Quilliot, Roger. La mer et les prisons. Paris, 1956.
38536.22.15	Rabelais, F. Les croniques admirables du puissant Roy Gargantua. Rochecorbon, 1956.
43538.77.6800	Rabiniaux, Roger. André Berry. Limoges, 1956.
38585.52	Racine, Jean. Confessions. London, 1956.
38583.3.22	Racine, Jean. Oeuvres complètes. v.1. Paris, 1956.
43752.41.100	Raimond, Fernande de. La fin des seigneurs blancs. Paris, 1956.
43752.57.61A	Ramuz, Charles Ferdinand. Lettres, 1900-1918. Lausanne, 1956. 2v.
FL 6139.56.10	Ravary, Bethe. Une conscience chrétienne devant la pensée religieuse. Paris, 1956.
43752.90.100	Raveton, Roland. La vie exilée. Paris, 1956.
43753.9.160	Reboux, Paul. Mes mémoires. Paris, 1956.
40573.14	Regard, Maurice. L'adversaire des romantiques. Paris, 1956. 2v.
43753.3.35	Régnier, P. Fêtes et nuages. 6. éd. Paris, 1956.
42515.34.45	Renan, Ernest. Renan, Taine et Brunetière à quelques amis italiens. Florence, 1956.
42587.51.45	Renard, Jules. Jules Renard par lui-même. Paris, 1956.
43552.4.2805A	René Char's poetry. Roma, 1956.
43753.59.3100	Renglet, Jean Claude. Le dialogue solitude à Monique S. Paris, 1956.
43753.60.100	Rennie, M. L'aigle d'argent. Paris, 1956.
37595.100	Revel, Bruno. Teati bilinqui delle origini. Milano, 1956?
FL 398.74.98	Richardson, J. Rachel. London, 1956.
43756.12.2700	Richter, Anne. The blue dog, and other fables for the French. Boston, 1956.
37562.292	Rickard, Peter. Britain in medieval French literature, 1100-1500. Cambridge, Eng., 1956.
40562.45.6	Ridel, Jean. Une amitié féminine de Lacordaire. Dijon, 1956.
40562.45.5	Ridel, Jean. Lacordaire et Madame Swetchine. Dijon, 1956.
42556.28.88	Rimbaud, Jean Arthur. Verše. Praha, 1956.
39586.23.10	Rivarol, Antoine. Écrits politiques et littéraires. Paris, 1956.
37569.207	Rodenbach, André. Condition de la poésie française en Flandre. Tournai, 1956.
43757.50.46	Rolland, Romain. Mémoires et fragments du journal. Paris, 1956.
43757.50.67	Rolland, Romain. Retour au palais Farnèse; choix de lettres. Paris, 1956.
43757.3.297	Romains, Jules. Le fils de Jerphanion. Paris, 1956.
40542.45	Romero Carranza, A. Ozanam e i suoi contemporanei. Firenze, 1956.
43757.83.2120	Rostand, Jean. Ce que je crois. Paris, 1956.
38525.84.10	Rotrou, Jean de. Venceslas. Saarbrücken, 1956.
42555.44.95	Roulet, Claude. Traité de poétique superieure. Neuchâtel, 1956.
FL 6048.37	Rousseau, J.J. The creed of a priest of Savoy. N.Y., 1956.
FL 6032.56	Rousseau, J.J. Du contrat social. Paris, 1956.
FL 6046.13.35	Rousseau, J.J. Emile for today. London, 1956.
37543.243.20	Rousseaux, André. Le monde classique. 4. série. Paris, 1956.
43757.92.2160	Rousselot, Jean. Une certaine Diane. Paris, 1956.
43757.96.130	Roy, Claude. Le soleil sur la terre. Paris, 1956.
43757.96.4710	Roy, Jules. The unfaithful wife. N.Y., 1956.
43761.5.4120	Sabatier, Robert. Boulevard. Paris, 1956.
43761.3.1030	Sabliaux, V. de. Le pied fourchu. Paris, 1956.
43761.31.705	Sagan, Françoise. A certain smile. 1st ed. N.Y., 1956.
43761.31.110	Sagan, Françoise. Un certain sourire. Paris, 1956.
43761.39.730	St. Exupéry, A. de. Un sens à la vie. 37. éd. Paris, 1956.

1956 - cont.

43761.39.160	St. Exupéry, A. de. St. Exupéry par lui même. Paris, 1956.
43761.39.106	St. Exupéry, A. de. Terre des hommes. 527. éd. Paris, 1956.
43761.45.100	Saintillac, Hector. L'ensorceleuse. Paris, 1956.
43761.48.150	Salacrou, Armand. Une femme, trop honnête. 3. éd. Paris, 1956.
43761.49.3100	Sallèles, Louis A. Boulevards et états d'âme (1912-1956). Paris, 1956.
43761.49.230	Salmon, André. Prikaz. Paris, 1956.
43761.49.210	Salmon, André. Sylvére. Paris, 1956.
41557.9.71	Sand, George. George Sand et Alfred de Musset. Monaco, 1956.
41557.9.130	Sand, George. Winter in Majorca. 2d ed. London, 1956.
43761.77.100	Sarraute, Nathalie. Portrait d'un inconnu, roman. Paris, 1956.
43761.78.745.5	Sartre, Jean Paul. Intimacy. London, 1956.
43761.78.758	Sartre, Jean Paul. Nekrassov. London, 1956.
43761.78.270	Sartre, Jean Paul. Nekrassov. 15. éd. Paris, 1956.
43761.90.2021	Sauvage, Tristan. Choix de poèmes (1949-1956). Paris, 1956.
41574.515	Savey-Casard, Paul. Le crime et la peine dans l'oeuvre de Victor Hugo. 1. éd. Paris, 1956.
V43500.297	Schaettel, Marcel. Pierres de lune. Bourges, 1956.
43763.2.1100	Schaettel, Marcel. Sonnets du no man's land. Paris, 1956.
43763.4.100	Schaltin, Raymond. Poèmes essentiels. Rodez, 1956-57. 4v.
43763.36.2122	Schehadé, Georges. Histoire de Vasco. 2. éd. Paris, 1956.
43763.37.2110	Schehadé, Laurice. Portés disparues. Paris, 1956.
43538.76.860	Scheidegger, Jean. George Bernanos romancier. Neuchâtel, 1956.
38585.23.75	Scherer, Jacques. Racine. v.1-2. Paris, 1956.
43620.2.345	Schlumberger, Jean. Madeleine et André Gide. 14. éd. Paris, 1956.
43763.38.260	Schlumberger, Jean. Passion. Paris, 1956.
43763.41.2100	Schwaller de Lubicz, Isha. Her-Bak, disciple de la sagesse egyptienne. Paris, 1956.
43765.32.130	Seghers, Pierre. Racines. Paris, 1956.
43765.76.2100	Serge, Jean. Elena et les hommes. Paris, 1956.
43765.75.100	Sernet, Claude. Étapes. Paris, 1956.
43765.76.110	Sernin, André. Icare, ou Comment on tue un écrivain. Paris, 1956.
43765.90.2100	Séveyrat, Aimé. Finie l'ére des chrysalides. Gap, 1956.
38546.49.20	Sévigné, Marie de R.C. Letters from Madame la marquise de Sévigné. 1st American ed. N.Y., 1956.
43768.21.100	Shedrow, A. Berceau sans promesses. Paris, 1956.
43769.54.790	Simenon, Georges. My friend Maigret. London, 1956.
43769.54.400	Simenon, Georges. Le petit homme d'Arkhaugelsk. Paris, 1956.
37568.150	Simon, P.H. Histoire de la littérature française du XX siècle. Paris, 1956. 2v.
43769.56.110	Simon, Pierre Henri. Les hommes ne veulent pas mourir. Paris, 1956.
43769.65.100	Sion, Georges. La malle de Pamela. Bruxelles, 1956.
39544.330	Sokolov, V.V. Vol'ter. Moskva, 1956.
37555.665	Sonet, Jean. Repertoire d'incipit des prières en ancien français. Genève, 1956.
37574.800	Soupault, P. Les deux cents plus beaux poèmes de la langue française. Paris, 1956.
43775.90.8100	Sourgens, J.M. Le feu sous la neige. Paris, 1956.
43757.50.10	Starr, W.T. Romain Rolland and a world at war. Evanston, Ill., 1956.
37574.140	Steele, Alan J. Three centuries of French verse, 1511-1819. Edinburgh, 1956.
42563.23.122	Steinmann, Jean. Léon Bloy. Paris, 1956.
43779.25.100	Sternberg, Jacques. La géométrie dans la terreur. Paris, 1956.
43697.75.830	Stiftung, F.V.S. zu Hamburg. Gedenkschrift zur Verleihung des Hansischen Goethe-Preises 1955. Hamburg, 1956.
37555.212.2	Suberville, Jean. Histoire et théorie de la versification française. Paris, 1956.
43738.1.815	Suire, Pierre. Le tourment de Péguy. Paris, 1956.
43780.69.790	Supervielle, Jules. In viaggio con Supervielle. Milano, 1956.
43780.69.345	Supervielle, Jules. Léscalier. Paris, 1956.
43787.29.120A	Tefri (pseud.). Les succès du docteur Olfa. Lausanne, 1956.
40556.23.40	Thévenaz-Schmalenbach, Cornelia. Joseph Joubert. Inaug. Diss. Genève, 1956.
43687.85.100	Thibauderie, Ivan de la. Langrottes et margouillats. Coutances, 1956.
38526.42.17	Thickett, D. Bibliographie des oeuvres d'Estienne Pasquier. Genève, 1956.
FL 6139.56.15	Thomas, J.F. Le pélagianisme de Jean-Jacques Rousseau. Paris, 1956.
42576.15.240	Thorlby, Anthony. Gustave Flaubert and the art of realism. London, 1956.
43617.59.800	Timbaldi Abruzzese, Eva. Il romanzo rurale di Maurice Genevoix. Torino, 1956.
43792.50.100	Tollet, Marcel. Des blancs, des noirs. Bruxelles, 1956.
43793.42.210	Triolet, Elsa. Le rendez-vous des étrangers. Paris, 1956.
37569.363	Trois poètes: Mariel Clarmont. Paris, 1956.
43793.67.720	Troyat, Henri. Amelie in love. N.Y., 1956.
43793.67.740	Troyat, Henri. The red and the white. N.Y., 1956.
42557.14.70	Underwood, V.P. Verlaine et l'Angleterre. Paris, 1956.
43822.14.100	Vacquin, Pierre. Flârtes et tambours. Paris, 1956.
43822.35.100	Vaguer, J.P. Les paysages vénéneaux. Paris, 1956.
40526.32.11	Vailland, Roger. Eloge du cardinal de Bernis. Paris, 1956.
37543.425	Valeri, Diego. Da Racine a Picasso. Firenze, 1956.
43822.48.1100	Valeri, Diego. Jeux de mots. Paris, 1956.
43822.49.430	Valéry, Paul. Collected works. v.1,3-5,7,9-13. N.Y., 1956- 10v.
37562.314	Valkhoff, M. Masterpieces of Old French literature. Johannesburg, 1956.
43545.4.4805	Vandromme, P. Robert Brasillach. Paris, 1956.
43822.75.100	Varel, André. Musiques dominantes. Paris, 1956.
41557.10.195	Varilhe, Jean de. Les années d'adolescence de George Sand. Guéret, 1956.
38527.9.33	Vauquelin de la Fresnaye, Jean. Les foresteries. Genève, 1956.
42582.3	Verne, Jules. Jules Verne. N.Y., 1956.
43824.3.1100	Vian, Boris. L'automne à Pékin. Paris, 1956.
43824.16.1110	Vidalie, Albert. La bonne ferte; roman. Paris, 1956.
43824.58.100	Vinaver, M. Les Coréens. Paris, 1956.

Chronological Listing

1956 - cont.

FL 6139.56.5 Voisine, Jacques. Jean-Jacques Rousseau en Angleterre à l'époque romantique. Paris, 1956.
FL 6139.56.5.2 Voisine, Jacques. Jean-Jacques Rousseau en Angleterre à l'époque romantique. Thèse. Paris, 1956.
39545.35.50 Voltaire, François Marie Arouet de. Candide. N.Y., 1956.
39544.28.90 Voltaire, François Marie Arouet de. Lettres. Textes nouveaux de la correspondance de Voltaire. Moscou, 1956. 2v.
39544.28.85 Voltaire, François Marie Arouet de. Lettres inédites à Constant d'Hermenches. Paris, 1956.
39545.125 Voltaire, François Marie Arouet de. Le taureau blanc. Lyon, 1956.
39545.125.2 Voltaire, François Marie Arouet de. Le taureau blanc. Paris, 1956.
39545.32.45 Voltaire, François Marie Arouet de. Zadig, ou La destinée. Genève, 1956.
37563.90 Weber, Henri. La création poétique au XVI siècle en France. Paris, 1956. 2v.
37563.92 Weber, Henri. La création poétique au XVI siècle en France. Thèse. Paris, 1956. 2v.
43833.20.705 Weil, Simone. The Iliad. Wallingford, Pa., 1956.
43833.41.100 Weingarten, Romain. Tomalnaut. Paris, 1956.
37530.111 Wenger, I. Zehn Jahre deutsche. Hamburg, 1956.
38585.16.230 Wheatley, K.E. Racine and English classicism. Austin, 1956.
43835.80.100 Wise, Conrad. Le massacre des innocents. Paris, 1956.
43845.13.100 Yacine, Kateb. Nedjma. Paris, 1956.
43852.89.160 Yourcenar, Marguerite. Les charités d'Alcippe. Liége, 1956.
43861.77.122 Zermatten, Maurice. La montagne sans étoiles. 2e éd. Paris, 1956.
42584.23.25 Zola, Emile. La république en marche. Paris, 1956. 2v.
42584.23.30 Zola, Emile. Zest for life. Bloomington, 1956.

1957

43522.7.100 Aberny, Jean. Poemás honnis. 1. ed. Cannes, 1957.
Htn 43554.2.1040* Académie...Paris. Discours prononcés dans la séance publique tenue. Paris, 1957.
43512.75.220 Achard, Marcel. Potate. Paris, 1957.
FL 360.100 Achard, Marcel. Rions avec eux. Paris, 1957.
43744.67.1370 Adam, international review. Marcel Proust. London, 1957.
43514.6.120 Adamov, Arthur. Paolo Paoli. 3. éd. Paris, 1957.
41522.18.320 Aguettant, Louis. Lecture de Baudelaire. Paris, 1957.
43538.35.100 Albert Béguin. Neuchâtel, 1957.
43522.17.100 Aldelbert, M. Les iles désertes. Paris, 1957.
43522.25.1102 Alexis, Jacques Stephen. Les arbres musiciens. 2. ed. Paris, 1957.
43522.98.110 Alyn, Marc. Cruels divertissements. Paris, 1957.
43522.98.100A Alyn, Marc. Le temps des autres. Paris, 1957.
43523.4.100 Amar, Gaston. Deux ans sur les mines. Paris, 1957.
43523.6.100 Amavis. L'éternel Paris. Paris, 1957.
V42582.2.45 Andreev, Kirill K. Tri zhizni Zhiulia Verna. Moskva, 1957.
43524.67.155 Anouilh, Jean. Antigone. Paris, 1957.
43524.67.797 Anouilh, Jean. Restless heart. London, 1957.
43524.67.795 Anouilh, Jean. The waltz of the toreadors. 1st American ed. N.Y., 1957.
43526.65.202 Apollinaire, Guillaume. Ombre de mon amour. Lausanne, 1957.
43528.22.100 Aréga, Leon. Pseudonymes. 2. éd. Paris, 1957.
43528.89.100 Arnothy, Christine. God is late. 1st ed. N.Y., 1957.
43528.89.1100 Arudy, France. Solderon. Paris, 1957.
43528.98.100 Arya. Le placard aux grenouilles. Paris, 1957.
43531.7.3100 Aubert, Claude. Terres de cendres. Genève, 1957.
43531.18.1170 Audiberti, Jacques. Le megére apprivoisee. 4. éd. Paris, 1957.
40517.7.3.10 Aulnoy, Marie C.J. de B. Contes de Saphir. Paris, 1957.
43535.35.21 Ayguesparse, Albert. Le vin noir de Cahors. Paris, 1957.
43535.54.300 Aymé, Marcel. La jument verte. Paris, 1957.
43535.54.290 Aymé, Marcel. La mouche bleue. 6e éd. Paris, 1957.
43535.54.310 Aymé, Marcel. Le puits aux images. 22e éd. Paris, 1957.
40597.29.4.85 Balzac, Honoré de. Le père Goriot. Paris, 1957.
40597.35.160 Balzac, Honoré de. La vieille fille. Paris, 1957.
41522.18.76 Bandy, W.T. Baudelaire devant ses contemporains. Monaco, 1957.
42563.23.124 Barbeau, Raymond. Un prophète luciferien. Paris, 1957.
42563.18.250 Barbier, Joseph. Les sources de La colline inspirée de Maurice Barrès. Nancy, 1957.
43738.1.260 Barbier, Joseph. Le vocabulaire. Paris, 1957.
43738.1.261 Barbier, Joseph. Le vocabulaire. Thèse principale. Paris, 1957.
43537.76.1100 Barjavel, René. Four de feu. Paris, 1957.
38542.26.10 Barnwell, H.T. Les idées morales et critiques de Saint Evremond. Paris, 1957.
42576.15.250 Bart, Benjamin F. Flaubert's landscape descriptions. Ann Arbor, 1957.
43537.77.3100 Barthes, Roland. Mythologies. Paris, 1957.
37574.830 Bartuschek, H. Der gallische Hahn. Berlin, 1957.
43537.82.110 Bassan, Jean. Nuls ve s'évadé. Paris, 1957.
43554.2.980 Bastien, Jacques. L'oeuvre dramatique de Paul Claudel. Reims, 1957.
43537.84.1100 Bataille, Georges. Le bleu du ciel. Paris, 1957.
41522.13.14.10 Baudelaire, Charles. Baudelaire. London, 1957.
41522.13.10 Baudelaire, Charles. La fanfarlo. Monaco, 1957.
41522.13.9.26A Baudelaire, Charles. Les fleurs du mal. Paris, 1957.
41522.13.9.24 Baudelaire, Charles. Les fleurs du mal. Paris, 1957.
41522.13.9.50 Baudelaire, Charles. La floraj de l'malbono. La Laguna, 1957.
43537.88.4100 Baudouy, Michel Aimé. La quadrelle Sarda. Paris, 1957.
43537.89.3100 Bauer, Anne M. La vigie aveugle. Paris, 1957.
43537.97.100 Bay, Paul. Miss Gorilla; roman. Spa, 1957.
37562.354A Bayrav, Süheylâ. Symbolisme médiéval: Béroul, Marie, Chrétien. Paris, 1957.
40532.6.5 Beaumarchais, Pierre A.C. de. La folle journée, ou Le mariage de Figaro. Paris, 1957.
43538.1.510 Beauvoir, Simone de. La longue marche. 30. éd. Paris, 1957.
43538.14.770 Beckett, Samuel. All that fall. London, 1957.
43538.14.150 Beckett, Samuel. Fin de partie. Paris, 1957.
43538.14.721 Beckett, Samuel. Murphy. N.Y., 1957.
43538.14.160 Beckett, Samuel. Tous ceux qui tombent. Paris, 1957.
37555.670 Béguin, Albert. Poésie de la présence de chrétien de Troyes à Pierre Emmanuel. Neuchâtel, 1957.

1957 - cont.

43744.67.1315 Benoist-Méchin, Jacque Gabriel Paul Michael. Retour à Marcel Proust. Paris, 1957.
43741.11.3800 Benoit, P.A. A propos des poèmes de la fille née sans mère. Alès, 1957.
43538.61.142 Benoît, Pierre. Erromango. Paris, 1957.
43538.61.150 Benoît, Pierre. Montsalvat. Paris, 1957.
43538.61.20 Benoît, Pierre. Oeuvres romanesques. Givors, 1957-59. 6v.
43538.61.4100 Benoit, Raymond. Les voix en chaine. Paris, 1957.
41592.31.10 Béranger, P.J. de. Sochineniia. Moskva, 1957.
43538.74.7100 Bergère, André. Sonatines et scherzos pour pulette à cordes. Paris, 1957.
43538.97.100 Bergin-le-Plan, Louis. Le rendez-vous de François Villon avec les poètes maudets. Paris, 1957.
43538.90.120 Berl, Emmanuel. La France irréalle. Paris, 1957.
43538.76.3105 Bernadi, François. Le vin de lune. 5. éd. Paris, 1957.
43538.76.103 Bernanos, Georges. Sous le soleil de Satan. Paris, 1957.
43538.76.1130 Bernard, Marc. La bonne humeur. 3. éd. Paris, 1957.
43538.76.5100 Bernard, Michel. Histoire de Martin et de Leannie. Paris, 1957.
43538.10.8100 Bernard-Massenat. Le masque creux. Paris, 1957.
43538.77.6105 Berry, André. Sonnets surréels. Limoges, 1957.
43538.77.8110 Berthet, Jean. Paroles sans romances, 1950-56. Paris, 1957.
40582.8.4.12 Beyle, Henri. De l'amour. Paris, 1957.
40582.5.5 Beyle, Henri. Feuillets inédits. Paris, 1957.
40582.19.20 Beyle, Henri. A Roman journal. N.Y., 1957.
40582.25.70 Beyle, Henri. Il rosso e il nero. Roma, 1957. 2v.
40582.25.17 Beyle, Henri. Le rouge et le noir. Paris, 1957. 2v.
38562.12.5 Bibliothèque Fontenelle, 1657-1757. Paris, 1957.
41522.16.10 Bibliothèque national, Paris. Charles Baudelaire. Exposition. Paris, 1957.
41596.2.20 Bibliothèque nationale, Paris. Alfred de Musset, 1810-1857. Paris, 1957.
42576.15.455 Bibliothèque nationale, Paris. Gustave Flaubert et Madame Bovary. Paris, 1957.
43540.99.21 Bizet, René. Choix de poèmes. Paris, 1957.
43550.58.840 Bjurström, C.G. Albert Camus. Stockholm, 1957.
43543.8.160 Blanchot, Maurice. Le dernier homme. Paris, 1957.
43543.8.3100 Blancotte, B. Cette lucarne qui mene au fond. Paris, 1957.
43543.8.2100 Blanquernon, Claude. Pierres du Hoggar. Paris, 1957.
43543.9.100 Blanzat, Jean. La Gartempe. Paris, 1957.
43544.112.100 Boileau, Pierre. Les magiciennes. Paris, 1957.
43697.52.854 Boisdeffre, Pierre. André Malraux. 4. éd. Paris, 1957.
43550.58.842 Bollinger, Renate. Albert Camus. Köln, 1957.
V43500.31 Bolsée, Berthe. Rosée d'octobre. Dison, 1957.
43544.51.1100 Boltanski, Luc. Le fusil. Paris, 1957.
43554.2.1320 Boly, Joseph. L'annonce faite à Marie [par] P. Claudel; étude et analyse. Paris, 1957.
38567.43 Bonfantini, Mario. L'art poétique. Napoli, 1957.
40575.1.12 Bonnerot, Jean. Un demi-siècle d'études sur Sainte-Beuve, 1904-1954. Paris, 1957.
43544.62.100 Bontemps, Elisabeth. Lil. Paris, 1957.
42563.36.65.22 Bordeaux, Henry. La robe de laine. Paris, 1957.
43544.76.100 Borel, Pierre Louis. Les idées. Paris, 1957.
43697.77.830 Borgal, Clément. Roger Martin du Gard. Paris, 1957.
43544.81.2180 Bosco, Henri. Barbache. 17. éd. Paris, 1957.
43544.81.2122 Bosco, Henri. Le mas théotime. Paris, 1957.
43544.81.2170 Bosco, Henri. Sabinus. Paris, 1957.
43544.89.2140A Bosquet, Alain. Premier testament. Paris, 1957.
43544.89.2142 Bosquet, Alain. Premier testament. 4. éd. Paris, 1957.
43544.108.110 Boulle, Pierre. E mc2 récits. Paris, 1957.
43544.108.715 Boulle, Pierre. The test. N.Y., 1957.
43544.89.3110 Bourniquel, Camille. Les abois. Paris, 1957.
43545.4.4200 Brasillach, Robert. La reine de Césarée. Paris, 1957.
37574.688 Bray, René. Anthologie de la poésie précieuse de Thibaut de Champagne à Giraudoux. Paris, 1957.
37569.230A Brée, Germaine. An age of fiction. New Brunswick, 1957.
43545.23.2100 Breitman, Michel. Le mal de Dieu. Paris, 1957.
FL 395.285 Bretty, Béatrice. La comédie-française à l'envers. Paris, 1957.
43545.42.120 Brisson, P. Propos de théâtre. 6. éd. Paris, 1957.
43626.22.820A Brodin, Pierre. Julien Green. Paris, 1957.
43823.75.2163 Bruller, Jean. Les animaux dénaturés. Paris, 1957.
43823.75.2210 Bruller, Jean. P.P.C. Paris, 1957.
37567.611 Brussels. Palais des Beaux-Arts. Le mouvement symboliste. Bruxelles, 1957.
37563.93 Buffum, Imbrie. Studies in the baroque from Montaigne to Rotrau. New Haven, 1957.
38514.23.90 Burger, André. Lexique de la langue de Villon. Genève, 1957.
43546.87.35 Butor, Michel. La modification. Paris, 1957.
43833.20.860 Cabaud, Jacques. L'expérience vécue de Simone Weil. Paris, 1957.
43550.10.100 Cabriès, Jean. Jacob. London, 1957.
37575.740 Cadix, Gaston. En Cevenne. Paris, 1957.
43550.50.1100 Caillier, Guy. Tant que tournera la terre, poèmes. Paris, 1957.
43550.58.220 Camus, Albert. L'exil et le royaume. 69. éd. Paris, 1957.
43550.58.730A Camus, Albert. The fall. 1. American ed. N.Y., 1957.
43550.58.722 Camus, Albert. The plague. N.Y., 1957.
43550.71.100 Capri, Agnès. Music-hall poésie. Paris, 1957.
43550.1.200 Carco, Francis. Rendez-vous avec moi-même. Paris, 1957.
43550.82.190 Cassou, Jean. Le Janus. Paris, 1957.
37562.358 Castellani, Arrigo Ettore. Bédier avait-il raison? Fribourg, 1957.
41564.55.87 Castex, Pierre. Vigny. Paris, 1957.
43550.85.100 Cathala, S. Meurtre d'un serin. 3. éd. Paris, 1957.
43550.98.105 Cayrol, Jean. La goffe, récit. Paris, 1957.
43551.59.102 Cendrars, Blaise. Du monde entier au coeur du monde. Paris, 1957.
43551.59.255 Cendrars, Blaise. Le Transsibérien. Paris, 1957.
43551.59.250 Cendrars, Blaise. Trop c'est trop. Paris, 1957.
43551.77.100 Certigny, H. Le bal masqué de Montparnasse. Paris, 1957.
43552.2.2100 Chabrol, Jean-Pierre. Fleur d'épine. 5e éd. Paris, 1957.
42515.38.5 Chadbourne, Richard MClain. Ernest Renan as an essayist. Ithaca, N.Y., 1957.
43552.2.3100 Chaffrol-Debillemont, Fernard. Suicides et misères romantiques. Paris, 1957.
43552.3.9260 Chamson, André. L'auberge de l'abime. 5e éd. Paris, 1957.
43552.3.9700 Chamson, André. A time to keep. London, 1957.
43552.7.7100 Chappuis, Pierre. Le soleil couronne et diamant. Paris, 1957.
43552.4.2230 Char, René. La bibliotheque est en feu. Paris, 1957.
43552.4.2021 Char, René. Poèmes et prose choisis. 3e éd. Paris, 1957.

Chronological Listing

1957 - cont.

43552.5.5100 Charpentreau, J. Les Jeux de l'espair. Paris, 1957?
40564.33 Chasles, Philarète. The legacy of Philarète Chasles. Chapel Hill, N.C., 1957.
42576.65.13.122 Chastel, Guy. J.K. Huysmans et ses amis. Paris, 1957.
43552.7.5100 Château, René. Cantiques sans Dieu. Paris, 1957.
40586.13.25 Chateaubriand, F.A.R. Atala. Berkeley, 1957.
43552.7.2100 Chazal, Malcolm de. Sens magique. Tananarive? 1957.
42576.12.40 Cherbonnel, Alice. My uncle and the curé. London, 1957.
43552.25.2106 Chevallier, Gabriel. Clochemerle-Babylone. 170e éd. Paris, 1957.
40517.44.12 Choderlos de Laclos, Pierre A.F. Dangerous acquaintances. Norfolk, Conn., 1957.
43552.65.100 Choisy, Maryse. Le serpent. Paris, 1957.
43552.65.110 Choisy, Maryse. Tes yeux m'ont vu. Paris, 1957.
43552.67.1100 Chouard, Claude Henri. L'étude intérieure. Paris, 1957.
43554.3.1100 Clairvaux, Henry. Oeil de mouche. Paris, 1957.
43554.2.735 Claudel, Paul. The essence of the Bible. N.Y., 1957.
43554.2.795 Claudel, Paul. Der Gnadenkranz. Einsiedeln, 1957.
43554.2.42 Claudel, Paul. Oeuvre poétique. Paris, 1957.
43554.67.1110 Cloup, François. L'ame prit la parole. Paris, 1957.
43556.1.425 Cocteau, Jean. La chapelle Saint Pierre. Monaco, 1957.
43556.1.420 Cocteau, Jean. La corrida du premier mai. Paris, 1957.
43556.1.435 Cocteau, Jean. La difficulté d'être. Monaco, 1957.
43556.1.440 Cocteau, Jean. Le grand écart. Paris, 1957.
43556.1.760 Cocteau, Jean. The holy terrors. N.Y., 1957.
43556.1.765 Cocteau, Jean. The imposter. N.Y., 1957.
43556.1.372 Cocteau, Jean. Le sang d'un poète. Monaco, 1957.
43554.2.1075 Coenen- Mennemeier, Brigitta. Der aggressive Claudel. Münster, 1957.
42576.65.13.119A Cogny, Pierre. Le Huysmans intime de Henry Ceard et Jean de Caldain. Paris, 1957.
43556.49.560 Colette, Sidonie Gabrielle. Chiens. Paris, 1957.
43556.49.765 Colette, Sidonie Gabrielle. My apprenticeships. London, 1957.
43556.51.100 Colombat, Armand. Poèmes. Paris, 1957.
43556.58.110 Conchon, Georges. Tous comptes faits. Paris, 1957.
40553.9.80 Constant de Rebecque, Benjamin. Le cahier rouge. Paris, 1957.
40553.9.75 Constant de Rebecque, Benjamin. Oeuvres. Paris, 1957.
40553.7.18A Constant de Rebecque, Benjamin. Le romantisme. Paris, 1957.
38575.37.15 Corneille, Pierre. L'illusion comique. Paris, 1957.
43556.82.720 Cossery, Albert. If all men were beggars. London, 1957.
43556.87.100 Cottereau, Roger. Manège. Paris, 1957.
39527.4.125 Couton, Georges. La poétique de La Fontaine. 1. éd. Paris, 1957.
43557.5.100 Craran, Arthur. Maintenant. Paris, 1957.
41522.18.310 Crépet, Jacques. Propos sur Baudelaire. Paris, 1957.
43557.24.1100 Cressot, Marcel. Musique pour deux saisons. Rodez, 1957.
43560.78.170 Curtis, Jean Louis. A la recherche du temps posthume. Paris, 1957.
43560.78.2100 Curvers, Alexis Théophille. Tempo di Roma. Paris, 1957.
43744.67.1310 Czoniczer, E. Quelques antécedénts de A la recherche du temps perdu. Genève, 1957.
43565.33.100 Dagneaux, P. Terrain vogue. Paris, 1957.
43565.41.65 Daix, Pierre. Réflexions sur la méthode de Roger Martin du Gard. Paris, 1957.
43554.2.1000 Daniel-Rops, Henry. Claudel tel que je l'ai connu. Strasbourg, 1957.
43565.60.1120 Daninos, Pierre. The secret of Major Thompson. N.Y., 1957.
42586.33.112 Darien, Georges. Bas les coeurs; 1870-1871. 2. éd. Paris, 1957.
43565.76.2100 Darmangeat, Pierre. Le temps de le Raison Ardente. Paris, 1957.
43565.89.115 Daumal, René. Petit théâtre de René Daumal. Paris, 1957.
37568.155 Declerck, R. Gestalten en gedachten. Antwerpen, 1957.
43753.58.2800 Decreus, J. Poesie et transcendance. Paris, 1957.
41543.22.55 Dédéyan, Charles. Gerard de Nerval et l'Allemagne. Paris, 1957. 3v.
43566.17.100 Dédéyan, Christian. Quatuor pour le temps des ténèbres. Tournai, 1957.
43566.29.1100 Defos, Bertrand. Simon le superbe. 7. éd. Paris, 1957.
43738.76.2800 Defrenne, M. Odilon-Jean Périer. Bruxelles, 1957.
43566.31.1100 Dega, Jean Pierre. Muguet du bois joli; poème romantique. Paris, 1957.
39545.21.15 Delattre, André. Voltaire l'impétueux essai presenté par R. Pomeau. Paris, 1957.
43566.48.6100 Del Castillo, Michel. Tanguy. Paris, 1957.
43566.48.7110 Del Corte, Daniela. Vers les cimes. v.1-4. Paris, 1957- 3v.
43566.49.7100 Delhaye de Marnyhac, Thérèse. La maison sans ame. Paris, 1957.
43566.52.1100 Delvaille, Bernard. Enfance, mon amour. Rodez, 1957.
FL 6139.57.5 Deregibas, Arturo. Il problema morale in Jean-Jacques Rousseau. Torino, 1957.
38585.16.270 Descotes, Maurice. Les grands rôles du théâtre de Jean Racine. 1. éd. Paris, 1957.
43566.81.1100 Des Ligneris, F. Fort Frédérick, roman. Paris, 1957.
43566.81.2100 Desmarest, M.A. Douce-amère. Paris, 1957.
43566.81.2120 Desmarest, M.A. Le fils Jan. Paris, 1957.
43566.81.5110 Desnos, Youki. Les confidences des Youki. Paris, 1957.
43566.82.7180 Destouches, Louis Ferdinand. D'un château à l'autre. Paris, 1957.
43566.82.7720.5 Destouches, Louis Ferdinand. Mea culpa...Semmelweis. 20. éd. Paris, 1957.
43567.25.100 Dheur, G. Vrai et usage de vrai. Paris, 1957.
43567.79.160 Dhôtel, André. Faraway. N.Y., 1957.
39564.15.5 Diderot, Denis. Le nevue de Rameau. Paris, 1957.
39564.19A Diderot, Denis. Salons. Oxford, 1957- 4v.
39564.15.15A Diderot, Denis. Le siècle des lumières. Paris, 1957.
43568.23.1100 Dieguez, M. de. Dieu est-il américain? Paris, 1957.
43569.21.110 Djebar, Assia. La soif. Paris, 1957.
43573.74.100 Dorcino, Jean. Pas de dragées pour le baptême. Paris, 1957.
38575.23.120 Dort, Bernard. Pierre Corneille, dramaturge. Paris, 1957.
37583.657 Le drame romantique. Paris, 1957.
43574.75.735 Druon, Maurice. The poisoned crown. N.Y., 1957.
43576.8.30 Dubois La Chartre, André. Journal intime d'Hercule. 6. éd. Paris, 1957.
43576.10.100 Dubus, Cyrille. Le poème du chaume. v.3. Paris, 1957.
43576.13.2106 Duchemin, J. Le chemin de Poitiers. 6. éd. Paris, 1957.
43576.6.435 Duhamel, Georges. Problèmes de l'heure. Paris, 1957.
42554.29.172 Dujardin, E. We'll to the woods no more. N.Y., 1957.
43576.53.2110 Dumay, Raymond. Vanina. 2. éd. Paris, 1957.

1957 - cont.

43738.1.805 Dupuy, Jean R. Un utopiste du passé. Aix-en-Provence, 1957.
43576.90.1110 Duvignaud, Jean. L'or de la République. 3. éd. Paris, 1957.
40515.14.20 Ehmer, Gisela. Die sensible Selbstdarstellung bei Julie de Lespinasse. Berlin, 1957.
43593.32.100 Engelmann, Jacques. Les amphigourdiers. Paris, 1957.
43597.61.100 Ernout, I. Jeux d'ombres. Paris, 1957.
43709.23.810 Escholier, Raymond. La neige qui brûle. Paris, 1957.
Mon 115.1 Espezel, Pierre d'. Presence et actualité de Montaigne. Paris, 1957.
43598.82.180 Estang, Luc. L'interrogatoire. Paris, 1957.
43599.41.120 Étiemble, René. L'énnemie publique. Paris, 1957.
37565.186 Etiemble, René. L'Orient philosophique du XVIII siècle. v.1-3. Paris, 1957-59.
43599.41.130 Étiemble, René. Le péché vraiment capital. Paris, 1957.
37567.444A Evans, David Owen. Social romanticism in France, 1830-1848. Oxford, 1957.
43601.23.100 Eveno, Lucien. Frissons et scintillements. Paris, 1957.
43606.9.5100 Fabre, Dominique. Charmants garçons. Paris, 1957.
43606.10.110 Fabre-Luce, Alfred. Une minute; roman. Paris, 1957.
43606.48.100 Falaise, Élisabeth. La source des rêves. Paris, 1957.
43606.76.3100 Farlane, Gilbert. Tous pour un. Paris, 1957.
43786.25 Fchecaja u Tam'pi, Gerald Félix. Feu le Brousse. Paris, 1957.
38554.527 Fénelon, F. de S. de la Mothe. Letters to men and women. London, 1957.
43607.74.100 Ferchaud, Suzanne. Le vent qui lève; poèmes. Paris, 1957.
43609.50.1100 Filippi, Louise. Pierres dures. Paris, 1957.
42576.20.23 Flaubert, Gustave. L'éducation sentimentale. Paris, 1957.
42576.28.92 Flaubert, Gustave. Madame Bovary. N.Y., 1957.
42576.28.90 Flaubert, Gustave. Madame Bovary. N.Y., 1957.
42576.28.95 Flaubert, Gustave. Madame Bovary. Paris, 1957.
42576.28.97 Flaubert, Gustave. Madame Bovary. Paris, 1957.
43610.25.4100 Fleury, François. Jours d'Arés; poèmes. Paris, 1957.
40515.17.50 Florian, Jean P.C. de. Lettres au Marquis A. de Florian, 1779-1793. Paris, 1957.
41574.525 Flottes, Pierre. L'éveil de Victor Hugo, 1802-1822. 8. éd. Paris, 1957.
43611.50.100 Follain, Jean. Tout instant. 2. éd. Paris, 1957.
39545.22.20 Folman, Michel. Voltaire et Madame Denis. Genève, 1957.
42557.14.85 Fongaro, Antoine. Bibliographie de Verlaine en Italie. Florence, 1957.
43611.75.1105 Forestier, Marie. Le détour. 5. éd. Paris, 1957.
43611.76.100 Forton, Jean. Cantemerle. Paris, 1957.
37596.50.3 Fournival, Richard de. Li bestiaires d'amours di Maistre Richart de Fornival e Li response du bestiaire. Milano, 1957.
37568.88.5 Fowlie, Wallace. A guide to contemporary French literature. N.Y., 1957.
43554.2.970 Fowlie, Wallace. Paul Claudel. London, 1957.
43554.2.972 Fowlie, Wallace. Paul Claudel. N.Y., 1957.
43556.1.890 Fraigneau, André. Cocteau par lui-même. Paris, 1957.
42576.62.22.42 France, Anatole. The gods are athirst. N.Y., 1957.
43612.4.100 France, Claire. Les enfants qui s'aiment. Paris, 1957.
43761.39.870 François, Carlo Roger. L'ésthétique d'Antoine de St. Exupéry. Neuchâtel, 1957.
37563.70.5A Françon, Marcel. Leçons et notes sur la littérature française du XVI siècle. Rochecorbon, 1957.
37596.10.181 Frappier, Jean. Chréstien de Troyes. Paris, 1957.
37596.10.180 Frappier, Jean. Chréstien de Troyes. Paris, 1957.
43612.24.100 Frère, Maud. L'herbe à moi. 3. éd. Paris, 1957.
37567.510 Frey, John A. Motif symbolism in the disciples of Mallarmé. Washington, 1957.
43612.42.100 Frié, Jacqueline Frédéric. Si peu de temps. Paris, 1957.
43613.64.100 Froment, Jeanne. Au fil de la vie. Paris, 1957.
43616.33.100 Gagliolo, F. Drigo. Paris, 1957.
43556.1.880A Galerie Matarasso, Nice. Images de Jean Cocteau. Nice, 1957.
43616.50.5100 Galls, Max Louis. L'age d'homme. Paris, 1957.
43616.58.110 Gandon, Yves. Petite suite d'été. Limoges, 1957.
43697.52.830 Gannon, E. The honor of being a man. Chicago, 1957.
FL 362.45 Garapon, Robert. La fantasie verbale et le comique dans le théâtre français du moyen âge. Paris, 1957.
43616.75.110 Garenne, A. L'amour vainqueur. Paris, 1957.
43616.79.130 Gascar, Pierre. L'herbe des rues. 16. éd. Paris, 1957.
43616.89.1103 Gauthier, Marie Joséphine. Orages désirés. 3. éd. Paris, 1957.
43527.3.810 Gavillet, André. La littérature au défi: Aragon surréaliste. Neuchâtel, 1957.
37574.840 Gennes, Renata de. Amours. Paris, 1957.
43538.14.800 Gessner, Niklaus. Die Unzulänglichkeit der Sprache. Zürich, 1957.
38524.874 Gill, Austin. Les ramonneurs. Paris, 1957.
43620.66.430 Giono, Jean. La bonheur fou. 61. éd. Paris, 1957.
37567.495 Giraud, Raymond. The unheroic hero in the novels of Stendhal. New Brunswick, 1957.
43620.74.1120 Giraudoux, Jean Pierre. Le mauvais charme. 6. éd. Paris, 1957.
41574.330 Glauser, A.C. Hugo et la poésie pure. Genève, 1957.
43622.41.700 Glissant, Edouard. The ripening. N.Y., 1957.
42586.64.10 Gobineau, Arthur de. Lettres persanes. Paris, 1957.
43625.19.330 Godoy, Armand. Dulcinée. Paris, 1957.
43625.49.180 Goll, Claire. Neue Blümlein des heiligen Franziskus. Darmstadt, 1957.
43625.49.155 Goll, Claire. Das Tätowierte Herz. Wiesbaden, 1957.
38551.145.5 Goré, Jeanne-Lydie. L'intinéraire de Fénelon. Grenoble, 1957.
43822.49.50 Got, Maurice. Assomption de l'espace. Paris, 1957.
43625.89.2100 Goudal, J. De mer et d'amour. 7. éd. Paris, 1957.
43556.49.850 Goudeket, Maurice. Close to Colette. N.Y., 1957.
43626.70.150 Gracq, Julien. The castle of Argol. Norfolk, Conn., 1957.
43626.22.260 Green, Julien. The transgressor. N.Y., 1957.
43626.23.1108 Grenier, Jean. Les grèves. 8e éd. Paris, 1957.
43626.23.1110 Grenier, Jean. Sur la mort d'un chien. Paris, 1957.
38528.1.30 Gringore, Pierre. La sottie du Prince des Sotz. Milano, 1957.
37596.10.200 Gsteiger, M. Die Landschaftsschilderungen in den Romanen Chrestiens de Troyes. Bern, 1957.
43628.23.150 Guéhenno, Jean. La foi difficile. Paris, 1957.
43628.24.2100 Guérande, Paul. Lamentable Clio. Paris, 1957.
43628.41.5110 Guillot, René. Tom-Toms in Kotokio. N.Y., 1957.
43628.85.700 Guth, Paul. The innocent tenant. London, 1957.
37596.10.175 Guyer, F.E. Chréstien de Troyes. N.Y., 1957.
42556.28.172 Hackett, Cecil A. Rimbaud. London, 1957.
43631.41.2100 Haïk, Farjallah. Jaumana. Paris, 1957.

Chronological Listing

1957 - cont.

42557.14.75	Hanson, Lawrence. Verlaine. N.Y., 1957.
37574.180	Hartley, Anthony. The Penguin book of French verse. Harmondsworth, 1957. 4v.
42577.4.49.145	Hartoy, Maurice d'. Guy de Maupassant inconnu. Paris, 1957.
38529.105	Hassell, James W. Sources and analogues of the Nouvelles récréations et joyeux. Chapel Hill, N.C., 1957-69. 2v.
37568.160	Hatzfeld, H. Trends and styles in twentieth century French literature. Washington, 1957.
37543.380	Hatzfeld, Helmut. Iniatiation à l'explication de textes français. München, 1957.
FL 6129.57	Healey, F.G. Rousseau et Napoléon. Genève, 1957.
43632.61.100	Henry, André. D'une voix chuchotée. Paris, 1957.
43632.76.150	Hériat, Philippe. Les Boussarde. Paris, 1957-68. 4v.
43738.1.810	Herriot, Edouard. Charles Péguy conférence donnée au théâtre municipal de Chartres. Angers, 1957.
43632.77.1100	Herta, Simon. Méditations au Golgotha. Paris, 1957.
41574.34.15	Heugel, J. Hugo, et le génie latin. Paris, 1957.
39566.170	Hinterhaeuser, Hans. Utopie und Wirklichkeit bei Diderot. Heidelberg, 1957?
43636.50.100	Hollier-Larousse, Jules. Les sentiers du destin. Paris, 1957.
43632.50.800	Hommage à Franz Hellens. Hommage à Franz Hellens. Paris, 1957.
43632.75.1800	Hommage des poétes à Jacques Hébertot. Paris, 1957.
37575.735	Hommage des poètes français aux poètes hongrois. Paris, 1957.
43554.2.990	Hoorn, H. Poésie et mystique. Genève, 1957.
41571.16.30	Hugo, Victor. Les misérables. Paris, 1957. 2v.
40597.2.415	Hunt, Herbert James. Honoré de Balzac. London, 1957.
42576.65.80.60	Huysmans, Joris Karl. Lettres inédites à Camille Lemonnier. Genève, 1957.
43643.23.2110	Ibels, J.C. Le sang de l'ange. Paris, 1957.
43652.46.110	Ikor, Roger. Mise au nef. Paris, 1957.
43654.7.100	Imbert, D. La Marie des sept péchés. Paris, 1957.
43659.67.120	Isou, Isidore (pseud.). Je vous apprendrai l'amour. Paris, 1957.
43667.14.280	Jacob, Max. Lettres aux Salacron. Paris, 1957.
42557.12.110	Jones, Percy M. Verhaeren. London, 1957.
43670.89.500	Jouhandeau, M. Carnets de l'écrivain. Paris, 1957.
43670.89.490	Jouhandeau, M. Réflexions sur la vieillesse et la mort. Paris, 1957.
43670.89.520	Jouhandeau, M. Théâtre sans spéctacle. Paris, 1957.
43670.94.350	Jouve, Pierre Jean. Mélodrame. Paris, 1957.
43670.98.110	Joyau-Dormoy, Alice. La saison éternelle. Fort-de-France, 1957.
43671.20.100	Judrin Roger. Boa-Boa. Paris, 1957.
42563.23.126	Juin, Hubert. Léon Bloy. Paris, 1957.
43671.51.100	Jullian, Philippe. Gilberte regained. London, 1957.
43673.19.100	Kédros, André. Le lit de procuste. Paris, 1957.
43673.75.1100	Kerhoas, Émilienne. Saint Cadov. Paris, 1957.
43673.76.2100	Kern, Alfred. Le clown. 11. éd. Paris, 1957.
43674.4.100	Khatchadourian, Alice. Le concert de la nuit. Paris, 1957.
43675.58.100	Kinds, Edmond. Les ornières de l'été. Paris, 1957.
37555.680	Klemperer, V. Moderne französische Lyrik. Berlin, 1957.
FL 398.42.10	Knapp, B.L. Louis Jouvet. N.Y., 1957.
42576.63.720	Kovaleva, I.S. Tvorchestvo Anatolia Fransa v gody pereloma. Leningrad, 1957.
42576.57.100	Krueger, C.O. Symbolic contrasts in the works of Pierre Loti. Missouls, 1957.
37562.295	Kukenheim, Louis. Guide de la littérature française du moyen âge. Leiden, 1957.
38526.26.79	Labé, Louise Charly. Das lyrische Gesamtwerk. Wiesbaden, 1957.
43687.9.3100	Labrderie-Roaldés, Guy. L'echelle enfouie. Paris, 1957.
43687.9.1100	Labruyère, Edith. L'anneau de Saturne. Paris, 1957.
37574.835.5	Lacroix de l'Isle, Robert. Poètes de Paris et de l'Île de France. Paris, 1957.
43687.24.100	Lafaye, Raymond. Pour monia. Paris, 1957. 3 pam.
38544.27.70	La Fayette, Marie M. La Princesse de Clèves. Paris, 1957.
41578.61.10	Lamartine, Alix. Les confidences de Madame de Lamartine. Paris, 1957.
43687.57.100	Lamy, Jacques. Fragments du temple entrevu. Paris, 1957.
43687.61.2100	Lanoë-Herpe, Jules. Sermur. Paris, 1957.
43687.61.1100	Lanoux, Armand. Yododo. Paris, 1957.
FL 396.20.10	Lapoint; Revue artistique et littéraire. Le théâtre national populaire. Souillar, 1957.
43687.74.15	Larbaud, Valéry. Oeuvres. Paris, 1957.
38543.19.52	La Rochefoucauld, François. Maxims. London, 1957.
42521.21	Lasserre, Maurice. Essai sur les poésies de Louis Veuillot. Paris, 1957.
43687.87.130	La Tour du Pin, Patrice de. Pepiniere de sapins de Noel. Paris, 1957.
FL 393.55	Laugh, John. Paris theatre audiences in the seventeenth and eighteenth centuries. London, 1957.
43687.89.5025	Laurentie, Henri. Choix de poèmes. Paris, 1957.
FL 377.180	Lawrenson, T.E. The French stage in the XVIIth century. Manchester, Eng., 1957.
43688.13.4100	Le Clercq, Pierre. En percevant. Paris, 1957.
43688.14.5100	Lecoq, Paul. Les yeux nus. Paris, 1957.
43688.19.100	Lédoux, Ph. La poudre aux moineaux. Paris, 1957.
43688.27.1100	Leféhure, Nadine. Les sources de la mer. 3e éd. Paris, 1957.
43688.34.2100	Le Guen, Jean. Le griot et l'echo. Paris, 1957.
38526.27.16	Lemaire de Belges, Jean. Le temple d'honneur et de vertus. Genève, 1957.
42577.4.70	Lemoine, F. Guy de Maupassant. Paris, 1957.
V43500.181	Lepaul, Jacquelyne. Le rhume des foins; poèmes. Paris, 1957.
43688.98.100	LeQuintrec, Charles. Les noces de la terre. Paris, 1957.
42515.15.5	Les Amitiés littéraires et artistiques. A. Poulet-Malassis. Alençon, 1957.
43688.88.130	Létraz, Jean de. On demande un ménage. Paris, 1957.
38537.38	Lewis, D.B.W. Doctor Rabelais. N.Y., 1957.
43761.31.810	Ligniéré, Jean. Françoise Sagan et le success. Paris, 1957.
43690.90.100	Livio, Robin. La terre est un gateau. Paris, 1957.
43692.63.100	Lloansi, Cyprien. Lumière d'Olivier. Paris, 1957.
43693.41.100	Loiselel, Pierre. Echantillons. Paris, 1957.
43744.67.1295	Louria, Yvette. La convergence stylistique chez Proust. Genève, 1957.
43694.8.110	Lubin, Armen. Les hautes terrasses. Paris, 1957.
43694.13.2100	Lucien, Henri. Le roman de Saint Savin. Paris, 1957.

1957 - cont.

43697.12.100	Machet, Marie Madeleine. Les fêtes du monde. Paris, 1957.
43697.14.115	MacOrlan, Pierre. Le gros rouge. Monte-Carlo, 1957.
43697.33.2100	Magnan, Jean Marie. La nuit d'Arles. Paris, 1957.
41578.135	Magnien, Emil. Lamartine et le Pelerinage Lamartinien en Maconnais. Macon, 1957.
40556.28.9	Maistre, Joseph de. Textes choisis et présentés par E.M. Cioran. Monaco, 1957.
42555.43.31	Mallarmé, Stéphane. Herodias. N.Y., 1957.
42555.44.80	Mallarmé, Stéphane. Le "live" de Mallarmé. Paris, 1957.
43697.2.2120	Mallet, Robert. Lapidé lapidaire. 4e ed. Paris, 1957.
43697.2.1735	Mallet-Joris, Françoise (pseud.). House of lies. N.Y., 1957.
43697.2.1100	Mallet-Joris, Françoise (pseud.). Le rempart des beguines. Paris, 1957.
41522.18.315	Manoll, Michel. La vie passionnée de Charles Baudelaire. Paris, 1957.
41568.26.70	Maple, H.L. Claude Tillier, 1801-1844. Genève, 1957.
43697.74.3140	Marceau, Félicien. Les belles natures. 17. ed. Paris, 1957.
43697.74.3150	Marceau, Félicien. L'oeuf, pièce en deux actes. Paris, 1957.
43697.76.8100	Marissel, André. L'homme et l'abime. Paris, 1957.
40535.30.40	Marivaux, Pierre Carlet de Chamblain de. La vie de Marianne. Paris, 1957.
43620.74.895	Marrill, René. Esthétique et morale chez Jean Giraudoux. Paris, 1957.
43697.79.6100	Martin, Jean Marie. Chansons pour une marionnette. Paris, 1957.
37569.245	Martin du Gard, Maurice. Les mémorables. Paris, 1957- 2v.
43697.78.5140	Martin Saint-René (pseud.). Céruléennes. Paris, 1957.
43792.90.820	Martineau, Henri. P.J. Toulet, collaborateur de Tilly. Paris, 1957.
43792.90.815	Martineau, Henri. P.J. Toulet et Arthur Machen. Paris, 1957.
43697.77.5100	Marty, Peské. Le bal des angoisses. Paris, 1957.
43697.86.3100	Mathieu, Jean. Deux chômeurs, roman. Bruxelles, 1957.
42584.25.235	Matthews, J.H. Les deux Zola. Genève, 1957.
42577.4.4.20	Maupassant, Guy de. Fin de siècle. Paris, 1957.
43697.88.732.5	Mauriac, François. Lines of life. London, 1957.
41539.40.5	Maurois, Andre. Three musketeers. London, 1957.
43697.89.795	Maurois, André. To an unknown lady. 1. éd. N.Y., 1957.
41539.40.10	Maurois, André. Les trois Dumas. Paris, 1957.
43697.89.4100	Maurois, Michelle. Les arapèdes. Paris, 1957.
43697.90.100	Mavel, Jean. De lys et d'ivoire. Rodez, 1957.
39566.260	May, Gita. Diderot et Boudelaire, critiques d'art. Genève, 1957.
43698.25.180	Meersch, M. van der. La compagne. Paris, 1957.
43698.35.130	Mégret, C. Le carrefour des solitudes. Paris, 1957.
FL 377.185F	Mélèse, Pierre. Le théâtre en France au XVIIe siècle. Paris, 1957.
37543.435	Ménard, Jean. De Corneille à Saint-Denys-Garneau. Montréal, 1957.
43698.58.100	Mendiri, Jacques de. Pensées pour l'actuel. Paris, 1957.
41555.2.15	Mérimée, Prosper. Romans et nouvelles. Paris, 1957.
37563.95	Merrill, R.V. Platonism in French renaissance poetry. N.Y., 1957.
43698.86.100	Métirrer, Pierre. Réalité; poèmes vivants. Paris, 1957.
43697.49.810	Michaël, Elizabeth. Joseph Malègue. Paris, 1957.
43698.200.210	Michaux, Henri. L'infini turbulent. Paris, 1957.
FL 6139.57.15	Mirabella, Tommaso. Fortuna di Rousseau in Sicilia. Caltanissetta, 1957.
39544.295	Mitford, Nancy. Voltaire in love. London, 1957.
43699.87.100	Mittet, Émile. Joies et rancoeurs. Paris, 1957.
43701.41.2104	Moitier, Suzanne. Le dragon du lac. 4. éd. Paris, 1957.
Mol 60.31.15	Molière, Jean Baptiste Poquelin. Eight plays. N.Y., 1957.
Mol 49.57	Molière, Jean Baptiste Poquelin. Molière par lui-même. Paris, 1957.
43822.49.1350	Mondor, Henri. Propos familiers de Paul Valéry. Paris, 1957.
43822.49.1050.5A	Mondor, Henri. Précocité de Valéry. 4e éd. Paris, 1957.
43701.59.1100	Monestier, Marianne. Kanaïok. Paris, 1957.
43701.60.2120	Monnier, Adrienne. Souvenirs du Londres. Paris, 1957.
43701.60.110	Monnier, Mathilde. Instants. Lausanne, 1957.
38513.69	Mons Passion play. Le mystère de la Passion joué à Mons en juillet 1501. Mons, 1957.
43886.15	Monsieur X et le mensonge. Paris, 1957.
Mon 32.57A	Montaigne, Michel de. The complete works of Montaigne. Stanford, 1957.
Mon 19.57	Montaigne, Michel de. Essais. Paris, 1957. 5v.
Mon 19.57.5	Montaigne, Michel de. Les essais. Paris, 1957.
Mon 28.64	Montaigne, Michel de. Sagesse de Montaigne. Paris, 1957.
43701.63.500	Montherlant, Henry de. Carnets. 16. éd. Paris, 1957.
43701.63.750	Montherlant, Henry de. Desert love. London, 1957.
43701.63.755	Montherlant, Henry de. The matador. London, 1957.
38575.93	Mony, Gabriel. La chanson de Rodrique. Nice, 1957.
43701.74.330	Morand, Paul. Fin de siècle. Paris, 1957.
43701.74.132	Morand, Paul. Ouvert la nuit. 2. éd. Paris, 1957.
43701.74.2110	Mordreuc, Jean. Le charoguard. Paris, 1957.
43701.75.1100	Moreau, Serge. La clé des nuits. Paris, 1957.
43701.87.100	Mottart, Hubert. Le septre et l'anneau. n.p., 1957.
43701.86.100	Moulin, Jeanine. Feux sans joie. Paris, 1957.
43701.89.3100	Moureau, Maurice. Touches et notes de poésie. Rodez, 1957.
43703.73.3120	Muray, Jean. Le marchand de Venise. Paris, 1957.
43703.80.170	Muselli, Vincent. Oeuvre poétique. Paris, 1957.
41596.23.30	Musset, Alfred de. A comedy and two proverbs. London, 1957.
37569.240	Nahas, Hélène. La femme dans la littérature existentielle. Paris, 1957.
42555.44.145	Nardis, Luigi de. Impressionismo di Mallarmé. Roma, 1957.
42555.44.147	Nardis, Luigi de. Mallarmé in Italia. Milano, 1957.
43705.86.100	Nathiu, Marcel. Carnet. Paris, 1957.
FL 6139.57	Nemo, Maxime. L'homme nouveau. Paris, 1957.
41543.17.3	Nerval, Gerard de. Les filles du feu. Paris, 1957.
41543.7.10	Nerval, Gerard de. Selected writings. N.Y., 1957.
43706.90.100	Neveu, Charlotte. Dona Quichotte. Paris, 1957.
42576.46.14.10	Newman, Pauline. Un romancier périgourdin. Paris, 1957.
40575.5.150	Nicolson, H.G. Saint-Beuve. London, 1957.
43707.17.100	Niderst, Alain. Le soleil et la mort. Paris, 1957.
41556.11.6	Nodier, Charles. Contes fantastiques. Paris, 1957. 2v.
43709.23.2100	Noël, Sean François. Théâtre. Paris, 1957.
43709.80.130	Nourissier, François. Le corps de Diane. Paris, 1957.
43723.18.720	Oldenbourg, Zoé. The awakened. N.Y., 1957.
43554.2.975	Ormesson, W. Paul Claudel et son fauteuil. Paris, 1957.

1957 - cont.

43729.85.110 Oster, Pierre. Solitude de la lumière. 4e éd. Paris, 1957.
43556.1.870A Oxenhandler, N. Scandal and parade. New Brunswick, N.J., 1957.
37574.90.7 The Oxford book of French verse. 2. ed. Oxford, 1957.
43737.34.220 Pagnol, Marcel. Souvenirs d'enfance. Monte Carlo, 1957. 3v.
43737.49.100 Palgen, Paul. Oratorio pour la mort d'un poète. Paris, 1957.
43737.59.110 Panneel, Henry. Les Fioretti du curé d'Ars. Paris, 1957.
43737.71.100 Papon, René. Le volcan. Paris, 1957.
43667.1.856 Parent, Monique. Francis Jammes. Paris, 1957.
43667.1.855 Parent, Monique. Rythme et versification dans la poésie de Francis Jammes. Paris, 1957.
43769.54.805 Parinaud, André. Connaissance de Georges Simenon. Paris, 1957.
38526.42.12.20 Pasquier, Étienne. Le monophile. Varese, 1957.
43737.89.1110 Paulhan, Jean. Un bruit de guêpe. Paris, 1957.
40516.60.110 Pauvert, J.J. L'affaire Sade. Paris, 1957.
43737.98.1100 Paysan, Catherine. La Pacifique. Paris, 1957.
43738.1.32 Péguy, Charles. God speaks. N.Y., 1957.
43738.1.22 Péguy, Charles. Oeuvres en prose. Paris, 1957-59. 2v.
43738.41.1100 Peignot, Jérôme. Jérômiades. Paris, 1957- 3v.
43738.48.100 Pellerin, Pierre. La possession de l'équateur. Paris, 1957.
43738.81.140 Perret, Jacques. Le caporal epinglé. Paris, 1957.
43738.81.21 Perret, Jacques. Histoires sous le vent. Paris, 1957.
43738.81.130 Perret, Jacques. Rôle de plaisance. 23e éd. Paris, 1957.
43738.81.123 Perret, Jacques. Salades de saison. 3e éd. Paris, 1957.
43738.78.170 Perse, Saint-John. Amers. Paris, 1957.
43738.90.100 Pevel, Henri. On a crevé le paravent. Paris, 1957.
43738.97.1160 Peyrefitte, Roger. Chevaliers de Malte. Paris, 1957.
43738.97.1730 Peyrefitte, Roger. The keys of St. Peter. N.Y., 1957.
43740.41.1100 Philip, Maurice. Maillons. Coutances, 1957.
V43500.243 Pic, Marcel. A la merci du feu. Paris, 1957.
43757.50.1115 Pichler, R. Romain Rolland. Leipzig, 1957.
37567.545 Pichois, Claude. L'image de la Belgique dans les lettres françaises de 1830. Paris, 1957.
43741.26.100 Pierre-Lambert, René. Ti et mi. Paris, 1957.
43741.25.150 Pieyre de Mandiargues, André. Astyanax. Viry-Chatillon, 1957.
43741.25.110 Pieyre de Mandiargues, André. Le musée noir. Paris, 1957.
43741.48.100 Pillendin, Roger. La belle jeunesse. Paris, 1957.
43744.67.1246 Piroué, Georges. Proust's way. London, 1957.
43742.3.105 Planchon, Michel. Compagnons de silence. 5e éd. Paris, 1957.
43742.41.200 Plisnier, Charles. Bruler vif. Paris, 1957.
37574.142 Poésies et dessins de Charles d'Orléans à Apollinaire, de Fouguet à Pecasso. Lausanne, 1957.
37574.910 Les Poètes français contre la guerre. Paris, 1957.
43743.41.100 Poirier, Jean M. Le prix du souvenir. Ottawa, 1957.
40532.46 Pollitzer, Marcel. Beaumarchais. Paris, 1957.
41596.4.110 Pommier, Jean. Alfred de Musset. Oxford, 1957.
40597.2.465 Pommier, Jean. L'invention et l'ecriture dans la Torpille d'Honoré de Balzac. Genève, 1957.
43743.75.140 Porché, Simone Benda. Sous de nouveaux soleils. Paris, 1957.
Mol 730.20 Poulaille, Henry. Corneille sous le masque de Molière. Paris, 1957.
43744.24.23.8A Prévert, Jacques. Paroles. Paris, 1957.
40522.9.41 Prévost, Antoine F. Histoire du chevalier des Grieux et de Manon Lescaut. Paris, 1957.
37567.500 Prevost, John C. Le dandysme en France. Genève, 1957.
38536.18.35 Rabelais, F. Oeuvres complètes. Paris, 1957. 5v.
38583.12.26 Racine, Jean. The best plays of Racine. Princeton, 1957.
43752.18.120 Radiguet, Raymond. Règle du jeu. Monaco, 1957.
42555.44.140 Ragusa, Olga. Mallarmé in Italy. N.Y., 1957.
43752.56.100 Ramounet, René. La rivage. Ales, 1957.
X Cg 43752.70.100 Rapin, Simone. L'année de l'amour. Bienne, 1957.
43552.4.2810 Rau, Greta. René Char. Paris, 1957.
43753.41.100 Reiner, S. Le caporal marche nu-tête. 5. éd. Paris, 1957.
42587.51.32 Renard, Jules. Lettres inédites. 4. éd. Paris, 1957.
42587.51.40 Renard, Jules. The sponger. London, 1957.
42587.51.50A Renard, Jules. Théatre complet. Paris, 1957.
43753.99.6100 Reynold, Gonzague de. Le chant d'une vie. Fribourg, 1957.
43756.11.100 Richer, Charline. L'evéntail. Paris, 1957.
42586.63.30 Rifaterre, Michael. Le style des Pléiades de Gobineau. Genève, 1957.
42556.28.54 Rimbaud, Jean Arthur. Oeuvres. Paris, 1957.
42556.28.56 Rimbaud, Jean Arthur. Oeuvres. Strasbourg, 1957.
43756.86.100 Rivière, Bertrande de. Chrysis. Paris, 1957.
43757.6.130 Robbe-Grillet, Alain. Dans le labyrinthe. Paris, 1957.
43757.6.120 Robbe-Grillet, Alain. La jalousie. Roma, 1957.
FL 398.52.50 Robichez, Jacques. Le symbolisme au théâtre. Paris, 1957.
37543.400 Robin, Eugène. Impressions littéraires. Bruxelles, 1957.
38537.25.235 Roe, Fredrick Charles. Sir Thomas Urguhart and Rabelais. Oxford, 1957.
FL 6119.56 Röehrs, Hermann. Jean-Jacques Rousseau. Heidelberg, 1957.
43757.49.110 Rolin, Dominique. L'epouvantail. 6. éd. Paris, 1957.
43757.50.70 Rolland, Romain. Correspondance, 1894-1901. Paris, 1957.
43757.50.72 Rolland, Romain. Thèse complementaire - Univ. de Paris. Paris, 1957.
43757.3.195 Romains, Jules. Une femme singulière. Paris, 1957.
43757.3.120A Romains, Jules. Pierres levées. Paris, 1957.
38525.12.25 Ronsard, Pierre de. Oeuvres complètes. v.7. Paris, 1957.
43757.79.100 Rosciszewska, Rita de. L'aventure; poèmes. Paris, 1957.
42514.28.90 Roudiez, L.S. Maurras jusqu'à l'action française. Paris, 1957.
43742.41.810 Roussel, Jean. La vie et l'oeuvre ferventes de Charles Plisnier. Rodez, 1957.
43757.92.2170 Rousselot, Jean. Agrégation du temps. Paris, 1957.
43757.92.2150 Rousselot, Jean. Les heureux de la terre. Paris, 1957.
43757.89.1100 Rousset, Jean Paul. Poaimes. Paris, 1957.
43757.96.150F Roy, Claude. Farandoles et fariboles. Lausanne, 1957.
43757.96.4160 Roy, Jules. Le fleuve rouge. Paris, 1957.
43757.96.4125 Roy, Jules. L'homme à l'épée. 5. éd. Paris, 1957.
43757.96.4140 Roy, Jules. Sept poèmes de ténèbres. n.p., 1957.
43554.2.1010 Roy, Paul-Émile. Claudel. Montréal, 1957.
37596.8.4 Rutebeuf. Oeuvres completes. v.1-2. Paris, 1957.
40516.60.70 Sade, D.A.F. de. La Marquise de Gange. Paris, 1957.
43761.31.120 Sagan, Françoise. Dans un mois. Paris, 1957.
43761.31.710 Sagan, Françoise. Those without shadows. 1st ed. N.Y., 1957.
43761.41.9100 St. Agrève, Marc. Le puits. Paris, 1957.

1957 - cont.

V43500.287 Saint-Clair, Georges. L'absence et les miroirs; poèmes. Paris, 1957.
43761.41.3100 St. Pierre, Michel de. Les écrivains. Paris, 1957.
40575.1.4 Sainte-Beuve, C.A. Vie. Paris, 1957.
43761.49.220 Salmon, André. Vocalises. Paris, 1957.
43761.56.21 Sandoz, Maurice Yves. Choix de poèmes. Monaco, 1957.
43761.1.100 Sandoz, Maurice Yves. Le labyrinthe. Paris, 1957.
43761.59.2100 Sandra, C. Mortvigne. Paris, 1957.
43761.77.120 Sarraute, Nathalie. Tropismes. Paris, 1957.
38537.25.225 Saulnier, V.L. Le dessein de Rabelais. Paris, 1957.
37562.300 Saulnièr, V.L. La littérature française du moyen âge. 4. éd. Paris, 1957.
37563.87.2 Saulnier, Verdun L. La littérature française de la renaissance. 4. éd. Paris, 1957.
43632.89.800 Savoret, André. Simples propos sur l'oeuvre de Jacques Heugel. Montrouge, 1957.
43757.50.1175 Scanno, Teresa di. Romain Rolland. Parma, 1957.
43763.4.110 Schaltin, Raymond. Quinzains et troisneufs, formes poétiques et modernes. Paris, 1957.
37567.616 Schaub-Koch, E. Contribução para o do fantastico no romance. Lisboa, 1957.
37555.675 Schossig, Alfred. Der Ursprung der Altfranzösischen Lyrik. Halle, 1957.
43763.39.2100 Schreiber, Boris. Le droit d'asile. Paris, 1957.
38514.27.10 Seaton, Ethel. Studies in Villon. Oxford, 1957.
43765.58.100 Senard, Pierre. Le regne de Venus. Paris, 1957.
43765.59.100 Sénéchal, Georges. Droit de cité. Vitry-sur-Seine, 1957.
43765.90.4100 Sevac, H. Poèmes parisiens. Paris, 1957.
39566.165 Seznec, Jean. Essais sur Diderot et l'antiquite. Oxford, 1957.
43769.11.1100 Sicard, Maurice Ivan. Aurélia; scènes de la vie fantastique. Paris, 1957.
42557.14.80 Sieper, Bernhard. Paul Verlaine. Herne, 1957.
43769.54.798 Simenon, Georges. The stowaway. London, 1957.
37569.40.200.5 Simon, P.H. La littérature du péche et de la grace. Paris, 1957.
43769.56.100 Simon, Pierre Henri. Les raisins verts. Paris, 1957.
43769.55.110 Simoncelly, Hermine. Trinité pour deux. Paris, 1957.
37574.696 Société de Poésie, Paris. Eventail. Paris, 1957.
43775.50.110 Sollers, Philippe. Le défi. Abbeville, 1957.
43775.95.100 Solore, C.G. Comme une odeur de nuit. 4. éd. Paris, 1957.
43775.96.100 Sorel, Claude. Le comédien de plume. Paris, 1957.
42577.4.39 Spaziani, Marcelo. Bibliographie de Maupassant en Italie. Florence, 1957.
43776.43.100 Spens, Willy de. Éléonore d'Aquitaine et ses troubadours. Paris, 1957.
37583.510 Stanton, Stephen Sadler. Camille, and other plays. N.Y., 1957.
43779.24.2103 Stéphane, Nelly. Les chercheurs. 6. éd. Paris, 1957.
39544.140.5 Stern, Jean. Voltaire et sa nièce. Paris, 1957.
43744.67.1285A Strauss, W.A. Proust and literature. Cambridge, 1957.
38526.19.25 Surin, Jean Joseph. Poésies spirituelles suivis des contrats spirituels. Paris, 1957.
43780.81.100 Susini Holden, (Mme.). Chienne de journée. Paris, 1957.
43620.2.355 Tanchot, Jacques. André Gide et la Cour d'Assises. Rouen, 1957.
43787.29.110 Tefri (pseud.). Cent réponses. Lausanne? 1957.
43787.50.100 Tellier, Marcel. Traduit du coeur. Rodez, 1957.
43788.24.1100 Théron, Germaine. Le secret merveilleux. 7e éd. Paris, 1957.
43550.58.830 Thody, Philip. Albert Camus. London, 1957.
42576.15.445 Thorlby, Anthony. Gustave Flaubert and the art of realism. New Haven, 1957.
41563.28.10 Toepffer, Rodolphe. Élisa et Widmer. Genève, 1957.
43792.74.1100 Torday, Sandor. Les miroirs se mirent. Paris, 1957.
43793.42.220 Triolet, Elsa. Le monument. 7e éd. Paris, 1957.
43538.99.21 Trois poètes. Paris, 1957.
43793.67.715 Troyat, Henri. Amelie and Pierre. N.Y., 1957.
37569.235 Tylden-Wright, David. The image of France. London, 1957.
37556.165A Ullman, Stephen. Style in the French novel. Cambridge, Eng., 1957.
42584.25.290 Untersteiner, Gabriella. L'oeuvre di Emile Zola e i suoi rapporti con Cézanne. Milano, 1957.
43822.50.122 Vailland, Roger. La loi, roman. Paris, 1957.
43822.49.750 Valéry, Paul. Cahiers. Paris, 1957-61. 29v.
43822.49.61 Valéry, Paul. Correspondance 1887-1933. 5e éd. Paris, 1957.
43822.49.192.2 Valéry, Paul. La jeune parque. Paris, 1957.
43822.49.18 Valéry, Paul. Oeuvres. Paris, 1957. 2v.
42581.33.42 Vallès, Jules. Un gentilhomme. Paris, 1957.
43611.5.120A Valloton, Henri. Alain-Fournier. Paris, 1957.
43822.51.2100 Valorbe, François. La vierge aux chimeres. Paris, 1957.
43822.55.100 Valton, André. Le banquet pantagruélique et poétique. Fontenay-le-Comte, 1957.
43697.88.845 Vandromme, Pol. La politique litteraire de François Mauriac. Paris, 1957.
37547.22.15 Vaneille, Jean Louis. Les patoisants bas-normands. Saint Lô, 1957-
43757.50.1170 Vanovskaia, T.V. Romen Rollan, 1866-1944. Leningrad, 1957.
37543.261.4 Van Tieghem, Philippe. Petite histoire des grandes doctrines littéraires en France. Paris, 1957.
43822.89.1100 Vaure, Jean Jacques. Sequences. Paris, 1957.
40527.19.15 Venzac, Géraud. Jeux d'ombre et de lumière sur la jeunesse d'André Chenier. 6. éd. Paris, 1957.
42557.20.7.5 Verlaine, Paul. Lettres inédites de Verlaine à Cazals. Genève, 1957.
42557.18.50 Verlaine, Paul. Poésies et proses. Paris, 1957.
42557.19.140 Verlaine, Paul. The sky above the roof. London, 1957.
43824.3.190 Vialar, Paul. Belada. Paris, 1957.
43824.3.200 Vialar, Paul. La grande meute. Paris, 1957.
43824.17.110 Viderot, Toussaint. Courage! Paris, 1957.
43824.6.130 Vigée, Claude. L'été indien. 4e éd. Paris, 1957.
43824.48.120 Vilallonga, José Luis de. L'heure dangereuse du petitquotin. Paris, 1957.
43824.51.100 Villemain, P. Confessions de Numida. Paris, 1957.
42547.19.5 Villiers de l'Isle Adam, Auguste. Oeuvres. Paris, 1957.
43824.58.2100 Vinant, Gaby. Poèmes et paradis. Paris, 1957.
43827.41.1100 Voillemot, Germaine. Les clés de l'adieu; poèmes. Paris, 1957.
FL 6139.57.10 Volpe, G. della. Rousseau e Marx e altri saggi di critica materialistica. Roma, 1957.
39545.35.52 Voltaire, François Marie Arouet de. Candide. Paris, 1957.
39545.46.3.20 Voltaire, François Marie Arouet de. L'ingénu. Genève, 1957.

Chronological Listing

1957 - cont.

39544.27.3.12	Voltaire, François Marie Arouet de. Lettres d'amour de Voltaire à sa nièce. Paris, 1957.
39543.25	Voltaire, François Marie Arouet de. Oeuvres historiques. Paris, 1957.
40597.2.425	Vouga, Daniel. Balzac malgré lui. Paris, 1957.
41522.18.325	Vouga, Daniel. Baudelaire et Joseph de Maistre. Paris, 1957.
43833.20.130	Weil, Simone. Ecrits de Londres et dernières lettres. 10e éd. Paris, 1957.
39566.160A	Wilson, A.M. Diderot. N.Y., 1957.
41522.18.330	Wisconsin. University. Memorial Library. Baudelaire. Madison, 1957.
43835.80.110	Wise, Conrad. La montagne de Zander. Paris? 1957.
43835.81.100	Wislenet, Paule. Le dépossédé; roman. Paris, 1957.
43697.75.840	Wolff, Gertrud. Der Todesgedanke im Drama Gabriel Marcel's. Erlangen, 1957.
43856.89.705	Yourcenar, Marguerite. Coup de grâce. N.Y., 1957.
43852.89.150A	Yourcenar, Marguerite. Feux. Paris, 1957.
43856.65.100	Yvon, Monique. Les pèlerins du destin, poèmes. Lyon, 1957.
43861.77.130	Zermatten, Maurice. Le lierre et le figuier. Bruges? 1957.
37596.10.185	Ziltener, Werner. Chréstien und die Aeneis. Graz, 1957.
42584.9.20	Zola, Emile. The abbé Mouret's sin. London, 1957.
42584.1.30	Zola, Emile. Chefs-d'oeuvre. Paris, 1957.
42584.13.30	Zola, Emile. Doctor Pascal. London, 1957.
42584.4.4	Zola, Emile. Ladies' delight. London, 1957.
42584.23.2.5	Zola, Emile. A love affair. London, 1957.
42584.23.83.2	Zola, Emile. The masterpiece. N.Y., 1957.
42584.12.32	Zola, Emile. Nana. N.Y., 1957.

1958

37595.7.30	Abailard, Pierre. The story of my misfortunes. Glencoe, Ill., 1958.
37575.148.5	Académie...Montpellier. Académie de Montpellier. Bas-Languedoc et Roussillon. Paris, 1958.
37575.148	Académie...Toulouse. Académie de Toulouse. Haut-Languedoc et Armagnac. Paris, 1958.
38539.90	Adam, Antoine. Romanciers du XVIIIe siècle. Paris, 1958.
37583.658.5	Adamov, Arthur. Théâtre de société. Paris, 1958.
42576.15.270	Alboreto, Luciano. Il rapporto vita poesia in Flaubert. Venezia, 1958.
43687.15.800	Alden, D.W. Jacques de Lacretelle. New Brunswick, 1958.
39574.27.30	Alembert, J. Le Rond d'. Einleitende Abhandlung zur Enzyklopädie, 1751. Berlin, 1958.
43523.4.3100	Amariu, Constantin. Le pauvre d'esprit, roman. Paris, 1958.
43523.5.2110	Amat, Robert. L'horizan s'affirme. Paris, 1958.
43523.5.2100	Amat, Robert. L'orgue solaire. Paris, 1958.
43524.3.100	Analis. Le prince des lys. Paris, 1958.
43524.67.799	Anouilh, Jean. Dinner with the family. London, 1958.
43524.67.798	Anouilh, Jean. Five plays. N.Y., 1958.
43524.67.220	Anouilh, Jean. Pauvres Bitos. Paris, 1958.
43524.67.122	Anouilh, Jean. Pièces roses. Paris, 1958.
43524.67.785	Anouilh, Jean. Time remembered. 1st American ed. N.Y., 1958.
37573.28	Anthologie des poètes français contemporains. Paris, 1958- 5v.
37575.209	Anthologie poétique de l'exposition. Bruxelles, 1958.
43697.88.850	Apfelbeck, Senta. François Mauriacs Einstellung zu Sünde. München, 1958.
43527.3.360	Aragon, Louis. La semaine sainte. Paris, 1958.
43528.12.100	Archimede. Poésies d'amour. Rome, 1958.
43528.61.2100	Arnold, Paul. Les dévayés, roman. Paris, 1958.
41522.18.370	Arnold, Paul. Das Geheimnis Baudelaires. Berlin, 1958.
43528.73.100	Arrabal, Fernando. Théâtre. v.1,3-6,7,8. Paris, 1958. 7v.
43531.17.100	Audet, Elaine. Soleil noir, poèmes. Paris, 1958.
43531.18.3100	Audibert, Jean Marie. La dame de Beyrouth. Paris, 1958.
43531.18.1190	Audiberti, Jacques. Infanticide préconisé. Paris, 1958.
43535.54.750	Aymé, Marcel. Across Paris. N.Y., 1958?
43554.2.1070	Babilas, W. Das Frankreichbild in Paul Claudels Personnalité de la France. Münster, 1958.
43537.11.3100	Baccouche, Hachime. Ma foi demeure; roman. Paris, 1958.
43537.14.110	Backer, A.M. de. L'herbe et le feu. Paris, 1958.
43697.75.850	Bagot, Jean Pierre. Connaissance et amour. Paris, 1958.
43697.75.130	Bagot, Jean Pierre. La soif (pièce en trois actes) précédée de Théâtre et mystère par Gaston Fessard. Paris, 1958.
43757.50.1225	Balakhonov, Viktor E. Romen Rollan v 1914-1924 gody. Leningrad, 1958.
40597.35.144	Balzac, Honoré. Splendeurs et misères des courtisanes. Paris, 1958. 2v.
40597.35.175	Balzac, Honoré de. La cabinet des antiques. Paris, 1958.
40596.13.140	Balzac, Honoré de. La comédie humaine. Paris, 1958. 11v.
40597.35.164	Balzac, Honoré de. Cousin Bette. N.Y., 1958.
40597.14.80	Balzac, Honoré de. Domestic peace, and other stories. Harmondsworth, 1958.
40597.35.87	Balzac, Honoré de. Illusions perdues. v.1-2. Paris, 1958.
40597.35.142	Balzac, Honoré de. Splendeurs et misères des courtisanes. Paris, 1958.
40597.86	Balzac, Honoré de. The stepmother. London, 1958.
40597.34.4	Balzac, Honoré de. Une ténébreuse affaire. Paris, 1958.
41522.2.16	Barbey d'Aurevilly, Jules. Lettres et fragments. Paris, 1958.
39596.32	Baridon, Silvio F. Le harmonies de la nature di Bernardin de St. Pierre. Milano, 1958. 2v.
43744.67.1345	Barker, R.H. Marcel Proust. N.Y., 1958.
42563.18.30	Barrès, Maurice. N'importe où hors du monde. Paris, 1958.
FL 1102.7	Barry, Félicien. Deux cent septante écrivains dialectaux du pays noir. Charleroi? 1958.
37572.75	Barthélemy, B. Textes choisis pour la lecture et l'explication. Paris, 1958-60. 5v.
41555.43.50	Baschet, Robert. Mérimée, 1803-1870. Paris, 1958.
43537.82.3100	Bastide, François Régis. Les adieux. N.Y., 1958.
43537.83.100	Bastien, André P. Domaines. Paris, 1958.
43537.88.1100	Bauchau, Henry. Geólogie. Paris, 1958.
41522.13.9.31	Baudelaire, Charles. The flowers of evil. N.Y., 1958.
41522.13.9.33	Baudelaire, Charles. The flowers of evil. N.Y., 1958.
41522.5.22	Baudelaire, Charles. Oeuvres. Paris, 1958.
43537.89.4100	Baudin, Suzanne. Le ciel frôla la terre. Paris, 1958.
43537.99.700	Bazin, Hervé. A tribe of women. N.Y., 1958.
43538.1.200.10	Béalu, Marcel. L'air de vie. Paris, 1958.

1958 - cont.

43554.2.942	Beaumont, Ernest. Les sens de l'amour dans le théâtre de Claudel. Paris, 1958.
43538.1.515	Beauvoir, Simone de. The long march. 1. ed. Cleveland, 1958.
43538.1.520	Beauvoir, Simone de. Mémoires d'une jeune fille rangée. Paris, 1958.
43538.14.782A	Beckett, Samuel. Endgame. N.Y., 1958.
43538.14.780	Beckett, Samuel. Endgame. N.Y., 1958.
43538.14.735A	Beckett, Samuel. From an abandoned work. London, 1958.
43822.49.1310	Bellivier, André. Henri Poincaré et Paul Valéry. Chevreuse, 1958.
40597.2.44	Benjamin, René. La prodigieuse vie d'Honoré de Balzac. Paris, 1958.
43538.61.56	Benoît, Pierre. De Koenigsmark à Montsalvat. Paris, 1958.
43538.61.170	Benoît, Pierre. La sainte vehme. Paris, 1958.
43538.62.4100	Bens, Jacques. Chanson recue. Paris, 1958.
43538.62.4110	Bens, Jacques. Valentin. Paris, 1958.
37583.658	Bentley, E.R. Let's get a divorce! and other plays. N.Y., 1958.
43538.91.110	Berimont, Luc. L'herbe à Tonnerre. Paris, 1958.
43538.10.54	Bernard, Jean J. Mon ami le théâtre. Paris, 1958.
43538.93.110	Berrin, Lucien. Le tisonnier des rêves. Paris, 1958.
43538.77.5100	Berry, Gaston. Le lys de sora. Paris, 1958.
43538.77.100	Berthet, Guy. L'amour s'en vient. Paris, 1958.
43538.77.2100	Bertin, Charles. Christoffel Columbus. Brussel, 1958.
43554.2.985	Berton, J.C. Shakespeare et Claudel. Génève, 1958.
41522.3.60	Bésus, Roger. Barbey d'Aurevilly. Paris, 1958.
40582.40.10	Beyle, Henri. The life of Henri Brulard. London, 1958.
40582.25.38	Beyle, Henri. The red and the black. N.Y., 1958.
43667.1.860	Bibliothèque Nationale, Paris. Francis Jammes. Paris, 1958.
37530.175	Bibliothèque Nationale, Paris. Répertoire collectif. Paris, 1958.
37595.34.30	Bibliothèque nationale, Paris. Mss. (Fr. 19152). Twelve fabliaux. Manchester, 1958.
40583.245	Billy, André. Ce cher Stendhal. Paris, 1958.
42557.14.90	Binet, Léon R. Verlaine à Aix-les-Bains. Paris, 1958.
43543.3.3100	Blanchard, Max. Rimes en short. Monte Carlo, 1958.
43552.4.2815	Blanchot, Maurice. La bête de Lascaux. Paris, 1958.
40583.260.5	Blin, Georges. Stendhal et les problèmes de la personnalité. Paris, 1958.
43544.17.100	Bodart, Roger. Le nègre de Chicago. Paris, 1958.
37597.26.62	Bodel, Jehan. Le jeu de Saint Nicolas. Oxford, 1958.
37568.165	Boisdeffre, P. de. Une histoire vivante de la littérature d'aujourd'hui. Paris, 1958.
43544.50.110	Bolloré, Gwenäel. Moira, la naufrageuse. Paris, 1958.
43544.50.100	Bolloré, Gwenäel. Propos interrompus. Paris, 1958.
40583.275	Bonfantini, M. Stendhal e il realismo. 1. ed. Milano, 1958.
43544.60.2110	Bonnefoy, Yves. Hier regnant désent. Paris, 1958.
41522.18.350	Bonzon, Alfred. La degradation des images dans la poésie Baudelairienne. São Paulo, 1958.
42563.36.255	Bordeaux, Henry. Mémoires secrets du chevalier de Rosaz. Paris, 1958.
40597.2.470	Borel, Jacques. Personnages et destins balzaciens. Paris, 1958.
43544.75.4100	Borel-Rosny, Robert. La rouguine au tapis. Paris, 1958.
43697.77.840	Borgal, Clément. Roger Martin du Gard. Paris, 1958.
43544.81.2185	Bosco, Henri. Bargabot. 3. éd. Paris, 1958.
37575.750	Bosquet, Alain. Les vingt meilleures nouvelles françaises. Paris, 1958.
38557.35.2	Bossuet, J.B. Letters of spiritual direction. London, 1958.
43544.86.100	Bouchéret, Roland. Hibernales. Paris, 1958.
40515.15.9	Bouissounouse, J. Julie de Lespinasse. Paris, 1958.
43544.108.720	Boulle, Pierre. The other side of the coin. N.Y., 1958.
43544.89.5100	Bounoure, Gabriel. Marelles sur le parvis. Paris, 1958.
43544.87.3146	Bourbon Busset, Jacques de. Fugue à deux voix; recit. 6. éd. Paris, 1958.
43544.87.4100	Bourdeillette, Jean. Reliques des songes. Paris, 1958.
42563.39.035	Bourgeois, André. La vie de René Boylesve. Genève, 1958.
37574.854	Bourgeois, Gaston. Poètes protestants d'aujourd'hui. Paris, 1958. 2v.
43544.113.100	Boussinot, Roger. L'eau du bain. Paris, 1958.
43545.4.4190	Brasillach, Robert. Notre avant-guerre. Paris, 1958.
38567.45A	Brody, Jules. Boileau and Longinus. Genève, 1958.
43823.75.2230	Bruller, Jean. Sur ce rivage. Paris, 1958- 3v.
39544.300	Brumfitt, J.H. Voltaire. London, 1958.
43738.1.820	Brussels. Bibliotheque Royale. Charles Péguy. Bruxelles, 1958.
38543.23.25	Bruzzi, Amelia. La Rochefoucauld. Bologna, 1958.
43546.87.55	Butor, Michel. L'emploi du temps. Paris, 1958.
43546.87.40	Butor, Michel. Le genie dulieu. Paris, 1958.
43546.87.45	Butor, Michel. Second thoughts. London, 1958.
43550.6.100	Cabanis, José. Les mariages de raison; roman. 8. éd. Paris, 1958.
43550.20.110	Cadou, Hélène. Cantate des nuits interieures. Paris, 1958.
43822.49.1305	Cain, L. Trois essais sur P. Valéry. Paris, 1958.
43550.48.120	Calet, Henri. Peau d'ours pour un roman. Paris, 1958.
37569.250	Callot, Emile. Cinq moments de la sensibilité française contemporaine. Annecy, 1958.
43550.58.716	Camus, Albert. Caligula and three other plays. 1. American ed. N.Y., 1958.
43550.58.230	Camus, Albert. Discours de Suède. 14. éd. Paris, 1958.
43550.58.750	Camus, Albert. L'envers et l'endroit. Paris, 1958.
43550.58.192	Camus, Albert. Le malentendu. Paris, 1958.
43550.58.723	Camus, Albert. The plague. N.Y., 1958.
43550.58.755	Camus, Albert. Récits et théâtre. Gallimard, 1958.
43550.58.745	Camus, Albert. Speech of acceptance upon the award of the Nobel prize for literature. 1. ed. N.Y., 1958.
43550.1.23	Carco, Francis. Poèmes en prose. Paris, 1958.
FL 395.290	Cardinue-Petit, Robert. Les secrets de la comédie française, 1936-1945. Paris, 1958.
42555.37.25	Carloni Valentini, Renata. Un poète présque oublié. Vimodrone? 1958.
37567.535	Carter, A.E. The idea of decadence in French literature. Toronto, 1958.
43535.54.800	Cathelin, Jean. Marcel Aymé. Paris, 1958.
43550.89.120	Cau, Jean. Mon village contés. Paris, 1958.
43550.89.110	Cau, Jean. Les paroissiens. Paris, 1958.
43550.89.100	Cau, Jean. Un testament de Staline. Paris, 1958.
43551.1.100	Céa, Claire. Epreuves. Paris, 1958.
42542.49.65	Céard, Henry. Lettres inédites à Emile Zola. Paris, 1958.
40542.37.5	Celier, Léonce. Federico Ozanam. 5. ed. Roma, 1958.
43551.59.21	Cendrars, Blaise. A l'aventure. Paris, 1958.

1958 - cont.

41522.18.345	The centennial celebration of Baudelaire's Les fleurs du mal. Austin, 1958.
43551.80.130	Cesbron, Gilbert. Il est plus tard que tu ne penses. Paris, 1958.
43552.2.2120	Chabrol, Jean-Pierre. Un homme de trop. Paris, 1958.
40524.32.50	Chadourne, Marc. Restif de la Bretonne. Paris, 1958.
43552.3.9270	Chamson, André. Nos ancêtres les Gaulois. Paris, 1958.
43552.4.9100	Chapuis, Michel. Bâtons rompus. 2e éd. Paris, 1958.
42556.28.285	Char, René. Le dernier couac. Paris, 1958.
43552.4.2220	Char, René. Sur la poésie. Paris, 1958.
38514.26.60	Charles d'Orleans. Charles d'Orleans. Paris, 1958.
37548.32.10F	Charlier, Gustave. Histoire illustrée des lettres française de Belgique. Bruxelles, 1958.
43552.4.3100	Charrier, René Albert. Sommeils. Avignon, 1958.
43552.5.1145	Chartier, Émile. Alain au lycée d'Alençon. Alençon, 1958.
43552.5.1180	Chartier, Émile. Les arts et les dieux. Paris, 1958.
43552.5.1061	Chartier, Émile. Correspondance avec Elie et Florence Halevy. Paris, 1958.
41522.3.65	Chastain, André. Un convive du Dîner d'athées de Barbey d'Aurevilly. Coutances, 1958.
40586.28.86	Chateaubriand, F.A.R. Mémoires d'outre-tombe. v.2. Paris, 1958.
40564.35	Chauvet, Victor. Manzoni, Stendhal. Catania, 1958.
43552.70.100	Chauviré, Jacques. Partage de la soif. Paris, 1958.
40526.32.12	Cheke, Marcus. The cardinal de Bernis. London, 1958.
40526.7.95	Chénier, André. André Chénier. Paris, 1958.
FL 363.33	Cherpack, Clifton. The call of blood in French classical tragedy. Baltimore, 1958.
43761.39.826	Chevrier, Pierre A. St. Exupéry. 4. éd. Paris, 1958.
42536.38	Chevrillon, André. Portrait de Taine. Paris, 1958.
FL 385.12.55	Chiari, Joseph. The contemporary French theatre. London, 1958.
37574.850	Chiari, Joseph. The Harrap anthology of French poetry. London, 1958.
42555.44.150.2	Chisholm, A.R. Mallarmé's L'après-midi d'un faune. Carlton, 1958.
42555.44.150	Chisholm, A.R. Mallarmé's L'après-midi d'un faune. Carlton, 1958.
40517.44.6	Choderlos de Laclos, Pierre A.F. Les liaisons dangereuses. Paris, 1958.
43552.69.110	Chraibi, Driss. De tous les horizons. Paris, 1958.
43553.54.100	Ciméze, Jean. Le coeur ébouillanté, suivi de Seconde lecture. Paris, 1958.
43554.2.796	Claudel, Paul. Images saintes de Bohême. V Římě, 1958.
43554.2.730	Claudel, Paul. A poet before the cross. Chicago, 1958.
43554.2.510	Claudel, Paul. Qui ne souffre pas. Paris, 1958.
43554.21.100	Clébert, Jean Paul. The blockhouse. 1st American ed. N.Y., 1958.
43554.23.3100	Clement-Dechamp, Emile. Au gré du veul. Paris, 1958.
43554.89.1100	Cluzel, M.E. Le droit de vivre. Paris, 1958.
43556.3.100	Coanet, Georges. De bas en haut. Paris? 1958.
43556.1.775	Cocteau, Jean. The miscreant. London, 1958.
43556.1.780	Cocteau, Jean. My journey round the world. London, 1958.
43556.1.770	Cocteau, Jean. Opium. N.Y., 1958.
43556.1.790	Cocteau, Jean. Paraprosodies précédées de sept dialogues. Monaco, 1958.
43556.1.430	Cocteau, Jean. La Salle des mariages. Monaco, 1958.
43556.49.570	Colette, Sidonie Gabrielle. Bêtes libres et prisonnières. Paris, 1958.
43556.49.770	Colette, Sidonie Gabrielle. Claudine in Paris. N.Y., 1958.
43556.49.65	Colette, Sidonie Gabrielle. Lettres à Hélène Picard. Paris, 1958.
43556.49.575	Colette, Sidonie Gabrielle. Notes marocaines. Lausanne, 1958.
37569.305	Colloque internationale des écrivains d'expression française. Le colloque internationale. Paris, 1958.
37548.205	Congres national de littérature comparée. Les Flandres dans les mouvements romantique et symboliste. Paris, 1958.
43756.90.835	Cook, Bradford. Jacques Rivière. Oxford, 1958.
40564.35.10	Cordié, Carlo. Romanticismo e classicismo nell'opera di Victor Chauvet. Messina, 1958.
37569.255A	Cornell, William Kenneth. The post-symbolist period. New Haven, 1958.
43574.70.805	Corot-Gélas, Georgette. Minou Drouet. Paris, 1958.
43556.89.2100	Couffin, André. Le bouge humain. Paris, 1958.
43556.89.1100	Cousin, Gabriel. L'ordinaire amour. 2e éd. Paris, 1958.
38575.23.117	Couton, Georges. Corneille. Paris, 1958.
43557.4.100	Crance, Gerard. Symphonie circuloire. Paris, 1958.
37595.90	Daix, Pierre. Naissance de la poesie française. Paris, 1958.
41592.10.40	Danilin, Iurii I. Beranzhe i ego pesni. Moskva, 1958.
43565.60.2100	Danilov, Joel. Les ondes du silence. Paris, 1958.
43565.60.1180	Daninos, Pierre. Les carnets du bon Dieu. Paris, 1958.
43565.61.100	Danoën, Émile. Le conseiller hippique. 4e ed. Paris, 1958.
43565.89.61	Daumal, René. Lettres à ses amis. Paris, 1958.
43565.90.3100	David, Jean. Les survivants. Paris, 1958.
43565.92.7110	Davray, Jean. Théâtre sans bornes. Paris, 1958.
39594.19.125	Dédéyan, Charles. Montesquieu et l'Angleterre. Paris, 1958.
43566.48.9110	Delahaye, Gilbert. Les enfants de minuit. Tournai, 1958.
43566.48.6700	Del Castillo, Michel. Child of our time. 1st American ed. N.Y., 1958.
43566.48.6110	Del Castillo, Michel. Le colleur d'offiches. Paris, 1958.
41566.36.4	Delécluze, E.J. Two loves in Rome. Garden City, 1958
43566.49.7110	Delhaye de Marnyhac, Thérèse. Savoir aimer. Paris, 1958.
43566.51.3100	Delpy, Jacqueline. La legende de l'homme. Paris, 1958.
43701.4.80	Delsemme, Paul. Un théoricien du symbolisme, Charles Morice. Paris, 1958.
43566.62.110A	Déon, Michel. Les gens de la nuit; roman. Paris, 1958.
43566.80.110	Des Cars, Guy. La chateau de la juive. Paris, 1958.
43566.80.1100	Deslandes, André. l'escalier. Paris, 1958.
43566.81.1110	Des Ligneris, F. Psyché 58. Paris, 1958.
43566.81.2110	Desmarest, M.A. Dis moi qui tu aimes. Paris, 1958.
43566.81.2130	Desmarest, M.A. La maison des Movettes. Paris, 1958.
43566.81.6100	Desnos, L. La fraîche. Paris, 1958.
38528.24.5	Despériers, Bonaventure. Cymbalum mundi. Manchester, 1958.
38526.12.55	Desportes, Philippe. Cartels et masquarades. Genève, 1958.
41592.10.10	Des Vallieres, Jean. Cannaissez-vous ce bon M. de Béranger. Paris, 1958.
39544.320	Diaz, F. Voltaire storico. Torino, 1958.
39564.9.20	Diderot, Denis. Le pour et le contre. Paris, 1958.
43569.21.100	Djebar, Assia. The mischief. N.Y., 1958.

1958 - cont.

43688.5.5800	Dormoy, Marie. Léataud. Paris, 1958.
43574.75.110	Druon, Maurice. Alexandre le Grand. Paris, 1958.
43574.75.725	Druon, Maurice. The royal succession. London, 1958.
43574.75.740	Druon, Maurice. Tistou of the green thumbs. N.Y., 1958.
38526.7.8	Du Bellay, Joachim. Joachim Du Bellay. Paris, 1958.
38526.6.18.15	Du Bellay, Joachim. Les regrets. Paris, 1958.
42545.28.800.2	Dubeux, Albert. La curieuse vie de Georges Courteline. Paris, 1958.
39578.6.5	Du Châtelet, G.É. Lettres. Genève, 1958. 2v.
43576.14.3100	Du Coffre, Marguerite. Ich suche. Köln, 1958.
43576.6.440	Duhamel, Georges. Le complexe de Théophile. Paris, 1958.
41538.28.12	Dumas, Alexandre. From Paris to Cadiz. London, 1958.
41538.28.10	Dumas, Alexandre. Travels in Switzerland. London, 1958.
43576.53.3100	Dumas, Lucien Henri. Amour, mélancolie. Paris, 1958.
43576.68.1100	Dupé, Gilbert. Les mal mariés célèbres. Paris, 1958.
43576.69.1110	Dupin, Jacques. Les brisants. Paris, 1958.
43576.71.4100	Dupont-Fromageot, Yves. Entrelacs. Paris, 1958.
43576.74.2150	Duras, Marguerite. Moderato cantabile. Paris, 1958.
43576.87.160	Dutourd, Jean. Le fond et la forme. v.1-3. Paris, 1958.
43581.89.110	Eaubonne, Françoise d'. Fort des femmes. Paris, 1958.
43761.39.885	Eitzenberger, Helmut. Antoine de St. Exupéry. München, 1958.
43592.41.110	Émié, Louis. Présenté par A. Loranquin. Rodez, 1958.
43592.53.280	Emmanuel, Pierre. Versant de l'Âge. Paris, 1958.
40522.30	Engel, Claire E. Le véritable Abbé Prévost. Monaco, 1958.
43598.11.100	Escande, Jean. Du flouze. Paris, 1958.
43598.82.2100	Escarpit, Robert. Les dieux du Patamba. Paris, 1958.
43601.41.100	Evian, Jeanne. Chants de Tahiti. Lyon, 1958.
43606.50.100	Fallet, René. Les vieux de la vieille. Paris, 1958.
43606.15.110	Fardoulis-Lagrange, Michel. Au temps de Benani. Paris, 1958.
43606.75.3100	Farges, Marcel. Nuit sans passeport, poèmes. Paris, 1958.
Mol 706.8.5	Fernandez, Ramon. Molière. N.Y., 1958.
43609.35.100	Figuéras, André. Poèmes patriotiques. Rodez, 1958.
43609.58.100	Finas, Lucette. L'échec; roman. Paris, 1958.
37574.865	Flammes vives, Paris. Banquet poétique de printemps. Aurillac, 1958.
42576.34.30F	Flaubert, Gustave. La queue de la poire et de la boule de Monseigneur. Paris, 1958.
43610.66.2110	Florenne, Yves. Le cavalier d'or. 4. éd. Paris, 1958.
37574.820	Flores, Angel. An anthology of French poetry from Nerval to Valéry. 1. ed. Garden City, 1958.
43538.5.3100	Fonson, Geneviève B. Babillage; poems. Paris, 1958.
43611.75.1110	Forestier, Marie. L'écran de fumée. Paris, 1958.
37574.860	Fouchet, Max P. De l'amour au voyage. Paris, 1958.
37597.26.65	Foulon, Charles. L'oeuvre de Jean Bodel. Rennes, 1958.
43612.4.110	France, Claire. Et le septième jour; roman. Montréal, 1958.
43612.4.112	France, Claire. Et le septième jour; roman. Paris, 1958.
FL 396.20	France. Embassy. United States. Theatre national populaire. N.Y., 1958.
42584.25.410	Franzen, Nils Olof. Zola et la joie de vivre. Stockholm, 1958.
40583.270	Frid, Iakov V. Stendal'. Moskva, 1958.
43616.41.2120	Gaillard, Robert. Le miel de la haine. Paris, 1958.
42515.37.35	Galaud, René M. L'âme celtique de Renan. 1. ed. New Haven, 1958.
43616.50.6100	Galunaud, G. El-l'Ben. La Courneuve, 1958.
43616.52.120	Galzy, Jeanne. Celle qui vient d'ailleurs. Paris, 1958.
43616.56.100	Gamo, Jean. Héresmédan. London, 1958.
43616.79.150	Gascar, Pierre. La barre de corail. 6. éd. Paris, 1958.
43616.79.140	Gascar, Pierre. Les pas perdue. 5. éd. Paris, 1958.
43616.81.100	Gaspar, Élisabeth. L'amour fantôme. Paris, 1958.
43616.88.100	Gatti, Armand. Le poisson noir. Paris, 1958.
43617.31.100	Gegauff, Paul. Une partie de plaisir. Paris, 1958.
43617.78.170	Genêt, Jean. L'atelier d'Alberto Giacometti. Décines, 1958.
43617.78.710	Genêt, Jean. The balcony. N.Y., 1958.
43617.78.160A	Genêt, Jean. Les nègres. Décines, 1958.
43617.77.2100	Germain, Gabriel. La lampe de Sala. Paris, 1958.
42554.26.820	Geslin, Olivier. Tristan Corbière, 1845-75. Bordeaux, 1958.
43620.2.79.17	Gide, André. Amyntas. London, 1958.
43620.2.55.45	Gide, André. The coiners. 3. ed. London, 1958.
43620.2.79.183	Gide, André. Correspondance: André Gide. Paris, 1958.
43620.2.79.175	Gide, André. Romans. Paris, 1958.
43620.39.100	Gillès, Daniel. L'état de grâce; roman. Paris, 1958.
43620.40.120	Gilliard, Edmond. Hymne terrestre, suivi de dialecte de l'architecte. Paris, 1958.
37555.535A	Gilman, Margaret. The idea of poetry in France. Cambridge, 1958.
43620.66.440	Giono, Jean. Angelo. Paris, 1958.
43620.66.285	Giono, Jean. Hortense, au Leau vive. Paris, 1958.
43620.74.775	Giraudoux, Jean. Duel of angels. London, 1958.
43620.74.780	Giraudoux, Jean. Elpénor. N.Y., 1958.
43620.74.702	Giraudoux, Jean. Four plays. N.Y., 1958.
43620.74.520	Giraudoux, Jean. La menteuse. Paris, 1958.
43620.74.530	Giraudoux, Jean. Portugal. Paris, 1958.
43620.74.525	Giraudoux, Jean. Un roi. Paris, 1958.
43620.74.26	Giraudoux, Jean. Théâtre. Paris, 1958. 4v.
39544.340	Girnus, Wilhelm. Voltaire. Berlin, 1958.
38526.48.38	Giudici, Enzo. Le opere minori di Maurice Scève. Parma, 1958.
43622.41.140	Glissant, Edouard. La lézarde. Paris, 1958.
42586.68.68	Gobineau, Arthur de. Correspondance, 1872-1882. Paris, 1958. 2v.
43625.17.100	Godel, Vahé. Homme parmi les hommes. Paris, 1958.
43625.27.155	Goffin, Robert. Oeuvres poetiques. Paris, 1958.
43625.51.100	Gogon, S. Angélique. Philadelphia, 1958.
43625.38.100	Gohier, Gerald. Otto John. Paris, 1958.
43625.48.30	Golay, Marthe. Lumière; poèmes. Paris, 1958.
43625.49.150	Goll, Claire. Chants peaux-rouges. Paris, 1958.
43625.78.100	Gorz, A. Le traître. Paris, 1958.
43625.89.1100	Goustille-Reinhart, Hélène. Fleurs solitaires. Rodez, 1958.
37547.95	Goy, Paul. Les poètes patois de la ville de Crest-en-Dauphiné. Crest, 1958.
43626.70.160	Gracq, Julien. Un balcon en forêt. Paris, 1958.
43626.70.140	Gracq, Julien. Liberté grande. 2e éd. Paris, 1958.
Mon 117.7	Gray, Floyd. Le style de Montiagne. Paris, 1958.
43780.69.800	Greene, Tatiana W. Jules Supervielle. Genève, 1958.
43744.67.1335	Gregh, Fernand. Mon amitié avec Marcel Proust. Paris, 1958.
43626.22.1700	Gregoire, Jean Albert. The money masters. London, 1958.
43626.22.1100	Gregoire, Jean Albert. Twenty-four hours at Le Mans. 1st ed. N.Y., 1958.

Chronological Listing

1958 - cont.

40597.2.455 Griftsov, B.A. Kak rabotal Bal'zak. Moskva, 1958.
43626.64.100 Grojnowski, Daniel. L'accord parfait. Paris, 1958.
43626.66.5110 Grosclaude, Pierre. Ces autres qui viendront. Paris, 1958.
FL 386.116 Grossvogel, David I. The self-conscious stage in modern French drama. N.Y., 1958.
43626.74.120.2 Groussard, Serge. La belle espérance. 2. éd. Paris, 1958.
43626.74.130 Groussard, Serge. Quartier chinois. Paris, 1958.
43574.41.805 Grover, Fréderic J. Drieu La Rochelle and fiction of testimony. Berkeley, 1958.
43628.43.110 Guigues, Louis Paul. La dernière chambre. Paris, 1958.
43628.42.3110 Guillaume, Louis. L'ancre de lumière. Rodez, 1958.
43628.42.3100 Guillaume, Louis. Hans ou Les songes vécus. Rodez, 1958.
42576.65.13.126 Guillemain, Charles. J.K. Huysmans et Lyon. Lyon, 1958.
40553.10.60 Guillemin, Henri. Benjamin Constant muscadin, 1795-1799. Paris, 1958.
43628.41.2110 Guiraud, G. Henri de. Helène des marais. Paris, 1958.
43752.57.880 Guisan, Gilbert. C.F. Ramuz. Genève, 1958.
FL 6134.2 Guyot, Charly. Un ami et défenseur de Rousseau. Neuchâtel, 1958.
43631.21.110 Haedrich, Marcel. Drame dans un miroir. Paris, 1958.
43741.2.800 Halaenwang, G. Avec René-Louis Piachaud. Genéve, 1958.
43554.2.1020 Halter, Raymond. La vierge Maire dans la vie et l'oeuvre de Paul Claudel. Tours, 1958.
43550.58.832A Hanna, Thomas. The thought and art of Albert Camus. Chicago, 1958.
43632.50.41 Hellens, Franz. Documents secrèts, 1905-1956. Paris, 1958.
43632.6.190 Henriot, Émile. Au bord du temps. Paris, 1958.
37543.405 Henriot, Émile. Neuf siècles de littérature française. Paris, 1958.
43632.76.3100 Hermies, Michel. La mauvaise grâce. Paris, 1958.
40592.84 Herold, J. Christopher. Mistress to an age. 1st ed. Indianapolis, 1958.
40517.75 Hilliard d'Auberteud, M.R. Miss McCrea. 1784. Gainesville, Fla., 1958.
42576.57.75 Hisar, Abdülhah Sinasi. Istanbul ve Pierre Loti. Istanbul, 1958.
43626.22.885 Hoesli, Silvia. Zum Problem der Angst im Werk von Julien Green. Schopfheim, 1958.
42525.8.88 Hoh, Friedrich. Ernst Hello. München? 1958.
43636.64.100 Hoog, Armand. Le dernier tonnerre. Paris, 1958.
43761.31.800 Hourdin, Georges. Le cas Françoise Sagan. Paris, 1958.
43556.49.855 Houssa, Nicole. Le souci de l'expression chez Colette. Bruxelles, 1958.
40556.28.80 Huber, Max. Die Staatsphilosophie von Joseph de Maistre in Lichte des Thomesmus. Basel, 1958.
41573.60 Hugo, Victor. La vie de Victor Hugo. Paris, 1958.
42576.65.28.7 Huysmans, Joris Karl. Down there. Evanston, 1958.
43620.74.890 Inskip, Donald. Jean Giraudoux. London, 1958.
FL 355.715 Institut d'études françaises, Saarbruecken. Catalogue de l'exposition. Le théâtre en France au Moyen-Âge. Sarrebruck, 1958.
43656.59.630 Ionesco, Eugène. Amédée. The new tenant. N.Y., 1958.
43656.59.625 Ionesco, Eugène. The chairs, a play. London, 1958.
43656.59.110 Ionesco, Eugène. Four plays. N.Y., 1958.
43656.59.621 Ionesco, Eugène. Plays. London, 1958-63. 8v.
43656.59.106 Ionesco, Eugène. Théâtre. v.2. Paris, 1958-
43659.88.715 Istrati, Panait. Kyra kyralina. Paris, 1958.
43667.11.112 Jaccottet, Philippe. L'ignorant. Paris, 1958.
43667.60.100 Janier, Raymond. Nos yeux s'étaient dit, poèmes. Paris, 1958.
38585.16.255 Jasinski, René. Vers le vrai Racine. Paris, 1958. 2v.
43670.24.100 Joel, Yves. Femme, mon ami. Paris, 1958.
43744.67.1322 Johnson, P.H. Proust recaptured. Chicago, 1958.
43744.67.1320 Johnson, P.H. Six Proust reconstructions. London, 1958.
43670.92.100 Jouffroy, Alain. A toi. 2. éd. Paris, 1958.
43670.89.61 Jouhandeau, M. Correspondance avec André Gide. Paris, 1958.
43670.89.540 Jouhandeau, M. Réflexions sur la vie et le bonheur. 7. éd. Paris, 1958.
43670.94.360 Jouve, Pierre Jean. Tombreau de Baudelaire. Paris, 1958.
43672.84.700 Katcha, Vahé. The hook. N.Y., 1958.
43672.85.100 Katherine, M. Suite persane. Paris, 1958.
43673.56.100 Kemp, R. Au jour le jour. Paris, 1958.
43673.56.110 Kemp, R. Discours de réception de Robert Kemp à l'Academie. Paris, 1958.
43673.78.110 Kerchove, Arnold de. La fureur et la grâce, poèmes. Paris, 1958.
43697.52.835 Kerudter, Fritz. André Malraux, die Suche nach einem neuen Menschenbild. München, 1958.
43673.83.169 Kessel, Joseph. Le lion. Paris, 1958.
37574.575 Klee-Palyi, Flora. Anthologie der Französischen Dichtung von Nerval bis zur Gegenwart. Wiesbaden, 1958.
43744.67.1365 Koehler, Erich. Marcel Proust. Göttingen, 1958.
FL 6139.58.5 Krafft, Olivier. La politique de Jean-Jacques Rousseau. Paris, 1958[1957]
40597.2.480 Kuhn-Meierhans, Doris. Le curé de Tours. Zürich, 1958.
43687.11.100 Lacaze, Raymond. Qu'on me pardonne d'en parler. Rodez, 1958.
38544.27.72 La Fayette, Marie M. La Princesse de Clèves. Paris, 1958.
39527.29.70 La Fontaine, Jean de. Fables. Paris, 1958-59. 2v.
42555.1.65 Laforgue, Jules. Poems. Berkeley, 1958.
38551.150 La Gorce, Agnès de. Le vrai visage de Fénelon. Paris, 1958.
43687.38.100 Lahille, J. Lettres d'un autre temps. Paris, 1958?
41578.85 Lamartine, Alphonse. Lamartine. Genève, 1958.
43620.2.375 Lambert, Jean. Gide familier. Paris, 1958.
43687.55.100 Lamoureux, Robert. La brune que voilà. Paris, 1958.
43822.49.1300 Lanfranchi, Geneviève. Paul Valéry et l'experience du moi pur. Lausanne, 1958.
43550.58.849 Lanfranchi, Geneviève. La secrète issue. Monte-Carlo, 1958.
40592.86 Lang, André. Une vie d'orages. Paris, 1958.
37530.170 Langlois, Pierre. Guide bibliographique des études littéraires. Paris, 1958.
43687.62.3100 Lanzmann, Jacques. Les passagers du Sidi-Brahim. Paris, 1958.
43687.77.2100 Larrive, Georges. L'autre face. Paris, 1958.
43524.67.815 Lassalle, J. Jean Anouilh. Rodez, 1958.
41543.22.85 La Tour Saint-Jacques. Gerard de Nerval. Paris, 1958.
43687.89.1140 Laurent, Jacques. L'Espagne et Juan. Paris, 1958.
43687.89.1130 Laurent, Jacques. Ici Clotilde. Paris, 1958.
43687.89.1150 Laurent, Jacques. Napoléon et Juan. Paris, 1958.

1958 - cont.

FL 396.54.10 Léautaud, Paul. Le théâtre de Maurice Boissard. 7. ed. Paris, 1958. 2v.
37566.117 Lebois, André. Admirable XIX siècle. Paris, 1958.
43688.13.100 Leclerq, Léna. Pomme endormie. Décines, 1958.
37556.170 Ledré, Charles. Histoire de la presse. Paris, 1958.
43738.78.700F Léger, Alexis S.-L. Seamarks. N.Y., 1958.
43688.42.100 Le Jeloux, Anne. La harpe du sentier. Paris, 1958.
43688.65.1100 Léonard, Raymond. Les heures algériennes; extraits. Ivry-sur-Seine, 1958-1960. 2v.
43688.77.1100 Léro, Yva. Doucherie. Martirique, 1958.
43744.67.1330 Le Sage, Laurent. Marcel Proust and his literary friends. Urbana, 1958.
40592.82.5 Levaillant, M. The passionate exiles. N.Y., 1958.
40553.10.48 Levaillant, Maurice. Les amours de Benjamin Constant. Paris, 1958.
FL 377.182 Lockert, Lacy. Studies in French-classical tragedy. Nashville, 1958.
37596.10.105 Lonin, Pierre. Prolégomènes à une édtion d'Yvain. Gap, 1958.
37597.8.5 Lorris, Guillaume de. De fragmenten van de tweede rose. Zwolle, 1958.
43694.11.2110 Lucas, Wilfrid Louis Eugène. La couronne de jois. Paris, 1958.
43694.11.4100 Lucasserie, Louis de. Le soleil et la mort, poèmes. Paris, 1958.
38585.43.12 Lugli, Vittorio. Interpretazione di Phèdre. Rocca san Casciano, 1958.
38514.165 Le Lyon coronné. Genève, 1958.
37564.267 Macchia, Giovanni. La fine dell' "Etá classica" e la litteratura francese agli. Roma, 1958?
37574.848 MacIntyre, C.F. French Symbolist poetry. Berkeley, 1958.
40535.32.40 McKee, K.N. The theater of Marivaux. N.Y., 1958.
43697.14.270 MacOrlan, Pierre. Babet de Picardie. Paris, 1958.
43697.14.1120 Macover, Alice. Pulsations. Monte-Carlo, 1958.
43697.14.1100 Macover, Alice. Signes, poèmes. Paris, 1958.
43545.4.4810 Madiran, Jean. Brasillach. Paris? 1958.
43697.48.1100 Malan, Pierre. La queue du paon. Paris, 1958.
43697.2.2140 Mallet, Robert. L'equipage au complet. 4e ed. Paris, 1958.
43697.52.2120 Malraux, Clara. La lutte isségale, roman. Paris, 1958.
37556.21.48 Manevy, Raymond. La presse française de Renaitdot à Rocheport. Paris, 1958.
43761.78.830 Manno, Ambrogio. L'esistenzialismo di Jean Paul Sartre. Napoli, 1958.
43697.61.6110 Manoll, Michel. Le vent des abimes. Nantes? 1958?
43697.61.2130 Mansour, Joyce. Les gisants satisfaits. Paris, 1958.
43697.61.3110 Mantrand, F. Les fievres de mars. Paris, 1958.
43697.62.100 Manuel, José. Des cris des ombres. Paris, 1958.
43550.58.827 Maquet, Albert. Albert Camus. N.Y., 1958.
43697.74.5100 Marceau, Alain. A la pointe des yeux. Montreal, 1958.
43697.74.3170 Marceau, Félicien. La bonne soupe. 5. ed. Paris, 1958.
43697.74.3705 Marceau, Félicien. The egg. London, 1958.
43697.75.190 Marcel, Gabriel. La dimension Florestan. Paris, 1958.
43697.75.710 Marcel, Gabriel. Three plays. 1st American ed. N.Y., 1958.
40529.28.10 Maréchal, Pierre S. Izbrannye ateist proizved. Moskva, 1958.
43697.75.9100 Margerit, Robert. La terre aux loups. Paris, 1958.
40535.27.50 Marivaux, Pierre Carlet de Chamblain de. Marivaux narratore e moralista. Napoli, 1958.
38523.6.30 Marot, Clement. L'adolescence clementine. Paris, 1958.
38523.10.30A Marot, Clément. Oeuvres. London, 1958- 5v.
FL 361.77 Marquet, Mary. Les impérissables. Paris, 1958.
43697.79.2100 Martenne, Thérèse de. La chaîne des douleurs, poèmes. Paris, 1958.
43697.77.7100 Martin-Chauffuv, Louis. L'écrivain et la liberté. Neuchâtel, 1958.
43697.78.5200 Martin Saint-René (pseud.). Immortelle. Paris, 1958.
43697.8.32 Masart, René. Echec au fisc. Paris, 1958.
43697.81.100 Massip, Renée. Les déesses, roman. Paris, 1958.
43697.82.130 Massis, Henri. Visages des idées. Paris, 1958.
38585.16.49 Maulnier, Thierry. Racine. 49e éd. Paris, 1958.
43697.88.480 Mauriac, François. Bloc-notes. Paris, 1958. 5v.
43697.88.510 Mauriac, François. Dieu et Mammon. Paris, 1958.
43697.88.160.2 Mauriac, François. Dieu et Mammon. Paris, 1958.
43697.88.560 Mauriac, François. La pierre d'achoppement. Monaco, 1958.
43697.88.797 Mauriac, François. Questions of precedence. London, 1958.
43697.89.5100 Mauroc, Daniel. Les jardins suffisent. Paris, 1958.
40587.110.8 Maurois, André. Chateaubriand. N.Y., 1958?
43697.89.135 Maurois, André. Climats. Paris, 1958.
43697.89.796 Maurois, André. September roses. London, 1958.
42514.28.76 Maurras, Charles. Lettres de prison. Paris, 1958.
43698.25.170 Meersch, M. van der. Masque de chair. Paris, 1958.
43698.58.3100 Menanteau, Pierre. Bestiaire pour un infant poète. Paris, 1958.
41555.23.20 Mérimée, Prosper. Colomba. Paris, 1958.
41555.26.5 Mérimée, Prosper. Stat'i o russkikh pisateliakh. Moskva, 1958.
43698.78.1100 Merville, Patrik. L'ennui. Paris, 1958.
43698.25.1100 Mex, Alphonse. L'idéal humain...et autres poèmes. Rodez, 1958.
38512.135 Mézières, Philippe de. Description of the Festum praesentalionis Beatae Mariae. New Haven, 1958.
40583.250 Michel, Francois. Études stendhaliennes. Paris, 1958.
43761.39.895 Migeo, Marcel. St. Exupéry. Paris, 1958.
43699.51.19 Milosz, Oscar Vladislas. L'amoureuse initiation. v.1-2,5,7,9-11. Paris, 1958- 7v.
41574.542' Miquel, Pierre. Hugo, touriste. Paris, 1958-
43699.77.100 Miroir, Jean. Pas d'amour pour elle. Paris, 1958.
43699.87.110 Mittet, Émile. Faisceau tournant. Paris, 1958.
Mol 191.40 Molière, Jean Baptiste Poquelin. Dom Juan. Oxford, 1958.
Mol 269.5.8 Molière, Jean Baptiste Poquelin. Tartuffo. Milano, 1958.
Mol 19.58 Molière, Jean Baptiste Poquelin. Théâtre. Paris, 1958. 4v.
43701.88.100 Monchet, Charles. Debus. Génève, 1958.
Mon 32.58 Montaigne, Michel de. Complete works. London, 1958.
Mon 55.5 Montaigne, Michel de. Giornale del viaggio di Michel de Montaigne in Italia. Firenze, 1958. 3v.
Mon 39.50 Montaigne, Michel de. Opyty. 2. izd. Moskva, 1958. 3v.
43701.80.1100 Montforez, Georges. Les enfants du Marais. Paris, 1958.
43701.63.510 Montherlant, Henry de. Don Juan. Paris, 1958.
37548.185 Mor, Antonio. Storia delle letterature del Belgio. Milano, 1958.
43701.74.340 Morand, Paul. Le prisonnier de Cintra. Paris, 1958.
FL 6139.58.15 Morando, Dante. Jean-Jacques Rousseau. Brescia, 1958.

Chronological Listing

1958 - cont.

43701.74.5100 Morchan, Frédéric. L'archivolte. Paris, 1958.
Mol 713.17.5 Mornet, Daniel. Molière. 5. éd. Paris, 1958.
43697.77.835 Moscow. Vsesoiuznaia gosudarst-vennaia biblioteka inostrannoi literatury. Rozhe Marten diu Gar. Moskva, 1958.
43701.89.1100 Mouloudji, Marcel. Chansons pour ma mélancolie. L'Arbalete, 1958.
43701.79.110 Moussy, Marcel. Si c'était vous. Paris, 1958.
41596.23.32 Musset, Alfred de. Comédies et proverbes. Paris, 1958. 2v.
43705.22.100 Naegelen, Marcel-Edmond. Avant que meure le dernier. Paris, 1958.
43706.74.110 Ner, Henri. Le sillage parfume. Paris, 1958.
41543.4.8 Nerval, Gerard de. Oeuvres. Paris, 1958.
41543.4.7A Nerval, Gerard de. Oeuvres. Paris, 1958. 2v.
43709.23.1100 Noël, Dominique. Symphonee en blanc. Paris, 1958.
43709.23.112 Noël, Marie. Le rosaire des joies. Paris, 1958.
43757.3.345 Norrish, Peter John. Drama of the group. Cambridge, Eng., 1958.
43709.85.100 Nothomb, Pierre. Aus de grâce. Paris, 1958.
43709.80.120 Nourissier, François. Bleu comme la nuit. Paris, 1958.
43709.80.140 Nourissier, François. Portait d'un indifférent. Paris, 1958.
37544.155 el Nouty, Hassan. Le Proche-Orient dans la littérature française. Paris, 1958.
37558.197 el Nouty, Hassar. Le Proche-Orient dans la littérature française. Paris, 1958.
43723.18.110 Oldenbourg, Zoé. Les irreductibles. Paris, 1958.
43723.50.100 Ollier, Claude. La mise en scene. Paris, 1958.
43833.20.890 Ottensmeyer, Hilary. Le thème de l'amour dans l'oeuvre de Simone Weil. Paris, 1958.
43731.85.100 Out-el-Kouloub. Ramza. Paris, 1958.
43737.74.1100 Paradis, Louis. Sentence le 21. Montréal, 1958.
43737.74.2100 Paraz, Albert. Le menuet du haricot. Genève, 1958.
43780.69.15 Paris. Bibliothèque Sainte-Geneviève. Collection Doucet. Jules Supervielle. Paris, 1958.
40542.17 Pativilca (pseud.). Federico Ozanam. Bilbao, 1958.
37595.34.20.5 Pauphilet, A. Poètes et romanciers du Moyen Âge. Paris, 1958.
43737.98.2100 Payen, Emile. Sarcasmes. Paris, 1958.
43738.1.78 Péguy, Charles. Temporal and eternal. London, 1958.
38526.43.5 Peletier, Jacques. Oeuvres poétiques. Rochecorbon, 1958. 2v.
43738.50.3100 Pelletier, René. Besançon, ville gauloise à la manière de Victor Hugo. Besançon, 1958.
37566.130 Perović, St. Iz radionice velikih majstora. Zagreb, 1958.
43738.81.1100 Perret, Vivette. Les absents, roman. Paris, 1958.
FL 6139.58.10 Petruzzellis, N. Il pensiero politico e pedagogico di G.G. Rousseau. 2. ed. Bari, 1958.
43738.97.150 Peyre, Joseph. Souvenirs d'un enfant. Paris, 1958.
43738.97.1745 Peyrefitte, Roger. Cavalieri di Malta. 2. ed. Firenze, 1958.
43738.97.1735 Peyrefitte, Roger. Special friendships. London, 1958.
43757.3.305 Pfeiffer, Rudolf. Les hommes de bonne volonté von Jules Romains. Winterthur, 1958.
37576.658 Picard, Gaston. Nouvelles 58. Paris, 1958.
43741.25.240 Pieyre de Mandiargues, André. Le Belvédére. Paris, 1958.
43741.25.120 Pieyre de Mandiargues, André. Le cadran lunaire. Paris, 1958.
43741.25.700 Pieyre de Mandiargues, André. The girl beneath the lion. N.Y., 1958.
Mol 810.7 Pighi, Lana. Molière e il teatro italiano in Francia. Bologna, 1958.
43741.59.100 Pingaud, Bernard. Le prisonnier. Paris, 1958.
43741.59.3160 Pinget, Robert. Baga. Paris, 1958.
43741.89.110 Piroué, Georges. Murir. Paris, 1958.
38514.57.20 Pisan, Christine de. The livre de la paire of Christine de Pisan. 's-Gravenhage, 1958.
43742.3.112 Planchon, Michel. Lumière noire. 2e éd. Paris, 1958.
43743.41.3100 Poirot-Delpech, Bertrand. Le grand dadais. Paris, 1958.
FL 398.19.10 Polletzeo, Marcel. Trois reines de théâtre. Paris, 1958.
FL 361.80 Pollitzer, Marcel. Grandes acteurs: leur vie, leurs amours. Paris, 1958.
41596.4.92 Pommier, Jean. Autour du drame de Venise: G. Sand et A. de Musset au lendemain de "Lorenzaccio". Paris, 1958.
43743.61.1100 Ponthier, François. Le phenix. Paris, 1958.
40539.15 Potocki, Jan. Manuscript trouvé à Saragosse. Paris, 1958.
43566.82.7810 Poulet, R. Entretiens familiers avec Louis Ferdinand Céline. Paris, 1958.
43743.89.1110 Poulet, Robert. Les ténèbres. Paris, 1958.
43743.89.3100 Poupeney, Norbert. Au vent des souvenirs. Paris, 1958.
43744.5.120 Prassinos, Gisèle. Le temps n'est rien. Paris, 1958.
41596.4.130 Prestreau, Georges. Alfred de Musset, sa famille et l'anjon. Angers, 1958.
43744.25.4100 Prévost, Alain. Bonne chance quand même. Paris, 1958.
40522.9.70 Prévost, Antoine F. Manon Lescaut. Paris, 1958.
43744.67.5100 Prous-Guillaumis, Jeanne. Puisque enfin je suis moi. Paris, 1958.
43744.67.51.3 Proust, Marcel. By way of Saint Beuve. London, 1958.
43744.67.51.2 Proust, Marcel. Marcel Proust on art and literature, 1896-1919. N.Y., 1958.
FL 396.50.4 Pruner, Francis. Le théâtre libre d'Antoine. Paris, 1958-
43750.20.130 Queffélec, Henri. Combat contre l'invisible. Paris, 1958.
43750.23.100 Queillé, Yvonne. Au vent qui me pousse. Paris, 1958.
43750.24.106 Queneau, Raymond. Exercises in style. London, 1958.
43750.24.1110 Querlin, Marise. Le plaisir des hommes; roman. Paris, 1958.
38585.43.15 Racine, Jean. Phaedra. Great Neck, 1958.
38585.43.17 Racine, Jean. Phaedra. San Francisco, 1958.
38583.12.30 Racine, Jean. Racine's mid-career tragedies. Princeton, 1958.
37562.303 Rasmussen, Jens. La prose narrative française de XVe siècle. Copenhague, 1958.
43752.82.110 Raspail, Jean. Le vent des pins. Paris, 1958.
43554.7.80 Ratinaud, Jean. Clemenceau. Paris, 1958.
37596.10.190 Reason, Joseph H. An inquiry into the structural style and originality of Chréstien's Yvain. Washington, 1958.
38525.26.25 Régnier, Mathurin. Oeuvres complètes. Paris, 1958.
37567.530 Reizov, B.G. Frantsuzskii istoricheskii roman v epokhu romantizma. Leningrad, 1958.
43753.58.130 Renard, M. L'invitation à la peur. Paris, 1958.
43753.59.1100 René, Claude. La nuit logique. Paris, 1958.
42578.31.115 Reul, X. de. Le roman d'un géologue. Bruxelles, 1958.
41542.4.85 Richardson, Joanna. Theóphile Gautier. London, 1958.
42556.28.78 Rimbaud, Jean Arthur. Bateau ivre. Das trunkene Schiff. Wiesbaden, 1958.

1958 - cont.

42556.28.58 Rimbaud, Jean Arthur. Oeuvres. Paris, 1958.
42556.28.90 Rimbaud, Jean Arthur. Poésies. Paris, 1958.
FL 6029.12 Ritzel, Wolfgang. Rousseaus Selbstverständnis in den Confessions. Wilhelmshaven, 1958.
43756.91.2100 Rivet, R. Lueurs aux vitres. Limoges, 1958.
43554.2.995 Roberto, Eugène. Visions de Claudel. Marseille, 1958.
43552.5.1820 Robinson, Judith. Alain. Paris, 1958.
43552.5.1822 Robinson, Judith. Alain. Thèse. Paris, 1958.
43757.12.120 Roblès, Emmanuel. L'horloge suivi de porferio. Paris, 1958.
43757.13.2100 Roche, Paul. Les chevaux de la nuit. Paris, 1958.
43757.13.1100 Rochefort, Christiane. Le repos deu guerrier. Paris, 1958.
43757.3.196 Romains, Jules. The adventuress. London, 1958.
39594.19.80 Rombaut, M.W. La conception stoïcienne du bonheur chez Montesquieu et chez quelques-uns de ses contemporains. Leiden, 1958.
37547.65 Rome, Palozzo Primoli. Hommage à commerce. Roma, 1958.
38525.17.20 Ronsard, Pierre de. Pierre de Ronsard. Paris, 1958.
41574.540 Roos, Jacques. Les idées philosophiques de Victor Hugo. Paris, 1958.
37556.4 Rossettini, Olga T. Les influences anciennes et italiennes sur la satire en France au XVIe siècle. Florence, 1958.
43757.91.2100 Rouquette, Yves. L'escriveire public. Toulouse, 1958.
43757.75.100 Rouré, Jacques. Tutti frutti. Paris, 1958.
FL 6042.58 Rousseau, J.J. Émile. Paris, 1958.
FL 6094.8.22 Rousseau, J.J. Les rêveries du promeneur solitaire. Paris, 1958.
41586.15.80 Rousseau, Laurier. Le Pinto de Népomucène Lemercier et la censure. Mayenne, 1958.
43757.92.2180 Rousselot, Jean. Présences contemporaines: rencontres sur les chemins. Paris, 1958.
43757.96.160 Roy, Claude. Le malheur d'aimer. Paris, 1958.
43758.9.100 Rubsel, Raoul S. Messages de l'enfer. Paris, 1958.
43758.24.110 Ruet, Noël. Le bouquet du sang. Loiret, 1958.
43761.5.4122 Sabatier, Robert. Boulevard. N.Y., 1958.
43761.5.4150 Sabatier, Robert. Canard au sang. Paris, 1958.
40516.60.75 Sade, D.A.F. de. Nouvelles exemplaires. Paris, 1958.
37567.620 Sailland, Maurice Edmond. Souvenirs littéraires et gastronomiques. Paris, 1958.
43761.39.170 St. Exupéry, A. de. Courrier sud. Paris, 1958.
43610.25.800 Saint-Jorre, Jean de. Fernand Fleuret et ses amis. Coutances, 1958.
43761.77.700 Sarraute, Nathalie. Portrait of a man unknown. N.Y., 1958.
FL 6029.10 Saussure, Hermine de. Rousseau et les manuscrits des Confessions. Paris, 1958.
43763.38.12 Schlumberger, Jean. Oeuvres. Paris, 1958. 7v.
43763.38.1100 Schneeberger, P.F. Emmanuelle ou Le doute. Paris, 1958.
43763.39.1100 Schneider, Marcel. L'escurial et l'amour, roman. Paris, 1958.
38537.50 Schrader, Ludwig. Pamarge und Hermes. Bonn, 1958.
43763.39.2110 Schreiber, Boris. Les heures qui restent. Paris, 1958.
38537.40 Screech, Michael Andrew. The Rabelaisian marriage. London, 1958.
43765.32.140 Seghers, Pierre. Les pierres. Paris, 1958.
42557.20.285 Seguin, Marc. Ce pauvre bonheur, la "dernière passion humaine" de Paul Verlaine. Paris, 1958.
40587.138 Sekrecka, M. Chateaubriand; jako teoretyk i krytyk literacki. Lublin, 1958.
37576.527 La serate di Médan. Milano, 1958.
43765.78.1100 Servain, Elisabeth. Cendres chaudes, chants de vie et de mort. Paris, 1958.
40517.44.80 Seylaz, Jean Luc. Les liaisons dangereuses et la creation romanesque chez Laclos. Genève, 1958.
40525.18 Shaw, Edward Pease. François-Augustin Paradis de Moncrif, 1687-1770. N.Y., 1958.
43769.11.1110 Sicard, Maurice Ivan. Les maudits; scènes de la vie révolutionnaire. Paris, 1958. 2v.
43769.11.100 Sicaud, Sabine. Poèmes. Paris, 1958.
43769.54.405 Simenon, Georges. Le voyageur de la Toussaint. Paris, 1958.
43769.56.2705 Simon, Claude. The grass. N.Y., 1958.
43769.56.2100 Simon, Claude. L'herbe. Paris, 1958.
43769.56.2120 Simon, Claude. Le vent. Roman. Paris, 1958.
43556.1.900 Simon, Karl. Jean Cocteau. Berlin, 1958.
43775.50.100 Sollers, Philippe. Une curieuse solitude. Paris, 1958.
43775.96.110 Sorel, Claude. Poésie et publicité. Paris, 1958.
FL 6049.22 Sorge, Giuseppe. Rousseau e la pedagogia sociale contemporanea. Mazara, 1958.
43775.89.1100 Soulat, Robert. Un nommé songe. Paris, 1958.
41522.18.90.3 Starkie, Enid. Baudelaire. Norfolk, 1958.
FL 6139.58 Starobinski, Jean. Jean-Jacques Rousseau. Paris, 1958.
43779.25.110 Sternberg, Jacques. L'employé. Paris, 1958.
41563.8 Sue, Eugène. Atar-gull. Paris, 1958.
42576.15.440 Suffel, Jacques. Gustave Flaubert. Paris, 1958.
43780.50.100 Sulivan, Jean. Le voyage intérieur. Paris, 1958.
37567.66.4 Symons, Arthur. The symbolist movement in literature. N.Y., 1958.
43785.75.105 Tardieu, Jean. L'éspace et la flûte. Paris, 1958.
43785.89.3100 Tauziac, Étienne. Poésies de chez nous, Périgord. Montauban, 1958.
43787.29.100 Tefri (pseud.). Nouvelles. Lausanne, 1958. 2v.
FL 6139.58.20 Temmer, M.J. Time in Rousseau and Kant. Genève, 1958.
43788.41.2100 Thiry, Marcel. Poésie, 1924-1957. Paris, 1958.
V43500.301 Thomas, Charles. Sixième heure; un cri dans le désert. Mouscron, 1958.
Mol 720.10 Thoorens, Léon. La vie passionée de Molière. Paris, 1958.
37568.170 Tison-Braun, M. La crise de l'humanisme. Paris, 1958. 2v.
40587.135 Trancia, Ennio. Chateaubriand. Brescia, 1958.
43793.67.730 Troyat, Henri. Strangers in the land. 1st ed. London, 1958.
43793.67.735 Troyat, Henri. Strangers on earth. N.Y., 1958.
43822.50.720A Vailland, Roger. The law. 1st American ed. N.Y., 1958.
43822.50.120 Vailland, Roger. La loi, roman. Paris, 1958.
43744.67.1380 Vallée, Claude. La féerie de Marcel Proust. Paris, 1958.
42581.33.8 Vallès, Jules. Jaçques Vingtras. L'enfant. Paris, 1958.
43822.58.100 Vandal, Linda. A cloche-coeur. Paris, 1958.
43574.41.810 Vandromme, P. Pierre Drieu La Rochelle. Paris, 1958.
43822.90.110 Vauthier, Jean. Les prodiges. Paris, 1958.
43823.2.30 Védrès, Nicole. L'exécuteur. Paris, 1958.
43823.2.40 Védrès, Nicole. Paris, le... Paris, 1958.
43823.81.100F Vella, Pierre. Maledicte. Paris, 1958.
43823.75.3100 Verdot, Guy. Demain à Pompei. Paris, 1958.

Chronological Listing

1958 - cont.

43823.76.1100	Vergnes, Georges. La vie passionnée de Guillaume Apollinaire. Paris, 1958.
42557.18.24	Verlaine, Paul. Poèmes saturniens. Paris, 1958.
42557.19.56	Verlaine, Paul. Sagesse. Liturgies intimes. Paris, 1958.
FL 6119.58	Vertsman, I.E. Zhan-Zhak Russo. Moskva, 1958.
43824.3.240	Vialar, Paul. Clara et les méchants. Paris, 1958.
43824.3.230	Vialar, Paul. Pas de pitié pour les cobayes. Paris, 1958.
43824.3.220	Vialar, Paul. Pas de temps pour mourir. Paris, 1958.
43824.3.210	Vialar, Paul. Le roman des oiseaux de chasse. Paris, 1958.
43824.7.105	Victor, P.E. Poèmes eskimo. Paris, 1958.
43824.16.1100	Vidalie, Albert. The moonlight jewelers. N.Y., 1958.
37542.45	Vier, Jacques. Littérature à l'emporte-pièce. Paris, 1958- 5v.
41564.29	Vigny, Alfred de. Mémoires inédits. 3. éd. Paris, 1958.
43824.51.1100	Villandry, A. La croisière de psyche. Paris, 1958.
43824.53.100	Villevieille, J. Le moulin de Bayard. Paris, 1958.
38514.20.90	Villon, François. Balladai. London, 1958.
38514.20.1	Villon, François. François Villon, un tableau synoptique. Paris, 1958.
38514.20.80	Villon, François. Poésies. Ballades. Strasbourg, 1958.
38514.18.35	Villon, François. Det stora testamentet. Stockholm, 1958.
43824.54.125	Vilmorin, Louise de. La lettre dans un tapi. Paris, 1958.
41574.545	Vincent, Paul. Victor Hugo entre les femmes et l'amour. Paris, 1958.
43826.3.120	Vlaminck, Maurice de. Le garde-fou. Paris, 1958.
39545.35.55	Voltaire, François Marie Arouet de. Candide. London, 1958.
39544.27.22	Voltaire, François Marie Arouet de. The love letters of Voltaire to his niece. London, 1958.
43828.41.100	Vrigny, Roger. Barbegal, récit. Paris, 1958.
43554.2.1035	Wahl, Jean André. Defense et elargissement de la philosophie. Paris, 1958.
37543.420	Wais, Kurt Karl P. Französische Marksteine von Racine bis Saint-John Peral. Berlin, 1958.
43830.48.100	Walder, Francis. Saint-Germain. 2e éd. Paris, 1958.
43832.51.100	Wallet, Régina. Le sang de la vigne. Paris, 1958.
37543.410	Waltz, Henriette. Explications françaises. Lyon, 1958.
38585.16.285	Weinrich, Harald. Tragische und komische Elemente in Racines Andromaque. Münster, 1958.
43833.41.3100	Weité, Pierre. L'adieu à l'Afrique. Paris, 1958.
37576.658.5	Widmer, Walter. Meistererzählungen des französischen Rokoko. München, 1958.
43837.49.100	Wolf, André. Les fleurs de l'exil. Paris, 1958.
43861.2.100	Zeraffa, Michel. Les daublures. Paris, 1958.
42584.1.32	Zola, Emile. Autres chefs-d'oeuvre. Paris, 1958.
42584.10.4	Zola, Emile. His Excellency. London, 1958.
42584.13.95	Zola, Emile. Mes voyages: Lourdes, Rome. Paris, 1958.
42584.19.13	Zola, Emile. Teresa Raquin. Torino, 1958.

1959

43538.76.805	Aaraas, Hans. Georges Bernanos. Oslo, 1959.
37595.9.110	Abailard, Pierre. Historia calamitatum. Paris, 1959.
37595.7.35	Abailard, Pierre. Istoriia moikh bedstvii. Moskva, 1959.
43552.26.800	Achard, M. Discours prononcés dans la séance publique tenue par l'Académie francaise. Paris, 1959.
40583.280	Adams, Robert M. Stendhal. N.Y., 1959.
43522.7.1100	Alberti, Henri. Les racines tordues. Paris, 1959.
43522.8.100	Albitre, Gilbert. L'ennui d'aimer; roman. Paris, 1959.
43522.15.100	Alcune, Roger. Lilial; ou, L'amandier, poésies. Paris, 1959.
43522.25.1120	Alexis, Jacques Stephen. L'espace d'un cillement; roman. Paris, 1959.
39594.19.85	Althusser, Louis. Montesquieu. Paris, 1959.
42553.32.85	Amiel, Henri F. Journal intime de l'année 1866. 5e éd. Paris, 1959.
42542.53.80	Anders, France. Jacques Copeau et le Cartel des Quatre. Paris, 1959.
37568.185	Andreev, L.G. Frantsuzskaia literatura, 1917-1956 gg. Moskva, 1959.
43524.21.100	Andro, J.C. Les vacances interdites. Paris, 1959.
43761.39.900	Angelet, Christian. Antoine de St. Exupéry. Brugge, 1959.
43524.67.125	Anouilh, Jean. L'hurluberlu, ou Le reactionnaire amoureux. Paris, 1959.
43524.67.792	Anouilh, Jean. Traveller without luggage. London, 1959.
43554.2.1080	Antoine, Gérald. Les cinq grandes odes de Claudel. Paris, 1959.
42563.21.107	Antoine, Louis. Un témoin de l'église: René Bazin. Paris, 1959.
43526.65.170.2	Apollinaire, Guillaume. Le poète assassiné. Paris, 1959.
43527.3.215	Aragon, Louis. Elsa. Paris, 1959.
43527.3.370	Aragon, Louis. J'abats mon jeu. Paris, 1959.
43527.3.730	Aragon, Louis. L'un ne va pas sans l'autre. Lyon, 1959.
43528.3.1100	Arnaud, Georges. L'enfer des humiliés. Paris, 1959.
43528.61.190	Arnoux, Alexandre. Marges du temps. Paris, 1959.
43528.73.110	Arrabal, Fernando. Baal Babylone; roman. Paris, 1959.
43529.80.100	Asselineau, Roger. Poésies incomplètes. Paris, 1959.
43531.18.1180	Audiberti, Jacques. L'effet Glapion; parapsychocomedie. Paris, 1959.
43531.9	Audiberti, Jacques. L'effet Glapion. Paris, 1959.
43531.19.2110	Audouard, Yvan. Cocagne. Paris, 1959.
43531.19.1100	Audra, A. Le lendemain des jours. Roder, 1959.
43532.23.160	Aveline, Claude. Le bestiaire inattendu. Paris, 1959.
43532.23.150	Aveline, Claude. Le poids du feu. Paris, 1959.
43535.54.182	Aymé, Marcel. Romans parisiéns. Paris, 1959.
41593.32.8.80	Bailly, Antoine. Pierre Dupont. Lyon, 1959.
43544.41.120	Baisdeffre, Pierre de. L'amour et l'ennui. Paris, 1959.
37555.536A	Balakian, Anna E. Surrealism. N.Y., 1959.
FL 398.49.34	Baldick, Robert. The life and times of Frédérick Lamaitre. Fair Lawn, N.J., 1959.
40563.22.15	Ballanche, Pierre Simon. La théodicée et la Virginie romaine. Genève, 1959.
37568.190	Balmas, E.H. Aspects et problèmes de la littérature contemporaine. Milano, 1959.
40597.35.165	Balzac, Honoré de. La cousine Bette. Paris, 1959.
40597.35.170	Balzac, Honoré de. L'envers de l'histoire contemporaine. Paris, 1959.
40597.19.40	Balzac, Honoré de. Eugénie Grandet. Paris, 1959.
40597.35.86	Balzac, Honoré de. Illusions perdues. Paris, 1959.
43738.1.270	Barbier, Joseph. La prière chrétienne...de Péguy. Paris, 1959.
43537.76.1110	Barjavel, René. Le diable l'emporte. Paris, 1959.
FL 398.6.20.10	Barrault, J.L. Nouvelles réflexions sur le théâtre. Paris, 1959.
37556.16.150	Barrillon, Raymond. Le cas Paris-soir. Paris, 1959.

1959 - cont.

40587.182.1	Bassan, Fernande. Chateaubriand et la Terre-Sainte. Paris, 1959.
40587.182	Bassan, Fernande. Chateaubriand et la Terre-Sainte. Thèse. Paris, 1959.
43537.84.2100	Bataille, Alfred. Arabesques. Paris, 1959?
38514.125	Baude, Henri. Dictz moraulx pour faire tapisserie. Genève, 1959.
41522.13.9.23	Baudelaire, Charles. Les fleurs du mal. Paris, 1959.
43537.98.2100	Bay, André. La carte du tendre. Paris, 1959.
43538.1.522	Beauvoir, Simone de. Memoirs of a dutiful daughter. 1. ed. Cleveland, 1959.
43538.14.775A	Beckett, Samuel. Krapp's last tape. London, 1959.
43538.14.755	Beckett, Samuel. Molloy. London, 1959.
FL 386.808	Beigbeder, M. Le théâtre en France depuis la libération. Paris, 1959.
38539.95	Bejart, M. Araspe. Avignon, 1959.
43538.49.100	Belen (pseud.). La géométrie dans les spasmes. Paris, 1959.
43538.51.2100	Belleval, Guy de. Jean des autres; roman. Paris, 1959.
43538.51.110	Belloni, Georges. Les chemins de gloire. Paris, 1959.
43538.61.180	Benoît, Pierre. Flamarens, roman. Paris, 1959.
43538.62.4120	Bens, Jacques. La plume et l'angre. 5. éd. Paris, 1959.
43538.75.130	Bergmans, Simone. Sébastien. Bruxelles, 1959.
42555.44.158	Bernard, Suzanne. Mallarmé et la musique. 2. éd. Paris, 1959.
37567.555	Bernard, Suzanne. Le poème en prose de Baudelaire. Paris, 1959.
43757.3.342	Berry, Madeleine. Jules Romains. Paris, 1959.
41522.58.8	Bertrand, Louis. Gaspard de la nuit. Monte-Carlo, 1959?
43538.82.3100	Bessette, Hélène. La Lour; roman. 2. éd. Paris, 1959.
43538.85.100	Bessonnet-Favre, C. Poèmes de la terre et des hommes de Francis Andé. Bruxelles, 1959.
40582.19.22	Beyle, Henri. A Roman journal. London, 1959.
40582.23.35	Beyle, Henri. Rome, Naples and Florence. London, 1959.
40582.25.19	Beyle, Henri. Le rouge et le noir. Paris, 1959.
40582.6.10	Beyle, Henri. Selected journalism from the English reviews. London, 1959.
41593.29.3.68	Bibliothèque nationale, Paris. Marceline Desbordes-Valmore. Paris, 1959.
43540.3.90	Billy, André. Le badaud de Paris et d'ailleurs. Paris, 1959.
40597.2.495	Billy, André. Balzac. Paris, 1959.
41555.43.45	Billy, André. Mérimée. Paris, 1959.
43697.88.855	Biltrau de Heredia, B. François Mauriac. Madrid, 1959.
37569.280	Blanchet, André. La littérature et le spirituel. Paris, 1959- 3v.
43543.8.180	Blanchot, Maurice. Le livre à venir. Paris, 1959.
43543.59.100	Blond, Georges. Les naufragés de Paris. Paris, 1959.
43543.67.110	Blondin, Antoine. Un singer en hiver. Paris, 1959.
43544.65.100	Blondin, Germaine. Le cahier d'Arlequin; poèmes. Paris, 1959.
43543.68.100	Blot, Jean. Les enfants de New York. 2. éd. Paris, 1959.
37597.26.70	Bodel, Jehan. Les fabliaux de Jean Bodel. Dakar, 1959.
43544.112.110	Boileau, Pierre. The evil eye. London, 1959.
37568.165.2	Boisdeffre, P. de. Une histoire vivante de la littérature d'aujourd'hui. Paris, 1959.
37569.295	Bolle, Louis. Les lettres et l'absolu. Genève, 1959.
43544.60.2130A	Bonnefoy, Yves. L'improbable. Paris, 1959.
43744.67.830	Bonnet, Henri. Marcel Proust de 1907 à 1914. Paris, 1959.
43550.58.240	Bonnier, Henry. Albert Camus. Lyon, 1959.
37563.99	Bonnot, Jacques. Humanisme et Pléiade. Paris, 1959.
37558.180	Bordeaux, Henry. Quarante ans chez les quarante. Paris, 1959.
43538.74.8100	Bordonove, G. L'enterrement du comte d'Orgaz. Paris, 1959.
43544.75.110	Borel, Marguerite Appeli. Les lettres. Paris, 1959.
41522.64.45	Borel d'Hauterive, Petrus. Champavert. Chicago, 1959.
43544.75.3100	Borgeaud, Georges. La vaiselles des évêques. Paris, 1959.
43544.81.150	Bory, Jean Louis. Usé par la mer. Paris, 1959.
43544.81.2720	Bosco, Henri. Barbache. London, 1959.
43544.81.2220	Bosco, Henri. Pierre Lampédouze. Paris, 1959.
43544.89.2150	Bosquet, Alain. Deuxième testament. Paris, 1959.
38557.31.25	Bossuet, J.B. Oraisons funèbres. Paris, 1959.
43544.108.725	Boulle, Pierre. Sacrilege in Malaya. London, 1959.
43544.113.110	Boussinot, Roger. Le sixième sens. Paris, 1959.
43544.88.4100	Boutron, Pierre Noël. Les colliers du nêve. Paris, 1959.
37543.430	Bray, Bernard. L'éxpression de l'inquiétude roman français dans le jeune. Groningen, 1959. 2 pam.
43620.2.79.185	Breachfeld, Georges I. André Gide and the Communist temptation. Geneve, 1959.
43698.200.805	Brechou, Robert. Michaux. 8. éd. Paris, 1959.
43550.58.855	Brée, Germaine. Camus. New Brunswick, 1959.
37555.685	Brée, Germaine. French poetry. N.Y., 1959.
43565.5.810	Breval, René. Philippe Daudet à bel. Paris, 1959.
43545.42.130	Brisson, P. Vingt ans de Figaro. 5. éd. Paris, 1959.
43550.58.847	Brisville, Jean A. Camus. 3. éd. Paris, 1959.
43545.63.100	Brochon, Pierre. Le canare ne chante plus. Paris, 1959.
42563.23.139	Bros, A.M. Léon Bloy à Logny-sur-Marne. Meaux, 1959.
43545.66.100	Brosse, Jacques. La chemise rouge. Paris, 1959.
43687.89.2800	Brunetière, Philippe. La Varende. Paris, 1959.
43546.75.100	Bureau, Jacques. Trois pierres chaudes en Espagne. Paris, 1959.
43547.75.100	Burgei, Maurice. En parte-a-faux. Paris, 1959.
43547.77.1100	Burnat, Jean. D'comme Dupont. Paris, 1959.
43547.77.2100	Buron, Nicole de. Los pies sobre el escritorio. Santiago de Chile, 1959.
38585.16.300	Butler, Philip. Classicisme et baroque dans l'oeuvre de Racine. Paris, 1959.
43546.87.50	Butor, Michel. A change of heart. N.Y., 1959.
43670.89.810	Cabanis, José. Jouhandeau. 3. éd. Paris, 1959.
38546.33.40	Callot, A. Pages d'histoire bourguignonne: Madame de Sévigné dans les vignes du seigneur à Saulieu en août 1677. Nuits, 1959.
43550.58.726.5	Camus, Albert. The rebel. N.Y., 1959.
43552.5.1825	Carbonara, C. L'arte e le arti secondo Alain. Napoli, 1959.
42557.12.130	Carneiró Leão, A. O culto da Ação em Verhaeren. Rio de Janeiro, 1959.
37567.90.10A	Cassagne, Albert. La théorie de l'art pour l'art en France. Paris, 1959.
43550.82.1100	Cassius de Linval, Paule. Reminiscences. Paris, 1959.
43550.82.200	Cassou, Jean. Le temps d'aimer. Paris, 1959.
43550.86.100	Castelane, J. Le léopard. Paris, 1959.
43550.98.170	Cayrol, Jean. Les corps etrangers. Paris, 1959.
42555.44.160	Cellier, Léon. Mallarmé et la morte qui parle. Paris, 1959.

Chronological Listing

1959 - cont.

43551.59.270 Cendrars, Blaise. Films sans images. Paris, 1959.
43551.80.140 Cesbron, Gilbert. Notre prison est un royaume. Paris, 1959.
43552.1.1100 Chaamba, Abdallah (pseud.). Le voyage des morts. Paris, 1959.
43552.2.2110 Chabrol, Jean-Pierre. Les innocents de Mars. Paris, 1959.
40517.4.5A Challes, Robert. Les illustres françaises. Paris, 1959. 2v.
43550.58.860 Champigny, Robert. Sur un héros païen. Paris, 1959.
43552.3.9280 Chamson, André. Devenir ce qu'on est. Namur, 1959.
43552.4.2780 Char, René. Poésies. Frankfurt, 1959.
43552.5.210 Chardonnę, Jacques. Le ciel dans la fenêtre. Paris, 1959.
43552.5.1155 Chartier, Emile. Le roi Pot. Paris, 1959.
37595.112 Chastel, André. Trésors de la poésie médiéval. Paris, 1959.
43552.65.120 Choisy, Maryse. Les iles s'enfuirent. Paris? 1959.
38546.95 Choleau, Jean. Le grand coeur de Madame de Sévigné. Vitré, 1959.
37595.36.7.15 Chrestien de Troyes. Erec et Énide. Bologna, 1959.
43552.76.100 Christian Yve, Guy. Les tentatives. Paris, 1959.
43552.93.100 Chweitzer, Lydia. La belle étoffe. Paris, 1959.
37530.186 Cioranescu, A. Bibliographie de la littérature française. Paris, 1959.
37574.770.5 Clancier, G.E. De Rimbaud au surréalisme. Paris, 1959.
39527.4.85.2 Clarac, Pierre. La Fontaine. Paris, 1959.
43554.2.75A Claudel, Paul. Lettres inedites de mon parrain Paul Claudel. Paris, 1959.
43556.1.61 Cocteau, Jean. Opéra. Paris, 1959.
43556.49.70 Colette, Sidonie Gabrielle. Lettres a Marguerite Moreno. Paris, 1959.
43556.49.718 Colette, Sidonie Gabrielle. The tender shoot. N.Y., 1959.
40553.9.67 Constant de Rebecque, Benjamin. Adolphe and The red note-book. London, 1959.
V43500.71 Coppieters de Gibson, Henri. Les mains de Pygmalion. Bruxelles, 1959.
40587.178 Cordiè, Carlo. Chateaubriand politico. Messina, 1959.
38574.28 Corneille, Pierre. Moot plays. Nashville, 1959.
38575.35.5 Corneille, Pierre. Sertorius. Genève, 1959.
42586.32.215 Coster, Charles de. Charles de Coster, journaliste. Bruxelles, 1959.
42586.32.60 Coster, Charles de. La legende et les aventures héroiques. Bruxelles, 1959.
38562.23.30 Counillon, J.F. Fontenelle. Fecamp, 1959.
39527.4.130 Couton, Georges. La politique de La Fontaine. Paris, 1959.
43550.58.845 Cruickshank, John. Albert Camus and the literature of revolt. London, 1959.
43560.78.2102 Curvers, Alexis Théophille. Tempo di Roma. 1st ed. N.Y., 1959.
39533.20.13 Cyrano de Bergerac. L'autre monde. Paris, 1959.
43565.7.100 Dabadie, Jean. Les dieux du foyer. Paris, 1959.
43565.41.140 Daix, Pierre. La rivière profonde. Paris, 1959.
43565.60.1705 Daninos, Pierre. Sonia, je t'adore. N.Y., 1959.
43565.77.100 Darribehaude, Jacques. Semelles de vent. Paris, 1959.
43565.89.700 Daumal, René. Mount Analogues. London, 1959.
42555.44.152 Davies, Gardner. Mallarmé et le drame solaire. Paris, 1959.
43565.92.7120 Davray, Jean. Le bruit de la vie. Paris, 1959. 4v.
43697.75.860 Davy, Marie. Un philosophe itinérant. Paris, 1959.
42587.27.80 Day, Hem. Bibliographie de Louise Michel, 1830-1905. Bruxelles, 1959.
42587.27.90 Day, Hem. Louise Michel, Jules Verne. Bruxelles, 1959.
43566.36.130 Deharme, Lise. Laissez-moi tranquille. Paris, 1959.
43566.42.790 Dejean, Georges. Las garras del maligno. México, 1959.
43738.1.825 Delaporte, Jean. Connaissance de Péguy. Paris, 1959. 2v.
43566.48.4800 Delbousquet, Germaine Emmanuel. Germaine Emmanuel Delbousquet, 1874-1909. Agen, 1959.
43566.48.6710 Del Castillo, Michel. The guitar. London, 1959.
43566.48.7100 Del Corte, Daniela. Des mystères du rosaire. Fontenay-le-Comte, 1959.
43566.49.3100 Delève, Ernst. Pura seta. Bruxelles, 1959.
43761.78.835 Dellevaux, Raymond. L'existentialisme et le théâtre de Jean Paul Sartre. 3. éd. Bruxelles, 1959.
43566.51.5100 Delperier, Michelle. Les enfants crucifiés. Paris, 1959.
43822.49.1345 Denat, A. L'art poétique après Valéry. Sydney, 1959.
43566.62.5100 Denuzière, Maurice. Les trois dés. Paris, 1959.
37543.548 Derche, Roland. Études de textes français. Paris, 1959.
43566.79.3100 Descrières, Yves. La glane en gerbe; rimailleries. Paris, 1959.
43566.81.2150 Desmarest, M.A. Les remparts de Saint-Paul. Paris, 1959.
38528.32.20A Despériers, Bonaventure. The mirrour of mirth and pleasant conceits . Columbia, S.C., 1959.
38526.13.60 Desportes, Philippe. Les amours de Diane. v.1-2. Genève, 1959.
43566.82.7200 Destouches, Louis Ferdinand. Balleto sans musique. Paris, 1959.
43566.82.3100 Detouches, C. La passion de Marie d'Agoult. Paris, 1959.
43568.6.100 Dib, Mohammed. Un été africain; roman. Paris, 1959.
43568.17.110 Didelot, R.F. Dernier Malin. Paris, 1959.
43568.17.120 Didelot, R.F. L'insolite. Paris, 1959.
39564.61.10 Diderot, Denis. Diderot et Falconet correspondance. Frankfurt, 1959.
39564.20.115 Diderot, Denis. Jacques, the fatlist and his master. N.Y., 1959.
39564.8.22 Diderot, Denis. Oeuvres esthétiques. Paris, 1959.
39564.20.5 Diderot, Denis. Regrets sur ma vieille robe et Lettre à une jeune mariée. 's-Gravenhage, 1959.
39564.11.30 Diderot, Denis. La religieuse. London, 1959.
43568.67.100 Diolé, Philippe. L'eau profonde; roman. Paris, 1959.
43765.41.3810 Doyon, René Louis. A la recherche du vrai à travers l'oeuvre de Claude Seignolle. Paris, 1959.
43574.75.745 Druon, Maurice. The curtain falls. London, 1959.
43574.75.120 Druon, Maurice. Les grandes familles. Paris, 1959.
43576.9.120 Du Bos, Charles. Choix de textes. Paris, 1959.
43576.29.100 Dufour, Liliane. Étape vers l'inconnu. Paris, 1959.
43576.6.248 Duhamel, Georges. Travail, ô mon seul repos. Paris, 1959.
41538.195 Dumas, Alexandre. Tangier to Tunis. London, 1959.
43576.54.2100 Dumesnil, R. Le rideau à l'Italienne. Paris, 1959.
40583.225.5 DuParc, Yves. Quand Stendhal relisait les Promenades. Lausanne, 1959.
42515.44.40 DuPasquier, Marcel. Edgar Quinet en Suisse. Neuchâtel, 1959.
43576.71.1100 Dupont, Denis. Premiers essais. Paris, 1959.
43576.71.110 Dupony, A. Roulez, tambours! Paris, 1959.
43576.74.2110 Duras, Marguerite. The square. N.Y., 1959.

1959 - cont.

40583.290 Dutourd, Jean. L'âme sensible. 11. éd. Paris, 1959.
43581.89.120 Eaubonne, Françoise d'. Je m'appelle Vristine. Paris, 1959.
43581.89.115 Eaubonne, Françoise d'. Le sous-marin de l'espace. Paris, 1959.
43581.89.100 Eaubonne, Françoise d'. Les tricheurs, roman. Paris, 1959.
43590.50.100 Ękman, Pierre A. Les enfants des collines. Paris, 1959.
43591.89.199 Éluard, Paul. Poésies. Paris, 1959.
43593.29.100 Enfoux, Janine. Cantique de l'amour. Paris, 1959.
43598.82.190 Estang, Luc. L'horloger du cherche-midi. Paris, 1959.
43538.76.880 Estève, Michel. Le seus de l'amour dans les romans de Bernanos. Paris, 1959.
38536.35 Facsimilé intéqral de l'un des trois éxemplaires conservés. Paris, 1959.
43606.50.110 Fallet, René. Une poignée de mains. Paris, 1959.
40515.2.34 Farnum, Dorothy. The Dutch divinity. London, 1959.
43607.76.7100 Fernandez, Dominique. L'écorce. Paris, 1959.
43744.67.1390A Ferré, André. Les années de collège de Marcel Proust. Paris, 1959.
42543.41.13 Feydeau, Georges. Du mariage au divorce. Paris, 1959.
43610.22.1100 Fleg, Daniel. Journal. Buchet, Chastel, 1959.
43610.23.100 Fleischman, Théo. Le peuple aux yeux clairs. Bruxelles, 1959.
40597.2.485 Folman, Michel. Honoré de Balzac. Genève, 1959.
43611.53.160 Fombeure, Maurice. Sous les tambours du ciel. Paris, 1959.
43625.19.818 Fontaine, Anne. Armand Godoy. Paris, 1959.
43611.61.100 Fontanet, Jean C. Qui perd gagne; roman. Neuchâtel, 1959.
37563.97 Forster, Elborg H. Die französische Elegie im 16. Jahrhundert. Köln, 1959.
37573.710 Fortini, Franco. Il movimento surrealista. 1. ed. Milano, 1959.
43611.76.110 Forton, Jean. Le grand mal. Paris, 1959.
43611.5.48 Fournier, Alain. The lost domain. London, 1959.
42515.38.15 France. Institut pédagogique national. Exposition Ernest Renan. Paris, 1959.
43612.4.4100 Francescat, Pierre. Le bonheur est sur l'autre rive; roman. Paris, 1959.
37563.70.7 Françon, Marcel. Leçons et notes sur la littérature française. 2. éd. Cambridge, Mass., 1959.
42584.25.216 Frandon, Ida Marie. La pensée politique d'Emile Zola. Paris, 1959.
37556.153 Frédérik, Pierre. Un siècle de chasse aux nouvelles. Paris, 1959.
43616.41.3100 Gaillard, J.C. Croix de bois. Paris, 1959.
43616.41.2140 Gaillard, Robert. Les mariés de l'exil. Paris, 1959.
43616.41.2130 Gaillard, Robert. Rayaume de la nuit. Paris, 1959.
43616.78.160 Gary, Romain. Lady L. N.Y., 1959.
43616.79.710 Gascar, Pierre. The seed. London, 1959.
43670.89.805 Gaulmier, Jean. L'univers de Marcel Jouhandeau. Paris, 1959.
43616.89.1110 Gauthier, Marie Joséphine. La patte et la main. Paris, 1959.
40586.28.64.5 Gautier, Jean Maurice. Le style des mémoires d'outre-tembe de Chateaubriand. Genève, 1959.
40586.28.64.7 Gautier, Jean Maurice. Le style des mémoires d'outre-tombe de Chateaubriand. Genève, 1959.
39544.325 Gay, Peter. Voltaire's politics. Princeton, 1959.
43617.59.160 Genevoix, Maurice. La framboise et bellehumeur. Paris, 1959.
43617.59.150 Genevoix, Maurice. Routes de l'aventure. Paris, 1959.
43617.82.100 Gennari, Genevieve. Journal d'une bourgeoise. Paris, 1959.
43538.1.430 Gennari, Geneviève. Simone de Beauvoir. Paris, 1959.
37569.275 Germain, André. Les croisés modernes. Paris, 1959.
37543.440 Geyl, Pieter. Franse figuren. Amsterdam, 1959.
43620.2.79.180A Gide, André. The correspondence of André Gide and Edmund Gosse. N.Y., 1959.
43620.2.55.40 Gide, André. The counterfeiters. N.Y., 1959.
43620.2.41.5 Gide, André. Pretexts. N.Y., 1959.
43620.2.79.143 Gide, André. Le Prométhée mal enchainé. Paris, 1959.
43620.2.79.170 Gide, André. So be it. 1. American ed. N.Y., 1959.
37574.710.10 Gide, André Paul Guillaume. Anthologie de la poésie française. Paris, 1959.
43620.50.1100 Gillaux, Max. Les violettes acides. Paris, 1959.
43620.49.2100 Gillet, Victor. Le jardin des regrets. Dijon, 1959.
43620.66.450 Giono, Jean. Domitien, suivi de Joseph à Dothan. Paris, 1959.
43620.66.205 Giono, Jean. Naissance de l'Odyssée. Paris, 1959.
43620.66.765 Giono, Jean. The straw man. 1. American ed. N.Y., 1959.
43620.74.1140 Giraudoux, Jean Pierre. Le pays sans chemins. Paris, 1959.
43620.74.1150 Giraudoux, Jean Pierre. Poeme ingénue. Paris, 1959.
43550.58.865 Girolamo, N. de. Albert Camus. Siena, 1959.
42555.44.166 Girolamo, Nicola di. Stéphane Mallarmé, Ouverture ancienne d'Herodiade. Siena, 1959.
42586.64.15 Gobineau, Arthur de. Les depeches diplomatiques du comte de Gobineau e Perse. Genève, 1959.
43625.48.2100 Golay, Jean. Les poèmes florentins. Marin, 1959.
43625.49.170 Goll, Claire. Un amour au quartier Latin. Paris, 1959.
42575.69.35 Goncourt, Edmond de. Journal. Paris, 1959. 4v.
43625.78.700 Gorz, A. The traitor. N.Y., 1959.
43626.70.700 Gracq, Julien. Balcony in the forest. N.Y., 1959.
43626.23.1123 Grenier, Jean. Les îles. Paris, 1959.
43628.23.160 Guéhenno, Jean. Sur le chemin des hommes. Paris, 1959.
43628.42.1100 Guillaume, Bernard. Vingt-quatre préludes, poèmes. Rodez, 1959.
42555.39.1192 Guillaume, Jean. Le mot-thème dans l'exégèse. Namur, 1959.
42555.39.1190 Guillaume, Jean. Le mot-thème dans l'exégèse de van Lerberghe. Bruxelles, 1959.
41574.291 Guillemin, H. Hugo et la sexualité. Paris, 1959.
43628.1.25 Guitry, Sacha. Théâtre. Paris, 1959-60. 15v.
42586.32.515 Gulo, Alois. Charles de Coster en Vlaanderen. Antwerpen, 1959.
37564.245 Haase, Erich. Einführung in die Literatur des Refuge. Berlin, 1959.
43631.2.57 Hamp, Pierre. La peine des hommes. Paris, 1959-
42556.28.275 Hanson, Elisabeth M. My poor Arthur. London, 1959.
43632.50.170 Hellens, Franz. Oeil-de-Dieu. Paris, 1959.
43632.50.200 Hellens, Franz. Petit théâtre aux chandelles. Paris, 1959?
43632.50.19 Hellens, Franz. Poésie complète (1905-1959). Paris, 1959.
38546.33.35 Hérard, Madeleine. Madame de Sévigné. Dijon, 1959.
43632.77.3100 Hermann, Claudine. L'étoile de David. Paris, 1959.

1959 - cont.

43632.89.1100 Heurtebize, Vital. Le bouffon triste, poèmes. Bordeaux, 1959.
41571.3.26 Hugo, Victor. L'oeuvre de Victor Hugo. Paris, 1959.
43638.53.130 Humbourg, Pierre. Les sentiers de l'automne. Paris, 1959.
40597.2.417 Hunt, Herbert James. Balzac's Comédie humaine. London, 1959.
42576.66.2.7 Huysmans, Joris Karl. Against nature. Harmondsworth, 1959.
43652.46.120 Ikor, Roger. Ciel ouvert. Paris, 1959.
43655.13.100 Inchakoff, B. Poèmes du long hiver et printemps fidèle. Paris, 1959.
43656.59.120 Ionesco, Eugène. Le rhinocéros. 1. éd. Paris, 1959.
43667.13.100 Jack, Muriel. Kalitka. Paris, 1959.
43667.14.62 Jacob, Max. Lettres à Marcel Béalu. Lyon, 1959.
43667.14.300F Jacob, Max. Méditation sur ma mort. Berne, 1959.
43667.14.1100 Jacqueneaux, Édith. Feu de sable. Le Mans, 1959.
37596.10.205 Jaeger, Hermann. Der Sinnbezirk der Fortbewegung. Erlangen? 1959.
43538.76.897 Jamet, Henry. Un autre Bernanos. Lyon, 1959.
43667.1.325 Jammes, Francis. Correspondance, 1898-1930. Paris, 1959.
43526.65.920 Jannine, Pasquale. La fortuna di Apollina+re in Italia. Milano, 1959.
43668.4.2100 Jean, Raymond. Les ruines de New York. Paris, 1959.
37567.565 Jensen, Christian A.E. L'evolution du romantisme l'année 1826. Genève, 1959.
38513.85 Jouhan. La farce du pauvre Jouhan. Genève, 1959.
43670.89.545 Jouhandeau, M. Les Argonautes. Paris, 1959.
43670.89.530 Jouhandeau, M. L'éternel procès. 2. éd. Paris, 1959.
43673.76.2110 Kern, Alfred. L'amour profane. Paris, 1959.
43673.83.170 Kessel, Joseph. The lion. N.Y., 1959.
40534.15.100 Keys, Allwyn Charles. Antoine Bret, 1717-92. Auckland, 1959.
43544.71.130 Kieffler, Rosemarie. Alchimie et toute-puissance. Génève, 1959.
43620.2.380 Krebber, G. Untersuchungen zur Ästhetik und Kritik André Gides. Geneve, 1959.
37562.295.2 Kukenheim, Louis. Guide de la littérature française du moyen âge. 2. éd. Leiden, 1959.
43687.11.110 Lacaze, Raymond. Poulido. Rodez, 1959.
37566.120 Lacretelle, Jacques de. Les maîtres et les amis. Namur, 1959.
38544.27.12 La Fayette, Marie M. Me. de la Fayette, par elle même. Paris, 1959.
39527.58 La Fontaine, Jean de. Bajky. Praha, 1959.
39527.10.10 La Fontaine, Jean de. Contes et nouvelles. Paris, 1959-60. 2v.
43687.32.100 Lagesse, Marcelle. La diligence s'eloigne à l'aube. Paris, 1959.
43687.53.2100 Lamarre, Lise. Precocités. Paris, 1959.
43620.2.365 Lamsfuss, G. Der Asthetizismus André Gides. Münster, 1959.
43687.58.3100 Landa, Michel L. Les cloches de plomb. Paris, 1959.
43687.58.2130F Landry, Charles François. Pour un peu plus d'humanité. Lausanne, 1959.
37564.240 Lang, Alfred. Gesellschaft und Wirtschaft Frankreichs im Spiegel der klassischen Literatur des 17. Jahrhundert (1660 bis 1715). Bonn, 1959.
43687.61.1130 Lanoux, Armand. A quoi jouent les enfants du bourreau? Paris, 1959.
43687.61.1135 Lanoux, Armand. La tulipe orageuse. Paris, 1959.
43606.76.830 La Rochefoucauld, Edmée. Léon-Paul Fargue. Paris, 1959.
38543.19.60 La Rochefoucauld, François. Maxims. N.Y., 1959.
43687.84.2100 Lataillade, Louis. Le groupe sud. Paris, 1959.
43687.89.1160 Laurent, Jacques. Les caprices de Caroline. Paris, 1959.
43687.89.170 Laurent, Jacques. Caroline Chérie. London, 1959.
43687.89.1710 Laurent, Jacques. Clotilde. N.Y., 1959.
43628.1.525 Lauwick, Hervé. Le merveilleux humour de Lucien et Sacha Guitry. Paris, 1959.
43687.89.2170 La Varende, Jean de. L'amour sacré et l'amour profane. Paris, 1959.
43687.89.2160 La Varende, Jean de. M. le Duc. Paris, 1959.
43822.49.1315 Lawler, James. Form and meaning in Valéry's Le cimetière marin. Carlton, 1959.
43688.5.5180 Léautaud, Paul. Bestiaire. Paris, 1959.
43688.5.5700 Léautaud, Paul. The child of Montmartre. London, 1959.
43574.89.800 Lebois, André. Druelle. Rodez, 1959.
43688.21.100 Lec, Emma. Le chant du grillon; poèmes, 1954-1959. Paris, 1959.
43738.78.710A Léger, Alexis S.-L. Anabasis. London, 1959.
43688.35.1100 Legueb, Marcel. Hélène, tu perdris Troie. Paris, 1959.
43744.67.1420 Le Point; revue artistique et litteraire. Universe de Proust. Souillac, 1959.
43688.98.110 LeQuintrec, Charles. Les chemins de Kergrist. Paris, 1959.
43620.74.900 LeSage, Laurent. Jean Giraudoux, his life and works. University Park, 1959.
43688.79.3110 LeSage, Roger. Go! Paris, 1959.
43688.79.100 Lescure, Pierre de. La saison des consciences. Paris, 1959.
37567.540 Lethève, Jacques. Impressionistes et symbolistes devant la presse. Paris, 1959.
Mol 712.10 Lewis, Dominic Bevan Wyndham. Molière; the comic mask. London, 1959.
40597.2.515 Le Yaouanc, M. Nosographie de l'humanité balzacienne. Paris, 1959.
40583.206.5 Liprandi, Claude. Sur un personnage du Rouge et le noir. Lausanne, 1959.
40583.178.10 Litto, Victor del. La vie intellectuelle de Stendahl. Paris, 1959.
43693.60.100 Longhy, Claude S. Le goût des sources. Paris, 1959.
43693.89.2100 Loubet, Guillaume. L'Hydre. Paris, 1959.
43524.67.825 Luppé, Robert de. Jean Anouilh. Paris, 1959.
FL 371.82 McKean, Mary F. The interplay of realistic and flamboyant art elements in the French mystères. Washington, 1959.
43697.14.1110 Macover, Alice. L'amazone. Paris, 1959.
43697.37.1100 Mahélin, Yves. Grandissante origine. Paris, 1959.
43697.41.3100 Maisongrande, H.G. Le cycle des Héretiers; poèmes. Paris, 1959.
42555.44.5 Mallarmé, Stéphane. Correspondance, 1862-1871. Paris, 1959. 3v.
42555.43.32 Mallarmé, Stéphane. Les noces d'Herodiade, mystère. Paris, 1959.
43697.2.1730 Mallet-Joris, Françoise (pseud.). Capé Céleste. N.Y., 1959.
43697.2.1130 Mallet-Joris, Françoise (pseud.). La chambre rouge. Paris, 1959.

1959 - cont.

43697.2.1110 Mallet-Joris, Françoise (pseud.). L'empire céleste. Paris, 1959.
43697.52.102 Malraux, André. Les conquérants. Paris, 1959.
43538.76.875A Manbrey, Pierre. L'expression de la passion intérieure dans le style de Bernanos Romancier. Washington, 1959.
43697.58.100 Manchon, Fernand. Variétés sur la rebellion algerienne. Constantine, 1959.
43697.61.3100 Mantraud, F. Sa espera. Paris, 1959.
37543.480 Maranini, L. Visione e personaggio secondo Flaubert. Padova, 1959.
FL 386.187 Marcel, Gabriel. L'heure théâtrale de Giraudoux à Jean-Paul Sartre. Paris, 1959.
43697.75.170 Marcel, Gabriel. Présence et immortalité. Paris, 1959.
43697.75.180A Marcel, Gabriel. Théâtre et religion. Lyon, 1959.
43667.1.865 Marie Margarita, Sister. La métrique de Francis Jammes vue dans le cadre de celle de ses contemporains et de ses prédécesseurs imédiats. Boston, 1959.
42563.23.132 Marie Saint-Louis de Gonzague, sister. Léon Bloy face à la critique. Bibliographie critique. Nashua, 1959.
40583.238 Marill, Francine. Stendhal. Paris, 1959.
40535.29.12 Marivaux, Pierre Carlet de Chamblain de. Le paysan parvenu. Paris, 1959.
40535.27.30 Marivaux, Pierre Carlet de Chamblain de. Théâtre choisi. Firenze, 1959-60. 2v.
43697.78.6100 Martin, Suzanne. Rue des vivants. Paris, 1959.
43792.90.825 Martineau, Henri. Le séjour de P.J. Toulet à Alger. Paris, 1959.
43697.82.140 Massis, Henri. De l'homme à Dieu. Paris, 1959.
43697.87.3100 Matveev, Michel. Ailleurs autrefois; roman. Paris, 1959.
43697.89.6100 Mauduit, Hyacinthe. L'héritier du ciel. Paris, 1959.
42577.4.2.5 Maupassant, Guy de. Bel-ami. Paris, 1959.
42577.4.29.30 Maupassant, Guy de. Pierre et Jean. Paris, 1959.
42577.1.38 Maupassant, Guy de. Short stories. London, 1959.
43697.88.3100 Mauriac, Claude. Le dîner en ville. Paris, 1959.
43697.88.490 Mauriac, François. Le fils de l'homme. Paris, 1959.
43697.88.65 Mauriac, François. Mémoires intérieurs. Paris, 1959.
43697.88.6100 Maurice, Margot. Les routes de la vie; poèmes. Paris, 1959.
43697.89.470 Maurois, André. Dialogues des vivants. Paris, 1959.
43697.89.480 Maurois, André. Portrait d'un ami qui s'appelait moi. Namur, 1959.
43697.89.4110 Maurois, Michelle. The sweetbread. N.Y., 1959.
39564.42 Mayer, Jean. Diderot, homme de science. Rennes, 1959.
43698.80.21 Mesers, Edward L.J. Poèmes, 1923-1958. Paris, 1959.
43556.1.910 Meunier, Micheline. Méditerranée. Paris, 1959.
41596.4.120 Meunier, Micheline. Trente-deux variations autour du nom d'Alfred de Musset. Paris, 1959.
43698.90.100 Mevel, Jean. Existence. Bordeaux, 1959.
43698.200.250 Michaux, Henri. Paix dans les brisements. Paris, 1959.
38513.45.5 Michel, J. Le mystère de la passion. Gembloux, 1959.
43699.51.61 Milosz, Oscar Vladislas. Textes inédits de O.V. de L. Milosz. Paris, 1959.
Mol 165.112 Molière, Jean Baptiste Poquelin. L'avare. London, 1959.
Mol 211.80.12 Molière, Jean Baptiste Poquelin. Les femmes savantes. Paris, 1959.
Mol 49.59 Molière, Jean Baptiste Poquelin. Maximes de Molière. La Haye, 1959.
Mol 19.59 Molière, Jean Baptiste Poquelin. Oeuvres complètes. Paris, 1959. 2v.
Mol 115.1.5 Molière, Jean Baptiste Poquelin. Skąpiec. Wrocław, 1959.
Mon 32.59 Montaigne, Michel de. Essays. Harmondsworth, 1959.
Mon 32.50 Montaigne, Michel de. Selected essays. N.Y., 1959.
43701.61.3100 Montargis, Jean. De tout et de rien. Paris, 1959.
43701.63.520A Montherlant, Henry de. Romans et oeuvres de fiction non théâtrales. Paris, 1959.
43701.74.350 Morand, Paul. Le lion écarlate. Paris, 1959.
37543.455 Morier, Henri. La psychologie des styles. Genève, 1959.
42556.28.256 Morrissette, Bruce A. La bataille Rimbaud. Paris, 1959.
43701.77.4100 Mortes, Claude. Ciels et brouillards. Paris, 1959.
42582.2.4 Moscow. Vsesoiuznaia gosudarstvennaia biblioteka. Inostrannoi literatury. Zhiul' Vern. Moskva, 1959.
43757.50.4 Moscow. Vsesoiuznaia Gosudarstvennaia Biblioteka Inostrannykh Literatur. Romen Rollan; bio-bibliograficheskii ukazatel'. Moskva, 1959.
43757.50.1180 Motyleva, Tamara L. Tvorchestvo Romena Rollana. Moskva, 1959.
43701.89.1110 Mouloudji, Marcel. La guerre buissonnière; roman. Paris, 1959.
43761.31.805 Mourgue, Gerard. Françoise Sagan. Paris, 1959.
43625.19.830 Mousel, Paul. Armand Godoy. Luxembourg, 1959.
43701.79.120 Moussy, Marcel. Les 400 coups. Paris, 1959.
43703.54.100 Mun, R. de. La mort d'un enfant. Paris, 1959.
43703.73.2100 Murat, Stéphane. La porte du sud. Paris, 1959.
37556.185 Nattier-Natanson, Evelyn. Les amitiés de la revue blanche et quelques autres. Vincennes, 1959.
38528.24.10 Needhart, Dorothea. Das Cymbalum mundi des Bonaventure des Periers. Genève, 1959.
41543.7.15 Nerval, Gerard. Oeuvres complémentaires. Paris, 1959- 4v.
41543.18 Nerval, Gerard de. Fortune's fool. London, 1959.
41543.6.20 Nerval, Gerard de. Les poètes du XVIe siècle. Cambridge, 1959.
42576.33.9.8 Neuenschwander-Naef, Claudia. Vorstellungswelt und Realität in Flauberts "Bouvard et Pécuchet". Winterthur, 1959.
43707.81.100 Nisin, Arthur. Un journal de Russie. Lausanne, 1959.
37562.305 Nolting-Hauff, Ilse. Die Stellung der Liebeskasuistik im höfischen Roman. Heidelberg, 1959.
43822.49.987 Noulet, Emilie. Suite valeryenne. Bruxelles, 1959. 2 pam.
37576.659.5 Nouvelle revue française. From the N.R.F. N.Y., 1959.
43714.5.110 Obaldia, René de. Le centenaire, roman. Paris, 1959.
43723.18.730 Oldenbourg, Zoé. The chains of love. London, 1959.
40597.2.475 Oliver, Edward. Balzac the European. London, 1959.
39535.68 L'ombre d'Amarante. Montpellier, 1959.
43626.22.840 Ott, Lydia. Das Erlebnis des Todes in den Erzählungen Julien Greens. Erlangen? 1959?
37543.465 The Oxford companion to French literature. Oxford, 1959.
43744.67.1360 Painter, George Duncan. Marcel Proust. London, 1959. 2v.
43744.67.1355 Painter, George Duncan. Proust; the early years. Boston, 1959-65. 2v.
43737.46.100 Pakrowan, Emich. La quatrième génération. Paris, 1959.
40583.305 Parma (City). Biblioteca palatina. Mostra Stendhaliana. Parma, 1959.
43738.41.185 Peisson, Edouard. Thomas et l'ange. Paris, 1959.

1959 - cont.

43738.49.1100 Pelegri, Jean. Les oliviers de la justice. Paris, 1959.
43738.62.100 Penzo, Berthe. Cerveau à la broche. Paris, 1959.
43701.63.885 Perruchot, Henri. Montherlant. Paris, 1959.
43738.97.1740 Peyrefitte, Roger. Knights of Malta. N.Y., 1959.
43740.3.100 Pham-Van-Ky. Les contemporains. Paris, 1959.
43740.64.100 Pholien, Georges. En lisant. Paris, 1959.
43741.25.140 Pieyre de Mandiargues, André. Feu de braise. Paris, 1959.
42563.23.130 Pijls, Pieter J.H. La satire littéraire dans l'oeuvre de Léon Bloy. Leiden, 1959.
42563.23.130.2 Pijls, Pieter J.H. La satire littéraire dans l'oeuvre de Léon Bloy. Leiden, 1959.
43741.59.3100 Pinget, Robert. Le fiston. Paris, 1959.
38546.100 Pirat, Yvonne. Madame de Sévigné. Paris, 1959.
43741.89.120 Piroué, Georges. Les limbes. Paris, 1959.
38514.58.30 Pisan, Christine de. Le livre de la mutacion de fortune. Paris, 1959. 2v.
43741.91.100 Pivot, Bernard. L'amour en vogue; roman. Paris, 1959.
38551.155 Pizzorusso, Arnaldo. La poetica di Fénelon. 1. ed. Milano, 1959.
43743.41.4100 Poilvet Le Guenn, Jean. Galons. Paris, 1959.
43743.41.3700 Poirot-Delpech, Bertrand. Fool's paradise. London, 1959.
41522.18.340 Porché, François. Baudelaire et la presidente. 2. éd. Paris, 1959.
37595.110 Pottier, Bernard. Antologia de textos del francés antiquo. Granada, 1959.
37565.126.5 Poulet, Georges. The interior distance. Baltimore, 1959.
43744.5.130 Prassinos, Gisèle. La voyageuse. Paris, 1959.
43744.25.4110 Prévost, Alain. Le chalutier Minium. Paris, 1959.
42515.22 Primoli, Joseph Napoléon. Pages inédites. Roma, 1959.
43628.1.520 Prince, Stéphane. Sacha Guitry hors sa légende. Paris, 1959.
V43500.249 Privat, Bernard. Au pied du mur, récit. Paris, 1959.
43638.55.800 Puel, Gaston. Edmond Humeau. Rodez, 1959.
43750.23.110 Queillé, Yvonne. Sur un air sempiternel; poèmes. Paris, 1959.
43750.24.250 Queneau, Raymond. Zazzie dans le métro. 114. éd. Paris, 1959.
43750.24.1100 Querlin, Marise. Condamné a vivre; roman. Paris, 1959.
38536.37 Rabelais, F. Le guart livre. Paris, 1959.
38536.18.41 Rabelais, F. Pantagruel. Genève, 1959.
38536.36 Rabelais, F. Pantagruel. Paris, 1959.
38536.18.40 Rabelais, F. Pantagruel de François Rabelais. Paris, 1959.
38537.44 Rabelais écrivain-médecin. Paris, 1959.
38585.43.60 Racine, Jean. Fedra. Milano, 1959.
38585.43.18 Racine, Jean. Phaedra. N.Y., 1959.
43752.18.15 Radiguet, Raymond. Oeuvres complètes. Paris, 1959. 2v.
43752.34.110 Ragon, Michel. Les Americains. Paris, 1959.
43752.38.1100 Rahnéma, Férydoun. Poèmes anciens. Paris, 1959.
43698.74.800 Rambach, Elisabeth. Die Mariendichtungen von Louis Mercier. Münster, 1959.
43752.57.62 Ramuz, Charles Ferdinand. Lettres, 1919-1947. Paris, 1959.
FL 6139.59 Rang, Martin. Rousseaus Lehre vom Menshen. Göttingen, 1959.
43752.8.100 Reboue, Edmond. Si toubib. Paris, 1959.
40575.5.155 Regard, Maurice. Sainte-Beuve. Paris, 1959.
43753.4.110 Régnier, Yves. Les voyages, roman. Paris, 1959.
42515.30.729.10 Renan, Ernest. Souvenirs d'enfance et de jeunesse. Paris, 1959.
43753.58.2110 Renard, J.C. En une seule vigne. Paris, 1959.
42587.51.50.2 Renard, Jules. Théatre complet. Paris, 1959.
42545.3.870 Renard, R. Maurice Maeterlinck et l'Italie. Paris, 1959.
40524.28.15 Restif de la Bretonne, Nicolas E. Monsieur Nicolas. Paris, 1959. 6v.
38537.1.3 Revue du seizième siècle. Table. v.1-19, 1913-1933. Genève, 1959.
43756.12.110 Richard, Marius. Mon ami Broque. Paris, 1959.
FL 398.7.80 Richardson, Joanna. Sarah Bernhardt. London, 1959.
37567.550 Ridge, George R. The hero in French romantic literature. Athens, 1959.
42556.28.89 Rimbaud, Jean Arthur. Vybor. Praha, 1959.
43757.6.125 Robbe-Grillet, Alain. Jealousy. London, 1959.
43757.6.705 Robbe-Grillet, Alain. Jealousy. N.Y., 1959.
43757.6.700 Robbe-Grillet, Alain. The voyeur. London, 1959.
37567.560 Robichon, Jacques. Le roman des chefs-d'oeuvre. Paris, 1959.
43757.12.130 Roblès, Emmanuel. L'homme d'avrile. Paris, 1959.
37556.190 Roger, Gaston. Maîtres du roman de terroir. Paris, 1959.
43757.50.690 Rolland, Romain. Chère Sofia. Paris, 1959. 2v.
43757.50.565 Rolland, Romain. Le voyage interieur. Paris, 1959.
43757.3.83 Romains, Jules. Boën, ou La possession des biens. Paris, 1959.
43757.3.48.5 Romains, Jules. Le dictateur. Quatre actes. 5. éd. Paris, 1959.
43757.3.288 Romains, Jules. Mémoires de Madame Chauvirel. Paris, 1959-60. 2v.
43757.3.276 Romains, Jules. Musse. Paris, 1959.
43757.58.100 Rondeau-Luzeau, Lucie. Les voix du mystère. Paris, 1959.
43761.78.825 Rooks, A.G. Jean-Paul Sartre's concepts of freedom and value. Natal, 1959.
FL 6001.959 Rousseau, J.J. Oeuvres complètes. Paris, 1959. 4v.
37574.875 Rousselot, Jean. Les nouveaux poètes français. Paris, 1959.
43757.93.130 Roussin, André. Comédies d'amour. Paris, 1959.
43757.93.1100 Rouveret, René. Si les fleuves parlaient. Paris, 1959.
43757.96.4130 Roy, Jules. Les belles croisades. Paris, 1959.
43761.13.130 Sachs, Maurice. Le voile de Veronique. Paris, 1959.
43761.31.140 Sagan, Françoise. Aimez-vous Brahms. Paris, 1959.
43761.32.100 Sage, Kay. Faut dire ce qui est. Paris, 1959.
43761.41.8100 St. Clair, Georges. L'automne et les courlis. Paris, 1959.
43761.41.2100 St. Marcoux, Jeanne. La guitare andalouse. Paris, 1959.
43761.49.2100 Salgas, Simone. Folles saisons. Paris, 1959.
41557.9.43.15 Sand, George. Lettres inédites de George Sand et de Pauline Viardat. Paris, 1959.
41557.9.58 Sand, George. Le voyage à Majorque de George Sand et seduc Chopin. Paris, 1959.
43761.77.705 Sarraute, Nathalie. Martereau. N.Y., 1959.
43761.77.149 Sarraute, Nathalie. Le planétarium. Paris, 1959.
43761.78.735.5 Sartre, Jean Paul. Nausea. Norfolk, 1959.
37563.87.5 Saulnier, Verdun L. La littérature française de la renaissance. 5. éd. Paris, 1959.
43780.5.810 Savet, Gabrielle. André Suarès. Paris, 1959.
41545.80 Scales, Derek P. Alphonse Karr. Genève, 1959.

1959 - cont.

38526.48.36 Scève, Maurice. Les hommes de la Renaissance. Paris, 1959.
38526.48.30.5 Scève, Maurice. Saulsaye. Cambridge, Mass., 1959.
38525.6.25 Schmidt, Albert M. L'amour noir. Monaco, 1959.
41522.20.80 Schmook, Gerard. Ein parijse beau onder Antwerpse jolikes. Gent, 1959.
41522.3.75 Schuetz, Günther. Barbey d'Aurevilly als Kritiker. Mainz, 1959.
43763.45.100 Schwarz-Bart, André. Le dernier des justes. Paris, 1959.
40515.2.36.5 Scott, Geoffrey. The portrait of Zélide. N.Y., 1959.
37556.175 Seguin, Jean Pierre. Nouvelles à sensations canards du XIXe siècle. Paris, 1959.
41543.22.75 Sénelier, Jean. Gerard de Nerval. Paris, 1959.
43628.1.515 Sereville, G. del. Sacha Guitry mon mari. Paris, 1959.
43765.77.100 Serreau, Geneviève. Le fondateur. Paris, 1959.
38575.23.112 Siciliano, Italo. Corneille. Venezia, 1959.
40587.140 Sieburg, Friedrich. Chateaubriand. Stuttgart, 1959.
43769.54.410 Simenon, Georges. Une confidence de Maigret. Paris, 1959.
43769.54.440 Simenon, Georges. Le roman de l'homme. Paris, 1959.
43769.54.668 Simenon, Georges. La vieille. Paris, 1959.
43769.56.2700 Simon, Claude. The wind. N.Y., 1959.
43769.56.3100 Simon, Jean Pierre. Terre de violence, roman. Paris, 1959.
43769.56.130 Simon, Pierre Henri. Portrait d'un officier. Paris, 1959.
43769.56.4100 Simonin, A. Touchez pas au grisbi. Paris, 1959.
42557.12.3 Simonson, Raoul. Oeuvres de Émile Verhaeren. Bruxelles, 1959.
43761.39.890 Smith, Maxwell A. Knight of the air. London, 1959.
40551.27 Spaemann, Robert. Der Ursprung der Soziologie aus dem Geist der Restauration. München, 1959.
43776.41.125 Spire, André. Poèmes juifs. Paris, 1959.
40593.22.5 Staël Holstein, Anne Louise. De la littérature considéreé dans ses rapports avec les institutions sociales. v.1-2. Genève, 1959.
43779.24.110 Stéphane, R. Une singulière affinité, roman. Paris, 1959.
43779.25.3100 Steuer, Raphaëla. David Rex; drame. Paris, 1959.
43779.67.100 Stoumon, M. Dans l'Alpille d'Or. Bruxelles, 1959.
43780.50.120 Sulivan, Jean. Bonheur des rebelles. Paris, 1959.
43780.50.110 Sulivan, Jean. Provocation. Paris, 1959.
43780.69.25 Supervielle, Jules. Poèmes choisis. Montevideo, 1959.
43780.69.335 Supervielle, Jules. Les suites d'une course. Paris, 1959.
43544.81.2805 Susini, Jean. Henri Bosco. Alès, 1959.
38542.12.20 Sutcliffe, Frank Edmund. Guez de Balzac et son temps. Paris, 1959.
38585.16.295 Tans, J.A.G. Vrijheid en voorbeschibbing bij Racine. Groningen, 1959.
42587.63.300 Testard, Maurice. Juliette à Sylvie. Paris, 1959.
43620.2.360 Teuler, Gabriel. Apres Gide. Paris, 1959.
40597.2.460 Teuler, Gabriel. Du côté de Balzac. Paris, 1959.
37568.200 Tfitzer, Leo. Marcel Proust. Torino, 1959.
43788.5.220 Tharaud, Jérôme. Contes de Notre Dame. Paris, 1959.
43788.24.1110 Théron, Germaine. L'arbre et l'écorce. Paris, 1959.
43788.41.5100 Thibon, Gustave. Vous serez comme des dieux. Paris, 1959.
43701.63.880 Thierry, Jean Jacques. Montherlant vu par des jeunes de 17 à 27 ans. Paris, 1959.
41557.10.205 Thomas, Edith. George Sand. Paris, 1959.
V43500.307 Thomin, René. Les chrysalides. Paris, 1959.
43788.25.110 Thoorens, L. La vie passionne de Honoré de Balzac. Paris, 1959.
37563.24.5 Tilley, Arthur A. The literature of the French renaissance. N.Y., 1959. 2v.
40534.40 Tissier, André. M. de Crac, gentilhomme garcon. Paris, 1959.
40546.24.5 Tocqueville, Alexis de. The European revolution and correspondence. Garden City, 1959.
43792.75.2700 Torres, Tereska. Not yet. London, 1959.
40597.2.500 Torres Bodet, J. Balzac. México, 1959.
43792.90.120 Toulet, Paul Jean. Lettres de P.J. Toulet et d'Émile Henriot. Paris, 1959.
43793.42.2100 Triolaire, I. Poèmes. Gap, 1959.
43793.42.240 Triolet, Elsa. L'âge de nylon. Paris, 1959. 3v.
43793.43.100 Tristan, Frédérick. Le Dieu des mouches. Paris, 1959.
43793.66.100 Trooz, Charles de. Le concert dans la bibliothèque. Bruxelles, 1959.
43793.67.240 Troyat, Henri. Les compagnons du coquelicot. Paris, 1959.
43793.67.745 Troyat, Henri. Elizabeth. N.Y., 1959.
37556.143.10 Turnell, Martin. The art of French fiction. London, 1959.
37556.143.12 Turnell, Martin. The art of French fiction. Norfolk, 1959.
37543.523 Université d'Aix-Marseilles. Faculté des lettres, Aix. Hommage au doyen Etienne Gros. Gap, 1959.
43822.50.130 Vailland, Roger. Les mauvais coups. Paris, 1959.
43822.50.725 Vailland, Roger. Monsieur Jean. 4e éd. Paris, 1959.
42543.62.100 Valentin, N. Mon père Léon Hennique. Paris, 1959.
37543.426 Valeri, Diego. Précis historique et anthologie de la littérature française. 11. éd. Milano, 1959.
37548.200 Vanwelkenhuyzen, Gustave. Vocations littéraires. Genève, 1959.
43823.48.100 Velan, Yves. Je. Paris, 1959.
42576.15.275 Vérard, René. Epilogue de "L'affaire Bovary". Rouen, 1959.
43823.75.4100 Vergez, Raoul. Les tours inachevées. Paris, 1959.
42557.18.705 Verlaine, Paul. Gedichte. Heidelberg, 1959.
42557.18.710 Verlaine, Paul. Poésies choisies. 2. éd. Roma, 1959.
42582.25.50 Verne, Jules. Le tour du monde en quatre-vingts jours. Paris, 1959.
43824.3.260 Vialar, Paul. La candinière de l'empereur. Paris, 1959.
43824.3.280 Vialar, Paul. Les quatre Zingari. Paris, 1959.
43824.3.270 Vialar, Paul. Le roman des bêtes de chasse. Paris, 1959.
43824.3.1130 Vian, Boris. Les batisseurs d'empire. Paris, 1959.
40583.285 Vianu, Tudor. Ideile lui Stendhal. Bucuresti, 1959.
41563.50.5 Vidocq, Eugène François. Les chauffeurs du nord. Paris, 1959.
37542.48 Vier, Jacques. Histoire de la littérature française. XVIe - XVIIe siècles. Paris, 1959.
37568.180 Vigorelli, Giancarlo. Carte francesi. Torino, 1959.
43824.48.100 Vilallonga, José Luis de. L'homme de sang. Paris, 1959.
43824.51.1110 Villandry, A. Meridien 40. Paris, 1959.
38514.20.7 Villon, François. Oeuvres. Paris, 1959.
43824.90.1130 Vivier, Robert. Chronos rêve. Bruxelles, 1959.
43826.3.130 Vlaminck, Maurice de. D'un lit dans l'autre. Monte-Carlo, 1959.
43827.41.1110 Voillemot, Germaine. L'oeil solaire, poèmes. Paris, 1959.
39545.35.60 Voltaire, François Marie Arouet de. Candide. Paris, 1959.
39545.55 Voltaire, François Marie Arouet de. La pucelle d'Orleans. Monte-Carlo, 1959?

Chronological Listing

1959 - cont.

37544.110 Vovard, André. Les turqueries dans la littérature française. Toulouse, 1959.

39545.4.11 Wade, Ira Owen. Voltaire and Candide. Princeton, 1959.

43830.48.120 Walder, Francis. Cendre et or. 7e éd. Paris, 1959.

43830.48.110 Walder, Francis. The negotiators. N.Y., 1959.

39544.335 Waldinger, René. Voltaire and reform in the light of the French revolution. Genève, 1959.

42584.25.265 Walter, Gerhard. Emile Zola. München, 1959.

43833.20.140 Weil, Simone. Leçons de philosophie. Paris, 1959.

37543.333 Widmer, Walter. Fug und Unfug des Übersetzens. Köln, 1959.

43512.23.100 Wielander, Angelus. Ein Tiroler Christenspiegel des 14. Affaltern am Albis, 1959.

43697.75.865 Wolf, Bernhard. Das ontologische Mysterium. München, 1959.

43845.13.120 Yacine, Kateb. Le cercle des représailles, théâtre. Paris, 1959.

43852.89.170 Yourcenar, Marguerite. Denier du rêve. Paris, 1959.

43538.76.925 Zamarriego, T. Tipología sacerdotal en la novela contemporánea: Bernanos, Maurlac, Geronella. Madrid, 1959.

43744.67.1405 Zéphir, J.J. La personalité humaine. Paris, 1959.

42584.2.5 Zola, Emile. Lettres inédites à Henry Céard. Providence, Rhode Island, 1959.

42584.23.19 Zola, Emile. Salons. Genève, 1959.

196-

43688.2.95 Belloni, Georges. La grande âme de Louis Le Cardonnel. Paris, 196-?

37583.302.1 Brenner, Clarence Dietz. Eighteenth-century French plays. N.Y., 196-?

V43550.58.780 Camus, Albert. Neznakomets. Paris, 196-?

43769.90.800 Canard, J. Daniel Sivet. Roanne, 196-?

42576.65.13.185 Cevasco, George A. J.K. Huysmans in England and America. Charlottesville, 196-.

37596.10.4.1 Chrestien de Troyes. Philomena. Concordances et index établis d'après l'édition. Liège, 196-.

42586.32.75 Coster, Charles de. La leggenda di Thyl Ulenspiegel. Milano, 196-?

43565.89.140 Daumal, René. Le Lyon rouge. Paris, 196-?

43526.65.985 Diviš, Vladimir. Apollinaire; chronique d'une vie. Paris, 196-.

41571.16.13 Hugo, Victor. Les misérables. N.Y., 196-?

43688.42.1100 Lejeune, Claire. La ganque et le feu. Paris, 196-.

43690.62.100 Linze, Georges. Manifestes poétiques, 1951-1961. Paris, 196-.

42578.31.330 Samopaloff, Andrée. Le nihiliste. Cleveland, 196-.

43824.3.1240 Vian, Boris. J'irai cracher sur vos tombes. n.p., 196-?

1960

43512.75.230 Achard, Marcel. L'amour est difficile. Paris, 1960.

43514.6.130 Adamov, Arthur. Les âmes mortes. Paris, 1960.

43517.2.110 Agadjanian, G. Le froid de l'enfer. Paris, 1960.

43522.25.2100 Alexandnan, Lucien. L'homme des lointains. Paris, 1960.

43522.25.1110 Alexis, Jacques Stephen. Romancero aux etoiles. Paris, 1960.

43522.50.100 Allen, Suzanne. L'êle du dedans. Paris, 1960.

43524.22.2100 André, Robert. Un combat opiniâtre. Paris, 1960.

43524.22.3100 Andries, A. De ci, de là et d'ailleurs. Bruxelles, 1960.

43524.67.235 Anouilh, Jean. Becket; or, The honor of God. N.Y., 1960.

43524.67.230 Anouilh, Jean. Becket, ou L'honneur de Dieu. Paris, 1960.

43524.67.775 Anouilh, Jean. The fighting cock. N.Y., 1960.

43524.67.240 Anouilh, Jean. Pièces costumées. Paris, 1960.

43526.24.100 Apesteguy, Pierre. Au nom du Père. Paris, 1960.

43526.65.300 Apollinaire, Guillaume. Chroniques d'art. Paris, 1960.

43526.65.117 Apollinaire, Guillaume. Le dossier d'Alcools. Geneve, 1960.

43527.3.380A Aragon, Louis. Les poetes. Paris, 1960.

43528.48.220 Arland, Marcel. A perdre haleine. Paris, 1960.

43528.48.215 Arland, Marcel. Je vaus écris. Paris, 1960.

43528.58.3100 Arnaud, Claude. Véronique. Paris, 1960.

43528.89.110 Arnothy, Christine. Pique-nique en Sologne. Paris, 1960.

43528.61.200 Arnoux, Alexandre. Zulma l'infidelle. Paris, 1960.

43761.78.845 Arntz, Joseph. Die liefde in de ontologie van Jean Paul Sartre. Nijmegen, 1960.

43528.73.700 Arrabal, Fernando. The automobile graveyard. N.Y., 1960.

37573.619.10 Association des écrivains combattants. Anthologie des écrivains morts à la guerre,1939-1945. Paris, 1960.

37565.165 Atkinson, Geoffroy. Le sentiment de la nature et le retour a la vie simple. Geneve, 1960.

42562.65 Aubanel, Henry. Camarguaises. Paris, 1960.

38527.22.5 Aubigné, Théodore Agrippa d'. Le printemps. Paris, 1960.

43531.78.100 Aury, Dominique. Literary landfalls. London, 1960.

43532.23.170 Aveline, Claude. C'est vrai, mais il ne faut pas le croire. Paris, 1960.

43535.54.330 Aymé, Marcel. Les tiroirs de l'inconnu. Paris, 1960.

43535.58.100F Aynard, R. Traversées. Paris, 1960.

42575.116 Baldick, Robert. The Goncourts. London, 1960.

43537.60.100 Ballet, René. Echec et mat. Paris, 1960.

37568.191 Balmas, E.H. Situazioni e profili. Milano, 1960.

43538.76.900 Baly, Joseph. Georges Bernanos. Paris, 1960.

40597.11.20 Balzac, Honoré de. Beatrix. Paris, 1960.

40597.6.1A Balzac, Honoré de. Correspondance. Paris, 1960-64. 5v.

40596.33 Balzac, Honoré de. Le curé de village. Paris, 1960.

40597.35.82 Balzac, Honoré de. Le médecin de campagne. Paris, 1960.

40597.29.4.90 Balzac, Honoré de. Le père Goriot. Paris, 1960.

40597.75.15 Balzac, Honoré de. Les petits bourgeois. Paris, 1960.

37556.7 Bar, Francis. Le genre burlesque en France au XVIIe siècle. Paris, 1960.

39545.4.16A Barber, William. Voltaire. London, 1960.

43537.77.5120 Baroche, Jacques. Le sang des vierges. Dijon, 1960.

41522.13.8.98 Baudelaire, Charles. Baudelaire. London, 1960.

41522.13.9.40 Baudelaire, Charles. Les fleurs du mal. Paris, 1960.

43537.99.160 Bazin, Hervé. Anom du fils. Paris, 1960.

37569.335 Bazjon, Louis. Mondes d'écrivains, destinées d'hommes. Paris, 1960.

43538.1.230 Béalu, Marcel. Contes du demi-sommeil. Perigueux, 1960.

40532.3.45 Beaumarchais, Pierre A.C. de. Beaumarchais par lui-même. Paris? 1960.

41563.33.15 Beaumont, Elie de. Mons. Cryptogame en zijn metamorphose. 's-Gravenhage, 1960.

43538.1.524A Beauvoir, Simone de. La force de l'âge. Paris, 1960.

43538.14.3100 Bechtel, Guy. En sortir au pas. Paris, 1960.

43538.14.180 Beckett, Samuel. La derniere bande. Paris, 1960.

1960 - cont.

43538.36.110 Béhaine, René. Pièces à conviction. Paris, 1960.

43538.49.120 Belen (pseud.). Et délivrez nous du mâle. Paris, 1960.

43538.49.110 Belen (pseud.). La reine des sabbats. Paris, 1960.

37568.205 Bémol, Maurice. Essai sur l'orientation des littératures de langue française au XXe siècle. Paris, 1960.

43822.49.1155 Bémol, Maurice. La méthode critique de Paul Valéry. Paris, 1960.

43538.61.200 Benoît, Pierre. Le commandeur. Paris, 1960.

43538.76.5110 Bernard, Michel. La plage. Paris, 1960.

43822.49.1340 Berne-Joffroy, André. Valéry. Paris, 1960.

43538.78.5100 Berry, Andrée Gabrielle. Le tombeau de Micheline; poèmes. Paris, 1960.

43538.77.9100 Bertoye, Achille. Deux existence tourmentees. Paris, 1960.

FL 1108.28.21 Bertrand, Jacques. Les oeuvres wallonnes. Charleroi, 1960.

43538.78.4100 Bertrand, Mirou. Fériale. Paris, 1960.

43538.82.3110 Bessette, Hélène. La route bleue. Paris, 1960.

43538.84.110 Bessy, Maurice. Car c'est Dieu qu'on enterre. Paris, 1960.

40582.12.70 Beyle, Henri. Armance; or Scenes from a Parisian salon in 1827. London, 1960.

40582.9.45 Beyle, Henri. The charterhouse of Parma. N.Y., 1960.

40582.65 Beyle, Henri. Féder. London, 1960.

43540.7.160 Bibescu, M.L. La nymphe Europe. Paris, 1960.

43540.3.95 Billy, André. L'allegretto de septième. Paris, 1960.

42575.112.10A Billy, André. The Goncourt brothers. 1st American ed. N.Y., 1960.

43822.49.1330 Blucher, Karl. Strategie des Geistes. Frankfurt, 1960.

41574.550 Blum-Manderieux, Arlette. Juliette Drouet et Victor Hugo. Paris, 1960.

43697.52.860 Blumenthal, Gerda. André Malraux. Baltimore, 1960.

43544.112.700 Boileau, Pierre. The tube. London, 1960.

43697.52.855 Boisdeffre, Pierre. André Malraux. 5. éd. Paris, 1960.

37547.100 Bordeaux, H. Portrait de la Savoie par ses écrivains. Thonon-les-Bains, 1960.

42563.36.315 Bordeaux, Henry. L'amour de la terre et de la maison. Paris, 1960.

42563.36.140 Bordeaux, Henry. Reflets de la montagne. Paris, 1960.

43544.74.4100 Borderie, Roger. Les moineaux de pluie. Paris, 1960.

43544.74.2100 Bordonove, Georges. Les lentations. Paris, 1960.

43544.81.160 Bory, Jean Louis. Musique. Paris, 1960.

43544.89.2160 Bosquet, Alain. Le mécréant; roman. Paris, 1960.

43544.88.2100 Boulanger, Daniel. Le gouverneur Polygame. Paris, 1960.

42555.44.162 Boulay, Daniel. L'obscurité esthétique de Mallarmé. Paris, 1960.

43544.88.5100 Boule de Gomme (pseud.). Vitamines d'estaminet. Poems. Paris, 1960.

43544.108.120 Boulle, Pierre. Un métier de seigneur. Paris, 1960.

43544.108.730 Boulle, Pierre. A noble profession. N.Y., 1960.

43544.87.3100 Bourbon Busset, Jacques de. Memoires d'un lion. Paris, 1960.

43757.3.350 Bourin, André. Connaissance de Jules Romains. Paris, 1960.

43544.89.3120 Bourniquel, Camille. L'ete des solitudes. Paris, 1960.

42554.49.1100 Bouvier, Jean Bernard. L'oeuvre de Jules Gross. Genève, 1960.

39533.20.30 Brandwajn, R. Cyrano de Bergerac. Warszawa, 1960.

43545.4.4210 Brasillach, Robert. Presence de Virgile. Paris, 1960.

43545.24.2100 Brest, Simon. Les yeux mangés. Rodez, 1960.

43545.24.155 Breton, André. Nadja. N.Y., 1960.

43545.24.775 Breton, André. Nadja. Neske, 1960.

43545.66.110 Brosse, Jacques. L'éphémère. Paris, 1960.

43823.75.2745 Bruller, Jean. For the time being. London, 1960.

42586.32.525 Brussels. Bibliotheque royale. Charles de Coster. Bruxelles, 1960.

43551.59.815 Buhler, J. Blaise Cendrars. Bienne, 1960.

43546.87.65 Butor, Michel. Degrés. Paris, 1960.

43546.87.70 Butor, Michel. Passing time. N.Y., 1960.

43546.87.60 Butor, Michel. Repertoire. Paris, 1960. 2v.

43546.87.62 Butor, Michel. Sobre literatura. Barcelona, 1960.

43550.6.110 Cabanis, José. Le bonheur du jour. Paris, 1960.

39534.32.4.10 Cadorel, Raymond. Scarron et la nouvelle espagnole dans le Roman comique. Aix-en-Provence, 1960.

43550.19.105 Cadou, René Guy. Hélène, ou Le règne végétal, 1944-1951. Paris, 1960.

38587.8.80 Calame, Alexandre. Regnard, sa vie et son oeuvre. Paris, 1960.

37547.18.1 Calmon, Jean. Essai de bibliographie du départment de lot. Supplement. pt. 1-3. Cahors, 1960-

43550.58.718 Camus, Albert. Caligula and three other plays. N.Y., 1960.

43550.58.21 Camus, Albert. Collected fiction. London, 1960.

43550.58.760 Camus, Albert. The possessed. N.Y., 1960.

43550.58.764 Camus, Albert. Resistance, rebellion, and death. N.Y., 1960.

41574.582 Carneiro Leão, Antonio. Victor Hugo no Brasil. 1. éd. Rio de Janeiro, 1960.

43550.83.1100 Castillou, Henry. La légion d'Oumrah. Paris, 1960.

43550.98.700 Cayrol, Jean. Foreign bodies, a novel. N.Y., 1960.

43550.98.180 Cayrol, Jean. Les pleurs et les déliés. Paris, 1960.

43551.59.11 Cendrars, Blaise. Oeuvres, édition complète. v. 2-7,8. Paris, 1960- 7v.

43551.59.253 Cendrars, Blaise. Saint Joseph de Cupertino. Paris, 1960.

43551.79.130 Césaire, Aimé. Ferrements. Paris, 1960.

43551.80.150 Cesbron, Gilbert. Avoir été. Paris, 1960.

43552.1.1110 Chaamba, Abdallah (pseud.). Le vieillard et l'enfant de 1958. Périgueux, 1960?

43552.1.110 Chabaneix, Philippe. Musiques du temps perdu. Paris, 1960.

42556.28.280 Chadwick, Charles. Études sur Rimbaud. Paris, 1960.

43538.76.930 Chaigne, Louis. Georges Bernanos. 3. ed. Paris, 1960.

37569.300 Chapsal, Madeleine. Les écrivains en personne. Paris, 1960.

43552.4.2023 Char, René. Anthologie. Paris, 1960.

43552.6.2100 Charreyre, Eugene. Fatima. Paris, 1960.

43552.5.1030 Chartier, Émile. Morceaux choisis. Paris, 1960.

43552.5.1185 Chartier, Émile. Les passions et la sagesse. Paris, 1960.

43552.5.6100 Charton, J.C. Le signe féminin, roman. Paris, 1960.

43552.15.100 Chazot, Jacques. Sophie Ripaille. Paris, 1960.

43552.18.120 Chédid, Andrée. Le sixième jour. Paris, 1960.

FL 398.13.12.2 Chevalier, Maurice. With love. Boston, 1960.

FL 398.12.10 Chevalier, Maurice. With love. Boston, 1960.

43552.25.2130 Chevallier, Gabriel. Les filles sont libres. Paris, 1960.

40517.44.15 Choderlos de Laclos, Pierre A.F. Les liaisons dangereuses. N.Y., 1960.

Chronological Listing

1960 - cont.

38514.29.5 Cigada, Sergio. L'opera poetica di Charles d'Orleans. Milano, 1960.
43554.1.30 Claude, Catherine. Le magot de Josepha. Paris, 1960.
43554.2.470 Claudel, Paul. Connaissance de l'Est! Paris, 1960.
43554.2.706 Claudel, Paul. The tidings brought to Mary. Chicago, 1960.
43554.2.200.10 Claudel, Paul. Two dramas. Chicago, 1960.
43788.41.2800 Clémeur, Marcel. L'oeuvre poétique de Marcel Thiry, du symbolisme à l'école du regard. Vieux-Virton, 1960.
43554.66.100 Clostermann, Pierre. Appui-feu sur l'oued Hallaïl. Paris, 1960.
43556.1.450 Cocteau, Jean. Guide à l'usage des visiteurs de la Chapelle Saint Blaise des Simples. Monaco, 1960.
43556.1.412 Cocteau, Jean. Jean Cocteau. Paris, 1960.
43556.1.202 Cocteau, Jean. Poésie critique. Paris, 1960. 2v.
37543.450 Cohn, Robert G. The writer's way in France. Philadelphia, 1960.
43556.49.505 Colette, Sidonie Gabrielle. La fleur de l'âge. Lausanne, 1960.
43556.49.737 Colette, Sidonie Gabrielle. Six novels. N.Y., 1960?
43556.58.120 Conchon, Georges. La lorriola de la Vicfaire. Paris, 1960.
37565.175 Congrès National de Littérature Comparée. Actes. [La France, La Bourgogne et la Suisse au XVIIIe siècle]. Paris, 1960.
43556.61.100 Constantineau, Gilles. Simples poèmes et ballades. Montréal, 1960.
37569.398 Controverses; theatre, roman, cinema. Paris, 1960.
43626.22.835 Cook, M.G. Hallucination and death as motifs of escape in the novels of Julien Green. Washington, 1960.
38576.12.42.50 Corneille, Thomas. Le berger extravagant. Genève, 1960.
38576.12.42.51 Corneille, Thomas. Le berger extravagant. Thèse. Genève, 1960.
43556.87.2100 Cotte, Jean Louis. Le sang des taureaux. Paris, 1960.
43556.89.3100 Cousseau, Jacques. Les singes. Paris, 1960.
37565.160 Cremonesi, C. Corso di letteratura francese. Milano, 1960.
43560.78.180 Curtis, Jean Louis. La parade. Paris, 1960.
37568.195 Curtius, Ernst R. Französischer Geist im zwanzigsten Jahrhundert. 2. Aufl. Bern, 1960.
42566.16.125 Dambska-Prokop, W. Le style indirect libre dans la prose narrative d'Alphonse Daudet. Krakow, 1960.
43565.60.1130 Daninos, Pierre. Un certain Monsieur Blot. Paris, 1960.
43565.89.7110 Dauphin, Marcel. Pierre Sully. Port-au-Prince, 1960.
43565.91.130 Davet, Michel. Biche et le roi de Naples. Paris, 1960.
43565.91.120 Davet, Michel. Éclatantes ténères. Paris, 1960.
43620.2.410 Davies, John C. A distinguished modern humanist. Armidale, 1960?
43566.50.2100 Debisle, Gérard. Rhapsodie caraïbe. Paris, 1960.
43701.63.890 Debrie-Panel, Nicole. Montherlant. Lyon, 1960.
37555.538 Décaudin, M. La crise des valeurs symbolistes. Toulouse, 1960.
43566.17.1100 Dedet, Christian. Le plus grand des taureaux. Paris, 1960.
43566.29.110 Defosse, Marcel. Le juge de Malte. Bruxelles, 1960.
43566.35.1100 Deguy, Michel. Fragment du cadastre. Paris, 1960.
FL 377.90 Deierkauf-Holsboer, Sophie Wilma. L'histoire de la mise en scène dans le théâtre français à Paris de 1600 à 1673. Paris, 1960.
42544.31.32 Delay, Jean Paul Louis. Discours de réception de M. Jean Delay à l'Academie Française et réponse de M. Pasteur Vallery-Radot. Paris, 1960.
43566.48.6720 Del Castillo, Michel. The disinherited. N.Y., 1960.
43566.48.6120 Del Castillo, Michel. La guitarra. Barcelona, 1960.
43566.51.6100 Delvolvé, Laure. Quand les carnassiers n'y sont pas; récit. Paris, 1960.
43566.62.5110 Denuzière, Maurice. Une tombe en Toscane. Paris, 1960.
43566.62.115 Déon, Michel. La carotte et le bâton. Paris, 1960.
40597.2.262 Descaves, Pierre. Balzac. Paris, 1960.
Mol 604.10 Descotes, Maurice. Les grands rôles du théâtre de Molière. Paris, 1960.
43566.78.1100 Des Forêts, Louis R. La chambre des enfants. Paris, 1960.
43566.80.1110 Deslandes, André. Le hasard abolit le hasard. Paris, 1960.
43566.81.1120 Des Ligneris, F. Bijoux, roman. Paris, 1960.
43566.81.2140 Desmarest, M.A. A la recherche de l'amour. Paris, 1960.
38526.13.65 Desportes, Philippe. Les amours d'Hippolyte. Genève, 1960.
43566.82.8100 Desse, G. Et sur cette pierre. Paris, 1960.
43566.82.7715A Destouches, Louis Ferdinand. Journey to the end of the night. N.Y., 1960.
43566.82.7115 Destouches, Louis Ferdinand. Nord, roman. Paris, 1960.
43567.79.170 Dhôtel, André. Le neveu de Pareucloud. Paris, 1960.
38526.7.50 Dickinson, G. Du Bellay in Rome. Leiden, 1960.
37543.485 Diéguez, M. de. L'écrivain et son langage. Paris, 1960.
43573.37.100 Dohet, Adelin Pierre. Tous dieux éteints. Bruxelles, 1960.
43538.5.805 Doisy, M. Belphégor et le clerc. Paris, 1960?
39566.180 Doolittle, J. Rameau's nephew. Genève, 1960.
43573.76.75 Dorgelès, Roland. Sous le casque blanc. Paris, 1960.
43573.89.2100 Douassot, Jean. Sens inverse. Paris, 1960.
37562.316 Dragonetti, Roger. La technique poétique des trouvères dans la chanson courtoise. Brugge, 1960.
43574.75.112 Druon, Maurice. Alexander. London, 1960.
38526.6.47 Du Bellay, Joachim. Les antiquitez de Rome et les regrets. Genève, 1960.
43576.87.2100 Dubit, Ernest. Domaines, les idées et les mots. Fribourg, 1960.
43576.8.35 Dubois La Chartre, André. Les amants de Schoenfelds. Paris, 1960.
43576.9.3100 Dubreuil, Aline. Ulysse et les sirènes. Paris, 1960.
42568.19.21.17 Ducasse, I.L. Poésies. 1. éd. Paris, 1960.
43552.14.100 Du Chazand, Henri. Printemps. Paris, 1960.
43576.13.2110 Duchemin, J. Rendez-vous sous l'horloge. Paris, 1960.
43576.6.775 Duhamel, Georges. Nouvelles du sombre empire. Paris, 1960.
41538.200 Dumas, Alexandre. Voyage en Russie. Paris, 1960.
43576.71.3100 Duploug, Fernand. L'homme de quarante ans. Paris, 1960.
43576.74.3100 Durand, C. Le bord de la mer. Paris, 1960.
43576.74.2170 Duras, Marguerite. Dix heures et demie du soir en été. Paris, 1960.
43576.74.2180 Duras, Marguerite. Hiroshima mon amour. Paris, 1960.
43576.74.2700 Duras, Marguerite. Moderato cantabile. N.Y., 1960.
43576.74.2160 Duras, Marguerite. Les viaducs de la Seine-et-Oise. Paris, 1960.
39594.3.50.10 Durkheim, E. Montesquieu and Rousseau. Ann Arbor, 1960.

1960 - cont.

40535.32.45 Durry, Marie J. A propos de Marivaux. Paris, 1960.
FL 394.122 Dussane, B. (Mme.). La comédie-française. Paris, 1960.
43576.90.1120 Duvignaud, Jean. La chasse à l'aigle. Paris, 1960.
42557.14.78 Eaubanne, Françoise. Verlaine et Rimbaud. Paris, 1960.
42557.14.77 Eaubonne, Françoise. La vie passionnée de Verlaine. Paris, 1960.
43581.89.130 Eaubonne, Françoise d'. Le temps d'apprendre à vivre. Paris, 1960.
43697.89.2800 Editions de minuit provocation à la desobéissance. Paris, 1960.
37574.907 Ekeloef, Gunnar. Hundra år modern fransk dikt. Stockholm, 1960.
43590.50.110 Ekman, Pierre A. Maria des quatre vents. Paris, 1960.
38524.152 Elledge, Scott. The continental model; selected French critical essays of the seventeenth century. Minneapolis, 1960.
37574.545.12 Éluard, Paul. La poésie du passé. Paris, 1960.
43592.41.120 Émié, Louis. Le volubilis. Villeneuve-sur-Lot, 1960.
43738.1.850 Emmerich, H. Nominalsuffixe im Sprachgebrauch Charles Péguys. Marburg, 1960.
43598.54.120 Esménard, Jean d'. Les chercheurs de amondes. Paris, 1960.
37573.316 Etiemble, René. Romanciers du XVIIIe siècle. Paris, 1960. 2v.
43780.69.805 Étiemble, René. Supervielle. Paris, 1960.
41522.18.365 Fairlie, Alison. Baudelaire. London, 1960.
43554.2.1060 Farabel, René. Le jeu de l'acteur. Paris, 1960.
43822.49.1255 Fehr, A.J.A. Les dialogues antiques de Paul Valéry. Leiden, 1960.
37544.80 Feigelson, Raph. Écrivains juifs de langue française. Paris, 1960.
FL 6139.60 Fetscher, Iring. Rousseaus politische Philosophie zur Geschichte des demokratischen Freiheitsbegriffs. Neuwied, 1960.
41592.8.10 Fischer, Jan O. Pierre-Jean de Béranger. 1. Aufl. Berlin, 1960.
42576.31.40 Flaubert, Gustave. Salammbô. Paris, 1960.
43611.50.110 Follain, Jean. Des heures. Paris, 1960.
43611.63.150 Fontaine, Anne. Henri Mondor. Paris, 1960.
43611.77.100 Fortin, Charles. Primitivité cosmique. Paris, 1960.
43611.76.120 Forton, Jean. L'épingle du jeu. Paris, 1960.
37583.660 Four modern French comedies. N.Y., 1960.
43611.90.100 Fourré, Maurice. Tête-de-Nègre. Paris, 1960.
FL 386.101 Fowlie, Wallace. Dionysus in Paris. N.Y., 1960.
42555.44.168 Fraenrel, Ernest. Les dessins trans-conscients de Stéphane Mallarmé. Paris, 1960.
43612.3.1100 Fraigneau, André. Les étonnements de Guillaume Francoeur. Paris, 1960.
37564.255 France. Archives. Documents du Minutier central concernant. Paris, 1960.
40546.27 France. Centre National de la Recherche Scientifique. Alexis de Tocqueville. Paris, 1960.
43550.58.880 France. Embassy. United States. Albert Camus, 1913-1960. N.Y., 1960?
43612.4.2100 Francolin, Claude. About de souffle. Paris, 1960.
37563.70.10 Françon, Marcel. Notes de cours. Cambridge, Mass., 1960.
43612.4.3100 Frank, Jean M. Journal d'un autre. Paris, 1960.
43616.41.2150 Gaillard, Robert. Marie des Isles. Paris, 1960- 7v.
43616.51.1100 Galtier-Boissière, Jean. Memoires d'un Parisien. Paris, 1960- 3v.
43616.60.100 Ganne, Gilbert. La panache blanc. Paris, 1960.
43616.78.705 Gary, Romain. A European education. N.Y., 1960.
43616.78.720 Gary, Romain. Nothing important ever dies. London, 1960.
43616.78.200 Gary, Romain. La promesse de l'aube. Paris, 1960.
43616.79.705 Gascar, Pierre. Beasts and men. N.Y., 1960.
43616.79.160 Gascar, Pierre. Soleils. Paris, 1960.
43616.81.110 Gaspar, Élisabeth. Les grilles du parc. Paris, 1960.
41542.31.25 Gautier, Théophile. Gentle enchanter. London, 1960.
43617.24.100 Geeraert, Robert Lucien. La corde à danser. Tournai, 1960.
43617.78.122 Genêt, Jean. Le balcon. 2. éd. Décines, 1960.
43617.78.715 Genêt, Jean. The balcony. N.Y., 1960.
43617.78.712 Genêt, Jean. The balcony. N.Y., 1960.
43617.78.155 Genêt, Jean. The blacks. London, 1960.
43617.78.162 Genêt, Jean. Les nègres. 2. éd. Décines, 1960.
43617.59.170 Genevoix, Maurice. Au cadran de mon clocher. Paris, 1960.
43617.59.180 Genevoix, Maurice. La dernière harde. Paris, 1960.
43617.59.190 Genevoix, Maurice. Vaincre à Olympie. Paris, 1960.
40597.2.490 George, Albert. Books by Balzac. Syracuse, N.Y., 1960.
37575.300 Gérard, Marcel. Anthologie française du Luxembourg. Luxembourg, 1960.
41522.18.380 Giacomelli Deslex, M. Appunti su Charles Baudelaire. Torino, 1960.
FL 398.69 Gianndi, Paul. La vie inspirée de Gerald Philipe. Paris, 1960.
43620.2.32.20 Gide, André. L'immoraliste. Paris, 1960.
43620.2.79.167 Gide, André. The return of the prodigal son. Logan, 1960.
43620.2.35.52 Gide, André. Two symphonies. N.Y., 1960.
43667.78.805 Giedion-Welcker, C. Alfred Jarry. Zürich, 1960.
43620.39.110 Gillès, Daniel. La termitiere. Paris, 1960.
43538.76.895 Gillespie, Jessie Lynn. Le tragique dans l'oeuvre de Georges Bernanos. Genève, 1960.
43620.67.700 Giovanni, José. The bread. London, 1960.
43622.41.150 Glissant, Edouard. Le sel noir. Paris, 1960.
43625.17.110 Godel, Vahé. Entre l'Arve et le Rhône. Genève, 1960.
43699.51.802 Godoy, Armand. Milosz. Paris, 1960.
43625.49.190 Goll, Claire. Klage um Ivan. Wiesbaden, 1960.
43625.45.2100 Golon, S. (pseud.). Indomptable Angélique. Paris, 1960.
42556.28.209.5 Graaf, Daniel. Arthur Rimbaud. Assen, 1960.
43697.88.860 Grall, Xavier. François Mauriac, journaliste. Paris, 1960.
43626.2.1030 Grandmougin, J. Noenoeil, homme d'état. Paris, 1960.
42584.25.245 Grant, Richard B. Zola's Son excellence Eugène Rougon. Durham, 1960.
43626.22.270 Green, Julien. Chaque homme dans sa nuit. Paris, 1960.
43626.23.4100 Grendel, Frédéric. Le traité de paix. Paris, 1960.
43626.23.2110 Grenier, Roger. La voie romaine. Paris, 1960.
43626.66.4100 Groote, Christian de. Adolescences. Paris, 1960.
43626.66.3100 Gros, Brigitte. Véronique dans l'appareil. Paris, 1960.
43626.74.140 Groussard, Serge. Jeunesses sauvages. Paris, 1960.
V43500.131 Guégan, Jane. Trace invisible de tes pas. Ixelles, 1960.
37595.108 Guiette, Robert. Fabliaux et contes. Paris, 1960.
42584.25.260 Guillemin, Henri. Zola. Paris, 1960.
43628.42.150 Guilloux, Louis. Les batailles perdues. Paris, 1960.
43628.85.120 Guth, Paul. Jeanne la mince. Paris, 1960.
43738.1.830 Guyon, Bernard. Péguy. Paris, 1960.

1960 - cont.

43631.16.100 Haddad, Malek. L'élève et la leçon. Paris, 1960.
43631.03.120 Haedens, Kléber. Salut au Kentucky. Paris, 1960.
41596.4.165 Haldane, Charlotte F. Alfred; the passionate life of Alfred de Musset. London, 1960.
Mol 270.35 Hall, H.G. Molière: Tartuffe. London, 1960.
43538.76.899 Hallen, Oskar. Georges Bernanos. Brugge, 1960.
42545.3.365 Halls, W.D. Maurice Maeterlinck. Oxford, 1960.
43632.76.4100 Hardy, René. Le bois des amants. Paris, 1960.
43697.52.840A Hartman, Geoffrey H. André Malraux. London, 1960.
43631.79.100 Hasard, M. Ça et lá. Monte Carlo, 1960.
43632.14.110 Hecquet, Stephen. Les collégiens, roman. Paris, 1960.
43632.20.100 Héduy, Philippe. Au lieutenant des Taglaïts. Paris, 1960.
43632.50.190 Hellens, Franz. Entre toutes les femmes. Paris, 1960.
43632.6.200 Henriot, Émile. On n'est pas perdu sur la terre. Paris, 1960.
37574.900 Hinderberger, H. Französische Symbolisten. Heidelberg, 1960.
43761.42.800 Hommage à Monique St. Helièr. Neuchâtel, 1960.
43528.86.800 Hort, Jean. Antonin Artaud. Genève, 1960.
43550.58.260 Hourdin, Georges. Camus le Juste. 2. éd. Paris, 1960.
41573.36.10 Hugo, Victor. Dieu (L'océan d'en haut). Paris, 1960.
41571.3.120 Hugo, Victor. Oeuvres. Lausanne, 1960-63. 24v.
37555.690 Huguenin, Daniel. Poésie et monde humain. Saint-Étienne, 1960.
43638.35.1100 Huguenin, Jean-René. La côte sauvage. Paris, 1960.
43757.50.1185 Hulia, O.P. Romen Rollan. Chernivtsi, 1960.
43638.51.100 Hulton, Nika. The witch. London, 1960.
43638.53.120 Humbourg, Pierre. Par une nuit sans lune. Paris, 1960.
43822.49.1355 Ingrosso, O. Note su Valéry. Bari, 1960.
43656.59.635 Ionesco, Eugène. The killer, and other plays. N.Y., 1960.
43656.59.130 Ionesco, Eugène. Rhinocéros. N.Y., 1960.
43667.14.145 Jacob, Max. Le laboratoire central. Paris, 1960.
43667.15.2100 Jacquemard, Simonne. Planant sur les airs. Paris, 1960.
42577.4.45 Janssen, Carl Luplan. Le décor chez Guy de Maupassant. Copenhagen, 1960-
39566.39 Johansson, J.V. Sur la correspondance littéraire. Göteborg, 1960.
43670.89.550 Jouhandeau, M. Cocu, perdu et content. Paris, 1960.
43670.94.370 Jouve, Pierre Jean. Proses. Paris, 1960.
43671.20.110 Judrin, Roger. Lampes de prison. Paris, 1960.
43527.3.820 Juin, Hubert. Aragon. Paris, 1960.
43671.51.110 Jullian, Philippe. Chateau-Bonheur. Paris, 1960.
43757.50.1195 Kaplan, M.S. Stilisticheskoe upotreblenie antonimov v romane Romena Rollana ocharovannaia chesha. Kazan, 1960.
39594.19.90 Kassem, Badreddine. Décadence et absolutisme. Droz, 1960.
39564.40 Kazarin, A.I. Ekonomicheskie vozzreniia Deni Didro. Moskva, 1960.
43673.78.130 Kerchove, Arnold de. La racine et l'oiseau. Paris, 1960.
43673.75.2100 Kerest, Franck. Les canons du ciel. Paris, 1960.
43673.76.2105 Kern, Alfred. The clown. N.Y., 1960.
43556.1.905 Kihm, Jean Jacques. Cocteau. Paris, 1960.
37530.180 Klein, Hans W. Die Fachbücherei des Neusprachlers. Dortmund, 1960.
43680.12.100 Kochnitzky, Leon. Les éphémérides. Aalter, Belgium, 1960.
41555.48.10 Kosko, Marja. Le thème de Mateo Falcone. Paris, 1960.
43681.21.100 Kréa, Henri. La révolution et la poésie. Paris, 1960.
43761.78.860 Kummer, Bernhard. Fehlentscheidung des deutschen Theaters. Lienau, 1960.
37596.17.10 Kundert-Forrer, V. Raoul de Houdenc. Bern, 1960.
38526.26.65 Labé, Louise Charly. De vijfentwintig sonnetten van Louïze Labé. Antwerpen, 1960.
42544.26.40 Labiche, Eugène. Nouveau théâtre choisi. Paris, 1960.
V43500.147 Labour, Magdeleine. Sabliers; poèmes. Nantes, 1960.
43687.12.100 Lachaumeric, Lila. La robe de lumière. Paris, 1960.
43687.15.2110 Lacrosil, Michèle. Sapotille et le serin d'argile; roman. Paris, 1960.
Mon 220.2 Lafon, Charles. Iconographie de Montaigne. Paris, 1960.
Mon 172.2 Lafon, Charles. Iconographie de Montaigne. Paris, 1960.
43687.37.1000 Laheffe, Pierre M. La mesure et l'imaginaire. Paris, 1960.
43687.41.100 Laigret, Christian. Le métis; roman. Paris, 1960.
43822.49.1325 Laitenberger, Hugo. Der Begriff der "Absence" bei Paul Valéry. Wiesbaden, 1960.
FL 386.177.3 Lalou, René. Cinquant'anni di teatro francese. Rocca San Casciano, 1960.
37569.115.8 Lalou, René. Le roman français depuis 1900. 8. éd. Paris, 1960.
43687.60.105 Lang, André. Bagage à la consigne. Paris, 1960.
43687.60.2100 Lange, Monique. Les plantanes. Paris, 1960.
43687.60.3100 Langfus, Anna. Le sel et le soufre. Paris, 1960.
37530.170.2 Langlois, Pierre. Guide bibliographique des études littéraires. Paris, 1960.
39544.46.15 Lanson, Gustave. Voltaire. Paris, 1960.
43550.58.945 La table ronde. Albert Camus. Paris, 1960.
43687.89.7100 Lauran, Annie. La machine a fait "Tilt". Paris, 1960.
43687.89.6100 Laureillard, Rémi. Hiclem. Paris, 1960.
43687.89.1190 Laurent, Jacques. Une affaire est une affaire. Paris, 1960.
43687.89.1180 Laurent, Jacques. Les passagers pour Alger. Paris, 1960.
43687.90.2100 Lavacourt, André. Les Français de la décadence. Paris, 1960.
43688.5.5155 Léautaud, Paul. Journal of a man of letters. London, 1960.
41522.3.70 Leberruyer, Pierre. au pays de J. Barbey d'Aurevilly. Coutances, 1960.
43688.7.2100 Lebesque, M. Chroniques du Canard. Paris, 1960.
43699.51.810 Lebois, A. L'oeuvre de Milosz. Paris, 1960.
43688.9.130 Lebrau, Jean. Jean Lebrau. Rodez, 1960.
43688.14.3150 Leclèrc, Tristan. Le tambour voilé. Paris, 1960.
43688.20.100 Leduc, Violette. Trésors à prendre. Paris, 1960.
43688.34.3100 Le Gouic, Gérard. À la fonte des Blés. Paris, 1960.
37544.82.2 Lehrmann, C. L'élément juif dans la littérature française. 2. éd. Paris, 1960- 2v.
43688.53.1100 Lemaitre, Maurice. Carnets d'un fanatique. Paris, 1960.
43619.23.800 Lepage, Albert. Michel de Ghelderode. Paris, 1960?
40512.46 LeSage, Alain René. Aventuras de Gil Blas de Santillana. Barcelona, 1960.
43688.79.1100 Lescure, Jean. Treize poèmes. Paris, 1960.
43527.3.815 Lescure, P. de. Aragon. Paris, 1960.
43688.82.110 Lesort, Paul André. G.B.K. Paris, 1960.
40587.42.15 Levaillant, Maurice. Chateaubriand. Paris, 1960.
41574.570 Levalley, Sylvie. Ruy Blas. Paris, 1960.
38526.20.80 Le Vert. Le docteur amoureux. Genève, 1960.
FL 362.32 Lewicka, Halina. La lanque et le style du théâtre comique. Warszawa, 1960. 2v.
43689.66.100 Lhôte, Jean Marie. Sédiment, poème. Paris, 1960.

1960 - cont.

37569.310A Library of Congress. Gertrude Clarke Whittall Poetry and Literature Fund. French and German letters today. Washington, 1960.
43690.48.100 Lilar, Suzanne. Le divertissement portugais. Paris, 1960.
43690.68.100 Lip, F. Poèmes dans la nuit. Paris, 1960.
43693.6.100 Loba, Aké. Kocoumbo, l'etudiant noir. Paris, 1960.
42576.65.13.128 Lobet, Marcel. J.K. Huysmans. Lyon, 1960.
43693.12.100 Lo Celso, André. Eclats dans les nuages. Paris, 1960.
43693.53.1100 Lombard, Ariane. Destinations. Paris, 1960.
42577.4.31.25 Los Angeles Public Library. Index to the stories of Guy de Maupassant. Boston, 1960.
43694.13.1100 Lucciani, Jean Pierre. Contes à dormir debout. Paris, 1960.
39566.175 Luppol, I.K. Deni Didro. Moskva, 1960.
37543.470 Macchia, Giovanni. Il paradiso della ragione. Bari, 1960.
41522.18.167 Macchia, Giovanni. La poetica di Baudelaire. Roma, 1960.
37543.495 Macchia, Giovanni. Storia della letteratura francese. Roma, 1960?
37556.200 McGhee, D.M. The cult of the conte moral. Menasha, 1960.
43697.14.300 MacOrlan, Pierre. Le rire jaune, suivi de la bête conquérante. Paris, 1960.
41556.47 Maixner, Rudolf. Charles Nodier et l'Illyrie. Paris, 1960.
43697.51.1100 Maloire, Albert. Ecrits dans le soleil. Paris, 1960.
43697.51.100 Malori, Jacques. Une traversée gratuite. Paris, 1960.
43697.74.120 Maran, René. Bertrand du Gueschin. Paris, 1960.
43792.1.40 Marchandeau, Marcel. Touny-Lérys. Paris, 1960.
43697.74.6100 Marchou, Gaston. Les temps imagines. Paris, 1960.
38526.32.4.5 Marguerite d'Angoulême. L'Heptaméron. Paris, 1960.
38526.32.30 Marguerite d'Angoulême. Petit oeuvre dévot et contemplatif. Frankfurt am Main, 1960.
43697.74.7100 Marie-Josèphe (pseud.). Arthurine. Paris, 1960.
43761.78.823 Marill, René. Jean-Paul Sartre. 5. éd. Paris, 1960.
43556.49.885 Marks, Elaine. Colette. New Brunswick, 1960.
43697.79.4100 Marnat, Jean. Primates, poèmes. Paris, 1960.
38523.12.30 Marot, Clément. L'enfer. 1. ed. Cambridge, Mass., 1960.
43697.78.7100 Marsolle, Edouard. Au clair de mon âme. Paris, 1960.
43697.74.4100 Martel, François. La colère noire; roman. Paris, 1960.
FL 396.20.5 Marteo, Gian. Il teatro poplare in Francia. Bologna, 1960.
41555.43.15 Mart'ianova, Elizaveta P. Ob otrazhenii russko-frantsuzskikh kulturnykh sviazei vo frantsuzskom iazyke i literature XIX veka. Khar'kov, 1960.
37567.614 Martino, P. Le naturalisme français, 1870-1895. 6. éd. Paris, 1960.
43697.88.3705 Mauriac, Claude. The dinner party. N.Y., 1960.
43697.88.798 Mauriac, François. The stuff of youth. London, 1960.
43697.89.2100 Maurienne (pseud.). Le deserteur. Paris, 1960.
43697.89.755 Maurois, André. The art of writing. London, 1960.
43744.67.1400 Maurois, André. Le monde de Marcel Proust. Paris, 1960.
43697.89.490 Maurois, André. Pour piano seul. Paris, 1960.
42514.28.205 Maurras, Charles. Charles Maurras. Lisboa, 1960.
38523.3.71 Mayer, C.A. La religion de Marot. Genève, 1960.
42563.23.140 Meer de Walcheren, P.B.A. van der. Alles is liefde. Brugge, 1960.
43698.25.735 Meersch, M. van der. Mash of flesh. London, 1960.
43698.52.110 Mélot du Dy, Robert. Choix de poésies, 1919-1956. Paris, 1960.
43698.52.21 Mélot du Dy, Robert. Trois recits. Bruxelles, 1960.
42584.25.270 Menichelli, Gian Carlo. Bibliographie de Zola en Italie. Florence, 1960.
43699.4.100 Miatlev, Adrian. Le sacrament du divorce. Paris, 1960.
43761.39.896 Migeo, Marcel. St. Exupéry. N.Y., 1960.
43761.48.800 Mignon, Paul L. Salacrou. Paris, 1960.
37544.71 Milner, Max. Le diable dans la littérature française de Cazotte à Baudelaire, 1772-1861. Paris, 1960. 2v.
43699.65.115 Miomandre, Francis de. Caprices, nouvelles. Paris, 1960.
41574.544 Miquel, Pierre. Avec Victor Hugo. Lefort, 1960.
43699.35.100 Miquet, Jacques. Vibrante jeunesse; poèmes. Paris, 1960.
42586.32.520 Mitskevich, B.P. Sharl' de Koster stanovlenie realizma v bel'giiskoi literature. Minsk, 1960.
Mol 191.45 Molière, Jean Baptiste Poquelin. Dom Juan. Paris, 1960.
Mol 196.5.10 Molière, Jean Baptiste Poquelin. The school for wives. London, 1960.
43538.76.885 Molnar, Thomas. Bernanos. N.Y., 1960.
43554.2.1050 Mondor, Henri. Claudel plus intime. Paris, 1960.
43701.59.140 Monfreid, Henri de. L'envers de l'aventure. Paris, 1960.
43701.60.2115 Monnier, Adrienne. Fableaux. Paris, 1960.
43701.60.2110 Monnier, Adrienne. Rue de l'Odéon. Paris, 1960.
43701.60.3100 Monnier, Jean Pierre. Les algues du fond. Paris, 1960.
43697.61.2140 Monsour, Joyce. Rapaces. Paris, 1960.
Mon 19.60 Montaigne, Michel de. Essais. Paris, 1960.
Mon 28.58.5 Montaigne, Michel de. Om böcker. Stockholm, 1960.
43701.61.3110 Montargis, Jean. Voyage autour de mon ombre. Paris, 1960.
43697.61.5100 Montéguès, J. Méditations d'un médecin. Paris, 1960.
43701.80.1110 Montforez, Georges. La presqu'île Martin. Paris, 1960.
43701.63.530 Montherlant, Henry de. Le cardinal d'Espagne. Paris, 1960.
43701.63.50 Montherlant, Henry de. Selected essays. London, 1960.
38585.16.280 Moore, Will G. Racine. London, 1960.
42582.2.80 Moré, Marcel. Le très curieux Jules Verne. Paris, 1960.
37557.76.50 Moreau, Pierre. La critique littéraire en France. Paris, 1960.
40587.230 Mourot, Jean. Chateaubriand. Paris? 1960.
40587.231 Mourot, Jean. Le génie d'un style: Chateaubriand. Paris, 1960.
43701.67.100 Moury, Alain. L'affaire d'une nuit. Paris, 1960.
43538.76.888 Mueggler, Rose M. Die menschlichen Beziehungen in Werke. Winterthur, 1960.
43703.75.110 Murciaux, Christian. Notre-Dame des désemparés. Paris, 1960.
43620.2.390 Murdock, Eleanor E. The critical reception of André Gide in Sweden. Cambridge, 1960.
42577.32.40 Murger, Henry. Vie de Bohème. London, 1960.
39527.4.135 Murques, Oditte. La Fontaine. Fables. London, 1960.
41596.23.35 Musset, Alfred de. Comédies et proverbes. Paris, 1960.
37543.538 Nardis, Luigi. Il soniso di Reims. Bologna, 1960.
43705.91.100 Navel, Georges. Chacun son royaume. Paris, 1960.
41543.7.20 Nerval, Gerard de. Oeuvres. v.2. v.1 lost. Paris, 1960.
43709.85.110 Nothomb, Pierre. Le chant du prince. Bruxelles, 1960.
43550.58.250 Nouvelle revue française. Hommage à Albert Camus. Paris, 1960.
43723.18.120 Oldenbourg, Zoé. Les brûlés. Paris, 1960.
40536.24.20 Orlando, Francesco. L'opera di Louis Ramond. Milano, 1960.

Chronological Listing

1960 - cont.

43729.85.120 Oster, Pierre. Un nom toujours nouveau; poèmes. Paris, 1960.
43737.12.2100 Pache, Jean. Poèmes de l'autre. Paris, 1960.
43737.34.230 Pagnol, Marcel. The days were too short. 1st ed. Garden City, 1960.
43737.34.222 Pagnol, Marcel. La gloire de mon père. Paris, 1960.
37573.74 Palmer, Ray E. French travellers in England, 1600-1900. London, 1960.
43737.58.100 Panafieu, Bruno. L'homme à l'odeur de poireau. Paris, 1960.
37555.545 Parent, Monique. Saint-John Perse et quelques devanciers. Paris, 1960.
43743.60.800 Paris. Bibliothèque Sainte Géneviève. Collection Doucet. Francis Ponge. Paris, 1960?
37556.15.200 Paris. École pratique des hautes études. Centre d'études des communications de masse. Deux enquêtes "Flash" sur la presse. Paris, 1960.
43822.49.1320 Parisier-Plottel, J. Les dialogues de Paul Valéry. Paris, 1960.
43737.77.110 Parmelin, Hélène. Le complexe de Filacciano. Paris, 1960.
43554.2.1110 Paul Claudel devant Tête d'Or. Paris, 1960.
43738.41.190 Peisson, Edouard. Le quart de nuit. Paris, 1960.
43738.50.130 Pellerin, J.V. Choix de poèmes. Paris, 1960.
43738.58.100 Pencalet, Marcel. Nos rives sont d'armor. Paris, 1960.
43738.76.4100 Périer, Delphine. La sonate écossaise. Paris, 1960.
43738.77.3100 Perrein, Michèle. Barbastre. Paris, 1960.
43738.78.180 Perse, Saint-John. Chronique. Paris, 1960.
43738.78.182 Perse, Saint-John. Chronique. Stockholm, 1960.
43738.78.788 Perse, Saint-John. Destierro. Santander, 1960.
43738.78.790 Perse, Saint-John. Jord vindar hav. Stockholm, 1960.
43738.78.23 Perse, Saint-John. Opere poetiche. Milano, 1960.
43738.97.170 Peyre, Joseph. Le plan du soleil, roman. Paris, 1960.
43738.97.1180 Peyrefitte, Roger. Du Vésuve à l'Etna. Paris, 1960.
43738.97.1190 Peyrefitte, Roger. Le spectateur nocturne. Paris, 1960.
43741.11.3120 Picabia, Francis. Dits. Paris, 1960.
43741.11.3110 Picabia, Francis. Revue publiée de 1917 à 1924. Paris, 1960. 2v.
43741.11.4100 Picard, Étienne. Dans les sentiers. Orleans, 1960.
43741.11.1100 Piccard, Eulalie. Pages choisies des Episodes de la grande tragédie russe. Neuchâtel, 1960.
43833.20.895 Piccard, Eulalie. Simone Weil. Paris, 1960.
41522.18.385 Pichois, C. Iconographie de Charles Baudelaire. Genève, 1960.
37573.684.1 Picon, Gaëtan. Panorama de la nouvelle littérature française. Paris, 1960.
43741.14.100 Picon, Gaëtan. L'usage de la lecture. Paris, 1960. 3v.
43741.25.180 Pieyre de Mandiargues, André. Cartolines et dédicaces. Paris, 1960.
43556.1.915 Pillaudin, R. Jean Cocteau tourne son dernier film. Paris, 1960.
43741.59.2100 Pineau, Christian. Mon cher député. Paris, 1960.
37569.330 Pingaud, B. Écrivains d'aujourd'hui. Paris, 1960.
43741.59.3120A Pinget, Robert. La manivelle. Paris, 1960.
43744.67.1247 Piroué, Georges. Proust et la musique du devenir. Paris, 1960.
43742.3.1100 Plaissy, Lucien. Chemins vers l'aube. Paris, 1960.
43765.41.3805 Plangue, Bernard. Un aventurier de l'insolite: Claude Seignolle. Perigueux, 1960.
37575.210 Poésie française de Belgique. Bruxelles, 1960?
43743.41.3120 Poirot-Delpech, Bertrand. La grasse matinée. Paris, 1960.
43743.41.5100 Poiteau, Émile. Aux jardins des muses. Paris, 1960.
41557.10.215 Poli, Annarosa. L'Italie dans la vie et dans l'oeuvres de George Sand. Paris, 1960.
43743.48.100 Poli, François. Gentlemen convicts. London, 1960.
43743.62.2110 Pons, Maurice. Le passager de la nuit. Paris, 1960.
42545.83.10 Ponsard, F. La comtesse d'Agouet et François Ponsard. Paris, 1960.
37555.695 Porter, Lambert C. La fatrasie et le fatras. Genève, 1960.
40539.15.5 Potocki, Jan. The Saragossa manuscript. 1st American ed. N.Y., 1960.
43626.22.830 Prévort, J.L. Julien Green, ou l'âme engagée. Lyon, 1960.
43744.67.47.5 Proust, Marcel. Remembrance of things past. N.Y., 1960? 2v.
43750.20.140 Queffélec, Henri. Frères de la brume. Paris, 1960.
43750.23.130 Queillé, Yvonne. Au rythme du vent de mer. Paris, 1960.
43750.24.726 Queneau, Raymond. Zazie. London, 1960.
43750.24.725 Queneau, Raymond. Zazie. 1. ed. N.Y., 1960.
38536.34 Rabelais, F. Rabelais. Paris, 1960.
43752.12.100 Rache, André. Les feux de la roue. Paris, 1960.
38583.12.27 Racine, Jean. Five plays. N.Y., 1960.
43752.57.885 Rapin, S. Hommage à Ramuz. Neuchâtel, 1960.
43752.82.100 Raspail, Jean. Welcome honorable visitors. N.Y., 1960.
42555.1.85 Reboul, Pierre. Laforgue. Paris, 1960.
40597.2.505 Reizov, Boris G. Bal'zak. Leningrad, 1960.
42587.52.27 Renard, Jules. Journal, 1887-1910. Paris, 1960.
43753.58.3100 Renauld-Krantz. La grâce. Paris, 1960.
43753.60.1100 Renault-Roulier, Gilbert. De sang et de chair. Paris, 1960.
43753.59.2100 René, Commandant (pseud.). Le soleil et le lion. Paris, 1960.
40524.28.8 Restif de la Bretonne, Nicolas E. Les nuits de Paris. Paris, 1960.
43744.67.1385 Revel, J.F. Sur Proust. Paris, 1960.
37555.542 Revol, Enrique L. Pensamiento arcaico y poesía moderna. Córdoba, 1960.
43619.24.820 Reynaud, J. Henri Ghéon, 1875-1944; étude de bibliographie. Paris, 1960.
43753.98.2100 Reynie, Charles. Les flammes mortes. Paris, 1960.
43753.99.6110 Reynold, Gonzague de. Mes memoires. Genève, 1960. 3v.
42575.75.5 Ricatte, Robert. La genèse de "La fille Elisa". Paris, 1960.
FL 6094.93 Ricattle, Robert. Reflexions sur les rêveries. Paris, 1960.
40597.2.530 Richard, Max. Louis Lambert et la métaphysique balzacienne. Paris, 1960.
43756.90.150 Rivière, Jacques. The ideal reader. N.Y., 1960.
FL 376.28 Roaten, Darnell. Structural forms in the French theater, 1500-1700. Philadelphia, 1960.
43757.49.120 Rolin, Dominique. Le lit. Paris, 1960.
43757.49.1100 Rolin, Gabrielle. Le secret des autres. Paris, 1960.
43757.3.230 Romains, Jules. Les hauts et les bas de la liberté. Paris, 1960.
38525.20.75 Ronsard, Pierre de. Ronsard. Paris, 1960.

1960 - cont.

43757.83.2130 Rostand, Jean. Discours de réception de Jean Rostand. Paris, 1960.
43757.89.2100 Rougier, Henry. L'or et la paille. Paris, 1960.
FL 6080.10 Rousseau, J.J. Jean-Jacques Rousseau et Malesherbes. Paris, 1960.
FL 6052.60 Rousseau, J.J. Julie. Paris, 1960.
FL 6077.9 Rousseau, J.J. Politics and the arts. Glencoe, Ill., 1960.
FL 6094.8.24 Rousseau, J.J. Les rêveries du promeneur solitaire. Paris, 1960.
43765.41.3800 Rousseaux, André. Terroirs et diableries de Claude Seignolle. Paris, 1960?
43757.93.140 Roussin, André. Comédies de famille. Paris, 1960.
43757.93.120 Roussin, André. Comédies de fantaisie. Paris, 1960.
43758.17.110 Rudel, Yves M. Telle était notre race. Paris, 1960.
43761.5.4160 Sabatier, Robert. La sainte force. Paris, 1960.
43761.31.130 Sagan, Françoise. Aimez-vous Brahms. 1st American ed. N.Y., 1960.
43761.31.150 Sagan, Françoise. Château en Suede. Paris, 1960.
37542.50 Saggi e ricerche di letteratura francese. 1. ed. Milano, 1960. 7v.
43761.48.125 Salacrou, Armand. Boulevard durand. Paris, 1960.
43761.48.160 Salacrou, Armand. Les idées de la nuit. Paris, 1960.
43761.49.2110 Salgas, Simone. Atalaya del sol. Paris, 1960.
43761.51.2100 Salomon, Xavier. Un homme à la porte. Paris, 1960.
40587.150 Salonne, M.P. Chateaubriand et les Dames de Plancoët. 2. éd. St. Brieuc, 1960.
41557.9.85 Sand, George. Lélia. Paris, 1960.
43761.58.1100 Sandier, Gilles. L'an n'aura plas d'hiver. Paris, 1960.
43761.77.715 Sarraute, Nathalie. The planetarium. N.Y., 1960.
43761.78.775 Sartre, Jean Paul. The devil and the good Lord. N.Y., 1960.
43761.78.707 Sartre, Jean Paul. Loser wins. London, 1960.
43761.78.285 Sartre, Jean Paul. Les séquestrés d'Altona. Paris, 1960.
43761.78.140 Sartre, Jean Paul. Théâtre. Paris, 1960-
39534.27.15 Scarron, Paul. Poesies diverses. v.2. Paris, 1960[1961]
37567.400.6 Schmidt, Albert M. La littérature symboliste. 6. éd. Paris, 1960.
43763.39.3100 Schmidt, William. L'affaire. Paris, 1960.
43763.39.1200 Schneider, Marcel. Le jeu de l'oie. Paris, 1960.
37562.306 Schon, Peter. Studien zum Stil der frühen französischen Prosa. Frankfurt, 1960.
43763.45.102 Schwarz-Bart, André. The last of the just. 1. American ed. N.Y., 1960.
42587.57.8 Schwob, Marcel. Spicilège. Paris, 1960.
43765.32.150 Seghers, Pierre. Piranese. Neuchâtel, 1960.
43765.41.3100 Seignolle, Claude. L'événement. Paris, 1960.
37569.315 Sérant, P. Le romantisme fasciste. Paris, 1960.
43765.76.3100 Serguine, Jacques. Le petit Lussard. Paris, 1960.
43765.90.3100 Séverin, Charles. L'agonie sans mort. Paris, 1960.
43769.51.100 Sils, Marie. Saint Georges et le dragon. Paris, 1960.
43769.49.100 Silvain, Pierre. La part de l'ombre. Paris, 1960.
43769.54.585 Simenon, Georges. Le coup de vague. Paris, 1960.
43769.54.420 Simenon, Georges. Le fils Cardinaud. Paris, 1960.
43769.54.425 Simenon, Georges. Les noces de Poitiers. Paris, 1960.
43769.56.2140 Simon, Claude. La route des Flandres, roman. Paris, 1960.
43769.56.120 Simon, Pierre Henri. Le somnambule. Paris, 1960.
37548.220 Société de belles-lettres de Lausanne. Belles lettres de Lausanne. Lausanne, 1960.
41596.53.50 Société d'emulation du Jura. Les cérémonies du deuxième centenaire de la naissance de Rouget de Lisle. Lons-le-Saunier, 1960.
42554.26.830 Sonnenfeld, Albert. L'oeuvre poétique de Tristan Corbière. Paris, 1960.
43775.96.120 Sorel, Claude. Europole. Paris, 1960.
37567.570 Spatz, I. Die französische Teufelsdarstellung von der Romantik bis zur Gegenwart. München, 1960.
43776.25.100 Sperling, Janine. La longue soirée. Paris, 1960.
40592.48 Staël Holstein, Anne Louise. Correspondance générale. Paris, 1960. 3v.
40592.47 Staël Holstein, Anne Louise. Lettres à Narbonne. Paris, 1960.
40592.45 Staël Holstein, Anne Louise. Lettres à Ribbing. Paris, 1960.
40592.43A Staël Holstein, Anne Louise. Lettres de Mme. de Staël. 2. vyd. Prague, 1960.
43779.4.100 Staines, Charles R. Constance. Paris, 1960.
39594.19.95 Stark, Werner. Montesquieu. London, 1960.
37569.285 Starkie, Enid. From Gautier to Eliot. London, 1960.
43779.25.120 Sternberg, Jacques. L'architecte. Illustrations de Topor. Paris, 1960.
43780.69.1100 Supervielle, Anne M. La guinta. Paris, 1960.
43780.81.1100 Susini, Marie. Le premier regard. Paris, 1960.
43780.82.100 Sussan, René. Les conflents. Paris, 1960.
43783.52.2100 Sylvain, Claude. Un dimanche à la campagne. Paris, 1960.
40597.2.510 Syracuse University. Honoré Balzac. Syracuse, 1960.
37543.515 Taha-Hussein, Minis. Présence de l'Islam dans la littérature. La Caire, 1960.
43526.65.925 Tangionge, G. I maggio ad Apollinaire. Roma, 1960.
43785.75.150 Tardieu, Jean. Poèmes à jouer. Paris, 1960.
43787.29.130 Tefri (pseud.). Au gravitor. Lausanne, 1960.
43787.55.100 Temkine Raymonde. Paul et Isabelle. Paris, 1960.
43788.5.210 Tharaud, Jérôme. Les contes de la Vierge. Paris, 1960.
43788.24.3100 Therame, Victoria. Morbidezza. Paris, 1960.
42586.63.35 Theren, R. L'Amadis de Gobineau. Montpellier, 1960.
43788.41.4100 Thibaudeau, Jean. Une cérémonie royale. Paris, 1960.
43788.41.3100 Thierry, J.J. La tentation du cardinal. Paris, 1960.
43538.61.805 Thiery, Hermann. Pierre Benoît ou l'eloge du Roman romanesque. Paris, 1960.
43761.78.850A Thody, Philip. Jean Paul Sartre. London, 1960.
43788.65.1100 Thomas, Henri. La dernière année. Paris, 1960.
43788.65.1110 Thomas, Henri. Histoire de Pierrot. Paris, 1960.
43788.65.130 Thomas, Henri. John Perkins. Paris, 1960.
37569.320 Three studies in modern French literature. New Haven, 1960.
43789.22.100 Tieghem, Olivier van. Les chats sauvages. Paris, 1960.
43789.49.110 Tillard, Paul. La racon des purs. Paris, 1960.
43789.82.100 Tissier, Jacques. Le gachis. Paris, 1960.
40546.20.15 Tocqueville, Alexis de. L'ancien régime et la révolution. Paris, 1960?
43792.16.100 Todd, O. La traversée de la Manche, roman. Paris, 1960.
43792.40.41 Toesca, Maurice. Trois semaines chaque année. Paris, 1960.
37562.310 Tourrier, A. Le courant réaliste dans le roman coutois en France au moyen âge. Paris, 1960.
43793.3.100 Tranchepain, Jacques. Vie. Paris, 1960.

Chronological Listing

1960 - cont.

43793.42.230 Triolet, Elsa. Elsa Triolet choisie par Aragon. Paris, 1960.
38525.36.30 Tristan L'Hermite, F. Choix de pages. Limoges, 1960.
43793.67.250 Troyat, Henri. La Barynia; roman. Paris, 1960.
43606.78.800 Troyat, Henri. Discours de reception a l'Académie Française. Paris, 1960.
38557.24.120 Truchet, Jacques. La prédication de Bossuet. Paris, 1960. 2v.
43795.77.100 Turon, Jean. C'était un adoloscent; roman. Paris, 1960.
37556.205A Ullman, Stephen. The image in modern French novel. Cambridge, Eng., 1960.
43822.50.730 Vailland, Roger The sovereigns. London, 1960.
43822.50.140 Vailland, Roger. La fête. Paris, 1960.
37574.912 Valeri, Diego. Lirici francesi. 1. ed. Milano, 1960.
43822.6.20 Vallotton, Benjamin. Comme volent les années. v.1,2-3. Lausanne, 1960-62. 2v.
43611.5.145 Vandamme, Jan. Alain-Fournier. Brugge, 1960.
43822.58.2100 Vandycke, Yvon. Les os creux, avec un complément de cinc linogravures. Ixelles, 1960.
43823.2.45 Védrès, Nicole. La bête lointaine, roman. Paris, 1960.
43823.2.50 Védrès, Nicole. Suite parisienne. Paris, 1960.
43823.75.170 Vercel, Roger. Au bont du môle. Paris, 1960.
37555.398 Verhesen, F. Voies et voix de la poésie française contemporaine. Bruxelles, 1960.
42557.20.25 Verlaine, Paul. Il dramma dell'uomo moderno nella poesia cristiana di Paul Verlaine [di] Attilio Galli. Ascoli Piceno, 1960.
42557.18.55 Verlaine, Paul. Poèmes. Paris, 1960.
43550.58.895 Vestre, Bernt. Albert Camus og menneskets revolte. Oslo, 1960.
43824.3.250 Vialar, Paul. Ligne de vie. Paris, 1960.
43824.16.2100 Vidal, Nicole. Emmanuel, ou Le livre de l'homme. Paris, 1960.
43824.17.100 Viderot, Toussaint. Pour toi, nègre mon frère. Monte-Carlo, 1960.
43824.6.140 Vigée, Claude. Les articles de la faim. Paris, 1960.
41564.1.4.10 Vigny, Alfred de. Daphné. Bologna, 1960.
43824.48.705 Vilallonga, José Luis de. The man of blood. N.Y., 1960.
43824.51.1120 Villandry, A. Eros-protée. Paris, 1960.
43824.50.1100 Villard-Gilles, Jean. La Venoge, et autres poèmes. Lausanne, 1960.
42547.22.25.2 Villiers de l'Isle Adam, Auguste. Axël. Paris, 1960.
42547.18.5.2 Villiers de l'Isle Adam, Auguste. L'Eve future. Paris, 1960.
38514.20.85A Villon, François. Complete works. N.Y., 1960.
43824.54.130 Vilmorin, Louise de. Le violon. Paris, 1960.
38585.16.290 Vinaver, Eugene. L'action poètique dans le théâtre de Racine. Oxford, 1960.
43824.59.2100 Vincent, J. Livre de l'amour. Paris, 1960.
40583.300 Vinogradov, Anatolii K. Stendal' i ego vremia. 2. izd. Moskva, 1960.
37595.97 Viscardi, A. Antologia dei narratori francesi del Medio Eno. Milano, 1960.
43526.65.930 Warres, R. Apollinaire. Lisbon, 1960.
37555.539 Weber, Jean Paul. Genèse de l'oeuvre poétique. Paris, 1960.
43833.7.100 Weker, Jean Paul. L'Orient extrême. Paris, 1960.
43822.49.1335 Whiting, Charles. Valéry, jeune poète. 1e éd. New Haven, 1960.
43757.3.338 Widdem, Werner. Weltbejahung und Weltflucht im Werke Jules Romains'. Genève, 1960.
43835.24.100 Wiesel, Eliezer. L'aube; recits. Paris, 1960.
FL 376.13 Wiley, William. The early public theatre in France. Cambridge, 1960.
43835.50.100 Willame, Georges. Sonnets. Namur, 1960.
43837.50.100 Wolf, Pierre René. A leur mesure. Paris, 1960.
43837.76.100 Worms, Jeannine. Un magnolia. Paris, 1960.
43841.90.100 Xavier, François. Le sexe et l'argent. Paris, 1960.
37556.210 Zeltner-Neukomm, Gerda. Das Wagnis des französischen Gegenwartromans. Reinbek, 1960.
42584.1.20 Zola, Emile. Romans. Lausanne, 1960. 24v.
42584.23.22 Zola, Emile. Les Rougon-Macquart. Paris, 1960- 5v.
43761.78.855 Zuidema, S.U. Sartre. Philadelphia, 1960.

1961

40597.2.535 Ablomievskii, D.D. Bal'zak. Moskva, 1961.
41522.18.445 Accaputo, N. L'estetica di Baudelaire e le sue fonti germaniche. Torino, 1961.
43514.6.140 Adamov, Arthur. Le printemps II. Paris, 1961.
43697.89.855 Adelhaefer, Inge. Die Interpretation englischen und amerikanischen Geistes in André Maurois' Werk. Berlin? 1961.
43514.24.100 Ades, Michèle. J'ai vecu là-bas. Paris, 1961.
41574.593 Alexandre, M. En marge d'un voyage romantique. Saint-Louis, 1961.
43744.67.1395 Allamand, Jules. Ce que Proust n'a pas dit. Paris, 1961.
41555.55.20 Allart de Méritens, Hortense. Lettere inedite a Gino Capponi. Genova, 1961.
42554.26.835 Angelet, C. La poétique de Tristan Corbière. Bruxelles, 1961.
41574.587 Angrand, Pierre. Victor Hugo raconté par les papiers d'Etat. Paris, 1961.
43524.67.255 Anouilh, Jean. La grotte. Paris, 1961.
43524.67.250 Anouilh, Jean. Léocadia. London, 1961.
43524.67.23 Anouilh, Jean. Nouvelles pièces noires. Paris, 1961.
43524.67.203 Anouilh, Jean. Pièces grinçantes. Paris, 1961.
43524.67.123 Anouilh, Jean. Pièces roses. Paris, 1961.
43527.3.735 Aragon, Louis. Holy week, a novel. N.Y., 1961.
42586.9.12.10 Arène, Paul. Contes et nouvelles de Provence. Paris, 1961.
43822.50.716 Arlet, Suzanne. Reflections sur la création littéraire. Paris, 1961.
43528.73.710 Arrabal, Fernando. Baal Babylon; a novel. N.Y., 1961.
43687.74.805 Association Internationale des Amis de Valéry Larbaud. Valéry Larbaud, notre ami. Moulins, 1961.
37566.135 Austin, L.J. Studies in modern French literature presented to P. Mansell Jones by pupils, colleagues and friends. Manchester, 1961.
43554.2.1140 Avré, Barna M. L'otage de Paul Claudel. Québec, 1961.
43535.54.350 Aymé, Marcel. Louisiane; pièce en quatre actes. Paris, 1961.
43535.54.755 Aymé, Marcel. The proverb and other stories. London, 1961.
43537.13.1100 Baccio, Jean. Frelons et abeilles. Paris, 1961.
42577.32.65 Baldich, Robert. The first Bohemian. London, 1961.

1961 - cont.

37568.190.2 Balmas, E.H. Aspects et problèmes de la littérature contemporaine. Milano, 1961.
40597.14.6.21 Balzac, Honoré de. César Birotteau. Paris, 1961.
40597.35.107.2 Balzac, Honoré de. Le colonel Chabert. Paris, 1961.
40597.35.107 Balzac, Honoré de. Le colonel Chabert. Paris, 1961.
40596.34 Balzac, Honoré de. Le curé de village. Bruxelles, 1961.
40597.87 Balzac, Honoré de. L'heritière de Birague. Paris, 1961.
37567.605 Barbagelata, H.D. Les grands romantiques français et le modernisme en Amérique latine. Paris, 1961.
42514.28.185 Barko, I.P. L'esthétique littéraire de Charles Maurras. Genève, 1961.
43537.74.2100 Barraud, Jean. Chants de mer. Paris, 1961.
FL 398.6.20.15 Barrault, J.L. Journal de Bord: Japon, Israël, Grèce, Yougoslavie. Paris, 1961.
FL 398.6.20.20 Barrault, J.L. Le phénomène théâtral. Oxford, 1961.
FL 398.6.20.25 Barrault, J.L. The theatre of Jean-Louis Barrault. N.Y., 1961.
42563.17.20 Barrès, Maurice. Le depart pour la vie. Paris, 1961.
43537.84.1110 Bataille, Georges. Le coupable. Paris, 1961.
41522.13.9.38 Baudelaire, Charles. The flowers of evil, and other poems. Charlottesville, 1961.
41522.5.25A Baudelaire, Charles. Oeuvres complètes. Paris, 1961.
41522.6.11 Baudelaire, Charles. Les paradis artificiels. Paris, 1961.
40532.15 Beaumarchais, Pierre A.C. de. Notes et reflexiones. Paris, 1961.
43538.14.170 Beckett, Samuel. Comment c'est. Paris, 1961.
43538.14.785 Beckett, Samuel. Happy days. N.Y., 1961.
43538.14.745A Beckett, Samuel. Poems in English. London, 1961.
43538.24.100 Beerblock, Maurice. La troisième fois et autres histoires. Bruxelles, 1961.
43697.75.845 Benoat, E. Gabriel Marcel. Brugge, 1961.
40597.2.555A Bérand, S.J. La genese d'un roman de Balzac. Paris, 1961. 2v.
38513.90 Bergerie de l'Agneau de France. Genève, 1961.
37583.661 Bermel, Albert. The genius of the French theater. N.Y., 1961.
43538.76.210 Bernanos, Georges. Français, si vous saviez. Paris, 1961.
43538.76.775 Bernanos, Georges. Oeuvres romanesques, suivis de dialogues des carmélities. Paris, 1961.
38525.22.45.100 Berry, André. Ronsard. Paris, 1961.
43538.77.7110 Berson, Simone. Pour le neilleur et pour le pire. Bruxelles, 1961.
43538.77.2103 Bertin, Charles. Christophe Colomb; piece en trois actes. Bruxelles, 1961.
43538.77.2110 Bertin, Charles. Journal d'un crime. Paris, 1961.
40582.9.30 Beyle, Henri. La chartreuse de Parme. Paris, 1961.
40582.3.13.5 Beyle, Henri. Lucien Leuwen. N.Y., 1961.
37596.10.162 Bezzola, Rito R. Liebe und Abenteuer im hofischen Roman. Hamburg, 1961.
43670.95.800 Bibliothèque Nationale, Paris. Louis Jouvet. Paris, 1961.
41542.2 Bibliothèque nationale, Paris. Théophile Gautier, 1811-72. Paris, 1961.
43540.9.100 Billetdoux, F. Brouillon d'un bourgeois. Paris, 1961.
43540.50.1100 Billetdoux, François. Théâtre. Paris, 1961. 2v.
41555.47.5 Billy, André. Hortense et ses amantes. Paris, 1961.
39527.4.145 Blavier-Paguot, Simone. La Fontaine. Paris, 1961.
43544.13.100 Bock, Paul Aloise. Les chemins de Rome. Paris, 1961.
42563.23.170 Bohet, Jeanine. Léon Bloy. Paris, 1961.
42547.22.110 Bollery, Joseph. La Bretagne de Villiers de l'Isle Adam. Saint-Brieuc, 1961.
43544.60.2140 Bonnefoy, Yves. La seconde simplicité. Paris, 1961.
43528.86.810 Bonneton, André. Le naufrage próphétique d'Antonin Artaud. Paris, 1961.
37569.325 Bonneville, G. Prophètes et témoins de l'Europe. Leyde, 1961.
37573.715 Borchardt, G. New French writing. N.Y., 1961.
42563.36.59 Bordeaux, Henry. La peur de vivre. Paris, 1961.
43544.74.3100 Bordier, Roger. Les blés; roman. Paris, 1961.
40597.2.545 Borel, Jacques. Le Lys dans la vallée et les sources profondes de la création balzacienne. Paris, 1961.
41522.18.390 Borgal, Clément. Baudelaire. Paris, 1961.
37567.590 Bornecyne, J. Henry. Réalisme et naturalisme. Paris, 1961.
43544.81.2230 Bosco, Henri. Un oubli moins profond. Paris, 1961.
38557.25.65 Bossuet, J.B. Oeuvres. Paris, 1961.
43765.31.800 Bouillier, H. Victor Ségalen. Paris, 1961.
43544.108.735 Boulle, Pierre. For a noble cause. London, 1961.
43545.2.110 Braibant, Charles. Un bourgeois sous trois républiques. Paris, 1961.
38575.23.73 Brasillach, Robert. Corneille. Paris, 1961.
43545.4.4220 Brasillach, Robert. Poètes oubliés. Lyon, 1961.
43545.4.4110.5 Brasillach, Robert. Les sept couleurs. Paris, 1961.
43550.58.870 Brée, Germaine. Camus. New Brunswick, N.J., 1961.
43697.77.845 Brenner, J. Martin du Gard. Paris, 1961.
43545.24.182 Breton, André. Ode à Charles Fourier. Paris, 1961.
FL 6119.61.5 Bretonneau, G. Valeurs humaines de Jean-Jacques Rousseau. Paris, 1961.
37556.215 Brombert, Victor. The intellectual hero. Philadelphia, 1961.
43545.67.100 Brousset, François. Flirt. Dijon, 1961.
43823.75.2742 Bruller, Jean. Freedom in December. London, 1961.
43823.75.2741 Bruller, Jean. Paths of love. N.Y., 1961.
43823.75.2220 Bruller, Jean. Sylva. Paris, 1961.
43545.89.4100 Brune, Jean. Cette haine qui ressemble a l'amour. Paris, 1961.
38514.23.94 Brunelli, Giuseppe Antonio. François Villon. Milano, 1961.
FL 6139.36.6 Brunello, Bruno. Gian Giacomo Rousseau, filosofo della politica. 2. ed. Bologna, 1961.
42555.1.95 Brunfaut, Marie. Jules Laforgue, les Ysaye et leur temps. Bruxelles, 1961.
37569.345 Bùi-Xuân-Bào. Naissance d'un héroïsme nouveau. Paris, 1961.
43667.1.880 Burght, Raymond van der. Francis Jammes. Bruxelles, 1961.
39534.1.32 Bussy-Rabutin. Histoire amoureuse des Gaules. Paris, 1961.
41522.18.375 Butor, Michel. Histoire extraordinaire. Paris, 1961.
43546.87.74 Butor, Michel. Mobile, study for a representation of the United States. N.Y., 1961.
43550.19.140 Cadou, René Guy. Le coeur définitif. Paris, 1961.
43550.19.130 Cadou, René Guy. Florilège politique. Paris, 1961.
43550.19.120 Cadou, René Guy. Poésie la vie entière. Fay-aux-Loges, 1961.
43550.41.100 Caillois, Roger. Ponce Pilate. Paris, 1961.
43550.49.100 Calendale, François. Demeure aux mews. Paris, 1961.

Chronological Listing

1961 - cont.

43550.58.726.15 Camus, Albert. The rebel; an essay on man in revolt. N.Y., 1961.
43550.58.765 Camus, Albert. Resistance, rebellion, and death. 1. American ed. N.Y., 1961.
FL 398.7.90 Castelol, André. Sarah Bernhardt. Paris, 1961.
42576.15.280 Castex, Pierre. Flaubert, "L'education sentimentale". Paris, 1961.
39545.20.5 Castex, Pierre. Voltaire. Paris, 1961.
43550.89.130 Cau, Jean. La pitié de Dieu. Paris, 1961.
43551.59.300 Cendrars, Blaise. Amours. Paris, 1961.
43551.79.150 Césaire, Aimé. Cadastre; poèmes. Paris, 1961.
Mol 750.27 Chabannes, Jacques. Mademoiselle Molière. Paris, 1961.
42563.70.5 Chabrillan, Celeste. Daughter of Paris. London, 1961.
FL 398.20.30 Chagny, André. Marquise de Parc créatrice du rôle d'Andromaque. Paris, 1961.
43554.2.1095 Chaigne, Louis. Paul Claudel. N.Y., 1961.
43554.2.1085 Chaigne, Louis. Vie de Paul Claudel et genése de son oeuvre. Tours, 1961.
37563.55.12 Chamard, Henri. Histoire de la Pléiade. Paris, 1961-1963. 4v.
43552.4.2025 Char, René. René Char. Paris, 1961.
43552.5.220 Chardonnę, Jacques. Femmes. Paris, 1961.
43552.5.1130A Chartier, Emile. Portraits de famille. Paris, 1961.
40586.35.10.5 Chateaubriand, F.A.R. Lettre à M. de Fontanes sur la campagne romaine. Genève, 1961.
40586.29.5 Chateaubriand, F.A.R. Memoirs. N.Y., 1961.
43552.5.7100 Chausse, C. La citadelle et la puissance de l'invention. Paris, 1961.
43701.63.900 Chevalley, Sylvie. Henry de Montherlant, homme de théâtre. Paris, 1961.
40587.155 Christophorov, Petr. Sur les pas de Chateaubriand en exil. Paris, 1961.
37555.372 Citron, Pierre. La poésie de Paris dans la littérature française de Rousseau à Baudelaire. Paris, 1961. 2v.
FL 6139.34.2 Cobann, Alfred. Rousseau and the modern state. Hamden, 1961.
43556.1.445 Cocteau, Jean. Cérémonial Espagnol du phénix. Paris, 1961.
43556.1.21 Cocteau, Jean. Leben und Werk. Wien, 1961. 2v.
43556.1.192 Cocteau, Jean. La machine infernale. Paris, 1961.
43656.59.800 Coe, Richard Nelson. Ionesco. Edinburgh, 1961.
38585.16.305 Coenen, Hans Georg. Elemente der Racineschen Dialoglechnik. Münster, 1961.
43556.49.707 Colette, Sidonie Gabrielle. Break of day. London, 1961.
43556.58.700 Conchon, Georges. The measure of victory. N.Y., 1961.
37562.318 Coppin, Joseph L. Amour et mariage dans la littérature française du nord au moyen âge. Paris, 1961.
40524.32.15 Courbin, Jean Claude. Restif et son oeuvre. Paris, 1961.
40546.7.10 Courier de Méré, Paul Louis. Pamphlets politiques choisis. Paris, 1961.
40534.33.6 Crébillon, Claude Prosper Jolyot de. Les égarements du coeur et de l'esprit. Paris, 1961.
39533.20.4.10 Cyrano de Bergerac. Histoire comique, contenant les états et l'empire de la lune et du soleil. Paris, 1961.
43565.53.100 Dambacourt, Georges. Les vespérales. Paris, 1961.
43556.49.890 Davies, M. Colette. Edinburgh, 1961.
43833.20.835.2 Davy, M.M. Simone Weil. Paris, 1961.
43566.82.7815 Debrie, D. Louis-Ferdinand Céline. Paris, 1961.
FL 6139.61.20 Dédéyan, Charles. Rousseau et la sensibilité littéraire. Paris, 1961.
43566.36.140 Deharme, Lise. Le années perdues. Paris, 1961.
43566.48.9100 Delahaye, Gilbert. Les racines du coeurs. Tournai, 1961.
40597.2.540 Delattre, G. Les opinions littéraires de Balzac. Paris, 1961.
37569.350 Delbaville, Paul. Poésie et sonorités. Paris, 1961.
43566.49.3110 Delève, Ernst. Je vous salue chéries. Bruxelles, 1961.
43566.50.4112 Della Faille, Pierre. L'homme inhabitable. 2. éd. Paris, 1961.
38539.98 Deloffre, F. Agréables conférences de deux paysans de Saint-Ouen et de Montmorency. Paris, 1961.
43554.2.1105 Dendooven, Lucien. Paul Claudel. Brugge, 1961.
42542.64.22 Descaves, Lucien. La maison anxieuse. Paris, 1961.
43566.81.7120 Desmeuzes, Jean. La mort dans l'amc, poèmes. Paris, 1961.
43566.82.1100 Desportes, Georges. Sous l'oeil fixe du soleil, poèmes masqués. Paris, 1961.
38526.12.45 Desportes, Philippe. Élégies. Genève, 1961.
43567.79.180 Dhôtel, André. Ma chère âme. Paris, 1961.
39564.8.10 Diderot, Denis. Philosophische Schriften. Berlin, 1961. 2v.
42545.3.835A Doneux, Guy. Maurice Maeterlinck; une poésie, une sagesse, un homme. Bruxelles, 1961.
40597.2.527 Donnard, J.H. Balzac; les réalités économiques. Paris, 1961.
40597.2.525 Donnard, J.H. La vie économique et les classes sociales dans l'oeuvre de Balzac. Paris, 1961.
43611.1.120 Donnay, M.T. Le Paul Fort que j'ai connu. Paris, 1961.
FL 364.100 Dorcy, Jean. The mime. 1st ed. N.Y., 1961.
37573.720 Dougherty, D.M. Perspectives de la littérature française. N.Y., 1961.
37543.580 Dresden, Samuel. La notion de structure. La Haye, 1961.
43574.75.760 Druon, Maurice. The lily and the lion. London, 1961.
43574.75.755 Druon, Maurice. The She-Wolf of France. N.Y., 1961.
38526.6.6 Du Bellay, Joachim. Oeuvres poétiques. Paris, 1961.
38526.6.50 Du Bellay, Joachim. Poems. Oxford, 1961.
43576.11.100 Dubrau, Louis. La belle et la bète. Bruxelles, 1961.
39578.6.10 Du Châtelet, G.E. Discours sur le bonheur. Paris, 1961.
43576.6.381 Duhamel, Georges. Tables de mon jardin. Paris, 1961.
42576.15.52 Dumesnil, René. La vocation de Gustave Flaubert. Paris, 1961.
38514.23.110 Dupont, Claude. Le thème de la solidarité humaine dans l'oeuvre de Villon. Alençon, 1961.
38551.160 Dupriez, B. Fénelon et la Bible. Paris, 1961.
43550.58.890 Durand, Anne. Le cas Albert Camus. Paris, 1961.
40583.315 Durand, Gilbert. Le décor mythique de la chartreuse de Parme. Paris, 1961.
43620.74.905 Durry, Marie J. L'univers de Giraudoux. Paris, 1961.
43576.87.170 Dutourd, Jean. Le déjeuner du lundi. Paris, 1961.
40583.290.5 Dutourd, Jean. The man of sensibility. N.Y., 1961.
42537.25 Duval, Elga J. Teodor de Wyzewa. Geneve, 1961.
43585.53.100 Ęeman, Jacques. Sillages et pistes. Bruxelles, 1961.
43592.41.130 Emié, Louis. Invention de l'amour. Villeneuve-sur-Lot, 1961.
43592.53.290 Ęmmanuel, Pierre. Evangeliaire. Paris, 1961.
FL 1106.8.2 En kértinéye dè fleûrs. 2. ed. Nivelles, 1961.
43598.82.200 Estang, Luc. Le bonheur et le salut. Paris, 1961.

1961 - cont.

43599.41.150 Étiemble, René. Blason d'un corps. Paris, 1961.
37569.384 Eustis, Alvin Allen. Marcel Arland, Benjamin Crémieux. Paris, 1961.
43538.76.935 Faij, Bernard. L'école de l'imprécation. Lyon, 1961.
43606.89.1700 Faux, Claude. The young dogs. N.Y., 1961.
43607.76.6100 Ferniot, Jean. Ļ'ombre portée. Paris, 1961.
37543.525 Fin du Moyen Âge et Renaissance. Anvers, 1961.
38526.67 Firnelie, Odet de. Les contens. Paris, 1961.
42576.33.15 Flaubert, Gustave. Sentimental education. London, 1961.
38562.21.10 Fontenelle, B. Le B. de. Lettres galantes. Paris, 1961.
43611.4.100 Fouchet, Max Pol. Demeure le secret. Paris, 1961.
37530.190 France. Archives Nationales. Les sources de l'histoire littéraire aux archives nationales. Paris, 1961.
FL 370.108 Frappier, Jean. Le théâtre profane en France. Paris, 1961.
43612.24.120 Frère, Maud. La delice. Paris, 1961.
40532.25.25 Frischauser, Paul. Beaumarchais, Wegbereiter der grossen Revolution. Hamburg, 1961.
39566.185 Gachev, D.I. Esteticheskie vzgeiady Didro. 2. izd. Moskva, 1961.
43620.2.405 Gagnebin, Laurent. André Gide nous interroge. Lausanne, 1961.
40532.50 Gaiffe, Felix. Beaumarchais. Paris, 1961.
40526.8.40 Gaiffe, Felix. Chénier: les bucoliques. Paris, 1961.
43616.50.8100 Galil (pseud.). Les mains coupeuses de mémoire. Paris, 1961.
43527.3.825 Garandy, Roger. L'intineraire d'Aragon. Paris, 1961.
43616.78.112 Gary, Romain. Education européenne. Paris, 1961.
43616.78.180 Gary, Romain. Johnnie Colier. Paris, 1961.
43616.78.715 Gary, Romain. Promise at dawn. 1. American ed. N.Y., 1961.
43616.78.730 Gary, Romain. The talent scout. 1. ed. N.Y., 1961.
43616.79.200 Gascar, Pierre. Le fugitif; roman. Paris, 1961.
41522.3.85 Gautier, Jean. J. Barbey d'Aurevilly, ses amours, son romantisme. Paris, 1961.
41542.19.10 Gautier, Théophile. Voyage en Russie. Paris, 1961.
37575.211 Geeraert, Robert L. La nouvelle poésie belge d'expression française. Tournai, 1961.
43617.24.110 Geeraert, Robert Lucien. Les printemps morts. Tournai, 1961.
43617.78.180 Genêt, Jean. Les paravents. Décines, 1961.
43617.82.700 Gennari, Genevieve. The other woman I am. N.Y., 1961.
43538.76.915 Georges Bernanos. Paris, 1961.
41564.55.105 Germain, François. L'imagination d'Alfred de Vigny. Paris, 1961.
43619.23.25 Ghelderode, Michel de. Seven plays. London, 1961.
FL 360.93.5 Gheon, Henri. The art of the theatre. N.Y., 1961.
43619.25.110 Gheorghiu, Georges. Homo Glacticus; roman. Paris, 1961.
37555.518 Gibson, R.D.D. Modern French poets on poetry. Cambridge, Eng., 1961.
43697.77.850 Gibson, Robert. Roger Martin du Gard. London, 1961.
43620.49.3100 Gille, Jules. Feux de fares; poèmes. Bruxelles, 1961.
43620.49.3110 Gille, Jules. Panier de pommes; poèmes. Bruxelles, 1961.
43620.49.3120 Gille, Jules. Simplicité; poèmes. Bruxelles, 1961.
43620.66.460 Giono, Jean. Crésus. Manosque, 1961.
43620.74.5100 Girard, Henri G. Mon procès. Paris, 1961.
43622.41.160 Glissant, Edouard. Monsieur Toussaint, théâtre. Paris, 1961.
42586.67.10 Gobineau, Arthur de. Mademoiselle Irnois. Paris, 1961.
38526.47.29 Gourier, F. Étude des oeuvres poétiques de Saint-Amant. Genève, 1961.
43626.70.170 Gracq, Julien. Préférences. Paris, 1961.
41543.35.30 Grandville, J.I.I.G. Aus einer anderen Welt. Dresden, 1961.
43626.5.5100 Gratiunt, Gilbert. Une fille majeure. Paris, 1961.
43626.22.735 Green, Julien. Each in his darkness. London, 1961.
FL 6139.61.5 Grimsley, Ronald. Jean-Jacques Rousseau. Cardiff, 1961.
43628.23.170 Guéhenno, Jean. Changer la vie. Paris, 1961.
Mol 560.28 Guibert, A.J. Bibliographie des oeuvres de Molière publiées au XVIIe siècle. v.1-2. and supplement. Paris, 1961. 3v.
FL 386.118A Guicharnaud, Jacques. Modern French theatre from Giraudoux to Beckett. New Haven, 1961.
43628.41.7100 Guiette, Robert. Seuils de la nuit. Paris, 1961.
37543.535.5 Guillemin, Henri. Éclaircissements. Paris, 1961.
43628.41.3130 Guillevic, Eugène. Le arnac, poème. Paris, 1961.
37568.210 Guissard, L. Écrits en notre temps. Paris, 1961.
39527.4.140 Guiton, Margaret. La Fontaine. New Brunswick, 1961.
37555.721 Gutmann, René A. Introduction à la lecture des poètes français. Paris, 1961.
40516.60.100 Gyser, René. De slecht befaande markies de Sade. Amsterdam, 1961.
43526.65.940 Hartwig, J. Apollinaire. Warszawa, 1961.
43566.82.7750 Haurez, M. Céline. Paris, 1961.
43632.50.210 Hellens, Franz. L'âge dur, 1957-1960. Paris, 1961.
43632.60.100 Hennart, Marcel. La voix de l'herbe. Paris, 1961.
37565.106 Henriot, Emile. Courrier littéraire, XVIIIe siècle. 9. éd. Paris, 1961. 2v.
43538.1.800 Henry, A.M. Simone de Beauvoir, ou L'échec d'une chretienté. Paris, 1961.
38527.60.10 Hoffmann-Harnisch, W. In dir selber suche den Sklaven. Bonn, 1961.
40553.9.81 Holdheim, William W. Benjamin Constant. London, 1961.
43556.1.920 Hommage à Jean Cocteau. Paris? 1961.
41573.66 Hugo, Victor. Dieu (Le seuil du gouffre). Paris, 1961.
41571.3.105 Hugo, Victor. Oeuvres poetiques complètes. Paris, 1961.
41574.14.35 Hugo, Victor. Post-scriptum de ma vie. Neuchâtel, 1961.
43638.35.1700 Huguenin, Jean-René. The other side of the summer. N.Y., 1961.
37567.575 Iknayan, M.M. The idea of the novel in France. Genève, 1961.
43652.46.140 Ikor, Roger. Si le temps. Paris, 1961. 4v.
43655.4.100 Inard d'Argence, Robert. Adalta, poèmes. Paris, 1961.
43822.49.1360 Ince, Walter Newcombe. The poetic theory of Paul Valéry. Leicester, 1961.
43667.14.215 Jacob, Max. Derniers poèmes en vers et en prose. Paris, 1961.
43667.53.1100 Jamati, Georges. La conquête de soi. Paris, 1961.
43761.78.900A Jameson, F. Sartre. New Haven, 1961.
43667.78.702A Jarry, Alfred. Ubu roi. Norfolk, 1961.
FL 6139.61.10 Jost, François. Jean-Jacques Rousseau Suisse. Fribourg, 1961. 2v.
40556.20.2 Joubert, Joseph. Joubert, 1754-1824. (Maximes et pensées). Paris, 1961.
43670.89.555 Jouhandeau, M. Animaleries. Paris, 1961.
43670.89.580 Jouhandeau, M. L'école des filles. Paris, 1961.

Chronological Listing

1961 - cont.

43670.89.51 Jouhandeau, M. Journaliers; 1957-1964. Paris, 1961-63. 16v.
41578.166 Journées européennes d'études Lamartiniennes. Actes du congrès. Macon, 1961- 3v.
43737.89.1800 Judrin, Roger. La vocation transparente de Jean Paulhan. Paris, 1961.
Mol 730.12 Jurgens, Madeleine. Quelques amis et protégés de Molière. n.p., 1961.
43672.59.100 Kane, Hamidou. L'ouverture ambiguë. Paris, 1961.
V43672.74.100 Kar, Catherine. Tatiane. Auxerre, 1961.
43538.14.810 Kenner, Hugh. Samuel Beckett. N.Y., 1961.
40532.53 Kerdik, Frits. Terloops ook drukker. 's-Gravenhage, 1961.
43673.78.2100 Kervan, Paul. Le bocal aux amulettes. Bruxelles, 1961.
43675.22.100 Kieffer, Jane. Cette sauvage lumière. Paris, 1961.
40583.324 Klostermann, Wolf. Der Wandel des Stendhalbildes. Kiel, 1961.
43680.48.100 Kolar, Jean M. La nouveau venu. Paris, 1961.
40517.44.85 Koppen, Erwin. Laclos Liaisons dangereuses in der Kritik. Wiesbaden, 1961.
37555.547 Krafft, Jacques Gustily. Poésie, corps et âme. Paris, 1961.
43681.65.100 Krôn, Marianne. Saisons. Paris, 1961.
37569.357 Kushner, Eva. Le mythe d'Orphée dans la littérature française contemporaine. Paris, 1961.
38526.26.76 Labé, Louise Charly. Oeuvres poétiques. Paris, 1961.
38563.22.40 Labrousse, Elisabeth. Inventaire critique de la correspondance de Pierre Bayle. Paris, 1961.
43687.13.100 Lacher, W. Le regard de Saturne. Lausanne, 1961.
43687.13.110 Lacher, W. Rueyres. Genève, 1961.
43687.15.2100 Lacrosil, Michèle. Cajou. Paris, 1961.
38544.27.455 La Fayette, Marie M. Isabelle ou le journal amoureux d'Espagne. Paris, 1961.
39527.8.25 La Fontaine, Jean de. Contes et nouvelles en vers. Paris, 1961.
39527.4.86 La Fontaine, Jean de. La Fontaine par lui même. Paris, 1961.
37571.80 Lagarde, André. Collection, textes et littérature. Paris, 1961- 6v.
38526.47.33.10 Lagny, Jean. Bibliographie des éditions anciennes des oeuvres. Paris, 1961.
43687.56.1100 Lamouche, André. L'aurore de l'amour. Paris, 1961.
FL 398.7.75 Lanco, Ivonne. Sarah Bernhardt. Paris, 1961.
40562.47 Langle de Cary, M. Prophète en son pays, Lacordaire, 1802-1861. Paris, 1961.
43687.74.17 Larbaud, Valéry. Oeuvres. Paris, 1961.
43687.80.2100 Lartéguy, Jean. Les prétoriens. Paris, 1961.
43687.83.1100 Las Vergnas, Raymond. Rendez-vous a Piccadilly. Paris, 1961.
40597.2.550 Laubriet, Pierre. Un catechisme esthétique. Paris, 1961.
40597.2.552 Laubriet, Pierre. L'intelligence de l'art chez Balzac. Paris, 1961.
39544.351 Lauer, R.Z. The mind of Voltaire. Westminster, Md., 1961.
43687.89.2180 La Varende, Jean de. Jean-Marie. Paris, 1961.
38525.21.33 Lebègue, Raymond. Ronsard. 3. éd. Paris, 1961.
37562.324 Lechner, G. Zur Zeit und zur Stilistischen. München, 1961?
43738.78.720 Léger, Alexis S.-L. On poetry. N.Y., 1961.
43738.78.120 Léger, Alexis S.-L. Poésie. Paris, 1961.
43688.34.3110 Le Gouic, Gérard. Dieu-le-douze. Paris, 1961.
43688.60.150 Leiris, Michel. Nuits sans nuit et quelques jours sans jour. Paris, 1961.
39544.350 Leithaeuser, J.G. Er Nannte sich Voltaire. Stuttgart, 1961.
42555.37.30 Lelleik, Lore. Der "Parnassier". Bonn, 1961.
40516.60.87 Lély, Gilbert. The Marquis de Sade. London, 1961.
40516.63.25 Ley, Francis. Madame de Kruedener et son temps. Paris, 1961.
40583.206.10 Liprandi, Claude. Au coeur du Rouge. Lausanne, 1961.
39544.354 Liubbinskii, V.S. Voltaire - Studien. Berlin, 1961.
39586.27.35 Loiseau, Yoan. Rivarol, suivi de Le vrai Laches. Paris, 1961.
37543.471 Macchia, Giovanni. Storia della letteratura francese. Torino, 1961.
43822.49.1365 Machon, Agnes. The universal self; a study of Paul Valéry. Toronto, 1961.
43822.49.1366 Machon, Agnes. The universal self. London, 1961.
43526.65.935 Mackworth, Cecily. Guillaume Apollinaire and the Cubist age. London, 1961.
43697.14.320 MacOrlan, Pierre. L'ancre de miséricorde. Paris, 1961.
43697.14.330 MacOrlan, Pierre. Sous la lumière froide. Paris, 1961.
43697.75.858 Maetze, W. Der Auffassung des Sozialen in Existenzphilosophie und Kultursoziologie. Berlin, 1961.
43833.20.910 Malan, I.R. L'énracinement de Simone Weil. Paris, 1961.
42555.43.86 Mallarmé, Stéphane. Mallarmé et son fils Anatole. Paris, 1961.
42555.43.7 Mallarmé, Stéphane. Oeuvres complètes. Paris, 1961.
42555.43.85 Mallarmé, Stéphane. Pour un tombeau d'Anatole. Paris, 1961.
43667.1.875 Mallet, Robert. Francis Jammes. Paris, 1961.
43667.1.885 Mallet, Robert. Francis Jammes. Paris, 1961.
43667.1.870 Mallet, Robert. Francis Jammes. Paris, 1961.
43697.2.1150 Mallet-Joris, Françoise (pseud.). Les personages. Paris, 1961.
43697.52.718 Malraux, André. The temptation of the West. N.Y., 1961.
43697.54.1110 Mamet, Magda. L'automne à mes semailles. Paris, 1961.
43697.60.100 Manier, B. Histoires d'ailleurs et de mille part. Bruxelles, 1961.
42563.37.125 Mansuy, Michel. Un moderne. Besançon, 1961.
43761.78.824 Marill, René. Jean-Paul Sartre. N.Y., 1961.
43761.39.802 Marill, René. St. Exupéry. Paris, 1961.
40535.27.33 Marivaux, Pierre Carlet de Chamblain de. Théâtre. Paris, 1961-62. 4v.
43697.77.6100 Martirerie, Andrée. Les autres jours; roman. Paris, 1961.
42576.15.290 Mason, G.M. Les écrits de jeunesse de Flaubert. Paris, 1961.
42514.28.81 Massis, H. Maurras et notre temps. Paris, 1961.
43697.82.150 Massis, Henri. Discours de réception de Henri Massis à l'Académie française. Paris, 1961.
43697.86.700 Masson, Loÿs. The shattered sexes, a novel. Great Neck, 1961.
43697.87.4100 Mattéi, G.M. Disponibles. Paris, 1961.
42577.1.8 Maupassant, Guy de. Oeuvres complètes illustrées. Lausanne, 1961-1962. 16v.
43697.88.3110 Mauriac, Claude. La marquise sortit. Paris, 1961.
43697.88.540 Mauriac, François. Le drôle. Paris, 1961.
43697.88.757 Mauriac, François. The Frontenacs. N.Y., 1961.

1961 - cont.

43697.88.730 Mauriac, François. Memoires intérieurs. N.Y., 1961.
43697.88.570 Mauriac, François. Le mystère frontenac. Paris, 1961.
43697.88.718 Mauriac, François. Second thoughts. Cleveland, 1961.
37573.726 Mauro, Walter. La resistenza nella literatura francese dalla 2 guerra mondiale all'Algeria. Roma, 1961.
FL 6139.61 May, G.C. Rousseau par lui-même. Paris, 1961.
42563.23.150 Meer de Walcheren, P.B.A. van der. Rencontres. Bruges, 1961.
43698.41.1100 Meillant, Henry. Poèmes à vivre. Toul, 1961.
43698.82.100 Messiaen, Alain. Cortège d'Euxerge. v.4-5. Paris, 1961-
43606.89.84F Mey, Ursula. Die Stellung von Gabriel Fauré. Erlangen? 1961.
40535.31.35 Meyer, Marlyse M. La convention dans le théâtre d'amour de Marivaux. São Paulo, 1961.
43620.2.400 Michaud, Gabriel. Gide et l'Afrique. Paris, 1961.
42566.16.140 Michel, L. Le langage méridinal dans l'oeuvre d'Alphonse Daudet. Paris, 1961.
42515.35.172.5 Millepierres, François. La vie d'Ernest Renan. Paris, 1961.
43699.75.1100 Mirande, Raymond. L'apparence et le feu. Bordeaux, 1961.
42545.28.9.38 Moinaux, Georges. The plays of Georges Courteline. London, 1961.
Mol 19.61 Molière, Jean Baptiste Poquelin. Théâtre. Paris, 1961-62. 2v.
40525.17.20 Moncrif, François A.P. de. Cats. London, 1961.
42555.44.65 Mondor, Henri. Autres précisions sur Mallarmé et inédits. Paris, 1961.
FL 355.95 Mongrédien, Georges. Dictionnaire biographique des comédiens français du XVIIe siècle. Paris, 1961.
43701.60.2021 Monnier, Adrienne. Dernières gazettes et écrits divers. Paris, 1961.
43701.61.3120 Montargis, Jean. Nous deux. Paris, 1961.
39594.14.4.5 Montesquieu, C.L. de S. The Persian letters. N.Y., 1961.
39568.25 Monty, Jeanne R. La critique littéraire de Melchior Grimm. Genève, 1961.
37564.250 Moore, W.G. French classical literature. London, 1961.
42513.48.30 Morcos, Saad. Juliette Adam. Thèse. Le Caire, 1961.
37555.300.5 Morier, H. Dictionnaire de poétique et de rhétorique. Paris, 1961.
40583.310 Moscow. Vsesoiuznaia gosudarstvennaia biblioteka innostrannykh literatury. Stendal'; bibliografiia russkikh perevodov i kriticheskikh literatury na russkom iazyke. Moskva, 1961.
41522.18.400 Mossop, D.J. Baudelaire's tragic hero. London, 1961.
38527.47.15 Mouflard, M.M. Robert Garnier, 1545-1590. La Ferté-Bernard, 1961-63. 3v.
43701.86.110 Moulin, Jeanine. Rue chair et pain. Paris, 1961.
43532.23.800 Mouret, Florentin. Les ouvrages de Claude Aveline. Paris, 1961.
43738.1.880 Mueller, Helmut. Charles Péguy und Corneille. München, 1961.
41574.575 Murav'eva, N.I. Guigo. Moskva, 1961.
43738.78.845 Murciaux, Christian. Saint-John Perse. Paris, 1961.
43703.80.805 Muselli, Vincent. Vincent Muselli. Paris, 1961.
42557.18.805 Nadal, Octave. Paul Verlaine. Paris, 1961.
37555.250 Nais, Hélène. Les animaux dans la poésie française de la Renaissance. Paris, 1961.
40527.24.80 Nardis, L. de. Saint-Lambert. Roma, 1961.
37572.80 Nelson, R. Aspects of French literature. N.Y., 1961.
41543.15.10 Nerval, Gerard de. L'Academie ou Les membres introuvables. Cambridge, 1961.
43706.90.1100 Neveu, Gerald. Un poète dans la ville. Grenoble, 1961.
41522.18.455 Nicoletti, G. Poesia in Baudelaire. Venezia, 1961.
41556.10.10 Nodier, Charles. Contes, avec des textes et des documents inédits. Paris, 1961.
37548.222 Nuffel, Roberto van. Poètes et polémistes: C. Beck. Bruxelles, 1961.
43712.84.100 Nyanai. La nuit de ma vie (1951) poèmes. Paris, 1961.
43723.18.130 Oldenbourg, Zoé. Les cites charnelles. Paris, 1961.
43723.18.735 Oldenbourg, Zoé. Destiny of fire. London, 1961.
37562.312 Oxford. University. Studies in medieval French. Oxford, 1961.
43744.67.1470 Pasquali, Costanza. Proust, Primoli, la moda. Roma, 1961.
43737.98.1110 Paysan, Catherine. Nous autres, les Sanchez; roman. Paris, 1961.
43738.81.160 Perret, Jacques. Nouvelles. Paris, 1961.
43738.78.184 Perse, Saint-John. Chronique. N.Y., 1961.
43738.78.22 Perse, Saint-John. Oeuvre poétique. Paris, 1961-62. 2v.
43738.97.1200 Peyrefitte, Roger. Le prince des Neiges, drame. Paris, 1961.
43740.3.110 Pham-Van-Ky. Perdre la demeure. Paris, 1961.
38585.18.60.10 Picard, Raymond. La carrière de Jean Racine. Paris, 1961.
38585.18.65.2 Picard, Raymond. Corpus Racinianum. Supplement. Paris, 1961.
43741.12.110 Picasso, Pablo. Trozo de piel, poema. Málaga, 1961.
43741.13.160 Pichette, Henri. Odes à chacun. Paris, 1961.
43741.13.170 Pichette, Henri. Tombeau de G. Philipe. Paris, 1961.
43741.25.160 Pieyre de Mandiargues, André. Cahier de poésie. v.1,3-4,5. Paris, 1961. 4v.
43741.59.2110 Pineau, Christian. La simple vérité, 1940-1945. Paris, 1961.
43741.59.3130 Pinget, Robert. Clope au dossier. Paris, 1961.
43741.59.3140 Pinget, Robert. Ici ou ailleurs, suivi de architruc. Paris, 1961.
43741.59.3110 Pinget, Robert. Monsieur Levert. N.Y., 1961.
43550.58.875 Pinnoy, M.B. Albert Camus. Brugge, 1961.
FL 1106.6 Piron, Maurice. Poètes wallons d'aujourd'hui. Paris, 1961.
FL 398.6.20.80 Poesio, Paolo Emilio. Jean Louis Barrault. Bologna, 1961.
43694.11.2805 Poilvet Le Guenn, J. La grande oeuvre architectural d'un poète inspiré. Paris, 1961.
37574.905 Pompidore, G. Anthologie de la poésie française. Paris, 1961.
43743.60.150 Ponge, Francis. Le grand recueil. Paris, 1961. 3v.
40539.15.10 Potocki, Jan. Die Handschrift von Saragossa. Frankfurt, 1961.
Mol 616.6.16 Présence de Molière. Cahiers de la compagnie Madeleine Renaud, Jean Louis Barrault. Paris, 1961.
FL 390.30F Prestigieux théâtres de France. Paris, 1961.
43524.67.820 Pronko, L.C. The world of Jean Anouilh. Berkeley, 1961.
42584.25.275 Puzikov, A.I. Emil' Zolia. Moskva, 1961.
43750.23.120 Queillé, Yvonne. Le printemps ça m'eblouit. Paris, 1961.
43750.41.100 Quillateau, C. Flaques de sel. Paris, 1961.
38585.19.9.8 Racine, Jean. Andromaque. Paris, 1961.
38585.43.20 Racine, Jean. Phaedra (Racine's Phèdre). N.Y., 1961.

1961 - cont.

38585.43.55 Racine, Jean. Phèdre. London, 1961.

38583.21 Racine, Jean. Three plays. Chicago, 1961.

43697.75.855 Ralston, Z.T. Gabriel Marcel's paradoxical expression of mystery. Washington, 1961.

43752.82.1105 Rassinier, Paul. Le mensonge d'Ulysse. 5. éd. Paris, 1961.

40532.48 Ratermanis, J.B. The comic style of Beaumarchais. Seattle, 1961.

40535.31.40 Ratermanis, J.B. Étude sur le comique dans le théâtre de Marivaux. Genève, 1961.

42515.30.729.15 Renan, Ernest. Souvenirs d'enfance et de jeunesse. Lausanne, 1961.

43753.59.2110 René, Commandant (pseud.). Mission confidentielle en Guinée. Paris, 1961.

43550.58.930 Revue des lettres modernes. Albert Camus. Paris, 1961. 2v.

42555.44.174 Richard, Jean Pierre. L'univers imaginaire de Mallarmé. Paris, 1961.

37567.596 Richard, Noel. A l'aube du symbolisme. Paris, 1961.

43822.49.1370 Richthofen, Erich von. Commentaire sur mon Faust de Paul Valéry. Paris, 1961.

37567.552 Ridge, George R. The hero in French decadent literature. Athens, 1961.

42556.28.69 Rimbaud, Jean Arthur. Oeuvres. Paris, 1961.

42556.28.57 Rimbaud, Jean Arthur. Rimbaud par lui-même. Paris, 1961.

43757.6.140 Robbe-Grillet, Alain. L'année dernière à Marienbad. Paris, 1961.

43757.50.1190 Robichez, Jacques. Romain Rolland. Paris, 1961.

43757.13.1200 Rochefort, Christiane. Les petits enfants du siecle. Paris, 1961.

43694.11.2800 Rodenboch, A. Wilfrid Lucas et son grand evangile d'amour chretien. Paris, 1961.

FL 6139.61.25 Roggerone, G.A. Le idee di Gian Giacomo Rousseau. Milano, 1961.

43757.50.771 Rolland, Romain. Rabindranath Tagore et Romain Rolland. Paris, 1961.

43757.3.294 Romains, Jules. Un grand honnete homme. Paris, 1961.

43757.3.263 Romains, Jules. Pour raison garder. Paris, 1961. 2v.

37556.18.50 Roncuzzi, Alfredo. La revista esprit ed Emmanuel Mounier. Roma, 1961.

FL 6139.61.15 Rota, Ghibaudi, S. La fortuna di Rousseau in Italia, 1750-1815. Torino, 1961.

43757.88.3120 Rougemont, Denis de. Comme toi-même. Paris, 1961.

41574.585 Rousselot, Jean. Le roman de Victor Hugo. Paris, 1961.

38525.6.15 Rousset, Jean. Anthologie de al poésie baroque française. v.1-2. Paris, 1961.

43757.93.100 Roussin, André. Comédies conjugales. Paris, 1961.

43757.93.110 Roussin, André. Les glorieuses. Monaco, 1961.

43757.98.1100 Roy, Francis Joachim. Les chiens; roman. Paris, 1961.

43761.31.715 Sagan, Françoise. Wonderful clouds, a novel. London, 1961.

43761.39.775 St. Exupéry, A. de. Regulus vel pueri soli sapiunt qui liber le petit prince inscribitur ab Augusto Haury. Latatiae, 1961.

43761.41.4100 Saintouge, Jacques A. Natales. Bruxelles, 1961.

37574.909 Sanavio, Piero. Poeti francesi d'Oggi. Roma, 1961.

42576.63.215 Sareil, Jean. Anatole France et Voltaire. Genève, 1961.

43761.78.780 Sartre, Jean Paul. The condemned of Altona. 1st American ed. N.Y., 1961.

43761.78.785 Sartre, Jean Paul. Sartre visita a Cuba. 2. ed. La Habana, 1961.

37566.142 Saulnier, Verdun L. La littérature française du siècle romantique. 6. éd. Paris, 1961.

43761.90.3110F Save, Michel. Icebergs de la mémoire. Dijon, 1961.

43761.90.3100F Save, Michel. Made in Magony. Lyon, 1961.

38526.48.31.5 Scève, Maurice. Délie, object de plus haulte vertu. Paris, 1961.

38526.48.33 Scève, Maurice. Poésies de Maurice Scève. Lausanne, 1961.

43752.57.890 Schaefer, W. Die Satzverknüpfung bei C.F. Ramuz. Marburg, 1961.

43763.36.2140 Schehadé, Georges. Le voyage. Paris, 1961.

37563.101 Schenda, R. Die französische Prodigienliteratur in der 2. Hälfte des 16. Jahrhunderts. München, 1961.

43761.78.875 Schlisske, G. Die Ontologie Jean-Paul Sartres als subjektiver Idealismus. München, 1961.

43591.89.815 Schmitz, K.H. Die Sprach der Farben in der Lyrik Paul Eluards. Erlangen, 1961.

37574.690 Seghers, Pierre. Le livre d'or de la poésie française. Verviers, 1961.

41522.3.90 Seguin, Jean P. Iconographie de Barbey d'Aurevilly. Genève, 1961.

37556.21.55 Seguin, Jean Pierre. L'information en France, à la fin du 15e siècle. Genève, 1961.

37596.8.20 Serper, Arié. Rutebeuf; poète satirique. Paris, 1961.

39594.15.20 Shackleton, R. Montesquieu. London, 1961.

37568.215 Shkunaeva, I.D. Sourememnaia frantzsuzskaia literatura. Moskva, 1961.

37567.585 Shroder, Maurice Z. Icazus. Cambridge, 1961.

43769.54.793 Simenon, Georges. The premier. London, 1961.

43769.56.700 Simon, Pierre Henri. An end to glory. 1. American ed. N.Y., 1961.

43550.58.885 Simon, Pierre Henri. Présence de Camus. Bruxelles, 1961.

38514.23.92 Simons, W.J. Portret van François. Baarn, 1961.

37596.106.10 Sletsjoe, Leif. Tre middelalderspill. Oslo, 1961.

38525.22.45.61 Sliver, Isidore. Ronsard and the Hellenic renaissance in France. St. Louis, 1961.

39544.356 Snethlage, Jacob. Voltaire. Den Haag, 1961.

43775.50.120 Sollers, Philippe. Le parc; roman. Paris, 1961.

43775.50.701 Sollers, Philippe. A strange solitude. London, 1961.

43775.50.700 Sollers, Philippe. A strange solitude. N.Y., 1961.

43775.2.35 Souvestre, Pierre. Fantômes P. Souvestre et M. Allain. Paris, 1961. 11v.

42556.28.178.5 Starkie, Enid. Arthur Rimbaud. London, 1961.

43779.4.1100 Starobinski, Jean. L'oeil vivant, essai. Paris, 1961-70. 2v.

37574.140.2 Steele, Alan J. Three centuries of French verse, 1511-1819. Edinburgh, 1961.

42556.22.800 Stutton, Howard. The life and work of Jean Richepin. Genève, 1961.

43780.5.67 Suarès, André. Correspondance. Paris, 1961.

43780.5.65 Suarès, André. Correspondance. Paris, 1961.

42584.25.310 Ternois, René. Zola et son temps. Dijon, 1961.

43550.58.831 Thody, Philip. Albert Camus, 1913-1960. London, 1961.

43788.65.1120 Thomas, Henri. La chasse aux trésors. Paris, 1961.

43788.65.1130 Thomas, Henri. Le promontori. Paris, 1961.

42576.15.450 Tillett, Margaret G. On reading Flaubert. London, 1961.

1961 - cont.

FL 6049.26 Tobiassen, Rolf. Nature et nature humaine dans l'Emile de Jean-Jacques Rousseau. Oslo, 1961.

Mon 130.6 Traeger, Wolf. Aufbau und Gedankenführung in Montaignes Essays. Heidelberg, 1961.

41574.580 Treskunov, M.S. Viktor Guigo. Izd. 2. Moskva, 1961.

43793.67.755 Troyat, Henri. The baroness. N.Y., 1961.

43793.67.750 Troyat, Henri. The brotherhood of the Red Poppy. N.Y., 1961.

37569.340 Truc, Gonzagne. Histoire de la littérature catholique contemporaine. Tournai, 1961.

37556.230 Uitti, Karl D. The concept of self in the symbolist novel. 's-Gravehhage, 1961.

42515.44.45 Vabre Pradal, Georgette. La dimension historique de l'homme. Paris, 1961.

43822.50.142 Vailland, Roger. Fête. N.Y., 1961.

43822.92.100 Vandercammen, Edmond. Poèmes choisis, 1931-1959. Paris, 1961.

37543.530 Van Tieghem, Philippe. Les influences étrangères sur la littérature française. Paris, 1961.

42576.43.60 Vanwelkenhuyzen, Gustave. Histoire d'un livre: "Un mâle" de C. Lemonnier. Bruxelles, 1961.

43626.22.845 Varga von Kibéd, Edmund. Die Welt- und Lebenserfahrung im Werk. München, 1961.

43823.75.190 Vercel, Roger. Vent de terre. Paris, 1961.

42557.20.300 Verlaine, Paul. Paul Verlaine a Arthur Rimbaud v překladech F. Hrubina. Praha, 1961.

42582.9.10 Verne, Jules. A journey to the center of the earth. Westport, 1961.

43824.16.1120 Vidalie, Albert. Le pont des arts. Paris, 1961.

41564.27.2 Vigny, Alfred de. Les destinées. Genève, 1961.

43824.48.110 Vilallonga, José Luis de. L'homme de plaisir, roman. Paris, 1961.

38514.18.40 Villon, François. Het goote testament. Utrecht, 1961.

43824.50.3100 Vilmain, Anne Marie. Terre et ciel. Paris, 1961.

37595.97.2 Viscardi, A. Filologia romanza. Milano, 1961.

43824.90.1100 Vivier, Robert. Le calendrier du distrait. Bruxelles, 1961.

39545.36.25 Voltaire, François Marie Arouet de. Candide, Zadig, and selected short stories. Bloomington, 1961.

39545.74 Voltaire, François Marie Arouet de. Les lettres d'Amabed de Voltaire. Paris, 1961.

39543.55 Voltaire, François Marie Arouet de. Mélanges. Paris, 1961.

39543.35 Voltaire, François Marie Arouet de. Les pages immortelles de Voltaire. Paris, 1961.

39544.28.16 Voltaire, François Marie Arouet de. Les peus belles lettres de Voltaire. Paris, 1961.

37595.87.5 Wagner, R.L. Textes d'étude. Genève, 1961.

43743.60.810 Walther, E. Francis Ponge: analytische Monographie. Stuttgart, 1961?

43835.24.120 Wiesel, Eliezer. Le jour; roman. Paris, 1961.

38525.22.45.105 Wilson, D.B. Ronsard. Manchester, 1961.

FL 6119.61 Wiuwar, Frances. Jean-Jacques Rousseau. N.Y., 1961.

37556.245 Xuriguera, Ramón. La idea de l'home en la novella francesa. Barcelona, 1961.

41522.3.80 Yarrow, Philip J. La pensée politique et religieuse. Genève, 1961.

42557.20.298 Zayed, Georges. La formation litteraire de Verlaine. Genève, 1961.

43761.39.822 Zeller, Renée C.T. La grande quête d'Antoine. Paris, 1961.

42584.23.65 Zola, Emile. Vingt messages inédits de Zola à Céard. Providence, 1961.

1962

43550.58.920 A Albert Camus, ses amis du livre. Paris, 1962.

43512.75.240 Achard, Marcel. L'amour ne paie pas. Paris, 1962.

43514.6.700 Adamov, Arthur. Two plays. London, 1962.

43522.90.100 Alvés, Michel. Entre les barricades. Paris, 1962.

43522.90.110 Alvés, Michel. Le pêcheur. Paris, 1962.

43522.98.120 Alyn, Marc. Délébiles. Neuchâtel, 1962.

38524.154 Alyn, Marc. Poètes du XVIe siècle. Paris, 1962.

43524.19.3100 André, Estelle. Herbier sentimental. Milano, 1962.

43667.14.815 Andreu, Pierre. Max Jacob. Paris, 1962.

42545.3.830 Andrieu, Jean Marie. Maeterlinck. Paris, 1962.

43537.99.800 Anglade, Jean. Hervé Bazin. Paris, 1962.

43524.67.270 Anouilh, Jean. La foire d'empoigne. Paris, 1962.

43524.67.213 Anouilh, Jean. Pièces brillantes. Paris, 1962.

43524.67.243 Anouilh, Jean. Pièces costumées. Paris, 1962.

43524.67.765 Anouilh, Jean. The rehearsal. N.Y., 1962.

43524.67.260 Anouilh, Jean. Les rendez-vous de Senlis. Paris, 1962.

43524.67.290 Anouilh, Jean. Tables. Paris, 1962.

FL 398.3.75 Antoine, A.P. Antonine, père et fils. Paris, 1962.

43526.65.801 Apollinaire, Guillaume. Apollinaire par lui-même. Paris, 1962.

43528.58.4100 Arnaud, Michel. Zoneilles. Paris, 1962.

43528.73.705 Arrabal, Fernando. Plays. London, 1962. 2v.

43531.19.130 Audry, Colette. Derrière la baignoire. Paris, 1962.

43531.48.100 Aulagnier, Pierre. Maré, Thécel, Pharès. 2. éd. Valence-sur-Rhône, 1962.

43531.77.100 Auroire, Georges. Nocturne. Paris, 1962.

37596.272 Avalle, d'Arco Silvio. Cultura e lingua francese delle origini nella passion di Clermont-Ferrand. Milano, 1962.

43532.23.122 Aveline, Claude. Le temps mort, suisi d'autres récits et de quelques. Paris, 1962.

43535.35.100 Ayguesparse, Albert. Selon toute vraisemblance. Bruxelles, 1962.

43535.54.760 Aymé, Marcel. The conscience of love. London, 1962.

43535.54.340 Aymé, Marcel. Les Maxibules. Paris, 1962.

Mon 168.3 Balmas, E.H. Montaigne e Padova e altri studi. Padova, 1962.

40596.40.5 Balzac, Honoré de. Le centenaire, ou Les deux Béringheld. Paris, 1962. 2v.

40597.35.230 Balzac, Honoré de. Clotilde de Lausignan. Paris, 1962. 2v.

40597.35.7 Balzac, Honoré de. Le vicaire des Ardennes. Paris, 1962. 2v.

42576.63.740 Bancquart, M C. Anatole France, polémiste. Paris, 1962.

43554.2.1115 Barbier, Joseph. Claudel, poète de la prière. Tours, 1962.

37568.220 Barjon, Louis. De Baudelaire à Mauriac. Tournai, 1962.

42563.16.13.30 Barrès, Maurice. La colline inspirée. Nancy, 1962.

43550.58.925 Barrier, M.G. L'art du récit dans l'étranger d'A. Camus. Paris, 1962.

43537.82.3110 Bastide, François Régis. La vie rêvee. Paris, 1962.

Chronological Listing

1962 - cont.

Mon 112.17	Batisse, F. Montaigne et la médicine. Paris, 1962.
41522.13.26	Baudelaire, Charles. Curiosités esthétiques. Paris, 1962.
41522.13.9.22	Baudelaire, Charles. Kvêty zla. Praha, 1962.
37576.662.5	Baüer, Gerard. Les moralistes français: La Rochefoucauld. Paris, 1962.
43537.99.710	Bazin, Hervé. In the name of the son. London, 1962.
43538.1.526	Beauvoir, Simone de. The prime of life. Cleveland, 1962.
43538.14.111	Beckett, Samuel. Molloy l'expulsé. Paris, 1962?
43744.67.1425	Bell, William S. Proust's nocturnal muse. N.Y., 1962.
39544.347	Bellugou, Henri. Voltaite et Frédéric II au temps de la Marquise du Châtelet. Paris, 1962.
43552.5.1815	Bénézé, G. Genéraux Alain. Paris, 1962.
40597.2.44.2	Benjamin, René. La vie prodigieuse de Balzac. Paris, 1962.
43538.61.1100	Benoît, Pierre. Trébin du patoès. Auxerre, 1962.
43538.2.1100	Benoit, Pierre André. Oreilles gardées. Paris, 1962.
43750.24.805	Bens, Jacques. Queneau. Paris, 1962.
43538.6.130	Berger, Yves. Le sud. Paris, 1962.
40583.332	Berges, Consuelo. Stendhal, su vida, su mundo, su obra. Madrid, 1962.
43538.77.4100	Bertrand, Mirou. Le chevalet féerique. Paris, 1962.
39544.252	Besterman, Theodore. Voltaire essays. London, 1962.
40582.12.56	Beyle, Henri. Armance. Paris, 1962.
40582.11.25	Beyle, Henri. Correspondence. Paris, 1962. 3v.
40582.38.80A	Beyle, Henri. Memoirs of a tourist. Evanston, 1962.
40582.33.5	Beyle, Henri. Les plus belles lettres de Stendhal. Paris, 1962.
40582.21.15	Beyle, Henri. Racine and Shakespeare. N.Y., 1962.
40526.8.50	Bibliothèque nationale, Paris. André Chénier, 1762-1794. Paris, 1962.
42563.16.4	Bibliothèque Nationale, Paris. Maurice Barrès, 1862-1923. Paris, 1962.
Mol 602.15	Billeter, Regula. Les valeurs spectaculaires dans l'oeuvre de Molière. Thèse. Boulogne, 1962.
43543.8.190	Blanchot, Maurice. L'attente. Paris, 1962.
38585.16.320	Blum, M. Le thème symbolique dans le théâtre de Racine. Paris, 1962. 2v.
FL 6138.94.5	Bocquillon, E. Jean-Jacques Rousseau, ce méconnu. Paris, 1962.
37597.26.63	Bodel, Jehan. Le jeu de Saint Nicolas. Bruxelles, 1962.
43544.18.140	Bodin, Jean. Louis le Grand. Paris, 1962.
37568.165.3	Boisdeffre, P. de. Une histoire vivante de la littérature d'aujourd'hui. Paris, 1962.
42563.18.242	Boisdeffre, Pierre de. Maurice Barrès. Paris, 1962.
37556.24.12	Boisdeffre, Pierre de. Où va le roman. Paris, 1962.
41522.18.36	Bonfantini, Mario. Baudelaire. 3. ed. Torino, 1962.
43544.60.4100	Boni, Nazi. Crépuscale des temps anciens. Paris, 1962.
42557.12.125	Borges, F. Émile Verhaeren. Antwerpen, 1962?
41574.589	Born, Émile. Victor Hugo. Paris, 1962.
41563.18.40	Bory, Jean L. Eugène Sue. Paris, 1962.
43544.81.170	Bory, Jean Louis. L'ordeur de l'herbe. Paris, 1962.
43544.89.2170	Bosquet, Alain. Maître objet. Paris, 1962.
38557.51.25	Bossuet, J.B. Élévations sur les mystères. Paris, 1962.
43544.108.740	Boulle, Pierre. The Chinese executioner. London, 1962.
43544.108.130	Boulle, Pierre. William Conrad. Paris, 1962.
42563.89.36	Bourges, Elémir. Elémir Bourges. Paris, 1962.
43544.88.110	Boussac de Saint-Marc, A. Cinq pièces. Paris, 1962.
43544.106.120	Boutelleau, G. Le grand ensemble. Paris, 1962.
37568.219	Bouvier, Émile. Les lettres françaises au XXe siècle. Paris, 1962.
42563.39.140	Boylesve, René. Profils littéraires; romanciers et poètes. Paris, 1962.
43545.1.2100	Brachetto, Roland. Ce silence dans mai. Génève, 1962.
42542.59.95	Braunstein, E. François de Curel et le théâtre d'idées. Genève, 1962.
43550.58.856	Brée, Germaine. Camus. Englewood, 1962.
37569.232	Brée, Germaine. The French novel from Gide to Camus. N.Y., 1962.
43545.22.1100	Brémond d'Ars, Ivonne de. Journal d'une antiquaire. Paris, 1962-64. 15v.
37569.40.16	Breton, André. Manifestes du surréalisme. Paris, 1962.
43545.39.2000	Briacq, Nicole. La Lande; récit. Paris, 1962.
43545.42.3110	Brisville, Jean Claude. La fuite au Danemark. Paris, 1962.
40583.13.5	Brombert, V.H. Stendhal. 1. ed. Englewood Cliffs, 1962.
43545.89.2100	Brudieux, André Roland. Le magasén aux accessoires. Bordeaux, 1962.
43823.75.2750	Bruller, Jean. Sylva. N.Y., 1962.
42576.15.300	Bruneau, J. Les débuts littéraires de Gustave Flaubert, 1831-1845. Paris, 1962.
41522.18.430	Brunelli, G.A. Charles Baudelaire e i Limbes 1851. Milano, 1962.
43738.1.835	Brunet, Frantz. La morale de Charles Péguy. Moulins, 1962?
37564.263	Bruzzi, Amelia. Studi sul barocco francese. Bologna, 1962.
Mol 702.10	Bulgakov, Mikhail Afanas'evich. Zhizh' gospodina de Mol'era. Moskva, 1962.
FL 6129.62	Burgelin, Pierre. Jean-Jacques Rousseau et la religion de Genève. Genève, 1962.
43538.76.910	Bush, William. Souffrance et expiation dans la pensée de Bernanos. Paris, 1962.
42577.4.49.155	Butler, A. Les parlers dirlectaux et populaires dans l'oeuvre de Guy de Maupassant. Genève, 1962.
43546.87.68	Butor, Michel. Mobile, étude pour une representation des États-Unis. Paris, 1962.
43550.6.120	Cabanis, José. Les cartes du temps. Paris, 1962.
43738.78.811	Caillois, Roger. Poétique de Saint-John Perse. Paris, 1962.
42581.31.5	Camp, Maxime du. Souvenirs littéraires. Paris, 1962.
43550.58.270	Camus, Albert. Carnets. Paris, 1962- 2v.
43550.58.11	Camus, Albert. Oeuvres complète. Paris, 1962. 6v.
43550.58.726.10	Camus, Albert. The rebel. N.Y., 1962.
43550.58.22	Camus, Albert. Théâtre récits nouvelles. Paris, 1962.
42584.25.320	Cantoni, Edda. Appunti sull'ideologia di Zola. Torino, 1962.
43550.75.100	Carême, Maurice. La grange bleue. Paris, 1962.
43550.75.110	Carême, Maurice. Pomme de Reinette. Paris, 1962.
43550.82.210	Cassou, Jean. Dernières pensées d'un amoureux. Paris, 1962.
43550.82.145	Cassou, Jean. Trente-trois sonnets. Paris, 1962.
43550.98.1100	Cazelles, Raymond. Vingt parapoèmes en forme de sonnetes. Paris, 1962?
42576.16.80	Cento, Alberto. La dotterina di Flaubert. Napoli, 1962.
42555.44.172	Chadwick, Charles. Mallarmé. Paris, 1962.

1962 - cont.

38546.105	Chaffanjon, A. La Marquise de Sévigné et sa descendance. Paris, 1962.
38526.10.14	Champier, S. Le livre de vraye amour. 's-Gravenhage, 1962.
43552.4.2790	Char, René. Fureur et mystère. 9e éd. Paris, 1962.
43552.4.2250	Char, René. La parole en archipel. Paris, 1962.
43552.5.230	Chardonne, Jacques. Détachements. Paris, 1962?
43738.78.820	Charpier, Jean. Saint-John Perse. Paris, 1962.
37556.18.75	Chatdain, Abel. Le monde et ses lectures sous la IVe république. Paris, 1962.
FL 6139.62.10	Château, Jean. Rousseau, sa philosophie de l'éducation. Paris, 1962.
43552.6.105	Chateaubriant, Alphonse de. Monsieur des Lourdinés. Paris, 1962.
41522.18.217	Chérix, Robert B. Commentaire des Fleurs du mal. 2. éd. Genève, 1962.
41522.18.216	Chérix, Robert B. Commentaire des Fleurs du mal. 2. éd. Genève, 1962.
40534.36.10	Cherpack, Clifton. An essay on Crébillon, fils. Durham, 1962.
42555.44.151	Chisholm, A.R. Mallarmé's Grand oeuvre. Manchester, 1962.
40517.44.14	Choderlos de Laclos, Pierre A.F. Les liaisons dangereuses. London, 1962.
37595.36.3.15	Chrestien de Troyes. Le chevalier de la charrette. Paris, 1962.
43552.80.100	Christophe, Lucien. Les cahiers publiés au front. León, 1962.
FL 6139.62	Ciampi, Vincenzo. Il problema educativo in Rousseau. Milano, 1962?
43554.2.45	Claudel, Paul. Oeuvre poétique. Paris, 1962.
43554.66.1100	Clot, René Jean. Le ramoneur de neige. Paris, 1962.
37595.99	Cluzel, Irénée. Les origines de la poésie. Paris, 1962.
43556.1.460	Cocteau, Jean. Le cordon ombilical. Paris, 1962.
43556.1.621	Cocteau, Jean. Four plays. London, 1962.
43556.1.470	Cocteau, Jean. Le requiem. Paris, 1962.
41557.10.230	Codroc'h, M. Répertoire des lettres publiées de George Sand. Paris, 1962.
43538.14.815	Cohn, Ruby. Samuel Beckett: the comic gamut. New Brunswick, 1962.
42542.53.74	Cologni, Franco. Jacques Copeau. Bologna, 1962.
38585.16.335	Congrès international Racinien. Actes du 1er congrès international Racinien. Uzès, 1962.
38527.105	Constans, Jacques de. Jacques de Constans. Genève, 1962.
41522.3.95	Corbière-Gille, Gizele. Barbey d'Aurevilly. Genève, 1962.
38575.34.15	Corneille, Pierre. La place royale. Paris, 1962.
42586.32.70	Coster, Charles de. La legende d'Ulenspiegel. Paris, 1962.
40532.52	Cox, Cynthia. The real Figaro. London, 1962.
43556.98.775	Coyné, André. Las vacaciones. Xalapa, 1962.
43761.78.865	Cranston, M.W. Sartre. Edinburgh, 1962.
43557.64.100	Cressanges, Jeanne. La feuille de betel. Paris, 1962.
FL 6119.40.3	Cresson, André. Jean-Jacques Rousseau; sa vie, son oeuvre, avec un exposé de sa philosophie. 3. éd. Paris, 1962.
37569.355	Cruickshank, John. The novelist as philosopher. London, 1962.
43560.78.190	Curtis, Jean Louis. Cygne sauvage. Paris, 1962.
39533.20.4.12	Cyrano de Bergerac. Histoire comique des états et empires de la lune. Paris, 1962.
39533.20.11	Cyrano de Bergerac. Oeuvres comiques. Paris, 1962.
39533.20.8	Cyrano de Bergerac. Voyages to the moon and the sun. N.Y., 1962.
VFL 6135.13	Czestochowa, Poland. Wystawa Życie i Dzieło Jana Jakuba Rousseau. Katalog wystawy 26.XI do 10.XII. Czestochowa, 1962.
43697.88.865	Czinczoll, J. Die christliche Tendenz in F. Mauriacs Roman "l'agneau". München, 1962.
43565.17.30	Dadelsen, Jean Paul de. Jonas. Paris, 1962.
43565.60.1710	Daninos, Pierre. A certain Monsieur Blot. N.Y., 1962.
43565.60.1140	Daninos, Pierre. Le jacassin. Paris, 1962.
37568.218	Declerck, R. Peidingen doorheen het franse geestesleven. Hasselt, 1962.
40583.320	Dédéyan, Charles. Stendhal chroniqueur. Paris, 1962.
43566.47.7110	Delamotte, Jean Paul. La communauté. Paris, 1962.
40583.337	Delfini, Antonio. Modena 1831. Milano, 1962.
37564.260	Demorest, Jean J. Studies in seventeenth-century French literature. Ithaca, N.Y., 1962.
43566.58.100	Dénes, Tibor. Oiseaux et mortels. Genève, 1962.
38575.23.106	Descates, Mauriel. Les grands rôles du théâtre. Paris, 1962.
42542.28.90	Descotes, Maurice. Henry Becque et son théâtre. Paris, 1962.
43566.81.4150	Desnos, Robert. Colixto, suivi de Coutrée. Paris, 1962.
43566.81.4112	Desnos, Robert. Domaine public. Paris, 1962.
43566.81.4160	Desnos, Robert. La liberté ou l'amour! Paris, 1962.
38526.12.60	Desportes, Philippe. Cléonice; dernières amours. Genève, 1962.
43566.82.7190	Destouches, Louis Ferdinand. Voyage au bout de la nuit. Paris, 1962.
43566.90.2100	Devilliers, C. Lieutenant Katia. Paris, 1962.
FL 6119.62.5	Dhôtel, André. Le roman de Jean-Jacques. Paris, 1962.
39564.21.50	Diderot, Denis. Tratado de lo bello. La Plate? 1962.
43568.24.700	Diesbach, Ghislain de. The toys of princes. N.Y., 1962.
43568.25.100	Dietrich, L. Le bonheur des tristes. Paris, 1962.
37567.598	Ditlevsen, Jytte. Inspirations italiennes dans les oeuvres. Tone, 1962.
43574.75.21	Druon, Maurice. Théâtre. v.1. Paris, 1962.
43576.8.1100	Dubillard, Roland. Naives hirondelles. Paris, 1962.
43576.9.4100	Du Bois, H. Scandale pour une sirène. Lyon, 1962.
40597.2.560	Ducourneau, Jean. Album Balzac. Paris, 1962.
43576.24.100	Duesberg, R. Les grenouilles. Paris, 1962.
43576.6.450	Duhamel, Georges. Problèmes de civilisation. Paris, 1962.
41538.205	Dumas, Alexandre. The flight to Varennes. London, 1962.
43576.74.2190	Duras, Marguerite. L'après-midi de Monsieur Unsiesmus. Paris, 1962.
43576.74.2153	Duras, Marguerite. Moderato cantabile. Paris, 1962.
38544.27.580	Durry, M.J. Madame de La Fayette. Paris, 1962.
43576.76.110	Durry, Marie-Jeanne. Mon ombre. Paris, 1962.
40597.2.570	Eaubonne, F. d'. Balzac que voici. Paris, 1962.
43581.89.140	Eaubonne, Françoise d'. L'échiquier du temps. Paris, 1962.
FL 6139.62.5	Eigeldinger, Marc. Jean-Jacques Rousseau et la réalité. Neuchâtel, 1962.
43591.89.350	Éluard, Paul. Éluard en die surrealisme. Kaapstad, 1962.
43591.89.61	Éluard, Paul. Lettres de jeunesse. Paris, 1962.
43697.49.820	Emery, L. Joseph Malègue, romancier inactuel. Lyon, 1962.

Chronological Listing

1962 - cont.

43632.6.800	Émile Henriot de l'Académie Française, 1889-1961. Paris, 1962?
42572.7.10	Erckmann, Emile. Contes et romans nationaux et populaires. Paris, 1962. 14v.
43598.82.210	Estang, Luc. D'une nuit noire et blanche. Paris, 1962.
37556.15.205	Estier, Claude. La gauche hebdomadaire, 1914-1962. Paris, 1962.
37556.238	Evnina, E.M. Sovremennyi frantzsuzkii roman, 1940-1960. Moskva, 1962.
43606.10.120	Fabre-Luc, Alfred. Vingt-cinq années de liberté. Paris, 1962-63. 3v.
42576.15.285	Fairlie, Alison. Flaubert. London, 1962.
43606.89.2100	Faucher, Jean. Alger la maudite. Paris? 1962.
40545.19	Fauriel, C.C. Fauriel in Italy. Roma, 1962.
38537.3.5	Febvre, Lucien. Le problème de l'incroyance au XVIe siècle; la religion de Rabelais. Paris, 1962.
43607.75.140	Ferdinand, Roger. Théâtre. Genève, 1962. 3v.
42576.35.32	Flaubert, Gustave. Les plus belles lettres de G. Flaubert. Paris, 1962.
FL 376.32	Forsyth, E. La tragédie française Jodelle à Corneille. Paris, 1962.
37555.392	Fournet, Charles. Poètes romantiques. Genève, 1962.
38514.23.96	Fox, John H. The poetry of Villon. London, 1962.
43612.4.120	France, Claire. Autour de toi Tristran. Paris, 1962.
43612.23.120	Frénaud, André. Il n'y a pas de paradis; poèmes. Paris, 1962.
39566.201	French, John. Diderot's treatment of dramatic representation in theater and painting. Ann Arbor, 1962.
43613.45.110	Frison-Roche, Roger. Lumière de l'Arctique. Paris, 1962- 2v.
37556.13.50	Gabriel-Robinet, Louis. Journaux et journalistes hier et aujourd'hui. Paris, 1962.
37548.133.2	Galand, Guy. Les lettres françaises de Wallonie. 2. éd. Charleroi, 1962.
43697.75.870	Gallagher, Kenneth. The philosophy of Gabriel Marcel. N.Y., 1962.
43616.78.190	Gary, Romain. Gloire à nos illustres pionniers. Paris, 1962.
43616.79.170	Gascar, Pierre. Vertiges du présent. Paris, 1962.
43616.82.1100	Gastines, Marie de. Miroitements. Paris, 1962.
43616.83.3110	Gasztold, Carmen Bernos de. Prayers from the Ark. N.Y., 1962.
43538.76.905	Gaucher, Guy. Georges Bernanos, ou L'invincible espérance. Paris, 1962.
41542.31.30	Gautier, Théophile. Les plus belles lettres de T. Gautier. Paris, 1962.
39534.22.80	Gegou, Fabienne. Antoine Furetière. Paris, 1962.
43617.78.121	Genêt, Jean. Le balcon. Décines, 1962.
43617.78.702	Genêt, Jean. The maids and Death Watch. N.Y., 1962.
43617.78.142	Genêt, Jean. Poèmes. 2. éd. Barbezat, 1962.
43617.78.720A	Genêt, Jean. The screens. N.Y., 1962.
FL 6119.62A	Geneva. Université. Jean-Jacques Rousseau. Neuchâtel, 1962.
43617.59.200	Genevoix, Maurice. Ceux de 14. Paris, 1962.
43550.58.910	Gennep, Frederik. Albert Camus. Amsterdam, 1962.
37575.765	Gershman, H. Anthology of critical preface to 19th century French novel. Columbia, 1962.
43619.23.31	Ghelderode, Michel de. Sortilèges et autres contes crépusculaires. Verviers, 1962.
43619.23.30	Ghelderode, Michel de. Sortilèges et autres contes crépusculaires. Verviers, 1962.
43620.2.79.197	Gide, André. Travels in the Congo. 2. ed. Berkeley, 1962.
43620.39.700	Gillès, Daniels. The Anthill. N.Y., 1962.
37573.18	Ginestier, P. Culture et civilisation françaises. Paris, 1962.
43620.66.470	Giono, Jean. Chroniques romanesques. Paris, 1962.
43620.66.131	Giono, Jean. Solitude de la pitié. Lausanne, 1962.
42554.26.840	Giovine, Esther. Bibliographie de Corbière, Lautredmont et Laforque en Italie. Firenze, 1962.
37568.123	Girard, M. Guide illustré de la littérature française moderne, de 1918. Paris, 1962.
43744.67.1410	Girard, R. Proust. Englewood Cliffs, N.J., 1962.
38526.48.38.5	Giudici, Enzo. Il rinascimento a Lione e la Délie di Maurice Scève. Napoli, 1962.
42586.65.10	Gobineau, Arthur de. Les conseils de Rabelais. Paris, 1962.
43625.17.120	Godel, Vahé. Quatre poèmes géométriques. Genève, 1962.
42563.18.270	Godfrin, J. Barrès mystique. Neuchâtel, 1962.
37558.155.5	Goldmann, L. Le dieu caché. Paris, 1962.
42575.68.5	Goncourt, Edmond de. Pages from the Goncourt journal. London, 1962.
43620.2.445	Got, Maurice. André Gide. Paris, 1962.
37574.185	Graham, Victor. Representative French poetry. Toronto, 1962.
37555.305.5A	Grammont, M. Petit traité de versification française. Paris, 1962.
37574.405.2	Grant, E.M. French poetry of the 19th century. 2. ed. N.Y., 1962.
42584.25.285	Grant, Elliott M. Notes on Germinal. Lyme, 1962?
42584.25.286	Grant, Elliott M. Zola's Germinal. Leicester, 1962.
38513.19.25	Gréban, Arnoul. The true mistery of the passion. London, 1962.
43626.41.1100	Grilhe, Gillette. Ombres; poèmes. Paris, 1962.
43574.41.806	Grover, Fréderic, J. Drieu La Rochelle. Paris, 1962.
37555.715	Grubbs, H.A. Introduction à la poésie française. Boston, 1962.
43550.58.935	Gudenschwager, E. Auffassung und Darstellung des Menschen in Albert Camus' Roman, La Peste. Mainz, 1962.
43628.23.112	Guéhenno, Jean. Caliban parle. Paris, 1962.
FL 6029.8.5	Guéhenno, Jean. Jean-Jacques. Paris, 1962. 2v.
43628.24.1100	Guérin, Daniel. Vautrin. Paris, 1962.
42555.39.1800	Guillaume, Jean. La poésie de van Lerberghe. Bruxelles, 1962.
42555.39.1802	Guillaume, Jean. La poésie de van Lerberghe. Namur, 1962.
42515.35.126	Guisan, Gilbert. Ernest Renan et l'art d'écrire. Genève, 1962.
43628.1.55	Guitry, Sacha. L'esprit. Paris, 1962.
43628.1.407	Guitry, Sacha. Si j'ai bonne mémoire. Paris, 1962.
43537.6.97	Guro, Irina R. Anri Barbius. Moskva, 1962.
43628.85.130	Guth, Paul. Jeanne la mince et l'amour. Paris, 1962.
FL 6129.62.5	Guyot, Charly. Plaidoyer pour Thérèse Levasseur. Neuchâtel, 1962.
43550.58.900	Haggis, Donald. Albert Camus. London, 1962.
42545.3.850	Hanse, J. Maurice Maeterlinck, 1862-1962. Paris, 1962.
43769.54.810	Hart, Willem A. De psychologie van Maigret. Utrecht, 1962.

1962 - cont.

38526.26.92	Harvey, Lawrence Elliot. The aesthetics of the renaissance love sonnet. Geneva, 1962.
43833.20.900	Hensen, Robert. Simone Weil. Lochem, 1962.
42554.55.15	Heredia, J.M. de. The trophies. London, 1962.
43632.89.1110	Heurtebize, Vital. A fleur de ciel. Paris, 1962.
43744.67.34	Hindus, M. A reader's guide to Marcel Proust. N.Y., 1962.
43538.14.805	Hoffman, F.J. Samuel Beckett: the language of self. Carbondale, 1962.
37562.319	Holmes, Urban. A history of Old French literature, from the origins to 1300. N.Y., 1962.
43763.38.800	Hosbach, J.D . Jean Schlumberger. Genève, 1962.
43538.1.815	Hourdin, G. Simone de Beauvoir et la liberté. Paris, 1962.
37543.540	Howard, E. Deutsch-französisches Mosaik. Zürich, 1962.
Mol 608.19	Hubert, Judd. Molière and the comedy of intellect. Berkeley, 1962.
41573.18.25	Hugo, Victor. La légende des siècles. Paris, 1962.
41571.3.115	Hugo, Victor. Oeuvres romanesques complètes. Paris, 1962.
41572.19	Hugo, Victor. Victor Hugo, témoin de son siècle. Paris, 1962.
42515.35.131	Huré, Anne. Entretiens avec Monsieur Renan. Paris, 1962.
43673.56.800	Huyghe, R. Discours de réception. Paris, 1962.
43620.2.156	Hytier, Jean. André Gide. 1. ed. N.Y., 1962.
43656.59.150	Ionesco, Eugène. Notes et contre notes. Paris, 1962.
43656.59.140	Ionesco, Eugène. La photo du Colonel. Paris, 1962.
42554.68.800	Ireson, J.C. L'oeuvre poétique de Gustave Kahn. Paris, 1962.
43527.3.830	Isbakh, Al. Abr. Lui Aragon; zhizn' i tvorchestvo. Moskva, 1962.
43667.14.310	Jacob, Max. Quatre problèmes à résoudre. Liège, 1962.
43667.15.2110	Jacquemard, Simonne. Le veilleur de nuit; roman. Paris, 1962.
43667.78.22	Jarry, Alfred. Tout Ubu. Paris, 1962.
41593.29.3.70	Jasenas, Eliane. Marceline Desbordes-Valmore devant la critique. Genève, 1962.
37555.735	Jauss, Hans Robert. Genèse de la poésie allegorique française au Moyen Age de 1180 à 1240. Heidelberg, 1962.
43668.4.3100	Jean-Charles, J. Les plumes du corbeau. Paris, 1962.
43670.38.100	Johnson, Robert. Concentricités. Paris, 1962.
FL 386.160	Jones, Robert Emmet. The alienated hero in modern French drama. Athens, 1962.
42514.28.190	Joseph, Roger. Le poète Charles Maurras. Paris, 1962.
FL 6129.62.10	Jost, François. Rousseau et la Suisse. Neuchâtel, 1962.
43670.89.511	Jouhandeau, M. Chroniques maritales. Paris, 1962.
43670.94.380	Jouve, Pierre Jean. La scène capitale. 3. éd. Paris, 1962.
43671.41.100	Juin, Hubert. Chroniques sentimentales. Paris, 1962.
41554.37.80	Kaye, Eldon. Charles Lassailly, 1806-1843. Genève, 1962.
43673.32.100	Kegels, Anne Marie. Haute vigne; poèmes. Bruxelles, 1962.
43757.50.1200	Kempf, Marcelle. Romain Rolland et l'Allemagne. Paris, 1962.
42576.15.425	Kenner, Hugh. Flaubert, Joyce and Beckett::The stoic comedians. Boston, 1962.
43761.78.870	Kern, Edith. Sartre; a collection of critical essays. Englewood Cliffs, 1962.
43626.22.850	Kerscher, R. Charaktere und Charakterzeichnung in den Romanen von Julien Green. München, 1962.
43674.4.110	Khatchadourian, Alice. Hémicycle. Paris, 1962.
43680.22.100	Koechlin, L. L'agende. Paris, 1962.
37562.321	Koehler, Erich. Trobadorlyrik und höfischen Roman. Berlin, 1962.
39527.60	Kohn, R. Le goût de La Fontaine. Paris, 1962.
43667.51.800	Kolbert, Jack. Edmond Jaloux et sa critique littéraire. Genève, 1962.
FL 6135.11	Konferetsiia, posviashchen 252 letiiu sodnia...Odessa, 1962. Tezisy. Konferents. posviashchennoi 250 letiiu sodnia rozhdeniia Zh. Zh. Russo, 1712. Odessa, 1962.
43680.81.100	Kosmann, Claude. Itinéraire. Itinerary. Itinerario. Paris, 1962.
37564.261	Krailsheimer, Alban. Studies in self-interest. Oxford, 1962.
37569.359	Krause, Gerd. Tendenzen im französischen Romanschaffen des Zwanzigsten Jahrhunderts. Frankfurt, 1962.
42557.25.800	Kuhn, Reinhard. The return to reality. Genève, 1962.
38526.26.5	Labé, Louise Charly. Louise Labé. Paris, 1962.
38527.60.8	La Boétie, Estienne de. Rassuzhdenie o dobrovol'nom rabstve. 2. izd. Moskva, 1962.
43687.9.100	Laborde, Lucien. Partage de la nuit. Paris, 1962.
37558.200	La Force, A. de C. En marge de l'académie. Paris, 1962.
41578.34.4	Lamartine, Alphonse. Raphäel. Neuchâtel, 1962. 2v.
43687.53.3100	Lambert, Claude. Le moins du monde. Liège, 1962.
43687.60.3110	Langfus, Anna. Les bagages de sable. Paris, 1962.
43687.60.3700	Langfus, Anna. The whole land brimstone. N.Y., 1962.
42584.25.202	Lanoux, A. Bonjour, Monsieur Zola. Paris, 1962.
43687.65.115	Lanza del Vasto, Joseph Jean. Approches de la vie intérieure. Paris, 1962.
43687.80.2130	Lartéguy, Jean. Les baladins de la Margeride. Paris, 1962.
43687.80.2700	Lartéguy, Jean. The centurions. 1st ed. N.Y., 1962.
43687.83.1110	Las Vergnas, Raymond. Cavalerie lourde. Paris, 1962.
43822.49.1420	Laurette, Pierre. Le thème de l'arbre chez Paul Valéry et Rainer Maria Rilke. Saarbrücken, 1962.
43687.89.2190	La Varende, Jean de. Le demi-solde. Paris, 1962.
37565.167	Lebois, A. Litterature sous Louis XV. Paris, 1962.
42556.28.305	Le Hardouir, Maria. Rimbaud, le transfuge. Lyon, 1962.
40575.5.170	Lehmann, A.G. Sainte-Beuve. Oxford, 1962.
37543.542	Le Meur, L. Panorama d'histoire de la littérature française. Paris, 1962.
41555.53	Léon, Paul. Mérimée et son temps. Paris, 1962.
42545.3.860	Lerberghe, C. Pelléas et Mélisande. Liège, 1962.
37576.662	Le Sage, Laurent. The French new novel; an introduction. University Park, 1962.
42576.63.725	Likhodzievskii, S.I. Anatol' Frans. Tashkent, 1962.
FL 397.111.18	Lilar, Suzanne. The Belgian theater since 1890. 3d ed. N.Y., 1962.
43550.56.800	Lindley, Jeanne. Seeking and finding. London, 1962.
43690.61.100	Linze, Jacques Gérard. Par le sable et par le feu. Roman, 1962.
37574.938	Lippens, Louis. Anthologie de poésie contemporaine, 1962. Bruxelles, 1962.
40583.178.12	Litto, Victor del. La vie intellectuelle de Stendhal. 2. éd. Thèse. Paris, 1962.
43693.20.30	Lo Duca, G. Journal secret de Napolean Bonaparte 1769-1869. Paris, 1962.

Chronological Listing

1962 - cont.

37597.9.18 Lorris, Guillaume de. The romance of the rose. N.Y., 1962.

43693.89.8100 Loumaye, Georges. Cent treize poèmes atroces. Bruxelles, 1962.

37557.70 Lucchini, Pierre. Les polémistes français depuis 1789. Paris, 1962.

40553.10.15 Luzi, Mario. Lo stile de Constant. Milano, 1962.

43697.42.100 Majault, Joseph. Les enfants du soir. Paris, 1962.

42555.43.50 Mallarmé, Stéphane. Les gossips de Mallarmé. Paris, 1962.

43697.2.1745 Mallet-Joris, Françoise (pseud.). The favourite. N.Y., 1962.

41574.594 Mallion, J. Victor Hugo et l'art architectural. Paris, 1962.

43697.52.800 Malraux, André. André Malraux. Paris, 1962.

43697.52.200 Malraux, André. Discours prononcé. Paris, 1962.

43697.51.3100 Malrieu, Jean. Vesper. Paris, 1962.

43697.58.1100 Manceaux, M. Un beau mariage. Paris, 1962.

43697.74.3180 Marceau, Félicien. Les cailloux. Paris, 1962.

43697.63.100 Marcotte, Gilles. Le poids de Dieu. Paris, 1962.

38537.51 Mardi, Enzo. Rabelais e il diritto romano. Milano, 1962.

37556.24.15 Margarido, A. O novo romance. Lisboa, 1962.

43538.76.920 Marie-Celeste, Sister. Le sens de l'agonie dans l'oeuvre de Georges Bernanos. Paris, 1962.

37568.108.10 Marill, René. Bilan littéraire du XXe siècle. Aubin, 1962.

43697.76.6130 Maritain, Raïssa. Notes sur le Pater. Paris, 1962.

37574.915 Marks, E. French poetry from Baudelaire to the present. N.Y., 1962.

42576.63.735 Marvaud, Jean. Anatole France. Paris, 1962.

42563.18.295 Massis, Henri. Barrès et nous. Paris, 1962.

43697.86.150 Masson, Loÿs. Le notaire des noirs. Paris, 1962.

42556.28.320 Matarasso, Henri. Vie d'Arthur Rimbaud. Paris, 1962.

40535.32.50 Matucci, M. L'opera narrativa di Marivaux. Napoli, 1962.

38526.36.62 Maucroix, F. de. Lettres. Grenoble, 1962.

38526.36.61 Maucroix, F. de. Lettres. Paris, 1962.

42577.4.28.27 Maupassant, Guy de. Notre coeur. Paris, 1962.

43697.88.3710 Mauriac, Claude. The marquise went out at five. N.Y., 1962.

43697.88.748 Mauriac, François. Cain, where is your brother? N.Y., 1962.

43697.88.550 Mauriac, François. Ce que je crois. Paris, 1962.

43697.88.382 Mauriac, François. Préséances. Paris, 1962.

37568.222 Maurois, André. De Proust à Camus. Paris, 1962.

43744.67.1415 Mein, Margaret. Proust's challenge to time. Manchester, 1962.

43698.58.5110 Ménard, J. Plages. Beauchemin, 1962.

42587.22.11 Ménard, Louis. Abandoné. Paris, 1962?

37567.608 Menichelli, G.C. Viaggiatori francesi reali o immaginari. Roma, 1962.

37564.262 Mercier, R. L'Afrique Noire dans la littérature française; les premières images, XVIIe-XVIIIe siècles. Dakar, 1962.

43698.75.7120 Merle, Robert. L'ile. Paris, 1962.

FL 6139.62.20 México. Universidad Nacional Coordinación de Humanidades. Presencia de Rousseau a los 250 años de su nacimiento y a los dos siglos de la aparición del Emilio y El contrato social. México, 1962.

43698.200.220 Michaux, Henri. Vents et poussières, 1955-1962. Paris, 1962.

40515.15.8 Mitchener, Margret. A muse in love. London, 1962.

42584.25.295 Mitterand, H. Zola, journaliste de l'affaire Manet à l'affaire Dreyfus. Paris, 1962.

43538.76.941 Moch, Léa. La sainteté dans les romans de Georges Bernanos. Paris, 1962.

42533.20 Mockel, Albert. Esthétique du symbolisme. Bruxelles, 1962.

43701.39.120 Mohrt, Michel. La prison maritime. Paris, 1962.

Mol 245.107 Molière, Jean Baptiste Poquelin. Le misanthrope. Paris, 1962.

Mol 60.48 Molière, Jean Baptiste Poquelin. The miser and other plays. Harmondsworth, 1962.

Mol 19.62 Molière, Jean Baptiste Poquelin. Théâtre complet. Lausanne, 1962. 5v.

43697.51.2100 Molle, Louis. Vie privee. Paris, 1962.

43701.63.915 Mondini, B. Montherlant du coté de Port-Royal. Paris, 1962.

43701.60.4100 Monieux, Marie. Le voyageur de janvier. Bruxelles, 1962.

43701.60.2130 Monnier, Adrienne. Les poesies. Paris, 1962.

Mon 19.62 Montaigne, Michel de. Essais. Paris, 1962. 2v.

Mon 19.62.10 Montaigne, Michel de. Essais. Paris, 1962-63. 5v.

Mon 19.62.5 Montaigne, Michel de. Oeuvres complètes. Paris, 1962.

39594.2.10 Montesquieu, C.L. de S. De l'esprit des lois. Paris, 1962. 2v.

43701.63.705 Montherlant, Henry de. The dream. London, 1962.

42513.48.31 Morcos, Saad. Juliette Adam. Beirut, 1962.

43701.75.7101 Moreau, Marcel J. Quintes. Paris, 1962.

43744.67.1430 Moss, Howard. The magic lantern of Marcel Proust. N.Y., 1962.

40587.159 Mourot, J. Études sur les premières oeuvres de Chateaubriand. Paris, 1962.

39527.61 Mourques, O. de. O Muse, fuyante proie. Paris, 1962.

41596.8.6 Musset, Alfred de. Poésies complètes. Paris, 1962.

39586.21.30 Myers, Robert. The dramatic theories of Elie-Catharine Fréron. Genève, 1962.

42576.15.310A Naaman, A.Y. Les débuts de Gustave Flaubert. Paris, 1962.

42576.15.311 Naaman, A.Y. Les débuts de Gustave Flaubert. Thèse. Paris, 1962.

42555.44.149 Nardis, Luigi de. L'ironia di Mallarmé. Roma, 1962.

43706.87.100 Nette (pseud?). Chansons de mon coeur. Paris, 1962.

37543.308.20 Neubert, Fritz. Französische Literaturprobleme. Berlin, 1962.

43550.58.915 Nguyen-Van-Huy, P. La métaphysique du bonheur chez A. Camus. Neuchâtel, 1962.

43707.14.1100 Nicolet, Arthur. Poèmes. Delémont, 1962.

43707.3.140 Nimier, Roger. D'Artagnan amoureux. Paris, 1962.

43707.3.130 Nimier, Roger. Le grand d'Espagne. Paris, 1962.

43709.85.130 Nothomb, Pierre. Les miracles, nouvelles. Bruxelles, 1962.

43725.41.100 Onimus, Jean. Face au monde actuel. Paris, 1962.

43738.1.242 Onimus, Jean. La route de Charles Péguy. Paris, 1962.

43554.2.1120 Oswald, W. Entwicklung und Funktion der Metaphorik in Claudels Tête d'Or. München, 1962.

43737.60.100 Pange, P.L.M. Comment j'ai vu 1900. Paris, 1962. 3v.

40583.328 Pellegrini, C. Stendhal e la Toscana. Firenze, 1962.

43738.78.777 Perse, Saint-John. Exile and other poems. 2d ed. N.Y., 1962.

1962 - cont.

42554.18.8 Petitbon, René. L'influence de la pensée religieuse indienne dans le romantisme et la parnasse; Jean Lahor. Thèse. Paris, 1962.

37567.621 Petitbon, René. Les sources orientales de Jean Lahor. Paris, 1962.

43738.98.1100 Peyre, Christiane. Une sociéte anonyme. Paris, 1962.

41522.18.415 Peyre, Henri. Baudelaire; a collection of critical essays. Englewood, 1962.

V43500.239 Peyre, Sully-André. Escriveto e la roso. Aigues-Vives, 1962.

43738.97.1170 Peyrefitte, Roger. Les fils de la lumière. Paris, 1962.

43741.12.705 Picasso, Pablo. Desire caught by the tail; a play. N.Y., 1962.

43741.13.180 Pichette, Henri. Dents de lait, dents de loup. Paris, 1962.

43753.90.800 Pierre Reverdy, 1889-1940. Paris, 1962.

43741.25.170 Pieyre de Mandiargues, André. Deuxième Belvedère. Paris, 1962.

43741.50.130 Pillionnel, J.H. Le puits et autres poésies, 1932-1960. Paris, 1962.

43741.59.3170 Pinget, Robert. L'inquisitoire. Paris, 1962.

38514.57.25 Pisan, Christine de. Christine de Pisan. Paris, 1962.

37564.151 Pizzarusso, A. La poetica del romanzo in Francia, 1660-1685. Rome, 1962.

43743.41.4110 Poilvet Le Guenn, Jean. Séquences pour une saga. Paris, 1962.

38585.57 Pommier, Jean. Tradition litteraire et modeles vivants dans l'Andromaque. Cambridge, 1962.

43743.62.1100 Pons, R. L'après-midi; suivi du déménagement, de journées et de l'enterrement. Paris, 1962.

43744.25.4120 Prévost, Alain. Les amoureux d'Euville. Paris, 1962.

43744.25.5100 Prévot, Gérard. Un prix Nobel. Paris, 1962.

FL 386.812 Pronko, Leonard Cabell. Avant-garde: the experimental theatre in France. Berkeley, 1962.

39566.194 Proust, Jacques. Diderot et l'encyclopédie. Paris, 1962.

43747.23.110 Puel, Gaston. Ce chant entre deux astres. 2. éd. Paris, 1962.

43750.20.160 Queffélec, Henri. Sous un ciel noir; récits. Paris, 1962.

43750.20.150 Queffélec, Henri. Tempête sur la ville d'Ys. Paris, 1962.

43750.23.140 Queillé, Yvonne. Sur mon coeur en bleu marine. Paris, 1962.

43750.24.270 Queneau, Raymond. Entretiens avec Georges Charbonnier. Paris, 1962.

43750.24.260 Queneau, Raymond. Les oeuvres complètes de Sally Mava. Paris, 1962.

38536.18.36 Rabelais, F. Oeuvres complètes. Paris, 1962. 2v.

38536.18.42 Rabelais, F. Pantagruel. Publié sur le texte définitif. Paris, 1962.

38536.39 Rabelais, F. Le tiers livre de F. Rabelais. Paris, 1962.

38585.19.9.10 Racine, Jean. Andromaque. Paris, 1962.

38585.20.11 Racine, Jean. Athalie. Paris, 1962.

38585.45 Racine, Jean. Jule Cesar. Paris, 1962.

38585.43.22 Racine, Jean. Phèdre. N.Y., 1962.

38583.6.35 Racine, Jean. Théâtre complet. Lausanne, 1962. 2v.

43752.90.1100 Ravard, Claude. Émaux d'amour. Paris, 1962.

FL 6139.62.15 Raymond, M. Jean-Jacques Rousseau. Paris, 1962.

37567.606 Reboul, Pierre. Le mythe anglais dans la littérature française sous la restauration. Lille, 1962.

38526.48.17 Reichenberger, K. Du Bartas und sein Schöpfungsepos. München, 1962.

FL 381.19 Reizov, B.G. Mezhdu klassitsizmom i romantizmom. Leningrad, 1962.

43753.61.100 Renoux, Alfred. Le grand test secret de Jules Verne. Paris, 1962.

40524.31.35 Restif de la Bretonne, Nicolas E. Les contemporaines. Paris, 1962. 3v.

40524.28.7 Restif de la Bretonne, Nicolas E. El Descubrimiento Austral por un Hombre Volador o y Dedalo Francés. Santiago de Chile, 1962.

40524.31.30 Restif de la Bretonne, Nicolas E. La vie de mon père. Paris, 1962.

43753.98.3100 Rey, Henri François. Les pianos mécaniques; roman. Paris, 1962.

43756.6.110 Ribaud, A. Le roi; chronique de la cour. Paris, 1962.

37567.601 Rièse, Laure. Les salons littéraires parisiens du Sd. Empire à nos jours. Toulouse, 1962.

39544.357 Rihs, Charles. Voltaire. Genève, 1962.

42556.28.67 Rimbaud, Jean Arthur. Rimbaud with plain prose translations of each poem. Harmondsworth, Middlesex, 1962.

43756.91.3700 Rivoyre, Christine de. The wreathed head. London, 1962.

43757.6.105 Robbe-Grillet, Alain. Les gommes. St. Amand, 1962.

43757.6.150 Robbe-Grillet, Alain. Instantanes. Paris, 1962.

43757.6.710 Robbe-Grillet, Alain. Last year at Marienbad. London, 1962.

43757.17.100 Rodet, Françoise. L'envers de feuilles; poèmes. Paris, 1962.

37568.225 Roger, Juan. Figuras de la literatura francesa contemporanea. Madrid, 1962.

43757.50.48 Rolland, Romain. Histoire d'une amitie. Paris, 1962.

43757.3.277 Romains, Jules. As it is on earth. N.Y., 1962.

42546.15.17 Rostand, Edmond. Die romanse oor die muur. Kaapstad, 1962.

43757.88.1100 Rouffanche, J. Dans la foule de gui. Paris, 1962.

FL 6003.6 Rousseau, J.J. A la rencontre de Jean-Jacques Rousseau. Genève, 1962.

FL 6002.962.5 Rousseau, J.J. Choix de textes. Paris, 1962.

FL 6022.62 Rousseau, J.J. Les confessions. Paris, 1962.

FL 6046.13.40 Rousseau, J.J. The Emile of Jean-Jacques Rousseau. N.Y., 1962.

FL 6081.5 Rousseau, J.J. Lettres écrites de la montagne. Neuchâtel, 1962.

FL 6062.5 Rousseau, J.J. Lettres sur la botanique. Paris, 1962.

FL 6005.22 Rousseau, J.J. The minor educational writings of Jean-Jacques Rousseau. N.Y., 1962.

FL 6002.962A Rousseau, J.J. Political writings. Oxford, 1962. 2v.

Htn FL 6095.10* Rousseau, J.J. Rousseau Juge de Jean-Jacques. Dialogues. Paris, 1962.

37543.544 Rousset, Jean. Forme et signification. Paris, 1962.

43757.93.150 Roussin, André. Comédies de la scène et de la ville. Paris, 1962.

41574.596 Russell, O.W. Étude historique et critique des Burgraves de Victor Hugo. Paris, 1962.

38526.7.55 Saba, Guido. La poesia di Joachim Du Bellay. Messina, 1962.

43761.31.160 Sagan, Françoise. Les violons parfois. Paris, 1962.

Chronological Listing

1962 - cont.

38542.23.5 Saint-Evremond, C. de M. de S.D. Oeuvres en prose. Paris, 1962. 4v.
43761.40.100 St. Gal de Prus, H. Galilée, carrefour du temps. Paris, 1962.
39578.35 Saint-Martin, Louis Claude. Le crocodile, ou La guerre du bien et du mal. Paris, 1962.
43761.50.100 Salis, J.R. de. Im Lauf der Jahre. Zürich, 1962.
Mol 270.36 Salomon, H.P. Tartuffe devant l'opinion française. Paris, 1962.
41557.9.73 Sand, George. Indiana. Paris, 1962.
43761.78.631 Sartre, Jean Paul. Literary and philosophical essays. N.Y., 1962.
43761.78.145 Sartre, Jean Paul. Théâtre. Paris, 1962.
37556.232 Sauerwein, Jules. Trente aus à la une. Paris, 1962.
37562.300.5 Saulnièr, V.L. La littérature française du moyen âge. 5. éd. Paris, 1962.
37563.87.6 Saulnier, Verdun L. La littérature française de la renaissance. 6e éd. Paris, 1962.
43620.2.435 Savage, C.H. André Gide. Paris, 1962.
43761.3.45 Savignon, André. Dans ma prison Le Londres. 2. éd. Bruxelles, 1962.
43763.37.110 Scheinert, David. Le mal du docteur Laureys. Bruxelles, 1962.
42577.4.29.70 Schniedt, A.M. Maupassant, par lui-même. Paris, 1962.
43550.58.905 Scott, Nathan. Albert Camus. London, 1962.
43757.50.64 Seché, Alphonse. Ces jours lointains. Paris, 1962.
39544.358 Séguin, J.A.R. Voltaire and the gentleman's magazine, 1731-1868. N.Y., 1962.
40587.140.5 Sieburg, Friedrich. Chateaubriand. N.Y., 1962.
41574.592 Simaika, Raouf. L'inspiration épique dans les romans de Victor Hugo. Genève, 1962.
43769.56.2710 Simon, Claude. The Flanders road. London, 1962.
43769.56.2150 Simon, Claude. Le palace, roman. Paris, 1962.
43769.56.140 Simon, Pierre Henri. Le jardin et la ville. Paris, 1962.
43750.24.800 Simonnet, Claude. Queneau déchiffré. Paris, 1962.
43769.65.110 Sion, Georges. La princesse de Chine. Bruxelles, 1962.
41557.10.225 Södergård, Ö. Essais sur la création littéraire de George Sand. Uppsala, 1962.
40583.330 Souka, Fatma. Les idées de Stendhal en matière d'art littéraire. Le Caire, 1962.
38526.48.170 Sponde, Jean de. Sonnet on love and death. Painesville, 1962.
40592.41 Staël Holstein, Anne Louise. Madame de Staël et le duc de Wellington; correspondance inédite, 1815-1817. Paris, 1962.
42556.28.178.10 Starkie, Enid. Arthur Rimbaud. N.Y., 1962.
37543.545 Style et littérature. La Haye, 1962.
43780.9.100 Subra, Marie France. Lettres anciennes. Paris, 1962.
42577.4.49.150 Sullivan, Edward. Maupassant. London, 1962.
38575.96 Sweetser, M.O. Les conceptions dramatiques de Corneille. Genève, 1962.
37567.191 Taha-Hussein, Mu'nis. Le romantisme français et l'Islam. Beirut, 1962.
40553.10.22 Talma, Julie C. (Mme.). Erotisch schimmenspel. Amsterdam, 1962.
42577.4.43.10 Tassart, François. Nouveaux souvenirs intimes sur Guy de Maupassant. Paris, 1962.
41596.51.40 Tersen, Émile. L'Internationale. Paris, 1962.
37568.216 Thiebaut, M. Entre les lignes. Paris, 1962.
43620.2.420 Thieny, Jean J. Gide. Paris, 1962.
43788.41.2110 Thiry, Marcel. Échec au temps. Bruxelles, 1962.
37577.37 Tréno, Robert. L'anti-France. Paris, 1962.
38525.35.35 Tristan L'Hermite, F. Poésies. Paris, 1962.
43793.67.260 Troyat, Henri. Les dames de Sibéria. Paris, 1962.
43793.67.760 Troyat, Henri. The encounter. N.Y., 1962.
38557.24.130 Truchet, Jacques. Bossuet panegyriste. Paris, 1962.
38557.24.120.10 Truchet, Jacques. Bossuet panégyriste. Paris, 1962.
43625.3.270 Uitti, Karl D. La passion littéraire de Remy de Gourmont. Princeton, 1962.
43822.50.735 Vailland, Roger. Turn of the wheel. N.Y., 1962.
43822.41.120 Vaillant-Couturier, Paul. Vers des lendemains qui chantent. Paris, 1962.
42581.33.9 Vallès, Jules. Le roman de Jacques Vingtras. Verviers, 1962. 3v.
43552.5.810 Vandromme, Pol. Jacques Chardonne: c'est beaucoup plus que Chardonne. Lyon, 1962.
43822.88.100 Vaucienne, François. Un rêve du jeune Jean Racine aux portes d'or de la Provence. Paris, 1962.
43822.90.1100 Vauthier, M. Faon l'héroique. Paris, 1962.
FL 6139.62.25 Velde, Isaac van der. De verhouding Rousseau-Locke. Groningen, 1962.
43761.78.880 Verhoeff, J.P. Sartre als toueelschrijver. Groningen, 1962.
42557.18.9 Verlaine, Paul. Oeuvres poétiques complètes. Paris, 1962.
43823.76.4100 Vernay, Andrée. Dernière terre. Paris, 1962.
38526.34.120 Vernay, Henri. Les divers sens du mot raison. Heidelberg, 1962.
37556.243 Vernois, Paul. Le roman rustique de George Sand à Ramuz. Paris, 1962.
FL 394.142 Versailles, France. Musée National. La comédie-française, 1680-1962. Paris, 1962.
43824.3.1110 Vian, Boris. L'arrache-coeur. Paris, 1962.
43824.3.1120 Vian, Boris. Je voudrais pas crever. Paris, 1962.
38523.3.85 Vianey, Joseph. Les epêtres de Marot. Paris, 1962.
43824.6.170 Vigée, Claude. Canaan d'exil. Paris, 1962.
43824.6.180 Vigée, Claude. Le poème du retour. Paris, 1962.
43824.6.160 Vigée, Claude. Révolte et louanges. Paris, 1962.
41564.24.15 Vigny, Alfred de. Chatterton. Bologna, 1962.
43824.48.112 Vilallonga, José Luis de. L'homme de plaisir. Paris, 1962.
42547.22.15A Villiers de l'Isle Adam, Auguste. Correspondance générale. Paris, 1962. 2v.
42547.17.20A Villiers de l'Isle Adam, Auguste. Correspondance générale de Villiers de l'Isle Adam et documents inédits. Paris, 1962. 2v.
39545.132.2 Voltaire, François Marie Arouet de. Essai sur les moeurs et l'esprit des nations. Paris, 1962.
37597.16.30 Wace, Maistre. La partie arthurienne du Roman de Brut. Paris, 1962.
43830.48.130 Walder, Francis. Une lettre de voiture. Paris, 1962.
42545.3.840 Warmoes, Jean. Maurice Maeterlinck. Bruxelles, 1962.
43526.65.875 Warnier, R. Un conte slave d'Apollinaire. Zagreb, 1962.
43833.20.621 Weil, Simone. Selected essays, 1934-1943. London, 1962.
41522.18.425 Wetherill, P.M. Charles Baudelaire et la poésie d'Edgar Allan Poe. Paris, 1962.
37558.203 Weygand, Maxime. L'année à l'academie. Paris, 1962.

1962 - cont.

43835.24.710 Wiesel, Éliezer. The accident. N.Y., 1962.
43524.67.830 Xans, Joseph Anna Guillaume. Toneel en leven; enkle beschouwingen over Anouilh. Groningen, 1962.
43852.89.190 Yourcenar, Marguerite. Sous bénéfice d'inventaire. Paris, 1962.
37530.188 Zambon, Maria R. Bibliographie du roman français en Italie au XVIIIe siècle. Firenze, 1962.
42584.4.3.10 Zola, Emile. Au bonheur des dames. Paris, 1962.
42584.23.400 Zola, Emile. Lazarc, suivi de Soeur des Pauvres. Neuchâtel, 1962.

1963

43512.13.100 Abirachid, R. L'Emerveillié. Paris, 1963.
42557.20.269 Adam, Antoine. The art of Paul Verlaine. N.Y., 1963.
37596.23.23 Adam (Mystery). Le mystère d'Adam. Genève, 1963.
39566.200 Akimova, A.A. Didro. Moskva, 1963.
41574.604 Albony, Pierre. La création mythologique chez Victor Hugo. Paris, 1963.
42562.60.8 Allais, Alphonse. La barbe et autres contes. Paris, 1963.
42562.60.15 Allais, Alphonse. Vive la vie! Paris, 1963.
38546.106 Allentuch, H.R. Madame de Sévigné. Baltimore, 1963.
43523.29.100 Amfreville, Henri d'. Fragments solaires. Neuchâtel, 1963.
40593.46 Andrews, W. Germaine. 1. ed. N.Y., 1963.
43524.19.2100 Andry, Marc. A quoi ça rime? Paris, 1963.
43524.67.300 Anouilh, Jean. Deux pièces roses. Paris, 1963.
43524.67.133 Anouilh, Jean. Pièces noires. Paris, 1963.
37574.721 Anthologie de poètes français actuels. Grenoble, 1963- 6v.
37575.780 Anthologie du XXeme anniversaire du Prix Max Rose de poésie. Bruxelles, 1963.
43526.65.794.5 Apollinaire, Guillaume. Pásmo. Praha, 1963.
43526.65.310 Apollinaire, Guillaume. Zwierzyniec albo Świta Orfeusza. Kraków, 1963.
43530.37.100 Atheros, Dominique. Le poète et l'amour. Monte-Carlo, 1963.
38526.48.244 Attal, J.P. Maurice Scève. Paris, 1963.
43531.18.1230 Audiberti, Jacques. Les tombeaux ferment mal. Paris, 1963.
43532.23.180 Aveline, Claude. Les reflexions de Monsieur F.A.T. Paris, 1963.
43537.12.1100 Bachelard, René. Noirs, mes amis. Paris, 1963.
43698.200.815 Badoux, L. La pensée de Henri Michaux. Zürich, 1963.
38526.8.6 Baif, Jean Antoine de. Le psautier de 1587. Paris, 1963.
43537.51.110 Ballot-Léna, Bernard. Poèmes, 1948-1956. Paris, 1963.
40597.29.1.20 Balzac, Honoré de. La maison du chat-qui-pelote. Paris, 1963.
41522.1.8 Barbey d'Aurevilly, Jules. Les diaboliques. Paris, 1963.
43738.1.840 Barbier, Joseph. L'Ève de Charles Péguy. Paris, 1963.
37544.120 Baroli, Marc. Le train dans la littérature française. Thèse. Paris? 1963.
42563.18.72 Barrès, Maurice. Mes cahiers, 1896-1923. Paris, 1963.
38585.16.330 Barthes, R. Sur Racine. Paris, 1963.
37556.22.60 Batailler, F. Analyses de presse. Paris, 1963.
38514.23.100 Battaglia, S. François Villon. Napoli, 1963.
38585.16.350 Baudouin, Charles. Jean Racine, l'infant du desert. Paris, 1963.
43537.97.110 Bay, Paul. De la terre au ciel; poésies. Bruxelles, 1963.
38563.7.5 Bayle, Pierre. The great contest of faith and reason. N.Y., 1963.
43538.1.530 Beauvoir, Simone de. La force des choses. Paris, 1963.
43538.14.2110 Beck, Béatrix. Le muet. Paris, 1963.
43538.92.100 Beckert, A. L'art du poème. Bruxelles, 1963.
43538.14.200 Beckett, Samuel. Dramatische Dicktungen. Frankfurt, 1963. 2v.
43538.14.788 Beckett, Samuel. Glückliche Tage und andere Stücke. Frankfurt, 1963.
43538.14.190 Beckett, Samuel. Oh les beaux jours. Paris, 1963.
43538.14.746 Beckett, Samuel. Poems in English. N.Y., 1963.
43538.14.795 Beckett, Samuel. Wie es ist. Frankfurt, 1963.
43701.63.910 Beer, J. de. Montherlant, ou L'homme encombré de Dieu. Paris, 1963.
43626.22.855 Benoot, Edgar. Julien Green. Brugge, 1963.
43750.24.810 Bergens, A. Raymond Queneau. Genève, 1963.
43538.6.720 Berger, Yves. The garden. N.Y., 1963.
43822.49.1415 Bergeron, Léandre. Le son et le sens dans quelques poèmes de Charmes de Paul Valéry. Gap, 1963.
40597.2.575 Bertault, Philippe. Balzac and the human comedy. N.Y., 1963.
43620.74.920 Best, Otto Ferdinand. Der Dualismus im Welt- und Menschenbild Jean Giraudoux das Verhältnis von Mann und Frau. München, 1963.
41564.55.115 Bibliothèque nationale, Paris. Alfred de Vigny, 1797-1863. Paris, 1963.
40522.10.5 Bibliothèque nationale, Paris. Manon Lescaut à travers deux siècles. Paris, 1963.
43540.9.710 Billetdoux, F. Chez Torpe. London, 1963.
43540.9.705 Billetdoux, F. Chin-chin. London, 1963.
43540.9.700 Billetdoux, F. A man and his master. London, 1963.
43540.3.100 Billy, André. Du noir sur du blanc. Paris, 1963.
42568.19.24.12 Blanchat, M. Lautréamont et Sade. Paris, 1963.
43697.52.885 Blend, C.D. André Malraux, tragic humanist. Columbus, 1963.
43543.63.100 Bloch, Pierre J. Rêve éveillé; poèmes. Rodez, 1963.
42555.44.180 Block, H. Mallarmé and the symbolist drama. Detroit, 1963.
37568.224 Bo, Carlo. Saggi e note di una letteratura. Milano, 1963.
43697.77.855 Boak, Denis. Roger Martin du Gard. Oxford, 1963.
43544.18.141 Bodin, Jean. Louis-le-Grand. Paris, 1963.
37568.228 Boisdeffre, P. de. Les écrivains français d'aujourd'hui. Paris, 1963.
37568.116.5 Boisdeffre, P. de. Métamorphose de la littérature. 5. éd. Paris, 1963. 2v.
43544.53.100 Bolsee, B. Cardiogramme. Belgique, 1963.
39566.196 Bonfantini, Mario. Introduzione alla lettura di Diderot. Torino, 1963.
43544.74.3700 Bordier, Roger. The golden plain. Boston, 1963.
43544.74.3710 Bordier, Roger. The golden plain. London, 1963.
43544.81.2240 Bosco, Henri. L'Épervier. Paris, 1963.
43544.89.2180 Bosquet, Alain. Un besoin de malheur; roman. Paris, 1963.
43544.108.115 Boulle, Pierre. Contes de l'absurde. Paris, 1963.
43544.108.745 Boulle, Pierre. Planet of the apes. N.Y., 1963.
43544.108.170 Boulle, Pierre. La planète des singes; roman. Paris, 1963.

Chronological Listing

1963 - cont.

43544.87.3110	Bourbon Busset, Jacques de. La grande conference. Paris, 1963.
43544.107.110	Boutron, Michel. Les liens; roman. Paris, 1963.
FL 6139.11.3	Boyd, William. The educational theory of Jean-Jacques Rousseau. N.Y., 1963.
39544.361	Brailsford, H.N. Voltaire. London, 1963.
42576.65.13.130	Brandreth, H.R.T. Huysmans. London, 1963.
43545.4.4011	Brasillach, Robert. Oeuvres complètes. Paris, 1963. 12v.
43620.2.470	Brée, Germaine. Gide. New Brunswick, 1963.
43545.23.110	Brenner, J. La féte au village. Paris, 1963.
43545.24.157	Breton, André. Nadja. Paris, 1963.
43537.6.100	Brett, Vladimir. Henri Barbusse, sa marche vers la clasté. Prague, 1963.
43545.63.1700	Brock, Mida. Poèmes. Paris, 1963.
37543.551	Brockmeier, P. Darstellungen der französischen Literaturgeschichte. Berlin, 1963.
43626.22.828	Brodin, Pierre. Julien Green. Paris, 1963.
FL 6139.63.5	Broome, Jack H. Rousseau; a study of his thought. London, 1963.
Mon 112.16	Brown, F.S. Religious and political conservatism. Geneva, 1963.
FL 374.11	Brown, Howard. Music in the French secular theater, 1400-1550. Cambridge, 1963.
FL 374.12	Brown, Howard. Theatrical chansons of the fifteenth and early sixteenth centuries. Cambridge, 1963.
43545.89.4110	Brune, Jean. Journal d'exil. Paris, 1963.
37563.102	Brunelli, Giuseppe A. Da Ronsard à Molière. Messina, 1963.
43699.51.815	Buge, J. Milosz en quête du divin. Paris, 1963.
43625.3.255	Burne, G. St. Rémy de Gourmont. Carbondale, 1963.
43546.87.72	Butor, Michel. Degrees. N.Y., 1963.
43546.87.76	Butor, Michel. Description de San Marco. Paris, 1963.
43546.87.36	Butor, Michel. La modification. Paris, 1963.
Mol 603.10	Cairncross, John. Molière bourgeois et libertin. Paris, 1963.
43550.51.100	Cali, F. Monsieur Thomas la Brévine. Paris, 1963.
43550.58.280	Camus, Albert. Albert Camus par lui-même. Paris, 1963.
43550.58.757	Camus, Albert. Carnets, 1935-1951. London, 1963-66. 2v.
43550.58.741	Camus, Albert. Exile and the kingdom. N.Y., 1963.
43550.58.702	Camus, Albert. Notebooks, 1935-1942. N.Y., 1963. 2v.
43550.70.1100	Capieu, Henri. Demeures. Paris, 1963.
41522.18.440	Carter, A.E. Baudelaire et la critique française, 1868-1917. Columbia, 1963.
42584.25.305	Carter, L.A. Zola and the theater. 1. ed. New Haven, 1963.
37557.79	Cary, Edmond. Les grandes traducteurs français. Genève, 1963.
43550.79.100	Cassagnau, Paul. Un nom pour t'appeler. Foutenoy-en-Puisaye, 1963.
FL 6139.54.5	Cassirer, E. The question of Jean-Jacques Rousseau. Bloomington, 1963.
41564.10.5	Castex, P. Vigny: Stello, Servitude et grandeur militaires. Paris, 1963.
37576.647.12	Castex, Pierre. Anthologie du conte fantastique français. 2. éd. Paris, 1963.
43744.67.1207	Cattaui, Georges. Proust perdu et retrouvé. Paris, 1963.
43550.89.700	Cau, Jean. The mercy of God. 1. ed. N.Y., 1963.
43550.89.140	Cau, Jean. Les parachutistes, precéde de Le amaître du monde. Paris, 1963.
43550.98.190	Cayrol, Jean. Le froid du soleil; roman. Paris, 1963.
41543.22.52	Cellier, Léon. Gerard de Nerval. Paris, 1963.
43551.59.104	Cendrars, Blaise. Du monde entier. Paris, 1963.
43551.79.160	Césaire, Aimé. La tragedie du Roi Christophe. Paris, 1963.
43551.80.160	Cesbron, Gilbert. Journal sans date. Paris, 1963. 2v.
37569.300.5	Chapsal, Madeleine. Quinze écrivains. Paris, 1963.
43552.4.2140.5	Char, René. Le marteau sans maitre. Paris, 1963.
43552.6.1100	Chargan, Maria. La lutte éternelle. Paris, 1963.
43552.5.1200	Chartier, Émile. Cahiers de Lorient. Paris, 1963-1964. 2v.
43552.5.1190	Chartier, Émile. Esquisses d'Alain (pseud.). Paris, 1963. 4v.
40586.17.25	Chateaubriand, F.A.R. Itinéraire de Paris à Jérusalem. Paris, 1963.
40586.28.90	Chateaubriand, F.A.R. Mémoires d'outre-tombe. Lausanne, 1963. 4v.
43757.50.1210	Cheval, René. Romain Rolland. Paris, 1963.
43552.25.2140	Chevallier, Gabriel. Clochemerle les Bains; roman. Paris, 1963.
43552.80.21	Christophe, Lucien. Poèmes, 1913-1963. Paris, 1963.
37555.719	Clancier, G.E. De Chénier à Baudelaire. Paris, 1963.
43554.2.26	Claudel, Paul. Paul Claudel, par lui-même. Paris, 1963.
43554.2.480	Claudel, Paul. Réflexions sur la poésie. Paris, 1963.
43709.3.840	Cocteau, J. La comtesse de Noailles - oui et non. Paris, 1963.
43556.48.100	Colas, Michel. La croix et le glaive. Paris, 1963.
43556.49.723	Colette, Sidonie Gabrielle. The blue lantern. London, 1963.
43556.49.725.10	Colette, Sidonie Gabrielle. Chéri. London, 1963.
43556.49.585	Colette, Sidonie Gabrielle. Lettres au petit corsaire. Paris, 1963.
42555.1.83	Collie, M. Laforgue. Edinburgh, 1963.
43556.55.100	Comiti, Jean Baptiste. Éclos la nuit. Paris, 1963.
43756.90.840	Coquoz, F.M. L'évolution religieuse de Jacques Rivière. Fribourg, 1963.
38575.70	Corneille, Pierre. Trois discours sur le poème dramatique. Paris, 1963.
FL 386.46.5	Corvin, Michel. Le théâtre nouveau en France. Paris, 1963.
37569.122	Crastre, Victor. Le drame du surrealisme. Paris, 1963.
42557.20.305	Cuénot, C. Le style de Paul Verlaine. Paris, 1963.
43744.67.1440	Daniel, G. Temps et mystification dans "A la recherche du temps perdu". Paris, 1963.
FL 383.195	Danilin, Iurii Iv. Parizhskaia kommuna i frantsuzskii teatr. Moskva, 1963.
43565.60.1170	Daninos, Pierre. Daninoscope. Paris, 1963.
43565.60.1150	Daninos, Pierre. Sonia, ou Le dictionnaire dse maux coulants. Paris, 1963.
43565.76.2110	Darmangeat, Pierre. Je crois en l'homme. Paris, 1963.
39544.366	Dassen, Julio. Voltaire, defensor de Juan Calas. Buenos Aires, 1963.
43565.90.130	Davignon, Henri. De la Princesse de Clères à Thérèse Desqueyroux. Bruxelles, 1963.

1963 - cont.

43833.20.905	Debidour, V.H. Simone Weil, ou La transparence. Paris, 1963.
40583.333	Dechamps, J. Amities stendhaliennes en Belgique. Bruxelles, 1963.
43566.17.2100	Dedet, Jean Marie. Polymnie prostituée. Paris, 1963.
40583.320.5	Dédéyan, Charles. L'Italie dans l'oeuvre romanesque de Stendhal. Paris, 1963. 2v.
43566.43.735	Dekobra, Maurice. The golden-eyed Venus. London, 1963.
43566.46.1100	Delanglade, Frédéric. A Lys et 12. Paris, 1963.
43620.2.350.5	Delay, J.P.L. The youth of André Gide. Chicago, 1963.
43566.48.6715	Del Castillo, Michel. Through the hoop. N.Y., 1963.
43566.52.170	Demaison, André. L'étoile de Dakar. Paris, 1963.
42576.36.180	Dénommé, R.T. The naturalism of Gustave Geffroy. Genève, 1963.
41542.4.95	Derosier, Marcel. Le souvenir de Théophile Gautier en Bigorre. Tarbes, 1963.
43566.78.1110	Des Forêts, Louis R. Le bavard. Paris, 1963.
43566.78.1700	Des Forêts, Louis R. The children's room. London, 1963.
38526.11.7.2	Desmarets de Saint Sorlin, Jean. Les visionnaires. Paris, 1963.
43611.5.165	Desonay, F. Le grand Meaulnes d'Alain-Fournier. Paris, 1963.
38526.12.76	Desportes, Philippe. Diverses amours et autres oeuvres meslées. Genève, 1963.
43566.82.7725	Destouches, Louis Ferdinand. Vive l'amnistie monsieur. Liège, 1963.
39594.19.140	Devletoglou, Nicos E. Montesquieu and the wealth of nations. Athens, 1963.
43567.79.190	Dhôtel, André. La tribu Bécaille. Paris, 1963.
43568.6.110	Dib, Mohammed. Ombre gardienne. Paris, 1963.
39564.8.65	Diderot, Denis. Contes. London, 1963.
39564.8.30	Diderot, Denis. Oeuvres politiques. Paris, 1963.
39564.15.20	Diderot, Denis. Opinions et paradoxes. Paris, 1963.
40587.158	Diéguez, Manuel de. Chateaubriand. Paris, 1963.
43568.67.110	Diolé, Philippe. L'Okapi. Paris, 1963.
43573.110	Dorgelès, Roland. An beau temps de la Butte. Paris, 1963.
43573.76.110	Dorgelès, Roland. Au beau temps de la Butte. Paris, 1963.
38575.23.100.15	Doubrovsky, Serge. Corneille et la dialectique du héros. Paris, 1963.
43573.89.3100	Doubrovsky, Serge. Le jour S, suivi de chronique américaine. Paris, 1963.
43573.89.6100	Doucet, R. D'ici et d'ailleurs. Paris, 1963.
38537.53	Doutenville, H. Rabelais dedans Touraine. Tours, 1963.
43574.75.715	Druon, Maurice. The glass coffin, and other stories. N.Y., 1963.
38526.48.17.10	Du Bartas, Guillaume de Salluste. Die Schöpfungswerke des Du Bartas. Tübingen, 1963.
37567.612	Dubois, J. Romanciers français de l'Instantane au XIXe siècle. Bruxelles, 1963.
43576.11.110	Dubrau, Louis. A la poursuite de Sandra. Paris, 1963.
43632.6.805	Dulière, A. Émile Henriot, sa vie, son oeuvre. Paris, 1963.
43576.74.2705	Duras, Marguerite. Ten-thirty on a summer night. N.Y., 1963.
FL 386.805.5	Dussane, Beatrix. J'étais dans la salle. Paris, 1963.
38547.16	Ehrmann, J. Un paradis désespéré. 1. éd. New Haven, 1963.
42554.30.8	Elskamp, M. Correspondance. Bruxelles, 1963.
43591.89.340	Éluard, Paul. Choix de poèmes. Paris, 1963.
43591.89.1110	Éluard, Paul. Le poète et son ombre. Paris, 1963.
38567.51	Emard, P. La Sainte-Chapelle du Lutrin. Genève, 1963.
43592.53.310	Emmanuel, Pierre. Le Gout de l'un. Paris, 1963.
43592.53.320	Emmanuel, Pierre. La nouvelle naissance. Paris, 1963.
43598.12.200A	Eschasseriaux, Bernard. Les dimanches de Ville-d'Avray; roman. Paris, 1963.
43598.86.621	Estivals, G. A gap in the wall. N.Y., 1963.
43604.19.130	Eydoux, Emmanuel. Pogrom; théâtre. Basel, 1963.
43606.10.130	Fabre-Luce, Alfred. Haute cour. Lausanne, 1963.
43606.10.700	Fabre-Luce, Alfred. The trial of Charles de Gaulle. N.Y., 1963.
43538.76.960	Fabrègues, J. de. Bernanos tel qu'il était. Tours, 1963.
43606.49.100	Falerne, J. Monsieur Duran de la Tour antiquaire. Paris, 1963.
43606.76.210	Fargue, Léon P. Poésies. Paris, 1963.
43697.52.870	Ferreira, V. André Malraux. Lisboa, 1963.
43609.58.700	Finas, Lucette. The faithful shepherd. N.Y., 1963.
37567.650	Fischer, Alexander. Das Vater-Sohn-Verhältnis in der französischen Literatur des 19. und 20. Jahrhunderts. Diss. München, 1963.
42576.35.28	Flaubert, Gustave. Extraits de la correspondance. Paris, 1963.
42576.20.30	Flaubert, Gustave. La première Éducation sentimentale. Paris, 1963.
37575.776	Flouquet, T.L. de. Anthologie de la troisième décade, 1950-60. Dilbeek, 1963.
43611.60.100	Fongy, L. de. Réalités. Nyon, 1963.
40592.92	Forsberg, R.J. Madame de Staël and freedom today. N.Y., 1963.
43757.92.805	Foucault, Michel. Raymond Roussel. Paris, 1963.
43538.76.945	Fraguière, M.A. Bernanos, fidèle à l'enfant. Fribourg, 1963.
Mol 706.9	France. Archives Nationales. Cent ans de recherches sur Molière. Paris, 1963.
42542.49.85	Frazee, R. Henry Céard, idéaliste de détrompé. Toronto, 1963.
43612.24.110	Frère, Maud. Les jumeaux millénaires; roman. Paris, 1963.
42556.28.315A	Frohock, Wilbur M. Rimbaud's poetic practice. Cambridge, 1963.
38512.11.5	Froissart, Jean. L'espinette amoureuse. Paris, 1963.
43614.12.100	Fuchs, Janine. Fibres de vie. Paris, 1963.
43550.58.940	Gadourek, C. Les innocents et les coupables. The Hague, 1963.
43550.58.942	Gadourek, C. Les innocents et les coupables. The Hague, 1963.
38557.24.140	Gaquère, François. Vers l'unité chrétienne. Paris, 1963.
43741.12.800	Garaudy, R. D'un réalisme sans rivages. Paris, 1963.
41574.602	Garcia Lyon, Virgina. Centenario de Los miserables de Victor Hugo. Santiago, 1963.
43616.74.2100	Gardye, Philippe. Matraque. Dessins de Lonchamp. Paris, 1963.
43616.79.180	Gascar, Pierre. Les moutons du feu. Paris, 1963.
43616.83.3100	Gasztold, Carmen Bernos de. Prayers from the Ark. London, 1963.
40526.8.65	Gausseron, Jacques. André Chénier et le drame de la pensée moderne. Paris, 1963.
41542.7.13	Gautier, Théophile. Le capitaine Fracasse. Lausanne, 1963.

Chronological Listing

1963 - cont.

43617.59.210 Genevoix, Maurice. Derrière les collines. Paris, 1963.
43538.1.430.2 Gennari, Geneviève. Simone de Beauvoir. Paris, 1963.
43620.2.69.40 Gide, André. André Gide. Paris, 1963.
43620.2.79.182 Gide, André. Correspondance, 1908-1920. Paris, 1963.
43620.2.53.8 Gide, André. Les faux-monnayeurs; roman. Paris, 1963.
43620.2.35.60 Gide, André. La symphonie pastorale and Isabelle. Harmondsworth, 1963.
40556.24.5 Gignoux, Claude Joseph. Joseph de Maistre; prophète du passé. Paris, 1963.
37557.78 Girard, A. Le journal intime. Paris, 1963.
43620.74.214 Giraudoux, Jean. Electre; pièce en deux actes. Paris, 1963.
43620.74.331 Giraudoux, Jean. La folle de Chaillot. Cambridge, Eng., 1963.
43620.74.623 Giraudoux, Jean. Judith. N.Y., 1963.
43620.74.785 Giraudoux, Jean. Plays. N.Y., 1963- 2v.
FL 6139.63.15 Gobbers, W. Jean-Jacques Rousseau in Holland. Gent, 1963.
42586.66.9.5 Gobineau, Arthur de. Nouvelles asiatiques. Paris, 1963.
43552.5.1835 Gontier, Georges. Alain à la guerre. Paris, 1963.
38514.30.10 Goodrich, Norma Lorre. Charles, duke of Orleans. N.Y., 1963.
Mol 607.13 Gossman, L. Men and masks: a study of Molière. Baltimore, 1963.
37567.60.10 Gourmont, Rémy de. Le livre des masques. Mercure, 1963.
37543.96.10 Gourmont, Rémy de. Promenades littéraires. Paris, 1963. 3v.
43626.22.280 Green, Julien. Pamphlet contre les catholiques de France. Paris, 1963.
43626.22.290 Green, Julien. Partir avant le jour. Paris, 1963.
39574.34 Grimsley, R. Jean d'Alembert, 1717-83. Oxford, 1963.
43628.23.190 Guéhenno, Jean. Notes. Paris, 1963.
37567.609 Guichard, L. La musique et les lettres en France du temps du Wagnerism. Paris, 1963.
Mol 607.11 Guicharnaud, J. Molière. Paris, 1963.
37548.221 Guiette, Robert. Écrivains français de Belgique au XIXe siècle. Paris, 1963.
42576.15.157 Guillemin, Henri. Flaubert devant la vie et devant Dieu. Paris, 1963.
43628.41.3150 Guillevic, Eugène. Sphior. Paris, 1963.
39544.360 Guiragossian, D. Voltaire's facéties. Genève, 1963.
40597.2.580 Gun, Willem H. van der. La courtisane romantique et son rôle dans la Comédie humaine de Balzac. Assen, 1963.
43554.2.1130 Guyard, M.F. Recherches claudeliennes autour des cinq grandes odes. Paris, 1963.
FL 6139.63.20 Haegi, Klaus Donat. Die politische Freiheit im Werk von Jean-Jacques. Winterthur, 1963.
37567.603 Hagberg, C.A. Fransk litteratur, 1836. Stockholm, 1963.
43631.49.2100 Haldas, Georges. Gens qui soupirent. Neuchâtel, 1963.
38526.52.85 Hall, Kathleen. Pontus de Tyard and his Discours philosophiques. London, 1963.
38514.23.105 Hansen, Karl Heinz. Holzschnitte zu den Balladen des François Villon. Hannover, 1963.
43556.1.930 Hellens, F. Adieu au poète Jean Cocteau. Liège, 1963.
43632.50.22 Hellens, Franz. Florilège poétique. Blainville-sur-Mer, 1963.
43738.78.825 Henry, A. Amers de Saint-John Perse. Neuchatel, 1963.
43632.77.3110 Hermann, Claudine. Le cavalier des steppes. Paris, 1963.
43632.77.4100 Herment, Georges. Seuil de terre. Ottigniés, 1963.
43697.52.875 Hoffmann, J. L'humanisme de Malraux. Paris, 1963.
42556.28.325 Houston, J.P. The design of Rimbaud's poetry. New Haven, 1963.
41573.9 Hugo, Victor. Dessinateur. Paris, 1963.
41571.3.110 Hugo, Victor. Oeuvres dramatiques complètes. Paris, 1963.
41572.20.10 Hugo, Victor. Quatre-vingt-treize. Paris, 1963.
41572.36.5 Hugo, Victor. Théâtre complète. Paris, 1963-64. 2v.
37556.17.5 Iakimovich, T.K. Frantsuzskii realisticheskii ocherk, 1830-1848 gg. Moskva, 1963.
Mon 178.14 Ilsley, M.H. A daughter of the Renaissance. The Hague, 1963.
43656.59.715 Ionesco, Eugène. Exit the King. N.Y., 1963.
43656.59.160 Ionesco, Eugène. Le roi se meurt. Paris, 1963.
43620.2.425 Ireland, George Wilhelm. Gide. Edinburgh, 1963.
42556.28.147 Izambard, Georges. Rimbaud tel que je l'ai connu. Paris, 1963.
43620.2.460 Jahhan, Razmond. André Gide et l'Orient. Paris, 1963.
43667.7.100 Jarlot, Gérard. Un chat qui aboie. Paris, 1963.
43697.88.870 Jensen, B. Diktning eller psykologi? Oslo, 1963.
37566.143 Jeune, Simon. De F.T. Graindorge à A.O. Barnabooth. Paris, 1963.
43524.67.840 Jolivet, P. Le théâtre de J. Anouilh. Paris, 1963.
37543.552 Jones, P.M. The assault on French literature. Manchester, Eng., 1963.
43670.94.21 Jouve, Pierre Jean. Poésie. Milano, 1963.
37568.229 Junod, Roger-Louis. Écrivains français du XXe siècle. Lausanne, 1963.
43672.59.700 Kane, Hamidou. Ambiguous adventure. N.Y., 1963.
43757.50.1205 Karczewska-Markiewicz, Zofia. Struktura Jana Kruzysztofa. Wrocław, 1963.
38528.19.5 Kasprzyh, K. Nicolas de Troyes. Warszawa, 1963.
38537.49 Keller, A.C. The telling of tales in Rabelais. Frankfurt, 1963.
43670.95.805 Kerien, W. Louis Jouvet, notre patron. Paris, 1963.
43673.77.2100 Kerraoul, Bernard de. Le poids des âmes, roman. Paris, 1963.
37569.360A Kesteloot, Lilyan. Les écrivains noirs de langue française. Bruxelles, 1963.
38537.48 Krailsheimer, Alban J. Rabelais and the Franҫiscans. Oxford, 1963.
40539.15.80 Krakowski, E. Le comte Jean Potocki. Paris, 1963.
37565.166 Kraus, Werner. Studien zur deutschen und französischen Aufklärung. Berlin, 1963.
38527.58.11 La Boétie, Estienne de. Discours de la servitude volontaire. Paris, 1963.
38527.58.5 La Boétie, Estienne de. Oeuvres politiques. Paris, 1963.
42584.25.43 Laborde, A. Trente-huit années près de Zola. Paris, 1963.
38563.22.41 Labrousse, Élisabeth. Pierre Bayle. La Haye, 1963-64. 2v.
38564.32.36 La Bruyère, J. de. Les caractères ou Les moeurs de ce siècle. Paris, 1963.
43687.35.100 Lahayé, Simone. Les rachetées, portraits et récits de bagne. Paris, 1963.
39566.197 Laidlaw, G.N. Elysian encounter. Syracuse, N.Y., 1963.
37555.201 Lalou, R. Histoire de la poésie française. 7. éd. Paris, 1963.

1963 - cont.

37569.115.9 Lalou, René. Le roman français depuis 1900. 9. éd. Paris, 1963.
41577.11.40A Lamartine, Alphonse de. Oeuvres poétiques complètes. Paris, 1963.
43687.60.3710 Langfus, Anna. The lost shore. London, 1963.
43687.61.1140 Lanoux, Armand. Quand la mer se retire. Paris, 1963.
43687.80.2120 Lartéguy, Jean. Le mal jaune. Paris, 1963.
43687.80.2710 Lartéguy, Jean. The praetorians. 1st American ed. N.Y., 1963.
43687.82.100 Lassalle, Jean Pierre. Le grand patagon; poèmes. Villefranche-de-Rouergue, 1963.
38514.23.97 Las Vergnas, Georges. François Villon. Paris, 1963.
43687.83.1120 Las Vergnas, Raymond. Le corbillard portugais; roman. Paris, 1963.
37565.169A Laufer, Roger. Style rococo. Paris, 1963.
43687.89.1210 Laurent, Jacques. Hortense 14-18. Paris, 1963-67. 5v.
37569.358 Lauwick, H. D'Alphonse Allais à Sacha Guitry. Paris, 1963.
43822.49.1390 Lawler, J.R. Lecture de Valéry. Paris, 1963.
43688.5.5021 Léautaud, Paul. Poésies. Paris, 1963.
43688.14.4100 Le Clézio, Jean Marie Gustave. Le procès-verbal. Paris, 1963.
37562.323 LeGentil, P. La littérature française du moyen âge. Paris, 1963.
FL 1022.10.5 Legge, Mary Dominica. Anglo-Norman literature and its background. Oxford, 1963.
43688.60.700 Leiris, Michel. Manhood: a journey from childhood into the fierce order of virility. N.Y., 1963.
43550.58.990 Leite, Antonio Roberto de Paula. Albert Camus; notas e estudo crítico. São Paulo, 1963.
43687.89.2805 Lelièvre, R. La Varende. Coutances, 1963.
43688.53.1120 Lemaitre, Maurice. Le temps des assis. Paris, 1963.
43688.65.2100 Léonard. Demain. Neuchâtel, 1963.
43688.97.100 Lépidis, Clément. La rose de Büyükada; roman. Paris, 1963.
37567.600A Levin, Harry. The gates of horn. N.Y., 1963.
43690.9.21 Libbrecht, Géo. Poésie, 1937-1962. Paris, 1963.
43690.55.100 Limbour, Georges. La chasse au mérou. Paris, 1963.
43693.53.2100 Lombard, J.C. Ta place. Paris, 1963.
43738.78.830 Loranquin, A. Saint-John Perse. Paris, 1963.
43694.41.100 Luissel, Jean. Via poussiere. Lavaur, 1963.
43574.41.815 Mabire, J. Drieu parmi nous. Paris, 1963.
FL 377.79 Macchila, G. La scuola dei sentimenti. Caltanissetta, 1963.
43526.65.936 Mackworth, Cecily. Guillaume Apollinaire and the Cubist age. 1st American ed. N.Y., 1963.
43617.78.805 McMahon, J.H. The imagination of Jean Genêt. New Haven, 1963.
42555.43.8 Mallarmé, Stéphane. Opere. Milano, 1963.
43697.2.1170 Mallet-Joris, Françoise (pseud.). Lettre à moi-même. Paris, 1963.
43697.52.2130 Malraux, Clara. Le bruit de nos pas. Paris, 1963. 3v.
43697.58.2100 Manan, J. Les mémoires de Bidasse d'après les célèbres chroniques. Paris, 1963.
40583.326 Maquet, Albert. Deux amis italiens de Stendhal. Lausanne, 1963.
42576.15.430 Maranini, Lorenza. Il 48 [i.e. quarantotto] nella struttura della "Education sentimentale" e altri studi francesi. Pisa, 1963.
43697.75.9110 Margerit, Robert. La révolution, roman. Paris, 1963- 4v.
43538.14.820 Marissel, A. Samuel Beckett. Paris, 1963.
43697.76.6150 Maritain, Raïssa. Journal de Raïssa. Paris, 1963.
43697.76.6142 Maritain, Raïssa. Le prince de ce monde. 2. ed. Bruges, 1963.
43620.74.910 Marrill, René. La Genèse du Siegfried de Jean Giraudoux. Paris, 1963.
43697.77.2100 Martel, A. Le mirivis des naturgies. Paris, 1963.
43697.78.9100 Martin, Vio. Visages de la flame. Neuchâtel, 1963.
39544.359 Mason, H.T. Pierre Bayle and Voltaire. London, 1963.
43697.81.110 Massip, Renée. La bête quaternaire; roman. Paris, 1963.
43611.5.170 Massis, Henri. Alain-Fournier sans Goncourt. Liège, 1963.
43556.1.925 Massis, Henri. De Radigue à Maritain; hommage à Cocteau. Liège, 1963.
43697.85.1100 Masson, G.A. L'hostellerie du Foyau. Bruxelles, 1963.
43697.89.7100 Mauget, I. Avec les gloires de mon temps. La Celle-Saint-Cloud, 1963.
43697.88.3120 Mauriac, Claude. L'agrandissement; roman. Paris, 1963.
43697.88.590 Mauriac, François. What I believe. N.Y., 1963.
43697.4.33.5 Mauriac, François. Young man in chains. N.Y., 1963.
43697.89.713 Maurois, André. The weigher of souls. N.Y., 1963.
43697.89.4120 Maurois, Michelle. L'oeil neuf. Paris, 1963.
37543.550 Mauron, Charles. Des métaphores obsédantes au mythe personnel. Paris, 1963.
42555.44.170 Mauron, Charles. Introduction to the psychoanalysis of Mallarmé. Berkeley, 1963.
37556.242 May, G.C. Le dilemme du roman au XVIIIe siècle. New Haven, 1963.
37555.717 Mazaleyrat, J. Pour une étude rythmique du vers français moderne; notes bibliographiques. Paris, 1963.
43698.58.5100 Ménard, J. Les myrtes. Montréal, 1963.
41555.7.80 Mérimée, Prosper. Lettres à Edward Ellice, 1857-1863. Paris, 1963.
42582.2.65 Métral, Maurice. Sur les pas de Jules Verne. Neuchâtel, 1963.
Mol 713.18 Meyer, J. Molière. Paris, 1963.
43698.200.720 Michaux, Henri. Light through darkness. N.Y., 1963.
43698.200.152 Michaux, Henri. Passages, 1937-1963. Paris, 1963.
43699.51.1100 Milon-Capitan, Jeanne. Si je suis, si je fus. Paris, 1963.
42584.25.335 Mitterand, Henri. Album Zola. Paris, 1963.
37557.76 Molho, R. La critique littéraire en France. Paris, 1963.
Mol 245.110 Molière, Jean Baptiste Poquelin. Le misanthrope. Paris, 1963.
Mol 269.3.15 Molière, Jean Baptiste Poquelin. Tartuffe. N.Y., 1963.
37564.28.12 Mongrédien, Georges. Les précieux et les précieuses. Paris, 1963.
43701.61.110 Monnier, Thyde. J'ai joué le jeu. Paris, 1963.
43701.58.100 Monod, S. Pastiches. Paris, 1963.
43701.63.560 Montherlant, Henry de. Le chaos et la nuit. Paris, 1963.
43701.63.565 Montherlant, Henry de. Discours de réception de M. Henry de Montherlant à l'académie française et réponse de M. le duc de Léuis Mirepoix. Paris, 1963.
43701.63.570A Montherlant, Henry de. Essais. Paris, 1963.
43701.63.415 Montherlant, Henry de. Le ville dont le prince est un enfant; trois actes. Paris, 1963.

Chronological Listing

1963 - cont.

43701.74.4100 Morax, R. Le théâtre du Jorat et René Morax. Lausanne, 1963.
42582.2.75 Moré, Marcel. Nouvelles explorations de Jules Verne. Paris, 1963.
43701.76.4100 Morin, Marcelle. Images d'Algérie. Rodez, 1963.
FL 6139.49.6 Mornet, Daniel. Rousseau. 5. éd. Paris, 1963.
43757.6.800 Morrissette, Bruce A. Les romans de Robbe-Grillet. Paris, 1963.
37574.911 Moulin, J. La poésie feminine. Paris, 1963. 2v.
43701.89.1120 Mouloudji, Marcel. Le petit vaincu. Paris, 1963.
43702.89.3100 Mouquin, F. Dans la mêlée. Paris, 1963.
43703.61.100 Muno, Jean. L'homme qui s'efface. Bruxelles, 1963.
43703.75.120 Murciaux, Christian. Pedro de Luna; roman. Paris, 1963.
43703.75.700 Murciaux, Christian. The unforsaken. London, 1963.
43538.76.950 Murray, S.M. La genèse de Dialogues des Carmélites. Paris, 1963.
43688.60.800 Nadeau, M. Michel Leiris et la quadrature du cercle. Paris, 1963.
37568.223 Nadeau, Maurice. Le roman français depuis la guerre. Paris, 1963.
43697.77.860 Narkir'er, F.S. Rozhe Marten diu Gar. Moskva, 1963.
38562.23.40 Nedeljković, D. Fontenel. Beograd, 1963.
37562.325 Nelli, René. L'Erotique des troubadours. Toulouse, 1963.
43706.50.100 Nelli, René. Point de langage. Paris, 1963.
38575.97 Nelson, R.J. Corneille, his heroes and their worlds. Philadelphia, 1963.
FL 6113.20 Neuchâtel. Catalogue de la correspondance. Neuchâtel, 1963. 2v.
38523.3.95 Neuhofer, Peter. Das Adjektiv als Stilelement bei Clément Marot. Wien, 1963.
42555.44.185 Nicolas, H. Mallarmé et le symbolisme. Paris, 1963.
43538.61.800 Nicolle, R. Pierre Benoît et Marcelle-Pierre Benoît. Paris, 1963.
37575.778A Nola, Jean Paul de. Les poètes de la rue des Sols. Paris, 1963.
43709.80.150 Nourissier, François. Un petit bourgeois. Paris, 1963.
43723.18.740 Oldenbourg, Zoé. Cities of the flesh. London, 1963.
43723.50.110 Ollier, Claude. Eté indien. Paris, 1963.
38525.106 Orlando, Francesco. Rotrou dalla tragicomedia alla tragedia. Torino, 1963.
43761.39.910 Pagé, Pierre. St. Exupéry et le monde de l'enfance. Montréal, 1963.
43737.34.240 Pagnol, Marcel. L'eau des collines. Paris, 1963. 2v.
40516.60.105 Pauvert, J.J. L'affaire Sade. Paris, 1963.
43591.89.820 Perche, Louis. Paul Eluard. Paris, 1963.
37555.553 Pfrommer, Walter. Grundzüge der Strophenentwicklung in der französischen Lyrik vom Baudelaire zu Apollinaire. Tübingen, 1963.
43740.41.2100 Philipe, Anne. Le temps d'un soupir. Paris, 1963.
43741.11.1011 Piccard, Eulalie. Collection des oeuvres complètes. v.1,2-3,4-5,6,10,16. Neuchâtel, 1963. 6v.
43741.25.190 Pieyre de Mandiargues, André. La motocyclette. Paris, 1963.
43741.25.200 Pieyre de Mandiargues, André. Le musée noir. Paris, 1963.
43741.25.220 Pieyre de Mandiargues, André. Sabine. Paris, 1963.
43741.59.3021 Pinget, Robert. Plays. London, 1963- 2v.
43741.66.100 Piot, André. Mémoires poétiques. Paris, 1963.
42557.12.135 Poortere, Carlo de. Bibliotheque Carlo de Poortere. Courtrai, 1963.
37574.917 Pornon, Charles. Anthologie (apocryphe) de la poésie française. Paris, 1963.
43744.67.1445 Poulet, G. L'espace proustien. Paris, 1963.
37568.230 Poulet, Robert. Aveux spontanés. Paris, 1963.
FL 398.49.31 Praag, M.M. De toneelspeler. 's-Gravenhage, 1963.
43744.24.22 Prévert, Jacques. Histoires d'autres histoires. Paris, 1963.
40522.9.42 Prévost, Antoine F. Histoire du chevalier des Grieux et de Manon Lescaut. London, 1963.
41574.595 Py, Albert. Les mythes grecs dans la poésie de Victor Hugo. Genève, 1963.
43750.24.280 Queneau, Raymond. Bords: mathématiciens. Paris, 1963.
38514.55.25 Quinze joyes de mariage. Les XV joyes de mariage. Genève, 1963.
38585.43.61 Racine, Jean. Fedra. 2. éd. Milano, 1963.
38585.35.10 Racine, Jean. Iphigénia. Harmondsworth, 1963.
38583.11.11 Racine, Jean. Lettres d'Uzès. Uzès, 1963.
43620.74.915 Raymond, Agnes G. Giraudoux devant la victoire et la défaite. Paris, 1963.
43753.4.100 Régnier, Yves. Les ombres. Paris, 1963.
FL 1108.243.105 Renard, Michel. Lès aventures dè Djan d'Nivèle èl fi dè s'pére. Naumur, 1963.
43753.90.2110 Réval, Gabrielle. Le royaume du printemps. Paris, 1963.
38557.24.125 Reynolds, E.E. Bossuet. 1. ed. Garden City, 1963.
43756.6.100 Ribaud, A. La cour (chronique du royaume). Paris, 1963.
41543.22.100 Richer, Jean. Nerval. Paris, 1963.
42556.28.206 Rickword, Edgell. Rimbaud, the boy and the poet. London, 1963.
43756.62.100 Rinval, Claude. Jusqu'à la limite de la chair. Paris, 1963.
39586.23.20 Rivarol, Antoine. Rivarol, par Jean Dutour. Paris, 1963.
43611.5.155 Rivière, I. Vie et passion d'Alain-Fournier. Monaco, 1963.
43756.90.111 Rivière, Jacques. Correspondance, 1907-1914. Paris, 1963.
43550.58.960 Rizobello, A. Albert Camus. Napoli, 1963.
43757.6.160 Robbe-Grillet, Alain. L'immortelle. Paris, 1963.
43757.6.170 Robbe-Grillet, Alain. Pour un nouveau roman. Paris, 1963.
43757.8.5100 Robin, Liliane. Le sortilège des Antille. Paris, 1963.
43822.49.1385 Robinson, J. L'analyse de l'esprit dans les cahiers de Valéry. Paris, 1963.
43757.13.1110 Rochefort, Christiane. Les stances à Sophie. Paris, 1963.
38525.20.28.8 Ronsard, Pierre de. Les amours. Paris, 1963.
43757.88.3700 Rougemont, Denis de. Love declared. N.Y., 1963.
FL 6024.20 Rousseau, J.J. Introduction à l'étude de Jean-Jacques Rousseau: les confessions, I-IV. Paris, 1963.
43757.92.122 Roussel, Raymond. Comment j'ai écrit certains de mes livres. Paris, 1963.
43757.92.176 Roussel, Raymond. La doublure. Paris, 1963.
43757.92.114 Roussel, Raymond. L'étoile au front; pièce en trois actes, en prose. Paris, 1963.
43757.92.192 Roussel, Raymond. Impressions d'Afrique. Paris, 1963.
43757.92.180 Roussel, Raymond. Locus solus. Lausanne, 1963.
43757.92.144 Roussel, Raymond. Nouvelles impressions d'Afrique. Paris, 1963.
43757.92.152 Roussel, Raymond. La vue. Paris, 1963.
43757.96.170 Roy, Claude. Léone, et les siens. Paris, 1963.
43757.96.4116 Roy, Jules. Retour de l'enfer. Paris, 1963.

1963 - cont.

43758.24.100 Ruet, Noël. Les sources dans le coeur. Paris, 1963.
43687.74.810 Ruggiero, Ortensia. Valéry Larbaud et l'Italie. Paris, 1963.
40516.60.22 Sade, D.A.F. de. De Sade quartet. London, 1963.
40516.60.76 Sade, D.A.F. de. Lettres choisies. Paris, 1963.
43761.31.180 Sagan, Françoise. Landru. Paris, 1963.
43761.31.170 Sagan, Françoise. La robe mauve de Valentine. Paris, 1963.
43591.89.855 Saint Denis, France. Musée Municipal d'Art et Histoire. Paul Eluard, 1895-1952. Saint-Denis, 1963.
37563.22.2 Sainte-Beauve, C.A. Tableau historique. Cambridge, 1963.
40575.39.5 Sainte-Beuve, Charles A. Selected essays. 1. ed. Garden City, 1963.
41557.9.28.15 Sand, George. Elle et lui. Neuchâtel, 1963.
43761.77.710 Sarraute, Nathalie. The age of suspicion. N.Y., 1963.
43761.77.160 Sarraute, Nathalie. Les fruits d'or. Paris, 1963.
41522.18.357 Sartre, J.P. Baudelaire. Paris, 1963.
43761.78.310 Sartre, Jean Paul. Les mouches, drame en trois actes. N.Y., 1963.
43761.78.716 Sartre, Jean Paul. The reprieve. Harmondsworth, 1963.
37564.264 Sassus, Jeannine. The motif of renunciation of love in the seventeenth century French novel. Washington, 1963.
37564.187.7 Saulnier, Verdun L. La littérature française du siècle classique. 7. éd. Paris, 1963.
37565.170 Saulnier, Verdun L. La litterature française du siècle philosophique. 7e éd. Paris, 1963.
37567.655 Sauro, Antoine. L'opposizione al romanticismo. Bari, 1963.
37567.607 Schmidt, A. La littérature symboliste, 1870-1900. 7. éd. Paris, 1963.
39585.5.80 Schnelle, K. Aufklärung und klerikale Reaktion. Berlin, 1963.
43620.2.440 Schoeler, C. von. Der mittelmeerische Geist André Gides. Tübingen, 1963.
39566.198 Schroeder, E. Diderot und die literarästhetische Tradition. Marburg, 1963.
43535.54.805 Scriabine, H. Les faux dieux. v. 1-2. Paris, 1963.
43765.22.100 Seers, E. Un manuscrit retrouvé à Kor-el-Fantin. Eleutheropolis, 1963.
43538.14.830 Seipel, H. Untersuchungen zum experimentellen Theater von Beckett und Ionesco. Bonn, 1963.
41568.17.30 Sénancour, Etienne Pivert de. Sur les générations actuelles. Genève, 1963.
43765.80.705 Serge, Victor (pseud.). Memoirs of a revolutionary, 1901-1941. London, 1963.
38546.36.30 Sévigné, Marie de R.C. Lettres. v.3. Paris, 1963.
43744.67.1435 Shattuck, Roger. Proust's binoculars. N.Y., 1963.
43769.54.700 Simenon, Georges. The iron staircase. London, 1963.
43769.54.796 Simenon, Georges. Maigret and the lazy burglar. London, 1963.
43769.54.743 Simenon, Georges. Pedigree. N.Y., 1963.
43769.56.2715 Simon, Claude. The palace. N.Y., 1963.
37544.115 Simon, Pierre H. Le domaine héröique des lettres françaises, Xe-XIXe siècle. Paris, 1963.
Mon 159.32 Snethlage, J.L. Montaigne. Den Haag, 1963.
FL 6135.12 Société des études robspierristes. Jean-Jacques Rousseau, 1712-1778. Gap, 1963.
37569.364 Soupault, P. Profils perdus. Paris, 1963.
38551.161 Spaemann, Robert. Reflexion und Spontaneität. Stuttgart, 1963.
43693.58.800 Spilleben, Willy. Emmanuel Looten, de Franse Vlaming. Lier, 1963.
43526.65.945 Steegmueller, F. Apollinaire. N.Y., 1963.
43779.24.4100 Steppe, André. Camarade Zolobine. Paris, 1963.
37543.553 Studi in onore di Carlo Pellegrini. Torino, 1963.
37555.332.2 Suchier, W. Französische Verslehre auf historischer Grundlage. 2. Aufl. Tübingen, 1963.
43697.89.865 Suffel, J. André Maurois. Paris, 1963.
38563.22.50 Talluri, Bruna. Pierre Bayle. Milano, 1963.
37569.362 Tans, Joseph. Romans lisibles et romans illisibles. Groningen, 1963.
41542.4.100 Tarbes, France. Musée Massey. Exposition Théophile Gautier, 1811-1872. Tarbes, 1963.
43787.29.140 Tefri (pseud.). Au Piladre. Paris, 1963.
41564.55.110 Teppe, J. Alfred de Vigny et ses amants. Paris, 1963.
37595.102 Terry, P.A. Lays of courtly love. 1. éd. Garden City, 1963.
FL 6039.17 Testa, Aldo. Meditazioni su Rousseau dal Contratto sociale al dialogo sociale. Bologna, 1963.
FL 396.90.20F Théâtres des Champs-Elysées, 1913-63. Paris, 1963.
40517.44.90 Thelander, D.R. Laclos and the epistolary novel. Genève, 1963.
43788.24.180 Thérive, André. La foire littéraire. Paris, 1963.
Mon 130.7 Thibandet, A. Montaigne. Paris, 1963.
42576.15.41.2 Thibaudet, A. Gustave Flaubert. Paris, 1963.
43788.41.2120 Thiery, Michel. La tentation d'Adam. 4e éd. Paris, 1958.
þ3788.41.2130 1 f Thiry, Marcel. Le festin d'attente. Bruxelles, 1963.
43788.41.2130 Thiry, Marcel. Le festin d'attente. Bruxelles? 1963.
43788.41.2140 Thiry, Marcel. Simul et autres cas. Bruxelles, 1963.
43788.65.1140 Thomas, Henri. Sous le lien de temps. Paris, 1963.
43792.19.100 Todrani, Jean. Je parle de l'obscur. Paris, 1963.
41563.30.20 Toepffer, Rodolphe. Voyages et aventures du Docteur Festes. Paris, 1963.
39596.31 Toinet, P. Paul et Virginie. Paris, 1963.
43792.76.100 Torma, J. Porte battante. Paris, 1963.
43792.77.100 Torreilles, Pierre. Corps dispersé d'Orphée. Neuchâtel, 1963.
43792.99.100 Torreilles, Pierre. Corps dispersé d'Orphée. Neuchâtel, 1963.
37548.223 Tougas, Gérard. Littérature romande et culture française. Paris, 1963.
40583.338 Trompeo, Pietro Paolo. Incontri di Stendhal. Napoli, 1963.
43793.67.270 Troyat, Henri. Une extrême amitie. Paris, 1963.
43793.67.340 Troyat, Henri. Sophie, ou La fin des combats; roman. Paris, 1963.
43799.5.200 Tzara, Tristan. Lampisteries. Paris, 1963.
Mon 178.8 Uildriks, Anne. Les idées littéraires de Mlle. de Gournay. Groningen, 1963?
43738.1.865 Vandamme, Jan. Charles Péguy. Brugge, 1963.
43822.92.110 Vandercammen, Edmond. Les sang partagé. Bruxelles, 1963.
43566.82.7825 Vandromme, P. Louis-Ferdinand Céline. Paris, 1963.
43619.23.805 Vandromme, P. Michel de Ghelderode. Paris, 1963.
37567.610 Van Tieghem, P. Le romantisme français. 7. éd. Paris, 1963.

1963 - cont.

37543.261.16 Van Tieghem, Philippe. Les grandes doctrines littéraires en France. 6. éd. Paris, 1963.

37555.255 Velikovskii, S.Iz. Poety frantsuzkikh revoliutsii 1789-1898. Moskva, 1963.

41578.167 Verdiers, Abel. Les amours italiennes de Lamartine. Paris, 1963.

37567.617 Vernois, Paul. La style rustique dans les romans champêtres après George Sand, problèmes de nature et d'emploi. Paris, 1963.

40587.160 Vial, André. Chateaubriand et le Temps Perdu. Paris, 1963.

43744.67.1480 Vial, André. Proust; structures d'une conscience et naissance d'une esthétique. Paris, 1963.

43824.16.3100 Vidal, Maurice. La vie qui passe. Paris, 1963.

37556.12.45 Vidiasova, L.M. Sovremennaia frantsuzskaia pechat. Moskva, 1963.

41564.10.20 Vigny, Alfred de. Stello. Montréal, 1963.

42547.21.10 Villiers de l'Isle Adam, Auguste. Cruel tales. London, 1963.

38514.20.100 Villon, François. Verzamelde gedichten. Amsterdam, 1963.

43620.2.475 Vitanović, Slobodan. Andre Žid i francusko klasično pozorište. Beograd, 1963.

38585.16.340 Vivaver, E. Racine et la poésie tragique. 2. éd. Paris, 1963.

41543.22.90 Vivier, M. Gerard de Nerval. Paris, 1963.

39545.35.70 Voltaire, François Marie Arouet de. Candide, vollständiger Text. Frankfurt, 1963.

39545.132 Voltaire, François Marie Arouet de. Essai sur les moeurs et l'esprit des nations et sur les principaux faits de l'histoire depuis Charlemagne jusqu'à Louis XIII. Paris, 1963. 2v.

39543.66 Voltaire, François Marie Arouet de. Politique de Voltaire. Paris, 1963.

39544.27.32 Voltaire, François Marie Arouet de. Select letters of Voltaire. London, 1963.

39545.130 Voltaire, François Marie Arouet de. Sermon du rabin akib. Jersey City, 1963.

39545.60.11 Voltaire, François Marie Arouet de. The sermon of the fifty. Jersey City, 1963.

37555.718 Voss, D. Die Majuskel bie französischen Lyrikern des 19. Jahrhunderts. Bonn, 1963.

FL 6139.63 Vossler, Otto. Rousseaus Freiheitslehre. Gottingen, 1963.

43828.41.110 Vrigny, Roger. La nuit de Mougins. Paris, 1963.

43538.1.810 Wasmund, Dagny. Der "Skandal" der Simone Beauvoir. München, 1963.

38585.16.325 Weinberg, B. The art of Jean Racine. Chicago, 1963.

FL 6139.63.10 Weissel, B. Von wem die Gewalt in der Staaten Herrührt. Berlin, 1963.

38537.25.240 Wickler, Franz Josef. Rabelais und Sterne. Bonn, 1963.

41568.1.80 Wieclawik, L. de. Alphonse Rabbé dans la mélée politique et littéraire de la restauration. Paris, 1963.

FL 6139.29.3 Wright, Ernest Hunter. The meaning of Rousseau. N.Y., 1963.

38575.95 Yarrow, Philip J. Corneille. London, 1963.

43852.89.702 Yourcenar, Marguerite. Memories of Hadrian, and reflections on the composition of memories of Hadrian. N.Y., 1963.

43852.89.200 Yourcenar, Marguerite. Le mystère d'Alceste. Paris, 1963.

42584.2.20 Zola, Emile. L'atelier de Zola. Genève, 1963.

42584.2.15 Zola, Emile. Lettres de Paris. Genève, 1963.

37562.322 Zumthor, P. Langue et techniques poétiques à l'époque romane. Paris, 1963.

1964

42545.3.875 Académie...Brussels. Académie royale de langue et littérature françaises. Bruxelles, 1964.

38524.150 Adam, Antoine. Les libertins au XVIIe siècle. Paris, 1964.

43514.6.150 Adamov, Arthur. Ici et maintenant. Paris, 1964.

42515.94 Aelberts, Alain V. Fatras; poèmes. Liège, 1964.

43822.49.1425 Aigrisse, Gilberte. Psychanalyse de Paul Valéry. Paris, 1964.

43522.6.100 Alba, Joseph. Ce chant qui nous entoure. Paris, 1964.

43522.7.2100 Albert-Birot, Pierre. Giabinoulor, épopée. Paris, 1964.

42562.60.3 Allais, Alphonse. Oeuvres complètes. Paris, 1964-1970. 11v.

42562.60.20 Allais, Alphonse. Le parapluie de l'escouade. Paris, 1964.

43524.67.796 Anouilh, Jean. Poor Bitos. London, 1964.

FL 396.50.8 Antoine, André. Memories of the theatre-libre. Coral Gables, 1964.

43526.65.700 Apollinaire, Guillaume. Alcools: poems, 1898-1913. 1st ed. Garden City, 1964.

43526.65.320 Apollinaire, Guillaume. Les diables amoureux. Paris, 1964.

43527.3.410 Aragon, Louis. Entretiens avec Francis Cremieux. Paris, 1964.

43527.3.195 Aragon, Louis. Le fou d'Elsa. Paris, 1964.

43527.3.400 Aragon, Louis. Il ne m'est Paris que d'Elsa. Paris, 1964.

43527.3.405 Aragon, Louis. Le voyage de Hollande. Paris, 1964.

38575.23.140 Arcine, Roland d'. Corneille, l'homme à travers l'oeuvre. Vienne, 1964.

38537.52 Artamonov, S.D. Fransua Rable. Moskva, 1964.

43528.86.72 Artaud, Antonin. Lettres à Génica Athanasiou. Paris, 1964.

40583.334 Atherton, J.H. Stendhal. London, 1964.

43709.85.805 Au pays de Nothomb. Vieux-Virton, 1964.

FL 6139.64.5 Baczko, Bronisław. Rousseau. Warszawa, 1964.

43537.18.1100 Badiou, Alain. Trajectoire inverse. Paris, 1964- 2v.

37563.104 Bady, René. L'homme et son institution de Montaigne à Berulle, 1580-1625. Paris, 1964.

FL 386.813 Baecque, Andée de. Le théâtre d'aujourd'hui. Paris, 1964.

38526.8.2 Baif, Jean Antoine de. Chansonnettes. Vancouver, 1964.

43527.3.840 Balashova, T.V. Tvorchestvo Aragona. Moskva, 1964.

40596.13.142 Balzac, Honoré de. Contes drolatiques. 2. éd. Paris, 1964.

40597.35.260 Balzac, Honoré de. Gambara. Paris, 1964.

40597.14.6.22 Balzac, Honoré de. Histoire de la grandeur et de la decadence de César Birotteau. Paris, 1964.

40597.35.240 Balzac, Honoré de. Massimilla Doni. Thèse. Paris, 1964.

40597.35.211 Balzac, Honoré de. Monographie de la presse parisienne. Paris, 1964.

40597.35.220 Balzac, Honoré de. Les paysans. Paris, 1964.

37566.13.8 Barbey d'Aurevilly, J.A. Le XIXe siècle des oeuvres et des hommes. Paris, 1964- 2v.

1964 - cont.

41522.2.3 Barbey d'Aurevilly, Jules. Oeuvres romanesques complètes. Paris, 1964-66. 2v.

41522.1.9 Barbey d'Aurevilly, Jules. The she-devils. London, 1964.

40597.2.600 Bardèche, Maurice. Une lecture de Balzac. Paris, 1964.

41522.18.460 Barlow, N.H. Sainte-Beuve to Baudelaire. Durham, N.C., 1964.

37568.232 Barrère, Jean Bertrand. Critique de chambre. Paris, 1964.

37569.374 Barrère, Jean Bertrand. La cure d'amaigressement du roman. Paris, 1964.

38585.16.331 Barthes, R. On Racine. 1. ed. N.Y., 1964.

43537.77.3110 Barthes, Roland. Essais critiques. Paris, 1964.

43611.5.180 Bastaire, J. Alain-Fournier. Paris, 1964.

41522.13.9.21 Baudelaire, Charles. Květy zla. Praha, 1964.

43537.89.5100 Baudot, Jean A. La machine à écrire mise en marche et programmée. Montréal, 1964.

43537.89.6100 Baudouin, Georges. Traduit de la mer. Bruxelles, 1964.

43537.89.1210 Bauër, Gérard. Chroniques, 1934-1953. Paris, 1964. 3v.

40583.335 Baumann, Carl. Literatur und intellektueller Kitsch. Heidelberg, 1964.

43761.78.885 Bauters, Paul. Jean-Paul Sartre. Brugge, 1964.

38563.5.5 Bayle, Pierre. Oeuvres diverses. Hildesheim, 1964-68. 4v.

37555.720 Bays, Gwendelyn. The Orphic vision. Lincoln, 1964.

43538.1.820 Béalu, Marcel. L'araignée d'eau et autres récits fantastiques. Paris, 1964.

38526.1.30 Beaulieu, E. Les divers rapportz. Genève, 1964.

40532.5.10 Beaumarchais, Pierre A.C. de. Le barbier de Séville. Firenze, 1964.

40532.14.30 Beaumarchais, Pierre A.C. de. Théâtre de Beaumarchais: Le barbier de Séville. Paris, 1964.

43538.1.535 Beauvoir, Simone de. Une mort très douce. Paris, 1964.

43538.14.792 Beckett, Samuel. How it is. London, 1964.

43538.14.790 Beckett, Samuel. How it is. N.Y., 1964.

43538.14.621 Beckett, Samuel. Play, and two short pieces for radio. London, 1964.

43538.14.747.2 Beckett, Samuel. Poesie in inglese. 2. ed. Torino, 1964.

37574.914 Bédouin, Jean Louis. La poésie surréaliste. Paris, 1964.

43538.35.1110 Beguin, Guy. Anamorphose. Bruxelles, 1964.

43538.35.1100 Beguin, Guy. Monsieur Faust, Madame et l'autre. Ixelles, 1964.

37555.722 Belaval, Yvon. Poèmes d'aujourd'hui. Paris, 1964.

37583.664 Benedikt, M. Modern French theatre: the Avant-garde, Dada, and Surrealism. 1. ed. N.Y., 1964.

43552.4.2820 Benoit, Pierre André. Bibliographie des oeuvres de René Char de 1928 à 1963. Paris, 1964.

FL 398.52.55 Béranger, Jacques. Une vie de théâtre. Bienne, 1964.

43757.6.815 Bernal, Olga. Alain Robbe-Grillet. Paris, 1964.

43538.76.785 Bernanos, Georges. Ultimi scritti politici. Brescia, 1964.

43538.77.2120 Bertin, Charles. Don Juan. Bruxelles, 1964.

41522.18.470 Bertocci, A.P. From symbolism to Baudelaire. Carbonade, 1964.

43757.50.1215 Bloch, J.R. Deux hommes se rencontvent. Paris, 1964.

42563.23.31 Bloy, Léon. Oeuvres. Paris, 1964. 10v.

37574.81 Boase, Alan Martin. The poetry of France. v.1,3-4. London, 1964. 3v.

37575.212 Bodart, Roger. Les poètes du bois de la Cambre. Paris, 1964.

43697.75.880 Börsenverein des Deutschen Buchhandels. Gabriel Marcel. Frankfurt, 1964.

FL 395.161 Boisanger, Claude de. Neuf mois à la comédie française. Paris, 1964.

37568.165.5 Boisdeffre, P. de. Une histoire vivante de la littérature. Paris, 1964.

FL 397.8.20 Boisson, F.A. Les douze colonnes de Louis. Bordeaux, 1964.

42576.15.325 Bollème, Geneviève. La leçon de Flaubert. Paris, 1964.

40535.31.15 Bonaccorso, Giovanni. Gli anni difficili di Marivaux. Messina, 1964.

37564.235.2 Bonfantini, Mario. La letteratura francese del XVII secolo. 2. éd. Napoli, 1964.

37543.565 Bonnet, Henri. De Malherbe à Sartre. Paris, 1964.

39566.205 Booy, J.T. de. Histoire d'un manuscript de Diderot. Frankfurt, 1964.

41522.18.465 Bopp, L. Psychologie des Fleurs du mal. v.1-2,3,4, pt.1-2. Genève, 1964. 5v.

43544.75.6100 Borel, Pierre Louis. De Péguy à Sartre. Neuchâtel, 1964.

43761.39.905 Borgal, Clément. St. Exupéry. Paris, 1964.

43544.101.120 Borne, Alain. La nuit me parle de toi. Limoges, 1964.

43544.89.2190 Bosquet, Alain. Les petites éternités. Paris, 1964.

43544.108.140 Boulle, Pierre. Histoires charitables. Paris, 1964.

43822.49.1410 Bourbon Busset, J. de. Paul Valéry. Paris, 1964.

43544.89.8100 Bourdeillette, Jean. La pierre et l'anémone. Paris, 1964.

42563.89.45 Bourges, Elémir. Les oiseaux s'envolent et les fleurs tombent. Paris, 1964.

43544.89.3130 Bourniquel, Camille. Le lac; roman. Paris, 1964.

43544.89.120 Bousquet, Joë. Lumière infranchissable pourriture. Lavaur, 1964.

FL 6129.64.5 Bovier, Gaspard. Journal du séjour à Grenoble de Jean-Jacques Rousseau. Grenoble, 1964.

FL 374.14 Bowen, B.C. Les caractéristiques essentielles de la farce française. Urbana, 1964.

43545.2.1100 Braekman, Hélène. Pierre à Briguet. Bruxelles, 1964.

43550.58.975 Brée, Germaine. Albert Camus. N.Y., 1964.

43550.58.872 Brée, Germaine. Camus. N.Y., 1964.

42556.28.211.5 Breton, André. Flagrant délit. Paris, 1964.

43545.24.1100 Breton, Jean. Dire non. Dijon, 1964.

43552.5.1845 Bridoux, Andre. Alain, sa vie, son oeuvre. Paris, 1964.

43545.41.4100 Briey, Martin de. Que la paix soit avec nous! Paris, 1964.

39544.363 Brooks, R.A. Voltaire and Leibniz. Genève, 1964.

43823.75.2204 Bruller, Jean. Le silence de la mer. Paris, 1964.

43554.2.1145 Brunel, Pierre. Le soulier de satin devant la critique. Paris, 1964.

43822.49.1556 Brunelli, Giuseppe Antonio. Introduzione alla poesia di Paul Valéry, da Solitude a Intermède, 1887-1892. v.1-2. Messina, 1964-65.

43545.92.100 Brutsch, Jean T. Madame Briboine et autres personnages. Genève, 1964.

43547.82.100 Busselen, Roland. Dénnis que je sois. Paris, 1964.

43744.67.1460 Butor, M. Les oeuvres d'art imaginaires chez Proust. London, 1964.

43546.87.32 Butor, Michel. Illustrations. Paris, 1964. 2v.

43550.6.170 Cabanis, José. Les jeux de la nuit. Paris, 1964.

1964 - cont.

43550.6.150 Cabanis, José. Plaisir et lectures. Paris, 1964. 2v.
43550.58.171 Camus, Albert. Le mythe de Sisyphe. Paris, 1964.
43550.58.970A Camus. Paris, 1964.
38514.166F Candille, Marcel. Étude du livre de vie active de l'hotel-Dieu de Paris. Paris, 1964.
43550.61.100 Cantraine, R. Une raison de mourir. Bruxelles, 1964.
42575.113 Caramachi, Enzo. Le réalisme romanesque des Goncourt. Pisa, 1964.
43550.58.965 Carruth, Hayden. After the stranger. N.Y., 1964?
43550.82.230 Cassou, Jean. La clef des songes. Lausanne, 1964.
43550.82.220 Cassou, Jean. Parti pris. Paris, 1964.
37563.79.5 Castor, G. Pléiade poetics. Cambridge, Eng., 1964.
39594.19.150 Cattaneo, Mario A. Le dottrine politiche de Montesquieu e di Rousseau. Milano, 1964.
43738.1.870 Cattaui, Georges. Péguy, témoin du temporel chrétien. Paris, 1964.
43550.98.172 Cayrol, Jean. Les corps etrangers. Paris, 1964.
42576.16.85 Cento, Alberto. La dottrina di Flaubert. 2. ed. Napoli, 1964.
43552.3.9290 Chamson, André. Comme une pierre qui tombe. Paris, 1964.
43552.4.2795 Char, René. Commune présence. Paris, 1964.
43552.4.2705 Char, René. Impressions anciennes. Paris, 1964.
43552.5.250 Chardonne, Jacques. Catherine; roman. Paris, 1964.
43552.5.215 Chardonne, Jacques. Demi-jour. Suite et fin du "Ciel dans la fenêtre". Paris, 1964.
Mon 113.18 Château, Jean. Montaigne, psychologie et pédagogue. Paris, 1964.
40586.5.22 Chateaubriand, F.A.R. Voyage en Amérique. Paris, 1964. 2v.
43552.7.1100 Chauveau, Jacqueline. Charette et l'epopée vendéenne. Paris, 1964.
43552.24.5100 Chesneau, Marc. Fragment du Journal poétique d'une âme, 1948-1965. Stockholm, 1964.
43738.1.875 Christophe, Lucien. Les grandes heures de Charles Péguy. Bruxelles, 1964.
43738.1.855 Christophe, Lucien. Le jeune homme Péguy. Brussels, 1964.
43738.1.925 Cimon, Paul. Péguy et le temps présent. Montréal, 1964.
43556.1.940 Clair, René. Inauguration du buste Jean Cocteau à Milly-la-Forêt (Chapelle Saint-Blaise des Simples) le vendredi 16 octobre 1964; discours. Paris, 1964.
38567.52 Clarac, Pierre. Boileau. Paris, 1964.
43554.2.452 Claudel, Paul. L'échange. Paris, 1964.
43554.2.405 Claudel, Paul. Letters from Paul Claudel, my godfather. Westminster, 1964.
43709.85.810 Clémeur, Marcel. L'esprit créateur de Pierre Nothomb. Vieux-Virton, 1964.
FL 6139.34.3A Cobban, Alfred. Rousseau and the modern state. 2. ed. Hamden, 1964.
43556.1.712 Cocteau, Jean. The infernal machine. Norfolk, Conn., 1964.
43538.14.845 Coe, Richard N. Beckett. Edinburgh, 1964.
FL 398.84.15 Collins, H.F. Talma. London, 1964.
37575.151.5 Comité Erckmann-Chatrian. Écrivains lorrains. Verdun, 1964.
43556.56.100 Compére, Gaston. Le signe infortuné. Bruxelles, 1964.
Mon 113.20 Conche, Marcel. Montaigne, ou La conscience heureuse. Paris, 1964.
43556.58.130 Conchon, Georges. L'état sauvage; roman. Paris, 1964.
40553.7.35 Constant de Rebecque, Benjamin. Écrits et discours politiques. Paris, 1964. 2v.
43556.77.2102 Corm, Charles. La montagne inspirée. 2e éd. Beyrouth, 1964.
38575.34.20 Corneille, Pierre. Le menteur. Paris, 1964.
37596.13.5 Coucy, G.C. Chansons attribuées au Chastelain de Couci. Paris, 1964.
40534.32.10 Crébillon, Claude Prosper Jolyot de. Crébillon fils. Paris, 1964.
43557.25.1100 Crevel, Bernard. Parce que...poesies. Paris, 1964.
43557.65.100 Croht-Legras, Rine. Les champs incultes. Paris, 1964.
42554.26.85 Cros, Charles. Oeuvres complètes. Paris, 1964.
42568.21.80 Crouzet, Marcel. Un inconnu du réalisme: Duranty, 1833-1880. Paris, 1964.
43701.63.920 Cruickshank, J. Montherlant. Edinbde urgh, 1964.
43554.2.1125 Czaschke, A. Der Cantique de Mesa. Münster, 1964.
37596.2.15 Damave, Helena. Die Sprache der Pilgerfahrt der träumenden Mönchs. Proefschrift. Haarlem, 1964.
43565.60.1160 Daninos, Pierre. Snobissimo ou Le désir de paraître. Paris, 1964.
43526.65.950 Davies, M. Apollinaire. Edinburgh, 1964.
43737.87.800 De la transparence en poésie. Lugano, 1964.
43540.3.800 Decreus, Juliette. Le prêtre dans l'oeuvre de André Billy. Paris, 1964.
41574.599 Dédéyan, C. Victor Hugo et l'Allemagne. Paris, 1964. 2v.
41574.600 Delalande, J. Victor Hugo. Paris, 1964?
43744.67.1465 Deleuze, Gilles. Marcel Proust et les signes. Paris, 1964.
43566.50.4100 Della Faille, Pierre. Autopsie de sodome. Paris, 1964.
40517.44.95 Delmas, André A. À la recherche des liaisons dangereuses. Paris, 1964.
43566.54.1100 Demez, Marie Antoinette. L'Adieu d'une larme, ou L'amour scaphandrire. Bruxelles, 1964.
37543.548.2 Derche, Roland. Études de textes français. 2. éd. Paris, 1964. 6v.
FL 360.101 Descotes, Maurice. Le public de théâtre et son histoire. Paris, 1964.
39566.202 Desne, Roland. Diderot et le neveu de Rameau. Paris, 1964?
43538.35.1800 Despert, Jehan. Guy Beguin, ou Le théâtre en liberte. Ixelles, 1964.
43566.90.150 Deval, Jacques. Les voyageurs; roman. Paris, 1964.
39564.8.8 Diderot, Denis. Ecrits philosophiques. Paris, 1964.
39564.15.50 Diderot, Denis. Eléments de physiologie. Paris, 1964.
39564.8.70 Diderot, Denis. Quatres contes. Genève, 1964.
37558.206 Didier, Robert. Isographie de l'académie française. Paris, 1964.
43573.76.37 Dorgelès, Roland. Les croix de bois. Paris, 1964.
40546.29A Drescher, S. Tocqueville and England. Cambridge, 1964.
43574.41.1100 Driessche, Andrée Model van den. De tes deux mains offertes. Bruxelles, 1964.
43574.41.170 Drieu La Rochelle, Pierre. Les chiens de paille. Paris, 1964.
43574.41.210 Drieu La Rochelle, Pierre. Le feu follet. Paris, 1964.
43574.41.200 Drieu La Rochelle, Pierre. Sur les écrivains. Paris, 1964.

1964 - cont.

43574.75.765 Druon, Maurice. The memoirs of Zeus. N.Y., 1964.
38526.6.785 Du Bellay, Joachim. Stesky. Praha, 1964.
43822.49.1400 Ducresne-Guillemine, Jacques. Études pour un Paul Valéry. Neuchâtel, 1964.
43576.6.102 Duhamel, Georges. Chronique des Pasquier. Paris, 1964. 2v.
37567.615 Duhamel, Roger. Aux sources du romantisme français. Ottawa, 1964.
43576.69.2100 Dupin d'Aniane, Charlotte R. La route de la joie. Clermont-Ferrand, 1964.
43576.71.4110 Dupont-Fromageot, Yves. Bergeries. Bruxelles, 1964.
43576.74.2200 Duras, Marguerite. La ravissement de Lol V. Stein, roman. Paris, 1964.
43581.89.150 Eaubonne, Françoise d'. Rêve de feu. Paris, 1964.
41574.601 Ecalle, Martine. Album Hugo. Paris, 1964.
42556.28.345 Eigeldinger, Marc. Rimbaud et le mythe solaire. Neuchâtel, 1964.
43589.32.100 Eigeldinger, Marc. Les voix de la forêt. Neuchatel, 1964.
43698.200.830 Engler, Winfried. Henri Michaux; das Michaux Bild, 1922-1959. Inaug. Diss. Tübingen, 1964.
43598.82.2110 Escarpit, Robert. Le litteratron. Paris, 1964.
43598.66.100 Esor. Un homme nouveau dans un monde nouveau. Anvers, 1964.
43599.13.1110 Etchart, Salvat. Les nègres servent d'exemple; roman. Paris, 1964.
37543.556 Etkind, Efin G. Pisateli Frantsii. Moskva, 1964.
43606.10.150 Fabre-Luce, Alfred. La bombe. Paris, 1964.
43606.10.140 Fabre-Luce, Alfred. Le procès de Haute Cour. Paris, 1964.
37556.16.100 Fajon, Étienne. En feuilletant L'Humanité. Paris? 1964.
38526.48.250 Falbe, A. Die Dichtung Maurice Scèves. Berlin, 1964.
43606.99.100 Faye, Jean-Pierre. L'écluse; roman. Paris, 1964.
37557.76.5 Fayolle, Roger. La critique littéraire. Paris, 1964.
38554.528 Fénelon, F. de S. de la Mothe. Letters. London, 1964.
38554.518.100 Fénelon, F. de S. de la Mothe. Letters of love and counsel. 1st American ed. N.Y., 1964.
43757.92.810 Ferry, Jean. Une autre étude sur Raymond Roussel. Paris, 1964.
37569.368 Fitch, Brian T. Le sentiment d'étrangeté chez Malraux, Sartre, Camus et S. de Beauvoir. Paris, 1964.
42576.33.10.7 Flaubert, Gustave. Bouvard et Pécuchet. Napoli, 1964-
42576.16.64 Flaubert, Gustave. Oeuvres. Lausanne, 1964. 18v.
42576.16.66 Flaubert, Gustave. Oeuvres complètes. Paris, 1964. 2v.
43538.14.840 Fletcher, John. The novels of Samuel Beckett. London, 1964.
43611.50.140 Follain, Jean. Appareil de la terre. Paris, 1964.
43526.65.980 Fonteyne, André. Apollinaire prosateur. Paris, 1964.
37574.860.5 Fouchet, Max P. La poésie française. Paris, 1964.
37576.15 Fourastié, Françoise. Les écrivains temoins du peuple. Paris, 1964.
43744.67.1450 Fowlie, Wallace. A reading of Proust. 1. ed. N.Y., 1964.
43761.39.945 France. Cour d'appel (Bastia). Audience solennelle d'installation de M. le PremierPrésident Marcel Armand. Melun, 1964.
38537.42.2A Francon, Marcel. Autour de la lettre de Gargantua à son fils. Cambridge, 1964.
42582.2.60 Franquinet, Edmond. Jules Verne en zijn wonderreizen. Zeist, 1964.
43612.23.130 Frénaud, André. André Frénaud. Milano, 1964.
43538.14.870 Friedman, Melvin J. Samuel Beckett. Paris, 1964.
43613.45.735 Frison-Roche, Roger. The raid. 1. ed. N.Y., 1964.
37555.723 Fukui, Y. Raffinement précieux dans la poésie française du XVIIe siècle. Paris, 1964.
Mol 173.6 Ganz, Hans U. Zur Quellenfrage des Bourgeois gentilhomme. Firenze, 1964.
43616.78.735 Gary, Romain. Hissing tales. 1. ed. N.Y., 1964.
43616.79.720 Gascar, Pierre. The fugitive. Boston, 1964.
43616.79.210 Gascar, Pierre. Le meilleur de la vie. Paris, 1964.
43616.79.715 Gascar, Pierre. Women and the sun. Boston, 1964.
38539.2.75 Gastaldi, Vittoria. Jean Pierre Camus, romantière barocco e vescovo di Francia. Catania, 1964.
43616.82.1110 Gastines, Marie de. Conquecigrues. Goudargues, 1964.
FL 394.108 Gautier, Jean Jacques. La comédie française. Paris, 1964.
40586.28.64.9 Gautier, Jean Maurice. Le style des mémoires d'outre-tombe de Chateaubriand. Genève, 1964.
FL 6059.21 Geller, Hermann. Die Funktion der Geständnisse in Rousseaus La nouvelle Héloise. Bonn, 1964.
43617.82.705 Gennari, Genevieve. Nostalgia. 1. American ed. N.Y., 1964.
37567.227 George, Albert J. Short fiction in France, 1800-1850. Syracuse, N.Y., 1964.
43617.74.1100 Gerardin, François. Vingt trois. Paris, 1964.
43617.86.100 Gers, José. Thalassa; poèmes. Bruxelles, 1964.
37575.765.5 Gershman, H. Anthologie des prefaces de romans français du XIXe siècle. Paris, 1964.
43620.2.79.181 Gide, André. Correspondance André Gide - Arnold Bennett. Genève, 1964.
43620.2.79.195 Gide, André. The trial. N.Y., 1964.
43620.2.44.5 Gide, André. Urien's voyage. London, 1964.
43620.2.79.200 Gide, André. The white notebook. N.Y., 1964.
43550.58.1010 Ginestier, Paul. La pensée de Camus. Paris, 1964.
43620.59.100 Ginet, Albert. Aux confins du silence et de la parole. Bruxelles, 1964.
42576.15.320 Giraud, R. Flaubert. Englewood Cliffs, 1964.
43620.74.621 Giraudoux, Jean. Three plays. 1. ed. N.Y., 1964.
41543.22.155 Girolamo, Nicola di. Miti e simboli napoletani nell'opera di Nerval. Bologna, 1964.
43620.75.1100 Giroux, Roger. L'arbre le temps. Paris, 1964.
40532.56 Giudici, Enzo. Beaumarchais nel suo e nel nostro tempo. Roma, 1964.
43622.41.170 Glissant, Edouard. Le quatrième siècle. Paris, 1964.
43625.7.100 Godefroy, Serge. Les loques; roman. Paris 1964.
43625.27.160 Goffin, Robert. Corps combustible. Paris, 1964.
37555.399 Goffin, Robert. Fil d'Ariane pour la poésie. Paris, 1964.
37558.156 Goldmann, L. The hidden God. London, 1964.
43625.48.3100 Goldstein, E. Madame E. Bourgmestre. Bruxelles, 1964.
43625.3.33.2 Gourmont, Rémy de. La culture des idées. Paris, 1964.
43626.70.132 Gracq, Julien. La littérature à l'estomac. Paris, 1964.
43626.1.1100 Grad, Jean. L'anneau pervers. Bruxelles, 1964.
38525.6.20 Graham, V.E. Sixteenth-century French poetry. Toronto, 1964.
43626.3.1100 Grandmont, Dominique. Histoire de dire, poèmes. Jarnac, 1964.
37567.623 Graño, César. Bohemian versus bourgeois. N.Y., 1964.
37565.68.6 Green, Frederick C. Eighteenth-century France, six essays. N.Y., 1964.

Chronological Listing

1964 - cont.

37566.144 Green, Frederick C. French novelists, from the Revolution to Proust. N.Y., 1964.
37565.68.3A Green, Frederick C. French novelists, manners and ideas, from Renaissance to the revolution. N.Y., 1964.
43626.22.45 Green, Julien. Diary, 1928-1957. 1st American ed. N.Y., 1964.
43626.22.300 Green, Julien. Milles chemins ouverts. Paris, 1964.
37556.22.75 Grenoble. Bibliothèque municipale. La presse Grenobloise, 1788-1888. Grenoble, 1964.
37556.250 Greshoff, C.J. Seven studies in the French novel. Cape Town, 1964.
43628.4.100 Guarini, Ferida. Le miroir sans tain. Neuchâtel, 1964.
43628.23.180 Guéhenno, Jean. Ce que je crois. Paris, 1964.
42587.58.85 Guérande, P. Le petit monde de la comtesse de Ségur. Paris, 1964.
43628.24.2110 Guérande, Paul. O.A.S. Métro. Paris, 1964.
Mol 607.10 Guicharnaud, J. Molière; a collection of critical essays. Englewood, 1964.
38526.26.87 Guidici, Enzo. Louise Labé e l'école lyonnaise. Napoli, 1964.
42584.25.325 Guillemin, Henri. Présentation des Rougon-Macquart. Paris, 1964.
43628.41.5700 Guillot, René. The children of the wind. London, 1964.
43611.5.160 Guiomar, M. Inconscient et imaginaire dans le Grand Meaulnes. Paris, 1964.
43628.1.140 Guitry, Sacha. Et puis voici des vers. Paris, 1964.
43628.1.130 Guitry, Sacha. Soixante jours de prison. Paris, 1964.
37556.127.5 Haedens, Kléber. Paradoxe sur le roman. Paris, 1964.
43631.21.120 Haedrich, Marcel. Le patron; roman. Paris, 1964.
42553.35.5 Halda, Bernard. Amiel et les femmes. Lyon, 1964.
43833.20.920 Halda, Bernard. L'évolution spirituelle de Simone Weil. Paris, 1964.
43631.49.3100 Halévy, Dominique. Celine ou la multiplication; histoire. Paris, 1964.
43631.54.100 Hamesse, P.P. La mesaventure. Bruxelles, 1964.
43524.67.835 Harvey, John. Anouilh; a study in theatrics. New Haven, 1964.
38513.14.11 Heinz, Annemarie. Der Wortschatz des Jean Mielot. Wien, 1964.
43632.41.102 Heitz, Robert Marie Charles. Souvenirs de jadis et de naguère. 2. éd. n.p., 1964.
40583.331 Hemmings, F.W.J. Stendhal, a study of his novels. Oxford, 1964.
43689.2810 Herbert, Michel. Bibliographie de l'oeuvre de Jean de La Varende accompagnée de nombreaux documents inédits. Paris, 1964. 3v.
43687.89.2810 Herbert, Michel. Biographie de l'oeuvre de Jean de La Varende accompagnée de nombreaux documents inédits. Paris, 1964. 3v.
37555.732 Hercourt, Jean. Éléments d'une poétique. Genève, 1964.
42524.38.80 Heurgon-Desjardins, A. Paul Desjardins et les décades de Pontigny. Paris, 1964.
40553.10.65 Hogue, Helen H.S. Of changes in Benjamin Constant's books on religions. Genève, 1964.
41572.42 Hugo, Victor. Avez-vous lu Victor Hugo? Paris, 1964.
41573.65 Hugo, Victor. Les contemplations. Paris, 1964. 2v.
41574.16.25 Hugo, Victor. Lettres à Juliette Drouet, 1833-1883. Paris, 1964.
41571.3.108 Hugo, Victor. Oeuvres poetiques. Paris, 1964.
41571.3.125 Hugo, Victor. Oeuvres politiques complètes. Paris, 1964.
41573.17.7.5 Hugo, Victor. Things seen. London, 1964.
FL 397.215.48.2 Huguenin, Auguste. La belle époque. 2e éd. Lausanne, 1964.
43638.35.1041 Huguenin, Jean-René. Journal. Paris, 1964.
40597.2.418 Hunt, Herbert James. Balzac's Comédie humaine. London, 1964.
42576.65.80.30 Huysmans, Joris Karl. La retraite de Monsieur Bougran. Paris, 1964.
39544.362 Iazykov, D.D. Vol'ter v russkoi literature, Sankt Peterburg, 1879. Ann Arbor, 1964.
43656.59.170 Ionesco, Eugène. La cantatrice chauve. Paris, 1964.
43656.59.700 Ionesco, Eugène. Notes and counter notes. N.Y., 1964.
43659.67.130 Isou, Isidore (pseud.). Les champs de force. Paris, 1964.
43659.67.31 Isou, Isidore (pseud.). Oeuvres de spectacles. Paris, 1964.
43667.14.102 Jacob, Max. La défense de Tartufe. Paris, 1964.
43667.14.320 Jacob, Max. Le terrain Bouchable. Paris, 1964.
43538.14.825 Jacobsen, J. The testament of Samuel Beckett. 1. ed. N.Y., 1964.
43554.2.1150 Jahier, Piero. Con Claudel, 1913-1955. Milano, 1964.
37567.9.15 James, Henry. French poets and novelists. 1st ed. N.Y., 1964.
43667.1.69 Jammes, Francis. Jeunes filles. Paris, 1964.
38523.41 Jannini, Pasquale Aniel. Tra momenti della poesia francese al tempo di Malherbe. Milano, 1964.
43667.61.100 Jans, Adrien. La tunique de Dieu. Bruxelles, 1964.
37569.371 Janvier, Ludovic. Une parole exigeante. Paris, 1964.
43667.78.140.5 Jarry, Alfred. L'amour absolu. Paris, 1964.
43667.78.180 Jarry, Alfred. Saint-Brieuc de choux. Paris, 1964.
FL 6139.64 Jean-Jacques Rousseau et son oeuvre. Paris, 1964.
37574.913 Jones, P.M. A book of French verse. London, 1964.
43670.89.815 Jouhandeau, Élise. Le bien de ronces. Paris, 1964.
43670.89.565 Jouhandeau, M. Chronique d'une passion. Paris, 1964.
41574.603 Journet, René. Le mythe du peuple dans Les misérables. Paris, 1964.
43670.94.22 Jouve, Pierre Jean. Poésie: les noces. Paris, 1964. 4v.
43757.50.1220 Karczewska-Markiewicz, Zofia. Romain Rolland. Warszawa, 1964.
39566.17 Kempf, R. Diderot et le roman ou Le démon de la presence. Paris, 1964.
42576.35.91 Kenner, Hugh. Flaubert, Joyce and Beckett. London, 1964.
43673.83.260 Kessel, Joseph. Discours de réception de M.J. Kessel. Paris, 1964.
43673.98.100 Keyser, Eugénie de. Le chien. Paris, 1964.
43550.58.950 King, A. Camus. Edinburgh, 1964.
43677.5.100 Klat, Hector. Du cèdre aux lys; poèmes. Beyrouth, 1964.
V43500.145 Klingsor, Tristan (pseud.). Second florilège. Blainville-sur-Mer, 1964.
FL 398.35.15 Knapp, B.L. That was Yvette. N.Y., 1964.
43680.92.105 Kowalski, Roger. Augurales. Montpellier, 1964.
43680.92.100 Kowalski, Roger. Le Ban. Paris, 1964.
43687.8.110 Labin-Bénichow, Gina. Ne pas laisser mourir. Paris, 1964.
38563.22.42 Labrousse, Élisabeth. Pierre Bayle: Hétérodoxie et rigorisme. La Haye, 1964.

1964 - cont.

38564.32.40 La Bruyère, J. de. Les caractères de Théophraste, traduits du grec avec les caractères ou Les moeurs de ce siècle. Paris, 1964.
39527.36.5 La Fontaine, Jean de. Luibov' psikhei i kupidona. London, 1964.
41522.18.54 Laforgue, R. L'échec de Baudelaire. Genève, 1964.
38526.47.33.15 Lagny, Jean. Le poète Saint-Amant. Paris, 1964.
43687.35.1100 La Haye, Marcel. La clef sous la porte; poèmes. Jarnac, 1964.
38526.22.17 La Perrière, G. de. Le théâtre des bons engins. Gainesville, Florida, 1964.
42584.25.315 Lapp, J.C. Zola before the Rougon-Macquart. Toronto, 1964.
43822.49.1081 La Rochefoucauld, Edmée de Fels. En lisant les cahiers de Paul Valéry. Paris, 1964-67. 3v.
38543.5.10 La Rochefoucauld, François. Oeuvres complètes. Paris, 1964.
43687.83.1130 Las Vergnas, Raymond. Cavalerie céleste; roman. Paris, 1964.
43687.85.1100 Lathis. L'organiste athée. Paris, 1964.
43687.90.110 Laude, Jean. Les plages de Thulé. Paris, 1964.
43687.89.2230 La Varende, Jean de. Coeur pensif. Paris, 1964.
43688.5.5132 Léautaud, Paul. Passe-temps. Paris, 1964.
43688.5.5190 Léautaud, Paul. Le petit ouvrage inachevé. Paris, 1964.
43688.9.1021 Lebois, André. Poèmes. Avignon, 1964.
43688.14.4700A Le Clézio, Jean Marie Gustave. The interrogation. N.Y., 1964.
43688.20.110 Leduc, Violette. La bâtarde. Paris, 1964.
38526.27.13.2 Lemaire de Belges, Jean. La concorde des deux langages. Cambridge, 1964.
43688.79.2110 Lescure, Jean. Images d'images. Paris, 1964.
43688.82.120 Lesort, Paul André. Les reins et les coeurs, roman. Paris, 1964.
37558.205 Lévis-Mirepoix, Antoine. Que signifie le parti des ducs à l'Académie? Paris, 1964.
43697.52.880 Lewis, R.W. Malraux. Englewood Cliffs, N.J., 1964.
43690.9.23 Libbrecht, Géo. Livres cachés; oeuvres complètes. v.1-6. Bruxelles, 1964-66. 5v.
43744.67.1455 Lowery, B. Marcel Proust et Henry James. Paris, 1964.
43565.5.815 Lucchini, P. Léon Daudet. Paris, 1964.
38527.61.15 Magny, Olivier de. Le odes amoureuses de 1559. Genève, 1964.
40556.26.65 Maistre, Joseph de. Du pape. Paris, 1964.
42555.44.6 Mallarmé, Stéphane. Correspondance Mallarmé-Whistler. Paris, 1964.
42555.43.17 Mallarmé, Stéphane. Mallarmé, par lui-même. Paris, 1964.
42555.44.10 Mallarmé, Stéphane. Recueil de nursery rhymes. Paris, 1964.
43697.2.1725 Mallet-Joris, Françoise (pseud.). A letter to myself. N.Y., 1964.
38575.98 Manters, Robert. Corneille critique son temps. Paris, 1964.
43697.74.3172 Marceau, Félicien. Théâtre. Paris, 1964.
43554.2.1160 Marcel, Gabriel. Regards sur le théâtre de Claudel. Paris, 1964.
43697.74.8100 Marill, Francine. Un temps pour souffrir; roman. Paris, 1964.
43546.87.80 Marill, René. Michel Butor. Paris, 1964.
38523.12.40 Marot, Clément. Clément Marot. Paris, 1964.
43697.76.9130 Martin du Gard, Maurice. Climat tempéré: maximes, caractères et confidences, 1933-1963. Paris, 1964.
43697.77.6700 Martinerie, Andrée. Second spring. Chicago, 1964.
40597.2.760 Martínez Estrada, Ezequiel. Realidad y fantasía en Balzac. Bahía Blanca, 1964.
43697.86.705 Masson, Loÿs. The overseer. 1st American ed. N.Y., 1964.
43697.88.3715 Mauriac, Claude. All women are fatal. N.Y., 1964.
43697.88.3160 Mauriac, Claude. La conversation. Paris, 1964.
43554.2.963 Maurocordato, A. Anglo-American influences in Paul Claudel. Génève, 1964.
43697.89.540 Maurois, André. De La Bruyère à Proust. Paris, 1964.
38557.55.85 Maximes et réfléxions de Bossuet sur la politique. Paris, 1964.
FL 6129.64 May, Gita. De Jean-Jacques Rousseau à madame Roland. Genève, 1964.
38514.70.10 Mazzariol, Emma S. Gli arrêts d'amour di Martial d'Auvergne. Venezia, 1964.
40597.2.700 Métadier, Paul. Balzac au petit matin. Paris, 1964.
Mon 123.7 Micha, Alexandre. Le singulier Montaigne. Paris, 1964.
43698.200.211 Michaux, Henri. L'infini turbulent. Paris, 1964.
40583.250.5F Michel, François. Fichier stendhalien. Boston, 1964. 3v.
41557.7.80 Mireaux, Émile. Un témoin critique de la monarchie bourgeoise et de la Révolution de 1848: Louis Reybaud. Paris, 1964.
39566.210 Moelbjerg, Hans. Aspects de l'esthetique de Diderot. København, 1964.
Mol 192.4 Molière, Jean Baptiste Poquelin. Don Juan. N.Y., 1964.
Mol 195.60 Molière, Jean Baptiste Poquelin. L'école des femmes. Paris, 1964.
Mol 166.4.10 Molière, Jean Baptiste Poquelin. The miser. N.Y., 1964.
Mol 19.64 Molière, Jean Baptiste Poquelin. Oeuvres complètes. Paris, 1964- 4v.
Mol 60.45 Molière, Jean Baptiste Poquelin. One act comedies of Molière. 1st ed. Cleveland, 1964.
43701.58.1100 Moncelet, Christien. Après le feu. Jarnac, 1964.
39533.20.35 Mongredien, Georges. Cyrano de Bergerac. Paris, 1964.
Mon 19.64 Montaigne, Michel de. Essais. v.1; v.2, pt.1-2. Paris, 1964. 3v.
Mon 30.64 Montaigne, Michel de. Selected essays of Montaigne. Boston, 1964.
39592.22 Montesquieu, C.L. de S. Oeuvres complètes. Paris, 1964.
43701.63.760 Montherlant, Henry de. Chaos and night. London, 1964.
42556.28.350 Morawska, Ludmiła. L'adjectif qualificatif dans la langue des symbolistes français. Poznan, 1964.
40575.5.175 Moreau, Pierre. La critique selon Sainte-Beuve. Paris, 1964.
FL 362.50 Morel, Jacques. La tragédie. Paris, 1964.
39566.203 Mornet, Daniel. Les cours de lettres, 1964-65. Paris, 1964.
42586.32.530 Moscow. Vsesoiznaia Gosudarstvennaia Biblioteka Inostrannoi Literatury. Sharl' de Koster; bibliograficheskii ukazatel'. Moskva, 1964.
43701.87.110 Mottart, Hubert. Le luth noir. Bruxelles, 1964.
38575.103 Muller, Charles. Essai de statisque lexicale. Paris, 1964.
37555.202 Nadal, Octave. A mésure haute. Paris, 1964.

Chronological Listing

1964 - cont.

37569.40.56 Nadeau, M. Histoire du surréalisme. Paris, 1964.
37597.47 Narcisus; poème du XIIe siècle. Paris, 1964.
38542.26.15 Nardis, Luigi de. Il cortegiano e l'eroe. Firenze, 1964.
43706.34.100 Négrié, Joseph. Contes et récits de le terre occitane. Paris, 1964.
41543.22.105 Nerval, Gerard de. Nerval, par lui-même. Paris, 1964.
41543.12.6 Nerval, Gerard de. Voyage en Orient. Paris, 1964.
42554.26.845 Newman, Pauline. Corbière, Laforgue, Apollinaire, ou le Rire en pleurs. Paris, 1964.
43550.58.1060 Nicolas, André. Une philosophie de l'existence: Albert Camus. Paris, 1964.
41522.18.495 Nies, Fritz. Poesie in prosaischer Welt. Heidelberg, 1964.
43824.3.1800 Noakes, Warren David. Boris Vian. Paris, 1964.
43709.23.130 Noël, Marie. Petit jour et souvenirs du beau mai. Paris, 1964.
43822.49.988 Noulet, Emilie. Suites; Mallarmé, Rimbaud, Valéry. Paris, 1964.
37565.168 Oblomievskii, D.D. Literatura frantsuzskoi revoliutsii. Moskva, 1964.
41556.48 Oliver, Alfred R. Charles Nodier. Syracuse, N.Y., 1964.
40597.2.585 Oliver, E.J. Honoré de Balzac. N.Y., 1964.
FL 6139.64.10 Orias, Arturo. Ethik und Staatsphilosophie bei Jean-Jacques Rousseau. n.p., 1964.
FL 6139.40.2 Osborn, A.M. Rousseau and Burke. N.Y., 1964.
37530.191 P.E.N. Club. Czechoslovakia. La littérature française en Tchecolovaquie. Prague, 1964.
43737.74.3130 Parain, Brice. Joseph. Paris, 1964.
43737.76.100 Paris, Jean. La maison de mon enfance. Paris, 1964.
37543.557 Paris. Collège de France. Six conférences. Nogent-le-Rotrou, 1964.
43752.57.895 Parsons, Clarence R. Vision plastique de C.F. Ramuz. Québec, 1964.
43552.5.1850 Pascal, Georges. Alain éducateur. Paris, 1964.
43738.12.100 Peches, Jean Marie. La rose des heures. Bruxelles, 1964.
43620.2.450 Perault, P.J. A propos d'Isabelle. Blairville-sur-Mer, 1964.
38563.30.5 Perrault, C. Parallele des anciens et des modernes en ce qui. München, 1964.
43738.77.5100 Perrelet, Olivier. Crise de rêves. Genève, 1964.
38524.146 Petroni, Liano. La commedia letteraria francese nella seconda metà de Cinquecento. Bologna, 1964.
40597.2.705 Petrova, Evgeniia A. Stanovlenie realizma Bal'zaka. Saratov, 1964.
37573.722 Peyre, H. Contemporary French literature. N.Y., 1964.
43738.97.180 Peyre, Joseph. Feu et sang de juillet. Paris, 1964.
43738.97.1750 Peyrefitte, Roger. The Prince's person. London, 1964.
37574.220 Picard, Raymond. La poésie française de 1640 à 1680. Paris, 1964.
43741.12.710 Picasso, Pablo. Wie man Wünsche beim Schwanz packt. Zürich, 1964.
43741.24.2100 Pierson-Piérard, Marianne. Plages. Bruxelles, 1964.
43822.49.1435 Pire, Francois. La tentation du sensible chez Paul Valéry. Bruxelles, 1964.
41574.598 Piroué, G. Victor Hugo romancier. Paris, 1964.
37569.375 Pistorius, Jiri. L'image de l'Allemagne dans le roman français. Paris, 1964.
38562.23.45 Pizzorusso, Arnoldo. Il ventaglio e il compasso. Napoli, 1964.
43743.60.700 Ponge, Francis. Die literarische Praxis. Olten, 1964.
37595.110.5 Pottier, Bernard. Textes médiévaux français et romans. Paris, 1964.
37565.178 Pozzo, Gianni M. La storia e il progresso nell'Illuminismo francese. Padova, 1964.
37569.367 Prémont, Laurent. Le mythe de prométhée dans la littérature française contemporaine. Québec, 1964.
40522.9.74 Prévost, Antoine F. Istoriia kavalera de Grie i Manon Lesko. Moskva, 1964.
43744.25.5021 Prévot, Gérard. Théâtre: La nouvelle Eurydice, La mise à mort, Guillaume Fischer. Paris, 1964.
FL 396.50.3 Pruner, Francis. Les luttes d'Antoine. Paris, 1964.
42584.25.330 Psichari, H. Anatomie d'un chef-d'oeuvre. Paris, 1964.
43750.2.100 Quaedvlieg, Phillippe. La chose qui vient de la mer. Liège, 1964.
43550.58.1030 Quilliot, Roger. L'univers théâtral et romanesque de'Albert Camus. Rodez, 1964.
43556.49.905 Raaphorst-Rousseau, Madeleine. Colette, sa vie et son art. Paris, 1964.
38536.24.5 Rabelais, F. Gargantua und Pantagruel. München, 1964. 2v.
38536.40 Rabelais, F. Le tiers livre. Genève, 1964.
38585.23.45 Racine, Jean. Bajazet. London, 1964.
43527.3.835 Raillard, G. Aragon. Paris, 1964.
43701.63.925 Rapke, Rudolf. Die Dramen Montherlants. Köln, 1964.
40597.2.605 Raser, George Bernard. Guide to Balzac's Paris. Choisy-le-Roi, 1964.
43737.83.800 Ratiu, Basile. L'oeuvre dramatique de Steve Passeur. Paris, 1964.
43752.94.700 Rawicz, P. Blood from the sky, a novel. 1. American ed. N.Y., 1964.
37543.281.5 Raymond, Marcel. Vérité et poésie. Neuchâtel, 1964.
43753.9.128 Reboux, Paul. A la manière de Baudelaire. Paris, 1964.
42515.30.546 Renan, Ernest. Ma soeur Henriette. Paris, 1964.
42587.52.29 Renard, Jules. Journal. N.Y., 1964.
43753.61.110 Renoux, Alfred. Jules Verne. Paris, 1964.
37596.38.15 Renzi, Lorenzo. Tradizione cortese e realismo in Gautier d'Arras. Padova, 1964.
37569.370 Richard, Jean Pierre. Onze études sur la poésie moderne. Paris, 1964.
42556.22.32 Richepin, Jean. Choix de poésie. Paris, 1964.
43756.27.100 Riffaud, Madelenie. De votre envoyee speciale. Paris, 1964.
43697.52.890 Righter, W. The rhetorical hero. London, 1964.
42556.28.85 Rimbaud, Jean Arthur. Opilý korab. 2. vyd. Praha, 1964.
43756.90.1110 Riverain, Achille. Aux couleurs de ma mélancolie. Bruxelles, 1964.
43756.90.1100 Riverain, Achille. Le manteau de plomb. Bruxelles, 1964.
43756.91.3100 Rivoyre, Christine de. Les sultans. Paris, 1964.
43757.6.715 Robbe-Grillet, Alain. The erasers. N.Y., 1964.
38513.93 Robert-Busquet, L. Farces du Moyen-Âge. Paris, 1964.
43697.77.865 Robidoux, Réjean. Roger Martin du Gard et la religion. Paris, 1964.
43688.69.800 Roc, Gil. A l'éconte des poètes wagneriens du siècle. Paris, 1964.
43757.13.4100 Roche, Denis. Les idées centésimales de Miss Elanize. Paris, 1964.

1964 - cont.

43757.50.280 Rolland, Romain. Fräulein Elsa. Paris, 1964.
43757.3.360 Romains, Jules. Ai-je fait ce que j'ai voulu? Paris, 1964.
41574.606 Romains, Jules. Inauguration du nouveau monument Victor Hugo à Paris...le mercredi 17 juin 1964. Paris, 1964.
43757.3.315 Romains, Jules. Lettres à un ami. Paris, 1964. 2v.
43546.87.85 Roudaut, Jean. Michel Butor. Paris, 1964.
43757.88.3710 Rougemont, Denis de. Dramatic personnages. N.Y., 1964.
43757.88.3125 Rougemont, Denis de. The myths of love. London, 1964.
43822.49.1395 Roulin, P. Paul Valéry. Neuchâtel, 1964.
FL 6022.64 Rousseau, J.J. Les confessions. Paris, 1964.
FL 6048.49.20 Rousseau, J.J. Profession de foi du Vicaire Savoyard. Paris, 1964.
FL 6094.8.26 Rousseau, J.J. Les rêveries du promeneur solitaire. Paris, 1964.
43697.88.885 Roussel, Bernard. Mauriac. Paris, 1964.
43757.92.132 Roussel, Raymond. La poussière de soleils; pièce en cinq actes et vingt-quatre tableaux. Paris, 1964.
43761.39.837 Roy, Jules. Passion et mort de St. Exupéry. Paris, 1964.
43761.13.642 Sachs, Maurice. Witches' sabbath. N.Y., 1964.
43761.31.190F Sagan, Françoise. Joxique Bernard Buffet. Paris, 1964.
40575.18.9 Sainte-Beuve, Charles A. Portraits of the seventeenth century. N.Y., 1964. 2v.
40575.18.24 Sainte-Beuve, Charles A. Portraits of the 18th century, historic and literary. N.Y., 1964. 2v.
37556.27.7 Saintsbury, George. A history of the French novel. N.Y., 1964. 2v.
43761.48.170 Salacrou, Armand. Comme les chardons; pièce sans entracte. Paris, 1964.
41557.10.18.20 Sand, George. Correspondance. Paris, 1964. 8v.
41557.9.72 Sand, George. Les lettres de George Sand à Sainte-Beuve. Genève, 1964.
43761.71.100 Saporta, Marc. Les invités; roman. Paris, 1964.
43761.6.25 Sarment, Jean. Poèmes. Paris, 1964.
43761.77.720A Sarraute, Nathalie. The golden fruits. N.Y., 1964.
43617.78.810 Sartre, J.P. Saint Genêt. London, 1964.
43761.78.290 Sartre, Jean Paul. Les mots. Paris, 1964.
43761.78.300 Sartre, Jean Paul. Qu'est-ce que la littérature? Paris, 1964.
43761.78.641A Sartre, Jean Paul. The words. N.Y., 1964.
37562.300.6 Saulnièr, V.L. La littérature française. 6. éd. Paris, 1964.
37569.376 Savage, Catharine. Malraux, Sartre, and Aragon as political novelists. Gainesville, 1964.
43763.36.3100 Schakovskoy, Zinaïda. Lumières et ombres. Paris, 1964.
37565.121 Schalk, Fritz. Studien zur französischen Aufklärung. München, 1964.
43822.49.1445 Schmitz, Alfred. Valéry et la tentation de l'absolu. Gembloux, 1964.
37543.555 Schneider, Marcel. La littérature fantastique en France. Paris, 1964.
43765.32.160 Seghers, Pierre. Nouvelles chansons et complaintes. Paris, 1964.
37556.21.56 Seguin, Jean-Pierre. L'information en France avant le périodique; 517 canards imprimés entre 1529 et 1631. Paris, 1964.
42587.58.40 Ségur, Sophie. L'auberge de l'ange-gardien. Paris, 1964.
42587.58.13 Ségur, Sophie. Un bon petit diable. Paris, 1964.
42587.58.30 Ségur, Sophie. La fortune de Gaspard. Paris, 1964.
42587.58.8.20 Ségur, Sophie. Les malheurs de Sophie. Paris, 1964.
42587.58.35 Ségur, Sophie. Nouveaux contes de fées pour les petits enfants. Paris, 1964.
42587.58.6.2 Ségur, Sophie. Les vacances. Paris, 1964.
43626.22.860 Semolue, Jean. Julien Green, ou l'obsession du mal. Paris, 1964.
43656.59.810 Sénart, Phillipe. Ionesco. Paris, 1964.
40524.46 Sentilly, de. Le rideau levé. v.1-2. Cythère, 1964.
37567.505.2 Siciliano, Italo. Il romanticismo francese da Prévost à Sartre. Firenze, 1964.
43769.54.783 Simenon, Georges. The blue room. 1. ed. N.Y., 1964.
43769.54.480 Simenon, Georges. Les dossiers de l'agence "O". Paris, 1964.
43769.54.788 Simenon, Georges. Five times Maigret. N.Y., 1964.
43769.54.470 Simenon, Georges. Maigret revient. Paris, 1964.
43769.54.728 Simenon, Georges. Maigret's special murder. London, 1964.
43769.54.460 Simenon, Georges. Les nouvelles enquêtes de Maigret. Paris, 1964.
43769.54.791 Simenon, Georges. The novel of man. N.Y., 1964.
43769.54.490 Simenon, Georges. Les petit docteur. Paris, 1964.
43769.54.450 Simenon, Georges. Signe Picpus. Paris, 1964.
37569.40.200.2 Simon, P.H. L'homme en procès: Malraux, Sartre. 6. ed. Paris, 1964.
FL 374.7 Sletsjoee, Leif. Franske profane middelalderspill. Oslo, 1964.
39594.19.110 Snethage, Jacob Leonard. Montesquieu. Den Haag, 1964.
FL 6119.64 Snethlage, Jacob L. Rousseau, stormvogel der revolutie. Den Haag, 1964.
43556.1.950 Société des Amis du Musée des Beaux-Arts de Nantes. Hommage à Jean Cocteau...Nantes, 21 mai au 15 juin 1964. Nantes, 1964.
43775.61.100 Sonkin, F. La dame. Paris, 1964.
42568.19.26 Soulier, Jean-Pierre. Lautréamont. Genève, 1964.
42544.30.86 Soupault, Philippe. Eugène Labiche. Paris, 1964.
38526.48.172 Sponde, Jean de. Poems of love and death. Edinburgh, 1964.
40592.40 Staël Holstein, Anne Louise. Madame de Staël. London, 1964.
FL 397.261 Steltz, Michael. Geschichte und Spielplan der Französischen Theater an Deutschen Fürstenhöfen in 17. und 18. Jahrhundert. München, 1964[1965]
43757.6.805 Stoltzfus, B.F. Alain Robbe-Grillet and the new French novel. Carbondale, 1964.
38585.16.345 Stone, John A. Sophocles and Racine. Genève, 1964.
FL 386.270 Surer, Paul. Le théâtre français contemporain. Paris, 1964.
43787.71.100 Teppe, Julien. La vie blette. Paris, 1964.
37583.210 Théâtre classique français. Paris, 1964-66. 12v.
37543.567 Theisen, Josef. Geschichte der französischen Literatur. Stuttgart, 1964.
43788.65.1150 Thomas, Henri. Le parjure, roman. Paris, 1964.
Mol 720.9 Thoorens, Léon. Le dossier Molière. Verviers, 1964.
43538.14.855 Tindall, William York. Samuel Beckett. N.Y., 1964.
40534.23.85 Tissier, André. Collin d'Harleville, 1755-1806. Paris, 1964-65. 2v.
43792.74.100 Tordeur, Jean. Conservateur des charges. Paris, 1964.
43792.92.100 Toulouse, Gilbert. Un été au Mexique. Paris, 1964.

1964 - cont.

43793.42.21	Triolet, Elsa. Oeuvres romanesques croisées d'Elsa Triolet et Aragon. Paris, 1964-65. 38v.
43793.67.280	Troyat, Henri. Le geste d'Ève. Paris, 1964.
37556.166	Ullman, Stephen. Style in the French novel. N.Y., 1964.
43822.50.150	Vailland, Roger. La truite. Paris, 1964.
43822.49.470	Valéry, Paul. Les essais de Paul Valéry; poèmes et proses. Paris, 1964.
42581.33.40	Vallès, Jules. Le tableau de Paris. Paris, 1964.
43822.51.4100	Valois, Michel. Des souvenirs...que le vent...poèmes. Paris, 1964.
43697.52.900	Vandegans, A. La jeunesse litteraire de André Malraux. Paris, 1964.
37562.328	Varvaro, Alberto. La narrativa francese alla metà del XII secolo. Napoli, 1964.
38585.16.355	Vaunois, Louis. L'enfance et la jeunesse de Racine. Paris, 1964.
43823.74.2100	Vercammen, Louky. La volière aux chimères. Bruxelles, 1964.
42557.20.6	Verlaine, Paul. Lettres inédites à Charles Morice. Genève, 1964.
41564.31.50	Vigny, Alfred. Les destinées. Paris, 1964.
41564.1.35	Vigny, Alfred de. Oeuvres complètes. Paris, 1964. 2v.
41564.1.40	Vigny, Alfred de. Vigny par lui-même. Paris, 1964.
43824.87.100	Vitrac, Roger. Dès-Lyre, poésies complètes. Paris, 1964.
39544.28.95	Voltaire, François Marie Arouet de. Lettres anglaises. Paris, 1964.
39544.28.40	Voltaire, François Marie Arouet de. Lettres philosophiques. Paris, 1964. 2v.
39545.46.10	Voltaire, François Marie Arouet de. Mahomet the prophet. N.Y., 1964.
37575.330	Walzer, Pierre O. Anthologie jurassienne. Porrentruy, 1964-65. 2v.
38575.99	Wanke, C. Seneca, Lucan, Corneille. Heidelberg, 1964.
42515.35.285.10	Wardman, H.W. Ernest Renan; a critical biography. London, 1964.
37569.373	Wautier, André. La poesie française contemporaine en Wallonie. Charleroi, 1964.
43833.41.5100	Weideli, Walter. Un banquier sans visage. Lausanne, 1964.
42576.15.380	Wetherill, Peter M. Flaubert et la création littéraire. Paris, 1964.
43835.24.700	Wiesel, Eliezer. The town beyond the wall. 1e éd. N.Y., 1964.
43554.2.1135	Willems, W. Paul Claudel. Bruxelles, 1964.
37562.326	Woledge, B. Répertoire des plus anciens textes. Genève, 1964.
40597.2.590	Wurmser, André. La comédie inhumaine. Paris, 1964.
43861.39.100	Zehoval-Bandalin, Iada. Tragédie et espoir d'Israël. Bruxelles, 1964.
42584.23.9.35	Zola, Emile. Germinal. Paris, 1964.

1965

43512.41.100	Abirached, Noukad. L'eclaircie; roman. Beyrouth, 1965.
37542.74	Abraham, Pierre. Manuel d'histoire littéraire de la France. Paris, 1965- 3v.
39544.365.5	Alatri, Paolo. Voltaire, Diderot e il "partito filosofico". Messina, 1965.
43522.36.100	Alhau, Max. Atteinte du songe. Goudargues, 1965.
41555.55.22	Allart de Méritens, Hortense. Nouvelles lettres à Sainte-Beuve, 1832-1864. Genève, 1965.
40597.2.680	Allemand, André. Honoré de Balzac. Paris, 1965.
40597.2.725	Allemand, André. Unité et structure de l'univers balzacien. Paris, 1965.
37569.40.206	Alquie, F. The philosophy of surrealism. Ann Arbor, 1965.
42553.32.92	Amiel, Henri F. Journal intime. Paris, 1965.
43523.66.100	Amoroso, Henri. Les sept péchés capitaux vus par un psychiatre. Paris, 1965.
43526.65.702	Apollinaire, Guillaume. Alcools. Berkeley, 1965.
43526.65.796	Apollinaire, Guillaume. Alkoholy života. Praha, 1965.
43526.65.797	Apollinaire, Guillaume. Básně-obrazy. Praha, 1965.
43526.65.710	Apollinaire, Guillaume. The heresiarck and co. 1st ed. Garden City, N.Y., 1965.
43526.65.11	Apollinaire, Guillaume. Oeuvres complètes. v.1-6. Paris, 1965. 8v.
43526.65.705	Apollinaire, Guillaume. Selected poems. Harmondsworth, 1965.
39566.215	Aquino, Pasquale d'. L'enciclopedismo e l'etica del Diderot. Salerno, 1965.
43528.2.130	Aragon, Louis. La mise à mort. Paris, 1965.
43527.3.406	Aragon, Louis. Le voyage de Hollande. 6. éd. Paris, 1965.
43528.48.105	Arland, Marcel. Le grand pardon. Paris, 1965.
40532.54	Arnould, Émile Jules François. La genèse du Barbier de Séville. Dublin, 1965.
43528.86.57	Artaud, Antonin. Antonin Artaud anthology. San Francisco, 1965.
37574.603	Aspel, Alexander. Contemporary French poetry. Ann Arbor, 1965.
37565.165.5	Atkinson, Geoffroy. The sentimental revolution. Seattle, 1965.
43531.18.1220	Audiberti, Jacques. Dimanche m'attend. Paris, 1965.
43531.18.1210	Audiberti, Jacques. Entretiéns avec Georges Charbonnier. Paris, 1965.
43688.5.5810	Auriant (pseud.). Une vipère lubrique; Paul Leautaud. Bruxelles, 1965.
38525.107	Baden, Jacqueline van. Rotrou, le héros tragigue et la révolte. Paris, 1965.
40553.10.75	Baelen, Jean. Benjamin Constant et Napoléon. Paris, 1965.
38537.55	Bakhtin, Mikhail M. Tvorchestvo Fransua Rable i narodnaia kul'tura sredrevekov'ia i Renessansa. Moskva, 1965.
37556.247	Balashova, T.V. Frantsuzskii roman 60-kh godov. Moskva, 1965.
43697.52.930	Balmas, Enea Henri. Le opere giovanili di André Malraux. Milano, 1965?
40597.14.68	Balzac, Honoré de. Droll stories; thirty tales. N.Y., 1965.
40597.19.50	Balzac, Honoré de. Eugénie Grandet. Paris, 1965.
40597.35.83	Balzac, Honoré de. Le médecin de campagne. Paris, 1965.
40596.7.4	Balzac, Honoré de. Oeuvres complètes. Paris, 1965. 24v.
40597.2.675	Barbéris, Pierre. Aux sources de Balzac. Paris, 1965.
43537.6.29.15	Barbusse, Henri. Le feu; journal d'une escouade, roman. Paris, 1965.
43551.80.800	Barlow, Michel. Gilbert Cesbron. Paris, 1965.
43537.77.4021	Barre, André. Symptomes; poèmes, 1943-1958. Rodez, 1965.
41574.283.15	Barrère, Jean Bertrand. Victor Hugo. Bruges, 1965.

1965 - cont.

42515.35.26.10	Barrès, Maurice. Huit jours chez M. Renan. Paris, 1965.
42563.16.3	Barrès, Maurice. Oeuvre. v.1-20. Paris, 1965. 10v.
39594.19.105	Baskin, Mark P. Montesk'e. Moskva, 1965.
42514.28.112	Beau de Loménie, Emanuel. Maurras et son système. Monsecret, Orne, 1965.
40532.6.20	Beaumarchais, Pierre A.C. de. Die Hochzeit des Figaro. Frankfurt, 1965.
43538.1.700	Beauvoir, Simone de. Force of circumstance. N.Y., 1965.
43538.14.210	Beckett, Samuel. Imagination morte, imaginez. Paris, 1965.
43538.14.798	Beckett, Samuel. Pronst. London, 1965.
40597.2.720	Béguin, Albert. Balzac lu et relu. Paris, 1965.
43538.48.100	Bellanger, Henri. Les noces de pierre. Fontenoy-en-Puisaye, 1965.
43698.200.820	Bellour, Raymond. Henri Michaux. Paris, 1965.
43761.39.925	Benedetto, Domenicantonio di. L'humanisme di A. de St. Exupéry. Sulmona, 1965.
43538.79.100	Bergot, Erwan. Mourir au Laos. Paris, 1965.
37568.54.4	Berl, Emmanuel. Mort de la morale bourgeoise, 1929. Paris, 1965.
43538.76.780	Bernanos, Georges. Georges Bernanos. Roma, 1965.
43744.67.998	Bersani, Leo. Marcel Proust; the fictions of life and of art. N.Y., 1965.
41522.58.18	Bertrand, Louis. Gaspard de la nuit. Paris, 1965.
41522.13.9.32	Besancon, France. Baudelaire. Les fleurs du mal. Concordances. Paris, 1965.
40582.21.16	Beyle, Henri. Racine et Shakespeare. Paris, 1965.
40582.25.75	Beyle, Henri. Scarlet and black. London, 1965.
43744.67.1485	Bibliothèque Nationale, Paris. Marcel Proust. Paris, 1965.
43554.2.1065	Blanc, André. Claudel. Paris, 1965.
37557.81	*Blessing, Marieluise. Der philosophische Dialog als literarische Kurstform von Renan bis Valery. Tübingen, 1965.
43744.67.1475	Błonski, Jan. Widzieć jasno w zachwyceniu. Warszawa, 1965.
42563.23.18.5	Bloy, Léon. Belluaires et Porchers, 1884-1894. Paris, 1965.
43538.76.965	Blumenthal, Gerda. The poetic imagination of George Bernanos. Baltimore, 1965.
37556.268	Bo, Carlo. Da Voltaire a Drieu La Rochelle. Milano, 1965.
43709.85.800	Bodart, Marie Thérèse. L'impromptu du Pont d'Oye avec Pierre Nothomb. Vieux-Virton, 1965.
37597.26.63.5	Bodel, Jehan. Le jeu de saint Nicolas. 2. éd. Bruxelles, 1965.
43620.66.845	Boisdeffre, Pierre de. Giono. Paris, 1965.
38567.43.10	Bonfantini, Mario. Boileau e la sue idee. Milano, 1965.
38567.54	Bonfantini, Mario. Le idee di Boileau. Torino, 1965.
37573.744	Bonheur, Gaston. Qui a cassé le vase de Soissons? Paris, 1965.
43617.78.815	Bonnefoy, Claude. Jean Genêt. Paris, 1965.
43544.60.2150	Bonnefoy, Yves. Pierre écrite. Paris, 1965.
43544.74.2110	Bordonove, Georges. Les Atlantes; roman. Paris, 1965.
43544.75.5100	Borel, Jacques. L'adoration; roman. Paris, 1965.
43544.101.130	Borne, Alain. Les fêtes sont fanées. Suivi de la dernière ligne. Genève, 1965.
43544.89.2200	Bosquet, Alain. La confession mexicaine; roman. Paris, 1965.
42576.65.13.157	Bossier, Herman. Geschiedenis van een romanfiguur. 2. uitg. Hasselt, 1965.
43544.87.3120	Bourbon Busset, Jacques de. La nuit salernes. Paris, 1965.
43544.114.100	Bourget-Pailleron, Robert. La demoiselle de la Closerie. Paris, 1965.
37544.122	Bourin, André. La France littéraire en zigzag. Bruxelles, 1965.
43544.94.132	Bove, Emmanuel. Journal écrit en hiver. Lausanne, 1965.
Mon 112.18	Bowman, Frank Paul. Montaigne: Essays. London, 1965.
Mol 270.37	Brandwajn, Rachmiel. Twarz i maska. Warszawa, 1965.
43545.5.1110	Brassens, Georges. Georges Brassens. Paris, 1965.
43545.24.100.6	Breton, André. Arcane 17 enté d'ajours. Paris, 1965.
43545.41.1021	Brière, Marie Christine. Liesses; poèmes. Rodez, 1965.
43827.89.800	Brion, Marcel. Discours de réception de Marcel Brion à l'Académie française et réponse de René Huyghe. Paris, 1965.
43545.41.5110	Brion, Marcel. L'enchanteur. Paris, 1965.
43545.41.5120	Brion, Marcel. Les escales de la haute nuit. Paris, 1965.
43550.58.1020	Brogan, Geoffrey. Albert Camus die Kunst in der Geschichte. Mainz, 1965.
43545.66.2100	Bronne, Carlo. Le bonheur d'Orphée; nouvelles. Bruxelles, 1965.
43823.75.2250	Bruller, Jean. Les chemins de l'être. Paris, 1965.
43822.49.1555	Brunelli, Giuseppe Antonio. Paul Valéry e il canzoniere, 1887-1892. Messina, 1965.
FL 6139.65.5	Bruno, Antonino. La formazione del pensiero politico di Rousseau. Catania, 1965.
38526.51.80	Bruzzi, Amelia. Il barocco nella poesia di Théophile de Viau. Bologna, 1965.
38543.23.30	Bruzzi, Amelia. Dai "Memoires" alle "Maximes" di La Rochefoucauld. Bologna, 1965.
43546.41.100	Buin, Yves. Les alephs. Paris, 1965.
43546.76.110	Burniaux, Constant. Poésie, 1922-1963. Paris, 1965.
43546.87.69	Butor, Michel. 6810000 litres d'eau par seconde. Paris, 1965.
43833.20.915	Cabaud, Jacques. Simone Weil. N.Y., 1965.
43550.44.100	Calef, Noel. Ascenseur pour l'echafaud. Paris, 1965.
43670.94.805	Callander, Margaret. The poetry of P.J. Jouve. Manchester, 1965.
43550.58.272	Camus, Albert. Carnets; mai 1935 - mars 1951. Paris, 1965.
43550.58.24	Camus, Albert. Collected plays. London, 1965.
43550.58.23	Camus, Albert. Essais. Paris, 1965.
40583.142.6	Caraccio, Armand. Stendhal. N.Y., 1965.
41522.18.475	Cargo, Robert. Concordance to Baudelaire's Les fleurs du mal. Chapel Hill, 1965.
43550.77.1700	Carrington, Leonora. La dama oval. México, 1965.
FL 6059.18	Carzou, Jean M. La conception de la nature humaine dans la nouvelle Héloise. Monte Carlo, 1965?
43550.82.240	Cassou, Jean. Entretiens avec Jean Rousselot. Paris, 1965.
43550.58.1045	Castex, Pierre Georges. Albert Camus et "l'Étranger". Paris, 1965.
37555.737	Cattaui, Georges. Orphisme et prophétie chez les poètes français 1850-1950. Paris, 1965.
43550.89.150	Cau, Jean. Le meurtre d'un enfant. Paris, 1965.
43550.98.220	Cayrol, Jean. Le coup de grâce. Paris, 1965.

Chronological Listing

1965 - cont.

43551.80.170 Cesbron, Gilbert. Entre chiens et loups. Paris, 1965.
43552.2.2130 Chabrol, Jean-Pierre. Les rebelles. Paris, 1965. 3v.
43552.3.1100 Chaigne, Louis. Reconnaissance à la lumière. Tours, 1965.
43552.2.8110 Chambon, Jean. Funeste; roman. Paris, 1965.
43552.3.9300 Chamson, André. La petite odyssée. Paris, 1965.
43552.4.2280 Char, René. L'âge cassant. Paris, 1965.
43552.4.2182 Char, René. Recherche de la base et du sommet. Paris, 1965.
43552.5.1220 Chartier, Émile. L'autre. Audin, 1965.
40585.430 Chateaubriand, F.A.R. Chateaubriand, par lui-même. Paris, 1965.
43552.18.160 Chédid, Andrée. Double-pays. Paris, 1965.
38516.4.26 Chesney, Kathleen. More poèmes de transition. Oxford, 1965.
43552.40.22 Chiha, Michel. La maison des champs. 2e éd. Beyrouth, 1965.
40517.44.21 Choderlos de Laclos, Pierre A.F. Opasnye sviazi. Leningrad, 1965.
37595.36.7.20 Chrestien de Troyes. Erec et Énide. Paris, 1965.
FL 367.5 Christout, Marie Françoise. Le merveilleux et le théâtre du silence en France à partie du XVIIe siècle. La Haye, 1965.
40534.30.5 Ciureanu, Petre. Crébillon. Genova, 1965.
43554.8.35 Clancier, Georges Emmanuel. Les incertains. Paris, 1965.
43554.8.30 Clancier, Georges Emmanuel. Terres de memoire. Paris, 1965.
43744.67.1525 Clarac, Pierre. Album Proust. Paris, 1965.
39527.63 Clarac, Pierre. Jean de La Fontaine. Paris, 1965.
43554.2.27 Claudel, Paul. Oeuvres en prose. Paris, 1965.
43554.5.2120 Clavel, Bernard. Qui m'emporte. Paris, 1965.
43554.5.2100 Clavel, Bernard. Le voyage du père; roman. Paris, 1965.
43554.5.1021 Clavel, Maurice. Saint Euloge de Cordoue. Paris, 1965.
37543.562 Clouard, Henri. Petite histoire de la littérature française des origines à nos jours. Paris, 1965.
43556.1.132 Cocteau, Jean. Thomas, l'imposteur. Paris, 1965?
37567.628 Coeuroy, André. Wagner et l'esprit romantique. Paris, 1965.
42555.44.250 Cohn, Robert Greer. Toward the poems of Mallarmé. Berkeley, 1965.
37596.10.210 Colby, Alice M. The portrait in twelfth-century French literature. Genève, 1965.
41557.10.240 Colin, Georges Emile. Bibliographie des premières publications des romans de George Sand. Bruxelles, 1965.
41522.3.115 Colla, Pierre. L'univers tragique de Barbey d'Aurevilly. Bruxelles, 1965.
38526.10.10.31 Colletet, Guillaume. Traitté de l'épigramme et Traitté du sonnet. Genève, 1965.
43556.50.3100 Collin, Bernard. Les milliers, les millions et le simple. Seine-et-Marne, 1965.
43556.58.705 Conchon, Georges. The savage state. 1st ed. N.Y., 1965.
40553.9.10 Constant de Rebecque, Benjamin. Choix de textes politiques. Utrecht, 1965.
40553.3.5 Constant de Rebecque, Benjamin. Wallstein, tragédie en 5 actes et en vers. Paris, 1965.
FL 360.102 Coppermann, Émile. Le théâtre populaire, pourquoi? Paris, 1965.
42554.26.150 Corbière, Tristan. A picture of Tristan. London, 1965.
40556.39.5 Cordelier, Jean P. La théorie constitutionnelle de Joseph Maistre. Paris, 1965.
38574.16.5 Corneille, Pierre. Writings on the theatre. Oxford, 1965.
40587.36.5 Courteuge, Charles. Touchante Pauline, amoureuse de Chateaubriand. Paris, 1965.
43738.75.1800 Courtot, Claude. Introduction à la lecture de Benjamin Péret. Paris, 1965.
38575.23.150 Currier, Peter. Corneille: Polyeucte. London, 1965.
39533.20.15 Cyrano de Bergerac. Lettres. Milano, 1965.
39533.20.14 Cyrano de Bergerac. Other Worlds. London, 1965.
43565.41.130 Daix, Pierre. L'accident. Paris, 1965.
43565.58.100 Danan, Alexis. Graffiti; poèmes. Blainville-sur-Mer, 1965.
41522.18.550 Daniel, Frank. Die Frau bei Baudelaire. Erlangen, 1965?
42586.33.120 Darien, Georges. La Belle France. Paris, 1965.
43565.90.3110 David, Jean. Assassin. Paris, 1965.
37564.265 Davidson, Hugh McCullough. Audience, words, and art. Columbus, Ohio, 1965.
43565.91.1100 Davy, Marie Magdeleine. Le berger du soleil. Paris, 1965.
43565.91.1110 Davy, Marie Magdeleine. La terre face au soleil. Neuchâtel, 1965.
43538.76.970 Debluë, Henri. Les Romans de Georges Bernanos. Neuchâtel, 1965.
43591.89.830 Decaunes, Luc. Paul Éluard, biographie. Rodez, 1965.
43576.9.835 Dédéyan, Charles. Le cosmopolitisme littéraire de Charles du Bos. v.1-3. Paris, 1965. 6v.
40513.38.5 Dédéyan, Charles. LeSage et Gil Blas. Paris, 1965. 2v.
38544.27.575.2 Dédéyan, Charles. Madame de La Fayette. 2. éd. Paris, 1965.
38585.59 Dédéyan, Charles. Racine et sa Phèdre. Paris, 1965.
43566.35.2100 Deguillaume, Jacques. Hippolyte le Grand. Rodez, 1965.
43566.48.4021 Delbousquet, Germaine Emmanuel. Coeur; poèmes. Rodez, 1965.
43566.48.6130 Del Castillo, Michel. Les aveux interdits. Paris, 1965. 2v.
38575.116 Delû-Bridel, Jacques. La préciosité, conception heroique de la vie. Bologna, 1965.
43566.77.3100 Deroisin, Sophie. Les jardins intérieurs; essai. Bruxelles, 1965.
43761.79.100 Desan, W. The marxism of Jean-Paul Sartre. Garden City, 1965.
43566.79.2100 Descarmes, Alain. Histoire satirique de la femme à travers les âges. LeMans, 1965?
43566.80.120 Des Cars, Guy. De cape et de plume. Paris, 1965.
43697.77.880 Descloux, Armand. Le Docteur Antoine Thibault. Thèse. Paris, 1965.
38528.24.6 Despériers, Bonaventure. Cymbalum mundi. N.Y., 1965.
43761.39.915 Devaux, André A. St. Exupéry. Paris, 1965.
42554.28.50 Dhôtel, André. La vie de Rimbaud; variétés. Paris, 1965.
39564.17.6 Diderot, Denis. Entretien entre d'Alembert et Diderot. Paris, 1965.
39564.10.78 Diderot, Denis. Nachtrag zu Bougainvilles Reise. Frankfurt, 1965.
37555.500.10 Diéguez, Manuel de. Essai sur l'avenir poétique de Dieu. Paris, 1965.
37575.151.2 Dimoff, Paul. Anthologie des poètes de Lorraine de 1700 à 1950. 2. éd. Nancy, 1965.
43573.76.100 Dorgelès, Roland. A bas l'argent! Paris, 1965.

1965 - cont.

43573.76.1100 Dorian, Jean Pierre. Coups de griffes, suivi d'une lettre au Général de Gaulle. Paris, 1965.
43573.89.4100 Doublet, Catherine. La courte paille. Paris, 1965.
37555.300.15 Dresse, Paul. Plaisir au vers; technique et rêve. Paris, 1965.
43574.41.700 Drieu La Rochelle, Pierre. The fire within. 1. American ed. N.Y., 1965.
38526.48.18.3 Du Bartas, Guillaume de Salluste. Bartas: his devine weekes and works, 1605. Gainesville, Florida, 1965.
43576.9.110 Du Bos, Charles. Approximations. Paris, 1965.
41543.22.110 Dubruck, Alfred. Gerard de Nerval and the German heritage. The Hague, 1965.
43757.50.1310 Duchatelet, B. La question du mariage dans Jean-Christophe de Romain Rolland. Groningen, 1965.
Mon 114.14 Duhamel, Roger. Lecture de Montaigne. Ottawa, 1965.
43738.1.890 Duployé, Pie. La religion de Péguy. Paris, 1965.
43576.74.4100 Durand, Pierre. Vingt ans. Paris, 1965.
43576.74.2115 Duras, Marguerite. Four novels. N.Y., 1965.
43576.74.2210 Duras, Marguerite. Théâtre. Paris, 1965. 2v.
43576.87.180 Dutourd, Jean. Le demi-solde. Paris, 1965.
43576.93.120 Duwez, Maurice. La boue des Flandres. Paris, 1965.
38585.62 Edwards, Michael. La Thébaide de Racine. Paris, 1965.
43591.89.825 Eglin, Heinrich. Liebe und Inspiration im Werke von Paul Éluard. Bern, 1965.
39594.19.155 Ehrard, Jean. Montesquieu, critique d'art. Paris, 1965.
41564.55.120 Eigeldinger, Marc. Alfred de Vigny: Un tableau synoptique de la vie et des oeuvres d'Alfred de Vigny et des événements artistiques. Paris, 1965.
37555.724 Elwert, Wilhelm Theodor. Traité de versification française des origines a nos jours. Paris, 1965.
42584.25.355 Emel'ianikov, Sergei P. Rugon-Makkary E. Zolia. Moskva, 1965.
43592.53.330 Emmanuel, Pierre. La face humaine. Paris, 1965.
43538.14.860 Esslin, Martin. Samuel Beckett: a collection of critical essays. Englewood Cliffs, N.J., 1965.
43538.76.980 Estéve, Michel. Bernanos. Paris, 1965.
42556.28.145.20 Étiemble, René. Nouveaux aspects du mythe de Rimbaud. Paris, 1965. 2v.
42582.2.90 Evans, I. Oliver. Jules Verne and his work. London, 1965.
43697.75.885 Ewijk, Thomas J.M. van. Gabriel Marcel, an introduction. N.Y., 1965.
43606.58.100 Fanchette, Jean. Identité provisoire; poèmes. Paris, 1965.
43606.89.4100 Fauquez, Arthur. Ambrosio tue l'heure. Malèves Ste-Marie, 1965.
43606.99.110 Faye, Jean-Pierre. Couleurs pliées. Paris, 1965.
43538.14.865 Federman, Raymond. Journey to chaos. Berkeley, 1965.
42515.38.35 Fini, Salvatore. Renan e l'Italia. San Severo, 1965.
43550.58.995 Fitch, Brian T. Albert Camus. v.1, pt.1-2. Paris, 1965. 2v.
42576.35.12 Flaubert, Gustave. Les lettres d'Egypte de Gustave Flaubert d'après les manuscrits autographes. Paris, 1965.
42576.35.33 Flaubert, Gustave. Lettres inédites de G. Flaubert à son éditeur Michel Levy. Paris, 1965.
42576.28.100 Flaubert, Gustave. Madame Bovary. 1. ed. N.Y., 1965.
42576.26 Flaubert, Gustave. Souvenirs. Paris, 1965.
43611.64.100 Fondane, Benjamin. L'éxode super flumina Babylonis. Veilhes, Tarn, 1965.
43620.2.455 Fowlie, W. André Gide: his life and art. N.Y., 1965.
42556.28.184 Fowlie, Wallace. Rimbaud. Chicago, 1965.
Mon 146.5A Frame, Donald Murdoch. Montaigne: a biography. 1. ed. N.Y., 1965.
42576.62.114 France, Anatole. Lettres inédites d'Anatole France à Jacques Lion. Paris, 1965.
38585.16.360 France, Peter. Racine's rhetoric. Oxford, 1965.
43538.35.800 Franck, Dorothée Juliane. La quête spirituelle d'Albert Béguin. Neuchâtel, 1965.
37563.70.8A Françon, Marcel. Leçons et notes sur la littérature française au XVIe siècle. 3. éd. Cambridge, Mass., 1965.
42582.2.85 Freedman, Russell. Jules Verne, portrait of a prophet. N.Y., 1965.
43612.24.130 Frère, Maud. Guido. Paris, 1965.
40535.31.50 Friedrichs, Friedhelm Alfred. Untersuchungen zur Handlungs- und Vorgangsmotivik im Werk Marivaux. Inaug. Diss. Heidelberg? 1965.
38527.29.5 Galzy, Jeanne. Agrippa d'Aubigné. Paris, 1965.
43616.53.21 Gambier, Gerard. Rocailles; nouvelles. Bruxelles, 1965.
43616.60.110 Ganne, Gilbert. Les hauts cris; roman. Paris, 1965.
37558.210 Garcon, Maurice. Le palais à l'académie. Paris, 1965.
43616.78.120 Gary, Romain. Frère Océan. Paris, 1965. 3v.
43616.78.745 Gary, Romain. The ski bum. N.Y., 1965.
43616.79.190 Gascar, Pierre. Les charmes. Paris, 1965.
43616.79.725 Gascar, Pierre. Lambs of fire. N.Y., 1965?
43616.90.110 Gaucheron, Jacques H. Les canuts. Paris, 1965.
42586.63.45 Gaulmier, Jean. Spectre de Gobineau. Paris, 1965.
43616.89.4100 Gautier, Yvonne. Mon enfance et elle, souvenirs. Paris, 1965.
37558.208 Gaxotte, Pierre. L'académie française. Paris, 1965.
43616.98.2100 Gayet Tancrède, Paul. Contes à pic. Paris, 1965.
43550.58.955 Gelinas, G.P. La liberté dans la pensée d'Albert Camus. Fribourg, 1965.
43617.78.102 Genêt, Jean. Haute surveillance. Paris, 1965.
43617.78.730 Genêt, Jean. Miracle of the rose. London, 1965.
43617.59.230 Genevoix, Maurice. Beau-françois. Paris, 1965.
39594.19.115 Gentile, Francesco. L'esprit classique nel pensiero del Montesquieu. Padova, 1965.
43611.5.185 Genuist, Paul. Alain-Fournier face à l'angoisse. Paris, 1965.
FL 6049.10.15 Gerdil, G.S. Reflections on education. Holborn, 1965.
37555.730 Gibaudan, René. La lyre mystérieuse: Gérard de Nerval, Aloysius Bertrand, Maurice de Guérin, Theophile Gautier. Paris, 1965.
43620.2.76.5 Gide, André. L'école des femmes. Paris, 1965.
43620.40.130 Gilliard, Edmond. La chasse de Pan. Genève, 1965.
43620.40.11 Gilliard, Edmond. Oeuvres complètes. Genève, 1965.
43620.66.480 Giono, Jean. Deux cavaliers de l'orage. Paris, 1965.
38526.48.38.12 Giudici, Enzo. Maurice Scève, bucolico e "Blasonneur". Napoli, 1965.
38526.48.38.10 Giudici, Enzo. Maurice Scève. Roma, 1965. 2v.
43656.59.825 Glukman, Marta. Eugène Ionesco y su teatro. Santiago de Chile, 1965.
42586.66.9.7 Gobineau, Arthur de. Nouvelles asiatiques. Paris, 1965.
37556.22.80 Godfrin, Jacqueline. Une centrale de presse catholique. Paris, 1965.
39533.22.95 Goebel, Gerhard. Zur Erzahltechnik in den "Histoires comigues" des 17. Jahrhunderts. Berlin, 1965.

Chronological Listing

1965 - cont.

43697.88.890 Goesch, Keith. François Mauriac, essai de bibliographie chronologique, 1908-1960. Paris, 1965.
43625.27.170 Goffin, Robert. Sablier pour une cosmogonie; poèmes. Bruxelles, 1965.
42575.68.10 Goncourt, Edmond de. Correspondance inédite, 1876-1896 d'Edmond de Goncourt et Henry Céard. Paris, 1965.
43743.48.1800 Goublet, Juliette. Léo Poldès: Le Faubourg. Aurillac, 1965.
43625.89.4100 Goudeket, Maurice. La douceur de vieillir. Paris, 1965.
38557.24.145 Goyet, Thérèse. L'humanisme de Bossuet. v.1-2. Paris, 1965.
43626.4.2021F Granoff, Katia. Cendres et reflets. Paris, 1965.
38527.49.10 Gras, Maurice. Robert Garnier, son art et sa méthode. Genève, 1965.
38526.17.105 Graville, Anne de. Le beau romant des deux amans Palamon et Arcita et de la belle et saige Emilia. Paris, 1965.
40535.32.60 Greene, Edward J. Marivaux. Toronto, 1965.
43626.23.2100 Grenier, Roger. Years in ambush. 1st American ed. N.Y., 1965.
43628.24.1110 Guérin, Daniel. Un jeune homme excentrique. Paris, 1965.
41593.33.60 Guérin, Maurice de. Maurice et Eugenié de Guérin. Paris, 1965.
41593.34.50 Guérin, Maurice de. Pages choisies. Manchester, 1965.
43750.24.820 Guicharnaud, Jacques. Raymond Queneau. N.Y., 1965.
43628.41.8021 Guichet, Robert. Partage d'aimer; poems. Rodez, 1965.
38526.26.89 Guidici, Enzo. Amore e follia nell'opera della Belle Cordière. Napoli, 1965.
43628.41.3160 Guillevic, Eugène. Poesias. Lisboa, 1965.
43552.5.1840 Halda, Bernard. Alain. Paris, 1965.
43538.76.975 Halda, Bernard. Bernanos, le scandale de croire. Paris, 1965.
37556.249 Halimi, André. Tous candidats à l'Élysée. Paris, 1965.
39532.13.17 Hamilton, Anthony. Mémoires du comte de Grammont. Paris, 1965.
39532.13.16 Hamilton, Anthony. Memoires of the comte de Grammont. London, 1965.
43566.82.3800 Hayman, David. Louis-Ferdinand Céline. N.Y., 1965.
43538.76.955 Hebblethwaite, P. Bernanos; an introduction. London, 1965.
43833.20.930 Heidsieck, François. Simone Weil. Paris, 1965.
37569.382 Heist, Walter. Genet und Andere; Exkurse über eine faschistische Literatur von Rang. Hamburg, 1965.
43632.50.230 Hellens, Franz. Les hors-le-vent. Liège, 1965.
43780.69.810 Hiddleston, James A. L'univers de Jules Supervielle. Paris, 1965.
40597.2.710 Hoffman, Léon-François. Repertoire geographique de la Comédie humaine. Paris, 1965. 2v.
43576.75.1800 Hommage à Georges Duret, 1887-1943. Poitiers, 1965.
43697.74.800 Hommage à René Maran. Paris, 1965.
43738.78.840 Honneur à Saint-John Perse. Paris, 1965.
43638.2.100 Huant, Ernest. Voyage en Assurs-Socyalie. Paris, 1965.
41573.69 Hugo, Victor. Un carnet des misérables, octobre-decembre 1860. Paris, 1965.
41572.53 Hugo, Victor. La poésie. Paris, 1965.
43638.35.1110 Huguenin, Jean-René. Une autre jeunesse. Paris, 1965.
43638.82.100 Husson, Jean H. Le cheval d'Herbeleau. Paris, 1965.
42576.65.45 Huysmans, Joris Karl. Là-haut, ou Notre-Dame de la Salette. Tournai, 1965.
43652.46.160 Ikor, Roger. Gloucq. Paris, 1965.
43656.59.705 Ionesco, Eugène. The bald soprano. N.Y., 1965.
37543.608 Itterbeek, Eugene van. Spreken en zwijgen. Hasselt, 1965.
43667.14.790 Jacob, Max. Wybór poezji. Warszawa, 1965.
38526.10.10.80 Jannini, Pasquale Aneil. Verso il tempo della ragione. Milano, 1965.
43667.78.191 Jarry, Alfred. Les antliaclastes. Paris, 1965?
43667.78.621 Jarry, Alfred. Selected works of Alfred Jarry. N.Y., 1965.
39527.4.150 Jasinski, René. La Fontaine et le premier recueil des Fables. Paris, 1965-66. 2v.
37543.265.2 Jasinski, René. Histoire de la littérature française. Paris, 1965-66. 2v.
43738.1.895 Jassem-Wilson, Nelly. Charles Péguy. London, 1965.
43785.98.100 Jay, Henri. Collinades; contes de Provence. Marseille, 1965.
43668.4.2110 Jean, Raymond. La littérature et la réel de Diderot au "nouveau roman". Paris, 1965.
FL 6139.65.10 Jean-Jacques Rousseau et l'homme moderne. Paris, 1965.
37561.27.5 Jeanroy, Alfred. Les origines de la poésie lyrique en France au moyen âge. 4e éd. Paris, 1965.
42576.63.800 Jefferson, Carter. Anatole France; the politics of skepticism. New Brunswick, N.J., 1965.
43668.50.100 Jelinek, Henriette. Portrait d'un séducteur. Paris, 1965.
43697.88.880 Jenkins, Cecil. Mauriac. Edinburgh, 1965.
38525.7.11 Jodelle, d'Estienne. Oeuvres complètes. Paris, 1965. 2v.
43670.50.100 Joliat, Yvette. Un évêché pour une danseuse. Delémont, 1965.
43670.89.570 Jouhandeau, M. Divertissements. Paris, 1965.
38524.147 Jourda, Pierre. Conteurs français du XVIe siècle. Paris, 1965.
43670.94.390 Jouve, Pierre Jean. Moires. Paris, 1965.
Mol 610.5 Jouvet, Louis. Molière et la comédie classique. Paris, 1965.
43591.89.1800 Jucker-Wehrli, Ursula. La poésie de Paul Éluard et le thème de la pureté. Zürich, 1965.
42555.60.80 Jullian, Philippe. Robert de Montesquiou, un prince 1900. Paris, 1965.
43576.6.820.5 Keating, Louis Clark. Critic of civilization. Lexington, 1965.
43673.83.270 Kessel, Joseph. The Bernan affair, a novel. N.Y., 1965.
43673.83.735 Kessel, Joseph. They weren't all angels. N.Y., 1965.
37547.14.15 Kirsch, Fritz Peter. Studien zur languedokischen und gaskognischen Literatur der Gegenwart. Wien, 1965.
43677.23.100 Klein, Guy. Les Culs bénis, ou Un trop fol amour. Montbard, 1965.
43677.66.110 Klossowski, Pierre. Le Baphomet. Paris, 1965.
43677.66.130 Klossowski, Pierre. Les lois de l'hospitalité. Paris, 1965.
40517.44.110 Knufmann, Helmut. Das Böse in der Liaisons dangereuses des Choderlos de Laclos. München, 1965.
43822.49.1550 Koehler, Hartmut. Poésie et profondeur sémantique dans La jeune parque. Nancy, 1965.
43680.59.100 Koné, Maurice. Au seuil du crépuscule. Rodez, 1965.
43761.77.800 Kranaké, Mimika. Nathalie Sarraute. Paris, 1965.

1965 - cont.

37565.180 Krauss, Werner. Perspektiven und Problems. Zur französische und deutschen Aufklärung und andere Aufsätze. Neuwied, 1965.
39544.364 Kuznetsov, Vitalii N. Vol'ter i filosofiia frantsuzskogo prosvesheheniia XVIII veka. Moskva, 1965.
43687.6.2100 Labagne, Henri. Lettre à un anecdotique. Ivry-sur-Seine, 1965.
42556.27.33.812 Lacretelle, Jacques de. Centenaire de Henri de Régnier. Paris, 1965.
38544.27.300 La Fayette, Marie M. Histoire de Madame Henriette. Paris, 1965.
37557.80 La Ferrière-Percy, Hector. Rapport sur les recherches faites à la bibliothèque impériale de Saint-Pétersbourg. Saint Pétersbourg, 1965.
39584.8 La Harpe, Jean François de. Correspondance inédite de Jean-François de La Harpe. Paris, 1965.
43687.60.3120 Langfus, Anna. Saute, Barbara. Paris, 1965.
43531.18.1250 La Nouvelle Revue Française. Hommage à Jacques Audiberti, 1899-1965. Paris, 1965.
37543.564 Lanson, Gustave. Essais de méthode. Paris, 1965.
43687.65.120 Lanza del Vasto, Joseph Jean. Noé. Paris, 1965.
43687.62.3110 Lanzmann, Jacques. Qui vive. Paris, 1965.
37547.103.5 Larat, Jean. Panorama des lettres en Auvergne. Clermont, 1965.
43687.80.2140 Lartéguy, Jean. Les tambours de bronze. Paris, 1965.
43687.80.2720 Lartéguy, Jean. Yellow fever. London, 1965.
38514.54.20 La Sale, Antoine de. Jehan de Saintré. Genève, 1965.
43697.88.875 Laurent, Jacques. Mauriac sous De Gaulle. Paris, 1965.
43628.1.530 Lauwick, Hervé. Sacha Guitry et les femmes. Paris, 1965.
43550.58.1075 Lazzari, Francesco. Camus e il cristianesimo. Napoli, 1965.
40556.50 Lebrun, Richard Allen. Throne and altar. Ottawa, 1965.
43688.14.4110 Le Clézio, Jean Marie Gustave. La fièvre. Paris, 1965.
43688.20.130 Leduc, Violette. L'affamée. Paris, 1965.
43688.20.120 Leduc, Violette. La bâtarde. N.Y., 1965.
43688.34.4100 Legray, Jacques. Le roman de la vie de Goethe. Paris, 1965.
37543.592 Le Hir, Yves. Analyses stylistiques. Paris, 1965.
37557.82 Leiner, Wolfgang. Der Widmungsbrief in der französischen Literatur (1580-1715). Heidelberg, 1965.
40516.60.115 Lély, Gilbert. Vie du Marquis de Sade. Paris, 1965.
37574.577 Lemaitre, Henri. La poésie depuis Baudelaire. Paris, 1965.
43688.98.120 LeQuintrec, Charles. Le mur d'en face; roman. Paris, 1965.
42576.46.9.30 Le Roy, Eugène. Nicette et Milou. Périgueux, 1965.
42576.63.785 Levaillant, Jean. Essai sur l'évolution intellectuelle d'Anatole France. Paris, 1965.
37542.55 Life and letters in France. London, 1965-70. 3v.
43690.55.110 Limbour, Georges. Les vanilliers. Lausanne, 1965.
43690.59.100 Lindon, Raymond. Quand la justice s'en mêle. Paris, 1965.
43690.61.120 Linze, Jacques Gérard. La conquête de Prague. Paris, 1965.
43738.78.800 Little, Roger. Word index of the complete poetry and prose of Saint-John Perse. n.p., 1965.
40583.178.15 Litto, Victor del. La vie de Stendhal. Paris, 1965.
37556.12.50 Livois, René de. Histoire de la presse française. Lausanne, 1965. 2v.
37565.172 Livre et société dans la France du XVIIIe siècle. v.2. Paris, 1965. 2v.
42556.28.412 Locker, Malka. Rimbaud; le poéte qui s'enfuit. 2. éd. Paris, 1965.
40526.8.25 Loggins, Vernon. André Chénier. Athens, 1965.
37597.9.18.5 Lorris, Guillaume de. Roman de la rose. Paris, 1965. 3v.
42555.58.85 Losito, Luigo. L'esordio letterario di Catulle Mendès. Bari, 1965.
43693.89.4021 Louis, Edner A. La porte s'ouvre; mes confidences à Marie-Jo. Port-au-Prince, 1965.
43693.89.5100 Louis, Gabriel. Portie civile contre la société. Paris, 1965.
43551.59.820 Lovey, Jean Claude. Situation de Blaise Cendrars. Neuchâtel, 1965.
42546.12.60 Lutgen, Odette. De pére en fils: Edmond et Jean. Paris, 1965.
37562.333 Lyons, Faith. Les éléments descriptifs dans le roman d'aventure au XIIe siècle. Genève, 1965.
37543.472 Macchia, Giovanni. Il mito di Parigi. Torino, 1965.
FL 6139.65 McDonald, Joan. Rousseau and the French revolution, 1762-1791. London, 1965.
43697.13.1100 Macle, Guy. Gaillardes et passagères. Saint-Ouen, 1965.
43697.14.380 MacOrlan, Pierre. Masques sur mesure. Paris, 1965.
43697.14.21 MacOrlan, Pierre. Mémoires en chansons. Paris, 1965.
42545.3.885 Maenner, Peter Johannes. Maurice Maeterlinck; Theatralische Repräsentation einer Philosophie im Zusammenhang der modernen Dramaturgie. Diss. München, 1965.
42545.05 Maeterlinck, Maurice. Poésies complètes. Bruxelles, 1965.
40556.27.50 Maistre, Joseph de. Works. N.Y., 1965.
43550.58.1015 Majault, Joseph. Camus. Paris, 1965.
43697.50.100 Mallat, Robert J. Poémes de la mort juive. Honfleur, 1965.
43697.2.1142 Mallet-Joris, Françoise (pseud.). Cordélia and other stories. N.Y., 1965.
43697.53.1100 Mambrino, Jean. Le veilleur aveugle. Paris, 1965.
43697.54.1100 Mamet, Magda. A l'écoute du temps. Paris, 1965.
43697.61.2150 Mansour, Joyce. Carré blanc. Paris, 1965.
43697.75.200 Marcel, Gabriel. Paix sur la terre. Paris, 1965.
43697.63.110 Marcotte, Gilles. Retour à Coolbrook. Paris, 1965.
Mon 108.9 Marcu, Eva. Répertoire des idées de Montaigne. Genève, 1965.
38526.34.531 Margarete of Austria. The chanson albums of Marguerite of Austria. Berkeley, 1965.
43697.76.6621 Maritain, Raïssa. Patriarch tree: thirty poems. Worcester, 1965.
40535.29.35 Marivaux, Pierre Carlet de Chamblain de. The virtuous orphan. Carbondale, 1965.
41595.2.81 Marseille-Lansiart, Monique. Lacenaire. Bourgoin, 1965.
43697.86.160 Masson, Loÿs. Le feu d'Espagne; roman. Paris, 1965.
43554.2.1155 Matheson, William Howard. Claudel and Aeschylus. Ann Arbor, 1965.
43620.2.279 Mauriac, Claude. Conversations with Andre Gide. N.Y., 1965.
43697.88.620 Mauriac, François. Nouveaux memoires intérieurs. Paris, 1965.

Chronological Listing

1965 - cont.

43697.88.724 Mauriac, François. Thérèse; a portrait in four parts. N.Y., 1965.
37568.235 Maurois, André. De Gide à Sartre. Paris, 1965.
43697.89.12 Maurois, André. Oeuvres. Paris, 1965. 5v.
40597.2.625.1 Maurois, André. Prométhée; ou, La vie de Balzac. Lausanne, 1965. 2v.
40597.2.625 Maurois, André. Prométhée; ou, La vie de Balzac. Paris, 1965.
41574.610 Maurois, André. Victor Hugo. Paris, 1965.
42514.28.235 Maurras, Hélène. Souvenirs des prisons de Charles Maurras. Paris, 1965.
41555.54.6 Meier, Harri. La carroza del santo sacramento de Próspero Merimé. Lima, 1965.
43698.75.8100 Mérens, Louis. Les français, fous, fous, fous. Paris, 1965.
43709.85.815 Mergeai, Jean. Pierre Nothomb; ou, Les paradis perdus. Vieux-Virton, 1965.
43698.98.700 Meynier, Yvonne. The school with a difference. London, 1965.
42555.44.113 Michaud, Guy. Mallarmé. N.Y., 1965.
43698.200.162 Michaux, Henri. La vie dans les plis, poèmes. Paris, 1965.
43698.200.230 Michaux, Henri. Wind und Staub. Olten, 1965.
38537.25.245 Michel, Pierre. Continuité de la sagesse française. Paris, 1965.
43757.6.820 Miesch, Jean. Robbe-Grillet. Paris, 1965.
43699.51.30 Milosz, Oscar Vladislas. Milosz. Choix de textes présenté par Jacques Buge. Paris, 1965.
42556.28.360 Missouri. Southwest Missouri State College. The William J. Jones Rimbaud collection. Springfield, 1965.
42533.20.5 Mockel, Albert. La correspondance entre Albert Mockel et Roger Desaise. Bruxelles, 1965.
43701.39.140 Mohrt, Michel. La campagne d'Italie. Paris, 1965.
43701.41.3100 Moinet, Bernard. Opium rouge. Paris, 1965?
43701.41.705 Moinot, Pierre. An ancient enemy. Garden City, 1965.
Mol 228.86 Molière, Jean Baptiste Poquelin. Le malade imaginaire. London, 1965.
Mol 19.65 Molière, Jean Baptiste Poquelin. Oeuvres complètes. Paris, 1965. 2v.
37565.72.10 Monglond, André. Le préromantisme français. Paris, 1965-1966. 2v.
Mol 713.20.5 Mongrédien, George. Recueil des textes et des documents du XVIIe siècle relatifs à Molière. Paris, 1965. 2v.
Mon 32.65 Montaigne, Michel de. Complete essays. Stanford, 1965.
Mon 19.65.5 Montaigne, Michel de. Essais. Paris, 1965. 3v.
Mon 19.65 Montaigne, Michel de. Les essais. Paris, 1965.
39594.9.60 Montesquieu, C.L. de S. Politique et Montesquieu. Paris, 1965.
43701.63.580 Montherlant, Henry de. La guerre civile, pièce en trois actes. Paris, 1965.
43701.61.2100 Montupet, Janiere. La rose amère. Paris, 1965.
37575.213 Mor, Antonio. Le più belle pagine delle letterature del Belgio. Milano, 1965.
43701.74.450 Morand, Paul. Nouvelles d'une vie. Paris, 1965. 2v.
43701.74.410 Morand, Paul. Tais-toi. Paris, 1965.
43701.75.7700 Moreau, Marcel J. The selves of Quinte. N.Y., 1965.
37567.629 Moreau, Pierre. Âmes et thèmes romantiques. Paris, 1965.
40587.97.5 Moreau, Pierre. Chateaubriand. Bruges, 1965.
43701.75.8100 Morhange, Pierre. Poèmes brefs. n.p., 1965.
43757.6.810 Morrissette, Bruce A. Alain Robbe-Grillet. N.Y., 1965.
40597.2.735 Moscow. Vsesoiuznaia gosudarstvennaia biblioteka inostrannoi literatury. Onore de Bal'zak. Moskva, 1965.
43556.1.935 Mourgue, Gérard. Jean Cocteau. Paris, 1965.
Mon 153.22 Mueller, Armand. Montaigne. Bruges? 1965.
43554.2.1200 Mueller, Klaus. Die Frühdramen Paul Claudels: l'Endormie, Fragment d'un drame, Tête d'Or, La Ville. Stuttgart, 1965.
43744.67.1535 Muller, Marcel. Les voix narratives dans la "Recherche du temps perdu". Genève, 1965.
41592.10.45 Murav'eva, Natal'ia I. Beranzhe. Moskva, 1965.
37555.647 Musser, Frederic O. Strange clamor; a guide to the critical reading of French poetry. Detroit, 1965.
37556.357 Mylne, Vivienne. The eighteenth-century French novel. Manchester, 1965.
38513.18.10 Le mystère de Saint Sébastien. Genève, 1965.
37569.40.57 Nadeau, M. The history of surrealism. N.Y., 1965.
37569.378 Narkir'er, Fedor S. Frantsuzskaia revoliutsionnaia literatura, 1914-1924. Moskva, 1965.
41543.12.13 Nerval, Gerard de. Aurélia. Paris, 1965.
42556.28.395 Nicoletti, Gianni. Rimbaud; una poesia del canto chiuso. Torino, 1965.
37568.233 Nimier, Roger. Journees de lectures. Paris, 1965.
43709.14.30 Noctuel. Dictionnaire français-rosse. Paris, 1965.
43709.80.110 Nourissier, François. Une histoire française. Paris, 1965.
40597.2.715 Nykrog, Per. La pensée de Balzac dans la Comédie humaine. Copenhague, 1965.
43550.58.1057 Onimus, Jean. Camus. 2. éd. Paris, 1965.
43728.18.100 Ordioni, Pierre. Le chant des ténèbres. Paris, 1965.
37558.204 Ormesson, Wladimir. Le clergé et l'académie. Paris, 1965.
43731.83.100 Osson-Essui, Denis. Vers de nouveaux horizons; roman. Paris, 1965.
42586.30.100 Pagés Larraya, Antonio. Gabriela de Coni y sus ficciones precursoras. Buenos Aires, 1965.
43737.34.250 Pagnol, Marcel. Le masque de fer. Paris, 1965.
FL 6139.39.2 Pahlmann, Franz. Mensch und Staat bei Rousseau. Berlin, 1965.
43744.67.1361 Painter, George Duncan. Marcel Proust. London, 1965. 2v.
43550.58.1035 Papamalamis, Dimitris. Albert Camus et la pensée grecque. Nancy, 1965.
43554.2.805 Paris. Bibliothèque Sainte-Genevieve. Collection Doucet. Paul Claudel; premières oeuvres, 1886-1901. Paris, 1965.
Mon 210.25 Paris. Lycée Montaigne. Montaigne en son temps à travers "Les Essais"; le voyage en Halie de 1580. Paris, 1965?
43556.1.955 Paris. Musée Jacques Mart-André. Jean Cocteau et son temps, 1889-1963. Paris, 1965.
43550.58.980 Parker, Emmett. Albert Camus, the artist in the arena. Madison, 1965.
43737.77.100 Parmelin, Hélène. Le voyage à Lucerne. Paris, 1965.
43550.58.1000 Passeri Pignoni, Vera. Albert Camus. Bologna, 1965.
43738.35.100 Pégue-Vérane, Gabrielle. Racines profondes. Lausanne, 1965.
43738.41.1110 Peignot, Jérôme. Grandeur et misères d'un employé de bureau. Paris, 1965.

1965 - cont.

43545.4.4820 Pellegrin, René. Un écrivain nommé Brasillach. Montsecret, 1965.
43738.59.100 Penent, Jacques Arnaud. Les temps morts. Paris, 1965.
43667.78.820 Perche, Louis. Alfred Jarry. Paris, 1965.
43738.75.100 Perec, Georges. Les choses. Paris, 1965.
43738.75.1110 Péret, Benjamin. Le déshonneur des poètes. Paris, 1965.
43744.77.1100 Péret, Benjamin. Vingt poèmes. Paris, 1965.
43738.85.1100 Petit, Henri. Les justes solitudes. Paris, 1965.
43738.97.1755 Peyrefitte, Roger. Les juifs. Paris, 1965.
41543.22.115 Peyrouzet, Edouard. Gerard de Nerval inconnu. Paris, 1965.
37557.76.35 Picard, Raymond. Nouvelle critique ou nouvelle imposture. Paris, 1965.
40583.340 Pieyre de Mandiargues, André. Beylamour. Paris, 1965.
43741.25.705 Pieyre de Mandiargues, André. The motorcycle. N.Y., 1965.
43741.25.210 Pieyre de Mandiargues, André. Porte devergondée. Paris, 1965.
43741.49.2100 Pilhes, René-Victor. La rhubarbe; roman. Paris, 1965.
43741.59.110 Pingaud, Bernard. L'amour triste. Paris, 1965.
43741.59.130 Pingaud, Bernard. Inventaire. Paris, 1965-
43741.59.120 Pingaud, Bernard. La scène primitive. Paris, 1965.
43741.59.3190 Pinget, Robert. Autour de Mortin. Paris, 1965.
43741.59.3200 Pinget, Robert. Quelqu'un. Paris, 1965.
43741.77.100 Piroué, Georges. Une si grande faiblesse. Paris, 1965.
38514.57.30 Pisan, Christine de. Ballades, rondeaux, and virelais. Leicester, Eng., 1965.
42542.64.13.20 Plat, Armand. Paul Déroulède. Paris, 1965.
43742.25.100 Pleynet, Marcelin. Comme; poésie. Paris, 1965.
37562.330 Poirion, Daniel. Le poète et le prince. Grenoble, 1965.
41557.10.255 Poli, Annarosa. George Sand vue par les italiens. Firenze, 1965.
38523.38.5 Ponge, Francis. Pour un Malherbe. Paris, 1965.
43743.60.21 Ponge, Francis. Tome premier. Paris, 1965.
43743.61.2100 Pontremoli, Pascal. Lapidaire. Paris, 1965.
43743.77.2100 Porquerol, Elizabeth. Les voix. Paris, 1965.
40539.15.15 Potocki, Jan. Rękopis znaleziony w Saragossie. Warszawa, 1965.
43743.98.460 Pozner, Vladimir. Le mors aux dents. Lausanne, 1965.
43744.24.23.9 Prévert, Jacques. Selections from "Paroles". Harmondsworth, 1965.
40522.9.75 Prévost, Antoine F. Histoire du chevalier des Grieux et de Manon Lescaut. Paris, 1965.
43688.14.3800 Pronger, Lester J. La poésie de Tristan Klimgsor, 1890-1960. Paris, 1965.
43656.59.805 Pronko, Leonard C. Eugène Ionesco. N.Y., 1965.
43744.67.74.10 Proust, Marcel. Choix de lettres. Paris, 1965.
43744.67.110 Proust. Paris, 1965.
43747.23.100 Puel, Gaston. Le cinquième chateau. Lavaur, 1965.
43750.24.201 Queneau, Raymond. Batons, chiffres et lettres. Paris, 1965.
43750.24.300 Queneau, Raymond. Le chien à la mandoline. Paris, 1965.
43750.24.320 Queneau, Raymond. Les derniers jours. Lausanne, 1965.
43750.24.290 Queneau, Raymond. Les fleurs bleues. Paris, 1965.
43761.39.920 Quesnel, Michel. St. Exupéry. Paris, 1965.
40587.55 Quillemin, Henri. L'homme des "Mémoires d'outre-tombe". Paris, 1965.
38536.36.5 Rabelais, F. Pantagruel. 2. éd. Genève, 1965.
43752.8.1100 Rabiniaux, Roger. Le soleil des dortoirs. Paris, 1965.
38585.47.16 Racine, Jean. Bérénice. London, 1965.
FL 397.311 Radulescu, Ion Horia. Le théâtre français dans les pays Roumaine, 1826-1852. Paris, 1965.
42547.22.120 Raitt, Alan William. Villiers de l'Isle Adam et le mouvement symboliste. Paris, 1965.
38525.22.45.42 Raymond, Marcel. L'influence de Ronsard sur la poésie française, 1550-1585. Genève, 1965.
41568.15.10 Raymond, Marcel. Sénancour; sensations et révélations. Paris, 1965.
42587.52.28 Renard, Jules. Journal, 1887-1910. Paris, 1965.
43753.98.3110 Rey, Henri François. Les chevaux masqués. Paris, 1965.
41557.5.10 Reybaud, Louis. Jérôme Paturot à la recherche. Paris, 1965.
38564.55.10 Richard, Pierre. La Bruyère et ses caractères; éssai biographique et critique. Paris, 1965.
43699.51.820 Richter, Anne. Milosz. Paris, 1965.
42556.28.68 Rimbaud, Jean Arthur. Correspondance, 1881-1891. Paris, 1965.
43744.67.1490 Riva, Raymond T. Marcel Proust. 1. ed. N.Y., 1965.
43757.6.180 Robbe-Grillet, Alain. La maison de rendez-vous. Paris, 1965.
43757.6.730 Robbe-Grillet, Alain. Snapshots, and, Towards a new novel. London, 1965.
43757.6.720 Robbe-Grillet, Alain. Two novels. N.Y., 1965.
43757.12.140 Roblès, Emmanuel. Plaidoyer pour un rebelle. Paris, 1965.
43744.67.1520 Rogers, Brian G. Proust's narrative techniques. Genève, 1965.
39594.19.130 Rosso, Corrado. Montesquieu moralista, dalle leggi al "Bonheur." Pisa, 1965.
43546.87.82 Roudiez, Léon. Michel Butor. N.Y., 1965.
43626.22.865 Rousseau, Guy Noël. Sur le chemin de Julien Green. Neuchâtel, 1965.
FL 6015.19 Rousseau, J.J. Correspondance complète. Genève, 1965. 14v.
FL 6070.4 Rousseau, J.J. Discours sur l'origine et les fondements de l'inégalité parmi les hommes. Paris, 1965.
43757.92.182 Roussel, Raymond. Locus solus. Paris, 1965.
43535.35.800 Rousselot, Jean. Albert Ayguesparse. Bruxelles, 1965.
37574.918 Rousselot, Jean. Poètes français d'aujourd'hui. Paris, 1965.
43757.92.2190 Rousselot, Jean. Route du silence. Goudargues, 1965.
37597.26.75 Ruelle, Pierre. Les congés d'Arras: Jean Bodel. 1. éd. Bruxelles, 1965.
42566.16.150 Sachs, Murray. The career of Alphonse Daudet. Cambridge, 1965.
40516.60.38 Sade, D.A.F. de. Français. Paris, 1965.
40516.60.52 Sade, D.A.F. de. Gesprek tussen een priester en een stervende, en andere teksten. Brugge, 1965.
43761.31.200 Sagan, Françoise. La chamade; roman. Paris, 1965.
43761.41.3110 St. Pierre, Michel de. Les nouveaux prêtres. Paris, 1965.
43761.77.1100 Sarrazin, Albertine. L'astragale; roman. Paris, 1965.
43761.78.625 Sartre, Jean Paul. The respectable prostitute - Lucifer and the Lord. Harmondsworth, Eng., 1965.
43761.78.790 Sartre, Jean Paul. Situations. N.Y., 1965.
43761.78.726 Sartre, Jean Paul. What is literature? N.Y., 1965.
37563.87.7 Saulnier, Verdun L. La littérature française de la renaissance. 7. éd. Paris, 1965.
43761.91.100 Savoy, Bernard. La fuite; roman. Paris, 1965.

Chronological Listing

1965 - cont.

40526.8.70 Scarfe, Francis. André Chénier, his life and work. Oxford, 1965.
38526.48.38.37 Scève, Maurice. Opere poetiche minori. Napoli, 1965.
41593.36.80 Schaerer-Nussberger, Maya. Maurice de Guérin. Paris, 1965.
43763.36.3110 Schakovskoy, Zinaïda. Une manière de vivre. Paris, 1965.
43763.36.2150 Schehadé, Georges. L'émigré de Brisbane. Paris, 1965.
Mol 270.38.5 Schérer, Jacques. Tartuffe; histoire et structure. Paris, 1965.
43697.77.870 Schlobach, Jochen. Geschichte und Fiktion in "l'été 1914" von Roger Martin du Gard. München, 1965.
43763.55.100 Schmitz, André. A voix double et jointe. Bruxelles, 1965.
37576.665 Schneider, Marcel. Histoires fantastiques d'aujourd'hui. Paris, 1965.
43538.14.850 Scott, Nathan Alexander. Samuel Beckett. London, 1965.
43765.32.170 Seghers, Pierre. Dialogue. Avec 2 photos par Fina Gomez. Paris, 1965.
37530.192 Séguin, J.A.R. French works in English translation. Jersey City, 1965. 8v.
41568.17.12 Sénancour, Etienne Pivert de. Obermann. Paris, 1965.
43769.49.110 Silvain, Pierre. La dame d'Elché. Paris, 1965.
43769.54.610 Simenon, Georges. La boule noire, roman. Paris, 1965.
43769.54.550 Simenon, Georges. Dimanche. Paris, 1965.
43769.54.575 Simenon, Georges. En cas de malheur. Paris, 1965.
43769.54.742 Simenon, Georges. The little saint. 1. ed. N.Y., 1965.
43769.54.799 Simenon, Georges. Maigret cinq: Maigret and the young girl. 1. American ed. N.Y., 1965.
43769.54.540 Simenon, Georges. L'ours en peluche. Paris, 1965.
43769.54.530 Simenon, Georges. Le passage de la ligne. Paris, 1965.
43769.54.520 Simenon, Georges. La patience de Maigret. Paris, 1965.
43769.54.500 Simenon, Georges. Le petit Saint. Paris, 1965.
43769.54.703 Simenon, Georges. A Simenon omnibus. London, 1965.
43769.54.625 Simenon, Georges. Strip-tease. Paris, 1965.
43769.54.600 Simenon, Georges. Les temoins. Paris, 1965.
43769.54.560 Simenon, Georges. Trois chambres à Manhattan. Paris, 1965.
43769.54.570 Simenon, Georges. Les volets verts. Paris, 1965.
43769.56.150 Simon, Pierre Henri. Histoire d'un bonheur; roman. Paris, 1965.
39566.204 Smietanski, Jacques. Le réalisme dans Jacques le fataliste. Paris, 1965.
43775.98.110 Sodenkamp, Andrée. Arivederci Italia; impressions d'Italie. Bruxelles, 1965.
43775.98.100 Sodenkamp, Andrée. Femmes des longs matins. n.p., 1965.
43775.50.125 Sollers, Philippe. Drame; roman. Paris, 1965.
43611.5.190 Sonet, Antoine. Le rêve d'Alain-Fournier. Gembloux, 1965.
43775.61.110 Sonkin, F. Admirable. Paris, 1965.
43775.97.100 Soréil, Arsène. Raisons vives. Bruxelles, 1965.
39533.22.16 Sorel, Charles. Histoire comique de Francion. Paris, 1965.
43775.90.7220 Soupault, Philippe. L'amitié. Paris, 1965.
37596.106.6 Sponsus. Sponsus; dramma delle vergini prudenti e delle vergini stolte. Milano, 1965.
40592.41.5 Staël Holstein, Anne Louise. The unpublished correspondence of Madame de Staël and the Duke of Wellington. London, 1965.
42555.44.178 Steland, Dieter. Dialektische Gedanken in Stéphane Mallarmés Diragations. München, 1965.
40583.336 Stendhal-Club. Première journée du Stendhal Club par Ernest Abravanel. Lausanne, 1965.
39533.22.90 Sutcliffe, Frank. Le réalisme de Charles Sorel. Paris, 1965.
42554.45.80 Theile, Wolfgang. René Ghil. Tübingen, 1965.
38526.49.25 Théophile de Viau. Prose. Torino, 1965.
43788.65.3100 Thomas, Charles. Alouettes. Coutances, 1965.
43822.49.1405 Thomson, Alastair. Valéry. Edinburgh, 1965.
39566.208 Tierno, Galvanl Enrique. Diderot como pretexto. Madrid, 1965.
41563.27.5 Toepffer, Rodolphe. Enter the comics. Lincoln, Nebr., 1965.
41557.10.74 Toesca, Maurice. Le plus grand amour de George Sand. Paris, 1965.
43792.51.100 Tolstoi, Catherine. Ce que savait la rose. Paris, 1965.
FL 390.115 Touchard, Pierre Aimé. Grandes heures de théâtre à Paris. Paris, 1965.
43545.90.800 Toupin, Paul. Les paradoxes d'une vie et d'une oeuvre. Montréal, 1965.
43793.3.2100 Trahard, Pierre. Césarion; satire. Paris, 1965.
43793.23.1100 Trenet, Charles. Un noir ebloiussant. Paris, 1965.
43793.67.290 Troyat, Henri. Les Eygletière. Paris, 1965.
43799.5.210 Tzara, Tristan. Les premiers poèmes. Paris, 1965.
40517.44.105 Ungarelli, Augusto. Un grande romanzo del settecento. Roma, 1965.
43554.2.1170 Vachon, André. Le temps et l'espace dans l'oeuvre de Paul Claudel. Paris, 1965.
43822.50.740 Vailland, Roger. The trout. 1st ed. N.Y., 1965.
37574.928 Valeri, Diego. Quaderno francese del secolo. Torino, 1965.
43822.49.3100 Valet, Paul. La parole qui me porte. Paris, 1965.
42581.33.32 Vallès, Jules. Les franc-parleurs. Paris, 1965.
43524.67.845 Vandromme, Pol. Au auteur et ses personnages. Paris, 1965.
42514.28.225 Vandromme, Pol. Maurras, l'eglise de l'ordre. Paris, 1965.
37556.21.60 Varin d'Ainvelle, Madeleine. La presse en France. Paris, 1965.
43823.2.42 Védrès, Nicole. Paris. 6e éd. Paris, 1965.
FL 375.85 Veil, Irene. Einige Personen der französischen Renaissancekomödie. Köln? 1965?
42557.18.9.2 Verlaine, Paul. Oeuvres poétiques complètes. Paris, 1965.
42557.18.9.5 Verlaine, Paul. Selected poems. London, 1965.
43824.3.1150 Vian, Boris. L'écume des jours. Paris, 1965.
43824.3.1210 Vian, Boris. Et on tuera tous les affreux. Paris, 1965.
43824.3.1160 Vian, Boris. L'herbe rouge; roman. Paris, 1965.
43824.3.1140 Vian, Boris. Théâtre. Paris, 1965.
37567.147.12 Viatte, Auguste. Les sources occultes du romantisme. 2e éd. Paris, 1965. 2v.
43824.16.2110 Vidal, Nicole. Emmanuel; a novel. N.Y., 1965.
37565.190 Vier, Jacques. Histoire de la littérature française, XVIIIe siècle. Paris, 1965- 2v.
41564.31.45 Vigny, Alfred de. Lettres à Philippe Soulet. Angoulême, 1965.
41564.7.7 Vigny, Alfred de. Servitude et grandeur militaires. Paris, 1965.
43824.48.1100 Vilar, Jean. Le dossier Oppenheimer. Genève, 1965.
43738.1.900 Villiers, Marjorie Howard. Charles Péguy. London, 1965.

1965 - cont.

42547.17.30 Villiers de l'Isle Adam, Auguste. Le prétendant. Paris, 1965.
42546.8.79 Violato, Gabriella. Bibiografie de Georges Rodenbach et de Albert Samain en Italie. Firenze, 1965.
43824.90.1110 Vivier, Robert. A quoi l'on pense. Bruxelles, 1965.
39543.67 Voltaire, François Marie Arouet de. The age of Louis XIV. N.Y., 1965.
39544.25.15 Voltaire, François Marie Arouet de. Mémoires pour servir à la vie. Paris, 1965.
39545.131 Voltaire, François Marie Arouet de. The philosophy of history. N.Y., 1965.
43824.3.1810 Vree, Freddy de. Boris Vian, essai. Paris, 1965.
43823.83.100 Vuillemin, Jules. Le miroir de Venise. Paris, 1965.
43744.67.1515 Waeber, Gottfried. Marcel Proust. München, 1965.
40597.2.670 Warneńska, Monika. Romantyczna podróż pana Honoriusza. Warszawa, 1965.
43761.78.890 Warnock, Mary. The philosophy of Sartre. London, 1965.
43833.20.710 Weil, Simone. Seventy letters. London, 1965.
43833.20.120.2 Weil, Simone. Venise sauvée. Paris, 1965.
43835.24.705 Wiesel, Eliezer. Dawn. N.Y., 1965.
42576.15.435 Wiesner, Gerlind. Untersuchungen zum Wortschatz von Gustave Flaubert. Inaug. Diss. Heidelberg? 1965?
37567.618 Wood, John Sinclair. Sondages, 1830-1848. Toronto, 1965.
43840.9.100 Wybot, Roger. Pourquoi Barabbas? Paris, 1965.
43761.78.895 Zehm, Günter Albrecht. Jean Paul Sartre. Velber, 1965.
37569.390 Zeltner-Neukomm, Gerda. Die eigenmächtige Sprache. Olten, 1965.
42584.23.27 Zola, Emile. J'accuse, ou La vérité en marche. Paris, 1965.

1966

38525.38.15 Abraham, Claude Kurt. The strangers. Gainesville, 1966.
38526.51.15 Adam, Antoine. Théophile de Viau et la libre pensée française en 1620. Genève, 1966.
40597.2.707 Adamson, Donald. The genesis of Le cousin Pons. London, 1966.
40597.2.730 Affron, Charles. Patterns of failure in La comédie humaine. New Haven, 1966.
43517.23.100 Agenor, Guy. Rubis, saphirs et topazes, poésies. Paris, 1966.
39574.27.10 Alembert, J. Le Rond d'. Discours préliminaire de l'encyclopédie. Paris, 1966.
43757.6.825 Alter, Jean. La vision du monde d'Alain Robbe-Grillet. Genève, 1966.
37556.4.5 Alter, Jean V. Les origines de la satire antibourgeoise en France. Genève, 1966. 2v.
43524.67.611 Anouilh, Jean. The collected plays. London, 1966- 2v.
41583.3 Antier, Benjamin. L'Auberge des Adrets. Grenoble, 1966.
43526.65.102 Apollinaire, Guillaume. Calligrammes. Paris, 1966.
43527.3.420 Aragon, Louis. Elegie à Pablo Neruda. Paris, 1966.
43591.89.835 Arcangeli Marenzi, Maria Laura. Linguaggio e poesia: Paul Eluard, Simone Weil, Antoine de Saint-Exupéry. Venezia, 1966.
43528.48.230 Arland, Marcel. Carnets de Gilbert. Paris, 1966.
43528.99.775 Arlet, Suzanne. Cisza i wołanie. Warszawa, 1966.
43528.89.120 Arnothy, Christine. Le jardin noir; roman. Paris, 1966.
43528.73.120 Arrabal, Fernando. Arrabal celebrando la ceremonia de la confusion. Madrid, 1966.
43529.8.35 Aspel, Pauline. Traversées. Crossings. Urbana, Ill., 1966.
43529.7.35 Astorg, Bertrand d'. La jeune fille et l'astronaute. Paris, 1966.
43530.84.100 Attal, Raoul. Le pain de la nuit. Boundary, 1966.
38527.29.6 Aubigné, Théodore Agrippa d'. Agrippa d'Aubigné...une étude. Paris, 1966.
38527.28.16 Aubigné, Théodore Agrippa d'. Les tragiques. Lausanne, 1966.
43531.18.2110 Audisio, Gabriel. A n'y pas coire, récits et portraits. Paris, 1966.
40542.16 Auge, Thomas E. Frederic Ozanam and his world. Milwaukee, 1966.
42586.33.800 Auriand (pseud.). Darien et l'inhumane comédie. Bruxelles, 1966?
37597.50 Avalle, d'Arco Silvio. Alle origini della letteratura francese i giuramenti di Strasburgo e la sequenza di Santa Eulalia. Torino, 1966.
38526.8.4 Baif, Jean Antoine de. Les amours de Francine. Genève, 1966. 2v.
43550.58.1025 Bakker, Reinout. Albert Camus. Baarn, 1966.
37569.40.76 Balakian, Anna E. Literary origins of surrealism. N.Y., 1966.
40597.24.10 Balzac, Honoré de. Histoire des Treize. Ferragus. Paris, 1966.
40597.28.20.5 Balzac, Honoré de. Le lys dans la vallée. Paris, 1966.
40597.12.60 Balzac, Honoré de. Nevedomyi shedevr. Moskva, 1966.
40597.32.85 Balzac, Honoré de. La rabouilleuse. Paris, 1966.
42563.18.310 Bancquart, Marie Claire. Les écrivains et l'histoire d'après Maurice Barrès. Paris, 1966.
37558.48.5 Barbey d'Aurevilly, Jules. Les quarante médaillons de l'académie, 1864. Paris, 1966.
37575.788 Barbier, Joseph. Notre-Dame des poètes. Saint Martin, 1966.
43757.50.1255 Barrère, Jean Bertrand. Romain Rolland: l'âme et l'art. Paris, 1966.
41574.283.10 Barrère, Jean Bertrand. Victor Hugo à l'oeuvre. Paris, 1966.
42576.15.340 Bart, Benjamin F. Madame Bovary and the critics. N.Y., 1966.
43537.77.3120 Barthes, Roland. Critique et verité. Paris, 1966.
43537.81.100 Basile, André. Le fil d'Ariane; poèmes. Paris, 1966.
40553.7.80 Bastid, Paul. Benjamin Constant et sa doctrine. Paris, 1966. 2v.
43537.84.110 Bataille, Michel. La ville des fous; roman. Paris, 1966.
Mon 112.22 Battista, Anna Maria. Alle origini del pensiero politico libertino: Montaigne e Charron. Milano, 1966.
43537.88.1110 Bauchau, Henry. La Déchirure. Paris, 1966.
43537.88.1120 Bauchau, Henry. La pierre sans chagrin. Lausanne, 1966.
41522.13.9.45 Baudelaire, Charles. Hořké propasti. Praha, 1966.
41522.5.28 Baudelaire, Charles. Oeuvres complètes. Paris, 1966. 3v.
43824.3.1805 Baudin, Henri. Boris Vian, la poursuite de la vie totale. Paris, 1966.
43537.99.170 Bazin, Hervé. Plumons l'oiseau. Paris, 1966.
37566.150 Beauchamp, Louis de. Le côté de Vinteuil. Paris, 1966.
43538.5.4100 Beauvais, Robert. Quand les Chinois. Paris, 1966.

Chronological Listing

1966 - cont.

43538.1.540 Beauvoir, Simone de. Les belles images. Paris, 1966.
43538.1.705 Beauvoir, Simone de. A very easy death. London, 1966.
43538.12.100 Béchu, Jean Louis. L'Acier, la rose, poèmes. Paris, 1966.
43538.14.230 Beckett, Samuel. Assez. Paris, 1966.
43538.14.794 Beckett, Samuel. Bing. Paris, 1966.
43538.14.220 Beckett, Samuel. Comédie et actes divers. Paris, 1966.
43538.14.125 Beckett, Samuel. En attendant Godot: pièce en deux actes. London, 1966.
43538.14.765 Beckett, Samuel. Imagination dead imagine. London, 1966.
43538.14.740.2 Beckett, Samuel. More pricks than kicks. 2. ed. London, 1966.
37574.927 Bédra. Les comédiens poètes. Paris, 1966.
43824.87.800 Béhar, Henri. Roger Vitrac. Paris, 1966.
43538.49.130 Belen (pseud.). Le réservoir des sens. Paris, 1966.
43538.51.1100 Belmont, Georges. Un homme au crépuscule; roman. Paris, 1966.
43538.98.100 Bengono, Jacques. La Perdrix blanche, trois contes moraux. Yaoundé, 1966.
43656.59.820 Benmussa, Simone. Eugène Ionesco. Paris, 1966.
43538.2.1110 Benoit, Pierre André. Le chemin resserré. Veilhes, 1966.
43554.2.1165 Berchan, Richard. The inner stage. East Lansing, 1966.
43538.1.835 Berghe, Christian Louis van den. Dictionnaire des idées dans l'oeuvre de Simone de Beauvoir. The Hague, 1966.
43538.91.120 Bérimont, Luc. Le bruit des amours et des guerres. Paris, 1966.
43538.77.7120 Berson, Simone. Le livre de Deborah. Bruxelles, 1966.
43538.77.2105 Bertin, Charles. Christophe Colomb. Bruxelles, 1966.
38585.58 Besançon, France. Université. Centre d'étude du vocabulaire français. Jean Racine, Phèdre. Concordances. Paris, 1966.
38575.28.25 Besançon, France. Université. Centre d'étude du vocabulaire français. P. Corneille. Le Cid. Paris, 1966.
43538.83.110 Bésus, Roger. Pour l'amour. Paris, 1966.
39527.5.15 Biard, Jean Dominique. The style of La Fontaine's fables. Oxford, 1966[1967]
42584.32.5 Bibliothèque Nationale, Paris. P.J. Hetzel, Paris, 1966. Paris, 1966.
43526.65.970 Billy, André. Avec Apollinaire, souvenirs inédits. Paris, 1966.
FL 1218.33.100F Blanc, François. Poésies en patois du Dauphiné. Grenoble, 1966.
43543.9.110 Blanzat, Jean. L'iguane. Paris, 1966.
43543.14.120 Bloch-Michel, J. Frosinia. Paris, 1966.
37569.418 Bloching, Karl Heinz. Die Autoren des literarischen "renouveau catholique" Frankreichs. Bonn, 1966.
42557.12.150 Bodart, Roger. Émile Verhaeren hier et aujourd'hui. Tournai, 1966.
43626.70.800 Boie, Bernhild. Haupt Motive im Werke...Gracqs. München, 1966.
38566.4.15 Boileau Despréaux, Nicolas. Oeuvres complètes. Paris, 1966.
43757.50.1260 Boissevain, W. Romain Rolland. Den Haag, 1966.
43544.41.1100 Boissonnas, Edith. L'embellie. Paris, 1966.
43744.67.1565 Bolle, Louis. Marcel Proust, ou Le complex d'Argus. Paris, 1966.
37566.158.2 Bonfantini, Mario. Ottocento francese. 2. ed. Torino, 1966.
43544.61.2100 Bonnard, Julien. Le fil d'Ariàne. Rodez, 1966.
43656.59.61 Bonnefoy, Claude. Entretiens avec Eugène Ionesco. Paris, 1966.
43544.61.21 Bonneton, André. Écho. Poems. Rodez, 1966.
39566.206 Bonneville, Douglas A. Diderot's Vie de Sénèque. Gainesville, 1966.
FL 6119.66 Borel, Jacques. Génie et folie de Jean-Jacques Rousseau. Paris, 1966.
43524.67.850 Borgal, Clement. Anouilh, la peine de vivre. Paris, 1966.
38526.47.33.20 Borton, Samuel L. Six modes of sensibility in Saint-Amant. The Hague, 1966.
43544.81.2270 Bosco, Henri. Le jardin des Trintaires. Paris, 1966.
43544.88.2110 Boulanger, Daniel. Les portes. Paris, 1966.
43544.108.160 Boulle, Pierre. Aux sources de la rivière Kwai. Paris, 1966.
43544.87.3130 Bourbon Busset, Jacques de. Journal. Paris, 1966. 4v.
38526.26.95 Brabant, Luc van. Louize Labé. Coxyde, Belgique, 1966. 2v.
43545.1.2110 Brachetto, Roland. Poèmes tunisiens. Paris, 1966.
43744.67.1236 Brée, Germaine. The world of Marcel Proust. Boston, 1966.
43545.23.4011 Bremond d'Ars, Eusèbe. Oeuvre poétique, 1888-1958. Paris, 1966.
43538.76.985 Bridel, Yves. L'esprit d'enfance dans l'oeuvre romanesque de Georges Bernanos. Paris, 1966.
43697.52.915 Brincourt, André. André Malraux ou le Temps du silence. Paris, 1966.
40516.60.125 Brochier, Jean Jacques. Le Marquis de Sade et la conquête de l'unique. Paris, 1966.
40516.60.120 Brochier, Jean Jacques. Sade. Paris, 1966.
42576.15.350A Brombert, Victor H. The novels of Flaubert. Princeton, 1966.
43512.12.800 Brosses, Marie Thérèse de. Entretiens avec Raymond Abellio. Paris, 1966.
43545.89.5100 Brucher, Roger. Chair de l'hiver. Bruxelles, 1966?
43823.75.2240 Bruller, Jean. Quota. N.Y., 1966.
43823.75.2260 Bruller, Jean. Quota ou Les Pléthoriens, roman. Paris, 1966.
43753.90.810 Brunner, Peter. Pierre Reverdy. De la solitude au mystère. Zürich, 1966.
Mon 112.19 Brush, Craig B. Montaigne and Bayle. The Hague, 1966.
42576.15.335 Buck, Stratton. Gustave Flaubert. N.Y., 1966.
42556.27.33.820 Buenzod, Emmanuel. Henri de Régnier; essai. Avignon, 1966.
37555.727 Burucoa, Christiane. D'autres horribles travailleurs. Millau, 1966.
43538.76.995 Bush, William. L'angoisse du mystère, essai sur Bernanos et Monsieur Ouine. Paris, 1966.
43550.6.180 Cabanis, José. L'age ingrant. Paris, 1966.
43550.6.190 Cabanis, José. La bataille de Toulouse; roman. Paris, 1966.
37567.645 Carassus, Émilien. Le snobisme et les lettres françaises de Paul Bourget à Marcel Proust. Thèse. Paris, 1966.
43550.74.1100 Cardon, Roger. Prométhée, ou Le mal du siècle. Paris, 1966.
43550.75.120 Carême, Maurice. La passagère invisible. Paris, 1966.
41543.22.135 Carofiglio, Vito. Nerval e il mito della Puretè. 1. ed. Firenze, 1966.
43550.98.200 Cayrol, Jean. Midi, minuit; roman. Paris, 1966.

1966 - cont.

43551.41.700 Ceillier, Philippe. To see the White Cliffs. London, 1966.
43551.59.330 Cendrars, Blaise. La banlieue de Paris. Paris, 1966.
43551.59.715 Cendrars, Blaise. Rum; a aventura de Jean Galmot. Lisboa, 1966.
43551.59.22 Cendrars, Blaise. Selected writings. N.Y., 1966.
43551.79.700 Césaire, Aimé. Im Kongo; ein Stück über Patrice Lumumba. Berlin, 1966.
43551.79.170 Césaire, Aimé. Une saison au Congo; théâtre. Paris, 1966.
43551.80.180 Cesbron, Gilbert. C'est Mozart qu'on assassine; roman. Paris, 1966.
43552.2.9100 Chaland, Paul. Le Chat-ours. Paris, 1966.
39586.19.3.25 Chamfort, S.R.N. Maksimy i mysli, kharaktery i anekdoty. Leningrad, 1966.
39533.8.20 Chapelain, Jean. Soixante-dix-sept lettres inédites à Nicolas Heinsius, 1649-1658. La Haye, 1966.
38526.10.8.29 Chappuys, Claude de. Poésies intimes. Genève, 1966.
43552.4.2270 Char, René. Retour amont. Paris, 1966.
43552.5.240 Chardonne, Jacques. Propos comme ça. Paris, 1966.
43552.6.3100A Charles-Roux, Edmonde. Oublier Palerme; roman. Paris, 1966.
42556.28.375A Charleville, France. Arthur Rimbaud dans les collections municipales de la bibliothèque et du musée. Charleville, 1966.
40586.21.14 Chateaubriand, F.A.R. Atala, René. Paris, 1966.
40586.28.92 Chateaubriand, F.A.R. Mémoires d'outre-tombe. 3. éd. Paris, 1966.
43552.24.4100 Chessex, Jacques. Le jeûne de huit nuits. Lausanne, 1966.
43552.25.2107 Chevallier, Gabriel. L'envers de "Clochemerle". Paris, 1966.
43552.69.120 Chraibi, Driss. Un ami viendra vous voir. Paris, 1966.
43553.71.21 Cipriani, Roland. Premiers poèmes. Paris, 1966.
37543.563 Clapton, G.J. Currents of thought in French literature. N.Y., 1966.
43554.2.490 Claudel, Paul. Au milieu des vitraux de l'Apocalypse. Paris, 1966.
43554.2.32.12 Claudel, Paul. Cinq grandes odes. Paris, 1966.
43554.5.2130 Clavel, Bernard. L'hercule sur la place. Paris, 1966.
43554.89.2100 Cluny, Claude Michel. Un jeune homme de Venise. Paris, 1966.
43556.1.788 Cocteau, Jean. The difficulty of being. London, 1966.
37555.726 Cohen, Jean. Structure du langage poétique. Paris, 1966.
42555.44.205 Cohn, Robert Greer. Mallarmé's masterwork. The Hague, 1966[1967]
40583.352 Colesanti, Massimo. Stendhal; la realtà e il ricordo. Roma, 1966.
43556.49.709 Colette, Sidonie Gabrielle. Autobiographie tirée des oeuvres de Colette. Paris, 1966.
43556.49.708 Colette, Sidonie Gabrielle. Earthly paradise; an autobiography. N.Y., 1966.
38576.12.42.90 Collins, David A. Thomas Corneille; protean dramatist. The Hague, 1966.
FL 386.46 Colnen-Mennemeier, Brigitta. Einsamkeit und Revolte. Dortmund, 1966.
43556.53.2100 Combet, Fernand. Schrumm Schrumm. Paris, 1966.
40583.386 Congrès stendhalien, 4th. Civitavecchia and Rome, 1964. Communications présentées au Congrès stendhalien de Civitavecchia. Firenze, 1966.
43556.77.3100 Cornuz, Jean Louis. Parce que c'etait toi...(roman). Neuchâtel, 1966.
FL 386.46.6 Corvin, Michel. Le théâtre nouveau en France. 2e ed. Paris, 1966.
43526.65.965 Couffignal, Robert. L'inspiration biblique dans l'oeuvre de Guillaume Apollinaire. Paris, 1966.
41574.614 Coulmas, Danae. Das Apokalyptische im lyrischen Werk Victor Hugos. Hamburg, 1966.
40546.7.15 Courier de Méré, Paul Louis. Pamphlets. Paris, 1966.
37569.426 Cranston, M. Enfance, mon amour. Berkeley, 1966.
X Cg 40534.33.9.2 Crébillon, Claude Prosper Jolyot de. La nuit et le moment. Paris, 1966.
43557.25.130 Crevel, René. Le clavecin de Diderot, 1932. Paris, 1966.
43560.78.200 Curtis, Jean Louis. La quarantine. Paris, 1966.
41555.44.15 Dale, R.C. The poetics of Prosper Mérimée. The Hague, 1966.
40517.44.120 Daniel, Georges. Fatalité du secret et fatalité du bavardage au 18e siècle. Paris, 1966.
37567.627 Danilin, Iurii I. Poety Parizhskoi Kommuny. Moskva, 1966.
43670.89.820 Danon, Jacques. Entretiens avec Élise et Marcel Jouhandeau. Paris, 1966.
43620.74.925 David, Aurel. Vie et mort de Jean Giraudoux. Paris, 1966.
37568.243 David, Jean. Le procès de l'intelligence dans les lettres françaises au seuil de l'entre-deux-guerres, 1919-1927. Paris, 1966.
43566.6.2100 Debotte, Jacqueline. Plus long temps que l'oubli. Rodez, 1966.
41543.22.125 Dédéyan, Christian. Nerval, pèlerin de la nuit, essai. Avignon, 1966.
43550.58.1070 Degenaar, Johannes. Die wêreld van Albert Camus. Johannesburg, 1966.
43566.35.100 Degny, Adeleine. Les condamnés. Paris, 1966.
40553.10.33 Deguise, Pierre. Benjamin Constant méconnu. Genève, 1966.
43566.35.1021 Deguy, Michel. Oui dire. Paris, 1966.
43744.67.1530 De Ley, Herbert. Marcel Proust et le duc de Saint-Simon. Urbana, 1966.
43566.50.4120 Della Faille, Pierre. Le grand alléluia. Millau, 1966.
43566.53.3100 Demdy, Henri. L'espoir ulcéré. Rodez, 1966.
43566.75.1100 Dereux, Philippe. Petit traité des épluchures. Paris, 1966.
43566.82.7011 Destouches, Louis Ferdinand. Oeuvres de Louis Ferdinand Céline. Paris, 1966- 5v.
43568.6.130 Dib, Mohammed. Le talisman, nouvelles. Paris, 1966.
39564.11.40 Diderot, Denis. Mémoires pour Catherine II. Paris, 1966.
39564.13.10 Diderot, Denis. Rameau's nephew, and d'Alembert's dream. Harmondsworth, 1966.
43757.50.1235 Diushen, Igor' B. Zhan-kristof Romena Rollana. Moskva, 1966.
41596.51.45 Dmitriev, Valentin G. Poet-kommunar. Moskva, 1966.
43656.59.815 Donnard, Jean Hervé. Ionesco dramaturge. Paris, 1966.
43554.2.1185 Donnard, Jean Hervé. Trois écrivains devant Dieu. Paris, 1966.
43574.41.220 Drieu La Rochelle, Pierre. Mémoirs de Dirk Raspe. Paris, 1966.
43636.55.800 Drion du Chapois, Ferdinand. Luc Hommel. Paris, 1966.
43617.78.820 Driver, Tom Faw. Jean Genêt. N.Y., 1966.
43574.70.110 Drouet, Minou. Du brouillard dans les yeux. Paris, 1966.
V43574.70.120 Drouet, Minou. La patte bleue. Paris, 1966.

1966 - cont.

38526.6.55	Du Bellay, Joachim. Les regrets. Genève, 1966.
43576.8.1110	Dubillard, Roland. Je dirai que je suis tombé; poèmes. Paris, 1966.
43576.8.1120	Dubillard, Roland. La maison d'os. Paris, 1966.
43576.12.1100	Ducharme, Réjean. L'avalée des avalés. Paris, 1966.
41538.53.65	Dumas, Alexandre. Les trois mousquetaires. Paris, 1966.
43576.74.2701	Duras, Marguerite. Moderato cantabile. London, 1966.
43576.74.2710	Duras, Marguerite. The sailor from Gibraltar. London, 1966.
43576.74.2215	Duras, Marguerite. Le vice-consul. Paris, 1966.
43576.77.1100	Durtal, Jean. Les coulisses de la politique: une femme temoigne 1932-1942. Paris, 1966.
38526.14.30	Du Ryer, Pierre. Scevole. Texte établi et présenté par Giancarlo Fasano. Bologna, 1966.
39544.373	Eberle, Josef. Voltaires Pucelle. Die Geschichte eines Gedichte. Aschaffenburg, 1966.
43587.1.100	Ega, Françoise. Le temps des madras. Paris, 1966.
FL 6029.14	Ellis, Madeleine. Rousseau's Venetian story. Baltimore, 1966.
43591.89.113	Éluard, Paul. Capitale de la douleur. Paris, 1966.
43592.53.340	Emmanuel, Pierre. Ligne de faite. Paris, 1966.
43744.67.1555A	Entretiens sur Marcel Proust, sous la direction de Georges Cattaui et Philip Kolb. Paris, 1966.
42572.40	Erckmann, Emile. Hugues le loup et autres contes fantastiques. Verviers, 1966.
43598.82.2700	Escarpit, Robert. The novel computer. London, 1966.
42556.28.145.6	Étiemble, René. Rimbaud. Paris, 1966.
43604.19.110	Eydoux, Emmanuel. Eliezer ben Yehouda. Basel, 1966.
41596.51.30	Ezhen Pot'e, sozdatel' gimna internatsional. Moskva, 1966.
42514.28.230	Fabrégues, Jean de. Charles Maurras et son action française. Paris, 1966.
43606.82.100	Fasquelle, Solange. L'air de Venise. Paris, 1966.
37568.239	Fay, Bernard. Les précieux. Paris, 1966.
43607.27.1100	Feldstein, Jean. Notes de voyage à travers l'Europe du XVe et du XVIe siècle. Paris, 1966.
38554.350.265	Fénelon, F. de S. de la Mothe. Fénelon on education. Cambridge, Eng., 1966.
37562.331	Ferrier, Janet Mackay. French prose writers of the fourteenth and fifteenth centuries. 1st ed. Oxford, 1966.
43550.58.2010	Fetzer, Peter. Themen naturhaften Daseins im Werk von Albert Camus. Tübingen, 1966.
37555.728	Finch, Robert. The sixth sense. Toronto, 1966.
43626.22.875	Fitch, Brian T. Julien Green. Paris, 1966.
42576.33.10.10	Flaubert, Gustave. Bouvard et Pécuchet. Paris, 1966.
42576.21.15	Flaubert, Gustave. Dictionnaire des idées reçues. Napoli, 1966.
42576.33.10.8	Flaubert, Gustave. Le second volume de Bouvard et Pécuchet. Paris, 1966.
37596.10.225	Foerster, Wendelin. Wörterbuch zu Kristian von Troyes sämtlichen Werken. 4. Aufl. Tübingen, 1966.
39544.376	Fontius, Martin. Voltaire in Berlin. Berlin, 1966.
43611.76.130	Forton, Jean. Les sables mouvants. Paris, 1966.
43611.88.130	Fougère, Jean. Les nouveaux bovidés. Paris, 1966.
43556.1.945	Fowlie, Wallace. Jean Cocteau. Bloomington, 1966.
43757.50.1270	France. Archives Nationales. Romain Rolland, sa vie, son oeuvre, 1866-1944. Paris, 1966.
37556.111.5	Friedrich, Hugo. Drei Klassiker des französischen Romans. 5. Aufl. Frankfurt, 1966.
42586.56.27	Fromentin, Eugène. Dominique. Paris, 1966. 2v.
42556.28.365	Fumet, Stanislas. Rimbaud; mystique contrarié. Paris, 1966.
43616.41.4021	Gaillard, Yann. Collection particulière. Paris, 1966.
42563.21.115	Galarneau, Joffre. René Bazin et le problème social. Paris, 1966.
37569.388	Ganne, Gilbert. Douze minutes de vérité. Paris, 1966.
43554.2.1190	Ganne, Pierre. Claudel, humour, joie et liberté. Paris, 1966.
38557.24.152	Gaquère, François. Le dialogue irénique Bossuet-Leibniz. Paris, 1966.
43616.78.210	Gary, Romain. Les mangeurs d'étoiles. Paris, 1966.
43616.79.1100	Gascht, André. Le Royaume de Danemark. Bruxelles, 1966.
43616.98.1110	Gay-Lussac, Bruno. La robe. Paris, 1966.
38526.34.125	Gelernt, Jules. World of many loves: the Heptaméron of Marguerite de Navarre. Chapel Hill, 1966.
43617.78.718	Genêt, Jean. The balcony. London, 1966.
43617.78.61	Genêt, Jean. Lettres à Roger Blin. Paris, 1966.
43617.78.725	Genêt, Jean. Querelle of Brest. London, 1966.
43617.59.2021	Genette, Gérard. Figures; essais. Paris, 1966. 2v.
43620.2.11	Gide, André. Self-portraits: The Gide/Valery letters. Chicago, 1966.
43757.50.1245	Gil'dina, Z.M. Romen Rollan i mirovaia kul'tura. Riga, 1966.
43554.2.1180	Gillet-Maudot, Marie Jeanne. Paul Claudel. Paris, 1966.
43527.3.845	Gindine, Yvette. Aragon, prosateur surréaliste. Genève, 1966.
43707.98.710	Ginsbourg, Ariel. Paul Nizan. Paris, 1966.
38537.59	Glauser, Alfred Charles. Rabelais créateur. Paris, 1966.
Mol 607.16	Glikman, Isaak D. Mol'er. Leningrad, 1966.
42586.64.6	Gobineau, Arthur de. Sons of kings. London, 1966.
42576.15.345	Gothot-Mersch, Claudine. La genèse de Madame Bovary. Paris, 1966.
43625.89.4700	Goudeket, Maurice. The delights of growing old. N.Y., 1966.
Htn 43625.3.25*	Gourmont, Rémy de. Selected writings. Ann Arbor, 1966.
43526.65.955	Grabska, Elżbieta. Apollinaire i teoretycy kubizmu w latach, 1908-1918. Warszawa, 1966.
43744.67.1540	Graham, Victor Ernest. The imagery of Proust. Oxford, 1966.
43626.3.3100	Grandjean, Jehanne. Shiragiku. Beppu, 1966.
42584.25.360	Grant, Elliott M. Emile Zola. N.Y., 1966.
43626.22.310	Green, Julien. Terre lointaine. Paris, 1966.
43538.76.990	Grégor, Paul. La conscience du temps chez Georges Bernanos. Zürich, 1966.
37567.624	Griffiths, Richard Mathias. The reactionary revolution: the Catholic revival in French literature, 1870-1914. London, 1966.
FL 6029.8.10	Guéhenno, Jean. Jean-Jacques Rousseau. London, 1966. 2v.
43752.57.900	Guers-Villate, Yvonne. Charles Ferdinand Ramuz; l'authenticité éthique et esthétique de l'oeuvre ramuzienne. Paris, 1966.
43628.41.3021	Guillevic, Eugène. Avec; poèmes. Paris, 1966.
43753.90.820	Guiney, Mortimer. La poésie de Pierre Reverdy. Genève, 1966.
43628.75.100	Gurgand, Jean Noël. Israéliennes. Paris, 1966.

1966 - cont.

Mol 607.15	Gutwirth, Marcel Marc. Molière ou L'invention comique. Paris, 1966.
43628.98.1100	Guyotat, Pierre. Éden, Éden, Éden. Paris, 1966.
43631.03.130	Haedens, Kléber. L'été finit sous les tilleuls. Paris, 1966.
43631.49.2110	Haldas, Georges. Boulevard des Philosophes, chronique. Lausanne, 1966.
Mon 148.2	Hallie, Philip Paul. The scar of Montaigne; an essay in personal philosophy. 1. ed. Middleton, Conn., 1966.
43527.3.850	Haroche, Charles. L'idée de l'amour dans Le fou d'Elsa et l'oeuvre d'Aragon. Paris, 1966.
37568.160.2	Hatzfeld, H. Trends and styles in twentieth century French literature. Washington, 1966.
43761.78.910	Haug, Wolfgang Fritz. Jean-Paul Sartre und die Konstruktion des Absurden. Frankfurt, 1966.
43632.50.220	Hellens, Franz. Objets. Paris, 1966.
43632.50.240	Hellens, Franz. Poétique des éléments et des mythes. Paris, 1966.
42584.25.191	Hemmings, F.W.J. Emile Zola. 2. ed. Oxford, 1966.
43757.92.815	Heppenstall, Rayner. Raymond Roussel: a critical guide. London, 1966.
FL 398.50.10	Hort, Jean. La vie héroique des Pitoëff. Genève, 1966.
FL 376.35	Huether, Jochen. Die monarchische Ideologie in den Französischen Römerdramen des 16. und 17. Jahrhunderts. München, 1966.
41571.3.130	Hugo, Victor. Oeuvres complètes. Lausanne, 1966- 38v.
42563.23.8.88	Husson, Odile. Lorraine et Afrique dans l'oeuvre de Louis Bertrand. Nancy, 1966.
37548.228	Huysmans, Camile. Quatre types: Le Renard et Vlenspiegel. Anvers, 1966.
43822.49.1181	Hytier, Jean. The poetics of Paul Valéry. 1st ed. Garden City, N.Y., 1966.
43656.59.710F	Ionesco, Eugène. The bald prima donna. London, 1966.
43656.59.180	Ionesco, Eugène. Délire à deux, essai de calligraphie sonore. Paris, 1966.
43659.88.180	Istrati, Panait. Opere alese. Bucuresti, 1966.
43744.67.1560	Jackson, Elizabeth R. L'evolution de la mémoire involontaire dans l'oeuvre de Marcel Proust. Paris, 1966.
42576.15.355	Jackson, Ernest. The critical reception of G. Flaubert in the United States, 1860-1960. The Hague, 1966.
43667.14.66	Jacob, Max. Lettres, 1920-1941. Oxford, 1966.
43667.15.2120	Jacquemard, Simonne. Éxploration d'un corps. Paris, 1966.
43667.1.315	Jammes, Francis. Correspondance de Francis Jammes et de Francis Vielé-Griffin (1893-1937). Genève, 1966.
37562.342	Jantzen, Hans-Günther. Untersuchungen zur Entstehung des altfranzösischen Prosaromans. n.p., 1966.
43538.14.875	Janvier, Ludovic. Pour Samuel Beckett. Paris, 1966.
43667.98.2100	Jayat, Sandra. Moudravi, ou Va l'amitié. Paris, 1966.
38512.142	Jean le Court, dit Brisebare. Le restor du paon. Genève, 1966.
37568.236	Jeanneau, Augustin. Petit guide de la littérature d'aujourd'hui. Paris, 1966.
43538.1.825	Jeanson, Francis. Simone de Beauvoir ou l'entreprise. Paris, 1966.
43550.58.1040	Jenne, Józef. Próba oceny Krytycznej Camusa. Londyn, 1966.
40583.327	Jones, Grahame C. L'ironie dans les romans de Stendhal. Lausanne, 1966.
42514.28.250	Joseph, Roger. J'ai vu condamner un juste au bagne. (Charles Maurras). Orleans, 1966.
40522.26	Josephsohn, Mirjam. Die Romane des Abbé Prévost als Spiegel des 18. Jahrhunderts. Thesis. Winterthur, 1966.
43757.50.1240	Josimović, Radoslav. Književni pogledi Romena Rolana. Beograd, 1966.
40556.20.5	Joubert, Joseph. Pensées. Paris, 1966.
43670.92.120	Jouffroy, Alain. Aube à l'antipode. Paris, 1966.
43670.89.575	Jouhandeau, M. Riposte à Roger Perfide. Liège, 1966.
43671.41.110	Juin, Hubert. Le repas chez Marguerite. Paris, 1966.
43538.1.830	Julienne-Caffié, Serge. Simone de Beauvoir. Paris, 1966.
37563.109	Jung, Marc-René. Hercule dans la littérature du XVIe siècle. Genève, 1966.
42555.44.195	Kansas. University. Museum of Art. Les mardis. Lawrence, 1966.
38525.22.45.110	Katz, R.A. Ronsard's French critics, 1585-1828. Genève, 1966.
37555.754	Keil, Erika. "Cantique" und "Hymne" in der französischer Lyrik seit der Romantik. Bonn, 1966.
37567.630	Keller, Luzuis. Piranèse et les romantiques français. Paris, 1966.
37595.36.3.20	Kelly, Frederick Douglas. Sens and conjointure in the Chevalier de la charrette. The Hague, 1966.
43673.77.2110	Kerraoul, Bernard de. Une grande conscience. Paris, 1966.
43673.83.252	Kessel, Joseph. Vent de sable. Paris, 1966.
42577.4.90	Kessler, Helmut. Maupassants Novellen. Braunschweig, 1966.
43673.98.110	Keyser, Eugénie de. La surface de l'eau. Paris, 1966.
43675.39.100	Kihm, Jean Jacques. Soixante-cinq poèmes d'amour. Paris, 1966.
43677.5.110	Klat, Hector. Ma seule joie, poèmes. Beyrouth, 1966.
42557.14.100	Knauth, Karl. Die poetische Bedeutung der Farbe in Verlaines Lyrik. Bonn, 1966.
43738.78.835	Knodel, Arthur. Saint-John Perse. Edinburgh, 1966.
43757.50.1265	Kobi, Emil Erich. Die Erziehung zum Einzelnen. Frauenfeld, 1966.
43680.12.110	Kochnitzky, Leon. Appogiatures. Bruxelles, 1966.
38563.29.80	Kortum, Hans. Charles Perrault und Nicolas Boileau. Berlin, 1966.
39544.371	Kotta, Nuçi. L'homme aux quarante écus; a study of Voltairian themes. The Hague, 1966.
42587.52.100	Kowzan, Tadeusz. Jules Renard i jego teatr. Wroclaw, 1966.
38525.6.30	Krailsheimer, Allan John. Three sixteenth-century conteurs. London, 1966.
43757.50.1110	Krampf, Miriam. La conception de la vie héroique dans l'oeuvre de Romain Rolland. Paris, 1966.
37573.318	Krauss, Werner. Antike und Moderne in der Literaturdiskussion des 18. Jahrhunderts. Selections in French. Berlin, 1966.
41543.22.120	Krüger, Manfred. Gerard de Nerval. Stuttgart, 1966.
40588.21.805	Laborde, Alice M. L'oeuvre de Madame de Genlis. Paris, 1966.
38526.27.8	La Ceppède, Jean de. Les théorèmes sur le sacré mystère de notre rédemption. Genève, 1966.
37556.11.20	Lacretelle, Jacques de. Face à l'événement, "Le Figaro", 1826-1966. Paris, 1966.

1966 - cont.

43687.26.1100	Laffay, Claire. Imaginaires. Paris, 1966.
37569.115.10	Lalou, René. Le roman français depuis 1900. 10. éd. Paris, 1966.
43554.2.1175	Landau, Edwin Maria. Paul Claudel. Velber, 1966.
43697.52.905	Langlois, Walter G. André Malraux: the Indochina adventure. N.Y., 1966.
39544.46.16	Lanson, Gustave. Voltaire. N.Y., 1966.
43687.62.3120	Lanzmann, Jacques. O rato da América. Lisboa, 1966.
43687.80.2725	Lartéguy, Jean. The hounds of hell. 1st ed. N.Y., 1966.
43687.80.2150	Lartéguy, Jean. Sauveterre, roman. Paris, 1966.
43620.2.780	Last, J. Mijn vriend, André Gide. Amsterdam, 1966.
37564.266	Lathuillère, Roger. La preciosité. Genève, 1966.
43687.90.1100	Launay, Pierre Jean. Aux portes de Trézène, roman. Paris, 1966.
43687.89.1200	Laurent, Jacques. La fin de Lamiel. Paris, 1966.
43687.89.2200	La Varende, Jean de. L'objet aimé. Paris, 1966.
43687.89.2210	La Varende, Jean de. La Varende, l'ami. Coutances, 1966.
43688.5.5061	Léautaud, Paul. Lettres à Marie Dormoy. Paris, 1966.
41596.4.135	Lebois, André. Vues sur le théâtre de Musset. Avignon, 1966.
37564.268	Lebois, André. XVIIe siècle; recherches et portraits. Paris, 1966.
43688.13.2021	Leclercq, François J. Du poème à la chansonnette. Niort, 1966. 3v.
43688.14.4120	Le Clézio, Jean Marie Gustave. Le déluge, roman. Paris, 1966.
43688.14.1021	Lecocq, Albert. Oeuvre poétique, suivie de poemes, de lettres et d'un texte inedits. Bruxelles, 1966.
40597.2.765	Lecour, Charles. Les personnages de la Comédie humaine. Paris, 1966. 2v.
41568.15.8	Le Gall, Béatrice. L'imaginaire chez Sénancour. Paris, 1966. 2v.
43688.60.21	Leiris, Michel. Brisées. Paris, 1966.
38512.89.3	Le ménagier de Paris. Le ménagier de Paris. Genève, 1966. 2v.
38514.170	Le monologue du franc archier de Baignolles. Le franc archier de Baignolles, suivi de deux autres monologues dramatiques. Genève, 1966.
38537.62	Leonarduzzi, Alessandro. F. Rabelais e la sua prospettiva pedagogica. Trieste, 1966.
43688.98.130	LeQuintrec, Charles. Stances du verbe amour, poèmes. Paris, 1966.
42576.46.8	Le Roy, Eugène. La damnation de Saint Guynefort. Périgueux, 1966.
43688.82.130	Lesort, Paul André. Vie de Guillaume Périer. Paris, 1966.
43744.67.1510A	Linn, John G. The theatre in the fiction of M. Proust. Columbus, 1966.
43690.61.130	Linze, Jacques Gérard. Le fruit de cendre. Paris, 1966.
37574.926	Lisowski, Jerzy. Antologia poezji francuskiej. Warszawa, 1966- 2v.
39586.19.16	List-Marzolff, Renate. Sebastien-Roch Nicolas Chamfort. München, 1966.
40583.178.20	Litto, Victor del. Album Stendhal. Paris, 1966.
37567.635	Lobet, Marcel. Le ceinture de feuillage. Bruxelles, 1966.
43693.58.110	Looten, Emmanuel. Exil inférieur. Paris, 1966.
37597.9.16.5	Lorris, Guillaume de. Der Rosenroman. Tübingen, 1966.
43693.82.100	Lossier, Jean Georges. Du plus loin. Neuchâtel, 1966.
37568.237	Lovtsova, Ol'ga V. Literatura frantsii, 1917-1965. Izd. 2. Moskva, 1966.
43697.14.135	MacOrlan, Pierre. La Vénus internationale. Paris, 1966.
43697.41.2021	Maisonneuve, Pierre. Poèmes d'un barbare; choix de poèmes écrits entre 1915 et 1964. Paris, 1966.
42555.43.4	Mallarmé, Stéphane. Poésies: poésies, choix de vers de circonstances. Paris, 1966.
42555.44.4	Mallarmé, Stéphane. Ein Würfelwurf. Olten, 1966.
43697.2.1180	Mallet-Joris, Françoise (pseud.). Les signes et les prodiges; roman. Paris, 1966.
37548.224	Mallinson, Vernon. Modern Belgian literature. 1830-1960. London, 1966.
43697.52.790	Malraux, André. Lockung des Okzidents. Berlin, 1966.
43620.2.171.2	Mann, Klaus. André Gide und die Krise des modernen Denkens. München, 1966.
40583.37.6	Martineau, Henri. L'oeuvre de Stendhal. Paris, 1966.
43697.79.1100	Martinez-Pagan, Antonio. Sous la poussière des étoiles; roman. Paris, 1966.
38524.36.5	Marty-Laveaux, C. La pléiade françoise. Genève, 1966. 2v.
42586.79.5	Mathé, Roger. Emile Guillaumin. Thèse. Paris, 1966.
37556.251	Matthews, J.H. Surrealism and the novel. Ann Arbor, 1966.
37574.930	Matthiews, J. An anthology of French surrealist poetry. London, 1966.
38575.23.155	Maurens, Jacques. La tragédie sans tragique. Paris, 1966.
43697.88.3130	Mauriac, Claude. L'oubli; roman. Paris, 1966.
43697.89.725	Maurois, André. The Chelsea way or, Marcel in England: A proustian parody. London, 1966.
37568.222.5A	Maurois, André. From Proust to Camus; profiles of modern French writers. 1st ed. Garden City, N.Y., 1966.
43697.89.63	Maurois, André. Lettre ouverte à un jeune homme sur la conduite de la vie. Paris, 1966.
40597.2.626A	Maurois, André. Prometheus. 1. ed. N.Y., 1966.
43697.89.49	Maurois, André. Soixante ans de ma vie littéraire. Périqueux, 1966.
41574.301	Maurois, André. Victor Hugo and his world. N.Y., 1966.
41522.18.500	Mauron, Charles. Le dernier Baudelaire. Paris, 1966.
43697.89.1110F	Mauron, Marie. Féerie des bois. Genève, 1966.
42514.28.21	Maurras, Charles. Lettres passe-murailles. Paris, 1966.
42584.25.400	Max, Stefan. Les métamorphoses de la grande ville dans les Rougon-Macquart. Paris, 1966.
43538.14.880	Mélèse, Pierre. Samuel Beckett. Paris, 1966.
43698.55.120	Memmi, Albert. La statue de sel. Paris, 1966.
43698.58.3110	Menanteau, Pierre. De chair et de feuilles, poèmes. Paris, 1966.
43757.50.1300	Mentel, Marianne. Romain Rolland und die bildende Kunst. Salzburg, 1966.
38585.66	Mercanton, Jacques. Racine. Paris, 1966.
43698.74.4100	Mercatrix. Poèmes gaulois. Paris, 1966.
41555.25	Mérimée, Prosper. The venus of Ille, and other stories. London, 1966.
Mon 123.8	Metschies, Michael. Zitat und Zitier Kunst in Montaignes Essais. Genève, 1966.
43591.89.1805	Meurand, Maryvonne. L'image végétale dans la poésie d'Eluard. Paris, 1966.
43694.11.2810	Mex, Alphonse. Dans la splendeur d'un chant de France. Caen, 1966.
37596.10.215	Micha, Alexandre. La tradition manuscrite des romans de Chréstien de Troyes. Genève, 1966.

1966 - cont.

43761.77.805	Micha, René. Nathalie Sarraute. Paris, 1966.
43698.200.825	Michaux, Henri. Dichtungen, Schriften. Frankfurt, 1966.
43698.200.130.5	Michaux, Henri. L'espace du dedans, pages choisies, 1927-1959. Paris, 1966.
43698.200.240	Michaux, Henri. Les grandes épreuves de l'esprit et les innombrables petites. Paris, 1966.
43699.13.100	Michel, Georges. Les timides aventures d'un laveur de carreaux. Paris, 1966.
FL 384.125	Mignon, Paul L. Le théâtre d'aujourd'hui de A jusqu'à Z. Paris, 1966.
FL 6139.66	Millet, Louis. La pensée de Jean-Jacques Rousseau. Paris, 1966.
37569.393	Mitchell, Bonner. Les manifestes littéraires de la belle époque, 1886-1914. Paris, 1966.
Mol 171.72	Molière, Jean Baptiste Poquelin. Le bourgeois gentilhomme. London, 1966.
FL 377.57	Mongrédien, Georges. La vie quotidienne des comédiens au temps de Molière. Paris, 1966.
Mon 37.60	Montaigne, Michel de. Saggi, a cura di Fausta Garavini. Milano, 1966. 2v.
43701.63.600	Montherlant, Henry de. Va jover avec cette poussière. Paris, 1966.
37568.240	Moore, Harry Thornton. Twentieth-century French literature. Carbondale, 1966. 2v.
41543.22.130	Moreau, Pierre. Sylvie et ses soeurs nervaliennes. Paris, 1966.
40597.2.745	Mount, Alan John. The physical setting in Balzac's "Comédie Humaine". Hull, 1966.
37555.725	Mourgues, Odette de. An anthology of French 17th century lyric poetry. London, 1966.
43701.99.100	Mozer, Hélène. Battement. Veilhes, 1966.
38546.110	Munk, Gerda. Madame de Sévigné et Madame de Grignan dans la correspondance et dans le critique. Utrecht, 1966.
43756.90.860	Naughton, Helen Thomas. Jacques Rivière; the development of a man and a creed. The Hague, 1966.
42576.15.360	Neale, Mary. Flaubert en Angleterre, étude sur les lecteurs anglais de Flaubert. Bordeaux, 1966.
Mol 614.3	Neri, Nicoletta. Molière e il teatro inglese della Restaurazione. Torino, 1966.
41543.14.5A	Nerval, Gerard de. Les chimères. Bruxelles, 1966.
41543.4.9	Nerval, Gerard de. Oeuvres. 4. éd. Paris, 1966-
43701.63.955	Neville, Daniel E. Henry de Montherlant; une revue de la critique de ses oeuvres. v.1-2. Lawrence, 1966-67.
43752.57.920	Nicod, Marguerite. Du realisme a la réalité. Genève, 1966.
43550.58.1050	Nicolas, André. Albert Camus ou le Vrai Prométhée. Paris, 1966.
43709.85.140	Nothomb, Pierre. Le buisson ardent; poèmes, 1957-1965. Paris, 1966.
43709.89.2100	Nougé, Paul. L'expérience continue. Bruxelles, 1966.
43714.5.120	Obaldia, René de. Théâtre. v. 2-4. Paris, 1966- 2v.
43538.14.925	Ohio State Unviersity, Columbus. Library. Nelson Algren and Samuel Beckett. Columbus, 1966?
43723.41.100	Olivier, Claude. Chimères et tourments. Angers, 1966.
37569.386	Onimus, Jean. La connaissance poétique. Paris, 1966.
39544.369	Orieux, Jean. Voltaire; ou, La royauté de l'esprit. Paris, 1966.
37565.173	Orlando, Francesco. Infanzia, memoria e storia da Rousseau ai romantici. Padova, 1966.
43737.12.2110	Pache, Jean. Analogies, poèmes 1958-1961. Neuchâtel, 1966.
42515.38.20	Paganelli, Don Sauveur. Ernest Renan, essai. Uzès, 1966.
38585.16.375	Paganelli, Don Sauveur. Jean Racine, essai. Uzès, 1966.
43737.65.110	Panet, Edmond. Les roses galactiques, vision et prophétisme. Paris, 1966.
43744.67.1500	Papers on Proust. Hollins, Va., 1966.
43741.59.800	Parain, Brice. Entretiens avec Bernard Pingaud. Paris, 1966.
42555.44.210	Park Ynhui. L'idée chez Mallarmé. Paris, 1966.
43737.79.100	Pascarel, Charles. Massacre du printemps. Paris, 1966.
38526.42.13.15	Pasquier, Étienne. Ecrits politiques. Textes réunis, publiés. Genève, 1966.
38526.42.13.12	Pasquier, Étienne. Lettres historiques pour les années 1556-1594. Genève, 1966.
43737.89.1011	Paulhan, Jean. Oeuvres complètes. Paris, 1966. 5v.
43737.98.1120	Paysan, Catherine. Les feux de la chandeleur, roman. Paris, 1966.
43822.49.1560	Perche, Louis. Valéry, les limites de l'humain. Paris, 1966.
37568.262	Perrone-Moises, Leyla. O nôvo romance francês. São Paulo, 1966.
43738.78.721	Perse, Saint-John. Two addresses. N.Y., 1966.
42563.23.185	Petit, Jacques. Léon Bloy. Paris, 1966.
37575.789	Peyrade, Jean. Approche de l'amour. Paris, 1966.
43740.41.2110	Philipe, Anne. Les rendez-vous de la colline. Paris, 1966.
37562.313	Pickford, Cedric Edward. Changing attitudes towards medieval French literature. Hull, 1966.
43741.25.260	Pieyre de Mandiargues, André. Soleil des loups. Paris, 1966.
43741.59.3151	Pinget, Robert. Graal flibuste. Paris, 1966.
43741.59.3705	Pinget, Robert. The inquisitory. London, 1966.
43741.59.3700	Pinget, Robert. Three plays. 1st American ed. N.Y., 1966.
43741.89.130	Piroué, Georges. Ces eaux qui ne vont nulle part. Lausanne, 1966.
43744.67.1545	Plantevignes, Marcel. Avec Marcel Proust; causeries, souvenirs sur Cabourg. Paris, 1966.
43701.59.800	Poisson, Georges M. Henry de Monfreid, le passionné de l'aventure. Paris, 1966.
V37543.589	Polanšćak, Antun. Od povjerenja do sumnje. Zagreb, 1966.
37562.332	Pollmann, Leo. Die Liebe in der hochmittelalterlichen Literatur Franckreichs. Habilitationsschrift. Frankfurt, 1966.
41557.10.250	Pommier, Jean J.M. George Sand et le rêje monastique, "Spiridion". Paris, 1966.
40539.15.30	Potocki, Jan. Parady. Warszawa, 1966.
41596.51.15	Pottier, Eugène. Oeuvres complètes rassemblées, présentées et annotées par Pierre Brochon. Paris, 1966.
41596.51.20	Pottier, Eugène. Pesni, stikhi, poemy. Moskva, 1966.
37566.149	Poulet, Georges. Trois essais de mythologie romantique. Paris, 1966.
43744.5.1100	Praz, Narcisse R. Peau de Moine. Neuchâtel, 1966.
43744.24.60	Prévert, Jacques. Fatras. Paris, 1966.
43744.41.3100	Privat, Bernard. Une nuit sans sommeil; roman. Paris, 1966.

Chronological Listing

1966 - cont.

42584.25.375 Proulx, Alfred C. Aspects épiques des Rougon-Macquart de Zola. The Hague, 1966.
43744.67.58.5 Proust, Marcel. Lettres retrouvées. Paris, 1966.
37556.20.100 Prunières, Bernard. La presse sans politique; étude systématique de la presse lue dans le Calvados. Paris, 1966.
43620.66.826 Pugnet, Jacques. Jean Giono. Paris, 1966.
43748.3.100 Py, Albert. L'homme rouge et son ombre cheval. [Poèmes]. Neuchâtel, 1966.
43750.24.310 Queneau, Raymond. Une histoire modèle. Paris, 1966.
43750.24.241 Queneau, Raymond. L'instant fatal. Précédé de Les Ziaux. Paris, 1966.
43750.24.251 Queneau, Raymond. Zazie dans le métro. Paris, 1966.
37567.640 Raimond, Marcel. La crise du roman, des lendemains du naturalisme aux années vingt. Paris, 1966.
43752.57.310 Ramuz, Charles Ferdinand. Jean-Luc persécuté. Lausanne, 1966.
37569.400 Random, Michel. Les puissances du dedans. Paris, 1966.
43620.74.916 Raymond, Agnes G. Jean Giraudoux: the theatre of victory and defeat. Amherst, 1966.
40597.2.810 Reboussin, Marcel. Balzac et le mythe de Foedora. Paris, 1966.
43833.20.925 Rees, Richard. Simone Weil; a sketch for a portrait. Carbondale, 1966.
42587.51.60 Renard, Jules. Dans la vigne de Jules Renard. Paris, 1966.
43753.75.30 Rerfer du Noble-Val, Helmic. Cocktail. Rodez, 1966.
43753.90.3100 Revel, Jean François. Contrecensures: politique, religion, culture en masse. Paris, 1966.
43756.7.120 Ribemont-Dessaignes, Georges. Théâtre: L'empereur de Chine, Le serin muet, Le bourreau du Pérou. Paris, 1966.
42556.28.51 Rimbaud, Jean Arthur. Complete works. Chicago, 1966.
43757.6.725 Robbe-Grillet, Alain. For a new novel. N.Y., 1966.
43757.6.735 Robbe-Grillet, Alain. La maison de rendez-vous. N.Y., 1966.
43757.13.1120 Rochefort, Christiane. Une rose pour Morrison. Paris, 1966.
FL 6139.56.27 Röhrs, Hermann. Jean-Jacques Rousseau. Vision und Wirklichkeit. 2. Aufl. Heidelberg, 1966.
43757.48.2100 Roland, Danielle. Rue des Canettes; roman. Tournai, 1966.
43757.50.1250 Rolland, Romain. Romain Rolland et le mouvement Florentin de La Voce. Paris, 1966.
38525.12.28 Ronsard, Pierre de. Les oeuvres de Pierre de Ronsard. Text de 1587. Chicago, 1966. 6v.
43822.49.1440 Rouart Valéry, Agathe. Paul Valéry. Paris, 1966.
FL 6032.66 Rousseau, J.J. Du contrat social. Paris, 1966.
43757.92.700 Roussel, Raymond. Impressions of Africa. London, 1966.
41574.609 Rousselot, Jean. Victor Hugo, phare ébloui. Paris, 1966.
43757.89.5100 Rouvres, Alain. Un coeur de pierre. Paris, 1966.
43566.82.7830 Roux, Dominiques de. La mort de Louis Ferdinand Céline; essai. Paris, 1966.
39566.209 Roy, Marie L. Die Poetik Denis Diderots. München, 1966.
43758.24.130 Ruet, Noël. Chants pour l'amour et la mort. Bruxelles, 1966.
37596.8.15 Rutebeuf. Rutebeuf: un tableau synoptique de la vie et des oeuvres de Rutebeuf. Paris, 1966.
43761.5.4170 Sabatier, Robert. Le chinois d'Afrique. Paris, 1966.
40516.60.48 Sade, D.A.F. de. Justine. N.Y., 1966.
40516.60.24 Sade, D.A.F. de. Selected letters. N.Y., 1966.
43761.31.210 Sagan, Françoise. Le cheval évanoui, suivi de l'écharde. Paris, 1966.
43761.39.180 St. Exupéry, A. de. Courrier sud. Vol de nuit. Terre des hommes. Paris, 1966.
43761.44.120 St. Soline, Claire. Les années fraiches. Paris, 1966.
43761.53.100 Samboo, Gopaljee. Un Indien à Paris. Paris, 1966.
41557.9.48.13 Sand, George. La mare au diable. Paris, 1966.
38563.19.10 Sandberg, Karl C. At the crossroads of faith and reason. Tucson, 1966.
43761.78.703 Sartre, Jean Paul. The age of reason. N.Y., 1966.
38526.48.31.7 Scève, Maurice. Délie. .Cambridge, Eng., 1966.
Mol 270.38 Schérer, Jacques. Structures de "Tartuffe". Paris, 1966.
42576.63.755 Schlumbohm, Dietrich. Der Aufstand der Engel. Hamburg, 1966.
43763.39.1110 Schneider, Marcel. La sibylle de Cumes. Paris, 1966.
43763.39.4100 Schritta, Alain Gérard. Chant dans la nuit. Paris, 1966.
38525.111 Schueler, Gerda. Die Rezeption der spanischen Comedia in Frankreich...Lope de Vega und Jean Rotrou. Köln, 1966.
39566.207 Schwartz, Jerome. Diderot and Montaigne. Genève, 1966.
42545.28.7.85 Schwarz, Martin. Octave Mirbeau, vie et oeuvre. The Hague, 1966.
37568.238 Sénart, Philippe. Chemins critiques, d'Abellio à Sartre. Paris, 1966.
41543.22.78 Sénelier, Jean. Un amour inconnu de Gerard de Nerval, avec des documents et des estampes inédits. Paris, 1966.
FL 385.80.50 Serreau, Geneviève. Histoire du "nouveau théâtre". Paris, 1966.
43765.78.100 Servais, Jean. Itinéraires; roman. Bruxelles, 1966.
43769.54.580 Simenon, Georges. Le confessional; roman. Paris, 1966.
43769.54.590 Simenon, Georges. L'horloger d'Everton. Paris, 1966.
43769.54.794 Simenon, Georges. The premier. 1. American ed. N.Y., 1966.
43769.54.368 Simenon, Georges. Quartier nègre. Paris, 1966.
43769.54.510 Simenon, Georges. Le train de Venise. Paris, 1966.
37568.150.5 Simon, P.H. Diagnostie des lettres françaises contemporaines. Bruxelles, 1966.
43620.66.850 Smith, Maxwell Austin. Jean Giono. N.Y., 1966.
37563.105 Smith, Pauline. The anti-courtier trend in sixteenth century French literature. Geneva, 1966.
43776.64.100 Spoerri, Daniel. An anecdoted topography of chance. N.Y., 1966.
37596.27.18 Sprissler, Manfred. Das rhythmische Gedicht Pater deus (11 Jht.) und das altfranzösische Aléxiuslied. Münster, 1966.
37563.107 Stage International d'Études Humanistes. Lumières de la Pléiade. Paris, 1966.
43779.24.5100 Stéphant-Beudeff, Joseph. De tribord à babord. Rodez, 1966.
38524.148 Stone, Donald. Four renaissance tragedies. Cambridge, 1966.
38525.21.35 Stone, Donald. Ronsard's sonnet cyles. New Haven, 1966.
38585.64 Strarre, Evert van der. Racine et le théâtre de l'ambiquité. Leiden, 1966.
40583.350 Strauss, André. La fortune de Stendhal en Angleterre. Paris, 1966.
37547.105 Suffran, Michel. Sur un génération perdue. Bordeaux, 1966.

1966 - cont.

37556.22.85 Sullerot, Evelyne. Histoire de la presse feminine en France, des origines à 1848. Paris, 1966.
38514.23.130 Süpek, Otto. Villon kis testamentumának keletkezése. Budapest, 1966.
43527.3.855 Sur, Jean. Aragon, le réalisme de l'amour. Paris, 1966.
43544.81.2810 Sussex, Ronald Thomas. Henri Bosco, poet-novelist. Christchurch, 1966.
43783.19.100 Sydol, Francis. Qui donc est mon prochain? Paris, 1966.
40597.2.59 Takayama, Tetsuo. Les oeuvres romanesques avortées de Balzac, 1829-1842. Tokyo, 1966.
43785.75.170 Tardieu, Jean. Conversation-sinfonietta. Paris, 1966.
43787.77.1100 Terna, Marieve. Au jardin de mon coeur. Paris, 1966.
43788.41.4110 Thibaudeau, Jean. Ouverture. Paris, 1966- 2v.
43788.41.1100 Thiery, Herman. Les dentelles de Montmirail. Bruxelles, 1966.
37543.566 Thimann, Ivor Cedric. A short history of French literature. 1. ed. Oxford, 1966.
43788.41.2150 Thiry, Marcel. Nondum jam non. Bruxelles, 1966.
40532.58 Thomasset, René. Beaumarchais, écrivain et aventurier. Paris, 1966.
37543.568 Tippetts, Marie. Les marines des peintres vues par les littérateurs de Diderot aux Goncour. Paris, 1966.
41557.10.260 Trepeznikova, Nataliia S. Zhorzh Sand - redaktor i sotrudnik zhurnala "Revue indépendante". Kazan, 1966.
43793.65.110 Trolliet, Gilbert. Laconiques. Paris, 1966.
43793.67.300 Troyat, Henri. Les Eygletière: La faim des lionceax; roman. v.2. Paris, 1966.
38526.52.18 Tyard, Pontus. Oeuvres poétiques complètes. Paris, 1966.
43799.5.205 Tzara, Tristan. Pamět člověka. Praha, 1966.
43688.5.5815 Uribe Arce, Armando. Léautaud y el otro. Santiago de Chile, 1966.
43822.49.800 Valéry, Paul. Básně. Praha, 1966.
42581.33.5.5 Vallès, Jules. L'enfant. Lausanne, 1966.
43822.92.120 Vandercammen, Edmond. Le jour est provisoire. Bruxelles, 1966.
43823.73.100 Véquaud, Yves. Le petit livre avalé; roman. Paris, 1966.
42557.11.65 Verhaeren, Émile. Gedichten. Lier, 1966.
42557.20.325 Verlaine, Paul. Prokletí básníci. V Praze, 1966.
42557.19.67 Verlaine, Paul. Verlaine, par lui-même. Paris, 1966.
43824.3.1180 Vian, Boris. Le dernier des métiers; saynète pour patronages. Paris, 1966.
43824.3.1170 Vian, Boris. Les fourmis. Couverture d'Alain Tercinet. Paris, 1966.
43824.3.1190 Vian, Boris. Trouble dans les Andains, roman inédit. Paris, 1966.
43824.16.700 Vidal, Nicole. Ring of jade. London, 1966.
43824.90.1120 Vivier, Robert. Un cri du hasard. Bruxelles, 1966.
39545.35.80 Voltaire, François Marie Arouet de. Candide. London, 1966.
39545.35.10 Voltaire, François Marie Arouet de. Candide. N.Y., 1966.
39545.37.14.5 Voltaire, François Marie Arouet de. Dialogues et anecdotes philosophiques. Paris, 1966.
42533.20.80 Warmoes, Jean. Albert Mockel, le centenaire de sa naissance. Bruxelles, 1966.
43833.20.150 Weil, Simone. Sur la science. Paris, 1966.
37567.350.5 Weinberg, Bernard. The limits of symbolism. Chicago, 1966.
43833.41.4100 Weiss, Otto G. La route de Berlin. Paris, 1966.
43687.74.815 Weissman, Frida. L'éxotisme de Valéry Larbaud. Paris, 1966.
43835.24.110 Wiesel, Éliezer. Le chant des morts; nouvelles. Paris, 1966.
43835.24.715 Wiesel, Éliezer. The gates of the forest. 1st ed. N.Y., 1966.
43835.37.100 Wilhem, Daniel Cerne. Poèmes. Neuchâtel, 1966.
43835.87.100 Wittig, Monique. The Opoponax. London, 1966.
43833.41.800 Wohmann, Gabriele. Theater von Innen. Olten, 1966.
43837.89.100 Wouters, Liliane. Le Gel. Paris, 1966.
43845.13.130 Yacine, Kateb. Le Polygone étoile. Paris, 1966.
42584.1.6 Zola, Emile. Oeuvres completes. v.1-12,15. Paris, 1966- 13v.

1967

43699.82.800 Académie française. Académie...Paris. Discours de réception à l'Académie française par Jean Mistler. Paris, 1967.
37569.402 Adereth, Maxwell. Commitment in modern French literature: a brief study of "littérature engagée". London, 1967.
FL 395.65 Alasseur, Claude. La comédie française au 18e siècle, étude économique. Paris, 1967.
43522.7.2021 Albert-Birot, Pierre. Poésie, 1916-1924. Paris, 1967.
39574.25.1 Alembert, J. Le Rond d'. Oeuvres et correspondance inédites de d'Alembert. Genève, 1967.
43522.25.4100 Alexandre, Marcel. Souvenirs du passé d'un enfant du Havre, de 1862 à 1960. Paris, 1967.
43522.25.3700 Alexandre, Philippe. The president is dead. London, 1967.
37557.76.15 Allemand, André. Nouvelle critique, nouvelle perspective. Neuchâtel, 1967.
43545.24.855 André Breton et le mouvement surréaliste. Paris, 1967.
37548.225 Andreev, Leonid G. Sto let bel'giiskoi literatury. Moskva, 1967.
43527.3.860 Andrievskaia, Aleksandra A. Nesobstvenno-priamaia rech' v Khudozhestvennoi proze Lui Aragona. Kiev, 1967.
43524.33.100 Anglade, Jean. Des chiens vivants. Paris, 1967.
43524.67.776 Anouilh, Jean. The fighting cock. London, 1967.
43526.65.798 Apollinaire, Guillaume. Stikhi. Moskva, 1967.
43526.65.715 Apollinaire, Guillaume. The wandering Jew, and other stories. London, 1967.
43527.3.430 Aragon, Louis. Blanche ou l'oubli. Paris, 1967.
39576.2.10 Argens, Jean Baptiste de Boyer. Mémories secrets de la république de lettres. Genève, 1967.
43620.2.785 Arland, Marcel. Entretiens sur André Gide [du 6 au 14 septembre 1964]. Paris, 1967.
43528.48.250 Arland, Marcel. La musique des anges. Paris, 1967.
43528.61.230 Arnoux, Alexandre. La double Hélène. Paris, 1967.
43531.19.2100 Audouard, Yvan. Les secrets de leur réussite. Paris, 1967.
42587.50.130 Auriant (pseud.). Exposition Hugues Rebell, 1867-1967. Nantes, 1967.
43532.23.210 Aveline, Claude. De. Paris, 1967.
43535.54.380 Aymé, Marcel. Enjambées. Paris, 1967.
43535.54.370 Aymé, Marcel. Le Minotaure. Paris, 1967.
43537.10.31 Baby, Yvonne. Qui, l'espoir. Paris, 1967.
43538.14.885 Backett at 60: a festschrift. London, 1967.
43744.24.90 Baker, William E. Jacques Prévert. N.Y., 1967.

Chronological Listing

1967 - cont.

40597.35.88	Balzac, Honoré de. Illusions perdues. Paris, 1967.
40597.29.4.95	Balzac, Honoré de. Le père Goriot. London, 1967.
40596.7.4.1	Balzac, Honoré de. Lettres à Madame Hanska. Paris, 1967. 4v.
40596.112.5	Balzac, Honoré de. Lost illusions. N.Y., 1967.
40597.35.84	Balzac, Honoré de. Le médecin de campagne. Paris, 1967.
40597.2.159.1	Bardèche, Maurice. Balzac, romancier. Genève, 1967.
38542.36	Barrin, Jean. Venus dans le cloitre. 1. éd. canadienne. Montréal, 1967.
42576.15.251	Bart, Benjamin F. Flaubert. Syracuse, 1967.
V38575.109	Bartkus, G. Kornelio teatras. Vilnius, 1967.
43537.84.1120	Bataille, Georges. L'Archangélique et autres poèmes. Paris, 1967.
43537.84.120	Bataille, Michel. L'Arbre de Noël. Paris, 1967.
43701.63.935	Batchelor, John W. Existence and imagination; the theatre of Henry de Montherlant. St. Lucia, 1967.
43526.65.960	Bates, Soctt. Guillaume Apollinaire. N.Y., 1967.
41522.13.14.6	Baudelaire, Charles. Charles Baudelaire in Selbstzeugnissen und Bilddokumenten. Reinbek, 1967.
41522.15.5	Baudelaire, Charles. Lettres inédites aux siens. Paris, 1967.
41522.18.520	Baudelaire. Paris, 1967.
43537.99.180	Bazin, Hervé. Le matrimoine; roman. Paris, 1967.
38544.27.595	Bazin de Bezons, Jean de. Vocabulaire de la Princesse de Clèves. Paris, 1967.
43538.14.2120	Beck, Béatrix. Cou coupé court toujours. Paris, 1967.
43538.14.799	Beckett, Samuel. Come and go; dramaticule. London, 1967.
43538.14.738	Beckett, Samuel. Eh, Joe. London, 1967.
43538.14.752	Beckett, Samuel. No's knife. London, 1967.
43538.14.50	Beckett, Samuel. A Samuel Beckett reader. London, 1967.
43538.14.240	Beckett, Samuel. Têtes-mortes. Paris, 1967.
FL 386.28	Behar, Henri. Étude sur le théâtre dada et surréaliste. Paris, 1967.
41522.18.540	Belleli, Maria Luisa. Introduzione alla lettura di Baudelaire. Torino, 1967. 4v.
37556.15.15	Bellet, Roger. Presse et journalisme sous le Second Empire. Paris, 1967.
37543.572	Bénichou, Paul. L'écrivain et ses travaux. Paris, 1967.
43538.75.9100	Bernanos, Michel. La Montagne morte de la vie. Paris, 1967.
43538.76.5120	Bernard, Michel. Brouage. Lausanne, 1967.
38525.37.2	Bernardin, Napoléon Maurice. Un precurseur de Racine. Genève, 1967.
43538.78.6100	Bert, Claude Andrée. Les Kibboutzniks, roman. Paris, 1967.
43620.2.800	Bertalot, Enrico Umberto. André Gide et l'attente de Dieu. Paris, 1967.
40597.2.796	Bertault, Philippe. Balzac. Paris, 1967.
38575.114	Besançon, France. Université. Centre d'étude du vocabulaire français. Pierre Corneille, Polyeucte, Concordances. Paris, 1967.
43538.82.3120	Bessette, Hélène. Les petites Lilshart. Paris, 1967.
38542.12.15	Beugnot, Bernard. J.L. Guez de Balzac. Montréal, 1967.
38526.2.3.5	Bèze, Théodore de. Abraham sacrifiant. Genève, 1967.
38585.16.380	Bibliothèque nationale, Paris. Jean Racine, Paris, 1967. Paris, 1967.
42584.32.7	Bibliothèque Nationale, Paris. P.J. Hetzel, un grande editore del XIX secolo. Milano, 1967.
40553.10.85	Bibliothèque nationale. Benjamin Constant. Paris, 1967.
43761.78.920	Biemel, Walter. Jean-Paul Sartre in Selbstzeugnissen und Bilddokumenten. Reinbek, 1967.
43761.78.923	Biemel, Walter. Jean-Paul Sartre in Selbstzeugnissen und Bilddokumenten. Reinbek, 1967.
37544.125	Bissoondoyal, Basdeo. India in French literature. London, 1967.
37556.20.150	Blanc-Rouquette, Marie Thérèse. La presse et l'information à Toulouse des origines à 1789. Toulouse, 1967.
FL 6119.67.5	Blanchard, William H. Rousseau and the spirit of revolt. Ann Arbor, 1967.
43543.8.1110	Blancpain, Marc. Ulla des antipodes. Paris, 1967.
37543.586	Blin, Georges. Leçon inaugurale faite le...13 janvier 1966. Nogent-le-Rotrou, 1967.
37556.258	Bo, Carlo. La crisi del romanzo francese nel'900. Milano, 1967.
37568.228.3	Boisdeffre, P. de. Les écrivains français d'aujourd'hui. 3. éd. Paris, 1967.
37556.24.11	Boisdeffre, Pierre de. La cafetière est sur la table. Paris, 1967.
40551.22	Bonald, L.G.A. de. En marge de la Sainte-Alliance, lettres de Bonald au Comte de Senfft. Paris, 1967.
43544.60.2160	Bonnefoy, Yves. Un Reve fait à Mantoue. Paris, 1967.
43544.66.100	Boos, Renée. Les aventures de Boule-de-Gomme. Lausanne, 1967.
43544.74.3120	Bordier, Roger. Un age d'or. Paris, 1967.
Mol 702.15	Bordonove, Georges. Molière génial et familiar. Paris, 1967.
41522.66.2	Borel, d'Hauterive, Petrus. Madame Putiphar. v.1-2. Genève, 1967.
40597.2.845	Borel, Jacques. "Seraphita" et le mysti cisme balzacien. Paris, 1967.
43544.75.5110	Borel, Jacques. Tata ou de l'Education, pièce moral et didactique en 2 actes et 3 tableaux. Paris, 1967.
43544.75.120	Borel, Marguerite Appeli. A travers deux siècles, souvenirs et rencontres (1883-1967). Paris, 1967.
41522.18.392	Borgal, Clément. Charles Baudelaire. Paris, 1967.
43544.81.2280	Bosco, Henri. Mon compagnon de songes. Paris, 1967.
43544.89.2210	Bosquet, Alain. Quatre testaments et autres poèmes. Paris, 1967.
FL 6070.80	Bosshard, Peter. Die Beziehungen zwischen Rousseaus Zweitem Discours und dem 90. Thesis. Zürich, 1967.
38557.31.35	Bossuet, J.B. Oraisons funèbres de Bossuet. Paris, 1967.
38557.54.40.5	Bossuet, J.B. Politique tirée des propres paroles de l'Ecriture Sainte. Genève, 1967.
43544.88.2120	Boulanger, Daniel. La nacelle, roman. Paris, 1967.
43544.108.750	Boulle, Pierre. My own River Kwai. N.Y., 1967.
43544.108.180	Boulle, Pierre. Le photographe. Paris, 1967.
43544.89.125	Bousquet, Joë. Lettres à Poisson d'Or. Paris, 1967.
43656.59.835	Bradesco, Faust. Le monde étrange de Ionesco. Paris, 1967.
42584.25.380	Brady, Patrick. L'oeuvre de Emile Zola. Roman sur les arts, manifeste, autobiographie, roman à clef. Genève, 1967.
37555.742	Braet, Herman. L'accueil fait au symbolisme en Belgique 1885-1900. Bruxelles, 1967.
43545.24.240	Breton, André. Les champs magnétiques, Suivis de Vous m'aublierez et s'il vous plaît. Paris, 1967.

1967 - cont.

43545.41.5130	Brion, Marcel. La musique et l'amour. Paris, 1967.
37543.570	Bronne, Carlo. Le promenoir des amis. Bruxelles, 1967.
43545.66.120	Brosse, Jacques. Cinq méditations sur le corps. Paris, 1967.
43545.24.865	Browder, Clifford. André Breton, arbiter of surrealism. Génève, 1967.
38537.70	Brown, Huntington. Rabelais in English literature. N.Y., 1967.
43823.75.2755	Bruller, Jean. La bataille du silence. Paris, 1967.
38514.23.94.10	Brunelli, Giuseppe Antonio. Saggi critici. Messina, 1967.
40556.48.10	Brunello, Bruno. Joseph De Maistre: politico e filosofo. Bologna, 1967.
41522.18.530	Brussels. Bibliothéque royale. Baudelaire en Belgique, avril 1864-juillet 1866. Bruxelles, 1967.
42586.63.38	Buenzod, Janine. La formation de la pensée de Gobineau et l'essai sur l'inégalité des races humaines. Paris, 1967.
43538.76.963	Burkhard, Willy. La genése de l'idée du mal dans l'oeuvre romanesque de G. Bernanos. Thèse. Zurich, 1967.
43546.76.120	Burniaux, Constant. L'odeur du matin. Bruxelles, 1967.
42555.62.55	Butler, John Davis. Jean Moréas; a critique of his poetry and philosophy. The Hague, 1967.
43546.87.38	Butor, Michel. Portrait de l'artiste en jeune singe. Paris, 1967.
43833.20.940	Cabaud, Jacques. Simone Weil à New York et à Londres, les quinze derniers mois, 1942-1943. Paris, 1967.
43550.39.100	Cahour, Michel. L'amour à froid. Paris, 1967.
43550.41.110	Caillois, Roger. Obligues. Montpellier, 1967.
43550.52.41	Calvet, Jean. Memoires de Mgr. Jean Calvet. Lyon, 1967.
43550.53.100	Camara, Sikhé. Poèmes de combat et de vérité. Honfleur, 1967.
43550.58.25	Camus, Albert. Lyrical and critical essays. London, 1967.
41522.18.620	Capasso, Aldo. Baudelaire quasi sconosciuto. Roma, 1967.
43550.70.100	Caplain, Jean Marie. L'ombre et la lumière, roman. Paris, 1967.
37543.626	Caramaschi, Enzo. Études de littérature française. Bari, 1967.
43550.75.2100	Cardinal, Marie. Cet été-la. Deux ou trois choses que je sais d'elle. Paris, 1967.
43550.76.100	Cariguel, Claude. L'insolence. Paris, 1967.
43626.22.870	Carrel, Janine. L'expérience du seuil dans l'oeuvre de Julien Green. Diss. Zürich, 1967.
41557.10.290	Carrère, Casimir. George Sand amoureuse. Paris, 1967.
43550.83.3100	Castex, Pierre. Lagardère, d'après Paul Féval père et fils. Paris, 1967.
40583.345	Castex, Pierre. Le rouge et le noir de Stendhal. Paris, 1967.
43550.83.1110	Castillou, Henry. Frontière sans retour, roman. Paris, 1967.
43538.14.950	Cattanei, Giovanni. Beckett. Firenze, 1967.
43744.67.1585	Cattaui, Georges. Marcel Proust. London, 1967.
43550.98.230	Cayrol, Jean. Je l'entends encore, roman. Paris, 1967.
43551.59.106	Cendrars, Blaise. Poésies complètes, 1912-1924. Paris, 1967.
42576.15.395	Cento, Alberto. Il realismo documentario nell'Education sentimentale. Napoli, 1967.
43552.1.2100	Chabannes, Jacques. Mon coeur au Canada. Paris, 1967.
43552.2.2150	Chabrol, Jean-Pierre. Les Fous de Dieu. Paris, 1967.
43552.2.2140	Chabrol, Jean-Pierre. L'illustre fauteuil et autres récits. Paris, 1967.
43552.2.2160	Chabrol, Jean-Pierre. Je t'aimerai sans vergogne. Paris, 1967.
37568.270	Champigny, Robert. Pour une esthétique de l'essai. Paris, 1967.
43552.3.9310	Chamson, André. La superbe; roman. Paris, 1967.
43744.67.1635	Chantal, René de. Marcel Proust, critique littéraire. Montréal, 1967. 2v.
43552.4.2221	Char, René. Sur la poésie. Paris, 1967.
43552.4.5130	Charbonneau, Robert. Chronique de l'âge a mer. Montreal, 1967.
43546.87.90	Charbonnier, Georges. Entretiens avec Michel Butor. Paris, 1967.
43552.6.6100	Charmont, Paul. Les Autrefois. Genève, 1967.
38514.64.35	Chartier, Alain. Le livre de l'esperance. Brest? 1967.
38526.10.8.10	Chassignet, Jean Baptiste. Le mespris de la vie et consolation contre la mort. Genève, 1967.
43552.5.4100	Chauffin, Yvonne. Le séminariste. Paris, 1967.
43552.13.120	Chaulot, Paul. Soudaine écorce. Paris, 1967.
43552.7.3100	Chavée, Achille. L'agenda d'emeraude. La Louvière, 1967?
43552.6.7100	Chazai, Louis. Petit florilège. Paris, 1967.
43552.24.5110	Chesneau, Marc. Second fragment du "Journal poétique d'une âme, 1948-1967. Paris, 1967.
43552.66.1100	Chonez, Claudine. Ils furent rois tout un matin. Paris, 1967.
42521.22	Christophe, Lucien. Louis Veuillot. Paris, 1967.
43553.3.11	Cingria, Charles Albert. Oeuvres complètes. Lausanne, 1967? 8v.
43553.3.110	Cingria, Charles Albert. Vingt-cinq lettres à Adrien Bovy, 1902-1908. Lausanne, 1967.
43554.2.32.15	Claudel, Paul. Five great odes. London, 1967.
43554.2.370.15	Claudel, Paul. Théâtre. Paris, 1967.
43554.2.462	Claudel, Paul. La ville. Thèse. Paris, 1967.
43554.5.1030	Clavel, Maurice. La Pourpre de Judée, ou Les délices du genre humain. Paris, 1967.
43556.1.735	Cocteau, Jean. My contemporaries. London, 1967.
43556.49.712	Colette, Sidonie Gabrielle. The pure and the impure. N.Y., 1967.
43556.50.4100	Colin, Gerty. Un tour au purgatoire. Paris, 1967.
43556.58.140	Conchon, Georges. L'apprenti gaucher. Paris, 1967.
42554.26.700	Corbière, Tristan. Corbière. Poems. Santa Barbara, 1967.
38546.109	Cordelier, Jean. Madame de Sévigné par elle-même. Paris, 1967.
43556.76.110	Cornélus, Henri. De sel et de terre. Bruxelles, 1967.
42576.15.365	Cortland, Peter. The sentimental adventure. The Hague, 1967.
43556.82.1100	Costantini, Pierre D. Aimons, Chantons, Sauvons la Corse. Bastia, 1967.
37556.260	Coulet, Henri. Le roman jusqu'à la révolution. Paris, 1967. 2v.
43557.66.150	Crommelynck, Fernand. Théâtre. Paris, 1967- 3v.
43560.78.210	Curtis, Jean Louis. Un jeune couple. Paris, 1967.
43560.87.110	Cuttat, Jean. Les couplets de l'oiseleur. [Poèmes]. Lausanne, 1967.
43565.17.70	Dadelsen, Jean Paul de. Tonah: selected poems. London, 1967.
43565.77.1100	Dartois, Yves. La mosaïque de Balsams, roman. Paris, 1967.

Chronological Listing

1967 - cont.

43565.90.4100 David, Marie Laure. L'echappée. Paris, 1967.
37543.281.80 De Ronsard à Breton, recueil d'éssais, hommages à Marcel Raymond. Paris, 1967.
43619.23.810 Deberdt-Malaquais, Elisabeth. La quête de l'identité dans le théâtre de Ghelderode. Paris, 1967.
43566.9.1100 Deblue, Henri. L'alter ego, pièce en trois actes. Lausanne, 1967.
43566.6.3021 Debray, Régis. La frontière. Suivi d'un jeune homme à la page. Paris, 1967.
43566.47.7100 Delamotte, Jean Paul. Sans hâte, cette nuit. Paris, 1967.
43738.1.935 Delaporte, Jean. Péguy dans son temps et dans le nôtre. Paris, 1967.
41593.27.60 Delille, est-il mort? Clermont-Ferrand, 1967.
42537.25.10 Delsemme, Paul. Teodor de Wyzewa et le cosmopolitisme littéraire en France à l'époque du symobolisme. Bruxelles, 1967?
43566.62.120 Déon, Michel. Mégalonose, supplément aux "voyages de Gulliver". Paris, 1967.
43566.62.125 Déon, Michel. Un parfum de jasmin. Paris, 1967.
43757.12.800 Depierris, Jean Louis. Entretiens avec Emmanuel Roblès. Paris, 1967.
38514.23.145 Deroy, Jean Prosper Theodorus. François Villon. Recherches sur le testament. La Haye, 1967.
37567.665 Descotes, Maurice. La légende de Napoléon et les écrivains français du XIXe siècle. Paris, 1967.
40597.2.755 Des Loges, Stéphanie. L'art structural de la narration dans la nouvelle de Balzac. Wrocław, 1967.
43788.41.815 Devaud, Marcel. Albert Thibaudet. Fribourg, 1967.
43567.79.200 Dhôtel, André. Lumineux rentre chez lui. Paris, 1967.
39564.23.10 Diderot, Denis. Sur l'art et les artistes. Paris, 1967.
43569.21.120 Djebar, Assia. Les alouettes naïves, roman. Paris, 1967.
43757.68.800 Djemil, Enyn. J. Guy Ropartz, ou La recherche d'une vocation. Le Mans, 1967.
37581.13 Dominique, P. François. Arlequin Hulla. v.1-10,12-13. Paris, 1967-72. 12 pam.
40534.16.28 Donnard, Jean Hervé. Le théâtre de Carmontelle. Paris, 1967.
41564.55.125 Doolittle, James. Alfred de Vigny. N.Y., 1967.
43573.76.120 Dorgelès, Roland. Lettre ouverte à un milliardaire. Paris, 1967.
43574.75.135 Druon, Maurice. Le bonheur des uns, nouvelles et récits. Paris, 1967.
38526.76 Du Bois-Hus, Gabriel. La nuict des nuicts, Les jour des jours, Le miroir du destin, ou La nativité du Daufin du Ciel. Bologna, 1967.
38514.23.140 Dufournet, Jean. Recherches sur le testament de François Villon. v.1-3. Paris, 1967-
43576.36.1100 Duhamelet, Geneviève. Encore un peu de temps, poèmes. Paris, 1967.
Mol 560.12 Dulait, Suzanne. Inventaire raisonné des autographes de Molière. Genève, 1967.
43576.72.1110 Dupuy, Jacqueline. Dialogue dans l'infini. Bruges, 1967.
43576.72.1100 Dupuy, Jacqueline. Dure est ma joie. Paris, 1967.
43576.74.2220 Duras, Marguerite. L'amante anglaise. Paris, 1967.
43544.97.800 Durieux, Adèle. Robert Boxus, écrivain Wallon. Gilly, 1967.
43576.78.100 Durussel, André. Le poids léger des jours, poèmes pour trois temps. Genève, 1967.
43576.87.190 Dutourd, Jean. Pluche ou l'Amour de l'art. Paris, 1967.
43697.52.935 Eggart, Dietmer. Das Problem der Einsamkeit und ihrer Überwindung im Romanwerk von André Malraux. Bamberg, 19
FL 6119.67 Einaudi, Mario. The early Rousseau. Ithaca, 1967.
42554.30.11 Elskamp, M. Oeuvres complètes. Avant pros de Bernard Delvaille. Paris, 1967.
41522.18.510 Emmanuel, Pierre. Baudelaire. Paris, 1967.
43592.53.350 Emmanuel, Pierre. Le monde est intérieur, essais. Paris, 1967.
43593.32.1100 Engelbach, Gérard. Poèmes. Paris, 1967.
43544.82.805 Ennetières, Elisabeth d'. Nous et les autres, souvenirs d'un tiers de siècle avec Jean de Boschère. Aurillac, 1967.
43598.14.100 Escoula, Yvonne. Six chevaux bleus. Paris, 1967.
43598.82.220 Estang, Luc. Le jour de Caïn. Paris, 1967.
43599.13.1100 Etchart, Salvat. Le monde tel qu'il est. Paris, 1967.
43599.13.100 Etcherelli, Claire. Elise, ou la vraie vie; roman. Paris, 1967.
37543.569 Éthier-Blais, Jean. Signets. v.1-2. Montréal, 1967.
37556.274 Eulenburg, Heilwig. Bewältigung des Leidens im Französischen Roman nach dem zweiten Weltkrieg. München, 1967.
42584.25.370 Euvard, Michel. Emile Zola. Paris, 1967.
43604.19.120 Eydoux, Emmanuel. Capitaine Alfred Dreyfus. Basel, 1967.
43604.19.150 Eydoux, Emmanuel. Le dernier Pourimspiel des orphelins du docteur Janusz Korczak. Basel, 1967.
39533.20.50 Ezba, Luciano. Magia e invenzione. Milano, 1967.
43606.10.170 Fabre-Luce, Alfred. L'homme journal, 1966-1967. Paris, 1967.
43620.2.790 Falk, Eugene. Types of thematic structure. Chicago, 1967.
43606.50.120 Fallet, René. Charleston, roman. Paris, 1967.
40516.60.130 Favre, Pierre. Sade, utopiste. 1. éd. Paris, 1967.
43606.99.120 Faye, Jean-Pierre. Le récit hunique, essai. Paris, 1967.
43757.92.820 Ferry, Jean. L'Afrique des impressions. Paris, 1967.
43609.83.100 Fisson, Pierre. Les automobiles. Paris, 1967.
42576.26.5 Flaubert, Gustave. Intimate notebook, 1840-1841. 1st ed. Garden City, 1967.
42576.34.35 Flaubert, Gustave. November. N.Y., 1967.
43538.14.890 Fletcher, John. Samuel Beckett's art. London, 1967.
43610.25.3100 Fleury, Edmond. Ils luttérent jusqu'à l'aube. Paris, 1967.
38575.23.160 Fogel, Herbert. The criticism of Cornelian tragedy; a study of critical writing from the seventeenth to the twentieth century. 1. ed. N.Y., 1967.
43611.53.190 Fombeure, Maurice. A chat petit, 1965. Paris, 1967.
42533.20.85 Fondation Charles Plisnier. Catalogue de l'exposition Albert Mockel. Bruxelles, 1967.
37569.405 Fontaine, François. La littérature à l'encan. Paris, 1967.
43611.4.110 Fouchet, Max Pol. Les Appels. Paris, 1967.
37543.585 Fowlie, Wallace. Climate of violence; the French literary tradition from Baudelaire to the present. N.Y., 1967.
42576.62.22.8 France, Anatole. Les dieux ont soif. London, 1967.
43612.30.100 Franco, Guy. Pas de visa pour Abidjan, récit. Toulouse? 1967.
40583.214.5 François-Poncet, Andre. Stendhal en Allemagne. Paris, 1967.
FL 370.106.2 Frank, Grace. The medieval French drama. Oxford, 1967.

1967 - cont.

43612.23.121 Frénaud, André. Il n'y a pas de paradis; poèmes, 1943-1960. Paris, 1967.
43612.24.1100 Frère, André. Nouvelles comédies à une voix. Paris, 1967.
43612.24.140 Frère, Maud. Le temps d'une carte portale. Paris, 1967.
43612.25.100 Freustié, Jean. Les collines de l'Est, nouvelles. Paris, 1967.
40583.270.2 Frid, Iakov V. Stendal'. Izd. 2. Moskva, 1967.
37569.380 Frohock, Wilbur Merrill. Style and temper; studies in French fiction, 1925-1960. Cambridge, 1967.
37569.380.5 Frohock, Wilbur Merrill. Style and temper. Oxford, 1967.
42563.23.190 Fumet, Stanislas. Léon Bloy, captif de l'absolu. Paris, 1967.
43616.9.100 Gabriel, Pierre. L'amour de toi. Veilhes, 1967.
43616.50.7100 Gallez, Jean-Paul. Féminaires. Paris, 1967.
43616.58.120 Gandon, Yves. Pour un Bourbon Collins. Paris, 1967.
38557.24.154 Gaquère, François. Le Dialogue irénique Bossuet-Paul Ferry à Metz (1652-1669). Paris, 1967.
43616.64.110 Garnier, Christine. L'essuie-glace; roman. Paris, 1967.
43616.78.1100 Garzarolli, Richard. Le grand nocturne. Lausanne, 1967.
43616.79.230 Gascar, Pierre. Auto. Paris, 1967.
43616.79.730 Gascar, Pierre. The best years. N.Y., 1967.
43616.82.100 Gasquet, Marie Girard. Une enfance provençale. Paris, 1967.
43616.88.110 Gatti, Armand. V comme Vietnam. Paris, 1967.
43616.89.5100 Gaulis, Louis. Capitaine Karagheuz. Lausanne, 1967.
43616.89.5110 Gaulis, Louis. Le serviteur absolu. Lausanne, 1967.
43550.58.1065 Gay-Crosier, Raymond. Les envers d'un échec. Paris, 1967.
43750.24.815 Gayot, Paul. Raymond Queneau. Paris, 1967.
43617.59.240 Genevoix, Maurice. La forêt perdue, roman. Paris, 1967.
41574.622 Georgel, Pierre. Léopoldine Hugo, une jeune fille romantique. Villequier, 1967.
43576.6.860 Georges Duhamel (1884-1966). Paris, 1967.
40566.7.5 Gerbod, Paul. Paul François Dubois, universitaire, journaliste et homme politique, 1793-1874. Thèse. Paris, 1967.
43619.23.27 Ghelderode, Michel de. Seven plays. N.Y., 1967.
43620.2.79.184 Gide, André. Correspondance, 1909-1951. Paris, 1967.
37596.27.20 Gierden, Karlheinz. Das altfranzösische Alexiuslied. Meisenheim, 1967.
40583.341 Gilman, Stephen. The tower as emblem. Frankfurt, 1967.
FL 6129.67 Gionnuzzi, Paolo. J.J. Rousseau e la chimica. Bari, 1967.
43620.66.520 Giono, Jean. Préface à "l'Iliade". Paris, 1967.
43620.74.790 Giraudoux, Jean. Plays. N.Y., 1967.
43620.74.550 Giraudoux, Jean. Siegfried. London, 1967.
43620.74.1160 Giraudoux, Jean Pierre. Le fils. Paris, 1967.
43531.18.1800 Giroud, Michel. Jacques Audiberti. Paris, 1967.
37555.200.10 Glauser, Alfred Charles. Le poème-symbole de Scène à Valéry. Paris, 1967.
42586.68.25 Gobineau, Arthur de. Les races et la République, introduction à une lecture de l'Essai sur l'inégalité des races humaines. Paris, 1967.
41596.4.140 Gochberg, Herbert S. Stage of dreams. The dramatic art of Alfred de Musset. Genève, 1967.
43625.27.180 Goffin, Robert. Le versant noir. Paris, 1967.
43538.1.235 Goldschmidt, Georges-Arthur. Un cas de flagrant délit; les contes de Marcel Béalu. Paris, 1967.
38514.30.25 Goodrich, Norma Lorre. Charles of Orleans; a study of themes in his French and English poetry. Genève, 1967.
40553.10.95 Gouhier, Henri. Benjamin Constant. Paris, 1967.
43625.3.53 Gourmont, Rémy de. Le joujou patriotisme. Paris, 1967.
43626.22.55 Green, Julien. Julien Green. Paris, 1967.
43626.22.745 Green, Julien. To leave before dawn. 1st ed. N.Y., 1967.
43626.66.1160 Grosjean, Jean. Elégies. Paris, 1967.
40583.368 Grün, Ruth. Hommes-copies, dandies and fausses passions. Genève, 1967.
43628.41.3170 Guillevic, Eugène. Euclidiennes. Paris, 1967.
43628.42.190 Guilloux, Louis. La confrontation. Paris, 1967.
43628.42.200 Guilloux, Louis. Cripure. Paris, 1967.
43628.41.9100 Guimard, Paul. Les choses de la vie, roman. Paris, 1967.
37542.58 Guth, Paul. Histoire de la littérature française. Paris, 1967- 2v.
40597.2.200.2 Guyon, Bernard. La pensée politique et sociale de Balzac. 2. éd. Paris, 1967.
42556.28.167 Hackett, Cecil A. Autour de Rimbaud. Paris, 1967.
43631.21.130 Haedrich, Marcel. L'entre-deux dieux. Paris, 1967.
42563.23.195 Hager, Ruth E. Léon Bloy et l'évolution du conte cruel. Paris, 1967.
43631.49.4100 Halet, Pierre. La butte de Satory. Paris, 1967.
43631.50.1100 Hallier, Jean-Edern. Le grand écrivain, roman. Paris, 1967.
38539.11.20 Hardee, A. Maynor. Jean de Lannel and the pre-classical French novel. Diss. Geneva, 1967.
43631.76.100 Hardy, René. La route des cygnes. Paris, 1967.
43631.89.1100 Haulot, Arthur. Espaces. Bruxelles, 1967.
43631.98.1100 Hazoumé, Roger Aralamon. Fleurs africaines, poèmes. Paris, 1967.
37562.346 Heger, Henrik. Die Melancholie bei den französischen Lyriken des Spätmittelalters. Bonn, 1967.
43632.50.23 Hellens, Franz. Arrière-saisons (1960-1967). Paris, 1967.
43632.50.270 Hellens, Franz. Célébration de la pomme. Le Jas du Revest-Saint-Martin, 1967.
43632.50.250 Hellens, Franz. Le dernier jour du monde, nouvelles fantastiques. Paris, 1967.
40597.2.775 Hemmings, Frederick William John. Balzac; an interpretation of La comédie humaine. N.Y., 1967.
43632.77.4110 Herment, Georges. Le poème enseveli. Veilhes, 1967.
39544.374 Heuvel, Jacques van den. Voltaire dans ses contes. Paris, 1967.
38551.165 Hillenaar, Henk. Fénelon et les jésuites. La Haye, 1967.
38543.24.20 Hippeau, Louis. Essai sur la morale de La Rochefoucauld. Paris, 1967.
41578.185 Hirdt, Willi. Studien zur Metaphorik Lamartines. München, 1967.
37556.270 Höhnisch, Erika. Das gefangene Ich. Heidelberg, 1967.
43633.28.100 Hoffmann, Georges. J'ai régné cette nuit, comédie en trois actes. Genève, 1967.
43550.58.2005 Hommage à Albert Camus. Paris, 1967.
43636.64.120 Hoog, Armand. Les deux côtes de la mer. Paris, 1967.
43638.2.110 Huant, Ernest. Le troisième triumvirat, fragments des mémoires de Gordien le Cybernétique. Paris, 1967.
41573.22.5 Hugo, Victor. Quatre-vingt-treize. Paris, 1967.
39533.8.33 Hunter, Alfred. Lexique de la langue de Jean Chapelain. Genève, 1967.
42576.65.80.40 Huysmans, Joris Karl. Lettres inédites à Jules Destrée. Genève, 1967.
43822.49.1185 Hytier, Jean. Questions de littérature. Genève, 1967.

Chronological Listing

1967 - cont.

42577.4.49.160	Ignotus, Pal. The paradox of Maupassant. London, 1967.
40583.360	Imbert, Henri François. Les métamorphoses de la liberté. Paris, 1967.
43656.59.50	Ionesco, Eugène. Journal en miettes. Paris, 1967.
43666.5	Izoard, Jacques. Aveuglement, Orphée. Bruxelles, 1967.
43761.77.815	Jaccard, Jean-Luc. Nathalie Sarraute. Zürich, 1967.
43667.11.21	Jaccottet, Philippe. Airs, poèmes, 1961-1964. Paris, 1967. 2v.
43667.14.340	Jacob, Max. L'homme de cristal. Paris, 1967.
43667.15.2150	Jacquemard, Simonne. A l'état sauvage, récits. Paris, 1967.
43667.15.2130	Jacquemard, Simonne. Navigation vers les iles, nouvelles. Paris, 1967.
43667.1.700	Jammes, Francis. Jammes. Poems. Santa Barbara, 1967.
43668.4.4100	Jean, Marie Louis. Au temps du Tonkin paisible. Paris, 1967.
43668.50.110	Jelinek, Henriette. La marche du fou. Paris, 1967.
43670.1.1100	Joachim, Paulin. Anti-Grâce. Paris, 1967.
37573.732	Jones, Cyril Meredith. Les lettres en France. N.Y., 1967.
43670.89.320.5	Jouhandeau, M. Chamin adour. Paris, 1967.
38523.3.56	Jourda, Pierre. Marot. 2. éd. Paris, 1967.
43671.41.120	Juin, Hubert. Un soleil rouge. Poèmes. Paris, 1967.
42557.12.145	Kalinowska, Zofia I. Les motifs décadents dans les poèmes d'Emile Verhaeren. Wrocław, 1967.
43672.58.100	Kanapa, Jean. Les Choucas ou quelques aspects de la vie de Fred Hopper dans l'hiver 1961-1962. Paris, 1967.
43672.84.100	Katcha, Vahé. Galia, roman. Paris, 1967.
43673.19.110	Kédros, André. Même un tigre. Paris, 1967.
43673.32.110	Kegels, Anne Marie. Les doigts verts. Bruxelles, 1967.
43673.78.120	Kerchove, Arnold de. Sensualité. Bruxelles, 1967.
43673.83.290	Kessel, Joseph. Les cavaliers. Paris, 1967.
37569.360.3	Kesteloot, Lilyan. Les écrivains noirs de langue française. 3. éd. Bruxelles, 1967.
43674.5.100	Khayr al-Din, Muhammad. Agadir. Paris, 1967.
41522.18.525	Kies, Albert. Études baudelairiennes. Louvain, 1967.
43675.58.110	Kinds, Edmond. Le temps des apôtres. Bruxelles, 1967.
43617.78.845	Kliess, Werner. Genêt. Velber, 1967.
FL 386.615	Knowles, Dorothy. French drama of the inter-war years, 1918-1939. London, 1967[1968]
43680.87.100	Kottelanne, Claude. Comment dire ce peu. Veilhes, 1967.
38537.66	Krailsheimer, Alban J. Rabelais. Paris, 1967.
43681.21.110	Kréa, Henri. Poèmes en forme de vertige. Paris, 1967.
38514.23.115	Kuhn, David. La poétique de François Villon. Paris, 1967.
43780.69.815	Kwiatkowski, Jerzy. Poezje bez granic. Kraków, 1967.
42544.28.15	Labiche, Eugène. The Italian straw hat, and The spelling mistakes. N.Y., 1967.
Mon 122.12	Lablénie, Edmond. Essais sur Montaigne. Paris, 1967.
43687.15.1021	Lacroix, Georgette. Mortes saisons; poèmes. n.p., 1967.
43687.100.100	Lacrosil, Michèle. Demain Jab-Herma. Paris, 1967.
38544.27.15	La Fayette, Marie M. Romans et nouvelles. Paris, 1967.
38544.27.310	La Fayette, Marie M. Vie de la Princesse d'Angleterre. Genève, 1967.
39527.29.90	La Fontaine, Jean de. Fables choisies. Paris, 1967.
39527.29.63.5	La Fontaine, Jean de. Le songe de vaux. Genève, 1967.
43687.53.4100	La Marque, B. Paris brûlera, récit des années, 1965 à 1975. Paris, 1967.
41578.28.15	Lamartine, Alphonse. Jocelyn, épisode. Paris, 1967.
43545.42.800	Lang, André. Pierre Brisson, le journaliste, l'écrivain, l'homme (1896-1964). Paris, 1967.
43687.60.2110	Lange, Monique. Cannibales en Sicile. Paris, 1967.
39533.20.40	Lanius, Edward W. Cyrano de Bergerac and the universe of the imagination. Genève, 1967.
42577.4.49.165	Lanoux, Armand. Maupassant le "Bel-ami". Paris, 1967.
43687.61.21	L'Anselme, Jean. The ring around the world: selected poems. London, 1967.
38543.10.50A	La Rochefoucauld, François. Maximes, suivies des réfléxions diverses. Paris, 1967.
38543.19.65	La Rochefoucauld, François. Réfléxions ou Sentences et maximes morales. Genève, 1967.
43687.80.2705	Lartéguy, Jean. The bronze drums. 1st American ed. N.Y., 1967.
43687.80.2160	Lartéguy, Jean. Les centurions. Paris, 1967.
43687.83.1140	Las Vergnas, Raymond. Meurtres à Quiberon, roman. Paris, 1967.
43687.89.1170	Laurent, Jacques. Au contraire. Paris, 1967.
43822.49.1422	Laurette, Pierre. Le thème de l'arbre chez Paul Valéry et Rainer Maria Rilke. Paris, 1967.
40553.10.80	Lausanne. Bibliothèque cantonale et universitaire. Benjamin Constant, 1767-1830. Lausanne, 1967.
43688.13.3100	Le Clec'h, Guy. L'aube sur les remparts, roman. Paris, 1967.
43688.14.4140	Le Clézio, Jean Marie Gustave. L'extase matérielle. Paris, 1967.
43688.14.4130	Le Clézio, Jean Marie Gustave. Terra amata. Paris, 1967.
42555.35.30	Leconte de Lisle, C.M.R. Leconte de Lisle, un tableau synoptique. Paris, 1967.
43688.20.700	Leduc, Violette. Thérèse and Isabelle. N.Y., 1967.
38514.23.120	Le Gentil, Pierre. Villon. Paris, 1967.
43688.49.1110	Lely, Gilbert. Ma civilisation, poèmes. Paris, 1967.
40516.60.117	Lély, Gilbert. Sade. Études sur sa vie. Paris, 1967.
43688.53.2021	Le Marois, Jean. La couronne d'Apollon. Poèmes. Genève, 1967.
42576.46.9	Le Roy, Eugène. Au pays des pierres. Périgueux, 1967.
37569.392	Le Sage, Laurent. The French new criticism; an introduction and a sampler. University Park, 1967.
43626.70.805	Leutrat, Jean Louis. Julien Gracq. Paris, 1967.
37566.160	Ley, Francis. Bernardin de Saint-Pierre; Mme de Staël, Chateaubriand, Benjamin Constant et Mme de Krudener. Paris, 1967.
43761.78.905	Lilar, Suzanne. A propos de Sartre et de l'amour. Paris, 1967.
43690.61.150	Linze, Jacques Gérard. L'etang-coeur. Paris, 1967.
43690.65.100	Lionel, Frédéric. L'affrontement. Neuchâtel, 1967.
37542.76A	A literary history of France. v.2-5. London, 1967- 4v.
40597.2.750	Lock, Peter W. Balzac: Le père Goriot. London, 1967.
37569.412	Loffler, Paul A. Chronique de la littérature prolétarienne française de 1930 à 1939. Rodez, 1967.
40597.9.20	Lorant, André. Les parents pauvres d'Honoré de Balzac. Thèse. Genève, 1967. 2v.
37597.9.25	Lorris, Guillaume de. The romaunt of the rose and Le roman de la rose. Oxford, 1967.
43620.74.930	Louw, Gilbert. La tragédie grecque dans les théâtre de Giraudoux. Nancy, 1967.
43694.11.3100	Lucain, Pierre Clotaire. Veillées guadeloupéennes. Paris, 1967.

1967 - cont.

43694.11.2120	Lucas, Wilfrid Louis Eugène. Mémoires, impressions, souvenirs, pensées et réflexions. Paris, 1967.
37544.130	Luchini, Albert Marie. Les chrétiens croient-ils encore au livre? Le livre de religion à la question. Paris, 1967.
43694.18.100	Ludin, Elohim. Ceux de Bizerte. Paris, 1967.
37562.338	Macchia, Giovanni. La letteratura francese dalla crisi del medioevo alla fine del Rinascimento. Roma, 1967.
43744.67.1600	Magnani, Loigi. La musica, il tempo, l'eterno nella "Recherche" di Proust. Milano, 1967.
43697.42.110	Majault, Joseph. La conférence de Genève; roman. Paris, 1967.
37568.250.2	Majault, Joseph. Littérature de notre temps. 2. éd. Tournai, 1967.
42555.43.95	Mallarmé, Stéphane. Vingt poèmes. Genève, 1967.
43697.2.1740	Mallet-Joris, Françoise (pseud.). Signs and wonders. N.Y., 1967.
43697.52.44	Malraux, André. Antimémoires. Paris, 1967.
43697.52.105	Malraux, André. Les conquérants. Paris, 1967?
43697.52.2705	Malraux, Clara. Memoirs. N.Y., 1967.
Mol 613.15	Mander, Gertrud. Jean-Baptiste Molière. 1. Aufl. Velber, 1967.
43697.74.3185	Marceau, Félicien. Un jour, j'ai rencontré la vérité. Paris, 1967.
43697.75.705	Marcel, Gabriel. Presence and immortality. Pittsburgh, 1967.
43697.75.210	Marcel, Gabriel. Le secret est dans les îles. Paris, 1967.
38526.32.48	Marguerite d'Angoulême. Geptameron. Leningrad, 1967.
38526.32.70	Marguerite d'Angoulême. Nouvelles. Paris, 1967.
43697.76.2110	Marill, René. Manuscrit enterré dans le jardin d'Éden. Bienne, 1967.
37544.135	Marquiset, Jean. Les gens de justice dans la littérature. Paris, 1967.
37568.260	Martin Du Gard, Maurice. Les libéraux, de Renan à Chardonne. Paris, 1967.
43697.79.8100	Marvaud, Jean. Printemps charentais. Versailles, 1967.
43697.81.120	Massip, Renée. Le rire de Sara. Paris, 1967.
37568.242	Massis, Henri. Au long d'une vie. Paris, 1967.
43545.24.890	Massot, Pierre de. André Breton ou le Septembriseur. Paris, 1967.
42556.28.370	Matarasso, Henri. Album Rimbaud. Paris, 1967.
43545.24.860	Matthews, J.H. André Breton. N.Y., 1967.
38585.43.65	Maulnier, Picary. Lecture de "Phèdre". Paris, 1967.
43697.88.70	Mauriac, François. Mémoires politiques. Paris, 1967.
43697.89.793	Maurois, André. The collected stories of André Maurois. N.Y., 1967.
43697.89.27	Maurois, André. D'Aragon à Montherlant. Paris, 1967.
43697.89.570	Maurois, André. Nouvelles directions de la littérature française. Oxford, 1967.
39566.260.2	May, Gita. Diderot et Boudelaire, critiques d'art. 2e ed. Genève, 1967.
43698.16.100	Medda, François. Le Molengui, roman. Paris, 1967.
41522.18.515	Melançon, Joseph. Le spiritualisme de Baudelaire. Montréal, 1967.
42555.45.75	Menard, Jean. Xavier Marmier et le Canada avec des documents inédits. Québec, 1967.
41574.616	Mercié, Jean Luc. Victor Hugo et Julie Chenay, documents inédits. Paris, 1967.
41555.2.18	Mérimée, Prosper. Romans et nouvelles. Paris, 1967. 2v.
43698.75.7130	Merle, Robert. Un animal doué de raison. Paris, 1967.
41522.17.23.20	Mermaz, Louis. Madame Sabatier. Lausanne, 1967.
43576.9.825	Mertens, Cornelis Joseph. Émotion et critique chez Charles Du Bos. Proefschrift. Nijmegen, 1967.
43698.200.725	Michaux, Henri. Michaux (poems). Santa Barbara, 1967.
43698.200.260	Michaux, Henri. La nuit remue. Paris, 1967.
43698.200.840	Michaux, Henri. Plume, précédé de Lointain intérieur. Paris, 1967.
43699.13.110	Michel, Georges. La promenade du dimanche. Paris, 1967.
43656.59.845	Mikheeva, Agnessa N. Kogda po stsene khodiat nosorogi. Moskva, 1967.
41522.18.505	Milner, Max. Baudelaire; enfer ou ciel, qu'importe! Paris, 1967.
43538.76.1000	Milner, Max. Georges Bernanos. Paris, 1967.
39544.370	Miró, César. Alzire et Candide, ou L'image de Perou chez Voltaire. Paris, 1967.
43545.22.805	Moisan, Clément. Henri Bremond et la poésie pure. Paris, 1967.
43701.1.40	Molaine, Pierre. Le sang. Paris, 1967.
Mol 60.50	Molière, Jean Baptiste Poquelin. Tartuffe and other plays. N.Y., 1967.
43701.59.160	Monfreid, Henri de. Les lionnes d'or d'Ethiopie. Paris, 1967.
39594.9.40	Montesquieu, C.L. de S. Essai sur le gout. 1. éd. Genève, 1967.
FL 6074.52	Moran, John H. On the origin of language; Jean-Jacques Rousseau, essay on the origin of languages. N.Y., 1967.
43701.74.440	Morand, Paul. Mon plaisir. Paris, 1967.
43701.99.1100	Moré, Marcel. Accords et dissonances, 1932-1944. Paris, 1967.
43701.75.7110	Moreau, Marcel J. Le chant des paroxismes, suivi de la Nukai. Paris, 1967.
39586.21.580	Mormile, Mario. Desfontaines et la crise néologique. Roma, 1967.
38514.130.5	Le mors de la pomme. Messina, 1967.
39566.72.5	Mortier, Roland. Diderot in Deutschland, 1750-1850. Stuttgart, 1967.
38585.68	Mourques, Odette de. Autonomie de Racine. Paris, 1967.
38585.63	Mourques, Odette de. Racine; or, The triumph of relevance. Cambridge, 1967.
38575.103.2	Muller, Charles. Étude de statistique lexicale. Thèse. Paris, 1967.
38575.103.2.2	Muller, Charles. Étude statistique lexicale. Thèse. Paris, 1967.
43703.50.21	Muller, Louis. Echos de mon pays. Porrentruy, 1967.
43703.61.110	Muno, Jean. L'île des pas perdus. Bruxelles, 1967.
43698.200.835	Murat, Napoléon. Henri Michaux. Paris, 1967.
37595.10.15	Murray, Albert Victor. Abélard and St. Bernard; a study in 12th century modernism. Manchester, 1967.
FL 397.70.5	Nattiez, Jean. La vie théâtrale des troupes ambulantes en Picardie. Amiens, 1967.
43707.98.110	Nizan, Paul. Paul Nizan, intellectuel communiste, 1926-1940. Paris, 1967.
43709.23.4100	Noël, Bernard. La face de silence. Paris, 1967.
FL 398.72	Nohain, Jean. Le Pétomane, 1857-1945. Paris, 1967.
40562.50	Nujens, Alvarus. Getuige voor de vrijheid. Lien, 1967.

Chronological Listing

1967 - cont.

43712.80.100 Nyssen, Hubert. Préhistoire des estuaires. Bruxelles, 1967.
43714.75.41 Obret, Muriel. Fragments d'un journal. Port-Louis, 1967.
37568.255 O'Brien, Justin. The French literary horizon. New Brunswick, 1967.
43723.50.120 Ollier, Claude. L'Échec de Nolan. Paris, 1967.
43723.50.130 Ollier, Claude. Navettes. Paris, 1967.
43538.14.910 Onimus, Jean. Beckett. Paris, 1967.
43725.41.110 Onimus, Jean. Interrogations autour de l'essentiel. Bruges? 1967.
FL 1029.66 L'ornement des dames, ornatus mulierum. Bruxelles, 1967.
43566.82.7835 Ostrovsky, Erika. Céline and his vision. N.Y., 1967.
43736.24.100 Ozeray, Jean Jacques. La tourmente du sentiment, poèmes. Paris, 1967.
40516.60.135 Pappot, G. De Markies de Sade. Amsterdam, 1967.
43737.77.120 Parmelin, Hélène. La gadgeture. Paris, 1967.
43737.77.1100 Paron, Charles Louis. Les vagues peuvent mourir. Paris, 1967.
43737.82.1100 Pasguier, Claude. Le jour du saigneur. Monte Carlo, 1967.
43737.86.100 Patient, Serge. Le mal du pays. Monte Carlo, 1967.
37562.334A Payen, Jean C. Le motif du repentir dans la littérature française médiévale. Thèse. Genève, 1967.
43737.98.1140 Paysan, Catherine. Histoire d'une salamandre. Levallois, 1967.
43737.98.1130 Paysan, Catherine. La musique du feu. Paris, 1967.
43738.41.1120 Peignot, Jérôme. L'amour a ses princes. Paris, 1967.
43738.49.1110 Pelegri, Jean. Les monuments du déluge. Paris, 1967.
37566.155 Pellegrini, Carlo. Letteratura e storia nell'Ottocento francese e altri saggi. Roma, 1967.
43738.49.2110 Pelletier Doisy, Jacqueline. Le domaine de hautefrâgne. Paris, 1967.
43738.49.2100 Pelletier Doisy, Jacqueline. L'étang de la breure. Paris, 1967.
43738.75.110 Perec, Georges. Un homme qui dort. Paris, 1967.
38526.27.5.261 Perkins, Jeanne G. Siméon La Roque, poète de l'absence, 1550-1615. Paris, 1967.
43738.77.7621 Perret, Christopher. Christopher Perret. Memorial volume. Genève, 1967.
43738.77.4100 Perry, Jacques. Vie d'un païen; roman. Paris, 1967. 3v.
43738.78.750 Perse, Saint-John. Birds. Durham, 1967.
43738.78.24 Perse, Saint-John. Saint-John Perse. Paris, 1967.
43738.98.2100 Peyramaure, Michel. Les Colosses de Carthage, roman. Paris, 1967.
43738.97.1760 Peyrefitte, Roger. The Jews. Indianapolis, 1967.
43738.97.1210 Peyrefitte, Roger. Notre amour. Paris, 1967.
38585.18.75 Picard, Raymond. Racine polémiste. Paris, 1967.
43741.11.1012 Piccard, Eulalie. Collection des oeuvres complètes. Neuchâtel, 1967-68. 10v.
41522.18.535 Pichois, Claude. Baudelaire. Études et témoignages. Neuchâtel, 1967.
43741.19.100 Pidoux, Edmond. Africaines. Neuchâtel, 1967.
43741.19.110 Pidoux, Edmond. Passage de la ligne. Roisel, 1967.
43741.24.2110 Pierson-Piérard, Marianne. Entre hier et demain, roman. Paris, 1967.
43741.25.250 Pieyre de Mandiargues, André. La marge. Paris, 1967.
40583.366 Pincherle, Bruno. In compagnia di Stendhal. (Beyle). Milano, 1967.
43741.59.3710 Pinget, Robert. Baga. London, 1967.
38514.57.35 Pisan, Christine de. Le livre du corps de policie. Genève, 1967.
42556.28.380 Plessen, Jacques. Promenade et poésie. Proefschrift. La Haye, 1967.
42568.19.27 Pleynet, Marcelin. Lautréamont par lui-même. Paris, 1967.
43742.89.100 Plumyène, Jean. Le complexe de gauche. Paris, 1967.
38514.30.20 Poirion, Daniel. Le lexique de Charles d'Orleans dans les ballades. Genève, 1967.
43761.78.915 Pollmann, Leo. Sartre und Camus; Literature der Existenz. Stuttgart, 1967.
37543.590 Pommier, Jean. Dialogues avec le passé, études et portraits littéraires. Paris, 1967.
43743.60.170 Ponge, Francis. Nouveau recueil. Paris, 1967.
43743.60.110.5 Ponge, Francis. Le parti pris des choses. Paris, 1967.
43743.60.160 Ponge, Francis. Le Savon. Paris, 1967.
43743.62.2120 Pons, Maurice. Rosa. Chronique fidèle des événements sur venus au siècle dernier dans la principauté de Wasquelham. Paris, 1967.
43743.61.2110 Pontremoli, Pascal. Le jonet der fer-blanc. Paris, 1967.
40524.32.55 Porter, Charles Allan. Restif's novels; or, An autobiography in search of an author. New Haven, 1967.
43743.89.1120 Poulet, Robert. Les sources de la vie. Paris, 1967.
43744.3.100 Praillet, Arthur. La flute d'herbe. Basse-Yutz, 1967.
43744.5.140 Prassinos, Gisèle. Les mots endormis. Paris, 1967.
43744.25.4130 Prévost, Alain. Le pont des absents. Paris, 1967.
43744.25.5110 Prévot, Gérard. La Haute note jaune, récit. Bruxelles, 1967.
43747.23.120 Puel, Gaston. La lumière du jour. Paris, 1967.
37567.660 Puzikov, Aleksandr I. Portrety frantsuzskikh pisatelei. Moskva, 1967.
43750.20.170 Queffélec, Henri. La voile tendue. Paris, 1967.
43750.24.730 Queneau, Raymond. Between blue and blue: a sort of novel. London, 1967.
43750.24.330 Queneau, Raymond. Courir les rues. Paris, 1967.
43738.1.940 Quoniam, Théodore. La pensée de Péguy. Paris, 1967.
38585.27.15 Racine, Jean. Britannicus. Cambridge, 1967.
38583.6.14 Racine, Jean. Complete plays. N.Y., 1967. 2v.
38583.6.40 Racine, Jean. Théâtre complet. Paris, 1967.
37556.256 Raimond, Michel. Le roman depuis la révolution. Paris, 1967.
43752.57.63 Ramuz, Charles Ferdinand. C.F. Ramuz, ses amis et son temps (Lettres de et à Ramuz). Lausanne, 1967- 6v.
43752.57.13 Ramuz, Charles Ferdinand. Oeuvres complètes. Lausanne, 1967- 20v.
43620.66.855 Redfern, W.D. The private world of Jean Giono. Durham, 1967.
43753.4.120 Régnier, Yves. Un monde aveugle. Paris, 1967.
43757.50.1305 Reinhardt, Hans. Romain Rolland's unveräffentlichte Dramen. München, 1967.
38544.27.590 Rémy, Jean-Charles. Madame de La Fayette. L'ésprit et les lettres. Lausanne, 1967.
40524.28.12 Restif de la Bretonne, Nicolas E. Le plus fort des pamphlets. Paris, 1967.
43753.99.7100 Rezvani, Serge. Les années-lumière, roman. Paris, 1967.
40515.2.36.10 Riccioli, Giovanni. L'esprit di Madame de Charrière. Bari, 1967.

1967 - cont.

40587.165 Richard, Jean-Pierre. Paysage de Chateaubriand. Paris, 1967.
43756.12.2100 Richter, Anne. Les locataires. Paris, 1967.
42556.28.73.5 Rimbaud, Jean Arthur. Illuminations. Genève, 1967.
43756.91.3705 Rivoyre, Christine de. The sultans; a novel. London, 1967.
41522.3.100 Rogers, Brian G. The novels and stories of Barbey d'Aurevilly. Genève, 1967.
43757.49.130 Rolin, Dominique. Maintenant. Paris, 1967.
43757.50.74 Rolland, Romain. Un beau visage à tous sens, choix de lettres de Romain Rolland. Paris, 1967.
43757.3.365 Romains, Gabrielle. Mes voyages avec Jules Romains. Paris, 1967-
Mol 163.10 Romer, Paul. Molières Amphitryon und sein gesellschaftlicher Hintergrund. Bonn, 1967.
43656.59.830 Ronge, Peter. Polemik, Parodie und Satire bei Ionesco. Bad Homburg, 1967.
38525.20.58 Ronsard, Pierre de. Lyrics of Pierre de Ronsard, Vandomois. Edinburg, 1967.
43620.2.795 Rossi, Vinio. André Gide; the evolution of an aesthetic. New Brunswick, 1967.
43757.89.7100 Roubaud, Jacques. E. Paris, 1967.
43752.57.905 Roud, Gustave. Avec Ramuz. Lausanne, 1967.
43757.91.2700 Rouquette, Yves. Lo poëta es una vaca; racònte. Lavit, 1967.
FL 6074.2.2 Rousseau, J.J. Essai sur l'origine des langues. Paris, 1967?
43757.96.4150 Roy, Jules. Les chevaux du soleil. Paris, 1967- 4v.
40583.354 Rude, Fernand. Stendhal et la pensée sociale de son temps. Paris, 1967.
43758.82.100 Russo, Antoine. Réflexions, sentiments, souvenirs de jeunesse (1956-1966). Paris, 1967.
FL 398.47.70 Rykova, Nadezhda I. Adrienna Lekuvrer. Leningrad, 1967.
40516.60.42 Sade, D.A.F. de. Voyage d'Italie, précédé des premières oeuvres, suivi de opuscules sur le théâtre. Paris, 1967.
38526.47.26 Saint-Amant, Marc Antoine Gérard. Oeuvres. v.2-3. Paris, 1967- 2v.
38542.20 Saint-Evremond. C. de M. de S.D. Lettres. Paris, 1967-68.
43761.41.1100 St. Gil, Philippe. Dialogues à une voix. Paris, 1967.
FL 376.8 Sakharoff, Micheline. Le héros, sa liberté et son efficacité. Paris, 1967.
43761.55.100 Samson, Jean Paul. Journals de l'an quarante. Montreux, 1967.
41557.9.31.15 Sand, George. La petite Fadette. Paris, 1967.
39544.375 Sareil, Jean. Essai sur Candide. Genève, 1967.
43761.77.170 Sarraute, Nathalie. Le silence, suivi de la mensonge. Paris, 1967.
43761.78.322 Sartre, Jean Paul. Bariona. 2e éd. Paris, 1967.
37556.310 Sasse, Klaus. Die Entdeckung der courtisan Vertueuse in der französischen Literatur des 18. Jahrhunderts. Hamburg, 1967.
41543.22.140 Schaeffer, Gérald. Le Voyage en Orient de Nerval. Neuchâtel, 1967.
43697.77.875 Schalk, David Louis. Roger Martin du Gard. Ithaca, 1967.
Mol 193.45 Scherer, Jacques. Sur le Dom Juan de Molière. Paris, 1967.
37563.75.5 Schmidt, Albert Marie. Études sur le XVIe siècle, avec les témoignages de François Mauriac et Marc Boegner. Paris, 1967.
43738.1.930 Schmitt, Hans Adolf. Charles Péguy; the decline of an idealist. Baton Rouge, 1967.
43763.39.1130 Schneider, Marcel. Entre deux vanités. Paris, 1967.
40597.2.805 Schneiderbauer, Anna Maria. Das Element des Daemonischen in Honoré de Balzacs Comédie humaine. München? 1967?
43538.14.935 Schoell, Konrad. Das Theater Samuel Becketts. München, 1967.
43763.45.110 Schwarz-Bart, Simone. La mulâtresse solitude. Paris, 1967.
37555.565.2 Scollen, Christine M. The birth of the elegy in France, 1500-1550. Genève, 1967.
38523.3.100 Screech, Michael A. Marot évangélique. Genève, 1967.
43687.74.820 Segonds, Jean P. L'Enfance bourbonnaise de Valéry Larbaud. Moulins, 1967.
43765.90.120 Sénac, Jean. Citoyens de beauté, poèmes. Rodez, 1967.
43765.80.706 Serge, Victor (pseud.). Memoirs of a revolutionary, 1901-1941. London, 1967.
43765.80.140 Serge, Victor (pseud.). Les révolutionnaires, romans. Paris, 1967.
43761.48.805 Silenieks, Juris. Themes and dramatic forms in the plays of Armand Salacrou. Lincoln, 1967.
43769.54.797 Simenon, Georges. An American omnibus. 1. ed. N.Y., 1967.
43769.54.635 Simenon, Georges. Le chat. Paris, 1967.
43769.54.754 Simenon, Georges. The confessional. London, 1967.
43769.54.455 Simenon, Georges. L'escalier de fer. Paris, 1967.
43769.54.620 Simenon, Georges. Lettre à mon juge, roman. Paris, 1967.
43769.54.768 Simenon, Georges. Maigret and the headless corpse. London, 1967.
43769.54.535 Simenon, Georges. Maigret et le voleur paresseux. Paris, 1967.
43769.54.771 Simenon, Georges. Maigret goes home. Harmondsworth, 1967.
43769.54.12 Simenon, Georges. Oeuvres complètes. Lausanne, 1967. 25v.
43769.54.11 Simenon, Georges. Oeuvres complètes. Lausanne, 1967. 38v.
43769.54.756 Simenon, Georges. The old men dies. 1. ed. N.Y., 1967.
43769.54.630 Simenon, Georges. L'Outlaw. Paris, 1967.
43769.56.2160 Simon, Claude. Histoire. Paris, 1967.
39596.33 Simon, Jean Jacques. Bernardin de St. Pierre ou Le triomphe de Flore. Paris, 1967.
37569.40.202 Simon, P.H. Témoins de l'homme. Paris, 1967.
38568.790.2 Simon, R. Lettres choisies de M. Simon. v.1-4. 2. éd. Frankfurt, 1967.
37562.340 Simone, Franco. Miscellanea di studi e ricerche sul Quattrocento francese. Torono, 1967.
43526.65.975 Simonis, Ferdinand. Die Lyrik Guillaume Apollinaires. Bonn, 1967.
37556.263 Sokolov, Valentin S. Pechat' narodnogo fronta i progressinvnaia frantsuzskaia literature. Leningrad, 1967.
43744.67.1580 Soupault, Robert. Marcel Proust, du côté de la médecine. Paris, 1967.
42576.15.370 Starkie, Enid. Flaubert::the making of the master. London, 1967.
38526.43.10 Staub, Hans. Le curieux désir; Scève et Peletier du Mans. Genève, 1967.
41543.22.175 Stierle, Karlheinz. Dunkelheit und Form in Gerard de Nervals "Chimères". München, 1967.

Chronological Listing

1967 - cont.

37595.106 Stimming, Albert. Lebensbericht. Auslieferung, 1967.
43779.77.1100 Stroheim, Erich von. Les feux de la Saint-Jean. v.1-2. Paris, 1967. 4v.
43756.90.865 Suffran, Michel. Jacques Rivière, ou La conversion à la clarité. Paris, 1967.
43780.50.130 Sulivan, Jean. L'obsession de Delphes. Paris, 1967.
43780.69.715 Supervielle, Jules. Selected writings. N.Y., 1967.
43780.69.720 Supervielle, Jules. Supervielle, Poèmes. Santa Barbara, 1967.
43780.75.100 Surdez, Raymond. Jeunesse, aller et retour. Genève, 1967.
43538.14.920 Tagliaferri, Aldo. Beckett e l'iperdeterminazione letteraria. 1. ed. Milano, 1967.
43761.39.935 Tavernier, René. St. Exupéry en procés. Paris, 1967.
FL 386.277 Temkine, Raymonde. L'entreprise théâtre. Paris, 1967.
38537.56 Tetel, Marcel. Rabelais. N.Y., 1967.
38526.49.10 Théophile de Viau. Théophile en prison et autres pamphlets. Paris, 1967.
38585.16.370 Tilley, Arthur. Three French dramatists: Racine, Marivaux, Musset. N.Y., 1967.
43785.12.100 Tôche, Pierre-Alain. Ventre des fontaines. Lausanne, 1967.
37573.460 Toesca, Maurice. Le chant romantique, anthologie. Paris, 1967.
41596.4.150 Tonge, Frederich. L'art du dialogue dans les comédies en prose d'Alfred de Musset. Paris, 1967.
43744.67.1550 Torres Bodet, Jaime. Tiempo y memoria en la obra de Proust. 1. ed. México, 1967.
43792.94.100 Tournier, Michel. Vendredi ou les Limbes du Pacifique. Paris, 1967.
43554.2.1195 Tricaud, Marie Louise. Le baroque dans le théâtre de Paul Claudel. Genève, 1967.
38525.35.55 Tristan L'Hermite, F. Les vers héroiques. Genève, 1967.
43793.65.100 Trolliet, Gilbert. Avec la rose. Genève, 1967.
39544.372 Trousson, Raymond. Socrate devant Voltaire, Diderot et Rousseau. Paris, 1967.
43793.67.310 Troyat, Henri. Les Eygletière: La malandre; roman. Paris, 1967.
43744.67.1570 Truffaut, Louis. Introduction à Marcel Proust. München, 1967.
38526.52.35 Tyard, Pontus. Les erreurs amoureuses. Genève, 1967.
42576.63.750 Tylden-Wright, David. Anatole France. London, 1967.
43822.50.160 Vailland, Roger. Oeuvres complètes. Lausanne, 1967. 12v.
37568.263 Vaksmakher, Moris N. Frantsuzskaie literatura nashikh dnei. Moskva, 1967.
FL 397.211 Vallon, Claude. Le dossier canadien du théâtre romand. Lausanne, 1967.
43554.2.1220 Varillon, François. Claudel. Paris, 1967.
FL 6049.24 Velde, Isaac Van der. Jean-Jacques Rousseau pedagoog. Amsterdam, 1967.
43823.75.770 Vercel, Roger. En dérive. Levallois-Perret, 1967?
42557.18.24.5 Verlaine, Paul. Les poèmes saturniens. Paris, 1967.
39566.212 Vernière, Paul. Diderot, ses manuscrits et ses copistes. Paris, 1967.
37555.740 Le vers français au 20e siècle, colloque organisé par le centre de philologie...de l'Université de Strasbourg du 3 mai au 6 mai 1966. Paris, 1967.
40587.160.5 Vial, André. Chateaubriand et une dame de Pierreclau. Paris, 1967.
43824.3.1705 Vian, Boris. Die Ameisen; sieben Erzählungen. Berlin, 1967.
43824.3.1200 Vian, Boris. Elles se rendent pas compte. Paris, 1967.
43824.3.1700 Vian, Boris. Froth on the daydream. London, 1967.
43824.3.1710 Vian, Boris. The generals' tea party. N.Y., 1967.
43738.1.945 Vigneault, Robert. L'univers féminin dans l'oeuvre de Charles Péguy. Bruges, 1967.
43824.48.130 Vilallonga, José Luis de. Allegro barbaro. Paris, 1967.
43824.54.135 Vilmorin, Louise de. L'Heure maliciôse. Paris, 1967.
37555.772 Vipper, Iurii B. Formirovanie klassitsizmo vo frantsusskoi poesii nachala XVII veka. Moskva, 1967.
43620.2.476 Vitanović, Slobodan. Andre Žid i francuski klasicizam. Beograd, 1967.
39545.102 Voltaire, François Marie Arouet de. Bog i luedi, stat'i, pamflety, pis'ma. Moskva, 1967. 2v.
39545.86 Voltaire, François Marie Arouet de. Romans et contes de Voltaire. Paris, 1967.
43827.91.1100 Voronca, Ilarie. Poèmes choisis. Paris, 1967.
38575.110 Voss, Harald. Corneille, oder das Werden einer menschlichen Ordnung. Bonn, 1967?
43822.49.1565 Wais, Karin. Studien zu Rilkes Valéry Übertragungen. Tübingen, 1967.
43832.52.100 Walter, Georges. Les enfants d'Attila. Paris, 1967.
43620.2.805 Watson-Williams, Helen. André Gide and the Greek myth. Oxford, 1967.
37596.10.220 Wehrli, Annegret. Semantische Untersuchung der Verben für Begehren, Gewähren, Versprechen, Ubergeben und Verweigern die Chrétien de Troyes. Zürich, 1967.
43833.41.120 Weingarten, Romain. L'été. Paris, 1967.
43656.59.850 Wendt, Ernst. Eugène Ionesco. 1. Aufl. Velber, 1967.
43833.82.100 Westphal, Eric. La Manifestation. Paris, 1967.
37575.792 Weverbergh, Julien. Jij goudgepuute lans. Amsterdam, 1967.
43697.52.910 Wilkinson, David Ormond. Malraux; and essay in political criticism. Cambridge, 1967.
37555.558 Wilson, Dudley Butler. Descriptive poetry in France from Blason to Baroque. N.Y., 1967.
37543.448 Yetkin, S.K. Edebiyatta akimlar. Istanbul, 1967.
43861.77.140 Zermatten, Maurice. La louve, pièce en 5 actes. Bienne, 1967.
43752.57.875.5 Zermatten, Maurice. Ramuz à Lens. Bienne, 1967.
42557.20.330 Zimmermann, Eléonore M. Magies de Verlaine, étude de l'évolution poétique de Paul Verlaine. Paris, 1967.

1968

37595.9.112 Abailard, Pierre. Historia calamitatum. n.p., 1968.
43512.75.250 Achard, Marcel. Gugusse. Paris, 1968.
37596.23.25 Adam (Mystery). Das altfranzösische Adamsspiel. München, 1968.
37596.23.15 Adam (Mystery). Le mystère d'Adam. Paris, 1968.
43526.65.865.5 Adéma, Marcel. Guillaume Apollinaire. Paris, 1968.
43522.25.110 Alexandre, Maxime. Mémoires d'un surréaliste. Paris, 1968.
37596.27.25 Aléxius, Saint. Légend. Das Leben des Heiligen Aléxius. München, 1968.

1968 - cont.

37596.27.15.2 Aléxius, Saint. Légend. La vie de Saint Aléxis. Genève, 1968.
37555.750 Alyn, Marc. La nouvelle poésie française. Les Hautes Plaines de Mane, 1968.
43522.98.130 Alyn, Marc. Nuit majeure. Paris, 1968.
38514.23.125 Anacker, Robert. François Villon. N.Y., 1968.
42542.1.24 Ancey, Georges. Théâtre. Paris, 1968.
43524.18.110 Andreau, Marianne. Carillon du temps perdu. Paris, 1968.
43744.67.1590 Andreev, Leonid G. Marsel' Prust. Moskva, 1968.
43524.19.1100 Andrieu, Jean Marie. Rien qu'un prêtre. Bruxelles, 1968.
43524.67.310 Anouilh, Jean. Eurydice, avec une notice...une analyse méthodique des textes choisis. Paris, 1968.
43526.65.330 Apollinaire, Guillaume. The poet assassinated. 1st ed. N.Y., 1968.
V43526.65.790 Apollinaire, Guillaume. Poezje wybrane. Wyd. 2. Warszawa, 1968.
43527.3.785 Aragon, Louis. Zu Lieben bis Vernunft verbrennt. Berlin, 1968.
43527.3.865 Arban, Dominique. Aragon parle avec Dominique Arban. Paris, 1968.
43528.48.218 Arland, Marcel. La nuit et les sources: Je vous écris. Paris, 1968.
38525.21.40 Armstrong, Elizabeth. Ronsard and the Age of Gold. London, 1968.
43528.89.130 Arnothy, Christine. Aviva; roman. Paris, 1968.
43528.86.11 Artaud, Antonin. Collected works. London, 1968- 3v.
42576.15.400 Asper-Bruggisser, Kathrin. Genèse du déterminisme de Gustave Flaubert. Zurich, 1968.
43775.97.800 Au pays de dure ardenne: Arsène Soreil. Vieux-Virton, 1968.
43531.7.3120 Aubert, Claude. L'unique belladone. [Poèmes]. Lausanne, 1968.
FL 6139.19.4.5 Babbitt, Irving. Rousseau and romanticism. Boston, 1968.
43537.13.1110 Baccio, Jean. Essaims. Rodez, 1968.
38527.30.10 Bailbé, Jacques. Agrippa d'Aubigné, poète des "Tragiques". Caen, 1968.
43537.1.2035 Baissette, Gaston. Isabelle de la garrigue; roman. Paris, 1968.
38537.55.5 Bakhtin, Mikhail M. Rabelais and his world. Cambridge, Mass., 1968.
43757.50.1275 Balakhonov, Viktor E. Romen Rollan i ego vremir. Leningrad, 1968.
40596.7.4.5 Balzac, Honoré de. Oeuvres complètes. Paris, 1968-71. 24v.
Mon 112.21 Baraz, Michaël. L'etre et la connaissance selon Montaigne. Paris, 1968.
39543.802.5 Barr, Mary M.H. Quarante années d'études Voltairiennes...1926-1965. Paris, 1968.
43537.77.6100 Barrault, Jean Louis. Rabelais. Paris, 1968.
41564.55.135 Bartfeld, Fernande. Vigny et la figure de Moïse. Paris, 1968.
43537.82.3130 Bastide, François Régis. La Forêt noire et le Troisième concerto. Paris, 1968.
43538.76.1010 Baude, Francine. Essai critique sur le roman de G. Bernanos, sous le Soleil de Satan. Diss. Lille? 1968?
41522.6.5 Baudelaire, Charles. L'art romantique, littérature et musique. Paris, 1968.
41522.13.27 Baudelaire, Charles. Curiosités esthétiques et autres écrits sur l'art. Paris, 1968.
41522.13.9.60 Baudelaire, Charles. Les fleurs du mal. Paris, 1968.
41522.13.9.18 Baudelaire, Charles. Les fleurs du mal. Paris, 1968-
41522.13.37 Baudelaire, Charles. Petits poèmes en prose. Paris, 1968.
41522.18.590 Baudelaire. Petit Palais. 23 novembre 1968-17 mars 1969. Paris, 1968.
43538.1.550 Beauvoir, Simone de. La femme rompue. L'age de discrétion. Paris, 1968.
43538.13.3110 Beckers, Alain. Les chorals spirituels. Paris, 1968.
43538.14.791 Beckett, Samuel. Cascando, and other short dramatic pieces. N.Y., 1968?
43538.14.250 Beckett, Samuel. Poèmes. Paris, 1968.
43538.100.100 Beer, Hélène. Holyland tours. Bruxelles, 1968.
37556.330 Belozubov, Leonid. L'Europe savante, 1718-20. Paris, 1968.
42576.65.13.165 Belval, Maurice M. Des ténèbres à la lumière. Thèse. Paris, 1968.
43538.101.100 Benacher, Elie. Suite judaïque. Paris, 1968.
43538.59.2120 Benedetto, André. Napalm. Honfleur, 1968.
43538.60.1100 Bénichoo, Aimé. Les Marranes. Paris, 1968.
43538.91.130 Bérimont, Luc. Un feu vivant. Paris, 1968.
43538.75.9110 Bernanos, Michel. The other side of the mountain. Boston, 1968.
43538.76.5130 Bernard, Michel. Les courtisanes. Paris, 1968.
43538.76.5140 Bernard, Michel. La négresse muette. Paris, 1968.
43538.75.1100 Berri, Claude. The two of us. N.Y., 1968.
43538.82.3130 Bessette, Hélène. Le divorce interrompu. Paris, 1968.
43538.83.120 Bésus, Roger. Le Maître, roman. Paris, 1968?
42563.23.200 Bibliothèque Nationale. Léon Bloy. Paris, 1968.
43701.63.940 Blanc, André. Montherlant, un pessimisme heureux. Paris, 1968.
37557.76.40 Blin, Georges. La cribleuse de blé, la critique. Paris, 1968.
39544.378 Bo, Carlo. Voltaire e dopo Voltaire. Milano, 1968.
43697.52.920 Boak, Denis. André Malraux. Oxford, 1968.
43544.17.110 Bodart, Roger. Le tour. Paris, 1968.
37568.165.7 Boisdeffre, P. de. Une histoire vivante de la littérature d'aujourd'hui. 7. éd. Paris, 1968.
43544.60.2700 Bonnefoy, Yves. On the motion and immobility of Douve. Athens, 1968.
43556.1.975 Borgal, Clément. Cocteau, Dieu, La mort, La poésie. Paris, 1968.
41522.3.105 Borneque, Jacques Henry. Paysages extérieurs et monde intérieur dans l'oeuvre de Barbey d'Aurevilly. Caen, 1968.
43761.78.935 Boros, Marie Denise. Un séquestré, l'homme sartrien. Paris, 1968.
43544.89.2220 Bosquet, Alain. Les tigres de papier. Paris, 1968.
39544.396 Bottiglia, William F. Voltaire; a collection of critical essays. Englewood Cliffs, N.J., 1968.
42542.35.30 Bouilhet, Louis. Lettres à Louise Colet. Rouen, 1968?
43544.88.2130 Boulanger, Daniel. La rose et le reflet. Paris, 1968.
43544.90.3100 Bourgeon, Roger. L'archevêgue des favelles. Paris, 1968.
43544.89.140 Bousquet, Joë. Le semé chemins. Limoges, 1968.
43544.105.120 Boyer, François. Jeux interdits. Paris, 1968.
41574.603.5 Brakhman, Sel'ma R. "Otverzhennye" Viktora Giugo. Moskva, 1968.
V38575.28.20 Brandwajn, Rachmiel. Corneille i jego "Cyd". Warszawa, 1968.

1968 - cont.

43545.4.4115 Brasillach, Robert. Le voleur d'étincelles. Paris, 1968.

43545.41.8100 Brideron, Jacques. Deux ans sous les hombes. Fontenay-le-Comte, 1968.

43545.41.9100 Brindeau, Serge. Où va la jour. Paris, 1968.

43545.41.9110 Brindeau, Serge. Poèmes pour quelque temps. Paris, 1968.

43545.41.5140 Brion, Marcel. Les miroirs et les gouffres. Paris, 1968.

43535.54.810 Brodin, Dorothy R. Marcel Aymé. N.Y., 1968.

40583.13.10 Brombert, Victor H. Stendhal: fiction and the themes of freedom. N.Y., 1968.

43556.1.965 Brown, Frederick. An impersonation of angels; a biography of Jean Cocteau. N.Y., 1968.

43823.75.2757 Bruller, Jean. The battle of silence. 1st ed. N.Y., 1968.

38543.22.40 Bruzzi, Amelia. La formazione delle Maximes di La Rochefoucauld attraverso le edizioni originali. Bologna, 1968.

43538.14.940 Büttner, Gottfried. Absurdes Theater und Bewusstseinswandel. Berlin, 1968.

V43761.39.930 Bukowska, Anna. St. Exupéry czyi parakodsy humanizmu. Warszawa, 1968.

38544.27.605 Burkart, Rosemarie. Die Kunst des Masses in Mme. de La Fayette's Princesse de Clèves. Bonn, 1968.

43546.76.130 Burniaux, Constant. D'humour et d'amour (journal d'un homme sensible. Paris, 1968.

43547.82.110 Busselen, Roland. Un quelqu'un. Paris, 1968.

Mon 112.20 Buton, Michel. Essais sur "les Essais". Paris, 1968.

V43550.10.105 Cabriès, Jean. Saint Jacob. Les Hautes Plaines de Mane, 1968.

42556.28.405 Caddau, Pierre. Dans le sillage du capitaine Cook ou Arthur Rimbaud le Tahitien. Paris, 1968.

38557.24.86 Calvet, Jean. Bossuet. Paris, 1968.

43524.67.860 Canaris, Volker. Jean Anouilh. 1. Aufl. Velber, 1968.

43550.74.2110 Caraco, Albert. Post mortem. Lausanne, 1968.

43697.52.945 Carduner, Jean René. La Création romanesque chez Malraux. Paris, 1968.

41522.18.545 Cargo, Robert T. Baudelaire criticism, 1950-1967; a bibliography. University, 1968.

43550.77.2100 Caroutch, Yvonne. Lieux probables; poèmes. Paris, 1968.

43697.88.895 Caspary, Anita-Marie. François Mauriac. St. Louis, 1968.

43550.83.1120 Castillou, Henry. La victorieuse, roman. Paris, 1968.

43554.2.1230 Cattaui, Georges. Claudel, le cycle des Coûfontaine et le mystère d'Israël. Paris, 1968.

43550.89.180 Cau, Jean. Le pape est mort. Paris, 1968.

43550.89.160 Cau, Jean. Le spectre de l'amour. Paris, 1968.

43550.89.170 Cau, Jean. Les yeux crevés. Paris, 1968.

43550.98.705 Cayrol, Jean. Mittag Mitternacht. (Roman. Uebersetzung aus dem Französischen). Olten, 1968.

43551.59.720 Cendrars, Blaise. Moravagine; a novel. London, 1968.

43551.59.13 Cendrars, Blaise. Oeuvres complètes. Paris, 1968-1971. 15v.

43551.61.100 Centa, Fuly di. Le manoir de la recontre. Paris, 1968.

43551.79.140.5 Césaire, Aimé. Return to my native land. Paris, 1968.

43551.80.200 Cesbron, Gilbert. Des enfants aux cheveux gris. Paris, 1968.

43551.80.210 Cesbron, Gilbert. Lettre ouverte à une jeune fille morte. Paris, 1968.

43552.1.1120 Chaamba, Abdallah (pseud.). Une adolescence au temps du Maréchal et de multiples aventures. Paris, 1968.

43552.2.2170 Chabrol, Jean-Pierre. Ma Déchirure, conte dramatique en seize tableaux. Paris, 1968.

42515.38.8 Chadbourne, Richard McClain. Ernest Renan. N.Y., 1968.

43620.2.850 Chadourne, Jacqueline M. André Gide et l'Afrique. Paris, 1968.

43552.3.9137 Chamson, André. Suite cévenole, romans. Paris, 1968.

43697.88.900 Chapon, François. François Mauriac, manuscrits. Paris, 1968.

43552.2.4100 Chapuis-Pampagnin, Daisy. Les résistants de l'ombre. Saint-Christol-les-Alés, 1968.

43552.6.3700 Charles-Roux, Edmonde. To forget Palermo. N.Y., 1968.

43552.5.1230 Chartier, Emile. Salut et fraternité. Paris, 1968.

40586.5.18 Chateaubriand, F.A.R. Voyage en Italie. Paris, 1968.

43552.6.9100 Chateauneu, Roger. Les Myrtes. Paris, 1968.

43552.7.2130 Chazal, Malcolm de. Poèmes. Paris, 1968.

42581.33.125 Chazelet, André. Jules Vallès ou l'Enfant révolté. Riom, 1968.

43552.18.170 Chédid, Andrée. Contre-chant. Paris, 1968.

43757.50.1211 Cheval, René. Romain Rolland's Begegnungen mit Österreich. Innsbruck, 1968.

43552.41.1700 Chirico, Giorgio de. Hebdomeras: a novel. London, 1968.

37596.10.2.30 Chrestien de Troyes. Arthurian romances. London, 1968.

43554.8.40 Clancier, Georges Emmanuel. Le pain noir. Paris, 1968.

43554.2.500 Claudel, Paul. Journal. Paris, 1968- 2v.

43554.5.2140 Clavel, Bernard. L'Espagnol. Paris, 1968.

43554.5.2110 Clavel, Bernard. La grande patience. Paris, 1968. 4v.

43554.5.2150 Clavel, Bernard. Malataverne. Paris, 1968.

43554.5.1040 Clavel, Maurice. Combat de franc-tireur pour une libération. Paris, 1968.

43554.21.110 Clébert, Jean Paul. Le silence, l'exil et la ruse. Paris, 1968.

43556.1.475 Cocteau, Jean. Faire-part. Paris, 1968.

43617.78.825A Coe, Richard Nelson. The vision of Jean Genêt. London, 1968.

43617.78.826 Coe, Richard Nelson. The vision of Jean Genêt. N.Y., 1968.

42577.4.80 Cogny, Pierre. Maupassant, l'homme sans Dieu. Bruxelles, 1968.

43556.37.120 Cohen, Albert. Belle du Seigneur. Paris, 1968.

43620.74.805 Cohen, Robert Carl. Giraudoux. Chicago, 1968.

43554.2.1255 Colliard, Lauro Aimé. Nouvelles recherches historiques sur Paul Claudel. Milano, 1968.

39577.6 Condorcet, Marie Jean Antoine. Oeuvres. Stuttgart, 1968. 12v.

40553.7.40 Congrès Benjamin Constant, Lausanne, 1967. Benjamin Constant. Paris, 1968.

40553.4.80 Constant de Rebecque, Benjamin. Benjamin Constant par lui-même. Paris, 1968.

43550.58.2050 Coombs, Ilona. Camus, homme de théâtre. Paris, 1968.

38574.30 Corneille, Pierre. Théâtre choisi de Corneille. Paris, 1968.

37564.272 Corsaro, Antonio. Astrattismo nella poesia francese del seicento e altri studi. Palermo, 1968.

43556.87.2110 Cotte, Jean Louis. Histoire d'eau, roman. Paris, 1968.

43556.87.2120 Cotte, Jean Louis. Occis soient-ils, roman. Paris, 1968.

38539.100 Crenne, Hilisenne de. Les Angovysses ou Loureuses qui procédént d'amours (1538). Paris, 1968-

FL 6039.19 Crocker, Lester G. Rousseau's Social contract. Cleveland, 1968.

1968 - cont.

FL 6129.68 Crocker, Lester Gilbert. Jean-Jacques Rousseau. N.Y., 1968-

37542.62 Cruickshank, John. French literature and its background. London, 1968- 5v.

43560.87.100 Cuttat, Jean. Frère lai. Lausanne, 1968.

42577.4.85 Danilin, Iurii I. Zhizn' i tvorchestvo Mopassana. Izd. 2. Moskva, 1968.

43565.60.1141 Daninos, Pierre. Le jacassin. Lausanne, 1968.

43565.74.100 Dard, Michel. Les années profondes, roman. Paris, 1968.

43565.81.100 Dasnoy, Albert. La longueur de temps. Bruxelles, 1968.

38525.21.45 Dassonville, Michel. Ronsard. Genève, 1968-

42566.19.8.100 Daudet, Alphonse. Tartarin of Tarascon. London, 1968.

43620.2.411 Davies, John C. Gide: l'immoraliste and la porte etroit. London, 1968.

43565.92.7150 Davray, Jean. Le désert, roman. Paris, 1968.

43566.6.3700 Debray, Régis. The frontier and A with-it young man. London, 1968.

43566.34.100 Degracia. Mariage mixte. Paris, 1968.

FL 396.39 Deierkauf-Holsboer, Sophie Wilma. Le théâtre de l'hôtel de Bourgogne. Paris, 1968-70. 2v.

43566.42.1100 Dejacques, Claude. A toi l'angoisse, à moi la rage, mai 68, les fresques de Nanterre. Paris, 1968.

43566.45.1100 Delaet, Jean. La petit herboriste. Bruxelles, 1968.

43566.50.4130 Della Faille, Pierre. Mise à feu, 04 le Jas du Revest Saint-Martin. Morel, 1968.

37556.262 Deloffre, Frédéric. La nouvelle en France à l'âge classique. Paris, 1968.

41542.4.105 Delvaille, Bernard. Théophile Gautier. Paris, 1968.

38514.23.150 Demarolle, Pierre. L'esprit de Villon, étude de style. Paris, 1968.

43566.76.4100 Deriex, Suzanne. L'enfant et la mort. Roman. Lausanne, 1968.

43566.81.4142 Desnos, Robert. Corps et biens. Paris, 1968.

43566.82.7745 Destouches, Louis Ferdinand. Castle to castle. N.Y., 1968.

42514.28.245 Detaille, Albert. Maurras en Provence. Marseille, 1968.

43568.6.140 Dib, Mohammed. La danse du roi, roman. Paris, 1968.

39564.8.23 Diderot, Denis. Oeuvres esthétiques de Diderot. Paris, 1968.

39564.4.10 Diderot, Denis. Oeuvres romanesques de Denis Diderot. Paris, 1968-69. 2v.

37569.403 Dimić, Ivan. La crise psychologique dans le roman français du 20e siècle. Thèse. Belgrade, 1968.

41596.37.55 Dolder, Charlotte. Le thème de l'être et du paraître dans l'itinéraire spirituel d'Alfred de Musset. Zürich, 1968.

41578.170 Domange, Michel. Le Petit monde de Lamartine. Evian, 1968.

43574.65.1100 Droit, Michel. L'écorché. Paris, 1968.

V43574.70.130 Drouet, Minou. La flamme rousse. Paris, 1968.

43574.75.140 Druon, Maurice. La fin des hommes. Lausanne, 1968-69. 3v.

43576.9.2130 Du Bouchet, André. Où le soleil. Paris, 1968.

43576.12.1110 Ducharme, Réjean. L'océantume. Paris, 1968.

38546.33.45 Duchêne, Roger. Mme. de Sévigné. Paris, 1968.

38526.80 Du Guillet, Pernette. Rymes. Genève, 1968.

42554.29.155.5 Dujardin, E. Les lauriers sant coupés. Saint Amand, 1968.

43576.50.100 Dulière, William L. Notes d'archéologie future. Louvain, 1968.

41538.16.20 Dumas, Alexandre. Le comte de Monte Cristo. Paris, 1968. 2v.

37568.268 Engler, Winfried. Französische Literatur im 20. Jahrhundert. Bern, 1968.

43822.49.1575 Entretiens sur Paul Valéry. Paris, 1968.

43598.82.2120 Escarpit, Robert. Paramémoires d'un gaulois. Paris, 1968.

43554.2.1210 Espiau de la Maëstre, André. Das göttliche Abenteuer. Salzburg, 1968.

43598.82.230 Estang, Luc. L'apostat. Paris, 1968.

37556.17.10 Estivals, Robert. L'avant-garde; étude historique et sociologique des publications périodiques ayant pour titre l'avangarde. Paris, 1968.

43599.38.100 Ęthier-Blais, Jean. Mater Europa. Paris, 1968.

42556.28.145.30 Etiemble, René. Le sonnet des voyelles de Rimbaud. Paris, 1968.

43604.19.140 Eydoux, Emmanuel. La mort d'un poète. Paris, 1968.

43606.10.160 Fabre-Luce, Alfred. Le général en Sorbonne. Paris, 1968.

40597.2.780 Faillie, Marie-Henriette. La femme et le Code civil dans La comédie humaine d'Honoré de Balzac. Paris, 1968.

40597.2.790 Fargeaud, Madeleine. Balzac et la Recherche de l'absolu. Paris, 1968.

37569.424 Fassbinder, Klara M. Der Versunkene Garten. Heidelberg, 1968.

43607.77.3021 Ferrare, Henri. Henry Ferrare, un ami de Max Jacob. Genève, 1968.

43607.77.2110 Ferron, Jacques. Contes. Montréal, 1968.

43697.77.890 Filipowska, Irena. Le tragique de l'individu dans les romans de Roger Martin du Gard. Poznan, 1968.

FL 398.49.40 Finkel'shtein, Elena L. Frederik-Lemetr. Leningrad, 1968.

41568.15.15 Fischler, Anita. Sensation ou raison, plaisir ou bonheur dans l'oeuvre d'Étienne Pivert de Sénancour. Thèse. Zürich, 1968.

43550.58.2037 Fitch, Brian T. Narrateur et narration dans L'étranger d'Albert Camus. 2. éd. Paris, 1968.

42576.35.38 Flaubert, Gustave. La correspondance de Flaubert. Columbus, 1968.

42576.28.102 Flaubert, Gustave. Madame Bovary. Paris, 1968.

42576.29 Flaubert, Gustave. Poésies de jeunesse inédites. Columbia, S.C., 1968.

42576.23.6.10 Flaubert, Gustave. La tentation de Saint-Antoine. Paris, 1968.

42576.15.375 Fletcher, John. A critical commentary on Flaubert's "Trois contes". London, 1968.

37557.76.20 Fowlie, Wallace. The French critic, 1549-1967. Carbondale, 1968.

43612.3.1110 Fraigneau, André. Le livre de raison d'un roi fou. Paris, 1968.

42576.62.2.7 France, Anatole. Balthasar. Thaïs. L'étude de nacre. Levallois-Perret, 1968.

42576.62.30.7 France, Anatole. Les désirs de Jean Servien. Levallois-Perret, 1968.

42576.62.118 France, Anatole. Lettres inédites d'Anatole France à Paul-Louis Couchoud et à sa femme. Paris, 1968.

42576.62.10.9 France, Anatole. Le lys rouge. Le jardin d'épicure. Levallois-Perret, 1968.

42576.62.12.2 France, Anatole. Le puits de Sainte Claire. Levallois-Perret, 1968.

Chronological Listing

1968 - cont.

42576.62.6.15 France, Anatole. La rôtisserie de la reine Pédauque. Levallois-Perret, 1968.
43612.4.1110 Francillon, Clarisse. Le carnet à lucarnes; roman. Paris, 1968.
43612.4.1120 Francillon, Clarisse. Vingt-neuf contes. Honfleur, 1968.
43619.23.815 Francis, Jean. L'eternal aujourd'hui de Michel de Ghelderode. Bruxelles, 1968.
43612.3.2100 Frank, Nino. Mémoire brisée. Paris, 1968. 2v.
43612.63.6110 Freminville, René Marie de la Poix de. Cet étrange Christophe Colomb. Paris, 1968.
43612.63.6140 Freminville, René Marie de la Poix de. Nuit et lumière de la mer; roman. Paris, 1968.
43612.23.140 Frénaud, André. La sainte face; poèmes. Paris, 1968.
37563.112 The French renaissance and its heritage: essays presented to Alan M. Boase by colleagues, pupils and friends. London, 1968.
43612.25.110 Freustié, Jean. Le droit d'aînesse. Paris, 1968.
Htn Mon 116.45.5* Friedrich, Hugo. Montaigne. Paris, 1968.
39534.20.15 Furetière, Antoine. Le Roman bourgeois. Paris, 1968.
43616.58.130 Gandon, Yves. Monsieur Miracle; roman. Paris, 1968.
43616.60.130 Ganne, Gilbert. Un fils unique; roman. Paris, 1968.
43616.76.1100 Garnier, Pierre. Perpetuum mobile. Paris, 1968.
43616.78.750 Gary, Romain. The dance of Genghis Cohn. N.Y., 1968.
43616.88.120 Gatti, Armand. La naissance. Paris, 1968.
43616.88.130 Gatti, Armand. La passion du général Franco. Paris, 1968.
43616.90.120 Gaucheron, Jacques H. Cahier grec, hommage à Ritsos. Paris, 1968.
43616.1.8110 Gautier, Jean Jacques. Une femme prisonnière. Paris, 1968.
43616.98.1120 Gay-Lussac, Bruno. L'ami. Paris, 1968.
43617.59.250 Genevoix, Maurice. Jardins sans murs, roman. Paris, 1968.
43545.4.4825 George, Bernard. Robert Brasillach. Paris, 1968.
43618.90.130 Gevers, Marie. Paravérités. Bruxelles, 1968.
39544.390 Giacomelli Deslex, Marcella. L'aggettivazione nei "contes" di Voltaire da Zadig a Candide. Torino, 1968.
43620.2.79.205 Gide, André. Correspondance. Paris, 1968. 2v.
43620.2.79.210 Gide, André. The notebooks of André Walter. N.Y., 1968.
43620.2.35.20 Gide, André. La symphonie pastorale. Paris, 1968.
40517.31.45 Ginguené, Pierre Louis. P.L. Ginguené journaliste et critique littéraire. Torino, 1968.
43620.66.490 Giono, Jean. Ennemonde et autres caractères. Paris, 1968.
43620.74.42.2 Giraudoux, Jean. Giraudoux par lui-même. Paris, 1968.
43620.74.1170 Giraudoux, Jean Pierre. Théâtre d'arrière-garde. Belle. Paris, 1968.
40536.24.10 Girdlestone, Cuthbert Morton. Louis François Ramond, 1755-1827. Paris, 1968.
37563.116 Giudici, Enzo. Spiritualismo e carnascialismo. Napoli, 1968.
43544.81.2815 Godin, Jean. Henri Bosco. Montréal, 1968.
43625.82.100 Gosset, René Pierre. Du Glizzard sur les magnolias. Paris, 1968.
43625.89.5100 Goustine, Luc de. Dix mai 1968, manifestation théâtrale en trois points et un schéma. Paris, 1968.
41574.612 Grant, Richard Bobson. The perilous quest. Durham, 1968.
43626.23.1140 Grenier, Jean. La vie quotietienne. Paris, 1968.
40587.232 Grevlund, Merete. Paysage intérieur et paysage extérieur dans les Mémoires d'outre-tombe. Paris, 1968.
43554.2.1225 Griffiths, Richard. Claudel. London, 1968.
FL 6119.68 Grimsley, Ronald. Rousseau and the religious quest. Oxford 1968.
38527.110 Gross-Kiefer, Esther. Le dynamisme cosmique chez Le Moyne. Thèse. Zurich, 1968.
43626.67.700 Groult, Benoîte. Feminine plural. London, 1968.
43822.49.1570 Grubbs, Henry Alexander. Paul Valéry. N.Y., 1968.
37548.230 Gsteiger, Manfred. Westwind. Bern, 1968.
43628.23.200 Guéhenno, Jean. La mort des autres. Paris, 1968.
38585.72 Guibert, Albert Jean. Bibliographie des oeuvres de Jean Racine publiées au XVIIIe siècle. Paris, 1968.
43628.42.4100 Guillao, Raymond. Prisons nègres pour l'Africain. Honfleur, 1968.
41543.4.32 Guillaume, Jean. Gérard de Nerval: Pandora. Namur, 1968.
41543.18.20 Guillaume, Jean. Gérard de Nerval: Pandora. Namur, 1968.
43554.2.1295 Guillemin, Henri. Le "Converti" Paul Claudel. Paris, 1968.
43628.41.3700 Guillevic, Eugène. Guillevic. Poems. Santa Barbara, 1968.
38514.23.135 Guiraud, Pierre. Le Jargon de Villon, ou le Gai savoir de la Coquille. Paris, 1968.
43628.85.61 Guth, Paul. Lettre ouverte aux idoles. Paris, 1968.
37543.595 Guyot, Charly. De Rousseau à Marcel Proust. Neuchâtel, 1968.
43752.57.930 Haggis, Donald R. C.F. Ramuz, ouvrier du langage. Paris, 1968.
43528.86.820 Hahn, Otto. Portrait d'Antonin Artaud. Paris, 1968.
43631.41.2110 Haïk, Farjallah. De chair et d'ésprit. Paris, 1968.
43631.49.2120 Haldas, Georges. Sans feu ni lieu. Lausanne, 1968.
43631.58.100 Handache, Gilbert. L'oeil de Cao Daï, roman. Paris, 1968.
43628.1.535 Harding, James. Sacha Guitry: the last boulevardier. London, 1968.
43538.14.905 Harrison, Robert. Samuel Beckett's Murphy: a critical excursion. Athens, 1968.
43631.85.100 Hatem, Amouar. Bétyles. Bienne, 1968.
43538.14.895 Hayman, Ronald. Samuel Beckett. London, 1968.
43632.50.260 Hellens, Franz. Essais de critique intuitive. Bruxelles, 1968.
43632.3.27 Hémon, Louis. Lettres à sa famille. Montréal, 1968.
43538.14.930 Hensel, Georg. Samuel Beckett. 1. Aufl. Velber, 1968.
43632.75.100 Herbart, Pierre. Souvenirs imaginaires, suivis de la nuit. Paris, 1968.
43632.74.100 Hercourt, Jean. Matière friable. Lausanne, 1968.
43632.77.5100 Herpe, François. Aux tentures du temps. Saint-Brieuc, 1968.
40534.16.24 Herrmann, Michael. Das Gesellschaftstheater des Louis Carrogis de Carmontelle. Meisenheim, 1968.
43620.2.820 Holdheim, William Wolfgang. Theory and practice of the novel. A study on André Gide. Genève, 1968.
43636.90.100 Hoveyda, Fereydoun. Le Losange. Paris, 1968.
43550.58.1085 Hoy, Peter. Camus in English. Wymondham, 1968.
43554.2.1215 Hubert, Marie Clotilde. Paul Claudel 1868-1955. Paris, 1968.
43638.8.100 Hubin, Christian. Le chant décapité la nuit. Bruxelles, 1968.
41574.507 Hugo, Adèle. Le journal d'Adèle Hugo. Paris, 1968- 2v.
41573.39.26 Hugo, Victor. La Belgique selon Victor Hugo. Bruxelles, 1968.

1968 - cont.

37542.60 Humanisme actif; mélanges d'art et de littérature offerts à Julien Cain. Paris, 1968. 2v.
FL 386.817 Iakimovich, Tat'iana Konstantinovna. Dramaturgiia i teatr sovremennoi Frantsii. Kiev, 1968.
43656.59.641 Ionesco, Eugène. Fragments of a journal. N.Y., 1968.
43656.59.190 Ionesco, Eugène. Présent passé, passé présent. Paris, 1968.
43656.59.720 Ionesco, Eugène. A stroll in the air. N.Y., 1968.
43538.1.840 Jaccard, Annie Claire. Simone de Beauvoir. Zurich, 1968.
37555.746 Jaccottet, Philippe. L'entretien des muses, chroniques de poésie. Paris, 1968.
43656.59.840 Jacobsen, Josephine. Ionesco and Genêt. 1. ed. N.Y., 1968.
37555.513 Janik, Dieter. Geschichte der Ode und der "Stances" von Ronsard bis Boileau. Bad Homburg, 1968.
43667.61.110 Jans, Adrien. Ivoiriennes. Paris, 1968.
43667.62.100 Janvier, Ludovic. La Balgneuse. Paris, 1968.
43667.78.705 Jarry, Alfred. The Ubu plays. London, 1968.
43591.89.845 Jean, Raymond. Paul Éluard par lui-même. Paris, 1968.
43668.4.2120 Jean, Raymond. La vive. Paris, 1968.
42536.42 Jeune, Simon. Poésie et système, Taine interprète de la Fontaine. Paris, 1968.
43701.63.930 Johnson, Robert Brown. Henry de Montherlant. N.Y., 1968.
37555.175.1 Jones, Percy Mansell. The background of modern French poetry. Cambridge, 1968.
43550.58.2025 Jonesco, Tony. Un homme, Camus et le destin. Paris, 1968.
FL 379.70 Joudoin, Eleanor Frances. Dramatic theory and practice in France, 1690-1808. N.Y., 1968.
43670.92.110 Jouffroy, Alain. Trajectoire, récit recitatif. Paris, 1968.
41522.18.555 Journées Baudelaire, Namur and Brussels, 1967. Journées Baudelaire. Actes du Colloque. Bruxelles, 1968.
43670.94.621 Jouve, Pierre Jean. An idiom of night: poems. London, 1968.
43697.52.925 Juilland, Ileana. Dictionnaire des idées dans l'oeuvre de André Malraux. The Hague, 1968.
37566.170 Juin, Hubert. Les incertitudes du réel. Bruxelles, 1968.
37565.182 Juin, Hubert. Les Libertinages de la raison. Paris, 1968.
43671.41.130 Juin, Hubert. Les trois cousines, roman. Paris, 1968.
43671.51.120 Jullian, Philippe. La fuite en Egypte. Paris, 1968.
42555.60.81 Jullian, Philippe. Prince of aesthetes: Count Robert de Montesquiou, 1855-1921. N.Y., 1968.
43671.61.1100 Junod, Roger Louis. Une ombre éblouissante; roman. Lausanne, 1968.
43538.76.815 Jurt, Joseph. Les attitudes politiques de Georges Bernanos jusqu'en 1931. Fribourg, 1968.
43550.58.1110 Kampits, Peter. Der Mythos vom Menschen. Salzburg, 1968.
43672.58.1100 Kancer, Serge. Les enfants de la colère. (Les loups dans la ville). Paris, 1968.
V40597.2.770 Karczewska-Markiewicz, Zofia. Ojciec Goriot Honoriusza Balzaka. Warszawa, 1968.
43673.84.100 Kateha, Vahé. La mort d'un juif. Paris, 1968.
37557.84 Kempf, Roger. Sur le corps romanesque. Paris, 1968.
43538.14.810.5 Kenner, Hugh. Samuel Beckett, a critical study. Berkeley, 1968.
43673.77.2120 Kerraoul, Bernard de. La carapace. Paris, 1968.
43673.83.295 Kessel, Joseph. Les amants du tage; roman. Paris, 1968.
43673.83.740 Kessel, Joseph. The horsemen. N.Y., 1968.
43556.49.900 Ketchum, Anne A. Colette; ou La naissance du jour. Paris, 1968.
43674.5.120 Khayr al-Din, Muhammad. Corps négatif, suivi de: Histoire d'un bon Dieu. Paris, 1968.
43674.67.100 Khoury, Venus. Terres stagnantes. Paris, 1968.
43744.67.1575 King, Adele. Proust. Edinburgh, 1968.
43617.78.840 Knapp, Bettina. Jean Genêt. N.Y., 1968.
37569.40.220 Kovač, Bohuslav. Alchýmia zázračného. 1. vyd. Bratislava, 1968.
V43550.58.1090 Kowalska, Amela. Dzuma Alberto Camusa. 1. wyd. Warszawa, 1968.
43680.92.120 Kowalski, Roger. Sommeils. Paris, 1968.
42584.25.390 Kranowski, Nathan. Paris dans les romans d'Emile Zola. Paris, 1968.
43620.2.810 Labuda, Alberta. Les thèmes de l'adolescence dans l'oeuvre d'André Gide. Poznán, 1968-69. 2v.
41595.2.15 Lacenaire, Pierre François. Memoire de Lacenaire. Paris, 1968.
Mon 122.10 LaCharité, Raymond C. The concept of judgment in Montaigne. The Hague, 1968.
38521.30.1 Lachèvre, Frédéric. Le procès du poète Thèophile de Viau. Genève, 1968. 2v.
FL 1048.177.102 Lacuve, Édouard. Fables en patois poitevin. 2. éd. Melle, 1968.
43687.50.1100 Lallement, Marcel. Une Famille Lorraine. Paris, 1968.
FL 366.36 Lang, Jack. L'état et le théâtre. Paris, 1968.
43687.65.130 Lanza del Vasto, Joseph Jean. Judas. Paris, 1968.
43687.62.3130 Lanzmann, Jacques. Les vangauguin, roman. Paris, 1968.
43687.74.230 Larbaud, Valéry. Beauté, mon beau souci. Paris, 1968.
38526.27.5.65 La Taille, Jean de. Saül le furieux, la famine, ou les gabéonites. Paris, 1968.
43687.89.2220 La Varende, Jean de. Dans le goût espagnol, suite romanesque. Paris, 1968.
37557.76.30A Lawall, Sarah N. Critics of consciousness. Cambridge, 1968.
43688.5.5065 Léautaud, Paul. Correspondance, 1912-1955. Paris, 1968.
43688.13.3110 Le Clec'h, Guy. Les jours de notre vie. Paris, 1968-
43688.14.4705 Le Clézio, Jean Marie Gustave. The flood. 1st American ed. N.Y., 1968.
43688.14.2100 Le Cog, Gabriel. Le Pastour au dur vitrail. Saint-Brieuc, 1968.
42555.36.22 Leconte de Lisle, C.M.R. La dernière illusion de Laconte de Lisle. Genève, 1968.
43688.20.140 Leduc, Violette. Thérèse et Isabelle. Paris, 1968.
37567.111.22 Lehmann, Andrew G. The symbolist aesthetic in France. 2. ed. Oxford, 1968.
43697.89.831 Lemâitre, George Édouard. Maurois, the writer and his work. N.Y., 1968.
43688.53.2100 Le Marois, Jean. La dernière nuit d'André Chémier. Genève, 1968.
43688.70.1100 L'Eplattenier, Gérald. La Colére d'Achille; poèmes. Genève, 1968.
43688.71.100 LePorrier, Herbert. La Demoiselle de Chartres. Paris, 1968.
43688.98.140 LeQuintrec, Charles. Le chemin noir, roman. Paris, 1968.
43690.33.100 Ligi, Isaac. Dans la peau d'un juif, récit. Aulnay-sous Bois, 1968.

1968 - cont.

43744.67.1630 Lins, Alvaro. A tecnica do romance em Marcel Proust. 3. ed. Rio de Janeiro, 1968.

43690.61.140 Linze, Jacques Gérard. La fabulation. Paris, 1968.

37542.68 Littérature française. v.1-2,6-8. Paris, 1968- 5v.

38525.6.5.5 Lockert, Lacy. More plays by rivals of Corneille and Racine. Nashville, 1968.

43693.18.700 Lodi, Maria. Charlotte Morel. London, 1968- 3v.

43611.5.195 Loize, Jean. Alain-Fournier, sa vie et le grand meaulnes. Paris, 1968.

40536.24.30 Lourdes. Musée Pyrénéen. Bibliothèque. Catalogue des ouvrages constituant la bibliothèque de Louis-François-Elisabeth Ramond, 1755-1827. Lourdes, 1968.

39594.19.120 Loy, John Robert. Montesquieu. N.Y., 1968.

43550.58.815.5 Luppé, Robert de. Albert Camus. 1. American ed. N.Y., 1968.

43694.97.100 Luxereau, François. Milieu du gué, suivi de Poèmes pour le Viet Nam. Honfleur, 1968.

FL 6039.18 McManners, John. The social contract and Rousseau's revolt against society. London, 1968.

43697.14.2100 Macouba, Auguste (pseud.). Eïa! Man-maïlle là! Honfleur, 1968.

40583.364 McWatters, K.G. Stendhal, lecteur des romanciers anglais. Lausanne, 1968.

43554.2.1265 Madaule, Jacques. Claudel et le langage. Bruges, 1968.

43556.1.970 Magnam, Jean Marie. Cocteau. Paris, 1968.

38527.61.9 Magny, Olivier de. Les gayetez (Recueil de poésie). Genève, 1968.

43761.39.950 Major, Jean Louis. Saint-Exupéry, l'écriture et la pensée. Ottawa, 1968.

38523.30.40 Malherbe, François de. Oeuvres poétiques. Paris, 1968. 2v.

43697.2.1115 Mallet-Joris, Françoise (pseud.). L'empire céleste. Paris, 1968.

43697.2.1190 Mallet-Joris, Françoise (pseud.). Trois âges de la nuit. Paris, 1968.

43697.52.45 Malraux, André. Anti-memoirs. N.Y., 1968.

43697.74.3190 Marceau, Félicien. Les Années courtes. Paris, 1968.

43697.74.8110 Marill, Francine. L'été finit en Israël, roman. Paris, 1968.

43697.76.6021 Maritain, Raïssa. Poèmes et essais. Paris, 1968.

40535.27.35 Marivaux, Pierre Carlet de Chamblain de. Théâtre complet. Paris, 1968. 2v.

42555.45.30 Marmier, Xavier. Journal, 1848-1890. Genève, 1968. 2v.

40516.60.140 Le Marquis de Sade. Paris, 1968.

43697.80.2100 Marti, Sandra. Le choix, roman. Paris, 1968.

40587.175 Martin-Chauffer, Louis. Chateaubriand. Paris, 1968.

FL 6139.68 Masters, Roger Davis. The political philosophy of Rousseau. Princeton, 1968.

43538.14.1005 Materialien zu Becketts "Endspiel". Frankfurt, 1968.

37557.76.55 Mattauch, Hans. Die literarische Kritik der frühen französischenZeitschriften, 1665-1748. 1. Aufl. München, 1968.

43697.86.2130 Maulnier, Thierry. La Défaite d'Annibal, suivi de la Ville au fond de la mer. Paris, 1968.

43697.88.3150 Mauriac, Claude. Théâtre: La Conversation. Ici, maintenant. Le Cirque. Les Parisiens du dimanche. Le Hun. Paris, 1968.

43697.88.767 Mauriac, François. Five novels. London, 1968[1969]

43697.88.730.5 Mauriac, François. The inner presence. Indianapolis, 1968.

43697.89.709 Maurois, André. Illusions. N.Y., 1968.

43697.89.580 Maurois, André. Les illusions. Paris, 1968.

42555.44.105.2 Mauron, Charles. Introdution à la psychanalyse de Mallarmé. 2e éd. Neuchâtel, 1968.

38585.43.24 Mauron, Charles. Phèdre. Paris, 1968.

37564.282 Mazon, Jeanne (Roche). Autour des contes de fées. Paris, 1968.

37563.122 Ménager, Daniel. Introduction à la vie littéraire du XVIe siècle. Paris, 1968.

43744.67.1615 Mendelson, David. Le verre et les objets de verre dans l'univers imaginaire de Marcel Proust. Paris, 1968.

43554.2.1240 Mercier-Campiche, Marianne. Le Théâtre de Claudel, ou la Puissance du grief et de la passion. Paris, 1968.

43698.200.711 Michaux, Henri. Selected writings; the space within. N.Y., 1968?

43699.13.130 Michel, Georges. L'agression. Paris, 1968.

43699.13.120 Michel, Georges. Les brevos. Paris, 1968.

43701.18.100 Modiano, Patrick. La place de l'étoilé. Paris, 1968.

Mol 19.68 Molière, Jean Baptiste Poquelin. Oeuvres complètes. Paris, 1968- 10v.

43701.59.2100 Monési, Irène. Une tragédie superflue, roman. Paris, 1968.

43701.59.170 Monfreid, Henri de. Abdi, enfant sauvage. Paris, 1968.

37567.670 Monglond, André. Pélerinages romantiques. Paris, 1968.

43701.60.1100 Monnier, Philippe. Mon village. Lausanne, 1968.

43701.63.120.70 Montherlant, Henry de. The girls. London, 1968. 2v.

38525.110 Morel, Jacques. Jean Rotrou, dramaturge de l'ambigüté. Paris, 1968.

43744.67.1610 Mouton, Jean. Proust. Paris, 1968.

43620.2.875 Moutote, Daniel. Le "Journal" de Gide et les problèmes du moi, 1889-1925. Paris, 1968.

38526.51.85 Müller, Gerhard. Untersuchung des poetischen Stils Théophiles de Viau. München, 1968.

42577.32.22 Murger, Henry. Scènes de la vie de Bohème. Grenoble, 1968. 2v.

41596.37.5 Musset, Alfred de. O castiçal, e dois provérbios. Pôrto Alegre, 1968.

41596.8.22 Musset, Alfred de. La confession d'un enfant du siècle. Paris, 1968.

37555.744 Le mysticisme dans la poésie française contemporaine. Anthologie. Tournai, 1968.

43822.49.1580 Nadal, André. Abeille spirituelle. Poème. Nîmes, 1968.

43705.41.100 Nailly, Charles. Péristyle (de la sincérité). Nogent-le-Rotrou, 1968.

43705.89.100 Naudin, Pierre. Les dernières foulées. Lausanne, 1968.

43744.67.1595 Newman, Pauline. Dictionnaire des idees dans l'oeuvre de Marcel Proust. The Hague, 1968.

37544.145 Newman, Pauline. Hélène de Sparte; la fortune du mythe en France. Paris, 1968.

42556.28.397 Nicoletti, Gianni. Rimbaud; una poesia del canto chiuso. 2. ed. Bari, 1968.

42584.25.385 Niess, Robert. Zola, Cézanne and Manet. Ann Arbor, 1968.

40532.59 Niklaus, Robert. Beaumarchais: Le barbier de Séville. London, 1968.

43707.3.150 Nimier, Roger. L'étrangère. Paris, 1968.

1968 - cont.

43709.23.3100 Noël, Denise. Pour un nouvel été. Paris, 1968.

43709.75.1110 Norge, G. Le vin profond. Paris, 1968.

43709.80.160 Nourissier, François. Le maître de maison. Paris, 1968.

37564.269 Oblomievskii, Dmitrii D. Frantsuzskii klassitsizm. Moskva, 1968.

43714.75.44 Obret, Muriel. D'une enfance. Port-Louis, 1968.

43723.18.141 Oldenbourg, Zoé. Argile et cendres. Paris, 1968.

43728.54.100 Ormesson, Jean d'. Les illusions de la mer. Paris, 1968.

38526.10.8.23 Ortali, Raymond. Un poète de la mort: Jean Baptiste Chassignet. Genève, 1968.

43550.98.800 Oster, Daniel. Jean Cayrol et son oeuvre. Paris, 1968.

37569.410 Pabst, Walter. Der moderne französische Roman. Berlin, 1968.

41555.36.10 Paevska, Anastasia V. Prosper Merime; bibliografiia. Moskva, 1968.

43620.2.270.5 Painter, G.D. André Gide. London, 1968.

43780.5.830 Paris. Musée Bourdelle. André Suarès, 1868-1948, 2 nov. - 2 dec., 1968. Paris, 1968.

43737.77.140 Parmelin, Hélène. Le diplodocus. Paris, 1968.

43737.77.130 Parmelin, Hélène. La femme-crocodile. Paris, 1968.

38526.46.400 Passerat, Jean. Les poésies françaises. Genève, 1968. 2v.

43554.2.1235 Paul Claudel, 1868-1968. Paris, 1968.

43737.89.4100 Paulus, Jean Olivier. Eläinih. 1. ed. Schlossberg, Belgium, 1968.

42555.44.220 Paxton, Norman. The development of Mallarmé's prose style. Genève, 1968.

43737.98.1150 Paysan, Catherine. Le nègre de Sables, roman. Paris, 1968.

43738.77.1100 Pérol, Jean. Le coeur véhément. Paris, 1968.

43757.50.1290 Pérus, Jean. Romain Rolland et Maxime Gorki. Paris, 1968.

43757.50.1285 Pesis, Boris A. Ot XIX k XX veka. Moskva, 1968.

43738.85.1110 Petit, Henri. La route des hommes. Paris, 1968.

43761.78.925 Peyre, Henri. Jean-Paul Sartre. N.Y., 1968.

43738.97.1220 Peyrefitte, Roger. Les américains, roman. Paris, 1968.

41595.55.80 Philippon, Albert. Les albums de Sophie-Aimée-Arménide de Montlivault. Tours, 1968.

43741.12.120 Picasso, Pablo. Les quatre petites filles, pièce en 6 actes. Paris, 1968.

43741.14.110 Picon, Gaëtan. Un champ de solitude. Paris, 1968.

43741.25.270 Pieyre de Mandiargues, André. Le marronnier. Paris, 1968.

37565.158 Pizzorusso, Arnaldo. Teorie letterarie in Francia. Pisa, 1968.

41522.18.615 Planche, Henry. La recherche de Baudelaire. Aix-les-Bains, 1968.

37575.215 La poésie contemporaine. Bruxelles, 1968.

37556.300 Pollmann, Leo. Der neue Roman in Frankreich und Lateinamerika. Stuttgart, 1968.

41522.13.9.61 Pommier, Jean. Autour de l'édition originale des Fleurs du mal. Genève, 1968.

43743.62.2130 Pons, Maurice. La passion de Sébastien N. Paris, 1968.

43522.7.2800 Pons, Max. Connaissance de Pierre Albert-Birot, témoignages, hommages, études, notes. Saint-Fronf-sur-Lémance, 1968.

43743.61.1110 Ponthier, François. Poigne-en-croce. Paris, 1968-69. 3v.

40539.15.35 Potocki, Jan. El manuscrito hallado en Zaragoza. Barcelona, 1968.

40539.15.40 Potocki, Jan. Rukopis', naidennaia v Saragose. Moskva, 1968.

43744.25.7100 Prévot-Leygonie, Augustin. Mademoiselle de la Talheyrie. Paris, 1968.

43761.78.930 Prince, Gérald Joseph. Métaphysique et technique dans l'oeuvre romanesque de Sartre. Genève, 1968.

43697.75.822 Prini, Pietro. Gabriel Marcel e la metodologia dell'inverificabile. Roma, 1968.

43656.59.806 Pronko, Leonard C. Eugène Ionesco. N.Y., 1968.

FL 386.816 Proskurnikovg, T.B. Frantsuzskaia antidrama. Moskva, 1968.

43744.67.4100 Prou, Suzanne. L'été jaune, roman. Paris, 1968.

43744.67.36 Proust, Marcel. Textes retrouvés. Urbana, 1968.

40532.60 Pugh, Anthony Roy. A critical commentary on Beaumarchais's Le mariage de Figaro. London, 1968.

41564.55.130 Quebedeau, Denise Bonhomme. Le collier theosophique d'Alfred de Vigny. Silverton, 1968.

43750.24.340 Queneau, Raymond. Battre la campagne. Paris, 1968.

43750.24.350 Queneau, Raymond. Le Vol d'Icare. Paris, 1968.

38585.23.48 Racine, Jean. Bajazet. London, 1968.

43752.38.1110 Rahnéma, Férydoun. Chant de délivrance. Honfleur, 1968.

43546.87.95 Raillard, Georges. Butor. Paris, 1968.

43752.57.715 Ramuz, Charles Ferdinand. Terror on the mountain. 1. ed. N.Y., 1968.

43659.88.800 Raydon, Édouard. Panaït Istrati, vagabond de genie. Paris, 1968.

43769.54.815 Raymond, John. Simenon in court. London, 1968.

43552.5.1860 Reboul, Olivier. L'homme et ses passions d'après Alain. Thèse. Paris, 1968.

43753.17.100 Réda, Jacques. Amen. Paris, 1968.

43538.14.915 Reid, Alec. All I can manage, more than I could. Dublin, 1968.

40583.362 Reizov, Boris G. Stendal'. Leningrad, 1968.

43753.90.201 Reverdy, P. La peau de l'homme. Paris, 1968.

37566.165 Reyes, Salvador. Peregrinajes literarios en Francia. Santiago de Chile, 1968.

37567.537 Richard, Noël. Le mouvement décadent: dandys. Paris, 1968.

43756.12.1100 Richaud, André de. La Douleur. Saint Martin, 1968.

38524.118 Rickard, Peter. La langue française au seizième siècle, étude suivie de textes. Cambridge, 1968.

42576.65.13.150 Ridge, George R. Joris-Karl Huysmans. N.Y., 1968.

40535.32.65 Rigault, Claude. Les domestiques dans le théâtre de Marivaux. Sherbrooke, 1968.

42556.28.390 Rimbaud. Paris, 1968.

43744.67.1640 Rivas, Marta. Un mito proustiano. Santiago de Chile, 1968.

43756.91.3110 Rivoyre, Christine de. Le petit matin, noman. Paris, 1968.

43757.7.7100 Robert, Jacques. Le dangereux été, roman. Paris, 1968.

43757.12.170 Roblès, Emmanuel. La croisière, roman. Paris, 1968.

43757.13.4110 Roche, Denis. Eros énergumène suivi du poème du 29 avril 62. Paris, 1968.

43550.58.2000 Roeming, Robert F. Camus; a bibliography. Madison, 1968.

37557.76.25 Romani, Bruno. La critica francese. Ravenna, 1968.

43757.50.1280 Romen Rollan. 1866-1966. Moskva, 1968.

42536.35.5 Rosca, Dumitru D. Influenţa lui Hegel asupra lui Taine teoretician al cunoaşterii şi al artei. Bucureşti, 1968.

1968 - cont.

43620.2.815 Rossi, Vinio. André Gide. N.Y., 1968.

FL 6074.3 Rousseau, J.J. Essai sur l'origine des langues où il est parlé de la mélodie et de l'imitation musicale. Bordeaux, 1968.

FL 6056.12 Rousseau, J.J. La nouvelle Héloise. University Park, 1968.

37569.408 Rousselot, Jean. Dictionnaire de la poésie française contemporaine. Paris, 1968.

37564.225.5 Rousset, Jean. L'intérieur et l'extérieur, essais sur la poésie et sur le théâtre au XVIIe siècle. Paris, 1968.

43757.89.6100 Roux, Dominique de. L'ouverture de la chasse. Lausanne, 1968.

43757.96.190 Roy, Claude. La dérobée. Paris, 1968.

43824.48.1800 Roy, Claude. Jean Vilar. Paris, 1968.

43757.96.180 Roy, Claude. La nuit est le manteau des pauvres. Paris, 1968.

42556.28.400 Ruff, Marcel A. Rimbaud. Paris, 1968.

43757.6.830 Sabato, Ernesto R. Tres aproximaciones a la literatura de nuestro tiempo: Robbe-Grillet, Borges, Sartre. Santiago de Chile, 1968.

40516.60.79 Sade, D.A.F. de. Juliette. 1st American ed. N.Y., 1968.

43761.31.220 Sagan, Françoise. Le garde du coeur, roman. Paris, 1968.

43761.31.720 Sagan, Françoise. The heart-keeper. London, 1968.

38526.47.31 Saint-Amant, Marc Antoine Gérard. Poésies baroques de Marc Antoine Gérard. Paris, 1968.

43761.44.2100 Salmon, André. Le monocle a deux coups, roman. Paris, 1968.

43761.49.250 Salmon, André. La négresse du sacré-coeur. Paris, 1968.

41557.9.44.25 Sand, George. Les maîtres sonneurs. Paris, 1968.

43701.74.805 Sarkany, Stéphane. Paul Morand et le cosmopolitisme littéraire. Paris, 1968.

43538.5.810 Sarocchi, Jean. Julien Benda, portrait d'un intellectuel. Paris, 1968.

43761.77.180 Sarraute, Nathalie. Entre lavie et la mort. Paris, 1968.

43538.76.1150 Sarrazin, Hubert. Bernanos no Brasil. Petrópolis, 1968.

43761.77.2101 Sartin, Pierrette. Une femme à part entière; roman. Paris, 1968.

43761.78.265 Sartre, Jean Paul. Le diable et le bon dieu. Paris, 1968.

43697.77.885 Savage, Catherine. Roger Martin du Gard. N.Y., 1968.

FL 6049.28 Scarlata, Giuseppe. La struttura del problema pedagogico nell' Emile di Jean Jacques Rousseau. Trapani, 1968.

39534.32.5.2 Scarron, Paul. The comical romance. N.Y., 1968.

41543.22.160 Schaerer, Kurt. Thematique de Gerard de Nerval. Paris, 1968.

43550.58.2060 Schaub, Karin. Albert Camus und der Tod. Zürich, 1968.

39544.386 Schick, Ursula. Zur Erzähltechnik in Voltaires "Contes." München, 1968.

40597.2.785 Schilling, Bernard Nicholas. The hero as failure; Balzac and the Rubempré cycle. Chicago, 1968.

43763.38.3011 Schlunegger, Jean Pierre. Oeuvres. Lausanne, 1968.

43763.38.2100 Schmidt, Claude. À travers la haie. Genève, 1968.

43763.39.1120 Schneider, Marcel. La nuit de longtemps. Paris, 1968.

43670.94.810 Schneider, Ursula. La quête du Nada dans l'oeuvre de Pierre Jean Jouve. Thèse. Zürich, 1968.

43763.2.52.2 Schopfer, Jean. Mayerling. London, 1968.

41556.50 Schulze, Joachim. Enttäuschung und Wahnwelt; Studien zu Charles Nodiers Erzählungen. München, 1968.

37556.20.90 Schwoebel, Jean. La presse, le pouvoir et l'argent. Paris, 1968.

40583.396 Schwyn, Walter. La musique comme catalyseur de l'émotion stendhalienne. Thèse. Zürich, 1968.

38537.64 Screech, Michael Andrew. Aspects of Rabelais's christian comedy. London, 1968.

43591.89.850 Ségalat, Roger Jean. Album Éluard. Paris, 1968.

43765.41.100 Seidner, Mireille. Les nouveaux lotophages. Tunis, 1968.

43528.86.805 Sellin, Eric. The dramatic concepts of Antonin Artaud. Chicago, 1968.

43765.90.110 Sénac, Jean. Avant-corps. Paris, 1968.

41543.22.75.5 Sénelier, Jean. Bibliographie nervalienne, 1960-67, et compléments antérieurs. Paris, 1968.

43765.89.110 Seuphor, Michel. Le monde est plein d'oiseaux. Lausanne, 1968.

43765.89.120 Seuphor, Michel. Paraboliques. Lausanne, 1968.

40522.28 Sgard, Jean. Prévost romancier. Paris, 1968.

43757.50.1295 Sices, David. Music and the musician in Jean-Christophe: the harmony of contrasts. New Haven, 1968.

43769.92.100 Sikorska, Andrée. Musique dans le noir, roman. Paris, 1968.

43769.54.732 Simenon, Georges. Maigret has doubts. London, 1968.

43769.54.714 Simenon, Georges. Maigret's pickpocket. London, 1968.

43769.54.778 Simenon, Georges. The move. 1. American ed. N.Y., 1968.

43769.54.778.5 Simenon, Georges. The neighbours. London, 1968.

43769.54.670 Simenon, Georges. La prison, roman. Paris, 1968.

43769.56.160 Simon, Pierre Henri. Le ballet de modène, suivi de entre confrères. Paris, 1968.

43565.60.805 Simon, Pierre Henri. Discours de remerciements et de reception à l'académie française...(Dainel-Rops). Paris, 1968.

37596.274 Simon de Pouille, chanson de geste. Genève, 1968.

37563.124 Simone, Franco. Umanesimo, Rinascimento, Barocco in Francia. Milano, 1968.

43775.50.130 Sollers, Philippe. Nombres; roman. Paris, 1968.

43775.50.705 Sollers, Philippe. The park. London, 1968.

43776.1.100 Spade, Henri. Les enfants de la guerre. Paris, 1968- 2v.

38585.16.385 Spillebout, Gabriel. Le vocabulaire, biblique dans les tragédies sacrées de Racine. Genève, 1968.

43556.1.961 Sprigge, Elizabeth. Jean Cocteau, l'homme et les miroirs. Paris, 1968.

43556.1.960 Sprigge, Elizabeth. Jean Cocteau: the man and the mirror. London, 1968.

40592.44 Staël Holstein, Anne Louise. De Staël-Du Pont letters. Madison, 1968.

40525.2.80 Stavan, Henry A. Gabriel Sénac de Meilhan. Paris, 1968.

42576.15.135.2 Steegmüller, F. Flaubert and Madame Bovary. N.Y., 1968.

38575.108 Stegmann, André. L'héroisme cornélien; genèse et signification. Thèse. Paris, 1968. 2v.

43779.25.130 Sternberg, Jacques. C'est la guerre, Monsieur Gruber. Paris, 1968.

37543.612 Strömberg, Kjell. Dikt och liv. Fransyska parnassvisiter. Stockholm, 1968.

37543.588 Studies in French literature presented to H.W. Lawton by colleagues. Manchester, Eng., 1968.

43780.50.140 Sulivan, Jean. Bonheur des rebelles. Paris, 1968.

43780.50.150 Sulivan, Jean. Consolation de la nuit, roman. Paris, 1968.

1968 - cont.

41564.55.140 Sungolowsky, Joseph. Alfred de Vigny et le dix-huitième siècle. Paris, 1968.

43780.69.780 Supervielle, Jules. Gedichte. Deutsch von Paul Celan. Frankfurt, 1968.

43785.53.100 Tamboise, Pierre Louis. Arnaout roi. Paris, 1968.

43785.75.160 Tardieu, Jean. Le fleuve caché, poésies, 1938-1961. Paris, 1968.

43785.75.700 Tardieu, Jean. The underground lovers, and other experimental plays. London, 1968.

43744.67.1605 Tarizzo, Domenico. Proust. Firenze, 1968.

43787.7.100 Tebelen, A. Mennan. L'inconscience du destin. Genève, 1968.

43761.77.810 Temple, Ruth Zabriskie. Nathalie Sarraute. N.Y., 1968.

38525.21.50 Terreaux, Louis. Ronsard, correcteur de ses oeuvres. Genève, 1968.

43526.65.1020 Themerson, Stefan. Apollinaire's lyrical ideograms. London, 1968.

43788.41.6100 Thinès, Georges. L'aporie. Bruxelles, 1968.

43524.67.855 Thody, Philip. Anouilh. Edinburgh, 1968.

43617.78.830 Thody, Philip. Jean Genêt; a study of his novels and plays. London, 1968.

43554.2.1270 Tissier, André. "Tête d'Or" de Paul Claudel. Paris, 1968.

43792.40.160 Toesca, Maurice. Le réquisitoire; roman. Paris, 1968.

41592.10.30 Touchard, Jean. La gloire de Béranger. Paris, 1968. 2v.

43620.2.835 Trahard, Pierre. "La porte étroite" d'André Gide. Paris, 1968.

43793.42.250 Triolet, Elsa. Écoutez-voir. Paris, 1968.

40556.48 Triomphe, Robert. Joseph de Maistre; étude sur la vie et sur la doctrine d'un matérialiste mystique. 1. éd. Thèse. Genève, 1968.

43793.65.120 Trolliet, Gilbert. Le fleuve et l'être; choix de poèmes. Neuchâtel, 1968.

43551.79.805 Trouillot, Hénock. L'intinéraire d'Aimé Césaire. Port-au-Prince, 1968.

43793.67.765 Troyat, Henri. An extreme friendship. 1st ed. N.Y., 1968.

43793.67.330 Troyat, Henri. Les héritiers de l'avenir, roman. Paris, 1968- 3v.

43793.67.320 Troyat, Henri. Tant que la terre durera; roman. Paris, 1968.

V40556.48.5 Trybusiewicz, Janusz. De Maistre. 1. wyd. Wernava, 1968.

43626.22.880 Uijterwaal, J. Julien Green, personnalité et création romanesque. Assen, 1968.

41522.18.585 Urruty, Jean. Le voyage de Baudelaire aux Mascareignes. Port-Louis, 1968.

43822.12.100 Vachey, Michel. C'était à Mégara, roman. Paris, 1968.

37556.320 Vachnadze, Georgii N. Pechat' piatoi respubliki 1958-1968 gg. Moskva, 1968.

FL 6059.22 Van Laere, François. Une lecture du temps dans la nouvelle Héloise. Neuchâtel, 1968.

42514.28.240 Vaulx, Bernard de. Charles Maurras. Moulins, 1968.

43591.89.840 Velikovskii, Samarii I. K gorizontu vsekh liudei. Moskva, 1968.

37596.278 Ver de Couloigne. Li ver de Couloigne, Du bon ange et du mauves. 1. Aufl. München, 1968.

42557.11.70 Verhaeren, Émile. Poèmes chrétiens de Verhaeren. Gembloux, 1968.

40517.44.115 Versini, Laurent. Laclos et la tradition. Paris, 1968.

37543.600 Vestdijk, Simon. Gallische facetten. Den Haag, 1968.

43824.3.290 Vialar, Paul. La cravache d'or, roman. Paris, 1968.

43824.3.1715 Vian, Boris. Heartsnatcher. London, 1968.

43824.3.1720 Vian, Boris. The Kuacker's ABC. N.Y., 1968.

43824.16.1130 Vidalie, Albert. Les Hussards de la Sorque. Paris, 1968.

41564.7.15 Vigny, Alfred de. Nevolia i velichie soldata. Leningrad, 1968.

43824.49.41 Vildrac, Charles. Pages de journal, 1922-1966. Paris, 1968.

43824.50.2100 Villanti, Paul Joseph Victor. Amour, bonheur et volupté. Nice, 1968.

41543.22.145 Villas, James. Gerard de Nerval; a critical bibliography, 1900 to 1967. Columbia, Mo., 1968.

42547.21.7 Villiers de l'Isle Adam, Auguste. Contes cruels. Paris, 1968.

42576.62.820 Virtanen, Reino. Anatole France. N.Y., 1968.

43824.90.1140 Vivier, Robert. Des nuits et des jours. Paris, 1968.

39545.35.90 Voltaire, François Marie Arouet de. Candide, ou L'optimisme. Genève, 1968.

39543.22 Voltaire, François Marie Arouet de. Les oeuvres complètes. Genève, 1968- 24v.

43656.59.855 Vos, Nelvin. Eugène Ionesco and Edward Albee. Grand Rapids, 1968.

43828.41.120 Vrigny, Roger. Fin de journée. Paris, 1968.

43833.41.130 Weingarten, Romain. Poèmes. Paris, 1968.

43833.98.1100 Weyergans, Franz. Mon amour dans l'île. Paris, 1968.

43833.98.1110 Weyergans, Franz. L'Operation, roman. Paris, 1968.

43835.24.621 Wiesel, Eliezer. Legends of our time. 1st ed. N.Y., 1968.

43835.24.140 Wiesel, Eliezer. Le Mendiant de Jérusalem. Paris, 1968.

43835.24.130 Wiesel, Eliezer. Zalmen ou la folie de Dieu. Paris, 1968.

43550.58.1080 Willhoite, Fred H. Beyond nihilism. Baton Rouge, 1968.

43835.50.1100 Williame, Élie. Reflets de la durée. Bruxelles, 1968.

42586.63.55 Young, E.J. Gobineau und der Rassismus. Meisenheim-an-Glan, 1968.

43852.89.220 Yourcenar, Marguerite. L'oeuvre au noir. Paris, 1968.

38526.26.100 Zamaron, Fernand. Louise Labé, dame de franchise. Paris, 1968.

43861.77.150 Zermatten, Maurice. Visages. Zürich, 1968.

43863.54.100 Zimmer, Bernard. Adaptations du théâtre antique. Paris, 1968-1969. 3v.

43863.54.110 Zimmer, Bernard. Théâtre. Paris, 1968-

42576.15.385 Zimmermann, Inge. Farbsymbolik und Handlungsstruktur im Romanwerk Flauberts. Bonn, 1968.

43554.2.1260 Zinke, Ludger. Paul Claudel. Würzburg, 1968.

42584.23.410 Zola, Emile. The debacle. London, 1968.

42584.23.78 Zola, Emile. Three faces of love. N.Y., 1968.

38551.170 Zovatto, Pietro. Fénelon e il quietismo. Udine, 1968.

38557.24.150 Zovatto, Pietro. La polemica Bossuet-Fénelon. Padova, 1968.

37564.280 Zuber, Roger. Les "Belles infidèles" et la formation du goût classique. Paris, 1968.

1969

43514.6.160 Adamov, Arthur. Off limits. Play in French. Paris, 1969.

39544.381 Adamski, Jerzy. Sekrety wieku oświecenia. Krakow, 1969.

42555.44.240 Agosti, Stefano. Il cigno di Mallarmé. Roma, 1969.

43519.53.100 Aima, Aymé. Thérèse Violette, roman. Besançon, 1969.

Chronological Listing

1969 - cont.

37543.620 Albouy, Pierre. Mythes et mythologies dans la littérature française. Paris, 1969.
37574.932 Alwyn, William. An anthology of twentieth century French poetry. London, 1969.
43523.67.100 Amouroux, Henri. Le Ghetto de la victoire. Paris, 1969.
43524.22.2110 André, Robert. L'amour et la vie d'une femme. Paris, 1969.
43524.33.110 Anglade, Jean. Le point de suspension. Paris, 1969.
43524.67.320 Anouilh, Jean. Cher Antoine; ou L'amour roté. Paris, 1969.
43524.86.100 Antier, Jean Jacques. La meute silencieuse; roman. Paris, 1969.
43526.65.61 Apollinaire, Guillaume. Lettres à Lou. Paris, 1969.
43526.65.340 Apollinaire, Guillaume. Poèmes à Lou. Paris, 1969.
43527.3.45 Aragon, Louis. Je n'ai jamais appris à écrire, ou Les incipit. Genève, 1969.
43528.17.100 Ardene, Claude. Longue est la nuit! Paris, 1969.
43697.89.875 Arland, Marcel. Discours de réception de Marcel Arland à l'Académie française et réponse de Jean Mistler. Paris, 1969.
43528.76.100 Arribat, Chantal. Noir et blanc. Paris, 1969.
43528.86.700 Artaud, Antonin. The Cenci. London, 1969.
39533.24.5 Assoucy, Charles. Les amours d'Apollon et de Daphné. Genève, 1969.
37556.366 Astier, Pierre A.G. La crise du roman français et le nouveau réalisme. Paris, 1969.
37574.950 L'atrium: grand prix de poésie du pays d'Arles; poèmes primés en 1969. Arles, 1969?
38527.17.30 Aubigné, Théodore Agrippa d'. Oeuvres. Paris, 1969.
38526.8.16 Augé-Chiquet, Mathieu. La vie, les idées et l'oeuvre de Jean Antoin e de Baif. Genève, 1969.
37562.352 Badel, Pierre Yves. Introduction à la vie littéraire du moyen âge. Paris, 1969.
40563.22.20 Ballanche, Pierre Simon. La vision d'Hébal. Genève, 1969.
37562.348 Balmas, Enea Henri. L'età del Rinascimento in Francia. Milano, 1969.
43537.74.3100 Barbier, Elisabeth. Ni le jour, ni l'heure; roman. Paris, 1969.
43537.77.1110 Baron, Jacques. L'an I du surréalisme. Suivi de l'an dernier. Paris, 1969.
43537.82.2110 Basson, Pierre. La Tête. Paris, 1969.
43537.84.140 Bataille, Michel. Une colere balanche; roman. Paris, 1969.
41522.14.45 Baudelaire, Charles. Baudelaire as a literary critic. University Park, Penn., 1969.
41522.6.35 Baudelaire, Charles. Jugendbriefe. Lettres inédites aux siens. Olten, 1969.
41522.13.36 Baudelaire, Charles. Petits poèmes en prose. Paris, 1969.
41522.14.50 Baudelaire as a love poet and other essays commemorating the centenary of the death of the poet. University Park, Penn., 1969.
43537.89.7100 Baudu, Antoinette. Sirocco en kabylie. Paris, 1969.
40587.180 Bazin, Christian. Chateaubriand en Amérique. Paris, 1969.
43550.58.2030 Bazin de Bezons, Jean de. Index du vocabulaire de "l'Étranger" d'Albert Camus.Paris, 1969.
38537.68 Beaujour, Michel. Le jeu de Rabelais. Paris, 1969.
40532.16.5 Beaumarchais, Pierre A.C. de. Correspondance. Paris, 1969- 2v.
43538.1.555 Beauvoir, Simone de. The woman destroyed. 1. American ed. N.Y., 1969.
43538.14.796 Beckett, Samuel. Film. N.Y., 1969.
40584.10.80 Beichel, Ursula. Alexandre Vinet. 1. Aufl. München, 1969.
43538.59.2100 Benedetto, André. Le petit train de Monsieur Kamodé. Honfleur, 1969.
43538.59.2110 Benedetto, André. Zone rouge, feux interdits. Honfleur, 1969.
41542.4.115 Benesch, Rita. Le regard de Théophile Gautier. Thèse. Zurich, 1969.
41522.18.570 Benjamin, Walter. Charles Baudelaire. Frankfurt, 1969.
37556.20.200 Bennett, Robert L. Les journaux de Caen, 1940-1944. Caen, 1969.
43538.62.4130 Bens, Jacques. Adieu Sidonie. Paris, 1969.
42554.30.15 Berg, Christian. Max Elskamp et le bouddhisme. Nancy, 1969.
43744.24.95 Bergens, Andrée. Jacques Prévert. Paris, 1969.
43538.75.3100 Bergonzo, Jean Louis. Les murs du havre. Paris, 1969.
43538.76.6110 Berl, Emmanuel. A contretemps. Paris, 1969.
43538.14.955 Bernal, Olga. Langage et fiction dans le roman de Beckett. Paris, 1969.
43538.76.240 Bernanos, Georges. Le lendemain, c'est vous! Paris, 1969.
43538.76.151.5 Bernanos, Georges. Monsieur Ouine. Paris, 1969.
43538.76.131 Bernanos, Georges. Nouvelle histoire de Mouchette. Paris, 1969.
40597.2.800 Besser, Gretchen R. Balzac's concept of genius. Genève, 1969.
39544.380 Besterman, Theodore. Voltaire. 1st American ed. N.Y., 1969.
38542.12.16 Beugnot, Bernard. J.L. Guez de Balzac. Supplement. Montréal, 1969.
37555.758 Beyer, Jürgen. Schwank und Moral. Heidelberg, 1969.
40582.25.80 Beyle, Henri. Red and black. N.Y., 1969.
40582.3.25.5 Beyle, Henri. Romans. Paris, 1969. 2v.
38526.2.3.6 Bèze, Théodore de. Abraham sacrifiant. N.Y., 1969.
38523.13.15 Bible. O.T. Psalms. French. Paraphrases. Les pseaumes de Clément Marot. Assen, 1969.
41578.190 Bibliothèque Nationale, Paris. Lamartine; le poète et l'homme d'État. Paris, 1969.
43526.65.1000 Bibliotheque Nationale. Apollinaire, Paris, 1969. Paris, 1969.
40587.170 Bibliothèque Nationale. Chateaubriand, le voyageur et l'homme politique. Paris, 1969.
38585.70 Biermann, Karlheinrich. Selbstentfremdung und Missverstandnis in den Tragödien Racines. Bad Homburg, 1969.
43540.34.102 Bigot, Muguette. Les voix de mon village. 2. éd. Huisseau-sur-Cosson, 1969.
40522.24 Billy, André. L'Abbé Prévost, auteur de Manon Lescaut. Paris, 1969.
40556.23.30 Billy, André. Joubert, énigmatique et délicieux. Paris, 1969.
43540.3.105 Billy, André. Propos du samedi. Paris, 1969.
43540.82.100 Bisson, Jean Pierre. Le matin rouge. Hanfleur, 1969.
37555.768 Blanchard, André. Trésor de la poésie baroque et precieuse. Paris, 1969.
43543.8.200 Blanchot, Maurice. L'entretien infini. Paris, 1969.
43544.19.700 Bodin, Paul. A young woman. N.Y., 1969.

1969 - cont.

37556.12.52 Boegner, Philippe. Presse, argent, liberté. Paris, 1969.
42563.18.240.2 Boisdeffre, Pierre de. Barrès parmi nous. Paris, 1969.
37568.228.4 Boisdeffre, Pierre de. Les écrivains français d'aujourd'hui. 4e éd. Paris, 1969.
37557.86 Bolléme, Geneviève. Les almanachs populaires aux XVIIe et XVIIIe siècles. Paris, 1969.
40597.2.830 Bonard, Olivier. La peinture dans la création balzacienne. Thèse. Genève, 1969.
37595.104 Boogaard, Nico H.J. Rondeaux et refrains. Paris, 1969.
43544.74.3110 Bordier, Roger. Le tour de ville. Paris, 1969.
43544.75.1100 Borel, Raymond C. L'Affaire Gregory, livre blanc, présenté et annoté. Paris, 1969.
42545.28.815 Bornecque, Pierre Henry. Le théâtre de Georges Courteline. Thèse. Paris, 1969.
43544.81.180 Bory, Jean Louis. Va dire au lac de patienter. Paris, 1969.
43544.82.61 Bosschère, Jean de. Lettres de La Châtre à André Lebois. (1939-1953). Paris, 1969.
43576.9.830 Bossière, Jacques. Perception critique et sentiment de vivre chez Charles Du Bos. Paris, 1969.
43822.50.805 Bott, François. Les saisons de Roger Vailland. Paris, 1969.
43554.2.1245 Bouchard, Isabelle. L'expérience apostolique de Paul Claudel d'après sa correspondance. Montréal, 1969.
38526.3.5.140 Bouchet, Jean. Epistres morales et familières du traverseur. N.Y., 1969.
43544.90.1100 Boujut, Pierre. Sang libre; poèmes. Paris, 1969.
43544.88.2150 Boulanger, Daniel. Retouches. Paris, 1969.
43544.88.2140 Boulanger, Daniel. Tchadiennes. Paris, 1969.
37574.946 Bourgeois, Gaston. Anthologie de l'Académie des poètes classiques. Paris, 1969.
43544.89.61 Bousquet, Joë. Correspondance. Paris, 1969.
43544.90.4100 Bouzekri, Marcelle. La codorniz. Paris, 1969.
43744.67.1235.2 Brée, Germaine. Marcel Proust and deliverance from time. 2. ed. New Brunswick, 1969.
42576.63.780 Bresky, Dusham. The art of Anatole France. The Hague, 1969.
37569.40.17 Breton, André. Manifestoes of surrealism. Ann Arbor, 1969.
43545.24.131 Breton, André. Les pas perdus. Paris, 1969.
43545.24.621 Breton, André. Selected poems. London, 1969.
43526.65.990 Breunig, Leroy C. Guillaume Apollinaire. N.Y., 1969.
37568.278 Broca, José Brito. Letras francesas. São Paulo, 1969.
43822.50.800 Brochier, Jean Jacques. Roger Vailland, tentative de description. Paris, 1969.
43545.66.2110 Bronne, Carlo. Bleu d'Ardenne. Bruxelles, 1969.
37556.266.2 Brooks, Peter Preston. The novel of worldliness: Crebillon, Marivaux, Laclos, Stendhal. Princeton, N.J., 1969.
43556.1.980 Brown, Frederick. An impersonation of angels. London, 1969.
43545.89.7100 Brunoy, Clément. Salyne, Roman. Paris, 1969.
43744.67.1625 Bucknall, Barbara J. The religion of art in Proust. Urbana, 1969.
42547.22.125 Buergisser, Peter. La double illusion de l'or et de l'amour chez Villiers de l'Isle Adam. Berne, 1969
43538.76.1155 Bush, William. Georges Bernanos. N.Y., 1969.
43780.5.825 Busi, Fréderick. L'ésthétique d'André Suarès. Wetteren, 1969.
43546.87.78 Butor, Michel. Essais sur le roman. Paris, 1969.
41522.18.376 Butor, Michel. Histoire extraordinaire. London, 1969.
43550.6.200 Cabanis, José. Des jardins en Espagne. Paris, 1969.
43550.58.26 Camus, Albert. Lyrical and critical essays. N.Y., 1969.
43688.7.810 Camus, André. Le centenaire de Philéas Lebesque. Grandvilliers, 1969.
43694.11.2815 Canivet, Louis. Un chant de France a l'heure du coeur. Rodez, 1969.
42557.20.335 Carter, Alfred Edward. Verlaine; a study in parallels. Toronto, 1969.
37555.568 Cave, Terence Christopher. Devotional poetry in France 1570-1613. London, 1969.
43550.98.240 Cayrol, Jean. Poésie-journal. Paris, 1969.
43550.98.4100 Cazenave, Georges. A l'ombre de mon pin. Paris, 1969.
43551.59.350 Cendrars, Blaise. Dites-nous, Monsieur Blaise Cendrars. Lausanne, 1969.
43551.59.340 Cendrars, Blaise. Inédits secrets. Paris, 1969.
37569.416 Cent écrivains français répondent au "questionnaire Marcel Proust". Paris, 1969.
39544.384 Centre Culturel Portugais, Paris. Voltaire et la culture portugaise. Paris, 1969.
43551.79.705 Césaire, Aimé. Return to my native land. Harmondsworth, 1969.
43551.79.180 Césaire, Aimé. Une tempête. Paris, 1969.
37542.72 Chaillet, Jean. Études de grammaire et de style. Paris, 1969. 2v.
41543.22.150 Chambers, Ross. Gerard de Nerval et la poétique du voyage. Paris, 1969.
43550.58.861 Champigny, Robert. A pagan hero. Philadelphia, 1969.
43552.4.2128 Char, René. Les matinaux, suivi de la Parole en archipel. Paris, 1969.
42556.28.375.1 Charleville, France. Arthur Rimbaud dans les collections municipales de la bibliothèque et du musée. Supplément. Charleville, 1969-
43822.49.1600 Charney, Hanna. Le scepticisme de Valéry. Paris, 1969.
40585.402 Chateaubriand, F.A.R. Oeuvres romanesques et voyages. Paris, 1969-
40586.5.23 Chateaubriand, F.A.R. Travels in America. Lexington, 1969.
40534.16.35 Chateaubrun, Jean B.V. de. The text and sources of Chateaubrun's lost Ajax. Frankfurt, 1969.
43552.18.180 Chédid, Andrée. L'autre. Paris, 1969.
43552.23.2100 Chenevière, Jacques. Daphné, ou l'Ecole des sentiments. Lausanne, 1969.
37574.934 Chevassus, Paul. Anthologie des jeunes poètes. Lyon, 1969. 2v.
42555.44.225 Cirolamo, Nicola di. Cultura e coscienza critica nell'Hérodiade di Mallarmé. Bologna, 1969.
43553.97.100 Cixous, Hélène. Dedans. Paris, 1969.
38585.16.80.2 Clark, Alexander Frederick Bruce. Jean Racine. N.Y., 1969.
37595.99.2 Cluzel, Irénée Marcel. La poésie lyrique d'oïl. 2. éd. Paris, 1969.
43556.37.130 Cohen, Albert. Les valeureux. Paris, 1969.
43556.50.4110 Colin, Gerty. Un si grand amour. Verviers, 1969.
43556.50.5100 Collin, Robert. Les Bassignots. Chaumont, 1969.

Chronological Listing

1969 - cont.

37567.720 Colloque d'Histoire Littéraire, École Normale Superieure de Saint-Cloud, 1966. Romantisme et politique, 1815-1851. Paris, 1969.
42565.57.20 Constant, A. Eliphas Lévi. 1. éd. Paris, 1969.
43620.2.840 Cordle, Thomas. André Gide. N.Y., 1969.
38575.31.30 Corneille, Pierre. Don Sanche d'Arragon. Paris, 1969.
38575.82 Corneille, Pierre. Seven plays. N.Y., 1969.
43556.82.2100 Coste, Didier. Journal exemplaire d'une enquête en province. Paris, 1969.
43556.89.4100 Couteaux, André. Un homme, aujourd'hui; roman. Paris, 1969.
40527.58 La Crèche. Besançon, 1969.
43557.64.110 Cressanges, Jeanne. La chambre interdite; roman. Paris, 1969.
43557.25.116 Crevel, René. L'esprit contre la raison. Paris, 1969.
43565.5.58 Daudet, Léon A. Paris, vécu. Paris, 1969.
FL 1098.55.11 David, Édouard. Oeuvres complétes...Amiens, musée de Picardie. Paris, 1969-
43620.2.855 Les débuts littéraires d'André Walter à l'immoraliste. (André Gide). Paris, 1969.
43619.23.820 Decock, Jean. Le théâtre de Michel de Ghelderode. Paris, 1969.
42582.2.50 Deesbach, Ghislain de. Le tour de Jules Verne en quatre-vingt livres. Paris, 1969.
43566.35.1110 Deguy, Michel. Figurations; poèmes, propositions, études. Paris, 1969.
43566.47.6100 Delarozière, Marie Françoise. Désert, ma citadelle. Paris, 1969.
43566.48.3100 Delcarte, Françoise. Sables. Paris, 1969.
43524.67.865 Della Fazia, Alba Marie. Jean Anouilh. N.Y., 1969.
37555.762 Delley, Gilbert. L'assomption de la nature dans la lyrique française de l'âge baroque. Berne, 1969.
37556.312 Dementev, E.G. Roman velikoi frantsuzskoi reloliutsii. Vladivostok, 1969.
43566.60.1100 Denis, Henri Pierre. Quelques nouvelles de Jessica. Paris, 1969.
40597.2.855 Denizot, Philippe M. Catalogue de la "Comédie humaine" de Balzac. Chinon, 1969.
37555.748 Denommé, Robert Thomas. Nineteenth-century French romantic poets. Carbondale, 1969.
43566.81.4170 Desnos, Robert. Fortunes. Paris, 1969.
43566.82.7755 Destouches, Louis Ferdinand. Rigodon par Louis-Ferdinand Céline. Paris, 1969.
39564.3.5 Diderot, Denis. Oeuvres complètes. Paris, 1969- 12v.
FL 6119.69 Dobinson, Charles Henry. Jean-Jacques Rousseau. London, 1969.
FL 386.63 Dominique, Léon. Le théâtre russe et la scène française. Paris, 1969.
38526.27.8.80 Donaldson-Evans, Lance K. Poésie et méditation chez Jean de La Ceppède. Genève, 1969.
37562.336 Donovan, Mortimor John. The Breton lay: a guide to varieties. Notre Dame, 1969.
43573.89.3110 Doubrovsky, Serge. La dispersion, roman. Paris, 1969.
40583.370 Doyon, André. Amitiés parisiennes de Stendhal. Lausanne, 1969.
43687.68.800 Drouillet, Jean. Hugues Lapaire, maître-poète de la terre de France. Avallon, 1969.
43576.8.1130 Dubillard, Roland. Le jardin aux betteraves. Paris, 1969.
38525.6.35 Dubois, Claude Gilbert. La poésie baroque...choix de poèmes. Paris, 1969. 2v.
43576.11.120 Dubrau, Louis. Les témoins. Bruxelles, 1969.
42568.19.21.13 Ducasse, I.L. Oeuvres complètes; les chants de Maldoror. Paris, 1969.
42576.12.100 Ducharme, Réjean. La fille de Christophe Colomb. Paris, 1969.
43576.12.1120 Ducharme, Réjean. La fille de Christophe Colomb. Paris, 1969.
39566.181 Duchet, Michèle. Entretiens sur "Le neveu de Rameau." Paris, 1969.
40517.23.12 Duclos, C.P. Les confessions du Comte de ***. Paris, 1969.
FL 398.20.16 Dullin, Charles. Ce sont les dieux qu'il nous faut. Paris, 1969.
42543.26 Dumas, Alexandre. Le Dossier "Tue-la!". Avignon, 1969.
43576.74.2230 Duras, Marguerite. Détruire, dit-elle. Paris, 1969.
43576.87.200 Dutourd, Jean. Petit journal, 1965-1966. Paris, 1969.
43576.90.2100 Duvert, Tony. Interdit de séjour. Paris, 1969.
42548.71.30 L'école des biches ou Moeurs des petites dames de ce temps. Paris, 1969.
38575.112 Eder, Klaus. Pierre Corneille und Jean Racine. 1. Aufl. Velber, 1969.
37565.184 Eighteenth century French studies: literature and the arts. Newcastle upon Tyne, 1969.
38585.80 Elliot, Revel. Mythe et legende dans le théâtre de Racine. Paris, 1969.
43591.89.166 Éluard, Paul. Poésie ininterrompue. Paris, 1969.
37568.272.2 Engler, Winfried. The French novel. N.Y., 1969.
43554.2.1250 Entretiens sur Paul Claudel, Cerisy-La Salle. Entretiens sur Paul Claudel. Paris, 1969.
43598.82.2130 Escarpit, Robert. Le fabricant de nuages, nouvelles. Paris, 1969.
37567.444.5 Evans, David Owen. Social romanticism in France, 1830-1848. N.Y., 1969.
43604.19.160 Eydoux, Emmanuel. Anéantir Israël. Théâtre. Basel, 1969.
43606.9.2100 Fabre-Luce de Gruson, Françoise. La clôture. Paris, 1969.
37575.707 Fau, Raymond. Rythmes et chansons pour le Seigneur, 110 chansons. Paris, 1969.
37556.15.50 Faucher, Jean André. Le quatrième pouvoir, la presse française de 1830 à 1960. Paris, 1969.
38514.23.170 Fife, Austin E. The life and poetry of François Villon. Logan, 1969?
37595.116 Finoli, Anna Maria. Artes amandi. Da Maître Elie ad Andrea Cappellano. Milano, 1969.
43538.76.982 Fitch, Brian T. Dimensions et structures chez Bernanos. Paris, 1969.
41522.18.625 Flavien, Jean. D'un Baudelaire à l'autre. Paris, 1969.
37597.10.15 Fleming, John V. The roman de la rose. Princeton, 1969.
43697.88.915 Flower, John, Ernest. A critical commentary on Mauriac's Le noeud de vipères. London, 1969.
43697.88.905 Flower, John Ernest. Intention and achievement: an essay on the novels of François Mauriac. Oxford, 1969.
43611.50.120 Follain, Jean. D'après tout. Paris, 1969.
43611.50.130 Follain, Jean. Exister. Paris, 1969.
43611.50.700 Follain, Jean. Transparence of the world: poems. N.Y., 1969.

1969 - cont.

38562.21.15 Fontenelle, B. Le B. de. Fontenelle und die Aufklärung. München, 1969.
42554.26.105 Forestier, Louis. Charles Cros, l'homme et l'oeuvre. Paris, 1969.
43611.4.120 Fouchet, Max Pol. Un jour, je m'en souviens; mémoire parlée. Paris, 1969.
40583.375 Fowlie, Wallace. Stendhal. N.Y., 1969.
38514.26.80 Fox, John Howard. The lyric poetry of Charles d'Orleans. Oxford, 1969.
37562.366 Fox, John Howard. The rhetorical tradition in French literature of the later Middle Ages. Exeter, 1969.
Mon 116.43 Frame, Donald Murdoch. Montaigne's Essais; a study. Englewood Cliffs, N.J., 1969.
42576.62.14.3 France, Anatole. L'anneau d'améthyste. Levallois-Perret, 1969.
42576.62.18.12 France, Anatole. Crainquebille. Putois. Riquet. Levallois-Perret, 1969.
42576.62.22.9 France, Anatole. Les dieux ont soif. Levallois-Perret, 1969.
42576.62.21.32 France, Anatole. L'île des pingouins. Levallois-Perret, 1969.
42576.62.4.3 France, Anatole. Jocaste et Le chat maigre. Levallois-Perret, 1969.
42576.62.8.7 France, Anatole. L'orme du mail. Levallois-Perret, 1969.
42576.63.22.10 France, Anatole. Le petit Pierre. Evreux, 1969.
42576.62.25.9 France, Anatole. La révolte des anges. Evreaux, 1969.
42576.62.20.6 France, Anatole. Sur la pierre blanche. Levallois-Perret, 1969.
42576.62.135.8 France, Anatole. La vie littéraire. Evreux, 1969- 3v.
Mon 116.50 Friedenthal, Richard. Entdecker des Ich. München, 1969.
37556.278 Frohock, Wilbur Merrill. Image and theme; studies in modern French fiction. Cambridge, 1969.
43616.12.100 Gachon, Lucien. Maria. Clermont-Ferrand, 1969.
43616.41.2160 Gaillard, Robert. Le sang du tigre. Paris, 1969.
41522.18.600 Galand, René M. Baudelaire; poétiques et poésie. Paris, 1969.
37543.604 Gallica: essays presented to J. Heywood Thomas by collegues, pupils, and friends. Cardiff, 1969.
43616.52.130 Galzy, Jeanne. La surprise de vivre. Paris, 1969.
43616.58.140 Gandon, Yves. Ginèvre. Levallois-Perret, 1969.
43616.58.100 Gandon, Yves. Ginèvre. Levallois-Perret, 1969.
38557.24.156 Gaquère, François. Les suprêmes appels de Bossuet à l'unité chrétienne, 1668-1691. Paris, 1969.
43616.77.1100 Garrabé, Michel. Le Déséquilibre. Honfleur, 1969.
43616.78.220 Gary, Romain. Adieu Gary Cooper. Paris, 1969.
41574.618 Gaudon, Jean. Le temps de la contemplation...Victor Hugo. Paris, 1969.
37575.793 Gavronsky, Serge. Poems and texts. N.Y., 1969.
41574.620 Gely, Claude. Victor Hugo, poète de l'intimité. Paris, 1969.
43617.78.200 Genêt, Jean. Funeral rites. N.Y., 1969.
43617.78.735 Genêt, Jean. Letters to Roger Blin; reflections on the theater. N.Y., 1969.
43617.78.775 Genêt, Jean. Der zum Tode Verurteilte. 1. Aufl. Hamburg, 1969.
43617.59.260 Genevoix, Maurice. Tendre bestiaire. Paris, 1969.
37569.40.45 Gershman, Herbert S. A bibliography of the surrealist revolution in France. Ann Arbor, 1969.
37569.40.46 Gershman, Herbert S. The surrealist revolution in France. Ann Arbor, 1969.
42586.32.535 Gheyselinck, Roger. De dood van taai geroddel. Antwerpen, 1969.
43822.49.1595 Giaveri, Maria Teresa. L'album de vers anciens di Paul Valéry. Padove, 1969.
43620.2.60.2 Gide, André. Saül; drame en 5 actes, 1896. Paris, 1969.
43524.67.870 Ginestier, Paul. Jean Anouilh. Paris, 1969.
43620.66.500 Giono, Jean. Une histoire d'amour. Manosque, 1969.
43620.74.555 Giraoudoux, Jean. Or dans la nuit. Paris, 1969.
43620.74.6100 Giraud, Pierre. L'enfant perdu, et autres contes. Paris, 1969.
43620.77.100 Girod, André. L'Ivrogne, poèmes. Paris, 1969.
42537.25.15 Girolamo, Nicola. Teodor de Wyzewa. Bologna, 1969.
43622.41.180 Glissant, Edouard. L'intention poétique. Paris, 1969.
42586.64.20 Gobineau, Arthur de. Lettres bresiliennes. Paris, 1969.
43550.58.2055 Goedert, Georges. Albert Camus et la question du bonheur. Luxemburg, 1969.
43625.27.190 Goffin, Robert. Faits divers. Paris, 1969.
43618.90.800 Goris, Jan Albert. Marie Gevers. Utrecht, 1969.
43550.58.1095 Grenier, Jean. Albert Camus, souvenirs. Paris, 1969.
FL 6139.61.7 Grimsley, Ronald. Jean-Jacques Rousseau; a study in self-awareness. 2. ed. Cardiff, 1969.
43628.22.100 Guénenno, Annie. L'épreure; récit. Paris, 1969.
43620.2.273A Guerard, Albert Joseph. André Gide. 2. ed. Cambridge, 1969.
43628.41.7110 Guiette, Robert. Ombres vives. Bruxelles, 1969.
43628.41.7021 Guiette, Robert. Poésie, 1922-1967. Paris, 1969.
42586.76.61 Guillaumin, Emile. Cent dix-neuf lettres d'Emile Guillaumin. Paris, 1969.
37543.535.10 Guillemin, Henri. Pas à pas. Paris, 1969.
43628.41.3621 Guillevic, Eugène. Selected poems. N.Y., 1969.
38514.23.160 Habeck, Fritz. François Villon, oder Die Legende eines Rebellen. Wien, 1969.
38551.175 Haillant, Marguerite. Fénelon et la prédication. Paris, 1969.
43631.49.2130 Haldas, Georges. Jardin des éspérances. Lausanne, 1969.
37569.420 Halimi, André. Trente-six écrivains...et leurs 4 vérités. Paris, 1969.
40583.380 Heisler, Marcel. Stendhal et Napoléon. Paris, 1969.
37556.12.55 Histoire générale de la presse française. Paris, 1969- 2v.
41557.10.265 Hommage à George Sand. Paris, 1969.
43697.52.940 Horvath, Violet M. André Malraux; the human adventure. N.Y., 1969.
37555.752 Houston, John Porter. The demonic imagination. Baton Rouge, 1969.
41572.24.12 Hugo, Victor. Les contemplations. Paris, 1969.
41571.16.35 Hugo, Victor. Les misérables. Paris, 1969. 2v.
43638.34.1100 Hugot, Noëlle. Symphonie sur le seuil. Honfleur, 1969.
41543.22.180 Humphrey, George René. L'esthétique de la poésie de Gerard de Nerval. Paris, 1969.
43638.76.100 Huriet, Michel. La fête de la dédicacé. Paris, 1969.
42576.66.3.15 Huysmans, Joris Karl. Against the grain. N.Y., 1969.
38512.2.10 Igly, France. Oton de Grandson. Travers, 1969.
43656.59.200 Ionesco, Eugène. Découvertes. Genève, 1969.

Chronological Listing

1969 - cont.

43656.59.725 Ionesco, Eugène. Hunger and thirst, and other plays. N.Y., 1969.

43656.59.1100 Ionesco, Joana. Mes années de lumière, roman vécu. Paris, 1969.

41578.180 Ireson, J.C. Lamartine: a revolution. Hull, England, 1969.

37568.274 Itterbeek, Eugène van. Tekens van leven. Brussel, 1969.

43667.7.1100 Jabès, Edmond. Elya. Paris, 1969.

43667.15.2140 Jacquemard, Simonne. L'Eruption des Krakatoa, ou Des chambres inconnues dans la maison. Paris, 1969.

38527.49.15 Jandorf, Gillian. Robert Garnier and the themes of political tragedy in the sixteenth century. Thesis. London, 1969.

42554.26.850 Jannini, Pasquale Aniel. Introduzione alla lettura de Les amours jaunes di Tristan Corbière. Roma, 1969.

43667.61.21 Jans, Adrien. Poésie 1924-1967. 1. éd. Paris, 1969.

43538.14.876 Janvier, Ludovic. Samuel Beckett par lui-même. Paris, 1969.

Mol 710.5 Jasinski, René. Molière. Paris, 1969.

37555.760 Jeanneret, Michel. Poésie et tradition biblique au XVIe siècle recherches stylistiques sur les paraphrases des "Psaumes", de Marot à Malherbe. Paris, 1969.

FL 376.34 Jeffery, Brian. French Renaissance comedy, 1552-1630. Oxford, 1969.

Mon 120.5 Jenzer, Carlo. Lebensnahe, Lebensferne und Realismus in den pädagogischen Ansichten von Michel de Montaigne. Bern, 1969.

39566.220 Joly, Raymond. Deux études sur la préhistorie du réalisme: Diderot. Québec, 1969.

42544.33.70 Joseph, Roger. Pour les fidèles de Jules Lemaître. Orléans, 1969.

39566.202.5 Josephs, Herbert. Diderot's dialogue of language? Columbus, 1969.

42555.62.60 Jouanny, Robert A. Jean Moréas, écrivain français. Paris, 1969.

37563.118 Joukovsky, Françoise. La gloire dans la poésie française et néolatine du 16e siècle. Genève, 1969.

43671.20.41 Judrin, Roger. Journal d'une monade, du 13 avril au 9 septembre 1968. Paris, 1969.

39568.23.15 Juettner, Siegfried. Grundtendenzen der Theaterkritik von Friedrich-Melchior Grimm (1753-1773). Wiesbaden, 1969.

FL 363.62 Kadler, Eric H. Literary figures in French drama, 1784-1834. The Hague, 1969.

43697.89.870 Keating, Louis Clark. André Maurois. N.Y., 1969.

43673.76.1100 Kermoal, Jacques. Le retour du général. Paris, 1969.

43673.78.1100 Kervyn de Marcke ten Driessche, Roger. Journal de bord. Bruxelles, 1969.

43674.5.110 Khayr al-Din, Muhammad. Soleil arachnide; poèmes. Paris, 1969.

43591.89.860 Kittang, Atle. D'amour de poésie. Paris, 1969.

37569.430 Knabenhans, Brigitte. Le thème de la pierre chez Sartre et quelques poètes modernes. Thèse. Zurich, 1969.

43528.86.815 Knapp, Bettina (Liebowitz). Antonin Artaud; man of vision. N.Y., 1969.

38585.16.390 Knight, Roy Clement. Racine. London, 1969.

FL 372.22F Konigson, Elie. La représentation d'un mystère de la passion à Valenciennes en 1547. Paris, 1969.

43823.75.2800 Konstantinović, Radivoje D. Vercors. Paris, 1969.

43761.39.933 Kwiatkowski, Władysław. Humanizm St. Exupéry'ego. Wyd. 1. Warszawa, 1969.

43687.9.2100 Laborde, Jean. L'héritage de violence. Paris, 1969.

37556.22.93 Lachat, François. Le pays d'Ernest Daucourt, 1873-1884. Fribourg, 1969.

39527.42.15 La Fontaine, Jean de. Voyage de Paris en limosin. Paris, 1969.

43550.58.2045 Lambert, B. L'epreuve littéraire aux concours des grandes écoles scientifiques; programme, 1970-1971. Villemomble, 1969.

37542.70 Lambert, B. L'épreuve littéraire aux concours des grandes écoles scientifiques. Villemomble, 1969. 2v.

43687.53.1120 Lambert, Jean. Le Plaisir de voir. Paris, 1969.

43757.12.805 Landi-Bénos, Fanny. Emmanuel Roblès ou, Les raisons de vivre. Honfleur, 1969.

43687.58.2140 Landry, Charles François. Baragne. Lausanne, 1969.

43687.65.140 Lanza del Vasto, Joseph Jean. L'homme libre et les ânes sauvages. Paris, 1969.

37558.150.10 La Rochefericauld, Edmée. Femmes d'hier et d'aujourd'hui. Paris, 1969.

37565.188 Launay, Michel. Introduction à la vie littéraire du XVIIIe siècle. Paris, 1969.

FL 6139.69.15 Launay, Michel. Jean-Jacques Rousseau et son temps. Paris, 1969.

37567.111.25 Lawler, James R. The language of French symbolism. Princeton, 1969.

41522.18.610 Leakey, F.W. Baudelaire and nature. N.Y., 1969.

43697.49.825 Lebrec, Jean. Joseph Malègue, romancier et penseur. Thèse. Paris, 1969.

FL 6139.69.10 Lecercle, Jean Louis. Rousseau et l'art du roman. Paris, 1969.

43688.14.4150 Le Clézio, Jean Marie Gustave. Le livre des fuites, roman. Paris, 1969.

43688.14.4710 Le Clézio, Jean Marie Gustave. Terra amata. London, 1969.

43688.34.1021 Legrand, Maurice. Poèmes amorphes. Paris, 1969.

43688.60.102 Leiris, Michel. Haut mal, suivi de autres lancers. Paris, 1969.

40575.5.190 Lejeune-Dehousse, Rita. Sainte-Beuve et l'Université de Liège. Liège, 1969.

43688.1.22 Leroux, Gaston. Chéri-Bibi. Évreux, 1969. 4v.

43688.1.36 Leroux, Gaston. Rouletabille. Levallois-Perret, 1969- 7v.

42576.46.7.2 Le Roy, Eugène. Le moulin du Frau. Paris, 1969.

40512.44.5 LeSage, Alain René. Histoire de Gil Blas de Santillane. Paris, 1969. 2v.

40512.60.1 LeSage, Alain René. Turcaret. London, 1969.

43690.9.100 Libbrecht, Géo. Géo Libbrecht. Bruxelles, 1969?

43690.65.110 Lionel, Frédéric. L'étreinte des masques. Neuchâtel, 1969.

37530.200 Littérature classique française. Tournai, 1969-

37543.632 Losfeld, Georges. Le livre des rencontres, Villon, d'Aubigné, Desportes, Malherbe. Paris, 1969.

37593.64.12.5 Luetgemeier, Gertrud. Beuträge zum Verständnis des "Jeu de la Feuillée" von Adam le Bossu. Thesis. Bonn, 1969.

40592.94 Luppé, Robert de. Les idées littéraires de Madame de Staël et l'héritage des lumières (1795-1800). Paris, 1969.

43761.78.940 McCall, Dorothy. The theatre of Jean-Paul Sartre. N.Y., 1969.

1969 - cont.

41522.18.580 Macchia, Giovanni. La critica letteraria di Baudelaire. Roma, 1969.

43697.12.1102 Machin, Paul René. Arc-en-ciel. 2e éd. Lure, 1969.

38514.28.10 McLeod, Enid. Charles of Orleans, prince and poet. London, 1969.

43697.14.13 MacOrlan, Pierre. L'ancre de miséricorde. Le quai des brumes. Genève, 1969.

43697.14.17 MacOrlan, Pierre. La cavalière Elsa. La Vénus internationale. Frontispice de Jim. Genève, 1969.

43697.14.12 MacOrlan, Pierre. Le chant de l'équipage. La bandera. Genève, 1969.

43697.14.192 MacOrlan, Pierre. Marguerite de la nuit. 1. ed. Genève, 1969.

43697.14.14 MacOrlan, Pierre. Montmartre, Les bandes, suivi de Parades abolies. Genève, 1969.

43697.14.16 MacOrlan, Pierre. Le nègre Léonard et maître Jean Mullin. Genève, 1969.

43697.14.430 MacOrlan, Pierre. Les pattes en l'air. 1 ed. Genève, 1969.

43697.14.232 MacOrlan, Pierre. Poésies documentaires complètes. 1. ed. Genève, 1969.

43697.31.1100 Magali, Andrée. Les Fiancés du petit lac. Paris, 1969.

43697.37.100 Mahé, Henri. La Bringuebale avec Céline. Paris, 1969.

37572.26.30 Maison, André. Anthologie de la correspondance française. Lausanne, 1969. 7v.

43822.49.1605 Maka-de Schepper, Monique. Le thème de La Pythie chez Paul Valéry. Paris, 1969.

43697.50.110 Mallat, Robert J. Saint-Dominque oú je meurs. Honfleur, 1969.

43697.52.220 Malraux, André. Romans: Les conquérants, La condition humaine, L'espoir. Paris, 1969.

43620.74.950 Mander, Gertrud. Jean Giraudoux. 1. Aufl. Velber, 1969.

40524.48.5 Marat, Jean Paul. Przygody młodego hrabiego Potowskiego. wyd. 1. Warszawa, 1969.

43697.74.3200 Marceau, Félicien. Le babour, pièce en deux parties. Paris, 1969.

43697.74.3210 Marceau, Félicien. Creezy. Paris, 1969.

38526.32.49 Marguerite d'Angoulême. Heptaméron. Budapest, 1969.

43697.79.9100 Marie-Jeanne (pseud.). Le labyrinthe. Paris, 1969.

43697.76.8021 Marissel, André. Choix de poèmes 1957-1968. Paris, 1969.

37555.766 Marissel, André. Poètes vivants; essai. Paris, 1969.

40535.15.110 Marivaux, Pierre Carlet de Chamblain. Journaux et oeuvres diverses. Paris, 1969.

43697.79.7100 Martin, Jean Claude. Moods. Monte Carlo, 1969.

43697.77.61 Martin du Gard, Roger. Lettres de Roger Martin du Gard à un jeune écrivain, 1953-1958. Paris, 1969.

43697.78.5170 Martin Saint-René (pseud.). Vitriks et Génowinn. Paris, 1969.

38537.74 Masters, George Mallary. Rabelaisian dialectic and the platonic-hermetic tradition. Albany, 1969.

37555.756 Matthews, J.H. Surrealist poetry in France. 1. ed. Syracuse, N.Y., 1969.

43697.88.5100 Matznett, Gabriel. La Caracole, chroniques polémiques, 1863-1968. Paris, 1969.

43620.2.845 Maucuer, Maurice. Gide, l'indécision passionnée. Paris, 1969.

43697.88.630 Mauriac, François. Un adolescent d'autrefois, roman. Paris, 1969.

39527.67 Mayer, Gerd Reiner. Die Funktion mythologischer Namen und Anspielungen in La Fontaines Fabelens. Bonn, 1969.

43697.98.1100 Mayeur, Pierre Xavier. La forêt du symbole, poèmes. Paris, 1969.

37563.114 Melanges d'histoire littéraire, XVIe-XVIIe siècle. Paris, 1969.

43550.58.2020 Melchinger, Christa. Albert Camus. 1. Aufl. Velbert, 1969.

43698.55.130 Memmi, Albert. Le scorpion; ou, La confession imaginaire. Paris, 1969.

37562.344 Ménard, Philippe. Le rire et la sourire dans le roman courtois en France au moyen âge. Genève, 1969.

43698.74.1100 Mer, Jacques. Poème pour la mort de Federico Garcia Lorca. Saint-Front-sur-Lémance, 1969.

43698.75.7710 Merle, Robert. The day of the dolphin, a novel. N.Y., 1969.

43698.77.100 Mertens, Pierre. L'Inde ou l'Amérique. Paris, 1969.

38526.51.90 Meyer-Minnemann, Klaus. Die Tradition der klassischen Satire in Frankreich. Bad Homburg, 1969.

Mon 123.9 Michel, Pierre. Montaigne. Bourdeaux, 1969[1970]

43699.12.1100 Michelet, Claude. La Grande muraille, roman. Paris, 1969.

38539.106 Millot, Michel. L'école des filles ou La philosophie des dames. Paris, 1969.

43699.51.63 Milosz, Oscar Vladislas. Soixante-quinze lettres inédites et sept documents originaux. Paris, 1969.

43699.98.100 Mizrahi, Rachel. Harry. Paris, 1969.

37543.602 Modern miscellany presented to Eugène Vinaver by pupils, colleagues and friends. Manchester, Eng., 1969.

37562.350 Moelk, Ulrich. Französische literarästhetik des 12. und 13. Jahrhunderts. Tübingen, 1969.

43701.39.150 Mohrt, Michel. L'ours des Adirondacks. Paris, 1969.

43701.50.100 Molinard, Barbara. Viens, nouvelles, précédées d'une preface de Marguerite Duras et suivies d'un récit improvisé. Paris, 1969.

43701.48.100 Moll-Collet, Simone. Cris et silences. Paris, 1969.

FL 377.57.1 Mongrédien, Georges. Daily life in the French theatre at the time of Molière. London, 1969.

40525.2.85 Monsembernard, Guy de. Sénac de Meilhan, 1736-1803. Auch, 1969.

Mon 19.69 Montaigne, Michel de. Essais. Paris, 1969. 3v.

Mon 16.03.5F Montaigne, Michel de. Essays, 1603. Facsimile. Menston, Eng., 1969.

39594.13.50 Montesquieu, C.L. de S. Lettres persanes de Montesquieu. Paris, 1969.

43701.63.610 Montherlant, Henry de. Les garçons. Paris, 1969.

37543.594 Moore, Will G. French achievement in literature. London, 1969.

38543.24.25 Moore, Will Grayburn. La Rochefoucauld, his mind and art. Oxford, 1969.

43701.74.460 Morand, Paul. Discours de réception de Paul Morand à l'académie française et réponse de Jacques Chastenet. Paris, 1969.

43701.99.1110 Moré, Marcel. La foudre de Dieu. Paris, 1969.

37556.15.210 Morin, Violette. L'écriture de presse. Paris, 1969.

37576.669 Morton, Miriam. Voices from France; ten stories by French Nobel prize winners. 1. ed. Garden City, N.Y., 1969.

43757.50.1105 Motyleva, Tamara L. Romen Rollan. Moskva, 1969.

1969 - cont.

40587.231.2 Mourot, Jean. Le génie d'un style: Chateaubriand. Paris, 1969.
43701.89.2100 Moustiers, Pierre. La paroi. Paris, 1969.
37543.596 Mueller, Armand. De Rabelais à Paul Valery. Paris, 1969.
41578.195 Musée Lamartine. Sur les pas de Lamartine, Mâcon, Musée Lamartine. Mâcon, 1969.
37568.223.1 Nadeau, Maurice. The French novel since the war. N.Y., 1969.
42576.15.390 Nadeau, Maurice. Gustave Flaubert. Paris, 1969.
43744.67.1505.5 Nathan, Jacques. Catations, reférences et allusions de Marcel Proust dans A la recherche du temps perdu. Paris, 1969.
38525.108 Nelson, Robert James. Immanence and transcendence; the theater of Jean Rotrou, 1609-1650. Columbus, 1969.
43620.2.825 Nersoyan, Hagop J. André Gide; the theism of an atheist. 1. ed. Syracuse, N.Y., 1969.
42568.19.45 Nesselroth, P.W. Lautréamont's imagery. A stylistic approach. Genève, 1969.
37556.360.2 Nicoletti, Gianni. Introduzione allo studio del romanzo francese nel Settecento. 2. ed. Bari, 1969.
41564.55.145 Nitschke, Uwe. Studien zum Schicksalsgedanken und seiner dichterischen Gestaltung bei Alfred de Vigny. Hamburg, 1969.
43709.75.1100 Norge, G. Les cerveaux brûlés. Paris, 1969.
37543.614 Nurse, Peter H. The art of criticism. Edinburgh, 1969.
37568.276 Nyssen, Hubert. Les voies de l'écriture. Paris, 1969.
43723.41.1100 Olivier-Lacamp, Max. Les feux de la colère. Paris, 1969.
43737.14.100 Pacora, Madou. Le pain du jour. Paris, 1969.
43737.34.132 Pagnol, Marcel. Marius. Monte-Carlo, 1969.
43737.75.1100 Parenteau Dencel, Jacques. Les saisons de l'enfance, poèmes. Paris, 1969.
37556.316 Pashchenko, Vadim Il'ich. Prsty kolonializmu in viiny. Kyiv, 1969.
43554.2.1290 La pensée religieuse de Claudel. Paris, 1969.
43538.14.960 Perche, Louis. Beckett, l'enfer à notre portée. Paris, 1969.
43738.75.1100 Péret, Benjamin. Oeuvres complètes. Paris, 1969.
43738.81.170 Perret, Jacques. La compagnie des eaux. Paris, 1969.
43620.2.860 Perry, Kenneth I. The religious symbolism of André Gide. The Hague, 1969.
43620.2.865 Petersen, Carol. André Gide. Berlin, 1969.
43626.22.890 Petit, Jacques. Julien Green. Paris, 1969.
37557.76.36 Picard, Raymond. New criticism or new fraud? Pullman, 1969.
43698.200.845 Place, Georges. Henri Michaux. Paris, 1969.
37574.940 Poèmes de la révolution, mai 1968. Paris, 1969?
43743.41.3110 Poirot-Delpech, Bertrand. Finie la comédie. Paris, 1969.
39544.275.4 Pomeau, René. La religion de Voltaire. Paris, 1969.
37543.606 Ponton, Jeanne. La religieuse dans la littérature française. Québec, 1969.
43743.75.1100 Poreaux, Denise. Cette année de la Montagne. n.p., 1969.
Mon 126.10 Povilloux, Jean Yves. Lire les essais de Montaigne. Paris, 1969.
43744.67.79.2 Proust, Marcel. Comment débuta Marcel Proust; lettres inédites. Paris, 1969.
43750.24.182 Queneau, Raymond. Chêne et chien. Paris, 1969.
43750.24.735 Queneau, Raymond. Icaro involato. Torino, 1969.
38536.36.6 Rabelais, François. Pantagruel. Paris, 1969.
38583.22 Racine, Jean. Abrégé de l'histoire de Port-Royal, suivi de la Thébaide et de Alexandre le Grand. Paris, 1969.
FL 398.81.30 Raillard, Jacques. Mes dix années à après de Cécile. Paris, 1969.
40526.34.80 Raitière, Anna. L'art de l'acteur selon Dorat et Samson, 1766-1863/65. 1. éd. Genève, 1969.
42555.1.100 Ramsey, Warren. Jules Laforgue. Carbondale, 1969.
37556.302 Reck, Rima D. Literature and responsibility; the French novelist in the twentieth century. Baton Rouge, 1969.
V37566.168 Reizov, Boris G. Frantsuzskii roman XIX veka. Moskva, 1969.
43526.65.995 Renaud, Philippe. Lecture d'Apollinaire. Lausanne, 1969.
40524.28.80 Restif de la Bretonne, Nicolas E. L'Anti-Justine de Rétif de La Bretonne. Paris, 1969.
43753.90.621 Reverdy, P. Selected poems. N.Y., 1969.
43550.58.2015 Rhein, Phillip H. Albert Camus. N.Y., 1969.
38512.143 Ribard, Jacques. Un ménestrel du 14e siècle: Jean de Condé. Genève, 1969.
37574.942 Richard, Gaston. Anthologie des poètes gadzarts. Paris, 1969?
40516.6.85 Rieger, Dietmar. Jacques Cazotte. Heidelberg, 1969.
FL 376.15.1 Rigal, Eugéne. Le théâtre français avant la période classique. Genève, 1969.
43756.35.100 Riguillaume. Les fleurs du soleil. Paris, 1969.
V42556.28.91 Rimbaud, Jean Arthur. Poezje wybrane. wyd. 1. Warszawa, 1969.
38526.47.20.5 Rivaudeau, André de. A man. Tragédie sainte. Genève, 1969.
43757.7.7110 Robert, Jacques. Si ma mémoire est bonne. Paris, 1969.
43757.8.5110 Robin, Liliane. Le piège. Paris, 1969.
43538.14.945 Robinson, Michael. The long sonata of the dead. London, 1969.
37569.414 Roger, Gaston. La grande alliance. Paris, 1969.
37542.78 Roger, Jacques. Histoire de la littérature française. Paris, 1969-70. 2v.
43757.50.76 Rolland, Romain. Gandhi et Romain Rolland: correspondance. Paris, 1969.
43757.50.1325 Romain Rolland (Hommage). Neuchâtel, 1969.
43757.53.1100 Romains, Gabrielle. Dix-neuf cent quatorze - dix-neuf cent dix-huit. Paris, 1969.
38525.20.21.2 Ronsard, Pierre de. Poésies choisies. Paris, 1969.
FL 6046.12.20 Rousseau, J.J. Émile. London, 1969.
VFL 6010.1 Rousseau, J.J. Traktaty. Moskva, 1969.
43757.89.8112 Roussel, Romain. Papa, tu me fais rire. 2. éd. Paris, 1969.
43757.96.20 Roy, Claude. Somme toute. Paris, 1969.
43757.96.200 Roy, Claude. Le verbe aimer et autres essais. Paris, 1969.
43757.96.4152 Roy, Jules. Les chevaux du soleil. Paris, 1969.
43824.3.1815 Rybalka, Michel. Boris Vian, essai d'interprétation et de documentation. Paris, 1969.
40516.60.41 Sade, D.A.F. de. Les infortunes de la vertu. Paris, 1969.
40516.60.25 Sade, D.A.F. de. Schriften aus der Revolutionszeit (1788-1795). Frankfurt, 1969.
43538.1.845 Saetre, Solveig. Kvinnen-det annet kjønn? Oslo, 1969.
43761.31.230 Sagan, Françoise. Un peu de soleil dans l'eau froide. Paris, 1969.

1969 - cont.

37567.685 Sagnes, Guy. L'ennui dans la littérature française de Flaubert à Laforgue, 1848-1884. Paris, 1969.
43761.40.4100 St. Ange (pseud.). Les cavaliers de mai. Paris, 1969.
42555.44.215 St. Aubyn, Frederic Chase. Stéphane Mallarmé. N.Y., 1969.
43761.41.7100 St. Phalle, Thérèse de. Le tournesol. Paris, 1969.
43701.63.945 Saint Robert, Philippe de. Montherlant le séparé. Paris, 1969.
40575.26.20 Sainte-Beuve, Charles A. Volupté. Paris, 1969.
43761.49.2130 Salgas, Simone. Le goupil. Lausanne, 1969.
Mol 619.15 Salzmann, Wolfgang. Molière und die lateinsche Komödie. Heidelberg, 1969.
41557.9.48.16 Sand, George. La mare au diable. François le Champi. Evreux, 1969.
43761.77.725 Sarraute, Nathalie. Between life and death. N.Y., 1969.
43761.77.3100 Sarte, Sylvie. Variations urbaines. Paris, 1969.
43761.78.330 Sartre, Jean Paul. Les communistes ont peru de la révolution. Paris, 1969.
43761.78.622.15 Sartre, Jean Paul. Huis clos, suivi de Les mouches. Paris, 1969.
37563.87.9 Saulnier, Verdun L. La littérature française de la Renaissance. 9e éd. Paris, 1969.
40535.31.45 Schaad, Harold. Le thème de l'être et du paraître dans l'oeuvre de Marivaux. Zürich, 1969.
FL 381.20 Schaefer, Rotraut. Das eindringen schlichter Sprache in das französische Alexandrenerdrama, 1740-1840. Göppingen, 1969.
43763.63.100 Schoendoerffer, Pierre. L'adieu au roi. Paris, 1969.
43538.14.851 Scott, Nathan Alexander. Samuel Beckett. London, 1969.
38526.14.131.80 Secret, François. L'ésotérisme de Guy Le Fèvre de La Bodevie. Genève, 1969.
43765.56.100 Semprum, Jorge. La deuxième mort de Ramon Mercader. Paris, 1969.
FL 6139.69.5 Shklar, Judith Nisse. Men and citizens. Cambridge, 1969.
38525.22.45.62 Silver, Isidore. The intellectual evolution of Ronsard. St. Louis, 1969.
43769.54.786 Simenon, Georges. Maigret takes the waters. London, 1969.
43769.54.637 Simenon, Georges. Maigret triumphant. London, 1969.
43769.54.782 Simenon, Georges. The prison. 1. ed. N.Y., 1969.
37575.214 Six jeunes poètes...Anthologie. Tournai, 1969.
41542.4.110 Smith, Albert Brewster. Ideal and reality in the fictional narratives of Théophile Gautier. Gainsville, 1969.
37567.695 La société française, 1815-1914. Paris, 1969.
43709.89.810 Sozzi, Giorgio P. Germain Nouveau. Urbino, 1969.
43776.1.110 Spade, Henri. La Polonaise. Paris, 1969.
37530.196 Spaziani, Marcello. Introduzione bibliografica alla lingua e alla letteratura francese. Palermo, 1969.
FL 6139.69 Spurlin, Paul Merrill. Rousseau in America, 1760-1809. University, 1969.
40592.37 Staël Holstein, Anne Louise. Korinna ili Italiia. Moskva, 1969.
41592.10.25 Staritsyna, Z.A. Beranzhe v Rossii XIX vek. Moskva, 1969.
37556.280 Stewart, Philip R. Imitation and illusion in the French memoir-novel, 1700-1750. New Haven, 1969.
43620.2.830 Stoltzfus, Ben Frank. Gide's eagles. Carbondale, 1969.
43769.56.2800 Sturrock, John. The French novel: Claude Simon, Michel Bulor, Alain Robbe-Grillet. London, 1969.
43611.5.200 Suffran, Michel. Alain-Fournier ou le mystère limpide, essai. Paris, 1969.
43780.69.61 Supervielle, Jules. Correspondance, 1936-1959. Paris, 1969.
43785.75.155 Tardieu, Jean. Poèmes à jouer. Paris, 1969.
43822.49.1590 Tauman, Léon. Paul Valéry ou le Mal de l'art. Paris, 1969.
43554.2.1280 Taviani, Ferdinando. La parabola teatrale. Firenze, 1969.
40524.1.17 Tencin, Claudine A.G. de. Mémoires du Comte de Comminge. Lille, 1969.
FL 397.111 Le théâtre contemporain de Belgique. Bruxelles, 1969.
43788.41.2170 Thiry, Marcel. Le jardin fixe. Lausanne, 1969.
43788.41.2160 Thiry, Marcel. Saison cinq, et quatre proses. Bruxelles, 1969.
41568.26.4 Tillier, Claude. Mon oncle Benjamin. Paris, 1969.
41578.175 Toesca, Maurice. Lamartine ou l'amour de la vie. Paris, 1969.
42587.57.85 Trembley, George. Marcel Schwob, faussaire de la nature. Thèse. Genève, 1969.
40597.2.815 Trost, Sigrid. Die Persönlichkeit im Umschwung der politischen Macht nach Balzacs Comédie humaine. Bern, 1969.
43793.67.282 Troyat, Henri. Le geste d'Ève. Paris, 1969.
43793.67.350 Troyat, Henri. La grive. Paris, 1969.
43620.2.4 Uzès. Musée Municipal. André Gide: exposition du centenaire. Uzès, 1969.
43822.50.170 Vailland, Roger. Écrits intimes. Paris, 1969.
43822.41.1100 Vaillard, Pierre Jean. Tu parles, Charles. Paris, 1969.
42581.33.18 Vallès, Jules. Oeuvres complètes. Paris, 1969. 4v.
43822.60.100 Vannier, Angèle. La nuit ardente, roman. Paris, 1969.
41574.626 Van Tieghem, Philippe. Dictionnaire de Victor Hugo. Paris, 1969.
41596.4.86 Van Tieghem, Philippe. Musset. Paris, 1969.
43822.74.1100 Vercel, Simone Roger. La fin du grand hiver. Paris, 1969.
43823.74.1100 Vercel, Simone Roger. La fin du grand hiver. Paris, 1969.
42557.18.9.4 Verlaine, Paul. Oeuvres poétiques. Paris, 1969.
43823.78.1120 Véry, Pierre. Les anciens de Saint Loup. Lausanne, 1969.
43823.78.1110 Véry, Pierre. Un grand patron, le guérisseur. Lausanne, 1969.
43824.3.1250 Vian, Boris. Textes et chansons. Paris, 1969.
43738.1.950 Viard, Jacques. Philosophie de l'art littéraire et socialisme selon Péguy et selon Balzac. Paris, 1969.
38514.20.17.10 Villon, François. Oeuvres. Evreux, 1969.
38514.20.11.5 Villon, François. Oeuvres. Paris, 1969. 2v.
43744.67.1660 Vizcaíno, José Antonio. Marcel Proust. Madrid, 1969.
38542.2.7.5 Voiture, Vincent. Lettres de Monsieur de Voiture: Lettres aux Rambouillet. Paris, 1969.
39544.382 Wade, Ira Owen. The intellectual development of Voltaire. Princeton, N.J., 1969.
40583.384 Weber, Jean Paul. Stendhal; les structures thématiques de l'oeuvre et du destin. Paris, 1969.
38567.56 White, Julian Eugene. Nicolas Boileau. N.Y., 1969.
37556.308 Wilhelm, Kurt. Der nouveau Roman. Berlin, 1969.
43546.87.100 Wolfzettel, Friedrich. Michel Butor und der Kollektivroman. Heidelberg, 1969.
43667.14.820 Wyss, Tobias. Dialog und Stille. Zürich, 1969.
38526.1.12 Young, Margaret. Guillaume des Autelz. Genève, 1969.
40553.10.105 Zampogna, Domenico. Benjamin Constant et Belle de Charrière. Messina, 1969.

1969 - cont.

42584.19.60 Zola, Emile. Pot-Bouille. Paris, 1969.
42584.19.14 Zola, Emile. Thérèse Raquin. London, 1969.
42584.23.28 Zola, Emile. Le ventre de Paris. Paris, 1969.
42584.25.395 Zola. Paris, 1969.
43870.43.621 Zuk, Georges. Georges Zuk: selected verse. San Francisco, 1969.

1970

43513.75.130 Acremant, Germaine (Paulain). Chapeaux gris, chapeaux verts; roman. Paris, 1970.
43514.6.170 Adamov, Arthur. Si l'été revenait. Paris, 1970.
37596.276 Alard de Cambrai. Le livre de philosophie et de moralité d'Alard de Cambrai. Paris, 1970.
38527.38.11 Alary, Jacques. L'imprimerie au 16e siècle: Etienne Dolet et ses luttes avec la Sorbonne. Genève, 1970.
39533.20.55 Alcover, Madeleine. La pensée philosophique et scientifique de Cyrano de Bergerac. Genève, 1970.
42562.60.25 Allais, Alphonse. Contes. Paris, 1970.
43522.98.2100 Alzon, Claude. Le Pionicat. Ol Marlieux, 1970.
43551.59.825 Amaral, Aracy A. Blaise Cendras no Brasil e os modernistas. São Paulo, 1970.
38585.16.415 Ambroze, Anna. Racine, poète du sacrifice. Paris, 1970.
43523.21.100 Amédée, Louis. Journal d'un jeune homme triste, ou l'Espoir retrauvé; roman. Paris, 1970.
43524.67.340 Anouilh, Jean. Ne réveillez pas madame. Paris, 1970.
43524.67.26 Anouilh, Jean. Nouvelles pièces grinçantes. Paris, 1970.
43524.67.755 Anouilh, Jean. Ornifle. 1st ed. N.Y., 1970.
43524.67.330 Anouilh, Jean. Les poissons rouges; ou, Mon père, a héros. Paris, 1970.
43524.67.161 Anouilh, Jean. La répétition; ou, L'amour puni. Paris, 1970.
43526.65.350 Apollinaire, Guillaume. Les exploits d'un jeune Don Juan. Paris, 1970.
43527.3.132 Aragon, Louis. Les beaux quartiers. Paris, 1970.
43527.3.391 Aragon, Louis. Le mouvement perpétuel. Paris, 1970.
43620.2.870 Archives et musée de la littérature. Présence d'André Gide. Bruxelles, 1970.
43528.48.270 Arland, Marcel. Attendez l'aube. Paris, 1970.
43824.3.1821 Armaud, Noël. Les vies paralleles de Boris Vian. Paris, 1970.
43544.60.2800 Arndt, Béatrice. La quête poétique d'Yves Bonnefoy. Thèse. Zürich, 1970.
43822.49.1585 Arnold, Albert James. Paul Valéry and his critics; a bibliography. Charlottesville, 1970.
43528.73.130 Arrabal, Fernando. L'enterrement de la sardine. Paris, 1970.
43528.86.14 Artaud, Antonin. Oeuvres complètes. Paris, 1970- 3v.
43528.86.14.5 Artaud, Antonin. Oeuvres complètes. Supplement. Paris, 1970.
40526.8.45 Aubarède, Gabriel d'. André Chénier. Paris, 1970.
37544.140 Aubéry, Pierre. Pour une lecture ouvrière de la littérature. Paris, 1970.
38527.28.17 Aubigné, Théodore Agrippa d'. Les tragiques. London, 1970.
41542.80.6 Audebrand, Philibert. Léon Gozlan: scènes de la vie littéraire, 1828-1865. Genève, 1970.
43545.24.900 Audoin, Philippe. Breton. Paris, 1970.
39566.9.1 Avezac-Lavigne, C. Diderot et la société du Baron d'Holbach. Paris, 1970.
43535.54.102 Aymé, Marcel. La Table-aux-Crevés. Paris, 1970.
FL 6139.70 Baczko, Bronisław. Rousseau. Wien, 1970.
38526.27.5.106 Baguenault de Puchesse, Gustave. Jean et Jacques de La Taille. Genève, 1970.
40597.2.840 Bakhmutskii, Vladimir Ia. "Otets Gorio" Balzaka. Moskva, 1970.
37555.536.1 Balakian, Anna E. Surrealism. N.Y., 1970.
40597.35.146 Balzac, Honoré de. A harlot high and low. Harmondsworth, Eng., 1970.
40597.35.124 Balzac, Honoré de. L'illustre Gaudissart. La muse du département. Paris, 1970.
40597.35.250 Balzac, Honoré de. Le secret des Ruggieri. Columbia, 1970.
38526.22.12.2 Banachévitch, N. Jean Bastier de La Péruse, 1529-1554. Genève, 1970.
40597.2.835 Barbéris, Pierre. Balzac et le mal du siècle. Paris, 1970. 2v.
39594.19.9.1 Barckhausen, Henri. Montesquieu, ses idées et ses oeuvres d'après les papiers de la Brède. Genève, 1970.
FL 398.7.95 Baring, Maurice. Sarah Bernhardt. Westport, 1970.
43538.14.970 Barnard, Guy Christian. Samuel Beckett: a new approach. London, 1970.
43537.77.6110 Barrault, Jean Louis. Jarry sur la Butte. Paris, 1970.
41574.283.20 Barrère, Jean Bertrand. Hugo. Paris, 1970.
43537.82.4100 Bastid, Paul. Ailleurs, poèmes. Paris, 1970.
37547.14.10 Bastit, Gaston. La Gascogne littéraire. Genève, 1970.
43537.84.1011 Bataille, Georges. Oeuvres complètes. Paris, 1970- 4v.
43537.89.8100 Baud-Bovy, Daniel. L'homme à la femme de bois. Genève, 1970.
41522.13.28 Baudelaire, Charles. Ausgewählte Gedichte. 1. Aufl. Frankfurt, 1970.
41522.18.560 Baudelaire, Charles. Letters from his youth. Garden City, N.Y., 1970.
41522.13.9.58 Baudelaire, Charles. Tsvety zla. 3. izd. Moskva, 1970.
43544.90.6100 Baurrec, Jean Roger. La brûlure. Paris, 1970.
38563.6.31 Bayle, Pierre. Projet et fragments d'un dictionnaire critique. Genève, 1970.
43537.99.190 Bazin, Hervé. Les bienheureux de la Désolation. Paris, 1970.
38544.27.595.5 Bazin de Bezons, Jean de. Étude de l'attribution de la Princesse de Clèves par des moyens de statistique du vocabulaire. Paris, 1970.
43701.63.950 Becker, Lucille. Henry de Montherlant; a critical biography. Carbondale, 1970.
43538.14.280 Beckett, Samuel. Le dépeupleur. Paris, 1970.
43538.14.260 Beckett, Samuel. Mercier et Camier. Paris, 1970.
43538.14.270 Beckett, Samuel. Premier amour. Paris, 1970.
43538.14.757 Beckett, Samuel. Residua; Prosadichtungen in drei Sprachen. 1. Aufl. Frankfurt, 1970.
43538.14.702 Beckett, Samuel. Waiting for Godot, tragicomedy in 2 acts. N.Y., 1970.
37574.914.1 Bédouin, Jean Louis. La poésie surréaliste. Paris, 1970.
43538.59.2130 Benedetto, André. Emballage, Le Havre 1970. Théâtre. Paris, 1970.

1970 - cont.

43538.59.2140 Benedetto, André. Rosa Lux, théâtre. Honfleur, 1970.
43538.59.1100 Bénézet, M. Biographies. A novel. Paris, 1970.
41543.22.170 Benichou, Paul. Nerval et la chanson folklorique. Paris, 1970.
39566.245 Bénot, Yves. Diderot: de l'athéisme à l'antecolonialisme. Paris, 1970.
38527.48.1 Bernage, Siméon. Étude sur Robert Garnier. Genève, 1970.
43538.76.5150 Bernard, Michel. La plage. Paris, 1970.
FL 360.105 Berrettini, Célia. Teatro francês. São Paulo, 1970.
38526.9.10 Bertaut, Jean. Recueil de quelques vers amoureux. Paris, 1970.
38585.16.410 Besançon, France. Université. Laboratoire d'analyse lexicologique. J. Racine, "Andromanque." Paris, 1970.
40582.8.4.13 Beyle, Henri. De l'amour. Paris, 1970.
40582.41.2 Beyle, Henri. Life of Rossini. N.Y., 1970.
37567.735 Bibescŭ, Marthe Lucie (Lahovary). Le confesseur et les poètes. Paris, 1970.
43620.2.885 Bibliothèque nationale, Paris. André Gide. Paris, 1970.
42586.63.50 Biddiss, Michael D. Father of racist ideology. London, 1970.
43697.75.890 Blázquez Carmona, Feliciano. Gabriel Marcel. Madrid, 1970.
38542.29.10 Blessebois, Pierre Corneille. Le Zombi du Grand-Pérou et autres oeuvres érotiques. Paris, 1970.
Mon 142.4 Blinkenberg, Andreas. Montaigne. København, 1970.
43543.67.120 Blondin, Antoine. Monsieur Jadis. Paris, 1970.
43543.89.1100 Blum, Suzanne. Ne savoir rien. Paris, 1970.
Mon 112.12.1 Boase, Alan Martin. The fortunes of Montaigne. N.Y., 1970.
43620.2.890 Boisdeffre, Pierre de. Vie d'André Gide, 1869-1951. Paris, 1970-
43544.48.100 Boldoduc, Michel. Les remontoirs. Paris, 1970.
40583.390 Bolster, Richard. Stendhal, Balzac, et le féminisme romantique. Paris, 1970.
43544.59.21 Bonheur, Gaston. Chemin privé; oeuvres poétiques (1930-1970). Paris, 1970.
38527.51.2 Bonnefon, Paul. Estienne de La Boétie. Genève, 1970.
43656.59.661 Bonnefoy, Claude. Conversations with Eugène Ionesco. London, 1970.
43544.60.2101 Bonnefoy, Yves. Du mouvement et de l'immobilité de Douve. Paris, 1970.
42563.33.100 Bordeu, Charles de. Le dernier maître. Pau, 1970.
43544.74.2120 Bordonove, Georges. Le chevalier Du Landreau. Paris, 1970.
43544.74.5100 Bordry, Paul. Étude et hypothèse sur la véritable fin dernière de "l'Histoire d'O". Paris, 1970.
43544.88.2160 Boulanger, Daniel. Mémoire de la ville. Paris, 1970.
43544.89.65 Bousquet, Joë. Lettres à Jean Cassou. Limoges, 1970.
37547.103.10 Bouvelot, Paule. L'Auvergne à travers la poésie auvergnate contemporaine. Aurillac, 1970?
39544.398 Bouvy, Eugène. Voltaire et l'Italie. Genève, 1970.
38585.16.401 Bowra, Cecil Maurice. The simplicity of Racine. Folcroft, 1970.
40535.31.20 Brady, Valentini Papadopoulow. Love in the theatre of Marivaux; a study of the factors influencing its birth, development, and expression. Genève, 1970.
37573.740 Brée, Germaine. Defeat and beyond; an anthology of French wartime writing, 1940-1945. N.Y., 1970.
43545.23.2110 Breitman, Michel. D'exil en exil. Paris, 1970.
43545.24.142 Breton, André. Point du jour. Paris, 1970.
37569.40.22 Breton, André. L'un dans l'autre. Paris, 1970.
43545.42.3120 Brisville, Jean Claude. Le rôdeur. Nora. Le récital. Paris, 1970.
43554.2.1305 Brodeur, Léo A. Le corps-sphère, clef de la symbolique Claudélienne. Montréal, 1970.
43556.1.995 Brosse, Jacques. Cocteau. Paris, 1970.
43545.67.1100 Broussard, Yves. Bestiaire des solitudes; poème. Bram, 1970.
Mol 702.11 Bulgakov, Mikhail Afanas'evich. The life of Monsieur de Molière. N.Y., 1970.
42554.26.855 Burch, Francis F. Tristan Corbière: l'originalité des Amours jaunes et leur influence sur T.S. Eliot. Paris, 1970.
39594.13.80 Cadalso, José. Defensa de la nación española contra la Carta persiana LXXVIII de Montesquieu. Toulouse, 1970.
43550.41.120 Caillois, Roger. Cases d'un échiquier. Paris, 1970.
43550.58.2075 Camus 1970. Sherbrooke, 1970.
42568.19.40 Caradac, François. Isidore Lucien Ducasse. Paris, 1970.
43761.39.955 Cate, Curtis. Antoine de St. Exupéry. N.Y., 1970.
39566.255 Catrysse, Jean. Diderot et la mystification. Paris, 1970.
37555.764 Caws, Mary Ann. The poetry of Dada and surrealism. Princeton, 1970.
42542.49.25 Céard, Henry. Une belle journée. Genève, 1970.
41522.18.630 Cellier, Léon. Baudelaire et Hugo. Paris, 1970.
43551.59.725 Cendrars, Blaise. The astonished man. London, 1970.
43551.79.190 Césaire, Aimé. Soleil cou-coupé. Nendeln, 1970.
43551.79.775 Césaire, Aimé. Ein Sturm. Berlin, 1970.
43552.1.1130 Chaamba, Abdallah (pseud.). Un voyage au Mont Athos. Paris, 1970.
43552.1.3100 Chabrièr, Agnès. La part des ténèbres; roman. Paris, 1970.
43552.2.2180 Chabrol, Jean-Pierre. Le Canon Fraternité. Paris, 1970.
43552.1.4100 Chabrun, Jean François. Les chantiers chimériques. Paris, 1970.
43552.3.1110 Chaigne, Louis. Itinéraires d'une espérance. Paris, 1970.
43552.2.8100 Chambon, Jean. La sentinelle; roman. Paris, 1970.
39586.19.3.6 Chamfort, S.R.N. Maximes et pensées: caractéres et anecdotes. Paris, 1970.
39586.19.3.10 Chamfort, S.R.N. Maximes et pensées. Suivies de mélanges de littérature et d'histoire. Paris, 1970.
43552.3.9320 Chamson, André. La tour de Constance; roman. Paris, 1970.
43556.1.999 Chanel, Pierre. Album Cocteau. Paris, 1970.
37555.83.2 Charbonnier, F. La poésie française et les guerres de religion (1560-1574). Genève, 1970.
43552.5.260 Chardonne, Jacques. Ce que je voulais vous dire aujourd'hui. Paris, 1970.
41578.156 Charvot, Louis. Aux confins du Dauphiné et de la Savoie. Montfleury, 1970.
43552.2.7100 Chasle, Raymond. Le corailleur des limbes. Honfleur, 1970.
39586.36.1 Chastellux, François Jean. Essai sur l'union de la poésie et de la musique. Genève, 1970.
37598.15.5 Chastie-musart. Chastie-musart. Roma, 1970.
40586.21.13 Chateaubriand, F.A.R. René. Genève, 1970.

Chronological Listing

1970 - cont.

40587.185 Chateaubriand today; proceedings of the commemoration of the bicentenary of the birth of Chateaubriand, 1968. Madison, 1970.
38551.43.8 Chérel, Albert. Fénelon au XVIIIe siècle en France. 1715-1820. Genève, 1970.
41574.638 Chételat, Emmanuel J. Les occidentales; ou, Lettres critiques sur Les Orientales de M. Victor Hugo. Paris, 1829. Paris, 1970.
43526.65.1005 Chevalier, Jean Claude. Alcools d'Apollinaire. Paris, 1970.
FL 398.12.20 Chevalier, Maurice. Les pensées de Momo. Paris, 1970.
40525.42.1 Chevalier de la Marmotte. Les songes du Chevalier de la Marmotte. pt.1. Paris, 1970.
FL 377.188 Chevalley, Sylvie Bostsarron. Album théâtre classique. Paris, 1970.
43554.5.2160 Clavel, Bernard. Le tambour du Bief. Paris, 1970.
43554.7.20 Clemenceau, Georges. Lettres à une amie; 1923-1929. Paris, 1970.
43554.23.1100 Clément, Michel. Confidences d'une prune. Montréal, 1970.
37574.944 Clodd, Alan. Collected verse translations. London, 1970.
43822.49.1610 Cloran, Émile M. Valéry face à ses idoles. Paris, 1970.
37576.670.5 Club des intellectuels français. Sélection 1970 de contes et nouvelles. Courbevoie, 1970.
43556.1.82 Cocteau, Jean. Lettres à André Gide. Paris, 1970.
43556.1.641 Cocteau, Jean. Professional secrets; an autobiography. N.Y., 1970.
43556.1.718 Cocteau, Jean. Two screenplays: The blood of a poet, The testament of Orpheus. London, 1970.
FL 6129.70 Cohler, Anne Meyers. Rousseau and nationalism. N.Y., 1970.
43556.49.27 Colette, Sidonie Gabrielle. Contes des mille et un matius. Paris, 1970.
43556.49.780 Colette, Sidonie Gabrielle. Places, by Colette. London, 1970.
37555.776 Colletet, Guillaume. Le parnasse français ou L'ecole des muses. Genève, 1970.
37547.14.1 Colletet, Guillaume. Vies des poètes gascons. Genève, 1970.
39527.75 Collinet, Jean Pierre. Le monde littéraire de La Fontaine. Paris, 1970.
43576.6.870 Comeau, Yvan. Georges Duhamel et la possession du monde jusqu'à la chronique des Pasquier. Thèse. Montréal, 1970.
43556.58.150 Conchon, Georges. Les honneurs de la guerre. Paris? 1970.
42514.28.89 Cormier, Aristide. Mes entretiens de prêtre avec Charles Maurras. Paris, 1970.
38576.12.42.55 Corneille, Thomas. Timocrate. Genève, 1970.
37567.440.1 Cornell, William Kenneth. The symbolist movement. Hamden, Conn., 1970.
FL 1018.46.100 Cotis-Capel. Raz-Bannes; poémes en langue normande. Coutances, 1970.
38528.14.85 Cottrell, Robert D. Brantôme: the writer as portraitist of his age. Genève, 1970.
37567.705 Couffignal, Robert. La paraphrase poétique de la "Genèse", de Hugo à Supervielle. Paris, 1970.
43556.89.5100 Coulonges, Georges. Le grand Guignol. Paris, 1970.
37576.670 Courtine, Robert J. Anthologie de la littérature gastronomique. Paris, 1970.
FL 6129.11.11 Courtois, Louis J. Le séjour de Jean-Jacques Rousseau en Angleterre, 1766-1767. Genève, 1970.
43550.58.1100 Les critiques de notre temps et Camus. Paris, 1970.
43554.2.1325 Les critiques de notre temps et Claudel. Paris, 1970.
42554.26.90 Cros, Charles. Oeuvres complètes. Paris, 1970.
37567.736 Cutler, Maxine G. Evocations of the eighteenth century in French poetry, 1800-1869. Genève, 1970.
39533.20.4.15 Cyrano de Bergerac. Voyage dans la lune. Paris, 1970.
37547.1.10 Daire, Louis François. Histoire littéraire de la ville d'Amien. Genève, 1970.
42546.12.65 Daladie, Maité. Lettre à ma niece sur Edmond Rostand. Toulouse, 1970.
43565.60.1210 Daninos, Pierre. Ludovic Morateur, ou, Le plus que parfait. Paris, 1970.
43565.89.130 Daumal, René. Tu t'es toujours trompé. Paris, 1970.
37543.640 De Jean Lemaire de Belges à Jean Giraudoux. Paris, 1970.
37567.710 Debré, Moses. The image of the Jew in French literature from 1800 to 1908. N.Y., 1970.
FL 1098.47.800 Debrie, René. Hector Crimon. Grandvilliers, 1970.
43566.42.2100 Déjean, Jean Luc. La feuille à l'envers. Paris, 1970.
38585.78 Delcroix, Maurice. Le sacré dans les tragédies profanes de Racine. Paris, 1970.
43744.67.1650.2 Deleuze, Gilles. Proust et le signes. 2. éd. Paris, 1970.
38512.150 Délivrance du peuple d'Israël. La délivrance du peuple d'Israël. 1. Aufl. München, 1970.
37548.234 Delmelle, Joseph. Panorama littéraire du Luxembourg. Vieux-Virton, 1970.
40516.60.145 Delpech, Jeanine. La passion de la Marquise de Sade. Paris, 1970.
41574.628 Delteil, Yvan. La fin tragique du voyage de Victor Hugo en 1843. Paris, 1970.
Mol 604.10.5 Descotes, Maurice. Molière et sa fortune littéraire. Saint-Médard-en-Julles, 1970.
38576.21.40 Desjardins, Marie C.H. Les désordres de l'amour. Genève, 1970.
40535.30.70 Desvignes-Parent, Lucette. Marivaux et l'Angleteer. Paris, 1970.
43567.79.210 Dhôtel, André. La maison du bout du monde. Paris, 1970.
43568.24.1100 Dieryck, Yves. Promenade en marge. Évreux, 1970.
43761.48.810 Di Franco, Fiorenza. Le théâtre de Salacrou. Paris, 1970.
42576.15.415 Digeon, Claude. Flaubert. Paris, 1970.
43697.52.950 Dorenlot, F.E. Malraux; ou, L'unité de pensée. Paris, 1970.
42563.23.210 Dotoli, Giovanni. Situation des études bloyennes. Paris, 1970.
43694.11.2820 Douenel, Henri. Les grandes orgues de Dieu. Paris, 1970.
40583.378 Dramińska-Joczowa, Maria. Wpływ ideologów na młodego Stendhala. Wrocław, 1970.
43538.14.985 Dreysse, Ursula. Realität als Aufgabe. Berlin, 1970.
37575.332 Dubacq, Jean. L'école de Rochefort. Paris, 1970.
42568.19.21.18 Ducasse, I.L. Oeuvres complètes de Lautréamont et Germain Nouveau. Paris, 1970.
37557.75.5 Duchêne, Roger. Realité vécue et art épistolaire. Paris, 1970.
40517.23.26 Duclos, C.P. Correspondance de Charles Duclos, 1704-1722. Saint Brieuc, 1970.
38528.20.15 Du Fail, Noël. Les baliverneries d'Eutrapel. Paris, 1970.
43535.54.816 Dumont, Jean Louis. Marcel Aymé et le merveilleux. Paris, 1970.

1970 - cont.

43576.74.2240 Duras, Marguerite. Abahn, Sabana, David. Paris, 1970.
43576.76.120 Durry, Marie-Jeanne. Eden; cinq actes. Paris, 1970.
41557.10.270 Dussault, Louis. George Sand. Montréal, 1970.
43576.90.2110 Duvert, Tony. Le voyageur. Paris, 1970.
42586.57.95 Eckstein, Marie Anne. Le rôle du souvenir dans l'oeuvre d'Eugène Fromentin. Zurich, 1970.
39598.50 Ehrard, Jean. De l'encyclopédie à la contre-révolution; Jean-François Marmontel, 1723-1799. Clermont-Ferrand, 1970.
37565.192 Ehrard, Jean. L'idée de nature en France à l'aube des lumières. Paris, 1970.
43545.24.831 Eigeldinger, Marc. André Breton. Neuchâtel, 1970.
43592.53.41 Emmanuel, Pierre. Autobiographies. Paris, 1970.
43592.53.360 Emmanuel, Pierre. Choses dites. Paris, 1970.
37556.355 Engler, Winfried. Texte zur französischen Romantheorie des 19. Jahrhunderts. Tübingen, 1970.
37569.446 Entretiens sur la paralittérature, Cerisy-la-Salle, 1967. Entretiens sur la paralittérature. 1er sept.-10 sept.1967. Paris, 1970.
43598.84.250 Estaunié, Édouard. La vie secrète. Évreux, 1970.
38544.27.615 Fabre, Jean. L'art de l'analyse dans la Princesse de Clèves. Paris, 1970.
43538.14.990 Federman, Raymond. Samuel Beckett: his works and critics. Berkeley, 1970.
42524.62 Felix, Jozef. Modernita súčasnosti. 1. vyd. Bratislava, 1970.
37543.624 Fellows, Otis Edward. Problems and personalities, from Voltaire to La nouvelle critique. Genève, 1970.
38554.518.44 Fénelon, F. de S. de la Mothe. Lettre à l'Académie, avec les versions primitives. Genève, 1970.
38554.518.47 Fénelon, F. de S. de la Mothe. Lettre à l'Académie. Genève, 1970.
43607.77.4100 Ferrière, Anette. Le squelette de Kazan. Paris, 1970.
42586.48.30 Féval, Paul H. Les mystères de Londres. Genève, 1970? 4v.
42543.41.30 Feydeau, Georges. Four farces. Chicago, 1970.
38585.16.395 Fingerhut, Margret. Racine in deutschen Übersetzungen des neunzehnten und zwanzigsten Jahrhunderts. Bonn, 1970.
43538.14.842 Fletcher, John. The novels of Samuel Beckett. 2. ed. London, 1970.
43538.76.1005 Flower, John Ernest. Georges Bernanos: Journal d'un curé de campagne. London, 1970.
38562.21.25 Fontenelle, B. Le B. de. The achievement of Bernard le Bovier de Fontenelle. N.Y., 1970.
38562.20.21 Fontenelle, B. Le B. de. Entretiens sur la pluralité des mondes. Paris, 1970.
42576.62.11.20 France, Anatole. Alfred de Vigny; étude. Poésies. Levallois-Perret, 1970.
42576.62.11.25 France, Anatole. Pages d'histoire et de littérature. Levallois-Perret, 1970.
42576.62.170 France, Anatole. Théâtre. Evreux, 1970.
43612.65.41 Frank, Bernard. Un siècle d'ebordé. Paris, 1970.
43612.24.150 Frère, Maud. L'ange avengle. Paris, 1970.
40532.25.22 Frischauser, Paul. Beaumarchais, adventurer in the century of women. Port Washington, 1970.
37544.150 Gachon, Lucien. L'écrivain et le paysan. Moulins, 1970.
43616.31.21 Gag, Francis. Théâtre niçois. Nice, 1970.
43616.33.1100 Gagnon, Alain. Le pour et le contre; nouvelles. Montréal, 1970.
43616.41.2170 Gaillard, Robert. La sultane de Jolo. Paris, 1970.
43616.53.1100 Gamarra, Pierre. La maison de feu. Évreux, 1970.
43616.53.1120 Gamarra, Pierre. L'or et le sang. Paris, 1970.
43616.53.1110 Gamarra, Pierre. Pauchkine. Bram, 1970.
41569.30 Gamiani, ou deux nuits d'excès. Paris, 1970.
41596.4.145 Ganne, Gilbert. Alfred de Musset, sa jeunesse et la nôtre. Paris, 1970.
43616.77.2100 Garreau, Albert. Inquisitions. Paris, 1970-
43616.78.41 Gary, Romain. Chien blanc. Paris, 1970.
43616.78.132 Gary, Romain. Tulipe. Paris, 1970.
43616.1.8120 Gautier, Jean Jacques. La chambre du fond. Paris, 1970.
41542.31.2 Gautier, Théophile. Poésies complètes de Théophile Gautier. Paris, 1970. 3v.
43616.89.7100 Gauzelin, Alain. L'ile mouvante. Paris, 1970.
43616.98.1130 Gay-Lussac, Bruno. Introduction à la vie profane. Paris, 1970.
38525.22.45.115 Gendre, André. Ronsard; poète de la conquête amoureuse. Neuchâtel, 1970.
43757.50.1315 Gersbach-Bäschlin, Annette. Reflektorischer Stil und Erzählstruktur. Bern, 1970.
43620.2.32.25 Gide, André. The immoralist. N.Y., 1970.
43620.2.35.21 Gide, André. La symphonie pastorale. Paris, 1970.
43620.66.510 Giono, Jean. L'Iris de Suse. Paris, 1970.
43552.5.1865 Giraud, Henri. La morale d'Alain. Toulouse, 1970.
41543.22.185 Girolamo, Nicola di. Nerval e la tematica delle Figlie del fuoco. Bologna, 1970.
42586.68.70 Gobineau, Arthur de. Gobineau: selected political writings. London, 1970.
37556.318 Godenne, René. Histoire de la nouvelle française aux 17e et 18e siècles. Genève, 1970.
38585.16.241 Goldmann, Lucien. Jean Racine. Paris, 1970.
37569.436 Goldmann, Lucien. Structure mentales et création culturelle. Paris, 1970.
38525.9.10 Gordon, Alexandre L. Ronsard et la rhétorique. Genève, 1970.
43761.78.945 Gore, Keith. Sartre: La nausée and Les mouches. London, 1970.
43625.76.100 Gorka, Stani. Les cavaliers de Guernica. Paris, 1970.
FL 6139.70.10 Gouhier, Henri. Les méditations métaphysiques de Jean-Jacques Rousseau. Paris, 1970.
42584.25.287 Grant, Elliott M. Zola's Germinal. Leicester, 1970.
40583.155.1 Green, Frederick Charles. Stendhal. N.Y., 1970.
38537.60 Greene, Thomas M. Rabelais; a study in comic courage. Englewood Cliffs, N.J., 1970.
38527.31.20 Griffiths, Richard. The dramatic technique of Antoine de Montchrétien. Oxford, 1970.
37596.103.100 Guillaume Le Vinier. Les poésies de Guillaume Le Vinier. Paris, 1970.
43628.41.3180 Guillevic, Eugène. Paroi. Paris, 1970.
38514.23.141 Guiraud, Pierre. Le testament de Villon. Paris, 1970.
38585.74 Gutwirth, Marcel. Jean Racine; un itineraire poétique. Montréal, 1970.
37593.64.2 Guy, Henry. Essai sur la vie et les oeuvres littéraires du trouvère Adam de la Halle. Genève, 1970.
42555.44.245 Haas, Doris. Flucht aus der Wirklichkeit. Bonn, 1970.
38544.27.610 Haig, Stirling. Madame de La Fayette. N.Y., 1970.

Chronological Listing

1970 - cont.

38526.3.5.201 Hamon, Auguste. Un grand rhétoriqueur poitevin; Jean Bouchet, 1476-1557? Genève, 1970.
42576.15.405 Hardt, Manfred. Flauberts Spätwerk. Frankfurt, 1970.
39533.20.45 Harth, Erica. Cyrano de Bergerac and the polemics of modernity. N.Y., 1970.
43538.14.965 Harvey, Lawrence Elliot. Samuel Beckett, poet and critic. Princeton, 1970.
37567.725 Heitmaun, Klaus. Der Immoralismus-Prozess gegen die französische Literatur im 19. Jahrhundert. Bad Homburg, 1970.
43632.50.280 Hellens, Franz. Cet âge qu'on dit grand. Bruxelles, 1970.
38526.46.360 Hester, Ralph M. A Protestant Baroque poet, Pierre Poupo. The Hague, 1970.
43632.89.2100 Heurté, Yves. La ruche en feu. Paris, 1970.
37596.10.230 Holmes, Urban Tigner. Chrétien de Troyes. N.Y., 1970.
43532.23.805 Hommage à Claude Aveline. Paris, 1970.
43636.89.140 Hougron, Jean. La gueule pleine de dents. Paris, 1970.
43626.22.2 Hoy, Peter C. Julien Green, 1900-; manuscrits, éditions originales, photographies, documents. Bibliographie. Oxford? 1970?
43626.22.1 Hoy, Peter C. Julien Green. Paris, 1970.
41574.624 Huas, Jeanine. Juliette Drouet; ou, La passion romantique. Paris, 1970.
41574.16.30 Hugo, Victor. Victor Hugo publie Les miserables. Paris, 1970.
37563.120 Humanism in France at the end of the Middle Ages and in the early renaissance. N.Y., 1970.
43527.3.875 Huraut, Alain. Louis Aragon, prisonnier politique. Paris, 1970.
40583.360.5 Imbert, Henri François. Stendhal et la tentation jauséniste. Genève, 1970.
43822.49.1362 Ince, Walter Newcombe. The poetic theory of Paul Valéry: inspiration and technique. 2nd ed. Leicester, 1970.
38526.21.100 Indermuehle, Werner. Essai sur l'oeuvre de Claude Hopil. Thèse. Zürich, 1970.
43656.59.210 Ionesco, Eugène. Jeux de massacre. Paris, 1970.
43620.2.425.5 Ireland, George William. André Gide: a study of his creative writings. Oxford, 1970.
37555.770 Ireson, J.C. Imagination in French romantic poetry. Hull, 1970.
37569.428 Isbakh, Aleksandr A. Vo glave kolonny. Moskva, 1970.
42576.65.13.160 Issacharoff, Michael. J.K. Huysmans devant la critique en France (1874-1960). Paris, 1970.
43667.11.120 Jaccottet, Philippe. Paysages avec figures absentes. Paris, 1970.
40597.2.875 Jacques, Georges. Le doigt de Dieu. Louvain, 1970.
38551.72.5 Janet, Paul. Fénelon, his life and works. Port Washington, 1970.
37555.18.2 Jasinski, Max. Histoire du sonnet en France. Genève, 1970.
37597.33.5 Jean de Condé. La messe des oiseaux et le Dit des jacobins et des fremeneurs. Paris, 1970.
38513.19.30 Jehan du Prier. Le mystère du Roy Advenir. Genève, 1970.
38525.22.45.120 Jones, Kenneth R. Wilson. Pierre de Ronsard. N.Y., 1970.
43670.89.1100 Jouffroy, Alain. La fin des alternances. Paris, 1970.
43670.89.620 Jouhandeau, M. Olympias, suivi de Antistia et de tout ou rien. Paris, 1970.
43526.65.1010 Journées Apollinaire, Stavelot, Belgium. Du monde européan à l'univers des mythes. Paris, 1970.
41556.39 Juin, Hubert. Charles Nodier. Paris, 1970.
43671.51.700 Jullian, Philippe. Flight into Egypt; a fantasy. N.Y., 1970.
43659.88.805 Jutrin-Klener, Monique. Panaït Istrati: un chardon déraciné, écrivain français, conteur roumain. Paris, 1970.
40524.32.60A Karmel, Alex. My revolution; promenades in Paris, 1789-1794, being the diary of Restif de la Bretonne. 1st ed. N.Y., 1970.
43672.84.110 Katcha, Vahé. Un nègre sur la statue de Lincoln. Paris, 1970.
42556.28.420 Kloepfer, Rolf. Sprachliche Konstituenten moderner Dichtung. Bad Homburg, 1970.
43556.1.985 Knapp, Bettina (Liebowitz). Jean Cocteau. N.Y., 1970.
40517.4.80 Knapp-Tepperberg, Eva Maria. Robert Challes Illustres françaises. Heidelberg, 1970.
43681.2.100 Kraemer, Jacques. Splendeur et misère de Minette la bonne Lorraine. Paris, 1970.
37530.198 Krauss, Werner. Französische Drucke des 18 Jahrhunderts in den Biliotheken der Deutschen Demokratischen Republik. v.1-2. Berlin, 1970.
40597.2.825 Kuchborskaia, Elizaveta P. Tvorchestvo Bal'zaka. Moskva, 1970.
38564.32.41 La Bruyère, J. de. Les Caractères de Théophraste. Évreux, 1970.
42555.1.2 Laforgue, Jules. Poésies complètes. Paris, 1970.
38526.27.15.7 Lamaire de Belges, Jean. Die Briefe des grünen Liebhaben. München, 1970.
43687.58.2160 Landry, Charles François. Bord du monde. Lausanne, 1970.
43687.58.2150 Landry, Charles François. Nouvelles méridionales. Lausanne, 1970.
39578.8.10 Lanson, Gustave. Le marquis de Vauvenargues. Genève, 1970.
40535.19.202 Lanson, Gustave. Nivelle de La Chaussée et la comédie larmoyante. 2. éd. Genève, 1970.
43687.65.150 Lanza del Vasto, Joseph Jean. Viatique et Enfances d'une pensée. v.1-2. Paris, 1970.
37575.460 LaRoche Folle, Jean de. Morale et maximes d'un simple, un guide dans la vie, sagesse. Guéret, 1970.
37568.282 La Rochefoucauld, Edmée de F. Courts métrages. Paris, 1970.
43687.82.1100 Lasseaux, Marcel. À s'y tromper. Paris, 1970.
38512.33.5 La Tour-Landry, Geoffrey de. Der Ritter vom Turn von den Exempeln der Gotsforcht vn Erberkeit. Basel, 1493. Unterschneidheim, 1970.
43687.89.1220 Laurent, Jacques. La Communarde; roman. Paris, 1970.
37596.94.1 Lavis, G. Les chansons de Blondel de Nesle. Liège, 1970?
37575.795 Le Brun, Annie. Les mots font l'amour, citations surréalistes. Paris, 1970.
37556.22.95 Leclerc, Joseph. Le cinéma, témoin de son temps. Paris, 1970.
43688.14.4160 Le Clézio, Jean Marie Gustave. La guerre. Paris, 1970.
43688.20.150 Leduc, Violette. La folie en tête. Paria, 1970.
43688.20.705 Leduc, Violette. In the prison of her skin. London, 1970.
FL 386.820 Lee, Vera G. Quest for a public. Cambridge, Mass., 1970.
41596.4.107 Lefebvre, Henri. Musset; essai. 2. éd. Paris, 1970.
43707.98.800 Leiner, Jacqueline. Le destin littéraire de Paul Nizan et ses étapes successives. Paris, 1970.

1970 - cont.

37542.64 Lemaître, Henri. La littérature française. Paris, 1970-72. 5v.
43688.77.3100 LeMarquet, Jacques. L'ile des pommes; (théâtre). Paris, 1970.
38527.5.1 Lemercier, Aimé Prosper. Étude littéraire et morale sur les poésies de Jean Vauquelin de la Fresnaye. Genève, 1970.
42557.20.256 Lepelletier, Edmond. Paul Verlaine, his life, his work. 1. American ed. N.Y., 1970.
43688.98.150 LeQuintrec, Charles. La marche des arbres. Paris, 1970.
43688.1.21 Leroux, Gaston. Romans d'aventures. Évreux, 1970- 3v.
43688.1.20 Leroux, Gaston. Romans fantastiques. v.2. Évreux, 1970-
42576.46.9.10 Le Roy, Eugène. Carnet de notes d'une excursion de quinze jours en Périgord. Paris, 1970.
42576.46.9.20 Le Roy, Eugène. Mademoiselle de la Ralphie. Paris, 1970.
40512.3.20 LeSage, Alain René. Le diable boiteux. 2. éd. Paris, 1970.
43689.24.100 Lherm, Gussy. Le secret de Roncevaux, roman historique. Brive, 1970.
37567.690 Lidsky, Paul. Les écrivains contre la commune. Paris, 1970.
40532.19.1 Lintilhac, Eugène. Beaumarchais et ses oeuvres. Genève, 1970.
37568.280 La littérature in France depuis 1945. Paris, 1970.
43620.2.880 Littlejohn, David. Gide. Englewood Cliffs, 1970.
43693.6.110 Loba, Aké. Les fils de Kouretcha. Paris, 1970.
37547.110 Longeon, Claude. Les écrivains foréziens du XVIe siècle. Saint-Étienne, 1970.
43693.74.41 Lorbais, Jean. Les cicatrices. Paris, 1970.
43693.74.100 Lorbais, Jean. Sans armure. Paris, 1970.
39566.235 Lough, John. The encyclopédie in eighteenth-century England, and other studies. Newcastle, 1970.
42514.28.260 Lubac, Paul de. Maurras face à Pascal. Privas, 1970.
37563.126 Macchia, Giovanni. La letteratura francese. Firenze, 1970. 2v.
43697.14.142 MacOrlan, Pierre. A bord de l'Étoile-Matutine. Genève, 1970.
43697.14.460 MacOrlan, Pierre. Le bataillon de la mauvaise chance. Le camp domineau. Genève, 1970.
43697.14.352 MacOrlan, Pierre. Le bataillonnaire. Genève, 1970.
43697.14.450 MacOrlan, Pierre. La maison du retour écoeurant; roman. Dinah miami; roman d'aventure. Le tueur no 2, roman policier. 1. éd. Genève, 1970.
43697.14.382 MacOrlan, Pierre. Masques sur mesure. 1 ed. Genève, 1970.
43697.14.440 MacOrlan, Pierre. Propos d'infanterie: Les poissons morts, La fin, Devant la meuse. 1. éd. Genève, 1970.
43697.14.425 MacOrlan, Pierre. Rues secrètes. Nuits aux bouges. Genève, 1970?
43697.14.15 MacOrlan, Pierre. Sous la lumiére froide: La pension Mary Stuart. Genève, 1970.
38527.61.7.5 Magny, Olivier de. Les cent deux sonnets des amours de 1553. Genève, 1970.
43697.2.200 Mallet-Joris, Françoise (pseud.). La maison de papier. Paris, 1970.
40517.44.130 Malraux, André. Le triangle noir. Paris, 1970.
43697.75.2021 Marcenac, Jean. L'amour du plus lointain; poèmes 1960-1970. Paris, 1970.
43697.75.2110 Marcenac, Jean. La patience des botocudos. Paris, 1970.
41522.18.595 Marchand, Jean José. Sur Mon coeur mis à nu de Baudelaire. Paris, 1970.
38526.33.1 Marguerite d'Angoulême. Marguerites de la Marguerite des princesses. N.Y., 1970. 2v.
38526.32.4.10 Marguerite d'Angoulême. Tales from the Heptaméron. London, 1970.
37569.422 Marill, René. Le roman d'aujourd'hui, 1960-1970. Paris, 1970.
40535.30.76 Marivaux, Pierre Carlet de Chamblain de. Le cabinet du philosophe. Genève, 1970.
40535.29.14 Marivaux, Pierre Carlet de Chamblain de. Udachlivyi krest'ianin, ili mennary 6-na. Moskva, 1970.
38514.70.15 Martial de Paris. Martines de la Vierge. Genève, 1970.
38514.69.15 Martial de Paris. Martines de la Vierge. Genève, 1970.
43697.78.5180 Martin Saint-René (pseud.). Le livre des guatrains. Paris, 1970.
43697.78.5021 Martin Saint-René (pseud.). Le livre des odes et autres formes de stances. Paris, 1970.
37564.52.1 Martino, Pierre. L'Orient dans la littérature française au 17e et au 18e siècle. Genève, 1970.
42577.1.40 Maupassant, Guy de. The complete short stories. London, 1970. 3v.
43556.1.1000 Mauriac, Claude. Une amitié contrariée. Paris, 1970.
43697.88.14 Mauriac, François. Oeuvres romanesques. Paris, 1970. 2v.
43697.89.641 Maurois, André. Memoirs, 1885-1967. London, 1970.
37543.550.1 Mauron, Charles. Des métaphores obsédantes au mythe personnel. Paris, 1970.
43697.97.1100 Maxime, Jean. La fête encercleé. Paris, 1970.
40516.50.21 Mercier, Louis S. Du théâtre; ou Nouvel essai sur l'art dramatique. Genève, 1970.
39594.19.135 Merry, Henry J. Montesquieu's system of natural government. West Lafayette, 1970.
43698.82.1100 Mestre, Philippe. Quand flambait le bocage. Paris, 1970.
FL 6139.70.5 Metelli Di Lollo, Carmela. Componenti anarchiche nel pensiero di J.J. Rousseau. Firenze, 1970.
43698.89.100 Meunier, Lucien. De sable et d'azur. Paris, 1970.
43699.12.1110 Michelet, Claude. Une fois sept. Paris, 1970.
43744.67.1645 Milly, Jean. Les pastiches de Proust. Paris, 1970.
43744.67.1645.5 Milly, Jean. Proust et le style. Paris, 1970.
43701.33.1100 Mogin, Jean. A chacun selon sa faim. Bruxelles, 1970.
43701.39.130 Mohrt, Michel. Un jeu d'enfer. Paris, 1970.
40583.372 Montello, Josué. Un maître oublie de Stendhal. Paris, 1970.
43526.65.1015 Morhange-Bégué, Claude. "La chanson du mal-aimé" d'Apollinaire. Paris, 1970.
39544.403 Morize, André. L'apologie du luxe au XVIIIe siècle et "Le mondain" de Voltaire. Genève, 1970.
43701.89.3110 Moureau, Maurice. Les morts-vivants. Honfleur, 1970.
43701.89.4100 Mourthé, Claude. La caméra. Paris, 1970.
43620.2.876 Moutote, Daniel. Les images végétales dans l'oeuvre d'André Gide. 1. éd. Paris, 1970.
40535.31.25 Muehlemann, Suzanne. Ombres et lumières dans l'oeuvre de Pierre Carlet de Chamblain de Marivaux. Berne, 1970.
37568.223.2 Nadeau, Maurice. Le roman français depuis la guerre. Paris, 1970.

1970 - cont.

43757.50.1320 Nedeljković, Dragoljub. Romain Rolland et Stefan Zweig. Thèse. Paris, 1970.
41543.7.11 Nerval, Gerard de. Selected writings. Ann Arbor, 1970.
43538.76.992 Nettelbeck, Colin W. Les personnages de Bernanos romancier. Paris, 1970.
37556.364 Netzer, Klaus. Der Laser des nouveau Roman. Frankfurt, 1970.
38528.18.5 Nicolas de Troyes. Le grand parangon des nouvelles nouvelles (choix). Paris, 1970.
38544.27.625 Niderst, Alain. "La Princesse de Clèves". Sens, 1970?
43709.23.3110 Noël, Denise. La lettre aux sortilèges. Paris, 1970.
43709.23.826 Noël, Marie. Marie Noël; une étude de André Blanchet. Paris, 1970.
43709.80.180 Nourissier, François. La crève. Paris, 1970.
40515.2.60 Nowinski, Judith. Baron Dominique Vivant Denon (1747-1825). Rutherford, 1970.
43550.58.2040 O'Brien, Conor Cruise. Camus. London, 1970.
43538.14.995 O'Hara, James Donald. Twentieth century interpretations of Molloy, Malone dies, The unnamable. Englewood Cliffs, N.J., 1970.
43723.18.150 Oldenbourg, Zoé. La joie des pauvres. Paris, 1970.
40553.10.110 Oliver, Andrew. Benjamin Constant, écriture et conquète du moi. Paris, 1970.
43550.58.1058 Onimus, Jean. Albert Camus and Christianity. University, 1970.
37558.235 Oster, Daniel. Histoire de l'académie française. Paris, 1970.
37562.364 Owen, Douglas David Roy. The vision of Hell: infernal journeys in medieval French literature. Edinburgh, 1970.
43737.34.260 Pagnol, Marcel. César. Monte-Carlo, 1970.
43737.34.141 Pagnol, Marcel. Fanny. Paris, 1970.
43737.34.11 Pagnol, Marcel. Oeuvres complètes. Paris, 1970- 12v.
43550.58.2070 Palomares, Alfonso. Albert Camus. Madrid, 1970.
Mon 126.5 Papíc, Marko. L'expression et la place du sujet dans les Essais de Montaigne. 1. éd. Paris, 1970.
43737.72.100 Papy-Sturm, Janine. Vibrer c'est déjà mourir. Paris, 1970.
43822.49.1615 Parent, Monique. Cohérence et résonance dans le style de Charmes de Paul Valéry. Paris, 1970.
38537.76 Paris, Jean. Rabelais au futur. Paris, 1970.
43737.77.150 Parmelin, Hélène. La manière noire. Paris, 1970.
41596.46.30 Parny, Évariste. Voina bogov. Leningrad, 1970.
43552.5.1850.5 Pascal, Georges. L'idée de philosophie chez Alain. Paris, 1970.
43554.2.1310 Paul Claudel zu seinem hundertsten Geburtstag. Stuttgart, 1970.
43737.89.1150 Paulhan, Jean. Les incertitudes du language. Paris, 1970.
43737.89.110 Pauwels, Louis. L'homme éternel. Paris, 1970.
43556.49.910 Pavlovic, M.B. Sidonie Gabrielle Colette. Beograd, 1970.
43697.52.955 Payne, Robert. A portrait of André Malraux. Englewood Cliffs, N.J., 1970.
38526.43.1 Peletier, Jacques. Oeuvres poétiques. Genève, 1970.
38564.62 Pellisson, Maurice. La Bruyère. Genève, 1970.
38526.43.21 Percheron, Luc. Pyrrhe. Genève, 1970.
38525.21.5.1 Perdrizet, Pierre. Ronsard et la réforme. Genève, 1970.
43738.77.1110 Pérol, Jean. Ruptures. Paris, 1970.
43744.67.1620 Peyre, Henri. Marcel Proust. N.Y., 1970.
43738.97.1230 Peyrefitte, Roger. Des français; roman. Paris, 1970.
42568.19.35 Peyrouzet, Edouard. Vie de Lautréamont. Paris, 1970.
37564.278 Picard, Raymond. Génie de littérature française, 1600-1800. Paris, 1970.
37564.274 Picard, Raymond. Two centuries of French literature, 1600-1800. London, 1970.
43741.12.715 Picasso, Pablo. The four little girls. London, 1970.
43741.14.120 Picon, Gaëtan. L'oeil double. Paris, 1970.
FL 376.11.1 Picot, Émile. Le monologue dramatique dans l'ancien théâtre français. Genève, 1970.
37563.21.2 Piéri, Marius. Le pétrarquisme au XVIe siècle: Petrarque et Ronsard. Genève, 1970.
43741.49.110 Pillement, Georges. Autres pièces cyniques. Paris, 1970.
37583.670 Pillement, Georges. Le théâtre d'aujourd'hui; de Jean-Paul Sartre à Arrabal. Paris, 1970.
43741.89.140 Piroué, Georges. La surface des choses. Lausanne, 1970.
43742.3.2100 Planté, Louis. Le destin de Marie Baradat. Pau, 1970.
43554.2.1285 Plourde, Michel. Paul Claudel; une musique du silence. Montréal, 1970.
43743.41.3130 Poirot-Delpech, Bertrand. La folle de Lituanie. Paris, 1970.
37556.300.5 Pollmann, Leo. Der französische Roman im 20. Jahrhundert. Stuttgart, 1970.
43761.78.916 Pollmann, Leo. Sartre and Camus; literature of existence. N.Y., 1970.
43743.55.100 Pommier, Jean. Le spectacle intérieur. Paris, 1970.
43743.61.3100 Ponty, Bernard. Le séquestre. Paris, 1970.
43892.11.5 Porche, Simone Benda. Mon nouveau testament. Paris, 1970.
37566.182 Portraits du prochain siècle. Paris, 1970.
42545.3.890 Postic, Marcel. Maeterlinck et le symbolisme. Paris, 1970.
43738.1.955 Prajs, Lazare. Péguy et Israël. Paris, 1970.
43761.78.950 Presseault, Jacques. L'être-pour-autrui dans la philosophie de Jean-Paul Sartre. Bruxelles, 1970.
43744.67.79.30 Proust, Marcel. Correspondance. Paris, 1970.
43744.67.47.10 Proust, Marcel. Time regained. London, 1970.
39566.230 Pruner, Francis. L'unite' secrète de "Jacques le fataliste." Paris, 1970.
43747.41.100 Puig, André. L'inachevé. Paris, 1970.
43750.23.1100 Quentin-Maurer, Nicole. Portrait de Raphaël. Paris, 1970.
43750.25.2100 Quéval, Jean. En somme. Poèmes. Paris, 1970.
43550.58.2065 Quilliot, Roger. The sea and prisons; a commentary on the life and thought of Albert Camus. University, 1970.
38536.42 Rabelais, F. Gargantua. 1. éd. Genève, 1970.
38539.6.20 Radouant, René. Guillaume du Vair. Thèse. Genève, 1970.
41555.43.55 Raitt, Alan William. Prosper Mérimée. London, 1970.
37569.432 Random, Michel. Le grand jeu. Paris, 1970. 2v.
40597.2.850 Raser, George Bernard. The heart of Balzac's Paris. Choisy-le-Roi, 1970.
37543.618 Raymond, Marcel. Être et dire. Études. (Recueil). Neuchâtel, 1970.
37555.52.22 Raymond, Marcel. From Baudelaire to surrealism. London, 1970.
43753.17.110 Réda, Jacques. Récitatif. Paris, 1970.
37596.7.20 Regalado, Nancy Freeman. Poetic patterns in Rutebeuf; a study in noncourtly poetic modes of the thirteenth century. New Haven, 1970.
42587.51.65 Renard, Jules. Oeuvres. Paris, 1970- 2v.

1970 - cont.

43753.99.7110 Rezvani, Serge. Théâtre. Paris, 1970.
41543.22.102 Richer, Jean. Nerval, expérience et création. 2e éd. Paris, 1970.
43756.31.100 Rigaut, Jacques. Écrits. Paris, 1970.
43757.6.740 Robbe-Grillet, Alain. The house of assignation. London, 1970.
43757.6.190 Robbe-Grillet, Alain. Projet pour une révolution à New York. Paris, 1970.
43757.7.7120 Robert, Jacques. La dragée haute; roman. Paris, 1970.
38514.180 Robertet, Jean. Oeuvres. Genève, 1970.
43757.8.1100 Robinet, André. Méditaire digest antifilouzofique. La Houssaye-en-Brie, 1970.
43757.12.180 Roblès, Emmanuel. Un printemps d'Italie; roman. Paris, 1970.
38526.10.8.28.1 Roche, Louis P. Claude Chappuys (?-1575). Genève, 1970.
FL 6139.70.15 Roggerone, Giuseppe Agostino. Studi su Rousseau. Lecce, 1970.
43757.50.22 Rolland, Romain. Textes politiques, sociaux, et philosophiques choisis. Paris, 1970.
43757.3.267 Romains, Jules. Amitiés et rencontres. Paris, 1970.
37556.358 Roman et lumière au XVIIe siècle. Paris, 1970.
38525.20.28.10 Ronsard, Pierre de. Les amours. Genève, 1970.
38525.18.8 Ronsard, Pierre de. Sonnets pour Hélène. Genève, 1970.
39594.19.132 Rosso, Corrado. Intorno a Montesquieu. Pisa, 1970.
38514.46.10 Roth, Oskar. Studien zum Estrif de fortune et vertu des Martin Le Franc. Bern, 1970.
41522.18.466 Rouger, Jean. Baudelaire et la vérité littéraire des Fleurs du mal. Paris, 1970.
42578.31.140 Roux, Paul. Le trésor de l'homme. Limoges, 1970.
43757.96.220 Roy, Claude. Poésies. Paris, 1970.
43544.108.800 Roy, Paulette. Pierre Boulle et son oeuvre. Paris, 1970.
43697.77.895 Roza, Robert. Roger Martin du Gard et la banalité retrouvée. Paris, 1970.
43758.17.120 Rudel, Yves M. Mon curé à l'heure du concile. Paris, 1970.
43758.18.100 Rudigoz, Roger. Armande ou le roman. Paris, 1970.
40516.60.5.5 Sade, D.A.F. de. Idée sur les romans. Paris, 1970.
40516.60.57 Sade, D.A.F. de. Journal inédit. Paris, 1970.
43761.31.240 Sagan, Françoise. Un piano dans l'herbe. Paris, 1970.
43761.41.2110 St. Marcoux, Jeanne. Le voleur de lumière. Paris, 1970.
43761.41.7110 St. Phalle, Thérèse de. Le souverain. Paris, 1970.
40575.20.11 Sainte-Beuve, Charles A. Galerie des femmes célèbres. Evreux, 1970?
40575.5.185 Sainte-Beuve, Lamartine; colloques, 8 novembre, 1968. Paris, 1970.
37564.276 Saisselin, Rémy Gilbert. The rule of reason and the ruses of the heart. Cleveland, 1970.
43761.49.2120 Salgas, Simone. La toupie. Paris, 1970.
43538.14.975 Samuel Beckett now. Chicago, 1970.
41557.9.42.30 Sand, George. Lettres à Alfred de Musset et Gustave Flaubert. Paris, 1970.
41557.8.140 Sand, George. Oeuvres autobiographiques. Paris, 1970- 2v.
43761.77.190 Sarraute, Nathalie. Isma; ou, Ce qui s'appelle rien. Paris, 1970.
43761.78.622.11 Sartre, Jean Paul. No exit (Huis clos) a play in one act and The flies (Les mouches) a play in three acts. N.Y., 1970.
42575.115 Sauvage, Marcel. Jules et Edmond de Goncourt, précurseurs. Paris, 1970.
43763.37.100 Scheinert, David. L'homme qui allait à Gotterwald; théâtre. Paris, 1970.
43763.38.4021 Schmidt, Albert Marie. Chroniques de réforme, 1945-1966. Lausanne, 1970.
37563.75.10 Schmidt, Albert Marie. La poésie scientifique en France au 16e siècle. Lausanne, 1970.
43822.49.1620 Schmidt-Radefeldt, Jürgen. Paul Valéry linguiste dans les Cahiers. Paris, 1970.
37543.630 Schober, Rita. Von der wirklichen Welt in der Dichtung. 1. Aufl. Berlin, 1970.
FL 386.821 Schoell, Konrad. Das französische Drama seit Zweiten Weltkrieg. Göttingen, 1970. 2v.
43763.63.700 Schoendoerffer, Pierre. Farewell to the king. London, 1970.
40536.28.21 Sedaine, Michel Jean. Théâtre. Genève, 1970.
41568.17.35 Sénancour, Étienne Pivert de. Libres méditations. Genève, 1970.
41568.15.20 Sénelier, Jean. Hommage à Sénancour. Paris, 1970.
43765.76.3110 Serguine, Jacques. La mort confuse. Paris, 1970.
43765.76.4100 Sermaise, Robert. Prélude charnel; roman. Paris, 1970.
43833.20.865 Sfamurri, Antonio. L'umanesimo cristiano di Simone Weil. L'Aguila, 1970.
39566.225 Shackleton, Robert. The encyclopédie and the clerks. Oxford, 1970.
37555.570 Shapley, C.S. Studies in French poetry of the fifteenth century. The Hague, 1970.
42576.15.410 Sherrington, R. Three novels by Flaubert; a study of techniques. Oxford, 1970.
43769.54.664 Simenon, Georges. Les autres. Paris, 1970.
43769.54.606 Simenon, Georges. Betty. Paris, 1970.
43769.54.645 Simenon, Georges. Les complices. Paris, 1970?
43769.54.650 Simenon, Georges. Feux rouges, roman. Paris, 1970.
43769.54.555 Simenon, Georges. La folle de Maigret. Paris, 1970.
43769.54.658.1 Simenon, Georges. Le grand Bob. Paris, 1970.
43769.54.660 Simenon, Georges. Je me souviens. Paris, 1970.
43769.54.656 Simenon, Georges. Maigret chez le coronet; roman. Paris, 1970.
43769.54.662 Simenon, Georges. Maigret et la vieille dame. Paris, 1970.
43769.54.652 Simenon, Georges. Maigret et le fantôme, suivi de Maigret hésite. Paris, 1970.
43769.54.595 Simenon, Georges. Maigret et le marchand de vin; roman. Paris, 1970.
43769.54.792 Simenon, Georges. Maigret's boyhood friend. London, 1970.
43769.54.666 Simenon, Georges. Les mémoires de Maigret. Paris, 1970.
43769.54.762 Simenon, Georges. November. London, 1970.
43769.54.642 Simenon, Georges. Le passager clandestin. Paris, 1970.
43769.54.648 Simenon, Georges. La porte. Paris, 1970.
43769.54.545 Simenon, Georges. Le président. Paris, 1970.
43769.54.41 Simenon, Georges. Quand j'étais vieux. Paris, 1970.
43769.54.640 Simenon, Georges. Le riche homme; roman. Paris, 1970.
43769.54.565 Simenon, Georges. Le train. Paris, 1970.
43769.54.616 Simenon, Georges. Le veuf. Paris, 1970.
43769.56.5100 Simonne, Jean Philippe. Les lois de l'été. Paris, 1970.
43697.88.910 Smith, Maxwell, Austin. François Mauriac. N.Y., 1970.

Chronological Listing

1970 - cont.

38523.12.80	Smith, Pauline M. Clément Marot, poet of the French renaissance. London, 1970.
43538.14.1000	Smuda, Manfred. Becketts Prosa als Metasprache. München, 1970.
37567.740	Solinas, Paolo. Notes sur le roman patriotique français de 1870 à 1914. Cagliari, 1970.
37556.314	Stackelberg, Jürgen. Von Rabelais bis Voltaire. München, 1970.
40592.42	Staël Holstein, Anne Louise. Madame de Staël et J.B.A. Sward; correspondance inédite (1786-1817). Genève, 1970.
43556.1.990	Steegmuller, Francis. Cocteau, a biography. 1st ed. Boston, 1970.
43779.23.100	Steiner, Jean François. Les Métègues. Paris, 1970.
40534.36.15	Sturm, Ernest. Crébillon fils et le libertinage au dix-huitième siècle. Paris, 1970.
37566.180	Tadié, Jean Yves. Introduction à la vie littéraire du XIXe siècle. Paris, 1970.
43656.59.860	Tarrab, Gilbert. Ionesco à coeur ouvert. Montréal, 1970.
38523.14.5	Theureau, Louis. Étude sur la vie et les oeuvres de Jean Marot. Genève, 1970.
43788.41.4120	Thibaudeau, Jean. Mai dix-neuf cent soixante-huit en France. Drama. Paris, 1970.
40517.44.125	Thody, Philip M.W. Laclos: Les liaisons dangereuses. London, 1970.
43788.65.1021	Thomas, Henri. Poésies: Travaux d'aveugle, Signe de vie. Paris, 1970.
40527.19.20	Toens, Ulrich. Studien zur Dichtung André Chéniers. Münster, 1970.
41596.4.155	Toesca, Maurice. Alfred de Musset, ou L'amour de la mort. Paris, 1970.
43792.75.2705	Torres, Tereska. The converts. London, 1970.
40597.2.865	Toulouse. Musée Paul Dupuy. La comedie humaine et ses objets. Toulouse, 1970.
37564.284	Tournand, Jean Claude. Introduction à la vie littéraire du XVIIe siècle. Paris, 1970.
43792.94.110	Tournier, Michel. Le roi des Aulnes. Paris, 1970.
43792.89.3100	Touroude, Georges. Les pavés de la haine. Paris, 1970.
37556.370	Tourteau, Jean Jacques. D'Arsène Lupin à San-Antonio; le roman policier français de 1900 à 1970. Paris, 1970.
Mol 253.8	Treloar, Bronnie. Molière: les Précieuses ridicules. London, 1970.
40583.388	Trout, Paulette. La vocation romanesque de Stendhal. Paris, 1970.
43822.12.110	Vachey, Michel. Amulettes maigres. Honfleur, 1970.
37564.286	Valle, Daniela dalla. La frattura. Ravenna, 1970.
42581.33.45	Vallès, Jules. La Commune de Paris. Paris, 1970.
43823.76.5100	Vermeil, Jules. Rose des marais; roman. Aire-sur-la-Lys, 1970.
FL 6074.80	Verri, Antonio. Origine delle lingue e civiltà in Rousseau. Ravenna, 1970.
FL 386.313	Versini, Georges. Le théâtre français depuis 1900. 1. éd. Paris, 1970.
43824.3.1230	Vian, Boris. Le loup-garou, suivi de douze autres nouvelles. Paris, 1970.
43824.3.1220	Vian, Boris. Théâtre inédit: Tête de Méduse. Paris, 1970.
43824.4.1100	Viat, Denys. Le coeur en bandoulière. Paris, 1970.
43824.6.190	Vigée, Claude. La lune d'hivers; récèt, journal, essai. Paris, 1970.
43824.50.1041	Villard-Gilles, Jean. Mon demi-siècle et demi. [Mémoires]. Lausanne, 1970.
41574.632	Villiers, Charles. L'univers métaphysique de Victor Hugo. Paris, 1970.
42547.16.5	Villiers de l'Isle Adam, Auguste. Axel. Dublin, 1970.
43824.54.21	Vilmorin, Louise de. Poèmes. Paris, 1970.
43824.54.1021	Vimereu, Paul. Tertres et cratères; recueil de nouvelles et extraits de carnets de guerre, 1914-1918. Abbeville, 1970.
43824.58.3100	Vincent, Edouard. Les Mureddu: la vie d'une famille sarde. Grenoble, 1970.
43528.86.825	Virmaux, Alain. Antonin Artaud et le théâtre. Paris, 1970.
39544.388	Vulliamy, Glwyn Edward. Voltaire. Port Washington, N.Y., 1970.
39594.19.145	Waddicor, Mark H. Montesquieu and philosophy of natural law. The Hague, 1970.
42558.80	Walzer, Pierre Olivier. La révolution des sept: Lautréamont, Mallarmé, Rimbaud, Corbière, Cros, Nouveau, Laforgue. Neuchâtel, 1970.
43554.2.1275	Waters, Harold A. Paul Claudel. N.Y., 1970.
43538.14.980	Webb, Eugene. Samuel Beckett: a study of his novels. Seattle, 1970.
43833.20.20.2	Weil, Simone. Cahiers. Paris, 1970.
43833.20.720	Weil, Simone. First and last notebooks. N.Y., 1970.
38526.47.33.25	Wentzloff-Eggebert, Christian. Forminteresse. 1e Aufl. München, 1970.
40597.1.5.1	Werdet, Edmond. Portrait intime de Balzac. Paris, 1970?
43833.98.1120	Weyergans, Franz. On dira, cet hiver; roman. Paris, 1970.
38527.49.20	Wierenga, Lambertus. La troade de Robert Garnier. Proefschrift. Assen, 1970.
43835.24.720	Wiesel, Eliezer. A beggar in Jerusalem. N.Y., 1970.
43835.24.150	Wiesel, Éliezer. Entre deux soleils. Paris, 1970.
42555.44.235	Williams, Thomas Andrew. Mallarmé and the language of mysticism. Athens, 1970.
43837.49.1100	Wolff, Philippe. La flippeuse. Paris, 1970.
43761.77.820	Wonderli-Müller, Christine B. Le thème du masque et les banalités dans l'oeuvre de Nathalie Sarraute. Thèse. Zürich, 1970.
40597.2.591	Wurmser, André. La comédie inhumaine. Paris, 1970.
43576.6.865	Zephir, Jacques J. Psychologie de Salavin de Georges Duhamel. Paris, 1970.

1971

38523.44	Abraham, Claude Kurt. Enfin Malherbe. Lexington, 1971.
37596.23.30	Adam (Mystery). Le jeu d'Adam. Paris, 1971.
41522.16.15	Aggeler, William F. Baudelaire, judged by Spanish critics, 1857-1957. Athens, Georgia, 1971.
42582.2.47	Andreev, Kirill K. Na poroge novoi ery. Moskva, 1971.
43524.33.120	Anglade, Jean. Un front de marbre; roman. Paris, 1971.
37573.410.5	Annales romantiques. Facsimile. v.1-12, 1823-36. Paris. Genève, 1971. 6v.
43527.3.737	Aragon, Louis. Paris peasant. London, 1971.
37567.738	Astier Loutfi, Martine. Littérature et colonialisme; l'expansion coloniale vue dans la littérature romanesque française, 1871-1914. Paris, 1971.

1971 - cont.

37565.165.10	Atkinson, Geoffroy. Prelude to the enlightenment: French literature, 1690-1740. London, 1971.
37595.119	Axton, Richard. Medieval French plays. Oxford, 1971.
43537.14.1100	Bacri, Roland. Poèmes: colère du temps. Paris, 1971.
43545.24.905	Balakian, Anna Elizabeth. André Breton. N.Y., 1971.
37567.739	Baldick, Robert. Dinner at Magny's. London, 1971.
42581.33.115	Bancquart, Marie-Claire. Jules Vallès. Paris, 1971.
43744.67.1665	Bardèche, Maurice. Marcel Proust, romancier. Paris, 1971.
43697.14.800	Barltaud, Bernard. Pierre MacOrlan. Paris, 1971.
43537.77.6700	Barrault, Jean Louis. Rabelais. 1st American ed. N.Y., 1971.
43550.58.1115	Barretto, Vicente. Camus; vida e obra. Rio de Janeiro, 1971.
43527.3.870	Becker, Lucille. Louis Aragon. N.Y., 1971.
37565.196	Beiträge zur französischen Aufklärung und zur spanischen Literatur. Berlin, 1971.
43538.76.61	Bernanos, Georges. Correspondance. Paris, 1971-
38575.23.157	Besançon, France. Université. Laboratoire d'analyse lexicologique. P. Corneille, "Cinna." Paris, 1971.
43619.23.825	Beyen, Roland. Michel de Ghelderode. Bruxelles, 1971.
40582.3.34	Beyle, Henri. Travels in the South of France. London, 1971.
40587.195	Bicentenaire de Chateaubriand. Paris, 1971.
40597.2.870	Bilodeau, François. Balzac et le jeu des mots. Montréal, 1971.
43543.3.2100	Blancpain, Marc. Le plus long amour. Paris, 1971.
43544.112.120	Boileau, Pierre. D'entre les morts. Genève, 1971.
43544.74.3130	Bordier, Roger. Les éventails; roman. Paris, 1971.
41522.64.50	Borel d'Hauterive, Petrus. Shampaver. Leningrad, 1971.
38526.10.8.2.5	Brach, Pierre de. Les amours d'Aymée. Genève, 1971.
43761.39.960	Breaux, Adèle. St. Exupéry in America, 1942-1943; a memoir. Rutherford, N.J., 1971.
39594.19.2	Bremer, Klaus-Jürgen. Montesquieus Lettres persanes und Cadalsos Cartas marruecas. Thesis. Heidelberg, 1971.
43823.75.2762	Bruller, Jean. The raft of the Medusa. 1st American ed. N.Y., 1971.
37544.95	Brunet-Jailly, Jean-Baptiste. Introduction à la practique de l'éxplication de texte. Stockholm, 1971.
42557.20.336	Carter, Alfred Edward. Paul Verlaine. N.Y., 1971.
37593.62.85	Cartier, Normand Raymond. Le bossu désenchanté. Étude sur le jeu de la feuillée. Genève, 1971.
43550.82.280	Cassou, Jean. Le voisinage des cavernes. Paris, 1971.
43545.24.895	Caws, Mary Ann. André Breton. N.Y., 1971.
43550.98.250	Cayrol, Jean. N'oubliez pas que nous nous aimons. Paris, 1971.
43551.80.220	Cesbron, Gilbert. Des leçons d'abîme. Paris, 1971.
43552.1.2110	Chabannes, Jacques. Printemps rouge; roman. Paris, 1971.
37556.22.89	Chabrol, Claude. Le récit féminin. The Hague, 1971.
37567.730	Chadwick, Charles. Symbolism. London, 1971.
43552.6.3110	Charles-Roux, Edmonde. Elle, Adrienne. Paris, 1971.
40586.21.75	Chateaubriand, F.A.R. Vie de Rancé. Paris, 1971.
37594.37	Chaurand, Jacques. Fou, dixième conte de la Vie des Pères. Genève, 1971.
42582.2.55	Chesneaux, Jean. Une lecture politique de Jules Verne. Paris, 1971.
43697.88.920	Le chrétien Mauriac. Paris, 1971.
43576.74.2800	Cismaru, Alfred. Marguerite Duras. N.Y., 1971.
43656.59.801	Coe, Richard Nelson. Ionesco. London, 1971.
38537.25.250	Coleman, D.G. Rabelais: a critical study in prose fiction. Cambridge, Eng., 1971.
38575.34.13	Corneille, Pierre. Pompée. London, 1971.
37556.22.100	Couperus, Marianne Constance. Un périodique français en Hollande; le glaneur historique, 1731-1733. Proefschrift. The Hague, 1971.
43556.89.7100	Coupry, François. Les autocoincés. Paris, 1971.
43822.49.1625	Les critiques de notre temps et Valéry. Paris, 1971.
43560.78.220	Curtis, Jean Louis. Le roseau pensant. Paris, 1971.
40545.7.5	Custine, Astolphe. Aloys; ou, Le religieux du Mont Saint-Bernard. Paris, 1971.
42554.64.801	Danilin, Iurii I. Zabytyi pamfletist. Moskva, 1971.
42586.33.130	Darien, Georges. L'epaulette. Paris, 1971.
42581.33.120	Delfau, Gérard. Jules Vallès, l'exil à Londres (1871-1880). Paris, 1971.
40535.32.38	Deloffre, Frédéric. Marivaux et le Marivaudage. 2. éd. Paris, 1971.
43566.54.2100	Demélier, Jean. Gens de la rue. Paris, 1971.
38526.48.15.5	Du Bartas, Guillaume de Salluste. Oeuvres. Toulouse, 1971-
42568.19.21.20	Ducasse, I.L. Oeuvres complètes. Paris, 1971.
43744.67.1675	Eggs, Ekkehard. Möglichkeiten und Grenzen einer wissenschaftlichen Semantik. Bern, 1971.
38537.80	Eldridge, Paul. François Rabelais, the great story teller. South Brunswick, 1971.
43738.78.850	Emmanuel, Pierre. Saint-John Perse: praise and presence. Washington, 1971.
39533.8.31	Fabre, Antonin. Lexigue de la langue de Chapelain. Genève, 1971.
43606.76.61	Fargue, Léon P. Correspondance, 1910-1946. Paris, 1971.
38526.32.61	Febvre, Lucien. Amour sacré, amour profane, autour de l'"Heptaméron". Paris, 1971.
38526.14.129	Filleul, Nicolas. Les théâtres de Gaillon. Genève, 1971.
42576.16.67	Flaubert, Gustave. Oeuvres complètes. Paris, 1971. 3v.
40515.47.5	Florian, Jean P.C. de. Six nouvelles. Mémoires d'un jeune Espagnol. Paris, 1971.
43744.67.1680	Florival, Ghislaine. Le désir chez Proust. Paris, 1971.
42576.63.20.10	France, Anatole. Vers les temps meilleurs: trente ans de vie sociale. Evreux, 1971. 4v.
FL 379.191	Gaiffe, Félix. Le drame en France au XVIIIe siècle. Paris, 1971.
40597.2.880	Galantaris, Christian. Les portraits de Balzac connus et inconnus, février-avril 1971. Paris, 1971.
43697.52.961	Galante, Pierre. Malraux. 1. ed. N.Y., 1971.
43697.77.900	Gallant, Melvin. Le thème de la mort chez Roger Martin du Gard. Paris, 1971.
38587.33	Garscha, Karsten. Hardy als Barockdramatiker. Frankfurt, 1971.
42556.28.417	Gascar, Pierre. Rimbaud et la commune. Paris, 1971.
43514.6.800	Gaudy, René. Arthur Adamov. Paris, 1971.
37569.440	Gauger, Rosemarie. Littérature engagée in Frankreich zur Zeit des Zweiten Weltkriegs. Göppingen, 1971.
43617.59.270	Genevoix, Maurice. Bestiaire sans oubli. Paris, 1971.
41522.18.635	Genovali, Sandro. Baudelaire, o della dissonanza. Firenze, 1971.
38546.33.50	Gérard-Gailly, Émile. Madame de Sévigné. Paris, 1971.

Chronological Listing

1971 - cont.

41574.630 Gerson, Noel Bertram. Victor Hugo: a tumultuous life. N.Y., 1971.

43620.2.79.179 Gide, André. Correspondance André Gide - François Mauriac, 1912-1950. Paris, 1971.

43620.48.61 Gilbert-Lecomte, Roger. Correspondance; lettres. Paris, 1971.

39566.250 Gorny, Léon. Diderot, un grand européen. Paris, 1971.

42547.22.130 Gourévitch, Jean Paul. Villiers de l'Isle Adam. Paris, 1971.

43626.22.320 Green, Julien. L'Autre. Paris, 1971.

43528.86.830 Greene, Naomi. Antonin Artaud. N.Y., 1971.

38526.17.30 Grévin, Jacques. César. Paris, 1971.

43626.74.150 Groussard, Serge. Taxi de nuit. Paris, 1971.

40583.392 Gutwirth, Marcel Marc. Stendhal. N.Y., 1971.

43554.2.1300 Harry, Ruth Naomi. Paul Claudel and Saint-John Perse. Chapel Hill, 1971.

37543.36.2 Hémon, Félix. Études littéraires et morales. Genève, 1971.

43538.14.1010 Hesla, David H. The shape of chaos. Minneapolis, 1971.

37544.90 Hesse-Fine, Evelyne. Études sur la thème de l'inceste dans la littérature française. Berne, 1971.

39544.400 Holmsten, Georg. Voltaire in Selbstzeugnissen und Bilddokumenten. Reinbek, 1971.

43636.89.150 Hougron, Jean. Les Asiates; roman. Paris, 1971.

37557.90 Howarth, William D. Explications: the technique of French literary appreciation. London, 1971.

42584.25.405 Iakimovich, Tat'iana K. Molodoi Zolia. Kiev, 1971.

40553.10.100 Jasinski, Béatrice W. L'engagement de Benjamin Constant. Paris, 1971.

38564.60 Jasinski, René. Deux accès à La Bruyère. Paris, 1971.

43668.4.120 Jeanson, Henri. En verve. Paris, 1971.

43668.60.100 Jenny, Laurent. Off; roman. Paris, 1971.

37567.658 Juden, Brian. Traditions orphiques et tendances mystiques dans le romantisme français (1800-1855). Paris, 1971.

43667.14.825 Kamber, Gerald. Max Jacob and the poetics of cubism. Baltimore, 1971.

41584.43.25 Kaye, Eldon. Xavier Forneret dit "L'homme noir" (1809-1884). Genève, 1971.

38526.7.60 Keating, Louis Clark. Joachim Du Bellay. N.Y., 1971.

43673.77.2130 Kerraoul, Bernard de. La réconciliation; roman. Paris, 1971.

37562.356 Klein, Karen Wilk. The partisan voice; a study of the political lyric in France and Germany, 1180-1230. The Hague, 1971.

43744.67.1670 Kopp, Richard L. Marcel Proust as a social critic. Rutherford, 1971.

37596.10.115 Kramer, Hans-Peter. Erzählerbemerkungen und Erzählerkommentare in Chrestiens und Hartmanns Erec und Iwein. Thesis. Göppingen, 1971.

43687.41.1100 Lainé, Pascal. L'irrévolution. Paris, 1971.

41578.35.140 Lamartine, Alphonse de. Alphonse de Lamartine ve Istanbul yazilari. Istanbul, 1971.

38543.10.52 La Rochefoucauld, François. Maximes. Genève, 1971?

38543.23.40 La Rochefoucauld, François. Memuary, maksimy. Leningrad, 1971.

43538.1.850 Lasocki, Anne-Marie. Simone de Beauvoir. La Haye, 1971.

40513.40 Laufer, Roger. Lesage. Paris, 1971.

FL 6119.71 Launay, Michel. Jean-Jacques Rousseau, ecrivain politique, 1712-1762. Cannes, 1971.

39534.23.1 Laurent, Émile. La journee des Madrigaux. Genève, 1971.

38537.84 Laurent, Marcel. Rabelais; le monde paysan et le langage auvergnat. Clemont-Ferrand, 1971.

41574.634 Lebreton-Savigny, Monique. Victor Hugo et les Américains (1825-1885). Paris, 1971.

42555.36.30 Leconte de Lisle, C.M.R. Leconte de Lisle: articles, préfaces, discours. Paris, 1971.

43620.74.940 Lemaître, Georges Edouard. Jean Giraudoux. N.Y., 1971.

43620.74.945 Lewis, Roy. Giraudoux: La guerre de Troie n'aura pas lieu. London, 1971.

41596.4.175 Lietz, Jutta. Studien zu den Novellen Alfred de Mussets. Hamburg, 1971.

38562.23.50 Lissa, Giuseppe. Cartesianesimo e anticartesianesimo in Fontenelle. Napoli, 1971.

43550.58.1105 Livi, François. Camus. Firenze, 1971.

43693.75.1100 Lorho, Robert. Les métamorphoses du biographe. Paris, 1971.

37597.9.30 Lorris, Guillaume de. The romance of the rose. Princeton, 1971.

37566.174 Macchia, Giovanni. I fantasmi dell'opera. Milano, 1971.

43744.67.1655 Marcel Proust, 1871-1922. N.Y., 1971.

38526.32.35 Marguerite d'Angoulême. Chansons spirituelles. Paris, 1971.

38526.34.31 Marquerite d'Angoulême. La coche. Genève, 1971.

39594.19.160 Mas, Enrico de. Montesquieu, Genovesi e le edizioni italiane dello Spirito delle leggi. Firenze, 1971.

43697.88.3041 Mauriac, Claude. Un autre De Gaulle; journal 1944-1954. Paris, 1971.

37556.340 Mercier, Vivian. The new novel from Queneau to Pinget. 1. ed. N.Y., 1971.

43698.200.270 Michaux, Henri. Poteaux d'angle. Paris, 1971.

Mol 196.5.15 Molière, Jean Baptiste Poquelin. The school for wives. 1st ed. N.Y., 1971.

FL 377.95 Moore, Will Grayburn. The classical drama of France. London, 1971.

43701.74.470 Morand, Paul. Venises. Paris, 1971.

37564.288 Nurse, Peter Harold. Classical voices: studies of Corneille, Racine, Molière, Mme de Lafayette. London, 1971.

43714.5.132 Obaldia, René de. Les richesses naturelles. Paris, 1971.

39566.240 O'Gorman, Donal. Diderot, the satirist. Toronto, 1971.

37543.638 Osburn, Charles B. The present state of French studies: a collection of research reviews. Metuchen, N.J., 1971.

39594.19.57 Oudin, Charles. Le spinozisme de Montesquieu. Genève, 1971.

43761.39.965 Ouellet, Réal. Les relations humaines dans l'oeuvre de St. Exupéry. Paris, 1971.

39566.265 Paitre, Fernand. Diderot biologiste. Genève, 1971.

38528.16.80 Pallister, Janis. The world view of Béroalde de Verville. Paris, 1971.

38526.42.10.70 Parmentier, Jean. Oeuvres poétiques. Paris, 1971.

43738.77.6700 Perrault, Gilles. Dossier 51; an entertainment. London, 1971.

43799.5.800 Peterson, Elmer. Tristan Tzara: dada and surrational theorist. New Brunswick, 1971.

43554.2.1315 Petit, Jacques. Claudel et l'usurpateur. Paris, 1971.

37555.774 Petrova, Injna I. Spivtsi svobody. Kyïv, 1971.

1971 - cont.

37565.194 Peyre, Henri. Qu'est-ce que le romantisme? Paris, 1971.

42553.35.10 Pfister, Susanne. Expansion et concentration dans la pensées d'Amiel. Berne, 1971.

37566.172 Pia, Pascal. Romanciers, poètes essayistes du XIXe siècle. Paris, 1971.

37563.128 Pineaux, Jacques. La poésie des protestants de langue française. Paris, 1971.

43743.41.6100 Poitou, Jean. D'un sexe à l'autre. Paris, 1971.

43544.81.2820 Poitras, Lionel. Henri Bosco et la participation au monde. Fribourg, 1971.

37556.300.1 Pollmann, Leo. La "nueva novela" en Francia y en Iberoamérica. Madrid, 1971.

43743.60.180 Ponge, Francis. La fabrique du pré. Genève, 1971.

37556.368 Positions et oppositions sur le roman contemporain; actes du colloque. Paris, 1971.

37557.76.60 Poulet, Georges. La conscience critique. Paris, 1971.

37556.22.90 Pourprix, Bernard. La presse gratuite. Paris, 1971.

37573.465 La psyché; choix de pièces en vers et en prose, 1826-30. Paris. Facsimile. Genève, 1971. 4v.

43750.24.360 Queneau, Raymond. On est toujours trop bon avec les femmes. Paris, 1971.

37556.351 Ratner, Moses. Theory and criticism of the novel in France from l'Astree to 1750. N.Y., 1971.

38525.5.35 Raymond, Marcel. La poésie française et la manièrisme, 1546-1610(?) Genève, 1971.

38543.23.45 Razumovskaia, Margarita V. Laroshfuko, autor Maksim. Leningrad, 1971.

43822.50.810 Recanati, Jean. Vailland. Paris, 1971.

41596.4.180 Rees, Margaret A. Alfred de Musset. N.Y., 1971.

38587.3.25 Regnard, Jean François. Oeuvres. v.2. Amsterdam, 1971.

FL 377.46 Reiss, T.J. Toward dramatic illusion; theatrical technique and meaning from Hardy to Horace. New Haven, 1971.

43756.11.1100 Ricardou, Jan. Révolutions minuscules. Paris, 1971.

37569.442 Ricardou, Jean. Pour une théorie du nouveau roman. Paris, 1971.

37567.718 Richard, Jean Pierre. Études sur le romantisme. Paris, 1971.

42557.20.345 Richardson, Joanna. Verlaine. London, 1971.

FL 398.47.75 Richtman, Jack. Adrienne Lecouvreur: the actress and the age. Englewood Cliffs, 1971.

43756.58.100 Rinaldi, Angelo. La maison des Atlantes; roman. Paris, 1971.

38526.48.38.40 Risset, Jacqueline. L'anagramme du désir. Roma, 1971.

41542.4.120 Rizza, Cecilia. Théophile Gautier, critico letterario. Torino, 1971.

43753.90.805 Rizzuto, Anthony. Style und theme in Reverdy's Les ardoises du toit. University, 1971.

43757.12.2110 Roché, Henri Pierre. Les deux anglaises et le continent. Paris, 1971.

43757.39.100 Rohou, Guy. Le bateau des îles. Paris, 1971.

43757.49.140 Rolin, Dominique. Les éclairs, roman. Paris, 1971.

42556.31.21 Rollinat, Maurice. Oeuvres. Paris, 1971-

37530.204 Ronge, Peter. Studienbibliographie Französisch; Beiträge zur bibliographischen Erschliessung der französischen Philologie. v.1-2. Frankfurt, 1971.

43626.22.895 Rose, Marilyn Gaddis. Julian Green, Gallic-American novelist. Berne, 1971.

43757.82.1100 Rossi, Pierre. Un soir à pise. Paris, 1971.

37562.362 Ryding, William W. Structure in medieval narrative. The Hague, 1971.

43761.31.725 Sagan, Françoise. Sunlight on cold water. London, 1971.

40575.50 Sainte-Beuve, Charles A. Literary criticism of Sainte-Beuve. Lincoln, 1971.

42576.15.420 Sartre, Jean Paul. L'idiot de la famille; Gustave Flaubert. Paris, 1971. 3v.

37573.515 Le scapin. Ser. 1-2,1885-86// Paris. Facsimile. Genève, 1971.

38526.48.34.1 Scève, Maurice. Oeuvres poétiques complètes. Paris, 1971. 2v.

38562.18.30 Schmidt, Christian. Fontenelles "Nouveaux dialogues des morts" als moralistisches Werk zwischen Preziosität und Aufklärung. Hamburg, 1971.

41522.3.120 Schwartz, Helmut. Idéologie et art romanesque chez Jules Barbey d'Aurevilly. München, 1971.

39544.394 Schwarzbach, Bertram Eugene. Voltaire's Old Testament criticism. Genève, 1971.

37594.50 Shapiro, Norman Richard. The comedy of eros. Urbana, 1971.

43769.54.654 Simenon, Georges. La mort de Belle. Paris, 1971.

43769.54.795 Simenon, Georges. Teddy bear. London, 1971.

43769.54.641 Simenon, Georges. When I was old. 1. ed. N.Y., 1971.

43769.56.2170 Simon, Claude. Les corps conducteurs. Paris, 1971.

43769.56.170 Simon, Pierre Henri. La sagesse du soir. Paris, 1971.

43775.50.141 Sollers, Philipe. L'écriture et l'expérience des limites. Paris, 1971.

43776.1.1100 Spaak, Claude. L'ordre et le désordre. Paris, 1971.

FL 6139.58.1 Starobinski, Jean. Jean-Jacques Rousseau. Paris, 1971.

37543.636 Strauss, Walter Adolf. Descent and return; the Orphic theme in modern literature. Cambridge, 1971.

40587.190 Switzer, Richard. Chateaubriand. N.Y., 1971.

37569.438 Tauber, Christian. Le thème de l'enfance dans la littérature actuelle. Thèse. Zurich, 1971.

37574.948 Taylor, Simon Watson. French poetry today. London, 1971.

37576.671 Textes. Suivi de la Mort de la littérature. Paris, 1971.

42587.27.95 Thomas, Edith. Louise Michel, ou La Vélleda de l'anarchie. Paris, 1971.

40583.398 Tillett, Margaret G. Stendhal. London, 1971.

42581.33.50 Vallès, Jules. The insurrectionist. Englewood Cliffs, N.J., 1971.

41578.112 Viallaneix, Paul. Lamartine. Paris, 1971.

43824.48.140 Vilallonga, José Luis de. Fiesta. Paris, 1971.

38567.58 Vitanović, Slobodan. Poetika Nikole Boaloa i francuski klasicizm. Beograd, 1971.

39543.70 Voltaire, François Marie Arouet de. Mélanges philosophiques. Paris, 1971.

43832.33.100 Wagner, Paul. Graine d'ortie. Paris, 1971.

Mol 623.10 Walker, H. Molière. N.Y., 1971.

37563.55.20 Wittschier, Heinz Willi. Die Lyrik der Pléiade. Frankfurt, 1971.

40583.400 Wood, Michael. Stendhal. London, 1971.

43761.39.940 Young, Michael Tomas. St. Exupéry; Vol de nuit. London, 1971.

1972

37563.104.5 Bady, René. Humanisme chrétien dans les lettres françaises: XVIe-XVIIe siècles. Paris, 1972.
38537.82 Bowen, Barbara C. The age of bluff: paradox and ambiguity in Rabelais and Montaigne. Urbana, 1972.
37563.55.25 Demerson, Guy. La mythologie classique dans l'oeuvre lyrique de la "Pléiade." Genève, 1972.
43566.82.7760 Destouches, Louis Ferdinand. North. N.Y., 1972.
42576.20.35 Flaubert, Gustave. The first sentimental education. Berkeley, 1972.
40517.4.85 Forno, Lawrence J. Robert Challe: intimations of the Enlightenment. Rutherford, N.J., 1972.
42576.15.460 Frey, G.W. Die ästhetische Begriffswelt Flauberts. München, 1972.
41557.10.285 Gerson, Noel Bertram. George Sand; a biography of the first modern, liberated woman. N.Y., 1972.
42575.118 Grant, Richard Babson. The Goncourt brothers. N.Y., 1972.
37567.737 Houston, John Porter. Fictional technique in France, 1802-1927. Baton Rouge, 1972.
42542.28.95 Hyslop, Lois Boe. Henry Becque. N.Y., 1972.
43668.4.41 Jeanson, Henri. Soixante-dix ans d'adolescence. Paris, 1972.
42544.28.20 Labiche, Eugène. La clé des champs. Paris, 1972.
41578.27.6 Lamartine, Alphonse de. Geneviève. Paris, 1972.
43701.63.620 Montherlant, Henry de. Le cardinal d'Espagne. Boston, 1972.
42576.15.390.5 Nadeau, Maurice. The greatness of Flaubert. N.Y., 1972.
37569.444 Roudiez, Leon Samuel. French fiction today. New Brunswick, N.J., 1972.
43761.5.4705 Sabatier, Robert. The safety matches. 1st ed. N.Y., 1972.
37557.76.45 Simon, John K. Modern French criticism. Chicago, 1972.
38525.36.9.1 Tristan L'Hermite, F. Le page disgracié. Paris, 1898. Nendeln, 1972.
38585.16.106 Vossler, Karl. Jean Racine. N.Y., 1972.
38537.86 Weinberg, Florence M. The wine and the will; Rabelais's Bacchic Christianity. Detroit, 1972.
42536.25 Weinstein, Leo. Hippolyte Taine. N.Y., 1972.
39566.161 Wilson, Arthur McCandless. Diderot. N.Y., 1972.
37562.360 Zumthor, Paul. Essai de poétique médiévale. Paris, 1972.